REDHOUSE YENİ
Türkçe - İngilizce
SÖZLÜK

NEW REDHOUSE
Turkish - English
DICTIONARY

REDHOUSE YAYINEVİ

FARMINGDALE PUBLIC LIBRARY
116 MERRITTS ROAD
FARMINGDALE, N.Y. 11735

ISBN 975-413-022-1

Redhouse Yeni Türkçe-İngilizce Sözlük
Editörler: V. Bahadır Alkım, Nazime Antel,
Robert Avery, Janos Eckmann, Sofi Huri,
Fahir İz, Mecdud Mansuroğlu, Andreas Tietze

© Copyright / Yayım Hakkı: Redhouse Yayınevi, 1968

Printing / Baskı — Binding / Cilt: UYCAN Tel.: (212) 276 23 58

13 th Edition On üçüncü Basım Aralık 1993 3000 Adet

90-34-Y-0099-1

REDHOUSE YAYINEVİ
Rızapaşa Yokuşu No. 50
Mercan 34450 İstanbul
Tel.: (212) 522 39 05 - (212) 522 14 98

Yazışma Adresi:
Posta Kutusu 142
Sirkeci 34432 İstanbul

REDHOUSE
YENİ
TÜRKÇE - İNGİLİZCE SÖZLÜK

Sir James Redhouse tarafından hazırlanıp, Amerikan Board Heyeti tarafından 1890'da «Kitab-ı Maani-i Lehçe» adıyle neşredilen Türkçe - İngilizce Lûgati esas tutarak hazırlanmış Yeni Türkçe - İngilizce Sözlük

Redhouse Yayınevi, İstanbul

NEW
REDHOUSE
TURKISH - ENGLISH DICTIONARY

A new dictionary based largely on the Turkish - English Lexicon prepared by Sir James Redhouse and published in 1890 by the Publication Department of the American Board.

Redhouse Press, Istanbul

Bu sözlüğün yeniden esaslı ve ilmî bir surette gözden geçirilip hazırlanabilmesini cömert yardımları sâyesinde mümkün kılan FORD VAKFI'na, Redhouse Yayınevi ve Amerika'daki merkezi olan «The United Church Board for World Ministries» en derin şükranlarını arzederler. Bu yardımlar hem malî bakımdan geniş ölçüde olmuş ve hem FORD VAKFI mensuplarının devamlı ilgisi, uzun bir süre devam etmesi gereken ve zaman zaman güçlükler gösteren bu çalışmanın gerçekleşmesine destek teşkil etmiştir.

The Redhouse Press and the United Church Board for World Ministries wish to express their heartfelt appreciation to the FORD FOUNDATION, which through generous grants has made it possible to carry out a thorough and scholarly revision of the dictionary. Their support has been financially substantial; and the sustained interest of concerned individuals within the Foundation has encouraged the Press through the strains of a necessarily long and complicated process.

TAHRİR HEYETİ   EDITORIAL COMMITTEE

        U. Bahadır Alkım

        Nazime Antel

        Robert Avery

        Janos Eckmann

        Sofi Huri*

        Fahir İz

        Mecdud Mansuroğlu (d. 1963)

        Andreas Tietze*

* Members of the Committee from the beginning.
* Başlangıçtan itibaren Heyette çalışanlar.

Aşağıda isimleri geçen şahıslara zahmetli araştırma, tashih, daktilo etme gibi hususlardaki yardımlarından dolayı pek müteşekkiriz.

Grateful thanks are due of the following people for painstaking checking, proofreading, and typing :

Handan Alkım
İbrahim Baş
Selime Hebel
Raife İz
Lâmia Kozlu
Franca Tonguç
Bercuhi Tüysüzyan

Matbaa tashihlerini doğruluk ve vuzuh bakımından gönüllü olarak gözden geçiren müteaddit eşhas arasında aşağıdaki isimleri, uzun bir süre devam eden değerli yardımlarından dolayı, minnetle zikretmeliyiz :

Among the many who have volunteered their services to check proof for accuracy and clarity, the following must be gratefully mentioned for their substantial services over an extended time :

Marion Jeffery
Mary Lou Johnson
M. E. Nadi

Osmanlıca imlâlar hattatımız Nur-i Osmaniye Camii Baş Müezzini **Recep Berk** tarafından yazılmıştır.

The Ottoman spellings were handwritten by the head muezzin of Nuri Osmaniye Mosque, **Recep Berk.**

Muhtelif sahalarda yardımlarına müracaat edilen mütehassıslardan bilhassa aşağıdaki zevat kendi sahalarındaki söz listeleri üzerinde değerli yardımlarda bulunmuşlardır :

Of the many specialists who have been called on for help in specific fields, the following especially deserve mention for sustained labors with special vocabulary lists :

Musiki	Hormoz Ferhat	Music
Musiki	Ethem Üngör	Music
Biyoloji, Botanik	Felix B. Minarovich	Biology and Botany
Tarih terimleri	Nejat Göyünç	Historical terms

ÖNSÖZ

Takriben yirmi yıllık bir hazırlığın mahsulü olan bu sözlük, bu nesle mensup ilim adamlarının eseri olmakla beraber, esas itibariyle, Sir James Redhouse tarafından kaleme alınıp 1890'da Yayınevimizce neşredilen, sonradan birçok defa basımı tekrarlanan ve son baskısı 1923'de yapılan esere dayanmaktadır. Tahrir Heyetimiz, Redhouse'un kendi devrinde faydalanma imkânını bulamadığı dil kaynaklarındaki malzemeyi de sözlüğe eklemiş ve arada geçmiş olan doksan yıla yakın bir zaman zarfında Türkçeye girmiş olan kelime ve ıstılahları da ithal etmiştir.

Sözlüğümüz, tek bir alfabetik dizinde hazırlanmış olan hem bir Osmanlıca - İngilizce hem de bir Türkçe - İngilizce sözlük niteliğindedir. Son iki yüzyıl zarfında bugünkü Türkiye'nin coğrafî sınırları içinde kullanılan standart Türkçenin hemen bütün kelimelerini ve deyimlerini mümkün olduğu kadar tam bir surette eserimize ithal etmeğe çalıştık. Gözden kaçma, yanılma ve yanlış hüküm verme dolayısiyle kitapta eksikler bulunabilir, ancak bunların asgarî hadde olduğunu da ümit etmekteyiz.

Taşra ağızlarında geçen kelime ve mânâlar, kullanılış sahaları tek bir bölgeye inhisar etmediği hallerde, ilâve edilmiştir. Türk atasözlerinin ve halk deyişlerinin mümkün olduğu nispette, muhtelif şekilleriyle gösterilmesine çalışılmıştır. Denizcilik, ziraat, spor, biyoloji ve botanik, tıp, anatomi, felsefe, tasavvuf ve mülkî idareye ait terimler, Arapça ve Farsça önek ve sonekler, Türkçe gramer şekilleri, argo ve halk deyişleri mütehassısların yardımıyle hususî kaynaklardan faydalanılarak takviye edilmiştir. Türkçeye giren ve tutunan yeni kelimelerin de sözlüğe dahil edilmesine ayrıca gayret sarfedilmiştir.

Günlük lisanda yer alan kelimeler, sadece kelime mânâlariyle değil, cümle içindeki kullanılış yerlerine göre de açıklanmıştır. Böylece birçok kelime sözlükte uzun maddeler halinde yer almaktadır (bk. **baş, göz, iç, iki, kara, ne, orta, su, şeytan, tas**). Sözlüğü hazırlarken, bibliyografyada da görüleceği gibi modern lûgatlar da dahil olmak üzere, elde mevcut bütün kaynaklardan istifade edilmiştir.

Nâşirler, ilim adamlarının, Redhouse Lûgatının eski metninden kayda değer hiçbir kelimenin çıkarılmaması hususundaki kanaatlerine iştirak etmişlerdir. Bununla beraber, yeni malzemeye yer açmak mülâhazasiyle bazı eski kelimelerin metin dışı bırakılmalarına lüzum hasıl olmuştur. Ümit edilir ki, Osmanlıca metinlerde nâdiren geçen veya farazî olarak mevcudiyeti düşünülen, hemen hepsi Arapça ve Farsça olan bu kelimeler bir kayıp teşkil etmiyecektir. Bu nevi kelimeleri ihtiva eden metinleri tetkik edecek bir ilim adamının çalışma masasında tafsilâtlı Farsça ve Arapça lûgatların zâten mevcut olacakları düşünülebilir. Nâdiren geçen bir kısım Türkçe kelimeler — yalnız, bugün bize kadar ulaşamamış kaynaklara sahip olduğu düşünülen — Redhouse'a istinaden itina ile muhafaza edilmiştir.

Bu sözlük, daha ziyade ilim adamlarını alâkadar edecek birçok hususları ihtiva etmektedir. Osmanlıca imlâların da verilmesi, bilhassa eski el yazmaları üzerinde ve diğer mevzularda araştırma yapanlara olduğu kadar, Osmanlıcada muhafaza edilmiş olup da, yeni imlâda kaybolmuş olan farklarla ilgilenen dilcilere de yardımcı olacaktır. Nâşirler, yakın bir gelecekte, ilim adamlarının istifadesine arzolunmak üzere, Osmanlıca imlâların kısaltılmış bir indeksini de yayınlamayı ümit etmektedirler.

Sözlükteki kelimelerin birçoğu, bugün günlük lisanda kullanılmaz hale gelmiştir. Bununla beraber, sözlük, bir kimsenin düşüncelerini ifade etmek için uygun İngilizce kelime ve ıstılahı seçmesi hususunda yardımcı olacak malzemeyi de ihtiva etmektedir.

Nâşirler, yakında, bu tafsilâtlı sözlükten, sadece günlük lisanda geçen kelimeleri seçerek, kısaltılmış bir Türkçe - İngilizce Redhouse Sözlüğü yayınlamayı da ümit etmektedirler.

Robert Avery

PREFACE

This dictionary, the product of nearly twenty years of preparation, is the work of scholars of this generation. But it rests solidly on the dictionary of Sir James Redhouse, particularly on the edition of 1890, which was reissued many times by our press, most recently in 1923. We have added materials from sources that were not available to Redhouse, and have included words and phrases that have come into use in the intervening years— now almost ninety years since the original manuscript was finished. Thus the dictionary is both an Ottoman-English and a Turkish - English dictionary in one alphabetical order.

The intention has been to include every word, and as nearly as possible every set phrase or locution, that has been used in standard Turkish as it has been spoken within the geographical area now called Turkey in the last two hundred years. There have been omissions through oversight, ignorance, or misjudgment, but it is hoped that they have been kept to a minimum.

Provincial words and meanings have been included if their use was not limited to one province. We have tried to list all proverbs and folk sayings that have come to our attention, many of them appearing several times with variant wordings. We have strengthened from special sources, and often with the help of specialists, the nautical and agricultural terms, musical terms, sports, Turkish grammatical forms, Persian and Arabic prefixes and suffixes, biological and botanical terms, medical and anatomical terms, philosophical, logical, and mathematical terms, slang and vulgarisms, historical terms (and especially terms from Ottoman history), religious and mystical terminology, and government and administrative terms both old and current. A special effort has been made to include all neologisms that have won any degree of acceptance.

The more common Turkish words are fully defined, not only as single words but in their contexts as phrases. Certain common words are therefore the subjects of extended articles. (See **baş, iç, iki, kara, ne, orta, su, şeytan, taş.**) In bringing the dictionary up to date all available sources have been used, including modern dictionaries as listed in the bibliography.

The editors have shared the concern of scholars that nothing of value should be dropped from the text of the old Redhouse dictionary. Perforce some entries have been omitted to make room for new material. It is hoped that the omitted words, nearly all Arabic or Persian words of rare or even merely hypothetical standing in Ottoman writing, will prove to be no loss. The texts where they might occur would be such that a scholar reading them would already have on his desk good Persian and Arabic dictionaries. A body of rare Turkish words has been carefully preserved, often on the sole authority of Redhouse himself, since he seems to have had informants and other sources no longer available to us.

This dictionary includes many features that are of interest chiefly to scholars. The indication of the old spellings in the Ottoman alphabet will be helpful especially to those reading old manuscripts or doing other research, and to linguists interested in distinctions preserved in the Ottoman and lost in the modern spellings. The publishers hope to produce, as a supplement to this dictionary, an abbreviated index of the Ottoman spellings for the convenience of such scholars.

Many of the words that are shown are no longer in common use. However the Turkish of today is given full attention, and a person may use this dictionary with confidence to help him choose the right English word or phrase to express his **thoughts.**

The publishers hope to produce in the near future a Shorter Redhouse Turkish-English Dictionary, retaining from this comprehensive dictionary only those materials that are in common use today.

Robert Avery

SIR JAMES REDHOUSE
(1811 - 1892)

Bu lûgate takaddüm eden 1890 tarihli Türkçe - İngilizce lûgat, Sir James Redhouse tarafından bütün bir ömür vakfedilerek meydana getirilmiştir. J. Redhouse Londra civarında doğmuş ve genç yaşında anne ve babasını kaybetmiştir. On beş yaşında iken Akdeniz'e müteveccihen gemiye binmiş ve İstanbul'a geldiği zaman Osmanlı Devletinin bir dairesinde desinatör olarak vazife almıştır.

Redhouse hemen Türkçe öğrenmeye koyulmuş ve Türkçe - İngilizce bir sözlük derlemeye başlamıştır. İstanbul'da sekiz yıl kaldıktan sonra Londra'ya dönmüş, baskıya verilmek üzere Türkçe - Fransızca - İngilizce bir sözlük hazırladığı sırada Bianchi'nin Türkçe - Fransızca lûgati intişar etmiştir. Bunun üzerine kendi lûgatinin neşrini geri bırakıp 1838'de Türkiye'ye dönmüş, önce Sadrıâzama sonra da Hariciye Nazırına mutemed tercüman olmuştur. Kendisinin bu görevi 1840'da Türk Bahriyesine nakledilmiştir. 1843'de İngiliz Sefarethanesi ile Osmanlı Devleti arasında mutemed bir irtibat tercümanı sıfatiyle on yıl süren görevine başlamıştır. Bu müddetin ilk kısmını 1847'ye kadar Erzurum'da geçirmiş, burada Türkiye ile İran arasında bir barış antlaşması ile nihayet bulan görüşmelere katılmıştır.

1853'de Redhouse, Türkiye'yi terkedip Londra'ya yerleşmiş, 1855'de «Osmanlıca Konuşma Dili Cep Kılavuzu = Vade Mecum of the Ottoman Colloquial Language» adlı, Kırım Savaşı vesilesiyle Türkiye'de bulunan İngiliz kara ve deniz birlikleri mensupları için kısa bir Türkçe el kitabı yayınlamıştır. 1856'da Londra'lı nâşir Quaritch Redhouse'dan hem İngilizce - Türkçe hem de Türkçe - İngilizce kısa bir sözlük hazırlamasını istemiştir. Kendisi 1880'de bu konu ile ilgili olarak şöyle demişti : «Eğer doğru hatırlıyorsam bu, dört veya beş aylık bir müddet zarfında tamamen yazılıp yayınlandı». Gerçekten bu sözlük tek bir ciltte birleştirilmiş olup İngilizce - Türkçe kısmının baş sahifesi 1856, Türkçe - İngilizce bölümününki ise 1857 tarihini taşımaktadır.

Redhouse, daha 1846'da Paris'de «Grammaire raisonnée de la langue ottomane» adlı eserini neşretmiş, bu arada Osmanlı Türkçesinde bileşik kelime teşkiline dair kaideleri de vermişti.

Türk halkının İngilizce eserlerden daha rahat bir surette faydalanarak neşriyat hazırlayabilmeleri için Türkiye'de oturan Amerikan misyonerlerine yardımda bulunmak maksadiyle, 1860 yılında Londra'da bir komite kurulmuş ve bu komite Redhouse'dan, İngilizce - Türkçe mufassal bir lûgat hazırlamasını istemişti. O sıralarda Londra'da oturan Newburyport (Massachusetts)'li bir Amerikalı olan William Wheelwright lûgatin derleme ve yayın masraflarını karşılamak üzere ikibin İngiliz lirası hibe etmişti. Redhouse da bu eserini sekiz aylık kesif çalışma neticesinde tamamladı. 1861'de yayınlanan kitap 47,000 İngilizce kelimenin Türkçe karşılığını vermekte idi. Bütün ilk baskı, neşir hakkı ve stereotip levhaları ile birlikte İstanbul'daki Amerikan Misyonu'na hibe edildi.

Yine o sıralarda Redhouse hayatının en büyük lûgatini hazırlama çabasına girişti. Osmanlı Türkçesi ile Arapça ve Farsçanın vokabüleri arasında belirli bir sınırın bulunmaması dolayısıyle, Osmanlı Türkçesinde eser kaleme alan bir müellifin bütün Arap ve Fars kelimelerini kullanabilmesi imkânını düşünerek — Kur'an'daki her kelimeyi, İran şairlerinden iktibasları ve bu üç dilden ata sözlerini de içine alan — Osmanlıca - Arapça - Farsça bir sözlüğü derlemeyi arzu etmekte idi.

1878'de Yakın - Doğu Misyon'undan Dr. E. E. Bliss Redhouse'u Londra'da ziyaret etti, dönüşünde de Neşriyat Dairesindeki yardımcıları ile görüştü. Neşriyat Dairesinin, daha mahdut sayıdaki Arap ve Fars kelimelerinden yalnız Osmanlıca ile yazılan eserlerde kullanılanlarını ihtiva edecek bir sözlüğü yayınlaması kararlaştırıldı; Redhouse, yeni şartlara uygun böyle bir müsveddeyi dört yıl içinde meydana getirdi. Kendisinin İstanbul'daki nâşirleri de derhal işe koyuldular; eserin tamamının takriben üçte birini teşkil eden ilk iki kısmı 1884'de yayınlandı. İngilizce «A Turkish and English Lexicon Shewing the English Significations of the Turkish Terms» ve Osmanlıca «Kitab-ı Maani-i Lehçe li-James Redhouse el-İngilizî» adındaki bu lûgatin tamamı ise on senelik bir tertip ve tashih çalışmasından sonra 1890'da neşredildi.

1890 baskısının önsözünde Redhouse şöyle demektedir : «... Bu eseri derlerken Bianchi'nin, Zenker'in ve Vefiq'in lûgatlerini rehber ittihaz ettim; bunlara ilâveten diğer menbalardan bir çok lüzûmlu kelime aldım, bazı hallerde Golius'a, Meninski'ye, Freytag'a, Lane'e ve ayni zamanda Calcutta Arapça Kamus'a, Kamusu Türki'ye, Farsça Kamus'a, Sihah yazmasına, Farsça Surah'ya, Vankulu'na, Şerefname'ye, Cihangiri'ye, Burhan'a, Şu'uri'ye, Reşidi'ye, Bahari-'Acem'e ve Giyas ül-Lûgat'e müracaat ettim, bu arada «Müntahabat-ı Lûgat-i Osmaniye» adlı tarafımca 1838 - 1841'de yazılmış olan bundan önceki kendi derlememi de unutmadım... Türkiye'den uzak kaldığım otuz yıl zarfında elimden gelen âzamî gayreti sarfettim ve bütün bu zaman içinde leksikografi ile meşgul oldum».

Hâlen British Museum'daki müsveddenin, muhtemelen her üç lisanın natamam fakat mufassal lûgatine ait olması muhtemeldir. 1890 baskısının müsveddesi İstanbul'da Redhouse Yayınevi'nde muhafaza edilmekte olup, gerek Redhouse'un ve gerek nâşirlerinin el yazıları ile yapılan tashihlerini ihtiva etmektedir.

Redhouse 1841'de Sultan'ın Nişanı İftihari ile taltif edildi. 1847'de de kendisine İran'ın Arslan ve Güneş Nişanı verildi. Cambridge Üniversitesi ise, Redhouse'a 1884'de Fahrî Edebiyat Doktorluğu pâyesini tevcih etti. Britanya İmparatorluğunun dış münasebetleri ile ilgili olarak Hanedana yaptığı hizmetlerine mükâfaten kendisine 1888 yılında Şövalye pâyesi verildi.

Sir James Redhouse 1892'de sekseninci yaş gününden hemen biraz sonra vefat etti.

SIR JAMES REDHOUSE

(1811 - 1892)

The Turkish-English dictionary of 1890 which lies behind this dictionary was the product of a lifetime of dedicated scholarship by Sir James Redhouse. He was born near London, and lost his parents while still young. At the age of fifteen he took ship for the Mediterranean, and when he reached Istanbul he got a job as a draftsman in an office of the Ottoman Government.

He set out immediately to learn Turkish, and began to compile a Turkish - English dictionary. After eight years in Istanbul he returned to London, and was preparing for the press a Turkish - French - English dictionary when the Turkish - French dictionary of Bianchi appeared. He postponed publication, and in 1838 returned to Turkey, where he became a confidential interpreter, first to the Grand Vizier, and afterwards to the Minister of Foreign Affairs. In 1840 he was transferred to the Turkish Admiralty. In 1843 he began a decade of service as the confidential medium of communication between the British Embassy and the Ottoman Government. The first part of this period, until 1847, he spent largely in Erzerum, where he participated in the negotiations that ended in a treaty of peace between Turkey and Persia.

He left Turkey in 1853 and settled in London. In 1855 he published a «Vade - Mecum of the Ottoman Colloquial Language», a simplified Turkish manual for members of the British army and navy units in Turkey at the time of the Crimean War. In 1856 the London publisher Quaritch asked him to prepare a short dictionary for both English - Turkish and Turkish - English. «If I remember rightly, it was written and published, complete, in about four or five months' time,» said Redhouse in 1880. This dictionary is in fact bound in one volume, with the date 1856 on the title page of the English - Turkish section, and 1857 on the title page of the Turkish - English.

Already in 1846 he had published in Paris his «Grammaire raisonée de la langue ottomane», giving among other things the rules for constructing compound words in Ottoman Turkish.

In 1860 a committee was formed in London for the purpose of assisting the American missionaries resident in Turkey to prepare publications that would make the resources of the English language more easily available to the Turkish people. The committee asked Redhouse to prepare an expanded dictionary from English to Turkish. An American who was then living in London, William Wheelwright of Newburyport, Massachusetts, donated two thousand pounds to cover the expenses of compiling and printing the work, and Redhouse finished it in eight months of intense labor. The book, which appeared in 1861, gáve the Turkish meanings of 47,000 English words. The whole first printing, together with the copyright and the stereotype plates, was donated to the American Board Mission Publication Department in Istanbul.

Meanwhile Redhouse was engaged in his greatest lexicographical endeavor. He recognised that the whole vocabulary of Arabic and of Persian was available to a writer of Ottoman Turkish, since there was no clear line dividing Ottoman Turkish from these languages; and he hoped to compile a complete dictionary of all three of the languages, including, for example, every word used in the Quran, as well as quotations from Persian poets, and proverbs in all three languages.

In 1878, Dr. E. E. Bliss of the American Board Mission in the Near East visited Redhouse in London, and on his return Bliss talked with his associates in the Publication Department. It was agreed that the Publication Department would publish a more limited dictionary, including only those parts of the Arabic and Persian vocabulary that had actually been used in Ottoman writing, and in four years Redhouse produced a manuscript according to the new specifications. His publishers in Istanbul began work immediately, and the first two sections, about a third of the total, appeared in 1884.

The complete dictionary appeared in 1890, after ten years of typesetting and proofreading. In English it was called «A Turkish and English Lexicon Shewing the English Significations of the Turkish Terms», and in Turkish, «Kitabı Maani-i Lehce li-James Redhouse el-İngilizi» :

In his preface of 1890, Redhouse says, «In compiling the present work, I have taken the vocabularies of Bianchi, Zenker, and Vefiq as my guides, adding many a necessary word from other sources, and occasionally consulting Golius, Meninski, Freytag, and Lane, as well as the Calcutta Arabic Qamus, the Turkish Qamus, a Persian Qamus, a manuscript Sihah, the Persian Surah, Vanqulu, the Sherefname, Jihangiri, Burhan, Shu'uri, Reshidi, the Bahari-'Ajem and the Giyasu-'l-lugat; not forgetting my own former compilation, entitled Muntakhamati-Lugati-Osmaniyye, written in 1838-41... I have done my best after an absence from Turkey of more than thirty years, during the whole of which I have been engaged in lexicography.»

The manuscript in the British Museum is presumably that of the incomplete but comprehensive dictionary of the three languages. The manuscript of the 1890 edition is preserved at the Redhouse Press in Istanbul, and shows emendations in the hand of Redhouse as well as of his editors.

Redhouse was awarded the Sultan's imperial order, the Nişanı İftihar, in 1841. In 1847 he was given the Persian order of the Lion and the Sun. Cambridge University gave him an honorary degree of Doctor of Letters in 1884. In 1888 he was made a Knight Commander of St. Michael and St. George, in recognition of services rendered to the (British) Crown in relation to the foreign affairs of the Empire. He died in 1892, soon after his eightieth birthday.

SEÇİLMİŞ BİBLİYOGRAFYA — SELECTED BIBLIOGRAPHY

Umumî Eserler — **General Works**

Ahterî (Mustafa bin Şemseddin-i Karahisarî): LÛGAT-İ AHTERÎ-İ CEDİD
480 s. Yer ve tarih gösterilmemiştir.

Bianchi, T. X. ve Kieffer, J. D.: ELSİNE-İ TÜRKİYE VE FRANSEVİYENİN LÜGATİ. DICTIONAIRE TURC-FRANÇAIS İki Cilt: xxx, 1097 ve 1320 s. 2. baskı Paris, 1850.

Heuser, Fritz: HEUSER-ŞEVKET TÜRKÇE VE ALMANCA LÛGAT
618 s. Wiesbaden, Harrassowitz, 3. baskı 1953.

Hony, H. C. TURKISH-ENGLISH DICTIONARY
xii + 419 s. Oxford, Clarendon Press, 2. baskı 1957.

Kadri, Hüseyin Kâzım: TÜRK LÛGATİ
4 cilt: xcix + 855, 982, 928, 894 s. İstanbul, Maarif Vekâleti, 1927-1945.

Meninski, Francisco à Mesgnien: LEXICON TURCICO-ARABICO-PERSICUM
3 cilt, 6079 s. Vienna, 1680.

Moran, A Vahid: TÜRKÇE-İNGİLİZCE SÖZLÜK, A TURKISH-ENGLISH DICTIONARY xv + 1462 s. İstanbul, Millî Eğitim Bakanlığı, 1945.

Naci, Muallim: LÛGAT-İ NACİ 960 s. İstanbul, Asır Matbaası, tarihsiz.

Özön, Mustafa Nihat: BÜYÜK OSMANLICA-TÜRKÇE SÖZLÜK
780 s. İstanbul, İnkılap Kitabevi, Genişletilmiş 3. Basım 1959.

Redhouse, James W.: KİTAB-I LEHCET ÜL-MAANİ Lİ-JAMES REDHOUSE EL-İNGİLİZÎ. A LEXICON, ENGLISH AND TURKISH.
ii + 12 + 827 s. Constantinople, American Mission 1861.

Redhouse, Sir James W.: KİTAB-I MAANİ-İ LEHCE Lİ-JAMES REDHOUSE EL-İNGİLİZÎ, A TURKISH AND ENGLISH LEXICON, SHEWING IN ENGLISH THE SIGNIFICATIONS OF THE TURKISH TERMS
viii + 2224 s. Constantinople, American Mission, 1890.

Sami, Şemseddin: KAMUS-İ TÜRKİ
1547 s. Der-Saadet, İkdam Matbaası, 1317 (1899).

Sami, Şemseddin: KAMUS EL-A'LAM
4 cild, 4830 s. İstanbul, Mihran Matbaası, 1306-1316 (1889-1898).

Türk Dil Kurumu: TÜRKÇE SÖZLÜK (Dördüncü Baskı)
xv + 808 s. İstanbul, Türk Tarih Kurumu Basımevi, 1966.

Vefik Paşa, Ahmed: LEHCE-İ OSMANİ, Tab'ı Cedid
2 cilt: 1455 s. Dersaadet, Mahmud Bey Matbaası, 1306 (1889).

Askerî — Military Terms

Ertung, Cemal : İNGİLİZCE-TÜRKÇE ASKERİ-TEKNİK LÛGAT
  80 s. İstanbul, Cemal Azmi Matbaası, 1947.

Bioloji, Botani — Biology and Botany

Ayaşlı, Sadullah : SALON ÇİÇEKLERİ ANSİKLOPEDİSİ
  68 s. + 123 resim. İstanbul, Aydın Matbaası, 1947.

Bedevian, Armenag K. : ILLUSTRATED POLYGLOTTIC DICTIONARY OF PLANT NAMES IN LATIN, ARABIC, ARMENIAN, ENGLISH, FRENCH, GERMAN, ITALIAN and TURKISH LANGUAGES. (NEBATAT LÛGATİ)
  XV 456 s. Cairo, Argus and Papazian Presses, 1936. (Yedi dilde indeksleri vardır. Ancak Türkçe terimler bazen bugünün nebatat mütehassısları tarafından kabul edilenlerden ayrıdır.)

Brauner, L. : NEBATLARIN METABOLİSMA FİZYOLOJİSİ
  VIII + 241 s. İstanbul, İstanbul Üniversitesi, 1939.

Devedjian, Karekin : PECHE ET PECHERIES EN TURQUIE
  169 s. Constantinople, Imprimerie de l'Administration de la Dette Publique Ottomane, 1926.

Ergene, Saadet : TÜRKİYE KUŞLARI (İstanbul Üniversitesi Fen Fakültesi Monografileri, Sayı 4)
  XX + 261 s. + 104 levha. İstanbul, İstanbul Üniversitesi Fen Fakültesi, 1945. (Tarif olunan bütün kuşların resimlerine ilâveten bu eserde indeksler vardır; indekslerden biri Lâtince, diğeri ise Türkçe isimlere dayanır).

Heilbronn, Alfred : İSPENÇİYARİ NEBATAT (PHARMAKOBOTANİK)
  XII + 182 s. İstanbul, İstanbul Üniversitesi, 1940.

Heilbronn, Alfred : NEBAT BİOLOGİSİ (BOTANİ) I Kısım
  145 s. İstanbul, İstanbul Üniversitesi, 1940.

Şerefeddin, Esad : NEBATAT-I SAYDALANİ. Tab-i Evvel.
  704 s. Der-Saadet, Matbaa-i Kader, 1328.

Denizcilik — Nautical Terms

Bapçum, İ. Etem : İNGİLİZCEDEN-TÜRKÇEYE DENİZCİLERE SÖZLÜK
  248 + IX s. İstanbul, İktisat Vekâleti Yüksek Deniz Ticareti Mektebi, 1938

Baran, Hayri : GEMİCİLİK
  VIII + 512 s. İstanbul, İktisat Vekâleti Yüksek Deniz Ticareti Mektebi, 1939

Nutki, (Süleyman) : ISTILÂHAT-I BAHRİYE
  100 levha. (İstanbul), Matbaa-i Bahriye, 1321.

Nutki, Süleyman : KAMUS-İ BAHRİ
  425 s. İstanbul, Matbaa-i Bahriye, 1333/1917

Thomson, William A. : HAND-BOOK OF NAUTICAL TERMS AND TECHNICAL AND COMMERCIAL PHRASES IN ENGLISH, ITALIAN, FRENCH AND TURKISH. (GEMİCİ TÂBİRLERİ, TEKNİK VE TİCARİ CÜMLELER KİTABI : İNGİLİZCE, İTALYANCA, FRANSIZCA VE TÜRKÇE)
  VII + 181 + X + 4 s. İstanbul, Osmanié Printing Works, 1892.

Felsefe   **Philosophy**

Çankı, Mustafa Namık : BÜYÜK FELSEFE LÛGATİ
    Cilt   I, VI + 792 s. İstanbul, Cumhuriyet Matbaası, 1954.
    »   II, 792 s. İstanbul, Aşıkoğlu Matbaası, 1955.
    »   III, 549 s. İstanbul, Nebioğlu Matbaacılık ve Kâğıtçılık Ltd. Ş.,1958.

Fennî, İsmail : FRANSIZCADAN TÜRKÇEYE LÛGATÇE-İ FELSEFE
    936 s. + VIII s. İstanbul, Matbaa-i Âmire, 1341

Tevfik, Rıza : MUFASSAL KAMUS-İ FELSEFE
    Cilt   I, 806 s.
    »   II, 400 s. İstanbul, Maarif-i Umumiye Nezareti, 1322/34

Tolun, Haydar : FELSEFE VOKABÜLERİ
    140 s. Bursa, Yeni Basımevi, 1934

Fen   **Science**

Arndt, Fritz : DENİZ KİMYA DERSLERİ I: UMUMİ VE ANORGANİK KISIM
    İkinci Bası 557 s. İstanbul, Üniversite Kitabevi, 1944

Arndt, Fritz ve Lütfi Ergener : DENEL ORGANİK KİMYA
    XX + 551 s. İstanbul, İstanbul Üniversitesi Yayınları, No. 329, 1947

Demiryollar Matbaası : FENNİ ISTILÂHAT LÛGATİ
    788 s. Haydarpaşa : Demiryollar Matbaası, 1928

Freundlich, E. Finlay ve W. Gleisberg : ASTRONOMİ
    11 + 480 s. İstanbul, İstanbul Üniversitesi, 1937

Milli Eğitim Bakanlığı : İLK VE ORTA ÖĞRETİM (FEN) TERİMLERİ, TÜRKÇE - OSMANLICA, OSMANLICA-TÜRKÇE, FRANSIZCA-TÜRKÇE
    Astronomi, 22 s. , 1939; Biyoloji 32 s. , 1937; Biyoloji, 55 s. , 1939; Botanik, 43 s. , 1937; Jeoloji, 37 s. , 1939; Kimya, 28 s. , 1939; Kimya Elemanları, 18 s. , 1937; Kimya, 42 s. , 1939; Matematik, 46 s. , 1937; Matematik, 57 s. , 1939; Mekanik, 13 s. , 1937; Zooloji, 25 s. , 1937; Zooloji, 20 s. , 1939.

Scipio, Lynn A. : ENGLISH-TURKISH TECHNICAL DICTIONARY (İNGİLİZCE - TÜRKÇE TEKNİK LÛGAT)
    224 s. İstanbul, Tsitouris Brothers, 1939

Tinghir, Ant. B. et Sinapian : FRANSIZCADAN TÜRKÇEYE ISTILÂHAT LÛGATI. DICTIONNAIRE FRANÇAIS - TURC DES TERMES TECHNIQUES DES SCIENCES, DES LETTRES ET DES ARTS.
    2 cilt : I, 423 s. II, 565 s. Constantinople, Imprimerie Lithographie K. Bagdadlian, 1891, 1892.

Güzel San'atlar   **Fine Arts**

Arseven Celâl Esad : FRANSIZCADAN TÜRKÇEYE VE TÜRKÇEDEN FRANSIZCAYA SAN'AT KAMUSU. DICTIONNAIRE DES TERMES d'ART FRANÇAIS - TURC, TURC - FRANÇAIS.
    269 - 60 s. İstanbul, Matbaa-i Amire, 1340 - 1349.

Arseven, Celâl Esad : FRANSIZCADAN TÜRKÇEYE SANAT LÛGATİ. DICTIONNAIRE d'ART FRANÇAIS - TURC.
185 s. Ankara : Alâaddin Kıral Basımevi, 1944.

Arseven, Celâl Esad : SANAT ANSİKLOPEDİSİ.
4 cilt : I, 592 s., İstanbul 1950 — Millî Eğitim Basımevi.
II, 593 - 1184 s. İstanbul 1947 — Millî Eğitim Basımevi.
III, 1185 - 1664 s. İstanbul 1950 — Millî Eğitim Basımevi
IV, 1665 - 2644 s. İstanbul 1952 — Millî Eğitim Basımevi.

Özbel, Kenan : EL SANATLARI I - XVI Kısımlar
C.H.P. Halkevleri Bürosu, Ankara — 1949.

Hukuk — Law

Agâh, Hüseyin : LÛGATÇE-İ ISTILÂHAT-I RESMİYE
73 s. İstanbul, Kitapçı Arakel, 1308.

Çubukçuoğlu, Zühtü : YENİ METNİ İLE ANAYASA VE YENİ KELİMELERİN İZAHLARI. 85 s. İstanbul, Kenan Matbaası, 1945.

Daniş, Hüseyin : FRANSIZCA - TÜRKÇE HUKUKİ VE MEDENİ LÛGAT
824 s. İstanbul, Kanaat Kütüphanesi, 1934.

Feyyaz, Celâl ve Feyzi Gürsel : HUKUK ISTILÂHLARI LÜGATİ (İkinci basılış).
400 s. İstanbul, Vakit Matbaası, 1943.

Galib, Hüseyin : KAMUS-İ HUKUK
269 s. İstanbul, Cemal Efendi Matbaası, 1305.

Millî Eğitim Bakanlığı : TÜRK HUKUK LÛGATİ
XV + 582 s. Ankara Maarif Vekilliği, 1944. (Tafsilâtlı hukuk terimlerini gösterir. Almanca, Fransızca, İngilizce ve Lâtince fihristleri vardır.)

Musiki — Music

Ataman, Mehmet Muhtar : MUSİKİ TARİHİ
373 s. Ankara, Millî Eğitim Bakanlığı, 1947.

İLERİ MUSİKİ MECMUASI. THE MUSIC MAGAZINE — Aylık Müzikoloji Dergisi
İstanbul, 1949 — 1968.

Tangor, Safa : MÜZİK
Cilt I, 64 s. İstanbul, Ahmet İhsan Basımevi Ltd., 1940.

Spor — Sports

Bükey, Kerim A. TENİS.
180 s. Ankara, Beden Terbiyesi Umum Müdürlüğü, Sayı 54, 1942.

Ergeneli, Nafiz ve Nuri Tuna : BEDEN TERBİYESİ MEVZUATI.
655 s. Ankara, Beden Terbiyesi Müdürlüğü, 1941.

Kodaman, Hulûsi : ZAR - KÂĞIT OYUNLARI VE HİLELERİ
262 s. İstanbul, Apa Yayınevi, 1944.

La Roux, Maxim (Çeviren : Tuna Baltacıoğlu) : ŞATRANÇ NASIL OYNANIR?
59 s. İstanbul, İkbal Kitabevi, 1946.

dent.	dentistry	dişçilik
dim.	diminutive	küçültme ismi
dip.	diplomacy	diplomasi
drivers' slang	drivers' slang	şoför argosu
drug.	druggist's term	eczacılık
E	English	İngilizce
econ.	economics	iktisad
e. g.	for example	meselâ
elec.	electricity	elektrik
embroidery	embroidery	el işleri
esp.	especially	bilhassa, özellikle
etc.	and so forth	ve saire
F	French	Fransızca
fam.	familiar	teklifsizce
fem.	feminine	müennes, dişil
fig.	figurative	mecazî
fin.	financial	malî
fine arts	fine arts	güzel sanatlar
folk.	folklore	halk bilgisi, folklor
forestry	forestry	ormancılık
furriery	furriery	kürkçülük
G	German	Almanca
geog.	geography	coğrafya
geol.	geology	jeoloji
geom.	geometry	hendese, geometri
Georgian	Georgian	Gürcü dilinde
Gk	Greek	Yunanca
gram.	grammar	gramer
gun.	gunnery	topçuluk
Heb	Hebrew	İbranice
hist.	history	tarih
histology	histology	histoloji, dokubilim
hort.	horticulture	bahçıvanlık, çiçekçilik
hum.	humorous	lâtife kabilinden, şaka
Hung	Hungarian	Macarca
i. e.	that is	yani
ins.	insurance	sigorta
intern.	international	milletlerarası
iron.	ironical	cinaslı, alay olarak
Isl. rel.	Islamic religion	İslâm dini
Ind	Indian	Hintçe
Ist.	Istanbul	İstanbul
It	Italian	İtalyanca
Jap	Japanese	Japonca
Jagatai	Jagatai	Çağatayca
jewelry	jewelry	kuyumculuk
joc.	jocular	şaka kabilinden
journ.	journalism	gazetecilik
L	Latin	Latince
law	law	hukuk

l. c.	lower case	küçük harf, miniskül
ling.	linguistics	dil bilgisi
lit.	literally	harfi harfine
literary	literary	edebî
literature	literature	edebiyat
logic	logic	mantık
lrnd.	learned	bugünkü halk dilinde kullanılmayan
mach.	machinery	makina işleri
Maliye term	Maliye term (term used in the Ottoman Ministry of Finance)	Maliye tâbiri
Malay	Malayan	Malezya dili
mar. com.	maritime commerce	deniz ticareti
mar. law	maritime law	deniz hukuku
math.	mathematics	matematik
mech.	mechanics	mihanik, mekanik
med.	medical	tıbbî
meteor.	meteorology	meteoroloji
mfg.	manufacturing	imalât
mil.	military	askerî
min.	mineralogy	mâdenler ilmi, mineraloji
mus.	music	musiki, müzik
myst.	mysticism	tasavvuf
myth.	mythology	mitoloji
n.	noun	isim
naut.	nautical	denizciliğe ait
neol.	neologism	yeni tâbir
num.	numismatics	sikkeler ilmi
obs.	obsolete	eski, kullanılmıyan
oft.	often	çok kere
onom.	onomancy	ismin harfleriyle fala bakmak
optics	optics	ışık kaideleri ilmi, optik
Or.	Oriental	Şark, Doğuya ait
Ott.	Ottoman	Osmanlı
P	Persian	Farsça
paint.	painting	resimcilik, ressamlık
pass.	passive (voice)	meçhul (edilgen) fiil
pathol.	pathology	hastalıklar ilmi, patoloji
ped.	pedagogy	çocuk terbiyesi, pedagoji
pharm.	pharmacology, pharmaceutics	eczacılık
phil.	philosophy	felsefe
phon.	phonetics	sesler ilmi, fonetik
phot.	photography	fotoğrafçılık
phys.	physics	fizik
physiol.	physiology	fizyoloji
pl.	plural	çoğul, cemi
poet.	poetic	şiirde kullanılan

poetry	poetry	şiir
pol.	politics	politika, siyaset
Pol	Polish	Leh dili
pop.	popular	halka mahsus
poss.	possessive	-in hali
print.	printing	matbaacılık
pros.	prosody	aruz, vezin tekniği
prov.	provincial	taşraya ait
psych.	psychology	psikoloji
Quranic	Quranic	Kur'an'a ait
rail.	railroad	demiryolu
refl.	reflexive (form)	dönüşlü fiil
rel.	religious	dinî
rhet.	rhetoric	retorik, belâgat ilmi
Romany	Romany	Çingene dili
Russ	Russian	Rusça
sc.	scientific	fennî
Serbo-Croatian	Serbo-Croatian	Sırb-Hırvat dili
sing.	singular	tekil, müfred
Sl	Slavic	Slav dili
soccer	soccer	futbol
sociol.	sociology	sosyoloji
Sp	Spanish	İspanyolca
sports	sports	spor
statistics	statistics	istatistik
stylistic	stylistic	üslûba ait
superl.	superlative	enüstünlük, tafdil
surg.	surgery	cerrahlık
T	Turkish	Türkçe
tailor.	tailoring	terzilik
tech.	technical	teknik
text.	textile	tekstil, dokumacılık
teleg.	telegraphy	telgrafçılık
theat.	theater	tiyatro
theol.	theology	ilâhiyat
U. S.	United States	Birleşik Devletler (Amerika)
usu.	usually	çok kere, ekseriyetle
var.	variant	başka türlüsü
verbal n.	verbal noun	mastar ismi, fiil ismi
vet.	veterinary	baytarlık
vulg.	vulgar	bayağı, âdi
w.	with	ile
wrestling	wrestling	güreş
zool.	zoology	zooloji

SÖZLÜĞÜN KULLANIŞ TARZI

1 — **Kelimelerin dizini:** Bütün kelimeler tek bir alfabetik dizin içinde verilmiştir. Filler ⇌**mek** ve ⇌**mak'**lar yazılmaksızın, köklerine göre sıralanmıştır. Herhangi bir madde içinde:

a) İlk olarak, kelimenin yalın haliyle karşılığı verilmiştir.

b) Türkçe veya İngilizcede bir tâbir olarak kullanıldığı hallerde, kelime hal ekleriyle birlikte gösterilmiştir.

c) Kelime, o kelime ile başlayan ibareler içinde, sonundaki hal ekleri dikkate alınmadan alfabetik sıraya tâbi tutularak gösterilmiştir.

d) Müştaklar, ayrı bir madde olarak alınmadıkları takdirde, alfabetik sıraya göre gösterilmişlerdir.

Şöyle ki:

    can   yalın halde kelime (a)

        candan   hal ekleri almış halde kelime (b)
        canım   hal ekleri almış halde kelime (b)
        can acısı   ibare içinde kelime (c)
        canını acıt⇌   ibare içinde kelime (c)
        canı ağzına gel⇌ ibare içinde kelime (c)

    dikiş

        dikişçi   esas kelime (a)
        dikişli   müştak (d)
        dikişsiz   müştak (d)

2 — **Bileşik kelimeler:** İbare olarak da kullanılabilen bileşik kelimeler umumiyetle ibare şeklinde gösterilmişlerdir, başka bir deyimle, bu gibi ibareler ilk kelimelerin altında madde-altı olarak verilmiştir.

Bazen bir bileşik kelime madde-başında kendi yerinde gösterilmiş ve ilk elemanının altında madde-altı olarak yazılan bu bileşik kelimeye asterisk işaretiyle bir atıf yapılmıştır.

Şöyle ki:

dikiz kelimesinin altında:

    dikiz aynası (Burada mânâ madde-altı olarak verilmiştir.)

ak kelimesinin altında :

    ak alem (Burada mânâ madde - altı olarak verilmiştir.)
    ak altın
    ak yol

kara kelimesinin altında :

    kara ağaç* (Bu bileşik kelimenin mânâsı, **kara** kelimesinin altında verilmeyip, asterisk, okuyucunun **karaağaç** maddesine müracaatını sağlar.)
    kara baş* (**karabaş** şeklinde müstakil bir madde olduğunu gösterir.)

3 — **Çekim halleri** : Sesli harf ile başlıyan bir ek ile teşkil edilmiş bir çekim hali, bazen kelimenin yalın halinden istidlâl edilemez. Bu gibi hallerde bir müphemiyet olduğu zaman, çekim hali kelimenin üstünde küçük punto yazıyla gösterilmiştir. Bu şekli okumak için asıl kelimenin son harfini atıp, küçük punto yazıdaki harfleri onun yerine koymak gerekir. Bazen, küçük punto ile yazılan ek'i esas kelime ile birleşmeden evvel, esas kelimenin birden fazla harfini atmak icap eder; bu değişikliklerin anlaşılması güç değildir.

Şöyle ki :

kavuk^{ğu} kavuk, kavuğu, kavuğa, kelimelerinin yerini tutar.
makbul^{lü} makbul, makbulü, makbule, kelimelerinin yerini tutar.
çekiç^{ci} Çekiç, çekici, çekice kelimelerinin yerini tutar.
mevzu^{uu} mevzu, mevzuu, mevzua, kelimelerinin yerini tutar.
şükür^{krü} şükür, şükrü, şükre, kelimelerinin yerini tutar.
kabahat^{ti} kabahat, kabahati, kabahate, kelimelerinin yerini tutar.

Fiillerin geniş zamanları, fiil köklerinin üzerine yapılan ufak punto harflerle gösterilmiştir. Kaide dışı hallerde, bir önceki sessiz harf de belirtilmiştir.

Şöyle ki :

kon= ^{ar} konmak ve konar kelimelerinin yerini tutar.
git= ^{der} gitmek ve gider kelimelerinin yerini tutar.
kal= ^{ır} kalmak ve kalır kelimelerinin yerini tutar.
gel= ^{ir} gelmek ve gelir kelimelerinin yerini tutar.
koşuş= ^{ur} koşuşmak ve koşuşur kelimelerinin yerini tutar.
düşür= ^{ür} düşürmek ve düşürür kelimelerinin yerini tutar.

4 — **Vokal Uzunluğu ve Vurgu** : Türkçe menşeli kelimeler umumiyetle kısa vokallere ve son hecede vurguya sahiptirler. Arapça veya Farsçadan alınan kelimelerin çoğu zaman bir veya birden fazla uzun vokalleri vardır. Bu gibi kelimelerde uzun vokaller çizği (—), kısa vokaller ise nokta (.) ile gösterilmiştir. Yine aynı şekilde, mutad Türkçe telâffuzların haricindeki vurgular bir kesme işareti (') ile belirtilmiştir.

Şöyle ki :

âdi (— —) iki uzun vokal.
zaten (—'.) bir vurgulu uzun, bir kısa vokal.
hazine (.—.) ikincisi uzun olan üç vokal.

Birçok kelimeler Türkçe ile kaynaşırken vokal uzunluğu bakımından değişikliklere uğramışlardır. Aslında mevcut olan **hemze** ve **ayn'ı** kaybeden kelimeler, bu farkı bazen uzun bir vokal ile telâfi etmişlerdir.

Şöyle ki :

Aslında **Cum'a** (..), sonradan **Cuma** (.—)
me'mur (.—), sonradan **memur** (—.)
şu'be (..), sonradan **şube** (—.)

Aynı şekilde, uzun vokaller zamanla kısalmıştır.

Şöyle ki :

Aslen **kitab** (.—) sonradan **kitap** (..)
Aslen **mal** (—) sonradan **mal** (.)

Bu cereyan hâlen devam etmekte olup, imlâda muhafaza edilmeyen farklar, telâffuzda da ortadan kaybolmaktadır.

Memur (.—) çoğu zaman (..) olarak telâffuz edilmektedir.
Tedbir (.—) de çoğu zaman (..) olarak telâffuz edilmektedir.

Umumiyetle, bu lûgatta sadece, iyice yerleşmiş vokal uzunluğu değişiklikleri kaydedilmiştir.

5 — Osmanlıca İmlâ : Osmanlıcayı yazmak için ufak değişikliklerle Arap alfabesi kullanılmıştır. Bu alfabenin yerini, 1928 yılında bugünkü Türk alfabesi almıştır. Lûgat, kelimelerinin 1928'den evvel kullanılan Osmanlıca imlâlarını göstermektedir. Arap ve Fars menşeli kelimelerin eski harflerde, umumiyetle tek bir doğru imlâ şekli bulunmaktadır. Birçok Türkçe ve Avrupa menşeli kelimelerin ise birden fazla yazılış şekli mevcut olup, bunlardan sadece en çok geçenleri gösterilmekle iktifa edilmiştir. Nâşirler, gelecekte, eski harflerle herhangi bir kitap veya elyazmasını tetkik edecek bir kimsenin bu lûgattaki kelimelere kolayca müracaatını sağlayacak kısaltılmış bir Osmanlıca imlâ indeksi yayınlamayı ümit etmektedirler.

6 — Tümleçler : Bu sözlükte eğik iki çizgi arasındaki harfler, fiillerin tümleçlerinin çekim hallerini gösterir.

Şöyle ki :

karış= /la/ : suyla karıştı; /a/ bu işe karışma.
çekin= /dan/ : ondan çekindim; günahtan çekinsinler.
işle= /ı/ : demiri işlediler.
kadar /a/ : ona kadar; duvara kadar.

7 — Kelimelerin menşeleri :

a) Kelimenin Türkçeye girdiği lisanı (kelimenin ilk menşei olmıyabilir) gösteren bir harf veya kısaltma ile,

b) Köşeli parantez içine alınan ve okuyucuya kelimenin menşeini daha iyi tanıtan diğer bir maddeye atfedici bir kelime ile, veya

c) Yine köşeli parantez içine alınan kelimenin Arapça veya Farsça şekli ile belirtilmiştir.

Şöyle ki:

mevlûd A Arapçadan alınmış.
rekor F Fransızcadan alınmış (Fransızca'ya İngilizceden girmiştir).
ikametgâh P Farsçadan alınmış, (Arapça bir kelimeden teşkil edilmiş olduğu halde).
hamam [hammam] kelimenin asla daha yakın şekli olan **hammam**'dan alınmış.
gurk [Persian **kurg**] Farsçadan değiştirilerek alınmış.

Türkçe menşeli, veya menşei meçhul, veya Türkçe takılarla meydana getirilmiş kelimelerin menşeleri gösterilmemiştir.

Şöyle ki:

Kayısı, hamamcı, ferahlık kelimelerinin menşeleri gösterilmemiştir.

8 — **Tasnifler** : Maddelerin çoğu, kelimelerin kullanılışına ve muayyen bir mânânın tatbik sahasına göre tasnife tâbi tutulmuştur. Belli başlı tasnif grupları, kısaltmalar cetvelinde verilmiş olup, kendi kendini izah eder mahiyettedir.

«Lrnd.» olarak tavsif edilen ve «learned» kelimesinin yerini tutan grup, bugün konuşulan Türkçe'de artık kullanılmıyan Osmanlıca kelime, şekil veya mânâları göstermek için verilmiştir. Bu kategoriye dahil olan bazı kelimeleri klâsik bir tahsile sahip kimseler hemen anlıyacaktır. Diğer bazıları ise, kullanılışları itibariyle o kadar nâdir ve muayyen sahalara münhasırdırlar ki, bugün hayatta olan herhangi bir kimsenin, bu gibi kelimelerin mânâlarını bulmak için bir lûgate müracaat etmesi icap eder.

9 — **Tarifler** : Tarifler, kelimenin esas mânâsı çoğu zaman başa alınmak suretiyle numaralanmıştır. Tek bir tarif içinde farklı mânâlar, birbirlerinden noktalı virgül, hemen hemen aynı mânaya gelen izahlar ise virgül ile ayrılmıştır.

10 — **Söz bölükleri** : Türkçe kelimeler, Lâtin gramerinin bölünüşlerine uymamaktadır. Sıfatlar rahatlıkla isim olarak (meselâ : büyüklerimiz), isimler sıfat olarak (demir boru), fiil kipleri sıfat olarak (gelecek sene) ve isim olarak (dükkânın geliri) kullanılır. Bu itibarla, lûgatte söz bölükleri gösterilmemiş, ancak kelimelerin (İngilizce karşılıklarının verilmesiyle), kullanılması caiz olan nevileri belirtilmiştir.

Bu lûgat, Redhouse'un Arapça fiil isimlerini bir harfi tarif ekliyerek ve gerundium olarak İngilizceye tercüme etme geleneğini devam ettirmektedir.

Şöyle ki:

te'lif a composing
istirham an asking for mercy

Bu tarz, mutad İngilizce üslûbuna göre pek de kullanışlı olmamakla beraber, kelimeyi tam olarak tarif etmek ve kelimeyi kendi muhtevası içinde tercüme etmek için en isabetli İngilizce fiili öne sürer.

11 — **İşaretler**: Lûgatte aşağıdaki işaretler kullanılmıştır :

—— **uzun çizgi**: Madde-başı kelimesinin yerini tutar ve madde-altlarında aynı kelimenin tekrarını önler.

Şöyle ki :

masraf
    ——ı çek= masrafı çekmek
    —— et= masraf etmek.

— **kısa çizgi** : bir önek veya sonek'i gösterir.

Şöyle ki :

—lar, —amiz, —kes   sonekler
bi—, ma—, na—   önekler.

= **eşit işareti** : Bu işaret bir fiil kök veya gövdesinin sonuna, bir fiil çekim ekinin başına ve kelime ortasına gelen bazı eklerin hem başına, hem de sonuna gelir.

Şöyle ki : **yap=**, **yaptıştırıl=**, **affet=** fiil görevleri.

=ıl=, =dır=, =n= fiilin ortasına gelen ekler.
=sin, =sınız, =dınız fiil çekim ekleri.

* **Asterisk** : okuyucuyu maddenin tek bir kelime ve alfabetik sıra içinde ait olduğu yerde ayrı bir madde halinde bulunduğu yere sevkeder.

Şöyle ki : **hoş**
    —— **beş*** : hoşbeş olarak asıl alfabetik sırasında bulunur.

12 — **Yanlışlar ve imlâ değişiklikleri** : Tereddüt veya dikkatsizlik neticesinde sözlükte yanlış ve imlâ değişikliklerinin mevcut olduğunun farkındayız. Bunların bazıları, şimdiden dikkatimizi çekmiş olup müteakip bir baskıda düzeltilmelerine çalışılacaktır. Meselâ : 1094 üncü sahifede «surprised» kelimesi, «surprized» olarak çıkmıştır. Sahife 417'deki «gusulhane» kelimesinin Osmanlıcasında fazla bir vav vardır. Sözlüğün son maddesi ise, bilinmeyen bir sebeple kelimenin menşei gösterilmeden basılmıştır.

Bazı şekillerde, dilin günlük kullanılışı müsaade ettiği nispette imlâ değişikliklerine müsamaha ettik. Şöyle ki : —**at** ile —**ât**, —**ane** ile—**âne** ,—**iyet** (..) ile —**iyet** (şeddeli) (—.) arasında belirli bir tercih yapmadık.

Bütün sözlük boyunca, mümkün olduğu kadar modern İngilizce imlâsına ve bilhassa Amerikan usullerine uyan bir imlâya sadık kalmaya çalıştık. Bununla beraber, yer yer Redhouse'tan alınmış olan eski yahut da, bilhassa İngiltere'de kullanılan bir imlâ şekli muhafaza edilmiş olabilir.

Bir kısım özel isimlerde Redhouse'tan ayrıldık; meselâ «Moslem» yerine «Muslim», «Qur'an» yerine «Quran» kelimelerini tercih ettik. Bazı Türkçe kelimelerin İngilizceleştirilmiş şekillerini doğrudan doğruya birer İngilizce kelime olarak kabul ettik; meselâ : **Ramazan, kadi, hodja** gibi. Okuyucu, eğer ilmî bir yayın hazırlıyacak olursa, milletlerarası transkripsiyon sistemini tatbik edebilir.

HOW TO USE THE DICTIONARY

1. Word order: All of the words are entered in one alphabetical order. Verbs are entered by their stems, without ═mek or ═mak. Within any main entry:

a) the simple word is defined first;

b) the word is shown with endings if there is an idiomatic usage in the Turkish or the English;

c) the word is shown in phrases that start with the word, arranged alphabetically without regard to endings on the main word;

d) any derivatives are shown, in their alphabetical order, unless they are separately treated as main words.

Thus :

can	simple word. (a)
candan	word with endings. (b)
canım	word with endings. (b)
can acısı	word in a phase. (c)
canını acıt═	word in a phase. (c)
canı ağzına gel═	word in a phase. (c)

dikiş

dikişçi	derivatives (d)
dikişli	
dikişsiz	

2. Compound words that can also be written as phrases are usually defined as phrases, that is, they are a subentry under the first word of the phrase. Occasionally a compound word is listed in its own place in the main entries, and a cross-reference is made to it as a subentry under the first element, with an asterisk mark.

Thus :

Under **dikiz,**
      dikiz aynası. (Defined as a subword in this place.)

Under **ak**
      ak alem (Defined as subwords in this place.)
      ak altın

Under **kara**

> **kara ağaç*** (This word is not defined as a subword of **kara**, but the asterisk refers the reader to the main entry **karaağaç**.)
>
> **kara baş*** (Defined as a main entry in the form **karabaş**.)

3. **Inflected forms**: An inflected word form constructed with an ending that begins with a vowel is sometimes impossible to deduce from the nominative. If there is any ambiguity about an inflected form, the inflected form is abbreviated in superscript. To read the form, drop the last letter of the original word, and substitute the letters of the superscript. Occasionally it is necessary to drop more than one letter of the original before adding the superscript ending, but these cases are self-evident.

Thus:

> **kavuk**[ğu] represents **kavuk, kavuğu, kavuğa**.
> **makbul**[lü] represents **makbul, makbulü, makbule**.
> **çekiç**[ci] represents **çekiç, çekici, çekice**.
> **mevzu**[uu] represents **mevzu, mevzuu, mevzua**.
> **şükür**[krü] represents **şükür, şükrü, şükre**.
> **kabahat**[ti] represents **kabahat, kabahati, kabahate**.

For verbs, the aorist is indicated in superscript letters. If there is any irregularity, the preceding consonant is also shown.

Thus:

> **kon=**[ar] represents **konmak, konar**.
> **git=**[der] represents **gitmek, gider**.
> **kal=**[ır] represents **kalmak, kalır**.
> **gel=**[ir] represents **gelmek, gelir**.
> **koşuş=**[ur] represents **koşuşmak, koşuşur**.
> **düşür=**[ür] represents **düşürmek, düşürür**.

4. **Vowel length and stress**: Words of Turkish origin usually have only short vowels and have a final stress accent. Words taken from Arabic or Persian often have one or more long vowels. For such words the long vowels are indicated by dashes and the short vowels by dots. Likewise, stress accents different from the regular Turkish pattern are indicated by an accent mark.

Thus:

> **âdi** (— —) has two long vowels.
> **zaten** (— .) has a long stressed first vowel and a short second vowel.
> **hazine** (. — .) has three vowels, and the second one is long.

Many words have undergone changes in vowel length as words have become assimilated into Turkish. Words that have lost original **hemza** or **'ain** have sometimes compensated by lengthening the associated vowel.

Thus:

> original **Cum'a** (..), more recent **Cuma** (. —)
> **me'mur** (. —), **memur** (— .)
> **şu'be** (..) **şube** (—˙.)

Also, long vowels are eventually shortened.

Thus:

    original **kitab** (.—), has become **kitap** (..)
    mal (—) has become **mal** (.)

This process is still going on, as distinctions no longer preserved in the spelling are being lost in the pronunciation.

Thus:

    memur (.—) is often heard as (..)
    tedbir (.—) is often heard as (..)

In general only well-established shifts in vowel length have been recorded in this dictionary.

5. **Ottoman spellings**: The Arabic alphabet, slightly modified, was used for writing Ottoman Turkish. This alphabet was replaced in 1928 by the present Turkish alphabet. The dictionary shows the Ottoman spellings of words that were in use before 1928. Words from Arabic and Persian generally have only one correct spelling in the old letters. Many Turkish and European words have more than one spelling; only the more common variants are shown. The publishers hope eventually to produce an abbreviated index to the Ottoman spellings, so that a person reading a book or manuscript in the old script may conveniently refer to the words in this dictionary.

6. **Complements**: In this dictionary the letters between slant lines indicate the case or cases in which the complements of a verb or postposition would appear.

Thus:

    karış= /la/ suyla karıştı; /a/ bu işe karışma
    çekin= /dan/ : ondan çekindim; günahtan çekinsinler.
    işle= /ı/ : demiri işlediler.
    kadar /a/ : ona kadar; duvara kadar.

7. **Derivations**: Derivations are indicated:

    a) By a letter or abbreviation showing the language from which the word came into Turkish (not the language of ultimate origin);

    b) By a word in brackets, referring the reader to another entry showing a more original form of the word;

    c) By a word in brackets that is labeled as being the Arabic or Persian form of the word.

Thus:

    mevlûd A taken from the Arabic.
    rekor F taken from the French (which had taken it from English).
    ikametgâh P taken from the Persian (although built on an Arabic word).
    hamam [hammam] derived from the more original **hammam**.
    gurk [Persian kurg] taken with alterations from the Persian.

Derivations are not shown for pure Turkish words, nor when the derivation is unknown, nor for words assimilated by adding Turkish suffixes.

Thus : **kayısı, hamamcı, ferahlık** are given without derivations.

8. Categories : For most words a category is given, showing the range of use of the word, or the range of application of a particular meaning. The common categories are listed with the table of abbreviations, and are self-explanatory.

The category «lrnd.», standing for the word «learned», is used to label Ottoman words, forms, or meanings that have not survived into modern spoken Turkish. Some words so labelled would be recognised by a person with a classical education. Others are so rare or specialized in their use that almost anybody now living would need to consult a dictionary to find their meaning.

9. Definitions: Definitions are numbered, usually with the primary meaning of the word first. Within a single definition related meanings are separated by semicolons, and nearly synonymous meanings are separated by commas.

10. Parts of speech : Turkish words do not fit neatly into Latin grammatical categories. Adjectives are used freely as nouns (**büyüklerimiz**), nouns as adjectives (**demir boru**), verbal forms as adjectives (**gelecek sene**) and as nouns (**dükkânın geliri**). Therefore there is no designation of parts of speech, but the range of permissible usage is indicated by the listing of the English equivalents.

This dictionary continues the practice of Redhouse in translating Arabic verbal nouns by the English gerund with an article.

Thus :

    telif a composing.
    istirham an asking for mercy.

This usage, while awkward in English, defines the word exactly, and suggests the most likely English verb to translate the word in its context.

11. Conventional signs : The following conventional signs have been used :

— **long dash :** stands for the main entry word, instead of repeating it for subentries.

Thus :

    masraf
        ——ı çek=   **masrafı çekmek.**
        —— et=   **masraf etmek.**

— **short dash :** indicates a prefix or suffix.

Thus :

    —**lar**, —**amız**, —**kes** suffixes.
    bi—, **ma**—, **na**— prefix.

= **equal sign :** This sign comes at the end of a verb root or stem, at the beginning of a verbal ending, and both before and after a verbal infix.

Thus :

    yap=, yapıştırıl=, affet= verbal stems
    =ıl=, =dır= verbal infixes
    =sın, =sınız, =dınız verbal endings

*   **asterisk** : refers the reader to the phrase written as a single word and shown as a main entry in its own place in the alphabetical order.

Thus :

    hoş
    —— **beş*** : look for **hoş beş** as a main word : **hoşbeş**.

12. **Errors and variations** : We are conscious that through hesitation or oversight errors and variations have appeared in the dictionary. A few of these have already come to our attention, and we will try to correct these and any others in a later edition. For example, on page 1094 the word «surprised» appears as «surprized». On page 417, the Ottoman spelling for **gusulhane** has an extra «vav». And the last entry in the dictionary is unaccountably left without a derivation.

We have allowed free variation in certain orthographical forms when the common usage of the language allows such variation. Thus we have made no consistent choice between —at and —ât, between —ane and —âne, between —iyet (..) and —iyet (with şedde) (—.)

The intention has been to use modern spellings throughout and to prefer American spellings to British. However an occasional spelling from Redhouse may preserve an older or a British form.

On some proper names we have modified the usage of Redhouse, preferring for example «Muslim» to «Moslem», and «Quran» to «Qur'an». We have accepted Anglicised versions of some Turkish forms as proper English words, as for example : Ramazan, kadi, hodja. The reader will make the necessary adjustments if he is preparing a scientific publication using an international transcription system.

REDHOUSE

YENİ
TÜRKÇE - İNGİLİZCE SÖZLÜK
NEW
REDHOUSE
TURKISH - ENGLISH DICTIONARY

A

a, A 1 *first letter of the alphabet.*
a 2 آ 1. *before noun, vocative in reproachful tone, e. g.,* **a efendim!** oh, my good sir! **a canım!** my dear! 2. *at end of sentence, confirms a retort or a remark, e. g.,* **geldim a!** Haven't I come, then!
a 3, **e** *after 2nd person conditional, imperative with impatient tone, e. g.,* **baksan a!** look here, then! **gelseniz e!** come, then!
a 4 (—) آ oh!
—a 5, **—e** • *A feminine (after emphatic consonants* **—a,** *otherwise* **—e,** *as in* **maşuka, Cemile.).**
—a 6 ا [**an** 6, **—en** 3] *adverb as in* **mutlaka.**
—a 7, **—e,** *after vowel* **—ya** 2, **—ye** 2 • ـه *dative* to, toward, on to, into, *e. g.,* **adama** to the man, **geline** to the bride, **masaya** to (on, on to, upon) the table, **testiye** into the pitcher.
=a 8, **=e,** *after vowel* **=ya** 3, **=ye** 3 • ـه *archaic, third person optative* he should, he may, *still used in expressions as* **hayrola, kolay gele.**
=a 9, **=e,** *after vowel* **=ya** 4, **=ye** 4 • ـه *adverb, used in expressions as* **güle oynaya, kala, ortaklaşa, diye.** *Gemination has reiterative or frequentative meaning, e. g.,* **vura vura** hitting again and again, **uyuya uyuya** sleeping overmuch, constantly sleeping, **güle güle** ever laughing.
[**aa—** *cf.* **ea—** .]
aah *colloq.* no!
âb 1 (—) آب P *lrnd.* 1. water; fluid; river; source, fountain; sap, juice; sap and soul of the universe; tears; sweat; urine; semen; broth; wine, drunkenness. 2. freshness, luxuriousness, vigor; grace, charm; radiance; dignified

look; sense of honor; virtue; chastity; excellence, rank, dignity; glory, fame; value; prosperity; health; splendor; polish, shine (of metal); luster, glitter; temper (of steel); diamond; precious stone; pearl; crystal; glass; mirror; sword, knife, dagger; mercury. 3. mercy, compassion, pity. 4. way, road; fashion, mode, rule, habit. **—ı âbistenî** 1. semen. 2. rain. 3. water for irrigation. **—ı ahmer** *poet.* 1. red wine. 2. tears of blood. **—u ateş** *poet.* calmness and anger, sedateness and vivacity of any kind. **—ı ateşin, —ı ateşmizaç, —ı ateşnâk, —ı ateşnüma, —ı ateşpare, —ı ateşreng, —ı ateşzede, —ı azerâsa, —ı azersa** *poet.* 1. wine. 2. hot tears. **—ı badereng** *poet.* tears of blood. **—ı baka** *poet.* water of life. **—ı baran** *poet.* rain, rain water. **—ı beste** *poet.* 1. ice; snow; hoarfrost; hail. 2. crystal; glass. 3. cold steel; sword, knife, dagger. **—ı ciger** *poet.* tears. **—ı cigerhun** *poet.* tears of grief. **—ı çeşm** *poet.* tears. **—u dane** *poet.* man's daily bread. **—ı dehan, —ı dehen** *lrnd.* 1. saliva, slaver, slobber. **—ı dendan** *lrnd.* 1. beauty of the teeth. 2. spittle. 3. thing spat out. **—ı dide** *poet.* 1. tears. 2. modest look. **—ı dide-i çeşm** *poet.* tears of the goblet, wine. **—ı efsürde** *lrnd.* 1. frozen water; ice; snow; hail. 2. jelly. 3. crystal; glass. 4. cold steel; sword, knife, dagger. **—ı engûr** *poet.* 1. grape-juice; must. 2. wine. **—ı erguvani** *poet.* 1. red wine. 2. tears of blood. **—ı eyyam** *poet.* 1. beauty of the days or time. 2. sunshine. **—ı füsürde** *var. of* **abı efsürde. —ı gerdende** *poet.* sphere, firmament, sky, heavens. **—ı germ** *lrnd.* 1. hot or warm water. 2. hot bath. 3. hot spring. **—u gil** *lrnd.* 1. the terraqueous globe. 2. the mortal body, the human frame. **—ı gure** *poet.* juice of unripe grapes. **—ı gûşt** *lrnd.* gravy, broth. **—ı harabat** *poet.* wine. **—ı haram** *lrnd.* the forbidden drink, wine. **—ı hasret** *poet.* tears of longing. **—ı hatır** *lrnd.* vigor of intellect, beauty of imagination. **—u hava** *lrnd.* climate. **—ı hayvan** *poet. same as* **abıhayat**. **—ı hazan** *poet.* autumnal rain. **—ı Hızır** water of life. **—ı hufte** *lrnd.* 1. stagnant water. 2. congealed water; ice, snow, hail, hoarfrost. 3. crystal, glass, goblet, bottle. 4. cold steel, sword, etc. in its scabbard. **—ı hurdenî** *lrnd.* drinking water. **—ı hurşid** *poet.* 1. sunlight. 2. fountain of life. **—ı huşk** *poet.* crystal, glass, cup, goblet, bottle. **—ı işret** *poet.* wine. **—ı kâr** *lrnd.* success, prosperity. **—ı kebud** *poet.* the Azure water, the China Sea, inhabited by mermaids. **—ı Kevser** the river Kevser (Kawthar) of Paradise, flowing with wine or nectar. **—ı küşade** *poet.* poor weak wine. **—ı la'li** *poet.* 1. wine. 2. tears. **—ı lûtf** (*lit.*, rain of kindness) *poet.* bounty, beneficence, benevolence. **—ı mervarid** *lrnd.* 1. luster of a pearl. 2. cataract of the eye. **—ı Meryem** 1. the purity, chastity, and holiness of the Virgin Mary. 2. grape must. 3. wine. **—ı meygûn** *poet.* 1. wine, tears. **—ı müncemid** *poet.* 1. frozen water; ice, snow, hail, hoarfrost. 2. crystal, glass; goblet, bottle. 3. sword, knife, dagger. **—ı nafi'** *poet.* red wine. **—ı nar** *poet.* red wine. **—ı nardan** *poet.* 1. juice of wild pomegranate. 2. red wine. 3. blood. 4. tears. **—ı nebat** *lrnd.* sap, juice, or luxuriance of a plant. **—ı neşat** *lrnd.* semen. **—ı puhte** *lrnd.* 1. boiled water. 2. broth. 3. jelly. **—u reng** *poet.* 1. freshness, beautiful skin (of a pretty face). 2. water and verdant beauty (of land). 3. beauty of style (in writing). 4. cosmetic paint, carmine, etc. **—ı rengin** *poet.* 1. colored water. 2. colored juice. 3. wine. 4. tears. **—ı revan** *lrnd.* running water. **—ı rez, —ı rezan** *poet.* wine. **A—ı Ruknabad** brook near Shiraz. **—ı siyah** *poet.* 1. the Deluge. 2. wine. 3. *med.* amourosia (disease producing blindness). **—ı sürh** *poet.* wine. **—ı şakayık** *poet.* 1. wine. 2. blood. **—ı şengerfi** *poet.* 1.wine. 2. tears. **—ı şirin** *lrnd.* water slightly sweetened as a drink. **—ı şor** *poet.* 1. salty, brackish, or hard water. 2. tears. **—u tab** *poet.* luster and sheen. **—ı tarab** *poet.* wine. **—ı telh** *poet.* 1. bitter water. 2. wine. 3. tears. **—ı yakut** *poet.* red wine. **—ı zehre** *poet.* 1. wine. 2. the light of dawn. **A—ı Zenderud** Zenderud (river of Ispahan). **—ı zer** *lrnd.* 1. goldwater, gold solution, gold leaf rubbed up with gum and used for gilding. 2. *poet.* golden-colored wine. **—ı zerd** *poet.* bitter tears of grief. **—ı zih** *poet.* tears. **—ı zindegânî, —ı zindegî** *poet.* water of life. **—ı zirkâh** *lrnd.* 1. water concealed by straws, which flows unperceived. 2. concealed or unacknowledged talent or merit. 3. intriguer, hypocrite. 4. intrigue; dissimulation, hypocrisy, and mischief. **—ı zülâl** *poet.* 1. pure, clear, sweet, fresh water. 2. crystal, glass.

âb 2 (—) آب *lrnd.* August (month).

aba 1 عبا آبا [**abâ 2**] 1. stout coarse woolen cloth. 2. cloak or coat made of such cloth. **— altından değnek göster**= to use an iron hand in a velvet glove. **— kebe** rough clothes. **— potur** baggy breeches of coarse cloth. **— terlik** slippers made of coarse cloth. **—yı yak**= *colloq.* to fall desperately in love.

abâ 2 (.—) عبا A *lrnd., same as* **aba 1.**

aba 3 آبا *prov.* 1. elder sister. 2. aunt.

aba= 4 آبا *prov.* to reject.

âba 5 (——) آبا A [*pl. of* **eb**] *lrnd.* 1. fathers. 2. male ancestors, forefathers. 3. *ancient astr.* spheres, the nine heavens; the seven celestial bodies (five planets and the sun and moon). **— ve ecdat, — vü ecdad** fathers and grandfathers, progenitors. **—yi mâneviye** spiritual fathers, moral guides. **—yi ulviye** the sublime fathers, the spheres, the planets.

abacı عبادى [*from* **aba 1**] maker or seller of coarse woolen cloth or garments. **— kebeci, sen neci?** *colloq.* Where do you come in? What concern is this of yours?

âbâd 1 (——) آباد A *lrnd.* [*pl. of* **ebed**] future eternities.

âbad 2 (——) آباد P *lrnd.* 1. prosperous, flourishing (place or person). 2. *when attached to name of a person forms a place-name*, e. g., Sultanabad. **— et**= to build up, to make prosperous, to develop (a site).

âbadan (———) آبادان P *lrnd.* prosperous, flourishing. **—î** (————) P, **—lık** 1. prosperity. 2. inhabited or cultivated place.

âbadi 1 (———) آبادى P kind of much valued yellowish glazed paper.

âbadi 2 (———) آبادى P *lrnd.* prosperity.

Abadile (.—..) عبادل A [*pl. of* **Abdullah**] *Isl. hist.* the 220 companions of the Prophet Muhammad who bore the name Abdullah.

abaî (.——) عبائى P *lrnd.* 1. made of homespun woolen cloth. 2. horse-cloth of homespun woolen.

abajur آباژور F 1. lamp-shade. 2. roller blind. **—cu** maker or seller of lampshades. **—lu** having a lampshade. **—luk** suitable for making lampshades (material).

abaka اباقا *prov.* uncle (father's brother).

abalı عبالى [**aba 1**] 1. wearing a homespun cloak. 2. poor, wretched. **—ya vur!** attack the weak.

aban= 1 آبانش /a/ 1. to lean forward

(against a person or thing), to push with the weight of one's body. 2. *slang* to live at someone's expense.
aban 2 (— —) آبان P *lrnd*. 1. eighth solar month of the Persian year, October. 2. tenth day of every month of the Persian solar year. 3. genius presiding over that day or month.
abandır=ᴵʳ آبانديرمك /ı,a/ *caus. of* **aban**= 1.
abanıkᵏᴵ *neol., ling.* consonant.
abani (— — —) آبانى fine cotton material embroidered with yellow silk, used for turbans.
abanla=ᴵʳ آبانلامق *prov.* to stride, pace out, measure by pacing.
abanos آبانوس [abnus] *var. of* **abanoz**.
abanosiye آبانوسيه [abnusiye] *bot., Ebenaceae*.
abanoz آبانوز [abnus] ebony. — **ağacı** ebony tree. — **gibi** black as ebony. — **kesil**= to become as hard as ebony. — **yürekli** hardhearted. — **cu** seller or worker of ebony. —**giller** *neol.; bot., Ebenaceae*.
abapuş (. — —) اباپوش P *lrnd*. 1. clad in homespun cloth. 2. poor.
abart=ᴵʳ آبارمق /ı/ *prov.* to exaggerate.
abaşo آباشو It *naut.* lower. — **babafingo** lower topgallant. — **gabya yelkeni** lower topsail.
âbatᵈᴵ آبات *var. of* **âbad** 1, 2.
abaza آبازه 1. Abkhasia. 2. Abkhasian. — **keçisi** domestic goat with long straight horns and long straight hair. —**ya var**= to practise selfabuse, masturbation. —**ca** Abkhasian (language).
abazan آبازان [habazan] *slang* craving, desperately hungry (sexual desire, etc.) —**lık** hunger, craving, libido.
abazi آبازى F *med.* abasia.
abbakᵏᴵ آبباق *prov.* extremely white.
Abbas 1 (. —) عباس A *man's name*. — **yolcu** One cannot detain someone who has to go.
abbas 2 (. —) عباس A *lrnd*. 1. habitually stern or frowning. 2. lion.
Abbasi (. — —) عباسى A Abbasid. —**yan**, —**yun** (. — — —) P *lrnd., pl.*
abbaz (— —) آب باز P *lrnd*. performer in the water, show-diver. —**î** (— — —) P aquatic sports, swimming, show-diving.
abdᵈᴵ عبد *same as* **abit** 2. —**i âciz**, —**i ahkar**, —**i kın** *can. law* slave whose parents are slaves. —**i me'zun** *can. law* slave who is allowed to trade so as to buy his own freedom.
abdal آبدال [ebdal] 1. degree in some dervish orders. 2. members of a semi-nomadic tribe in Anatolia and Central Asia who make their living by playing music at weddings, etc. 3. *same as* **aptal**.
abdan (— —) آبدان P *lrnd*. 1. vessel for water. 2. watering pot. 3. pond, tank, reservoir.

abdar (— —) آبدار P *lrnd*. 1. full of water. 2. juicy, succulent. 3. in full sap, green and luxuriant (plant). 4. lustrous, brilliant. 5. well-tempered (sword, etc.), polished, keen. 6. in good circumstances of body or estate (a man). 7. beautiful, graceful. 8. agreeable, pleasant.
abdendan (— . —) آبدندان P *lrnd*. 1. fool, dupe, sucker, easily plucked. 2. kind of delicious pear. 3. kind of pomegranate. 4. kind of sweet.
abdest (— .) آبدست P *same as* **aptes**.
abdestan, abdestdan (— . — —) آبدستان آبدستدان P *lrnd*. ewer for ablutions.
Abdi 1 عبدى *man's name, short for* **Abdullah** or any other name beginning with **Abd**-.
abdi 2 (. —) عبدى A *lrnd*. pertaining to slaves, servile.
abdiâciz (. . — .) عبد عاجز P your humble servant.
abdiahkar (. . — —) عبد احقر P *lrnd*. your humble servant.
abdih (— .) آبده P *lrnd*. giver of grace, beauty and luster; ornament. —**i dest** one who graces the chief seat in an assembly; *esp.*, the Prophet Muhammad.
abdiyet (. . — .) عبديت A *lrnd*. servitude, bondage, slavery.
Abdo, Abdulᵘᴵ عبدو عبدال *man's name* (short for Abdullah or any other name beginning with **abd**-.)
Abdullah عبدالله A (*lit.*, God's servant) *man's name*.
Abdurrahman (. . . —) عبدالرحمن A *man's name*.
abdülaziz (. . . —) عبدالعزيز A 1. *w. cap.*, *man's name, esp. of the Ottoman Sultan Abdulaziz*, 1861-69. 2. *var. of* **abdülleziz**.
abdülbatn عبدالبطن A *lrnd*. a slave to his belly, glutton.
abdülleziz (. . . —) عبداللذيذ [habbül'aziz] earth almond.
abdüsselâm (. . . —) عبدالسلام [yebruhussanem] mandrake, *bot., Mandragora officinarum*.
abdüsselâtin (. . . —) عبدالسلاطين [habbüsselâtin] croton tiglium seeds.
abe آبه [a 2, be 2] *prov.* hey!
abede • عبد A *lrnd., pl. of* **âbid** 1.
âbekᵏᴵ (— .) آبك P *lrnd*. 1. rivulet. 2. mercury.
abendam (— . —) آب اندام P *lrnd*. graceful of figure.
Aber 1 (— .) عابر A Heber (the great-grandson of Noah).
aberasyon آبراسيون F *astr.* aberration. — **elipsi** aberrational ellipse. — **sabiti** constant of aberration.
aberat (. . —) عبرات A *lrnd., pl. of* **abre**.

abes عبث A 1. vain, useless; futility. 2. absurd, unreasonable; nonsense, absurdity. 3. *lrnd.* an occupying oneself uselessly. — **söyle=** to talk rubbish, to talk when no good result can be looked for. —**le uğraş=** to exert oneself in vain. — **yere** in vain, to no purpose.

Abese عبس A *name of the 80th Sura of the Quran.*

abesen ('..) عبثاً A *lrnd.* fruitlessly, in vain.

abgâh (——) آبگاه P *lrnd.* 1. pond, water tank. 2. the side between the ribs and hip, the hypochondriac region of the abdomen.

abgine (——.) آبگینه P. *lrnd.* 1. rock-crystal. 2. glass. 3. diamond. 4. vessel of crystal or glass. 5. sword, knife, dagger. 6. tears. 7. lover's heart.

abgir (——) آبگیر P *lrnd.* 1. hollow place where water collects, pool, pond, ditch. 2. weaver's brush for sprinkling the yarn in the loom.

abgûn (——) آبگون P *lrnd.* 1. waterlike. 2. water-colored, azure. 3. sky. 4. bright (sword-blade, etc.). 5. starch (of wheat, rice, etc.).

abhane (——.) آبخانه P *lrnd.* water closet, privy, urinal.

abher عبهر A *lrnd.* 1. narcissus, jonquil. 2. jasmine. 3. cock'scomb, *bot.*, *Celosia cristate.* 4. plump and tender person or thing. —**î** (..—) P like narcissus; pertaining to the narcissus.

abhiz (——) آبخیز P *lrnd.* 1. sudden flow of water, flash flood, inundation. 2. spring of water. 3. land where springs are found. 4. canal, aqueduct, conduit.

abhur (——.) آبخور P *lrnd.* 1. water-drinker. 2. food and water, meat and drink; daily bread. 3. lot, destiny. 4. vessel for drinking water. 5. watering place.

âbhurd (——.) آبخورد P *lrnd.* 1. one who has drunk water. 2. short stay, halt for refreshment. 3. *same as* **abhur**[2-5].

âbhurde (——..) آبخورده P *lrnd.* 1. who has drunk water. 2. irritated, swollen and inflamed as result of contact with water (wound, sore).

âbhust (——.) آبخست P *lrnd.* 1. marshy island in a river. 2. channel excavated by water; rivulet. 3. cucumber, watermelon.

abıca *obs.*, *var. of* **amca**.

âbıhayat (——..—) آب حیات P 1. water of life. 2. elixir. 3. liquor, raki. — **içmiş** healthy and young-looking in spite of advanced age.

abık[kı] 1 آبیق *prov.* cryptorchid.

abık[kı] 2 (——.) آبق A *lrnd.* fugitive, runaway, absconding (slave).

âbıru (——.—) آبرو [**âbru**] *poet.* 1. radiance of the face, gracefulness, beauty. 2. honor, glory, celebrity; honest pride. 3. modesty, shame. — **dök=** to implore humbly, to humiliate oneself in a servile manner.

abi 1 آبی *Ist. slang for* **ağabey**, elder brother.

âbi 2 (——) آبی A *lrnd.* who refuses compliance, will not do or take (something).

âbî 3 (——) آبی P *lrnd.* 1. pertaining to water, aqueous, aquatic. 2. light blue, sky-blue. 3. quince. 4. variety of grape.

âbid 1 (—.) عابد *cf.* **âbit** 1.

âbid 2 (—.) آبد A *lrnd.* 1. permanent, perpetual; eternal.

âbid 3 (.—) عبید A *lrnd.*, *pl. of* **abd**.

âbidane 1 (—..—.) عابدانه P *lrnd.* devoutly, as a servant of God; devout (action).

abîdane 2 (.—..—.) عبیدانه P *lrnd.* humbly, devotedly; humble (service, etc.).

âbide 1 (—..) آبده [based on **âbid** 2] monument, memorial; edifice.

âbide 2 (—..) عابده A *lrnd.*, *fem. of* **âbid** 1.

âbidevi (—..—) آبدوی [**âbide** 1] monumental.

=abil=, **=ebil=**, *after vowel* **=yabil=**, **=yebil=** to be able to, *e. g.*, **okuyabilirim** I can read.

âbile (—..) آبله P *lrnd.* 1. pustule, pimple. 2. a little blister. 3. bubble (on water or wine). —**i ruh-i felek** (*lit.*, pimple on the cheek of the sky) *poet.* star.

âbir 1 (—.) عابر A *lrnd.* 1. that passes, goes, travels along. 2. that crosses, passes over. 3. weeping. 4. *Arabic gram.* past, perfect, preterite tense.

abîr 2 (.—) عبیر A *lrnd.* perfume and salve made of saffron, musk, ambergris, and perfumed oils. —**i nebatî** natural ambergris. —**fişan** (.—.—) P fragrant. —**şemim** (.—.—) P odoriferous. —**te'sir** (.—.—) P sweet-smelling, fragrant as ambergris.

abis F *sc.* abyss (of the sea). —**al** abyssal, bottomless.

âbist (—.) آبست , **âbistan** (—.—) آبستان , **âbiste** (—..) آبسته P *poet.* pregnant, with child, with young.

âbisten (—..) آبستن P *lrnd.* pregnant. —**i feryadhân** (*lit.*, the groaning pregnant one) the sighing harp or lute. —**gâh** (—..—) P 1. womb, vagina. 2. *poet.* the word. 3. lying in chamber. 4. place of concealment. 5. privy. —**î** (—..—) P pregnancy.

âbişhur (—..) آبشخور P *lrnd.* 1. watering place, drinking place. 2. drinking-vessel. 3. daily bread, food. 4. short halt or stay for refreshment. 5. lot, destiny.

âbit[di] 1. (—.) عابد [**âbid** 1] 1. servant. 2. worshipper. 3. devotee.

abit[bdi] 2 عبد [**abd**] 1. servant. 2. *law* slave. 3. worshipper; human being.

âbkâr (— —) آبکار P *poet.* 1. water-carrier, water bearer. 2. cup-bearer. 3. vintner; wine-seller. 4. wine-drinker.
abkarî (..—) عفری A (*lit.*, pertaining to fairyland) *lrnd.* 1. wonderful, fine, beautiful. 2. rich carpet. 3. mere lie.
Abkasî (..—) عفسی A *hist.* pertaining to the Arabian tribe of Abdulqais.
âbkend (—.) آبکند P *lrnd.* 1. dry, hollow channel scooped out by a rush of water; watercourse. 2. hollow worn by water; pond.
âbkeş (—.) آبکش P *lrnd.* 1. water-drawer. 2. water-carrier. 3. cup-bearer. 4. wine-drinker.
abla آبلا 1. elder sister (also used in addressing respectfully girl or woman, *esp.*, of older age). 2. *obs.* fore-woman (of female slaves in a family). 3. *pop.* (a man's own) wife. 4. *prov.* lesbian. **—cı** *prov.* lesbian.
ablak[kı] آبلق [eblak] round, chubby (face). **— çehreli, — yüzlü** chubby-faced.
ablalık[ğı] آبلالق the condition and quality of being an older sister, elder sistership. **— et=** /a/ to behave like an elder sister (toward someone).
abli آبلی Gk *naut.* gaff-balancer rope of a trysail, vang. **—yi bırak=, —yi kaçır=** *pop.* to lose one's self control, to be perplexed, to get confused.
abluka (..'.) آبلوقه It blockade. **—ya al=** /ı/ to subject to a blockade. **—yı boz=** to break the blockade. **— et=** /ı/ to blockade. **—yı feshet=** to discontinue the blockade. **— filosu** blockading squadron. **— hattı** line of blockade. **— ilânı** declaration of blockade. **— kaçağı** blockade-runner. **—yı kaldır=** to raise the blockade. **—yı yar=** to run the blockade.
âbnak[kı] (— —) آبناک P *lrnd.* 1. watery, wet. 2. juicy, sappy.
abnus (— —) آبنوس P *lrnd.* ebony. **—î** (— — —) P 1. of ebony. 2. like ebony, ebon, black. 2. seller or worker of ebony. **—iye** (— — —.) *bot., Ebenaceae.*
abone آبونه F 1. subscriber. 2. subscription. 3. subscription fee. **— bedeli, — ücreti** subscription fee. **—yi kes=** to cancel one's subscription. **— ol=** /a/ to subscribe (to). **— şeraiti** terms of subscription. **—yi yenile=** to renew one's subscription. **—lik** state and condition of being a subscriber.
aboniman آبونمان F 1. subscription. 2. season ticket. **— sigortası** *insurance* floating policy.
aborda (..'.) آبوردا It *naut.* alongside! **— et=, — ol=** /a/ to go alongside (another ship, pier, etc.).
abortif آبورتیف F *med.* abortive.
abortus (..'.) آبورتوس L *med.* abortion.
abosa (..'.) آبوصه It *naut.* avast! **— et=** *slang* to stop, to halt.

abr عبر A *lrnd.* 1. a going along or across. 2. an interpretation of a dream. 3. consideration, examination. 4. a shedding tears; grieving, mourning.
abra 1 آبرا *prov.* tare.
abra= 2 آبرامق *prov.* to manage, steer (*esp.*, a boat or ship).
âbrah (— —), **âbrahe** (— —.) آبراه آبراهه P *lrnd.* canal, conduit, aqueduct, pipe of water.
abrân (.—) عبران A *lrnd.* weeping, tearful, mourning.
abraş آبراش [ebreş] 1. speckled, dappled, piebald (horse). 2. having colorless spots (face, leaf). 3. leprous. **—lık** leprosy.
abraz آبراز *prov.* sterile-born (cattle).
abre عبره A *poet.* tear.
âbreside (—.—.) آبرسیده P *lrnd.* damaged by water.
abrık[ğı] آبرق *prov.* leaning over.
abrıl= آبرلمق *prov.* to lean over.
Abril آبریل Gk *prov.* April.
abrile آبریله It *naut.* clew up the main-sail! clew up the fore-sail!
âbriz (— —) آبریز P *lrnd.* 1. ewer, water-jug, pitcher; watering-pot. 2. bucket. 3. sink, sewer, cesspool. 4. privy, urinal. 5. chamber pot.
âbru, âbruy (— —) آبرو آبروی P same as âbıru.
abs عبس A *lrnd.* looking cross, frowning, sternness of countenance.
âbsalan (— — —) آبسالان P *lrnd.* garden, park.
abse آبسه *var.* of **apse**.
absent آبسنت *var.* of **apsent**.
âbseyr (—.) آبسیر P *lrnd.* easy-paced, smooth-paced (saddle beast).
absid آبسید F *arch.* apse.
absorbe آبسوربه F *sc.* absorbed. **— et=** to absorb.
absorpsyon آبسورپسیون F *sc.* absorption.
abstre آبستره F *phil.* abstract.
âbsuvaran (—.— —) آب سواران P *poet.* (*lit.*, water riders) bubbles floating on water or wine.
âbşar (— —) آبشار P *lrnd.* waterfall, cascade.
âbşinas (—.—) آب شناس P *lrnd.* 1. water diviner. 2. one who distinguishes the qualities of water. 3. pilot, one who knows the shallows, etc. 4. one who knows ways and rules.
âbtab 1 (— —) آبتاب P *poet.* 1. splendor. 2. the sun. 3. daylight, daytime. 4. wine. 5. the universal soul.
âbtab 2 (— —) آبتاب P *poet.*, same as **âbu tab.**
âbtabe (— —.) آبتابه P *lrnd.* 1. pot for pouring water; ewer. 2. kettle.

abu آبو *prov.* ah!, oh!
abukat[ıı] آبوكات *prov., var. of* **avukat**.
abuksabuk[ğu] آبوقہ صابون *colloq.* nonsensical, incoherent (talk). — **konuş**=, — **söyle**= to talk nonsense.
abula et=[der] آبولا ایتمك *slang* to rob (a person) by sudden attack.
abuli آبولی F *psychiatry* abulia.
abullabut[du] آبوللابوط *colloq.* boorish; dunce. —**luk** boorishness.
aburcubur آبورجبور 1. a variety of food eaten haphazardly. 2. haphazard, confused, incongruous.
abus (. —) عبوس A 1. cross-looking, grim, frowning. 2. evil, distressing (day).
abusülvech (. —..) عبوس الوجه A *lrnd.* grim faced, sour faced, stern looking.
Abuzettin Bey ابوزالدین بك *slang* dandy.
[abü- see under abu-]
âbverz (—.) آب ورز P *lrnd.* swimmer.
âbyar (— —) آبیار P *lrnd.* waterer, irrigator. —**î** (— — —) P 1. occupation of an irrigator; irrigation, watering. 2. *fig.* help. —**ii himmetinizle** with your kind help.
âbzih (—.) آبژه P *poet.* 1. rivulet or trickle into a stream. 2. water flowing from a corner of the eye.
ac 1 *cf.* **aç 1**.
âc 2 آج P *lrnd.* tamarisk.
âc 3 (—) عاج A *lrnd.* 1. ivory. 2. beautiful teeth. 3. tortoise shell.
acaba (. ..) عجبا A 1. *in a question* I wonder if. 2. oh indeed!
acâc (. —) عجاج A *lrnd.* 1. flying dust. 2. rising smoke. 3. fools.
=**acağı** آجغی *cf.* =**acak**.
=**acağım,** =**eceğim,** *after vowels* =**yacağım,** =**yeceğin** =**ecek** (*pl.* =**acağınız,** =**eceğiniz**) *colloq.* future second person you will.
acaib (. —) عجائب A [*pl. of* **acîbe**] *lrnd.* 1. strange things, wonders. 2. *cf.* **acayip**. —**i seb'a** the Seven Wonders of the World.
acaibat[ıı] (. —. —) عجائبات A *lrnd. pl. of* **acaib**. — **tuzu** *colloq.* sodium sulfate.
acaibî (. —. —) عجائبی [**acaib**] *obs.* short jacket.
acaiz (. —.) عجائز A *pl. of* **acuz, acuze**.
=**acak**[ğı], =**ecek**[ği], *after vowel* =**yacak**[ğı], =**yecek**[ği] جمی ایمش ه مجك 1. future or intentional participle going to, *e. g.,* **çalışacağım** I am going to work, I shall work, **gelmeyeceksiniz** you are not going to come, you will not come, **oturacak değilim** I don't intend to sit, **geçecekti** he was going to pass, **acınacak hal** pitiable condition, **çalışacak adam** the man who is going to work, who will work, who may

work, who has to work, who is willing to work. 2. *particiğle indicating purpose* to, *e. g.,* **gidecek yer** a place to go, **kesecek bıçak** a knife to cut, **okuyacak kitap** a book to read. 3. *with personal suffix, future infinitive* that I (you, he, etc.) will, *e. g.,* **Kalacağınız doğru mu?** Is it true that you will stay? **Gideceğimizi söyledik.** We said that we would go. 4. *with personal suffix and dative suffix instead of, e. g.,* **Ayıplıyacağınıza kendiniz yapın.** Instead of finding faults, do it yourself. **Bekleyeceğime kalkıp gideyim.** Instead of waiting, I had better go.
âcal[lı] (— —) آجال A *lrnd., pl. of* **ecel**.
A'câm (. —) اعجام A *lrnd., pl. of* **Acem 2**.
acar 1 آجار [*Arabic* a'cer] *prov.* 1. clever, cunning. 2. bold, fearless. 3. hardy, plucky. 4. new.
âcar 2 (— — —) آجار A *lrnd., pl. of* **ecr**.
Acaride (. —. —.) عجارده A *name of an ancient Muslim sect*.
acayip[bi] عجایب [**acaib**] 1. strange, queer, curious. 2. how strange!, curious!, how odd! —**lik** strangeness, queerness, oddity.
a'câz (. —) اعجاز A *lrnd., pl. of* **aciz 3** 1. posterior parts of the body, buttocks. 2. trunks of trees. 3. *pros.* second hemistichs of couplets; last feet of second hemistichs; last words in rhyming prose.
a'ceb 1 عجب ا A *lrnd.* most wonderful, very marvelous.
aceb 2 عجب A *lrnd.* 1. wonder, astonishment. 2. wonder, marvel. 3. surprising, astonishing. — **acîb** a strange thing, marvelous, wonderful.
aceb 3 عجب [**aceb 2**] *var. of* **acep**.
acebülacaib, a'cebülacaib (. —. . —.) عجب العجائب A *lrnd.* wonder of wonders, marvel of marvels.
acelacayip عجب العجائب [**acebülacaib**] *pop.* very odd, strange, queer.
acele عجله A 1. hurry, haste, undue haste, precipitancy. 2. urgent. 3. hasty, hurried (action). 4. in haste, in a hurry, urgently, hastily. —**ye boğ**= /ı/ to use haste to cloud the issue. — **et**= to make haste, to be in a hurry. —**ye gel**= to be done in a hurry and therefore carelessly. —**ye getir**= /ı/ to profit from another's need for haste. — **ile** in a hurry, hastily. — **işe şeytan karışır** *proverb* Great haste makes waste. —**si var** urgent. —**si yok** there is no hurry about it, not urgent. —**ci** who is always in a hurry, hustler, impatient. —**cilik** the habit of hurrying, hastiness.
aceleten (. ...) عجلة A *lrnd.* hastily, hurriedly.

Acem 1 |Acem 2| 1. a Persian. 2. *pop.* non-Persian native of Iran, *esp.*, a Shiite Turk from Azerbaijan. — **çapkını** *obs.* horse for hire to ride around town. — **gömleği** kind of shirt. — **halısı** Persian carpet. — **kaması** straight, broad, double-edged dagger. — **kılıcı** two-edged sword. — **kılıcı gibi iki tarafa kes=** to be a double-dealer, double-faced. — **kösteği** *Or. bookbinding* a fine piece of leather used to fasten the cover on the back of the book. — **külâhı** Persian black lambskin cap. — **mübalağası** excessive exaggeration. — **pilâvı** rice stewed with meat.

Acem 2 A *lrnd.* the non-Arabs, the non-Arabic speaking nations, *esp.*, the Persians.

acem 3 [Acem 1] *Or. mus.* 1. the note f". 2. a **makam** starting with f" and ending with a'.

a'cem 4 A *lrnd.*, 1. speaking Arabic incorrectly, barbarous, foreigner. 2. dumb, speechless, mute.

acemaşiran (...— —) *Or. mus.* 1. the note f'. 2. a **makam** starting with f" and ending with f'.

acembuselik[ġi] (..—..) *Or. mus.* a **makam** combining **acem** and **buselik**.

acemice (..'.) [Acem 1] in Persian; Persian; the Persian language.

acemi 1 [acemi 2] untrained, inexperienced, raw; novice; recruit. — **ağa** *hist.* title given to a rank of eunuchs serving in the Sultan's Harem. — **Arap** an untaught negro slave. — **beygir** gelding in training or not broken in. — **çaylak** *colloq.* clumsy, awkward person. — **çaylak bu kadar uçar** (*lit.* That is how an untaught kite can fly.) That's all you can expect from a clumsy fellow. — **efrad** recruits. — **er** recruit. — **erat** recruits. — **nefer** recruit. — **oğlan** *Ott. hist.* a conscript boy selected and brought up, later to join the Janissaries.

acemi 2 (..—) A. *lrnd.* 1. a barbarous speaker of Arabic. 2. foreign to the Arabs, barbarian. 3. a Persian.

a'cemî 3 (..—) A 1. who does not speak Arabic well. 2. not in good Arabic.

acemice (..—'.) [acemi 1] clumsily, awkwardly, ineptly.

acemilik[ġi] (..—.) lack of experience, awkwardness, clumsiness. — **çek=** to suffer from inexperience.

Acemistan (...—) P *pop.* Persia.

acemkürdî (...—) *Or. mus.* **makam** starting like **acem**, then using b' instead of b' (seğah), and ending on a'.

acenta, acente (..'.) It *com.* 1. agent, representative. 2. agency. — **muavini** subagent. —**lık**, —**lik** *com.* agency.

acep [aceb 3] I wonder!

Acer (—.) A Hagar (the mother of Ishmael).

a'cez A *lrnd.*, *superl.* of **âciz 1.**

acezan (..—) A *lrnd.* inability.

aceze A *lrnd.*, *pl.* of **âciz 1.**

acı 1 1. bitter, acrid; rancid, sour; gone off; turned (butter). 2. brackish, hard, salt, briny (water). 3. biting, tart, pungent, sharp, hot (pepper, etc.). 4. painful, heart-rending, pitiable, dismal. 5. reproachful, scathing, harsh, acrimonious, caustic. — **acı** bitterly, sarcastically; sharply, hard. — **ağaç***. — **çiğdem** meadow saffron, *bot., Colchicum autumnale.* — **dil** bitter words, reproaches. — **hâtıra** sad, painful memory. — **kahve** coffee made with little sugar. — **marul***. — **patlıcanı kırağı çalmaz** *proverb* (*lit.* The bitter egg-plant does not get frost-bitten.) A worthless vessel does not get broken. — **pelin***. — **renk** lurid color. — **ses** sharp noise; heart-rending cry. — **soğan, kuru ekmek** reduced to bread and raw onions, in very poor circumstances. — **soğuk** bitter cold. — **söyle=** to tell the painful truth unsparingly. — **söz** hard words, reproaches, complaints. — **su** hard, brackish water; *joc.* wine. — **şikâyet** bitter complaint. — **yonca***.

acı 2 1. pain, ache, smart. 2. grief, sorrow. — **acıyı, su sancıyı (bastırır)** *proverb* One fire burns out another's burning; one's pain is lessened by another's anguish. — **çek=** to be in pain, to suffer. —**sını çek=** /ın/ to suffer for something, to pay the penalty of an action. —**sını çıkar=** /ın/ to compensate oneself for (something), to take revenge for (something). — **görmüş** gone through suffering. —**yı tatmıyan tatlıyı anlıyamaz** *proverb* He who has not tasted bitterness cannot completely appreciate happiness. —**sı tepemden çıktı** it hurt terribly, I nearly passed out. — **yitimi** *neol., path.* analgesia.

acı=' 3 1. to hurt, to give pain, to feel sore, to ache. 2. /a/ to pity, to feel compassion for, to grudge (a thing), to feel sorrow for (its loss or waste). 4. to become bitter; to become rancid (butter, oil).

acıağaç[cı] bitter wood, quassia.

acıbadem (..—.) 1. bitter almonds. 2. *slang* cunning, shrewd, hardboiled. 3. *w. cap., name of a quarter near Kadıköy, Istanbul.* — **badem kurabiyesi** macaroon, almond cooky.

acıbakla 1. tonka bean. 2. lupine. 3. horse bean, tick bean.

acıca somewhat bitter, bitterish.

acıçaça آجی باجا kind of fish.

acıdülekᵗⁱ آجی دولك squirting cucumber, *bot.*, *Ecballium.*

acıelma آجی الما bitter purging apple, colocynth.

acıgıcı آجی گیجی *prov.* sorrel, *bot.*, *Rumex acetosa.*

acıhıyar آجی خیار 1. bitter cucumber, colocynth. 2. squirting cucumber.

acılgın آجی یلغنه bitter tamarisk, *bot. Tamaris orientalis.*

acıkᵗⁱ 1 آجیق آجی *prov.* 1. grief, sorrow, mourning. 2. anger, rage. —ı **tut**= to get angry, to become furious.

acıkᵗⁱ 2 آجیق [azıcık] *pop.* a little, a wee bit.

acık=ⁱʳ 3 آجیقمق to feel hungry. —**tım** I am hungry.

acıklan=ⁱʳ آجیقلنمق to grow sad, to become mournful.

acıklı آجیقلی 1. touching, pathetic, sad, tragic. 2. who has experienced much grief. — **komedi** tragicomedy.

acıksın=ⁱʳ آجیقسنمق *prov.* to be troubled, to feel sorry.

acıktır=ⁱʳ آجیقدرمق /ı/ to make hungry, to give a keen appetite.

acılan=ⁱʳ, **acılaş**=ⁱʳ آجیلانمق آجیلاشمق 1. to turn sour or rancid. 2. to become irritated, to grow angry, to get annoyed.

acılat=ⁱʳ آجیلاتمق /ı/ to render bitter.

acılı آجیلی 1. grieved, sorrowful, mourning. 2. having a bitter taste.

acılıkᵗⁱ آجیلق *n.* of **acı** 1.

acıma آجیمه pity, compassion.

acımarul آجی مارول dandelion, *bot., Taraxacum.*

acımsı آجیمسی bitterish.

acımtırakᵗⁱ آجیمتراق somewhat bitter, bitterish. —**lık** slight bitterness.

acın 1 آجن *obs.* of starvation, of hunger (to die).

acın=ⁱʳ 2 آجینمق to feel sorrow, to grieve.

acınacakᵗⁱ آجینه جق pitiable, deplorable, miserable.

acınaklı آجیناقلی pitiable, stirring compassion.

acındır=ⁱʳ آجیندرمق /ı, a/ to arouse compassion for. **kendine acındır**= to make (somebody) pity oneself, to arouse pity for oneself.

acıpelin آجی پلین wormwood, *bot., Absinthium.*

acır آجیر *var.* of **acur** 1.

acırakᵗⁱ آجیراق somewhat bitter, bitterish.

acırga آجیرغه horseradish.

acırgan=ⁱʳ آجیرغانمق /a/ *obs.* to feel compassion.

acış=ⁱʳ آجیشمق *prov.* 1. to feel pain, to suffer. 2. to express sorrows to each other.

acıt=ⁱʳ آجیتمق /ı/ 1. to cause pain, to hurt (a part of the body). 2. to make bitter (food); to leave a bitter taste (in the mouth); to cause to turn (butter, etc.).

acıttır=ⁱʳ آجیتدرمق /ı/ to let be hurt (a part of the body).

acıyonca آجی یونجه *bot.* kind of clover.

acîb 1 (.—) عجیب A same as **acip**.

âcib 2 (—.) عاجب A *lrnd.* 1. surprising, wonderful. 2. very pleasing.

acîbe (.—.) عجیبه A *lrnd.* 1. strange thing, wonder. 2. curiosity; monstrosity.

acîbeihilkatᵗⁱ (.—. ....) عجیبه خلقت **acibei-tablat** (.—. ...—.) عجیبه طبیعت A *lrnd.* monster, monstrosity.

âcil 1 . (—.) عاجل A 1. hasty, speedy, swift (person). 2. transitory, fleeting. 3. ready, prompt, immediate, urgent, pressing.

âcil 2 (—.) آجل A *lrnd.* referred to a future term or time, deferred, postponed, future.

âcilâne (—.—.) عاجلانه P *lrnd.* 1. in haste. 2. pertaining to the present.

âcile 1 (—..) عاجله A *lrnd.* the present fleeting life.

âcile 2 (—..) آجله A *lrnd.* eternity; anything that relates to a future life.

âcilen 1 (—´..) عاجلاً A 1. in haste, urgently, promptly. 2. in ready money. 3. now, without delay. 4. in this present life.

âcilen 2 (—´..) آجلاً A *lrnd.* at a fixed future time, when the time comes.

acîn (.—) عجین A *lrnd.* 1. kneaded. 2. dough, paste.

acinî (.——) عجینی A *sc.* like paste in consistency.

acipᵇⁱ (.—) عجیب [acîb 1] *lrnd.* 1. very wonderful; wondrous. 2. very queer, strange.

âcir (—.) آجر A *law* lessor, renter, who receives rent.

aciyo (´..) آجیو It *var.* of **acyo**.

âciz (—.) عاجز A 1. unable, incapable, helpless, impotent; weak, powerless, destitute. 2. poor, humble. —**leri** *archaic, in polite correspondence* your humble servant. — **kal**= /dan/ to be unable, to be at a loss, to give up in despair.

acizᶜᶻⁱ 2 عجز [acz 1] inability, impotence; weakness, helplessness; *law* insolvency. — **hali** *law* state of insolvency. —**e karşı sigorta** credit insurance.

acizᶜᶻⁱ 3 عجز [acz 3] *lrnd.* 1. rump; buttocks. 2. last part, *esp.*, the final letter of a word or the last word of a verse or sentence. — **kemiği** *anat., os sacrum.*

âcizane (—.—.) عاجزانه P 1. humbly, modestly, unworthily; if I may be so presumptuous. 2. *in polite conversation with 1st person singular, e. g.,* **taraf-ı âcizanemden**

by myself, by me.

âcizî 1 (—.—) عاجزى P *lrnd.* pertaining to a poor and humble person, *esp.*, pertaining to your humble servant; my.

âcizî 2 (—.—) عاجزى P *lrnd.* 1. inability, weakness. 2. humbleness.

âciziyet (—.—.) عاجزيت A *lrnd.* 1. inability, incapacity. 2. poverty, humility.

âcizlik[i] (—..) عاجزلك 1. inability, 2. humbleness.

acm عجم A *lrnd.* 1. a testing by biting (for hardness or softness). 2. a trying, testing (sword). 3. dotting of Arabic letters.

acma (.—) عجما A [*fem. of* **a'cem** 4.] *lrnd.* 1. who speaks barbarous Arabic; foreign; Persian. 2. dumb, *esp.*, a dumb brute. 3. daytime service of worship. 4. treeless (country).

acn عجن A *lrnd.* 1. a kneading. 2. a placing one's fists on the ground in the act of rising from a prostration.

acûl[ü] (.—) عجول A always in a hurry, very impetuous, impatient. **—âne** (.——.) P *lrnd.* hastily, precipitately.

acun *neol.* cosmos, universe. **—sal** cosmic.

acur 1 آجُر [**acûr 2**] hairy cucumber, *bot.* variety of *cucumis melo.*

acûr 2 (.—) عجور A *same as* **acur 1.**

acuz (.—) عجوز A *lrnd.* 1. old woman. 2. the world.

acuze (.—.) عجوزه A 1. old woman. 2. a spiteful, foul-mouthed, treacherous old hag; shrew, vixen. 3. the world. **—i Ferhad** *Or. literature* the old woman who announced to Ferhad, falsely, the death of Shirin thereby driving him to suicide. **—lik** 1. the quality, disposition or acts of an old woman. 2. malicious act.

âcüssinn[nnî] (—..) عاج السن A *anat.* dentine, *substantia eburnea.*

acyo (.'.) آجيو It *fin.* agio, premium. **—cu** a person dealing with agiotage. **—culuk** agiotage, speculative dealing in securities.

acz 1 عجز A *same as* **aciz 2.**

acz 2 عجز A *same as* **aciz 3.**

aczî (.—) عجزى A *anat.* sacral.

aczül'esed عجز الاسد A *astr.* the constellation Corvus.

aczülgurab (...—) عجز الغراب A *astr.* the star η Corvi.

aç[cı] **1** آچ 1. hungry. 2. covetous, insatiable, greedy. 3. hungry (soil). 4. *obs., and in certain phrases* hunger. **— acına** on an empty stomach, without food. **— açık** hungry and homeless. **— aman bilmez** *proverb* The hungry know no mercy. **— ayı oynamaz** (*lit.,* a hungry bear will not dance) If you want a man to work well, first feed him. **— bırak**═ to starve (a person), to let go hungry. **— biilaç, — ve biilaç** wretched and miserably destitute. **— çıplak** without food and clothing, hungry and destitute. **— diril**═ *obs.* to go hungry. **—a dokuz yorgan örtmüşler de uyuyamamış** *proverb* You can't sleep if you are hungry. **— doymam, tok acıkmam sanır** *proverb* Every person thinks that his present condition will never change. **— dur**═ to remain without food. **— esner, âşık gerinir** *proverb* A person's movements betray his condition. **— gözlü*. — ile dost olma, yemem der de sömürür** *proverb* Don't associate with a hungry person, he will say «I don't eat» and he will drain you to the dregs. **— ile eceli gelen söyleşir** *proverb* (*lit.* He whose death-bell has tolled deals with the hungry) A hungry man is an angry man. **— kal**═ to go without food. **— karnına** while hungry, with an empty stomach. **—ın karnı doyar, gözü doymaz** *proverb* A starved person's stomach may be filled, but his eyes will look for more. **—ından karnı gurlar, başında nergis parlar** *prov.* (*lit.* From hunger his belly rumbles, a narcissus glows on his head.) He starves at home but keeps up a pretentious show. **— kiminle olsa savaşır** *proverb* A hungry man will fight anybody. **— ko**═, **— koy**═ *same as* **aç bırak**═. **—ın koynunda ekmek durmaz** *proverb* (*lit.* Bread will not stay in the bosom of a hungry man.) He who is in need cannot save money. **— köpek fırın deler** *proverb* A hungry dog will break through the wall of the oven. **— kurt aslana saldırır** *proverb* A hungry wolf will attack a lion. **— kurt gibi** ravenous as a wolf. **— kurt yavrusunu yer** *proverb* A hungry wolf will eat his own cub. **—ından öl**═ to die of hunger, to starve. **— ölmez, gözü kararır** *proverb* A hungry person does not die, but gets dizzy. **— susuz** deprived of food and water, starving. **— taksir** fasting, very hungry. **— tavuk darıyı düşünde görür** *proverb* (*lit.* A hungry hen dreams of grain.) One imagines what one wishes. **— tavuk kendini arpa ambarında sanır** *proverb* (*lit.* A hungry hen imagines herself in a granary.) Some people live by illusions. **— uyuz ve kan kuduz** *obs.* starving. **— yanından kaç** Beware of the hungry.

aç═[ar] **2** آچ I. /ı/ 1. to open. 2. to open up (a door or window in a wall). 3. to open (a road). 4. to open, draw aside, lift, drop (veil, etc.). 5. to open, clear away, break through (obstruction). 6. to clear, break up (ground). 7. to take by force, conquer; to break in, to burgle. 8. to uncover. 9. to open out, spread out, unfold. 10. to set, spread, unfurl (sail, flag). 11. to roll out (paste).

12. to untie, undo (knot, etc.). 13. to unlock; to unbar, unlatch. 14. to unravel. 15. to solve (difficulty, etc.). 16. to turn on, switch on. 17. to call, ring up (telephone). 18. to widen (interval, step, etc.). 19. *naut.* to steer off; to open to sea. 20. to explain more fully. 21. to open, begin (conversation, war, etc.). 22. to disclose. 23. to clean, rub up (rusty thing); to polish, furbish (metals, etc.). 24. to clean, whiten (laundry). 25. to make lighter (color). 26. to suit, become (a person), to lighten the complexion of a person,(as dress, color, etc.). 27. to sharpen, cut (pen, pencil). 28. to whet, sharpen (appetite). II. 1. to open (flower, leaves, etc.). 2. to clear up, become fine (sky, weather). 3. *slang* to go away. 4. /dan/ to bring up (subject, matter) in conversation. —**tı ağzını yumdu gözünü** he poured out an unrestrained diatribe. — **başı!** *slang* Scram! — **gözünü açarlar gözünü** If you are not careful you will be made to suffer for it. —**ıl, madık kutu** *colloq.* a person who keeps his knowledge to himself, an uncommunicative person. —**ma kutuyu, söyletme kötüyü** Don't bring up the subject, otherwise you will hear things you don't want to hear.

açacak[¹] آچَجَك 1. any tool used for opening, e. g., **konserve açacağı** can opener. 2. *prov.* key.

açalya (ˊ..) آچَالِیَه Gk *bot.* azalea.

açan 1 آچَان *neol., anat.* tensor, extensor.

açan 2 آچَان *prov., var. of* **haçan.**

açar 1 آچَار *prov.* key, picklock.

açar 2 (——) آچَار *prov.* pickle or preserve of any kind as a condiment. 2. mixture of any kind.

'Açe آچَه *geog.* Achin (in northern Sumatra). — **Sultan** *hist.* Achinese Sultan.

açelya (ˊ..) آچَلِیَه *var. of* **açalya.**

açevele (...ˊ.) آچَوَرَه It *naut.* sprit. — **donanım** sprit rigging. — **gönderi** sprit boom. — **palangası** sprit tackle. — **pruva!** brace up the head yards!

açgözlü آچگوزلو covetous, greedy, insatiable. — **daya çocuğu** *colloq.* greedy child. —**lük** covetousness, greediness. —**lük et**= to behave very greedily.

açı آچی *neol., sc.* angle. — **ortay.** — **uzaklığı** *astr.* angular distance.

açıcı آچیجی 1. that which opens, opening, opener. 2. *anat.* extensor.

açık[¹] آچیق 1. open; the open. 2. uncovered; naked. 3. wide. 4. public. 5. unenclosed. 6. not roofed over. 7. clear, cloudless, fine. 8. light (shade of color). 9. impudent, obscene, saucy; free (in manner or conduct), frank. 10. plain (language), not in cipher. 11. plain, audible, distinct, well-articulated (voice). 12. vacant; unoccupied; unemployed; vacancy. 13. vacant space; a vacant or blank interval. 14. a deficit, a balance on the wrong side. —**ında,** —**larında** *naut.* off..., offshore... —**ta** 1. in the open air; outdoors. 2. *naut.* in the offing, offshore. 3. unemployed. 4. on half pay. —**tan** 1. from a distance. 2. extra, outside one's regular income. — **açık** openly, frankly. —**tan açığa** quite openly, publicly, without any attempt at secrecy. — **ağız** *obs.* babbler, imbecile. — **ağız aç kalmaz** *proverb* (*lit.* He who opens his mouth is fed.) In order to get something, one has to ask for it. — **alınla** with frank face, with a clear conscience. — **artırma** sale by public auction. — **ateş** *mil.* direct fire. — **ayak** *obs.* with big strides. — **baş** 1. bareheaded; bald. 2. licentious. 3. Imeretian (Caucasus). —**ta bırak**= /ı/ to leave in the open, to cause to be homeless or unemployed, to leave one without a home or a job. — **bono ver**= /a/ to give a blank check; to give full freedom to act in one's name. — **ciro** *fin.* blank endorsement, general endorsement. —**a çık**= 1. to be removed from one's office. 2. to be known, to come out. —**ı çık**= /ın/ to have a deficit (employee). —**a çıkar**= public administration to remove from office. — **deniz** *law* high seas. — **dur**= to stand aside; not to interfere. — **düş**= 1. *naut.* to fall away (from a fleet, etc.). 2. *wrestling Turkish style* to have one's navel uncovered (and, consequently, to be counted out). —**ta eğlen**= *naut.* to wait offshore without dropping anchor. — **eksiltme** public auction by underbidding. — **elli** open-handed, generous, liberal. — **fikirli** broad-minded, enlightened, liberal-minded. — **gel** *slang* 1. Stand away. 2. come on, out with it! — **göz***. — **hava** open air, outdoor, fresh air, clear weather. — **hava tiyatrosu** open-air theater. — **hece** *phon., pros.* open syllable. — **huy** a free and easy, careless, somewhat impudent habit of mind. — **itibar** *fin.* overdraft. —**ta kal**= to have lost one's home or job, to be out in the cold. —**ı kapat**= to meet the deficit. — **kapı** 1. open door. 2. a hospitable person; hospitality. — **kapı bırak**= *fig.* to leave the door open (for further negotiation). — **kapı siyaseti** *dipl.* open diplomacy. — **kaş** wide-spaced eyebrows. — **konuş**= to be frank, to talk frankly. — **kredi** *com.* open credit, blank credit. — **liman** *mil.* an unprotected port. —**lar livası** *ironical* the unemployed. — **maaşı** half-pay. — **mektup** open letter. — **meşrep***. — **ordugâh** *mil.* bivouac. — **rey** open vote. — **saçık***. — **satış** *com.* public sale.

—**tan satış** *com.* short sale. — **söyle=** to speak clearly, openly, frankly. — **söz** plain words, unadorned truth. — **sözlü** outspoken (person). — **şehir** *mil.* open city. — **teşekkür** public acknowledgment. — **tohumlular** *bot.*, Gymnospermae. — **ver=** to have a deficit. —**a ver=**, —**a vur=** to bring into the open, to reveal, to disclose. — **yer** vacancy.

açıkça (..'.) آچیقجَه frankly, clearly, openly, plainly. —**sı** to tell the truth, frankly speaking, in plain words.

açıkgöz آچیقگوز clever, sharp, smart, shrewd. —**lük** sharpness; slyness. —**lük et=** to be shrewd, to jump at an opportunity.

açıkla=ᵣ آچیقلامق 1. /ı/ to disclose, to reveal; to make public, to announce; to explain. 2. *obs.* to become public (concealed matter), to be divulged. —**ma** explanation, statement. —**mada bulun=** to make a statement.

açıklıkᵏ¹ آچیقلیق 1. *abstr. n.* of **açık**. 2. uncoveredness. 3. unenclosedness. 4. being without a roof. 5. clearness, cloudlessness. 6. lightness (shade in color). 7. freedom, sauciness; indecency. 8. plainness, unmistakableness, clearness. 9. distinctness (articulation). 10. vacantness, blankness. 11. opening, door, window, aperture, gap, blank space. 12. clear, cloudless weather. 13. space, distance; open space. 14. *astr.* azimuth.

açıkmeşrepᵇ¹ آچیقمشرب overfree, licentious (woman).

açıksaçıkᵏ¹ آچیق صاچیق 1. immodestly dressed, insufficiently clothed. 2. indecent. —**lık** indecency.

açıl=ᵣ آچیلمق 1. to be opened, to open. 2. to come open, to open of its own accord; /a/ to open out (as a window into the garden). 3. to be dispersed. 4. to vanish (darkness, sleep). 5. to be cleaned. 6. to clear (weather). 7. to open (flower). 8. to cheer up, be refreshed; to recover. 9. to become relaxed in manner, unembarrassed, at ease. 10. /a/ to confide (in), to disclose one's secret (to). 11. to become more spacious. 12. /a/ *naut.* to shove off, push off. 13. /dan/ come up (in conversation). 14. to become vacant (post). 15. to be extravagant, to overspend. —**ır kapanır** collapsible, folding. —**ıp saçıl=** 1. to dress immodestly (woman). 2. to spend money lavishly. —**ım** *neol.*, *astr.* declination. —**ış**, —**ma** opening; inauguration; *mil.* deployment. —**ış bilânçosu** *com.* annual opening balance.

açım آچیم opening, inauguration; *prov.* prelude.

açımla=ᵣ /ı/ *neol.* to comment.

açın 1 *neol.* discovery.
açın=ᵢᵣ **2** *neol.*, *biol.* to develop. —**dır=** *math.*, *biol.* to develop. —**dırma** development. —**ık** *ling.* vowel. —**ım** *math.*, *biol.* development.
açınla=ᵣ *neol.* /ı/ to discover.
açıortay *neol.*, *geom.* bisector.
açısal *neol.*, *geom.* angular. —**hız** angular velocity.
açkı آچقی 1. polishing wax; polish. 2. smith's tool used for widening a hole. 3. *prov.* key. — **makinası** *leather mfg.* polishing machine. — **tahtası** goldsmith's board in making gold leaf. —**cı** polisher. —**la=** /ı/ to polish. —**lı** polished.
açlıkᵏ¹ آچلیق 1. hunger. 2. starvation, famine. 3. appetite, greed. — **çek=** to hunger; to endure poverty. — **grevi** hunger strike. —**tan nefesi kok=** to be poverty-stricken. —**tan öl=** to perish from hunger, to starve.
açma آچمه 1. opening. 2. a clearing. 3. hole made in the leg of a mutton carcass when hung for flaying. 4. kind of puff paste bun. —**lık** detergent.
açmaz , آچماز 1. reserved, secretive. 2. difficult position (chess, checkers). 3. difficult situation, dilemma, impasse. 4. *slang* trick. —**a düş=** *slang* to get into a tight corner. —**a getir=** *slang* /ı/ to deceive, to dupe. — **oyna=** *slang* /a/ to trick. —**lık** secretiveness.
açtır=ᵢᵣ آچدیرمق /a, ı/ *caus.* of **aç=** 2.

ad 1 آد 1. name, appellation. 2. proper name; first name. 3. name, fame, repute, reputation. — **al=** to make a name for oneself. —**ını bağışla=** to tell one's name (when asked). —**ınızı bağışlar mısınız?** May 'I know your name, please? —**ı bat=** to be forgotten, not to be talked of any more. —**ı batası**, —**ı batasıca** *a mild curse.* —**ı belirsiz** unknown, of obscure origin. —**ı bile okunma=** /ın/ to be insignificant, to have no influence. —**ı bozul=** /ın/ to lose one's good name. —**ı çık=** /ın/ to be talked about; to gain a bad reputation. — **çıkar=** *archaic* to gain fame. —**ı geçen** aforesaid, afore-mentioned. — **kal=** /ın/ to be remembered after one is dead. —**ı kale alınma=** /ın/ to have no influence. — **kazan=** to make a name for oneself. — **ko=** *archaic* to leave lasting fame. — **ko=**, — **koy=** /a/ to name, give a name. —**ı kötüye çık=** /ın/ to gain a bad reputation. — **san** name and fame. —**iyle saniyle** by one's well-known name. — **tak=** /a/ to nickname. — **ur=** /ı/ *archaic* to name, give a name. —**ı üstünde** as the name implies, the name tells you all.

—ı var 1. famous. 2. existing only by name; having an undeserved reputation. **— ver=** /a/ to name, to give a name.

ad=ᵃʳ 2 آدمى to step (a step), to make (steps).

Âd 3 (—) عاد A *man's name; mythical ancestor of an ancient people in Arabia who were exterminated for refusing to accept the message of a prophet.*

ad^ddı 4 عَدّ A *lrnd.* number; enumeration. **—den efzun** beyond number; incalculable. **— et=** *cf.* **addet=**. **— ol=** *cf.* **addolun=**.

ada 1 آده آرا آله 1. island. 2. division of a town, city block. **A—lar** the Princes' Islands near Istanbul. **— balığı** tench, *zool.* *Tinca tinca.* **— çayı***. **A—lar denizi** the Archipelago, the Aegean Sea. **— soğanı***. **— tavşanı** rabbit, *zool.*, *Oryctolagus cuniculus.* **— yavrusu** a kind of small fishing-boat in the Bosporus.

ada=ʳ 2 آرامس /a,ı/ 1. to vow, to give (to). 2. to vow, promise, pledge. **— bana, adayım sana** *proverb* (*lit.* Pledge me and I shall pledge you.) Scratch my back and I will scratch yours.

ada=ʳ 3 آراس *archaic* to give a name.

âda 4 (.—) اعدا A *lrnd., pl. of* **adu**.

âdab (— —) آداب A *cf.* **âdap. —ı muaşeret** rules of good manners, etiquette. **—a mugayir** against the rules of good society. **—ı umumiye** common decency.

adacık^ğı آدهجيق 1. islet. 2. *anat.* insula.

adaçayı^nı آراچايى garden sage, *bot.*, *Salvia officinalis.*

âdad (.—) اعداد A *lrnd., pl. of* **aded**. **—ı asliye** *gram.* cardinal numbers. **—ı kesriye** *gram.* fractional numbers. **—ı müsellese** *math.* triangular numbers. **—ı mütebayine** *math.* prime numbers. **—ı rütbiye** *gram.* ordinal numbers. **—ı tevziiye** *gram.* distributive numbers.

adadiyoz آرا ديوز *slang* a tough, ruffian.

adak^ğı 1 آراق 1. vow. 2. promise. 3. menace, threat. 4. votive offering. **— ada=, — et=** 1. to vow. 2. to promise, to threaten.

adak^kkı 2 ادقّ A *lrnd.* more subtle, finer; most minute, very slender, thinnest.

adaklı آراقلى 1. vowed, promised. 2. *prov.* fiancé, fiancée.

adal^lıı اضل A *lrnd., superl. of* **dâl** 7.

adalât (..—) عضلات A *lrnd., pl. of* **adale**.

adale عضله A *anat.* muscle. **—li** muscular, strong, brawny. **—lilik** muscularity.

adalet^tı (.—.) عدالت A justice, equity. **A— Bakanı** Minister of Justice. **A— Bakanlığı** Ministry of Justice. **—ayin** (.—..—) P *lrnd.* just. **—kâr** (.—.—) P *lrnd.* just. **—kârane** (.—.——.) P *lrnd.* just, equitable (act); justly, equitably. **—kârî** (.—.——) P *lrnd.* justice. **—li** just, equitable. **—siz** unjust, inequitable. **—sizlik** injustice, inequity.

adalı آداولى 1. islander. 2. *w. cap.* Aegean islander.

adalî (..—) عضلى A *anat.* muscular.

adam آدم [**âdemî 1**] 1. man, human being. 2. man. 3. person, individual. 4. servant, employee; agent, representative. 5. a good, honest, well-mannered person. 6. personage. 7. one, *as in*, **—ın güleceği gelir**. One would laugh. 8. my good fellow. **— başına** for each, per person. **— beğenme=** to be hypercritical (of persons). **— boyu** man's height. **— çekiştir=** to slander. **—a dayanma ölür, duvara dayanma yıkılır** *proverb* Do not rely on man, he may die; do not lean against the wall, it may fall down. **—a dön=** to improve. **— et=** /ı/ to make a man (of someone), to bring up well. **— evlâdı** a person of good family and upbringing. **— gibi** properly, like a gentleman. **—ına göre** according to person, considering the qualities of each person. **— içine çık=** to mix with people. **— kaldır=** to kidnap, to abduct. **— oğlu** 1. *same as* **— evlâdı**. 2. human being, man. **— ol=** to become a fine, upstanding man. **— olmaz** incorrigible, hopeless. **— otu***. **— öldür=** *law* to commit homicide, manslaughter; to kill somebody. **— sarrafı** a fine judge of character, a good judge of people. **—dan say=** /ı/ to give consideration to someone, not to disregard, not to overlook. **— sen de** don't worry. take it easy. never mind. **— taslağı** lout. **— vur=** to commit murder. **— yerine koy=** /ı/ to count someone a person of moment or consequence. **—akıllı** (..′...) properly, thoroughly, fully. **—cağız** 1. little man. 2. poor fellow. 3. *fam.* fellow. **—casına** (..′...) like a human being; in a proper manner. **—cık** little man. **—cıl** 1. tame. 2. *prov.* attacking or killing men (beast); shy, not used to men (beast); *neol.* misanthrope. **—cılayın** *same as* **adamcasına**. **—lık** humanness, humanity; humaneness, manliness, virtue.

adamotu آدم اوتى *bot.* mandrake.

adamsı آدهمسى like an island.

adamsız آدمسز without help, servantless. **—lık** lack of domestic help.

adan=ᵘʳ آرانى *pass. of* **ada=** 2 and 3.

âdap^bı (— —) آداب [**âdab**] [*pl. of* **edeb**] regular customs and observances, rules of good manners. **— ve erkân** customary observance or practice. **—ı muaşeret, —ı umumiye** *cf.* **âdab.**

adaptasyon آداپتاسيون F 1. adaptation (of

a novel or play). 2. an adapted work (novel or play), *esp.* one changed to fit local conditions.

adapte آداپته F adapted (novel or play). **— et=** to adapt (novel or play).

adasoğanı[nı] آداصوغانی squill, sea onion, *bot.*, *Scilla maritima.*

adaş 1 آداش one having the same name, namesake.

adaş=[ır] **2** آداشمك to vow mutually.

adat=[tı] **1** آداتمك /a,ı/ *caus. of* **ada=** 2 and 3.

âdat 2 (— —) عادات A [*pl. of* **âdet** 1] *lrnd.* customs, usages, practice, habits. **—ı ticariye** commercial practice.

âdat 3 (— —) اعداد *var. of* **âdad**.

adavet (. — .) عداوت A enmity, hostility, hatred. **—i diniye** religious antipathy.

aday *neol.* candidate. **—lık** candidacy. **—lığını koy=** to put forward one's candidacy for office.

adcı *neol., phil.* nominalist. **—lık** nominalism.

add عد *cf.* **ad** 4.

addet=[der] عد ایتمك /ı/ to count, deem, esteem. 2. *obs.* to count, calculate.

addolun=[ur] عد اولنمق *pass. of* **addet=**.

aded عدد A 1. number, sum, total, amount. 2. numeral, figure. 3. unit, *as in* **yedi aded kitap** seven books. **—i âşari** *math.* decimal. **— ferd** *math.* odd number. **—i kesri** *math.* fractional number. **—i murabba** *math.* square number. **—i mükaab** *math.* cubic number. **—i mükesser** *math.* fractional number. **—i mürekkeb** composite number. **—i müretteb** total membership (parliament, etc.). **—i müzehheb** golden number (of a year in the Metonic lunar cycle). **—i rüus** *can. law* total of potential heirs. **—i sahih** *math.* whole number. **—i silsile-i alelvilâ** *math.* arithmetical progression. **—i tam** *math.* whole number. **—i zevc** *math.* even number. **—en** (. . .) A *lrnd.* numerically.

adedî (. . —) عددی A 1. numerical. 2. *law* capable of enumeration. **— sıfat** numerical adjective. **—yat** (. . — —) *law* things that may be counted.

âdel اعدل A *lrnd., superl. of* **âdil** 1.

adele 1 عدل A *lrnd., pl. of* **âdil** 1.

adele 2 عضل *var. of* **adale**.

âdelü'l-âdilîn (. . . — . —) اعدل العادلین A *lrnd.* the Most Just One, God.

âdem 1 (—.) آدم [**âdemî** 1] archaic for **adam** 1.

Âdem 2 (—.) آدم Adam. **— Baba Adam. — oğlu** sons of man, men. **— oğlu çiğ süt emmiştir** *proverb* (lit. The son of Adam has been fed on raw milk.) Man can never be trusted completely.

adem 3 عدم A 1. non-existence, nothingness; annihilation; death. 2. lack, absence. [*For compounds, see* **ademiemniyet — ademivücud.**]

âdeman (—.—) آدمان P [*pl. of* **Âdem** 2] men, mankind.

âdemhur (—.—) آدمخور P *lrnd.* man-eating, anthropophagous.

âdemî 1 (—.—) آدمی A archaic human being, man, human.

Âdemî 2 (—.—) آدمی A *lrnd.* 1. pertaining to Adam. 2. Adamite.

ademî (. . —) عدمی A *lrnd.* pertaining to nonexistence.

ademiemniyet (. . . . —) عدم امنیت P insecurity, lack of confidence.

ademiicra (. . ′ . . —) عدم اجرا P *com.* nonexecution.

ademiiktidar (. . ′ . . . —) عدم اقتدار P incapacity; *med.* impotence.

ademiimkân (. . ′ . . —) عدم امکان P impossibility.

ademiimtizac (. . ′ . . . —) عدم امتزاج P incompatibility, disagreement, disharmony, discord.

ademiirtibat[tı] (. . ′ . . . —) عدم ارتباط P disjunction, disconnection, lack of communication.

ademiistikrar (. . ′ . . . —) عدم استقرار P *biol.* instability, fluctuation, variability.

ademiistima[aı] (. . ′ . . . —) عدم استماع P *law* inadmissibility of an action, having no point in law.

ademiiştiha (. . ′ . . . —) عدم اشتها P lack of appetite.

ademiitaat[tı] (. . ′ . . —.) عدم اطاعت P disobedience.

ademiitimad (. . ′ . — . —) عدم اعتماد P lack of confidence, distrust; *pol.* nonconfidence. **— reyi** vote of nonconfidence.

ademikabiliyet[tı] (. . ′ . — . — .) عدم قابلیت P incapability, incapacity.

ademikabul[lü] (. . ′ . . —) عدم قبول P *fin.* nonacceptance.

ademikifaye (. . ′ . . — .) عدم کفایة P in **— kararı** *pol.* vote that a debate has been insufficient.

ademimerkeziyet (. . ′ . . . . —) عدم مرکزیت P *pol.* decentralization.

ademimesuliyet (. . ′ . . — — .) عدم مسئولیت P *law* nonresponsibility, nonliability.

ademimevcudiyet (. . ′ . . — — .) عدم موجودیت P nonexistence.

ademimutabakat (. . ′ . . — . —) عدم مطابقت lack of coordination, incoherence.

ademimuvaffakıyet (. . ′ . . . . — .) عدم موفقیت P unsuccessfulness, failure.

ademimüdahale (. . ′ . — . .) عدم مداخله P *pol.* nonintervention, noninterference.

ademimüsavat (. . ′ . . — —) عدم مساوات P

ademimüşabehet

com. disparity, inequality.
ademimüşabehet (..′..—..) عدم مشابهت P dissimilarity, lack of resemblance.
ademiriayet[ti] (..′..—.) عدم رعایت P law nonobservance, violation, disregard.
ademisalâhiyet[ti] (..′..——.) عدم صلاحیت P law noncompetency.
ademitaayyün (..′....) عدم تعین P phil. indeterminism.
ademitahayyüz (..′....) عدم تحیز P phil. impenetrability.
ademitecavüz (..′..—.) عدم تجاوز P pol. nonaggression.
ademitediye (..′..—.) عدم تأدیه P fin. nonpayment, default.
ademiteessür (..′....) عدم تأثر P psych. apathy.
ademitekerrür (..′....) عدم تکرر P nonrecurrence.
ademitenafüz (..′..—.) عدم تنافذ P phil. impenetrability.
ademitenasüb (..′..—.) عدم تناسب P disproportion.
ademitenazur (..′..—.) عدم تناظر P asymmetry, lack of symmetry.
ademiteslim (..′..—) عدم تسلیم P com. nondelivery.
ademivücud[du] (..′..—) عدم وجود P nonexistence.
âdemiyan (—.—) آدمیان P lrnd., pl. of **âdemî** 1. —e (—.—.) P 1. human; humane (act). 2. humanely.
âdemiyet 1 (—.—.) آدمیت A lrnd. humanity, humaneness; manliness.
ademiyet 2 (..—.) عدمیت A lrnd. quality of nonexistence.
âdemkârî (—.——) آدم کاری man-made, artificial.
âdemlik[ği] (—..) آدملک archaic for **adamlık**.
adenit آدنیت F med. adenitis, glandular inflammation.
âder (—.) آدر P lrnd., var. of **âzer**.
aderans آدرانس F med. adhesion.
ades عدس A lrnd. lentil, bot., Lens culinaris.
adese. عدسه A 1. lens. 2. rare a single lentil. 3. med. malignant measles, black measles, rubeola maligna. —**i ayniye** 1. anat. lens. 2. optics ocular (lens) —**i meriye** optics objective (lens).
adesî (..—) عدسی A lenticular.
adesiye (..—.) عدسیه A [fem. of **adesî**] 1. lrnd. lenticular. 2. lrnd. lentil soup; lentil stew. 3. lrnd. bat's droppings used as medicine. 4. med. malignant measles.
adesülmâ (...—) عدس الما A duckweed, water lentil, bot., Lemna minor.
âdet 1 (—.) عادت A custom, practice, usage; habit. —**i ağnam** Ott. hist. sheep tax. — **ve ahlâk** law customary usage, moral standards. —**i belde** local custom. — **çıkar**= to start a custom. — **edin**= /ı/ to acquire a habit, to form a habit. —**e mugayir** contrary to custom. —**i müstemirre** lrnd. unbroken custom. — **üzere** according to practice, customarily, as usual. — **yerini bulsun diye** for the sake of formality, as a gesture.
âdet 2 (—.) عادت [**âdet** 1] menses. — **gör**= to menstruate. —**ten kesil**= to come to the end of menses, to undergo menopause.
adet[di] 3 عدد var. of **aded**.
âdeta (—′.—.) عادتا A 1. almost, in fact, simply. 2. obs. customarily, as usual. 3. cavalry walking.
âdetçe (..′.) عادتچه conventionally, according to custom; as usual, according to wont.
âdetullah (—..—) عادت الله A lrnd. the rules and practices of divine origin governing the universe; natural law.
adezyon آدزیون F med. adhesion.
adha (.—) اضحی A lrnd., rel. animals sacrificed at the Feast of Sacrifice (**Kurban Bayramı**).
adım آدیم 1. step (in walking). 2. measure, pace. —**larını aç**= to stride. — **adım** step by step. — **at**= to take a step. —**ını atama**= to be unable to restrain oneself (from doing something). — **atla** sport hop, skip and jump. — **atma** taking a step. — **attırma**= not to allow to put a foot outside the house. — **başına, — başında** at every step. —**larını sıklaştır**= to quicken one's step. —**ını tek al**= to move with caution. —**ını tetik al**= to watch one's step. — **uydur**= to fall in step; fig. to fall in line, to fit in (with). —**la** 1. to pace. 2. /ı/ to measure by steps. —**lık** in compounds as **beş** —**lık** five paces long, five paces away.
âdi 1 (——) عادی A 1. customary, habitual, usual, everyday. 2. ordinary, inferior. 3. vulgar, mean, common. — **alacaklar** com. law unsecured debt. — **gün** week day, working day. — **iflâs** com. law nonfraudulent bankruptcy. — **şirket** com. law unincorporated association.
Âdi 2 (——) عادی A 1. pertaining to the ancient tribe of Ad. 2. lrnd. ancient, prehistoric.
adid 1 (.—) عدید A lrnd. numerous.
adid 2 (.—) عدید A lrnd. 1. number, amount, total. 2. stranger counted as belonging to a tribe or family. 3. equal, alike.
adîde (.—.) عدیده A lrnd. [fem. of **adid** 1] numerous, a great many.
adidülhasa (.—..—′) عدید الحصی A lrnd.

, as many as the pebbles, innumerable.
âdil 1 (—.) عادل A 1. just, equitable. 2. lrnd. devious. 3. w. cap., man's name.
adil[dll] **2** عدل [adl] lrnd. 1. justice, equity, integrity. 2. equivalent, fair price.
adîl 3 (.—) عديل A lrnd. equal, like, match.
âdilâne (—.—.) عادلانه P 1. justly, equitably. 2. equitable (act).
âdilî (—.—) عادلى P lrnd. justness, equitableness.
âdilik[ël] (—..) عاديلك vulgarity, meanness.
âdillik[ël] (—..) عادللك justness, equitableness.
adim (.—) عديم A lrnd. lacking, wanting.
adimülihtimal[ll] (.—...—) عديم الاحتمال A lrnd. improbable, impossible.
adimüliktidar (.—...—) عديم الاقتدار A lrnd. impotent, powerless.
adimülimkân (.—..—) عديم الامكان A lrnd. impossible.
adimülmisal[ll] (.—..—) عديم المثال A lrnd. unmatched, unequalled.
adîmülvefa (.—..—′) عديم الوفاء A lrnd. 1. faithless, disloyal. 2. unresponsive, not returning affection.
adimünnazir (.—.—) عديم النظير A lrnd. matchless, peerless, unequalled, unrivalled.
adimüssani (.—.——) عديم الثانى A lrnd. unique, peerless.
Adin[dni] عدن var. of **Adn**.
Adisababa آديس بابا 1. capital of Ethiopia. 2. l. c., a card game.
adit[dl] (.—) عديد var. of **adid 1**.
âdiyat[ll] (———) عاديات A lrnd. customary and habitual things.
âdiye 1 (——.) عاديه A lrnd., fem. of **âdi 1**.
âdiye 2 (——.) عاديه A lrnd. injustice; hindrance.
adl[ll] عدل A same as **adil 2**. — **ü dad** P lrnd. justice and equity.
adla=[r] **1** آدلامق /ı/ to give a name (to)
adlâ[âi] **2** (.—) اضلع A [pl. of **dılı**] 1. anat. ribs. 2. geom. sides, edges (of a figure) 3. math. roots (of numbers).
adlan=[ır] آدلانمق 1. to be named. 2. to make a name for oneself.
adlı آدلى 1. named, called. 2. famous, celebrated. — **adınca** each one by name. — **adiyle** by his well-known name. — **sanlı famed, celebrated**.
adlî (.—) عدلى A 1. judicial, juridical. 2. w. cap., pen name of Sultan Mahmut II. 3. a gold coin of the time of Sultan Mahmut II. — **âmir** law president of a court martial. — **hata** legal error. — **muamele** law judicial proceedings. — **muzaheret** law legal aid,

action in forma pauperis. — **sicil** law record of previous convictions. — **subay** mil. provost marshal, prosecuting officer. — **tâkibat** law prosecution. — **tasfiye** com. law winding-up, liquidation. — **tebligat** law communication sent by a court. — **tıp** forensic medicine. — **yardım** law commission to take evidence.
adliye (—.—.) عدليه A 1. judicial, juridical. 2. administration of justice. 3. w. cap. Department of Justice, Ministry of Justice. 4. a gold coin of the time of Sultan Mahmud II. 5. the Shiah branch of Islam (a Shiite usage). — **mahkemeleri** ordinary courts of justice. A— **Nazırı** Minister of Justice. A— **Nezareti** Ministry of Justice. A— **Sarayı** Courthouse. A— **Vekâleti** Ministry of Justice. A— **Vekili** Minister of Justice. —**ci** specialist in judicial affairs.
Adn عدن A Eden.
adres آدرس F address. — **kitabı**, — **rehberi** directory, address-book. — **sahibi** addressee.
Adriyatik[ël] ادرياتيك F Adriatic Sea.
adsız آدسز 1. nameless. 2. unknown, without fame, obscure, undistinguished. 3. infamous, illfamed. — **parmak** ring finger.
adu (.—) عدو var. of **aduv**. —**yi can** mortal enemy.
adud عضد 1. anat. upper arm, humerus. 2. lrnd. supporter. 3. lrnd. strength, might, ability.
adudi (..—) عضدى A anat. humeral, brachial.
adudüddevle عضد الدول A hist. Supporter of the State (title of a high dignitary).
adudülcasi (...——) عضدالجانى A astr. the star β Herculis.
adudülmültehib (......') عضد الملتهب A astr. the star α Cephei.
=**adur**=, =**edur**=, after vowel =**yadur**=, =**yedur**= in imperative and optative forms, indicates continuance of action, e. g., Siz yazadurun, ben şimdi gelirim. You go on writing, I shall be back presently. O giyinedursun, biz arabayı getiririz. Let her go on dressing, while we bring out the car. Ben yazıyı okuyadurayım, sen kitapları hazırla. Let me go on reading this article; meanwhile you get the books ready.
adut[du] عضد var. of **adud**.
aduv[vvü] عدو A lrnd. enemy, foe.
aduvvüllah (...——) عدوالله A lrnd. enemy of God.
adüv[vvü] عدو var. of **aduv**.
adventis آدونتيس F anat. adventitia.
adyende (—..) آدينده P lrnd. rainbow.
aerolit ارولت astr. aerolite.

aerop^{bd} اءروپ   F biol. aerobe.
af^{tfı} 1 عفو   [af 2] 1. forgiving; forgiveness, pardon. 2. exemption, excusing from some duty. 3. dismissal, discharge. — buyurunuz! I beg your pardon! — dile= to apologize, to beg pardon of. —ı umumî amnesty, general pardon.
af^{fvi} 2 عفو   [afv] lrnd., same as af 1.
afacan آفا جان   [âfetican] gamin, urchin; naughty, wild, restless (child).
afaf (.—) عفاف , afafet (.—.) عفافت A lrnd. abstaining (from offense), chastity, continence, self-restraint.
âfak^{kı} (——) آفاق A lrnd., pl. of ufk.
afakan آناقان var. of hafakan.
âfakgir (———) آفاقگیر P lrnd. world-conquering, ruling the universe.
âfakî 1 (———) آفاقی [based on Arabic] 1. futile, superficial (talk). 2. phil. objective. — hukuk law law.
âfaki 2 (———) آفاقی A lrnd. who comes to Mecca from a distant place; who goes from Mecca to a distant place; who belongs to a distant region, foreign; vagrant, vagabond.
afaki 3 آناقی F med. aphakia.
âfakilik^{ĝı} (———.) آفاقیلك 1. objectivity. 2. superficiality.
afal afal آفال آفال [aval 1] colloq. bewildered, stupefied (look, expression), puzzled. — bak= to look stupidly, to be taken aback.
afalla=^r آفاللامق [aval 1] colloq. to be bewildered, amazed, taken aback; to be disconcerted.
afallahuanh (..—..) عفا الله عنه A lrnd. may he be forgiven (said of a deceased person, and by a writer of himself, esp. in the signature to a fetva.)
afallaş=^{ır} آفاللاشمق same as afalla=.
afallaştır=^{ır}, afallat=^{ır} آفاللاشدیرمق آفاللاتمق /ı/ colloq. to astonish, puzzle, confuse.
afara عفاره [Arabic 'afara] prov. grain residues from sifting, mixed with chaff, earth, etc. —cı thresher who receives the residue in payment.
afaret^{tı} (.—.) عفاریت A lrnd. diabolical malice and cunning, malignity.
afarit (.——) عفاریت A lrnd., pl. of ifrit.
afaroz آفاروز [aforos] 1. slang driving away, banishment. 2. same as aforos.
âfat 1 (——) آفات pl. of âfet 1. —ı semaiye Godsent calamities, disasters.
afat 2 آفات colloq. for âfet 2.
afatla=^r آفاتلامق colloq. 1. to scold and storm; to curse and swear. 2. to blab.
afatlan=^{ır} آفاتلانمق colloq. 1. to be fidgety, to worry. 2. to work oneself into a passion, to lose one's head.
afatlat=^{ır} آفاتلاتمق colloq. /ı/ to

plague, torment, drive mad.
afazi آفازی F med., psych. aphasia.
afel آفل F astr. aphelion.
afele عفله A path. vaginal hernia; blocked state of the vagina. — ol= to have the vagina blocked by rupture or swelling. —zede P path. whose vagina is blocked by rupture or swelling.
afen عفن A lrnd. putrefaction, rotting; putridity, stench. —î (..—) A pertaining to putridity.
âferide (—.—.) آفریده P lrnd. created; creature. —gân (—.—.) P pl.
âferidgâr (—.——) آفریده کار P lrnd. the Creator.
aferim آفریم آفرم colloq. for âferin 1.
âferin 1 (—'..) آفرین P bravo!, well done! — al= school to receive an honorable mention. — oku= /a/ archaic to applaud.
âferin 2 (—.—) آفرین P lrnd. who creates, creator.
âferinende (—.—..) آفرینده P lrnd. who creates, creator.
âferinhan (—.—.) آفرین خان P lrnd. who praises, applauder.
âferiniş (—.—.) آفرینش P lrnd. 1. creation. 2. creature.
âfet 1 (—.) آفت A 1. calamity, disaster, catastrophe. 2. path. affection.
âfet 2 (—.) آفت [âfat 1] 1. person of bewitching beauty. 2. w. cap., woman's name.
âfetican (—..—) آفت جان P lrnd. woman of ravishing beauty.
âfeticihan, âfetidevran (—...—) آفت جهان آفت دوران P lrnd. woman of ravishing beauty, bewitching the whole world.
âfetzede (—...) آفتزده P lrnd. victim of a calamity, disaster-stricken. —gân (—...—) P pl.
aff عفو cf. af 1.
affet=^{der} عفو ایتمك [af 1] /ı/ 1. to forgive (act). 2. to excuse (person). 3. to pardon (convict). 4. to excuse, give leave. 5. to dismiss, to discharge. —ersiniz I beg your pardon; excuse me; I am sorry. —mişsiniz siz onu! get along with you!
affolun=^{ur} عفو اولنمق [af 1] pass. of affet=. —maz unpardonable, inexcusable.
Afgan (.—) آفغان Afghan. —ca the Afghan language, Pushtu, Pashto. —istan (.—.—) Afghanistan. —lı an Afghan.
afi آفی slang pretension, ostentation, swagger. — kes=, — sat=, — yap= to give oneself airs, to swagger, to show off.
afif (.—) عفیف A 1. chaste, uncorrupted, abstentious. 2. w. cap., man's name.
âfil (—.) آفل A lrnd. going down

sinking, setting (sun).
afili آفِلی *slang* swaggering, ostentatious, showy.
afise (.—.) عَفیسه A dish made from boiled bread, sugar, butter, and dates.
afiş آفیشه F poster, placard, bill. **— yazısı** *print.* poster type.
afitap[bı] (—.—) آفتاب [aftab] *poet.* sun; *fig.* beautiful face. **—i âlemtâb** the world-illumining sun.
afiv[tvı] عفو *var. of* **afv**.
afiyet (—.—.) عافیت A health. **—inize** your health, sir. **—le** (*lit.*, with good health) 1. with a good appetite (to eat). 2. good luck, good bye. **—te, —üzre** in good health. **— bul=** to regain health, recover. **—ola, — olsun** I hope you enjoy(ed) it, bon appétit; good health, may it do you good. (said to a person eating, drinking, or coming from bath, shaving, etc.). **— şeker olsun** bon appétit. I hope you enjoy(ed) it.
afoni آفُنی F *path.* aphonia.
aforizim[zmı] آفُرِزم F aphorism.
aforos, aforoz آفُروس آفُرُوز Gk. 1. excommunication, anathema. 2. excommunicated Christian. **— et=** /ı/ to excommunicate. **— oku=** to pronounce excommunication (on), to anathematize, to label as accursed. **— ol=** to be excommunicated. **—la=** /ı/ to excommunicate. **—lu** excommunicated.
afortiyori L *phil.* a fortiori, all the more.
afrâ 1 (.—) عفرا A *lrnd.* 1. fox-colored, tawny. 2. moonlit (night).
afra 2 (.—) عَفرا عَفر A *lrnd.* 1. cock's hackles. 2. mane.
afrazi آفرازی F *psych.* aphrasia.
Afrika (.'.) آفریقا It Africa. **—lı** African (person).
afrodizyak[kı] F *physiol.* aphrodisiac.
afs 1 عَفس A *lrnd.* 1. a folding, doubling, bending; twisting. 2. constriction, puckering, squeezing.
afs 2 عَفس, **afsa** عَفسه A *lrnd.* 1. nutgall, oak apple. 2. the oak that produces nutgalls, *bot.*, *Quercus infectoria*.
afsun (.—.) آفسون P 1. charm, spell, enchantment. 2. crafty tale, eloquent, persuasive discourse. **—cu** sorcerer, enchanter, conjurer. **—culuk** sorcery, enchantment. **—la=** /ı/ to bewitch, to enchant. **—lu** bewitched, enchanted.
Afşar آفشار 1. *name of Turkoman tribe in Anatolia and Iran.* 2. *l. c.*, *prov.* adroit, clever, quick.
aft آفت F *path.* aphta. **— humması** aphtous fever.
âftab (—.—) آفتاب P *lrnd.* the sun.
âftabe (—.—.) آفتابه P *lrnd.* ewer.

âftabgâh (—.—.) آفتابگاه P *lrnd.* 1. sunny place. 2. sunny day.
âftabgerdek[ğı] (—.—..) آفتابگردك P *lrnd.* 1. sunflower. 2. chameleon.
âftabgir (—.—.) آفتابگیر P *lrnd.* parasol.
âftabî (—.—.) آفتابی P *lrnd.* 1. solar. 2. awning, sunshade.
âftabnâk[kı] (—.—.) آفتابناك P *poet.* sunny.
âftabperest (—.—..) آفتابپرست P *lrnd.* 1. sun worshipper. 2. sunflower; any flower supposed to follow the motion of the sun. 3. chameleon, *zool.*, *Cameleo vulgaris*.
âftabru (—.—.) آفتابرو P *poet.* with a face bright as the sun, beaming, fair.
âftabruh (—.—.) آفتابرخ P *poet.* with cheeks of a bright hue, rosy-cheeked.
âftave (—.—.) آفتاوه P *lrnd.*, *var. of* **aftabe**.
aftos افتوس Gk *slang* sweetheart, mistress.
aftospiyos آفتوسپیوس Gk *slang* worthless, unimportant. **— iki tavuk bir horoz** hocus-pocus!
aftoz آفتوز *var. of* **aftos**.
afüv[vvü] عفو A *lrnd.* 1. always forgiving. all-forgiving (God).
afv عفو *lrnd.*, *same as* **af 1**. **— anilkısas** *can. law* renunciation of the right of retaliation.
afve عفوه A 1. *can. law* blood-money, blood-price. 2. *lrnd.* scum in a cooking pot.
afyon افیون P 1. opium. 2. *w. cap.*, *short for* **Afyonkarahisar** (city in Anatolia). **—u patla=** /ın/ to be frightened into consciousness, to be startled. **— ruhu** laudanum. **— tiryakisi** opium addict.
afyonkeş افیونکش [*based on Persian*] opium addict.
afyonlu افیونلو 1. containing opium. 2. showing the effects of opium intoxication. 3. *w. cap.* native of Afyonkarahisar (city in Anatolia).
âgâh (—.—) آگاه P 1. aware, informed, cognizant. 2. wary, vigilant. 3. *w. cap.*, *man's name*. **— et=** /ı/ 1. to make aware, to inform. 2. *in monasteries of the Mevlevi order* to awaken (for morning prayer). **— ol=** /a/ to be aware (of), to know. **—î** (—.—) P *lrnd.*, **—lık** 1. cognizance; knowledge, news, notice, information. 2. wariness, vigilance.
aganta (..'.) آغانطه It *naut.* hold on, avast. **— burina burinata.** haul out the bowlines. **— et=** to hold fast, to haul taut. **— iskota** all sheets aft; **— prasya burina** braces and bowlines.
agar 1 آغار F *biol.* agar, agar-agar.
agar[rrı] **2** اغر A *var. of* **ağar 2**.
âgaz (—.—) آغاز P *lrnd.* beginning, start. **— et=** /a/ to begin, to commence.

âgaze (— —.) آغازه P *Or. mus.* the opening notes of a song.
âgazgâh (— — —) آغازگاه P *lrnd.* place and time of commencement, origin; God as from whom all things take their beginning.
âgazkâr (— — —) آغازکار P *lrnd.* beginning, start.
âgeft (—·) آگفت P *lrnd.* sorrow, affliction.
âgeh (—.) آگه P *lrnd., var. of* **âgah.**
âgehî (—.—) آگهی P *lrnd., var. of* **âgâhî.**
âgen (—.) آگن P *lrnd.* stuffing, filling (of a pillow).
âgenc (—.) آگنج P *lrnd.* filled, stuffed, crammed.
âgende (—..) آگنده P *lrnd.* filled, stuffed, crammed.
âgene (—..) آگنه P *lrnd.* stuffing, lining.
âgeniş (—..) آگنش P *lrnd.* stuffing, padding, wadding.
âgift (—.) آگفت P *var. of* **âgeft.**
aglütinasyon آغلوتیناسیون F *biol.* agglutination.
aglütinin آغلوتینین F *biol.* agglutinin.
agnozi آغنوزی F *psych.* agnosia.
agnostisizm آغنوستیسیزم F *phil.* agnosticism.
agorafobi آغورافوبی F *psych.* agoraphobia.
agrafi آغرافی F *psych.* agraphia.
agrandisman آغراندیسمان F *phot.* enlargement.
agranülositoz F *path.* agranulocytosis.
agreje F *university* supplementary assistant professor.
agu, agucukᵏᵘ آغو آغوجق *nursery* little darling (baby). **— bebek** darling little babe
âgûn (— —) آگون P *lrnd.* inverted, reversed; upside-down.
âguş (— —) آغوش P 1. embrace, bosom. 2. armful.
ağ 1 آغ net. **— at=** to cast a net. **— iğnesi** netting needle. **— ör=** to make a net. **— tabaka** *anat.* retina. **—a tutul=** to be caught in a web.
ağ 2 آغ small piece of cloth inserted where the leg seams of pants meet, crotch.
ağ 3 آغ *prov. for* **ak 1.**
ağ=ᵃʳ **4** آغمق *archaic* 1. to rise in the air, mount. 2. to weigh down (scale, etc.).
ağa آغا 1. *rural* lord, master. 2. local big landowner, Agha. 3. Mister (used in addressing an illiterate person). 4. *obs.* head male servant in a great man's household. 5. *hist.* Agha (title formerly given to certain officers, *esp.* of the Janissaries). 6. *prov.* elder brother; paternal uncle. **— baba** 1. father (in addressing a person to whom the title Agha is due). 2. grandfather; oldest man in the family.

— bey*. — çadırı *hist.* tent of the Agha of the Janissaries. **A— Divanı** *Ott. hist.* Council of the Agha Janissaries. **—lar eğleniyor** the great are having a good time while the poor suffer. **— gedikleri** *Ott. hist.* suite of the Agha of the Janissaries. **— kapısı** *Ott. hist.* office and official residence of the Agha of the Janissaries. **A— Paşa** *Ott. hist.* the Agha of the Janissaries (when holding the rank of a vezir).
ağabani *var. of* **ağbani.**
ağabey آغابك elder brother (used also, familiarly, as title of respect in addressing nonrelated persons). **—lik** elder brotherhood, state of being elder brother. **—lik et=** /a/ to act as an elder brother (toward), to father.
ağac آغاج *cf.* **ağaç.**
ağacıkᵏ¹ آغاجق *dim. of* **ağa.**
ağaçᶜ¹ **1** آغاج 1. tree. 2. wood, timber; wooden. 3. pole, wooden pillar; stick. 4. wooden tool, handle, etc. **— balı** *prov.* resin. **—a balta vurmuşlar, sapı bendendir demiş** *proverb* They struck at the tree with an axe; the tree said: the handle is made from my wood. **— bayramı** Arbor Day. **— buda=** to prune trees. **—a çıksa pabucu yerde kalmaz** (*lit.* Should he climb a tree, his shoes wouldn't stay on the ground.) He is very smart; he knows what he is up to. **— çileği. — çivi** treenail, wooden peg. **— damarı** grain of wood. **A— Denizi** name of the forest extending from İzmit to the Sakarya valley. **— dik=** to plant trees. **— fulü** mock orange, syringa, *bot., Philadelphus Cotonarius*. **— garnitür** print. wooden fittings. **— hamuru** wood pulp. **— işleri** woodwork. **— kabuğu** bark. **— karası** black resin exuded from certain trees. **— kavunu*. kes=** to fell trees. **— kömürü** charcoal. **— kurdu** wood-boring maggot. **— lâlesi** tulip tree, *bot., Liriodendron lulipifera*. **— püsü** resin. **— sütleğeni** tree spurge, tree Euphorbia. **— şakayıkı** tree peony. **—a tapma** tree-worship. **— üzümü** *prov.* mulberry. **— yaprağı ile güler** *proverb* (*lit.* The tree rejoices when it has its leaves.) A person is happy when surrounded by loved ones. **— yaşken iğilir** *proverb* Twist the wand while it is green; train while the mind is pliant.
ağaçᶜ¹ **2** آغاج *prov.* an old measure of distance, league.
ağaççıkᵏ¹ آغاججق 1. a little tree, pet tree. 2. pet wooden toy.
ağaççileğiⁿ¹ آغاج چیلگی raspberry, *bot., Rubus ideus*.
ağaçkakan آغاج قاقان woodpecker, *zool., Picus*.
ağaçkavunuⁿᵘ آغاج قاوونی citron, *bot., citrus medica*.
ağacla=ʳ آغاجلامق /1/ 1. to afforest. 2. to

cover with timber (pit, etc.). 3. *obs.* to beat with a stick. **—n=** *pass.* **—ndır=** /ı/ to afforest. **—ndırma** afforestation.

ağaçlı اغاجلو A having trees, wooded. **— yol** road lined with trees, avenue.

ağaçlık[1] اغاجلق 1. full of trees, well wooded. 2. wood, copse, bush.

ağacsıl *neol., sc.* arboreal.

ağalan=[ɪʳ] اغالنمق to play the Agha; to become proud and assuming; to lord it over.

ağalık[1] اغالق 1. state and condition of being an Agha. 2. generosity, nobility. 3. pride, conceit. **— hakkı** *hist.* due received by the agha in the case of escheat and reissuance of state land.

ağani (.——) اغانی A *lrnd., pl. of* **uğniye.**

ağar=[ɪʳ] 1 اغارمق 1. to turn gray, white (hair, sky). 2. to become bleached, whiten. 3. to loom in the distance. 4. to become pale, faded. **—ma** 1. a becoming gray or white. 2. dawn.

ağar[ʳⁿ] 2 اغر A *lrnd.* 1. very self-confident and presumptuous. 2. white, bright. 3. with a white spot on the forehead (horse). 4. having a beard that covers the face. 5. noble, generous, eminent. 6. white-hot (day). **—rı gurret** most fair and open faced, guileless.

ağart=[ɪʳ] اغارتمق /ı/ *caus. of* **ağar=** 1.

ağartı اغارتی 1. whiteness; hardly visible grayness in the dark. 2. *prov.* dairy products.

ağaşte (.. —) اغشته P *lrnd.* smeared, anointed; mixed (with). **—i hun u hak** smeared with blood and earth.

ağavat (. . —) اغوات [**ağa, -at** 3] *hist., pl. of* **ağa** 2, 5.

ağayan (.. —) اغایان [**ağa, -an** 9] *obs., pl. of* **ağa** 2, 5.

âgaz (——) اغاز 1. *var. of* **âgaz.** 2. *Or. mus.* the beginning of a melodic line.

ağba (. —) اغبا A *lrnd., pl. of* **gabi.**

ağbani (. ——) اغبانی *var. of* **abani.**

ağber اغبر A *lrnd.* dust-colored, 2. tarnished; overclouded.

ağbes اغبس A *lrnd.* dust-colored, ash-colored, drab, dingy white.

ağbiyâ (.. —) اغبیا A *lrnd., pl. of* **gabi.**

ağcık[1] اغجیك *anat.* reticulum.

ağda اغده [**akide** 2] semisolid confection made of sugar or grape juice, thick syrup. **— yapıştır=** to apply this confection as a depilatory. **—cı** 1. dealer in **ağda.** 2. (*lit.*, man who pulls hairs with **ağda**) bore. **—lan=, —laş=** to become the consistency of thick syrup. **—landır=, —laştır=** /ı/ *caus. of* **ağdalan=.** **—lı** 1. of the consistency of thick syrup. 2. bombastic, florid, highflown.

ağdar (. —) اغدار A [*pl. of* **gadr**] *lrnd.* wrongs, frauds, acts of injustice.

ağdık[1] اغدیك *prov.* 1. fault, blemish; faulty, bad. 2. too weighty, very heavy.

ağdır=[ɪʳ] اغدرمق /ı/ *prov., archaic* 1. to make a thing rise up. 2. *prov.* to weigh heavy on one side.

ağfal[1] (. —) اغفال A [*pl. of* **gufl**] 1. waste lands, wildernesses. 2. unmarked, doubtful things.

Ağferülgafirin (... —. —) اغفر الغافرین A *lrnd.* (*lit.,* the most pardoning of all pardoners) God.

ağı 1 اغی poison, venom. **— ağacı** oleander, *bot., Nerium oleander.* **— otu** hemlock, *bot., Conium maculatum.*

ağı 2 اغی *obs.* silk cloth. **— kurdu** *obs.* Spanish fly, *zool., Lytta vesicatoria.*

ağıd اغیت *cf.* **ağıt.**

ağıl 1 اغیل 1. sheep fold. 2. halo. **— resmi** *hist.* tax on sheepfolds.

ağıl=[ɪʳ] 2 اغیلمق *same as* **ağın=.**

ağıla=[ʳ] اغیلامق to poison. **—n=** *pass.* **—t=** *caus. of* **ağıla=.**

ağılı اغیلو poisonous, venomous. **— baldıran** poison hemlock.

ağıllan=[ɪʳ] اغیللنمق 1. to gather in a fold (flock). 2. to become surrounded with a halo (moon).

ağıllık[1] اغیللك enclosed place used as a fold or pen.

ağım اغیم prominent part of the instep. **—lı** high in the instep.

ağın=[ɪʳ] اغینمق to roll in the dust or grass (horse, etc.).

ağına=[ʳ] اغیناسی *var. of* **ağın=.** **—t=** /ı/ *caus.*

ağır 1 اغیر 1. heavy, weighty; hard. 2. grave, severe, dangerous. 3. sedate, dignified, serious, earnest. 4. valuable, precious; elaborate. 5. ponderous, tedious. 6. sharp, stinging (words), strong (curse). 7. strong (liquor). 8. indigestible, unwholesome, rich (food). 9. foul, fetid (smell). 10. slow; dull. 11. stupid; lazy. 12. hard (of hearing). 13. *obs.* weight. **—ınca** equal to its weight. **— adam** 1. serious-minded man. 2. bore, dull person. **— ağır** slowly. **— ağır gel** *naut.* ease the helm. **— aksak** *Or. mus.* a rhythmic pattern of nine beats with a signature of 9/4. **— aksak semai** *Or. mus.* a rhythmic pattern often of ten beats with a signature of 10/4. **— al=** to act unhurriedly. **—dan al=** 1. to take it easy. 2. to act reluctantly. **—ından at=** *prov.* to swagger. **— ayak** heavy with child. **— bas=** 1. to weigh heavily. 2. to have strong influence, to be influential, to have weight. 3. /ı/ to oppress, as a nightmare. **— basmayınca yeyni kalkmaz** *proverb* (*lit.* The scale pan with the light weight will not ağır= rise until the heavy weight presses the other pan down.) The worthless will not move ere the strong uses his influence. — **canlı** lazy, inactive, sluggish. — **ceza***. — **davran=** to act slowly, move slowly. — **dilli** foul-mouthed, vituperative, scurrilous. — **düyek** *Or. mus.* a rhythmic pattern of 8 beats with a signature of 8/4. — **elli** heavy-handed. — **elli dul karı alır** *proverb* The heavy-handed marries a widow. — **esvap** expensive clothes. — **evfer** *Or. mus.* a rhythmic pattern of nine beats with a signature of 9/4. — **ezgi fıstıkî makam** *colloq.* slowly, slow and sure, unhurriedly, taking one's time, ponderously. — **gel=** /a/ to come hard (to), to be found difficult. —**ına git=** /ın/ to give offence, hurt the feelings. — **hapis** penal servitude, imprisonment with hard labor. — **hava** 1. unhealthful climate. 2. lugubrious melody. 3. *prov.* kind of slow dance. — **ihmal** *law* gross negligence. — **iş** hard work. — **işit=** to be hard of hearing. — **kanlı***. — **kazan geç kaynar** *proverb* (*lit.* A heavy cauldron boils late) Great things are done slowly. — **kol köprüsü** *mil.* heavy bridge. — **kusur** *law* gross negligence. — **küre***. — **mal** expensive goods. — **ol!** go slowly! — **otur=** to be costly, to work out to be expensive. — **otur ki bey desinler!** *proverb* Behave with dignity so that you may be respected. — **para cezası** *law* fine. **kendini** — **sat=** to agree only after many entreaties, to sell oneself high, to make a point of one's own importance. — **semaî** *Or. mus.* 1. *name of a musical form*. 2. a rhythmic pattern of 10 beats. — **sıklet** *sport* heavy-weight. — **silâh** *mil.* heavy arms. — **söyle=** to use hard words. — **sözler** hard words. — **şarkı** elaborate Oriental song. —**ını takın=** to put on a grave demeanor, conduct oneself with gravity and decorum. — **topçu** *mil.* heavy artillery. — **vurgu** *ling.* grave accent. — **yaralı** seriously wounded, gravely injured. — **yongayı yel kaldırmaz** *proverb* (*lit.* The wind will sweep away a heavy chip.) He who has power weathers the storm.

ağır=[r] آغِرمِ *obs., var. of* **anır=**.

ağırbaşlı آغِرباشلو serious-minded, dignified, sedate. —**lık** serious-mindedness, dignity, sedateness.

ağırca آغِرجَه somewhat heavy.

ağırceza (—..—) آغِرجزا *short for* — **mahkemesi** criminal court for major cases. — **işleri** *law* indictable offences.

ağırkanlı آغِرقانلو indolent, sluggish, slow. —**lık** indolence, sluggishness.

ağırküre *neol.* barysphere.

ağırla=[r] آغِرلَه /ı/ 1. to treat with marks of respect and distinction (guest). 2. to become heavy. 3. to slow down. 4. *obs.* to become smelly.

ağırlama آغِرلامَه 1. *verbal n.* 2. *Or. mus.* another name given to the «yürük aksak» rhythmic pattern.

ağırlan=[r] آغِرلانى 1. to be treated with respect and distinction (guest). 2. to become heavy. 3. to become sedate, discreet, dignified. —**dır=** *caus. of* **ağırlan=**.

ağırlaş=[r] آغِرلاشى to become heavy, etc. (*cf.* meanings of **ağır**). —**tır=** *caus.*

ağırlat=[r] آغِرلتى /ı,a/ *caus. of* **ağırla=**.

ağırlık[tı] آغِرلِق 1. weight, heaviness, weightiness; *phys.* gravity. 2. a weight used in weighing. 3. slowness of motion or action. 4. indigestibility. 5. foulness, stench. 6. costliness. 7. sedateness, gravity, serious-mindedness. 8. hardness of hearing. 9. stupidity. 10. fatness. 11. severity of a disease. 12. unhealthiness. 13. baggage, luggage; *mil.* train. 14. money, jewellery, clothes, etc., presented to the bride by the bridegroom, according to previous agreement. 15. nightmare. — **bas=** /a/ 1. for a nightmare to oppress one. 2. for sleepiness to overcome one. 3. for apprehension to overcome (one). — **et=** *obs.* to treat with honor and respect (guest). — **kütlesi** *astr.* gravitational mass. — **merkezi** *phys.* center of gravity.

ağırlıklu آغِرلِقلُو *obs.* esteemed, honored.

ağırsa=[r], **ağırsın=**[ar] آغِرساَم آغِرصنى /ı/ *prov.* to find burdensome; to treat as a burden (guest).

ağırşak[tı] آغِرشاق 1. spindle whorl. 2. cap-shaped disk. —**lan=** *obs.* to become round and more or less prominent; to produce a round prominence.

ağış *sc.* ascending movement, rise.

ağıt[dı] آغِت *prov.* dirge, lament, funeral song; wailing, keening, lamentation. — **et=**, — **kopar=**, — **yak=** to wail, lament for the dead. —**çı** wailer, mourner, wailing woman.

ağız[ğzı] 1 آغِز 1. mouth. 2. opening; entrance; mouth (of a river); muzzle (of a gun). 3. edge, rim (of a cup); brink (of a precipice); cutting edge (of a knife, etc.); bit (of a key); point (of a pen). 4. a fill, *as in* **ikinci** — the second fill (of an oven); a time *as in* **çamaşırı üç — yıkadım** I washed the laundry three times. 5. style of speech, way of talking; language, dialect, vernacular, *as in* **külhanbey ağzı** slang, **Anadolu ağzı** Anatolian dialect. 6. style of singing, *as in* **Urfa ağzı** the Urfa style of singing. 7. talk, language; persuasive words. —**dan** orally; by word of mouth. —**iyle** personally (to tell). —**ını aç=** 1. to open one's mouth. 2. to speak up. 3. to start to say hard things, to give vent to one's feelings. —ını **açacağına gözünü aç!** Don't stand gaping, open your eyes! —**ını açıp gözünü yum=** to pour out an unrestrained diatribe. —**ı açık** 1. open, without a cover (receptacle). 2. gaping idiot, stupid. 3. kind of open shelf or showcase. —**ı açık ayran delisi** idiot. —**ı açık kal=** to be open-mouthed with astonishment. — **açma=**, —**ını açma=** not to open one's mouth, to be silent, to hold one's tongue, to shut one's eyes and not see. — **açtırma=** to give no opportunity to talk. — **ağza** 1. mouth to mouth, face to face (to talk). 2. brimful. —**ı ağzına** brimful, quite full. — **ağza dolu** quite full, brimming. —**ı ağzına kavuşma=** *prov*. to be very happy. — **ağza ver=** to put heads together and talk. —**dan ağza yayıl=** to be spread from mouth to mouth (rumor). —**a alınmaz** 1. inedible, unpalatable. 2. obscene, very vulgar, unmentionable. — **alışkanlığı** habit of saying (what one's mouth is used to utter). —**ına alma=** not to mention, not to let pass one's lips. — **ara=**, —**ını ara=** to sound out (a person). —**ının aşı olma=** to be beyond one's capacity. — **at=** *obs*. to brag. —**ı aya gözü çaya bak=** *colloq*. to do things in a haphazard way. —**ına bak=** /ın/ to hang on one's lips; to obey blindly. —**ından baklayı çıkar=** to put aside considerations and speak out, to let the cat out of the bag. —**ında bakla ıslanma=** not to be able to keep a secret. —**ına baktır=** to have great charm in talking. —**ından bal ak=** (*lit*., to have honey flowing from one's lips) to talk sweetly. — **ballandır=** /ı/ to sweeten one's mouth, to find pleasure in talking of enviable things. —**ını bıçak açma=** to be too distressed to talk, have one's mouth sealed with grief. — **bir et=** to agree to say the same thing. — **biriktir=** *obs*., *same as* **ağız bir et=**. — **birliği et=** to agree. —**ı boş** indiscreet, unable to keep a secret. —**ını boz=** to use bad language, to swear, vituperate. —**ı bozuk** 1. foulmouthed, scurrilous. 2. *obs*. hardmouthed (horse). —**ı büyük** pretentious, talking big. —**ı cıvık** *prov*. garrulous, indiscreet. — **çak=** /a/ *obs*. to flatter. —**ı çarpık** wry-mouthed. —**ı çarpıl=** 1. for one's mouth to become crooked. 2. to put on a sulky face. —**ını Çarşamba pazarına çevririm** (*lit*. I shall turn your mouth into the Wednesday market.) I shall punch you in the mouth (if you say it). —**ı çelikli** inveterate talker. — **çevresi** *obs*. gold or silver-embroidered guest napkin. —**ından çıkanı kulağı işitme=** not to realize what one says, to be carried away by one's temper. —**ına çöp koymamış ol=** not to have eaten a thing. —**ını da-**

ğıt= /ın/ 1. to swear. 2. to hit someone in the mouth (for saying something). — **dalaşı** quarrel, row. —**ı değiş=** to change one's attitude (in speaking). — **değişikliği** variety in food. —**ını dik=** (*lit*., to sew one's mouth) to shut up like a clam. —**ı dili bağlan=** to be tongue-tied. —**ı dili kuru=** to talk oneself dry. — **dil verme=** to be too ill to talk. —**ında dili yok** taciturn, quiet, never objecting, peaceable. —**ı doğrusuna git=** to follow one's nose, to go straight, to behave unconcernedly. —**dan dolma** muzzleloader. —**dan dolma malûmat** hearsay information. — **dolusu küfür** unrestrained swearing. —**ından dökül=** 1. to be said unconvincingly, half-heartedly (words). 2. to be evident from one's words (lie). —**a düş=** to be in everybody's mouth, to be a subject of common gossip, to have one's reputation spoiled. —**ından düşürme=** /ı/ to talk about constantly. —**ını düzelt=** to watch one's way of talking, to shift to politer talk. — **et=** /a/ to try to persuade; to talk in a theatrical manner, to swagger. —**ını faraş gibi aç=** to answer back impudently. —**ına geleni söyle=** 1. to talk without thinking, to prattle. 2. to scold or swear unreservedly. —**ında gevele=** to mumble. —**ı gevşek** blabberer, garrulous, indiscreet. —**ından girip burnundan çık=** /ın/ to get around someone with persuasive words. —**ına girecek gibi yaklaş=** /a/ to come too close to someone. —**ına göre olma=** to be an unsuitable subject for discussion as being too exalted for the speaker. —**ının harcı olma=** /ın/ to be far above one to talk about (person) —**ı havada** with head in the air (walking); conceited (in one's talking), braggish; asking for a fantastic price. —**ını havaya aç=** to be left in the cold, not to get a thing. —**ını havaya aç, götünü bayıra!** heaven forbid. —**ını hayra aç!** don't say such an ill-omened thing! heaven forbid! don't say it. —**ının içine bak=** /ın/ to hang on someone's lips. — **iğ=** /a/ to ask a favor, to beg. 2. to pucker one's mouth. —**dan işitme** hearsay. —**ından kaçır=** /ı/ to let slip (words). —**ına kadar** up to the brim, full. —**ı kalabalık** garrulous, babbling out many things at a time. — **kalabalığı** flow of words. — **kalabalığına getir=** /ı/ to confuse (the issue) by a flow of words. —**ının kalayını ver=** /ın/ *slang* to rebuff brusquely. —**dan kap=** to snatch a secret out of one. —**ını kapa=**, —**ını kapat=** 1. to close the mouth, shut up, be silent. 2. to close someone's mouth, to silence; to bribe into silence. —**dan kapma** learned by ear. — **karası** slander, calumny. —**ı kara** 1. who enjoys giving bad news, morbid. 2. who intrigues, backbites. —ı **bir karış açık kal=** to gape with astonishment. **—ının kaşığı olma=** /ın/ to be far above one to talk about (person). — **kavafı** tough talker. — **kavgası** quarrel, altercation, battle of words. **—ına kilit vur=** to lock someone's lips, to silence. **—ını kiraya mı verdin?** Why don't you say something? **—ı kok=** to have bad breath. **—ını kokla=** /ın/ obs. to sound someone out. **—ının kokusunu çekmek, —ının kokusunu dinle=** /ın/ to put up with someone's caprices. **—ı köpür=** to foam at the mouth. **—dan kulağa** from mouth to mouth. **—ı kulaklarına var=** to grin from ear to ear, to be extremely pleased. **—ı kulağına yakın** prov. who talks in a thoughtful and considerate way. **—ın kurusun** (lit. May your mouth dry out.) Shut up. Stop it. (said to one who predicts evil things). **—iyle kuş tutsa** no matter what he does (he will not succeed or be appreciated). **— kuşağı** naut. rail. **—ından lâf al=** /ın/ to get information out of one, to wangle words out of someone. **—ında lâf çiğne=** to beat around the bush. **—ından lâf kaçır=** to let slip, to let a secret out unintentionally. **—ınıza lâyık** delicious, I wish you could have it too (food). **— mızıkası** mouth organ. **— otu** obs. priming, primer (of a gun). **—ının otunu ver=** /ın/ prov. to give someone his due. **—ının ölçüsünü al=** to be reproved for saying something, to get as good as one gives. **—ının ölçüsünü ver=** /a/ to give someone the deserved answer, to give someone a piece of one's mind. **—ını öpeyim!** I should like to kiss your mouth for bringing such good news. **—ına bir parmak bal çal=** /ın/ (lit., to let lick honey from one's finger) to try to put someone off by promises or petty gains. **—lara bir parmak bal ol=** to become a subject of gossip. **— patlangıcı** bubble gum. **—ının payını al=** to have a bitter experience, to be greatly disappointed, to get bitten. **—ının payını ver=** /a/ same as **—ının ölçüsünü ver=**. **—ı pek** secretive. **—ının perhizini ver=** /a/ to silence. **— persengi** the usual theme of one's discourse, subject constantly harped upon. **—ı pis** foulmouthed. **—ını poyraza aç=** slang to be left in the cold, not to have a share in. **— sakızı** subject of constant talk. **—dan sakız avla=** to try to extract information from a person. **—ının salyaları ak=** to desire longingly. **— sat=** to brag, boast. **—ı sıkı** secretive, discreet. **—ını silip otur=** (lit., to wipe one's mouth and to sit). 1. to act as if nothing had happened. 2. to give up (protecting, etc.), not to say anything any more. **—iyle söyle=** to say it oneself. **—ından söz al=** /ın/ 1. same as **—ından lâf al=**. 2. to obtain a promise. **—ında söz çiğne=** to beat around the bush. **—ından söz kaçır=** same as **—ından lâf kaçır=**. **— suyu** saliva. **—ının suyu ak=** to have a strong desire for something. **—ının suyunu akıt=** /ın/ to make one's mouth water. **—ı sulan=** same as **—ının suyu ak=**. **—ı süt kok=** (lit., to have one's mouth smell of milk) to be immature, young. **— şakası** joke, jesting. **—ını şapırdat=** to smack the lips. **— tamburası** Jew's harp. **— tamburası çal=** colloq. to say disconcerting things. **—ına taş almış** (lit. He has a pebble in his mouth.) He keeps a stubborn silence. **— tadı** harmony, peace (in family or community). **— tadiyle** with full enjoyment, with no disharmony. **—ının tadını al=** /dan/ to have had a bitter experience (with). **—ının tadını bil=** to be a gourmet. **—a tat, boğaza feryat!** (lit., taste to the mouth, wail to the throat) delicious, but scanty (food). **— tavanı** palate. **—ı teneke kaplı** (lit., with one's mouth lined with tin) insensitive to hot food. **—ını tıka=** /ın/ to stop someone's mouth. **—ını topla** Shut up. Don't be impudent. **—ında torba mı var?** (lit. Do you have your mouth in the fodder-bag?) Can't you say something? **—ı torbaya yakın** easy to get along with, good-natured. **—ını tut=** to hold one's tongue. **—ında tükürüğü kuru=** to have one's mouth dry from repeating a thing many times. **— tütünü** chewing tobacco. **— üşür=** obs. to agree in advance to say the same thing. **—ı var dili yok** same as **—ında dili yok**. **—ın var olsun!** I am very glad to hear it. **—ı varma=** to be reluctant to say something, not to have the heart to say it. **—ına yakışmıyor** It is not like you to say that. **—ı yan=** /dan/ to have a painful experience (with). **— yap=** to try to explain away a matter. **— yarı** obs. saliva, spittle. **—ını yay=** to broaden one's mouth (impudent manner of talking). **—ını yele aç=** slang to be left in the cold, not to get what one expects. **—ından yel alsın** (lit. May the wind take it from your mouth.) Heaven forbid! **—ını yırtarım** Hold your tongue. Stop it or I'll hit you. **—ı yok** quiet, mild of speech; unable to speak for oneself, helpless. **—ını yokla=** /ın/ to sound out (a person). **—ını yor=** to talk uselessly, to waste time with one's talking. **—ı yukarda** charges high prices. **—ı yüksel=** to demand higher prices. **— yüreğin artığını söyler, — yüreğin taşkınını söyler** proverb When the heart is full, the mouth cannot keep silent. **—ına bir zeytin ver, ardına bir tulum tut!** (lit. Put an olive in its mouth, hold a skin-bag to its bottom.) Give a trifle and expect plenty!

ağız[gz1] 2 آغز آغِیز آغُز 1. colostrum, beestings. 2. cream (of milk).

ağızla=ʳ آغزلامق /ı/ 1. to mouth a thing, make a mouth to it. 2. *naut.* to fix in an opening (spar, etc.). 3. *naut.* to reach the entrance (of a port, etc.).

ağızlaş=ʳ آغزلاشمق *anat.* to anastomose. **—ma** anastomosis.

ağızlat=ʳ آغزلاتمق /ı/ *caus. of* **ağızla=**.

ağızlık⁶¹ آغزلق 1. mouthpiece (of pipe, trumpet, etc.). 2. cigarette-holder. 3. appliance to put into or over the mouth of an animal, muzzle. 4. cover of leaves put over a full fruit-basket. 5. stone ring put over the mouth of a well. 6. *prov.* funnel. 7. *obs.* the top part of a fluid. **—çı** maker of cigarette-holders.

ağızsız آغزسز overbashful, soft-spoken, submissive.

ağla=ʳ آغلامق 1. to weep, shed tears, cry. /a/ 2. to weep, mourn (for). 3. to complain; to whine. 4. to shed tears (tree). **—rsa anam ağlar, kalanı yalan ağlar** (*lit.*, it is only my mother who would weep, the tears of all the others would be false) 1. Only a mother's tears are true. 2. No one else would suffer but myself. **—mıyan çocuğa meme vermezler** *proverb* No one feeds the baby that does not cry. **—ma ölü için, ağla diri için** *proverb* Cry not for the dead but for the living. **— sıkla=** to weep and lament.

ağlağan آغلاغان *obs.* crybaby, tearful.

ağlâl¹¹ (. —) اغلال A *lrnd., pl. of* **gul**.

ağlama آغلامه weeping, crying; lamentation. **A— Duvarı** Wailing Wall.

ağlamaklı ol=ʳ, **ağlamalı ol=**ʳ آغلامقلی اولمق آغلاملی اولمق to feel like crying.

ağlamış آغلامش tearful, whining. **— suratlı** always wearing a mournful face.

ağlamsa=ʳ, **ağlamsı=**ʳ آغلامسامق آغلامسیمق to whine, whimper.

ağlamsık⁶¹ آغلامسق whining, whimpering, tearful.

ağlaş=ʳ آغلاشمق 1. to weep together. 2. to lament together.

ağlat=ʳ 1 آغلاتمق /ı/ *caus. of* **ağla=**. **—ırsa Mevlâm bir gün güldürür** *proverb* If the Lord causes me to weep, He is sure to make me laugh some day.

ağlat 2 (. —) اغلاط A *lrnd., pl. of* **galat**.

ağlayık⁶¹ آغلایق *obs., same as* **ağlamış**.

ağlayış آغلایش weeping; complaint.

ağlâz اغلاظ A *lrnd., superl. of* **galiz**.

ağleb اغلب A *lrnd., superl. of* **galib**. **—i ihtimal** (…… —) P most probably, in all probability.

ağlef اغلف A *lrnd.* 1. encased. 2. uncircumcised. 3. hard, inaccessible to the truth. 4. abounding in comforts.

ağlık⁶¹ آغلغی *prov. for* **aklık**.

ağma آغمه *obs.* 1. ascension, rise. 2. star. 3. shooting star.

ağmad (. —) اغماد A *lrnd., pl. of* **gımd**.

ağman آغمان *prov.* fault, blemish.

ağna 1 (. —) اغنی A *lrnd., superl. of* **gani**.

ağna 2 (. —) اغنا A *lrnd.* paraphernalia of a bride.

ağna=ʳ 3 آغنامق *var. of* **ağına=**.

ağna=ʳ 4 آغنامه *prov., same as* **anla=**.

ağnak⁶¹ اغناق *obs.* place where animals may roll in the dust.

ağnam (. —) اغنام A [*pl. of* **ganem**] *obs., Maliye term.* 1. sheep; cattle. 2. sheep tax, cattle tax. **— bacı** *obs.* sales tax on cattle. **— müdürü** *obs.* director of the cattle tax office. **— rüsumatı** *obs.* taxes of various kinds paid on sheep and goats. **— vergisi** cattle tax, sheep tax.

ağnat=ʳ 1 آغناتمق /ı/ *var. of* **ağınat=**.

ağnat=ʳ 2 آغناتمق *prov., same as* **anlat=**.

ağniya (.. —) اغنیا A *lrnd., pl. of* **gani**.

ağniye اغنیه A *lrnd.* [*pl. of* **gına**] songs, canticles; singing.

ağo آغو *prov., same as* **ağa**.

ağraz 1 (. —) اغراض A *lrnd., pl. of* **garaz**.

ağraz 2 (. —) اغراض A *lrnd., pl. of* **garz**.

ağreb اغرب A *lrnd., superl. of* **garib**.

ağrel اغرل A *lrnd.* 1. uncircumcised. 2. plentiful, fruitful, abundant.

ağrı 1 آغری ache, pain; throb, spasm; *usu. pl.* throes of childbirth, labor, travail. **—sı tut=** for birth pains to commence, to commence labor. **— ver=** /a/ to hurt.

ağrı=ʳ 2 آغریمق 1. to ache, hurt, throb with pain. 2. *obs.* to suffer pain; to grieve.

Ağrı 3 آغری *geog.* 1. Ararat. 2. *name of a vilayet in Eastern Anatolia.* **— dağı** Mount Ararat.

Ağrıboz آغریبوز Gk 1. Euboea. 2. Chalkis, Euripos.

ağrık⁶¹ 1 آغرق 1. *obs.* ache. 2. *prov.* sick person.

ağrık⁶¹ 2 آغرق *prov.* heavy things, baggage.

ağrıklı آغرقلی 1. continuously aching. 2. diseased.

ağrılı آغریلی aching, painful.

ağrıma آغریمه sheep disease causing loss of wool.

ağrısız آغریسز painless. **— başa kaş bastı** (*lit.* A head with no ache is bothered by the eyebrow.) He who has no worries invents them. **— baş mezarda gerek** *proverb* Only death ends all troubles. **— baş yastık istemez** *proverb* A healthy person needs no coddling.

ağrıt=ʳ آغریتمق /ı/ to hurt, to cause to ache.

ağribe اغربه A *lrnd., pl. of* **gurab** 1.

ağribetül'arab اغربة العرب A (*lit.*, the crows of

the Arabs) *hist.* certain famous dark-skinned heroes of ancient Arabic history, born of black mothers.

ağsa=ᵣ اَغْسَامَ آ *obs. for* **aksa**= 1.
ağsakᵏ¹ اَغْسَاك آ *obs. for* **aksak.**
ağsan (.—) اغْصَان A *lrnd., pl. of* **gusn.**
ağsat=ᵣ اَغْصَانِمِ آ *obs. for* **aksat**= 1.
ağsı *neol., anat.* reticular.
ağsır=ᵣ اَغْرَس آ *prov. for* **aksır**=. —ᵢk *prov. for* **aksırık.** —t= *prov. for* **aksırt**=.
ağşiye اغْشِيَه A *lrnd., pl. of* **gışa.**
ağtaş اغْطَش A *lrnd.* 1. dark. 2. weak-eyed.
ağtiye اغْطِيَه A *lrnd., pl. of* **gıta.**
ağu 1 آغُو *archaic for* **ağı** 1.
ağu 2 آغُو *var. of* **agu.** —**cuk** *var. of* **agucuk.**
âğulᵘ (——) آغُول P *lrnd.* side-glance; angry look.
ağula=ᵣ آغُولَامَ *archaic for* **ağıla**=.
ağulu آغُولُو *archaic for* **ağılı.**
Ağustos آغُسْتُوس آغُسْطُوس L August. —**ta bokun mu dondu?** *vulg.* How can you complain of cold on such a warm day? — **böceği** 1. cicada. 2. chatterbox. —**ta suya girse balta kesmez buz olur** (*lit.,* If he went into the water in August, the water would freeze so hard that an axe could not break it.) He is always unfortunate; he has no luck at all.
ağuş (——) آغُوش *var. of* **aguş.**
ağvalˡˡ (.—) اغْوَال A *lrnd., pl. of* **gul.**
ağvar (.—) اغْوَار A *lrnd., pl. of* **gar** 2.
ağvat (.—) اغْوَاط A *lrnd., pl. of* **gait.**
ağyar (.—) اغْيَار A [*pl. of* **gayr**] 1. *poet.* others, strangers; rivals, all those who are connected with the beloved except the lover himself. 2. *myst.* those other than God.
ağyed اغْيَد A *lrnd.* 1. lithe, tender, pliant. 2. drowsy.
ağyer اغْيَر A *lrnd., superl. of* **gayur.**
ağzab اغْضَب A *lrnd., superl. of* **gazûb.**
ağziye اغْزِيَه A *lrnd., pl. of* **gıza,** victuals, food.
ah 1 (——) آه A, P آخ 1. ah!, oh!; alas! 2. sigh, groan. — **al**=, —**ını al**= to be cursed by someone for one's cruelty, to have caused tears. — **çek**= to sigh. —**ını çek**= /ın/ to suffer for the tears one has caused to others, to get one's deserts for a wicked deed. —**ı çık**= /ın/ for the tears of the injured to turn against the evildoer. — **deyip ah işit**= to be left to one's grief, to sigh and moan. — **deme ki düşmanın oh demesin** *proverb* Don't cry lest your enemies rejoice. — **u elem** pain and suffering. — **u enin** sighs and groans. — **et**= to sight. — **u feryad** sighs and laments. — **u figan** sighs and wailings. —**a gel**= to get one's deserts for wicked deeds. —**ı göklere çık**= for one's sighs to reach heaven. —**ı kalma**= /ın/ for the tears of the oppressed not to go in vain. — **min-el-aşk!** Alas, for love! — **min-el-mevt!** Ah cruel death! (often on tombstones). — **u nale** sighs and laments. — **of de**= to keep sighing. —**ı serd** *poet.* deep sigh, heart-rending sigh. —**ı tut**= /ın/ *same as* —**ı çık**=. —**ına uğra**=, —**a uğra**= /ın/ *same as* —**ını çek**=. — **vah,** — **u vah** sighs and laments. —**ı yerde kalma**= /ın/ *same as* —**ı kalma**=. — **u zar** sighs and tears.
ah 2 اخ A *lrnd.* brother. — **billiban** foster brother. — **lieb** half brother by the father. — **liebeveyn** full brother. — **liüm** half brother by the mother.
ah=ᵃʳ 3 احْمَس *prov. for* **ak**= 2.
aha آها *prov.* here, there.
ahabᵇᵇ¹ احَبّ A *lrnd., superl. of* **habib, muhib.**
ahabir (.——) اخَابِير A *lrnd.* various kinds of information.
ahabîs (.—.) اخَابِيث A *lrnd., pl. of* **ahbes.**
Ahabiş 1 (.—.) اخَابِيش A *lrnd.,* [*pl. of* **Ahbeş**] Abyssinians.
Ahabiş 2 (.——) اخَابِيش A *lrnd.* [*pl. of* **uhbuş**] Abyssinians.
ahaci (.——) اخَاجِي A *lrnd., pl. of* **uhciye.**
âhad 1 (——) آحَاد A [*pl. of* **ehad**] 1. *math.* units. 2. *lrnd.* individuals. — **hanesi** *math.* unit column.
ahad 2 احَد *var. of* **ehad.**
ahadᵈᵈ¹ 3 احَدّ A *lrnd., superl. of* **hâd** 2.
âhadinas (——.—) آحَادِنَاس P *lrnd.* a person of the common people.
ahadis (.——) اخَادِيث A Hadiths. —**i nebeviye** traditions of the sayings of the Prophet Muhammad.
ahadiyetᵗⁱ (..—.) احَدِيَّت *var. of* **ehadiyet.**
ahaffᶠᶠⁱ احَفّ A *lrnd., superl. of* **hafif.**
ahakᵏᵏ¹ احَقّ A *lrnd., superl. of* **hak** 1. truest, very right.
ahalˡⁱ (—.—) آهَال P *lrnd.* rubbish, trash.
ahali (.——) اهَالِي A inhabitants, population, the people. — **mübadelesi** exchange of population.
aharʳʳ¹ 1 احَرّ A *lrnd., superl. of* **har 5, 6.**
ahar 2 آهَار [**âhar** 4] dressing, finish (for cloth), size (for paper).
âhar 3 (—.) آخَر A *lrnd.* another, other. — **bir kimse** another person.
âhar 4 (——) آهَار P *same as* **ahar** 2.
aharla=ᵣ آهَارْلَامَ /ı/ to size, dress, finish (paper or cloth). —**n**= *pass.* —**t**= *caus.*
aharlı آهَارْلِي dressed, sized, finished (paper, cloth).
ahasˢˢⁱ 1 احَصّ A *lrnd., superl. of* **hasis** 1.
ahasˢˢⁱ 2 احَصّ A *lrnd.* extra special, peculiar; choice; intimate.
ahasin (.—.) اخَاسِن A *lrnd., pl. of* **ahsen.**
ahatᵈⁱ 1 آحَاد *var. of* **âhad** 1.
ahatᵈⁱ 2 احَد *var. of* **ehad.**

ahavatᵗⁱ (..—) آهوات A *lrnd.* sisters. **A—ı Hud** *collective name for the 6th, 7th, and 10th Suras of the Quran.*
ahavi (..—) اُخَوي A *lrnd.* brotherly, sisterly, fraternal.
ahbâb (.—) اَحباب A *lrnd., pl. of* **hib.**
ahbapᵇⁱ اَحباب [**ahbâb**] acquaintance; friend. **— çavuşlar** *colloq.* pals, cronies, chums. **—ça konuş=** /la/ to be on friendly terms (with). **— ol=** /la/ to strike up a friendship with. **—lık** acquaintance, friendship. **—lık et=** /la/ to be on friendly terms (with).
ahbar 1 (.—) اَحبار A *lrnd., pl. of* **hibr 1.**
ahbar 2 (.—) اَخبار A information; news; narratives, traditions, chronicles. **—î** (.——) A *obs.* chronicler.
ahbes اَخبث A *lrnd., superl. of* **habis 1.**
ahbeseyn اَخبثين A *lrnd.* the two excrements of the body, urine and feces.
Ahbeş اَحبش A *lrnd.* the Ethiopians; an Ethiopian.
ahbiye اَخبيه A *lrnd., pl. of* **hıba.**
ahbun اَخبون Arm *prov.* manure.
ahcar (..—) اَحجار A *lrnd., pl. of* **hacer 1.**
ahçı اَچى [**aşçı**] 1. cook. 2. keeper of a small restaurant. **— başı** head-cook, chef. **— dükkânı** small restaurant, eating-house. **— iskambili** kind of card game. **— kadın** woman cook. **— yamağı** kitchen boy. **—lık** profession of a cook; art of cooking, cookery, cuisine. **—lık et=** to be a cook by profession, to work as a cook, to be a chef.
ahdᵈⁱ **1** عهد A *lrnd., same as* **ahit. A—i Atik*.**
ahd 2 عهد A *lrnd.* 1. a recently fallen shower. 2. first rain of the season.
ahdaᵃⁱ اَضدع A *lrnd., superl. of* **hadi 3.**
ahdân (.—) اَحدان A *lrnd., pl. of* **hıdn.**
ahdar اَخضر A *lrnd.* green.
ahdas 1 (.—) اَحداث A *lrnd., pl. of* **hades 1.**
ahdas 2 (.—) اَحداث A *lrnd., pl. of* **hades 2.**
ahdeb اَحدب A *lrnd.* 1. hunchbacked, humpbacked, gibbous. 2. difficult, perplexing, crooked.
ahden عهداً A *lrnd.* by treaty, promise, oath.
ahdet=ᵈᵉʳ عهد ايتمك [**ahit**] /a/ to engage solemnly, to contract to do, to pledge, to promise with an oath, to vow.
ahdgüsil عهدگسل P *lrnd.* breaking one's promise.
ahdî (.—) عهدى A *law* pertaining to a treaty, stipulated by a pact, contractual. **— tarife** customs tariff applied under treaty.
Ahdiatikᵏⁱ (...—) عهد عتيق P *obs.* the Old Testament.
Ahdiceditᵈⁱ (...—) عهد جديد P *obs.* the New Testament.

ahdipişin (..——) عهد پيشين P *lrnd.* former days, days gone by.
ahdlaş=ⁱʳ عهدلاشمق *var. of* **ahitleş=.**
ahdli عهدلى *var. of* **ahitli.**
ahdname (.—.) عهدنامه P *var. of* **ahitname.**
ahdolsun عهد اولسون [**ahit**] I swear! I vow!
ahdüpeyman (...—) عهد و پيمان P *poet.* solemn oath.
ahekᵏⁱ (—.) آهك P *lrnd.* 1. lime, plaster. 2. depilatory made of lime and arsenic. **—i sadef** shell-lime. **—i siyah** Roman cement. **—i tefte** quicklime.
ahen 1 (—.) آهن P *lrnd.* 1. iron; steel. 2. *poet.* steel weapon, sword.
[*For compounds, see* **ahenicüft - aheniter.**]
Ahen 2 آهن *geog.* Aachen.
ahen aşiyan (—.—.—) آهن آشيان P *lrnd.* thimble.
ahencame (—.—.) آهن جامه P *lrnd.* 1. chain mail, coat of mail, armor. 2. iron bands fastened around a heavy box.
ahencan (—.—) آهن جان P *lrnd.* ironhearted, tried in adversity.
ahençub (—.—) آهن چوب P *lrnd.* iron skewer, spit for roasting.
ahendig (—.—) آهن ديك P *lrnd.* iron pot, cauldron.
ahendil (—..) آهن دل P *lrnd.* brave, courageous, dauntless.
ahene (—..) آهنه P *lrnd.* iron ring.
aheng (—.) آهنگ P *lrnd.* 1. *same as* **ahenk.** 2. act of drawing along, extension. 3. line, row, series. 4. curve, arch; crown of an arch or dome. 5. supporting wall. 6. design, purpose, intention; prepared, fitted, eager. 7. tuning; tuned, in tune. 8. introductory chords, overture. 9. melody, tune, music; concord, symphony, harmony. 10. custom, habit, fashion, usage; canon, regulation, rule. 11. perseverance, persistence. 12. speed, haste, quickness, agility. **— et=** 1. to set about; to set out. 2. to enjoy oneself. 3. to make merry with music and dancing, etc.; to sing. 4. to tune an instrument. 5. to prepare for, to undertake.
ahengdar (—.—) آهنگدار P *same as* **ahenktar.**
ahenger (—..) آهنگر P *lrnd.* blacksmith.
ahengerî (—..—) آهنگرى P *lrnd.* smith's craft.
ahengî (—.—) آهنگى P *lrnd.* 1. preparedness. 2. consonance, harmony.
ahenha, ahenhay (—.—) آهنها آهنهاى P *lrnd.* difficult to restrain, strong, restive (horse).
ahenî (—.—) آهنى P *lrnd.* 1. iron, made of iron. 2. hard.
ahenicüft (—...) آهن جفت P *lrnd.* plowshare.
ahenigâv (—..—) آهن گاو P *lrnd.* plowshare.
aheniham (—..—) آهن خام P *lrnd.* pig iron.

ahenin (—.—) آهنین P *poet.* 1. iron, made of iron. 2. hard, strong. **—can** (—.——) P *poet.* ironhearted, unfeeling, cruel, inured to distress. **—ciğer** (—.—..) P *poet.* brave and enduring, intrepid. **—duş** (—.——) P *poet.* strongbacked, sturdy.

aheninerm (—...) آهن نرم P *lrnd.* soft iron.

aheninkaba (—.—.—) آهنین قبا P *lrnd.* coat of mail.

aheninkemer (—.—..) آهنین کمر P *poet.* 1. girdle. 2. brave warrior.

aheninpençe (—.—..) آهنین پنجه P *poet.* 1. ironhanded, strong, powerful. 2. iron hand with strong springs, on which athletes exercise their grip.

aheninreg (—.—.) آهنین رگ P *poet.* muscular (horse).

ahenisebz (—...) آهن سبز P *lrnd.* well-tempered steel.

aheniserd (—...) آهن سرد P *poet.* 1. cold iron. 2. the human heart.

aheniter (—...) آهن تر P *lrnd.* well-tempered steel.

ahenk[ɡi] (—.) آهنك [**aheng**] 1. harmony, accord, agreement. 2. music, musical party. **—i ezelî** predetermined harmony, preestablished harmony. **— kaidesi** the rule of vowel harmony. **—i savait** vowel harmony. **— tahtası** *mus.* sounding board.

ahenkaba (—..—) آهن قبا P *lrnd.* plate armor, coat of mail.

ahenkeş (—..) آهن کش P *lrnd.* magnet.

ahenkle=[r] (—...) آهنكلمك /ı/ to tune. **—n=** *pass.* **—ş=** to accord, get into time with others. **—ştir=** to bring into accord, to harmonize. **—t=** *caus.* of **ahenkle=**.

ahenkli (—..) آهنكلی in tune, harmonious; in accord, in order.

ahenksiz (—..) آهنكسز inharmonious, discordant, out of tune. **—lik** lack of harmony, discord.

ahenktar (—.—) آهنكدار [**ahengdar**] harmonious, in tune, in accord.

ahenpare (—.—.) آهن پاره P *lrnd.* piece of iron.

ahenpaye (—.—.) آهن پایه P *lrnd.* rest on which a spit turns.

ahenreg (—..) آهن رگ P *poet.* strong, sinewy (horse).

ahenrüba (—..—) آهن ربا P *lrnd.* magnet.

ahensa, ahensay (—.—.) آهن سا ، آهن سای P *lrnd.* file, rasp.

aher 1 (—.) آخر *var.* of **âhar 3.**

aheste (—..) آهسته P 1. slow. 2. gentle. 3. calm. 4. low, soft (voice). **— aheste** slowly; gently; softly. **— beste** slowly, taking one's time.

ahestegi (—..—) آهستگی P *lrnd.* 1. slowness. 2. gentleness. 3. calmness. 4. softness (of voice).

ahestelik[ɡi] (—...) آهسته لك *same as* **ahestegi.**

ahesteray (—..—) آهسته رای P *poet.* calm in judgment, of moderate views, wise.

ahesterev (—...) آهسته رو P *poet.* going slowly, walking gently.

ahestesuhan (—....) آهسته سخن P *poet.* softspoken; low-voiced.

ahfa (.—) اخفا افغا A [*superl.* of **hafi**] *lrnd.* most secret.

ahfad 1 (.—) اضفاد A *cf.* **ahfat.**

ahfadiyelik[ɡi] (.—...) اضفادیه لك *colloq.* suitable to be handed down to future generations.

ahfat[di] (.—) اضفاد [**ahfad**] grandsons, grandchildren.

ahfeş 1 اخفش A *lrnd.* weak-eyed, day-blind, nyctalops.

Ahfeş 2 اخفش A *name of various Arabian grammarians.* **—in keçisi gibi başını salla=** (*lit.*, to nod like Ahfesh's goat) to agree senselessly with everything another person says.

ahger اخگر P *lrnd.* live coal, ember.

ahgül اخگل P *lrnd.* chaff, awn, beard of wheat, etc.

ahı اخی *var.* of **ahî.**

ahılık[ɡi] اخیلك *var.* of **ahilik.**

ahım şahım آهم شاهم *colloq.* beautiful, bright, especially good. *usu. in* **— bir şey değil** of no particularly striking beauty, value, quality.

ahır 1 (—.) آخر [**ahur**] stable, shed, barn.

âhır 2 (—.) آخر *var.* of **âhir 1.**

ahır=[ır] **3** آخرمق *obs.* to hack, to cough slightly, to expectorate.

ahırla=[r] آخرلامق to become stiff from staying too long in the stable.

Ahısha, Ahıska آخضخه *geog.* Akhaltsikhe (Caucasus).

ahi اخی [*Arabic* (.—)] brother (in a religious fraternity or trade guild). **A—ler** the Akhis (urban fraternity ruling over parts of Anatolia in late Seljuk times).

Ahibaba اخی بابا *hist.* dervish of an order centered in Kırşehir, visitor to the guilds of various trades, *esp.*, of tanners and saddlers.

ahibba (..—) احباء A beloved friends, sweethearts.

ahîd (.—) عهید A *lrnd.* bound by a promise, confederate, ally.

ahihte (—.., ——.) آهخته آهیخته P *poet.* unsheathed, drawn (sword).

ahil (—.) آهل A *lrnd.* 1. inhabited, peopled. 2. having a family. 3. sociable, domesticated, tame.

ahilik[ɡi] اخیلك 1. the institution, organization, or quality of an Akhi (*cf.* **ahi**). 2. generosity, chivalry.

ahillâ (..—) اهلّة A *lrnd., pl. of* **halil** 1.
ahille اهلّة A 1. *lrnd., pl. of* **hilal**. 2. toothpicks.
âhin (—.) آهن A *lrnd.* inherited wealth.
âhir 1 (—.) آخر A 1. last, latter. 2. last part, end. 3. at the end, at the last. —**i berdelacuz** *calendar* storm usually occurring about March 17th. —**i eyyam-ı matar** *calendar* storm usually occurring about May 12th. — **nefes** the last breath. — **ol**= to come to an end, to finish. —**i sittei sevir** *calendar* storm usually occurring about April 26th. —**i siyah-ı bevarih** *calendar* storm usually occurring on July 9th. —**i sukutu evrak** *calendar* storm usually occurring about December 9th. — **zaman** the end of time. **A— Zaman Peygamberi** the Last Prophet, Muhammad.
ahir 2 (.—) اخر A *lrnd.* last, hindmost.
âhirbin (—.—) آخربين P *lrnd.* farsighted, prudent.
âhire (—..) آخره A *fem. of* **âhir** 1.
ahiren (—´..) 1 آخراً A *lrnd.* lastly, at last, finally.
ahîren 2 (.—´.) اخيراً A *lrnd.* lastly, recently.
ahiret (—..) آخرت A *same as* **ahret**. —**lik** *same as* **ahretlik**.
âhirikâr (—..—) آخركار P *lrnd.* 1. the issue, result, end of a matter. 2. finally, at length.
âhirîn (—.—) آخرين A *lrnd.* the latter ones, the last ones.
âhirül'emr (—...) آخرالامر A *lrnd.* finally, at last, at length.
ahitʰᵈⁱ عهد [ahd] 1. injunction, solemn request; imperial decree. 2. agreement, pact, treaty, covenant. 3. oath, promise, engagement. 4. space of time, period, epoch; reign. — **al**= /dan/ to receive a promise. [*For compounds, see* **Ahdiatik — ahdüpeyman**.]
ahitleş=ⁱʳ عهدلشمك to enter into a solemn agreement with one another.
ahitli عهدلو bound by a promise, treaty or oath.
ahitname (..—.) عهدنامه [ahdname] (written) pact, treaty; character, privilege; capitulations (in the Ottoman Empire).
âhiz 1 (—.) آخذ A *lrnd.* receiver, one who receives.
ahizʰᶻⁱ 2 اخذ [ahz] *lrnd.* a taking, receiving; seizure, capture, exaction. [*For compounds, see* **ahziasker - ahzukaz**.]
âhize (—..) آخذه A *elec.* receiver, receiving set.
ahkad (.—) احقاد A *lrnd., pl. of* **hıkd**.
ahkâm (.—) احكام A 1. judicial sentences, judgments 2. commands, ordinances, decrees, statutes, laws, gists of laws, stipulations, requirements, provisions (of a law, etc.). 4. inferences from omens, etc.; absurd suppositions. 5. *colloq.* conceit, false pride. —**ı âmire** *law* imperative provisions. — **çıkar**= *colloq.* to put forward absurd suppositions. — **defteri** *Ott. adm.* book kept by each government office, in which pertinent regulations, decrees, etc., were written. —**i nahiye** *law* prohibitions. —**ı şahsiye** *law* personal statute. —**ı şer'iye** statutes of the Muslim canonical law. —**ı tefsiriye** *law* variable rules, non-compulsive provisions.
ahkar احقر A most humble; very contemptible.
ahkem احكم A *lrnd.* most stable, very firm.
Ahkemülhakimîn (...—.—) احكم الحاكمين A the Firmest of Judges, God.
ahlâ 1 (.—) احلى A *lrnd.* very sweet, sweetest.
ahla=ʳ 2 آهلامق To sigh. —**yıp ohla**= to sigh and moan.
ahlâb (.—) احلاب A *lrnd., pl. of* **hilb**.
ahlâbünnisa (.—..—) احلاب النساء A *lrnd.* woman chasers.
ahlad *cf.* **ahlat** 1. احلد
ahlâf 1 (.—) احلاف A *lrnd., pl. of* **hilf** 1.
ahlâf 2 (.—) احلاف A *lrnd., pl. of* **halef**.
ahlâkᵏⁱ 1 (.—) اخلاق A 1. morals, morality; ethics. 2. virtues, good qualities. 3. conduct, manners; character. — **ve âdap** *law* morals. — **ve âdaba aykırı muameleler** *law* acts offending against good morals. — **bozukluğu** moral corruption. — **dersi** lesson in behavior. — **dışı** amoral. —**ı hamîde** laudable moral qualities. —**ı hasene** good moral qualities. — **hocası** teacher of morals. — **kaidesi** moral principle, rule of morals. —**ı umumiyeye tecavüz** *law* offence against good morals. —**ı zemime** bad moral qualities.
ahlâkᵏⁱ 2 (.—) اخلاقیه A *lrnd., pl. of* **halak**.
ahlâkçı (.—.) اخلاقجی 1. moralist. 2. *school slang* teacher of ethics.
ahlâkdışı (.—..) *neol.* amoral. —**lık** amoralism.
ahlâkiyat (.———) اخلاقيات A ethics.
ahlâkiyet (.———.) اخلاقيت A morality.
ahlâkiyun (.———) اخلاقيون A moralists, ethicists.
ahlâkî (.——) اخلاقی A moral, ethical.
ahlâklı (.—.) اخلاقلی of good conduct, decent. —**lık** good conduct, decency.
ahlâksız (.—.) اخلاقسز immoral, dissolute. —**lık** immorality, vice.
ahlâm (.—) احلام A *lrnd., pl. of* **hulm**.
ahlâs اخلص A *lrnd.* most pure, unadulterated.
ahlatᵈⁱ, ᵗⁱ 1 اخلاط Gk 1. wild pear. 2. wild pear-tree. 3. boor. — **ağa** boor, fool, clown. —**ın iyisini ayılar yer** *proverb* (*lit.* The best wild pears are eaten by the bear.) Fortune favors fools.

ahlat 2 اخلاط A *physiol.* the humours of the body. **—ı erbaa** the four humours (blood, phlegm, yellow bile, black bile). **—ı fâside** morbid humours. **—ı rediye** corrupted humours.

ahlât 3 اغلاط A *lrnd., superl. of* **mahlut.**

ahmaiye (..—.) احمیة A *in* **adale-i —** *anat.* scalenous.

ahmakᵍⁱ احمق A stupid, foolish; dote, fool, idiot. **— ıslatan** (*lit.,* drenching the fool) drizzle, very light rain. **—ça** 1. somewhat foolish. 2. foolishly, stupidly. **—lık** stupidity, foolishness.

ahmalⁱⁱ (.—) احمال A *lrnd., pl. of* **haml.**

Ahmed 1 احمد A man's name; one of the names of the Prophet Muhammad.

ahmed 2 احمد A *lrnd.* most laudable, gratefully commemorable.

Ahmedî (..—) احمدی A *lrnd.* Belonging to Ahmed; Mohammadan.

Ahmediye 1 (..—.) احمدیة A 1. *name of several orders of dervishes.* 2. *obs.* The Sultan Ahmed Mosque in Istanbul.

ahmediye 2 (..—.) احمدیة A kind of richly ornamented old Turkish velvet.

ahmer احمر A *lrnd.* red.

ahmeran (..—), **ahmereyn** احمران احمرین A *lrnd.* (*lit.,* the two red things) 1. wine and flesh. 2. gold and saffron.

ahmerlikᵍⁱ احمرلك redness, ruddiness.

Ahmetᵈⁱ احمد *var. of* **Ahmed 1.**

ahna (.—) احنا A *lrnd.* 1. bent, bowed, curved. 2. inclined, affectionate.

ahnas (.—) احناس A *lrnd., pl. of* **hins.**

ahnef احنف A *lrnd.* bow-legged, crook-legged.

ahnes احنس A *lrnd.* snub-nosed, pug-nosed.

Ahnuh (.—) اخنوخ Bib. the patriarch Enoch.

ahr عهر A *lrnd.* debauchery, ribaldry.

ahram 1 (.—) احرام A *lrnd., pl. of* **harem.**

ahram 2 (.—) احرام A *lrnd., pl. of* **harîm.**

ahrar (.—) احرار A *lrnd., pl. of* **hür.**

Ahrariye (.——.) احراریة A *name of an order of dervishes related to the Nakshibendi order.*

ahras (.—) احراس A *lrnd., pl. of* **haris 3.**

ahraz احرس [**ahres**] *prov.* dumb, mute, inarticulate. **—ın dilinden anası anlar** *proverb* Only a mother understands the speech of the mute.

ahreb 1 احرب A *pros.* verse in which the measure **mefâîlü** is replaced by **mef'ûlü.**

ahreb 2 احرب A *lrnd., superl. of* **harab.**

ahrec احرج A *lrnd.* piebald, black and white in patches.

ahrem احرم A *pros.* verse starting with a measure shortened by one syllable.

ahres احرس A *lrnd.* dumb, mute.

ahreş احرش A *lrnd.* 1. rough to the touch, scabrous. 2. rough-scaled (lizard, etc.). 3. roughbacked (camel, etc.). 4. new-minted (coin).

ahret آخرت [**ahiret**] the other world beyond the grave, hereafter, the next world. **— adamı** a man who is not of this world, otherworldly person. **— babası** adoptive father. **— evlâdı** adopted child. **—e git=** to die. **— hakkını helâl et=** to renounce one's claim for past favors or grievances (otherwise settled on Judgment Day.) **— kardeşi** adopted brother, adopted sister. **—i kazan=** to secure one's place in heaven. **— korkusu** the fear of the Last Judgment. **— oğlu** adopted son. **—te on parmağım yakasında olsun** May my ten fingers be on his collar in the next world (said to call down judgment on someone on the Last Day, to claim something from someone at the Last Judgment). **— suali** 1. the examination on the Day of Judgment. 2. harassing interrogation. **— yolculuğu** death. **—ini yap=, —ini zenginleştir=** to acquire merit in God's sight.

ahretlikᵍⁱ آخرتلك 1. adopted orphan brought up as a servant. 2. pertaining to the other world, otherworldly.

ahriyan (..—) اخربان, **âhriyan** (—.—) آخربان P *lrnd.* goods and chattels, household furniture.

ahrüf احرف A *lrnd., pl. of* **harf.**

ahsas (.—) احساس A *lrnd., pl. of* **his.**

ahseb احسب A *lrnd.* 1. most calculated, suitable, fitting. 2. leprous. 3. red-haired, roan-colored, tawny.

ahsem احسم A *lrnd.* 1. flat and broad-nosed. 2. broad (sword). 3. lion.

ahsen احسن A *lrnd.* most beautiful, very good, better, best. **—i takvim** *Isl. theol.* (*lit.,* the most excellent pattern) the form of man as created.

ahsentü (´..) احسنت A *lrnd.* well done!, bravo!

Ahsenülhalikîn (...—.—) احسن الخالقین A *theol.* the most beneficient of creators, God.

ahsenülvecheyn احسن الوجهین A *lrnd.* the better of the two alternative methods.

ahsır=ʳ, **ahsur=**ᵘʳ اخسرمه *prov. for* **aksır=.**

ahşa 1 (.—) احشا A *anat.* intestines, bowels, guts; viscera.

ahşa 2 (.—) اخشی A *lrnd.* very frightening, most dreadful.

ahşab 1 (.—) احشاب A *lrnd., pl. of* **haşeb.**

ahşab 2 *cf.* **ahşap.**

ahşam 1 اخشم [*Middle Persian*] *prov. for* **akşam.**

ahşam 2 (.—) احشام A *lrnd., pl. of* **haşem.**

ahşamın (.'.) اخشامین *obs.* in the evening.

ahşapᵇⁱ احشاب [**ahşeb**] wooden, made of timber (house, ship, bridge).

ahşeb اخشب A *lrnd.* 1. wooden. 2. coarse, hard. 3. severe. 4. high rugged mountain.
ahşen اخشن A *lrnd., superl. of* **haşin**.
ahşic (.—) اخشیج , (——) آخشیج P *lrnd.* opposite, contrary.
ahşican (.———) اخشیجان , (———) آخشیجان P *lrnd.* 1. the opposites. 2. the four elements.
ahşig (.—) اخشیگ , (——) آخشیگ P *lrnd., var. of* **ahşic**.
ahşigân (.———) اخشیگان , (———) آخشیگان P *lrnd., var. of* **ahşican**.
ahtab (.—) اططاب A *lrnd., pl. of* **hatab**.
ahtabos اختبوس , **ahtabot** اختبوت Gk *obs. for* **ahtapot**.
ahtapot[tu, du] آختاپود آغاناپوت اختاپوط , اختپوط Gk 1. octopus, cuttlefish. 2. polyp or similar tumor. 3. *slang* hanger-on, sponger.
ahtar 1 (.—) اخطار A *lrnd., pl. of* **hatar**.
ahtar=[ır] **2** اخترمه افتارمه *prov. for* **aktar**= 1.
ahte (—.) آخته P *lrnd.* 1. drawn (sword). 2. castrated.
ahter اختر P *lrnd.* 1. star. 2. fortune. **—i dünbaledar** comet. **A—i Kâviyan** *name of the ancient Persian ensign, originally a blacksmith's apron.* **—i suhte** *same as* **—suhte**. **—gû** (..—) P astrologer. **—suhte** (..—.) P one whose star is lost in the sun's rays, *i. e.* unfortunate. **—şinas** (...—) P who knows the stars, astronomer. **—şümar** (...—), **—şümür** P astronomer, astrologer.
ahtlaş=[ır] عدم کشی *var. of* **ahitleş**=.
ahu 1 (——) آهو P 1. gazelle, antelope. 2. graceful boy; beautiful girl. 3. eye like velvet. **—yu ateşîn** *astr.* Aries. **— bakışlı** gazelle-eyed, velvet-eyed. **—yu bezm** the subject of the toasts of a convivial party. **—yı Çin** *poet.* the musk-deer of China. **—yı dünbalekeşide** *poet.* eye elongated at the outer corner with antimony, doe-look. **—yu felek** *poet.* 1. the sun. 2. the sign Aries. **— gözlü** gazelle-eyed. **—yu havarî** *poet.* the sun. **—yu Hotan** *poet.* the sun. **—yu ner** *poet.* 1. male antelope. 2. black and white cloud. **—yu sefid** *poet.* a fair beauty. **—yu simîn** *poet.* fair-skinned beauty. **—yu siyah** *poet.* black antelope. **—yu şir-efgen** *lrnd.* 1. beautiful young person. 2. bewitching eye. **—yu Tatar** *poet.* the musk-deer of Tartary. **—yu zerîn** *poet.* 1. the sun. 2. flagon, cup.
ahu 2 (——) آهو P *lrnd.* blemish, fault, vice.
ahubaba آهوبابا [ahibaba] 1. friendly old man. 2. *same as* **ahibaba**. 3. old man who smokes a lot.
ahubeçe (——..) آهوبچم P *poet.* fawn.
ahubere (——..) آهوبره P *poet.* fawn. **—i felek** 1. the sun. 2. the sign Aries.

ahuçeşm (——.) آهوچشم P *poet.* with beautiful large eyes like a gazelle.
ahudil (——.) آهودل P *poet.* timid, fearful.
ahududu آهوطودى اهودت [ahu, dut] raspberry, *bot.* Rubus idaeus.
ahugân (———) آهوكان P *poet.* fawns.
ahumade (———.) آهومادە P *lrnd.* doe, hind, female gazelle.
ahun (——) آهون P *lrnd.* pit, underground gallery.
ahunber (——.) آهونبر P *lrnd.* 1. miner; well-digger. 2. housebreaker, burglar.
ahund (—.) آهوند P *lrnd.* theologian, preacher, schoolmaster in Iran.
ahupa, ahupay (———) آهوپا آهوپاى P *poet.* fleet of foot.
ahur (——) آهور P *lrnd., same as* **ahır 1**.
ahuşitab (——.—) آهوشتاب P *poet.* swift as a gazelle.
ahval[ii] (.—) احوال A conditions, circumstances; affairs, event. **— ahkâmı değiştirir** rules change according to circumstances. **—i âlem** world affairs, state of the world. **—i hâzıra** present state of affairs, present circumstances, status quo. **—i mutade** the usual state of affairs, ordinary circumstances. **—i sıhhiye** health conditions. **—i siyasiye** political conditions. **—i şahsiye** *law* civil status. **—i şahsiye sicili** register of births, deaths, and marriages. **— ve şerait** *law* the circumstances. **—i umumiye** general conditions.
ahvat اخوط A *lrnd.* 1. most comprehensive. 2. very prudent, most cautious.
ahvaz (.—) احواض A *lrnd., pl. of* **havz**.
ahvec احوج A *lrnd., superl. of* **muhtac**.
ahvef احوف A *lrnd., superl. of* **mahuf**, **muhif**.
ahvel احول A *lrnd.* 1. squint-eyed. 2. most crafty.
ahver 1 احور A *lrnd.* 1. having beautiful eyes with large pupils. 2. intellect.
Ahver 2 احور A *lrnd.* the planet Jupiter.
ahya (.—) احیا A *lrnd.* the living. **— ve emvat** the quick and the dead.
ahyaf (.—) اخیاف A *lrnd.* 1. different things. 2. uterine brothers or sisters. 3. feet of hills, valley slopes. 4. *Arabic pros.* distich composed alternately of words all of dotted and then all of undotted letters.
ahyal[ii] (.—) اخیال A *lrnd., pl. of* **hayl**.
ahyan (.—) احیان A *lrnd., pl. of* **hin 2**.
ahyanen (.—'.) احیاناً A *lrnd.* from time to time, now and then, occasionally.
ahyar (.—) اخیار A *lrnd.* good (men); virtuous; kind, beautiful.
ahyat (.—) اخیاط A *lrnd., pl. of* **hayt**.
ahyaz (.—) احیاض A *lrnd., pl. of* **hayz 2**.
ahyer اخیر A *lrnd.* better, best.

ahz اخذ *cf.* **ahiz 2.**
ahzab (.—) احزاب A *lrnd., pl. of* **hizb**.
ahzan (.—) احزان A *poet., pl. of* **hüzn**.
ahzar 1 (.—) احزار A *lrnd., pl. of* **hazer**.
ahzar 2 اخضر A *lrnd., var. of* **ahdar**.
ahzem احزم A *lrnd.* 1. most prudent, very cautious. 2. thick in the waist.
ahzer اخزر A *lrnd.* small and narrow-eyed, twinkling.
ahzet=^der اخذ ايتمك [**ahiz 2**] /ı/ to take, receive.
ahziasker اخذ عسكر P *obs.* a recruiting, enlistment. — **şubesi** recruiting office.
ahziintikam (....—) اخذ انتقام vengeance. — **et=** /dan/ to take vengeance.
ahzisar (..—) اخذ ثار P *lrnd.* vengeance. — **et=** to take revenge, to revenge oneself.
ahzugirift اخذ وگرفت P *law* apprehension. — **et=** /ı/ to apprehend, to arrest. — **müzekkeresi** warrant of arrest.
ahzuistifa (....—) اخذ واستيفا P *geom., logic* exhaustion.
ahzuita (..——) اخذ واعطا P buying and selling, commerce, business, trade. — **et=** to do business, to trade.
ahzukabz اخذ و قبض P *law* collection (of a sum), encashment. — **et=** to receive into one's possession, to collect, to cash.
aib (—.) آئب A *lrnd.* 1. who returns. 2. who turns to God. 3. setting (sun, etc.).
aid 1 (—.) عائد A *var. of* **ait**.
âid 2 (—.) آيد A *lrnd.* declining (day).
aid 3 (—.) عائد A *lrnd.* 1. that returns. 2. which accrues, redounds. 3. who visits a sick person.
aidat (—.—) عائدات A 1. subscription (to a society). 2. revenues, income, allowance. 3. remuneration. 4. agency fee (shipping).
aide (—..) عائده A *lrnd.* 1. income, revenue, profit. 2. advantage, utility. 3. favor; gift.
aidiyet^ti (—..—) عائديت A state of belonging (to a person), interest, concern.
aiffa (..—) اعفا, **aiffe** عفه A *lrnd., pl. of* **afif**.
âih (—.) عائه A *lrnd.* morally corrupt or suspect.
âihe (—..) عائهه A *lrnd.* shout, clamor.
aik^kı (—..) عائق A *lrnd.* that hinders; impediment, hindrance, obstacle. — **ol=** to be an impediment, to hinder.
aika (—..) عائقه A *lrnd.* hindrance, impediment, obstacle.
aikka عقا A *lrnd., pl. of* **akik 2**.
âil (—.) عائل A *lrnd.* 1. who supports his family. 2. who has a large family. 3. poor, necessitous, needy. 4. not in equipoise (balance). 5. deviating, swerving. 6. insufficient to furnish the shares of all the heirs (inheritance). 7. exceeding, in excess. 8. hard, distressing.
aile (—..) عائله A 1. family. 2. wife. — **bahçesi**, — **gazinosu** amusement place where only soft drinks should be served. — **cüzdanı** *banking* savings account. — **doktoru** family doctor. — **efradı** members of a family. — **hukuku** family law. — **ismi** family name, surname. — **mallari** *law* family property. — **meclisi** *law* family council. — **ocağı** home, the family hearth. — **reisi** head of the family, *law, pater familias.* — **şirketi emvali** *law* joint family property. — **vakfı** *Isl. law* pious foundation left to the benefit of the family. — **vesayeti** *law* family guardianship. — **yurdu** *law* family home. — **yuvası** home, family. —**ce** (—..) as a family. —**lik** *same as* **ailevî**.
ailevî (—..—) عائلوى *neol.,* based on Arabic regarding the family, private, domestic.
ain (—.) عائن A *lrnd.* 1. spectator, beholder, looker-on. 2. possessed of the evil eye. 3. running water.
aine 1 (—..) آئنه A *lrnd.* times, seasons. **her** — at all times, always.
aine 2 (—..) آئنه A *lrnd.* easy and short (stage of night journey).
aine 3 (—..) عائنه A *lrnd.* 1. visible body. 2. troop, flock, herd.
ainne عنه A *lrnd., pl. of* **inan 3**.
ais (—.) عائث A *lrnd.* lion.
aise (—..) آئسه A *lrnd.* who is past childbearing.
aiş (—.) عائش A *lrnd.* that lives, living; living comfortably.
aişe (—..) عائشه A *lrnd.* 1. *cf.* **aiş**. 2. *w. cap.* woman's name; name of the Prophet Muhammad's second wife.
ait^di (—.) عائد A /a/ concerning, relating to; pertaining to, belonging to. — **ol=** /a/ to concern, relate; to belong to.
aiz 1 (—.) عائذ A *lrnd.* that takes refuge.
aiz 2 (—.) عائز A *lrnd.* poor, necessitous.
aiz 3 (—.) عائض A *lrnd.* 1. who gives in exchange. 2. compensatory.
aizza (..—) اعزا, **aizze** عزه A *lrnd., pl. of* **aziz 1**.
aj (—) آژ P *lrnd.* rest, repose, ease.
ajan آژان F agent (of a firm or of a political organization). —**lık** agency.
ajanda آژاندا F agenda.
ajans آژانس F 1. agency; news agency. 2. news bulletin.
ajene (—..) اژنه P *lrnd., same as* **ajine**.

ajeng (—.) آڭَنْكْ P *lrnd.* wrinkle, fold, crease of the skin.

ajfendakki (—.—) آڭْفَنْدَاك P *poet.* rainbow.

ajigği (——) آڭِكْ P *lrnd.* wrinkle, fold, crease of the skin.

ajih (——) آڭِحْ P *lrnd.* discharge from the eyes.

ajine (——.) آڭِنَه P *lrnd.* steel pick used for notching millstones.

ajir 1 (——) آڭِرْ P *lrnd.* intelligent; awake, alert, vigilant; ready, prepared.

ajir 2 (——) آڭِرْ P *lrnd.* 1. pond, lake. 2. noise, sound; cry; shout.

ajirakki (———) آڭِرَاك P *lrnd.* noise, sound; cry; shout.

ajug (—.) آڭُكْ P *lrnd.* prunings, loppings, clippings.

ajur آڭُورْ F embroidery openwork. **—lu** open-worked.

akkı **1** آق 1. white. 2. clean, unsullied. 3. unblemished, beaming with honest pride (face). 4. white of the eye. 5. white of an egg. 6. white speck (in the eye). **—ı ak karası kara** white-skinned, black-eyed, black haired. **— akçe** silver money. **— akçe kara gün içindir** *proverb* White money is for a black day. **— alaca** having white spots. **— alem** *hist.* standard of the Ottoman sultans. **— altın** platinum. **— Arap** Arab. **— aş** sweet dish of rice flour and chicken's white meat. **— balıkçıl** great white heron. **— behmen** white behen, *bot., Centaurea behen.* **— benizli** of a fair complexion. **— biber** white pepper. **— çam** silver fir, *bot., Picea pectinata.* **— çöpleme** white hellebore, *bot., Veratrum album.* **— demir** wrought iron. **— düş**= /a/ 1. to begin to turn gray (hair, beard). 2. to have a white speck (eye). **— ev** the white tent of respected families among nomad tribes. **— göt kara göt geçit başında belli olur** (*lit.*, white buttocks, black buttocks, at the crossing they become evident) *proverb* There is a time when one's real character comes to light. **— göz** *prov.* coward. **— gözlü** hard-hearted, cruel, deceitful. **— gün ağartır, kara gün karartır** *proverb* Happy times gladden the heart; sorrow makes one gloomy. **—ı karayı seç**= to be old enough to know black from white. **—la karayı seç**= to have a very hard time. **— koyunu gören içi dolu yağ sanır** (*lit.* He who sees the white sheep thinks the inside of it is full of fat.) *proverb* Appearances can deceive. **— mika** white mica. **— oda** bridal chamber. **— pak*.** **— porselen** very white Chinese porcelain. **— saçlı** white-haired. **— sakal** elder in a community. **— sakal, kara sakal** all, high and low, rich and poor. **— sakallı** 1. white-bearded. 2. an elder of a village. **— sakallısından tut yok sakallısına kadar** young and old, all the people. **— sinir** sinew, tendon, nerve, yellow fibrous tissue. **— şeker kara şeker, bir damarı soya çeker** (*lit.*, White sugar, black sugar, one of its veins takes after its ancestors.) *proverb* Inheritance shows eventually. **— tilki** arctic fox, *zool., Alopex lagopus.* **— toz ağacı** aspen, *bot., Populus tremula.* **— yakut** white sapphire. **— yol** the Milky Way. **— yüz ile** honorably.
|For other compounds see **akağa - akzar**|

ak=ar **2** آقمق 1. to flow; to be shed. 2. to glide. 3. to ooze, to trickle, to drip; to leak. 4. to spread and blend as dye in washing. 5. to fray, to unravel (textiles). 6. /a/ *prov.* to have a liking (for). **—masa da damlar** (*lit.,* even if it does not flow, at least it drips) A small income (profit) is better than none at all. **—acak kan damarda durmaz** *proverb* One cannot escape fate. **—mış kumaş** frayed material.

âkkı **3** (—) آكْ P *lrnd.* 1. vice, defect, blemish. 2. calamity, misfortune.

âkkkı **4** (—) عاق A *lrnd.* undutiful to parents, disobedient.

akkkı **5** عقّ A *lrnd.* 1. cleft, furrow. 2. a cleaving, splitting; rending, slitting. 3. sacrificing a sheep, etc., on the birth of a child.

akkkı **6** عقّ A *lrnd.* unfilial.

akkkı **7** علاق A *lrnd.* 1. a hindering. 2. a delaying, putting off. 3. an interrupting. 4. a wearying of one with repetition. 5. a silencing in argument, etc. 6. beating, flogging 7. a wasting away by fever. 8. sultriness, a being windless (day).

Akkkı **8** علك A name of an Arab tribe.

aka آقا *prov., var. of* **ağa**.

akabbi **1** عقب |akb| 1. *anat.* heel; hock. 2. end; issue, result. 3. space after; time next after. 4. succeeding thing. 5. issue, descendants, offspring; *can. law* grandchildren from sons. **—ı leşker** rear-guard.

akab 2 عقب A *lrnd.* tendons, sinews.

akabe 1 عقبه A *lrnd.* 1. steep mountain road, pass. 2. *w. cap.*, Aqaba (name of a Red Sea port). 3. *w. cap. name of a summit between Mina and Mecca.* **A—i Sâni** *Isl. hist.* the second secret night meeting of the Prophet Muhammad with seventy men of Medina who swore to fight in his defense. **A—i Ulâ** *Isl. hist.* the first secret night meeting of the Prophet Muhammad with notables of Medina.

akabe 2 عقبه A *lrnd., anat.* sinew, tendon.

akabi (..—) عقبى A *anat.* calcancal.

akabince (...—.) عقبنجه |akab 1| in one's immediate rear, immediately behind one.

akabinde عقبنده |akab 1| immediately after, subsequently.

akabinden عقبندن [akab 1] 1. from behind one. 2. immediately after one.

akaç^cı neol. drain pipe. **—la=** to drain. **—lama** drainage. **—lama havzası** drainage basin.

âkad 1 اعقد A lrnd. 1. most knotted, most coagulated. 2. curly-tailed. 3. curly-horned. 4. stuttering, hesitating.

ak'ad 2 اقعد A lrnd. near in descent to an ancestor of a remote period, the intervening links having been very long-lived men.

akademi آقادمی F academy.

akademya (..'.) آقادمیا Gk same as **akademi**.

akağa آق آغا hist. white eunuch of the Sultan's palace. **A—lar Kapısı** the official residence and office of the white eunuchs in the Great Palace.

akağaç^cı آق آغاج kind of birch; kind of maple.

akağan آقاغان overflowing; fickle, changeable, unstable.

akaid (.—.) عقائد A theol. doctrines, tenets of faith, religious precepts, fundamental articles of faith, dogmas. **— kitabı** catechism.

akaik^kı (.—.) عقائق A lrnd., pl. of **akik 1, akika**.

akail (.—.) عقائل A lrnd., pl. of **akıle**.

akaim 1 (.—.) اقائم A lrnd., pl. of **akvam**.

akaim 2 (.—.) عقائم A lrnd., pl. of **akim, akime**.

akair (.—.) عقائر A lrnd., pl. of **akar 3**.

akais (.—.) عقائص A lrnd., pl. of **akisa**.

akait^dı (.—.) عقائد var. of **akaid**.

akaju آقاژو F mahogany.

akak^kı **1** آقاق prov. river bed; water course.

akak^kı **2** (.—.) عقاق A lrnd. unfilial conduct.

ak'ak^kı **3** عقعق A lrnd. magpie, zool. Pica caudata.

akak^kı **4** عقق A lrnd. 1. a being forked (lightning). 2. a being pregnant (beast).

ak'aka عقعقه A lrnd. 1. chatter, chattering (magpie). 2. rustling, crackling (of tissue).

akakıya (.—.—) اقاقیا A lrnd. tannin of the acacia.

â'kal^lı **1** اعقل A lrnd. most intelligent, most wise.

akal^llı **2** اقلّ A lrnd. 1. less, least, very little, very few; very small in value, very humble. 2. at the very least. **—i kalil** the least of the little. **— ma yekûn** the least possible. **—i müddet** the shortest space of time.

akala آق عله kind of cotton plant.

akalli اقلّی [akal 2] at least, at the least.

akalliyet (..—.) اقلیت A minority. **—ler** the minorities, esp. the non-Muslim communities in Turkey. **—in hakları** law minority rights. **—ler hukuku** law law and rights of minorities. **—te kal=** to be in the minority. **— mektepleri** schools of non-Muslim communities in Turkey. **—lerin temsili** minority representation.

akam 1 (.—) عقام A lrnd. 1. barren, childless. 2. unrelenting, ruthless; perverse. 3. disastrous (illness, war).

akam 2 عقم var. of **akm**.

akamber آق عنبر ambergris.

akamet (.—.) عقامت A sterility, barrenness. **—e uğra=** to fail, to come to naught.

akan آقان [ak= 2] that runs, flowing. **— sular durur** /a/ that leaves no place for objection, that clinches the argument. **— yıldız** meteor, shooting star.

akanim (.——) اقانیم var. of **ekanim**.

akap^bı عقب var. of **akab 1**.

akar 1 آقار [ak=2] 1. which runs, flowing. 2. leaking, leaky. 3. prov. brook, stream, rivulet. **— su** 1. running water. 2. cf. **akarsu. — sular durur** same as **akan sular durur. — yakıt** neol. liquid fuel. **— yıldız** same as **akan yıldız. —ı yok kokarı yok** colloq. having no special fault, quite all right, it's fine.

akar 2 (.—) عقار A 1. law real estates, landed property. 2. rented out accomodation or similar source of revenue.

akar 3 (.—) عقار A lrnd. barrenness, sterility.

akar 4 عقر A lrnd. being glued to the spot with fright, consternation; misfortune.

akarat^tı (.——) عقارات A immovable estate, pieces of landed property. **—ı mevkufe** the landed property endowment of a pious foundation.

akarca آقارجه prov. 1. running water. 2. permanently flowing fountain. 2. path. flux, fistula.

akaret 1 (.—.) عقارت A 1. piece of landed property that yields a revenue. 2. leased accommodation, shop or the like.

akaret 2 (.—.) عقارت A lrnd. barrenness, sterility.

akarib 1 (.—.) اقارب A lrnd. nearest kinsmen.

akarib 2 (.—.) عقارب A lrnd., pl. of **akreb 2**.

akarsu^yu آقارصو 1. diamond necklace. 2. same as **akar su**.

akas 1 عقص A lrnd. disagreeableness, ill temper, stinginess. 2. a being twisted over the ears (ram's horn).

akâs 2 عكس A *lrnd.* stubbornness, unmanageableness.
akasır (. —.) اقاصر A *lrnd.*, *pl. of* **aksar**.
akasi (. — —) اقاصى A *lrnd.*, *pl. of* **aksa 2**.
akasim (. — —) اقاسيم A *lrnd.*, *pl. of* **aksam 1, uksume**.
akasis (. — —) اقاصيص A *lrnd.*, *pl. of* **kıssa**.
akasma آقه آصمه 1. white bryony, *bot. Bryonia dioica*. 2. *name of several white-flowering climbers*.
akasya (..'.) آقاسيا F locust, *bot.*, *Robinia pseudoacacia*.
akatı[ı] (. —.) اقاطع A *lrnd.*, *pl. of* **kati**.
akati[ıı] (. — —) اقاطيع A *lrnd.*, *pl. of* **akta**.
akavil (. — —) اقاويل A *lrnd.*, *pl. of* **akval 1**.
akavim (. — —) اقاويم , (. —.) A *lrnd.*, *pl. of* **akvam**.
akaz[zzi] اقز A *lrnd.* 1. feathered (arrow). 2. featherless (arrow).
akb اقب A *lrnd.*, *same as* **akab 2**.
akbaba آق بابا 1. vulture. 2. *prov.* daisy. **—ya dön=** *colloq.* to become whitehaired.
akbah اقبح A *lrnd.*, *superl. of* **kabih**.
akbalık[tı] آق بالق *name of several kinds of fresh-water fish*; kind of sea fish, *zool.*, *Lucioperca*.
akbasma آق باصمه *path.* cataract.
akbenek[tı] آق بنك *path.* white speck in the eye.
akbiye اقبيه A *lrnd.*, *pl. of* **kaba 2**.
akciğer آق جكر lungs. **— borucuğu** *anat.* bronchiole. **— borusu** *anat.* bronchus. **— göbeği** *anat.* pulmonary hilum. **— keseciği** *anat.* pulmonary vesicle. **— petekleri** *anat.* pulmonary alveoli. **— veremi** *path.* pulmonary tuberculosis. **— zarı** *anat.* pleura **—liler** *zool.*, *Pulmonata*.
akça 1 آقچه آقى off-white, whitish, pale, faded. **— kanat** *prov.* sandfly.
akça 2 آقچه آقى [akça 1] *var. of* **akçe**.
akçaağaç[cı] آقچه آغاج maple. **—giller** *bot.*, *Aceraceae*.
akçaarmudu[nu] آقچه آرمودى fine-flavored summer pear.
akçakavak[tı] آقچه قواق white poplar, *bot.*, *Populus alba*.
akçapak[tı] آقچه پاك kind of fish, *zool.*, *Blicca bjoerkna*.
akçapakça آقچه پاكچه not bad looking (woman).
akçe آقچه [akça 2] 1. *hist.* small silver coin, asper (the basic unit of the older Ottoman money system, one third of a para). 2. money. **— adama akıl öğretir** *proverb* Money makes one wise. **—si ak olanın bakma yüzü karalığına** *proverb* Money makes up for most things. **— etmez** of no value, worthless. **—nin gittiğine bakma, işin bittiğine bak** *proverb* Don't spare your money if you wish your work done. **—nin gümüş olduğunu bilmiş** (*lit.*, he has found out that the asper is of silver) He is so clever as to know the obvious. **— kes=** to strike coins. **— kesesi** *obs.* purse. **— tahtası** a money changer's cash board. **—si ucuz olanın kendi kıymetli olur** *proverb* The generous man is liked. **—nin yüzü sıcaktır** *proverb* (*lit.* The face of money is warm.) The sight of money disarms. **—li** rich, wealthy. **—li adamdan dağlar korkar** *proverb* (*lit.* The mountains are afraid of the wealthy.) Money is power. **—lik** worth one asper, of small value. **—siz** penniless; without money. **—sizlik** pennilessness.
akçıl اقچل آقچيل whitish, faded; unpleasantly white.
akd[dı] عقد A *lrnd.* 1. *same as* **akit 2**. 2. knot, a tying. 3. arch, vault. 4. a place of figures in notation; decade. 5. opinion, belief, judgment, thought. 6. a bending down the fingers in counting or in archery. 7. a forming fruit, budding (tree); a developing breasts (girl). 8. a congealing, thickening (liquid).
akda (. —) عقدا A *lrnd.* 1. tongue-tied, who has a speech impediment (woman). 2. female slave.
akdah (. —) اقداح A *lrnd.*, *pl. of* **kadeh**.
akdam 1 (. —) اقدام A *lrnd.*, *pl. of* **kadem**.
akdam 2 *var. of* **akdem**.
akdar 1 (. —) اقدار A *lrnd.*, *pl. of* **kader, kadr**.
akdar=[ır] 2 اقدرمك *var. of* **aktar=** 1.
akdarı آق دارى millet, *bot.*, *Panicum miliaceum*.
akdem اقدم A *lrnd.* 1. former, more ancient. 2. foremost in place. **—i mülûk-ü zaman** the most outstanding of all the princes of the time.
akdemce (..'.) اقدمجه not long ago; a little while ago.
Akdeniz آق دڭز the Mediterranean (including the Aegean). **— adaları** the Archipelago. **— boğazı** the Dardanelles. **—e kaptan Mısıra sultan** very haughty, excessively proud, ostentatious.
akder 1 اقدر A *lrnd.*, *superl. of* **kadir 2**.
akder 2 اقدر A *lrnd.* 1. short-necked, short in stature. 2. that places his hind feet in the tracks of his forefeet (horse).
akdes اقدس A *lrnd.*, *superl. of* **kaddus, kuddus, mukaddes**.
akdet=[der] عقد ايتمك [akd 1] /ı/ 1. to tie. 2. to conclude (bargain), to settle (matter), to contract (marriage). 3. to hold (meeting), to set up (council).
akdiken آق ديكن buckthorn, *bot.*, *Rhamnus catharticus*.
akec (—.) آكج P *lrnd.* hook.
a'kef اعكف A *lrnd.*, *superl. of* **âkif**.
akek[ki] عكك A *lrnd.* sultry humid weather.

akenhaᵃ¹ علنكع A *lrnd.* male demon, ghoul.
aker عكر A *lrnd.* 1. a thickening, becoming turbid. 2. dregs, sediment. 3. filth, dirt.
akeş عكش A *lrnd.* a becoming matted together, mattedness.
akf عكف A *lrnd.* 1. hindering, detention. 2. a cleaving to.
akfa (.—) اقفا A *lrnd.*, *pl. of* **kafa**.
akfalˡˡ (.—) اقفال A *lrnd.*, *pl. of* **kufl**.
akfar (.—) اقفار A *lrnd.*, *pl. of* **kafr**.
akfas (.—) اقفاص A *lrnd.*, *pl. of* **kafes**.
akfed اقفد A *lrnd.* 1. club-footed. 2. that goes on the tips of his hoofs (horse).
akfer اقفر A *lrnd.* barren, desert.
akfi (.—) اقفى, **akfiye** اقفيه A *lrnd.*, *pl. of* **kafa**.
akfize اقفزه A *lrnd.*, *pl. of* **kafiz**.
akfulˡⁱ اقفل A *lrnd.*, *pl. of* **kufl**.
akgömlekᵏⁱ آق كوملك *anat., tunica albuginea*.
akgöt آق گوت stonechat, *zool., Saxicola torquata*.
akgünlükᵏᵘ, **akgünnük**ᵏᵘ آق گونلك frankincense, olibanum.
akhardal آق خردل white mustard, *bot., Sinapis alba*.
akher اقهر A *lrnd.*, *superl. of* **kahhar, kahir**.
akı 1 *var. of* **ahı**.
akı 2 *neol., phys.* flux, flow.
âkıb 1 (—.) عاقب A *lrnd.* 1. follower, successor. 2. the Successor of the Prophets: the Prophet Muhammad.
akıb 2 عقب A *lrnd., var. of* **akb**.
âkıbet (—..) عاقبت A 1. end, latter part. 2. consequence, outcome, result. 3. *log.* consequence. 4. ultimately, finally. —**bin** (—..—) P *lrnd.* who foresees consequences, foresighted. —**binî** (—..—) P, —**binlik** *lrnd.* foresight, prudence. —**endiş** (—...—) P *lrnd.* far-sighted, prudent. —**endişî** (—...—) P, —**endişlik** *lrnd.* prudence.
akıbetül'emr (—....) عاقبة الأمر A *lrnd.* 1. end of the matter, the long and short of it. 2. finally.
akıbüşşeytan (....—) عقب الشيطان A *lrnd.* a mode of sitting up on the heels, forbidden in worship.
akıcı آقيجى [ak=] 1. fluid, liquid. 2. fluent. — **sessiz** *phon.* liquid consonant. —**lık** 1. fluidity. 2. fluency.
âkıd 1 (—.) عاقد A *var. of* **âkid 1**.
akıd 2 عقد A *lrnd., var. of* **akid 2**.
akılᵏˡ **1** عقل [akl 1] 1. reason, intelligence; wisdom, discernment, discretion. 2. mind, comprehension; memory. 3. idea, opinion, thought. 4. prudence. 5. age of discretion, maturity. —**dan** from memory, by imagination. —**ımda** I haven't forgotten it, I have it in mind. —**ınca** 1. according to his intelligence. 2. according to his own lights, well-meaning but blundering. — **akıldan üstündür (ta arşa varınca)** There is always another mind that is superior, it always pays to consult others. — **al=** /dan/ to seek advice (from), to consult (a person). —**ı al=** /ı/ 1. to grasp, comprehend. 2. to believe in the possibility (of). —**ını al=** 1. to scare out of one's wits. 2. to cause one to lose one's head. — **almaz** unbelievable, inconceivable. —**ı başında** 1. intelligent, serious-minded. 2. in one's right mind. —**ını başına al=** *same as* —**ını başına topla=**. —**ını başından al=** to cause one to lose one's head. —**ını başına devşir=** *same as* —**ını başına topla=**. —**ı başına gel=** 1. to come to. 2. to come to one's senses, to sober down. 3. to think the better of it. —**ını başına getir=** 1. to recall oneself to one's senses. 2. to think the better of it. —**ı başından git=** to lose one's senses, to go out of one's mind. —**ı başından bir karış yukarı** thoughtless, foolish, absent-minded. —**ını başına topla=** 1. to come to one's senses, to collect oneself. 2. to gather one's wits together, to think and consider well. —**nla bin yaşa!** what a bright idea! (said sarcastically when a person gives a completely impossible idea or suggestion). —**ını boz=** to lose one's reason, to go mad. —**ını bulandır=** 1. to suggest a new possibility. 2. to confuse one's mind. —**ını çal=** /ın/ to enchant, fascinate; charm, captivate. —**ı çalık** crazy, irresponsible. —**ını çel=** /ın/ to dissuade from a good intention, to cause one to give up a decision, to lead astray. —**ından çık=** to slip one's mind. —**ından çıkar=** to dismiss from one's mind, to forget all about it, to give up the idea. —**ınla çok yaşa!** good for you!, well thought!, there's brains for you! — **danış=** /a/ to ask advice, to consult. — **defteri** *colloq.* notebook. —**ını değiştir=** to change one's mind. — **dişi** wisdom tooth. —**ına dokun=** /ın/ to unbalance. —**ı dur=** to be perplexed, dumbfounded. —**ına düş=** *prov.* to come into one's mind, to be remembered, to strike one. —**ı er=** /a/ to understand, to grasp. — **erdireme=** /a/ to be unable to grasp. —**ına es=** to strike (sudden idea), to occur (to some one, as a sudden impulse). — **et=** /ı/ to think (of). —**ı fikri** /da/ all his thoughts (are fixed on something). — **fukarası** idiot, stupid. —**dan gayrımüsellah** short of brains, feeble minded. —**ından geç=** to pass through one's mind (idea), to occur to one's mind. —**ından geçir=** /ı/ to happen to think (of). —**ına gel=** 1. to occur to one's mind. 2. to recur to one's memory. —**a gelen başa gelir** *proverb* What one fears always happens. —**ına geleni yap=** to act according to one's whims. —**ına getir=** 1. /ı,ın/ to remind

(someone). 2. /ı/ to recollect, remember, call to mind, recall. **—ı git=** to be perplexed. **—ı gözünde** *obs.* whose mind does not go beyond what his eyes see, not very imaginative. **— hastalığı** mental disease. **— hastanesi** hospital for mental diseases. **— hastası** insane person. **—ına hiffet getir=** to go mad. **— hocası** adviser, mentor, master (usually ironic). **— için tarik birdir** *proverb* There is only one way for the wise. **—ının iki çekirdeği eksik** *prov.* half-wit. **— ile fetva verilmez** *proverb* Even an intelligent person cannot make pronouncements; one has to live through an experience. **—ını kaçır=** to go mad, to go out of one's mind. **—ında kal=** to stay in one's mind, to be borne in mind, remembered. **— kârı değil** unreasonable, unwise, not done by an intelligent person. **—ı karış=** to be perplexed, to get one's mind muddled up. **—ını kaybet=** to lose one's mind. **—ı kes=** to decide, judge, or form an opinion. **—ı kısa** half-witted. **—ına koy=** /ı/ to have made up one's mind. **— kumkuması, — kutusu** a mine of wisdom (person). **—ının mıhı eksik** *prov.* half-witted. **—ı okkadan dört yüz dirhem eksik** (*lit.*, whose intelligence lacks 400 dirhems in the **okka**) feeble-minded. **— olmayınca başta kuru kafa neyler?** If there is no brain in the head, what can the empty skull do? **— olmayınca başta ne kuruda biter ne yaşta** *proverb* (*lit.* If there is no brain in the head, it will grow neither in the dry nor in the wet.) There is no cure for stupidity. **—ı oyna=, —ını oynat=** to go mad. **— öğret=** /a/ to give advice. **— para ile satılmaz** Brains cannot be bought with money. **—ları pazara çıkarmışlar, herkes gene kendi aklını beğenip almış** *proverb* (*lit.* Opinions were offered for sale in the market, everybody chose and bought his own again.) Everybody sticks to his own opinion. **—ını perişan et=** to upset one's mind. **—ını peynir ekmekle yemiş** (*lit.*, who has eaten wisdom with bread and cheese) who has lost his head, who acts foolishly. **— sat=** to give unwanted advice. **—ına sığdırama=** /ı/ to be beyond one's comprehension. **—ı sıra** *same as* **aklınca. —ına sin=** to sink into one's mind. **—ı sonradan gel=** to be wise after the event. **— sor=** /a/ to ask advice. **—ına şaşayım!** I am surprised at you!, have you no brains? **—ını şaşır=** to lose one's head, to go crazy. **—ı tepesinden yukarı** thoughtless, foolish, absent-minded. **— terelelli** freakish, frivolous (person). **—ına turp sıkayım!** (*lit.* Let me squeeze radishes on your brain.) 1. What a fool you are! 2. I don't want your advice. **—da tut=** /ı/ to bear in mind. **—ına uy=** /ın/ 1. to act according to someone's way of thinking. 2. to follow one's whim. **— var iz'an var, — var**

mantık var, — var yakın var 1. With a little bit of intelligence one can understand it. 2. Why don't you use your brains? **— ver=** /a/ to give advice. **— bir vezirdir, gönül bir padişah** (*lit.* The mind is a vizier, the heart is a sultan.) The heart may or may not do what the mind advises. **—a yakın** reasonable, sensible (word). **— yaşta değil baştadır** *proverb* Intelligence does not go by age. **—ı yat=** /a/ for one's mind to accept a matter, to be convinced. **—a yelken et=** to let oneself go, to follow one's fancy. **—ına yelken et=** to go crazy. **— zayıflığı** mental deficiency. **—ından zoru var** There is something wrong with his mind.

âkıl[ii] 2 (—.) عاقل A rational, intelligent, wise, prudent. **— ve baliğ** who possesses legal discretion.

âkıl[ii] 3 (—.) عاقل A *can. law* relation or companion of a homicide who is bound to contribute towards the payment of blood-money.

âkılâne (—.—.) عاقدنه P 1. wisely, intelligently, prudently. 2. wise, intelligent, prudent (act).

akılcılık[ft] *neol., phil.* rationalism.

âkıle 1 (—..) عاقل A *psych.* mental faculty, reason.

âkıle 2 (—..) عاقل A *can. law* the body of relations or companions of a homicide bound to pay the blood money.

akılgın آقل يغن white tamarisk, *bot., Tamarix mannifora.*

akıllâ (..—) اقلّ A *Irnd., pl. of* **kalil.**

akıllan=[ir] |*based on* **akıl** 1| to become wiser after some bitter experience. **—maz** incorrigible.

akıllı عقلی عقللو reasonable, wise, intelligent, prudent, clever. **— davran=** to act wisely. **— düşman akılsız dosttan yeğdir** *proverb* A wise enemy is better than a foolish friend. **— evlât neylesin malı, akılsız evlât neylesin malı?** *proverb* Inherited wealth is not necessary to the wise son and of no use to the unwise. **— geçin=** to pass for a wise man. **— köprüyü arayıncayadek deli suyu geçer** *proverb* While the careful man looks for the bridge, the impetuous one has crossed the water. **— ol da deli sansınlar** *proverb* Act wisely and care not if you are called a fool. **— uslu** sober-minded, wise. **—ca** intelligently, wisely, cleverly. **—lık** intelligence, cleverness. **—lık et=** to act intelligently.

akılsız عقلسز unreasonable, foolish. **— başın ayak çeker zahmetini, — baştan ne çeker sefil ayak, — iti yol kocatır** *proverb* Little wit in the head makes much work for the feet. **—lık** folly, foolishness.

akım *neol.* current, trend.

akın آقین آقن 1. rush, torrential flow. 2. raid. **— akın** rushing and surging in crowds. **— çap=** *obs., same as* **akın et=**. **— et=** /a/ to make a raid, to attack and pillage. **— sal=, — saldır=, — ver=** /a/ *obs., same as* **akın et=**. **—cı** 1. raider. 2. *hist.* a special corps of light cavalry whose duty was to pillage the enemy. 3. pioneering, crusading. **—cılık** incursion, raiding.

akındırık[kı] آقندریه *prov.* resin.

akıntı آقنتی آقنتی 1. current, flow. 2. *path.* flux, flow. 3. *arch.* inclination. **A— Burnu** name of a point on the Bosphorus near Arnavutköyü. **— çağanozu** current crab (said sarcastically of a person who has a conspicuous crookedness in his body). **— demiri** *naut.* kedge anchor. **—ya kürek çek=** (*lit.,* to row against the current) to waste one's efforts. **— midyesi** the common, reddish-brown mussel, *zool., Mytilus edulis.* **— payı** *naut.* leeway. **— zaviyesi** *naut., aero.* drift angle. **—lı** having a current. **—sız** still (water).

âkır (—.) عاقر A *lrnd.* barren, sterile.

âkırkarha (—..—) عاقر قرما A pellitory of Spain, *bot., Anacyclus pyrethrum.*

akış 1 آقیش flow, course, current. **— aşağı** downstream. **— yukarı** upstream.

akış='' **2** آقیشمی to flow all together.

akışkan *neol., phys.* fluid.

akıt='' آقیتمی /ı/ to cause to flow, to pour, to shed. **—ma** 1. *verbal n.* 2. cast (iron, etc.). 3. blaze (on a horse). 4. *prov.* pancake. **—tır=** /ı/ *caus. of* **akıt=**.

akib 1 (—.) عاقب *var. of* **akıb 1**.

akib 2 عقیب A *lrnd.* 1. follower; following, consequent. 2. time or space immediately after.

âkibet (—..) عاقبت *var. of* **âkıbet**.

akibinde (.—..) عقیبنده [**akîb 2**] /ın/ immediately after, on the heels (of), in consequence (of).

âkid 1 (—.) عاقد A *lrnd.* 1. who ties; who knots. 2. congealing. 3. who holds a meeting. 4. *law* contracting party, party to a contract.

akîd 2 (.—) عقید A *lrnd.* bound by compact, ally, confederate.

akîd 3 (.—) عقید A *lrnd.* coagulated, thickened, congealed.

akide 1 (.—.) عقیده 1. an article of faith, dogma. 2. religious faith, creed. **—yi boz=** to act contrary to one's faith. **—si bozuk** loose in religious convictions. **—si pâk** whose belief is sound.

akide 2 (.—.) عقیده A sugar candy. **— şekeri** sugar candy.

âkideyn (—..) عاقدین A *law* both contracting parties.

âkidîn (—.—) عاقدین A *law* the contracting parties, the signatories.

akidülkerem (.—...) عقید الکرم A *lrnd.* generous, very liberal.

akidüllisan (.—..—) عقید اللسان A *lrnd.* tongue-tied.

âkif (—.) عاکف A *lrnd.* 1. assiduous, persevering. 2. assiduous in devotion. 3. *w. cap., man's name.* **A— Paşa kaidesi** a style of writing in Arabic characters.

akik[kı] **1** (.—) عقیق A 1. carnelian, agate. 2. *poet.* red wine; profuse tears from reddened eyes. **—i nâb** *poet.* 1. pure wine. 2. the sweetheart's lip. **—ı Yemenî** carnelian from Yemen.

akik[kı] **2** (.—) عقیق A *lrnd.* 1. watercourse, deeply scooped-out ravine, valley scooped out by a stream; pool of water in a ravine. 2. hair shorn from newborn infants or animals. 3. flash of lightning. 4. sword. **—ı âlâ** the Upper Ravine of Medina.

akik[kı] **3** (.—) عکیك A *lrnd.* oppressively hot and humid (day); oppressiveness of humidity.

akika (.—.) عقیقه A *lrnd.* 1. watercourse, canal, river. 2. slip of cloth torn off. 3. prepuce cut off in circumcision. 4. hair shorn from newborn infant or animal; the ceremony of shaving the hair of an infant on the sixth day after birth. 5. sheep slaughtered as a thank-offering at a birth, etc. 6. flash of lightning piercing the clouds. 7. soft date stone.

âkil 1 (—.) آکل A *lrnd.* 1. eater; eating, consuming. 2. corrosive. 3. who receives bribes. 4. embezzler.

âkil 2 (—.) عاقل *var. of* **âkıl 2,3**.

akîl 3 (.—) عقیل A *lrnd.* 1. very reasonable, wise. 2. *w. cap., man's name.*

âkile (—..) آکله A *lrnd.* 1. eating; corrosive. 2. phagedenic ulcer; canker. 3. rust.

âkilnefsehü (—....) آکل نفسه A *lrnd.* kind of gum, euphorbium.

âkilülbeşer (—....) آکل البشر A *lrnd.* cannibal.

âkilülcerad (—...—) آکل الجراد A *lrnd.* who lives on grasshoppers.

âkilül'esmak[kı] (—...—) آکل الأسماك A *zool.* piscivorous, fish-eating.

âkilülhaşarat (—....—) آکل الحشرات A *zool.* insectivorous, insect-eating.

âkilülhaşayiş (—...—) آکل الحشائش A *zool.* herbivorous, plant-eating.

âkilülhevam (—...—) آکل الهوام A *zool.* insectivorous, insect-eating.

âkilülhububat (—...——) آکل الحبوبات A *zool.* grain-eating.

âkilülkül (—...) آکل الكل A *zool.* omnivorous.

âkilüllahm (—...) آکل اللحم , **âkilüllühum** (—...—) آکل اللحوم A *biol.* carnivorous, flesh-eating.

âkilünnebat (— ... —) آكلُ النبات A *zool.* herbivorous, plant-eating.

âkilüssemek[ki] (— ....) آكل السمك A *zool.* fish-eating.

akim (. —) عقيم A *lrnd.* 1. sterile, barren (woman), childless (man). 2. fruitless, unproductive; unsuccessful. 3. that brings no rain (wind), *esp.* west wind, also northwest wind. 4. sultry and windless (day). 5. ruthless (battle). — **kal**= to fail, to come to nought (plan).

akir 1 (. —) عقير A *lrnd.* 1. cut, wounded. 2. hocked, hamstrung. 3. barren, childless.

akir 2 عكر A *lrnd.* thick, foul, dreggy, turbid.

akîre (. — .) عقيره A *lrnd.* 1. voice of a singer, weeper or reader. 2. wounded leg; wounded (beast). 3. slain nobleman.

akis[ksi] 1 عكس [aks 1] 1. reverse; reversion. 2. reflection; reverberation; echo. 3. the contrary, opposite. 4. *sc.* inversion. 5. *log.* conversion. —**ini iddia et**= to assert the contrary. — **kabiliyeti** *sc.* reversibility. —**ini söyle**= to contradict. —**ler uyandır**= to awaken an echo, to arouse reactions (in the press, etc.).

âkis 2 (— .) عاكس A *lrnd.* reflected.

akis 3 عكس A *lrnd.* perverse, obstinate, bad-tempered.

akîs 4 (. —) عكيس A *lrnd.* layer (of a vine, etc.).

akisa (. — .) عقيصه A *lrnd.* lock, plait of long hair.

âkise (— ..) عاكس A *sc.* reflector.

akisse اقصّه A *lrnd., pl.* of **kıssıs**.

âkit[di] 1 (. —) عاقد A *var.* of **âkid** 1.

akit[kdi] 2 عقد [akd] 1. compact, treaty, agreement, contract. 2. conclusion of a compact. 3. marriage. —**i bey** *com. law* conclusion of a bargain. —**in bozulması** cancellation or violation of a contract. —**ten doğan borçlar** contractual obligations. —**ten doğan mesuliyet** contractual responsibility. —**e ehliyet** capacity for contract. —**i istikraz** *law* contraction of a loan. —**i ittifak** *pol.* conclusion of an alliance. —**i meclis** holding of a meeting. —**i muahede** *pol.* conclusion of a treaty. —**i mukavele** *law* conclusion of a contract. —**i nikâh** conclusion of a marriage contract. — **serbestîsi** freedom of contract. — **va'di** *law* preliminary agreement. — **yeri kanunu** *law lex loci contractus.* —**i zimmet** *Isl. law* the acceptance of a subject status in a Muslim state by a non-Muslim.

akite et[der] آكیته اتمك F *com.* /ı/ to receipt.

akk *cf.* **ak** 5-8.

Akkâ (. —) عكّا A Acre.

akkâm (. —) عكّام A 1. *hist.* Arab attendant of the caravan which conveyed the Sultan's yearly gifts to Mecca and Medina. 2. *lrnd.* tent-pitcher and baggage muleteer; attendant in charge of a traveller's palanquin. — **başı** *hist.* head of the Arab attendants of the caravan carrying the Sultan's gift to the Holy Cities.

akkan [ak 1, kan] *neol., anat.* lymph. — **düğümü** *anat.* lymph node, lymph gland.

akkar 1 (. —) عقّار A drug, medicinal herb.

akkâr 2 (. —) عكّار A *lrnd.* 1. one who feigns flight and then returns to the charge. 2. *name of an Arab tribe.*

akkâs (. —) عكّاس A *obs.* photographer. — **başı** Court Photographer.

akkâse (. — .) عكّاسه A a codex whose pages are of different color in the margin.

akkavak[ğı] آق قواق white poplar, abele, *bot.*, *Populus alba.*

akke 1 عكّه A *lrnd.* 1. sultriness. 2. first heat of a fever. 2. sand heated by the sun.

Akke 2 (.'.) عكّه A *var.* of **Akkâ.**

akkefal آق كفال bleak, *zool., Alburnus.*

Akkerman آق كرمان *geog.* Akkerman, Alba Julia, Cetatea Alba (in Bessarabia).

akkın آققين *prov.* gently sloping, smooth.

akkor آق قور *sc.* incandescent. —**luk** incandescence, white heat.

Akkoyunlu آق قوينلو *hist.* the Turkoman dynasty of the White Sheep reigning in Azerbaijan after Timur's inroad.

akkuyruk[ğu] آق قويروق green tea.

akl 1 عقل A *cf.* **akıl** 1.

akl[lı] 2 عقل A *can. law* blood money, fine; the payment of a fine.

akla=[r] آقلامق آقلن /ı/ 1. to whiten. 2. to mark with white. 3. to clear any one's honor. 4. to fair-copy (writing). 5. to clear, refine, draw liquid off from the sediment.

aklâm (. —) اقلام A 1. *calligraphy in Arabic characters* the styles of calligraphical writing. 2. *obs.* government offices. —**ı devlet** government offices. —**ı sitte** the six styles of writing (**rik'a, muhakkak, sülüs, reyhani, nesih, tevkiî**).

aklan 1 آقلان *prov.* 1. slope, incline. 2. stream, water course.

aklan=[ır] 2 آقلانمق آقلن *pass.* or *refl.* of **akla**=.

aklat=[ır] آقلاتمق آقلت /ı/ *caus.* of **akla**=.

akldar (. —) عقلدار P *lrnd.* reasonable.

aklef اقلف A *lrnd.* uncircumcised.

aklen (.'.) عقلاً A by reason and judgment. — **ve naklen** by reason and tradition.

aklet=[der] عقل اتمك *var.* of **akıl et**= (**akıl** 1).

aklı آقلی spotted with white. — **karalı** black and white.

aklık[ğı] آقلق 1. whiteness. 2. white speck (on the eye, forehead, etc.). 3. white face-paint.

aklî (. —) عقلي A pertaining to the mind

aklibaliğ

mental. — **hastalık** mental disease. — **muvazene** mental balance, sanity.
aklibaliğ (..—.) عقل بالغ P *lrnd.* mature mind.
aklievvel عقل اول P *theol.* the First Cause, the Creator. 2. *myst.* the state of union with God. 3. natural intelligence; very intelligent.
aklihayvanî (...——) عقل حيوانى P *phil.* instinct.
akliilâhî (...——) عقل الهى P *theol.* the Divine Intellect.
akliinsanî (...——) عقل انسانى P *phil.* human intellect.
aklikül[lü] عقل كل P *theol.* 1. the Universal Intellect being the first entity created. 2. the angel Gabriel. 3. the Prophet Muhammad.
aklimaad (...—) عقل معاد P *theol.* meditation on the life to come.
aklimaaş (...—) عقل معاش P *lrnd.* sense of economy.
aklimutlak[kı] عقل مطلق P *theol.* the Absolute Intellect, the Creator.
aklımücerred عقل مجرد P *theol.* the Sole Intellect, the Creator.
aklimüstefad (....—) عقل مستفاد P *theol.* the portion of the Absolute Intellect given to man.
aklinefsani (...—.) عقل نفسانى P *phil.* instinct.
aklirahmani (...——) عقل رحمانى P *theol.* the Divine Intellect.
aklisani (..——) عقل ثانى P *theol.* the carnal mind.
akliselim (...—) عقل سليم P common sense. — **sahibi** sensible person.
aklişeytanî (...——) عقل شيطانى P *theol.* the diabolical intellect.
akliyat (.——) عقليات matters solved by reasoning and not settled by tradition.
akliye (.—.) عقليه A 1. mental. **emraz-ı akliye** mental diseases; department for mental diseases (in a hospital). 2. *phil.* rationalism. —**ci** psychiatrist, neurologist, specialist in mental diseases.
akliyun (.——) عقليون A *phil.* rationalist philosophers. — **felsefesi** rationalism.
akm عقم A *lrnd.* barrenness, sterility.
akma 1 آقر [ak= 2] 1. flowing, gliding. 2. *prov.* pitch, tar. — **hançer** grooved dagger.
akma 2 آقر *var. of* ağma 3.
akmadde [ak 1, madde] *neol., anat.* white matter.
akman آقمان *prov.* clean, decent.
akmar 1 (.—) اقمار A *lrnd., pl. of* kamer.
akmar 2 (.—) اقمار A *lrnd., pl. of* kamir.
akmer اقمر A *lrnd.* 1. pale blue, pale slate, gray. 2. beautiful as the moon.
akmî (.—) عقمى A *lrnd.* obsolete, unintelligible.

akmisa اقمصه A *lrnd., pl. of* kamis.
akmişe اقمشه A 1. stuffs, materials. 2. rugs, carpets, etc.
aknan (.—) اقنان A *lrnd., pl. of* kın 3.
akne F *path.* acne.
akolât[dı] F *print.* half-brace.
akoli F *path.* acholia.
akomodasyon F *physiol.* accomodation (of the eye).
akonit[ti] آقونيت F aconite, *bot.,* Aconitum.
akonitin آقونتين F aconite (drug).
akont F *com.* installment, partial payment.
akord آقورد F *cf.* akort.
akorda (.'.) آقورده F *mus.* state of being in tune. —**cı** piano tuner.
akordeon آقوردیون F 1. *mus.* accordion. 2. accordion pleats.
akordet=[der] آقورد ايتمك /ı/ to tune (musical instrument).
akort[du] آقورد [akord] *mus.* state of being in tune. — **anahtarı** tuning-key. —**u bozuk** 1. out of tune. 2. inharmonious, discordant. —**çu** piano tuner.
akoryon آقوريون F *microbiol.* Achorion.
akov آقو *Sl* a certain measure for liquids and grains formerly used in the Balkan countries.
akova ('..) آقوا [akva] *naut.* awash.
akoz et=[der] آقوز ايتمك *Gk slang* to shut up.
akörtü *neol., anat.* aponeurosis.
akpak[kı] آق پاق very white, very clean.
akr 1 عقر A *lrnd.* 1. a cutting, wounding. 2. a hamstringing, hocking. 3. a slaughtering, killing, destruction. 4. a chafing the back of a beast (saddle). 5. an impeding, delaying.
akr[rı] **2** عكر A *lrnd.* a turning away, *esp.,* a turning as in flight and then wheeling again to the charge.
akra[aı] **1** اقرع A *lrnd.* 1. bald. 2. sharp and fine-tempered (sword). 3. very brave, bravest, very warlike.
akra 2 (.—) اقرا A *lrnd., pl. of* akîr 1.
akraba (..—) اقربا [akriba] a relative; relatives. —**nın akrabaya akrep etmez ettiğin** *proverb* A scorpion does not do the harm one relative does another. —**lık** kinship, relationship.
akrak[ğı] اقرا obs. whiter.
akran (.—) اقران A 1. equals, peers. 2. equal, peer, match. 3. equal in age or rank. —**lık** equality in age or standing.
akras (.—) اقراص A *lrnd., pl. of* kurs 1.
akreb 1 عقرب *cf.* akrep.
akreb 2 اقرب A *lrnd.* very near, nearest. —**i mekniyat** *law* nearest cited.
akrebe عقربه A *lrnd.* 1. female scorpion. 2. a quick, intelligent female slave. 3. double hook, pothook. 4. shoe latchet.

akrebek^{ği} عقربك P *lrnd.* 1. a little scorpion. 2. hour hand (watch).
akrebî (..—) عقربى A *zool.* pertaining to the scorpion, scorpioid. **—ye** *Scorpionida.*
akreditif اكرديف F *com.* 1. letter of credit. 2. bank credit.
akrep^{bi} عقرب |akreb| 1. scorpion. 2. *w. cap., astr.* Scorpio. 3. hour hand (clock). 4. a children's disease. 5. *slang* policeman, cop. **—ler** *zool.*, *Scorpionida.* **A— burcu** *astr.* the sign Scorpio. **— kuyruğu bıyık** mustache with ends curved upwards.
akret عقرت A *lrnd.* barrenness, sterility.
akriba (..—) اقربا A *lrnd.* near relatives.
akride اقرده A *lrnd., pl. of* **kırd.**
akriha اقرحه A *lrnd., pl. of* **karah.**
akrobat آقروبات F acrobat. **—lık** acrobatics.
akromatopsi F *psych.* achromatopsia, color blindness.
akromegali F *path.* acromegaly.
akropol^{lü} F *hist.* acropolis.
akrostiş F *pros.* acrostic.
aks^{si} 1 عكس *cf.* **akis 1.**
aks 2 عفص A *lrnd.* a braiding and looping up long hair.
aks 3 F *mech.* axle.
aksa=^r 1 آقسامه آقسى 1. to limp, hitch. 2. to have a hitch, to stall.
aksa 2 (.—) اقصا A *lrnd.* 1. remotest, very distant; uttermost. 2. *log.* extreme. **—yi bilâd** the most distant countries, the ends of the earth.
aksak^{ği} آقساق آقسو آقناق 1. limping, lame; lopsided. 2. *Or. mus.* a rhythmic pattern of nine beats with a signature of 9/8. 3. *print.* not well filled (page). **— fahte, — perişan** *Or. mus.* kinds of time. **— semâî** *Or. mus.* a rhythmic pattern of ten beats with a signature of 10/8. **—lık** lameness; lopsidedness.
aksal'eb (...) اقصى الأب A *can. law* the first ancestor who was a Muslim.
aksam 1 (.—) اقسام A 1. parts, portions, divisions. 2. *mech.* spare parts. **—ı kelâm** *gram.* parts of speech. **—ı rihve** *anat.* soft parts.
aksam 2 (.—) اقسام A *lrnd., pl. of* **kasem.**
aksam 3 اقصم A *lrnd.* 1. having the foreteeth broken. 2. *pros.* the foot **mefâiletün** reduced by contraction into **fâiletün.**
aksan آقسان F accent, stress; style of pronunciation.
aksar اقصر A *lrnd., superl. of* **kasir 2.**
aksat=^{ır} 1 آقصائى اقصى /ı/ *caus. of* **aksa**= 1.
aksat 2 اقسط A *lrnd.* 1. very just, most equitable. 2. spindle-shanked.
aksata |ahzuita| *vulg.* business, buying and selling. **— et**= to do business, to buy and sell.

Aksayışark^{kı} (.—..) اقصاى شرق P the Far East.
akse 1 آقسه F *path.* fit, attack.
akse 2 عكس |based on Arabic| *neol., physiol.* reflex.
aksendaz (..—) عكس انداز P *lrnd.* which throws back a reflection, reflecting; re-echoing.
akseptans E , **akseptasyon** F *com.* acceptance.
akset=^{der} عكس ايتمك |aks 1| 1. to be reflected, reverberated, echoed. 2. /a/ to come to the hearing of a persen. 3. *obs.* to revert, invert; to reflect. **—tir**= /ı/ to reflect, reverberate, echo.
aksır=^{ır} آقسرمق to sneeze.
aksırık^{ği} آقسرق a sneeze. **— tıksırık** continual sneezing and coughing. **—lı tıksırıklı** sneezing and coughing, old and in bad health.
aksırış آقسريش a sneezing, sneeze.
aksırt=^{ır} آقسرتمق to cause to sneeze.
aksırtıcı آقسرتيجى sneeze-provoking, sternutatory.
aksi (.—) عكسى |aks 1| 1. opposite, contrary. 2. adverse, unlucky. 3. perverse, peevish,. cross. **— delil** counterproof. **— gibi** *colloq.* unfortunately. **— git**= to go wrong (things). **— halde** in the contrary case, otherwise. **— mütalâa** contrary opinion, opposition. **— şeytan!** damned! **— takdirde** otherwise. **— tesadüf** unfortunate coincidence; by an unfortunate coincidence. **— tesir** countereffect, the opposite effect. **—tesir***.
aksilik^{ği} (.—.) عكسيلك 1. an unfortunate incident, misfortune, hitch. 2. crossness, obstinacy, peevishness. **— et**= to make difficulties.
aksimürekkep^{bi} عكس مركب P *log.* contraposition.
aksine عكسنه 1. to the contrary. 2. contrary, counter. 3. unfortunately. 4. /ın/ contrary to, in opposition to. **— git**= /ın/ to go exactly contrary, to run counter (to). **— hareket et**= /ın/ to act against, to violate (law).
aksiseda (...—) عكس صدا P echo.
aksiseğirdim |based on **aks 1**| *neol., gun.* recoil.
aksişems عكس شمس P *astr.* solar reflection.
aksitesir (...—) عكس تأثير P *sc., econ.* reaction.
aksiyom آقسيوم F *math.* axiom.
aksiyometre (..../.) F *naut.* axiometer.
aksiyon 1 آقسيون F *com.* share, stock. **— ve obligasyon borsası** stock exchange.
aksiyon 2 آقسيون F *sc.* action. **— akımı** *physiol.* action current. **— kuvantumu** *sc.* Planck's constant. **— türbünü** *mech.* action turbine.
aksiyoner آقسيونر F *com.* shareholder.
aksolun=^{ur} عكس اولنمق *pass. of* **akset**=.
akson آقسون F *biol.* axon.

aksöğüt

aksöğüt^du آق سوگود white willow, *bot.*, *Salix alba*.
aksu آق صو *path.* cataract.
aksungur آق سنغر white falcon, *zool.*, *Falco rusticolus*.
aksül'amel عکس العمل A reaction.
aksülümen آق سلمن *chem.* sublimate.
aksünger آق سونگر pumice.
akşam آخشام آخشام [ahşam] 1. evening, *esp.*, the sunset-hour, the time of the first evening prayer. 2. in the evening. 3. last night. —a this evening, tonight. —ları every evening, of an evening. — ahıra, sabah çayıra said of those who have no thought in life except eating and sleeping. —dan akşama every evening. —ı bul= to last until evening. —a doğru toward evening. —ı et= to stay until evening. — ezanı the call to prayer at sunset. — gazetesi evening paper. — günü the departing day, afternoon and evening. — güneşi the evening sun, the setting sun. —lar hayrolsun good evening. —ın işini sabaha bırakma Never put off till tomorrow what may be done today. —dan kalma, —dan kalmış having a hangover. — karanlığı dusk. —a karşı toward evening. —dan kavur sabaha savur *said of those who spend all their earnings thoughtlessly*. — namazı the evening worship. — sabah constantly, any old time. —a sabaha at any moment. —dan sonra merhaba! rather late! Why didn't you say it at the time? — sularında round about evening. —ı şerifleriniz hayırlar olsun! good evening. — üstü, — üzeri toward evening. — vakti in the evening. — yediğini sabaha unut= to be very absent-minded. — yemeği supper, dinner.
akşamcı آخشامجی 1. one who drinks every evening, habitual drinker. 2. *obs.* one who goes to bed early. —lık the habit of drinking every evening. —lık et= to drink regularly every evening.
akşamla=ʳ آخشاملمك 1. to draw towards evening, to get late in the day. 2. to stay until evening. 3. to spend the evening (in a place). —t= *caus.*
akşamlayın, akşamleyin (.ʼ..) آخشاملین in the evening.
akşamlık^ği آخشاملق 1. special to evening use. 2. evening dress.
akşamlı sabahlı آخشاملو صباحلو morning and evening, always.
akta^aı 1 اقطاع A *lrnd.* flocks.
akta^aı 2 اقطع A *lrnd.* one whose hand is amputated. 2. deaf.
aktab (.—) اقطاب A *lrnd.* 1. shafts, axles. 2. poles. 3. chiefs, leaders, centers of influence. 4. chief saints.
aktaeyn اقطعین A *lrnd.* the two most trenchant things, the sword and the pen.

aktan (.—) اقطان A *lrnd.*, *pl.* of **kutn**.
aktar=ʳ 1 آقترمق اقتارمن /ı/ 1. to turn over, to turn upside down. 2. to transfer from one place to another; to move from one receptacle to another. 3. to plow. 4. to unsaddle, to unhorse (rider); to throw down. 5. to retile (roof). 6. to take over from another book (passage). 7. *prov.* to pour. 8. *prov.* to read through from end to end (the Quran). 9. *prov.* to seek, to look (for).
aktar 2 اقتار اقطار |**attar 1**| herbalist, dealer in small wares.
aktar 3 (.—) اقتار A *lrnd.*, *pl.* of **kutr**.
aktar 4 (.—) اقطار A *lrnd.* 1. sides, margins. 2. regions, districts; spaces. 3. diameters.
aktar 5 (.—) اقطار A *lrnd.*, *pl.* of **katre**.
aktarıl=ʳ آقتاریلمق *pass.* of **aktar**= 1.
aktariye آقطاریه [**attariye**] herbalist's wares.
aktarlık^ği آقطارلق the trade of a herbalist.
aktarma آقترمه 1. a turning over. 2. transshipment. 3. change (of trains, etc.). 4. retiling (of a roof). 5. *hist.* prize (ship). 6. *com.* transit (not subject to customs duties). — bileti transfer ticket. — eşyası *com.* goods in transit. — et= /ı/ to transfer, transship. — treni connection train. — yap= to change (trains, etc.). —lı having a connection (train, etc.).
aktart=ʳ آقتارتمق /ı/ *caus.* of **aktar**= 1.
aktavşan آق طاوشان jerboa, *zool.*, *Jaculus jaculus*.
aktet=^der *var.* of **akdet**=.
aktı آقتی *obs.* fee for piecework.
aktif آقتیف F *com.* active; assets.
aktivizm آقتیویزم F *phil.* activism.
aktör آقتور F *theat.* actor. —lük the art and profession of an actor.
aktris آقتریس F *theat.* actress.
aktüalite آقتوالیته F 1. actuality. 2. newsreel.
aktüel آقتوئل F modern, contemporary.
aktüer F *insurance* actuary.
akub 1 (.—) عقوب A *lrnd.* successor (in any good work).
akûb 2 (.—) عکوب A *lrnd.* dust.
akuk^ku (.—) عقوق A *lrnd.* 1. undutiful to parents. 2. pregnant (beast). 3. soft (date stone).
akul^lü (.—) عقول A *lrnd.* 1. intelligent. 2. astringent (medicine). 3. taking shelter in inaccessible mountains (beast).
akur (.—) عقور A *lrnd.* biting (dog, etc.). —ane (.——.) P like a biting dog.
akustik^ği آقوستیك F 1. acoustical. 2. acoustics.
akümülatör آکومولاتور F *elec.* storage battery.
akva 1 (.ʼ.) اقوا It *same as* **akova**.
akva 2 (.—) اقوی A *lrnd.* stronger, strongest, very strong.

akvalⁱⁱ **1** (. —) اقوال A *lrnd.* words, opinions; agreements.
akvalⁱⁱ **2** (. —) اقوال A *hist.* kings (of the Himyarites).
akvam (. —) اقوام A *lrnd.* peoples, nations.
akvaryum آقوارْيوم F aquarium.
akvas (. —) اقواس A *lrnd.* 1. bows. 2. *geom.* arcs.
akvatⁱⁱ (. —) اقوات A *lrnd., pl. of* **kut 1**.
akvatinta (. . .´. .) It aquatint.
akve عكوه A *lrnd.* 1. the middle of a thing. 2. the waist in its thickest part. 3. root (of the tongue, tail, etc.). 4. twisted sinew used as a whip.
akved اقود A *lrnd.* 1. bull-necked. 2. avaricious. 3. long (mountain).
akvem اقوم A *lrnd., superl. of* **kavîm**.
akveriyat (. . — —) اقوريّات A *lrnd.* great calamities.
akves اقوس A *lrnd.* bowed, curved, bent.
akviya (. . —) اقويا A *lrnd.* the strong, the powerful.
akya (.´.) آقيا leer fish, *zool.*, *Lichia amia*.
akyad (. —) اقياد A *lrnd., pl. of* **kayd**.
akyalⁱⁱ (. —) اقيال A *hist.* kings (of the Himyarites).
akyaz (. —) اقياظ A *lrnd. pl. of* **kayz**.
akyel (.´.) آقيل *prov.* west or southwest wind.
akyuvar *neol., anat.* leucocyte, white blood corpuscle.
akz^{zi} عكز A *lrnd.* 1. a leaning on a staff. 2. a planting a spear in the ground.
akza (. —) اقضى A *lrnd.* most authoritative in judgment. **—yı kuzât-ül-Müslimîn** the most authoritative of Muslim judges.
akzar 1 (. —) اقذار A *lrnd.* filthy things.
akzar 2 *neol., anat.* fascia.
akziye اقضيه A *lrnd.* 1. judgments, decrees. 2. fates.
al 1 آل 1. vermilion, flame scarlet, red. 2. bay (horse). 3. rouge. **— al crimson. —ı al moru mor, —ı alına moru moruna** flushed, purple in the face. **— bayrak** the Turkish flag. **— elmaya taş atan çok olur** There are always those who will be jealous of and try to harm a worthy person. **—lar giy=** 1. to wear red. 2. to rejoice. **— giymedim ki alınayım** Why should I take offense since I have done no such thing? **— gömlek ya yeninden ya yakasından** (*lit.* A crimson shirt will show either at the cuffs or at the collar.) The truth will out. **— kanlara boyan=** to be soaked in blood, to become blood-stained. **— kiraz üstüne kar yağmış** A most unexpected thing may happen. **— sancak** the Turkish flag. **— vala** *prov.* scarlet silk gauze veil. **— yanak** ruddy-cheeked. **— yuvar***.

âlⁱⁱ **2** آل P [al 1] *poet.* fiery red, vermilion. **—i muasfer** yellowish red, orange-colored.
al 3 آل *prov.* trick, fraud. **— et=** /a/ to trick, to deceive.
âlⁱⁱ **4** (—) آل P |al 3| *poet.* fraud, deceit, treachery. **— eyle=** /a/ to deceive.
alⁱⁱ **5** (—) آل A *lrnd.* family (in the broad sense); dynasty, line. **—i abâ** the Prophet and his family. **A—i Abbas** the Abbaside dynasty. **A—i Cengiz** the dynasty of Jengiz Khan. **—ü evlâd** the whole family. **A—i İmran Sûresi** *name of the third Sura of the Quran*. **A—i Osman** the Ottoman dynasty. **A—i Resul** the family of the Prophet Muhammad. **A—i Selçuk** the dynasty of the Seljuks. **A—i Timur** the Timuride dynasty.
âlⁱⁱ **6** (—) آل A *lrnd.* morning or evening haze, mirage.
al=^{ir} **7** آلمق I. /ı/ 1. to take, get, procure, obtain. 2. to buy, purchase. 3. to receive. 4. to accept. 5. to take in, contain; to include, understand. 6. to seize, grasp, carry away; to capture, conquer. II. 1. to start. 2. to catch; to take fire. 3. to take effect (contagion). 4. to take (graft). 5. to set (dye). 6. to grow. **—dı** *before a name, romantic folk literature* began (to recite). **kendini alama=** /dan/ to be unable to refrain (from). **—ır mısın akideyi miski pahasına?** *verse* (*lit.* Do you buy sugar-candies at the price of musk sugar?) Would you buy a valuable thing at a low price? **— Allahım kulunu zaptet delini** *colloq.* He is crazy. **— beraber** *naut.* Give way together. **—a bildiğine*. — birini vur öbürüne** The one is no better than the other. **— cevabını otur aşağı** *ironically* Now you're answered. **—dı fitili** (*lit.*, His wick has taken fire.) He is on tenterhooks (with doubts or anxiety); he is greatly provoked; he is in a rage. **— iskeleyi** *slang* Scram! **— kaşağıyı gir ahıra, yarası olan gocunsun** (*lit.* Take the currycomb and go into the stable; let him who has an itch scratch himself.) Evil be to him who thinks it. **— külâh ver külâh** same as **al takke ver külâh — bir kürek** *naut.* pull a stroke. **—ma mazlûmun âhını çıkar âheste âheste** *proverb* Don't provoke the curse of the oppressed, it will take effect sooner or later. **— sana** There Take it. **— sana bir daha** Here is another one for you. **— takke ver külâh** 1. struggling, tumbling with one another. 2. becoming very intimate with one another. **—ıp ver=** 1. to quarrel. 2. to scold, grumble. 3. to be full of excitement. 4. to play and joke. **—ıp vereme=** /la/ to keep pestering (someone) without a reason. **—ıp yürü=** to make headway.
âlâ 1 (— —) اعلى A 1. very good, excellent,

first rate, best quality. 2. *lrnd.* higher, highest.

ala 2 آلا آر 1. spotted, speckled. 2. pied, variegated. — **bula** motley. — **geyik** fallow deer, *zool., Dama dama*. — **kuru** *prov.* half dry. — **kuş** 1. *obs.* peacock. 2. *prov.* noisy fellow, brawler. — **sığın** fallow deer, *zool., Dama dama*.

[For other compounds, see **alabacak - alakarga**.]

ala 3 آر *prov., var. of* **elâ**.

ala 4 آر *prov.* kind of hood used by a bird hunter to conceal his head and face.

âlâ 5 (— —) آر P *lrnd.* reddish color.

-âlâ 6 (— —) آر P *lrnd.* soiled, contaminated.

ala 7 آر Get on! — **ala hey!** exclamation used to produce prolonged noise, esp. during a circumcision.

alâ 8(. —) عمل A *lrnd.* sublimity, exaltation, superiority, eminence.

ala'ayyi takdîrin (..—..—.) علی ای تقدیر A *lrnd.* in every possible case.

alabacak[1] آلا با یاجاق horse with white feet.

alâbahtek (.—'..) علی بختك A *lrnd.* see what luck brings, try your luck.

alabalık[1] آلا بالیق speckled trout, *zool., Trutta fario*.

alabanda (..'.) آلابانده It *naut.* 1. side (of a ship); bulwarks. 2. the guns on one side of a man-of-war. 3. broadside. 4. hard (a-port, a-starboard). 5. *slang* a scolding. — **astarı** side sheeting. — **ateş** broadside. — **et=** /ı/ to put hard over (helm). — **iskele** hard a-port. — **sancak** hard a-starboard. — **ver** /a/ *slang* to scold severely. — **ye=** *slang* to get a good scolding.

alabaş الا باش *prov.* kind of cabbage.

alabildiğine آلابیلدیكنه to the utmost; at full speed.

alaborina (..'.) آلابورینه It *naut.* before the wind, on a bowline.

alabros F *hairdressing* crew cut.

alabura (..'.) آلا بورا [albura] *naut.* a capsizing, overturn. — **et=** 1. to cross (yard). 2. to hoist (flag). 3. to overturn (boat). — **ol=** to capsize, to turn turtle, to keel over (boat).

alaca 1 آلاجه 1. motley, speckled, variegated; piebald (horse). 2. striped stuff. 3. *prov.* a variegated kind of grapes. — **ağaçkakan** the great spotted woodpecker, *zool., Dendrocopus major*. — **balıkçıl** squacco heron, *zool., Ardeola ralloides*. — **baykuş** tawny owl, *zool., Strix aluco*. — **bayrak** *Ott. hist.* the four cavalry divisions of the Janissaries. — **bulaca** blotched and daubed incongruously. — **doğan** peregrine falcon. — **dostluk** fickle friendship.

— **gölge** penumbra. — **karanlık** twilight. — **karga** rook, *zool., Corvus frugilegus*. — **menekşe** *same as* **hercayi menekşe**. — **tavuk** the great gray shrike, *zool., Lanius excubitor*.

alaca 2 آلاجه in — **verece** the handing over and taking over of the purchased object.

alacak[1] آلاجق 1. *com.* money owed to one, credit. 2. *law* claim, chose in action. — **dâvası** *law* personal action. — **ı olsun!** I'll make him pay for it!, I'll show him! — **senedi** *com. law* document evidencing the debt. — **ına şahin, vereceğine karga** an eager creditor but a laggardly debtor. — **ın temliki** *law* transfer of claims. — **ına tut=** /ı/ to take on account. — **ım var** /dan/ (someone) owes me money, *com.* I am (someone's) creditor. — **la verecek ödenmez** *proverb* A debt you owe can't be paid by a debt owed to you. — **lan=** *com.* to be credited. — **landır=** /ı/ to credit.

alacaklı آلاجقلی creditor. — **bakiye** credit balance. — **lar heyeti** board of creditors. — **taraf** credit side.

alacala= آلاجه لامق /ı/ to speckle, spot, blotch, to mark with variegated colors. — **n=** to become speckled, variegated. — **t=** *caus. of* **alacala=**.

alacalı آلاجه لی motley, speckled; piebald (horse). — **bulacalı** mixed colored. — **kumtaşı** grit.

alacalık[1] آلاجه لق 1. multicoloredness, motleyness. 2. double-facedness, double-dealing, double-crossing.

alacehri آلاجهری berries used for the preparation of a dye (speckled buckthorn berries), fruit of *Rhamnus infectoria* or *Reseda Luteola*.

alâcenahil'istical (.—.—...—') علی جناح الاستعجال A *lrnd.* on the wings of haste, hastily.

alacık[1], **alaçık**[1], **alaçuk**[1] آلاجق آلاچق آلاچوق 1. felt-covered round tent of the nomads. 2. hut made of brushwood.

aladı آلادی *prov.* haste, hurry.

alâevfaz (.—.—) علی اوفاز A *lrnd.* in great haste.

alaeyyihalin (.—..—.) علی ای حال A *lrnd.* in any event.

a'lâf 1 (.—) اعلاف A *lrnd., pl. of* **alef**, fodder, hay; straw.

alâf 2 (— —) آلاف *lrnd.* thousands.

alafranga (..'.) آلافرنغه It European style (hour, calendar); in the Occidental way, European. — **lık** imitation of European ways.

alagarson آلا غارسون F *hairdressing* boyish bob.

alâgayrilkıyas (.—...—) علی غیر القیاس A *lrnd.* contrary to expectation.

alahalihi (.——..) علی حال A *lrnd.* in the same condition, unchanged.

alâhaza (.———) علىهذا A *lrnd.* thereupon.
alâhazattakdir (.——..—) علىهذاالتقدير A *lrnd.* in this case.
a'lâhazret (.—..) علىحضرت P *lrnd.* His most exalted majesty (the Shah).
alâhide (.—..), **alâhidetin** (.—...) علىحده ، علىحدهٍ A *lrnd.* separately, singly, apart.
alâif (.—.) علائف A *lrnd.*, *pl. of* **ulûfe.**
alaik[kı] 1 (.—.) علائى A *lrnd.* relations, connections.
alaik[kı] 2 (.—.) علائى A *lrnd.*, *pl. of* **alika.**
alâim (.—.) علائم A *lrnd.* signs, miracles. **—i cevviye** atmospherical phenomena.
alâimisema (.—...—) علائمسما P rainbow.
Alâiye (.——.) علائيه *former name of the seaport Alanya.*
alak[gı] 1 آلاق *prov.* hut.
alak[kı] 2 علق A *lrnd.* 1. anything that hangs. 2. a thing by which a thing hangs. 3. rent, torn by a catching thorn. 4. sufficiency of support, maintenance. 5. attachment. love. 6. pertinacity. 7. clot of coagulated blood. 8. leech.
alâka 1 (.—.) علاقة A 1. connection, tie, relationship. 2. attachment, affection; *poet.* love. 3. interest. 4. *law* lieu, claim. **— duy=** /a/ to be interested (in), to fall in love (with). **— et=** /a/ *obs.* to fall in love (with). **— göster=** /a/ to take an interest (in). **—sını kes=** /la/ to break off relations (with). **— uyandır=** to arouse interest.
alaka 2 *var. of* **aleka.**
alâkabahş (.—..) علاقةبخش P *lrnd.* interesting.
alâkadar (.—.—) علاقةدار P 1. connected; concerned, involved. 2. interested. **—lar** those concerned, the interested parties. **— et=** /ı/ 1. to interest. 2. to concern. **— ol=** /a/ to show interest (in), to be interested (in); to be concerned (with).
alâkadaran (.—.—) علاقةداران P *lrnd.* those concerned, the interested parties.
alâkadrilhâl (.—..—) علىقدرالحال A *lrnd.* according to condition or capacity.
alâkadrilkifaye (.—...—.) علىقدرالكفاية A *lrnd.* according to ability.
alâkadrilimkân (.—...—) علىقدرالامكان A *lrnd.* as far as possible.
alâkadril'istitaa (.—....—) علىقدرالاستطاع A *lrnd.* as far as possible.
alâkadrissia (.—....) علىقدرالسعة A *lrnd.* as far as possible.
alâkadrittaka (.—..—.) علىقدرالطاقة A

lrnd. according to power or ability; as far as one can endure.
alâkalı (.—..) علاقلى 1. connected; involved, concerned. 2. *archaic* in love.
alakarga آلاقارغا jay, *zool.*, *Garrulus glandarius.*
alâkart آلاقارت F *restaurant* a la carte.
alâkasız (.—..) علاقسز uninterested, indifferent. **—lık** lack of interest, indifference.
alâkavlin (.—..) علىقولٍ A *lrnd.* according to one assertion.
alakbulak[gı] *var. of* **allakbullak.**
alâkıye 1 (.—.—.) علاقية A *lrnd.* 1. persistent. 2. devotedly attached.
alâkıye 2 (.—.—.) علاقية A *lrnd.* surname.
alâkıye 3 (..—.) *var. of* **alekıye.**
alâkilaittakdireyn (.—.—..—.) علىكلاَ - التقديرين - A *lrnd.* according to either one of the two suppositions, in both cases.
alako[r], **alakoy**[ar] آلاقوىم ، آلاقوى *var. of* **alıko=, alıkoy=.**
alâküllihal (.—..—), **alâküllihalin** (.—..—.) علىكلحال A *lrnd.* in any case.
— geçin= to live at a subsistence level.
alal[ır] آلالمك *obs.* to redden, to blush.
âlâlık[gı] 1 (.—.) اعلالوه |âlâ 1| superiority, excellence.
alalık[gı] 2 آلالوه |ala 2| spottedness, speckledness.
a'lâm 1 (.—) اعلام A *lrnd.* 1. marks, signs. 2. ornamented border on cloth. 3. milestones, signposts, waymarks. 4. mountains. 5. flags, banners. 6. chiefs, princes. 7. proper names.
âlâm 2 (——) آلام A *lrnd.* pains, sorrows.
alâm 3 (.—) علام A *lrnd.*, *pl. of* **alâmet 1.**
Alaman آلامان It *same as* **Alman.**
alamana (...'.) آلامانة 1. small lugger; fishing smack. 2. large trawlnet.
Alamanya (...'.) آلامانية It *same as* **Almanya.**
alâmelainnas (.—.—.—) علىملأالناس A *lrnd.* in public, before the world.
alâmeratibihim (.—.—...) علىمراتبهم A *lrnd.* according to their rank.
alâmet 1 (.—.) علامت A 1. sign, mark, symbol, characteristic. 2. wonder, miracle. **—i farika** trade-mark. **—i mümeyyize** characteristic. **—i şerife** the Monogram of the Sultan.
alâmet 2 (.—.) علامت |alâmet 1| monstrous, enormous.
alâminüt آلامينوت F prepared in a minute (dish).
alan 1 آلان 1. open space, sheltered plateau among mountains; clearing in a forest, glade. 2. *neol.* square (in a town); airport;

alan field, arena. 3. *neol.* sphere (of action, etc.). 4. *phys.* field. 5. *geom.* area.

alan 2 آلان [al= 7] who takes, receives, buys; purchaser; *com.* consignee, payee (bill of exchange).

alânî (.——) علنى A *lrnd.* 1. public, open, manifest. 2. plain-spoken, straightforward.

alâniyet (.——.) علنيت A *lrnd.* 1. publicity, notoriety. 2. a speaking or acting publicly. **—en** (.——´..) A publicly, openly.

alantalan, alantaran آلان تالان آلان تاران in utter confusion. **— et=** /1/ to mess up, to make a mess (of).

alâportekiz آلا پورتکیز It *naut.*, in **— piyan bağı** seizing.

alar=ʳ آلارمق *prov.* to redden.

alarga (.´.) آلارغا It *naut.* 1. Push off. Keep away! Keep clear. 2. at some distance, in the offing; offing, open sea. 3. *slang* keep off. **— dur=** *slang* to keep off. **— et=** /1/ to put out to sea (ship). **— ol=** to push off, to shove off; to keep off, to keep clear. **— tut=** /1/ *naut.* to hold off. **—da yat=** to be anchored offshore (ship).

alârm آلارم F *mil.* alarm; state of alarm, state of emergency (during an air raid). **— işareti** alarm signal.

alâs (——) آلاس P *lrnd.* charcoal.

alâsülseyilleyl (.—....) على مضى الليل A *lrnd.* about two thirds through the night.

alaşa آلاشه 1. wild, unbroken or ill-trained; restive. 2. trained to bear the packsaddle.

alaşağı et=ᵈᵉʳ آل آشاغى ایتمك [al= 7, aşağı] *colloq.* to tear down (in a concerted effort), to overthrow, to depose; to knock down.

alaşıkᵗⁱ آلاشیه *obs.* trimming around the edge of a garment, border.

alaşım *neol., chem.* alloy.

alât (——) آلات A *lrnd.* 1. tools, implements, instruments, equipment. 2. organs of the body. **—ı cinsiye** *anat.* sex organs. **— ve edevat** tools and implements, outfit, stock. **—ı harb** arms, instruments of war. **—ı nâriye** firearms. **—ı rasadiye** instruments for observation (astronomical, meteorological, etc.). **—ı tenasüliye** *anat.* genital organs.

alata آلاتا *prov.* stray (sheep, etc.).

alâtarikilhezel (.—.—...) على طریق الهزل A *lrnd.* satirically.

alâtarikil'istişare (.—.—...—.) على طریق الاستشاره A *lrnd.* by way of consultation.

alâtarikutte'vil (.—.—..—) على طریق التاویل A *lrnd.* trying to explain away.

alaten, alatenli آلاتن آلاتنلى [ala 2, ten 1] *obs.* leprous.

alatenlikᵗⁱ آلاتنلك *obs.* leprosy.

alatla=ʳ آلاتلامق *prov.* to hurry.

alaturka .(...´.) آلاتورقه It 1. Turkish style (hour, calendar); in the Turkish way. 2. Turkish music. **—cı** lover of Turkish music; partisan of Turkish music.

alatya آلاتیه brown or black variety of Angora wool.

alâüddevle (.—...) علاءالدوله A *hist.*, honorific title in the Seljuk Empire.

alav آلاو *prov., var. of* **alev**.

alâva (.——) علاوى A *lrnd., pl. of* **ilâve**.

alâvechil'icaz (.—..——) على وجه الايجاز A *lrnd.* briefly.

alâvechil'umum (.—...—) على وجه العموم A *lrnd.* all, universally.

alâvechittedkik (.—...—) على وجه التدقيق A *lrnd.* by way of investigation.

alâvefkılmatlûb (.—...—) على وفق المطلوب A *lrnd.* as desired.

alâvefkılmurad (.—...—) على وفق المراد A *lrnd.* as desired, at pleasure, *ad libitum*.

alavere, alavira (...´.) آلاویره 1. utter confusion, rumpus, jumble. 2. passing or throwing a thing from hand to hand. 3. *naut.* gangway for loading coal. 4. *naut.* downhaul. 5. *prov.* deal, transaction. 6. *com.* stock jobbering, agiotage. **— dalavere çevir=, — dalavere yap=** to play a dirty trick. **— tulumbası** suction pump. **—ci** *com.* stock jobber, speculator.

alay 1 آلاى Gk 1. *mil.* regiment. 2. procession; parade. 3. festive ceremony, celebration. 4. troops in line. **bir —** a great quantity, a large number. **— alay** in troops, in companies. **— arabası** State coach of the Sultan. **— bağla=** to draw up troops in formation; to line up for battle. **— başı** *Ott. hist.* colonel of the corps of bombardiers. **— beyi** 1. *hist.* military rank connected with fief. 2. *formerly* commander of the gendarmes. **— çavuşu** *formerly* kind of sergeant at arms; halberdier of the escort of the Sultan; marshal of the procession at state occasions. **—a çıkar=** /1/ to transfer to the troops (from a military school). **— elbisesi** uniform, parade kit. **— emini** *formerly* adjutant and paymaster of a regiment. **— esvabı** *same as* **alay elbisesi**. **— geçir=** 1. to review troops. 2. to pay no attention, to be absent-minded. **— göster=** to pass in review. **—ı hümayun** sovereign's parade. **— imamı** *mil.* Muslim chaplain. **— kâtibi** secretary of a regiment. **— komutanı** regiment commander. **A— Köşkü** name of a pavilion near the Grand Palace, formerly used by the Sultans to watch parades. **— kur=** *same as* **alay bağla=**. **— mahkemesi** military tribunal of a regiment. **— meydanı** parade ground. **— ol=** to get into formation. — **sancağı** regimental flag. — **sancakları** flags for dressing ships, celebrations, etc. — **tâlimi** regimental drill. — **topu** regimental fieldpiece. —**i vâlâ** in a procession, with great pomp.

alay 2 آلای [alay 1] mockery, ridicule, teasing. —**a al=** /ı/ to make fun (of), to ridicule, to laugh (at). — **et=** /la/ to make fun (of), to ridicule, to mock. — **geç=** *slang* to make fun (of). — **için** for fun, as a joke. — **kes=** *slang* to make fun (of). —**ında ol=** /ın/ not to take seriously, to take as a joke. —**cı** 1. mocker. 2. mocking, derisive.

alâye (. — .) علایه A *lrnd.* high place, height.

alayı^nı (.′..) آلایی [alay 1] *colloq.* all of them, the whole lot. — **bir elin ipliği** *prov.* They are all cut from the same cloth.

alayim (. — .) علایم *var. of* **alaim.**

alâyiş 1 (— —.) آلایش [alâyiş 2] *lrnd.* pomp, display, show.

alâyiş 2 (— —.) آلایش P *lrnd.* defilement, pollution, contamination.

alaylı 1 آلایلی [alay 1] 1. stately, spectacular. 2. officer risen from the ranks.

alaylı 2 آلایلی [alay 2] mocking.

alaymalay آلای مالای [alay 1] all together, the whole lot. — **yukarıya!** *naut.* all hands on deck!

alaz 1 آلاز *prov.* flame, blaze.

alaz 2 آلاز *prov.* wide apart, sparse (trees, etc.).

alazla=^r آلازلامق /ı/ 1. to scorch, singe. 2. to brand. —**ma** 1. a scorching. 2. *prov.* erythema. —**n=** 1. to be scorched, to be singed. 2. to be branded. 3. to become inflamed.

alâzur^rru (. — .) علی ضرّ A *only in* — **al=** /ı/ *can. law* to marry as a second wife.

alb 1 *var. of* **alp 1.**

alb^bi **2** عب A *lrnd.* 1. mark, wound, scar. 2. a rugged, rocky spot.

albas=^ar آل باصمق 1. to be stricken with puerperal fever. 2. to be troubled by a nightmare (woman after childbirth). —**ma**, —**tı** puerperal fever.

albatr F *geol.* alabaster.

albay *neol., mil.* colonel; navy captain. —**lık** *mil.* colonelcy; navy captaincy.

albeni (.′..) آلبنی charm, attractiveness, allure.

albora, albura (..′.) آلبوره It *same as* **alabura**.

albüm آلبوم F album.

albümin آلبومین F *biochem.* albumin.

alca آلجه 1. reddish. 2. chestnut bay (horse).

alçacık^ğı آلچاجق 1. rather low. 2. very low.

alçak^ğı آلچاق 1. low. 2. vile, mean, low, base; stingy; cowardly. 3. short in stature. 4. *obs.* humble. —**tan al=** to react in a soft, friendly manner. — **arz** *geog.* low latitude. — **eşeğe kim olsa biner** *proverb* It's the willing horse that gets exploited. — **gönüllü*.** —**tan görüş=** to talk quietly and in a friendly manner. — **harf** *print.* inferior letter. — **herif** rascal, mean fellow. — **ses** 1. low voice. 2. low tone. — **tazyik** low pressure. — **uçan yüce konar, yüce uçan alçak konar** *proverb* He who flies low lands high, he who flies high lands low. — **voltaj** *elec.* low tension. — **yerde tepecik kendisini dağ sanır** *proverb* A small hill on a low plain imagines itself a mountain. — **yerde yatma sel alır, yüksek yerde yatma yel alır** *proverb* Don't be at the top or at the bottom, or you will suffer.

alçakça 1 آلچاقجه rather low.

alçakça 2 (..′.) آلچاقجه meanly, in a cowardly way.

alçakgönüllü آلچاق گوكللو humble, unpretentious, modest. —**lük** humility, modesty.

alçakla=^r آلچاقلامق *obs.* 1. to become low, to stoop; to go down in the world. 2. /ı/ to despise, contemn. —**n=** to stoop to baseness, to become mean and vile. —**t=** /ı/ to lower.

alçaklık^ğı آلچاقلق 1. lowness. 2. despicableness, vileness; stinginess; cowardice. 3. shortness of stature. 4. *obs.* humility.

alçal=^ır آلچالمق 1. to become low. 2. to stoop. 3. to degrade oneself. —**t=** 1. to lower, reduce, 2. to humiliate, abase.

alçarak^ğı آلچارق somewhat low, dwarfish.

alçı 1 آلچی plaster of Paris. —**ya koy=** /ı/ *surg.* to put in a plaster cast. — **taşı** gypsum.

alçı 2 آلچی the flat side of a knucklebone (used in games).

alçıla=^r آلچیلامق /ı/ to cover with plaster of Paris. —**n=** *pass.* —**t=** *caus. of* **alçıla=.**

alda=^r آلدامق /ı/ *prov., same as* **aldat=.**

aldağaç^cı, **aldağan** آلداغان *obs.* deceitful.

aldan=^ır آلدانمق 1. /a/ to be deceived, duped, taken in (by). 2. to be wrong, mistaken.

aldanç^cı آلدانج *obs.* easily deceived, soft, dupe.

aldangıç^cı آلدانغج *prov.* trick, tricky device, sharp practice.

aldanık^ğı آلدانق *prov.* duped.

aldanış آلدانش, **aldanma** آلدانمه deception, a being deceived.

aldaş=^ır آلداشمق *obs.* to deceive mutually.

aldat=^ır آلداتمق /ı/ to cheat, deceive, dupe. —**an** who deceives, cheater, imposter, shark. —**ıcı** deceptive. —**ıl=** *pass. of* **aldat=.** —**ış,**

—ma deception, fraud. **—maca** tricky. **—maca yok!** no cheating!
aldayıcı آلدایجی *prov.* deceptive.
aldayış آلدایش *prov.* deception, fraud, trick.
aldığına آلدیغنه *var. of* **alabildiğine**.
aldır=ᵘʳ آلدیرمق آلدرمق 1. /ı,a/ (*caus. of* **al=** 7) to cause or allow to take, fetch, buy. 2. /a/ to mind, to pay attention (to). **—ış etme=** /a/ not to mind, not to pay any attention (to). **—ışsız** indifferent, callous, unheeding. **—ma!** *colloq.* Never mind. Don't worry. **—mamazlıktan gel=** to pay no attention, not to care. **—maz** indifferent, callous. **—mazlık** indifference.
âle 1 (—.) آلَ P *lrnd.* muskroot, root of spikenard (*Nardostaghys jatamansi*).
âle 2 (—.) عالٍ A *lrnd., pl. of* **ail**.
âle 3 (—.) عالَ A *lrnd.* shelter from sun or rain.
aledderecat (....—) علی الدرجات A *lrnd.* in degrees, in all shades.
aleddevam (...—) علی الدوام A *lrnd.* continuously.
alef علف A *lrnd.* 1. grass, fodder, straw, forage, provender. 2. daily bread. **—i şimşir** a prey to the sword.
alefzar (..—) علفزار P *lrnd.* pasturage, a field where forage is collected.
alekᵏ¹ *var. of* **alak** 2.
aleka علقة A 1. *path.* clot of blood, coagulum. 2. *zool.* leech.
alekıye (..—.) علقیة A *zool., Hirudinea*.
alekî (..—) علقی A 1. *path.* coagulated, clotty. 2. *zool.* hirudine, hirudinean, pertaining to leeches.
aleksi F *psychiatry* alexia, word blindness.
alel'acaib (...—.) علی العجائب A queer, strange, odd.
alelacayipᵇⁱ (...—.) علی العجائب [**alel'acaib**] queer, odd.
alelacele علی العجله A hastily, hurriedly, in haste.
alelâde (..—.) علی العادة A ordinary, usual.
alel'ağleb علی الأغلب A *lrnd.* for the most part.
alel'amya (...—) علی العمیا A *var. of* **alel'imya**.
alel'ekser علی الأکثر A *lrnd.* often, usually, for the most part.
alelfevr علی الفور A *lrnd.* at once, immediately.
alelgafle علی الغفلة A *lrnd.* 1. unexpectedly, all of a sudden. 2. being caught unawares.
alelhadise (..—..) علی الحادثة A *phil.* epiphenomenon.
alelhadisiye (..—.—.) علی الحادثیة A *phil.* epiphenomenalism.
alelhafa (...—) علی الخفا A *lrnd.* secretly.

alelhesab (...—) علی الحساب A *com.* on account (payment).
alelhusus (...—) علی الخصوص A especially.
alel'ıtlak (...—) علی الإطلاق A *lrnd.* absolutely; indiscriminately; without exception.
alel'icmal (...—) علی الإجمال A *lrnd.* succinctly, briefly, in abstract.
alel'ihtisar (....—) علی الإختصار A *lrnd.* briefly, in brief.
alel'immiya, alel'imya (...—) علی العمیاء *lrnd.* blindly, without thinking.
alel'infirad (....—) علی الإنفراد A *lrnd.* singly, one by one, one at a time.
alel'istimrar (....—) علی الإستمرار A *lrnd.* incessantly, continuously.
alel'iştirak (....—) علی الإشتراک A *lrnd.* in partnership, in common.
alelittifak (....—) علی الإتفاق A *lrnd.* unanimously.
alel'ittisal (....—) علی الإتصال A *lrnd.* continuously, unremittingly, incessantly; in connection.
alelkaide (..—..) علی القاعدة A *lrnd.* by rule, as a rule.
alelkıyas (...—) علی القیاس A *lrnd.* in comparison.
alel'umum, alelûmum (...—) علی العموم A generally, in general, commonly.
alel'usul, alelûsul (...—) علی الأصول A 1. as a rule, as a formality. 2. duly, in due form.
alelvilâ (...—) علی الولاء A *lrnd.* successively.
âlem 1 (—.) عالم A 1. world; universe. 2. class of beings, realm; *nat. hist.* kingdom. 3. state, condition. 4. field, sphere. 5. *fig.* a world by itself. 6. people, the public. 7. merrymaking, festivity. **—de** 1. would that! how I wish! *as in* **Âlemde o burada olsaydı!** Would that he were here! 2. for all the world, *as in* **Âlemde bir daha oraya gitmem!** I would not go there again for anything in the world! **ne —desiniz?** How are you getting on? **—i mi** /ın/ What sense is there (in)? Did it have to happen now! *e. g.,* **Şimdi gece yarısı; şarkı söylemenin âlemi mi?** It is midnight; what a time to start singing! **kendi —inde** immersed in one's own world, not concerned with things going on about one. **—i âb** *poet.* drinking party. **—in ağzına bir parmak bal ol=** to be an object of gossip. **—in ağzında sakız ol= —in ağzının sakızı ol=** to be a matter of common talk. **—in ağzı torba değil ki büzesin** (*lit.* People's mouths are not bags that can be tied.) You cannot prevent people from gossiping. **—i asgar** *myst., same as* **âlem-i sağır**. **—i azamet** the high empyrean heaven, the residence of Omnipotence. **—i bâki** the eternal world. **—i bâlâ** the world above, heaven. **—i bâtın** *myst.* the

inner world. **—i beka** the eternal world, the other world. **—i berzah** *myst.*, *same as* **âlem-i misal**. **—i ceberut** 1. *myst.* the heaven above the starry firmament and immediately under the high empyrean heaven. 2. God's divine power over all things. **—e cellât lâzım, benim neme lâzım** (*lit.* If people want an executioner, why should I be the one?) Why should I do the hard task, why not someone else? **—i diğer** *myst.* the other world. **—i ekber** *myst.*, *same as* **âlem-i kebir**. **—i emr** *myst.* the world of unconditioned existence. **—i ervah** 1. the world of the spirits. 2. the spiritual world. **—i esbab** the material world, this life. **—i fâni**, **—i fenâ** the transitory world. **—i firkat** *poet.* separation. **—i gayb** the invisible world, the future world. **—i hâb** *poet.* sleep. **—i halk** all creation. **—i hayvanat** *nat. hist.* the animal kingdom. **—i İslâm** the Muslim world. **—de itibar zenginle güzeledir** In this world, respect is to the rich and beautiful. **—i kebir** the whole world (the heavens and the earth), the macrocosm. **—i kevn ü fesad** *myst.* the world of existence and dissolution, this world. **—i kudsî** *myst.* the empyrean heaven. **—i kübra** *myst.*, *same as* **âlemi kebir**. **—i lâhut** *myst.* the empyrean heaven. **—i mâna** *myst.* 1. the invisible world, the spiritual world. 2. dream. **—e maskara olmaktan meydan süpürgesi olmak yeğdir** *proverb* It is better to be a broom in a dervish convent than a laughingstock to the world; it is better to do humble work and be respected, rather than be a laughingstock by pretentious dealings. **—i melekût** *myst.*, *same as* **âlem-i ceberut**. **—i menam** *poet.* dreams, the world of dreams. **—i misal** *myst.* the world of ideas, *i. e.*, the world between the spiritual and the material world, in which the ideas (mind and spirit) dwell before entering the world of the body. **—i nasıl tanırsın, kendin gibi** *proverb* (*lit.* How do you imagine the world? Like yourself) A person's opinion of others betrays his own character. **—i nâsût** *myst.* the world of man. **—i nebatat** *nat. hist.* the vegetable kingdom. **—i rüya** *poet.* the world of dreams. **—i sabavet** *poet.* infancy. **—i safa** *poet.* the world of pleasure, pleasures. **—i sağır** *myst.* the lesser world, the microcosm; man. **—i suğra** *myst.*, *same as* **âlem-i sağır**. **—i suri** *myst.* the visible world. **—i süflî** *myst.* this world, the earth. **—i şehadet** *myst.* the visible world. **—i şems** *lrnd.* the solar system. **—i ulvî** *myst.* the world above, heaven. **—i zevk u safa** *lrnd.* world of pleasure; merrymaking, drinking party.

alem 2 عَلَمْ A 1. *lrnd.* mark by which a thing is known, sign. 2. *archaic* flag, banner. 3. *lrnd.* landmark, guide-post, beacon. 4. *lrnd.* a figured border of a garment. 5. *lrnd.* high mountain. 6. *gram.* proper name; epithet. 7. metal device (crescent and star, etc.) on top of a minaret, cupola of a mosque, or on a flagstaff, etc. **—i hümayun** *Ott. hist.* the imperial standard. **—i nebi** *Ott. hist.* the sacred banner of the Prophet which is unfurled in case of a Holy War. **— ol=** /a/ to become the distinctive name (of a person or species). **—i saadet** *Ott. hist.*, *same as* **alemi nebi**.

a'lem 3 اعْلَم *lrnd.* most learned.

âlemane (—.—.) عالَمانَهْ P *lrnd.* special to the world; worldly; earthly.

âlemara (—.——) عالَمْ آرا P *lrnd.* world-adorning.

alemdar (..—) عَلَمْدار P *hist.* 1. standard-bearer. 2. an officer of the Janissaries.

alemdarî (..——) عَلَمْداری P *hist.* the rank of a standard-bearer.

âlemefruz (—..—) عالَمْ افْروز *poet.* world-illuminating.

âlemeyn (—.—) عالَمَیْن A *lrnd.* the two worlds, this world and the next.

âlemgîr (—.—) عالَمْگیر P *poet.* 1. world-conquering. 2. filling the world (fame).

âlemî 1 (—.—) عالَمی A *lrnd.* pertaining to the world, worldly, earthly.

âlemî 2 (—.—) عالَمی [**âlemî 1**] *lrnd.* man, mortal.

âlemî 3 (..—) عَلَمی A *gram.* pertaining to a proper name; epithetic.

âlemîn (—.—) عالَمین A *lrnd.*, *pl. of* **âlem 1**.

âlemiyan (—.——) عالَمیان *lrnd.* the inhabitants of the world, the mortals, men, mankind.

âlemiyane (—.——.) عالَمیانَه P *lrnd.* like a human being; shrewd, clever (act); knavishly, knavish (act).

alemiyet (..—.) عَلَمیَّت A *gram.* quality of a proper name.

âlemnüma (—..—) عالَمْنُما P *lrnd.* showing the world.

âlempenah (—..—) عالَمْپَناه P *archaic* the Refuge of the Universe (a title of the Sultan).

âlempenahî (—..——) عالَمْپَناهی *lrnd.* 1. the quality of a sovereign, sovereignty. 2. sovereign.

âlemsuz (—.—) عالَمْسوز P *poet.* setting the world on fire.

âlemşümul[lu] (—..—) عالَمْشُمول P *lrnd.* world-wide, universal.

âlemtab (—.—) عالَمْتاب P *poet.* world-illuminating.

alemülcins عَلَمُ الْجِنْس A *lrnd.* generic noun derived from a proper noun.

alen علن A *lrnd.* a becoming published, publicity.
alenen (..'..) علناً A publicly, openly.
alenî (..—) علنى A public, open. — **müzayede** public auction. — **satış** public sale.
aleniyet (..—.) علنیّت A publicity.
alerji آلرژى F *path.* allergy.
alerjik[ži] آلرژیك F *path.* allergic.
alerre'svel'ayn علی الرأس والعین A *lrnd.* (lit., upon the head and the eye) at your service!, with pleasure!
alerrüus (...—) علی الرؤوس A *Maliye* term per capita (tax), poll tax.
alessabah (...—) علی الصباح A *lrnd.* in the morning.
alesseher علی السحر A *poet.* at dawn, at daybreak.
alesseviye (...—.) علی السویة A *lrnd.* equally, to all alike.
alert F *mil.* 1. state of alarm (during an air-raid). 2. alarm, alert, air-raid signal.
aleste (..'.) آلسته It 1. *naut.* ready!, stand by! 2. *slang* ready. — **tiramola!** about ship! ready about!
âlet (—.) آلت A 1. tool, implement, instrument, device. 2. apparatus, machine. 3. instrument, means, agent. 4. *anat.* organ. —**i câriha** *law* any object used for wounding or stabbing. — **işler el övünür** *proverb* The tool does the work; the hand gets the credit. — **ol**= /a/ to be an instrument (to), to lend oneself (to), to act as a stooge (for). —**i tecfif** *chem.* desiccator. —**i tenasül**, —**i tenasüliye** genital organ.
alettafsil (...—) علی التفصیل A *lrnd.* in detail.
alettahkik (...—) علی التحقیق A *lrnd.* definitely, for sure.
alettahmin (...—) علی التخمین A *lrnd.* on estimation, at a guess, approximately.
alettahsis (...—) علی التخصیص A *lrnd.* especially.
alettakdir (...—) علی التقدیر A *lrnd.* on estimation.
alettedric (...—) علی التدریج A *lrnd.* by degrees, gradually.
alettemadi (...——) علی التمادی A *lrnd.* continuously, incessantly.
alettertib (...—) علی الترتیب A *lrnd.* in due order, regularly; successively.
alettetali (...—–) علی التتالی A *lrnd.* in uninterrupted succession.
alettevali (...—) علی التوالی A *lrnd.* successively; continuously.
alev آلو 1. flame. 2. pennant (on a lance, etc.). — **al**= to catch fire; to flare up in a passion. — **alev** aflame, blazing. — **cihazı** *mil.* flame thrower. — **kesil**= to blaze up; to flare up in a passion. — **saçağı sardı** The fire has reached the roof, things have gone too far.
alevgir (..—) آلوگیر [alev+gir] *lrnd.* flaming.
Alevî (..—) علوی A 1. *hist.* descendant of the Caliph Ali. 2. Alawi (partisan of the Caliph Ali). — **tac** white woolen headdress with twelve segments worn by the chiefs of the Bektashi order. —**lik** Alawiism. —**yan** (..——) P descendants of the Caliph Ali.
alevkeş آلوکش [alev+keş] *poet.* spitting flames.
alevlen=[ir] علولنمك آلولنمك 1. to break out in flame, to become blazing. 2. to grow violent, to increase in intensity. 3. to flare up in anger. —**dir**= /ı/ *caus.* —**mez** nonflammable.
alevli آلولو 1. in flames, flaming. 2. furious, violent.
aleyh 1 علیه A used only in dative and locative against, e. g., **aleyhte** against, in opposition; **aleyhimize** against us. —**inde bulun**= to be hostile (to), to take a contrary stand; to talk against, to backbite. —**e dön**= to take up a contrary position. —**ine dön**= to turn against one; turn to one's disadvantage.
aleyhasselâm (....—) علیها السلام A peace be upon her! (said of a prophetess).
aleyhdar (..—) علیهدار P same as **aleyhtar**.
aleyhilgufran (....—) علیه الغفران A *rel. formula* on whom be God's pardon.
aleyhilla'ne علیه اللعنة A *rel. formula* curses be on him!
aleyhirrahme علیه الرحمة A the mercy of God be upon him! (said of a deceased Muslim).
aleyhisselâm (....—) علیه السلام [abbrev. عم] A peace be upon him! (formula used of a prophet).
aleyhtar علیهدار [aleyhdar] opponent; opposed. —**lık** opposition.
aleykesselâm (....—) علیک السلام A *archaic* peace be upon thee!
aleykümselâm (....—), **aleykümüsselâm** (.....—) علیکم سلام علیکم السلام A peace be upon you (said in reply to the Muslim greeting **selâmünaleyküm**).
alfabe الفبا F 1. alphabet. 2. primer.
alfabetik[ži] الفبتیك F alphabetical.
algarina (..'.) الغارینا It *naut.* sheer hulk, floating crane, crane barge.
algı 1 آلغی *prov.* 1. purchase. 2. booty. 3. tax. 4. ladle used for collecting the raw opium that trickles from the incised capsules of the poppy.
algı 2 *neol., psychol.* perception. —**cılık** perceptionism.
algıla=[r] [algı 2] *neol., psychol.* to perceive.
algımsalgım آلغم صالغم [alâimsema] *prov.* rainbow.

algın آلغین *prov.* 1. pale, limp, sickly, wan. 2. love-stricken, enamoured.
algit=ᵈᵉʳ آل گیتدی *prov.* to carry off.
algoncar (..—) آلغنجا P *bot.* morello cherry, bullace.
algoritma (...˙.) آلغوریتما F *math.* algorithm, algorism.
algûn (——) آلگون , **algûne** (——.) آلگونه P *lrnd.* rouge.
=alı. **=eli,** *after vowel* **=yalı** 3, **=yeli** ملی الی *since, as in*, **bulalı** since finding, **Ben buraya geleli onu görmedim** I have not seen him since I came here.
alıc *cf.* **alıç.**
alıcı آلیجی 1. customer. 2. *radio, telephone* receiver. 3. *prov.* the Angel of Death. — **gözüyle bak=** to look carefully, and with interest. — **kuş** bird of prey. — **kuşun ömrü az olur** *proverb* A bird of prey does not live long. — **melek** the Angel of Death. — **verici** *colloq.* one who takes back a present he has given.
alıçᶜⁱ آلیج 1. Neapolitan medlar, *bot., Crataegus azarolus*, or its fruit. 2. mountain ash, *bot., Sorbus aucuparia*, or its fruit.
alıkᵗⁱ آلیق آلوق 1. crazy, imbecile, silly. 2. *prov.* saddle-cloth. 3. *prov.* old clothes, rags. — **alık bak=** to stare stupidly. —**laş** to become imbecile. —**laştır** /ı/ *caus.* —**lık** stupidity, imbecility.
alıko=ʳ آلیقومه |al=7, ko=| /ı/ to detain, to keep. —**n=**, —**nul=** *pass.*
alıkoy=ᵃʳ آلیقویمی /ı/ *same as* **alıko=**.
alım 1 آلیم 1. a single act of taking. 2. the quantity taken at one time. 3. purchase. 4. *obs.* money owed to one, credit. 5. capacity; quickness of mind. 6. range (gun, etc.); eyeshot. 7. attraction, attractiveness. —**ını al=** /ın/ *prov.* to get the measure of. — **satım** purchase and sale; business, trade.
=alım 2, **=elim,** *after vowel* **=yalım** 3, **=yelim** 3 آلم یلم الم ملم *let us, e. g.,* **bakalım** let us see, **gidelim** let us go, **yapmıyalım** let us not do it.
alımlı آلملی 1. attractive. 2. *prov.* quick of mind, intelligent. 3. capacious. 4. *obs.* creditor.
alımsız آلمسز unattractive, ugly, plain.
alınⁱⁿⁱ 1 آلین آلن 1. forehead, brow. 2. *mining* face. —**ında** right in front, *as in* **güneşin alnında** right in the sun, in the direct sun. ˋ—**ı açık** having nothing to be ashamed of, blameless. —**ı açık yüzü ak** *same as* **alnı açık**. —**ının akiyle** honorably, without a blemish. —**ını çat=** to frown, scowl. — **çatkısı**, — **çatması** fillet, band round the head. —**ının damarı çatlamış** brazen-faced. — **ı davul derisi** unabashed, shameless. — **doğruları** *math.* frontal lines. — **düzlemi** *neol., math.* front plane. —**ımın kara yazısı** my luckless destiny. —**ını karışlarım!** 1. I'll show you! (used for a threat). 2. I dare you! — **kası** *anat.* frontal muscle. — **kemiği** *anat.* frontal bone. —**ından öp=** to kiss on the forehead (in admiration, etc.). — **teri dök=** to sweat (over), to toil. — **teriyle kazan=** to earn with hard work, to earn with the sweat of one's brow. — **yazısı***.
alın=ⁿ 2 آلنی 1. *pass. of* **al=** 7. 2. /a or dan/ to take offence (at). 3. /a/ *obs.* to be charmed, enchanted, enraptured (by).
alıngan آلنغان touchy, easily offended, susceptible. —**lık** touchiness, susceptibility.
alınlı آلنلی آلینلی 1. who has a large forehead. 2. brazen-faced, impudent, shameless.
alınlıkᵗⁱ آلنلق آلینلق 1. ornament worn on the forehead. 2. inscription on the front of a building. 3. *arch.* pediment, frontal.
alınyazısıⁿⁱ آلن یازیسی the writing on the forehead, *i. e.,* the decree of Providence upon each individual; destiny.
alırlıkᵗⁱ *neol., psychol.* receptivity.
alış 1 آلش آلیش 1. a taking, receiving. 2. purchase, a buying. — **fiatı** purchase price. — **veriş***.
alış=ⁿ 2 آلیشمی /a/ 1. to become accustomed (to), to get used (to); to become familiar (with), to become trained. 2. to become tame. 3. to get to working smoothly. —**mış kudurmuştan beterdir** *proverb* A habit is worse than madness.
alış=ⁿ 3 آلیشمی *prov.* to catch fire.
alış=ⁿ 4 آلیشمی *obs.* to Buy from each other. آلیشید آلیشیب آلیش آلشه
alışıkᵗⁱ 1 1. /a/ accustomed (to), used (to). 2. tame. 3. working smoothly. — **müşteri** a regular customer. —**lık** 1. habit, force of habit. 2. skill, good training.
alışıkᵗⁱ 2 آلیشیق *obs.* money owed (to one).
alışıl=ⁿ آلشلمی /a/ *pass. of* **alış=** 2.
alışkan آلشقان accustomed; tame. —**lık** force of habit, by custom, out of convention.
alışkın آلشقین /a/ used (to), accustomed (to). —**lık** habitude, force of habit.
alıştır=ⁿ آلشدیرمه آلشدرمه /ı, a/ 1. to accustom (to), to let acquire a habit. 2. to train; to domesticate. 3. to make work smoothly. 4. to allow to get used (to).
alıştır=ⁿ 2 آلشدرمه /ı/ *prov., caus. of* **alış=** 3.
alıştır=ⁿ 3 آلشدرمه /ı/ *colloq.* to make lukewarm.
alışveriş آلش ویرش آلیش ویریش 1. buying and selling, business, trade, commerce; shopping. 2. dealings, relations. — **et=** /la/ 1. to do business, to traffic. 2. to have dealings (with). —**i olma=** /la/ to have no

alız dealings (with), not to have anything to do (with).

alız آلز prov. lean, thin, sickly.

âli 1 (— —) عالی A 1. high, exalted, sublime. 2. w. cap., man's name. **A— Askerî Şura** Supreme Defense Committee, Army Council.

ali 2 (. —) علی A lrnd. 1. high, exalted, noble. 2. w. cap. the Most High. 3. w. cap., man's name. **A— kız** colloq. tomboy. **A— Paşa vergisi** colloq. a present which is taken back. **A— Veli** Tom, Dick, and Harry.

âli 3 (— —) آلی |based on Arabic| phil. instrumental, technical.

âlibaht (— —..) عالی بخت P lrnd. of exalted fortune.

âlicah (— — —) عالی جاه P lrnd. high in rank.

âlicenab, âlicenap[bı] (— —. —) عالی جناب P noble-hearted, magnanimous. **—lık** noble-heartedness, magnanimity.

alicengiz علی جنگیز only in **— oyunu** a dirty trick.

alif (. —) علیف A lrnd. kept in the stable and fed with fodder.

âlifıtrat (— —..) عالی فطرت P lrnd. of noble nature.

Aligurna (...'.) آلغورنا It obs., geog. Leghorn, Livorno.

âligüher (— —..) عالی گهر P lrnd. of noble essence.

âlih (—.) آله A lrnd. astonished, stupefied.

âlihe 1 (— ..) آلهه A lrnd. gods, goddesses, deities.

âlihe 2 (— ..) الهة |based on Arabic| lrnd. goddess.

âlihimem, âlihimmet (— —..) عالی همم عالی همت P lrnd. noble, gracious.

alik[kı] (. —) علیب A lrnd. barley, fodder for horses.

alika (. —.) علیفه A lrnd. 1. camels sent for bringing grain. 2. nosebag for fodder.

âlikadir[dri] (— —..) var. of **âlikadr**.

âlikadr[rı] (— —.) عالی قدر P lrnd. highly esteemed, noble.

alikıran علی قران only in **— baş kesen** colloq. bully, despot.

alikorna, alikurna (...'.) علی قورنه |Aligurna| obs. Leghorn paper.

alil (. —) علیل A 1. permanently invalid. 2. lrnd. sick, diseased.

âlim 1 (— .) عالم A 1. learned, wise; scholar, savant. 2. lrnd. who knows, knowing.

alîm 2 (. —) علیم A lrnd. 1. very learned, wise, knowing. 2. omniscient (God).

alîm 3 (—.) ألم A lrnd. grieving, pained, suffering.

âlimakam (— —. —) عالی مقام P lrnd. of high position, of high rank.

alimallah (.´..—) علم الله A 1. God knows. 2. by God!

âlimane (— —.) عالمانه P scholarly; in a scholarly manner.

âlimekân (— —. —) عالی مکان P lrnd. of high position, of high rank.

âlimlik[ki] (— ..) عالملك learning, scholarship.

âlişan (— — —) عالیشان P lrnd. illustrious, most noble.

âlitebar (— —. —) عالی تبار P lrnd. of noble descent.

alivre آلیوره F com. to be delivered. **— satış** time bargain.

âliyat (— — —) آلیات |based on Arabic| obs. technology.

âliye 1 (— ..) عالیه A lrnd. 1. high, elevated, exalted. 2. upper part. 3. w. cap. the Highlands of Arabia.

Âliye 2 (— —.) عالیه name of a dervish order belonging to the **Halvetiye**.

aliye 3 (. —.) علیة A 1. lrnd. very high, exalted. 2. w. cap., woman's name.

aliyül'a'lâ (. —. . —) علی الأعلا A lrnd. of the very best quality.

alizeler آلیزه لر F geog. trade winds.

aljezi آلژزی F path. algesia.

alkali آلقالی F chem. alkali.

alkalik[ki] آلقالیك F chem. alkaline.

alkaloit[di] آلقالوئید F chem. alkaloid.

alkam علقم A lrnd. 1. colocynth. 2. anything bitter.

alkame علقمه A lrnd. 1. bitterness. 2. colocynth. 3. w. cap., man's name.

alkım |algımsalgım?| neol., rainbow.

alkış آلقش 1. acclamation, cheer, applause. 2. prov. blessing; praise. **— çavuşları** hist. court officials whose task was to acclaim the sovereign on certain occasions. **— et=** /a/ to acclaim, to praise. **— tufanı** great applause, torrent of applause. **— tut=** /a/ to cheer. **— ver=** /a/ obs. to praise. **—çı** applauder, flatterer. **—çılar** claque. **—la=** /ı/ to acclaim. **—n=** pass. of **alkışla=**.

alkol[lü] آلقول F alcohol.

alkolik[ki] آلقولیك F alcoholic.

alkolizm آلقولیزم F alcoholism.

alkollü آلقوللی containing alcohol; intoxicating.

alla=[r] آللمق in **— pulla=** colloq. /ı/ to decorate, to deck out.

allâf (. —) علاف A lrnd. furnisher of provender; forager.

Allah (. —) الله A 1. God. 2. O God!, How wonderful! Really! **—ım!** My God! **—tan** happily, luckily, fortunately. **— acısın** /a/ May God have pity on him! Only God can help him. **— acısını unutturmasın** May God spare you from a greater sorrow (said when one is subjected to a great loss or grief). — **adamı** a man of God. — **akıllar versin!** /a/ I am surprised at you (him, etc.). — **Allah!** goodness gracious! — **aşkına!** for heaven's sake (expressing amazement or imploration). — **aratmasın** May God spare you from having something worse (said when one is discontented). — **bağışlasın** /ı/ God bless him (her, them). (i. e. someone's child or loved person). — **bana, ben de sana** I shall pay you my debt when I can. —**ın belâsı** a curse of God, nuisance, pest; unbearable, dreadful. — **belânı vermesin!** /ın/ euphemism for **Allah belânı versin!** — **belânı versin!** God curse you! — **beterinden esirgesin!** /ı/ May God protect from worse trouble! — **bilir** God knows, who can tell? —**ın bildiğini kuldan ne saklayım?** Why should I hide from man what is known to God? What's the use of making a secret of it! —**a bin şükür** Thank God. May God be praised! — **bir!** by the one God! — **bir, söz bir** I give my word for it. —**tan bulsun** Let God punish him. — **büyüktür** 1. God is sure to punish one someday for an injustice. 2. Let us rely on God. — **canını almasın!** /ın/ euphemism for **Allah canını alsın.** — **canını alsın** God curse you. —**ın cezası** same as **Allahın belâsı.** — **cezanı versin** same as **Allah belânı versin.** — **dağına göre kar verir** proverb (lit., God sends the snow according to the mountain.) A person has enough strength for his troubles. — **dokuzda verdiğini sekizde almaz** proverb (lit., God does not take away at the age of eight, what he has given to be taken at the age of nine) Nobody dies before his time. Destiny cannot be altered. — **ecir sabır versin!** /a/ May God give patience. (said for condolence). — **eksik etmesin** /ı/ May we not suffer his loss. —**a emanet** May God protect (him, etc.) — **emeklerini eline vermesin** May God grant that your effort be fruitful and not in vain. —**ın emriyle Peygamberin kavliyle** according to the will of God and the word of the Prophet (said when a woman is asked in marriage). — **encamını hayır eyleye** /ın/ May God bring him (it) to a happy end. — **esirgesin!** God forbid! — **etmesin!** God forbid! — **gani gani rahmet eylesin** /a/ May God have abundant mercy upon him! (said for a dead person). — **gazabı** the scourge of God, evildoer. — **gecinden versin** /a/ May God ordain it to be late (used when mentioning death). — **göstermesin!** God forbid! —**ın günü** every single day. — **hakkı için** in God's name. —**a havale et**= /ı/ to leave to God (punishment, revenge). — **hayırlar versin** God turn it to goodness. — **herkesin gönlüne göre verir** proverb God gives to every person according to his heart's desire. —**ın hikmeti** by divine decree, strange coincidence. — **ıslah etsin** /ı/ May God reform him. —**a ısmarladık** Good-bye (said by the person leaving). — **için** verily, truly, impartially, to be fair; ironically oh, indeed! — **ikisini bir yastıkta kocatsın** May they have a happy life together (said for a newly married couple). — **imdat eylesin** /a/ May God help (you, etc.). — **imhal eder, ihmal etmez** proverb God delays, but neglects not. — **inandırsın** May God cause you to believe me. — **insanın aklını alacağına canını alsın** It is better to die than to lose one's mind. — **isterse** God willing. —**ın işine karışılmaz** God knows best. — **iyiliğini versin** euphemism for God damn you! —**ın izniyle** God willing. —**a kal**= to be left to chance. — **bir kapı kaparsa bin kapı açar** proverb Whenever God closes one door, he opens a thousand. — **kardeşi kardeş yaratmış, kesesini ayrı yaratmış** proverb God has created brothers as brothers, but He has created them with separate purses. — **kavuştursun** /ı/ May God unite you again. (said to those remaining behind after another has departed on a journey). — **kazadan belâdan esirgesin,** — **kazadan belâdan saklasın** God protect you from all evil. — **kerim** God is gracious; trust in God. —**tan kork** (lit., fear God.) How can you! What a shame! —**tan korkmaz** disgraceful, cruel, ruthless. — **korusun!** God forbid! — **lâyığını versin** /ın/ May God give (him, you) his deserts. euphemism for Damn you (him)! — **mübarek etsin** God bless (him, etc.). — **müstahakkını versin** same as **Allah lâyığını versin.** — **nasip eyliye** May God grant it. — **ne verdiyse** whatever God has given (modest expression in reference to food). —**ın öldürmediğini kimse öldüremez** proverb Nobody can kill a person whom God spares. — **ömürler versin** May God give you a long life. (used for greeting and thanking). — **övmüş te yaratmış** /ı/ (He etc.) is marked out by God (said about a beautiful person). — **rahatlık versin** /a/ Good night! — **rahmet etsin,** — **rahmet eylesin** /a/ May God have mercy on him (said for a dead person). —**ın rahmetine kavuş**= (lit., to meet with God's mercy) to die. — **razı olsun** /dan/ May God be pleased (with you etc.). God bless (you, him, etc.). — **rızası için** for God's sake. — **sabır versin** /a/ May God give patience. (said to one who has incurred a loss, etc.). — **sağ gözü sol göze muhtaç etmesin** (lit. May God cause not the right eye to need the left eye) God save one from needing another's help! — **saklasın!** /dan/ God forbid! — **selâmet versin!** /a/ May God protect (him, etc.). —**ını seven tutmasın** going or running in great haste. **—ı seversen** for the love of God. **— şaşırtmasın** /ı/ May God protect one from sin. **— son gürlüğü versin** May God keep one healthy and in one's right mind in old age. **—a şükür!** Thank God! **— taksiratımızı affetsin** /ın/ May God forgive us. **— tamamına erdirsin** May God bring it to a happy conclusion (said of an event, affair, etc.). **— toprağı kadar ömür versin!** /a/ May God give you as much life as the earth covering him. (used when someone is compared favorably with a dead person), May you live long. **— versin** 1. May God help you (said to a beggar when one does not give him anything). 2. May you enjoy it, I am so glad. **— vere de** God grant (that), I hope (that). **— vermesin!** /ı/ God forbid! **— verince kimin oğlu kimin kızı demez** proverb God in His giving makes no distinction between persons. **— vergisi** God's gift, innate talent. **— yapısı** a work of God, not man-made. **— yarattı deme=** (lit., not to say 'God has created him') to have no mercy (beating someone). **— yardımcısı olsun** /ın/ God help him (said of a person in a desperate position). **— yazdı ise bozsun** May it never happen (said when one does not wish to do a certain thing wished for him). **— yürü kulum deyince** When God wishes someone success (his success knows no bounds). **— ziyade etsin** May God give you abundantly (said by the guest after a meal).

allahlık⁸¹ آللهلق 1. the quality of being God. 2. harmless, simple man, simpleton. 3. left to God, unpredictable.

allahsız آللهسز atheist; heretic.

Allahua'lem (.—...) اللّه اعلم A lrnd. God knows best; Heaven only knows.

Allahuekber (.—...) اللّه اکبر A God is most great! (used in worship and as a battle-cry).

Allahutaalâ (.—..—) اللّه تعالی A God, whose majesty be exalted; God the Most High. **— ve takaddese** God, may He be exalted and accounted holy.

allâk⁸¹ 1 آللاک |from Arabic 'allak 2| 1. untrustworthy, fickle. 2. deceitful.

allâkᵏⁱ 2 (.—) علاک A lrnd. seller of chewing gum.

allakbullak⁸¹ آللق بوللق confused, topsy-turvy. **— et=** /ı/ to make a mess (of), to set in confusion.

allâm (.—) علّام A lrnd. 1. omniscient, all-knowing. 2. very learned.

allâme (.—.) علّامه A 1. exceedingly learned. 2. lrnd. well versed in genealogies.

allâmî (.—ˉ) علّامی A lrnd. pertaining to a very learned man.

allâmulguyub (.—..—) علّام الغیوب A lrnd. the omniscient knower of all hidden things.

allasen (...) colloq. for **Allahı seversen.**

allaşkına (..·..), **allaşkınıza** (..·...) colloq. for **Allah aşkına.**

allegro It. mus. allegro.

allem kallem et=ᵈᵉʳ آللّم قلّم ایتمك , also **allem et=. kallem et=** to try all sorts of things (to gain one's ends).

allı آللی mixed with red, partly red; wearing red. **— pullu** colorful and decked out with spangles, showily dressed. **— yeşilli** red and green (dress, etc.).

allık⁸¹ آللق 1. redness, flame color. 2. rouge.

alma 1 آلما a taking, receiving, buying.

alma 2 آلما prov. for **elma.**

almacık⁸¹ آلماجق prov. head of the thigh-bone, knuckle-bone.

almaçᶜⁱ neol., elec. receiver.

Alman آلمان |Alaman, with influence of F| German.

almanak⁸¹ آلماناق F almanac.

Almanca (..·.) آلمانجه the German language, German.

Almanlaş=ⁱʳ آلمانلشمق to be Germanized.

Almanya (..·.) آلمانیه ،آلمانیا |Alamanya| Germany. **—lı** from Germany, a German.

almaş 1 neol. 1. phil. alternative. 2. permutation. 3. exchange of posts between two officials.

almaş=ⁱʳ 2 آلماشمق prov. 1. to exchange. 2. to take turns. **—ık** 1. used by taking turns. 2. sc. alternate. **—tır=** /ı/ to use by taking turns.

almazlan=ⁱʳ آلمازلانمق obs. to refuse to take, to refrain from taking.

alnaçᶜⁱ آلناچ prov. front, the side facing the onlooker.

alnı cf. **alın** 1.

alo آلو F hello (used in telephone conversation).

alonj F com. allonge, rider.

alopati F med. allopathy.

alopesi F path. alopecia.

aloritmi F path. allorhythmia.

alotropi F chem. allotropy.

alösemi F path. aleukemia.

alpᵖⁱ 1, **alp**ᵇⁱ آلب archaic hero, brave, heroic.

Alpᵖⁱ 2 آلب usu. pl. the Alps. **— keçisi** chamois.

alpaka (..·.) آلپاقا F 1. zool. alpaca. 2. alpaca cloth.

alplık⁸¹ آلبلق |alp 1| archaic heroism.

alşimi آلشیمی F alchemy.

alşimist آلشیمیست F alchemist.

alt آلت space or place beneath a thing; bottom, underside; lower part; lower, inferior. **—ına** under, beneath, below, e. g., **Ayakları-**

nızı masanın altına koyunuz Put your feet under the table. —ında under, beneath, below, *e. g.*, **Ayaklarım masanın altındadır.** My feet are under the table. —ından from beneath, from underneath, *e. g.*, **Ayaklarınızı masanın altından çekiniz** Remove your feet from underneath the table. —ına al= /ı/ to throw down (in wrestling, etc.). —tan al= to assume a humble attitude. —ı alaylı üstü kalaylı showy on the outside, but poor underneath. — alta one under the other. —tan alta in an underhand way. — alta üst üste 1. rough and tumble (fight). 2. in a close embrace, in a bear hug. — aşağı vur= /ı/ to cast down, to overthrow, to conquer. — başında /ın/ near, next. — başından /ı/ from the very bottom (of). —ından Çapanoğlu çık= /ın/ to take a bad turn unexpectedly. — çenesinden girip üst çenesinden çık= /ın/ to get round someone with persuasive words. —ını çiz= /ın/ to underline. — dudak lower lip, underlip. — et= /ı/ to overwhelm, conquer. —ına et= to foul one's clothes or bed. —tan gel= *same as* **alttan al=**. —ından girip üstünden çık= /ın/ 1. to squander, to spend recklessly (a fortune). 2. to disorder completely, to disarray. —a gittim diye yerinme, üste çıktım diye sevinme Rejoice not in victory nor be discouraged in defeat (for neither last). —ını ıslat= to wet one's underclothes or bed. —ına kaçır= to be unable to control one's bowels. —ında kal= /ın/ to have no retort (to another's statement); to be unable to reply; to remain under obligation. —ta kal= to be defeated. —ta kalanın canı çıksın *proverb* Woe to the defeated! — kasa *print.* lower case. — kat first floor. —ı kaval üstü şişane ˙ (*lit.*, smoothbore below, and rifled above) wearing ill-assorted clothes. — ol= /a/ to be conquered, to be overcome (by). — taraf 1. the lower part; the underside. 2. remainder, rest, sequel. 3. all that is involved (is only), *e. g.*, **Niçin bu kadar üzülüyorsunuz? Alt tarafı ön kuruş!** What are you making such a fuss about? It is only a matter of a few cents. — tarafı Çapanoğlu çık= *same as* **altından Çapanoğlu çık=.** — tarafı çıkmaz sokak (*lit.* The outcome is a blind alley.) It leads nowhere. — tetik halfcock notch of a gun. — tetiğe al= /ı/ to halfcock (gun). — uc *same as* **alt taraf**[2, 3] — üst*. —ını üstüne getir= /ın/ to upset, to turn upside down, to confuse; to search; to leave no stone unturned. — yan 1. the lower side. 2. *same as* **alt taraf**. — yüz the lower side, the lower surface.

|*For other compounds, cf.* **altabaşo - altüst**.|

altabaşo (. . . .) آلتا باشو |alt, abaşo] *naut.* foot (of a sail).

altakıntı آلت آقنتی *phys. geog.* undercurrent.
altala= آلتا لامه *prov.* to overcome.
altamga (. . .) آلتمغا *hist.* vermilion stamp, the cipher of the family of Jengiz Khan.
altbilinç[ci] *neol.*, *psych.* the subconscious. —sel subconscious.
altcins آلت جنس *biol.* subgenus.
altçene آلت چكه *anat.* the lower jaw. — kemiği jaw, mandible.
altçı آلتچی *obs.* the first wife (in polygamy).
altderi آلت دری *biol.* derma.
alternatif F *sc.* alternative. — akım *elec.* alternating current. — borç *law* alternative obligation.
alternator, alternatör F *elec.* alternator.
altes آلتس F His Highness.
altev آلت اور *prov.* ground floor; room on the ground floor.
altfamilya (. . . .) آلت فاميليا *biol.* subfamily.
altı آلتی six. —da bir one sixth. — ok the six arrows (emblem of the Republican People's party). — okka et= /ı/ to manhandle by lifting repeatedly by arms and legs.
|*For compounds, cf.* **altıatar - altıyüz**.|
altıatar آلتی آتار *prov.* sixshooter.
altıgen *neol.*, *geom.* hexagon.
altık[ı] *neol.*, *phil.* subaltern. —lama subalternation.
altıkardeş آلتی قارداش *astr.* the constellation of Cassiopeia. (*cf.* **zat-ı kürsi**).
altıköşe آلتی كوشه *geom.* hexagon.
altılı آلتیلی *cards* six.
altılık[ı] آلتیلیك 1. pertaining to six. 2. *obs.* six-piaster piece.
altın 1 آلتین آلتون 1. gold. 2. gold coin. 3. golden. — adını bakır et= to turn one's gold to dross. — adı pul ol= /ın/ for one's good name to be disgraced. — anahtar her kapıyı açar *proverb* Money talks. — ateşte, insan mihnette belli olur *proverb* Gold is proved by fire, man by suffering. — babası moneybags, Croesus. — bilezik gold bracelet; *fig.* a craft on which one can rely in all circumstances to earn one's living. — çiçeği buttercup, crowsfoot, *bot.*, *Ranunculus acris*. — devri the most prosperous epoch. — eli bıçak kesmez The rich cannot be defeated. — esası *econ.* gold standard, gold basis. — kakma inlaid with gold. — kamışı loosestrife, *bot.*, *Lysimachia*. — kaplama gold-plated. — karşılık *econ.* the gold reserve kept by the national bank against the bank notes in circulation. — kartal golden eagle, *zool. Aquila chrysaetos*. — kaydı *com.* gold clause. — kes= *colloq.* to be very rich. — kestir= *prov.* to buy gold ornaments in great quantity for the bride. —ın kıymetini sarraf bilir *proverb* (*lit.* The money-changer knows the worth

of gold.) A good thing is appreciated by the expert. **— kozak** *hist.* cylindrical gold case in which a letter from the Sultan was sent to a foreign potentate. **— kökü** ipecacuanha root. **— leğene kan kus=** to live in misery in spite of great wealth. **A— Ordu** *hist.* the Golden Horde. **— otu** hart's tongue fern, *bot. Scolopendrium vulgare.* **— pas tutmaz** *proverb (lit.* Gold does not rust.) A good character cannot be harmed by slander. **— rıhı** powdered gold leaf used on important documents. **A— Sahili** the Gold Coast. **— sarısı** golden blonde, titian. **— suyu** *aqua regia;* gilding wash, liquid gold. **— şartı** *com.* gold clause. **— topu gibi** like a golden ball (said for a pretty, healthy child). **— tutsa, toprak olur, —a yapışsa elinde bakır kesilir** said of a very ill-fortuned person.
|For other compounds, cf. **altınbaş - altıntop.**|
altın 2 آلتن *obs.* lower, inferior.
altınbaş 1. gold-headed. 2. kind of melon. 3. *prov.* owl. **— kefal** golden gray mullet, *zool. Mugil auratus.*
altıncı sixth.
altıncık[¹] 1. small gold coin. 2. corn marigold, *bot. Chrysanthemum segetum.* **—lar** the beloved money.
altınla=[¹] /ı/ to ornament with gold, to gild. **—n=** *pass.* **—t=** /ı/ *caus.*
altınlı 1. containing gold; ornamented with gold. 2. rich.
altınoluk[¹¹] 1. golden gutter (on the roof of the Kaaba). 2. kind of striped fabric.
altıntabak[¹] buttercup, crowfoot, *bot., Ranunculus acris.*
altıntop daffodil, *bot., Narcissus pseudonarcissus.*
altıparmak[¹] 1. six-fingered. 2. large kind of bonito. 3. rich cloth with stripes in six colors.
altıpatlar six-shooter, revolver.
altışar six at a time, six each. **— altışar** by sixes.
altıyüz six hundred.
altkarşıt[ᵈ] *neol., phil.* subcontrary.
altla=[ʳ] /ı/ *neol., phil.* to subsume. **—ma** subsumption.
altlık[¹] 1. support, base. 2. pad put under a paper for writing.
altlı üstlü including the upper and the lower part.
altmış sixty.
altmışaltı cards sixty-six (name of a card game). **—ya bağla=** /ı/ *slang* to put (someone) off with promises.
altmışar sixty each, sixty at a time.

— altmışar by sixties.
altmışıncı sixtieth.
altmışla=[ʳ] to reach sixty.
altmışlık[¹] 1. pertaining to sixty. 2. sixty years old, sexagenarian. 3. sixty-para piece.
alto (.′.) It *mus.* alto.
altsınıf *biol.* subclass.
altşube *biol.* subbranch.
alttakım *biol.* suborder.
altun *archaic for* **altın 1. —î** (.——) gold colored.
altüst upside down, topsy-turvy, in utter confusion. **— böreği** *pastry* turnover. **— et=** /ı/ to upset, to run upside down, to make untidy.
alû 1 (——) P *lrnd.* plum, plum-tree.
alu 2 *obs.* miserable, base.
alubalu (———) P *lrnd.* sour cherry.
alubuhara (——.——) P *obs.* dried plum from Bukhara or Iran.
aluçe (——.) P *lrnd.* small plum; cherry; bullace, sloe; currant.
-alud (——) P *lrnd.* soiled with, contained with, *e. g.,* **hunalud.**
alûde (——.) P *lrnd.* soiled, contaminated. **— et=** /ı/ to soil. **—dâmen** (——.——.) P whose skirts are soiled; contaminated with sin, guilty, wicked. **—gi** (——.——) P pollution, contamination.
alûfe (.—.) A *lrnd.* fodder, provender.
aluğde (—..) P *poet.* furious.
alûvyon F *geol.* alluvion.
alüfte 1 (—..) P *poet.* troubled, distressed; love-stricken.
alüfte 2 |**alüfte 1**| harlot, prostitute.
alüftegân (—..—) P *lrnd.* pl. of **alüfte 1.**
âlüh (—.) P *poet.* eagle.
alül'âl[¹¹] (—.—) A *lrnd.* highest of the high, best of the good.
alüminyom, alüminyum F aluminum, aluminium.
alveol[¹¹] F *anat.* alveole, alveolus.
alveoler F *anat.* alveolar.
alya (.—) A *lrnd.* 1. high place, height, eminence. 2. sky.
alyans F wedding ring.
alyon |*from the name of a nineteenth century wealthy person*| *slang* very rich.
alyuvar *neol., anat.* red blood corpuscle, erythrocyte.
am 1 female genital organ. **— biti** crab louse. *zool., Phthirus pubis.*

=am 2, =em, *after vowel* =yem 2, =yem 3, ٫ا *archaic for* =ayım, *etc.* let me, *e. g.*, kalam! Let me stay.

âm 3 (—) عام A *lrnd.* solar year. —ı kabil, —ı mukbil next year.

âm^mmı 4 (—) عامّ A *lrnd.* general, universal; common, public.

am^mmı 5 عمّ A *lrnd.* paternal uncle.

ama 1 اما |amma| but, yet, still.

âmâ, a'mâ 2 (. —) اعمی ' اما A blind.

=ama= 3, =eme=, *after vowel* =yama= 3, =yeme= 1. not to be able to, *e. g.*, yapamadım I was not able to do it; gelememişti He had not been able to come.

amâ 4 (. —) عمی A loss of eyesight; blindness.

amâ 5 (. —) عماء A *lrnd.* 1. rain clouds. cumuli. 2. contention.

amacgâh (— — —) اماجگاه P *lrnd.* 1. place on which a target is fixed. 2. the world (in which men are butts for the shafts of fortune).

amaç^cı 1 آماج 1. *prov.*, *var. of* alnaç. 2. *same as* amaç 2.

amaç^cı 2 (— —) آماج P 1. aim. 2. target; butt on a mound used as target. 3. *obs.* the twenty-fourth part of a parasang.

âmade (— — .) آماده P *lrnd.* ready, prepared. —gi (— — . —) P readiness, preparation.

amah (— —) آمه P *lrnd.* swelling. tumor.

amaik^kı (. — .) عمائن A *lrnd., pl. of* amik.

amaim (. — .) عمائم A *lrnd., pl. of* imame 1.

amair (. — .) عمائر A *lrnd.* buildings; public buildings. —i hayriye buildings for public charity.

âmak^kı, a'mak^kı (. —) اعماق A *lrnd.* depths; profundities.

amakat^tı (. — .) عماقت A *lrnd.* depth; profundity.

âmal^lı, a'mal^lı 1 (. —) اعمال A 1. works, deeds, actions. 2. *lrnd.* dependencies of a city. —i erbaa *math.* the four arithmetical operations. A—i Rüsül *Bib., obs.* the Acts of the Apostles.

âmâl^lı 2 (— —) آمال A *lrnd.* aspirations, ambitions, desires, hopes.

amale (. — .) عمال A *lrnd.* workman's wages.

âmâlık^kı (— — .) اعمالی |âmâ 1| blindness.

Amalik^kı (. — —) عمالیین , Amalika (. — . .) عمالقة *Bib. hist.* the Amalekites.

Amaliki (. — — —) عمالیقی *Bib. hist.* an Amelekite.

a'mam (. —) اعمام A *lrnd., pl. of* am 5.

aman (. —) آمان |eman| 1. oh! ah! mercy! help! for goodness sake! 2. mercy. — aralık verme= /a/ not to give any respite. — bul= to escape; to be saved. — de= to ask for quarter, to surrender. — derim! don't you do it! beware of doing such a thing, *e. g.*, dağa çıkacakmışsın, aman derim! I heard you were going to climb the mountain; don't you do it! — dile= /dan/ to ask for quarter. — diyene kılıç kalkmaz *proverb* No sword is lifted against one who asks for quarter. — gayret! keep on! hold on! —a gel= to come to terms, to give in. —a getir= /ı/ to bring to terms, to beat to their knees. — iste= *same as* aman dile=. —ını kes= /ın/ *obs.* to cut off all hope from. —ını tüket= /ın/ *obs.* to exhaust, to cause to despair. — verme= /a/ to show no mercy (to). — zaman bilme=, — zaman dinleme= to listen to no protests. —ı zamanı yok there is no trying to get out of it, you must.

amanallah (. — . —) آمان الله oh God! my God!

amanat عمانت |emanet| *prov.* 1. *same as* emanet. 2. not well set, in danger of slipping or falling.

amanın (. — .' .) امانن oh! ah! help!

amansız آمانسز merciless.

a'mar 1 (. —) اعمار A *lrnd.* lifetimes, lives.

âmar 2 (— —) آمار P *lrnd.* 1. calculation, computation, account. 2. investigation, scrutiny.

amâr 3 (. —) عمار A *pl. of* amare.

amare (. — .) عماره A *lrnd.* 1. symbol of chieftainship set up in a tent or on a headdress, etc., by a chief. 2. gesture of respect for a symbol of dignity or its owner.

amas (— —) آماس P *lrnd.* swelling, tumor.

amaside (— — — .) آماسیده P *lrnd.* swollen.

Amasya (. .' .) آماسیه Amasia (town in Anatolia). —nın bardağı, biri olmazsa biri daha Nothing is indispensable.

amatör اماتور F amateur.

amayicibilli (. — . . . —) عمای مجبلی P *lrnd.* congenital blindness.

amayielvan (. — . . —) عمای الوان P *psych.* color blindness.

amayiidrak^kı (. — . . —) عمای ادراک P *psychopath.* agnosia.

ambak^tı *prov.* green shell (of a walnut). —la= /ı/ to shuck (walnuts).

ambalaj آمبالاژ F packing, package. — kâğıdı wrapping paper, packing paper. — yap= /ı/ to pack, to wrap up.

ambale آمبالا F crammed, blocked, stuffed (mind).

ambar انبار ، آمبار |enbar| 1. storehouse, store room, store. 2. granary; grain bin, grain cellar. 3. *naut.* hold. 4. bin for measuring sand,

ambargo 56

stones, etc. 5. shipping firm, — **ağzı** *naut.* hatchway. — **ağzı çerçevesi** coamings of the hatchway. —**da duran sıçan aç kalmaz** *proverb* The rat in the storehouse does not go hungry. — **faresi** very fat. — **kapağı** *naut.* hatch. — **memuru** storekeeper. —**cı** storekeeper.
ambargo (..'.) آمبارغو F embargo. —**yu kaldır**= /dan/ to lift the embargo (from). — **koy**= /a/ to impose an embargo (on).
amber عنبر A 1. ambergris. 2. *poet.* scent, perfume, fragrance. 3. *lrnd.* shield of whaleskin; shield. 4. *man's or woman's name.* — **balığı** spermaceti whale. — **çiçeği** musk mallow, *bot., Hibiscus abelmoschus.* —**i eşheb** *lrnd.* ambergris. —**i Şahri** ambergris of Shahr in southern Arabia. —**i ter** P *poet.* fresh ambergris; anything fresh and fragrant. **A—abad** (..—) P *poet., name of a mythical city.* —**agin** (..—) P *poet.* full of ambergris; fragrant. —**bar** (..—) P *poet.* fragrant. —**baris** barberry, *bot., Berberis vulgaris.* —**bu** (..—) P *poet.* smelling of ambergris; fragrant. —**buy** (..—) 1. *same as* **amberbu.** 2. sweet sultan, *bot., Amberboa moschata.* 3. a valued kind of fragrant rice. —**efşan** (...—) P 1. *poet.* diffusing fragrance. 2. *Or. mus., name of a mode.* —**i** (..—) *lrnd.* 1. pertaining to ambergris; perfumed with ambergris. 2. seller of ambergris. 3. pertaining to the Anberite tribe. 4. skillful guide (like the Anberites). —**in** (..—) P *poet.* perfumed with ambergris; fragrant. —**iye** (..—.) 1. liquor. 2. musk okra, *bot., Abelmoschus moschatus.* —**li** mixed with ambergris; perfumed with ambergris. —**sa** (..—) P *lrnd.* resembling ambergris. —**şemim** (...—) P *poet.* fragrant as ambergris.
ambliyopi F *path.* amblyopia.
amboli F *path.* embolism.
amca عمو جا آمو جا |am 5| paternal uncle (familiarly used in addressing an older man). —**baba yarısı** A paternal uncle is half a father. —**m dayım, hepsinden aldım payım** I have suffered enough from relatives. — **kızı** paternal girl cousin. — **oğlu** paternal boy cousin. — **lık** 1. unclehood. 2. step-uncle. —**zade** (..—.) cousin (child of one's paternal uncle).
amd عمد A *lrnd.* purpose, deliberate intention; *law* premeditation. —**en** (.'.) A *law* intentionally, on purpose.
amed (—.) آمد P *obs.* 1. 'arrived' (sign used in official registers to mark the arrival of incoming documents, etc.). 2. coming, arrival. 3. income, revenue. 4. importation; what is imported.
amedci (—..) آمدجی |amed| *Ott. hist.* the receiver general of provincial correspondence addressed to the Grand Vezier.
amede (—..) آمده P *lrnd.* 1. come, arrived; happened. 2. repartee, impromptu.
amedengâh (—..—) آمدنگاه P *lrnd.* a place to which people usually come, rendezvous.
amedenî (—..—) آمدنی P *lrnd.* 1. who is to come; which is to happen. 2. income, impost, revenue; requisite, fee.
amedenilaklakᵏˡ (—.....) آمدنی لقلق P *calendar* arrival of the storks (February 28).
amedî (—.—) آمدی P *same as* **amedci.** —**i divanı humayun** 1. *same as* **amedci.** 2. clerks of the **amedci's** office.
amediye (—.—.) آمدیه *obs.* import duty.
amedreft (—..) آمد رفت P *lrnd.* 1. arrival and departure, coming and going. 2. income and expenditure.
amedşüd (—..) آمد شد P *lrnd.* arrival and departure, coming and going.
amel 1 عمل A 1. act, action, work, deed; practice, performance. 2. *obs.* government office; province of administration. 3. *Arabic gram.* government of a word in a sentence. 4. *math.* operation. —**i bâtıl** inane deed. —**e gel**= to take effect, to be enforced. —**e getir**= /ı/ to put into execution; to enforce. —**i Kayseri** Caesarean operation. — **oluna** Let it be done, *Fiat* (formula used by the Sultans on decrees). —**i salih** good work, pious deed.
amel 2 عمل |amel 1| diarrhea. — **hapı** laxative pill. — **ol**= to have diarrhea.
ameldar (..—) عملدار P *obs.* 1. magistrate. 2. tax-collector.
amele عمله A 1. worker, workman. 2. *obs.* governors, magistrates; tax-collectors. — **hukuku** labor legislation. — **partisi** *obs.* Labor party.
amelehü (.'...) عملهٔ A *inscribed on works of art:* made by, *fecit.*
amelen (.'..) عملاً A *lrnd.* in deed, in effect, in action.
amelî (..—) عملی A 1. practical, applied; acquired by practice. 2. *obs.* artificial, manufactured.
amelimanda عمل مانده |amelmande| incapable of work, invalided, retired (servant).
ameliyat 1 (..——) عملیات |ameliyat 2| surgical operation. — **et**= /ı/ to operate (on). — **ol**= to be operated upon.
ameliyat 2 (..——) عملیات A *lrnd.* practical performances; deeds, acts.
ameliyathane (..——.) عملیاتخانه |ameliyat 1| operating room (in a hospital).
ameliye (..—.) عملیه A 1. process, procedure, operation. 2. *lrnd., fem. of* **amelî.**
amelli عمللی |amel 1| 1. that does,

practices, acts. 2. *obs.* who holds a government office; which has provinces.

amelmande (.. — .) عَمَل‌نَادَه P *lrnd.*, same as **amelimanda**.

amelsiz عَمَلسِز 1. inert. 2. who does not practice what he professes.

amen (— .) آمَن A *lrnd.*, *superl. of* **âmin**, **emin**.

amenajman F management (of forest or mine).

amenna (— . —) آمَنّا A 1. *rel. formula* we believe. 2. admitted, agreed.

amenore F *path.* amenorrhea.

amentü (— . .) آمَنت A *rel. formula* I believe in, credo. — **billâhi vahdehü lâ şerike lehü** I believe in God alone, who has no associate.

Amerika (.. ' . .) آمَریقا It America. — **Birleşik Devletleri** the United States of America. —**lı** an American. —**lılaş=** to become Americanized. —**lılaştır=** /ı/ to Americanize.

Amerikan آمَریقان It 1. American. 2. *l. c.* unbleached, coarse calico. — **sığırı** moose. —**vari** (.... — —) in the American fashion.

ameş عَمَش A *lrnd.* weakness of sight and a watering of the eyes.

ametçi (— . .) آمَدجی *var. of* **amedci**.

ametist F *min.* amethyst.

amevi (.. —) عَموی A *lrnd.* 1. pertaining to a paternal uncle or aunt, avuncular. 2. pertaining to a blind person.

amfi (.'.) آمفی F dissecting room or lecture room arranged with rising tiers of seats, amphitheater.

amfibol[lü] F *min.* amphibole.

amfiteatr F *archae.* amphitheater.

amforik[ɛi] F *med.* amphoric.

amfoter F *chem., phys.* amphoteria.

amha (. —) عَمها A *lrnd.* having no landmarks (desert, etc.); thoroughly bewildering.

âmî 1 (— —) عامی A *lrnd.* 1. annual. 2. of the same year. 3. in its first year, yearling.

âmî 2 (— —) عامی P *var. of* **âmmî 1**.

ami 3 (. —) عمی A *lrnd.* blind; ignorant.

amib F *cf.* **amip**.

amibiye (.. — .) آمیبیه *zool.*, *Amoebina*.

Amid 1 (— .) آمِد *hist.* the town of Diyarbakır.

amid 2 (.. —) عمید A *lrnd.* 1. very sick. 2. lovesick.

amid 3 (. —) عمید A *lrnd.* 1. chief, leader, general. 2. principal point.

a'mide اَعمِدَه A *lrnd., pl. of* **amud**.

amiği (— — —) آمیغی P *lrnd.* real, material, not figurative.

âmih 1 (— .) عامه A *lrnd.* perplexed, bewildered.

amih 2 عمه A *lrnd.* confused, perplexed.

amihte (— — .) آمیخته P *lrnd.* 1. mixed, mingled; combined. 2. compound, composite, complex. 3. associated, intimate, familiar.

amihtegi (— — . —) آمیختگی P *lrnd.* 1. mixture. 2. sociability.

amik[kı] (. —) عمیق A deep, profound. **A— ovası** *name of a plain east of Antioch.*

amil 1 (— .) عامل A 1. factor, agent, motive, reason, cause. 2. *Arabic gram.* governing (word). — **ol=** /da/ to have an effect (upon), to be of consequence (in).

amil 2 (— .) آمل A *lrnd.* hoping, longing for.

amil 3 (— .) عامل A 1. *Arabic hist.* governor, high administration officer. 2. *Ott. hist.* intendant of finance, collector of revenues.

amil 4 (— .) عامل A *lrnd.* workman; manufacturer.

amil 5 (— .) عامل A *lrnd.* who acts, acting. — **bizzat** self-operative.

amile (— . .) عامله A *lrnd.* 1. foot, leg. 2. the part of the shaft nearest to the iron head of a spear.

amim (. —) عمیم A *lrnd.* 1. abundant. 2. universal, general.

amimülihsan (. — . . —) عمیم‌الاحسان A *lrnd.* doing good to every one.

âmin 1 (— —) آمین A amen. — **alayı** *obs.* ceremony performed by a class when a new pupil begins school. — **de=** to agree, assent.

âmin 2 (— .) آمن A *lrnd.* 1. safe, secure. 2. sure, confident. 3. trusty, trustworthy.

amin 3 F *chem.* amine.

âminen (— ' . .) آمناً A *lrnd.* 1. safely, in safety. 2. confidently, without misgivings.

âminhan (— — —) آمین‌خوان P *lrnd.* who says amen; who approves readily.

amip[bi] | **amib** | *zool.* amoeba.

âmir (— .) آمر A 1. /ı/ commanding, who gives orders; imperative, necessitating. 2. commander. 3. superior, chief. —**i adli** president of court-martial. — **hükümler** *law* imperative provisions. —**i ita** *fin. adm.* official who authorizes that a payment be made. — **ve memur** the superior and the subordinate officials. —**i mücbir** *law* extortioner.

amir 2 (— .) عامر A *lrnd.* 1. in a good state of repair; cultivated; inhabited, flourishing. 2. belonging to the government, Imperial.

amîr 3 (. —) عمیر A *lrnd.* populous, flourishing; cultivated.

amiral[lü] آمیرال F admiral. — **gemisi** flagship. —**lık** admiralship, admiralty.

âmirane (— . — .) آمرانه P commandingly, imperiously; imperious (way, action).

amire 1 (— . .) عامره A *cf.* **amir 2**.

amîre 2 (. — .) عمیره A *cf.* **amîr 3**.

âmirlik**ᵗⁱ** (— ..) آمرلك |âmir 1| authority, superiority in rank.
amitoz F *biol.* amitosis.
amiyane (— . — .) عاميانه P vulgarly; vulgar (term).
âmm 1 A *cf.* âm 4.
amiyotrofi F *path.* amyotrophy.
amiz 1 (— —) آميز P *lrnd.* 1. mixture, combination; compound. 2. a frequenting, association. 3. copulation.
-amiz 2 (— —) آميز P *lrnd.* mingling with, mixed with, *as in* hakaretamiz, tehdidamiz.
amize (— — .) آميزه P *lrnd.* 1. mixed; mixture. 2. sprinkled with gray. 3. copulation. 4. temperament, constitution.
amizemu (— — . —) آميزمو P *poet.* whose hair is sprinkled with gray.
amiziş (— — .) آميزش P *lrnd.* 1. mixture, alloy. 2. sociableness.
amk**ᵏⁱ** عمق A *lrnd.* 1. depth. 2. remote part (of a desert).
amm عم A *cf.* am 5.
amma (.' —) اما A 1. but, yet, still. 2. how, *e. g.*, — koşuyor! How he does run! — ba'd *archaic* now to our subject (the clause by which a writer, after pious ascriptions, ordinarily introduces his subject). — da *same as* amma². — da yaptın ha! — yaptın! How can it be! Not really!
ammal**ⁱⁱ** (. —) عمال A *lrnd.* assiduous at work.
ammame (. — .) عمامه |imame 2| *lrnd.* turban.
ammar (. —) عمار A *lrnd.* 1. who causes all to prosper, benevolent; cultivator. 2. mason; architect. 3. *w. cap.*, man's name.
ammat (. —) عمات A *lrnd., pl. of* amme 4.
amme 1 (— .) آمه A *lrnd.* cleaving through the skull, laying bare the brain (wound).
âmme 2 (— .) عامه A *lrnd.* 1. common, universal, general. 2. commonalty, the public; the vulgar masses, the common people. — davası *law* public prosecution. — efkârı public opinion. —i enam the whole human race. — hizmeti public service. — hukuku *law* public law. — idaresi *law* public administration on a territorial basis. — iktidarı *law* executive power of the authority. — işletmeleri public works. — malları public property. — menfaati public interest. — müesseseleri public institutions, institutions of public utility. — nizamı kaideleri *law* rules of public policy. — sigortası national insurance.
amme 3 عم A section of the Quran. — cüzü section of the Quran that begins with the 78th sura and contains all the short suras to the end of the book, formerly used as the second Arabic reading book in schools. — dersi *formerly*, second class of Quran reading.
amme 4 عمة A |*fem. of* am 5| *lrnd.* paternal aunt.
âmmeten (—' . .) عامة A *lrnd.* generally, universally.
âmmî 1 (— —) عامى A *lrnd.* common, vulgar.
ammi 2 عمى |am 5| *prov.* paternal uncle.
âmmülmenafi**ⁱⁱ** (— .. — .) عام النافع A *lrnd.* of universal utility.
amnezi F *psychiatry* amnesia.
amniyon F *anat.* amnion.
amonyak**ᵗⁱ** آمونياك F *chem.* ammonia.
amora (. .'.) آموره *var. of* amura.
amoralizm آمورالیزم F *phil.* amoralism.
amoroz آموروز F *path.* amaurosis.
amorti (. .'.) آمورتى F 1. *com.* a paying off. 2. *lottery* the smallest prize. — et= /ı/ *com.* to amortize, to redeem, to pay off.
amortisman آمورتيزمان F *com.* amortization. — akçesi sinking fund.
amortisör F *auto.* shock absorber.
amper F *elec.* ampere.
ampermetre (...'.) F *elec.* amperemeter.
ampes *slang* hashish, dope.
ampirik**ᵗⁱ** F *phil.* empirical.
ampirizm F *phil.* empiricism.
ampiyem F *path.* empyema.
amplifikatör F *radio* amplifier.
ampul**ⁱⁱⁱ** آمپول F 1. electric bulb. 2. *med.* ampule. 3. *anat.* ampulla.
ampütasyon F *med.* amputation.
amr 1 عمر A *lrnd., var. of* ömr.
Amr 2 عمرو A man's name, esp., fictitious name used in legal treatises together with the name Zeyd for the names of plaintiff and defendant in cases cited.
amran (. —) عمران A *lrnd.* 1. the two cuffs of a garment. 2. the two tonsils.
ams عمس A *lrnd.* gloominess (of the day).
amşa (. —) عمشا A *lrnd.* 1. weak and watery (eye). 2. weak-sighted, bleary-eyed (woman).
Amu 1 (— —) آمو P the river Oxus. — Derya the river Oxus.
amu عمو |am 5| paternal uncle.
amuca عموجه *prov. for* amca.
amud (. —) عمود A *lrnd.* 1. tent-pole; column, pillar, post, obelisk. 2. mace, truncheon. 3. beam (of a balance). 4. stick, staff, wand, baton. 5. stock (of a cross-bow, rifle, etc.). 6. ridge on the side of a weapon. 7. chief, military leader, commander. 8. *cf.* amut. —u fıkari *anat.* vertebral column.
amude (— — .) آموده P *lrnd.* collected, strung; prepared; adorned.

amuden (. —́ .) عَمُودًا A *geom.* perpendicularly, vertically; at right angles.
amudî (. — —) عَمُودِيّ A *geom.* perpendicular, vertical; rectangular.
amudussalib (. — . . —) عَمُودُ الصَّلِيب A *lrnd.* the upright timber of the Cross.
amudussubh (. — . .) عَمُودُ الصُّبح A *lrnd.* spreading light of the dawn, morning beam.
amudül'asar (. — . . —) عَمُودُ الاِعْصَار A *lrnd.* sand spout.
amudülbatn (. — . .) عَمُودُ البَطن A *anat.* 1. medial line of the abdomen. 2. vertebral column; the back.
amudülkalb (. — . .) عَمُودُ القَلب A *anat.* the arch of the aorta.
amudüllisan (. — . . —) عَمُودُ اللِّسَان A *anat.* the raphe of the tongue.
amudüssühr (. — . .) عَمُودُ السُّحر A *anat.* root of the lung (pulmonary artery, veins, and bronchi).
amuhte (— — .) آمُوخْتَه P *lrnd.* taught, instructed.
amuhtegân (— — . —) آمُوخْتَگَان P *lrnd.* those who are taught. —ı **ezelî** those who are taught from eternity (prophets, seers, and saints).
amulü (. —) عَمُول A *lrnd.* hardworking.
amura (. .́ .) آمُورَه It *naut.* let fall and set (the lower sails)! — **et**= to let fall and set (the lower sails). — **yakası** jewel leech.
Amure (— — .) آمُورَه ı A *obs.* Gomorrah.
Amuriye (. — — .) عَمُورِيَّة A *hist. geog.* Amorium (ancient city in Asia Minor).
amus (. —) عَمُوس A *lrnd.* 1. difficult, perplexing. 2. perverse and stupid. 3. fierce.
amutdu (. —) عَمُود A |amud| *geom.* a perpendicular, an upright. — **indir**= /a/ to drop a perpendicular on to a given line.
-amuz (— —) آمُوز P *lrnd.* teaching; taught, *e. g.*, **edebamuz, hikmetamuz, kâramuz.**
amuzende (— — . .) آمُوزَنْدَه P *lrnd.* 1. teacher. 2. pupil.
amuzgâr (— — —) آمُوزْگَار P *lrnd.* teacher.
amuzî (— — —) آمُوزِی P *lrnd.* teacher's profession.
amuziş (— — .) آمُوزِش P *lrnd.* 1. a learning. 2. a teaching, instruction.
amüle (— . .) آمُل P *bot.* myrobalan tree.
âmülfil (. — .) عَامُ الفِيل A *hist.* the year of the Elephant (the year, about 570 A.D., when an Abyssinian governor attacked Mecca with an army including elephants).
amürz (— .) آمُرْز , **amürza** (— . —) آمُرْزَا P *lrnd.* remitting, absolving, forgiving.
amürzende (— . . .) آمُرْزَنْدَه P *lrnd.* forgiver.
amürzgâr (— . —) آمُرْزْگَار P *lrnd.* forgiver, pardoner; God, the forgiver of sins.

âmürzgâri (— . — —) آمُرْزْگَارِی P *lrnd.* forgiveness.
amürziş (— . .) آمُرْزِش P *lrnd.* a forgiving, pardon.
amüs (— .) آمُس A *lrnd.*, *pl.* of **ems.**
Amvas (. —) عَمْوَاس A Emmaus (in Palestine).
amya (. —) عَمْيَاء A *lrnd.* blind (woman).
amyant F asbestos.
amzade (. — .) عَمْزَادَه P *lrnd.*, same as **amcazade.**
an 1 (—) آن A moment, instant. —ı **daim** the everpresent eternity of God. **bir — evvel** as soon as possible. —ı **vahitte** in a single moment.
an=ar **2** آنْمَك /ı/ 1. to call to mind, to remember; to think (of). 2. to talk (of), to mention.
ân 3 (—) آن P *poet.* beauty, grace, elegance.
an 4 آنْ *prov.* mind, perception, memory.
an 5 آنْ *prov.* balk, boundary (between fields).
-an 6 ا *adverb, as in* **mahsusan, zaten.**
an 7 *cf.* **ol 1.**
=**an 8,** =**en,** *after vowel* =**yan 3,** =**yen 2** ان ی *present participle, e. g.*, **kalan** staying, that stays, **çeken** pulling, that pulls.
-an 9, *after* -a, -e, -gân ان گان P *lrnd.*, *plural of rational beings, e. g.*, **zenan** women, **kapudanan** admirals, **çavuşan** sergeants, **bendegân** slaves.
annni **10** عَنّ A *lrnd.* 1. a bridling (horse). 2. a reining in (horse).
an- 11 عَن A from; on account of; after; *e. g.*, **an'asl, ancehlin, ankarib.**
ana 1 آنا انا انا 1. mother (the form **anne** is preferred in Istanbul). 2. *after a name, appellation or respect for women saints, e. g.*, **Meryem Ana.** 3. main part; principle, main, fundamental, basic. 4. *fin.* capital, stock; principal. —**m!** oh! dear! —**sı ağla**= *colloq.* to go through hardship. —**sını ağlat**= /ın/ *colloq.* to give one great trouble, to give one a hard time. —**sının ak sütü gibi helâl olsun** May it be as lawful a property to him as his own mother's milk. — **akçe** *fin.* principal. —**m anam dediği hamam anası, kel Fatma değil mi?** (*lit.*, She whom he is bragging about as his mother, is she not Baldheaded Fatma, the keeper of the women's bath-house?) He is overpraising (a person). — **arma** *naut.* lower rigging. —**mın aşı tandırımın başı** (*lit.*, my mother's cooking, my seat by the fire) home sweet home! — **ata** *prov.* parents. —**n atan kim? Yakın komşun.** *proverb* Who is your father and mother? Your neighbor. — **ata sofrasında büyümemiş** (*lit.*, not brought up at

ana

the table of one's parents) mannerless. **—m avradım olsun** *vulg.* *(lit.*, may my mother become my wife) I swear! **— baba** parents, father and mother. **—m babam!** *slang* dear! my! oh my! **— baba bir** having the same father and mother. **— baba duası almış** blessed by his parents. **— baba evlâdı** 1. a beloved child. 2. somebody's child, a human being **— baba günü** a state of great confusion and crowdedness, pandemonium. **— baba ile iftihar olmaz** *proverb* It does not do one any good to boast of one's parents. **—sına babasına pay veren** snapdragon, *bot.*, *Antirrhinum*. **—sına bak kızını al, kenarına bak bezini al** *proverb* When you marry consider the mother of the girl, when you buy cloth look at its border. **—nın bastığı yavru incinmez** *proverb* A mother's tread does not harm her young. **—sını bellerim!** *vulg.* I'll show him! **— bir** born of the same mother. **— cadde** main road. **— çizgi** *geom.* generatrix, generant. **—sının çocuğu** like mother like child. **—sı danası** *colloq.* his mother and the rest of the family. **— defter** the principal book, ledger. **— dil** *ling.* a language from which other languages are derived. **— dili** mother tongue. **— direk** *naut.* lower mast. **—dan doğma** 1. stark naked. 2. from birth, naturally, congenital. **—sından doğduğuna pişman** sorry to have been born, feeling very miserable. **— doğru** *same as* **ana çizgi**. **—m ekmeğine kuru, ayranına duru demem** I would never call my mother's bread dry, nor my mother's buttermilk thin. I would never be disloyal to my home. **—sından emdiği süt burnundan (fitil fitil) gel=** (*lit.*, to have one's mother's milk come out of one's nose like candle wicks) to go through extreme hardship. **— evlâdı atmış, yâr başında tutmuş** *proverb* The mother has driven out her child; the beloved has taken him to her bosom. True love is even stronger than a mother's love. **—ndan evvel ahıra girme!** *vulg.* Don't go into the stable before your mother enters. Don't overstep your elders. **— gibi yâr olmaz, Bağdat gibi diyar olmaz** *proverb* No friend like a mother, no country like Baghdad. **— güverte** *naut.* main deck. **— hat** *railway* main line, trunk line. **— hatlar** the main lines, the outline. **—nın ilki olmaktan dağlarda tilki olmak yeğdir** *proverb* Better to be a fox on the mountains than a firstborn. **—sının ipliğini pazara çıkarmış, —sının ipliğini satmış** (*lit.*, having sold his mother's yarn in the market) scoundrel, wretch. **— kadın** matron managing a woman's bathhouse. **—sı Kadir gecesi doğurmuş** born on the Night of Power, fortunate, very lucky. **— kara*. —sının karnında dokuz ay on gün nasıl durmuş?** (*lit.* How did he stay in his mother's womb for nine months and ten days?) He is very impatient. **— kesir** *math.* generant fraction. **— kız** mother and daughter. **—sının körpe kuzusu** mother's darling. **— kucağı** mother's bosom. **—lar kundağa sarmamış** (*lit.*, not swaddled by mothers) very crafty, very smart. **—lar kusuru** an unworthy mother. **— kuzusu** dear child, poor dear. **—sının kuzusu** mother's darling. **— lağım** main sewer. **— mal*. — mektebi** kindergarten, nursery school. **—sının mihrinden geçer, bundan geçmez** He would renounce his mother's dowry, but not this claim. **—ları ne ki danaları ne olsun?** Children take after their mothers (in a bad sense). **—sının nikâhını iste=** to charge an outrageous price. **— oğul** mother and son. **—mın öleceğini bilsem kulağı dolusu darıya satardım** *prov.* (*lit.* If I knew that my mother was going to die, I would sell her for her ear's full of millet.) If a loss is certain, it is better to make a small profit from it. **— över, baba sever** *proverb* A mother demonstrates her love; a father does not. **— para** *fin.* principal. **—mızı rüşvetle işret ağlatır** *proverb* Bribery and drink cause our mothers to weep. **—sını satayım!** damn it! **—n seni bu gün için doğurdu** This is the day for which you were born; show what you can do. **— seren** *naut.* lower yard. **—sı soğan babası sarmısak, kendi gülbeşeker çıktı** (*lit.* His mother is an onion, his father garlic, he himself has turned out to be rose jelly.) He does not resemble his parents. **— sütü** breast-milk. **— şasi** *auto.* chassis. **— tarafından** on the mother's side. **—lar taş yesin** (*lit.* Mothers may eat stone) Mothers do not think of themselves. **— vatan** home, mother country. **—n yahşi baban yahşi** your mother is fine, your father is good (used for persuading someone to do something). **— yarısı** like one's mother. **— yasa*. — yelkenler** *naut.* lower sails. **—sı yerinde** as old as one's mother. **— yiğidin kalkanıdır** *proverb* The mother is a shield to the hero. **— yol** main road. **— yönler** the cardinal points of the compass. **— yurt** *same as* **ana vatan**.

ana 2 بٲ cf. **ol. 1**.
ânâ 3 (— —) اِنٲ A *lrnd.*, *pl. of* **ena**.
ânâ 4 (. —) انٲ A *lrnd.* trouble, fatigue, distress.
a'nab (. —) اعناب A *lrnd.*, *pl. of* **ineb**.
anacık^t¹ اناجيك little mother, darling mother.
anaç^c¹ اناج اناج 1. full grown (young beast). 2. capable of becoming a mother. 3. able to take care of his own interest; experienced, shrewd. **—la=** to reach maturity. **—lık** maturity; shrewdness.
anadil (. — .) عنادل A |*pl. of* **andelib**| *poet.* nightingales.

Anadollu آناطولیلی *var. of* **Anadolulu.**
Anadolu (..'..) آناطولی Gk Anatolia.
— **Hisarı** Anadolu Hisar, *name of a castle and place on the Bosporus.* —**lu** an Anatolian.
anaerki[ni] *neol., sociol.* matriarchy. —**l** matriarchal.
anaf (— —) آناف A *lrnd., pl. of* **enf.**
anafet (.—.) عنافت A *lrnd.* roughness, severity, grimness.
anafilâksi F *biol.* anaphylaxis.
anafor 1 آنافور Gk countercurrent, eddy.
anafor 2 آنافور Gk *slang* extra profit, illicit gain, something got for nothing. —**cu** one who seeks to make illicit gains, parasite.
anaforla=[r] **1** آنافورلامق to form a countercurrent, to eddy.
anaforla=[r] **2** آنافورلامق /ı/ to gain in an illicit way; to steal.
anahtar آناختار، انختار Gk 1. key. 2. wrench, spanner. 3. electric switch; interrupter. 4. *mus.* key. — **ağası** *hist.* the Agha of the Keys, a steward of the Sultan's palace. — **ağzı** the warded edge of the bit of a key. — **deliği** key hole. — **dili** bit, web (of a key). — **dişi** notch (on the bit of a key). — **memesi** the end of the pin of a key. — **taşı** *arch.* keystone (of an arch). — **uydur=** /a/ to match up a key (to a lock).
a'nak[kı] **1** (.—) اعناق A *lrnd.* 1. necks. 2. trunks of trees. 3. internodal portions of stems or stalks. 4. dust clouds raised by the wind.
a'nak[kı] **2** اعنق A *lrnd.* 1. long-necked. 2. marked with white in the neck.
anak[kı] **3** آناق *prov.* 1. memory. 2. souvenir.
anak[kı] **4** (—.) آنق A *lrnd.* very charming, most pleasing.
anak[kı] **5** (.—) عناق A *lrnd.* 1. she-kid. 2. calamity. 3. disappointment. 4. the middle star in the Great Bear, § *Ursae Majoris.*
anakara *neol., geog.* continent.
anakat[tı] (.—.) عناقت A *lrnd.* disappointment, failure.
anakib (.—.), (.——) عناكيب A *lrnd., pl. of* **ankebut.**
anakid (.——) عناقيد A *lrnd., pl. of* **unkud.**
anakul'arz (.—..) عناق الارض A *lrnd.* black lynx, *zool., Caracal melanotis.*
anal F *anat.* anal.
analık[tı] آنالق 1. maternity, motherhood. 2. stepmother; adoptive mother; motherly woman, matron. — **et=** /a/ to be a mother (to). — **sigortası** maternity insurance.
analitik[ti] F analytical.
analiz آناليز F analysis. —**le=** /ı/ to analyse.

analjezi F *med.* analgesia.
analoji آنالوژی F analogy.
anamal *neol., econ.* capital. —**cı** capitalist. —**cılık** capitalism.
anamnez F *med.* anamnesis. case history.
ânân 1 (——) آنان P *lrnd.* those.
anân 2 (.—) عنان A *lrnd.* clouds.
ananas آناناس It pineapple. —**giller** *bot., Bromeliaceae.*
an'anat[tı] (..—) عنعنات A *lrnd.* traditions.
an'ane 1 عنعنه A 1. tradition. 2. *lrnd.* a reciting the names of the transmitters of a hadith; such a series of names of authorities. —**siyle** with all its details.
anâne 2 (.—.) عنانه A *lrnd.* cloud.
ananet (.—.) عنانت A *lrnd.* sexual impotence.
an'anevi (...—) عنعنوی [*based on* **an'ane 1**] traditional. —**ye** (...—.) traditionalism.
anansefali F *biol.* anencephaly.
anarı اكارى *prov.* the other side, to the other side; on the other side, beyond, the space beyond. — **beri** to and fro, back and forth.
anarşi آنارشی F anarchy.
anarşist آنارشيست F anarchist.
anarşizm آنارشيزم F anarchism.
ânas (——) آناس A *lrnd., pl. of* **ins.**
anasanlı *neol., sociology* metronymic.
anasır (.—.) عناصر A *lrnd., pl. of* **unsur.** —**ı erbaa** the four elements.
an'asl عن اصل A *lrnd.* by origin, originally.
anason آناسون، اناسون [**anison**] anise, *bot., Pimpinella anisum;* aniseed.
anastomoz F *anat.* anastomosis.
ânat (——) آنات A *lrnd.* 1. moments. 2. nuances.
anatomi آناتومی F anatomy.
anatomik آناتوميك F anatomical.
anavata (...'.) *embroidery* raised satin stitch in colored thread.
anayasa *neol., pol. law* constitution.
|**anb-** see **amb-.**|
anbean (—.—) آن بآن P *lrnd.* with every moment, more and more, gradually; incessantly.
anca 1 (.'.) آنجه 1. *archaic* according to him. 2. *archaic* that much, so much. — **beraber kanca beraber** sticking together no matter what happens.
anca 2 (.'.) آنجه *var. of* **ancak.**
anca 3 (——) آنجا P *lrnd.* there; thither; that place.
ancak (.'.) آنجق، آنجه، آنجاق 1. only, solely, merely; just; hardly, barely. 2. but, on the other hand, however.
ancaleyin آنجه لين *var. of* **ancılayın.**

ancanibi (.—..) عَنْ جَانِبِ A *lrnd.* from, on the part of.

ancarı اِنْجَارِى *prov.* where?

ancehlin عَنْ جهل A *lrnd.* from ignorance, unknowingly.

ancelika (..′..) آنْجَلِيقَه It *bot.* angelica.

ancılayın آنجِلاين archaic thus, in that manner; to that degree, that much; according to him.

an cihan (—.—) آنْ جِهَان P *lrnd.* the other world.

ançizle=ʳ آنْچِزلَه مك *slang* to go away, to leave.

ançüez آنْچُوَه ز Sp anchovy.

an çünan (—.—) آنْچُنَان P *lrnd.* thus, so; in like manner, like that.

ançüviz *var. of* **ançüez**.

and آنْد *cf.* **ant**.

anda آنْدَه archaic 1. *cf.* **ol** 1. 2. there; thither.

andaçᶜⁱ آنْدَاچ *prov.* souvenir.

andakᵏⁱ آنْدَق archaic 1. at once, instantly. 2. so much, that much, to that degree.

andan آنْدَن archaic 1. *cf.* **ol** 1. 2. thereafter. — **gerü** thereafter.

andavallı آنْدَاوَالِى *slang* fool, idiot, imbecile.

andelib (..—) عَنْدَلِيب A *poet.* nightingale.

andem 1 (—.) آنْدَم P *lrnd.* thereupon, then; immediately, at once.

andem 2 عَنْدَم A *lrnd.* red dye, *esp.*, dragon's blood, sapan, or bukkum wood.

andemi F endemic.

andet=ᵈᵉʳ آنْدِتْمَكْ to take an oath, to swear.

andıkᵏⁱ آنْدِيق kind of hyena.

andır=ʳ آنْدِرْمَق |*caus. of* **an=** 2.| 1. /a,ı/ to bring to mind, to remind (someone of). 2. /ı or obs. a/ to remind (of), to bear a resemblance (to). —**an** *logic* analogue. —**ış** *logic* analogy.

andız آنْدِز elecampane, *bot.*, *Inula helenium*. — **otu** *same as* **andız**.

andiç=ᵉʳ آنْدِچْمَك to take an oath. —**ir=** /a/ to make swear an oath (someone).

andilya (..′.) Gk endive, *bot.*, *Lichorium endivia*.

andlaş=ʳ آنْدلاشْمَق *var. of* **antlaş=**.

andlı آنْدلِى *var. of* **antlı**.

andojen F *physiol.* endogenous.

ane 1 *prov., var. of* **anne**.

-ane 2, after vowel **-yane** (—.) آنه P *lrnd.* in the manner of, like, *forming adjective or adverb, e. g.*, **şahane bir yürüyüş** a majestic gait, **nazikâne konuşuyor** he talks politely.

ane 3 (—.) عانَه A *anat.* 1. pubis. 2. the hair of the pubic region.

ane 4 (—.) عَانَه A *lrnd.* 1. *w. cap.* Ana (town on the Euphrates, the Anatha of the Roman Empire). 2. female wild ass; herd of wild asses. 3. group of stars in the body of Capricorn.

anela (.′.) آنَلَه It *naut.* ring (of an anchor).

anemi آنَمِى F *path.* anemia.

anemon آنَمُون F anemone.

anen (—′.) آنًا A *lrnd.* at a moment.

anenfeanen (—′..—′.) آنًا فَآنًا A *lrnd.* at successive moments, incessantly; occasionally; with every moment, more and more.

anestezi F *med.* anesthesia.

anet عَنَت A *lrnd.* 1. distress, hardship. 2. perdition. 3. depravity; sin; error; fornication, adultery. 4. harm, mischief; oppression. 5. contention.

anevrizma (...′.) Gk *path.* aneurysm.

Aneze عَنَزِه A 1. *man's name*. 2. *name of an Arab tribe*. 3. *l. c.* Syrian camel with a single hump.

anf عَنف A *var. of* **unf**.

anfizem F *path.* emphysema.

an gafletin (..′..) عَنْ غَفْلَةٍ A *lrnd.* inadvertently.

angaje آنْگَاژَه F occupied. —**et=** /ı/ to employ.

angajman آنْگَاژْمَان F *com.* engagement. —**a gir=** to enter an engagement, to bind oneself.

angarya, angarye (..′.) آنْغَارْيَه آنْغَارْيَا Gk 1. forced labour, corvee; drudgery. 2. *mil.* fatigue duty. 3. *intern. law* angary. 4. unwillingly, perfunctorily. — **dinle=** /ı/ to listen carelessly and in a perfunctory manner.

angeh (—.) آنْگَه P *lrnd.* then; at that time.

angı آنْغِى *prov.* souvenir; memory; fame.

angıçᶜⁱ آنْغِيچ *prov.* side panel of slats for a horse cart.

angıd *cf.* **angıt**.

angıdı آنْغِيدى ruddy, brick-colored.

angıl آنْغِل *prov.* famous.

angır=ʳ آنْغِرْمَق *prov., var. of* **anır=**.

angıtᵈⁱ آنْغِت 1. ruddy shelduck, *zool.*, *Casarca ferruginea*. 2. *colloq.* fool, idiot.

angıtı آنْغِتِى *var. of* **angıdı**.

Anglikan آنْگلِيكَان F Anglican. — **kilisesi** the Anglican Church, the Church of England.

Anglosakson آنْگلوسَاكْسُن F Anglo-Saxon.

angudi (..—) *var. of* **angıdı**.

angutᵈᵘ *var. of* **angıt**.

anhaminha (.—.—) عَنْهَا مِنْهَا |**anha, minha**| A *lrnd.* this and that; finally.

anı 1 آنى *cf.* **ol** 1.

anı 2 *neol., psych.* memory.

anıkᵏⁱ *neol.* apt, inclined, disposed, ready. —**la=** /ı/ 1. to prepare, to dispose. 2. *psych.* to reproduce (memory). —**lık** aptitude,

inclination, disposition, readiness.
anıl=ır آكُلُس pass. of **an**= 2.
anıl anıl آكُل اكُل آكُلِين اكُل 1. purlingly, gurgling. 2. slowly, gently, quietly.
anılca obs. gently, slowly. **—cık** gently, slowly.
anımsa=ᵣ /ı/ neol., psych. to remember faintly.
anın آنك cf. **ol 1.**
anır=ᵣ آكَرَمِسى آكَرِمِسى 1. to bray. 2. vulg. to brag, to talk big. **—t**= /ı/ caus.
anış آكَش |**an**= 2| a remembering, remembrance, commemoration.
anıtᵈ¹ 1 آكَت var. of **angıt**.
anıtᵈ¹ 2 neol. monument. **— kabir** mausoleum; w. cap. tomb of Atatürk in Ankara. **—sal** monumental.
anız آكَز اكَز stubble.
âni 1 (— —) آنٍ A instantaneous, momentary; sudden; suddenly.
âni 2 (— —) آنٍ P myst. belonging to other than God; having an individual existence.
a'nî 3 (. —) اعنى A lrnd. I mean, that is to say, to wit, namely.
âni 4 (— .) عانٍ A lrnd. 1. humble, submissive. 2. captive. 3. distressed. troubled.
anî 5 (. —) عنّى A lrnd. occupied (with), solicitous (about).
ânid 1 (— .) عانِد A lrnd. obstinate, perverse.
anîd 2 (. —) عنيد A lrnd. obstinate, insubordinate.
ânide (—'—.) آنِيَه instantly, at once, all of a sudden.
anidroz F path. anhydrosis.
anîf 1 (. —) عنيف A lrnd. violent, rough, brusque.
ânif 2 (— .) آنف A lrnd. preceding. **—en** (—'..) A above, before, in the preceding passage.
anifülbeyan (—...'—) آنفاليبان A lrnd. aforementioned
anifüzzikr (—...) آنفالذكر A lrnd. mentioned above.
anikᵏ¹ (. —) عنيق A lrnd. 1. neck. 2. embracing with the arms around the neck.
anila (..'.) آنِلَ var. of **anela**.
anilgıyab (...—) عن الغياب A lrnd. 1. in absence, in absentia. 2. not having personally met.
anilmerkez عن المركز A phys. centrifugal.
animizm آنِمِزم F phil. animism.
ânis 1 (— .) آنِس A lrnd. sociable, familiar.
ânis 2 (— .) عانِس A lrnd. middle-aged and unmarried, old maid, old bachelor.
anison آنِسون انِسون Gk same as **anason**.
aniye (—..) آنِيَه A lrnd., pl. of **ina**.

aniz (.—) عنيز A lrnd. afflicted, suffering.
anjin آنجِين F path. angina.
anjiom F path. angioma.
Anka 1 (. —) عنقا A 1. Phoenix (a mythical bird of enormous size). 2. fabulously rich. **— bezirgân** archaic very rich merchant. **— gibi** nonexistent. **— gönüllü** generous-hearted.
anka 2 (. —) عنقا A lrnd. calamity, misfortune.
Ankara (.'.) آنغره Ankara, formerly Angora. **— keçisi** Angora goat. **— kedisi** Angora cat. **— yünü** Angora wool.
ankarib (..—) عن قريب A lrnd. in the near future, soon.
ankariya (.'..) عن قريه var. of **angarya**.
ankasdin, ankastın (.'.) عن قصد A on purpose, deliberately.
ankebut (..—) عنكبوت A 1. poet. spider; spider's web. 2. lrnd. fine thread (in an optical instrument). 3. lrnd. rete (of an astrolobe). **—î** (..——) A spiderlike; arachnoid. **—iye** (..——.) 1. fem. of **ankebuti**. 2. anat. the arachnoid membrane. 3. spiders, zool., Arachnida.
ankes F com. cash in hand, cash balance.
ankesman F com. paying in, collection (of a payment).
anket آنكِت F inquiry.
ankıtᵈ¹ آنفت var. of **angıt**.
ankiloz F path. ankylosis.
ankonsinyasyon F com. on consignment.
ankudî (..—) عنقودى var. of **angıdı**.
ankutᵈᵘ عنقود var. of **angıt**.
anla=ᵣ آكُلَمَس 1. /ı or dan/ to understand, comprehend. 2. /ı/ to find out. 3. /dan/ to know (about), have knowledge (of). 4. /dan or ı/ to appreciate, enjoy. 5. /dan/ to respond (to). **senin anlıyacağın** the long and the short of it is. **—r anlamazdan korkulur** Fear him who feigns ignorance. **—dımsa Arap olayım** colloq. I don't understand it at all. **—dın mı kazın ayağını?** colloq. Do you get the hang of it? **—yana sivri sinek saz, anlamıyana davul zurna az** proverb To a person who has understanding, the mosquito sounds like a musical instrument; to him who does not understand, drums and pipes are not sufficient. **—yanla taş taşı, anlamıyanla bal yeme** Carrying stones together with an understanding person is better than eating honey with someone who has no understanding. **—dık yel değirmeni, amma suyu nereden?** All right, I understand now what a windmill is, but, how do you get the water? (said when someone shows

anlak

by a stupid question that he has not understood the explanation).
anlakᵏ¹ *neol., psych.* intelligence.
anlam *neol., psych.* meaning, sense. **—daş** *ling.* synonymous. **—sal** *ling.* semantic.
anlan=ⁱʳ آکلنمر *obs., pass. of* **anla=**.
anlar آکلر *cf.* **ol 1**.
anlaş=ⁱʳ آکلشمر /la/ 1. to understand each other. 2. to come to an understanding, to come to an agreement. **—amamazlık** 1. disagreement. 2. misunderstanding.
anlaşıl=ⁱʳ آکلشلمر *pass. of* **anla=**. **—an** it appears that. **—dı** all right, spare your words, O. K. **—dı Vehbi'nin kerrakesi** Now it is clear; now I see through it. **—maz** incomprehensible, unintelligible.
anlaşma آکلشمه agreement, understanding; pact, treaty. **— akdet=** to make an agreement. **—ya var=** to come to an agreement.
anlaşmazlıkᵏ¹ آکلشمازلق 1. disagreement, incompatibility. 2. misunderstanding.
anlat=ⁱʳ آکلتمر /ı, a/ 1. to explain. 2. to relate, tell. 3. to describe. **—ıl=** *pass.* **—ım, —ış** manner of telling, way of describing. **—ışa göre fetva verilir** *proverb* The fetva is pronounced according to the way the matter is presented. The result depends on the presentation of the case. **—tır=** /a, ı/ *caus. of* **anlat=**.
anlayış آکلایش understanding, intelligence. **—lı** intelligent, understanding. **—sız** insensitive, inconsiderate, lacking in understanding.
anlıkᵏ¹ *neol., phil.* intellect. **—çılık** *phil.* intellectualism. **—sal** *phil.* intellectual.
anlı şanlı آنلی شانلی renowned, glorious, famed.
ann *cf.* **an 10**.
anna=ʳ *prov., var. of* **anla=**.
annaçᶜ¹ *prov., var. of* **alnaç**.
anne آننه |ana 1| mother. **—ciğim** dear mother. **—lik et=** /a/ to be a mother (to someone).
anneanne آننه آننه grandmother, mother's mother.
annı *prov., var. of* **alnı**.
anod F *same as* **anot**.
anofel آنوفل F *zool.* anopheles.
anomal¹¹ آنومال F *sc.* anomalous.
anomali آنومالی F anomaly.
anonim آنونیم F anonymous. **— şirket** *com.* joint stock company.
anoreksi F *path.* anorexia.
anorganikᵏ¹ F *sc.* inorganic.
anormal¹¹ آنورمال F abnormal.
anotᵈᵘ |anod| F *elec.* anode.
anozmi F *path.* anosmia.
anra=ʳ آکرامر *archaic* to roar (lion).

ansal *neol., psych.* mental.
ansala=ʳ آکسالامر /ı/ *archaic* to mimic, mock.
ansamimilkalb (..—..) عن صميم القلب A *lrnd.* from the bottom of the heart.
ansar (.—) انصار A *lrnd., pl. of* **nâsır 1**, 1. *lrnd.* helpers, assistants, auxiliaries, abettors. 2. *hist., w. cap.* those inhabitants of Medina who invited the Prophet Muhammad and his adherents to their city, and were the first to take up arms on behalf of Islam. **—î** (.——) A belonging to the Ansar.
ansefalit F *path.* encephalitis.
ansıla=ʳ آکسلامر *var. of* **ansala=**.
ansır=ⁱʳ آکصرمر *prov., var. of* **aksır=**.
ansız 1 آنسز *archaic* without him, her, it.
ansız 2 آنسز sudden; suddenly. **—ca** suddenly. **—da** *archaic* suddenly. **—ın** (.'..) suddenly, all of a sudden. **—lık** suddenness.
ansiklopedi آنسیكلوپدی F encyclopedia.
antᵈ¹ آنت oath. **—ını boz=** to violate one's oath. **— et=, — iç=** *cf.* **and içmek**. **— sı=** *obs.* to break an oath. **— ver=** /a/ 1. to administer an oath. 2. to urge one on by binding him with an oath.
Antakya (..'.) انطاکیه geog. Antioch.
Antalya (..'.) آنطالیه geog. Antalya, *hist.* Adalia.
antant¹¹ F 1. agreement. 2. *w. cap.* Entente. **— kal=** *com.* to come to an understanding.
Antarktikᵏ¹ آنتارقتیک F *geog.* Antarctic.
anten آنتن F 1. *zool.* antenna. 2. *radio* antenna.
antena (.'.) آنتنا It *naut.* the yard of a lateen sail.
Antepᵇ¹ (.'.) عینتاب geog. Aintab (now Gaziantep). **a— fıstığı** pistachio. **a— fıstığıgiller** *bot., Pistacia Anacardiaceae.*
anter 1 عنتر A *lrnd.* gadfly, *zool., Tabanus.*
Anter 2 عنتر A Antar, hero of a famous Arabic romance.
antere 1 عنتره A *lrnd.* 1. a stabbing, piercing with a spear. 2. a rushing into peril, impetuosity, valor. 3. the buzzing (of flies).
Antere 2 عنتره A *man's name, esp.* Antara, son of Sheddad, an ancient Arabic poet, the prototype of the popular hero Antar (*cf.* **Anter 2.**).
anteri 1 انتری |anterî 2| *prov. for* **entari**.
anteri 2 (..—) عنتری A *lrnd.* 1. *w. cap.* pertaining to Antar (*cf.* **Anter 2.**). 2. bodice, long-sleeved jacket.
anterit F *path.* enteritis.
anterlin F *print.* lead, space line.
antet آنتت F letterhead. **—li kâğıt** stationery with letterhead.
antijen F *biol.* antigen.

antika (..´.) انتقا آنتیقا آنتیقه It
1. antique; relic of an ancient time; objet d'art.
2. *embroidery* hemstitch. 3. *print.* Roman.
4. *colloq.* queer, funny, eccentric. **—cı** dealer in antiques. **—lık** *colloq.* eccentricity, queerness.
antikor F *biol.* antibody.
Antiller آنتیللر *geog.* the Antilles. **Büyük —** the Greater Antilles. **Küçük —** the Lesser Antilles.
antilop[bu] آنتیلوب F *zool.* antelope.
antimon آنتیمون G *chem.* antimony.
antimuvan F *chem.* antimony.
antin *slang* prostitute.
antipati آنتیپاتی F antipathy.
antipatik آنتیپاتیك F antipathetic.
antipirin آنتیپیرین F *pharm.* antipyrine.
antipot[du] آنتیپود F *geog.* antipode.
antisepsi آنتیسپسی F *med.* antisepsis.
antiseptik[ti] آنتیسپتیك F *med.* antiseptic.
antişambr آنتیشامبر F antechamber.
antitez آنتیتز F *phil.* antithesis.
antitoksin آنتیتوكسین F *biol.* antitoxin.
antlaş=[ır] آندلاشمق 1. to swear an oath with another. 2. to swear an oath with others. **—ma** solemn agreement, pact. **—tır=** *caus.* of **antlaş=**.
antlı آندلی bound by an oath, under a vow, sworn.
antoloji آنتولوژی F anthology.
antraks آنتراكس F *path.* anthrax.
antrakt آنتراكت F *theat.* intermission, interval.
antrasit آنتراسیت F *min.* anthracite.
antre آنتره F 1. entrance, doorway. 2. admission fee.
antrenman آنترنمان F *sport* exercise, training.
antrenör آنترنور F *sport* trainer.
antrepo آنترپو F *com.* bonded warehouse.
antrkot آنتركوت F butchery beef from the top of the ribs.
antropi آنتروپی F *phys.* entropy.
antropoloji آنتروپولوژی F anthropology.
antropometri آنتروپومتری F anthropometry.
antropomorf آنتروپومورف F anthropomorphous.
anud (.—) عنود A *same as* **anut**. **—ane** (.-.—.) P *lrnd.* stubbornly, obstinately; stubborn, obstinate (act).
anun انڭ آنڭ *cf.* **ol** 1.
anunçün آنڭچون ازڭچون *archaic* therefore.
anus (´..) L *anat.* anus.
anut[du] (.—) عنود |anud| obstinate, stubborn.
anüf (—.) آنف A *lrnd., pl.* of **enf**.
anüite F *fin.* annuity.
anük[tü] (—.) آنك P *lrnd.* 1. lead. 2. tin, pewter.
anüri F *path.* anuria.

anve عنوه A *lrnd.* force, violence.
anveled عن ولد A *law* leaving issue (at death).
Anvers آنورس F *geog.* Antwerp.
anversaten F *textile* sateen.
anvet عنوت A *var.* of **anve**.
anveten (.´..) عنوةً A *lrnd.* by force.
anyedin (..´.) عن یدین A *lrnd.* by hand.
anyet عنیت A *lrnd.* difficulty, distress.
anz عنز A *lrnd.* 1. she-goat; she-ibex; she-gazelle. 2. female eagle, vulture, hawk, or heron. 3. the star ſ Aurigae.
anzarot عنزروت |enzerut| *slang* raki, arrack.
anze عنزه A *lrnd.* she-goat; she-gazelle.
aort F *anat.* aorta.
ap[bı] (—) *var.* of **âb** 1.
apaçık[ğı] (.´..) آپاچیق آپاچق 1. quite open, wide open. 2. quite manifest, very clear, evident.
apak[ğı] (.´.) آپاق pure white, all white.
apalak[ğı] آپالاق plump, fat, chubby (child).
apandis آپاندیس F *anat.* appendix.
apandisit آپاندیسیت F *path.* appendicitis.
apansız (.´..) آپانسز آپانسیز quite unexpectedly, without warning, all of a sudden. **—da** *archaic* suddenly. **—ın** quite unexpectedly, suddenly.
apar=[ır] آپارمق *prov.* /ı/ 1. to carry away; to make off (with). 2. to bring, to fetch.
apartıman, apartman آپارتمان F 1. apartment house. 2. apartment, flat.
apar topar آپار طوپار very suddenly (leaving), headlong.
apaş آپاش F a Parisian tough, French gangster.
apaşikâr (.´...) آپاشكار evident, very clear.
apati آپاتی F *path.* apathy.
apayrı (.´..) آپایری quite separate, completely different.
apaz آپاز Arm 1. cupped hand. 2. handful. **—la=** /ı/ to grasp (with the hand).
apazlama آپازلاما *naut.* abreast (wind).
aperitif F aperitif, appetizer.
apış 1 آپش آپیش 1. space between the two legs when set astraddle. 2. the inner side of a leg. **—ını aç=** to open one's legs asunder, sit or stand astraddle. **— arası** the space between the legs; *anat.* perineum.
apış=[ır] 2 آپشمق 1. to open the legs apart and stand or sit astraddle. 2. to give up, to stand helpless. **—ak** *same as* **apşak**. **—ık** with legs astraddle; too tired to move (horse, etc.). **—ıp kal=** to be completely bewildered.
apışlık[ğı] آپشلق gore, gusset (in knickers or trousers at the fork of the legs).

Red 5.

apıştır=" آیشدیرمس caus. of **apış=** 2.; *naut.* to lie on two anchors somewhat apart from one another.

apiko (..'.) آییقو It 1. *naut.* apeak. 2. *slang* ready, alert, quick; excellent.

aplikasyon آپلیقاسیون F *embroidery* applique.

apne F *path.* apnea.

apolet آپولت F epaulet.

apopleksi آپوپلکسی F *path.* apoplexy

aport آپرت F *hunting* fetch it. (order given to a dog).

apostrof آپوستروف F apostrophe.

apraksi آپراقسی F apraxia.

apre آپره F *textile* dressing, finishing. **—ci** finisher, dresser.

apse آپسه F *path.* abscess.

apsent آپسنت F absinthe.

apsis آپسیس F *geom.* abscissa.

apşak[¹] آپشاق 1. bowlegged. 2. sluggish; too tired to move, fagged out.

aptal آبدال |apdal| stupid; simpleton, fool. **—ca** stupidly; stupid (act). **—ca balık** bleak, blay, *zool., Alburnus.* **—laş=** to become stupid. **—laştır=** /ı/ to render stupid. **—lık** stupidity, foolishness. **—lık et=** to act like a fool. **—sı** somewhat stupid, naive.

aptes آپتس |abdest| 1. ritual ablution; the state of canonical purity. 2. bowel movement; feces. **— al=** to perform an ablution. **— boz=** to relieve nature, to ease oneself. **— bozan** unarmed tapeworm, beef tapeworm, *zool., Taenia saginata.* **— bozan otu** great burnet, *bot., Poterium officinale.* **—i bozul=** /ın/ to lose the state of canonical purity (by an easement of nature, escape of wind, pus, semen, etc.) **—i gel=** /ın/ to want to relieve nature. **—inde namazında ol=** to be faithful in performing one's religious duties. **—inde şüphesi olma=** /ın/ to have full confidence in oneself. **— tazele=** to renew one's ablution. **— ver=** *colloq.* /a/ to scold.

aptesane, apteshane (..—.) آبدستخانه P water closet, toilet.

aptesli آبدستلی purified by an ablution (person).

apteslik[¹] آبدستلك 1. *obs.* light kind of robe, easily tucked up over the elbows, used in ablutions. 2. room for the performance of ablutions.

aptessiz آبدستسز 1. not purified by an ablution, in a state of canonical pollution (person). 2. profligate, uninhibited. **— yere basma=** to be too particular or fastidious.

apul apul آپول آپول waddingly, saunteringly.

ar 1 (—) عار A 1. shame. 2. bashfulness; shyness; modesty. **— belâsı** the curse of being forced to consider what people will say for the sake of one's reputation. **— çekmekten bâr çek-** mek evlâdır *proverb* Better hardship than shame. **— damarı çatla=** to lose all sense of shame. **— dünyası değil kâr dünyası** This is a world of profit, not a world of scruple. **— et=** to be ashamed. **— gözden, kâr yüzden anlaşılır** *proverb* Modesty is reflected in the eyes, success in the face. **— namusu peynir ekmekle yemiş** (*lit.,* who has eaten virtue and honor with bread and cheese) altogether shameless. **— namus tertemiz** utterly shameless. **—ı satmış namusu kiraya vermiş** (*lit.,* who has sold honor and hired out virtue) who has lost all sense of shame. **— yılı değil, kâr yılı** leaving aside all sense of shame where one's interest is concerned. **— yiğidin kamçısıdır** *proverb* A sense of shame drives a man to exert himself.

ar 2 F are (100 m.²).

ar=" 3 آرمق *prov.* to be exhausted.

-ar 4, -er 5 *after vowel and* **-m, -şar, -şer** شار شر ¹ *suffixed to cardinals, forms distributive numerals, e. g.,* **onar** ten each; *repeated, distributive numeral adverb, e. g.,* **ikişer ikişer** two by two, two at a time.

-ar 5, -er 6, *cf.* **-r 2.**

-ar= 6, **-er=** 7 مك لك *suffixed to color and a few other adjectives* to become, *as in* **ağar=, sarar=, karar=, göğer=, morar=, yaşar=.**

=ar= 7, **=er=** *suffixed to some monosyllabic verbal stems ending in* **-k** *or* **-p,** *causative, as in* **çıkar=, çöker=, kopar=.**

ara 1 ارا آرا 1. the space between, distance; interval, gap; interstice; intermediate, intermediary. 2. state of relation, footing (between two persons). **—da*. —dan*. —sına** between, *e. g.,* **sobayı pencere ile kapı arasına koyalım** Let us put the stove between the window and the door. **—sında** 1. between, *e. g.,* **soba pencere ile kapı arasındadır** The stove is between the window and the door. 2. among, *e. g.,* **halk arasında** among the people. **—sından** 1. from between, *e. g.,* **sobayı pencere ile kapı arasından kaldırınız** Remove the stove from between the window and the door. 2. from among, *e. g.,* **halk arasından** from among the people. 3. through, *e. g.,* **yol ormanlar arasından geçiyor** The road goes through woods. **—ya*. —ları açık** They are not on friendly terms; their friendship is broken. **—ları açıl=** /ın/ for their relations to be severed, for their good relations to be spoiled. **—larına al=** /ı/ 1. to surround, to hem in. 2. to let someone join (one's group). **— ara** from time to time. **— ayı** the 11th lunar month **Zilka'de** (coming between **Şeker Bayramı** and **Kurban Bayramı**). **— bağı** septum (of the nose). **— bilançosu** *com.* interim balance-sheet. **—larını boz=** /ın/ to spoil their friendship, to create a rift (between)

—**larını bul**= /ın/ to reconcile, to settle a dispute (between). — **bulucu** mediator. —**larında dağlar kadar fark var** There are mountains of difference between them; they are as different as black and white. — **duvar** partition, dividing wall. —**larını düzelt**= /ın/ to reconcile. —**larına gir**= /ın/ to meddle; to come between (two people or parties). —**ya git**= to be lost; to be sacrificed. —**sı hoş olma**= /ın, la/ not to like. —**larında kan ol**= /ın/ to have a blood feud (between). — **kapı** communicating door. —**larına kara çalı gibi gir**= to spoil the friendship between two people. —**larından kara kedi geçmiş** /ın/ (*lit*. A black cat has passed between them.) They have quarrelled. — **kararı** *law* provisional decision (of a court). —**larına karış**= /ın/ to mix (with). — **kesit***. —**sı kesme** kind of outdoor game. — **limanı** maritime com. port of call. — **nağmesi** *same as* **aranağme**. — **sıra***. —**sını soğut**= /ın/ to delay (a thing) so that it is forgotten. —**larından su sızmaz** /ın/ to be very close friends. —**ları şekerrenk** /ın/ Their relations are strained; they are not too friendly. — **taksimi** *Or. mus.* taksim between two pieces of a **fasıl** (usually played against a rhythmic-melodic drone). — **ver**= /a/ to pause, make a break; to stop, cease. — **yatı** halting place for the night. — **yerde** *same as* **arada**.
|*For other compounds see* **arabeyin** — **arasöz 1.** *And under* **arada, aradan, araya.**|
ara=ᵣ 2 آرا آرام آره آلام /ı/ 1. to seek, look (for), hunt (for). 2. to search 3. to long (for), to miss. 4. to ask (for), to demand, to inquire (after); to visit. —**ma!** 1. too much to expect. 2. *prov.* Never mind. —**yıp bul**= /ı/ to seek and find, to find. 2. to ask (for trouble). —**makla bulunmaz** It is an exceptional occasion, a godsend. —**yan Mevlâsını da bulur, belâsını da** *proverb* 1. Seek and you shall find. 2. One finds what one is looking for. —**yıp tara**= /ı/ to search thoroughly, to comb, to go through with a fine-tooth comb.
âra 3 (— —) آرا A *lrnd.* 1. opinions. 2. votes. —**yı umumiye** *pol.* plebiscite, referendum.
-ara 4 (— —) آرا P *lrnd.* which adorns, who embellishes, *e. g.*, **meclisâra, dilâra**.
ara 5 (. —) عرا A *lrnd.* 1. region, neighborhood. 2. courtyard. 3. wall; walled enclosure, garden, date orchard.
arâ 6 (. —) عرى A *lrnd.* 1. nudity, nakedness. 2. wild, bare tract, desert.
Arab 1 عرب A *lrnd*: 1. the Arabs. 2. *cf.* **Arap**. —**ı arabiye, —ı âribe** the genuine Arabs. —**ı müsta'ribe, —ı müteârribe** people of foreign or mixed descent, naturalized among the Arabs.
A'rab 2 (. —) اعراب A *lrnd.* Arabs of the desert, Bedouins.
ârab 3 (— —) آراب A *lrnd., pl. of* **irb 1**. —**ı seb'a** the seven parts (that are on the ground in canonical prostration, *i. e.*, forehead, hands, knees, feet).
araba 1 عرابه عربه ارابه آرابه 1. carriage, wagon, cart. 2. car, automobile. 3. carload, wagonload. — **çatalı** pole of an ox-wagon. —**yı çek**= *colloq.* to clear out, to get off. — **devrilince yol gösteren çok olur** *proverb* After the cart is upset, there are many who offer advice. —**sını düze çıkar**= (*lit.*, to reach even ground with one's cart) to overcome difficulties. — **ile tavşan avlanmaz** *proverb* (*lit.* One cannot hunt rabbits from a wagon.) There is no success without labor. — **kırılınca yol gösteren çok olur** *same as* **araba devrilince yol gösteren çok olur**. — **koş**= to hitch the horses to a carriage. — **körüğü** hood of a carriage. — **kösteği** lock chain to the wheel of a coach. — **kullan**= to drive a car. — **oku** pole of a carriage. —**nın ön tekerleği geçtiği yerden arka tekerleği de geçer** *proverb* (*lit.* Where the front wheel of a carriage passes, the back wheel passes, too). If one person has been able to accomplish something, then others can too. — **vapuru** car ferry.
araba 2 عربة A *lrnd.* pontoon used in bridges on the Tigris.
arabacı عرباجى ارابه جى عربه جى آرابه جى 1. driver (of a cart, wagon, coach, etc.). 2. a maker of wheeled vehicles, cartwright. —**lık** the profession of a driver.
arabalıkᵗⁱ آرابه ليق 1. wagon house, cart shed. 2. cartload, wagonload.
araban (.. —) عربان P a mode in Oriental music.
Arab arba (...—) عرب عربا , **Arab aribât** (....—) عرب عربات , **Arab aribe** عرب عربة A *lrnd.* the genuine Arabs.
arabat 1 (. — —) عربات A *lrnd., pl. of* **arabe**.
arabat 2 (.. —) عربات A *lrnd., pl. of* **araba** 2.
arabe (. — .) عربة A *lrnd.* 1. bag for covering the teats of a sheep or goat, to prevent them from being sucked. 2. obscene talk.
arabeskᵏⁱ F *art* arabesque.
arabeyinʸⁿⁱ آربين *anat.* diencephalon.
Arabi 1 (.. —) عربي A Arabian, Arabic; Arabic, the Arabic language. — **aylar** the months of the Arabic lunar calendar.
A'rabi 2 (. — —) اعرابي A a nomad Arab, Bedouin.
Arabistan (...—) عربستان P Arabia.

— **inciri** sycamore fig, *bot., Ficus sycomorus*.
Arabiyat (..——) عربيات A *lrnd.* Arabic studies.
Arabiye (..—.) عربيه A *lrnd.* 1. *fem.* of **Arabi** 1. 2. the Arabic language.
Arabiyet (..—.) عربيت A *lrnd., same as* **Arabiyat**.
arabun (..—) عربون A *lrnd.* earnest money, something given to bind a contract.
aracı آراجى آره جى mediator, go-between. **—lık** mediation, intervention.
araçᶜⁱ *neol.* means, medium; tool. **—lı** indirect. **—sız** direct.
arada آراده ارده [**ara** 1| in between. **bir —** in one place; at the same time, together. **— bir** from time to time, now and then. **— çıkar** /ı/ to get a thing done while doing other work. **— git=** to pass unnoticed. **— kal=** to suffer for mixing up in a dispute, to suffer as the third in an argument, to be left in the lurch. **— kayna=** to pass unnoticed; to go in vain (other things having happened). **— sırada** from time to time, occasionally, now and then.
aradan آردن ارد ن [**ara** 1] in between (of time). **—̣ çık=** to withdraw from a group; to wash one's hands of a matter. **— çıkar=** /ı/ to get (something) done in order to get it out of the way.
A'raf 1 (.—) الاعراف A *Isl. theol.* place separating Paradise from Hell.
a'raf 2 (..—) اعراف A *lrnd., pl.* of **örf**.
Arafat (..—) عرفات A Arafat, a hill near Mecca known as a place of pilgrimage.
arafet (.—.) عرافت A *hist.* guild wardenship.
arais (.—.) عرائس A *lrnd., pl.* of **arus** 1, **aruse**.
araiş (.—.) عرائش A *lrnd., pl.* of **ariş** 1, **arişe**.
araiz (.—.) عرائض A *lrnd., pl.* of **ariza**.
=arak 1, **=erek** 1; *after vowel* **=yarak** 2, **=yerek** *forms adverbial verb form with the meaning of concurrency, e. g.,* **konuşarak geldik** *we came talking.*
arakᵏⁱ 2 عرق A *lrnd.* 1. perspiration. 2. alcoholic liquor, raki. **—ı cebin** sweat of the brow. **—ı infial** perspiration caused by unpleasant emotion.
a'rakᵏⁱ 3 (.—) اعراق A *lrnd., pl.* of **ırk**.
arakᵏᵏⁱ 4 ارق A *lrnd., superl.* of **rakik**.
araka Gk variety of peas.
arakçı آراقچى *slang* thief, pilferer.
arakçin (..—) عرقچين P linen cap worn under a turban.
arakdar (..—) عرقدار P *lrnd.* sweating, perspiring.

arakesitᵈⁱ *neol., geom.* intersection.
arakı اراقى عرق |**arak** 2| *prov.* raki.
arakıye (..—.) عرقيه A soft felt cap.
araki 1 (.——) عراقى A *lrnd., pl.* of **arkuve**.
araki 2 (..—) عرقى A *physiol.* sudatory, causing sweating.
arakib (.——) عراقيب A *lrnd., pl.* of **urkub**.
arakla=ʳ آراقلامق /ı/ *slang* to steal, pilfer.
araknakᵏⁱ (..—) عرقناك P *lrnd.* sweating excessively.
arakriz (..—) عرقريز P *lrnd.* dripping with perspiration.
arala=ʳ آرالامق الالمق /ı/ 1. to separate. 2. to space, to open out. 3. to leave ajar (door); to half open. **—n=** *pass. and refl.*
aralaş=ʳ آرالاشمق *same as* **aralan=**. **—tır=** *caus.* of **aralaş=**.
aralat=ʳ آرالاتمق *caus.* of **arala=**.
aralıkᵏⁱ آرالق ارلق 1. space, opening, interval, gap. 2. time, interval, moment. 3. corridor. 4. toilet, water closet. 5. ajar, half-open. 6. *w. cap.* December. **bir —** for a while, some time. **— aralık** from time to time, now and then; at intervals, spaced. **— ay** the lunar month **Zilkade. A— ayı** December. **— bırak=** 1. to leave a space. 2. /ı/ to leave ajar, half-open. **— et=** /ı/ to half-open. **—a git=** to be spent in vain. **— ver=** /a/ to stop (working, etc.), to discontinue, to interrupt.
aralıklı آرالقلى spaced, having intervals.
aram (—..) آرام P *poet.* rest, repose, quiet. **—ı can** heart's ease; the beloved. **—ı dil** soul's rest; the beloved. **— et=** to rest, repose.
arama آرامه 1. search, exploration. 2. *law* search, searching. **— emirnamesi, — müzekkeresi** search warrant.
arambahş (——.) آرامبخش P *poet.* peace-giving, soothing.
aramcu (———) آرامجو P *poet.* longing for tranquility; peace-seeker.
aramet (.—.) عرامت A *lrnd.* obstinacy, malignance.
aramgâh (———) آرامگاه, **aramgeh** (——.) آرامگه P *poet.* place of repose, retreat.
Aramî 1 (———) آرامى A Aramean; Aramaic.
aramî 2 (———) آرامى P *lrnd.* peace, calmness, repose, rest.
aramîde (———.) آراميده P *poet.* rested, quieted, reposing.
aramiş (——.) آرامش P *lrnd.* repose, quiet, rest.
aramkâr (———) آرامكار P person living lazily and tranquilly.

aramsaz (———) آرامْسازْ P poet. resting, reposing; dwelling.

aramzar (———) آرامْزارْ P poet. place of rest.

aran=" آرَنَمْ 1. pass. of **ara**= 2. 2. to search one's own clothes and pockets. 3. colloq. to look for trouble.

aranağme (.'...) آرانغَمْ 1. Or. mus. instrumental ritornello in a vocal piece. 2. fig. refrain, oft-repeated words.

aranıl=" آرانْلَمْ pass. of **ara**= 2.

arantaran آرانْ طارانْ same as **alantalan**.

"**Arap**ᵇ¹ عرب |Arab 1| 1. Arab. 2. Negro. 3. l. c., slang negative (photograph). — **Araba yüzün karadır demiş** One Negro said to the other: «How black your face is!» — **ardında!** The black man is behind you (said to children as a restraint). — **atı** Arabian horse. — **atının yanında duran ya huyundan ya suyundan** pro-\verb (lit. The horse that stands beside the Arabian horse acquires something of its nature.) People influence each other by contact. — **bacı** Negro nurse, mammy. — **bocusu** naut. parbuckle. — **çakmağı** wooden apparatus for producing fire by friction. — **çorap** colloq. Negroes. — **darısı** buckwheat, bot.,Fagopyrum esculentum. — **dilini çıkarmış gibi** (lit., as if a Negro had stuck out his tongue) loud red. — **doyuncaya yer, Acem çatlayıncaya** proverb An Arab eats until he is full; a Persian eats until he bursts. — **inciri** prickly pear, bot., Opuntia vulgaris. — **oğlu** son of an Arab, of Arabian descent; Arab. — **sabunu** soft soap. — **saçı** 1. fuzzy hair. 2. tangled affair, mess. — **şerbeti** decoction of hot spices to induce perspiration, an intoxicating fumigatory used /by Negroes. — **teli** tambourine without cymbals. — **Üzengi** name of a giant bogey in fairy tales. — **zamkı** gum Arabic.

Arapça (.'.'.) عربجَه 1. the Arabic language, Arabic. 2. in the Arabian fashion. 3. unintelligible. —**dır değil mi? Uydur uydur söyle!** (lit., It's Arabic, isn't it? Make up words and talk!) You can say what you want where nobody can check you. —**laştır**= /ı/ to Arabicize.

arar 1 (. —) عرار A lrnd., bot. yellow oxeye.

ar'ar 2 عرعر A 1. juniper, bot., Juniperus communis. 2. juniper tree, bot., Callitris quadrivalvis.

araret (. — .) عراراتْ A lrnd. 1. ill-temper. 2. lordly eminence.

ararot آرارُوتْ E arrowroot.

Aras 1 ارس Aras; hist. Araxes river.

a'ras 2 (. —) اعراس A lrnd., pl. of **urs**.

a'ras 3 (. —) اعراص A lrnd., pl. of **arsa** 1.

arasat" 1 (.. —) عرصاتْ A 1. pl. of **arsa** 1. 2. w. cap., Isl. theol. place where the resurrected are to assemble on the Day of Judgment.

arasıra آرا صِرَه '.—.. now and then, from time to time, occasionally.

arasız آراسِزْ uninterrupted, continuous; continuously.

arasif (. — —) عراصيف A lrnd., pl. of **ursuf**.

arasöz neol. digression.

arasta آراسْتَه |raste| 1. shops of the same trade built in a row. 2. obs. campfire, sutler's camp.

arastakᵉ¹ آراسْتاكْ Arm prov. ceiling, beams supporting the flat roof.

araste (———.) آراسْتَه P lrnd. prepared, arranged; decorated, adorned. —**gi** (———.—) P abst. n. —**lik** arrangement; decoration.

araş=" 1 آرَشَمْ /ı/ obs. to seek one another.

a'raş 2 (. —) اعراشْ A lrnd., pl. of **arş** 2.

araştır=" آراشْتَرمَم ارشْتَرمَم /ı/ 1. to seek carefully. 2. to search thoroughly, to investigate, to explore. —**ıcı** explorer, investigator; searching. —**ma** investigation, research, exploration.

arat=" 1 آراتَمْ /ı,a/ caus. of **ara**= 2.

arat 2 (. —) عراتْ A var. of '**ara** 5.

arattır=" آراتْدَرمَم /ı, a/ caus. of **arat**= 1. 2. caus. of **ara**= 2.

araya آرايا |ara 1| in between. — **al**= /ı/ to surround, to hem in. **bir — gel**= to come together, to meet in one place, to gather. — **gir**= to meddle, intervene. — **git**= to be lost, to be the victim (in a confusion, etc.). — **koy**= /ı/ to have (a person) intervene, to have someone act as intermediary. — **söz bırak**= to start gossip.

arayende (———..) آرايَنْدَه P lrnd. who adorns, ornamenting; decorator.

arayıcı آرايِجَى |ara 2| 1. seeker; seeking. 2. searcher; searching. 3. beachcomber. 4. one who makes a living by combing dumps. 5. obs. garbage collector. 6. customs inspector. — **fişeği** kind of firecracker.

arayış آرايِشْ a seeking; a searching.

arayiş (———.) آرايِشْ P lrnd. adornment, embellishment, decoration.

âraz 1 (———) آراضْ A lrnd., pl. of **arz** 1.

a'raz, âraz 2 (. —) اعراضْ A pl. of **araz** 5, med. symptoms.

a'râz 3 (. — —) اعراضْ A lrnd., pl. of **arz** 3.

a'râz 4 (. — —) اعراضْ A lrnd., pl. of **ırz**.

araz 5 عرضْ A 1. med. symptom. 2. phil. nonessential attribute; accident. . fortuitous event. 3. theol. worldly goods, property; any kind of wealth except gold and silver.

araza ارضه A *lrnd.* woodworm; white ant, termite.
arazan (..) عرضا A *phil.* accidentally.
arazat 1 (..—) الارضات A *lrnd., pl. of* **arz 1**.
arazat 2 (.—.) عراضت A *lrnd.* broadness, breadth, width.
arazbar (..—) عرضبار P *Or. mus.* a **makam** starting with g" and ending on a'. — **buselik** a **makam** starting like **arazbar** and ending like **buselik**.
arazi 1 (.——) اراضى A 1. land. 2. territory. 3. real property, estate, estates. —**i âmire** *can. law* cultivated land. — **arabası** jeep, land-rover. —**i gamire** *can. law* cultivable waste land. —**i haraciye** *can. law* land, subject to the payment of the **harac**. — **hukuku** land law. —**i mahlûle** *can. law* lands reverting to the state through escheat. —**i memlûke** *can. law* lands held in fee simple, freehold lands. —**i metruke** *law* abandoned or ownerless lands. —**i mevat** *law* dead lands, uncultivated and unappropriated. —**i mevkufe** *can. law* lands possessed in mortmain. —**i mezrua** *law* arable land. —**i milkiye** *hist.* private domain lands of the Sultan's estates. —**i miriye** *can. law* crown lands, state-owned lands distributed to individuals. —**i öşriye** *can. law* tithe lands, lands subject to the payment of tithes. — **sahibi** landowner. — **tatbikatı** *mil.* field exercise. — **terki** cession of territory. — **vergisi** land tax. — **vitesi** *auto.* auxiliary gearshift (in jeeps).
a'razî 2 (.——) الاراضى A *phil.* incidental, accidental, casual.
arazî 3 (..—) عرضى A 1. *phil.* accidental, extrinsic, adventitious. 2. *theol.* pertaining to worldly goods.
arazîn, arazun (..—) ارضين A *lrnd., pl. of* **arz 1**.
arbede عربده A 1. uproar, riot, row, tumult, noisy quarrel. 2. *lrnd.* quarrelsomeness. —**cu** (...—) P quarrelsome. —**kâr** (...—) P quarrelsome.
arbitraj آربيتراژ F *fin.* arbitration.
arca (.—) عرجاء A *lrnd.* 1. lame, limping. 2. hyena.
arce عرج A *lrnd.* declivity, inclination, bias.
arcele عرجيل A *lrnd.* herd, flock.
ard 1 آرد *cf.* **art 1**.
ard 2 (—) آرد P *lrnd.* flour.
ard=[ar] **3** اردصن /i/ *prov.* to hang, suspend.
arda 1 آردا 1. *obs.* target pole. 2. *hist.* long staff (of certain officers).
arda 2 عرضه آرده lathe chisel.
ardabe (——.) آراب P *lrnd.* soup, stew.
ardala آردال 1. large camel bell.
2. pillion, cushion for a beast's back.
ardalı اردالو carrying a long staff, as a beadle, tipstaff, verger.
ardarda آردآرده one after another.
ardbiz (——) آردبيز P *lrnd.* 1. flour sifter. 2. flour sieve.
ardıç[cı] آرديج آرديج آرديج juniper, *bot., Juniperus*. — **katranı** juniper tar, oil of cade. — **kuşu** fieldfare, *zool., Turdus pilaris*. — **sakızı** gum juniper. — **suyu** gin, Hollands. — **tohumu** juniper berries.
ardıl *neol., phil.* consecutive.
ardın ardın آردين اردين اردن backwards.
ardınca (..'.) اردنج behind, following (him). — **ol=** *archaic* to pursue; to seek (to).
ardıradan آرديرادن *obs.* from behind.
ardışık[ı] *neol., math.* consecutive.
ardiye ارضيه |arziye| *com.* 1. warehouse. 2. warehousing charge, storage rent.
ardlaş=[r] *var. of* **artlaş=**.
ardoda *neol., anat.* posterior chamber.
arduvaz F slate. — **kapla=** /a/ to slate.
|**areb** *see* **arab**|
a'rec 1 اعرج A *lrnd.* lame, limping.
arec 2 عرج A *lrnd.* a becoming lame, lameness.
arec 3 (—.) آرج P *lrnd.* elbow.
arecan (..—) عرجان A *lrnd.* limping gait, lameness.
a'ref 1 اعرف A *lrnd.* 1. most knowing, very intelligent. 2. best known.
a'ref 2 اعرف A *lrnd.* 1. maned; flowing-maned, long-maned. 2. crested.
Arefat (..—) عرفات *var. of* **Arafat**.
arefe 1 عرفه |Arefe 2| *same as* **arife 1**.
Arefe 2 عرفه A Arafa, hill near Mecca, on top of which a **hutbe** is annually delivered on the eve of Kurban Bayram.
arekâniye (..——.) عركانيه A *lrnd.* coarse, stout woman.
arekiye (..—.) عركيه A *lrnd.* adulteress.
arem عرم A *lrnd.* speckledness, mixture of white and black.
areme 1 عرم A *lrnd.* heap.
areme 2 عرم A *lrnd., pl. of* **arim 1**.
aremgâh (—.—) آرمگاه P *poet., var. of* **aramgâh**.
aremide (—.—.) آرميده P *poet.* rested, reposed. —**gi** (—.—.—) P state of rest, tranquillity.
aremrem عرمرم A *lrnd.* numerous army.
aren 1 F arena.
aren 2 (—.) آرن P *poet.* elbow.
arena (.'.) آرنا It scouring sand.
arenc (—.) آرنج P *poet.* elbow.
arende (—..) آرنده P *lrnd.* who brings, carrier.

areng (—.) آرَنگ P poet. elbow.
areometre (....'.) F phys. areometer.
ares عرس A lrnd. 1. a cleaving (to). 2. exhaustion.
areste (—..) آرَسته P poet., var. of **araste**.
arf عرف A lrnd. smell, fragrance.
arfa (.—) عرفا A lrnd. 1. maned. 2. hyena.
arfec عرفج A lrnd. kind of thorny tree.
argaçᶜⁱ آرغاج ارغاج woof, weft. —**la**= /ı/ to woof (a cloth), to weave in its woof. —**lan**= pass. of **argaçla**=.
argalı آرغالی argali, zool., Ovis ammon.
argı=ʳ آرغینی ارغینی obs. to grow thin, become emaciated.
argıd cf. **argıt**.
argın 1 آرغین archaic weak, feeble, tired. —**lık** weakness, fatigue, exhaustion.
argıtᵈⁱ ارغیت prov. mountain pass, neck, ridge between two valley heads.
argo آرغو F slang, cant.
arı 1 آری آرو bee; wasp. —**lar** zool., Hymenoptera. — **bal alacak çiçeği bilir** proverb (lit. A bee knows from which flower to take honey.) A clever person knows where his profit lies. — **beyi***. — **biti** an insect parasite on bees and wasps. — **çiçeği** honeywort, bot., Cerinthe retorta. — **gibi** like a busy bee, busily. — **gibi sok**= to sting like a bee. — **götü** small rose bud. — **iğnesi** bee-sting. — **kovanı** 1. beehive. 2. foxglove, bot., Digitalis purpurea. — **kovanı gibi işle**= to be greatly frequented, to buzz like a beehive. — **kuşu** bee eater, zool., Merops apiaster. — **otu** moon trefoil, tree medick, bot., Medicago arborea.
arı 2 آری prov. clean; pure; sc. pure. — **duru** very clean. — **eteklü** archaic chaste. — **kil***. — **sili** clean.
arı=ʳ 3 آریمی آرمس prov. 1. to become clean. 2. to recover health.
arıbeyiⁿⁱ آری‌بگی queen bee.
arıca آریجه prov. clean.
arıcı آریجی beekeeper. —**lık** apiculture.
arıdıl=ʳ آریدلمی archaic for **arıtıl**=.
arıkᵏⁱ 1 آرق آرو prov. lean, thin. — **ata kuyruğu da yüktür** proverb To the lean horse even its own tail is a burden. — **öküze bıçak olmaz** proverb A lean ox need not fear the butcher's knife.
arıkᵏⁱ 2 آرق var. of **arı** 2.
arıkᵏⁱ 3 آرق prov., var. of **ark** 1.
arık=ʳ 4 آریقمی prov. to grow lean.
arıkil آریکل min. kaolin.
arıkla=ʳ 1 آریقلامی prov. to grow lean.
arıkla=ʳ 2 آریقلامی /ı/ prov. to clean, purify. —**n**= pass.
arıklan=ʳ آریقلانمی prov. to grow scraggy. —**dır**= /ı/ caus.
arıklat=ʳ 1 آریقلاتمی /ı/ caus. of **arıkla**= 1.
arıklat=ʳ 2 آریقلاتمی /ı/ caus. of **arıkla**= 2.
arıklıkᵏⁱ 1 آریقلق leanness, thinness.
arıklıkᵏⁱ 2 آریقلق cleanness, purity.
arıl=ʳ آریلمی same as **arı**= 3.
arılıkᵏⁱ 1 آریلق place for bees, beehouse, beehive.
arılıkᵏⁱ 2 آریلق prov. cleanness, purity.
arın=ʳ آرینمی to become clean, to be purified.
arış 1 آریش |**arış** 2| 1. pole (of an oxcart). 2. bow collector (of a trolley car).
arış 2 آریش weaving warp.
arış 3 ارش |**erş**| obs. cubit (measure from the tip of the middle finger to the elbow).
arışla=ʳ 1 آریشلامس /ı/ to set with a warp (loom).
arışla=ʳ 2 آریشلامس /ı/ to measure in cubits.
arıt=ʳ آریتمی /ı/ to clean, cleanse, purify. —**ıl**= pass.
ârız 1 (—.) عارض A 1. phil. happening, accidental; event, accident. 2. lrnd. impeding, obstructing. — **ol**= /a/ to happen, occur, befall.
ârız 2 (—.) عارض A poet. cheek.
ârız 3 (—.) عارض A lrnd. gift, present.
ârız 4 (—.) عارض A meteor. heavy cloud, stratus.
ârıza 1 (—..) عارضه A 1. defect, failure, breakdown, obstruction. 2. phil. accident. 3. unevenness, roughness (of the country). 4. lrnd., fem. of **ârız** 1.
ârıza 2 (—..) عارضه A poet. cheek.
ârızalı (—...) عارضه‌لی 1. defective, out of order. 2. uneven, rough, rugged, broken (country).
ârızan (—'..) عارضاً A phil. accidentally, casually.
ârızaten (—'...) عارضةً A phil. accidentally.
ârızî (—.—) عارضی A phil. accidental, casual. —**yet** (—.—.) casual nature.
âri 1 (—.) عاری A 1. /dan/ bereft (of), free (from), lacking. 2. lrnd. naked, bare. 3. simple, unadorned (prose, without rhyme or measure).
Ari 2 (——) آری [based on Sanskrit] Aryan (language).
âri 3 (——) آری P poet. yes indeed! truly.
ârib (—.) عارب A lrnd. pure-blooded, genuine (Arab).
âric 1 (—.) عارج A lrnd. 1. lame, limping. 2. that mounts, ascending.

aric

aric 2 (.—) عَرِيج A *lrnd.* lame; badly arranged.

ârif 1 (—.) عَارِف A 1. knowing, wise, sagacious; versed, skilled, expert. 2. w. cap., man's name. **—i billâh** *myst.* who has attained to true knowledge of God. **— isen bir gül yeter kokmaya, cahil isen gir bahçeye yıkmaya** *proverb* (*lit.* If you are wise one rose is enough for you to smell, if you are ignorant you will go into the garden and destroy it.) A word to the wise is enough. **—e bir işaret yeter** *proverb* A hint is enough for the wise **— olan anlasın** He who is wise will understand. **—e tarif ne lâzım?** The wise need no explanation.

arif 2 (.—) عَرِيف A *lrnd.* 1. renowned, known. 2. who knows well, expert. 3. adept (in spiritual mysteries or occult science). 4. *obs.* warden of a guild. 5. *obs.* monitor (in a school).

ârifane 1 (—.—.) عَارِفَانَه P *lrnd.* 1. wise, sagacious (act); sagaciously, knowingly. 2. skilful, expert (act); expertly.

arifane 2 (..—.) عَرِيفَانَه [**herifane**] 1. picnic or entertainment to which each partaker contributes. 2. one's share in such feast, etc. **—ci** partaker in such a picnic.

arife 1 عَرْف [**arefe 1**] eve. **— çiçeği** impatient child who wears his Bairam presents on the day before Bairam. **— divanı** *Ott. hist.* Court reception on the eve of a religious feast. **— günü** the day before a Bairam. **— günü yalan söyleyenin bayram günü yüzü kara olur** *proverb* He who tells a lie on the day before Bairam will be shamed the next day.

arife 2 (—..) عَارِف A kindness, favor, gift, bounty.

arifi (.——) عَرِيفِى P **ariflikᵏⁱ** *obs.* 1. guild-wardenship. 2. the functions of a monitor in a school.

arig (——) آرِيغ P *lrnd.* grudge, hatred, malice.

arikᵏⁱ (.—) عَرِيب A *lrnd.* 1. of noble descent; full-blooded (horse). 2. light-hearted, generous.

arike (.—.) عَرِيكَ A *lrnd.* 1. remnant of a camel's hump. 2. nature, disposition, temperament.

ârim 1 (—.) عَارِم A *lrnd.* cross, disagreeable.

arim 2 عَرِم A *lrnd.* obstinate and self-willed.

arin (.—) عَرِين A *lrnd.* 1. thicket, jungle. 2. the haunt of a wild beast. 3. courtyard (of a house). 4. eminence, greatness. 5. strength. 6. cooing (of a dove).

arina (.'..) *var. of* **arena**.

arine (.—.) عَرِينَه A *lrnd.* the haunt of a wild beast.

aris (.—) عَرِيس A *lrnd.* bridegroom.

Aristatalis (—.———) آرِسْطَا طَالِيس A *lrnd.* Aristotle. **—iye** (—.———.) *phil.* Aristotelianism.

Aristo ارسطو A Aristotle. **—culuk** *phil.* Aristotelianism.

aristokrasi ارستوقراسى F *pol.* aristocracy.

aristokratᵘ ارستوقرات F *pol.* aristocrat. **—lık** aristocracy.

ariş 1 (.—) عَرِيش A *lrnd.* 1. booth, shed. 2. alcove, summer-house. 3. trellis. 4. howdah, litter.

ariş 2 (.—) عَرِيش A *prov.* carriage shaft.

arişe (.—.) عَرِيشَه A *lrnd.* trellis, vine arbor.

aritmetikᵏⁱ F 1. arithmetic. 2. arithmetical. **— dizi** *math.* arithmetical series, arithmetical progression.

aritmi F *path.* arythmia.

ariva (..'.) آرِوَا It *naut.* up aloft!, away aloft!

ariya 1 (.'..) *var. of* **arya 1**.

ariya 2 (.'..) *var. of* **arya 2**.

ariye (.—.) عَرِيَه A *lrnd.* 1. palm-tree stripped of its fruit. 2. date-palm reserved for home consumption when the produce of an orchard is sold. 3. date-palm especially assigned to a person for the fruit season.

ariyet (——.) عَارِيَت A 1. a borrowed thing. 2. *law* loan, gratuitous loan. 3. *can. law* a thing the usufruct of which is gratuitously abandoned to someone. 4. a temporary thing, stopgap, makeshift; *naut.* jury. **—en** (——'..) as a loan, for temporary use. **—î** (—'.—.) P *lrnd.* temporary, makeshift.

ariyetsaray (——..—) عَارِيَت سَرَاى P *lrnd.* the temporary dwelling place, this world.

ariyüşşekl (——..) عَارِ الشَّكْل A *lrnd.* amorphous.

ariz (.—) عَرِيض A *lrnd.* wide, broad. **— u amik** at great length, in great detail.

ariza (.—.) عَرِيضَه A *lrnd.* petition; letter.

arizülbitan (.—..—) عَرِيض البَطَان A *lrnd.* rich, wealthy.

Arjantin آرژَانْتِين F *geog.* Argentina. **—li** an Argentine.

arkᵏⁱ 1 آرْق irrigation trench, canal.

årkᵏⁱ 2 F 1. *arch.* arch. 2. *elec.* arc. **— lâmbası** arc lamp.

arkᵏⁱ 3 عَرْق A *lrnd.* 1. a rubbing and squeezing something with the hands to make it soft. 2. a scraping, fretting, crushing. 3. a chafing or cutting his side with his leg joint until the flesh appears (camel). 4. a trying one with misfortune.

arka آرْقَا ارْق آرْفَا 1. the back. 2. back part, rear, back side, back face, reverse; hind, back. posterior. 3. the space behind, beyond.

4. powerful friend, backer, supporter. 5. that follows, sequel, the remaining part. 6. a backload (of something). **—dan** from behind, in the back; behind the back. **—sına** /ın/ behind, e. g., **Şemsiyeyi kapının arkasına koy** Put the umbrella behind the door. **—sında** /ın/ 1. behind, after, e. g., **Şemsiye kapının arkasındadır** The umbrella is behind the door. 2. after, e. g., **Bu işin arkasındayım** I am after this job. **—sından** /ın/ 1. from behind, e. g., **Sandalyeyi kapının arkasından çek** Take the chair away from behind the door. 2. after, e. g., **Çocuğun arkasından koş** Run after the child. **—sına al=** /ı/ to shoulder, to take on one's back. **—sını al=** /ın/ to bring to an end. **— arka** backwards. **—sı arkasına, — arkaya** one after the other. **—dan arkaya** behind the back, secretly. **— arkaya ver=** to back each other, to join forces. **—ya at=** /ı/ to put off, delay. **— beyin** anat. metencephalon. **—da bırak=** /ı/ to leave behind. **—sını bırakma=** /ın/ to follow up, to stick (to). **— çantası** knapsack. **— çevir=** /a/ to turn one's back (on), to shun. **— çık=** /a/ to befriend, to back. **—sına düş=** /ın/ 1. to follow (a matter). **—sı gelme=** /ın/ to be discontinued. **—sını getireme=** /ın/ to be unable to accomplish (a matter). **—ını göreyim** I'll be glad to see the back of you; off with you! **—da kal=** to stay behind; to be left behind. **—da kalan kazadan korkma** proverb No need to fear an accident which has passed. **— kalanlar** those who are left behind (relatives of a deceased person). **—sı kavi** 1. warmly dressed. 2. who has strong backing. **—sı kesil=** /ın/ to cease, to be cut off. **—da koy=** /ı/ to leave behind. **—nı kürke, kapını Türke alıştırma** proverb Do not accustom your back to a fur coat, do not accustom a country fellow to frequent your home as a guest. **— lâmbaları** automobile rear lights. **—sı mihrapta** who has strong support. **— ol=** /a/ to protect, to back, to give support (to). **—sı pek** same as **arkası kavi**. **— plânda** in the background, of minor importance, in indefinite suspense (proposal). **— sahife** print. verso, reverse page, left-hand page. **—sı sıra** /ın/ following, right after, on his heels. **— sokak** back street. **—dan söyle=** to talk behind someone's back, to backbite. **—sından teneke çal=** /ın/ (lit., to make a noise by banging on a tin can) to chase somebody off with shouted insults. **— üstü yat=** to lie on one's back. **—sı var** to be continued (newspaper serial). **—sını ver=** /a/ to lean one's back (against). **—sı yere gelme=** /ın/ not to be defeated, invincible. **—sını yere getir=** /ın/ to bring another's back to the ground, to defeat. **—sı yufka** There is not much to follow (said of food at table). **—sında yumurta küfesi yok ya, dönüverir** (lit. He does not have a basket full of eggs on his back, so he can turn easily.) There is nothing to prevent him from changing his mind.

arkacı آرقه جى prov. supporter, backer.
arkaç[c1] آرقاچ prov. rounded, flattish hill top.
arkadaş ارقه داش آرقه داش آرقه داش comrade, companion, friend, colleague, fellow. **— değil arka taşı** harmful companion. **— ol=** to become friends. **—ça** like friends, in a friendly manner. **—lık** comradeship, friendship.
arkala=[r] آرقه لامق ارقه لمق /ı/ 1. to take on one's back. 2. prov. to back, to support, to protcet. **—n=** /a/ prov. to lean (upon), to find support (in). **—t=** /a,ı/ caus. of **arkala=**.
arkalı ارقه لى آرقه لى 1. broad-backed. 2. who has a supporting friend, who has backing.
arkalıç[c1] آرقه ليچ porter's saddle, porter's frame.
arkalık[ğı] ارقه لق آرقه لق 1. porter's saddle. 2. kind of jacket covering only the back. 3. carrier (of a bicycle). 4. back (of a chair).
arkasız آرقه سز آرقاسز 1. having no back, backless. 2. having no protector, lacking a backer. **— olanın ayağına vurmuşlar, vay arkam demiş, karnına vurmuşlar, yine vay arkam demiş.** proverb (lit. The one who had no backing was hit on the foot, he cried: «Oh, my back!»; he was hit in the stomach, again he cried, «Oh, my back!») Any misfortune may befall one who has no protector.
Arkeen F geol. Archaean.
arkegon F bot. archegonium.
arkeolog F archaeologist.
arkeoloji F archaeology.
arketip F archetype.
arkın آرقن prov. weak; soft, low (voice).
arkırı prov. for **aykırı**.
arkoz F geol. arkose.
Arktik[ği] آرقتیک F Arctic. **— kuşak** Arctic Zone.
Arktika (´..) آرقتیقه L the Arctic Region.
arkun آرقون archaic, same as **arkın**. **— arkun** slowly, softly, gently. **—cacık, —cak** slowly, softly.
arkurı, arkuru آرقورى آرقورو archaic for **aykırı**.
arkuva ارقوه A lrnd. wooden crosspiece at the mouth of a leather bucket.
arlan=[ır] (—..) عارلانمق to feel ashamed, to be ashamed. **—dır=** caus. **—maz** brazenfaced, unabashed.
arlı (—.) عارلو عارلى bashful.
arm عرم A lrnd. obstinacy, headstrongness, pigheadedness.

arma 1 (`.'.`) آَرْما آَرَم F coat of arms, armorial bearings.

arma 2 (`.'.`) آَرْما آَرَم It 1. *naut.* rigging. 2. *slang* jewelry worn on the person. 3. *slang* scolding. —**yı al=** to unrig (ship). —**yı doldur=** to tauten the standing rigging. — **donat=** to rig. — **et=** /ı/ to rig (ship). — **soy=** to unrig.

armador آَرْمادُور It *naut.* 1. rigger. 2. experienced seaman. — **çeliği** belaying pin.

armadora (`..'.`) آَرْمادُوره It *naut.* pinrack.

armağan آَرْمَغَان |ermağan| 1. gift, present brought from far. 2. commemorative volume. — **et=** /a, ı/ to make a present (of).

arman (— —) آَرْمَان P *poet.* regret, disappointment, unfulfilled desire. —**î** (— — —) P regretful, disappointed, grieved.

armator, armatör آَرْمَاتُور F *naut.* 1. rigger. 2. ship-owner.

armatur F *elec.* armature.

=**armışçasına** cf. =**rmışçasına**.

=**armış gibi** cf. =**rmış gibi**.

armoda (`.'.`) آَرْمُودا Gk *naut.* rope to guide the tackle for catting or fishing the anchor.

armonik[gi] آَرْمُونِيك F, **armonika** (`...'.`) آَرْمُونِيقا It 1. harmonica. 2. accordion.

armonyum آَرْمُونْيُوم F harmonium.

armoz آَرْمُوز Gk *naut.* seam, joint (between planks).

armud آَرْمُود cf. **armut**.

armuda (`.'.`) آَرْمُوده var. of **armoda**.

armudî (`..—`) آَرْمُودِى |based on **armud**| pear-shaped. — **altın** pear-shaped coin or medal worn as an ornament or amulet suspended round the neck or on the crown of a child's cap.

armudiye (`..—.`) آَرْمُودِيَه |based on **armud**| *same as* **armudî altın**.

armut آَرْمُود |emrud| 1. pear. 2. *slang* fool, imbecile, blockhead. — **ağacı** pear tree. — **ağacı elma vermez** *proverb* (*lit*. A pear tree bears no apples.) You can't expect a person to do what is not natural to him. —, **ağacından uzak düşmez** (*lit*. The pear does not fall far from the tree.) Like father like son. — **altını** *same as* **armudî altın**. —**un iyisini ayılar yer** *same as* **ahlatın iyisini ayılar yer**. — **kurusu** dried pears. — **piş ağzıma düş!** Pear, get ripe and fall right into my mouth! (said of one who expects things to fall into his lap without doing anything about it himself). —**un sapı var, üzümün çöpü var** *proverb* (*lit*. The pear has its stem, the grape has its pedical.) There is always something wrong.

armuz آَرْمُز var. of **armoz**.

Arnavut[du] آَرْناوُود Gk Albanian. — **bacası** *arch.* dormer window. — **beli** gardener's digging fork. — **besası** an agreement sure to be quickly broken. — **biberi** red pepper. — **darısı** millet. — **derzi** *arch.* pointing of a rough stone wall. — **elması** delicious kind of apple imported from Albania. — **kaldırımı** rough cobblestone pavement. — **peyniri** a rich, ball-shaped kind of cheese from Albania. — **zarı** kind of top-shaped, five-faced die. —**ça** Albanian (language).

Arnavutluk[gu] آَرْناوُودْلُك 1. Albania. 2. the character of an Albanian. —**ğu tuttu** the Albanian blood in him flared up and he acted with impulsive violence.

arnı *prov.*, var. of **alnı**.

arnika (`.'.`) آَرْنِيقه L arnica, mountain tobacco, *bot.*, *Arnica montana*.

arnuk[gu] آَرْنُوك *obs.* tired.

arozöz آَرُوزُوز F watering cart, sprinkler.

arpa آَرْپا ارپا barley. — **arpa bit by bit**; in small bits. —**sı az gel=** not to have had enough (punishment, etc.). — **boyu fairy-tales** very short distance; the slightest bit. — **mı buğday mı?** boy or girl? — **eken buğday biçmez** *proverb* He who sows barley cannot reap wheat. — **ektim darı çıktı** (*lit.*, I sowed barley, millet grew) I did not get what I expected; it was a disappointment. — **emini** *Ott. adm.* comptroller of the supplies of barley for Istanbul and the Sultan's stables. — **naibi** *Ott. adm.* a substitute comptroller of the barley supplies. — **suyu** *hum.* beer. — **şehriye**, — **şehriyesi** grain-shaped macaroni. — **unun yoksa tatlı dilin de mi yok?** (*lit.* Even if you don't have any barley flour, don't you have at least a sweet tongue?) It does not cost anything to be nice. — **verilmiyen at kamçı zoruyla yürümez** *proverb* A horse cannot be made to go with the whip if it has not been properly fed.

arpacı آَرْپَجِى ارپه جى |arpa| seller of barley. — **kumrusu** kind of domestic ringdove. — **kumrusu gibi düşün=** to be deep in thought, to brood.

arpacık[gi] آَرْپَجِك ارپه جك 1. sty (on the eyelid), *path.* hordeolum. 2. front sight (of a gun). — **soğanı** shallot, *bot.*, *Allium ascalonicum*.

arpağan آَرْپَغَان ارپاغان kind of wild oats.

arpala=[r] آَرْپَلَه ارپه لامق 1 to treat with barley. 2. to become sick from overfeeding with barley, or from diseased barley (horse). —**ma** a disease of a horse's leg.

arpalık[gi] آَرْپَلِك ارپه لق 1. field suitable for growing barley; fertile soil. 2. barley bin; granary for barley. 3. *Ott. adm.* kind of fief; stipend. 4. mark on the cutting surface of a horse's nippers by which his age can be known, but which wears away with old age.

arra (. —)   عَرّا   A *lrnd.* virgin.
arrade (. — .)   عَرّادَه   A *lrnd.* small ballista, catapult.
arraf (. —)   عَرّاف   A *can. law* 1. diviner, soothsayer, esp. one who finds lost or stolen things. 2. astrologer. 3. physician.
arras (. —)   عَرّاص   A *lrnd.* 1. with thunder and lightning (cloud). 2. flashing, gleaming.
ars *var. of* **as** 4.
arsa 1   عَرْصَه   A 1. plot of vacant land, building land. 2. *lrnd.* courtyard, open field, country. **—ı âlem** the world. **—ı arasat** place of assembly on the Day of Judgment. **—ı kârzar**, **—i merdanegi** *poet.* battlefield. **—ı şatranç** *lrnd.* chessboard.
=**arsa** 2 *cf.* =**rsa**.
arsen   آرسن   G *same as* **arsenik**.
arsenik[ği]   آرسنیك   F *chem.* arsenic.
arsıulusal *neol.* international.
arsız   آرسز   1. shameless; impudent, insolent; saucy, troublesome, spoiled (child); bold, pushing, importunate. 2. vigorous (plant), encroaching. **— neden arlanır, çul da giyse sallanır** *proverb* A shameless person is never abashed, he swaggers even when in rags. **— pirsiz** utterly shameless. **—ın yüzüne tükürmüşler, yağmur yağıyor demiş** *proverb* They spat in the face of the shameless man, and he said, «It is raining.» **—ca** unabashedly, impertinently; impertinent (action). **—lan=** to become troublesome, importunate, overbearing, impudent, shameless. **—laş=** to become impudent. **—lık** 1. shamelessness, impudence, insolence; boldness, importunity. 2. encroaching vigor (plant).
arslan   آرسلان   *var. of* **aslan** 1.
arslanî (. . —)   آرسلانی |*based on* **arslan**| *lrnd., same as* **aslanlı**.
arş 1   آرش   F *mil.* march!
arş 2   عرش   A 1. throne. 2. throne of God; the Ninth Heaven. 3. *lrnd.* booth, temporary shed; alcove, summer-house; trellis, roof, ceiling, canopy. 4. *lrnd.* bier. 5. *lrnd.* bird's nest. **—ı âlâ** the throne of God; the Empyrean. **—ı Cevza** *astr.* the stars in the constellation Lepus, beneath the feet of Orion. **— ü ferş** heaven and earth. **—ı mecîd** the throne of God.
arş 3, 4, 5   آرش   *var. of* **arış** 1, 2, 3.
arşak[ği] آرشاك *prov., var. of* **ağırşak**.
arşaşıyan (. — . —)   عرش آشیان   P *lrnd.* nestling at the foot of the divine throne (dead saint).
arşe   عرشه |*based on* **arş** 2| *lrnd.* elevated deck, poop (of a ship).
arşın   آرشین   1. ell, yard (Turkish measure of length of about 28 inches, 68 cm., now in disuse). 2. yardstick. 3. iron scraper for cleaning dough and flour from a baker's trough. **—ları aç=** *slang* to walk with big strides. **—ı büyük** long-legged. **—la sat=** /ı/ to sell by the yard. **—a vur=** /ı/ to measure by the yard. **—la=** /ı/ 1. to measure by the yard. 2. to walk with big strides, to stride along. **—lık** 1. sold by the yard (cloth). 2. measuring one yard in length.
arşidük[kü]   آرشیدوك   F archduke.
arşidüşes   آرشیدوشس   F archduchess.
arşipel   آرشیپل   F *geog.* archipelago.
arşiv   آرشیو   F archives.
arşiyan (. . —)   عرشیان   P *lrnd.* angels who carry the throne of God.
arşülcevza (. . . —)   عرش الجوزا   A *astr.* the constellation Lepus.
arşüssimak[kı] (. . . —)   عرش السماك   A *astr.* stars of the constellation Corvus, below Spica.
arşüssüreyya (. . . . —)   عرش الثریا   A *astr.* a group of stars beneath the Pleiades.
art[dı] 1   آرت   1. back, hinder part, behind, rear; hind. 2. the space behind. 3. sequel, end. **—ına** *same as* **arkasına**. **—ınca*. —ında, —ından** *same as* **arkasında, arkasından**. **—ını al=** /ın/ 1. to complete. 2. *archaic, mil.* to surround. **— aradan** from the back, from the rear; in a roundabout way, indirectly. **—ı arası kesilmeden** incessantly, uninterruptedly. **— arda*. —ı arası gelme=** not to come to an end. **—a at=** /ı/ to postpone. **—ından atlı mı geliyor?** Why all this hurry? **—ını boşla=** /ı/ to give up trying. **—ına düş=** /ın/ to pursue, follow. **—ından eski pabuç at=** /ın/ to throw an old slipper (after someone for good luck or in token of contempt). **— eteğinde namaz kılınır** (*lit.* One might perform the ritual prayer on the back skirt of her dress.) She is of exemplary virtue. **—ını getir=** /ı/ to complete, to bring to an end. **—ına kadar aç=** /ı/ to have a wide open (door). **— kafa** *anat.* occiput. **—ından sapan taşı yetişmek** (*lit.* A stone from a sling could not catch up with him.) He is running very fast. **—ı sıra** immediately following him. **—ında yüz köpek havlamıyan kurt kurt sayılmaz** *proverb* (*lit.* A wolf is not a real wolf, unless there are a hundred dogs barking at his back.) No strong man is without his critics.
art=[ar] 2   آرتمق   1. to increase. 2. to be more than what is needed, to be in excess. 2. to remain over, to be left over.
artağan   آرتاغان   *prov.* increasing, multiplying.
artakal=[ır]   آرته قالمق   /dan/ to remain over (from).
artal[li]   عرطل   A *lrnd.* enormous, disproportionately big, gargantuan.

artaliyet (..—.) عرطليت |based on **artal**| *lrnd.* enormousness.
artçı آرجى *mil.* rear guard.
arter آرتر *F anat.* artery.
arteriyoskleroz *F path.* arteriosclerosis.
artezyen آرتزين *F* deep well, artesian well.
artı *neol., math.* plus.
artıkᵍ¹ **1** آرتق، آرتق، آرتقين 1. left, remaining over; remnant, residue; *pl.* leftovers. 2. superfluous, redundant. — **eksik** without considering whether it is too much or too little. — **gün** leap day. — **mal göz çıkarmaz** *proverb* A little extra does no harm. — **yıl** leap year, bissextile.
artık 2 (.'.) آرتیه، ارتق، آرتق 1. *in initial or final position* now, well then; (not) any more, (no) longer, *e. g.*, **Yeter artık!** Enough now! **Artık gelmez** He won't come after this (it is too late). 2. *isolated* what next?
artıklıkᵍ¹ ارتقلق superabundancy.
artıkrakᵍ¹ آرتفراق *obs.* more.
artıl='' آرتل *pass. of* **art**= 2.
artımlı آرتملى fully swelling (rice, etc.).
artır='' ارترمق، آرتيرمق، آرتيرمه /ı/ 1. to let become more, to make increase, to augment. 2. to leave some over purposely, to economize, to save. 3. to offer more (for), to bid more (at an auction). —**ıl**= *pass.* —**ılmış** *mus.* augmented (interval). —**ış**= /ı/ *archaic* for several bidders to raise by higher bids (price). —**ma** sale by auction.
artış آرتش increase, augmentation.
artist آرتست *F* 1. actor, actress, artist in a show. 2. artistic.
artlaş='' آرتلاشمق to lag behind gradually.
artrit آرترت *F path.* arthritis.
artropati *F path.* arthropathy.
artsız arasız آرتسز آراسز uninterrupted, perpetual; continually.
arttır='' ارتيرمق، آرتيرمه *var. of* **artır**=.
Aruba (.——) عروبا *A lrnd.* the Seventh Heaven, the Empyrean.
arufe (.—.) عروف *A lrnd.* very wise, learned.
aruğ (——) آروغ , (—.) آرغ *P lrnd.* belch, eructation. —**zen** (——.) *P* one who belches.
arun (——) آرون *P lrnd.* good qualities and habits (of a man).
arus 1 (.—) عروس *A lrnd.* bride. —**u Adn** *poet.* 1. moon. 2. a youth of Paradise, handmaid. —**u Arab** *poet.* the temple of Mecca, the Kaaba. —**u cihan** *poet.* 1. world; wealth, power. 2. the planet Venus. —**u çerh** *poet.* the sun. —**u felek** *poet.* the sun. —**u huşkpistan** *poet.* 1. barren woman. 2. the disappointing world. —**u haveri**, —**u ruz** *poet.* the sun. —**u Şam** *poet.* the city of Damascus.

arus 2 (.—) عروس *A lrnd.* bridegroom.
arus 3 (.—) عروس *P lrnd.* 1. *name of one of the eight treasures of Khusrev Parvis.* 2. *alchemy* sulfur.
arusan (.——) عروسان *P lrnd.* brides. —**ı bağ**, —**ı çemen** *poet.* flowers of the field. —**ı huld** *poet.* the houris of Paradise.
arusane (.——.) عروسانه *P lrnd.* bridal, like a bride.
aruse (.—.) عروسه *A lrnd.* bride.
arusekᵏ¹ **1** (.—.) عروسك *P lrnd.* 1. little bride. 2. doll. 3. firefly; glowworm. 4. sheowl. 5. small kind of catapult.
arusekᵍ¹ **2** عروسك |**arusek 1**| very brilliantly iridescent greenish and rose-colored mother-of-pearl used for inlaid ornamentation. —**li** ornamented with such mother-of-pearl.
arusî 1 (.——) عروسى *A lrnd.* pertaining to a bridegroom or bride, bridal.
arusî 2 (.——) عروسى *P lrnd.* wedding feast, nuptials. —**iye** *Ott. hist.* a tax on weddings.
aruz (.—) عروض *A* 1. prosody, *esp.* the prosody of the classical Arabic-Persian tradition. 2. meter. 3. *pros.* the last foot of the first hemistich of a distich. 4. *lrnd.* side; road. 5. *lrnd.* tenor of a discourse. 6. *lrnd.* ridgepole of a long tent. 7. *w. cap., name of Mecca and Medina with their territories.*
aruzî (.——) عروضى *A lrnd.* 1. prosodic. 2. prosodist.
arv عرو *A lrnd.* a shuddering from fever.
arvana اروانا *prov.* she-camel.
arvatᵈ¹ *var. of* **avrat 1**.
arya 1 (.'.) آريا It *mus.* aria.
arya 2 (.'.) آريا It *naut.* Down from aloft. — **et**= to dip (flag, sail). — **kürek** Boat the oars.
arz 1 ارض *A* 1. the earth. 2. *lrnd.* land, region, country, territory. 3. *lrnd.* the soil (of a country). 4. *lrnd.* plot of land. —**ı harac** *can. law* land conquered by the sword and subject to the payment of tribute. **A—ı Kenan** Canaan. —**ı meskûn** the inhabited world. **A—ı Mev'ud** the Promised Land. —**ı mîrî** *can. law* land owned by the Islamic community and distributed to individuals. **A—ı Mukaddes** the Holy Land. —**ı öşriye** *can. law* soil annexed by agreement and subject to the payment of a tithe.
arz 2 عرض *A* 1. presentation, demonstration, showing. 2. a submitting something to one's superior; *Ott. hist.* a writ of the Grand Vizier addressed to the Sultan. 3. *com.* offer. —**ı bendegi et**= /a/ to present one's duty (to a superior). —**ı cemal** /a/ a showing one's fair face. —**ı didar** /a/ a showing one's face to an admirer. —**ı endam** a showing oneself.

— et=*. —ı hal*. —ı hizmet /a/ an offering of one's services. —ı hulus /a/ a presenting one's regards. —ı hüner a showing one's skill. —ı hürmet, —ı ihtiram /a/ a presenting one's respects. —ı leşker a presenting one's troops for inspection. —ı mafizzamir a representation of what is in the mind. —ı mahzar collective petition, round robin. —ı müddea law a statement of one's claim. —ı müveddet a showing affection. —ı nedamet an expressing of regret. — odası Ott. hist. a large hall in a public building where the Grand Vizier or other high personage held a court; the Sultan's audience hall in the Grand Palace. — u talep, — ve talep econ. supply and demand. —ı tâzimat a presenting one's respects. —ı ubudiyet a presenting one's homage. arzuhal*.

arz 3 عرض A 1. geog. latitude. 2. lrnd. width; broadside of a thing. 3. lrnd. mountain, mountain slope. 4. lrnd. bank of clouds. 5. lrnd. army. —ı cenubî geog. south latitude. — dairesi geog. parallel of latitude. — derecesi geog. degree of latitude. —ı kevkeb geog. latitude of a star. —ı şimalî geog. north latitude.

arza عرضه P 1. presentation, representation, submission of a matter. 2. levee. 3. parade.

arza aynin (...'.) عرض عين A lrnd. before one's eyes.

arzadaşt (..—) عرض داشت P lrnd. petition.

arzan (.'.) عرضاً A 1. in width. 2. across, transversally, intersecting. 3. geog. in latitude.

arzanî (.—) عرضانى A transversal.

arzdaşt (..—) عرض داشت P lrnd. petition, memorandum.

arzet=der عرض اتمك |arz 2| /ı,a/ 1. to present. 2. to submit, to tender. 3. to offer.

arzgâh (.—) عرضگاه P lrnd. place where people or troops assemble for a court, review, etc.

arzıhalⁱⁱ (..—) عرض حال P same as arzuhal. Arzıtilekᵗⁱ neol., astr. Mercury.

arzi 1 (.—) ارضى A 1. pertaining to the soil. 2. earthly. 3. terrestrial.

arzi 2 (..—) عرضى A latitudinal; transversal.

arziyat (.——) ارضيات A geology.

arziye (.—.) ارضيه A 1. fem. of arzi 1. 2. same as ardiye.

arzlı عرضلو 1. having the breadth of. 2. geog. having the latitude of.

arzolun=ur عرض اولنمق pass. of arzet=.

arzu 1 (..—) آرزو |arzu 2| 1. wish, want, request. 2. desire, longing. 3. w. cap., woman's name. — çek archaic to long. — et= /ı/ to wish (for), to want; to long (for), to desire. —sunda ol= /ın/ to have a wish (to do something). — üzerine on request.

arzu 2 (——) آرزو P lrnd., same as arzu 1.

arzuhalⁱⁱ (..—) عرض حال |arzıhal| petition, written application. — encümeni obs. Committee on Petitions. — hakkı law right of petition. — ver= to present a petition. —ci 1. obs. an officer who receives petitions. 2. writer of petitions, street letter writer. 3. petitioner.

arzukeş (——.) آرزوكش P lrnd. wishful, desirous, longing.

arzula=ʳ آرزولامق /ı/ 1. to desire, wish (for), long (for). 2. archaic to be bound (for).

arzullahi (..—.) ارض الله A in — vâsia God's earth is endless (used of waste land).

arzulu آرزولو desirous, wishing, longing.

arzuman آرزومان prov. desire.

arzumend (——.) آرزومند P lrnd. desirous. —i (——.—) P desire; wishfulness.

as 1 آس F cards ace.

as 2 (—) آس A lrnd. myrtle.

as=ᵃʳ 3 آصمق /ı/ 1. to hang up, to suspend. 2. to hang (a criminal). 3. slang to neglect, to play truant, to delay payment (of a debt). —tığı astık kestiği kestik (lit. The one whom he hangs is hanged; the one whom he slays is slain.) What he says goes. —ıp kes= /ı/ to exercise tyranny.

as 4 آص prov. weasel; ermine.

as 5 (—) آس P lrnd. 1. mill. 2. ground grain.

asˢˢⁱ 6 (—) عاسّ A lrnd. who patrols; patrol, guard, night watchman.

asˢˢⁱ 7 عسّ A lrnd. 1. a fretting round a thing (moth). 2. a biting (snake). 3. a bothering, importuning.

asˢˢⁱ 8 عسّ A lrnd. a going around, patrolling; a prowling; round, patrol.

as 9 in neologisms sub- as in asteğmen.

asâ 1 (.—) عصا A 1. scepter, staff, stick, baton. 2. lrnd. a beating. —yı dik= to insist and wait persistently (in order to force an issue). A—yı Musa the rod of Moses.

-âsâ 2 (——) آسا P lrnd. 1. like, similar (to), resembling, as in cennetâsâ. 2. quieting, tranquillizing; quiet, tranquil, as in dilâsâ.

âsâ 3 (——) آسا P lrnd. 1. a yawning, yawn. 2. gravity, dignity.

a'sâ 4 (.—) اعصا A lrnd., pl. of asâ 1.

âsab 1 (.—) اعصاب A pl. of asab 2.

asab 2 عصب A 1. same as âsap 1. 2. lrnd. sinews, fibrous tissue. 3. lrnd. stems of twining plants.

asabani (..—.) عصبانى A lrnd. nerve-like; tendinous.

asabe 1 عَصَبَة A lrnd. 1. nerve. 2. sinew, fiber. 3. stem of a twining plant.
asabe 2 عَصَبَة A 1. the tall cylindrical part of a fez. 2. arch. reglet.
asabe 3 عَصَبَة A 1. can. law the body of a deceased person's collateral relations to whom no definite portion of the inheritance is assigned by canonical law and who become residuary legatees after the assigned portions have been paid over. 2. lrnd. the agnates of a deceased person. 3. lrnd. league, coalition for the protection of another person. — **bigayrihi** female relation or relations whose legal share in the inheritance drops to half the amount if they have brothers. — **binefsihi** male heir or heirs, between whom and the deceased all the links are males. — **maagayrihi** relation or relations (sister, etc.) who receive a share only after all legal portions have been paid over. **—i nefsiye** same as **asabe binefsihi**. **—i nesebiye** heir or heirs by consanguinity. **—i sebebiye** heir or heirs by indirect relationship, whereby a former owner becomes heir to his enfranchised slave or vice versa.
asabî 1 (..—) عَصَبِي A 1. nervous, irritable, on edge. 2. anat. neural. 3. biol. tendinous; pertaining to a climbing plant.
asabi͡ 2 (.—.) اصابع A 1. anat. fingers; toes. 2. obs. inches, digits. **—i Firavun** kind of branching coralline or stone, found in the Red Sea. **—i Hürmüs** bot. finger of Hermes, Hermodactylus.
asabî 3 (..—) عَصَبِي A 1. can. law pertaining to one's collateral relations. 2. lrnd. pertaining to one's party.
asabiî (.—.—) اصابعي A anat. pertaining to fingers, digital.
asabil (.—.) اصابل A lrnd., pl. of **ıstabl**.
asabileş=ⁱʳ (..—..) عَصَبِيلَشْمَك |asabî 1| to get nervous, be irritated. **—tir**= /ı/ caus.
asabilikᵍⁱ (..—.) عَصَبِيلِك nervousness, irritability.
asabiülazara (.—...—.) اصابع العزاره A lrnd. variety of long grape.
asabiülfeteyat (.—....—) اصابع الفتيات A lrnd. kind of sweet basil.
asabiye (..—.) عَصَبِيَّة A 1. fem. of **asabi 1, 3**. 2. nervous diseases. 3. neurology, neuropathology. **—ci** nerve specialist, neurologist, neuropathologist.
asabiyet 1 (..—.) عَصَبِيَّت A 1. nervousness, irritability. 2. biol. the quality of a nerve; tendinousness.
asabiyet 2 (..—.) عَصَبِيَّت A 1. can. law consanguinity. 2. lrnd. party zeal; patriotism.
asabiyülcenah (..—..—) عَصَبِيّ الجناح A zool. neuropteron.
âsâd (— —) آساد A lrnd., pl. of **esed**.

asadıkᵏ¹ (.—.) اصادود A lrnd., pl. of **esdak**.
Asaf 1 (—.) آصَف A 1. man's name. 2. Asaph, name of the vizier of King Solomon. 3. l.c. minister, grand vizier.
asaf 2 صف A bot. caper-bush, Capparis spinosa.
asafane (—.—.) آصفانه P lrnd. vizierial; vizierially.
asafî (—.—) آصفي A lrnd. vizierial.
asafir (.——) عَصافِير A birds, zool., Passeres.
asafirülmünzir (.——...) عَصافِير المُنذِر A Persian hist. an excellent kind of camel used by the ancient Persian kings.
âsafrey (—..) آصف رأى P lrnd. having the judgment of Asaph, of sound opinion (vizier).
âsaftedbir (—..—) آصف تدبير P lrnd. wise in his decisions like Asaph (vizier).
asagir (.—.) اصاغِر , **asagire** (.—..) اصاغِرَه A lrnd. the very small, the smallest ones.
asahʰʰ¹ اصح A lrnd., superl. of **sahih**.
asahib (.——) اصاحِب A lrnd. lords, owners, masters; friends, companions.
asaib (.—.) عَصائِب A lrnd., pl. of **isabe**.
asair (.—.) عَصائِر A lrnd., pl. of **asire**.
asakᵏ¹ عسى A lrnd. 1. adherence. 2. assiduity, perseverance. 3. a dunning. 4. ill nature, malice.
asakir (.—.) عَساكِر A lrnd., pl. of **asker**. **—i bahriye** navy troops. **—i berriye** land troops. **—i cerrar** marauding soldiers. **—i hassa** Ott. hist. the Imperial guard. **—i mansurei Muhammediye** Ott. hist., name of a military body founded by Mahmud II. **—i muavine** auxiliary troops. **—i muntazama** regular troops. **—i nizamiye** Ott. hist. soldiers doing their first military service. **—i redife** Ott. hist. reserve troops. **—ı şahane** the Imperial Ottoman army.
asako=ʳ, **asakoy=**ᵃʳ آصمه قومق آصمه قويمق |as= 3| archaic /ı/ to leave hanging, to hang.
asal 1 neol. basic, fundamental. **— analiz** chem. immediate analysis. **— sayı** math. prime number.
âsâlⁱⁱ **2** (— —) آسال A lrnd. features, characteristics (of a man).
âsâlⁱⁱ **3** (— —) آسال P lrnd. foundation, structure, frame.
âsâlⁱⁱ **4** (— —) آصال A lrnd. late afternoons.
a'sal 5 (.—) امال A lrnd., pl. of **asel**.
a'sal 6 اعصال A lrnd. 1. crooked, gnarled; crook-legged, curly-tailed. 2. intricate, difficult, troublesome.

asalakᵏ¹ آسالاق 1. *biol.* parasite. 2. *prov.* parasite, sponger. —**lık** *biol.* parasitism.
asalet (. —.) اصالت A 1. nobility, nobleness. 2. a performing the duties of an office, by right and not as substitute; definitive appointment. 3. *lrnd.* rootedness, firmness.
asaleten 1 (. —́ . .) اصالةً A *law* acting as principal and not as a representative, *in propria persona*.
asaleten 2 (.́ . . .) اصلةً A *lrnd.* totally, wholly, entirely.
asaletlû (. — . .) اصالتلو archaic noble, of noble birth (used as epithet with certain titles, *esp.*, of ambassadors and other foreign dignitaries, particularly in formal correspondence).
âsam 1 (— —) آسام A *lrnd., pl. of* **ism** 2.
asamᵐᵐ¹ 2 اصم A *lrnd.* 1. deaf. 2. deaf to reason. 3. *math.* surd, irrational. 4. *Arabic gram.* whose second and third radicals are the same (root).
a'sam 3 اعلم A *lrnd.* 1. white in the forelegs (stag). 2. having a white feather in the wing (crow).
asam 4 عصم A *lrnd.* a being marked with white in a foreleg.
asammiyet (. . — .) اصمّیت │based on **asam** 2│ *med.* surdity (in percussion).
asan (— —) آسان P *lrnd.* 1. easy. 2. light, easily borne. —**gir** (— — —) P easily taken, easily captured. —**î** (— — —) P, —**lık** 1. facility, ease. 2. lightness.
asansör آسانسور F elevator, lift.
âsapᵇ¹ 1 (— —) اعصاب │**âsab** 1│ *anat.* nerves. — **bozukluğu** nervous disturbance. —**ı bozul=** /ın/ to get nervous, to be upset. —**ına dokun=** /ın/ to get on one's nerves, to irritate.
asapᵇ¹ 2 عصب │**asab** 2│ *anat.* nerve.
âsar 1 (— —) آثار A *lrnd.* 1. traces, marks, tracks. 2. remains, relics. 3. monuments (left behind), works, buildings, books written, oeuvres. 4. histories, traditions, legends. —**ı atika***. —**ı kalemiye** the writings (of an author). —**ı mehdiye** *astr.* nutation.
asar=ⁱʳ 2 آسرمك *prov.* to grow.
a'sâr 3 (. —) اعصار A *lrnd., pl. of* **asr** 1.
asâr 4 (. —) عثار A *lrnd.* troublesome matter, unlucky affair.
asar 5 عثر A *lrnd.* dust, flying dust.
asar 6 عثر A *lrnd.* refuge, shelter.
asare 1 (— — .) آساره P *lrnd.* computation, calculation; account.
asare 2 عصره A *lrnd.* flying dust, dust cloud.
asaret (. — .) عسارت A *lrnd.* 1. hardness, difficulty; grievousness. 2. harshness.
asarıatika (— — . . — .) آثار عتیقه P antiquities, ancient monuments.
asârrai (. . — —) عصا الرعی A *bot.* knotgrass, polygonum.
asas 1 عسس A *var. of* **ases** 1, 2.
as'as 2 عثعث A *lrnd.* 1. bare hilltop. 2. buttock. 3. soft earth. 4. intrigue, corruption.
asatıb (. — .) اصاطب, **asatıl** (. — .) اصاطل *lrnd., pl. of* **ıstabl**.
asavi (. . —) عصوی A *lrnd.* pertaining to a stick.
asavid (. — —) عصاوید A *lrnd., pl. of* **ısvad**.
asavidülharb (. — — . .) عصاوید الحرب A *lrnd.* men who will not desert their comrades in battles.
asavidüzzalam (. — — . . —) عصاوید الظلام A *lrnd.* thick darkness.
-âsây (— —) آسای P *var. of* **-âsâ** 2.
asayiş (— — .) آسایش P 1. public order, public security. 2. *lrnd.* repose, rest, tranquility, ease. — **et=** *lrnd.* to rest, repose. —**perver** (— — . . .) P peace-loving, promoting public security.
asb عصب A *lrnd.* 1. a binding, band, bandage. 2. strangulation (of the testicles). 3. fillet, handkerchief, turban. 4. a being obligatory. 5. *pros.* replacement of the foot **mefâilatün** by **mefâilün**. 6. climbing plant. 7. kind of mottled cloth, plaid.
asbağ (. —) اصباغ A *lrnd., pl. of* **sıbg**.
asbah (. —) اصباح A *lrnd., pl. of* **subh**.
asban (— —) آسبان P *lrnd.* miller.
asbaşkan *neol.* deputy chief, vice-president.
asbe عصبه A *lrnd.* cleft, chasm in a mountain.
asbest آسبست F asbestos.
asbi (. —) عصبی, **asbiye** عصبیه A *lrnd., pl. of* **sabi** 1.
asbur اصبور *var. of* **aspur**.
asced عسجد A *lrnd.* 1. gold. 2. gems.
ascedî (. . —) عسجدی A *lrnd.* fullblooded (horse, camel).
asda (. —) اصدا A *lrnd., pl. of* **sada**.
asdaf (. —) اصداف A *lrnd., pl. of* **sadef**.
asdağ (. —) اصداغ A *lrnd., pl. of* **sudg**.
asdakᵏ¹ اصدق A *var. of* **esdak**.
asdar اصدار *var. of* **astar** 1.
asdıka (. . —) اصدقا A *lrnd., pl. of* **sadik**, *lrnd.* friends.
│For /asef/ *cf.* /asaf 1│
asefat (. . . —) عسفات A *lrnd.* agony of death.
asel عسل A *lrnd.* 1. honey; honeylike juice; juice of fresh dates. 2. sweet gum exuding from some trees; honeydew. —**i Davud** kind of balsam. —**i lübna** 1. gum benzoin. 2. storax. —**i musaffa** clarified honey. —**i rims** manna from *Tamarix mannifera*. —**i temr** thick juice of ripe fresh dates. —**i urfut** gum of *Acacia urfuta*.

aselân (..—). عسلان A *lrnd.* 1. a quivering (spear). 2. a running with wide steps and flexures of the body.

aseli (..—) عسلي A *lrnd.* 1. honeylike; honey-colored. 2. *hist.* a distinguishing piece of yellow cloth which the Jews were compelled to wear on the shoulder.

aseliyet (..—.) عسليت |*based on* **aseli**| *lrnd.*, *abstr. n. of* **aselî**.

asen عثن A *lrnd.* smoke, vapor.

asenkron F *phys.* asynchronous.

asepsi F *med.* asepsis.

aseptik[ß¹] F *med.* aseptic.

a'ser 1 اعسر A *lrnd.*, *superl. of* **asir 2**, **asîr 1**.

a'ser 2 اعسر A *lrnd.* 1. left-handed. 2. unlucky, inauspicious. — **yeser** ambidextrous.

aser 3 عسر A *lrnd.* left-handedness.

aserat (..—) عثرات A *lrnd.*, *pl. of* **asre**.

aserî عثري A *lrnd.* watered by rain only (sown field).

ases 1 عسس A *hist.* guard, night-watchman, policeman. — **başı** *hist.* chief policeman, captain of the guard.

ases 2 عسس A *lrnd.*, *pl. of* **as 6**.

asese عسسة A *lrnd.*, *pl. of* **as 6**.

asesiye عسسية *Ott. hist.* night-watchman's fee collected from the shopkeepers.

asetilen F *chem.* acetylene.

aseton آسه تن F *chem.* acetone.

asf[fı] **1** عسف A *lrnd.* 1. oppression, tyranny; unjust seizure. 2. death agony.

asf 2 عصف A *lrnd.* 1. a blowing with violence (wind). 2. a rushing along. 3. a carrying off, destroying. 4. an earning, gaining a living.

asf 3 عصف A *lrnd.* the green blades of growing grain.

asfa (.—) اصفى A 1. purest. 2. most sincere.

asfaf (.—) اصفاف A *lrnd.*, *pl. of* **saf 2**.

asfalt آسفالت F asphalt.

asfar (.—) اصفار A *lrnd.*, *pl. of* **sıfr**.

asfe 1 عسفة A *lrnd.* 1. puff of wind, gust. 2. whiff of odor.

asfe 2 عصفة A *lrnd.* blade of growing grain.

asfen (..) اسفنا A *lrnd.* by unjust seizure.

asfer اصفر A *lrnd.* yellow, sorrel; sallow.

asfiksi F *path.* asphyxia.

asfiya (..—) اصفيا A *lrnd.*, *pl. of* **safi 2**. 1. sincere friends. 2. saints.

asfur 1 اصفر |*usfur*| *same as* **aspur**.

asfur 2 (.—) عصفر *var. of* **usfur**.

asgar اصغر A *lrnd.* smallest, littlest.

asgarî (..—) اصغري |*based on* **asgar**| minimum, least.

ashab, ashap[bı] (.—) اصحاب A 1. *Isl. hist.* companions and disciples of the Prophet. 2. *lrnd.* companions, fellows, associates. 3. *lrnd.* possessors, masters; possessors (of), men (of). —ı **aba** the Prophet and his family. —ı **âmâl** covetous, ambitious people. —ı **A'raf** *Isl. theol.* the spirits who tenant battlements between Heaven and Hell. —ı **câh** men of rank. —ı **Cahîm** inhabitants of Hell, the damned. —ı **cennet** the people of Paradise, the blessed. —ı **devlet** 1. people of wealth. 2. dignitaries. —ı **emlâk** landowners. —ı **feraiz** *can. law* close relatives who are entitled to a share in the inheritance. —ı **hayr** philanthropists, benefactors. —ı **itibar** people of reputation, the well-esteemed. —ı **kalem** civil functionaries. A—ı **Kehf** *myth.* the Seven Sleepers. —ı **kiram** *Isl. hist.* the companions and disciples of the Prophet. —ı **matlûb** *law* the body of creditors (of a bankrupt). —ı **menâsıb** holders of high offices. —ı **mesâlih** people who come on official business (to a public office). —ı **namus** people jealous of their honor. —ı **nâr** the damned (demons and condemned souls). —ı **rivayet** narrators of legends, stories, etc. —ı **salib** *hist.* the crusaders. —ı **servet** the wealthy. —ı **süyuf** men of the sword. —ı **şimal** *rel.* the damned. —ı **tahric** theologians who educe canonical decrees from the Quran and Hadith. —ı **tedbir** wise planners, thoughtful administrators. —ı **temyiz** theologians who are able to distinguish between traditions of strong and of weak foundation. —ı **tercih** theologians who have the authority to select the best variant of a tradition. —ı **tevarih** annalists, historians. —ı **yemin** *rel.* the blessed.

ashar (.—) اصحار A *lrnd.*, *pl. of* **sıhr**.

ası 1 عصي *var. of* **assı**.

=**ası 2**, =**esi**, *after vowels* =**yası**, =**yesi** سى-سي *archaic future participle, still used in expressions:* 1. *in curses, as:* **kör olası adam** the cursed man, may he go blind. 2. *with possessive and* **gel=**, *for the conceiving of a wish. as* **sizi göresim geldi** I long to see you; I miss you very much.

ası 3 عاصي *prov. for* **âsi 1**.

asıcı اسيجي that hangs, that suspends, suspensory.

âsif (—.) عاصف A *lrnd.* blowing, boisterous, tempestuous.

âsife (—..) عاصفة A *lrnd.* 1. *fem. of* **âsıf**. 2. storm, gale.

asıhha (..—,...) اصحا A *lrnd.*, *pl. of* **sahih**.

asık[ğı] اسيق hanging. — **çehre**, — **surat** sulky face. — **yüzlü** sulky, surly.

asıl[sh] **1** اصل [asl] 1. origin; original; originally. 2. original (from which a copy is made). 3. essence (of a thing), essential, real, true; fundamental, essentially. 4. family stock, radical stock. 5. capital stock. 6. *lrnd.* base, basis. 7. *lrnd.* root. **—ında** originally; essentially. **—ı astarı yok** It is quite unfounded, it is not true. **—ına bakılırsa** the truth of the matter (is). **—ı çavşir** opopanax root (a dye). **—ı esası yok**, **—ı faslı yok** It iş quite unfounded. **—ını inkâr eden haramzade** *proverb* He who rejects his origin is a bastard. **—ı meyyit** *law* the male forebears of the deceased. **—ı nesli belirsiz** whose origin is not known, of obscure background. **— sayılar** *gram.* cardinal numbers. **—ı vakf** *law* integral property of a religious foundation. **—ı var** It is substantially true; it is founded on fact. **—ı yok** It is not true. **—ı yok astarı yok**, **—ı yok faslı yok**, **—ı yok nesli yok** It is void of all truth, entirely unfounded.

asıl=[ır] **2** اصطیلی /a/ 1. *pass. of* **as= 3**. /a/ 2. *refl. of* **as= 3**, to hang. 3. to pull one's full weight. 4. to stretch out, lean over. 5. to hang on, to cling (to), to insist. **—acak**, **—ası** gallows bird. **—acak, suya boğulmaz** *proverb* A gallows bird will not get drowned.

asılı 1 اصلی آصیلو آصیلی hanging, suspended. **— vadi** *phys. geog.* hanging valley.

asılı 2 اصیلو *var. of* **assılı**.

asılık[gi] عاصیلی *prov. for* **âsilik**.

asılış آصیلیش, **asılma** *verbal n. of* **asıl= 2**.

asılsız اصلسز unfounded; insubstantial, trifling.

asılzade (.. — .) اصلزاده P |aslzade| nobleman, aristocrat, peer. **—lik** nobility, peerage.

âsım (—.) عاصم A *lrnd.* 1. chaste, virtuous. 2. defender, protector. 3. defended, protected. 4. *w. cap.*, man's name.

âsime (—..) عاصمه A 1. *lrnd.* well defended. 2. *w. cap.* Medina. 3. capital town, metropolis. **=asın**, **=esin**, *after vowels* **=yasın**, **=yesin**, *pl.* **=sınız** *etc. second person of optative, e. g.*, **Sana ev verdim ki oturasın** I gave you a house so that you might live in it.

asıntı آصنتی 1. a delaying. 2. *colloq.* unpaid debt. **—da bırak=** /ı/ to delay, to leave in the air.

asır[srı] **1** عصر [asr 1] 1. century. 2. age, time, period, era. **—ı hazır** the present century. **—ı saadet** the era of the Prophet.

asır[srı] **2** عصر [asr 2] *Isl. rel.* the time of the midafternoon service of worship. **—ı evvel** hour of worship in the early afternoon. **—ı sani** hour of worship in the midafternoon.

asırdide (.. — .) عصر دیده |P asrdide| *lrnd.* age-old.

âsıre (—..) آصره A *lrnd.* 1. tent rope, tether. 2. tie, relationship; grace, favor.

âsi 1 (— —) عاصی A 1. rebellious, refractory; rebel. 2. sinner. 3. *lrnd.* obstinately bleeding (vein). **— hurma** gingerbread tree, *bot.*, *Hyphaene thebaica*. **— hurma zamkı** gum bdellium.

Asi 2 (— —) عاصی A *geog.* Orontes (river).

asî 3 (. —) عصّی A *lrnd.* very rebellious.

asî 4 (. —) عصی A *lrnd.* fit, suitable, worthy.

âsi 5 (— —) آسی A *lrnd.* physician, doctor, surgeon.

âsi 6 (— —) آسی A *lrnd.* grieved, mourning, sorrowful.

asi 7 (— —) آثی A *lrnd.* corrupt, perverse, wicked.

asib 1 (— —) آسیب P *lrnd.* 1. collision. 2. misfortune, accident.

asîb 2 (. —) عصیب A *lrnd.* oppressively hot (day).

asid F *same as* **asit**.

aside آسیده عصیده |A. — .| dish made of ground meat, okra, and flour.

asidoz آسیدوز F *path.* acidosia.

âsif 1 (. —) آسف A *lrnd.* sorry, regretful.

asîf 2 (. —) عسیف A *lrnd.* laborer, hired workman.

asil 1 (. —) اصیل A 1. noble, aristocratic. 2. definitively appointed, permanent (official); performing the duties of an office by right and not as a substitute. 3. *law* principal (as distinguished from an agent). 4. *lrnd.* rooted, firm. 5. *lrnd.* sound (of judgment), intelligent. **— azmaz** *proverb* Once a noble always a noble.

asil 2 (. —) اصیل A *lrnd.* 1. late afternoon, evening. 2. death, destruction.

âsil 3 (— .) عاسل A *lrnd.* 1. who collects honey; honeybee. 2. that contains honey. 3. wolf. 4. quivering (spear).

asilâne (. — — .) اصیلانه F nobly; noble (act).

asilbent[di] اصلبنت عسلبنت |aseli lübna| *pharm.* 1. gum benzoin. 2. storax.

asile (. —) A *lrnd.* 1. late afternoon. 2. death, destruction. 3. the whole (of a thing).

âsilik[gi] (— — .) عاصیلك |âsi 1| 1. rebelliousness; rebellion. 2. sinfulness.

asilzade (. — — .) اصیلزاده *var. of* **asılzade**.

âsim .(—.) آثم A *lrnd.* offender, criminal, sinner.

âsime (— — .) آسیمه , (— ..) آسیمه P *poet.* confused, bewildered, stupefied, giddy.

âsimegi (— — . —) آسیمگی P, **âsimelik**[gi] (— ...)

âsimesar *poet.* confusion, bewilderment, giddiness.
âsimesar (— —.—) آسِيمَسار, âsimeser (— —..) آسِيمَسر P *poet.* confused, bewildered.
asimptot F *geom.* asymptote.
âsin (—.) آسِن A *lrnd.* stinking, fetid.
asîr 1 (.—) عَسِير A *lrnd.* 1. difficult, hard, arduous; distressing.
asîr 2 (.—) عَثِير A *lrnd.* stumbling, falling.
asîr 3 عَسِر A *lrnd.* 1. hard, fast, tight. 2. difficult; distressing.
asîr 4 (.—) عَصِير A *lrnd.* pressed, squeezed, expressed; juice.
âsir 5 (—.) آسِر A *lrnd.* one who relates; recorder (of traditions).
asîre (.—.) عَسِيره A *lrnd.* expressed juice or oil.
asis (.—) عَسِيس A *lrnd., pl. of* as 6.
asistan آسِستان F assistant (of a professor). —lık assistantship.
asit[di] آسِت |asid| *chem.* acid.
asitan 1 (—.—) آسِتانِه P *lrnd.* 1. threshold. 2. royal court. 3. a lying supine. —ı refi mekân *Ott. hist.* the court of the Sultan (to which petitions were addressed).
asitan 2 (—.—) آسِتانات P *lrnd.* horoscope.
asitane (—.—.) آسِتانه P *lrnd.* 1. threshold. 2. *w. cap., Ott. hist.* Istanbul. 3. main dervish convent. A— kaymakamı *Ott. hist.* substitute for an absent grand vizier. A—i Saadet, A—i Saadetaşiyane *Ott. hist.* the Sultan's court; Istanbul. —li *obs.* native of Istanbul.
asitborik[gi] آسِتبوریك F *chem.* boric asid.
asitfenik[gi] آسِتفنك F *chem.* carbolic acid.
|*for* /asiya/ *cf.* /asya/|
asiye (— —.) آسِيه A *bot.* Myrtaceae.
ask[kı] آسك F *bot.* ascus.
askarid آسكاريد F *zool.* ascarid, Ascaris.
askat *neol., math.* submultiple.
asker عَسكَر A 1. soldier; soldiers, army. 2. *obs.* mass of people, multitude. 3. *slang* money. —e al= /ı/ to enlist, to recruit. —e çağır= /ı/ to call up to military service. — çantası soldier's knapsack. — çek= *obs.* to lead an army (somewhere). —e davet call to enlistment. —e git= *same as* — ol=. — kaçağı deserter. — ol= to join the army, to be called up to military service. — tayını soldier's ration. — topla= to raise an army. — yaz= /ı/ to enroll, enlist (in the army). —ce soldierly, befitting a soldier, military (act).
askergâh (..—) عَسكَرگاه P *lrnd.* military camp.
askerî (..—) عَسكَری A military, pertaining to the army. — adlî hâkim president or member of court-martial. — bando military band. — ceza hukuku military penal law. — fesat *law* mutiny. — harekât military operations. — heyet military mission. — hizmet military service. — karakol military guard. — mahkeme military court, court-martial. — mıntaka military zone. — mükellefiyet compulsory military service, the obligation of military service. — suç *law* military offense. — temyiz mahkemesi supreme military court.
askerice (..—'.) عَسكَرجه from a military standpoint.
askerileş=[ir] عَسكَرلشمك to become militarized. —tir= /ı/ *caus.*
askeriye (..—.) عَسكَريّه A the armed forces.
askerlik[gi] عَسكَرلك 1. soldiership. 2. military service. —ten ihraç dishonorable discharge. — mükellefiyeti *same as* askerî mükellefiyet. — şubesi recruiting office. —ten tecrit demilitarization.
askı آسقی 1. anything by which another thing is suspended, hanger; suspenders, braces; clothes hanger; coat rack; *med.* sling; silkworm's cocoon; *arch.* kingpost. 2. anything suspended, hangings, pendant; bunch of fruit hung up to ripen; hanging bowl for flowers; pendant of a necklace, etc.; *arch.* ornament suspended from a vault; *hist.* prize hung on the wall of a coffee house where a contest of bards took place. 3. suspension; a posting of bills, etc.; banns; display of presents hung up, *esp.,* of a trousseau. —ya al= /ı/ 1. to prop up temporarily (building, for repairs). 2. *naut.* to hang on board (disabled ship, for moving her). —da bırak= /ı/ to leave in the air, in doubt, to shelve (a matter). —ya çık= 1. to start spinning cocoons (silkworm). 2. to be posted (banns, etc.). —da kal= to remain in suspense. — üzümü grapes conserved by hanging them up in bunches.
askıcı آسقیجی 1. dealer in suspenders or coat hangers. 2. man who arranges decorative hangings in bridal chambers. 3. dealer in lockets, amulets, charms, etc. 4. *colloq.* person who hangs back and delays in payment of debts, slow in paying back.
askılı آسقیلی having a suspender or hanger. — yatak hammock.
asl اَصل A *same as* asıl 1. — ü fer root and branch.
aslâ 1 (.'—) اَصلا |aslan 2| never, by no means. — ve kat'a never, never!
aslâ[a] 2 اَصلع A *lrnd.* bald; bare.
aslâb (.—) اَصلاب A *lrnd., pl. of* sulb 1.
aslah 1 اَصلح A *lrnd.* most correct, best, very fine.

aslahallah (...—) اصلح الله A *lrnd.* may God amend.

aslan 1 آصلان اصلان 1. lion, *zool.*, *Felis leo*. 2. brave man. 3. *Ott. hist.*, title used for a Sultan by his mother. **— ağzı** 1. stone faucet in the shape of a lion's head. 2. snapdragon, *bot.* Antirrhinom. **— ağzında ol=** to be in the lion's mouth (said when something is very difficult to obtain). **— gibi** like a lion, strongly built (person). **— kuyruğu** common motherwort, *bot.*, *Leonurus cardiaca*. **— ölüsünden tilkinin dirisi yeğdir** *proverb* Better to be a living fox than a dead lion. **— payı** the lion's share. **— pençesi** lion's foot, lady's mantle, *bot.*, *Alchemilla*. **— postunda yakışır** *proverb* (*lit.* It befits a lion to sit still on his skin.) A person should keep his dignity. **— sütü** raki. **— sütü emmiş** fed on lion's milk (said of a hero). **— yürekli** lion-hearted.

aslan 2 (´.) اصلا A originally; fundamentally, essentially, basically.

aslancı اسلانجى lion keeper.

aslangiller *zool.* Felidae.

aslanhane (..—.) اسلانخانه lion house (in a zoo, etc.).

aslanlan=" اسلانلانمق to become a very lion of bravery.

aslanlı آسلانلو *hist.* designation of coins showing the figure of a lion.

aslen (´.) اصلا *cf.* **aslan 2**.

aslıkᵍ¹ اصلى impervious (female).

aslî (.—) اصلى A fundamental, essential, principal, radical, original. **— aded** *gram.* cardinal number. **— âza** true member (of a society, etc.). **— ceza** *law* principal punishment. **— cihetler** *geog.* the cardinal points. **— cümle** *gram.* main clause. **— dâva** *law* principal claim; principal action. **— haklar** *law* fundamental rights. **— maaş** *Maliye* term basic salary (of which the actually paid salary is a multiple). **— nüsha** original text. **— sayı sıfatı** *gram.* cardinal number.

asliye (.—.) اصليه A *in* **— mahkemesi** court of first instance.

aslül'asaf اصل الأصف A *pharm.* caper plant root.

asmᵐ¹ **1** عَصْم A *lrnd.* a setting crookedly (broken bone); a broken bone's joining unevenly.

asm 2 عصم A *lrnd.* 1. a binding (the head of a waterskin). 2. protection, safeguards. 3. an earning a livelihood.

asma 1 آصمه vine, grape-vine, *esp.*, on a trellis. **— çubuğu** vine stem, shoot of a vine. **— kabağı** a very long edible variety of gourd. **— kütüğü** vinestock. **— yaprağı** vine leaf.

asma 2 آصمه a suspending, hanging; suspended, pendulous. **— kandillik** large metal hoop suspended from the ceiling, to which lamps are attached (*esp.*, in mosques). **— karar** *Or. mus.* melodic dominant. **— kat** mezzanine. **— kilit** padlock. **— köprü** 1. suspension bridge. 2. drawbridge. **— oda** elevated alcove. **— pusula** *naut.* telltale compass, hanging compass. **— saat** wall clock.

asmagiller *neol.*, *bot.* Vitaccae.

asmalıkᵍ¹ آصمه لق 1. place planted with vines. 2. vine suitable for climbing on a trellis.

asman (— —) آسمان P *lrnd.* heaven, the heavens, sky. **—ı berin** the highest heaven. **— u risman** What a reply! (used when an impertinent or evasive answer is given to a sensible question). **—cunî** (— — — —) P 1. sapphire, hyacinth. 2. sky-blue azure. **—dere** (— —..) P *poet.* the Milky Way, galaxy. **—e** (— —.) P *poet.* ceiling; roof. **—gûn** (— — —) P *poet.* sky blue. **—gûni** (— — — —) P *poet.* sky blueness, azure. **—i** (— — —) P same as **asümani**. **—izeban** (— — —.—) P *poet.* angel-tongued. **—paye** (— — —.) P exalted as the heavens. **—peyvend** (— —..) P reaching to the sky.

asmar (— —) آسمار P *lrnd.* myrtle, *bot.*, *Myrtus communis*.

asmet اصمت A *lrnd.* silent, speechless, tongue-tied.

Asmuğ (— —) آسموغ P Zoroastrianism, name of a demon supposed to sow dissension.

asnam (.—) اصنام A *lrnd.*, *pl.* of **sanem**.

aso (´.) آسو It cards ace.

aspiratör اسپيراتور F vacuum cleaner.

aspur اصپور |**asfur 1**| 1. safflower, bastard saffron, *bot.*, *Carthamus tinctorius*. 2. red dye extracted from safflower.

asr 1 عصر A *cf.* **asır 1**.

asr 2 عصر A *cf.* **asır 2**.

asr 3 عصر A *lrnd.* a pressing, squeezing, wringing.

asr 4 عصر A *lrnd.* a forcing, dunning (a debtor).

asr 5 عصر A *lrnd.* watered only by rain (field).

asr 6 عصر A *lrnd.* a slipping, stumble, fall.

Asr 7 عصر A *myth.*, name of a tribe and country of demons.

asra 1 اصره obs. yonder.

asra=ʳ **2** اصرا /ı/ obs. to protect, take care of, guard.

asran (.—) عصران A *Isl. rel.* the two times of afternoon service of worship.

asrane (.—.) عصرانه P *Isl. rel.* the afternoon service of worship.

asre عثره A *lrnd.* slip, lapse, fall, stumble; mistake, sin.

asrem اصرم A *lrnd.* 1. poor man

encumbered by a numerous family. 2. maimed in the ear.
asret=[der] عصراىتݘك |asr 3| /ı/ to press, squeeze; to express, to wring out.
asri 1 (.—) عصرى |based on asr 1| 1. modern; up to date. 2. continuing for ages. **—leş=** to become modernized. **—leştir=** /ı/ to modernize. **—lik** modernness, modernism, fashionableness.
asrî 2 (.—) عصرى |based on asr 2| Isl. rel. pertaining to the afternoon service of worship.
assal[i] (.—) عتّال A lrnd. collector or vendor of honey.
assale (.—.) عتّالە A lrnd. 1. honeybees. 2. beehive.
assar (.—) عتّار A lrnd. 1. oil presser. 2. presser of grapes.
assas (.—) عسّاس A lrnd. 1. nightwatch. 2. wolf.
assı آصى archaic profit, benefit. **— et=** to be of use. **—ya ver=** /ı/ to lend on interest. **—lan=** /dan/ to profit (from). **—landır=** /ı/ caus. of **assılan=**. **—lı** profitable, advantageous. **—sız** useless.
assubay neol., mil. noncommissioned officer.
astan (——) آستان P var. of **asitan 1**.
astane (——.) آستانە P var. of **asitane**.
astar 1 آستار |P .—| 1. tailor. lining. 2. priming, undercoat (paint). 3. Ott. hist. brown cloth wrapped around the headgear of certain officers. 4. prov. ceiling. **— kapla=**, **— koy=** /a/ to line (coat, etc.). **— vur=** /a/ to apply an undercoat (of paint). **—ı yüzünden pahalı** The accessories cost more than the thing itself.
astar 2 Romany, in **— et=** /ı/ slang to have sexual intercourse (with).
astarla=[r] آستارلا- ا ستارلەمق /ı/ 1. to line (coat, etc.). 2. to apply an undercoat (of paint). **—n=** pass. **—t=** caus. of **astarla=**.
astarlı آستارلى 1. tailor. lined. 2. having an undercoat (paint).
astarlık[ɪ] آستارلق 1. material for lining. 2. paint used as undercoating.
astasım neol., phil. episyllogism.
asteğmen neol., mil. second lieutenant.
asteni آستنى F path. asthenia.
aster (—.) آستر P lrnd., var. of **astar 1**.
astım آستم F path. asthma. **—lı** asthmatic.
astır=[r] آستدرمك /a,ı/ caus. of **as= 3**[1, 2].
âsti (——) آستى P poet. sleeve.
astigmatizm آستغماتيزم F path. astigmatism.
âstin (——) آستين , (—.) P poet. sleeve.
astine (——.) آستينە P poet. egg.
astinefşan, astinfeşan (———.) آستين فشان آستينفشان

P poet. who refuses, shrugging off.
astma آستما Gk path. asthma.
astragan آستراغان F astrakhan.
astrofizik[i] آسترو فيزيك F sc. astrophysics.
astronom آسترونوم F sc. astronomer.
astronomi آسترونومى F sc. astronomy.
astronomik[i] آسترونوميك F sc. astronomical.
astronot F sc. astronaut.
astropika (.'...) neol., geog. subtropics.
astropikal[i] (.'...) neol., geog. subtropical.
asub (.—) اصوب A lrnd. 1. queen bee. 2. prince, chief, lord.
asude (——.) آسوده P quiet, tranquil, at rest. **—dil** (——..) P poet. tranquil at heart, free from care. **—gi** (——.—) P lrnd. repose, quietness, rest. **—hal** (——.—) P poet. tranquil, rested. **—hatır** (——.—.) P poet. tranquil in mind. **—lik** (——..) quiet, repose, rest.
asuf 1 (.—) عروف A lrnd. 1. violent, unjust. 2. one who loses his way.
asuf 2 (.—) عصوف A lrnd. 1. very violent (wind). 2. swift (camel).
asuğde (—..) آسغده P lrnd. 1. ready, prepared. 2. half-burned, charred (wood).
asum 1 (.—) عروم A lrnd. working diligently for his living.
asum 2 (.—) عصوم A lrnd. voracious, greedy.
asuman (—.—) آسمان |asman| same as **asüman**.
asumani (—.——) آسمانى |asmani| same as **asümani**.
Asur 1 (——) آثور Assyria.
asur 2 (——) عاثر A lrnd. pitfall, pit for catching wild beasts.
asur 3 (.—) عثر A lrnd. apt to trip, wont to stumble.
Asuri (——) آثورى Assyrian.
asus (.—) عسوس A lrnd. 1. that prowls by night in quest of prey. 2. not shy of approaching men (woman).
âsüd (—.) آسى A lrnd., pl. of **esed**.
asüfte (—..) آسفتە P poet. firebrand, quenched brand.
âsüman (—.—) آسمان |asman| poet. the heavens, sky. **—î** (—.——) P 1. celestial, heavenly. 2. sky-colored, azure. 3. angel.
asvaf (.—) اصواف A lrnd., pl. of **suf**.
Asvan (.—) اسوان Aswan. **— taşı** min. syenite.
asvat (.—) اصوات A 1. lrnd., pl. of **savt**. 2. reputations.
asve اثوه A lrnd. long lock of hair.
asveb اصوب A lrnd., superl. of **musib, saib 1**.
asvef اصوف A lrnd. woolly.

asy عَصْی A *lrnd.* rebelliousness; rebellion.
Asya 1 (.'.) آسْیا It Asia. **—yı vusta** Central Asia.
asya 2 (— —) آسْیا , **asyab** (— —) آسْیاب P *lrnd.* mill.
asyaban (— — —) آسْیابان P *lrnd.* miller.
asyaf (. —) اصْیاف A *lrnd., pl. of* **sayf**.
Asyai (— — —) آسْیائی |*based on* **Asya 1**| Asiatic style.
Asyalı آسْیالی Asiatic (person).
asyazene (— — . .) اسْیازنه P *lrnd.* pick for sharpening millstones.
asyun (— —) آسْیون P *poet.* bewildered, confused, giddy.
aş 1 آش cooked food; pilaf; soup. **— damı** *prov.* kitchen. **— deliye kaldı** (*lit.* The food is left to the fool.) The person who does not get involved in an argument profits. **— er=***. **— evi** 1. small restaurant. 2. *prov.* kitchen. **—ın koyusunda, işin kıyısında** eager for food, but laggardly for work. **— olsun!** Bon appêtit! (said to children). **— otu** *prov.* herbs used in making soup. **— pişti bayram geçti** (*lit.* The food has been cooked; the feast is over.) The festivities are over, back to normal. **— pişti, kaşık üstüne dikildi** (*lit.* The food is cooked; the spoon is planted on top of it.) All is ready. **— taşınca kepçeye paha olmaz** *proverb* When the food has boiled over, the ladle is worthless. **—ta tuzu bulun=** (*lit.,* to have a pinch of salt in the food) to make a contribution, however small. **—ından yemedim, tütsüsünden kör oldum** (*lit.* I have not eaten his |its| food; I have been blinded by his |its| smoke.) I got nothing but trouble for my pains in connection with him (or it). **— yer=** *same as* **aşer=**.
aş=ᵃʳ **2** آشْمَق 1. /ı/ to pass (over), to go (beyond). 2. /ı/ to surpass, exceed. 3. /a/ to cover (stallion, etc.). 4. *slang* to disappear, slip away.
aşˢˢⁱ **3** عُش A *lrnd.* bird's nest.
aşa=ʳ **1** آشامَق /ı/ *prov.* to eat, to swallow.
aşâ 2 (. —) عَشا A *lrnd.* supper. **A—yı Rabbani** *Christ. rel.* the Lord's Supper, Eucharist.
aşâ 3 (. —) عَشا A *lrnd.* weakness of sight; night blindness.
a'şa 4 (. —) اَعْشی A *lrnd.* 1. purblind, weak-sighted. 2. night-blind.
a'şab (. —) اَعْشاب A *lrnd.* herbs, simples.
aşabet (. — .) عَشابَت A *lrnd.* grassiness, luxuriance of herbage.
aşağa اَشاغَه archaic for **aşağı**.
aşağı آشاغی 1. down, downwards; lower, inferior; mean, common; the lower part; downtown; the space below; the latter part. 2. *obs.* down (designating non-Ottoman Europe). **—da** below; downstairs **—dan** from below; less. **—ya** down, downwards. **— al=** /ı/ to pull down, bring down. **—dan al=** to sing small, to adopt a humble attitude. **— Almanca** Low German. **— at=** /ı/ not to pay any attention (to), to disregard. **— gör=** /ı/ to look down (upon), to despise. **— kal=** /dan/ to fall short (of). **— koysan pas olur, yukarı koysan is olur** *proverb* (*lit.* If you put it on a low place it becomes rusty; if you put it on a high place it becomes sooty.) One can't seem to do anything right. **— kurtarmaz** /dan/ Nothing less will do. **— mal** goods of inferior quality. **— omurgalılar** *zool.* inferior vertebrata. **— tabaka** mob, lower class. **— tut=** /ı/ to look down (upon), to despise. **— tükürsem sakalım, yukarı tükürsem bıyığım** If I spit downwards there is my beard, if I spit upwards there is my mustache. **— var=** *obs.* to add up. **— yukarı** approximately, more or less; to and fro, up and down. **bir — bir yukarı** to and fro, up and down (*cf.* **beş aşağı beş yukarı**). **... aşağı ... yukarı** *in expressions like* **Hasan aşağı Hasan yukarı** It's «Hasan» all the time; nothing but «Hasan». **—ca** somewhat low. **—ki** the lower one; the one below; the undermentioned, the following. **—la=** 1. to come down, deteriorate, to become cheap. 2. /ı/ to lower; to degrade, to treat as inferior. **—n=** *pass., refl.* **—t=** /ı/ *caus. of* **aşağıla=**. **—lı yukarılı** having an upper and a lower part; downstairs and upstairs. **—lık** baseness, meanness, vulgarity; mean, ordinary, vulgar, banal.
aşair (. — .) عَشائر A *lrnd., pl. of* **aşiret**.
aşakᵍⁱ **1** اَشَك *obs.* low; humble.
aşakᵏᵏⁱ **2** اَشَق A *lrnd., superl. of* **şak 3**.
aşakᵏⁱ **3** عَشَك A *lrnd., pl. of* **aşaka**.
aşaka عَشَكه A *lrnd.* a twining plant, ivy.
aşam 1 (— —) آشام P *lrnd.* food; drink.
-aşam 2 (— —) آشام P *lrnd.* drinking, *as in* **hunaşam**.
aşama *neol., mil.* rank.
aşamideni (— — — . —) آشامیدنی P *lrnd.* something drinkable.
âşar (. —) اَعْشار A *lrnd.* 1. *pl. of* **öşür**. 2. *pl. of* **aşir 1**.
aşarat (. . —) عَشَرات *var. of* **aşerat**.
âşarî (. — —) عَشاریة A decimal.
a'şaş (. —) اَعْشاش A *lrnd., pl. of* **aş 3**.
aşaşet (. — .) عَشاشَت A *lrnd.* leanness.
aşat=ᵗʳ آشاتْمَق /a,ı/ *prov., caus. of* **aşa= 1**.
aşavet (. — .) عَشاوَت A *lrnd.* night-blindness; weakness of sight.
aşaya (. — —) عَشایا A *lrnd., pl. of* **aşî 1, aşiye**.
aşçı آشْچی cook. **—başı** 1. head cook, chef.

2. *Ott. hist.* captain of the Janissaries.

aşebe عَشَبه A *lrnd.* 1. old and shriveled. 2. short and lean.

aşebî (..--) عَشَبِى |based on Arabic| *bot.* herbaceous. **—ye** (..—.) herbaceous plants.

aşer=ᵉʳ آش يَرمَلك to have capricious desires, *esp.* concerning food (pregnant woman).

aşerat (..—) عَشَرات A *math.* the tens (the numbers occupying the next place to the left of the units).

aşere عَشَره A *lrnd.* 1. ten. 2. *math.* a ten (number to the left of the unit).

aşeş عَشَش A *lrnd.* leanness.

aşevîⁿⁱ 1 (.'..) آشْاُورى *cf.* **aş 1**.

aşevî 2 (..—) عَشرى A *lrnd.* pertaining to the evening.

aşhane (.—.) آشْخانَه P 1. kitchen. 2. cookshop.

aşı آشى آشُو 1. *med.* vaccination, inoculation. 2. *hort.* a grafting, budding; scion, graft, bud (put into the stock). 3. *hort.* artificial pollination. **— boyası***. **— çeliği** *hort.* grafting shoot. **— iğnesi** *med.* hypodermic needle. **— kâğıdı** certificate of vaccination. **— kalemi** *hort.* cutting used for grafting. **— memuru** vaccination officer. **— ol=** to be inoculated. **— şehadetnamesi** certificate of vaccination. **— taşı***. **— tuttu** 1. *med.* The vaccination has taken. 2. *hort.* The graft has taken. **— vur=**, **— yap=** /a/ 1. *hort.* to graft, bud. 2. *med.* to inoculate.

aşıboyasıⁿⁱ آشى بوياسى red ochre.

aşıcı آشىجى 1. vaccinator. 2. *hort.* grafter (of trees).

âşıkᵏ¹,ᵍ¹ 1 (—.) عاشِك A 1. lover; in love. 2. *myst.* enraptured; enraptured saint, dervish. 3. wandering minstrel, bard, troubadour. **— âlemi kör, dört yanını duvar sanır** *proverb* The enamored imagines all people blind and himself surrounded by walls. **—a Bağdat ırak değildir, —a Bağdat sorulmaz** For one who is in love even Baghdad is not too far to go. **—ın hali kalinden belli olur** *proverb* The lover's words betray his condition. **—lar kahvesi** coffee house frequented by wandering minstrels. **— ol=** /a/ to fall in love (with). **— olan karda gezer, izini belli etmez** *proverb* (*lit.* The enamored walks in the snow without leaving traces.) Love makes one very clever in hiding one's steps. **—a rüsvaylık kendi belâsıdır** *proverb* The lover's disgrace is of his own making. **—ı şeyda** *poet.* madly in love, desperate lover. **—a ya sabır ya sefer gerek** *proverb* The enamored must either suffer patiently or go away. **— yolunu şaşırmış embroidery** meander. **—ı zâr** *poet.* tearful lover.

aşıkᵍ¹ 2 آشِك آشِيك knucklebones. **— at=** 1. to play at knucklebones. 2. /la/ to vie, compete (with). **—ı bey oturt=**, **—ı cuk oturt=**, **—ı çift oturt=** 1. to throw the knucklebones into winning position. 2. to strike it rich. **— çıkıntısı** *anat.* ankle, *malleolus*. **— kemiği** *anat.* anklebone, *astragalus, talus*. **— oyna=** to play at knucklebones.

aşıkᵍ¹ 3 آشِيك *arch.* purlin, horizontal beam.

aşık=ⁱʳ 4 آشِيقْمَق *archaic* to hurry.

âşıka (—..) عاشِقَه A woman in love.

âşıkane (—.—.) عاشِقانَه P amorously; amorous (act, condition).

âşıkdaş (—..) عاشِقْداش *var.* of **âşıktaş**.

âşıkî (—.—) عاشِقى P *poet.* the condition of a lover, love, passion.

âşıklı (—..) عاشِقْلى *colloq.* lover; in love.

âşıklıkᵍ¹ (—..) عاشِقْلِك *abstr. n.* of **âşık** 1.

âşıktaş (—..) عاشِقْداش sweetheart, whom one flirts with. **—lık** flirtation, amourette, love affair. **—lık et=** to flirt.

aşıktır=ⁱʳ آشِيقدرمَق /ı/ *archaic* to speed up, accelerate.

aşıl=ⁱʳ آشِلمَق *pass.* of **aş=** 2.

aşıla=ʳ آشِلامَق /ı/ 1. *med.* to inoculate, vaccinate. 2. *hort.* to graft, bud. 3. to refrigerate by putting into cold water or on ice. 4. to infect. 5. /a,ı/ inculcate, instill (ideas). **—ma** 1. *verbal n.* 2. *hort.* newly grafted tree. 3. cooled. **—n=** *pass.* of **aşıla=**. **—t=** /ı/ *caus.* of **aşıla=**. **—ttır=** /a,ı/ *caus.* of **aşılat=**.

aşılı آشِلى 1. inoculated, vaccinated. 2. grafted.

aşın=ⁱʳ آشِنمَق to wear away, to become worn away by friction, to be corroded, to be eroded. **—dır=** /ı/ *caus.* **—dıran** *chem.* corrosive. **—dırma** *geol.* erosion. **—ma** corrosion; *com.* wear and tear; *geol.* erosion. **—ma payı** *com.* amortization.

aşır=ⁱʳ 1 آشِرمَق آشِيرمَك /ı/ 1. /dan/ to pass (over a high place). 2. /dan/ to carry away secretly, to steal (from); to smuggle; to purloin, plagiarize. 3. /a/ to carry away hurriedly (to a place). 4. to get rid (of), to send away (disliked person). 5. to escape (an evil).

aşırˢʳ¹ 2 عُشْر *var.* of **aşir** 4.

aşıramento (...'..) آشِرامَنتو [based on **aşır=** 1] *joc.* a stealing.

aşırı آشِرى آشورى آشُرى 1. excessive, extreme; excessively, extremely. 2. over, beyond. 3. every other, *as in* **gün aşırı**. **— derecede** excessively. **— doyma** *sc.* supersaturation. **— duyu** *psych.* hyperesthesia. **— git=** to go beyond bounds, to overshoot the mark, to exceed the limit. **— sigorta** overinsurance.

— **uzay** *geom.* hyperspace.
aşırıl=ᵗʳ آشِرِلْمَٰ *pass. of* **aşır**= 1.
aşırılıkᵍ¹ آشِرِلِغِي *excess.*
aşırla=ʳ آشِرلَامَٰ /ı/ *prov.* sewing to overcast.
aşırma آشِرمَـ 1. *verbal n. of* **aşır**= 1. 2. passed over, conveyed over. 3. smuggled; stolen. 4. a belt put over another one for safety. 5. *arch.* purlin. 6. *Or. costume* the part of a woman's veil wrapped around the forehead. 7. *prov.* bucket.
aşırt=ᵗʳ آشِرتْـَ آشُرْتَ /ı/ *caus. of* **aşır**= 1. —ma *same as* **aşırma**.
aşısız آشِيسِز 1. unvaccinated. 2. ungrafted.
aşıtaşıⁿ¹ آشى طاشى *min.* crude ochre.
aşi 1 (. —) عَشِى A *lrnd.* evening from sunset to nightfall; afternoon from the middle of the sun's decline to nightfall.
âşi 2 (— —) عاشِى A *lrnd.* 1. pasturing in the evening; dining in the evening. 2. going (toward), approaching.
aşi 3 (. —) عَشِى A *lrnd.* weaksighted, purblind.
aşib 1 (— —) آشِيب P *lrnd.* terror, affliction; confusion.
âşbi 2 (. —) عاشِب A *lrnd.* 1. plentiful in herbage (land). 2. pasturing (beast).
aşib 3 عَشِب, **aşîb 4** (. —) عَشِيب A *lrnd.* rich in herbs, verdant.
aşifte آشفته |**aşüfte**| prostitute.
aşihe (— —.) آشِيهه P *lrnd.* neigh.
aşikᵏ¹ (. —) عَشِيى A *lrnd.* lover; very lovingly fond.
aşikâr (— . —) آشكار |**aşkâr 2**| manifest, evident, clear, open.
aşikâra (— . — —) آشكارا |**aşkâra**|,
aşikâre (— . — .) آشكاره |**aşkâre 1**| *same as* **aşikâr**.
aşikârlıkᵍ¹ (— . — .) آشكارلِق openness, publicity, manifestness.
Aşil آشِيل F *myth.* Achilles. — **kirişi** *anat.* Achilles tendon.
aşili F *path.* achylia.
aşina 1 (— . —) آشنا |**âşnâ 1**| 1. familiar, well-known. 2. acquaintance. 3. /a/ *lrnd.* knowing, acquainted (with). 4. the one you know (used when one does not want to mention the name).
-**aşina 2** (— . —) آشنا |**âşnâ 1**| *lrnd.* knowing, *as in* **lisanaşina**.
aşinalıkᵍ¹ (— . — .) آشنالِق 1. acquaintance, intimacy. 2. gesture of salutation. 3. *lrnd.* expertness. — **et**= /a/ 1. to greet by a gesture, to bow. 2. to offer friendly attentions.
aşinayi (— . — —) آشنايى |**aşnayi 1**| *lrnd.* acquaintance; friendship.
aşirˢʳ¹ **1** عَشر |**aşr**| portion of ten verses in the Quran.

âşir 2 (— .) عاشِر A 1. *lrnd.* tenth. 2. *hist.* collector of tithes, tither.
aşir 3 (. —) عَشِير A *lrnd.* 1. a tenth, tenth part. 2. one tenth of a **kafiz** (about 8 square yards).
aşir 4 (. —) عَشِير A *lrnd.* intimate friend, companion; spouse.
aşiran (. — —) عَشِيران 1. *Or. mus.* the note e'. 2. *obs.* a **makam** of Turkish music. — **maye** *Or. mus.* composite **makam** starting with the makam **maye** followed by **aşiran**. — **zemzeme** *Or. mus.* an old compound **makam**.
âşire (— . .) عاشِره A *lrnd.* 1. *fem. of* **âşir 2**. 2. every tenth verse of the Quran; a special mark indicating a subdivision of ten verses in the Quran. 3. any one of the ten primary pinions of a bird's wing.
âşiren (— ' . .) عاشِراً A tenthly.
aşiret (. — .) عَشِيرت A tribe; nomadic tribe.
aşiyan (— . —) آشيان |**aşyan**|, **aşiyane** (— . — .) آشيانه |**aşyane**| *lrnd.* 1. nest. 2. house, abode.
a'şiye 1 اعشِيه A *lrnd.*, *pl. of* **aşâ 3**.
aşiye 2 (. — .) عَشِيه A *lrnd.* the evening from sunset to nightfall.
aşkᵏ¹ عَشق |**ışk**| love, passion; *myst.* ecstatic love of God. — **ına** for the sake of, *as in* **Allah aşkına**. — **ınıza!** your health! (drinking one's health). — **ağlatır dert söyletir** *proverb* Love makes one cry; trouble makes one talk. — **ı cismani** sensual love, carnal love. — **ı domal**= *vulg.* to get excited. — **ı Eflâtunî** Platonic love. — **et**=, — **eyle**= 1. *archaic* to salute. 2. *same as* **aşket**=*. — **a gel**= to become exulted. — **ı ilâhî** divine love. — **ile** with great zeal. — **ı niyaz et**= *myst. orders* to salute (the sheikh, etc.). — **ola!** — **olsun!** 1. well done! bravo! 2. too bad of you! how awful! (used in reproach). — **olmayınca meşk olmaz** *proverb* Without love and enthusiasm no real mastership can be attained. — **ı ruhanî** spiritual love. — **la şevkle** whole-heartedly, with great zeal.
aşkar 1 عَشقر A *lrnd.* ruddy-skinned and reddish-haired; chestnut, sorrel.
aşkâr 2 (— —) آشكار P *lrnd.*, *same as* **aşikâr**.
aşkâra (— — —) آشكارا P *lrnd.*, *same as* **aşikâr**.
aşkâre 1 (— — .) آشكاره P *lrnd.*, *same as* **aşikâr**.
aşkâre 2 (— — .) آشكاره P *lrnd.* cook.
aşkbaz (. —) عَشقباز |**ışkbaz**| *lrnd.* feigning lover, gallant, coquette, flirt. — **î** (. — —) P, — **lık** gallantry, flirtation, coquetry.

aşkdaş عشقداش *same as* **âşıktaş**.

aşkefza (..—) عشق افزا P *Or. mus.* the şed on the Hüseyni-aşiran note E of the kürdî makam.

aşket=[der] عشق اتمك /a/ to land (a blow on the face).

aşkın عشقين 1. excessive; /dan/ exceeding, surpassing. 2. /ı/ having passed, over, beyond, *as in*, **yetmişi aşkın bir adam** a man over seventy. 3. *phil.* transcendent. — **sigorta** overinsurance. — **taşkın** overexcitable, overemotional.

aşkî (.—) عشقى [ışki] pertaining to love, amorous.

aşktaş عشقداش *same as* **âşıktaş**.

aşla=[r] آشلا T *var. of* **aşıla=**.

aşlık[ı] آشلق T *prov.* meant for cooking; provisions, foodstuffs; cereals.

âşnâ 1 (——) آشنا P *lrnd., same as* **aşina 1**.

âşnâ 2 (——) آشنا P *poet.* swimmer, swimming.

aşnab (——) آشناب P *poet.* swimmer.

aşna fişne آشنا فيشنه *colloq.* coquetry, flirting.

aşnager (——.) آشناگر P *poet.* swimmer.

aşnagerî (——.—) آشناگرى P *poet.* aquatic prowess; swimmer's art, swimming.

aşnav (——) آشناو P *var. of* **aşnab**.

aşnayi 1 (———) آشنايى P *same as* **aşinayi**.

aşnayi 2 (———) آشنايى P *poet.* aquatic prowess, swimmer's art, swimming.

aşnu آشنو *obs.* old, ancient.

aşoz آشوز T *Gk naut.* rabbet.

aşpez (—.) آشپز P *lrnd.* cook.

aşpezî (—.—) آشپزى P *lrnd.* cookery.

aşr[rı] عشر A *lrnd.* 1. ten. 2. decade, ten days. 3. *same as* **aşir 1**. **—i ahar** the last decade (of a lunar month). **—i evsat** the middle decade (of a lunar month). **—i evvel** the first decade (of a lunar month).

aşrhan (.—) عشرخوان P *lrnd.* 1. reciter of a portion of the Quran. 2. deposed from office.

aşşab (.—) عشاب A *lrnd.* collector and seller of medicinal herbs, herbalist.

aşşar (.—) عشار A *lrnd.* collector of tithes.

aştır=[ır] آشدرمق /ı/ to pair (beasts, in breeding).

aşti (——) آشتى P *lrnd.* peace, reconciliation, concord. **—bahşay** (——.—) P peace-giving. **—hure** (——..) P reconciliation feast. **—saz** (————) P pacificatory, pacifying, peacemaker. **—sazi** (—————) P *abstr. n.*

aşub 1 (——) آشوب P *lrnd.* confusion, tumult, disturbance.

-aşub 2 (——) آشوب P agitating, exciting, disturbing, *as in* **dilaşub, şehraşub**.

aşubengiz (——.—) آشوب انگيز P *poet.* producing tumult, inciter of discord.

aşubgâh (———) آشوبگاه P *poet.* place of confusion.

aşufte (——.) آشفته P *var. of* **aşüfte**.

aşuğ آشوغ T Arm |*from* **âşık 1**[1]| Armenian minstrel.

Aşura (———) عاشورا , عاشوراء (.——) عشرا عشورا A *Isl. rel.*, name of the tenth day of Muharrem.

aşure عشوره [Aşura] sweet dish made of cereals, sugar, raisins, etc. — **ayı** the month of Muharrem. — **günü** 10th of Muharrem.

aşuz *var. of* **aşoz**.

aşüfte (—..) آشفته P *poet.* beside one's self, agitated, excited, bewildered; violently in love. **—gi** (—..—) P, **—lik** agitation, excitement, bewilderment; passionate love.

aşv عشو A *lrnd.* 1. an eating supper; a putting out to pasture in the evening (beast). 2. a traveling by night.

aşvades آشوادس T *Gk zool.* cockle, shellfish, *Cardium edule.*

aşve عشوه A *lrnd.* the shades of evening, darkness.

aşy عشى A *lrnd.* a supping; a giving supper.

aşyan (——) آشيان P *lrnd.* 1. nest. 2. abode.

aşyane (——.) آشيانه P *lrnd.* 1. nest. 2. abode.

at 1 آت T 1. horse. 2. stallion. **—tan aktar=** /ı/ *archaic* to unhorse. **—ı alan Üsküdarı geçti** (*lit.* The one who has taken away the horse has long passed Üsküdar.) It is far too late. **— anası, —lar anası** mannish woman with large features. **— arıklıkta, yiğit gariplikte** *proverb* A horse's noble qualities come out when he is underfed, a man's when he is away from home. **— arkasına gel=** *archaic* to mount a horse. **—la arpayı bozuştur=, —la arpayı döğüştür=** (*lit.*, to cause barley and horse to fight) to sow discord among close friends. **—a arpa yiğide pilâv** *proverb* The horse wants his barley, the man his pilaf. To each his own. **— at olunca sahibi mat olur** *proverb* By the time a horse is broken in, the owner is worn out. **—a bakma dona bak, içindeki cana bak** *proverb* When you buy a horse do not look at his present condition, rather consider his color and his spirit. **— balığı** 1. hippopotamus. 2. sheatfish, *zool., Silurus glanis.* **— başı beraber** neck and neck; on the same level. **— beslenirken, kız istenirken** *proverb* The horse should be sold while being fattened, the maiden should be given away in marriage while she has suitors. **—a bin=** to mount a horse; to ride a horse. **—a binmeden ayaklarını salla=** (*lit.*, to dangle one's legs before mounting the horse) to count one's chickens before they are hatched. **— binenin, kılıç kuşananın** *proverb* The horse belongs to the one who mounts him, the sword to the one who girds himself with it. **—a binen nalını mıhını arar** *proverb* (*lit.* He who mounts a horse examines shoes and nails.) One must be prepared before one starts. **— binicisini bilir** *proverb* The horse knows his rider. **— boynuna düş=** *archaic* to lean forward over the neck of the horse (for speed). **—ını boz at yanına bağlama, ya huyun huylanır ya tüyün** *archaic proverb* Do not tie your horse near to a wild horse; he will pick up his habits. **— bulunur meydan bulunmaz, meydan bulunur at bulunmaz** *proverb* (*lit.* When there is a horse, there isn't a polo field; when there is a polo field, there is no horse.) There is always something lacking. Opportunities do not come when they are needed. **— cambazı** 1. horse dealer, horsemonger. 2. horse trainer, horsebreaker. 3. equestrian performer, show-rider. **— cambazhanesi** circus. **— cambazlığı** 1. a dealing in horses. 2. horse training, horse breaking. **— çalındıktan sonra ahırın kapısını kapat=** to shut the stable door after the horse has gone. **— çatlat=** to ride a horse to death. **— donu** 1. color of a horse. 2. *hist.* horse armor. **—a dost gibi bakmalı, düşman gibi binmelidir** *proverb* One should take care of a horse like a friend, but ride him like an enemy. **—tan düşene yorgan döşek, eşekten düşene kazma kürek** *proverb* He who falls from a horse needs a doctor; he who falls from a donkey is buried. **— elin, torba emanet, bizim dahdaha ne var?** Let us not worry about other people's business. **—a et ite ot yedir=** (*lit.*, to give meat to the horse, grass to the dog) to give the wrong thing to the wrong person. **— görünce aksar, su görünce susar** He starts limping at the sight of a horse; he gets thirsty at the sight of water (said of a person who wants whatever he sees). **— hırsızı gibi** like a horse thief (said of a person with the apperance of a ruffian). **— ile avratta uğur vardır** a horse and a wife can bring luck. **—tan inip eşeğe bin=** (*lit.*, to dismount from a horse and to mount a donkey) to suffer a come-down. **— kafalı** stupid. **—ta karın, yiğitte burun** *proverb* A big belly is a good feature in a horse, a big nose in a man. **— kasnısı** giant fennel, *bot.*, *Ferula communis*. **— kestanesi** horse chestnut, *bot.*, *Aesculus hippocastanum*. **— kılı** horse hair. **— koş=** /ı,a/ to harness (horse to carriage). **— koştur=** /a/ same as **at oynat=**. **— koşusu** horse race. **— kuyruğu** 1. horse's tail. 2. mare's tail, *bot.*, *Hippuris vulgaris*. 3. false horse-tail, *bot.*, *Equisetum arvense*. **— meydanı** hippodrome. **— nalı** horseshoe. **—a nal çakıldığını görmüş, kurbağa da ayağını uzatmış** *proverb* (*lit.* The toad saw the horse being shod and it also stretched out its foot.) To each his place. **— oğlanı** groom. **— oynat=** 1. to make a horse prance. 2. to show one's skill. **—ın ölümü arpadan olsun!** (*lit.* Let the horse's death be from barley.) It is not worth depriving oneself of something one likes, for fear of bad consequences. **— ölür itlere bayram olur** *proverb* When the horse dies the dogs feast. **— ölür meydan kalır, yiğit ölür şan kalır** *proverb* (*lit.* The horse dies, the polo field remains; the hero dies, his fame remains.) Fame only is permanent. **— pazarı** horse market.. **— sahibine göre eşer** *proverb* The horse's speed depends on his rider. **— sineği** forest fly, *zool.*, *Hippobosca equina*. **— solucanı** *zool.*, *Ascaris megalocephala*. **— sülüğü** horse-leech, *zool.*, *Haemopsis sangui sorba*. **— sür=** to urge on a horse. **— takımı** harness. **— tep=** *archaic* to rush the horse. **— teper katır teper ara yerde eşek ölür** *proverb* (*lit.* The horse kicks, the mule kicks, the donkey dies between the two.) When the mighty fight, the weak suffer. **—ın tepmezi, itin kapmazı olmaz** *proverb* There is no horse without a kick; there is no dog without a bite. **— uşağı** groom. **— yarışı** horse race. **— yiğidin yoldaşı** *proverb* The horse is the hero's companion. **—ın yürük ise bin de kaç!** (*lit.* If you have a fleet horse, mount and flee.) Take to your heels. **— yürümekle yol alır, kibar vermekle ün alır** *proverb* Fame grows from a good man's giving. **—ı zapteden gemdir** *proverb* It is the bit that controls the horse.

at=ᵃʳ 2 رَمْيٌ 1. /ı/ to cast, throw; to throw away; to throw out; to drop; to throw down; to put in, store (provisions); to throw off (clothes); to throw over (scarf); to eject, ejaculate. 2. /ı/ to fluff, shoot, fire, fire off, blow up. 3. /ı/ to throw with a carder's bow (cotton). 4. /ı/ *colloq.* to empty (glass). 5. /ı,a/ to postpone (to another time), to leave (for another time). 6. to splinter, break, crack. 7. to go off, explode, blow up. 8. to beat, pulsate (heart, artery). 9. *colloq.* to boast, swagger; to tell yarns, to tell exaggerated stories, to lie. 10. to fade. **—ma din kardeşiyiz, — martini Debreli Hasan!** **—ma Recep!** *slang* come, come, don't swagger. **—ıp savur=** *colloq.* to swagger. **—tığı taşı yerine vardır=** to hit the target, to accomplish what one has begun. **—tığı tırnak bile olma=** /ın/ (*lit.*, not to be worth even a nail clipping) to be very inferior (to someone). **—ıp tut=** to rant, declaim; to boast, swagger, brag. **—tığını vur=** always to hit the mark, to succeed in every enterprise. **—tığını vurur, tuttuğunu koparır** He always gets what he wants.

-at 3 (—) ات , *after vowels* **-vat** (—) وات A |*pl. of* **—a 5, —at 5, —e, —et**| 1. *plural, as in* **haşarat, gelişat**. 2. *name of sciences, as in* **hayvanat, nebatat** |**ilm-i hayvanat, ilm-i nebatat**|. 3. *concrete result of an action, as in* **icraat, tatbikat.**

at[d1] **4** آت *var. of* **ad 1.**

-at[ti] **5** *after non-emphatic consonants* ت —et A *var. of* **—a 5.**

at[tti] **6** عتّ A *lrnd.* 1. repetition. 2. reprimand, reproach.

at[ttı] **7** عتّ A *lrnd.* a slitting, tearing, rending.

ata 1 آتا 1. ancestor. 2. *archaic* father. 3. *w. cap., short for* **Atatürk**. **— ana** *archaic* father and mother. **—lara babam öldü demişler, iş başına düşmüş demiş, anam öldü demişler, öksüz olmuşsun demiş** *proverb* By his father's death a man is left with more responsibilities, but a mother's loss is irretrievable. **— bey*. — dostu oğula mirastır** *proverb* A father's friend is the best inheritance. **— sözü, —lar sözü** *proverb.*

ata=[r] **2** /ı/ *neol.* to appoint.

ata 3 (.—) عطاء A *lrnd.* 1. a giving, munificence; gift, donation, favor. 2. *w. cap., man's name.*

atab عطب A *lrnd.* a perishing, destruction, death.

atabey آتابك *Seljuk hist.* 1. a prince's tutor. 2. minister; commander; regent. **A—ler** the Atabeg dynasty.

atacılık[ğı] *neol., biol.* atavism.

atad (.—) عتاد A *lrnd.* 1. readiness, preparedness. 2. implements, apparatus, outfit. 3. large cup.

ataerki[ni] *neol., sociol.* patriarchy.

a'taf 1 (.—) اعطاف A *lrnd., pl. of* **atıf 2.**

a'taf 2 اعطف A *superl. of* **atuf.**

atah (.—) عتاه A *var. of* **atahet.**

atahe (.—.) عتاهه A *lrnd.* 1. foolish, stupid. 2. erring, sinning.

atahet (.—.) عتاهت A *lrnd.* imbecility, insanity.

atahiye (.— ..) عتاهيه A *lrnd., same as* **atahe.**

atahiyet (.— ..) عتاهيت A *lrnd.* imbecility, madness.

ataib (.—.) اطايب A *lrnd., pl. of* **atyeb.**

ataik[kı] (.— .) عنايين A *lrnd., pl. of* **atika.**

atair (.—.) عتاير A *lrnd., pl. of* **atire.**

atak[ğı] **1** آتاق 1. rash, audacious, reckless. 2. boastful.

atak[kı] **2** (.—) عتاق A *can. law* emancipation (of a slave), manumission.

atakat[ti] (.—.) عتاقت A *lrnd.* 1. emancipation, manumission. 2. a growing old, age.

ataklık[ğı] آتاقلق *abstr. n. of* **atak 1.**

ataksi F *path.* ataxia.

atakuş (.— —) عطاكوش P *lrnd.* beneficient.

atal[li] **1** عطل A *lrnd.* 1. uncovered part of the body. 2. neck. 3. body. 4. stature, figure, beauty of person.

atal[li] **2** عطل A *lrnd.* 1. lack of ornaments (woman). 2. want, deficiency, privation. 3. lack of occupation, idleness.

atalet (.—.) عطالت A idleness, inertia. **— kanunu** *phys.* principle of inertia.

atalık[ğı] آتالق 1. *abst. n. of* **ata 1**. 2. *archaic* guardian, tutor; elderly man.

ataman آتامان *hist.* ataman, hetman.

atan=[ır] آتانی *pass. of* **ata=** 2.

atanib (.— —) اطانيب A *lrnd., pl. of* **ıtnabe.**

atardamar *neol., anat.* artery.

ataş 1 *prov., var. of* **ateş 1.**

ataş 2 عطش A *same as* **ats.**

ataşa (.— —) عطاشى A *pl. of* **atşan.**

ataşe آتاشه F *dipl.* attaché.

Atatürk[kü] آتاتورك Kemal Atatürk, founder and first president of the Turkish Republic. **—çü** adherent of Atatürk and his doctrine. **—çülük** Atatürk's political doctrine.

atavik[ği] آتاويك F *biol.* atavistic.

atavil (.—.) اطاول A *lrnd., pl. of* **atvel.**

atavizm آتاويزم F *biol.* atavism.

ataya (.— —) عطايا A *lrnd., pl. of* **atiyye.**

atb[bi] عتب A *lrnd.* 1. anger, vexation. 2. reproach.

atba[aı] اطبع A *lrnd.* 1. most filthy. 2. most to one's taste.

atbak[kı] (.—) اطباق A *lrnd., pl. of* **tabak 1.**

atbal[li] (.—) اطبال A *lrnd., pl. of* **tabl.**

atban (.—) عتبان A *lrnd.* anger, vexation, reproach.

atbıka اطبقه A *lrnd., pl. of* **tabak 1.**

atçağız تجغز little horse.

ateb عتب A *lrnd., pl. of* **atebe.**

atebat (..—) عتبات A *lrnd.* 1. thresholds. 2. steps. 3. shrines.

atebatülmevt (..—..) عتبات الموت A *lrnd.* death throes.

atebe عتبه A *lrnd.* 1. threshold. 2. step,

ateşengiz

stair. 3. *mus.* fret (of a lute). 4. rugged slope. 5. hardship, difficult matter. **—i âliye, —i seniye, —i ulya** *Ott. hist.* the Imperial Threshold (capital or court of the Sultan).

ateh *A psych.* dotage, senility. **— getir=** to become senile, to reach one's second childhood. **—i kablelmiad** *dementia praecox,* senility.

atel 1 *F surg.* splint.

atel 2 *A lrnd., pl. of* **atele.**

atel 3 *A lrnd.* haste to do evil, evil propensity.

atele *A lrnd.* 1. crowbar, wrench, mattock. 2. stout Persian archery bow. 3. clod of earth.

atelye *F* 1. workshop. 2. studio.

ateme *A lrnd.* the first third of the night.

aterina (...'.) *Gk* sand smelt, *zool., Atherina presbyter.*

ateş 1 [**âteş 2**] 1. fire, heat; light for a cigarette. 2. *mil.* fire! 3. fever, temperature. 4. vivacity, vehemence, zeal, ardor, exuberance. **— aç=** /a/ *mil.* to open fire (on). **— al=** 1. to catch fire, to take fire. 2. to get furious. 3. to fall in love. **— alma=** to misfire, fail. **— almağa mı geldiniz?** Have you come to get fire? (said to a visitor who stays a very short time) Why so soon? **— ateşle söndürülmez** *proverb* One cannot put out fire with fire. **—e atıl=** to throw oneself into the fire, to risk one's life blindly. **— bacayı sardı** (*lit.* The fire has caught the chimney.) Things have got beyond control. **— balığı** sardine, *zool., Alosa sardina.* **—le barut bir yerde olmaz** *proverb* (*lit.* Fire and powder cannot stay together.) It is dangerous to leave young people together. **— bastı** /a/ I went hot all over. **— baskını** *mil.* fire attack. **— başı** fireside. **— böceği** firefly, glowworm. **— böceği görse yangın sanar** (*lit.* When he sees a firefly he thinks a fire has broken out.) He always makes the worst of things. **— çak=** to strike fire. **—e düş=** to fall into danger, to get hustled. **—i düştü** His temperature has gone down. **— düştüğü yeri yakar** *proverb* (*lit.* The fire burns the place where it falls.) A calamity only really affects its immediate victim. **— et=** /a/ to fire (on, gun). **— geçmez** fireproof. **— gemisi** *hist.* fire ship. **— gibi** 1. very hot. 2. very quick, active, agile, intelligent. **— gömleği** erysipelas; St. Anthony's fire. **—ten gömlek** a shirt of fire; ordeal. **—e göster=** /ı/ to heat slightly by holding to the fire. **— hattı** *mil.* firing line. **— kayığı** large rowing boat. **— kenarı kış gününün lâlezarıdır.** *proverb* The fireside is winter's tulip garden. **— kes** cease fire. **— kesil=** to blow one's top.

— kırmızısı fiery red. **—e körükle git=, —e kürekle git=** to throw oil on the fire. **—e mukavim** fireproof. **— olmıyan yerde duman çıkmaz** *proverb* No smoke without fire. **— olsa cirmi kadar yer yakar** (*lit.* If he were fire, he could not burn more than he reaches.) He cannot do much harm. **—le oyna=** to play with fire. **— pahasına** very expensive. **—le pamuğun oyunu olmaz** *proverb* (*lit.* Fire and cotton cannot play together) *same as* **Ateşle barut bir yerde olmaz.** **— püskür=, — püskürt=** /a/ to spit fire, to be very angry. **— saçağı sardı** (*lit.,* The fire has caught the eaves.) Things have gone beyond control. **— sahası** *mil.* firing zone. **—le su hatıra bakmaz** *proverb* Fire and water make no exceptions. **— tuğlası** fire brick. **—e tut=** /ı/ 1. to heat slightly by holding to the fire. 2. to subject to a volley of bullets. **— tutmıyan yer** artillery dead angle. **— tutuştur=** to light a fire, to kindle a fire. **—i uyandır=** to make a fire burn up. **— ver=** /a/ to set on fire, to burn. **—e ver=** /ı/ 1. to set on fire. 2. to play havoc (with). **—e vur=** /ı/ *archaic* to set on fire, to burn up. **— yak=** to light a fire. **—e yan=** to suffer a loss, to go through a great misfortune. **—ine yan=** /ın/ to suffer because of someone else.

ateş 2 (—.) *P poet.* 1. fire. 2. desire, appetite, love. 3. rage. 4. light, lustre, beauty. **—i aşk** love, passion. **—i dil** fire of the heart, passion. **—i farisî** erysipelas; pimple on the lip. **—i firkat** the pain of separation. **—i hasret** the pain of longing. **—i sevda** love, passion. **—bar** (—.—) *P poet.* raining fire, flaming. **—baz** (—.—) *P* 1. playing with fire. 2. pyrotechnist. 3. *Mevlevi order* cook. **—bazî** (—.——) *P* pyrotechnics; fireworks.

ateşçi *naut.* fireman, stoker. **—lik** work of a stoker.

ateşdan (—.—) *P lrnd.* 1. fireplace. 2. chafing dish.

ateşdem (—..) *P poet.* whose voice is heartrending.

ateşdide (—.—.) *P lrnd.* gone through fire, undergone suffering.

ateşdil (—..) *P poet.* passionate.

ateşefruz (—..—) *P lrnd.* 1. that lights a fire. 2. tinder; small firewood.

ateşefşan (—..—) *P poet.* scattering fire.

ateşek[kı] (—..) *P lrnd.* 1. small fire. 2. lightning. 3. firefly. 4. syphilis.

ateşengiz (—..—) *P* 1. *poet.* burning, inflaming. 2. *lrnd.* firebrand. 3. *lrnd.* incendiary, mischief-maker.

ateşfam (—.—) آتش فام P *poet.* fire-colored, red.
ateşfeşan (—..—) آتش فشان P *var. of* **ateşefşan**.
ateşgâh (—.—) آتشگاه P 1. fireplace. 2. fire temple.
ateşgede (—...) آتشگده P |**ateşkede**| *lrnd.* fire temple.
ateşgire (—.—.) آتشگیره P *lrnd.* 1. fire irons. 2. tinder.
ateşgûn (—.—) آتشگون P *poet.* fire-colored, red.
ateşhane (—.—.) آتشخانه P *lrnd.* 1. fire temple. 2. hearth.
ateşhar (—.—) آتش خوار P *lrnd.* 1. who receives bribes. 2. tyrant.
ateşhatır (—.—.) آتش خاطر P *lrnd.* 1. quick to fall in love, of fiery temperament. 2. having a quick mind.
ateşhıram (—..—) آتش خرام P *poet.* fiery-footed.
ateşhiz (—.—) آتش خیز P *poet.* burning, inflaming.
ateşî 1 (..—) آتشی fire-colored, red.
ateşî 2 (—.—) آتشی P *lrnd.* 1. pertaining to fire, fiery, like fire. 2. hellish, infernal; demon, devil; damned soul.
ateşin (—.—) آتشین P *lrnd.* fiery. —**mizac** (—.—.—) P of fiery temperament. —**zeban** (—.—.—) P who has a fiery tongue.
ateşistan (—..—) آتشستان P *poet.* region of fire.
ateşkede (—...) آتشکده P *same as* **ateşgede**.
ateşle=ʳ آتشلمك /ı/ to set fire (to), to ignite. —**me** *mech.* ignition. —**me odası** *mech.* combustion chamber. —**n=** 1.*pass. of* **ateşle=**. 2. to become enraged. 3. to become violent (quarrel, etc.). —**ndir=** *caus. of* **ateşlen=**.
ateşli آتشلی 1. fiery; vivacious, fervent. 2. having a fever; connected with fever. — **silâhlar** firearms.
ateşlikᵍⁱ آتشلك 1. firepan, small brazier. 2. place fit for lighting fire. 3. fit for burning; firewood. 4. fit for hell.
ateşnakᵏⁱ (—.—) آتشناك P *poet.* fiery.
ateşnihad (—..—) آتش نهاد P *poet.* of fiery temperament.
ateşpare (—.—.) آتش پاره P *poet.* 1. spark of fire, an ember. 2. bright, vivacious. 3. quarrelsome.
ateşpay (—.—) آتش پای P *poet.* quick; restless, mettlesome.
ateşperest (—...) آتش پرست P fire-worshipper; Zoroastrian. —**î** (—...—) P *lrnd.* —**lik** fire-worship.

ateşreng (—..) آتش رنگ P *poet.* fire-colored, red.
ateşriz (—.—) آتش ریز P *poet.* pouring fire, seditious.
ateşsuhan (—...) آتش سخن P *lrnd.* fiery-tongued, who uses inflammatory language.
ateştab 1 (—.—) آتشتاب P *poet.* 1. shining like fire; burning like fire. 2. who lights a fire.
ateştabᵇ¹ **2** (—..) آتش طبع P *lrnd.* of a fiery temperament.
ateşzar (—.—) آتش زار P *poet.* field of fire.
ateşzeban (—..—) آتش زبان P *same as* **ateşinzeban**.
ateşzede (—...) آتش زده P *lrnd.* fire-stricken.
ateşzen, ateşzene (—.., —...) آتش زنه P *lrnd.* flint-and-steel, tinderbox.
atet عنت A *lrnd.* coarse language, roughness of speech.
atf 1 عطف A *cf.* **atıf 2**.
atfᶠⁱ **2** عنف A *lrnd.* a plucking out.
atfalˡⁱ (.—) اطفال A *var. of* **etfal**.
atfan (.'.) عطفاً A *var. of* **atfen**.
atfe عطفه A *lrnd.* bead worn to secure love.
atfen (.'.) عطفاً A /a/ based on, referring to.
atfet=ᵈᵉʳ عطف ایتمك /a, ı/ 1. to attribute, ascribe, impute. 2. to direct, to turn, to incline favorably. 3. *gram.* to join conjunctively.
atfi (.—) عطفی A *gram.* conjunctive, copulative.
atgı آتغی *var. of* **atkı**.
atgiller *neol., zool., Equidae*.
athʰⁱ عته A *lrnd., var. of* **ateh**.
athalˡⁱ اطحل A *lrnd.* ash-colored.
athar (.—) اطهار A |*pl. of* **tahir 1**| *lrnd.* the pure.
ather اطهر A *lrnd.* most pure.
atıbba (..—) اطبّا , **atıbbe** اطبّه A *lrnd., same as* **etibba**.
atıcı آتیجی 1. throwing; *anat.* ejaculatory. 2. marksman, good shot. 3. braggart, swaggerer. 4. carder of cotton.
âtıf 1 (—.) عاطف A *lrnd.* 1. turned (toward), favorably inclined, kind. 2. *gram.* conjunctive, copulative. 3. *w. cap., man's name*.
atıfᶠⁱ **2** عطف A 1. reference (to another page, etc). 2. favorable inclination, favor. 3. *lrnd.* a turning and facing. 4. *lrnd.* a bending, folding, doubling. 5. *gram.* a joining by a conjunction; conjunction. 6. *econ.* imputation. —**ı beyan** *gram.* supposition. —**ı inan et=** *lrnd.* to turn the reins (towards), to turn in a new direction. — **ve isnad** *law* imputation.

—ı **nazar**, —ı **nigâh** glance, look. — **rabıtası** *gram.* coordinating conjunction. —ı **tefsir** *gram.* a hendiadys. —ı **zimam et⸗** same as **atfı inan et⸗**.

atıfet (—..) عاطفت A *lrnd.* 1. affection, sympathy, pity, benevolence, protection. 2. *w. cap.*, *woman's name*. —**kâr** (—..—) P kind, benevolent.

atık[ki] **1** آتیق *prov.* small churn.

âtık[ki] **2** (—.) عاتق A *law* emancipated, manumitted.

âtık[ki] **3** (—.) عاتق A *lrnd.* 1. fully-fledged (bird). 2. nubile (girl). 3. noble, fleet (horse). 4. old (wine, etc.).

âtık[ki] **4** (—.) عاتق A *anat.* 1. upper part of the back. 2. shoulder.

atıl⸗[ır] **1** آتیل 1. *pass.* of **at⸗** 2. 2. /a/ to cast oneself (upon), to precipitate oneself (upon). —**an ok geri dönmez** *proverb* (*lit.* A sped arrow never comes back.) What's done can't be undone.

âtıl 2 (—.) عاطل A 1. idle, vacant, inactive, inert. 2. *phys.* inert. 3. composed of undotted letters (distich in Arabic script). —**âne** (—.—.) P *lrnd.* lazily, idly.

atılgan آتیلغان dashing, bold, reckless, plucky. —**lık** audacity, boldness.

atılım *psych.* élan, dash.

atılış آتیلیش , **atılma** آتیلمه *verbal n.* of **atıl⸗** 1.

atım 1 آتیم *artillery* 1. discharge; round. 2. range (of gun). 3. charge of powder. —**lık** the quantity of powder for one charge. **bir —lık barudu kalmış** (*lit.* He has only one more charge of powder left.) He is at the end of his resources.

âtım 2 (—.) عاطم A *lrnd.* perishing, dying.

âtır 1 (—.) عاطر A *poet.* 1. sweet-smelling, fragrant, scented. 2. gracious, noble.

atır 2 عطر A *lrnd.* sweet-smelling, fragrant.

âtıs (—.) عاطس A *lrnd.* 1. sneezing. 2. dawn.

atış 1 آتیش *verbal n.* of **at⸗** 2. — **meydanı** *mil.* shooting field, range.

atış⸗[ır] **2** آتیشـ 1. /ı, la/ to throw at each other. 2. /la/ to abuse one another, quarrel. 3. /la/ to indulge in repartee. 4. /a/ to talk as if nothing had happened (quarrelling children).

âtış 3 (—.) عاطش A *lrnd.* thirsty.

atış 4 عطش A *lrnd.* thirst.

atıştır⸗[ır] آتیشدیرمق 1. /la,ı/ *caus* of **atış⸗** 2. 2. *colloq.* /ı/ to bolt (food), to gobble (food). 3. to begin to rain or snow slowly.

âti 1 (——) آتی A 1. future. 2. following (in writing).

âti 2 (——) عافی A *lrnd.* proudly disobedient and rebellious.

ati 3 (.—) عتی A *lrnd.* proud, overbearing.

atid (.—) عتید A *lrnd.* ready, prepared.

atide (.—.) عتیده A *lrnd.* scent-box.

atif (.—) عطیف A *lrnd.* gentle, mild, tractable (woman).

âtih (—.) عاته A *lrnd.* who takes a pleasure in molesting.

atik[ki] **1** آتیك agile, swift, alert.

atîk[ki] **2** (.—) عتیق A 1. *archaic* ancient, old. 2. *lrnd.* beautiful; noble, excellent. 3. *w. cap., surname of the Caliph Abu Bakr.*

atîk[ki] **3** (.—) عتیق A *can. law* freed, emancipated, manumitted (slave).

âtik[ki] **4** (—.) عاتك A *lrnd.* 1. bright, red, yellow. 2. limpid, clear; unmixed, pure. 3. excellent, valued, prized.

atika (.—.) عتیقه A *lrnd.* 1. freed, manumitted (female slave). 2. beautiful.

atikiyat (.———) عتیقیات [*based on* **atik 2**] archaeology.

atiklik[ği] *abstr. n.* of **atik 1**.

atîl (.—) عتیل A *lrnd.* hired laborer, servant.

âtim 1 (—.) عاتم A *lrnd.* dilatory; tardy, late.

atîm 2 (.—) عطیم A *lrnd.* perishing.

at'ime 1 اطعمه A *lrnd.* food; dishes.

atime 2 (.—.) اطیمه A *lrnd.* hearth, fireplace.

Atina (..'.) آتینه Gk Athens. —**lı** an Athenian.

atîr (.—) اطیر A *lrnd.* fault, offense, crime.

atire (.—.) عتیره A *hist.* victim sacrificed by the ancient pagan Arabs in the month of Rajab.

atît[u] (.—) اطیط A *lrnd.* creaking sound.

âtiyen (—'—.) آتیاً A *lrnd.* 1. in future. 2. later, below, later on (in writing).

atiyülbeyan (—...—) آتی البیان A *lrnd.* about to be explained.

atiyüzzikr (—...—) آتی الذکر A *lrnd.* about to be mentioned, mentioned below, following, undermentioned.

atiyye (.—.) عطیه A *lrnd.* gift from a superior to an inferior. *wakf law* honorary office. — **et⸗** /a,ı/ to give (to an inferior). —**i şahane** *Ott. hist.* bounty granted by the Sultan on accession, the birth of a prince, etc.

atk[ki] **1** عتك A 1. *can. law* emancipation, manumission (slave). 2. *lrnd.* a being or becoming old, age. 3. *lrnd.* a biting, seizing with the teeth.

atk[ki] **2** عتك A *lrnd.* 1. a cleaving;

atkestanesigiller

adherence; permanence. 2. a being or becoming dark red, or brown with age (bow).
atkestanesigiller *neol., bot.* Aesculaceae.
atkı اتقى 1. shawl, stole. 2. *textile* woof, weft. 3. *prov.* pitchfork. 4. slipper strap. 5. *arch.* breastsummer (of a door etc.). —la= /ı/ *textile* to weave in the woof.
atkuyruğugiller *neol., bot.,* Equisetaceae.
atlıⁱⁱ اتل A *lrnd.* a dragging along violently.
atla=ʳ آتلامق ا طلامق 1. to jump; /a/ to jump (on, upon, into); /dan/ to jump (from, out of), to leap (over, through). 2. /ı/ to jump (over); to skip, omit, pass over (in reading, etc.). 3. *journalism* to miss out on the news.
atlama آتلاما *verbal n. of* atla=.
— **taşı** stepping-stone.
atlambaçᶜⁱ آتلامباج leaping, jumping (children's game).
atlan=ⁱʳ 1 آتلانمق ا طلانمق *pass. of* atla=.
atlan=ⁱʳ 2 آتلانمق ا تلنمق *archaic* 1. to mount a horse. 2. to get a horse. 3. to become a horse. 4. to rear (horse). —dır= /ı/ *caus.*
atlangıçᶜⁱ آتلانغيج stepping-stone.
Atlantikᵏⁱ آطلانتيك F Atlantic.
atlas 1 اطلس A satin. — **dikişi** diamond pattern quilting. —**ı gerdun** *poet.* sky.
atlas 2 آطلس F atlas (maps).
Atlas 3 آطلس Atlas mountains. **a**— **çiçeği** crab cactus, *bot.,* Epiphyllum. — **Denizi** Atlantic Ocean.
atlas 4 آطلس L *anat.* atlas.
atlasçiçeğigiller *neol., bot.,* Cactaceae.
Atlasi (..—) اطلسى [*based on* Atlas 3] *archaic* Atlantic.
atlaslı آطلسلى lined with satin, covered with satin.
atlat=ⁱʳ آتلاتمق 1. /a,ı/ *caus. of* atla=. 2. /ı/ to have a narrow escape (from), overcome (illness, etc.). 3. /ı/ to get rid (of a person with empty promises), to put off. —ış, —ma *verbal n.*
atlayış آتلايش *verbal n. of* atla=.
atlaz *var. of* atlas 1.
atles 1 اطلس A *lrnd., var. of* atlas 1.
atles 2 اطلس A *lrnd.* old, worn, threadbare, worn smooth by wear.
atlesî (..—) اطلسى A *lrnd.* of satin.
atlet آتلت F 1. athlete. 2. sleeveless undershirt.
atletikᵍⁱ آتلتيك F athletic.
atletizm آتلتيزم F athletics.
atlı آتلى 1. horseman, rider; mounted, riding on horseback. 2. having a horse. — **araba** horse wagon, cart. — **ases** 1. *Ott. hist.* mounted guard. 2. *colloq.* busybody, very active and bold woman. — **karaca** *archaic for* **atlı karınca 1.** — **karınca** 1. merry-go-round. 2. large ant. — **tramvay** horse-drawn tram.
atliye طلى A *lrnd., pl. of* tıla 1.
atm 1 الطم A *lrnd.* stricture, narrowing.
atmᵐⁱ 2 عتن A *lrnd.* slowness, tardiness, lateness, laziness.
atma 1 آتمه 1. *verbal n. of* at= 2. 2. *arch.* crosspiece. 3. *rail.* sleeper.
atmâᵃⁱ 2 (.—) اطماع A *lrnd., pl. of* tama.
atmaca آتماجه hawk, *zool.,* Accipiter.
atmasyon آتماسيون [*based on* atma 1] *slang* lie, swagger, exaggeration. —**cu** liar, swaggerer.
atmık *neol., biol.* sperm.
atmosfer آتموسفر F *sc.* atmosphere. —**ik** atmospheric.
atolⁱⁱ F *geog.* atoll.
atom آتوم F *chem.* atom. — **bombası** atomic bomb. —**al** atomic. —**culuk** *phil.* atomism.
atölye آتولیه F *var. of* atelye.
atrʳⁱ عتر A *lrnd.* 1. sacrifice, slaughtering. 2. stiffness (spear). 3. vibration (spear).
atrab (.—) اطراب A *lrnd.* joys, rejoicings, festivities.
atraf (.—) اطراف A *var. of* etraf.
atrar (.—) اطرار A *lrnd., pl. of* turre.
atreş اطرش A *lrnd.* deaf; hard of hearing.
atrıka اطرق A *lrnd., pl. of* tarîk 1.
atrina (..'.) *var. of* aterina.
atrofi آتروفى F *path.* atrophy.
atrukᵏᵘ اطروك A *lrnd., pl. of* tarîk 1.
ats عطس A *lrnd.* 1. a sneezing. 2. daybreak.
atse عطسه A *lrnd.* sneeze. —**i anberin** a whiff of fragrance. —**i çah** an echo from a well. —**i keman** the twang of an archery bow. —**i subh**, —**i şeb** daybreak, dawn. —**i tiğ** the whir of a sword in striking.
atsız 1 آتسز horseless.
atsız 2 آدسز *var. of* adsız.
ats عطش A *lrnd.* 1. thirst, a being thirsty. 2. desire, longing. —**ı garam** thirst for love.
atşa (.—) عطشى A *lrnd.* 1. *fem. of* atşan. 2. *pl. of* atşan.
atşan (.—) عطشان A *lrnd.* 1. thirsty. 2. desirous.
attalⁱⁱ (.—) عتال A *lrnd.* porter.
attar 1 (.—) عطار A *lrnd.* 1. perfumer. 2. *same as* **aktar 2.**
attar 2 (.—) عتار A *lrnd.* 1. brave; spirited (horse). 2. rough, desolate (place).
attari (.——) عطارى P *lrnd.* the business of a perfumer or herbalist.

attariye (. — —.) عطارِيه |based on **attar 1**| same as **aktariye**.
attarlık[1] (. —.) عطارلوه lrnd., abstr. n. of **attar 1**.
attas (. —) عطّاس A lrnd. who sneezes habitually.
attır=[r] آتدِرمَم آتَدِرمِه آنَدِرمَس /a,ı/ caus. of **at= 2**.
atub (. —) عتوب A lrnd. obdurate, contumacious, impervious to reproof.
atuf (. —) عطوف A lrnd. 1. affectionate, kindly inclined. 2. snare, trap. 3. w. cap., man's name.
atufet (. —.) عطوفت A lrnd. kindness, favor. **—li, —lû** (. —. —) archaic kind, benevolently inclined (form of address used in letters to high dignitaries and also to friends).
atufi (. — —) عطوفى |based on **atuf**] lrnd. kind, benevolently inclined (in expressions of respect).
atuh (. —) عتوه A lrnd. imbecile, senile.
atun (— —) آتون P lrnd. governess, female teacher for girls.
atvad (. —) اطواد A lrnd., pl. of **tavd**.
atvak[ı] (. —) اطواك A lrnd., pl. of **tavk**.
atvar (. —) اطوار A var. of **etvar**.
atvas (. —) اطواس A lrnd., pl. of **taus, tavus**.
atvel اطول A lrnd. very long, longest, very tall, tallest.
atyab (. —) اطياب A lrnd., pl. of **tib**.
atyar (. —) اطيار A lrnd., pl. of **tayr**.
atyeb اطيب A lrnd., superl. of **tayyib**.
atyebeyn اطيبين A lrnd. the two most delicious things (variously defined as eating and sleeping, milk and dates, strength and appetite, etc.).
atyer اطير A lrnd., superl. of **tair**.
av 1 آو 1. hunt, hunting, chase. 2. game, prey; catch (fish); booty. **— ara=** 1. to look for game. 2. to look for something to lay hands on. **— avla=** to hunt. **—a bin=** archaic to mount a horse and go hunting. **— çantası** game-bag. **—a çık=** to go out hunting. **— çiftesi** double-barreled hunting gun. **— eti** game. **—a giden avlanır** proverb The hunter became the hunted. **— havası** 1. good hunting weather. 2. thieves' opportunity. **— hayvanı** game. **— hukuku** game laws. **— köpeği** hunting dog, hound. **— kuşu** 1. hawk used in fowling. 2. game bird. **— takımı** hunting equipment. **— tezkeresi** shooting license. **— tüfeği** shotgun. **— uçağı** fighter plane. **— yeri** hunting ground.
âv 2 (—) آو P var. of **âb 1**.
âva 1 (— —) آوا P lrnd., var. of **avaz 1**.
âva 2 (— —) آوا P lrnd. cooked food, soup, stew.

avacim (. —.) عواجم A lrnd. teeth.
avaciz (. —.) عواجز A lrnd., pl. of **âciz 1**.
a'vad 1 (. —) اعواد A lrnd., pl. of **ud 1**.
avadan آوادان prov. set of tools. **—cılar** Ott. hist. certain class of servants in the Sultan's palace.
avadanlık[1] **1** آوادانلق 1. an artificer's set of tools. 2. prov. a woman's jewelry. 3. carpentry fillet, molding. 4. slang, glans penis.
avadanlık[1] **2** (— — —.) آوادانلق P |avadan| archaic cultivated, inhabited place.
avadi (. — —) عوادى A lrnd. that run, assail or transgress, esp., evils that assail men.
avah (— —) آواخ P poet. oh! alas!
avaid (. —.) عوائد A 1. can. law fees, revenues. 2. lrnd. favors, gifts, kindnesses.
avaik[ı] (. —.) عوائك A lrnd., pl. of **aika**.
avakıb (. —.) عواقب A lrnd. 1. ends, conclusions. 2. consequences. **—ı hasene** a good end (of life).
avakır (. —.) عواقر A lrnd., pl. of **âkır, âkıre**.
aval 1 آوال Kurd slang fool, simpleton. **— aval bak=** to stare stupidly.
aval[li] **2** F com. endorsement of bill of exchange by third party.
avali (. — —) عوالى A lrnd., pl. of **âliye 1**.
avalim (. —.) عوالم A [pl. of **âlem 1**.] lrnd. worlds.
a'vam 1 (. —) اعوام A [pl. of **âm 3**] lrnd. years.
avam 2 (. —) عوام [A **avamm**] 1. the common people, populace, the vulgar. 2. rabble, mob. 3. the commons. **A— Kamarası** the House of Commons. **— takımı** the rabble. **—ca** vulgar (expression, act).
avamfirib (. —. —) عوام فريب P lrnd. demagogue. **—ane** (. — . — —.) P demagogically; demagogical (act).
avamil 1 (. —.) عوامل A 1. lrnd. factors, motives. 2. Arabic gram. governing words.
avamil 2 (. —.) عوامل A lrnd., pl. of **amile**.
avampesend (. —..) عوام پسند P lrnd. admired by the vulgar, of low taste. **—ane** (. —..—.) P according to vulgar taste; vulgar (act).
a'van 1 (. —) اعوان A lrnd., pl. of **avn 2**.
avan 2 (. —) عوان P 1. prov. bully, brute. 2. archaic policeman; executioner.
avan 3 (. —) عوان A lrnd. 1. middle-aged woman, matron. 2. middle-aged female beast (mare, cow).
avanak[ı] آواناك Arm gullible, simpleton. **—lık** gullibility.

avanan (. — —) عوانات P *lrnd.*, *pl. of* **avan 2**. —ı **felek** the seven planets (as arbiters of fate).

avanid (. — .) عوانِد A *lrnd.*, *pl. of* **ânid 1.**

avanis (. — .) عوانِس A *lrnd.*, *pl. of* **ânis 2.**

avans آوانس F *com.*, *mech.* advance. — **al**= /ı/ to have an advance; /ı/ to have in advance. — **ver**= /a,ı/ to advance (money).

avanta (. . . .) آوانتا *colloq.* illicit profit; anything got without payment. —**cı** one who makes illicit gains, parasite.

avantüriye F adventurer.

avar 1 *prov.* vegetable.

Avar 2 آوار *hist.* Avar.

avar 3 (— —) آوار P *lrnd.* account, bill.

avar 4 (. —) عوار A *lrnd.* defect, blemish, fault.

avara 1 (. . .) آوارا Gk *naut.* shove off! — **et**= /ı/ to shove off.

avara 2 آوارا [**avare 1**] 1. *mech.* loose, free-running. 2. *prov.* useless, fruitless. — **kasnak** loose pulley. — **kolu** switch lever.

avarce, avarçe (— — . —) آوارجه P *lrnd.* cashbook; diary, journal, register.

avare (— — .) آواره P 1. idle, out of work. 2. exiled, vacant, wandering; roaming wildly about (eyes), wild (looks). — **dolaş**= to drift about. — **et**= /ı/ to keep from working. — **ol**= to be idle.

avaregi (— — . —) آوارگی P *lrnd.* 1. exile, vagrancy, wandering. 2. ruin, desolation, wretchedness.

avarelik[si] (— — . .) آوارهلك *abstr. n. of* **avare.**

avareser (— — . .) آوارهسر P *lrnd.* unfettered, unrestricted.

avarız 1 (. — .) عوارض A levy, extraordinary tax. — **akçası** extraordinary local levy. —**i divaniye** *Ott. hist.* extraordinary taxes. — **vakfı** pious foundation out of whose accrued income extraordinary taxes and other expenses of a village or community were paid.

avarız 2 (. — .) عوارض A *lrnd.* 1. defects; obstacles. 2. *phil.* accidents. 3. *geog.* relief. —ı **cismaniye** bodily infirmities. —ı **müktesebe** *law* acquired defects or hindrances (such as drunkenness, dissipation). —ı **semaviye** *law* inherent defects or hindrances (such as insanity, death). —ı **zemin** *geog.* relief.

avarız 3 (. — .) عوارض A *lrnd.*, *pl. of* **ârız 3.**

avarızcı (. — . .) عوارضجى collector of extraordinary taxes.

avari (. — —) عوارى A *lrnd.*, *pl. of* **ariyet.**

avarif (. — .) عوارف A *lrnd.*, *pl. of* **ârife 2.**

Avarin آوارين A *hist.* Navarino (now Pylos).

avarya (. . .) آواريه It *maritime law* average.

a'vas 1 الاعوص A *lrnd.* 1. unintelligible, abstruse (verse). 2. terrible, uncouth. 3. difficult, hard, intricate.

avas 2 عوص A *lrnd.* hardness, difficulty.

avasıf (. — .) عواصف A *lrnd.*, *pl. of* **âsıfe.**

avasım (. — .) عواصم A 1. *lrnd.*, *pl. of* **âsıme.** 2. *hist.* the towns and castles of Northern Syria and Cilicia (being the defenses of Aleppo against the Byzantines and the Crusaders).

avasi (. — —) عواصى A *lrnd.*, *pl. of* **âsi 1.**

avasir (. — —) عواثير A *lrnd.*, *pl. of* **asur 2.**

avaşir 1 (. — .) عواشر A *lrnd.*, *pl. of* **âşire.**

Avaşir 2 (. — —) عواشير A *pl. of* **Aşura.**

avatıf 1 (. — .) عواطف A *lrnd.* kindnesses, favors.

avatık[kı] (. — .) عواتق A *lrnd.*, *pl. of* **âtık 2, 3, 4.**

avatıl (. — .) عواطل A· *lrnd.*, *pl. of* **âtıl 2.**

av'ava, av'ave عوعوه A *lrnd.* 1. bark, barking. 2. vociferous abuse.

avaz 1 (— —) آواز P 1. cry, shout, clamor. 2. *lrnd.* voice, sound, noise. 3. *lrnd.* tone, note. 4. *lrnd.* echo. 5. *lrnd.* report, rumor; fame.

avaz 2 آواز [**avaz 1**] *only in* — **avaz bağır**= to shout loudly, to yell. — **çek**= *archaic* to sing. —ı **çıktığı kadar** at the top of his voice. **bir** —ı **yerde, bir avazı gökte** *colloq.* crying greatly with pain.

a'vaz 3 (. — .) الاعواض A *lrnd.*, *pl. of* **ivaz.**

avaz 4 (. —) عواز A *lrnd.* dislike, aversion.

avaze (— — .) آوازه P *var. of* **avaz 1.**

avazil (. — .) عوازل A *lrnd.*, *pl. of* **âzil 2.**

avazir (. — —) عوازير A *lrnd.*, *pl. of* **azur 3.**

avazlı (— — .) آوازلو آوازلى 1. having a voice or tone. 2. loud-voiced, bellowing. —**ca** rather loud.

avca (. —) عوجا A *lrnd.*, *fem. of* **a'vec 1.**

avcar *prov.* materials (for cooking); utensils.

avcı آوجى 1. hunter, huntsman. 2. *mil.* skirmisher, light infantry soldier, rifleman. — **avında, yolcu yolunda gerek** *proverb* (*lit.* The hunter should go about his hunt, the traveller should get on his way.) One should be about one's business. — **başı** Ott. hist. 1. chief hunter of the court. 2. an officer of the Janissaries. — **bölüğü** light infantry company. — **çantası** game bag. — **çukuru** mil. rifle pit. — **hattı** mil. line of skirmishers. — **hendeği** mil. fire trench. — **kedi** a good mouser. — **köpeği gibi yeler unmaz** Like a hound, he always runs and never gets fat. — **kuş** bird of prey. — **mangası** mil. skirmishing platoon. — **ne kadar hile bilse, ayı o kadar yol bilir** proverb The hunter may know many tricks, but the bear knows as many paths. — **otu** bot. Adonis. **A— Sultan Mehmet** Ott. hist. Sultan Mohammad IV. — **uçağı** fighter plane. — **zağarı** 1. hunting dog, hound. 2. sycophant, toady, hanger-on.

avcılıkᵍⁱ آوجیلِس huntsmanship, hunting, shooting. — **et=** to hunt.

avdᵈⁱ عود A lrnd. 1. return. 2. visit (to the sick). 3. repetition. 4. a swerving.

avdaz archaic var. of **abdest**.

avdet 1 عودت A return. — **et=** to return.

avdet=ᵈᵉʳ **2** عودت ایتمك lrnd. 1. to return. 2. to pay a visit. 3. to repeat. 4. to swerve.

Avdetî (..—) عودتی [based on **avdet**] lrnd. Dönme, Dunmeh.

avdetname (..—.) عودت نامه P dipl. letter of recall.

a'vec 1 اَعوج A lrnd. 1. crooked, curved, bent, awry. 2. cross, perverse.

avec 2 عوج A lrnd., abstr. n. of **a'vec 1**.

a'ved اعود A lrnd. more profitable, most beneficial.

avel slang, var. of **aval 1**.

aven 1 F geog. sink, pothole.

âven 2 (—.) آون A lrnd. very calm, most tranquil.

avend (—.) آوند P lrnd. 1. vessels, pots and pans. 2. proof, trial.

avene عونه [based on **avn 2**] helpers, accomplices, gang.

aveng (—.) آونگ P lrnd. 1. clothes-line; line on which bunches of grapes are hung up to dry. 2. things hanging on a line.

avengân (—.—) آونگان P lrnd. suspended on a line, pendulous.

a'ver 1 اعور A lrnd. 1. blind in one eye; squint-eyed. 2. anat., coecum, blind gut. 3. crooked, bad, disagreeable, abominable. 4. useless, inexperienced, incompetent. 5. obliterated, effaced. 6. ill-equipped, lacking in necessities; without water (desert). 7. motherless. 8. unlucky, unsuccessful.

-aver 2 (—.) آور P lrnd. that brings, that causes, that possesses, as in **cengâver**, **dilâver**.

aver 3 عور A lrnd. blindness of one eye.

a'ver 4 اعور A lrnd. nit, louse-egg.

averce, averçe (—..) آورجه P var. of **avarce, avarçe**.

averd 1 (—.) آورد P poet. battle, fight.

averde (—..) آورده P lrnd. 1. brought. 2. related, narrated.

averdenî (—..—) آوردنی P lrnd. suitable for a present.

averdgâh (—.—) آوردگاه P poet. battlefield.

averdgeh (—..) آوردگ P var. of **averdgâh**.

avez 1 عوذ A lrnd. 1. refuge. 2. dislike.

avez 2 عوز A lrnd. poverty, want.

avfᶠⁱ عوف A lrnd. a hovering and circling round a thing (bird).

avgın آوغین P prov. subterranean water-channel, covered conduit.

âvi 1 (——) آوی A lrnd. who comes, goes, gets to a place, takes to an abode.

âvi 2 (——) عاوی A lrnd. barking, yelping, howling.

avihte (——.) آویخته P lrnd. suspended, hanging. **—gî** (——.—) P suspension.

avîl (.—) عویل A lrnd. wail, cry, lament.

âvine (—..) آونه A lrnd., pl. of **evan**, times; moments; seasons.

âvineten (—'...) آونةً A lrnd. repeatedly, occasionally.

avir عور A lrnd. morally corrupt.

avis (.—) عویص A lrnd. hard to understand, difficult.

avitaminoz F path. avitaminosis.

aviye (.—.) عویه A lrnd. a howling, barking, howl.

aviz 1 (——) آویز P lrnd. 1. pendant. 2. a place or thing on which anything hangs.

-aviz 2 (——) آویز P lrnd. that suspends, adheres, as in **dilâviz, sahtaviz**.

avize 1 (——.) آویزه P 1. chandelier. 2. pendant to an earring; earring; pendant. **— ağacı** bot. Yucca. **—i gûş** poet. earring.

avize 2 (——.) آویزه P lrnd. tenacious adherent, parasite, flatterer.

avizgin (——.) آویزگن P lrnd. importunately clinging person or thing.

aviziş (——.) آویزش P lrnd. act of clinging, adhering, holding suspended.

avizo F navy dispatch boat.

avkᵏⁱ عوق A lrnd. delay, impediment, hindering. **— u te'hir et=** /ı/ to hinder and delay.

avka=ʳ آوقاماسی, **avkı=**ʳ آوقنمان prov. /ı/ 1. to crush, crumble with the hand. 2. to rub (laundry). **—la=** /ı/ to crumble; to rumple. **—t=** /a, ı/ caus. of **avkala=**.

avkın var. of **avgın**.

avlⁱⁱ **1** عول A lrnd. 1. a supporting a family. 2. a having a large family to maintain.

3. a becoming poor, poverty. 4. *can. law* an inheritance's being insufficient to furnish the canonical shares. 5. unevenness of a balance. 6. a swerving.

avl[li] 2 عول A *lrnd.* 1. cry, lament. 2. cause of anxiety. 3. troublesomeness, vexatiousness (of a matter). 4. one to whom one has recourse in trouble.

avla 1 *var. of* **avlağı**.

avla=[r] 2 آولامق /ı/ 1. to hunt, shoot. 2. to deceive, dupe.

avlağı *prov.* hedge, fence of brushwood.

avlak[ğı] آولاق hunting ground; place where game abounds.

avlan=[ır] آولانمق 1. *pass. of* **avla=** 2. 2. to go hunting. **—ıl=** 1. *same as* **avlan=**[1]. 2. *pass. of* **avlan=**[2]. **—ış** verbal n. of **avlan=**.

avlat=[ır] آولاتمق /a, ı/ *caus. of* **avla=** 2.

avle عول A *lrnd.* cry, lament.

avlı *var. of* **avlu**.

avlî (.—) عولى A *can. law* concerning an inheritance in which the canonical shares exceed the total.

avlu عولو آولو آولى Gk court, courtyard.

avm[mi] عوم A *lrnd.* a swimming.

avn[ni] 1 عون A *lrnd.* help, aid, assistance. **—i ilâhî** divine aid.

avn[ni] 2 عون A *lrnd.* 1. assistant, servant. 2. guard, armed attendant; executioner.

avni (.—) عونى A 1. pertaining to divine aid. 2. w. cap., *man's name; pen-name of Sultan Mehmed II, the Conqueror*.

avniye (.—.) عونيّة [based on **avnî**] *Ott. hist.* kind of hooded, long-sleeved raincoat.

avra 1 (.'.) L *path.* aura.

avra 2 (.—) عورا A *fem. of* **a'ver** 1.

avrad *cf.* **avrat**.

avrana *var. of* **arvana**.

avrat[dı] 1 عورات آورات [avret] *prov.* 1. woman. 2. wife. **— al=** to take a wife. **—ı âr zapteder, er zaptetmez** *proverb* It is the sense of decency that restrains a woman, not the fear of her husband. **—la atı emanet verme!** *proverb* Do not entrust your wife or your horse to anybody. **— boşa=** to divorce, repudiate a wife. **— malı başa tokmaktır** *proverb* (*lit.* A wife's dowry is a blow on the head.) A woman makes her dowry a cause of constant reproach to her husband. **— pazarı** *hist.* female slave market.

avrat 2 (.—) عورات A *lrnd., pl. of* **avret**.

avret عورت A 1. privy parts. 2. parts of the body that, by religious law, have to be covered. 3. *lrnd.* time of the day when people usually undress. 4. *lrnd.* anything usually kept concealed from public view. 5. woman; wife. 6. *lrnd.* weak part in a regiment fortress, or frontier. **— yerleri** privy parts, pudendum. **—çe** womanly, womanish (act, etc.).

avrı=[r] آوريمق *archaic* 1. to curve, bend, warp, curl up. 2. to be bent, curved, curled. **—k** curved, bent, curled, warned. **—klık** *abstr. n.* **—l=** *same as* **avrı=**. **—lı** *same as* **avrık**.

âvriz (——) آوريز P *var. of* **âbriz**.

Avrupa (..'.) آوروپا اوروپا Gk Europe. **—î** European style.

Avrupalı آوروپالى European. **—laş=** to become Europeanized. **—laştır=** /ı/ to Europeanize.

avruz آوروز [âvriz] chamber pot.

Avs عوص A 1. *man's name*. 2. *hist., name of an Arabian tribe*.

avsec, avsece عوسجه A *bot.* boxthorn, *Lycium halimifolium*.

Avşer *var. of* **Afşer**.

avuç[cu] آووج آوج 1. the hollow of the hand (palm and fingers); the full grasp of the hand. 2. handful. **— aç=** to beg, to go begging. **— avuç** by the handful, lavishly. **— dolusu** handful; plenty. **—u gidişiyor** His palm is itching (taken as an omen that the person will receive money). **— ısır=** to bite the palm of the hand (in emotion). **— içinde** at one's command. **—unun içine al=** /ı/ to take into one's possession, to take complete command (of). **—unun içi gibi bil=** /ı/ to know thoroughly. **— içi kadar** very small, narrow (place). **—u kaşınıyor** *same as* **avucu gidişiyor**. **—umu koklamadım ki** How was I to know? **— unu** the miller's share of flour. **—unu yala=** (*lit.,* to lick one's palm) not to be able to get anything.

avuçla=[r] آووجلامق آووچلامق /ı/ 1. to grasp. 2. to take by handfuls; to measure by handfuls. **—t=** /a,ı/ *caus.*

avuçlu آووچلو that has a palm.

avukat آووقات It 1. lawyer, solicitor, advocate, barrister. 2. fluent talker, loquacious; able to convince and defend. **—lık** advocacy, barristership.

avun=[ur] آوونمق 1. to have the attention distracted. 2. /la/ to let oneself be put off; to be consoled. 3. *prov.* to conceive (cow, etc.). **—dur=** 1. /ı,la/ to console. 2. *prov., caus. of* **avun=**[3].

avurt[du] آوورت آوورد آوورد 1. hollow inside the cheek. 2. the movable part of the cheek. 3. *colloq.* threatening way of speaking, boastfulness, airs. **—u avurduna çökmüş** with sunken cheeks. **— dağıt=** to go about shouting at people, threatening. **— et=, — kes=** to give oneself airs, to talk threateningly and braggingly. — **öttür=** *archaic* to chatter. — **sat=** *same as* **avurt et=**. — **şişir=** 1. to puff out the cheeks. 2. to be conceited. — **ur=** *archaic* to chat. — **u yelli** *prov.* talkative, boasting. — **u yırtık** *obs.* garrulous. — **zavurt et=** *same as* **avurt et=**. — **la=** *colloq.* to talk braggingly, to boast. — **laş=** /la/ *archaic* to talk (with). — **lu** puffed up, conceited, bombastic.

Avustralya (...'.) آوستراليه اوستراليا آوسترالیا It Australia. — **lı** an Australian.

Avusturya (...'.) آوستريا آوستريه It Austria. — **lı** an Austrian.

avut=ᵘʳ آوتُن آوتُن /ı/ 1. to distract, divert. 2. to put off with promises, to delude. 3. to amuse and quieten (infant). — **ma** *verbal n.* — **tur=** /a,ı/ *caus. of* **avut=**. — **ul=** *pass. of* **avut=**.

avuz=, =**evuz**, *after vowel* =**yavuz**, — **yevüz**, *archaic, same as* =**alım 2**, *etc.*

avva (. —) عَوّاء A *lrnd.* 1. that barks much (dog). 2. *astr.* Boötes. 3. *astrol.* the 13th lunar mansion.

avvac (. —) عَوّاج A *lrnd.* dealer or worker in ivory.

avvad (. —) عَوّاد A *lrnd.* lutist.

avvam (. —) عَوّام A *lrnd.* 1. a good swimmer. 2. swift (horse).

avye عَوْيَه A *lrnd., var. of* **aviye**.

avzᶻⁱ **1** عَوْذ A *lrnd.* a taking refuge, seeking protection.

avz 2 عَوْض A *lrnd., var. of* **ivaz**.

ay 1 آی 1. moon. 2. month. 3. crescent. 4. *poet.* beautiful face. — **ağılı** halo of the moon. — **da âlemde bir** very rarely, once in a long while. — **dan aya** monthly, once in a month. — **aydın**, — **aydını** moonlight. — **aydın hesap belli** absolutely clear, as clear as daylight. — **baklavası** crescent-shaped pastry. — **balta** *hist.* crescent-shaped battle-axe. — **bastı** /ı/ The moon has struck him (said of a lunatic having a fit). — **başı** the first of the month. — **başı***. — **çiçeği***. — **dede** *child language* the moon. — **dedeye misafir ol=** *joc.* to sleep in the open. — **demir** cooper's adze. — **doğdu** 1. new moon, 2. *w. cap.,* man's name. — **a doğ veya doğayım de=** to say to the moon: Rise or I shall rise instead. *(folk-tale expression used of a very beautiful girl.)* — **doğuşundan, insan yürüyüşünden bellidir** *proverb* The month can be predicted by the way the new moon rises; you can tell a man by his walk. — **ı günü tamam oldu** Her time is come, she is near childbirth. — **hali** time of menstruation. — **ışığında ceviz silkilmez** *proverb* (*lit.* One should not shake down walnuts on a moonlit night.) There are things that have to be done in secret. — **ın kaçı?** What day of the month is it? — **karanlığı** clouded moon. — **köpüğü** *archaic* selenite, moonstone. — **ın ondördü gibi** like the full moon, very beautiful (person). — **parçası** a beauty. — **tabya** *fort.* lunette. — **tutulması** eclipse of the moon. — **var yılı besler, yıl var ayı beslemez** *farmer's proverb* Some months furnish enough for the whole year; some years don't even give a month's supply. — **da yılda bir** very rarely. — **da yılda bir namaz, onu da şeytan komaz** He would perform the prayer once in a blue moon, and even then the devil would not let him (said for a neglectful person). — **yıldız** star and crescent (Turkish emblem).

ay 2 آی 1. exclamation of surprise, oh! *e. g.,* **Ay, burada biri var!** Oh, someone is here! 2. exclamation of pain, oh! *e. g.,* **Ay, ayağım!** Oh, my foot!

ay=ᵃʳ **3** آیمَق 1. to come to, to awake. 2. *archaic* to bring to.

ayʸʸⁱ **4** عَیّ A *lrnd.* 1. a bending (bow, etc.); a twisting. 2. a dog's howling.

ayʸʸⁱ **5** عَیّ A *lrnd.* puzzled, unable to find a way to act, impotent.

aya 1 آیَه 1. the palm of the hand. 2. *archaic* scale of a balance. — **çal=**, — **çatlat=** *archaic* to clap the hands.

âya 2 (— —) آیا P *poet.* 1. I wonder. 2. maybe, perhaps, perchance.

aya 3 آیا Gk holy, *as in* **Ayasofya**.

aya=ʳ **4** آیامَق /ı/ *prov.* to respect, to honor.

aya 5 (. —) عَیاء A *lrnd.* 1. unable, impotant. 2. incurable.

a'yad (. —) اعیاد A *lrnd., pl. of* **îd**.

ayağ آیاغ *same as* **eyağ**.

ayail (. — .) عَیائل A *lrnd., pl. of* **iyal**.

ayakᵍⁱ آیاق 1. foot. 2. leg. 3. base, pedestal, plinth; *arch.* pillar. 4. bottom. 5. pedal (of a sewing machine, etc.); shaft (of the loom). 6. *geog.* tributary; mouth (of a stream), outlet (of a lake). 7. step. 8. stair; rung (of a ladder). 9. gait, walking-speed. 10. *prov.* conduct, way of acting 11. «stand-up», *as in* **ayak birahanesi**, **ayak satıcısı**. 12. *folk poetry* rhyme, rhymeword. 13. foot (measure). 14. *same as* **ayağ**. **bir — ğı** *as in* **bir ayağı plajda** He is at the beach all the time. — **ta** standing, erect; on one's feet. — **tan** on the hoof (of livestock for slaughter). — **aç=** in a meeting of folksingers, to throw in a verse to which the other party has to respond with a similar verse. — **ını al=** /ı/ *prov.* to backbite, slander. — **ını alama=** /dan/ to be unable to refrain (from). — **ı alış=** /ın, a/ to get used to frequenting. — **altı***. — **ının altında** /ın/ as though under one's feet

ayak

(said of panoramic view). **—ının altına al=** /ın/ to thrash; to give a hiding, to thrash. **—lar altına al=** to trample (upon), to disregard. **—ının altında dolaş=** /ın/ to get under one's feet, to be in the way. **— altında kal=** to be trodden under foot. **—ının altına karpuz kabuğu koy=** /ın/ (lit., to put a piece of watermelon rind under someone's foot) to lay a trap (for), to intrigue (against), to cause to fall. **—ının altına sabun kalıbı koy=** prov. (lit., to place a cake of soap under someone's feet) to cause to fall, to trap. **—ını at=** /a/ to go (to), to arrive (at). **— ayak** archaic step by step. **— ayak üstüne at=** to cross the legs. **— bağı** 1. impediment, hindrance (as family obligations). 2. wedlock. **—ının bağını çöz=** /ın/ to divorce (one's wife). **—ına bağ vur=**, **—ını bağla=** /ın/ to hinder. **—ı bağlı** in wedlock (woman). **— bas=** 1. /a/ to arrive (at), to enter. 2. to insist. **— bastı parası** tax paid on arrival at a place. **—lar baş oldu, başlar ayak** The first have become last, the last first; the social order is reversed, and upstarts rule. **—ına baş ur=** /ın/ archaic to prostrate oneself (before someone). **—tan bırak=** /ı/ archaic to paralyse (legs), to cripple. **— bileği** ankle, anat., tarsus. **— birahanesi** (quoted under ayak[11]). **—larım birbirine dolaşıyor** My feet get in each others' way. I keep stumbling over my feet. **—ının birini çekme=** /dan/ not to sever one's relations completely, not to stop frequenting altogether. **—ı cıvık** prov. being always on the go, unstable. **—ına çabuk** swift of foot, quick, agile. **—ını çabuk tut=** to hurry, to walk quickly. **—ını çek=** /dan/ to stop frequenting. **—ını çel=** /ın/ to trip up. **—larını çıkar=** to take off one's shoes. **bir —ı çukurda** having one foot in the grave. **— değiş=, — değiştir=** 1. to change his pace (horse). 2. to get into step by changing one's foot (in marching). **—ını denk al=** to be on one's guard. **— dire=** to insist, to put one's foot down. **— divanı** Ott. hist. a council held in haste, in the Sultan's presence. **—a dokunmadık taş olmaz, başa gelmedik iş olmaz** proverb (lit., There is no stone that cannot hit the foot.) There is nothing that can't happen to one. **—ına dolan=, —ına dolaş=** to boomerang, to recoil on oneself. **—ında donu yok, başına fesleğen takar** (lit. She has no underwear, but she adorns her hair with sweet basil.) She likes to show off regardless of her poverty. **—ın dur=** archaic, **—ta dur=** to stand, to remain standing. **—a düş=** archaic to fall; to fall into misery, to be prostrated. **—ına düş=** /ın/ to prostrate oneself (before someone), to cast oneself at the feet (of). **—tan düş=** archaic to lose one's strength, to become destitute; to fall into misery, to be prostrated. **—ı düze bas=** to step on level ground, to get out of trouble. **—ının etini ye=** prov. to wear one's feet out. **bir — evvel** as soon as possible. **— freni** foot brake. **—ına gel=** /ın/ to come to one by itself (any desired thing). **—ları geri geri git=** to be reluctant, to trail one's feet. **—ına git=** /ın/ to visit personally (as an act of modesty). **—ını giy=** to put on one's shoes. **—ı ile** with one's own foot, on one's own volition. **—ı ile gelene ölüm olmaz** proverb He who gives himself up is not put to death. **—ına ip tak=** /ın/ to backbite. **— işi** work done by one who engages in small business deals and errands with no fixed office or shop. **— izi** footprint. **— kabı*. —ına kadar gel=** /ın/ to show modesty by visiting. **—ı kademli** who brings good luck. **—ta kal=** not to find a seat; to remain standing. **—a kaldır=** /ı/ 1. to cause to stand up. 2. to wake up, to stir up, to alarm, arouse, to bring one to one's feet. **—a kalk=** 1. to stand up, rise to one's feet. 2. to recover and get out of bed. 3. to rebel. **—ına kapan=** /ın/ to cast oneself at the feet (of); to implore mercy. **—ına kara su in=** to get one's feet worn out with standing. **—ı karıncalı** of suspicious conduct (woman). **— kavafı** one who walks around engaged in a suspicious business. **—ını kaydır=** /ın, dan/ to cause (a person) to lose his job. **—ını kes=** /dan/ to stop frequenting. **—ını kes=** /ın, dan/ to stop someone from frequenting. **— kirası** messenger's fee. **—ı köke iliş=** (lit., to be tripped up by a root) to hit an obstacle. **— kösteğini kes=** prov. to cut the fetters (symbolical performance when a child begins to learn to walk). **— makinası** treadle sewing-machine. **— mühürle=** myst. orders to put the big toe of the right foot over that of the left (posture of respect). **— naibi** Ott. hist. assistant judge. **— öp=** to kiss the foot, to implore. **—ı özengide** (lit., having the foot in the stirrup) ready to go. **—ına pabuç olama=** to be beneath another in station or worth. **— parmağı** toe. **— patırtısı** 1. a tramping of feet. 2. a mere threat, a vain attempt at coercion. **—lara sal=** /ı/ archaic to trample under foot, to humiliate. **—ına sarıl=** /ın/ same as ayağına kapan=. **— satıcısı** peddler, hawker. **— sesi** footstep. **—ınıza sıcak su mu dökelim, soğuk su mu dökelim?** What shall I pour on your feet, hot water or cold water? (expression of delight at the arrival of a rare visitor). **—ına sıkı** a good walker, a fast walker. **—ı suya er=** finally to understand, to realize. **— sürt=** to walk around a great deal. **— sürü=** to drag one's feet. **—ını sürüyerek gel=** to drag one's foot in coming (said of a person whose arrival is followed by many other visitors). **—ı şaş=** ˙ to take a false step, to make a false move. **— takımı** rabble, mob. **— talimi** *mil.* step drill. **— tarağı** *anat., metatarsus.* **— taşı** 1. pumice-stone used at a bath to abrade the soles of the feet. 2. slab of stone at the foot of a staircase, which serves as a horseblock. 3. the channeled slab of an eastern toilet. 4. *archery* column in memory of the farthest shot, erected where the archer stood. **—ı taşa dokun=** to hit an obstacle. **—ına taş dokunsa benden bilir** (*lit.* If his foot hits against a stone, he blames it on me) He always blames me for everything. **— tavışı, — tavuştusu** *archaic* clatter of feet; muffled footsteps. **— tedavisi** *med.* treatment given in the outpatient clinic of a hospital. **— teri** (*lit.*, sweat of the foot) fee paid to a person for a job that involves walking; doctor's fee for a home visit. **—ını tetik al=** to be on one's guard. **—ına tez** swift of foot. **— torno** *naut.* leading-block. **—ının tozuyla** with the dust on one's feet, just arrived. **— turabı** (*lit.*, the dust of the feet) a very humble person. **—ınızın turabı olayım** I beseech you. **— ucu** 1. foot (of the bed). 2. *astr.* nadir. **—ı uğurlu** who brings good luck. **— uydur=** /a/ 1. to fall in step; to keep in step (with). 2. to invent a matching second line (folk-singer). **— üstü, — üzeri** without sitting down, in haste. **—ı yanmış it gibi** like a dog with a burned foot (said for someone who keeps going from place to place). **—ı yere basma=** to walk with one's feet in the air, to feel very happy. **— yolu** toilet, water-closet. **—ını yorganına göre uzat=** to stretch one's feet according to one's quilt.

[*For other compounds, see* **ayakaltı - ayaktaş.**]

ayakaltıⁿⁱ آیاقآلتی much frequented (place).
ayakçakᵍⁱ آیاقچاق *prov.* 1. footstool. 2. ladder. 3. pedal (of a machine).
ayakçı آیاقچی *prov.* 1. servant who runs errands. 2. worker hired for a certain period.
ayakçın آیاقچین *prov.* treadle (of a loom).
ayakkabıⁿⁱ آیاققابی shoe, boot; footwear. **—larını çevir=** /ın/ to turn round the shoe left at the door by a visitor (so that he may leave quickly). **— dar olunca dünya geniş olmuş ne fayda?** *proverb* (*lit.* If one's shoes pinch, what good does it do that the world is large?) One small trouble spoils the whole pleasure. **—cı** seller of shoes, dealer in shoes; shoemaker. **—cılık** shoe trade; shoemaking.
ayakkaplar *pl., var. of* **ayakkabı.**
ayakla=ʳ آیاقلامق /ı/ 1. to measure by pacing (distance). 2. to trample (on). 3. to put a leg or foot (to a

thing). **—n=** 1. to get on one's feet. 2. to rise in remonstrance, to rebel. 3. to acquire a foot or leg. **—ndır=** /ı/ *caus. of* **ayaklan=.** **—nma** rebellion, revolt, mutiny. **—t=** *caus. of* **ayakla=.**
ayaklı آیاقلو 1. having a foot or leg, footed. 2. long-legged. 3. on foot, movable, ambulatory. **— bardak** wineglass. **— canavar** 1. person who keeps going around. 2. mischievous child. **— divan** *same as* **ayak divanı.** **— kütüphane** (*lit.*, a walking library) very learned person. **— mani** *folk.* kind of rhymed couplet. **— tercüman** interpreter accompanying travellers.
ayaklıkᵍⁱ آیاقلق 1. thing special to the foot. 2. thing used in place of a foot or leg. 3. place to step on. 4. pedal, treadle. 5. stilt. 6. footplate, base (of a column). **— cambazı** walker on stilts.
ayakman *prov.* clog, patten.
ayaksız آیاقسز footless; legless. **—lar** *zool.* apoda.
ayaktaş آیاقداش companion; accomplice.
ayalˡⁱ (.—) عیال [iyal] 1. wife. 2. household (of a man).
ayala=ʳ آیالامق /ı/ *prov.* to grasp with the palm of the hand. **—ma** 1. *verbal n.* 2. handful.
ayalı آیالو having a palm (hand).
ayan 1 (.—) اعیان A, **âyan** (— —) A 1. notables; chiefs. 2. senators; the Senate. 3. *obs.* chief man in a village or town. **— âzası** senator. **— başı** *obs.* the chief notable of a town or village. **— u eşref** notables, nobility. **— meclisi** the Senate. **—ı sâbite** *phil.* latent realities.
a'yan 2 (.—) اعیان A *lrnd., pl. of* **ayn 3.**
ayan 3 (.—) عیان [iyan] plain, clear, manifest, evident. **— beyan** very clear.
Ayandon آیاندون Gk St. Anthony. **— fırtınası** *calendar* St. Anthony storm (name of a storm in midwinter, about January 29th).
âyanlıkᵍⁱ (.—.) اعیانلق 1. the quality or functions of a notable. 2. senatorship.
a'yar 1 (.—) اعیار A *lrnd., pl. of* **ar 1.**
ayar=ⁱʳ **2** آیارمق 1. *archaic* to go astray. 2. /ı/ *prov., var. of* **ayart=.**
a'yar 3 (.—) اعیار A *lrnd., pl. of* **ayr.**
ayar 4 عیار [iyar] 1. a regulating (clock, machinery), fixing, setting, adjusting (camera, etc.). 2. accuracy, correctness (scales, clock, etc.); standard weight; standard purity (gold, silver). 3. standard (of a measure); grade, degree of fineness, carat (gold, silver). 4. quality, character (person). 5. solder. **—ı bozuk** 1. out of order, not regulated (clock,

ayart= etc.). 2. of bad character. **— damgası** hallmark, assayer's mark. **—dan düş=** to fall below standard in fineness. **— et=** /ı/ 1. to regulate, fix, set, adjust. 2. to test for fineness, to assay (gold, silver). **—a vur=** /ı/ to test on the touchstone (gold, silver). **—cı** assayer; gauger. **—la=** /ı/ 1. to regulate, fix, set, adjust. 2. to assay, test, gauge. **—lama** adjustment. **—lan=** pass. of **ayarla=**. **—lat=** /a,ı/ caus. of **ayarla=**. **—lı** 1. regulated (clock). 2. tested and correct; of standard fineness. **—lı bomba** time-bomb. **—sız** 1. not regulated, out of order. 2. unassayed; below standard.

ayart=[r] آیارتمی /ı/ 1. to lead astray, pervert. 2. to incite to leave one's employment for another. **—ıl=** pass. **—tır=** /a, ı/ caus. of **ayart=**.

Ayas آیاس man's name.

Ayasofya (...'.) آیاصوفیه Gk Hagia Sophia. **—da dilenir, Sultan Ahmed'de zekât verir** He begs at Hagia Sophia and gives alms at Sultan Ahmed Mosque (said of a poor but extravagant person).

Ayastefanos (...'..) آیاستفانوس Gk former name of Yeşilköy near İstanbul.

Ayasuluğ, Ayasuluk[ğu] آیاسولوغ Gk former name of the town of Selçuk near the site of ancient Ephesus.

ayat (——) آیات A lrnd. 1. verses of the Quran. 2. signs, wonders. **—ı muhkemat** unambiguous verses of the Quran. **—ı mütesabihat** ambiguous verses of the Quran.

ayaz 1 آیاز 1. frost on a cold winter's night; dry cold, nip in the air. 2. cloudless, clear weather. 3. bare, bald. 4. w. cap., man's name. **— al=** to get nothing. **—a kal=** to miss something by being too late. **—da kal=** 1. to be exposed to frost. 2. to wait in vain. **— kes=** to be exposed to the cold for a long time. **A— Paşa kola çıktı, A— Paşa kol geziyor** (lit. Ayaz Pasha is going the rounds.) It is freezing weather. **— vurmuş** frost-bitten.

=ayaz= 2, **=eyaz=**, after vowel **=yayaz=**, **=yeyaz=** nearly, almost, all but, e. g., **bayılayazdım** I almost fainted.

ayazla=[r] آیازلامی 1. to spend the night exposed to severe cold; to become cold in the frost. 2. to wait in vain. 3. to become clear and cold (weather). **—n=** same as **ayazla=**. **—t=** /ı/ caus. of **ayazla=**.

ayazlı, ayazlık[ğı] 1 آیازلو chilly and clear (night, weather).

ayazlık[ğı] 2 آیازلو prov. porch, veranda.

ayazma (...) آیازمه Gk sacred fountain of the Greeks.

ayb[bı] عیب A lrnd., same as **ayıp**.

aybaşı[nı] آی باشی menstruation. **— görmek** to menstruate. **—sı tut=** to have a fit of bad temper.

aybcu (.—) عیبجو P lrnd. censorious, critical. **—luk** abstr. n. **—yi** (.——) P censoriousness.

aybçin (.—) عیبچین P lrnd. faultfinding, censorious. **—î** (.——) P a faultfinding.

aybeay آی بای month by month, monthly.

aybet=[der] 1 عیب اتمك /ı/ archaic to blame.

aybet 2 عیبت A lrnd. fault, defect.

aybgû, aybgûy (.—) عیبگوی P lrnd. slanderer, tale-bearer. **—luk** abstr. n. **—yî** (.——) P a slandering, tale-bearing.

aybnak[kı] (.—) عیبناك P lrnd. faulty, blemished; defective.

ayboci آی بوجی naut. heave aback!

ayçiçeği[ni] آی چیچکی sun-flower, bot., Helianthus annuus.

aydaş prov. thin, weak, puny.

aydın 1 آیدن 1. luminous, light; bright and lustrous, sparkling; lucid, clear. 2. archaic light, source of light. 3. neol. enlightened, intellectual. 4. w. cap., man's name. 5. w. cap., name of a town and province in southwestern Asia Minor. 6. w. cap., Or. mus. the **aksak** rhythmic pattern that is somewhat like the **yürük**. **A— ili** hist. the province of Aydın.

aydın=[ır] 2 prov. 1. /a/ to grumble, to complain. 2. to chatter, to babble.

aydınlan=[ır] آیدینلنمی 1. to become luminous, to brighten up. 2. to become clear. **—ma** 1. illumination. 2. clarification.

aydınlat=[ır] آیدینلاتمی /ı/ 1. to illumine, illuminate. 2. to clarify, explain. **—ma** 1. illumination. 2. clarification.

aydınlı آیدینلی 1. luminous, light. 2. w. cap., a man of Aydın.

aydınlık[ğı] آیدینلك 1. luminous, bright; light, daylight. 2. clear, brilliant; clearness. 3. arch. light shaft; opening for light. **— feneri** arch. lantern. **—lı** lighted; light-giving.

aydos Gk naut. dogwatch.

ayefan (..—) عیفان A lrnd. a loathing, dislike.

ayeft (—.) آیفت P lrnd. petition, necessity, need.

ayekân (..—) عیکان A lrnd. a rolling the shoulders as one walks.

ayel عیل A lrnd. an idle story that does not concern the hearer.

ayelân (..—) عیلان A lrnd. a being unable to find a thing lost.

a'yen 1 اعین A lrnd. most evident, very clear.

a'yen 2   ‎عَيِن‎   A *lrnd.* large-eyed.

ayen 3   ‎عين‎   A *lrnd.* 1. large-eyedness. 2. a buying back a thing for less than one had charged for it, as a means of covering up of a usurious profit on money lent.

ayenan (..—)   ‎عينان‎   A *lrnd.* 1. a flowing with tears. 2. a having abundant water (mill).

ayende (—..)   ‎آينده‎   P *lrnd.* 1. coming, that comes. 2. next, the next in the future. — **ve revende** coming and going; travellers, passengers. —**gân** (—..—)   P   *pl.* 1. arrivals. 2. newborn babes.

ayet (—.)   ‎آيت‎   A 1. verse of the Quran. 2. *lrnd.* sign, wonder, miracle. —**i kerime** sacred verse (*i.e.*, any verse of the Quran). —**i maksud** the 62nd verse of the 41th Sura of the Quran («Obey God and obey the Apostle and those in authority from among you».) —**i tergib** a verse where the joys of heaven are mentioned. —**i terhib** a verse where the sufferings of hell are mentioned.

ayetan (—.—)   ‎آيتان‎   A *Isl. rel.* the two verses constituting the profession of faith.

ayetli (—..)   ‎آيتلی‎   having a verse of the Quran inscribed on it. — **altın** gold medal bearing a verse of the Quran.

ayetülhıfz (—...)   ‎آيت الحفظ‎   A verse of the Quran inscribed on amulets for protection against evil.

Ayetülkürsi (—...—)   ‎آيت الكرسی‎   A the 256th verse of the 2nd Sura of the Quran.

Ayetülmevaris (—...——)   ‎آيت المواريث‎   A the 12th verse of the 4th Sura of the Quran.

Ayetünnur (—..—)   ‎آيت النور‎   A the first verse of the 24th Sura of the Quran.

ayf[n]   ‎عيف‎   A *lrnd.* 1. a hovering (bird). 2. dislike.

ayfan (.—)   ‎عيفان‎   A *lrnd.* who dislikes; disgusted.

ayfe   ‎عيفه‎   A *lrnd.* 1. wheel of a hovering bird. 2. a suck at the breast of a childbearing woman in order to remove the obstruction of milk.

aygın baygın   ‎آيغين بايغين‎   languid; languidly.

aygır   ‎آيغير‎   1. stallion. 2. unruly person, rough fellow. 3. *prov.* shoe, skid (of a carriage).

aygırî (..—)   ‎آيغری‎   P same as **aygırlık**.

aygırlan=[r]   ‎آيغرلنمق‎   1. to become a stallion. 2. to act like a stallion; to behave violently. —**dır=** /ı/ *caus.*

aygırlık[§1]   ‎آيغرلق‎ ‎آيغرلوغ‎   1. quality and behavior of a stallion. 2. unruliness, violence. 3. horse fit to be a stallion.

aygırsa=[r] *prov.* to be in heat (mare).

aygıt *prov.* tool; *neol., sc.* instrument, apparatus.

ayı   ‎آيو‎ ‎آيی‎   1. bear. 2. stupid, clumsy fellow. — **balığı** seal, *zool., Phoca*. — **boğan** great big fellow, giant. — **dutu** *prov.* blackberry. — **gülü** garden peony, *bot., Padus officinalis*. —**ya kaval çal=** (*lit.*, to play the shepherd's pipe to the bear) to try in vain to explain something to a blockhead. —**nın kırk hikâyesi varmış, hepsi ahlat üstüne** *proverb* The bear knows forty stories; they are all about wild pears (used insultingly for a person who keeps harping on one subject). — **kulağı** auricula, bear's ear, *bot., Primula auriculata*. — **pavuryası** kind of crab, *zool., Dromia vulgaris*. — **pençesi** bear's breech, *bot., Acanthus mollis*. — **tabanı** clumsy, clownish man. — **üzümü** bearberry, *bot., Arctopus uva-ursi*. —**yı vurmadan postunu sat=** to count one's chickens before they are hatched.

ayıb *cf.* **ayıp**.

ayıcı   ‎آيوجی‎ ‎آيجی‎   1. bear leader. 2. rough fellow.

ayıgiller *neol.*, bears, *zool., Ursidae*.

ayık[§1]   ‎آيوق‎ ‎آيق‎   who is in full possession of his senses, sober, recovered from fainting.

ayıkla=[r]   ‎آيقلامق‎   /ı/ to clear of refuse, to clean, pick, sort (rice, vegetables, etc.). — **şimdi pirincin taşını!** The situation has become helplessly confused. —**ma** selection. —**n=** *pass. of* **ayıkla=**.

ayıklat=[r]   ‎آيقلاتمق‎   /a, ı/ *caus. of* **ayıkla=**.

ayıklık[§1]   ‎آيقلق‎   state of soberness; recovery from fainting, etc.

ayıl=[r]   ‎آيلمق‎   to recover from stupor or drunkenness, to come to. —**t=** /ı/ *caus.*

=**ayım**, =**eyim**, *after vowel* =**yayım 1**, =**yeyim**, *colloq. after* **a, e** =**yım 2**, =**yim 2**, *let me, may I, e. g.,* **gideyim** Let me go. **kalayım mı?** May I stay?

ayın 1   ‎عين‎   [ayn 1] *var. of* **ayn 1**.

=**ayın 2**, =**eyin** *archaic for* =**ayım**, etc.

ayın bayın *archaic* utterly confused, amazed.

ayınka (..'.) *slang* smuggling of tobacco. —**cı** tobacco smuggler.

ayıp[b1]   ‎عيب‎   [ayb] 1. shame, disgrace; shameful, disgraceful, unmannerly. 2. fault, defect. — **ara=** to keep finding faults. — **dâvası** *law* action of warranty regarding defects of property sold. —**a karşı tekeffül** *law* warranty regarding default. **bir — ört=** to serve to cover a defect, to fill a gap. —**ını yüzüne vur=** /ın/ to tell someone's fault to his face.

ayıpla=[r]   ‎عيبلامق‎   /ı/ to find fault (with), blame, censure, criticize. —**n=** *pass.* —**t=** /a, ı/ *caus. of* **ayıpla=**.

ayıplı   ‎عيبلی‎   faulty, defective.

ayıpsın=[r]   ‎عيبسنمق‎   /ı/ to look upon as shameful.

ayıpsız free from defect, perfect. — **dost arıyan dostsuz kalır** *proverb* He who wishes to find a faultless friend remains friendless.

ayır=ʳ /ı/ 1. to part, separate, sever; to divide. 2. to choose, pick, select. 3. to distinguish; to discriminate. 4. to set apart. —**aç** *neol.*, *chem.* reagent. —**an** *neol.*, *phys.* dispersive.

ayırdet=ᵈᵉʳ /ı, dan/ to distinguish, discern; to discriminate. —**ilir** discernible. —**ilmez** indiscernible.

ayırıcı 1. that separates, who picks, separator. 2. distinctive.

ayırım act of separating; point of separation, bifurcation.

ayırma *verbal n.* of **ayır=**.

ayırt 1 *neol.*, *phil.* characteristic. — **et=** *cf.* **ayırdet=**.

ayırt=ⁱʳ **2** /a, ı/ *caus.* of **ayır=**.

ayırtla=ʳ /ı/ *prov. same as* **ayıkla=**. —**n=** *pass.* —**t=** /a,ı/ *caus.* of **ayırtla=**.

ayırtlaş=ⁱʳ *archaic* to part; to get away, to leave.

ayırtlat=ⁱʳ *caus.* of **ayırtla=**.

ayıtᵈⁱ **1** agnus-castus, *bot.*, *Vitex agnus-castus*.

ayıt=ᵈⁱʳ **2** /ı/ *prov.* 1. to say, to tell. 2. to recite.

ayıtla=ʳ /ı/ *prov.*, *var.* of **ayırtla=**.

ayi- 1 Gk holy, *as in* **Ayiyani** St. John (of the Greek church).

ayi 2 (.—) A *lrnd.* puzzled, perplexed.

ayid *same as* **ayıt 1**.

ayin 1 (—.) *var. of* **ayin 2**.

ayin 2 (——) P 1. rite, religious musical service; act of worship. 2. ceremony. 3. *Mevlevi order* music played during worship. 4. *lrnd.* custom; law; way, manner, fashion. 5. *lrnd.* a decking with flags. —**i Cem**, —**i Cemşid** 1. drinking orgy. 2. *Bektashi order* a ceremony of worship. —**i ruhani** church worship. —**i şerif** *Mevlevi order* a composition in four sections played during the **semâ**.

ayinbend (——.) P *lrnd.* decoration with flags.

ayine (——.) P *lrnd.* mirror. —**i âlemnüma** 1. *poet.*, *same as* **ayinei İskender**¹. 2. *myst.* the heart of the Perfect Man. —**i ârız** *poet.* beautiful cheek. —**i asman** *poet.* the sun. —**i billûr** crystal mirror. —**i çerh** *poet.* the sun. —**i Çin**, —**i Çinî** mirror of polished metal. —**i devran** wheel of fortune. —**i gitiefruz** *poet.* the sun. —**i gitinüma** 1. *poet.*, *same as* **ayinei İskender**¹. 2. *myst.* the heart of the Perfect Man. —**i haverî** *poet.* the sun. —**i Huda** *myst. poet.* the human heart. —**i İskender** 1. the mirror of Alexander the Great (which, placed on an island, was used for the observation of ships). 2. *poet.* the sun. —**i maksud** *same as* **âyeti maksud**. —**i şeşcihet** *myst.* 1. the heart of the Prophet Muhammad; the heart of the saint. 2. vision. —**i vicdan** conscience. —**i zânu** *lrnd.* knee-cap, patella bone. —**i zerin** *poet.* the sun. —**dan** (——.—) P case for a mirror. —**dar** (——.—) P *hist.* mirror-bearer (in a palace). —**efruz**, —**füruz** (——..—) P polisher of mirrors. —**ru** (——.—) P *poet.* whose face is shining like a mirror. —**saz** (——.—) maker of mirrors. —**zeday** (——..—) P polisher of mirrors.

ayinhan (———) P *Mevlevi order* singer in a religious service.

ayinperest (——..) *lrnd.* scrupulously observant of rites and ceremonies.

ayise (—..) A *var. of* **aise**.

aykᵏ¹ A *lrnd.* hindrance, a delaying.

ayka A *lrnd.* 1. sea-shore. 2. yard of a house.

ayke A *lrnd.* wood, thicket.

aykırı 1. across, crosswise; *naut.* athwart. 2. in the opposite direction; running against; incongruous. 3. /a/ contrary (to), against, not in accordance with. 4. inclined, sloping, slanting. 5. perverse, ill-natured, ill-tempered. — **git=** to swerve from a given direction; /a/ to oppose, provoke. — **katmanlaşma** *geol.* discordant stratification. —**la=**, —**laş=** to take on an athwart position. —**lık** *abstr. n.* of **aykırı**.

aylᵘ A *lrnd.* 1. a proudly strutting, strut. 2. a roaming, wandering. 3. a being burdened with a large family. 4. poverty, an impoverishing. 5. a being unable to find one's way.

ayla 1 *neol.* 1. halo. 2. *anat.*, areola. 3. *w. cap.*, woman's name.

ayla=ʳ **2** *prov.* 1. to revolve. 2. to slip, glide down. 3. to become a month; to have lasted a month.

aylâ 3 (.—) A *lrnd.*, *pl.* of **âil**.

aylakᵏ¹ 1. idle, unemployed. 2. *prov.* day-laborer; farm-hand who works in return for food. 3. *prov.* gratis, for nothing. — **durmaktan aylak işlemek yeğdir** *proverb* Better to work in return for food than to stay idle.

aylakçı 1. casual laborer. 2. *Ott. hist.* temporarily hired seaman in the navy. —**lık** work done by a casual laborer.

aylaklıkᵍ¹ آیلاق لنی idleness, unemployment.
aylan⁼ⁱʳ آیلانمی 1. to become a moon; to become crescent shaped; to become a satellite and revolve. 2. to become a month old. 3. *prov.* to circle, eddy, wheel. 4. *prov.* to lounge about idly. —**dır**⁼ /ı/ *caus.* —**ma** *verbal n.* of **aylan**=.
aylat⁼ⁱʳ آیلاتمی /ı/ *caus.* of **ayla**= 2.
aylaz آیلاز *same as* **haylaz**. —**lık** *abstr. n.*
ayle 1 عائل [**aile**] *var. of* **aile**.
ayle 2 عيل A *lrnd., pl. of* **âil** 2.
aylet عيلت A *lrnd.* poverty, need.
aylı آیلی that has a moon.
aylıkᵍ¹ آیلق 1. monthly. 2. monthly pay or salary. 3. a month old; of a month's duration; enough for a month. —**çı** who lives on a monthly salary. —**lı** paid monthly.
aymᵐⁱ عيم A *lrnd.* a suffering from lack of milk.
ayma (.—) عيما A *lrnd., fem. of* **ayman**.
ayman (.—) عيمان A *lrnd.* suffering from lack of milk.
aymet عيمت A *lrnd., same as* **aym**.
aynⁿⁱ 1 عين ع A *Arabic script, name of the letter* ع (The letter is the 18th letter of the Arabic alphabet, or, the 21st letter of the enlarged Arabic alphabet as used in Persian and Turkish. It occurs in Arabic loan words, where it is pronounced as a slight glottal stop. In the Turkish Latin alphabet it is occasionally indicated by an apostrophe between consonant and vowel. ع has the numerical value of 70 in chronograms. In astronomical works it is used as an abbreviation for **içtima** and for **terbi**. In the margin of the Quran it denotes the end of a section of ten verses. Before a quotation of poetry it marks a hemistich). —**i betra** the sign hemze in Arabic script (ء). —**leri çatlat**= to pronounce the letter ع with a guttural sound. —**i mühmele**, —**i sa'fas** *names of the letter* ع .
aynⁿⁱ 2 عين A 1. *used only with possessive suffix* self; an exact copy, counterpart. 2. *law* thing, *res.* 3. *phil.* essence. 4. coin, cash, ready money. —**iyle** 1. in exactly the same way, likewise. 2. in kind (payment). —**ini al**=, —**ini çıkar**= /ın/ to take a copy (of). —**i hakikat** the truth itself, the very truth. —**i hata** a complete mistake. —**i hikmet** wisdom itself, the right thing. —**i isabet** the very thing to do. —**i keramet** a very miracle. —**i mazmun** *law* thing for which indemnity is obligatory. —**i mevkuf** *can. law* object of a pious donation (wakf).
aynⁿⁱ 3 عين A *lrnd.* 1. eye; look, glance. 2. eye-hole (needle, etc.). 3. bud. 4. lookout, scout, spy. 5. bullion. 6. touch of the evil eye. 7. scale (of a balance). —**i bahıka** a blind eye whose mate has its sight. —**i bakar** *same as* **aynülbakar**. —**i ibret** consideration of the example of others. —**i inayet** 1. a look of favor. 2. favor. —**i iyan** a spiritual vision of realities. —**i mürekkeb** *biol.* composite eye. —**i vahid** one-eyed.
aynⁿⁱ 4 عين A *lrnd.* spring, source. —**i hayat** fountain of life.
ayna آینه [**ayine**] 1. mirror, looking glass; speculum. 2. *naut.* telescope. 3. *naut.* quadrant, sextant; theodolite. 4. panel (of a door or wainscot). 5. *naut.* the surface of a whirlpool. 6. knee-cap (of a horse). 7. *slang* perfect; very well. 8. spider crab, *zool.*, *Maia squinado*. 9. lathe-head. — **camı** plate glass. — **gibi** mirror-like; lustrous; clean, bright. — **sırrı** silvering of a mirror. — **taşı** ornamental slab of a fountain. —**cı** 1. maker of mirrors, seller of looking-glasses. 2. mirror-bearer (in a palace or public bath). 3. trickster; fortune-teller with a mirror. 4. lookout man with a telescope; observer with a quadrant or sextant. —**lan**= to become like a mirror.
aynalı آینه لی آینه لی آینه لو 1. fitted with mirrors. 2. paneled. 3. *slang* beautiful. 4. *hist., name given to a certain type of gold coins.* — **dolap** wardrobe fitted with mirrors. — **sazan** mirror-carp, *zool.*, *Cyprinus carpio*. — **yazı** calligraphy decorative writing in symmetrical arrangement, with repetition in the opposite direction.
aynalıkᵍ¹ آینالق *naut.* backboard.
Aynaroz آینه روز [**Aynoroz**] Mount Athos.
aynasız آیناسز *slang* 1. bad, unpleasant. 2. policeman. 3. loaded (dice).
aynekᵏⁱ عينك P *lrnd.* eye-glasses, spectacles. —**dan** (..—) P spectacle case.
aynelyakin (...—) عين اليقين A *lrnd.* with certainty.
aynen (.'.) عيناً A 1. exactly, textually. 2. in kind (payment). 3. in ready money.
aynıⁿⁱ عينى [**ayn** 2] 1. same, identical. 2. exactly. — **kapıya çıkar** It comes to the same thing. — **şekilde** in the same way, likewise. — **zamanda** at the same time, simultaneously; meanwhile. —**lık** identity, sameness.
ayni 1 عينى *var. of* **aynı**.
ayni 2 (.—) عينى A 1. *phil.* essential, genuine, real, concrete. 2. in kind. — **akit** *law* real contract. — **borçlar** *law* real obligations. — **dâva** *law* action in rem. — **haklar** *law* real rights. — **mesuliyet** *law* real obligation — **sermaye** *com.* capital in kind. — **statü** *law* real statute. — **teminat** *law* specific security. — **yardım** aid in kind

ayni 3 (. —) عَيْنِيّ A *anat*. pertaining to the eye, ocular.

aynisafa (... —) عين صفاء [*based on* **aynussafa**] field marigold, *bot*., *Calendula arvensis*; pot marigold, *bot*., *Calendula officinalis*.

ayniyat (. — —) عَيْنِيّات A *adm*. goods, chattels, property, belongings. — **muhasebesi** accountancy regarding physical property.

ayniye (. —.) عَيْنِيّه A 1. *short for* **rüsum-u ayniye**. 2. *short for* **eşyayı ayniye**.

ayniyet (. —.) عَيْنِيّت [*based on* **ayn 2**] identity, sameness.

Aynoroz آینوروز *Gk same as* **Aynaroz**.

aynussafa (... —) عين الصفاء A *same as* **aynisafa**.

aynülbakar عين البقر A 1. ox-eye daisy, *bot*., *Chrysanthemum Leucanthemum*. 2. mountain tobacco, *bot*., *Arnica montana*. 3. damask plum.

aynülfi'l عين الفعل A *Arabic gram*. the second radical of a stem.

aynülhayat (... —) عين الحياة A *lrnd*. spring of life.

aynülhir[ri] عين الهر A *min*. cat's eye.

aynülkemal[li] (... —) عين الكمال A *lrnd*. piercing look that kills, the evil eye.

aynüllâme (.. —.) عين اللّامة A *lrnd*. the evil eye.

aynürrami (.. — —) عين الرامي A *astr*. the star 32 *Sagittarii*.

aynüsseretan (.... —) عين السرطان A *biol*. crab's eye.

aynüssevr عين الثور A *astr*. α *Tauri*, Aldebaran.

aynüşşems عين الشمس A 1. *min*. kind of precious stone. 2. *w. cap*. Heliopolis (town in Egypt).

ayol (.'.) آیول [**ay oğul**] well!, you!, say!

ayr[ri] عَیر A *lrnd*. 1. wild ass, *zool*., *Asinus onager*. 2. midrib of a leaf; prominent ridge on a flat surface. 3. each of the long muscles of the back on either side of the spinal column. 4. the tragus of the ear, with the adjacent part of the helix. 5. pupil of the eye.

ayran آیران 1. a cool drink made of yoghurt and water. 2. buttermilk. — **budalası**, — **delisi** simpleton. —**ım ekşidir diyen olmaz** *proverb* (*lit*. No one will say, «My buttermilk is sour.») Nobody confesses to the shortcomings of his own work. —**ı kabar**= /ın/ to boil up, to get angry, to take on airs, to get excited. —**ı yok içmeğe atla gider sıçmağa** *vulg*. He has no buttermilk to drink, but he goes on horse-back to relieve himself (said of a poor person who loves showing off).

ayrı آیری 1. separate, apart, alone. 2. different, distinct. — **ayrı** one by one, separately. — **basım**, — **basma** off-print, reprint. — **baş çek**= *prov*. to go one's own way. — **çanakyapraklılar** *bot*. dialysepalous plants. — **düş**= to become separated from each other. —**sı gayrısı olma**= 1. to have all things in common. 2. to make no discriminations. — **seçi ol**= to divide out (shares). — **seçi yap**= to discriminate. — **taç yapraklılar** *bot*., *Dialypetalae*. — **tut**= /ı/ to make a distinction (between), to discriminate (between).

ayrıca 1 (.'..) آیریجه in addition, also, further, moreover.

ayrıca 2 آیریجه somewhat apart.

ayrıcalık[ğı] *neol*., *sociol*. privilege.

ayrıç[cı] 1. *prov*. bifurcation, parting of the ways. 2. *neol*. chapter.

ayrık[ğı] 1 آیریق *same as* **ayrık otu**. — **otu** couch grass, *bot*., *Agropyron repens*.

ayrık[ğı] 2 آیریق 1. wide apart. 2. *log*. disjunctive. 3. *prov*. other; (in negative context) any more, no more.

ayrıksı *prov*. different.

ayrıl=[ir] آیریلمق 1. *pass. of* **ayır**=. 2. to part, to separate from one another. 3. to crack, split, open; /a/ to split (into). 4. to depart. —**amaz** inseparable; *phil*. inherent.

ayrılan=[ir] آیریلمغن to separate; to be separated.

ayrılaş=[ir] آیریلاشمق 1. to become separated. 2. to grow different. —**ma** *neol*., *phil*. differentiation. —**tır**= /ı/ *caus*.

ayrılı آیریلی having something separate. — **gayrılı** having separate property.

ayrılık[ğı] آیریلیق 1. separation; isolation; absence; *phil*. disjunction; *law* judicial separation. 2. difference. — **çeşmesi** a fountain outside of a town where travellers take leave of their friends; *w. cap*., name of a fountain in Kadıköy, Istanbul, where the pilgrim caravans used to set out on their journey. — **dâvası** *law* action for judicial separation. — **kargası** jay, *zool*., *Garrulus glandarius*.

ayrılır آیریلیر separable.

ayrılış, آیریلیش **ayrılma** آیریلمه separation, severance.

ayrılmaz آیریلماز *same as* **ayrılamaz**.

ayrılt=[ir] آیریلتمق *caus. of* **ayrıl**=.

ayrım 1. *var. of* **ayırım**. 2. *neol*., *phil*. difference. —**laş**= *biol*., *phil*. to become differentiated. —**sal** *neol*., *phil*. differential; *chem*. fractional.

ayrıntı *neol*. detail, accessory.

ayrış=[ir] آیریشمق 1. *prov*. to separate, to cease from partnership. 2. *neol*., *chem*. to be decomposed. —**abilir** *chem*.

decomposable. —ım *chem.* decomposition. —tır= /ı/ *chem.* to decompose.
ayrıt^(dı) *neol., geom.* edge.
ayruk^(ğu) آيردو *prov., var. of* **ayrık** 2. —ça *archaic* different; differently. —sı= *archaic* to become different, to change. —sıt= /ı/ *caus. of* **ayruksı=**.
aysberg E *geog.* iceberg.
ayş^(si) عيش A *lrnd.* life; pleasant life, gay life. —**i dehruze** a life of ten days duration (*i.e.*, the short life in this world). **— u işret, — u nûş** life and enjoyment, jollity and drinking.
Ayşe عايشه [**Aişe**] *woman's name.* **— kadın fasulyesi** kind of French bean.
ayşuşe (. —.) عيشوشه A *lrnd.* pleasant life, agreeable living.
aytal^(li) عيطل A *lrnd.* tall and gracefully slim.
ayun (. —) عيون A *lrnd.* evil-eyed.
a'yün اعين A *lrnd.*, *pl. of* **ayn** 3, 4.
ayva آيوه آيوا quince. **— ağacı** quince tree, *bot., Cydonia vulgaris.* **— çekirdeği** 1. quince seed. 2. tea rose pink. **— lûabı** quince seed jelly. **— murabbası** quince marmalade. **— rengi** sallow as a quince. **— tüyü** 1. the fuzz on a quince. 2. fuzz on a youth's cheek.
ayvadana آيوه طنه آيوا ضنه Gk wormwood, *bot., Artemisia herba alba.*
ayvalık^(ğı) آيوالي 1. quince orchard. 2. *w. cap.,* name of a town in western Anatolia.
ayvan *prov., var. of* **eyvan.**
ayvaz آيواض عيواظ 1. footman, man servant in a mansion. 2. *navy* hospital aid on a ship. 3. *w. cap., man's name, esp.,* name of the beautiful youth in the popular story of **Köroğlu.** **— kasap hep bir hesap** It makes no difference.
ayyab (. —) عياب A *lrnd.* fault-finding, censorious. **—e** (. — .) very censorious.
ayyal^(li) (. —) عيال A *lrnd.* conceitedly swaggering, strutting.
ayyan (. —) عيان A *lrnd.* 1. unable to find a way to act, puzzled. 2. tired, fatigued.
ayyar (. —) عيار A *lrnd.* 1. cheat, rogue, knave, tricky vagabond. 2. *archaic* sharp, sprightly. —î (. — —) P deceit, imposture, knavery.
ayyaş (. —) عياش A 1. alcoholic, drunkard. 2. *lrnd.* one fond of good living and merriment. —**lık** habitual drunkenness, dipsomania.
ayyefan, ayyifan (.. —) عيفان A *lrnd.* given to loathing, fastidious.
ayyil 1 عيل A *lrnd.* poor, needy.
ayyil 2 عيل A *lrnd.* man's household; member of one's household.

ayyire عيّره A *lrnd.* abundance of cattle or property the sight of which overwhelms the eyes.
ayyuk^(ku) (. —) عيّوق A 1. *astr.* Capella. 2. the highest point of the heavens. **—a çık=** to reach the highest sky, to become terribly loud. **—a çıkar=** /ı/ 1. to raise to the skies, to vaunt. 2. to raise to the skies (cry, lament, etc.).
az 1 آز few; a few; not much, little, small; not enough; scarcely, rarely, seldom. **bir —***. **— adam değil** He is quite a man, he is remarkable. **— az** gradually, slowly, little by little. **—dan az** very few, extremely little. **—ı bilmiyen çoğu hiç bilmez** *proverb* He who does not appreciate the little will not appreciate the much. **— bir şey** only a little. **— buçuk** scanty, hardly enough; somewhat. **— bul=** /ı/ to consider insufficient. **— buz değil** It is quite something; it is no small matter. **— çok** more or less. **—a çoğa bakma=, — çok deme=** to be satisfied with what one gets. **—ı çoğa say=, —ı çoğa tut=** to regard the little as much, to take the will for the deed. **— daha** almost, nearly, all but. **—a demişler: nereye gidiyorsun? Çoğun yanına! demiş** *proverb* (*lit.* They asked the little: Where are you going? It said: To join the much.) The majority decides. **— fena değil** really very bad; very good. **— gel=** to be not enough. **— gitti uz gitti, dere tepe düz gitti** *fairy tales* He went uphill and down dale. **— gör=** /ı/ to consider insufficient. **— günün adamı değil** He is a man who looks back on a rich life full of experience. **— işten çok iş çıkar** *proverb* The business starts simply; it gets harder later. **— iş değil** The work is not to be underrated. **— işlek** unproductive. **— kaldı, — kalsın** almost, nearly, all but. **— olsun öz olsun, — olsun uz olsun** little but good. **— söyler öz söyler, — söyler uz söyler** He speaks little but well. **— sözlü** reticent. **— tamah çok ziyan getirir** *proverb* A little greed causes great loss. **— veren candan çok veren maldan verir** *proverb* He who gives little gives from his heart; he who gives much gives from his wealth. **— ye de bir uşak tut!** If you must have help, you had better eat little and hire a servant. **— yenmez, çok artmaz** What seems little turns out to be more than enough; what seems a lot proves to be just enough.
az=^(ar) 2, *archaic* **az**=^(ur) آزمر 1. to act outrageously, to become unmanageable, mad, furious (wind, sea), wild (dog), excited, threatening; to be in flood (river). 2. to become infected (wound). 3. to assume alarming proportions, to grow anomalously,

âz

become monstrous. 4. to become grimy, soiled deeply, rubbed in, uncleanable (dirty clothes). 5. to be a halfbreed. 6. *archaic* to go astray; /dan/ to fall asunder; /ı/ to lose (one's way). 7. *archaic* to be spoiled.

âz 3 (—) آز P *lrnd.* greed, covetousness.

âz^zz1 **4** (—) عاضّ A *lrnd.* that bites, biting.

az^zz1 **5** عضّ A *lrnd.* a nipping, snapping, biting.

az^zz1 **6** عظّ A *lrnd.* 1. throwing or knocking to the ground, overthrow. 2. prostration, an overwhelming (calamity).

âza 1 (— —) اعضا [a'za 2] 1. member of a council, society, etc. 2. limb, member of the body.

a'za 2 (. —) اعضاء A 1. *anat.* members, limbs, organs. 2. members (of a council, etc.), fellows (of a society). **—i dahiliye** *anat.* internal organs. **—i fahriye** honorary members.

aza 3 (. —) عزا A *lrnd.* 1. condolence. 2. a mourning, lamenting. 3. patience under a loss by death.

aza 4 (. —) عزا A *lrnd.* assertion of the relationship of son to a person, a calling one the son (of so and so).

azab 1 (. —) عذاب A *same as* **azap 1.**

azab 2 عذب *cf.* **azap 2.**

a'zab 3 (. —) اعذب A *lrnd.*, *pl.* of **azeb 3.**

a'zab 4 اعضب A *lrnd.* slit-eared, dock-eared, having one horn broken (beast).

azacık^g1 (.'..) آزه جیه *var.* of **azıcık.**

azad 1 (— —) آزاد P *lrnd.* 1. free, not enslaved. 2. free-born, of noble lineage; virtuous, righteous. 3. free, unencumbered, untrammeled; free from any defect, ailment, sorrow, etc. **— et=** /ı/ to free, emancipate, manumit; to liberate, relieve. **— etme** *law* manumission. **— kabul etmez bendeniz** *polite letter style* (*lit.*, your servant who accepts no freedom) your obedient servant. **— ol=** *pass.* of **azad et=**.

a'zad 2 (. —) اعضاد A *lrnd.* 1. *pl.* of **adud, azd 1, azıd, azud 2, ızd, uzd, uzud.** 2. tracts, regions, parts. 3. bordering stones (of a wall or road).

azad 3 (. —) عضاد A *lrnd.* short and thickset.

azaddiraht (— —..) آزاد درخت P margosa tree, pride of India, *bot.*, *Melia azadirachta.*

azade (— —.) آزاده P 1. free, untrammeled. 2. /dan/ free, released (from). 3. *lrnd.* excellent, noble. 4. *pros.* hemistich expressing in itself a complete idea. **—dil** (— —..) P *poet.* whose heart is free from all care and desire. **—gi** (— —. —) P *abstr. n.* of **azade. —ser** (— —..) P *poet.* who is free from care.

azadî (— — —) آزادى P *lrnd.*, *abstr. n.* of **azad 1.**

azadmerd (— — .) آزاد مرد P *lrnd.* a man free from worldly ties. **—i** (— —. —) P *abstr. n.*

azafir (. — —) اظافير A *anat.* nails, claws.

azah (—.) آزح P *lrnd.* wart.

azahane (. — —.) عزا خانه P *lrnd.* house of mourning and condolence.

azahi (. — —) اضاحى A *lrnd.*, *pl.* of **udhiye.**

azahik^ki (. — —) اضاحيك A *lrnd.*, *pl.* of **uzhuke.**

azaim 1 (. —.) عظائم A *pl.* of **azime 1.**

azaim 2 (. —.) عزائم A *lrnd.*, *pl.* of **azime 4.**

azaim 3 (. —.) اعزّا A *lrnd.*, *pl.* of **azime 5, azimet 2.**

azaimhan (. — . —) عزائم خوان P *lrnd.* conjurer; exorcist.

azaimullah (. — .. —) عزائم الله A *theol.* divine statutes and decrees.

Azak^g1 آزاق Azov. **— denizi** the Sea of Azov. **— eyeri** sweet sedge, *bot.*, *Acorus Calamus.*

azal=^ır **1** آزالمق to become less, to lessen, diminish, to be reduced, lowered, decreased.

azal^li **2** (— —) آزال A *lrnd.* times without beginning.

azal^li **3** عضل A *lrnd.*, *pl.* of **adale.**

âzalık^g1 (— —.) آزالق membership.

azalil (. — —) اضاليل A *lrnd.* errors.

azalt=^ır آزالتمق /ı/ to lessen, reduce, lower, decrease. **—ıl=** *pass.*

âzam 1 (—.) اعظم [a'zam 2] greatest, largest.

a'zam 2 اعظم A *lrnd.* very exalted (in rank), highest, greatest.

azam 3 اضم A *lrnd.* 1. hate, malevolence. 2. envy. 3. anger, animosity.

azamat 1 (.. —) عظمات A 1. greatness. 2. the great, chiefs.

azamat 2 (.. —) اضمات A *lrnd.*, *pl.* of **azam 3.**

azamet 1 عظمت A 1. greatness, grandeur, majesty. 2. pomp. 3. arrogance, conceit. **— sat=** to give oneself airs.

azamet 2 (. —.) عظامت A *lrnd.* 1. greatness, vastness. 2. grandeur, a being imposing, momentous.

azametfüruş (.... —) عظمت فروش P *lrnd.* arrogant, conceited.

azametli عظمتلى 1. grand, great,

august. 2. pompous. 3. arrogant, conceited.
azametlû (...—) عظمتلو archaic majestic, grand (as a title of the Sultan).
âzami (—.—) اعظمى |âzam 1|. greatest, maximum, utmost; to the fullest degree. **— derecede, — olarak** to the utmost.
âzamiyet (—.—.) اعظميّت |based on **âzam 1**| 1. maximum value, maximal degree. 2. *math.* the sign > (greater than).
azamut (..—) عظموت A *lrnd.* the ineffable greatness (of God).
azan (——) آذان A *lrnd.*, pl. of **üzn, üzün,** ears. **—üddüb** (——..) A mullein, *bot., Verbascum.* **—ül'anz** (——..) A water plantane, mad-dog weed, *bot., Alisma Plantago-aquatica.* **—ülcedi** (——..—) A ribwort, ribgrass, *bot., Plantago lanceolata.* **—ül'erneb** (——...) A hare's ear, *bot., Bupleurum retundifolium.* **—ülfil** (——.—) A elephant's ear, *bot., Caledium esculentum.* **—ülkıssıs** (——..—) A navelwort, pennywort, *bot., Cotyledon umbilicus.*
azap[bi] **1** (.—) عذاب |azab 1| 1. pain, torment, torture. 2. *archaic* punishment. **—ı cehennem** the torments of hell. **— çek=** to suffer torment. **—ı kabir** the torment of the grave (inflicted on sinners by the questioning angels). **— ver=** /a/ to cause pain, to torment.
azap[bi] **2** عزب |azeb 3| 1. *hist.* soldier of a certain class, *esp.*, a marine. 2. *prov.* farm hand, farm laborer. **A— kapısı** location near the docks on the Golden Horn, Istanbul.
azar 1 آزار |âzar 2| scolding, reprimand. **— işit=** to be scolded.
âzar 2 (——) آزار P *lrnd.* molestation, vexation, injury, annoying, teasing, tormenting.
-azar 3 (——) آزار P that hurts, injures, annoys, torments, as in **dilâzar, merdümazar.**
Azar 4 (——) آزار A *lrnd.* March.
a'zar 5 (.—) اعذار A *lrnd.*, pl. of **özr.**
azar[rn] **6** اضرّ A *lrnd., superl.* of **muzır.**
azar azar آزار آزار little by little.
âzardide (———.) آزارديده P *lrnd.* who has been hurt, injured, annoyed, molested.
âzarende (——..) آزارنده P *lrnd.* that hurts, vexes, afflicts; tormentor.
âzari 1 (———) آزارى P *lrnd.* 1. injuriousness. 2. trouble, annoyance, affliction.
azari 2 (.——) عذارى A *lrnd., var.* of **azara.**
âzariş (——.) آزارش P *lrnd.* a hurting, molestation, annoyance.
azarla=[r] آزارلامق آزارلاماق /ı/ to scold, reprimand, rebuke. **—n=** *pass.* **—t=** *caus.* of **azarla=.** **—yış** *verbal n.* of **azarla=.**
âzarmend (—..) آزارمند P *lrnd.* hurt, vexed, annoyed, afflicted. **—i** (——.—) P injuredness, affliction.
âzarresan (——.—) آزاررسان P *lrnd.* hurtful, injurious.
âzarreside (——.—.) آزاررسيده P *lrnd.* hurt, injured, annoyed, afflicted.
azat[dı] **1** آزاد |azad 1| a setting free; dismissal (from school). **— buzat, beni cennet kapısında gözet!** Be free and await me at the Gate of Paradise! (said when releasing a captive bird). **— vakti** time of recess (in school).
azat 2 (.—) عذات A *lrnd.* good, rich, upland soil.
azatla=[r] آزادلامق آزادلاماق /ı/ 1. to free, liberate, enfranchise, manumit. 2. to dismiss (from school). **—ma** freed, freedman. **—n=** *pass.* of **azatla=.**
azatlı آزادلو freed, manumitted freedman.
azatlık[ğı] آزادلوق 1. freedom from slavery, liberty. 2. fit to be set free. 3. *Ott. hist.* retirement pay of the black eunuchs of the Sultan's harem.
azatsız آزادسز 1. unfreed, still enslaved. 2. who will not accept his freedom.
azaz 1 (.—) عزاز A *lrnd.* hard ground.
azaz 2 (.—) عضاض A *lrnd.* bit, bite.
azazet (.—.) عزازت A *lrnd.* 1. greatness, strength, might, glory. 2. difficulty, scarcity; value.
Azazil (.——) عزازيل A *a name of the* Devil.
azb[bi] **1** عذب A *lrnd.* pleasant to drink, sweet, agreeable.
azb 2 عزب A *lrnd.* unmarried state, celibacy.
azb 3 عضب A *lrnd.* 1. a cutting off. 2. a beating, striking. 3. a reproaching vehemently. 4. a using one up (disease).
azb 4 عضب A sharp (tongue).
azba 1 (.—) ضبى A *lrnd., pl.* of **zabi.**
azba 2 (.—) عزباء A *lrnd.* single, unmarried (woman).
azba 3 (.—) عضباء A *lrnd.* 1. *fem.* of **a'zab 4.** 2. *w. cap., name of the single she-camel of the Prophet Muhammad.*
azbu[uu] ضبع A *lrnd.* hyenas.
azbülbeyan (...—) عذب البيان A *lrnd.* sweet in expression, eloquent.
azca آزجه rather little, somewhat few.
azcık[ğı] (.'.) آزجق *var.* of **azıcık.**
azd 1 عضد A *lrnd., var.* of **adud.**
azd 2 عضد A *lrnd.* 1. help, assistance. 2. a cutting, lopping.
azde (—.) آزده P *var.* of **azede.**
azdır=[r] آزديرمق آزديرماق /ı/ 1. to allow to become serious (a small evil), to cause to get out of hand. 2. to allow to smart (wound). 3. to cause to become grimy, uncleanable (dirty

a'zeb 110

laundry). 4. to lead astray (morally); to make lose one's way. 5. to spoil by overkindness (child). **—ıl=** pass.

a'zeb 1 اعذب A lrnd., superl. of **azb 1**.

azeb 2 عذب A lrnd. 1. floating particles in water, motes. 2. the afterbirth.

azeb 3 عذب A 1. lrnd. bachelor; grass widower. 2. same as **azap 2**.

azebe 1 عذبة A lrnd. 1. a particle of impurity floating in water. 2. tail-end, tip, handle.

azebe 2 عزبة A lrnd. unmarried woman, spinster; grass widow.

azebî (..—) عزبي A lrnd. generous, noble-minded.

azede (—..) آزده P lrnd. 1. dyed, tinged. 2. pricked (with some pointed instrument).

a'zel 1 اعزل A lrnd. 1. separate, isolated. 2. unarmed, defenseless.

azel 2 عذل A lrnd. reproof, blame, censure.

azele عذلة A lrnd., pl. of **âzil 2**.

azemat (..—) عزمات A lrnd., pl. of **azme**.

azeme عزمة A pl. of **âzim 3**.

azer 1 (—.) آذر P lrnd. fire.

Azer 2 (—.) آزر A name of Abraham's father.

Azer 3 (—.) عازر A Bib. Lazarus.

azerahş (—..) آذرخش P lrnd. thunderbolt.

Azerbaycan (—.—) آذربایجان geog. Azerbaijan. **—lı** Azerbaijani.

azergede (—...) آذرگده P [azerkede] poet. fire temple.

azergûn (—.—) آذرگون P poet. flame-colored, fiery red.

Azerî (—.—) آذری P Azerbaijani. **—ce** the Azerbaijani language.

azerkede (—...) آذرکده P same as **azergede**.

azerkiş (—.—) آذرکیش P lrnd. fire-worshipper.

azerm (—.) آزرم P lrnd. 1. modesty, bashfulness, virtue. 2. mildness, gentleness, sweetness.

azermcu (—.—) آزرمجو P lrnd. well-conducted, decorous, modest; gentle-mannered.

azerperest (—...) آذرپرست P lrnd. fire worshipper.

azerşin (—.—) آذرشین P poet. salamander.

azeryun (—.—) آذریون P same as **azergûn**.

azevat (..—) عذوات A lrnd., pl. of **azat 2**.

azf[fi] **1** عزف A lrnd. the low sound of moaning of demons in the desert.

azf[fi] **2** عزف A lrnd. a stringed musical instrument.

azfar (.—) اظفار A anat. nails; claws.

azfarüttib (.—.—) A drug., ungues odorati; onycha.

azfendak[ki] (—.—) آزفندك P var. of **ajfendak**.

azgan (.—) اضغان A lrnd., pl. of **zığn**.

azgas (.—) اضغاث A lrnd. 1. bunches. 2. muddles. **—ı ahlâm** confused dreams.

azgaş=[ır] آزغاشمق archaic to get into a heated argument, to quarrel violently. **—tır=** caus.

azgın آزغین 1. excessively fierce and wild, ferocious, mad; excessively wicked, depraved, disobedient, rebellious; excessive, unbounded; in flood. 2. whose wounds tend to smart (body). 3. archaic stray, astray. **—lık** excessiveness, fierceness; depravity.

azha 1 (.—) اضحی A var. of **adha**.

azha 2 (.—) اضحی A lrnd. silver-grey (horse).

azhar 1 (.—) اظهار A lrnd. noons.

azhar 2, azher اظهر A lrnd. most evident. **— mineşşems** clearer than the sun.

azhur اظهر A lrnd., pl. of **zahr 2**.

azı آزی 1. molar tooth. 2. tusk (of a boar). 2. prov. one of the two pegs protruding downwards from each of the bottom rafters of a primitive ox cart (**kağnı**), by which the body of the cart is kept on the axle. **— dişi** molar tooth.

azıcık[ğı] (.'..) آزیجیق just a little bit. **— aşım kavgasız başım** modest living and peaceful mind.

azıd عضد A lrnd., var. of **adud**.

azık[ğı] آزیق 1. provisions. 2. archaic food. **—çı** sutler; forager. **—çılık** sutlery; foraging. **—lan=** to provide oneself with provisions; to eat. **—landır=** /ı/ caus. of **—lan=**. **—lı** 1. supplied with provisions. 2. well off, living in comfort. 3. hospitable, charitable. **—lık** 1. provisions. 2. a receptacle for provisions, bag, nosebag. 3. place abounding in forage.

azılı آزیلو 1. furnished with tusks; having molar teeth. 2. ferocious, wild; tough and dangerous. 3. tusked wild bear. **— domuz** tusked wild bear.

azım[zmı] عظم [azm 2] anat. bone. **—ı aciz** os sacrum. **—ı adesî** lenticular bone, os lenticulare. **—ı adud** humerus. **—ı akab** os calcaneum. **—ı âne** pubis bone, os pubis. **—ı cebhî** frontal bone, os frontale. **—ı cidarî** parital bone, os parietale. **—ı dıl'î** os costale. **—ı enfî** nasal bone, os nasale. **—ı fahız** femur. **—ı gırbalî** ethmoid bone, os ethmoidale. **—ı hanek** palatine bone, os palatinum. **—ı harkafa** os ilium. **—ı kâb** astragalus. **—ı kafa** occipital bone, os occipitale. **—ı kass**

sternum. —ı **kasaba** *tibia*. —ı **ketif** shoulder blade, *scapula*. —ı **kûbere** *radius*. —ı **lâmi** tongue bone, *hyoides*. —ı **mik'a** plowshare bone, *vomer*. —ı **rıdfa** kneepan, kneecap, *rotula, patella*. —ı **rikâbî** stirrup bone, stapes. —ı **sutgi** temporal bone, *os temporale*. —ı **şaziye** *fibula*. —ı **terkova** clavicle, *clavicula*. —ı **us'us** *coccyx*. —ı **vecenî** zygomatic bone, *os zygomaticum*. —ı **vetedî** sphenoid, *os sphenoidale*. —ı **zend** *cubitus, ulna*. —ı **zıfri** *os unguis*.

azımsa= آزیساسه , **azımsı=** آزیمسی /ı/ to regard as too little.

azın azın آزن آزن *archaic* little by little, slowly.

azınlık[ⁿ] *neol.* minority. —**lar** the minorities, *esp.*, the non-Muslim communities in Turkey.

azınsı= آزنسی *prov., var. of* **azımsı=**.

azırga= آزرغه /ı/ *archaic* to regard as little, to belittle. —**n=** *prov.* 1. /ı/ to regard as little. 2. to be stingy, mean.

azırra (..—) اضرّا A *lrnd.*, *pl. of* **zarir**.

azış= آزشمه 1. to grow vehement, to become worse. 2. to grow exasperated with each other. 3. *archaic* to lose one another. —**tır=** *caus.*

azıt= آزتمه 1. to become unmanageable, wild, excited. 2. /ı/ to lose (one's way); to let go out of hand; to cause to overgrow; to allow to smart (wound); to make go astray, to let fall into vicious deeds.

azi 1 (— —) آزی A *lrnd.* wave.

azi 2, azî (.—) عذی A *var. of* **azy.**

azi 3 (.—) عزی A *lrnd.* patient, enduring.

âzib 1 (—.) عازب A *lrnd.* bachelor, unmarried.

azîb 2 (.—) عزیب A *lrnd.* bachelor, unmarried.

azide (——.) آزیده P *lrnd.* pricked (with a sharp-pointed instrument).

azif (.—) عزیف A *lrnd., same as* **azf 1.** —**i ra'd** the distant rumble of thunder.

azife (—..) آزفه A *lrnd.* 1. that which is to come, which is near. 2. death; resurrection, the future state.

aziğ (— —) آزیغ P *lrnd.* aversion, disgust, abhorrence.

azih عزه A *lrnd.* not fond of music, women, and amusement; morose.

azihe (.—.) عضیهه A *lrnd.* lie, calumny.

azil[ⁿ] **1** عزل |azl 1| 1. dismissal, discharge from office; dismissed, discharged from office. 2. *lrnd.* onanism. — **et=***. — **ol=**, — **olun=***.

âzil 2 (—.) عاذل A *lrnd.* faultfinding, faultfinder.

âzil 3 (—.) عاذل A *lrnd.* a blood vessel connected with menstruation.

azîle (.—.) عضیل A *lrnd.* muscle.

azim 1 (.—) عظیم A 1. great, vast, immense. 2. powerful, magnificent, glorious. 3. *archaic* very much, greatly.

azim[zmi] **2** عزم [azm 1] 1. determination, resolution. 2. *lrnd.* a setting out, beginning, undertaking. — **et=***. —**i rah**, —**i sefer** a setting out on a journey.

âzim 3 (—.) عازم A *lrnd.* 1. who sets out on a journey. 2. resolved to do (something), determined. —**i dâr-ı beka ol=** to die. — **ol=** 1. to set out. 2. to decide on something. —**i sefer ol=** 1. to set out on a journey. 2. to decide on a journey.

azîm 4 (.—) عزیم A *lrnd.* determined run, dash.

azîme 1 (.—.) عظیمه A *lrnd.* important affair; great sin; grievous calamity.

âzime 2 (—..) آزمه A *lrnd.* biting; bitter, disastrous (year).

âzime 3 (—..) آزمه A *lrnd.* canine tooth.

azîme 4 (.—.) عزیمه A *lrnd.* reproach, censure, reproof.

azîme 5 (.—.) عزیمه A *lrnd.* incantation, spell; charm, amulet. — **oku=** to recite an incantation.

azimet (.—.) عزیمت A 1. a setting out, departure. 2. *var. of* **azîme 5**. — **et=** to set out on a journey.

azimkâr (..—) عزمکار [based on **azim 2**] determined, resolute. —**ane** (..— —.) P resolutely, with determination.

azimli عزملی determined, resolute.

azimut F *astr.* azimuth.

azimülkadr[ri] (.—..) عظیم القدر A *lrnd.* great in power.

azimüşşan (.—.—) عظیم الشان [based on Arabic] *lrnd.* most glorious.

azimüttecalid (.—..— —) عظیم التجالید A *lrnd.* large-limbed, large-bodied.

âzin 1 (—.) آذن A *lrnd.* 1. who permits. 2. porter, doorkeeper. 3. bail, surety.

âzin 2 (—.) آذن P *lrnd.* 1. ceremony, pageant. 2. general illumination with flags, etc.

azine (— —.) آذینه P *lrnd.* Friday.

azir 1 (.—) عزیر A *lrnd.* 1. excuse, apology. 2. who makes an excuse, apologist, defender.

azir 2 (.—) عزیر A *lrnd.* rent paid for the pasture of a field after its crop has been gathered.

âzire 1 (—..) آزیره A *lrnd., pl. of* **izar 3**.

azire 2 عذره A *lrnd.* 1. courtyard. 2. human excrement.

âzire 3 (—.) عزیره A *lrnd.* feast.

aziye (.—.) عذیه A *lrnd.* rich upland soil.

aziz

aziz 1 (.—) عَزِيز A 1. dear, beloved. 2. saintly, holy, sacred; saint. 3. *lrnd.* rare, high-priced, precious, highly esteemed. 4. *lrnd.* glorious, great; powerful, mighty. 5. *w. cap.*, *man's name.* **A—i Hakîm** the powerful and wise God. **A—i Mısr** the powerful Prince of Egypt (used *esp.*, for Potiphar and Joseph). **— ol!** May you be always esteemed! **A—i Zuintikam** the powerful and jealous God.

aziz 2 (.—) عَضّ A *lrnd.* 1. a snapping, biting; bite. 2. companion, one of the same age.

azizan (.——) عَزِيزان P *lrnd.*, *pl. of* **aziz 1.**

azize (.—.) عَزِيزه A *fem. of* **aziz 1.**

Aziziye (.——.) عَزِيزِيّه [*based on* **Aziz 1⁵.**] 1. *name of a quarter of the city of Aleppo.* 2. *former name of two towns in Anatolia, now called* **Emirdağ** *and* **Pınarbaşı**, *respectively.* **a— fes** broad-bottomed, narrow-crowned fez with short tassel, as worn in the time of Sultan Abdulaziz.

azizlik^gi **1** عَزِيزلِك practical joke, trick played for fun.

azizlik 2 (.—.) عَزِيزلِك *abstr. n. of* **aziz 1.** **— et=** /a/ to play a trick (on a friend for fun).

azk^ki عَزْك A *lrnd.* palm-tree laden with dates.

azl^li **1** عَزْل A *same as* **azil 1.**

azl^li **2** عَذْل A *lrnd.* a blaming, censuring; blame, reproof.

azl^li **3** عَضْل A *lrnd.* a preventing, *esp.*, a wrongfully forbidding a girl to marry.

azlaf (.—) اظلاف A *lrnd.*, *pl. of* **zılf.**

azlâl^li (.—) اظلال A *lrnd.* shades, shadows.

azlem اظلم A *lrnd.* 1. darkest. 2. most unjust, very tyrannical.

azlet=^der عَزْلِيتْمَك [**azil 1**] /ı/ to dismiss from office.

azlık^gi آزْلِق 1. paucity, scarcity. 2. minority.

azlol=^ur, **azlolun=**^ur عَزْل اولمه، عَزْل اولونمه [**azil 1**] *pass. of* **azlet=.**

azm^mi **1** عَزْم A *same as* **azim 2.**

azm 2 عَظْم A *same as* **azım.**

azm^mi **3** عَضْم A *lrnd.* 1. a biting; a champing. 2. a reproaching, chiding; a reviling; a driving away with menaces or reproaches.

azm 4 عَظْم A *lrnd.* 1. winnowing fork. 2. grasp of an archery bow. 3. root of the tail.

azma 1 آزْما 1. monstrous; monstrosity. 2. hybrid, half-bred.

-azma 2 (——) آزْما P *lrnd.* experienced in, *as in* **kârazma.**

azma 3 (.—) اظلما A *lrnd.* 1. dried up, parched. 2. one who has brown and bloodless gums. 3. black; dusky, tawny.

azmak^gi آزْماق 1. body of water left over from an inundation; marshy depression. 2. artificial or temporary stream of water resulting from the overflow of a river.

azman آزْمان 1. enormous, overgrown; an extra large specimen. 2. hybrid. 3. *prov.* castrated (animal). 4. heavy log.

-azmay (——) آزْماى P *var. of* **-azma 2.**

-azmayi (———) آزْمايى P *lrnd.*, *abstr. n. of* **-azma 2.**

azmayiş (——.) آزْمايش P *lrnd.* experienced; proof, trial.

azme عَزْمه A *lrnd.* 1. intention, resolution. 2. duty.

azmen 1 (.'.) عَزْمًا A *lrnd.* resolutely, determinedly.

azmen 2 اضْمَن A *lrnd.* 1. most comprehensive. 2. most trustworthy as a surety.

azmend (—.) آزْمند A *lrnd.* greedy, covetous.

azmet=^der **1** عَزْم ايتْمَك [**azim 2**] 1. /a/ to resolve (upon), to decide firmly. 2. *lrnd.* to start off (on a journey).

azmet 2 عَزْمت A *lrnd.* resolution, determination.

azmi 1 (.—) عَزْمى [*based on* **azm 1**] 1. pertaining to resolution. 2. *w. cap.*, *man's name.*

azmi 2 (.—) عَظْمى A *anat.* of bone, osseous.

azmude 1 (——.) آزْموده P *lrnd.* that has been tried, proved, known by experience.

-azmude 2 (——.) آزْموده P *lrnd.* experienced in, *as in* **kârazmude.**

azmudegi (——.—) آزْمودگى P *lrnd.* experience.

azmun (——) آزْمون P *lrnd.* proof, trial, experiment.

aznavur آزْناوور Georgian 1. *prov.* terror inspiring, dark-faced, sour-faced. 2. *archaic* chief, head.

aznif اَزْنيف Arm kind of domino (game).

azoik^gi F *geol.* azoic.

azot آزوت F *chem.* nitrogen.

azoti (..—) آزوطى [*based on* **azot**] *chem.* nitrogenous. **—yet** (..—.) nitrate.

azotlu آزوتلى *chem.* nitrogenous.

azr^ri عَذْر A *lrnd.* a forbidding, prevention.

azra (.—) عَذْرا A *lrnd.* 1. virgin. 2. *astr.*, Virgo. 3. unbored pearl. 4. an iron instrument of torture. 5. *backgammon* a throw of two dice making seven points. 6. *w. cap.*, *woman's name, esp.*, *Vamık's sweetheart in the epic poem of Vamık and Azra.* 7. Medina.

Azrail (.——) عَزْرائيل, (.—.) عَزْرَئيل A Azrael (name of the angel of death).

azrar (.—) اَضْرار A *lrnd.* harms, losses, injuries.

azref اظرف A *lrnd., superl. of* **zarif.**

azub (. —) عزوب A *lrnd.* 1. abstaining from eating and drinking because of excessive fatigue (beast). 2. unsheltered.

a'zud 1 اعضد A *lrnd., pl. of* **adud, azd, azıd, azud 2, ızd, uzd, uzud.**

azud 2 عضد A *lrnd., var. of* **adud.**

azuf 1 (. —) عزوف A *lrnd.* food.

azuf 2 (. —) عزوف A *lrnd.* abstaining, averse.

azuğ (— —) آزوغ P *lrnd.* a lopping, trimming. 2. prunings, loppings (of trees).

azuka (— —.) آزوقه P *lrnd.* provisions.

a'zum 1 اعظم A *lrnd., pl. of* **azm 2.**

azum 2 (. —) عزوم A *lrnd.* 1. determined, resolute, persevering. 2. aged she-camel with some remains of strength. 3. old woman.

azum 3 (. —) عضوم A *lrnd.* hardy, robust.

azumet (. —.) عزومت A entertainment, feast.

âzur 1 (— —) آزور P *lrnd.* avaricious, greedy.

azur[rru] **2** اضر A *lrnd., pl. of* **zarra 1.**

âzur 3 (— —) آذور A *lrnd.* inflammation of uvula and fauces, pain in the throat.

azuz (. —) عضوض A *lrnd.* 1. bite, thing to be eaten. 2. given to biting. 3. severe, distressing (circumstance). 4. tyrannical.

azürde (— ..) آزرده P *lrnd.* hurt, annoyed, offended, rebuked, afflicted. —**dil** (— ...) P hurt at heart, sorrowful. —**gi** (— .. —) P pain, grief, affliction, annoyance. —**lik** (— ...) *abstr. n. of* **azürde.**

azv[vi] عزو *lrnd.* imputation, a falsely imputing. — **et**=, —ı **töhmet et**= /a,ı/ to impute.

azva (. —) اعضوا A *lrnd., pl. of* **zav.** *cf.* **edva.**

azvay اضواء aloes (drug).

azver (—.) آزور P *var. of* **âzur 1.**

azvî (. —) عزوى [based on **azv**] *lrnd.* imputative.

azviyat (. — —) عزویات [based on **azv**] *lrnd.* unproved imputations.

azy[yı] عزى A *lrnd.* watered by rain only (field).

ayzaf (. —) اضیاف A *lrnd., pl. of* **zayf.**

ayzak[kı] اضیق A *lrnd., superl. of* **zayyık.**

âzz 1 (—) عاض *cf.* **âz 4.**

azz 2 (—) عاض *cf.* **az 5.**

azz 3 عظ *cf.* **az 6.**

azza عضه A *lrnd.* a single act of biting, bite.

azzab (. —) عضاب A *lrnd.* abuser, reviler.

azzaf (. —) عزّاف A *lrnd.* rumbling, noisy with thunder (cloud).

azzal[li] (. —) عزّال A *lrnd.* railer, accuser, faultfinder.

azze ismühü (.'. .'..) عزّ اسمه A May His name be glorified.

azze nasruhu (.'. .'..) عزّ نصره A May His assistance (to him) be powerful.

azze ve celle (.'. . .'.) عزّ و جلّ A May He be honored and glorified.

B

b, B *second letter of the alphabet.* (As an abbreviation **B.** stands for **Bay**).

baᵃⁱ **1** (—) بْ A *Arabic script, name of the letter* ب (This letter is the 2nd letter of the Arabic alphabet, pronounced as **b**. In chronograms, it has the numerical value of 2. In dates, it is the abbreviation for **Receb**, or it stands as a symbol for Monday. In astronomical works, it stands for *Gemini*). **—i Arabiye, —i ebced, — muvahhade** the Arabic, or single-dotted ب , (as opposed to **—i Farisiye, —i müsellese, —i Tasiye** the Persian, or three dotted پ which is pronounced P).

ba 2 (—) بْ P *lrnd.* with, *e. g.*, **ba dostan telattuf, ba düşmanan müdara** with friends affability, with enemies simulated friendliness. **ba sened** with receipt, with document, **ba tapu** with title deed.

ba 3 بَ Gk oh!, oh, indeed!

baᵃⁱ **4** (—) بَاع A *lrnd.* 1. fathom, measure of the two arms extended. 2. nobility, rank.

baa (—.) باع A *lrnd.*, *pl. of* **bayi**.

baakᵏⁱ (.—) بهان A *meteor.* rain cloud.

Baalbekᵏⁱ بعلبك Baalbek, Heliopolis.

Baalzebub (...—) بعل زبوب *Heb.*, **Baalzebul**ⁱⁱⁱ Gk *Bib.* Beelzebub.

bab 1 (—) باب A *lrnd.* 1. chapter. 2. branch, field; class, kind, category. 3. respect, relation. 4. *Arabic gram.* aspect. 5. *onomancy* alphabet. **—ı kebir** *onomancy* the Persian alphabet of 29 letters. **—ı sagir** *onomancy* the Arabian alphabet of 22 letters, contained in the **ebced** formula. **—ı tahkir** *Arabic gram.* depreciatory noun form.

bab 2 (—) باب A *lrnd.* 1. gate, door. 2. public building, office; palace. 3. *Maliye term* unit (for buildings). 4. passage; mountain pass; strait. 5. *anat.* portal vein, *vena portae.* 6. *myst.* spiritual leader, chief saint; *w. cap.*, title of the founder of the Babi sect. **—ı adalet** the administration of justice, the courts. **—ı âli*. —ı asafi** *obs.* the palace of the Grand Vizier. **B—ı Askerî** *Ott. hist.* the offices of the Ministry of War. **B—ı Defteri** *Ott. hist.* the offices of the Ministry of Finance. **—ı devlet** civil service. **—ı fetvapenahi** the office of the Sheikh ul Islam. **B—ı Hümayun** the Imperial Gate (name of the outermost big gate of Topkapı Saray). **— mahkemesi** *obs.* a certain lower court in Istanbul. **—ı meşihat** the office of the Sheikh ul Islam. **— naibi** *obs.* head of a certain lower court in Istanbul. **B—ı Saadet** 1. the Gate of Happiness (name of the innermost big gate of Topkapı Saray). 2. the Court of the Sultan. 3. Istanbul. **B—ı Selâm** the Gate of Peace (name of the second big gate of Topkapı Saray). **B—ı Seraskerî** *Ott. hist.* Offices of the Minister of War. **B—ı Şerif** *Mevlevi order* the gate of Mevlana Jalaleddin Rumi's mausoleum in Konya. **B—ı Zaptiye** *Ott. hist.* Offices of the Minister of Police.

bab 3 (—) باب *archaic* good luck; fortunate. **— tut=** /ı/ to hold auspicious.

bab 4 (—) باب P *lrnd.* worthy, deserving, suitable.

bab 5 (—) باب P *lrnd.* 1. father. 2. spiritual father.

baba 1 بابا 1. father. 2. elderly man; venerable man (often used after name). 3. elder of a religious order, sheikh. **—m!** 1. my, my! 2. *between two imperatives, exclamation over something that does not seem to end, e. g.,* **koş babam koş!** Run, run, run!

— **adam** a fatherly, kind man. — **anne***. —**nın aşık kemiğine!** on your father's knucklebone! (used in abuse). —**dan babaya** ancestral. — **bir** of the same father but of a different mother. — **bucağı** property inherited from ancestors. — **değil, tırabzon babası** said of a good-for-nothing father. — **dostu** paternal friend, old friend of the family. —**sının hayrına değil ya!** not just for love. —**sı hık demiş, burnundan düşmüş** colloq. He is just like his father. — **hindi** turkey cock. — **hindi gibi kabar=** to swell like a turkey cock. — **incir** large fig. —**dan kalma**, —**dan miras** inherited from the father. — **mirası mum gibidir** Inherited wealth melts like a candle. — **ocağı** family home. —**dan oğula** from father to son. —**sının oğlu** Like father like son. —**sı oğluna bir bağ bağışlamış, sonra oğlu babasına bir salkım üzüm vermemiş** proverb The father gave the son a vineyard; later the son denied his father a bunch of grapes. —**na rahmet!** Bless your father! — **tahir** cf. **tahir**. — **tarafından** on the father's side, paternal. — **torik** joc. large bonito. — **yiğit***. — **yurdu** family homestead.

baba 2 بابا 1. naut. bollard; bitt. 2. stout post of a staircase, newelpost. 3. knob. — **tatlısı** kind of fritter.

baba 3 بابا kind of nervous fit said to be characteristic of negro slaves; fit of dogged obstinacy. —**sı tut=**, —**ları üstünde ol=** /ın/ to have a fit.

baba 4 بابا prov., var. of **veba**.

baba 5 (— —) بابا P lrnd. 1. father. 2. grandfather. 3. head of an order, sheikh.

babaanne بابا آننه father's mother, paternal grandmother.

babacan بابا جان good-natured; nice elderly man.

babaçᶜⁱ باباچ 1. big (turkey cock or other fowl). 2. swaggering, big.

babaçko (.'.) باباچقو slang stout (woman).

babadya (.'.) archaic var. of **papatya**.

babafingo (...'.) بابافینغو Gk naut. topgallant. — **çubuğu** topgallant mast. — **grandi** main topgallant. — **sereni** topgallant yard. — **yelkeni** topgallant sail.

babakoru بابا قورى veined agate cut so that the veins run horizontally across the surface; jasponyx.

babaköş, babakûş بابا كوش blindworm, zool., Anguis fragilis.

babal prov., var. of **vebal**.

babalı 1 بابالى having a father. — **fırın has çıkarır** A father's oven produces good bread (said regarding a young man who spends his father's money).

babalı 2 بابالى 1. having a nervous fit (negro slave). 2. irritable, irascible.

babalıkᵍⁱ بابالق 1. fatherhood. 2. stepfather; father-in-law; adoptive father. 3. simple old man. — **dâvası** law affiliation proceedings. — **et=** /a/ to act as a father (to).

babayane (— — —.) بابایانه P lrnd. fatherly, paternal (act, manner); like a father.

babayani (.. —'.) بابایانى [**babayane**] unpretentious, free and easy (man). —**lik** abstr. n.

babayiğitᵈⁱ بابا یگیت brave lad, strong fellow; brave, virile. —**lik** braveness, virility.

baber (—.) بابر P 1. var. of **bebr**. 2. w. cap., Babur (name of a Mogul emperor).

babet (—.) بابت A lrnd. 1. item. 2. respect, relation. 3. a suitable thing. 4. prov. class, category. —**le=** /ı/ to classify.

Babıâli (—. — —) باب عالى P 1. hist. the Sublime Porte (the Central Office of the Imperial Government of the Ottoman Empire in Istanbul, comprising the offices of the Grand Vizier, the Minister of Foreign Affairs, and the Council of State). 2. name of a quarter in Istanbul that has a concentration of publishers.

Babil (—.) بابل A Babylon, Babel. — **kulesi** the tower of Babel.

Babilhane (—. — .) بابلخانه P same as **babulhane**.

Babilî (—. —) بابلى A lrnd. 1. Babylonian. 2. l. c., seductive, lewd.

Babulˡᵘ بابل var. of **Babil**.

babulhane (.. — .) بابولخانه, **babulluk**ᵍᵘ بابوللق archaic brothel.

babulhaneci keeper of a brothel.

babune (— — .) بابونه P, **babunec** (— — .) بابونج A camomile, bot., Anthemis nobilis.

babur (—.) بابر var. of **baber**.

Babül'ebvab (—. . —) باب الابواب A lrnd., geog. Darband.

Babül'esvakᵏⁱ (—. . —) باب الاسواق A lrnd. straits of Gibraltar.

Babüssaada (—. . —.) باب السعاده A var. of **Babı Saadet**. — **ağası** hist. head eunuch of the Sultan's harem.

Babüzzukakᵏⁱ (—. . —) باب الزقاق A lrnd. Straits of Gibraltar.

babzen (—.) بابزن P lrnd. spit, skewer.

bac (—) باج P hist. 1. tribute; tax. 2. toll. —**ı bazar** Ott. hist. market dues. — **u harac** tribute and contribution, duties, taxes. —**ı kırtıl** Ott. hist. pasture dues. —**ı tamga** hist. a kind of sales tax. —**ı ubur** hist. transit duty.

baca باجا 1. chimney; flue; naut. funnel. 2. skylight; smoke hole. 3. shaft; mine shaft; sewer ventilator. 4. prov. flat roof. 5. prov. lamp-chimney. — **aydınlığı**

skylight. **— başı** projecting ledge around the mantle of a fireplace. **—sı eğri amma tütünü doğru çıkar** (*lit.* The chimney is crooked, but the smoke comes out straight.) Don't bother about details. **— kulağı** side shelf of a fireplace. **— külâhı** chimney cap, cowl. **— süpürücü** chimney sweep. **— tomruğu** *arch.* the part of the chimney rising above the roof. **—sı tütmez** whose chimney does not smoke, poor, desolate.

bacak[g1] **1** باجانه. cards jack, knave.

bacak[g1] **2** باجانه. 1. leg. 2. shank. **— kadar** tiny, small (child), very short (person). **— kalemi** shank bone, *anat., tibia.* **—lı** 1. legged. 2. long-legged. 3. *obs.* Dutch ducat. 4. *print.* ascending or descending (letter). **—lı yazı** large, plain script. **—sız** 1. short-legged, dwarfish. 2. insignificant, miserable.

bacaluşka (...'.) بجالشقه. It *mil. hist.* basilisk (kind of gun).

bacanak[g1] باجاناه. the husband of one's wife's sister.

bacban (——) باجبان P *lrnd.* collector of tolls.

bacdar (——) باجدار P *lrnd.* collector of tolls.

baceng (—.) باجنك P *lrnd.* small window.

bacgâh (——) باجكاه P *lrnd.* toll-house.

bacgir (——) باجگیر P *lrnd.* collector of tolls.

bacgüzar (—.—) باجگزار P *lrnd.* tributary; taxable.

bacı باجى 1. negro nurse. 2. *prov.* elder sister; sister. 3. *prov.* wife. 4. *myst.* orders, title of respect given to the sheikh's wife.

bacınak[g1] باجیناه *var. of* **bacanak**.

baç[c1] باچ *same as* **bac**.

bad[d1, di] **1** (——) باد P *poet.* 1. wind. 2. air. 3. breath. 4. sigh, moan, groan. 5. *myst.* the aid of God. 6. pride, haughtiness. 7. praise. **—ı afet** wind of calamity. **—ı aheng** melody, tune. **—ı aşk** passion of love. **—ı bahar** breeze of spring. **— u bid** nothing. **—ı bürut** pride, airs, conceit. **—ı cem** wind obedient to Solomon. **—ı ecel**, **—ı fena** death. **—ı giysu** pride, airs, affectation. **—ı hava** 1. *hist.* law of the country (*i. e.,* when a criminal is apprehended and punished in any place of which he is not a native). 2. *Ott. hist.* kind of revenue. 3. *same as* **bedava**. **—ı hazan** the wind of autumn. **—ı herze** nonsense. **—ı İsa**, **—ı Mesih** 1. the healing breath of Jesus. 2. able physician. 3. a sovereign remedy. **—ı neva** melody, tune. **—ı nevruz** spring breeze. **—ı saba** 1. zephyr. 2. *myst.* divine influence of grace. **—ı sarsar** violent, cold storm. **—ı seher** morning breeze. **—ı semum** the poisonous wind of the desert. **—ı serd** 1. cold wind. 2. deep sigh. **—ı subh** morning breeze. **—ı Süleyman** 1. the wind that wafted king Solomon wherever he wished. 2. majesty, magnificence. **—ı şurta** fair, favorable wind.

bad 2 (——) باد P *var. of* **bade 1.**

-bad 3 (——) باد P *lrnd.* let it be, it, *as in* **mübarekbad, selâmetbad.**

ba'd- 4 بعد A *lrnd.* after, *as in* **ba'dezin.**

-bada (——) بادا P *lrnd., var. of* **-bad 3.**

badad (——) باداد P *lrnd.* with equity, justly; just, equitable.

badaluşka (...'.) بدالشقه *var. of* **bacaluşka.**

badam (——) بادام P *poet.* 1. almond. 2. beautiful eye. **—ı dümağz** almond with two kernels. **—î** (————) P almond-shaped.

badana 1 بادانه limewash, whitewash. **— et=** /ı/, **— vur=** /a/ to whitewash.

badana=[r] **2** بادناس /ı/ *archaic* to whitewash.

badanacı بادناجى whitewasher.

badanala=[r] بادنالا /ı/ to whitewash. **—n=** *pass.* **—t=** /a,ı/ *caus.*

badanalı بادنالى whitewashed.

badaş 1 بادش |padaş ?| *same as.* **bağdaş 2.**

badaş=[r] **2** بادشم *same as* **bağdaş=** 3.

badaver, badaverd (——.) بادآور P *lrnd.* 1. windfall, riches acquired without labor. 2. *name of one of the treasures of Khusrau Parwiz.* 3. *a mode in Oriental music.*

badban (——) بادبان P *lrnd.* sail. **—ı ahdar** the blue firmament.

badbanküşa (——.—) بادبانكشا P *lrnd.* that spreads sail. **—yı azimet ol=** to set out on a journey.

badbedest (—..) بادبدست P *lrnd.* empty-handed, poor, frustrated.

badbiz (——) بادبیز P *lrnd.* fan.

badderkef[ffi] (—..) بادركف P *lrnd.* poor, penniless; disappointed.

bade 1 (—.) باده P *poet.* 1. wine. 2. cup, bowl, glass of wine. **—i canbahş** life-giving wine. **—i gülfam**, **—i gülgûn**, **—i gülreng**, **—i hamra** red wine. **—i mest** strong wine. **—i nab** clear wine. **—i sadsale** century-old wine. **— süz=** to drink wine.

ba'de- 2 (.'.) بعد A *lrnd.* after, *as in* **ba'de haza.**

ba'de bu'din (.'.'.) بعد بعد A *lrnd.* so long afterwards.

badefra, badefrah (—.—) بادافرا بادافراه P *lrnd.* punishment, retribution.

badefürüş (—..—) باده فروش P *lrnd.* seller of wine.

badegüsar (—..—) باده گسار, **badehar** (—.—) باده خوار P *poet.* drinker of wine.

ba'deharabilbasra (...—...) بعد خراب البصره A

lrnd. when it is too late (*lit.*, after the destruction of Basra).

ba'de haza (.'. — —) بعد هذا A *lrnd.* after this.

ba'dehu (.'..) بعده A *lrnd.* afterwards, then.

badekeş (— ..) باده‌کش P *lrnd.* wine-drinker.

ba'del'asr بعد العصر A *lrnd.* after the hour of afternoon service.

ba'del'eda (...—) بعد الأداء A *lrnd.* 1. after (a thing) is performed. 2. after a payment is made.

ba'del'icra (...—) بعد الاجراء , **ba'del'ifa** (..— —) بعد الايفاء A *lrnd.* after (a thing) is performed.

ba'del'imza (...—) بعد الامضاء A *lrnd.* after the signature.

ba'delliya velleti (...— ..—) بعد اللیا والتی A *lrnd.* after a great deal of trouble and noise.

ba'delvuku[uu] (...—) بعد الوقوع A *lrnd* after the event, *ex post facto*.

ba'delyevm بعد اليوم A *lrnd.* henceforth, from now on.

badem (—.) بادم P *almond* (tree and fruit). — **ağacı** almond tree, *bot.*, *Prunus amygdalus*. — **ezmesi** almond paste, marchpane, marzipan. — **göz** almond eye. — **helvası** kind of sweet made with almonds. — **içi** almond kernels. — **kurabiyesi** macaroon. — **kürk** fur made up of the legs only of fox's skins. — **sübyesi** drink made of pounded almonds, almond milk. — **şekeri** 1. sugared almonds. 2. *slang* bullet. — **yağı** almond oil.

ba'dema (.'. —) بعد ما A *lrnd.* henceforth.

bademcik[gi] بادمجك tonsil, *anat.*, *amygdala*. —**leri al**=, —**leri çıkar**= to remove the tonsils.

bademî (—.—) بادمی P pertaining to almonds; almond-shaped.

bademli (—..) بادملو containing almonds.

bademlik[gi] (—..) بادملك almond orchard.

badenuş (—.—) باده‌نوش P *poet.* wine-drinker.

badepalâ (—.——) باده‌پالا P *lrnd.* wine-strainer.

badeperest باده‌پرست P *poet.* lover of wine, drunkard.

badepeyma, badepeymay (—..—) باده‌پیما P *poet.* wine-drinker.

baderna (.'.) بادرنه It *naut.* keckling. — **et**= /l/ to keckle.

ba'desselâm (...—) بعد السلام A *lrnd.* after salutation (initial formula in letters).

ba'dettahiye (...—.) بعد التحية A *lrnd.* after due salutation.

ba'dettahkik (...—) بعد التحقيق A *lrnd.* after investigation.

ba'dettecribe بعد التجربة A *lrnd.* after experience; *phil.*, *a posteriori*.

ba'deza (..—) بعد ذا A, **ba'de zalike** (.'. —'..) بعد ذلك A, **ba'dezan** (..—) بعد آزان P *lrnd.* after that, afterwards.

ba'dezin (..—) بعد ازین بعد ازاین P *lrnd.* henceforth, hereafter.

ba'dezzeval[li] (...—) بعد الزوال A *lrnd.* after noontime, p.m.

badgân (——) بادگان P *lrnd.* keeper, guardian; treasurer.

badgâne (——.) بادگانه P *lrnd.* latticed window.

badgerd (—.) بادگرد P *lrnd.* 1. dust cloud. 2. whirlwind.

badgir (——) بادگیر P *lrnd.* opening for ventilation.

Badgis (——) بادغیس name of a district in northwest Afghanistan.

badgünd (—.) بادگند , **badhaye** (——.) بادخایه P *lrnd.* 1. swollen testicle. 2. inguinal hernia.

badherze (—..) بادهرزه P *lrnd.* incantation employed by housebreakers to lull the people of the house to sleep.

badıç[cı] بادج *Arm prov.* pod.

badi 1 بادی *prov.* duck. — **badi yürü**= to waddle.

badi 2 (——) بادی A *lrnd.* 1. that originates, causes; author, originator. 2. beginning; a beginning. 3. conspicuous, apparent. —**i emirde** in the beginning. —**i nazarda** at first glance. — **ol**= /a/ to be the cause (of).

badi 3 (——) بادی A *lrnd.* dwelling in the wilderness; peasant.

badi 4 (——) بادی P *lrnd.* 1. pertaining to the wind; windy; aerial, airy. 2. inconstant.

ba'di 5 (.—) بعدی [based on **ba'd-** 4] *phil.*, *a posteriori*.

badiebed'in (—...'.) بادی ابدی A *lrnd.* first of all.

badih (—.) بادہ A *lrnd.* unexpected, sudden; unexpected visitor.

badihe (—..) بادھہ A *lrnd.* 1. unexpected event. 2. *myst.* sudden inspiration of the heart.

badik[gi] بادیك 1. *slang* bandy-legged, waddling. 2. *prov.* duck; gosling. —**le**= to waddle.

badilcan (—.—) بادلجان P *var. of* **badincan**.

badilücan (—..—) بادل وجان P *lrnd.* with heart and soul.

badin (—.) بادن A *lrnd.* 1. large-bodied, bulky, fat. 2. stiff with age, old.

bad'inan (—.—) باعنات P *poet.* swift, fleet (horse).

badincan, badingân (—.—) بادنجان بادنگان P *lrnd.* eggplant, *bot.*, *Solanum melongena*. —ı

badincaniye

ahmer tomato, *bot., Lycopersicum esculentum*. **—ı berrî**, **—ı deştî** wild eggplant, *bot., Solanum cordatum*. **—ı tiryaki** burweed, clotweed, *bot., Xanthium strumarium*.

badincaniye (—.——.) باذنجانية [based on **badincan**] *bot., Solanaceae*.

badir (—.) بادر A *lrnd*. 1. who strives to do instantly. 2. happening suddenly. 3. full (moon); full-grown (lad); ripe (fruit).

badire (—..) بادرة A *lrnd*. 1. unexpected event; misfortune, calamity. 2. anything said or done off-hand; repartee.

badiülemr (—...) باديء الأمر A *lrnd*. the first beginning of the matter.

badiye 1 (—..) بادية A *lrnd*. desert, wilderness. **—i gul** the desert of demons, *i. e.* the world. **—i tih** the desert of the wanderings of the Israelites.

badiye 2 (—..) بادية P same as **badya**.

badiyenişin (—...—) بادية نشين P *lrnd*. inhabiting the wilderness.

badiyepeyma (—...—) بادية پيما P *lrnd*. journeying in the wilderness; swift horse, traveller.

badiyül'emr (—...) بادي الأمر A *lrnd.*, var. of **badiülemr**.

badiyürrey (—...) بادي الرأي A *lrnd*. the first thought, intuitive opinion.

badkeş (—.) بادكش P *lrnd*. 1. large fan; punkah. 2. bellows.

badkirdar (—.—) بادكردار P *poet*. swift, fleet, nimble.

badmesir (—.—) بادمسير P *poet*. swift as the wind.

badmühre (—..) بادمهره P *lrnd*. stone said to be taken from the skull of the viper and to absorb poison from snake wounds.

badnüma (—.—) بادنما P *lrnd*. vane, weather-cock.

badpa (——) بادپا P *poet*. swift as the wind, fleet (horse). **—yı vehm** quick of conception, of a lively imagination.

badpeyma (—.—) بادپيما P *poet*. 1. swift; swift steed. 2. wandering; traveller, wanderer. 3. pauper, vagabond.

badreftar (—.—) بادرفتار P *poet*. going like the wind, swift, fleet.

badrencbuye (—.—.) بادرنجبويه A *lrnd*. balm, *bot., Melissa officinalis*.

badreng (—.) بادرنك P *lrnd*. 1. citron. 2. lemon balm, lemon thyme. 3. fleet horse.

badrise (——.) بادريسه P *lrnd*. flywheel of a spindle.

badser (—.) بادسر P *lrnd*. proud, vain, affected.

badseyr (—.) بادسير P *poet*. travelling like the wind, swift, fleet.

badsüvar (—.—) بادسوار P *poet*. 1. fleet horse. 2. fleet horseman.

badviz (——) بادويز P *lrnd*. fan.

badya (.'.) باديه [**badiye 2**] wide and shallow bowl, tub.

badzehr (—.) بادزهر P 1. bezoar-stone, *esp.* the one said to be found in the serpent. 2. antidote for poison.

badzen (—.), **badzene** (—..) بادزن P *lrnd*. fan.

-baf (—) باف P *lrnd*. who weaves, as in **zerbaf**.

bafende (—..) بافنده P *lrnd*. weaver.

bafon بافون German silver.

bafte (—.) بافته P *lrnd*. 1. woven. 2. interwoven, *esp.* silk or gold or silver thread, spangles, *etc.* worked on cloth.

bagaj باغاژ F 1. luggage, baggage. 2. *auto*. trunk. **—a ver=** /ı/ to check (baggage), to book (luggage).

bagal[li] بغل P *lrnd*. 1. armpit; inner part of the upper arm. 2. embrace with one arm. 3. side of a hill or mountain. 4. groin.

bagalbend (—...) بغلبند P *lrnd*. band passed around the body under the armpits.

bagalek[ki] بغلك P *lrnd*. glandular swelling under the armpit or in the groin, bubo.

bagalgir (..—) بغلگير P one who supports by holding the upper arm. **—î** (..——) P *abstr. n.*

bagalteri (...—) بغلترى P *lrnd*. sweat of shame, feeling of confusion, bashfulness.

bagam (—.) باغم P *lrnd*. sad, sorrowful.

bagat (——) باغات P *lrnd*. gardens, orchards; vineyards.

bagelat (..—) بغلات A *lrnd., pl.* of **bagle**.

baggal[li] (.—) بقّال A *lrnd*. owner and hirer out of mules; muleteer.

bagi 1 (——) باغى A *lrnd*. 1. rebellious; rebel. 2. wicked; sinner. 3. who desires; seeker. **—yi nisin** 1. seeker after women. 2. young man.

bagi 2 (——) باغى P *lrnd*. grown in a garden.

bagi 3 (.—) بغى A *lrnd*. 1. sinning (woman), adulterous; adulteress; prostitute, harlot. 2. female slave. 3. female singer.

bagistan (—.—) باغستان P *poet*. park; tract of country containing gardens.

bagiy[sy1] *ver*. of **bagy**.

bagiyane (—.—.) باغيانه P *lrnd*. in a rebellious way; wickedly.

bagiye 1 (.—.) بغيه A *lrnd*. advance guard, reconnoitering party.

bagiye 2 (.—.) بغيه A *lrnd*. a thing desired.

bagiz (.—) بغيض A *lrnd*. 1. malevolent,

inimical; hater, enemy. 2. hated, odious, hateful.
bagˡⁱ بغل A *lrnd.* mule.
bagle بغلى A *lrnd.* she-mule.
bagy بغى A *lrnd.* 1. a striving after, desiring excessively. 2. an acting wickedly, oppression, rebellion, sin. 3. a woman's committing fornication or adultery; harlotry. — **et=** 1. to act wickedly, tyrannically, rebelliously. 2. to commit adultery or fornication.
bağ 1 باغ 1. tie, bond; string, lace; bandage; *naut.* knot. 2. bunch; bundle. 3. connection, link; affection. 4. impediment, restraint. 5. *gram.* conjunction. 6. *anat.* ligament. — **doku** *anat.* connective tissue. — **fiil** *gram.* gerund. — **kuşak** *arch.* binding-piece.
bağ 2 (—) باغ *P* 1. vineyard. 2. *poet.* garden, orchard. 3. *poet.* world, sphere (as the scene of happening in poetry). **—ı Adn** the Garden of Eden. — **arala=** to prune the vines. **—ı bahar** *poet.* 1. spring-garden. 2. down or dark hair of youth. — **bahçe** vineyards and orchards. **—ı bedi** *poet.* paradise. — **belle=** to hoe a vineyard over. **—ı bihişt** garden of paradise. — **boz=** to harvest grapes. — **bozumu** vintage. — **bozumu fırtınası** *calendar* a storm occurring about the 1st of October. — **buda=** to prune a vineyard. **—ı cennet** garden of paradise. **—ı cihan** *poet.* the world. **—ı cinan** paradise. — **çubuğu** vine shoot; vine cutting. **—ı dehr** *poet.* the world. — **dik=** to plant a vineyard. **—ı firdevs**, **—ı huld** *poet.* paradise. **—ı İrem** garden of Iram; *poet.* earthly paradise. **—ı kuds** *poet.* paradise. — **kütüğü** vine stock. **—ı naim**, **—ı refi**, **—ı Rıdvan** *poet.* paradise. — **tavası** pan in which grape juice is boiled down to a syrup.
bağ=ᵃʳ 3 باغمى /ı/ to lay a spell (upon), to charm.
bağa باغا بغا 1. tortoise shell; made of tortoise shell or similar material. 2. *obs.* generic name of batrachians and chelonians. — **gözlük** horn-rimmed spectacles.
bağaltakᵍⁱ بغلطاق *P* 1. *prov.* jacket. 2. *lrnd.* headdress. 3. *lrnd.* part of horse armor.
bağana باغانه بغنه بغانه *obs.* astrakhan. — **kürkü** fur of astrakhan lambskin. — **resmi** tax paid on lambskins used for astrakhan fur.
bağarsıkᵍⁱ *prov., var. of* **bağırsak**.
bağban (——) باغبان *P poet.* gardener. **—î** (———) *P lrnd.* horticulture.
bağcı باغجى grape grower. **—lık** viniculture.
bağçe (—.) باغچه *P lrnd., same as* **bahçe**.
bağçevan (—.—) باغچوان *P lrnd., same as* **bahçıvan**.
bağda 1 *prov.* a tripping (with the foot in wrestling).
bağda=ʳ 2 باغدامى /ı/ *obs.* to intertwine; to embrace; to cross (legs).
bağdaçᶜⁱ بغداج *var. of* **bağdaş 1**.
Bağdad (.—) بغداد A *same as* **Bağdat**. **—î** (.——) A 1. pertaining to Baghdad, of Baghdad, from Baghdad. 2. *l. c., arch.* lath and plaster work.
bağdala=ʳ باغدالامى بغدالامى /ı/ *prov.* to entwine one's leg around an opponent's leg so as to trip him in wrestling.
bağdan=ʳ باغدانمى *pass. of* **bağda= 2**.
bağdaş 1 بغداش a sitting cross-legged in Oriental fashion. — **kur=** to sit cross-legged.
bağdaş 2 بغداش [badaş 1] companion, comrade.
bağdaş=ʳ 3 باغداشمى /la/ 1. to suit, to agree, to get along well (with). 2. *obs.* to embrace one another. 3. *prov.* to sit cross-legged.
Bağdatᵈⁱ بغداد A Baghdad. — **çıbanı** Aleppo button. — **gibi diyar, ana gibi yar olmaz** *proverb* There is no country like Baghdad; there is no friend like one's mother. — **hâli, — harap** *joc.* (*lit.*, Baghdad is devastated.) The stomach is empty, I am hungry; the wine cup is empty. — **köşkü** the Baghdad Kiosk in the Palace. — **mahallebisi** kind of milk pudding mixed with pounded almonds and pistachios. — **mâmur** *joc.* (*lit.*, Baghdad is in its prime.) My stomach is full; the wine cup is brimming. **—ı tamir et=** *joc.* (*lit.*, to rebuild Baghdad) to eat one's meal. — **tatlısı** kind of sweet dish made of apricots, sugar, almonds, and cream. **—lı** native of Baghdad.
bağı باغى *archaic* spell, charm.
bağıcı باغجى *same as* **bayıcı**.
bağıl *neol.* 1. dependent, conditional. 2. *phys.* relative.
bağıldakᵍⁱ باغلده *var. of* **bağırdak**.
bağım, bağın *neol.* dependence. **—laşım, —laşma** interdependence. **—lı** dependent. **—lılık** dependence. **—sız** independent. **—sızlık** independence.
bağıntı *neol.* relation. **—cılık** *phil.* relativism. **—lı** *phil, gram.* relative. **—lık** relativity.
bağırᵍʳⁱ **1** بغر باغر 1. bosom, breast. 2. heart. 3. *archaic* liver, lungs. 4. middle part (of an archery bow), saddle (of a mountain). **—lar** *neol., anat.* viscera. **—ı açık** with one's shirt opened. **—ına bas=** /ı/ to embrace, to take to one's heart, to enfold. **—ı baş, —ı başlu** *archaic* having a bleeding heart, greatly distressed. **—ını doğra=, —ını ez=** /ın/ to

bağır= cause intense pain (to). **—ı göçük** hollow-chested. **—ı hûn et=, —ı kan et=** /ın/ to cause the heart to bleed, to pain greatly. **—ı kara** 1. afflicted, sorrowful. 2. kind of bird. **—ı katı** hard-hearted. **—ına taş bas=** to bear suffering with great patience. **—ının yağı eri=, —ı yan=** to endure great suffering. **—ı yanık** heartsick, who has suffered greatly. **— yeleği** *archaic* jacket worn under armor.

bağır=ᴵʳ **2** باغرمه بغرمه to shout, yell, cry out. **—ıp çağır=** to clamor, to shout about.

bağır bağır باغرباغر loudly, at the top of one's voice, *only in* **— bağır=** to shout at the top of one's voice.

bağırdakᵏⁱ باغرداق بغرداق the strap with which an infant is fastened into its cradle.

bağırış 1 باغرش *verbal n. of* **bağır= 2.**

bağırış=ᴵʳ **2** باغرشمك *same as* **bağrış=.**

bağırsakᵏⁱ باغرصاغه بغرسانه *same as* **barsak.**

bağırt=ᴵʳ باغرتمك /ı/ *caus. of* **bağır= 2.**

bağırtı باغرتى outcry, shout, yell.

bağırtlakᵏⁱ باغرتلاق بغرتلاق Pallas's sand grouse, *zool.*, *Syrrhaptes paradoxus.*

bağış *neol.* grant, donation.

bağışıkᵏⁱ *neol., biol.* immune. **—la=** /ı/ to immunize. **—lama** immunization. **—lık** immunity.

bağışla=ʳ باغشلامق بغشلمق /a,ı/ 1. to give gratis, to donate. 2. to forgive, to pardon. 3. not to take away, to spare (life). **—ma** *verbal n.* **—n=** *pass. of* **bağışla=. —t=** /a,ı/ *caus. of* **bağışla=. —yıcı** forgiving; forgiver. **—yış** *verbal n. of* **bağışla=.**

bağlᵘ بغل A *lrnd.* mule.

bağla 1 باغلا *prov.* dam, weir.

bağla=ʳ **2** بغلامق باغلامه 1. /ı,a/ to tie, fasten, bind; to connect. 2. /ı/ to fetter, tie up, chain; to bandage; to wrap up; to tie, make a knot. 3. /ı/ to conclude, to end up (speech, etc.); /ı,a/ to make secure (by contract, etc.). 4. /ı,a/ to assign (salary, etc.); to invest (capital), to engage (money); *irrigation* to let flow (water). 5. /ı/ to obstruct; to paralyse, frustrate (luck, etc.); *archaic* to shut, lock (door). 6. /ı/ to be covered (with a layer of something), to form (skin, crust, scum, etc.); to form (seeds, head, fruit); to draw up (line of battle). 7. /ı/ *prov.* to compose (song, etc.).

bağla=ʳ **3** باغلامه بغلامه /ı/ to bind by a charm or spell.

bağlaçᶜⁱ *neol., gram.* conjunction.

bağlama باغلامه 1. *verbal n. of* **bağla= 2.** 2. tied, bound. 3. folk instrument with three double strings, played with a plectrum. 4. *mech.* coupling. 5. *arch.* crossbar. 6. *ling.* liaison. **— limanı** *naut.* port of registry, home port.

bağlan 1 باغلانت *var. of* **baklan.**

bağlan=ᴵʳ **2** باغلنمك باغلانمه 1. *pass. of* **bağla= 2.** 2. /ı/ *obs.* to tie on or around oneself. **—ıl=** *same as* **bağlan= 2¹. —ış** *verbal n. of* **bağlan= 2.**

bağlantı باغلانتى tie, connection.

bağlaş=ᴵʳ باغلاشمق to unite, to get tied to one another.

bağlat=ᴵʳ باغلتمه باغلتمك /a,ı/ *caus. of* **bağla= 2.**

bağlayıcı باغلايجى tying, binding connecting.

bağlayış باغلايش *verbal n. of* **bağla= 2.**

bağlı 1 باغلو باغلى بغلو 1. bound, chained; /a/ tied, fastened, attached (to), connected (with). 2. having ties, strings, etc. 3. /a/ dependent (on). 4. /a/ faithful, devoted (to). 5. *archaic* closed, locked.

bağlı 2 باغلو باغلى bewitched, spell-bound, *esp.*, so as to be impotent in marriage.

bağlı 3 باغلى باغلو containing vineyards.

bağlıkᵏⁱ باغلى piece of ground suitable for a vineyard; tract with many vineyards.

bağlılıkᵏⁱ باغليلق 1. *abstr. n. of* **bağlı 1**, devotion, attachment. 2. *neol.* correlation. **— endeksi** *statistics* coefficient of correlation.

bağrış=ᴵʳ باغرشمه باغرشمك 1. to cry out together. 2. to yell at each other. **—ma** *verbal n.* **—tır=** *caus. of* **bağrış=.**

bağsaᵃⁱ (. —) بغشا A *lrnd.* mixed crowd, mob.

bağsere بغشره A *lrnd.* confusion, tumult.

bağşış باغشش *prov., var. of* **bahşiş.**

bağtakᵏⁱ بغتاق بغطاق P 1. *obs.* high cap worn by certain women in the Sultan's harem. 2. *obs.* robe. 3. long cloth or shawl wrapped around the chest and waist, sometimes around the head, and sometimes around an infant.

bağteten (´ . .) بغتة A *lrnd.* suddenly.

bağvan (— —) باغوان P *var. of* **bağban.**

bağyaz (. —) بغياز P *lrnd.* present made on occasion of pleasure to oneself as when buying a new house.

bağza (. —) بغضا A *lrnd.* violent, rancorous hatred; extreme spite and ill will.

bağzar (— —) باغزار P *poet.* garden, park; place full of gardens.

bah 1 بَهْ 1. nonsense!, impossible! 2. *prov.* of course.

bah 2 (—) بَاهْ A *lrnd.* 1. coitus. 2. lust, sexual desire, libido.

bah 3 بَخْ A *lrnd.* good! excellent! **— bah!** bravo, bravo!

baha 1 (. —) بها P *same as* **paha.**

baha 2 (—.) باهَا A *lrnd.* 1. enclosed court, yard; area. 2. great body of water.

bahaber (—..) باخبر P *lrnd.* 1. informed. 2. intelligent. 3. cautious, circumspect.

bahacı با غی: *same as* **pahacı**.
bahadır, bahadir, bahadur (. — .) بهادر P *poet.* brave, gallant, valiant; champion, hero. **—an** (. — . —) *pl.* **—lan=** to become brave, to assume the airs of a hero. **—landır=** *caus.* of **bahadırlan=**. **—lık** bravery, heroism, gallantry.
bahadurane (. — . — .) بهادرانه P *poet.* brave (act); gallantly.
bahaduri (. — . —) بهادری P *poet.* valor, bravery.
Bahai (. — —) بهائی P Bahai. **—lik** Bahaism.
bahak^{kı} بهق A *lrnd.* a having a purulent and sunken eye.
bahal^{li} بهل A *lrnd., same as* **buhl**.
bahalan=^{ır}, **bahalaş=**^{ır} (. — . .) بها لانمق بها لاشمق *same as* **pahalan=, pahalaş=**.
bahalı بها لو بها لی: *same as* **pahalı**.
bahane (. — .) بهانه P 1. pretext, excuse. 2. *lrnd.* defect, fault. 3. *lrnd.* motive, cause. **—siyle** under the pretext (of). **— ara=** to seek a pretext, to try to find an excuse. **— bul=** 1. to find a pretext. 2. /a/ to find fault (with). **— et=** /ı/ to use as an excuse. **—ci** who always makes excuses.
bahanecu (. — . — .) بهانه جو P *lrnd.* who seeks a pretext.
bahanefuruş (. — . . —) بهانه فروش P *lrnd.* who makes pretexts.
bahaneperdaz (. — . . —) بهانه پرداز P *lrnd.* who invents excuses.
bahar 1 بهار [bahar 2] 1. spring; season of verdure and flowers. 2. flowers, blossoms; verdure. **—ı başına vur=** 1. to be lightly dressed in cold weather. 2. to become too coquettish. **— faslı, — mevsimi** the spring season. **— noktası** *astr.* vernal point.
bahar 2 بهار [bahar 3] spices.
bahar 3 (. —) بهار P *lrnd., same as* **bahar 2**.
bahar 4 بخر A *lrnd.* fetidness of breath.
baharan (. — —) بهاران P *poet.* spring, spring days.
baharat بهارات [Arabic . — —] spices.
baharcı بهارجی 1. spice-merchant. 2. lover of spices.
baharî (. — —) بهاری P *poet.* pertaining to the spring, vernal.
baharin (. — —) بحارین A *lrnd., pl.* of **buhran**.
baharistan (. — . —) بهارستان P *poet.* 1. spring. 2. place of verdure and blossom.
bahariye (. — — .) بهاریه [based on **bahar 1**] 1. *poetry* ode in praise of the spring season. 2. *Ott. hist.* suit of clothes distributed to certain Janissary officers in the spring.
baharlı بهارلو بهارلی: flavored with spice, spiced.
bahati (. — —) بخاتی A *lrnd., pl.* of **buhti**.

bahatic (. — .) بخاتع A *lrnd., pl.* of **buhtec**.
bahça با غچه *prov., var.* of **bahçe**.
bahçe با غچه باغچه [bağçe] 1. garden; park. 2. garden café. **— kekiği** garden thyme, *bot., Thymus Vulgaris*. **— kızılkuyruğu** European redstart, *zool., Phoenicurus phoenicurus*. **— mimarisi** garden architecture. **— ötleğeni** garden warbler, *zool., Sylvia borin*. **— teresi** garden cress, *bot., Lepidum sativum*. **—cik** small garden. **—li** having a garden or gardens. **—lik** 1. place full of gardens. 2. plot for a garden. 3. *naut.* quarter gallery in an old warship.
Bahçesaray باغچه سرای Bakhchi-sarai (in the Crimea).
bahçıvan باغچه وان [bağçevan] gardener. **— kovası** watering can. **—lar ocağı** *Ott. hist.* the gardeners' quarters in the Sultan's palace. **— tarağı** rake. **—lık** gardening, horticulture.
bahe (. —) باهه A *lrnd.* court, courtyard.
bahem (. —) باهم P *lrnd.* with one another, together.
bahhal^{li} (. —) بخّال A *lrnd.* very avaricious, stingy, miserly.
bahhar (. —) بحّار A *lrnd.* sailor.
bahhas (. —) بحّاث A *lrnd.* 1. investigator, researcher. 2. disputant, controversialist.
bahhat (. —) بختّات A *lrnd.* dealer in or possessor of Bactrian camels.
bahık^{kı} (. —) باهق A *lrnd.* blind in one eye; who has one eye sunk in the socket.
bahıkul'ayn (. — . . .) باهق العین A *lrnd.* blind in one eye.
bahıred (. — . .) باهرد P *lrnd.* intelligent.
bahız (. —) باهظ A *lrnd.* hard to bear, unbearable.
bahıza (. — . .) باهظه A *lrnd.* heavy calamity.
bahi 1 (. — —) باهی A *lrnd.* 1. beautiful, glorious. 2. empty, deserted. 3. wide-mouthed (well).
bahi 2 (. — —) باهی A *lrnd.* venereal, sexual; aphrodisiac; lascivious, lustful.
bahi 3 (. —) بهی A *hist.* a coin with the monogram ج stamped on it.
bahide (. — .) باهیده P *lrnd.* 1. carded. 2. unwound from the cocoon (silk).
bahil 1 (. —) بخیل A avaricious, stingy.
bahil 2 (. —) باخل A *lrnd.* miserly, avaricious.
bahil 3 (. —) باهل A *lrnd.* 1. free, unrestrained. 2. without occupation. 3. unarmed. 4. unmarried.
bahilik et=^{der} باهیلك اتمك to be ready to fly at and kill.
bahir 1 (. —) باهر A *lrnd.* 1. bewildered, confounded. 2. stupid, idiotic. 3. impudent, lying. 4. bright, vivid (red).
bahir 2 (. —) باهر A *lrnd.* 1. manifest,

bahir

evident. 2. that overcomes, superior; that outshines, excellent. 3. a vein in the skin of the head.

bahirʰʳⁱ 3 بحر [**bahr**] same as **bahr** 1, 2.

bahire (. —.) بحيره A Arabian hist. In pre-Islamic times a slit-eared she-camel or sheep left to wander and vested with a sacred character.

bahisʰˢⁱ 1 بحث [**bahs** 1] 1. subject, topic. 2. wager, bet. 3. lrnd. search, investigation, inquiry. 4. lrnd. argument, dispute, controversy, debate. — **aç**= /dan/ to bring up (a subject). —**i âhar**, —**i diger** another matter, different question. — **et**=*. —**i geçen** aforementioned. —**e giriş**= /ına/ to bet, wager. —**i kapa**= to close the subject. —**i kaybet**= to lose the wager. — **mevzuu** subject, matter. — **mevzuu ol**= to be dealt with, discussed, treated (matter). — **mevzuu olma**= to be out of the question. —**i müşterek** pari-mutuel, totalizator, betting. — **tut**=, — **tutuş**= /la/ to bet, wager.

bahis 2 (—.) باحث A lrnd. 1. who investigates; researcher. 2. /dan/ that treats (of a subject).

bahkᵏⁱ بخى A lrnd. a losing one eye.

bahlˡⁱ بخل A lrnd., same as **buhl**.

bahmal باغمال [**mahmel**] obs. velvet.

bahname (——.) باغنامه P pornography, obscene writing.

bahrʳⁱ 1 بحر A lrnd. 1. sea. 2. large lake; large river. 3. very learned man; very generous man. 4. the gape of a bow. **B**—**i Ahmer** the Red Sea. **B**—**i Ahzer** 1. the Indian Ocean. 2. poet. vault of heaven. — **u ber** poet. land and sea. **B**—**i Ebyaz** the Mediterranean. **B**—**i Esved** the Black Sea. **B**—**i Ezrak** the Nile. **B**—**i Faris** the Persian Gulf. **B**—**i Harezm** Lake Aral, Aral Sea. **B**—**i Hazer** the Caspian Sea. —**i ilm**, —**i irfan** sea of wisdom. **B**—**i Kulzüm** 1. the gulf of Suez. 2. the Red Sea. **B**—**i Mağrib** 1. the Mediterranean. 2. the Atlantic Ocean. **B**—**i Meshur** Isl. rel. the Enchanted Sea (the waters under the throne of God). **B**—**i Muhit** the Ocean. **B**—**i Muhit-i Atlasi** the Atlantic Ocean. **B**—**i Muhit-i Hindî** the Indian Ocean. **B**—**i Muhit-i Kebir** the Pacific Ocean. —**i muhitî** geog. oceanic. **B**—**i Mutavassıt** the Mediterranean. **B**—**i Müncemid-i Cenubi** the Antarctic Ocean. **B**—**i Müncemid-i Şimalî** the Arctic Ocean. —**i rahm** anat., fundus uteri. **B**—**i Rum**, **B**—**i Sefid** the Mediterranean. **B**—**i Siyah** the Black Sea. **B**—**i Umman** the Sea of Oman. **B**—**i Zulumat** the Atlantic Ocean.

bahrʳⁱ 2 بحر A pros. class of meters. —**i basit**, —**i cedid**, —**i hafif**, —**i hezec**, —**i kâmil**, —**i medid**, —**i muzari**, —**i müctes**, —**i mütedarik**, —**i mütekarib**, —**i recez**, —**i remel**, —**i seri**, —**i tavil**, —**i vafir** names of the more common classes of meters (For the definitions, see the second word of each compound).

bahrʳⁱ 3 بحر A lrnd. a making wide or spacious.

bahran (ʹ.) بحرا A by sea.

bahreyn بحرين A 1. lrnd. the two seas (i. e. the Mediterranean and the Black Sea). 2. w. cap., Bahrein.

bahrî 1 (.—) بحرى A 1. maritime, marine. 2. nautical, naval. 3. lrnd. sailor, mariner. — **iklim** geog. oceanic climate. — **musademe** collision at sea. — **musadere** mar. law prize.

bahrî 2 بحرى [**bahrî** 1 ?] kingfisher, zool., Alcedo atthis.

bahriye 1 بحريه [**bahriye** 2] navy. — **askeri** naval forces (sailors, mariners, etc.). — **feriki** Ott. hist. vice-admiral. —**i harbiye** navy. — **meclisi** Ott. hist. naval board, Board of Admiralty. — **mektebi** naval officers' school. — **nazırı** minister of marine. — **nezareti** ministry of marine. — **silâhendazı** marine. —**i ticariye** merchant fleet. — **tüfekçisi**, — **tüfekçi askeri** marine. — **zâbiti** naval officer.

bahriye 2 (.—.) بحرية A 1. fem. of **bahrî** 1. 2. zool., Thalassinidea.

bahriyeli بحريلى sailor in the navy; naval officer.

bahriyun (.——) بحريون A [pl. of **bahrî** 1] lrnd. sailors, seamen.

bahsˢⁱ 1 بحث A same as **bahis** 1.

bahsˢⁱ 2 بخس P lrnd. 1. withered, shrivelled, shrunk; withering, shrivelling, contracting; a being scorched by fire. 2. melted; a melting away, wasting away.

bahsˢⁱ 3 بخس A lrnd. 1. deficient, fraudulent; fraud, a defrauding by deficient measure. 2. grown without artificial irrigation (seed).

bahsan (.—) بحسان P same as **bahs** 2.

bahset=ᵈᵉʳ بحث ايتمك 1. /dan/ to treat (of a subject), to talk (about), to mention. 2. /ına/ to wager, bet. 3. lrnd. to discuss.

bahsî 1 (.—) بحثى [based on **bahs** 1] phil. discursive.

bahsî 2 (.—) بخسى P 1. withered; ripe for the sickle. 2. melted.

bahsî 3 (.—) بخسى A lrnd. grown on land not irrigated (grain).

bahside (.—.) بخسيده P lrnd. 1. withered, decayed; wrinkled, shriveled. 2. melted away. 3. injured; afflicted, grieved. 4. alarmed, agitated, anxious. 5. wasted, changed for the worse in appearance.

bahş 1 بخش P lrnd. 1. giving. 2. a forgiving. 3. share; portion, part, fragment.

4. destiny, lot. —i kalenderî a giving away generously.
-bahş 2, -bahşa (. —) بخش P 1. giving, as in hayatbahş, ruhbahşa. 2. forgiving, as in hatabahş.
bahşayende (. — ..) بخشاینده P lrnd. 1. who gives; bountiful; giver. 2. who forgives, merciful.
bahşayiş (. —.) بخشایش P lrnd. 1. a giving, bestowing; gift, bounty. 2. a pardoning, forgiveness.
bahşayişger (. — ..) بخشایشگر P lrnd. merciful; God, the forgiver of sin.
bahşende بخشنده P lrnd., same as bahşayende.
bahşet=der بخشاتمك /a,ı/ lrnd. 1. to give. 2. to forgive, remit.
bahşiş بخشش P 1. tip, baksheesh. 2. lrnd. a giving; gift, present; given as a present. 3. lrnd. a forgiving, sparing. — atın dişine bakılmaz proverb Never look a gift horse in the mouth. — ver= /a/ to tip.
bahşude (. —.) بخشوده P lrnd. 1. pardoned (by God). 2. given, bestowed.
baht 1 بخت P 1. luck, fortune, destiny. 2. good fortune, good luck. —ınıza It depends on how lucky you are. —ı açık lucky. —ı açıl= /dan/ to become lucky (in). —ı bağlı to have no luck (in finding a husband). —a bağlı mukavele law aleatory contract. —ı bed bad luck, ill fortune. —ı bidar good fortune. —ı dü mahe lrnd. temporary good luck, fickle fortune. — işi a matter of luck, a turn of fortune. —ı kara unlucky. — körlüğü ill fortune. —ına küs= to be cross with one's luck, to become bitter. — olmayınca başta ne kuruda biter ne yaşta proverb If you have no luck, nothing avails. —ı siyah, —ı şum poet. ill fortune. —ı yaver good luck.
baht[u] 2 بخت A lrnd. pure, unadulterated.
bahtaver (. —.) بختاور P lrnd. fortunate, lucky.
bahtbergeşte بخت برگشته P lrnd. unfortunate.
bahte 1 (—.) باخته A lrnd. 1. who has hazarded and lost. 2. lost (in a game).
bahte 2 بخته P lrnd. three-year-old ram.
bahtek[ki] بختك P lrnd. 1. ill fortune. 2. w. cap., name of the vizier of Anushirvan.
bahter (—.) باختر , bahter بختر P lrnd. 1. the West. 2. archaic the East. 3. w. cap., Bactria.
bahtere بختره A lrnd. stately gait.
bahterî (.. —) بخترى A lrnd. 1. one who has a handsome person and a stately gait. 2. conceited, haughty.
bahthufte بخت خفته P lrnd. whose fortune is asleep, unlucky.
bahtiyar (.. —) بختیار P 1. lucky, fortunate; happy. 2. w. cap., man's name. —âne (.. — —.) P lrnd. luckily, happily; lucky, happy (manner).
bahtiyari 1 (.. — —) بختیارى P lrnd. good fortune, prosperity, happiness.
Bahtiyarî 2 (.. — —) بختیارى P Bakhtiari (member of the Bakhtiari tribe in Iran).
bahtiyarlık[ğı] بختیارلق prosperity, good fortune; happiness.
bahtlı بختلى fortunate, lucky.
bahtmend بختمند P lrnd. fortunate. —î (. . —) P good fortune.
bahtsız بختسز unfortunate, unlucky, ill-starred. —lık ill fortune; unhappiness.
bahtver بختور P lrnd. fortunate.
bahur 1 (— —) باحور A lrnd. the heat of the dog-days.
bahur 2 (. —) بخور A lrnd., same as buhur 2.
bahuri (— — —) باحورى A lrnd. critical (time of a fever).
bahurşişe (. — —.) بخور شیشه P lrnd. 1. censer. 2. perfume sprinkled on the fire to scent a room.
bahurülberber (. — ...) بخور البربر A orpine, tree orpine, bot., Telephium imperati.
bahurül'ekrad (. — .. —) بخور الاکراد A hog's fennel, bot., Peucedanum officinale.
bahus (. —) بحوث A lrnd. who minutely inquires and scrutinizes.
bahusus (—. —) بخصوص P especially.
bahyazi (. — —) بخیازى P lrnd. small gift such as a worn garment, given to a servant or pauper.
bahye بخیه P lrnd. seam, esp. a seam in thick leather or in a quilted garment. —zen P stitcher, seamer, quilter.
bai (—.) باع A lrnd., var. of bâyi.
baid 1 (. —) بعید A lrnd. 1. remote, far off, distant. 2. extensive. 3. improbable, farfetched.
baid 2 (. —) باعد A lrnd. remote, distant.
baidül'ahd[di] (. — ..) بعید العهد A lrnd. of ancient date.
baidülgavr (. — ..) بعید الغور A lrnd. 1. profound, unfathomable. 2. keen of intellect, of profound knowledge.
baika (— ..) بائقه A lrnd. calamity, misfortune.
bain (—.) بائن A lrnd. 1. evident, plain. 2. definitively divorced (woman); definitive (divorce). 3. separate, divided, distinct.
bair 1 (. —) بائر A lrnd. 1. perishing, perished, extinct. 2. waste (land), uncultivated.
bair 2 (. —) بعیر A lrnd. camel; esp. full-grown male camel.
bais 1 (—.) باعث A lrnd. 1. cause, motive.

bais 124

2. God, the Creator and the inspirer of prophecy; revealer, inspirer. 3. raiser from the dead. 4. awakener from sleep. 5. producer, maker. 6. deputer, nominator; who sends. **— u bâdi** the cause and inducement (of); the causer and originator. **—i hayatım** the cause of my life, *i. e.,* my father. **—i hüzn** causing sorrow, sad. **—i leyl ü nehar** 1. the creator of night and day, God. 2. the sun. **— ol=** /a/ to cause, to be the cause (of).
bais 2 (.—) بَعِيث A *lrnd.* 1. person sent, messenger, envoy. 2. army, expedition, body of troops.
baisiyet (—.—.) باعِثيّت [based on bais 1] *phil.* causativity.
bait (—.) بايِت A *lrnd.* 1. that stays overnight. 2. stale.
baiz (—.) بايِض A *lrnd.* that lays eggs, oviparous.
bajdar (——) بازدار P *lrnd., var. of* **bacdar.**
bak=[ar] **1** بَقمى 1. /a/ to look, to look (at), to pay attention (to), to consider; to face (towards). 2. /a/ to examine (patient, etc.), to investigate, to look (into). 3. to look (at, for the purpose of selecting); /a/ to look (for). 4. /a/ to take care (of), to look (after), tend; to treat (patient); to be in charge (of). 5. /a/ to depend (on). 6. /a/ to look (to for guidance); to be dependent (on, for living, etc.). 7. /a/ to verge (on another color). **—!** 1. Look. Mind. I give you warning. 2. *mil.* Attention! **—alım** 1. Let us see; we'll see. 2. Well now! oh! *e. g,.* **Gel bakalım!** Well now, come! **Ne yaptın bakalım?** Well, what did you do? **—sana!**, **—sanıza!** Look here! say! **—arsan bağ olur, bakmazsan dağ olur** *proverb* If you take care of it, it will become a vineyard; if you neglect it, it will become waste land. **—an göze yasak olmaz** *proverb* You cannot prevent an eye from looking. **—ma ile öğrenilseydi köpekler kasap olurdu** *proverb* If one could learn simply by watching, dogs would be butchers. **—a kal=** to stand in astonishment or bewilderment. **—ar kör** 1. a blind man whose eyes appear normal. 2. one who looks at things distractedly, one who is unaware of what is going on around him.
bak[ki] **2** (—) بالك P *lrnd.* fear, dread, terror; timidity, shyness. **— ü perva** fear and dread.
bak[kkı] **3** بَق A *lrnd.* 1. gnat, mosquito, *zool., Culex pipiens.* 2. bedbug, *zool., Cimex lectularius.*
baka 1 اِنا قَ بَقَ *archaic, var. of* **bağa.**
baka 2 (.—) بَقاء A *same as* **beka.**
bakabunga, bakabunka (...'.) بَقابُونغه

[**bekâbunka**] brooklime, *bot., Veronica beccabunga.*
bakacak[ği], **bakacık**[ği] بَاقَجِي *prov.* lookout, observation place.
bakaça (.'.) بَقاجه It woodcock, *zool., Scolopax rusticola.*
bakak[kı] (.—) بَقاق A *lrnd.* talkative, garrulous, loquacious.
bakalarya, bakalera (...'.) بَقالاريا It *naut.* counter timber. **— lumbarları** sternports of a man-of-war.
bakalit[di] F Bakelite.
bakalorya F baccalaureate, bachelor's degree.
bakalyaro (...'.) بَقاليارو Gk bacalao, codfish, *zool., Gadus Callarias.*
bakan *neol.* minister, state secretary. **B—lar Kurulu** Council of Ministers.
bakanak[ği] بَقانه 1. cloven hoof. 2. dewclaw, false hoof. 3. cushion under the toe of a camel's foot.
bakanlık[ği] *neol.* ministry.
bakar بَقَر A *lrnd.* 1. ox, *zool., Bos.* 2. a bovine; the bovine species. 3. cattle. 4. stupid.
bakara 1 باقارا F baccarat.
bakara 2, bakare بَقَره A *lrnd.* cow; ox; a bovine.
bakari (..—) بَقَرى A *zool.* bovine.
bakariye (..—.) بَقَريّة A 1. *fem. of* **bakari.** 2. *zool.* the bovine species.
bakavet (.—.) بَقاوت A *lrnd.* 1. a looking attentively, attention. 2. expectation. 3. a taking care (of).
bakaya (.——) بَقايا A 1. *lrnd.* remnants. 2. arrears, outstanding taxes. 3. *mil.* absentee conscript.
bakbak[kı] (.—) بَقباق A *lrnd.* garrulous; a talkative man.
bakça باقچه *prov., var. of* **bahçe.**
bakemal[li] (—.—) باكَمال P *lrnd.* perfect, excellent.
bakı 1 باقى 1. *archaic* inspection; care, treatment. 2. *geog.* exposure. **— kulu** *obs.* tax inspector.
bâkı[ii] **2** (—.) باقى A *lrnd.* spotted black and white, speckled, mottled.
bakıa (—..) باقعه A *lrnd.* 1. calamity, misfortune. 2. very intelligent (man). 3. very cautious bird.
bakıcı باقيجى 1. attendant, guard; nurse. 2. soothsayer, fortuneteller. **—lık** 1. a nursing. 2. a fortunetelling.
bakıl=[ır] **1** باقيلمق *pass. of* **bak= 1.**
bakıl 2 (.—) باقل A *lrnd.* 1. sprouting forth, becoming visible. 2. producing verdure (ground). 3. *w. cap., name of a proverbially stupid man,* Simple Simon.
bakılâ (.—.—) باقلا A *lrnd.* the common

broad-bean, *bot., Faba vulgaris.* **—yı kıptı** sacred bean, Pythagorean bean, *bot., Nelumbium speciosum.*

bakılâe (—.—.) باقلائه A *lrnd.* a single broad-bean.

bakılâi (—.——) باقلائى A *lrnd.* pertaining to the bean, *bot., fabaceous.*

bakılanî (—.——) باقلانى A *lrnd.* seller of beans.

bakıle (—..) باقلى , **bakıllâ** (—.—) باقلى A *lrnd.,* vars. of **bakılâ.**

bakım باقم 1. care, attention, upkeep. 2. viewpoint, point of view. 3. glance, look. **bir —a** in one respect. **— evi** nursing home, polyclinic; créche, hospital for children. **— yurdu** asylum for the destitute.

bakımcı باقمجى *prov.* soothsayer.

bakımlı باقملى well cared-for, well-kept.

bakımsız باقمسز neglected, unkempt, disorderly. **—lık** neglect, lack of good care.

bakın= باقن to look about.

bakır 1 باقر 1. copper; of copper. 2. copper coin. 3. copper kitchen utensils. **— çağı** *hist.* Bronze Age. **— çal=** to be contaminated with verdigris (food). **— kaplama** copperplated. **— kırı** shade of gray (horse). **— oksidi** *chem.* copper oxide. **— pası** verdigris. **— rengi** copper-red. **— sulfatı** *chem.* copper sulfate. **— taşı** *min.* malachite. **— tel** copper wire. **— tuzu** *chem.* copper sulfate.

bâkır 2 (—.) باقر A *lrnd.* 1. that cleaves, rips. 2. who diligently investigates. 3. w. cap., surname of the fifth of the twelve imams of the Shiite Muslims.

bakırcı باقرجى coppersmith.

bakırhane (..—.) باقرخانه copper workshop.

bakış 1 باقش glance, look; view. **— noktası** *opt.* point of sight, point of vision. **— zaviyesi** visual angle.

bakış= 2 باقشم to look at one another; to look around in bewilderment. **—ık** *neol.* symmetrical. **—ım** *neol.* symmetry. **—ımsız** *neol.* asymmetric. **—tır=** /ı/ 1. *caus.* of **bakış= 2.** 2. to look searchingly (into).

bakıyat (—.—) باقيات A *lrnd.* things that remain permanently, enduring things. **—ı salihat** good works the effects of which will endure.

bakıye (—.—.) بقيّه A 1. remainder, remnant, residue; arrears (of a debt), balance. 2. *lrnd.* truly durable thing. 3. quarter granted to an adversary. **—i matlûp** *com.* credit balance. **—i ömr** *poet.* the rest of one's life. **—ler usulü** *phil.* method of residues.

bakıyetullâh (.—..—) بقيّة الله A *lrnd.* thing permanent in God's sight, good work leading to eternal happiness.

bakıyetüsselef (.—....) بقيّة السّلف A *lrnd.* those who still uphold the old virtues.

bakıyetüsseyf (.—...) بقيّة السّيف , **bakıyetüssüyûf** (.—...—) بقيّة السّيوف A *lrnd.* remnants of a defeated army.

bakıyevi (.—.—) بقيوى [based on **bakıye**] residual; *geol.* detrital.

baki 1 (——) باقى A 1. enduring, permanent, everlasting. 2. not yet ended, still valid. 3. *lrnd.* remaining; remnant, surplus; *math.* remainder. **— kal=** to remain over; to survive. **— selâm** *formula used at the end of letters* I have nothing to add but greetings.

baki 2 (——) باكى A *poet.* 1. weeping; wailing. 2. raining (cloud); *meteor.* rain cloud; nimbus.

baki[li] 3 (.—) بقيع A *lrnd.* grove, forest.

bakil (.—) بقيل A *lrnd.* productive of plants (land).

bakir 1 (—.) باكر [based on Arabic] virginal, untouched. **— orman** virgin forest.

bakir 2 (—.) باكر A *lrnd.* early.

bakir 3 (—.) بقير A *lrnd., pl.* of **bakara 2.**

bakiran (—.—) باكران P *lrnd.* virgins. **—ı bihişt** the houris of paradise.

bakire (—..) باكره [based on Arabic] virgin, maiden.

Bakiülgarkad (.—...) بقيع الغرقد A name of the cemetery of Medina.

bakiye 1 (—..) باقيه A *fem.* of **baki 1,** remaining, eternal.

bakiye 2 بقيّه A *Or. mus.* interval of a small minor second equal to the Pythagorean limna.

bakiye 3 (—..) باكيه A *lrnd., fem.* of **baki 2.**

bakka بقّه A 1. *gnat.* mosquito. 2. bed-bug.

bakkal[li] 1 بقّال [bakkal 2] grocer. **—a bırakma!** *colloq.* Don't put it off (said when one says, **bakalım** leaving something in suspense). **— çakkal** grocers and the like. **— dükkânı** grocery, general store. **— kâğıdı** thick and ugly-looking paper. **— tavanı** *arch.* ceiling with the beams in the open.

bakkal[li] 2 (.—) بقّال A *lrnd.* greengrocer.

bakkaliye (.——.) بقّاليه [based on **bakkal 1**] 1. groceries. 2. grocery store.

bakkallık[li] بقّاللق business or occupation of a grocer.

bakkam بقّم A, بقّام logwood, *bot., Haematoxylon campechianum.*

bakkar (.—) بقّار A *lrnd.* dealer in cattle, drover.

bakkari (.——) بقّارى A *lrnd.* 1. pertaining to a cattle-dealer or herdsman. 2. stout stick, cudgel.

baklⁱⁱ بقل A *lrnd.* herbage; vegetable; green.

bakla بقله |**bakılâ**| 1. broad-bean, horsebean. 2. link of a chain. 3. round spot (on the skin of a horse), dapple. **—yı ağzından çıkar=** to put aside all considerations and speak out. **— at=** to throw beans (for fortunetelling). **— çiçeği** of a dirty yellowish white color. **— dök=** *same as* **bakla at=**. **— falı** fortunetelling by throwing beans. **— kırı** dappled gray. **—giller** *neol., bot., Leguminosae*. **—msı** bean-shaped.

baklan بقمدك, **baklankaz** بقمدت نقاز *obs.* ruddy shelduck, *zool., Casarca ferruginea*.

baklava بقلوا باقلوا بقلوا sweet pastry generally cut into diamond-shaped pieces. **— alayı** *Ott. hist.* festivity held in the Sultan's palace during Ramazan, at which baklava was distributed to the Janissaries. **— biçimi** diamond-shaped, rhombus-shaped. **— börek (yanında)** very easy (in comparison with). **— dilimi** diamond-shaped, rhombus-shaped.

bakle بقله A *lrnd.* 1. succulent plant. 2. purslane, *bot., Portulaca oleracea.*

bakliyat (. — —) بقليات pulses (beans, etc.).

bakliye بقليه [based on **bakla**] *bot., Leguminosae.*

bakmazlan=ⁱʳ بقمزلنمر *archaic* to refuse to look; to pretend not to look.

bakraçᶜⁱ باقراج 1. copper bucket. 2. plunger (of a pump). **— dili** valve in the plunger (of a pump).

baksımat, baksimatᵗⁱ بقسمات A *archaic, same as* **peksimet.**

bakteri F *bot.* bacterium. **—ler** bacteria. **—giller** *neol., bot., Bacteriaceae.*

bakteriyemi F *path.* bacteremia.

bakteriyolog F bacteriologist.

bakteriyoloji F bacteriology.

baktır=ⁱʳ باقديرمه باقدرمه /a,ı/ *caus. of* **bak=** 1. **—ıl=** *pass.* **—t=** *same as* **baktır=.** **—tıl=** *pass.*

Bakû (. —) باكو *geog.* Baku. **—lu** native of Baku.

bakur (— —) باقور, **bakure 1** (— —.) باقوره A *lrnd.* horned cattle.

bakûre 2 (— —.) باكوره A *lrnd.* first fruit of a season.

bakva (. —) بقوا, **bakya** (. —) بقيا A *lrnd.* mercy, quarter granted to an adversary.

bakyaz باقياز *var. of* **bağyaz.**

bal 1 بال honey. **— ağzı** virgin honey. **— alacak çiçeği bul=** to find the person from whom to profit. **— arısı** honeybee, *zool., Apis mellifera.* **— ayı*.** **— başı** 1. the purest honey. 2. honey sherbet. **— demekle ağız tatlılanmaz** *proverb* (*lit.* The mouth does not become sweet by mentioning honey.) Talking is not enough. **— dök te yala** Pour out honey and lick it (used to describe an immaculate place). **— gibi** 1. like honey, very sweet. 2. in spite of it all, very well. 3. all the more. **— gümeci** 1. honeycomb. 2. *embroidery* honeycomb pattern. **— kabağı** 1. sweet yellow gourd, winter squash, *bot., Cucurbita maxima.* 2. *slang* stupid fellow, blockhead. **— kapanı** *Ott. hist.* building in Istanbul in which the honey trade was centered (between Tahtakale and the Egyptian Bazaar). **— mumu*.** **— özü** *bot.*, nectar. **— peteği** honeycomb. **— rengi** honey-colored. **— sağ=** to take honey (from the hive). **— tutan parmağını yalar** *proverb* (*lit.* One who touches honey licks his finger.) One who has something to do with a big deal will get some profit out of it for himself. **— yemez*.**

balⁱⁱ **2** (—) بال P *poet.* 1. wing. 2. arm. 3. height, growth.

balⁱⁱ **3** (—) بال A *lrnd.* 1. heart, mind, soul, spirits. 2. condition, state. 3. care, solicitude.

balⁱⁱ **4** (—) بال A *lrnd.* kind of large fish.

ba'lⁱⁱ **5** بعل A *lrnd.* 1. husband, spouse. 2. lord, master; owner. 3. *w. cap., Bib.* Baal.

Balⁱⁱ **6** (—) بال F *geog.* Basle.

bala 1 بالا *prov.* child, babe; young animal.

bala 2 بالا *archaic, var. of* **vala 2.**

balâ 3 (— —) بالا P *lrnd.* 1. high, exalted, elevated, supreme; tall. 2. the upper portion (of something), summit, crown (of the head); hill, mountain. 3. height, stature, length. **—da bahsi geçen** mentioned above. **— rütbesi** *cf.* **rütbei bâlâ.**

bala 4 (— —) بالا P *lrnd.* horse led for parade.

balaban بالابان بالابان 1. *prov.* husky, strong person. 2. tame bear. 3. a small wind instrument used in Turkistan. 4. bittern, *zool., Botaurus stellaris.* 5. goshawk, *zool., Accipiter gentilis.* 6. *archaic* large drum; stout drumstick. **—lan=, —laş=** to become very large.

balâd F *poetry* ballad.

balâdest (— — —.) بالادست P *lrnd.* 1. the chief seat in a room. 2. superior, winner, uppermost. **—î** (— —. —) P 1. superiority. 2. oppression.

baladur بالادور It packer of opened bales in the customhouse.

balâhane (— — — .) بالاخانه P *lrnd.* upper room.

balakᵍⁱ بالاق *prov.* 1. young animal, cub. 2. buffalo calf.

balalayka (. . ́ .) بالالايقا Russ balalaika.

balama بالاما Romany the caricaturized type

of a Greek or European in the popular theater.
balân (— —) بالان P *lrnd.* 1. porch, hall. 2. trap, snare.
balançina (...´.) بالنجينه It *naut.* boom lift.
balâne (— —.) بالانه P *lrnd.* porch, hall.
balânişin (— —.—) بالانشين P *lrnd.* sitting high, occupying the chief seat. **—i mesned-i saltanat** seated upon the royal throne.
balansine (...´.) بالانسينه It *var. of* **balançina**.
balâpervaz (— —.—) بالاپرواز P *lrnd.* high-flying; highflown, haughty, pretentious.
balâr (— —) بالار P *lrnd.* 1. main beam of a roof; joist, rafter. 2. son dutiful to his mother.
balârev (— —.) بالارو P *lrnd.* high-flying, lofty.
balast F 1. *rail.* ballast, gravel. 2. *naut., aero.* ballast.
Balat بالاط *Gk* 1. *name of a quarter in Istanbul on the Golden Horn.* 2. *name of a village on the Menderes River near the site of ancient Miletus.*
balata (..´.) F *auto.* brake lining. **—lı levha** clutch-plate, clutch-disk.
balâter (— —.) بالاتر P *lrnd.* higher, superior.
balâterîn (— —.—) بالاترين P *lrnd.* highest.
balatinos بلاطينوس L *Eur. hist.* a palatine.
balayı[n1] بالآيى honeymoon.
balballan=[r] بالبالنمك *prov.* to speak thickly. **—dır**= *caus.*
balcı بالجى dealer in honey.
balçak[ğ1] بالچاق guard of a sword hilt.
balçık[ğ1] بالچيق wet clay, mud. **— hurma, — hurması** crushed dates. **— inciri** crushed dry figs. **—la**= /ı/ to plaster or soil with clay. **—lan**= *pass., refl.* **—landır**= *caus. of* **balçıkla**=. **—lat**= /ı/ *caus. of* **balçıkla**=. **—lı** mixed with wet clay, soiled with clay, muddy.
baldak[ğ1] بالداق *archaic* suspensory ring of a sword scabbard or belt.
baldır بالدر ، بالدور ، بالدر 1. *anat.* calf; back of the shank (in quadrupeds). 2. *archaic* stem (of a plant). **— bacak** not properly dressed. **—ı çıplak** 1. barelegged. 2. rowdy, rough, ruffian. **—ımın etini yerim de kasaba minnet etmem** I would rather eat the flesh of my own leg than ask a favor of the butcher. **—ı kara** maidenhair fern, *bot., Adiantum capillus Veneris.* **— kemiği** tibia; fibula. **— patlatan** *wrestling* tactic in which pressure is applied to the adversary's calf. **— siniri** tendon of the calf.
baldırak[ğ1] بالدراق ، بالدرك lower part of the leg of trousers.
baldıran بالدران ، بالدران poison hemlock, *bot., Conium maculatum.*
baldırgan بالدرغان asafetida plant, *bot., Ferula assafoetida.*
baldız بالدوز ، بالديز ، بالدز sister-in-law, wife's sister.
bale 1 باله F ballet.
ba'le 2 بعله A *lrnd.* 1. wife, spouse. 2. mistress, lady owner.
balena (.´.) بالنا It *same as* **balina**.
balet It ballet.
balgam بلغم A, بالغم 1. mucus, phlegm. 2. *ancient physiol.* phlegm. **— at**=, **— bırak**= to drop a malicious hint. **—ı cıssı** white thick phlegm. **— söken** *med.* expectorant. **— taşı** kind of semiprecious stone.
balgami (..—) بلغمى A 1. mucous, phlegmy. 2. *archaic* phlegmatic. **— mizaç** of phlegmatic temperament. **— taş** *same as* **balgam taşı**. **— yeşim** green-veined jasper; verdantique.
balgamlı بلغملى mucous, phlegmy.
balgarise بلغاريسه *var. of* **bargarisa**.
balık[ğ1] بالق ، باليق fish. **—lar** 1. *zool.*, Pisces. 2. *astr.*, Pisces. **— adam** skin diver. **— ağı** fishing net. **— ağzı** *prov.* snapdragon, *bot., Antirrhinum.* **— avı** fishing. **— avla**= to fish. **— baştan kokar** *proverb* (*lit.* The fish begins to stink at the head.) Corruption starts at the top. **—a çık**= to go out fishing. **— çorbası** fish soup. **— dişi** fishbone (as carving material). **— emini** *Ott. hist.* collector of dues on fish brought to market in Istanbul. **— eti** flesh of fish. **— etinde** nicely covered, neither thin nor fat (woman). **— ezmesi** fish paste. **— kaçtı** *name of a game in which people sit on the floor in a circle and one person tries to catch an object passed around under their knees.* **— kanadı** *fin.* **— kartalı** osprey, *zool., Pandion haliaetus.* **— kavağa çıkınca** (*lit.*, when the fish climbs the poplar tree) never. **— kılçığı** 1. fishbone. 2. herringbone (ornament). **— kulağı** shell of a maritime snail or mussel. **— nefsi** spermaceti. **— oltası** fishing line. **— otu** 1. fish-poison. 2. cocculus indicus plant, *bot., Anagallis paniculata.* **— paçası** jelly of stewed fish. **— pastırması** dried or smoked fish. **— pazarı** fish market. **— pilâkisi** dish of well-spiced cold fish. **— pilâvı** rice stewed with fish. **— pulu** fish scale. **— sepeti** basket trap for fish. **— sırtı** camber, ridge; ridged, hogbacked (road, roof). **— suyu** fish broth. **— tavası** fried fish. **— tohumu** *cocculus indicus,* seeds used to stupefy fish. **— tut**= to fish, to angle. **— tutkalı** isinglass. **— yağı** 1. fish oil. 2. cod liver oil. **— yumurtası** 1. fish roe. 2. dried and smoked roe of the gray mullet.
balıkçı بالقجى ، باليقجى fisherman, fisher; fish

peddler. — **bağı** *naut.* fisherman's bend. — **gemisi** fishing smack. — **kayığı** fishing boat, fishing barge.

balıkçıl 1 با يقجيل با لعجيل heron, egret, bittern; *zool.* any bird of the *Ardeidae* family, *esp.*, European heron, *Ardea cinerea*.

balıkçıl 2 *neol., zool.* piscivorous.

balıkçılıkᵍⁱ با لعجيليى fishery, fishing.

balıkçın با لعجين با لعجين 1. *var.* of **balıkçıl 1**. 2. tern, *zool., Sterna hirundo*.

balıkçır با لعجير *var.* of **balıkçıl 1**.

balıkhane (..—.) با لعخانه با لعقانه central establishment for the marketing and taxation of fish. — **kapısı** *Ott. hist.*, name of one of the gates of the Topkapı Sarayı, through which functionaries were sent for banishment or execution.

balıkla=ʳ با لعقلمد to writhe in agony.

balıklağa, balıklakᵍⁱ با لعقلاغ با لعقلاغ good fishing ground.

balıklama با لعقلمد 1. *sports* with a pike dive; pike dive. 2. headlong.

balıklava با لعقلاوه با لعقلاوه با لعقلاوه 1. same as **balıklağa**. 2. *geog., w. cap.*, Balaklava.

balıklı با لعقلى با لعقى 1. containing fish. 2. *w. cap.*, name of a place in Istanbul known for its Greek monastery and hospital.

balın با لين |balin| round cushion.

bali 1 (— —) با لى A *lrnd.* 1. old, worn-out, threadbare. 2. who tests.

baliⁱⁱ **2** (—.) با لع A *lrnd.* that swallows.

balide (— —.) با ليده P *lrnd.* grown, increased.

baligan mabelâğ (—'..—'.) با لغاً مابَلغ A *lrnd.* amply.

baliğ 1 (—.) با لغ A *lrnd.* 1. amounting (to), attaining. 2. adolescent. 3. adult. 4. perfect, mature; *myst.* arrived at spiritual perfection. 5. who delivers a message. — **ol**= /a/ to amount (to), to reach.

baliğ 2 (—.) با لغ P *lrnd.* 1. drinking horn. 2. cup of wine.

balin (— —) با لين P *lrnd.* pillow, cushion.

balina (.'.) با لنه |balena| 1. whale, *zool., Balaena*. 2. whalebone. — **çubuğu** whalebone. —**giller** *neol.*, whales, dolphins, *zool., Cetacea*.

balinperest (— —..) با لين پرست P *lrnd.* lazy; sluggard.

balistikᵍⁱ F *mil.* ballistics.

baliş (—.) با لش P *lrnd.* 1. pillow, cushion. 2. sack of money; a sum of gold (8 1/2 miskals, about 45 grams). 3. hasp, staple. 4. growth, development. —**çe** (—..) P little cushion; pad; bustle-pad.

balişt (—.) با لشت P *lrnd.* cushion, pillow. —**çe** (—..) P same as **balişçe**.

balkan با لقان با لقان 1. *geog., w. cap.*, Balkan. 2. thickly wooded mountain range. **B—lar** the Balkans. **B— dağları** the Balkan mountains. **B— memleketleri** the Balkan countries. **B— yarımadası** the Balkan Peninsula. **B—lı** native of the Balkans. —**lık** mountainous, thickly wooded.

balkı=ʳ با لعمى با لعمى *prov.* 1. to flash; to glitter. 2. to experience a sudden twinge of pain.

Balkız با لعبز Gk name of the ruins of ancient Cyzicus on the Sea of Marmara.

balkon با لقون It balcony.

balkur=ᵘʳ با لعمر *archaic var.* of **balkı**=.

balküşa (—.—) با لكشا P that takes wing, flying.

balla=ʳ با لامد /ı/ to honey, to mix with honey; to spread honey (on). —**n**= 1. *pass.* 2. to become honey; to become thick like honey. —**ndır**= /ı/ 1. *caus.* of **ballan**=². 2. to praise extravagantly, to make one's mouth water (for).

ballı با لى 1. containing honey, honeyed. — **börek** honey bun; *fig.* a very delicious thing.

ballıbaba با لى بابا dead-nettle, *bot., Lamium*. —**giller** *neol., bot., Lamiaceae*.

balmumcu با لموجى seller of beeswax.

balmumuⁿᵘ با لموى با لموى 1. wax, beeswax. 2. sealing wax. — **çiçeği** wax flower, *bot., Hoya carnosa*. — **tekerleği** round cake of beeswax. — **yapıştır**= /a/ to mark (words).

balo (.'.) با لو It ball, dance. — **iskarpinleri** pumps, dress shoes.

balon با لون It or F 1. balloon. 2. *chem.* retort. — **balığı** putter or swellfish, *zool., Tetraodon spadiceus*. — **barajı** *mil.* balloon barrage. — **sepeti** basket of a balloon. — **uçur**=, — **uçurt**= to let out a trial balloon. — **usturmaça** *naut.* round fender. —**cu** 1. balloon-seller. 2. balloon operator; aeronaut. —**la**= /ı/ *naut.* to balloon out, to swell (sail).

balotaj F *pol.* ballotage, run-off election.

baloz با لوز Gk low-class café chantant.

balsamiye (..—.) با لساميه *var.* of **belsemiye**.

balsıra با لصره honeydew; mildew.

balta با لط 1. ax, hatchet; battle ax. — **as**= /a/ *colloq.* to pester, to annoy, to keep on (at); to threaten, to blackmail. — **değmemiş**, — **girmemiş**, — **görmemiş** never out, untouched (forest, hair). — **ile yonulmuş** unpolished, uncouth, rough. — **ol**= /a/ to pester, to keep on (at), to harass. — **resmi** *Ott. hist.* slaughter tax. **bir** —**ya sap olma**= not to stick to any job, to fail to enter a career. —**yı taşa vur**= to put one's foot in it, to make a blunder.

baltabaş با لط باش *naut.* straight-stemmed.

baltaburun بالطبرون 1. *naut.* straight-stemmed. 2. hooknosed, having a huge nose.

baltacı بالطجى 1. maker or seller of axes. 2. woodcutter. 3. fireman equipped with an ax. 4. *Ott. hist.* halberdier attached to the Sultan's palace. 5. *obs., mil.* sapper. **— kethüdası** *Ott. hist.* lieutenant colonel of the corps of halberdiers.

baltacık⁽ᵍⁱ⁾ بالطجىى 1. hatchet, adze. 2. rynd of a millstone.

baltala⁼ʳ بالطلمق /ı/ 1. to sabotage, to paralyze, to frustrate, to block, to wreck, to torpedo. 2. to strike with an ax, to hew down, to hack to pieces. 3. to cup. **—ma** *verbal n.* **—madan git=** 1. to act violently, to handle roughly. 2. to pronounce words barbarously.

baltalı بالطلو 1. furnished with an ax. 2. armed with a halberd. 3. *obs.* sapper.

baltalık⁽ᵍⁱ⁾ بالطلو 1. district in which the inhabitants of a village have the right of woodcutting. 2. *forestry* coppice, copse.

Baltık⁽ᵍⁱ⁾ بالطيق F the Baltic. **— denizi** the Baltic Sea.

balu (— —) بالو P *lrnd.* brother.

balua (— — .) بالوع A *lrnd.* sink for refuse water; drain, sewer.

baluğ (— .) بالغ P *var. of* **balığ** 2.

balvar (— —), **balver** (— .) بالور P *poet.* winged; strong-winged.

balya (´.) بالى It *com.* bale. **— yap=** /ı/ to bale, to make into bales.

balyaçı بالياجى *var. of* **baylaç**.

balyadur بالادور *var. of* **baladur**.

balye (´.) بالية *var. of* **balya**.

balyemez باليمز It *Ott. hist.* long-range battering gun or its projectile.

balyos, balyoz 1 بالوس [baylos] *hist.* Bailo, the Venetian Resident at the Porte. **— hanı** *Ott. hist.* building in Istanbul where all foreign delegations were housed (at Çemberlitaş).

balyoz 2 بالوز Gk sledge hammer. **— gibi** very heavy.

Ba'lzebub (..—) بعلزبوب, **Ba'lzebul**⁽ˡⁱⁱ⁾ (..—) بعلزبول *vars. of* **Baalzebub, Baalzebul**.

balzen (— .) بالزن P *lrnd.* striking the wings, flying.

bam (—) بام P *lrnd.* 1. roof, flat roof. 2. ceiling. 3. morning, daybreak. 4. *mus.* the lowest string of an instrument. **—ı bedi** the ninth heaven. **—ı bülend** 1. high roof, lofty building. 2. sky. **—ı çeşm** eyelid. **B—ı Dünya** the Roof of the World, the Pamirs. **—ı ferah**, **—ı hazra** the sky. **—ı Mesih** the heaven of the Messiah, the fourth heaven. **—ı refi**, **—ı revakı bedi** the ninth heaven. **— sesli** bass-voiced. **— teli***. **—ı vesi** the ninth heaven. **—ı zamane** the lowest heaven.

bambaşka (´..) بامشقه quite different.

bambu بامبو F *or* E bamboo.

bambuk⁽ᵍᵘ⁾ بنبك. Gk *archaic* cotton.

bambul 1 بانبل kind of beetle harmful to the fields. **— otu** heliotrope, turnsole, *bot.*, *Heliotropium europaeum*.

bambul 2 بانبل *var. of* **banyol**.

bamdad (— —) بامداد, **bamdadan** (— — —́) بامدادان P *poet.* at dawn:, dawn.

bamdadi (— — —) بامدادى P *poet.* early, matutinal.

bamdadpegâh (— — .—) بامدادپگاه P *poet.* at dawn, at daybreak.

bame (— .) بامى P *lrnd.* long beard.

bamgâh (— —) بامگاه P *poet.* dawn, morning; at dawn.

bamteli⁽ⁿⁱ⁾ بام تلى [bam] 1. *mus.* string giving the lowest sound in stringed instruments. 2. the part of the beard on the lower lip; imperial. 3. vital point, sore spot. **—ne bas=**, **—ne dokun=** /ın/ to vex, to annoy.

bamya, bamye (´.) بامى، باميه A 1. gumbo, okra, *bot.*, *Hibiscus esculentus*. 2. *vulg.* penis. **—cı** 1. grower or seller of okra. 2. *Ott. hist.* member of one of the two parties of **cirit** players and athletes, attached to the Sultan's palace.

ban 1 بانك [beng] henbane, *bot.*, *Hyosciamus niger*. **— otu** *same as* **ban 1**.

ban 2 بان Serbo-Croatian *hist.* ban (title).

ban 3 (—) بان P 1. horseradish tree, *bot.*, *Moringa aptera*. 2. *poet.* tall and graceful. 3. gum labdanum. **— cevizi** seeds of horseradish tree. **— yağı** oil of ban.

ban 4 بان P *archaic* 1. loud cry, call. 2. call to prayer, azan.

-ban 5 (—) بان P keeper, *as in* **bağban**.

ban⁼ᵃʳ **6** بائن /ı,a/ to dip (into).

bana 1 بكا to me (*cf.* **ben 1**). **— bak!** Look here! **— mısın deme=** /a/ to show no reaction (to). **— dokunmıyan yılan bin yaşasın** *proverb* The snake that does not touch me can live a thousand years for all I care. **— göre hava hoş** I don't care. **— kalırsa** as far as I am concerned; if it were up to me.

bana 2 بان Serbo-Croatian *obs.* hot spring; saline bath.

banak⁽ᵍⁱ⁾ باناك Arm *prov.* dish consisting of bread soaked in gravy.

Banaluka بنالوق 1. Banja Luka (in Yugoslavia). 2. *embroidery* kind of applique work.

banavele (...́.) باناوله [bonavela] *only in* **— deliği** *naut.* lubber's hole.

band بانت F *elec., med.* band, tape. **— izole** insulating tape.

banda (´.) باندا It band (of musicians).

bandaj باندژ F 1. *med.* bandage. 2. *rail.* tire.

bandara (´..) باندارہ *var. of* **bandıra**.
bandır=ir باندیرمك /ı,a/ to dip (into).
bandıra (´..) باندیرہ ، باندرا It *naut.* flag, colors, **—lı** having a flag; sailing under the colors (of).
bandırma 1 باندرمه sweet made of grape juice and walnuts or almonds.
Bandırma 2 (´..) باندرما Gk Bandırma, the ancient Panormus. **— taşı** *min.* boracite.
bandırollü باندرول F stamped paper wrapped around monopoly articles to show tax paid.
bando 1 (´.) باندو [**banda**] band (of musicians).
bando 2 (´.) باندو It *naut.* let go!
baneva (—.—) بانوا P *lrnd.* rich, wealthy.
banggi (—) بانگ P *lrnd.* loud call; cry; loud noise. **—ı Allah, —ı namaz** call to prayer. **—ı revarev** 1. blast of a trumpet announcing the approach of a great man. 2. the second blast of the trumpet announcing the Day of Judgment.
bangır bangır بانغر بانغر sobbingly. **— ağla=** to weep aloud. **— bağır=** to shout loudly.
bangla=r بانگلی *same as* **banla=**.
bango (´.) بانغو Gk cabinetmaker's workbench.
bangaboz بانغابوز *slang* fool, simpleton, idiot.
bangzen (—.) بانگزن P *lrnd.* 1. crier. 2. muezzin.
banıl=ır بانلمك *pass. of* **ban=** 6.
bani (——) بانى A *lrnd.* who builds, builder, founder. **—i mebanii Müslimanî** *hist.* founder of the edifices of Islam (laudatory term applied to Muslim rulers or theologians).
bank 1 بانق F bank, banker's office. **B—ı Osmani** *obs.* the Imperial Ottoman Bank.
bank 2 بانق It *or* G bench (in a public place).
bank 3 بانق E *naut.* bank, sandbank.
banka 1 (´.) بانقه ، خنقه It bank, banker's office. **— akseptasyonu** bank acceptance. **— cüzdanı** passbook, bankbook. **— çeki** banker's bill, bank bill. **— hesabı** bank account. **— iskontosu** bank rate, bank discount. **— kredisi** bank credit. **— memuru** bank official. **— muameleleri** banking transactions, banking business. **—ca muteber** bankable. **— şubesi** branch bank. **—ya yatır=** /ı/ to deposit (in a bank).
banka 2 خنقه ، بانقه It *hist.* rowers' bank (in a galley).
bankacı (´..) بانقه جى banker. **—lık** banking. **—lık hukuku** law of banking.
banker بانقر It 1. banker. 2. *colloq.* very rich.
bankeş (—.) بانكش P *lrnd.* 1. that coos. 2. male pigeon kept for his cooing.
bankır bankır بانغر بانغر *var. of* **bangır**.

bangır.
bankiz F *geog.* ice field, ice pack.
banknot بانقنوط F bank bill, banknote, paper money. **— ihracı** issue of banknotes.
banko (´.) بانقو It *gambling* «bank!»
banla=r بكلمى [**ban 4**] 1. *prov.* to cry out; to make a loud noise; to crow, to hoot. 2. *archaic* to recite the ezan, to call to prayer.
banliyö (´..) بانليو F suburb. **— treni** suburban train, commuter's train.
bant F *var. of* **band**.
banu (——) بانو P *lrnd.* 1. lady, princess, grand dame. 2. mistress of household. 3. bride. 4. *w. cap.*, woman's name. 5. flask, decanter. **—yi meşrik** the sun. **—yi Mısr** Potiphar's wife (Zeliha).
banyo (´.) بانيو It bath; bathtub; bathroom; spa, watering place. **— et=, — yap=** to take a bath; to bathe.
banyol بانيول It *Ott. hist.* bagnio, prison of the galley slaves.
bapbi (—) باب [**bab 1**] *same as* **bab 1**.
bar 1 بار F night club.
bar 2 (—) بار P *lrnd.* 1. burden, load; cargo. 2. quantity forming a load. 3. baggage. 4. foetus. 5. produce of a tree (fruit, leaves or flowers). 6. sorrow, grief. 7. gape of a bow (when drawn for a shot). 8. *name of one of the eight treasures of Khusrau Parwiz.* **— ü bengâh** luggage, baggage, movables, effects. **—ı giran** heavy load. **— ol=** /a/ to be a burden (on a person).
bar 3 بار Arm *prov.* kind of folk dance (Eastern Anatolia).
bar 4 بار F *print.* virgule.
bar 5 بار Arm *prov.* 1. tarnish, dirt. 2. fur (on the tongue).
bar 6 (—) بار P *lrnd.* God. **—ı Huda** God the Lord.
bar 7 (—) بار P *lrnd.* 1. court, reception chamber of a dignitary; audience, levee. 2. pomp, display, state, magnificence. 3. leave, permission; access, admittance.
bar 8 (—) بار P *lrnd.* time, turn. **— bar** repeatedly, time after time. **—ı evvel** the first time.
barrn **9** (—) بار A *lrnd.* 1. good, righteous; just, true. 2. tender, dutiful; kind, affectionate. 3. *law* true to his oath. 4. true (word), truly spoken (promise).
Bar 10 بار *geog.* Bar, Antivari.
-bar 11 (—) بار P *lrnd.* raining down, pouring out, *as in* **eşkbar**.
-bar 12 (—) بار P *lrnd.* place abounding in, *as in* **rudbar**.
ba'r 13 بعر A *lrnd.* dung (when dropped in separate balls).
barabar *prov. for* **beraber**.

barah (— —) بارە P *var. of* **berah** 3. **—i** (— — —) P *abstr. n.*
baraj باراژ F 1. dam, barrage. 2. *mil.* barrage. 3. *school slang* the lowest passing grade (in an examination). **—ı aş=**, **—ı geç=** to pass (the examination).
barakᵍⁱ 1 بارانى بارانو *obs.* plush; long-piled cloth.
barakᵍⁱ 2 باراك براك *prov.* long-haired dog.
baraka (..'.) بركة It hut, shed.
baran 1 باران *prov.* 1. row of vines. 2. furrow.
baran 2 (— —) باران P *lrnd.* 1. rain, shower. 2. *myst.* an outpouring of God's spirit on the heart. **—dide** (— — —.) P 1. that has been caught in the rain. 2. who has gone through many an experience. **—i** (— — —) P 1. rain coat. 2. pertaining to rain. **—zede** (— — ..) P drenched with rain.
barata باراتا It 1. *obs.* kind of cloth cap. 2. Turk's-cap lily.
baratarya (...'.) باراتاريه It *mar. law* barratry.
baraver (— —.) باراور P *lrnd.* 1. laden. 2. fruitful (tree).
barbar 1 باربار F barbarian; barbarous. **—ca** barbarously, brutally. **—lık** barbarism, brutality.
bar bar 2 بار بار *var. of* **bağır bağır.**
barbarişka (...'.) باربارشقه It *naut.* stopper, rolling hitch.
Barbaros باربا روس It Barbarossa (surname of the admiral under Suleiman the Magnificent).
barbata (..'.) باربطه It *mil.* parapet.
barber (—.) باربر P *lrnd.* carrying a load; porter.
barberdar (—.—) باربردار P *lrnd.* 1. lifting up a load; porter. 2. patient, obedient.
barbet باربت F *naut.* barbette.
barbunya (..'.) باربونيه Gk 1. red mullet, *zool., Mullus barbatus.* 2. small reddish kind of shelled bean. **— fasulyesi** small reddish kind of shell bean.
barbut باربوت gambling kind of dice game.
barbüngâh (—.—) باربونگاه P *lrnd.* place where a load is laid down.
barça (.'.) بارجه It *hist.* ancient warship, large galley.
barçakᵍⁱ بارچاق same as **balçak.**
barda باردا cooper's adze.
bardacıkᵍⁱ بارداجق 1. small cup. 2. *prov.* kind of fresh fig.
bardakᵍⁱ باردك باردوق برداق 1. cup, mug, goblet, glass. 2. *prov.* jug, pitcher. **— altı** doily to put under cups or glasses. **—tan boşanırcasına** pouring heavily (rain). **— eriği** apricot-shaped large kind of plum. **bir — suda fırtına** tempest in a teacup. **—çı**

maker or seller of mugs; servant who has charge of the drinking cups.
bardan (— —) باردان P *lrnd.* 1. receptacle for goods, cupboard, chest, saddlebag. 2. wine flagon, decanter.
bardar (— —) باردار P *lrnd.* 1. laden. 2. pregnant. 3. fruitful (tree).
bare 1 (—.) بارە P *var. of* **bar** 8.
bare 2 (—.) بارە P *var. of* **baru.**
bare 3 (—.) بارە P *poet.* curl, ringlet.
ba're 4 بعرە A *lrnd.* single pellet of dung.
bareh (—.) بارە P *var. of* **barah. —i** (—.—) P *var. of* **barahi.**
barekallah (—..—), **barekallahu** (—..—.) بارك الله A *lrnd.* 1. may God bless! 2. wonderful!
barem بارم F 1. classification and advancement system for the salaries of state officials. 2. ready reckoner. **— kanunu** law regulating the salaries of state officials.
barende (—..) بارنده P *lrnd.* that rains, raining.
bareng (—.) بارنگ P *lrnd.* colored, beautifully colored. **— ü buy** beautifully colored and fragrant.
bargâh (— —) بارگاه P *lrnd.* place of audience, court. **—ı âm** hall of public audience. **—ı has** privy presence chamber. **—ı Kibriya** presence of the Almighty.
bargam بارغام fish of the bass family.
bargarisa (...'.) بارغاريسه It *naut.* sponson.
bargeh (—.) بارگە P *var. of* **bargâh.**
bargir (— —) بارگير P *lrnd.* 1. carrying a load. 2. beast of burden; baggage horse.
barha (— —) بارها P *lrnd.* time after time, often.
barhana [**barhane**] *prov.* baggage, luggage, movables.
barhane (— —.) بارخانە P *lrnd.* 1. storehouse, store room. 2. baggage, movables (including cattle and servant); the whole cargo of a caravan. **— gibi** like a barn (room).
barhuda (—.—) بارخدا P *lrnd.* 1. God the Lord. 2. king, prince.
barı 1 [**baru**] *prov.* garden wall, fence.
barı=ʳ 2 بارى *prov.* /ı/ to shelter, to protect.
barın=ʳ بارين 1. /da/ to take shelter (in). 2. to live, to get along. **—ak** shelter. **—dır=** /ı, da/ *caus. of* **barın=. —ış, —ma** *verbal n. of* **barın=. —ma limanı** *naut.* port of emergency.
barış 1 بارش reconciliation, peace. **— et=**, **— görüş ol=**, **— ol=** to make peace (with one another), to become reconciled.
barış=ʳ 2 بارش to be reconciled, to make peace (with one another). **—ık** at peace, reconciled. **—ıklık** mutual peace, reconciliation, harmony. **—ma** reconciliation. **—tır=**

/ı/ to reconcile, to make peace (among).
—**tırıcı** peacemaker, conciliator; conciliatcry.
bari 1 (ˈ.) بارى |bari 3| at least, for once.
bari 2 (— —) بارى A the Creator, God.
—**i taalâ** the Creator, may He be exalted!
bari 3 (— —) بارِ P lrnd. once, a time.
bariii **4** (—.) بارع A lrnd. 1. that overtops; that excels, eminent, preeminent. 2. beautiful, handsome. 3. intelligent and witty, superior. 4. victorious. 5. good, proper.
barid (—.) بارِد A lrnd. 1. cold; chilly and unpleasant; frigid, chilling. 2. pleasant and cool. 3. sharp (sword). 4. blunt (sword).
baridülmizac (— … —) باردالمزاج A lrnd. having a cold temperament, of forbidding disposition.
bariğ (—.) بارغ A lrnd. who lives in ease and plenty, fortunate.
barih 1 (—.) بارح A lrnd. hot summer wind in Arabia.
barih 2 (—.) بارح A lrnd. 1. angry; perverse, obstinate, reverse, inverse. 2. passing from the right side of the hunter to the left side (game), inauspicious, unfortunate.
bariha (— . .) بارحه A lrnd. last night; yesterday.
barikkı **1** (—.) بارق A lrnd. shining, glittering, flashing; flashing with lightning (cloud).
barikki **2** (— —) باريك P lrnd. 1. slender, slim; thin in texture, fine, small-grained. 2. acute, subtle, penetrating.
barika (— . .) بارقة A lrnd. 1. flashing sword; sword. 2. flashing of lightning; flashing of weapons. 3. myst. sudden illumination of the mind by inspiration.
barikanüma (— … —) بارق نما P lrnd. flashing, gleaming.
barikatdı F barricade.
barikbin (— — —) باريك بين P lrnd. sharp-sighted; discerning, intelligent.
barîkris (— — —) باريك ريس P lrnd. 1. who spins fine yarns. 2. who splits hairs, subtle.
barilik, barim باريلك prov., var. of **bari 1.**
barisfer F geol. barysphere.
baristaruniye (—.— — —.) بارسطارونيه
[based on Arabic] bot., Verbenaceae.
bariş (—.) بارش P lrnd. rain, shower.
baritdı (—.) بارد var. of **barid.**
baritin F min. barite.
bariton باريتون F mus. baritone.
bariz (—.) بارز A 1. manifest, evident. 2. lrnd. prominent, projecting; who gives forth into the open air.
barkkı بارك only in **ev bark.**
barka 1 (ˈ.) بارقه It barge.

Barka 2 (ˈ.) بارقه geog. Cyrenaica.
barkalonga (— … .) بارقه لونقه Sp naut., hist. small Spanish gunboat.
barkan F geog. crescent-shaped travelling sand-dune, barkhan.
barkeş (—.) باركش P lrnd. 1. bearing a burden, loaded; porter. 2. patient, obedient.
barkı=r بارقى var. of **balkı=.**
barklan=ır بارقلانـ only in evlen= barklan=.
barklı بارقلى only in evli barklı.
barko (ˈ.) بارقو It naut. bark, barque.
barkobestiya (— … .) باركوبستيا It naut., hist. barkentine.
barlâm بارلام hake, zool., Merluccius vulgaris.
barmakgı برمق prov. for **parmak.**
barname (— —.) بارنامه P lrnd. customs declaration.
baro (ˈ.) بارو F law bar, the body of lawyers.
barokku F art hist. baroque.
barometre (— … ˈ.) بارومتره F, **barometro** بارومترو It barometer.
baron بارون F baron (European title).
baroskop باروسقوب F phys. baroscope.
bars بارس archaic, var. of **pars 1.**
barsakgı بارصاق [bağırsak] intestine, bowel, gut. — **askısı** anat. mesentery. — **iltihabı** path. enteritis. — **kazıntısı** colloq. last child of a family.
barsam بارسام var. of **varsam.**
barsama بارسامه mint-like plant used in cookery.
barsat (— —) بارسات P lrnd. monsoon.
bartıl |bertil 1| prov. bribe.
baru (— —) بارو P lrnd. 1. well; rampart of a castle. 2. tower in a castle wall; castle fortress.
barud (— —) بارود P [barut] lrnd., var. of **barut.** —î (.— —) P slate-colored, dark gray.
barut بارود Gk 1. gunpowder. 2. quick to anger, vehement. —**la ateş bir yerde durmaz** cf. **ateşle barut bir yerde olmaz.** — **fabrikası** powder mill. — **fıçısı** (gibi) dangerous place where a fight or trouble could start at any moment. — **gibi** irascible. — **hakkı** mil. powder charge. — **kabağı** obs. powder flask. — **kesil=**, — **ol=** to fly off into a temper. —**la oyna=** to play with fire. — **veznesi** powder flask. —**çu** powder maker. —**çu başı** obs. director of the government powder mills. —**hane** (. . — .) powder mill. —**luk** powder flask, powder horn.
barver (—.) بارور P lrnd. fruitful, plentiful.
baryum (ˈ.) باريوم G chem. barium.
bas=ar **1** باصمه 1. /a/ to tread (upon), to stand (on); /ı,a/ to set (the foot,

on); /a/ to enter (upon a year or age). 2. /ı or a/ to press; to weigh down. 3. /ı/ to impress, stamp; to print; to coin. 4. /ı/ to swoop down (upon), to overwhelm, overpower; to raid, attack suddenly, surprise; to flood. 5. to arrive suddenly (crowd), to crowd in; to set in (darkness, cold, pain). 6. /ı/ to let off suddenly, to bring down (a blow), to let out (cry). 7. to settle, sag (building). 8. /ı/ to sit (on eggs). —! 1. Step back! (for a horse); Back up the car! 2. *slang* Be gone! Off with you! **—ıp git=** *colloq.* to walk off. **—tığı yerde ot bitmez** Where he passes no grass grows.

ba's[sı] 2 بعث *A lrnd.* 1. a rising from the dead; God's raising the dead in the general resurrection. 2. a causing to arise. 3. a sending, mission. 4. *Isl. hist.* detachment, small company of men sent on a mission or on a warlike excursion. **—i emvat** resurrection of the dead.

basadora (...'.) باصادوره It *naut.* footrope.
basafa (—.—) با صفا P *lrnd.* pure, sincere.
basair (.—.) بصائر *A lrnd.*, *pl. of* **basiret**.
basak[ğı] *prov.* step (of stairs).
basal[lı] بصل *A* 1. *bot.* bulbous root, bulb. 2. *lrnd.* onion, *bot., Allium cepa*.
basala, basale بصل *A* 1. *bot.* bulb, bulbous root. 2. *lrnd.* onion. **—i ihliliye** *anat.* bulb of the urethra. **—i sisaiye** *anat.* bulb of the spinal chord, *medulla oblongata*. **—i şemmiye** *anat.* olfactory bulb, *bulbus olfactorius*.
basaliye (..—.) بصليّه |based on basal| *bot., Allium*.
basalülfar (...—) بصل الفار *A* squill, *bot., Scilla maritima*.
basalüzzaferan (.....—) بصل الزعفران *A* saffron, crocus, *bot., Crocus sativus*.
basalüzzi'b بصل الذئب *A* fair-haired hyacinth, *bot., Muscari comosum*.
basamak[ğı] بصمق ياصمه من باصامه باصا مات 1. step, stair; round (of a ladder), rung. 2. running board (of an automobile). 3. *arith.* place occupied by a digit within a decimal figure. 4. *algebra* order.
basamaklı باصاماقلی having steps. **— damarlar** *anat.* scalariform vessels. **— ızgara** step grate.
basaman (———) باسامان P *lrnd.* 1. rich, wealthy; well-stocked, well-furnished; prosperous, successful. 2. well-arranged; ornamented, adorned. 3. numerous, multitudinous. 4. strong, powerful. 5. prudent, moderate, wise, sagacious. 6. honest, virtuous, good.
basar بصر *A* 1. *biol.* sight, vision. 2. *poet.* eye. 3. *lrnd.* mental perception, mind, intelligence. **—ı müzdeviç** *opt.* binocular vision.

basaret (.—.) بصارت *A lrnd.* 1. a seeing, perceiving. 2. mental perception.
basarık[ğı] باصارق باصارنه *var. of* **basırık**.
basarî (..—) بصری *A psych.* visual; *anat.* optical.
basarna *prov.* lever, jack.
basarülhak[kkı] بصر الحق *A lrnd.* the visual power of God.
basavab (—.—) با صواب P *lrnd.* correct, right.
basbasa بصبصه *A lrnd.* 1. a wagging the tail (dog). 2. a cringing, fawning.
basbayağı (.'...) باس بياغی 1. very common, ordinary. 2. altogether, entirely. 3. simply, in no unusual way.
ba'se بعثه *A lrnd.* 1. a raising from the dead. 2. a sending, mission.
baseng (—.) با سنك P *lrnd.* 1. heavy. 2. powerful, great.
ba'set=[der] بعثتمك /ı/ *lrnd.* 1. to raise from the dead. 2. to send on a mission.
basgı با صغی باصغر باصغی *archaic, var. of* **baskı**.
bası *neol.* printing, impression.
basıcı باصیجی 1. that presses. 2. *neol.* printer.
basık[ğı] 1 باسق 1. low (ceiling), having a low ceiling. 2. low in stature, squat, dwarfish. 3. pressed down, compressed. 4. *obs.* mumbling (pronunciation).
basık[kı] 2 (—.) باسق *A lrnd.* 1. tall, full-grown (palm). 2. eminent, noble-minded.
basıklık[ğı] باسقلق 1. *abstr. n. of* **basık** 1. 2. *astr.* oblateness.
basıl=[ır] باصیلمق باصیلمه *pass. of* **bas=** 1.
basılı باصیلی printed.
basılış, basılma باصیلمه باصیلش 1. *verbal n. of* **basıl=**. 2. *print.* impression.
basım *neol.* printing, impression. **— evi** printing house, press. **—cı** printer.
basın *neol.* press, newspapers. **— ateşesi** press attaché. **— toplantısı** press conference.
basınç[cı] 1. *neol., phys.* pressure. 2. *archaic* oppression.
basıölçer *neol., phys.* manometer.
basır 1 (—.) باصر *A lrnd.* who sees; who perceives, who comprehends readily; sharp-sighted, quick-sighted.
basır=[ır] 2 باصرمق /ı/ *prov.* 1. *same as* **bastır=**. 2. to bar, bolt (gate, door). 3. to fill up (a well).
basıra (—..) باصره *A* 1. *biol.* eyesight, vision. 2. *lrnd.* eye.
basırgan=[ır], **basırgın=**[ır] باصرغنمق *obs.* to have a nightmare.
basırık[ğı] باصرق *prov.* 1. treadle (of a loom), pedal. 2. strong bar, bolt etc., of a gate.
basış باصش *abstr. n. of* **bas=** 1.
basıt (—.) بسط *var. of* **basit** 2.

basıta (—..) باسطة var. of **basita** 1.
basil 1 F bacillus.
basil 2 (—.) باسل A lrnd. 1. brave, courageous. 2. grim, stern, frowning.
basilik[kı] (—.—) باسيليق A anat. basilic vein.
basillemi F path. bacillemia.
basim (—.) باسم A lrnd. who smiles or laughs gently, smiling.
basir (.—) بصير A lrnd. 1. the all-seeing God. 2. seeing, perceiving. 3. discerning, sagacious, penetrating.
basiret (.—.) بصيرت A 1. discernment, understanding, insight. 2. caution, circumspection, watchfulness; care, attention. 3. lrnd. signal, warning, admonition. 4. lrnd. shield, buckler. **—i bağlan=** for one's insight to fail one, to be blind (to a danger). **—li** possessed of discernment or foresight, sagacious; cautious, circumspect, watchful. **—siz** lacking discernment, devoid of foresight, blind. **—sizlik** abstr. n.
basit 1 بسيط [basit 4] simple, easy, plain. **— cümle** gram. simple sentence. **— kelime** gram. simple word, simplex. **— kesir** math. simple fraction. **—i rakkas** phys. simple pendulum. **— usul-ü muhakeme** law summary proceedings, summary procedure. **— zaman çekimi** gram. indicative.
basit 2 (—.) باسط A lrnd. 1. that opens, spreads, stretches out. 2. extended; long.
basit 3 (.—) بسيط A 1. same as **basit 1**. lrnd. 2. spread out, extended; level; spacious; plane; surface, superficies. 3. liberal, generous. 4. smiling, cheerful. 5. eloquent. 6. element. 7. spirit. 8. pros. the meter **müstef'ilün failün müstef'ilün failün** (——.—) (—.—) (——.—) (—.—).
basita 1 (—..) باسطة A anat. extensor.
basita 2 (.—.) بسيطة A lrnd. 1. sundial. 2. plain; surface, superficies. 3. the earth. 4. elementary substance.
basitülkef[ffi] (—...) باسط الكف A lrnd. beggar.
basitülyed (—...) باسط اليد A lrnd. invested with power, exercising control.
Bask[kı] **1** Basque.
bask[kı] **2** بسق A lrnd. a spitting.
basketbol[lü] F sports basketball.
baskı باصقى 1. press. 2. constraint, restraint. 3. printing; edition, number of copies printed. 4. stamp (for printing fabrics). 5. tailor. hem. 6. lever (of a press, etc.). **— altında** under discipline, under pressure. **— kalıbı** print stamp. **— kolu** pump handle. **— makinası** printing press. **—cı** 1. one who presses. 2. stamper of fabrics. 3. operator of a printing press. 4. rail. brakeman.
baskıç[cı] باسقيچ prov. staircase, stairs; ladder.

baskın باصقين باصقون باصقى بصقين 1. unexpected attack, raid; unexpected visit. 2. /dan/ more powerful, overpowering, superior; heavy, oppressing; pressed down. **— alayı** raid by people of the neighborhood on a disorderly house. **— çık=** /dan/ to get the upper hand, to be superior. **— et=** /a/ to surprise, to swoop down (upon). **— gel=** to be heavy, to seem irresistible. **—a uğra=** to be raided, to be attacked by surprise. **—a uğrat=** /ı/ to raid, to attack by surprise. **— ver=** to be attacked by surprise. **— yap=** /a/ to attack by surprise, to swoop down (on or upon). **—lık** abstr. n. of **baskın**².
baskısız باصقيسز undisciplined, uncontrolled. **— büyü=** to grow up without discipline or control. **— yongayı yel alır, yel almazsa el alır** (lit. A weightless chip is wafted away by the wind, if not by the wind by people.) A child not kept under control is easily led astray.
baskül F weighing machine; scales.
basma باصمه 1. verbal n. of **bas=** 1. 2. printed. 3. print, printed cloth, calico. 4. geol. transgression. 5. a card game. **— kalıp**[pı]* **— saat** repeating watch, repeater. **—cı** maker or dealer in printed material. **—hane** (..—.) obs. printing establishment, press.
basmakalıp[bı] (..'..) باصمه قالب 1. pressure-molded. 2. stereotyped. 3. conventional, cliché.
baso (.'.) باصو It mus. bass. **— tutma** bass accompaniment.
Basra (.'.) بصره geog. Basra. **— körfezi** Persian Gulf.
bassal[lı] (.—) بصّال A lrnd. onion grower; seller of onions.
bassas (.—) بصّاص A lrnd. flashing, sparkling.
bassasa (.—.) بصّاصه A lrnd. eye.
bast[tı] **1** بسط A lrnd. 1. a spreading out; a stretching forth, expanding. 2. explanation, an expounding. 3. a making glad. 4. a banishing shyness, a putting one at ease. 5. God's supplying the means of subsistence. **—ı makal et=** to talk at length, to expound. **—ı mukaddemat et=** to introduce a subject, to make preliminary remarks. **—ı yed et=** 1. to stretch out the hand; to undertake, to do; to perform benefactions. 2. to raise the hand (against another); to exercise authority (over another).
bast 2 بسط A lrnd. intoxicating preparation of hemp.
basta (.'.) It naut. avast!
bastal بسطال باسطال var. of **pastal**.
bastan (——) باستان P poet. 1. ancient, of yore, bygone, past. 2. the world.
bastar (——) باستار P lrnd. and what

do you call it! (used as an expletive). — u **bistar** so and so.

bastarda (..'.) بَا سْتَارِدَه باسطارده It same as **baştarda**.

bastat[tı] بَسْطَت A *lrnd.* 1. extensiveness, spaciousness; width, length, height. 2. erudition, knowledge; superiority, preeminence. 3. increase, growth.

bastet=[der] بَطْ ايتْمَكْ /ı/ *lrnd.* to expound, to tell in detail.

bastı بَاصدِى 1. vegetable stew. 2. fillet, ribbon.

bastıbacak[ğı] بَاصدِى بَاجَاق 1. shortlegged, bandylegged. 2. gamin, urchin.

bastık[ğı] بَاسْتِى *prov.* grapejuice mixed with starch and made into thin layers and dried.

bastır=[ır] بَاصدرمق 1. /ı,a/ *caus.* of **bas**= 1. 2. *same as* **bas**= 1[2, 4, 5, 6]. 3. /ı/ to suppress, extinguish; to appease. 4. /ı/ to hem. 5. /ı/ *naut.* to splice. 6. /ı/ to surpass. 7. /ı/ *wrestling* to force down. —**ıl**= *pass.* —**ım** *neol., phil.* coercion.

bastırma بَاصدِرْمَه 1. *verbal n.* of **bastır**=. 2. *prov.*, *same as* **pastırma**.

bastika (..'.) بَاصْدِيقَه It *naut.* snatchblock.

bastiyon بَاسْتِيونْ It *or* F *mil.* bastion.

baston 1 بَاسْتُونْ It walking stick, cane. — **fırancalası** French bread. — **yutmuş gibi** as stiff as a poker.

baston 2 بَاسْتُونْ It *naut.* 1. boom, studdingsail boom. 2. flying jib boom.

bastondiflok[ğu] بَاسْتُونْ دِيفْلُوك It *naut.* jib boom.

basur (— —) بَاصُورْ A, بَاصُور 1. piles, hemorrhoids. 2. ulcer or tumor causing hemorrhage. — **memesi** hemorrhoidal swelling. — **otu** pilewort, lesser celandine, *bot., Ranunculus Ficaria*.

basuri (— — —) بَاصُورِى A *anat.* hemorrhoidal.

ba'sü ba'delmevt (.'. ...) بَعْث بَعْدَ الْمَوْت A *lrnd.* resurrection.

baş 1 بَاشْ 1. head, *anat.*, caput. 2. knob; bulb (of a plant); cyme. 3. lump (of cheese, crude sugar, etc.). 4. skein, hank (of silk, etc.). 5. head, *e. g.,* **yüz baş koyun** 100 head of sheep. 6. summit, top; pyramidal heap above a full measure of grain; the top of a liquid; cream, top milk. 7. *naut.* prow, forepart, bow. 8. beginning, commencement; first, initial. 9. river head, spring. 10. beginning of a chapter, paragraph, etc. 11. end, extremity. 12. head, chief; leader; warden (of a guild or craft); main, chief, principal. 13. *Turkish style wrestling* first class. 14. *com.* agio, premium on bills, etc. 15. at, by the side of, near, *e. g.,* **sofra başı** at the table, **havuz başı** by the pond's side. **ocak başı** near the fireplace. —**ına** 1. at, to, *e. g.,* **Makinenin başına geldi** He came to the machine. 2. per, *e. g.,* **koyun başına** per sheep. —**ında** 1. at, near, around, *e. g.,* **masa başında** at the desk, around the table. 2. on his hands, *e. g.,* **Başında üç çocuk var** He has three children on his hands. He has to support three children. 3. at every, *e. g.,* **saat başında** at the end of every hour, for every hour. —**ından** 1. from its beginning, *e. g.,* **başından sonuna kadar** from beginning to end. 2. away from, *e. g.,* **başımdan git!** Go away (from me)!, Leave me alone! —**ta** first of all, most of all. —**tan** from the beginning, from the start. —**ını acemi berbere teslim eden cebinden pamuğu eksik etmesin** *proverb* He who entrusts his head to an inexperienced barber must carry cotton in his pocket. —**ını aç**= 1. to uncover one's head (*esp.,* as a gesture initiating prayer or imprecation). 2. /ın/ to open up (a subject of talk), to give an inkling (of). —**ı açık** 1. bareheaded. 2. clear, evident, obvious. 3. overfree, unceremonious; shameless. —**ı açık kâtip** eloquent, ingenious and highly ornamental writer. —**ı açıl**= for the head to go bald. —**ını ağrıt**= /ın/ to give a headache (to); to annoy by talking a lot. —**ını alama**= /dan/ 1. to be too busy (with). 2. not to be able to escape (from some ill). — **alıp baş ver**= to wage a bitter fight. —**ını alıp git**= to go away, to leave by oneself. —**ının altından çık**= /ın/ to be hatched out in someone's head (plot); to come out (of a person), to be caused (by). —**ı araya git**= to be the one to suffer (in other people's disputes). —**tan aş**=, —**ından aş**= to be too much for someone, to overwhelm. —**tan aşağı** from top to bottom, from head to foot, from end to end, throughout. —**ından aşağı kaynar sular dökül**=, —**ından aşağı bir kova su dökül**= to have a terrible shock, to meet with sudden excitement. —**ından aşkın** too much for someone (work, worry). —**ına at**= /ın/ to throw in (someone's) face. —**ından at**= to get rid (of). —**ı ateşe yan**= to get the worst of it. —**ında ateş yan**= to be in great distress. —**tan ayağa (kadar)** from head to foot, altogether. — **ayak, ayak baş oldu** The high and the low have changed places. —**ı bacadan aşmadı ya** After all, her head has not reached the chimney yet (said for a girl whose marriage age has not passed). — **bağı** 1. head band, fillet. 2. *naut.* bow fast, head fast. — **bağla**= 1. to bind up the head. 2. /ın/ to fasten the head; to attach one to some regular business; to marry one to another. —**ı bağlı** 1. fastened by the head; attached. 2. betrothed, married

—a baş 1. *archaic* from end to end. 2. *archaic* face to face. 3. **başabaş***. **—tan baş** *prov.* excellent, of first quality. **—tan başa** from end to end, entirely. **—ı başa çat=** to put heads together. **— belâsı** nuisance, troublesome person or thing. **—ına belâ getir=**, **—ına belâ sar=**, **—ını belâya sok=**, **—ını belâya uğrat=** /ın/ to bring trouble (upon). **—ımla beraber** with great pleasure, gladly. **— bezi** handkerchief. **—ı bez olsun yaşı yüz olsun** Provided it is a woman, it does not matter how old she is. **— bilmez** unbroken (horse). **—ına bit=** /ın/ to be a nuisance (to). **— bodoslaması** *naut.* stempost. **— bostanda bitmez** *proverb* (*lit.*, Heads do not grow in vegetable-gardens.) One does not take unnecessary chances with one's life. **— boy** best quality. **— ve buğ**, **— buğ***. **— bul=** to pay, to leave a profit. **—ına buyruk** independent. **—ı bütün** *prov.* married (woman). **—ından büyük işlere kalk=**, **başından büyük işlere karış=** to undertake things that are beyond one's powers, to bite off more than one can chew. **—ına çadır yık=** /ın/ to bring catastrophe (upon one). **—ına çal!** /ı/ Hit your head on it! (used when giving something contemptuously). **— çanağı** *prov.* dome of the skull, skull. **—ının çaresine bak=** to take care of one's own affairs oneself, not to leave things to others. **— çat=** *archaic* to put heads together. **— çek=** 1. /a/ to head (movement, dance). 2. /a/ *archaic* to rebel (against). 3. /dan/ *archaic* to part (from). **—ını çel=** /ın/ *naut.* to divert from her course. **— çevir=** /dan/ to turn away (from). **— çıbanı** scrofulous pustule on the head in children. **—a çık=** to succeed, to be accomplished. **—a çık=** /la/ to cope (with), to handle, master, control. **—ına çık=** /ın/ to plague, to become a nuisance (to). **—tan çık=** to get out of control, to be led astray, to be corrupted. **—a çıkar=** /ı/ to bring to a successful issue, to accomplish. **—tan çıkar=** /ı/ to lead astray, to corrupt, seduce. **—ına çorap ör=** /ın/ to plot (against someone), to get (someone) into trouble. **— damar** main artery. **—ı darda** in straitened circumstances, in trouble, in need. **—ı dara gel=** to get into trouble, to find oneself in a difficult situation. **—ında değirmen çevir=** /ın/ to harass, to torment. **— denizi** *naut.* head-on sea, waves from ahead. **—ına dert aç=**, **—ına dert çıkar=** /ın/ to cause trouble (to). **—ının derdine düş=** to have enough trouble of one's own. **—ını derde sok=**, **—ını derde uğrat=** 1. to get into trouble, to bring trouble upon oneself. 2. /ın/ to get someone into trouble. **—ına devlet kuşu kon=** to have a stroke of great luck. **—ını dik tut=** to hold the head high. **—ı dinç** without trouble, at ease, peaceful. **—ını dinle=** to rest. **—ına dola=** /ı, ın/ to burden, to saddle (some one with something). **—ı dön=** to feel dizzy. **—ına dön=**, **—ında dön=** /ın/ to dance attendance (on). **— dönmesi** dizziness, giddiness, vertigo. **—ını döv=** to beat one's head in despair. **—ı dumanlı** dazed, drunk; crazed with love. **— edeme=** /la/ not to be able to cope (with). **— eğ=** 1. to bow. 2. /a/ to bow one's head, to submit (to). **—ına ekşi=**, **—ında ekşi=** /ın/ to become a burden (to), to be a permanent and unwelcome nuisance. **— eldeyken** while still living. **— et=** 1. *cf.* **baş edeme=**. 2. /a/ to make a sign (to) by moving the head. 3. /ı/ to accomplish. **—ının etini ye=** /ın/ to nag (at), to plague constantly with a demand. **—ını ez=** /ın/ to crush. **—a geç=** to occupy the foremost place. **—ına geç=** /ın/ to become the chief (of). **—ından geç=** 1. /ın/ to happen, to occur (to), *e. g.,* **Başımdan bir hâdise geçti** I had an experience. **—tan geç=** 1. to be willing to give one's life. 2. *archaic* to despair of life. **—ına geçir=** /ı, ın/ to pull (the roof) down on one, to bring down (on), to make a great row. **—a gel=**, **—ına gel=** /ın/ to happen (to), to befall. **—a gelen çekilir** *proverb* One has to take what comes. **—ına gelen pişmiş tavuğun başına gelmedi** /ın/ incredible things have happened (to). **— gidince ayak payidar olmaz** *proverb* When the head is gone, the foot cannot hold on. **—ı göğe değ=**, **—ı göğe er=** to rejoice greatly; to find happiness. **—ı göl ayağı sel** *prov.* He may blunder all he likes! **— göster=***. **— götür=** *archaic* to lift up the head. **— göz et=** /ı/ to marry to one another. **— göz ol=** to marry. **—ı gözü sadakası** alms given for one's safety. **—ını gözünü yar=** /ın/ 1. to handle roughly (in fighting). 2. to use badly (language, etc.) **—a güreş=** 1. *Turkish style wrestling* to contest the first class. 2. to take up the most difficult side of a thing. **—ına hal gel=** /ın/ to have great trouble. **—ına hasır yak=** to complain, to be in despair. **—ı havada** high-headed, proud. **—ı havalan=** to be distracted by love affairs. **—ı hoş ol=** /la/ to like, to be fond (of). **— humması** cerebral fever. **—ı için** /ın/ for the sake of, *used in imploring, e. g.,* **evlâdının başı için** for the sake of your child. **—a ilet=** /ı/ *archaic* to accomplish. **—ını inan=** /a/ to trust one's life (to). **— indir=** *archaic* 1. to bow the head. 2. /a/ to submit (to). **—ına indir=** /ı, ın/ *same as* **başına geçir=**. **—tan inme** very sudden, coming out of the blue. **—ına iş aç=**, **—ına iş getir=** /ın/ to cause trouble (to). **—ı kaba** *archaic, same as*

başı kabak. **—ı kabak** bare-headed, bald-headed. **—ına kak=** /ı, ın/ to remind one reproachfully (of a kindness done to him), to rub in (a favor done to someone). **—ından kalsın!** May it remain after you! (imprecation referring to possessions). **— kaldır=** 1. /a. karşı/ to rebel (against). 2. to raise one's head, to revive. **— kaldırma=** /dan/ to be engrossed (in work). **—tan kalma** left over from someone else. **—ı kapalı** secret; in a covert way. **— kasarası** *naut.* forecastle. **—ını kaşımağa eli değme=**, **—ını kaşımağa vakti olma=** to be swamped with work. **—ında kavak yelleri es=** to be woolgathering. **— kayusu** *archaic* fear for one's life. **—ım kazan oldu** My head is drumming (as the result of noise and uproar). **—ım kel mi benim?** What is wrong with me? why am I left out? **— kes=** to bow the head in greeting, to bow. **—ını kes=** /ın/ to behead. **—tan kıça haber yok** No one knows what the other one does. **— kıç vur=** *naut.* to pitch and scend. **—ına kına yak=** to dye one's hair with henna (as a gesture of joy). **— kır=** to bow. **—ı kız=** to get furious. **— ko=** *archaic* 1. /a/ to stake one's life (on). 2. /a/ to submit (to). 3. to bow down, to prostrate oneself. **—ına ko=** /ı/ *archaic* to leave alone, to abandon. **—ını koltuğunun altına al=** to do something at the risk of one's life. **—ından· kork=** to fear for one's life. **— koş=** 1. /a/ to do wholeheartedly, to enter heart and soul (into an enterprise). 2. /a/ *archaic* to join. 3. /ı,a/ *archaic* to appoint chief (to an army). 4. /la/ *archaic* to race (with). **— köşe** seat of honor. **—ını kurtar=** to save one's life. **—ı nare yan=** to suffer as a result of one's meddling. **—ından nikâh geç=** to have married. **— okut=** *myst. orders* to undergo a certain service of penitence. **—ını okut=** /ın/ to have prayer recited (over a sick person). **— ol da eşek başı ol** *proverb* One should always try to be at the head. **— omuzluğu** *naut.* bow. **—ını ortaya koy=** to challenge death, to risk one's life. **— oyna=** *archaic* to play with one's life. **—ıyla oyna=** to play with one's life, to invite danger. **— öğren=** to be trained to the rein. **— öğret=** /a/ to break to the rein. **—ı önünde** with downcast eyes, modestly reserved. **— örtüsü** *same as* **başörtü.** **— paçası** jelly of sheep's heads. **—ına patla=** /ın/ to burst on one's head (storm), to fall to one's lot. **—ı pek** 1. obstinate, hard-headed. 2. stupid, unintelligent. **— pilâvı** rice cooked with sheep's head. **— reis** *Ott. hist.*, title of the superintendent of the **bostancı** *guards in the 19th century.* **— ruznamçeci** *Ott. hist.* director of the registry of the imperial treasury.

—ınız sağ olsun! May your life be spared! (formula of condolence). **— sağlığı** condolence. **— sal=** *archaic* to shake one's head. **— salla=** /a/ to nod, to agree (with). **—ına sar=** /ı, ın/ to burden, saddle (someone with something). **—ından sav=** /ı/ to get rid (of). **—tan savma** in order to get rid of it, carelessly, in a negligent, perfunctory way. **— sedir** Turkish sofa on which the most honored guest is seated; seat of honor. **—ı sert** hard-headed, obstinate. **—ı sığınım** *neol., ling.* proclisis. **—ı sıkıl=** to be in distress; to be hard up. **—ı sıkış=** to have more work than one can handle. **—ına soğuk geç=** to have a cold in the head, to act stupidly. **—ından soğuk su dökül=** to be overwhelmed with a sudden disappointment. **—ını sokacak yer** a place to lay one's head. **—ı sondalık** *neol., ling.* hysteron-proteron. **—a sür=** *prov.* to last to the end. **— tacı** crown; a greatly respected and loved person. **— tası** skull. **—ı taşa değ=** to realize the hardships of life. **—ına taş dik=** to erect a tombstone over one. **—ı taşa gel=** *same as* **başı taşa değ=.** **—ını taştan taşa vur=** to knock one's head against the wall in great repentance. **—ını taşa vur=** to repent greatly. **—ına teller takın=** to rejoice greatly. **—tan tırnağa** from tip to toe. **—ına tokmak ol=** /ın/ to keep one under restraint. **—ına toprak!** Earth be upon you! (imprecation). **—ına toprak koy=**, **—ına toprak saç=** to cover one's head with earth (gesture of mourning). **— tut=** *naut.* to steer her course. **—ı tut=** to have a headache. **— tüyü** 1. crest feather. 2. plume. **— ur=** *archaic* to touch the ground with the head, to prostrate oneself. **—ına ur=** *archaic* to put on the head. **— üstü** *naut.* forecastle deck. **— üstüne!** with pleasure! **—ı üstünde taşı=**, **—ı üstünde tut=** /ı/ to respect greatly, to hold very precious. **—ı üstünde yeri ol=** /ın/ to be highly venerated or loved (by). **—ını ütüle=** /ın/ *slang* 1. to reprimand. 2. to nag. **—a var=** 1. /ı/ *prov.* to accomplish, finish. 2. *archaic* to be accomplished, to come to an end. **— ver=** 1. to come into ear (grain). 2. to appear, to come out. 3. /a/ to give one's life (for). 4. /a/ to give him his head (horse). 5. *fin.* to allow a premium on a bond. **— vergisi** poll tax. **—ına vur=** 1. /ın/ to hit on the head. 2. to go to one's head (drink etc.); to produce giddiness (fumes). **—ına vur ağzından lokmasını al!** Hit him on the head and take away the food from his mouth! (used to describe a very good natured person). **— yarılır börk (fes) içinde, kol kırılır yen içinde** *proverb* (*lit.* The head is wounded within the cap; the arm breaks inside the sleeve.) Private

things should not be made public. — **yastığı pillow**. **—ı yastık yüzü görme=** not to have a moment's rest. **— yazısı** fate, destiny. **—ında yazılı ol=** /ın/ to be the destiny (of). **—ını ye=** /ın/ to be the cause of the death (of), to kill. **—ı yerine gel=** to recover one's senses, to get rested. **—a yetir=** /ı/ prov. accomplish, to bring to an end. **—ına yık=** /ı,ın/ 1. to pull down (on one, upon one). 2. to throw (a burden on someone). **—ı yukarda** proud, conceited. **—ına yular geçir=** /ın/ to get complete control (of someone). **—ına zindan et=** /ı,ın/ to make a place feel like a prison (to someone).
[For further compounds, see **başabaş - başyukarı**.]
baş 2 1. poet. wound. 2. archaic boil.
başa 1 archaic var. of **paşa**.
başa 2 same as **beşe**.
başabaş 1. only just enough, with the ends only just meeting. 2. com. at par. **—tan aşağı** below par, at a discount. **— çık=**, **— gel=** to come out just right. **—tan yukarı** above par, at a premium.
başağa Ott. hist. head agha (a high dignitary in the palace of the Sultan's mother).
başağrısı[nı] 1. headache. 2. trouble, nuisance. **— ver=** /a/ to be a nuisance (to), to cause worry (to).
başak[gı] 1. ear (of grain), spike. 2. grain, fruit, etc., left over by the reapers, gleanings. 3. ornamental plait of grain hung up to bring luck. 4. archaic arrow-head. **— bağla=** to come into ear. **— et=** to glean. **— kılavuzu** top kernels in an ear ear or grain. **— tut=** to come into ear. **—çı** gleaner. **—la=** to glean. **—lan=** to come into ear, to ear. **—landır=** caus. of **başaklan=**. **—lı** 1. eared, in ear. 2. with gleanings left (field, etc.). **—sız** earless, spikeless.
başalkışçı Ott. hist. the head acclaimer.
başaltı[nı] 1. naut. compartment under the forecastle, steerage. 2. Turkish style wrestling second class.
başama obs. a woman's muffler or coif for the head.
başamiral[li] admiral-in-chief.
başar=[ır] /ı/ 1. to bring to a successful conclusion, to accomplish, achieve. 2. archaic to manage, to control.
başarı neol. accomplishment; success.
başarıl=[ır] pass. of **başar=**.
başarılı successful.
başart=[ır] /ı, a/ caus. of **başar=**.

başasistan chief intern (in a hospital).
başaşağı 1. head-first, headlong. 2. upside-down. 3. archaic downstream. **— et=** /ı/ to turn upside-down, to reverse.
başat[dı] neol., biol., phil. dominant.
Başbakan neol. Prime Minister, premier. **— yardımcısı** Deputy Prime Minister. **—lık** 1. office of Prime Minister, premiership. 2. the Prime Minister's office (building).
başbakı kulu Ott. hist. tax inspector.
başbaltacı Ott. hist. head of the halberdier corps.
başbart same as **başbert**.
başbaşa tete-à-tete, face to face. **— kal=** to stay alone (with). **— ver=** to put heads together, to consult; to join efforts. **— vermeyince taş yerinden kalkmaz** proverb Union is strength.
başbert archaic ringworm, tetter, porrigo.
başbölükbaşı Ott. hist. a high-ranking officer in the Janissary corps.
başbuğ commander, chief, leader, chieftain.
başcüce Ott. hist. chief dwarf in the Sultan's palace.
başçağız 1. small head. 2. head of a boil.
başçavuş 1. mil. sergeant-major. 2. Ott. hist. an officer of the Janissary corps.
başçı seller of cooked sheep's heads.
başçık[ğı] 1. small head; small knob. 2. anat. capitulum. 3. bot. anther.
başdefterdar (... —) Ott. hist. administrator of finance.
başdeveci Ott. hist. chief cameleer (high officer in the Janissary corps).
başdilsiz Ott. hist. chief mute (in the Sultan's palace).
başdöndürücü dazzling, vertiginous, stupefying.
başe (—.) P lrnd. sparrow-hawk, zool., Accipiter nisus. **—i felek** 1. poet. the sun. 2. astr. the constellations Aquilla and Lyre.
başefendi head clerk in a government office.
başeski 1. Ott. hist. a Janissary petty officer. 2. Ott. hist. officer of the white eunuchs in the Sultan's palace. 3. obs. oldest servant in a mansion.
başgedikli mil. sergeant-major.
başgöster=[ir] to show oneself, to appear, arise, break out, begin.
başhademe head servant.

başhalife (..—.) باش خليفه Ott. hist. chief clerk.
başhamlacı باش حملجى Ott. hist. chief oarsman in the Sultan's palace.
başhane باشخانه Ott. hist. storehouse for sheep heads and trotters.
başharf باش صرف print., calligraphy initial.
başhaseki (.—..) باش خاصكى Ott. hist. 1. a high officer of the Janissary corps. 2. an officer of the palace guard.
başhekim باش حكيم head doctor (of a hospital).
başıboş باشى بوش left untethered; untied, free, independent, without occupation. — **bırak=** /ı/ to leave untethered, to leave uncontrolled, to leave to oneself. — **kal=** to be left free, to be independent.
başıbozukˢⁱ باشى بوزوق 1. civilian. 2. irregular (soldier).
başıkᵏ¹ (—.) باشك A lrnd. sparrow-hawk, zool., Accipiter nisus.
başın=ⁱʳ باشنمق prov. to toss the head in contempt, disgust, or refusal.
başikbalⁱⁱ (..—) باش اقبال Ott. hist. chief favorite in the Sultan's harem.
başir (—.) باشر A lrnd. 1. that brings glad tidings. 2. who rejoices at good news.
başka باشقه 1. other, another, different. 2. /dan/ except, apart (from), other (than). 3. archaic apart, alone, independent. —**sı** another, someone else. — **başka** 1. separately, one by one. 2. different. — **biri** another, someone else. — **çıkar=** /ı/ archaic to make a master (apprentice).
başkaca باشقه جه 1. somewhat different. 2. otherwise, further.
başkadın باش قادين Ott. hist. the first wife of the sultan.
başkalan=ⁱʳ باشقه لانمق same as **başkalaş=**. —**dır=** /ı/ caus.
başkalaş=ⁱʳ باشقه لاشمق to become altered, to change, to grow different. —**ım** neol., geol. metamorphism. —**ma** neol., biol. metamorphosis.
başkalıkˢⁱ باشقه لق 1. state of being different, differentness. 2. alteration, change.
başkan neol. president; chairman; chief. —**lık** presidency; chairmanship.
başkarakollukçu باش قره قوللقجى Ott. hist. a petty officer of the Janissary corps.
başkâtipᵇⁱ (.—.) باش كاتب head clerk.
başkentᵗⁱ, ᵈⁱ neol. capital (of a country).
Başkırdistan (...—) باشغردستان Bashkiria.
Başkırtᵈⁱ باشغرد Bashkir. —**ca** Bashkir (language).
başkilise باش كليسه cathedral.
başkomutan neol. commander-in-chief, supreme commander. —**lık** supreme military command.

başkonsolos باش قونسولوس consul general. —**luk** consulate general.
başkullukçu باش قوللقجى Ott. hist. an officer in the kitchen of the Sultan's palace.
başkumandan باش قوماندان commander-in-chief.
başla=ʳ باشلامق 1. /a/ to begin, commence, start. 2. knitting to cast on. 3. /ı/ archaic to head, to lead.
başlahana باشلهنه cabbage, bot., Brassica oleracea capitata.
başlala باش للا Ott. hist. a prince's chief tutor.
başlama باشلامه verbal n. of **başla=**. — **fiili** gram. inceptive verb, inchoative verb.
başlan=ⁱʳ باشلانمق 1. /a/ pass of **başla=**. 2. to develop a head, cyme, bulb (plant).
başlangıçᶜⁱ باشلانغيج a beginning, start, commencement, preface, foreword. — **noktası** starting-point; geom. origin. — **sür'ati** phys. initial velocity.
başlanıl=ⁱʳ باشلانيلمق /a/ pass. of **başla=**.
başlanma باشلانمه verbal n. of **başlan=**.
başlat=ⁱʳ باشلاتمق /ı, a/ caus. of **başla=**. —**ıl=** /a/ pass.
başlayıcı باشلايجى beginner.
başlayış باشلايش 1. a beginning. 2. mode of beginning. 3. chess opening.
başlı 1 باشلى 1. headed; having a head, knob, etc. 2. naut. dipping at the bow (vessel). — **cıvata** head bolt. — **değnek** knobbed staff. — **somun** headed nut. — **vida** head screw.
başlı 2 باشلى poet. wounded.
başlıbaşına باشلى باشنه separate, independent, in itself; independently, by himself, on his own.
başlıca باشليجه principal, chief, main.
başlıkˢⁱ باشلق 1. cowl, cap, headgear; bridal head-dress; crown; helmet; head-harness. 2. capital (of a column); truss (of a post supporting a beam). 3. war head (of a torpedo). 4. title; headline; crosshead, heading (of a column); heading, superscription; caption (of a page). 5. hub, nave (of a wheel). 6. headship, presidency. 7. money paid by the bridegroom to the bride's family. — **tasması** noseband of a bridle.
başmabeyinci (.—...) باش مابينجى Ott. hist. Lord High Chamberlain.
başmakᵍⁱ باشماق prov. shoe; slipper. —**ı şerif** the holy shoe (of the Prophet).
başmakale (..—.) باش مقال journ. editorial.
başmakçı باشماقجى prov. 1. shoemaker. 2. person in charge of shoes that are taken off at the door of a mosque.
başmaklıkᵍⁱ باشماقلق Ott. hist. fief

başman

conferred on the royal women of the Sultan's House.
başman *neol.* primate. **—lık** *phil.* primacy.
başmimar (..—) باش معمار *Ott. hist.* chief architect of the court.
başmuallim باش معلّم headmaster.
başmuharrir باش محرّر *journ.* editor, editorial writer, leader writer. **—lik** editorship.
başmuhasebe (..—..) باش محاسبه chief treasurer's office.
başmukabele (..—..) باش مقابله *Ott. hist.* head clerk in the checking office of the Treasury.
başmurahhas باش مرخّص chief delegate.
başmurakıp[b1] (..—.) باش مراقب *fin.* controller-in-chief.
başmusahib (..—.) باش مصاحب *Ott. hist.* chief servant in the private chambers of the Sultan.
başmüddeiumumi (.....——) باش مدّعی عمومی attorney general. **—lik** office of the attorney general.
başmüdür باش مدير director general.
başmüfettiş باش مفتّش chief inspector.
başmüşavir (..—.) باش مشاور chief counsellor, chief advisor.
başöğretmen *neol.* school principal.
başörtü باش اورتو kerchief, head-scarf. **—lü** kerchiefed.
başpapaz باش پاپا chief priest, highest priest (Christian).
başpare (.—.) باش پاره 1. ornamental knob; knob on the mouthpiece of a narghile; the mouthpiece for instruments such as the ney, etc. 2. butt (of an arrow).
başparmak[§1] باش پارمق thumb; great toe.
başpehlivan باش پهلوان wrestling champion (of Turkey).
başpiskopos باش پسقوپوس archbishop.
başrol[lü] باش رول *theat.* leading role, lead.
başsağı[s1] *neol.* condolence.
başsahife باش صحيفه title page.
başsavcı *neol.* attorney-general.
başsayfa same as **başsahife**
başsız باش سز 1. headless. 2. having no chief. **—lık** lack of government; anarchy.
başşehbender باش شهبندر *obs.* consul general.
başşehir[hri] باش شهر capital (of a country).
baştankara (..—.) باش طنقره 1. *naut.* ashore stem on. 2. headlong, plunged (into). 3. *prov.* drunk. 4. great titmouse, *zool.*, *Parus major.* **— et=**, **— git=** 1. *naut.* to go ashore stem on. 2. to throw oneself headlong into something as a last hope. 3. to run aground, to be stranded, to be sunk.
baştarda, baştarde باشتارده It *obs.*, *naut.* bastard, small war-galley. **—yı humayun** *Ott. hist.* flag ship.

baştaş باش طاش *archaic* companion, comrade.
baştene, baştina باشتنه Sl *Ott. hist.* kind of hereditary land tenure.
başucu[nu] باش اوجی 1. head end (of a bed). 2. *astr.* zenith. **—nda** /ın/ at the bedside, near, close to, *e. g.*, **Hastanın başucunda oturuyor** He is sitting at the patient's bedside.
başülke *neol.* the home country (of an empire).
başvekâlet (..—.) باش وكالت same as **başbakanlık.**
başvekil (..—) باش وكيل prime minister, premier. **—lik** premiership.
başvur=[ur] باش وورمه 1. /a/ to knock the head (against); to take (the bait, fish). 2. /a/ to have recourse (to), to apply (to). 3. *naut.* to pitch and scend.
başyaver (.—.) باش ياور *mil.* first aide-de-camp.
başyazar *journ.* editor, editorial writer, leader writer.
başyazı *journ.* editorial.
başyemek[ği] باش يمك main dish, main course.
başyukarı باش يوقارى upstream.
bat=[ar] 1 باتمق 1. /a/ to sink; to be plunged (into); to be badly soiled (with). 2. to set (sun, etc.). 3. to be lost sight (of); *naut.* to run aground, to founder; to be lost (money), to go to pieces, to perish; to go bankrupt, to be ruined. 4. /a/ to enter deeply, to penetrate; to become ingrown (nail). 5. /a/ to hurt. **—tı balık yan gider** *colloq.* come what may (said when one is in trouble and does not care or fear the worst). **—a çıka** dragging oneself along.
bat[tı] 2 بط A *lrnd.* 1. duck; goose. 2. wine flagon, large cup. **—ı mey, —ı sahba, —ı surhabzay, —ı şarab** wine flagon. **—ı zer** *poet.* the sun.
bat[tı] 3 بط A *lrnd.* incision, a ripping open.
bataet[ti] (.—.) بطاءت *lrnd.* slowness.
bataih (.—.) بطائح A *lrnd.*, pl. of **batiha.**
bataik[k1] (.—.) بطائك A *lrnd.*, pl. of **bitaka.**
batain (..—.) بطائن A *lrnd.*, pl. of **bitane.**
batak[ğı] باتاق 1. swampy, boggy; swamp, marsh. 2. floundering, unstable, unsound (business). 3. pond; tank for immersion (in a bathhouse, to perform the Jewish rites). 4. bowl for taking water out of a jar. **—çı** fraudulent borrower; bankrupt; swindler, cheat, crook. **—çılık** *abstr. n.* **—hane** (..—.) gambling den; den of thieves; *slang* joint. **—lı** marshy (area).
bataklık[ğı] باتاقلق bog, marsh, swamp, fen, moor. **— baştankarası** marsh titmouse, *zool.*, *Parus palustris.* **— baykuşu** short-eared owl, *zool.*, *Glareola pratincola.* **— kuşları** tern-like marsh birds, *zool.*, *Glareolidae.* **— serçesi**

Spanish sparrow, *zool., Passer hispaniolensis.*
— süseni yellow iris; yellow water-flag, *bot., Iris pseud-acorus.*
batal[li] بَطَل A *lrnd.* hero, valiant man.
Batalese (. — ..) بَطَالِسَة A *lrnd., hist.* the Ptolemys.
batalet 1 (. — .) بَطَالَت A *lrnd.* 1. idleness, unemployment, disuse. 3. a trifling in speech, jesting.
batalet 2 (. — .) بَطَالَت A *lrnd.* bravery, heroism, valor.
batanet (. — .) بَطَانَت A *lrnd.* 1. bigbelliedness. 2. gluttony.
batar 1 باتار *prov.* pain, pang.
batar 2 بَطَر A *lrnd.* 1. contempt, disdain. 2. insolence, pride, conceit. 3. ingratitude toward God, returning no thanks for prosperity.
bátarik[ki] (. — .) بَطَارِكَة , (. — —) بَطَارِنَة **batarika** (. — ..) بَطَارِقَة A *lrnd., pl. of* **batrik.** 1. *Eastern church* patriarchs. 2. *Byzantine hist.* patricians.
bataris (. — .) بَطَارِس P *lrnd.* fern, *bot., Pteris.*
batarya, batarye (. .′ .) باتاريه It 1. *artillery* battery. 2. *naut.* the guns of one deck, on one side of a ship; also, the halfdeck reserved for them. 3. *elec.* battery.
— ye= to get a good scolding.
batha (. —) بَطْحَاء A *lrnd.* wide and pebbly torrent channel; *w. cap., name of the lowest part of the valley of Mecca.*
batı باطى 1. west; western. 2. *w. cap.,* West, Occident; Western, Occidental. 3. westwind. **— karayel** *naut.* west-northwest. **— kerte karayel** *naut.* west by north. **— kerte lodos** *naut.* west by south. **— lodos** *naut.* west-southwest.
batıcı باتيجى stinging, pricking, hurting.
batık[ği] باتيق 1. sunk, sunken, hollow. 2. submerged (submarine). 3. wrecked, ruined.
— gözlü hollow-eyed.
bâtıl (—.) باطل A 1. vain, null and void, idle, non-valid, absurd, false; falsehood, lie. 2. *lrnd.* the devil. **— itikat** superstition; false belief.
batılı باطلى western, occidental; Western; Westerner.
batıllık[ği] (— ..) باطللق *abstr. n. of* **bâtıl.**
bâtın 1 (— .) باطن A 1. *myst.* the inner man; the hidden, spiritual essence. 2. *lrnd.* the inside, interior; inward, internal. 3. *myst.* God.
batın[tnı] **2** بطن [**batn 1**] 1. *anat.* abdomen. 2. gestation, *e. g.,* **Bir batında iki çocuk doğurdu** She gave birth to two children at a time. 3. link in a pedigree, generation. 4. *lrnd.* inside, interior, middle; hidden mystical meaning.

bâtınen (— ′ . .) باطناً A inwardly; mystically.
bâtıni (— . —) باطنى A inner, interior, intrinsic, hidden, esoteric.
batıniye (— . — .) باطنيّة A *Isl. Theol.* the Batinites (school attributing special importance to the interpretation of the hidden meaning of the Quran).
batınperest بطن‌پرست P *lrnd.* bellyworshipping, gluttonous.
batır 1 باطر *var. of* **batur.**
batır=[ir] **2** باتيرمق /ı/ 1. *caus. of* **bat=** 1. 2. to stick (into), to prick. 3. to lose (capital, fortune). 4. to speak ill (of), to decry. 5. to kill secretly, to cause to disappear mysteriously.
batır 3 بَطَر A conceited, contemptuous.
batırıl=[ir] باتيريلمق *pass. of* **batır=** 2.
batırt=[ir] باتيرتمق /ı, a/ *caus. of* **batır=** 2.
batısal *neol.* western.
batış 1 باتيش *verbal n. of* **bat=** 1.
batış 2 (— .) باطش A *lrnd.* that seizes and acts violently, gallant, vigorous.
batışülbâtışin (— .. — . —) باطش البطشين A *lrnd.* man in the prime of life.
batıye (— ..) باطيه A *lrnd.* jar, earthen vessel.
bati 1 (. ′ .) باتِ It *naut.* end for end!
— et= /ı/ to reverse (the rope in a tackle).
bati 2 (. —) بطى A *lrnd.* slow; slothful, lazy; dilatory; tardy, late.
batiha (. — .) بطيحه A *lrnd.* wide, pebbly torrent channel.
batik 1 F *text.* batik, battik.
batik[ki] **2** (— .) باتيك A *lrnd.* sharp, keen (sword).
batin (. —) بطين A *lrnd.* 1. large-bellied. 2. well-stuffed.
batir (— .) باتر A *lrnd.* 1. sharp, keen (sword), sharp sword. 2. that lops off.
batiş (. —) بطيش A *lrnd.* powerful, stern, impetuous in assault.
batiülhareke (. — . ...) بطى الحركة A *lrnd.* slow in motion.
batiülhazm, (. — ..), **batiyülinhizam** (. — ...—) بطى الهضم، بطى الانهضام A *physiol.* slow to digest, indigestible.
batiülmizac (. — .. —) بطى المزاج A *lrnd.* temperamentally slow.
batkın باتقين 1. sunk, swallowed up, plunged. 2. thrust in; depressed, hollow, deep. 3. lost, sunk; ruined, bankrupt. **—lık** *abstr. n.*
Batlamyos بطلميوس A Ptolemy (the astronomer and geographer).
batma باتمه 1. *verbal n. of* **bat=** 1. 2. *prov.* manger, crib.
batman بطمان باطمان باتمان batman (weight varying from 2 to 8 okes (5-30 lbs.), used in Turkey until 1931).

batn 1 بطن A 1. *same as* **batın 2**. 2. *lrnd.* clan, subdivision of a tribe.

batn 2 بطن A *lrnd.* the broader side of a feather.

batnan ba'de batnın (.´. .´. .´.) بطناً بعد بطن A *lrnd.* generation after generation.

batni (. —) بطنى A *anat.* abdominal; ventral.

batokᵏᵘ باتوق E *naut.* buttock.

batone F *anat.* rod (in the retina).

batpazarıⁿⁱ بات بازارى *lrnd.*, *same as* **bit pazarı**.

batr بطر A *lrnd.* a splitting, slitting, incision.

batrikᵏⁱ (. —) بطريق A *lrnd.* 1. Eastern church patriarch. 2. Byzantine *hist.* patrician.

batriki 1 (. — —) بطريقى A *lrnd.*, Eastern church patriarchal.

batrikî 2 (. — —) بطريقى P, **batrikiyet** (. — — .) A *lrnd.*, Eastern church patriarchate.

batş بطش A *lrnd.* 1. a seizing, carrying away by force. 2. aggressive force, strength, vigor, sternness.

batta بطة A *lrnd.* duck; goose.

battalʰ **1** بطّال [battal 2] 1. large and clumsy, over-size. 2. *obs.* large-sized thick writing paper polished on one side only and used in public offices for rough drafts. 3. useless, worthless; void, non-valid, abrogated, canceled; obsolete, out of use (document consigned to the archives). 4. unemployed, idle. — **boy** *print.* over-size; 57×82 cm. (paper). — **çek**= /a/, — **et**= /ı/ to cancel officially (document). — **kâğıt** double folio. — **ol**= to be canceled; to be out of date.

battalʰ **2** (. —) بطّال A *lrnd.* brave, heroic, champion, hero. **B— Gazi** name of a legendary hero who fought against the Byzantines in Asia Minor.

battaniye بطّانيه [Arabic **battaniya**] blanket.

battır=ⁱʳ بات تند رمس *obs.*, *var. of* **batır**= 2.

batur باتور *prov.* brave, valiant, hero.

batuta (.´.) It *gambling* kind of card trick in baccarat.

baus (— —) باموث A *lrnd.*, Christian church 1. Easter. 2. prayer said on Easter Monday.

bauz (. —) بعوض , **bauza** (. — .) بعوضه A *lrnd.* mosquito, gnat.

bav باو training for the chase; the quality of a well-trained dog, hawk, etc. **—cı** trainer of hunting dogs, etc.

baver (—.) باور P *lrnd.* belief, faith, assent, acceptance. — **kıl**= /a/ to believe.

bavlı 1 باولى 1. trained for the chase. 2. lure used to train a dog or hawk for the chase.

bavlı=ʳ **2** باولمس to become well-trained for the chase. **—t**= /ı/ to train for the chase.

bavul باوول It suitcase, trunk.

bavurcu باورجى *archaic* cook.

bavücud (—. —) باوجود P *lrnd.* in spite of this, nevertheless, notwithstanding.

Bavyera (.´.) باويره It *lrnd.* Bavaria. **—lı** Bavarian.

Bay 1 *neol.* Mr., Mister, Sir.

bay 2 باى 1. *prov.* rich. 2. *archaic* prince, chief.

bay 3 (—) باى [bay 2] *poet.* rich. — **u geda** the rich and the poor.

bay=ᵃʳ **4** بايمق *prov.*, *same as* **bağ**= 3.

bayağı 1 بايغى 1. ordinary, common, plain. 2. mean, vulgar, banal. 3. *archaic* previous, of old. — **gün** weekday. — **kesir** *math.* common fraction, vulgar fraction. **—laş**= to become vulgar. **—lık** *abstr. n. of* **bayağı**.

bayağı 2 (. .´.) بايغى quite, simply, e. g., **Bayağı beğendim.** I simply liked her. I have to admit I quite liked her.

bayak *prov.* just a little while ago.

bayam *prov.*, *same as* **payan**.

Bayan *neol.* Miss; Mrs., Mistress; madame, lady.

Bayas باياس *archaic for* **Payas**.

bayat بايات [bait] stale, not fresh, old.

bayatî (. — —) باياتى *Or. mus.* one of the oldest and most used **makams**. It is a composition of the **uşşak** 4th and **puselik** 5th. — **araban** a combination of **bayati** and **araban**. — **araban - buselik** a combination of these three **makams**. — **buselik** a **makam** starting like **bayati** and ending like **buselik**.

bayatla= باياتلامق to become stale. **—t**= /ı/ *caus.*

Bayazıtᵈⁱ˒ᵗⁱ [Bayezid] بايزيد name of a district in Istanbul.

bayekdiger (—. —.) بايكديگر P *lrnd.* with one another, together.

Bayezid بايزيد 1. *same as* **Bayazıt**. 2. *hist.*, man's name. 3. *same as* **Doğu - Bayazıt**.

baygân (— —) بايگان P *lrnd.* guardian.

baygın بايغين 1. fainted; unconscious. 2. who feels faint; faint, languid; amorous. 3. drooping (plant). — **baygın** languidly, amorously. **—lık** *abstr. n. of* **baygın**. **—lık geçir**= to feel faint, to be overcome.

bayı=ʳ بايمق *prov.* to become rich.

bayıcı بايجى sorcerer, witch.

bayık بايق *prov.* really, indeed, truly.

bayıl=ⁱʳ باييلمق 1. to faint, to feel faint. 2. /a/ to be thrilled (with), to be enraptured (by), to like greatly. 3. to droop (plant). 4. /ı/

slang to pay (money). —ış, —ma *verbal n.* —t= /ı/ to make faint; *med.* to narcotize.
bayın *prov.* spoiled (child).
bayındır 1 بایندر rich and prosperous, cultivated, developed. —lık *abstr. n.* **B—lık Bakanlığı** Ministry of Public Works.
Bayındır 2 بایندر 1. name of an ancient Turkish tribe. 2. name of a town southeast of İzmir.
bayır 1 بایر 1. slope; slight rise, ascent. 2. hill. — **aşağı** downhill. — **kuşu** wood lark, *zool.,* Lullula arborea. — **turpu** 1. horseradish, *bot.,* Cochlearia armoracia, Armoracia rusticana. 2. vulgar fellow. —**cık** slight slope.
bayır=[ir] **2** بایر *var. of* **bayı=**.
bayıt=[ir] بایت /ı/ *caus. of* **bayı=**.
bâyi[ii] (—.) بایع A 1. seller on commission, *esp.* licensed retailer of monopoly goods, tobacconist. 2. wholesale distributor of newspapers. 3. supplier. 4. *law* seller, selling party. 5. *lrnd.* seller, vendor; buyer.
bayiiye (—.—.) بایعیه [*based on* **bayi**] *obs.* sales tax.
bayin (—.) باین *var. of* **bain**.
bayiste (—..) بایسته P *lrnd.* necessary; proper, fitting. —**i hestî** necessarily existing (God).
bayistî (—.—) بایستی P *lrnd.* necessity.
Baykal 1 بایقال Baikal. — **denizi**, — **gölü** Lake Baikal.
baykur (.—) بایقور A *lrnd.* herd of oxen.
baykuş بایقوش بایغوش بایقوش owl. —**lar** owls, *zool.,* Strigidae.
baylaç[cı] بایلاج It *hist.* 1. office of a bailo, European consulate in Turkey. 2. custom tax collected by a bailo.
baylan *prov.* spoiled (child).
baylık[ğı] باییلق 1. *prov.* wealth, opulence. 2. *obs.* uterus.
baylos بایلوس Gk *hist.* bailo.
bayrak[ğı] بایراق بیرق 1. flag, standard, colors. 2. *obs.* foreign flag. — **aç=** 1. to unfurl a flag; to display a flag, *esp.* for recruiting volunteers. 2. to break out in open revolt. —**ları aç=** to become abusive and insolent. — **askeri** *hist.* volunteer serving in the navy for one summer season. — **çek=** to hoist the flag. — **dik=** to plant a flag. — **direği** flagstaff, flagpole. — **esası** *law* the law of the flag. — **göster=** to show the colors. —**ı indir=** to lower the flag, to dip the flag; to haul down the flag, to strike the colors. — **resmi** *Ott. hist.* present made by a newly appointed vizier to the person who brings him the horse-tail pennant. —**ı yarıya indir=** to fly the flag at half-mast. —**lı** with a flag. —**lık** 1. bunting. 2. *obs.* the number of militiamen attached to a flag.

bayrakdar (..—), **bayraktar** بایراقدار بیراقدار *archaic* standard bearer.
bayram بایرام بیرام 1. religious festival, Bairam; national holiday; festival, festivity. 2. *w. cap., man's name.* — **alayı** *hist.* the Sultan's riding to a mosque in stately procession on the morning of the Bairam feast. — **arifesi** the eve of Bairam. — **ayı** the month of Shawwal of the Arabic calendar. —**dan bayrama** rarely, once in a blue moon, on occasion. — **ertesi** after Bairam. — **et=** to feast, to rejoice exceedingly. — **günü** on the day of Bairam. —**ınız kutlu olsun**, —**ınız mubarek olsun** happy Bairam!, happy feast! — **namazı** morning service on the first day of Bairam. —**dan sonra bayramın mubarek olsun!** (*lit.* Happy Bayram! after the Bayram is over) too late. — **şekeri** candy offered to visitors on Bairam days. — **tebriki** congratulation for Bairam; greeting card for Bairam. — **topu** gun fired on Bairam days. — **üstü** just before Bairam. — **yap=** *same as* **bayram et=**. — **yeri** fair grounds.
bayramî (..—) بیرامی [*based on* **bayram**] *lrnd.* 1. belonging to Bairam. 2. belonging to the Bayramiye order.
Bayramiye (..—.) بیرامیه [*fem. of* **bayrami**] name of a dervish order founded by Hacı Bayram Veli in Ankara about 1400 A. D.
bayramlaş=[ır] بایراملشمك /la/ to exchange Bairam good wishes.
bayramlık[ğı] بایراملیق 1. fit for Bairam. 2. Bairam present. 3. one's best dress.
baysungur, baysunkur بایصونغور بایسونغر بای صونغور 1. a bird of prey. 2. *hist., man's name.*
baytak[kı] **1** بیطاق *var. of* **beydak**.
baytak[kı] **2** بیطاق *var. of* **paytak 1**.
baytal بایتال بیطال *prov.* mare.
baytar بیطار (.—), بطر A veterinary surgeon, veterinarian.
baytara بیطاره A *lrnd.* the veterinary art.
baytarî 1 (..—) بیطارة , (.——) بیطری A veterinary.
baytarî 2 (..—) بیطری (.——) بیطری P *lrnd.* the veterinary art.
baytariye (..—.) بیطریة , (.——.) بیطاریة A veterinary department.
baytarlık[ğı] بیطارلق بیطارلیق the veterinary art or profession.
baz 1 F 1. *chem.* base. 2. *math.* base.
-baz 2 (—) باز P playing with, *as in* **canbaz, hokkabaz.**
baz 3 (—) باز A 1. *lrnd.* falcon, hawk. 2. *prov.* sturdy fellow.
baz 4 (—) باز P *lrnd.* 1. back, backwards; behind. 2. again, anew. 3. open, openly. 4. apart; alone; distinct.

ba'z 5 بَعْض A *lrnd.* part, portion.
bazalⁱⁱ F *chém.* basic. **— metabolizma** *phys.* basal metabolism.
bazalt F *geol.* basalt.
ba'zan (.'.) بَعْضاً A, **bazan** (—'.) sometimes, now and then.
bazar (——) بازار P *archaic* market.
bazargân (———) بازارگان P *archaic* merchant.
bazari 1 (———) بازاری P *lrnd.* 1. pertaining to a market; bought or sold in a market. 2. market-man.
bazari 2 (———) بازاری P *lrnd.* weeping, wretched.
bazaverd (——.) بازآورد P *lrnd.* gift.
bazban (——) بازبان P *archaic* falconer, hawker.
bazdar 1 (——) بازدار P *archaic* falconer.
bazdar 2 (——) بازدار P *lrnd.* who keeps back.
bazdariye (———.) بازداری [based on **bazdar 1**] *lrnd.* falconry.
bazdaşt (——) بازداشت P *lrnd.* a holding back, detaining, concealing.
bazdid (——) بازدید P *lrnd.* 1. return-visit. 2. investigation. 3. reappearance.
bazek (—.) بازک P *lrnd.* little hawk, merlin, sparrow hawk.
bazen 1 بازن F same as **pazen**.
ba'zen 2 (.'.) بَعْضاً A, **bazen** (—.) same as **ba'zan**.
bazende (—..) بازنده P *lrnd.* who plays; dancer.
bazgeşt (—.) بازگشت P *lrnd.* 1. return. 2. repentance; desisting. 3. past quarrel, a dispute that has taken place between two people in the past. 4. *myst.* orders kind of recital of a litany.
bazgeşte (—..) بازگشته P *lrnd.* 1. returned. 2. desisting, shunning; repenting.
bazgûn (——), **bazgûne** (——.) بازگون، بازگونه P *lrnd.* reverse, perverse.
bazhah (——) بازخواه P *lrnd.* 1. one who asks back, who demands the restitution of something. 2. who inquires.
bazhane (——.) بازخانه P *lrnd.* falcon cage.
bazhast 1 (——) بازخاست P *lrnd.* resurrection.
bazhast 2 (——) بازخواست P *lrnd.* 1. demand for restitution. 2. inquiry. 3. the last judgment.
bazhiz (——) بازخیز P *lrnd.* resurrection.
ba'zı 1 (.'.) بَعْضِ [**ba'z 5**], **bâzı** (—.) 1. some, certain; some of, *e. g.*, **bâzısı** some of them. 2. sometimes. **— bâzı** now and then, from time to time.
bazı 2 بازی [**bazu**] same as **pazı 2**.

bazıⁱⁱ **3** (—.) باضع A *lrnd.* 1. that cuts, cutting, sharp, keen (sword). 2. that quenches thirst.
bazıa (—..) باضعة A 1. *law* head wound slightly grazing the skin with no actual bleeding.
bazıkᵏⁱ (—.) بازک A *lrnd.* sagacious, quick in sagacity.
bazi 1 (——) بازی A *lrnd.* 1. who despises, dislikes. 2. foul-mouthed, scurrilous.
baziⁱⁱ **2** (—.) بازیع A *lrnd.* handsome, intelligent, useful (lad).
bazi 3 بازی A *lrnd.* hawk, falcon.
bazi 4 (——) بازی P *lrnd.* 1. play, amusement; dancing; game. 2. trick, deceit, knavery.
baziçe (——.) بازیچه P *lrnd.* 1. plaything, toy, doll. 2. laughingstock.
bazigâh (———) بازیگاه P *lrnd.* place for games or amusement.
baziger (———.) بازیگر P *lrnd.* 1. acrobat. 2. dancer. 3. player, actor.
bazigûş (———) بازیگوش P *lrnd.* cheerful, playful.
baziğ (—.) بازیغ A *lrnd.* 1. who draws blood, who sacrifices. 2. just erupting (tooth). 3. just rising (heavenly body).
bazih (—.) بازخ A *lrnd.* 1. high. 2. proud, haughty.
bazikᵏⁱ (—.) بازک A *lrnd.* cutting, keen (sword).
bazil 1 (—.) بازل A *lrnd.* 1. who expends, liberal. 2. who exerts himself.
bazil 2 (—.) بازل A *lrnd.* 1. cutting its first tushes (camel, about 9 years old). 2. erupted (camel's tush). 3. mature in age, experience and judgment.
bazile (—..) بازلة A *surg.* instrument for puncturing.
bazir 1 (—.) بازر A *lrnd.* 1. sower. 2. spreader of rumors. 3. great talker, garrulous babbler.
bazir 2 (—.) بازر A *lrnd.* sowing, sower.
bazirgân (—.—) بازرگان P *archaic* merchant. **— başı** 1. warden of the merchants' guild. 2. merchant. **—î** (—.——) P *lrnd.* trade.
bazitᵈⁱ F *bot.* basidium.
baziver (——.) بازیور P *lrnd.* adorned, ornamented.
bazlama, bazlamaçᶜⁱ**, bazlambaç**ᶜⁱ بازلاما، بازلاماج، بازلامباج *prov.* flat bread baked on an iron sheet.
bazmande (——.) بازمانده P *lrnd.* 1. remaining, left behind, relic. 2. surviving, survivor. 3. incapacitated. **—gi** (——.—) P *abstr. n.*
bazofil F *biol.* basophilic.

bazoka (..'.) F *mil.* bazooka.
bazpes (—.) بازپس P *lrnd.* backwards.
bazpiç (——) بازپیچ P *lrnd.* 1. beads hung over a cradle as a plaything. 2. swing; hammock.
bazpürs (—.) بازپرس P *lrnd.* repeated inquiry, inquiry.
bazr بظر A *anat.* clitoris.
bazra (.—) بظرا A *lrnd.* whose clitoris is large and not amputated.
bazu (——) بازو P *lrnd.* 1. *anat.* upper arm, humerus. 2. strength. 3. *myst.* the divine will. **—yu himmet** effort, endeavor.
bazubend (——.) P, **bazubent**[di] (—..) بازوبند 1. armlet, brassard. 2. amulet worn on the upper arm.
bazudiraz (——.—) بازودراز P *lrnd.* 1. whose power is far-reaching. 2. tyrannical. 3. meddling.
bazuküşade (——.—.) بازوکشاده P *lrnd.* suppliant, petitioner.
bazur (——) بازور P *lrnd.* strong, powerful.
bazuvend (——.) بازوند *var.* of **bazubend**.
bazza (—.) بزّه A *lrnd.* soft-skinned and plump (woman).
be 1 1. *name of the letter* b. 2. *var.* of **ba 1**.
be 2 به 1. in vocatives expressing reproach, oh, you, *e. g.*, **be kadın!** O woman! 2. *vulg.* in terminal position, hey!, you fellow, I say! *e. g.*, **Neredesin be?** Hey, where are you?
be- 3 ب به [**be- 4**] 1. by, *as in* **ay be ay**. 2. to, *as in* **yüz beyüz**.
be- 4 به P *lrnd.* 1. with. 2. by. 3. in, at. 4. to, into. 5. on, upon. 6. according. 7. from, for, through.
beanşart ki (.—..) به آن شرط که P *lrnd.* on condition that, providing.
bebe *prov.* baby.
bebecik[ği] بِچِک little baby, little darling.
bebek[ği] بِبَک 1. baby. 2. doll. 3. pupil of the eye. 4. w. cap., *name of a district of Istanbul on the Bosphorus*.
Beberuhi (...'.) بِبِروحی *name of the funny dwarf in the Turkish shadow puppet show*.
bebga (.—) بِغا A *lrnd.* parrot.
bebgaiye (.——.) بِغائیه [*based on* **bebga**] *psych.* psittacism.
bebirlen=[ir] بِبِرلنمک *prov., same as* **böbürlen**=.
bebr بِبر P 1. leopard, *zool.*, *Felis pardus*. 2. tiger, *zool.*, *Felis tigris*.
Bec بِج *var.* of **Beç**.
beca (.—) بِجا P *lrnd.* in place, proper, fitting. **— nabeca** without consideration, at random.
becalet (.—.) بِجالت A *lrnd.* 1. imposing aspect, stateliness. 2. portliness, corpulence.
becanibi (.—'..) بِجانب P *lrnd.* toward.
becari (.——), **becarim** (.—.) بِجارم

A *lrnd.* calamities, misfortunes.
becayiş (.—.) بِجایش 1. *adm.* exchange of offices between two officials. 2. *psych.* transference. **— et**= /ı/ to exchange with one another (officer).
becbece بِجبِجه A *lrnd.* lullaby or other noises made to soothe a baby.
becek[ği] *prov.* corner.
becelleş=[ir] بِجللشمك /la/ *colloq.* to wrangle.
becene بِجنه *prov.* deserted (place).
becer=[ir] بِجرمك /ı/ 1. to carry out successfully, to manage cleverly. 2. to make a fine job of it (used ironically). **—ikli** skillful, adroit, resourceful. **—iklilik** skill, adroitness, dexterity. **—iksiz** maladroit, clumsy. **—iksizlik** *abstr. n.* **—il**= *pass. of* **becer**=. **—iş**, **—me** *verbal n. of* **becer**=. **—t**= /ı,a/ *caus. of* **becer**=.
becid بِجد P *prov.* 1. in earnest. 2. pressing, important.
beciheti (...'.) بِجهت P *lrnd.* by reason of; for the purpose of; in relation to.
becil (.—) بِجیل A *lrnd.* 1. imposing of aspect, majestic, venerable. 2. corpulent, portly; big, gross.
becir (.—) بِجیر A numerous, many; much, plentiful.
becit[di] بِجد [**becid**] 1. *prov.* hurriedly, quickly; urgent. 2. *archaic* strongly, greatly; repeatedly. 3. /a/ *archaic* given (to), eager (for). **—le**= /ı/ *archaic* to take seriously, to give oneself (to some work).
beclet بِجلت A *lrnd.* handsome appearance, beauty.
Beç[ci] بِچ Hung *hist.* Vienna. **— tavuğu** guinea fowl, *zool., Numida meleagris*.
beçce بِچّه P *var. of* **beçe 2**.
beçe 1 بِچه *archaic, var. of* **peçe**.
beçe 2 بِچه P 1. *poet.* child, infant; boy, youth. 2. *hist.* slave boy, page. 3. *lrnd.* young of an animal. **—i hor** *poet.* precious stone or metal. **—i hunin** *poet.* bitter tears. **—i hurşid** *poet.* precious stone or metal. **—i kûy** *lrnd.* foundling, bastard. **—i nev** 1. new-born infant. 2. young animal. 3. young shoot of a plant. **—i tavusu ulvi** *poet.* 1. the sun; day. 2. the moon. 3. fire. 4. ruby; garnet.
beçebaz (..—) بِچهباز P *lrnd.* sodomite.
beçedan (..—) بِچهدان P *lrnd.* womb, uterus.
beçedar (..—) بِچهدار P *lrnd.* 1. having young. 2. pregnant.
beçegân (..—) بِچگان P *lrnd., pl. of* **beçe 2**. **—ı dide** *poet.* tears.
Beçli, Beçlu بِچلی *hist.* Viennese.
bed 1 بد P 1. ugly, unseemly. 2. *lrnd.* bad, evil, ill. **— gel**= /a/ to look ugly, to seem unbecoming (to). **—ine git**= /ın/ to vex,

bed   146

annoy. **— görün=** /a/ to look ugly (to the eye).

bedᵈⁱ **2** بدء A *lrnd.* 1. a beginning, commencing. 2. a producing; production, creation. 3. *psych.* threshold. **—i besmele** *hist.* first reading lesson of a prince. **— et=*. —i tahliye** *com.* beginning of the unloading of the cargo.

bedᵈⁱ **3** بدع A *lrnd.* an originating, invention, creation. **— et= 2.***

beda (.—) بدا A *lrnd.* sudden thought, idea; a thought's suddenly occurring to one.

bedaatⁱⁱ (.—.) بداعت A *lrnd.* 1. novelty, innovation. 2. wonder.

bedad (.—) بداد A *lrnd.* 1. a sallying forth to battle, *esp.* in a man-to-man fight. 2. a contributing to a fund. 3. share, lot, portion.

bedaet (.—.) بداءت A *lrnd.* 1. a becoming visible, appearing. 2. an entering the mind (idea).

bedahet 1 (.—.) بداهت [based on Arabic] obviousness.

bedahet 2 (.—.) بداهت A *lrnd.* 1. improvisation; faculty of speaking extempore; impromptu, extempore. 2. suddenness, unexpectedness; unexpected event. 3. first occurrence, beginning. **—en** (.—´..) A extemporaneously, extempore.

bedahlâkᵏⁱ (..—) بداخلاق P morally depraved, immoral (person).

bedahş بدخش P *poet.* balas ruby.

Bedahşan (..—) بدخشان *geog.* Badakhshan.

bedahşani (..——) بدخشانی **bedahşi** (..—) بدخشی P *lrnd.* 1. of Badakhshan. 2. balas ruby.

bedahter بداختر P *lrnd.* ill-starred, unfortunate.

bedahu (.——) بداهو P *lrnd.* very wicked, vicious.

bedaiⁱⁱ (.—.) بداع A *same as* **bedayi.**

bedaih (.—.) بدائه بدایه A *lrnd., pl. of* **bedihe.**

bedaihül'ukulⁱⁱ (.—...—) بدائع العقول A *lrnd.* the first-fruits of intellectual exertion; impromptu remarks.

bed'alef بدعلف P *lrnd.* that eats unclean things.

bedamuz (.——) بدآموز P *lrnd.* 1. ill-taught, ill-bred. 2. who teaches others bad things.

bedan (.—) بدان P *lrnd.* 1. with that. 2. for that purpose.

bedanet (.—.) بدانت A *lrnd.* a becoming fat; corpulency, obesity.

bed'asl بدأصل P *lrnd.* of a bad stock.

bedava (.—.) بدا هوا [badı hava] gratis, for nothing, free. **— sirke baldan tatlıdır** *proverb* Vinegar that costs nothing is sweeter than honey. **—cı** one who wants to get things for nothing.

bedavaz (.——) بدآواز P *lrnd.* having an ugly voice.

bedavet 1 (.—.) بداوت A *lrnd.* 1. nomad life, Bedouinism, nomadism. 2. desert, wilderness.

bedavet 2 (.—.) بداوت A *lrnd.* the first that appears.

bedavi (.——) بداوی A *lrnd.* belonging to the desert; living in the desert.

bedavra (.´.) *prov., var. of* **pedavra.**

bedaya (.——) بدایا A *lrnd., pl. of* **bedie.**

bedayiⁱⁱ (.—.) بدایع A *lrnd.* 1. novelties, curious and precious things. 2. beautiful sayings, rhetorical embellishments. **—i lâfziye** *rhet.* verbal embellishments. **—i ma'neviye** *rhet.* embellishments depending on the sense.

bed'âyin (.——) بدآیین P *lrnd.* 1. ill-bred, wicked, perverse. 2. of perverse practice, heretic.

bedbaht بدبخت P unlucky, unfortunate, unhappy. **—lık** unhappiness.

bedbin (.—) بدبین [based on Persian] pessimistic. **—lik** pessimism.

bedbu (.—) بدبو P *lrnd.* ill-odored, fetid, stinking.

bedcelev بدجلو P *lrnd.* obstinate, refractory (horse).

bedçehre بدچهره P *lrnd.* ugly.

bedçeşm بدچشم P *lrnd.* 1. evil-eyed. 2. covetous. 3. shying (horse).

beddalⁱⁱ (.—) بقال A *lrnd.* grocer.

beddimağ (..—) بددماغ P *lrnd.* capricious, obstinate.

beddua (..—) بددعا P curse, imprecation, malediction. **— al=** to be an object of malediction. **— et=** /a/ to curse.

beded بدد A *lrnd.* 1. power, ability. 2. barter, exchange.

bed'eda (..—) بدادا P *lrnd.* unmannerly, uncouth.

bedel بدل A 1. /a/ equivalent (of). 2. value, worth; price. 3. /a/ substitute (for); in lieu of, for, in exchange for, *e. g.*, **buna bedel** in lieu of that, instead. 4. *hist.* sum paid for exemption from military service; military substitute who serves for some other person. 5. *obs.* commutation sometimes paid to civil or military officers in lieu of rations. 6. *myst.* saint. 7. *gram.* nonexplicative opposition. **—i askerî** *obs.* tax levied on non-Muslim Ottoman subjects in lieu of military service. **—i a'ver** *lrnd.* a poor exchange (taking bad for good). **—i bendedir** *fin.* value in myself (inscribed on certain drafts). **—i cizye** *Ott. hist.* annual tribute paid by Walachia, Moldavia, and the

Republic of Ragusa. **—i ferağ** *law* equivalent paid for the purchase of an estate. **—i has** *obs.* fee paid to civil servants as a substitute for a fief. **—i hesaptadır** *fin.* 'credit to be placed to account' (formula inscribed on an endorsed bill of exchange). **—i icare** *law* rent. **— ile ferağ** *law* cession of property in exchange for some benefit. **—i kabzedilmiştir** *fin.* value received (inscribed on checks). **—i kitabe** *rel. law* the stipulated fee for emancipation, stated in a contract between the slave and his owner. **—i mahlûlât** *Ott. hist.* fee received at the transfer of a reverted fief to a new holder. **—i mayetehallel** *biol.* the equivalent of the energies used up by the body. **—i misil** *law* the just, legal, customary equivalent. **—i mükâtebe** *same as* **bedeli kitabe. —i nakdî** *obs.* sum paid for exemption from military service. **—i nükûl** *com.* forfeit. **—i nüzl** *obs.* local tax for the maintenance of a billeting office. **—i öşr** *obs.* an equivalent for the tithe, collected from land alienated from agricultural use. **—i rakabe** *same as* **bedeli kitabe. —i şahsi** *obs.* person hired by another as a military service substitute. **—i tahsil içindir** *fin.* 'value to be collected in cash' (formula inscribed on the checks). **—i tamamen ödenmiş aksiyon** *fin.* paid up share. **—i teminat içindir** *fin.* value to stand as a specific guarantee (inscribed on checks). **—i terhin içindir** *fin.* value standing against surety (inscribed on checks). **—i tesviye edilmiş hisse senedi** *fin.* 'paid-up share. **— tut=** *Ott. hist.* to pay someone for having him be a substitute for military service. **—i zeamet** *obs.* compensatory salary paid to a person dispossessed of his fief.

bedelci *obs.* 1. one who has paid to be exempted from his military service. 2. agent for procuring military substitutes.

bedelen (.'..) A /a/ *lrnd.* in lieu of, in exchange for.

beden 1 A 1. body. 2. trunk, principal part. 3. *mil.* wall (of a castle). 4. *naut.* bight (of a rope). 5. *naut.* shank (of an anchor). 6. *fishing* lower end part of the line. **—inden** out of one's own pocket. **— arası** space between battlements on a castle wall. **— bağı** *naut.* rolling hitch. **— cezası** *law* corporal punishment. **— duvarı** *arch.* main outer wall. **— muayenesi** *mil.* physical examination. **— mükellefiyeti** compulsory labor. **— sağlamlığı** *mil.* physical fitness. **— terbiyesi** physical training.

bed'en 2 (.'..) A *lrnd.* first, at first, as a beginning.

bed'endiş (..—) P *lrnd.* malevolent, malicious.

bedene A *lrnd.* fat camel or ox sacrificed at Mecca in discharge of a vow.

bedenen (..'.) A 1. physically. 2. *lrnd.* in person; personally.

bedenî (..—) A 1. physical, corporal, somatic. 2. corporeal, bodily. 3. *lrnd.* fat, bulky, corpulent.

bedenli 1. having a body. 2. large-bodied, corpulent. 3. walled (castle).

bedenos Gk kind of grouse.

bedensel *neol.* physical, corporeal.

beder P *lrnd.* out of doors; out, forth, away.

bedest P *lrnd.* span (measure).

bedestan (..—) , **bedesten** |bezistan| 1. the central building in the Covered Market in Istanbul (market where antiques, objets d'art, jewelry, etc., are sold). 2. vaulted and fireproof part of a bazaar where valuable goods are kept.

bed'et=^{der} **1** |bed 2| *lrnd.* 1. /a/ to begin, to start, to set about (to). 2. to make a beginning, to commence action.

bed'et=^{der} **2** |bed 3| *lrnd.* /ı/ to create, invent.

bed'et 3 A *lrnd.* beginning, commencement, the first of a thing. **—en** (.'..) A at first, first.

bedevat (..—) A *lrnd.*, pl. of **bedv 1.**

bedevi (..—) A 1. Bedouin. 2. *lrnd.* pertaining to the desert or open country; nomadic. **—lik** Bedouinism.

Bedeviye (..—.) name of an order of dervishes.

bedeviyet |based on **bedevi**| Bedouinism.

bedfal^{li} (.—) P *lrnd.* inauspicious.

bedfercam (..—) P *lrnd.* ending badly, doomed.

bedfial^{li} (..—) P *lrnd.* mischievous, evil-doing.

bedgevher P *lrnd.* wicked by nature, ill-natured.

bedgirdar (..—) [Persian **bedkirdâr**] *lrnd.* evil-doer, malefactor.

bedgû, bedgûy (.—) P *lrnd.* slanderer, detractor.

bedgüher P *same as* **bedgevher.**

bedgüman (..—) P *lrnd.* 1. suspicious, always suspecting evil. 2. malevolent, ill-willed.

bedhah (.—) P malevolent, malicious. **—i** (.——) P *lrnd.*, **—lık** malevolence, malice, enmity.

bedhal^{li} (..—) P *lrnd.* in bad circumstances, miserable.

bedhu, bedhuy (.—) P *lrnd.*

bad-tempered; ill-natured, of bad character, vicious.

bedi͡i 1 (.—) بَدِع A *lrnd.* 1. new, novel, newly invented, novelty. 2. wonderful, hitherto unseen or unheard. 3. originator, inventor, introducer; the Creator. **B—i sanî** God the Originator and Maker of all things.

bedi͡i 2 (.—) بَدِع A *rhet.* the science of the figures of speech.

bedî 3 (.—) بَدى P *lrnd.* badness, wickedness.

bedi 4 (.—) بَدء A *lrnd.* first, beginning.

bedia (.—.) بَدِيع A *lrnd.* 1. creation of art. 2. novelty, wonderful thing, marvel. 3. *rhet.* fanciful expression, ornament of speech. 4. *w. cap., woman's name.*

bedid 1 (.—) بَديد P *lrnd.* manifest, visible.

bedid 2 (.—) بَديد A *lrnd.* 1. pad for one side of a packsaddle. 2. saddlebag. 3. like, equal, match.

bedid 3 (.—) بَديد A *lrnd.* open, uncultivated plain.

bedidar (.——) بَديدار P *lrnd.* manifest, visible.

bedide (.—.) بَديدە A *lrnd.* 1. alike, match, equal. 2. calamity, evil.

bed'ie (.—.) بَدءە A *lrnd.* 1. a beginning, a first occurrence. 2. faculty of extemporizing or of repartee; impromptu.

bedihe (.—.) بَديهە A *lrnd.* 1. a first beginning. 2. impromptu verse, an extempore elegant or flowery remark. 3. intuitive perception, intuitive and sound judgment; *phil.* axiom. **—gû** (.—.—) P *lrnd.* who in talking finds elegant expressions.

bedihî (.——) بَديهى A 1. self-evident, obvious. 2. *lrnd.* extempore.

bedihiyat (.———) بَديهيات A self-evident facts; *phil.* axioms.

bedihiyet (.——.) بَديهيت |based on **bedihi**| self-evidence, obviousness.

bedii (.——) بَدعى |based on **bedi 2**| 1. esthetic. 2. *lrnd.* rhetorical. **—at** (.———) A esthetics.

bedil (.—) بَدل A *lrnd.* substitute, equivalent, alternative; vicar, representative.

bedin 1 (.—) بَدن A *lrnd.* corpulent, bulky, fat.

bedin 2 (.—) بَدن P *lrnd.* to this, with this, in this.

bedir^dri —. |**bedr**| full moon. **— hali** full (of the moon). **—i kâmil, —i tam** full moon.

bedirik^gi *var. of* **bedrik.**

bediülcemal^li (.—..—) بَديع الجمال A *lrnd.* of rare beauty, exquisitely beautiful.

bedkâr (.—) بَدكار P *lrnd.* wicked, sinful.

bedkirdar (..—) بَدكردار P *same as* **bedgirdar.**

bedkiş (.—) بَدكيش P *lrnd.* impious, inhuman.

bedlehçe بَدلهجە P *lrnd.* ill-tongued, foul-mouthed.

bedleş=^ir بَدلشمك to grow ugly, disagreeable.

bedligâm (..—) بَدلگام P *lrnd.* hard-mouthed, headstrong; rebellious, unruly.

bedlik^gi بَدلك 1. ugliness. 2. wickedness, worthlessness; wicked action.

bedlika (..—) بَدلقا P *lrnd.* ugly-faced.

bedmaye (.—.) بَدمايە P *lrnd.* of bad character, wicked.

bedmest بَدمست P *lrnd.* intoxicated, badly drunk. **—î** (..—) P intoxication, drunken stupor. **—lik** *abstr. n.*

bedmezheb بَدمذهب P *lrnd.* 1. blasphemous. 2. sectary.

bedmihr بَدمهر P *lrnd.* unloving, unkind.

bedmizac (..—) بَدمزاج P *lrnd.* bad-tempered.

bednam (.—) بَدنام P *lrnd.* ill-famed.

bednihad (..—) بَدنهاد P *lrnd.* wicked, of bad character.

bednijad (..—) بَدنژاد P *lrnd.* ill-born, of base descent.

bedniyet (.—.) بَدنيت P *lrnd.* ill-intentioned.

bedpesend بَدپسند P *lrnd.* 1. who approves of what is bad. 2. whom the bad like. 3. difficult to please.

bedr —. A *lrnd.* 1. *same as* **bedir.** 2. handsome youth. 3. *w. cap.* Badr (small town southwest of Medina, scene of a battle in the time of the Prophet Muhammad).

bedraka بَدرقە P *lrnd.* 1. escort, guide. 2. spiritual teacher, monitor.

bedram (.—) بَدرام P *lrnd.* 1. wild, shy, timid (beast). 2. obstinate, intractable (horse).

bedran (.—) بَدران P *lrnd.* who drives cattle badly, who conducts matters badly.

bedre بَدرە A 1. *prov.* pail. 2. *lrnd.* water-skin. 3. *obs.* purse; purse containing 1000 pieces of silver; purse containing 7000 pieces of gold.

bedreftar (..—) بَدرفتار P *lrnd.* going badly, of bad conduct.

bedreg بَدرگ P *lrnd.* of bad stock, malevolent.

bedrek^gi بَدرك *var. of* **bedrik.**

bedreng بَدرنگ P *lrnd.* 1. of bad color. 2. of bad character.

bedrik^gi بَدرك *prov.* tuft of corded cotton wool ready for spinning, prepared by rolling it around a short stick.

bedrud (.—) بَدرود P *lrnd.* farewell.

bedruzgâr (.——) بَدروزگار P *lrnd.* 1. unfortunate, wretched. 2. bad, wicked.

bedsigâl^li, **bedsikâl**^li (..—) بَدسكال P *lrnd.* malignant, malevolent.

bedsiret (. —.) بد سيرت P *lrnd.* of bad ways, of ill-repute.

bedsuret (. —.) بد صورت P *lrnd.* ugly, monstrous.

bedşekl بد شكل P *lrnd.* deformed, ill-shaped, ugly.

bedter بدتر P *lrnd.* worse.

bedterin (. . —) بدترين P *lrnd.* worst.

bedtıynet[ti] بد طينت P *lrnd.* of bad character, malignant.

beduh (. —) بدوح A *obs.* word used for luck and safety charms.

bed'urrey بد الرأى A *lrnd.* first thought, first opinion.

bedv 1 بدو A *lrnd.* thought, idea.

bedv 2 بدو A *lrnd.* open, uncultivated country.

bedzeban (. . —) بد زبان P *lrnd.* ill-tongued, foul-mouthed.

bedzehre بد زهره P *lrnd.* timid, cowardly.

befc بج P *lrnd.* spittle accidentally thrown out while speaking.

befş بفش P *lrnd.* pomp, magnificence.

-beft بفت P woven, *as in* zerbeft.

beftere بفتره P *lrnd.* falconer's lure; decoy-bird.

befteri (. . —) بفترى P *lrnd.* weaver's reed, sley.

bega (. —) بغا P *lrnd.* passive sodomite.

begâh (. —) بگاه P *var. of* pegâh. [/begal/ *see* /bagal/.]

beganuş (. — —) بغا نوش P *lrnd.* quick-going horse.

begavet (. —.) بغاوت A *lrnd.* wickedness, injustice, disobedience, rebellion.

begaya 1 (. — —) بغايا A *lrnd.* advanced guards, scouts.

begaya 2 (. — —) بغايا A *lrnd.*, *pl. of* bagi 3.

begayet (. —.) بغايت P extremity, exceedingly.

begaz (. —) بغاز P *lrnd.* wedge.

begazat[ti] (. . —.) بغاضت A *lrnd.* hatefulness.

begeh بگه P *var. of* begâh.

begonya (. . .) بغونيا L begonia. —**giller** *neol., bot.*, Begoniaceae. —**siye** *bot.*, Begoniaceae.

begter بگتر P *lrnd.* steel breastplate, cuirass; plate or scale armor.

begteri (. . —) بگترى P *lrnd.* armorer, maker of scale or plate armor.

begterpuş (. . —) بگترپوش P *lrnd.* clad in scale or plate armor.

beğ بگ *archaistic spelling variant of* bey 1. [/beğ/ *see* /bey/.]

beğen=[ir] بگنمك /1/ 1. to like, admire; to approve (of), to be pleased (with). 2. to choose; to prefer. — **beğendiğini** Choose whatever you like.

beğendi بگندى [hünkâr beğendi] dish made of eggplants, baked in the coals, mashed and served with meat.

beğendir=[ir] بگندير مك /1, a/ *caus. of* beğen=. —**il=** *pass.*

beğenil=[ir] بگنيلمك *pass. of* beğen=.

beğeniş بگنش, **beğenme** بگنمه *verbal n. of* beğen=.

beğir=[ir] بگير مك *prov.* to bleat.

beh به A *lrnd.* Good! Wonderful, bravo!

beha 1 (. —.) بها *lrnd., var. of* baha 1.

beha 2 (. —.) بها A *lrnd.* 1. beauty, comeliness. 2. a being accustomed, familiarity.

behacet (. —.) بهجت A *lrnd.* beauty.

behagir (. — —) بهاگير P *lrnd.* precious, expensive, costly.

behaim (. —.) بهايم A *lrnd., pl. of* behime.

behak[kı] بهق A *path.* mild kind of leprosy.

behakkı بحقى P *lrnd.* for the love of, by, *e. g.*, **behakkı Huda** for the love of God.

behakulhacer بهق الحجر A *bot.* lichen.

behalil (. — —) بهاليل A *lrnd., pl. of* bühlûl.

behane (. —.) بهانه *var. of* bahane.

behar (. —) بهار *poet., var. of* bahar 1.

beharic (. —.) بهارج A *lrnd.* base coins.

behcet بهجت A *lrnd.* 1. cheerfulness, joy, happiness. 2. beauty, brightness of complexion. 3. *w. cap., man's name*.

behem بهم P *lrnd.* together, with one another. — **amihte** mixed together.

behemehal (. .'. —) بهمحال P in any case, no matter what happens, for sure, come what may.

behemzede بهم زده P *lrnd.* jumbled together, thrown into confusion.

beher بهر P to each, per, *e. g.*, **beher gün** daily, per day, per diem. —**i** each one, apiece.

beherhal (. . —) بهرحال P in any case.

behey بهى in *vocative expressing irritation*, O, *e. g.*, **behey adam!** O man!

behhat (. —) بهات A *lrnd.* slanderer, calumniator.

behî (. —) بهى A *lrnd.* 1. beautiful, elegant, graceful. 2. *obs.* excellent (in addressing certain officials).

behic (. —) بهيج A *lrnd.* 1. cheerful, radiant. 2. beautiful, comely; bright-colored. 3. *w. cap., man's name*.

behil بهل P *lrnd.* lawful; permitted or given by the owner.

behime (. —.) بهيمه A *lrnd.* 1. brute, wild beast. 2. quadruped; domestic ruminant.

behimî (. — —) بهيمى A *lrnd.* animal (instincts), bestial, brutish.

behimiyet (. — .) حيميت | based on **behimî** | *lrnd.* animal instinct, bestiality, brutishness.

behir (. —) بهير A *lrnd.* out of breath, panting; asthmatic.

behire (. — .) بهيره A *lrnd.* 1. noble, esteemed (woman). 2. slender, delicate (woman). 3. *w. cap.*, *woman's name*.

behired بخرد P *lrnd.* intelligent, intelligently.

behişt بهشت *var. of* **bihişt**.

behite (. — .) بهيته A *lrnd.* infamous lie, slander, calumny.

Behiye (. — .) بهيه A *woman's name*.

behle بهله P, **behli** بهلى *obs.* falconer's leather gauntlet for carrying a hawk.

behlûl[tü] (. —) بهلول 1. *var. of* **bühlûl**. 2. *w. cap.*, *man's name*.

behman (. —) بهمان P *lrnd.* some one, such and such.

behme بهمه A *lrnd.* lamb; kid; young calf.

Behmen بهمن P 1. Bahman (name of a genius in ancient Persian religion). 2. *man's name; name of Artaxerxes Longimanus*. 3. Persian calendar January; second day of each month. 4. *l. c., bot.* behen root, *radix behen*.

behod بخود P *lrnd.* by oneself.

behr 1 بهر A *lrnd.* 1. distance. 2. distress, misfortune; disappointment. 3. rays of light, radiance.

behr 2 بهر P *lrnd., var. of* **behre**.

Behram (. —) بهرام P 1. *man's name*; Bahram (name of a Sassanid King of Persia). 2. Bahram (name of an angel in the ancient Persian religion). 3. *lrnd.* the planet Mars.

behre بهره P *lrnd.* share, lot, part, portion.

behredar (. . —) بهره‌دار P, **behremend** بهره‌مند P, **behrever** بهره‌ور P *lrnd.* one who has a share, sharer, sharing.

behresiz بهره‌سز /dan/ having no share (of), lacking (in).

behreyab (. . —) بهره‌ياب P *lrnd.* one who finds a share, partaker.

behri بهرى P *lrnd.* for, for the sake of, *e. g.*, **behri Huda** for God's sake.

beht بهت A *lrnd.* 1. amazement, bewilderment. 2. lie, falsehood; slander, calumny.

behut[tü] (. —) بهوت A *lrnd.* given to calumny.

behükmi بحكم P *lrnd.* by the decree of, *e. g.*, **behükmi kader** by the decree of destiny.

Behzad (. —) بهزاد [bihzad] *man's name; name of a famous Persian painter*.

beis[si] بأس [be's 1] harm. — **yok** Never mind! No harm!

bej بژ F beige.

bek[ki] **1** E *football* back.

bek[ki] **2** F gas burner.

bek 3 *prov.* lookout.

beka (. —) بقا A 1. a lasting, enduring, remaining. 2. perpetualness, permanency, eternalness. 3. *myst.* the annihilation of self or of self-seeking by an eternal union with God, together with a missionary vocation to mankind. — **bul=** to last, to be permanent. **—ı ruh** immortality of the soul.

bekabunka (. . . '. .) بكا بونقه It *same as* **bakabunga**.

bekâm (. —) بكام P *lrnd.* 1. in accordance with one's wish. 2. satisfied, contented.

bekâmet (. — .) بكامت A *lrnd.* 1. dumbness. 2. a refraining from speaking.

bekâr 1 (. —) بكار A 1. single, unmarried, bachelor. 2. grass widower. — **odaları** inn where rooms are let to provincials who come to work in town.

bekar 2 F *mus.* the sign, ♮ natural.

bekâr 3 (. —) بكار P *lrnd.* 1. at work. 2. useful, advantageous.

bekâret (. — .) بكارت A 1. virginity, maidenhood. 2. maidenhead, hymen.

bekârlık[ğı] (. — .) بكارلق bachelorhood, celibacy. — **sultanlık** *proverb* A bachelor's life is a king's life.

bekaya (. — —) بقايا *var. of* **bakaya**.

bekçi بكچى watchman; night-watchman; guard; lookout. — **köşkü** room on the top of a high tower as lookout for fires. — **kulesi** watchtower, fire-guard tower. —**lik** watchman's duty.

bekef بكف P *lrnd.* in the palm of the hand.

bekem بكم A *lrnd.* 1. dumbness. 2. a refraining from speech.

beker 1 بكر A *lrnd.* early morning, between dawn and sunrise.

beker 2 بكر A *lrnd.* promptness of action, speediness.

bekere بكره A *prov.* pulley.

bekî (. —) بكى A *lrnd.* who weeps much.

bekil (. —) بكيل A neat, fastidious in dress and deportment.

bekîm (. —) بكيم A *lrnd.* 1. dumb. 2. silent. 3. unable to express himself.

bekir 1 بكر A *lrnd.* 1. who habitually rises early. 2. *w. cap.*, *man's name*.

bekir 2 (. . —) بكير A *lrnd.* early riser.

Bekke بكه *ancient name of Mecca*.

bekle=[r] بكله‌مك /ı/ 1. to wait (for), to await, expect, to look (for). 2. /dan/ to expect (from). 3. to guard, to watch (over), to attend.

bekleme بكله‌مه *verbal n.* — **kulübesi** *mil.* sentry box. — **müddeti** *mar. law* lay days. — **odası**, — **salonu** waiting room.

beklen=[ir] بكلنمك *pass. of* **bekle=**. **—medik** unexpected. **—ti** *same as* **bekleme**.

bekleş=[ir] بكلشمك to wait together. **—tir=** /ı/ *caus*.

beklet=[ir] بكلتمك /ı/ caus. of **bekle=**. **—il=** pass. of **beklet=**. **—tir=** caus. of **beklet=**.
bekleyici بكلى يجى one who waits or watches.
bekleyiş بكلى يش waiting.
bekmaz (.—) بكماز var. of **bigmaz**.
bekmez بكمز prov., var. of **pekmez**.
bekr بكر A lrnd. young camel, from its second to its fifth or ninth year.
bekre بكره A lrnd. the grooved wheel of a pulley or block; pulley; block.
bekri 1 بكرى habitual drinker. **B— Mustafa** 1. name of a famous drunkard, hero of many anecdotes. 2. drunkard.
Bekrî 2 (.—) بكرى A hist. 1. descendent of the first caliph Abu Bakr. 2. one belonging to an Arabic tribe called Banu Bakr.
bekrilen=[ir] بكريلنمك to become a habitual drunkard. **—dir=** /ı/ caus.
bekrilik[ği] بكريلك habitual drunkenness.
beksemad, beksemat, beksimet بكسمات بكسماد vars. of **peksimet**.
Bektaşi (.— —) بكتاشى 1. dervish of the Bektashi order; belonging to the Bektashi order. 2. person politely contemptuous of orthodoxy. **— babası, — dervişi** dervish of the Bektashi order. **— musikisi** religious music used by the Bektaşi order. **— sırrı** deep mystery. **— taşı** min. Oriental alabaster. **— üzümü** gooseberry, bot., Ribes grossularia. **—lik** Bektashiism.
bektaşimeşreb (.— — ..) بكتاشى مشرب religiously free thinking.
bekûnek[ki] (.—.) بكونك P lrnd. wooden sword.
bekûr (.—) بكور A lrnd. early.
bekûri (.— —) بكورى P lrnd. 1. blindly. 2. in despite.
bel 1 بل ل. 1. waist. 2. loins; the small of the back. 3. the middle of the back (of an animal). 4. sperm. 5. pass in a mountain ridge. 6. naut. midship body. **—i açıl=** to lose control over the evacuation of urine. **— ağrısı** lumbago. **— bağla=** /a/ to rely (upon), to trust. 2. archaic to prepare resolutely for an undertaking. **—ini bük=** /ın/ to bend double (years, trouble); to weigh heavily (on), to ruin. **—ini doğrult=** to recover. **—i gel=** to have a discharge of sperm. **—inden gel=** /in/ to be the child (of). **— gevşekliği** med. incontinence. **— gibi ak=** to flow in a column as thick as one's waist. **—i ince** small in the waist. **— kemiği** 1. backbone, spine. 2. basic part, pillar. **—ini kır=** /ın/ to ruin, cripple. **— kündesi** Or. style wrestling tactic in which the opponent is grasped on both sides of the waist, turned by pressure applied to the umbilical region and thrown to the ground. **— mühresi** vertebra. **— omuru** anat. lumbar vertebra. **— soğukluğu** path. gonorrhoea. **— ver=** to bulge, to sag.
bel 2 بل ل. P 1. spade. 2. digging fork. 3. lrnd. oar, paddle.
bel 3 بل ل. prov. mark, sign.
bel[ʼi] **4** بلع A lrnd. 1. swallowing. 2. astr. absorption.
belâ 1 (.—) بلا A 1. calamity, misfortune, evil, trouble. 2. lrnd. trial, proof, test. **— ara=** to look for trouble. **—ya bak ki** the trouble is that. **—yı berzah** great calamity. **—sını bul=** to get into trouble; to get one's deserts. **—ya çat=** to run into trouble. **—sını çek=** /ın/ to suffer (for some deed). **— çekmeyince bal yenmez** proverb No pleasure without effort. **— çıkar=** to make trouble, to cause a row. **—ya düş=** to run into trouble; to encounter calamity. **— geliyorum demez** proverb Misfortune comes without warning. **—ya gir=** to run into trouble. **—yı muazzam** dreadful calamity, great trouble. **—lar mubareki** the last straw (said for a trouble that comes on top of a series of misfortunes). **— oku=** to curse. **—yı satın al=** to invite trouble. **—yı sav=** to drive trouble away, to escape from trouble. **—yı siyah** unbearable misfortune. **—ya sok=** /ı/ to cause trouble, to get into trouble. **—ya tutul=, —ya uğra=** to meet with misfortune, to get into trouble.
belâ 2 بلا A lrnd. decay, threadbareness.
belâbil (.—.) بلابل A lrnd., 1. pl. of **belbal**. 2. pl. of **bülbül**.
belâdet (.—.) بلادت A lrnd. stupidity, stolidity.
belâdır (.—.), **belâdur** (.— —) بلادر بلا دور P marking nut, bot., Semicarpus Anacardium.
belâduri (.—.—) بلادورى P lrnd. an electuary composed of anacardium.
belâgat[tı] **1** (.—.) بلاغت A 1. eloquence. 2. rhetoric.
belâgat 2 (.——) بلاغت A lrnd. slander, backbiting, gossip.
belâgatfüruş (.—..—) بلاغت فروش P lrnd. who makes a show of eloquence.
belâgatmeşhun (.—..—) بلاغت مشحون lrnd. eloquent.
belâgatnişan (.—..—) بلاغت نشان lrnd. eloquent.
belâgatperdaz (.—..—) بلاغت پرداز lrnd. who cultivates eloquence.
belâgatpira (.—..—) بلاغت پيرا P lrnd. who adorns eloquence, eloquent.
belâgatşiar (.—..—) بلاغت شعار P lrnd. eloquent.

belâgerdan (. —. —) بلاگردان P *lrnd.* that wards off evil (alms, etc.).

belâğ (. —) بلاغ A *lrnd.* 1. arrival (letter, message, etc.). 2. an arriving at the age of puberty. 3. delivery of a message, etc. 4. message; anything brought by a messenger. 5. sufficiency.

belâh بلح A *lrnd.* unripe dates.

belâhet (. —.) بلاهت A stupidity, foolishness; *psych.* idiocy.

belâk[kı] بلق A *lrnd.* 1. a being piebald, checkered with black and white. 2. a having the legs white as high as the thighs (horse). 3. bewilderment, astonishment.

belâkeş (. —.) بلاکش P *lrnd.* going through much suffering.

belâki[iı] (. —.) بلافح A *lrnd.*, pl. of **belka 2, belkaa.**

belâl[lı] (. —) بلال A *lrnd.* 1. water; moisture. 2. a sip of water enough to moisten the mouth.

belâlet (. —.) بلالت A *lrnd.* moisture, humidity.

belâlı (. —.) بلالى 1. calamitous, troublesome. 2. afflicted with evil. 3. *vulg.* bully.

belâli[iı] (. — —) بلاليع A *lrnd.*, pl. of **bellâa, bellûa.**

belâlik[kı] (. — —) بلاليك A *lrnd.* barren sandy plains, deserts.

Bel'am (. —) بلعام *Bib.* Balaam.

bel'ame بلعمه A *lrnd.* a swallowing, devouring.

belâs (. —) بلاس A *lrnd.* haircloth, sackcloth.

belâya (. — —) بلايا A *lrnd.* 1. calamities, afflictions, troubles, ills. 2. trials, proofs, tests.

belâzede (. —. .) بلازده P *lrnd.* smitten with misfortune, unfortunate.

belâzır, belâzur (. —.) بلاذر A same as **beladır.**

belbal[lı] (. —) بلبال A *lrnd.* anxiety, anguish, grief, perturbation of mind.

bel bel بل بل perplexedly, amazedly, stupidly, *only in* — **bak=** to look perplexed.

belbele 1 بلبله P *lrnd.* 1. drinking vessel with a spout. 2. gurgling of water when poured from a bottle.

belbele 2 بلبله A *lrnd.* 1. *same as* **belbal.** 2. confusion of voices, hubbub.

belci بلجى 1. maker or seller of spades. 2. worker who tills the soil with a spade or digging fork.

Belcika بلجيقه F *archaic for* **Belçika.**

Belçika بلجيقه [Belcika] Belgium. —**lı** Belgian. — **Kongosu** Belgian Congo.

beldar (. —) بلدار P *mil. hist.* pioneer.

belde بلده A 1. city. 2. *lrnd.* country. 3. *astrol.* the twenty-first lunar mansion (the space between the constellations Sagittarius and Capricorn, the place of the sun on the shortest day). — **devleti** *hist.* city-state. — **kadısı** *obs.* judge. —**i tayyibe** *lrnd.* 1. Medina. 2. Istanbul. 3. Jerusalem.

bele=[r] بلمك /1/ *prov.* 1. to smear, soil; /a/ to dip (into flour, etc.) 2. to swaddle.

belec بلج A *lrnd.* 1. space between the two eyebrows. 2. cheerfulness, gladness, happiness.

beled 1 بلد A *lrnd.* 1. country, region, district. 2. city, town, village. 3. *w. cap.*, name of an ancient town near Mosul. —**i haram** Mecca. **B— Suresi** name of the ninetieth Sura of the Quran.

beled 2 بلد P *lrnd.* who is entirely familiar with a place; guide.

beled 3 بلد A *lrnd.* plummet, sounding lead.

beledî 1 (. . —) بلدى A 1. municipal. 2. kind of locally-made cotton material. 3. *lrnd.* belonging to a town, local; town-made. 4. *lrnd.* native (to a region).

beledi 2 بلدى kind of fish, *zool.*, Squalius cephalus.

belediye بلديه [dairei belediye] municipality. **B—ler Bankası** state-owned bank making loans to municipalities. — **dairesi** town hall. — **encümeni** municipal corporation. — **Kanunu** law that determines the status of the various communities. — **meclisi** town council. — **reisi** mayor. — **reisliği** mayoralty. — **seçimi** municipal election.

belediyet 1 (. . —.) بلديت [based on **beledî 1**] *lrnd.* 1. municipal state, civic state. 2. civilization. 3. quality of being native to a region; localness.

belediyet 2 (. . —.) بلديت [based on **beled 2**] *lrnd.* thorough knowledge (of a place).

beleh بله A *lrnd.* stupidity, silliness; idiocy.

belek بلك *prov.* 1. mountain pass. 2. swaddling clothes. 3. sign, mark. 4. present, gift.

belel بلل A *lrnd.* 1. moisture, humidity. 2. abundance of the comforts of life. 3. beauty, freshness; prosperity, splendor.

belen 1 بيلان، بلان، بلن *prov.* 1. mountain pass; steep torrent-bed in a mountain pass. 2. mountainous region.

belen=[ir] **2** بلنمك *pass. of* **bele=.**

belend بلند P *var. of* **bülend.**

belengmüşk[kü] بلنگمشك P *lrnd.* a wild, aromatic plant.

beler=[ir] بلرمك to be wide open, to stare (eyes). —**i kal=** to remain staring (eyes). —**t=** /1/ to open wide in terror (eyes).

belesan (. . —) بلسان A *lrnd.* 1. balm, balsam. 2. balsam tree, *bot.*, Commiphora *opobalsamum.* — **yağı** balm of Gilead, Mecca balsam. **—la=** /ı/ to anoint with balsam.

beleş A *slang* gratis, for nothing. **—ten** for nothing. **—e kon=** to take possession of something without having to pay for it. **—çi** one who gets something for nothing, sponger.

bel'ét=ᵈᵉʳ /ı/ to swallow; to devour.

belgᵍⁱ A *lrnd.* 1. eloquent. 2. that reaches a destination or maturity.

belge *neol.* document, certificate. **—cilik** diplomatics. **—le=** /ı/ to document.

belgi *prov.* sign, mark, ensign.

belgin *neol., phil.* precise. **—lik** precision. **—siz** imprecise.

belgisiz *neol.* indeterminate, vague; *gram.* indefinite.

belgitᵈⁱ *neol.* receipt; evidence. **—le=** /ı/ *phil.* to demonstrate.

Belgrad Belgrade. **— Ormanı** name of a forest near the European shore of the Bosphorus.

Belh Balkh.

belha (. —) A *lrnd., fem. of* **ebleh.**

beli (.´.) P *prov.* yes.

belid (. —) A *lrnd.* 1. stupid, dull, unintelligent. 2. heavy, slow, lazy (beast).

beligane (. — .) P *lrnd.* eloquently.

Beligrad *archaic for* **Belgrad.**

Beligradcıkᵍⁱ *geog.* Belogradchik in Northeast Bulgaria.

beliğ (. —) A *lrnd.* 1. eloquent. 2. complete, full, great (endeavor, etc.).

beliğᵍⁱ 1. *prov.* plait, tress. 2. *prov.* mark, sign. 3. *archaic* quiver including compartment for a bow.

belil (. —) A *lrnd.* 1. cold and damp (wind). 2. just enough to moisten; insignificant in quantity.

belile (. — .) P, **belilec** (. — .) A belleric myrobalan, bedda nut tree, *bot., Terminalia Bellerica;* bedda nut.

belin *prov.* bewilderment, terror.

Belinas (. — —) A *var. of* **Belinus.**

belinle=ʳ to be startled with fear, to be frightened, to wake from sleep with sudden fright, to start with terror. **—n=** *prov., same as* **belinle=. —ndir=, —t=** /ı/ *caus.*

Belinus (. — —) A Apollonius (name of two ancient Greek philosophers).

belir=ʳ 1. to appear, to become visible. 2. *same as* **beler=. —iş** *verbal n.*

belirle=ʳ *neol., phil.* to determine. **—me** determination. **—yen** determinative.

belirli *neol.* determined.

belirsiz 1. unknown, uncertain, indefinite, undetermined. 2. imperceptible.

belirt=ⁱʳ /ı/ 1. *caus. of* **belir=.** 2. to state, to make clear. 3. *phil.* to determine. **—en** determinative.

belirti *neol.* sign, symptom.

belirtikᵍⁱ *neol., phil.* explicit.

belirtme *verbal n. of* **belirt=,** determination.

belitᵈⁱ *neol., phil., math.* axiom.

beliye (. — .) A *lrnd.* 1. evil, trouble, affliction, calamity. 2. sore trial, temptation. 3. *ancient Arabian hist.* female animal left to starve on the grave of its owner so that he may use it in the other world.

belka 1 (. —) A 1. *fem. of* **eblak.** 2. *w. cap., name of a region in northern Jordan; name of a castle in the same region.*

belkaᵃⁱ **2** , **belkaa** A *lrnd.* waste, desert land, wilderness.

belki P 1. perhaps, maybe. 2. *archaic* but rather. **— de** it may even be that...

belkiliğim *vulg., var. of* **belki.**

belkim *vulg., var. of* **belki.**

Belkis (. —) [**Bilkis**] the Queen of Sheba.

bellâᵃⁱ (. —) A *lrnd.* exceedingly voracious.

bellâa (. — .) A *lrnd.* sewer, drain.

bellâdon F *pharm.* belladonna extract.

bellân (. —) A *lrnd.* 1. hot bath. 2. attendant at a hot bath.

bellâs (. —) A *lrnd.* maker or seller of sackcloth.

belle=ʳ **1** /ı/ 1. to observe well so as to impress on one's mind; to commit to memory, to learn by heart. 2. to suppose, to think. 3. *prov.* to look up, to visit.

belle=ʳ **2** /ı/ to dig over with a spade or fork.

bellekᵍⁱ 1. *neol., psych.* memory. 2. *prov.* things learned and remembered.

belleme 1 *verbal n. of* **belle=** 1, 2.

belleme 2 1. numnah, horse-blanket. 2. *prov.* kind of short woolen jacket.

bellen=ⁱʳ , **bellenil=**ⁱʳ *pass. of* **belle=** 1, 2.

bellet=ⁱʳ /a,ı/ *caus. of* **belle=** 1, 2.

belleyiş *verbal n. of* **belle=** 1, 2.

belli 1. evident, obvious, known, clear; visible. 2. *neol.* certain, definite. 3. *archaic* well-known, notorious, famous. **— başlı** 1. eminent, notable, well-known; main, chief. 2. definite, proper. **— belirsiz** hardly visible. **— bil=** /ı/ *archaic* to know well, to be sure (of). **— et=** /ı/ to show, to be unable to conceal. **— olmaz** You can never tell; one never knows.

bellisiz بلمسز بلیسز unknown, uncertain; imperceptible. **—lik** *abstr. n.*

bellûa (. —.) بَلوع A sewer, drain.

bellûr (. —) بَلور A *var. of* **billevr.**

bellûrin (. — —) بَلورین *P poet.* of rock-crystal or cut-glass, crystalline.

bellût 1 (. —) بَلوط *A lrnd.* 1. acorns, oakmast. 2. oak, *bot., Quercus.*

bellut^du **2** بَلود *prov., var. of* **bellût 1.**

bellûtiye (. — —.) بَلوطیه *A bot.,* Cupuliferae.

bellûtul'arz (. —..) بَلوط الأرض *A* wall germander, *bot., Teucrium chamaedrys.*

bellûtulmelik^ki (. —...) بَلوط الملك *A* chestnut, *bot., Castanea sativa.*

belsem بَلسم *A lrnd.* balsam. **—î** (..—) *A lrnd.* balsamic. **—iye** (..—.) *bot.,* Balsaminaceae.

belû^uu (. —) بَلوع *A lrnd.* large, deep and wide; that can receive much (receptacle).

Belûcistan (. —. —) بَلوچستان (...—) *geog.* Baluchistan.

bel'um (. —) بَلعوم [bül'um] *anat.* gullet, esophagus.

belv بَلو *A lrnd.* trial, test.

belva (. —) بَلوى *A lrnd.* trial, ordeal, test; affliction, adversity.

bem 1 بَم *A lrnd.* 1. the lowest string of an instrument. 2. low note; base, deep (sound).

bembeyaz (. ..) بَم بياض *pure* white, snow-white.

bemol^lü بَه مول *F mus.* flat.

bemr بَمر *var. of* **bebr.**

ben 1 بَن (genitive **benim**, dative **bana**, *pl.* **biz** 1) I. **— ağa sen ağa bu ineği kim sağa?** I am an Agha, you are an Agha, who should then milk the cow? **—im diyen** who thinks he can do everything, *e. g.*, **benim diyen kimse bu işi başaramaz** It is not for everybody to accomplish this thing. **— ben de=** to keep saying I, to be egotistic. **—i bilen kurt yesin** (*lit.* I would rather be eaten by the wolf that knows me.) If I have to suffer, I would rather suffer at the hands of a person I know. **— derim bayram haftası, o der mangal tahtası** I say the feast week; he understands the stove base (said to describe a complete misunderstanding of a statement). **— hadımım derim, o oğuldan uşaktan nen var der** I say I am a eunuch; he asks me how many children I have (said when a person shows no understanding for the other's situation). **— isterim bacımdan, bacım ölür acından** I am expecting help from my sister, but my sister herself is starving (said when help is expected from the wrong person). **— sana hayran, sen cama tırman.** Love should not be one-sided. **— şahımı bu kadar severim** That is as far as my love for my master goes (said when too great a sacrifice is expected from one). **—deki yara elde duvar deliği** (*lit.* My wound is to others like a crack on the wall.) No one can really understand what others suffer.

ben 2 بَن 1. mole; beauty spot. 2. freckle; speck (in the eye); speckle (on the skin of ripening grapes). **— düş=** to have a speck appear (eye); to become speckled.

ben 3 بَن [ban 3] *same as* **ban 3.** **— ağacı** horse radish tree, *bot., Moringa aptera.*

ben 4 *prov.* bait.

ben 5 بَن *P lrnd.* harvest, stack of produce.

benadık^kı (. —.) بَنادق *A lrnd., pl.* of **bunduk 1.**

benadik^kı (. — —) بَنادیق *A lrnd., pl.* of **bunduk 2.**

benadir (. —.) بَنادر *A lrnd., pl.* of **bender**, seaports.

benadire (. —..) بَنادره *A lrnd., pl.* of **bündar 2.**

benaik^kı (. —.) بَنائك *A lrnd., pl.* of **benika.**

benam (. —) بَنام *P* 1. named, *e.g.*, **Rüstem namiyle benam bir adam** a man by the name of Rüstem. 2. famous. **—ı Yezd** in the name of God.

benan (. —) بَنان *A lrnd.* 1. fingertips. 2. fingers.

benasır (. —.) بَناصر *A lrnd., pl.* of **bınsır.**

benat (. —) بَنات *A lrnd.* 1. daughters; girls. 2. dolls. **—ı dehr** misfortunes of life. **—ı Havva** daughters of Eve, women. **—ı na'şı kübra** *astr.* Big Dipper; the outer three stars of the Big Dipper. **—ı na'şı suğra** *astr.* Little Dipper; the outer three stars of the Little Dipper. **—ı sadr** fruits of genius, inspirations. **—ı Verdan** cockroaches.

benban (. —) بَنبان *P lrnd.* superintendent of a farm.

benc بَنج *A lrnd.* henbane, *bot., hyosciamus niger.* **—i deştî** 1. wild henbane. 2. purple-flowered thorn-apple, *bot., Datura fastuosa.*

bence (.'.) بَنجه according to me, for me, as to me.

benci (..') بَنجی one who talks constantly about himself.

bencil *neol.* selfish.

bencileyin (.'...) بَنجیلیین *archaic* like me, such as I.

bencilik^ği بَنجیلیك selfishness, egotism; *phil.* egoism, solipsism. **— yitimi** *psych.* depersonalization.

bend 1 ‎بند‎ P *lrnd.* 1. bond, tie, fastening; chain; captivity; impediment. 2. knot in a cord; separating knot in a rosary; node in a plant; joint, articulation, seam; portion between two nodes. 3. bale, bundle, pack. 4. piece of deceit, fraud, imposture, hypocrisy, stratagem; wrestling trick, manoeuver. 5. *same as* **bent 1**. 6. *same as* **bent 2**. — **ü best et**= /ı/ to tie and fasten. — **et**=*.

bend 2 ‎بند‎ A *lrnd.* 1. banner, flag. 2. province.

-bend 3 ‎بند‎ P 1. that is bound or confined, *as in* **kalebend, prangabend**. 2. that binds, *as in* **köşebend**.

bendab (.—) ‎بنداب‎ P *lrnd.* 1. dyke, dam. 2. reservoir of water formed by damming.

bendbaz (.—) ‎بنديات‎ P *lrnd.* ropedancer.

bende ‎بنده‎ P *lrnd.* slave; servant; bondsman; subject. —**leri** (*lit.*, their servant) your servant (deferentially for I). —**niz** your humble servant, I. —**i halkabegûş** slave marked with an earring, unredeemable slave.

bendegân (..—) ‎بندگان‎ P *lrnd.* 1. pl. of **bende**. 2. those who are in the service of a ruler.

bendegi (..—) ‎بندگی‎ P *lrnd.* bondage, slavery; service; condition of a subject; devotion, worship.

bendehane (..—.) ‎بندهخانه‎ P *lrnd.* 1. my house (term of humility). 2. slave quarters.

bendelik[ti] ‎بندهلك‎ *same as* **bendegi**.

bendenevaz (...—) ‎بندهنواز‎ P, **bendenüvaz** (...—) *lrnd.* kind to one's servants.

bendeperver ‎بندهپرور‎ P *lrnd.* who cherishes his servants, who protects his subjects.

bendeperverane (....—.) P *lrnd.* worthy of one who cherishes his servants (act).

bendeperverî (....—) ‎بندهپروری‎ P *lrnd.* kind treatment of one's servants or subject.

bender ‎بندر‎ P *lrnd.* 1. trading port. 2. commercial town, emporium.

benderek[ti] ‎بندرك‎ *learned corruption for* **mendirek**.

bendergâh (..—) ‎بندرگاه‎ P *same as* **bender**.

bendeş ‎بندش‎ *prov.* equal, like, similar. —**lik** equality, similarity. —**siz** unequalled.

bendet=[der] ‎بندتمك‎ /ı/ *poet.* to tie, to bind; to captivate.

bendezade (..—.) ‎بندهزاده‎ P *lrnd.* 1. son of your slave (*i. e.* my son). 2. child of one's slave or servant.

bendgâh (.—) ‎بندگاه‎ P *lrnd.* joint, articulation.

bendî (.—) ‎بندی‎ P *lrnd.* captive; Muslim captive in the hands of unbelievers.

bendiban, bendivan (.——) ‎بندیبان‎ P *lrnd.* jailer.

bendiyan (.——) ‎بندیان‎ P *pl. of* **bendî**.

benefsec ‎بنفسج‎ A *lrnd.* 1. violet, *bot.*, *Viola odorata*. 2. violet color.

benefsecülkilâb (.....—) ‎بنفسجالكلاب‎ A *lrnd.* dog violet, *bot.*, *Viola canina*.

benefsecî (...—) ‎بنفسجی‎ A *lrnd.* violet-colored.

benefşe ‎بنفشه‎ P *lrnd.* 1. violet, *bot.*, *Viola odorata*. 2. violet-colored.

benefşegûn (...—) ‎بنفشهگون‎ P *poet.* violet-colored. —**mehd** (...—.) P *poet.* heaven and earth. —**tarem** (...——.) P *poet.* the sky.

benefşî (..—) ‎بنفشی‎ [*based on* **benefşe**] *lrnd.* violet-colored.

benek[ti] **1** ‎بنك‎ [**benek 2**] small spot, speck, freckle. — **benek** speckled. —**le**= /ı/ to spot, speckle, to mark with spots. —**len**= *pass*. —**lendir**= /ı/ *caus*. —**leş**= to become a spot. —**let**= *caus. of* **benekle**=.

benek[ki] **2** ‎بنك‎ P *lrnd.* 1. berry of turpentine tree. 2. pimple; drop of perspiration on the face. 3. incipient cavity. 4. satin woven with silver thread.

benekli ‎بنكلی‎ spotted, speckled. — **ballıbaba** spotted deadnettle, *bot.*, *Lemium maculatum*. — **hani balığı** kind of fish, *zool.*, *Paracentropristis hepatus*. — **kırlangıç balığı** gray gurnard, *zool.*, *Trigla milvus*.

benevbet ‎بنوبت‎ P *lrnd.* in turns, alternately, taking turns, alternating. — **timar** *Ott. hist.* military fief held jointly.

benevi (..—) ‎بنوی‎ A *lrnd.* filial.

beneviş ‎بنویش‎ *same as* **meneviş**.

beng ‎بنگ‎ P 1. henbane, *bot.*, *Hyoscyamus niger*. 2. extract of henbane, hemp leaves, or other plants, used as intoxicant.

bengâh (.—) ‎بنگاه‎ P 1. dwelling. 2. iron chest. 3. tent and baggage of a grandee.

Bengal ‎بنگال‎, **Bengâle** (.—.) ‎بنگاله‎ Bengal.

bengi 1 kind of folk dance.

bengi 2 (.—) ‎بنگی‎ P *lrnd.* 1. addict of an intoxicant like the extract of henbane, hemp leaves, or other plants. 2. pertaining to henbane. —**lik** *abstr. n.* —**lik otu** thornapple, *bot.*, *Datura Stramonium*.

bengi 3 *neol.* eternal. —**le**= /ı/ to eternalize. —**lik** eternity. —**su** water of life.

beni- (.—) ‎بنی‎ A *lrnd.* the sons of, *e. g.*, **B— Abbad** the Abbadides. **B— Abbas** *hist.* the Abbasides. **B— Âdem** sons of Adam, mankind. — **beşer** mankind. **B— İsrail** children of Israel, the Jews. — **nev** mankind. **B— Nuh** sons of Noah, mankind. **B— Ümeyye** *hist.* the Umayyads.

beniçincilik[ti] *neol., phil.* egocentricity.

benika (.—.) ‎بنيقه‎ A *lrnd.* gusset, gore.

benim بَنُوم بَنُم my; mine. — **Arap oynadı** gambler's slang I am having a spell of good luck. — **için** for me. —**ki** mine. —**le** with me.

benimse=ʳ بَنْسَه مَلك /1/ to appropriate to oneself, to make one's own, to consider one's own; to identify oneself (with), to take up seriously.

benimsi=ʳ بَنْسِيلَك var. of **benimse=**.

benin (. —) بَنِين A lrnd. sons; children.

beninle=ʳ بَنْلَيلَك var. of **belinle=**.

benizⁿᶻⁱ بَنِز color of the face. —**i ağar=**, —**i at=** to grow pale in the face. —**i bozul=** to become pale from illness. —**i geç=**, —**inde kan kalma=**, —**i kül gibi ol=** to turn very pale in the face, for the blood to drain from the face. —**i sarar=**, —**i sararıp sol=**, —**i sol=** to become pale from illness. —**i uç=** to go suddenly pale in the face.

benlen=ⁱʳ, **benleş=**ⁱʳ بَنلَشَك 1. to become marked with moles, spots, specks, or freckles. 2. to begin to show spots of color (ripening grapes, etc.).

benleştir=ⁱʳ بَنلَشْتِرَمَك /1/ caus. of **benleş=**.

benli بَنلُو spotted, freckled; having a mole; having spots of color (ripening grapes, etc.).

benlikᵍⁱ بَنلِك 1. conceit, inordinate self-esteem. 2. egotism. 3. personality, ego. —**inden çık=** to change one's personality. — **dâvası** self-assertion. — **ikileşmesi** psych. splitting of the personality. —**çi** who has inordinate self-esteem, conceited. —**çilik** abstr. n.

benmari F [**bain-marie**] double boiler.

benna (. —) بَنّا A lrnd. builder, architect, mason.

bennakᵏⁱ (. —) بَنّاك hist. a peasant who holds little or no land.

bentᵈⁱ 1 بَنْد [**bend** 1] 1. dam, dyke, weir, barrage. 2. reservoir.

bentᵈⁱ 2 بَنْد [**bend** 2] 1. paragraph; article. 2. newspaper article. 3. stanza in a poem; the single rhyme part of each stanza, preceding the recurrent couplet, or couplet with recurrent rhyme.

benu- (. —) بَنُو A lrnd., same as **beni-**.

benun (. —) بَنُون A lrnd. sons; children.

benül'ahyaf (. . . —) بَنُولْ اَحْيَاف A law uterine brothers, half brothers or half sisters on the mother's side.

benül'allât (. . . —) بَنُولْ الْعَلَّات A law half brothers or half sisters on the father's side.

Benül'anber بَنُولْ العَنْبَر A hist., name of an Arab tribe in the time of the Prophet.

benül'âyan (. . . —) بَنُولْ اعْيَان A law children who have the same father and mother.

benvan (. —), **benven** بَنُوَان P vars. of **benban**.

benze=ʳ بَنْزَه مَلك بَنْزَه مَلك /a/ to resemble, to look like, to seem like. —**ye benzeye yaz, benzeye benzeye kış olur** Imperceptible changes in time lead to the opposite. —**me** resemblance. —**n=** /a/ archaic to pretend to resemble (some other person or thing).

benzer بَنْزَر similar, like; resembling. —**ce** somewhat resembling. —**lik** similarity, resemblance.

benzeş 1 بَنْزَش archaic, same as **bendeş**.

benzeş=ⁱʳ 2 بَنْزَشْمَك to resemble each other. —**im**, —**me** neol. assimilation. —**tir=** /1/ caus. of **benzeş=**.

benzet=ⁱʳ بَنْزَتْمَك /1,a/ 1. caus. of **benze=**, to liken (to). 2. to mistake (for). 3. to compare (with). —**il=** pass. of **benzet=**. —**iş** verbal n. of **benzet=**. —**me** 1. verbal n. of **benzet=**; rhet. simile. 2. imitated, false.

benzeyiş بَنْزَه يِش بَنْزَيِش verbal n. of **benze=**.

benzin بَنْزِن F gasoline, petrol; benzine. — **deposu** 1. gas tank. 2. filling station, gas station. — **göstergesi** fuel gauge. — **memesi** carburetor jet. — **motoru** gasoline engine. — **otomatiği**, — **pompası** pump that feeds gasoline into the carburetor. —**ci** keeper of a filling station.

benzolˡⁱ بَنْزول F chem. benzol.

ber 1 بَر P lrnd. 1. breast, bosom; teat. 2. embrace. 3. memory. 4. fruit, produce, seed, grain; profit, result, utility. 5. country, region.

ber 2 بَر P lrnd. superior.

ber 3 بَر prov. pen for sheep-milking.

berʳʳⁱ 4 بَرّ A lrnd. 1. land; continent. 2. wilderness, desert. —**i atîk** the Old World. — **ü bahr** land and sea. —**i cedid** the New World. —**i Şam** same as **Berrüşşam**.

berʳʳⁱ 5 بَرّ A lrnd. 1. good, faithful, pious, upright, true. 2. w. cap. God.

berʳⁱ 6 بَرء A lrnd. 1. a creating, creation. 2. a being free, safe, out of danger; freedom from connection, responsibility, or claim.

ber- 7 بَر P lrnd. on, in, according to, e. g., **ber âyini pişin** according to ancient usage. **ber minvali muharrer** in the way written above, as stated above. — **takdir***. [For compounds see **bervechi-**.]

-ber 8 بَر P lrnd. that carries, as in **emirber**, **nameber**.

bera (. —) بَرا A lrnd. a being free, safe, out of danger.

beraa (. —.) بَراء A var. of **beraat** 2.

beraat 1 (. — —) بَرائَات A lrnd., pl. of **beraet**.

beraatᵗⁱ 2 (. —.) بَرا عَت A lrnd. superiority, excellence. —**i istihlâl** rhet. the expressing of the main theme of a work of writing in the first introductory sentences.

beraber (.—.) بَرابَر P 1. /la/ together; accompanying. 2. /la/ equal; level, in a line, abreast, even; uniform. 3. *lrnd.* exactly. **—ince, —inde** together; with one. **—e bit=** *sport* to finish in a dead heat. **— düşüp kalk=** to live together. **—e kal=** *sport* to draw, to tie. **—ine var=** /ın/ *archaic* to go forth to meet (someone). **—ce** together. **—le=** /ı/ to make equal, alike, in line (with), to make even, uniform. **—leş=** to become equal (to). **—leştir=** *caus.* of **beraberleş=**. **—lik** *abstr. n.* of **beraber**; *games* draw; unity, cooperation.

berabıt (.—.) بَرابِط A *lrnd., pl.* of **berbat 2**.

berabih (.—.) بَرابِح A *lrnd., pl.* of **berbah**.

Berabir (.—.), **Berabire** (.—..) بَرابِر، بَرابِرة A *lrnd., pl.* of **Berber 2**.

beracim (.—.) بَراجِم A *lrnd., pl.* of **bürcüme**.

beraet (.—.) بَرائت، بَراءَة A *law* acquittal, innocence, non-guilt. **— et=** to be acquitted. **— ettir=** /ı/ to acquit. **—i zimmet** freedom from obligation, responsibility, or guilt.

beragis (.——) بَراغِث A *lrnd., pl.* of **bürgus**.

berah 1 (.—) بَراح A *lrnd.* open, uncultivated, and treeless tract of country.

berah 2 (.—) بَراح A *lrnd.* a quitting, departure, flight.

berah 3 (.—) بَراه P *lrnd.* 1. on the road. 2. correct, proper.

Berahim (.—.), **Berahime** (.—..) بَراهِم A *lrnd.* Brahmans.

berahin (.——) بَراهين A *lrnd.* proofs.

berakan (..—) بَرَقان A *lrnd.* 1. a lightning, flashing with lightning, gleaming, glittering, sparkling. 2. a menacing, blustering.

beraki[ii] (.—.) بَرقِع A *lrnd., pl.* of **burku 1**.

ber'akis, ber'aks بِعَكس P *lrnd.* on the contrary, inversely.

Beramike (.—..) بَرامِكة A *lrnd.* the Barmecides.

berangar (.——) بَرانغار P *lrnd.* the right wing of an army.

beranis (.—.) بَرانس A *lrnd., pl.* of **bürnüs**.

berari (.——) بَراري A *lrnd.* deserts, waste lands.

beras بَرص A *lrnd.* 1. leprosy. 2. white patch of hair grown over an old wound in an animal's coat.

berasin (.—.) بَراسن A *lrnd., pl.* of **bürsün**.

beraslı بَرصلى *lrnd.* leprous.

berat 1 (.—) بَرات [beraet] patent, warrant, title of privilege. **—ı âlişan, —ı hümayun, —ı şerif** *Ott. hist.* royal or imperial diplomas, letters or privileges.

berat 2 (.—) بَرات [beraet] *in* **— gecesi, — kandili** the sacred night between the 14th and the 15th day of the month Shaban.

Berat 3 بَرات Berat (town in Albania).

beratil (.——) بَراطيل A *lrnd., pl.* of **bertil 1**.

beratlı بَراتلى holder of a patent; privileged. **— tüccar** *obs.* privileged merchants; privileged merchant.

beravat (.——) بَراوات *var.* of **berevat**.

beraver (.—.) بَراوَر P *lrnd.* fruit-bearing, fruitful.

beraya (.——) بَرايا A *lrnd.* 1. the free citizens of the Muslim state. 2. mankind; creatures.

berayı- (.—.) بَراي P *lrnd.* for, for the sake of, by reason of, *e. g.,* **— malûmat** as an information, for your information. **— maslahat** on business. **— tenezzüh** for pleasure.

beraz (.—) بَراز A *lrnd.* 1. open plain, large field. 2. human excrement.

berazban (.——) بَرازبان P *lrnd.* the shank of a blade, which enters the handle.

berazih (.—.) بَرازخ A *lrnd., pl.* of **berzah**.

berazihül'iman (.—..——) بَرازخ الإيمان A *lrnd.* points of faith not yet fully grasped or accepted, debatable ground between doubt and belief.

berazik[ki] (.——) بَرازك A *lrnd., pl.* of **berzik**.

berazin (.——), بَرازين A *lrnd., pl.* of **birzevn**.

berazvan (.——) بَرازوان P *var.* of **berazban**.

berbad (.—) بَرباد P destroyed, scattered, lost.

berbah بَرباه A *lrnd.* 1. water conduit, sewer. 2. earthen water pipe. 3. *anat.* epididymis.

berbar (.—.) بَربار P *lrnd.* upper room.

berbaris (.——) بَرباريس A barberry tree, *bot., Berberis vulgaris*.

berbat[di] 1 بَرباط [berbad] 1. soiled, filthy; very bad, dreadful, disgusting. 2. spoiled, injured, ruined.

berbat 2 بَرباط A *lrnd.* kind of lute. **—nevaz** (...—) P lute-player.

berbatlık[gi] بَرباطلك *abstr. n.* of **berbat 1**.

berbatzen بَرباطزن P *lrnd.* lute-player.

berbend بَربَند P *lrnd.* girdle; breastband; band to hold an infant in its cradle.

berber 1 بَربَر It barber; hairdresser. **— aynası** 1. hand-mirror. 2. pear-shaped, ovoid.

— **balığı** threadfin *zool.*, *Anthias sacer*.
— **dükkânı** barber's shop.
Berber 2 بَرْبَر A a Berber. — **kabaili** the Berber tribes. —**ce** the Berber language.
berberhane (..—.) بَرْبَرْخانَه [based on **berber 1**] barber's shop.
Berberî (..—) بَرْبَرى A a Berber.
berberis بَرْبَريس *var. of* **berbaris**.
Berberistan (...—) بَرْبَرِسْتان the Berber country, Barbary.
Berberiye (..—.) بَرْبَرِيَّه A *lrnd.* Barbary.
berberlik[ti] بَرْبَرْلِك the profession of a barber; hair dressing. —**e başla**= to flatter exaggeratedly.
berca (.—) بَرْجا P *lrnd.* in place, proper.
berceste بَرْجَسْتَه P *lrnd.* 1. beautiful, fine, elegant. 2. proper, befitting. 3. salient, prominent, conspicuous.
Bercis (.—) بَرْجيس *var. of* **Bircis**.
berçide (.—.) بَرْچيدَه P *poet.* gathered, collected.
berçin (.—) بَرْچين P *poet.* gathering; gatherer.
berd بَرْد A cold, coldness; coolness.
berdar 1 (.—) بَرْدار P *lrnd.* hung; crucified. — **et**= /ı/ to execute by hanging, to hang. — **ol**= to be hanged.
berdar 2 (..—) بَرْدار P *var. of* **bardar**.
-**berdar 3** (.—) بَرْدار P *lrnd.* that raises, that upholds, *as in* **barberdar, fermanberdar**.
-**berdari** (.——) بَرْدارى P *lrnd.* forms abstract nouns of compounds with -**berdar 3**, *as in* **fermanberdari**.
berdaşte (.—.) بَرْداشْتَه P *lrnd.* 1. raised, exalted. 2. removed.
berde بَرْدَه P *lrnd.* captive; slave; servant. —**gân** (..—) P *pl.*
berdegi (..—) بَرْدَگى P *lrnd.* captivity; slavery, bondage.
berdel'acuz (...—) بَرْدُالْعَجوز A calendar, name of a cold spell in mid-March.
berdevam (..—) بَرْدَوام P continuing, going on. — **ol**= to continue.
berdî (.—), **berdiye** (.—.) بَرْدى بَرْدِيَه A papyrus plant, *bot.*, *Cyperus papyrus*.
berduş (.—) بَرْدوش P *lrnd.* on the shoulders.
berdveselâm (...—) بَرْدوسَلام A ribwort, *bot.*, *Plantago*.
bere 1 بَرَه 1. bruise. 2. concavity caused by a blow, dent.
bere 2 بَرَه F beret.
bere 3 بَرَه P *lrnd.* 1. lamb; young (of an animal). 2. *astr.* Aries. —**i ab wave**. —**i dümaderî** favorite of fortune, well off. —**i felek** *astr.* Aries.
bereç 1 بَرَچ A *lrnd.* 1. conspicuousness; anything elevated or well known. 2. a being naturally widely open so as to show the white all round the iris (eye). 3. a living in luxury.
bereç 2 بَرَچ A *lrnd.* beautiful boy.
bered بَرَد A *lrnd.* hail, hail-storm.
berefşan (..—) بَرَفْشان *Or. mus.* a rhythmic pattern having 32 beats with signatures of 32/8, 32/4, 32/2.
bereh بَرَه P *var. of* **berah 3**.
Brehmen بَرَهْمَن P, A Brahman.
berehne بَرَهْنَه P *lrnd.* bare, naked.
berehnegi (...—) بَرَهْنَگى P *lrnd.* nakedness, nudity.
Berehut[tü] (..—) بَرَهوت name of a deep precipice in Hadhramaut supposed to be the abode of the souls of unbelievers.
bereket بَرَكَت A 1. abundance, plenty; increase; fruitfulness. 2. blessing; divine gift. 3. Fortunately, thank heavens! —**i içinde** Never mind its small quantity; it has the blessing of abundance. —**ini gör** May you see its increase. — **versin!** 1. May God give you blessed increase. Thank you. 2. Fortunately, thank heaven! —**len**= to be blessed with increase and fertility. —**lendir**= /ı/ *caus.* of **bereketlen**=. —**li** blessed; fruitful; fertile; abundant. —**li olsun!** May it be plentiful (said to a person who is eating or working in the fields, etc.) —**siz** not blessed; unfruitful; scanty.
berele=[r] بَرَلَه /ı/ to bruise; to batter, dent. —**n**= *pass.* —**ndir**= /ı/ *caus.* —**t**= /ı/ *caus. of* **berele**=.
bereli 1 بَرَلى bruised; battered, dented.
bereli 2 بَرَلى [**bere 2**] wearing a beret.
berencen بَرَنْجَن P *lrnd.* ornamental metal ring worn on the wrist, arm, or ankle.
berencmüşk[kü] بَرَنْجْمُشْك P *var. of* **belengmüşk**.
berendaz (..—) بَرَنْداز P *lrnd.* removing.
berende بَرَنْدَه P *lrnd.* carrying; carrier.
berendek[ki] بَرَنْدَك P *lrnd.* small, low hill.
berere بَرَرَه A *lrnd.*, *pl. of* **bar 9**.
bereş بَرَش A *lrnd.* white speck on the fingernail on the skin; freckle; small spot of white hairs on a horse's coat.
berete بَرَتَه *var. of* **barata**.
berevat (..—) بَرَوات [based on **berat 1**] *lrnd.* patents, warrants, privileges.
berf بَرْف P *lrnd.* snow. —**ab** (.—) P snow water; water cooled with snow. —**dan** (.—) P 1. icehouse. 2. vessel for cooling water. —**dar** (.—) P snowy.
berferağ (..—) بَرْفَراغ P *lrnd.* in repose, at leisure, unoccupied.
berg 1 بَرْگ P *lrnd.* dam, weir.
berg 2 بَرْگ P *poet.* 1. leaf. 2. apparatus, appliances, gear; arms. 3. wealth. 4. power, ability. 5. talent, genius, intellect. 6. dress, costume. 7. melody, harmony, music. — **ü bar**,

— ü ber leaf and fruit; wealth. **—i çeşm** eyelid. **—i gül** rose petal. **—i hazan** autumn leaf. **— ü neva, — ü saz** means of subsistence. **—i sebz, —i ter** 1. fresh leaf. 2. a poor man's offering.

bergab (.—) برغاب P lrnd. dam, reservoir.

Bergama (.'..) برغمـ geog. Bergama; hist. Pergamum.

bergamot برغموت F bergamot, bot., Citrus bergamia.

bergbid (.—) برگ بيد P lrnd. 1. willow leaf. 2. willow leaf shaped spear head.

bergdar (.—) برگدار P lrnd. 1. leafy. 2. possessed of means.

bergendi برگندى It hist. brigantine (ship).

bergeşte برگشته P lrnd. turned, topsy-turvy; ruined, broken.

bergeşteahter برگشته اختر P lrnd. unlucky, unfortunate.

bergeştegi (...—) برگشتگى P lrnd. change, inversion; reverse, misfortune, ruin.

bergeştehal[ii] (...—) برگشته حال P lrnd. most afflicted.

berggâh (.—) برگ گاه P lrnd. stalk, bit of chaff.

bergriz (.—), **bergrizan** (.——) برگ ريز برگ ريزان P poet. fall, autumn.

bergüstüvan (...—) برگستروان P lrnd. 1. neck armor for a horse. 2. coat of mail; breastplate.

bergüzar (..—) برگذار P lrnd. present, gift, souvenir.

bergüzide (..—.) برگذيده P lrnd. selected, choice. **—gi** (..—.—) P abstr. n.

berh 1 برح A lrnd. evil, distress, trouble.

berh 2 برح P lrnd. a little, small quantity, bit.

berhabe (.—.) برحوابه P lrnd. mattress.

berhane (.—.) برخانه P [var. of **barhane**] unpractically large mansion, rambling house.

berhar (.—) برخوار P lrnd. one having a share.

berhaste (.—.) برخاسته P lrnd. 1. that has risen up. 2. risen; swollen. 3. sprouted and up through the soil. 4. grown-up. 5. become audible (sound). 6. departed.

berhava (..—) برهوا P blown up. **— et=** /ı/ to blow up. **— ol=** 1. to explode; to be blown up. 2. to be destroyed, frustrated.

berhayat (..—) برحيات P living, alive.

berhe برهه A lrnd. interval, space of time.

berhem برهم P lrnd. together; confused, jumbled; perplexed. **—hurde** P in collision, dashed together. **—zede** P knocked into a heap, jumbled together. **—zen** P that knocks together, that confuses.

Berhemen برهمن P var. of **Berehmen**.

berhene برهنه A lrnd. establishment of proof.

berheten minezzeman (.'.....—) برهة من الزمان A lrnd. for a certain space of time.

berhihte برخيخته (.—.) برخيخته P lrnd. 1. educated; chastised, punished. 2. drawn up, drawn out; drawn together for an attack.

berhor برخور P var. of **berhar**.

berhordar, berhurdar (..—) برخوردار P 1. same as **berhudar**. 2. sharer, participator; sharer in happiness. **—i** (..——) P prosperity, success, happiness.

berhudar (..—) برخدار [berhordar] happy, prosperous, successful. **— ol** God bless you, thank you. **—lık** happiness, prosperity, success.

beri 1 برى 1. hither, here; near, hithermost; the hither side, this side (of). 2. /dan/ since, e. g., **dünden beri** since yesterday; for (space of time), e. g., **üç aydan beri** for three months. **—de** on this side, nearer. **— anarı** var. of **anarı beri**. **— gel** come nearer, come here. **— öte** prov., var. of **öte beri**. **— taraf** this side.

beri 2 (.—) برى A lrnd. 1. /dan/ free (from), clear, absolved, innocent, guiltless (of). 2. sound, right; free from ill propensities, deeds, or false beliefs. **— et=** /dan/ to free (from).

beri 3 (.—) برى A lrnd. cut, pared, chipped into shape, shaped out, fashioned, roughly shaped, but not yet finished (arrow).

beria (.—.) بريعه A lrnd. 1. beautiful woman. 2. w. cap., woman's name.

beriberi F path. beriberi.

berid (.—) بريد A lrnd. 1. postal system; mail. 2. messenger carrying mail; post boy who travels with a courier; animal carrying post. 3. stage between two posthouses; distance originally of about 6, subsequently 10 or 12 miles. 4. the gait of a post horse. **—i felek** astr. moon; Saturn.

berik[kı] **1** (.—) بريك A lrnd. sparkle, glitter, flash.

berik[kı] **2** (.—) بريك A lrnd. blessed, that brings blessing.

beriki بريكى the nearest, the nearer one; this one; the last mentioned.

berin 1 (.—) برين P lrnd. on this, upon this; according to this.

berin 2 (.—) برين P poet. sublime, supreme. **—daire** (.——..) P the sky. **—süfre** (..—.) P the sky.

berişim (.—.) بريشم P lrnd. 1. silk. 2. silken string of a lute.

beriyat (.——) بريات A lrnd., pl. of **beriye**.

beriye (.—.) بريّه A lrnd. creature;

berk created things; human being; the Creation.

berk[ki] **1** بَرْك prov. 1. hard, strong, solid, firm, fast, tight; strongly, tightly. 2. steep, rugged.

berk[ki] **2** بَرْق A lrnd. lightning, flash of lightning. **—ı revan** swift horse. **—ı Yemani** sword from Yemen.

berk[ki] **3** بَرْك var. of **berg 2**.

berk[ki] **4** بَرْك A lrnd. 1. herd of camels lying down. 2. the part of a camel's breast on which he lies. 3. breast.

berkarar (..—) بَرقَرار P lrnd. 1. stable, durable, constant, established. 2. according to the decision.

berkefşan (..—) بَرقافْشان P lrnd. scattering flashes of lightning.

berkemal[li] (..—) بَركمال P lrnd. perfect; perfectly, in perfection.

berkendaz (..—) بَرقانداز P lrnd. 1. that darts lightning. 2. musketeer.

berkende بَركَنده P lrnd. dug up, eradicated.

berkeşide (..—.) بَركَشيده P lrnd. drawn (sword).

berki=[r] **1** بَركِمَك prov. to harden, to become solid.

berki 2 (.—) بَرقى A lrnd. 1. like lightning. 2. electrical.

berkin=[ir], **berkiş=**[ir] بَركِنمَك prov., same as **berki= 1**.

berkiştir=[ir], **berkit=**[ir] بَركِشتيرمَك /ı/ to render solid, to harden.

berklen=[ir] بَركلَنمَك prov. to become hard, firm, tight, solid. **—dir=** /ı/ caus.

berklik[ği] بَركليك prov., abstr. n. of **berk 1**.

berkuk[ku] (.—) بَرقوق A lrnd. prune, apricot.

berlâm بَرلام hake, zool., Merluccius vulgaris.

bermah (.—) بَرماه, **bermahe** (.—.) بَرماهه, **bermeh** بَرمه P lrnd. gimlet, auger, drill.

bermurad (..—) بَرمُراد P lrnd. 1. having one's wish come true, satisfied, happy. 2. according to one's wishes.

bermutad (..—) بَرمُعتاد P lrnd. as usual.

berna (.—) بَرنا P lrnd. 1. young man, youth. 2. beautiful, elegant.

bernah (.—) بَرناه var. of **berna**.

bernai (.—) بَرنائى P lrnd. youth, youthfulness; folly, inexperience.

bernak[ki] (.—) بَرناك P var. of **berna**.

bername (.—.) بَرنامه P lrnd. superscription, title, heading.

bernas (.—) بَرناس P lrnd. ignorant, thoughtless; ignorance, thoughtlessness.

berniye (.—.) بَرنيه A lrnd. large-mouthed jar.

berpa, berpay (.—) بَرپا، بَرپاى P lrnd. 1. standing, erect. 2. revolted.

berr cf. **ber 4, 5**.

berrade (.—.) بَرّاده A lrnd. vessel for cooling water.

berrak[kı] (.—) بَرّاق A clear, limpid; lrnd. flashing, gleaming, brilliant.

berraka (.—.) بَرّاقه A 1. of brilliant complexion (woman). 2. who shows her beauty by glimpses (woman).

berraklan=[ır] (.—..) بَرّاقلانمَك to become clear, limpid, bright. **—dir=** /ı/ caus.

berraklık[ğı] (.—.) بَرّاقليق clearness, limpidity, brilliance.

berrakussenaya (.—..——) بَرّاقُ الثَنايا A lrnd. whose front teeth gleam.

berrani (.——) بَرّانى A lrnd. 1. outer, exterior; external. 2. pertaining to the country, rustic. 3. foreign; foreigner; outsider. 4. who does not consider himself bound by religious laws.

berren (.'.) بَرًّا A lrnd. by land.

berreyn بَرّين A lrnd. the two continents (Europe and Asia).

berrî (.—) بَرّى A lrnd. 1. belonging to land, terrestrial. 2. belonging to the wilderness, wild, uncultivated. **— iklim** geog. continental climate.

berriye (.—.) بَرّيّه A lrnd. desert.

Berriyetüşşam (.—..—) بَرّيّةُ الشّام, **Berrüşşam** (..—) بَرّالشّام A the Syrian Desert.

bersa (.—) بَرصا A lrnd., fem. of **ebras**.

bersam (.—) بَرسام P same as **birsam**.

bersat (.—) بَرسات P var. of **barsat**.

bersem بَرسَم P lrnd. wand held by a fire-worshipper at his rites.

berş بَرش A obs. narcotic made of hemp leaves and laudanum or opium with syrup.

berşa (.—) بَرصا A lrnd., fem. of **ebreş**.

Berşaves (.—.) بَرشاوش P astr. Perseus.

bert 1 بَرت 1. tetter, ringworm. 2. affected with tetter or ringworm. **— baş** scald-headed. **— sakal** whose beard has partly fallen off from tetter.

bert=[er] **2** بَرتمَك /ı/ to sprain (a joint).

bertakdir (..—) بَرتقدير P lrnd. on the supposition that.

bertaraf بَرطَرف P aside, out of the way. **— et=** /ı/ to get rid (of), to remove, to do away (with). **— ol=** pass.

berteng بَرتَنگ P lrnd. girth; surcingle; breastband for fastening an infant in its cradle.

berter بَرتَر P lrnd. higher. **—in** (..—) P highest.

bertik[ği] بَرتيك sprained.

bertil 1 (.—) بَرطيل A lrnd. 1. pick for notching a millstone. 2. crowbar. 3. stepping stone at the mouth of a well. 4. bribe.

bertil=ⁱʳ 2, **bertin**=ⁱʳ برتلك. برتنك *refl. or pass. of* **bert**= 2.

beru (.—) برو. *archaic, var. of* **beri** 1.

berud (.—) برود. A *lrnd.* that cools and refreshes; anything cool.

berumend (.—.) برومند. P *lrnd.* 1. fruitful. 2. advantageous, profitable. 3. fortunate, prosperous, flourishing, happy, rich.

Berut بروت. [*Arabic* .—] *var. of* **Beyrut**.

berüferud (...—) برو فرود. P *lrnd.* up and down, up hill and down dale.

bervakᵏ¹ (.—) بروك بردان. **bervaka** برواقا. A 1. asphodel, *bot.*, *Asphodelus ramosus*. 2. *lrnd.* Arabian shrub that becomes green in cloudy weather and is therefore a proverbial symbol of thankfulness.

bervechi- برو چی. P *lrnd.* in the manner of, by way of, *e. g.*, **bervechi âti** in the following manner; **bervechi bâlâ** as stated above; **bervechi iştirak** *law* by way of partnership; **bervechi meşruh, bervechi muharrer** as aforesaid; **bervechi peşin** in advance; **bervechi ta'cil** in a hasty manner; **bervechi tafsil** in detail; **bervechi zir** as stated below; in the following manner.

bervefkᵏ¹ بروفق. P *lrnd.* according to. **—i murad** as desired.

berver برور. P *lrnd.* 1. fruitful. 2. in fruit. 3. pregnant.

berz 1 برز. P *lrnd.* agriculture, husbandry.

berz 2 برز. A *lrnd.* upright, trustworthy, intelligent and of winning manners.

berzah برزخ. A 1. *geog.* isthmus. 2. state of anxiety or suffering. 3. *lrnd.* state of mental fever and excitement endured by a lover. 4. *lrnd.* person or thing that causes anxiety; pest, torment. 5. *lrnd.* obstacle, barrier, obstruction. 6. *lrnd.* interval, connecting stage; intermediate state of the soul after death and before the final judgment; the grave. 7. *myst.* religious teacher. 8. *myst.* this world, corporal existence.

berze برزه. P *lrnd.*, *same as* **berz** 1.

berzede برزده. P *poet.* gathered, collected.

berzegâv (..—) برزه گاو. P *lrnd.* ox that draws the plow.

berzen برزن. P *lrnd.* 1. street; quarter of a town. 2. the fields, plain, desert.

berzgâr (.—), **berzger** برزگار. برزگر. P *lrnd.* farmer, husbandman. **—î** (..—) P agriculture, farming.

berzî (.—) برزی. A *lrnd.*, *same as* **berz** 2.

berziger (.—.) برزیگر. A *same as* **berzgâr**.

berzikᵏ¹ (.—) برزیك. A *lrnd.* troop, body of men.

berzin (.—) برزین. P *lrnd.* fire.

be's 1 بأس. A 1. *same as* **beis**. 2. *lrnd.* might, power; prowess, valor. **— ve satvet** might and valor.

besˢˢⁱ 2 بثّ. A *lrnd.* a spreading, dissemination, scattering; a raising dust in clouds.

bes 3 بس. P 1. *lrnd., prov.* enough! hold! 2. *lrnd.* very, sufficiently; much, many, sufficient.

be'sa 1 (.—) بأساء. A *lrnd.* want; distress, calamity, evil.

besa 2 (.'.) بسا. Alb agreement, compact.

besa 3 (.—) بسا. P *lrnd.* enough! many, much.

besabis (.—.) بسابس. A *lrnd., pl. of* **besbes**.

besait (.—.) بسائط. A *lrnd.* elementary substances.

besalet (.—.) بسالت. A *lrnd.* courage, valor. **—li** brave, daring.

besamet (.—.) بسامت. [*based on Arabic*] *lrnd.* smiling countenance, radiance.

besanı- (.—.) بسانی. P *lrnd.* in the form of, after the manner of.

besat (.—) بساط. A *lrnd.* open, level tract of country.

besatet (.—.) بساطت. A *lrnd.* 1. easiness of speech, eloquence. 2. simplicity, plainness.

besatin (.——) بساتین. A *lrnd.* gardens.

besatinî (.———) بساتینی. A *lrnd.* gardener; market gardener.

besavend (.—.) بساوند. P *lrnd.* 1. the last consonant in a verse, on which the rhyme is based. 2. similar; parallel.

besbaic (.—.) بسباج. A polypody, wallfern, goldenlocks, *bot.*, *Polypodium vulgare*.

besbase (.—.) بسباس. A *lrnd.* mace of nutmegs.

besbedava (.'.—.) بس بداوا. absolutely gratis.

besbelli (.'..) بسبللی. quite obvious, very clear; quite evidently.

besberaber (.'.—.) بس برابر. entirely even with another.

besbes بسبس. A *lrnd.* desert.

besbese بسبسه. A *lrnd.* 1. dissemination, scattering. 2. a raising dust in clouds.

besbeter (.'..) بسبتر. even worse.

besdil بسدل. *var. of* **pestil**.

besebelli بسه بللی. *var. of* **besbelli**.

besen بسن. A *lrnd.* lovely, beautiful.

besend, besende بسند. P *lrnd.* 1. sufficient, enough. 2. perfect. 3. contented, satisfied.

besendekâr (...—) بسندکار, **besendkâr** (..—) بسندکار. P *lrnd.* contented, satisfied. **—î** (...——) P content, contentment.

besfaic (.—.) بسفائج. A *var. of* **besbaic**.

besgûy (.—) بسگوی. P *lrnd.* talkative, loquacious.

besi 1 بسی. 1. a fattening, a feeding up

besî (domestic animal); fatness. 2. place where animals are fattened. 3. *biol.* nutrition. 4. a prop or shim put underneath something to even it up. **—ye al=**, **—ye çek=** /ı/ to set to fatten (beast). **—ye koy=** /ı/ same as **besiye al=**. **— örü** *neol., bot.*, albumen.

besî 2 (. —) بسى P *lrnd.* abundance, multitude; many, plenty.

besic (. —) بسيج P *lrnd.* readiness, preparation; necessaries.

besidoku *neol., bot.* endosperm.

besil 1 (. —) بسيل [based on **besalet**] *lrnd.* brave, valiant.

besil 2 (. —) بسل A *lrnd.* stern, grim, frowning.

besile=ʳ 1 بسيله مك /ı/ same as **besle=**.

besile 2 (. — .) بسيله P *lrnd.* kind of bean.

besili بسيلى fatted, fat, fleshy, well-fed (animal).

besîm (. —) بسيم A *lrnd.* smiling, cheerful of countenance.

besin *neol., biol.* aliment.

besîr (. —) بسير A *lrnd.* many, much.

besirek[ğı] male hairy camel, offspring of a male Bactrian and a female African camel.

basisuyu[nu] *neol., bot.* sap.

besk[kı] بسك A *lrnd.* 1. a breaking through a dam (torrent). 2. a bursting forth (tears). 3. gap broken by a torrent in a bank.

beskele بسكله P *lrnd.* wooden latch or bar of a door.

besl 1 بسل A *lrnd., var. of* **besil 2**.

besl 2 بسل A *lrnd.* 1. prevention, restraint, detention. 2. reproof, blame, scolding.

besle=ʳ بسله مك /ı/ 1. to feed, nourish. 2. to fatten (beast). 3. to keep, support, maintain. 4. to prop so as to even something up, to reinforce, to fill up. **— kargayı oysun gözünü** Feed the crow and it will pick out your eyes (said when someone returns evil for good). **—me** 1. *verbal n. of* **besle=**. 2. fattened; fed, supported. 3. girl servant brought up in the household. **—n=**, **—nil=** *pass. or refl. of* **besle=**. **—niş**, **—nme** *verbal n. of* **beslen=**. **—nme havzası** *geog.* basin of a river, catchment area, drainage area, watershed. **—t=** /ı/ *caus. of* **besle=**. **—yici** nutritive; nutritious; feeder, supporter. **—yiş** *verbal n. of* **besle=**.

besli بسلى *var. of* **besili**.

besm بسم A *lrnd.* a smiling, smile.

besmele بسمله A the formula **bismillahirrahmanirrahim**. **— çek=** to pronounce this formula. **— de=** to start by pronouncing this formula. **— oku=** to recite the above formula.

besmelehan (. . . —) بسمله خوان , **besmelekeş** بسمله كش P *lrnd.* who recites the formula **bismillahirrahmanirrahim**.

besmelesiz بسمله سز 1. without pronouncing the formula **bismillahirrahmanirrahim**. 2. good-for-nothing, bad (person); bastard.

bespaye (. —.) بس پايه P polybody, wallfern, goldenlocks, *bot.*, *Polypodium vulgare*.

besr بسر , **besre** بسره A *path.* pimple, pustule.

besrek[ğı] بسرك *var. of* **besirek**.

bessam (. —) بسّام A *lrnd.* who smiles much.

best بست P *lrnd.* 1. a binding. 2. bond, obstacle, band. 3. sanctuary, asylum. **— ü bend et=** /ı/ to bind.

beste 1 بسته P 1. a vocal composition consisting of four verses each followed by the same melodic passage. 2. *pros.* poem of two couplets. **— bağla=** /a/ to compose the music (for).

beste 2 بسته P *lrnd.* 1. bound, fastened; fettered; prisoner. 2. obstructed, blocked; shut, locked, barred. 3. under obligation; obligatory; arranged, concluded, agreed to. 4. congealed, coagulated; benumbed. 5. that has set or taken form (young fruit). 6. under a spell and sexually impotent. 7. bundle, bale, package.

besteci بسته جى *mus.* composer.

bestedem بسته دم P *lrnd.* who cannot breathe, breathless.

bestegi (. . —) بسته گى P *lrnd., abstr. n. of* **beste 2**.

bestehisar (. . . —) بسته حصار *Or. mus.* an archaic **makam** of the eighteenth century.

beste-ısfahan بسته اصفهان *Or. mus.* a **makam** of the 13th or 14th centuries formed by the addition of the **kürdi** to the **ısfahan makam**.

bestekâr (. . —) بسته كار P *mus.* composer.

bestele=ʳ بسته له مك /ı/ *mus.* 1. to compose. 2. to set to music (poem).

besteleb بسته لب P *poet.* with sealed lips.

bestenî (. . —) بسته نى P *lrnd.* 1. fit to be bound. 2. thing used as a bond. 3. ice cream, water ice.

bestenigâr (. . . —) بسته نگار P *Or. mus.* a very ancient compound **makam**, composed by the addition of **segâh** to the bottom of the **saba makam**.

besterahm بسته رحم P *lrnd.* barren (woman).

besul[lü] (. —) بسول A *lrnd.* brave, valiant.

besur (. —) بسور A *lrnd.* stern-looking, frowning, grim.

besye F *fin.* bear.

beş بش five. **— aşağı beş yukarı** after some bargaining. **—te bir** one fifth. **—i bir arada**, **—i bir yerde**, **—i birlik** ornamental coin worth five gold Turkish pounds. — **çifte** boat with five tiers of rowers. — **darplı sofyan** *Or. mus.* a fast rhythmic pattern of five beats. — **kardeş** the hand with the five fingers (used in a slap). — **köşe** pentagon. — **para etmez** worthless. — **paralık** worth a penny. — **parmak** 1. chaste tree, *bot., Vitex Agnus-castus.* 2. starfish. — **parmak bir değil** *proverb* Men are not all alike. — **parmak otu** cinquefoil, *bot., Potentilla reptans.* — **vakit namaz** the complete schedule of daily prayers.

beşaat[ti] (.—.) A *lrnd.* 1. a being bitter, a tasting bad. 2. fetidness of the breath. 3. ill temper, irritability.

beşair (.—.) A *lrnd.*, *pl.* of **beşaret 1, bişaret, büşaret.**

beşam (.—), **beşame** (.—.) A *lrnd.* balm of Gilead, balsam of Mecca, *bot., Commiphora oppobalsamum.*

Beşanika (.—..) [based on **Boşnak**] *lrnd.* the Bosnians.

beşaret 1 (.—.) A *lrnd.* good news; announcement of good tidings; pleasure caused by good news. — **et=** /ı/ to announce as good news. **B—i Meryem** *Christ. rel.* Feast of the Annunciation.

beşaret 2 (.—.) *colloq.* very ugly, repulsive.

beşaret 3 (.—.) A *lrnd.* beauty, comeliness.

beşaretlen=[ir] to receive good news.

beşaşet (.—.) A *lrnd.* cheerfulness; cheerful reception. —**li** cheerful, smiling.

beşbeter *colloq.*, *var. of* **besbeter.**

beşbıyık[ği] *prov.* medlar.

beşe *prov.* elder brother, elder.

beşem A *lrnd.* 1. a suffering from indigestion. 2. weariness, disgust.

beşer 1 five each, five apiece. — **beşer** by fives.

beşer 2 A *lrnd.* man, mankind.

beşer 3 A *lrnd., same as* **beşere.**

beşere A *anat.* scarfskin, epidermis.

beşerevi (...—) [based on **beşere**] *anat.* epidermal.

beşerî 1 (..—) A human. — **coğrafya** anthropogeography. — **ilimler** humanities and social sciences.

beşerî 2 (..—) A *anat.* epidermal.

beşeriyat[ti] (..——) [based on **beşerî 1**] anthropology.

beşeriyet (..—.) [based on **beşerî 1**] 1. mankind, humanity. 2. human nature.

beşgen *neol., geom.* pentagon.

beşi[ii] (.—) A *lrnd.* nauseous, foul-breathed; coarse, unpleasant, disagreeable.

beşibirlik[ği] ornamental coin worth five Turkish gold pounds.

beşik[ği] 1. cradle. 2. *mil.* gun carriage. 3. *naut.* ship's cradle. — **alayı** *hist.* "procession of the cradle" a ceremony in the Sultan's Palace on the occasion of the birth of a royal prince. — **kertiği,** — **kertme** betrothed while still an infant. — **örtüsü** *arch.* gable roof. — **sandalye** rocking chair. —**çi** maker and seller of cradles.

Beşiktaş name of a district of Istanbul.

beşim A *lrnd.* 1. suffering from indigestion. 2. weary, disgusted.

beşinci the fifth.

beşir (.—) A *lrnd.* 1. messenger of good news; evangelist; prophet. 2. pleasing in countenance, cheerful. 3. *man's name.*

beşiz quintuplets. —**li** fivefold.

beşleme division into five parts.

beşli 1. fivefold, having five parts. 2. *folk poet.* five-line stanza, quintain. 3. *mus.* quint. 4. *card games* the five. 5. *Ott. hist.* Janissary with daily allowance of 5 aspers, employed in accessory services of the army.

beşlik[ği] 1. pertaining to five. 2. five-piaster piece; worth five piasters. — **simit gibi kurul=** to give oneself exaggerated airs.

beşluyan (..—) *Ott. hist., pl.* of **beşli**[5].

beşme post of a woodworker's lathe.

beşpençe starfish, *zool., Asterias.*

beşşak[kı] (.—) A *lrnd.* mendacious, untruthful; liar.

beşşaş (.—) A *lrnd.* always cheerful and smiling.

beştaş children's game jackstone, five stones.

beşuş (.—) [based on *Arabic*] *lrnd.* of cheerful countenance, smiling. —**âne** (.——.) P cheerfully, smilingly.

beşyüz five hundred. —**üncü** five-hundredth.

bet[ti] **1** *var. of* **bed 1**[1].

bet 2 used only in — **beniz** color of the face. —**i benzi ağarmıştı** His face was very pale. —**i benzi at=** to grow pale from fear. —**i benzi kalmamış,** — **benzi uçmuş** He has no color left in his face.

bet 3 used only in — **bereket** abundance. —**i bereketi kalmadı** It has grown scarce; it is spent quickly.

bet[tti] **4** A *lrnd.* 1. a cutting off or through. 2. decision, conclusion.

bet[tti] **5** A *lrnd.* kind of shawl for the neck.

betahsis (..—) P *lrnd.* especially, particularly.

betekrar (..—) P *lrnd.* again, anew.

betat (.—) بَتات. A *lrnd.* 1. provisions and necessaries for a journey. 2. household effects, furniture.

betel=ⁱʳ بتلك. *colloq.* to grow rude, to become offensive.

betenha (..—) بَتنها. P *lrnd.* sole, separate.

beter بَتر. P worse.

beterca (..—) بَترجا. P *lrnd.* 1. vulva. 2. anus. 3. the space under the tip of the fingernail.

beti *neol.* figure.

betil (.—) بتيل. A *lrnd.* 1. cut off. 2. same as **betul**.

betile (.—.) بتيله. A *lrnd.*, same as **betul**.

betim *neol., phil.* description. —**le**= /ı/ to describe. —**sel** descriptive. [/bet/ see /bed/]

beton بتون. F building concrete. — **karıştırıcı** cement mixer.

betonarme بتون آرمه. F building reinforced concrete.

betr بَتر. A *lrnd.* 1. a cutting off entirely. 2. a docking (the tail).

bettar (.—) بَتّار. A *lrnd.* very sharp (sword).

bettat (.—) بَتّات. A *lrnd.* maker or vendor of neck scarves.

bette بَتّه. A *lrnd.* most certainly, most decidedly.

betukᵏᵘ 1 (.—) بتوك. A *lrnd.* very sharp (sword).

betukᵏᵘ 2 (.—) بتوك. P *lrnd.* round wooden tray.

betulⁱⁱ (.—) بتول. A *lrnd.* 1. virgin who has no desire for marriage. 2. woman who consecrates herself to the sole service of God. 3. *w. cap.* the Virgin Mary; the Prophet's daughter Fatima.

beturakᵏⁱ (.——) بتورك. P *lrnd.* subterranean granary.

bevadi (.——) بوادى. A *lrnd., pl. of* **badiye 1**.

bevadih (.—.) بوادة. A *lrnd., pl. of* **badihe**.

bevadir (.—.) بوادر. A *lrnd., pl. of* **badire**.

bevah (.—) بواه. A *lrnd.* publicity.

bevahan (.—'.) بواها. A *lrnd.* publicly, openly.

bevahid (.—.) بواحد. A *lrnd.* evils, calamities, misfortunes.

bevahir (.——) بواهير. A *lrnd., pl. of* **bahur 1**.

bevais (.—.) بوائس. A *lrnd., pl. of* **bais 1**.

bevaki 1 (.——) بواقى. A *lrnd.* 1. things that remain, remainders, remnants. 2. permanently lasting, eternal things.

bevaki 2 (.——) بواك. A *lrnd., pl. of* **bakiye 2**.

bevaliⁱⁱ (.——) بوالع. A *lrnd., pl. of* **balua**.

bevar (.—) بوار. A *lrnd.* destruction, death.

bevarid (.—.) بوارد. A *lrnd., pl. of* **barid**.

bevarih (.—.) بوارح. A *lrnd., pl. of* **barih 1**.

bevarikᵏⁱ (.—.) بوارق. A *lrnd., pl. of* **barika**.

bevasir (.——) بواسير. A *lrnd., pl. of* **basur**.

bevaşikᵏⁱ (.—.) بواشق. A *lrnd., pl. of* **başık**.

bevatın (.—.) بواطن. A *lrnd., pl. of* **bâtın 1**.

bevatir (.—.) بواتر. A *lrnd., pl. of* **batir**.

bevazi 1 (.——) بوازى. A *lrnd., pl. of* **bazi 3**.

bevaziⁱⁱ **2** (.—.) بواضع. A *lrnd., pl. of* **bazıa**.

bevazih (.—.) بوازخ. A *lrnd., pl. of* **bazih**.

bevazil (.—.) بوازل. A *lrnd., pl. of* **bazil 2**.

bevilᵛⁱⁱ بول [bevl] urine.

bevl بول A *lrnd.* 1. same as **bevil**. 2. a passing water. — **et**= 1. to urinate, to pass water. 2. /ı/ to void by the urethra.

bevldan (.—) بولدان P *lrnd.* 1. chamber pot. 2. urinal.

bevle بوله. [based on **bevl**] *chem.* urea.

bevlî (.—) بولى. A *physiol.* urinary; *chem.* uric.

bevliye (.—.) بوليه. A 1. urology. 2. *lrnd., fem.* of **bevlî**. —**ci** urologist.

bevrakᵏⁱ بورك A *var. of* **burak 2**.

bevsa (.—) بوصاء. A *lrnd.* handsomely formed, full-buttocked (woman).

bevş بوش A *lrnd.* 1. multitude, mob. 2. the noise of a multitude.

bevvab (.—) بوّاب. A *lrnd.* 1. gatekeeper, doorkeeper, porter; usher, chamberlain. 2. *anat.* pylorus. —**ı mide** *anat.* pylorus. —**an** (.——) P *pl.* —**î** (.——) A pertaining to a porter —**in** (.——) A *pl. of* **bevvab**.

bevvalⁱⁱ (.—) بوّال. A *lrnd.* one who passes water much; enuretic.

bevvapᵇⁱ (.—) بوّاب. *var. of* **bevvab**. —**lık** *lrnd.* post or occupation of a doorkeeper.

bey 1 بك. 1. gentleman, Sir; *after name* Mr., Mister. 2. prince, ruler, chieftain; chief, head, master. 3. notable, country gentleman. 4. *card games* ace. 5. *games*, name of one of the sides of a knucklebone. 6. *obs.* decoy bird used for catching wild hawks in nets. — **armudu** a large, fine variety of pear. — **baba** father (used also for other respected elderly persons). — **balığı** a fish of the cod family. — **börkü** *obs.*, name of a flower; coxcomb, *bot.*, Celosia cristata. —**lere inanma, suya dayanma** *proverb*

Do not rely upon the protection of a person of high position.

beyʸ¹ 2 بَيْع· A *same as* **beyi**. **— bil'isticrar** *law* sale in small quantities, for which inclusive payment is received afterwards. **— bil'istiğlâl** *law* sale on the condition that the selling party may rent the object sold and that it becomes his property again when he has fully paid back its price in rent. **— bilmücazefe** *law* lump sale. **— bilvefa** *law* sale with power of redemption. **— darbetilgais** sale in advance of a pearl-diver's find. **— darbetilkanıs** sale in advance of a hunter's catch. **— ü ferağ** *law* alienation, sale. **— habelihabele** *law* sale of an unborn animal. **— ilkailhacer** *ancient Arabic law* sale by throwing a stone. **— ma lem yukbaz** *law* sale without delivery. **— men yezid** *law* sale by auction. **— ü şira** *law* purchase and sale, commerce, trade. **— ü şira et=** to buy and sell, to trade.
[*For other compounds, see* **beyi**]

bey'a بَيْعَه· A *lrnd*. 1. sale; purchase. 2. a shaking of hands to conclude a bargain. 3. a touching the hand or making other token in acknowledging allegiance to a sovereign.

beyaban (.——) بَيَابَان P *lrnd.* desert, wilderness.

beyabaniyat (.————) بَيَابَانِيَات A *astr.* the extra-zodiacal fixed stars.

beyadıkᵏ¹ (.—.) بَيَادِه , **beyadıka** (.—..) بَيَادِفَ A *lrnd., pl. of* **beydak**.

beyadir (.—.) بَيَادِر A *lrnd., pl. of* **beyder**.

beyan 1 (.—) بَيَان A 1. declaration, expression. 2. *rhet.* clearness, distinctness; clear style; language; discourse. 3. *rhet.* the part of rhetorics dealing with comparison and metaphor. 4. *gram.* explanation. **— et=** /ı/ to express, declare, announce. **—ı hal et=** to explain about oneself. **—ı istikra** *rhet.* the addition of a phrase to a foregoing word, explaining it in an inductive way. **—ı tağyir** *rhet.* an explanation that modifies the sense, as an alternative or exception. **—ı takrir** *rhet.* a confirmatory explanation as «all, everyone». **—ı tebdil.** *rhet.* an explanation which changes the sense of the foregoing word. **—ı tefsir** *rhet.* an exegetical explanation. **—ı zaruret** *rhet., law* an expression of one's thought by a sign, silence, or by context.

bey'an 2 (.—) بَيْعًا· A in the expression **— fî bey' vâhid** *law* two sales in one (*e. g.,* You will have this for a lira, if you sell me that for two.)

beyanat (.——) بَيَانَات A statement, declaration.

bey'ane (.—.) بَيْعَانَه P *lrnd.* earnest money.

beyanî (.——) بَيَانِي A *lrnd.* 1. explanatory, expository. 2. pertaining to the part of rhetorics dealing with comparison and metaphor; a specialist of this science.

beyanname (.——.) بَيَانْنَامَه declaration, written statement; *com.* manifest.

beyarıkᵏ¹ (.—.) بَيَارِق *lrnd., pl. of* **bayrak**.

beyat 1 (.—) بَيَات A *lrnd.* a being, doing, happening by night.

bey'atᵗⁱ 2 بَيْعَت· A *var. of* **bey'a**.

beyatıra (.—..) بَيَاطِرَه A *lrnd., pl. of* **baytar**.

beyati (.——) بَيَاتِي *var. of* **bayati**.

Bey'atül'akabe بَيْعَةُ الْعَقَبَه· A *Isl. hist.* the Pact of the Pass (name of either of the two pacts between the Prophet and certain converts from Medina before the Hegira).

Bey'atülharb بَيْعَةُ الْحَرْب· A *Isl. hist.* the second Pact of the Pass (name of the pact between the Prophet and seventy men from Medina, who promised to protect him, if necessary, by the sword).

Bey'atünnisa (....—) بَيْعَةُ النِّسَاء· A *Isl. hist.* the first Pact of the Pass (name of the pact between the Prophet and twelve men from Medina, who expressed allegiance without pledging themselves to protect him by the sword; this oath was ultimately converted into an oath for female converts only).

Bey'atürrıdvan (....—) بَيْعَةُ الرِّضْوَان· A *Isl. hist.* the Pact of Hudaibiya (name of the oath of allegiance taken by the followers of the Prophet on a certain occasion).

beyaz 1 بَيَاض [**beyaz** 2] 1. white; white spot. 2. fair-skinned. 3. fair copy. 4. blank paper. 5. *slang* heroin. **—ın adı var esmerin tadı** *proverb* Dark-skinned women are lovelier than fair-skinned ones. **— balıkçıl** great white heron, *zool., Egretta alba.* **— ciro** *com.* blank endorsement. **—a çek=** /ı/ to make a fair copy (of). **—a çıkar=** /ı/ to clear (from accusation). **— diken** hawthorn, *bot., Crataegus oxyacantha.* **— et=** /ı/ to make a fair copy (of). **— göz balığı** kind of sea fish, *zool., Maena.* **— iş** simple white embroidery. **— kadın ticareti** white slave trade. **— karaman** kind of fat-tailed sheep whose meat is considered superior. **— kurt** kind of acorn barnacle, *zool., Balanus.* **— kurtluca** spindlewort, *bot., Atractylis gummifera.* **— mukallit** olivaceous warbler, *zool., Hippolais pallida.* **— perde** motion picture screen. **— peynir** soft white cheese. **B— Saray** the White House. **— üzerinde irade** *Ott. hist.* Sovereign Command.

beyaz 2 (.—) بَيَاض A *lrnd.* 1. whiteness, white color. 2. the white of an egg. 3. light (of day).

beyazımsı بَيَاضِيمْسِى , **beyazımtırak**ᵏⁱ بَيَاضِيمْتِرَاق whitish.

Beyazıtᵈˡ˒ ᵗˡ بایزید *var. of* **Bayazıt**.
beyazir (. — .) بایضر A *lrnd., pl. of* **beyzer**.
beyazire (. — ..) بایضرة A *lrnd., pl. of* **beyzar**.
beyazlan=ⁱʳ بیاضلنمق to become white.
beyazlat=ⁱʳ بیاضلتمق /ı/ to whiten, bleach. **—ıl**= *pass*.
beyazlıkᵍⁱ بیاضلق *abstr. n. of* **beyaz 1**.
beyceğiz بیکجگز, **beycik**ᵍⁱ بیکجک 1. young man, young gentleman. 2. pet prince, little prince.
beyd بید. A *lrnd*. a perishing, perdition, destruction, extinction, disappearance.
beyda (. —) بیدا A *lrnd*. desert, barren wilderness.
beydakᵏⁱ بیدق A *lrnd*. 1. pawn in chess. 2. foot traveler; foot soldier.
beyder بیدر. A *lrnd*. 1. threshing floor. 2. stack of grain at a threshing floor.
beydudet (. — .) بیدودت. A *lrnd., same as* **beyd**.
beyefendi (.′...) بک افندی sir; after name Mister, Mr.
beyerkiⁿⁱ *neol*. aristocracy.
beygare (. — .) بیغاره. P *lrnd*. reproach, reproof.
beygir بیکیر, بارگیر [**bargir**] 1. horse; packhorse, cart horse. 2. gelding. **— değirmeni** mill turned by horse power. **— gibi** clumsy, awkward, stupid. **— gücü**, **— kuvveti** *mech*. horsepower. **— otu** pewter grass, horsetail, *bot.*, *Equisetum arvense*. **—ci** one who hires out horses; man in attendance on hired horses. **—li** horse-driven.
beyhude 1 (. — .) بیهوده P in vain; useless, vain. **— yere** unnecessarily. **—lik** uselessness, purposelessness.
beyhude 2 (. — .) بیهوده, **beyhüde** بهده. P *lrnd*. scorched, singed.
beyiʸⁱ بیع. [**bey 2**] *law* sale, bargain; purchase. **—i bat** definite, irrevocable sale. **—i bâtıl** non-valid sale. **—i caiz** legal sale. **—i fâsid** a sale that might be valid but for some minor default. **—i gayrilâzım** sale that reserves the right of redemption. **—i gayrimün'akid** nonvalid sale. **—i lâzım** sale without right of redemption. **—i mekruh** a legal, but morally odious sale. **—i mevkuf** sale requiring confirmation by a third person. **—i muhtelifün fih** sale in which the article sold is disputed. **—i mukayaza** sale against payment in goods, barter. **—i mutlak** sale with payment and delivery at the time. **—i mübadele** barter. **—i mün'akid** perfected sale. **—i müstahab** sale made for charity. **—i nafiz** sale not requiring confirmation by a third person. **—i sahih** valid sale. **—i teati** sale without legal formula, consisting of the mere exchange of goods and money. **—i telcie** fictitious sale. [*For other compounds see* **bey 2**]

beyinʸⁿⁱ بین. 1. brain. 2. mind; brains, intelligence. **—im attı** I got angry, I was furious. **—i bâlâ** *joc*. head. **— bırakma**= /da/ to leave no brains (in), to tire greatly, to bewilder. **—im bulandı** 1. I was dazed. ˜2. I smelled a rat. **—i çürük** crazy, unreasonable. **—i dağınık** scatter-brained. **—im delindi** It shook my brain (great noise). **— edisi** *psychol*. cerebration. **— humması** *path*. brain fever. **— kabuğu** *anat*. cortex of the brain. **— kızartması** fried brain, brain fritters, baked brains. **— omurilik sıvısı** *neol., anat*. cerebrospinal fluid. **— patlat**= to split one's brains (over). **— salatası** brain salad, boiled brain with olive oil and lemon. **—e sar**= to feel very deeply. **—im sarsıldı** *same as* **beynim delindi**. **—i sulan**= to grow senile, to have water on the brain. **— tavası** *same as* **beyin kızartması**. **—ine vur**= to go to the head (drink). **—inden vurulmuşa dön**= to be greatly upset (by an unexpected event). **— zarları** *anat*. meninges. **—cik** *anat*. cerebellum. **—li** having brains, brainy. **—sel** *neol*. cerebral. **—si** *neol*. cerebroid. **—siz** brainless, stupid. **—sizlik** brainlessness, stupidity.
beyitʸᵗⁱ بیت. [**beyt 1**] *pros*. couplet, distich. **—i musarra'** couplet of two rhyming verses. **—i tam** a perfect distich.
bey'iye (. — .) بیعیه. [*based on* **bey 2**] *com*. commission, retailer's premium. **— tezkeresi** certificate of sale.
Beykoz بیکوز. *name of a district of Istanbul*. **— işi** Beykoz ware (Turkish imitation of Venetian glass).
beyle=ʳ بکلمك /ı/ *archaic* to appoint as ruler. **—n**= to impose oneself as ruler.
beylerbeyi بکلربکی 1. *Ott. hist*. governor-general. 2. *w. cap., name of a district in Istanbul*. **—lik** 1. office of a governor-general. 2. province ruled by a governor-general.
beyli بکلی *archaic* having a ruler.
beylikᵍⁱ بکلك. 1. rank of a ruler; principality, region ruled over by a ruler. 2. the quality of a respected gentleman. 3. belonging to the government, state-owned. 4. conventional, stereotyped, commonplace. 5. thin, small soldier's blanket. **— çeşmeden su içme!** (*lit*. Do not drink from the public fountain.) Beware of becoming a government employee. **— gemi** *Ott. hist*. government ship. **— kaşık aşsız, kârgir bina taşsız kalmaz** *proverb* (*lit*. The government spoon is never without food; a stone building is never without stone.) A government employee will never suffer hunger. **— fırın has çıkarır** *humorous* It is a profitable

thing to be a government employee. — **sarhoş** habitual drunkard. — **sat=** to give oneself the airs of a little lord. — **tuğla** building kind of thin brick. — **vermekle, yiğitlik vurmakla** *proverb* It befits a lord to give; it befits the valiant to strike.

beylikçi علكجى. *Ott. adm.* head of the government chancery office. — **kesedarı** the principal lieutenant of the head of the chancery office.

beyn بين. A *Irnd.*, *same as* **ara 1**.

beynamaz بى نماز. *var. of* **binamaz**.

beyne- بين. A *Irnd.* between; among; inter-.

beynebeyn بين بين. A *Irnd.* between the two, intermediate.

beyneddıl'î (...—) بين الضلعى. A *anat.* intercostal.

beynehu (.'..) بينه. A *in the expression* — **beynallah,** — **ve beynallah** between him and God, known only to him and God.

beynehüma (...—) بينهما. A *Irnd.* between the two of them, the relations between them.

beynel'adale بين العضل. A *anat.* intermuscular.

beynel'akran (...—) بين الاقران. A *Irnd.* between equals.

beynelfakdi velvücud (...'. ..—) بين الفقد والوجود. A *Irnd.* between non-existence and existence.

beynelhalk بين الخلق. A *Irnd.* among the people.

beynelhavfi verreca (.... ..—) بين الخوف والرجاء. A *Irnd.* between fear and hope.

beynelhücrevi (....—) بين الحجروى. A *anat.* intercellular.

beynel'ihvan (...—) بين الاخوان. A *Irnd.* among brethren.

beynelmedareyn (...—.) بين المدارين. A *geog.* intertropical.

beynelmilel بين الملل. A international.

beynel'ulema (....—) بين العلماء. A *Irnd.* among the learned.

beynel'üdeba (....—) بين الادباء. A *Irnd.* among the cultured.

beynennas (..—) بين الناس. A *Irnd.* among the people.

Beynennehreyn بين النهرين. A *Irnd.*, *geog.* Mesopotamia.

beynennevmi velyakaza (...'. ....) بين النوم واليقظ. A *Irnd.* between sleep and waking.

beynessemai vel'arz (...—'...) بين السماء والارض. A *Irnd.* between heaven and earth.

beynezzevceyn بين الزوجين. A *law* between man and wife.

beyni بينى *archaic for* **beyin**.

beynnunet (.—.) بينونت. A *Irnd.* 1. reparation. 2. a going away to a distance. —**i âzamiye** *astr.* digression.

Beyoğlu بك اوغلى Beyoğlu, Pera, *name of* a district of Istanbul.

Beyrut (.'.) بيروت. [*Arabic* .—] Beirut.

beyt 1 بيت. A *same as* **beyit**.

beyt 2 بيت. A *Irnd.* 1. house, habitation. 2. room; closet, case, compartment. 3. family; household. 4. division (in a mathematical table, etc.) 5. *astrol.* sign of the Zodiac. 6. a figure in geomancy. —**i ankebut** spider's web. —**i halfi** *biol.* posterior cavity. —**i iddet** *law* the matrimonial home. —**i kuddami** *biol.* anterior cavity. —**i mamur** 1. the Kaaba. 2. the prototype of the Kaaba in the seventh heaven. —**i muazzam** the Kaaba. —**i mukaddes** 1. Jerusalem. 2. the Aksa Mosque at Jerusalem. 3. *myst.* a heart free from attachments save love of God. —**i mutbak** *pros.* verse whose first hemistich ends in the middle of a word. —**i muzlim** *optics* camera obscura. —**i münir** *optics* camera lucida. —**i şerif** the Kaaba.

beytullah (..—) بيت الله. A 1. the Kaaba. 2. Mecca. 3. the house of God, place of worship. 4. *myst.* the heart of the perfect man.

beytutet (.—.) بيتوتت. A *Irnd.* a passing the night. — **et=** to pass the night.

beytül'ahzan (...—) بيت الاحزان. A *poet.* the house of sorrows; Jacob's tent after the loss of Joseph; this world; the human breast.

beytül'arus (...—) بيت العروس. A *poet.* bridal chamber.

beytül'atik[kı] (...—) بيت العتيق. A *Irnd.* the Kaaba.

beytülferağ (...—) بيت الفراغ. A *Irnd.* toilet, privy.

beytülharam (...—) بيت الحرام. A *Irnd.* the Kaaba.

beytülhelâ (...—) بيت الخلا. A *Irnd.* toilet, privy.

beytülhikme بيت الحكمة. A *Irnd.* a heart in love with God.

Beytüllahm بيت اللحم. A *Bib.* Bethlehem.

beytülmal[lı] (..—) بيت المال. A *can. law* the public treasury; the branch of the public treasury that is concerned with the canonical division of inheritance. —**ci** *Ott. hist.* an officer concerned with the canonical distribution of inheritances.

beytürruhm بيت الرحم. A *Irnd.* the Kaaba.

beyü (.—) بيو. P *Irnd.* bride.

beyugani (.———) بيوكانى. P *Irnd.* wedding feast.

bey'ussadakat (....—) بيع الصدقات. A *can. law* sale of something receivable as alms.

bey'ussarf (..—) بيع الصرف. A *can. law* exchange of coin for coin, money-changing.

bey'ussulh بيع الصلح. A *can. law* sale by suit before a judge, the seller admitting the plaintiff's claim.

beyuz (.—) بَيُوض۔ A *lrnd.* 1. that lays many eggs. 2. oviparous.

bey'üddeyn biddeyn بَيْعُ الدَّيْنِ بِالدَّيْنِ۔ A *can. law* exchange of a debt for a debt (The debtor becomes indebted to another who assumes the obligation to the creditor.)

bey'ül'ayne بَيْعُ العِينَه۔ A *can. law* 1. a simulated sale through which a loan against interest is concealed. 2. same as **bey'üsselem**.

bey'ülberaet anil'ayb (...—. ...) بَيْعُ البَراءَةِ عَنِ العَيْبِ۔ A *can. law* sale on warranty of soundness.

bey'ül'edyan (...—) بَيْعُ الأدْيَان۔ A *can. law* sale against immediate payment, with no immediate delivery of the goods.

bey'ülgarer بَيْعُ الغَرَر۔ A *can. law* a speculative sale of anything which the seller does not have, but hopes to obtain.

bey'ülhasat (...—) بَيْعُ الحَصَاة۔ A *can. law* sale by casting a pebble to indicate the thing sold, or the thing agreed to be bought.

bey'ülhibe بَيْعُ الهِبَه۔ A *can. law* sale disguised as a gift with the understanding that an equivalent gift shall be returned.

bey'ül'ikale (...—.) بَيْعُ الإِقَالَة۔ A *can. law* sale in which the thing sold reverts to the seller.

bey'ül'ilka (...—) بَيْعُ الإِلْقَاء۔ A *can. law* 1. same as **bey'ülmünabeze**. 2. same as **bey'ülhasat**.

bey'ülkâli (..——) بَيْعُ الكَالِي۔ A *can. law* 1. contract to deliver at a future time a certain article of sale, the price being paid down at once. 2. sale on credit. — **bilkâli** sale in which both delivery and payment are deferred.

bey'ülmazmun (...—) بَيْعُ المَضْمُون۔ A *can. law* sale of a child or a beast yet unborn.

bey'ülmelkuh (...—) بَيْعُ المَلْقُوح۔ A *can. law* sale of the future progeny of a male beast.

bey'ülmuaveme (...—..) بَيْعُ المُعَاوَمَه۔ A *can. law* sale of the produce of a fixed area during a specified time for a sum paid down.

bey'ülmugabene (...—..) بَيْعُ المُغَابَنَه۔ A *can. law* fraudulent sale.

bey'ülmuhakâle (...—..) بَيْعُ المُحَاقَلَة۔ A *can. law* an exchange of growing grain for grain already in store.

bey'ülmuhatara (...—..) بَيْعُ المُخَاطَرَة۔ A *can. law* sale subject to a contingency.

bey'ülmukayaza (...—..) بَيْعُ المُقَايَضَه۔ A *can. law* barter.

bey'ülmurabaha (...—..) بَيْعُ المُرَابَحَه۔ A *can. law* sale with a profit.

bey'ülmuvazaa (...—..) بَيْعُ المُوَاضَعَه۔ A *can. law* fictitious transaction.

bey'ülmülâmese (...—..) بَيْعُ المُلَامَسَه۔ A *can. law* sale under an old Arabian custom by which a customer could secure an article at his own price if he could manage to touch it.

bey'ülmünabeze (...—..) بَيْعُ المُنَابَذَه۔ A *can. law* 1. sale under an old Arabian custom by which the seller threw the article on the customer, letting him have it at his own price. 2. same as **bey'ülhasat**.

bey'ülmüsaveme (...—..) بَيْعُ المُسَاوَمَه۔ A *can. law* sale by bargaining, without question as to cost price.

bey'ülmuztar[rr] بَيْعُ المُضْطَر۔ A *can. law* an extortionate sale of the necessities of life.

bey'ülmüzabene (...—..) بَيْعُ المُزَابَنَه۔ A *can. law* exchange of an unknown quantity for a quantity known or unknown.

bey'ülvazia (...—.) بَيْعُ الوَضِيعَه۔ A *can. law* sale at a loss.

bey'ülvefa (...—) بَيْعُ الوَفَاء۔ A *can. law* sale with reservation of a right to repurchase.

bey'ünnüs'e بَيْعُ النَّسِيئَه۔ A *can. law* sale on credit.

bey'üsselef بَيْعُ السَّلَف۔ A *can. law* 1. sale concluded on condition that money be lent by one to the other. 2. same as **bey'ülkâli**.

bey'üsselem بَيْعُ السَّلَم۔ A *can. law*, same as **bey'ülkâli**.

bey'üssirar (...—) بَيْعُ السِّرَار۔ A *can. law* sale by a secret agreement.

bey'üssünya (...—) بَيْعُ الثُّنْيَا۔ A *can. law* sale in lump of an unknown quantity, with the exception of a named definite quantity.

bey'üşşirke بَيْعُ الشِّرْكَة۔ A *can. law* sale of a share in partnership.

bey'ütteati (...——) بَيْعُ التَّعَاطِي۔ A *can. law* sale in agreement but without fixing price or quantity.

bey'üttelcie بَيْعُ التَّلْجِئَه۔ A *can. law* fictitious sale.

bey'ütterazi (...——) بَيْعُ التَّرَاضِي۔ A same as **bey'ütteati**.

bey'üttevliye بَيْعُ التَّوْلِيَه۔ A *can. law* transfer of purchases to another buyer.

beyya[a] (.—) بَيَّاع۔ A *lrnd.* seller, vendor.

beyyi[i] بَيِّع۔ A *lrnd.* 1. seller; dealer. 2. buyer; customer.

beyyin بَيِّن۔ A *lrnd.* distinct, evident, manifest.

beyyinat (..—) بَيِّنَات۔ A *lrnd.* clear, manifest things.

beyyine بَيِّنَه۔ A 1. *law* proof, evidence, argument. — **külfeti** *law* burden of proof.

beyyinussadakat[u] (....—.) بَيِّنَةُ الصِّدَاقَة۔ A *lrnd.* of manifest truth.

beyyinülhilâf (....—) بَيِّنَةُ الخِلَاف۔ A *lrnd.* of manifest falseness.

beyz بَيْض۔ A *lrnd.* 1. eggs. 2. iron helmets.

beyza 1 (.—) بَيْضَا۔ A *lrnd.* 1. *fem.* of **ebyaz**. 2. black paper. 3. the sun. 4. desert, wilderness. 5. evil, misfortune, calamity

6. *myst.* the first manifestation or emanation of the Godhead in creation. 7. *w. cap.*, frequent place name in Arabic countries.

beyza 2 بيضه‎ A *lrnd.* 1. egg. 2. iron helmet. 3. *path.* headache, *cephalalgia congestiva.* 4. testicle. 5. the midst, heart, or body of a people or country. **—i aftab** *poet.* the sun. **—i anka** an extremely rare thing. **—i ateşin, —i çerh** *poet.* the sun. **— der külâh** egg in the cap (in jugglery); game of hunt the egg; man's head; the human heart. **—i hâkî** the world, terrestrial globe. **—i kâfur** *poet.* 1. snow. 2. the sun. 3. the moon. 4. lightning; thunderbolt. **—i mahi** fish spawn; fish roe; botargo; caviar. **—i subh** *poet.* the sun. **—i zer, —i zerin** 1. *poet.* the sun. 2. an ancient Persian oval gold coin of the Achaemenid dynasty.

beyzabazî (..——) بيضه بازى P *lrnd.*, children's game egg-breaking.

beyzade (.—.) بيك زاده 1. prince; son of a nobleman. 2. nobleman, aristocrat. 3. lavish fop. **—lik** *abstr. n.*

beyzaha (..—) بيضها P *lrnd.*, pl. of **beyza 2**. **—yi zerin** *poet.* stars.

beyzar (.—) بيزار A *lrnd.* 1. falconer. 2. husbandman, farmer. 3. *same as* **beyzer.**

beyzatussayf بيضة الصيف A *lrnd.* the hottest part of summer.

beyzatüddik[kl] (...—) بيضة الديك A *lrnd.* 1. cock's egg (which he is supposed to lay once in his life; it is employed as a test of virginity). 2. a very rare or impossible thing.

beyzatülbeled بيضة البلد A *lrnd.* 1. ostrich egg. 2. chief of a city; much respected or dreaded person. 3. truffle; mushroom.

beyzatül'enuk[kl] (....—) بيضة الأنوق A *lrnd.* 1. eagle's egg. 2. very rare thing.

beyzatülhar[rn] بيضة الحر A *lrnd.* great heat.

beyzatülhıdr بيضة الخدر A *lrnd.* virgin.

beyzatül'islâm (....—) بيضة الإسلام A *lrnd.* 1. the people of Islam. 2. the territory of Islam. 3. the vital center of Islam.

beyzatülkayz بيضة القيظ A *lrnd.* the hottest part of summer.

beyzatül'ukr بيضة العقر A *lrnd.*, *same as* **beyzatüddik.**

beyzatünnehar (....—) بيضة النهار A *lrnd.* daylight.

Beyzavi (.——) بيضاوى A *lrnd.* native of a place named **Beyza**; *name of the author of a famous Arabic commentary on the Quran.*

beyze بيضه *var. of* **beyza 2**.

beyzer بيزر A *lrnd.* fuller's beetle; big club.

beyzevi (..—) بيضوى A *lrnd.* oval, elliptical.

beyzi (.—) بيضى A oval. *geom.* ellipse; elliptical.

bez 1 بز [**bez 2**] 1. linen or cotton material, cloth. 2. piece of cloth, diaper, dustcloth. **—den bebek** 1. rag doll. 2. lazy, useless person. **— çöz=** to take out the cloth from the loom. **— kaplı** cloth-bound (book). **— manika** *naut.* hose; wind sail. **— tezgâhı** loom.

bez[zzl] **2** بزّ A *lrnd.* 1. cloth, linen. 2. furniture, drapery, clothing.

bez=[er] **3** بزمك /dan/ to get tired (of), to become disgusted (with).

bez 4 بيض A *lrnd.* [**beyz**] 1. *anat.* gland. 2. an inflamed gland, an indurated cyst.

beza 1 (.—) بذاء A *lrnd.* a being or becoming obscene or abusive in speech, abusiveness, scurrility.

bez'a 2 بضعه A *lrnd.* piece of meat cut off.

bezaat[ti] **1** (.—.) بضاعت A *lrnd.* smartness, handsomeness, intelligence (of a young man).

bezaat[ti] **2** (..—) بضعات A *lrnd.*, pl. of **bez'a 2**.

bezadi (.——) بزادى P *lrnd.* beryl.

bezağ بزغ P *lrnd.* 1. frog. 2. dam; dammed reservoir for water.

bezağa بزغه P *lrnd.* lizard.

bezai[ii] (.—.) بضائع A *lrnd.* goods, wares.

bezare (.—.) بظاره A *lrnd.*, *anat.* clitoris.

bezaz (.—) بزاز A *lrnd.* slovenliness, untidiness, squalor.

bezazet (.—.) بزازت [**bizazet**] *lrnd.* the drapery or furniture business.

bezbaz (.—) بزباز P *lrnd.* mace (the outer covering of the nutmeg).

bezci بزجى cloth-seller.

bezdir=[ir] بزديرمك /ı/ to sicken, to disgust, to weary.

bezdirme بزديرمه kind of flat bread.

beze 1 بزه Gk *prov.* lump of dough.

beze 2 بزه P *lrnd.* sin, crime.

beze=[r] **3** بزه مك /ı/ to deck, adorn, embellish.

beze 4 بزه [**beyza**] *prov.* gland; inflamed gland.

beze 5 بزه F macaroon.

bezek بزك ornament; decoration. **—çi** 1. lady's maid. 2. professional adorner of women. 3. decorator.

bezel *neol., physiol.* glandular.

bezelya, bezelye (.'..) بزليه Gk pea, peas.

bezen 1 بزن ornament, embellishment.

bezen=[ir] **2** بزنمك *pass., refl. of* **beze= 3**. **—dir=** /ı/ *caus.* **—iş, —me** *verbal n. of* **bezen=**.

bezer بزر A *lrnd.* garrulousness, loquacity.

bezesten *var. of* **bezistan.**

bezeyiş بزه ييش *verbal n. of* **beze= 3**.

bezg[sl] بزغ A *lrnd.* 1. bloodletting, phlebotomy; scarification. 2. the sunrise.

bezgin بزگين disgusted, wearied; discouraged, depressed. **—lik** weariness, lethargy.

bezî 1 (.—) بزى A lrnd. obscene, foul-mouthed.

bezi[ii] **2** (.—) بزع A lrnd. handsome and intelligent (youth).

bezik[gi] بزلك F card games bezique.

bezim (.—) بزم A lrnd. calm, restrained, self-possessed.

bezir 1 بزر |**bezr 1, 2**| 1. linseed oil. 2. flaxseed. **— mürekkebi** black ink made of burned linseed oil. **— yağı** linseed oil.

bezir 2 بزر A lrnd. 1. loquacious, talkative. 2. who cannot keep a secret, blab. 3. spendthrift.

bezîr 3 (.—) بزير A lrnd. 1. slanderer. 2. who cannot keep a secret, blab.

bezirci بزرجى dealer in linseed oil.

bezirgân بزرگان |**bazirgân**| 1. greedy merchant. 2. Jewish shopkeeper or peddler. 3. archaic merchant.

bezirger بزرگر |**bezrger**| lrnd. farmer, plowman, sower.

bezirhane (..—.) بزرخانه linseed oil press; linseed oil mill.

bezistan (..—) بزستان P lrnd. 1. cloth market. 2. same as **bedestan**.

beziş بزش verbal n. of **bez= 3**.

bezk[ki] بزك A lrnd. a spitting.

bezl 1 بذل A lrnd. a spending freely; gift, present. **—i can et=** to give one's life. **—i cehd, —i himmet, —i makdur, —i mechud** a doing one's very best, exertion. **—i nefs et=** to expend oneself, to use all one's energies, to exert oneself.

bezl 2 بذل A med. puncture, a puncturing.

bezla (.—) بزلاء A lrnd. calamity, dreadful misfortune.

bezle بزله P lrnd. witticism, bon mot, pleasantry, epigram.

bezlegû (..—) بزله گو P lrnd. wit, jester.

bezlengeç[ci] بزلنگج , **bezlengiç**[ci] بزلنگيج same as **bizlengeç**.

bezlet=[der] بزل ايتمك /1/ lrnd. to spend freely, to give generously.

bezm بزم P poet. banquet; convivial meeting, feast. **—i Cem** drinking party. **—i elest, —i ezel** the day of creation of man. **—i işret, —i mey, —i safa** drinking party. **—i tarab** Or. mus. a **makam** of Nihavend character which was never popular. **—i vuslat** feast of union (of lovers).

bezmara (.——) بزم آرا P 1. a mode in Oriental music. 2. poet. adorning the party.

bezmaverd (.—.) بزماورد P lrnd. dish of meat balls.

bezme بزمه verbal n. of **bez= 3**.

bezmefza (..—) بزم افزا P poet. that increases the pleasure of a banquet.

bezmgâh (.—) بزمگاه , **bezmgeh** بزمگه P poet. banqueting place.

bezr 1 بزر A lrnd. 1. seed; sown seed. 2. a sowing seed. 3. dissemination, a scattering. 4. offspring.

bezr 2 بزر A lrnd. 1. seed. 2. flaxseed.

bezrek[ki] بزرك P lrnd. small seed.

bezrgâr (.—) بزرگار , **bezrger** بزرگر P same as **bezirger**.

bezrgeri (..—) بزرگرى P lrnd. husbandry.

bezrülbenc بزر البنج A pharm. seeds of henbane, Hyosciamus seeds.

bezrülkaz[zzi] بزر القز A lrnd. silkworm's eggs.

bezrülkettan (...—) بزر الكتان A lrnd. flaxseed.

bezul[lü] (.—) بذول A lrnd. liberal, generous.

bezur (.—) بذور A var. of **bezîr 3**.

bezv بذو A lrnd. obscenity, foulmouthedness.

bezzar 1 (.—) بذار A lrnd. 1. sower of seed. 2. spendthrift.

bezzar 2 (.—) بزار A lrnd. dealer in flaxseed or linseed oil.

bezzaz (.—) بزاز A lrnd. cloth merchant.

bezzazane (.——.) بزازانه P lrnd. commonly sold in the market, common, stale.

bezzazistan (.—.—) بزازستان P lrnd. market hall.

bıcılgan بجلغان , **bıcırgan** بجرغان vet. scratches; cracked heel of a horse.

bıçak[gi] بيچاق 1. knife. 2. book binding guillotine. **— ağzı** the sharp edge of a knife. **— bıçağa** knife to knife; at daggers drawn. **— çek=** /a/ to threaten with a drawn dagger. **— eğe** knife-shaped file. **— gibi kes=** /ı/ to cut off, to stop at once (pain). **— kemiğe dayandı** It has reached the limit, it cannot be endured any longer. **— kınını kesmez** proverb (lit. A knife does not cut its sheath.) Authorities do not use their power against their own folk. **— sırtı kadar fark** a hairbreadth's difference. **— sil=** to finish off a job. **— silimi** outset, start. **— yarası onulur, dil yarası onulmaz** proverb A knife wound heals; a wound caused by words does not. **— ye=** to receive a knife wound. **—çı** cutter. **—çılık** the making and selling of knives. **—la=** /ı/ to stab, to knife. **—laş=** to fight with knives. 1. having a knife, armed with a knife, 2. Ott. hist. servant in the office of the pantry at the Imperial Palace.

bıçılgan بجلغان same as **bıcılgan**.

bıçırgan بجرغان 1. same as **bıcırgan**. 2. steel burnisher used to polish the inner surfaces of holes drilled in metals.

bıçkı بجقى ٠ بجقى ٠ بيجقى 1. two-handed saw, bucksaw. 2. saddler's knife. — **tozu** sawdust. —**cı** 1. sawyer. 2. maker or seller of bucksaws. —**cık** small saw; small knife. —**hane** sawmill.

bıçkın بجقين slang rascal, rowdy.

bık=ᵃʳ بقمق /dan/ to tire (of), to get bored (with), to grow tired (of a thing once liked). —**ıl=** pass. —**ış** verbal n. of **bık=**.

bıkkın بقغين disgusted, bored, tired. —**lık** boredom, disgust.

bıkma بقمه verbal n. of **bık=**.

bıktır=ⁱʳ بقدرمق ٠ بقدرمس /ı, dan/ caus. of **bık=**.

bıldır (´.) بلدير ٠ بلد ٠ بيلد ٠ بولد ٠ بيلدير archaic last year.

bıldırcın بلدرجين ٠ بلدرمجين ٠ بلدبرجين ٠ بلدمجين ٠ جين 1. quail, zool., Coturnix Coturnix. 2. plump little woman. — **fırtınası** calendar a storm early in September. — **otu** monk's-hood, bot., Aconitum Napellus.

bıldırki بلدركى prov. of last year.

bınar بكار ٠ بيكار archaic, var. of **pınar**.

bıngıl bıngıl بكيل ٠ بغيل fat and quivering like jelly.

bıngılda=ʳ بغلدامق to quiver like jelly. —**k** fontanel. —**t=** /ı/ caus. of **bıngılda=**. —**yık** same as **bıngıldak**.

bınsır بنصر A anat. 1. the fourth finger, ring finger. 2. the fourth toe.

bıraga براغه var. of **braga**.

bırak=ⁱʳ براقمق ٠ برقمق 1. /ı/ to leave; to quit, abandon; to let go (of), to relinquish, abandon, release; to allow, tolerate; to grow (beard); to fail (in an examination). 2. /ı,a/ to put, put down; to deposit; to entrust; to bequeath; to put off, postpone (until). 3. to come unstuck (glued part). —**ıl=** pass. —**ıntı** 1. leavings, refuse. 2. deposit; driftwood. 3. jetty, artificial breakwater. —**ış**, —**ma** verbal n. of **bırak=**. —**ma** left; released. —**tır=** /ı, a/ caus. of **bırak=**. —**tırıl=** pass. of **bıraktır=**.

bıranda (.´.) برانده var. of **buranda**.

bıttih (.—) بطيخ, **bıttiha** (.—.) بطيخه A lrnd. melon; muskmelon.

bıttihî (.——) بطيخى A lrnd. 1. pertaining to the melon. 2. grower or seller of melons.

bıyıkᵏⁱ بييق ٠ بيق 1. mustache. 2. whiskers (of a cat). 3. tendril. 4. naut. spritsail yard. — **altından gül=** to laugh up one's sleeve. —**larını balta kesmez ol=** /ın/ to become unmanageable, to have no fear or restraint left. — **bur=** 1. to twist the mustache. 2. to swagger, to show oneself off to the girls. —**ları ele al=** to grow up (young man). — **falına**

var= to pull broodingly at one's mustache. —**ına gül=** /ın/ to make fun (of). —**ını okut=** to have the hodja read a prayer over one's newly growing mustache. —**ını sil=** to consider some job finished and stop following it up. —**ı terle=** to have the mustache start growing (youth). —**ı yelli** conceited, proud. —**lan=** to grow a mustache. —**lı** having a mustache, mustached. —**lı baştankara** bearded titmouse, zool., Panurus biarmicus.

bızdıkᵍⁱ بزدك Arm slang child.

bızıkᵍⁱ 1 بزك prov. anus.

bızık=ⁱʳ 2 بزيقمق prov. 1. to feel oppressed. 2. to cheat.

bızıkçı بزيقجى same as **mızıkçı**. —**lık** abstr. n.

bızır بظر [bazr] anat. clitoris.

bızla=ʳ بزلامق to calve.

bızlangıçᶜⁱ بزلنغيچ ٠ بزلنكيچ same as **bizlengeç**.

bi- 1 ب A lrnd. by, with, through, in, as in binefsihi, bizatihi.

bi- 2 (—) فى P lrnd. without, as in bibehre, biçare.

bia 1 (—.) بيعه A lrnd. mode of selling, buying, or bargaining.

bia 2 (—.) بيعه A lrnd. church; synagogue.

biab (——) بى آب P lrnd. 1. waterless, dry, arid; sapless; juiceless. 2. lusterless. 3. ashamed, shameful; shameless, dishonorable.

biadᵈᵈⁱ (—.) بى عد P lrnd. innumerable, countless.

biadil (—.—) بى عديل P lrnd. matchless, unequalled.

bialˡⁱ (.—) بعال A lrnd., pl. of **ba'l** 5.

biaman (—.—) بى آمان P lrnd. merciless, pitiless.

biar 1 (.—) بنا ٠ بيا A lrnd., pl. of **bi'r** 3.

biar 2 (——) بى عار P lrnd. shameless.

biaram (———) بى آرام P lrnd. restless, peaceless.

biasl (—.) بى اصل P without foundation. — **u esas** without foundation, quite unfounded.

biatᵗⁱ (—.) بيعت [bey'at 2] oath of allegiance, homage. — **et=** /a/ to take an oath of allegiance, to do homage (to).

biavnillâhi (...—´.) بعون الله A lrnd. with the help of God.

biaynihi (..´..) بعينه A lrnd. exactly so, in the very same way; exactly, fully resembling.

bibaht (—.) بى بخت P lrnd. unlucky.

bibakᵏⁱ (——) بى باك P lrnd. fearless, intrepid.

biban (———) بيبان A lrnd., pl. of **bab** 2.

bibasiret (—.—.) بى بصيرت P lrnd. lacking discernment, blind, ignorant.

bibedel

bibedel (—..) بی بدل P lrnd. 1. matchless, unequalled. 2. without payment.
bibeha (—.—) بی بها P lrnd. 1. invaluable, priceless. 2. valueless; gratis.
bibehre (—..) بی بهره P lrnd. 1. /dan/ who has no share (in); bereft (of), lacking. 2. poor, destitute; unfortunate.
biber 1 بیبر 1. pepper, bot., Piper nigrum. 2. pepper, bot., Capsicum. — **ağacı** pepper tree, bot., Schinus. — **dolması** stuffed peppers. — **tanesi** peppercorn. — **turşusu** pickled green peppers.
biber 2 (—.) بی بر P lrnd. without fruit, barren.
biberg (—.) بی برگ P poet. 1. leafless. 2. without means.
biberiye 1 (..—.) بیبریه rosemary, bot., Rosmarinus officinalis.
biberiye 2 (..—.) بیبریه |based on **biber 1**| bot., Piperaceae.
biberle=ʳ بیبرله /ı/ to pepper. **—n=** pass., refl. **—t=** caus. of **biberle=**.
biberli بیبرلی 1. peppered, peppery. 2. expensive.
biberlikᵍⁱ بیبرلك 1. pepper shaker, pepperbox, pepper pot; pepper mill. 2. bed of garden peppers.
biberon بیبرون F feeding bottle.
bibi 1 بیبی |bibi 3| prov. paternal aunt.
bibi 2 بیبی prov. turkey.
bibi 3 (——) بیبی P archaic lady.
bibliyografi بیبلیوغرافی F, **bibliyografya** (....'.) بیبلیوغرافیا It bibliography.
biblo ('.) بیبلو F knicknack, trinket, objet d'art.
bica (——) بیجا P lrnd. out of place, wrong, unseasonable.
bicad 1 (.—) بجاد A Arabian cloak or upper garment of striped cloth.
bicad 2 (——) بجاد , **bicade** (—.—.) P بجاده lrnd. 1. deep red precious stone. 2. ruby lip, lip.
bicademizab (——..—) بجاده مذاب P poet. red wine; blood.
bicadi (.——) بجادی A lrnd. beryl, garnet.
bican (——) بیجان P lrnd. 1. lifeless; spiritless; listless. 2. submissive. 3. valiant.
bicikᵍⁱ بجك prov. breast; teat.
bicişkᵏⁱ بجشك P lrnd. physician; surgeon.
biç=ᵉʳ بچمك /ı/ to cut; to cut up, to cut out (timber, cloth); to reap, mow.
biçare (——.) بیچاره P 1. poor, wretched. 2. lrnd. without hope, without remedy. **—gân** (——.—) P lrnd., pl. of **biçare**. **—gi** (——.—) P lrnd. helplessness; need, necessity. **—lik** (——..) 1. wretchedness, misery. 2. lrnd. helplessness, hopelessness.

—var (——.—) P lrnd. helpless, destitute, miserable.
biçekᵍⁱ بچك prov. cutting instrument, cutter.
biçerbağlar بچرباغلر agr. reaping machine.
biçerdöğer بچردوگر agr. combine.
biçici بچیجی 1. tailor's cutter. 2. reaper, mower.
biçil=ⁱʳ بچلمك pass. of **biç=**. **—miş kaftan** /a/ fitting well, just the right thing, cut out (for).
biçili بچلی cut, cut through, reaped, mown, cut out.
biçim بچم 1. shape, form; way, manner. 2. elegant form, well-proportioned shape. 3. tailor. cut. 4. harvest. **—ine getir=** /ı/ to find a convenient occasion (for). **—e sok=** /ı/ to give shape (to). **— vakti** harvest time; hay time. **—li** well-shaped, well-cut, trim. **—lik** fit for reaping; land set apart for reaping. **—siz** ill-shaped, ugly.
biçin بچین archaic harvest. **—lik** same as **biçimlik**.
biçiş بچش verbal n. of **biç=**.
biçişkᵏⁱ بچشك P var. of **bicişk**.
biçki بچكی tailor. cutting out (clothes).
biçme بچمه 1. verbal n. of **biç=**. 2. cut, cut out; estimated. 3. neol., geom. prism.
biçtir=ⁱʳ بچدرمك /ı, a/ caus. of **biç=**.
biçun (——) بیچون P lrnd. absolute, eternal, divine, inexplicable (God). **— u çira** absolute (God).
bidᵈᵈⁱ **1** بد A lrnd. equal, similar, like.
bid 2 (——) بید P poet. willow. **—i giryan** weeping willow. **—i ham** fresh wood of aloes, wood of Aquilaria Agallochum the perfume of which is developed only after being buried for a long time. **—i Mecnun**, **—i muleh** weeping willow, bot., Salix babylonica. **—i müşk** Egyptian willow, bot., Salix aegyptiaca. **—i piyade**, **—i revan** weeping willow. **—i surh**, **—i Taberî** a species of willow. **—i üşer mudar**, bot., Calotropis gigantea.
bid 3 (——) بد P lrnd., Hindu rel. Veda.
bid 4 (——) بد A lrnd., pl. of **beyda**.
bidaᵃⁱ بدع A lrnd., pl. of **bid'at**.
bidaa (.——) بضاعة var. of **bizaat**.
bidad 1 (——) بیداد P lrnd. injustice, oppression, cruelty.
bidad 2 (.——) بداد A lrnd. 1. a contributing to a general fund. 2. barter, exchange.
bidadger (——.) بیدادگر P lrnd. tyrant, oppressor.

bidalⁱⁱ (.—) بيال A lrnd. exchange, barter.
bidar 1 (——) بيدار P poet. 1. awake; active, attentive, alert, wary, circumspect. 2. experienced; enlightened.
bidar 2 (.—) بيدا A lrnd. 1. quickness in action. 2. an outstripping.
bidarbaht (——.) بيدابخت P poet. fortunate, lucky.
bidardil (——.) بيدادل P poet. vigilant, alert; enlightened.
bidari (———) بيداری P abstr. n. of **bidar 1**.
bid'atⁱⁱ بدعت A 1. innovation. 2. heresy. 3. can. law apocryphal, uncanonical text. —**i hasane** useful innovation. —**i seyyie** pernicious innovation.
bidayetⁱⁱ (.—.) بدايت A a beginning, commencement. — **mahkemesi** court of first instance, lower court. —**en** (.—´..) A at the beginning, initially.
bidbaf (——) بيدباف P lrnd. wicker-worker, basket maker; cane-worker.
bidberg (—.) بيدبرگ P lrnd. 1. willow leaf. 2. willow-leaf-shaped arrow head; arrow with willow-leaf shaped head.
biddefeat (.·..—) بالدفعات A repeatedly, time and again.
bidencir (—.—) بيدانجير P lrnd. castor-oil plant, bot., Ricinus cummunis. —**i Hatai** croton-oil plant, bot., Croton tiglium.
bider 1 بذر [bezr 1] prov. seeds.
bider 2 بدر A lrnd., pl. of **bedre**.
biderd (—.) بيدرد P poet. untroubled; having no worry.
biderman (—.—) بيدرمان P poet. hopeless, without remedy.
bidest بدست var. of **bedest**.
bidester (—..) بيدستر P lrnd. beaver, zool., Castor fiber.
bidestüpa (—..—) بيدست‌وپا P lrnd. powerless.
bideva (—.—) بيدوا P poet. incurable, hopeless.
bidevlet (—..) بيدولت P lrnd. unfortunate, unhappy.
bidil (—.) بيدل P poet. 1. timid, lacking heart, pusillanimous. 2. dejected, dispirited. 3. in love. 4. heartless, destitute of affection.
bidimağ (—.—) بيدماغ P lrnd. brainless.
bidin (——) بيدين P lrnd. irreligious, unbeliever, infidel.
bidireng (—..) بيدرنگ P lrnd. without delay, at once; quick.
bidiriğ (—.—) بيدريغ P lrnd. 1. unsparing, liberal. 2. readily accepted, not refused.
bidist بدست P var. of **bedest**.

bidistan (—.—) بيدستان P lrnd. willow grove.
bidmuş (——) بيدموش, **bidmüşk**ᵘ (—.) بيدمشك P lrnd. a fragrant shrub.
bidon بيدون F oil drum, metal barrel.
Bidpay (——) بيدپای P name of a mythical Indian philosopher and minister of state connected with the so-called Aesop's fables collected in the Sanskrit Hitopadesa, the Arabic Kalila ve Dimna, the Persian Enverî Süheylî, and the Turkish Humayunname.
biduht (—.) بيدخت P lrnd. the planet Venus.
biecmaihim (..´...) بأجمعهم A lrnd. all together, the whole lot.
biedeb (—..) بأدب P lrnd. 1. ill-mannered, rude. 2. impudent. —**ane** (—..—.) P 1. rudely. 2. impudently, shamelessly.
bieman (—.—) بأمان P var. of **biaman**.
biemrillah (...—) بأمرالله A lrnd. by the decree of God.
bienbaz (—.—) بأنباز P lrnd. without partner.
biencam (—.—) بأنجام P lrnd. infinite, boundless.
biesrihi (..´..) بأسره A lrnd. with all its appurtenances, all together.
bieyyihal (...—) بأی حال A lrnd. under any circumstances, without fail.
bifaide (——..) بيفائده P lrnd. purposeless, useless, futile.
bifazlihi (..´..) بفضله A lrnd. by His grace.
biftekᵗⁱ بفتك F beefsteak, steak.
bifütur (—.—) بفتور P lrnd. fearless, careless.
biga (.—) بغا A lrnd. a committing adultery (woman).
bigâh (——) بيگاه P lrnd. unseasonable, out of place.
bigalⁱⁱ 1 (.—) بغال A lrnd., pl. of **bagl**.
bigalⁱⁱ 2 (.—) بغال A lrnd., pl. of **bagle**.
bigam (—.) بيغم P lrnd. free from sorrow.
bigâne (——.) بيگانه P 1. /a/ stranger (to), detached (from); unpracticed (in). 2. lrnd. strange, foreign, unknown; stranger, foreigner. — **vü aşna** strangers and acquaintances; myst. the uninitiated and adepts. — **vü hiş** strangers and relatives. —**gi** (———.—) P lrnd. 1. foreignness, a being a stranger. 2. myst. spiritual unconcern for worldly things. —**huy** (———.—) P lrnd. cold and distant, shy, unsociable, reserved. —**lik** abstr. n.
bigaraz (—..) بيغرض P disinterested.
bigat (.—) بغات A lrnd. a taking by surprise, unexpected arrival.

bigaye (— —.) بغایه P *lrnd.* endless, boundless; much.
bigayret (—..) بغیرت P *lrnd.* inert, spiritless, lifeless.
bigayri hakkin (.ʹ. ʹ.) بغیر حق A *lrnd.* without any right, unjustly.
bigi گی *archaic var. of* **gibi**.
bigiran (—.—) بیگران [bikeran] *lrnd.* inestimable, infinite, boundless.
bigmaz (.—) بگماز P *poet.* wine; cup of wine; banquet.
bigüman (—.—) بیگمان P *lrnd.* doubtless, sure.
bigünah (—.—) بیگناه P *lrnd.* innocent, guiltless.
bih 1 به P *lrnd.* good, excellent; better; well.
bih 2 به P *lrnd.* quince.
bih 3 به A *lrnd.* by, with, through, in him or it, *as in* **mamulün bih**.
bih 4 (—) بیخ P *lrnd.* 1. root; rhizome. 2. base, foundation. 3. origin. **— u bün** root and stalk.
biha (.—) بها A *fem. of* **bih 3**.
bihab (——) بیخواب P *lrnd.* sleepless.
bihaber (—..) بیخبر P /dan/ *lrnd.* unaware (of), ignorant (of).
bihad[dd¹] (—.) بیحد P *lrnd.* boundless, immense, limitless.
bihakkin (.ʹ.) بحق A *lrnd.* 1. rightly. 2. fully, truly.
biham (.—) بهام A *lrnd., pl. of* **behme**.
bihamat (.——) بهامات A *lrnd.* herds of calves or kids, flocks of lambs.
bihamdillâhi (...—ʹ.) بحمدالله A *lrnd.* thanks be to God; with the help of God.
bihan (.—) بهان P *lrnd.* the good; good men.
bihanüman (——.—) بیخانمان P *lrnd.* 1. homeless. 2. destitute.
bihar (.—) بحار A *lrnd.* seas, oceans.
bihareket (—...) بی حرکت P *lrnd.* motionless.
bihasbirrütbe بحسب الرتبه A *lrnd.* according to rank.
bihasıl (——.) بحاصل P *lrnd.* with no result, unprofitable; fruitless, barren.
bihaver (——.) بیخ آور P *lrnd.* rooted, firmly established.
bihaya (—.—) بی حیا P *lrnd.* impudent, shameless.
bihayat (—.—) بی حیات P *lrnd.* lifeless.
bihbud (.—) بهبود P *lrnd.* 1. sound, healthy. 2. good; holy.
bihdane (—.—) به دانه P *lrnd.* quince seeds.
bihemal[li] (—.—) بیهمال P *lrnd.* peerless.

bihemta (—.—) بیهمتا P *lrnd.* incomparable, unequaled.
bihengâm (—.—) بیهنگام P *lrnd.* unseasonable, out of place, unfitting.
bihesab (—.—) بیحساب P *lrnd.* innumerable, countless.
bihgüzin (..—) بهگزین P *lrnd.* 1. who selects the best. 2. money-changer.
bihi 1 به A *var. of* **bih 3**.
bihî 2 (.—) بهی P *lrnd.* goodness, virtue.
bihî 3 (.—) بهی P *lrnd.* quince.
bihicab (—.—) بی حجاب A *unabashed*, shameless.
bihin (.—) بهین P *lrnd.* better; best.
bihired (—..) بیخرد P *lrnd.* stupid, unintelligent.
bihiss[ssi] (—.) بی حس P *lrnd.* insensitive, callous.
bihişt بهشت P *lrnd.* paradise; heaven. **—i dünya** the earthly paradise. **—aşyan** (..——) P dwelling in paradise. **—hıram** (...—) P departed to paradise. **—î** (..—) P heavenly, celestial. **—nişin** (...—) P dwelling in paradise, sainted. **—sima** (..——) P of heavenly countenance. **—zar** (..—) P a place like paradise in beauty.
bihken (—.) بیخ کن P *lrnd.* who eradicates, pulls up by the roots.
bihred بخرد P *lrnd.* intelligent. **—î** (..—) P wisdom, intelligence.
bihte (—.) بخته P *lrnd.* sifted, bolted, screened.
bihter بهتر P *lrnd.* better. **—î** (..—) P superiority. **—în** (..—) P best.
bihud (—.) بیخود P *lrnd.* insensible, stupefied, stunned, perplexed; enraptured.
bihude (——.) بیهوده P *lrnd., same as* **beyhude 1**. **—gi** (———.—) P uselessness, futility. **—gû** (——.—) P who talks to no purpose. **—hand** (——..) P who laughs without cause. **—kâr** (———.—) P who occupies himself in useless efforts.
bihudi (—.—) بیخودی P, **bihudluk**[lu] بیخودلی *lrnd., abstr. n. of* **bihud**.
bihudud (—.—) بی حدود P *lrnd.* boundless, without boundaries.
bihuş (——) بیهوش P *lrnd.* insensible, unconscious; bewildered. **—î** (———) P unconsciousness; bewilderment.
bihuzur (—.—) بی حضور P *lrnd.* uneasy, disturbed, restless, irritated. **—luk** *abstr. n.*
bihümal[li] (—.—) بیهمال P *var. of* **bihemal**.
bihüner (—..) بیهنر P *lrnd.* unskillful; ignorant.
bihzad (.—) بهزاد P *lrnd.* 1. noble by birth. 2. legitimate, lawfully born.

biibaretiha (..—'..—) بعبارتها A lrnd: verbally, word for word.

biihtiyar (—..—) بى اختيار P lrnd. involuntarily.

biihtiyat (—..—) بى احتياط P lrnd. heedless, uncircumspect.

biiktidar (—..—) بى اقتدار P lrnd. incapable, powerless, impotent.

biilac (—.—) بى علاج P lrnd. without remedy, incurable.

biilâç[cı] (—..) بى علاج [biilac] *only in* **aç biilâç**.

biinayetillâh (..—..—) بعناية الله A lrnd. by the grace of God.

biinsaf (—.—) بى إنصاف P lrnd. merciless, tyrannical, cruel.

biintiha (—..—) بى إنتها P lrnd. endless, infinite; infinitely.

biirtiyab (—..—) بى ارتياب P lrnd. doubtlessly.

biiştibah (—..—) بى إشتباه P lrnd. undoubtedly, surely.

biitibar (—..—) بى إعتبار P lrnd. unesteemed.

biitidal[li] (—..—) بى إعتدال P lrnd. unjust, unequal; immoderate.

biiznillâh (...—) بإذن الله , **biiznillâhi taalâ** (...—. .—) بإذن الله تعالى A with the permission of God, God willing.

bika[ı] 1 (.—) بقاع A lrnd., pl. of **bika** 2, **buk'a** 1. B—**kelb** *name of a place near Damascus*.

bik'a 2 بقعه A lrnd., var. of **buk'a** 1.

bikâm (——) بيكام P lrnd. unsuccessful, disappointed, frustrated.

bikan (——) بقان A lrnd., pl. of **buk**.

bikâr (——) بيكار P lrnd. unoccupied, idle.

bikarar (—.—) بى قرار P lrnd. 1. inconstant, unsettled. 2. impatient, restless.

bikarbonat بيقاربونات F chem. bicarbonate.

bikayd (—.) بى قيد P lrnd. unrestrained; independent, carefree.

bikemübiş (—..—) بيكم وبيش , **bikemükâst** (—..—) بيكم وكاست P lrnd. neither more nor less, accurately.

bikeran (—.—) بى كران P lrnd. immense, boundless; endless.

bikes (—.) بى كس P lrnd. having nobody, friendless; without kith or kin. —**i** (—.—) P, —**lik** (—..) abstr. n.

bikıyas (—.—) بى قياس P lrnd. incomprehensible, enormous, immense.

bikir[kri] بكر [bikr] virginity, maidenhood.

bikr بكر A lrnd. 1. virgin. 2. first offspring of a female (human or animal). 3. first fruit; the first of anything.

bikran (.—) بكران P lrnd. —**ı bihişt** virgins of paradise, houris. —**ı çerh** 1. stars and planets. 2. houris.

bikrî (.—) بكرى |based on **bikr**| lrnd. pertaining to a virgin.

bikusur (—.—) بى قصور P lrnd. faultless.

bil 1 (—) بيل lrnd., var. of **bel** 2.

bil=[ir] 2 بلمك . بلك /ı/ 1. to know; to be informed, aware; to understand. 2. to learn; to hear; to recognize; to guess. 3. to consider, deem; to think, believe, suppose; to hold responsible; /ı,dan/ to believe to be the cause. 4. to experience; to appreciate, value. 5. *after* =a=, =e= to be able to, *e. g.,* **yapabilmek** to be able to do. —**emedin** at most. —**erek** knowingly, on purpose. —**meden** not knowing, unintentionally. —**e bile** with full knowledge of the consequences. —**e bile lâdes** with full knowledge of the disadvantageous consequences. —**diğinden kalma**=, —**diğini oku**= to insist on having one's own way. —**miş ol** know well, hear this. —**diğinden şaşma**= to go one's own way, not to listen to others.

bilâ- (.—) بلا A lrnd. without.

bilâbedel (.—..) بلا بدل A lrnd. gratis, for nothing.

bilâd (.—) بلاد A lrnd., pl. of **belde**, **beled** 1. —**ı aşere** Ott. hist. the 10 towns of a high category of judgeships; Izmir, Eyub, Khania, Aleppo, Thessalonike, Sofia, Trabzon, Galata, Jerusalem, Larissa. —**ı erbaa** Ott. hist. the 4 towns of the highest category of provincial judgeships: Edirne, Bursa, Damascus, Cairo. —**ı hâraciye** Ott. hist. tributary territories. —**ı isnaaşere** Ott. hist. the 12 towns of a certain category: Adana, Erzurum, Baghdad, Beirut, Diyarbakir, Ruschuk, Sarajevo, Sivas, Tripoli, Aintab, Chankiri, Marash. —**ı selâse** Ott. hist. Istanbul, Eyub, and Üsküdar.

bilâder (.—.) بلادر colloq., var. of **birader**.

Bilâdülcebel (.—...) بلاد الجبل A geog. Media.

Bilâdülcerid (.—..—) بلاد الجريد A name of a district in Central Tunisia.

Bilâdürrum (.—.—) بلاد الروم A Anatolia.

bilâfark (.—.) بلا فرق A lrnd. without difference, similarly.

bilâfasıla (.—..) بلا فاصل A lrnd. uninterruptedly, continuously.

bil'afiye (.—..) بالعافيه A lrnd. in good health, happily.

bilâğ (.—) بلاغ A lrnd. an exerting oneself to the utmost, striving.

bilâhara (.—..) بالآخره A later, at a later time.

bilâimhal (.—.—) بلا امهال A lrnd. without delay, immediately.

bilâistisna (. — .. —) بلا استثناء A *lrnd.* without exception.

bilâkayduşart (. — ...) بلا قید و شرط A *law* unconditionally.

bilâkis (.'..) بالعکس A on the contrary.

bilâl[ir] **1** (. —) بلال A 1. var. of **belâl**. 2. *w. cap.*, man's name.

bilâl[li] **2** (. —) بلال A *lrnd.* a visiting one's relatives; a sending a message or present to one's relatives.

bilâmucip (. — — .) بلا موجب A *lrnd.* without reason, without motive.

bilâmüddet (. — ..) بلا مدت A *lrnd.* indefinitely, for an indefinite time.

bilâmüzakere (. — . — .) بلا مذاکره A *lrnd.* without discussion.

bilânço (.'.) بیلانچو It balance; balance sheet.

bilârdo (.'.) بیلاردو [**bilyardo**] billiards.

bil'asale (.. — .) بالاصاله A *law* acting as principal and not as a representative.

bilâsebeb (. — ..) بلا سبب A *lrnd.* without cause.

bilâşek (. — .) بلا شك A *lrnd.* without doubt.

bilâtaksir (. — . —) بلا تقصیر A *lrnd.* having no fault.

bilâtashih (. — . —) بلا تصحیح A *lrnd.* uncorrected.

bilâta'vik (. — . —) بلا تعویق A *lrnd.* without delay.

bilâteehhür (. — ...) بلا تأخر A *lrnd.* without loss of time, without delay.

bilâteemmül (. — ...) بلا تأمل A *lrnd.* without considering.

bilâtehir (. — . —) بلا تأخیر A *lrnd.* immediately, without delay.

bilâteklif (. — . —) بلا تكلیف A *lrnd.* unceremoniously, informally.

bilâtereddüd (. — ...) بلا تردد A *lrnd.* unhesitatingly.

bilâteşbih (. — . —) بلا تشبیه A *lrnd.* not that it compares, far from being alike.

bilâtevanin (. — . — .) بلا توانی A *lrnd.* without delay, energetically.

bilâücret (. — ..) بلا اجرت A *lrnd.* unpaid; free of charge.

bilâvasıta (. — — ..) بلا واسطه A directly.

bilbedahe (.. — .) بالبداهه A *lrnd.* extempore, extemporaneously.

bilcümle (.'..) بالجمله A all, entire; entirely.

bildar (— —) بیلدار P *lrnd.* 1. delver, digger. 2. oarsman, rower.

bildik[gi] بیلدیك. acquaintance. — **çık=** to turn out to have been formerly acquainted.

bildir[ir] بیلدیریرك بیلدیر مك بیلدی ملك /ı,a/ *caus.* of. **bil=** 2 to communicate, to make known. —**il=** *pass.* of. —**iş**, —**me** *verbal n.* of **bildir=**. —**me kipi** *neol., gram.* indicative mood.

bile 1 بیله 1. even, *e. g.*, **Çocuklar bile duydu** Even the children have heard of it. 2. already, *e. g.*, «**Ne zaman gidecek?**» «**Gitti bile**» «When will he leave?» «He's gone already.»

bile 2 بیله *prov.* together. —**since** together with him.

bile 3 بیله *var.* of **bilye**.

bile=[r] **4** بیلمك. بیلر. بیلەلك. /ı/ to sharpen, whet, grind.

bilece (..'.) بیله جه. *prov.* together, in company (with).

bileği بیلكی بیلەگی بیلگی بیلگو whetstone, hone, grindstone. — **çarkı** circular grindstone. — **taşı** whetstone. —**ci** knife-grinder.

bilek[gi] **1** بیلك 1. wrist. 2. pastern (in an animal). — **bilek ak=** to flow in a column as thick as one's wrist. —**ine güven=** to trust to one's fists. —**inin hakkı ile** /ın/ purely by his own ability and work. — **kuvveti** the strength of one's fists. — **saati** wrist watch. —**inde altın bileziği var** /ın/ He has a profitable handicraft.

bilek[ki] **2** بیلك P *lrnd.* 1. anything new and elegant. 2. gift.

bilek[ki] **3** (— .) بیلك P *lrnd.* 1. small spade, hoe. 2. broad arrowhead; arrow with broad head.

bilekçe بیلكچه *archaic* 1. handcuff, manacle. 2. fetter for the ankle. 3. wrist; pastern.

bilekçik[gi] بیلكچك small wrist.

bileme بیله مه *verbal n.* of **bile=** 4.

bilen 1 بیلن *var.* of **belen 1**.

bilen=[ir] **2** بیلنمك. *pass.* of **bile=** 4. —**il=** *pass.* of **bile=** 4. —**me** *verbal n.* of **bilen=** 2.

bileş=[ir] *neol., phil., gram., sc.* to form a compound. —**en** *phys.* component. —**ik** compound. —**ik faiz** *math.* compound interest. —**ik göz** *biol.* composite eye. —**ik kelime** *gram.* compound word. —**ik kesir** *math.* compound fraction. —**ik yaprak** *bot.* compound leaf. —**im** *phil., gram., sc.* composition. —**ke** *phys.* resultant. —**tir=** /ı/ *phil., gram., sc.* to compose.

bilet=[ir] **1** بیلتمك /ı/ *caus.* of **bile=** 4.

bilet 2 بلت [**bilyet**] ticket. — **gişesi** ticket office, booking office; box office. —**çi** ticket collector.

bileyici بیلەیجی knife-grinder.

bileyiş بیلەیش بیلەیشە *verbal n.* of. **bile=** 4.

bilezik[gi] بیلەزیك

بيلزيك. بيرزيك. 1. bracelet. 2. metal ring around a column, gun, etc. 3. ring-shaped stone forming the top of a well. 4. narrow ring of white hairs round the shank of a horse. 5. *slang* handcuffs. —çi maker and seller of bracelets.

bilfarz بالفرض A *lrnd.* supposing; supposedly.
bilfiil بالفعل A *lrnd.* actually, in fact.
bilfikrissakib (...—.) بالفكر الثاقب A *lrnd.* with penetrating thought.
bilge بیلگه *prov.* learned.
bilgi بیلگو بیكو بیلگی 1. knowledge; learning. 2. science, branch of science. 3. information. 4. *archaic* diviner, seer. — edin= to take notice; to be informed; to obtain information.
bilgiçᵍⁱ بیلگیچ 1. pedant; pedantic. 2. *archaic* sage, man of learning. —lik pedantry.
bilgili بیلگیلی well-informed; learned.
bilgilikᵍⁱ بیلگیلك mark, sign.
bilgin *neol.* savant, scholar, scientist.
bilgudüvvi vel'âsâl (....—.—) بالغدو والآصال A *lrnd.* mornings and evenings, early and late.
bilhassa (⸱ ..) بالخاصه A especially; particularly. — **ve bilhassa** above all.
bilhayr بالخیر A *lrnd.* in good health, with good luck.
bili بر *archaic* knowledge.
bil'icab (.——) بالایجاب A *lrnd.* of necessity.
bilici بیلیجی knowing, knower.
bil'ifa (.——) بالایفا A /ı/ *lrnd.* doing, performing; paying.
bil'iftihar (...—) بالافتخار A *lrnd.* proudly, feeling proud.
bil'ihtimam (...—) بالاهتمام A *lrnd.* carefully, with great care.
bil'ihtisar (...—) بالاختصار A *lrnd.* briefly, in short.
bil'ihtiyar (...—) بالاختیار A *lrnd.* by choice, willingly.
bilikᵍⁱ بیلك بیلیك *prov.* knowledge; intelligence.
bil'iktibas (...—) بالاقتباس A /dan/ *lrnd.* quoting (from).
bil'iktifa (...—) بالاكتفا A /la/ *lrnd.* being content (with).
bil'iktisab (...—) بالاكتساب A /ı/ *lrnd.* gaining, obtaining.
bil'iktiza (...—) بالاقتضا A *lrnd.* of necessity.
bil'iltica (...—) بالالتجا A /a/ *lrnd.* taking refuge (in), trusting.
bil'iltifat (...—) بالالتفات A *lrnd.* courteously, with courtesy.
bil'iltimas (...—) بالالتماس A *lrnd.* supporting favorably; with a recommendation.

bil'iltizam (...—) بالالتزام A *lrnd.* 1. on purpose. 2. of necessity.
bilim *neol.* science. —**sel** scientific.
bilimtay *neol.* academy.
bil'imtihan (...—) بالامتحان A *lrnd.* by examination, by passing an examination.
bil'imtisal (...—) بالامتثال A /a/ *lrnd.* following the example (of), conforming (to).
bil'imtizac (...—) بالامتزاج A /la/ *lrnd.* blending, fitting in (with).
bil'imza (..—) بالامضا A *lrnd.* having signed, signing.
bilinⁱʳ بیلینك *pass.* of **bil**= 2.
bilinçᵉⁱ *neol., psych.* the conscious. — **altı** the subconscious.
bilindikᵍⁱ *neol., algebra* known.
bilinemezcilikᵍⁱ *neol., phil.* agnosticism.
bil'infaz (..—) بالانفاذ A /ı/ *lrnd.* executing.
bil'infirad (...—) بالانفراد A *lrnd.* separately, individually.
bil'infisal (...—) بالانفصال A /dan/ *lrnd.* being separated, withdrawing from.
bil'inkısam (...—) بالانقسام A *lrnd.* by being divided.
bil'inkişaf (...—) بالانكشاف A *lrnd.* by coming to light, being discovered.
bilinme بیلنمه *verbal n.* of **bilin**=.
bilinmedik (..⸱ ..) بیلنمدك 1. unknown. 2. *algebra* unknown.
bil'inşirah (...—) بالانشراح A *lrnd.* cheerfully, with a glad heart.
bil'intac (..—) بالانتاج A /ı/ *lrnd.* concluding, finishing.
bil'intihab (...—) بالانتخاب A *lrnd.* by election; by choice.
bil'intikal (...—) بالانتقال A /dan/ *lrnd.* being transferred (from), having passed to someone (from).
bil'intisab (...—) بالانتساب A /a/ *lrnd.* joining, adhering.
bil'irad (.——) بالایراد A *lrnd.* by income.
bil'irae (..—.) بالارائه A /ı/ *lrnd.* by showing, demonstrating.
bil'irkâb (..—) بالارکاب A /a/ *lrnd.* embarking (on); mounting.
bilirkişi *neol., law* expert.
bil'irsvel'istihkak (......—) بالارث والاستحقاق A *lrnd.* by inherited right.
bil'is'af (..—) بالاسعاف A /ı/ *lrnd.* by fulfilling, granting.
bil'isbat (..—) بالاثبات A /ı/ *lrnd.* by proof, having proved.
bil'iskât (..—) بالاسکات A /ı/ *lrnd.* having silenced; having convinced.
bil'isnad (..—) بالاسناد A /ı/ *lrnd.* by imputation (of), accusing.

bil'israf (..—) بالإسراف A /ı/ lrnd. by spending, squandering.

bil'istical (...—) بالإستعجال A lrnd. hastily, in haste.

bil'isticar (..——) بالإستيجار A /dan/ lrnd. by renting (from).

bil'isticvab (...—) بالإستجواب A lrnd. upon interrogation.

bil'istida (...—) بالإستدعاء A /ı/ lrnd. by request (of), requesting.

bil'istidlâl (...—) بالإستدلال A /dan/ lrnd. by deduction, deducing, inferring (from).

bil'isti'fa (...—) بالإستعفا A /dan/ lrnd. by resignation, resigning (from).

bil'istifsar (...—) بالإستفسار A /ı/ lrnd. by inquiring (after).

bil'istihbar (...—) بالإستخبار A lrnd. by asking for information.

bil'istihdam (...—) بالإستخدام A /ı/ lrnd. by employing, taking into service.

bil'istihsal (...—) بالإستحصال A /ı/ lrnd. by producing, obtaining.

bil'istiklâl (...—) بالإستقلال A lrnd. independently, absolutely.

bil'istikmal (...—) بالإستكمال A /ı/ lrnd. by completing, concluding.

bil'istilzam (...—) بالإستلزام A /ı/ lrnd. requiring, rendering necessary.

bil'istimlâk (...—) بالإستملاك A lrnd. by expropriation.

bil'istintak (...—) بالإستنطاق A lrnd. by cross-examination, interrogating.

bil'istisna (...—) بالإستثنا A /ı/ lrnd. by exception (of), exempting.

bil'istişare (...—.) بالإستشاره A lrnd. by consultation.

bil'istizan (..——) بالإستيزان A /dan/ lrnd. by obtaining permission.

biliş 1 بلیش، بلیش، بلیش . verbal n. of **bil= 2**.

biliş 2 بیش . archaic acquaintance, friend.

biliş=ir **3** بلشمك، بلشمك . to become mutually acquainted.

bil'iş'ar (..—) بالإشعار A /ı/ lrnd. by communicating, giving information (about).

bilişikġi بلشك . prov. acquaintance, acquainted. **—lik** abstr. n.

bilişil=ir بلشلمك . pass. of **biliş= 3**.

bilişlikġi بلشلك . abstr. n. of **biliş 2**.

bilişme بلشمه . verbal n. of **biliş= 3**.

biliştir=ir بلشدرمك . /ı/ caus. of **biliş= 3**. **—il=** pass.

bil'iştira (...—) بالإشترا A /ı/ lrnd. by purchasing, having purchased.

bil'iştirak (...—) بالإشتراك A lrnd. jointly, in participation.

bil'ita (..—) بالإعطا A /ı, a/ lrnd. by giving, having given.

bil'itiraf (...—) بالإعتراف A /ı/ lrnd. by confessing, having confessed.

bil'itiraz (...—) بالإعتراض A /a/ lrnd. by objecting (to).

bil'ittifak (...—) بالإتفاق A lrnd. unanimously.

bil'ittihad (...—) بالإتحاد A lrnd. unitedly, in unison.

bilkasd بالقصد A lrnd. on purpose, designedly.

bilkeşf بالكشف A /ı/ lrnd. on investigation (of), having investigated.

Bilkis (.—) بقيس A same as **Belkis**.

bilkuvve بالقوه A lrnd. virtual, potential; virtually, potentially.

bilkülliye (..—.) بالكلّيه A lrnd. totally, entirely.

billâh (.—), **billâhi** (.'—.) بالله ، **billâhil'azîm** (.—..—) بالله العظيم A by God!

billevr بلور A lrnd., same as **billûr**.

billit (.—) بلّيت A lrnd. 1. silent, taciturn. 2. wise, prudent.

billûr (.—) بلّور A 1. rock-crystal. 2. cut-glass. 3. sc. crystal. **— cisim** anat. crystalline lens. **— gibi** 1. very clear (water). 2. very fair and pretty (neck, arms). **B— Köşk** the 'Crystal Palace' (name of a famous collection of fairy tales). **— mühre** calligraphy glass ball for polishing paper. **—cu** maker or seller of cut-glass ware. **—î** (.——) A lrnd. 1. of rock-crystal. 2. of cut glass. 3. like crystal, crystalline. 4. maker or seller of cut-glass ware. **—iye** (.——.) A 1. cut-glass ware. 2. a sweet pastry. **—laş=** chem. to crystallize. **—laşma** crystallization. **—laştır=** to crystallize. **—su** neol., chem. crystalloid.

bilme بلمه . verbal n. of **bil= 2**.

bilmece بلمجه . riddle; puzzle.

bilmemezlikġi بلمزلك . assumed ignorance. **—ten gel=**, **—e vur=** /ı/ to pretend not to know.

bilmerre بالمرّه A lrnd. at once.

bilmez بلمز . who does not know, ignorant. **—den gel=**, **—e vur=** to play the ignorant, to assume an air of ignorance. **—celik** neol., rhet. pretended ignorance as a figure of speech. **—le=** /ı/ neol. to show up the ignorance (of). **—len=** to pretend not to know, to feign ignorance. **—lik** ignorance. **—likten gel=** to pretend ignorance.

bilmukabele (..—..) بالمقابل A in return, in reciprocation; in retaliation.

bilmuvacehe (..—..) بالمواجهه A /ı/ lrnd. by confronting.

bilmünakasa (..—..) بالمناقصه A com. by underbidding.

bilmünasebe (..—..) بالمناسبه A *lrnd.* in this connection.
bilmünavebe (..—..) بالمناوبه A *lrnd.* alternately, by turns.
bilmüşahede (..—..) بالمشاهده A *lrnd.* by observation.
bilmüşavere (..—..) بالمشاوره A *lrnd.* on consultation.
bilmüzakere (..—..) بالمذاكره A *lrnd.* by discussion.
bilsam (.—) بلسام A *var.* of **birsam 2**.
bil'umum (.'.—) بالعموم A in general, on the whole; all.
bilûtfihi (..'.) بلطفه A *lrnd.* by the favor of God.
bilüzum (—.—) بللزوم P *lrnd.* unnecessary.
bilv بلو A *lrnd.* worn out; grown old and experienced.
bilvasıta (.'—..) بالواسطه A indirectly.
bilvekâle (..—.) بالوكاله A *lrnd.* as a substitute, as a proxy.
bilvesile (..—.) بالوسيله A *lrnd.* profiting by the occasion, taking this opportunity.
bilya (.'.) بليه It *same as* **bilye**.
bilyardo (..'.) بليارو It *same as* **bilârdo**.
bilye (.'.) بليه [bilya] 1. *children's game* marble. 2. *mech.* ball of a ball bearing. —li yatak *mech.* ball bearing.
bilyet بليت, **bilyeto** (..'.) بليتو It *obs.* ticket.
bilyon بليون F a thousand million, (U.S.) billion.
bim (—) بيم P *lrnd.* 1. fear, dread, terror. 2. danger.
bimağz (—.) بيمغز P *lrnd.* brainless, stupid, inconsiderate.
bimahal[li] (—..) بيمحل P *lrnd.* out of place.
bima'na (—.—) بيمعنا P *lrnd.* absurd, unreasonable, meaningless.
bima'nahu (..—.) بمعناه A *lrnd.* having the same meaning, the same, ditto.
bimanend (——.) بيمانند P *lrnd.* peerless, unmatched.
bimar (——) بيمار P 1. *lrnd.* sick, ill. 2. *poet.* languishing (eye). —ciğer (——..) P *poet.* sick at heart. —çeşm (——..) P languid-eyed. —dar (———) P attendant on the sick, nurse. —dil (——.) P *poet.* sick at heart.
bimare (——.) بيماره P *lrnd.* sick, infirm, ill.
bimarhane (———.) بيمارخانه P *archaic* 1. hospital. 2. lunatic asylum.
bimarhiz (———) بيمارخيز P *lrnd.* convalescent.

bimari (———) بيماری P *lrnd.* sickness, infirmity. —i barik tuberculosis.
bimaristan (———.—) بيمارستان P *lrnd.* 1. hospital. 2. lunatic asylum.
bimarpursi (———.—) بيمارپرسی P *lrnd.* visitation of the sick.
bimaye (———.) بيمايه P *lrnd.* poor, indigent.
bimeal[li] (—.—) بيمآل P *lrnd.* absurd, senseless.
bimecal[li] (—.—) بيمجال P *lrnd.* impotent, powerless, weak.
bimekân (—.—) بيمكان P *lrnd.* homeless.
bimer (—.) بيمر P *lrnd.* innumerable, countless.
bimerhamet (—...) بيمرحمت P *lrnd.* pitiless, ruthless.
bimeze (—..) بيمزه P *lrnd.* insipid, tasteless.
bimihr (—.) بيمهر P *lrnd.* unkind, loveless.
biminnet[ti] (—..) بيمنت P *lrnd.* 1. who does not remind one offensively of favors conferred, gracious. 2. not accompanied with any offensive taunt; not implying an obligation, disinterested. 3. without the necessity of asking, without entreaty.
bimisal[li] (—.—), **bimisl** (—.—) بيمثل بيمثال P *lrnd.* incomparable, unequalled, peerless, nonpareil.
bimnak[ki] (——) بيمناك P *poet.* afraid, frightened.
bimuhaba (—.——) بيمحابا P *lrnd.* fearlessly, unrestrainedly, impertinently.
bimübalât (—.——) بيمبالات P *lrnd.* carelessly, inconsiderately.
bimüdanî (—.——) بيمدانی P *lrnd.* matchless.
bimürüvvet (—...) بيمروت P *lrnd.* ungenerous.
bin 1 بيك thousand. —de per thousand. —lerce, —lerle thousands of. — belâ ile with the greatest difficulty. — belâdan artakalmış gone through many adventures. — bir a great many, all kinds of. —de bir scarcely, very rarely. — bir ayak bir ayak üstüne a closely packed crowd. B— bir direk the cistern of the thousand columns at Istanbul. B— bir Gece Masalları The Arabian Nights stories. —i bir paraya abundant, very many. — can ile with heart and soul. — dereden su getir= to make all sorts of excuses. — göz otu*. — işçiye bir başçı There must be generals, too. — işit bir söyle! *proverb* Listen much, say little. — kat manifold; much. — nasihatten bir musibet yeğdir *proverb* One bad experience is better than many words of

counsel. — **ölçüp bir biçmeli** Check the length before you cut the cloth. **—i bir paraya** a great many, very numerous. **— renge gir=** to use a thousand subterfuges. **— pişman ol=** to be very sorry, to regret greatly. **— tarakta bezi ol=** /ın/ to have many projects at once. **—in yarısı beşyüz** Half of a thousand is five hundred (said to a brooding person, with the meaning: You don't gain anything by thinking too hard.) **— yaşa!** May you live a thousand years!, Long life to you! **— yıl günahkâr, bir gün tövbekâr** Repentance makes up for many years of sin.

bin=er 2 بنمك. /a/ 1. to mount, get upon, embark, board. 2. to ride (a horse, a bicycle, in a car, to travel (on a boat)). 3. to overlap. 4. to be added (to). **—diği dalı kes=** to cut the ground from under one's own feet.

bin 3 بن A *lrnd.* son of, *as in* **Ahmed bin Mehmed** Ahmed, the son of Mehmed.

-bin 4 (—) بين P *lrnd.* seeing, that sees, *e. g.*, **cihanbin, hurdebin 2.**

bin 5 (—) بن A *lrnd.* region, district.

bina 1 (.—) بناء A 1. building, edifice, structure; ship on the stocks. 2. *Arabic gram.* form; indeclinability of the termination (of Arabic words); indeclinable Arabic word. 3. *lrnd.* construction; a nourishing the body (food); a constructing (a poem) on a given rhyme. 4. *can. law* consummation of marriage. **— emini** *Ott. hist.* official in charge of constructions. **— et=** /ı/ 1. to build, construct. 2. /ı,a/ to base (upon). **—i Hak** *lrnd.* God's creature. **— vergisi** house tax.

bînâ 2 (——) بينا. P *lrnd.* 1. seeing. 2. perceiving, sagacious.

binaberan (.—.—), **binaberin** (.—.—) بناً برين بناً بران. P *lrnd.* because of that, therefore.

binadil (——.) بينا دل. P *lrnd.* whose heart perceives the truth.

binaen (.—.) بناءً A /a/ *lrnd.* in consequence (of). **—alâzâlik, —aleyh** consequently, therefore.

binager (.—.) بناگر P *lrnd.* builder.

binagûş (.——) بناگوش var. of **bünagûş.**

binam (——) بی نام P *lrnd.* nameless, anonymous.

binamaz (—.—) بی نماز P 1. one who does not perform the daily worship. 2. *can. law* precluded from the daily worship on account of canonical uncleanness.

binasib (—.—) بی نصیب P *lrnd.* destitute, poor.

binaullah (.—.—) بناء الله A *lrnd.* God's creature.

binayi (———) بنایی. P *lrnd.*, *abstr. n.* of **bînâ 3.**

binayirefte (———..) بینایی رفته. P *lrnd.* whose sight is gone, blind.

binazîr (—.—) بی نظیر. P *lrnd.* matchless, unequalled.

binbaşı بك باشى. 1. *mil.* major. 2. *navy* commander. 3. *air force* squadron leader. **—lık** rank of major.

binbirdelik otunu بك بر دلك اوتی St. John's wort, *bot.*, *Hypericum perforatum.*

bincişkki بنجشك P *lrnd.* sparrow.

bindallı بك دالی purple velvet embroidered with silver thread.

bindir=r بندرمك. 1. /ı,a/ *caus. of* **bin= 2.** 2. /a/ to collide (with), to ram, to run (into). **—il=** *pass. of* **bindir=.** **—ilmiş kıt'a** motorized troops. **—iş** *verbal. n.*

bindirme بندرمه 1. *verbal n. of* **bindir=.** 2. characterized by overlapping or resting on another thing. 3. *arch.* corbel. **— limanı** *mil.* port of embarkation. **— rampası** loading ramp.

binefsihi (.´..) بنفسه. A *lrnd.* 1. of himself; spontaneous. 2. personally, in person.

binekgi 1 بنك saddle beast; used for riding on. **— arabası** cab, carriage. **— atı, — beygiri, — hayvanı** saddle horse. **— taşı** horse block.

binekki 2 (—.) بنك. P *lrnd.* pupil of the eye.

binemekki (—..) بی نمك. P *lrnd.* unseasoned; insipid, saltless, tasteless.

binende (—..) بیننده P *lrnd.* 1. that sees, possessed of sight; beholder. 2. eye. 3. provident, sagacious. 4. who looks (for), hopes, expects. **—gi** (—..—) P *abstr. n.*

bineng (—.) بی تنگ P *lrnd.* shameless, disreputable.

biner بیڭر. a thousand each.

bineva (—.—) بی نوا. P *lrnd.* 1. poor, destitute; beggar. 2. silent. **—i** (—.——) P, **—lık** (—.—.) *abstr. n.*

bineyitdi بنه گیت Gk *prov.* board with hollows for carrying bread to and from the oven.

bingân (—.) بنگان. P *same as* **pingân.**

Bingazi (.——) بنغازی. *geog.* Benghazi.

bingeş=ir بنگشمك *prov.* 1. to ride together on one horse. 2. to mount on one another, to get on top of one another.

bingöz otunu بنگوز اوتی. scammony, *bot.*, *Convulvulus Scammonia.*

bini 1 بنی. *prov.* 1. *verbal n. of* **bin= 2.** 2. anything mounted or ridden. 3. lath overlapping the edge of a door/wing. **—ye gel=, —ye yara=** to be adapted to riding; to be fit to be ridden.

bini 2 (——) بینی. P *lrnd.* 1. nose.

2. snout. 3. tip, point. 4. promontory, cape; projecting edge of a mountain.
binici بینیجی ٬ بنجی rider; good horseman. **—lik** horsemanship, horse-riding. **—lik okulu** riding school.
binihaye, binihayet (—.—.) بہ نہایہ ٬ بینہایہ P *lrnd.* endless, infinite.
binil=[lr] بینلك ٬ بنلك *pass. of* **bin**= 2.
bininci بکنجی the thousandth.
biniş 1 بینیش ٬ بنش ٬ بینش ٬ بنش
1. *verbal n. of* **bin**= 2. 2. *Ott. hist.* a riding in state. **—i humayun** the Sultan's riding in state.
biniş 2 بینش It *Ott. hist.* long cloak worn by certain dignitaries.
biniş 3 (—.) بینش P *lrnd.* vision, sight.
binişan (—.—) بی نشان P *lrnd.* without mark, without trace.
binit[dl] بنت ٬ بنت. *prov.* saddle beast. **—li** rider.
biniyaz (—.—) بینیاز P *lrnd.* independent, self-sufficient.
binlik[ği] بیكلك 1. a thousand-lira note. 2. large wine bottle holding 1000 drams. **— tesbih** rosary of 1000 beads.
binme بنمه. 1. *verbal n. of* **bin**= 2. 2. overlapping.
binnefs بالنفس A *lrnd.* in person, personally.
binnetice (..—.) بالنتیجه A *lrnd.* consequently, as a result.
binnisbe بالنسبه A *lrnd.* relatively.
bint بنت A *lrnd.* 1. daughter, girl; daughter of, *e. g.,* **Ayşe bint Hasan** Ayşe, the daughter of Hasan. 2. doll. **—i amm** the daughter of one's paternal uncle. **—i lebun** she-camel two years old. **—i mıhaz** she-camel entering its second year. **—iyet** (.—.) daughterhood, daughterly state.
bintülcebel بنت الجبل. A *lrnd.* echo.
bintülfikr بنت الفكر. A *lrnd.* 1. thought. 2. poetry.
bintülhabiye (..—..) بنت الحابیه. A,
bintül'ineb بنت العنب A *poet.* wine.
bintüşşefe بنت الشفه. A *poet.* word, speech.
binye بنیه. *var. of* **bünye**.
bipayan (———) بی پایان P *lrnd.* infinite, endless, immense.
biper u bal[li] (—. . —) بی پر و بال P *lrnd.* destitute, without resources.
biperva (—.—) بی پروا P intrepid, fearless; without scruple, fearlessly.
bir 1 بر. 1. one; a, an; unique; one, same, equal, alike. 2. once. 3. only, mere; merely; just. 4. so, in such a way. **— abam var atarım nerde olsa yatarım** It is all the same to me; can stay anywhere. **— ağızdan** in unison, with one voice. **— ağızdan çıkan bir orduya yayılır** Rumors start from a single tongue. **— alay** a great quantity, a large number. **— an evvel** as soon as possible. **— ara** for a moment, *as in,* **toplantı esnasında o bir ara içeri girdi** While the meeting was going on he came in for a moment. **— arada** 1. all together. 2. at the same time. **— araya gel**= to come together; to come at the same time, to clash. **— araba söz** a load of words, unnecessary talk. **— aralık** *same as* **bir ara**. **— atımlık barutu kal**=, **— atımlık barutu ol**= to have only very little left (resources). **— avuç** a handful. **— baba dokuz oğlu besler, dokuz oğul bir babayı besliyemez** *proverb* One father feeds nine sons; nine sons cannot feed one father. **— bakıma** in one way, in one respect. **— baş** *prov.* straight on, directly. **— başına** all alone, all by oneself. **—e bin kat**= to exaggerate, to make much of a trifle. **— bir** one by one. **— boy** once. **— cihetten** in one way, in a way. **— çala** *prov.* for an instant. **— çırpıda** at one stretch, without interruption, at once. **— çiçekle yaz olmaz** *proverb* One blossom does not make a summer. **— çift sözüm var** /a/ I have a word or two to say (to). **— çöplükte iki horoz ötmez** *proverb* Two cocks cannot crow on one dunghill. **— daha**, **— dahi** 1. once more, once again. 2. one more. **— dalda durma**= to be fickle, to change constantly. **— damla** 1. very little. 2. very small (child). **— de** in addition, also. **— dediğini iki etme**= /ın/ to do everything another person asks for, to fulfill every wish (of). **— defa** once. **— defalık** for once only. **— deli bir kuyuya taş atmış, kırk akıllı çıkaramamış** *proverb* One fool threw a stone into a well; forty wise men could not get it out. **— derece** to a certain degree. **— dereceli intihap** *pol.* direct election. **— deri bir kemik** very thin, only skin and bones. **— dirhem et bin ayıp örter** One ounce of plumpness covers a thousand defects. **— dokun bin ah dinle kâse-i fağfurdan** When you come to know people, you find that they have their own troubles. **— düziye** continuously, incessantly. **— elden idare edil**= to be under one administration. **— elle verdiğini öbür elle al**= to give with one hand and take with the other. **— eyyam** for a while. **— gel**= to come out even. **— getir**= /ı/ to bring out even. **— gömlekten baş çıkar**= to put shoulder to shoulder, to join hands, to cooperate. **— gör**= /ı/ to regard as equal, not to discriminate. **— gözü gül**= to have mixed feelings. **— gözü kör, bir kulağı sağır et**= to make oneself half deaf and blind. **— gûna** a kind; any kind. **— gün** one day; some day. **— gün evvel** as soon as

possible. — **günün beyliği beylik** Better to enjoy oneself for one day than not at all. — **hoş** strange, queer. — **hoş ol=** to feel embarrassed. — **içim su** very pretty woman. — **içim suya git=** to sell very cheap. — **iki** one or two, very few. — **iki demeden** at once; quickly, without hesitating. — **iki derken** then all of a sudden; suddenly. — **ipte iki cambaz oynamaz** Two cunning men cannot play tricks on one another. — **iştir oldu** It is too bad, but what has happened has happened. — **kalemde** at once, at one effort. — **kapıya çık=** to come to the same thing. — **kararda,** — **karar üzere** unvaryingly, in the same state. — **kat daha** twice as much; still more. — **kere** 1. once. 2. for once. — **kerecik** just once. — **koşu** at one stretch, quickly. — **koyundan iki post çıkmaz** proverb One cannot get two hides out of one sheep. — **Köroğlu bir Ayvaz** just husband and wife (and no one else). — **kötünün yedi mahalleye zararı var** proverb One bad person harms seven districts. — **kulağından girip öbüründen çık=** to go in one ear and out the other. — **lokma bir hırka** (lit., a mouthful of bread and a coat) living modestly. — **miktar** a little, some. — **misli art=** to double. — **nice** a good many. — **o kadar da** the same amount. — **ol=** to join forces, to unite. — **oldu amma pir oldu** It has happened only once, but properly. — **olmuş ki** She is in a very bad state. — **örnek** of a pattern, the same. — **paralık et=** /1/ to disgrace. — **parça** 1. a little, a bit; a moment. 2. one piece, a whole. — **sıçrarsın çekirge, iki sıçrarsın çekirge, üçüncüde girersin ele** (lit. O grasshopper, you may jump once, you may jump twice, but at the third jump you will be caught.) You can't always trust to luck. — **sıkımlık canı ol=** to be very frail. — **sürçen atın başı kesilmez** proverb They do not behead the horse for stumbling once. — **sürü** heaps of, lots of. — **şey** something. — **şeyler** something or other, a lot of things. — **şeye benzeme=** to be very bad. — **şey değil** Don't mention it; you are welcome. — **şeyler ol=** to become strange; to put on airs. — **şeye yarama=** to be good for nothing. — **tahtada** at once, at one effort. — **takrip,** — **takrip ile** somehow, in some way. — **tarafa bırak=** /1/ to put on one side. — **tarikle** obs. by some means. — **taşla iki kuş vur=** to kill two birds with one stone. — **tuhaf ol=** to feel strange, to have a strange sensation. — **tut=** /1/ to regard as equal, not to discriminate. — **türlü** 1. somehow, in one way or another. 2. with negative verb in no way. 3. after conditional clause just as bad, e. g., **gitsem bir türlü, gitmesem bir türlü** Whether I go or not, it is just as bad. — **uğurdan** archaic 1. all together. 2. all at once. — **vakit,** — **vakitler** at one time. — **var bir yok** at one moment there, at the next not; transitory. — **varmış bir yokmuş** 1. in fairy tales once upon a time. 2. It is past and gone. — **voltalı** naut. second futtock. — **yana** aside from, apart from, e. g., **bütün bunlar bir yana** aside from all this. — **yastığa baş koy=** to be husband and wife. — **yastıkta koca=** to have a long life together (husband and wife). — **yaşıma daha girdim** I am very much surprised; we live and learn! — **yiyip bin şükret=** to be very thankful. — **yol** prov. once. — **yola çık=** to come to the same thing. — **zaman,** — **zamanlar** at one time.

bir^rri 2 بِرّ A lrnd. 1. righteousness, piety, performance of duty. 2. kindness, favor; present, gift, bounty. 3. the mercy and grace of God. 4. future bliss, the joys of heaven; heaven. 5. truth, truthfulness, faithfulness, honesty.

bi'r 3 بِئْر A lrnd. well, pit.

bira 1 (.'.) بيرَه. It beer. — **fabrikası** brewery. — **mayası** barm, yeast.

bira 2 (.—) بِرَا A lrnd., pl. of **berî 2**.

birader (.—.) بِرَادَر P 1. brother. 2. old fellow! — **ender** lrnd. stepbrother, half brother. — **hande** lrnd. adopted brother. — **i rızai** lrnd. foster brother. — **âne** (.—.—.) P lrnd. brotherly, fraternal. — **î** (.—.—) P, — **lik** (.—..) lrnd. fraternity, brotherhood. — **zade** (.—.—.) P brother's child.

birah (——) بِيراه P lrnd. 1. roadless. 2. gone astray. 3. dissolute, unprincipled.

birahane (..—.) بِيرَخَانَه beerhouse.

birahe (——.) بِيرَهِ P lrnd. 1. blind alley. 2. place where there is no road or path.

birahi (———) بِيرَهِى P lrnd. 1. roadlessness. 2. deviation from the right way. 3. state of excommunication. 4. action contrary to faith or rule; infraction; impropriety.

birahm (—.) بِىرَحْم P lrnd. merciless, cruel.

birasya (..'.) بِراسْيَا It same as **prasya**.

biraz 1 بِرَاز a little, some. — **dan** in a little while; a little later.

biraz 2 (.—) بِرَاز A lrnd. 1. a warrior's advancing out of the ranks to meet a foe in single combat. 2. a going forth alone to ease nature.

birbir- بِرْبِر only with possessive suffix each other, e. g., **birbirimizi tanıyoruz** We know each other. **birbirinize bakınız** Look at each other. **birbirinden öğrendiler** They learned from one another. **birbirlerini anlamıyorlar** They do not understand each other.

—inin ağzına tükürmüşler gibi as though they had decided to say exactly the same thing. —i ardınca one after the other. —ine düş= to start quarrelling. —ine düşür= /ı/ to set at loggerheads. —ine geç= 1. to start quarrelling. 2. to get entangled. —ine gir= 1. to start quarrelling. 2. to be stirred up. —inin gözünü çıkar= to fight bitterly. —inin gözünü oy= to be at daggers drawn with one another. —ine kat= /ı/ to set at loggerheads. —ini takip eden successive.

bircilikᵍⁱ neol., phil. monism.
bircinsten ہمجنست homogeneous.
Bircis (.—) برجيس A lrnd. 1. the planet Jupiter. 2. she-camel abounding with milk.
birçenekliler neol., bot., Monocotyledoneae.
birçenetli neol., bot. univalve.
birçokᵍᵘ بیرچوق many, a lot (of).
birden بردن 1. at once, suddenly. 2. at a time, in one lot.
birdenbire (.'..) بردن بر suddenly.
birdirbir بردربر children's game leapfrog.
birdun (.—) بردون P lrnd. violent, mettlesome stallion.
bire بره prov. 1. same as be 2. 2. exclamation of surprise oh!, ah!
birebir (.'.) بربر most efficacious (remedy).
biregü بركو archaic someone, somebody; another.
bireh (—.) بره P var. of birah.
Birehmen برهمن var. of Berehmen.
birekᵏⁱ برك A lrnd., pl. of birke.
bireng (—.) برنك P lrnd. 1. colorless. 2. spotless. 3. the uncolored outline or sketch of a picture. 4. myst. the divine essence. —î (—.—) P colorlessness.
birer برر one each, one apiece. — birer singly, one by one. — ikişer one or two each.
bireşim neol. synthesis. —sel synthetic.
Biretülfürat (—...—) بيرة الفرات A archaic the town of Birejik.
birevcikli neol., bot. monoecious.
birey 1 (—.) بیرأى P lrnd. imprudent.
birey 2 neol. individual. —cilik individualism. —leme phil. individuation. —leştir= /ı/ to individualize. —lik individuality. —sel individual adj.
birez برز prov., var. of biraz 1. —ce a little.
Birgevi (..—) برگوى lrnd. man born in Birgi.
birgez ('.) برگز archaic once, one time. —den all at once, all together. —in once, at one time.
biriⁿⁱ برى one of them; one person, someone, e. g., **biri geldi** Someone came. **biri gider biri gelir** One goes; the other comes. —birini one another, each other. — yer biri bakar, kıyamet ondan kopar When there are haves and have-nots, a clash is unavoidable.
biricikᵍⁱ بریجك 1. unique, the only. 2. archaic once, only once.
biriçᶜⁱ بریچ E card games bridge.
birikᵍⁱ **1** بریك E naut. brig (two-masted square-rigged vessel).
birik=ⁱʳ **2** بریكمك 1. to come together, to assemble; to accumulate; to collect, to form a puddle, a mass, a heap. 2. archaic to unite. —inti assemblage; accumulation; mass. —me verbal n. of birik=. —tir= /ı/ to gather, assemble; to collect; to accumulate, to save up (money). —tiril= pass. of biriktir=.
birim neol. unit.
birin birin برن برن archaic one by one.
birinc برنج P same as pirinç 1, 2. —i Kâbülî the fruit of Embelia ribes.
birincasf (..—) برنجاسف P lrnd. mugwort, bot., Artemisia vulgaris.
birinci برنجى 1. the first. 2. first quality. — elden com. at first hand. — ferik hist. lieutenant general. — gel= to be first (in a race). — hamur best quality paper. B— Kânun December. — kaptan naut. captain. — mevki first class (in a train etc.), cabin class (on a ship). — mülâzim first lieutenant. B— Teşrin October. — zabit navy officer next in rank to the captain. — zaman geol. paleozoic era. — zar bot. primine.
birincil neol. primary.
birincilikᵍⁱ برنجيلك first rank, first place, championship.
biring برنك P lrnd. kind of myrobalan.
birisiⁿⁱ بریسى same as biri.
biriskᵏⁱ بریسك F card games brisque.
birişte بریشته P lrnd. fried, grilled, roasted, baked.
biriya (—.—) بریا P lrnd. sincere; sincerely.
biriyantin بریانتین [briyantin] brilliantine.
birizola (...) بریزولا It same as pirzola.
birkaç برقاج a few, some, several.
birke برکه A lrnd. 1. pool; cistern. 2. breast; the part of a camel's breast that rests on the ground when he crouches at rest. 3. can. law relatives entitled to compensation in a case of manslaughter. —i lâciverd poet. sky.
birleş=ⁱʳ **1** برلك /ı/ to make one; to believe in the unity (of). —n= to become one.
birle 2 برله archaic with.
birleş=ⁱʳ برلشمك to unite; to meet; to agree. —en geom. concurrent. —ek neol., anat. commissure. —ik united, joint. B—ik Amerika Devletleri United States of America. B—ik Arap Cumhuriyeti United Arab

Republic. —im *verbal n. of* **birleş=**, union, *com. law* consolidation. —**me değeri** *chem.* valence. **B—miş Milletler** United Nations. —**tir=** /ı/ *caus. of* **birleş=**. —**tirme borusu** *mech.* joint, coupling.

birlet=ᵗʳ بر لنّت. /ı/ *caus. of* **birle=** 1. —**il=** *pass.*

birli بر لى. card games ace.

birlikᵍⁱ بر لك. 1. unity, oneness; accord. 2. sameness; identity; equality; similarity. 3. union; association; corporation; *mil.* unit. 4. one (piaster or lira) piece. 5. *mus.* whole (note). —**te** together, in company. —**te çalış=** to cooperate, to collaborate. —**te dâva** *law* joinder of parties. —**te hareket** *mil.* combined operation. —**te kefil** *law* joint surety. —**te öğretim** coeducation. —**te sigorta** joint insurance. —**siz** disunited, divided.

Birmanya (..´.) بىرمانيا. It Burma. —**lı** Burmese.

biro, birov بر و. بر و. Hung *Ott. hist.* village mayor.

birreca (..—) بالرجاء A /ı/ *lrnd.* 1. requesting. 2. hoping (for).

birrefah velbenin (..—..—) بالرفاه والبنين A *lrnd.* with happiness and children! (Arabic congratulation on marriage).

birrıza (..—) بالرّضاء A *lrnd.* willingly.

birrivaye (..—.) بالرّوايه A *lrnd.* according to report.

birsam (.—) برسام A 1. *psych.* hallucination. 2. *lrnd.* pleurisy.

birtakım بر طاقم some, a certain number of.

birterimli *neol.*, algebra monomial.

birteviye (.´...) برتوى. *var. of* **biteviye**.

biruh (——) بىروح *P lrnd.* lifeless, soulless.

birun (——) بىرون, (.—) برون *P lrnd.* 1. out; outer, exterior; outside the exterior surface (of a thing); the exterior (of a person or thing). 2. /dan/ more, exceeding, surpassing. 3. the public apartments of an Eastern house. 4. *Ott. hist.* central public administration with offices outside the Palace.

biruni (———) بىرونى *P lrnd.* 1. external. 2. the outside. 3. excluded.

biruyi (———) بىروىى *P lrnd.* shamelessness.

biruz 1 (——) بىروز *P* unfortunate.

biruz 2 (——) بىروز *P lrnd.* beryl.

bir zec (——.) بىرزع A *lrnd.* turquoise.

biruzi (———) بىروزى *P lrnd.* 1. destitute of daily bread. 2. misfortune.

birümmetiha (..´...—) برتها, **birümmetihi** (..´....) برتنه A *lrnd.* with all its appurtenances, entirely.

biryan (.—) بىريان *P lrnd.* roasted, broiled, fried or baked food.

biryedim بىريديم strawberry tree, *bot.*, *Arbutus unedo*.

birze, birzed (—.) بىرزد. بىرزه *P pharm.* galbanum.

birzevn بىرزون. A *lrnd.* common work horse, not of Arabian blood.

bisaman (———) بىسامان *P lrnd.* poor, destitute.

bisan (——) بىسان *P lrnd.* matchless, unequalled.

bisat (.—) بساط A *lrnd.* 1. mat; carpet; bed; cushion. 2. cloth or leather chess board. 3. office or selling stand improvised by spreading out a mat, carpet, etc. —**ı felek** the terrestrial globe. —**ı hâk** *poet.* the surface of the earth. —**i kevn u mekân** the whole world, the universe. —**ı setrenc** chessboard.

bisati (.——) بساطى A *lrnd.* 1. seller of mats, carpets, etc. 2. peddler, stallkeeper.

bi'se بئس A *lrnd.* how bad!, how miserable!

bisebat (—.—) بىثبات *P lrnd.* inconsistent, frivolous.

bisebeb (—..) بىسبب *P lrnd.* unmotivated, having no cause.

biser 1 (—.) بىسر *P lrnd.* 1. headless. 2. vagabond. — **ü bün** with no head or tail, nonsense. — **ü pa** totally destitute. — **ü saman** destitute, miserable.

biser 2 (—.) بىسر *P lrnd.* kind of hawk.

biserakᵏⁱ (—.—) بىسراك *P lrnd.*, *same as* **besirek**.

bisere (—..) بىسره *P var. of* **biser 2**.

biserekᵍⁱ بىسرك *same as* **besirek**.

bi'set بعثت A *lrnd.* mission.

bisiklet بىسكلت F bicycle. — **bölüğü** *mil.* cycle corps.

biskivi, bisküvit بىسكوى F biscuit, cracker.

bismi- بسم A *in rel. formulae* in the name of, e. g., **bismişah** (..—) Bektashi order of dervishes in the name of the King (i. e. Ali).

bismil بسمل *P* 1. *archaic* clean, pure. 2. *lrnd.* slaughtered in the name of God (for food); slain. 3. *lrnd.* long-suffering; meek, gentle.

bismilgâh (..—) بسملگاه, **bismilgeh** بسملگه *P* 1. *lrnd.* slaughterhouse, butchery. 2. *poet.* place where a lover is exposed to cruel treatment by his love.

bismillâh, bismillâhi (..—), (..—´.) بسم الله A in the name of God. — **de=**, — **ile başla=** to start an undertaking by invoking the name of God.

bismillahirrahmanirrahim (..—..—..—) بسم الله الرحمن الرحيم A *rel. formula* in the name of God, the Compassionate, the Merciful.

bismilşüde بسم شده P poet. sacrificed, slaughtered.
bist (—) بیست P lrnd. twenty.
bistah (——) بسناع P lrnd. 1. rash, dauntless, bold. 2. impudent, insolent.
bistam (.—) بسّام P lrnd. red coral.
bistar (——) بسنار P lrnd., only in **bastar u bistar**.
bistegânî (—.——) بستگانی P lrnd. allowance paid on the 29th of each month.
bister بستر P lrnd. bed, mattress, pillow.
bisteraheng (..—.) بسترآهنگ P lrnd. coverlet, quilt.
bisturi بستوری F surg. bistoury.
bistüm (—.), **bistümin** (—.—) بستمین بستم P twentieth.
bisud (——) بسود P lrnd. useless, purposeless; in vain.
bisükûn (—.—) بسکون P lrnd. restless, peaceless.
Bisütun (—.—) بستون P 1. name of d mountain in Persia. 2. poet. the heavens.
bisyar (.—) بسیار P lrnd. much, numerous; very; often. —**ber** (.—.) P very fruitful. —**gû** (.——) P talkative, garrulous. —**husp** (.—.) P slothful, lethargic. —**î** (.——) P plenty, abundance. —**kes** (.—.) P who has many friends or dependents.
biş 1 بش archaic, var. of **beş**.
biş 2 (—) بش P /dan/ lrnd. more, other; excess.
biş 3 بيش A, P lrnd. monkshood, bot., Aconitum Napellus.
biş=ᵉʳ **4** بشّك prov., var. of **piş**= 2.
bişaibe (——..) بی شائبه P lrnd. 1. without doubt. 2. pure, immaculate, without blemish.
bişaret (.—.) بشارت var. of **beşaret 1**.
bişbaha (.—.) بش بها P lrnd. high-priced, valuable, precious.
bişbahar (—.—) بش بهار P lrnd. house-leek, bot., Sempervivum tectorum.
bişe (—.) بيشه P lrnd. forest, wood, thicket.
bişekᵏᵏⁱ (—.) بی شك P lrnd. without doubt, doubtless. — **ü şüphe** unquestionably, undoubtedly.
bişekib (—.—) بشکیب P lrnd. impatient.
bişekilᵏˡⁱ (—..) بشکل chem. amorphous.
bişerm (—.) بی شرم P lrnd. shameless, indecent.
bişi 1 بشی prov. kind of pastry.
bişi 2 بيشی P lrnd. excess, increase. [/biş/ see /piş/.]
bişkel, bişkele, bişkine بشكل P lrnd. skeleton key, crook used for opening and locking the bolt of a door.

bişkûlˡⁱⁱ (.—) بشکول P lrnd. intelligent; expeditious, assiduous.
bişmuş (——) بيش موش P lrnd. mouse, feeding on monkshood and whose flesh is an antidote to that poison.
bişr بشر A lrnd. cheerfulness of countenance.
bişter (—.) بيشتر P /dan/ lrnd. more, still more.
bişuur (—.—) بی شعور P lrnd. unconscious; thoughtless.
bişümar (—.—) بی شمار P lrnd. innumerable.
bişüphe (—..) بی شبهه P lrnd. doubtless.
bit 1 بت 1. louse, zool., Pediculus. 2. louse, parasite on plants or animals. —**i kanlan**= to become well off. — **otu** lousewort, bot., Pediculus. — **pazarı** used goods market. — **sirkesi** nit. — **yeniği** doubtful point, tender spot, hidden blemish.
bit=ᵉʳ **2** بتمك 1. to end, come to an end; to be settled. 2. to be all gone; to be exhausted; to be ruined; to be very frightened. 3. /a/ colloq. to be fascinated (by).
bit=ᵉʳ **3** بتمك 1. to grow, sprout. 2. archaic to come into existence.
bita (.'.) بطا It naut. bitt. —**ya vur**= /ı/ to bitt, to put around a bitt.
bitab (——) بی تاب P same as **bitap**. — **u takat** utterly exhausted. —**i** (———) P fatigue, tiredness, exhaustion.
bitah (.—) بطاح A lrnd., pl. of **batha**.
bitahammül (—...) بی تحمل P lrnd. impatient.
bitaka (.—.) بطاقة A lrnd. 1. price label. 2. letter sent by a carrier pigeon.
bitakatᵘ (——.) بی طاقت P lrnd. powerless, impotent.
bitaksir (—.—) بی تقصیر P lrnd. without defect, without fail.
bitakva (—.—) بی تقوا P lrnd. unholy; sinful.
bitamamiha (..—'.—) بتماما, **bitamamihi** (..—'..) بتمامه A lrnd. completely.
bitan 1 (.—) بطان A lrnd., pl. of **batin**.
bitan 2 (.—) بطان A lrnd. strap, girth.
bitane (.—.) بطانة A lrnd. 1. lining of a garment. 2. intimate friend, confident. 3. secret.
bitapᵇⁱ (——) بی تاب [bitab] exhausted, feeble. — **düş**= to get exhausted.
bitaraf (—..) بی طرف P neutral; impartial. —**âne** (—..—.) P impartially. —**laştır**= /ı/ to neutralize. —**lık** neutrality.
bite 1 (.'.) بته var. of **bita**.
bite 2 بته var. of **pide**.

bitedbir (—.—) بى تدبير P lrnd. improvident, imprudent.

biteemmül (—...) بى تأمل P lrnd. inconsiderate, thoughtless.

bitefavüt (—.—.) بى تفاوت lrnd. not differing from each other, not in contradiction with each other.

bitehaşi (—.——) بى تحاشى P lrnd. fearlessness, rashness.

bitehevvür (—...) بى تحور P lrnd. cool, prudent, cautious.

bitek[si] بنك. *prov.* fertile.

bitekellüf (—...) بى تكلف P lrnd. without ceremony; unceremoniously, in a free and easy way.

bitemyiz (—.—) بى تمييز P lrnd. undiscerning, indiscreet.

bitenahi (—.——) بى تناهى P lrnd. endless, infinite.

bitereddüd (—...) بى تردد P lrnd. unhesitating, sure.

bitevakkuf (—...) بى توقف P lrnd. without stopping, incessantly.

bitevfik[ki] (—.—) بى توفيق P lrnd. destined to failure.

bitevi (´...) بتوى 1. continuously, incessantly. 2. *archaic* whole, in one piece. —**ye** (´...) continuously. —**yelik** continuousness.

bitey *neol.* flora.

biti 1 بتى. *prov.* written document; book; notebook; letter.

biti=ᴵʳ 2 بتمك *archaic* to be destined, to be decreed.

bitik[si] 1 بتك. 1. exhausted, worn out, broken down. 2. *slang* in love.

bitik[si] 2 بتك. same as **biti** 1. —**çi** *archaic* secretary.

bitik[si] 3 بتك. *archaic* contiguous.

bitim بتم ending, end. —**li** *neol.* finite. —**siz** *neol.* infinite.

bitir=ᴵʳ 1 بتيرمك. /ı/ 1. to finish, complete, terminate. 2. to accomplish. 3. to exhaust; to kill; to destroy.

bitir=ᴵʳ 2 بتيرمك. *caus.* of **bit**= 3.

bitiril=ᴵʳ بتيريلمك. *pass.* of **bitir**= 1.

bitirim بتيريم. 1. *prov.* end, conclusion. 2. *slang* smart, topping. — **yeri** *slang* gambling den. —**ci** owner of a gambling den.

bitiriş بتيريش. *verbal n.* of **bitir**= 1, 2.

bitirme بتيرمه *verbal n.* of **bitir**= 1, 2. — **pazarı** 1. bargain in the lump. 2. final offer in bargaining, or an offer to close out the remaining stock.

bitirmiş بتيرمش. *colloq.* experienced, versed in all vices; cunning.

bitiş 1 بتش. *verbal n.* of **bit**= 2, 3.

bitiş=ᴵʳ 2 بتشمك. 1. to become contiguous, to join, to grow together. 2. to be contiguous, to adhere.

bitişik[si] بتشك. contiguous, adjacent, joining; attached; next door. — **çanakyapraklı** *bot.* gamosepalous. — **ikizler** Siamese twins. — **kelimeler** two words written together. — **nizam** city planning continuous row system (not semi-detached). — **taçyapraklı** *bot.* gamopetalous. —**lik** contiguity.

bitişim *neol., ling.* agglutination.

bitiştir=ᴵʳ بتشديرمك. /ı/ *caus.* of **bitiş**=. —**il**= *pass.* of **bitiştir**=. —**me** *verbal n.* of **bitiştir**=.

bitit=ᵈᵘʳ بتيدمك *archaic.* to decree, destine, ordain.

bitki 1. *neol.* plant. 2. *prov.* produce, product, yield. — **bitleri** *zool.* phytophthora. —**lenme** *geog.* vegetation. —**msi** plant-like, phytoid. —**msi hayvanlar** *zool., Phytozoa*.

bitkin بتكين. exhausted, worn out, very tired. —**lik** exhaustion.

bitkisel *neol.* vegetable, vegetal.

bitle=ᵉʳ بتله مك. بتلك. 1. /ı/ to delouse, to clear of lice. 2. *slang* to angle for a quarrel. —**n**= 1. to become lousy, to get lice. 2. to clear oneself of lice. —**t**= /ı/ *caus.* of **bitle**=¹.

bitli بتلو. 1. infested with lice, lousy. 2. *slang* penniless. — **baklanın kör alıcısı olur** *proverb* (lit. Wormy horsebeans find a blind buyer.) There will always be someone who cares even for the most unattractive.

bitme بتمه. *verbal n.* of **bit**= 2, 3.

bittabi (´..) بالطبع A lrnd. naturally, of course.

bittahkik (´.—) بالتحقيق A /ı/ lrnd. having investigated, verified.

bittahsis (´.—) بالتخصيص A lrnd. especially, particularly.

bittamam (´.—) بالتمام A lrnd. completely, fully.

bittav بالطوع A lrnd. voluntarily.

bittavassut (´...) بالتوسط A lrnd. upon intervention. — **kabul** *com. law* acceptance supra protest, acceptance for honor. — **tediye** *com. law* payment by intervention.

bitterazi (´.——) بالتراضى A lrnd. by mutual consent.

bittesir (´.—) بالتأثير A elec. by induction.

bitüm بتوم F *min.* bitumen.

bitüvan (—.—) بى توان P lrnd. impotent, weak.

bityare (.—.) بتياره. P *var.* of **petyare**.

biümid (—.—) بى اميد P lrnd. hopeless, desperate.

biüre بيوره F only in — **testi** *biochem.* biuret test.

biv (—) بِو P *lrnd.* moth, worm, maggot.
bivabet (.—.) بوابت A *lrnd.* office and duty of a gatekeeper, usher, or chamberlain.
bivaktü (—.) بی وقت P *lrnd.* untimely, unseasonable.
bivare (——.) بواره P *lrnd.* poor, without weight or influence; destitute, friendless.
bivaye (——.) بوايه P *lrnd.* 1. destitute, poor, deprived. 2. independent, without want. —**gi** (———.) P *abstr. n.*
bivaz (——) بواز P *lrnd.*, bat, *zool.*, *Vespertilio.*
bive (—.) بوه P *lrnd.* 1. widow; widower. 2. stranger; poor, destitute. 3. squirting cucumber, *bot.*, *Ecballium.*
bivefa (—.—) بی وفا P *lrnd.* faithless, insincere, ungrateful. —**î** (—.——) P, —**lık** faithlessness, insincerity.
bivegi (—.—) بوگى P *lrnd.* widowhood.
biver (—.) بور P *lrnd.* myriad, 10,000.
bivezen (—..) بوه زنى P *lrnd.* widow.
bivukuf (—.—) بی وقوف P *lrnd.* ignorant, uninformed.
bivücuddü (—.—) بی وجود P *lrnd.* non-existent.
biyaaʾ بيع A *lrnd.*, *pl. of* **bia** 2.
biyaban (.——) بيابان P *same as* **beyaban**. —**î** (.———) P *lrnd.* wild, savage. —**neverd** (.——..) P *lrnd.* travelling in the desert. —**nişin** (.———.) P *lrnd.* living in the desert; hermit.
biyea (..—) بياعا A *lrnd.*, *pl. of* **beyyi**.
biyel بيل F *mech.* tire-rod, pushrod, crank arm. — **başı** big end.
biyografi بيوغرافى F biography.
biyokimya بيوكيميا [based on **kimya**] biochemistry.
biyoloji بيولوژى F biology.
biyopsi بيوپسى F *med.* biopsy.
biz 1 بز we; *in formal or modest speech* I. —**den** 1. from us; one of us. 2. *slang* sly, crafty. —**ler** we. — **bize** by ourselves, without any strangers in our midst. —**den iyiler** the djinns.
biz 2 بز awl.
biz 3 بز *archaic for* **bez** 1.
bizzʾi 4 بضع A *lrnd.* small number (from 3 to 9).
-**biz** 5 (—) بز P *lrnd.* sifting, *as in* **fitnebiz**.
biz=er 6 بزك *archaic for* **bez**= 3.
biz 7 (—) بيض A *lrnd.*, *pl. of* **beyza** 1, **ebyaz**.
bizaaʾ 1 بضع A *lrnd.*, *pl. of* **bez'a** 2, **biz'a** 2.
biz'a 2 بضعه A *lrnd.*, *var. of* **bez'a** 2.
bizaattü (.——) بضاعت A *lrnd.* 1. dealer's stock in trade; capital. 2. man's stock of ability, capacity, etc.
bizan (——) بيزان A *lrnd.*, *pl. of* **baz** 3.
Bizans بيزانس F Byzantium. —**lı** Byzantine.
bizar 1 (——) بيزار P *lrnd.* 1. tired; weary, disgusted, sick (of). 2. healed, absolved; clear of annoyance. — **et**= to weary, distress. — **ol**= /dan/ 1. to be wearied (by). 2. to be clear (of), free (of).
bizar 2 (.—) بزار A *lrnd.*, *pl. of* **bezr** 1.
bizarî (———) بيزارى P, **bizarlık**kı (——.) بيزارلق. *abstr. n. of* **bizar** 1.
bizatiha (.—ʹ.—) بذاتها A *fem. of* **bizatihi**.
bizatihi (.—ʹ..) بذاته A *lrnd.*, *phil.* in himself, in itself, of itself, by itself.
bizaz (.—) بذاذ A *lrnd.*, *var. of* **bezaz**.
bizazettü (.—.) بذاذت A *same as* **bezazet**.
bizce بزجه according to us, in our opinion, as far as we are concerned.
bizcileyin (ʹ...) بزجيلين *archaic* like us.
bizeban (—.—) بيزبان P *lrnd.* mute, dumb.
bizevallı (—.—) بيزوال P *lrnd.* imperishable.
bizim بزم our; ours. — **için** for us. —**ki** ours.
bizişkki بزشك P *lrnd.* physician, surgeon. —**î** (..—) P medical practice, practice of a surgeon.
biziya (—.—) بيضيا P *lrnd.* dark, obscure, without light.
bizle=r 1 بزله /ı/ to stick an awl into, to pinch with an awl.
bizle 2 بزله A *lrnd.* everyday.
bizlengeçci, **bizlengiç**ci بزلنگيچ *prov.* goad.
bizmut بزموت F *chem.* bismuth. — **kaymağı** nitrate of bismuth.
bizo F *print.* kind of quoin.
bizran (.ʹ) بضرا A *lrnd.* without retaliation (murder).
bizzarure (..—.) بالضروره A *lrnd.* forcedly, by necessity.
bizzat (.ʹ—) بالذات A personally, in person.
blânko (ʹ.) It *com.* blank (check).
blefarit F *path.* blepharitis.
blenoraji F *path.* blennorrhea.
blero F *painting* badger-hair brush; softener, blender.
blokku بلوك F 1. *building* block, concrete block. 2. writing pad. 3. *print.* block, patent block. 4. *pol.* bloc. — **inşaat** construction of apartment buildings in groups. — **usulü** *rail.* block system.
bloke بلوكه F *com.* closed (account); stopped (check). — **et**= /ı/ to close, to stop.
blokhavs E *mil.* blockhouse.
bloknot F memorandum block, writing pad.
blöf بلوف F bluff. — **yap**= to bluff.
bluz بلوز F blouse.

boa F 1. *zool.* boa. 2. feather-boa.
bobin بربين F *phys., mec.* reel; *text.* bobbin, spool; *phot.* roll of film, spool; *elec.* coil. — **kâğıdı** *print.* paper in rolls.
bobstil بربستيل. *slang* dandy; *vulgar* snob.
boca 1 (.'.) بوجه. *var. of* **poca.**
boca (.'.) بوجا in — **et**= /ı/ *colloq.* to turn over, cant over, to tilt.
bocala=ʳ بوجالامـ [**pocala**=] 1. to falter, to act in a confused manner. 2. *same as* **pocala**=.
boci, bocu 1 (.'.) بوجى. *same as* **boca 2.**
bocu 2 بوجو. *prov.* kind of small dog, turnspit dog.
bocukᵍᵘ **1** بوجوك. *prov.* pig, hog. — **kırımı** hog slaughtering.
bocukᵍᵘ **2** بوجوك [**bojuk**] *obs.* Christmas.
bocurgatᵈ¹ بوجورغات. [**boci+ırgat**] *naut.* capstan, crab.
bocurum بوجوروم. Ck *naut.* jigger (sail).
bodoslama بردوسكه Gk 1. *naut.* stempost; sternpost. 2. *slang* nose. —**dan**•*slang* from the front.
bodrum بودروم. بدروم. Gk 1. subterranean vault, dungeon, cellar. 2. *w. cap.* Bodrum, the ancient town of Halicarnassus. — **katı** basement. — **palas** *colloq.* basement.
boduçᶜᵘ بودچ. *prov.* vessel with a handle and spout.
bodukᵍᵘ بردك. *prov.* 1. camel colt. 2. buffalocalf.
bodur بودر. بودور. بوطر short, squat; dwarf. — **çapak** white bream *zool., Blicca bjoerkna.* — **hurma ağacı** dwarf palm, *bot., Chamaerops humilis.* — **meşe** British oak, red oak, *bot., Quercus robur.* — **söğüt** dwarf willow, *bot., Salix herbacea.* — **tavuk her gün piliç** (*lit.* A dwarf hen will always stay a chicken.) Small women always look young. —**lan**= to become short, dwarf, low, squat. —**landır**= /ı/ *caus.* —**luk** shortness of stature.
boğ 1 بغ. *prov.* bundle.
boğ=ᵃʳ **2** بوغمـ /ı/ 1. to choke, strangle. 2. to suffocate. 3. /a/ to drown (in). 4. to constrict by binding. 5. /a/ to overwhelm (with); to conceal (under a flood of words, jokes, etc.) 6. *slang* to cheat, dupe.
boğa بغا. بوغا. 1. bull. 2. *w. cap., astr.,* Taurus. — **dikeni** milk thistle, *bot., Silybum Marianum.* — **döğüşü,** — **güreşi** bullfight. — **yaprağı** fleawort, *bot., Plantago Psyllium.*
boğaça (.'.) بوغاچه. بوغچه *var. of* **poğaça.**
boğada (.'.) بوغاده. It a preparing the laundry with a lixivium, lyeing.
boğanakᵍ¹ بوغاناق *var. of* **boğunak.**

boğasa=ʳ بوغاصه *prov.* to come in heat (cow).
boğası 1 بوغاصى. *prov.* kind of twill; twilled cotton used for linings.
boğası=ʳ **2** بوغاصى. *var. of* **boğursa**=².
boğata (.'.) بوغاطه. بوغاته It *naut.* dead-eye for a lanyard.
boğaz بوغاز. بوغز 1. throat; gullet, esophagus. 2. neck (of a bottle, etc.). 3. *furriery* the fur of the throat. 4. mountain pass. 5. strait; *w. cap.,* the Bosphorus. 6. mouth of a river. 7. food, board, maintenance; a mouth to feed; eating, food; appetite. 8. sore throat. **B—lar** the Straits, the Bosphorus and the Dardanelles. — **aç**= to break up the ground around a tree. —**ı açıl**= to develop an appetite. — **ağrısı** sore throat. — **alan** *prov.* acrid, irritating the throat (food). —**ından artır**= to save money by economy on food. —**ında bırak**= /ı/ to make stick in one's throat (food), to spoil one's enjoyment. — **boğaza gel**= to fly at one another's throats, to have a violent quarrel. —**ını çıkar**= to earn just enough for one's food. — **derdi** the care for one's living. —**ına dizil**= to stick in one's throat (food, because of worry, etc.) — **dokuz boğum** One should know how to hold one's tongue. — **doldur**= to fill up the earth around a plant. —**ına dur**=, —**ında dur**= to stick in one's throat (food; because of worry, etc.) —**ına düşkün** gourmet; fond of good food. —**ı ele ver**= *archaic* to be caught. —**ından geçme**= to stick in one's throat (food, because one has one's dinner spoiled by the absence of someone). **B— hisarı** *hist.* the Castle of the Dardanelles. **B— içi*.** —**a in**= to affect the throat (catarrh). —**ına kadar** up to one's neck. —**ında kal**= *same as* **boğazına dur**=. — **kavgası** struggle for a living. —**ından kes**= *same as* **boğazından artır**=. —**ını kes**= /ın/ to cut the throat (of). **B— kesen*.** —**ı kısıl**= to get a hoarse throat. —**ı kuru**= to get very thirsty. **B—lar meselesi** *pol.* the question of the Straits. — **ol**= to have a sore throat. — **ola!** *colloq.* bon appétit! **B—lar rejimi** *pol.* régime of the Straits. —**ına sarıl**= /ın/ to get at someone's throat. —**ını sık**= /ın/ 1. to throttle, choke. 2. to press hard (for a debt, etc.). —**ı tok** 1. satiated. 2. contented, having no greed. — **tokluğuna** for one's food only (work, service). —**ını yırt**= to shout at the top of one's voice.
Boğaziçiⁿⁱ بوغازايچى. the Bosphorus.
Boğazkesen بوغازكسن *hist.* the castle of Rumeli Hisarı on the Bosphorus.
boğazla=ʳ بوغازلامـ. بغزلمـ /ı/ to slaughter (by cutting the throat). —**ma** *verbal n.* —**n**= *pass. of* **boğazla**=. —**nış,** —**nma** *verbal n.* —**ş**= to cut each other's

throats, to fight violently. —**t=** /ı/ *caus. of* **boğazla=**.
boğazlayan بوغازلیان. 1. slaughterer. 2. cut-throat. 3. *w. cap.*, Bogazlayan (town in the Vilayet of Yozgat).
boğazlayış بوغازلایش. *verbal n. of* **boğazla=**.
boğazlı بوغازلی. 1. great eater; eating much. 2. *w. cap.* native of the Bosphorus.
boğazlıkᵍⁱ بوغازلوٴ. 1. belonging to the throat. 2. belonging to food.
boğazsız بوغازسز. having small appetite; who eats little.
boğça بوغچه. *same as* **bohça**.
Boğdan بوغدان. بغدن Sl 1. *hist.* Moldavia. 2. Bogdan (Slavonic personal name). — **beği** *hist.* prince of Moldavia. —**lı** *hist.* Moldavian.
boğday بغدای. *var. of* **buğday**.
boğdur=ᵘʳ بوغدرمه, بوغدورمه. /ı,a/ *caus. of* **boğ=** 2.
boğma بوغمه. 1. *verbal n. of* **boğ=** 2. 2. strangulated, choked; stifled, smothered, suppressed. 3. *prov.* kind of baggy trousers.
boğmaca بوغماجه, بوغمجه. *path.* croup; *laryngismus stridulus.* — **öksürüğü** whooping-cough, *pertussis.*
boğmakᵍⁱ بوغمق, بوغمهك. 1. node, joint, articulation. 2. *archaic* necklace, collar fitting closely round the neck; wooden or iron collar applied to criminals. 3. *prov.* heavy rain, torrent. — **kemikleri** *anat.* phalanges. —**lı** noded, jointed, knotty. —**lı hayvanlar** *zool.*, Articulata. —**lı kuşu** calandra lark, *zool.*, *Melanocorypha calandra.*
boğmukᵍᵘ بوغموك. *archaic* necklace.
boğucu بوغیجی. suffocating.
boğukᵍᵘ بوغوك. 1. hoarse, raucous. 2. muffled. — **boğuk** 1. hoarsely. 2. with a muffled sound. — **sesli** hoarse-voiced, gruff-voiced. —**lan=** to become hoarse and gruff (voice). —**landır=** /ı/ *caus. of* **boğuklan=**.
boğul=ᵘʳ بوغلمق. 1. *pass. of* **boğ=** 2. 2. to be drowned, to drown. 3. to become hoarse or smothered (voice). 4. *engine of auto.* to be flooded. —**ma, —uş** *verbal n.*
boğum بوغم, بوغوم. 1. knot, joint, node. 2. internode, segment between two joints. 3. *anat.* ganglion. 4. *obs.* inch. — **boğum** divided by articulations, knotty, nodose. —**lama** articulation. —**lan=** to form a joint. —**landır=** /ı/ *caus.* —**lu** having nodes, knotted, jointed. —**luca** somewhat nodose. —**suz** free from nodes, jointless.
boğun 1 بوغن. *prov. var. of* **boğum**.
boğun=ᵘʳ 2 بوغنمق. *archaic* to choke from vexation and the like.
boğunakᵍᵘ بوغناق. *archaic* 1. strangled, suppressed; hoarse, gruff. 2. *same as* **boğmak**³. —**lı** torrential (rain).

boğuntu بوغنتی. 1. oppression, suffocation. 2. *slang* a cheating, duping. —**ya getir=** /ı/ *slang* to squeeze money out (of someone). — **yeri** *slang* gambler's den.
boğursa=ʳ, **boğursı=**ʳ بوغورساماق, بوغورسیماق. *prov.* 1. to come in heat (she-camel). 2. *same as* **boğasa=**.
boğurtlakᵍⁱ بوغرتلاق. *prov.* windpipe, larynx. — **kuşu** *prov., var. of* **bağırtlak**.
boğuş 1 بوغش. *verbal n. of* **boğ=** 2.
boğuş=ᵘʳ 2 بوغشمق. 1. to be involved in a violent fight, to be at each other's throat. 2. to quarrel, fight.
boğuz بوغوز. *archaic for* **boğaz**.
bohça بوغچه, بوحچه. 1. bundle in a wrapper. 2. square wrapper for a bundle. 3. *prov.* square shawl. 4. small bale of fine tobacco. 5. *slang* buttocks. —**sını bağla=** to pack up one's traps. — **baha** *hist.* customary present sent by civil servants in the provinces to their superiors in the capital. — **böreği** kind of bundle-shaped pastry. — **et=** /ı/ to wrap up in a bundle. — **gönder=** *prov.* to send presents in a bundle. —**sını koltuğuna ver=** /ın/ to sack, to fire. —**cı** woman peddler selling female garments, linen, etc. —**la=** /ı/ to wrap up in a bundle. —**lan=** *pass. of* **bohçala=**. —**lat=** /ı,a/ *caus. of* **bohçala=**.
bohur بوهر. *same as* **buğur** 1.
bojukᵍᵘ بوژوك. Sl *obs.* Christmas.
bokᵏᵘ بوق. *vulg.* 1. dung, feces, excrement, ordure. 2. dirt, rubbish; worthless, bad. 3. *min.* scoria, dross. —**tan** made of rubbish, worthless, bad. — **at=** /a/ to throw dirt (on), to slander. —**a bas=** to get into a mess. —**u bokuna** in vain, for nothing. —**unda boklavat bul=** /ın/ to overestimate, to praise undeservedly. — **böceği** dungbeetle, scarabaeus, *zool.*, *Scarabaeus sacer.* — **bulaştır=** /a/ *same as* **bok at=**. — **canına olsun!** damn you! —**u cinli** restless, nervous. —**unu çek=** /ın/ to suffer the evil consequences (of an action). —**u çık=** /ın/ to come to light, to be discovered (the ugly side of a thing). —**unu çıkar=** /ın/, — **et=** /ı/ to spoil. —**unda inci ara=** /ın/ *same as* **bokunda boklavat bul=**. —**u kuru=** /ın/ to be frightened to death. —**tan künet** worthless, a mere nothing. — **püsür** 1. rubbish. 2. details. — **sineği** dung fly. —**un soyu** damned! — **sür=** to slander, to throw mud (at). —**unu temizle=** /ın/ to clean up the mess another has caused. — **tulumu** very fat. — **ye=** to say or do something wrong, to blunder, to put one's foot in it. — **yedi başı** meddler. — **yemenin âlâsı**, — **yemenin Arapçası**, — **yemenin gülpembesi** a major blunder. — **yiyen keşkülünü yanında taşır** He who wishes to do as he

pleases must provide for himself. — **yoluna git=** to lose one's life for nothing, unnecessarily.

bokça 1 بوقچه. *vulg.* quite bad.

bokça 2 بغچه. بوقچه. *var. of* **bohça**.

bokçu بوقچى. 1. dealer in dung. 2. cleaner of cesspools.

bokla=[r] بوقلامق. /ı/ 1. to soil, befoul. 2. to spoil, mismanage; to bring disrepute (upon). **—n=** *pass.* **—t=** /ı,a/ *caus. of* **bokla=**.

boklu بوقلى. 1. soiled with dung; filthy. 2. *min.* containing scoriae, slags, or ashes. 3. *vulg.* disagreeable. **—ca bülbül** wren, *zool.*, *Troglodytes troglodytes*.

bokluk[ğu] بوقلق. 1. dunghill. 2. filthy place. 3. state of disorder, bad state.

boks بوقس. F *sports* boxing. **— et=**, **— yap=** to box.

boksör بوقسور. F *sports* boxer.

bol 1 بول. 1. wide and loose-fitting; too large. 2. abundant, ample, copious. **— ağızdan** exaggeratedly (talking). **— biç=** /ı/ to estimate lavishly. **— bol** amply, abundantly, generously. **— bol yiyen bel bel bakar** He who squanders his money is left empty-handed. **— bolamat** *colloq.* amply, abundantly, in abundance. **— doğra=** *colloq.* 1. to spend lavishly. 2. to be lavish in promises. **— keseden at=** to make extravagant promises, to scatter promises around. **— paça** slovenly, untidy. **— paçadan at=** *same as* **bol keseden at=**. **— şekilli** *chem.* polymorphous.

bol[lü] **2** بول. G claret cup, fruit punch.

bol[lü] **3** بول. E *sports* bowls.

bol=[ur] **4** بولمق. *archaic* to be.

bola بولا. *prov.* the wife of one's paternal uncle.

bola ki بولدكه بولكه. [**bol=** 4] *prov.* 1. maybe, perhaps. 2. would that.

bolal=[ır] بولالمق. *prov.* 1. to become wide or loose. 2. to become abundant. **—t=** /ı/ *caus.*

bolamadı بولامادى *prov.* 1. ample, in abundance. 2. wide, loose.

bolay ki بولايكه. *var. of* **bola ki**.

bolca بولجه. 1. somewhat wide. 2. rather amply, fairly abundant.

bolero بولرو. F bolero.

boliçe (..´.) بوليچه. Jewish woman.

bollan=[ır] بوللنمق. *same as* **bollaş=**.

bollaş=[ır] بوللشمق. 1. to become wide, loose-fitting, loose. 2. to become plentiful, abundant. **—tır=** /ı/ *caus.*

bollat=[ır] بوللتمق. /ı/ *same as* **bollaştır=**. **—ıl=** *pass. of* **bollat=**. **—tır=** /ı,a/ *caus. of* **bollat=**.

bolluk[ğu] بوللق. 1. wideness, looseness. 2. abundance, plenty; plenteous (country).

—ta büyümüş grown up in the midst of plenty, luxurious, prodigal, wasteful.

Bolşevik[ği] بولشويك. Russ Bolshevik. **—lik** Bolshevism.

bom بوم. *slang* lie. **— at=** to lie.

bomba 1 (.´.) بومبا. بومبه. It 1. bomb. 2. barrel; bomb-shaped metal container. **— gibi** *slang* in good condition. **— gibi patla=** to explode like a bomb (in fury). **— patlat=** *slang* to commit a theft. **—cı** bombardier; maker of bombs. **—la=** /ı/ to bomb.

bomba 2 (.´.) بومبه. It *same as* **bumba**.

bombarda (..´.) بومباردە. It *obs.* mortar vessel, bomb ketch.

bombardıman بومباردمان. F bombardment, bombing. **— uçağı** bomber.

bombires بومبيرس. It *naut.* bowsprit.

bombok[ku] (.´.) بومبوق. *vulg.* very bad, utterly spoiled.

bombon بومبون. F candy.

bomboş (.´.) بومبوش. quite empty.

bomcu بومجى. *slang* liar.

bonaça (..´.) بوناجه. It *naut.* calm, tranquility of weather.

bonatire بوناتيره. F *print.* press-proof.

bonavela (...´.) بوناولا. It *same as* **banavele**.

boncuk[ğu] بونجوق. 1. bead. 2. *colloq.* Negro, Negress. 3. *naut.* parrel truck. **— gibi** bead-like (eyes). **— illeti** infantile convulsions; fit. **— mavisi** turquoise blue. **—çu** dealer in beads.

bonfile بونفله. F *butchery* sirloin steak.

bonjur بونژور. F 1. morning coat. 2. good morning!

bonmarşe بونمارشه. F department store.

bono (.´.) بونو. It *com.* bond, bill.

bonservis بونسرويس. F letter of recommendation, certificate of good service.

bop بوب. Sl *poker* ante.

bor 1 بور. F *chem.* boron.

bor 2 بور. [**bur 1**] *prov.* unbroken ground, waste land.

bora (.´.) بورا. It 1. storm, squall, tempest. 2. violent scolding. **— patlat=** to be furious, to break out in a fury, to storm. **—ya tutul=**, **— ye=** to get a good scolding.

borağan بوراغان. *var. of* **burağan**.

borak[kı] بوراق. [**burak 2**] borax.

boraks بوراقس. F *chem.* borax.

boran بوران. *var. of* **buran**.

borani بورانى. [**burani**] dish of stewed and fried vegetables.

borasit بوراست. F *min.* boracite.

borat بورات. F *chem.* borate.

borazan بورازان. [**boruzen**] *mil.* 1. trumpet. 2. trumpeter. **— başı** first trumpeter. **—cı** trumpeter.

borç[cu] بُرج. 1. debt; loan. 2. duty; obligation. 3. *bookkeeping* debit. **—a** on credit, as a loan. **— al=** /ı/ to borrow (money). **— altına gir=** to incur a debt. **—u as=** to neglect one's debt. **—a bat=** to be deep in debt. **— bini aşıyor** The debts have piled up. **— et=** to get into debt. **— gırtlağa çıktı** The debts have reached the limit. **—a gir=** to get into debt. **— harç** debts. **—lar hukuku** law of obligation, *jus obligationum*. **— ikrarı** *law* acknowledgement of liability. **—unu kapat=** to settle one's debt. **— muamele** *com.* loan business. **— olarak** as a loan. **—unu öde=** to pay one's debt. **— ödenir, kira ödenmez** Better to get into debt to buy a house than forever to remain a tenant. **— paçasından akıyor** He is sunk in debt. **— para** loan. **— senedi** *com.* certificate of debt, note of hand. **— ver=** /ı,a/ to lend (money). **— vermekle tükenir, yol yürümekle** *proverb* One gets rid of one's debts by paying them, even though little by little. **— yiğidin kamçısıdır** *proverb* A debt drives one to work harder. **—lan=** to get into debt, to become indebted. **—landır=** /ı/ 1. *caus.* 2. *com.* to debit, to charge. **—lu** debtor; /a/ indebted, under obligation.

borda 1 (ˈ.) بُردَه. It *naut.* 1. board, broadside. 2. beam. **—da** abeam. **—dan** from abeam. **— ateşi** broadside (fire). **— borda** *slang* side by side. **— bordaya** broadside to broadside, alongside. **— feneri** side light. **—ya gel=** to come alongside. **— hattı** line of battleships moving abreast. **— iskelesi** accomodation ladder.

borda 2 (ˈ.) بُردَا. بُردَه. It *naut.* attack upon a ship by a boarding party. **— et=**, **—la=** /ı/ to board (an enemy ship).

bordo (ˈ.) بُردو. F 1. claret red. 2. Bordeaux wine.

bordro (ˈ.) بُردرو. F list, register, roll; payroll; docket.

borina (..ˈ.) بُرنا. It *same as* **burina**.

borineta (...ˈ.) بُرنته. It *same as* **burinata**.

bornoz, bornuz بُرنوز *var. of* **burnuz**.

borsa (ˈ.) بُرسه. It stock-exchange, exchange, bourse. **— acentası** exchange broker. **— bülteni** market report. **— fiatı** stock-exchange quotation. **— muamelesi** stock-exchange operation, exchange transaction. **— oyunu** speculation.

borsuk[gu] بُرسوق. بُرسون. بُرصن. *var. of* **porsuk 1, 2.**

bortla=[r] بُرتلامن *prov.* to foal (camel).

boru بُرو. بُرى. بُره. 1. pipe, tube. 2. *mus.* horn; natural trumpet. 3. speaking trumpet; phonograph horn. 4. *slang* nonsense, empty talk; bad, in a bad state. 5. *slang* vain, boaster. **— anahtarı** pipe wrench. **— bileziği** ornamental ring put around a stove pipe. **— mu bu?** *slang* Do you think that is nothing? **— çal=** to sound a trumpet. **—yu çal=** to be successful. **— çiçeği** downy thorn-apple, *bot.*, *Datura metel*; morning-glory, *bot.*, *Ipomoea purpurea*; mallow bindweed, *bot.*, *Convulvulus althaeoides*. **— değil** That's no small matter! **— dirseği** elbow, elbow-shaped pipe. **— döşe=** to lay pipes. **— hattı** pipe line. **— kabağı** oblong kind of gourd. **— kelepçesi** pipe clip. **—suna ot tıka=** to silence, to stop (a garrulous person). **—su öt=** *colloq.* to have authority, to be influential. **—cu** 1. maker or seller of pipes, tubes, horns, or trumpets. 2. trumpeter; horn-blower. 3. leader of the pump squad. **—cuk** *anat.* tubule, tubulus. **—msu** *biol.* tubiform.

boruzen بُرزن. بُرزن. [**boru + -zen**] *lrnd., same as* **borazan**.

bos بُص *only in* **boy bos**.

bosa (ˈ.) بُصا. بُصه. It *naut.* stopper to a cable. **— zinciri** top chain.

Bosna (ˈ.) بُسنه. Bosnia. **— sarayı** Sarajevo.

Bosnak[gı] بُسناق. [**Bosniyak**] *same as* **Bosniyak**.

Bosnevi (..—) بُسنوی. [*based on* **Bosna**] *lrnd.* a Bosnian.

Bosniyak[gı] بُسنیاق. Sl a Bosnian. **—ca** Bosnian, Serbo-Croatian (language).

bostan بُستان. [**büstan**] 1. vegetable garden, kitchen garden. 2. *prov.* melon. 3. *obs. a* **makam** *in Turkish music*. **— beli** gardener's spade with a very long handle. **— beygiri** horse that turns a water wheel. **— beygiri gibi dön=** to be busy going around all day. **— dolabı** noria, water wheel for irrigation. **— korkuluğu** 1. scarecrow. 2. a mere puppet. **— patlıcanı** large kind of eggplant. **— tahtası** a plant bed in a kitchen-garden.

bostancı بُستانجی. 1. market gardener, vegetable gardener. 2. *Ott. hist.* member of the Imperial guard. **— baratası** *Ott. hist.* high red cloth cap worn by the Imperial guards. **— başı** *Ott. hist.* commander of the Imperial guards, who had jurisdiction over the shores and waters of the Bosphorus and was frequently charged with the execution of grandees. **— ocağı** *Ott. hist.* the corps of the Imperial guards.

boş بُش. 1. empty, empty-handed; hollow; blank; uninhabited; vacant (post); free, not engaged (seat); not in use (machine); unsown, uncultivated (land); divorced (woman); *print.* space. 2. futile, frivolous, of no effect, useless; ignorant, superficial (person). 3. unoccupied, at leisure; unemployed, out of work, idle; idleness. 4. loose, slack (rope); looseness, slack; loose, not tethered; unaware, careless.

—ta unemployed, idle. —una in vain, uselessly. — al= *naut.* to slack. —a al= /ı/ 1. to prop up temporarily (building, for repairs). 2. *mech.* to uncouple, to ungear. —unu al= /ın/ to tauten (rope), to take in the slack. — atıp dolu tut=, — atıp dolu vur= to hit the mark at a venture, to hit upon (the truth) at a guess. — barsak *anat.* jejunum. — boğaz*. — boşuna, —u boşuna quite in vain, uselessly. — böğür*. — bulun= to be taken unawares, to do or say something without thinking. — çalış= to run on no load, to run light (machine). — çık= lottery to hit a blank. —a çık= to come to naught. — çuval ayakta durmaz *proverb* (*lit.* An empty sack cannot stand up.) A person without capacity does not succeed. — dön= to come back empty-handed. — dur= to be unoccupied, to idle. — durma sigortası unemployment insurance. — düş= /dan/ to be considered as divorced (from her husband). — gez= to wander about idle; to be unemployed. — gezenin baş kalfası, — gezenin boş kalfası good-for-nothing, vagabond, loafer. —a git= 1. to be in vain, to be of no use. 2. to miss the mark. — işle= *same as* boş çalış=. — kafalı silly, addlepated. — kâğıdı written declaration of divorce (given to a woman by her husband). — ko=, — koy= /ı/ to leave to himself. —a koydum dolmadı, doluya koydum almadı However I try to do it, it still does not work. — küp brainless fellow. — lâf karın doyurmaz *proverb* Empty words do not fill the stomach. — ol! I divorce you! (formula pronounced by the husband). — otur= to sit idle, to be unoccupied. — vakit 1. spare time. 2. leisure. — ver= /a/ *slang* not to bother (about), to take no notice (of). — yere 1. in vain. 2. groundlessly, without reason.

boşa=^{r} بوشامه /ı/ 1. to repudiate, divorce (one's wife). 2. *obs.* to set loose (an animal).

boşal=^{ır} بوشالں. 1. to be emptied; to empty itself, to run out; to be poured out (of, into). 2. to be discharged (gun); to unwind itself, to be unwound (rope); to run down (spring of a clock, etc.). 3. to become free, to become vacant. 4. to come out in haste (crowd). —ış, —ma *verbal n.* evacuation. —t= /ı/ *caus.* of boşal=. 1. to empty; to pour. 2. to discharge (gun). 3. to evacuate; to render vacant, to vacate. 4. to unload, to discharge (cargo or ship); to disembark, to land (troops). —taç *neol.* exhaust pump. —tıl= *pass.* of boşalt=. —tım *neol., physiol.* excretion. —tma *verbal n.* of boşalt= discharge. —tma havzası *geog.* drainage basin. —tma limanı port of discharge. —tma müddeti *mar. com.* laydays. —ttır= /ı,a/ *caus.* of boşalt=.

boşan=^{ır} بوشانر. 1. /dan/ to be divorced (from). 2. /dan/ to be loosed, to be set at large; to break loose; to break through its barriers (fluid). 3. to be discharged by accident (firearm). 4. /dan/ to burst forth (tears, blood). 5. to burst fort in a torrent of complaint or invective; to pour out one's heart. —ış, —ma *verbal n.* divorce. —ma dâvası suit for divorce. —mış divorced.

boşat=^{ır} بوشاتر. 1. /ı, a or dan/ *caus.* of boşa=. 2. /ı/ *prov., var.* of boşalt=. —ıl= *pass.* of boşat=.

boşayış بوشایش. *verbal n.* of boşa=.

boşboğaz بوشبوغاز. garrulous, indiscreet; blab. —lık idle talk. —lık et= to talk indiscreetly.

boşböğür بوش بوگور. *anat.* side, flank.

boşla=^{r} بوشلاں. /ı/ 1. *slang* to neglect; to let alone. 2. *prov.* to let go, loose. —n= *pass.* —t= /ı,a/ *caus.* of boşla=. —yış *verbal n.* of boşla=.

boşluk^{ğu} بوشلق. *abstr. n.* of boş; blank; cavity; *phys.* vacuum.

Bosnak^{ğı} بوسناق [Bosnak] a Bosnian. —ca Bosnian, Serbo-Croat (language).

bot 1 بوت E *naut.* boat.
bot 2 بوط F boot.
botanik^{ği} بوتانیك. F botany. —çi botanist.
botin بوتین F *same as* potin.
botla=^{r} بوتلاں. to foal (camel).
botur بوطور [batır 3] *prov.* proud, insolently vain.
boturak^{ğı} بوتراق. *var.* of pıtrak.
boturlan=^{ır} بوطورلنر. *prov.* to display arrogance and insolence.
boturluk^{ğu} بوطورلق. *abstr. n.* of botur.
bovata (.´.) بواطه *var.* of boğata.
boy 1 بوی 1. height; stature. 2. length. 3. size. 4. edge (of a road), bank (of a river). 5. *prov.* sort, quality. — al= to grow in height; to shoot up. —u beraber, —una beraber, —unca beraber as tall as himself. — boy assorted, of various sizes; of various qualities. —dan boya all over, from end to end. — çek= to grow in height. —a çek= to shoot up (child). — çukuru *mil.* standing trench. —u devrilsin! I wish he'd fall down dead! — et= /ı/ to sort out according to sizes. — göster= to show oneself. —u kısa short of stature. — kürkü full-length fur coat. —unun ölçüsünü al= to get one's deserts, to learn by painful experience. — ölçüş= /a/ to compete (with). — sür= to grow in height. — tut= not to be out of one's depth (water). —u uzun 1. tall; long. 2. snake. —u uzun yer distant place. — ver= not to be beyond one's

depth (water). **—a yet=** *archaic* to grow tall.

boy 2 بوى clan, branch of a tribe. **— beyi** chieftain of a clan.

boy 3 بوى. seeds of fenugreek. **— otu** fenugreek, *bot.*, *Trigonella Foenumgraecum*. **— tohumu** *same as* **boy 3**.

boya 1 بویه ٬ بویا 1. paint; dye; color; make-up. **— ağacı** cam-wood, barwood, *bot.*, *Baphia nitida*. **— al=** to take paint (wood, etc.); to take a dye (fabric). **—sı atmış** faded. **— kalem** colored pencil. **— kökü** madder root, the root of *Rubia tinctorum*. **— maddesi** *biol.* pigment. **— otu** dyer's madder, *bot.*, *Rubia tinctorum*. **— resim** painting. **— sür=** /a/ to paint. **— tabancası** spray-gun, air-brush. **— tut=** *same as* **boya al=**. **— tuttu** The dye has set. **— vur=** /a/ to paint. **—sı vur=** /ın/ to run (color, dye).

boya=ᵣ 2 بویهمس ٬ بویاموس /ı,a/ to paint, to dye, to color (a thing a certain color).

boyacı بویاجى 1. dyer; house-painter. 2. dealer in paints. 3. shoeblack. **— kedisi gibi**, **— köpeği gibi** dyed in all colors, crudely colored. **— küpü** dyer's vat. **— küpü değil** It is not a dyer's vat where one can just dip things in and take them out again. (Things cannot be done properly in haste.) **—lık** 1. dyeing; house-painting. 2. trade in paints. 3. business of a shoeblack.

boyahane (..—.) بویاخانه dye-house, dyer's shop.

boyala=ᵣ بویالامق /ı/ to cover with paint.

boyalı بویالى painted, colored, dyed.

boyama بویامه 1. *verbal n. of* **boya=** 2. 2. colored, painted, dyed. 3. colored kerchief. **— resim** painting, colored drawing.

boyan 1 بویان *prov.*, *var. of* **biyan 2**.

boyan=ᵣ بویانمق /a/ 1. *pass. of* **boya=** 2. 2. *refl. of* **boya=** 2. 3. to use makeup. **—ık** painted; dyed.

boyar بویار. Sl *hist.* boyar, landed nobleman of Wallachia, etc.

boyasız بویاسز unpainted; undyed, uncolored; unpolished (shoe); without makeup.

boyat=ᵣ بویاتمق /ı,a/ *caus. of* **boya=** 2. **—ıl=** *pass.*

boy bos بوى بوص stature. **—u yerinde** tall and well made.

boyca (.'.) بویجه 1. as regards height. 2. lengthwise, longitudinally. **— evlâdı var** He has grown-up children. **— günaha gir=** to go deep into sin.

boydaş بویداش 1. of the same height, equal in stature. 2. equal.

boykot بویقوط E boycott. **—çu** boycotter.

boyla=ᵣ بویلامق /ı/ 1. *colloq.* to be rushed (to), to end up (at). 2. to traverse lengthwise; to pace off lengthwise. 3. to measure the length or height (of). 4. to fall prone (upon the ground).

boylam *neol.*, *astr.* longitude.

boylan=ᵣ بویلانمق 1. to grow in stature, to increase in length or height. 2. *pass. of* **boyla=**. **—ıp boslan=** to grow and develop into handsome proportions. **—dır=** /ı/ *caus. of* **boylan=**¹.

boylaş=ᵣ بویلاشمق 1. *same as* **boylan=**¹. 2. to be sorted into lengths, qualities, or classes. **—tır=** /ı/ *caus.*

boylat=ᵣ بویلاتمق /a,ı/ *caus. of* **boyla=**.

boylu بویلی tall, high; long. **— boslu** tall and well-developed, handsome. **— boyunca** 1. at full length. 2. from end to end.

boymul بویمول 1. hen harrier, *zool.*, *Circus pyaneus*. 2. marsh harrier, *zool.*, *Circus aeruginosus*.

boyna (.'.) بوینه [**boyuna 3**] *naut.* scull. **— et=** to scull. **— palası** blade of a scull.

boynuz بوینوز 1. horn, antler, made of horn. 2. horn, trumpet. 3. cupping horn. 4. antenna (of insects, etc.). **— ağacı** Judas tree, *bot.*, *Cercis siliquastrum*. **— çek=** /a/ *med.* to cup. **— çiçeği** flower of the Judas tree. **— dik=** *same as* **boynuz tak=**. **— otu** hellebore, *bot.*, *Helleborus*. **— tak=** 1. to become a cuckold. 2. /a/ to make a cuckold (of). **— vur=** /a/ to gore. **—ları yaldızla=** *same as* **boynuz tak=**. **—cuk** *anat.* cornicle. **—lan=** to become horned, to grow horns. **—lu** horned. **—suz** hornless, polled.

boysuz بویسز. short in stature.

boyunʸⁿᵘ **1** بویون ٬ بوین ٬ سوین 1. neck. 2. *geog.* pass, defile. **—una al=** /ı/ to take upon oneself. **—u altında kalsın!** May he die! **—u armut sapına dönmüş** He has grown very thin. **—una at=** /ı, ın/ to put (the blame on a person). **—una atıl=** /ın/ to fall on somebody's neck. **— atkısı** scarf, neckerchief. **— bağı** necktie, tie. **—una bin=** /ın/ to pester, to dun. **— borcu** a binding duty. **— bur=** to wring the neck. **— buran** wryneck, *zool.*, *Jynx torquilla*. **—u burulu** *archaic*, *same as* **boynu bükük**. **— bük=**, **—unu bük=** 1. to bow the neck. 2. to show humility. **—u bükük** destitute, unhappy, sorrowful. **— çemberi** the ridge of the collar-bones. **— çeviren** *same as* **boyun buran**. **—una el bırak=** /ın/ to embezzle. **— iğ=** /a/ to submit; to humiliate oneself (before). **—u iğri** *same as* **boynu bükük**. **—unu kaşı=** to be embarrassed. **— kemiği** cervical section of the vertebral column. **— kes=** 1. to bow

Red 13.

boyun

the head. 2. /a/ to submit. —**unu kes**= /ın/ to behead. —**um kıldan ince** I am ready to accept any decision, ready to comply with anything. — **kır**= *same as* **boyun kes**=. —**u kopsun!** May he die! — **kökü** base of the neck. —**una sarıl**= /ın/ to embrace. — **tut**= /a/ 1. to stand up (against). 2. *archaic* to submit. —**u tutul**= to have a stiff neck. —**unu uzat**=, —**unu ver**= /a/ to surrender; to submit. —**unu vur**= /ın/ to behead, decapitate. — **yatağı** *mech.* plummer block.

boyunʸⁿᵘ 2 بُويُون. *archaic* bail, surety, security (person).

boyuna 1 بويُونَه lengthwise; longitudinally.

boyuna 2 (.'..) بويُونَه *colloq.* incessantly, continually.

boyuna 3 (..'.) بويُونَه It *same as* **boyna**.

boyunca (..'.) بويُونجَه 1. lengthwise. 2. along, *e. g.*, **sahil boyunca** along the shore. 3. throughout, *e. g.*, **ömür boyunca** throughout one's life.

boyundurukᵗᵘ بويُوندُورُوق 1. yoke. 2. *wrestling* headlock. — **altında** under the yoke, reduced to servitude. — **hakkı** *hist.* a kind of land tax. —**a vur**= /ı/ 1. to put under the yoke. 2. to reduce to servitude. — **yeke** *naut.* rudder with yoke.

boyunlu بويُونلُو having a neck, necked.

boyunlukᵗᵘ بويُونلُق 1. thing worn around the neck. 2. *hist.* neckguard for a horse.

boyutᵈᵘ *neol.* dimension.

boz 1 بُوز. 1. gray; roan, color of a horse's coat produced by the mixture of white and red hair; *prov.* speck of gray color (eye); *prov.* light blond, fair. 2. rough, waste, uncultivated (land). — **ayı** brown bear, *zool.*, *Ursus arctos*. — **camgöz** cow shark, *zool.*, *Hexanchus griseus*. — **doğan***. — **kır***. — **kurt** grey wolf. — **madde** *anat.* gray matter.

boz=ᵃʳ **2** بُوزَر. 1. /ı/ to undo, disintegrate; to take to pieces, take down (tent), demolish, scrap; to cut for alteration (garment); to change (money). 2. /ı/ to spoil, put out of running order; to ruin, destroy; to upset (stomach, plans, etc.), to disturb (peace). 3. /ı/ to throw into confusion; to disorganize; to defeat, rout (army). 4. /ı/ to deform; to taint; to make putrid; to adulterate; to deprave, corrupt; to cause to wither; to make thin and pale. 5. /ı/ to obliterate, deface, erase, cross out; to break (oath), to cancel (agreement); to break (custom); *law* to quash (by cassation). 6. /ı/ *colloq.* to disconcert, put out of countenance; to embarrass, humiliate, to cause to lose face. 7. /ı/ to violate, deflower. 8. /ı,a/ to turn into (a joke). 9. to change for the worse (weather). 10. *colloq.* to go mad; /la/ to be crazy (about).

boza بُوزَه. boza (beverage made of fermented millet). — **ol**= *var. of* **bozum ol**=. —**cı** maker or seller of boza. —**hane** shop where boza is made.

bozar=ⁱʳ بُوزَرسم. بُوزَرسم. 1. to turn pale. 2. to take on a gray color. —**t**= /ı/ *caus.*

Bozbaba بُوزبابا. Hagios Strati (island near Lemnos).

bozbakkalˡⁱ بُوزبَقَّال. fieldfare, *zool.*, *Turdus pilaris*.

bozca بُوزجَه. 1. grayish. 2. uncultivated soil. **B— Ada** *geog.* Tenedos.

bozdağan, bozdoğan 1 بُوزداغان. iron war-mace. — **armudu** variety of pear.

bozdoğan 2 بُوزدوغان. بُوزطوغان 1. merlin, *zool.*, *Falco aesalon*. 2. *w. cap.*, name of a town in Southwest Anatolia. **B— kemeri** name of an aqueduct in Istanbul.

bozdur=ᵘʳ بُوزدورسم. بُوزدِيرِمِم. /ı,a/ *caus. of* **boz**= **2**.

bozgun بُوزغُون. بُوزغِين 1. rout, defeat. 2. routed, defeated. 3. *archaic* demolished, deranged, destroyed, spoiled. — **düş**= to be defeated in an argument. —**a uğra**= to be routed, to be defeated. —**a uğrat**= /ı/ to rout, defeat. — **ver**=, — **ye**= to be defeated, to be routed. —**cu** defeatist. —**culuk** defeatism. —**luk** state of confusion and defeat.

bozkır بُوزقِير. 1. steppe. 2. pale gray (horse).

bozla=ʳ بُوزلادِم. *prov.* to bellow, to low (cow, camel).

bozlakᵏⁱ **1** بُوزلاق. *prov.* kind of folk song.

bozlakᵏⁱ **2** بُوزلاق. grayish.

bozlukᵗᵘ بُوزلُق. grayness, gray color.

bozma بُوزمَه. 1. *law* cassation, abrogation, quashing. 2. /dan/ made out (of); pervert, proselyte; descendant of mixed blood. —**cı** one who buys old things and uses the materials; ship-breaker; demolisher of buildings; dealer who uses the material of old jewelry.

bozrakⁱⁱ بُوزراق. grayish, light gray.

bozucu بُوزوجى. 1. demolisher, spoiler; demolishing, spoiling. 2. ship-breaker.

bozukᵗᵘ **1** بُوزُوق. بُوزوق. 1. broken, destroyed; spoiled, gone bad. 2. out of order, out of repair. 3. bad, depraved, corrupt; bad (weather). 4. change, small change. — **çehre** upset and worried looking face. — **düzen** in a disorderly state, out of order. — **para** small change.

bozukᵗᵘ **2** بُوزُوق. 1. *folk mus.* kind of lute. 2. musical piece of corrupt tradition.

bozuklukᵗᵘ بُوزُوقلُق. 1. *abstr. n.*; vice; defeat. 2. *com.* small change.

bozul=ⁿʳ بوزولمق . 1. *pass. of* **boz=** 2. 2. to become spoiled, tainted, putrid; to become depraved, corrupt; to wither; to become thin and sallow. 3. to be disconcerted, to look vexed, to look annoyed. **—ma** 1. *verbal n.* 2. *same as* **bozma²**. **—uş** *verbal n. of* **bozul=**.
bozum بوزم . 1. *slang* embarrassment, humiliation, discomfiture. 2. *slang* a going broke. 3. *verbal n. of* **bozul=**. **— et=** *slang* to embarrass. **— havası çalıyordu** *slang* An atmosphere of embarrassment prevailed. **— ol=** *slang* to be embarrassed, to lose face.
bozumca بوزومجه *kind of lizard.*
bozumsu بوزومسى , **bozumturak**ᵏⁱ بوزمتراى . grayish, somewhat gray.
bozumtukᵏᵘ بوزمتق *prov., same as* **bozumsu**.
bozuntu بوزنتى . 1. *colloq.* discomfiture, embarrassment. 2. *colloq.* caricature (of), mere parody (of). 3. old materials, scrap, refuse.
bozuş 1 بوزش . *verbal n. of* **boz=** 2.
bozuş=ⁿʳ **2** بوزشمق . to break with one another. **—ma** *verbal n.* **—tur=** /ı/ *caus. of* **bozuş=**. **—uk** on unfriendly terms. **—ukluk** *abstr. n.*
bozyürükᵏᵘ بوزيوروك *sandsnake, zool., Eryx.*
böbrekᵏⁱ ببرك . بوبرك [**böğrek**] kidney. **— iltihabı** *path.* nephritis. **— leğeni** *anat.*, pelvis renalis. **— yağı** suet.
böbürlen=ⁱʳ ببورلنمك to assume an arrogant air. **—dir=** /ı/ *caus.*
böce بوجه . *prov., var. of* **böcek**.
böcekᵏⁱ بوجك . 1. little creeping beast, vermin, bug, beetle, worm. 2. *zool.* insect. 3. louse. 4. lobster; crayfish. 5. *hist.* police spy, detective. **— başı** *Ott. hist.* chief of the detective department of the police. **— çıkar=** to hatch silkworms. **— gibi** 1. dark-skinned and tiny (child). 2. disgusting; frightful. **— kabuğu** greenish blue with a metallic luster. **—çil** *biol.* insectiverous. **—len=** to become infested with vermin. **—li** infested with vermin.
böcü بوجو . 1. bogey, bugbear. 2. scarecrow.
böcükᵏᵘ بوجك . *prov., var. of* **böcek**.
böğ بوك . a kind of venomous spider, *zool.*, *Galeodes*.
böğetᵈⁱ بوكت . *var. of* **büğet**.
böğler بوكلر . *zool.*, *Solifugal.*
böğrekᵏⁱ بوكرك . *archaic for* **böbrek**.
böğrülce بوكرولجه *same as* **börülce**.
böğrüş=ⁿʳ بوكروشمك to bellow together.
böğürᵍʳⁿ **1** بوكر . 1. side, flank. 2. sidepiece of a saddle frame.
böğür=ⁿʳ **2** بوكرمك to bellow, to low.
böğürlü بوكرلو .

long in the flank (beast).
böğürme بوكرمه . *verbal n. of* **böğür=** 2.
böğürt=ⁿʳ بوكرتمك /ı/ *caus. of* **böğür=** 2.
böğürtlen بوكرتلن . بكرتلن 1. bramble, blackberry, *bot.*, *Rubus Jruticosus*. 2. *slang* vomit. **—lik** thicket of brambles.
böğürtü بوكرتو . bellow, roar.
böğürücü بوكروجى . bellowing; bellower.
böğürülce بوكرولجه same as **börülce**.
böke بوكه . *prov.* champion.
böl=ᵉʳ بولمك . 1. /ı/ to separate. 2. /ı,a/ to divide (into portions). **—dür=** /ı, a/ *caus.*
böle بوله . *prov.* cousin.
bölen *neol., math.* divisor.
bölge بولكه . 1. *prov.* line of division; section. 2. *sc., mil.* region, zone. **— başkanı** *sport* team captain. **— komutanı** *mil.* section commander. **—sel** *neol., sc.* regional.
bölme بولمه . 1. *verbal n. of* **böl=**; *math.*, division. 2. partition, dividing wall. 3. compartment. 4. *naut.* bulkhead. 5. divided, partitioned, separated. **—cik** *anat.* trabecula. **—li** having compartments, partitioned.
bölü *neol., math.* divided by, e. g., **üç bölü dört** 3 ÷ 4 or 3/4.
bölücü بولجى . dividing, that divides; divider.
bölükᵏᵘ بولوك . 1. *mil.* company. 2. *mil.* squadron. 3. *hist.* detachment, squad. 4. part, division, subdivision; compartment. 5. group, body (of men). 6. *math.* order. 7. one of two braids of hair. 8. district composed of several villages of Turkish nomads in Persia. **— ağası** 1. *hist.* a lieutenant commanding a wing of a company. 2. captain of gendarmes. **— başı** 1. *hist.* captain of the Janissaries. 2. *obs.* sergeant of police. 3. stevedore, section leader. **— bölük** in groups. **—e çık=** *Ott. hist.* to be assigned to service in the court cavalry (Janissary). **— emini** *obs., mil.* quartermaster, paymaster. **— halkı** *Ott. hist.* cavalry troops of the Janissary corps. **— komutanı** *mil.* captain. **— pörçük** in bits.
bölükân (..—) بولوكان . *lrnd., pl. of* **bölük**.
bölükât (..—) بولوكات . *lrnd., pl. of* **bölük**, *same as* **bölük halkı**. **—ı seb'a** *Ott. hist.* the Turkish military forces in Egypt, organized in seven companies.
bölüklü بولوكلو . 1. containing subdivisions, partitioned. 2. *Ott. hist.* Janissary pertaining to a certain company.
bölüm بولوم . 1. *verbal n. of* **böl=**. 2. portion, slice, part, division. 3. *math.* quotient. 4. *mil.* disposition of forces. **—le=** *neol.* to divide into classes, to classify.
bölün=ⁿʳ بولنمك . 1. *pass. of* **böl=**. 2. *refl. of* **böl=**. **— bilme=** *math.* divisibility. **—en** *math.* dividend. **—me** 1. *verbal n. of* **bölün=**

2. *biol.* division. **—mez** indivisible. **—tü** part, section.
bölüş 1 بولش. *verbal n. of* **böl=**.
bölüş=ᵘʳ **2** بولشمك. /ı/ to divide among themselves, to share out. **—me** *verbal n.* **—tür=** /ı, a/ *caus. of* **bölüş=**.
bön 1 بون. imbecile, simple, foolish. **— bön bak=** to stare foolishly.
bön 2 بون. [**bün 2**] *prov.* ground coffee.
bönlükᵍᵘ بونلك. imbecility, simple-mindedness.
bönsü=ʳ بونسمك. *prov.* to behave like an imbecile. **—n=** /ı/ to treat as an imbecile.
börekᵍⁱ بورك. flaky pastry with thin layers of cheese or other filling. **—çi** maker or seller of **börek**.
börkᵏᵘ برك، بورك. 1. *prov.* kerchief. 2. *hist.* tall felt cap of the Janissaries. **—çü** *obs.* maker or seller of felt caps.
börkenekᵍⁱ 1. *neol., biol.* parson's nose. 2. *prov.* cap, rain hood.
bört=ᵉʳ بورتمك. to roast slightly (intransitive). **—tür=** /ı/ to roast slightly.
börtü böcekᵍⁱ بورتو بوجك. vermin.
börü بورى. *archaic* wolf.
börülce بورجه. cow pea, black-eyed bean, *bot., Dolichos sesquipedalis, vigna sinensis*.
böy بى. *var. of* **böğ**.
böyle بويله. so, this, in this way; such. **—si** such a one, this kind. **— böyle** 1. in this way (often used to avoid repeating reported speech). 2. by and by, gradually. **— gelmiş böyle gider** It has always been this way and it will always be. **— iken** while this is so, notwithstanding the circumstances. **— olunca** it being thus, in this case. **—ce, —cene, —likle** thus.
bradikardi برادىقارضى. F *path.* bradycardia.
braga (´.) براغة, **brago** (´.) براغو. It *obs., naut.* breeching of a ship's gun.
bragot براغوت. It *naut.* brace block of the foreyard and mainyard.
brakil براقيل. It *naut.* heel chain of the jib boom.
brakisefalⁱⁱ براقيسفال. F *anthropometry* brachycephalic.
branda (´.) برانده. It *same as* **buranda**.
bravo (´.) براوو. It, F bravo!, well done!
bre برى. *same as* **bire**.
Brehmen برهمن. *var. of* **Birehmen**.
Brezilya (´.´.) برزيليا. 1. Brazil. 2. *l. c.* brazilwood, *bot., Caesalpinia echinata*.
brıçka (´.) برچقا. Russ buggy.
briç برج. E card games bridge.
brikᵏⁱ بريك. F *naut.* brig.
briket بريكت. F briquette.
Britanya (´.´.) بريتانيا. It Britain.
briyantin برىانتين. F brilliantine.
brom 1 بروم. F *chem.* bromine.

brom 2 بروم. F *bot.* brome grass.
bromür بروميور. F *chem.* bromide.
bronş برونش. F *anat.* bronchus. **—çuk** bronchiole.
bronşit برونشيت. F *path.* bronchitis.
bronz برونز. F bronze.
broş بروش. F brooch.
broşür بروشور. F brochure.
brovning براونينك. E Browning (gun).
Brüksel بروكسل. F Brussels. **— lâhanası** Brussels sprouts.
brüt بروت. F *com.* gross (weight, total).
buⁿᵘ **1** بو. (*All oblique cases are based on* **bun—**, *pl.* **bunlar**, *archaic* **bular**) this. **— ağza kayık yanaştırmam** I don't give a damn. **— anda** at present. **— arada** 1. meanwhile. 2. among other things, in passing. 3. *archaic* here. **— asıl** *archaic* such, of this kind. **— bakımdan** in this respect; from this point of view. **— cihetle, — cihetten** in this respect; from this point of view. **— cümleden** as an instance of this. **— cümle ile** nevertheless. **— da geçer yahu** This too will pass; nothing is permanent. **— defa** this time; and now. **— fakir** this poor man (*i. e.*, I). **— gez** *archaic* this time, this once. **— gibi** such, of this kind, like this. **— gün*. — haysiyetle** in this respect. **— hususta** in this respect. **— işte bir hikmet var.** There must be a vital reason for it. **— itibarla** therefore, consequently. **— kabilden** of this sort. **— kadar*. — merkezde** 1. in this sense, to this effect. 2. more or less like this. **— münasebetle** in this connection. **— ne perhiz, bu ne lâhana turşusu** what a contrast!, how inconsistent! **— resme, — resmile** *archaic* thus. **— sevdadan vazgeç** You'd better give it up. **— suretle** in this way, thus. **— takdirde** in which case, in this case. **— yakınlarda** 1. recently. 2. in the near future. **— zeminde** in this sense, to this effect.
[*For other compounds, see* **buna 1, bunda, bundan, bunun**.]
bu 2 (—) بو. P *lrnd.* 1. odor, perfume, aroma, flavor. 2. slight trace, touch (of). 3. hope, desire, expectation. **—yu ümid** the faintest hope. **—yu vefa** the hope of finding reciprocal love, the hope of loyalty.
-bu 3 (—) بو. P *lrnd.* scented, *as in* amberbu.
bu- 4 (—) بو. A *var. of* **ebu-**, *as in* **Bubekr.**
Bubekr (—.) بوبكر. *var. of* **Ebubekr**.
buberdekᵏⁱ (—..) بوبردك. P *lrnd.* nightingale.
bubon بوبون. F *path.* bubo.
bubu (—̄—) بوبو. P *lrnd.* hoopoe, *zool.,* *Upupa epops*.

bucakᵗⁱ بجاݨہ بڄجانہ 1. corner, nook. 2. *adm.* subdistrict. 3. *archaic* angle. 4. *w. cap., hist.* southern Bessarabia; Bessarabia. — **bucak ara=** /ı/ to seek in every hole and corner. — **bucak kaç=** /dan/ to run away trying to hide (from). **bir —a tıkıl=** to be tucked up in a corner. **—lı** 1. that has corners. 2. *archaic* that has angles. 3. *w. cap., hist.* a Bessarabian.

bucarda (..'.) بوجارده F road *making* tool for roughening the surface of newly laid cement, bush-hammer.

bucurgat بوجرغات *var. of* **bocurgat.**

buçᶜᵘ *neol.* end, limit.

buçuğar بو بوجغر *archaic* one half each.

buçukᵍᵘ بو بجوڠ، بوجوق، بجوك، بجوك 1. and a half, *e. g.*, **iki buçuk** two and a half, **saat iki buçuk** It is half past two. 2. *prov.* half. 3. *archaic* a half asper. **—çu** *Ott. hist.* officer whose job was to shower coins over the crowd on certain occasions. **—lağı** *prov.* half measure. **—lu** having halves or fractions (account).

bu'd 1 بعد. A *lrnd.* 1. distance; remoteness. 2. *Or. mus.* interval between two notes. 3. improbability, absurdity. 4. profundity of view, penetration. 5. *phys.*, dimension. 6. *astr.* the horary angle of a heavenly body; declination of a heavenly body. 2. *myst.* estrangement from the divine truth. **—u akreb** the nearest distance, the least elongation. **—u bâid** great distance. **—u eb'ad** the greatest distance, maximal elongation. **—u hakikî** *astr.* true distance. **—u ittisal** *astr.* the apparent distance between the centers of two heavenly bodies when in contact. **—u kutb** *astr.* polar distance, codeclination. **—u küsufî** *astr.* the distance from the sun within which a planet is lost to sight in the solar rays. **—u meftur** distance in absolute space, natural distance. **—u muaddel** *astr.* the horary angle of a heavenly body from the east or west horizon. **—u mukavvem** *astr.* tabulated distance. **—u müzevva** *astr.* angular distance. **—u ru'yet** apparent distance. **—u semtürre's** *astr.* zenith distance. **—u tamamî** *naut.* nautical distance.

bud 2 بود. *cf.* **but 1.**

bud 3 (—) بود P *lrnd.* existence, being.

buda=ʳ **1** بودامق /ı/ 1. to prune, to lop; to trim. 2. *wrestling* to prevent from gripping.

Buda 2 ('.) بودا. Buddha.

budacıkᵗⁱ بوداجق *dim. of* **budak.**

budakᵍⁱ بوداق، بوده، بوداغ 1. knot (in timber), burr. 2. *archaic* branch, twig. — **deliği**, **— gözü** knothole. **— özü** young shoot. **—lan=** 1. to become knotty. 2. to send forth shoots. **—landır=** /ı/ *caus. of* **budaklan=**. **—lı** gnarled, knotty.

budala بودالا بداله [**büdelâ**] 1. foolish, imbecile; fool. 2. crazy (about), *e. g.*, **sinema budalası** crazy about movies. **— yerine koy=** *colloq.* to take one for a fool. **—ca** stupidly; stupidly done. **—lan=** to become stupid. **—landır=** /ı/ *caus. of* **budalalan=**. **—lık** 1. foolishness, stupidity. 2. craze, madness.

budama بودامه. *verbal n. of* **buda=** 1.

bu'dan 1 (.—) بعدان A *lrnd., pl. of* **baid 1.**

budan=ᵘʳ **2, budanıl=**ᵘʳ بودانمه. *pass. of* **buda=**. **—ış** *verbal n. of* **budan=**.

budantı بودانتی loppings, prunings.

Budapeşte (...'.) بودا پشت. Budapest.

budat=ᵘʳ بوداتمه /ı/ *caus. of* **buda=**.

budayıcı بودایجی. pruner of trees.

budayış بودایش. *verbal n. of* **buda=**.

bu'de 1 بعده A *lrnd.* 1. distance. 2. prudence, penetration.

bude 2 (—.) بوده P *lrnd.* existent.

bu'den 1 ('.) بعدا A *lrnd.* in point of distance.

buden 2 (—.) بودا P *lrnd.* being, existence.

budeni (—.—) بودنی P *lrnd.* possible; future; likely to happen; fore-ordained.

Budin ('.) بودین. *geog.* Buda.

Budist بودیست F Buddhist.

Budizm بودیزم F Buddhism.

budun *neol.* people, nation.

budunbetim *neol.* ethnography.

budunbilim *neol.* ethnology.

bueda (..—) بعدا A *lrnd., pl. of* **baid 1.**

bufa ('.) بوفه. lamprey, *zool.*, *Petromyzon*.

bufüruş (—.—) بوفروش. P *lrnd.* vender of scents, perfumer.

buga (.—) بغاء. A *lrnd.* a desiring, endeavoring.

bugas (.—) بغاث. A *lrnd.* certain birds that are not hunted.

bugat (.—) بغات A *lrnd.* rebels; bandits.

bugün بوکون. today. **—lerde** in these days. **—e bugün** unquestionably, sure enough (used in emphatic speech). **— buldum bugün yerim, yarına Allah kerim** *colloq.* Today I have found food, so I will eat today; tomorrow is in God's hands. **—den tezi yok** right away. **— yarın** at any time, soon. **—kü** of today, today's. **—lük** for today.

buğ 1 بغ. *var. of* **buğu 1.**

buğ 2 بغ. *archaic* leader, chieftain, commander.

buğa بغا. *var. of* **boğa**.

buğaça (.'.) بوغاچه *var. of* **boğaça.**

buğata (.'.) بوغاته *var. of* **boğata.**

buğaza (..—) بغضاء A *lrnd., pl. of* **bagız.**

buğda بغدا prov. for **buğday**.
buğday بغدای ، برغدای 1. wheat. 2. weight grain (72 to a miskal). — **biti** wheat weevil. — **ekmeğin yoksa buğday dilin de mi yok?** If you cannot give what you are asked for, at least act in a friendly way. — **pası** wheat rust; wheat mildew. — **rengi** darkish (skin). —**cık** goat grass, bot., Aegilops ovata. —**cıl** a bird of the thrush family, zool., Luscinia svecica cyanecula. —**giller** neol., bot., Gramineae, Poaceae. —**sı meyva** neol., bot., caryopsis.
buğlan=ᵣ برغلنم. var. of **buğulan**=.
buğra بوغرا. adult male camel.
buğu بوغو ، بوغی 1. vapor, steam, fog; vapor settled on glass, etc. 2. moisture, dew on fruit, «the bloom». — **bağla**= to become fogged, to be steamed up (window pane). —**ya otur**= to take a vapor bath. —**da pişir**= /ı/ to stew.
buğulan=ᵣ برغولانمق to be steamed up, to mist over (glass, etc). —**dır**= /ı/ caus.
buğulu بوغولی fogged, steamed up; covered with dew (fruit).
buğur 1 بوغور. adult male Bactrian camel. —**sa**= same as **boğursa**=.
buğur 2 بوغور. [bu uğur] archaic then, now.
buğyan (.—) بغیان A lrnd. seekers, strivers.
buğyet بغیت A lrnd. a desiring, seeking.
buğz بغض A hatred, spite, malevolence, rancor, enmity, ill will. —**et**= /a/ to hate.
buh (—) بوه. A lrnd. great horned owl, eagle owl, zool., Bubo bubo.
buhaçᶜⁱ بوهاچ Sl owl.
buhar 1 بخار. [buhar 2] steam, vapor. — **gemisi** steamship. — **makinası** steam engine.
buhar 2 (.—) بخار. A lrnd. vapor; effluvium, exhalation, fumes.
Buhara (.—́—) بخارا geog. Bukhara, Bokhara. — **halısı** Bokhara (rug).
Buhari 1 (.——) بخاری. A native of Bukhara.
buhari 2 (.——) بخاری. P prov. chimney.
buharlan=ᵣ بخارلانمق. 1. to vaporize, to evaporate. 2. to be exposed to steam. 3. to give out steam. —**dır**= /ı/ caus.
buharlaş=ᵣ بخارلاشمق. to evaporate, to vaporize. —**ma** evaporation. —**tır**= /ı/ to vaporize.
buharlı بخارلی. steamy, vaporous.
buhası بخاسی var. of **boğası 1**.
buhelâ (..—) بخلا. A lrnd. misers.
buheyre بحیره. A geog. small sea; lagoon; lake. —**i dem'iye** anat. lachrymal sac.
buhlˡⁱ بخل. A lrnd. avarice, stinginess.
buhran (.—) بحران A crisis. —**ı ceyyid** path. salutary crisis. — **geçir**= 1. to go through a crisis. 2. to have a fit of nerves. —**ı kâmil**, —**ı mahmud** path. salutary crisis. — **noktası** phys. critical points. —**ı redi** path. unfavorable crisis. — **suhuneti** phys. critical temperature. —**ı tahallül** path. salutary crisis. — **vergisi** emergency tax. —**ı zeveban**, —**ı zübul** path. unfavorable crisis, followed by dissolution. —**î** (.——) A sc. critical. —**lı** (.—.) sc. critical.
buhş بخش. A lrnd. hole; central hole of an astrolabe.
buht بخت. A lrnd. Bactrian camel.
buhtec بختج. A lrnd. decoction; grape juice boiled down to a syrup.
buhti (.—) بختی. A lrnd. Bactrian camel.
Buhtnasr بخت نصر , **Buhtunnasr** بختالنصر A Nebuchadnezzar.
buhuᵘᵘ 1 (.—) بخوع. A lrnd. a humbling oneself, submission.
buhu 2 بوهو. var. of **puhu**.
buhulˡⁱ (.—) بخول. A lrnd. 1. avarice. 2. stinginess.
buhur 1 (.—) بحور. A lrnd., pl. of **bahr 1, 2**.
buhur 2 (.—) بخور. [bahur 2] incense, fumigatory. —**u Meryem** cyclamen, bot., Cyclamen europaeum.
buhur 3 بخور. same as **buğur 1¹**.
buhurcu (.—.) بخورجی. dealer in incense.
buhurdan (.——) بخوردان. [buhur 2, -dan] 1. censer. 2. incense box. —**lık** censer.
buhurla=ᵣ بخورلامق. /ı/ to fumigate with incense. —**n**= pass. —**t**= /ı,a/ caus. of **buhurla**=.
buhurlu بخورلو impregnated with incense.
buhurlukᵍᵘ بخورلوك 1. censer. 2. incense box.
buhus (.—) بخوس. A lrnd., pl. of **bahs 3**.
buhuş (.—) بخوش. A lrnd., pl. of **buhş**.
buhutet (.—.) بخوتت. A lrnd. purity, unadulteratedness.
buji بوژی F 1. mech. spark plug. 2. med. bougie.
bukᵏᵘ (—) بوق. A lrnd. 1. horn, trumpet; blast of a horn. 2. conch shell. 3. blab, indiscreet person. 4. nonsense, foolish.
buk'a 1 بقعه A lrnd. 1. plot of land, district, region. 2. spot, patch. 3. large building, edifice.
buka 2 (—.) بوقا. A lrnd., same as **buk**.
bukadar بوقادار. بوقدر. 1. this much, that much, so many. 2. That's all. 3. odd, e. g., **yetmiş bukadar yıl** seventy-odd years. —**ı da fazla** That's too much; that is going too far. —**a kadar** to that degree. — **kusur kadı kızında da bulunur** Nothing can be perfect.
bukağı بوقاغی ، بوقغی fetter; hobble. —**la**= /ı/ to fetter. —**lan**= passive of **bukağıla**=. —**lat**= /ı/ caus. of **bukağıla**=.

—lı furnished with a fetter, fettered. **—lık** pastern.

bukal بُقَال Gk bottle for wine or beer.

bukalemun 1 بُوقَلَمُون [bukalemun 2] 1. chameleon, zool., *Chamaeleon vulgaris*. 2. fickle person.

bukalemun 2 (—..—) بُوقَلَمُون P lrnd. 1. fickle, capricious, changeable, 2. particolored, variegated; iridescent; shot silk. 3. chameleon. 4. turkey, zool., *Meleagris gallopavo*. 5. fickle fortune, changeable world. 6. the everchanging vegetation of the fields. 7. kaleidoscope. 8. tortoise.

bukame (.—.) بُغَام A lrnd. 1. refuse of wool. 2. stupid man, idiot.

bukat (——) بُوقَات A lrnd., pl. of **buk**.

buket بُوكَت F bunch of flowers, bouquet.

bukkar (.—) بَقَّار A lrnd., pl. of **bakare**.

bukle بُوكْل F curl of hair, lock.

Bukrat (.—) بُقْرَاط A Hippocrates, the physician. **—î** (.——) A Hippocratic. **—iyun** (.———) A adherents of the Hippocratic school of medicine.

bukul (.—) بُقُول A lrnd., pl. of **bakl**.

bukva (.—) بُقْوَا A var. of **bakva**.

bukya (.—) بُقْيَا A var. of **bakya**.

bul= بُولْمَق 1. /ı/ to find; to discover; to invent. 2. /ı/ to reach, to hit; to meet (with). 3. /ı,a/ to find (fault, with), to blame (on). 4. *naut.* to run aground (ship). **—up buluştur=** to be adroit in providing. **—dukça buna=** not to find anything enough, always wishing for more.

bula 1 بُولا prov. elder sister.

bula= 2 بُولامَق 1. /ı, a/ to roll (in flour); to besmear, bedaub (with); to smear (on). 2. /ı/ archaic to stir, mix.

bul'aceb بُو الْعَجَب A lrnd. 1. wonderful thing. 2. juggler, conjurer.

bulada بُولادا Gk prov. chicken.

bulak 1 بُولاه prov. spring, fountain. **— otu** watercress, bot., *Nasturtium officinale*.

Bulak 2 بُولاق Boulaq (quarter of Cairo).

bulama بُولامَه 1. a semi-solid molasses of boiled grape juice. 2. verbal. n. of **bula=** 2. 3. smeared.

bulamaç بُولامَاچ thick soup made with flour, butter and sugar.

bulan= بُولانمَق 1. to become turbid; to become cloudy. 2. to be stirred, to be upset. 3. pass. of **bula=** 2. **—dır=** /ı/ caus. of **bulan=**. **—dırış** verbal n.

bulanık بُولانِق turbid; cloudy; dim. **— suda balık avla=** to fish in muddy waters. **—lık** abstr. n. **—sı** somewhat turbid.

bulanış بُولانِش, **bulanma** بُولانمَه verbal n. of **bulan=**.

bulantı بُولانتى 1. nausea. 2. turbidity.

bular بُولَر archaic, pl. of **bu 1**.

bulaş= بُولاشمَق 1. to be smeared, to become dirty. 2. /a/ to soil, to become smeared (on), to be sticky. 3. /a/ to pass by contagion (disease). 4. /a/ to be involved (in an affair). 5. /a/ to stick (to, troublesome person); to pester. 6. /a/ to take in hand (work). **—ıcı** contagious (disease).

bulaşık بُولاشِق 1. smeared, bedaubed, soiled; tainted. 2. contagious (disease). 3. compromising, troublesome. 4. smear, blotch, daub, stain, smudge. 5. dirty dishes. **— bezi** dish cloth. **— deniz** dangerous waters (because of mines). **— gemi** ship with a foul bill of health. **— makinası** dishwasher (machine). **— patente** naut. foul bill of health. **— suyu** dishwater. **—çı** dish washer. **—lık** abstr. n. of **bulaşık 1-3**.

bulaşıl= بُولاشِلمَق pass. of **bulaş=**.

bulaşış بُولاشِش verbal n. of **bulaş=**.

bulaşkan بُولاشقان sticky, adhesive.

bulaşma بُولاشمَه verbal n. of **bulaş=**; ling. contamination.

bulaştır= بُولاشدِرمَق /ı,a/ caus. of **bulaş=**.

bulat= بُولاتمَق /ı,a/ archaic, caus. of **bula=** 2².

bulayıcı بُولايِجى one who smears or plasters.

bulayış بُولايِش verbal n. of **bula=** 2.

buldok بُولدوك F bulldog.

buldumcuk ol= بُولدُمجُق اُولمَق pop. to lose one's head in joy at having found something greatly desired.

buldur= بُولدُرمَق /ı,a/ caus. of **bul=**.

Buleheb (—..) بُو لَهَب var. of **Ebuleheb**.

Bulgar بُولغَار 1. a Bulgarian. 2. hist. a Volga-Bulgarian; the country of the Volga-Bulgarians; the city Bolgar on the Volga. 3. l. c. Russian leather, Bulgar. **—ca** Bulgarian (language).

bulgari (..—) بُلغَارى [based on **Bulgar**] 1. small kind of guitar. 2. Russian leather.

Bulgaristan (...—) بُلغَارِستان [based on **Bulgar**] Bulgaria.

bulgu neol. a finding, discovery; invention.

bulgur بُولغُور 1. boiled and pounded wheat. 2. snow in small, hard grains. **— pilâvı** dish of boiled pounded wheat. **—cu** dealer in pounded wheat. **—cuk** snow in small, hard grains. **B—lu** name of a village east of Üsküdar. **B—luya gelin mi gideceksin?** (lit. Are you going as a bride to Bulgurlu?) Why are you in such a hurry?

bulgusal neol., phil. heuristic.

bulheves بُو الْهَوَس P var. of **ebülheves**.

bulma بولمه. *verbal n. of* **bul=**.
bulmaca بولمه جه crossword puzzle.
bulti (. —) بلطى. A Nile perch, *zool.*, *Lates niloticus*.
bulucu بولیجی. that finds, capable of finding.
bulum بولوم. *verbal n. of* **bul=**.
bulun 1 بولون *archaic* captive, prisoner.
bulun=ᵘʳ **2** بولنش 1. *pass. of* **bul=**. 2. /da/ to find oneself, to be found, to be present, to exist, to be; to take part (in); to be (at), to be busy (with); *with verbal nouns, e. g.*, **ricada bulun=** to make a request. 3. /a/ to be available for help (to). **—dur=** /ı/ *caus*. **—durul=** *pass. of* **bulundur=**. **—ma** *verbal n. of* **bulun=**. **—maz** unobtainable, not to be found; rare, choice. **—maz Hint kumaşı** a very rare, excellent thing. **—tu** 1. a rare find. 2. foundling. **—ul=** *pass. of* **bulun=**². **—uş** *verbal n. of* **bulun=**.
buluş 1 بولیش *verbal n. of* **bul=**. 1. invention; discovery. 2. original thought.
buluş=ᵘʳ **2** بولشمی. to come together, to meet.
buluşlu بولشلی. clever, resourceful.
buluşma بولشمه meeting.
buluştur=ᵘʳ بولشدرمق /ı/ *caus. of* **buluş= 2**. **—ma** a bringing together (two people).
bulut بولوط. بولت. بولوت 1. cloud. 2. *slang* dead drunk. **— gibi** dead drunk. **—tan nem kap=** to be very touchy, or suspicious. **—unu ver=** *slang* to become dead drunk. **—lan=** to become cloudy. **—landır=** /ı/ *caus. of* **bulutlan=**. **—lu** cloudy; turbid, opaque. **—su** *astr.* nebulous, nebular. **—suz** cloudless, clear.
bulûz بلوز. *var. of* **blûz**.
bulvar بولوار. F boulevard.
bum 1 (—) بوم A *lrnd.* owl.
bum 2 (—) بوم P *lrnd.* 1. country, region; one's home, country. 2. ground, groundwork of embroidered cloth. 3. nature, character, disposition.
bumba (. .) بومبه [**bomba 2**] *naut.* spanker boom.
bumbar بونبار [**mumbar**] 1. large gut for sausages. 2. sausage made of rice and meat stuffed in a large gut. 3. weatherstripping. **—lık** sausage stuffing.
bumburuşukᵏᵘ بوم بوروشد. very creased, wrinkled all over.
bun 1 بوڭ. *prov.* distress, depression, calamity, trouble, great need.
bun- 2 بوڭ. *cf.* **bu 1**.
buna 1 بوڭا 1. *dative of* **bu 1**. 2. *archaic* hither. **— binaen** hence, for this reason. **— gelince** as to this. **— mebni** hence, for this reason. **— mukabil** on the other hand.
buna=ʳ **2** بوناسمق. بوڭاسمق to enter

upon dotage, to become imbecile.
bunakᵏ¹ بوڭاق. in second childhood, dotard. **—lık** dotage.
bunal=ᵘʳ بوڭالمق. بوكلمق 1. /dan/ to be stupefied (with smoke, trouble, talk). 2. to be bored, depressed. **—ım edebiyatı** beat literature. **—ım gençliği** crazy, mixed up kids. **—ış**, **—ma** *verbal n. of* **bunal=**. **—t=** /ı/ to stupefy. **—tıcı** stupefying. **—tış**, **—tma** *verbal n. of* **bunalt=**.
bunama بوڭاما *verbal n. of* **buna= 2**, dotage, second childhood.
bunamış بوڭامش dotard. **—lık** *abstr. n.*
bunar بكار *archaic*, *var. of* **pınar**.
bunat=ᵘʳ بوڭاتمق /ı/ *caus. of* **buna= 2**.
bunca (.´.) بونجه. 1. this much, so much. 2. *archaic* in this way. **— zaman** for such a long time.
buncağız بونجغز. this poor little thing.
buncılayın بونجیلایین *archaic* 1. so much, this much. 2. like this, such.
bunda بونده. 1. *locative of* **bu 1**. 2. *archaic* here; hither.
bundan بوندن. 1. *ablative of* **bu 1**. 2. *archaic* from here. **— akdem**, **— akdemce** before this; formerly, before. **— başka** besides; moreover. **— böyle** henceforth. **— dolayı** therefore. **— iyisi can sağlığı** What more do you want? This is the best one can have. **— nâşi**, **— ötürü** therefore. **— sonra** 1. after this. 2. henceforth, from now on.
bundukᵏᵘ **1** بندق A *lrnd.* 1. filbert, hazelnut; various species of nuts. 2. cannon ball, bullet, missile. 3. crossbow; musket, matchlock. **—u hindî** nicker nut, seed of *Caesalpinia bonduc*.
bundukᵏᵘ **2** (. —) بندوق. A *lrnd.*, *same as* **bunduk 1**²,³.
bunduka بندقه A *lrnd.* 1. nut, hazelnut. 2. ball, missile, bullet. 3. pellet of indurated feces in the bowels.
bundukçu بندقچی. *archaic* 1. pellet-shooting crossbow-man. 2. matchlock-man.
bundukdar (. . —) بندقدار [**bunduk 1**, **-dar**] *same as* **bundukçu**.
bunduki (. . —) بندقى A *hist.* Venetian sequin.
bundukiye (. . — .) بندقیه A *hist.* musket; crossbow for shooting pellets.
bungun بوڭغن *prov.* oppressive; sad, distressing.
bunlar بونلر *pl. of* **bu 1**.
bunlu بوڭلی *archaic* depressing, distressing, sad.
bunsuz بونسز without this.
bunu بونی *accusative of* **bu 1**.
bunucukᵏᵘ بونیجق *colloq.* this little thing.
bunun بونڭ *possessive of* **bu 1**. **—la beraber**,

—la birlikte nevertheless. — burası this very place. — için therefore. — üzerine thereupon.
bur 1 (—) بُرْ. A lrnd. waste land; unfit for cultivation, rough.
bur 2 (—) بُرْ. A lrnd., pl. of bair 1, in — ve hınziyan good-for-nothing and infamous.
bur 3 (—) بُرْ. P lrnd. roan. —u ebreş red roan.
bur=ᵃʳ 4 بُرْمَسْ /ı/ 1. to twist, to screw; to wring. 2. to castrate by strangulation of the neck of the scrotum. 3. to gripe (bowels). 4. to cause an acrid feeling in the mouth. 5. archaic to wind, wrap (around). —a bura oyna= to dance with violent contortions.
bura (.́.) بُورَا بُرَا [bu, ara] this place, this spot. cf. also burada, buradan, burası, buraya.
buracık^{ğı} بُورَاجِقْ. this small place.
burada بُورَادَه. here.
buradan بُورَادَنْ. from here, hence.
burağan بُورَاغَانْ. whirlwind, an eddying tempest of wind, rain, or snow.
Burak^{kı} 1 (.—) بُرَاقْ. A traditional name of the horse which carried the Prophet Muhammad for his ascension. —ı Cem lrnd. the wind called up by King Solomon to carry him and his throne.
burak^{kı} 2 (—.) بُورَقْ. A lrnd. borax.
burak=ᵘʳ 3 بُورَقْمِ. archaic, var. of bırak=.
buraki (—.—) بُورَقِي. A lrnd. pertaining to borax.
burakulhabbazin (—...——) بُورَة الخَبَّازِينْ A lrnd. baking soda.
burakussağa (—..—.) بُورَن الصَّاغْ A lrnd. pure borax.
buralı بُورَلي. native of this place.
buram buram بُورَامْ بُورَامْ in whirls (snow), in clouds (smoke), in great quantities (smell, sweat).
buran بُورَانْ var. of burağan.
buranca (.́.) بُورَانْجَ. Gk great mullein, bot., Verbascum Trapsus.
burancina (...́.) بُورَانْجِنَ. It naut. metal lining of the pinhole of a blocksheave.
buranda (.́.) بُرَانْدَا [branda] naut. sailor's hammock. — bezi canvas.
burani (———) بُورَانِي. P lrnd., same as borani.
buranice بُورَانِجَ. Sl dugout canoe used by fishermen in the Balkans.
buraniye (———.) بُورَانِيَه. A same as borani.
burası^{nı} بُورَاسِي. 1. this place. 2. this particular, this.
buraya بُورَيَه. here, hither.
burc بُرْج. A 1. tower; bastion. 2. constellation of the zodiac, sign of the zodiac. 3. astrol. planetary house, mansion. —u âbî Aquarius. —u akreb Scorpio. —u ateşî, —u azerî igneous sign (Aries, Leo, Sagittarius). —u bâdî aerial sign (Gemini, Libra, Aquarius). — u baru towers and walls (of a castle). —u bere Aries. —u büz, —u cedi Capricornus. —u cenubî southern sign (Libra to Pisces). —u cevza Gemini. —u delv Aquarius. —u esed Leo. —u hâkî terraneous sign (Taurus, Virgo, Capricornus). —u hamel Aries. —u harifî autumnal sign (Libra, Scorpio, Sagittarius). —u hilâl Cancer. —u hoşe Virgo. —u hût Pisces. —u kavs Sagittarius. —u mizan Libra. —u rebiî vernal sign (Aries, Taurus, Gemini). —u sayfî estival sign (Cancer, Leo, Virgo). —u seretan Cancer. —u sevr Taurus. —u sünbüle Virgo. —u süreyya Pleiades. —u şeref astrol. the house of honor or exaltation of any planet. —u şetvi hibernal sign (Capricornus, Aquarius, Pisces). —u şimalî northern sign (Aries to Virgo). —u terazu Libra.
burcu burcu بُرْجِي بُرْجِي. fragrantly, smelling sweetly.
burç^{cu} 1 بُرْج. var. of burc.
burç^{cu} 2 بُرْج. بُرج. prov. 1. mistletoe, bot., Viscum album. 2. shoot, sprout.
burçak^{ğı} بُرْچَاق. common vetch, bot., Vicia sativa.
burda (.́.) بُورْدَه. var. of burada.
burdur=ᵘʳ بُورْدُرْمَسْ /ı,a/ caus. of bur= 4.
bure (—.) بُورَه. P lrnd. borak.
burgaç^{cı} بُورْغَاج. بُرْغَاج. 1. twist, bend; twisted, bent, crooked, screwed. 2. involved, confusing (speech). —lan= to become twisted, sinuous, involved.
burgas بُورْغَاسْ var. of burgus.
burgaşık^{ğı} بُورْغَاشِقْ. archaic twisted, crooked.
burgata (.́.) بُورْغَاتَ. It naut. unit of measure for the circumference of a rope (about one inch).
burgaz بُرْغَازْ بُورْغَازْ. var. of burguz.
burgu بُورْغُو بُرْغُو. 1. auger, gimlet. 2. corkscrew. 3. prov. screw. 4. peg to tighten a string in stringed instruments. 5. archaic torture screw. 6. archaic kind of trumpet. —cu maker or seller of screws; shipbuilding worker at screwing planks.
burgul 1 بُورْغُولْ [burgul 2] prov., same as bulgur.
burgul^{lü} 2 (.—) بُرْغُولْ. P lrnd., same as bulgur.
burgula=ᵣ بُورْغُولَامَسْ بُرْغُولَمَسْ. /ı/ to bore with a gimlet. —n= 1. pass. 2. prov. to make kicking movements with his legs (baby).
burgulu بُورْغُولُو. 1. furnished with screw, gimlet, or borer, threaded. 2. screwed.

burgus, burguz برغوس برغوز Gk archaic castle, tower.
burhan برهان var. of **bürhan**.
buri 1 (— —) بوری A lrnd. 1. rush or reed mat. 2. gray mullet.
buri 2 (— —) بوری A lrnd. gone to the bad (boy).
burina (.'.') بورینه [borina] naut. bowline. — **patası** bowline bridle. — **yakası** leach.
burinata (...'.) بوریناته [borineta] naut. topgallant bowline.
buriya (— . —) بوریا P lrnd. mat woven of rushes or reeds.
buriyabaf (— . — —) بوریاباف P lrnd. weaver of rush mats.
burjuva بورژوا F sociol. bourgeois.
burjuvazi بورژوازی F sociol. bourgeoisie.
burk=ᵃʳ برقمن بوقمن 1. /ı/ to sprain (joint). 2. same as **burkul**=. 3. /ı/ archaic to twist.
burkaᵃⁱ برخ A var. of **burku 1**. —**ı kühli** poet. darkness.
burkaküşa (...—) برخكش P lrnd. lifter of veils. —**yı esrar** who unravels mysteries.
burkuᵘᵘ **1** برخ A lrnd. 1. lady's veil. 2. door curtain of the Kaaba at Mecca. 3. firmament; first, fourth or seventh heaven.
burkuᵘᵘ **2** (.—) برقوع A lrnd. lady's veil.
burkukᵏᵘ (.—) برقون A the wild apricot.
burkulˡᵘ **1** برقول var. of **burgul**.
burkul=ᵘʳ **2** بورقمن to be sprained. —**muş** sprained. —**uk** castrated by twisting. —**uş** verbal. n. of **burkul**=.
burkut=ᵘʳ برقتمن /ı/ to sprain. —**uş** verbal n.
burlağan بورلغان prov. water eddy, whirlpool.
burlota (.'.') بورلوته It naut. fire ship.
Burma 1 بورمه geog. Burma.
burma 2 بورمه 1. verbal n. of **bur**= 4. 2. screwed, twisted, spiral; screw, anything having a screw thread; screw thread; screw, convolution; formed by twisting. 3. gripe of colic. 4. castrated by twisting. 5. tap, faucet, cock. 6. prov. bracelet. — **sarık** turban with thick coils. —**la**= 1. to make into a spiral. 2. to furnish with a screw thread. —**lı** 1. having a spiral. 2. furnished with a screw thread. —**lı tüfek** gun with a twisted barrel, rifled gun.
burnaz بورناز large-nosed, hawk-nosed.
burnus, burnuz بورنس برنوز [bürnüs] 1. Arabian cloak, burnous. 2. bathrobe.
burs بورس F scholarship, bursary.
Bursa (.'.) بورسه برسه geog. Bursa, the ancient Prusia.
Bursavi (.——), **Bursevi** بورساوی [based on **Bursa**] native of **Bursa**.
burt=ᵃʳ بورتمن same as **burtar**=.
burtar=ⁱʳ بورتارمه /ı/ archaic to contort (face). —**t**= /ı,a/ caus.
burtukᵍᵘ بورتوق puckered, wrinkled, creased; pucker, wrinkle, crease.
burtul=ᵘʳ بورتمن to become puckered, wrinkled, contorted.
burtın بورتون It hist. kind of large warship.
burtuş=ᵘʳ بورتشمن to be wrinkled, contorted. —**uk** puckered, wrinkled, contorted.
buru بورى 1. gripe of colic. 2. prov. pains of childbirth.
burucu بوروجى that twists.
burukᵍᵘ بوروق 1. acrid, astringent, puckery. 2. twisted, sprained; twist, sprain. —**luk** abstr. n.
burul=ᵘʳ بورولمه 1. pass. of **bur**= 4. 2. to twist oneself about, to writhe. —**ma** verbal n. —**muş** 1. twisted, screwed. 2. castrated by twisting.
burulu بورولو 1. twisted, screwed. 2. /a/ wound (around). 3. strangled; castrated by strangulation of the scrotum.
burum بوروم 1. twist, contortion. 2. gripe of the bowels. — **burum** 1. all in twists, contorted. 2. repeatedly griped.
burunʳⁿᵘ **1** بورون برون 1. nose. 2. beak, bill. 3. tip, pointed end. 4. headland, cape, point. 5. pride, arrogance. — **boku** prov. dirt of the nose. — **boşluğu** anat. nasal cavity. — **bur** /a/ to curl the nostrils in disdain, to turn one's nose up (at). — **buruna** close together, very close. — **buruna gel**= /la/ to run (into). — **bük**= /a/ to turn one's nose up (at). — **u büyü**= to become conceited. —**u büyük** arrogant, conceited. —**unu çek**= 1. to sniff. 2. colloq. not to get anything. —**una çık**= /ın/ to become unbearable (to). — **deliği** nostril. —**unun dibinde** under one's very nose, very near at hand. —**unun dikine git**= to go one's way not caring for other people's advice. — **direği** anat. nasal septum. —**umun direği kırıldı** The bad smell suffocates me. —**umun direği sızladı** I felt pained. —**unun doğrusuna git**= same as **burnunun dikine git**=. —**um düştü** The bad smell has suffocated me. —**undan düşmüş** /ın/ very like him or her, resembling greatly, the very image (of). —**undan düşen bin parça olur** Anything that falls from his nose breaks into a thousand pieces (said for a person in a very bad temper). —**undan fitil fitil gel**=, —**undan gel**= to be spoiled completely (pleasure). — **una gel**= /ın/ to become unbearable (to). —**undan getir**= /ın/ to spoil the pleasure (of a person). —**una gir**= to

come too close (to a person). **—u havada conceited**, nose-in-the-air. **—una hırızmayı tak=** /ın/ (*lit.* to put a ring in one's nose) to twist around one's finger. **—u kabar=** to become conceited. **—u Kafdağında** very conceited. **— kanı** bright scarlet color. **—undan kan damlayıncaya kadar çalış=** to exhaust oneself with work. **—u kana=** to bleed from the nose. **—u kanamadan** without being hurt, without· the slightest scratch. **— kanadı** *anat.*, ala of the nose. **— kemiği** *anat.* nasal bone, *os nasale*. **—undan kıl aldırma=** to be very conceited and unapproachable; untouchable. **—unu kır=** /ın/ to humiliate. **— kıvır=** /a/ to turn one's nose up (at), to sniff (at). **—unda kok=** *same as* **burnunda tüt=**. **— nezlesi** rhinitis. **— otu** *obs.* snuff. **— perdesi** nasal septum. **—unu sıksan canı çıkar** He is greatly distressed. **—unu sil=** to blow one's nose. **—unu sok=** /a/ to poke one's nose (into). **—undan solu=** to be greatly enraged. **—unu sür=** /a/ *same as* **burnunu sok=**. **—unu sürt=** to eat humble pie. **—u sürtül=** to learn one's lesson through a humiliating experience. **— şişir=** to swell with pride. **— tapası** *mil.* nose fuze. **—umda tütüyor** I long for him. **—unun ucunda** under one's nose, very close. **—unun ucunu görme=** to be blind with pride. **—unun ucundan ilerisini görme=** to be unable to see further than one's nose. **—undan yakalan=** to be well and truly caught. **—unun yeli harman savuruyor** The wind from his nose could winnow wheat (said of a very conceited person). **— zarı** nasal tissue.

burun=ᵘʳ 2 بورون. to gripe with colic.
buruncukᵍᵘ بورنجق ،بورونجك. *dim.* of **burun**.
buruncuna (...ˊ.) بورنجنه. *var.* of **buruncina**.
burundalıkᵍⁱ بروندالق ،بورنداليق
burundarukᵍᵘ ،برونداروق **burunduk**ᵍᵘ بوروندوق،
burundurukᵍᵘ بوروندوروق
same as **burunsalık**.
burunlu بورنلو ،بورونلو 1. that has a nose; pointed. 2. proud, arrogant.
burunsalıkᵍⁱ
بورنصالق ،بورونصالق ،برونصالق ،برونصاليق. device fixed on the nose of an animal; switch for holding the muzzle, lip, or nose; ring, toggle, or loop passed through the cartilage of the nose or lip.
burunsuz بورنسز ،بورونسز. 1. having no nose, point, etc. 2. having a very small or flat nose. 3. having forward control (automobile), cab over engine.
buruntu بورنتى. griping in the bowels, colic.
Burusa بروسه. *archaic for* **Bursa**.
buruş 1 بورش ،بوروش. 1. pucker, wrinkle, crumple, corrugation. 2. *verbal n.* of **bur=** 4. 3. *prov.* dried fruit. **— buruş ol=**, **— yarış ol=** to become very crumpled.
buruş=ᵘʳ 2 بوروشمك ،بروشمك to become puckered, wrinkled, crumpled, ruffled.
buruşko (..ˊ.) بوروشقو ،بروشقو. It rough in taste, tart, but lively and fresh (wine).
buruşma بورشمه ،بوروشمه verbal *n.* of **buruş=** 2.
buruştur=ᵘʳ بوروشدرمك ،بروشدرمك ،بروشديرمك /ı/ to pucker, wrinkle, crumple, ruffle, contort.
buruşukᵍᵘ بوروشوق ،بوروشيق ،بروشوق ،بروشيق. puckered, wrinkled, crumpled, contorted, shrivelled, ruffled; pucker, wrinkle, crumple, crease.
bus 1 بس. *prov.*, *var.* of **püs**.
bus 2 (—) بوس. P *lrnd.* a kissing; kiss. **— et=***.
-bus 3 (—) بوس. P *lrnd.* kisser, kissing, as in **damenbus**.
bus 4 (—) بوص. A *lrnd.* 1. color, complexion. 2. buttocks; fullness in buttocks of a woman.
busakᵏⁱ (.—) بصاق. A *lrnd.* spittle, saliva when spit out.
busakulkamer (.—...) بصاق القمر. A *lrnd.* selenite, moonstone.
busara (..—) بصرا. A *lrnd.*, *pl.* of **basir**.
busat بساط. *archaic*, *var.* of **pusat**.
buse (—.) بوسه. P *lrnd.* 1. kiss. 2. *myst.* worldly pleasure; emotion of divine love and rapture evoked in the heart of a devotee.
buseca, busecay (—.—) بوسه جا ،بوسه جاى. P *poet.* a place usually kissed.
buseçin (—.—) بوسه چين. P *poet.* gathering kisses.
busegâh (—.—) بوسه گاه. P *poet.* 1. a place usually kissed. 2. royal apartment.
busekᵏⁱ (—.) بوسك. P *poet.* little kiss.
buselikᵍⁱ 1 (—.—) بوسليك. P Or. *mus.* 1. the note b'. 2. **makam** starting with a', c" or e", stressing c", and ending on a'. **— aşiran makam** composed of the **makams buselik** and **aşiran**.
buselikᵍⁱ 2 (—..) بوسه لك. worth a kiss (thing).
buset=ᵈᵉʳ بوس ايتمك. to kiss.
-busi (——) بوسى. P *lrnd.*, *abstr. n.* of **-bus** 3, as in **damenbusi**.
buside (———.) بوسيده. P *lrnd.* 1. who has kissed. 2. that has been kissed.
bust بسط. A *lrnd.*, *pl.* of **bisat**.
bustan (——) بوستان. P *lrnd.*, same as **bostan**.
bustanefruz (——.—) بوستان افروز. P *lrnd.* cockscomb, *bot.*, *Celosia cristata*.

bustani (———) بُسْتانی. P lrnd.
1. horticultural; cultivated. 2. gardener.
3. *Ott. hist.* member of the corps of the Imperial guard.

bustanpira (————) بُسْتان پیرا. P lrnd. gardener.

bustanseray (——.—) بُسْتان سرای. P lrnd. pavillion or palace in a garden.

busu بُوصُو archaic for **pusu**.

buş 1 بُوش. E mech. bushing.

buş 2 (—) بُوش. P lrnd. kind of eye salve gathered from the hooves of sheep, and imported from Derbend on the Caspian.

buş=ar 3 بُوشی. /ı/ archaic to become angry (with).

buşu بُوشو. archaic anger.

butdu 1 بُوت. thigh, leg of meat, rump.

butt'u 2 بطء. A lrnd. slowness.

buta بُوطه [bute] archaic 1. same as **pota**. 2. archery target.

Butalib (——.) بُوطالب. var. of **Ebutalib**.

butayn بُطين. A lrnd. 1. anat. ventricle. 2. astrol., ventriculus Arietis (the second lunar mansion).

bute (—.) بُوته. P lrnd. 1. shrub. 2. young animal; child. 3. crucible. 4. butt for shooting at.

buteyn بُطين. var. of **butayn**.

butimar (———) بُوتیمار. P lrnd. heron, egret, bittern.

butkal بُوتقال. It wine bottle, beer bottle.

butllü بطل. A lrnd., same as **butlan**.

butlan (.—) بُطلان. A 1. law invalidity, nullity, voidness. 2. lrnd. worthlessness, uselessness. — **dâvası** law action for nullity, action for voidance.

butlukgu بُوتلو. archaic 1. short breeches. 2. thigh-piece in armor.

butm بُطم. A var. of **butum**.

butnan (.—) بُطنان. A lrnd., pl. of **batn 1**.

butrakgu بُطراق. var. of **pıtrak**.

butullü (.—) بُطول. A lrnd., same as **butlan**.

butulet (.—.) بُطولت. A lrnd. bravery, valor.

butum بُطم. A prov. seeds of turpentine tree, *Pistacia terebinthus*.

butun 1 (.—) بُطون. A lrnd., pl. of **batn 1**.

butun 2 (——) بُطون. A lrnd. 1. a being hidden (in). 2. a becoming intimate (with).

butut (.—) بُطوط. A pl. of **bat 2**.

Butürab (——.—) بُوتُراب. A var. of **Ebütürab**.

buullü (.—) بُعول. A lrnd., pl. of **ba'l 5**.

buulet (.—.) بُعولت. A. lrnd. 1. a marrying. 2. a becoming owner.

buus (.—) بُعوث. A lrnd., pl. of **ba's 2**.

buutbu'du بُعد. [bu'd] phys. dimension. —**lu** dimensional.

buy 1 (—) بُوی. P var. of **bu 2**.

buy=ar 2 بُویس. prov. to freeze to death.

buya (——) بُویا. P 1. poet. sweet-smelling, fragrant. 2. lrnd. foul-smelling, fetid.

Buyahya (—.—) بُویحیی. var. of **Ebuyahya**.

buyan 1 بُویان. prov., same as **meyan 1**.

buyan 2 (——) بُویان. P same as **buya**.

buydan (——) بُویدان. P lrnd. perfume box.

buydar (——) بُویدار. P lrnd. 1. odorous, fragrant. 2. fetid. 3. hunting by scent (dog).

buyefzar (—.—) بُوی افزا. P lrnd. spice, seasoning.

buyfürüş (—.—) بُوی فروش. P lrnd. seller of perfumes.

buyiş (—.) بُویش. P lrnd. a smelling.

buymaderan (——.—) بُوی مادران. P lrnd. southernwood, bot., *Artemisia*.

buyperest (—..) بُوی پرست. P lrnd. 1. hunting by scent; hound; cheetah. 2. parasite.

buyrukgu بُویروق، بُویرُق، بُویوروق. 1. command, decree. 2. /a/ archaic commanding (over). — **kulu** in charge of the execution of an order. — **tut=** to obey orders.

buyrul=ur بُویرلمق، بُیرلمق. pass. of **buyur=**. —**ma**, —**uş** verbal n.

buyrultu بُیرلدی، بُویرلدی، بُیرلدی. Ott. hist. mandate, rescript; nomination paper for a lower official; patent or safe-conduct addressed to whom it may concern. —**cu** clerk who engrosses and issues mandates, nomination papers, and patents.

buysuz (——) بُوی سوز. P lrnd. censer, chafing-dish.

[/buyur/ see /buyr/.]

buyur=ur بُویرمق، بُیورمق. 1. /1,a/ to order to be done, to decree. 2. /a/ to command, rule (over). 3. *in respectful speech:* /a/ to come, enter, pass; /ı/ to take, have, eat, drink; /ı/ to say, utter. 4. *in respectful speech, after verbal noun* to be so kind (as to), to condescend, to deign (to), e. g., **teşrif buyur=** same as **teşrif et=**. —**dum** Ott. hist. mandate, written order. —**sunlar**, —**un**, —**unuz** Please. Come in. Sit down. Help yourself. —**un cenaze namazına!** Come to the funeral service! (used to express the sudden realization of a desperate situation). — **et=** /ı/ to show in, to invite (to sit down, to eat, etc.). —**ma** verbal n. of **buyur=**. —**t=** caus. of **buyur=**. —**tu** same as **buy-rultu**. —**ucu** who gives orders; lazy fellow fond of ordering others about. —**uş** verbal n. of **buyur=**.

buz 1 بُوز. 1. ice. 2. very cold. — **adası**

iceberg. — **akıntısı** ice stream. — **bağla=** to become covered with ice, to freeze. — **çiçeği** ice plant, bot., *Mesembryanthemum crystallinum*. **—lar çözüldü** 1. The ice broke up. 2. The ice was broken; the atmosphere warmed up. — **dağı** iceberg. **B— denizi** Polar Sea, Arctic Sea. — **dolabı** refrigerator, icebox. — **gibi** 1. icy, very cold. 2. *colloq*. in very good condition, clean and fresh; fat and firm (meat). 3. *colloq*. regular, good and proper, e. g., **buz gibi hırsız** He is a regular thief. — **gibi soğu=** /dan/ to lose one's affection completely (for). — **kes=** to freeze, to feel very cold. — **kesil=** 1. to freeze, to be frozen. 2. to be stunned. — **kıran** icebreaker. — **mıhı** sharp-headed nail used in winter on boot soles or horseshoes to check slipping. — **parçası** ice block. — **tabakası** sheet of ice. — **tut=** to be covered with ice, to freeze. — **üstüne yazı yaz=** to write on ice (used to express a useless effort). — **yalağı** geog. cirque, corrie.

buzʳᵘ 2 بُضع. A lrnd. 1. coition. 2. vulva.
buzʳᵘ 3 بُضع. A lrnd. woman's dower from her husband.
buzağı بوزاغو. بزاغى. بوزاغى calf (not yet weaned); fawn. — **burnu** great snapdragon, bot., *Antirrhinum majus*. **—la=** to calve. **—lat=** /ı/ caus. of **buzağıla=**. **—lık** 1. place where calves are penned. 2. last month of a season when calves begin to graze; last hay of the season, used to feed the calves.
buzare (.—.) بظاره. A 1. anat. clitoris. 2. lrnd. fleshy excrescence in the middle of the upper lip.
buzhane (.—.) بوزخانه. [buz 1, hane] 1. ice house; ice factory. 2. cold storage plant.
buzine (——.) بوزينه, (—..) P lrnd. monkey.
buzla=ʳ بوزلا. /ı/ 1. to ice over; to strew with ice, to freeze. 2. to cloud (polished surface). **—n=** pass. or refl. **—ndır=** caus. of **buzla=**.
buzlu بوزلو. 1. iced; mixed with ice. 2. clouded, dulled in polish; frosted (glass). — **cam** frosted glass.
buzlukᵏᵘ بوزلوك. ice house.
buznine (——.) بوزنينه. P same as **buzine**.
buzuᵘᵘ (.—.) بضوع A lrnd., pl. of **buz** 3.
buzul neol., geog. glacier. — **devri** glacial period, ice age. — **kar** névé, firn. — **taş** moraine.
buzur (.—.) بظور. A lrnd., pl. of **bazr**.
buzuzatᵘ (.—.) بضوضت. A lrnd. a being soft-skinned.
büber بُبر. var. of **biber** 1.
bü'bu (.—.) بؤبؤ. A lrnd., same as **bü'bü** 3.

bü'bü بؤبؤ. A lrnd. 1. essence, substance. 2. middle, center; pupil of the eye. 3. learned man.
bü'bü'ül'ayn بؤبؤالعين. A lrnd. pupil of the eye.
bücr بُجر. A lrnd. 1. evil, mischief; calamity. 2. marvellous thing, momentous event.
büculᵘ (.—) بجول. A lrnd. 1. ease, richness, comfort. 2. joyfulness.
bücür بجور. short (of stature), squat.
büdᵈᵈᵘ بُد. A lrnd. escape; means of escape; possibility of avoiding some disagreeable thing.
büdelâ (..—) بدلا. A 1. pl. of **bedîl**. 2. myst. a degree higher than that of the **ebdal**. 3. Ott. hist., title given to certain wandering dervishes.
büdn بدن. A lrnd. a fattening, fatness, corpulence.
büduᵘᵘ (.—) بدوع. A, **büduat**ᵘ (.—.) بدوعت. [based on Arabic] lrnd. a being or becoming eminent, excellency.
büdur 1 (.—) بدور. A lrnd. 1. pl. of **bedr**. 2. pl. of **bedre**.
büdur 2 (.—) بدور. A lrnd. 1. a striving to outdo. 2. an exerting oneself to the utmost. 3. a happening unexpectedly.
büdün 1 بدن. A fatness.
büdün 2 بدن. A lrnd. 1. pl. of **bedin** 1. 2. pl. of **bedene**.
büdüvᵛᵛᵘ بدو. A lrnd. appearance, manifestation.
büfe بوفه. F buffet.
büge بوگه, **büğelek**ᵉᵏ بوگه لك. prov. gadfly, zool., *Tabanus bovinus*. — **sokmuşa dön=** to rage as if stung.
büğetᵈ بوگت. prov. weir.
büğü بوگو. same as **büyü** 1.
bühlûlᵘ (.—) بهلول. A lrnd. 1. merry, cheerful, laughing; jester. 2. fool; stupid. 3. noble, excellent, princely.
bühr بُهر. A lrnd. 1. difficulty of breathing; asthma. 2. a being out of breath, panting.
büht 1 بُهت. A lrnd. lie, falsehood.
büht 2 بُهت. P lrnd. a planet's motion in a given time.
bühtan (.—) بهتان. A false accusation, calumny. — **et=** /a/ to accuse falsely, to calumniate. **—amiz** (.——) P lrnd. calumniatory (words). **—cı** (.—.) calumniator, slanderer. **—endaz** (.—.—) P who casts aspersions; calumniator. **—zede** (.—..) P calumniated, smeared.
bühur (.—) بهور. A lrnd. 1. a shining brightly and eclipsing the light of the stars (moon). 2. brightness, splendor.
bükᵏᵘ 1 بوك. prov. 1. thicket, jungle. 2. brambles.
bük=ᵉʳ 2 بوكمك /ı/ 1. to bend. 2. to twist,

bükâ

curl, contort. 3. to fold. 4. to spin; to twine.
bükâ (.—) بُكا A *lrnd.* a weeping.
— et= to weep.
bükât (.—) بُكات A *lrnd., pl. of* **baki 2**.
büken *anat.* flexor.
büklüm بوكلوم [**büklüm**] 1. coil, twist; curl. 2. fold; *anat.* plica. **— büklüm in curls, curly.**
bükm بُكم A *lrnd., pl. of* **ebkem**.
bükman (.—) بُكمان A *lrnd., pl. of* **bekîm**.
bükme بوكمه 1. *verbal n. of* **bük=** 2. 2. bent, crooked; folded, twisted; twined, spun. 3. *tailor.* cord used as a trimming.
bükre بُكره A *lrnd.* early morning.
Bükreş (.'.) بُكرش Bucharest.
büktür=ᵘʳ بوكدرمك /a,ı/ *caus. of* **bük=** 2.
bükûr (.—) بُكور A *lrnd.* a rising and working between dawn and sunrise.
bükûriyet (.—.—.) بُكوريت A *lrnd.* primogeniture.
bükücü بُكيجى bending, twisting; twister; spinner; *anat.* flexor.
bükükᵘ بوكك bent, twisted.
bükül=ᵘʳ بوكولمك 1. *pass. of* **bük=** 2. 2. *refl. of* **bük=** 2. **—me** *verbal n.*
bükülü بوكولو bent, crooked, twisted, curled, spun.
bükülükᵘ بلك ولك P *lrnd.* 1. unequal. 2. ignorance.
bükülüm بوكولوم *same as* **büklüm**.
bükülüş بوكولش *verbal n. of* **bükül=**.
büküm بوكوم 1. *verbal n. of* **bük=** 2. 2. twist, twine, curl, torsion, bend, fold.
bükün 1 بوكون 1. *archaic* fold, crease. 2. *neol., gram.* flexion.
bükün=ᵘʳ **2** بوكنمك *prov.* to writhe (with pain); to curl up (person).
büküntü بوكنتى bend, fold, twist. 2. *tailor.* hem.
büküş بوكش *verbal n. of* **bük=** 2. [/bül/ *see* /ebül/.]
bül- بول A *var. of* **ebül-**.
bülâᵘ بُلاع A *lrnd.* voracious, greedy.
bülâh بُلاه A *lrnd.* large kind of exotic bird.
bülâlᵘ (.—) بُلال A *lrnd., var. of* **belâl**.
bülbül بُلبل P 1. nightingale, *zool., Luscinia megarhynchos.* 2. any singing bird of the warbler or oriole family. 3. *myst.* prophet; the Prophet. 4. *naut.* hook of a tackle. **—ü altın kafese koymuşlar; «ah vatanım» demiş** *proverb* (lit. They kept the nightingale in a gold cage, but still he moaned, «oh my sweet home!») There is no place like home. **— çanağı gibi** tiny (bowl). **—ün çektiği dili belâsıdır** *proverb* All trouble comes from not holding one's tongue. **— dişi** kind of fine needlework.

—ü genc *lrnd.* owl. **— gibi** fluently, in an unrestrained way (talk). **—ü nâlân** *poet.* lamenting nightingale. **—ü şeyda** *poet.* love-stricken nightingale. **— yuvası** a pastry somewhat like baklava.
bülbüle بُلبله A *lrnd.* jug with a spout.
bülbüli (..—) بُلبلى P *lrnd.* 1. wine cup. 2. wine.
büldan (.—) بُلدان A *lrnd.* 1. cities. 2. countries.
bülega (..—) بُلغا A *lrnd., pl. of* **beliğ**.
bülend بُلند P *lrnd.* 1. high, elevated. 2. tall, lofty. 3. exalted in rank. 4. loud. **—ahter** P high-starred, prosperous, lucky. **—avaz** (..——) P 1. loud-voiced. 2. of high repute. **—bâlâ** (..——) P tall. **—bin** (..—) P 1. who has high ambitions. 2. whose mind is engaged on holy things. **—ce** somewhat high, tall, or lofty. **—himmet** P highminded. **—î** (..—) P 1. height; tallness; loftiness; peak, summit, ridge. 2. maturity; greatness, sublimity, eminence. **—iktidar** (....—) P of surpassing might, puissant. **—pâye** (..—.) P of exalted rank. **—per** P high-flying, soaring. **—pervaz** (...—) P 1. high-flying. 2. ambitious. 3. bragging, presumptuous. **—ter** P higher; taller; louder. **—terin** (...—) P highest, tallest, loudest.
bülgûne (..—.) بُلگونه P *lrnd.* rouge.
bülh بُله A *lrnd., pl. of* **belha, ebleh**.
bülkatᵘ بُلقت A *lrnd.* variety of color; piebaldness.
bülkefd, bülkefde بُلقفده P *lrnd.* bribe (to a judge).
bülten بُلتن F bulletin.
bülûc (.—) بُلوج A *lrnd.* 1. a breaking forth (dawn). 2. a becoming manifest (truth).
Bülûcistan (.—.—) بُلوجستان *same as* **Belûcistan**.
Bülûçᶜᵘ **1** (.—) بُلوج 1. a Baluchi. 2. Baluchistan rug.
bülûçᶜᵘ **2** (.—) بُلوج P *lrnd.* 1. ornament for a roof ridge. 2. clitoris.
bülûd (.—) بُلود A *lrnd.* a settling (in a place).
bülûğ (.—) بُلوغ A 1. puberty. 2. *lrnd.* a reaching the age of discretion; maturity. 3. *lrnd.* a reaching, attaining, arriving; a being near arrival. **—a er=** to attain the age of puberty. **—u kemal** fullness of moral perfection.
bülûğiyet (.——.) بُلوغيت A *lrnd.* adult age, puberty.
bül'um بُلعوم , (.—) بُلعم A *lrnd., same as* **bel'um**.
bümum (.—) بُموم A *lrnd., pl. of* **bem 2**.
bün 1 بُن P *lrnd.* 1. base, foundation; bottom; trunk; root. 2. tip, extremity.

3. issue, result. **—ü bagal** armpit. **—ü bînî** 1. tip of the nose. 2. base of the nose. **—ü cah** bottom of a well. **—ü dendan** 1. root of a tooth. 2. extreme effort. **—ü gûş** 1. hollow behind the ear. 2. innermost cavity of the ear. 3. utmost attention. **—ü huşe** 1. stalk of a bunch of grapes. 2. stalk of an ear of grain. **—ü nahun** 1. base of a fingernail, quick. 2. utmost endeavor. **—ü ran** groin.

bün[nnü] **2** بُنّ. A lrnd. coffee beans.

-bün 3 بُن P lrnd. tree, bush, as in **gülbün**.

bünagûş (.——) بناگوش P lrnd. 1. lobe of the ear. 2. ridge of the mastoid bone.

bünagûşi (.———) بناگوشى. P lrnd. box on the ear; admonition.

bünaver (.—.) بناور P lrnd. 1. based, grounded, rooted. 2. boil, carbuncle.

bündar 1 (.—) بندار P lrnd. 1. based, rooted; well-established, firmly settled. 2. wealthy. 3. speculator; forestaller, engrosser.

bündar 2 (.—) بندار. P lrnd. 1. same as **bündar 1**[3]. 2. merchant in precious stones.

büne بنه. P lrnd. 1. household stuff, goods and chattels. 2. baggage train, including women, children, cattle, and servants.

büngâh (.—) بنگاه P lrnd. 1. strongroom, safe. 2. habitation, dwelling.

bünlâd (.—) بنلاد P lrnd. foundation, base (of a wall).

bünlü بنلو having a base.

bünud (.—) بنود A lrnd., pl. of **bend 2**.

bünüvvet بنوّت A lrnd. sonship.

bünyad (.—) بنياد. P lrnd. 1. foundation, base. 2. construction of a building. 3. building, edifice. **—ger** (.—.) P builder.

bünyan (.—) بنيان A lrnd. 1. building, edifice. 2. construction of a building. **— et=** /I/ to construct.

bünye بنيه. A 1. structure. 2. lrnd. building, edifice. 3. lrnd. construction of a building.

bünyevi (..—) بنيوى. [based on Arabic] structural.

bür[rrü] **1** بر. A lrnd. wheat (as a species).

bür[rü] **2** بر. A lrnd. 1. same as **ber 6**[2]. 2. cure.

-bür 3 بر. P lrnd. that cuts, as in **nahunbür**.

büra (.—) برا. A lrnd., pl. of **beri 2**.

bürade (.—.) براده. A lrnd. filings; dust rubbed off from any material.

bürail (.—.) برائل. A lrnd. feathers round the neck of a cock.

büraya (.—.) بريه. A lrnd. 1. chip, shaving, paring; nail paring. 2. dregs, refuse.

bürc برج. A same as **burc**.

bürcas (.—) برجاس. P lrnd. mark to shoot at.

bürcüme برجمه. A 1. knuckle; finger joint. 2. middle toe of a bird.

bürçek[gi] بورچك , **bürçük**[gü] بورچوك. archaic curl of hair.

bürd 1 برد. P lrnd. riddle, puzzle.

bürd 2 برد. A lrnd. blanket used by the Arabs as a wrap. **—ü hazremî** blanket made in Hadhramaut. **—ü muhattat** striped blanket. **—ü Yemanî** blanket made in Yemen.

bürdbar (.—) بردبار P lrnd. patient; forebearing. **—i** (.——) P, **—lık** patience.

bürde 1 برده. P lrnd. 1. carried, borne; carried off. 2. who has conquered, gained. 3. conquered, beaten.

bürde 2 برده. A same as **bürd 2**.

bürdek[ki] بردك. P lrnd. enigma, puzzle.

bürdi (.—) بردى. A lrnd. maker or seller of Arabian blankets.

bürdüşşebab (...—) بردالشباب. A lrnd. youthful beauty.

büre بره. archaic same as **pire 1**.

bürea (..—) برءا. A lrnd., pl. of **berî 2**.

bürem برم. A lrnd., pl. of **bürme 2**.

bürende برنده. P lrnd. that cuts; that kills.

bürgus (.—) برغوث. A lrnd. flea.

bürgü برغو. prov. kerchief; veil; woman's cloak.

bürhan (.—) برهان. A 1. theol., law proof, evidence. 2. log. indisputable argument, argumentum ad rem. 3. Rifai order a wounding oneself in religious ecstasy. **—ı innî** argument a posteriori. **—ı kat'î** decisive argument. **—ı limmî** argument from material cause to material effect. **—ı Mesih** the Messiah's proof (raising the dead, healing the sick, etc.). **—ı mizanî** logical argument, proof. **—ı raci** a begging the question. **—ı süllemî** the «ladder argument» used in considering the infinite. **—ı tatbik** the argument of supra-application, used in considering the infinite. **—ı tezayüf** the argument of correlation, used in considering the infinite. **—ı türsi** a theorem used to prove the finiteness of space.

bürhani (.——) برهانى. A lrnd. of the nature of a proof, demonstrative, decisive.

bürhe برهه. A var. of **berhe**.

büride (.—.) بريده. P lrnd. 1. cut, cut off, severed, cropped; felled. 2. circumcised. 3. interrupted; prevented, obstructed. 4. broken; sundered, torn away. 5. cut out (clothes). 6. travelled over (space). 7. who has broken the ties of friendship.

büridedüm (.—..) بريده دم. P lrnd. 1. dock-tailed. 2. unlucky.

büridegi (.—.—) بريدگى. P lrnd., abstr. n. of **büride**.

bürideser (.—..) بريده سر. P lrnd. decapitated.

büridezeban (.—..—) بريده زبان. P lrnd.

bürkân

1. whose tongue has been cut out. 2. mute; silenced.
bürkân (.—) بُركان A *lrnd.* volcano. —**î** (.— —) A volcanic.
bürke بُركه A *lrnd.* seagull.
bürme 1 بُرمه *prov.* woman's cloak.
bürme 2 بُرمه A *lrnd.* pot, kettle; cauldron for cooking.
bürnüs بُرنس A 1. high hat or cap formerly worn by the Arabs of North Africa. 2. Arabian cloak, burnous.
büro بُرو F office.
bürokrasi بُروقراسى F bureaucracy; red tape.
bürran (.—) بُرّان P *lrnd.* sharp, cutting.
bürre بُرّه A *lrnd.* grain or plant of wheat.
bürri (.—) بُرّى A *lrnd.* 1. pertaining to wheat, wheaten. 2. dealer in wheat.
bürsün بُرسن A *lrnd.* 1. hand, palm. 2. paw; claw; sole of a paw or claw.
büru 1 (.—) بُروء A *lrnd.* 1. creation. 2. recovery, cure. 3. a becoming free of anything undesirable.
büru[uu] **2** (.—) بُروع A *lrnd.* 1. excellence, perfection. 2. a conquering, victory.
büruc (.—) بُروج A *lrnd.* turrets. —**u sabite** the signs Taurus, Leo, Scorpio, Aquarius.
bürud (.—) بُرود A *lrnd., pl. of* **bürd 2**.
bürudet (.—.) بُرودت A coolness, cold; unfriendly relations; loss of interest. —**engiz** (.—..—) P *lrnd.* exciting coolness, displeasing.
büruk[ku] **1** (.—) بُروق A *lrnd.* lightnings.
büruk[ku] **2** (.—) بُروق A *lrnd.* 1. a flashing, glittering. 2. a menacing. 3. a rising (star).
büruk[kü] **3** (.—) بُروك A *lrnd.* 1. *pl. of* **berk 4**. 2. group of stars forming Libra and Scorpio.
büruk[kü] **4** (.—) بُروك A *lrnd.* 1. reclining position (camel). 2. a crouching, kneeling (beast). 3. a remaining, sojourning. 4. a being assiduous.
bürut[tu] (.—) بُروت P *lrnd.* mustache.
büruz (.—) بُروز A *lrnd.* 1. an issuing forth. 2. manifestation.
bürü=[r] بُرومك /ı/ 1. to cover up, fill (smoke, a room etc.). 2. to wrap, enfold.
bürülü بُرولو wrapped, enfolded, enveloped.
bürüm بُروم 1. *prov.* roll, fold. 2. *bot.* involucre.
bürümcek[ği]**, bürümcük**[ğü] بُرومجك 1. kind of crepe made of raw silk. 2. outer threads of the silkworm's cocoon. 3. *bot.* involucel.
bürüme بُرومه 1. *verbal n. of* **bürü=**. 2. wrapped up; enveloped in verbiage. —**den iş gör=** to act carelessly and hastily.
bürün=[ür] بُرونمك 1. /ı/ to wrap around oneself. 2. /a/ to wrap oneself up (in). 3. /a/ to be filled (room, etc. with smoke). 4. *pass. of* **bürü=**.
bürüncek[ği]**, bürüncük**[ğü] بُرونجك *var. of* **bürümcek**.
bür'üssaa (..—.) بُرء الساعه A *lrnd.* immediate cure, instantaneous remedy.
bürüyücü بُروجى that wraps; enveloping.
bürüyüş بُرويش *verbal n. of* **bürü=**.
bü'sa (.—) بُؤسى A *lrnd.* 1. distress, poverty. 2. calamity, misfortune.
büsak[kı] (.—) بُساق A *lrnd.* spittle.
büsbütün (.'..) بُسبوتون altogether, wholly, completely.
büselâ (..—) بُسَل A *lrnd., pl. of* **basil 2**.
büskül بُسكل A *lrnd.* the hindermost horse in a race.
büslet بُسلت A *lrnd.* celebrity, renown.
büsr بُسر A *lrnd.* 1. unripe fruit. 2. full-grown but unripe dates. —**e** A full-grown but unripe date.
büssed بُسَّد P *lrnd.* coral.
büssedîn (..—) بُسَّدين P *lrnd.* 1. of coral. 2. like coral; red, coral.
büst بُست F *fine arts* bust.
büstan (.—) بُستان A *lrnd.* garden.
büsuk[ku] (.—) بُسوك A *lrnd., pl. of* **besk**.
büsul[lü] (.—) بُسول A *lrnd.* a frowning, looking stern.
büsur 1 (.—) بُسور A *path.* pustules, pimples. —**u balgamiye** phlegmatic pustules. —**u demeviye** sanguinous pustules.
büsur 2 (.—) بُسور A *lrnd.* a looking stern, grimness.
büsut بُسط A *pl. of* **bisat**.
büşaret (.—.) بُشارت A *lrnd., var. of* **beşaret 1**.
büşr بُشر A *lrnd.* good news.
büşra (.—) بُشرى A *lrnd.* 1. good news. 2. Gospel.
büşur (.—) بُشور A *lrnd.* 1. a giving good news. 2. a being rejoiced.
büt بُت P *lrnd.* 1. idol; image; statue. 2. beautiful boy; beautiful girl. 3. *myst.* God; spiritual teacher. 4. *myst.* fleshly lust; self-love.
bütçe بُتجه F budget. — **müzakeresi** *pol.* budget debate.
bütek[ki] بُتك P *lrnd.* little idol.
Büthal[li] (.—)**, Büthale** (.—.) بُتخال P *lrnd., name of an idol temple*.
büthane (.—.) بُتخانه P *lrnd.* 1. idol temple. 2. house of one's beloved. 3. tavern; brothel.
bütkede بُتكده P *lrnd.* 1. idol temple. 2. tavern.
bütnigâr (..—) بُتنگار P *lrnd.* painter.
bütperest بُتپرست P *lrnd.* idolator.
bütperestî (...—) بُتپرستى P *lrnd.* idolatry.

bütşiken بت شکن P. *lrnd.* destroyer of idols, iconoclast.
bütteraş (..—) بت تراش P *lrnd.* carver of idols.
bütün بتون، بوتون، بسون 1. whole, entire, total, complete; whole, unbroken, undivided; *before plural form* all; the whole, entirety; wholly, altogether. 2. *neol., math.* total, sum total. — **bütün** totally, altogether. —**ce** entirely. —**cülük** *phil.* integralism. —**le**= /ı/ to complete; to make complete, to mend, repair. —**leme** *verbal n.* —**leme imtihanı** makeup examination, examination to complete a conditional grade. —**len**= 1. *pass.* of **bütünle**=. 2. *refl.* of **bütünle**=. —**let**= /ı,a/ *caus.* of **bütünle**=. —**lük** *law* universality of the law.
büus (.—) بوؤس A *lrnd.* a becoming distressed.
büuz (.—) بوؤز A *lrnd.*, *pl.* of **baz** 3.
büval[ii] (.—) بوال A *lrnd.* incontinence of urine; diabetes.
büve بوه , **büvelek**[ti] بوه لك *vars.* of **büğe, büğelek**.
büvet[di] بوگت *var.* of **büğet**.
büveyt بويت A *lrnd.* 1. little house, hut. 2. little division.
büviş بوهش P *lrnd.* 1. existence. 2. a coming into being; birth; occurrence.
büye, büyelek[ti] برگك *vars.* of **büğe, büğelek**.
büyeyz بييض [based on Arabic] *biol.* ovule.
büyu[uu] (.—) بيع A *law* sales; purchases; barters, exchange; commercial transactions. —**u bâtıla** non-valid sales. —**u faside** *pl.* of **bey'i fasid** *see* **beyi**. —**u sahiha** valid sales.
büyud (.—) بيود A *lrnd.* 1. perdition, destruction. 2. extinction, disappearance. 3. a setting of the sun.
büyun 1 (.—) بيون A *lrnd.*, *pl.* of **bin** 5.
büyun 2 (.—) بيون A *lrnd.* separation.
büyut (.—) بيوت A *lrnd.* 1. houses, habitations. 2. families, households.
büyutat (.——) بيوتات A *lrnd.* 1. aggregations of habitations. 2. noble families.
büyuz 1 (.—) بيون A *lrnd.* perdition, death, a being killed.
büyuz 2 (.—) بيوض A *lrnd.*, *pl.* of **beyz**.
büyü 1 بوگی، بو جی، بوجو *spell*, incantation, sorcery; charm. — **boz**= to break a spell. — **otu** thornapple, *bot.*, Datura Strammonium. — **otu ruhu** spirit or tincture of Datura, *spiritus strammonii*. —**süne tavşan başı** A hare's head against his spell! (expression used to break a spell). — **yap**= /a/ to practice sorcery, to cast a spell (against).
büyü=[r] 2 بيومك، بيوماك، بويماك to grow; to grow up; to become large; to increase in size, rank, or importance. —**müş te küçülmüş** grown small again after having grown up (said for a child who talks and acts like a grown-up person).
büyücek[ti] بيوجك *somewhat large.*
büyücü بوكو جی، بيوجی، بويجی *sorcerer,* witch. —**lük** sorcery, witchcraft.
büyük[tü] بيوك، بوبك، بويوك 1. great; large, big; great, high in rank; important, serious. 2. older, elder, eldest. —**ler** 1. the great; *w. cap.*, the great saints of old. 2. adults. — **abdest** *same as* **büyük aptes**. B— **Ada** the largest of the islands in the Marmara near Istanbul. — **akıntı** a current of the Bosphorus. — **amiral** full admiral, (in England) Admiral of the Fleet, First Sea Lord. — **ana**, — **anne** grandmother. — **aptes** 1. *Isl. rel.* full ablution. 2. bowel movement. — **ata** *archaic* grandfather. — **atardamar** *anat.* aorta. B— **ayı** *astr.* Big Dipper, *Ursa Major*. — **ayrıkotu** Bermuda grass, dog's tooth grass, *bot.*, *Cynodon dactylon*. — **baba** grandfather. — **baldıran** poison hemlock, *bot.*, *Conium maculatum*. — **balık küçük balığı yutar** *proverb* A big fish swallows a little fish. — **baston** *naut.* jib boom. — **başın derdi büyük olur** *proverb* Great heads have great troubles. — **baş hayvanlar** cattle (cows, buffaloes, horses). — **başlı** 1. large-headed. 2. intelligent. — **bayram** the Great Bairam (Kurban bayramı). B— **Britanya** Great Britain. —**ten büyüğe** *law* from the eldest member of the family to the next eldest member (inheritance). B— **Çekmece** *name of a place west of Istanbul*. — **çıkma** *Ott. hist.* series of advancements of officials on the occasion of the the new sultan's enthronment. — **defter** *com.* ledger. B— **Değirmenlik** the island of Melos. B— **Dere** *name of a district of Istanbul, situated on the Bosphorus*. B— **devletler** the Great Powers. — **elçi** ambassador. — **erkânı harbiye** *mil.* supreme general staff. — **flok** *naut.* jib. — **gözdemiri** *naut.* the best bower anchor. — **hanım** the elder or eldest lady of the house. — **harf** capital letter, capital. — **Hindistan cevizi** coconut. — **ısırgan otu** stinging nettle, large nettle, *bot.*, *Urtica dioica*. — **ikramiye** first prize. B— **İskender** Alexander the Great. — **kafalı** very intelligent. — **karga** raven, *zool.*, *Corvus corax*. — **kasa** *com.* central pay office. — **kervançulluğu** European curlew, *zool.*, *Numenius arquata*. — **kısım** *mil.* the bulk (of an army). — **komutanlık** *mil.* high command. — **lokma ye, büyük söz söyleme** Don't be too sure of yourself. — **martı** herring gull, *zool.*, *Larus argentatus*. B— **Mevlût ayı** *pop.* the lunar month **Rebiülevvel**. B— **Millet Meclisi**

the Grand National Assembly (of Turkey). **— mirahôr** *Ott. hist.* grand master of the Sultan's horse. **— mücennep** *Or. mus.* interval twice bigger than the **bakkiye**, equal to 8 **komas**; it is shown by the relationship 65536/59049. **B— Okyanus** Pacific Ocean. **— orta** *Turkish style wrestling* third class. **— oyna=** *gambling* to play for high stakes. **— öksürük** *prov.* whooping cough. **— ölçüde** on a large scale. **— önerme** *log.* major premise. **— Paskalya** Easter. **— peder** grandfather. **— sakakuşu** pelican. **— sayılar kanunu** *statistics* law of large numbers. **— söyle=** to talk big; to boast. **— söz** big talk. **— sözüme tövbe!** I hate to talk big, but... **— terim** *log.* major term. **— tonoz demiri** *naut.* stream anchor. **— toy kuşu** great bustard, *zool.*, *Otis tarda.* **— tövbe, — tövbe ayı** *pop.* the lunar month **Cemaziyülevvel. — tut=** /ı/ to esteem highly. **— valide** grandmother. **— yemin** solemn oath, binding oath.

büyükçe بیوکچه. somewhat large.
büyükle=ʳ بیوکله. /ı/ *archaic* to esteem highly. **—n=** to become proud. **—ndir=, —t=** /ı/ to make great.
büyüklükᵏᵘ بیوکلك. *abstr. n. of* **büyük**; size. **— göster=** to show generosity, to act nobly.
büyükse=ʳ بیوکسه. /ı/ to enlarge, to overrate. **—me çoğulu** *neol., gram., pluralis majestatis.*
büyüksün=ᵘʳ بیوکسنه. to feel important.
büyüle=ʳ بویوله. /ı/ to bewitch; to charm. **—n=** *pass.*
büyült=ᵘʳ بیولتمك. /ı/ *var. of* **büyüt=**.
büyülü بویولو. bewitched; charmed, enchanted, magic.
büyüme بیومه. 1. *verbal n. of* **büyü=** 2. grown.
büyün=ᵘʳ بیونمك. *archaic* to grow large.
büyüt=ᵘʳ بیوتمك. /ı/ 1. to enlarge. 2. to exaggerate. 3. to bring up (child). **—eç** *neol.* magnifying glass. **—me** 1. *verbal n. of* **büyüt=**, enlargement, *phot.* blowup, enlargement. 2. foster child. **—ül=** *pass. of* **büyüt=**. **—üş** *verbal n. of* **büyüt=**.
büyüyüş بیویش. *verbal n. of* **büyü=** 2.
büz=ᵉʳ 1 بوزمك. /ı/ to gather, to constrict, to pucker.
büz 2 بز. P *lrnd.* goat. **—ü kûhî** mountain goat, *zool.*, *Capra aegagrus.*
büzakᵏı (. —) بزاق. A *lrnd.* spittle, saliva when spit out.
büzakülkamer (. —...) بزاق القمر. A *lrnd.* selenite, moonstone.

büzban (. —) بزبان. P *lrnd.* goatherd.
büzdekle=ʳ بوز دکله مك. *prov.* to behave in a miserable way.
büzdil بزدل. P *lrnd.* timid, cowardly.
büzdükᵏᵘ بوزدك. 1. puckered. 2. anus. **—le=** /ı/ to constrict, pucker.
büzdür=ᵘʳ بوزدرمك. 1. /ı,a/ *caus. of* **büz=** 1. 2. /ı/ *same as* **büz=** 1.
büzgale (. —.) بزغاله. P *lrnd.* kid. **—i felek** *astr.* Capricornus.
büzgen *neol., anat.* sphincter.
büzgü بوزگی. *tailor.* smocking, shirr. **—lü** smocked, shirred.
büziçe (. —.) بزیچه. P *lrnd.* kid.
büzme بوزمه. 1. *verbal n. of* **büz=** 1. 2. drawn together by means of strings (bag).
büzmuy (. —) بزموی. P *lrnd.* goat's hair.
büzr بزر. A *lrnd., pl. of* **bezur**.
büzuğ (. —) بزوغ. A *lrnd.* 1. a rising (sun). 2. an appearing through the gum (tooth).
büzulᵘ (. —) بزول. A *lrnd.* an appearing through the gum in the ninth year (camel's tush).
büzur 1 (. —) بزور. A *lrnd.* seeds.
büzur 2 (. —) بزور. A *lrnd., pl. of* **bezr** 2.
büzuri (. — —) بزوری. A *lrnd.* dealer in seeds.
büzuz (. —) بزوز. A *lrnd., pl. of* **bez** 2.
büzuzet (. — .) بزوزت. A *lrnd.* slovenliness, untidiness, neglect.
büzükᵏᵘ بوزوك. 1. contracted, constricted, puckered. 2. anus. 3. *slang* courage.
büzül=ᵘʳ بوزولمك. 1. *pass. of* **büz=** 1. 2. *refl. of* **büz=** 1, to shrink, shrivel up. 3. to crouch, to draw one's body together, to cower. **—üp kal=** to shrink into one's shoes. **—me, —üş** *verbal n.*
büzürg بزرگ. P *lrnd.* 1. great, large. 2. tall. 3. elder, eldest; adult. 4. powerful, eminent; superior, chief. 5. holy. 6. *Or. mus.* a **makam** existing for more than three centuries but seldom used; it is composed of the fifths of the **hüseyni, puselik** and **rast makams. —ân** (. . —) P *pl.* **—âne** (. . — .) P befitting a great man, grand. **—dil** P great-hearted, high-minded. **—himmet** P high-minded. **—î** (. . —) P greatness. **—meniş** P 1. noble-minded. 2. proud, haughty. **—sal** (. . —) P aged. **—vâr** (. . —) P powerful; noble, illustrious; holy. **—vârâne** (. . — — .) P befitting a great man, noble. **—vâri** (. . — —) P greatness, eminence; nobility; sincerity. **—zâde** (. . — .) P highborn.

C

c, C the third letter of the alphabet.

—ca 1, —ce after unvoiced consonants **—ça, —çe** با جه diminutive of adjectives somewhat, as in **sarıca** somewhat. yellow, yellowish.

—ca 2, —ce, after unvoiced consonants **—ça, —çe,** preceded by stressed syllable 1. after adjective, adverb -ly, e. g., **güzelce** nicely, **sersemce** stupidly. 2. after noun or pronoun, adverb according to, e. g., **sayıca** according to number, in number, **bence** according to me, **aklınca** according to his way of understanding; like, after the manner of, e. g., **hayvanca** like a beast; in the degree of, e. g., **boyumca** with all my height; as, e. g., **ailece** as a family, with all the family. 3. after plural or collective noun by (followed by passive verb), e. g., **meclisçe karar verildi** It was decided by the assembly. 4. after name of nation or country in the language of, e. g., **İngilizce** in English, **İngilizce bir kitap** an English book; the language of, e. g., **İngilizce** English, the English language.

ca 3 (—) با P lrnd. 1. place, time, occasion. 2. rank, office.

caadet (. —.) جعادت A lrnd. a being crisp, curly (hair).

caba جابا جابه جبا 1. gratis, for nothing. 2. thrown into the bargain; and what's more, into the bargain. Ott. hist. landless peasant; landless bachelor subject to feudal taxation. **—dan** gratis. **— resmi** Ott. hist. feudal dues collected from landless bachelors. **—cı** sponger, parasite.

ca'be جعبه A lrnd. 1. quiver. 2. case, box, cabinet.

cabeca (—.—) جابجا P lrnd. here and there.

ca'bedar (..—) جعبه دار P lrnd. 1. quiver-bearer to an archer. 2. archer.

ca'besaz (..—) جعبه ساز P lrnd. musical box, barrel-organ.

cabi (——) جابی A rel. law collector of the revenue of a pious foundation. **—lik** occupation of a **cabi**.

Cabilka (—.—) جابلقا P 1. lrnd. a (mythical) city in the extreme east with a thousand gates. 2. myst. first stage of mankind's striving toward the absolute.

Cabilsa (—.—) جابلسا P 1. lrnd. a (mythical) city in the extreme west with a thousand gates. 2. myst. the ultimate goal of human endeavor, where the absolute and the qualified meet. (cf. **Cabilka**).

cabir (—.) جابر A lrnd. 1. forcing, who forces. 2. who joins and mends what is broken; who sets a fracture or dislocation. **—i küll-i kesîr** Restorer of all that is broken, God.

cablus (——) جابلوس P lrnd. flatterer. **—î** (———) P flattery, adulation.

cacık[1] جاجیق salad made of yoghurt, garlic, and chopped cucumber or lettuce.

cacim (—.) جاجم P lrnd., same as **cicim**.

ca'd[dı] جعد A lrnd. 1. crisp, curly (hair). 2. curl, lock, ringlet. 3. crookedness. **—i kalem** 1. ink adhering to the pen. 2. beautiful calligraphy. 3. witty words flowing from a writer's pen.

cadalos, cadaloz جادالوز spiteful old hag. **—luk** spitefulness, spite.

cadde جادّه A main road in a city, thoroughfare. **—yi tut=** slang to clear out.

cadı جادی [cadu] 1. witch; wizard. 2. vampire.

3. hag. **— kazanı** den of intrigues. **—lan=** to become a witch, wizard, hag or vampire. **—landır=** /ı/ caus. of **—lan=**. **—lık** witchcraft, magic; spell.

cadib (—.) جاذب A lrnd. censorious.

cadu (——) جادو P lrnd. 1. same as **cadı**. 2. witchcraft, sorcery. 3. poet. beautiful eye. **—fen** (——.) P skilled in witchcraft. **—ger** (——.) P witch, sorcerer. **—geri** (——.—) P witchcraft, magic. **—hayal** (——.—) P whose imagination bewitches the hearer. **—hayalî** (——.——) P specter, illusion. **—küş** (——.) P that kills sorcerers, wizards or witches. **—küşan** (——.—) P men sent out by İskender to kill sorcerers and magicians. **—suhan** (——..) P poet; eloquence. **—yane** (——-.) P like a sorcerer. **—vi, —yi** (——-) P witchcraft. **—zeban** (——.—) P having eloquent speech; poet.

caf جاف com. slang C.I.F.

cafcaf جاف جاف, **cafcuf** جاف جوف 1. pomp, pompousness, showiness. 2. highsounding vain talk. **—lı, —lu** pompous, showy, elegant.

ca'fer جعفر A lrnd. 1. small stream, rivulet. 2. w. cap., man's name. **C—i Sadık** Ja'fer the Truthful (sixth of the twelve Imams of the Shias).

cafi (—.) جافى A lrnd. cruel, savage, unfeeling.

cagir (——) جاگير P lrnd. holding, occupying a place. **— ol=** to occur, take place; to exist.

cagüzin (——.—) جاگزين P lrnd. choosing a residence. **— ol=** to select a place and live there.

cağ جاغ prov. 1. spoke of a wheel. 2. banister. 4. knitting needle.

cağıl cağıl جاغل جاغل humming and booming. **cağılda=**ʳ جاغلدامق to hum and boom. **—t=** /ı/ caus.

—cağız, —ceğiz after unvoiced consonents **—çağız, —çeğiz** جغز جكز diminutive often implying endearment or pity dear little, poor little, e. g., **kızcağız** dear little girl.

cah (—) جاه A lrnd. rank, office, high position, dignity.

cahd جحد A lrnd. obstinate denial.

cahız (—.) جاحظ A lrnd. large and prominent (eyeball); having staring eyes.

cahid 1 (—.) جاهد A lrnd. assiduous, striving.

cahid 2 (—.) جاحد A lrnd. who denies obstinately.

cahil (—.) جاهل A 1. ignorant; ignoramus. 2. illiterate, uneducated. 3. inexperienced, untaught. 4. not knowing, ignorant (of), e. g., **bu işin cahiliyim** I know nothing about this. 5. unenlightened as to the true faith. **—i munsif** ignorant but reasonable (who admits ignorance and seeks for correction). **—e söz anlatmak, deveye hendek atlatmaktan güçtür** proverb It is easier to make the camel jump a ditch than get something into an ignorant head. **—âne** (—.—.) P ignorantly.

cahilî (—.—) جاهلى A lrnd. 1. of ignorance. 2. pertaining to pre-Islamic Arabian paganism.

cahiliye (—.—.) جاهليّه A pre-Islamic Arabian paganism; the time of pre-Islamic Arabian paganism.

cahiliyet (—.—.) جاهليّت A 1. same as **cahiliye**. 2. abstr. n. of **cahil 1**. **—i cehlâ** the deepest depth of ignorance (state of the pagan Arabs and others before Islam was promulgated).

cahillikᵗⁱ (—..) جاهللك ignorance; folly. **— et=** to act foolishly.

cahim (.—) جحيم A 1. lrnd. hell; hell fire. 2. theol. the fifth or sixth in descent of the seven pits of hell. **—î** (.——) A infernal, pertaining to hell.

cahiyen (—'..) جاهياً A lrnd. openly, publicly.

cahiz (—.) جاحظ A lrnd. 1. high, tall. 2. bold; irritable, passionate.

cahs جحش A lrnd. 1. a scratching, lacerating. 2. a killing. 3. a trick.

cahud (.—) جحود A lrnd. 1. obstinate denier. 2. hist. Arabian Jew obstinately denying the mission of the Prophet.

caiʰ (—.) جائع A same as **cayi**.

caif (—.) جائف A lrnd. penetrating deeply (stab).

cail 1 (—.) جائل A lrnd. moving in a circle.

cail 2 (—.) جاعل A lrnd. 1. creating; the Creator. 2. making, rendering.

cair (—.) جائر A lrnd. 1. deviating. 2. unjust; tyrant.

caiz (—.) جائز A 1. proper, right, allowable; possible, feasible. 2. rel. lawful, permitted. **— gör=** /ı/ to approve (of). **—at** (—.—) A lawful things.

caize (—..) جائزه A 1. hist. reward given to a poet for a laudatory poem. 2. lrnd. favor. 3. obs. quotation mark. 4. obs. mark made on a document in a public office, indicating that it has been examined.

—cakᵗⁱ **1, —cek**ᵗⁱ جك جك added to some adjectives (final -k being dropped), diminutive somewhat, e. g., **büyücek** somewhat large.

—cakᵗⁱ **2, —cek**ᵗⁱ جك جك added to some nouns, adverb as, e. g., **evcek** as a family, with all the people of the house.

caka جاقا جاغا slang showing off, swagger,

ostentation. — **sat=**, — **yap=** to swagger, show off. **—cı** swaggerer. **—lı** showy, ostentatious.

cakcaka بغمغمه A *lrnd.* loud and continuous clatter.

caket جاكت F *same as* **ceket**.

ca'lî 1 (.—) P, **cali** (——) جعلی artificial, false, insincere.

cali 2 (——) جالی A *lrnd.* 1. that cleans, furbishes. 2. shining, polished; evident, manifest. 3. who banishes; who emigrates.

calib (—.) جالب A *lrnd.* 1. that draws, attracting. 2. that brings. **—i dikkat** attracting attention. **—i merhamet** causing pity.

calif (—.) جالف A *lrnd.* 1. that pares, strips, tears off. 2. who pulls out.

Calinus (———) جالینوس A Galen, the physician.

calip[bl] (—.) جالب *same as* **calib**.

calis (—.) جالس A *lrnd.* sitting. — **ol=** to sit, to be sitting.

ca'liyet (.—.), **caliyet 1** (——.) جعلیّت *lrnd.* artificialness, insincerity.

caliyet 2 (—..) جالیت A *lrnd.* 1. that cleans; who banishes. 2. *the people banished by the Caliph Omar from* **Cezire**.

calk[kı] جلق A *obs.* masturbation. — **çal=** to practice masturbation.

Calut (——) جالوت A Goliath.

cam 1 جام [**cam 2**] 1. glass; of glass. 2. window pane; window. — **çerçevesi** window sash. **—ı çerçeveyi indir=** to go berserk. — **evi** groove of a window sash. — **fabrikası** glassworks. — **geçir=** /a/ to glaze (window). — **gibi** glassy. — **göbeği***. — **göz***. — **kırığı** glass fragment. — **sileceği** *auto.* windshield wiper. — **tak=** /a/ to fit in glasses or panes. — **yuvası** *same as* **cam evi**.

cam 2 (—) جام P *poet.* 1. cup, goblet, glass; cup of wine. 2. glass mirror. 3. lens; spyglass. 4. glass. 5. *myst.* any position in life. **—ı Cem**, **—ı Cemşid** 1. the mythical cup of Jamshid renowned in poetry. 2. mythical mirror that reflects all events. **—ı cihannüma** 1. mythical mirror that reflects the world. 2. astrolabe. 3. telescope. 4. the human heart. **—ı fena** the cup of death. **—ı gitinüma** *same as* **camı cihannüma**.

camadan جامادان [**camedan**] 1. *prov.* double-breasted waistcoat, usually of embroidered velvet. 2. *naut.* reef (in a sail). — **astarı** *naut.* reef bend. — **bağı** *naut.* reef-knot. — **bağla=** *naut.* to reef; to take in a reef. **—ı fora et=** *naut.* to shake out a reef. — **halatı** *naut.* reef point. — **matafyonu** *naut.* reef cringle. — **vur=** *same as* **camadan bağla=**.

camat (——) جامات A *lrnd.*, *pl. of* **cam 2**, cups, goblets.

cambaz جانباز [**canbaz**] 1. acrobat; rope dancer. 2. circus rider; roughrider. 3. horse dealer. 4. swindler. **—hane** circus. **—lık** occupation and quality of a trick rider or acrobat.

camcı جامجی glazier. — **macunu** putty.

came 1 (—.) جامه P *lrnd.* 1. garment. 2. cloth. 3. sheet. 4. wrapper; wrap. **—i ahiret**, **—i fena** shroud, winding sheet. **—i hâb** bed. **—i hurşid** 1. anything that obscures the sun. 2. *myst.* the body as covering up the soul.

came 2 (—.) جامه P *var. of* **cam 2**[1].

camedan (—.—) جامه‌دان P *lrnd.* chest for holding clothes.

camedar (—.—) جامه‌دار P *hist.* officer of the Janissaries in charge of the wardrobe of the Agha.

camegâh (—.—) جامه‌گاه P *obs.* dressing room in a Turkish bath.

camegi (—.—) جامگی P *lrnd.* 1. material for a garment. 2. allowance.

camehane (—.—.) جامه‌خانه P *lrnd.* wardrobe; chest for clothes.

camekân (—.—) جامه‌کان P 1. shop window; show case. 2. anything built with glass panes. 3. dressing-room of a Turkish bath. **—lı** fitted with glass panes.

camekiye (—.—.) جامه‌کیّه [*based on* **camegi**] *hist.* allowance given to persons employed in pious foundations.

cameşuy (—.—) جامه‌شوی P *lrnd.* 1. laundryman. 2. *same as* **çamaşır**.

camgöbeği[ni] جام‌گوبگی glass-green.

camgöz جام‌گوز 1. toke, shark, *zool.*, *Galeus canis*. 2. stingy, miser.

camğul[lu] (——) جامغول P *lrnd.* scamp; rogue.

camıs, camız جامیس جامیز *prov.*, *var. of* **camus**.

cami[ii, iyi] **1** (—.) جامع A mosque; mosque in which Friday and feast day *prayers are performed. **—i kebir** *lrnd.* principal mosque. — **musikisi** religious music pertaining to the mosque; it is choral music containing the following forms: **salât** (various), **tekbir**, **tevşih, naat, mahfil sürmesi, tesbih, savt, mi'raciye, mevlid, ezan**. — **ne kadar büyük olsa imam yine bildiğini okur** *proverb* (*lit.* No matter how big the mosque, the prayer-leader recites what he knows.) It is useless to try to persuade an obstinate person. **—i şerif** *term of reverence* the holy mosque. — **yıkılsa da mihrap yine yerinde kalır** Even though the mosque is ruined its mihrab stands erect (said of a person who is still beautiful in old age).

câmi[ii] **2** (—.) جامع A *lrnd.* /ı/ that

camia

collects, unites, brings together; embracing, containing, holding. 2. *w. cap.* God, who unites in Himself all divine attributes. 3. *rhet., tertium comparationis.* 4. general compendium (name of books).

camia (—..) جامعه A group, body, community. **C— Suresi** *name of the twenty-sixth sura of the Quran.*

camid (—.) جامد A *lrnd.* 1. frozen, congealed, solidified. 2. stationary, quiescent. 3. cataleptic. 4. dead; lifeless, inanimate. 5. inert, dull. 6. incontestable, valid. 7. *gram.* primitive, underived. 3. *Arabic gram.* defective verb.

camidülkef[fſl] (—...) جامد الكف A *lrnd.* close-fisted, stingy.

camidülmal[ll] (—..—) جامد المال A *law* inanimate chattel, property.

camih (—.) جامح A *lrnd.* 1. unmanageable (horse). 2. who acts inconsiderately.

camiiyet[u] (—.—.) جامعيت [based on **câmi 2**] *lrnd.* comprehensiveness, universality.

camiülhayr (—...) جامع الخير A *lrnd.* having all good qualities.

camiülkemalât (—...—) جامع الكمالات A *lrnd.* who unites in himself all perfections.

camiül'ulûm (—...—) جامع العلوم A *lrnd.* learned in all sciences.

camla[=r] جاملامق /ı/ to fit with glass. **—n=** 1. *pass.* 2. to become glass. **—ndır=** /ı/ *caus.* of **camlan=**[2]. **—t=** /ı/ *caus.* of **camla=**.

camlı جاملى fitted with glass.

camlık[gı] جاملق place shut in with glass.

camsı *neol.* glasslike; *anat.* vitreous.

camus (——) جاموس A water buffalo, *zool., Bubalus.*

camuş جاموش *prov., var.* of **camus**.

can 1 جان [**can 2**] 1. soul. 2. life. 3. person, individual. 4. energy, zeal, vigor; vitality, strength. 5. *myst. orders* brother, friend; disciple. 6. dear, lovable. **—dan** sincerely, wholeheartedly; sincere, cordial. **—ım** darling, my dear, my good fellow (often used in reproach or objection). **cânım** precious, lovely, e. g., **cânım avizeyi kırdı** He broke the lovely chandelier. **—ı acı=** to feel pain. **— acısı** acute pain. **—ını acıt=** /ın/ to cause acute pain. **—ı ağzına gel=** to be frightened to death. **—ını al=** /ın/ to take someone's life, to kill. **— alacak nokta** the crucial point. **— alıp can ver=** to be in agony; to be in great distress. **—alıcı***. **— arkadaşı** close companion, intimate friend. **— at=** /a/ to desire strongly. **—ını bağışla=** /ın/ to spare someone's life. **—la başla** with heart and soul. **— başıma sıçradı** *archaic* I was much frightened; I was beside myself with fear. **— bayılması** faintness. **— beraber** very dear. **— besle=** to feed oneself well. **—ından bez=** to be tired of one's life. **— boğazdan geçer**, **— boğazdan gelir** *proverb* One cannot live without food. **—ı boğazına gelmiş** on the point of death. **—ı burnundan gel=** to be extremely exhausted. **— cana** in close companionship. **— cana baş başa** every one for himself. **—a can kat=** to enliven, to delight greatly. **—ı canına sığma=** to feel very impatient. **— cebinde** very frail (person). **—ı cehenneme!** To Hell with him! **— ciğer, — ciğer kuzu sarması** very dear, intimate. **— cümleden aziz** One's life is more precious than everything else. **— çabası** *prov.* struggle for existence. **—ı çek=** /ı/ to long (for). **—ı çekil=** to feel exhausted. **— çekiş=** to be in the throes of death. **— çekişmedense ölmek yeğdir** *proverb* Better to die than to suffer the agony of death. **—ı çık=** 1. to die. 2. to get very tired. **—ı çıkasıca** May the devil take him! **— çıkmayınca huy çıkmaz** *proverb* He will never change his habits. **— damarı** vital point, most sensitive spot. **— dayanma=** /a/ to be intolerable. **—ına değ=** /ın/ 1. to please greatly. 2. to cause joy to the spirit (of a deceased person). **— derdine düş=** to struggle for one's life. **— direği** *mus.* soundpost (in a violin). **—ını dişine al=, —ını dişine tak=** to make desperate efforts. **— düşmanı** mortal enemy. **— eriği***. **— evi***. **—ına ezan oku=** /ın/ *slang* to kill, to destroy. **— feda!** /a/ one would give one's life (for)!, most welcome! **—dan geç=** to give up the ghost. **—ına geç=** to become intolerable. **—a gel=** *obs.* to come to life. **—ı gel=** to be refreshed, to revive. **—ı gelip git=** 1. to undergo fits of fainting. 2. for one's heart to hover between hope and despair. **— gitmeyince canan ele girmez** *proverb* One does not attain one's love unless one gives up one's life. **—ım hakkı için** by my soul. **— halatı** *naut.* life line. **— havliyle** in a desperate attempt to save one's life. **—ı hulkumuna gel=** to be on the point of death. **—ımın içi** my darling. **—ı içine sığma=** to feel very impatient. **—ının içine sokacağı gel=** /ı/ to feel a strong wave of love (for). **—ı iste=** /ı/ to desire. **—ın isterse** If you will; I don't care. **—ına işle=** to touch to the quick. **— kalma=** /da/ to have all the life drained out (of). **—ına kâr et=** *same as* **canına yet=**. **—ına karîm olsun!** /ın/ May he suffer for it. **—ına kasdet=** /ın/ to plot against someone's life. **—a kasıt** *law* intention of murder. **— kaygısına düş=** to fight for one's very life. **—ına kıy=** /ın/ to kill. **— korkusu** fear of death. **— kulağı ile dinle=** to be all ears; /ı/ to listen intently (to).

— **kurban!** /a/ *same as* **can feda!** —**ını kurtar=** 1. to save one's life. 2. /ın/ to save someone's life. — **kurtaran***. — **kurtaran yok mu!** help! — **kuşu** soul. —**ına minnet!** What more could one want! So much the better! —**ına oku=** /ın/ 1. to harass. 2. to destroy, to ruin. — **oyunu** venture in which life is at stake. — **pazarı** a matter of life and death. —**ı pek** enduring, tough, unbroken by suffering. —**ına rahmet!** /ın/ Peace be on his soul! —**ın sağ olsun!** Don't you worry. — **sağlığı** health. —**ını sık=** /ın/ to annoy. — **sıkıcı** annoying; boring. —**ı sıkıl=** /a/ 1. to be bored (by). 2. to be annoyed, vexed (by). — **sıkıntısı** annoyance; boredom. —**ımı sokakta bulmadım** I didn't find my life on the street; I don't want to risk it. —**ına susa=** 1. to want to die. 2. /ın/ to thirst for someone's blood. —**ına tak de=**, —**ına tak et=** to become intolerable. — **tart=** *archaic* to be in the throes of death. —**ı tatlı** fond of comfort, afraid of disturbances. —**ı tez** quick; hustler. —**ına tükürdüğümün**, —**ına üfürdüğümün** damned. — **ver=** to die, to perish. —**ını yak=** /ın/ to hurt; to cause suffering (to). —**a yakın** lovable; agreeable, pleasant. —**ı yan=** to feel pain. —**ına yandığımın** damned. —**ı yanan eşek attan yüğrük olur** *proverb* He who has had a painful experience will make extra efforts. —**ı yerine gel=** to recover, to be refreshed. —**ına yet=** to become intolerable. —**ı yok mu?** Doesn't he count, too? — **yoldaşı** congenial companion.
can 2 (—) جان P *lrnd.* 1. soul; heart. 2. life. 3. weapon. 4. wind. —**ı aziz** one's own life. —**ı can** 1. God. 2. the truth of Islam. 3. dear friend. — **u dilden**, — **u gönülden**, — **u yürekten** with all one's heart and soul, most sincerely.
can[nnı] **3** (—) جان A *lrnd.* the djinns or demons. — **ebü can** father of the race of the djinns.
canâ (——) جانا P *poet.* O friend! darling!
canaferin (——.—) جان آفرین P *lrnd.* 1. who creates life. 2. life-giving, refreshing.
canalıcı جان آلیجی the Angel of Death.
canan (——) جانان P 1. *poet.* belovéd. 2. *myst.* the Belovéd (God). 3. *lrnd.*, *pl.* of **can 2**.
canane (——.) جانانه P *poet.* beloved.
canavar جانا وار [**canvar**] 1. wild beast, rapacious animal. 2. *prov.* boar, wild hog; wolf. 3. brute, brutal wretch, monster. — **balığı** great white shark, *zool.*, *Corcharodon cacharias*. — **düdüğü** siren. — **otu** broomrape, *bot.*, *Orobanche*. — **otugiller** *bot.*, *Orobanchaceae*. — **ruhlu** having a monstrous character, murderous, inhuman. —**lık** savagery, ferocity.

canaver (——.) جان آور P *lrnd.* alive.
canazar (———) جان آزار P *lrnd.* cruel, inhuman.
canbahş (—.) جانبخش P *lrnd.* 1. life-bestowing; resuscitating. 2. who pardons a forfeited life.
canbaz (——) جانباز P *lrnd.* 1. who stakes his life, venturesome. 2. *same as* **cambaz**. 3. *Ott. hist.* special troops employed in dangerous enterprises. —**î** (———) P intrepidity.
canbeleb (—..) جان بلب P *lrnd.* at death's door, dying.
candade (——.) جان داده P *lrnd.* lover.
candar (——) جاندار P *lrnd.* 1. alive, animate. 2. quick, active, powerful. 3. animal, living creature. 4. guard. —**î** (———) P life, animation.
candarma (..'.) جاندارما *var.* of **jandarma**.
cane (—.) جانه P *var.* of **can 2**.
canefşan (—.—) جان افشان P *lrnd.* /a/ who devotes his life (to).
canefza (—.—) جان افزا P *lrnd.* soul-reviving.
caneriği جان اریگی a variety of green plum.
canevi جان اوی the seat of life (heart, pit of the stomach), the vital spot.
canfersa (—.—) جان فرسا P *lrnd.* irksome, intolerable, annoying.
canfes جانفس A fine taffeta.
canfeza (—.—) جان فزا جانفزا P 1. *var.* of **canefza**. 2. *Or. mus.* a **makam** five or six centuries old which has not been popular; it is composed of the **saba** and **acemaşiran** adding the four of **kürdi** to the end.
canfişan (—.—) جان فشان P *var.* of **canefşan**.
cangâh (——) جانگاه P *lrnd.* the seat of life, life's core.
cangeza (—.—) جان گزا P *lrnd.* gnawing at the soul, deadly, mortal.
cangıl cungul جنغل جونغل dingdong.
cangüdaz (—.—) جانگداز P *lrnd.* soul-melting, consuming.
cangüsil (—..) جانگسل P *lrnd.* heart-breaking, depressing.
cangüzar (—.—) جانگذار P *lrnd.* penetrating the heart; heart-breaking.
canhıraş (—.—) جانخراش P *lrnd.* soul-rending, disagreeable.
cani 1 (——) جانی A 1. *law* criminal. 2. murderer.
cani 2 (——) جانی P *lrnd.* 1. vital; spiritual. 2. heartily loved, cordial.
canib (—.) جانب A *lrnd.* 1. side. 2. direction. 3. party (to a transaction). —**inden** on the part of. —**ine** towards. —**dar** (—.—) P *mil.* flank guard. —**eyn** (—..) A *law* the two parties (to a transaction)

canih

—î (—.—) A *math., anat.* lateral.
canih (—.) جانح A *lrnd.* 1. inclined, biased. 2. who goes over to a sect or party. 3. sinner; offender.
Canik جانیك *formerly, a district with its center in Samsun.* — **elması** kind of small, fragrant apple.
canişin (—.—) جانشین P *lrnd.* substitute (person); successor.
caniyane (—.—.) جانیانه P criminal (act).
cankâh (——) جانكاه P *lrnd.* depressing the spirit, afflicting, cruel.
cankurtaran جان قرتاران 1. life-saving, life-saver. 2. *obs.* kind of sail. — **arabası** ambulance. — **filikası** lifeboat. — **kemeri** lifebelt. — **otomobili** ambulance. — **raketi** life-rocket. — **simidi** life buoy. — **yeleği** lifebelt.
canlan=ᵣ جانلنمق 1. to come to life; to be refreshed. 2. to become active. —**dır=** /ı/ to enliven, refresh.
canlı جانلی 1. living, animate; living creature, living being. 2. lively, alive, brisk, active; vigorous. 3. *in compounds* fond of, *as in* **para canlısı**. — **bebek** pretty as a doll. — **canavar** very naughty and mischievous. — **cenaze** like a living corpse, wan and worn-out. —**laştırma** *rhet.* personification. —**lık** liveliness, vigor.
cannisar (—.—) جان نثار P *lrnd.* devoting his life.
canperver (—..) جان پرور P *lrnd.* soul-nourishing.
canrüba (—.—) جان ربا P *lrnd.* soul-ravishing. —**yi** (—.——) P charm; lethal quality.
cansız جانسز 1. lifeless; spiritless, dull. 2. listless.
cansipar (—.—) جان سپار P *lrnd.* who sacrifices life. —**ane** (—.——.) P self-sacrificing (act). —**î** (—.——) P exposure to life; devotion to a cause.
cansitan (—.—) جانستان P *lrnd.* soul-ravishing, alluring; killing, fatal. —**î** (—.——) P allurement; murder.
cansuz (——) جانسوز P *lrnd.* soul-inflaming, heart-consuming.
canşikâr (—.—) جانشكار P *lrnd.* life-taking; the angel of death, Azrael.
canvar (——) جانوار, **canver** (—.) جانور P *lrnd.* 1. living. 2. animal, beast.
car 1 جار [icar] *same as* **çar 2**.
car 2 جار *prov.* precipice.
car 3 جار *prov.* cry, call; proclamation by a public crier. — **çek=**, — **et=** to cry out, to proclaim in public.
car 4 جار A *lrnd.* neighbour.
carʳⁿ **5** جارّ A *lrnd.* 1. that pulls, drags, stretches. 2. *Arabic gram.* preposition.

carcar جار جار *colloq.* 1. chatterbox, noisy fellow. 2. noisily.
carcı جارجی *prov.* public crier; herald.
cardın جردون A *prov.* rat.
carıs جاریس A *prov.* 1. who disgraces others, who shows others up. 2. disgraced. — **et=** to disgrace. —**lan=** to become shrewish or abusive. —**landır=** /ı/ *caus. of* **carıslan=**. —**lık** 1. disgrace. 2. shrewishness (in a woman).
cari (——) جاری A *lrnd.* 1. current, in force, present. 2. usual, customary; valid. 3. that occurs, happens. 4. flowing, running, moving. 5. *calligraphy,* a style in Arabic script. — **fiat** current price. — **hesap** current account.
carih (—.) جارح A 1. *law* that wounds, wounding. 2. *lrnd.* that rebuts, annuls.
cariha (—..) جارحه A *lrnd.* 1. limb, member. 2. *zool.* rapacious animal.
carim (—.) جارم A *lrnd.* who sins; criminal delinquent.
cariye (—..) جاریه A female slave; concubine.
carla=ᵣ جارلامق *colloq.* to shout, to talk vociferously. —**t=** /ı/ *caus.*
carmakᵗⁱ, **carmakçur** جارمجور Arm *slang* raki, arrack.
cart جارت tearing noise, ripping noise. — **cart öt=** *colloq.* to brag. — **curt et=** *colloq.* to scatter threats about. — **kaba kâğıt!** *slang* Brag away!
carta (ʹ.) جارطه A *vulg. fart.* — **çek=** to fart. —**yı çek=** to die.
caru جارو *archaic* call, cry. — **çal=** to cry out, to call.
carub (——) جاروب P *lrnd.* broom. —**keş** (——.) P sweeper; *hist.* sweeper of the sanctuary in Mecca. —**zen** (——.) P sweeper.
carullah (—.—) جارالله A *Isl. rel.* person who makes Mecca his residence.
cascavlakᵗⁱ (ʹ..) جاص جاولاق completely bald.
caselikᵏⁱ (—.—) جاثلیں A Christian provincial archbishop.
-casına, -cesine جسنه like, as, *e. g.,* **kabacasına** rudely, **delicesine** foolishly.
casi (——) جاثی A *lrnd.* kneeling; seated.
Casiye (—..) جاثیه A *lrnd.,* name of the forty-fifth sura of the Quran.
casus (—.) جاسوس [Arabic ——] spy. —**î** (———.). P *lrnd.,* —**luk** espionage.
cav=ᵃʳ جاومق *prov.* to deviate, to go astray.
cavalacosti (—..ʹ.), **cavalacoz** جاوالوجوز *slang* worthless.
cavcav جاوجاو *pop.* bad coffee made from reused grounds.
cavers (—.) جاورس P *lrnd.* millet.

cavi (——) جاوى A *calligraphy* kind of hard reed pen used for very fine writing.

cavid (——) جاوید, **cavidan** (———) جاودان جاویدات P *poet.* eternal.

cavidane (———.) جاودانه P *poet.* eternal, eternally.

cavidani (————) جاودانى P *poet.* 1. eternity. 2. eternal.

cavidanseray (—.—.—) جاودان سراى P *poet.* Paradise.

cavla=[r] جاولامق *slang* to die.

cavlak[ğı] جاولاق *colloq.* bald; naked; hairless, featherless. **—ı çek=** *slang* to die.

cavşır جاوشیر [*Arabic* ——] same as **çavşır**.

cay=[ar] 1 جایمق /dan/ to go back (on), to change one's mind.

cay 2 (—) جاى P same as **ca 3**. **—ı iştibah** a matter of doubt. **—ı karar** place where one settles. **—ı mülâhaza** matter to be considered. **—ı sualdir** It is questionable, doubtful. **—ı ümid** 1. giving room for hope. 2. being hoped for.

caydır=[ır] جایدیرمق /ı, dan/ *caus. of* **cay=** 1.

caygâh (——) جایگاه P *lrnd.* 1. place. 2. rank, dignity, station.

caygir (——) جایگیر P *lrnd.* 1. occurring, taking place. 2. established, settled.

cayıl=[ır] جایلمق *pass. of* **cay=** 1.

cayır cayır جایر جایر 1. furiously, fiercely (to burn). 2. *slang* by force. **— yan=** to burn furiously.

cayırda=[r] جایردامق to hiss, creak, crackle, roar (fire, door, etc.) **—t=** /ı/ *caus.*

cayırtı جایرتى جایردى a hissing, creaking crackling, tearing, roaring noise. **—yı bas=**, **—yı kopar=** to start shouting furiously.

cayi[iı] (—.) جایع جائع A *lrnd.* hungry; starving.

cayma جایمه *verbal n. of* **cay=** 1. **— tazminatı** forfeit money.

çaynişin (—.—) جاى نشین P *lrnd.* successor.

caz جاز E jazz; jazz band.

cazbant (.'.) جاز بانت E jazz band.

cazgır جازغیر *Or. style wrestling* person who announces the wrestlers and recites a prayer before a contest.

cazır cazır جازر جازر with a crackling noise (to burn).

cazib (—.) جاذب A *cf.* **cazip**.

cazibe (—..) جاذبه A 1. charm, attractiveness. 2. *phys.* attraction. 3. *phys.* gravity; gravitation. **—i arz** gravity, terrestrial gravitation. **—dar** (—..—) P, **—li** attractive.

cazim (—.) جازم A *lrnd.* 1. who asserts, or resolves. 2. who acts or speaks decidedly upon conjecture. 3. *Arabic gram.* that makes the last consonant of a word quiescent.

cazip[bi] (—.) جاذب [**cazib**] 1. attracting, attractive. 2. alluring.

cazu (——) جاذو P *var. of* **cadu**.

-ce 1 جه *cf.* **-ca 1, 2**. **— hali** *gram.* equative.

ce 2 جه *baby talk* boo! **— de=** to pop in, to pay a very short visit.

ceb جیب *cf.* **cep**.

cebabire (.—..) جبابره A *lrnd.*, *pl. of* **cebbar**.

ceban (.—) جبان A *var. of* **cebban**.

cebanet (.—.) جبانت A cowardliness, cowardice.

cebban (.—) جبّان A *lrnd.* cowardly.

cebbar (.—) جبّار A 1. tyrant; tyrannical. 2. powerful, able. 3. *theol.* all-compelling (God). **—ane** (.——.) P tyrannically. **—î** (.——) P, **—lık** (.—.) overbearing tyranny.

cebe جبه P *hist.* armor, cuirass, coat-of-mail; munitions of war. **—ci** *Ott. hist.* armorer attached to a special military corps. **—hane** (..—.) P *prov.*, same as **cepane**.

cebel جبل A *lrnd.* 1. mountain, hill. 2. mountainous country. **C—i Bereket** *name of a former district of the province of Adana*. **C—i Cudi** *Mount Judi in Southeast Turkey where according to a tradition Noah's Ark rested*. **C—i Düruz** 1. *Mount Lebanon*. 2. *name of a district on Mount Lebanon*. **—i hindî** bastard hemp, *bot., Datisca cannabina*. **C—i Lübnan** *Mount Lebanon*. **C—i Tarık**[*]. **— topçusu** *mil.* mountain artillery. **—i Tur** 1. *Mount Sinai*. 2. *Ott. hist.*, *term used for a mountainous area in the vilâyet of Mardin*. **—i Zühre** *anat.*, *mons Veneris*.

cebeli 1 جبلى Ott. hist. 1. soldier provided by the retainer of a military fief in fulfilment of his obligations. 2. local mounted police.

cebelî 2 (..—) جبلى A pertaining to mountains.

cebelistan (...—) جبلستان P mountainous region.

Cebelitarık[kı] (...—.) جبل طارق *geog.* Gibraltar.

cebelleş=[ir] جبللشمك *same as* **cedelleş=**.

cebellezi (..'..) جبللزى *slang* a pocketing, grabbing. **— et=** to appropriate what does not belong to one.

cebellokum جبل لوقوم جبل لقوم amethyst.
Cebellüsselc جبل الثلج A Anti-Lebanon.

cebepuş (...—) جبه پوش P *lrnd.* clad in plate-armor.

ceberî (..—) جبرى A *phil.* one who believes in predestination, fatalist. **—ye** (..—.) doctrine of fatalism.

ceberut (..—) جبروت A *lrnd.* 1. God's majesty and dominion. 2. pride, arrogance

cebhane

3. *myst.* a certain high stage in a mystic's development. **— âlemi** God's divine power over all things; the highest heaven. **— makamı, — menzili** state of direct relation with the divine attributes.

cebhane (.—.) مبحَنه same as **cepane**.

cebhe جبهه A *lrnd.*, same as **cephe**. **—sa, —say** (..—) P one who rubs his forehead on the ground; beseeching, entreating. **—sayi** (..——) P earnest entreaty.

cebhî (.—) جبهى A *anat.* frontal.

cebîn 1 (.—) جبين A timid, cowardly.

cebîn 2 (.—) جبين A *lrnd.* forehead. **—fersa** (.—.—) P, **—sa** (.——) P who rubs his forehead in prostration. **—sayî** (.———) P earnest entreaty.

cebir[brl] جبر [**cebr**] 1. algebra. 2. compulsion, constraint, force. 3. *phil.* predestination. 4. *lrnd.* a joining anything broken; a mending, restoration. **—i âdi** *math.* elementary algebra. **—i âlâ** *math.* advanced algebra. **—i hatır et=** *lrnd.* to make up for an offense. **— ile** by force. **— kullan=** to use force. **—i mâfât** *lrnd.* a making up for something lost. **— muadelesi** *math.* algebraic equation. **— ve mukabele** *math.* algebraic equation; algebra. **—i nefs et=** to restrain oneself, to use self-restraint. **—i noksan et=** *lrnd.* to make up a deficiency. **— ü taaddi** *law* compulsion and violation of rights.

cebîre (.—.) جبيره A *surg.* splint.

cebirsel *neol.* algebraic.

cebr جبر A same as **cebir**.

cebraheng (.—.) جبرآهنگ P *pharm.* seeds of yellow turpeth.

Cebrail (.——) جبرائيل A the Archangel Gabriel.

cebren (.'.) جبرا A by force, under constraint, compulsorily.

cebret=[der] جبرت 1. /1,a/ to compel, constrain, force, coerce. 2. /ı/ *lrnd.* to mend, join, repair, restore.

cebrî (.—) جبرى A 1. compulsory, forced. 2. algebraic; algebraist. 3. *phil.* predestinarian. **— aded** *math.* algebraic number. **— hücum** *mil.* forced assault. **— icra** *law* compulsory execution. **— mecmu** *math.* algebraic sum. **— muamele** act of violence. **— satış** *law* compulsory sale. **— taarruz** *mil.* forced attack. **— tasfiye** *com.* compulsory liquidation. **— tedbirler** violent measures. **— yürüyüş** *mil.* forced march.

cebriye (.—.) جبريه A *phil.* fatalism.

cecim ججم *prov.*, same as **cicim**.

ced[ddl] **1** جد A 1. grandfather. 2. forefather. **—i âlâ** the first ancestor, founder of a family, eponym. **— beced** from ancestor to ancestor, throughout past generations. **—i fasid** male ancestor through a female line. **—ine rahmet** Blessed be your ancestor! **—i sahih** ancestor in the direct male line.

ced[d'l] **2** جدع A *lrnd.* 1. a mutilating by cutting off a part of the body. 2. a keeping in prison.

cedavil[ll] (.—.) جداول A *lrnd.*, pl. of **cedvel**.

ceddani (.——) جدّانى [based on Arabic] *biol.* atavistic.

ceddaniyet (.——.) جدّانيت [based on **ceddani**] *biol.* atavism.

cedde جدّه A *lrnd.* 1. grandmother. 2. female ancestor.

cedden (.'.) جدّا A *lrnd.* from a grandfather or ancestor; ancestrally.

cedel جدل A 1. dispute, argument. 2. *phil.* dialectics. 3. *log.*, *argumentum ex hypothesi.* **— et=** to dispute pertinaciously. **— ve hilâf ilmi** science of disputation as a branch of jurisprudence. **—gâh** (..—) P contest-ground. **—î** (..—) A 1. dialectical. 2. controversial; controversialist. **—î-i mücib** one who answers controversially. **—î-i sail** one who opens the controversy. **—leş=** to argue, dispute, debate.

ceder جدر A *path.* swelling; tumor (in the throat).

cederi (..—) جدرى A *path.* smallpox, variola. **—i bakarî** cowpox. **—i kâzib** chickenpox. **—i muhtelit** smallpox in which some of the pustules each evolve a second pustule. **—i muzaıf** confluent smallpox.

cedgâre (.—.) جدگاره P *lrnd.* different roads; conflicting opinions.

cedi جدى [**cedy**] 1. *astr.* Capricornus. 2. *lrnd.* kid (in its first year).

cedid (.—) جديد A *lrnd.* 1. new; modern. 2. *pros.* the meter **fâilâtün fâilâtün müstef'ilün** (—.—— : —.—— : ——.—). **— mücedded** *obs.* quite new. **—an** (.——) A *dual of* **cedid** (*lit.*, the two new things) night and day. **—en** (.—'.) A newly.

cedir (.—) جدير A *lrnd.* worthy, fit, suitable.

cedvar (.—) جدوار A *bot.* zedoary, *bot., Curcuma Zedoaria.* **—î** (.——) A 1. pertaining to zedoary. 2. emmenagogue.

cedvel جدول A same as **cetvel**.

cedy جدى A same as **cedi**.

cefa (.—) جفا A 1. cruelty, oppression. 2. unkindness, harshness. 3. suffering, pain. 4. *myst.* God's hiding himself from a devotee. **— çek=** to suffer, to be subject to suffering. **— et=** /a/ to inflict pain, to torment. **— gör=** to suffer. **—cû** (.——) P *poet.* cruel. **—dide** (.——.) P *poet.* long-suffering. **—hây** (.——) P *poet.* unkind; cruel. **—kâr**

(. — —) P 1. cruel; tormentor. 2. long-suffering. —**keş** (. —.) P lrnd. long-suffering. —**pişe** (. — —.) P lrnd. tyrannical, cruel.

ceffelkalem (.´...) مَقْتًا نَفَم A offhand (to write).

cefin[fni] مَفْن [cefn] A anat. eyelid.

cefir[fri] جَفْر A same as **cifir**.

cefn جَفْن A same as **cefin**.

ceft جَفْت P prov. nut shell; acorn shell.

-ceğiz جَغِز cf. **-cağız**.

cehabize (. — ..) جَهَابِزَة A lrnd. 1. cunning bankers and money-changers. 2. men of intelligence and experience.

cehalet (. — .) جَهَالَات A 1. ignorance; inexperience. 2. lrnd. a being unenlightened by the true faith, misbelief. —**i müstetemme** lrnd. crass ignorance.

cehamet (. — .) جَهَامَات A lrnd. 1. coarseness of features with wrinkling and ugliness. 2. crabbedness, severity of expression.

cehan (. —) جَهَان P lrnd., var. of **cihan**.

ceharet (. — .) جَهَارَت A lrnd. a having a distinctly audible voice; loud voice.

cehaz (. —) جَهَاز A var. of **cihaz**.

cehd جَهْد A same as **cehit**. — **et=** to strive, to exert oneself.

cehele جَهَلَة A lrnd., pl. of **cahil**.

cehende جَهَنْدَة P lrnd. that springs, leaps or jumps.

cehennem جَهَنَّم A 1. hell, Gehenna. 2. hot and disagreeable place. — **azabı** hellish torture. —**in bucağı**, —**in dibi** very far, end of the world. — **gibi** like hell, hellish, infernal, very hot. —**e kadar yolu var** He can go to hell for all I care. — **kütüğü** hardened sinner. — **ol!** Go to hell! —**e postu ser=**, —**e seccadeyi yay=** to spread one's mat in hell, to be a permanent sinner. — **taşı** lunar caustic, silver nitrate. — **zebanisi** demon of hell. —**î** (. . .—) A hellish, infernal. —**lik** 1. worthy of hell, deserving hell. 2. furnace or stokehole of a Turkish bath.

ceheşan (. . —) جَهَشَان A lrnd. a running in fright to a protector.

cehil[hli] جَهْل [cehl] lrnd. ignorance. —**i basit** admitted ignorance. —**i mürekkep** ignorance masquerading as wisdom.

cehir (. —) جَهِير A lrnd. 1. loud, outspoken (word, etc.); sonorous. 2. pleasing, graceful.

cehit[hdi] جَهْد [cehd] effort, striving, endeavor.

cehiz (. —) جَهِيز P lrnd., same as **çeyiz**.

cehl جَهْل A same as **cehil**.

cehlâ (. —) جَهْلَا A lrnd., fem. of **echel**.

cehm جَهْم A lrnd. morose, cross, disagreeable; moroseness, grimness.

cehmülvech جَهْم الوجه A lrnd. grim, cross-looking.

cehr جَهْر A lrnd. a speaking audibly, distinctly, publicly.

cehre جَهْرَه P 1. spindle; spindleful of yarn. 2. yarn reel.

cehren (.´.), **cehreten** (.´..) جَهْرَةً. A lrnd. aloud; publicly.

cehri 1 جَهْرِي 1. yellow weed, dyer's weed, bot., Reseda Luteola. 2. buckthorn, bot., Rhamnus.

cehri 2 (. —) جَهْرِي [based on **cehr**] lrnd. read aloud, spoken publicly.

cehş جَحْش A lrnd., same as **ceheşan**.

ceht جَهْت cf. **cehit**.

Cehud 1 (. —) جُهُود P lrnd. the Jews.

cehud 2 (. —) جُهُود A lrnd. painstaking, hard-working.

cehûl[lü] (. —) جَهُول A lrnd. extremely ignorant or foolish; wrong in opinion or conduct. —**âne** (. — —.) P most ignorantly.

cehûm (. —) جَهُوم A lrnd. weak, impotent.

-cek[ği] 1 جَك cf. **-cak 1**.

-cek 2 جَك cf. **-cak 2**.

ceket جَاكَت [caket] jacket.

celâ (. —) جَلَا A lrnd. a leaving one's country. —**yi vatan et=** to migrate.

celâbib (. — —) جَلَابِيب A lrnd., pl. of **cilbab**.

celâcil (. —.) جَلَاجِل A lrnd., pl. of **cülcül**.

celâdet (. —.) جَلَادَت A lrnd. bravery, courage, intrepidity. —**li**, —**şiar** (. — ..—) P brave and enduring.

celâfet (. —.) جَلَافَت A lrnd. rudeness, coarseness, vulgarity.

celâil (. —.) جَلَائِل A pl. of **celile**.

celâl[li] (. —) جَلَال A 1. glory, majesty of God. 2. wrath, rage (of God); any divine attribute of might or wrath (as distinguished from **cemal**). 3. w. cap., man's name.

celâlet (. —.) جَلَالَت A lrnd. majesty, greatness. —**lu**, —**meab** (. — ..—) P His Majesty.

Celâlî (. — —) جَلَالِي A Ott. hist. Jalali rebel. — **takvim** Jalalaean calendar (a little-used calendar based on an era beginning 1079 A. D.). — **tarih** date according to the Jalalaean calendar. —**yane** (. — — —.) P suited to a Jalali rebel; rebellious. —**ye** (. — —.) A name of a Muslim sect.

celâllen=[lr] جَلَاللن to get into a towering rage. —**dir=** /ı/ caus.

celâlli جَلَاللى awe-inspiring and quick-tempered.

celâsin جَلَاسِن brave and efficient. —**lik** courage and efficiency.

celb جَلْب A same as **celp**.

celbe جَلْبَه net bag used by hunters.

celbet=[der] جَلْبَت /ı/ 1. to attract. 2. to let come, procure; import; law to summon

celd جلد A *law* flogging, flagellation. —et= to flog.

celeb 1 جلب A same as **celep 1**.

celeb 2 جب P *lrnd.* 1. courtesan. 2. noise, tumult.

celebe جلبه A *lrnd.* clamors, sounds, confused murmurs.

celed جلد A *lrnd.* 1. hard, level ground. 2. a being hardy, enduring, energetic; patient energy.

celep^bi 1 جلب |celeb 1| 1. drover, cattle dealer. 2. *Ott. hist.* man risen from servitude to a high office in the Sultan's palace. 3. female African camel. —çi, —keş P drover.

celep^bi 2 جلب *prov.* rough, coarse, awkward.

celesat (..—) جلسات . A *lrnd., pl. of* **celse**.

celf جلف A *lrnd.* 1. a peeling; skin or surface of a thing. 2. a wounding, slashing with a sword.

celfin جلفين *prov.* young hen, chicken.

celi (.—) جلى A *lrnd.* 1. obvious, public, open to view. 2. *calligraphy* a spectacular style of writing.

celib (.—) جليب A *lrnd.* imported or taken from place to place.

celid 1 (.—) جليد A *lrnd.* strong, sturdy, energetic.

celid 2 (.—) جليد A *lrnd.* hoarfrost. —î (.——) A pertaining to or like hoarfrost.

celil (.—) جليل A 1. *lrnd.* great, glorious, illustrious. 2. *obs.* illustrious (in titles of respect).

celilülmüşaş (.—..—) جليل المشاش A *lrnd.* great of soul, noble of disposition.

celis (.—) جليس A *lrnd.* companion, comrade.

cellâd (.—) جلّاد A same as **cellât**. —ı felek *poet.* angel of death. —iye executioner's fee.

cellât^di جلّاد |cellâd| 1. executioner. 2. very cruel person. 3. *lrnd.* public scourger. —lık executioner's office; cruelty, villainy.

celle celâlehü (.'. .—'..) جلّ جلاله A *rel. formula* May His glory be exalted!

celp^bi جلب |celb| 1. attraction. 2. a causing to come; procuring; an importing; *law* summons; *mil.* call. —name (.—.) P *law* summons, written citation.

celse جلس A 1. *pol.* session. 2. *law* hearing, sitting (of the court). 3. *lrnd.* an act of sitting. —yi aç= to open the session. —yi hafife *lrnd.* short rest. —yi hafiye 1. *pol.* secret session. 2. *law* a hearing in camera. —yi kapa=, —yi tatil et= to close the session.

celve جلوه A *obs.* first unveiled presentation of a bride to her husband at the wedding; present given by the husband on this occasion.

celvet جلوت A *myst.* a coming out of retreat with ceremonies after a period of seclusion. C—iye (..—.) name of an order of dervishes.

cem^m'i 1 جمع A *lrnd.* 1. cf. **cemi 1**. 2. collection; mass, group. 3. *rhet.* proposition in which two or more subjects have one predicate. 4. *law* inclusion of a general and a particular subject in one category or judgment. 5. *log.* distribution of a term; generalization; sentence that in fact contains two propositions. 6. *myst.* ecstatic state of mind in perceiving the unity of God. —i gayri zevil'ukul *Persian gram.* plural form for non-rational beings. —i kesret *Arabic gram.* plural of large numbers. —i kıllet *Arabic gram.* plural of small numbers. —i leşker et= to levy troops. —i mükesser *Arabic gram.* broken plural. —i müşterek *Arabic gram.* plural form common to small and large numbers. —i sahih, —i salim, —i tashih *Arabic gram.* regular plural. —i teksir *Arabic gram.* broken plural. —i zevil'ukul *Persian gram.* plural form for rational beings.

Cem 2 جم P 1. name of a legendary king of ancient Persia, Jemshid. 2. name of Solomon. 3. name of Alexander the Great.

cem^mmi 3 جمّ A *lrnd.* multitude, concourse. —i gafir great multitude.

cemaat^ti 1 (.—.) جماعت . A 1. congregation; assembly. 2. religious community. 3. crowd. 4. *Ott. hist.* regiment of Janissaries. 5. *geomancy* figure in which all four regions are pairs.

cemaat 2 (.——) جماعات . *lrnd., pl. of* **cemaat 1**.

cemad (.—) جماد A *lrnd.* inanimate thing. —î (.——) A pertaining to the inanimate world.

cemahir (.——) جماهير A *lrnd., pl. of* **cumhur**.

cemal^li (.—) جمال A 1. beauty, grace. 2. perfection (of God). 3. *myst.* manifestation of the Divine perfection; any divine attribute of mercy, grace and kindness. —î (.——) A pertaining to beauty, grace and goodness. C—iye (.——.) name of an order of dervishes.

cem'an (.'.) جمعاً A as a total, in all. —yekûn sum total.

cem'aniye (.——.) جمعانية [based on Arabic] *sociol.* collectivism.

Cemazilevvel (.—...) جمادى الاول same as **Cemaziyelevvel**.

Cemaziyel'ahır, Cemaziyül'ahır (.—..—.) جمادى الآخر ، جمادى الآخر [Cumadel'ahır] name of the 6th month of the Arabian lunar year.

Cemaziel'evvel, Cemaziyül'evvel (. — — ....) جمادى الأول ، جمادى الأولى [Cumadel'evvel] name of the 5th month of the Arabian lunar year. **—ini bilirim** I know all about him (things that are not to a person's credit).

cemcah '(.—) جمّ جاه ، جمّى P lrnd. exalted in station as king Jem, august, glorious, imperial.

cemed جمد A lrnd. 1. ice; snow. 2. frozen, congealed, set (fluid).

cemekᵍⁱ جمك prov. iron point at the end of a long stick, used by plowmen for breaking up clods and for scratching off mud.

cemel جمل A lrnd. he-camel. **—ilbahr, —ülmâ** (. . . —) A 1. whale. 2. swordfish.

cemerat (. . —) جمرات A lrnd., pl. of **cemre**.

cem'et⁼ᵈᵉʳ جمع ، ـنك /ı/ 1. math. to add up (account). 2. lrnd. to collect, bring together.

cemiᵐ'ⁱ 1 جمع |cem 1| 1. gram. plural. 2. math. addition; sum, total.

cemiⁱⁱ 2 (.—) جميع A lrnd. all; the whole. **—i nâs** all mankind, every man.

cem'î 3 (.—) جمعى A 1. social, collective; social. 2. gram. pluralizing, plural.

cemia جمعيه A lrnd. people gathered together, group of people.

cemian (.—'.) جميعًا A lrnd. entirely, as a whole, altogether.

cemil (.—) جميل A lrnd. 1. praiseworthy, admirable. 2. charming, beautiful. 3. all-gracious (God). 4. w. cap., man's name. **—at** (.— —) A admirable acts or deeds.

cemile (. —.) جميله A 1. kind act, favour. 2. w. cap., woman's name.

cemilen⁼ⁱʳ جميلنك gram. to form a plural (word). **—dir**⁼ /ı/ caus.

cemiyet 1 جمعيت [cem'iyet 2] 1. society, association. 2. social. society, social body. 3. gathering, assembly. 4. wedding. **C—i Akvam** League of Nations. **— hayatı** social life. **—i hayriye** charitable society. **—ler hukuku** law of corporations. **— hürriyeti** freedom of association. **— sahibi** the person who holds the wedding. **—gâh** (. . . —) P lrnd. place of meeting.

cem'iyet 2 (. — .) جمعيت A 1. gram. plural character (of a word). 2. myst. the quality of mind that enables the devotee to be in full communication with God. 3. lrnd. composure, tranquillity of mind. **—i hatır** lrnd. composure of mind.

cemmalⁱⁱ (.—) جمّال A lrnd. camel owner; camel driver.

cemmaş (.—) جمّاش A lrnd. who addresses or touches women in an impudent manner; rake.

cemmaz (.—) جمّاز A lrnd. lively, mettlesome (beast).

cem'ol⁼ᵘʳ, **cem'olun**⁼ᵘʳ جمع اولمه ، جمع اولنمه pass. and refl. of **cem'et**⁼.

cemre جمره A 1. increase of warmth supposed to fall from the sun, successively, into air, water, and earth in February. 3. lrnd. small pebble. 4. Isl. rel. heap on which the pilgrims to Mecca cast pebbles. 5. path. boil.

cemreviye (. . —.) جمرويّه [based on **cemre**] poetry poem written in celebration of the first signs of spring.

Cemşasb (.—) جمشاسب P name of Jemshid, Solomon, and a son of Jemshid.

Cemşid (.—) جمشيد P name of a legendary king of ancient Persia. **—i Mahî, —i Mahigir** 1. Solomon when he was in exile without his magic ring. 2. the sun when in the sign Pisces.

cem'ülcemᵐ'ⁱ جمع الجمع A 1. Arabic gram. plural of plural. 2. myst. the stage when a mystic sees God in every object.

cenab (.—) جناب A 1. term of reverence majesty. 2. lrnd. side; place. **C—ı Hak** God. **C—ı hilâfetpenahi** His Majesty the Caliph. **C—ı Kibriya, C—ı Lemyezel, C—ı Vacib-ül-vücud** God.

cenabet (.—.) جنابت A 1. Isl. rel. uncleanliness, ritual impurity; unclean, impure (person). 2. vulg. foul, disgusting. **—li** canonically impure. **—lik** 1. canonical impurity. 2. hatefulness.

cenah (.—) جناح A 1. mil. wing of an army. 2. wing (of a building). 3. lrnd. wing; fin; arm; wing (of a door); casement (of a window). **— topu** mil. flank gun. **—eyn** (. — .) A lrnd. two sides.

cenan (.—) جنان A lrnd. heart, soul, mind.

cenapᵇⁱ (.—) جناب [cenab] term of respect, as in **elçi cenapları** His Excellency the Ambassador.

cenaze (.—.) جنازه A 1. corpse. 2. funeral. **— alayı** funeral procession. **— arabası** hearse. **— gibi** very pale. **—sini kaldır**⁼ /ın/ to bury. **— marşı** funeral march. **— namazı** prayer performed at the funeral. **— salâsı** funeral prayer.

cenb جنب A 1. lrnd. side. 2. anat. pleura.

cenbî (.—) جنبى A 1. lrnd. lateral. 2. anat. pleural.

cenbiye جنبيه A curved Arabian dagger.

cendekᵍⁱ prov. carcass.

cendel جندل A lrnd. stone, rock, boulder.

cendere جنده‌ره P 1. press, screw; wine press; mangle; bookbinder's press. 2. depressingly narrow place. 3. lrnd. narrow valley, gorge. **— altında** under pressure, under torture. **— baklavası** kind of sweet pastry. **—ye koy**⁼

/ı/ to put under pressure, to torture.
cenef جنف A *lrnd.* 1. a deviating (from the right way). 2. an acting unjustly; unjust.
ceneral جنرال It *obs.* general (of a European army).
Ceneviz جنویز It 1. the Genoese. 2. Genoa. **—li** a Genoese.
Cenevre (..'.) جنوره It 1. Geneva. 2. *obs.* gin.
ceng جنگ P *lrnd.*, same as **cenk**. **— ü cidal** fight, combat. **—i zergeri** mock fight.
cengâh (.—) جنگاه P *lrnd.* field of battle.
cengâver (.—.) جنگاور P *lrnd.* warlike, heroic; hero, warrior. **—ane** (.—.—.) P warrior-like. **—î** (.—.—) P, **—lik** (.—..) quality of a warrior; heroism.
cengazmude (.——.) جنگ آزموده P *poet.* experienced in war, veteran.
cengbaz (.—) جنگ باز P *poet.* warlike; warrior, hero.
cengcu (.—) جنگجو P *lrnd.* warrior, hero; quarrelsome, pugnacious.
cenge جنگه *prov.* 1. very small ember or spark of fire. 2. firefly.
cengel جنگل P jungle. **—istan** (...—) P forest, thicket.
cengî (.—) جنگی P *lrnd.* warlike, military.
Cengiz جنگیز Jenghiz Khan (the great Asiatic conqueror of the thirteenth century). **—iyan** (..——) *pl.* descendants and subjects of Jenghiz.
cenib (.—), **cenibe** (.—.) جنیب A *lrnd.* 1. led horse. 2. tractable, easy to lead. 3. stranger; foreign.
cenibet (.—.) جنیبت A *lrnd.*, same as **cenib**. **—dar** (.—.—) P, **—keş** (.—..) P leader of a horse of state.
cenin (.—) جنین A foetus; embryo. **—i kâzib** pseudopregnancy. **— kesesi** amnion. **—ı sakıt** abortion; abortive fruit. **— suyu** amniotic liquor.
cenkˢⁱ جنك [ceng] 1. battle, combat. 2. war; strife. **— arabası** *hist.* battle chariot. **— çekici** *obs.* hammer-shaped mace. **— eri** warrior, champion. **— et=** /la/ to fight. **— meydanı** battlefield. **—çi** warlike; warrior. **—leş=** /la/ to fight; to quarrel. **—leştir=** /ı/ *caus.*
cennat (.—) جنات A *lrnd.*, *pl. of* **cennet**.
cennet جنت A 1. paradise, heaven. 2. *lrnd.* garden, park. **C—i Adn** Garden of Eden. **C—i A'lâ** Highest Heaven. **—i a'mal** *theol.* the materialistic concept of Paradise. **—e bile delilsiz girilmez** Even Heaven is not entered without a helper. **—i ef'al** same as **cenneti a'mal**. **—i kalb** *theol.* the spiritual concept of Paradise. **'—in kapısını aç=** to be worthy of Heaven (through a good deed). **—ten kovul=** to be expelled from Paradise. **— kuşu** 1. bird of Paradise. 2. an innocent babe who is evidently not long for this world. 3. good man. **—i nefs** same as **cenneti a'mal**. **— öküzü** good-hearted but simple person, an innocent. **—i ruh**, **—i sıfât** same as **cenneti kalb**. **— taamı** food of paradise, e. g., pumpkin, squash. **—i vesile** *lrnd.* highest heaven. **—i zat** same as **cenneti kalb**. **—âsa** (..——) P *lrnd.* like paradise. **—aşyan** (..——) P *lrnd.*, **—li** dwelling in paradise, deceased. **—lik** destined for heaven, deserving of heaven. **—makam** (...—), **—makar**, **—mekân** (...—) P *lrnd.* dwelling in paradise, deceased, of happy memory. **—nazîr** (...—) P *lrnd.* resembling paradise.
Cennetüddünya (....—) جنة الدنیا A *lrnd.* earthly paradise, i. e., Damascus.
cennetünnaim (....—) جنة النعیم A *lrnd.* Paradise, Heaven.
Cenova (.'..) جنوه It -Genoa. **—lı** Genoese.
centilmen جنتلمن E gentleman. **— anlaşması** gentleman's agreement. **—ce** gentlemanlike. **—lik** gentlemanliness.
centiyane (.——.) جنتیانه A gentian, *bot.*, *Gentiana lutea*.
cenub (.—) جنوب A same as **cenup**. **—u garbî** southwest. **—u şarkî** southeast. **—en** (.—'.) A *lrnd.* southward, to the south, from the south. **—î** (.——) A southern. **C—î Amerika** South America.
cenupᵇᵘ (.—) جنوب [cenub] south. **— arz** *geog.* southern latitude.
cepᵇⁱ جیب [ceyb] 1. pocket. 2. *mil.* pocket. **—ine at=** /ı/ to pocket. **—inden çıkar=** /ı/ to be far superior (to). **—i delik** penniless, broke. **—ini doldur=** to fill one's pockets, to accumulate wealth. **—e el at=** to reach for one's pocket. **— feneri** flashlight, torch. **— harçlığı** pocket money. **—i humayun** *obs.* the privy purse of the Sultan. **—ine indir=**, **—ine koy=** /ı/ to pocket. **— kruvazörü** navy pocket cruiser. **—i para gör=** to earn money. **— saati** pocket watch. **— tabancası** pocket pistol. **— zırhlısı** navy pocket battleship.
cepane, cephane (.—.) جبخانه [cebehane] 1. ammunition, munitions. 2. powder magazine. 3. armory, storehouse for arms, arsenal. 4. *slang* opium. **— arabası** ammunition wagon, caisson. **— gemisi** navy munition ship. **— toparlağı** artillery ammunition limber. **— treni** *mil.* ammunition train. **—yi tüket=** to exhaust one's supplies. **—lik** ammunition store.
cephe جبهه [cebhe] 1. front (of a building, etc.). 2. *mil.* front. 3. *lrnd.* forehead. **—den** frontally, from the front; frontal. **— al=** /a karşı/ to take sides (against). **— değiştir=**

to shift the front. **— gerisi** behind the lines. **—yi geri al=** *mil.* to withdraw the front line. **— harbi** front line war. **— hattı** front line, the lines. **— hatları** *mil.* front lines. **— hücumu** frontal attack. **—ye sok=** /ı/ *mil.* to bring up to the front. **— taarruzu, —den taarruz** *mil.* frontal attack. **—yi yar=** to break through the lines.

cepken جپكن same as **çepken**.

cer[rri] **1** جرّ A 1. *mech.* a pulling, dragging; traction. 2. *lrnd.* attraction. **— atelyesi** railway repair shop. **—i eskal** 1. a dragging heavy bodies; jack, crane, derrick. 2. dynamics. **— kabiliyeti** haulage capacity. **—i kelâm et=** *lrnd.* 1. to invite discourse for some interested purpose. 2. to be prolix in discourse. **— kuvveti** force of traction. **—i miyah** hydrodynamics.

cer[rri] **2** جرّ [cer 1] the custom of theology students (formerly) of making money through serving as itinerant preachers and prayer leaders in villages during the months Rajab, Shaban, and Ramadan. **—e çık=, —e git=** to go on a working trip (theology student). **— hocası** theology student on a working trip.

cer[rri] **3** جرّ A *Arabic gram.* a putting a noun in the genitive; the vowel that characterizes the genitive. **—i civar** *Arabic gram.* a putting in the genitive by reason of proximity, in defiance of strict rule.

cer[r'i] **4** جرع A *lrnd.* a drinking by sips, a sipping.

cerab (.—) جراب A 1. *lrnd.* leather bag. 2. *anat.* scrotum.

cerabe (.—.) جرابه A *anat.* follicle.

cerabülkalb (.—..) جراب القلب A *anat.* pericardium.

cerad (.—) جراد A *lrnd.* 1. locusts. 2. looters, plunderers.

cerahat[ti] (.—.) جراحت [cirahat] matter, pus. **— bağla=, — topla=** to suppurate. **—len=** to suppurate. **—li** suppurated.

cerahor جراخور [çerahar] *Ott. hist.* one of a class of workmen employed on the repairs of fortresses.

ceraid (.—.) جرائد A *lrnd.* pl. of **ceride**.

ceraim (.—.) جرائم A *lrnd.*, pl. of **cerime**.

cerair (.—.) جرائر A *lrnd.*, pl. of **cerire**.

ceran جران *prov.,* var. of **ceylân**.

ceraskal[li] (..—) جرا نقال *colloq.,* var. of **cerri eskal**, cf. **cer 1**.

cerban (.—) جربان A *lrnd.* mangy.

cerbeze جربزه A 1. readiness of speech. 2. presence of mind, quick-wittedness. 3. *lrnd.* wiliness. **—li** go-ahead; loquacious; able to get what he wants by talking.

cerbua (.—.) جربوع A jerboa (a rodent).

cercer جرجر A *prov.* flail.

cerda (.—) جردا A *lrnd.* 1. bare, nude. 2. hairless. 3. bare of vegetation.

cerde جرده [ceride] *hist.* escort of Arab horsemen that accompanies the Mecca pilgrims. **—ci** horseman of the escort of the pilgrims.

cereb جرب A *path.* mange, scabies. **—î** (..—) A scabious. **—iye** (..—.) A *zool.* Acarina.

cerek[ği] جراك *prov.* pole.

cereme جرمه *var.* of **cerime**.

ceren جرن *prov.,* var. of **ceylân**.

ceres جرس A 1. *lrnd.* small bell hanging from an animal's neck. 2. *myst.* a divine warning to the heart. **—hay-ı zerin** P (*lit.,* the golden bells) stars. **—iye** (..—.) A *bot.,* Campanulaceae.

cereyan (..—) جريان A 1. current; draught; *elect.* current. 2. course of events. 3. movement, tendency, trend. **—ı aç=** *elec.* to turn on the current. **—ı daimî** *elec.* direct current, D.C. **— et=** to happen, occur, to take place. **—ı kes=** to break the current. **—ı mütenavip** *elec.* alternating current, A.C. **— müvellidi** *elec.* generator.

cerh جرح A *law* 1. a wounding. 2. refutation. 3. rejection of testimony by a judge.

cerha جرحه [ceriha] wound.

cerhet=[der] جرحت /ı/ 1. to wound. 2. to refute, rebut.

cerhî (.—) جرحى A *lrnd.* wounded. **—ye** (.—.) *path.* traumatism.

ceri (.—) جرى A *lrnd.* bold, brave, valiant.

ceride (.—.) جريده A 1. *lrnd.* journal, newspaper. 2. *obs.* account book, register; memorandum book. **— kalemi** *obs.* census office. **—i nüfus** *obs.* register of births.

cerih (.—) جريح A *law* wounded.

ceriha (.—.) جريحه [based on *Arabic*] *lrnd.* wound. **—dar** (.—.—) P wounded.

cerim (.—) جريم A *lrnd.* guilty; criminal.

cerime (.—.) جريمه A 1. penalty. 2. *law* fine. 3. *lrnd.* sin, crime. **—sini çek=** /ın/ to pay the penalty (of).

cerire (.—.) جريره A *lrnd.* fault, crime, transgression.

cerm جرم A *lrnd.* 1. a cutting off; a clipping. 2. a committing a crime, trespassing.

Cermen جرمن F *hist.* Teuton.

cerr جرّ cf. **cer 1-3**.

cerrah (.—) جرّاح A 1. surgeon. 2. *obs.* dresser of wounds. **— başı** *Ott. hist.* the chief surgeon of the Imperial Court. **— mili** surgeon's probe. **—î** (.——) A surgical. **—iye** (.——.) A 1. surgery. 2. surgical ward. **—lık** (.—.) surgery.

cerrar (.—) جرّار A *lrnd.* 1. bold,

importunate, troublesome (beggar). 2. numerous and powerful (army). **—ı kûçe u bazar** an importunate street beggar.

cerrare (.—.) جَرّارَه A poet. ringlet of hair.

cerrarlık[ti] (.—.) جَرّارلِك abstr. n. of **cerrar**.

cerre جَرّه A prov. earthenware jar.

cerret=[der] جَرّيتمك /ı/ mech. to pull, drag.

ces[ssi] جَسّ A 1. med. palpation. 2. lrnd. a scrutinizing.

cesamet (.—.) جَسامَت A 1. bulkiness, hugeness. 2. size, importance. **—li** (.—..) huge, bulky.

cesaret (.—.) جَسارَت A courage. **— et**= /a/ to venture, to dare. **—ini kır**= /ın/ to discourage. **—len**= to take courage. **—lendir**= /ı/ to encourage. **—li** courageous, bold. **—siz** (.—..) timid.

cesed جَسَد A cf. **ceset**. **—î** (..—) A lrnd. bodily, corporeal. **—iyet** (..—.) lrnd. corporeality.

ceset[di] جَسَد [cesed] 1. corpse, body. 2. lrnd. body (of man or animal). 3. lrnd. physical body. 4. myst. form, idea, prototype.

cesim (.—) جَسيم A lrnd. 1. great, bulky, huge. 2. important, serious.

-cesine جَسينه cf. **-casına**.

cest جَست P poet. leap, jump. **— ü çalâk** agile, quick.

ceste ceste جَسته جَسته P lrnd. little by little, by installments.

cesur (.—) جَسور A brave, courageous, bold. **—ane** (.——.) P bravely. **—luk** (.—.) bravery, courage.

ceşn جَشن P lrnd. banquet; feast; social entertainment. **C—i Meryem** the Virgin Mary's feast (provided for her by a palm tree on her flight to Egypt). **—saz** (.—) P who makes a feast, rejoicing and feasting.

cetvel جَدوَل [cedvel] 1. list in tabulated form, register, schedule. 2. column in a list. 3. ruler. 4. marginal line around a page. 5. irrigation canal. **— tahtası** ruler.

cev[vvi] 1 جَو A 1. meteor. atmosphere. 2. lrnd. space. **—i hava** atmosphere.

cev 2 جَو P lrnd. barley.

cevab (.—) جَواب A cf. **cevap**. **— alelcevab**, **—ı cevab** lrnd. reply to an answer; law rejoinder. **—ı kat'î** lrnd. decisive reply, categorical answer. **—ı müskit** lrnd. silencing reply. **—ı red** lrnd. refusal. **—ı şâfi** lrnd. satisfactory answer. **—ı şart** lrnd. consequent to a condition. **—en** (.—'.) A in reply. **—î** (.——) A replying. **—name** (.——.) P written reply, answering letter. **—nüvis** (.—.—) P lrnd. secretary.

cevad 1 (.—) جَواد A lrnd. liberal, generous.

cevad[ddı] 2 (.—) جَوادّ A lrnd., pl. of **cadde**.

cevahir (.—.) جَواهِر A [pl. of **cevher**] jewelry. **— yumurtla**= to make speech blunders. **—î** (.—.—) A lrnd. jeweller.

cevaiz (.—.) جَوائِز A lrnd., pl. of **caize**.

cevami[ii] (.—.) جَوامِع A lrnd., pl. of **cami** 1, 2, **camia**.

cevamid (.—.) جَوامِد A lrnd., pl. of **camid, camide**.

cevamis (.——) جَواميس A lrnd., pl. of **camus**.

cev'an 1 (.—) جَوعان A lrnd. hungry, famished.

cevan 2 (.—) جَوان P poet., same as **civan**. **—âne** (.——.) P peculiar to youth. **—baht** (.—.) P fortunate; brave. **—î** (.——) P youth, youthfulness.

cevanib (.—.) جَوانِب A lrnd., pl. of **canib**. **—i erbaa** the four sides, all sides.

cevanmerd (.—.) جَوانمَرد P lrnd. 1. brave, manly. 2. generous, noble. **—î** (.—.—) P braveness, generosity.

cevap[bı] (.—) جَواب [cevab] 1. answer, reply. 2. law defense. **— al**= to receive an answer. **—ı dayat**=, **—ı dik**= to be ready with an answer. **— et**= archaic to answer; to say. **— lâyihası** law statement of defense. **— ver**= /a/ to answer, to reply (to). **—landır**= /ı/ to answer. **—laş**= to exchange replies. **—laştır**= /ı/ caus. **—lı** 1. having an answer. 2. reply paid (telegraph). **—sız** unanswered.

cevari (.——) جَوارى A lrnd., pl. of **cariye** 1.

cevarih (.—.) جَوارِح A pl. of **cariha**.

cevasis (.——) جَواسيس A lrnd., pl. of **casus**.

cevaz (.—) جَواز A lrnd. 1. permissibility, lawfulness. 2. possibility, feasibility, probability. 3. permission; passage, transit. **— göster**= /a/ to allow, permit. **—ı istihdam kararı** rehabilitation (of an official). **—ı kanunî** lawfulness. **—ı şer'î** canonical lawfulness. **— ver**= /a/ to allow, permit.

cevazib (.—.) جَواذِب A lrnd., pl. of **cazibe**, attractive; attractions.

cevbecev, cev cev جَوبَجَو P lrnd. grain by grain, a little at a time, bit by bit.

cevd جَود A lrnd. abundant shower of rain.

cevdet جَودَت A lrnd. 1. goodness, superiority. 2. kindness, generosity. **—i fehm**, **—i zihn** excellence of intellect, shrewdness, capacity.

cevelân (..—) جَولان A lrnd. 1. a wandering up and down, a walking around. 2. circulation. **— et**= 1. to wander up and down. 2. to circulate, to revolve. **—gâh** (..——) P place where circuits are made, orbit; battlefield; arena; hunting ground. **—ger** (..—.) P horseman who careers around as in a fight.

cevere بَرْوَ A *lrnd.* 1. who deviate, who err. 2. who act unjustly.

cevesan (..—) بَرْسَان A *lrnd.* 1. a seeking and inquiring diligently after news. 2. an examining minutely.

cevf جَوْف A 1. *biol.* cavity. 2. *lrnd.* cavity; interior space. **—i a'lâ** *biol.* thoracic cavity. **—i arz** *geol.* the cavity inside the earth. **—i batni, —i esfel** *biol.* abdominal cavity; *anat.* ventral cavity. **—i fem** *anat.* cavity of the mouth. **—i galsami** *biol.* bronchial cavity. **—i leyl** *poet.* middle of the night. **—i mide** *anat.* gastric cavity. **—i nuhai** *anat.* medullar cavity. **—i sadri** *anat.* cavity of the chest. **—î** (.—) A *anat.* pertaining to a cavity, internal.

cevher جَوْهَر A 1. jewel, gem. 2. precious thing or person. 3. ability, capacity, good quality. 4. ore. 5. *phil.* essence, substance. 6. *anat.* substantial, substance. 7. *onomancy* dotted letter. 8. *obs.* damascening of a sword blade. **—i ebyaz** *anat., substantia alba.* **—i ferd** 1. *phys.* atom. 2. *poet.* the beloved; the lips of the beloved. **—i kül** *myst.* the essence of the universe. **—i mücerred** *myst.* the spiritual essence of the universe. **—i sincabî** *anat., substantia grisea,* gray matter. **—i ulvi** *myst.* 1. spheres. 2. a spirit. 3. fire. **—i vahid** *phil.* monad. **— yumurtla=** same as **cevahir yumurtla=**. **—dar** (..—) P *lrnd.* 1. set with jewels. 2. damascened. 3. gifted, capable. 4. in which only the dotted letters count (chronogram). **—füruş** (...—) P *lrnd.* jeweller; selling jewels. **—î** (..—) 1. pertaining to jewels. 2. dealer in jewels. 3. *phil.* substantial, essential. **—in** (..—) P *lrnd.* 1. made of jewels; set with jewels. 2. in which only the dotted letters count (chronogram). **—iye** (..—.) A *phil.* substantialism. **—iyun** (..——) *phil.* substantialists. **—li** 1. made of jewels; set with jewels. 2. gifted, capable.

cevir[vrı] جَوْر same as **cevr**.

ceviz جَوْز [cevz] 1. walnut. 2. *naut.* knot. **— ağacı** walnut tree, *bot., Juglans regia;* of walnut wood. **— boya** walnut stain. **— içi** shelled walnuts. **— kabuğu** nutshell. **— kabuğu doldurmaz** very unimportant, slight. **— kır=** 1. to behave improperly, to do the wrong thing. 2. to have a good time. **— oyunu** kind of pitch-and-toss. **— sucuğu** sweet made of grape juice and walnuts. **— yağı** walnut oil. **—giller** *bot., Juglandaceae.* **—lik** orchard of walnut trees, walnut grove.

cevr جَوْر A 1. *poet.* injustice, tyranny, oppression. 2. *myst.* a hindering a devotee from spiritual progress. **— ü cefa** torture, torment. **— et=** /a/ to torment, torture. **—pişe** (.—.) P *lrnd.* unjust, cruel, tyrannical.

cevs جَوْس same as **cevesan**.

cevşen جَوْشَن A *obs.* coat of mail, cuirass. **—duz** (..—) P maker of cuirasses. **—güdaz** (...—) P breaker of cuirasses. **—güzar** (...—) P, **—hay** (..—) P armor-piercing. **—puş** (...—)P clad in mail, cuirassier. **—şikâf** (..—) P armor-splitting. **—li** clad in a cuirass.

cevval[II] (.—) جَوَّال A 1. active, lively. 2. *lrnd.* rover; much-travelled.

cevvî جَوِّي A *lrnd.* nux vomica.

cevz جَوْز A *lrnd.* walnut. **— ber günbed** P walnut on a dome (said for labor in vain). **—i bevva** nutmeg. **—i erkam** earth chestnut, *bot., Carum bulbocastanum, Conopodium denudatum.* **—i ermanyus** butter and eggs, *bot., Linaria vulgaris.* **—i gendüm** name of a fungus. **—i hindi** coconut. **—i masil** downy thorn-apple, *bot., Datura Metel.*

cevza (.—) جَوْزَا A *astr.,* Gemini.

cevziye جَوْزِيَّة A *bot., Juglandaceae.*

cevzuttarfa جَوْزُالطَّرْفَا A fruit of tamarisk.

cevzuttib (..—) جَوْزُالطِّيب A *lrnd.* nutmeg.

cevzülkay جَوْزُالقَيْ A nux vomica.

cevzülkevsel جَوْزُالكَوْسَل A physic nut.

cevzürret[tt], **cevzürrette** جَوْزُالرَّتّ جَوْزُالرَّتَّة A Indian soapnut tree, *bot., Sapindus trifoliatus.*

cevzüsserv جَوْزُالسَّرْو A *lrnd.* cypress cone.

ceyb جَيْب A 1. *anat., geol.* sinus; *math.* sine. 2. *lrnd.* bosom (of garment), neck opening of shirt or garment. 3. *lrnd.* pocket. **—i a'zam** *geom.* sine of 90°. **—i kavs** *geom.* sine of an arc. **—i murakabe** posture of meditation. **—i sabr** patient endurance. **—i tamam** *math.* cosine. **—î** (.—) A *math.* pertaining to a sine.

ceyda (.—) جَيْدَا A *lrnd.* who has a long, graceful neck.

Ceyhun (.—) جَيْحُون A *geog.* Oxus river (Amu Darya).

ceylân جَيْلَان [ceyran] gazelle, antelope, *zool., Antilope dorcas.*

ceyran جَيْرَان *prov.,* same as **ceylân**.

ceyş جَيْش A *lrnd.* army, expeditionary force.

ceyyid جَيِّد A *lrnd.* good, excellent.

ceza (.—) جَزَا A 1. punishment; fine; penalty. 2. retribution, recompense. 3. *gram.* apodosis; *log.* consequence to a condition. **—yı ağırlatıcı sebepler** *law* aggravating circumstances. **— al=** /dan/ to fine. **—yı amel** retribution for a deed. **—sını bul=** to meet one's due punishment, to get one's deserts. **—ya çarpıl=** to be fined. **—ya çarptır=** /ı/

cezair

to fine; to punish. — **çek**= to serve a sentence. —**sını çek**= /ın/ to suffer (for a deed), to get one's deserts. — **evi** prison. — **gör**= to be punished. —**yı hafifletici sebepler** *law* extenuating circumstances. — **hukuku** criminal law. —**nın infazı** *law* execution of the sentence. —**ya kal**= to stay in after school, to be kept in. — **kanunu** criminal code. — **kararnamesi** *law* certificate of penalty (in the summary criminal jurisdiction of justices of the peace). — **kes**= /a/ to fine. — **mahkemesi** criminal court. —**yı mucip** punishable. — **muhakeme usulü** *law* penal proceedings, criminal procedure. —**yı nakdî** fine. — **sahası** *sports* penalty area. —**yı seza** due punishment, deserts. —**yı Sinimmar** *lrnd.* the reward of Sinimmar (who in recompense for having built a beautiful palace for a king was hurled from its battlements, to prevent him from ever making a better). —**nın sukutu** *law* quashing of the conviction. —**yı şart** *gram.* apodosis. —**nın takdiri** *law* determination of punishment. —**nın tebdili** *law* commutation of sentence. —**nın tecili** *law* suspension of sentence. — **ver**= 1. /a/ to punish; to fine. 2. to pay a fine. — **vuruşu** *sports* penalty kick. — **yaz**= /a/ to fine. — **ye**= to be punished; to be fined. —**en** (. ´.) A as a punishment, by way of punishment. —**î** (. —) A *law* penal. —**î şart** *com. law* penalty.

cezair (. —.) جَزَائِر A *lrnd., pl. of* **cezire**. **C—i Bahrisefid** the Islands of the Aegean Archipelago (name of a province of the Ottoman Empire). **C—i Garb** Algiers. **C—i Halidat** Canary Islands. **C—i Mülûk** Molucca Islands. **C—i Saadet** Canary Islands. **C—i Seb'a, C—i Yunan** Ionian Islands.

cezalan=ır (. —..) جَزَالَنْمَق to be punished. —**dır**= (. —...) /ı/ to punish.

cezalet (. —.) جَزَالَت A 1. *rhet.* high-sounding quality (of a word); beauty of diction, purity of speech. 2. *lrnd.* keenness of intellect; soundness.

cezalı (. —.) جَزَالِي punished; fined. — **bilet** ticket plus fine.

Cezayir (. —.) جَزَائِر [cezair] Algiers; Algeria. — **dayısı** *hist.* the Dey of Algiers. — **dayısı gibi kurul**= to be puffed up. — **menekşesi** periwinkle, *bot., Vinca rosea*. — **ocağı** *hist.* the organization of the Janissaries of Algiers. —**li** an Algerian.

cezb جَذْب A *lrnd.* 1. a drawing; attraction. 2. allurement, an enticing. 3. suction. — **ü def** attraction and repulsion.

cezbe جَذْبَه A ecstasy, rapture. —**ye gel**= to be enraptured. — **halinde** in ecstasy, in rapture.

cezbet=der جَذْب ایتمك /ı/ 1. to draw, to attract. 2. *lrnd.* to imbibe.
cezebat (..—) جَذَبَات A *lrnd., pl. of* **cezbe**.
cezîl (.—) جَزِيل A *lrnd.* bountiful, large, abundant.
cezimzmi *same as* **cezm**.
cezirzri 1 جَذْر [cezr 1] *math., bot., ling.*, root. —**ini çıkar**= /ın/ *math.* to find the root (of). — **işareti** *math.* radical sign.
cezirzri 2 جَزْر [cezr 2] ebb.
cezire (. —.) جَزِيرَه A 1. *w. cap.*, Mesopotamia. 2. *lrnd.* island.
Ceziretül'arab (. —....) جَزِيرَةُ الْعَرَب A the Arabian peninsula.
cezm جَزْم A 1. *Arabic script* the sign which, placed over a consonant, shows that no vowel follows. 2. *Arabic gram.* word with no vowel after the last consonant. 3. *calligraphy* straight-nibbed reed pen. 4. *lrnd.* definite resolution, decision. 5. *lrnd.* a cutting, severing.
cezme جَزْمَه A *same as* **cezm 1**.
cezmet=der جَزْم ایتمك /ı/ *lrnd.* 1. to decide, resolve (on). 2. to cut through, cut off. 3. *Arabic script* to make a consonant quiescent.
cezpbi *same as* **cezb**.
cezr 1 جَذْر A *same as* **cezir 1**. —**i amudi** *bot.* taproot. —**i ârızi** *bot.* adventitious root. —**i asam** *math.* irrational root. —**i dereni** *bot.* tuberous root. —**i havai** *bot.* aerial root. —**i mantık** *math.* rational root. —**i mikâb** *math.* cube root. —**i murabba** *math.* square root. —**i mükeab** *math.* cube root. —**i natık** *math.* rational root. —**i rişî** *bot.* fascicular root. —**i tam** *math.* rational root. —**i vetedî** *bot.* taproot.
cezr 2 جَزْر A *same as* **cezir 2**. —**i kâmil** low water at spring tide. — **ü med** the tides. —**i nakıs** low water at neap tide.
cezrî (.—) جَذْرِي [based on cezr 1] radical. —**ye** *pol.* radicalism.
cezuuu (. —) جَزُوع A *lrnd.* impatient; lamenting, complaining.
cezub (. —) جَذُوب A *lrnd.* attracting, attraction.
cezve جَذْوَه pot with long handle for making Turkish coffee.
cezzab (. —) جَذَّاب A *lrnd.* exceedingly attractive.
cezzar (. —) جَزَّار A *lrnd.* 1. camel butcher. 2. cruel, bloodthirsty.
-cı, -ci, -cu 3, -cü, *after unvoiced consonants* **-çı, -çi, -çu, -çü** جِي one habitually or professionally occupied with, *as in,* **gazeteci, kapıcı, kahveci, yolcu**.
cıbıl جِبِل *prov.* naked.
cıbır جِبِر *prov.* poor, broke.

cıcıkᵏ¹ جيجى *used only in* —ını çıkar= /ın/ to wear out, to damage by use.

cıda جدا *archaic* lance, spear, javelin.

cıdav جداو *vet.* 1. withers. 2. saddle gall.

cıgara (. ́.) جيغاره [**çigara**] cigarette. — iç= to smoke a cigarette.

cığa جيغا *prov., var. of* **ciga**.

cığan جفان *prov.* miser, stingy. [for /cığıl/ see /cıvıl/.]

-cıkᵏ¹, **-cik**ᵏ¹, **-cuk**ᵏᵘ, **-cük**ᵏᵘ, *after unvoiced consonants* **-çık**ᵏ¹, **-çik**ᵏ¹, **-çuk**ᵏᵘ, **-çük**ᵏᵘ صى جاك. 1. *diminutive,* little, pet, *e. g.,* **Ayşecik** little **Ayşe**, **kuzucuk** pet lamb. 2. *added to adjectives denoting littleness,* very, *e. g.,* **incecik** very thin, very fine, **kısacık** very short.

cılasın جلاسين *same as* **celasin**.

-cılayın, -cileyin جلايين جليين *archaic adverbial suffix* as, according to, after the manner of, *e. g.,* **bencileyin, buncılayın**.

cılber جلبر *var. of* **çılbır** 1, 2.

cılgar جلغار *var. of* **cıvgar**.

cılız جليز puny, thin, undersized.

cılk جلق 1. rotten, addled (egg). 2. inflamed, festering (wound). — çık= 1. to be addled (egg). 2. to come to naught (affair).

cılkava جلقوا fur made of pieces from the back of the neck of wolves or foxes.

cılklanⁱʳ= جلقلنمك to become addled (egg).

cıllıkᵏ¹ جللق *same as* **cıcık**.

cımbakuka (. . .́.) جيمبا قوقا *colloq.* ill-formed, thin person.

cımbar جيمبار *same as* **cimbar**.

cımbız جيمبيز Gk 1. tweezers. 2. *text.* burling iron.

cınakᵏ¹ جيناق *prov.* claw.

cıncıkᵏ¹ جينجق *prov.* glass ware.

cırboğa جرپوغا *var. of* **cerbua**.

cırcır جرجر 1. creaking sound. 2. babbler. 3. ratchet borer, drill. — böceği cricket, *zool.,* *Gryllus.* — et= 1. to creak. 2. to babble.

cırgına (. .́.) جرغينه *It only in* — et= /ı/ *naut.* to fish (a yard).

cırılda=ʳ جرلدامق to make a creaking, buzzing noise. —t= /ı/ *caus.*

cırıltı جرلتى creaking noise.

cırla=ʳ جرلامق 1. to creak; to chirp. 2. to babble. —k 1. having a screeching voice; shrew. 2. cricket, *zool., Gryllus.* 3. shrike, *zool., Lanius.* —n= 1. to make a screeching noise. 2. to grumble. —t= /ı/ *caus. of* **cırla**=. —yık *same as* **cırlak**.

cırnakᵏ¹ جرناق *prov.* claw.

cırt جرت harsh, screeching sound.

cırtavı جرتاوى braggart.

cırtla=ʳ جرتلامق to make a scraping, screeching noise. —k braggart. —t= /ı/ *caus. of* **cırtla**=.

cısˢ¹ جصّ A *lrnd.* gypsum, plaster; chalk.

cıssî (. —) جصّى A *sc.* cretaceous, calcarious.

cıva جيوا *var. of* **civa**.

cıvadra (. .́.) جيوادره *It naut.* bowsprit. — **bastonu** jib boom. — **çanaklığı** bee. — **sereni** spritsail yard.

cıvata (. .́.) جواطه *It* bolt; tree nail. — **anahtarı** wrench. — **somunu** screw nut.

cıvdır=ⁱʳ جودرمك *prov.* to go mad.

cıvgar جيوغار Gk additional pair of animals attached in front of another pair pulling a plow or a gun; whiffletree, swinging bar.

cıvı=ʳ جيويمق 1. to become soft and sticky (fruit, etc.). 2. to become impertinent, to become unpleasantly silly.

cıvıkᵏ¹ جيويق 1. soft, sticky, greasy. 2. impertinent, impudently familiar, unpleasantly silly. — **mantarlar** *bot., Mixomycetes.* —la= 1. /a/ to make soft and sticky by squeezing. 2. *same as* **cıvı**=². —lan= 1. *pass.* 2. *same as* **cıvı**=².

cıvıl cıvıl جيول جيول with a soft, gurgling sound, twittering.

cıvılda=ʳ جيويلدامق to chirp, chirrup, twitter. —n= *same as* **cıyılda**=. —ş= to chirp together.

cıvıltı جيويلتى, **cıvırtı** جيورتى a chirping sound, a twittering.

cıvıt=ⁱʳ جيوتمك 1. *same as* **cıvı**=. 2. /ı/ *caus. of* **cıvı**=.

cıyak cıyak جياق جياق with a shrill voice (to screech).

cıyırda=ʳ جييردامق to make a noise when torn (paper, cloth).

cıyırtı جييرتى sound as of cloth tearing.

cız 1 جيز 1. sizzling noise. 2. *baby language* fire; anything hot. — et= *same as* **cızla**=.

cız=ᵃʳ **2** جيزمك *prov. for* **çiz**=.

cızbız جزبيز grilled meat. — **köfte** grilled meat ball.

cızdam جزدام *same as* **cızlam**.

cıziktır=ⁱʳ جزقترمك *same as* **çiziktir**=.

cızılda=ʳ جزلدامق *var. of* **cızırda**=.

cızır cızır جزر جزر with a sizzling noise.

cızırda=ʳ جزردامق to sizzle, creak, splutter. —t= /ı/ *caus.*

cızırtı جزرتى a sizzling, creaking noise.

cızla=ʳ جزلامق 1. to make a sharp, sizzling noise. 2. to have a pang.

cızlam جزلام *slang* flight. —ı çek= to flee.

cızlan=ⁱʳ جزلنمك *same as* **cızla**=.

cızlat=ⁱʳ جزلتمك /ı/ *caus. of* **cızla**=.

-ci جى *cf.* **-cı**.

cib جب *prov.* wholly, entirely.

cibah (. —) جباه A *lrnd., pl. of* **cebhe**.

cibalⁱⁱ (. —) جبال A *lrnd., pl. of* **cebel**.

cibavet (.—.) جِبايَتْ A *rel. law* rent collection for a pious foundation.
cibayet (.—.) جِبايَتْ A 1. *adm.* imposition and collection of a tax. 2. same as **cibavet**.
cibillet جِبِلَّتْ A same as **cibilliyet**.
cibillî (..—) جِبِلّى A innate, natural, inborn.
cibilliyet (..—.) جِبِلِّيَّتْ [*based on* **cibilli**] natural disposition, nature, temperament, character. **—siz** ignoble.
cibin جِبِنْ *prov.* fly; mosquito.
cibinlik[ti] جِبِنْلِكْ 1. mosquito net. 2. *obs.* place where mosquitos abound.
cibre (.'.) جِبْرَه Gk residue of pressed grapes or other fruit.
Cibril (.—) جِبْرِيل A *var. of* **Cebrail**.
cibriya (..—) جِبْرِيا , **cibriyet** (.—.) A *lrnd.* pride, haughtiness.
cibs جِبْس A *min.* gypsum; plaster of Paris.
cibt جِبْت A *lrnd.* 1. idol. 2. soothsayer; sorcerer; sorcery, witchcraft; spell.
cici جِيجِى *baby language* 1. good, pretty; nicely, properly; pretty thing. 2. toy, plaything. **—m!** my dear! **— anne** grandma. **— el** right hand.
cicibici جِيجِى بِيجِى , **cicili bicili** جِيجِيلى بِيجِيلى glaringly ornamented, gaudily decked out with trifles.
cicim جِيجِمْ rug woven on a hand loom, with designs added by embroidering.
cicoz جِيجوز 1. *slang* All gone. Nothing left. 2. *slang* Run away. Let's run away. 3. *prov.* kind of children's game. **—la** *slang* to flee, run away.
cid[ddi] 1 جِدّ A *lrnd.* earnestness; a doing one's best. **— ü cehd et=** to use all diligence.
cid 2 (—) جِيد A *lrnd.* long slender, beautiful neck, *esp.* front of the neck, throat.
cida جِدا same as **cıda**.
cidal[li] (.—) جِدال A *lrnd.* 1. fight, combat. 2. contention, dispute. **—cu** (.——) P contentious.
cidar (.—) جِدار A 1. *biol., mech.* wall. 2. *lrnd.* wall. **—î** (.——) A *anat.* parietal.
cidav جِداو same as **cıdav**.
Cidde (.'.) جِدّه *geog.* Jidda.
cidden (.'.) جِدّاً A in earnest, seriously, truly; greatly.
ciddî (.—) جِدّى A serious, earnest; true, real. **—ye al=** /ı/ to take seriously. **—leş=** to become serious. **—lik** seriousness.
ciddiyat (..—) جِدّيات A *pl.* serious things.
ciddiyet (..—.) جِدّيَّتْ A seriousness, earnestness.
cife (—.) جِيفَه A *lrnd.* carcass; disgusting thing. **—gâh** (—.—) P place of carcasses (i. e., the world).
cifir[fri] جِفْر [**Cifr**] onomancy.
Cifr جِفْر A *name of an Arabic theological book ascribed to Ali and in use as a source of esoteric knowledge of all things past, present, and future.*
cifre جِفْرَه It *obs.*, same as **şifre**.
cifrî (.—) جِفْرى A *lrnd.* pertaining to onomancy; onomantist. **—yat** (..—) A things pertaining to onomancy; books on onomancy.
ciga جِغا جِيغا بِغا بِغا *archaic* plume worn by princes and women, egret.
ciger جِگَر P *lrnd.* 1. same as **ciğer**. 2. middle of a thing. 3. courage. **—aşam** (..——) P *lrnd.* afflicted, sad. **—bend** P *lrnd.* 1. liver, lights and heart. 2. son; dear, darling. **—cuş** (..—) P *lrnd.* what stirs or moves the heart powerfully. **—dar** (..—) P *lrnd.* plucky, brave. **—duz** (..—) P *poet.* heart-piercing. **—gâh** (..—) P *poet.* heart. **—güdaz** (...—) P *poet.* grievous. **—hare** (..—.) P *lrnd.* 1. cruel, hard-hearted. 2. deeply afflicted. 3. witch, sorcerer. **—hay** (..—) P *lrnd.* afflicted, sorrowing. **—hun** (..—) P *poet.* heart-broken. **—pare** (..—.) P *poet.* darling. **—rend** P distressing. **—suz** (..—) P *poet.* tormenting. **—tab** (..—) P *lrnd.* 1. grievous. 2. who is grieved; who suffers from bilious fever. **—teşne** P *poet.* parched with thirst.
ciğer جِگَر |**ciger**| 1. liver. 2. lungs. 3. heart, affections. 4. one's child; darling. **— acısı** sorrow caused by the loss of one's child. **— ağrısı** a disease of sheep. **—i ağzına geldi** His heart came into his mouth. **—i beş para etmez** despicable. **—ini dağla=**, **—ini doğra=** /ın/ to cause great suffering (to). **—ine geç=** /ın/ to hurt deeply. **— hastalığı** tuberculosis. **—ine işle=** /ın/ to hurt deeply. **—i kebap ol=** to suffer greatly. **—imin köşesi** darling; beloved child. **—ini oku=** /ın/ to penetrate into one's thoughts. **— otu** lichen, *bot., Cetraria*. **— parçası** beloved child. **— perdesi** the layers of the peritoneum that envelop the liver. **—i sızla=** to feel great compassion. **—lerini sök=** /ın/ to treat very cruelly. **— tavası** fried liver. **—ini yak=** /ın/ to cause great suffering (to). **—i yan=** 1. /dan/ to suffer greatly (from). 2. /a/ to feel great compassion (for).
ciğerci جِگَرجى seller of liver and lungs. **— sırığı** very tall person.
ciğerköşe جِگَرگوشه [Persian *jigargosha*] darling, beloved child.
cihad (.—) جِهاد A 1. *Isl. rel.* holy war. 2. *lrnd.* religious endeavor. 3. *lrnd.* endeavor, effort. 4. *myst.* warfare against self. **—ı asger** the lesser warfare (i. e., war against infidels). **—ı ekber** the great warfare (i. e., the struggle in one's own heart to reduce it to meek submission to the divine ordinances). **— fet-**

vası a fatwa declaring a war sacred. **—ı mukaddes** holy war. **—î** (. — —) A pertaining to holy warfare. **C—iye** *Ott. hist.*, name of an Ottoman coin used in 1811. **—pişe** (. — —.) P *lrnd.* veteran in the holy war.

cihan (. —) جهان P 1. world; universe. 2. all the world, everybody. **— cihan** *lrnd.* abundant, copious. **— harbi** world war. **—aferin** (. — —. —) P *lrnd.* world-creating; Creator. **—ara** (. — — —) P *poet.* world-adorning. **—âver** (. — —.) P *poet.* mighty, wealthy; valiant. **—bân** (. — —) P *lrnd.* keeper of the world; God. **—bânî** (. — — —) P *lrnd.* empire, sovereignty; sovereign, king. **—bîn** (. — —) P *lrnd.* 1. seeing the world; eye; traveller. 2. dear child. 3. telescope. **—cû** (. — —) P *lrnd.* aspiring to possess the world. **—dâr** (. — —) P *lrnd.* ruling the world, emperor. **—dàrâne** (. — — —.) P *lrnd.* in the manner of a monarch, sovereign. **—darî** (. — — —)P *lrnd.* 1. sovereignty. 2. imperial. **—dide** (. — —.) P *lrnd.* that illumines the world. **—gerd** (. —.) P *lrnd.* that goes around the world. **—gîr** (. — —) P *lrnd.* 1. world conqueror. 2. that fills the world, world-wide. **—gîrî** (. — — —) P *lrnd.* 1. world conquest. 2. imperial, royal. **—î** (. — —) P *lrnd.* mundane, worldly. **—iyan** (. — — —) P *lrnd.* mortals. **—key** (. — .) P *lrnd.* ruler of the world. **—küşâ** (. — . —) P *lrnd.* world-subduing. **—mutâ** (. — . —) P *lrnd.* obeyed by the whole world. **—neverd** (. — ..) P *lrnd.* that goes around the world; great traveller. **—nümâ** (. — . —) P 1. roof terrace with extensive view. 2. *lrnd.* showing the whole world. **—penah** (. — . —) P *lrnd.* shelter of the world, great monarch. **—pu** (. — —) P *lrnd.* that goes about the world. **—sâlâr** (. — — —) P *lrnd.* powerful monarch; general. **—sitân** (. — . —) P *lrnd.* world-conquering. **—suz** (. — —) P 1. *poet.* world-inflaming (sun). 2. *lrnd.* world-afflicting (tyrant). **—şümûl** (. — . —) P world-embracing, world-wide, global. **—tâb** (. — —) P *poet.* which lights and warms the world (sun).

cihar 1 (. —) چهار [çehar] dice games four.

cihar 2 (. —) جهار A *lrnd.* 1. a speaking plainly and audibly. 2. a showing, disclosing; a being known, a being public. **—en** (. — '.) A loudly, publicly.

cihat (. —) جهات A *lrnd.*, *pl.* of **cihet**. **—ı asliye** 1. *rel. law* the principal services and duties of a pious foundation. 2. *geog.* cardinal points. **—ı erbaa** *geog.* the four cardinal directions. **—ı fer'iye** *rel. law* accessory duties and services of a pious foundation. **—ı gayrızaruriye** *rel. law* facultative services of a pious foundation. **— idaresi** *obs.* administration of the personnel of religious services. **—ı selâse** the three dimensions. **—ı sitte** the six directions (before, behind, right, left, above, below). **—ı zaruriye** *rel. law* the obligatory duties and services of a pious foundation.

cihaz (. —) جهاز A 1. apparatus, equipment; *anat.* system. 2. *lrnd.* trousseau. **—ı asabî** *anat.* nervous system. **—ı basarî** *anat.* visual system. **—ı deveranî** *anat.* circulatory system. **—ı elektrikî** *phys.* electrical apparatus. **—ı hazmî** *anat.* digestive system. **—ı müfriğ** *anat.* excretory system. **— sigortası** dowry insurance. **—ı tenasülî** *anat.* genital system. **—ı teneffüsî** *anat.* respiratory system.

cihet جهت A 1. side, direction, quarter; point of the horizon. 2. point, matter, aspect, point of view. 3. *log.* mode (of a modal proposition); motive, reason, means. 4. *rel. law* office, post, prebend (in a pious foundation). **bir —ten** in one respect. **—i askeriye** the military authorities. **—i camia** *log.* connecting circumstance. **—i maişet** means of subsistence. **— tâyini** orientation. **— tevcihi** *rel. adm.* appointment to office.

-cik[gi] جك *cf.* **-cık**.

cil (—) جيل A *lrnd.* 1. people, nation, race. 2. generation.

cilâ (. —) جلا A 1. polish, luster, gloss, finish. 2. polish, polishing wax; varnish. 3. *lrnd.* a cleansing, refurbishing, burnishing. 4. *slang* sweet taken together with hashish. **— et=** /ı/ *lrnd.* to cleanse, furbish. **— ver=** /a/, **— vur=** /a/, **— yap=** /ı/ to polish. **—bahş** (. —.) P *lrnd.* giving luster. **—cı** polisher; burnisher. **—dâde** (. — —.) P *lrnd.* polished **—dâr** (. — —) P *lrnd.* glossy, polished, shining. **—ger** (. —.) P *lrnd.* polisher; burnisher. **—dâde** (. — —.) P *lrnd.* polished. **—lan=** *pass.* **—lat=** /ı,a/ *caus.* of **cilâla=**. **—lı** polished, burnished, glossy. **—lı taş devri** Neolithic age.

cilânger (. —.) جلانگر P *lrnd.* locksmith.

cilâsin جلاسين *same as* **celâsin**.

cilbab (. —) جلباب A *lrnd.* woman's cloak.

cilban (. —) جلبان A *prov.* chickling vetch, bitter vetch, *bot.*, *Lathyrus sativus*; common vetch, lints, tare, *bot.*, *Vicia sativa*.

cilbend جلبند [Persian **cildband**] *obs.* portfolio, large pocketbook; folder.

cild جلد A *cf.* **cilt**. **—ger** P *lrnd.* bookbinder. **—î** (. —.) A *med.* cutaneous, pertaining to the skin. **—iye** (. — .) 1. skin diseases. 2. dermatology; dermatological ward.

-cileyin جليين *cf.* **-cılayın**.

cilgar جلگار *var.* of **cıvgar**.

cilt[di] جلد [cild] 1. skin. 2. a binding (of a

book); volume. 3. *lrnd.* hide; leather. — **hastalığı** skin disease. — **tezgâhı** *bookbinding sewing-press.* —**çi** bookbinder. —**le**= /ı/ to bind (book). —**len**= *pass.* —**let**= /a/ *caus.* of **ciltle**=. —**li** 1. bound. 2. in volumes. —**siz** unbound.

cilve 1 جلوه [**cilve 2**] coquettery, coquettish airs, grace. — **kutusu** coquettish; coquette. — **yap**= to put on coquettish airs.

cilve 2 جلوه A manifestation (of fate). 2. *myst.* God's manifestation of Himself to a saint. 3. same as **celve.** 4. *lrnd.* splendor, beauty.

cilvefürûş (...—) جلوه فروش P *lrnd.* coquettish.

cilvegâh (..—) جلوه گاه P *lrnd.* seat of beauty.

cilvekâr (..—') جلوه کار P *lrnd.* coquettish.
cilvelen=ⁱʳ جلوه لنمك to put on coquettish airs.
cilveleş=ⁱʳ جلوه شرك to flirt.
cilveli جلوه لى coquettish.
cilvenüma (...—) جلوه نما P *lrnd.* manifesting a coquettish beauty.

cilvepenah (...—) جلوه پناه P *lrnd.* resplendent.

cilveperdaz (...—) جلوه پرداز P *lrnd.* of perfect loveliness, beautiful.

cim 1 جم [**cim 2**] *Arabic script, name of the letter* . — **karnında bir nokta** *colloq.* ignorant person.

cim 2 جم. A *lrnd., Arabic script, name of the letter* ج. (This letter is the fifth letter of the Arabic, sixth letter of the Ottoman Turkish alphabet, pronounced as j. In chronogram, it has the numerical value of 3.) —**i Arabiye** the Arabic, or single-dotted ج. (pronounced j). —**i Farisiye** the Persian, or three-dotted ج , *i. e.,* the letter چ (pronounced ch as in 'child').

cimaᵃⁱ (.—) جماع. A sexual intercourse, coition, cohabitation. ± **et**= to have sexual intercourse.

cimalˡⁱ (.—) جمال. A *lrnd., pl. of* **cemel.**
cimbakuka (...'.) جمبا قرق *same as* **cımbakuka.**

cimbar . ـ جمبر. *text.* stretcher on a loom.
cimbistra (.'.) جمبستره Gk 1. tweezers. 2. *surg.* small forceps.

cimcime جمجمه *prov.* small and delicious watermelon.

cimdallı جمدالى *kind of card game.*
cimnastikᵇⁱ جمناستیق F gymnastics.
cimri جمرى miser; mean, parsimonious. —**len**= to become mean. —**lendir**= /ı/ *caus.* of **cimrilen**=. —**lik** meanness, stinginess.

cin 1 جن [*Arabic* **cinn**] djinn, genie, demon, sprite, evil spirit. — **ağacı** deodar, Himalayan cedar, Indian cedar, *bot., Cedrus*

Deodara. — **Ali** very cunning fellow. —**leri ayağa kalk**=, —**leri başına çık**=, —**leri başına toplan**= to become furious. —**ler cirit oynuyor** The djinns throw javelins there (said for a completely deserted place). — **çarp**= /a/ to be smitten by a djinn. — **darısı** popcorn. — **fikirli** clever, ingenious, shrewd. — **gibi** agile, clever, quick. —**göz** shrewd, clever. — **ifrit kesil**=, — **ifrit ol**= to become very angry. —**leri kalk**= *same as* **cinleri ayağa kalk**=. — **mısırı** popcorn. — **saçı** dodder, *bot., Cuscuta.* **C— Suresi** *name of the 72nd sura of the Quran.* — **taifesi** the demons. —**ler top oynuyor** The djinns play ball there (said for a completely deserted place). —**i tut**= to become furious. — **yavrusu** mischievous little child, imp, urchin.

cin 2 جين E gin.
cinaî (.——) جنائى A criminal. —**yat** (.———) A criminology. —**yet** (.——.) A criminality.

cinan (.—) جنات A *lrnd., pl. of* **cennet.** —**üd-dünya** the four earthly paradises, *e. g.,* (1) Ubulla meadows of Basra; (2) Sogdiana, or the vale of Samarkand; (3) the pass of Bewwan in Aljezira; (4) the vale of Damascus.

cinas (.—) جناس A 1. *poetry* play upon words, paronomasia, pun. 2. equivocal allusion.

cinayat (.——) جنایات A *lrnd., pl. of* **cinayet.**

cinayet (.—.) جنایت A 1. *law* crime. 2. murder. —**bilim** *neol.* criminology. —**kâr** (.—.—) P *lrnd.* criminal.

cinci جنجى. exorcist.
Cingen [**çingân**] *prov. for* **Çingene.**
cingil جنگل Gk one stalk in a bunch of grapes.
cinistan (..—) جنستان P *lrnd.* fairyland.
cinli جنلى haunted; possessed by a demon.
cinnet جنت A insanity, madness. — **getir**= to go mad, to become insane. —**i maniyai inhitatiye** *psychiatry* manic-depressive insanity. —**i mütenavibe** *psychiatry* cyclothymic condition, circular insanity.

cinni 1 (.—) جنى A djinn, demon.
cinnî 2 (.—) جنى A *lrnd.* demoniacal.
cins جنس A 1. sort, type, kind, variety, category. 2. *biol., log.* genus. 3. sex; *gram.* gender. 4. race, stock, family, breed. 5. of good race, thoroughbred. — **arası** *psych.* intersexual. — **cins** of various kinds, assorted. — **cinse çeker** *proverb* Like father like son. — **ismi** *gram.* common noun. —**i lâtif** the fair sex. — **ve nev'** genus and species. —**el** *neol.* sexual. —**î** A sexual. —**iyet** A, —**lik** sex; sexuality. —**likbilim** *neol.* sexology. —**liksiz** asexual.

cinsül'ecnas (...—) جنس الاجناس A *log.* summum genus.

cip^{bi} E jeep.
cirah (. —) جراع A lrnd., pl. of **cürh**.
cirahat^{ti} (. — .) جراحت A lrnd. 1. wound. 2. surgery. **—bend** (. — ..) P 1. surgeon. 2. surgical bandage.
ciran (— —) جيران A lrnd., pl. of **car** 4.
ciranta (. .′.) جرا نظر It com. endorser.
Circis (. —) جرجيس A St. George (in Islamic tradition).
ciret (— .) جيرت A lrnd. neighborliness.
cirit^{di} جريد [Arabic **carīd**] stick used as a dart in the mounted game of jereed; the game of jereed. **—ci** seller or maker of jereed sticks; jereed player.
cirm جرم A 1. size, volume. 2. astr. body. **—i semavi** heavenly body.
ciro (.′.) جيرو It com. endorsement. **— bankası** clearing bank. **— et=** 1. com. to endorse. 2. /a/ slang to pass on, to transfer (to).
cirriye (. — .) جرّيّة A biol. 1. crop of a bird. 2. gizzard. 3. reticulum.
cisim^{smi} جسم [cism] 1. sc. body; material thing, matter. 2. lrnd. human body. 3. geomancy the earth. **—i azm** anat. diaphysis. **—i basit** phil. simple substance, element. **—i beyzi** geom. ellipsoid. **—i billûri** biol. crystalline lens. **—i cemadi** inorganic body. **—i cevherî** elementary substance; constitutional parts. **—i Eflâtunî** geom. Platonic body. **—i felekî** Ptolomaic astr. heavenly body. **—i havai** gaseous substance. **—i hayvanî** animal body. **—i lâtif** supernatural body. **—i nâmî** organic body. **—cik** biol. corpuscle. **—len=** to embody, to take a material form, to solidify.
cism جسم A same as **cisim**.
cismani (. — —) جسمانى A lrnd. 1. corporeal. 2. material. **— ceza** law corporal punishment. **— zarar** law bodily harm. **—yet** (. — — .) A 1. corporeality. 2. materiality.
cismen (.′.) جسمًا A lrnd. 1. as regards the body. 2. in size.
cismî (. —) جسمى A lrnd. 1. solid. 2. corporeal. **—yet** A 1. solidity. 2. corporeality; materiality.
cisr جسر A lrnd. bridge. **—i atik** obs. the Old Bridge. **—i cedid** obs. the New Bridge (names of the bridges over the Golden Horn). **—eyn** A lrnd. the two bridges (over the Golden Horn).
civa (.′.) جيوه [Persian **cıwa**] mercury, quicksilver. **— gibi** very restless, mercurial. **— merhemi** mercury ointment. **— yakısı** mercurial plaster. **—lı** containing mercury.
civan′ (. —) جوان [cevan 2] poet. 1. young, youthful; young man, youth. 2. handsome young man. **—ım** my young fellow. **— kaşı** embroidery zigzag ornament. **— perçemi** yarrow, bot., Achillea Millefolium. **—lık** youth, youthfulness. **—merd** same as **cevanmerd**. **—merdlik** bravery; generosity.
civar (. —) جوار A neighborhood, vicinity, environments, surroundings; neighboring. **—ı Hakka peyvest ol=** lrnd. to die and go to heaven. **—iyet** (. — — .) A neighborhood, closeness.
civarina (. . .′.) جوارينا It naut. windlipper, cat's-paw.
civata (. .′.) same as **cıvata**. جواط
civciv جوجو 1. chick. 2. a chirping (of birds); chatter, noise. **—li** noisily; lively, crowded.
civelek^{ği} جبوه لك 1. colloq. lively, playful, coquettish. 2. obs. young, strong, and active lad; young camel. 3. hist. youth in the service of the Janissaries,
[For /civil/ and /civir/ see /cıvıl/.]
ciyadet (. — — .) جيادت A lrnd. excellence, freshness, cleanness.
ciyak ciyak جياه جياه var. of **cıyak cıyak**.
ciyef جيف A lrnd., pl. of **cife**.
ciz=^{er} 1 جيزمك prov., var. of **çiz=**.
ciz^{z′i} 2 جذع A lrnd. trunk, bole, shaft of a tree; beam, log; bot. stipe.
Cizvit^{ti} جزويت F Jesuit.
cizye جزيه A can. law capitation tax collected from non-Muslims. **—dar** (. . —) P collector of the capitation tax. **—güzar** (. . . —) P person subject to capitation tax.
coğrafi (. — —) جغرافى A sc. geographical. **— arz** geographical latitude. **—yün** (. — — —) A geographers.
coğrafya (. .′.) جغرافيا [A . — . —] geography. **—cı** geographer.
cokey جوكى F jockey.
conta (.′.) جونتا It mech. 1. joint. 2. packing.
cop^{bu} جوب [çub] 1. billy, truncheon. 2. prov. stick.
corum جوروم shoal, school of fish.
coş=^{ar} جوشمك 1. to become exuberant, to become enthusiastic. 2. to become violent (wind), to rise (river), to boil up; archaic to overflow. **—ku** neol. enthusiasm.
coşkun جوشقون 1. ebulliant, exuberant, enthusiastic. 2. gushing, violent, vehement. **—luk** 1. ebullience, exuberance, enthusiasm. 2. vehemence, violence.
coştur=^{ur} جوشدرمك /ı/ caus. of **coş=**.
covino (.′..) جوينو It slang smart, dandy.
cömert^{di} جومرد [civanmerd] generous, liberal, munificent. **—in eli tutulmaz** proverb You can't prevent anybody from being generous. **—lik** generosity, liberality, munificence.

cönkᵍᵘ بونلك 1. a codex in which the line of writing is parallel to the seam. 2. manuscript collection of folk poems.

cuᵘᵘ **1** (—) جوع A *lrnd.* hunger, starvation. **-u bakar, -u kelbî** *path.* bulimia, canine hunger.

cu 2 (—) جو P *poet.* stream, brook.

-cu 3 جى *cf.* **-cı.**

-cu 4 (—) جو P that seeks, that desires, *as in* **harbcu.**

cud (—) جود A *lrnd.* liberality, munificence.

cudam جودام *prov.* wretch. miserable fellow.

Cudi (— —) جودى *cf.* **Cebeli Cudi.**

-cuğaz, -cüğez جغز *archaic for* **-cağız, -ceğiz.**

cuğd جعد P *poet.* owl.

Cuha (— —) جوحا جوحى A *name of a boy about whose pranks and drolleries the Arabs tell many stories.*

cukᵍᵘ **1** بلك *children's game* the winning position of the thrown knucklebone.

cukᵍᵘ **2** جوك *slang* hashish.

-cuk-ᵍᵘ **3** جك *cf.* **-cık.**

culah (— —) جولاه P *archaic* weaver. **—ek** little weaver; spider.

culâkî (—.—) جولقى [Persian colahî] *lrnd.* devotee who wears sackcloth; religious mendicant.

culban (.—) جلبان *var. of* **cilban.**

culha جولها [Persian culaha] *prov.* weaver.

Cuma 1 (.—) جمعه [Cum'a 2] Friday. **— alayı** *hist.* the Sultan's procession to the mosque for the Friday noon service. **bir —sı eksik** *colloq.* idiotic. **— ertesi** *same as* **Cumartesi. — selâmlığı** *same as* **— alayı.**

Cum'a 2 جمعه A *lrnd., same as* **Cuma 1. — Suresi** *name of the 62nd Sura of the Quran.*

Cumadelâhire (—.—..), **Cumadiyül'ahir** (.—..—.), جمادى الآخره A *lrnd., same as* **Cemaziyel'ahır.**

Cumadelûlâ (.—..—.), **Cumadiyül'evvel** (.—....) جمادى الأول جمادى الأولى A *lrnd., same as* **Cemaziyel'evvel.**

Cumalıkᵍⁱ (.—.) جمعلى *pertaining to Friday.*

Cumartesi جمعه ارتسى Saturday.

cumba (.'.) جومبه bay window.

cumbadak (.'..) جومبه دان جومبه داق splash! (noise produced by a sudden fall into water).

cumbul cumbul جومبول جومبول 1. *noise produced by a liquid slopping about.* 2. too watery (food).

cumbulda=ʳ جومبولده to make a gurgling sound (slopping fluid).

cumbultu جومبولدى gurgling, splashing sound. [For /cumbur/ see /cumbul/.]

cumhur (.—) جمهور A the mass of the people, the public; the nation; crowd. **— başkanı** president of the republic. **— cemaat** in a crowd. **—u hükema** the learned, the sages. **— ilâhisi** *rel. orders* a kind of hymn sung in unison in the **dergâhs** of **tekkes** other than those of the Mevlevi and Bektashi orders. **—a muhalefet kuvvei hatadandır** It is a mistake to go against the mass. **— reisi** president of the republic. **—u üdeba** the literary world. **—î** (.—.—) A republican.

cumhuriyet (.—.—.) جمهوريت A republic. **C— Halk Partisi** the Republican People's Party. **C—çi Köylü Millet Partisi** the Republican Peasant National Party. **—çi** republican. **—çilik** republicanism. **—perver** (.—.—...) P republican.

cumuᵘᵘ (.—) جموع A *lrnd., pl. of* **cem 1,** crowds, troops.

cunda (.'.) جونده It *naut.* peak (of a gaff); arm-end of a yard. **—ya bin=** to take charge (of affairs, etc). **— yelken** studding sail.

cunta (.'.) جونطه *var. of* **conta.**

cup جپ plop! (noise produced by a fall into water).

cuppadak (.'..) جوپ ده same as **cumbadak.**

cura 1 جورا 1. *mus.* the smallest variety of the **bağlama.** 2. kind of shrill wind instrument. 3. small, shrill-voiced hawk. 4. puny, undersized.

cura 2 جرعه [cür'a] *slang* the last puff of a cigarette.

curcuna (.'.) جرجونه 1. noisy dance in a drunken revel, carousal. 2. noisy confusion, confused medley. 3. *Or. mus.* the 10/16 or 10/8 degree of the **aksaksemai** rhythmic pattern of 10 beats. **—ya çevir=, —ya döndür=** *same as* **curcunaya ver=. —ya kalk=** *slang* to start a row; to quarrel. **—yı kopar=** to shout and quarrel. **—ya ver=** /ı/ to cause a great uproar (in a place).

curnal جورنال It report of an informer. **— et=** /ı/ to denounce, report, inform (against). **—cı** delator, denouncer, informer.

curp جرپ *var. of* **cup.**

cuş (—) جوش P *poet.* 1. a boiling, bubbling; ebullition, fermentation, effervescence; an overflowing. 2. outbreak, commotion, attack; enthusiasm. **— et=** to boil over; to become violently agitated. **—a gel=** to come to the boiling point; to become agitated. **— u huruş** excitement, commotion, enthusiasm. **— u huruş et=** to boil up and rush violently.

cuşacuş (—.—.) جوشاجوش P *poet.* full of excitement.

cuşan (— —) جوشان P *poet.* 1. boiling; fermenting. 2. agitated, excited.

cuşaver (— —.) جوشآور P *poet.* exciting.

cuşide (— —.) جوشيده P *lrnd.* 1. in

ebullition, violently agitated. 2. roused, excited. **—gi** (— —. —) P outbreak. **—mağz** (— —..) P passionate, excited; wary.

cuşiş (—.) بوشش P lrnd. ebullition; commotion, excitement.

cuy (—) جوی P var. of **cu 2**.

cuya, cuyan (— —) جويا جويان P lrnd. that seeks; that longs for, desires.

cuybar (— —) جويبار P poet. river, stream.

cuyende (— ..) جوينده P poet. seeking; seeker.

-cü cf. **-cı.**

cübbᵇᵘ جبّ A lrnd. 1. well. 2. dungeon. **—ü Yusuf** Joseph's well.

cübbe جبّه A same as **cüppe.**

cübena (.. —) جبنا A lrnd., pl. of **cebin 1.**

cübn جبن A caseous, cheesy.

cüce جوجه dwarf. **— balaban** little bittern, zool., Ixobrychus minutus. **— baykuş** scops owl, zool., Otus scops. **— karabatak** pygmy cormorant, zool., Phalacrocorax Pygmaeus. **— kartal** booted eagle, zool., Hieraetus pennatus. **— martı** little gull, zool., Larus minutus. **— sıvacı kuşu** nuthatch, zool., Sitta europaea and other varieties. **— sinekyutan** red-breasted flycatcher, zool., Muscicapa parva. **— yıldızlar** astr. dwarf stars. **—lik** dwarfishness.

cücükᵗᵘ جوجوک prov. 1. bud, young shoot. 2. heart of an onion. 3. tuft of beard, «imperial». 4. chick. 5. sweet and tender.

cüda (. —) جدا P separated, separate, remote. **— cüda** lrnd. one by one, separately. **— düş=** /dan/ to be separated (from). **—gâne** (. — —.) P lrnd. separately. **—lık** —**yi** (. — —) P lrnd. separateness, separation.

cüfa (. —) جفاء A lrnd. 1. froth, scum. 2. useless, vain thing.

cüftᵗᵘ جفت P lrnd., same as **çift. —ü betul** Isl. rel. the «Husband of the Virgin» (name given to the Caliph Ali).

cüfte جفته P lrnd., same as **çifte.**

-cüğez جك cf. **-cuğaz.**

cühelâ (.. —) جهلاء , **cühhal**ᵘ (. —) جهّال A lrnd., pl. of **cahil. — takımı** the ignorant people.

Cühud (. —) جهود P lrnd. the Jews. **— baklası** Egyptian lupine, bot., Lupinus termis. **—ane** (. — —.) P Jewish. **—î** (. — —) P 1. Jew; Jewish. 2. Judaism.

-cükᵗᵘ جك cf. **-cık.**

cül جل A lrnd. horse-cloth.

cülâb (. —) جلاب A lrnd. 1. rose-water. 2. demulcent, julep.

cülâh (. —) جلاه P var. of **culâh.**

cülbaf (. —) جلباف P lrnd. weaver of horsecloths.

cülcül جلجل same as **cülcüle.**

cülcülân (.. —) جلجلان A lrnd. coriander seed; sesame seed. **—ı kalb** 1. innermost part. 2. deep concern of the heart.

cülcüle جلجله A lrnd. 1. small cymbal of a tambourine. 2. small bell.

cülencübin (... —) جلنجبين A lrnd. rose jam.

cülesa (.. —) جلساء A lrnd., pl. of **celîs.**

cüllenar (.. —) جلّنار A lrnd. pomegranate flowers.

cülnesrin (.. —) جلنسرين A dogrose, bot., Rosa canina.

cülus (. —) جلوس A 1. accession to the throne. 2. lrnd. a sitting. **—u humayun** Ott. hist. the accession of a sultan to the throne. **—î** (. — —) A pertaining to a royal accession. **—iye** (. — —.) A poetry poem in praise of a royal accession to the throne.

cüman (. —) جمان A lrnd. 1. pearls. 2. woman's belt, ornamented with beads.

cümban (. —) جنبان P lrnd. moving, shaking, stirring.

cümbür cemaat جمبور جماعت [cumhur cemaat] all together, the whole crowd.

cümbüş جنبش [Persian cunbis] 1. merry-making, revel; jollity. 2. kind of mandolin with metal body. 3. lrnd. motion, agitation. **— et=** to revel, to enjoy oneself with noisy merriment. **—lü** exciting, merry.

cümcüme جمجمه A anat. skull.

cümel 1 جمل A lrnd., pl. of **cümle. —i hikemiye** aphorisms.

cümel 2 جمل A lrnd. calculation by use of the letters of the alphabet as numerals.

cümhur (. —) جمهور same as **cumhur.**

cümle 1 جمله A 1. gram. sentence, clause. 2. a total, whole; system, group. **—i asabiye** anat. nervous system. **—i asliye** gram. main clause. **—i cezaiye** gram. apodosis. **—i fi'liye** gram. verb clause. **—i hikemiye** aphorism. **—i ihbariye** gram. indicative clause. **—i inzaiye** gram. imperative or optative clause. **—i ismiye** gram. noun clause. **—i istidrakiye** gram. adversative clause. **—i istifhamiye** gram. interrogative clause. **—i kevkebiye** astr. constellation. **—i lenfaviye** anat. lymphatic system. **—i muteriza** gram. parenthetical clause. **—i mütemmime** gram. subordinate clause. **—i sempatii kebir** anat. sympathetic system. **—i şartiye** gram. conditional clause. **—i şartiyei faraziye** gram. hypothetic conditional clause. **—i tabia** gram. subordinate clause. **—i tamme** gram. complete sentence. **—i tefsiriye** gram. appositional clause. **—i vasfiye** gram. adjectival clause. **—i zarfiye** gram. adverbial clause.

cümle 2 (.'.) جمله [cümle 1] all. **—miz** all

cümlecik

of us, we all. **— âlem** all the world, everybody. **— kapısı** main door.

cümlecikᵍⁱ جمله بك. *gram.* clause.

cümleten (.'..) جملة A all together. **— Allaha ısmarladık** Goodby, everyone.

cümud (.—) جمود A *lrnd.* 1. coagulation. 2. *med.* rigor; catalepsy.

cümudiye (.——.) جموديّة A 1. glacier. 2. iceberg. **— dili** *geol.* glacier. **— sirki** *geol.* corrie. **— sürgüsü** *geol.* rock bar.

cünd جند A *lrnd.* troops, military force.

cündi (.—) جندى A 1. expert horseman. 2. *hist.* soldier, warrior. **—lik** horsemanship.

cünha جنحه A *law* misdemeanor, serious offense. **— sahibi** culprit.

cünub (.—) جنوب A *lrnd., pl. of* **cenb**.

cünud (.—) جنود A *lrnd., pl. of* **cünd**.

cünun (.—) جنون A *psychiatry* madness, insanity. **—u devrî** periodical mania, cyclic insanity. **—u gayrimutbık** *law* intermittent insanity. **— getir=** to become insane, to go mad. **—u mutbık** *law* confirmed insanity. **—u sebni** furious madness. **—u şebab** dementia praecox.

cünüb جنوب A canonical uncleanness.

cüppe جبّه [**cübbe**] robe worn by imams, judges, barristers and professors, with full sleeves and long skirts. **—ci** maker or seller of **cüppe**.

cür'a جرعه A *poet.* 1. gulp. 2. the last gulp of a drink. 3. *myst.* hidden mysteries manifested only to those who have attained a high grade of sanctity. **—dan** (..—) P *lrnd.* small water bottle carried by a traveller. **—nuş** (..—) P *lrnd.* who drinks. **—riz** (..—) P *lrnd.* kind of ewer with a spout.

cür'et جرأت A 1. boldness, courage. 2. insolence, impudence. **— et=** to dare, venture.

cür'etkâr (..—) جرأتكار P 1. bold, courageous. 2. insolent, impudent. **—âne** (..——.) P 1. boldly. 2. impudently.

cür'etlen=ⁱʳ جرأتلن to become bold. **—dir=** *caus.*

cür'etli جرأتلى 1 .bold. 2. insolent.

cür'etsiz جرأتسز timid. **—lik** timidity.

cür'etyab (..—) جرأتياب P *lrnd.* bold; impudent.

cürh جرح A *law* wound.

cürm جرم A *cf.* **cürüm**. **—nak** (.—) P *lrnd.* guilty, criminal.

cürsume (.—.) جرثومه, **cürsüme** جرثمه A 1. *biol.* germ. 2. *lrnd.* root, rootstock, rhizome; source, base, origin.

cüruf (.—) جروف A scoria, slag; dregs, sediment; scum.

cüruh (.—) جروح A *lrnd., pl. of* **cürh**.

cürümʳᵐᵘ جرم A crime, guilt; *law* felony, offense, misdemeanor. **—ü cinayet resmi** *feudal law* tax exacted by the feudal lord from known criminals. **—ünü inkâr et=** *law* to plead not guilty. **— isnadı** *law* imputation of crime. **— işle=** to commit a crime. **—ünü itiraf et=** *law* to plead guilty. **—ü meşhut** *law* crime caught in the act. **—ü meşhut halinde** *law* caught in the act. **—ü meşhut yap=** /a/ to lay a trap to catch someone red-handed. **— tasnii** a framing a person. **—e teşebbüs** attempt at crime, attempted crime.

cüsam (.—) جسام A *lrnd.* nightmare.

cüseym, cüseyme جسيم، جسيمه A *biol.* corpuscle.

cüsse جثّه A a bulky body; volume. **—dar** (..—) P, **—li** big bodied, bulky, voluminous.

cüstucu (..—) جست وجو P *lrnd.* a seeking, searching.

cüsuᵘᵘ (.—) جسوع A *lrnd.* stinginess, meanness.

cüvan (.—) جوان *var. of* **cevan**.

cüyuş (.—) جيوش A *lrnd., pl. of* **ceyş**.

cüzᶻʼᵘ جزء A 1. part, section, fragment, piece, particle; element, component. 2. a thirtieth part of the Quran; section of the Quran separately bound. 3. separately published section of a book; booklet. 4. *phys.* atom. 5. *math.* aliquot part. 6. *geom.* degree. 7. *pros.* metrical foot. 8. *myst.* a finite being, as a part of the universal whole. 9. *law* a lineal male descendant; female descendant. **—ü ced** *law* a lineal male descendant of the paternal grandfather. **—ü eb** *law* a lineal male descendant of the father. **—ü ferd** *phys.* atom. **—ü ferdî** *phil.* atomic. **—ü ferdiye** *phil.* atomism. **—ü ictima** *astrol.* the longitude of conjunction of two heavenly bodies. **—ü istikbal** *astrol.* the longitude of the point of opposition. **— kesesi** ornamented leather or cloth bag or holder for carrying a section of the Quran. **—ü lâyetecezza** *lrnd.* indivisible part. **—ü meyyit** *law* a lineal male descendant of the deceased. **—ü mütemmim** *sc.* integral part, component. **—ü müzahhaf** *pros.* contracted or expanded foot. **—ü salim** *pros.* an unaffected, whole foot. **—ü tam** *sc., mil.* unit.

cüzaf (.—) جزاف A *law* a buying and selling by guess as to quantity.

cüzam (.—) جزام A leprosy, Hanson's disease. **—hane** (.——.) leprosarium. **—lı** leprous; leper.

cüzbend جزبند P 1. *obs.* portfolio. 2. *lrnd.* bookbinder.

cüzdan جزدان portfolio, pocketbook.

cüzeyr جزير A *bot.* rootlet, radical, rhizoid.

cüzeyre جزيره A 1. *geog.* islet. 2. *anat.* insula.

cüzhan (.—) جزء خوان P reader or reciter of the Quran.

cüz'i (.—) جزئى A 1. insignificant, trifling, small. 2. *lrnd.* partial, fragmentary. 3. *phil.* particular, not universal; a particular or individual thing. 4. *phys.* elementary. 5. *log.* a particular or singular term. **—yi hakikî** 1. *phil.* a true particular, an individual thing. 2. *log.* word denoting an individual thing. **—yi izafi** 1. *phil.* a relative particular, a species. 2. *log.* word denoting a species. **— küsuf** *astr.* partial eclipse. **—ce** somewhat little, rather insignificant. **—yat** (..—) A 1. trifles, insignificant things. 2. *phil.* particular things, individual things. 3. *log.* particular or singular terms. 4. *lrnd.* special or particular sciences, branches of universal science, as medicine, astronomy, etc. 5. *Ptolemaic astr.* secondary spheres. **—yat-ı umur** insignificant happenings. **—yet** A *abst. n. of* **cüz'i**.

cüzur (.—) جزور A *lrnd., pl. of* **cezr 1**.

cüzvi جزوى P *obs.* a little.

Ç

ç, Ç the fourth letter of the alphabet.

-ça چه *cf.* **-ca 1, 2**.

çaba چابا 1. *prov.* worry; effort. 2. *phil.* effort.

çabala= چابالامق چابالامه چابا طه to strive, to struggle, to do one's best.

çabalama چابالامه a striving, effort. **— kaptan ben gidemem** It's no use, captain; I can't go (said of a worn-out old vessel or a tired person).

çabalan= چابالانمق to thrash arms and legs, to flounder.

çabalat= /ı/ *caus. of* **çabala=**.

çabucacık (.'...) چابوجاجيق quickly.

çabucak (.'..) چابوجاق جبجه چابوجه quickly.

çabuk چابك چابون جبجه quick, fast, swift, hasty; quickly, speedily, soon. **— çabuk quickly. — ol!** Be quick! Hurry up. **—laş=** to gain speed. **—laştır=** /ı/ to speed. **—luk** quickness; speed, haste.

çabük (—.) چابوك P *lrnd.* 1. quick, swift, speedy; soon, quickly. 2. agile, adroit. **—dest** (—..) P adroit, dextrous. **—hiram** (—..—) P swift-paced. **—i** (—.—) P swiftness, agility. **—pa** (—.—) P swift of foot. **—rev** (—..) P swiftly-moving. **—rikâb** (—..—) P swift-riding. **—suhan** (—...) P quick at rejoinders. **—süvar** (—..—) P 1. good rider, excellent horseman. 2. racing jockey. 3. courier. **—süvarî** (—..—) P horsemanship.

çaç (—) چاچ P *lrnd.*, same as **çeç 1**.

çaça 1 چاچه sprat, *zool., Clupea sprattus; Spratella sprattus phalerica*.

çaça 2 (.'.) چاچه Gk 1. *naut.* experienced sailor. 2. *slang* woman who keeps a brothel.

çaçaron چاچارون It *colloq.* wearisome chatterer. **—luk** chattering, empty talking.

çaçi (——) چاچى P poet. made in the ancient city of Chach in Transoxiana (bow).

çader (—.) چادر P *lrnd.*, same as **çadır**[1, 2]. **—nişin** (—..—) P *lrnd.* tent-dweller; nomad. **—şeb** (—..) P *lrnd.* bed sheet.

çadır چادر [**çader**] 1. tent, pavilion. 2. *prov.* kind of cloak worn by women in the East, chuddar. 3. *prov.* umbrella. 4. *obs.* balloon. **— ağırsağı, — başı** cap or truck of a tentpole fixed outside to keep the rain out. **— bezi** tent canvas. **—ı boz=** to strike a tent. **— çanağı** truck at the top of the tentpole, which holds the canvas. **— çiçeği** bindweed, cornlily, *bot., Convolvulus arvensis*. **— direği** tentpole. **— eteği** flap of a tent. **— göbeği** same as **çadır çanağı**. **— kanadı** movable flap of a tent. **— kazığı** tentpin, tentpeg. **— kur=** to pitch a tent. **— mehterleri** *Ott. hist.* special troop in charge of the Sultan's tent during military expeditions. **— tablası** flat wooden disc on the top of a tentpole. **— tekerleği** same as **çadır ağırsağı**. **— topu, — topuzu** ornamental ball surmounting a tent. **— uşağı** 1. gum ammoniacum. 2. dorema, gum ammoniacum plant, *bot., Dorema ammoniacum*.

çadırcı چادرجى tentmaker. **Ç—lar** the Market of the Tentmakers (name of a street in the Covered Market of Istanbul).

çadırî چادرى a particular color of green.

çağ 1 چاغ 1. time. 2. age, period. 3. the right time (for something). 4. maturity; strength; stature. **— aç=** to open a period.

çağ 2 جاغ |çah| *prov.* sink, drain.
çağ 3 جاغ *prov.* pole.
çağa جاغا *prov.* infant.
çağala جغالە |Persian cagala| same as **çağla**.
çağana جاغنە جغنە |Persian .—.| *Or. mus.* 1. rattle composed of metal discs mounted on a wire, used by dancers in beating time. 2. small metal castanet. 3. small tambourine.
çağanak[ⁱ] جاغناك same as **çağana**.
çağanoz جاغنوز crab.
Çağatay جاغتای جغتای Jagatai, Chagatai. **—ca** in Jagatai.
çağdaş جاغداش contemporary.
çağıl çağıl جاغل جاغل جغل جغل burbling, murmuring (of water).
çağılda=ʳ جاغلامق to burble, murmur (water). **—t=** /ı/ *caus.*
çağıltı جاغلتی the plash, burble, murmur of running water among rocks.
çağır=ʳ 1 جاغرمق 1. /ı/ to call; to invite; to summon. 2. to shout, to call out. 3. to sing.
çağır 2 جاغر *archaic* wine.
çağırgan جاغرغان *prov.* noisy, clamorous.
çağırıl=ʳ جاغرلمق same as **çağrıl=**.
çağırış, çağırma جاغرش جاغرمە a calling, call; summons.
çağırt=ʳ جاغرتمق /ı,a/ *caus. of* **çağır=** 1.
çağırtka جاغرتقە 1. field cricket. 2. common grasshopper.
çağırtkan جاغرتغان decoy bird.
-çağız جغز *cf.* **-cağız**.
çağla 1 جغلا جاغلا جغلە |çağala| 1. green almond eaten in the shell. 2. unripe fruit. **— yeşili** almond green.
çağla=ʳ 2 جاغلامق to burble, purl, plash (falling water). **—ma** *verbal n.*
çağlan=ʳ جاغلانمق to reach one's prime. **—dır=** /ı/ *caus.*
çağlar جاغلار same as **çağlıyan**.
çağlat=ʳ جاغلاتمق /ı/ *caus. of* **çağla=** 2.
çağlayan جاغلايان same as **çağlıyan**.
çağlayık[ⁱ] جغلايق جاغلايق bubbling spring; hot spring.
çağlayış جاغلايش *verbal n. of* **çağla=** 2.
çağlı جاغلی in one's prime; well-built, healthy, sturdy, strong.
çağlık[ⁱ] جاغلق *prov.* room with drainage for bathing.
çağlıyan جاغليان waterfall; cascade.
çağrı *neol.* 1. *mil.* call (to arms); notice, announcement. 2. *gram.* vocative. **— hali** *gram.* vocative case.
çağrıl=ʳ جاغرلمق *pass. of* **çağır=** 1.
çağrış=ʳ جاغرشمق 1. to call out together, to shout together. 2. to sing in unison. **—ım** *neol., psych.* association. **—tır=** /ı/ *caus. of* **çağrış=**.

çağşağı جغشاغی *prov.* child's rattle.
çah (—) جاه P *poet.* 1. well; shaft sunk in the earth. 2. pit, dungeon. **—ı Babil** the Pit of Babylon (where Harut and Marut are confined until Judgment Day). **—ı Bijen** the well in which Bizhan was imprisoned by Afrasiyab, according to Firdausi's Shahnameh. **—ı gabgab** dimple under the chin. **—ı nisyan** the pit of forgetfulness, oblivion. **—ı pest** deep pit, *i. e.*, the world. **—ı Rüstem** the pit into which Rustem was decoyed, according to Firdausi's Shahnameh. **—ı sitarecu** astronomer's well. **—ı Yusuf** the well into which Joseph was cast by his brothers. **—ı zekan, —ı zeneh, —ı zenehdan** dimple on the chin. **—ı zic** astronomer's well. **—ı zulmani** dark pit, *i. e.* the world; body, flesh.
çahcu (——) جاهجو P *lrnd.* 1. welldigger. 2. cleaner of wells. 3. grapnel for recovering things fallen into a well.
çahken (—.) جاهكن P *lrnd.* welldigger.
çahsar (——) جاهسار P *lrnd.* well's mouth.
çahyüz (—.) جاهيوز P *lrnd.* grapnel for recovering things fallen into a well.
çaiye جائيە *bot.*, Theaceae; Ternstroemia.
çak=ᵃʳ 1 جاقمق 1. /ı/ to drive in with blows (nail); to nail on; to tether to a pin. 2. /ı/ to strike (fire, blow); to snap (teeth); *slang* to snap (salute); to fire (gun). 3. /dan/ *slang* to understand; /ı/ *slang* to notice, perceive. 4. /ı,a/ *slang* to palm off (false coin, etc.); *archaic* to tell (on), denounce, to inform (against). 5. to flash (lightning). 6. *slang* to drink, carouse. 7. *school slang* to fail (in an examination).
çak 2 جاق noise produced by clash of metals.
çakᵏⁱ **3** (—) جاك P *lrnd.* 1. rent, slit; gash; crack, fissure; cracked, fissured. 2. a clashing. 3. daybreak. **— çak** tattered and torn. **— et=** /ı/ to rend, tear; to crack, split. **—i giriban et=** to rend one's clothes (in despair). **— ol=** *pass. of* **çak et=**.
çak 4 جاق *prov.* exactly, precisely, *e. g.*, **çak boğazıma geldi** It came right to my throat.
çakâçakᵏⁱ (———) جاكاجاك P *lrnd.* 1. noise; clash of arms. 2. full of rents, wounds, etc.
çakal جقال جاقال 1. jackal, *zool.*, Canis aureus. 2. *slang* sly, cunning; mean; wretch. **— eriği** sloe, *bot.*, Prunus spinosa. **—lar gibi ulu=** to howl like jackals, to shout and cry violently.
çakaloz جقالوز جاقالوز *hist.* kind of swivel gun.
çakar جقار *fishing* kind of dragnet for catching mackerel.
çakaralmaz جاقارآلماز 1. rusty old gun. 2. good-for-nothing.

çakçak[ġı] **1** چاقپامه sound of repeated resonant blows.

çakçak[kı] **2** (— —) چالق چالق P lrnd. clash of swords.

çakdar (— —) چاكدار P lrnd. torn, cracked, split, burst.

çaker (— .) چاكر P lrnd. servant. **—iniz** your humble servant. **—i kemine** *archaic* most humble servant. **—ane** (— . — .) P *term of respect* of this humble servant. **—hane** (— . — .) P *term of respect* my humble home. **—i** (— . —) P 1. *term of respect* of this humble servant. 2. *same as* **çakerlik**. **—lik** servitude. **—nüvaz** (— . . —), **—perver** (— . . .) P who is kind to his servants. **—zade** (— . — .) P *term of respect* your servant's son.

çakı چاقى [*Persian* **çaku**] pocket knife, clasp knife. **— gibi** dextrous, intelligent, very sharp.

çakıcı 1 چاقيجى maker or seller of knives.

çakıcı 2 چاقيجى 1. *colloq.* habitual tippler. 2. *slang* boxer; scamp.

çakıl 1 چاقل 1. pebble. 2. gravel. **— döşe=** /a/ to pave with pebbles; to gravel. **— ocağı** gravel pit. **— pidesi** flat cake baked on hot pebbles. **— taşı** rounded pebble.

çakıl=[r] **2** چاقلمق *pass. of* **çak=** 1.

çakılda=[r] چاقلدامق to clatter.

çakıldak[ġı] چاقلداق 1. rattle. 2. mill clapper; mill hopper. 3. ball of dried dung hanging on a beast's tail. 4. ceaseless talker.

çakıldat=[r] چاقلدتمق /ı/ *caus. of* **çakılda=**.

çakılı چاقيلى fixed, nailed (to something).

çakıllı چاقللى having pebbles; gravelled.

çakıllık[ġı] چاقللق 1. pebbly place; place paved with pebbles. 2. gravel pit.

çakıltı چاقلدى clattering, rattling noise.

çakım, çakın چاقيم 1. flash of lightning. 2. *verbal n. of* **çak=** 1. **bir —lık** enough for one lighting (match).

çakır 1 چاقر 1. grayish blue, gray with blue streaks (eyes); having grayish blue eyes. 2. goshawk, *zool.*, *Accipiter gentilis.* **— dikeni** burdock, *bot.*, *Arctium tomentosum*; burr, the fruit of burdock. **— doğan** *same as* **çakır**[2]. **— kanat** teal, *zool.*, *Anas crecca.* **— pençe** having a hawk-like grip, clawing, grasping.

çakır 2 چاقر *archaic* wine.

çakır 3 چاقر *prov.*, name of a folkdance.

çakırcı چاقرجى falconer.

çakır çukur چاقرچقور 1. with a rattling noise; rattling noise. 2. very broken (ground), full of potholes.

çakırdak[ġı] چاقرداق *var. of* **çakıldak**.

çakırkeyf چاقركيف half tipsy, somewhat drunk.

çakış 1 چاقش *verbal n. of* **çak=** 1.

çakış=[r] **2** چاقشمق 1. to fit into one another. 2. to collide with one another. 3. to compete in improptu verse.

çakıştır=[r] چاقشدرمق *colloq.* 1. to drink, to booze. 2. /ı/ *caus. of* **çakış=** 2. 3. /ı/ *prov.* to place side by side for comparison.

çakma چاقمه 1. *verbal n. of* **çak=** 1. 2. nailed on. 3. *jeweller's art* embossed; mold for embossing. 4. *prov., same as* **çakmak** 4.

çakmak[ġı] چاقمق 1. pocket lighter. 2. steel for striking on a flint. 3. trigger, flintlock. 4. a kind of pustule on the face. **— çamuru** muddy substance applied to pustules. **— taşı** flint. **— tekne** priming-pan of a flintlock gun. **— tiftik** short mohair of first quality.

çakmakçı چاقمقچى 1. maker or seller of flints. 2. maker or repairer of flintlock guns.

çakmaklı چاقمقلى flintlock gun.

çakozla=[r] چاقوزلامق /ı/ *slang* to understand, to see into.

çakrak[ġı] چاقراق a kind of sheep, bred for mutton.

çakşağı چاقشاغى *same as* **çağşağı**.

çakşır, çakşur چاقشير trousers secured round the waist in folds, and sewn to light leather boots at the ankles. **—lı** with feathered shanks (pigeon).

çaktır=[r] چاقدرمق /ı,a/ *caus. of* **çak=** 1.

çal=[ar] **1** چالمق 1. /ı,a/ to strike, to give (a blow, to); to throw, to knock (down); to smear (butter), to apply (salve); to mix (into), to add (flour) to soup. 2. /ı/ to move continuously and energetically (broom, shovel); to sweep (dust); to cut on the bias (cloth); *archaic* to strike off, cut off (head); *archaic* to delete. 3. /ı/ to knock (on a door); to play (musical instrument, tune); to strike (the hour). 4. to strike (of a clock), to ring (of a bell), to play (of a record player or radio). 5. /ı/ to affect in some detrimental way (sun, frost, wind, smoke, verdigris, acid). 6. /ı/ to steal. 7. /a/ to have a flavor or smell (of), to have a tinge (of), to smack (of); to be tinged with an accent (of, manner of talking). **—ıp almaca** at random, hastily. **—a çala ezgisini getir=** to attain one's aim by keeping at something long enough. **—ıp çırp=** to steal continuously. **—ma elin kapısını, çalarlar kapını** *proverb* Don't cause trouble or you will have trouble. **—ıp kes=** /ı/ to cut off. **—madan oyna=** 1. to be very jolly. 2. to be always ready (to do something).

çal 2 چال *prov.* bare hill.

çala چاله *prov.* old, worn out.

çalâk[kı] (— —) چالاك P lrnd. agile, swift.

çalakalem چالاقلم with a swift pen, writing swiftly.

çalakamçı چال قامچى lashing out with a whip.
çalakaşık چال قاشیق lapping up with a spoon.
çalakılıç چال قیلیچ dealing out sword-blows in all directions.
çalakırbaç چال قیربا ج same as **çalakamçı**.
çalâki (— — —) چالاکى P lrnd. agility, swiftness.
çalakürek چال کورك rowing hard.
Çalap چالاب archaic God.
çalapa چالاپه It 1. pharm. jalap. 2. jalap plant, bot., Ipomoea jalappa.
çalapaça چالاپاچه dragging along (someone), with pushing and pulling.
çalapala چالا پالا with all one's force.
çalar چالار equipped with a striking mechanism (clock). — **saat** 1. chiming clock. 2. alarm clock.
çalçene چالچنه chatterbox.
çaldır= چالدرمق /ı,a/ caus. of **çal=** 1.
çalgı چالغى 1. musical instrument. 2. instrumental music. — **âleti** musical instrument. — **çağanak** with music and merry-making. — **çal=** to play music. — **sandığı** obs. barrel organ. — **takımı** band, orchestra.
çalgıcı چالغىجى musician, instrumentalist. — **otu** hedge mustard, bot., Sisymbrium officinale. —**lık** music-playing (as a profession); the profession of a musician.
çalgılı چالغىلى offering musical entertainment (restaurant, etc.).
çalgın چالغىن prov. paralyzed.
çalı چالى bush, shrub. — **bülbülü** whitethroat warbler, zool., Sylvia communis. — **bülbülleri** warblers, zool., Sylviidae. —**dan çalıya sıçra=** to jump from one thought to another. — **çırpı** sticks, thorns, and brambles. — **dikeni** Christ's-thorn, Jerusalem thorn, bot., Paliurus aculeatus. — **fasulyesi** string beans with large edible pods and small beans. — **gibi** thick and rough (hair). — **horozu** capercaillie, zool., Tetrao urogallus. — **kavak** pollarded poplar, the branches of which are used for wickerwork. — **kuşu** goldcrest kinglet, zool., Regulus regulus. — **süpürgesi** besom, broom made from heath.
çalık چالیق 1. crooked, awry. 2. slanting; bevelled. 3. deranged; deranged in the mind. 4. that moves sideways (horse). 5. prov. scarred in the face; scar. 6. obs. whose name is struck out from the roll.
çalılık چالیلیق thicket, bushes, brush-wood.
çalım چالیم 1. swagger, strut, affected dignity. 2. the curved cutting part, edge of a scimitar. 3. sport a dodging in dribbling the ball. 4. naut. bow, bow line (of a vessel). — **et=** same as **çalım sat=**. —**ına getir=** /ı/ 1. to find a convenient occasion (for). 2. to bring into its proper trim. — **sat=** to strut, swagger. —**lı** 1. pompous; stuffed shirt. 2. naut. narrow-built and with a high bow.
çalın= چالینمق pass. of **çal=** 1.
çalış= چالیشمق 1. to work. 2. /a/ to study. 3. to try, strive. 4. archaic to fight. —**ıp çabala=** to strive hard, to endeavor, to do one's best.
çalış 2 چالیش 1. verbal n. of **çal=**. 2. archaic fight, battle.
çalışkan چالیشقان hard-working, diligent. —**lık** diligence.
çalışma چالیشما a working, work; study. **Ç— Bakanlığı** Ministry of Labor.
çalıştır= چالیشدرمق /ı/ caus. of **çalış=** 1.
çaliş (—.) چالیش P lrnd. 1. elegant gait; stateliness. 2. battle; enmity.
çalka= چالقامق /ı/ 1. to agitate, shake. 2. to toss about. 3. to rinse; to wash out (mouth). 4. to turn the stomach (milk); to cause indigestion (milk). 5. to disturb and addle (egg of brooding hen). 6. to beat (eggs), to churn (milk). —**la=** /ı/ same as **çalka=**. —**lan=** same as **çalkan=**. —**lat=** /ı,a/ caus. of **çalkala=**. —**n=** 1. pass. of **çalka=**. 2. to sway about; to move about restlessly. 3. to be rough (sea). 4. to be agitated (with rumors). —**nış=** verbal n.
çalkantı چالقانتى 1. agitation. 2. nausea; violent disturbance of the heart or mind. 3. beaten eggs. 4. refuse remaining in a sieve. 5. neol., phil. fluctuation, agitated.
çalkap چالقاب prov. at a glance. — **gör=** to catch a glimpse (of).
çalkar چالقار 1. gin for separating seeds from cotton. 2. upsetting the stomach. 3. purgative.
çalkat= چالقاتمق /ı,a/ caus. of **çalka=**.
çalkatura prov. registration of cattle.
çalma چالما 1. verbal n. of **çal=** 1. 2. stolen. 3. beaten up, shaken, mixed. 4. drink made of yoghurt. 5. obs. kind of turban. 6. chiselled (metal object). 7. prov. head scarf. 8. omelet.
çalpa= چالپامق /ı/ prov., var. of **çalka=**.
çalpara چالپاره [çarpare] 1. castanet. 2. disc acting as a valve in a chain pump. 3. lady crab, zool., Portunus puber. —**lı tulumba** chain pump.
çalyaka چال یقا seizing someone by the collar. — **et=** /ı/ to collar (person).
çam چام pine, bot., Pinus. — **baştankarası** coal titmouse, zool., Parus ater. — **devir=** to put one's foot in it, to make a blunder. — **fıstığı** pine nut. — **fıstık ağacı** Italian stone pine, bot., Pinus Pinea. — **mantarı** agaric, bot., Polyporus officinalis. — **pürü** fallen pine needles. — **sakızı** 1. pine resin. 2. a bore who sticks to one. — **sakızı, çoban armağanı** small

present. — **yarması gibi** a giant of a fellow.

çamariva (..´.) جاما ریوا It *naut.* all hands aloft! — **et=** to go aloft.

çamaşır جاماشیر جماشیر [**cameşuy**] 1. underclothing, underwear. 2. linen, bed linen. 3. laundry. — **ağası** *hist.* keeper of linen (in the Sultan's Palace). — **as=** to hang out the laundry. — **değiştir=** to change one's underclothes. — **ipi** clothes line. — **kazanı** boiler (washing). — **makinası** washing machine. — **mengenesi** mangle. — **sık=** to wring out the laundry. — **teknesi** washtub. — **ustası** keeper of linen (in a great house). — **yıka=** to do the laundry, to wash.

çamaşırcı جماشیرجی washerwoman; laundryman. — **kadın** washerwoman, laundress. — **usta** *Ott. hist.* woman superintendent of the Sultan's linen.

çamaşırhane (...—.) جماشیرخانه laundry room, wash house.

çamaşırlık[¹] جماشیرلق 1. laundry room. 2. underclothing material.

çamça (.´.) جمجه roach (small fresh water fish), *zool., Rutilus rutilus.*

çamçak[¹] جمجق جامجاق 1. wooden bowl for drinking water. 2. large wooden ladle.

çamçarşı جام چارشی all round, on all four sides.

çame (—.) جامه P *lrnd.* 1. verse, poetry; ode. 2. speech, discourse. **—dan** (—.—) P eloquent; orator. **—gû** (—.—) P singer of odes; poet.

çamış جامش [**camuş**] *prov.* unruly, restive, obstinate (horse).

çamlı جاملی covered with pines.
Çamlıca جاملیجه name of a hill near Üsküdar.
çamlık[¹] جاملق pine grove.

çamoka, çamuka (..´.) جاموقه kind of sardine, *zool., Atherina hepsetus.*

çamur جامور 1. mud, mire; muddy. 2. mixture of clay, etc.; mortar; plaster. 3. *slang* mean wretch. — **at=** /a/ to sling mud (at), to slander. **—a bas=** to get involved in a dirty job. **—a bula=** /a/ to disgrace, to soil. **—a bulaş=** to get involved in a dirty job, to come up against mean people. **—dan çekip çıkar=** /ı/ to save someone from a disreputable situation. — **deryası** all over mud. **—a düş=** to sink in the mire of life. **—u karnında, çiçeği burnunda** very fresh. — **sıçrat=** to splash with mud; to soil. — **sıva=** /a/ to throw mud (at), to soil. **—a taş at=** to invite abuse from an impudent and aggressive person.

çamurla=[ʳ] جامورلامق /ı/ 1. to soil with mud. 2. cover with accusations. **—n=** 1. *pass.* 2. *reflex.* **—ndır=** *caus.*

çamurlaş= جامورلاشمق 1. to become mud. 2. to become aggressive.

çamurlat=[ʳ] جامورلاتمق *caus. of* **çamurla=**.
çamurlu جامورلی muddy, miry.
çamurluk[ᵍᵘ] جامورلق 1. muddy place. 2. gaiters. 3. mudguard.

çamuş جاموش [**şemus**] *same as* **çamış**.

çan جان 1. large bell. 2. gong. — **çal=** 1. to ring the bell. 2. to make a great fuss about something. — **çiçeği** bell-flower, *bot., Campanula.* — **çiçeğigiller** *bot., Campanulaceae.* — **kulesi** belfry, bell tower. **—ına ot tıka=** /ın/ to silence. — **tokmağı** clapper, tongue of a bell.

çanak[¹] جناق جانق جنش جاناق 1. earthenware pot. 2. *bot., anat.* calyx. — **aç=** same as **çanak tut=**. — **gibi** large (mouth). — **çömlek** pots and pans. — **mehtabı** *obs.* festive illumination of a ship by means of fire in pots. **—ına ne doğrarsan kaşığına o çıkar** You reap what you sow. — **tut=** /ı/ 1. to beg. 2. to invite (insult, quarrel, etc.). — **üzengi** *obs.* cylindrical stirrup. — **yalayıcı** toady. — **yaprağı** *bot.* sepal. **—cı** potter; seller of pottery.

Çanakkale جناق قلعه *name of a town and province on the Dardanelles.* — **Boğazı** the Dardanelles.
çanaklık[¹] جناقلق *naut.* top of a mast. — **mavnası** *naut.* cheek of the lower mast.
çanaksı *neol., biol.* calyciform.
çancı جانجی bell ringer, sexton.
çançan جان جان a repeated clanging and jangling. — **et=** to chatter loudly and endlessly.
çandır جاندر 1. sheep of mixed breed. 2. *prov.* of mixed breed.
çane (—.) جانه P *lrnd.* 1. lower jaw; chin. 2. pertinacity in talk.
çanga جانغه *prov.* small copper bucket.
çangıl çungul جانغل جونغل , **çangır çungur** جانغر جونغر with a clanging noise; with a harsh, grating voice.
çangırda=[ʳ] جانغرداموق to clang continuously, to jangle. **—t=** /ı/ *caus.*
çangırtı جانغردی clanking, jangling sound.
Çankırı (.´..) جنغری *name of a town and province north of Ankara.*
çanlı جانلو جانكی furnished with a bell or gong. — **şamandıra** *naut.* bell buoy.
çanlık[¹] جانكلق 1. bell tower. 2. belfry.
çanta جانطه جنته جانته bag, case, valise, pouch, knapsack, handbag, briefcase, purse, suitcase, kit. — **çiçeği** slipperwort, *bot., Calceolaria integrifolia.* **—da keklik** in hand, in the bag. **—cı** 1. maker of or dealer in bags, etc. 2. *hist.* purse-bearer of the Sultan.
çantal جانطال *prov.* gown opening in front and with the skirt divided into three loose flaps.

çap[p] **1** جاپ 1. diameter. 2. *mil.* caliber. 3. caliber, scale, size. 4. plan showing size and boundaries of a plot, extracted from the cadastral map. **—tan düş=** to be undersized. **—ına getir=** /ı/ to create a favorable occasion (for). **— hesabı** *print.* estimate of size based on calculation of average line. **— ölçer** caliper rule. **— pergeli** calipers, caliper compass. **— tuğla** square bricks accurately molded.

çap=[ar] **2** جاپمن *prov.* 1. to run, trot, canter, gallop. 2. to ride fast. 3. /ı/ to raid, to pillage.

çapa 1 جاپه چاپا چپه چپ It 1. hoe. 2. a hoeing (of a crop).

çapa 2 چپه چاپا چاپ چپ It *naut.* 1. palmed anchor; palm of an anchor; anchor sign. 2. bilge plank.

çapacı جاپه جى 1. hoer. 2. maker or seller of hoes. 3. *hist.* a military sapper and miner; villager bound to such duty and free from taxes.

çapaçul چاپاچول *colloq.* untidy, slovenly, disordered.

çapak[g] **1** چاپاق جاپاق چپق 1. rheum from the eyes, crust round the eyes. 2. fin, beard (of casting); wire-edge, burr. **— kalemi** chisel for removing rough edges.

çapak[g] **2** چاپاق جاپاق چپق bream, *zool.*, Abramis brama.

çapaklan=[r] چاپاقلنمق to become gummy (eye).

çapaklı چاپاقلى 1. that has a crust of dried rheum on the eyelids. 2. that has a fin or burr; *print.* having a flaw in the casting (letter).

çapala=[r] چاپاله چپاله چپله طى /ı/ to hoe. **—n=** *pass.* **—t=** /ı,a/ *caus. of* **çapala=**.

çapalı چاپالو چاپالى furnished with a hoe.

çapan چاپان *same as* **çapar.**

Çapanoğlu چاپان اوغلى name of the family of a feudal chieftain of central Anatolia in the 18th and 19th centuries. **—nun aptes suyu** weak and muddy-looking tea.

çapar چاپار 1. *archaic* mounted courier. 2. *prov.* speckled, piebald; albino, pock-marked. 3. *naut.* kind of small craft. **— ulak** *archaic* mounted courier.

çaparı چاپارى It fishing line with many hooks.

çaparız چاپارز چاپارز چاپارس [paçarız] 1. obstacle, entanglement. 2. *naut.* athwart-hawse. **— gel=** to block the road; to create a difficulty. **—a getir=** *slang.* to entrap. **—lan=** to become perverse, to become difficult. **—lı** having obstacles, thorny. **—lık** entanglement.

çapavul چاپاول *archaic* raider.

çapıl=[r] چاپلمق *pass. of* **çap=** 2.

çapın=[r] چاپنمق *archaic* 1. to wander aimlessly about. 2. to hurry, to hasten, to run.

çapkın چاپقن چاپغن چاپغين چاپيقن چپقن 1. rake, debauchee, roué; naughty, coquettish. 2. rascal; mischievous (child). 3. *archaic* swift (horse). **—lık** profligacy, debauchery, rascality.

çapla=[r] چاپلامق چاپلى /ı/ to gauge the diameter (of); to calibrate. **—n=** *pass.* **—t=** /ı,a/ *caus. of* **çapla=**.

çapla 2 چاپلا steel chisel to scrape off metal.

çaplı چاپلى چاپلو 1. having the diameter; calibered. 2. large-sized, of large caliber; bulky, huge-bodied.

çaplus (— —) چاپلوس P *var. of* **cablus.**

çaprak[g] چاپراق *archaic* saddle-cloth.

çaprast چاپراست [Persian .—] *same as* **çapraz.**

çapraş=[r] چاپراشمق to become tangled, to become complicated. **—ık** involved, intricate, tangled.

çapraz چاپراز چاپرز [**çaprast**] 1. crosswise, transversal. 2. diagonally; *geom.* diagonal. 3. *tailor.* double-breasted. 4. three-cornered file; crosscut file; sawset, saw file. 5. *anat.* decussation, intersection, chiasma. 6. *phil.* crucial. 7. a metal clasp to a girdle; belt fastening with a metal clasp; frog fastening. 8. *Or. style wrestling* kind of clinch. 9. table of a backgammon board. **—a al=** *Or. style wrestling* to take in a clinch. **— gaga** crossbill, *zool.*, Loxia curvirostra. **— kerteriz** *naut.* cross bearings.

çaprazlama چاپرازلامه 1. crosswise; diagonally. 2. *rhet.* chiasmus.

çaprazlaş=[r] چاپرازلاشمق to become entangled.

çaprazlı چاپرازلى 1. that has clasps or frogs for fastening. 2. who wears a clasped belt.

çaptır=[r] چاپدرمق /ı/ *caus. of* **çap=** 2.

çapuk[gu] چاپوق *var. of* **çabuk.**

çapul چاپول چابل plunder, booty, spoil; marauding expedition, raid, sack. **— et=** /ı/ to pillage, sack.

çapula چاپوله [Persian **pacıla**] *prov.* kind of light sandal.

çapulcu چاپولجى raider, pillager. **—luk** pillage, looting.

çapulla=[r] چاپوللامق /ı/ to sack, pillage, plunder. **—n=** 1. *pass.* 2. to get plunder or spoil.

çaput چاپوت [Persian **cağbut**] *prov.* 1. rag. 2. coarse cloth.

çar 1 چار Russ. *hist.* czar, tsar.

çar 2 چار [car 1] *prov.* shawl, scarf, kerchief, wrapper.

çar 3 (—) چار P *lrnd.* four.

çar 4 (—) چار P *poet., same as* **çare.**

çar'ahsic (— — —) چار آخشيج P, **çar'ahur** (— — .) چار آخر P *lrnd.* the four elements.

çar'aktar (— . —) چار آقطار P *lrnd.* 1. the four cardinal points of the compass. 2. all directions.

çarbaliş (— — .) چار بالش P *lrnd.* 1. throne. 2. corner seat of honor. 3. the four elements. 4. the world. **—i erkân** 1. the four natural qualities (heat, cold, dryness, moisture). 3. the first four caliphs.

çarcihet (—..) چار جهت P lrnd. the four sides.

çarcuyıfıtret (——...) چار جوى فطرت P lrnd. the four temperaments (sanguine, choleric, melancholy, phlegmatic).

çarçabuk (.'..) چار چابون very quickly.

çarçeşm (—.) چار چشم P lrnd. 1. four-eyed, wearing spectacles. 2. having a spot over each eye (beast). — **ile** eagerly (to expect).

çarçube (——.) چار چوبه P lrnd. frame.

çarçur چار چور a squandering. — **et=** /ı/ to squander.

çardak[s1] چار داق چار طاق [**çartak**] 1. light structure consisting of posts and a roof of branches; trellis, bower. 2. hist. office of the overseer of trades. — **çorbacısı** hist. colonel of the 56th regiment of Janissaries.

çardeh (—.) چارده P lrnd. 1. fourteen. 2. full moon. —**üm** (—..) P fourteenth.

çarduval[ll] (—.—) چار دوال P lrnd. four-thonged whip.

çare (—.) چاره P 1. way, means, device. 2. remedy, cure; help. —**sine bak=** /ın/ to see (to), to settle. — **bul=** /a/ to find a remedy, to find a means (for). — **yok** no use, no good trying, useless.

çar'ebru (—.—) چار ابرو P lrnd. with a slight mustache (boy).

çarecu (—.—) چاره جو P lrnd. who seeks for a remedy.

çarejdeha (—..—) چار اژدها P, **çar'erkân** (—.—) چار اركان P, **çar'esbab** (—.—) چار اسباب lrnd. the four elements.

çareperdaz (—..—) چاره پرداز P lrnd. remedial.

çaresaz (—.—) چاره ساز P who applies a cure, a provider of remedy.

çaresiz (—..) چاره سز 1. inevitable; inevitably, of necessity. 2. irreparable, incurable. —**lik** helplessness; lack of means; urgency; poverty.

çareviç[s1] چاره ويج Russ. hist. czarevitch, tsarevitch.

çareyab (—.—) چاره ياب P lrnd. who finds a remedy; who finds a means.

çargâh (——) چارگاه P 1. Or. mus. a simple makam which is the basic scale of Turkish music and equals the major scale in Western music. 2. the note in the third space (c- do) of the staff. 3. lrnd. the four directions.

çargâme (——.) چارگامه P lrnd. 1. ambling nag. 2. a game of athletic leaping.

çargûşi (———) چارگوشى P poet. four-lipped wine-flagon.

çarh چرخ P 1. same as **çark**. 2. circular motion; mil. turn (in infantry drill). 3. Mevlevi order a turn on the left foot (in whirling). 4. poet. sky; destiny. 5. lrnd. circular argument. —**ı abkeşi** lrnd. Persian water wheel. —**ı abnus** lrnd. the Ninth Sphere. —**ı ahengerî** lrnd. blacksmith's grindstone. —**ı ahzar** lrnd. the blue vault of heaven. —**ı atlas**, —**ı berîn** lrnd. the Ninth Sphere. —**ı çaharum** lrnd. the Fourth Sphere. — **çevir=** to move in a circle, to mill. —**ı devvar** lrnd. the revolving sphere of heaven. —**ı esîr** lrnd. the Ethereal Sphere. — **et= mil.** to make a turn, to wheel. —**ı felek** 1. sphere of heaven; destiny. 2. same as **çarkıfelek**. —**ı gaddar** poet. cruel fate. —**ı kebud** poet. azure sky. —**ı kinesaz** poet. bad luck. —**ı lâciverd**, —**ı mina** poet. azure sky. —**ı nigûn** poet. adverse fortune. —**ı nühüm** lrnd. the Ninth Sphere. —**ı sitemkâr** poet. cruel fate.

[For other compounds, see **çerh**.]

çarha چرخه P 1. circling of light troops in front of the main body of a force. 2. lrnd., same as **çarh**. — **cengi** skirmish. — **topu** a piece of light field artillery. —**cı** skirmisher. —**lan=**, —**laş=** to skirmish. —**laştır=** /ı/ caus.

çarhaye (——.) چارخايه P lrnd. bold, brave, manly.

çarhendaz (..—) چرخ انداز P hist. cross-bowman.

çarık[s1] چاروق چاريق چاروغ چاريغ 1. rawhide sandal. 2. drag, skid, shoe (for a carriage wheel). 3. slang pocketbook. —**ı çek=** to put on one's boots, to start off. — **çürük** same as **çürük çarık**. —**çı** maker or seller of rawhide sandals.

çarıklı چاريقلى 1. wearing rawhide sandals. 2. boor. — **diplomat**, — **erkânıharp** a boorish fellow who shows unexpected shrewdness.

çariçe (.'.) چاريچه Russ. hist. czarina.

çark[kı] چرخ چارك [**çarh**] 1. wheel (of a machine). 2. lathe. 3. mech. flywheel. 4. naut. paddle wheel. 5. grindstone. 6. machine; press. 7. hist. crossbow, catapult. 8. same as **çarh**[2, 3]. —**ı bozul=** to have one's affairs upset, to meet with misfortune. —**a çektir=** /ı/ to put to the grindstone. —**ı döndü** His luck has turned to the bad. —**ına et=** /ın/ term of abuse to spoil. — **gemisi** paddle-wheel steamer. — **işi** machine-made. — **işlet=** 1. to work a machine. 2. to work a scheme for one's own advantage. —**ına oku=** /ın/ term of abuse to spoil. —**a tut=**, —**a ver=** /ı/ to put to the grindstone.

çarka چارقه var. of **çarha**.

çarkçı چرخجى 1. naut. engineer, mechanic. 2. knife-grinder. — **başı** naut. chief engineer. —**lık** knife-grinding; occupation of an engineer.

çarkıfelek چرخ فلك [**çarhı felek**] 1. passion

flower, *bot., Passiflora.* 2. *fireworks* Catherine wheel. **—giller** *bot., Passifloraceae.*

çarkla= بر قلدرمق برقلوی /ı/ to turn in a lathe. **—n=** *pass.* **—t=** *caus.* of **çarkla=**.

çarklı چارقلی برقلو provided with paddle wheels. **— vapur** paddle-wheel steamer.

çarköşe (—..) چارکوشه P *lrnd.* 1. four-cornered. 2. the four directions; all sides. 3. *geom.* square; quadrilateral. 4. square shawl or kerchief. 5. square leather or matting, used as a table for food.

çarlık[ğı] چارلق *hist.* czardom, tsardom.

çarliston چارلستون E 1. *dance* Charleston. 2. *slang* fop, dandy. **— biber** an oblong variety of green pepper.

çarmader (— —.) چارمادر P *lrnd.* the four elements.

çarmağz (—.) چارمغز P *lrnd.* walnut.

çarmezheb (—..) چارمذهب P *lrnd.* the four orthodox schools of Islam.

çarmıh چارمیخ [**çarmik**] 1. *hist.* cross on which criminals were nailed. 2. trestles and rope, used by rope-dancers. 3. *lrnd.* sodomy. **—a ger=** /ı/ to crucify.

çarmih (— —) چارمیح P *lrnd.*, same as **çarmıh**[1,2]; *lrnd.* sodomy. **—i hayat** 1. the four elements. 2. the four humours of the body.

çarmik[ği] چارمیسی چارموں [**çarmih**] *naut.* shroud.

çarnaçar (— — —) چار ناچار P willy-nilly, of necessity, whether one likes it or not.

çarp=[ar] چارپمق 1. /a/ to bump, to hit, to dash (against), to run (into), to collide (with). 2. /ı,a/ to hit, knock, strike (against). 3. /ı/ to strike, smite, paralyze, distort (evil spirit); to affect violently, to strike (sun, disease); to go to the head (wine). 4. /ı/ *slang* to pinch; to carry off. 5. to bang (door); to beat (heart, pulse); to palpitate, to throb (heart). 6. /ı,la/ *math.* to multiply (by). 7. /ı,a/ *prov.* to wash by shaking and beating (rug, in water).

çarpa (— —) چارپا P *lrnd.* quadruped; beast of burden.

çarpan چارپان 1. *math.* multiplier. 2. greater weever (fish), *zool., Trachinus draco.* **—lara ayır=** *math.* to factor.

çarpana چارپانا *prov.* worn old shoe.

çarpara چارپاره [**çarpare**] castanet.

çarpare (— —.) چارپاره P *Or. mus.* percussion instrument made of hard wood used in dance music.

çarpere (—..) چارپره P *lrnd.* four-feathered (arrow).

çarpı *neol., math.* multiplication sign.

çarpık[ğı] چارپیق چارپیسی 1. crooked, bent; warped; slanting, deviating; awry. 2. smitten by an evil spirit; paralysed. **— ayak** whose arrival brings bad luck. **— çurpuk** crooked, deformed. **—lık** crookedness; deformity.

çarpıl=[ır] چارپلمق 1. *pass.* of **çarp=**. 2. to become crooked, bent, warped, slanting. **—an** *neol., math.* multiplicand. **—ış, —ma,** *verbal n.* of **çarpıl=**.

çarpım *neol., math.* product. **— tablosu** multiplication table.

çarpın=[ır] چارپنمق to struggle or knock about with the arms or limbs. **—dır=** /ı/ *caus.* **—ma** *verbal n.*

çarpıntı چارپنتی 1. palpitation, throbbing. 2. a beating (of waves).

çarpış=[ır] چارپشمق 1. to clash; to collide. 2. to fight. **—ma** 1. clash; collision. 2. conflict; fight. **—tır=** /ı/ *caus.* of **çarpış=**.

çarpıt=[ır] چارپتمق /ı/ to make crooked, to distort (face).

çarpma چارپما 1. *verbal n.* of **çarp=**. 2. that closes on being slammed (lock). 3. beaten, produced by beating. 4. embossed (silverware). 5. stolen. 6. large five-pointed fishhook.

çarptır=[ır] چارپدرمق چارپتدرمق /ı,a/ *caus.* of **çarp=**.

çarsu (— — —) چارسو P *lrnd.* 1. square, market place. 2. crossroad, intersection. 3. the four directions, four sides.

çarşaf چارشاف چارشف [**çarşeb**] 1. bed sheet. 2. women's outdoor overgarment. **— gibi** calm (sea). **—a gir=** to reach the age of wearing the overgarment (girl). **— kadar** very large (handkerchief, etc.). **—lı** wearing a **çarşaf**. **—lık** material for bed sheets, etc.

Çarşamba چارشنبه [**çarşenbih**] Wednesday. **— karısı** the Wednesday Witch (an evil spirit that haunts on Wednesday nights). **— karısı gibi** like a witch, untidy and ugly.

çarşeb (—.) چارشب P *lrnd.* bed sheet.

Çarşembih (— ..) چارشنبه P *lrnd.*, same as **Çarşamba**.

çarşı چارشی چارشو [**çarsu**] shopping district, down-town region, the bazaars, market quarter. **— ağası, — başı** *obs.* warden of trades. **—ya çık=** to go shopping. **— ekmeği** common bread (as sold in shops). **— esnafı, — halkı** tradesmen. **— hamamı** public bath. **— pazar** shopping district, shops. **—lı** tradesman.

çarta (— —) چارتا P *lrnd.* four-stringed lute.

çartak[ğı] (— —) چارطاق P *lrnd.*, same as **çardak**.

çartar (— —) چارتار same as **çarter**.

çartekbir (—.—) چارتکبیر P *lrnd.* the four calls of **Allahü ekber,** made at burials or at taking a vow of renunciation.

çarter چارتر E *com.* charter.

çarüm (—.) چارم , **çarümin** (—.—) چارمین P *lrnd.* fourth.

çarüminbam (—.——) جارمين بام P lrnd. fourth heaven.

çar'üstad (—.—) جار استاد P lrnd. the four elements.

çarva (——) جار وا P var. of **çarpa**. **—dar** (————) P one who owns and lets out beasts of burden.

çaryar (——) جار يار P lrnd. the first four caliphs. **—ı güzin** same as **çaryar**.

çaryek[ki] (—.) جار يك P lrnd. one fourth, quarter.

çasar (——´) جاسار ، جاسار Hung emperor (of the Holy Roman Empire).

-çasına cf. **-casına**.

çaşıt[dı] جاشيت ، جاشود ، جاشيد ، جاشد prov. spy. **—la=** /ı/ to spy, to observe secretly. **—lık** the acts and quality of a spy; spying.

çaşni (——) جاشنى P lrnd., same as **çeşni**.

çaşnigir (————) جاشنيگير P hist. taster to a prince. **— usta** Ott. hist. woman who tasted all food placed before the Sultan in the harem.

çat=[ar] 1 جاتمق 1. /ı/ to stack (arms, etc.); to jerrybuild; to tack together, to baste together. 2. /ı,a/ to tie (around the head); to load (on a beast). 3. /a/ to collide (with), knock (against), to bump up (against); to meet (with trouble), to come up (against a difficulty); to scold, to be cross (with), to rebuke aggressively; to acquire favor through flattery; prov. to meet, to run (into).

çat 2 جات sudden sharp noise, clack. **— çat et=, — çut et=** to make a sharp, repeated knocking sound. **— kapı** There was a sudden knock at the door. **— orada, çat burada, çat kapı arkasında** He goes around and gossips all the time. **— pat** 1. a little, some (ability in speaking a language). 2. now and then.

çat 3 جات prov. juncture.

çatadak جاتدق with a sudden cracking noise.

çatak[ğı] 1 جاتاق 1. involved, intricate. 2. attached, twinned(fruit). 3. quarrelsome.

çatak[ğı] 2 جاتاق ، جتق ، جتاق ، جاتاق line of intersection of two slopes. **— çutak** tumbledown, dilapidated.

çatal جاتال ، جتال 1. fork; pitchfork; forked. 2. prong; branch of a forked object. 3. bifurcation. 4. having a double meaning. 5. involved, difficult. 6. hoarse (voice). 7. naut. jaw of a gaff or boom. 8. naut. breasthook in a ship's timbers. 9. artillery bracket, ladder. **— ağız** geog. delta. **— anahtar** a turn-screw key with two points or edges. **— avuç** double handful. **— bayrak** Ott. hist. the yellow and red forked flag of the Janissaries. **— bel** digging fork. **— bıçak** knives and forks, silver. **Ç— burgaz** obs. for **Lüleburgaz**. **— çekiç** claw hammer. **— çutal** 1. hoarse (voice). 2. very complicated. **— gör=** to see double. **— kasa** naut. rope end with double eye. **— kazık** complicated affair the outcome of which is doubtful. **— ok** thills of a horse carriage. **— pin** mech. fork pin. **— sakal** forked beard. **— tırnak** cloven hoof. **— tırnaklı** cloven-footed. **— yeri** bifurcation. **—lan=** to fork, to become forked. **—landır=** /ı/ caus. **—laş=** 1. to fork, to become forked. 2. to become complicated. **—laştır=** /ı/ caus. **—lı** 1. forked. 2. difficult, complicated. 3. gram. disjunctive. **—lık** 1. forkedness. 2. bifurcation. 3. complexity.

çatana (..´.) جطنه small steamboat.

çatı جاتى 1. gable roof; roof. 2. framework, skeleton; scaffolding. 3. neol., anat. pubis. 4. the arch of the thighs (of a horse). 5. prov. rope. **— altı, — arası, — katı** attic. **— kirişi** rafter. **— mahyası** arch. hip of the roof. **— makası** arch. principal rafter of a roof. **— merteği** arch. rafter. **— oku** arch. ridgepole of the roof. **— penceresi** dormer window. **— tabanı** wall plate supporting the roof.

çatık[ğı] جا تيق ، جا تق ، جتق ، جتيق 1. fitted together, joined. 2. stacked. 3. frowning, sulky, stern (face). **— kaş** beetle brows. **— kaşlı** beetle-browed. **— suratlı, — yüzlü** sulky face, scowling.

çatıl=[ır] جاتلمق 1. pass. of **çat=** 1. 2. to have the legs give way and spread out in exhaustion (horse). 3. to stand thunderstruck.

çatır çatır جاتر جاتر ، جاطر جاطر 1. with a cracking or crashing noise. 2. by force; like it or not.

çatır çutur جاتر جوتر with a crackling or crashing noise.

çatırda=[r] جاتردامق 1. to make a crackling or crashing noise. 2. to chatter (teeth). **—t=** caus.

çatırtı جاتردى crackling noise.

çatış=[ır] جاتشمق 1. to clash, collide. 2. to have a quarrel, a clash. 3. to be in conflict, to clash (interests, ideas). 4. to fit into one another (joints). 5. to mate (dogs, etc.). **—ık** contradictory, clashing. **—kı** neol., phil. antinomy, contradiction. **—ma** verbal n. of **çatış=**. **—tır=** /ı/ caus. of **çatış=**.

çatkı جاتقى 1. bandage round the head. 2. mil. stack of rifles. 3. frame, skeleton. 4. a basting. **—lık** pole connecting the yokes of oxen.

çatkın جا تقين ، جا تقين 1. protégé, favorite. 2. frowning (eyebrows). **—lık** 1. intimate familiarity of an inferior. 2. grumpiness, sour looks.

çatla=[r] جاتلامق ، جتلامق 1. to crack, split. 2. to burst with impatience. 3. to die from overeating, exhaustion, etc. 4. to break (wave) **—sa** no matter how hard one tries, at the very

çatlak

most. **—yası** deserving to burst, damned, darned. **— patla=** to burst with impatience or anger.

çatlak باتلاق مِتدره 1. split, slit, fissured; crack, fissure, crevice. 2. chapped (hand). 3. hoarse (voice). 4. cracked (in the brain). 5. breaker, surf. 6. print. vertical succession of blanks. **— ses** hoarse voice.

çatlama باتلمه verbal n. of **çatla=**; bot. dehiscence.

çatlat= باتلتمق /ı/ caus. of **çatla=**.

çatlayış باتلیش verbal n. of **çatla=**.

çatma باتمه 1. verbal n. of **çat=** 1. 2. put up hastily; framework. 3. brought close together; basted. 4. silk brocade. **— kaş** eyebrows that join, beetle brows.

çatra patra (. . . .) باتره باتره Gk incorrectly and brokenly (speaking a foreign language).

çattır= باتتیرمق /ı,a/ caus. of **çat=** 1.

çav 1 باو 1. prov. fame. 2. archaic news.

çav 2 باو hist. Mongol paper money.

çav 3 باو prov. penis (of a horse, camel, etc.).

çav= ar 4 باومق same as **cav=** 2.

çavalya (. . .) باوالیا [cuvaliye] lidded fish basket.

çavdar باودار ـ چودر ـ جودار rye, bot., Secale cereale. **— mahmuzu** ergot of rye.

çavlan= باولنمق archaic to become famous, to be noised abroad.

çavlı باولی obs. young, untrained hawk.

çavşır باوشیر [Arabic causır] pharm. opapanax gum.

çavun باوون leather whip.

çavuş باووش 1. mil. sergeant. 2. guard. 3. hist. halberdier of the bodyguard of the Sultan; herald, messenger; musician of the Palace. **— başı** hist. chief of the corps of halberdiers of the Sultan's bodyguard. **— kuşu** hoopoe, zool., Upupa epops. **— oku** archery arrow that whistles in flight. **— üzümü** variety of large, white grape, Chasselas, sweetwater. **—an** (. . —) P lrnd., pl. of çavuş. **—luk** occupation of a sergeant.

çay 1 چای Chin 1. tea; tea plant, bot., Thea sinensis; Camellia thea. 2. tea party, reception.

çay 2 چای brook, rivulet, stream. **— bin olur çeşme bir, ahbap bin olur candan bir** proverb There are many brooks, but only one fountain; one has many friends, but only one intimate friend. **—dan geçip derede boğul=** same as **denizi geçip çayda boğul=**. **—ı görmeden paçaları sıva=** to roll up one's trousers before reaching the stream. **— gözleri** headsprings of a stream. **— kenarında kuyu kaz=** to give oneself unnecessary trouble.

çayan چایان prov., same as **çıyan**.

çaycı چایجی 1. seller of tea; tea merchant. 2. keeper of a tea shop. 3. drinker of tea, person who is fond of tea.

çaydan, çaydanlık چایدان ـ چایدانلق teapot.

çaygiller neol., bot., Ternstroemia.

çayhane (. — .) چایخانه tea house, tea room.

çayır چایر 1. meadow; pasture. 2. pasture grass; green fodder, fresh fodder. **— çekirgesi** great green grasshopper, zool., Acrida viridissima. **— çimen** green meadows. **— doğanı** Montagu's harrier, zool., Circus pygargus. **— güzeli** love grass, tickle grass. bot., Eragrostis major. **— incir kuşu** meadow pipit, zool., Anthus pratensis. **— kebabı** dish of pieces of meat stewed with vegetables. **— kuşu** lark, zool., Alauda arvensis. **— mantarı** common mushroom, bot., Agaricus campestris. **— mücveri** kind of omelette mixed with ground meat, onions, fennel, and cheese. **— otu** 1. grass; green fodder. 2. timothy grass, bot., Phleum pratense. **— peyniri** cream cheese. **— soğuğu** a spell of cold days in May. **— tirfili** meadow clover, bot., Trifolium pratense. **— yulafı** oat grass, bot., Triticum ovatum.

çayır çayır چایر چایر var. of **cayır cayır**.

çayırla= چایرلامق 1. /ı/ to pasture. 2. to graze. 3. to become ill from grazing. **—n=** to graze. **—t=** /ı/ caus. of **çayırla=**.

çayırlı چایرلی containing meadows.

çayırlık چایرلق meadowland pasture.

çaylak چایلاق 1. kite, zool., Milvus. 2. colloq. avaricious person; obstinate beggar. 3. hist. hanger-on at the Porte, sent out to convey news of appointments, etc., and living by presents from those interested.

-çe 1 چه cf. **-ca 1, 2**.

-çe 2 چه P lrnd., diminutive suffix, as in divançe, kemençe, leğençe.

çeç 1 چچ [çaç] heap of winnowed grain.

çeç 2 چچ P 1. winnowing fork. 2. coarse sieve for separating grain from chaff.

Çeçen چچن the Chechen people; an individual of the Chechen people. **— kazağı** cossack of the Don. **—ce** the Chechen language.

çedene چدنه linseed.

çedik چدیك prov. morocco slipper. **— pabuç** lady's house slippers. **—çi** maker or seller of slippers.

çeft چفت prov., var. of **ceft**.

çegane (. — .) چگانه lrnd., var. of **çağana**.

çeğin eni چگین same as **çiğin**.

-çeğiz چگیز cf. **-cağız**.

Çeh 1 چه Czech.

çeh 2 چه P var. of **çah**.

çehar (. —) چهار P lrnd., same as **çar 3**. **—deh** (. — .) P fourteen. **—deh masum** the 14 innocents (i. e., the Prophet, his daughter

Fatima, and the 12 imams). —**dehüm** (. — ..) P fourteenth. —**gâne** (. — —.) P fourfold. —**mağz** (. —.) P walnut. —**üm** (. —.) P fourth. —**üm manzar** the fourth heaven.

Çehçe (.ˊ.) چمسی Czech (language).

çehiz چهیز [cihaz] same as **çeyiz**.

Çehli چهلی obs. Czech.

çehre چهره [çihre] 1. face, countenance; aspect, appearance. 2. sour face. —**si bozul**= to look upset. — **çat**=, — **eğ**=, — **et**= to make a wry face. — **fıkarası**, — **züğürdü** ugly-looking. —**li** sulky-faced. —**siz** ugly-faced.

çek=ᵉʳ 1 چكمك I. 1. /ı/ to pull, draw; to tug (at rope, etc.); to haul, drag; to draw (lot); to draw on (boots, trousers); naut. to tow; to transport, transfer; archaic to march, send out (an army). 2. /ı, dan/ to take away, to save (from a bad habit); to withdraw (money); to recall, to withdraw (an army); to extort (money); to clear (goods at the customs' office); to draw (goods from the market); to draw off (fluid from a barrel); 3. /ı/ to extract (tooth); to draw (sword, pistol); to distill (spirits); to take a copy (of). 4. /ı,a/ to draw, attract (iron, as a magnet; attention). 5. /ı/ to absorb (moisture); to inhale; to sniff; to sip (hot soup); slang to drink. 6. /ı,a/ to stretch out, extend; to construct (wall); to dig (ditch); to hang (curtain). 7. /ı,a/ to draw, trace (a line); to apply (kohl); to draw up in due form (written document, bill of exchange, protest); to send (telegram). 8. /ı,a/ to apply (paint); to cover (with a veil, etc.); 9. /ı/ to photograph, take a photograph (of); to grind (coffee, grains); /ı,a/ to put (on the scales), to weigh; to have a certain weight; /ı,a/ to sew (on a sewing machine). 10. /ı/ to bear (weight); to bear (expense); to endure, suffer, undergo (pain, excitement). 11. /ı,a/ to ill-treat (with blows); to give (banquet); to present (with). 12. /ı,a/ to give a meaning (to), to interpret. 13. /ı/ to utter (a long-drawn sound, cry, musical note). 14. /ı,a/ to mate, to pair for breeding. 15. /ı/ sport to kick (ball). 16. /ı/ gram. to inflect, decline, conjugate (a word). II. 1. to suffer; /dan/ to undergo trouble (because of). 2. to shrink (material). 3. to move, start off (coachman, driver, boatman). 4. to draw (stove, flue). 5. to take (so many hours, to travel), to be at such and such distance. 6. to have (a certain number of days, months). 7. to expose (to an examination, cross-examination). 8. /a/ to resemble (one's father, etc.). —**eme**= /ı/ to be jealous (of). —**!**, — **arabanı**! colloq. Clear out! Get out! Off with you! —**ip çekiştir**= /ı/ to gossip maliciously (about a person), criticize. —**ip çevir**= /ı/ to manage (a house), to keep in order (a person). —**ip çıkar**= /ı/ to pluck out. —**ip git**= to go away. — **kuyruğunu** colloq. Get the hell out of here. —**iver kuyruğunu**! /ın/ slang You can't expect any good (from). —**eceğimiz var** /dan/ We will have trouble (with).

çekᵏⁱ 2 چك E fin. check. — **defteri** check-book.

Çekᵏⁱ 3 چك P Czech.

çekâçakᵏⁱ (. — —) چكاچاك, **çekâçek**ᵏⁱ چكاچك, **çekçak**ᵏⁱ چكچاك P vars. of **çakaçak**.

çekçekᵍⁱ چكچك small four-wheeled hand-cart.

çekecekᵍⁱ چكه جك shoe-horn.

çeke düzen چكه دوزن archaic for **çeki düzen**.

çekekᵍⁱ چكك prov. slip (for a boat).

çekele=ʳ چكه لمك /ı/ to pull gently and repeatedly.

çekeleve چكه له وه Gk archaic sailing-craft with two short forward-leaning masts.

çekelez چكه لز prov. squirrel.

çekeme=ᵉ چكه مه مك cf. **çek**= 1. —**zlik**, —**mezlik** envy, jealousy.

çeki چكی 1. a weight of 250 kilos (firewood). 2. obs. large rough balance for weighing wood, etc. 3. obs. a weight for silk, etc., of about 300 gm. 4. prov. head scarf. — **düzen** tidiness, orderliness. — **düzen ver**= /a/ to put in order, to tidy up, to array. —**ye gelme**= 1. to be very heavy; to be unbearable. 2. to be disorderly, untidy. — **taşı** obs. stone weight of 180 okkas (230 kilos). — **taşı gibi** 1. very heavy, ponderous. 2. very slow, lazy.

çekici 1 چكیجی weigher of firewood, etc.

çekici 2 چكیجی 1. attractive. 2. pulling, dragging.

çekiçᶜⁱ چكیچ hammer. — **balığı** hammerhead shark, zool., Sphyrna zygaena malleus. — **kemiği** anat. hammer, malleus. —**hane** steamhammer shop of a factory. —**le**= /ı/ to hammer. —**len**= pass. —**let**= /ı,a/ caus. of **çekiçle**=.

çekide (. —.) چكیده P poet. dropped, oozed out.

çekikᵍⁱ چكیك 1. slanting (eyes). 2. drawn out. 3. drawn in.

çekil=ⁱʳ چكیلمك 1. pass. of **çek**= 1. 2. /dan/ to withdraw, draw back, recede; to draw off, to get away; to retire, resign. 3. to shrink, contract.

çekile=ʳ چكیلمك /ı/ to weigh by the **çeki**. —**n**= pass. —**t**= /ı,a/ caus. of **çekile**=. —**yici** weigher by **çeki**.

çekiliş, çekilme çekilme 1. verbal n. of **çekil**=. 2. geol. regression. 3. mil. withdrawal.

çekilmez چكیلمز unbearable, intolerable.

çekim چكیم 1. single act of drawing. 2. quantity drawn at a time. 3. graceful, well-proportioned shape. 4. *neol., phys., astr.* attraction. 5. *neol., gram.* inflection, declination, conjugation. 6. *slang* a sniff (of heroin). **— eki** *gram.* termination. **—le=** /ı/ 1. *gram.* to inflect, decline, conjugate. 2. *phys.* to attract. **—li** graceful, well-proportioned; attractive. **—se=** /dan/ *neol.* to refrain (from). **—ser davran=** *neol.* to abstain from voting.

çekimsiz چكمسز 1. ill-proportioned, clumsy; unattractive. 2. *neol., gram.* indeclinable.

çekin=[ir] چكنمك 1. /dan/ to feel hesitant to do something because of respect (for a person) or fear (of a person); to draw back or hold back through fear, scruple, or dislike (from doing something). 2. /ı/ *archaic* to long (for). **—meden** without hesitation or bashfulness. **—dir=** /ı, dan/ *caus.* of **çekin=**.

çekingen چكنكن shy, timid, bashful, modest, reserved. **—lik** reservedness; shyness.

çekinik *neol., biol.* recessive.

çekirdek[gi] چكردك 1. pip, seed, stone of a fruit. 2. *neol., sc.* nucleus. 3. *mil.* cadre. 4. *obs.* grain (goldsmith's weight). **— eri** *mil.* cadreman. **— fiziği** nuclear physics. **— içi** kernel. **— kahve** coffee beans. **— özü** *biol.* nuclein. **— özsuyu** *biol.* nuclear sap. **—ten yetişme** trained for something from the cradle. **— zarı** *biol.* nuclear membrane. **—çik** *biol.* nucleolus. **—len=** to form seeds, to seed (plant). **—li** having seeds. **—siz** having no seeds. **—siz kuru üzüm** seedless raisin, sultana.

çekirge چكرگه 1. grasshopper, locust. 2. cricket. **— kuşu** starling, *zool., Sturnus vulgaris*. **— suyu** water put out to attract birds for the annihilation of locusts.

çekiş=[ir] 1 چكشمك 1. to quarrel, dispute; to pull one another in a quarrel. 2. /ı/ to draw mutually. **—e çekişe pazarlık et=** to haggle, to bargain hard. **—ici** quarrelsome. **—me** *verbal n.*

çekiş 2 چكش 1. *verbal n.* of **çek=** 1. 2. *verbal n.* of **çekiş=** 1. **—ten düş=** to diminish in speed (engine).

çekiştir=[ir] /ı/ 1. *caus.* of **çekiş=**. 2. to pull at both ends. 3. to criticize maliciously, to backbite. **—iş, —me** *verbal n.*

çekme چكمه 1. *verbal n.* of **çek=** 1; *phys.* traction. 2. drawer, till. 3. drawn; pulled on. 4. overalls. 5. *prov.* boot. **— burun** straight, handsome nose. **— demir** rolled iron. **— kat** penthouse. **— sac** rolled plate. **— tel** rolled wire.

çekmece چكمجه 1. drawer, till. 2. ornamental casket, coffer; small chest of drawers, desk. 3. *archaic* small port of refuge. 4. *hist.* drawbridge. **—ci** maker or seller of desks, caskets, etc.

çekmen *neol., biol.* sucker.

Çekoslovak[kı] چكوسلواق a Czechoslovakian.

Çekoslovakya چكوسلواقيا *geog.* Czechoslovakia.

çektir=[ir] چكدرمك /ı, a/ *caus.* of **çek=** 1.

çektiri چكدرى *hist.* war galley with sails and oars.

çektirme چكدرمه 1. *verbal n.* of **çektir=**. 2. large boat with sails and oars, for transporting goods. 3. *hist., same as* **çektiri**.

çekum L *anat.* caecum.

çeküll *neol., phys.* plumb line.

çel=[er] چلمك /ı/ 1. to divert. 2. to turn up (the ends or sides of a thing). 3. *same as* **çal=** 1[1,2]. **—dir=** /ı,a/ *caus.*

çelebi چلبى 1. well-bred, educated; gentleman, man of refinement. 2. *hist.* prince; *after names, title of respect for man (in later times, often for non-Muslims)*. 3. *title of the leader of the Mevlevi order*. 4. *prov.* husband's brother. 5. kind of backgammon. **—lik** 1. politeness; gentility. 2. quality and manners of a **çelebi**.

çelek[gi] چلك *prov.* bucket.

çelem چلم *prov.* turnip.

çelenk[gi] چلنك 1. wreath; garland. 2. *obs.* aigrette; plume as head ornament.

çelep[bi] چلب *var.* of **çalap**.

çeler=[ir] چلرمك *prov.* to die of indigestion (cattle).

çelik[gi] 1 چليك steel. **— gibi** very strong. **— levha** steel plate.

çelik[gi] 2 چليك 1. diverted; turned aside. 2. persuaded. 3. *var.* of **çalık**[1,2].

çelik[gi] 3 چليك 1. short piece of tapered wood. 2. cat (in tipcat). 3. *hort.* cutting. 4. *naut.* belaying-pin, marline spike; carling; pin, fid. 5. *Mevlevi order* stock for flogging, whipping post. **— başı** *naut.* throat (of a sail). **— çomak** tipcat. **—le=** /ı/ to fix with pins or spikes. **—li** furnished with a bevelled or tapering pin, spike, etc.

çelim چليم 1. stature, form. 2. swagger, affected dignity. **—li** gracefully shaped, in good condition. **—siz** in poor condition, puny, thin and ugly. **—sizlik** puniness.

çelipa (. — —) چليپا P *lrnd.* crucifix, the cross.

çeliş=[ir] *neol., log.* to be in contradiction. **—ik** contradictory. **—me** contradiction. **—mezlik** contradiction. **—mezliğe düş=** to contradict each other (of people).

çelme چلمه 1. *verbal n.* of **çel=**. 2. trip (with the foot). **— at=, — tak=** /a/ to trip up. **—le=** to trip with the foot.

çeltik[gi] چلتك 1. rice in the husk. 2. rice field. **— fabrikası** rice mill. **—çi** rice grower. **—çilik** rice growing. **—li**

marshy land cultivated as rice-fields.

çeman (. —) چمان P *poet.* walking with swinging, graceful airs.

çember چنبر P 1. hoop; flat ring of wood or iron; rim of a wheel; child's hoop; ring-shaped. 2. metal strip (round a case, crate, etc.). 3. fortune, Fortune's wheel. 4. *neol., geom.* circumference. 5. *mil.* encirclement, ring. 6. *prov.* neck scarf; head scarf. 7. *Or. mus.* a great rhythmic pattern with 24 beats, with signatures of 24/4, 24/2. **— çevir=** to trundle a hoop. **—i felek** *lrnd.* 1. vault of heaven. 2. zodiac. 3. Fortune's wheel. **— geçir=** /a/ to put hoops (to). **— içine al=** /ı/ *mil.* to encircle. **— kayık** kind of round-sterned craft. **—i mina** *same as* **çemberi felek.** **— sakal** round trimmed beard. **— yemeni** head kerchief. **—le=** /ı/ 1. to hoop. 2. *mil.* to encircle. **—let=** /ı,a/ *caus.* **—li** hooped; furnished with hoops.

Çemberlitaş چنبرلی طاش the «Burnt Column» in Istanbul.

çemçe چمچه *same as* **çömçe.**

çemen 1 چمن Arm 1. cumin, *bot., Cuminum cyminum.* 2. condiment prepared from ground fenugreek seeds, red pepper, and garlic, used as the coating of **pastırma**. **— otu** fenugreek, *bot., Trigonella Foenumgraecum.*

çemen 2 چمن P *poet., same as* **çimen 1**. **—ara** (.. — —), **—bend** P gardener. **—efruz** (... —) P 1. wild red anemone. 2. bright flower. **—î** (.. —) P deep green. **—zar** (.. —) P green meadow, grassy plot.

çemkir=ʳ چمكیرمك /a/ *prov.* 1. to scold, to give a rude answer. 2. to bark.

çemre=ʳ چمره مك /ı/ *prov.* to tuck up (one's garments, trousers, or sleeves). **—k** 1. tucked up; with garments tucked up. 2. quick and nimble. **—le=** *same as* **çemre=**. **—n=** 1. to tuck up one's garments, trousers, or sleeves. 2. to get ready (for some action). **—t=** /ı,a/ *caus. of* **çemre=**.

çenar (. —) چنار P *poet., same as* **çınar.**

çenber چنبر *same as* **çember.**

çend چند P *lrnd.* 1. how much; how many. 2. several, some.

çendan (. —) چندان P *lrnd.* so much; so many. **— ki** 1. however much, however often. 2. although.

çene چنه جَكَ [çane] 1. jaw; jaw bone. 2. chin. 3. eloquence; loquacity; chatter; prattling. 4. *mech.* jaw. 5. *naut.* forefoot. **—sini aç=** 1. to start talking. 2. /ın/ to give opportunity to talk, to loosen someone's tongue. **— altı** 1. the underside of the chin. 2. double chin; dewlap. **— altı bezi** *biol.* maxillary gland. **— altı kayışı** *mil.* chin strap. **— at=** to drop one's jaw in dying, to die. **—sini bağla=** /ın/ to tie up the jaw (of a person after death). **—sini bıçak açma=** to be tongue-tied because of great sorrow. **— çal=** to chat, to gossip. **— çukuru** dimple on the chin. **—si düşük** garrulous, very talkative, having a wagging tongue. **— kavafı** persistent talker. **— kemiği** jaw bone. **—ye kuvvet** by dint of talking. **—si kuvvetli** great talker. **—si oyna=** to keep eating. **—n pırtı!** Shut up! Stop talking! **— sakızı** a saying that is always in one's mouth, something repeated constantly. **— sat=** to chatter. **—sini tut=** to hold one's tongue. **—n tutulsun!** Curse your tongue! (for saying this). **— ucu** chin. **— yarıştır=** /la/ to engage in endless conversation. **— yor=** to chatter incessantly.

çenebaz (.. —) چنه باز [çene, -baz 2] chatterer, talker; garrulous.

çenekᵍⁱ *neol.* 1. *anat.* mandible. 2. *bot., zool.* valve.

çeneli چنه لو 1. having a chin. 2. talkative; forceful speaker.

çenetᵈⁱ 1. *neol., bot.* valve. 2. *prov.* one half of a twin object (like kernel of almond, shell of mussel).

çeng چنگ P *lrnd.* 1. hand; paw; claw of a bird of prey. 2. *same as* **çenk.** 3. curved, crooked. **— ü çegâne** musical entertainment. **—i dehen** Jew's harp. **—i Meryem** rose of Jericho, *bot., Anastatica Hierichuntina.* **—i Rumi** *astr.* Lyra.

çengâlˡⁱ (. —) چنگال P *lrnd.* hand; paw of a beast; claw of a bird of prey.

çengel چنگل P 1. hook; hooked, crooked. 2. *lrnd.* claw. 3. *Turkish style wrestling* a hooking one's foot around the opponent's foot. **—e as=** /ı/ 1. to hang up on a hook. 2. to impale on a hook. **— beygiri** *obs., mil.* the foremost pair of horses drawing a gun. **—e gel=** to come to the gallows, to be hanged. **—de kokmuş etim yok** I have no spoiled meat on the hook (*i. e.,* I am in no hurry to have my daughter married as her age is not yet past). **— sakızı** chewing gum made from the juice of a thistle (galactites). **—i tak=** /a/ to get one's claws (into), to get hold (of), to be a nuisance (to), to keep pestering. **—cik** *anat., hamulus.* **—le=** /ı/ 1. to hook, to fasten with a hook. 2. to impale on a hook. **—li** hooked. **—li iğne** safety pin.

çengi چنگی public dancing girl. **— kolu**, **— takımı** a troop of dancing girls.

Cengiz چنگیز *same as* **Cengiz.**

çenkᵍⁱ چنك [çeng] the simple form of the present-day harp which goes back to primitive times; although it was very popular among Turks it was abandoned in the 18th century.

çenkî (.—) چنکی P a çenk player.
çenkharbî چنك حربى Or. mus. a rhythmic pattern of 10 beats with signatures of 10/8, 10/4.
çent=ᵉʳ چنتمك /ı/ 1. to notch, nick. 2. to mince (onions, etc.).
çentikᵍⁱ چنتك 1. notched, slightly incised. 2. notch, slight incision. **—le**= /ı/ to notch. **—len**= 1. *pass.* 2. to become notched. **—let**= /ı,a/ *caus.* of **çentikle**=.
çentil=ⁱʳ چنتلمك *pass.* of **çent**=.
çenttir=ⁱʳ چنتدرمك *caus.* of **çent**=.
çep چپ P *lrnd.* 1. left, left-hand; the left-hand side; on the left. 2. false note in music; false (note). **— ü rast** 1. left and right. 2. unsteadiness.
çepçevre (.'..), **çepeçevre** (..'..) چپ چوره all around.
çepel چپل P 1. dirt, mud; filthy, foul, dirty, muddy, disagreeable. 2. mixed, adulterated; wheat mixed with impurities. **—le**= /ı/ to soil, spoil; to adulterate. **—len**= 1. to become filthy, muddy, disagreeable. 2. *pass.* of **çepelle**=. **—li** muddy. **—lik** filth, mud; disagreeableness, filthiness.
çependaz چپ انداز P *lrnd.* fraud; fraudulent, treacherous.
çeper چپر P 1. *prov.* wall; fence. 2. *neol., sc.* wall.
çepiçᶜⁱ چپیچ year-old goat.
çepin چپین It *prov.* gardener's hoe, small hoe.
çepiş چپش same as **çepiç**.
çepken چپکن stout jacket the sleeves of which are slit, leaving the arms free.
çeplus (.—) چپلوس P *var.* of **cablus**.
Çepni چپنى member of a Turkish tribe in Anatolia with early connections with the Bektashi order.
çepreşikᵍⁱ چپرشك، چپره شك same as **çapraşık**.
çera (.—) چرا P *poet.* pasture. **—ca** (.——) P, **—gâh** (.——) P place of pasture. **—ger** (.—.) P herbivorous.
çerağ (.—) چراغ *lrnd., var.* of **çirağ**.
çerahar (.——) چرا خوار, **çerahur** (.—.) چرا خور P *lrnd.* 1. place of pasture. 2. grazing (animal), herbivorous.
Çerakise (.—..) چراكس [based on **Çerkes**] *lrnd.* the Circassians.
çerazar (.——) چرازار P *poet.* meadow, pasture.
çerb چرب P *lrnd.* 1. fat, plump. 2. greasy, oily; unctuous, persuasive. 3. superior, predominant. **— u huşk** fat and lean, rich and poor, plentiful and scant. **—dest** P expert, dexterous; wise, intelligent.
çerbe چربه P *lrnd.* 1. fat, grease. 2. oiled paper.

çerbgû (.—) چرب گو P *lrnd.* smooth-spoken, bland.
çerbî (.—) چربى P *lrnd.* 1. fatness, plumpness. 2. glibness of tongue.
çerbiş چربش P *lrnd.* fat, grease, drippings.
çerbpehlu (..—) چرب پهلو P *lrnd.* 1. in good condition, fat. 2. kind, generous.
çerbzeban (..—) چرب زبان P smooth-tongued; glib-tongued.
çerçeve چرچوه [**çarçube**] frame; window frame, sash; border; shaft (of a loom). **— kâğıdı** thick, coarse, white paper, used as oilpaper for windows. **—ci** maker or seller of frames. **—le**= /ı/ to frame. **—len**= *pass.* **—let**= /ı,a/ *caus.* of **çerçevele**=. **—li** framed.
çerçi چرچى peddler.
çerçive چرچیوه *var.* of **çerçeve**.
çerde چرده *lrnd.* 1. color, complexion of skin. 2. dark complexion.
çerden çöpten چردن چوپدن made of rubbish, flimsy.
çerehor چره خوار [**çerahar**] *same as* **cerehor**.
çerende چرنده P *lrnd.* herbivorous.
çerez چرز [Persian **caras**] hors d'oeuvres, appetizer; tidbits, snack. **—len**= 1. to eat tidbits. 2. to take advantage of opportunities. **—lik** fit to be eaten as an appetizer; tidbits.
çerge, çergi چرگى Gk 1. small, makeshift tent, gipsy's tent. 2. *hist.* marqee used as a porch to a royal encampment. **— çerisi** gipsies. **—nişin** (...—) P tent-dweller.
çerh چرخ P *lrnd., same as* **çarh. —ab** (.—) P Persian waterwheel. **—gâh** (.—) P hall where whirling dervishes perform. **—î** (.—) P 1. pertaining to a wheel; revolving, circular (motion). 2. pertaining to the spheres, celestial. **—saz** (.—) P 1. who makes wheels. 2. who turns in a circle. **—zen** 1. crossbowman. 2. who rotates.
çeri چرى *hist.* army, troops. **— başı** 1. gipsy chief. 2. *hist.* commander of troops. **— çek**= *archaic* to conduct troops. **— düz**= *archaic* to raise an army.
Çerkes چرکس *same as* **Çerkez. —î** (..—) P 1. of Circassian manner. 2. Circassian coat, with a tight-fitting body and full skirts.
Çerkez چرکز [**Çerkes**] a Circassian. **— tavuğu** ground chicken with bread, walnuts and red pepper-sauce. **—ce** Circassian (language).
çermikᵍⁱ چرمیك Arm *prov.* hot spring.
çertikᵍⁱ چرتك *prov.* a part of a bunch of grapes.
çerviş چرویش [**çerbiş**] 1. inferior cooking fat. 2. *archaic* the juicy part of a cooked dish.
-çesine چسنه *cf.* **-casına**.
çespan (.—) چسبان P *lrnd.* suitable, worthy.
çeşide (.—.) چشیده P *lrnd.* 1. who has tasted. 2. which has been tasted.

çeşitdi چشیت 1. kind, sort, variety. 2. assortment. 3. *biol.* variety. 4. *com.* sample. — **çeşit** assorted. — **düz**= to procure an assortment of things. — **kenar** *geom.* of unequal sides. —**le**= /ı/ to increase the variety (of).

çeşitli چشیدلی assorted; different. —**lik** assortment, variation, change.

çeşm چشم P *poet.* 1. eye. 2. sight; look; observation; perception. 3. hope, expectation. 4. evil eye. 5. *myst.* the divine beauty. —**i ahu** doe-eyed. —**i bed** evil eye. —**i bed dur!** P Far be the evil eye! —**i biab** 1. lackluster eye. 2. shameless eye; shamelessness. —**i bülbül** 1. kind of precious Turkish-made glassware. 2. *obs.* kind of spotted material. —**i dümbaledar** eye with the corner painted so as to look longer. —**i frengî** spectacles. —**i gazel** 1. gazelle's eye. 2. cup of wine. —**i giryan** tearful eye. — **ü gûş** eye and ear, attention. —**i habide** sleepy eye. —**i handan** smiling eye. —**i horos** 1. red wine. 2. ruby lips. —**i hunbar**, —**i hunfişan**, —**i hunhar**, —**i hunriz** cruel eye. —**i ibretle bak**= /a/ to take a lesson (from). —**i İsmail** an upturned eye of resignation and despair like those of Ishmael when about to be sacrificed by Abraham. —**i mahmur** languid eye. —**i mest** 1. drunken eye; languid eye. 2. *myst.* divine mystery of which a glimpse is vouchsafed to a saint. —**i mizan** 1. scale of a balance. 2. pivot hole in which the beam of a balance plays. —**i nergis** 1. corona of a narcissus flower. 2. beautiful eye. 3. *myst.* a saint's concealment of his high beatitude from the eyes of men. —**i nerm** 1. soft, kind eye. 2. shameless eye. 3. beardless lad (used by lewd men). —**i Simail** *same as* **çeşmi İsmail**. —**i sitareşümer** sleepless eye. —**i siyah** black eye; black-eyed. —**i suzen** 1. eye of a needle. 2. narrow passage. —**i şeb** 1. moon. 2. star. —**i şebpeyma** sleepless eye. —**i terazu** *same as* **çeşmi mizan**. —**i zağ** blue eye, bluish-gray eye. —**i zanu** knee cap. —**i zuğal** live coal. —**an** (. —) P *pl. of* **çeşm**. —**aru** (. — —) P amulet against the evil eye. —**aviz** (. — —) P 1. woman's veil. 2. blinkers; fly guards of leather strips put over a horse's eyes. —**bend** P 1. bandage for the eyes. 2. fascination of the eyes. —**bendek** P game of blindman's buff. —**beste** P whose eyes are bewitched. —**dan** (. —) P socket of the eye. —**daşt** (. —) P hope, expectation.

çeşme چشمه P 1. fountain with spout. 2. *lrnd.* spring of water. 3. *lrnd.* eye of a needle. 4. *lrnd.* vaulted arch. 5. *lrnd.* sun. — **burması** fountain tap. —**ye gitse çeşme kuruyacak** If he went to the fountain, the fountain would run dry *said of a very unlucky person.* —**i haverî** *lrnd.* sun. —**i hayvan** *lrnd.* fountain of life. —**i Hızır** *lrnd.* fountain of life. —**i simab** *poet.* moon; sun; day. —**i terazu** *same as* **çeşmi mizan**. —**i tiregûn** *poet.* night. —**sar** (. . —) P, —**zar** (. . —) P *poet.* district abounding with springs.

çeşmhane چشمخانه P *lrnd.* socket of the eye.

çeşmhorde چشم خورده P *lrnd.* struck by the evil eye.

çeşmnişin (. . —) چشم نشین P *lrnd.* permanently visible.

çeşmpiş (. —) چشم پیش P *lrnd.* modest, bashful.

çeşmreside (. . —.) چشم رسیده P *lrnd.* struck by the evil eye.

çeşmter چشم تر P *lrnd.* moist-eyed; weeper.

çeşmzahm چشم زخم P *lrnd.* a blow from the evil eye.

çeşmzed چشم زد P *lrnd.* 1. twinkle of an eye. 2. amulet against the evil eye.

çeşni چشنی [**çaşni**] 1. flavor, taste. 2. small portion eaten to judge the flavor of a thing. 3. sample, specimen. 4. *lrnd.* the first note or two, sounded by a musician before playing a tune. —**sine bak**= /ın/ to test the flavor (of), to taste. — **tut**= bakery to keep a sample of the dough.

çeşnici چشنیجی 1. *hist.* taster in the sultan's court. 2. assayer (in a mint). — **başı** 1. *hist.* chief taster at the Sultan's court. 2. chief assayer (in a mint). 3. man who frequently changes wives.

çeşnilen=ir چشنیلنمك to become properly flavored. —**dir**= /ı/ *caus.*

çeşnili چشنیلی 1. tasty; properly flavored. 2. fired by means of a percussion cap.

çete (.'.) چته Sl band of rebels, brigands, etc. — **harbi** guerrilla warfare. — **reisi** guerrilla chieftain. —**ci** member of a band; raider. —**cilik** a raiding, marauding.

çetele (.'..) چتل It tally, tally stick. — **çek**= to keep tally. —**ye dön**= to become scarred, notched. — **tut**= *same as* **çetele çek**=.

çetin چتین 1. hard, difficult. 2. perverse, intractable. — **ceviz** hard nut. —**leş**= to become hard. —**leştir**= /ı/ *caus.* —**lik** hardness, difficulty.

çetr چتر P *lrnd.* 1. tent. 2. umbrella, parasol. 3. chuddar.

çetrefil چترفیل 1. confused, complicated. 2. speaking badly (a language); badly constructed (sentence).

çetükgü چتك *archaic* cat.

çevgân (. —) چوگان P 1. polo stick. 2. *lrnd.* hooked stick; hook drumstick; hooked

çevgen

stick with a suspended ball as an emblem of royalty. 3. *myst.* the circumstances of life (as tossing man about like a ball). — **topu** polo ball. **—baz** (.——) P *lrnd.* polo player. **—dar** (.——) P *lrnd.* servant who carries the polo stick. **—zen** (.—.) P *lrnd.* one who strikes with a polo stick.

çevgen مُرگن *var. of* **çevgân.**

çevikᵍⁱ مُرِلِك مُبيرلِك [çabük] 1. nimble, agile, swift. 2. *mil.* mobile.

çevir=ⁱʳ مُبِورِ ملك مُبورِ ملك 1. /ı/ to turn, turn round; to rotate, spin; to roast on the spit. 2. /ı, la/ to surround, encircle, enclose (with). 3. /ı/ to send back, to return (something not accepted); /ı, dan/ to stop (someone going his way). 4. /ı/ to manage. 5. /ı, a/ to change, transform (into); to translate (into). 6. to change (into, weather, wind). 7. *neol.* to translate. — **kazı yanmasın** Turn the goose on the spit so that it won't burn. *i. e.* Change the subject (said ironically in reaction to an evasive reply). **—geç** *neol., elec.* switch. **—i** *neol.* translation. **—ici** 1. that turns something. 2. *anat.* rotator. **—iş** *verbal n. of* **çevir=**.

çevirme مُورمه 1. *verbal n. of* **çevir=**. 2. lamb, etc., roasted on the spit. 3. sweet made of sugar and fruit juice. — **hareketi** *mil.* encircling movement, outflanking maneuvre. — **kolu** *mech.* crank.

çevirt=ⁱʳ مُبيرتمك /ı,a/ *caus. of* **çevir=**. [*in many compounds,* **çevir=** *equals* **döndür=**.]

çevlikᵍⁱ مُرلك *prov., var. of* **çevrik.**

çevre مُور، مُور، مُور، 1. surroundings. 2. circle (of society). 3. *geom.* circumference; periphery, circuit, contour. 4. *sociol.* environment, milieu. 5. *geog.* perimeter. 6. embroidered kerchief. — **açı** *neol., geom.* inscribed angle. — **al=** /ı/ *archaic* to surround, encircle. — **kası** *neol., anat.* orbicularis. — **yan** *archaic* all sides, surroundings. **—l** *neol.* 1. *geom.* circumferential. 2. *sociol.* environmental. **—le=** /ı/ to surround, encircle, enclose; to circumscribe. **—len=** *pass.*

çevren *neol., geog., astr.* horizon.

çevresel *neol.* 1. *anat.* peripheral. 2. *sociol.* marginal.

çevri *neol., geog.* whirlwind; whirlpool. — **yazı** *ling.* transcription, transliteration.

çevrikᵍⁱ مُورلك 1. turned; turned around. 2. surrounded; enclosed. 3. whirlwind; whirlpool; waterspout.

çevril=ⁱʳ مُورلمك *pass. of* **çevir=**. **—i** surrounded.

çevrim *neol., phys.* cycle. **—sel** cyclic.

çevrin=ⁱʳ مُورِنمَك /ı/ *archaic* to go (around).

çevrinti مُورِنتی مُورِنتی 1. circular motion, rotation, whirl. 2. whirlwind; whirlpool. 3. refuse sifted out of winnowed corn. **—li** having whirling wind, dust, water, etc.

çevriş مُورِش *var. of* **çerviş.**

çeyiz جهاز [cehiz] trousseau. — **alayı** procession carrying a bride's trousseau in state to her husband's house. — **çemen** the complete trousseau. — **halayığı** *obs.* slave girl given to a bride as part of her dowry. **—le=** /ı/ to furnish with a trousseau. **—len=** *pass.* **—li** having a dowry. **—lik** suitable for a trousseau (material, etc.)

çeyne=ʳ چيكنه ملك *archaic for* **çiğne=**.

çeyrekᵍⁱ چيرك [çaryek] 1. a quarter, one fourth; quarter of an hour. 2. five piastres. — **ses** *mus.* quarter tone; the Turkish tonic scale has 24 unequal intervals. **—çi** *obs.* itinerant butcher.

çeyrekle=ʳ چيركله ملك /ı/ to bend and stretch the limbs (of a baby, in exercising movements).

çez=ᵉʳ چزمك *prov., var. of* **çöz=**.

-çı چى *cf.* **-cı.**

çıban چبان boil, abscess, pustule. — **ağrışağı** the sore and swollen part of a boil. — **başı** 1. head of a boil or pustule. 2. a delicate matter. **—ın başını kopar=** to bring matters to a head. — **çıkar=** to have a boil. — **dök=** to be covered with boils, to develop many pustules. **—lı** having boils.

çıbıkᵍⁱ چبق *var. of* **çubuk.**

çıfıt چفيت [Cühud] contemptuous Jew; mean, stingy; malicious. — **çarşısı** a place in a very confused state, messy place. — **orucu** a long drawn-out affair. **—lık** the quality of a Jew.

çıfıta (..'.) چفوته [çifuta] *naut.* 1. blocks, cradle (in a dry dock). 2. ropes by which a ship's cradle is held in launching.

çığ 1 چغ avalanche.

çığ 2 چغ *archaic* loud noise; cry.

çığ 3 چغ *prov.* basket-work; screen; partition in a tent.

çığa چغا چیغا *var. of* **çuka 2.**

çığıltı چغلتی confused noise of animals crying together.

çığır 1 چغیر چغر 1. rut, track; path. 2. way. — **aç=** to open a new road, to start a new method. **—ından çık=** to go off the rails, to go off the tracks.

çığır=ⁱʳ **2** چغرمق /ı/ *prov. for* **çağır= 1.**

çığırtkan چغرتقان 1. *same as* **çağırtkan.** 2. tout, noisy advertiser, runner. **—lık** a being a noisy advertiser.

çığırtma چغرتمه small, primitive fife.

çığış=ⁱʳ چغشمك *archaic* to rattle, clatter, rustle

çığıştı جِغِشْتُی ,جِغِشْت *archaic* rustling, rattling noise.

çığıt^(dı, tı) جِغِیت ,جِغِت ,جِغِد ,جِغِنِیت ,جِغِیت ,جِغِت ,جِغِت *prov.* freckles.

çığlık^(ğı) جِغِلق ,جِغِلغ cry, loud cry, scream. **— at=, —ı bas=, — kopar=** to utter a loud scream. **—çı** professional moaner, lamenter, keener.

çığrıl=^(ır) جِغِرِلْمَه *prov.*, *var. of* **çağrıl=**.

çığrış=^(ır) جِغِرِشْمَه *prov.*, *var. of* **çağrış=**.

çık=^(ar) 1 جِغْمَه ,جِغْمَغ 1. /dan/ to go out; to move out (of a house); to start off (from a place); to get out, slip one's memory; to leave (job, hospital); to pass out (of a school); to be subtracted (from). 2. /dan/ to come out; to issue from (fluid, smell); to result; to be made, produced (from); to be got out (of sufficient cloth, dress). 3. to go out; to set out; to get out; to come off (part); to be dislocated (limb), to run (color); to pass by, to be over (season). 4. to come up, spring up, appear, come into view; to come out, be issued (book, money); to break out (fire, storm, war, epidemic); to get about (rumor); to rise (sun, moon); to come into use; to be issued (order, law); to be announced (promotion); to turn out to be, to prove; to come to pass, to come true. 5. /a/ to go up, ascend; to climb; to increase, rise (fever, price); to amount (to), to cost. 6. /a/ to lead (to); to fall to one's lot; to run (color). 7. /a/ to show oneself (to); to appear (before the court); to apply in person (to a high official). 8. /a/ to compete (with). 9. /a/ *theat.* to act the part (of). 10. /dan/ to incur the expense (of a sum of money). 11. to have a bowel movement. 12. to raise one's bid. 13. /ı/ *slang* to fork out, pay up (money); *card games* to play (a trump, etc.). **—madık canda ümit var** *proverb* While there's life, there's hope. **—a gel=*. —ıp git=** to go away.

-çık^(ğı) 2 جِق *cf.* **-cık**.

çıkagel=^(ır) جِقَه گَلك to appear suddenly.

çıkar=^(ır) 1 جِقَارْمَه ,جِقَارَه ,جِقَارْمَق /ı/ 1. *caus. of* **çık=** 1; /dan/ to take out, extract, expel, bring out, push out, send out; to remove; to strike out, omit; to export; to publish; to unload, land; to take off, throw off (garment); to raise; to produce; /dan/ to derive, deduce; to make out, decipher, get the sense (of); /dan/ to subtract. 2. to vomit. 3. to last to the end (of a season, etc.). 4. /ı, dan/ to vent one's anger (on somebody). 5. to cause to appear (as), *as in* **haklı çıkar=, yalancı çıkar=**. **—ıp at=** to throw off (clothes). **—ıl=** *pass. of* **çıkar=**.

çıkar 2 جِقَار profit, advantage, interest. **—ına bak=** to follow one's selfish interest. **—ı yok** leads nowhere. **— yol** a course that leads somewhere, way out. **—cı** always looking for gain.

çıkarma جِقَارْمَه *verbal n. of* **çıkar=** 1; *math.* subtraction; *mil.* landing.

çıkarsama *neol.*, *phil.* inference.

çıkart=^(ır) جِقَارْتَنِی ,جِقَارْتْمَه ,جِغِز تَنی /ı/ 1. *caus. of* **çıkar=**. 2. *same as* **çıkar=**^(1, 2).

çıkartı *neol.*, *biol.* excrement.

çıkartıl=^(ır) جِقَارْتِلْمَه *pass. of* **çıkart=**.

çıkartma جِقَارْتْمَه 1. *verbal n. of* **çıkart=**. 2. decalcomania, decal.

çıkı جِقِی *prov.* small bundle.

çıkık^(ğı) جِقِق ,جِقِیق 1. dislocated, out of joint; dislocation. 2. projecting, protruding; projection, salient part. **— sar=** to bandage a sprain. **—çı** bonesetter.

çıkıl=^(ır) جِقِلْمَه *pass. of* **çık=** 1.

çıkım جِقِم ,جِقِیم *archaic* 1. *verbal n. of* **çık=**. 2. rebuke, vituperation.

çıkın جِقِن ,جِقِین 1. knotted bundle. 2. purse full of money. **—la** /ı/ to bundle.

çıkıntı جِقِنْتِی ,جِقِنْدَه ,جِقِنْدَق 1. projecting part, salient part. 2. marginal note. 3. *anat.* process. 4. opium of inferior quality. 5. *slang* cigarette. **—lı** varied in outline with salients or projections.

çıkırık^(ğı) جِقِرِق *same as* **çıkrık**.

çıkış 1 جِقِش ,جِقِیش 1. *verbal n. of* **çık=** 1. 2. *mil.* sally, sortie. 3. *horse races* start. 4. *Turkish style wrestling* the wrestlers' entrance into the arena. 5. scolding. **— et=** to make a spirited start (horse in a race). **— noktası** starting point, point of departure. **— yap=** to scold.

çıkış=^(ır) 2 جِقِشْمَه 1. /a/ to rebuke, scold. 2. to suffice. 3. /a or la/ to compete (with), to enter into rivalry (with). **—ma** *verbal n.* **—tır=** /ı/ *caus. of* **çıkış=**.

çıkla جِقْلَه *prov.* purely, completely.

çıkma جِقْمَه 1. *verbal n. of* **çık=** 1. 2. *arch.* overhang. 3. set of towels used upon emerging from a Turkish bath. 4. projection; promontory. 5. marginal note. 6. come out; appeared. 7. /dan/ separated (from a group). 8. *hist.* advancement from service in the palace to the Janissary regiment. **—lı** having a projection or a bay window.

çıkmaz جِقْمَز ,جِقْمَاز 1. that does not come out. 2. blind alley, impasse, dead-end street. **— ayın son çarşambası** February 30th, a time that never comes. **—a gir=** to come to an impasse **— leke** indelible stain. **— sokak** blind alley. **— yol** 1. blind alley. 2. policy that leads to failure. **—lık** *phil.* aporia problem without an answer.

çıkolata (...´.) چیقولاته [**çokolâto**] same as çikolata.

çıkrık[¹] چیغریق چغرق چغره [**cehre**] 1. spinning wheel. 2. pulley, winding wheel. 3. lathe. —**çı** lathe operator.

çıkşağı چیقشاغی prov. yo-yo.

çılan چیلان kind of jujube, fruit of *Zizyphus jujuba*.

çılbır 1 چلبر dish of poached eggs with yogurt.

çılbır 2 چلبر leading rein.

çıldır=[ʳ] چیلدرمق to go mad, to lose one's wits. —**asıya** madly.

çıldır çıldır چلدر چلدر brightly. —**bak**= to look with bright, shining eyes.

çıldırmış چیلدرمش crazy, gone mad.

çıldırt=[ʳ] چیلدرتمق /ı/ caus. of çıldır=.

çılgava چیلغوه var. of cılkava.

çılgın چلغین چلغین چلغین mad, insane, raving. —**ca** madly. —**lık** madness, insanity.

çılkafa, çılkava چلقفا same as cılkava.

çıltak[¹] چیلتاق prov. quarrelsome, clamorous.

çıma (´.) چیمه It *naut*. rope's end; hawser or other rope let overboard. —**at**=, —**ver**= to let a rope overboard. —**cı** quayside hand.

çımariva (...´.) چیما ریوا It *naut*. aloft! —**et**= to go aloft.

çımbar چیمبار var. of cimbar.

çımkır=[ʳ] چمقرمق to evacuate feces in a watery jet (bird). —**ık** 1. bird's feces. 2. prov. gardener's watering pot.

çınak[¹] چیناق prov. claw. —**la**= /ı/ to scratch.

çınakop[ᵇᵘ] چینا قوب young of the seafish *Temnodon saltator* (**lüfer**), 10-15 centimeters long.

çınar چنار [**çenar**] plane-tree, *bot.*, *Platanus orientalis*. —**kökü** root wood of plane tree, used by cabinetmakers. —**giller** *bot.*, *Platanaceae*. —**lık** grove of plane trees.

çın çın چین چین chinking sound. —**öt**= 1. to resound with a chinking noise. 2. to be quite empty.

çıngar چینغار Gk *slang* quarrel, noisy dispute, row. —**çıkar**= to start a quarrel.

çıngı چنغی prov. spark.

çıngıl چنغل var. of cingil.

çıngırak[¹] چینغراق چینغراق چینغراق چینغراق چینغراق small bell. —**ı çek**= *slang* to die. —**sesli ötleğen** kind of warbler, *zool.*, *Sylvia curruca*. —**lı** furnished with bells. —**lı yılan** rattlesnake, *zool.*, *Crotalus*.

çıngır çıngır چینغر چینغر tinkling sound. —**öt**= to give a tinkling sound.

çıngırda=[ʳ] چینغرداسمق to give out a tinkling sound, to tinkle. —**k** same as çıngırak. —**t**= /ı/ caus. of çıngırda=.

çıngırtı چینغرتی tinkling sound.

çınkı چنقی same as çıngı.

çınla=[ʳ] چینلامه چینلامق 1. to give out a ringing or clinking sound. 2. to ring (ear). —**ma** verbal n. —**t**= /ı/ caus. of çınla=.

çınokop چینوقوب same as çınakop.

çınra=[ʳ] چنرامق *archaic* to ring. —**ğu**, —**k** small bell. —**t**= /ı/ caus. of çınra=.

çıplak[¹] چیبلاق 1. naked, nude; bare. 2. destitute, poverty-stricken. 3. *hist.* sailor of a certain category in the early Ottoman navy. —**at** pauper. —**gözle** with the naked eye. —**mülkiyet** *law* bare ownership (without right of use or profit). —**sazan** leather carp. —**tel** naked wire. —**lık** nakedness.

çıplan=[ʳ] چیبلانمق to become bare.

çıplat=[ʳ] چیبلاتمق /ı/ to strip, to denude.

çıra چیرا چره [**çirağ**] 1. chip of pitch pine wood. 2. prov. oil lamp; light.

çırağ چراغ var. of çirağ.

çırağan (.—.—) چراغان var. of çirağan.

çırak[¹] چراق [**çirağ**³] 1. apprentice. 2. pupil, novice. 3. person brought up as a servant in a great household and later married off and set up in life. —**çık**= to leave service with provision for the future; to complete apprenticeship. —**çıkar**=, —**et**= /ı/ caus. —**yetiştir**= to train apprentices; /ı/ to train as an apprentice. —**lık** 1. apprenticeship. 2. apprentice's fee.

çırakma چراقمه [**çirağpa**] 1. lamp bracket. 2. candlestick.

çırakman چراقمان [**çirağbane**] decoy light for fish. —**lara çık**= to become furious, to get into a rage.

çırala=[ʳ] چیرالامق /ı/ to kindle with pitch-pine (fire); to incite (quarrel).

çıralı چیرالی resinous. —**çam** pitch pine.

çıramoz چیراموز *fishing* iron grill at the end of a long pole projecting from a boat and used as a torch holder in fishing by night.

çırbır چربر same as çılbır 1.

çırçıl چیرچیل It *naut.* hooks (for lifting barrels).

çırçıplak[¹] (´..) چیرچیبلاق stark naked.

çırçır چرچر 1. cotton gin. 2. trickling spring. 3. field cricket. 4. creaking noise; incessant babbler. 5. same as çırçıl. —**balığı** kind of seafish, *zool.*, *Cremilabrus*.

çırgına et=[ᵈᵉʳ] چیرغینه /ı/ var. of cırgına et=.

çırılçıplak[¹] (..´..) چیریل چیبلاق stark naked.

çırlak[¹] چیرلاق var. of cırlak.

çırnık[¹] چیرنیق Sl *hist.* kind of boat used on the Danube.

çırp=[ar] چیریمق 1. /ı/ to beat with short, repeated blows; to beat (carpet); to clap (hands); to flutter (wings); to rinse (laundry), to full (fabrics). 2. /ı/ to trim, clip (the ends of something). 3. /ı/ to mark with a chalk-line. 4. /ı/ to pinch. 5. to palpitate (heart).

çırpı چرپی 1. chip, shaving, clipping, dry twigs. 2. chalk-line, dyed cord used like a chalk-line; sawing mark on a log. 3. flat ruler. 4. process of bleaching and fulling; liquid used in bleaching. — **çek=** same as **çırpı çırp=**. —**dan çık=** to overstep the mark; to go too far. — **çırp=** to mark a straight line with a chalk-line. — **ipi** 1. carpenter's chalk-line. 2. mason's leveling line. — **tut=** to apply a line to see whether a thing is straight. —**cı** fuller, rinser. —**cı taşı** flat stone on which clothes are beaten while being washed.

çırpıl=ır چرپلمق pass. of **çırp=**.
çırpın=ır چرپنمق 1. to flutter (with the wings), to struggle (with the arms). 2. to be all in a fluster, to struggle desperately.
çırpıntı چرپنتی 1. palpitation. 2. flurry. 3. slight agitation (of the sea). 4. driftwood, etc., cast ashore by the waves. —**lı** slightly agitated (sea).
çırpış=ır چرپشمق /ı/ to flutter (birds).
çırpıştır=ır چرپشدرمق /ı/ 1. to write off hastily; to do carelessly and hastily. 2. to tap, to beat lightly. —**ma** 1. verbal n. 2. scribbled hurriedly; done hastily and carelessly.
çırpma چرپمه 1. verbal n. of **çırp=**. 2. kind of hemming stitch. 3. Turkish style wrestling a stemming back the opponent's hand.
çırptır=ır چرپدرمق /ı,a/ caus. of **çırp=**.
çıtıı چیت crack, cracking sound. — **et=** to make a cracking sound. — **kuşu** wren, zool., Troglodytes troglodytes. — **yok** there is not a sound to be heard.
çıta (ˊ.) چیته lath, long narrow strip of wood.
çıtakğı چتاق 1. boor; rough, brutal country fellow. 2. Turk from the Balkans, having a peculiar Turkish pronunciation. 3. prov. quarrelsome, ill-tempered.
çıtarı 1 چتاری kind of brocade made of silk mixed with cotton.
çıtarı 2 چتاری kind of seabream, zool., Box salpa.
çıtçıt چیتچیت colloq. snap fastener.
çıtılgı چتیلغی archaic dense wood, jungle.
çıtı pıtı چتی پتی dainty, delicate and lovely.
çıtır çıtır چتر چتر with a crackling sound.
çıtırda=ır چتردامق to crackle, to make a crackling noise. —**t=** /ı/ caus.
çıtır pıtır چتر پتر with a sweet babble (said of the talking of a child), prattling.
çıtkırıldım چیتقرلدم 1. over-delicate, fragile; over-sensitive. 2. dandy, effeminate.
çıtla=ır چتلامق 1. to crackle, to make a crackling noise. 2. prov. to burst open (bud), to split open (fruit). —**t=** 1. /ı/ caus. 2. /ı,a/ to drop a hint (about).
çıtpıtıı چیت پیت small toy explosive that goes off when stepped on.
çıvga چوغا prov. thin, lean.
çıvgar چوغار var. of **cıvgar**.
çıvgın چوغین prov. sleet.
çıyan چیان 1. centipede, zool., Scolopendra. 2. a disgusting blond person. — **otu** common polypody, bot., Polypodium vulgare. —**cık** bistort, snake weed, bot., Polygonum bistorta.
çız=ar چیزمك var. of **çiz=**.
-çi 1 چی cf. **-cı**.
çi- 2 (—) چه P lrnd. what? e. g., **çifaide**.
çiçe چیچه prov. aunt.
çiçekğı 1 چیچك 1. flower, blossom. 2. pattern of a fabric showing flowers. 3. colloq. fickle and tricky person. 4. chem. flowers (of sulphur). 5. print. ornament. — **aç=** to bloom, to come into flower, to blossom. — **bahçesi** flower garden. — **balı** flower honey. — **biti** plant louse, aphid, green fly. —**i burnunda**, —**i burnunda çamuru karnında** very fresh, brand new. — **demeti** bunch of flowers. — **durumu** bot. inflorescence. — **gibi** neat, very clean. — **gibi açıl=** to bloom like a flower; to exhibit premature or unexpected development of character. — **inciri** coarse, green fig. — **kokusu** 1. smell of flowers. 2. flower perfume. — **kopar=** to pick flowers. — **lahanası** Brussels sprouts. — **muhasebesi** a simple manner of keeping accounts. — **pazarı** flower market. — **sapçığı** bot. pedicel. — **sapı** bot. peduncle. — **suyu** orange flower water. — **tarhı** flower bed. — **tozu** bot. pollen. — **ver=** to flower, to produce flowers. — **yağı** essential oil from flowers; neroli oil; sunflower oil. — **yaprağı** bot. bractea. **Bir** —**le yaz olmaz** proverb One flower doesn't make a summer.
çiçekğı 2 چیچك [**çiçek 1**] smallpox, variola. — **aşısı** vaccination, inoculation for smallpox. — **bozuğu** pock-mark; pock-marked. — **çıkar=**, — **dök=** to have smallpox. — **hastalığı** smallpox, variola.
çiçekçi چیچكجی florist. —**lik** floriculture.
çiçeklen=ır چیچكلنمك to flower, to come into flower, to blossom. —**dir=** /ı/ caus.
çiçekli چیچكلی 1. in flower, in bloom. 2. ornamented with flowers. — **bitkiler** bot., Phanerogamia.
çiçeklikği چیچكلك 1. vase, flower vase; flower stand. 2. flower garden. 3. flower bed. 4. flower house; conservatory. 5. bot. receptacle.

çiçeksi=ʳ *neol., chem.* to effloresce. **—me** *chem., path.* efflorescence.
çiçeksiz چیچکسیز without flowers. **— bitkiler** *bot.,* Cryptogamia.
Çiçilya (..'.) چیچیلیه It *archaic* Sicily.
çide (—.) چیده P gathered, picked, plucked.
çifaide (.'—..) چه فائده P *lrnd.* what use? What good is it?
çifçi چفجی *var. of* çiftçi.
çiflik^gi چفلك *var. of* çiftlik.
çift چفت [cüft] 1. couple, pair; double. 2. duplicate. 3. pair of oxen yoked to a plow. 4. *watch-making* pair of fine pincers; *print.* pincers. 5. *math.* even (number). 6. *archaic* fellow, mate. 7. *lrnd.* peer, equal. **— aded** *math.* even number. **— atlı** two-horse. **— beygiri** plow-horse. **— çift** in pairs, by pairs. **— çubuk** agriculture, farming. **— çubuk sahibi** owner of an estate, wealthy in landed property. **— dudaksıl** *neol., ling.* bilabial. **— düğmeli** *tailor.* double-breasted. **— hatlı** *rail.* double-track. **— kanatlı** folding (door, window). **— kanatlı tayyare** *aero.* biplane. **— karineli** *naut.* double-keeled. **— koş=** to harness the beasts to the plow. **—e koş=** /ı/ to harness to the plow (beast). **— meclis sistemi** *pol.* two-chamber system. **— motörlü** *aero.* twin-engined. **— önlü** *tailor.* double-breasted. **— parmaklılar** *zool., Artiodactyla.* **— pencere** double window. **— sayı** *math.* even number. **— sür=** to plow. **— sütun** *print.* double column. **— mi tek mi?** odd or even? **— uskurlu** *naut.* twin-screw. **— yıldızlar** *astr.* double stars.
çiftçi چفتجی farmer, agriculturalist. **—nin karnını yarmışlar, kırk tane gelecek yıl çıkmış** *proverb* A farmer always counts on the future. **—lik** agriculture, farming, husbandry.
çifte چفته [cüfte] 1. double, paired. 2. kick with both hind feet at once (horse, etc.). 3. double-barreled gun, shotgun. 4. pair of oars; double-oar boat. 5. pair of whorls on a horse's forehead. **— at=** to lash out with both hind feet at once. **— dürbün** binoculars. **— düyek** *Or. mus.* a great rhythmic pattern with 16 beats, with signatures of 16/8, 16/4. **— gülle** *hist.* 1. double shot. 2. bar shot. **— hamam** public bath having two divisions, one for men, the other for women. **— harf** *print.* double letter, ligature. **— kâğıt** *slang* doped cigarette. **— kanatlılar** *zool., Diptera.* **— kanca bağı** *naut.* blackwall hitch. **— kavrulmuş** 1. twice-roasted. 2. kind of small-cut, hard Turkish delight. 3. hard-boiled (person). **— kumrular** two inseparable chums. **← nağra, — nâra** *Or. mus., popular name for* **kudüm. — sigorta** *com.* double insurance. **— sofyan** *Or. mus., name given to the high degree of* **yürük** 9/16 *in the* **aksak** *rhythmic pattern.* **— şamdan** two-branched candlestick. **— tatar** *hist.* couriers dispatched in pairs. **— telli** *name of a kind of dance special for women, and the wordless music to this dance.* **— vergi** *fin.* double taxation. **—hane** pairing cage for birds. **—le=** /ı/ 1. to kick with both hind feet at once. 2. *naut.* to cast a second anchor (vessel moored on one anchor). **—leş=** to kick each other with both hind feet at once. **—li** 1. kicking (horse). 2. marked in the forehead with a pair of whorls (horse). 3. ill-omened, unlucky. 4. treacherous. **—lilik** malicious treachery, perfidy.

çifter çifter چفتر چفتر in pairs.
çiftle=ʳ چفتله /ı/ to pair, to mate (beasts). **—n=** 1. *pass.* 2. to become a pair. **—ndir=** /ı/ *caus.*
çiftleş=ⁱʳ چفتلش 1. to become a pair. 2. to mate. **—me** a mating. **—tir=** /ı/ *caus. of* çiftleş=.
çiftlik^gi چفتلك 1. farm, agricultural estate. 2. *abstr. n. of* çift. 3. plot of 20 - 30 acres, that can be cultivated with a single plow. **— sahibi** farm owner.
çifuta (..'.) چفوطه *same as* çıfıta.
çigara (..'.) چغاره It *obs., same as* cıgara.
çigûne (.—.) چگونه P *lrnd.* what kind, what sort, how? **—gi** (.—.—) P nature, manner, circumstance.
çiğ 1 چیگ 1. raw, uncooked. 2. crude, soft, fresh, green (person). 3. crude, out of place, unfitting (act, words). 4. ugly and clashing, crude (color). 5. *prov.* immature, unripe (fruit); uncultivated (land). **— bak=** to look around in an uncouth and boorish manner. **— çiğ ye=** /ı/ to devour, to tear to pieces (in great rage); to nourish a great enmity against someone. **— iplik** unprocessed yarn. **— köfte** dish made of ground meat, pounded wheat and red pepper. **— kömür** half-burnt charcoal. **— toprak** soil left without cultivation for a long time. **— yemedim ki karnım ağrısın** I have done no wrong, so I have nothing to fear.
çiğ 2 چیگ *same as* çiy.
çiğde چگده 1. jujube tree, *bot., Zizyphus sativus.* 2. jujube.
çiğdem چگدم crocus, meadow saffron, *bot., Colchicum.* **—giller** *bot., Colchicaceae.*
çiğdene چگدنه board of resinous pine wood.
çiğin^gni چگن *prov.* shoulder.
çiğit^di چگت cotton seed.
çiğlik^gi چگلك *abstr. n. of* çiğ 2.
çiğne=ʳ چگنه [çeyne=] /ı/ 1. to chew, masticate. 2. to trample down, to tread under foot; to run over (person in car accident). **—yip geç=** /ı/

to neglect in passing by, not to look up while visiting in the neighborhood. **—k** *archaic* much trodden (path). **—me** chewing, mastication. **—me kası** *anat.* masseter. **—mik** food masticated and then fed to a baby. **—n=** *pass.* of **çiğne=**. **—t=** /ı,a/ *caus.* of **çiğne=**. **—tici** *anat.* masticatory.

çiğse=ᵣ, çiğsi=ᵣ بیگسه مك بیگسامك بیگسیمك *same as* **çise=** 2.

çiğzin=ᵣ بیگزنمك *archaic* to turn, turn around. **—dir=** /ı/ *caus.*

çihacet (. —.) چه حاجت P *lrnd.* what need?

çihar (. —) چهار [çehar] *dice games* four. **— ü dü** four and two. **— ü se** four and three. **— ü yek** four and one.

çihil چهل P *lrnd.* 1. forty. 2. many. **—üm** fortieth.

çihre چهره P *lrnd.* face. **—küşa** (... —) P *lrnd.* 1. portrait painter. 2. who unveils a lady. **—nüma** (... —) P *lrnd.* 1. who shows her face (lady). 2. that occurs (event). **—perdaz** (... —) P *lrnd.* portrait painter, sculptor. **—perdaz-ı cihan** *poet.* the sun.

-çikᵍⁱ 1 جك *cf.* -cık.

çikᵍⁱ 2 چیگ *prov.* the hollow face of a knucklebone.

çiklet چیكلت E chewing gum.

çikolata (...'.) چقولاته چیقولاته [çokolâto] chocolate.

çil 1 چیل 1. freckle, speckle; freckled, speckled. 2. spot (on a mirror). **— horoz** speckled cock. **— keklik** gray partridge, *zool.*, *Perdrix cinereus.*

çil 2 چیل 1. ruffled grouse, *zool.*, *Bonasa.* 2. francolin; *zool.*, *Francolinus.* **— ardıcı** reed warbler, *zool.*, *Acrocephalus arundinaceus.* **— yavrusu gibi dağıl=** to scatter like a covey of partridges.

çil 3 چیل shiny, bright (coin). **— akçe** new and shiny coin.

çil 4 چل P *same as* **çihil**.

çilâv (. —) چلاو P dish of boiled rice.

çile 1 چله [çille] 1. ordeal, trial, suffering. 2. period of severe trial; period of religious retirement with fasting; *myst. orders* period of forty days during which a novice has to fast and engage in religious exercises, before admission to an order of dervishes. 3. a feeding a horse in a dark stable for a certain period to make it strong; healthy condition of a horse. **— çek=** 1. to pass through a severe trial, to suffer greatly. 2. to pass through a forty-day novitiate. **—den çık=** to get very furious, to lose control of one's temper. **— çıkar=** *same as* **çile doldur=**. **—den çıkar=** /ı/ to infuriate. **—i dey** *lrnd.* forty days of most severe winter. **—si doldu** His suffering has come to an end. **— doldur=** to be going through a period of severe trial. **—ye gir=** *myst. orders* to enter on a forty-day novitiate. **— kır=** *myst. orders* to break off the religious exercises before the period is over. **—i merdan** *myst. orders* 1. novitiate of dervishes. 2. the trials of a pious man. **—ye soyun=** *same as* **çileye gir=**.

çile 2 چله 1. hank, skein. 2. *archery* bowstring.

çilecilikᵍⁱ چله جیلك *phil.* asceticism.

çilehane (.. —.) چله خانه 1. *myst. orders* cell where the novice undergoes his ordeal. 2. place of suffering.

çilekᵍⁱ چیلك چلك چیلك strawberry, *bot.*, *Fragaria vesca.* **— reçeli** strawberry jam.

çilekeş چله كش [Persian **cillakas**] 1. sufferer, endurer; suffering. 2. engaged in religious retirement.

çilelen=ⁱʳ چله لنمك *prov.* to gain strength by good feeding (horse).

çileli چله لی 1. suffering, enduring. 2. full of suffering. 3. *prov.* well-fed (horse).

çileşiken چله شكن [Persian **cillasikan**] *myst. orders* one who breaks off the religious exercises before the period is over.

çilingir چلنگیر چیلنگیر [cilânger] 1. locksmith. 2. *slang* burglar, lockbreaker. **— sofrası** *colloq.* small table with raki and light snacks.

çille چله P *lrnd., same as* **çile 1**.

çillen=ⁱʳ چلنمك چیللنمك to become freckled, speckled, spotted. **—dir=** /ı/ *caus.*

çilli چللی چیللی freckled, speckled, spotted.

çiltiyan چلتیان *var. of* **çintiyan**.

çilüm چلم P *same as* **çihilüm**.

çim 1 چیم garden grass, lawn. **— tohumu** grass seed. **— tut=** to become grassy.

çim 2 چیم چم [Persian —] Arabic script, name of the letter چ. (This letter is the 7th letter of the Persian and Ottoman-Turkish alphabet, pronounced as ch. In chronograms, it has the numerical value of 3.)

çim=ᵉʳ 3 چمك *prov.* to dip down (in water), to duck under water; to wash by pouring water over oneself.

çimbakuka (...'.) چمبا قوقه *same as* **cimbakuka**.

çimbar چمبار *same as* **cimbar**.

çimdi=ᵣ چمدیمك *archaic, same as* **çimdikle=**.

çimdikᵍⁱ چمدك چیمدیك pinch. **— at=**, **— bas=** /a/ to pinch. **— dikişi** kind of quilting stitch. **— pidesi** kind of pastry. **—le=** /ı/ to pinch with the fingers. **—len=** *pass.* **—let=** *caus.* of **çimdikle=**.

çimdir=ᵣ چمدرمك *caus.* of **çim= 3**.

çimen 1 چمن [çemen 2] meadow, lawn, turf. **—lik** meadow land.

çimen 2 چمن *var. of* **çemen 1**.
çimento (..'.) چمنتو It cement.
çimlen=ᴵʳ چملنمك چملنمك 1. to sprout, to germinate. 2. to become covered with grass. 3. to get bits of profit out of other people's affairs. **—dir=** /ı/ *caus.* **—me** *bot.* germination.
çimre=ʳ چمره چمر *var. of* **çemre=**.
çimşir چمشیر *var. of* **şimşir**.
Çin 1 چین [Çin 2] China. **— ayvası** Japanese quince, *bot.*, *Cydonia japonica*. **— baklası** Tonka bean, *bot.*, *Dipteryx odorata*. **— mavisi** china blue. **— mürekkebi** India ink. **— ördeği** mandarin, *zool.*, *Aix galericulata*. **— tavuğu** Cochin fowl.
Çin 2 (—) چین P *lrnd.* China. **— ü Maçin** the land of China.
çin 3 (—) چین P *poet.* 1. fold, plait, wrinkle. 2. curl, twist. 3. ripple. **—i cebin**, **—i ebru**, **—i pişani** frown.
-çin 4 (—) چین P *lrnd.* picking, collecting, *as in* **arakçin, damençin**.
çin 5 چین ﻣﯩﻨﻚ ﻣﻠﻚ archaic real, all, completely. **— sabah** very early in the morning.
çin 6 چین *prov., var. of* **çiğin**.
çinakopᵇᵘ چنا قوپی *same as* **çınakop**.
çinbar, çinber چنبر - چنبا *same as* **cimbar**.
Çince (.'.) چینجه Chinese, the Chinese language.
çine (—.) چینه P *poet.* a pecking of food (bird). **—dan** (—.—) P bird's crop.
çinerarya (..'.) چیناریا It seaside ragwort, *bot.*, *Cineraria maritima*.
çinever (—..) چینه ور P *lrnd.* food-pecking (bird).
Çingân (.—) چنگان, **Çingâne** (.—.) چنگانه *lrnd.*, **Çingâr** (.—) چنگار *obs.*, **Çingen** *prov., same as* **Çingene**.
Çingene چنگانه 1. gypsy; the Gypsies. 2. *l. c.* mean, miserly fellow. **— ahtapotu** 1. proud flesh of a wound. 2. *path.* polyp. **— beyi** *Ott. hist.* appointed head of the Gypsies. **— borcu** petty debts. **— çalar, Kürt oynar** The Gypsy plays, the Kurd dances (said of 1. a place where there is complete disorder, 2. persons, one worse than the other). **— çergesi** 1. Gypsy tent. 2. dirty and miserable-looking place. **— çergesinde musandıra aranmaz** *proverb* No use looking for fine furniture in a gypsy tent. **— çorbası** confusion. **— düğünü** 1. Gypsy wedding. 2. disorderly gathering. **— karısı** Gypsy woman. **— kavgası** noisy quarrel. **— kızı** Gypsy girl; dancing girl. **— palamudu** young of bonito (fish). **— pavuryası** a small kind of crab, *zool.*, *Carcinus maenas*. **— pembesi, — sarısı** bright pink or yellow. **—ce** 1. Gypsy-like. 2. Romany. **—lik**

1. meanness, miserliness. 2. paltriness, shabbiness. 3. vagabondage.
çingil چنگل *same as* **cingil**.
çini 1 چینی [Çinî 2] encaustic tile, glazed tile; porcelain; made of encaustic tiles; encaustic, glazed. **— İznik'i** *hist.* İznik (Nicaea) where tiles were made. **— mavisi** cobalt blue. **— mürekkebi** India ink. **— soba** tiled stove.
Çinî 2 (——) چینی P *lrnd.* Chinese.
çinici چینیجی maker of tiles. **—lik** the art of tile-making.
çinili چینیلی tiled, decorated with encaustic tiles. **Ç—li İznik** *obs.* Iznik (the ancient Nicaea). **Ç—li Köşk** the Tiled Kiosk (Sultan's Kiosk in the grounds of the Sultan's palace in Istanbul).
Çinizlikᵍⁱ چینیزلك *var. of* **çini İznik'i**.
çinkâri (———) چنکاری *text.* in the Chinese style (fabric).
çinko (.'.) چنقو چنقو It 1. zinc; zinc sheet. 2. zinc plate, zincograph. **— tuzu** *chem.* zinc sulfate.
çinkograf چنقوغراف G zincographer.
çinkografi چنقوغرافی G zincography.
çinle=ʳ چنلمك چنلامك *چله ملك* *var. of* **çınla=**.
Çinli چینلی a Chinese.
çintiyan 1 چنتیان *prov.* kind of trousers made of coarse fabric, worn by peasant women.
çintiyan 2 چنتیان *prov.* kind of dagger or scimitar. **— kılıç** broadsword, scimitar.
çipil چپیل 1. bleary, gummy, dirty (eye); blear-eyed. 2. *same as* **çepel**. 3. *prov.* swampy, boggy; swampy place. **—lik** 1. bleareyedness. 2. swampy place.
çipo (.'.) چیپو It *naut.* anchor stock. **— çemberi** stock band of an anchor. **— kalktı** The anchor's atrip.
çipura (..'.) چپورا gilt head bream, *zool.*, *Chrysophrys aurata*.
çir 1 چیر Arm *prov.* dried prunes or apricots.
çir 2 (—) چیر P *lrnd.* valiant, bold; victorious.
çıra (.—) چرا P *lrnd.* 1. why? 2. the why and wherefore, reason.
çırağ (.—) چراغ P *lrnd.* 1. lamp, light, candle, torch. 2. teacher, guide. 3. client, dependent. **—ı çeşm** light of the eye. **— dinlendir=** *myst. orders* to put out the light. **— uyandır=** *myst. orders* to light a torch, lamp, candle, etc. **—an** (.——) P 1. lamps. 2. illumination on festive occasions. **Ç—an Sarayı** name of a palace in Istanbul (burned down in 1910). **—bane** P lampstand, candlestick. **—bere** P 1. oil lamp. 2. lamp stand. **—dan** (.——) P lamp stand. **—ek** P 1. little lamp. 2. glowworm. **—küş** (.—.) P 1. extinguisher of light. 2. who holds secret

gatherings at which the lights are blown out and all present give themselves to licentiousness. —**pa** (. — —), —**paye** (. — —.) P lamp stand. —**perhiz** (. —. —) P lantern. —**püf** (. —.) P *same as* **çirağküş.**

çire (— .) مير P *lrnd.* 1. brave, strong. 2. victorious. 3. high. 4. quick, swift, nimble. —**dest** P skillful, dexterous. —**gî** (— . —) P *abstr. n. of* **çire.** —**kâr** (— . —) P quick, clever and bold. —**zeban** (— . . —) P eloquent.

çiriş چريش [**seriş**] 1. shoemaker's and bookbinder's paste made of powdered asphodel root; paste, glue; *text.* size. 2. powdered asphodel root. — **çanağı gibi** sticky and foul tasting (mouth). — **otu** asphodel, *bot.*, *Asphodelus*. —**le**= /ı/ to smear with paste. —**len**= *pass.* —**lendir**= /ı/ *caus.* —**let**= /ı,a/ *caus. of* **çirişle**=. —**li** pasted; pasty, gluey; *text.* sized.

çirk[ki] چرك P 1. *lrnd.* dirt; rust. 2. *prov.* pus, matter; ear-wax; mucus. 3. *prov.* manure. 4. *prov.* deposit in a pipe stem or cigarette-holder. —**i dünya** *lrnd.* worldly vanities.

çirkâb (. —) چركاب P *lrnd., same as* **çirkef.**

çirkalud (. — —) P *lrnd.* soiled, filthy, dirty.

çirkef چركف [**çirkâb**] 1. filthy water, foul water. 2. sink, sewer. 3. very disgusting person, despicable fellow. —**e basma, üstüne sıçrar** Beware of dealing with a despicable person, for you will have trouble. — **kuyusu** cesspool. — **suyu** dirty water, foul water. —**e taş at**= to throw a stone into muddy water, *i. e.* to invite the abuse of an insolent person.

çirkin 1 چركين چركين [**çirkin 2**] ugly, unbecoming; shameful, disgusting.

çirkin 2 (. —) چيركين P *lrnd.* 1. soiled, filthy. 2. *same as* **çirkin 1.**

çirkince 1 (...') چيركينجه rather ugly.

çirkince 2 (..'.) چيركينجه in an ugly manner.

çirkinle= چيركينله مك 1. to become ugly. 2. /ı/ to call ugly. —**n**=, —**ş**= to become ugly. —**ştir**=, —**t**= /ı/ to make ugly, to spoil the appearance (of).

çirkinlik[ki] چيركينلك ugliness.

çirkinse=, **çirkinsi**= چيركينسه مك /ı/ to consider ugly.

çirklen=[ir] چركلنمك *prov.* to become soiled, befouled.

çirklet=[ir] چركلتمك *prov.* /ı/ to soil, befoul.

çirkli چركلو *prov.* dirty, soiled; purulent; rusty.

çiroz چيروز Gk 1. salted and dried thin mackerel. 2. very thin person.

çirtik[ki] چرتك *prov.* 1. a snapping of the fingers. 2. small stalk forming part of a bunch of grapes. — **çal**= to snap one's fingers in dancing.

çise 1 چيسه drizzle.

çise=[r] **2**, **çisele**=[r] چيسه مك to drizzle.

çisi=[r] چيسيمك to drizzle. —**nti** drizzle. —**ntili** drizzly.

çist (—) چيست P *lrnd.* What is? What is it?

çistan (— —) چيستان (. —), چيسنان P *lrnd.* enigma, riddle.

çiş چيش nursery 1. urine. 2. evacuation of urine. — **et**= to urinate. —**i gel**= to want to go to the toilet. —**li** wetted.

çit 1 چيت hedge; fence of hurdles; fence.

çit 2 چيت P 1. chintz, printed cotton cloth. 2. *prov.* head kerchief.

çitari چيتارى *same as* **çıtarı 1, 2.**

çitavr چيطور P *lrnd.* how? in what manner?

çiten چيتن *prov.* wicker basket.

çiti چيتى a rubbing in washing (laundry). —**le**= /ı/ 1. to rub in washing. 2. *prov.* to sew together tightly. —**li** rubbed in washing (laundry).

çitiş=[ir] چيتشمك 1. to interlace, to become matted together. 2. to close well (teeth). —**ik** interwoven, tangled. —**me** *ling.* crasis. —**tir**= /ı/ *caus. of* **çitiş**=.

çitle=[r] چيتله مك /ı/ to hedge, to enclose with a wicker fence.

çitlembik[ği] چيتلنبك terebinth berry. — **ağacı** 1. terebinth tree, turpentine tree, *bot.*, *Pistacia terebinthus*. 2. Oriental nettle-tree, *bot.*, *Celtis tournefortii*. — **gibi** small and dark (girl).

çitlen=[ir] چيتلنمك *pass. of* **çitle**=. —**dir**= /ı/ *caus.*

çitli چيتلى hedged in.

çitlik[ği] چيتلك 1. boughs for fencing. 2. place enclosed with hedges.

çitmik[ği] چيتمك *prov.* 1. small stalk forming part of a bunch of grapes; small bunches of grapes left in a vineyard after the harvest. 2. small quantity, a pinch.

çiv=[er] چيومك *same as* **cav**= **2.**

çivgar چيوغار *var. of* **cıvgar.**

çivi چيوى 1. nail. 2. peg, pin. — **başı** nail head. — **çak**= to drive in nails. — **çeken** nail puller. — **çiviyi söker** *proverb* One nail drives out another. — **gibi** 1. healthy, strong. 2. stiff with cold (finger). — **kes**= *colloq.* to feel very cold, to freeze. — **yazı**, — **yazısı** cuneiform script. — **yukarı** *Or. style wrestling* at bringing the opponent to the floor head-down with the legs in the air.

çivili (. — —) چيويلى indigo blue.

çivile=[r] چيويله مك 1. to nail. 2. *slang* to stab. 3. *prov.* practice of exorcising a disease by nailing it to the wall. —**me** *sport*

dive with the feet foremost. —n= 1. *pass. of* **çvile**=. 2. to be fixed to the spot. —t= /ı,a/ *caus. of* **çivile**=.
çivili جیویلی 1. nailed. 2. having nails. — **köpekbalığı** spiny shark, *zool.*, *Echinorhinus spinosus.*
çivit^(dl) جوید ، جیوید ، جیویت ، جیود indigo, washing-blue, blue bag. — **fidanı** indigo plant, *bot.*, *Indigofera tinctoria.* — **otu** woad, *bot.*, *Isatis tinctoria.* —**le**= /ı/ 1. to dye with indigo. 2. to blue (laundry). —**li** blued (laundry).
çiy چیی dew. — **düştü**, — **yağdı** Dew has fallen. —**li** dewy. —**se**= *prov.* to drizzle, to fall like dew.
çiz=^(er) 1 چیزمك /ı/ 1. to draw (line); to mark; to score. 2. to sketch, to draw (drawing). 3. to cross out, cancel, strike off. 4. to scratch, scarify.
çiz 2 چیز P *lrnd.* thing, something, anything.
çizdir=^(ir) چیزدیرمك /ı,a/ *caus. of* **çiz**= 1. —**t**= /ı,a/ *caus.*
çizek^(kl) چیزك P *lrnd.* small thing, trifle, a little.
çizelge *neol.* printed form for filling in statistics, etc.
çizge *neol.* diagram, graph, curve.
çizgi چیزگی 1. line; dash. 2. stripe; striation. 3. scratch, scar. — **çakısı** forestry marking knife. — **resim** drawing. —**le**= /ı/ to lineate.
çizgili چیزگیلی 1. marked with lines, ruled. 2. striped; *sc.* striated. 3. scratched, slightly cut. — **çek** *fin.* crossed check. — **kas** *neol.*, *anat.* striated muscle. — **külte** *geol.* striated rock. — **mercan balığı** kind of sea-bream, *zool.*, *Pagellus mormyrus.*
çizgin=^(ir) چیزگینلك same as **çiğzin**=.
çizgisel *neol.*, *sc.* linear.
çizi چیزی same as **çizgi**.
çizik^(kl) چیزك 1. line; scratch. 2. marked with scratches; scarified; *sc.* striated. —**li** scored with lines, lined; marked with scratches.
çiziktir=^(ir) چیزكدیرمك /ı/ to scrawl.
çizil=^(ir) چیزلمك *pass. of* **çiz**= 1.
çizili چیزلی 1. ruled, lined. 2. marked, scratched. 3. drawn, delineated. 4. canceled, crossed out.
çizinti چیزنتی *prov.* scratch.
çizme 1 چیزمه high boot, top boot. — **ile tandıra gir**= to act in a boorish, unmannerly fashion. — **kalıbı** boot last, boot tree. — **kulağı** bootstrap. — **den yukarı çık**= to meddle with things one does not understand.
çizme 2 چیزمه 1. *verbal n. of* **çiz**= 1. 2. marked, scratched.

çizmeci چیزمه‌جی bootmaker.
çizmeli چیزمه‌لی wearing high boots.
çoban چوبان [**çuban**] 1. shepherd, herdsman. 2. rustic, boor. **Ç— Adası** the island of Caso, Kasos. — **aldangıcı**, — **aldatan** goatsucker, nightjar, *zool.*, *Caprimulgus europaeus.* — **armağanı çam sakızı** *proverb* A shepherd's present is pine resin (expression of modesty, in giving a present). — **çantası** shepherd's-purse, *bot.*, *Capsella Bursa-pastoris.* — **değneği** 1. shepherd's staff, crook. 2. knot grass, *bot.*, *Polygonum aviculare.* — **düdüğü** water plantain, *bot.*, *Alisma.* — **iğnesi** shepherd's needle, *bot.*, *Geranium.* — **itikadı** simple and firm faith. — **kalkıtan** caltrop, *bot.*, *Santoria calcitrapa.* — **kebabı** stew of meat and vegetables. — **köpeği** sheep dog. — **köpeği gibi ne yer ne yedirir** He is like a sheep dog; he doesn't eat nor does he let others eat (said of a very stingy person). — **mayası** milkwort, *bot.*, *Polygala.* — **minaresi** kind of grass. — **püskülü** holly, *bot.*, *Ilex aquifolium.* — **püskülügiller** *bot.*, *Aquifoliaceae.* — **süzeği** catchweed, goose-grass, *bot.*, *Galium Aparine.* — **tarağı** teasel, *bot.*, *Dipsacus fullonum.* — **taşı** name of a certain large and fine diamond in the sultan's treasure. — **tuzluğu** barberry, *bot.*, *Berberis vulgaris.* — **yıldızı** *var. of* **çolpan** 1. — **yolu** sheep track.
çobanlık^(ğı) چوبانلق 1. occupation of a shepherd. 2. shepherd's pay. — **et**= /a/ to shepherd.
çocuk^(ğu) چوجوق 1. child, infant; childish. 2. boy. 3. human foetus. —**tan al haberi** A child will tell the truth. — **aldır**= to have one's child aborted. — **arabası** baby carriage. — **babası** father. — **bahçesi** 1. children's park. 2. play pen. — **bakımı** child care. — **bakımevi** creche, day nursery. — **bezi** diaper. — **bilim** *neol.* pedagogy. — **büyüt**= to bring up children. — **canlısı** child lover. — **dispanseri** children's clinic. — **doğur**= to give birth to a child. — **düşür**= to have an abortion. — **düşürme** abortion, miscarriage. **Ç— Esirgeme Kurumu** Society for the Protection of Children. — **getir**= to give birth to a child. — **gibi** in a childish manner, child-like. — **hastalığı** children's disease. — **hekimi** pediatrician. —**a iş buyuran ardınca kendi gider** *proverb* He who sends a child on an errand, in the end has to go himself. — **mahkemesi** juvenile court. — **maması** baby food. — **odası** nursery. —**u ol**= /ın/ to have a child, to give birth to a child. — **oyuncağı** 1. toy. 2. child's play; matter of no consequence. — **peydahla**= to be with child (unmarried woman). — **yap**= to bear a child, to have children. —**un yediği helâl, giydiği haram** Money spent on food for a child

is well spent; if spent for clothing it is wasted. **— yetiştir=** to bring up children. **— zammı** child allowance. **—cağız** poor little child. **—ça** (. ́.) childish (act). **—laş=** to become childish; to enter into one's second childhood. **—lu** having children. **—luk** 1. childhood. 2. childishness; folly. **—su** childish.

çoğaçᶜⁱ چوغاج *prov.* sun, sunshine; sunny place.

çoğal=ᵘʳ چوغالمق to increase, multiply, to become abundant. **—t=** /ı/ to increase, augment, make abundant.

çoğan چوغان *same as* **çöven** 1.

çoğuⁿᵘ چوغى 1. the greater part, the majority. 2. most, most of. 3. mostly, usually.

çoğul *neol., gram.* plural. **—la=** /ı/ to form the plural (of). **—lan=** to form a plural.

çoğumsa=ʳ چوغمساماق /ı/ to consider to be too much or many.

çoğun, çoğunca چوغنجه (. ́.) *prov.* often.

çoğunlukᵍᵘ *neol.* majority. **—la** by the majority of votes.

çoğurcukᵍᵘ چوغرجى *prov.* starling, *zool.*, Sturnus.

çoha چوها چوما *same as* **çuha**.

çokᵍᵘ 1 چوب 1. much, great (in amount), long (in duration); too much; very; often; the greater part, the most of a thing. 2. many; too many. **—tan** 1. for a long time. 2. a long time ago. **—tanki** that dates from a long time ago, old, ancient. **—u***. **— ayaklılar** *zool.*, Myriapoda. **—tan beri** for a long time. **— bilen çok yanılır** *proverb* He who knows much is often wrong. **— bilmiş** 1. wiseacre, know-all, cunning. 2. precocious. **— çok** at most, at the most. **— defa** often. **— düzlemli** *neol., geom.* polyhedral. **— evli** polygamous. **— evlilik** polygamy. **— fazla** far too much. **— fazlı** *elec.* polyphasal. **— geçmeden** before long, soon. **— gel=** /a/ to be too much (for); to seem too much (to). **— git=** to go too far. **—u gitti azı kaldı** Most of it is over; the end is near. **— gör=** 1. /ı/ to consider to be too much. 2. /ı, a/ to grudge (a person a thing). **— heceli** *ling.* polysyllabic. **— hücreli** *biol.* multicellular. **—a kalmaz** before long. **— karılı** polygynous. **— karılılık** polygyny, polygamy. **— kere** often, frequently. **— kocalı** polyandrous. **— kocalılık** polyandry. **— köşeli** *geom.* polygonal. **— kutuplu** *elec.* multipolar. **—a mal ol=** to cost too much. **— naz âşık usandırır** *proverb* To go too far in feigning unwillingness wearies the wooer. **— ol=** to go too far. **—a otur=** to cost too much. **— safhalı** *elec.* polyphasal. **— söyle=** to talk too much. **— sürmez** It will not last long, before long. **— şey!** Marvellous! Wonderful! You don't say so! **— tanrıcılık** polytheism. **— taraflı** *law* multilateral. **— tasım** *neol., log.* polysyllogism. **— terimli** *algebra* polynomial. **— vakit** often, frequently. **—a var=** to cost too much. **—a varmaz, —a varmazdan** soon, before long. **— vecihli** *geom.* polyhedral. **— yaşa!** long live! **— yaşıyan bilmez, çok gezen bilir** *proverb* One does not learn by living long, but by travelling much. **— yüzlü** *geom.* polyhedral; polyhedron. **— zaman** often. **—u zarar, azı karar** It is always good to be moderate. **— ziyade** far too much.

çok=ᵃʳ 2 چوقمق *archaic* to crowd together, to flock.

çoka 1 چوقا *var. of* **çuka** 2.

çoka 2 چوقا *same as* **çuha**.

çokal 1 چوقال *archaic* 1. coat of mail, plate-armor; quilted jacket worn as defensive armor. 2. horse armor.

çokal 2 چوقال Gk 1. thickly glazed coarse pottery. 2. thick coarse glazing.

çokallı 1 چوقالى in armor.

çokallı 2 چوقالى thickly and coarsely glazed.

çokça چوقجه somewhat abundant, quite numerous, a good many.

çokçulukᵍᵘ *neol., phil.* pluralism.

çokgen *neol., geom.* polygon.

çoklaş=ᵘʳ چوقلشمق to become numerous, to increase. **—tır=** /ı/ *caus.*

çoklukᵍᵘ چوقلى 1. abundance, multiplicity. 2. crowd. 3. often; mostly.

çokmakᵍᵘ چوقماق, **çokman** چوقمان, **çokmar** چوقمار *archaic* 1. mace. 2. hornless sheep. 3. mastiff. 4. sluggard, worthless fellow.

çokolato (. . ́.) چوقولاتو It *obs., same as* **çikolâta**.

çokra=ʳ چوقرامق to boil violently with a loud bubbling noise. **—ğan** copious spring. **—t=** /ı/ *caus.*

çoksa=ʳ, **çoksan=**ᵘʳ, **çoksu=**ʳ, **çoksun=**ᵘʳ چوقسان چوقسامق چوقسنمق /ı/ to consider to be too much or many.

çoku=ʳ چوقومق *archaic* /ı/ to peck, to bill.

çokum, çokuntu *prov.* a gathering group.

çokuş=ᵘʳ چوقوشمق *prov.* 1. to put noses together, as animals in eating out of one trough. 2. to flock together, to crowd together.

çolakᵍᵘ چولاى having one arm missing or paralyzed; crippled in one hand.

çolpa چولپا 1. clumsy, uncouth, untidy. 2. untidy about the feet and legs. 3. galloping or cantering with the left foot foremost (horse). **—lık** clumsiness.

Çolpan 1 چولپان *astr.* Venus.

çolpan 2 چولپان *same as* **çolpa**³.

çoluk çocukᵍᵘ چولوق چوجوق 1. household, family, wife and children. 2. children, pack of children. **—a karış=** to become a family man. — **sahibi** a man with a family.

çomakᵏⁱ بوماك بومه ممود يمال 1. cudgel, truncheon. 2. short, thick stick. 3. the larger drumstick. 4. stick, bat (in tipcat). 5. *anat.* rod (of the retina). **—dar** *hist.* 1. warrior armed with a mace. 2. squire who carries his lord's mace.

çomar بومار 1. mastiff, large watchdog. 2. *prov.* hornless sheep. 3. *slang* old saloon-keeper.

çomrukᵏᵘ بومروك *prov.* stump of a broom.

çomur بومور *prov.* common turnip, *bot.*, Brassica rapa.

çop بوپ *same as* **cop.**

çopra بوپره 1. backbone of a fish. 2. impenetrable thorn-patch. **— balığı** loach, *zool.*, Cobitis.

çopur بوپور 1. pock-marked; pock marks. 2. *archaic* freckle. 3. *archaic* fallow deer, *zool.*, Dama dama; spotted antelope.

çopurina (...ˊ.) بوپورينه kind of sea-fish.

çor بور *prov.* disease, illness.

çorakᵏⁱ بوراك 1. arid, barren. 2. brackish, bitter (water). 3. impervious kind of clay used for spreading on flat roofs of houses. 4. saltpeter bed. **—lık** barrenness.

çorapᵇⁱ بوراپ [*Arabic* **jaurab**] stocking, sock, hose. **— bağı** garter, suspender. **— makinası** stocking loom, knitting machine. **— ör=** 1. to knit socks. 2. *cf.* **başına çorap ör=**. **— söküğü gibi** one following the other in rapid succession, easily and quickly. **— şişi** knitting needle. **—çı** maker or seller of stockings, hosier.

çorba بوربه [**şorba**] 1. soup. 2. medley, mess. **—arpası** bruised barley used for soups. **—ya dön=** to become a mess. **—ya döndür=**, **— et=** /ı/ to make a mess (of). **— gibi** confused, in a mess. **— içmeğe çağır=** to invite to a meal. **— kâsesi** soup bowl. **— kaşığı** tablespoon. **—da maydanozu ol=**, **—da tuzu bulun=** to contribute a small share (to a general expense).

çorbacı بورباجى 1. maker or seller of soup. 2. person fond of soup. 3. Christian notable in Turkish towns. 4. *slang* boss. 5. *hist.* colonel of the Janissaries. 6. *obs.* official receiver and entertainer of guests in a village or town.

çorbalıkᵏⁱ بورباليك suitable for making soup.

çorlu بورلو *prov.* diseased, ill.

çortan, çortun بورتن *prov.* roof gutter.

çotira (..ˊ.) بوتيره trigger fish, *zool.*, Balistes capriscus.

çotra (ˊ.) بوتره It flat wooden bottle. **— balığı** *same as* **çotira**.

çotukᵏᵘ بوتوك *prov.* 1. tree stump. 2. stock of a vine.

çotur بوتور flat (nose); flat-nosed.

çotura (.ˊ..) بوتوره *same as* **çotra**.

çödür=ᵘʳ, **çöğ=**ᵍᵉʳ **çöğdür=**ᵘʳ چودرمك چودور مك *prov.* 1. to spurt, jet. 2. to squirt urine in a jet.

çöğel=ⁱʳ چوكلك *prov.* to raise the head, to rise up.

çöğen 1 چوكان *same as* **çöven 1**.

çöğen 2 چوكان *prov.*, *var.* of **çevgân**.

çöğündür چوكندر *var.* of **çükündür**.

çöğür 1 چوكور *archaic* popular instrument similar to **kopuz** played with a plectrum. **— şairi** bard, minstrel.

çöğür 2 چوكور *prov.* thorny bush.

çöğürcü چوكورجى *same as* **çöğür şairi**.

çök=ᵉʳ **1** چوكمك 1. to collapse, fall down in a heap, fall in; to give way. 2. to cave in, to become sunk and hollow; to be doubled up (back); to be prostrated by age or fatigue, to break down. 3. to kneel down (camel); to crouch down; *colloq.* to sit down. 4. to settle, to be precipitated. 5. to fall, to envelop (darkness); to descend upon one (sorrow).

çök 2 چوك *archaic, only in* **— et=**, **— ur=** to kneel down.

çökekᵏⁱ چوكك *prov.* hollow ground, depression, bog.

çökel=ⁱʳ *neol.*, *chem.* to settle, to precipitate.

çökelekᵏⁱ چوكلك 1. *prov.* cheese made of skimmed milk, curds. 2. *neol.*, *chem.* precipitate.

çökelikᵏⁱ چوكلك *same as* **çökelek**¹.

çökelt=ⁱʳ /ı/ *neol.*, *chem.* to precipitate.

çökelti *neol.*, *chem.* precipitate.

çöker=, **çökert=** چوكرمك چوكرتمك /ı/ 1. to make kneel down (camel). 2. to cause to collapse. **—il=** *pass.*

çökkün چوككن broken down, collapsed; *psych.* depressed. **—lük** breakdown; depression.

çökme چوكمه 1. *verbal n.* of **çök= 1**. 2. broken down, fallen in. 3. *geog.* subsidence (of earth).

çöktür=ᵘʳ چوكدرمك /ı/ *caus.* of **çök= 1**.

çökükᵏᵘ چوكك 1. collapsed, fallen in. 2. caved in, sunk, sunk in; prostrated by age. **— saha** *geog.* depression.

çöküntü چوكنتى 1. *verbal n.* of **çök= 1**¹. 2. debris, wreckage. 3. sediment, deposit. 4. *geol.* subsidence (of earth).

çöküş 1 چوكش *verbal n.* of **çök= 1**.

çöküş= 2 چوكشمك to kneel down together; *colloq.* to sit down together.

çöl چول 1. desert; arid, barren. 2. waste land, wilderness. **— fareşi**, **— sıçanı** jerboa, *zool.*, Dipus. **—lük** desert tract of country; mixed with desert tracts (land); arid, barren.

çölmekᵏⁱ چولمك *archaic*, *same as* **çömlek**. **— kaynat=** to plot mischief.

çölpe, çölpekᵏⁱ چولپه *same as* **çolpa**.

çömçe چومچه *prov.* ladle. **— gelin** large, crud

doll carried about in a ceremony as a rain charm.

çömel=ir بو ملمك to squat down on one's heels. **—t=** /ı/ caus.

çömez بو مز 1. one who follows blindly in his master's ways. 2. *hist.* impoverished theology student who served his teacher in return for board and tuition.

çömlekği بو ملك earthen pot. **— hesabı** calculation of an illiterate person; crude scheme. **— kebabı** meat roasted in a pipkin.

çömlekçi بو ملكجى potter. **— çamuru, — kili** potter's clay. **—lik** pottery, potter's occupation.

çönge بو نكَ *archaic* 1. blunt, dull. 2. weak (eyesight).

çöngel=ir بو نكَلمك *archaic* 1. to become blunt. 2. to weaken (eyesight). **—t=** /ı/ caus.

çöngü بو نكو *same as* **çönge**.

çöppü بو پ 1. chip, straw. 2. stalk, peduncle of a fruit. 3. sweepings, litter, rubbish, trash, garbage. **— arabası** garbage truck. **— atlama=** not to miss the slightest thing, to be very attentive. **— atlamaz** meticulous, punctilious. **— çatan** person who acts as go-between in a marriage, matchmaker. **— çatan böyle çatmış** This marriage was so destined. **—ten çelebi** very thin person. **— çıkaran** *obs.* garbage man. **—ten direk** unsound undertaking. **— dubası** boat for garbage disposal. **— gibi** very thin, skinny. **— kalem** kind of stonecutter's chisel. **— kapan** *archaic* ember. **— kebabı** pieces of meat and eggplant grilled on spits of wood and then cooked lightly. **— kutusu, — tenekesi** garbage can.

çöpçini (. — —) بو پچينى [**çubu çinî**] *drug.* chinaroot, root of *Smilax china*.

çöpçü بو پچى 1. scavenger, sweeper. 2. garbage collector. **—lük** scavengery.

çöpleme بو پلو bear's foot, *bot., Helleborus foetidus*.

çöplen=ir بو پلنمك 1. to pick up scraps for a meal. 2. to get bits of profit out of other people's affairs.

çöplü بو پلو 1. that has a stalk. 2. mixed with sticks and straws. 3. littered; full of sweepings. **—ce bülbül** *same as* **bokluca bülbül**.

çöplükğü بو پلك 1. rubbish heap, place for dumping garbage. 2. filthy place. **— horozu** pleasure addict lacking in good taste.

çöpür بو پور *prov.* 1. combings, cardings. 2. mohair, hair of the Angora goat.

çörçil بو رچيل E *mil.* soldier's boot.

çörçöppü, **çör**rü, **çöp**pü بو ر بو پ 1. sticks and straws, twigs. 2. sweepings, rubbish. 3. odds and ends. **çörden çöpten** flimsy, of unsound structure, jerry-built.

çördekği بو ردك *naut.* 1. tye of a topsail yard. 2. halyard.

çördükğü بو ردك 1. hyssop, *bot., Hyssopus officinalis*. 2. *prov.* wild pear, *bot., Pirus communis, var. achras*.

çörekği بو رك 1. round cake or loaf, commonly sweetened; kind of bun. 2. *prov.* bread. 3. ring-shaped bread. 4. disc (of sun, moon). 5. coil, spiral; *naut.* coil of a rope end, grommet. **— otu** *same as* **çöreotu**. **—çi** maker or seller of cakes or buns. **—hane** *obs.* royal bakery. **—len=** to coil oneself up (serpent). **—lik** dough or flour fit for making cakes.

çöreotunu بو ره اوت [**çörek otu**] black cumin; seeds of *Nigella sativa*.

çörten بو رتن *same as* **çortan**.

çöv=er بو مك *var. of* **çöğ=**.

çöven 1 بو ون soapwort, *bot., Saponaria officinalis*. **— otu** soapwort.

çöven 2 بو ون *prov., var. of* **çevgân**.

çöz=er 1 بو زمك /ı/ 1. to untie, unfasten, unbutton; *naut.* to unbend (sail). 2. to unravel, disentangle, undo (knot); to solve (problem). 3. *text.* to arrange on the loom (warp). 4. *prov.* to expel prematurely (animal fetus). **— bakalım!** *slang* off with you!

çöz 2 بو ز *prov., butchery* suet covering the intestines.

çözdür=ür بو زدرمك /ı; a/ *caus. of* **çöz=**.

çözgü بو زكو 1. *text.* warp. 2. striped cotton sheeting. **—le=** /ı/ to furnish with the warp (loom). **—len=** *pass.* **—let=** /ı, a/ *caus. of* **çözgüle=**. **—lü** furnished with a warp.

çözgün بو زكون 1. untied, unfastened. 2. disentangled. 3. soft (snow).

çözme بو زمه 1. *verbal n. of* **çöz=** 1. 2. kind of cotton sheeting.

çözü بو زو *same as* **çözgü**¹.

çözükğü بو زك 1. loose, untied. 2. unraveled. 2. *math.* solved (problem).

çözül=ür بو زلمك 1. *pass. of* **çöz=** 1. 2. *slang* to run away. 3. *mil.* to withdraw from contact with the enemy, to disengage one's troops. **—me** *verbal n.* **—üş** *verbal n. of* **çözül=**; *literature* denouement.

çözüm *neol., math.* solution. **—le=** /ı/ *phil., gram., chem.* to analyze. **—leme** analysis. **—sel** analytic.

çözüntü بو زنتى 1. ravellings. 2. broken fragments of ice floating on a river. 3. débacle, disintegration, breaking up.

çözüş=ür بو زشمك *sc.* to dissociate.

-çu چى *cf.* **-cı**.

çub (—) بو ب P *lrnd.* 1. rod, stick; cudgel; staff. 2. corporal punishment with a stick, castigation, flogging. 3. wood, timber, log; piece of wood; firewood. **—u çinî** *same as*

çuban

çöpçini. —u edeb a beating. —u Hüdai divine chastisement. —u yasa bastinado stick.
çuban (——) چوبان P lrnd., same as çoban. —î (———) P 1. quality of a shepherd. 2. shepherd's pay. 3. clownishness, boorishness.
çubbend (—.) چوب بند P lrnd. scaffold, trellis, frame of wood.
çubdar (——) چوبدار P hist. usher bearing a staff.
çubdest (—.) چوبدست P lrnd. walking stick; wand.
çube (—.) چوبه P lrnd. stick; piece of wood.
çubek[ki] (—.) چوبك P lrnd. little stick.
çubhor (——) چوبخوار P lrnd. 1. timber worm. 2. beaten, drubbed.
çubi, çubin (——) چوبى چوبين P lrnd. wooden.
çubkâri (————) چوبكارى P lrnd. a beating.
çubpare (——.) چوب پاره P lrnd. piece of wood.
çubuk[gu] چبوق مسن چبوك 1. rod, bar; wand, staff; the smaller drumstick; text. shaft stave (on a loom). 2. long tobacco pipe; pipe stem. 3. young branch, shoot, twig; forestry sapling. 4. stripe or rib in a tissue. 5. naut. upper mast. 6. obs. measure of length (about 14 feet). — aşısı hort. grafting. — demiri iron in rods or bars. — iç= to smoke a long pipe. — takımı mouthpiece of a tobacco pipe. —u tellendir=, —unu tüttür= 1. to smoke one's pipe. 2. to take it easy.
çubukçu چبوقچى 1. maker or seller of pipe stems. 2. hist. servant in charge of smoking pipes.
çubukla=[r] چبوقلامق /ı/ to beat (carpet). —n= pass. —t= /ı, a/ caus.
çubuklu چبوقلى 1. furnished with rods. 2. striped, ribbed (cloth). 3. w. cap., name of a district on the Bosphorus.
çubukluk[gu] چبوقلق closet where pipes are kept.
çubyasak[ki] (—.—) چوب ياساق P lrnd. staff of office, mace.
çuçur چوچور same as çırçır balığı. — azmanı kind of seafish.
çuğd چغد P poet. owl.
çuğundur چغندر P same as çükündür.
çuha چوخا [Persian chukha] broadcloth. Ç— adası the isle of Cerigo, Kythera. — arşını obs. measure of about 28 inches, for measuring cloth, etc. — çiçeği cowslip, bot., Primula veris. — çiçeğigiller bot., Primulaceae. — kapla= /a/ to face with broadcloth.
çuhacı چوخاجى draper. — arşını obs. cloth-seller's ell (about 28 inches).
çuhadar (..—) چوخادار P hist. lackey, footman. — zerdesi dish of sweet gourd and sugar.

-çuk[gu] چوك cf. -cık.
çuka 1 چوقا چوغا var. of çuha.
çuka 2 چوقا چوغا Sl sterlet (caviar sturgeon), zool., Acipenser ruthenus.
çukundur چقندر P var. of çuğundur.
çukur چقور چغور چوقور 1. pit, hollow, cavity, dent, hole, depression; depressed, hollowed out, hollow, sunk. 2. sink, cesspool. 3. dimple. 4. colloq. grave. 5. slang buttocks. 6. geog. fosse, ravine, glen. — aç= to dig a pit. Ç—Bostan name of an ancient reservoir near the mosque of Sultan Selim in Istanbul. —a düş= to fall into trouble. —unu kaz= /ın/ to plot (against). Ç—ova the littoral plain of Cilicia. —ca somewhat depressed. —cuk small cavity; dimple. —lan=, —laş= to become hollowed, depressed. —laştır=, —lat= /ı/ caus. —lu furnished with pits, hollows; dented. —luk 1. hollowness, depression. 2. place abounding in pits. 3. geog. depression.
çul چول [cül] 1. haircloth. 2. horsecloth. 3. rough, badly made clothes. — çuval haircloth sack. — çürüt= to sit a long time (visitor). —u düz= to become well-dressed. —u tut= to grow rich. — tutmaz spendthrift, shiftless.
çulâh (.—) چولاه var. of culâh.
çulâki چولاكى Gk kind of coarse cloth.
çulha چولها [Persian julaha] 1. weaver. 2. prov. loom. — çukuru pit under the loom. — kuşu penduline titmouse, zool., Remiz pendulinus. — tarağı weaver's reed, sley. — tezgâhı hand loom. —lık business of a weaver.
çulla=[r] چوللامق 1. /ı/ to furnish with a horsecloth, to cover with a horsecloth. 2. /ı/ to cook in a closely covered vessel. 3. naut. to break right over a ship (waves).
çullama چوللاما 1. food cooked in a closely covered vessel. 2. dish of meat covered with dough.
çullan=[ır] چوللانمق 1. pass. of çulla=. 2. /üstüne/ to fall (upon), to hurl oneself (upon).
çullu چوللو covered with a horsecloth.
çulluk[gu] چوللوق woodcock, zool., Scolopax rusticola.
çulpa چولپا same as çolpa.
Çulpan چولپان same as Çolpan 1.
çulsuz چولسز 1. having no horsecloth. 2. colloq. untidily and poorly dressed.
çultar, çultarı چولتار چولتارى prov. quilted cloth placed over a saddle for protection.
çumça چومچه same as çömçe.
çun (—) چون P lrnd. 1. how? 2. like, as. 3. when. 4. as, since, because. — ü çira the why and wherefore, a questioning.
çunin (—) چونين P var. of çünin.

çurcal چورجال obs. lanyard to the hammer of a cannon.
çurçar چورچار same as **çarçur**.
çurçur چورچور same as **çırçır balığı**. **—cu gambler's slang** gambler who has little money.
çuval چوال [Persian **juwal**] 1. sack. 2. slang fat (person). **— bezi** sacking, hessian. **— gibi** 1. rough (material). 2. loose, untidy (clothes). **bir — inciri berbat et=** to undo everything by a gaffe, to upset the applecart.
çuvaldız چوالدز [Persian **juwal-duz**] 1. packing needle. 2. jeweler's art kind of a flat file. 3. obs. a measure for the thickness of a column of flowing water.
çuvaliye چوالیه small flat wicker basket without handles.
çuvalla=ᵣ چواللە school slang to fail the class.
-çü 1 چو cf. **-cı**.
çü 2 چو P lrnd. 1. as, like. 2. when.
-çükᵍᵘ **1** چوك cf. **-cık**.
çükᵏᵘ **2** چوك penis.
çükündür چوكوندور [**çukundur**] prov. beet.
çükür چوكور Gk prov. hoe combined with axe.
çün 1 چون P var. of **çun**.
-çün 2 چون archaic for, e. g., **benümçün** for me.
çünan (. —) چنان P lrnd. like that, such; so.
çünin (. —) چنین P lrnd. like this, such; so.
çünki چونكە P, **çünkü** 1. because, for. 2. archaic as, since.
çürü=ᵣ چوروملك 1. to rot, decay, putrify, to go bad. 2. to be worn out, to become unsound (material). 3. to be worn out, to be demoralized. 4. to be refuted, to lose its value (argument, claim). 5. to be bruised, discolored.

çürükᵍᵘ چوروك 1. rotten, decayed, putrid; addled, bad (egg); carious (tooth); bad, of inferior value (money); irrecoverable (investment). 2. unsound (material); frail, of delicate health; unreliable, not dependable (person); untenable, worthless (claim). 3. bruised, discolored; bruise, ecchymosis. 4. mil. rejected as unfit (recruit); disabled (soldier). **— çarık** rotten. **—e çık=** mil. to be invalided out (soldier); to be discarded as useless. **—e çıkar=** /ı/ mil. to invalid out (soldier); to discard as useless. **— gaz** auto. exhaust. **— iple kuyuya inilmez** proverb (lit. One cannot descend into a well with a rotten rope.) You can't undertake anything with a person who is not reliable. **— istim** steam engine waste steam. **— merdivenle dama çıkılmaz** proverb (lit. One cannot climb to the roof on a bad ladder.) Don't undertake anything with an unreliable person. **— su** naut. dead water. **— tahtaya bas=** to fall into a trap. **— vesikası** mil. certificate of disability. **—çül** neol., biol. saprophyte.
çürüklükᵍᵘ چوروكلك 1. abstr. n. of **çürük**. 2. pit for leaving garbage, etc., to rot. 3. common grave, charnel pit.
çürüt=ᵘʳ چوروتمك /ı/ caus. of **çürü=**. **—ül=** pass.
çüst چست P lrnd. 1. quick, fleet, numble. 2. tight, firm, strong. 3. tight-fitting, narrow. 4. fit, suitable. 5. elegant, comely. **—î** (. —) P abstr. n.
çüş چوش 1. whoa! (used for ordering a donkey to stop). 2. vulg. Stop it! Look out! What a boor! (exclamation used when some one behaves boorishly).
çüt چت Kurd prov., same as **çift**.
çütre (.̇.) چتره var. of **çotira**.

D

d, D *the fifth letter of the alphabet.*
da 1, de, *after unvoiced consonants* **ta 1, te** دَ (written as a separate word, but always following another word; it is **da, ta** after syllable with back vowel, **de, te** after syllable with front vowel, the stress being upon the preceding syllable.) 1. *too, also, e. g.,* **Ben de geleceğim** I shall come, too. **O da bizi gördü** He, too, saw us. **Orada kitap ta var, kâğıt ta** There are books there, and also paper; you will find there both books and paper. 2. *conjunctive particle, sometimes equalling* and, *e. g.,* **Sen de kim oluyorsun?** And besides, who are you? **Sen reçeteyi getir de ilâcı ben bulurum** You just bring me the prescription and I'll find the medicine. **Durdu durdu da bugün tam işim varken geldi** He left it till now and then he had to go and come today when I was so busy. **Konuşur da konuşur** He talks and talks. **Çocuk «Şeker de şeker!» diye tutturdu** The child kept asking for candy. **«Yapmam da yapmam!» diyor** He insists he won't do it. He keeps saying, «I won't do it.»
-da 2, -de, *after unvoiced consonants* **-ta, -te** دَ *locative,* 1. *in, at, on, upon, e. g.,* **masada** on the table; **çekmecede** in the drawer; **Ağustosta** in August; **saat dörtte** at four o'clock; **teyzemde** at my aunt's; **yemekte** at table. 2. *within, in, e. g.,* **dört saatte gidiyor** He goes there in four hours; it takes him four hours to go there; **bütün senede iki kere** twice within the whole year. 3. *in the possession of, with, e. g.,* **anahtar bende** I have the key. 4. *having, of, e. g.,* **seksen yaşında bir adam** a man of eighty; **dört metre boyunda bir pencere** a window four meters long. 5. *in fractions, denominator, e. g.,* **dörtte biri** one fourth.

—da= 3, —de= دامه د ه ملك *following onomatopoeics ending in* -r *or* -l (but with reduction of the geminate forms to singles) to produce the sound of, *as in* **çatırda=, gürülde=.**
da[ai] **4** (—) دا A *lrnd.* disease, illness. **—i merak** hypochondria.
[*For other compounds, see* **dauzzaby — daüzzi'b.**]
daavi (.——) دعاوى A *lrnd., pl. of* **dâva.** **— nâzırı** *obs.* minister of justice.
daban طبا *prov., var. of* **taban 1.**
dabbe (—.) دابّ A *lrnd.* beast; saddle beast.
Dabbetülarz (—...) دابّة الارض A *Isl. rel.,* miraculous creature expected to appear in the last days of the world.
dablin دابلين E *naut.* doubling, lining of extra plates.
dâd 1 (—) داد P *lrnd.* 1. cry for redress, complaint; cry; wail, lamentation. 2. justice, equity; Justice! right, portion, share. 3. redress; retribution, vengeance. 4. a giving; sale, delivery. **—ını al=** to obtain one's right; to take one's revenge; /ın/ to avenge. **— bir feryat iki** I am utterly in despair. I can't stand it any more. **— ü feryad** lamentation, cries; a wailing. **—a gel=** 1. to show pity, to soften. 2. to come for justice.
dad 2 داد P *lrnd.* 1. a giving; sale, delivery. 2. gift; liberality, munificence. **—ı Hak, —ı Hüda** a gift of God; talent. **— ü sitad, — ü sited** a selling and buying, trade, commerce.
-dad 3 (—) داد P *lrnd.* given by, *as in* **hudadad.**
dad 4 ضاض A *name of the letter* ض (15th letter of the Arabic, 18th letter of the

Ottoman Turkish alphabet, in Turkish pronounced as z, less commonly d. In chronograms, it has the numerical value of 800). **—ı mu'ceme** the dotted ض .

dada 1 دادا P *lrnd.* child's nurse.
dada 2 دادا *prov.* infant, baby.
dada= ³ دادامق *prov.* to scatter bird bait.
dadaferid (— —.—) داد آفريد , **dadaferin** (— —.—) داد آفرين P *lrnd.* creator of justice, God.
dadan=" دادانمق /a/ 1. to acquire a taste (for), to overdo (a thing one grows fond of). 2. to get into the habit of visiting too frequently. **—dır=** /ı, a/ *caus.*
dadar (— —) دادار P *var. of* **dadaver.**
dadaş داداش *prov.* 1. brother. 2. comrade, pal. 3. young man, youth.
dadaver (— —.) داد آور P *lrnd.* 1. distributor of justice, just ruler. 2. God.
dadbahş (—.) دادبخش P *lrnd.* 1. dispenser of justice. 2. God.
daddih (—.) داددە P *lrnd.* 1. giver of gifts. 2. giver of justice; God.
-dade (—.) داده P *lrnd.* 1. who has given, *as in* **dildade.** 2. given, delivered, paid, *as in* **karardade, rızadade.**
dader (—.) دادر P *lrnd.* brother. **—ane** (—.—.) P brotherly.
dadferma (—.—) دادفرما P *lrnd.* 1. administering justice; just ruler. 2. God.
dadgâh (— —) دادگاه P *lrnd.* seat of judgment; court of justice.
dadger (—.) دادگر P *lrnd.* 1. doer of justice; just ruler. 2. God.
dadgir (— —) دادگير P *lrnd.* 1. just; just ruler. 2. God. 3. avenger.
dadgüster (—..) دادگستر P *lrnd.* 1. just. 2. God. **—i** (—..—) P justice.
dadhah (— —) دادخواه P *lrnd.* suitor for justice, complainant. **—î** (— — — —) P *abstr. n.*
dadı دادى [*Persian* **dadu**] child's nurse. **—lık** occupation of a nurse. **—lık et=** /a/ to look after (a child).
dadres (—.) دادرس P *lrnd.* 1. who comes to one's help. 2. just. 3. who revenges.
dafıkⁱ (—.) دافق A 1. *anat.* ejaculatory. 2. *lrnd.* that bursts forth in a flood (water, tears).
dafıka (—..) دافقة A *anat., canalis ejaculatorius.*
dafiⁱⁱ (—.) دافع A 1. /ı/ *lrnd.* that repels, wards off. 2. God. **—i humma** *med.* antipyretic. **—i taaffün** *med.* antiseptic. **—i tayyare** *mil.* antiaircraft.
dafia (—..) دافعة A *lrnd., phys.* repulsion.
dafire (.—.) ضفيرة *anat.* plexus.
dagalⁱⁱ دغل A *lrnd.* suspicious act, trick. **—baz** (..—) P trickster.

dağ 1 طاغ باغ 1. mountain. 2. heap, mound. **—larca** *archaic* in heaps. **— adamı** 1. mountaineer, highlander. 2. boor; rough fellow. **— alası** kind of trout, *zool., Salmo alpinus.* **—lar anası** a great big woman. **— ardıcı** sandarach tree, *bot., Callitris quadrivalvis.* **— ayısı** boorish fellow, rough fellow. **— babaları** bramble, *zool., Fringilla montifringilla.* **—da bağın var, yüreğinde dağın var** Wealth does not mean being free from care and worries. **— başı** 1. mountain top, summit. 2. wild, remote place. **— bataryası** *mil.* mountain battery. **— boğazı** gorge, mountain defile. **— burnu** projecting shoulder of a mountain. **—da büyümüş** uncouth, boorish. **— çayı** *same as* **ada çayı. —a çık=** 1. to climb a mountain. 2. to take to the hills. **— çileği** wild fruit resembling strawberry. **— dağa kavuşmaz, insan insana kavuşur** *proverb* (*lit.* Mountains don't meet: men do.) Separated friends may meet some day. **— dağ üstüne olur, ev ev üstüne olmaz** *proverb* (*lit.* Mountain can stand upon mountain, but house cannot stand upon house.) Two families cannot live in one house. **—lar dayanmaz** /a/ Even mountains could not stand (it), *i. e.* It is beyond human endurance. **— deviren** like a bull, clumsy, boorish. **— doğura doğura bir fare doğurmuş** The mountain labored and gave birth to a mouse. **—lara düş=** to become completely destitute. **— elması** crab apple. **— eriği** wild prune; sloe, bullace. **— eteği** foothills, skirts of a mountain. **— geçidi** mountain pass. **—dan gelmiş** uncouth, boorish. **—dan gelip bağdakini koğ=** to be a newcomer and to treat the old-timers rudely. **—ların gelin ablası, —ların gelin anası** 1. bear. 2. bear-like woman. **— gibi** 1. huge, tall and strong. 2. in enormous quantities. **— ispinozu** bramble, *bot., Fringilla montifringilla.* **— kadar, —lar kadar** enormous. **—a kaldır=** /ı/ to kidnap, to elope with, run away with, to seize and take to the mountains (person). **— keçisi** chamois, *zool., Rupicapra.* **— kedisi** wildcat; chaus. **— kerevizi** mountain parsley, *bot., Petroselinum oreoselinum.* **— kılavuzu** mountain guide. **— kıt'ası** *mil.* Alpine troops. **— kitlesi** *geol.* massif. **— kolu** *geog.* branch chain of mountains. **— kulanı** wild ass. **—daki kuşun kırkı bir akçeye** It is easy to brag about things unachieved. **— kuyruksallıyanı** gray wagtail, *zool., Motacilla cinerea.* **— mersini** whortleberry, bilberry, *bot., Vaccinium Myrtillus.* **—ların misafir aldığı mevsim** summer. **— muharebesi** *mil.* mountain battle. **— parçası gibi** great big (person). **— payesi** lateral branch of a mountain. **— savaşı** *mil.* mountain warfare. **— serçesi** tree sparrow, *zool., Passer* *montanus*. **— sıçanı** marmot. **— sırtı** mountain ridge. **— silsilesi** mountain range. **— sporu** mountain sport, Alpinism. **—ların şenliği** 1. bear. 2. boorish fellow. **— taş** 1. all around, as far as the eye can see. 2. in great quantities. **—lara taşlara** God preserve us from it! (expression used when a calamity is mentioned.) **— tavuğu** hazel grouse, hazel hen, *zool.*, *Tetrastes bonasia*. **— tepesi** mountain peak. **— topu** mountain gun. **— topçusu** mountain artillery. **— yalımı** steep mountain slope. **— yürümezse abdal yürür** *proverb* If the mountain does not go to the Prophet, the Prophet must go to the mountain.

dağ 2 داغ [dağ 3] 1. brand made with a hot iron; *med.* cautery, cauterization. 2. branding iron. **— bas=**, **— vur=**, **— yak=** /a/ to impress a brand (upon), to brand.

dağ 3 (—) داغ P *lrnd*. 1. scar; inward grief, pang. 2. mark, trace; spot, stain; freckle; tattooed mark. 3. blemish; *poetry* tautology. 4. *poetry*, name of the poet mentioned at the end of his poem. **— ber dağ** *poet.* wound upon wound. **— ber dil** *poet.* with a wound in the heart. **—ı cigersuz** *poet.* heart-rending pain. **— dağ** *lrnd.* marked with scars. **—ı derun**, **—ı dil** *poet.* grief, sorrow, pang. **—ı elem** *poet.* pain. **—ı gulâmî** *lrnd.* brand on a slave. **—ı hasret**, **—ı hicran** *poet.* great yearning. **—ı ışk** *poet.* pain of love. **—ı nihan** *poet.* secret pain. **—ı zinde** *poet.* open wound, bleeding wound.

dağar 1 طغار *prov.* 1. earthen vessel with wide top. 2. earthen brazier. 3. *obs.* large measure of grain.

dağar 2 طاغار، طغار *prov.* leather skin or cloth bag slung over the shoulder, large pouch.

dağarcıkᵏⁱ طاغارجمه، طغارجمه pouch carried over the shoulder by shepherds, hunters, etc. **—ındakini çıkar=** to come out with one's plan. **—ı yüklü** he has great knowledge.

dağcı داغجى mountaineer, mountain climber, Alpinist. **—lık** mountaineering, Alpinism.

dağdağa دغدغه P tumult, turmoil, confusion; trouble. **—lı** tumultuous, noisy, confused; troublesome.

dağdağan طاغدغان، داغدغان *prov.* water elder, *bot.*, *Viburnum Opulus*.

dağdar (——) داغدار P 1. *poet.* having an open wound; suffering. 2. *lrnd.* branded; spotted, stained; blemished.

-dağı دغى *archaic*, same as **-daki**.

dağıl=ᵘʳ داغلى، طاغلى 1. scatter; to disperse, separate. 2. to spread; to be disseminated (rumors). 3. to fall to pieces; to be dissolved. 4. to become untidy. 5. *pass.* of **dağıt=**. **—ın!** *mil.* Dismissed! **—ım** 1. *psych.* dissociation. 2. *chem.* dispersion.

dağılış داغيليش distribution.

dağılma داغيلمه *verbal n.* of **dağıl=**; distribution, dispersal, strewing, scattering.

dağın=ᵘʳ طاغنى *archaic*, same as **dağıl=**.

dağınıkᵍⁱ طاغنيه 1. scattered, dispersed. 2. untidy; disorganized. **— nizam** *mil.* extended order, dispersed formation. **—lık** untidiness; dispersion.

Dağıstan داغستان، طاغستان *geog.* Dagestan, Daghestan near the Caspian Sea. **—lı** of or from the Daghestan country.

dağıt=ᵘʳ طاغتمى /ı/ 1. to scatter, disperse. 2. to distribute, serve out. 3. to disorder (room). 4. to break to pieces. 5. to dissolve (business firm, parliament). 6. *print.* to distribute (type). **—ıl=** *pass.* **—ım**, **—ış**, **—ma** *verbal n.* of **dağıt=**. **—tır=** /ı, a/ *caus.* of **dağıt=**.

dağî (.—) داغى [dağ 1, —î] 1. Or. *mus.* a vocal musical work having the character of **uzun hava**. 2. *lrnd.* highlander; boor. **— bayati** *obs.* a **makam**.

dağla=ʳ داغلمى /ı/ 1. to brand. 2. to burn (sun, wind). 3. *med.* to cauterize. 4. to wound (feelings).

dağlağı داغلغى *prov.* 1. branding iron. 2. cauterizing iron. **— düğmesi** knot of a cauterizing iron.

dağlan=ᵘʳ داغلنمى *pass.* of **dağla=**.

dağlat=ᵘʳ داغلتمى /ı, a/ *caus.* of **dağla=**.

dağlı 1 داغلى 1. mountaineer, highlander. 2. *card games* king.

dağlı 2 داغلى 1. branded. 2. scarred. 3. sore, hurt to the quick.

dağlıçᶜⁱ داغليچه kind of stump-tailed sheep.

dağlıkᵍⁱ طاغلوه، داغلوه mountainous, hilly (country).

dağukᵍᵘ طاغوره، داغوره *archaic* scattered, dishevelled.

dağzen (—.) داغزن P *poet.* wounding, hurting deeply.

dah ده giddap! (command to a beast to go forward). **— et=** /ı/ to turn (one) out like a beast.

daha داها، دها 1. more, further; *arith.* and, plus, *e. g.*, **üç, iki daha** three plus two; /dan/ *comparative*, than, *e. g.*, **bizden daha küçük** smaller than us. 2. still, *e. g.*, **Vakit daha erken** It is still early; *with negative verb*, not yet. 3. only, *e. g.*, **Daha bu sabah gördüm** I saw him only this morning. **— neler!** Whatever next! How absurd! **—sı var** That is not all.

dahalet (.—.) دخالت [based on Arabic] same as **dehalet**.

dahame, dahamet (. —.) ضخامت ضخام A biol. hypertrophy.

dahaya (. — —) ضحايا A lrnd., pl. of dahiye 2.

dahdah ده ، ده ، دا ، ده child's language giddap (horse, donkey).

Dahhak[ki] ضحّاك P name of a legendary king of ancient Persia, notorious for his cruelty.

dahi 1 دخی A 1. also, too, even, e. g., O dahi söyledi He said it, too; even he said it. 2. archaic, same as daha; and; /dan/ other (than).

dâhi 2 (— —) داهی A 1. genius, man of genius. 2. lrnd. very cunning person.

Dâhi 3 (— —) داحی A God (who spreads out the heaven and the earth).

dahik[ki] (— .) ضاحك A lrnd. who laughs, laughing.

dahil 1 (— .) داخل A 1. the interior, inside. 2. including, e. g., **vergi dahil** including tax. 3. lrnd. that enters. 4. hist., name of a degree in the hierarchy of schools of canonical law. —**i esnan** same as **dahili kur'a**. — **et**= /ı/ to insert; to include. —**i kur'a** mil. of military age. —**i memleket** inside the country. — **ol**= /a/ 1. to be inserted, included (in). 2. to go (in), to enter. —**i rahm** med. intrauterine.

dahîl 2 (. —) دخيل A lrnd. 1. person admitted to intimacy; person seeking protection with another person. 2. the true character, thoughts, intention (of a man); the inner, true state (of a case). 3. pros. single consonant standing between a long a and the principal letter of a rhyme.

dahile (— ..) داخله A lrnd. 1. the inside, interior; heart, mind, thoughts. 2. gram. prefix.

dahîlek (. — .) دخيلك A ancient Arabian law formula I take refuge in Thee.

dahilen (— ..) داخلاً A lrnd inwardly, internally. — **mersum** geom. inscribed.

dahilî (— . —) داخلی A inner, internal. — **harb** civil war. — **hastalıklar** path. internal diseases. — **hizmet talimatnamesi** mil. internal regulations. — **istihale** geol. endomorphism. — **işler** home affairs, domestic affairs. — **karakol** mil. military police in a military school, etc. — **merkez** biol. hypocentrum. — **müşahede** psych. introspection. — **nizamname** internal regulations; pol. standing orders. — **piyasa** econ. home market. — **ticaret** econ. home trade. — **zaviye** geom. internal angle.

dahiliye (— . — .) داخليه A 1. adm. home affairs; ministry of home affairs. 2. path. internal diseases; ward for internal diseases. 3. department of buildings and grounds. 4. lrnd., fem. of **dahilî**. — **müsteşarı** adm. undersecretary of state for home affairs. — **mütehassısı** internal diseases specialist. — **nâzırı** minister of the interior, secretary of state for the home department. — **nezareti** ministry of the interior, ministry of home affairs, Home Office. — **subayı** mil. officer employed in the administration of a military school, hospital, etc. — **şefi** supervisor of buildings and grounds. — **vekâleti** ministry of the interior. — **vekili** minister of the interior. — **zabiti** same as **dahiliye subayı**.

dahim (. —) ضخيم A lrnd. large, corpulent.

dahiyane (— . — .) داهيانه P of genius (act); in the manner of a genius.

dahiye 1 (— . .) داهيه A lrnd. 1. calamity. 2. same as **dâhi 2**.

dahiye 2 (. — .) ضحيّة A lrnd. sacrificial beast.

dahl[li] دخل A 1. connection, relationship. 2. lrnd. revenue, income, profit; tradesman's cash box. 3. lrnd. a blaming; blemish, stain, vice. — **et**= /a/ to interfere (with); to blame. — **ü harc** income and expenditure. —**i ol**= /da/ to be connected (with); to have to do (with).

dahla=[r] داحلمك /ı/ to start up (a beast).

dahm ضخم A lrnd. huge, corpulent.

dahme 1 دخمه F lrnd. 1. vault, tomb, mausoleum. 2. charnel-house of the Parsees.

dahme 2 دخمه [dahme 1] lrnd. Roman candle; firecracker.

dahmeküşa (. . . —) دخمكنا P gravedigger.

dahra ضخره [dehre] prov. billhook.

dahve ضحوه A lrnd. early forenoon. —**i kübra** the later part of early forenoon. —**i suğra** the earlier part of early forenoon.

dai 1 (— —) داعی A lrnd. 1. one who prays. 2. phil. motive, cause. 3. one who calls; one who calls to religion, missionary. —**leri**, —**niz** your well-wisher, i. e. I, he (formerly especially used among members of the schools of canonical law).

dai 2 (. —) دعی A 1. can. law adopted son; claimant for recognition as a son. 2. lrnd. invited guest; invited.

daim (— .) دائم A 1. enduring, lasting, permanent. 2. always.

daima (— . —) دائماً A always, continually.

daimî (— . —) دائمی [based on **daim**] 1. constant, permanent, perpetual. 2. pop. constantly. — **encümen** standing committee. — **kadro** permanent staff. — **ordu** standing army. —**lik** permanency.

daimiyet (— . — .) دائميت [based on **daimî**] lrnd. permanency.

daimül'eyyam, daimülkarar, daimülkıyam (— . . . —) دائم الايام دائم القرار دائم القيام A lrnd. for all times; perpetual, permanent.

dain (—.) دائن A *law* creditor.
dair 1 (—.) دائر [**dair 2**] /a/ about, concerning, relating to, *e. g.*, **buna dair** about this.
dair 2 (—.) دائر A *lrnd.* revolving; circulating. **— ve sair** travelling.
daire (—..) دائره A 1. circle; circumference. 2. department; office; district; apartment, flat; range, limit. 3. *mus.* tambourine. 4. *lrnd., fem. of* **dair 2**. **—i aide** *adm.* the department concerned. **—i arz** *geog.* parallel. **—i azime** *naut.* great circle. **—i bahriye** *obs.* office of the navy. **—i belediye** 1. ward of a city. 2. police jurisdiction. **— bıçkısı** circular saw. **— çevresi** *geom.* circumference, periphery of a circle. **—i evvelüssümut** *astr.* prime vertical. **—i faside** *log.* vicious circle. **—i husuf** *astr.* ecliptic. **—i imkânda ol=** to be possible. **—i inkılâp** *astr.* tropic. **—i intihabiye** *pol.* electoral district, constituency. **—i irtifa** *astr.* circle of altitude, almacantar. **— kavsi** *geom.* arc of a circle. **—i kaza** *law* jurisdiction. **— kesmesi** *geom.* sector of a circle. **—i meyl** *astr.* circle of declination. **— muhiti** *geom.* circumference. **—i muhitiye** *bot.* pericycle. **—i muhtelife** *pros.* class of Arabian meters, containing **tavil, medid, basît**. **—i mutelife** *pros.* a class of meters. **—i müçtelibe** *pros.* class of Arabian meters, containing **remel, recez, hezec**. **— müdürü** office director. **—i müştebihe, —i müttefika** *pros.* classes of Arabian meters. **—i nısfünnehar** *astr.* meridian. **— parçası** *geom.* segment of a circle. **—i resmiye** *adm.* government office. **—i saa** *astr.* hour circle. **—i sadaret** *hist.* office of the grand vizier. **—i sagire** *naut.* small circle. **—i semt, —i semtiye** *astr.* vertical circle, azimuth circle. **—i suğra** same as **dairei sagire**. **—i tecyib** *astr.* circle from which an astrolabe is divided by sines. **—i tenvir** *astr.* circle of illumination. **—i tul** *geog.* meridian. **—i uzma** same as **dairei azime**. **—ci** 1. maker or seller of tambourines. 2. tambourine-player. **—li nişangâh** *mil.* ring sight.
dairen (—'..) دائراً A *lrnd.* 1. in a circle. 2. /ı/ around, surrounding. **— madar** all round.
dairesal (—...) *neol., geom.* circular.
dairetülbüruc (—....—), **dairetüşşems** دائرة البروج دائرة الشمس A *astr.* ecliptic.
dairevi (—..—) دائروى [based on **daire**] circular.
dairezen (—...) دائرزن P *lrnd.* tambourine player.
daiyan (—.—) داعیان P *lrnd., pl. of* **dai 1**.
daiye (—..) داعیه A *lrnd.* motive, intention; desire.
dak^kı 1 دقّ A *lrnd.* 1. a beating, tapping,

knocking. 2. pulverization. **—ı bab et=** to knock on the door. **— et=** /ı/ 1. to beat, tap. 2. to pound.
-dak 2 دك *prov.* unto, as far as, until, *e. g.*, **burayadak** as far as here.
dakaik^kı (.—.) دقائق A *pl. of* **dakika 1, 2**.
dakı 1 دقى *archaic, same as* **dahi 1**.
-dakı^y1 **2** دكى *archaic, same as* **-daki**.
-daki^ni, **-deki**^ni, after unvoiced consonants **-taki**^ni, **-teki**^ni ده كى that is in, on, with, etc., *e. g.*, **odadaki masa** the table in the room; **evdekini getir** Bring the one that is in the house. **sizdeki ayna** the mirror that you have.
dakik^kı 1 (.—) دقيق A 1. exact, particular, painstaking, thorough. 2. *lrnd.* subtle, fine, minute; thin, slender.
dakik^kı 2 (.—) دقيق A *lrnd.* flour, meal.
dakika 1 (.—.) دقيقه A 1. minute. 2. *geom.* minute. **—sında** instantly, at once. **—sı dakikasına** punctually, exactly on time. **—sı dakikasına uymaz** very changeable; temperamental.
dakika 2 (.—.) دقيقه A *lrnd.* subtle point. **—bîn** (.—.—), **—dân** (.—.—), **—senc** (.—..), **—şinas** (.—..—) P well-informed.
dakikî (.——) دقيقى [based on **dakik 2**] *bot.* farinaceous.
dakiklik^ği (.—.) دقيقلق abstr. n. of **dakik 1**.
dakka *var. of* **dakika 1**.
daktilo ('...) داقتيلو F 1. typist. 2. a typing. 3. typewriter. **— et=** /ı/ to type. **— ile yazılmış** typewritten.
daktilografi داقتيلوغرافى F typewriting.
daktiloskopi داقتيلوسقوپى F dactyloscopy.
dak tut=^ar دق طوتمق /a/ *archaic* to blame, to criticize; to object (to).
dal 1 دال طال 1. branch, bough, twig. 2. branch, ramification, subdivision. 3. *prov.* horn. **—ları bastı kiraz** cherries weighing down the branches (cry of street-seller of cherries). **— boy** thinly clad. **— budak sal=** 1. to shoot out branches. 2. to grow, spread. **—dan dala atla=** to be unsteady, to jump from one thing to the other. **—dan dala kon=** to be fickle, inconstant. **bir —da durma=** to be fickle, capricious, unsteady. **— gibi** slender; graceful; lightly dressed. **— sal=, — sür=** to push out branches.
dal=^ar 2 دالمق طالمق 1. /a/ to dive, to plunge (into); to be plunged (in thought, occupation). 2. /a/ to enter suddenly, to plunge in. 3. to become absorbed, distracted; to fall asleep, to drop off, to doze; to become unconscious (sick person). 4. *Or. wrestling* suddenly to bend down and catch the lower part of the opponent's body.
dal- 3 دال طال 1. bare, naked, *as in*

dalkılıç. 2. without turban (headgear), *as in* **dalfes.**

dal⁴ دال طال *prov.* back; shoulder. **—ına bas=** /ın/ to irritate. **—ına bin=** /ıń/ to put pressure (on), to pester.

dalᴵⁱ 5 دال طال [*Arabic* **—**] *Arabic script, name of the letter* د (This letter is the 8th letter of the Arabic, 10th letter of the Ottoman Turkish alphabets, pronounced as **d.** In chronograms, it has the numerical value of 4).

dalᴵⁱ 6 (—) دال A *lrnd., same as* **dal 5. —i ebced, —i mühmele** the letter د.

dâlᴵᴵᴵ 7 (—) دال A /a/ *lrnd.* that points out, indicates; indicative (of).

dâlᴵᴵᴵ 8 (—) ضال A *lrnd.* astray, lost, erring, perverted.

dala=ʳ طالاموه دالاموه /ı/ 1. to bite (dog, bear). 2. to sting, prick; to burn, cauterize; to scratch; to chafe.

dalabı=ʳ طالابییه دالابیس *prov.* to flatter.

dalak§ⁱ 1 دالاق طالاق 1. spleen, milt. 2. *prov.* honeycomb with its honey. 3. *prov.* certain position of the knucklebone in the game. **— iltihabı** *path.* splenitis. **— ol=** to have inflammation of the spleen. **— otu** germander, *bot., Teucrium.* **— şişmesi** *path.* enlargement of the spleen.

dalakᵏⁱ 2 دلق A *lrnd.* dervish's cloak. **—puş** (..—) P 1. clad in shreds. 2. dervish.

dalâlᴵⁱ (.—) ضلال A *lrnd., same as* **dalâlet.**

dalâletᵗⁱ (.—.) ضلالت A *rel.* error, state of being astray, corruption. **—e düş=** to go astray, to be corrupted.

dalan (— —) دالان P *lrnd.* vestibule, hall.

dalapᵇⁱ دالاب heat (in female animals). **—a gel=** to be in heat (mare).

dalaş 1 طالاش dogfight, fight.

dalaş=ʳ 2 طالاشمق to fight savagely (dogs); to quarrel violently. **—kan** *archaic* quarrelsome, pugnacious. **—tır=** /ı/ *caus. of* **dalaş=.**

dalavera, dalavere (..ʹ.) دالاوره *colloq.* 1. trick, manoeuvre, intrigue. 2. thingumy, what's-its-name. **— çevir=** to plot, intrigue. **—ci** intriguer, trickster.

dalda دالده *prov.* 1. shadow. 2. sheltered place; shelter.

daldır=ʳ طالدیرمق 1. /ı/ *caus. of* **dal=** 2. 2. /ı/ *hort.* to layer (a shoot of plant). 3. *colloq.* to become distracted.

daldırma طالدیرمه 1. *verbal n.* 2. *hort.* layered (branch); layer.

daldız دالدیز *prov.* 1. sharp cutting tool used for hollowing out wood. 2. beekeeper's tool for extracting honeycombs from the hive.

dalfes دالفس fez without a turban.

dalga طالغه دالغه 1. wave, ripple; undulation, corrugation; watering (on silk); wave (of hair); *elec.* wave. 2. *slang* distraction. 3. *slang* trick; hidden purpose; thing, contraption; affair. 4. *slang* dope. **—yı başa al=** 1. *naut.* to breast the waves. 2. to face (dangers). **— boyu** *elec.* wave length. **— dalga** in waves; in light and dark (colors). **—ya düş=** *slang* 1. to fall into a trap. 2. to be absent-minded. **— geç=** *slang* 1. to woolgather. 2. /a/ to make fun (of) in a covert way. **—ya gel=** *slang* to happen in a moment of distraction. **—ya getir=** *slang* to get done in a moment of another person's distraction. **— gibi gel=** to come continuously and in torrents. **— kalk=** for the waves to rise. **— kıran** breakwater. **—sı ol=** /la/ *slang* to have a love affair with. **— uzunluğu** *elec.* wave length.

dalgacı دالغجی *colloq.* 1. woolgatherer. 2. one who gets out of doing work, laggard. 3. trickster. **—cı Mahmut** *same as* **dalgacı.**

dalgalan=ʳ دالغالنمق 1. to undulate, to wave. 2. to become rough (sea). 3. to become corrugated (metal sheet); to become watered (silk); to become uneven (dye). **—dır=** /ı/ *caus.*

dalgalı دالغالی 1. rough (sea); undulated. 2. corrugated (metal). 3. watered (silk). **— akım** *elec.* alternating current. **— arazi** undulating ground. **— borçlar** *fin.* floating debt. **— sigorta** *com.* floating insurance policy.

dalgıçᶜⁱ طالغیج دالغیج 1. diver. 2. grebe, *zool., Columbus.* **—lık** occupation of a diver.

dalgın دالغین طالغین 1. absent-minded, plunged in thought. 2. unconscious (sick person), comatose. **— uyku** deep sleep. **—lık** 1. absent-mindedness. 2. lethargy.

dalı دالی *same as* **dal 4. —dan gel=** to come from behind.

dalız [**dehliz**] *neol., anat.* vestibule.

daliye (— — .) دالیة [*based on* **dal 5**] *anat.* deltoid.

dalkavuk§ᵘ طالقاوون دالقاوون 1. toady, flatterer, buffoon. 2. parasite, sycophant. **—luk** sycophancy; flattery.

dalkılıç دالقیلیج طالقیلیج 1. with naked sword. 2. *archaic* swordsman; swashbuckler.

dallan=ʳ دالانمق 1. to shoot out branches, to branch out. 2. to ramify and become complicated. **—ıp budaklan=** *same as* **dallan=.** **—dır=** /ı/ *caus. of* **dallan=.**

dalle (—.) دالّ A *math.* determinant.

dallı دالّی 1. branched, ramified. 2. ornamented with branches, etc. (printed cotton). **— budaklı** ramified; intricate.

dalma دالما طالما *verbal n. of* **dal=** 2.

Dalmaçya دالماجیه *geog.* Dalmatia.

daltaban طالطبان بالطبان 1. destitute, tramp, wretched. 2. *archaic* barefoot.

daltaşak طال طاشاق *vulg.* stark naked.

daluyku بال اویقر *archaic* deep sleep.

dalya 1 طاليا (..) F dahlia, *bot., Dahlia.*

dalya 2 طاليا (..) It *com.* completed (used when, in counting, the standard number, usually 10 or 100, is reached).

dalyan 1 طاليان باليان Gk enclosure of nets fixed on poles used for catching fish; weir for fishing. — **nöbetçisi** lookout on the observation pole of a fishing enclosure. — **tarlası** place where a fishing enclosure is set up.

dalyan 2 طاليان *archaic, var. of* **İtalyan**; *now only in* — **gibi** well-built, athletic. — **tüfeği** *obs.* kind of musket.

dalyancı طاليانجى fisherman at a **dalyan** station.

dalyarak[ⁿ] طال یاراق 1. *vulg.* stark naked. 2. *archaic* with drawn weapon. 3. silly fool; blockhead.

dam 1 طام دام 1. roof. 2. roofed shed; outhouse; stable. 3. *prov.* house. 4. *slang* prison, jail. — **aktar=** to repair the roof by overhauling the tiles. — **ı al=** to roof a building. — **altı** *arch.* loft, attic, garret. — **a at=** /ı/ *slang* to put in prison. — **dan çardağa atla=** to jump from one subject to another. — **deresi** *arch.* roof valley. — **dan düşer gibi** in an abrupt and out-of-place manner (question, remark). — **dan düşen halden bilir** He who falls from the roof knows how it feels. One can only sympathize if one had had the same experience. — **kapağı** *arch.* hinged skylight. — **koruğu** wallpepper, creeping jack, *bot., Sedum acre.* — **koruğugiller** *bot., Crassulaceae.* — **üstünde saksağan, vur beline kazmayı!** *joc.* What nonsense!

dam 2 دام F 1. lady partner (in dance). 2. *games* queen.

dâm 3 (—) دام P *poet.* snare, trap. — **a düş=** to fall into a trap.

dâm 4 (—) دام P *lrnd.* non-rapacious beast.

dam=ar **5** طاميى *archaic* to drip.

dama (..) دام با ما It 1. game of checkers. 2. *checkers* king; King! — **çık=** *checkers* to become a king (man). — **de=** 1. to give up, accept defeat. 2. to come to an end, to be exhausted. 3. *checkers* to cry «King!». — **oyunu** the game of checkers. — **pulu** *checkers* man. — **tahtası** checkerboard. — **taşı** *checkers* man. — **taşı gibi oynat=** /ı/ to move constantly from place to place, to shift around.

damacana (...) داماجانا [damicana] demijohn.

damacı داماجى checkers player.

damad (——) داماد P *same as* **damat**.

damak[ⁿ] طاماق دامان 1. palate. 2. barb of a fishhook. 3. projecting catch in the bolt of a lock. 4. projection in the middle of a horse's bit. 5. inflammation of the palate. — **eteği** *anat.* soft palate. — **ını kaldır=** to press the palate up with a finger (done to a frightened person in order to prevent bad consequences). — **kemeri** *anat.* palatine vault. — **kemiği** *anat.* palatine bone, palatine. — **ı kuru=** to feel very thirsty. — **sessizi** *ling.* palatal. — **lı** 1. having a palate. 2. barbed. — **lı diş** set of false teeth furnished with a palate. — **lı iğne** barbed fishhook. — **sıl** *neol., ling.* palatal.

damalı (...) داما لى checkered.

daman (——) دامان P *same as* **damen**.

damar دامار طامار 1. blood-vessel, vein; *anat.* vessel, vas. 2. vein, streak (of a mineral); *mining* vein, lode. 3. vein (in a leaf). 4. obstinacy. 5. vein of temperament, streak. — **ına bas=** /ın/ to irritate. — **ı bozuk** of a low breed, vile, mean, low. — **ını bul=** /ın/ to find the weak spot (in a person). — **ı çatlamış** shameless, brazen-faced. — **ına çek=** /ın/ to take (after one's father, etc.). — **daraltan** *physiol.* vasoconstrictor. — **ı depren=**, — **ı depreş=** to become obstinate and difficult. — **ına dokun=** /ın/ to irritate. — **genişleten** *physiol.* vasodilator. — **gevşemesi** *path.* aneurysm. — **ını gıcıkla=** /ın/ to flatter the pride (of a person). — **ına gir=** /ın/ to find the weak spot (in a person). — **ına işle=** /ın/ to get deep (into a person, habit, etc.). — **ı kırık** shameless. — **ı kurusun!** /ı/ Damn his bad habit! — **sertleşmesi** *path.* arteriosclerosis. — **tabaka** *anat.* chorioid coat. — **ı tut=** to become obstinate; to become furious. — **lı** 1. vascular. 2. veined. 3. have swollen veins. 4. obstinate. — **sız** 1. having no veins. 2. shameless.

damasko (..) داماسقو It 1. damask. 2. imitation Damascus steel.

damat[ⁿ¹] (——) داماد [damad] 1. son-in-law; bridegroom. 2. man married into a royal family. — **vekili** proxy who executes a contract of marriage for the bridegroom.

dame (——) دام A *lrnd.* May it be lasting, in formulas like: — **iclâlühü** May his honor last. — **ikbalühü** *Ott. hist.* May his prosperity last (formula used in official documents when a vizier or similar high official is mentioned). — **izzühü** May his glory be lasting. — **kadrühü** *Ott. hist.* May his rank last (formula used in official documents when a judge is mentioned). — **mecdühü** May his grandeur endure. — **mülkühü** May his dominion be lasting. — **sirruhu** May he sleep in peace. — **uluvvuhu** *Ott. hist.* May his exaltation last (formula used in official documents when a Sheikhul-Islam or other high dignitary is mentioned).

damen (—.) دامن P *poet.* 1. skirt (of a garment). 2. outskirts (of a place). 3. *calligraphy* tail (of a letter). **—i afv** forgiveness. **—i alude** unchasteness. **— dermiyan et=** to tuck up the garment, to prepare (for work). **—i huşk** chastenesss, purity. **—bus** (—.—) P who kisses the skirt (of a superior). **—busî** (—.——) P kissing of the skirt. **—çin** (—.—) P who tucks up his skirts. **—efşan** (—..—) P who abandons. **—gir** (—.—) P who takes hold of the skirt of a person (as supplicant or as an opponent). **—keş** (—..) P 1. /dan/ who pulls his skirts away (from). 2. who trails his skirts proudly.

damet (—.) دامت A *lrnd.* May it be lasting, *in formulas like*: **— maalîhu** May his excellency be permanent. **— saadetühü** May his happiness be lasting.

damga دامغا طمغا تمغا 1. instrument for stamping, stamp, rubber-stamp. 2. mark, stamp; hallmark; brand; stigma. **— bas=** /a/ to stamp. **— kanunu** stamp act. **— pulu** revenue stamp. **— resmi** stamp duty. **— vur=** /a/ to stamp. **—cı** clerk who affixes stamps. **—la=** /ı/ 1. to mark with a stamp. 2. to cancel (stamps). 3. to brand. 4. to stigmatize. **—lan=** *pass.* **—lat=** *caus. of* **damgala=**.

damgalı دامغه لی 1. stamped, marked. 2. branded. 3. stigmatized. **— eşek** *contemptuously* known to everybody. **— kâğıt** stamped paper.

damgazede دامغازده marked with a stamp.

damıt= /ı/ *neol., phys.* to distill. **—ık** distilled. **—ma** distillation.

damızlıkᵃ¹ داميزلق داميزلو 1. kept for propagating (seed, etc.). 2. ferment, yeast. 3. beast kept for breeding.

damia (—..) دامعه A *can. law* superficial head wound.

damicana (...'.) داميجانه It *obs., same as* **damacana**.

damiğa (—..) دامغه A *can. law* head wound that cleaves through the skull into the brain.

damir (—.) دامر A *lrnd.* perishing, perished, lost.

damiye (—..) دامیه A *can. law* head wound in which blood collects.

damla 1 داملا طاملا طامله 1. drop; *med.* drops. 2. very small quantity, bit. 3. medicine dropper. 4. paralytic stroke. 5. gout. **bir — çocuk** very small child, a mite of a child. **— damla** drop by drop, little by little. **— gel=**, **— in=** /a/ to have a stroke. **— sakızı** superior kind of mastic. **— taş** drop-shaped precious stone. **— yakut** fine kind of ruby.

damla=ʳ **2** داملامق طاملامق 1. to drip. 2. to come in suddenly. **—ya damlaya göl olur** *proverb* Little by little one saves a lot.

damlalı طاملالو paralytic.

damlalıkᵃ¹ طاملالوق 1. medicine dropper. 2. eavestrough. 3. *arch.* dripstone, drip molding.

damlat=ʳ طاملاتمق *caus. of* **damla= 2**.

damping دامپينغ E *com.* sale; dumping.

damzır=ʳ طامزرمق طرزمق /ı/ *prov.* to let drip, to drop; to give little by little. **—t=** /ı/ *same as* **damzır=**.

-dan 1, -den, *after unvoiced consonants* **-tan, -ten** دن 1. from; out of, of; because of, due to; since. *e. g.*, **İstanbul'dan** from Istanbul; **yünden yapılmış** made of wool; **Yağmurdan gecikti** He was late because of the rain; **yazdan** since summer. 2. through, by, by way of, *e. g.*, **Kapıdan girdi** He came in through the door. 3. than, *e. g.*, **bundan büyük** larger than this.

dan 2 دان sharp sound, ding. **— dan** bang, bang (sounds of shooting).

-dan 3 (—) دان P receptacle of, case of, *as in* **gülâbdan, sürmedan**.

-dan 4 (—) دان P who knows, *as in* **nüktedan**.

dan 5 (—) دان P *poet., var. of* **dane**.

dan 6 طاك *prov.* 1. astonishment, amazement. 2. amazing. **—a gel=** to be amazed.

dan 7 طاك *prov., var. of* **tan 1**.

dan=ᵃʳ **8** طانمق /a/ *archaic* to be amazed (at). **—a kal=** to be amazed.

dan=ᵃʳ **9** طانمق /a/ *archaic* to consult.

dana 1 طنا طانه دانه دانا weaned calf. **— ayağı** 1. calf's-foot, *bot., Arum maculatum*. 2. dumb-cane, *bot., Dieffenbachia seguine*. **— baş** stupid, doltish. **— burnu** 1. mole cricket, *zool., Gryllotalpa*. 2. calf's snout, lesser snapdragon, *bot., Antirrhinum Orontium*. 3. *path.* whitlow. **— eti** veal. **—lar gibi bağır=** to baw. **— kıran otu** kind of hellebore. **—nın kuyruğu kopacak** The crucial moment will come; the worst will happen.

dana 2 (——) دانا P *lrnd.* wise, learned; omniscient. **—dil** (——.) P having wisdom. **—yan** (———) P the learned, the wise. **—yî** (———) P wisdom, learning.

-dan beri, -den beri, *after unvoiced consonants* **-tan beri, -ten beri** دن بری 1. since, *e. g.*, **geçen seneden beri** since last year. 2. for, *e. g.*, **Onu beş günden beri görmedim** I have not seen him for five days.

dandini (.'..) داندینی 1. expression used when dandling a baby. 2. in a mess, in complete disorder, untidy. **— bebek** *colloq.* childish, flippant person. **— beyim, hoppala paşam** expression used about a person who is fond of being pampered and flattered.

dan dun دان دون bang, bang (sounds of shooting.). **—a git=** *same as* **tantuna git=**.

dane (—.) دانه P 1. *artillery* shell, cannon ball; bullet. 2. *prov.*, *same as* **tane 1**. 3. grain (gold weight). 4. *poet.* bait for catching birds. 5. *lrnd.* one's daily bread, food.

danecin (—.—) دانه چین 1. who picks grains. 2. who gets small profits out of something.

danende (—..) داننده P *lrnd.* knowing, wise; omniscient (God).

dang (—) دانگ P *obs.* small weight.

dangalak[ā] دانغالاوه طانغالاوه loutish person, boor, blockhead; stupid.

dangıl dungul دانغل دونغل boorish and talking with a broad provincial accent.

[/da/ see /ta/]

danış=[ır] دانشمو طانشمو 1. /ı, a/ to consult (about), to ask advice (of, about). 2. /ı/ to confer (about), to discuss.

danışık[ā] دانشیق *archaic* 1. consultation; conversation. 2. a pretending to agree with one another for some ulterior motive. — **et=** /ı/ *archaic* to confer, discuss. **—çı** *archaic* counselor. **—lı döğüş** 1. sham fight. 2. put-up job.

danışma دانشمه information; inquiry. — **bürosu** information office.

danışman 1 *neol.* counselor, advisor.

danışman 2 طانشمان [**danişmend**] *archaic* learned man; learned.

danıştay *neol., adm.* council of state.

danıştır=[ır] دانشتیرمو طانشتیرمو /ı, a/ *caus.* of **danış=**.

Danimarka (...'.) دانیمارقه *geog.* Denmark. **—lı** Dane.

daniska (.'.) دانیسقه *colloq.* the finest, the best (of), *e. g.*, **O, bu işin daniskasını bilir** He knows all the ins and outs.

daniş (—.) دانش P *lrnd.* 1. knowledge, learning. 2. science. — **ve bîniş** learning and knowledge. **—ger** (—..) P learned, wise.

danişmend (—..) دانشمند 1. *archaic* learned man, learned in the law. 2. *obs., can. law* assistant functionary in a court.

danişver (—..) دانشور P *lrnd.* learned, wise.

Daniye دانیه L *archaic* Denmark.

dank دانق *only in* **kafasına dank de=**, **kafasına dank et=** to dawn (upon one), finally to be brought home (to one).

danla=[r] طا گلامو /ı/ *archaic* to be amazed (at).

-danlık[ā], *sometimes also* **-denlik**[ā] دانلق [**-dan 3**] receptacle of, *as in* **çaydanlık, iğnedenlik, yağdanlık.**

dans دانس F dance, *esp.* European dancing. — **et=** to dance.

dansa=[r] دانسامو /ı/ *prov.* to blame.

-dan sonra, -den sonra, *after unvoiced consonants* **-tan sonra, -ten sonra** دن صوكره 1. after (an event), *e. g.*, **bundan sonra** after this. 2. *archaic* after (so much time), *e. g.*, **üç günden sonra** after three days.

dansöz دانسوز F woman dancer.

dantel, dantelâ (.'.) دانتل دانتلا F lace, lacework. — **ağacı** lace tree, *bot.*, *Lagetta lintearia*.

dapa دپا *archaic* toward, *e. g.*, **tamu dapa** towards Hell.

dapdaracık[ā] داپدراجق very narrow.

dar 1 دار طار 1. narrow; tight. 2. scant, scanty. 3. difficulty, straits; difficult; with difficulty, only just, barely. **— açı** *neol., geom.* acute angle. **—a boğ=** /ı/ 1. to take advantage of the difficult situation (of someone). 2. to bring pressure (on), to rush. **—da bulun=** to be in financial difficulty. **—a dar, — darına, —ı darına** very narrowly, barely, only just. **— dirlik** *archaic* scanty living, poverty. **—a düş=** to fall upon hard times. **— fikirli** narrow-minded. **—a gel=** 1. to come to a pinch. 2. to be done in a hurry, to occur in a rushed and inopportune moment. **— gelirli** of small income, in the lower income bracket. **—a getir=** /ı/ to put pressure (upon), to rush, hurry. **— hat** *rail.* narrow-gauge line. **— kafalı** narrow-minded. **—da kal=** to be in need. **— kurtul=** to have a narrow escape. **— sesli** *ling.* close vowel. **— tıkız** fat, bloated.

dar 2 (—) دار A *lrnd.* 1. dwelling place; region, country; world. 2. house, mansion, habitation, abode. **—ı adl** *can. law* the Islamic world. **—ı ahiret** the other world. **—ı ahzan** *same as* **beytül'ahzan**. **—ı beka** the other world. **—ı cihan** this world. **— u diyar** house and home, one's country. **—ı dünya** this world. **—ı eman** *can. law* non-Islamic country under protection of an Islamic ruler. **—ı fena, —ı gurur, —ı hüzn, —ı ibtilâ** this world. **—ı naim** Paradise. **—ı ridde** *can. law* apostatic country. **—ı şeş der** this world. **—ı şurayı askerî** *Ott. hist.* Council of the Ministry of War. **—ı ukba** the world to come. **—ı zimmet** *same as* **darı eman**.

[*For other compounds see* **darülaceze, — Darüttıbaatil' âmire**.]

-dar 3 (—) دار P *lrnd.* that has, possesses, holds, *as in* **defterdar, hazinedar, maldar**.

dar 4 (—) دار P *lrnd.* 1. gallows, gibbet. 2. beam, rafter; pole. 3. wood; timber. 4. tree. 5. *myst. orders* place in the center of the hall of ceremonies in a convent of Bektashi dervishes, where the penitant member confesses his sins.

dara 1 (..) طارا دارا Gk *com.* tare, allowance of weight. **—sını al=** /ın/ to deduct the tare (of). **—sı alınmış** good for little. **—ya at=**, **—ya çıkar=** /ı/ to disregard, to take no notice (of). **—sını çıkar=** /ın/ to deduct the tare (of). **— taşı** stone put into a balance to counterpoise a receptacle, before it is filled.

Dara 2 (— —) دارا P 1. *hist.* Darius. 2. *lrnd.* king, sovereign; God.

daraat¹¹ (. — .) ضراعت A *lrnd.* meekness, humility, submissiveness. **— et=** to act with submission. **—name** (. — . — .) P humble letter.

daraba درابه A *prov.* 1. board fence. 2. board cover for a shop front.

daraban (. . —) ضربان A *physiol.* pulsation; palpitation, throbbing. **—ı dehr** *lrnd.* the strokes of time.

darabat (. . —) ضربات *lrnd.*, *pl.* of **darbe**.

daracıkᵏ¹ (.´. .) طارجیق small and narrow.

darağacıᵐ¹ دارآغاجى [dar 4] 1. gallows. 2. *naut.* shear legs, shears.

daral=ˡʳ طارلمه دارلمه 1. to become narrow, tight; to shrink. 2. to become scanty; to become restricted, to be reduced. **—ma** *verbal n.*; *path.* stenosis. **—t=** /ı/ *caus.* of **daral=**. **—tı** *verbal n.* of **daral=**, *anat.* isthmus. **—tılı** *ling.* constrictive.

darat (— —) دارات P *lrnd.* pomp, magnificence.

Daray (— —) داراى P *var.* of **Dara 2**.

darayi (— — —) داراى P 1. *obs.* kind of silk stuff. 2. *lrnd.* sovereignty; *w. cap.* Godhead.

darb ضرب A *lrnd.* 1. a hitting, striking, beating; blow. 2. force, violence, severity. 3. a coining money. 4. *same as* **zarb**. 5. *pros.* last foot of the second hemistich of a distich. 6. *mus.* stroke (in beating time). 7. *log.* deduction. 8. sort, kind, species. **—ı dest** force of arms, strength of hand. **—ı feth** *Or. mus.* the largest rhythmic pattern as a single unit which beats 88 times with signatures of 88/4, 88/2. **— lülesi** large tap placed somewhere along a main pipe to control the flow of water. **—ı mesel***. **—ı Türkî** *Or. mus.* a fast rhythmic pattern of 18 beats used in religious vocal compositions with signature of 18/4. **—ı unûk et=** /ı/ *lrnd.* to behead.

darbaz (— —) داربازْ P *lrnd.* rope-dancer.

darbe ضربه A blow, stroke. **—i hükûmet** *pol.* coup d'état.

darbeci (. . —) ضربجى A *lrnd.* false or grossly alloyed (coin).

darbele=ʳ ضربلك /ı/ 1. to injure. 2. to sabotage. 3. to deal blows (to).

darben (.´.) ضرباً A *lrnd.* by blows; by force.

darbet=ᵈᵉʳ ضربايتمك 1. /ı/ to hit, strike. 2. /ı/ to cut off; to cut open (vein, tumor). 3. /ı/ to coin (money). 4. /ı/ *same as* **zarbet=**. 5. to pulsate, throb, palpitate.

darbeyn (. —) ضربين *Or. mus.* a combination of two rhythmic patterns of the same speed class.

darbhane (. — .) ضربخانه P *same as* **darphane**. **D—i Âmire** *Ott. hist.* the Imperial Mint. **— emini** *Ott. hist.* Master of the Mint.

darbımesel ضرب مثل P proverb.

darbız داربيز A *prov.* moist, heavy (soil).

darbuka (. .´.) داربوقه [*Arabic* . — .] *Or. mus.* a rhythmic instrument made in the shape of an earthenware pitcher with a skin covering the bottom. It is used in popular music; more recently this instrument is also made of metal.

darbuy (— —) داربوى P *lrnd.* agalloch, eaglewood.

darbülhicab (. . . —) ضرب الحجاب A 1. *hist.* the command that placed all free adult Muslim females under the veil. 2. *lrnd.* the act of putting a Muslim female under the veil.

darbzen ضربزن P *hist.* kind of gun, falconet.

darçin (— —) دارچين P *lrnd.*, *same as* **tarçın**.

dardağan 1 طار طغان طار طغان دارغان *archaic* scattered. **— sarık** *Ott. hist.* turban with the folds irregularly wound.

dardağan 2 طارطغان دارطغان *prov.*, *same as* **dağdağan**. **— darısı saç=** /a/ to wish evil (on a person).

darende (. — . .) دارنده P *lrnd.* possessor; bearer, one who holds.

dareyn (— .) داريْن A *lrnd.* this world and the next.

dargın دارغين طارغين طارغون دارغون cross, angry. **—lık** anger, irritability.

darı دارى طارى 1. millet. 2. *prov.* maize, corn. **—sı başınıza!** May your turn come next! (for a happy event).

darık=ʳ دارِيقمق *prov.* to be in difficulty, in straits.

darıl=¹ʳ طارلمق دارلمق /a/ 1. to become cross, angry (with), to be offended. 2. to scold. **—gan** easily hurt. **—ış** to become cross with one another. **—maca yok!** No offense! **—t=** /ı/ to offend, to make cross.

darib (. —) ضارب A *lrnd.* that beats, strikes, hits. **—i müştereki asgar** *math.* least common multiple.

darifülfül (— . . .) دار فلفل [Persian **darfilfil**] long pepper, *bot.*, *Piper longus*.

darir (. —) ضرير *same as* **zarir**.

darlan=ʳ, **darlaş=**ʳ دارلنمه طارلشمه طارلنمه دارلشمه 1. to become narrow. 2. to become tight. 3. to become scant, limited.

darlaştır=ʳ, **darlat=**ʳ دارلشدرمق دارلتمق /ı/ to make narrow.

darlıgan=ᵗʳ دار یغنا نمی /dan/ archaic to be depressed (by); to be distressed.

darlıkᵍⁱ طارلوه دارلو 1. abstr. n. of **dar 1**. 2. poverty, need, trouble.

darmadağan, darmadağın طار مر طغان 1. in utter confusion. 2. all over the place. **— ol=** to be scattered, to be put into confusion.

darpᵇⁱ ضرب var. of **darb**.

darphane ضربخانه P mint.

darrûmi (— — —) دار رومی P drug. tormentil, bot., Tormentilla officinalis.

darsini (— — —) دار صینی P drug. cassia bark, bark of Cinnamomum Cassia.

darşiş'an (— — — —) دار شیشعان P the aromatic bark of Myrica Sapida.

daru (— —) دارو P lrnd. drug, medicine; remedy.

daruberd (— — .) دار برده P poet. 1. power, strength; pomp. 2. battle.

daruddarb (— . .) دار الضرب A lrnd. mint.

darufürüş (— — . —) دارو فروش P lrnd. druggist, chemist.

daruga (— — .) داروغه P hist. mayor, local magistrate.

darugir, darukûb (— — — —) دار و کوب P poet. 1. tumult, conflict. 2. pomp, pride.

darül'aceze (— . . . .) دار العجزه A poorhouse.

darül'akakir (— . . — —) دار العقاقیر A hist. storeroom for drugs in a hospital.

Darülbedayiⁱⁱ (— . . — .) دار البدایع A former name of the City Theater of Istanbul.

Darül'elhan (— . . —) دار الالحان A former name of the Istanbul Conservatory.

darülfena (— . . —) دار الفنا A lrnd. this transitory world.

darülfünun (— . . —) دار الفنون A obs. university.

darülhadis (— . . —) دار الحدیث A hist. school where the traditions of Islam are taught.

darülharb (— . .) دار الحرب A can. law the countries outside the dominion of Islam.

darülharekât (— . . . —) دار الحرکات A mil. war operation area.

Darülhilâfe (— . . — .) دار الخلافه A 1. Ott. hist. Istanbul. 2. l.c. city where the seat of the caliph is.

darülhuffaz (— . . —) دار الحفاظ A hist. school where children are taught the Quran by heart.

darülhuld (— . .) دار الخلد A lrnd. Paradise.

darül'islâm (— . . —) دار الاسلام A can. law dominion of Islam.

darülkütüb (— . . .) دار الکتب A archaic library.

darülmuallimat (— . . . . —) دار المعلمات A obs. women teachers' training college.

darülmuallimin (— . . . . —) دار المعلمین A obs. teachers' training college.

darülmülk (— . .) دار الملک A obs. capital (of a kingdom).

darül'ulûm (— . . —) دار العلوم A lrnd., obs. university.

darüssaade (— . . — .) دار السعاده A Ott. hist. the palace of the Sultan. **— ağası** chief black eunuch of the Sultan's palace.

darüssair (— . . —) دار السعیر A lrnd. hell.

darüssaltana (— . . . .) دار السلطنه A 1. Ott. hist. Istanbul. 2. lrnd. capital city.

darüsselâm (— . . —) دار السلام A lrnd. 1. Paradise. 2. w. cap. Bagdad.

Darüşşafaka (— . . . .) دار الشفقه A name of a school for orphans in Istanbul.

darüşşifa (— . . —) دار الشفاء A archaic hospital; lunatic asylum.

darütta'lim (— . . —) دار التعلیم A lrnd. school.

darüttebar (— . . —) دار التبار A lrnd. hell.

Daruttıbaatil'âmire (— . . — . . — .) دار الطباعه العامره A Ott. hist. the Imperial Printing House.

das (—) داس P poet. sickle. **—ı zerrin** new moon. **—u dalûs** (— . . —) 1. rubbish; rabble. 2. foolish; base.

dasitan (— . —) داستان [Persian **dastan**] archaic, same as **destan**. **—î** (— . — —) P literature epical.

dasnikᵍⁱ داسنی slang pimp.

-daş, rarely **-deş,** after unvoiced consonants **-taş 4** داش fellow with regard to..., companion concerning, as in **dindaş, meslektaş, yoldaş**.

daşte (— .) داشته P lrnd. 1. had, that has had. 2. worn out, old.

datura (— — .) دا تو ره P lrnd. thornapple, bot., Datura.

dauzzaby داء الظبی A lrnd. the disease of being faultless.

dauzzarair (— . . — .) داء الضرائر A lrnd. the disease of rival wives, jealousy.

daülcümud (— . . —) داء الجمود A path. catalepsy.

daül'efrenc (— . . . —) داء الافرنج [based on Arabic] lrnd., path. syphilis.

daülfil (— . —) داء الفیل A lrnd., path. elephantiasis.

daülhanazir (— . . — —) داء الخنازیر A lrnd., path. scrofula, king's evil.

daülkelb (— . .) داء الکلب A path. rabies, hydrophobia.

daülkiram (— . . —) داء الکرام A lrnd. the disease of the generous: poverty.

daülküulˡᵘ (— . . —) داء الکحول [based on Arabic] path. alcoholism.

daülmerakᵏⁱ (— . . —) داء المراه A path. 1. hypochondria. 2. melancholia.

daülmülûkᵏᵘ (— . . —) داء الملوک A path. gout.

daüssa'leb (— . . . .) داء الثعلب A path. alopecia, baldness.

daüsseher (— . . .) داء السهر A path. insomnia.

daüssıla (— . . .) داء الصله A homesickness, nostalgia.

daütteşhir (—..—) راء التشهير [based on Arabic] *path.* exhibitionism.

daüzzi'b (—..) راء الذئب A *lrnd.* hunger.

dav 1 داو [dav 2] 1. *games* turn, move. 2. *card games* stake; a doubling one's stake. — **sür=** to double the stake.

dav 2 (—) داو P *lrnd.* 1. a drinking the health of a person; a refilling a glass to drink someone's health. 2. *same as* **dav 1**.

da'va (.—) A, **dâva** (——) دعوى دعوا 1. *law* suit, lawsuit, action. 2. *law* trial. 3. claim; assertion, allegation; complaint, quarrel. 4. proposition, thesis; problem, cause, matter, question; *math.* theorem; *math.* problem. — **aç=** /aleyhine/ to bring suit (against), to file a complaint (against). —**arzuhali** *law* petition. —**ya bak=** *law* to hear a case. — **başı** main argument. —**sında bulun=** /ın/ to claim, *e. g.,* **peygamberlik dâvasında bulun=** to claim to be a prophet. —**nın dinlenmesi** *law* hearing of an action. —**ya ehliyet,** — **ehliyeti** *law* capacity of suing and being sued. — **et=** /ı/ 1. *law* to bring a suit (against). 2. *archaic* to claim, demand. —**yı faslet=** *law* to settle a litigation. —**dan feragat et=** *law* to withdraw an action. —**sını gör=** /ın/ *law* to hear the case (of); to settle the case (of). —**yı hâdise** *law* incidental claim emerging from an action. — **hakkı** *law* right of action. —**yı hallet=** 1. *law* to settle a litigation. 2. to solve a problem. —**sına hizmet et=** /ın/ to serve the cause (of). —**yı ıslâh et=** *law* to amend an action. —**nın ihbarı** *law* third party notice. — **ikame et=** *same as* **dâva aç=**. —**ya müdahale** *law* intervention; joinder. —**nın nakli** *law* transfer of a case for hearing in another court. —**nın reddi** *law* dismissal of action, judgment of nonsuit. —**nın sukutu** *law* discontinuance of action. — **takip et=** *law* to conduct an action in court. — **talebi** *law* bill of complaint. —**ların tefriki** *law* severance of actions. —**sını tut=** /ın/ to take the side (of), to adhere to the cause (of). —**dan vazgeç=** 1. *law* to withdraw an action, to abandon the prosecution of an action. 2. to give up a claim. — **vekili** *law* lawyer, person admitted to practice law and, in smaller towns, to conduct litigation in court.

dâyacı دعواجى *law* plaintiff, claimant; litigant. —**n Bursa'ya gitti** No one is appearing against you; case dismissed. —**n kadı ise yardımcın Allah olsun** If your plaintiff is the judge himself, may God be your helper!

dâvalaş='ır دعوالاشمن to start litigation against each other.

dâvalı دعوالى 1. *law* defendant. 2. *law* in dispute, contested. 3. *law* litigant. 4. preten-tious; *literature* serving a cause, proclaiming an idea.

davar داوار 1. sheep or goat; sheep or goats. 2. *archaic* goods, possessions. —**cık** child's go-cart.

da'vat (.—) دعوات A *lrnd.* 1. prayers, benediction. 2. *pl. of* **davet**.

daver (—.) داور P *lrnd.* 1. ruler, king; magistrate, governor. 2. *w. cap.* God. —**i asman,** —**i azam** God. —**i devran** monarch of the world. —**ane** (—.—.) P like a sovereign; befitting a valiant great person. —**î** (—.—) P 1. dominion; jurisdiction. 2. trial, judgment.

davet (—.) دعوت [Arabic da'wat] 1. invitation; party, feast. 2. call; request; *law* summons; *com.* convocation. — **et=** /ı/ 1. to invite, call, summon; to convoke. 2. to invite, provoke. 3. request. —**e icabet et=** 1. to accept an invitation. 2. to accede to a request. —**çi** person sent to invite. —**iye** (—.—.) 1. written invitation, invitation card. 2. *law* summons, citation; subpoena. 3. *archaic* present given to one who brings an invitation. —**li** invited; invited guest. —**siz** uninvited. —**siz misafir** uninvited guest; unexpected visitor.

davlı داولى *prov.* piece of leather for a pair of sandals.

davlumbaz طاولنباز طاولومباز [tablbaz] 1. paddlebox. 2. chimney hood. 3. *slang* behind, rump. 4. *archaic* kettledrum.

davran='ır طاورانمق داورنمق 1. to bestir oneself, rouse to action. 2. to act, to behave. 3. /a/ to make (for), to reach (for). —**ma!** Don't stir; don't move or I shoot! —**ış** behavior, attitude.

Davud 1 (—.) داود A David.

davud 2 (—.) داود *mus.* tuning to the note A. —**î** (———) bass voice. —**î ney** *mus.* large variety of nay **(ney)**.

davul طاوول داول [tabl] 1. a rhythmic instrument made of a large and rather wide wooden hoop covered on both sides with donkey hide. It is beaten with a stick on one side and on the other (the right side) with a mallet. It is a national instrument usually played with a **zurna**. 2. *slang* behind, rump. — **çal=** 1. to beat the drum. 2. to explain, *e. g.,* **bir saattir davul çalıyorum hâlâ anlıyamadın** I have been talking about it for a whole hour, but you still don't understand. —**u biz çaldık, parsayı başkası topladı.** We did the job and took all the trouble; others benefited from it. —**a dön=** to swell. — **döv=** *same as* — **çal=**. — **gibi** swollen. — **onun omuzunda çomak başkasının elinde** He is only a figurehead; someone else pulls the strings. —**un**

davulbaz

sesi uzaktan hoş gelir *proverb* Distance lends enchantment. **— tozu, minare gölgesi** *joc.* drum powder, minaret shadow (quack medicine). **— zurna ile** with drum and pipe, with pomp, with flourish of trumpet.

davulbaz داول باز |**tablbaz**] *archaic* 1. drummer. 2. small drum hung at the saddle.

davulcu داولجى drummer.

davulga 1 طاولغا *prov.* strawberry tree, *bot.*, *Arbutus Unedo.*

davulga 2 داولغا *archaic* helmet.

daya=" دايامه طايامه 1. /ı/ to prop up, shore up. 2. /ı, a/ to lean (against), to rest (on); to base (on); to hold (against); to draw up (against). 3. /ı, a/ to thrust resolutely, to fling offensively (at, argument). 4. /ı/ to present immediately, *e. g.*, **istifayı dayadı** He presented his resignation without delay (in anger or protest). **—yıp döşe=** /ı/ to furnish completely (house).

dayakᵍ¹ دايا طايه طاياه 1. a beating. 2. prop, support, shore. 3. *archaic* stick. **— arsızı** child hardened by beating and hence impudent. **— at=** /a/ to give a beating. **— cennetten çıkmadır** The stick is from Paradise. Thrashing is the best means of education. **— cezası** corporal punishment. **— kaçkını** one who deserves flogging. **— vur=** /a/ to put up a prop (to), to prop, to shore up. **— ye=** to get a thrashing. **— yoksulu** one who invites a thrashing. **—çı** *naut.* worker whose job is to shore up ships. **—la=** /ı/ to support with props, to shore up. **—lama** *arch.* a shoring. **—lan=** *pass.* of **dayakla=**. **—lat=** /ı, a/ *caus.* of **dayakla=**. **—lık** 1. deserving a beating. 2. suitable as a prop.

dayalı طايالى 1. /a/ leaning against. 2. propped up, shored. **— döşeli** completely furnished (house). **— yan** *mil.* supported flank.

dayama طايامه 1. *verbal n.* of **daya=**. 2. *prov.* sheep pen, fold. 3. *prov.* kind of flat bread. 4. *prov.* advanced money, credit. **— merdiven** ladder.

dayan=" طيانمه طايانمه دايانمه 1. /a/ to lean (against, on); to push, press (against, on); to rest, to be based (on, upon); to be backed (by), to rely (on, upon); to confide, trust (in). 2. to resist, hold out; to endure, last; /a/ to support, tolerate. 3. /a/ to be drawn up (against); to arrive at the door (of), to appear in a threatening way. 4. /a/ to set (about a thing) energetically, *e. g.*, **Böreğe dayandı** He fell upon the pastry. **Şoför gaza dayandı** The driver stepped on the gas. 5. to sit up in bed. **—ak** 1. support, base. 2. *neol., phil.* substratum. **—dır=** /ı/ *caus.* of **dayan=**. **—gaç** 1. prop, support. 2. *obs.* prop with crosspiece, used to lean against while sitting. **—gan** that resists, bears, endures.

dayanıkᵍ¹ دايانق *obs.* resistance, endurance, firmness. **—lı** strong, lasting, enduring, resistant. **—sız** 1. weak, not resistant, not enduring. 2. *chem.* unstable.

dayanılmaz دايانيلماز 1. irresistible. 2. unbearable.

dayanış 1 دايانش *verbal n.* of **dayan=**.

dayanış=" 2 *neol.* to act with solidarity. **—ma** *neol.* solidarity.

dayanma دايانمه *verbal n.* of **dayan=**. **— müddeti** lifetime (of an object). **— noktası** *phys.* point of support.

dayat=" دايا تمه طايا تمه 1. /ı, a/ *caus.* of **daya=**. 2. to insist on getting something done one's own way. **—ıl=** *pass.* **—tır=** /ı, a/ *same as* **dayat=**.

daye (—.) دايه P *archaic* child's nurse. **—gî** (—.—) P *Irnd.* the duties of a child's nurse. **—lik** state and occupation of a **daye**.

dayı 1 دايى طايى 1. maternal uncle (familiarly used in addressing an older gentleman). 2. *colloq.* protector; protection, pull. 3. *slang* policeman. 4. *hist.* dey. **—sı dümende** *colloq.* He has powerful protectors. **—lık** state of being an uncle. **—zade** (..—.) cousin (son or daughter of one's maternal uncle).

dayı 2 دايى *prov.* good, pleasant.

dayin (—.) داين *var.* of **dain**.

daz داز طاز 1. bald-headed; bald. 2. bare (country). **— kafalı** bald-headed.

dazara dazar, dazara dazır دازاره دازر دازاره دازر in great hurry, speedily (to run).

dazla=ʳ دازلامه /ı/ *prov.* to find fault (with).

dazlakᵍ¹ طازلاق دازلاق 1. bald. 2. bare, barren (country). **— kafalı** bald-headed.

dazlıkᵍ¹ طازلق داز لق baldness; bald-headedness.

de=" 1 ديمك /ı, a/ 1. to say (to); to produce the sound (of); to mention (to), to tell; to think, to be of the opinion. 2. to give a name (to), to call. **—me!** You don't say so; oh, don't! **—me=** not to pay attention, not to heed, *e. g.*, **Kar, kış demez denize girer** Whether it snows or is cold, he always goes for a swim in the sea. **—medim mi?** I told you so. **—mek** 1. coming to mean, *e. g.*, **Bu ne demek?** What does this mean? «**Oiseau**», **Fransızcada kuş demektir** «Oiseau» means bird in French. 2. **demek***. **—rken** 1. while saying, while trying to, when intending to. **Dama çıkayım derken düştü** As he was trying to climb to the roof, he fell. 2. *in initial position*, just at that moment; then. **—sene** *colloq.* that means, then, that is to say, i. e. **diye***. **—diği dedik** 1. his word is law, *e. g.*, **Kumandanın dediği dediktir** What the commander says goes. 2. obstinate, insistent; authoritative. **—diği**

dedik, çaldığı düdük, —diği dedik, düdüğü düdük He always gets what he wants; he always wants to have his own way. **—r demez** *prov.* just at that moment, suddenly, so saying. **—yip geçme** don't underrate, don't underestimate, *e. g.*, **nezle deyip geçme** Don't underrate a cold. **—meğe gel=** to come to mean. **—yip gel=** /ı/ *prov.* to come especially to see (someone). **—meğe getir=** to imply, not to say in so many words. **—me gitsin!** wonderful, indescribable, *e. g.*, **Öyle bir düğün oldu ki deme gitsin!** What a grand wedding it was. **—meğe kalma=** no sooner than, as soon as.

de 2 دە *cf.* **da 1.**
-de 3 دە *cf.* **-da 2.**
=de= 4 دە *cf.* **=da=** 3.
de 5 دە دى *prov.* now then!, come on!
|/dea/ see /daa/.|
|/deb/ see /teb/, /dep/ see /tep/.|

de'b داب A *lrnd.* custom, habit, manner.
debagatᵗⁱ (. —.) دباغت |Arabic **dibağa**| 1. a tanning. 2. tanner's trade. **— et=** /ı/ to tan.
debar (. —) دبار A *lrnd.* perdition.
debbabe (. —.) دبابه A *hist.* siege tower.
debbağ (. —) دباغ A *lrnd.*, same as **tabak.**
debbe دبه A *prov.* large copper jug.
debboy دبوى |depo| same as **deppoy.**
debbus (. —) دبوس A *lrnd.* mace.
debdebe دبدبه P pomp and circumstance, display, state. **—li** magnificent.
debe دبه P *prov.* suffering from hernia, ruptured. **— taşak** scrotal hernia; suffering from scrotal hernia.
debelen=ⁱʳ دبهلنمك *prov.* 1. to struggle and kick about while lying on one's back. 2. to struggle desperately.
debelikᵍⁱ دبهلك *prov.* rupture, hernia.
Deberan (..—) دبران A *astr.* Aldebaran.
debir (. —) دبير A *lrnd.* 1. scribe, clerk. 2. chancellor. 3. school master. **—i encüm, —i felek** *astr.* Mercury. **—istan** (. —.—) P 1. school. 2. record office.
debistan (..—) دبستان P *lrnd.* school.
debr دبر A *lrnd.* 1. rear. 2. *rel.* the latter part of the time when a service can be performed.
debrayaj دبرياژ F *auto.* clutch pedal.
Debre دبره Debar, Dibra (in Albania).
debur (. —) دبور A *lrnd.* 1. west wind. 2. *myst.* outburst of passion that leads to sin.
Decace (. —.) دجاجه A 1. *astr.* Cygnus. 2. *l.-c., lrnd.* hen; cock.
Deccalˡⁱ (. —) دجّال A 1. *Isl. rel.* Dadjdjal (a legendary personage in Mohammedan eschatology). 2. *lrnd.* impostor; Antichrist.

ded دد P *poet.* ferocious, wild beast. **— ü dâm** wild beasts.
dede دده 1. grandfather. 2. old man. 3. *myst. orders* sheikh. **—si koruk yemiş, torunun dişi kamaşmış** *proverb* The grandfather ate sour grapes; the grandchild's teeth were set on edge. The sins of the father are visited upon the son and the son's sons. **— kuşağı** *prov.* rainbow. **— külâhı** conoidal dervish hat.
Dedeağaçᶜⁱ دده آغاج *geog.* Alexandroupolis.
dedikodu ديديقودى gossip, tittle-tattle; backbiting. **— et=, — yap=** to gossip about people; to backbite. **—cu** gossiper; scandalmonger. **—lu** 1. gossipy (news). 2. tricky (affair).
dedir=ⁱʳ ديديرمك /ı, a/ *caus. of* **de=** 1.
dedirgin ديديرگين دديرگين same as **tedirgin.**
dedirt=ⁱʳ ديديرتمك /ı, a/ same as **dedir=.**
def 1 دف P same as **tef 1.**
defᶠⁱ **2** دفع A 1. repulsion, a pushing back, driving away. 2. *lrnd.* refutation; *law* defense. **—i belâ** a warding off of evil. **—i belâ kabilinden** in order to ward off an evil, to get rid of a nuisance; insincerely, unwillingly. **— et=*. —i gam** a cheering oneself up. **—i hacet** a relieving nature. **—i meclis et=** *lrnd.* to dismiss an assembly. **—i münazi için** *law* in order to get rid of claimants. **—' ol=*. — ü ref et=** to cure and remedy. **—i şüphe et=** to remove a doubt from one's mind. **—i taaffün** *med.* antisepsis. **—i tabi** *obs.*, **—i tabii** bowel movement, motion. **— ü tard** *mil.* a repelling.
defᶠⁱ **3** دف A same as **def 1.**
defa 1 دفعه A time, turn, *e. g.*, **üç defa** three times. **— ve defa** time after time, repeatedly, again and again.
defa 2 (.'.) دفعه A *colloq.* again, once more; *mil.* repeat! (fire).
defaat (..—) دفعات A *lrnd., pl. of* **defa** 1. **—la** repeatedly.
defain (.—) دفائن A *lrnd., pl. of* **define.**
def'aten (.'..) دفعة A *lrnd.* all at once; in one payment, in a lump sum.
defatir (.—.) دفاتر A *lrnd., pl. of* **defter.**
def'et=ᵈᵉʳ دفع ايتمك /ı/ 1. to repel, push back, repulse, drive away. 2. to expel, eject. 3. *lrnd.* to refute.
deffaf (.—) دفّاف A *lrnd.* 1. maker or seller of tambourines. 2. tambourine player.
deffafe (.—.) دفّافه A *lrnd.* girl tambourine player. **—i felek** the planet Venus.
deffeteyn دفّتين A *lrnd.* 1. the two covers of a book. 2. folder, miniature folded and mounted on covers.
defiʳⁱ دفع *var. of* **def 2. — supabı** *mech.* exhaust valve.

defin 1 دَفن |defn| burial, interment.
defin 2 (. —) دَفين A lrnd. buried, interred.
define (. — .) دَفينه A buried treasure; treasure; treasure-trove.
deflâsyon دفلاسيون F econ. deflation.
defle=ᵉʳ دَفعلامك /ı/ colloq. to drive away.
defn دَفن A cf. **defin** 1.
defne (.'.) دَفنه Gk sweet bay, laurel; bot., Laurus nobilis. — **balığı** fish cooked or dried with bay leaves. — **tohumu** bayberries. — **yaprağı** 1. bay leaf. 2. young of the seafish Temnodon saltator (lüfer), less than 10 centimeters long. — **giller** bot., Lauraceae.
defnet=ᵈᵉʳ دَفن ايتمك /ı/ to bury, inter.
def'ol=ᵘʳ دَفع اولمه 1. to be removed, go away. 2. colloq. to clear out, to go. —! colloq. Off with you! Get out!
defter دَفتَر A 1. notebook, copybook, exercise book. 2. register, inventory; fin. adm. tax roll; pl., hist. the rolls. 3. com. account book, book. — **aç=** to open a subscription list. —**i âmal** Isl. rel. list of an individual's good and bad acts. —**i a'mali doldur=** to be a great sinner. —**ini dür=** /ın/ archaic to settle the account (of), to kill. — **emini** hist. director of the registry of landed property. — **et=** /ı/ to register. —**e geçir=** /ı/ to enter in the book. —**i hâkani** Ott. hist. main register of revenues of the Ottoman Empire. —**i kabart=** to run deep into debt. —**i kapa=** to close a subject. —**i kebir** com. ledger. — **tut=** com. to keep the books. — **tutma** com. bookkeeping. —**ini yap=** /ın/ to prepare an inventory (of). —**e yaz=** /ı/ colloq. to mark down as a fool.
defterdar (. . —) دَفتَردار P 1. director of the financial administration of a province. 2. Ott. hist. minister of finance. — **kapısı** Ott. hist. ministry of finance. —**lık** office of the director of finance of a province.
defterhane (. . — .) دَفتَرخانه P Ott. hist. 1. office of the registry of landed property. 2. archives in which land registers are preserved.
defterî (. . —) دَفتَرى A lrnd. pertaining to a register.
def'üddefᶠⁱ دَفع الدَفع A law refutation of a defense.
defzen دَفزَن P lrnd. tambourine player.
değ=ᵉʳ دَكمك 1. /a/ to touch. 2. /a/ to hit, reach, attain. 3. to be worthwhile; /a/ to be worth (cost, trouble). 4. /a/ archaic to befit. —**dir=** /ı, a/ caus.
değenekᵍⁱ دَكَنك archaic, same as **değnek**.
değer دَكَر 1. value; worth. 2. price. — **biç=** /a/ to evaluate, to fix the price (of). — **bilir** appreciative. — **koy=** /a/ same as **değer biç=**. — **kuramı** phil. theory of values, axiology. — **paha** econ. just price. — **ver=** /a/ to esteem, appreciate. —**len=** to gain value, to become valuable. —**lendir=** /ı/ 1. caus. 2. to appraise. 3. com. to realize the value (of). —**li** valuable; talented, worthy, estimable. —**siz** worthless.
değgin /a/ neol. concerning.
değil دَكل 1. final not, e. g., **Memnun değil** He is not pleased. 2. isolated no. 3. initial, or in anticipation of verb not only, let alone, e. g., **Değil arkadaşlarını** (or **Arkadaşlarını değil**), **babasını bile ziyaret etmedi** He didn't come to see his father, let alone his friends. 4. after locative, not caring, e. g., **Bu işin parasında değilim** It isn't the money involved I care about. — **mi ki** since, e. g., **Değil mi ki gelirim dedi, mutlaka gelir** Since he said he would, he is sure to come.
değim دَكيم 1. verbal n. of **değ=**. 2. neol. value; merit, virtue. —**li** neol. worthy. —**siz** neol. unworthy.
değin 1 دَكين /a/ until, e. g., **bugüne değin** until today, up to now.
değin=ⁱʳ 2 دَكنمك /a/ archaic to attain.
değin=ⁱʳ 3 دَكنمك /a/ to touch (on a subject).
değir=ⁱʳ دَكرمك /ı/ prov., caus. of **değ=**; to pass on (message).
değirmen دَكرمَن 1. mill. 2. grinder, grinding machine. 3. slang watch. — **beygiri gibi dolaş=** to be busy all day walking around. — **çakıldağı** clapper of the mill-hopper. — **çarkı** mill wheel. — **deresi** millrace. — **hakkı** certain amount of flour left to the miller as part of the milling fee. — **kanadı** sail of a windmill; paddle of a watermill. —**de sakal ağart=** to be inexperienced and immature. —**in suyu nereden geliyor?** Where does the expense come from? Who pays for it? — **taşı** millstone. — **taşı kadar** very large. —**ci** miller. —**cilik** miller's trade. —**lik** 1. place where there are many mills. 2. millstone quarry.
değirmi دَكرمى 1. round, circular. 2. square (cloth). —**le=** /ı/ 1. to make circular. 2. to make square. —**len=**, —**leş=** to become round and flat. 3. to become square. —**let=** /ı, a/ caus. of **değirmile=**. —**lik** roundness.
değirt=ⁱʳ دَكرتمك /ı, a/ caus. of **değir=**.
değiş=ⁱʳ 1 دَكشمك 1. to change, to become different, to become altered, to vary; to change, to be replaced; to change one's clothes, to change. 2. /ı/ to change for another, to substitute; /ı, la or a/ to exchange, barter (for). —**en**, —**ici** variable, changeable.
değiş 2 دَكش exchange. — **et=** /ı/ to exchange. — **tokuş** exchange, barter.
değişikᵍⁱ دَكشك 1. changed, different; novelty. 2. varied. 3. exchanged, substituted; prov. changeling. 4. prov. two families' mutually giving each other their

daughters in marriage. — **tarife** *com.* sliding scale tariff. —**lik** change, variation, alteration. —**lik olsun diye** for a change.

değişil=ⁱʳ دكشلك *pass. of* **değiş**= 1².

değişim 1. *verbal n. of* **değiş**= 1. 2. *math.* variation. — **et**= *naut.* to change (wind).

değişinim *neol., biol.* mutation.

değişke *neol.* modification.

değişken 1. changeable. 2. *math.* variable.

değişkin *neol.* modified.

değişme دكشمه *verbal n. of* **değiş**= 1.

değişmez دكشمز unchangeable, invariable; constant, stable; *phil.* immutable. — **doku** *bot.* permanent tissue.

değiştir=ⁱʳ دكشدرمك 1. /ı/ to change. 2. /ı, a/ to exchange (for). —**geç** *neol., chem.* converter. —**il**= *pass. of* **değiştir**=. —**me personeli** *mil.* replacements. —**t**= /ı, a/ *caus. of* **değiştir**=.

değme 1 دكمه 1. *verbal n. of* **değ**=. 2. *chem.* contact.

değme 2 دكمه every, any, *e. g.,* — **adam bu işi yapamaz** Not every man can do it.

değmede (..'..) دكمده *colloq.* probably not, unlikely.

değnekᵍⁱ دكنك 1. stick, rod, cane, wand. 2. a beating with a stick. — **cennetten çıkmıştır** *proverb* The cane is heaven-sent. — **çal**= /a/ to beat with a stick. — **gibi** very thin, thin as a lath. —**çi** *hist.* foreman; head of a guild. —**li** *hist.* doorkeeper. —**li kavas** shrew, quarrelsome person.

değşincilikᵍⁱ *neol., biol.* mutationism.

değşir=ⁱʳ 1 دكشرمك *archaic, same as* **devşir**=.

değşir=ⁱʳ 2 دكشرمك /ı/ *archaic* to change, to alter.

değzin=ⁱʳ دكزنمك *archaic* 1. to turn; circulate. 2. /ı/ to go (around).

deh 1 ده Giddap! (command to a beast to go forward).

deh 2 ده P *lrnd.* ten. — **hezar** ten thousand.

deha 1 (.—) دها A genius.

deha 2 (.'.) دها *prov.* There it is.

dehakâr (.——) دهاكار P *lrnd.* having genius.

dehalet (.—.) دخالت [*based on Arabic*] a taking refuge. — **et**= /a/ to take refuge (with).

-de haliⁿⁱ *neol., gram.* locative.

dehan (.—), **dehen** دهان د دهن P *lrnd.* mouth, orifice. —**bend** P mouth-veil; muzzle.

dehirʰʳⁱ دهر *var. of* **dehr.**

dehle=ʳ دهله مك /ı/ 1. to urge on (a beast). 2. *slang* to fire, to turn out.

dehliz دهليز [*Persian* **dihliz**] 1. entrance-hall, corridor. 2. *anat.* ear-passage; vestibule.

dehna (.—) دهنا A *lrnd.* extensive desert without water.

dehr دهر A *lrnd.* world, fortune, time. **D— Suresi** *name of the seventy-sixth sura of the Quran.*

dehre دهره P *prov.* reaping hook, billhook.

dehrî (.—) دهری A *phil.* materialist, atheist; materialistic, atheistic. —**iye** (.—.) A *phil.* materialism, atheism. —**iyun** (.——) A *phil.* materialists, atheists.

dehruzi (.——) دهروزی P *lrnd.* 1. ten days old. 2. transitory.

dehşet دهشت A 1. terror, horror, dread, awe. 2. marvelous. —**e düş**= to be horrified. —**âver** (..—.) P, —**efşan** (...—) P, —**engiz** (...—) P *lrnd.* terrible, dreadful. —**li** terrible, dreadful; formidable, marvelous.

dehüm, dehümin (..—) دهم دهمين P *lrnd.* tenth.

dejenere دژنره F degenerate.

dekᵏⁱ **1** دك *prov.* trick, ruse. —**e düşür**= /ı/ to play a trick (on).

dek 2 دك *archaic* like, similar to.

dek 3 دك /e/ until, as far as.

dek 4 دك *archaic for* **tek 2.**

dek 5 دك *archaic, same as* **tek 4.**

Dekadanlar دكادانلر F 1. the Decadénts (name given by its opponents to the literary school of **Servetifünun**). 2. the Decadents (a school of French writers at the end of the 19th century).

dekagram دكاغرام F *phys.* decagram.

dekaikᵏⁱ (.—.) دقائق A *same as* **dakaik.**

dekalitre (..'.) دكاليتره F *phys.* decaliter.

dekametre (...'.) دكامتره F *phys.* decameter. — **kare** square decameter. — **küb** cubic decameter.

dekan دكان G dean of a University faculty. —**lık** dean's office.

dekar دكار F land measurement of a thousand square meters, .247 acres (*cf.* **dönüm**).

Dekartçı دكارتجی *phil.* Cartesian. —**lık** Cartesianism.

-deki *cf.* **-daki.**

dekolte دكولته F 1. low-cut, low-neck; decolleté. 2. licentious, immodest, indecent.

dekont دكونت F *fin.* statement of account.

dekor دكور F *theat.* décor, setting; scenery.

dekovil دكوويل F narrow gauge railroad.

dekzede دكزده P *lrnd.* who has shaved off all hair from his face.

del=ᵉʳ دلمك /ı/ to make a hole (in), to pierce, to bore, to hole. —**ip geç**= /ı/ to pierce through.

delâil (.—.) دلائل A *lrnd., pl. of* **delil.** **D—i Hayrat** *name of a Muslim prayer book.*

delâlet (.—.) دلالت A 1. a guiding, guidance. 2. mediation. 3. indication; denotation; signification. — **et**= /a/ 1. to act as a guide. 2. to indicate. 3. to be instrumental (in), to act as an intermediary.

deldir= دلدیرمك /ı, a/ caus. of **del=**.
delege دلگه F delegate, representative.
delfin دلفین Gk 1. astr. Dolphin. 2. obs. dolphin, porpoise, zool., Delphinus delphis.
delgi neol. drill, gimlet.
deli 1 دلی دلو 1. insane, lunatic; fool, idiot; mad, maniac; crazy, wild. 2. eccentric, whimsical. 3. foolish, thoughtless; rash, foolhardy. 4. brave, heroic. 5. harmful, strong. —**si** crazy about, too fond of, e. g., **çocuk delisi** very fond of children, crazy about children. — **alacası** motley, variegated. — **bal poisonous honey.** — **balkabağından olmaz ya!** How foolish, how mad! — **balta** cruel person. — **bayrağı aç=** to fall madly in love. — **bozuk** unbalanced, fitful; inconstant. — **divane ol=** /diye/ to be crazy (about), to go crazy (over). — **dolu** thoughtless, inconsiderate. — **duman** foolhardy, reckless, daredevil. —**nin eline değnek ver=** to give the whip hand to a harmful person. — **fişek** unbalanced, flippant. —**ye her gün bayram** Every day is a holiday for a fool (said about out-of-place rejoicing or festivity). — **ırmak** wild and torrential river. — **kanlı*.** — **kızın çeyizi gibi** in wild disorder; tasteless clothing monotonous in color and style. — **olmak işten bile değil** It drives one crazy. — **orman** 1. a vast and dense forest. 2. w. caps., name of a region in Dobrudja. — **otu** yellow alison, bot., Alyssum. — **pazarı** colloq. in a pickle; state of great disorder. — **poyraz** violent north wind. — **pösteki sayar gibi** like a fool who counts the hairs of a skin (said of useless and tedious work). — **Raziye** crazy person; flippant girl. — **saçması** utter nonsense. — **saraylı,** — **saraylı gibi** oddly decked out in tawdry finery.
deli 2 دلی دلو [delil³] Ott. hist. irregular trooper of the guides. — **başı** leader of irregular cavalry.
delice 1 (..'.) دلیجه crazily, madly; crazy, mad (act).
delice 2 دلیجه 1. somewhat mad, crazy. 2. wild (plant). 3. darnel, rye grass, bot., Lolium temulentum. 4. ergoted rye. 5. kind of falcon. — **doğan** hen harrier, zool., Circus cyaneus; hobby, zool., Falco subbuteo. — **mantar** poisonous mushroom.
delikᵍⁱ دلیك 1. hole, opening, orifice; pierced, bored; anat. foramen. 2. slang prison. — **aç=** /da/ to hole, to pierce, to bore. — **büyük, yama küçük** The need is greater than the means. — **deşik** full of holes. — **deşik** —**et=** to cover with holes all over, to perforate badly. — **kapa=** to meet a need, to come in handy. —**e tık=** /ı/ slang to put into jail.
delikanlı دلیقانلی دلیغانلی youth, young man; young and sprightly. —**lık** youth; youthfulness.

delikli دلیكلی having a hole, having holes, perforated. — **taş** sink. — **tuğla** perforated brick. —**ler** zool., Foraminifera.
deliksiz دلیكسز without a hole. — **uyku** sound sleep, sleep of the just.
delil (.—) دلیل A 1. proof, evidence; indication, sign; phil. argument. 2. lrnd. guide. 3. same as **deli 2**. — **başı** same as **deli başı**. —**i bürhanî** phil. demonstrative argument. —**i cedeli** phil., ex-concesso argument. —**i ilzamî** phil. convincing evidence. — **ittihaz et=** /ı/ phil. to use as proof of an inference. —**i kat'î** phil. absolute evidence. —**i naklî** phil. testimony received from a valid authority. —**lerin takdiri** law estimation of evidence. —**i vücut** phil. ontological argument.
delilen=ⁱʳ دلیلنمك to become mad, eccentric. —**dir=** /ı/ caus.
delilî (.——) دلیلی A phil. evidential, inferential.
delilikᵍⁱ دلیلك madness, insanity; mania; foolishness, folly, eccentricity. — **et=** to act foolishly, to act unwisely. —**e vur=** 1. to pretend madness. 2. to give oneself up to folly out of despair.
delim دلیم archaic much, many, a great deal.
delin=ⁱʳ دلینمك 1. pass. of **del=**. 2. to become worn through; to burst.
delir=ⁱʳ دلیرمك to go mad, become insane. —**t=** /ı/ caus.
delişmen دلیشمن spoiled and irresponsible, lacking in balance, over-impulsive.
delkᵏⁱ **1** دلك A 1. phys. friction. 2. lrnd. a rubbing with the hand, friction.
delkᵏⁱ **2** دلك var. of **dalak 2**.
delket=ᵈᵉʳ دلك اتمك /ı/ to rub.
dellâkᵏⁱ (.—) دلّاك A lrnd., same as **tellâk**. —**iye** tip given to the masseur in a public bath.
dellâlˡˡ (.—) دلّال A lrnd., same as **tellâl**. —**e** (.—.) A procuress. —**iye** (.—.̣.) fee given to a crier or broker.
delme دلمه 1. verbal n. of **del=**. 2. bored, pierced, perforated, punched. 3. prov. waistcoat. — **makinası** punching machine.
delta (.'.) دلتا F geog. delta. — **kası** anat. deltoid muscle.
delv دلو A 1. astr. Aquarius. 2. lrnd. bucket.
dem 1 دم A 1. blood, hemorrhage; menstrual blood. 2. lrnd. blood feud; homicide. — **gel=**, — **kaybet=** to have a menstrual hemorrhage. — **resmi** hist. slaughter tax. —**i şiryani** anat. arterial blood. —**i veridî** anat. venous blood.
dem 2 دم P a being steeped (tea). —**i gel=** to become steeped (tea).
dem 3 دم P poet. 1. breath; gust, blast. 2. drone. 3. sip, draught. 4. Bektashi order

wine, raki. 5. sigh; murmur; exlamation. 6. *mus.* the bass sounds of the **ney**. 7. talk; boastful talk. 8. odor, fumes. 9. point; edge. **— al=** to rest and take breath. **—i ateşîn** 1. fiery blast. 2. burning sigh. **— çek=** 1. to sing long and sweetly (nightingale), to warble. 2. to drink wine. **— çıkar=** /da'n/ to play (flute). **— ü dud** 1. vapor and smoke. 2. vigor, energy, fire. **—i ejderha** dragon's mouth; jaws of danger. **—i germ** 1. hot breath. 2. heated words. **—i İsa** the life-giving breath of Jesus. **—i kalem** 1. point of a pen. 2. scratching sound of a pen. **—i nerm** 1. soft breath. 2. soft words. **—i serd** 1. cold breath. 2. despairing sigh. 3. disagreeable words. **— sür=** to lead a happy life. **—i tiğ** edge of a sword. **— tut=** /a/ *Or. mus.* the constant accompaniment in tonic and dominant of a **makam** during performance. **—i vâpesin** last breath. **— vur=** /dan/ to talk (about a thing) somewhat pretentiously.

dem 4 P *poet.* instant; time. **—inde** at the right time. **— bedem** from time to time. **—i seher, —i subh**, time of dawn. **— sür=** to lead a happy life. **—i şam** eventide. **—i teslim** 1. time of death. 2. silence; obedience, resignation.

dem^(m'i) **5** A *lrnd.* tears. **—i Eyyub** Job's tears, *bot., Coix Lachryma-Jobi.*

dem'a A *lrnd.* tear.

demadem (.—.) P *lrnd.* from time to time, now and then.

demagog F demagogue.

demagoji F demagogy.

demağ (.—) P *lrnd.* palate.

deman 1 (.—) P *lrnd.* raging, roaring.

dem'an 2 (.—) A *lrnd.* overflowing; filled with tears.

demar (.—) A *lrnd.* destruction, death.

demarşör F *auto.* starter.

dembaz (.—) P *lrnd.* 1. talker, boaster. 2. wheedler.

dembedem (.'..) P *lrnd.* from time to time, now and then.

dembeste P *lrnd.* dumbfounded, breathless from amazement.

demdeme 1 P *lrnd.* 1. drum, tom-tom, clamor, turmoil. 2. fame, renown, rumor. 3. fraud, deceit, falsehood.

demdeme 2 A *lrnd.* 1. anger, rage; angry talk. 2. a talking angrily against someone. 3. enraged destruction.

deme verbal n. of **de=** 1. **—m o deme değil, —m o demek değil** *prov.* That is not my meaning; that's not what I mean.

demeç^(ci) *neol.* speech; statement. **—te bulun=** to make a statement.

demek so, thus, therefore, in this cases e. g., **demek yarın gelecek** So he's coming tomorrow after all. **demek şehir çok sıcaktı** Then the town was really hot. **— ki, — oluyor ki** that means, that means to say.

demet Gk 1. bunch, bouquet (flowers); bundle. 2. sheaf (of grain). 3. *phys.* bundle (of rays). 4. *bot.* corymb. **— demet** in bunches, in sheaves. **—le=** /ı/ to tie in sheaves, in bunches. **—len=** *pass.* **—let=** /ı, a/ *caus. of* **demetle=**.

demevi (..—) A 1. sanguine (temperament); full-blooded. 2. *lrnd.* pertaining to the blood. **—yet** (..—.) A sanguineness, full-bloodedness.

demgirifte P *lrnd.* 1. inflamed. 2. tainted, malodorous.

demgüzar (..—) P *lrnd.* 1. one who passes the time; one who lives. **— ol=** /la/ to make a pastime (of).

dem'î 1 (.—) A *lrnd.* pertaining to tears, lachrymose.

demi^(m'i) **2** *var. of* **dem 6.**

demide (.—.) P *lrnd.* 1. expanded, full-blown. 2. blossomed, sprouted, come forth.

demin (.'.) just now, a second ago. **—cek, —cik** just a moment ago. **—den** just now, a second ago.

demir 1. iron; made of iron; iron part of anything. 2. anchor. 3. fetters, irons. 4. bar (of a door). 5. *pl.* grille (of a window). 6. *shoe-making* heelplate. **— ağacı** ironwood, *bot., Sideroxylon oxycaritha.* **— al=** *naut.* to weigh anchor; to move. **— aralığı** *elec.* air-gap (of dynamo). **— at=** 1. to cast anchor, to anchor. 2. to overstay one's welcome. **— ayısı** manatee, sea cow. **— baş*. — bırak=** to anchor. **— boku** iron slag. **— bozan** *obs.* antimony. **— çirki** iron slag. **— diken** caltroy, *bot., Tribulus terrestris.* **— don** *archaic* armor. **— döğ=** to beat iron. **— gibi** 1. strong, iron-like. 2. very cold (thing). **— gömlek** *archaic* armor. **— kaldır=** *naut.* to weigh anchor. **— kapan** magnet. **D— kapı** iron gate; *w. cap., geog.* Iron Gates, *name of various mountain passes in Turkey, Hungary and U.S.S.R.* **— karıncası** vermicular markings on iron. **— kazık** polar star, pole star. **D— kırat** *prov., corruption of* **Demokrat. — kırı** iron grey (horse). **— kırmızısı** iron oxide red, tarragona. **— leblebi** difficult to handle, to understand; unbearable thing, unbearable task. **— pası** 1. iron rust. 2. iron rust color. **— perde** iron curtain; *w. cap., pol.* Iron Curtain. **— resmi** anchorage, anchor dues. **— suyu** water for tempering iron. **— tara=** *naut.* to drag the anchor. **— taş** *mil. hist.* iron ball. **— tavında,**

demirbaş

dilber çağında *proverb* Strike the iron while it is hot; marry off the girl while she is young. **—i tavında döğ=** to strike while the iron is hot. **— tozu** iron filings. **— üzerinde** *naut.* anchored. **— üzerinde yat=** *naut.* to lie at anchor. **— vur=** /a/, **—e vur=** /ı/ to put in chains. **— yastığı** *naut.* anchor lining. **—de yat=** *naut.* to be anchored, moored. **— yeri** *naut.* mooring, anchorage. **— yolu***. **— yongası** iron scrap.
demirbaş 1. fixtures and equipment. 2. old timer; unchanging (thing). 3. inflexible; obstinate. **— erzak** *mil.* reserve ration. **— eşya** inventory stock. **D— Şarl** *hist.* Charles XII of Sweden. **— tâyinat** *mil.* reserve ration, D ration.
demirci 1. ironworker, smith. 2. ironmonger. **— körüğü** forge billows, blower. **— mengenesi** smith's vise. **— ocağı** smith's forge, smithy. **—lik** blacksmith's profession.
demirhane (..—.) ironworks.
demirhindi |temri hindî| tamarind, *bot., Tamarindus indica*.
demirî (..—) iron-grey.
demirle=ʳ /ı/ 1. to anchor. 2. to bolt and bar (door).
demirli 1. anchored. 2. containing iron, ferriferous. 3. chained; bolted. **— kil** *geol.* ferruginous clay.
demiryol, demiryoluⁿᵘ railroad, railway. **— makası** railway switch.
demkeş P *lrnd.* 1. that draws breath. 2. cooing dove; singer; accompanying singer. 3. who drinks wine.
demle=ʳ /ı/ to steep, to brew. **—n=** 1. to be steeped (tea). 2. to drink (wine etc.). **—ndir=** /ı/ same as **demle=**.
demli 1. well steeped (tea). 2. intoxicated.
demlikᵍⁱ tea-pot.
demografi F demography.
demokrasi F democracy.
demokrat F democrat; democratic. **—lık** state of being a democrat.
demren same as **temren**.
demriye same as **temreyi**.
demsaz (.—) P *lrnd.* confident, friend, intimate, boon companion. **—î** (.——) P intimacy, confidence.
-den 1 *cf.* **-dan 1.**
den=ⁱʳ **2** *pass. of* **de= 1.**
denaet (.—.) A baseness, meanness, cowardice, vileness. **—kâr** (.—.—) P mean, vile. **—kârane** (.—.——.) P meanly, cowardly.
denanir (.——) A *lrnd., pl. of* **dinar**.
denaset (.—.) A *lrnd.* a being soiled; pollution, defilement.

-denberi *cf.* **-danberi.**
dendan (.—) P *lrnd.* 1. tooth. 2. serration (of an Arabic letter). **—i bülûğ** wisdom tooth. **—ı saadet** *Isl. rel.* piece of Muhammad's tooth broken off during the battle of Uhud.
dendane (.—.) P *lrnd.* tooth; serration.
dendanmüzd (.—.) P *lrnd.* money and other things distributed to the guests at a feast.
dendene A *lrnd.* 1. a buzzing, humming (of flies). 2. a muttering.
dene 1 *prov., var. of* **tane 1.**
dene=ʳ **2** /ı/ 1. to test, to try, to experiment; to attempt. 2. to tempt. **—k** *archaic* proved, tried. **—me** 1. test, trial. 2. essay. **—n=**, **—nil=** *pass. of* **dene=**.
denes A *lrnd.* pollution; a being soiled, polluted.
denet=ⁱʳ **1** /ı, a/ *caus. of* **dene= 1. —il=** *pass.*
denet 2 *neol.* control, supervision. **—çi** controller, supervisor. **—le=** /ı/ to check, oversee.
deney *neol., sc.* experiment. **— kap** *chem.* test tube. **— üstü** *phil.* transcendental.
deneyim *neol., phil.* experimentation.
deneysel *neol., phil.* experimental. **—cilik** experimentalism.
deng 1 *cf.* **denk 1.**
deng 2 P *lrnd.* amazed, confused; astonished, confounded; stupid, ignorant.
dengâdeng (.—.) P *lrnd.* in equipoise; equal.
denge *neol., sc.* equilibrium. **—le=** /ı/ balance. **—siz** out of balance.
-den haliⁿⁱ *neol., gram.* ablative.
deni (.—) A *lrnd.* base, vile, mean, despicable.
denil=ⁱʳ *pass. of* **de= 1.**
denilikᵍⁱ (.—.) meanness, vileness.
denis A *lrnd.* soiled, dirty.
deniş=ⁱʳ *prov., var. of* **değiş=**.
deniz 1. sea; ocean; large lake; *in compounds* marine, maritime, nautical, naval. 2. waves; high sea; a swell. **—in açığı** the offing. **—e açıl=** to put (out) to sea. **— alası** sea trout, *zool., Trutta fario*. **— albayı** *navy* captain. **— aldı** /ı/ (It) has been washed overboard; (it) has been washed out to sea. **— altı***. **— amı, — anası** jellyfish. **— aşırı** overseas. **— aşırı ticaret** overseas trade. **— ataşesi** naval attaché. **—in attığı enkaz** *law* jetsam. **— aygırı** sea horse, *zool., Hippocampus*. **— ayısı** sea cow, manatee, *zool., Trichechus manatus*. **—de balık** a bird in the bush, a thing not in one's possession or power. **—deki balığın pazarlığı olmaz, —deki**

balığa tava hazırlanmaz *proverb* Don't heat the frying pan before the fish is caught. — **banyosu** sea bathing. — **baskını** *geog.* 1. high tide; neap tide; flood tide. 2. tidal wave. 3. bore, eagre. 4. inroad of the sea. — **basması** *geol.* an inroad made by the sea's eroding the land. — **binbaşısı** *navy* Commander. **—den bir katre** a drop in the ocean. — **buzulu** iceberg, ice-floe. — **canavarı** sea monster. — **çakısı** razor clam, *zool.*, *Solen* **—den çıkmış balık** a fish out of water; all confused. — **çulluğu** sanderling, *zool.*, *Crocethia alba.* — **dantelâsı** *zool.* millepore. — **derya** 1. the immense seas. 2. all around, as far as the eye can see. — **derya ayak altında** lying at one's feet like a vast panorama. — **durdu,** — **düştü** The sea has died down. —**e düşen yılana sarılır** *proverb* A drowning man will clutch at a straw. —**e elverişli** *naut.* seaworthy. — **eri** *navy* seaman. — **eriştesi** *same as* — **kadayıfı.** — **feneri** lighthouse. — **ganimetleri** *law* sea prize. **—den geçip çayda boğul=** to cross the sea safely and to be drowned in a stream; to succeed in solving major problems, but be unable to solve the minor ones. — **gergedanı** narwhal, *zool.*, *Monodon monoceros.* — **gibi** as vast as the ocean. —**e gir=** to go swimming, to go sea-bathing. —**e gitse kurutur** Even his presence makes things go wrong. He is always awkward; he always brings bad luck. — **güzeli** red drum, red fish, *zool.*, *Sciaena.* — **hamamı** an enclosure for sea-bathing. — **haritası** sea chart. — **hasaratı** average. — **haydutluğu** piracy. — **hırsızı** pirate. — **hıyarları** holothurians, *zool.*, *Holothuriae.* — **hortumu** waterspout. — **hukuku** maritime law. — **iğnesi** European pipefish, *zool.*, *Syngnathus acus.* —**e indir=** /ı/ to launch (ship). — **ineği** sea cow. — **kabarıyor** The sea is becoming rough. — **kadayıfı** badderlocks, *bot.*, *Alaria esculenta.* — **kanunnamesi** maritime code. — **kazası** shipwreck, accident at sea. — **kenarı** seashore. — **kestanesi** sea urchin, *zool.*, *Echinus.* — **kırlangıcı** tern, *zool.*, *Sterna hirundo.* — **kızı** mermaid, siren. — **kızları** sirens, *zool.*, *Sirenia.* **—leri kolla!** *naut.* Ease the ship! — **köpüğü** meerschaum. — **kredisi** maritime credit. — **kulağı** lagoon. — **kulubü** yacht club. **—de kum onda para** He has lots of money. — **kurdu** sea wolf, an old salt. —**i kurut=** to be pessimistic, to be discouraging. — **kuvvetleri** naval forces. — **lâleleri** sea lilies, *zool.*, *Crinoidea.* — **mahkemesi** Admiralty Court. — **marulu** sea lettuce, *bot.*, *Ulva Lactuca.* — **mili** sea mile. — **muharebeleri hukuku** *law* of naval warfare. — **musadere mahkemesi** *law* prize court. **D—**

Müsteşarı Undersecretary of State for the Navy. **D— Müsteşarlığı** Navy Department. **D— Müzesi** Naval Museum. — **nakliyatı simsarı** shipping broker. — **nakliyat şirketi** ocean shipping company. — **otu** seaweed. — **ödüncü** *com.* loan on bottomry. — **pıhtısı** jellyfish. — **razıyanesi** samphire, sea fennel, *bot.*, *Crithmum maritimum.* — **salyangozu** periwinkle. — **sathı** sea surface; sea level. — **sazı** a kind of rush, *bot.*, *Juncus maritimus.* — **serveti** *law* property on the high seas. — **sigortası** maritime insurance. —**e su götür=,** —**e su taşı=** 1. to carry water to the sea. 2. to give a small present to a rich man. — **subayı** naval officer. — **şakayıkları** sea anemones, *zool.*, *Actiniaria.* **D— Şûrası** Admiralty Council. — **tarağı** dredging-machine. — **tavşancılı** osprey, *zool.*, *Pandion haliaetus.* — **tayyaresi** seaplane, hydroplane. — **tehlikesi** *com.* sea risks. — **tekesi** shrimp; prawn. — **tezgâhı** stocks, shipyard. — **ticareti hukuku** maritime law. — **topçuluğu** naval artillery. — **tutması** seasickness. — **uçakçılığı** naval aviation. — **üssü** naval base. — **yarbayı** *navy* commander. — **yolları** maritime line. — **yosunu** seaweed. — **zabıtası** maritime police. **—de zabıt ve musadere** *law* right of prize.

denizaltı[y1] **1** دكز آلتی *navy* a submarine.
denizaltı[n1] **2** دكز آلتی submarine; submerged; deep-sea (current).
denizci دكزجی 1. seaman, sailor. 2. seaworthy. **—lik** 1. sailing, navigation, ocean transportation. 2. sea sports. 3. seaworthiness.
denizel *neol.*, marine; naval. — **oluşuk** *geol.* sea formation.
denizlik[gi] دكزلك 1. *naut.* sloping board of a boat to keep water out. 2. *arch.* sloping board under a window.
denizsel *neol.* maritime.
denk[gi] **1** دنك *var. of* **dang.**
denk[gi] **2** دنك 1. bale; half a horse-load; large package. 2. in equilibrium, in proper balance; trim; counterpoise; equal; suitable; match; *math.* equivalent. — **bağla=** to fasten the bales. — **boz=** to open bales of merchandise. —**i dengine** everyone to his match. — **et=** /ı/ to balance; *naut.* to trim (a boat). — **gel=** /la/ to balance, to be in equipoise. —**ine getir=** /ı/ 1. to balance, to harmonize. 2. to choose the right moment (for). —**i ile karşıla=** 1. to retaliate; to pay one in his own coin. —**e koy=** /ı/ *slang* to pawn. — **taşı** *obs.* ballast stone; pebble, stone used as a weight. —**le=** /ı/ 1. to make up in bales. 2. *naut.* to trim (boat). —**lem** *neol. math.* equation. —**lemler sistemi** *math.* simultaneous equations. —**len=** 1. *pass. of* **denkle=.** 2. *same as* **denkleş=.** —**leş=** to become properly balanced, to

become evenly trimmed. **—leştir=** /ı/ 1. *caus. of* **denkleş=**. 2. *prov.* to find, to put together (money). **—let=** /ı, a/ *caus. of* **denkle=**.

denkserlik[gi] *neol., phil.* equity.

denli دكلى *prov.* 1. good-natured, tractable, careful. 2. staid, grave, serious, important. **— densiz söz söyle=** to talk out of turn.

-denlik[gi] دنلك *cf.* **-danlık**.

denlû دكلو *archaic* thus, so, like, as (degree, manner).

densiz دكسز lacking in manners and consideration, of no weight. **—len=** to act in an inconsiderate and unbecoming manner. **—lik** inconsiderateness.

-den sonra دن صوكره *cf.* **-dan sonra**.

denşir=[ir] *neol., chem.* to denature. **—en** *chem.* denaturant.

denyo (´.) دنيو Romany *slang* stupid, idiot, fool, ass.

deontoloji ديونتولوژى F *phil.* deontology. |/dep/ *see* /tep/.|

deplek[gi] دپلك *archaic* small drum.

depo دپو F 1. depot. 2. warehouse, store. 3. *slang* a living storehouse of knowledge etc. **— et=** /ı/ to store. **— mevcudu** stock.

depor دپور F *com.* backwardation.

depozito (...'.) دپوزيتو F deposit, security.

deppoy دپوى |depo| *mil.* depot, quartermaster's store.

deprem *neol.* earthquake. **—sel** seismal, seismic.

depresyon دپرسيون F *med., psych.* depression.

der=[er] 1 ديرمك /ı/ to pick (flower), to pick up, gather, collect. **—ip devşir=** /ı/ to gather together.

der 2 در *prov.*, *same as* **ter** 1.

der 3 در P *lrnd.* 1. door, gate. 2. house, palace. 3. mountain pass. **D—i Aliye** *same as* **Deraliye**.

der- 4 در P *lrnd.* in, into *as in* **derambar, dercep, dertop**. **— an nefes** at that instant.

-der 5 (—) در P *lrnd.* that tears, as in **safder**.

dera (.—) درا P *lrnd.* bell.

deraguş (.——) در آغوش P embracing, embrace. **— et=** /ı/ to embrace, to clasp.

derahim (.—.) دراهم A *lrnd.*, *pl. of* **dirhem**.

derahş درخش P *same as* **dirahş**.

derakab (´..) درعقب P immediately afterwards, instantly.

Deraliye درعليه |Deri Aliye *under* **der** 3| *hist.* The Sublime Porte.

derambar (..—) درانبار P *lrnd.* stored, in stock. **— et=** /ı/ to store, to put in stock.

deraviş (.——) درويش A *lrnd.*, *pl. of* **derviş**.

derayende (.—..) داريښنده P *lrnd.* talkative, chatterbox.

derban (.—) دربان P *lrnd.* doorkeeper, porter. **—ı felek** *poet.* sun.

derbar (.—) دربار P *lrnd.* residence, court. **D—ı devletkarar, D—ı saadetkarar** the court of the Sultan; Istanbul.

derbeder دربدر P 1. vagrant, tramp. 2. untidy, slovenly, disorderly, irregular. **—i** (...—) P, **—lik** vagrancy, mendicancy.

derbend دربند P *lrnd.* 1. door-fastener. 2. chained, fastened, in bonds. 3. *same as* **derbent**.

derbent[di] دربنت |derbend| 1. mountain pass, defile. 2. *archaic* fortress commanding a mountain pass; guardhouse at a pass. **— ağzı** entrance of a defile. **—çi** *archaic* pass-guard, custom house officer.

derbest, derbeste دربست P *lrnd.* 1. closed door. 2. closed, covered; fastened. 3. mute, silent.

derc 1 درج A 1. insertion, inclusion. 2. *archaic* roll of paper, scroll. **— et=***.

derc 2 درج P *lrnd.* manuscript illuminated with figures; writing on illuminated paper.

dercengievvel درجنگ اول |based on Persian| *lrnd.* first of all, at first.

dercep درجيب |der- 4, cep| *only in* **— et=** /ı/ *joc.* to pocket, to make off with.

dercet=[der] درج ايتمك /ı/ to insert, to include.

derd درد P *same as* **dert**. **—i derun, —i dil** *poet.* heartache. **—i hicran** *poet.* pain of separation. **—i ışk** *poet.* love-sickness. **—i nihan** *poet.* secret pain. **—i ser** *poet.* headache, trouble. **—i şikem** *lrnd.* bowel pains, pangs.

derda (.—) دردا P *poet.* Alas, woe is me!

derdaşam (.——) درد آشام P *poet.* troubled, sorrowful.

derd'aşina (.—.—) درد آشنا P *lrnd.* who sympathizes with one's trouble.

derdengiz (..—) دردانگيز P *poet.* painful.

derdest دردست P *lrnd.* 1. in hand, seized, in the possession of. 2. at hand, in readiness. 3. arrest. **— et=** /ı/ to arrest, to seize. **—i tasarruf** in one's possession.

derdhorde دردخورده P *poet.* sorrowful, pained.

derdir=[ir] درديرمك /ı; a/ *caus. of* **der=** 1.

derdkeş دردكش P *lrnd.* suffering, unhappy.

derdmend دردمند P *lrnd.* unfortunate, poor, miserable. **—ane** (.—.) P miserably.

derdnâk[ki] (.—) دردناك P *poet.* pained, sorrowing, afflicted.

derdzede دردزده P *lrnd.* afflicted, sorrowing, pained, ill.

dere دره P 1. valley. 2. stream, rivulet. 3. *arch.* roof valley. **— beyi***. **— iskorbiti** bullhead, *zool., Cottus gobio*. **— kayası** fresh water goby, *zool., Gobio fluviatilis.* **— kumrusu** collared turtledove, *zool., Streptopelia decaocto.* **— otu** dill, *bot., Anethum graveolens.* **— pisisi** English flounder, *zool., Fleuronectes flesus.* **— tepe** up hill and down dale. **— tepe düz git=** to keep on going incessantly. **—den tepeden konuş=** to hold a rambling conversation.

derebey, derebeyi^ni د ر ه بكی 1. feudal lord; local potentate; despot. 2. bully. **— kesil=** to lord it over people; to take on a bullying attitude.

derebeylik^ği د ر ه بكلك 1. local despotate. 2. *neol.* feudalism.

derecat (..—) در جات A 1. *lrnd., pl. of* **derece.** 2. *law* instances.

derece در جه A 1. degree, grade. 2. rank, degree. 3. thermometer. 4. *lrnd.* step, stair. **— al=** 1. to take the temperature. 2. to be placed (in a competition). **— derece** 1. by degrees; of various degrees. 2. graduated, graded. **—i hararet** temperature. **—i imkânda ol=** *lrnd.* to be possible. **—i inhilâl** *chem.* degree of dispersion. **—i kemal** degree of perfection. **—i kevkep** *astr.* longitude of a heavenly body. **— tenzili** reduction in the salary scale. **—si var mı?** Does he have a temperature? **—li** graded. **—li deneykap** *neol., chem.* graduated test tube. **—siz** beyond measure, extreme.

derek^ği درك *prov.* cupboard; drawer.

derekât (..—) در کات A *pl. of* **dereke.**

dereke در که A *lrnd.* 1. a stage (in a descending line of order). 2. a low stratum. 3. pit of hell.

derekî 1 (..—) در کی |based on **dereke**| *biol., psych.* regressive.

derekî 2 (..—) در قی A *anat.* thyroid.

deren در ن A *bot., path.* tubercle.

derende در نده P *lrnd.* that tears or rends, rapacious, fierce.

derenî (..—) در نی A *path.* tuberculous.

dergâh (.—) در گاه P *lrnd.* 1. court of a king. 2. dervish convent. **—ı âli** *Ott. hist.* the Sultan's court. **—ı ilâhi, —ı izzet** the throne of grace at which prayers are offered. **—ı muallâ** *Ott. hist.* the Sultan's Court.

derge=^r در گه /ı/ *archaic* to gather. **—n=, —ş=** to gather, to assemble.

dergeh در گه P *var. of* **dergâh.**

dergi *neol.* periodical, review, magazine.

dergin *neol.* compiled, codified.

dergûş (.—) در گوش P heard; remembered. **— et=** /ı/ to hear; to remember.

derhal (.'.) در حال [P .—] at once, immediately.

derhar در خور P *lrnd.* worthy, fit, becoming.

derhast در خواست P *lrnd.* request, prayer, petition. **— et=** /ı/ to ask (for).

derhatır (.—.) در خاطر [der- 4, hatır] *only in* **— et=** /ı/ *lrnd.* to remember.

derhayal (..—) در خیال [der- 4, hayal] *only in* **— et=** /ı/ *lrnd.* to imagine, visualize.

derhem در هم P *lrnd.* 1. perplexed, bewildered; distorted. 2. mixed, confused. **— berhem ol=** to be all mixed up, to be confused.

deri 1 د ر ی 1. skin, hide. 2. leather. **— altı** *anat., med.* subcutaneous. **— bağla=** to heal (sore). **— bıçağı** bookbinder's knife. **—si dikenliler** *zool., Echinodermata.* **— hastalığı** skin disease. **— kaplı** leather-bound (book). **bir — bir kemik, —si kemiğine yapışmış** skin and bones, skinny. **— pişmesi** *tanning* ripening of the hides. **— sanayii** manufacturing of leather goods. **—sine sığma=** to be too big for one's skin. **—sini yüz=** /ın/ 1. to flay, skin. 2. to rob, strip. 3. to torture.

derî 2 (.—) د ر ی P *lrnd.* 1. pertaining to the mountains. 2. *w. cap.,* Dari (an Iranian dialect).

dericilik^ği د ر یجیلك leather manufacturing.

deriçe (.—.) در یچه P *lrnd.* 1. small door, trapdoor, wicket. 2. window.

deride (.—.) در یده P *lrnd.* rent, torn. **—çeşm** (.—..) P shameless, saucy-eyed. **—dehan** (.—..—) P indiscreet in speech, outspoken.

deril=^ir د ر یلك 1. *pass. of* **der=** 1. 2. *archaic* to gather, assemble.

derilen=^ir د ر ینلنك to heal.

derim 1 د ر یم *verbal n. of* **der=** 1.

derim 2 در یم *prov.* framework of a felt tent. **— evi** felt tent.

derin 1 د ر ن د ر ین 1. deep; depth. 2. profound. **—den** from far away (sound); from the depths. **—den derine** 1. from far away (sound). 2. minutely. **— düşün=** /ı/ to consider seriously. **— su** *naut.* deep water; deepwater.

derin- 2 (.—) در ین P *lrnd.* in this, *e. g.,* **—suret** in this case, then.

derincek^ği د ر ینجك *archaic* fine head scarf.

derinlemesine د ر ینلمه سنه in depth.

derinlen=^ir, **derinleş=**^ir د ر ینلنك د ر ینلشك to become deep. **derinlendir=, derinleştir=** /ı/ *caus.*

derinlet=^ir د ر ینلتك /ı/ to deepen.

derinlik^ği د ر ینلك 1. depth; depths; deepness. 2. profundity. **—ine** in depth. **— dümeni** *submarine* horizontal rudder.

derinti در ینتی *archaic* 1. gathered from here and there, scraped together. 2. mass of rubbish. 3. mob; corps of irregular troops.

deriş=^ir *neol., chem.* to be concentrated. **—ik** concentrated. **—me** concentration.

derk^ki د ر ك A *lrnd.* 1. comprehension,

derkafa (..—) در قفا P lrnd. close on the heels (of a fugitive).

understanding. 2. acquisition; attainment. — et=*.

derkâr (.—) دركار P lrnd. 1. manifest, evident. 2. occupied, busy; in operation.

derkemend دركمند P only in — et= /ı/ lrnd. to noose, snare.

derkemin (..—) در كمين P lrnd. in ambush.

derkenar (..—) در كنار P lrnd. 1. marginal note, postscript. 2. in a margin, on the edge of a thing, at the side. 3. in the bosom, in the embrace, in one's arms. — et= /ı/ 1. to note in the margin. 2. to embrace.

derket=^der درك ايتمك /ı/ lrnd. 1. to comprehend, understand. 2. to acquire; to attain.

derle=^r درلمك ديرلمك /ı/ to gather together, collect. —yip topla= to gather together, tidy up (room, etc.) —n= 1. pass. of **derle**=. 2. refl. of **derle**=.

derli toplu درلي طوپلي tidy; well coordinated.

derman (.—) درمان P poet. 1. remedy, medicine, cure, specific. 2. strength, power, energy. — ara= to seek a remedy. — bul= /a/ to find a remedy (for). — ol= /a/ to be a remedy, cure (for).

dermande (.—.) درمانده P lrnd. distressed, helpless, broken-down, worn out. —gâh (.—.—) P the poor and destitute. —gî (.—.—) P misery, poverty, exhaustion.

dermansız (.—.) درمانسز 1. exhausted, feeble, debilitated. 2. poet. irremediable, incurable, beyond remedy. — dert incurable disease. —lık incurability, debility.

derme درمه gathered, collected together. — çatma hastily put up, jerry-built; scraps, odds and ends. — devşirme archaic hastily collected together.

dermeyan (..—) درميان P lrnd. in the midst, under discussion; up for discussion. — et= /ı/ 1. to bring forward for consideration. 2. to produce, to display.

dernek^ği درنك 1. association, society, club. 2. gathering, assembly; place of assembly. 3. prov. wedding feast; public amusement.

derneş=^ir درنشمك archaic to gather together.

dernezd درنزد P lrnd. 1. near. 2. with, among. —i ekâbir in the opinion of the great.

derpiş (.—) درپيش P only in — et= /ı/ lrnd. 1. to put forward, submit, consider, bear in mind. 2. to explain. 3. to anticipate, suggest.

derrak^kı (.—) درّاك A lrnd. very intelligent, penetrating.

derri (.—) درّى A lrnd. bright, shining.

ders درس A 1. lesson, class, lecture; example, moral. — al= /dan/ to take lessons (from); to learn a lesson (by). —i âm archaic 1. public lecture in a mosque. 2. theological lectures. — anlat= to give a lesson (to a class etc.). —i as= to play truant from a lesson, to pass up a class. — çalış=, —e çalış= to study. — de= archaic to teach. — et= archaic to study. — gör= /dan/ to be taught (by). — göster= /a/ to teach. — halkası archaic a circle of students assembled for lesson. —i ibret a warning from an example. — kesimi end of school term. — ver= /a/ 1. to give a lesson (to). 2. to teach (someone) not to do the same thing again.

Dersaadet (..—.) درسعادت |Persian **dar-i sa'adat**| Ott. hist. Istanbul.

dersane (.—.) درسخانه var. of **dershane**.

dershân (.—) درسخوان P lrnd. student, pupil.

dershâne (.—.) درسخانه P classroom, schoolroom, place of instruction (less formally regulated than a school).

dersî (.—) درسى A lrnd. pertaining to lessons.

dersiye درسيه A obs. lesson fee; school fees.

dert^di درد |**derd**| 1. pain, suffering, malady, disease, illness. 2. affliction, woe, trouble, sorrow, grief, cares, worries; annoyance, grievance. 3. colloq. tumor, boil. —ini aç= /a/ to confide one's troubles (to). —e çat= to run into trouble. — çek= to suffer. —ini çek= /ın/ to suffer (for another person or thing); to be left to hold the baby. — değil It's no trouble. —e **derman** cure, remedy. —e dert kat= to pile one trouble on another. —ini deş= /ın/ to stir up one's troubles. —e deva cure, remedy. — dök= to pour out one's troubles. —e düş= to fall into trouble. —ine düş= /ın/ to be deeply occupied with something special. —e gir= to get into trouble. —i günü his special thought, his obsession. —ini Marko Paşaya anlat No one will listen to your woes. — ol= /a/ to become a worry (to). — ortağı fellow sufferer. —e sok= /ı/ to cause trouble (for). — üstü, murat üstü Relief will follow the suffering. — yan=, —ini yan= to complain; /a/ to pour out one's troubles (to a person). —ine yan= /ın/ to suffer for.

dertlen=^ir درتلنمك 1. /a or dan/ to be pained (by), to be sorry (because of). 2. prov. to become ill. —dir= /ı/ caus.

dertleş=^ir درتلشمك /la/ to have a heart to heart talk (with); to pour out one's grievances. —tir= /ı/ caus.

dertli درتلى 1. pained; sorrowful, wretched. 2. sick. 3. aggrieved, complaining.

der top درطوپ |**der 4, top**| colloq., only in

— **et=** /ı/ to gather together. — **ol=** 1. to roll into a ball. 2. to be gathered together.
deruhde دروهده P, **deruhte** دروهته assumed, undertaken. — **et=** /ı/ to undertake, to take upon oneself. —**ci** obs. contractor.
derun (.—) درون P lrnd. inside, interior; heart, mind, soul. — **u birûn** internal and external, outside and in. —**bin** (.——) P obs. med. endoscope. —**dâr** (.——) P grudging, malevolent, spiteful.
derunec (.—.) درونج A leopard's bane, bot., Doryanthes Pardalianches. —**i akrebî** heliotrope, bot., Heliotropium europaeum.
derunî (.——) درونى P lrnd. 1. internal, inner; mental, spiritual. 2. cordial, sincere. 3. phil. intrinsic.
derunperver (.—..) درون پرور P lrnd. 1. generous, brave, noble-hearted. 2. heart-winning.
derunriş (.——) درون ريش P lrnd. wounded, offended; heartsore, careworn.
dervaze (.—.) درواز ه P lrnd. door, gate. —**i gûş** poet. earhole. —**i nûş** poet. mouth. —**bân** (.—.—) P gatekeeper; sentry.
dervend درو ند P, **dervent**di درو نت var. of **derbent**.
derviş 1 درويش [derviş 2] 1. dervish; one who has renounced the world. 2. poor; humble, simple, contented, tolerant. —**in fikri neyse zikri de odur** One cannot keep off the subject that is on one's mind.
derviş 2 (.—) درويش P lrnd., same as **derviş 1**. —**i abapuş** a cloaked dervish. —**i dilriş** a heartsore dervish —**i sultandil** the poor man with the heart of an emperor, the Prophet. —**an** (.——) P lrnd. dervishes. —**âne** (.———.) P in the manner of a dervish. —**î** (.——) P lrnd., —**lik** the quality of a dervish; modesty, contentment. —**meşrep** P, —**nihad** (.—.—) P having the temperament of a dervish, unconventional; simple, tolerant, modest.
derya (.—) دريا P 1. sea, ocean; a large body of water. 2. myst. God, the source and goal of all things. 3. very learned man. —**yi adem** the sea of nothingness, the world. —**yi ahdar**, —**yi ahzar** poet. sky. — **beyi** early Ott. hist. Admiral. **D**—**yı Hind** lrnd. the Indian Ocean. — **kalemi** Ott. hist. central office handling certain affairs of the province of the Archipelago. —**yi lâl** wine cask. —**yi ummân** the ocean.
deryab (.—) دريا ب P lrnd. who knows, knowing.
deryabar (.——) دريا بار P lrnd. 1. sea, ocean, 2. seaport.
deryabend (.—.) دريا بند P lrnd. port, haven.
deryaçe (.—.) دريا چه P lrnd. small sea; lake, pool.
deryadil (.—.) دريا دل P poet. large-hearted, magnanimous, tolerant.
deryaî (.——) دريا يى P lrnd. of the sea, marine.
deryakeş (.—.) دريا كش P poet. insatiable drunkard.
deryaneval (.—.—) دريا نوال P lrnd. bounteous as the sea, very generous.
deryanuş (.——) دريا نوش P same as **deryakeş**.
deryuz (.—), **deryuze** (.—.) دريوز ه دريوز P lrnd. begging, beggary; act of supplication, prayer, request.
derz درز A 1. anat. suture. 2. lrnd. seam. 3. lrnd. wall pointing. —**i iklilî** anat. coronal suture. —**i kışrî** anat. squamous suture. —**i lamî** anat. lambdoidal suture. —**i seffudî** anat. obeloid suture. —**i sehmî** anat. sagittal suture, parietal suture.
derzi (.—) درزى P lrnd. tailor.
derzincir (..—) درزنجير P poet. in chains.
desais (.—.) دسائس A lrnd., pl. of **desise**.
desam (.—), **desame** (.—.) دسام [disam] anat., valvula. —**ı iklilî** valvula mitralis. —**ı sînî** valvula semilunaris.
desatin (.——) دساتين A lrnd., pl. of **destan**.
desatir (.——) دساتير A lrnd., pl. of **düstur**.
desdeğirmi دس دگرمى quite round (circle).
desem دسم A lrnd. 1. grease, fat, dripping. 2. greasy dirt, filthy grease.
desen دسن F 1. design; ornament. 2. art drawing.
desigram دسيگرام F decigram.
desilitre (...) دسيليتره F deciliter.
desimalli دسيمال F math. decimal.
desimetre (...) دسيمتره F decimeter. — **kare** F square decimeter. — **küp** F cubic decimeter.
desise (.—.) دسيسه A lrnd. trick, device, plot, intrigue. —**ci** same as **desisekâr**.
desisekâr (.—.—) دسيسه كار P trickster, intriguer, cheat. —**âne** (.—..——.) P tricky, intriguingly. —**lık** trickery.
desiseli دسيسه لى tricky, deceitful.
desister دسيستر F decistere.
deskere دسكره P lrnd., same as **teskere**.
despot دسپوت Gk 1. despot. 2. Greek Orthodox Church despot. 3. hist., title of Christian rulers. —**hane** (..—.) Greek Orthodox Church office and residence of a despot. —**luk** quality or rank of a despot.
dessam (.—), **dessame** (.—.) دسّام دسّامه vars. of **desam**, **desame**.
dessas (.—) دسّاس A lrnd. intriguer, trickster; intriguing, deceitful.
dest دست P poet. 1. hand; hand and arm.

dostadest

2. hand's-breadth; handful. 3. grasp, possession. 4. handle; pestle. 5. seat of honor. 6. power, might; superiority. 7. *myst.* God's omnipotence. **—i ahenin** iron hand; might. **—i gayb** hand of fate. **—i izdivacını talep et=** /ın/ to ask for (a girl's) hand in marriage. **—i Musa** the sun. **— u pa** hand and foot. **—i yar** helping hand, support, protection.

destadest (.—.) دستادست P *lrnd.* 1. hand in hand. 2. *com.* ready money.

destalây (.——) دستآلای P *lrnd.* soiled hand.

destâmuz (.——) دستآموز P *lrnd.* 1. accustomed to the hand, tame. 2. bird trained to hunt; skillful, dexterous.

destan (.—) دستان P 1. epic, epic poem. 2. *folk literature* ballad, song. 3. *poet.* song (of birds). 4: *archaic* history, tale, fable. 5. *lrnd.* fraud, imposture. 6. *w. cap., poet.* Zal (the father of Rustam). **— gibi** very long (letter, etc.). **—ger** (.—.) P *lrnd.* deceiver, impostor.

destanzen (.—.) دستان زن P *lrnd.* 1. story-teller. 2. bard. 3. musician.

destar (.—) دستار P 1. turban, muslin band wrapped around a headgear. 2. *lrnd.* napkin, tablecloth; handkerchief. **—i humayun** *hist.* Sultan's turban. **— suyu** *Mevlevi order* water into which the end of the sash of Mevlana's turban has been dipped (used for healing). **—i şerif** *Mevlevi order* turban used by the Mevlevi dervishes. **—i Yusufi** *Ott. hist.* special kind of Sultan's turban.

destaran (.——) دستاران P *lrnd.* small gratuity given to a tradesman's assistant or to an artisan before work is done.

destarbaha (.—.—) دستاربها P *Ott. hist.* small gratuity paid to certain officials.

destarbendan (.—.—) دستاربندان P *lrnd.* turban wearers; judges, lawyers, doctors; dervishes.

destarçe (.—.) دستارچه P *lrnd.* 1. small turban. 2. handkerchief.

destarhan (.——) دستارخوان P *lrnd.* 1. tablecloth. 2. food sent on a tray.

destari (.——) دستاری [based on **destar**] *lrnd.* maker of turbans.

destarpuş (.——) دستارپوش P *lrnd.* wearing a turban.

destaviz (.——) دستاویز P *lrnd.* 1. small present from an inferior. 2. a clutching, seizing, firm hold.

destbaz (.—) دستباز P *lrnd.* active, dexterous, skillful.

destbedest دست بدست P *lrnd.* 1. hand in hand. 2. from hand to hand.

destbend دستبند P 1. *lrnd.* handcuff, manacle. 2. bracelet.

destberdehan (...—) دست بردهان P *lrnd.* whose hand is on his mouth (in grief, despair, or rage).

destberencen دست برنجن P *lrnd.* bracelet.

destberser دست برسر P *lrnd.* whose hands are on his head; perplexed; in despair.

destbersine (..—.) دست برسینه P *lrnd.* with the hands clasped on the bosom in an attitude of respect, ready for service.

destbeste دستبسته P *lrnd.* 1. whose hands are bound; prisoner, captive. 2. close-fisted, avaricious.

destbus (.—) دستبوس P *lrnd.* 1. a kissing of hands. 2. who kisses the hand. **—i** (.——) P a kissing of hands.

destbürd دستبرد P *lrnd.* 1. superiority, superior skill. 2. victory, conquest.

destçalâk[ki] (.——) دست چالاک P *lrnd.* light-fingered; thief.

destçub (.—) دست چوب P same as **desteçub**.

destdiraz (..—) دست دراز P *lrnd.* 1. with long hands. 2. rapacious, oppressive.

deste 1 دسته P 1. bunch, bouquet; packet. 2. dozen. 3. a quire of paper; *Turk. art* a packet containing ten sheets of gold leaf. 4. *Or. wrestling* the lowest of the five grades into which wrestlers are divided. 5. *lrnd.* handle, hilt; the neck of a guitar or violin; pestle. **— başı** choice specimen put on the top of a package of goods. **— deste** by dozens, in packets, in heaps.

deste 2 دسته It only in **— et=** *naut.* to ride hard.

desteçub (..—) دسته چوب P *lrnd.* stick, staff.

destefgen دست افکن P *lrnd.* 1. servant, subject; weak. 2. keepsake; memorandum, sketch, note.

destefşan (..—) دست افشان P *lrnd.* 1. who emotionally waves his hands and arms about. 2. dancer.

destefşar (..—) دست افشار P *lrnd.* held and squeezed in the hand; kind of compressible gold and a ball made of it.

destefzar (..—) دست افزار P *lrnd.* hand implement, tool.

destegül دسته گل P *lrnd.* long-sleeved cloak of a dervish.

destek[gi] دستک P 1. support; prop; beam used as a prop. 2. *naut.* crutch. 3. *lrnd.* tiny hand. **— bağı** *anat.* sustentaculum. **— doku** *biol.* support tissue. **— koy=**, **— vur=** /a/ to put a prop, shore or support (to something). **—le=** /ı/ to prop, to support. **—len=** *pass.* of **destekle=**. **—li** supported, propped.

destekzen دستک زن P *lrnd., mus.* one who beats time.

destemora (...'.) دستامورا It *naut.*

cap of a mast, lower mast cap. — **zivanası** mast head tenon.

destenbuye (..—.) دستنبویه P *lrnd*. 1. pomander. 2. small fragrant species of melon.

destendaz (..—) دستانداز P *lrnd*. 1. who waves his hands about; dancer; swimmer; archer. 2. pickpocket. 3. oppressor.

destere دسترە P *same as* **testere**.

desteseng دستسنگ P *lrnd*., *fine arts* small pestle for mixing paint, etc.

destevrencen دستاورنجن P *lrnd*. bracelet.

destfüruş (..—) دستفروش P *lrnd*. hawker, peddler.

destgâh (.—) دستگاە P *lrnd*., *same as* **tezgâh**.

destgir (.—) دستگیر P *lrnd*. 1. who takes by the hand; helper, protector, patron; saint. 2. taken by the hand. 3. prisoner.

desthat[tu] دست خط P *lrnd*. 1. one's own handwriting. 2. signature.

desthun (.—) دستخون P *lrnd*. «blood throw» (at dice when a gamester has staked his head or a limb of his body).

desti دستی [P .—] *prov., same as* **testi**.

destimal[li] (..—) دستمال [*Persian* **dastmâl**] *lrnd*. napkin, handkerchief.

destine (.—.) دستینه P *lrnd*. 1. bracelet. 2. autograph. 3. neck of a guitar or lute.

destkâr (.—) دستکار P *lrnd*. 1. handwork, a work of art. 2. workman; artisan. **—î** P *lrnd*. 1. handmade. 2. art; trade.

destkeş دستکش P *lrnd*. 1. who withdraws his hand; who abandons, who throws in his hand. 2. who puts forth his hand, beggar. 3. led by the hand; who leads by the hand. 4. prisoner, captive. 5. glove. 6. pay, hire.

destmal[li] (.—) دستمال P *lrnd*., *same as* **peştemal**.

destmaye (.—.) دستمایه P *lrnd*. capital, stock in hand.

destmerd دستمرد P *lrnd*. a friend in need.

destnüvişt دست نوشت P *lrnd*. one's own handwriting; signature.

destpak[ki] (.—) دستپاك P *lrnd*. 1. clean-handed, with unsoiled hands. 2. empty-handed. 3. handkerchief, towel.

destpeyman (..—) دستپیمان P *lrnd*. dowry.

destrenc دسترنج P *lrnd*. 1. manual work. 2. hire for service.

destres دسترس P *lrnd*. who obtains, attains, succeeds. — **ol=** /a/ to attain (to), to arrive (at).

destroyer (..'.) دستروییر E *navy* destroyer.

destur 1 (.'—) دستر [**destur 2**] 1. Make way! 2. with your permission, by your leave. **—un** begging your pardon (used before mentioning something considered improper).

destur 2 (.—) دستر P 1. permission; leave. 2. *Persian hist.* prime minister; vezir, counselor of state; high priest of the Zoroastrians. — **al=** 1. to obtain permission. 2. to get leave. **—u a'zam, —u mükerrem** *hist.* His Excellency the Prime Minister. **—u müracaat** *lrnd*. leave to return. **—unu tutama=** *pop*. not to be able to hold one's water. — **ver=** /a/ 1. to allow, to permit. 2. to give leave.

destursuz دستورسز without permission; without leave. — **bağa gireni sopa ile kovarlar** It is improper to enter any place without permission.

destvane (.—.) دستوانە P *lrnd*. 1. bracelet. 2. glove; gauntlet.

destyab (.—) دستیاب P *lrnd*. successful, victorious; success, victory.

destyar (.—) دستیار P *lrnd*. friend, helper, assistant. **—i** (.——) P help, assistance.

destzen دستزن P *lrnd*. starting, commencing.

-deş 1 دش *var. of* **-daş**, *as in* **kardeş**.

deş=[er] **2** دشمك /1/ 1. to lance (boil). 2. to open up (a painful subject). **—ele=** /1/ to scratch up (the ground). **—ik** pierced, burst open; hole. **—il=** *pass. of* **deş=**. **—im**, **—me** *verbal n. of* **deş=**.

deşne دشنە P *poet*. dagger. **—i subh** the rays of morning sunlight.

deşt دشت P *lrnd*. desert, waterless plain. **—i fena** *poet*. this world. **D—i Kıpçak** *hist.* the Sarmatian Steppe, the country of the Golden Horde. **—î** (.—) P wild, found in the desert.

deştir=[ir] دشدرمك /1, a/ *caus. of* **deş= 2**.

detay دتای F detail.

detektör دەتکتور F *elec*. detector.

determinant دترمینانت F *math., biol.* determinant.

determinizm دترمینیزم F *phil.* determinism.

detonatör دەتوناتور F *mil.* detonator.

dev دیو P 1. ogre; demon, fiend; devil. 2. giant; gigantic. — **adımlarıyla ilerle=** to make gigantic progress. — **anası** 1. ogress; female demon. 2. monstrous (woman). — **aynası** convex mirror, magnifying mirror. **kendini dev aynasında gör=** to have inflated ideas about oneself. — **gibi** enormous, huge, gigantic. — **yıldız** *astr.* giant star.

deva (.—) دواء A remedy, medicine, cure. **—yı kül** panacea, all-healing medicine.

devab[bbı] (.—) دواب A *lrnd*., *pl. of* **dabbe**.

devadev (.—.) دوادو P *lrnd*. a running hither and thither.

devahi (.——) دواهی A *lrnd*., *pl. of* **dahiye 1**.

devahil (.——.) دواخل A *lrnd*., *pl. of* **dahile**.

devahin (.——) دواخین A *lrnd*., *pl. of* **duhan**.

devai 1 (.——) دوائی A *lrnd*. pertaining to drugs, medicinal.

devai 2 (.——) دواعی A *lrnd*., *pl. of* **daiye**.

devair (.—.) دوائر A 1. offices, departments. 2. *lrnd.* circles. **—i mütevaziye** *geom., astr.* concentric circles; parallels of latitude, parallels of declination. **—i müttehidetülmerakiz** *geom.* concentric circles.

devali (.——) دوالي A *lrnd.* 1. *anat.*, pl. of **daliye**. 2. varicose.

devalib (.——) دوالیب A *lrnd.*, pl. of **dulab**.

devalüasyon دوالواسیون F devaluation.

devam (.—) دوام A 1. continuation. 2. duration. 3. a frequenting, attendance. 4. constancy, assiduity. **—!** Go on. **— et=** 1. to last, to go on. 2. /a/ to continue, to keep on; to carry on, to go on (with). 3. /a/ to attend, follow (classes). 4. /dan, a kadar/ to extend (from, to). 5. to persevere. **—ı var** to be continued (article or serial).

devamlı دوامی 1. continuous, lasting, unbroken, uninterrupted, steady. 2. constant, assiduous; regular.

devamsız دوامسز 1. without continuity. 2. inconstant. 3. irregular (in attendance). **—lık** lack of continuity or perseverance; irregular attendance at work, absenteeism.

devan (.—) دوان P *poet.* running, that runs.

devanapezir (.——.—) دواناپذیر P *lrnd.* incurable.

devar (.—) دوار A *lrnd.* giddiness, vertigo.

devasa (.——) دیواسا [divâsâ] *lrnd.* gigantic, giant-like.

devat (.—) دوات A *lrnd.*, same as **divit**. **—dar** (.——) P *hist.* Keeper of the Inkstand (title of a vizierial secretary).

devavin (.—.—) دواوین A *lrnd.*, pl. of **divan** 3.

deve دوه camel. **— bağırtan** steep and stony road. **—nin başı!** *colloq.* stuff and nonsense! incredible! **—ye bin=** *slang* to take dope. **— bir akçeye, deve bin akçeye** When you have no money you can't buy a thing no matter how cheap it is; when you have money you buy it however expensive it is. **— boynu** 1. *geog.* low pass over a mountain ridge. 2. S or U-shaped tube. **—den büyük fil var** There is always one mightier. **— dağarcığı** he-camel's faucal bag. **— dikeni** 1. thistle, *bot.*, Carduus. 2. camel's thorn, *bot.*, Alhagi Maurorum. **— dişi** having large grains (wheat), having large seeds (pomegranate). **— döşlü** hollow-bellied (horse). **— dudaklı** drooping-lipped. **—yi düze çıkar=** to overcome difficulties, to get on the smooth road. **— ekmeği** *prov.* carob, locust bean. **— elması** eryngo, *bot.*, Eryngium. **— gibi** huge and awkward (person). **—yi gördün mü? Yeden görsün!** I haven't seen a thing. I know nothing about it (said by someone who wants to avoid all responsibilities). **— gözü** kind of large sweet grapes. **—si hacı** Only his camel is a pilgrim (said of a person who has made the pilgrimage to Mecca but has remained unaffected). **—yi hamudu ile yut=** to take everything, lock, stock, and barrel. **— hamuru** a ball of dough given to a camel; any indigestible food. **—ye hendek atlat=** to try to do an impossible or very difficult thing. **— hörgücü** camel's hump. **— kenesi** camel tick. **— kini** a great and lasting hatred, deep-seated rancor. **— kinli** vindictive as a camel, never forgetting or forgiving an injury. **— kolu** *mil.* camel brigade. **— köçeği, — köşeği** sucking camel colt, very young camel. **— kulağı** common sanicle, *bot.*, Sanicula. **—de kulak** a drop in the ocean. **— kuşu*. — mesti** skin of a camel's foot. **—nin nalı!** *same as* **devenin başı! — nalbanda bakar gibi** *joc.* with a look of blank astonishment. **— ol=** to disappear (money, etc.). **— otu** wild oat grass, *bot.*, Danthonia Forskalii. **—ye ot lâzımsa, boynunu uzatsın** Nothing worthwhile is got without some trying. **— tabanı** 1. colt's foot, *bot.*, Yussilago Farfara. 2. *archaic* large wine cup. 3. *archaic* striding walk. **— tımarı** hasty and shoddy work. **— tüyü** 1. camel hair. 2. camel colored. **— yap=** /ı/ to embezzle. **—yi yardan uçuran bir tutam ottur** By running after a petty attraction a whole enterprise can be brought to disaster. A small incident may cause a great disaster. **— yuları** *Or. wrestling* a holding the opponent's head sideways by the chin under one's arm. **— yürekli** coward. **— yürüyüşü** slow but constant work.

deveci دوه جی 1. camel driver. 2. camel owner. **—ler** *Ott. hist.*, name of the first five regiments of Janissaries.

devecik[ti] دوه جك *archaic* chameleon.

devekuşu[nu] دوه قوشی ostrich, *zool.*, Struthio camelus.

devende دونده P *lrnd.* running, that runs about; which flows.

deveran (..—) دوران 1. *biol.* circulation. 2. *astr.* revolution. 3. *lrnd.* a going around. **—ı dem** *biol.* blood circulation. **— mihveri** *astr.* axis of rotation. **— müddeti** *astr.* period of rotation. **—î** (..—) A 1. circulatory. 2. circulating, revolving.

devha دوحه A *lrnd.* 1. a large tree with spreading branches. 2. grove, thicket, orchard.

Devhatüzzeheb دوحة الذهب A *Isl. rel.* the Golden Tree (title given to the Caliph Ali).

devi (.—) دوی A *lrnd.* 1. continued confused sound, hum, buzz; rumble, roar. 2. a ringing in the ear.

devim *neol., sc.* movement, motion.

devin=[ir] دوینمك 1. *neol., sc.* to move. 2. *prov.*

to struggle, to kick about. —dir= /ı/ caus.
devinduyum *neol., psych.* kinesthesia, kinesthesis. —sal kinesthetic.
devingen *neol., sc.* mobile. — **damar** *physiol.* vasomotor.
devinirlikği *neol., phil.* motility.
devirvri **1** د و ر [devr] 1. period, epoch, era. 2. cycle. 3. turn, tour, revolution; *sc.* period; *astr.* period of revolution. 4. *sc.* circuit, circumference, periphery. 5. *com.* transfer, a turning over. 6. *Mevlevi order* a ritual whirling. 7. *Isl. myst.* cycle of existence passing out from the Divine Reality down through the Arc of Descent and then back into the godhead in the form of the Perfect Man. 8. *Or. mus.* rhythmic cycle. — **basamak** *arch.* step of spiral stairs. — **devir** by turns, in cycles, in periods. — **sür**= to live happily and in prosperity.
[For other compounds, see **devr**.]
devir=ir **2** دويرمك د د رمك د ديرمك /ı/ 1. to overturn, knock down, turn over, turn upside down; to throw down, overthrow; to upset, capsize. 2. to tilt to one side. 3. to drink down, toss off (in drinking). 4. to turn on a lathe.
devirli دورلى *sc.* periodic.
devirt=ir دورتمك /ı/ *caus.* of **devir**=. —til= *pass.*
devit=ir /ı/ *neol.* to move, to put into action. —ken *phil.* motor.
devlet دولت A 1. state; government; power; dynasty. 2. prosperity, good luck, success; high rank. —çe on the part of the government. —le Good luck to you (said to the departing guest). — **adamı** statesman. D—**i Aliye**, D—**i Aliyei Osmaniye** the Ottoman Empire. —**ler arası** international; intergovernmental. —**ler arası hukuku** international law. —**ler arası idare hukuku** international administrative law. —**ler arası ticaret hukuku** international commercial law. D—**i Behiyei İran** the Kingdom of Iran. — **borçları** public debt, national debt. —**i döndü** His fortune has declined. — **düşkünü** who has seen better days. — **emlâki** public property. — **erkânı** ministers and high officials. —**in esas hakları** *law* fundamental rights of States. D—**i Fahîme** *obs.* illustrious state (complimentary title applied to any Power, except Turkey and Persia). — **hazinesi** state treasury, Exchequer. — **hizmeti** government service, public service, civil service. —**ler hukuku** *law* the law of nations. —**ler hususî hukuku** international private law. — **ve ikbal ile** Good luck to you (said to a departing guest). —**ler konfederasyonu** confederation of states. — **kuşu** unexpected good luck, windfall. — **memuru** government official. — **muameleleri** acts of state. D—**i Osmaniye** the Ottoman Empire. — **reisi** head of the State. — **ricali** ministers and high officials. D— **Şurası** Council of State. — **tahvilâtı** state bonds. —**ini tep**= to destroy one's own good luck. —**ler umumî hukuku** international law, law of nations. — **varidatı** public revenues. —**çi** partisan of state control. —**çilik** étatisme, state control.
devlethane (..—.) دولتخانه P house of prosperity (a polite reference to somebody else's house).
devlet'iktiran (....—) دولت اقتران P *lrnd.* prosperous, fortunate.
devletleştir=ir دولتلشدرمك /ı/ to nationalize, to bring under state control. —**me** nationalization.
devletli دولتلو 1. prosperous, fortunate; wealthy. 2. most excellent (title given to Sultans and ministers). 3. *prov.* owl.
devletlû (..—) دولتلو *archaic* illustrious, excellent (formerly applied to officials of the first and highest class). — **fahametlû** illustrious and excellent (title given to the Grand Vizier). — **siyadetlû** illustrious and of noble descent (title given to the Grand Sherif of Mecca).
devletmeab (...—) دولتمآب P *same as* **devletli**.
devletmedar (...—) دولتمدار P *lrnd.* center of greatness; great (king, etc.).
devletmend دولتمند P *lrnd.* prosperous, fortunate; wealthy.
devletsiz دولتسز unlucky, unfortunate.
devletyab (..—) دولتياب P *lrnd.* prosperous, fortunate.
devonikği دوونيك P *geol.* Devonian.
devr دور A *lrnd., same as* **devir** 1. —**i afitab** *astr.* solar cycle. —**i âlem** a going round the world, globe-trotting. —**i aşari calendar** cycle of ten years. —**i bâtıl** *log.* reasoning in a circle. —**i çerh** *poet.* motions of the heavens. —**i daim** a moving in a closed circle; *phys.* perpetual motion. —**i daim tulumbası** *auto.* water pump. —**i dilârâ** *poet.* age of happiness. —**i ekdah** *poet.* a circling of wine cups. —**i isnaaşerî** *calendar* twelve-year cycle (formerly used by Turks and Persians). —**i felek** *poet.* vicissitudes of fortune. —**i gûşmal** times of repressions, days of calamity and distress. —**i gül** *poet.* rose blossom time. —**i hindî** *Or. mus.* a minor rhythmic pattern of seven beats with signature of 7/8. —**i içtimai** *astr.* cycle based on sun-moon conjunctions (i. e., month). —**i ihtiyari** 12 day cycle of lucky and unlucky days. —**i ikbal** period of prosperity and good fortune. —**i inhitat** *hist.* period of decline, era of

devr decadence. **—i kamerî** *astr.* lunar cycle. **—i kasdi** *path.* crisis. **—i kebir** 1. *Or. mus.* a major rhythmic pattern of 28 beats with signature of 28/4. 2. *Mevlevi order* ritual exchange of good wishes on Bayram days. **—i kebise** *calendar* embolismic cycle. **—i mi'cerî** 1. *astr.* the moon's orbit. 2. *lrnd.* life in this present world. **—i muhasebe** *adm.* the turning over of affairs by a resigning official to his successor. **—i nücumî** *astr.* astral cycle. **—i rahavi** *obs.* revolution in a horizontal plane. **—i revan** *Or. mus.* a fast rhythmic pattern composed of 14 or 26 beats. **D—i Saadet** *Isl. hist.* period of the lifetime of the Prophet Muhammad. **—i sabık** *pol., ancien regime; hist.* reign of the previous sultan. **—i sabık yarat=** *pol.* to hold the civil service personnel responsible for the wrongs of a bygone régime. **—i saltanat** reign (of a sultan). **—i senevî** anniversary. **—i sittinî** *calendar* cycle of 60 years. **—i şemsî** *astr.* solar cycle. **—i şer'î** *can. law* fictitious sale of property in order to avoid open violation of the law against usury. **—i tefrih** *path.* incubation period. **— ü temlik** *law* transfer. **—ü teselsül** *law* vicious circle in a legal action, admitting of no decision. **— ü teslim** *adm.* the turning over of affairs by a resigning official to his successor. **— i tezayüd** *path.* development period of an illness. **—i turan** *Or. mus.* a rhythmic pattern of seven beats. **—i zaman** lapse of time.

devr 2 دور P *lrnd.* repetition of a lesson.

devran (.—) دوران [deveran] 1. time, age, epoch. 2. *poet.* wheel of fortune, fate. 3. *myst. orders* the turning of dervishes with their arms on the shoulders of one another during the performance of **tekke** music. **— sür=** to live happily in prosperity.

devre 1 دوره A 1. period; term, epoch. 2. session (of Parliament etc.); cycle. 3. *elec.* circuit. 4. *sc.* rotation, revolution.

devre 2 دوره *prov.* wrong; in the wrong way, upside down.

devrent[dı] دورنت *var.* of **dervent**.

devret=[der] دورهتمك 1. /ı, a/ to turn over, to transfer. 2. *lrnd.* to revolve, to circulate.

devrhan دورخوان P *lrnd.* person whose duty is to keep on reciting the Quran.

devrî (.—) دورى [based on **devr**] *sc.* 1. pertaining to rotation, rotatory. 2. periodical, periodic, cyclical. **— halle** *astr.* periodic solution.

devrik[gı] دوریك folded, turned back on itself. **— cümle** *neol., gram.* inverted order of words. **— yaka** turn-down collar.

devril=[ir] دوریلمك 1. *pass.* of **devir=** 2. 2. to capsize; to be overthrown (government).

devrim دوریم 1. folding; curve, bend. 2. *neol.* revolution; reform. **—ci** *neol.* revolutionary; progressive.

devrisi دوریسی *prov.* next, following (day, year).

devriye 1 دوریه [devriye 2] *mil.* patrol; police beat. **— gez=** to go the rounds.

devriye 2 (.—.) دوریّه A *Isl. rel.* 1. a rank among cadis. 2. *myst.* poem on the Creation.

devrnüma (..—) دورنما P *lrnd.* diorama; panorama.

devşir=[ir] دوشیرمك 1. to collect, to gather, to pick. 2. to roll up, to fold. **—il=** *pass.*

devşirim دوشیریم *verbal n.* of **devşir=**. **—li** compact, put together, tidy. **—siz** badly put together, untidy.

devşirme دوشیرمه 1. *verbal n.* of **devşir=**. 2. *Ott. hist.* recruiting of boys for the Janissary corps; a boy so recruited.

devvar (.—) دوّار A *sc.* revolving, rotating.

Dey دی P *lrnd.* 1. Persian calendar, name of the tenth month of the solar year. 2. winter; December.

deycur (.—) دیجور A *lrnd.* darkness; dark (night).

deydan (.—), **deyden** دیدان A *lrnd.* custom, habit, way.

deyi 1 1. *neol., psych.* ability of expression, language. 2. *phil.* logos.

deyi 2 دی *prov.,* same as **diye**.

deyim *neol.,* idiom, phrase, expression.

deyiş دیش 1. *verbal n.* of **de=** 1. 2. kind of folk poem or song.

deymumet (.—.) دیمومت A *lrnd.* permanence, perpetuity, continuity.

deyn دین A *law* debt, obligation; incumbent duty, obligatory act.

deynunet (.—.) دینونت A *law* a trial at law with conviction and sentence; a being judged, found guilty and sentenced.

deyr دیر A *lrnd.* 1. monastery, convent; church, temple. 2. *myst.* this world. 3. *poet.* tavern. **—i mihnet** this world of suffering. **—i mugan** 1. temple of the magi. 2. tavern. **—anî** (.——) A pertaining to a monastery.

deyre دیره *prov.* open-fronted dress with side-slit skirt.

deyrhane (.—.) دیرخانه P same as **deyr**[1].

deyrî (.—) دیری A *lrnd.* pertaining to a monastery.

deyü دیو *archaic,* same as **diye**.

deyyan (.—) دیّان A *lrnd.* requiter of good and evil; judge, ruler, especially, God, the supreme ruler.

deyyar (. —) ديّار A *lrnd.* 1. inhabitant of a convent, monk. 2. anyone.

deyyus (. —) ديّوث A *vulg.* pander, cuckold. **—luk** profession of a pander.

dezenfekte ده ن ف ه نطفه F disinfected. **— et=** /ı/ to disinfect.

-dı 1, -di, -du, -dü, د ط same as **-tı 4** *as in* **patırdı, lakırdı.**

=di 2, =di 2, =du, =dü, *after unvoiced consonants* **=tı 2, =ti 2, =tu 2, =tü 4,** *after vowels* **=ydı, =ydi, =ydu, =ydü** (. .́) يدى يد [idi] 1. *at the end of sentence* he (she, it) was, *e. g.,* **hava güzeldi.** The weather was fine. 2. *in enumerations, e. g.,* **kalemdi, kâğıttı, filândı, falandı derken masraf büyüdü** Pencils, paper, odds and ends, all together, it came to quite a sum.

=dı 3, =di, =tı, *etc.* 3rd person of perfective past, *e. g.,* **geldi** He came. He has come. **düştü** He fell. He has fallen.

dıbabiye (. — —.) ضبابيّه [*based on Arabic*] *zool.,* Sauria.

dıbıkᵏᶦ ديبيس [dıbk] *prov.* 1. sticky matter. 2. birdlime. **—lı** smeared with birdlime. **—lık** stickiness.

dıbkᵏᶦ دبق A *lrnd., same as* **dıbık.**

dığdığı ديغدىغى دغ دغى who pronounces r like ğ; who stutters over d and t.

=dık 1, =dik, =tık, =ydık, *etc.* (. .́) *pl. of* **=dım 1,** *etc.* يديك ديك دك يدك

=dıkᵏᶦ **2, =dik, =tık,** *etc.* دك ديك 1. *participle referring to an action conceived as realized, as in* **bildik, tanıdık;** *cf.* **=madık;** *with possessive suffix, e. g.,* **okuduğum kitap** the book I am reading, the book I have read. **gördüklerini anlat!** Say what you see. Say what you have seen. **oturduğumuz ev** the house we live in. 2. *with possessive suffix, verbal noun in which the action is conceived as realized, e. g.,* **geldiğini öğrendim** I have heard that he has come. I heard that he had come. **düştüğünü gördüm** I saw him fall.

=dık 3, =dik, =tık, *etc.* ديك دك *pl. of* **=dım 2,** *etc.*

dıkᵏᵏᶦ **4** دقّه A *lrnd.* 1. wasting of the soft tissues of the body. 2. hectic fever.

dıkakᵏᶦ (. —) دقاق A *anat.* ileum.

=dıkça, =dikçe, =tıkça, *etc.* دكجه 1. each time that, *e. g.,* **aklıma geldikçe** Every time I think of it. 2. the more, *e. g.,* **düşündükçe kızıyorum** The more I think of it the angrier I become. 3. as long as, *e. g.,* **sen ısrar ettikçe** as long as you insist. 4. *in paronomasia* more and more, *e. g.,* **azıttıkça azıttı** He got more and more out of hand.

=dıkta, =dikte, =tıkta, *etc. archaic* while, when, *e. g.,* **buraya geldikte** when he (you, etc.) came here.

=dıktan başka, =dikten başka, *etc.* دقدن بشقه besides, after, *e. g.,* **bunu kabul ettikten başka** not only did he (you, etc.) accept, but.

=dıktan sonra, =dikten sonra, *etc.* دقدن صوكره after, *e. g.,* **gittikten sonra** after having left, after he (you, etc.) has (had) left.

dılᶦᶦ ضلع same as **dılı.**

dılakᵏᶦ دودو clitoris.

dılıᶦᶦ ضلع [dıl] 1. *geom.* side. 2. *biol.* rib. 3. *math.* square root; square 4. *lrnd.* segment of a globular figure. **—ı kâzib** *anat.* false rib. **—ı mücessem** *geom.* edge. **—ı zaviye** *geom.* side of an angle.

dıl'î (. —) ضلعى A *anat.* costal.

=dım 1, =dim 1, =ydım, *etc.* دم يم [idim] (. .́) I was, *e. g.,* **yoktum** I was not there; **hastaydım** I was sick; **bendim** It was I.

=dım 2, =dim 2, *etc.* دم 1st. *person singular of past, e. g.,* **aldım** I bought, I have bought; **düştüm** I fell, I have fallen.

dımdızlakᵏᶦ (. .́.) ديم دزلاق *colloq.* 1. bare, naked, bald. 2. destitute; empty-handed.

Dımışkᵏᶦ دمشق A same as **Dimişk.**

=dın 1, =din, =tın, =ydın, *etc.* (. .́.) دك يدك [idin] 2nd person singular, familiar style, you were, *e. g.,* **yoktun** You were not there. **hastaydın** You were sick.

=dın 2, =din, =tın, *etc.* دك 2nd person singular of past, familiar style, *e. g.,* **bekledin** You waited; you have waited; **düştün** You fell; you have fallen.

=dınız 1, =diniz, =tınız, =ydınız, *etc.* (. .́..) دكز [idiniz] *pl. of* **=dın 1,** *etc.*

=dınız 2, *etc., pl. of* **=dın 2,** *etc.*

=dır 1, =dir, =tır, *etc.* (. .́.) در 1. *at the end of sentence* is, is indeed, *e. g.,* **azdır** It is little. **yapacaktır** He is indeed going to do it. 2. *attached to noun before final verb, expressive element stressing the noun, e. g.,* **bir kıyamettir koptu** A frightful tumult started.

=dır⁼ᵗ **2, =dir=, =tır=,** *etc., causative* to make, to have, to cause, *as in* **yaptır=, yazdır=, vurdur=, çıkartır=.**

Dıraçᶜᶦ دراچ Durazzo (in Albania.)

dıragon دراغون *var. of* **dragon.**

dırahoma (. .́..) دراهومه *var. of* **drahoma.**

dırav دراو *slang* money.

dırdır دردر در در a continuous grumbling; nagging. **— et=** to grumble, to nag. **—cı** grumbler, nagger.

dırdırı دردرى *same as* **dırdırcı.**

dırılda=ʳ, **dırıldan=**ʳ دريلدامق دريلدانمق to whine and annoy continuously.

dırıltı دريلتى درلتى 1. a grumbling snarling; wearisome talk. 2. squabble. **— çı**

kar= to cause a squabble. **— et=** 1. to make an annoying noise. 2. to grumble; to nag; to talk in a tiresome way.

dırlan=ᵗʳ درلانمق درلانمق to complain, to talk annoyingly.

dırlaş=ᵗʳ درلاشمق درلاشمق to squabble in undertones.

dış ديش طيش طش outside, exterior; outer appearance; outer covering; external, outer; foreign; *geom.* circumscribed. **—ında** /ın/ outside of, *e. g.*, **bunun dışında** outside of this. **—tan** external, externally; *phil.* adventitious. **— açı** *geom.* exterior angle. **— ağaları** *Ott. hist.*, *title given to some high officials.* **— başkalaşım** *neol., geol.* exomorphism. **— bükey** *neol., sc.* convex. **— deniz** ocean. **— deri** 1. *histology* ectoderm. 2. *bot.* exodermis. **—a dönük** *psych.* extrovert. **—a dönüm** *psych.* extroversion. **—ı eli yakar, içi beni yakar** Don't be deceived by appearances. **— haberler** foreign news. **— hat** external line; *mar. com.* international line (calling at foreign ports); international line (telephone). **—ı hayhaylı, içi vayvaylı** Things are seldom what they seem. **— hazine** *Ott. hist.* State treasury. **— işleri** foreign affairs. **D— İşleri Bakanı** Minister of Foreign Affairs. **D— İşleri Bakanlığı** Ministry of Foreign Affairs. **—ı kalaylı, içi vayvaylı** *same as* **dışı hayhaylı, içi vayvaylı.** **— kapak** *bookbinding* outside cover. **— kapının mandalı** a very distant relative. **— lâstik** *auto.* shoe (of tire). **— lenfa** *neol., anat.* perilymph. **— merkez** *neol., geol.* epicenter. **— merkezli** *neol., geom.* eccentric. **— merkezlik** *neol., geom.* eccentricity. **— meydancı** Mevlevi order, title given to the dervish who introduces the initiates to the sheikh. **—a patlama** *ling.* explosion. **— plâzma** *biol.* ectoplasm. **— ters açı** *neol., geom.* alternate exterior angle. **— ticaret** foreign trade. **— yan** *anat.* lateral. **— yarıçap** *neol., geom.* exterior radius of a regular polygon. **— yürek zarı** *anat.* pericardium. **— yüz** outside, exterior; outer surface; appearance.

[**dışarda, dışardan,** *vars. of* **dışarıda, dışarıdan.**]

dışarı طيشارو طشارو ديشارى ديشارو دشارى دشاره 1. out; the outside, exterior. 2. the space outside; out of doors; outdoor. 3. the provinces (as opposed to the capital); the country (as opposed to town). 4. foreign lands, abroad. **—da** outside; abroad. **—dan** from the outside; from abroad. **—sında** /ın/ outside of, *e. g.*, **bunların dışarısında** outside of these. **—ya** outside, out, towards the outside; abroad. **— çık=** 1. to go out. 2. to go to the toilet, to defecate. **—dan evlenme** *sociol.* exogamy. **— git=** 1. to go out; to go into the provinces. 2. to go abroad. **— uğra=** 1. to protrude (eyes). 2. to rush out. **— vur=** 1. /ı/ to show, manifest. 2. to show on the outside (spot); to appear, become manifest (illness). **— yaz** *gambler's slang* Write it down as a win. **—lı** provincial, rustic. **—lık** *same as* **dışarlık.**

dışarlakᵍⁱ ديشارلاق projecting, protruding.

dışarlıkᵍⁱ ديشارلق the provinces.

dışıkᵍⁱ *neol., geol., chem.* scoria.

dışınlı *neol., phil.* extrinsic.

dışkı *neol., biol.* feces. **—lık** *biol.* cloaca.

dışlıkᵍⁱ ديشلك طشلى *prov.* peace, calmness, quietness. **—sız** restless. **—sızlık** restlessness.

dışrakᵍⁱ *neol., phil.* exoteric.

dızdıkᵍⁱ دزدك *only in* **—ının dızdığı** a distant relative.

dızdızcı دزدزجى *slang* kind of pickpocket; swindler. **—lık** swindling.

dızgal دزغال *slang* beard. **—lı** bearded.

dızık=ᵗʳ دزيقمق *prov.* to run.

dızılda=ʳ, **dızıldan=**ᵗʳ دزلدامق دزلدانمق to hum, to buzz. **dızıldat=** /ı/ *caus. of* **dızılda=.**

dızıltı دزلتى دزلدى a continued humming, buzzing.

dızla=ʳ دزلامق 1. to hum, to buzz. 2. *slang* to swindle.

dızlakᵍⁱ دزلاق دزلاو طزلاق *colloq.* bald, naked. **—lık** baldness, nakedness.

dızlan=ᵗʳ دزلانمق طزلانمق to keep on humming or buzzing to oneself.

dızman دزمان طزمان *prov.* big, huge.

dızmır دزمير *prov.* obstinate.

-di 1 دى *cf.* **-dı 1.**
=di 2 دى *cf.* **=dı 2.**
=di 3 دى *cf.* **=dı 3.**
di 4 (—) دى P *lrnd.* yesterday.

diam (.—), **diamet** (.—.) دعامت A *lrnd.* 1. pillar, post. 2. prop, stay, buttress, support. 3. a notable, a pillar of the State.

diayet (.—.) دعايت A *lrnd.* call, summons, invitation.

dib ديب *cf.* **dip.**

diba (——) ديبا P 1. brocade; silk tissue. 2. *poet.* velvety skin and complexion.

dibace (——.) ديباجه *lrnd.* A preface, foreword; prologue. **—bend** (——..) P composer of a preface.

dibağ (.—) دباغ A *lrnd.* tan-liquor.

dibekᵍⁱ ديبك large stone or wooden mortar. **— kahvesi** coffee ground in a mortar. **—hane** (..—.) pounding mill.

dibelik دبلك *archaic* completely, entirely.

dibet ديبت E *obs.* kind of strong woolen material, tibet.

dibkᵏⁱ دبى A *var. of* **dıbk.**

dibs دبس A *lrnd.* boiled juice of grapes or other fruit.

Dicle (' .) دجل A Tigris River.

did=ᵉʳ 1 دیه مك *cf.* **dit=**.

did 2 (—) دید P *lrnd.* 1. a seeing, sight, view, contemplation. 2. *myst.* a spiritual contemplation of God in his glory.

didan (— —) A *lrnd.*, *pl. of* **dud 2**. **—ı em'a** intestinal worms. **—ı haytiye** threadworms. **—ı şeritiye** tapeworms.

didar (— —) P *lrnd.* 1. face, countenance. 2. sight, ocular power. 3. eye. 4. interview, meeting. **—bin** (— — —) . P who beholds the countenance (of another).

dide 1 (— .) دیده P *lrnd.* 1. eye, sight. 2. *myst.* omniscience. **—i giryan** the tearful eye. **—ler ruşen!** I wish you joy; congratulations.

-dide 2 (— .) دیده P *lrnd.* 1. that has seen or experienced, *as in* **asırdide, cihandide**. 2. that has been seen or experienced, *as in* **nâdide**.

dideban (— . —) دیدبان P *lrnd.* watchman, sentry. **—anı âlem** the seven planets. **—ı çeharüm** the sun. **—ı felek** 1. the sun. 2. the planet Saturn.

didebaz (— . —) دیدباز P *lrnd.*1.whose eyes are open. 2. who rolls the eyes, who sends glances.

dideberah (— . . —) دیدبراه P *lrnd.* whose thoughts are on the road; on the lookout, impatient, expectant.

didebidar (— . — —) دیدبیدار P *lrnd.* wide awake, sleepless.

didedar (— . —) دیددار P *lrnd.* 1. sentry, scout. 2. vigilant.

didedûz (— . —) دیددوز P *lrnd.* who fixes his eyes on something.

didegâh (— . —) دیدگاه P *lrnd.* outlook; observatory.

didegân (— . —) دیدگان P *lrnd.* 1. eyes. 2. who has seen or experienced.

didepuş (— . —) دیدپوش P *lrnd.* 1. veiling the eyes. 2. bribe.

dideriz (— . —) دیدریز P *lrnd.* that tires the eye.

dideşur (— . —) دیدشر P *lrnd.* a stroke of the evil eye.

didik didik دیدك دیدك picked into fibers and filaments. **— et=** /ı/ 1. to pick into fibers. 2. to pull to pieces. **— ol=** to go to pieces.

didikle=ʳ دیدكله مك /ı/ 1. to pick into fibers and shreds. 2. to tear to pieces.

didil=ⁱʳ دیدیلمك *pass. of* **dit=**.

didin=ⁱʳ دیدینمك 1. to toil, to wear oneself out. 2. to fret.

didirgin دیدرگین *same as* **tedirgin**.

didiş=ⁱʳ دیدیشمك /la/ to quarrel continuously, to live like a cat and dog, to bicker.

didişimci *neol., phil.* eristic.

didişken دیدیشكن 1. quarrelsome. 2. untiring.

didon دیدون F 1. *colloq.* Frenchman. 2. *slang* snob. **— sakal, — sakallı** wearing an 'imperial'.

difana (. ' .) دیفانا G double or triple fishing net.

diferansiyel دیفرانسیل F *auto.* differential gear.

difraksiyon دیفراكسیون F *phys.* diffraction.

difteri دیفتری F *med.* diphtheria.

difüzör دیفوزور F *phys.* diffuser.

dig (—) دیگ P *lrnd.* kettle, cauldron.

digal (. —) دغال A *lrnd.*, *pl. of* **dagal**.

diger (— .) دیگر P *lrnd.*, *same as* **diğer**. **—bar** (— . —) P another time, again. **—bin** (— . —) P, **—endiş** (— . . —) P altruist, unselfish. **—gûn** (— . —) P altered, changed in color or appearance. **—kâm** (— . —) P altruist, unselfish. **—ruz** (— . —) P the next day.

diğer دیگر [diger] 1. other, the other; different. 2. next, succeeding. **— biri** another; some one else.

diğren دیگرن Gk *prov.* pitchfork.

dih 1 ده P *lrnd.* village, hamlet.

-dih 2 ده P *lrnd.* that gives, *as in* **fermandih**.

dihan (. —) دهان A *lrnd.*, *pl. of* **dühn**.

dihat (. —) دهات P *lrnd.*, *pl. of* **dih 1**.

dihende دهنده P *lrnd.* that gives; a giver.

dihim (. —), (— —) دهیم P *lrnd.* crown, diadem.

dihistan (. . —) دهستان P *lrnd.* a country of villages.

dihiş دهش P *lrnd.* a giving; gift; alms.

dihkan (. —) دهقان P *lrnd.* 1. cultivator. 2. headman of a village. **—î** (. — —) P pertaining to the country; villager, peasant.

Dihli دهلی *obs.* Delhi.

dihliz (. —) دهلیز P A *lrnd.*, *same as* **dehliz**.

dij دژ P *lrnd.* 1. bad, wicked; angry. 2. ugly, horrible. **—aheng** (. — .) P evil-intentioned, malicious.

dijem دژم P *lrnd.* 1. sad, melancholy. 2. mad. 3. angry, furious. 4. drunk.

dijhim (. —) دژخیم P *lrnd.* 1. surly, malignant. 2. jailer, executioner.

dijkâm, (. —), **dijkâme** (. — .) دژكام دژكامه P *lrnd.* 1. angry, furious. 2. abstemious, chaste. 3. eunuch.

dikᵏⁱ **1** دیك 1. perpendicular. 2. straight, upright, stiff (in standing). 3. steep. 4. intent, fixed, penetrating (look). 5. *geom.* right. 6. obstinate, contrary. **— açı** *geom.* right-angle. — **adam** an unyielding, uncompromising man. — **âlâsı** *colloq.* the very utmost (derogatory). — **aşağı** straight down. — **bakışlı** staring angrily, sharp looking. — **baş**, — **başlı** obstinate, pig-headed. — **biçme** *geom.* right prism. — **burun** porbeagle shark, *zool.*, *Lamma Cornubica.* — **dik bak=** /a/ to stare angrily, to look fixedly (at). — **dikine** straight up, up a steep incline. —**i dikine** utterly opposed. — **dörtgen** *geom.* rectangle. — **dur=** to stand upright. —**ine git=** to do just the opposite of what one is asked; to be pig-headed. — **kafalı** pig-headed, obstinate, cussed. — **kenar** *geom.* right side. — **mizaç** 1. an arbitrary disposition. 2. irritable, fussy. — **rüzgâr** *naut.* head wind. — **ses** a sharp voice or sound; harsh voice. — **silindir** *math.* right cylinder. — **söz** sharp, angry words. — **sözlü** rudely outspoken. — **traş**, —**ine traş** 1. a shaving against the grain. 2. *colloq.* utterly boring talk. — **tut=** /ı/ to hold straight, upright. — **üçgen** *geom.* right triangle. — **yamuk** *geom.* trapezoid with one right angle. — **yokuş** steep ascent.

dik=ᵉʳ 2 د َ ك ِ ل /ı/ 1. to sew; to stitch; to make (dress, etc). 2. *naut.* to splice.

dik=ᵉʳ 3 د ِ ك َ ل /ı, a/ 1. to erect, to set up; to stick (a thing into a thing). 2. to plant. 3. to stare, to fix (the eyes upon an object). 4. to prick up (ears). 5. to drain, drink off (a cup). 6. to stand on end (hair).

-**dik** 4 د ِ ك ْ *cf.* -**dık** 1.
=**dik**ᵍⁱ 5 د ِ ك ْ *cf.* =**dık** 2.
=**dik** 6 د ِ ك ْ *cf.* =**dık** 3.
dikᵏⁱ 7 (—) د ِ ك ْ A *lrnd.* cock, rooster. —**i ebyaz** *Isl. myth.* the cock of paradise.
=**dikçe** د ِ ك ْ چ ه *cf.* =**dıkça.**
dikeçᶜⁱ د ِ ك ْ چ *prov.* prop.
dikel د ِ ك َ ل Gk *prov.* long-handled digging-fork.
diken د ِ ك َ ن 1. thorn; spine. 2. thorny plant, thornbush. — **çalıbülbülü** white-throated warbler, *zool.*, *Sylvia communis.* — **çıkıntı** *anat.*, *processus spinalis.* — **dudu** blackberry. — **üstünde otur=** to be on tenterhooks. —**ce** stickleback, *zool.*, *Gasterostens aculeatus.* —**len=** to become thorny.
dikenli د ِ ك َ ن ْ ل ي thorny, prickly. — **balık** stickleback, *zool.*, *Gasterosteus aculeatus.* — **çütre balığı** filefish, *zool.*, *Stephanolepis ocheticus.* — **dülger balığı** dory, John dory, *zool.*, *Zeus faber.* — **öksüz balığı** armed gurnard, *zool.*, *Peristedion cataphractum.* — **tel** barbed wire. — **yılan** death adder, *zool.*, *Acanthophis.*
dikenlikᵍⁱ د ِ ك َ ن ْ ل ك place with many thorns and brambles.

dikensi د ِ ك َ ن ْ س ي spinoid, spinelike. — **çıkıntı** *anat.*, *processus spinalis.*
dikensiz د ِ ك َ ن ْ س ز without thorns; spineless. — **gül bahçesine çevir=** to root out all opposition. — **gül olmaz** *proverb* There is no rose without a thorn. —**siz kalkan** brill, kind of flat fish, *zool.*, *Rhombus laevis.*
dikey *neol.*, vertical; *geom.* perpendicular.
dikgen *neol.*, *geom.* orthogonal.
dikici د ِ ك ي ج ي 1. cobbler. 2. *hist.* tent-pitcher. 3. *obs.* seamstress.
dikikᵍⁱ د ِ ك ِ ك same as **dikili.**
dikil=ⁱʳ د ِ ك ِ ل 1. *pass.* of **dik=** 2, 3. 2. /a/ to post oneself (at a place).
dikili د ِ ك ِ ل ي 1. sewn; stitched; *naut.* spliced. 2. planted, set. 3. set up, erected. **bir — ağacı yok** He doesn't have a stick in this world. — **taş** erect stone monument; obelisk.
dikim د ِ ك ِ م *verbal n.* of **dik=** 2, 3. —**hane** (..—.) workshop for sewing clothes.
dikiş د ِ ك ِ ش 1. seam. 2. *surg.* stitch. 3. *anat.* suture, sutura. 4. *verbal n.* of **dik=** 2, 3. — **dik=** to sew. **bir —te iç=** /ı/ to drink off at a draught. — **iğnesi** sewing needle. — **kaldı** almost, *e. g.*, **yanmasına dikiş kaldı** It almost burned; it was saved from burning by a hair's breadth. — **kutusu** sewing box. — **makinası** sewing machine. — **payı** tailor. seam allowance. — **tutturama=** to be incapable of keeping a post, to be unable to settle down to a job. — **yeri** 1. seam. 2. *med.* stitch scars. — **yurdu** needlework and dress-making school. —**çi** dress-maker, sewing-woman. —**li** sewed, stitched; spliced. —**siz** seamless.
dikitᵈⁱ *neol.*, *geol.* stalagmite.
dikiz د ِ ك ِ ز Romany *slang* look; sly, roguish look; glance. — **aynası** 1. mirror of a car. 2. observation mirror. — **et=**, — **geç=** /ı/ to watch intently, to stare (at). —**ci** *slang* a look-out man (burglar). —**le=** /ı/ to observe intently, stare (at).
dikkatᵗⁱ د ِ ق ّ ت A 1. careful attention. 2. Take care! Look out! 3. *lrnd.* finesse, subtlety. —**e al=** /ı/ to take note (of), to take into consideration. —**i çek=** /a/ to draw, call attention (to). — **dağınıklığı** *psych.* aprosexia. — **et=** 1. /a/ to pay attention (to). 2. to be careful. — **kesil=** to be all ears, to be all attention. —**e şayan** remarkable, worthy of attention.
dikkatli د ِ ق ّ ت ل ي attentive, careful, painstaking; carefully made. —**ce** attentively, carefully, painstakingly.
dikkatsiz د ِ ق ّ ت س ز careless, inattentive; thoughtless. —**lik** carelessness, inattentiveness, thoughtlessness.

dikleme, diklemesine دیکلمه و دکلمه سنه perpendicularly.

diklik[gi] دیكلك ۔ *abstr. n. of* **dik** 1. **— et=** to be obstinate.

dikme دیكمه 1. *verbal n. of* **dik=** 2, 3. 2. seedling, young plant. 3. derrick; prop; single spar crane. 4. *geom*. perpendicular. **— ayağı** *geom.* foot of a perpendicular. **— taş** a stone pillar. **—li** propped, shored-up; furnished with a derrick.

dikmen دیكمن *arch.* peak, summit.

dikse دیكسه *prov.* a tree covered with bird-lime, specially set up on an open plain, at a time when migratory birds are passing over.

diktatorya (...'.) دیكتاتوریا dictatorship.

diktatör دیكتاتور F dictator. **—lük** dictatorship.

dikte 1 دیكته F dictation. **— et=** /ı, a/ 1. to dictate (letter). 2. to dictate to (order). **=dikte** 2 دیكته *cf.* **=dıkta**.

=dikten başka دیكدن باشقه *cf.* **=dıktan başka**.

=dikten sonra دیكدن صوكرا *cf.* **=dıktan sonra**.

diktir=[ir] دكدرمك ۔ دیكدرمك ۔ دیكدیرمك *caus. of* **dik=** 2, 3.

dil 1 دل ۔ دیل 1. tongue; language; dialect. 2. promontory, spit. 3. bolt of a lock; tenon of a mortise; *prov.* key. 4. index of a balance. 5. *naut.* sheave of a block or pulley. 6. reed of a wind instrument. 7. *hist.* military intelligence from a foreign country; prisoner of war expressly taken for the obtaining of information. **—i açıl=** to start talking. **—i ağır** stammerer; whose tongue is heavy. **—i ağırlaş=** to begin to speak with difficulty (sick person). **— ağız verme=** not to be able to talk, to be too ill to talk. **— al=** *hist.* to take a prisoner for information. **— altı** 1. pustule under the tongue. 2. pip (in fowls). **— altı bezi** *biol.* sublingual gland. **—inin altında bir şey var** There is something he hasn't come out with yet. **—inin altındaki baklayı çıkar=** to speak out what is in one's mind without any consideration. **— altı siniri** *anat.* hypoglossal nerve. **— avcısı** spy. **— bağı** 1. frenum under the tongue. 2. hush money. **—ini bağla=** /ın/ to silence. **—i bağlı** 1. tongue-tied. 2. silenced. **— balığı** sole, *zool., Solea vulgaris*. **— basan** *med.* spatula; depressor. **— belâsı** trouble caused by not holding one's tongue. **— bilgisi** *neol.* grammar. **— bilim** *neol.* linguistics. **— bilmez** one who does not speak Turkish. **—i bir karış** impudent, who answers back. **—i bir karış dışarı çıkmak** to get very tired of walking or running on a hot day. **— bozuntusu** jargon. **— buran** astringent. **—i çal=** to speak with an accent. **— çıkar=** to put out the tongue in defiance or mockery. **—i çıkık** idiot, fool. **—i çözül=** to start to talk; to find one's tongue. **—im damağıma yapışmış** My tongue is sticking to the roof of my mouth; I am very thirsty. **— damak** *prov.* who has a sweet tongue. **—lere destan ol=** to be on everybody's tongue. **—i dışarı çık=** to pant. **—den dile dolaş=** *same as* **—e düş=**. **—ine dola=** /ı/ to keep on and on (about a thing). **—de dolaş=, —lerde dolaş=** to be the subject of common gossip. **—i dolaş=** to mumble (from fear, etc.). **— dök=** /a/ to try to talk someone round. **—i döndüğü kadar** as much as he could explain. **— dönme=** to be unable to get one's tongue round a word. **—e düş=, —lere düş=** to become a subject of common talk. **—inden düşürme=** /ı/ to keep on and on (about a thing). **— ebesi** talkative; chatter-box. **—i ensesinden çekilsin** May his tongue be pulled out (curse). **—ini eşek arısı soksun** May his tongue be stung by a hornet (curse said of a person who makes an unpleasant remark). **—ini fare mi yedi?** Have you lost your tongue? **—e gel=** 1. to start to talk. 2. to be a subject of common talk. **—e gelmez** indescribable. **—e getir=** /ı/ to cause to talk. **—de gez=, —lerde gez=** to be disreputable; to be a subject of common talk. **—i her şeye dön=** to be always ready to speak ill of others. **—ini ısır=** to bite one's tongue (to ward off the evil eye). **—le ikrar et=** /ı/ to confirm by word of mouth. **—ine inmiş** 1. He has paralysis of the tongue. 2. He has lost his tongue. **— kavgası** quarrel. **— kayması** slip of the tongue. **—in kemiği yok** The tongue has no bones, *i. e.* One can say anything one likes. **—ini kes=** to shut up. **—ine kıl dolaşmamış** He is smooth of speech. **—ini kıs, otur!** Shut up; be quiet. **—i kısa** *slang* helpless, lacking the courage to speak (because of a fault). **—e kolay** easy to say (but actually difficult). **— koy=** to interfere; to butt in. **—i kurtlu** *prov.* who speaks ill of others, gossiper. **—inden kurtulamazsın** Beware of his tongue; he will never leave you alone. **—i kuru=** 1. to be very thirsty. 2. to exhaust oneself talking. **—in kurusun!** Curse your tongue! **D— Kurumu** Philological Society. **— malası** pointed trowel. **— oğlanı** *hist.* a student-interpreter who is learning the language of the country. **— otu yemiş** *prov.* chatterbox, great talker. **—i pabuç kadar** impudent and tactless in talking back. **—e perhiz et=** to be discreet, to keep a secret. **—ine perhiz etmez** He can't hold his tongue. **—in persengi** a thing frequently on one's tongue, always being repeated. **— peyniri** cheese made in long strips. **—ini peynir ekmekle mi yedin?** What's wrong with your tongue? Why don't you say something? (said to one who keeps silent

dil

where he should speak). **—ine sağlam ol=** 1. to be discreet. 2. to avoid bad language. **—i sarmaş=** to splutter in speaking. **—iyle sok=** /ı/ to wound with the tongue. **—lerle tarif olunamaz** indescribable. **— tut=** *hist.* to capture an enemy for the sake of information. **—ini tut=** to hold one's tongue. **— tutukluğu** *psych.* anarthria, inability to articulate words. **—i tutul=** to be tongue-tied. **—iyle tutul=** to be caught out by one's own words. **—in tutulsun!** Curse your tongue! **—imde tüy bitti** I am sick of saying it over and over again. **— ucu** tip of the tongue. **—imin ucunda dolaşıyor** I am holding myself back from saying it. **—imin ucuna geldi** 1. I nearly let it out. 2. It is on the tip of my tongue; I can't find the right word. **—inin ucunda ol=** to be on the tip of one's tongue, to slip one's memory. **—i uzadı** His tongue is getting too long; he doesn't know his place; he forgets himself. **— uzat=** /a/ to malign, to defame. **—i uzun** impudent, insolent, **— üşür=** *archaic* to talk all at once. **—im varmıyor** I can't bring myself to say it. **—e ver=** /ı/ to divulge, to denounce. **—ine vird et=** /ı/ to keep on repeating (something). **— yarası** a being hurt by someone's biting tongue. **—ine yavuz** *prov.* great talker. **—in yettiği kadar** as much as one can explain. **—ini yut=** to be overcome by great surprise or fear; to appear to have lost the use of one's tongue. **—ine yürük** *prov.* great talker. **—i zifir** who uses bad language, foul-mouthed.

dil 2 دل P *poet.* 1. heart, mind, soul. 2. courage. 3. desire, intention. **— bağla=** /a/ to be in love (with). **—i bikarar** troubled heart, restless heart. **— ü can** heart and soul. **—i divane** foolish heart. **—i hâk** heart of the earth; grave. **—i nalân** sad heart, weeping heart. **—i sengin** stony heart. **— ver=** /a/ to fall in love (with).

dil=ᵉʳ **3** دلمك /ı/ to cut into slices.

dilâgâh (.——) دل آگاه P *poet.* vigilant, provident, prudent.

dilâra (.——) دل آرا P 1. *poet.* beloved, sweetheart. 2. *Or. mus.* a **makam** no longer used.

dilâram (.——) دل آرام P *poet.* 1. heart-soothing. 2. lovely woman, sweetheart.

dilâsa (.——) دل آسا P *poet.* 1. tranquil at heart. 2. mind-soothing.

dilâşub (.——) دل آشوب P *poet.* 1. that perturbs the heart. 2. sad.

dilâşüfte (.—..) دل آشفته P *poet.* love-stricken heart.

dilâver (.—.) دلاور P *lrnd.* brave, courageous. **—î** (.—.—) P, **—lik** valor, bravery, courage.

dilâviz (.——) دل آویز P 1. *poet.* heart-ravishing. 2. *Or. mus.* a **makam** no longer used.

dilâzad (.——) دل آزاد P *poet.* heart-whole and fancy free.

dilâzar (.——) دل آزار P *poet.* heart-tormenting, cruel.

dilâzürde (.—..) دل آزرده P *poet.* broken-hearted; offended.

dilbaz (.—) دلباز P *poet.* 1. eloquent; pleasant talker. 2. flirt, coquettish. **—î** (.——) P, **—lık** flirtation, coquettry.

dilbend دلبند P *poet.* heart-binding, beloved.

dilber دلبر P 1. beautiful woman, beloved. 2. heart-captivating. **— dudağı** kind of Turkish pastry. **— kâkülü** sweet-smelling artemisia. **—âne** (..—.) P *lrnd.* in a coquettish manner. **—len=** to grow pretty. **—lik** beauty.

dilbeste دلبسته P *poet.* in love; greatly attached (to).

dilcikᵍⁱ دلجك 1. *anat.* clitoris. 2. pip (of fowl). 3. *bot.* ligula. 4. *prov.* uvula.

dilcu (.—) دلجو P *poet.* 1. captivating; beloved; desirable. 2. *myst.* God.

dildade (.—.) دلداده P 1. *poet.* beloved; lover. 2. *obs.* kind of bandeau worn across the forehead. **—firib** (.—..—) P *poet.* who deceives lovers.

dildar (.—) دلدار P *poet.* 1. possessing the heart, beloved. 2. *myst.* God, the beloved of his saints. 3. *Or. mus.* a **makam** no longer used.

dilduz (.—) دلدوز P *poet.* that pierces the heart.

dile=ʳ دیلمك /ı/ 1. to wish (for), to desire, long (for). 2. to ask (for), to beg, to request.

dilefgâr (..—) دل افگار P *poet.* heartbroken.

dilefruz (..—) دل افروز P *poet.* heart-rejoicing.

dilekᵍⁱ دیلك 1. wish; thing wished for. 2. request, petition, demand. **— et=** /ı/ *archaic* to wish (for), to ask (for). **— kipi** *neol., gram.* optative. **—çe** *neol.* petition. **—li** who has a wish; who has a request to make.

dilen=ⁱʳ دیلنمك /ı, dan/ to beg (as a mendicant); to ask (for).

dilenci دیلنجی beggar. **— çanağı** beggar's alms bowl. **— çanağı gibi** full of odds and ends. **— çanağından para çal=** to rob a beggar. **— değneğine dön=** to become very thin. **—ye hıyar vermişler iğri diye beğenmemiş** When they gave the beggar a cucumber he complained because it was crooked. **—nin totbası dolmaz** Beggars are never satisfied. **— vapuru** steamer that calls at every landing-stage. **—lik** begging, mendicancy, beggary. —**lik et**= to go about begging.

dilendir=ᵗʳ /a, 1 or 1/ *caus.* of **dilen**=.

dilet=ᵗʳ /1, a/ *caus.* of **dile**=.

dilfeza (..—) P *poet.* heart-rejoicing.

dilfigâr (..—) P, **dilfikâr** (..—) P *poet.* wounded at heart; broken-hearted; sad.

dilfirib (..—) P *poet.* heart-alluring, charming.

dilfüruz (..—) 1. *poet.* heart-cheering. 2. *Or. mus.* a **makam** no longer used.

dilgerm P *poet.* 1. animated, warm-hearted; full of desire; in love. 2. angry.

dilgir (.—) P *poet.* 1. that saddens the heart. 2. offended, mortified, angry.

dilgoz *slang* stupid, foolish, blockheaded.

dilgüdaz (..—) P *poet.* heart-melting, sad.

dilhah (.—) P *poet.* heart's desire, beloved object.

dilhar (.—) P *poet.* irritating to the feelings, annoying.

dilharab (..—) P *poet.* heartbroken, sad.

dilharaş (..—) P *same as* **dilhıraş**.

dilhaste P *poet.* sick at heart, sad, sorrowful.

dilhaş (.—) P *poet., same as* **dilhoş**.

dilhıraş (..—) P *poet.* heartrending, horrible.

dilhoş P *poet.* happy at heart, contented, glad.

dilhun (.—) P *poet.* very sad, sorrowful.

-di'li geçmiş zaman *neol., Turk. gram.* past tense containing the morpheme /dı/.

dilim 1. slice; strip. 2. *arch.* foil. — **dilim** in slices, in strips. —**le**= /1/ 1. to cut into slices. 2. to separate an orange into its segments. —**let**= /1, a/ *caus.* —**li** cut up into strips or slices.

dilinim *neol., geol.* cleavage.

dilir (.—) P *poet.* brave, courageous, fearless. —**ane** (.——.) P bravely; brave (act). —**î** (.——) P, —**lik** bravery, gallantry.

dilkeş P 1. *poet.* heart-attracting, amiable; beloved. 2. *Or. mus.* a **makam** no longer in use. — **haveran** *Or. mus.* a **makam** starting with e″ and ending on f′ sharp.

dilkeşide (..—.) P *Or. mus.* a **makam** starting with e′ and ending on d.

dilki *same as* **tilki**.

dilkûb (.—) P *poet.* heart-tormenting, heart-breaking, heart-rending.

dilkûr (.—) P *poet.* blind-hearted.

dilküşa (..—) P *poet.* 1. joy-giving, pleasant; beloved. 2. *Or. mus.* a **makam** beginning like **şetaraban** and ending on g′.

dille=ʳ /1/ *archaic* 1. to touch or lick with the tongue. 2. to censure, to backbite.

dillen=ᵗʳ 1. to loosen one's tongue, to begin to talk; to become over-talkative; to talk rudely or indiscreetly. 2. to become a subject of gossip. —**dir**= /1/ *caus.* of **dillen**=.

dilleş=ᵗʳ *archaic* to talk (with someone); to have a conversation together. —**tir**= /1/ *caus.* of **dilleş**=.

dilli 1. talkative. 2. tongued; bolted; sheaved. — **düdük** chatterbox, talkative person. — **düdük et**= /1/ to spread (gossip, rumor).

dilmaçᶜ¹ *archaic* interpreter, dolmetscher, dragoman. —**lık** functions and quality of an interpreter.

dilme 1. *verbal n.* of **dil**= 3. 2. square pole.

dilmeçᶜ¹ 1. *archaic, arch.* lobe. 2. *prov.* slit up the sides of a long robe.

dilmürde P *poet.* stony-hearted, unfeeling.

dilnişin (..—) P 1. *poet.* agreeable, pleasing; deep in one's heart. 2. *Or. mus.* a compound **makam** two centuries old.

dilnüvaz (..—) P *poet.* soothing, comforting the heart; beloved. —**î** (..——) P, —**lık** flattery, heart-soothing act.

dilpesend P *poet.* agreeable, pleasing; beloved.

dilpezir (..—) P *poet.* agreeable, amiable, soothing to the heart; beloved.

dilriş (.—) P *poet.* wounded to the heart, sorrowful.

dilrüba (..—) P 1. *poet.* heart-ravishing; beloved. 2. *Or. mus.* an old **makam**.

dilsaz (.—) P *poet.* heart-pleasing, heart-warming, kind.

dilsir (.—) P *poet.* contented, satisfied.

dilsitan (..—) P *poet.* heart-stealing.

dilsiz dumb, mute. —**lik** dumbness.

dilsuhte P *poet.* afflicted, sore at heart.

dilsuz (.—) P 1. *poet.* heart-inflamed; moving, sad. 2. *Or. mus.* an old **makam**.

dilşad (.—) P *poet.* happy, contented, glad.

dilşikâf (..—) دل شکاف P poet. heartbreaking.

dilşikâr (..—) دل شکار P poet. captivating the heart; beloved.

dilşiken دل شکن P poet. heartbreaking.

dilşikeste دل شکسته P poet. heartbroken, disappointed.

dilşüde دل شده P poet. who has lost his heart in love.

dilşüküfte دل شکفته [P **dilşigufta**] poet. pleased, happy, glad.

dilteng دل تنگ P poet. distressed, sad, mournful. —**î** (..—) P distress.

dilteşne دل تشنه P poet. yearning, desirous.

dilyekî (..—) دل یکی P lrnd. 1. unanimity. 2. concord, mutual sympathy.

dilzede دل زده P poet. wounded; hurt, in love.

dilzinde دل زنده P poet. 1. revived, refreshed. 2. open-minded, alert; knowing.

-dim 1 دم cf. **-dım 1**.

=dim 2 دم cf. **=dım 2**.

dima (.—) دماء A pl. of **dem 1**.

dimağ (.—) دماغ A brain, mind; intelligence. —**âşüfte** P lrnd. crazy. —**çe** P anat. cerebellum. —**î** (.——) A cerebral.

dimdik (.′.) دیمدیك bolt upright, erect, stiff.

dimi دیمی Gk text. fustian.

Dimişk[k¹] دمشق A archaic Damascus. —**i Şam** Damascus. —**î** (..—) A 1. from Damascus; native of Damascus. 2. l. c. damascene.

Dimne دمنه A Dimnah name of a jackal in the Fables of Bidpai.

Dimyat (.—) دمیاط A geog. Damietta. —**a pirinc giderken evdeki bulgurdan ol=** to lose what one has in the effort to get more or better.

din 1 (—) دین A 1. religion; belief; faith; creed. 2. the Islamic faith. 3. Isl. theol. Last Judgment. —**i bâtıl** false religion. —**i bir uğruna** for the sake of Islam. —**i bütün** sincerely religious, entirely given to the Islamic faith and observing its laws. —**değiştir=**, —**inden dön=** to change one's religion. —**inden döner, dâvasından dönmez** He would sooner give up his religion than his claim. **bir —de durma=** to be constantly changing one's mind. —**i hak** the true religion of Islam. —**in hâmisi** defender of the faith. —**hürriyeti** religious freedom. —**iman hak getire** There's not a spot of religion in him. —**den imandan çık=** to become utterly exasperated. —**i İslâm** the Muslim religion. —**i İsa** Christianity, the Christian faith. —**i Musa** Judaism. —**Muhammed dini, ekmek buğday ekmeği, yol Halep yolu** Choose only the very best. —**i mübin** the Muslim religion. **D— Suresi** name of the 107th sura of the Quran. —**i tabii** inherent religiosity. —**e yan=** to have compassion on. —**yıkılmazsa düşman yıkılmaz** Unless your enemy's religion is destroyed, he will not be destroyed. —**i yiyip imanı arkasına atmış** He has lost all sense of goodness and decency.

din 2 دین F phys. dyne.

din 3 (—) دین P lrnd. 1. name of the 24th day of the month. 2. rel. the angel who has charge of the pen.

din=[er] **4** دینمك 1. to cease, stop; to die down, get better, calm down. 2. archaic to rest.

=din 5 دین cf. **=dın 1**.

=din 6 دین cf. **=dın 2**.

dinamik[ti] دینامیك F dynamics; dynamic.

dinamit دینامیت F dynamite.

dinamizm دینامیزم F dynamism.

dinamo (.′.) دینامو F dynamo.

dinamometre (.....′.) دینامومتره F dynamometer.

dinar 1 (——) دینار A dinar (Arabic gold coin; monetary unit of Iran).

dinar 2 دینار Sl dinar (monetary unit of Jugoslavia).

dinc دینج cf. **dinç**. —**el=** to regain one's vigor. —**elt=** /ı/ caus. —**elten** neol., med., psych. sthenic.

dincierki neol. theocracy.

dinç[cl] دینچ 1. vigorous, robust, active. 2. clear, calm, untroubled, unruffled. —**lik** 1. vigor, vivacity, robustness. 2. peace, serenity.

dindar (——) دیندار P religious, devout, pious. —**ane** (———.) P religiously, devoutly, piously; devout, pious (act). —**î** (———) P lrnd., —**lık** religiousness, devotion, piety.

dindaş (—.) دینداش coreligionist.

dindir= دیندیرمك /ı/ caus. of **din= 4**.

dinek[ği] دینك prov. halting place, resting-place.

dinel=[ir] دینلمك prov. 1. to get to one's feet; to remain standing. 2. to crop up (a matter). 3. /a/ to take a stand (against).

dinen (—′.) دیناً A lrnd. from the religious point of view.

dineri, dineyri (.′..) دینری It card games diamonds.

dinfürûş (—.—) دین فروش P lrnd. hypocrite; hypocritical.

dingil دینگل 1. axle, axle-tree.

dingilde=[r] دینگلدەمك to make a rattling clatter. —**t=** /ı/ caus.

dingin neol. 1. chem. passive. 2. extinct (volcano). 3. calm. 4. exhausted. —**lik** chem. passivity.

dinî (——) دینی A religious, pertaining to religion.

-diniz 1 دینیز cf. **-dınız 1**.

=diniz 2 دِگِز cf. =dınız 2.
dinle=ᵣ 1 دِيكْلَمَكْ ،كُولَمَكْ ،دِيكُولَمَكْ /ı/ 1. to listen to, to hear. 2. to pay attention to, to obey, to conform to.
dinle=ᵣ 2 دِيكْلَمَكْ only in başını dinle=, kafasını dinle= to take a rest in a quiet place; kendini dinle= 1. same as başını dinle=. 2. to be always preoccupied with one's health.
dinleme دِيكْلَمَه a listening. — âleti mil. sound locator. — hizmeti mil. listening service.
dinlen=ᵢᵣ 1 دِيكْلَنْمَكْ to take a rest, to rest, to relax. —dir= /ı/ 1. caus. 2. colloq. to extinguish, put out (light, fire). —dirilmiş old (wine); fallow (ground).
dinlen=ᵢᵣ 2, dinlenil=ᵢᵣ دِيكْلَنِلْمَكْ ،دِيكْلَنْمَكْ pass. of dinle= 1.
dinlenme دِيكْلَنْمَه rest, relaxation; recreation.
dinlet=ᵢᵣ دِيكْلَتْمَكْ /ı or ı, a/ 1. caus. of dinle= 1, 2. 2. to bore by talking or singing too much. 3. to sing a song well. —il= pass. —tir= /ı, a/ 1. caus. of dinlet=. 2. same as dinlet=.
dinleyici دِيكْلَيِجِى ،دِيكْلَيِيجِى 1. listener. 2. eavesdropper. —ler audience.
dinpenah (—.—) دِين پَنَاه P lrnd. defender of the faith.
dinperver (—..—) دِين پَرْوَر P lrnd. pious. —î (—..—) P piety.
dinsiz دِينْسِز 1. irreligious, unbelieving, atheist. 2. cruel. —in hakkından imansız gelir Set a thief to catch a thief. —lik 1. atheism, irreligion. 2. cruelty.
dinşiken (—..) دِين شِكَن P lrnd. sacrilegious.
dip^ᵇˡ دِيب 1. bottom; foot, lowest part; the back; base. 2. anus. 3. pieced-together fur. 4. prov., name of several root vegetables. 5. archaic origin, root. —ten buda=, —inden buda= /ı/ 1. to cut from the bottom. 2. to nip in the bud. —i bul= to find bottom (in sounding). —ini bul= /ın/ to exhaust (a stock). — çal= prov. to shake and roll the buttocks (in dancing). —e çök= to sink to the bottom, to be deposited. —ine darı ek= /ın/ to exhaust entirely, to finish. — dede prov. great grandfather; ancestor. — demiri the iron heel of a lance. — deniz archaic ocean. — diş wisdom tooth. — doruk completely, from head to foot. —e düz yık= /ı/ prov. to level with the earth. —ine gel= to be coming to an end. — göster= to drain to the dregs. —ine in= to be near its end. —ten inkâr et= to deny completely. —ten kapuya prov. completely, from end to end. — karpuzu watermelon growing near the root of the vine, whose seeds are good for sowing. —i kırmızı balmumu ile çağırmadım ya After all, I didn't ask you (him) to come. — koçanı counter-foil. —ten kopar= /ı/ to root out, to uproot. — sömür= to drink to the dregs. —inden traş a clean shave; a close haircut. —i tut=, —ine yan= cookery to burn.

dipçik^ᵍⁱ دِيپ چِك butt of a rifle. — demiri heel piece of the stock of a rifle. — kuvvetile by force. — vur= to knock down with the butt of a rifle.

dipdiri دِيپ دِيرى 1. full of life, energetic. 2. safe and sound.

diplarya (..'.) دِيپْلَارْيَا Gk kind of small plaice (fish).

diple=ᵣ دِيپْلَمَكْ slang to fail (a class in school).

diploma (..'.) دِيپْلُومَا L diploma; degree. —lı graduate; qualified.

diplomasi دِيپْلُومَاسِى F pol. diplomacy.

diplomat دِيپْلُومَات F diplomat.

diplomatik^ᵍⁱ دِيپْلُومَاتِيك F diplomatic.

diplomatlık^ᵍⁱ دِيپْلُومَاتْلِق 1. diplomacy. 2. profession of a diplomat.

dipsiz دِيپْسِز 1. bottomless. 2. unfounded, false. 3. unfathomable. — kile spendthrift. — kile boş ambar It's useless, futile. — testi spendthrift, squanderer. —lik bottomlessness; groundlessness.

-dir 1 دِر cf. -dır 1.

=dir 2 دِرْمَكْ cf. =dır= 2.

dir^ʳ¹ 3 دِرْع A lrnd. coat of armor.

dir 4 (—) دِير P lrnd. 1. slow; sluggish. 2. late, tardy. — dir 1. slowly. 2. at long intervals; very late. — u zûd slowly or quickly; sooner or later.

dirahş دِرَخْش P lrnd. sparkle, glitter, splendor.

dirahşan (..—) دِرَخْشَان P lrnd. shining, sparkling, glittering. — ol= to shine, sparkle, glitter, to flash.

dirahşende دِرَخْشَنْدَه P lrnd. shining, refulgent.

diraht دِرَخْت P lrnd. tree, plant, shrub, bush. —ı Meryem "Mary's tree" (the tree under which the Virgin Mary is said to have rested during the flight to Egypt). —ı Vakvak mythical tree with fruit resembling men's heads.

diran (——) دِيرَان A lrnd. houses, mansions.

dirayet (.—.) دِرَايَت A comprehension, sagacity, subtlety of intellect.

dirayetkâr (.—.—) دِرَايَتْكَار P lrnd. shrewd, quick of comprehension. —âne (.—.—.) P cleverly, intelligently; shrewd (act). —kâri (.—.—) P intelligence.

dirayetli دِرَايَتْلِى intelligent, shrewd.

dirayetmend (.—..) دِرَايَتْمَنْد P lrnd., same as dirayetli.

dirayetsiz دِرَايَتْسِز stupid, unintelligent. —lik stupidity.

diraz (.—) دِرَاز P lrnd. 1. long talk. 2. far, distant; deep. —dest (.—.) P 1. long

dire armed; rapacious; tyrannical. 2. clever, dextrous, victorious. **—düm** (. — .) P long-tailed beast. **—gûş** (. — —) P. 1. donkey. 2. hare. **—î** (. — —) P, **—lık** 1. length, lengthiness; tallness. 2. distance; deepness.

dire=ᵣ دِرَ ساك دِرَ ه ساك 1. /ı, a/ *only in* **ayak dire**=. 2. *prov.* to prop (against).

direfş درفش P *lrnd.* 1. flag, banner. 2. cobbler's awl, pricker. **—i kâviyan** the ancient royal banner of Persia, originally the leather apron of the blacksmith Kava.

direfşan (. . —) درفشان P *lrnd.* 1. fluttering, waving in the wind. 2. shining, flashing.

direkᵏⁱ 1 دیرك column, pillar; upright post or pole; mast; flagstaff. **— astarı** *naut.* cheek of a mast. **— dibi** *naut.* mast base. **— direk bağır**= to shout at the top of one's voice. **— gibi** tall as a post.

direkᵏⁱ 2 دِرك *pop., var. of* **direkt**.

direkli دیركلی having columns, posts, poles, or masts. **— iryal**, **— riyal** *hist.* pillar dollar.

direklikᵏⁱ دیركلك a tree fit to become a column, post or mast.

direksiyon دیركسیون F *auto.* steering-wheel; steering mechanism; steering. **— boşluğu** play in the steering. **—u kır**= to swing the wheel over. **— mili** steering column. **— simidi** steering wheel.

direkt دیرەكت F direct; nonstop. **— masraflar** through rate. **— tevcih** *artillery* direct laying.

direktif دیرەكتیف F instructions, orders. **— al**= /dan/ to take orders or instruction (from). **— ver**= /a/ to give orders (to), to direct.

direm درم P *lrnd.* 1. *var. of* **dirhem**. 2. cash, money. **—güzin** (. . . —) P money-changer, banker.

diren 1 دیرن *var. of* **diğren**.

diren=ᵢᵣ 2 دیرنمك to put one's foot down, insist.

dirençᶜⁱ *neol., phys.* resistance.

direng درنگ P *lrnd.* 1. delay, tardiness, hesitation. 2. a staying, rest; peace. 3. eternity.

direnim *neol., psych.* obstinacy.

direş=ᵢᵣ دیرشمك *prov.* to resist; to be determined.

direv درو P *lrnd.* harvest, reaping. **—ger** P reaper, harvester.

direy *neol., biol.* fauna.

direzin 1 دیرەزین *var. of* **drezin**.

direzin 2 دیرەزین *prov., weaving* weft. **— sök**= to go to and fro.

dirgen دیرگن *var. of* **diğren**.

dirgür=ᵤᵣ دیرگورمك /ı/ *archaic* 1. to revive, to bring back to life; to raise from the dead. 2. to animate.

dirhem درهم A 1. drachma (400th part of an okka). 2. *hist.* drachma (silver coin). **— kadar**

a small quantity, very little. **—lik** *hist.* tube-like box for measuring gunpowder.

diri دیری 1. alive, living. 2. vigorous, energetic, lively. 3. fresh. 4. undercooked.

diriğ (. —) دریغ P *lrnd.* 1. Alas!, Ah!, Woe! 2. regret, repentance. 3. refusal. **— et**= /ı, dan/ to refuse, to withhold (from).

diriğa (. — —) دریغا P *lrnd.* alas!, ah! **— ki** It is a pity!

diriksel *neol., biol.* animal, physiological. **— ısı** animal heat.

diril=ᵢᵣ دیریلمك 1. to return to life; to come to life, to be revived, to gain fresh vigor. 2. *archaic* to live.

dirilikᵏⁱ دیریلك *abstr. n. of* **diri**.

dirilt=ᵢᵣ دیریلتمك /ı/ *caus. of* **diril**=. **—me** vivification.

dirim دیریم 1. *only in* **ölüm dirim**. 2. *neol.* life. **— ağacı** *anat.* arbor vitae. **— konisi** *bot.* cone of vegetation. **—li** *sc.* living. **—sel** *neol., sc.* vital.

dirin (— —) دیرین P *lrnd.* ancient, old.

dirine (— — .) دیرینه P *lrnd.* 1. ancient, old. 2. lasting, permanent.

dirisa, **dirise** (. .' .) دیریسه It *naut., artillery* the training (of a gun). **— et**= 1. /ı/ to train (gun, on something). 2. to change (wind).

dirlikᵏⁱ دیرلك 1. peace, peaceful living together. 2. *prov.* comfortable living, wealth. 3. *hist.* revenue granted as a living. 4. *archaic* life. **— düzenlik** a harmonious living together, peace. **— et**= 1. /la/ *prov.* to get along (with). 2. *archaic* to live. **— sahibi** *obs.* who possesses the means of subsistence. **—li** 1. easy to get on with (person). 2. *prov.* rich, well off. **—siz** 1. lacking peace and harmony. 2. cantankerous, ill-tempered, difficult to get on with. 3. *prov.* indigent.

dirre درّه A *lrnd.* 1. whip, scourge. 2. an outpouring.

dirsekᵏⁱ دیرسك 1. elbow. 2. knee (of timber), bend (of a river), elbow (in a pipe); crank. **— çevir**= /a/ to drop (someone). **— çıkıntısı** *anat.* olecranon. **— çürüt**= (*lit.,* to wear out the elbows with studying) to be occupied with one's studies for a long period of time. **— kemiği** *anat.* cubit. **—li** having an elbow or bend. **—li payanda** *mil.* shouldered buttress. **—lik** armor elbow guard, cubitiere.

diruz (— —) دیروز P *lrnd.* yesterday.

diryakᵏⁱ 1 (. —) دریاق A *lrnd., same as* **tiryak**.

diryakᵏⁱ 2 (. —) دریاك P *lrnd., same as* **tiryak**.

disam (. —) دسام A *lrnd.* plug, stopper, bung.

-disar (. —) دسار [*based on Arabic*] *lrnd.* full of, *as in* **merhametdisar**.

disiplin دیسیپلین F 1. discipline. 2. branch of knowledge; *academic curriculum* branch of instruction, subject. **—siz** undisciplined.

disk[ki] دیسك F 1. *sport* discus. 2. *mech*. disk; *auto*. clutchplate, clutch disk.

dismenore دیسمنوره F *path*. dysmenorrhoea.

dispanser دیسپانسر F welfare center for treatment of out-patients.

dispeç[cı] دیسپچ F *mar. ins.* average adjustment.

dispepsi دیسپپسی F *path*. dyspepsia.

dispne دیسپنه F *path*. dyspnea.

distal[li] دیستال F *anat*. distal.

distribütör دیستریبیوتور F *elec*. distributor, make-and-break.

distrofi دیستروفی F *path*. dystrophy.

disüri دیسوری F *path*. dysuria.

diş دیش 1. tooth; tusk. 2. tooth (of a saw, comb); cog (of a wheel); ward (of a key); serration (of a line, letter); thread (of a screw). 3. clove (of garlic); head (of cloves). 4. *slang* dope. **— aç=** /ı/ to serrate, to thread. **— ağrısı** toothache. **—ten artar, işten artmaz** *proverb* Better to save money by economical living than to try to make more out of one's job. **— bademi** soft-shelled almonds. **— bakımı** dental care. **— başı** *obs*. crown of a tooth. **— bile=** /a/ to watch for a chance to take revenge (on), to have a bitter grudge (against). **— budak*. — buğdayı** 1. wheat boiled and mixed with sugar, etc., and distributed on the occasion of an infant's cutting the first tooth. 2. kind of large-grained wheat. **— çatırdaması** a chattering of the teeth. **— çek=** to extract a tooth. **—ini çek=** /dan/ *prov*. to give up (doing a thing). **— çıkar=** 1. to cut teeth. 2. to pull out a tooth. **— çukuru** *anat*. socket of a tooth. **— çürüğü** *path*. tooth decay, caries. **—ine dayan=** /ın/ to stand firm against the assault (of trouble). **—ine değme=** to be very little (food). **— diş** 1. having many teeth, notches, cogs; teethed; serrated. **—e diş** tooth for tooth, retaliation. **—e dokunur** worthwhile. **—leri dökül=** to lose one's teeth through age. **— eti** *anat*. gum. **— fırçası** toothbrush. **— geçireme=** /a/ to be unable to defy or harm. **—e gelir** an easy prey. **— gıcırdat=** to gnash the teeth. **—ine göre** to one's taste. **— göster=** /a/ to bare one's teeth, to threaten. **— hekimi** dentist. **— hilâli otu** toothpick bishop's-weed, *bot*., *Ammi Visnaga*. **— kamaştır=** to set the teeth on edge. **— karıştıracak** toothpick. **— kemiği** *anat*. dentine. **— kır=** *slang* to doctor a cigarette. **— kirası** *hist*. presents given to guests after a meal, *esp.* in Ramazan. **—inin kovuğuna bile gitme=, —in kovuğunu doldurma=** to be very little in quantity. **— kökü** root of a tooth. **— macunu** toothpaste. **— otu** toothwort, leadwort, *bot*., *Plumbago*. **— otugiller** *neol*., *bot*., *Plumbaginaceae*. **— özü** *anat*. dental pulp. **— sessizi** *neol*., *phon*. dental. **—ini sık=** to set one's teeth, to endure, bear. **— siniri** *anat*. dental nerve. **—ini sök=** /ın/ to draw the teeth (of something, somebody); to render harmless. **— suyu** dental rinse. **— tabibi** dentist. **— tacı** *anat*. crown of a tooth. **— tak=** /a/ 1. to fit out with false teeth. 2. *colloq*. to have one's teeth (into a person). **— takımı** false teeth, dentures. **— taktır=** to be fitted out with false teeth. **—inden tırnağından artır=** to save money by working hard and making self-sacrifices. **—i tırnağı döküldü** He grew old in the same service. **—ini tırnağına kat=** to work tooth and nail. **— tozu** tooth powder. **—i tut=** to have a toothache. **— yuvası** *anat*. tooth socket.

dişbudak[ğı] دیشبوداق ash tree, *bot*., *Fraxinus ornus*.

dişçi دیشچی 1. dentist. 2. *slang* a trader in teeth taken from tombs. **—lik** dentistry.

dişe=[r] دیشه مك *prov*. to roughen a millstone with a pick. **—n=** *pass*.

dişengi دیشنگی *prov*. 1. toothed pick for roughening millstones. 2. chippings made when roughening millstones.

dişi دیشی 1. female, she-, mate. 2. soft, yielding. **— anahtar** hollow key. **— aslan** lioness. **— burma** female screw. **— demir** soft iron. **— iğnecik** *naut*. brace of a rudder. **— kasnı** *drug*. galbanum melted and strained. **— kopça** an eye for a hook. **— kuştur yuvayı yapan** *proverb* It's the female that builds the nest. **— kuşkonmaz** wild asparagus, *bot*., *Asparagus acutifolius*. **— organ** *bot*. pistil. **— rumî kökü** apple of the earth, *bot*., *Aristolochia rotunda*. **— söz** soft words. **— vida** female screw. **—li** provided with a female, mated. **—lik** female sex.

dişindirik[ği] دیشندریك *prov*. kind of halter tied to the jaw of a horse.

dişle=[r] دیشله مك /ı/ 1. to bite, nibble, gnaw. 2. to tooth, serrate.

dişlek[ği] دیشلك having protruding teeth.

dişlen=[ir] دیشلنمك *pass*. of **dişle=**. **—t=** /ı, a/ *caus*. of **dişle=**.

dişli دیشلی 1. toothed, serrated; notched, jagged; *mech*. cogwheel. 2. having sharp teeth; able to cause harm. 3. formidable, influential; able to get things done. **— çark** sprocket, cogwheel. **— grupu** *mech*. train of gears. **— kas** *anat*. serratus muscle. **— tırnaklı** very aggressive and fierce, red in tooth and claw. **— tren** cog railway.

dişsel *neol*., *biol*., *gram*. dental.

dişsiz ديشسز 1. toothless. 2. unserrated, smooth. **—lik** toothlessness.

dit=der دتمك ددملك ديتمك /ı/ 1. to card, tease (cotton, wool). 2. to tear to pieces. **—tir=** /ı, a/ caus.

div (— —) ديو P lrnd., var. of **dev**.

divalli ديوال ∙ [düval] gold and silver thread embroidery over cardboard, on rich material.

divan 1 ديوان F divan, sofa, couch.

divan 2 (— —) ديوان P 1. Council of State. 2. hist. the holding of a Court; public sitting (of governor, council, judge). 3. mus. a form used in Turkish music and folk music. **—ı ahkâmı adliye** Ott. hist. first civil court, established in 1868. **D—ı Âli** law High Court of Justice. **D—ı Âlii Askerî** Military High Court. **D—ı âm** hist. public audience, public court. **— amedcisi** Ott. hist. the receiver-general of provincial correspondence addressed to the Grand Vizier. **— beyi** Ott. hist. the head of a corps of heralds and messengers specially attached to the Grand Vizier as chief of the Divan and often employed on important missions. **— beylikçisi** Ott. hist. title of one of a coordinate pair of officers of state at the Porte (the other being the **amedci**). **— çavuşu** Ott. hist. a member of a corps of heralds and messengers specially attached to the Grand Vizier as chief of the Divan and often employed on important missions. **—a çek=** /ı/ to summon into one's presence. **— dur=** to stand in a respectful position with hands folded in front. **— efendisi** Ott. hist. the official secretary of a Vizier or of the governor of a province. **— günü** Ott. hist. Council or Court day. **—ı hakanî** Ott. hist. a Council of State presided over by the Sultan. **—ı harb** Court Martial. **—ı harbi örfî** Court Martial during a state of siege. **—ı has** Ott. hist. special Council presided over by the Sultan. **—ı haysiyet** law Court of honor. **D—ı hümayun** Ott. hist. the Imperial Chancery of State under the direction of the **Beylikçi**. **—ı ilâhî** Divine Day of Justice. **—ı istinaf** obs. Superior Court of Appeal. **— kalemi** Ott. hist. the office of the Imperial chancery presided over by the **Beylikçi efendi**. **— kâtibi** Ott. hist. Secretary of the Council of State. **— kovan** obs. an intrusive frequenter of Councils. **— kur=** to hold a council or court. **— malı** obs. public money; public revenue; a treasury claim. **—ı Muhasebat** adm. audit office. **— odası** large and spacious room, hall. **— oldu** The council has met. **—ı padişahî** Ott. hist. a council presided over by the Sultan or by a vizier. **— rahtı** obs. parade costume. **—ı riyaset Turk. Parliament** board composed of the Speaker, his three deputies and his secretaries. **— sazı** the largest **bağlama** used in folk music. **— sinisi** very large round metal tray used for banquets. **— sür=** Ott. hist. to hold a council (expression used in the Palace). **— taburu** mil. parade. **—ı temyiz** law Supreme Court of Appeal. **—ı temyiz-i askerî** Military Supreme Court of Appeal. **— ver=** Ott. hist. to give orders and instructions. **— yeri** obs., naval hist. poop deck (where councils used to take place). **D— Yolu** "Divan Road" (one of the main thoroughfares of Istanbul).

divan 3 (— —) ديوان P literature a poet's collected poems arranged alphabetically, divan. **— edebiyatı** hist. of Ott. literature classical school of poetry. **— şairi** hist. of Ott. literature a poet of the classical school. **—ce** P literature a small divan.

divane (— — .) ديوانه P foolish, insane; half-witted; crazy. **—gi** (— — . —) P, **—lik** foolishness; madness.

divangâh (— — — —) ديوانگاه P lrnd. place where a court is held, hall.

divanhane (— — — .) ديوانخانه P lrnd. 1. hall of audience. 2. a large hall in a house.

divanî (— — —) ديوانى P 1. pertaining to the imperial divan. 2. calligraphy (Arabic script) a style of large handwriting used in the imperial chancery. **— celisi** calligraphy a large variety of **divanî** writing. **— kırması** calligraphy a simplified variety of **divanî** writing.

divar (— —) ديوار P lrnd., same as **duvar**.

divasa (— — —) ديواسا P lrnd., same as **devasa**.

divbeçe (— . .) ديوبچه P lrnd. a little giant.

divcame (— — .) ديوجامه P lrnd. lion's skin worn by warriors.

divcan (— — —) ديوجان P lrnd. reckless, daring; hard-hearted.

divçe (— .) ديوچه P lrnd. 1. a little imp. 2. any small and destructive worm or grub; as the clothes moth, the weevil, or the bookworm. 3. leech.

divgir (— —) ديوگير P lrnd. 1. who captures demons. 2. captured by demons; insane.

divî (— —) ديوى P lrnd. 1. demonical. 2. devilishness.

divikgi ديويك zool. termite; white ant.

divit دوت ديويت دوات [Persian davet] hist. a pen-case, often combined with an ink-holder, worn in the girdle by scribes. **—çi** maker or seller of pen-cases.

divlah (— — —) ديولح P lrnd. place haunted by demons.

divlekgi ديولك var. of **düvelek**.

divzede (— . .) ديوزده P struck by a demon; smitten with palsy or madness.

diyabaz دیاباز F *geol.* diabase.
diyabet دیابت F *med.* diabetes.
diyafram دیافرام F *anat., phys., mech.* diaphragm. — **kası** *anat.* phrenic muscle.
diyagram دیاغرام F diagram.
diyak[kı] دیاك Sl *hist.* deacon, *esp.* a Roman-Catholic deacon (among Slavonians). **—ça** *obs.* Latin.
diyaklâz دیاقلاز F *geol.* diaclase.
diyakoz (.ˈ.) دیاقوز Gk *Christ.* Churches of the East deacon.
diyalâj دیالاژ F *geol.* diallage.
diyalektik[ği] دیالكتیك F *phil.* dialectic.
diyalel دیالل F *log.* dialellus.
diyaliz دیالیز F *chem.* dialysis.
diyalog[ğu] دیالوگ F dialogue.
diyanet (. —.) دیانت A *lrnd.* 1. religiosity, piety, devoutness. 2. religion. **D— İşleri Müdürlüğü** Department of Religious Affairs (in Turkey). **—kâr** (. —.—) P, **—li** *lrnd.* religious, devout, pious.
diyanî (. — —) دیانى [based on Arabic] only in **— tesis** *law* religious foundation, pious endowment.
diyapazon دیاپازون F *mus.* 1. diapason, pitch. 2. tuning-fork.
diyar (.—) دیار A a country, land. **—ı adem** *lrnd.* the other world. **—ı gurbet** foreign lands; strange lands. **—ı küfr** *lrnd.* non-muslim lands. **—ı Rum** *archaic* the Ottoman Empire.
diyare دیاره F *med.* diarrhea.
diyari (...ˈ) دیارى Gk *slang* two-piaster piece.
diyaset (. —.) دیاثت [based on Arabic] *lrnd.* a being a pander or contented cuckold.
diyatom دیاتوم F *bot.* diatom.
diye دیه [de= 1] *following direct speech* 1. if direct speech is followed by a verb designating verbal expression, other than **de=**, this element is obligatory, sometimes it can be rendered by saying, *e. g.*, "**Dur!**" **diye bağırdı** He shouted, "Stop!" "**Olmaz!**" **diye itiraz etti** He objected, saying, "I don't agree". 2. thinking that, hoping that, fearing that, pretending that, *e. g.*, **Gücenirsiniz diye bir şey demedim** I didn't say anything, thinking that you might be offended. **Eğleniriz diye gittik** We went hoping that we would amuse ourselves.
diyet 1 دیت A blood money. **—i muğallaz** *can law* blood-money payment of a hundred pregnant she-camels.
diyet 2 دیت F *med.* diet.
diyez دیز F *mus.* sharp.
diyoptri دیوپترى F *phys.* diopter.
diyorit دیوریت F *geol.* diorite.
diz 1 دیز knee. **— ağırşağı** *archaic* kneepan, patella bone. **— ardı** *anat.* hollow of the knee. **— bağı** *anat.* the tendon of the knee. **—lerinin**

bağı çözül= to give way at the knees (from fear etc.), to be very frightened. **D— bağı Nişanı** Order of the Garter. **— boyu** up to the knees, knee-deep; all-pervading. **— çök!** *mil.* Down on your knees!, Kneel down! **— çök=** to kneel, to kneel down. **— çöktür=** /a/ to make one kneel down; to bring to his knees, to force to his knees, to subdue. **— çukuru** *mil.* shallow rifle pit. **— çürüt=** *archaic* to study hard. **—i dibinde** at one's feet. **— dize** knee to knee. **— donu** *Or. wrestling* knee-length leather trousers. **— döv=** to be bitterly sorry. **—e gel=** to fall on one's knees; to abase oneself. **— kapağı** kneepan, kneecap. **— kapağı kemiği** *anat.* rotula. **—lerine kapan=** /ın/ to fall at somebody's feet in supplication. **—leri kesil=** to feel exhausted, to feel one's knees giving way. **—lerini kırarak selâm ver=** to curtsy. **— öp=** to kiss the knees of a superior in entreaty. **— üstü** kneeling, on the knees. **—e var=** same as **dize gel=**.
diz=[er] 2 دیزمك /ı/ 1. to line up, to arrange in a row or series; to string (beads, etc.). 2. to set up (type).
diz 3 دیز P *lrnd.* castle, fort.
dizanteri دیزانترى F *path.* dysentery.
dizbarko (.ˈ.) دیزبارقو It 1. unloading (of a ship). 2. unloading and port charges.
dizdar (. —) دیزدار P *lrnd.* warden of a castle; constable.
dizdir=[ir] دیزدیرمك /ı, a/ *caus.* of **diz=** 2.
dizel دیزل F *mech.* diesel (engine).
dizge 1 *neol., phil.* system.
dizge 2 دیزگی *archaic* 1. that reaches to the knee (clothing). 2. garter. **— çorap** knee-length socks.
dizgi دیزگى *print.* composition, a setting up of type.
dizgin دیزگین rein, bridle. **—leri başkasına kaptır=** to let another take control. **—e çarp=** /ı/ same as **dizgine vur=**. **— çek=** to draw rein, to stop. **—lerini ele al=** /ın/ to use the rein (of), to control. **—leri ele ver=** to let another take control. **—ini kıs=** /ın/ to hold in check. **— kullan=** to draw in the reins. **—i topla=**, **—leri topla=** to rein in, to check off. **—e vur=** /ı/ to silence, to check, to control. **—siz** uncontrolled, unbridled.
dizi دیزى 1. line, row, series. 2. string (of beads). 3. a file (of soldiers). 4. *math.* progression. **— kemikleri** *anat.* phalanges.
dizici دیزیجى 1. bead-threader. 2. typesetter, compositor.
dizil=[ir] دیزلمك *pass.* of **diz=** 2.
dizile=[r] دیزیله مك /ı/ to line up, to arrange in a row.

dizili دِيزِيلُو دِيزِيلُمْ دِيزِيلِى arranged in a line or row.
dizilme, diziliş دِيزِيلْمَه دِيزِلْمَه دِيزِلِشْ دِيزِيلِيشْ verbal n. of dizil=.
dizin neol. index.
dizin dizin 1 دِيزِينْ دِيزِينْ on the knees. — yürü= to walk on one's knees.
dizin dizin 2 دِيزِينْ دِيزِينْ archaic in lines, in rows, in strings.
diziş دِيزِيشْ verbal n. of diz= 2.
dizlik[ği] دِزْلِكْ دِيزْلِكْ knee-breeches, drawers reaching to the knee.
dizme دِيزْمَه دِيزْمَه 1. verbal n. of diz= 2. 2. arranged, lined. — makinası print. typesetting machine.
do دُو F mus. do; C.
doblin دُوبْلِينْ It naut. slack (of a rope or sail).
dobra dobra ('. '.) دُوبْرَا دُوبْرَا Sl bluntly, frankly.
Dobravenedik[ği] دُوبْرَه وَنَدِيكْ Sl hist. Ragusa, Dubrovnik.
doca دُوجَه It hist. the Doge of Venice.
doçent دُوچَنْتْ University lecturer, assistant professor.
doçentlik[ği] دُوچَنْتْلِكْ lecturership, assistant professorship. — imtihanı examination to qualify as a university lecturer. — travayı inaugural dissertation.
dogma ('.) دُوغْمَا E or G phil. dogma. —cılık neol. dogmatism.
dogmatik[ği] دُوغْمَاتِيكْ F phil. dogmatic.
dogmatizm دُوغْمَاتِيزْمْ F phil. dogmatism.
doğ=[ar] دُوغْمَقْ 1. to be born, to come into the world. 2. to rise (sun, etc.). 3. to come to pass, to happen. —madık çocuğa kaftan biçilmez proverb You should not cut out a coat for a child still unborn. —duğuna pişman tired of life, unhappy, miserable.
doğa neol., sc. nature. — üstü supernatural. —ca natural. —cılık phil. 1. naturalism. 2. naturism.
doğaç[cı] neol., psych. inspiration. —lama, —tan improvisation.
doğal neol. natural. — hâl sc. natural state. —cılık phil. naturalism.
doğan دُوغَانْ falcon, hawk. zool., falco. — burunlu hawk-nosed. —cı falconer. —cıbaşı Ott. hist. chief falconer of the Sultan.
doğdur=[ur] دُوغْدُرْمَقْ /ı/ caus. of doğ=.
doğma دُوغْمَه 1. verbal n. of doğ=. 2. /dan/ born; risen (above the horizon). — büyüme native, born and bred (in a place).
doğra=[r] دُوغْرَامَقْ /ı/ to cut into slices or pieces; to carve.
doğram دُوغْرَامْ a slice. — doğram in slices, in pieces.
doğrama دُوغْرَامَه 1. verbal n. of doğra=.

2. carpenter's work. —cı carpenter. —cı kalemi rabbeting chisel. —cılık carpentry.
doğran=[ır] دُوغْرَانْمَقْ pass. of doğra=.
doğrat=[ır] دُوغْرَاتْمَقْ /ı, a/ caus. of doğra=.
doğru 1 دُوغْرُو 1. straight; direct; math. straight line. 2. right, correct, true; honest, loyal, straightforward; correctly; truth. 3. /a/ toward, towards; about, around (time); /dan/ from, e. g., aşağıdan doğru from below. —dan directly. —su the truth of the matter; to speak honestly, to be quite frank about it. — adam honest man, just man. — akım elec. direct current. —dan ayrılma= not to leave the path of righteousness. — barsak anat. rectum. — bul= /ı/ to approve (of). — çık= to come true, to prove to be right, to come out right. — çizgi geom. straight line. —dan doğruya directly; direct. —dan doğruya dâva law direct claim. — doğru dosdoğru the exact truth (of the matter). —ya doğru iğriye iğri de= always to tell the truth. — dur= 1. to stand straight. 2. to sit still, to be quiet. — dürüst properly. — hat 1. geom. straight line. 2. rail. trunk line; through train. — kılıç broadsword. — orantılı math. direct proportional. — otur= to sit still, to be quiet, to sit properly. — parçası geom. segment of a line. — posta through, non-stop. — rota naut. direct course. — söyle= to speak the truth. —yu söyliyeni dokuz köyden kovarlar proverb The man who tells the truth is driven out of nine villages. — söyliyenin tepesi delik olur proverb He who tells the truth gets holes in the head. — söze akan sular durur, — söze can kurban The truth is precious even when it hurts. — söze ne denir? That is the way it is, and that is the end of the matter. —dan şaşma! Keep straight ahead (avoid temptation). — yol 1. main street, high street. 2. direct way. 3. the right way.
doğru 2 ('.) دُوغْرُو 1. directly. 2. isolated that's right, true.
doğruca (.'.) دُوغْرُوجَه straight, directly.
doğruculuk[ğu] neol., phil. veracity.
doğrul=[ur] دُوغْرُولْمَقْ 1. to straighten out; to be straightened. 2. to sit up. 3. /a/ to direct oneself (towards). 4. to be righted; to be put right. 5. pop. to be earned.
doğrula=[r] دُوغْرُولَامَقْ /ı/ to corroborate, confirm. —n= 1. pass. 2. to become straight. —t= caus. of doğrula=.
doğrult=[ur] دُوغْرُولْتْمَقْ /ı/ 1. to make straight, to straighten. 2. /ı, a/ to direct. 3. to make right, to straighten out. 4. pop. to earn (money). —maç neol., elec. rectifier. —man neol., geom. directrix.
doğrultu neol., sc. direction.
doğrulu neol., geom. rectilinear.

doğruluk[gu] طوغرولی دوغرولی abstr. n. of **doğru**.
doğrulum neol., biol. tropism.
doğrusal neol. 1. math. linear 2. geom. rectilinear. — **denklem** math. linear equation.
doğu 1 دوغو طوغی 1. east; eastern. 2. w. cap. the East, the Orient; the eastern provinces of Turkey. **D— Bayazıt** town in Eastern Anatolia.
doğu 2 دوغی طوغی prov. small-eared (sheep or goat).
doğum دوغوم طوغوم 1. birth; year of birth. 2. confinement. 3. chem. nascency. — **evi** maternity hospital. — **hali** chem. nascent condition. — **sancıları** labor pains. — **sigortası** law maternity insurance. — **yap**= to give birth to a child. —**lu** born in such and such a year, e. g., **39 doğumlu** born in '39 (1939).
doğur=[ur] طوغورمق دوغورمق /ı/ to give birth to; bear (children); to foal; to litter (cat, etc.); to bring forth; to breed. —**anlar** zool. the viviparous animals. —**gan** prolific, fecund. —**ma** verbal n. of **doğur**=. —**t**= 1. /ı, a/ caus. of **doğur**=. 2. /ı/ to assist at childbirth. —**tucu** neol., phil. maieutic, maieutical. —**tuculuk** neol., phil. maieutics. —**uş** verbal n. of **doğur**=.
doğuş دوغوش طوغوش verbal n. of **doğ**=. —**tan** innate; from birth. —**lu** archaic well-born, noble. —**tancı** neol., phil. nativist. —**tancılık** neol., phil. nativism.
doj دوژ F hist. the doge of Venice.
dok[ku] **1** دوق E dock, wharf.
dok[ku] **2** دوق E text. duck (for sail-cloth).
doka (ʹ.) دوقا var. of **duka 1, 2**.
dokan=[ır] دوقانمق prov., same as **dokun**= 1.
doksan دوقسان طقسان ninety. —**ar** ninety each. —**ıncı** ninetieth. —**lık** ninety years old.
doktor دوقتر F physician; doctor. —**lu** gamblers' slang marked card.
doktora (.ʹ.) دوقترا F doctorate.
doktorluk[gu] دوقترلغی 1. doctorate. 2. profession of a doctor.
doktrin, دوقترین F doctrine.
doku=ʳ **1** دوقومق طوقومق /ı/ 1. to weave. 2. prov. to hit (the tree for collecting fruit); archaic to hit, to drive in (nail).
doku 2 neol., biol. tissue. —**bilim** histology.
dokum neol., biol. texture.
dokuma دوقومه طوقومه 1. verbal n. of **doku= 1**. 2. woven (tissue); cotton cloth. —**cı** weaver. —**cılık** textile industry.
dokun=ᵘʳ **1** دوقونمق طوقونمق /a/ 1. to touch, to come in contact (with); to feel. 2. to handle, meddle (with). 3. to concern, to bear a relation (to). 4. to affect, to harm; to have an effect on (good, evil); to vex, to tease; to move, to touch (the heart). 5. to bite (fish).

—**u dokunuver**= /a/ slang to pummel.
dokun= **2** دوقونمق طوقونمه pass. of **doku= 1**.
dokunaç[cı] neol., biol. tentacle.
dokunaklı طوقناقلی طوقناقی 1. moving, touching. 2. biting, piquant. 3. strong (tobacco, etc.). — **rüzgâr** naut. kind of strong wind.
dokundur=ᵘʳ دوقوندرمق طوقوندرمه /ı, a/ 1. caus. of **dokun**=. 2. to mention in a covert way, to hint (at). —**ul**= pass.
dokunma دوقونمه طوقونمه 1. verbal n. of **dokun**= 1, 2. 2. biol., psych. touch, sense of touch.
dokunsal neol., biol. tactile.
dokunulmaz دوقونلمز untouchable. —**lık** neol., pol. immunity.
dokunum neol., biol., psych. sense of touch.
dokunuş دوقونش طوقونش verbal n. of **dokun**= 1, 2.
dokurcun طقورجین طوقورجین prov. 1. thatched stack of hay, grain, etc. 2. kind of game, played with small stones or shells.
dokuş 1 دوقوش طوقوش archaic, verbal n. of **doku**= 1.
dokuş=ᵘʳ **2** دوقوشمق طوقوشمه same as **tokuş**=.
dokut=ᵘʳ دوقوتمق طوقوتمه /ı, a/ caus. of **doku**= 1. —**tur**= /ı, a/ vulg., same as **dokut**=. —**ul** pass. of **dokut**=.
dokuyucu دوقویجی weaver.
dokuyuş دوقویش طوقویش verbal n. of **doku**= 2.
dokuz دوقوز طوقوز nine. — **ayın çarşambası bir araya geldi** Nine months of Wednesdays all at once. There is too much to do. — **babalı** colloq. whose father is unknown. — **canlı** lit. having nine lives (cat), having great resistance for hardships, very tough. — **doğur**= 1. to be greatly anxious with expectation. 2. to go through great difficulties. — **doğurt**= /a/ to hustle, to bring pressure upon one. — **düğüm altında** very carefully guarded (money). — **körün bir değneği** the only support (of a large household). — **köyden koğulmuş** expelled from everywhere. —**unda ne ise doksanında da odur** He will always be the same; he will never improve. — **oturak otur**= naut. to run heavily aground. — **taş** a kind of game played with small stones or shells. — **yorgan eskit**= to have a very long life. —**ar** nine each. —**ar dokuzar** by nines. —**la**= /ı/ to make it nine, to increase to nine. —**lan**= to become nine. —**lu** 1. containing nine. 2. card games the nine (card). —**uncu** ninth.
dol=ᵃʳ دولمق طولمه 1. to become full; to fill; to swell; to become completed; /a/ to fill (a place). 2. to be near exploding (with anger), to be exasperated. 3. naut. to become taut (rope); archaic to be drawn (bow).

dola=[r] طولامق دولامق /ı, a/ to wind, wrap (round).
dolab (.—) دولاب P same as **dolap 1-3**.
dolak[fi] طولوق دولاق puttee.
dolam طولم one turn of any coiled thing; fold of a turban.
dolama 1 طولمه دولمه 1. verbal n. of **dola=**. 2. twisted, wound, wrapped round. 3. prov. kind of apron; kind of jacket, dolman.
dolama 2 طولمه دولمه whitlow. — **otu** thyme-leaved nailwort, bot., Paronychia serpyllifolie.
dolamaç[ci] دولاماج prov., same as **dolambaç**.
dolaman دولمان طولمان same as **dolama 1**[3]. —**lı** 1. dressed in a **dolaman**. 2. Ott. hist. in full dress, nof on camping (Janissary).
dolambaç[ci] طولمباج دولمباج 1. winding (road). 2. anat. cochlea, labyrinthus. —**lı** meandering road.
dolamık[fi] طولامیق prov. trap, net, snare.
dolan 1 طولان دولان deceit, deception, usually in **yalan dolan**.
dolan=[r] **2** دولنمق 1. /a/ to wind round (a thing); to surround, encircle. 2. to go round in a circle, to revolve; to wander around.
dolandır=[r] **1** دولاندرمق /ı/ to cheat (someone) out of his money; to defraud. —**ıcı** embezzler, swindler. —**ıcılık** fraud, swindle.
dolandır=[r] **2** دولاندرمق /ı/ caus. of **dolan= 2**.
dolangıç[ci] طولانغیج prov. pipit, zool., Anthus.
dolap[bi] طولاب دولاب [dolab] 1. cupboard; wardrobe. 2. any revolving thing; turnstile; water - wheel; tread-mill; merry - go - round; musical box; obs. revolving wall locker for passing food, etc. without contact. 3. stall in the Covered Market in Istanbul. 4. colloq. trick, plot, intrigue. — **beygiri gibi dönüp dur=** to go in circles like a miller's horse. —**ı bozul=** to go awry (business). — **çevir=** colloq. to set a snare, trap. — **çivisi** medium-sized nail. — **dönüyor** colloq. A plot is hatching. —**a gir=** colloq. to be duped, trapped, taken in. — **kur=** same as **dolap çevir=**. — **saat** grandfather clock. —**a sok=** /ı/ colloq. to dupe, trap, take in; intrigue. —**çı** 1. plotter, intriguer. 2. cupboard maker. —**lı** 1. furnished with cupboards. 2. naut. furnished with a binnacle. 3. tricky, deceitful.
dolâr دولار F dollar.
dolaş=[r] **1** دولاشمق طولاشمق 1. to go around; to go round about; to wander; to get around (news); /ı/ to patrol (soldier); to go on the beat (police); to go a round of visits. 2. to become entangled, confused. 3. /a/ to wind (round a thing). 4. /a/ prov. to tease.
dolaş 2 دولاش archaic obstacle, tangle; involved, entangled.
dolaşık[fi] دولاشیق 1. intricate, confused. 2. round-about (way), meandering (road). —**lık** entanglement, intricateness, crookedness.
dolaşıl=[r] دولاشلمق pass. of **dolaş=**.
dolaşım neol., biol. circulation.
dolaşma دولاشمه verbal n. of **dolaş=**.
dolaştır=[r] دولاشدرمق /ı, a/ caus. of **dolaş=**. —**tırıl=** pass. دولاشدرلمق.
dolay neol. surroundings, outskirts, suburbs; environment.
dolayı دولایی 1. /dan/ because of, on account of, due to, e. g., **harbden dolayı** because of the war. 2. archaic roundabout, all around. —**sıyle** 1. by reason of, on account of, owing to, e. g., **bayram dolayısıyle** on account of the feast. 2. indirectly; consequently.
dolaykutupsal neol., astr. circumpolar.
dolaylı neol. indirect. — **tümleç** gram. indirect object.
dolaysız neol. direct.
doldur=[r] طولدرمق دولدرمق /ı/ 1. to fill; to fill up; /ı, a/ to fill (into). 2. to stuff. 3. to complete (sum or period of time). 4. to load (firearm); to prime (person with information); to charge (accumulator). 5. to foul (the clothes of a child). 6. naut. to let the wind fill (sails); to tauten (slack rope). —**ma** 1. verbal n. 2. filled, filled up, in. —**t=** /ı, a/ caus. of **doldur=**. —**ul=** pass. of **doldur=**.
dolerit دولریت F neol., geol. dolerite.
dolgu دولغو dent. filling.
dolgun طولغون دولغون 1. filled, stuffed, full. 2. high (salary). 3. plump. 4. ready to burst (with anger or sorrow). —**luk** 1. fullness. 2. vexation.
dolikosefal دولیقوسفال F biol. dolichocephalic.
dolma دولما طولما 1. verbal n. of **dol=**. 2. filled up (with earth or stones); reclaimed (land). 3. stuffed; stuffed vegetables. 4. slang lie, made-up story. — **duvar** timber-frame wall filled in with bricks. — **kalem** fountain-pen. —**cı** slang trickster, cheat. —**lık** fit for stuffing (tomatoes, etc.).
dolman دولمان var. of **dolaman**.
dolmuş طولمش دولمش 1. taxi or boat which only starts when it is filled up with passengers. 2. full, filled, stuffed. — **nöbeti** obs. the regular fare for each passenger in an omnibus-boat. — **ok** archaic arrow on a drawn bow, ready to be shot. — **yap=** to carry passengers in a pooled taxi.
dolomi دولومی F geol. dolomite.
dolu 1 طولو دولو 1. full, filled; /la/ filled (with), full (of). 2. lo ded (gun). 3. solid (not hollow). 4. archaic cup. —**su** the contents of, e. g., **bir bardak dolusu süt** a glass of milk. — **ay** archaic full moon. — **çek=** to draw a winner (in a lottery). —**yu çek=** archaic to drain a cup of wine.

— **dizgin** giving the horse its head; at full speed, galloping. —**ya koydum almadı, boşa koydum dolmadı** I was puzzled; I found no solution to the problem. — **zar** *gamblers' slang* loaded dice.

dolu 2 (.ˊ.) طولو دولو plentiful, in abundance.

dolu 3 طولو دولو hail, hailstorm. — **yağ=** to hail.

doluk=ᵘʳ طولوقمق *prov.* to be filled with tears (eyes).

dolun دولون full (moon).

doluş 1 دولوش *verbal n. of* **dol=**.

doluş=ᵘʳ **2** طولوشمق /a/ to crowd (into a place).

domağı دوماغی *var. of* **dumağı**.

domal=ᵘʳ طوماليق دوماليق 1. to rise, stand out, project as a bump or tumor. 2. to bend down with the seat sticking out.

domalan دومالان 1. truffle, *bot., Tuber.* 2. *prov.* tumor, abscess.

domalıçᶜⁱ طوماليج *prov.* 1. protuberance; rounded and projecting. 2. protruding (eyes).

domalt=ᵘʳ طوما لتمق دوما لتمق /ı/ *caus. of* **domal=**.

domanıçᶜⁱ دومانيج *same as* **domalıç**.

domates دوماتس Gk tomato.

dombay طومباى *prov.* water buffalo.

dombaz طومباز *same as* **tombaz**.

domino (.ˊ.) دومينو 1. It dominoes (game). 2. domino (costume).

Dominyon دومينيون F *geog.* Dominion.

domuz طوموز دوموز 1. pig, swine; wild boar, *zool., Sus scrofa.* 2. obstinate; cunning and selfish; spiteful, malicious. —**una 1.** out of spite. 2. thoroughly. — **ağırşağı** 1. sowbread *bot., Cyclamen europaeum.* 2. truffle, *bot., Tuber.* — **arabası** 1. truck, low four-wheeled vehicle. 2. *mil., hist.* a military shield on wheels. — **ayağı** 1. *mil., hist.* caltrop. 2. *mil., hist.* wormer used for withdrawing the charge from a gun. 3. land caltrops, *bot., Tribulus terrestris.* — **ayrığı** creeping dog's-tooth grass, *bot., Cynodon dactylon.* — **balığı** porpoise, *zool., Delphinus delphis.* — **budu** a leg of pork, ham. — **burnu** *med.* kind of whitlow. — **damı** 1. gallery of a mine supported by wooden props; *archaic* covered gallery in a fortification. 2. pigsty. — **derisi** pigskin. — **ekmeği,** — **elması** *same as* **domuz ağırşağı.** — **gibi** 1. obstinate, vicious, pigheaded. 2. boorish, coarse. 3. strong, healthy. — **gibi çalış=** to work like mad. —**un gok dediği yer** a very distant place. — **kılı** hog's bristle, bristles. —**dan kıl çek=,** —**dan kıl kopar=** to wangle something out of a stingy person. — **kuyruğu irtibat teli** *mil.* pig's-tail connection. — **pastırması** bacon. — **sucuğu** pork sausage. — **şeridi** pork tapeworm, *zool., Taenia solium.* — **tırnağı** *naut.* crowbar, jemmy; worm, chain stopper clew. — **topu** a kind of torture binding legs and hands together in a ball. — **yağı** lard. — **yavrusu** young hog, porkling, piglet. —**ca** (.ˊ.) swinishly; very maliciously. —**giller** wild pigs, *zool., Suidae.* —**lan böceği** the bombardier beetle, *zool., Brachinus crepitans.* —**lan=** to become pigheaded. —**luk** 1. swinish behavior. 2. viciousness, maliciousness. 3. pigsty.

don 1 طون دون frost, a freezing. —**a çek=** to freeze, to have frost. —**lar çözüldü** The frost is thawing. — **havası** frosty weather. — **yağı** tallow. — **yağı ile pekmez** incompatible (people).

don 2 طون دون 1. pair of drawers, underpants. 2. coat, color (of a horse). 3. *archaic* clothing, garment.

don=ᵘʳ **3** طونمق دونمق 1. to freeze, to become frozen; to be frozen to death; to feel extremely cold. 2. to solidify, to set (concrete, etc.); to be petrified with horror. —**a kal=** to be petrified with horror, to freeze on the spot.

don 4 دون Gk *only in* — **ağacı** *naut.* mainrail, roughtree-rail, bulwark, stanchion; top timbers.

donan=ᵘʳ طونانمق to deck oneself, to be decked out, illuminated, ornamented, equipped. —**ım** *naut.* rigging.

donanma دونانمه طونانمه 1. *verbal n. of* **donan=**. 2. fleet, naval force, navy. 3. illumination. — **fişeği** rocket.

donat=ᵘʳ طونتمق دونا تمق /ı/ 1. to deck out, to ornament; to equip; to dress (ship). 2. *slang* to abuse, to insult. 3. *archaic* to dress, to clothe, array. —**an** *mar. law* shipowner. —**anın mesuliyeti** *mar. law* shipowner's liability.

donatı *neol.* equipment; fitting.

donatıl=ᵘʳ طونا تلمق *pass. of* **donat=**.

donatım *neol.* equipment; *mil.* ordnance.

donatma طونا تمه دونا تمه 1. *verbal n. of* **donat=**. 2. outfitting of a ship. — **iştiraki** *mar. law* collective ship ownership.

donattır=ᵘʳ دونا تدرمق /ı, a/ *caus. of* **donat=**.

dondur=ᵘʳ طوندرمق دوكدرمق /ı/ *caus. of* **don= 3**.

dondurma دوكدرمه 1. *verbal n. of* **dondur=**. 2. ice cream. 3. made to freeze, frozen, set, solidified. — **kutusu,** — **makinası** ice cream freezer. — **taş** artificial stone, concrete. — **yap=** to make ice cream. —**cı** ice cream seller.

donki دوكى E *naut.* donkey-engine.

donlukᵍᵘ دونلق Ott. *hist.* 1. clothing-money (formerly allowed to soldiers, etc.). 2. a length of cloth given to soldiers.

donma طونمه دوكمه 1. *verbal n. of* **don= 3**.

donra

2. solidified; frozen. **— karton** carton pierre. **— noktası** *phys.* freezing point.
donra طوگره *prov.* 1. dandruff. 2. a layer of dirt on the body.
donsuz طونسز دونسز 1. having no underwear. 2. destitute, poverty-stricken; *sans culottes;* vagabond.
donuca, donucu طونیجم دونیجی *prov.* tetanus.
donuk^{ğu} طوقونه دونوق 1. frozen, cold, frigid, torpid. 2. dim, dull, lusterless. **— cam** frosted glass. **—lan=** 1. to become frosted, frigid. 2. to become dim. **—landır=** /ı/ *caus. of* **donuklan=**. **—laş=** *same as* **donuklan=**. **—luk** dimness, dullness.
donuz طوكز طوقوز *prov., same as* **domuz**.
dopdolu طوب طولو full up, chockful.
doru طورى chestnut with dark mane, tail, and fetlocks (horse).
doruk^{ğu} طوروق summit (of a mountain); top (of a tree). **— çizgisi, — hattı** *geog.* topline. **—la=** /ı/ *prov.* to heap up, to pile up.
dorum دوروم *prov.* camel colt.
dosa (´.) دوسه *naut.* gangplank. **— tahtası** gangplank.
dosdoğru طوس طوغرى straight; straight ahead; perfectly correct.
dost 1 دوست [**dost 2**] 1. friend; friendly. 2. lover; mistress. 3. *myst.* God. **— ağlatır düşman güldürür** *proverb* Friends criticize; enemies flatter. **—lar alışverişte görsün diye** for the sake of appearances, in order to appear busy. **—un attığı taş baş yarmaz** *proverb* Friendly criticism does no harm. **— başına** May the same befall all my friends. **— başa, düşman ayağa bakar** *proverb* A friend sees your face; a critical person sees your feet (shoes). **—lar başından ırak** May God spare all my friends (formula used when recounting some gruesome misfortune). **—a düşmana karşı** publicly, for all the world to see. **— edin=** to make friends; /ı/ to make one's friends. **— gani** *Or. mus.* a **makam** no longer used. **— kara günde belli olur** *proverb* When you are in trouble you find out who your friends are. **— ol=** to become friends. **— sözü acıdır** *proverb* A friend's criticism hurts. **—lar şehit biz gazi** Let them run the risk; we'll take the credit. **—la ye iç, alışveriş etme** *proverb* Don't mix business with friendship.
dost 2 (—) دوست P *lrnd., same as* **dost 1**. **—u mecazî** *myst.* the beloved. **—ân** (——) P *pl. of* **dost**. **—âne** (——.) P friendly (action); in a friendly manner.
dostça دوستچه *same as* **dostane**.
dostdar (——) دوستدار P *lrnd.* lover; friend.
dostgâh (.—) دوستگاه P *Or. mus.* a **makam** no longer used.

dostî (——) دوستى P *lrnd.* friendship.
dostluk^{ğu} دوستلوق friendship. **— et=** 1. to be friends. 2. /a/ to do a favor. **bir — kaldı** This is the last one (said by a shopkeeper or by somebody who offers something). **— kantarla, alışveriş mıskalla** Business is business.
dosya (´.) دوسیه F file, dossier.
doy=^{ar} دویمق 1. to become filled and satiated (with), to have enough (of food, etc.). 2. to become tired (of); to be sick (of).
doygun دویغون satiated, who has satisfied all his needs, saturated. **—luk** satiation, a being completely satisfied, saturation.
doyma دویما 1. satiety. 2. *sc.* saturation. **—mış** *sc.* unsaturated.
doymaz دویماز insatiable; greedy. **—lık** insatiability; greed.
doymuş دویمش *sc.* saturated.
doyum دویوم 1. satiety. 2. *archaic* booty. **— olmaz** /a/ One cannot have enough (of it). **—lu** 1. satisfying, satiating. 2. *archaic* rich with spoil. **—luk** 1. amount sufficient to satisfy. 2. *archaic* plunder, spoil, booty.
doyun=^{ur} دویونمق *archaic* to satisfy oneself (with food etc.)
doyur=^{ur} دویورمق /ı or ı, a/ 1. to fill, satisfy, satiate. 2. /ı/ *sc.* to saturate. **—an** *phys.* saturant. **—ul=** *pass.*
doz دوز F *med.* dose. **—unu kaçır=** /ın/ to overdo.
döğ=^{er} دوگمك *same as* **döv=**.
dök=^{er} دوكمك /ı/ 1. to pour; to shed (tears, leaves); to spill; to empty, throw out, throw away; to purge (worms); *slang* to fail (students in an examination). 2. /ı, a/ to pour (into); to pile up (troops); to spend freely (money, on something). 3. to cast (metal); to form in a mold, to mold. 4. to develop (skin eruptions). 5. /ı, a/ to turn, change (into a joke, etc.); to set down (on paper).
dökme دوكمه 1. *verbal n. of* **dök=**. 2. poured; cast (metal). **— benzin** petrol in bulk. **— su ile değirmen dönmez** *proverb* You can't turn a millwheel with water from pails. **— taş** granite, serpentine and other igneous stone (especially when formed in columns). **—ci** founder, metal worker. **—cilik** craft of founding, metal working.
döktür=^{ür} دوكديرمك 1. /ı, a/ *caus. of* **dök=**. 2. *slang* to give an elegant performance (in writing, dancing, speaking, etc.). 3. *slang* to oscillate the body in a belly dance.
dökül=^{ür} دوكلمك *pass. of* **dök=**. **dökülüp saçıl=** 1. to undress; to throw off one's clothes. 2. to spend lavishly. 3. to unburden oneself; to make a clean breast of it; to pour it all out. **—me** *verbal n. of* **dökül=**.

döküm دوكوم 1. *verbal n.* of **dök**=. 2. enumeration (in an account). 3. *slang* rags. —**hane** foundry. — **kalıbı** casting mould. —**lü** well-fitting (clothes).

dökün=ᵘʳ دوكنلك to throw water over oneself.

döküntü دوكنتو 1. remains, remnants, leavings, debris, remainder; straggler. 2. scum of the earth, the dregs. 3. skin eruption. 4. reef (in the sea), *archaic* mole, breakwater. 5. *com.* deficiency in weight; short weight. —**lük** rocky place in the sea.

döl دول 1. seed, germ, fetus, semen. 2. race, stock, origin. 3. *prov.* son; young; child. — **al**= to breed from an animal. — **ayı** *prov.* March. — **dök**= to set (of fruit, of vegetables after the blossom has fallen). — **dökümü** breeding season; spring. — **döş** children, descendants, family, progeny. — **eşi** afterbirth. —**den kal**= to be past breeding, to be past child-bearing. — **tut**= to become pregnant (animal). — **ver**= to bring forth young. — **yatağı** womb, *anat.* uterus. — **yolu** *anat.* vagina.

dölcekᵍⁱ, **dölcel** دولجك دوبل *prov.* 1. about to foal (mare). 2. prolific, fertile, fruitful, productive.

dölekᵍⁱ دولك *prov.* 1. steady, stable, enduring; serious, balanced, dignified, composed. 2. even, flat. — **dur**= to sit quietly (child). —**lik** seriousness, dignity, composure.

dölen=ⁱʳ دولنلك *prov.* 1. to be at ease; to relax; to calm down. 2. to settle down; to act steadily. 3. to increase. 4. to be put in order (affairs).

dölle=ʳ دوللسك /ı/ *biol.* to inseminate, fertilize, fecundate. —**me** insemination, fertilization, fecundation. —**n**= *pass.* of **dölle**=. —**nme** fecundation.

dölsüz دولسز childless, heirless; without young.

dölütᵈᵘ *neol., biol.* fetus.

dön=ᵉʳ دونلك 1. to go round, to spin, circle, roll, pivot. 2. to turn round; /a/ to turn (toward); /ı/ to turn (round a corner); /dan/ to swerve (from a course); to change one's mind; to fail to keep an agreement; /dan, a/ to turn back, to return; to change faith, to be converted. 3. /a/ to change, be changed, transformed (into). 4. to fail an examination; not to pass one's class. —**dür**= /ı/ *caus.* —**dürül**= *pass.* —**eç** *neol., phys.* rotor.

dönekᵍⁱ دونك fickle; untrustworthy; *slang* who always fails his examinations. —**lik** fickleness.

dönel 1 *neol., geom.* rotatory.

dönel=ⁱʳ 2 دونلك to begin to decline.

dönem *neol.* period of time.

dönemeçᶜⁱ دونمج road bend, curve. —**li** winding, curved (road).

döner دونر turning, revolving, pivotal. — **delilik** *neol., psych.* circular insanity. — **eklem** *neol., anat.* trochoid, pivotal joint. — **kapı** revolving door. — **kebap** meat roasted on a revolving vertical spit. — **kemik** *anat.* radius. — **koltuk** swivel chair. — **merdiven** spiral stairs. — **sermaye** *econ.* circulating capital.

döngel دونگل medlar, *bot., Pirus germanica*.

dönme دونمه 1. *verbal n.* of **dön**=; sc. rotation. 2. /dan/ converted to Islam (from another faith); *w. cap.* member of a Jewish community who were converted to Islam in the 17th century. — **dolap** 1. revolving cupboard. 2. revolving wheel (at a fun-fair). 3. waterwheel.

dönükᵍᵘ دونوك with one's back turned; turned, changed, altered.

dönül=ᵘʳ دونلى *pass.* of **dön**=.

dönüm دونوم *verbal n.* of **dön**=; a turn, a turning. 2. land enough to plow in a day. 3. a measure of land (forty by forty arshins, 940 m², about 1/4 acre). — **noktası** turning point.

dönüş 1 دونش *verbal n.* of **dön**=, return.

dönüş=ᵘʳ 2 /a/ *neol., phil., geom., biol.* to change, to be transformed.

dönüşlü دونشلى *gram.* reflexive (verb).

dönüştür=ᵘʳ *neol.* /ı, a/ *caus.* of **dönüş**= 2. —**üm** transformation.

dönüşüm *neol.* transformation. —**cülük** transformism.

dönüşün دونشين *prov.* on the return, when returning; after the return.

dörd- دورد- *cf.* **dört**. —**er** four each. —**er dörder** by fours; four at a time.

dördül دوردل *prov.* square.

dördün *neol., astr.* quarter.

dördüncü دوردنجى fourth. — **zaman** *geol.* quarternary era.

dördüz دوردوز 1. quadruplet. 2. *sc.* quadrigeminal. — **yumurcaklar** *neol., bot.* quadrigeminal tuberus. —**lü** of four parts; with four branches.

dörtᵈᵘ دورت four. — **adımlık yer** close by. — **ana** *archaic* the four elements. — **ayağı bir yere getir**= to be over-zealous. — **ayak***. — **ayak üstüne düş**=, — **ayak üzerine düş**= to land on all fours; to be very lucky; to get out of trouble easily. — **ayaklı** quadruped, beast. — **başı mamur** in perfect condition, prosperous, flourshing. — **başlı** *anat.* quadriceps. —**te bir** one fourth, a quarter. — **bir tarafı**, — **bir yanı** all around it, on all sides of it. — **cihar** backgammon a throw of two fours giving the right to make four moves of four. — **darplı sofyan** *Or. mus.*

a fast rhythmic pattern of four beats. **— dön=** /ı/ to search desperately for a remedy. **— duvar** an empty house or room. **— duvar arasında kal=**, **— duvar içinde kal=** to be shut in. **— elle sarıl=**, **— elle yapış=** /a/ to clutch (at), to hold fast (to); to stick heart and soul (at). **— elli** *zool.* quadrumanous. **— gözle bekle=** /ı/ to wait eagerly (for). **— göz bir evlât için** A child needs all the care of both parents. **— işlem** *neol., math.* the four arithmetical operations. **— kapı selâmı** Bektashi order kind of salutation. **—॔ kaşlı** 1. with a budding mustache (youth). 2. whose eyebrows are bushy or joined together. **— kat** fourfold. **— katlı** four storied; fourfold. **— kenar** *neol., geom.* quadrilateral. **— kitap** the four sacred books, i. e. the Pentateuch, the Psalms, the Gospels, and the Quran. **— kollu** four-armed; four-threaded; four-stranded (rope); four-handled. **— kolluya bin=**, **— kolluya çık=** *slang* to die. **— köşe, — köşeli** four-cornered, four-sided; square. **— köşe tekerlek** *colloq.* a hopeless business. **— mezhep** the four orthodox schools of Islam: Hanefi, Shafi'i, Maliki and Hanbeli. **— nal** gallop. **— nala git=** to go at full gallop. **— nala kaldır=** /ı/ to cause to gallop (horse). **— nala kalk=** to start galloping. **— taraftan** on all sides. **— ucunu koyuver=** to let things go, to let things slide; to lose heart entirely, to give up. **— üstüne, — üstü dört** perfect. **— üstü murat üstü** in perfect condition, prosperous, flourishing. **— yanına bak=, — yana bakın=** to look all around. **— yanı deniz kesil=** to fall into a hapless plight. **— yol ağzı** crossroad, junction. **— yüzlü** *neol., geom.* tetrahedron.

dörtayak[ʰ] دورت آیاق 1. quadruped. 2. on all fours.

dörtgen *neol., geom.* quadrangle. **— biçme** quadrangular prism.

dörtlü دورتلی *cards* four.

dörtlük[ᵗᵘ] دورتلك 1. quatrain. 2. *mus.* quarter note.

döş دوش *prov.* 1. breast, bosom. 2. flank (of a beast). **— eti** breast (mutton), brisket (beef), scrag end of meat.

döşe=ʳ دوشه مك /ı/ 1. to spread, lay down (floor, pavement, carpet, etc.). 2. to floor, to pave. 3. to furnish (room, house). **—yip daya=** /ı/ to furnish completely (room, house).

döşek[ᵗⁱ] دوشك 1. mattress, bed. 2. *naut.* flooring (of a boat). 3. *naut.* futtock. 4. a thin layer of concrete, etc. **— döşe=** to spread out a bed. **— minderi** wool under-mattress. **—li** 1. having a bed. 2. broad and flat-bottomed (boat). 3. having a broad base; well-settled, solidly based. **—lik** 1. bedding; a quantity

sufficient for a bed; bed-ticking. 2. a place in which beds are kept. 3. *naut.* timber used as flooring in a ship.

döşeli دوشه لی 1. furnished. 2. floored, paved. **— dayalı** fully furnished (house).

döşeme دوشه مه 1. floor, pavement. 2. furniture; upholstery. **— kapağı** *arch.* trap-door. **— kirişi** *arch.* floor joist. **—॔ takımı** set of furniture. **— zarı** *arch.* stone underlayer of marble pavement. **—ci** furniture-dealer, upholsterer. **—cilik** upholstery. **—li** furnished.

döşen=ⁱʳ دوشنمك 1. *pass.* of **döşe=**. 2. to dilate upon a subject in a criticizing way; /a/ to scold. 3. *colloq.* to take to one's bed, to be bedridden.

döşet=ⁱʳ دوشتمك /ı, a/ *caus.* of **döşe=**. **—tir=** /ı, a/ 1. *caus.* of **döşet=**. 2. *caus.* of **döşe=**.

döv=ᵉʳ دوگمك /ı/ 1. to beat; to thrash, flog; to thresh (grain); to hammer, forge; to pound (coffee, pepper); *prov.* to knock continually (at). 2. to bombard. **—dür=** /ı, a/ *caus.*

döveç[ⁱ] دوه ج *prov.* 1. mortar. 2. pestle.

döven دون flail; threshing machine.

döver دور Gk *prov.* pillar, rafter.

döviz دوبز F 1. foreign exchange. 2. motto, device, slogan or welcome, inscribed on a decorative ribbon or poster. 3. placard. **— takyidatı** *fin.* exchange control.

dövme دوگمه 1. *verbal n.* of **döv=**. 2. tattoo. 3. wrought (iron, etc). 4. *prov.* dehusked wheat.

dövül=ᵘʳ دوگلمك *pass.* of **döv=**. **—me** *verbal n.* of **dövül=**. **—müş** beaten; ground.

dövün 1 دوگون *prov.* 1. tattoo. 2. burnt incision, constantly kept open by replaceable chick peas, thought to be effective in drawing off pain. **— döğ=** to tattoo.

dövün=ᵘʳ 2 دوگونمك 1. to beat oneself; to scourge, flagellate oneself. 2. to show excessive sorrow and repentance. **—dür=** /ı/ *caus.* of **dövün=**.

döviş 1 دوکش *verbal n.* of **döviş=** 2; fight. **—te yumruk sayılmaz** (*lit.* Separate blows are not counted in a fight.) Once in on a big project you must go along with it all the way.

döviş=ᵘʳ 2 دوکشمك /la/ to fight, struggle. **—ken** quarrelsome; bellicose, combative. **—tür=** /ı, la/ to make fight (with one another). **—ücü** fighter.

dragoman دراغمان Gk *archaic* dragoman.

dragon دراغن F 1. dragoon. 2. *slang* penniless, pauper; scum.

drahoma (..ˊ.) دراخما Gk dowry (used referring to Greeks and Armenians).

Dral dede دال ددـه *colloq., only in* **—nin**

düdüğü gibi naked, helpless, disappointed, left in the cold.

dram درام F drama.

dramatik[t¹] دراماتيق F 1. dramatic. 2. tragic, painful, sad.

drednot دردنوت E dreadnought.

drenaj درناژ F med. drainage.

drezin درزين F rail. plate layer's trolley.

drise (.'.) دريسه var. of **dirisa**.

droseragiller neol., bot. Droseraceae.

[/du/ see /tu/.]

=du 1, =dü دو 1. cf. =dı 1. 2. archaic for =dı 1, =di, e. g. inildü, takıldu.

=du 2 دو cf. =dı 2.

=du 3 دو cf. =dı 3.

dua (.—) دعا A prayer. —**lar** archaic God bless you!, Goodbye! —**sını al**= /ın/ to have the blessing (of a person). — **et**= to pray; to pray for somebody in gratitude. —**yı me'sur** lrnd. a prayer traditionally handed down.

duacı دعاجى 1. one who prays. 2. an official of a mosque especially appointed to recite prayers. —**nız** your humble servant. — **çavuşu** same as **selâm çavuşu**.

duagû (.——) دعاگو P same as **duacı**.

duahan (.——) دعاخوان P 1. one who prays. 2. myst. orders one who ends the ceremony of **zikr** with prayers.

duaülcevşen '(.—...) دعاءالجوشن A hist., name of a prayer used on entering battle.

duba (.'.) دوبه 1. pontoon; buoy. 2. flat-bottomed barge. — **gibi** very fat.

dubar دوبار G mullet (fish).

dubara 1 (.—'.) دوبارە [dubare] deuce (at dice).

dubara 2 (..'.) دوبارە [dubara 1] colloq. trick; intrigue. —**ya düş**=, —**ya gel**= to be taken in, to be tricked. —**cı** trickster, liar.

dubare دوباره P lrnd. twice.

duble دوبله F a 'double' (beer, spirits).

ducret[ti] ضجرت A lrnd. distress, depression, anxiety.

duçar (——) دوچار P lrnd. /a/ subject (to), afflicted (with). — **ol**= /a/ to be subject (to), to be afflicted (with).

dud 1 (—) دود P lrnd. 1. smoke. 2. breath. 3. anguish, sadness. —**i âh** 1. sigh. 2. malediction. —**i ciger** sighs. —**i çerag** 1. lampblack. 2. the student's midnight oil. —**i dil** sigh. —**i dimağ** conceit, arrogance. —**i hâm** the dense smoke of green wood.

dud 2 (—) دود A lrnd. worm. —**i ibrişim** silkworm.

dudak[ğı] دوداق lip. — **boyası** lipstick. — **bur**=, —**ını bük**= to distort one's mouth as when about to weep. — **bük**= to curl one's lip (in a sneer, disdain, etc.). —**ı çatlamış** His lips are parched. — **çukuru** the groove in the upper lip. — **dudağa** lip to lip. — **ısır**= to bite one's lip in astonishment. — **kıpırdat**= to open one's lips, to utter a word. — **payı bırak**= not to fill to the brim. — **sarkıt**= to sulk. — **sessizi** neol., phon. labial. —**ı yarık** hare-lipped. **bir** —**ı yerde, bir dudağı gökte** having enormous lips (in folk tales, about negroes).

dudâlud (———) دودآلود P lrnd. 1. smoked; perfumed. 2. sorrowful. 3. affected with hallucinations.

dudefgen, dudefken (—..) دودافگن P lrnd. 1. that throws out smoke. 2. who enchants by incense; bewitching, enchanting.

dudgirifte (—...) دودگرفته P lrnd. smoked, smoky.

dudhane (——.) دودخانه P lrnd. 1. hearth, fireplace. 2. house, family, race.

dudi (——) دودى A anat. vermiform.

dudkeş (—.) دودكش P lrnd. chimney, smoke hole.

dudman (——) دودمان P lrnd. household, family lineage, clan. **D**—**ı Bektaşiye** Ott. hist. the corps of Janissaries.

dudpeymay (—.—.) دودپيماى P lrnd. sending forth volumes of smoke or sighs.

dudu دودو [tuti] 1. colloq. old Armenian woman. 2. archaic, title given to women. — **burnu hotoz** archaic kind of headgear for women. — **dilli** talkative, pleasant talker. — **kuşu** 1. parrot. 2. pretty, light-headed chatterbox (woman).

duğ (—) دوغ P lrnd. yogurt; buttermilk.

duha (.—) ضحى A lrnd. the earlier part of the forenoon. **D**— **Suresi** name of the ninety-third sura of the Quran.

duhan (.—) دخان A lrnd. 1. smoke. 2. tobacco. — **gümrüğü emini** Ott. hist. head of the tobacco custom office. **D**— **Suresi** name of the forty-fourth sura of the Quran. —**cı başı** Ott. hist. keeper of the tobacco of the Commander of the Janissaries. —**î** (.——) A 1. pertaining to or resembling smoke. 2. tobacco-colored.

duht دخت P same as **duhter**.

duhte (—.) دوخته P lrnd. 1. sewn, stitched. 2. pierced, skewered, nailed.

duhter دختر P lrnd. 1. girl, maiden; daughter. 2. female slave. —**i âfitap** poet. wine. —**i hum** poet. red wine. —**i rez** poet. wine. —**i ruzgâr** worldly events. —**î** (..—) P girlhood, maidenhood.

duhul[lü] (.—) دخول A lrnd. 1. entering, entrance. 2. penetration. 3. law a man's consummating the sexual act. — **hakkı** right of free entrance.

duhuliye (.——.) دخوليه A 1. entrance fee. 2. import duty. — **resmi** import tax.
=**duk** 1 دك cf. =**dık** 1.
=**duk**ᵍᵘ 2 دك cf. =**dık** 2.
=**duk** 3 دك cf. =**dık** 3.
duka 1 (.ˈ.) دوقه It archaic duke. **D— denizi** hist. the Tyrrhenian Sea. —**lık** dukedom.
duka 2 (.ˈ.) دوقه It archaic ducat.
=**dukça** دقچه cf. =**dıkça**.
=**dukta** دقته cf. =**dıkta**.
=**duktan başka** دقتن باشقه cf. =**dıktan başka**.
=**duktan sonra** دقتن صوكره cf. =**dıktan sonra**.
dul دول طول widow; widowed; widower. — **aptal otu** spurge olive, bot., Daphne Nezereum. — **avrat otu** burdock, bot., Arctium tomentosum. — **kal**= to be widowed.
dulâb (——) دولاب P lrnd. water-wheel.
dulda دولده prov. shade; sheltered place. —**lan**= /a/ to take refuge (under).
dullukᵍᵘ دوللمی طوللمی widowhood.
dulukᵍᵘ, **dulun** 1 دولك prov. temple (of the head).
dulun=ᵘʳ 2 دولنمك prov. 1. to disappear. 2. to set (sun, star).
=**dum** 1 دم cf. =**dım** 1.
=**dum** 2 دم cf. =**dım** 2.
duma, dumağı دوماغی دما prov. cold in the head.
duman دومان 1. smoke; fumes; smoky, full of smoke. 2. fog, mist, haze. 3. condensation (on a glass of cold water). 4. bloom (on a fruit). 5. speck, opacity (in the eye). 6. slang bad, hopeless (state, condition). 7. slang hashish. — **attır**= /a/ colloq. to ruin; to defeat completely. —**ı doğru çıksın** Let the chimney be crooked, as long as it draws. — **sal**= to emit smoke. —**ı üstünde** very fresh, brand new.
dumancı دومانجی slang one who makes lots of money out of next to nothing.
dumanla=ʳ دومانلسمك /ı/ to smoke (something or some place). —**n**= 1. pass. 2. to become smoky; to be filled with smoke; to acquire bloom (fruit); to become cloudy (eyes); to be confused (mind). —**ndır**= caus. of —**n**=.
dumanlı دومانلی 1. smoky, fumy; misty, dim. 2. colloq. tipsy.
dumansız دومانسز smokeless. — **barut** smokeless powder.
dumbaz دومباز same as **tombaz**.
dumdum دوم دوم E dumdum bullet.
dumlu دوملو archaic cold.
dumru دومرو archaic tambourine.
dumur (.—) ضمور A phys. atrophia. —**a uğra**= to be atrophied.

=**dun** 1 دن cf. =**dın** 1.
=**dun** 2 دن cf. =**dın** 2.
dun 3 (—) دون A lrnd. 1. low; base, vile. 2. lower, inferior. —**î** (——) P, —**luk** abstr. n.
=**dunuz** 1 دكز cf. =**dınız** 1.
=**dunuz** 2 دكز cf. =**dınız** 2.
dur=ᵘʳ 1 دورمق طورمس 1. to stop; to become motionless, to cease from motion; to be stopped. 2. to stand; to lie, to be (somewhere); to sit still; to wait; to remain; /üzerinde/ to dwell (upon a subject); prov. to reside, stay, live. 3. to last, endure; to continue to be; following verb + =**a** cf. =**adur**=; following verb + =**ip** cf. =**ıp dur**=. 4. to suit, to go, e. g., **Tablo bu duvarda nasıl durdu?** How does the picture look (go) on this wall? 5. to take up an attitude (toward somebody or something), e. g., **Bana karşı soğuk durdu** He met me coolly. 6. prov. to stand up. **Dur!** 1. Wait! Stop! 2. archaic Stand up. —**ma,** —**madan** continually, continuously. —**up dinlenmeden** ceaselessly, continuously, unceasingly. —**up dur**= to stand solidly. —**du durdu da** after having postponed the matter again and again, e. g., **durdu durdu da en iyisini buldu**. He waited long, but finally he got the best one. —**du durdu da turnayı gözünden vurdu** He waited long but finally made a good shot, a good stroke of business. —**up dururken** with no reason, without provocation. —**a kal**= to stand bewildered or aghast. — **otur yok,** — **yok otur yok** not a moment's peace, all hurry and bustle.
=**dur** 2 در cf. =**dır** 1.
=**dur**= 3 دیر cf. =**dır**= 2.
dur 4 (—) دور P lrnd. 1. far, far-off, distant. 2. absent. — **u diraz** at full length, at great length.
duraçᶜⁱ دراج طوراج [dürrâç] francolin (bird).
duradur (———) دور ادور P lrnd. 1. far and away. 2. long-continued. 3. prolix.
durağan neol. fixed, stable.
durakᵍⁱ دوراك طوراق 1. stop (bus, tram). 2. halt, pause. 3. prov. stationary, not in motion. 4. pros. caesura. 5. a form in religious Turkish music; tonic note. 6. archaic place, residence. — **evferi** Or. mus. a rhythmic pattern of 21 beats. — **su** stagnant water. — **yeri** 1. bus-stop; streetcar stop. 2. pause, stopping-place in reading.
durakla=ʳ دوراقلامق 1. to pause, to come to a stop. 2. to hesitate. —**ma** 1. pause. 2. hesitation. 3. mil. standstill.
duraklı دوراقلی phys. stationary.
duraksa=ʳ دوراقسامق to hesitate.
dural neol., phil. static.

durala=ʳ طورالامس دورالاس 1. to pause, to come to a stop. 2. to hesitate.

durbaş (——) دورباش P *archaic* 1. a cudgel, mace etc. for keeping back the mob. 2. Off! Away! Stand back!

durbin (——) دوربین P 1. *lrnd.* far-sighted, provident. 2. *archaic*, same as **dürbün**.

durdur=ᵘʳ طوردیرمه دوردرمه /ı/ *caus.* of **dur=**1¹.

durendiş (—.—) دورانديش P *lrnd.* far-sighted, prudent. **—lik** prudence.

durgun دورغون طورغون 1. calm, quiet. 2. subdued, fatigued. 3. stagnant, stationary; dull. **— mevsim** dead season, dull season. **—luk** 1. calmness, heaviness, dullness. 2. stagnation. 3. perplexity.

durgur=ʳ طورغورمه /ı/ *archaic* 1. *caus.* of **dur=** 1. 2. to set up, to build.

durgut=ᵘʳ دورغتمق /ı/ *archaic, caus.* of **dur=** 1.

duriba ضربت A *lrnd.* It was struck (inscription on coins).

durma دورمه طورمه *verbal n.* of **dur=** 1.

durmuş دورمش طورمش stagnant, stale. **— et** meat which has been kept for some time. **— oturmuş** experienced and settled down.

duru دورو طورو 1. clear, limpid. 2. *prov.* watery. **— su** settled, clear water.

durubuemsalⁱⁱ (.—..—) ضروب أمثال A *lrnd.* proverbs.

durugel=ⁱʳ طوروگلك دوروگلك *archaic* to get up, to rise.

durukᵍᵘ 1 *neol., phys.* stator.

duruk=ᵘʳ 2 طوروقمق دوروقمق *archaic* to hesitate.

duruksa=ʳ, **duruksı=**ʳ طورو قسامه دورو قسیمه to hesitate.

durul=ᵘʳ طورولمه دورولمه 1. to become clear and limpid. 2. to settle down.

durula=ʳ طورولامه دورولامه /ı/ to rinse. **—n=** *pass.* **—t=** /ı, a/ *caus.* of **durula=**.

durult=ᵘʳ طورولتمه دورولتمه /ı/ *caus.* of **durul=**.

durulukᵍᵘ طورولوك clearness, limpidity.

durum دوروم طوروم 1. state, situation, position. 2. behavior, attitude.

durumsa=ʳ طوروماسه دوروماسه to hesitate.

durur=ᵘʳ دوررمه *archaic, caus.* of **dur=** 1.

duruş 1 دوروش طوروش 1. *verbal n.* of **dur=** 1. 2. *phil.* attitude.

duruş= 2 دوروشمه طوروشمه /la/ *archaic* to confront one another (in argument or combat).

duruşma *neol., law* a hearing in a lawsuit. **— hazırlığı** *law* preliminary proceedings.

durut=ᵘʳ دورتمه *prov., caus.* of **dur=** 1².

duş 1 دوش F shower.

duş 2 (—) دوش طوش P *lrnd.* 1. shoulder. 2. last night.

duş 3 دوش طوش *archaic* 1. face to face. 2. direction. **— gel=**, **— ol=** /a/ to meet, come across.

duşakᵍⁱ دوشاق *prov.* fetter, hobble, clog. **—la=** /ı/ to fetter (a beast).

duşine (——.) دوشینه P *lrnd.* last night.

duşize (——.) دوشیزه P *lrnd.* maid, virgin. **—gî** (——.—) P 1. virginity. 2. the hymen.

duşmalⁱⁱ (——) دوشمال P *lrnd.* towel.

dut 1 دوت طوت [**tut** 1] 1. mulberry, *bot., Morus*. 2. *slang* tipsy, very drunk. **— gibi** *slang* greatly ashamed. **— kurusu** dried mulberries. **— kurusu ile yar sevilmez** You can't win your love with dried mulberries. **— rakısı** mulberry brandy. **— yemiş bülbüle dön=** to be tongue-tied, to become sad and quiet.

dut=ᵃʳ 2 دوتمن *prov. for* **tut=**.

dutlukᵍᵘ دوتلق 1. mulberry garden. 2. full of mulberry trees.

duvakᵍⁱ دووان طوان 1. veil; bride's veil. 2. *prov.* stone or earthenware lid of a large jar. **—ına doyma=** to have no chance of enjoying one's married life (said of a young widow). **— düşkünü** a newly married woman who becomes a widow, young widow. **—lı** having a veil, veiled.

duvar دیوار [**divar**] wall. **— arpası** wall barley, *bot., Hordeum murinum*. **— askısı** clothes rack. **— ayağı** *arch.* the foot or foundation of a wall. **— ayak** *arch.* engaged pier, piedroit. **— çek=** to build a wall. **— çevir=** /a/ to build a wall around. **— dayağı** *arch.* pole, etc. used as wall support. **— dişi** *arch.* notch, scarf-joint. **— eteklığı** *arch.* plinth, dado. **— gibi** 1. stone-deaf. 2. very solid. **— halısı** wall rug. **— ilânı** poster, placard. **— kâğıdı** wallpaper. **— kaplaması** *arch.* dressing (of stone, etc.). **— kemik** *anat.* parietal bone. **—ı nem, yiğidi gam yıkar** *proverb* Worry exhausts even a strong person. **— ör=** to put up a wall. **— pabucu** *arch.* footing (of a wall). **— resmi** wall painting, fresco. **— saati** wall clock. **— semeri** *arch.* coping (of a wall). **— tırmaşık kuşu** wall creeper, spider-catcher, *zool., Tichodroma muraria*. **—a yazıyorum** Mark my words; some day you will see that I am right. **—cı** 1. bricklayer, stonemason. 2. *slang* burglar. **—cılık** bricklaying. **—la=** /ı/ to wall in. **—lan=** *pass.* of **duvarla=**. **—lat=** /ı, a/ *caus.* of **duvarla=**. **—lı** walled, walled up.

duy=ᵃʳ 1 دویمق طویمق /ı/ 1. to hear; to learn (of). 2. to feel, to perceive, to be aware of.

duy 2 دوی F *elec.* contact socket, holder (of electric light bulb).

duyar *neol., psych., biol.* sensible. **—ga** *neol.*

biol. antenna. **—lık** *neol., psych., biol.* sensibility.

duygu دویغو طویغو 1. sense, sensation; sentiment, feeling; perception. 2. *archaic* a thing heard, seen or perceived; information, knowledge. **—daş** *neol., psych.* sympathizer. **—daşlı** sympathetic. **—daşlık** sympathy. **—la** /ı/ *neol., psych.* to affect, move, touch. **—lan=** *neol.* to be affected, moved, touched. **—lanım** *neol., psych.* affection. **—lu** sensitive. **—sal** *neol., psych.* affective. **—suz** numb, insensitive; callous, unfeeling, hard-hearted.

duyma دویما طویم *verbal n. of* **duy=** 1, sensation.

duymaz دویماز طویماز 1. deaf. 2. insensitive; lacking in perception. **—lık** insensibility. **—lıktan gel=** to pretend not to have heard; to be deaf to entreaties.

duynak[gı] دویناق *archaic* nail, claw, hoof.

duysal *neol., physiol.* sensorial, sensory.

duyu *neol., physiol.* sense.

duyul=[ur] طویولمق دویولمق *pass. of* **duy=** 1. **—ur** *neol., psych.* perceptible.

duyum دویوم طویوم *verbal n. of* **duy=** 1, *neol., psych.* sensation. **— eşiği** *neol., psych., physiol.* threshold of consciousness. **— ikiliği** *neol., psych.* synesthesia. **— ölçer** *neol., psych.* esthesiometer. **— yitimi** *neol., psych.* anesthesia. **—culuk** *neol., phil.* sensualism. **—sal** *neol., psych.* sensorial. **—samazlık** *neol., psych.* apathy.

duyur=[ur] دویورمق طویورمق /ı, a/ *caus. of* **duy=** 1. **—ul=** *pass. of* **duyur=**.

duyusal *neol.* 1. *ling.* affective. 2. *psych.* sensitive.

duyuş دویوش طویوش 1. *verbal n. of* **duy=** 1. 2. *psych.* impression. **— vurgusu** *neol., ling.* affective accent.

-duz (—) دوز P that sews, pierces, *as in* **çuvalduz, zerduz.**

duzah (—.) دوزخ P *lrnd.* 1. hell. 2. *myst.* society of the worldly. **—î** (—.—) P *lrnd.* hellish. **—iyan** (—.——) P *lrnd.* the fallen angels.

duzak[gı] دوزاق *same as* **tuzak.**

duziko (′..) دوزیقو Gk raki.

=dü 1 دو 1. *cf.* **=dı** 1. 2. *cf.* **=du** 1.

=dü 2 دو *cf.* **=dı** 2.

=dü 3 دو *cf.* **=dı** 3.

dü 4 دو P *lrnd.* two. **— beş*** **— vü nim** two and a half.

düadü (..—.) دوادو P *lrnd.* two by two.

düalizm دوالیزم F *phil.* dualism.

düb[bü] دب A *lrnd.* bear. **—i asgar** *astr.* the Little Dipper. **—i ekber** *astr.* the Big Dipper. **—i şimalî** Russia.

dübara (.—.) دوبارا P *var. of* **dubara** 1.

dübare (.—.) دوباره P *var. of* **dubare.**

dübbiye (.—.) دبیه A bears, *zool.*, Ursidae.

dübeş دوبش [dü + beş] backgammon fives at dice.

dübeyt, dübeyti (..—) دوبیت دوبیتی P *pros.* poem consisting of four hemistichs, two distichs.

dübiraderan (..—.—) دوبرادران P *lrnd.* 1. *astr.* the two stars. β, γ, in the Little Dipper. 2. golden eagle.

düble دوبل F *in* **— et=** cards to double.

dübr دبر A *lrnd.* the hinder part of anything, the back of the body; space or direction behind the rear; the buttocks; the anus.

dübur (.—) دبور A *lrnd.* 1. adversity, misfortune. 2. a coming behind, bringing up the rear.

dübür دبر A *var. of* **dübr.**

düca دجی A *lrnd.* darkness.

dücace (.—.) دجاجه A *lrnd., same as* **decace.**

dücaciye (.——.) دجاجیه A *zool.*, Gallinaceae.

dücihan (..—) دوجهان P *lrnd.* the two worlds.

düden دودن *prov.* chasm.

düdil دودل P *lrnd.* 1. undecided, inconstant. 2. hypocritical, two-faced.

düdük[ğü] دودك دودوك 1. whistle; pipe; flute. 2. long, hollow tube. 3. siren. 4. *slang* silly fellow. **—ü çal=** to succeed; to rejoice over success. **— gibi** shrill (voice). **— gibi kal=** to be left entirely alone (through one's own fault). **— gibi kıyafet** too tight clothes. **— kemiği** a long bone of an arm or leg. **— makarnası** macaroni. **— öttür=** to blow a whistle; to sound the siren. **—çü** fifer, piper. **—le=** *slang* to injure someone's honor, to deflower, to know sexually. **—lü tencere** pressure cooker.

düello (.′.) دوئللو F duel.

düesbe دواسبه P *lrnd.* 1. who travels with all speed. 2. courier, messenger.

düfuf (.—) دفوف A *lrnd., pl. of* **def 3.**

dügâh (.—) دوگاه P Or. *mus.* 1. one of the oldest compound **makams.** 2. name of the "A" note in the second space on the staff. **—ı acem** a makam having no sample today. **—ı hicaz** a makam having no sample today. **—ı kadim** a makam having no sample today. **— puselik** an old compound **makam.**

dügâne (.—.) دوگانه P *lrnd.* double, dual, twin. **—i vacib** the two obligatory acts of worship in a service.

dügûne (.—.) دوگونه P *lrnd.* 1. of two varieties. 2. in two manners.

düğ=[er] دوگلمك /ı/ *archaic* to knot.

düğe دوگه *same as* **düve.**

dügelekği, **düglek**ği دوگ لك *same as* **düvelek**.
düğme دوگمَ 1. button; bud; pimple; nipple. 2. electric switch. —**ci** maker or seller of buttons. —**le**= /ı/ to button up. —**len**= *pass. of* —**le**=. —**let**= /ı, a/ *caus. of* **düğmele**=. —**li** buttoned, buttoned up.
düğü دوگو *prov.* 1. broken rice. 2. the fine parts of boiled and pounded wheat (**bulgur**). —**cük** 1. fine **bulgur**. 2. snow falling in small hard flakes.
düğüm دوگوم knot; bowknot; *sc.* knot. — **aç**= to untie a knot. — **bağla**= to tie a knot. — **noktası** crucial point, vital point. — **ol**= to get knotted. — **yeri** crucial point. —**le**= /ı/ to knot, to tie in a knot. —**len**= 1. *pass. of* **düğümle**=. 2. to become knotted, to become a knot. —**let**= /ı, a/ *caus. of* **düğümle**=. —**lü** knotted, tied in knots.
düğün دوگون wedding feast; circumcision feast. — **bayram** merry-making, feast. — **çiçeği** buttercup, ranunculus, *bot.*, *Ranunculus*. — **çiçeğigiller** *bot.*, *Ranunculaceae*. — **çorbası** soup made of bouillon, flour, etc. — **dernek** festival, merry entertainment. — **dernek, hep bir örnek** Always the same old thing. — **et**= to rejoice. — **evi** house where a wedding feast takes place. — **evi gibi** crowded and noisy (place). — **pilâvı ile dost ağırla**= to entertain at another's expense; to take credit for what has been done by others. — **soygunu** *Ott. hist.* female servant at a wedding feast who had to put off her outer garments so that she could move with ease in waiting upon guests. — **yap**= to hold a wedding.
düğüncü دوگونجى *prov.* wedding guest.
düğürcü دوگورجى *prov.*, *var. of* **dünürcü**.
düğürcükğü دوگورجك *var. of* **düğücük**.
dühat (.—) دهات *A lrnd.*, *pl. of* **dâhi** 2².
dühn دهن *A lrnd.* oil, ointment, unguent.
dühnülban (..—) دهن البان *A drug.* oil of ben.
dühnülbelesan (....—) دهن البلسان *A drug.* balm of Gilead or Mecca.
dühnülfücl دهن الفجل *A drug.* oil from the seed of *Raphanus oleiferus*.
dühnülhırvaʾı دهن الخروع *A drug.* castor-oil.
dühur (.—) دهور *A lrnd.*, *pl. of* **dehr**.
dühül دهل P *lrnd.* drum. —**baz** (..—) P 1. drummer. 2. small drum used by falconers. —**deride** (...—.) P disgraced.
=**dük** 1 دك *cf.* =**dık** 1.
=**dük** 2 دك *cf.* =**dık** 2.
=**dük**ğü 3 دك *cf.* =**dık** 3.
dükḱü 4 دك F duke.
=**dükçe** دكچه *cf.* =**dıkça**.
dükeli دكلى *archaic* all.
dükkân دكان [A .—] 1. shop. 2. *slang* gambling house. — **aç**= to set up business, to open shop. — **fiatı** selling-price. — **sahibi** owner of a shop. —**cı** shopkeeper.
dükkânçe (.—.) دكانچه P *lrnd.* small shop.
dükruvar دوكروار F *com.*, *del credere*.
=**dükte** دكته *cf.* =**dıkta**.
=**dükten başka** دكتن باشقه *cf.* =**dıktan başka**.
=**dükten sonra** دكتن صوكره *cf.* =**dıktan sonra**.
dülâ (.—) دولا P *lrnd.* two-fold, doubled; double.
dülbend دلبند P *lrnd.* 1. *same as* **tülbent**. 2. turban. — **ağası** *Ott. hist.* the valet in charge of turban muslins. —**dar** (..—) P *Ott. hist.* groom of the muslins.
Düldül 1 دلدل A Duldul (name of the Prophet's mule).
düldül 2 دلدل *prov. for* **dürbün**.
dülekği دلك *var. of* **düvelek**.
dülger دولگر [**dürger**] 1. carpenter. 2. builder. — **bağı** *naut.* kind of knot. — **balığı** John dory. —**lik** carpentry.
dülûkḱü (.—) دلوك A *lrnd.* sunset.
=**düm** 1 دم *cf.* =**dım** 1.
=**düm** 2 دم *cf.* =**dım** 2.
düm 3 دم P *lrnd.* tail. —**i gâv** 1. oxtail. 2. scourge, lash. 3. long trumpet. —**i gürg** false dawn; twilight.
düm 4 دم P *Or. mus.* a word used in beating time, spoken as the right hand beats.
dümağz دمغز P *lrnd.* double-kerneled.
dümballi (.—), **dümbale** (.—.) دمبال دمباله P *lrnd.* tail. —**i çeşm** outer corner of the eye.
dümbe دمبه P *lrnd.* 1. tail. 2. posterior, buttocks.
dümbekki دمبك P *lrnd.* 1. little tail. 2. tomtom.
dümbelekği طنبلك دمبلك [**dümbek**] 1. a rhythmic instrument made of two earthenware or wooden bowls one end of which is covered with a skin, chiefly used in Anatolia. It is played either with the fingers or sticks. 2. *colloq.* stupid fellow. 3. *slang* catamite. —**çi** drummer.
dümbüride (..—.) دم بريده P *lrnd.* dock-tailed.
dümdar (.—) دمدار P *mil.* rear guard.
dümdüz دوم دوز 1. quite smooth, quite level; absolutely straight. 2. plain, simple (fellow).
dümen دومن It 1. rudder. 2. *slang* trick. — **bedeni** *naut.* shank of the anchor. — **dinle**= *naut.* to answer her helm (ship). — **dolabı** *naut.* rudder wheel, steering wheel. —**i eğri** zigzagging. —**i elinde ol**= /ın/ to be in charge (of), to pull the strings. — **evi** wheel-house, rudder case. — **iğnesi** *naut.* pintle of the rudder. — **kır**= to change directions, to veer. —**i kır**= *slang* to go away, to slip away. — **kullan**= to steer. — **neferi**

dümmel

slang the last or laziest pupil. **— suyu** the wake of a ship. **— suyundan git=** /ın/ to follow in someone's wake. **— tut=** to steer. **— yap=** *slang* /a/ to deceive, to trick somebody. **— yekesi** tiller. **— yelpazesi** back-piece of a rudder. **—ci** 1. steersman. 2. *slang* the last or laziest pupil. 3. *slang* shill.

dümmel ضُمَّل A *lrnd.* boil, abscess.

dümuᵘᵘ (. —) ضُمُوع A *lrnd.*, *pl. of* **dem 5**.

dün 1 دُن 1. yesterday. 2. the past. **— akşam** last evening, yesterday evening. **— bir bugün iki** So soon! In such a short time! **—den bugüne** in a short time, overnight. **—den bugün güzelsin** You are more beautiful today than yesterday (said in flattery). **— değil evvelki gün** the day before yesterday. **—den hazır** over-eager, only too glad, just waiting for it. **—den ölmüş** listless, spiritless. **—den razı**, **—den teşne** *same as* **dünden hazır**. **— yumurtadan çıkmış, bugün kabuğunu beğenmiyor** Hatched only yesterday, and he despises the shell today.

dün 2 دُن دُونْ *archaic* night. **— baskını** night raid. **— buçuğu** midnight. **— ü gün** night and day. **— içi** night, night time.

=**dün 3** دُن *cf.* =**dın 1**.

=**dün 4** دُن *cf.* =**dın 2**.

dün=ᵉʳ 5 دُونْلَك *archaic* to rise up in the air.

düne=ʳ دُونَلَك *archaic*, *same as* **tüne=**.

dünim (. —) دُنِيم P *lrnd.* in halves, in two, divided.

dünit دُونِيت F *geol.* dunite.

dünkiⁿⁱ, dünküⁿᵘ دُنْكِى yesterday's. **— çocuk** too young; a raw person, young and inexperienced. **— gün** yesterday.

dünle, dünleden دُنْلَه دُنْلَه دَن *archaic* at night, in the night.

dünün دُونِين *archaic* during the night. **— günün** night and day.

dünür دُونُر دُكُر دُكُور 1. the father-in-law or mother-in-law of one's child. 2. woman sent out to inquire about a prospective bride and to lead the marriage negotiations. **— gez=** to search for a suitable bride for a suitor. **— git=** to go and see a girl and ask for her hand on behalf of another. **—cü** *same as* **dünür²**.

dünürlükᵍᵘ دُونُرلُك 1. relationship between two persons connected by intermarriage of blood-relations of each. 2. deputy-suitorship.

=**dünüz 1** دُكِز *cf.* =**dınız 1**.

=**dünüz 2** دُكِز *cf.* =**dınız 2**.

dünya (. —) دُنيا A 1. world, Earth. 2. this life. 3. everyone, people. **—da** never in this world, *e. g.*, **—da gitmem** I would not go for the whole world. **— adamı** man of the world. **— âlem** all the world, everybody. **—yı anla=** to understand life, to be mature. **— başına yıkıldı** His world went all to pieces. **—lar benim oldu** I felt on top of the world. **— bir araya gelse** in no circumstances, in no way. **— bir kararda durmaz** Things may change. **—nın çivisi kopmuş** The world has gone mad. **—yı dûn** *lrnd.* this world. **— durdukça** for ever and ever. **— duydu** Everybody heard about it. **—dan el etek çek=** to give up all worldly things. **— evi** marriage. **— evine gir=** to get married. **—dan geç=** to retire from the world, to lose touch with life. **—ya gel=** to be born. **—ya getir=** /ı/ to give birth (to). **—ya gözlerini kapa=** to die. **—yı gözü görmüyor** He is so overwhelmed that he doesn't care about anything else. **— gözüyle gör=** /ı/ to see (somebody) before one dies. **— güzeli** a ravishing beauty. **—dan haberi yok** 1. He knows nothing about it. 2. He is too innocent, inexperienced. **— Hazreti Süleyman'a kalmamış** Vanity of vanities, all is vanity. **—nın kaç bucak olduğunu ona gösteririm** I'll show him! **— kadar** a whole world, a great lot. **—ya kazık kakacak değil ya** He's got to die some day; no one lives forever. **— kelâmı etmedi** He didn't say a word; he didn't open his mouth. **— kurulalıdan beri** since Adam's day. **—nın malı dünyada kalır** You can't take your worldly goods with you (when you die). **—nın öbür ucu** the far end of the world. **—nın parası** a lot of money. **— penceresi** *prov.* the eyes. **—nın tahammülü yok** It's not worth while to worry about things in this world. **—da tasasız baş bostan korkuluğunda bulunur** No one is free from worries in this world. **—yı tut=** to spread all over the world. **— tükenir, yalan tükenmez** There is no end to people's lying. **—nın ucu uzundur** Life is full of all sorts of experiences. **—sı uygun** wealthy, well-to-do. **— varmış** How wonderful! (expression of relief). **— bir yağlı kuyruktur, yiyebilene aşk olsun!** *proverb* The world is full of profitable things, provided that one knows how to get them. **— zindan ol=** /a/ to be in great distress.

dünyalıkᵍⁱ دُنيالِك worldly goods, wealth; money.

dünyaperest (. — . .) دُنياپَرَست P worldly-minded, materialist.

dünyevî (. . —) دُنيَوى A worldly.

düpdüz, düpedüz دُپدُز دُپەدُز 1. quite level, absolutely flat; very straight. 2. sheer.

düpüldü, düpürdü دُپُلدُ دُپُردُ *archaic* noise.

dür=ᵉʳ 1 دُرلَك دُرلَك /ı/ to fold, roll up.

dürʳʳᵘ **2** دُرّ A *lrnd.* pearl. **—i Aden** pearl of Aden. **—i giranmaye** precious and big pearl. —i hoşab fine pearl. —i manzum strung pearls. —i meknun hidden pearl. —i nab shining white pearl. —i nasüfte 1. virgin pearl, unbored pearl. 2. virgin. 3. an original poetic concept. —i nefid a string of pearls. —i sadefnişin a pearl which is still in its mother of pearl. —i semin precious pearl. —i sirab large pearl. —i şehdane large pearl. —i şehvar magnificent pearl. —i yegâne a matchless pearl. —i yekdane 1. rare pearl. 2. The Prophet Muhammad. —i yekta rare pearl, pearl of great price. —i yetim 1. rare pearl. 2. the Prophet Muhammad.

=dür 3 دُرّ cf. =dır 1.
=dür 4 دُرّ cf. =dır 2.
dürbün دوربين [Persian durbin] fieldglass, telescope.
dürc درج A lrnd. 1. a little casket for jewels, etc. 2. a pretty mouth.
dürd درد P poet. sediment, lees, dregs.
dürdane (.—.) دردانه P lrnd. pearl.
dürdaşam (.——) دردآشام P poet. who drains to the dregs.
dürdî (.—) دردى P lrnd. dregs.
dürdkeş دردكش P poet. who drains to the dregs.
dürdür=ür دوردرمك /ı, a/ caus. of dür= 1.
dürefşan (..—) درافشان P var. of dürrefşan.
düreng دورنك P lrnd. 1. of two colors. 2. double-faced, hypocrite; inconstant, fickle.
dürer درر A poet. 1. pl. of dür 2. 2. eloquent sayings. 3. tear-drops. 4. white teeth. —bar (..—) P that pours forth eloquent sayings.
dürger دركر P lrnd., same as dülger.
dürlü درلو prov., same as türlü.
dürme درمه 1. verbal n. of dür= 1. 2. prov. cabbage.
dürraa (.—.) درّاعه A lrnd. upper garment for men, long robe.
dürraçı (.—) درّاج A francolin.
dürraki (.—.) درّاقى [Persian durragin] nectarine.
dürrat (.—) درّات A lrnd., pl. of dürre.
dürre درّه A lrnd. 1. single pearl. 2. pretty word, eloquent saying. 3. tear-drop.
dürrefşan (..—) درافشان P lrnd. 1. pearl-scattering. 2. sweetly-prattling (mouth). 3. eloquent. 4. weeping (eye).
dürt=er دورتمك /ı/ 1. to prod, to goad. 2. to stimulate, to incite. 3. archaic to rub, to apply (ointment, etc.).
dürtlengiçi دورتلنكيج prov. ox goad.
dürttür=ür دورتدرمك /ı, a/ caus. of dürt=.
dürtü دورتو archaic goad. neol., psych. drive, motive.
dürtükle=r دورتوكلمك /ı/ 1. to prod slightly and continually. 2. to incite, to encourage.
dürtül=ür دورتولمك pass. of dürt=.
dürtün=ür دورتونمك archaic to rub on oneself (ointment etc.).
dürtüş 1 دورتوش verbal n. of dürt=.
dürtüş=ür 2 دورتوشمك /la/ to push or prod one another gently. —le=, —tür= /ı/ same as dürtükle=.
düru (.—) دورو P lrnd. 1. two-faced. 2. double-faced, deceitful.
dürud (.—) درود P lrnd. 1. prayer, thanksgiving, blessing. 2. salutation, greeting. — oku= to recite the formula of salutation in worship.
düruğ (.—) دروغ P lrnd. false, untrue; untruth, lie. —âmiz (.———) P false.
dürus (.—) دروس A lrnd., pl. of ders.
düruy (.—) دروى P same as düru. —î (.——) P insincerity, double-dealing, hypocrisy.
Düruz (.—) دروز lrnd., pl. of Dürzi, the Druse people.
düruze (.—.), düruzi (.——) دروزه دروزى P lrnd. 1. two days old, of two days duration. 2. ephemeral, transitory.
dürü دورى prov. wedding present.
dürül=ür دورولمك pass. of dür= 1.
dürüm دوروم 1. verbal n. of dür= 1. 2. prov. roll, fold, pleat. 3. prov. piece of flat bread formed into a roll or fold and eaten with food which is taken up from the plate on this roll. —ü bozulmamış brand-new. — dürüm folded, pleated. bir — kaymak a roll of clotted cream.
dürüst درست P 1. correct, honest, straightforward, open. 2. lrnd. accurate. — ayar (...—) P archaic 1. of standard fineness. 2. of perfect integrity. —î (..—) P, —lük 1. correctness, validity. 2. soundness; healthiness.
dürüş=ür دورشمك archaic 1. to strive, to apply oneself diligently. 2. to struggle, to fight.
dürüşt درشت P coarse, harsh, severe, brutal. —len= to become rough, coarse, hard.
dürüt=ür دورتمك /ı/ 1. prov. to invent, fabricate (a lie). 2. archaic to create.
Dürzi (.—) درزى A Druse. — Dağı Mount Lebanon.
dürzü درزو [Dürzi] vulg. scoundrel, mean fellow.
düse دوسه P double three (in backgammon).
düstur (.—) دستور A lrnd. 1. code of laws. 2. norm, rule. 3. pharm. codex. —i (.—.) A normative. —ül'amel rule, formula, guiding principle. —ül'edviye obs., pharm. codex.
düsur (.—) دثور A lrnd. a being

obliterated, effaced, worn out; oblivion, forgetfulness.

düş=ᵉʳ **1** دوشمك 1. to fall, fall down; to be overthrown (government), to be deposed (ruler); to be aborted (child); to decline in wealth, power, esteem, to fall away in health, to fall on evil days; to decrease, fall (in value), to drop (fever); *archaic* to fall (in battle) 2. /a/ to fall (into, upon); to be thrown (on), *naut.* to drift (to port or starboard); to pass (into a worse state), to fall (into a dangerous or difficult condition); to come, to land (at), to end up (at); to be located (in relation to something else); to pass by inheritance (to), to be transferred by lot (to), to fall to one's lot; to fall (on a certain day); to beset (doubt, fear); to appear (gray hairs in beard, freckles on face). 3. /dan/ to fall, to drop (from); to show a deficiency (in), *as in* **ayardan düş=, çaptan düş=, elden ayaktan düş=, kuvvetten düş=.** 4. /a/ to befit, become; to concern; to be incumbent (upon). 5. /a *or* üzerine/ to show interest (in), to show sympathy (for), to take (to), to fall (for), to be addicted (to). 6. to give the impression of being (odd, silly, etc. words or acts), *e. g.,* **Bu söz kaba düştü** These words were rude. 7. *colloq.* to be chanced upon, to be found, *e. g.,* **Bu fırsat her zaman düşmez** This opportunity does not always come. 8. /ı, dan/ to subtract, deduct. **—enin dostu olmaz** *proverb* People do not befriend those who have fallen into adversity. **—e kalka** struggling along, with difficulty. **—üp kalk=** /la/ to live together (with). **—mez kalkmaz bir Allah** No one is so great that he may not fall some day.

düş 2 دوش *prov.* dream; vision. **— az=** to have a seminal emission during sleep. **— gör=** to have a dream.

düşah (.—) دوشاخ P *lrnd.* 1. two-branched, bifurcated, forked; fork. 2. double-pointed arrow. 3. kind of pillory.

düşelekᵍⁱ دوشلك *archaic* share, lot.

düşembe, düşenbih دوشنبه P *archaic* Monday.

düşes دوشس F duchess.

düşeş دوشش P 1. sixes (at dice). 2. *slang* windfall; bargain.

düşey *neol., sc.* vertical.

düşize (.—) دوشیزه P *lrnd., var. of* **duşize.**

düşkü *neol., phil.* incident.

düşkün دوشكون 1. fallen. 2. fallen on hard times. 3. /a/ addicted (to). 4. Bektaşi order a member who has committed a sin against the rule of the order and is in an 'excommunicated' state. **—lük** 1. decay, poverty. 2. excessive fondness or addiction.

düşman دوشمان دشمن P 1. enemy, foe, antagonist. 2. one who consumes much (of something), *e. g.,* **pilâv düşmanı** a great pilaf eater. **— ağzı** calumny. **— çatlat=** to be in fortunate circumstances occasioning the envy and discomfiture of one's enemies. **— düşmana gazel okumaz, — düşmana mevlût okumaz, — düşmana yasin okumaz** Expect no praise from an enemy. **—ın karınca ise de hor görme!** Don't underestimate the enemy. **—lık** enmity, hatred, antagonism.

düşme دوشمه *verbal n. of* **düş= 1;** *phys.* fall.

düşmen دوشمن P *poet., same as* **düşman.**

düşnam (.—) دشنام P *lrnd.* abuse, invective. **— et=** /a/ to abuse, vituperate. **— dihende** P 1. abuser. 2. index finger.

düşsel *neol., psych.* oneiric.

düşükᵍü دوشوك 1. fallen, drooping. 2. low (price, quality). 3. misconstrued (sentence), unrefined (style of writing). 4. *neol., med.* miscarriage. **— ateş** *path.* subnormal temperature. **— basınç** *meteor.* depression. **—lük** looseness (of style); faultiness (of rhyme etc.); fall (in prices).

düşül=ᵘʳ دوشولمك *pass. of* **düş= 1.**

düşüm دوشوم *archaic* a large wooden štamp used by tithe collectors.

düşümdeş=ⁱʳ *neol., phil.* to coincide.

düşümdeşlikᵍⁱ *neol., phil.* coincidence.

düşün=ᵘʳ دوشونمك 1. /ı/ to think (of), to reflect (over); to think over, to ponder (over); to think out. 2. to be gloomily pensive, to be sad. **—üp taşın=** to think over carefully, to consider at length.

düşünce دوشونجه 1. thought, idea. 2. reflection, observation, consideration. 3. anxiety worry. **bir — aldı** /ı/ (He) began to get worried. **—li** pensive, thoughtful; worried. **—siz** thoughtless, inconsiderate. **—sizlik** thoughtlessness.

düşündür=ᵘʳ دوشوندورمك /ı *or* ı, a/ *caus. of* **düşün=.**

düşünme دوشونمه *verbal n. of* **düşün=.**

düşünül=ᵘʳ دوشونولمك *pass. of* **düşün=.**

düşünür *neol.* thinker.

düşünüş دوشونوش way of thinking.

düşür=ᵘʳ دوشورمك /ı/ *caus. of* **düş=.** **—t=** /ı, a/ *caus. of* **düşür=.** **—tül=** *pass. of* **düşürt=.**

düşüş دوشوش *verbal n. of* **düş= 1.**

düşütᵈü *neol., med.* miscarried foetus.

düşvar (.—) دشوار P *lrnd.* difficult, hard. **—hû** (.——) P ill-tempered. **—î** (.——) P, **—lık** difficulty. **—pesend** (.—..) P hard to please. **—zay** (.——) P producing with pain.

düt دوت sound imitating a whistle or a siren.

düta (.—) دوتا P *lrnd.* 1. doubled; in two layers. 2. bent.

düttürü (.'..) دوت ـ ـ 1. oddly dressed

tightly dressed. 2. odd or tight dress. 3. *archaic* garrulous. **D— Leylâ** one whose clothes are too tight and too short.

düvalⁱⁱ (.—) دوال P *lrnd.* 1. strap or thong of hide or leather. 2. stirrup leather. 3. fraud, deceit, trick.

düvazdeh (.—.) دوازده P *lrnd.* twelve. **D— İmam** the 12 imams of the Shiites.

düve دوه heifer.

düvel دول A *lrnd.*, *pl. of* **devlet**¹. **—i muazzama** *intern. law* the Great Powers. **—i mütehabbe** *Ott. hist.* the powers on terms of mutual friendship with the Ottoman Empire.

düvelekᵏⁱ دوللك *prov.* 1. kind of small melon. 2. unripe melon.

düveli (..—) دولى *lrnd.* concerning states, interstate.

düven *var. of* **döven**.

düvist (.—) دويست P *lrnd.* two hundred.

düvüm, düvümin (..—) دوميں P *lrnd.* second.

düyekᵏⁱ دويك P *Or. mus.* rhythmic pattern of 8 beats with signatures of 8/8, 8/4.

düyun (.—) ديون A *lrnd.*, *pl. of* **deyn**. **—u gayrımuntazama** floating debts. **D—u Umumiye** the Public Debts (of the Ottoman Empire). **—ât** (.——) A liabilities, debts.

düyüm, düyümin (..—) دويم P *lrnd.*, *vars. of* **düvüm**.

düz 1 دوز 1. smooth, even; flat, level; level place, a plain. 2. straight. 3. uniform, plain-colored, without ornament; plain, simple. **— arazi** level ground. **— atkı** *arch.* lintel. **— ayak** 1. without stairs, on one floor. 2. on a level with the street. **— güverte** *naut.* flushdeck. **— kalem** straight-edged chisel. **— kanadlılar** *zool.* Orthoptera. **— nefes et=** /l/ *slang* to get the better (of), to defeat, to knock out, to wind. **— oluş** *biol.* orthogenesis. **— perçin çivisi** countersunk rivet. **— piyan-bağı** *naut.* flat seizing. **— sesli** *phon.* unrounded vowel. **— su** *naut.* waters with flat bottom, shallows. **— taban***. **— tümleç** *neol., gram.* direct object. **— uçuş** level flight. **— yüzlü eklem** *neol., anat.* arthrodia.

düz 2 دوز brandy made of grapes.

düz=ᵉʳ **3** دوزمك /l/ 1. to arrange, to compose; to prepare, to bring together; *archaic* to mend, to put to rights. 2. to invent (tale, etc); to counterfeit, to forge. 3. *slang* to know carnally. **—üp koş=** /l/ *archaic* 1. to arrange, to compose. 2. to adorn, embellish.

düzce (.'.) دوزجه flatly, simply. **—si** frankly, to tell the truth.

düzd دوزد *lrnd.* thief; robber. **—efşar** (..—) P abettor of thieves; receiver. **—î** (..—) P theft; robbery.

düzdide (.—.) دوزديده P *lrnd.* 1. stolen 2. stealthy, furtive.

düzdür=ᵘʳ دوزدرمك /l, a/ *caus. of* **düz= 3**.

düze *neol.* dose.

düzeban (..—) دوزبان P *lrnd.* 1. double-tongued. 2. deceitful, hypocrite. **—î** (..——) P double-tonguedness; hypocrisy.

düzeçᶜⁱ *neol., phys.* level (instrument).

düzekᵏⁱ *prov.* plain ground on a slope.

düzel=ⁱʳ دوزلمك to improve and reach a right and proper condition; to be improved; to be put in order, to be settled. **—t=** /l/ *caus. of* **düzel=**. **—til=** *pass. of* **düzelt=**.

düzem *neol., chem.* dosage.

düzen دوزن 1. order, harmony, regularity. 2. orderliness, neatness. 3. *mus.* harmony, a being in tune. 4. ruse, trick, lie. **— akçası** *Ott. hist.* money paid to Janissary recruits. **—i bozuk** out of order; out of tune. **— kur=** to set a trap; to contrive. **— ver=** /a/ to put in order; to tune. **—baz** (..—) liar, cheat, trickster. **—bozan** death. **—ci** *same as* **düzenbaz**. **—geç** *neol., phys.* regulator. **—le=** /l/ to put in order. **—leşik** *neol., phil.* coordinate. **—li** in order, orderly, tidy; in tune. **—lik** order, peace, harmony. **—siz** out of order, untidy, out of tune. **—sizlik** disorder, untidiness. **—teker** *neol., phys.* flywheel (of engine).

düzet=ⁱʳ دوزتمك /l/ *same as* **düzelt=**.

düzgü *neol., phil.* norm. **—lü** normal.

düzgün دوزكون 1. smooth, level, regular, in order. 2. correct. 3. old-time makeup, face paint. 4. *neol., math.* regular. **— beşgen** *neol., geom.* regular pentagon. **— et=** *archaic* to smooth, to level. **— hareket** *neol., phys.* uniform motion. **— sür=** to use face paint. **—cü** *obs.* 1. makeup woman. 2. cosmetics seller. **—le=** /l/ to make up with face paint (face). **—lü** made-up with face paint. **—lük** 1. order, regularity. 2. the state of being in tune or in accord. 3. *obs.* cosmetics box.

düzgüsel *neol., phil.* normative.

düzgüsüz *neol., phil.* abnormal.

düzine (.'.) دوزينه It dozen.

düzle=ʳ دوزلمك /l/ to smooth, to flatten, to level.

düzlem *neol., geom.* plane. **— açı** plane angle. **— geometri** plane geometry. **— küre** planisphere.

düzleme دوزلمه *verbal n. of* **düzle=**. **— ruhlusu** *phys.* spirit level; water level (instrument).

düzlen=ⁱʳ دوزلنمك to become smooth, flat, level. **—dir=** /l/ *caus.*

düzlet=ⁱʳ دوزلتمك /l/ *caus. of* **düzle=**. **—il=** *pass. of* **düzlet=**.

düzlükᵗü د و ز لك 1. smoothness, flatness, levelness. 2. evenness, uniformity. 3. plainness, straightforwardness. 4. flat level, plain.

düzme د و ز مه 1. verbal n. of **düz=** 3. 2. made-up, false, counterfeit, sham. **—ce** counterfeit, made-up, false. **—ci** trickster.

düztaban د و ز طبان 1. flat-footed. 2. ill-omened man. 3. *naut.* rabbet plane.

düzül=ür د و ز لملك د و ز و لملك *pass. of* **düz=** 3.

düzüm د و ز م *Or. mus.* rhythmic pattern.

düzüne (. ′.) د و ز ينه *var. of* **düzine.**

E

e 1 the sixth letter of the alphabet.
e 2 Enough! Well, all right. Oh! (surprise).
e 3 *cf.* **a 3.**
-e 4 *cf.* **-a 5.**
=e 5 *cf.* **=a 7.**
=e 6 *cf.* **=a 8.**
=e 7 *cf.* **=a 9.**
eabid (. —.) اعا بد A *lrnd., pl. of* **abd,** servants.
eacîb (. — —) اعا جيب A *lrnd., pl. of* **ucube.** **—i dehr** marvels of the world.
eacim (. —.) اعا جم A *lrnd., pl. of* **a'cem 1, acemî 2.**
eadallah (. — . —) اعاد الله A *lrnd.* God cause him to return!
eadi (. — —) اعا دى A *lrnd., pl. of* **âda 4,** enemies.
eali (: — —) اعا لى A *lrnd., pl. of* **âlâ 1.**
eammmi عم ا A *lrnd., superl. of* **âm 4.**
eanallah (. — . —) اعان الله A *lrnd.* May God help (him).
Earib (. — —) اعا ريب A *lrnd., pl. of* **A'rab 3,** nomadic Arab tribes.
eariz (. — —) اعا رض A, (. —.) *lrnd., pl. of* **aruz 1.**
easir (. — —) اعا صير A *lrnd., pl. of* **i'sar,** hurricanes, tornadoes, whirlwinds, sandstorm.
eazzzi عز ا A *lrnd., superl. of* **azir.**
eazım (. —.) اعا ظم A *lrnd., pl. of* **a'zam 3.** **—i ahibbâ** the dearest of friends. **—i millet** the great men of the nation. **—i ricâl** the highest state officials. **—i üdebâ** the highest literary men.
eaz'Allah (. . . —). **eazzellahu** (. . . —.) اعز الله A *lrnd.* May God exalt and glorify.

eb ا ب A *lrnd.* father. **—i müşfik** kind father.
ebaanced (. — . .) ابا عن جدّ ا [*based on Arabic*] *lrnd.* from the time of one's ancestors, for many generations.
ebabil (. — —) ابا بيل A *lrnd.* 1. large flight of birds. 2. legendary birds that destroyed the army of Abraha, an Ethiopian general who attacked Mecca. 3. "the souls of the damned", birds that fly low up and down the Bosphorus without alighting, manx shearwaters. 4. mountain swift.
eb'ad 1 (. —) ابعا د A 1. size. 2. *lrnd., pl. of* **bu'd 1,** dimensions. **—ı binihaye** *lrnd.* infinite dimensions. **—ı selâse** *lrnd.* the three dimensions.
eb'ad 2 ابعد A *lrnd., superl. of* **baid 1.**
ebadid (. — —) ابا ديد A *lrnd.* scattered, dispersed.
ebaid (. — .) ابا عد A *lrnd., pl. of* **eb'ad 2.**
ebalis (. — .), **ebalise** (. — . .) ابا لس ابا لسه A *lrnd., pl. of* **iblis.**
ebarikki (. — —) ابا ريق A *lrnd., pl. of* **ibrik.**
ebatdi (. —) ابعد *var. of* **eb'ad 1.**
ebatil (. — —) ابا طيل A *lrnd.* vanities, vain, false, groundless things.
ebayi (. — —) ابا ى *kind of saddle-housing* or horsecloth.
ebbar (. —) ابّا ر A *lrnd.* maker or seller of needles.
ebbaz (. —) ابّا ز A *lrnd.* leaping, springing, bounding (deer); leaper, springer.
ebbed'Allah, ebbedallahu ابّد الله A *lrnd.* May God cause to endure for ever. **— mecdühu!** May his honor endure for ever.

ebced اَبجَد A *lrnd.* the first word in the mnemonic formula giving the arrangement of the Arabic letters according to their numerical value (the ancient order) (ا = 1, ب = 2, ج, د = 3, etc.). — **hesabı** enumeration by letters of the alphabet.

ebcedhan (..—) ابجَد خوان P *lrnd.* a learner of the alphabet.

ebdaᵃⁱ ابدَع A *lrnd., superl. of* **bedi 4**.

ebdalˡⁱ 1 (.—) ابدال A *lrnd., pl. of* **bedil**.

ebdalˡⁱ 2 (.—) ابدال A *lrnd.* 1. *pl. of* **bedel**. 2. saintly men through whom God continues the world in existence. —**an** (.——) *pl.*

ebdan (.—) ابدان A *lrnd., pl. of* **beden 2**.

ebe ابە 1. midwife; obstetrician. 2. the one who is 'it' in children's games. 3. *prov.* grandmother. — **arı** *prov.* queen bee. — **bulguru** *prov.* powdered snow. — **geçti**, —**m geçti** *prov.* leapfrog. — **gümeci**, —**m gümeci***. — **hekim** doctor who tends a woman during pregnancy and delivery. — **iskemlesi** *prov.* delivery chair. — **kuşağı**, —**m kuşağı** rainbow. — **örekesi** *prov., same as* **ebe iskemlesi**. —**nin örekesi** *colloq.* pack of nonsense. — **pisiği** the awned ear of some grasses. —**lik** midwifery; obstetrics.

ebed ابد A future eternity.

ebeda (.'.—), **ebeden** (.'..) ابدا ، ابدً A *lrnd.* 1. ever, eternally. 2. *followed by negative verb* never.

ebedgâh (..—), **ebedhane** (..—.) ابدگاه ، ابدخانە P *lrnd.* tomb, grave.

ebedî (..—) ابدى A eternal, never-ending. —**leştir=** /ı/ to eternalize. —**lik** eternity.

ebediyen (..—.) ابدياً A eternally, in perpetuity.

ebediyet (..—.) ابديت A eternalness, neverendingness.

ebedkıyam (...—), **ebedmüddet** ابدقيام ، ابدمدت P *lrnd.* eternal.

ebedpeyvend, **ebedpeyvest** ابدپيوند ، ابدپيوست P *lrnd.* reaching to eternity, eternal.

ebedelâbad (...——) ابدالآباد A *lrnd.* to all eternity; world without end.

ebegümeciⁿˡ ابەگوممجى mallow, *bot., Malva sylvestris.* —**giller** *bot., Malvaceae.*

ebenanced, **ebenanceddin** ابًا عن جد A *same as* **ebaanced**.

eber⁼ⁱʳ ابەرمك /ı/ *prov.* 1. to bring. 2. to carry away.

eberʳʳⁱ ابر A *lrnd.* most pious, very just.

ebetᵈⁱ ابد *same as* **ebed**.

ebeveyn ابوين A parents.

ebgalˡⁱ (.—) ابغال A *lrnd., pl. of* **bağl**.

ebgaz (.—) ابغاض A *lrnd., pl. of* **bugz**.

ebhalˡⁱ ابخل A *lrnd., superl. of* **bahil 1**.

ebhar 1 (.—) ابحار A *lrnd., pl. of* **bahr 1**.

ebhar 2 ابخر A *lrnd.* stinking breath (man).

ebhas (.—) ابحاث A *lrnd., · pl. of* **bahs 1**. —**i müşkile** difficult matters.

ebher ابهر A *anat.* aorta.

ebhire ابخرە A *lrnd., pl. of* **buhar**.

ebhur ابحر A *lrnd., pl. of* **bahr 1**, seas.

=**ebil**= 1 ابيل *cf.* =**abil**= 2.

ebil 2 (.—) ابيل A *lrnd.* Christian monk, priest, elder.

ebilülebilîn (.—..——) ابيل الابيلين A *lrnd.* the Priest of Priests (i. e. Jesus Christ).

ebka- (.—) ابقى A *lrnd.* May God cause (him) to last.

ebkâr (.—) ابكار A *lrnd., pl. of* **bikr**.

ebkem ابكم A *lrnd.* dumb. —**iyet** dumbness.

eblâğ ابلغ A *lrnd., superl. of* **beliğ**.

eblakᵏⁱ ابلق A *lrnd.* 1. piebald (horse), black and white. 2. *same as* **ablak**. —**ı akuk** a pregnant piebald stallion, *i. e.* an impossibility. —**ı çarh** day and night time; fortune (good or bad). —**süvar** (...—) P valiant warrior.

ebleh ابله A stupid, foolish, imbecile. —**an** (..—) P the stupid ones. —**ane** (..—.) P stupidly; stupid, silly (act). —**firib** (...—) P deceiving the fools. —**î** (..—) P foolishness, folly, stupidity. —**iyet** (..—.) foolishness, stupidity.

ebna (.—) ابناء A *lrnd.* 1. *pl. of* **bin 1**, **ibn**, sons. 2. men, people. —**yi Âdem**, —**yi beşer** mankind. —**yi cins** fellow men. —**yi dehr** opportunists. —**yi sebil** travelers, wayfarers. —**yi sipahiyan** *Ott. hist.* cavalry corps. —**yi zaman** 1. men of the present age. 2. timeservers.

ebniye ابنيە A *lrnd., pl. of* **bina 1**. —**i hassa** *Ott. hist.* imperial buildings; public buildings. —**i hayriye** charitable foundations. —**i sultaniye emini** *Ott. hist.* overseer of the Sultan's buildings.

ebr ابر P *poet.* cloud. —**i bahar** cloud of spring. —**i bârân** rain cloud. —**i ihsan** cloud of bounty. —**i mürde** sponge. —**i nisan** vernal clouds, cold rain. —**i rahmet** rain cloud. —**i seher** morning cloud. —**i sünbülgûn** black cloud.

ebrac (.—) ابراج A *lrnd., pl. of* **burc**.

ebralûd (.——) ابرآلود P *lrnd.* cloudy.

ebrar (.—) ابرار A *lrnd., pl. of* **bar 9**. —**i ümmet** the good people of a nation.

ebras (.—) ابرص A *lrnd.* leprous.

ebred ابرد A *lrnd., superl. of* **barid**.

ebreş ابرش A *lrnd., same as* **abraş**.

ebrişem (.—.) ابريشم P *lrnd., same as* **ibrişim**.

ebrkâr (.—) ابركار P *lrnd.* astonished, amazed.

ebru 1 (.—) اَبْرُو P poet. eyebrow.
ebru 2 (.—) اَبْرُو P 1. marbling (of variegated paper); marbled (paper), of different colors. 2. watering (of fabrics). — **ebru** red in waves (cheek). —**cu** maker of marbled paper.
ebruferah (.—.—) اَبْرُوفَرَاح P lrnd. cheerful, affable. —**î** (.—.——) P cheerfulness, generosity.
ebrula= اَبْرُولَامَق /ı/ to marble (paper).
ebruli (.——) اَبْرُولِى , **ebrulu** اَبْرُولُو 1. marbled (paper). 2. watered (fabric). — **kâğıt** marbled paper. — **karanfil** picotee, bot., Dianthus Caryophyllus.
ebruvân (.——) اَبْرُوَان P lrnd. the two eyebrows.
ebsar (.—) اَبْصَار A lrnd., pl. of **basar**.
ebtal[li] (.—) اَبْطَال A lrnd., pl. of **batal**.
ebter اَبْتَر A lrnd. 1. docktailed. 2. left without a child (man). 3. useless, unprofitable (man or thing). 4. pros. reduced in a special way from four syllables to two.
ebu- (.—) اَبُو A lrnd. the father of. E— **Bekr** Abu-Bakr (the first caliph); man's name. — **cabir** bread. E— **Cehl** 1. Father of Ignorance (nickname given by the Prophet Muhammad to one of his greatest enemies). 2. ignorant. — **cehil hurması** fruit of the doom palm. — **cehil karpuzu** 1. colocynth, bitter apple, bot., Citrullus colocynthis. 2. ignorant. E— **Eyyub** camel. E— **Hafs** surname of the Caliph Omar. E— **Hanifa** surname of the founder of the Hanafite school. — **kalemun** same as **bukalemun**. — **kışır** zool., Squalius cephalus. E— **Leheb** 1. name of the Prophet Muhammad's uncle. 2. unbeliever.
Ebu Nüvas (.— .—) اَبُو نُوَاس A Abu Nuwas (Arab poet about whom many anecdotes are told).
Ebussuud (.—.—) اَبُو السُعُود A 1. famous sheikh ul-Islam of Suleyman the Magnificent. 2. man's name. — **efendinin gelini**, — **efendinin torunu** very devout person.
Ebutalib (.——.) اَبُو طَالِب A lrnd. 1. surname of the father of the Caliph Ali. 2. beggar.
Ebu Yahya (.—.—) اَبُو يَحْيَى A lrnd. Angel of Death.
ebul- A lrnd. the father of, e. g., **ebulbeşer**. [/ebul/ see /ebül/.]
ebül'aceb اَبُو العَجِيب A lrnd. 1. conjurer. 2. time, fortune.
ebülbeşer اَبُو البَشَر A lrnd. father of men, Adam.
ebülburun اَبُو البُرُون [based on Arabic] lrnd., joc. a large-nosed man.

Ebülfeth اَبُو الفَتْح A lrnd. the Conqueror, Fatih Mehmet II.
ebülfuzul[li] (...—) اَبُو الفُضُول A lrnd. meddlesome fool.
ebülheves اَبُو الهَوَس A lrnd. adventurer.
Ebülhevl اَبُو الهَوْل A lrnd. the Sphinx of Egypt.
Ebülhikem اَبُو الحِكَم A lrnd. the Father of Wisdom, original surname of **Ebucehl**.
ebülvakt[li] اَبُو الوَقْت A lrnd. man of principles who is not influenced by the changes of the time.
Ebütürab (...—) اَبُو تُرَاب A nickname given to Ali by the Prophet Muhammad.
ebüzzeheb اَبُو الذَهَب A lrnd. very rich.
ebvab (.—) اَبْوَاب A lrnd., pl. of **bab 1, 2**. —**ı rahmet** God's doors of mercy.
ebval[li] (.—) اَبْوَال A lrnd., pl. of **bevl**.
ebvibe اَبْوِبَه A lrnd., pl. of **bab 1, 2**.
ebyat[li] (.—) اَبْيَات A lrnd., pl. of **beyt 1**.
ebyaz اَبْيَض A lrnd. white.
ecahil اَجَاهِل A lrnd., pl. of **echel**.
ecanib (.—.) اَجَانِب A, **ecanip**[bi] (.—.) strangers, foreigners.
ecdat[dı] (.—) اَجْدَاد A pl. of **ced**, grandfathers, ancestors.
ece اِجَه 1. prov. elder brother; elder sister. 2. archaic old man; archaic chief, great (person).
=**eceğin** cf. =**acağın**.
=**ecek**[ği] cf. =**acak**.
ecel 1 اَجَل A 1. the appointed hour of death, death. 2. lrnd. an appointed term, end of a period fixed beforehand. —**den aman olursa** If we live long enough. — **beşiği** 1. suspended cradle for a workman. 2. merry-go-round. 3. unsafe, death-trap (vehicle). — **beşiği gibi** very dangerous. —**i gelmiş** His hour of death has come. — **geldi cihane baş ağrısı bahane** One has to die; illness is a pretext. —**i gelen köpek cami duvarına siyer** (lit. A dog whose time of death has come urinates against the mosque wall.) One who is seeking his own ruin does something provoking. —**i kaza** accidental death. —**i mev'ut**, —**i müsemma** natural death. —**iyle öl=** to die a natural death. —**ine susamış** foolhardy. — **teri dök=** to be in mortal fear.
ecel[lli] **2** اَجَلّ A lrnd., superl. of **celil**. —**li mahlukat** the highest of all creatures, man.
ecelacayip var. of **acelacayip**.
ecelreside (...—.) اَجَل رَسِيدَه P lrnd. moribund.
ecem اَجَم A lrnd. thickets, woods, forests.
ecfan, **ecfün** اَجْفَان A lrnd., pl. of **cefn**.
echel اَجْهَل A superl. of **cahil**, most ignorant.
echer اَجْهَر A lrnd. 1. very beautiful (person). 2. day-blind.

echize اجهزه A lrnd., pl. of **cihaz**.
eci اجی prov. 1. elder sister. 2. grandmother.
ecil^(cll) **1** اجل [ecl] lrnd. cause, reason.
ecil 2 (. —) اجیل A lrnd. deferred, postponed until a fixed future time.
ecille اجله A lrnd. men of great rank, power, or esteem.
ecinne 1 اجنه A lrnd., pl. of **cin 1**.
ecinne 2 اجنه A lrnd., pl. of **cenin**.
ecinni اجنی [cinni 1] djinn, evil spirit. **— askeri** archaic mob. **—ler top oynuyor** deserted.
ecir^(eri) **1** اجر [ecr] 1. reward, recompense. 2. remuneration, pay, wage. **—i misil** law just price; adequate pay. **—i müsemma** law agreed price. **— sabır dile**= /a/ to offer one's condolences.
ecir 2 (. —) اجیر A lrnd. day laborer. **—lik** wage-earning; labor.
eciş bücüş اجش بوجش out of shape, crooked, distorted. **— yazı** scrawl, bad handwriting.
ecl اجل A same as **ecil 1**.
eclâf (. —) اجلاف A lrnd. rowdies, rabble, hooligans, mob.
ecmain (.. —) اجمعین A lrnd. all, all together.
ecmel اجمل A lrnd. most beautiful, very good.
ecnad اجناد A lrnd., pl. of **cünd**.
ecnas (. —) اجناس A lrnd., pl. of **cins**. **— akçe** mixed moneys, coins of various kinds. **—ı muhtelife** various kinds.
ecnebi (.. —) اجنبی A stranger, foreigner, alien; strange, foreign. **— parası** foreign exchange. **—lik**, **—yet** quality of a foreigner, alienness.
ecnibe اجنبه A lrnd. sides, parts, margins.
ecniha اجنحه A lrnd., pl. of **cenah**.
ecr اجر A same as **ecir 1**.
ecram (. —) اجرام A lrnd., pl. of **cirm**. **—ı felekiye**, **—ı semaviye**, **—ı ulviye** heavenly bodies.
ecreb اجرب A lrnd. having the itch, mangy.
ecred اجرد A lrnd. hairless, bare (man).
ecsad (. —) اجساد A lrnd., pl. of **cesed**. **—ı seb'a** the seven metals: gold, silver, tin, lead, iron, copper and the Chinese speculum metal.
ecsam (. —) اجسام A lrnd., pl. of **cism**.
ecsem اجسم A lrnd. very bulky, most stout.
ecvaf (. —) اجواف A lrnd., pl. of **cevf**.
ecvef اجوف A lrnd. 1. hollow, empty (in the middle). 2. empty-headed, good-for-nothing. 3. Arabic gram. hollow (root).
ecvibe اجوبه A lrnd., pl. of **cevab**.
ecyaf^(fı) (. —) اجیاف A lrnd., pl. of **cife**.
ecyal^(lı) (. —) اجیال A lrnd. generations.
ecza 1 (. —) اجزا A 1. drugs, chemicals. 2. lrnd., pl. of **cüz**. **—cı** chemist, druggist, pharmacist. **—cılık** pharmacy. **—hane** drugstore, pharmacy. **—lı** prepared with chemicals; containing chemicals. **—lı tüfek** gun used with percussion caps.
eczane (. —.) اجزاخانه var. of **eczahane**.
eczem اجذم A lrnd. mutilated in the arm, hand, or fingers.
eçhel اجهل var. of **echel**.
eçsam (. —) اجسام var. of **ecsam**.
eçsad^(dı) (. —) اجساد var. of **ecsad**.
eda 1 (. —) ادا P 1. affected voice or manner, affectation. 2. insolence, haughty airs. 3. style, manner.
eda 2 (. —) اداء A 1. law a paying, payment; performance, an acquitting oneself of (a duty). 2. lrnd. a pronouncing, articulating (word or letter). **—yı deyn** a paying of a debt. **— et=** 1. law to pay (a debt); to perform (a duty). 2. lrnd. to articulate (word or letter).
edak^(kkı) ادق var. of **adak 2**.
edalı (. —.) ادالی 1. gracious, charming. 2. affected. 3. having an air.
edam Allahü (. —. —.) ادام الله A lrnd. May God make eternal.
edani (. — —) ادانی A lrnd. vile men, low people.
edat (. —) ادات A gram. particle. **—ı istifham** interrogative particle.
eddai (.' — —) الداعی A lrnd. your humble servant.
Eddeberan (... —) الدبران A astr. Aldebaran, the Bull's Eye.
eddua (.. —) الدعاء A lrnd. prayers, blessings; farewell, goodby.
ede prov. elder brother.
edeb ادب A cf. **edep**. **—i kelâm** euphemism. **—amuz** (.. — —) P lrnd. educating. **—ane** (.. —.) P lrnd. respectfully, politely; polite, respectful (act).
edebhane (.. —.) ادبخانه P lrnd. a toilet.
edebî (.. —) ادبی A literary.
edebiyat (.. — —) ادبیات A literature. **E—ı Cedide** the name of a Turkish literary school at the end of the 19th Century. **E—Fakültesi** Faculty of Arts, college of literature and arts. **—ı Osmaniye** the Ottoman literature. **—çı** man of letters.
edebiyyun (.. — —) ادبیون A lrnd. men of letters.
edeme ادمه A biol. derma.
edep^(bı) ادب [edeb] 1. breeding, manners, politeness, respect, modesty; rule, custom, mode of action. 2. lrnd. training, education, accomplishments, literature. **—i edepsizden öğren!** Bad manners teach good manners. **— erkân** good manners, rules and customs.

edepsiz

— et= to be ashamed. — göster= /a/ to teach good manners. — öğret= /a/ 1. to teach good manners. 2. to inflict punishment. —tir söylemesi Excuse the expression. —ini takın Behave yourself; where are your manners? — yahu! Shame on you! — yeri private parts. — yolu *archaic* toilet. —len= to become well-behaved. —li well-behaved, well-mannered.

edepsiz اديسز ill-mannered, rude, shameless, insolent. —ce (..'.) with bad manners, impertinently. —lik bad manners, rudeness, impertinence.

eder ايدر price, *e. g.* **Bu kumaşın ederi 100 liradır.** The price of this cloth is 100 liras.

edevat (..—) ادوات A tools, instruments, implements.

edhan (.—) ادهان A *lrnd.*, *pl.* of **dühn.**

edhem ادهم A *lrnd.* black (horse).

Edhemiye ادهميه A *name of a sect founded by Ibrahim ibn Adham.*

edhine ادهنة A *lrnd.*, *pl.* of **duhan.**

edi *only in* — **ile büdü** two tiny or helpless people.

edib (.—) اديب A 1. literary man; writer. 2. polite, gentlemanly. —**ane** (.——.) P 1. worthy of a literary man, in a literary manner. 2. in a polite and gentlemanly manner.

edikᵍⁱ ادك *prov.* kind of soft, unsoled houseboot.

edil=ⁱʳ ايديلمك *pass.* of **et=** 2.

edilgen *neol., gram.* passive.

edilgi *neol., Aristotelian phil.* passion; effect.

edilgin *neol., phil.* resulting.

edille ادلة A *lrnd., pl.* of **delil.** —**i asliye,** —**i erbaa,** —**i şer'iye** *can. law* the four fundamentals of canonical law: Quran and hadith, Sunna, consensus of the learned, analogy.

edim 1 ادم A *lrnd.* 1. tanned hide, leather. 2. face, surface (of the earth).

edim 2 *neol., phil.* act. —**sel** *phil.* actual.

edin=ⁱʳ ادينمك 1. /ı/ to get, procure, acquire. 2. /la/ to keep at somebody; to get into the habit of bothering or talking about someone. —**ilmiş** *biol.* acquired. —**me** *verbal n.* of **edin=.**

edipᵇⁱ (.—) اديب *var.* of **edib.**

Edirne (..'.) ادرنه *geog.* a town in Thrace, formerly Adrianople. — **kapı** the Edirne Gate (one of the gates of Istanbul).

ediş اديش *verbal n.* of **et=.**

ed'iye ادعيه A *lrnd., pl.* of **dua.** —**i hayriye** benedictions, blessings.

edmiga ادمغة A *lrnd., pl.* of **dimağ.**

edna (.—) ادنى *lrnd.* 1. lowest, of most ordinary quality. 2. the least, smallest, most trifling.

ednas (.—) ادناس A *lrnd., pl.* of **denes.**

Edremit ادرميد a town in Western Anatolia (the ancient Adramyttium).

=edur= *cf.* **=adur=.**

edva (.—) ادواء A *lrnd.* lights. —**i bahriye** *naut.* St. Elmo's fire, corposant.

edvar (.—) ادوار A *lrnd.* 1. *pl.* of **devr.** 2. *Or. mus.* books about musical rules.

edviye ادويه A *lrnd., pl.* of **deva.**

edyan (.—) اديان A *lrnd., pl.* of **din** 1.

ef'a افعى A *lrnd.* viper, adder.

efahim (.—.) افاخم A *lrnd., pl.* of **efham.**

efai (.——) افاعى A *lrnd., pl.* of **ef'a.**

efail (.——) افاعيل A *lrnd., pl.* of **ef'ile.**

ef'alⁱⁱ (.—) افعال A *lrnd., pl.* of **fiil.** —**i akliye** 1. operations of the mind. 2. verbs expressing an opinion. —**i akliye inhitatı** *path.* psycholepsy. —**i hasene** good works. —**i muzırra** harmful deeds. —**i seyyie** evil deeds.

efanin (.——) افانين A *lrnd.* 1. numbers of varieties. 2. groups of branches.

efavic (.—.) افاوج A *lrnd.* quantities of troups; crowds, masses.

efayikᵏⁱ (.—.) افائك A *lrnd.* lies, slanders, calumnies.

efazallahu افاض الله A *lrnd.* May God shower down (blessings).

efazıl (.—.) افاضل A *pl.* of **efzal.**

efdalⁱⁱ افضل A *lrnd.* superior; preferable.

efdaliyet افضليت A *lrnd.* superiority, preeminence.

efe افه 1. swashbuckling village dandy; member of West Anatolian Zeybeks. 2. *prov.* elder brother. — **sat=,** — **yap=** to swagger, to boast and bluster.

efektif F *fin.* cash, ready money.

efelik افه لك swagger, dash.

efendi (..'.) افندى Gk 1. gentleman; gentlemanly. 2. master. 3. *Ott. hist.*, title given to literate people, members of the Clergy, Ottoman princes, army officers up to major. —**m** 1. Yes (as an answer to a call). 2. I beg your pardon? What did you say? 3. *added to a sentence for politeness.* **E—miz** 1. Muhammad. 2. the Ottoman Sultan. 3. our Master (spiritual or by authority). — **adam,** —**den adam** gentleman. — **baba** 1. elderly gentleman. 2. father (or child's address to his father). — **biçimi fes** fez of a certain style. — **dairesi** *Ott. hist.* clerical office of the Janissaries. — **efendi** in a well-behaved way. — **gibi yaşa=** to live like a gentleman. —**ler götürsün!** May he die! — **kapısı** same as **efendi dairesi.** —**m nerede ben nerede!** How far you are from understanding me! —**me söyliyeyim** and, 'um', er (pause-filler in speech). —**lik** gentlemanly behavior.

effakᵏⁱ (.—) افاك A *lrnd.* slanderer; liar

Efgan 1 (.—) افغان same as **Afgan**.
efgan 2 (.—) افغان P *lrnd.* moan, groan,
Efganistan (.—.—) افغانستان same as **Afganistan**.
-efgâr (.—) افگار P *lrnd.* wounded, *as in* **dilefgâr**.
-efgen افگن P *lrnd.* that casts away, that throws down, *as in* **esbefgen, kûhefgen**.
efgende افگنده P *lrnd.* thrown out, down or away. **—gi** (...—) P *abstr. n.*
efham 1 افخم A *lrnd.* very great, most illustrious.
efham 2 (.—) افهام A *pl. of* **fehm**.
efhem افهم A *lrnd.* quick in understanding, intelligent.
ef'i (.—) افعی *var. of* **ef'a**.
ef'ide افئده A *lrnd.* hearts.
ef'ile افعل [based on Arabic] *pros.* verse foot (.—— *or* —.—.).
efil efil افل افل blowing gently (wind).
efkâr 1 (.—) افکار A 1. thoughts, ideas; intentions. 2. *colloq.* worry, anxiety. **—ını boz=** /ın/ to pervert, to lead one to change his mind unfavorably. **— dağıt=** to cheer oneself up, to drown one's sorrows. **— et=** to worry. **—ı umumiye** public opinion.
efkar 2 افقار A *lrnd., superl. of* **fakir** 1. **—ı fukara** the poorest of the poor.
efkârlan= to worry.
efkârlı افکارلی worried, anxious.
Eflâk[kı] **1** (.'.) افلاق *hist.* 1. Walachia. 2. the Walachians. **— beyi** Walachian prince.
eflâk[kı] **2** (.—) افلاک A *lrnd., pl. of* **felek**. **—ı cüziye** the lesser spheres. **—ı külliye** the greater spheres, encircling the earth. **—ı seb'a** 1. the Seven Spheres. 2. *Isl. Myst.* The Seven Attributes (life, knowledge, power, will, hearing, sight, speech). **—e ser çekmiş** reaching the sky, very tall, very high.
eflâkî (.——) افلاکی A *lrnd.* 1. celestial, pertaining to the spheres. 2. who studies the motions and the influences of the spheres. 3. who believes in the influences of the spheres as arbiters of worldly events.
eflâkiyan (.—.—) افلاکیان P *lrnd.* 1. stars, planets. 2. astronomers; astrologers; believers in the influences of the spheres. 3. worshippers of the spheres.
eflâkşinas (.—.—) افلاکشناس P *lrnd.* versed in the motions and influence of the spheres; astronomer.
Eflâtun 1 (.——) افلاطون A 1. Plato. 2. learned man. **—u Cihan** a very wise man.
eflâtun 2 (.—.) افلاطون lilac-colored.
Eflâtunhikmet (.——..) افلاطون حکمت P *lrnd.* equal to Plato in wisdom.
eflâtuni (.———) افلاطونی P lilac-colored.
eflâz (.—) افلاذ A *lrnd.* 1. *pl. of* **filze**.

efles افلس A *lrnd.* very poor, broke. **—i nâs** the poorest among men.
efnan (.—) افنان A *lrnd.* 1. sorts, varieties, kinds. 2. branches, twigs. **—ı elvan** varieties of colors.
efniye افنیه A *lrnd.* courtyards.
efrad (.—) افراد A *lrnd.* 1. *pl. of* **ferd**. 2. *cf.* **efrat**. **—ını câmi ağyarını mâni** uniting all the main points and leaving out what is not pertinent. **—ı nâs** the ordinary people.
efrah (.—) افراح A *lrnd.* rejoicings; joyfulness.
efrahte (.—.) افراخته P *lrnd.* raised, elevated.
efras (.—) افراس A *lrnd., pl. of* **feres**.
Efrasiyab (.—.—) افراسیاب P Persian poet., name of a Turanian hero.
efraşte (.—.) افراشته P same as **efrahte**.
efrat[dı] (.—) افراد [efrad] *mil.* private soldiers; recruits.
-efraz 1 (.—) افراز P *lrnd.* raising, exalting, *as in* **serefraz**.
efraz 2 (.—) افراض A *lrnd.* person versed in reciting the Quran.
Efrenc افرنج A *lrnd.* Frank, European; the Franks. **—î** (..—), **—iye** (..——) A European. **—iyun** (..——) A Europeans. **—müşk** P sweet basil.
efrend افرند P *lrnd.* beauty, splendor, pomp.
Efreng افرنگ P *obs.*, same as **Efrenc**. **—î** (..—) European.
Efrikiye (.——.) افریقیه A *hist.*, a district in the province of Tunis.
efruğ (.—) افروغ P *lrnd.* rays of the sun; beams of the moon; light of a candle.
efruhte (.—.) افروخته P *lrnd.* lighted; alight; burning. **—gi** (.—.—) P *abstr. n.*
-efruz (.—) افروز P *lrnd.* burning; illuminating; adorning, *as in* **âlemefruz, meclisefruz**.
efruze (.—.) افروزه P *lrnd.* 1. wick. 2. fuel.
efruzende (.—..) افروزنده P *lrnd.* bright, shining; one who sets on fire.
efsa (.—) افسا P *lrnd.* enchanter.
efsah افصح A *lrnd., superl. of* **fasih**.
efsane (.—.) افسانه P 1. tale, myth, fable; legend. 2. *lrnd.* tale, story, narrative. **— efsun** idle talk, chitchat. **—cu** (.—.—) P *lrnd.* idle talker, fantast. **—gû** (.—.—) P *lrnd.* story-teller, teller of tales. **—nüvis** (.—..—) P *lrnd.* writer of stories. **—perdaz** (.—..—) P *lrnd.* story-teller; who invents stories. **—vî** (.—.—) P legendary.
efsar (.—) افسار P *lrnd.* halter, headstall.
efsay (.—) افسای P *var. of* **efsa**.
efsed افسد A *lrnd., superl. of* **fasid**.

efsentin (..—) انسنتين A wormwood, *bot.,* Artemisia Absinthium.
efser افسر P *poet.* crown, diadem.
efsun (.—) افسون P *lrnd., same as* **afsun**.
—**ger** (.—.) P witch, sorcerer; charmer.
efsus (.—) افسوس P *poet.* 1. a wrong, injury; pity. 2. Ah! Alas!
efsürde افسرده P *lrnd.* 1. frozen; congealed. 2. cold. 3. that lacks love, joy, vivacity; insipid. —**can**, —**dil** P one whose soul is dead to love or joy. —**gân** (...—) P those whose souls are frozen to any feeling. —**gî** (...—) P coldness, insipidness. —**hatır** (...—.) P dispirited. —**mağz** P stupid. —**revan** (....—) P *same as* **efsürdedil**.
-**efşan** (.—) افشان P *lrnd.* dispersing, scattering, spreading, diffusing, *as in* **gülefşan, hunefşan.**
-**efşar** (.—) افشار P *lrnd.* squeezing, pressing. *e. g.,* **zer-i destefşar** gold pure and soft enough to be molded in the hand.
efşürde افشرده P *lrnd.* squeezed, pressed (juice).
efşüre افشره P *lrnd.* expressed juice.
eftamintokofti (.....) افتامينتوقوفتى *Gk slang* lie, fib.
eftimun (..—) افتيمون A lesser dodder, clover dodder, *bot., Cuscuta Epithymum.*
efvac (.—) افواج A *lrnd., pl. of* **fevc**.
efvah (.—) افواه A *lrnd.* 1. mouths. 2. spices, perfumes. —**ı nariye** firearms.
efyal (.—) افيال A *lrnd.* elephants.
efyun (.—) افيون P *lrnd., same as* **afyon**.
efza' 1 افزا A *lrnd.* terrors, fears.
-**efza** 2 (.—) افزاع P *lrnd.* increasing, augmenting, *as in* **behcetefza, ruhefza.**
efzalⁱⁱ افضل A *lrnd., same as* **efdal**.
efzayiş (.—.) افزايش P *lrnd.* increase, augmentation.
-**efzud** (.—) افزود P *lrnd.* augmenting, *as in* **dehşetefzud**.
efzude (.—.) افزوده P *lrnd.* increased, augmented.
efzun (.—) افزون P *lrnd.* increasing, increased; much, many; /dan/ more (than). —**î** (.——) P 1. increase. 2. multiplicity, abundance; excess.
egavla=ʳ Arm /ı/ *slang* to get, to take hold of.
Ege اگه [*based on Greek*] 1. Aegean Sea. 2. West Anatolian littoral. —**denizi** Aegean Sea.
egemen *neol.* sovereign. —**lik** sovereignty.
eger, egerçi اگرجى *vars. of* **eğer, eğerçi**.
egval (.—) اغوال A *lrnd., pl. of* **gûl** 1.
egvar (.—) اغوار A *lrnd.* caves, caverns; cavities.
egzama, egzema (..'.) اگزما [**ekzema**] *path.* eczema

egzost, egzoz اگزوس E *mech.* exhaust. —**borusu** exhaust pipe. —**kolektörü** exhaust manifold. —**supapı** escape valve.
eğ=ᵉʳ اگمك /ı/ *same as* **iğ=**.
eğdir=ⁱʳ اگديرمك /ı/ *same as* **iğdir=**.
eğe 1 ايگه file (tool). —**vur=** /a/ to file.
eğe 2 اگه *anat.* rib. —**ler arası** intercostal. —**kemiği** rib.
eğe 3 اگه *prov.* 1. master, owner. 2. elder brother.
eğele=ʳ اگه لمك /ı/ to file (with a file). —**n=** *pass.* —**t=**, —**ttir=** *caus. of* **eğele=**.
eğer اگر P if; whether.
eğerçi اگرجى P *lrnd.* though, although.
eğiçᶜⁱ اگيج *prov.* forked stick for picking fruit.
eğikᵍⁱ 1. *same as* **iğik**. 2. *neol., geom.* oblique. —**prizma** oblique prism. —**lik** inclination.
eğil=ⁱʳ اگيلمك *same as* **iğil=**.
eğinᵍⁿⁱ اگين *prov.* back, shoulders. —**ine bin=** /ın/ to bully.
eğindirikᵍⁱ اگنديريك *prov.* 1. back cover. 2. cape collar.
eğinim *neol., psych.* inclination.
eğinti اگنتى filings.
eğir=ⁱʳ 1 اگيرمك /ı/ to spin.
eğir 2 اگير 1. sweet flag, *bot., Acorus calamus.* 2. orris, *bot., Iris florentina.* —**kökü** orris root.
eğir 3 اگير [*Arabic* **cakar**] *prov.* bee bread, propolis. —**mumu** propolis.
eğirici اگيريجى spinner; spinning.
eğiril=ⁱʳ اگيريلمك *pass. of* **eğir=** 1.
eğirme اگيرمه *verbal n. of* **eğir=** 1.
eğirt=ⁱʳ اگيرتمك /ı, a/ *caus. of* **eğir=** 1.
eğirtmeçᶜⁱ اگيرتميج *prov.* spindle; spinning wheel.
eğit=ⁱʳ /ı/ *neol.* to educate. —**im** education. —**imli** educated. —**men** educator. —**menlik** instructorship. —**sel** educational.
eğle=ʳ اگله /ı/ *prov.* 1. to retard, to delay. 2. to amuse.
eğlen=ⁱʳ اگلنمك 1. to have a good time, to amuse oneself, to enjoy oneself. 2. /la/ to make fun (of), to joke (with). 3. *prov.* to stop, stay, wait, loaf.
eğlence اگلنجه amusement, entertainment, diversion; joke; plaything, toy. —**li** amusing, agreeable, diverting, entertaining. —**lik** tidbits, appetizers (nuts, etc.).
eğlendir=ⁱʳ اگلنديرمك /ı/ *caus. of* **eğlen=** 1, 3.
eğlenti اگلنتى amusement, feast, party.
eğleş=ⁱʳ اگلشمك *prov.* 1. to stop, to delay. 2. to stay, to dwell.
eğme اگمه *same as* **iğme**.
eğre اگره *prov.* saddlecloth.

eğrek⁽ᵗⁱ⁾ اگرك prov. 1. pond, pool; backwater of a stream. 2. shady refuge for flocks.

eğrelti اگرلتى bracken, fern, *bot.*, *Pteris aquilina*. — otu same as eğrelti. — otugiller *bot.*, *Filicineae*.

eğreti اگرتى same as iğreti.

eğri اگرى same as iğri. [/eğri-/ see /iğri-/.]

Eğriboz اگربوز *geog.* Negropont (ancient Euboea); the town of Euripos (ancient Chalkis).

eğrim اگریم same as eyrim.

eğsi اگسى var. of eksi 2.

eğsinim *neol., psych.* inclination.

eh 1 اه indicating half-hearted acceptance All right. Very well. *e. g.*, **Eh, gidelim artık** Well, let's go.

eh 2 (—) اه *colloq., indicating impatience* Oh, well enough. *e. g.*, **Eh, anladık artık!** Too much talk!

ehab⁽ᵇᵇⁱ⁾ اصب A *lrnd.* most beloved, dearest. **—i ehibba** the best beloved of friends. **—i emval** the most valued property (*cf.* **ahab**.)

ehabir (.——) اصابر var. of **ahabir**.

ehad اصد A *lrnd.* 1. unit. 2. individual person. 3. One (God). — **aşer** A eleven.

ehadiyet⁽ᵗⁱ⁾ (..—.) اصدیّت A *Isl. rel.* oneness, unity; the oneness of God.

-e hali⁽ⁿⁱ⁾ *neol., gram.* dative.

ehali (.—.) اصالى A same as **ahali**.

ehdab (.—) اصداب A *lrnd.* eyelashes.

ehdaf (.—) اصداف A *lrnd.*, *pl.* of **hedef**.

ehdeb اصدب A *lrnd.* whose eyelashes are long and drooping.

ehem⁽ᵐᵐⁱ⁾ اهمّ A *lrnd.* most important.

ehemmiyet اهمیّت A importance. **—le** attentively, carefully; with interest. — **ver=** /a/ to consider seriously. **—li** important. **—siz** unimportant.

ehibba (..—) اصبّا A *lrnd.*, var. of **ahibba**.

ehil⁽ʰⁱⁱ⁾ 1 اهل [ehil 2] qualified, efficient, able. **—i** /ın/ versed (in).

ehil⁽ʰⁱⁱ⁾ 2 اهل [ehl] *lrnd.* 1. people, community. 2. men (of letters, science, etc). 3. *prov.* husband; wife. **—i aba** the Prophet and his family. **—i ahiret** the dead. **—i aruz** prosodists. **—i arz** demons, the djinns. **—i badiye** bedouins. **—i basiret** prudent, sagacious. **—i belâgat** talebearer, busybody. **—i beyt** the Prophet's family. **—i bid'at** a man or a sect that follows religious innovations. **—i büyutat** members of noble tribes. **—i cehennem** the people of hell, the damned. **—i cennet** saint, one destined for Paradise. **—i dil** P 1. an understanding, tolerant, good-natured person. 2. a man of God. **—i divan** *Ott. hist.* officials of the Imperial Chancery. **—i dünya** man of the world. **—i ehvâ** schismatics, heretics. **—i fesad** intriguer, mischievous plotter; scoundrel, villain. **—i Hak** *myst.* man of God. **—i hak u yakîn** wise, contemplative, pious. **—i hakikat** *myst.* devout person. **—i hal** *myst.* a mystic. **—i heva** licentious, libertine. **—i hey'et** astronomers, stargazers. **—i hibre** *law* expert. **—i hikmet** philosopher, philosophers. **—i hiref, —i hirfet** craftsman. **—i hüner** skillful. **—i ırz** respectable. **—i idrak** intelligent, sagacious. **—i iffet** respectable, chaste, modest. **—i iman** religious. **—i irfan** man of knowledge, learned. **—i İslam** Muslim; Muslims. **—i ittika** pious, devout. **—i kal** man who follows only the outward show of religion. **—i kalem** clerks of the government offices. **—i kanaat** easily contented. **—i kelâm** eloquent; orator. **—i kerem** liberal, generous. **—i keyf** one who seeks his own pleasure. **—i kıble** a Muslim. **—i kitab** people of the book, *i. e.*, Muslims, Christians, Jews. **—i kubûr** the dead. **—i mahşer** those who will rise at the Judgment Day. **—i mâna** same as **ehli hal**. **—i mansab** high official; minister. **—i marifet** 1. having some particular talent. 2. *myst.* those who have attained to an inner knowledge of God. **—i merakib** 1. mounted travellers. 2. seafarers. **—i muhasebe** accountant. **—i naîm** inhabitants of Paradise, the Blessed. **—i namus** honorable, of good repute. **—i nar** the damned. **—i nazar** possessed of insight. **—i nifak** hypocrites. **—i nücum** astrologers. **—i perde** a veiled, chaste woman. **—i rey** person of judgment. **—i Rum** *hist.* Ottomans. **—i safa** pure in heart. **—i salah** righteous, devout. **—i salîb** crusaders. **—i servet** the wealthy, rich. **—i sûk** market traders. **—i sülûk** follower of a sect. **—i sünnet** the Sunnis. **—i şia** the Shiites. **—i tahkik** a man of exact science; philosopher, doctor. **—i takva** pious, devout. **—i tarik** member of a religious order; dervish. **—i tasavvuf** mystic, anchorite; a teacher or follower of the Sufi doctrines. **—i tedbir** wise counselor, wise administrator. **—i teslis** Christians. **—i tevarih** historians. **—i tevhid** monotheists; Muslims. **—i vukuf** *law* expert. **—i yakin** *myst.* one who has attained to the knowledge of divine truth. **—i zevk** 1. a pleasure-lover. 2. *myst.* one who has found divine spiritual delight. **—i zimmet** non-Muslim subjects of a Muslim state.

ehl اصل A *cf.* **ehil 1, 2**.

ehlî (.—) اصلى A tame, domestic, domesticated. **—leş=** to become tame. **—leştir=** /ı/ to tame. **—lik** tameness.

ehliyet 1 (.—.) اصلیّت A *lrnd.* tameness.

ehliyet 2 اصلیّت [based on **ehil 1**] 1. efficiency, capacity, competency. 2. *pop.*, same as

ehliyetname. — **imtihanı** qualifying test. —**li** capable, talented, fit for office. —**name** (...—.) P certificate of competence; driver's license. —**siz** incapable, incompetent, unqualified. —**sizlik** incapacity, disqualification.

ehlullah (..—) اهل الله A lrnd. men of God; saints.

ehnâme (.—.) اهنامه P lrnd. trifle, useless thing.

ehram (.—) اهرام A 1. Pyramid; lrnd. the Pyramids. 2. geom. pyramid. —**ı gayrı muntazam** geom. irregular pyramid. —**ı kaim** geom. right pyramid. —**ı mail** geom. oblique pyramid. —**ı muntazam** geom. regular pyramid. —**ı nâkıs** geom. frustrum of a pyramid. —**î** geom. pyramidal.

Ehremen, Ehrimen اهرمن P lrnd. Satan, devil; seducer.

ehtar (.—) اهطار A lrnd., var. of **ahtar**.

ehva (.—) اهوا A lrnd., pl. of **heva**.

ehvalⁱⁱ (.—) اهوال A lrnd., pl. of **hevl**.

ehvel اهول A lrnd. most terrifying.

ehven اهون A 1. cheap, inexpensive. 2. the better (of two poor alternatives). 3. lrnd. easiest. — **kurtul**= to get away, get off cheaply. —**i şer** (lrnd. —**i şerreyn**) the lesser of two evils. —**iyet** cheapness. —**leştir**= /ı/ 1. to cheapen. 2. to make easier (things). —**lik** cheapness.

ehviye اهويه A lrnd., pl. of **hava**. —**i lâtife** sweet melodies.

ehya (.—) اهيا A lrnd., same as **ahya** 1.

ehyan (.—) احيان A lrnd., pl. of **hin**.

ehzab (.—) احزاب A lrnd., pl. of **hizb**.

eimme ائمه A lrnd., pl. of **imam**. —**i din** religious authorities. —**i erbaa** Isl. rel. the founders of the four orthodox schools of Islam. —**i esma** Isl. rel. the seven chief names of God. —**i isnaaşer** Isl. rel. the Twelve Imams. —**i izam** Isl. rel. religious leaders.

eizze اعزه A same as **aizze**.

ejdeha (..—) اژدها P lrnd., var. of **ejder**.

ejder, ejderha (..—) اژدر ـ اژدرها P dragon. — **gibi** terrifyingly monstrous. —**i kahir** dragon of death. —**i münakkaş** 1. variegated dragon. 2. strong, brave, but merciless person.

ekᵏˡ 1 اك 1. joint, join; seam, scar, knot (tree). 2. a piece joined on to another piece to lengthen or widen it. 3. gram. suffix, affix, prefix. —**ler** bot., annexa. —**ini belli etme**= to cover up, dissimulate; not to give oneself away. — **dalaş ol**= colloq. to bother (someone), to pester. → **kök** bot. adventitious root. —**ten pükten** made up of odd pieces. — **sigorta** an insurance taken out to cover two risks. — **yeri** seam, scar; body joint.

ek=ᵉʳ 2 اكله /ı/ 1. to sow. 2. /ı, a/ to sprinkle (salt); scatter. 3. to drop, leave behind one; slang to put off, to leave in the cold. 4. slang to spend, to throw about (money). 5. slang to kill. 6. /ı, a/ slang to hit, strike, to rain blows upon. —**tiğini biç**= to reap what one sows.

=**ek**ᵍⁱ 3 cf. =**k**.

ekâbir (.—.) اكابر A the great; important people; VIPs. —**i devlet** the influential men of a country's administration. — **kapısı** colloq. government offices; homes of important people

ekalⁱⁱⁱ اقل A same as **akal** 3.

ekalim (.——) اقاليم A lrnd., pl. of **iklim**. —**i seb'a** the seven Ptolemaic climes, the whole habitable earth.

ekalliyet (..—.) اقليت A same as **akalliyet**.

ekanim (.——) اقانيم A Christ. theol., pl. of **uknum**. —**i selâse** the Holy Trinity.

ekarib 1 (.—.) اقارب A same as **akarib** 1.

ekârim (.—.) اكارم A lrnd., pl. of **ekrem**.

Ekâsire (.—..) اكاسره hist. Chosroes, kings of Persia; lrnd. kings, sovereigns.

ekavil (.—.) اقاول A lrnd., same as **akavil**. —**i bâtıla** empty words.

ekâzib (.——) اكاذب A lrnd., pl. of **ükzube**.

ekbad (.—) اكباد A lrnd., pl. of **kebed**.

ekbah اكبح A lrnd., same as **akbah**.

ekbent same as **entbent**.

ekber اكبر A lrnd. 1. greatest, very great, most high. 2. older, oldest. — **evlât hakkı** law right of primogeniture.

Ekberiye (..—.) اكبريه A lrnd.; name of a Dervish order.

ekdar (.—) اكدار A lrnd., pl. of **keder**.

eke اكه prov. 1. old, aged, mature. 2. experienced, wise, clever.

ekele=ʳ 1 اكله /ı/ prov. to sprinkle (salt, pepper, etc.)

ekele 2 اكله lrnd., pl. of **âkil** 1, gourmets.

ekfa (.—) اكفا A lrnd., pl. of **küfv**.

ekfan (.—) اكفان A lrnd., pl. of **kefen**.

ekhâlⁱⁱ 1 (.—) اكحال A lrnd., pl. of **kühl**.

ekhalⁱⁱ 2 اكحل A lrnd. one who uses antimony to beautify his eyes.

ekid (.—) اكيد A lrnd. 1. strong, firm. 2. definite, clear-cut. —**en** (.'—.) A definitely, urgently.

ekil=ⁱʳ 1 اكله pass. of **ek**= 2.

ekilᵏˡⁱ 2 اكل [ekl] lrnd. an eating. — **ü şürb** 1. eating and drinking. 2. an embezzling.

ekili اكيلى sown.

ekilme اكلمه verbal n. of **ekil**= 1.

ekim اكيم 1. verbal n. of **ek**= 2. 2. neol. October. — **ayı** October.

ekin اكين 1. crop; growing grain. 2. sowing of seed. — **bağı** a sheaf of corn. — **biç**= to reap, harvest. — **biti**, — **böceği** harvest bug, zool., Curculionidae. — **iti gibi** stuck up, haughty. — **kargası** cornfield rook, *zool., Corvus frugilegus.* — **vakti** seedtime. **—ci** sower, cultivator; farmer. **—cilik** farming, husbandry. **—lik** 1. arable land. 2. grain fields. 3. flowerbed. **—lü** *Ott. hist.* having arable land (peasant).

ekinoks اكينوقس L *astr.* equinox.

ekip[pl, bl] اكيب F team, crew, gang, company. [/ekis/ see /eks/.]

ekkâl[ll] (. —) اكّال A *lrnd.* 1. voracious, glutton. 2. corrosive caustic.

ekl[ll] اكل A same as **ekil** 2. — **et**=*.

eklâmsi اكلامسى F *med.* eclampsia.

ekle=[r] اكلەمك ، اكلمك 1. /ı, a/ to join on (piece), to add (to); /ı/ to join a piece on (to). 2. /ı, a/ *slang* to hit, bash.

eklem *neol., anat.* joint, articulation. — **bacaklılar** *zool., Arthropoda.* — **bağı** interarticular ligament. — **kapsülü** articular cartilage.

ekleme اكلمه 1. *verbal n.* of **ekle**=. 2. added, joined on. — **otu** pewter grass, horsetail, *bot., Equisetum arvense.* **—li** joined up, patched.

eklemle=[r] *neol.* /ı, a/ or /ı, la/ to articulate (with). **—n**= *pass.*

eklen=[lr] اكلنمك /ı/ *pass.* of **ekle**=. **—ti** *neol., gram.* suffix.

eklet=[lr] 1 اكلتمك /ı, a/ *caus.* of **ekle**=.

eklet=[der] 2 اكل ايتمك [ekl] /ı/ *lrnd.* to eat.

ekli اكلو pieced, put together.

ekmam 1 (. —) اكمام A *lrnd., pl.* of **küm** 2, sleeves.

ekmam 2 (. —) اكمام A *lrnd., pl.* of **kim**, calyxes of buds.

ekme اكمه *verbal n.* of **ek**= 2.

ekmek[şi] 1 اكمك ، اتمك 1. bread. 2. food; subsistence, livelihood; job. — **ağacı** bread tree, breadfruit tree, *bot., Artacarpus.* — **aslanın ağzında** (*lit.* The bread is in the lion's mouth.) It is very difficult to make a living. **—ini ayağile tepti** (*lit.* He has kicked his bread with his foot.) He has lost a good job or a good opportunity through his own fault. — **ayvası** a kind of quince. **—i bütün** *prov.* He has enough for his needs and is obliged to no one. — **çarpsın!** May bread strike me if I don't speak the truth (oath). — **çeşnisi** bread standard. — **çiğnemeden yutulmaz** *proverb* You have to chew the bread to swallow it. **—i dizinde** ungrateful. — **düşmanı** *slang* wife. **—e el bas**= to swear (on bread). — **elden su gölden** living on others. **—inden et**= to take the bread out of another's mouth. — **gibi**, — **gibi aziz** as essentially valuable as daily bread. — **içi** inside of a loaf, crumb. — **kabuğu** crust of a loaf. — **kadayıfı** a sweet made of bread dough baked and soaked in sugar syrup. **—ini kana doğra**= to undergo terrible hardship. — **kapısı** the place where one works for one's living. — **karnesi** bread ration card. **—ini kazan**= to earn one's daily bread. **—ine koç** *obs.* hospitable, generous, liberal. — **küfü** *bot., penicillium.* **—ine mani ol**= to prevent someone from earning his living. — **narhı** fixed price of bread. **—inden ol**= to lose one's job. — **parası** cost of bread; modest livelihood. — **somunu** a loaf of bread. **—ini taştan çıkarır** (*lit.* He can make bread out of a stone.) He can always turn his hand to something. — **ufağı** crumbs of bread. **—ine yağ sür**= /ın/ unintentionally to give an advantage.

ekmekçi اكمكچى baker, bread seller. — **başı** *Ott. hist.* head of the court bakers. — **küreği gibi dili var** He has a tongue as long as a baker's shovel. — **tebeşiri** a baker's score kept with chalk marks. **—lik** baker's trade.

ekmeklik[şi] اكمكلك 1. suitable for bread making (flour, etc.). 2. *colloq.* job furnishing adequate livelihood. 3. *slang* job involving no work where one lives off another. 4. *gambling slang* someone who is easy game.

ekmel اكمل A *lrnd., superl.* of **kâmil.** **—i enbiya** the Prophet Muhammad. **—iyet** (.. —.) perfection. **—âne** (.. —.) P in a perfect manner, faultlessly.

eknaf (. —) اكناف A *lrnd.* 1. sides, borders, edges. 2. regions, districts.

eknan (. —) اكنان A *lrnd., pl.* of **kin.**

eknun (. —) اكنون P *lrnd.* now, at the present.

ekolâli F *psych.* echolalia.

ekoloji F *biol.* ecology.

ekonoma اقونوما F *law* place where goods are sold at wholesale prices to workers and their families.

ekonomi اقونومى F economy.

ekopraksi اقوپراقسى F *psych.* echopraxia.

ekrad (. —) اكراد A *lrnd., pl.* of **kürd.**

ekran اكران F *psych.* screen.

ekre اكره same as **eğre.**

ekreh اكره A *lrnd., superl.* of **kerih.**

ekrem اكرم A *lrnd., superl.* of **kerim.** **—âne** (.. —.) P generously. **—iyet** (.. —.) generosity.

ekrem-ül-ekremin (..... —) اكرم الاكرمين A *lrnd.* the most generous one, God.

ekrem-ül-ümem اكرم الامم A *lrnd.* the best of the peoples, the Muslims.

eksantrik[şi] اكسانتريك F eccentric; out of center. — **mili** *mech.* eccentric rod.

eksarh اكسارح Gk *Or. Christian Church* exarch. **—hane** residence of the exarch, exarchate.

eksekuvatür اكسكواتور F *law* official warrant

ekselâns

to enforce a judgment of a foreign court or an arbiter's award.

ekselâns اکرملانس F Excellency.

eksen Gk 1. *neol.*, *sc.* axis. 2. *prov.* axle of a two-wheeled ox cart. —**el** axial.

ekser 1 اکسر large nail, spike. — **kes=** to make nails.

ekser 2 (.'.) اکثر [ekser 3] same as **ekseri**.

ekser 3 اکثر A *lrnd.* 1. *superl.* of **kesir** 2. 2. majority, the greater part.

ekseri (.'..) اکثری [ekser 3] most.

ekseriya (.'..—) اکثریا A usually, mostly, for the most part.

ekseriyet اکثریّت [*Arabic* ..—.] majority. —**le** generally, usually, mostly. —**i âra** majority of votes. —**i mutlaka** absolute majority.

ekserle=ʳ اکرله /ı/ - *prov.* to nail. —**n=** *pass.* —**t=** *caus.* of **ekserle=**.

eksi 1 *neol., math.* minus.

eksi 2 اکسی *prov.* half-burned piece of wood.

eksi=ʳ **3** اکسیمك /ı/ archaic, same as **eksilt=**.

eksibe اکسبه A dune, sand-dune.

eksikᵏⁱ اکسیك 1. lacking, wanting, absent, defect, missing; /dan/ less (than). 2. deficient, incomplete, defective, imperfect; deficit. — **akça** coin of short weight. — **çık=** to be lacking (in weight, etc.). — **doğ=** to be born before time. —**, doldur=** to fill the gap. —**ini doldur=** /ın/ to make good a deficiency. — **etek** *prov.* woman. — **etme=** /ı/ always to have, never to omit; to keep always in stock. — **gedik** small necessities; deficiencies. —**ini gediğini tamamla=** to provide what is necessary; to complete the parts which are missing. — **gel=** not to be enough. — **olma!** May you always abide! Thank you, very kind of you. — **olma=** always to turn up. — **olmasın!** God bless him! — **olsun!** No, thank you! (refusing contemptuously). — **olma, bayır turpu gibi!** Well done! (said contemptuously). —**ini tamamla=** /ın/ to complete what is lacking, to fill the gap. —**i yok gediği yok** perfect, complete, not lacking anything.

eksikli اکسكلو archaic 1. deficient, defective. 2. needy, poor.

eksiklikᵍⁱ اکسكلك 1. deficiency, defectiveness. 2. absence, lack.

eksiksiz اکسكسز 1. complete, perfect. 2. permanent, never lacking.

eksil=ʳ اکسلمك 1. to decrease, to grow less. 2. to disappear. —**en** *math.* subtrahend. —**me** diminution; *math.* decrease. —**t=** /ı/ to diminish, to reduce. —**tme** 1. *verbal. n.* 2. a putting up to tender.

eksiz اکسز 1. seamless, all one piece. 2. *gram.* without a suffix.

eksper اکسپر F *com.* expert, valuer.

ekspres اکسپرس F express train.

ekstra اکسترا F best quality. — **ekstra** the very best.

ekstrafor اکسترافور F dress-making straight or bias binding.

ekşi 1 اکشی 1. sour, tart; acid. 2. sour-faced. — **aş** *prov.* meat stew with plums. — **suratlı** sour-faced. — **yemedim ki karnım ağrısın** I haven't done anything to be sorry about. — **yoncagiller** *bot.*, Oxalidaceae. —**li** sour, sour-flavored. —**lik** acidity, tartness. —**msi** sourish. —**mtrak** sourish.

ekşi=ʳ **2** اکشیمك 1. to turn sour, to become acid. 2. to ferment. 3. to be upset (stomach). 4. to become cross or disagreeable. 5. *slang* to be disconcerted. —**me** *verbal n.* —**t=** *caus.* of **ekşi=**.

ektaf (.—) اکتاف A *lrnd.*, *pl.* of **kitf**.

ekti اکدی *prov.* 1. parasite. 2. tame, docile.

ektir=ⁱʳ اکدیرمك /ı, a/ *caus. of*- **ek=** 2.

ekûlᵘ̈ (.—) اکول A *lrnd.* greedy, voracious, gluttonous. —**âne** (.——.) P in a greedy manner. —**î** (.——) P gluttony.

ekvan (.—) اکوان A *lrnd.*, *pl.* of **kevn**.

ekvar (.—) اکوار A *lrnd.* 1. large herds or droves. 2. saddles. 3. hives. 4. blacksmiths' forges.

ekvator اکواتور F equator. —**al** *neol.* equatorial.

ekvaz (.—) اکواز A *lrnd.* cups; pots.

ekyalᵘ̈ (.—) اکیال A *lrnd.*, *pl.* of **keyl**.

ekyas (.—) اکیاس A *lrnd.*, *pl.* of **kis 1**.

ekzema اکزما F same as **egzema**.

ekzos, ekzost var. of **egzost**.

el 1 ال 1. hand. 2. forefoot. 3. handwriting, hand. 4. interference, assistance; power. 5. one discharge (of a fire-arm). 6. deal (of cards). —**de** 1. in hand, in possession. 2. in hand, in course of being made. 3. won over. —**iyle** via, care of (c/o). — **aç=** to beg for alms. —**i açık** generous, open-handed. —**i ağır** 1. slow; slow worker. 2. heavy-fisted. —**ine ağır** slow; slow worker. —**i ağır işi pâk** *prov.* slow but sure. —**i ağzında kal=** to be astonished. —**den ağıza yaşa=** to live from hand to mouth. — **al=** /dan/ 1. *myst. orders* to receive permission to inititate others. 2. *econ. hist.* to become a master craftsman. —**den al=** /ı/ to buy straight from the producer or maker. —**ine al=** /ı/ to take in hand, to take charge (of). —**ini al=** archaic, same as **elini tut=**. —**e alınır** in good condition, useful. —**e alınmaz** 1. in very bad condition. 2. obscene. —**altı** archaic followers

—i altında, —inin altında 1. at his disposal. 2. handy, within reach. 3. in his power. — altından in an underhanded manner, secretly. — arabası 1. wheelbarrow. 2. *school slang* masturbation. —i armut devşirmiyor ya! He can hit back; he can defend himself. Why doesn't he do something? —'at= /a/ to lay hands (upon), to seize. —de avuçta bir şey kalmadı There is (was) nothing left; absolutely cleared out. —de avuçta nesi varsa everything he possesses. —e avuca sığmaz out of hand, very mischievous, uncontrollable. — ayası palm of the hand. —i ayağı bağlı not free to act, having the hands tied. —i ayağı buz kesil= 1. to be very cold. 2. to be cold with excitement. —ini ayağını çek= /dan/ 1. to cease to frequent (place). 2. to cease doing (something). — ayak çekildi The place is deserted; everyone has retired. —ine ayağına düş= /ın/ to implore. —den ayaktan düş= to be crippled by illness or old age. —i ayağı düzgün sound in wind and limb. —ine ayağına kapan= /ın/ to implore. —ini ayağını kes= 1. /dan/ to stop going (to some place.) 2. /dan, ın/ to stop somebody from coming (to a place). —ine ayağına sarıl= /ın/ to implore. —i ayağı tutar well and strong, in good health. —i ayağı tutmaz 1. crippled. 2. feeble. — bağla= to join the two hands in front of the body in an attitude of respect. —ini bağla= /ın/ to tie someone's hands. —e bak= to practice palmistry. —ine bak= /ın/ 1. to depend on another for one's living. 2. to look at someone's hands to see what has been brought. — bas= /a/ to swear (by placing one's hand on something sacred). — başı *prov.* leader in a game. —i bayraklı quarrelsome, insolent and abusive person. — bebek gül bebek spoiled, coy. —i belinde 1. alert, ready for action. 2. spoiling for a quarrel. — bende! *children's game* You're it! — benim, etek senin! *archaic* I am a petitioner, you are a benefactor. — bezi hand towel. — bıçkısı a small hand saw. —ini bırakıp ayağını, ayağını bırakıp elini öp= /ın/ 1. to implore vehemently. 2. to kiss someone's hand as a sign of great joy. —de bir soon to happen. — birliği cooperation. — bombası hand grenade. —i boş 1. empty-handed; *archaic* poor. 2. unemployed, idle. —i boş dön=, —i boş gel= to return empty-handed. —i böğründe kal= to feel utterly helpless and discouraged. — bul= to find a helping hand. —inde bulun= /ın/ to be owned (by). —i çabuk, —ine çabuk a person who gets things done quickly. —ini çabuk tut! Be quick! Hurry up! — çabukluğu dexterity, sleight of hand. — çabukluğu marifet sleight of hand, legerdemain. — çal= *archaic* to clap the hands. — çek= /dan/ to withdraw, give up, relinquish. — çektir= /a, dan/ *caus.* —den çık= 1. to go out of one's possession. 2. to be out of one's hands. —den çıkar= /ı/ to sell, to dispose (of). — çırp= to clap the hands. —i daldan kay= to feel let down and deserted. — damarlı yaprak *bot.* palmate leaf. —i dar, —i darda to be in straitened circumstances. —i değ= /a/ to find the time and place to do. —imde değil It's not in my prerogative; I can't help it. — değirmeni coffee mill, coffee grinder. — değiştir= to change hands. — değmemiş intact; untouched by hand. —lerin dert görmesin! May your hands never see any trouble! (said in gratitude to someone who has helped.) —ini dişle= *archaic* to gnaw one's fist in frustration. —imde doğdu I've known (him) since he was born. — döğüşü fisticuffs; barefisted fighting. —den düşme secondhand (purchase). —den düşürme= /ı/ to use continually. —i düzgün dexterous. —inde ekşi= /ın/ *colloq.* to go flat in someone's hands (project delayed for too long a time). — ele hand in hand. — elde baş başta *colloq.* bereft of everything. —den ele dolaş= to circulate, to pass from hand to hand, to change hands many times. — ele tutuş= to take each other by the hand. — elden üstündür arşa varıncaya kadar *proverb* Everyone has his master. — el üstünde kimin eli var? *children's game* "Whose hand is on top?" (played by piling hands on the back of a bending child who has to guess whose hand is on top of the pile). —den ele gez= to go about, to circulate, to pass from hand to hand, to change hands many times. — ele ver= to join forces, cooperate. — eli yur, el de yüzü *proverb* (*lit.* One hand washes the other, and the hand the face.) We all need each other. — emeği 1. hand work, labor. 2. what is received for the labor of one's hands. — ense *Turk. wrestling* a hold whereby the opponent's throat and back of neck are pinioned. — ense çek= to withdraw completely. — erimi *obs.* arm's length. —i ermez gücü yetmez helpless in the face of a difficult situation. — et= /a/ to sign (to someone) to come. —de et= /ı/ to obtain; to gain possession (of). —ini eteğini çek= /dan/ to be through with something, to withdraw. — etek çekildikten sonra when all have retired. —ine eteğine doğru pure, well-conducted, decent. — etek öp= 1. to implore. 2. to flatter. —ine eteğine sarıl= /ın/ to plead and implore. — etek tut= *myst. orders* to join the Way. — feneri flashlight. — freni *mech.* hand brake. —e geç= to be caught, to come into one's possession. —e geçmez not easily come by. —den geçir= /ı/ to review, go over something. —e geçir= /ı/ to get hold (of), to obtain. —den gel= 1. to be within one's capabilities. 2. *slang* to tip, to give a little extra. —e gel= 1. to come in handy. 2. to be old enough to be carried in arms (baby). —inden geleni arkasına koymasın Let him do his worst for all I care. —den gel bakalım *slang* Come on, hand over! (money). —den geldiği kadar as much as possible —i geniş generous, liberal. —i genişle= to come into money. —e getir= /ı/ *same as* ele geçir=. —de gez=, —lerde gez= to be very popular. —e gir= *archaic, same as* ele geç=. —den git= to be lost, to pass out of one's hand. —ini göğsüne koy= to be fair, to act conscientiously. —i hafif skillful, light of touch. —inin hamuru ile erkek işine karışma! Don't meddle in things which only concern men. —den hibe *law* executed gift. —inden hiç bir şey kurtulmaz There is nothing he can't do. — ilânı handbill. —iyle koymuş gibi bul= to find something very easily. — ile tutulur tangible. — işi handwork; handmade. —inden iş çıkmaz slow-working, incapable of finishing a job. —i işte gözü oynaşta His mind is busy elsewhere while he is working. — kadar very small. —de kal= to be left over (money or goods). —ine kal= to be left in somebody's hands. — kaldır= 1. to raise a hand. 2. /a/ to lift the hand (to strike). —i kalem tutar able to express himself in writing. — kat= /a/ to interfere, to have a hand (in). — kavuştur= *same as* — bağla=. — kavşur= *archaic, same as* — kavuştur=. —inden kaza çıktı He was the unwilling cause of an accident. — kes=, —i kes= /dan/ to give up. —ini kes= /dan, ın/ to stop somebody from doing something. —lerine kına yaksın (*lit.* Let her apply henna to her hands.) Now she can rejoice (said ironically). —i kırıl= to get used to a job. —i kırılsın! May he break his arm! —i kısa *slang* awkward, incapable. — kiri something one can easily give up. —ini kolunu bağla= /ın/ to prevent from action. —i kolu bağlı kal= to have the hands tied, not to be able to do what one wants. —ini kolunu sallaya sallaya gel= to come empty-handed. —ini kolunu sallaya sallaya gez= to walk about without fear. — koy= /a/ to lay hands upon, to seize. —i koynunda 1. harmless (person). 2. helpless; unemployed. —i koynunda kal= *same as* eli böğründe kal=. —inin körü! What nonsense! Shut up! —i kulağında about to happen, just around the corner. — kumbarası *mil.* hand grenade. —i maşalı impudent and quarrelsome. —den ne gelir? What's to be done? What can one do? —i nurdan kopsun! *archaic* May his hands be blessed. —i ol= /da/ to have a hand (in something). —ini oynat= to tip, to give money. — öpmekle ağız aşınmaz It costs one nothing to show respect. —i pek stingy, close-fisted. — pençe divan dur= to stand in an attitude of respect, with joined hands; to stand ready to receive orders. — peşrevi *slang* a patting, caressing. —ine sağlık! Well done! — salla= to wave (the hand). —imi sallasam ellisi başımı sallasam tellisi I have only to beckon. — san'atı handcraft. —im sende! *children's game* You're it! —ini sıcak sudan soğuk suya sokmaz She doesn't lift a finger to help. — sık= to shake hands. —i sıkı close-fisted, mean. —i silâh tutan capable of bearing arms. — sok= /a/ to interfere (with), to put one's oar (in). —i sopalı bully. — suyu water for washing the hands. —ine su dökemez He is much inferior. — sür= /a/ to touch. — şakası playful pushing and pulling. — tarağı *anat.* metacarpus. —i tartısız 1. having no sense of measure. 2. inconsiderate, rash. —i terazili *archaic* expert, sure-handed. — teskeresi stretcher. —de tut= /ı/ to keep in reserve. —inden tut= /ın/ to help, protect. — ulağı messenger boy; a helper. —i uz *archaic* skilled, clever with his hands. — uzat= 1. to stretch out the hand; /a/ to extend the hand (to); to reach (for); to lay hands (on). 2. /a/ to help, to give a helping hand. — uzluğu skill. —i uzun thief. — üstünde gez= to be very popular. — üstünde tut= /ı/ to treat with great respect and honor. —im varmaz /a/ I haven't got the heart (to do it). —de var bir *math.* and carry one. — ver= 1. /a/ to help, lend a hand. 2. *see* elver=. 3. /a/ *prov.* to shake hands. 4. /a/ *myst. orders* to give permission to initiate others. —e ver= /ı/ to give away; to hand over, betray. —inle ver, ayağınla ara You cannot expect him to pay his debt quickly. —ini veren kolunu alamaz If you give him your hand you will lose your whole arm. —i vergili *prov.* generous. — vur= /a/ *prov.* to touch, to lay hand (to work). bir —i yağda bir eli balda She has all she needs; she lives in comfort and luxury. —im yakanda! I shall hold you responsible. You'll pay for it! —lerim yanıma gelecek I can't lie; I must tell the truth (for I shall die some day). —i yat= /a/ to get used (to work). —i yatkın skilled, having a knack. — yazısı handwriting. — yazması manuscript. — yordamı a groping. —i yordamlı *archaic* clever with his hands, deft. **— yu=** /dan/ *archaic* to abandon, to withdraw (from). **—ler yukarı!** Hands up! **—i yüzü düzgün** fairly pretty.

el 2 ال 1. stranger, alien; person not belonging to the family or tribe; others. 2. people; *archaic* tribe; *archaic* country, region. 3. *archaic* tribesman, relation, friend. **— ağzı ile kuş tutulmaz** You should rely first on yourself. **—in ağzı torba değil ki büzesin** You can't stop people from talking. **— âlem*.** **— ârı düşman gayreti** keeping up appearances, face-saving. **—den ayrıksı** *prov.* quite different from others. **— beğenmezse yer beğensin** *prov.* Death is better than dishonor. **— beyi** *hist.* ruler over a region. **— elin aynasıdır** People watch each other's doings. **—in geçtiği köprüden sen de geç** Do as others do. **—le gelen düğün bayram** A trouble shared is a trouble halved. **—den gelen öğün olmaz** Don't rely on others. **— gün** people, others. **—e güne karşı** in the face of others. **— iyisi** *prov.* good to others (but not to his own family). **— kapısı** a stranger's house (as a servant's working place). **— kazanıyla aş kaynat=** to use other people's work for some selfish advantage. **— oğlu** any stranger. **—den vefa zehirden şifa** One can't expect kindness from strangers. **—e verir talkını, kendi yutar salkımı** Practice what you preach. **— mi yaman bey mi yaman?** The people are more powerful than the ruler.

el- 3 ال A *lrnd.*, definite article in Arabic words, as in **elfatiha**.

elâ 1 (..—) الا hazel (eyes).

elâ 2 الا A *poet.*, a vocative exclamation. **— ey!** Now know that...

el'aceb العجب A *lrnd.* How strange.

el'aceletü mineşşeytan (..... ...—) العجلة من الشيطان A *lrnd.* Haste is of the Devil.

el'âcile (.—..) الاجل *lrnd.* the future state, life after death.

elâdo الادو Gk *only in* **— et=** /ı/ *slang* to snatch away.

lelâlem (.—.) ايل عالم [el 2, âlem 1] people, all the world, everybody.

el'aman (..—) الامان A 1. I am fed up! Enough! 2. *lrnd.* pardon, mercy. **— çağır=** to cry for help.

el'ân (.'.) الان [Arabic .—] A now, at present; still.

elâstikği الاستيك F elastic. **—î** (...—) elastic. **—iyet** elasticity.

el'avzü billâhi (... .—.) العوذ بالله A *rel. formula* Refuge is in God.

elbab (.—) الباب A *lrnd.*, *pl. of* **lüb 2**.

elbaki (.——) الباقي A *lrnd.* 1. the Eternal One, the eternal. 2. finally, as to the rest.

elbasir (..—) البصير A *lrnd.* the All-seeing One, God.

elbediii (..—) البديع A *lrnd.* God, the Creator.

elbet, elbette (.'., .'..) البته A certainly, decidedly, surely.

elbise (.—., ...) البسة [Arabic .—.] clothes, garments, dress, suit (of clothes).

elcar sümmeddar (.— ..—) الجار ثم الدار A *lrnd.* first the neighbor, then the house, *i. e.* choose a house with regard to the surrounding people.

elcasi (.——) الجاثي A *astr.* Hercules.

elcebbar (..—) الجبار A 1. *astr.* Orion. 2. *lrnd.* God the Compelling; God the Restorer of the poor.

elceğiz الجيز a very small hand. **—imle yaptım** I did it with my own hand.

elcekği *prov.* glove.

Elcezire (..—.) الجزيرة A *geog.* Mesopotamia.

elcikği الجك *prov.* glove.

elçi الجي ambassador, envoy, minister. **—ye zeval olmaz** An envoy cannot be blamed for his mission. **—lik** 1. the quality and functions of an envoy. 2. embassy; legation.

eldiven الديوان الدوان الدون الدوان glove. **—ci** glover; glove-seller.

ele= r الملك الملك /ı/ 1. to sift, to sieve. 2. to search carefully, to select. 3. *slang* to rob. 4. *slang* to exhaust, finish.

elebaşı الرباشي 1. ringleader, chief of a bandit gang. 2. captain (in a game).

eleğim sağma الگيم صاغم [alaimi sema] *pop.* rainbow.

eleji الژي F *poetry* elegy.

elekği الك fine sieve. **—ini boğazına geçir=** to lose everything one has. **—ten geçir=** /ı/ 1. to sift. 2. to examine minutely. **—çi** 1. sieve-maker. 2. gypsy woman. **—le=** /ı/ *archaic* to sift.

elektrikği الكتريك F 1. electricity. 2. *obs.* electric. **— balığı** torpedo, electric ray fish. **—çi** electrician. **—î** *phys.* electric. **—iyet** *phys.* electricity. **—le=** /ı/ to electrify. **—leme** electrification. **—len=** *pass. of* **elektrikle=**. **—li** electric; live (wire).

elektrolit F *phys.* electrolyte.

elektroliz F *phys.* electrolysis.

elektromıknatıs *phys.* electromagnet.

elektromotor F *phys.* electromotor; electromotive. **— kuvvet** electromotive force.

elem الم A 1. pain; ailment; affliction. 2. sorrow, care. **— çek=** to suffer. **— ver=** to give pain; to ache; to smart; to cause suffering.

eleman الرمان F 1. member of personnel, staff member, trained worker. 2. *sc.* element. 3. *elec.* battery cell.

eleme الالم ‎ 1. *verbal n.* of **ele=**. 2. sifted; selected. **— imtihanı** preliminary examination.

elemya, elemye (..'.) الميّ الكّ ‎ *Gk prov.* winding apparatus for skeining yarn.

elemzede المزده ‎ *P* struck with pain; afflicted, suffering.

elen= 1 النك ‎ *pass.* of **ele=**.

Elen 2 الرن ‎ *F* Greek, Hellenic; Hellene.

Elenika النيقا ‎ *Gk* modern Greek as used by the literate; literary language. **—sını bil=** /ın/ to know the best (of).

elerki[ni] *neol.* democracy.

elest, elestü الت ‎ *A Isl. rel.* "Am I not (your Lord)?" (God's question to Adam at his creation.)

eleştir=[ir] *neol.* /ı/ to criticize. **—im** criticism. **—imci** critic. **—imcilik** criticism, art of criticism.

elet=[ir] 1 التك ‎ /ı, a/ *caus.* of **ele=**.

elet=[ir] 2 ايتلك ‎ *prov., var.* of **ilet=**.

elez[zzi] الذ ‎ *A superl.* of **leziz**.

eleze *var.* of **eneze**.

elf الف ‎ *A lrnd.* a thousand. **—i evvel** *Isl. hist.* the first thousand years after the Hejira. **—i sani** *Isl. hist.* the second thousand years after the Hejira.

elfaf (.—) الغاف ‎ *A lrnd.* thickly entangled trees, thickets.

elfatiha (.—..) الفاتحة ‎ *A Isl. rel.*, name of the opening chapter of the Quran.

elfaz (.—) الفاظ ‎ *A lrnd., pl.* of **lâfız**. **—ı müştereke** 1. words with several meanings. 2. words common to several languages. **—ı müteradife** synonymous terms.

elfirak (..—) الفراق ‎ *A lrnd.* How painful to be separated! Farewell.

elfiye (.—.) الفية ‎ *A pros.* poem of a thousand couplets.

elgaraz الغرض ‎ *A lrnd.* in a word, in short.

elgaz (.—) الغاز ‎ *A lrnd., pl.* of **lûgaz**.

elgin الكين ‎ *archaic* stranger; strange, foreign.

elhac[cci] (.—) الحاج ‎ *A* before names, *lrnd.* the pilgrim.

elhad (.—) الحاد ‎ *A lrnd., pl.* of **lahd**.

elhak[kı] الحق ‎ *A lrnd.* truly, really, indeed.

elhal (.—) الحال ‎ *A lrnd.* in fact.

elhaletü hazihi (.—.. .—..) الحالة هذه ‎ *A lrnd.* at the present time, now.

Elhamd الحمد ‎ *A lrnd.*, a name for the first sura of the Quran.

elhamdülillah الحمد لله ‎ *A lrnd.* Thank God! Glory be to God! Wonderful!

elhan (.—) الحان ‎ *A lrnd., pl.* of **lahn**.

elhap[bı] الحب ‎ [based on Arabic **habt** 1] children's game in which the one who keeps the longest silence wins. **—ı boz=** to break the silence.

elharezmî, elharzemî (.—.—) الخوارزمي ‎ *A lrnd., phil.* algorism.

elhasıl (.'—.) الحاصل ‎ *A* in short, to sum up.

Elhayyülkayyum (....—) الحي القيوم ‎ *A lrnd.* the ever-living and self-sustaining God.

elhazer الحذر ‎ *A lrnd.* Beware! Be careful!

elhükmü lillah (... .—) الحكم لله ‎ *A lrnd.* Judgment is with God.

=eli *cf.* **=alı**.

elif 1 الف ‎ *A* Arabic alphabet, name of the letter *l* (It has the numerical value of 1.) **— ba***. **—i bilmez** illiterate. **—ini bilmez** /ın/ He doesn't know the first thing (about it). **—i elifine** exactly, just. **— gibi** upright; slender. **—i görse direk sanır, —i görse mertek sanır** (*lit.* If he saw an **elif** he would think it was a post.) He is completely illiterate. **—i iklim** *lrnd.* the first of the seven climates, the equatorial climate. **—i kûfiyan** *lrnd.* 1. the Cufic **elif**. 2. anything bent or crooked. 3. penis. **—ten yeye kadar** from a to z.

elif 2 (.—) اليف ‎ *A lrnd.* intimate, familiar, sociable.

elifba (..—), **elifbe** الفبا ‎ *A* the Arabic alphabet.

elifî (..—) الفي ‎ *A* 1. *same as* **elifî şalvar**. 2. *lrnd.* tall, erect, straight as an **elif**. **— nemed** Mevlevi order of dervishes belt. **— sumat** Mevlevi order of dervishes dining mat. **— şalvar** kind of baggy trousers. **— taç** Bektashi order of dervishes kind of headgear.

elifiye (..—.) الفية ‎ *A pros.* poem with the initial letters of the couplets arranged alphabetically.

elifli الفلي ‎ marked with the letter **elif**. **— kiraz** variety of cherry marked with a dark red line.

elik[ği] الك ‎ *prov.* mountain goat; ibex.

=elim 1 *cf.* **=alım** 2.

elim 2 (.—) اليم ‎ *A* painful, grievous, deplorable.

elindelik[ği] *neol., phil.* free will.

elips *F* 1. *math.* ellipse. 2. *gram.* ellipsis.

el'iyazubillah (..—..—) العياذ بالله ‎ *A lrnd.* God forbid!

elkab (.—) الالقاب ‎ *A lrnd., pl.* of **lâkab**.

elken الكن ‎ *A lrnd.* who stutters; stammerer. **—kün** *P* that makes (an adversary) stammer.

elkıssa القصة ‎ *A lrnd.* in short, to cut a long story short.

Ellât[tı] (.—) اللات ‎ *A Isl. hist.*, name of the idol worshipped at Ta'if, destroyed by order of the Prophet Muhammad.

elle=[r] الملك ‎ /ı/ to handle, feel with the hand, touch with the hand. **—me** 1. *verbal n.* 2. hand-picked, selected. **—me mangal kömürü**

1. handpicked charcoal. 2. *slang* scoundrel. **—n=** *pass. of* **elle=**.

elleş=ⁱʳ الّٰشك *archaic* /la/ 1. to shake hands; to take each other by the hand. 2. to try one another's strength by hand grips. 3. to come to blows. **—tir=** /ı/ *caus*.

elli الّٰى fifty. **— altı** *slang* slap; a beating. **— dirhem otuz** *slang* very drunk.

ellikᵍⁱ الّٰلك *prov.* 1. glove. 2. device protecting the hand (of reapers).

ellilikᵍⁱ الّٰلك 1. fifty years old. 2. a banknote for fifty liras, etc.; a coin of fifty piasters.

ellinci الّٰيني fiftieth.

ellişer الّٰشر fifty each; fifty at a time.

elma الما apple. **— baş** crested grebe, *zool.*, *Podiceps cristatus*. **— dibi kürk** fur made of the border of the fox skin. **— gibi** red (cheek). **— göz kurdu** *entom.*, *Authonomus pomorum*. **— kürk** fur made of the cheek pieces of fox skin. **bir —nın bir yarısı biri bir yarısı biri** as like as two peas. **— şarabı** cider.

elmacıkᵍⁱ الماجك 1. high part of the cheek, cheek bone, zygomatic bone. 2. ball of the hip joint.

elmalıkᵍⁱ المالو apple orchard.

elmas الماس [*Persian* .—] 1. diamond. 2. diamond glass cutter. 3. very precious, beloved; beautiful. **—çı** seller or cutter of diamonds.

elmasiye (.—..) الماسيه [*based on Arabic*] fruit jelly.

elmaspare (.——.) الماسپاره P *lrnd.* 1. a piece of diamond. 2. very brilliant person.

elmastıraş الماستراش [*Persian* .—.—] 1. diamond glass cutter. 2. cut glass, cut diamond. 3. who cuts diamonds.

elmelikül'allâm (.....—) الملك العلام A *lrnd.* God, the Omniscient Ruler.

elminnetülillah (.....—) المنة لله A *lrnd.* thanks be to God.

elöpen *prov.* lizzard.

elsen السن A *lrnd.* very eloquent.

elsine, elsün السنه السن A *lrnd., pl. of* **lisan**. **—i selâse** the three languages (Turkish, Persian, Arabic).

eltaf 1 (.—) الطاف A *lrnd., pl. of* **lûtf**.

eltaf 2 الطف A *superl. of* **lâtif**.

elti التى sister-in-law (wife of the husband's brother).

elvah (.—) الواح A *lrnd., pl. of* **levh**.

elvan (.—) الوان A *lrnd., pl. of* **levn**. **— elvan** *pop.* all kinds. **— şekeri** candies of various kinds and colors.

elveda (..—) الوداع A farewell, goodby.

elver=ⁱʳ الوربك 1. to be enough, to suffice. 2. to be convenient, to be suitable. 3. *archaic* to happen. **—ir!** That's enough!

elveriş الوريش *verbal n. of* **elver=**. **—li** 1. suitable, convenient. 2. sufficient. 3. profitable. **—siz** unsuitable, inconvenient.

elviye الويه A *lrnd., pl. of* **liva**.

elyaf (.—) الياف A *pl. of* **lif**.

elyakᵏⁱ اليق A *superl. of* **lâyık**.

elyevm اليوم A *lrnd.* today, at the present time.

elzem الزم A most necessary, indispensable. **—iyet** (..—.) *lrnd.* extreme necessity.

em=ᵉʳ 1 امك 1./ı/ to suck; to absorb. 2. *slang* to press out, to profit (from). **—e eme iliğini kurut=** /ın/ to suck to the very marrow, to exhaust (someone). **—diği sütü burnundan getir=** /ın/ to cause one to suffer. **—diği sütü haram et=** /a/ to curse one by wishing that the very milk that nourished him as a baby may become a curse.

em 2 ام *prov.* medicine, remedy. **— sem** *archaic* medicine, remedy. **—e seme yarama=** *archaic* to be useless.

=em 3 *cf.* **=am 2**.

em'a (.—) امعا A *anat.* intestines, bowels. **—i galiza** large intestine. **—i rakika** small intestine.

emacid (.—.) اماجد A *lrnd., pl. of* **emced**.

emakin (.—.) اماكن A *lrnd., pl. of* **mekân**.

eman (.—) امان A *lrnd., same as* **aman**.

emanat (.——) امانات A *lrnd., pl. of* **emanet**. **—i mukaddese, —i mübareke, —i şerife** P Islamic sacred relics.

emanet (.—.) امانت A 1. a trust, anything entrusted to another for safekeeping. 2. *Ott. hist.* government office receiving or paying out government money. 3. *archaic* trustworthiness, faithfulness. **— et=** /ı, a/ to entrust, to commit to another. **— hesabı** deposit account. **—e hıyanet** breach of trust, embezzlement. **—çi** depositary. **—dar** (.—.—) P *lrnd., same as* **emanetçi**.

emaneten (.—'..) امانتاً A 1. on deposit; as a trust, for safekeeping. 2. on government account, not by farming out.

emanetkâr (.—.—) امانتكار P *lrnd.* trustworthy.

emanetullah (.—..—) امانة الله A *lrnd.* charge laid upon one by God (subordinates or needy persons).

emani (.——) امانى A *Ott. hist.* 1. to whom quarter has been given. 2. who is an alien under protection in the land of Islam.

emarat (.——) امارات A *lrnd., pl. of* **emare**.

emare (.—.) اماره A *lrnd.* 1. sign, mark, token; indication. 2. *law* circumstantial evidence.

emaret (.—.) امارت A *hist.* 1. chieftainship, leadership. 2. territory of a chief.

emasil (.—.) اماثل A *lrnd.* best, most eminent, peers, nobles.

embriyoloji F embryology.
embriyon F *anat.* embryo.
emcad (. —) اَمْجَادٌ A *lrnd.*, *pl.* of **macid**.
emced اَمْجَدٌ A *lrnd.*, *superl.* of **mecîd**.
emcek[gi], **emcik**[gi] اَمْجِيكْ ، اَمْجَكْ *prov.* teat; nipple.
emdir=[ir] اَمْدِيرْمَكْ /1, a/ *caus.* of **em**= 1. **=eme= 1** *cf.* **=ama= 3**
eme 2 اَمَة A *can. law* female slave.
emece *var.* of **imece**.
emeç[cl] *neol., bot.* mycelium.
emed[ddi] اَمَدّ A *lrnd.*, *superl.* of **medid**.
emeddallah (. . . —) اَمَدَّ اللهُ A *lrnd.* May God prolong...
emek[gi] اَمَكْ 1. work, labor. 2. trouble, pains. — **birliği** cooperation. — **çek=** to work hard, to take great pains. —**iyle ekmeğini kazan=** to work for one's living. —**i geç=** /a/ to contribute efforts in some accomplishment. — **gör=** *archaic* to work hard, to labor. —**i hebaya gitti** All his efforts came to nought. — **olmadan yemek olmaz** One has to work in order to get what one wants. — **sarfet=**, — **ver=** /a/ to work hard, to labor (at), to take great pains (with). — **ye=** *archaic* to work hard, to labor. — **yerde kalmaz** Hard work is never in vain. —**çi** *neol.* worker, laborer; proletarian.
emekle= اَمَكْلَمَكْ 1. to crawl on all fours (baby or infirm person). 2. to attempt, to try (as a beginner). —**t=** /ı/ *caus.*
emekli اَمَكْلِى *neol.* retired (official).
emeksiz اَمَكْسِزْ effortless, without work. — **evlât** *prov.* stepchild.
emektar (. . —) اَمَكْدَارْ old and faithful servant, old and loyal official; veteran. —**lık** *abstr. n.*
emektaş اَمَكْداشْ fellow worker, comrade.
emel اَمَلْ A 1. desire, wish; hope, aspiration; ambition, longing, coveting. 2. object of desire; ideal.
emen=[ir] اَمَنْمَكْ *prov.* to take trouble, to take pains.
emer[rri] اَمَرّ A *lrnd.* most bitter; very unpleasant.
Emevî (. . —) اَمَوِى A Omayyad. —**ye** *pl.*
emhar (. . —) اَمْهَارْ A *lrnd.*, *pl.* of **mihr**.
e mi اَمِى Mind you! Will you? *e. g.*, **Unutma, e mi!** Don't forget, will you! **Çabuk gel, e mi!** Come quickly, will you?
emici اَمِيجِى sucking, sucker.
emik[gi] اَمِكْ ، اَمِيكْ *prov.* bruise produced by sucking.
emil=[ir] اَمِلْمَكْ *pass.* of **em=** 1.
emin (. —) اَمِينْ A 1. safe, secure; free from doubt. 2. sure, certain; strong, firm. 3. trustworthy. 4. steward, custodian, trustee. 5. *Ott. hist.* superintendent, head of a department. 6. God. —**i beytülmal**, —**i hazine** *Ott. hist.* imperial treasurer. —**i kadi** *Ott. hist.* trustee of a judge. —**i mahzen** *Ott. hist* Superintendent of the Imperial storehouse. — **ol=** /dan/ to be sure (of). — **ol!** Believe me! —**i vahy**, —**i vahyullah** the Prophet Muhammad. —**î** (. — —) P, —**lik** *abstr. n.* of **emin**.
emir[mri] 1 اَمْرْ [emr] 1. order, command; decree. 2. *lrnd.* matter, business; event, case. — **al=** /dan/ to receive orders (from). —**i âli** *Ott. hist.* imperial rescript (firman). —**e amade** ready, at one's service. — **atlısı** *mil.* mounted orderly. —**i bilmaruf** an injunction to act and speak kindly or righteously. — **eri** *mil.* orderly. — **et=***. —**i gaib** *gram.* 3rd *pers.* of *the imperative.* —**i Hak** God's decree, *i. e.* death. —**e hazır** ready, at one's disposal. —**i hazır** *gram.*, 2nd person of the imperative. — **kipi** *gram.* imperative mood. — **kulu** one who has to obey orders. — **limanı** port of call. —**i maruf** *Isl. rel.* the command to do what is right and lawful in the eyes of God and man. —**e muharrer senet** *fin.* promissory note. —**i mübin** *lrnd.* a self-evident matter. —**e müheyya** same as —**e amade**. — **neferi** *mil.*, same as **emir eri**. —**i sami** *Ott. hist.* an order emanating from the Grand Vizier. — **sıygası** *gram.*, same as **emir kipi**. — **subayı** *mil.* adjutant. —**i şerif** *Ott. hist.* the imperial decree, the Sultan's order. — **şer'in** I am ready to accept the decision of the canonical law. —**i vaki** *fait accompli*, accomplished fact. — **ver=** /a/ to order, command. —**ine ver=** /ı, ın/ to put under one's order.
emîr 2 (. —) اَمِيرْ A 1. prince, chief, leader, ruler, commander. 2. *lrnd.* descendant of the Prophet Muhammad. **E—i âbı hayvan** the Prophet Khidr. —**i ahur** *hist.* Master of the Horse. —**i alem** *Ott. hist.* pasha of the lowest grade; officer who invested the princes of Moldavia and Wallachia. —**i hac** same as **emîrülhac**. —**i Mekke** *Ott. hist.*, title given to the governors of Mecca who were descendants of the Prophet. —**i nahl** *lrnd.*, title given to the Caliph Ali. — **sar=** *obs.* to wear the green turban in sign of descent from the Prophet Muhammad. —**i zenburan** *lrnd.* queen bee.
emirane (. — —.) اَمِيرَانَه P princely, imperial (act); imperially.
emirber اَمِرْبَرْ P *mil.* orderly; bearer of an order.
emircik[gi] اَمِرْجِكْ kingfisher, halcyon, *zool.*, *Alcedo atthis.* — **kuşu** same as **emircik**.
emire (. — .) اَمِيرَه A *lrnd.* woman leader, princess. — **âşık** cock's-comb, *bot.*, *Celosia cristata.*

emirî (. — —) اميری P lrnd., same as **emirlik**.
emirlikᵍⁱ (. — .) اميرلك 1. principality. 2. the quality of a commander.
emirname (.. — .) امرنامه P decree; written command. **—i sâmi** vizierial letter directed to any government functionary.
emirülbahr (. — ..) اميرالبحر A hist. naval commander, admiral.
emirülceyş (. — ..) اميرالجيش A hist. military commander, general-in-chief.
emirülhacᶜᶜⁱ (. — ..) اميرالحج A Ott. hist. commander of the great caravan of pilgrims to Mecca appointed by the Sultan.
Emirülmüminin (. — ... —) اميرالمؤمنين A Commander of the Faithful (title of the Caliphs).
emirülümera (. — ... —) اميرالامراء A Ott. hist. commander of commanders (title given to a pasha).
emirzade (. — — .) اميرزاده P lrnd. son of a commander.
emisyon اميسيون F 1. fin. issue. 2. radio transmission.
emiş kamış اميش قامش familiar, intimate.
emiş karış اميش قاريش اش قارش archaic 1. intermingled. 2. familiar, intimate.
emkine امكنة A lrnd., pl. of **mekân**.
emlâh 1 (. —) املاح A lrnd., pl. of **milh**.
emlâh 2 املح A lrnd., superl. of **melih**.
Emlâh-ül-Arab املح العرب A the Prophet Muhammad.
emlâkᵏⁱ (. —) املاك A pl. of **mülk**. **—i emiriye** same as **emlâki miriye**. **—i hassa**, **—i humayun** Ott. hist. lands belonging to the Sultan. **—i mevkufe** donated lands, bestowed property. **—i milliye** national property, state lands. **—i miriye** hist. crown lands, public property.
emle=ʳ املك /ı/ prov. to heal, to cure.
emles املس A lrnd. smooth.
emlikᵍⁱ املك prov. sucking lamb.
emma (. —) اما A lrnd., same as **amma**.
emmar (. —), **emmare** (. — .) امّار امّاره A lrnd. imperious, commanding.
emme امّ verbal n. of **em=** 1. **— borusu** mech. induction pipe, inlet manifold. **— supapı** mech. inlet valve. **— tulumba** suction pump.
emmeçᶜⁱ neol., phys. aspirator, suction pump.
emmi عمّی [ammi 2] prov. 1. paternal uncle. 2. familiar mode of address.
emn امن A lrnd. safety, security; assurance, faith, confidence. **— ü eman** safety, security. **— ü selâmet** peace and security.
Emnabad (. — —) امن آباد P hist. name of a palace at Fındıklı on the Bosphorus.
emniyet امنيت [based on Arabic] 1. safety, freedom from fear, security. 2. confidence, belief. 3. pop. the police, the law. **— altına al=** to make safe. **— âmiri** chief of the police office. **—i âmme** lrnd. public security. **— bölgesi** mil. safety zone. **— et=** 1. /a/ to trust (in). 2. /ı, a/ to entrust to someone's care. **— haddi** safety limit. **— hattı** mil. safety line. **— horozu** mil. safety hammer (of a gun). **— kademesi** mil. security échelon. **— kemeri** safety belt. **— mesafesi** security distance. **— müdürü** chief of police. **— müfrezesi** mil. security detachment, security patrol. **— payı** margin of safety. **— sahası** mil. safety zone. **E— Sandığı** name of a credit institution which makes loans on the security of real estate or valuables. **— somunu** lock nut. **—i suiistimal** law embezzlement; breach of confidence. **— supapı** mech. safety valve, bypass valve. **— tedbiri** security measure, safety precaution. **— tertibatı** mech. safety gear. **E—i Umumiye** Ott. hist. Public Security, the police. **—bahş** P lrnd. inspiring confidence and security. **—bahşî** (. ... —) P abstr. n. **—li** trustworthy, reliable; safe. **—siz** unsafe, insecure; distrustful, untrustworthy. **—sizlik** lack of confidence; untrustworthiness.
emoraji اموراژی F path. hemorrhage.
emoroid امورویده F path. hemorrhoids, piles.
empermeabl امپرميابل F raincoat, water-proof; mackintosh.
emperyalist امپرياليست F pol. imperialist; imperialistic.
emperyalizm امپرياليزم F pol. imperialism.
empresyonizm امپرسيونيزم F art impressionism.
emprevizyon امپرویزيون F law want of foresight.
emprime امپريمه F text. printed silk material.
emr امر A cf. **emir 1**. **— ü ferman menlehül'emrindir**, **— ü ferman veliyül'emrindir** Ott. hist. And to command belongs unto him to whom all commanding belongs (phrase commonly used in concluding letters).
emraz (. —) امراض A path., pl. of **maraz**. **—ı akliye** mental diseases. **—ı asabiye** nervous diseases. **—ı bevliye** urinary diseases. **—ı dahiliye** internal diseases. **—ı efrenciye** venereal diseases. **—ı intaniye** infectious diseases. **—ı nisaiye** gynecological diseases. **—ı sariye** contagious diseases. **—ı zühreviye** venereal diseases.
emre امره archaic lover.
emred امرد A lrnd. beardless; young. **—perest** P pederast, sodomite.
emret=ᵈᵉʳ امرتمك /ı, a/ to order, to command.
emrî (. —), **emriye** (. — .) امری امريه A lrnd. pertaining to order, imperative.
emrud (. —) امرود P lrnd. pear.
ems امس A lrnd. yesterday.
emsalⁱⁱ (. —) امثال A 1. similar cases.

emsalsiz

2. *math.* coefficient. 3. *lrnd.*, *pl. of* **mesel**. **— göster=** to show precedent. **—i hikemiye** maxims, aphorisms. **—i kesiresine nail olasınız** Many happy returns of the day! (said at feast days). **—i misillû** as in similar cases; in like manner. **—i nâmesbûk** unprecedented. E**—i Süleyman** *Bib.* Proverbs of Solomon. **—i yok** matchless, peerless, unequaled, nonpareil.

emsalsiz امثال ' matchless, peerless, unequaled.

emsar (.—) امصار [*pl. of* **mısr**] A *lrnd.* large towns, cities. **— ü bilâd** great cities and towns.

emsile امثلة A 1. *lrnd.*, *pl. of* **misal**. 2. *Arabic gram.* paradigms for derivation, conjugation or declension; book on accidence.

emtar (.—) امطار A *lrnd.*, *pl. of* **matar**.

emtia امتعة A *lrnd.* goods, wares, merchandise, commodity.

emvac (.—) امواج A *lrnd.*, *pl. of* **mevc**.

emvah (.—) امواه A *lrnd.*, *pl. of* **mâ 2**.

emval^{ii} (.—) اموال A *law*, *pl. of* **mal**. **—i bâtına** possessions that can be concealed (such as gold, silver). **—i emiriye** crown property. **—i eytam** orphan's property. **—i gayrimenkule** real estate. **—i menkule** movables, movable goods. **—i metruke** abandoned property. **—i umumiye** public property. **—i zahire** possessions that cannot be concealed (such as land, buildings).

emvat (.—) اموات A *lrnd.* the dead.

emyah (.—) امياه A *lrnd.*, *pl. of* **mâ 2**.

emyal^{ii} (.—) اميال A *lrnd.*, *pl. of* **mil 1, 2**.

emza (.—) امضى A *lrnd.* very current; most penetrating, very sharp.

emzice امزجة A *lrnd.*, *pl. of* **mizac**.

emzik^{ği} امزيك 1. pacifier, comforter. 2. baby's bottle, feeding bottle. 3. *prov.* spout. 4. *prov.* cigarette-holder. 5. *slang* hookah, narghile. **—çi** *prov.* milk nurse, wet nurse. **—li** 1. having a spout. 2. with a child at the breast (woman).

emzir=^{ir} امزرمك /ı/° 1. to suckle, to give suck. 2. *slang* to siphon out gasoline from a car. **—il=** *pass.* **—iş** *verbal n. of* **emzir=**. **—t=** /ı, a/ *caus. of* **emzir=**.

en 1 اڭ *before adjective* most. **— aşağı**, **— az**, **— azdan** at least. **— baştan** from the very beginning. **— büyük ortak tam bölen** *math.* highest common divider. **— evvel** first of all. **— küçük ortak kat** *math.* lowest common multiple. **— sonra** last of all, lastly. **— ziyade mazharı müsaade devlet şartı** *intern. law* most-favored-nation clause.

en 2 اڭ ، انك width, breadth. **—ince**, **—ine** in width, breadthwise, crosswise, transversally. **—ine boyuna** 1. in length and breadth. 2. tall and well-built. 3. fully. **—ine boyuna çek=** /ı/ 1. to make it long drawn out. 2. to explain away. **—ine boyuna ölçüp biç=** /ı/ to consider in detail. **—ine çektik, boyuna çektik, nihayet buna karar verdik** /ı/ We considered it from all angles and then decided on this. **—ine kalın bağırsak** *neol.*, *anat.* tranverse colon. **—i sonu** the long and the short of it. **—inde sonunda** in the end, at last.

=en 3 *cf.* **=an 8**.

-en 4 A *lrnd.*, adverb, as in **muhtemelen, muvakkaten**.

en=^{er} **5** انك *prov.*, same as **in= 1**.

en 6 اناك ، انك *archaic* complexion.

ena (.—) انا A *cf.* **ene**.

enabib (.——) انابيب A *lrnd.*, *pl. of* **ünbube**.

Enacil (.——) اناجيل A *lrnd.*, *pl. of* **İncil**. **—i erba'a** the four Gospels.

enafis (.—.) انافس A *lrnd.*, *pl. of* **enfes**.

Enahid (.——) اناهيد P *lrnd.*, *astr.* Venus.

enai (.——) انائى A *lrnd.* egoistic, egotistical.

enaiyet (.——.) انائيت A *lrnd.*, same as **enaniyet**.

En'am 1 (.—) انعام A collection of verses from the Quran, including the **Sure-i En'am**. **— Suresi** *name of the sixth sura of the Quran*.

enam 2 (.—) انام A *lrnd.* mankind, the human race.

enamil (.—.) انامل A *lrnd.*, *pl. of* **enmile**.

enaniyet (.—..) انانيت A *lrnd.* egoism; pride, selfishness.

enar (.—) انار P *lrnd.* pomegranate.

enarallahu (.—.—.) انارالله A *lrnd.* May God enlighten! **— kabrühu** May God make his tomb radiant.

enaşid (.——) اناشيد A *lrnd.*, *pl. of* **ünşude**.

enayi (.—.) انايى [enai] *slang* fool, idiot. **— boğ=** to deceive a fool. **— dümbeleği** a prize idiot. **—lik** foolishness.

enba (.—) انباء A *lrnd.*, *pl. of* **nebe**.

enbâhûn (.——) انباهون P *lrnd.* castle, fortification.

enban (.—), **enbane** (.—.) انبانه ، انبان P *lrnd.* bag, wallet of hide or leather.

enbar (.—) انبار P *lrnd.*, same as **ambar**.

enbaşte (.—.) انباشته P *lrnd.* filled, stuffed, crammed.

enbaz (.—) انباز P *lrnd.* 1. partner, shareholder. 2. companion, associate; fellow, mate. **—î** partnership, association.

enbiya (..—) انبيا A *lrnd.*, *pl. of* **nebi**.

enbube (.—.) انبوبه P *sc.* pipe, tube; spout. **—i teneffüsiye** *anat.* respiratory tube.

enbubî (.——) انبوبى A *sc.* tubular, tubiform.

enbuh (.—) انبوه P *lrnd.* 1. much, many; crowded; numerous. 2. full. **—î** (.——) P abundance.

encad (.—) اِنجاد A lrnd., pl. of **necd**.
encam (.—) اِنجام P lrnd. end, extremity, termination; conclusion of an act; ultimate state, result of an act. — **bul**=, **—a er**= to end, to terminate, to result. **—ını hayretsin** May God bring about a happy ending (said when the outcome is in doubt). **—ı kâr** finally, at the end. **—pezir** (.—.—) P finished, concluded.
encas (.—) اِنجاس A lrnd., pl. of **neces**.
encekᵍⁱ اِنجك var. of **enik** 1.
encere اِنجره P lrnd. nettle.
ences اِنجس A lrnd., superl. of **neces, necis**.
encikᵍⁱ اِنجيك var. of **enik** 1.
encir (.—) اِنجير P lrnd., var. of **incir**.
encüm اِنجم A lrnd., pl. of **necm**.
encümen اِنجمن P meeting, council, committee. **—i adlî** council of justice. **—i daimî** permanent council. **E—i Dâniş** Ott. hist. Academy of Science (of Istanbul); academy, learned society. **—i kehkeşan** lrnd. the milky way. **—i gerdünpeymâ** lrnd. the seven planets. **—i sûr** lrnd. festive gathering. **—i ülfet** lrnd. club. **—gâh** P lrnd. place of assembly. **—sipah** P poet. having troops as numerous as the stars. **—sûz** P poet. that burns up the stars (sun).
encüre اِنجمُره A lrnd. nettle.
encüriye اِنجميرة A 1. bot., Urticaceae. 2. path. urticaria, nettle-rash.
enda (.—) اِندا A lrnd., pl. of **neda**.
endad (.—) اِنداد A lrnd., pl. of **nid**.
endaht اِنداخت [Persian .—] mil. a firing, discharge (of a firearm); a throwing. **— et**= 1. to fire, to shoot, to discharge. 2. slang to have a sexual discharge.
endahte (.—.) اِنداخته P lrnd. fired, discharged, thrown.
endam (.—) اِندام P shape, figure, stature; body. **—aynası** full-length mirror. **—ı nihanî, —ı piş** lrnd. the privy parts. **—ı sîm** poet. fair, snow-white. **—ı şerm** lrnd. the privy parts. **—harek** (.—— .) P lrnd. back-scratcher. **—lı** well-proportioned, graceful. **—sız** ill-proportioned, shapeless, graceless.
-endaz (.—) اِنداز P lrnd. who throws, that discharges, e. g., **lengerendaz, tîrendaz**.
endaze (.—.) اِندازه P 1. measure; proportion. 2. obs. a measure of length of about 26 inches. **—sini al**= /ın/ to estimate the ability (of a person); to estimate the importance and consequences (of a matter). **—si bozuk** ill-proportioned; not in proper order. **— çıkar**= shipbuilding to make a mold. **—ye gelmez** inestimable, measureless, immeasurable; unreasonable. **— güvertesi** shipbuilding floor of the mold loft. **—ye vur**= /ı/ to measure; to calculate, to consider. **—hane** (.—.—.) P shipbuilding mold loft. **—le**= /ı/ to measure; to estimate. **—len**= pass. **—siz** 1. out of order, irregular; ill-proportioned. 2. uncalculated.
endbentᵈⁱ اِندبنت same as **entbent**.
-ende اِنده P lrnd., active participle of Persian verbs, e. g., **hanende, sazende**.
endekᵏⁱ اِندك P lrnd. 1. small number; few. 2. small quantity, little. **— endek** little by little, gradually.
endeks اِندكس F index, econ. cost-of-living index.
endeksale (..—.) اِندك سال P lrnd. young.
endeksuhan اِندك سخن P lrnd. 1. taciturn. 2. in short, in fine.
endekşümar (...—) اِندك شمار P lrnd. few in number.
Endelüs اِندلس A cf. **Endülüs**.
ender 1 اِندر A very rare.
ender 2 اِندر P lrnd. upon, within, as in **hayret ender hayret, kat ender kat**.
ender 3 اِندر P lrnd. in, into.
enderun (..—) اِندرون P lrnd. 1. women's apartments of a palace, gynaeceum; w. cap. same as **Enderun-i Hümayun**. 2. the interior of a thing. **E— ağaları** Ott. hist. the eunuchs of the Sultan's palace. **E—i Hümayun** Ott. hist. the ladies' apartments in the Sultan's palace; the Sultan's private apartments; the Palace, the part of the Palace that was under the Sultan's private administration. **E— Mektebi** Ott. hist. Palace School.
enderunî (..——) اِندروني P lrnd. 1. inner, interior. 2. pertaining to the palace.
endir=ⁱʳ اِندير مك /ı/ prov., same as **indir**=.
endirekt F indirect. **— ateş** artillery indirect firing.
-endiş (.—) اِنديش P lrnd. who thinks, e. g., **akıbetendiş, durendiş**.
endişe (.—.) اِنديشه P 1. care, anxiety, perplexity. 2. worry; fear, suspicion. 3. lrnd. thought, consideration, reflection. **— et**= to worry, to be anxious. **—kâr** (.—.—) P lrnd. thoughtful, anxious. **—kârî** (.—..—) P lrnd. anxiety, thoughtfulness. **—len**= to become anxious. **—lendir**= /ı/ caus. **—li** anxious, troubled; thoughtful.
endişenakᵏⁱ (.—.—) اِنديشه ناك P lrnd. thoughtful, anxious. **—i** (.—..—) P thoughtfulness, anxiety.
endişesiz (.—..) اِنديشه سز carefree, unworried, calm. **—lik** calmness, unworriedness.
endişnâkᵏⁱ (.——) اِنديشناك P lrnd. thoughtful, anxious.

-endud 1 (.—) اندود P *lrnd.* coated, painted, encrusted with, *e. g.,* **zerendud.**
endud 2 (.—) اندود P *lrnd.* plaster, gilding, coating.
enduh (.—) اندوه P *lrnd.* care, anxiety, trouble, grief. **—gîn** (.——) P, **—nâk** (.——) P anxious, sorrowful, oppressed with care.
enduhte (.—.) اندوخته P *lrnd.* 1. collected, heaped up, massed. 2. acquired, gained.
-enduz (.—) اندوز P *lrnd.* that collects, acquires, *e. g.,* **zulmetenduz, ibretenduz.**
endüksiyon اندوكسيون F 1. *phil.* induction. 2. *elec.* induction. **— bobini** *elec.* induction coil, field magnet coil.
endüktör اندوكتور F *elec.* inductor.
Endülüs اندلس A *geog.* Andalusia.
endüstri اندوستري F industry.
endüvi F *elec.* armature (of dynamo).
ene 1 انا A *lrnd.* I; *phil.* ego.
ene=ᵣ 2 انا /ı/ to castrate.
eneiye (..—.) انائيه A *lrnd., phil.* solipsism.
eneiyet (..—.) انائيت A *lrnd.,* same as **enaniyet.**
enekᵍⁱ **1** اناك *prov.* plow-handle.
enekᵍⁱ **2** اناك *prov.* castrated.
enekᵍⁱ **3** اناك *archaic* lower jaw. **— çukuru** dimple.
enekle=ᵣ اناكلمك /ı/ *archaic* to castrate. **—t=** /ı, a/ *caus.*
enelhak انا الحق A *Isl. myst.* I am God (the statement for which Mansur-al-Hallaj was condemned to death).
enen=ⁱʳ اننمك *pass. of* **ene= 2.**
enerji انرژي F energy.
enerjikᵍⁱ انرژيك F energetic.
enet=ⁱʳ انتمك /ı, a/ *caus. of* **ene= 3.**
enez, eneze انز، انزه *colloq.* feeble, weak; incapable.
enf انف A *lrnd.* 1. nose. 2. cape; promontory. 3. tip, end, point.
enfaᵃⁱ انفع A *lrnd., superl. of* **nafi.**
enfalˡⁱ (.—) انفال A *lrnd.* spoils, booty.
enfar (.—) انفار A *lrnd., pl. of* **nefer.**
enfas (.—) انفاس A *lrnd., pl. of* **nefes.** **—ı hayriye** *rel.* the blessed and healing breath of the saints. **—ı madude** the numbered breaths, human life. **—ı Mesih** the life-giving breath of Jesus. **—ı müşkbar** sweet words.
enfeksiyon انفكسيون F *path.* infection.
enfes انفس A delightful, delicious, very good.
enfî (.—) انفي A *anat.* pertaining to the nose.
enfiye انفيه [*based on Arabic*] snuff. **— çek=**, **— kullan=** to take snuff. **— kutusu** snuffbox. **—ci** maker or seller of snuff.
enflâsyon انفلاسيون F *econ.* inflation.
enflüanza (...) انفلونزا F *path.* influenza.

enfraruj انفرارژ F *phys.* infrared. **— ışınlar** infrared rays.
enfüs انفس A *lrnd., pl. of* **nefs 1.** **— ü afak** *phil.* subjectivism and objectivism.
enfüsî (..—) انفسي [*based on* **enfüs**] *phil.* subjective.
enfüsiye (..—.) انفسيه A *phil.* subjectivism.
engâre (.—.) انگاره P *lrnd.* tale, story, fiction; legend, tradition. **—gû** (.—.—) P story-teller.
engebe انگبه Gk *prov.* unevenness of ground; broken ground, rough country. **—li** steep and broken (ground). **—lik** undulating ground.
engebin (..—) انگبين P *lrnd.,* same as **engübin.**
engeçᶜⁱ انگچ *prov.,* same as **yengeç.**
engel انگل 1. obstacle, difficulty, handicap. 2. *prov.* rival, one who is in one's way. **— imtihanı** *school* repetition of the **ikmal imtihanı. —e kal=** *school* to be required to take a makeup examination. **— ol=** /a/ to hinder, to prevent. **—siz** without hindrance, unimpeded; without a competing rival.
engelyun (..—) انگليون P *lrnd.* 1. *w. cap.* the New Testament. 2. *w. cap.,* name of the book of Mani. 3. shot silk cloth of seven colors. 4. chameleon.
enger sakızıⁿⁱ انگر صاقيزي same as **çengel sakızı.**
engerekᵍⁱ انگرك adder, viper, *zool.,* Pelias berus, Vipera. **— otu** viper's bugloss, *bot.,* Eclium.
Engerus (..—) انگروس L same as **Engürus.**
engihte (.—.) انگيخته P *lrnd.* excited, raised, stirred up.
engin 1 انگين 1. open, wide, vast, boundless. 2. the high sea, the open sea, offing. **—e çık=** *naut.* to make for the offing. **—den git=** *naut.* to keep off shore.
engin 2 انگين *prov.* 1. low, ordinary; cheap. 2. base, mean.
enginar انگنار Gk artichoke, *bot.,* Cynara Scolymus.
enginlikᵍⁱ انگينلك *abstr. n. of* **engin 1.**
enginsel *neol., bot.* pelagic.
engişt انگشت P *lrnd.* charcoal; charred wood. **—ger** charcoal-burner.
-engiz (.—) انگيز P *lrnd.* exciting, stirring, *e. g.,* **fitulengiz.**
engizisyon انگيزيسيون F the Inquisition. **— sistemi** *law* inquisitorial system.
engiziş (.—.) انگيزش P *lrnd.* excitement.
engûr (.—) انگور P *lrnd.* grape.
engûrekᵏⁱ انگورك P *lrnd.* 1. a little grape. 2. pimple, boil. **—i çeşm** pupil of the eye.
engübin (..—) انگبين P *lrnd.* honey. **—fâm** P honey-colored.
Engürü انگورى *archaic* Ankara.
Engürüs انگروس Hung *archaic* 1. Hungary.

2. Hungarian; Hungarians. **—lü** a Hungarian.

engüşt انگشت P *lrnd.* 1. finger. 2. toe. 3. pivot; spoke of a wheel. **—i âfitab** sunbeam. **—i arus** kind of grape. **—i âsya** pivot of a millstone. **— bedendan** amazed, astonished. **— berdehan-ı hayret, — berleb** amazed, bewildered. **—i bînâm** the fourth finger. **—i büzürg** thumb. **—i dirâz** middle finger. **—i halka** the ring-finger. **—i hasret** finger bitten in bereavement. **—i hata** the finger that points at mistakes. **—i hayret** finger bitten in astonishment. **—i kihin** little finger; little toe. **—i kûçek** little finger. **—i mihîn, —i miyane** middle finger. **—i muhannâ** finger painted with henna. **—i ner** thumb. **—i nîl** ignominy; poverty. **—i peşimani** finger bitten in regret. **—i semin** thumb. **—i sütürk** thumb. **—i şek, —i şehadet** forefinger of the right hand. **—i tahayyür** finger bitten in astonishment.

engüştane (..—.), **engüştene** انگشتانه P *lrnd.* thimble.

engüşter, engüşteri (...—), **engüşterin** (...—) انگشترين انگشترى انگشتر P *lrnd.* 1. finger ring. 2. thimble.

engüştkeş انگشت كش , **engüştnüma** (...—) انگشت نما P *lrnd.* pointed out, famous; pointed at, infamous.

engüştvane (..—.) انگشتوانه P *lrnd.*, same as **engüştane**.

enha (.—) انحاء A *lrnd., pl. of* **nahv**.

enhar (.—), **enhür** انهر , انهار A *lrnd., pl. of* **nehir**.

enhas اخس A *lrnd.* most inauspicious.

enik[t1] **1** انك , انيك *prov.* pup, cub, whelp, the young of a carnivorous animal.

enîk[k1] **2** (.—) انيس A *lrnd.* beautiful, excellent, charming.

enikle=[r] انكله مك *prov.* to bring forth young (beast).

enikonu انى قونو quite; thoroughly.

enin (.—) انين A *lrnd.* a moaning; moan, whine, groan.

enis (.—) انيس A *lrnd.* friend, companion, familiar, acquaintance of the same temper or disposition.

enisan (.——) انيسان P *lrnd.* 1. lie. 2. joke, jest; senseless words.

enise (.—.) انيسه A *lrnd., fem. of* **enis**.

eniş انش prov., same as **iniş**.

enişte (.´.) انشته sister's or aunt's husband.

enjeksiyon انژكسيون F injection. **— natürel** *slang* sexual intercourse.

enjektör انژكتور F *mech.* injector.

enkas انقص A *lrnd.* very deficient, most defective.

enkaz (.—) انقاض A wreckage; debris; ruins. **—ı remime** rotten wreckage.

enker انكر A *lrnd.* very unpleasant, most disagreeable.

enkiha انكحه A *lrnd., pl. of* **nikâh**.

enlem *neol., geog.* latitude.

enli انلو wide, broad. **—len=, —leş=** to become broad, to widen. **—lik** breadth.

enmile انمله A *lrnd.* fingertip.

enmuzec (.—.) انموذج A *lrnd.* sample, specimen; pattern, model, type. **—i evvel** *metaphysics* archetype.

ensa انسا A *lrnd.* forgettings, oblivions.

ensab (.—) انساب A *lrnd., pl. of* **neseb**.

ensac (.—) انساج A *lrnd., med., pl. of* **nesc**.

ensaf 1 (.—) انصاف A *lrnd., pl. of* **nısıf**.

ensaf 2 انصف A *lrnd., superl. of* **munsif**.

ensal[ll] (.—) انسال A *lrnd., pl. of* **nesl**.

ensar (.—.) انصار A *lrnd., var. of* **ansar**.

ense انسه 1. back of the neck. 2. back, behind. 3. *slang* buttocks. **—sine bin=** /ın/ to worry, persecute, to tyrannize. **—sinde boza pişir=** /ın/ *slang* to drive hard, to over-tire and torment. **— çukuru** hollow at the back of the neck between the two splenii muscles. **—den gel=** to come up from behind. **—sinden git=** /ın/ to follow close upon. **—si kalın** 1. stiff-necked, obstinate. 2. well-off; carefree; influential. **— kemiği** 1. occiput. 2. vertebrae of the neck. **— kökü** nape of the neck. **— kökünden gel=** /ın/ to be very close behind. **— mıhı** atlas (bone). **— sertliği** *path.* stiff neck. **—sine vur, ekmeğini elinden al** Hit him on the neck and take the bread out of his hand (said of a very mild person). **— yap=** to lead a comfortable and lazy life. **—sine yapış=** /ın/ to seize, to collar.

enseb انسب A *lrnd., superl. of* **münasib**.

ensele=[r] انسه له مك /ı/ *slang* to seize by the neck, to collar. **—n=** *pass.*

enser اكثر *prov., same as* **ekser 1**.

ensice انسجه A *lrnd., pl. of* **nesc**.

ensiz انسز narrow. **—lik** narrowness.

enspektör انسپكتور F inspector.

enstalâsyon انستلاسيون F *elec.* installation.

enstantane انستانته F *phot.* snapshot.

enstitü انستيتو F institute.

entak[k1] انطق A *lrnd., superl. of* **natuk**.

entari انطارى A loose robe; dress. **—lik** material for a robe.

entbent[dl] انت بند *colloq.* confused, ashamed, disconcerted. **— ol=** to be taken aback.

entelektüel انتلكتوئل F intellectual.

entelekya (.´.) انتلكيا L *phil.* entelechy.

entere انتره F interest, advantage.

enteresan انتره سان F interesting.

entereso (...´.) انتره سو It *obs.* interest, advantage. **—cu** (....—) egoist, opportunist.

enterlin اِنْتَرلين F same as **anterlin**.
enternasyonalˡⁱ اِنْتَرْناسيونال F 1. international. 2. pol. International.
enterne اِنْتَرْنَه F mil. interned. — **et=** to intern.
entertip اِنْتَرْتيب F print. composing machine, Intertype.
enterüptör اِنْتَروپتور F elec. interruptor, switch.
entimem اِنتيمم F phil. enthymeme.
entipüften اِنتيپوفتن slang flimsy, rubbishy; empty (words); insignificant.
entrika (. ́.) اِنْتريقه It intrigue; trick. — **çevir=** to intrigue, to scheme. **—cı** schemer, trickster.
enüstünlükˢü neol., gram. superlative degree.
envaᵃⁱ (.—) اِنواع A lrnd., pl. of **nevi**.
envanter اِنوانتر F com. inventory.
envar (.—) اِنوار A lrnd., pl. of **nur**.
enver اِنور A lrnd., superl. of **münir**.
enyab (.—) اِنياب A lrnd., pl. of **nâb 2**.
enzar (.—) اِنظار A lrnd., pl. of **nazar**. **—ı umumiye** the public eye.
enzeh اِنزه A lrnd., superl. of **nezih**.
enzerut اِنزروت A sarcocolla, bot., Sarcocolla.
enzime اِنظمه A lrnd., pl. of **nizam**.
eosen F geol. Eocene.
epçetᵈⁱ same as **ebced**.
epey (. ́.) اِپَى 1. pretty well. 2. a good many, a good deal of. **— oldu** a long time ago. **—ce** pretty well, fairly; to some extent.
epher var. of **ebher**.
epidemi اِپيدمى F epidemic.
epifitⁱⁱ F bot. epiphyte.
epikˢⁱ اِپيك F epic, epical.
Epikürcülükˢⁱⁱ phil. Epicureanism.
epistemoloji F phil. epistemology.
epitelyum L biol. epithelium.
epkem var. of **ebkem**.
eple=ʳ اِپلمك /ı/ archaic to consider, to think over, to reflect upon. **—t=** /ı, a/ caus.
epope اِپوپه F literature epic, epic poem.
epri=ʳ 1 اِپريمك prov. 1. to wear thin, to grow threadbare. 2. to fall to pieces (overcooked meat).
epri=ʳ 2 اِپريمك archaic to speak through the nose.
epsem اِپسم archaic 1. dumb, speechless. 2. quiet, silent. **— ol=** to be silent.
epyun (.—) اِپيون P lrnd., same as **afyon**.
er 1 اِر 1. male. 2. brave man, manly man; capable man, clever man; man (of knowledge, art, etc.). 3. neol., mil. private. 4. prov. husband. **— başı** obs. headman, spokesman, leader, captain (of a multitude). **— bezi** neol., anat. testicle. **— boşalt=** archaic to unhorse a rider. **— çiçeği** Bektashi order any dervish or person acceptable to the Baba. **—e git=** prov. to marry (a man). **— kişi** 1. man, adult. 2. a manly man. **— lokması er kursağında kalmaz** proverb A gentleman repays good with good. **— meydanı** field of contest (for brave men). **— oğlu er** a real son of a hero. **— oyunu birdir** once is enough; no need to try again. **—e var=** prov. to marry (a man). **—e ver=** prov. to give in marriage (woman).
er=ᵉʳ 2 اِرمك 1. /a/ to attain; to reach. 2. to arrive at maturity; ripen. 3. to reach spiritual perfection.
er 3 اِر prov. early; soon. **— geç** early or late, sooner or later.
er 4 اِر P lrnd., var of **eger**.
-er 5 cf. **-ar 4**.
=er 6 cf. **=r 2**.
=er= 7 cf. **=ar=** 6.
=er= 8 cf. **=ar=** 7.
era اِرا L era, significant date.
eracif (.——) اِراصيف A lrnd., pl. of **ercaf**, **ürcufe**.
eracih (.——) اِراجيح A lrnd., pl. of **ürcuhe**.
eraciz (.——) اِراجيز A lrnd., pl. of **ürcuze**.
eraik (.—.) اِرائك A lrnd., pl. of **erike**.
erakim (.——) اِراقيم A lrnd., pl. of **erkam**.
eramil (.—.) اِرامل **eramile** (.—..) اِراملة A lrnd. widows, poor women.
Eramine (.—..) اِرامنة A lrnd., pl. of **Ermeni**.
eranib (.—.) اِرانب A lrnd., pl. of **erneb**.
erat neol., mil. privates, recruits.
erazi (.——) اِراضى A var. of **arazi 1**.
erazil (.—.) اِرازل A lrnd., pl. of **erzel**.
erbaᵃⁱ (.—) اِرباع A lrnd., pl. of **rub'**.
erbaa اِربعه A lrnd. four. **—mie** four hundred.
erbab (.—) اِرباب A 1. same as **erbap**. 2. lrnd., pl. of **rab**.
erbabül'akâkiz (.—..——) اِرباب العكاكيز A lrnd. magistrates.
erbain (..—) اِربعين A 1. forty days of midwinter (Dec. 22nd - Jan. 30th). 2. myst. orders forty-day penitence. 3. lrnd. forty. **— çıkar=** myst. orders to undergo a forty-day period of penitence. **—e gir=** myst. orders to go into a forty-day retreat.
erbapᵇⁱ (.—) اِرباب [erbab] 1. expert. 2. people concerned with. **—ı bilir** Connoisseurs will appreciate it. **E—ı Divan** Ott. hist. members of the council of state or board of administration. **—ı fen** lrnd. men of science. **—ı garez** lrnd. interested, selfish people. **—ı hacat** lrnd. men of affairs. **—ı himmet** lrnd. high-minded, liberal persons. **—ı hired** lrnd. sages. **—ı hiref** lrnd. craftsmen, artisans. **—ı hüner** talented; skilled people. **—ı kalem** men of the pen, writers;

clerks, secretaries. —ı **maali** *lrnd.* grandees, notables. —ı **mâna** *myst.* mystics, men of God. —ı **namus** *lrnd.* men of honor. —ı **safayı bâtın** *myst.* the pure in heart. —ı **san'at** craftsmen, artisans. —ı **servet** wealthy people, the rich. —ı **seyf** *lrnd.* military men. —ı **suhan** *lrnd.* eloquent orators. —ı **sülûk** *lrnd.* observers of religious precepts, devout. —ı **tagallüb** *lrnd.* superiors; conquerors. —ı **temkin** *lrnd.* men of dignity and self-possession. —ı **temyiz** *lrnd.* men of discrimination; prudent. —ı' **ticaret** merchants, business men. —ı **timar** *hist.* possessors of small military fiefs. —ı **vukuf** *law* experts. —ı **yakin** *lrnd.* men of spiritual knowledge.

erbaş *neol., mil.* noncommissioned officer.

erbaun (..—) اربعون A same as **erbain**.

Erbıa (..—) اربعاء A *lrnd.* Wednesday.

ercaf (.—) ارجاف A *lrnd.* false rumor, disquieting and baseless talk.

ercah ارجح A *lrnd.* most preferable. —**iyet** (..—.) A superiority.

ercel ارجل A *lrnd.* 1. large-footed. 2. most manly.

ercevan (..—) ارجوان A *lrnd.*, same as **erguvan**.

ercik[gi] *neol., bot.* stamen.

Erciyas, Erciyaş, Erciyeş ارجيش Mount Argaeus near Kayseri.

ercmend ارجمند P same as **ercümend**.

ercül ارجل A *lrnd., pl.* of **ricl**.

ercümend ارجمند [**ercmend**] *lrnd.* worthy, estimable.

erdeb اردب [**irdeb**] *lrnd.* a grain measure of about five bushels, ardeb.

Erdel اردل *Ott. hist.* Transylvania.

erdem اردم virtue. —**li** virtuous.

erden *neol.* 1. virgin. 2. intact, untouched. —**lik** virginity.

Erdeşir (..—) اردشير P names of several kings of ancient Persia. —**i ceng** brave warrior. —**ane** (..——.) P like a warrior.

=**erdi** *cf.* =**rdi**.

erdir=[ir] ارديرمك /ı, a/ *caus.* of **er**= 2.

Erdün اردن *var.* of **Ürdün**.

erek[gi] 1 *neol., phil.* aim, end, goal. —**bilim** teleology. —**çilik** finalism. —**lik** finality. —**sel** final. —**sel neden** the final cause.

=**erek** 2 *cf.* =**arak** 1.

Erendiz *neol., astr.* Jupiter.

erenler ارنلر 1. those who have arrived at the divine truth. 2. *mode of address among dervishes.* 3. *archaic* men. —**in sağı solu olmaz** You never can tell; he is unpredictable.

erfa[al] ارفع A *lrnd., superl.* of **refî** 2.

erfane *var.* of **arifane** 2.

erg[gi] 1 *phys.* erg.

erg[gi] 2 ارك P *lrnd.* citadel.

ergab ارغب A *lrnd.* most desirable.

erganun (..—) ارغنون P *lrnd., mus.* organ.

ergavan (..—) ارغوان P *lrnd.*, same as **erguvan**.

ergeç[ci] ارگچ *prov.*, same as **erkeç**.

ergen ارگن youth of marriageable age, bachelor. —**e karı boşaması kolaydır** It is easy to talk. —**lik** 1. bachelorhood. 2. youthful acne.

ergi=[r] *neol., phys.* to melt. —**me** fusion.

ergin ارگين mature, ripe, adult; *law* major. —**leş**= to mature. —**lik** maturity; *law* majority, coming of age.

ergiveç[ci] ارگيوج *prov., var.* of **evirgeç**.

erguvan ارغوان [**ergavan**] Judas-tree, *bot.*, Cercis Siliquastrum. —**î** (..——) P purple. —**î balıkçıl** purple heron, *zool.*, Ardea purpurea.

ergür=[ür] ارگورمك *archaic, caus.* of **er**= 2.

erham 1 (.—) ارحام A *lrnd.* 1. *pl.* of **rahm**. 2. relations, kindred, kith and kin. —**ve ensab** *law* kin and relations.

erham 2 ارحم A *lrnd., superl.* of **rahîm**.

erhamürrahimin (...—.—) ارحم الراحمين A *rel.* the most compassionate of merciful ones, God.

erhas ارخص A *lrnd., superl.* of **rahis**.

eri=[r] ارمك 1. to melt, to become liquid, to dissolve. 2. to pine away. 3. to wear out (textiles.) 4. to be greatly embarrassed.

erib (.—) اريب A *lrnd.* intelligent.

eriğen ارگن which melts easily; dissolving (in the mouth).

erik[gi] اريك plum. —**ağacı** plum tree.

erike (.—.) اريكه A *lrnd.* 1. throne. 2. raised platform for reclining upon. —**nişin** sitting on the throne.

eril *neol., gram.* masculine.

erim اريم ارم the space which a thing can reach or attain; a reach.

erime ارمه dissolution, fusion, melting. —**noktası** melting point.

erim erim ارم ارم only in —**eri**= to be totally worn out, to be exhausted.

erimez ارمز *chem.* insoluble.

erimiş ارمش *chem.* dissolved.

erin=[ir] 1 ارنمك *prov.* to be too lazy, to feel lazy.

erin 2 *neol.* mature, adult.

erincek[gi] ارنجك *prov.* 1. lazy. 2. shy, bashful.

erinç[ci] *neol.* peace, rest.

erir ارر *phys.* soluble. —**lik** solubility.

eristik[gi] F *phil.* eristic.

eriş 1 اريش verbal n. of **er**= 2.

eriş=[ir] 2 ارشمك 1. /a/ to reach, to arrive (at); to attain. 2. to mature. —**im** 1. *verbal n.* 2. *neol.* communications. —**kin**

adult, mature. —**kinlik** adulthood, maturity. —**me** verbal n. of **eriş**=.

erişte ارشته |rişte| vermicelli.

eriştir=ir ارشدرمك /ı, a/ caus. of **eriş**= 2.

erit=ir ارتمك /ı/ 1. caus. of **eri**=. 2. to squander (money). —**en** neol., phys. solvent. —**il**= pass. of **erit**=.

eriyikği neol., phys. solution.

erkki 1 neol. power, faculty; authority.

erkki 2 ارك P lrnd. citadel (of a fortress), often the abode of a prince or governor.

erkam (. —) ارقام A lrnd., pl. of **rakam**. —**ı divaniye** the finance cipher. —**ı hindiye** Arabic numbers. —**ı müş'ire** index numbers.

erkân (. —) اركان A 1. great men, high officials, pillars of the State, etc. 2. main points, basic principles, fundamentals, essentials (in religion, science, etc.). 3. rules of conduct. 4. lrnd., pl. of **rükn**. —**ı devlet** ministers of state and great functionaries. —**ı harb** mil. General Staff. —**ı harb zabiti** mil. staff officer. —**ı harbiye** mil. general staff. — **kürkü** Ott. hist. fur coat worn by ministers and high officials. —**ı memurin** high officials. — **minderi** sitting cushion for a guest of honor.

erke neol., phys. energy.

erkeçci اركج he-goat, billy-goat.

erkekği اركك 1. man; male. 2. manly, courageous, virile, honest and true. 3. prov. husband. 4. good, hard (iron, copper). 5. mech., carpentry male. — **anahtar** solid-stemmed key. — **canlısı** who is always running after men (woman). — **iğnecik** naut. pintle of a rudder. — **kasnı** drug. galbanum in tears or in lumps. — **kopça** a hook for an eye. — **organ** bot. stamen. — **rumî kökü** birthwort, bot., Aristolochia longa.

erkekçe (. .' .) اركگ manly, in a manly manner, manfully.

erkeklikği ارككلك 1. masculinity; manliness, virility, courage. 2. male sex, sexual potency.

erkeksi اركگسی tomboyish, masculine (woman).

erken 1 اركن early. —**ce** rather early, a little early, somewhat early. —**ci** early riser; early comer. —**den** early.

=**erken 2** cf. =**rken**.

erketeci اركته جی Gk slang look-out man (for a burglar or cheat).

erkin neol., phil. free. —**cilik** liberalism. —**lik** liberty.

erlik ارلك manliness, courage, bravery. — **suyu** semen.

erme ارمه verbal n. of **er**= 2.

ermel ارمل A lrnd. widower.

ermende ارمنده P lrnd. reposing, resting, at rest.

Ermeni (. . —) ارمنی A Armenian. — **gelini**

gibi kırıt= 1. to hang back, to be slow in doing something. 2. to be affected, to attitudinize. —**ce** Armenian (language).

Ermenistan (. . . —) ارمنستان Armenia.

=**ermiş** cf. =**rmış**.

=**ermişçesine** cf. =**rmışçasına**.

=**ermiş gibi** cf. =**rmış gibi**.

erneb ارنب A lrnd. hare, rabbit.

eros (.' .) اروس G psych. love. —**al** neol. erotic. —**allık, erosçuluk** neol. eroticism.

erre اره P lrnd. saw. —**hane** P sawmill. —**keş** P maker or seller of saws.

=**erse** cf. =**rsa**. ارسه

erselikği biol. hermaphroditism.

erş ارش A can. law fine, blood money (for a wound).

erşed ارشد A . lrnd., superl. of **raşid, reşid**.

ertak ارتاق Arm slang Let's go.

erte ارته archaic 1. the next, the following (day, week, etc.); the morrow. 2. morning. — **gece** day and night. —**ki** tomorrow's. —**le**= 1. to become the next day (night). 2. to begin the next day (person). 3. to be left to the next day; /ı/ to postpone.

ertesi ارتسی 1. the next, the following (day, week, etc.), e. g., **ertesi yıl** the year after. 2. the day after, e. g., **bayram ertesi** the day after the feast.

erür=ür ارورمك /ı, a/ archaic, caus. of **er**= 2.

erüzzzü اروز A lrnd. rice.

ervah (. —) ارواح A lrnd., pl. of **ruh**. —**ı habise** evil spirits. —**ı lâtife**, —**ı tayyibe** good spirits, angels.

Ervam (. —) ارواﻢ A lrnd., pl. of **Rum**.

eryah (. —) ارياح A lrnd., pl. of **rih**.

erz 1 ارز A lrnd. cedar. —**i Lübnan** cedar of Lebanon.

erz 2 ارز |erüz| lrnd. rice.

erzakkı (. —) ارزاق A provisions, stored food.

erzalli (. —) ارذال A lrnd., pl. of **rezil**.

erzan (. —) ارزان P lrnd. 1. inexpensive, abundant. 2. worthy, valued. 3. permitted, fit, proper, due. — **buyur**= /ı/ to permit, allow, grant. —**beha** (. —.—) P low, cheap price. —**î** (. — —) P abstr. n.

erzel ارذل A superl. of **rezil**.

erzen ارزن P lrnd. millet.

erzenin (. . —) ارزنین P lrnd. cornbread.

erziş ارزش P lrnd. worth, value, price.

es=er 1 اسمك 1. to blow. 2. /a/ to come suddenly to mind. —**ip savur**= 1. to blow and raise the dust. 2. to storm and bluster.

es 2 اس musical sign for a rest.

es'ab اصعب A lrnd., superl. of **sa'b**.

esabii (. — —) اسابيع A lrnd., pl. of **üsbu**:

es'ad اسعد A lrnd., superl. of **said**.

esafil (. — .) اسافل A lrnd., pl. of **esfel**. —**i nâs** mob, rabble, scum.

esalib (.——) اساليب A lrnd., pl. of **üslûb**.
esame (.—.) اسامى [esami] Ott. hist. muster roll of the Janissaries. — **çal**= to be left out of the muster roll. —**si okunmaz** same as **esamisi okunmaz**. —**li** 1. registered in the muster roll. 2. shrewish, quarrelsome.
esami (.——) اسامى A lrnd., pl. of **ism** 1. —**si okunmaz** of no consequence, unimportant (person).
esanid (.——) اسانيد A lrnd., pl. of **isnad**, attributions (of things) to authors or reporters.
esans اسانس F perfume, essence, attar. —**çı** seller of perfumes.
es'ar (.—) اسعار A lrnd., pl. of **si'r** 1.
esaret (.—.) اسارت A slavery, captivity.
esarir (.——) اساریر A lrnd., pl. of **esrar** 1. 1. lines, wrinkles. 2. beauties, beautiful features of a face or cheeks.
esarun (.——) اسارون A asarabacca, wild nard, bot., *Asarum europecum*.
esas 1 (.—) اساس A 1. foundation, base, basis. 2. the true state (of a thing). 3. fundamental principle, essence, the essentials; essential, real, basic. — **itibariyle** as a matter of fact, in principle, essentially, basically. — **nizamname** statute. — **olarak** same as **esas itibariyle**. —**ı yok** untrue, without foundation.
esas 2 (.—) اساس A lrnd. goods, effects, chattels. —**ı beyt** household goods, furniture and utensils.
esasen (.—.) اساسا A fundamentally, from the beginning. 2. anyhow.
esasi (.——) اساسى A fundamental, basic.
esaslan=ır (.—..) اساسلنمق 1. to be founded, to be established. 2. to become firm, to gain ground. —**dır**= caus.
esaslı (.—.) اساسلى 1. authentic, true, reliable; sound, solid, concrete. 2. fundamental, principal; radical; main. — **surette** fully, thoroughly; radically.
esassız (.—.) اساسسز unfounded, baseless, false, untrue.
esatin (.——) اساطين A lrnd., pl. of **üstüvane**, columns, pillars. —**i ulemâ** pillars of knowledge.
esatir (.——) اساطير A legends, tales, stories, myths; mythology. —**i evvelin** lrnd. tales of the men of old.
esatiz (.—.), esatize (.—..) اساتذه A lrnd., pl. of **üstaz**.
esb اسب P lrnd. 1. horse. 2. chess knight. —**i sabareftar** a horse that is swift as the wind. —**i tâzi** Arabian horse, swift horse.
esbab (.—) اسباب A law, pl. of **sebeb**. —**ı mâzeret** exculpation. —**ı muhaffife** extenuating circumstances. —**ı mücbire** *force majeure*. —**ı müşeddide** aggravating circumstances.

esbak⁽ᵏⁱ⁾ اسبق A lrnd. former, late, sometime.
esbat (.—) اسباط A lrnd., pl. of **sıbt**.
esbefgen اسب افگن P lrnd. bold, brave.
esbran (.—) اسبران P lrnd. who urges his horse.
esbsüvar (..—) اسبسوار P lrnd. riding a horse, on horseback; rider.
esbtâz (.—) اسبتاز P lrnd. who makes his horse run.
esca⁽ᵃⁱ⁾ (.—) اسجاع A lrnd., pl. of **sec'** 1.
esdad (.—) اسداد A lrnd., pl. of **sed**.
esdak⁽ᵏⁱ⁾ اصدق A lrnd., superl. of **sadık**.
Esdakülkailîn (...—.—) اصدق القائلين A lrnd. the most Truthful of Speakers, God.
esed اسد A lrnd. 1. lion. 2. hero. **E— burcu** the constellation Leo. —**î** (.—) A 1. pertaining to the lion. 2. Ott. hist. silver piaster of the Seljuk Sultans of Konya. —**î guruş** hist. money of Holland.
Esedullah (...—) اسد الله A rel. the Lion of God, the Caliph Ali.
esef اسف A regret. — **et**= /a/ to be sorry, to feel regret (for), to pity. —**le** regretfully.
esefa (..—) اسفا P lrnd. It's a pity; alas!
esefhan (..—) اسف خوان P lrnd. who sorrows, who keeps regretting.
esefnak⁽ᵏⁱ⁾ (..—) اسفناک P lrnd. sorrowful, regretful.
esen 1 اسن *archaic* healthy, well, sound, robust. —**le**= /ı/ to bid farewell, to wish health and happiness. —**leş**= to bid each other farewell. —**lik** health, soundness.
esen⁽ⁿⁿⁱ⁾ 2 اسن A lrnd. the oldest, most aged.
eser اثر A 1. work, work of art, written work. 2. trace, sign, mark; chem. trace. 3. the Hadith. 4. pl. monuments, remains. 5. lrnd. effect. —**i cedit** foolscap paper. —**i İstanbul** Istanbul ware.
esfar 1 (.—) اسفار A lrnd., pl. of **sefer**.
esfar 2 (.—) اسفار A lrnd., pl. of **sifr**.
esfel اسفل A lrnd., superl. of **sefil**. —**i nâs** the vilest of all men.
esfelüssafilin (...—.—) اسفل السافلين A lrnd. 1. the lowest of the low. 2. the deepest pit of hell.
esha (.—) اسخى A lrnd. very liberal, most munificent.
eshab (.—) اصحاب A lrnd., same as **ashab**.
esham (.—) اسهام A fin. share.
eshar (.—) اسحار A lrnd., pl. of **seher** 1.
eshiya (..—) اسخياء A lrnd., pl. of **sahi** 2.
-esi ـه‌سى cf. -ası 2.
esik⁽ᵍⁱ⁾ neol., geol. fault, break (in a lode).
es'ile اسئله A lrnd., pl. of **sual**.
esim (.—) اثيم A lrnd. culpable, guilty, sinful.
esin 1 neol. 1. morning breeze. 2. inspiration.
=esin 2, =esiniz cf. =asın.

esinti اسنتى breeze; light wind. **—li** 1. breezy. 2. capricious, unpredictable.

esir 1 (.—) اسير A 1. slave. 2. prisoner of war, captive. **— almaca** children's game prisoners' base. **— düş=** to be taken prisoner. **—i firaş** bedridden. **— pazarı** slave market. **— ticareti** slave trade.

esir 2 (.—) اثير A anc. sc. ether, aether.

esir=[ir] **3** اسيرمك prov. 1. to be in heat. 2. to be drunk.

esirane (.——.) اسيرانه P lrnd. slavishly, servile.

esirci اسيرجى slave trader. **—lik** slave trade.

esirge=[r] اسيركمك /ı, dan/ 1. to spare, to protect (from). 2. to grudge; to withhold (from). **—me** verbal n. **—n=** pass. of **esirge=**.

esirî (.——) اثيرى A anc. sc. ethereal, aethereal.

esirik[ği] اسيريك prov. in heat (beast), violent, unmanageable.

esirlik[ği] (.—.) اسيرلك captivity, slavery.

esirme neol., psych. ecstasy.

eskal[li] **1** (.—) اثقال A [pl. of **sıkl**] lrnd. 1. weights. 2. burdens, baggage.

eskal[li] **2** اثقل A lrnd., superl. of **sakil**.

eskam (.—) اسقام A lrnd., pl. of **sakam 1**.

eskatologya (....·.) اسقاتولوژيا L phil. eschatology.

eski 1 اسكى 1. old, ancient. 2. former, ex-; veteran. 3. old, worn out; second-hand. **—den** formerly, in old days, in the past. **—ler** 1. the ancients. 2. old things. **— ağza yeni taam, — ağza yeni kaşık** New food for an old mouth (said when eating something for the first time that year). **E— Ahit** the Old Testament. **—den beri** since the old times, all along, for a long time past. **— çamlar bardak oldu** Times have changed; things are not what they were. **— defterleri karıştır=** to dig out old accounts, to delve into the past. **E— Dünya** the Old World (Europe, Asia and Africa). **— göz ağrısı** an old flame. **— hale getirme** law entire restitution. **— hamam eski tas** the same old thing, just the same as ever. **— hayratı da berbat et=** to make something worse by trying to improve it. **— kafalı** old-fashioned (person). **—den kalma** time-honored, old. **— kurt** old hand. **— kütük** an old, experienced man. **— maden** 1. genuine material. 2. real, old chinaware. **—si olmıyanın yenisi olmaz** Those that have no old clothes can't possibly have really new ones. **— pabuç** trifle. **— püskü** old and tattered things, castoffs. **— toprak** healthy and well-preserved person of the old generation. **E— Zeğra** geog. Stara Zagora (in Bulgaria). **E— zaman** hist. antiquity. **— zamanda** in the past, in the old days.

eski=[r] **2** اسكيمك 1. to wear out, become old. 2. to get old in service. **—ci** 1. dealer in secondhand wares, itinerant buyer of junk. 2. cobbler. **—leş=** to become old. **—lik** oldness, ancientness. **—t=** /ı/ 1. caus. 2. to wear to pieces, to use up. **—til=** pass. of **eskit=**.

eskrim اسقريم F sports fencing.

eslâf (.—) اسلاف A lrnd., pl. of **selef**.

esle=[r] اسلمك /ı/ archaic to take notice (of), to obey.

eslem اسلم A lrnd., superl. of **sâlim**.

esliha اسلحه A lrnd., pl. of **silâh**. **—i cariha** hand weapons (daggers, etc.). **—i memnua** prohibited arms. **—i nâriye** firearms.

esma 1 (.—) اسماء A lrnd., pl. of **isim**. **—yi âdad** gram. numerals; cardinal numbers. **—yi celâl** Isl. rel. the names of God. **— çek=** to use prayer beads to recite the names of God. **—yi hasna** the names of God. **—yı üzerine sıçrat=** to look for trouble, to bring trouble upon oneself.

esma 2 (.—) اسمى A lrnd., superl. of **sami**.

esma[aı] **3** (.—) اسماع A lrnd. ears.

esmah اسمح A lrnd. most munificent, most generous.

esmak[ki] (.—) اسماك A lrnd., pl. of **semek**.

esman (.—) اثمان A lrnd., pl. of **semen 2**.

esmar 1 (.—) اثمار A lrnd., pl. of **semer 2**.

esmar 2 (.—) اسمار A lrnd., pl. of **semer 3**.

esmender اسمندر P lrnd., same as **semender**.

esmer اسمر A 1. darkskinned, swarthy. 2. dark, brown. **—leş=** to become darkskinned. **—let=** /ı/ to cause to be brown. **—lik** darkness, brownness.

esna (.—) اثناء A lrnd. interval, course, time. **—sında** during, while; in the course of. **—yi ikamette** in the course of one's stay. **—yi rahta** in the course of the journey, en route.

esnaf 1 اصناف [esnaf 2] A 1. trades, guilds. 2. tradesman, artisan. 3. slang prostitute; pander. **— ağzı** sales talk. **— cemiyeti** artisans' association. **— loncası** guild. **— zihniyeti** commercial-mindedness, mentality of a shopkeeper. **—lık** tradesman's calling.

esnaf 2 اصناف A lrnd., pl. of **sınıf**.

esnah (.—) اسناح A lrnd., pl. of **sinh**. **—ı nücum** astrol. stars outside the lunar mansions. **—ı rieviye** anat. pulmonary cells.

esnam (.—) اصنام A lrnd., pl. of **sanem**.

esnan (.—) اسنان A lrnd. 1. pl. of **sin**. 2. equals.

esne=[r] اسنه مك 1. to yawn; to gape. 2. to stretch and recover shape. 3. to bend, to give (board, etc.); to stretch (material).

esnek[ği] اسنك 1. elastic. 2. prov. gag or muzzle, snaffle-bit. **—lik** elasticity.

esnet=ᶦʳ اِسْنَتْمَكْ /ı/ caus. of **esne**=.
esneyiş اِسْنَيِشْ verbal n. of **esne**=.
esniye اَثْنِيَه A lrnd., pl. of **sena**.
espapᵇᶦ pop., var. of **esvap**.
espri اِسْپْرِى F wit, clever remark, joke. **—li** witty (story).
esr اَسْر A lrnd. a capturing, a taking prisoner.
esraᵃᶦ اَعْرَع A lrnd., superl. of **seri 1**.
esrar 1 (.—) اَسْرَار A 1. mystery. 2. secrets. **— kutusu, — küpü** secretive person.
esrar 2 اَسْرَار [**esrar 1**] hashish. **— çek**= to smoke hashish. **— kabağı, — nargilesi** hubble-bubble (for smoking hashish). **— tekkesi** opium den.
esrarengiz (.—.—) اَسْرَارَ انْگيزْ P lrnd. mysterious.
esrarkeş اَسْرَارْ كَشْ P smoker of hashish, hashish addict.
esre اَسْرَه A Arabic script vowel point for i. **—le**= /ı/ to supply with the i vowel point. **—li** having the vowel point for i.
esri=ʳ اِسْرِيكْ archaic to get drunk.
esrikᵍᶦ اِسْرِيكْ prov. 1. drunk. 2. overexcited. **—lik** drunkenness.
essah صَحْ [**asah**] prov. really, truly.
esselâ (..—) اَلصَّلَا A lrnd. Come and try! (an expression of challenge.)
esselâm (..—) اَلسَّلَامْ A lrnd. greetings. **— aleyk, —ün aleyk, — aleyküm, —ün aleyküm** Greetings to you.
estaᵃᶦ اَسْطَع A lrnd., superl. of **sâti 2**.
estağfurullah (..'...) اَسْتَغْفِرُ اللهْ A (lit. I ask pardon of God.) Don't say so, not at all, don't mention it (phrase used in reply to an expression of thanks, exaggerated praise, or self-criticism.)
estampᵖᶦ F art print, engraving.
estampaj F archeol. squeeze.
estar 1 (.—) اَسْطَار A lrnd., pl. of **satır**.
estar 2 (.—) اَسْتَار A lrnd. 1. lining. 2. cover; curtain.
estek köstek et= اَسْتَكْ كوسْتَكْ اِتْمَكْ colloq. to make all sorts of excuses to get out of doing something.
ester 1 G chem. ester. **—leş**= to esterify.
ester 2 اَسْتَر P lrnd. mule. **—bân** (..—) P muleteer.
estetikᵍᶦ اَسْتَتِيكْ F phil. aesthetics; aesthetic. **—çi** aesthetician.
estir=ᶦʳ اَسْدِيرْمَكْ /ı/ caus. of **es**= 1.
esuf (.—) اَسُوفْ A lrnd. tender-hearted; sorrowful, sad.
esvakᵏᶦ (.—) اَسْوَاك lrnd., pl. of **suk**.
esvapᵇᶦ (.—) اَثْوَابْ A clothes, garment. **—çı** ready-made clothes merchant, secondhand clothes dealer. **—çı başı** Ott. hist. keeper of the wardrobe (of the Sultan). **—lık** material for making clothes.

esvar (.—) اَسْوَار A lrnd., pl. of **sur 1**.
esved اَسْوَدْ A lrnd. black. **—eyn** the two black ones, the snake and the scorpion.
esyaf (.—) اَسْيَافْ A lrnd., pl. of **seyf**.
eş 1 اَشْ 1. one of a pair, mate, fellow. 2. husband; wife. 3. a similar thing, a thing that matches another, a match. **— dost** friends and acquaintances. **— tut**= /ı/ to choose as a partner. **—i yok** peerless.
eş=ᵉʳ **2** اَشْمَكْ /ı/ 1. to dig up slightly, to scratch (the soil). 2. to search and investigate.
eş=ᵉʳ **3** اَشْمَكْ archaic 1. to gallop (horse). 2. /a/ to go (to war or other duty). **—ip yort**= to walk about. **—miş yortmuş** experienced.
eşaim (.—.) اَشْائِمْ A lrnd. people who bring bad luck.
Eşaire (.—..) اَشَاعِرَه A Isl. rel. those who belong to the order of the religious leader **Ebul-Hasan-il-Eş'arî**.
eşanlam, eşanlamlı neol. synonymous.
eş'ar 1 (.—) اَشْعَار A lrnd., pl. of **şiir**.
eş'ar 2 (.—) اَشْعَار A lrnd., pl. of **şa'r**. **—ı guddeviye** bot. glandular hairs. **—ı mümissa** bot. absorbing hairs.
eş'ar 3 اَشْعَر A lrnd. the best of poets. **—i nâs** the best reciters among the people. **—i zaman** the best poets of the time.
eşarpᵇᶦ اَشَارْپْ F scarf; stole.
Eşaya (..—) اَشَعْيَا A Bib. Isaiah.
eşbah 1 (.—) اَشْبَاحْ A lrnd., pl. of **şebah**.
eşbah 2 (.—) اَشْبَاه A lrnd., pl. of **şibh**.
eşbası neol., geog. isobar.
eşbeh اَشْبَه A lrnd. 1. superl. of **şebih**. 2. brave, manly man.
eşbiçim, eşbiçimli neol., chem. isomorphous. **—lik** isomorphism.
eşcaᵃᶦ اَشْجَع A lrnd., superl. of **şeci**.
eşcan (.—) اَشْجَانْ A lrnd. sorrows, troubles.
eşcar (.—) اَشْجَار A lrnd., pl. of **şecer**.
eşdeğer neol., sc. equivalent. **—lik** equivalence.
eşedᵈᵈᶦ اَشَدْ A lrnd., superl. of **şedid**.
eşekᵍᶦ اَشَكْ 1. donkey, ass. 2. vulg. ass; silly, stupid, perverse person; stupid and vulgar. **— arısı** wasp, zool., Vespa; hornet, zool., Vespa crabo. **— at olmaz, ciğer et olmaz** You can't make a donkey into a horse, nor liver into meat. **— balığı** obs. dried codfish. **— başı mısın?** Why don't you use your authority? What are you there for? **— başı mıyım?** Why don't you ask my opinion? What do you take me for? **— büyüdü, semeri küçüldü** He has grown out of all his clothes. **— cenneti** slang prison. **— dâvası** asses' bridge, pons asinorum. **— derisi gibi** very thick and coarse. **— dikeni** thistle, milk thistle, bot., Galactites tomentosa. **—i düğüne çağırmışlar, ya su lâzımdır ya odun demiş** proverb When a donkey is invited to a

eşel

wedding he can only think that people want him to carry wood and water. **—ten düşmüş karpuza dön=** *slang* to be shocked. **— eyeğili** *prov.* 1. obstinate, perverse. 2. lazy, sluggish. **— gibi** like an ass; vulgar, thoughtless. **—e gücü yetmiyen semerini döver** *proverb (lit.* He who is unable to beat the donkey beats its packsaddle.) People take out their revenge on the subordinates of a powerful person. **— herifin damadı** You son-in-law of a donkey. You old fool! **— hıyarı** squirting cucumber, *bot., Ecballium Elaterium.* **— hoşaftan ne anlar?** What does a donkey know about fine foods? **— inadı** stubborn as a mule. **— kadar** grown up, big. **— kadar oldu** It's time he grew up. **— kengeri** carline thistle, *bot., Carlina vulgaris.* **— kulağı** field scabious, *bot., Knautia arvensis.* **—in kulağını kesmekle küheylân olmaz** A donkey does not become a thoroughbred by getting its ears cut short. **— kulaklı** long-eared. **— kurdu** wood louse. **—in kuyruğu gibi ne uzar ne kısalır** Like a donkey's tail, it does not change its length. **— lâlesi gibi açıl=** *obs.* to be bold and impertinent. **— marulu** sow thistle, milk thistle, *bot., Sonchus oleraceus.* **— oğlu eşek!** Donkey son of a donkey! **— oyunu** horseplay. **— pastırması** fatless, bad quality preserved meat. **— sırtı** *arch.* gable roof. **— sineği** gadfly, horsefly, *zool., Tabanus.* **— sudan gelinceye kadar döv=** /ı/ to give (someone) a beating. **— sülüğü** horse leech. **— şakası** coarse practical joke. **—e ters bindir=** /ı/ to pillory, to expose. **— turpu** wild radish, *bot., Raphanus Raphinistrum.* **— zeytini** a large type of olive. **—ce, —cesine** stupidly; asinine, utterly stupid (act). **—ci** donkey driver. **—çik** donkey foal. **—çilik** occupation of a donkey driver. **—len=** to make an ass of oneself. **—lik** folly, utter stupidity.

eşel[III] A *lrnd.* withered in the arm.

eşele=[r] /ı/ 1. to scratch and scrabble. 2. to seek out and inquire into. **—me** *verbal n.*

eş'em A *lrnd.* most unlucky, most inauspicious.

eşer[rri] A *lrnd., superl. of* **şerir**.

eşfak[kı] 1 A *lrnd., superl. of* **şefik**.

eşfak[kı] 2 (.—) A *lrnd.* kind deeds, compassionate acts. **—ı şâmile** kindnesses shown to all people.

eşfakengiz (.—.—) P *lrnd.* touching, effecting.

eşgal[ıı] 1 (.—) A *lrnd., pl. of* **şuğl**.

eşgal[ıı] 2 A *lrnd., superl. of* **meşgul**.

eşha (.—) A *lrnd., superl. of* **şehî** 1.

eşhad (.—) A *lrnd., pl. of* **şâhid**.

eşhas (.—) A *pl. of* **şahs**; characters (of a play or novel), *dramatis personae.*

eşheb A *lrnd.* grey (horse).

eşhedü A *Isl., rel. formula* 'I bear witness'. **— billâh!** by God! **— enne lâ ilâhe illâllah** I bear witness that there is no god but God.

eşher A *lrnd., superl. of* **meşhur, şehîr**.

eşhür A *lrnd., pl. of* **şehr** 1. **—ül hac, —ül malûmat** the four sacred months (Shawwal, Zulkade, Zulhijje, Muharrem).

eşi'a A *lrnd., pl. of* **şua**.

eşidda (..—) A *lrnd., pl. of* **şedid**.

eşik[ğı] 1. threshold. 2. bridge (of a stringed instrument). **— ağası** *Ott. hist.* lord chamberlain. **—ini aşındır=** /ın/ to frequent constantly. **—e çık=** *archaic* to go to the toilet. **—ine gel=** /ın/ to petition. **—ine yüz sür=** to go to a great person to pay one's respects.

eşil=[ır] *pass. of* **eş** 2. **—me** *verbal n.*

eşin=[ır] to scratch and paw the earth (animal).

eşineğitim *neol.* coeducation.

eşinzaman *neol., phys.* synchronous. **—lık** synchronism.

eşirra (..—) A *lrnd., pl. of* **şerir**.

eşit[ıı] *neol.* equal, match, the same. **—çi** *phil.* egalitarian. **—çilik** *phil.* egalitarianism. **—lik** equality. **—sizlik** inequality.

eşk[kı] P *poet.* tears, tear, weeping.

eşkâl[ıı] (.—) A *lrnd., pl. of* **şekl**.

eşkalûd (.—.—) P *lrnd.* tearful.

eşkar A *lrnd.* red-haired (man); dun (horse).

eşkbar (.—) P *poet.* tearful, lachrymose.

eşkefşan (..—) P *poet.* shedding tears, very tearful, weeping.

eşkenar *neol., geom.* equilateral. **— dörtgen** equilateral quadrangle, parallelogram. **— parelelyüz** rhombohedron. **— üçgen** equilateral triangle.

eşkere *prov., var. of* **aşikâre**.

eşkıya (..—) A 1. brigand. 2. *lrnd., pl. of* **şakî** 1. **— gibi** wild-looking (individual). **—lık** banditry, brigandage; rebellion.

eşkin cantering. **—ci** *Ott. hist.* mounted feudal yeoman; irregular cavalryman.

eşkriz (.—) P *poet.* tearful, weeping.

eşkver P *poet.* tearful.

eşle=[r] /ı/ to pair, to match. **—n=** *pass.* **—ndir=** /ı/ *caus.* **—nik** *neol., math.* conjugate. **—ş=** /le/ to pair; to mate, to couple. **—ştir=** /ı/ *caus. of* **eşleş=**.

eşlik[ği] 1. *abstr. n. of* **eş** 1. 2. *neol., mus.* accompaniment.

eşme 1. *verbal n. of* **eş=** 2. 2. scooped

out, shallowly dug. 3. shallow well, waterhole.
eşmel اَشْمَل A *lrnd., superl. of* **şâmil**.
eşnaʾ اَشْنَع A *lrnd., superl. of* **şenî**.
eşneb اَشْنَب A *lrnd.* having fine teeth (man).
eşofman F *sports* sweat pants and sweatshirt.
eşraf (. —) اَشْراف A 1. notables of a town or village. 2. *lrnd., pl. of* **şerif**.
eşrâk[kı] (. —) اَشْراك A *lrnd., pl. of* **şerik, şirk**.
eşrar (. —) اَشْرار A *lrnd., pl. of* **şerir**.
eşrat (. —) اَشْراط A *lrnd., pl. of* **şerat**. —ı saat signs of approaching doom.
eşref اَشْرَف A *lrnd., superl. of* **şerif**. —i evkat the most propitious time. —i mahlûkat the pearl of creation, man. — saat propitious moment, opportune time. —î (..—) name of an old Ottoman gold coin.
eşria اَشْرِعَة A *lrnd., pl. of* **şira'** 3.
eşribe اَشْرِبَة A *lrnd.* drinks, beverages.
eşsıcak *neol., sc.* isotherm.
eşsiz اَشْسيز 1. unmatched, unequalled; unique, peerless. 2. unpaired.
eşteprem *neol., geol.* isoseismal.
eştir[ir] 1 اَشْتِرْمَك /ı, a/ *caus. of* **eş**= 2.
eştir[ir] 2 اَشْتِرْمَك /ı/ *archaic, caus. of* **eş**= 3.
eşüd[ddü] اَشُدّ A *lrnd.* strength, vigor of life.
eşvak[kı] 1 (. —) اَشْواق A *lrnd., pl. of* **şevk** 1.
eşvak[kı] 2 (. —) اَشْواق A *lrnd., pl. of* **şevk** 3.
eşvat (. —) اَشْواط A *lrnd., pl. of* **şavt**, circuits in running races, or esp., circumambulations of the Kaaba at Mecca.
eşya 1 (. —) اَشْيا A 1. things, objects. 2. furniture; luggage; belongings; goods; goods and chattels. — ağırlığı *mil.* baggage train. —yı ayniye goods turned over to the customs authorities as payment in kind of customs fees.
eşya 2 (. —) اَشْيَاع A *lrnd., pl. of* **şia**.
eşyah (. —) اَشْيَاخ A *lrnd., pl. of* **şeyh**.
eşyalı (. —.) اَشْيَالى furnished.
eşyeb اَشْيَب A *lrnd.* white-haired, aged.
eşyükselti *neol., geog.* contour line.
eşzaman *neol., phys.* isochronal. —lık isochronism.
et 1 اَتْ 1. flesh. 2. meat. 3. fleshy part of fruit, pulp, *bot.* sarcocarp. — bağla= to begin to heal (wound). — baltası meat hatchet. — beni small, colored, fatty excrescence on the body. — bezi gland. —i budu yerinde plump. —ine dolgun plump, well-fleshed. —e gömül= to grow into the flesh (fingernail). — kafalı blockhead, stupid. — kanat *prov.* a kind of bat. — kesimi, — kırımı *Chr. rel.* Shrove Tuesday, Mardi gras. — kurdu flyblow, maggot in meat. — lokması a meat dish. E— Meydanı *hist.* name of a square in the Aksaray quarter of Istanbul, where the Janissaries had barracks. —i ne budu ne 1. very lean and thin. 2. too small and unimportant. — oburlar *neol., zool., Carnivora*. —i senin kemiği benim (*lit.* His flesh is yours; his bones are mine.) Be as rough as you want with him (said by a parent to a schoolmaster). — sineği blowfly. — suyu 1. broth of meat, bouillon. 2. gravy. — şeftalisi clingstone peach. — tahtası chopping board. —le tırnak arasına girilmez One should not interfere in the family matters of others. — tırnaktan ayrılmaz You can't separate close relatives or friends. —le tırnak gibi very closely related. — tırnak ol= to become close relatives. — toprak soft, reddish-brown earth. — tutma= not to put on flesh. — uru wen, fleshy tumor. — yaran *path.* deep-seated whitlow. — yemeği dish of meat.
et=[der] 2 اَتْمَك 1. to do, to make. 2. to amount to; to be worth. 3. /ı, dan/ to deprive (of). 4. *nursery language* to have a bowel movement. —tiğini buldu He got his deserts. —tiği hayır ürküttüğü kurbağaya değmez He is more of a hindrance than a help; he causes more harm than good. —tiği ile kal= to be left with nothing but the shame of it (when a design against another has not come off). —tiği yanına kal=, —tiği yanına kâr kal= to get away with (a bad deed).
-et 3 ت *cf.* **-at** 5.
etajer اَتاجَر F set of shelves (in a room), whatnot, dresser (with set of shelves).
etamin اَتامين F coarse muslin.
etba[aʾ] (. —) اَتْباع A *lrnd.* 1. followers. 2. attendants, servants.
etbauttabiîn (. —.—.—) اَتْباعُ التّابِعين A *lrnd.* the disciples of those who learned from companions of the Prophet.
etbent *same as* **entbent**.
etçil *neol., biol.* carnivorous.
etek[ği] اَتَك 1. skirt (of a dress). 2. foot (of a mountain). —i arı *archaic* honest (woman). — bağı *archaic* belt worn to lift the skirt. — belde ready. —i belinde active, industrious (woman). — bezi a wrapping for an infant's legs. — çek= /dan/ to give up, to abandon. — dolusu skirtful, heaps, lots. —ine düş= /ın/ to fall at somebody's feet, to entreat. —i düşük dirty, sloppy, slovenly. — etek heaps, loads. —ini göstermez strictly honest (woman). —leri ıslık çal= to be overjoyed. —ini öp= /ın/ 1. to kiss the skirt (of a superior). 2. to flatter, to toady. — öpmekle ağız aşınmaz no harm in being very respectful (to a superior). — pisliği illegitimate intercourse, dishonesty. —ine sarıl= /ın/ to entreat, to implore. —i savruk untidy, sloppy. — silk= /dan/ to break off relations (with). — tahtası skirting-board (in a toilet). —teki taşı dök= *slang* to be reconciled, to stop

etem

quarrelling. **—i temiz** honest (woman). **—leri topla=** to gather up one's skirts. **—leri tutuş=** to be exceedingly alarmed. **—ine yapış=** /ın/ to entreat, to implore. **—leri zil çalıyor** He is exceedingly glad. **—le=** /ı/ 1. to kiss somebody's skirt. 2. to flatter. **—li** skirted. **—lik** 1. skirt, frock. 2. material for a skirt.

etemᵐᵐⁱ اَتَمّ A lrnd., superl. of **tam**.

etene 1. neol., biol. placenta. 2. prov. placenta (of an animal).

eter اَتَر F chem. ether.

etfalˡⁱ (. —) اَطْفَال A lrnd., pl. of **tıfl**. **—i bağ** poet. young plants, fresh flowers.

etfaiye اَطْفَائِيَه var. of **itfaiye**.

etibba (. . —) اَطِبَّاء A lrnd., pl. of **tabib**. **— odası** Chamber of Physicians, Medical Council. **—yi hâssa** Ott. hist. physicians of the palace.

etiket اَتِيكَت F 1. label, ticket. 2. etiquette.

etimoloji اَتِمُولُوژِى F ling. etymology.

etimolojikᵗⁱ اَتِمُولُوژِيك F ling. etymological.

etioloji اَتِيُولُوژِى F phil., med. etiology.

etken neol. 1. phil., chem. agent. 2. gram. active.

etkıya (. . —) اَتْقِيَاء A lrnd., pl. of **taki** 2.

etki 1 neol. effect, influence.

etki=ʳ 2 /a/ neol., chem. to act (upon).

etkile=ʳ neol. /ı/ to effect, to have influence (upon).

etkili neol., phil. /ı/ effectual. **—lik** phil. efficacy.

etkime neol. action.

etkin neol., sc. active. **—ci** activist. **—ci okul** active school. **—cilik** phil. activism. **—lik** phil., chem. activity.

etli اَتْلِى 1. fleshy, plump. 2. pulpy, fleshy (fruit). 3. meaty, cooked with pieces of meat. **— börek** kind of pastry with ground meat. **— butlu** plump. **— canlı** very healthy, sturdy, ruddy with health (person). **— ekmek** Konya's famous variety of flat bread baked with ground meat, tomatoes, etc. **—ye sütlüye karışma=** to avoid being involved. **— yaprak** bot. fleshy leaf.

etme اَتْمَه verbal n. of **et=** 2.

etmekᵗⁱ اَتْمَك archaic for **ekmek**.

etmen neol., phil., math. factor.

etnografya (. . . .) اَتْنُوغْرَافِيَا It ethnography.

etnoloji اَتْنُولُوژِى F ethnology.

etrab (. —) اَتْرَاب A lrnd. equals in age, contemporaries; companions.

etraf (. —) اَطْرَاف A 1. sides; all sides, world around; surroundings. 2. relatives. 3. anat. extremities, limbs. **—ına** /ın/ around, e. g., **masanın etrafına dizildiler** They lined up around the table. **—ında** /ın/ around, e. g., **evin etrafında bir bahçe var** Around the house there is a garden. **ateşin etrafında dönüyorlar** They turn around the fire. **—iyle** in all detail. **—ını al=** /ın/ to surround. **—ında dört dön=** /ın/ to run (after), to hover (around), to pay great attention (to). **— ve eknaf** the surrounding country. **—lı** detailed. **—lıca** in a detailed manner, in detail.

Etrâkᵏⁱ (. —) اَتْرَاك A lrnd., pl. of **Türk**.

etribe اَتْرِبَه lrnd., pl. of **türab**.

etsiz اَتْسِز 1. fleshless; meatless. 2. thin.

Ettahiyat (. . — —) اَلتَّحِيَّات A name of a certain Muslim canticle.

Ettev'eman (. . . —) اَلتَّوْأَمَان A lrnd., astr. the sign of Gemini.

ettir=ⁱʳ اَتْدِرْمَك /ı, a/ caus. of **et=** 2. **—gen** gram. causative, factitive. **—il=** pass. of **ettir=**. **—t=** /ı, a/ caus. of **ettir=**. **—til=** pass. of **ettir=**.

etüv F 1. sterilizer. 2. drying-out cupboard.

etvar (. —) اَطْوَار A lrnd., pl. of **tavr**. **— ve evza** mode of conduct, way of acting.

eüzü billâh (. —. . —) اَعُوذُ بِاللّٰه rel. formula I take refuge in God. God forbid. Far be it from us.

ev اَو 1. house, dwelling-place. 2. home, household. 3. office, institution, as in **basım evi**. 4. prov. clan, family. 5. Ott. hist. apartment of a prince and his mother in the Sultan's palace. 6. archaic tent. **— aç=** 1. to set up house. 2. to keep a house (brothel). **— alma komşu al** Neighbours are of first importance. **— altı** 1. underground cellar. 2. ground floor. **—de arama** law house search. **—e bak=** 1. to look for a house. 2. to keep house. **— bark** household. **— bark sahibi** family man. **— bas=** to raid a house. **— bekçiliği et=** to be obliged to stay at home. **— boz=** to break up a home. **— doktoru** family doctor. **— ekmeği** homemade bread. **— eşyası** furniture, effects. **— gailesi** worries of a house. **— halkı** household, family. **— hayvanı** domestic animal. **—deki hesap çarşıya uymaz** Things don't turn out as one reckons. **— ıssı** archaic landlord, host. **— idaresi** housekeeping. **— işi** housework. **bir — işlet=** to run a brothel. **— kadını** housewife. **— kirası** rent, house rent. **— kumaşı** homemade material. **—deki pazar çarşıya uymaz** Things don't turn out as one reckons. **— reisi** law head of the house, head of the family. **— reisliği** law authority over the family. **— sahibesi** hostess. **— sahibi** 1. host. 2. landlord. **— sahibi kadın** landlady. **— sahibi mülk sahibi hani bunun ilk sahibi** proverb It is futile to be proud of one's possessions. **— san'atları** domestic arts and crafts. **—i sırtında** homeless; vagabond. **—lere şenlik** Happiness over homes! (expression used while mentioning death or a calamity.) **— takımı** household, family. **— tut=** to hire a house. **— yapıcı** homemaker. **— yemeği** homemade food. **— yık=** to break up a home.

evabid (. —.) اوابد A *lrnd., pl. of* **âbide.**

evahir (. —.) اواخر A *lrnd.* 1. *pl. of* **âhir** 1. 2. the last ten days of a month. **—i ömründe** towards the end of his life.

evail (. —.) اوائل A *lrnd.* 1. *pl. of* **evvel.** 2. the first ten days of a month.

evamir (. —.) اوامر A *lrnd., pl. of* **emr.** **E—i Aşere** *obs., Bib.* the Ten Commandments. **— kalemi** *Ott. hist.* office for vizierial letters.

evan (. —) اوان A *lrnd., pl. of* **an** 1. **—ı şebab** youth.

evâni (. — —) اوانى A *lrnd.* vessels, dishes. **—i sîm ü zer** silver and gold dishes.

evasıt (. —.) اواسط A *lrnd.* 1. *pl. of* **evsat.** 2. the middle ten days of a month.

-evbar (. —) اوبار P *lrnd.* who consumes, which devours, *e. g.*, **merdümevbar, ömrevbar.**

evbaş (. —) اوباش A *lrnd.* low fellows; the rabble. **—ân** (. — —) A the rabble. **—î** (. — —) P the character or conduct of a blackguard.

evc اوج A *lrnd.* 1. summit, apogee. 2. *astr.* aphelion. 3. *same as* **eviç. —i bâlâ** climax. **—i huzî, —i nihavendî, —i puselik** *cf.* **eviç.**

evca[aî] (. —) اوجاع A *lrnd., pl. of* **veca.** **—ı şedide** intense pains.

evcara (. — —) اوجآرا P *Or. mus.* a şed makam produced by transferring the scale of the **zirgüleli hicaz** to the **ırak** pitch.

evce (´.) اوجه with the whole family.

evceb اوجب A *lrnd., superl. of* **vacib.** **—i vecaib** the most necessary thing.

evceğiz اوجغز a little house.

evceh اوجه A *lrnd.* most beautiful; most proper; very noble. **—i akval** the most appropriate words.

evcek[ği] (´.) اوجك same as **evce.**

evcgir (. —) اوجگير P *lrnd.* who occupies the apogee.

evci اوجى 1. weekly boarder. 2. who stays home.

evcik[ği] اوجك small house.

evcil اوجل domesticated.

evcimen, evciment[di] اوجمن home-lover.

evç[ci] *var. of* **evc.**

evdiye اودیه A *lrnd., pl. of* **vadi** 1.

evedi اودى *prov., same as* **ivedi.**

eveğen 1. *neol., med.* acute (illness). 2. *prov.* hasty, fast.

evel اول *var. of* **evvel.**

ever=[ir] اورمك /ı/ *prov.* to give in marriage (daughter); to marry (son).

evet اوت 1. yes, certainly. 2. *archaic* but, however. **— efendimci** yes-man.

evfa (. —) اوفاء A *lrnd.* 1. most loyal. 2. most sufficient.

evfak[kı] اوفق A *lrnd., superl. of* **muvafık.**

evfer اوفر A *lrnd.* 1. most abundant, very numerous. 2. *Or. mus.* rhythmic pattern of nine beats used especially in Mevlevi music. **—i Mevlevi** a rhythmic pattern.

evham (. —) اوهام A *pl. of* **vehm.** **— getir=, —a kapıl=** to imagine things; to be hypochondriac. **—lı** hypochondriac; full of suspicions.

evhaş اوحش A *lrnd.* most wild, very unsociable.

evhen اوهن A *lrnd.* very weak, most feeble.

eviç[vci] اوج [evc] *Or. mus.* an ancient makam. **— aşirân** a compound makam approximately six or seven centuries old. **— gerdaniye** an extinct makam. **— hûzî** *same as* **eviç aşiran. — muhalif** an extinct makam. **— maklub** an extinct makam. **— nihavend** an extinct makam. **— puselik** a compound makam approximately two centuries old.

evidda (.. —) اودّاء A *lrnd.* loving friends. **—yi kadime** old friends.

evin اوين *prov.* kernel; grain of wheat.

evir=[ir] اويرمك /ı/ 1. *neol.* to change, to alter. 2. *archaic* to turn. **—ip çevir=** /ı/ to turn round and round. **—e çevire döğ=** /ı/ to thrash soundly. **—geç** *prov.* baker's shovel. **—me** 1. *verbal n. of* **evir=.** 2. *neol., log.* conversion. **—t=** /ı/ *neol.* 1. *chem.* to invert. 2. *phys.* to reflect. **—tik** *neol., chem.* inverted. **—tim** *neol.* 1. *chem.* inversion. 2. *phys.* reflection.

ev'iye اوعيه A *biol., anat.* vessels, veins, ducts. **—i demeviye** blood vessels. **—i haşebiye** ligneous veins. **—i helezoniye** spiral veins. **—i lenfaiye** lymph vessels. **—i meni** *anat., vesiculae seminales.* **—i münakkata** *bot.* punctate ducts. **—i nâkile** *bot.* conductor veins. **—i süllemiye** *bot.* scalariform vessels.

-evjen اوژن P *lrnd.* who or which overthrows, *as in* **şirevjen, merdevjen.**

evkaf (. —) اوقاف A 1. pious foundations; estates in mortmain. 2. the government department in control of estates in mortmain. **E—ı Hümayun** *Ott. hist.* Imperial estates in mortmain; department of control of these estates. **E—ı Hümayun Hazinesi** *Ott. hist.* Treasury of the Imperial Estates in Mortmain. **E— Nazırı** *Ott. hist.* the minister of mortmain estates. **E— Umum Müdürlüğü** Administration of Estates in Mortmain.

evkâr (. —) اوکار A *lrnd., pl. of* **vekr.**

evkat (. —) اوقات A *lrnd., pl. of* **vakt.** **—ı hamse** the five canonical times for Islamic

evked

worship. —**güzâr** (. — . —) P who passes his time.

evked اوﻛﺪ A lrnd. very firm, most authentic. —**i evâmir** the firmest orders.

evlâ (. —) اوﻟﻰ A lrnd. 1. most suitable, best. 2. /dan/ better (than).

evlâd (. —) اوﻻد A, **evlât**ᵈⁱ 1. child; son. 2. children; descendants. —! (.'.) Poor creature! —**ım!** My child! My son! — **acısı** grief for one's deceased child. —**ı butun** law children of one's daughter. — **canlısı** very fond of his or her children. —**ını dövmiyen dizini döver** proverb He who does not spank his child will regret it. — **edin=** 1. /ı/ to adopt a child. 2. to become a parent. — **ü ıyâl** wife and children, family. —**ı inas** daughters. —**ı sadriye** law a woman's own children. — **sahibi ol=** to become a parent. —**ı sulbiye** law one's own children. —**ı üm** law children of the same mother. —**ı vatan** children of the country. —**ı zuhur** law one's own children and the children of one's son. —**ı zükûr** sons.

evlâdiye (. — — .) اوﻻدﯾﻪ law heirloom. —**lik** a thing that will last for several generations, heirloom.

evlâdiyet (. — — .) اوﻻدﯾﺖ A lrnd. condition of being a direct descendant.

evlâtlıkᵍⁱ اوﻻدﻟﻖ 1. adopted child. 2. foster child. 3. abstr. n. of **evlâd**. —**a kabul et=** /ı/ to adopt. —**tan tardet=** /ı/ to disown (child).

evlekᵍⁱ اوﻟﻚ Gk 1. furrow (in a field). 2. a quarter of a **dönüm**. 3. water-channel, drainage-ditch. 4. slang a ten-lira note.

evlen=ⁱʳ اوﻟﻨﻤﻚ to get married; /le/ to marry. — **barklan=** to marry and have a household. —**dir=** /ı/ caus. —**dirme memuru** marriage registration official, registrar.

evlenme اوﻟﻨﻤﻪ marriage. — **akdi** law marriage, ceremony of marriage. — **dairesi** marriage registration office, registry office. — **kâğıdı** marriage certificate. — **mukavelesi** marriage contract, marriage settlement. — **sigortası** law marriage insurance, dowry insurance. — **tellâllığı** law marriage brokage, negotiation of marriage. — **vâdi** law promise of marriage.

evleviyet اوﻟﻮﯾﺖ A lrnd. preference. —**le** so much the sooner, all the more.

evli اوﻟﻰ married. — **barklı** married and having a household. — **evine köylü köyüne dağıldı** Everybody went to his own place. — **kadın** married woman. —**lik** state of being married. —**lik birliği** law conjugal community.

evliya (. . —) اوﻟﯿﺎء A 1. Muslim saint; saintlike person. 2. lrnd., pl. of **veli**. — **devesi** woodlouse. — **otu** bot., Hedysarum. —**yı umur** lrnd. heads of the administration.

evliyalıkᵍⁱ اوﻟﯿﺎﻟﻖ 1. sainthood; saintliness.

2. fitted to be a saint; innocent, ingenuous. — **sat=**, — **tasla=** to pass as a saint.

evliyaullah (. . — . —) اوﻟﯿﺎءﷲ A lrnd. saints.

evolüsyon F phil. evolution.

evrad 1 (. —) اوراد A |pl. of **vird**| Isl. rel. portions of scripture recited at stated times.

evrad 2 (. —) اوراد A lrnd., pl. of **verd 1**.

evrakᵏⁱ (. —) اوراق A 1. documents, papers. 2. lrnd., pl. of **varak**. — **evrak** in sheets. —**ı halkaviye** bot. verticillate leaves. — **kalemi** record office, registry. — **mahzeni** place where archives are kept. —**ı matbua** law printed publications. —**ı metrûke** papers left behind by a deceased person. — **müdürü** Keeper of Archives in a state office. —**ı müsbite** law document of proof. —**ı müteakıbe** bot. alternate leaves. —**ı mütekabile** bot. opposite leaves. —**ı nakdiye** paper currency, paper money. — **olarak** in sheets. —**ı resmiye** official documents. —**ı umumiye** state archives.

evram (. —) اورام A lrnd., pl. of **verem**.

evran, evren 1 اورن prov. 1. dragon, monster. 2. great; saint. 3. time.

evren 2 neol. universe. —**bilim** neol., phil. cosmology. —**doğum** neol., phil. cosmogony.

evrencen اورﻧﺠﻦ P lrnd. ornamental ring; bracelet. —**dest** P bracelet; armlet. —**pay** (. . . —) P anklet.

evreng اورﻧﻚ P poet. throne. —**nişin** (. . . —) P enthroned, reigning.

evrensel neol. universal.

evride اورده A anat., pl. of **verid**.

evrikᵍⁱ neol., phil., math. inverse.

evril=ⁱʳ اورﯾﻠﻤﻚ pass. of **evir=**. —**ir** neol., phil. convertible.

evrim neol., phil., biol., evolution. —**cilik** evolutionism. —**len=** to evolve.

evrişikᵍⁱ neol., log. converse.

evsaᵃⁱ اوﺳﻊ A lrnd. most extensive, very large, plentiful.

evsaf (. —) اوﺻﺎف A lrnd., pl. of **vasf**. —**ı hamide** praiseworthy qualities.

evsah (. —) اوﺳﺎخ A lrnd., pl. of **vesah**.

evsan (. —) اوﺛﺎن A lrnd. idols.

evsat 1 اوﺳﻂ A 1. lrnd. middle, middling; phys. mean (temperature). 2. Or. mus. a rhythmic pattern of twenty-six beats.

evsat 2 (. —) اوﺳﺎط A lrnd., pl. of **vasat**. 1. middles; middle things. 2. medium, moderate things.

evse=ʳ, **evsele=**ʳ, **evsi=**ʳ اوﺳﻤﻚ اوﺳﯿﻤﻚ prov. to winnow.

evşen اوﺷﻦ A lrnd. toady, sycophant.

evtad (. —) اوﺗﺎد A lrnd., pl. of **veted**. —**ı arz** hills and mountains. —**ı bilâd** princes and chief men. —**ı fem** teeth.

evtan (. —) اوﻃﺎن A lrnd., pl. of **vatan**.

evtar (. —) اوتار A lrnd., pl. of **veter**. —ı âcile urgent needs.

-evüz cf. **-avuz**.

evvab (. —) اوّاب A lrnd. who turns frequently to God in prayer; sincere penitent.

evvah (. —) اوّاه A lrnd. 1. one who often sighs. 2. merciful, compassionate. 3. earnest believer. 4. one who prays much.

evvel اوّل A 1. first; before, earlier, of old. 2. the first part, the beginning. 3. log. antecedent. —**den** beforehand, previously. —**i**, —**leri** formerly. — **âhir**, — **ve âhir** from the very beginning, always. — **ve âhirini bilirim** I know him very well. — **Allah** with God's help; certainly. — **Allah sonra sizin sayenizde** Thanks first to God and then to your help. — **bahar** spring. —**i bed** lrnd. first of all. — **beevvel** first of all, before anything else. — **emirde** first of all. — **hesap sonra kasap** Count your money before you plan your shopping. — **selâm sonra kelâm** First greet, then talk. — **taam sonra kelâm** First eat, then talk (dictum of good manners). — **zaman** old times.

evvelâ ('. —) اوّلا A firstly, in the first place; to begin with.

evvel-be-evvel اوّل باوّل A first of all.

evvelce (.'.) اوّلجه previously, formerly.

evvelen اوّلاً A lrnd. first.

evvelî (. . —) اوّلی A lrnd. first, original, primary.

evvelin (. . —) اوّلین A lrnd. the ancients, who are or were first. — **ve âhirîn** the ancients and people of today.

evveliyat (. . . —) اوّلیات A 1. antecedents. 2. lrnd. first elements, principles, rudiments; preamble.

evveliyet (. . —.) اوّلیت A priority; primacy.

evvelki اوّلکی 1. the former. 2. the (year, month, week) before last. — **gün** the day before yesterday.

evvelsi اوّلسی pop., same as **evvelki²**.

evvel-ül-evâil (. . . . —.) اوّل الاوائل A lrnd. the first of all things.

evvelûn (. . —) اوّلون A lrnd. the first (people).

evzaᵃ¹ (. —) اوضاع A lrnd. 1. gestures. 2. acts, conduct, behavior. 3. position, postures. —ı **baride** cold behavior.

evzah اوضح A lrnd., superl. of **vazıh**.

evzan (. —) اوزان A pl. of **vezn**.

evzar (. —) اوزار A pl. of **vizr**.

ey 1 ای O, e. g., **ey şair!** O poet!

ey 2 ای Here there! What are you doing!

eya (. —) ایا A lrnd. Hey there!

eyadi (. — —) ایادی A lrnd., pl. of **yed**.

—**i nâsda** in the hands of men, in the hands of the public.

eyağ (. —) ایاغ P poet. drinking cup.

eyalat (. — —) ایالات A lrnd., pl. of **eyalet**. —ı **mümtaze** the autonomous provinces of the Ottoman Empire.

eyalet (. —.) ایالت A 1. province. 2. principality.

eyamin (. —.) ایامن A lrnd., pl. of **eymen**. 1. prosperous, fortunate, auspicious things. 2. right hands; right sides.

=**eyaz**= cf. =**ayaz**=.

eye 1 ایه same as **eğe 1**.

eye 2 ایه prov., same as **eğe 3¹**.

eyeği ایگی prov. rib.

eyer ایر saddle. — **baltası** battleax carried on the saddle. — **kaltağı** saddletree. — **kap**= to saddle. — **karpuzu** cantle of a saddle. — **kâsesi** seat of a saddle. — **kaşı** saddlebow, pommel. — **kolanı** saddlegirth. — **vur**= /a/ to put on a saddle. — **vurgunu** saddle-galled. —**ci** saddler, maker of saddles. —**le**= /ı/ to saddle. —**len**= to be saddled. —**let**= /ı, a/ caus. of **eyerle**=. —**li** saddled. —**siz** unsaddled, saddleless, bareback.

eyi ایی var. of **iyi**.

=**eyim** cf. =**ayım**.

=**eyin** cf. =**ayın**.

eyit=ᵉʸᵈᵘ̈ʳ ایت var. of **ayıt**=.

eyle=¹ ایله 1. to make, to do. 2. archaic to say.

eyle 2 ایله archaic, var. of **öyle**. — **olsa** in that case, then.

eylem neol. 1. action. 2. operation. —**li** fully appointed (lecturer). —**siz** acting (lecturer).

Eylûlᵘ̈, **Eylül** (. —) ایلول A September.

eyman (. —) ایمان A lrnd., pl. of **yemin**.

eymen 1 ایمن A lrnd. 1. right (as opposed to left). 2. righthanded. 3. fortunate, happy, prosperous; auspicious. 4. very secure, most trustworthy.

eymen= **2** ایمنك 1. prov. to feel shy, to be timid. 2. /dan/ archaic to be terrified (of).

eymün ایمن A lrnd., pl. of **yemin**.

eyn ایـن A lrnd. Where? — **elmefer** Whither can I fly?

eyrekᵍⁱ ایرك prov., same as **eğrek**.

eyreti ایرتی same as **iğreti**.

eyrim ایریم prov. saddlepad.

eyser ایسر A lrnd. 1. lefthanded. 2. very easy; most moderate. 3. very propitious. —**i eyyam** 1. the most propitious of times; happy days. 2. favorable winds.

eytam (. —) ایتام A lrnd., pl. of **yetim**. — **sandığı** orphan's fund. — **ve eramil** orphans and widows (receiving a pension from the government).

eytişim neol., phil. dialectic.

Eyüp^(bü) ایـّوب [Eyyub] 1. Job. 2. *name of a suburb of Istanbul.*

eyvah (.—) ایوه Alas! **—lar olsun!** What a pity! I am sorry.

eyvallah (ʹ.—) ایوﷲ *pop.* 1. Thanks. 2. Goodby. 3. All right. **— de=** /a/ not to object (to), to agree (to), to accept (everything). **— etme=** /a/ not to want to be obliged (to anyone).

eyvan (.—) ایوان P 1. *arch.* liwan, three-walled vaulted antechamber, open at the front. 2. *lrnd.* upper hall. **—ı mah** Ptolemaic *astr.* lunar sphere. **E—ı Kisra** the palace of the King of Persia. **—ı simabî**, **—ı zerkârî** *poet.* vault of heaven.

eyvay (.—) ایوای A *archaic, poet.* Alas.

eyyam (.—) ایّام A 1. time, period. 2. *naut.* favorable wind. 3. *lrnd., pl. of* **yevm;** prosperous days, better days. 4. *lrnd.* power, influence. **bir —** a while, at one time, for a while. **— adamı** opportunist, insincere man. **—ı âdiye** *lrnd.* weekdays. **— ağası** *same as* **eyyam efendisi. —ı Arab** *hist.* the noted days and battles of the old Arabians. **—ı aşer** *Isl. rel.* the first ten days of Muharrem. **—ı aza** *lrnd.* the days of mourning. **—ı bahur** dog days. **—ı bukalemun** *lrnd.* changeable times. **—ı cem** *Isl. rel.* the four days on which Mecca pilgrims visit Mina and Arafat. **— efendisi** opportunist, timeserver. **— görmüş** who has seen better days. **— hava** fine weather with a fair wind. **—ı madudat** *Isl. rel.* the last three days of the Feast of Sacrifice. **—ı malûmat** *Isl. rel.* the first ten days of the month **Zulhicce. — ola!** May wind and weather be favorable to you. **— reisi** opportunist, timeserver. **— sürmüş** who has seen better days. **—ı şeanin** *Chr. rel.* Palm Sunday and two or three following days. **—ı tercil** *lrnd.* the days of sacrifice in pagan times. **—ı teşrik** *same as* **ˏeyyamı madudat.**

eyyar (.—) ایّار A *lrnd.* May (month).

eyyedallahu (...—.) ایّدﷲ A *lrnd.* May God strengthen.

Eyyub (.—) ایّوب A Job. **—u Ansari** *hist., name of an Arab Commander reported to have died outside Istanbul.*

eyyüha (..—) ایّتها A *lrnd.* O you!

eyzan (ʹ.) ایضاً A *lrnd.* likewise, also.

ez-^(er) **1** ازمك /ı/ 1. to crush, to pound; to bruise. 2. to suppress, to reduce to impotence. 3. *slang* to spend. **— de suyunu iç!** It is absolutely worthless, it is useless.

ez- 2 از P *lrnd.* of, from, out of, as in **ezhercihet.**

eza (.—) اذا A torture, torment, pain; annoyance, vexation. **— çek=, — gör=** to suffer pain, to suffer injustice.

ez'af 1 (.—) اضعاف A *lrnd., pl. of* **zı'f.**

ez'af 2 (.—) اضعف A *lrnd., superl. of* **zaif.**

ezafir (.——) اظافر A *lrnd.* fingernails.

ezan (.—) اذان A *Isl. rel.* call to prayer, the azan. **— oku=** to recite the azan.

ezancümle (.—..) ازآن جمله P *lrnd.* for example.

ezanî (.——) اذانى [*based on* **ezan**] pertaining to the azan. **— saat** the hour as reckoned from sunset.

ezber ازبر P 1. by heart. 2. a learning by heart; lesson to be learned by heart. **—den, —e** 1. by heart. 2. without knowing. **—den bil=, —e bil=** /ı/ to know thoroughly. **—e git=** to proceed blindly. **—e iş gör=** to act without due knowledge. **—e konuş=** to talk without knowledge. **—den oku=** /ı/ to recite by heart. **—e öğren=** /ı/ to learn by heart. **—ci** who learns parrot fashion. **—le=** /ı/ to learn by heart, to commit to memory. **—len=** *pass. of* **ezberle=. —let=** /ı, a/ *caus. of* **ezberle=.**

ezcanüdil (.—..) از جان و دل P *lrnd.* with heart and soul.

ezcümle (ʹ...) ازجمله P for instance.

ezdad (.—) اضداد A *lrnd., pl. of* **zıd.**

ezdir=^(ir) ازدرمك /ı, a/ *caus. of* **ez= 1.**

ezel 1 ازل A *lrnd.* past eternity, time without beginning. **—den** from eternity.

ezel^(lli) **2** اذلّ A *lrnd., superl. of* **zelil.**

ezelî (..—) ازلى A eternal. **— ve ebedî** eternal in the past and eternal in the future. **—lik, —yet** past eternity.

ezgi ازگى 1. tune, note, melody. 2. style, tempo. **—ci** discontented (person).

ezgil ازگیل *prov.* medlar (a fruit).

ezgin ازگین 1. crushed, bruised, smashed. 2. trampled under foot; oppressed, tyrannized. **—lik** feeling of hunger; feeling of faintness.

ezhan (.—) اذهان A *lrnd., pl. of* **zihn. —ı nâs** public opinion.

ezhar 1 (.—) اذخار A *lrnd.* provisions, stores.

ezhar 2 (.—) ازهار A *lrnd., pl. of* **zehr 2.**

ezher ازهر A *lrnd.* shining, bright; **—ül levn** having a shining countenance, beautiful; white.

ezheran (..—), **ezhereyn** ازهران ازهرین A *lrnd.* sun and moon.

ezhercihet ازهرجهت P *lrnd.* from all points of view, all around.

ezıkka ازقّه A *lrnd., pl. of* **zukak.**

ezi (.—) اذى A *lrnd.* hurt, injured; hurtful; annoying.

ezici ازیجى crushing, overwhelming.

ezik^(ği) ازك 1. crushed. 2. bruised and squashed (fruit). **—lik** 1. *abstr. n.* 2. feeling of hunger or faintness.

ezil=ᴵʳ ازلك ازلمك pass. of **ez**= 1. —**ip büzül**= to show signs of embarrassment.
ezille ازلّه A lrnd., pl. of **zelil**.
ezimme ازمّه A lrnd., pl. of **zimam**.
ezin (. —) ازين P lrnd. such as; this; from this.
ezincümle (. — ..) ازين جمله P lrnd. as an instance of this.
ezinpiş (. — —) ازين بيش P lrnd. henceforth.
ezinti ازنتى ازينتى ازندى unpleasant, sinking, fainting sensation about the stomach and heart.
eziyet اذيت A torment, torture; cruelty, ill treatment, injury, pain, hurt, fatigue, suffering. — **çek**= to suffer fatigue, pain, tyranny. — **et**= /a/ to torment, to torture. — **ver**= /a/ to cause pain or great trouble (to).
eziyetkâr (. . . —) اذيتكار P tormenter. —**âne** P cruelly.
eziyetli اذيتلى hard, painful, vexatious, tiring, trying.

ezkadim (. . —) ازقديم P lrnd. from time of old.
ezkâr (. —) ازكار lrnd., pl. of **zikr**.
ezkaza (. . —) ازقضا P by accident, by chance.
ezkiya 1 ازكياء A lrnd., pl. of **zeki** 1.
ezkiya 2 (. . —) ازكياء A lrnd., pl. of **zeki**.
ezman (. —) ازمان A lrnd., pl. of **zemen**.
ezme ازمه 1. verbal n. of **ez**= 1. 2. crushed, pounded; paste.
ezmine ازمنه A lrnd., pl. of **zaman** 1.
eznab (. —) ازناب A lrnd., pl. of **zeneb**.
eznev ازنو P lrnd. again, anew.
Ezrail عزرائيل A var. of **Azrail**.
ezrakᵏⁱ ازرق A lrnd. blue.
ezrar (. —) ازرار A lrnd. buttons.
ezserinev ازسرنو P lrnd. afresh, anew.
ezvac (. —) ازواج A lrnd., pl. of **zevc**.
ezvakᵏⁱ (. —) ازواق A lrnd., pl. of **zevk**.
ezyalˡⁱ (. —) ازيال A lrnd., pl. of **zeyl**.

F

f, F seventh letter of the alphabet.
fa 1 فا F mus. fa. — **anahtarı** mus. bass clef.
fa 2 (—) A Arabic script name of the letter ف (This is the 20th letter of the Arabic, the 23rd of the Ottoman alphabet. In chronograms, it has the numerical value of 80.) —**i fiil** Arabic gram. the first radical (of a root).
faalˡⁱ (. —) فعّال A active. — **âza**, — **üye** active member (of a society). —**âne** (. — —.) P actively.
faale (. — .) فعلة A lrnd. workers, laborers.
faaliyet (. — —.) فعاليت A activity. —**te** active, working, running. — **sahası** 1. field of activity. 2. com. line of business.
fabrika (. .'.) فابريقه It factory, plant, works. — **işi** machine-made. —**cı** factory owner, manufacturer.
fabrikator It, **fabrikatör** F فابريقاتور com. factory owner, manufacturer.

faciˡⁱ (—.) فاجع A lrnd. distressing, horrible.
facia (—..) فاجعه A 1. calamity. 2. drama, tragedy. —**engiz** (—. . .—) P, —**lı** tragic.
facianüvis (—. . .—) فاجعه نويس P obs. dramatist, tragedian.
facir (—.) فاجر A lrnd. dissolute, sinning; adulterous.
faça 1 (.'.) فاچه It naut. a ship's facing the wind with the topsail aback. — **et**= to back the topsail.
faça 2 فاچا It 1. slang face. 2. gambler's slang the card at the bottom of a pack.
façeta (..'.) فاچته It jewelry facet (of a precious stone).
façuna (..'.) فاچنه It naut. a serving, whipping (of a rope). — **et**= /ı/ to serve, whip (rope). — **maçulası**, — **maçunası** serving mallet.
fadıl (—.) فاضل A var. of **fazıl**.
fagosit F physiol. phagocyte.

fağfur (. —) فغفور P 1. *poet.* the Emperor of China. 2. *lrnd.* porcelain. **—i Çin** *poet.* the Emperor of China. **—î** (. — —) P *lrnd.* chinaware; of porcelain, porcelain. **—iye** chinaware.

fahamet (. —.) فخامت A *lrnd.* glory, grandeur. **—lû** (. —. —) *archaic* illustrious, His Highness (formerly used about grand viziers, foreign princes, and the Khedive).

fahametpenâh (. —.. —) فخامتپناه P great, eminent.

fahaşet (. —.) فحاشت A *lrnd.* indecency, obscenity.

fahham (. —) فحّام A *lrnd.* 1. charcoal seller. 2. charcoal burner.

fahhar (. —) فخّار A *lrnd.* habitual boaster.

fahır[hrı] فخر [fahr] *lrnd.* glory, pride, excellence. **—i âlem**, **—i kâinat** the Glory of the World (i. e., the Prophet).

fahız[hzı] فخذ [fahz] *anat.* thigh.

fahim 1 (. —) فاخم A *lrnd.* great, grand, illustrious.

fahim[hmi] **2** فهم *var. of* **fahm**.

fahimane (. — —.) فخيمانه P *lrnd.* illustrious, glorious (in titles).

fahir[hri] **1** فخر [fahr] *same as* **fahır**.

fahir 2 (—.) فاخر A *lrnd.* 1. sumptuous, splendid. 2. who glories in his deeds. 3. *w. cap.*, man's name.

fahire (—..) فاخره A *lrnd.*, *fem. of* **fahir 1, 2**.

fahiş (—.) فاحش A 1. excessive, exorbitant. 2. *lrnd.* obscene, immoral. **— cezai şart** *law* excessive penalty. **— faiz** *law* usurious interest. **— fiat** exorbitant price, *law* unlawful price. **— hata** gross error.

fahişe (—..) فاحشه A 1. harlot, prostitute. 2. *lrnd.*, *same as* **fahiş**.

fahl فحل A *lrnd.* eminent man.

fahm فحم A 1. *chem.* carbon. 2. *lrnd.* charcoal, coal. **—i hayvani** animal charcoal. **—i nebati** vegetable coal. **—i türabi** pit coal, mineral coal. **—î** (. —) A *chem.* carbonic. **—iyet** (. —.) *chem.* carbonate.

fahr فخر A *same as* **fahır**. **—i Edhemi**, **—i Hüseynî** *Bektashi order* kinds of dervish headgear.

fahri (. —) فخرى A honorary (title, member), volunteer. **—yat** (. — —) A honorary deeds, objects of pride.

fahriye (. —.) فخريه A *literature* poem of self-glorification.

fahriyen (. —.) فخريا A *lrnd.* honorary; without payment.

fahs فحص A *lrnd.* investigation, examination.

fahşa (. —) فحشاء A *lrnd.* obscene behaviour, immorality.

fahte (—.) فاخته P 1. *poet.* ring-dove; turtle-dove. 2. *Or. mus.* a rhythmic pattern of 20 beats.

fahur (. —) فخور A *lrnd.* 1. self-glorifying. 2. big, large. **—ane** (. — —.) P boastingly; self-glorifying (manner).

fahz فخذ A *same as* **fahız**. **—î** (. —) A *anat.* femoral.

faide (—..) فائده A *lrnd.* 1. *same as* **fayda**. 2. didactic anecdote, moral tale. 3. *archaic* interest. **—cu** (—.. —) P interest-seeker. **—mend** (—...) P profitable, useful.

faik[ki] (. —.) فائق A 1. superior. 2. *lrnd.* excellent. **—iyet** (—. —.) superiority.

fail (—.) فاعل A 1. agent, author; *law* author (of a crime), perpetrator. 2. *gram.* subject. **—i asli** *law* principal author (of a crime). **F—i Hakikî** the Real Actor, God. **—i muhtar** *law* free agent. **F—i Mutlak** the Absolute Actor, God. **—i müstakil** *law* the sole author (of a crime). **—i müşterek** *law* accomplice, associate.

failî (—. —) فاعلى A *lrnd.*, *law* acting, active, efficient. **—yet** (—. —.) *lrnd.* 1. effect, effectiveness; *phil.* efficiency, activity. 2. *gram.* quality of being the subject.

faiz 1 (—.) فائض A 1. interest. 2. *lrnd.* abundant, copious. **— al=** to charge interest. **—i basit** simple interest. **—in faizi** compound interest, interest on interest. **— fiatı** rate of interest. **— getir=** to yield interest. **— haddi** limit of the rate of interest. **— hesabı** computation of the interest. **—i işle=** to yield interest. **—le işlet=** /ı/ to invest on interest. **—i müfred** simple interest. **—i mürekkep** compound interest. **— nispeti** rate of interest. **— öde=** to pay interest. **— ver=** to allow interest. **—e ver=** /ı/ to lend on interest. **—e yatır=** /ı/ to put out at interest. **— yürüt=** to calculate interest.

faiz 2 (—.) فائز A *lrnd.* successful, fortunate. **— ol=** to succeed; /a/ to attain.

faizci (—..) فائضجى usurer, money lender.

faizlen=[ir] (—...) فائضلن to bear interest, to yield interest.

faizli (—..) فائضلى at interest, interest-bearing.

faizsiz (—..) فائضسز free of interest.

fak[kı] فخ [Arabic fakhkh] *prov.* snare, trap. **—a bas=** to be deceived, to be duped. **—a bastır=** /ı/ *caus.*

faka (—.) فاقه A *lrnd.* poverty. **—i şedide** great need.

fakahet[ti] (. —.) فقاهت A *lrnd.* expertise in the canon law of Islam. **—li** expert in the canon law of Islam. **—lû** (. —. —) title given to experts of the canon law of Islam.

fakar (. —) فقار A *lrnd.* vertebrae. **—i** (. — —) A vertebral.

fakat فقط A 1. but, however. 2. *archaic*

only, merely. **—i makati yok** No excuses accepted.
fakd نَقْد A *lrnd.* lack, absence. **—i nakd** lack of money.
fakfon فاقفون German silver.
fakı فاقى [**fakih**] *prov.* learned man (in the village).
fakıa (—..) فاقعه A *lrnd.* misfortune, calamity.
fakır فقر *var. of* **fakr**.
fakîd (.—) فقيد A *lrnd.* missing, lost.
fakih (.—) فقيه A expert in the canon law of Islam.
fâkihe (—..) فاكهه A *lrnd.* fruit.
fakihetüşşita (—....—) فاكهة الشتاء A *lrnd.* fire (for heating).
fakir 1 فقير [**fakir 2**] 1. poor, needy, pauper; beggar; poor fellow. 2. your humble servant. **— düş=** to become poor. **— fukara** the poor. **—in tesellisi ölümdür** *proverb* Only death ends a poor man's troubles.
fakir 2 (.—) فقير A 1. fakir. 2. dervish. 3. *lrnd.*, *same as* **fakir 1**. **—i vakîr** *lrnd.* poor and crushed by adversity. **—ane** (.——.) P poorly.
fakirhane (.——.) فقيرخانه P the house of your humble servant, *i. e.* my house.
fakirleş=ir فقيرلشمك to become poor.
fakirlikgi فقيرلك poverty.
fakr فقر A *lrnd.* poverty, need, want. **— u fâka** utter poverty, destitution. **—ı hal kâğıdı** certificate of poverty. **— u sefalet** utter poverty. **—ı tam** *myst.* complete union with God. **— u zaruret** utter poverty, destitution. **—i fahri** «My poverty is my pride» (saying of the Prophet).
fakrüddem فقرالدم A *path.* anemia.
faksimil F, **faksimile** L *print.* facsimile.
faktör فاكتور F *sc.* factor.
fakulya (../.) فاكوليا Gk *arch.* spandrel.
fakülte (../.) فاكولته F college of a university, school of a university.
falli **1** فال [**fal 2**] 1. fortune (fate, destiny). 2. fortune-telling, soothsaying. **— aç=** to tell fortunes by cards. **— at=** to cast lots. **— bak=**, **—a bak=** to tell fortunes. **—ına bak=** /ın/ to tell someone's fortune. **— dik=** *obs., same as* **fal tut=**. **— taşı gibi aç=** /ı/ to open wide (eyes). **— tut=** to seek a sign or omen from the Book.
falli **2** (—) فال [*Arabic* fa'l] 1. omen, augury. 2. *same as* **fal 1**. **—i hayr** good omen.
falakkı فلك A *lrnd.* 1. stocks (punishment). 2. dawn. 3. all creation. **F— Suresi** name of the 113th sura of the Quran.
falaka فلقه A 1. a staff with a loop of rope let through two holes, by which the feet of a culprit are held up for the bastinado. 2. *naut.*

short rope spliced on a rope or yard for holding it in position. **—ya çek=** /ı/, **— vur=** /a/, **—ya vur=**, **—ya yatır=**, **—ya yık=** /ı/ to subject to a bastinado.
falakacı فلقه جى *Ott. hist.* one of the men in the retinue of the Grand Vizier who administered the bastinado to any wrongdoers the Grand Vizier happened to see while touring through the streets. **— başı** captain of the **falakacı** group.
falan فلان [**fülân**] *colloq.* 1. so and so. 2. and so on, etc. 3. and such like; about, approximately. **— falaka**, **— falan**, **— festekiz**, **— feşmekân**, **— fıstık**, **— filân**, **— fistan**, **— fişman** *same as* **falan²**. **—ca** *same as* **falan¹**. **—ıncı** the so-manyeth. **—istan** such and such a land.
falcı فالجى fortune-teller. **—lık** fortune-telling.
falçeta (../.) فالچته It shoe-making curved shoe knife.
falic (—.) فالج A *lrnd.* paralysis; hemiplegia.
falih (—.) فالح A *lrnd.* lucky, successful.
falname (.—.) فالنامه P oracular book used in fortune-telling.
falso 1 (./.) فالصو It 1. false note. 2. *colloq.* blunder, false step. **— et=**, **— ver=** to make a blunder, to put one's foot in it. **— yap=** 1. to play a false note. 2. to make a slip.
falso 2 (./.) فالصو It *naut.* jury. **— patrisası** jury backstay.
falya, falye (./.) فاليه It touch-hole, vent of a muzzle-loading gun. **— çivile=** to spike a gun. **— deliği** touch-hole. **— iğnesi** pricker, priming-needle. **— otu** priming of a fire-arm. **— teknesi** priming-pan. **— ver=** *archaic* 1. to spring a leak. 2. to have its touch-hole worn out (gun).
falûz (——), **faluzec** (——.) فالوذ فالوذج *lrnd., vars. of* **palude**.
falzen (—.) فالزن P *lrnd.* soothsayer, fortune-teller, diviner.
fam 1 (—) فام P *lrnd.* color.
-fam 2 (—) فام P *lrnd.* colored, *as in* **gülfam, minafam**.
familya (./.) فاميليا It 1. wife. 2. family; *biol.* family.
fan=ar فانمق *prov.* to become old and worn out.
fanatikgi فاناتيك F fanatic.
fanatizm فاناتيزم F fanaticism.
fanfan فان فان 1. unintelligible (chatter). 2. talking like a toothless old person. **— böceği** bombardier beetle.
fanfar فانفار F 1. brass band. 2. flourish (of trumpets), fanfare.
fanfin فان فين *pop.* foreign-sounding talk. **— et=** to talk in a foreign language.

fangri Gk bream, *zool.*, *Pagrus*.

fanıkᵍⁱ (فانق) *prov.* old and worn out.

fâni (——) فانى A transitory, perishable. **— dünya** the transitory world.

fanilâ (.'.) فانيلا فانـُر It 1. flannel undershirt. 2. *obs.* flannel.

fanilikᵍⁱ (——.) فانيلك transitoriness, perishability.

faniyet (——.) فانيت |*based on* **fânî**| transitoriness.

fanso (.'.) فانسو var. of **falso** 1, 2.

fanta (.'.) فانت blue titmouse, *zool.*, *Parus caeruleus*.

fantazma (.'.) فانتازم Gk *psych.* phantasm.

fantazi فانتازى *var. of* **fantezi**[1].

fantaziya 1 (..'..) فانطازيه It 1. *mus.* fantasia. 2. fantasia (equestrian performance).

fantaziya 2, fantaziye (.'..) فانطازيا فانازيه Gk 1. phantasy, fancy, imagination. 2. pomp and parade. 3. kind of satin. 4. *same as* **fantezi**[1].

fantezi فانتزى F 1. fancy, de luxe, pompous. 2. fancy, imagination. **— harf** *print.* any type that is not Roman.

fanus 1 (—.) فانوس [**fanus 2**] 1. glass cover; cup-shaped glass cover over the light holes in the cupola of a bath. 2. lamp glass.

fanus 2 (——) فانوس A *lrnd.* 1. lantern. 2. lighthouse. **—i gerdan, —i hayal** 1. painted gauze shade that revolves with the heat of the lamp. 2. the revolving spheres.

fanya (.'.) فانى Gk wide-meshed part of a fishnet.

far 1 فار F headlight.

far 2 (—) فار A *lrnd.* mice, rats.

farʳʳ **3** (—) فارّ A *lrnd.* 1. fugitive, deserter. 2. *law* who on the point of death divorces his wife.

farad F *elec.* farad.

faraon F *card game* faro.

faraş فراش [**ferraş**] dust pan. **— gibi**, **— kadar** very large (mouth).

faraza (.'.—) فرضا [**farzen**] supposing, let us suppose.

farazi (..—) فرضى |*based on Arabic*| hypothetical.

faraziyat (..——) فرضيات [**farziyat**] *pl. of* **faraziye**.

faraziye (..—.) فرضيه |*based on Arabic*| hypothesis, supposition, assumption.

farbala (.'..) فاربالا F *tailor.* furbelow.

fare (—.) فاره A 1. house mouse, *zool.*, *musculus*. 2. brown rat, *zool.*, *Rattus norvegicus*. **—ler cirit oynuyor** «The mice are playing jereed» (said of a deserted place). **— deliği** 1. mouse hole. 2. hiding place. **— deliğine sığmamış, bir de kuyruğuna kabak bağlamış** The mouse could not squeeze into its hole and, to make matters worse, it had tied a pumpkin to its tail (said to describe an additional complication to an already difficult situation, or when an uninvited guest takes a friend along, too). **— düşse başı yarılır** completely empty. **— kapanı** mouse trap. **— kulağı** mouse ear hawkweed, *bot.*, *Hieracium Pilosella*. **— kuyruğu eğe** round file. **— zehiri** rat poison.

farfara (.'..) فارفاره |*based on Arabic*| windbag; braggart. **—cı** braggart. **—lık** idle bragging.

farı=ʳ فارى *prov.* 1. to grow old. 2. to get tired; /dan/ to get tired (of).

farıkᵏⁱ (—.) فارق , **farıka** (—..) فارقه A *vars. of* **farik, farika**.

farıt=ⁱʳ فارى /ı/ *prov., caus. of* **farı=**.

fariğ (—.) فارغ A *lrnd.* 1. free from work, at leisure, at peace. 2. /dan/ exempt (from); free (from). 3. *law* who conveys (property). **— ol=** 1. to cease from work. 2. /dan/ to cede, renounce.

fariğülbalˡⁱ (—..—) فارغ البال A *lrnd.* carefree.

fariğülhalˡⁱ (—..—) فارغ الحال A *lrnd.* in good circumstances, well off.

farikᵏⁱ (—.) فارق *lrnd.* distinguishing, separating, distinctive.

farika (—..) فارقه A *same as* **alâmeti farika**. **—vi** (—..—) characteristic, typical, distinguishing.

farilˡⁱ فاريل E *fishing* border rope for furling a net.

farinks فارنكس L *anat.* pharynx.

faris (—.) فارس A *lrnd.* 1. rider on a horse, skillful rider. 2. *w. cap.* Persia.

Farisî (—.—) فارسى A 1. the Persian language; Persian. 2. *lrnd.* a Persian. **—ce** *pop., same as* **Farisî**[1].

farisiyat (—.——) فارسيات A *lrnd.* 1. Persian literature. 2. Persian writings (of a poet).

fariza (.—.) فريضه A *same as* **feriza**.

farkᵏⁱ فرق A 1. difference. 2. discrimination. 3. *lrnd.* parting of hair; head; summit. **— et=***. **— gör=, — gözet=** to discriminate, to treat differently; to differentiate. **—ı küllî** great difference. **—ında ol=** /ın/ to notice, to be aware (of). **— olun=***. **—ı tam** *Isl. myst.* the condition of a saint who abandons all earthly ties and is entranced in union with God. **— tut=** *same as* **fark gör=**. **—ına var=** /ın/ to notice, to become aware (of).

farket=ᵈᵉʳ فرق ايتمك 1. /ı/ to notice, realize, perceive. 2. to differ, to make a difference.

farklı فرقلى 1. different. 2. better; dearer. **— tarife** *com.* differential price list. **—ca** 1. slightly different. 2. slightly better.

farkolun=ᵘʳ فرق اولنمق *pass. of* **farket=**.

farksız فرقسز 1. without any difference, same, equal; /dan/ same (as), identical (with) 2. without discrimination. 3. indistinct, imperceptable.

farmason فارماسون F 1. freemason. 2. *pop.* atheist. —**luk** freemasonry.

fars 1 فارس F 1. farce, mockery, comedy. 2. *theat.* farce.

Fars 2 (—) فارس P the province of Fars in Persia.

Farsî 1 (— —) فارسى P *lrnd.*, same as **Farisî**.

farsi 2 فارسى *arch.*, carpentry with the corner cut off.

farş فارش Gk *naut.* bottom planks.

fart فرط A *lrnd.* excess, overdoing, exaggeration. —**ı enaniyet** *psych.* egotism, overselfishness. —**ı hassasiyet** *psych., path.* oversensitiveness. —**ı mesai** overwork. —**ı muhabbet** doting love, too much love. —**ı nezaket** overpoliteness, scrupulous politeness. —**ı semen** *path.* adiposity. —**ı tağdiye** over-feeding. —**ı teessür** excessive grief. —**ı zekâ** great intelligence.

farta furta فارتا فورتا same as **fart furt**. —**sı yok**, —**sız** tactless, inconsiderate; awkward, clumsy.

fart furt فارت فورت *colloq.* brag; empty threats. — **et=** to brag; to throw about threats, to throw one's weight about. —**çu** braggart.

faruk^(ku) (— —) فاروق A *lrnd.* 1. who discriminates between right and wrong. 2. *w. cap, title* given to the Caliph Omar. —**ane** (— — —.) P justly, fairly.

farz فرض A 1. *rel.* obligatory act. 2. binding duty. 3. *lrnd.* supposition, hypothesis. —**ı ayn** *rel.* duty applicable to all. — **et=*. —ı kifaye** *rel.* a duty the observance of which, by some, will absolve the rest. —**ı muhal** supposing the impossible that... — **oldu** It has become a necessity; it has become a «must». — **sahibi** *can. law* legatee of the first degree.

farzen (.'.) فرضاً A *lrnd.*, same as **faraza**.

farzet=^(der) فرض ایتمك /ı/ to suppose, to imagine.

farziyat (..—) فرضيات A *lrnd.*, same as **faraziyat**.

Fas 1 فاس A *geog.* 1. Morocco. 2. Fez.

fas 2 فاس F *photography* front-view. —**tan resim** full-face portrait.

fas^(ssı) **3** فص A *lrnd.* gem cut for setting.

fasafiso (...'.) فاصه فيصو *slang* empty words, nonsense, trash.

fasahat^(tı) (.—.) فصاحت A same as **fesahat 1**.

fasamen F lorgnette.

fasarya (.'.) فاسارىا Gk *slang* nonsense, trash.

fasat^(dı) فاصات F *arch.* façade.

fasd فصد A *lrnd.* a lancing a vein; phlebotomy.

faseta (..'.) فاسته F facet (of a precious stone). —**lı** facetted.

fasıl^(slı) **1** فصل |**fasl**| 1. chapter, section. 2. *Or. mus.* a concert program all in the same **makam**. 3. *lrnd.* season. 4. *lrnd.* act (of a play). 5. *lrnd.* gossip; slander. 6. *lrnd.* solution. —**ı bahar** *poet.* spring. — **heyeti** *Or. mus.* orchestra. —**ı müşterek** *geom.* intersection; edge. —**ı rebi** *poet.* spring.

fasıl 2 (—.) فاصل A *lrnd.* separating, dividing.

fâsıla (—..) فاصله A interval; interruption. — **ver=** to make a break; /a/ to interrupt. —**lı** intermittent, interrupted. —**sız** continuous, uninterrupted; incessantly.

fasid (—.) فاسد A *lrnd.* vicious; perverse. — **daire** vicious circle.

fasih (.—) فصيح A correct and clear (speech); eloquent, fluent. —**âne** (.— —.) P clearly and distinctly; correctly and fluently.

fasihülkelâm (.—..—) فصيح الكلام A *lrnd.* eloquent.

fasik^(kı) (—.) فاسق A *lrnd.* 1. impious; depraved. 2. sinner.

fasikül فاسيكول F fascicule.

fasile (.—.) فصيله A 1. *bot.* family. 2. *lrnd.* family; category. —**i fülfüliye** *bot.*, Piperaceae. —**i haşhaşiye** *bot.*, Papaveraceae. —**i hayzuraniye** *bot.*, Junceae. —**i kibritiye** *bot.*, Lycopodiaceae. —**i lahmiye** *bot.*, Crassulaceae. —**i salibiye** *bot.*, Cruciferae. —**i sanevberiye** *bot.*, Coniferae. —**i sencariye** *bot.*, Boraginaceae. —**i şakikiye** *bot.*, Ranunculaceae. —**i şefeviye** *bot.*, Labiatae. —**i zeytuniye** *bot.*, Oleaceae.

fasiyes F *geol.* facies.

fasl فصل A same as **fasıl 1**.

fasla فصله |**fasıla**| *math.* abscissa.

faslı فاسى Moroccan.

fasone فاصونه F *text.* figured (with woven-in design).

fassad (.—) فصاد A *lrnd.* phlebotomist.

fassal^(lı) (.—) فصال A *lrnd.* slanderer, detractor.

fasulya, fasulye (..'.) فاصوليه Gk. bean. — **mı dedin?** *slang* «Did you say beans?» (said to someone who has been talking nonsense). — **gibi kendini nimetten say=** to think oneself very important, to put on airs. —**cı** *gambler's slang* scorer.

fasya فاسيا L *anat.*, fascia.

faş (—) فاش P *lrnd.* divulged, well known. — **et=** /ı/ to divulge, to betray (a secret). — **ol=***.

faşır faşır فاشر فاشر pss! pss! (noise of boiling water or urinating).

faşî (— —) فاشى A *lrnd.* divulged.

faşist فاشيست It Fascist.

faşol=ur فاش اولمه to become known and talked of.
fatanet (.—.) فطانت A same as **fetanet**.
fâtıkki (—.) فاتر A lrnd. who rends, rips or tears; who solves. — **u râtık-ı umur** a good manager of affairs.
Fatımî (—.—) فاطمی A hist. Fatimid. **—ye** the Fatimid dynasty.
fatır (—.) فاطر A lrnd. the Creator. **F—a Suresi** name of the 35th sura of the Quran.
fatih (—.) فاتح A 1. conqueror. w. cap. Mehmet II, the Conqueror. 3. lrnd. that opens.
Fatiha (—..) فاتحه A Isl. rel. the opening chapter of the Quran. — **oku**= 1. to recite the **Fatiha**. 2. to give up hope. **—han** (—..—) reciter of the **Fatiha**.
fatihan (—.—) فاتحان P lrnd., pl. of **fatih**. — **evlâdından** descendant of a family that came in with the Conquest.
Fatihülebvab (—...—) فاتح الابواب A 1. Isl. rel. the Opener of Doors, God. 2. l. c., a conqueror of cities. 3. name given to Mehmed II, on conquering Constantinople.
fatikki (—.) فاتك A lrnd. who assails boldly; daring, venturesome.
fatin 1 (.—) فطين A lrnd. very intelligent.
fâtin 2 (—.) فاتن A lrnd. seducer, corrupter.
fatir 1 (—.) فاتر A lrnd. weak, languid, tired.
fatîr 2 (.—) فطير A lrnd. 1. unleavened (bread). 2. unworked, immature, crude.
fatura (..'.) فاطوره A It invoice. — **tanzim et**= to make out an invoice.
fava (.'.) فاوا Gk mashed broad beans.
favori فاوری F 1. whiskers. 2. horse racing the favorite.
favul فاول E football foul.
fay 1 فای F geol. fault.
fay 2 فای F text. faille.
fayda فایده [faide] profit; use; advantage. **—sı dokun**= to come in useful, to help. — **yok** It's no use; there is nothing to be done. **—cıl** neol., phil. utilitarian. **—cılık** neol., phil. utilitarianism. **—lan**= /dan/ to profit (by); to make use (of). **—lı** useful, profitable, advantageous. **—sız** useless, vain.
fayrap فایراپ E naut. Fire up! — **et**= 1. naut. to get up steam. 2. slang to open fully.
faysal فیصل A var. of **feysal**.
fayton فایطون F phaeton.
faz فاز F phys. phase.
fazahatti (.—.) فضاحت lrnd. shameful act.
fazazet (.—.) فظاظت A rudeness, hardness; using bad language.
fazıl (—.) فاضل A lrnd. 1. virtuous. 2. superior.

faziha (.—.) فظیحه A lrnd. shameful act.
fazilet (.—.) فضیلت A virtue, goodness, grace; merit. **—lû** (.—.—) Ott. hist., the official title of high canonical functionaries. **—mend** (.—..) P lrnd. virtuous, gracious. **—perver** (.—...) P virtuous, good.
fazl فضل A lrnd. 1. excess. 2. generosity. 3. virtue, grace. 4. superiority. **—ı Hak ile** by the grace of God. **—ı müşterek** math. interval of an arithmetic progression.
fazla فضلا A 1. excessive; superfluous. 2. remainder. 3. /dan/ more (than). 4. too much; very much; too many. 5. a lot; plenty. **—siyle** amply; abundantly. — **gel**= to be too much. — **git**= to go too far; to overdo. — **mal göz çıkarmaz** There is no harm in having a little extra. — **olarak** furthermore; moreover, besides. **—laş**= to increase. **—lık** excess; abundance; surplus.
fe name of the letter **f**.
febiha ('.—) A lrnd. Well and good! So much the better.
fecaatti (.—.) فاعت [based on Arabic] calamity, tragedy, catastrophe.
fecayiti (.—.) فجایع A lrnd., pl. of **facia**.
fecere فجره A lrnd., pl. of **facir**.
feciti (.—) فجیع A tragic; painful; terrible.
fecia (.—.) فجیعه A lrnd. tragedy; calamity.
fecircri فجر [fecr] dawn. **F—i Âti** «Dawn of the New Age» (literary school about 1900-1910). **—i kâzib** false dawn. **—i sadık** the true dawn, beginning shortly before sunrise. **F— Suresi** name of the 89th sura of the Quran. **—i şimalî** aurora borealis, the northern lights.
fecr فجر A same as **fecir**.
feda (.—) فدا [fida] sacrifice; a sacrificing. — **et**= /ı/ to sacrifice. — **ol**= to be sacrificed. — **olsun!** Let it be sacrificed! (said by the person who relinquishes).
fedaî (.—.—) فدائی P one ready to sacrifice his life, volunteer. **—lik** self-sacrifice. **—yan** (.—.—) P self-sacrificing (persons).
fedakâr (.—.—) فداکار P self-sacrificing; devoted, loyal. **—ân** (.—.—) P loyal and devoted persons. **—âne** (.—.—.) P in a devoted manner. **—î** (.—.—) P loyalty. **—lık** 1. self-sacrifice, devotion. 2. great difficulties and expense.
feddan (.—) فدان A acre measure (in Syria and Egypt).
fedre •—. فدره P arch. mat laid on the roof and daubed with clay.
feemma فاما A lrnd. and then as to (so and so).
feharis (.—.) فهارس A lrnd., pl. of **fihris**.
fehavi (.—.—) فحاوی A lrnd., pl. of **fehva**.
fehd فهد P lrnd. hunting-panther, leopard.
fehham (.—) فهام , **fehim 1** (.—) فهیم

A *lrnd.* quick on the uptake.
fehim 2 فهيم A *same as* **fehm**.
fehm فهم A *lrnd.* comprehension, understanding. — **et=** /ı/ to understand, comprehend.
fehmî (. —) فهمى A *lrnd.* pertaining to understanding.
fehmsaz (. —) فهمساز P *lrnd.* intelligible, reasonable.
fehüvelmatlûb (. . . . —) فهو المطلوب A *lrnd.* that is exactly what is wanted.
fehva (. —) فحوى A *lrnd.* tenor, import. —**sınca** as the saying goes, according to (the saying).
feillâ فئلّا A *lrnd.* otherwise.
fek[kki] **1** فك A *anat.* jaw. —**i âlâ** upper jaw. —**i esfel** lower jaw.
fek[kki] **2** فك A *lrnd.* 1. a severing, detaching, separation. 2. a solving (a difficulty). — **et=***. —**i hacz** *law* release from distress. —**i mühr** 1. a breaking a seal. 2. *law* removal of seals. —**i rabıta** a breaking off of relations. —**i rakabe** *law* manumission. —**i rehn** *law* release from pledge. —**i şefe** *poet.* a parting of the lips.
fekahet (. —.) فكاهت A *lrnd.* joyousness, jolliness.
fekat فقط A *same as* **fakat**.
fekçe فكچه | *based on Persian* | *biol.* mandible.
fekke فكّه A *lrnd.* breach, gap.
fekket=[der] فك ايتمك |**fek 2**| /ı/ *lrnd.* to sever, detach, separate; to break open; to undo, raise.
fekkî (. —) فكّى A *anat.* maxillary.
fekül F *chem.* fecula.
felâcerem (. —..) فلاجرم A *lrnd.* without fail.
felâh (. —) فلاح A 1. prosperity, happiness. 2. deliverance. — **bulma=** to be in a hopeless state.
felâhan (. —.) فلاحن , (. ——) فلاحان P *lrnd.* sling (for missiles).
felâhat[li] (. —.) فلاحت |*Arabic* **filaha**| *lrnd.* agriculture.
felâhyab (. ——) فلاحياب P *lrnd.* prosperous, happy.
felâket (. —.) فلاكت | *based on Arabic* | disaster, calamity, catastrophe. —**e uğra=** to meet with a disaster. —**i uzma** dreadful calamity. —**dide** (. —.—.) P calamity-stricken. —**li** disastrous. —**zede** (. —...) P victim of a disaster. —**zedegân** (. —...—) P victims of a disaster.
felâsife (. —..) فلاسفه A *lrnd.*, *pl. of* **feylesof**.
felat (. —) فلات A *lrnd.* waterless waste, desert.
Felâtun (. ——) فلاطون P *same as* **Eflâtun**.

felç[ci] فلج | *based on Arabic* | *path.* 1. paralysis. 2. hemiplegia. — **isabet et=** /a/ to have a stroke. —**i kısmî** partial paralysis. —**i nısfî** hemiplegia. —**e uğra=** 1. to be paralyzed. 2. to have a stroke. —**e uğrat=** /ı/ to paralyze.
feldispar (.'.) فلدسپار F *geol.* feldspar.
feldmareşal[li] (.'. ...) فلدمارشال F *mil.* field marshal.
felek[gi] **1** فلك |**felek 2**| 1. firmament, heavens; *Ptolemaic astr.* revolving sphere of heaven. 3. fate, destiny. — **bana bunu çok gördü** Fate has denied me this. —**in çemberinden geçmiş** broken on the wheel of fate. — **düşkünü** unfortunate, unlucky. —**ten bir gün çal=** (*lit.*, to steal a day from fate) to have a very enjoyable day. —**ten kâm al=** to have a very good time. — **kimine kavun yedirir, kimine kelek** Fate smiles on some and frowns on others. —**e küs=** to be downhearted, sick at heart, weary. —**in sillesine uğra=**, —**in sillesini ye=** to suffer the blows of fate.
felek[ki] **2** فلك A *lrnd.*, *same as* **felek 1**. —**i aksa**, —**i a'lâ**, —**i Atlas**, —**i a'zam** *Ptolemaic astr.* the ninth sphere, empyrean. —**i büruc** *Ptolemaic astr.* the eighth sphere. —**i cevzehr** *Ptolemaic astr.* the outer concentric sphere of the moon. —**i eflâk** *same as* **feleki a'lâ**. —**i esfel** *Ptolemaic astr.* the lowest sphere. —**i hamil** *Ptolemaic astr.* the deferent of a planet. —**i kül** *Ptolemaic astr.*, Primum mobile. —**i musavver**, —**i mükevkeb**, —**i sevabit** *Ptolemaic astr.* the eighth heaven. —**i tedvir** *Ptolemaic astr.* epicycle of a planet.
felek[gi] **3** فلك *var. of* **felenk**.
felekcah (. . —) فلك جاه P *poet.* enthroned in heaven.
felekdebdebe فلك دبدبه P *lrnd.* surrounded with attendants as numerous as the stars.
felekî (. —.) فلكى A *lrnd.* celestial, heavenly; astronomical. —**yat** (.. ——) A astronomy; astrology. —**yun** (.. ——) A astronomers, astrologers.
felekmeşreb فلك مشرب P fickle; untrustworthy.
felekseyr فلك سير P *lrnd.* moving fast (like the spheres).
felekzede . . — . فلكزده P *lrnd.* unfortunate, unlucky, victim of fate.
Felemenk[gi] ('. ..) فلمنك E 1. Holland, Netherlands. 2. *obs.* Fleming, Dutchman; Dutch. — **altını** *hist.* Dutch ducat. — **kasası** *naut.* Flemish eye. — **taşı** rose diamond; diamond cut and polished in Holland. —**çe** Dutch, the Dutch language. —**li** Dutchman.
felenk[gi] فلنك Gk *naut.* 1. crosspiece of timber on the ways of a launching ship. 2. boat chock.
felevat[ti] (.. —) فلوات A *lrnd.* waterless wastes, deserts.
felfelek[gi] فلفلك |**ferferek**| 1. kind of small

felhan

butterfly. 2. *fig.* doubt, *as in* **içime felfelek sokma** Don't raise doubts in my mind.
felhan (. —) فلهان A *prov.* plowed land left fallow for a period of time.
felihaza (.. — —) فلهذا A same as **felizalike**.
felizalike (.. — ..) فلذلك A *lrnd.* therefore, wherefore.
fellâh (. —) فلّاح A 1. fellah; Arab villager; Arab; Negro. 2. *lrnd.* agriculturist. — **gibi** black like a Negro.
fellek fellek, fellik fellik فلك فلك running hither and thither. — **ara=** /ı/ to search high and low (for).
fels فلس A *lrnd., biol.* fish scale.
felsefe فلسفه A philosophy. — **yap=** to philosophize. —**i ûlâ** metaphysics.
felsefi (.. —) فلسفى A philosophical. —**yat** (.. — —) . A *lrnd.* philosophical sciences.
fem[mmi] فم [*Arabic* fam] 1. *obs.* muzzle of a gun. 2. *lrnd.* mouth; opening, orifice. —**i cenubi** *astr.* the star ∝ *Piscis Australis.* —**i esed** 1. ancient *astr.* the eighth lunar mansion. 2. *lrnd.* dangerous strait. —**i feres** *astr.* the star ε *Pegasi.* —**i hut** *astr.* the star ∝ *Piscis Australis.* —**i kıytas** *astr.* the star Ceti. —**i mide** *anat.* pylorus. —**i nehr** *lrnd.* mouth of a river. —**i rahm** *anat., os uteri.* —**i semeke** *astr.* the star β *Piscium.* —**i tinîn** *astr.* the star μ or γ *Draconis.*
feminist فمينيست F feminist.
feminizm فمينيزم F feminism.
femmî (. —) فمّى [*based on* fem] *anat.* oral.
fen[nni] فنّ A 1. science; branch of science. 2. *lrnd.* sort, variety, category. — **adamı** scientist. —**ini al=** /ın/ to master the technique (of). —**i derya** *lrnd.* seamanship. — **erbabı** the scientists. — **fakültesi** college of science. —**i harb** *lrnd.* the art of war. — **heyeti** technical commission. — **işleri müdürlüğü** technical department of a municipality. — **kıt'ası** *mil.* technical service unit. —**i kimya** *lrnd.* chemistry. —**i madeniyat** *obs.* mineralogy. —**i menafiül'âza** *obs.* physiology. —**i mimarî** *obs.* architecture. —**i saydelani** *obs.* pharmacy, pharmaceutics. —**i tabakatül'arz** *obs.* geology. —**i tedavi** *obs.* therapeutics. —**i terbiyei etfal** *obs.* pedagogy. —**i teşrih** *lrnd.* anatomy. —**i tıb** *lrnd.* medicine. —**i ziraat** *lrnd.* agronomy.
fena 1 (. —) فنا [**fena 2**] 1. bad; evil. 2. ill, sick. — **bak=** /a/ to glare angrily (at). —**ya çek=** /ı/ to take (something) in a bad sense. — **et=** to do evil; to do the wrong thing; /ı/ to treat badly, to punish (used in threatening someone). — **git=** to go badly. —**sına git=** to be exasperated. — **gözle bak=** /a/ to look daggers (at). — **halde** badly. — **kalpli** wicked. — **kokulu** smelly, bad-smelling, fetid, stinking. — **muamele** *law* ill treatment. — **muamele et=** /a/ to treat harshly. — **ol=** to feel bad; to feel faint. —**ya sar=** to take a turn for the worse. —**ya var=** to get worse; to end up badly. — **yakalan=** to be badly caught. —**ya yor=** /ı/ to interpret unfavorably.
fena 2 (. —) فنا A *lrnd.* death, extinction, annihilation. — **bul=** to die; to come to an end.
fenaca (. —.) فناجه rather bad, somewhat bad.
fenadik[kı] (. —.) فنادق A *lrnd., pl. of* fındık.
fenafilâşk[kı] (. —..) فنا فى العشق *myst.* annihilation in divine love.
fenafillâh (. —. —) فنا فى الله A *myst.* annihilation in God.
fenalaş=[ır] (. —..) فنالاشمق 1. to get worse, to deteriorate. 2. to turn faint. —**tır=** /ı/ *caus.*
fenalık[ğı] (. —.) فنالق 1. badness, evil. 2. injury, harm. 3. a fainting. — **et=** /a/ to harm. — **geçir=** to feel ill. — **gel=** /a/ to faint.
fenagâh (. — —) فناگاه P the transitory abode, this world.
fenapezir (. —. —) فناپذير P *lrnd.* transitory. — **ol=** to perish.
fenar فنار Gk *lrnd., same as* **fener**.
fenayab (. — —) فناياب P *lrnd.* transitory.
fend فند [fen] trick, ruse, feint.
fener فنر [fenar] 1. lantern; street lamp. 2. lighthouse. 3. coffee tray with handle on top. 4. *mech.* pinion (of a shaft). 5. *arch.* lantern light, lantern turret, lantern. 6. *naut.* crown knot. — **alayı** torchlight procession. — **balığı** angler, anglerfish, *zool., Lophius piscatorius.* — **çek=** to light the way with a lantern. — **dikişi** *bookbinding* kind of stitch. — **direği** lamp post. — **dişli** *mech.* truncated conical cogwheel. — **dubası** *naut.* light buoy. — **gemisi** *naut.* lightship. — **gövdesi** *lathe-shop* headstock of a lathe. **F—ler idaresi** Lighthouse Board, *in England* Trinity House. — **kasnak** *lathe-shop* cone pulley of a lathe. — **memuru** lighthouse keeper. — **mili** *lathe-shop* spindle of a lathe, mandrel. —**i nerede söndürdün?** Where did you put your lantern out? (said jokingly to one who arrives late in the morning). — **resmi** *naut.* lighthouse dues. — **şamandırası** *naut.* light buoy.
fenerci فنرجى 1. lighthouse keeper. 2. lamplighter.
fenerli فنرلى 1. *w. cap., Ott. hist.* Phanariot, member of the old Greek aristocracy in Istanbul. 2. *slang* long-bearded man. — **matkap** drill driven by a toothed wheel.
fenik[ği] **1** G pfennig (German money).

fenik=ⁱʳ 2 فنلك *prov.* to be stupefied, oppressed, worried, annoyed.

Fenike (..'.) فنيك *hist.* Phoenicia. **—li** Phoenician.

feni'melmatlûb (....—) فنعم المطلوب A *lrnd.* that was just what was wanted.

fenlen=ⁱʳ فنلنك to know more than befits one's age (girl).

fennen (.'.) فنّاً A scientifically; as regards science, technically.

fennî (.—) فنّي A scientific, technical, expert. **— ıstılah, — tabir** technical term.

fenniyat (.——) فنّيات |based on Arabic| technology.

fenolˡü F *chem.* phenol.

fenomen فنومن F *phil.* phenomenon. **—izm** F phenomenalism.

fentᵈⁱ فند *var. of* **fend.**

feodalˡⁱ فوردال F *hist.* feudal.

feodalite فوردالية F *hist.* feudalism.

fer 1 فر P 1. radiance, luster, brightness. 2. *lrnd.* pomp, display. **— ü şevket** *lrnd.* pomp and circumstance.

ferʳʳⁱ 2 فرع A 1. *phil.* branch, subdivision. 2. *Or. mus.* a rhythmic pattern of 16 beats. 3. *lrnd.* branch, bough, limb. **—i fiil** *gram.* participle.

ferʳʳⁱ 3 فرّ A *lrnd.* flight, a running away.

ferace (.—.) فراجه |fereci| 1. dustcoat formerly worn by Turkish women when they went out. 2. *archaic* cloak worn by **ulema** on ceremonial occasions. **—len=** to put on a **ferace. —li** wearing a **ferace. —lik** material suitable for a **ferace.**

ferade ferade فراده فراده *archaic* one by one, singly.

feradis (.——) فراديس A *lrnd., pl. of* **firdevs.**

feragatˡⁱ (.—.) فراغت A 1. self-sacrifice, abnegation. 2. *law* renunciation, abandonment (of a right), cession, waiver; abdication. **—le** devotedly. **—i caiz olmıyan** *law* inalienable. **— et=** /dan/ *law* to renounce, abandon, cede; to abdicate (from). **—i nefs** self-sacrifice, abnegation. **— sahibi** altruistic, unselfish. **—kâr** (.—.—) P self-sacrificing, self-denying.

ferağ (.—) فراغ A 1. *law* cession (of property), transfer. 2. *lrnd.* a withdrawing from work, a being unoccupied, a being free from care, leisure. **— anilcihat** *can. law* an abandoning one's rights to a revenue from a pious foundation. **—ı bal** *lrnd.* ease, freedom from anxiety. **— bilmuvazaa** *law* fictitious transfer. **— bilvefa** *law* temporary transfer of property as security. **— et=** /dan/ *law* to cede, to withdraw (from). **—ı fasid** *law* invalid transfer. **— harcı** conveyance fee. **—ı hâtır** *lrnd.* ease, tranquillity, peace of heart.

— ü intikal *law* transfer. **— ve intikal harcı** conveyance fee. **— ve intikali kabil olmıyan** *law* inalienable. **—ı kabil** *law* transferable. **—ı kat'î** *law* unconditional transfer, absolute transfer of property. **—ı sahih** *law* legally valid transfer.

ferah 1 فرخ |Persian .—| spacious, open, roomy, wide. **— ferah** easily, abundantly.

ferah 2 فرح A *lrnd.* cheerfulness, gladness. **—aver** (..—.) P, **—bahş** P imparting joy or gladness, exhilarating. **—efza** (...—) P *same as* **ferahfeza.**

ferahem (.—.) فراهم P *lrnd.* 1. collected, gathered. 2. together, much, many.

ferahfeza (...—) فرح فزا P 1. *lrnd.* mirth increasing. 2. *Or. mus.* a compound **makam** approximately two centuries old.

ferahi (.——) فراحي P 1. crescent-shaped metal collar plate formerly worn by police guards. 2. *hist.* gorget.

ferahla=ʳ, **ferahlan=**ⁱʳ فراحله 1. to become spacious or airy; to clear up. 2. to become cheerful, to feel relieved. **—dır=** /ı/ *caus.*

ferahlıkᵍⁱ فراحلق 1. spaciousness, airiness. 2. cheerfulness, relief.

ferahnâkᵏⁱ (..—) فرحناك P *lrnd.* 1. cheerful. 2. *Or. mus.* a compound **makam** a century and a half old.

ferahnüma فرحنما *Or. mus.* a **şed makam** named by the famous musician H. S. Arel.

ferahrev (.—.) فراغ رو P *lrnd.* 1. walking fast. 2. hasty. 3. spendthrift.

ferahru (.——) فراغ رو P *lrnd.* smiling, cheerful looking.

ferahzâr (..—) فرحزار A *Or. mus.* an extinct **makam.**

feraid (.—.) فرائد A *lrnd., pl. of* **ferid, feride.**

Feraine (.—..) فراعنه A *lrnd., pl. of* **Firavn.**

feraiz (.—.) فرائض A *lrnd., pl. of* **feriza. — ilmi** *can. law* the science of dividing an inheritance.

feramin (.——) فرامين A *lrnd., pl. of* **ferman.**

feramûş (.——) فراموش P *lrnd.* forgetfulness, neglect. **— et=** /ı/ to forget, overlook, neglect. **—i** (.————) P forgetfulness, forgetting.

fer'an, fer'en (.'.) فرعاً A *lrnd.* as a side issue, as a secondary matter.

feraset 1 (.—.) فراست |firaset| 1. sagacity, intuition. 2. understanding.

feraset 2 (.—.) فراست A *lrnd.* horsemanship.

ferasetli فراستلي sagacious, sharp-witted.

feraşet (.—.) فراشت |based on **ferraş**|

feravân *hist.* titular office of sweeper of the mosques of Mecca and Medina, held by some high functionary at Istanbul, etc., the actual duties being performed by the servants. — **beratı** imperial warrant conferring the **feraşet**. — **bohçası** parcel of presents sent by the titular sweeper at Istanbul to his substitutes in Mecca and Medina.

feravân (.——) فراوان P *same as* **firavân**.

feraz 1 (.—) فراز P *lrnd.* 1. above, up, upwards, uphill. 2. height, altitude, ascent; rising slope.

-feraz 2 (.—) فراز P *lrnd.*, in compounds that raises, *as in* **serferaz**.

ferbih فربه P *lrnd.* fat, plump. —**î** (..—) P, —**lik** fatness.

ferbiyûniye (.———.) فربيونيه A spurge, *bot.*, *Euphorbiaceae*.

ferc فرج A *anat.* vulva.

fercâm (.—) فرجام P *lrnd.* end, conclusion, issue. —**gâh** (.——) *poet.* the final resting place, grave, tomb.

ferce فرجه *lrnd.*, *var of* **fürce**.

ferd فرد A 1. person, individual; member. 2. *literature* unrhymed couplet. 3. *lrnd.* single; unique; peerless; odd (number). —**i âferide**, —**i vâhid** *lrnd.*, *followed by negative verb* not a single soul, none, nobody.

ferda (.—) فردا P *lrnd.* the morrow, the next day; future; eternity; the Day of Judgment. —**sı gün** next day. —**ya sal=** /ı/ to postpone, to put off.

ferdaferd (.—.) فردافرد P *lrnd.* individually, one by one.

ferdaniye (.——.) فردانيه |*based on Arabic*| *phil.* individualism.

ferdaniyet (.——.) فردانيت |*based on Arabic*| *lrnd.* solitariness; uniqueness.

ferdasız (.—.) فرداسز *lrnd.* futureless, without prospects; hopeless.

ferde فرده A *lrnd.* 1. a female. 2. bale, bag of merchandise.

ferden (.'.) فردًا A individually, one by one; personally. — **ferdâ**, — **ferden** individually, separately.

ferdî (.—) فردى |*based on* **ferd**| individual; personal. — **olarak** individually. — **teşebbüs** personal initiative. —**leştir=** /ı/ *phil.* to individualize.

ferdiye (.—.) فرديه |*based on* **ferd**| *phil.* individualism.

ferdiyet (.—.) فرديت |*based on* **ferdî**| *lrnd.* individuality. —**çi** *phil.* individualist. —**çilik** *phil.* individualism.

ferdiyül'esâbi[ii] (.—..—.) فردى الاصابع *zool.* perissodactyl.

fere فره *prov.* 1. chick of a game bird. 2. chicken.

ferec فرج A *lrnd.* dissipation of care or grief; ease; joy.

fereci (..—) فرجى A *archaic, same as* **ferace**[2].

feres فرس A 1. *astr.* Pegasus. 2. *lrnd.* horse; *chess* knight. —**i âzam**, —**i ekber** *astr.* Pegasus. —**i evvel** *astr.*, *Equuleus*. —**i sanî** *astr.* Pegasus. —**î** (..—) A *zool.* equine.

feresülbahr فرس البحر A *lrnd.* hippopotamus.

Feresülhayat (....—) فرس طيبة A *Isl. rel.*, name of Gabriel's steed.

ferez فرز *prov., same as* **firez**.

ferfene *prov., var. of* **herifane**.

ferfere فرفره A *same as* **farfara**.

ferferek[gi] فرفرك P whirligig, pinwheel.

Ferhad (.—) فرهاد P *Isl. literature*, name of a famous lover.

ferhan (.—) فرحان A *lrnd.* cheerful, happy.

Ferhar (.—) فرخار P 1. *poet.*, name of a city remarkable for the beauty of its inhabitants and a number of idols; name of an idol-temple where beautiful girls devoted themselves to worship. 2. *l. c.*, *lrnd.* ornament, decoration.

Ferhat[d1] **1** فرهاد *var. of* **Ferhad**.

ferhat[ti] **2** فرحت A *lrnd.* joy, cheerfulness.

ferheng فرهنگ P, **ferhenk**[gi] *lrnd.* 1. dictionary, lexicon (especially Persian). 2. knowledge, wisdom.

ferhunde فرخنده P *lrnd.* auspicious, lucky. —**fal** (...—) P, auspicious, lucky, fortunate. —**gî** (...—) P auspiciousness, happiness; fortune. —**pâ** (...—) P of auspicious footstep; fortunate. —**tâli** lucky, fortunate.

feri[i] **1** فرع *var. of* **fer 2**.

fer'i 2 (.—) فرعى A *lrnd.* derived, secondary; subordinate; accessory. — **ceza** *law* accessory punishment. — **fail** *law* accessory. — **haklar** *law* accessory rights.

feri 3 فرى E *same as* **feribot**.

-ferib (.—) فريب P *lrnd.*, *same as* **firib**.

feribot فريبوت E train ferry; car ferry.

ferid (.—) فريد A *lrnd.* single, unique, incomparable. —**i dehr** unique in the world.

feride (.—.) فريده A 1. *lrnd.* unique, incomparable. 2. *w. cap.*, *woman's name*.

Feridun (.——) فريدون P *Persian literature*, name of a famous Persian king. —**fer** P glorious as Feridun.

ferifte فريفته P *lrnd., same as* **firifte**.

ferih (.—) فرح A *lrnd.* cheerful, joyous. — **fahur** in abundance, in comfort (to live).

ferik[k1] **1** (.—) فريه |**ferik 4**| *obs.*, *mil.* Divisional General.

ferik[gi] **2** فريك |*Persian* **faruk**| *prov.* chick, chicken; young of a game bird. — **elması** kind of apple.

ferik[gi] **3** فريك |*Arabic* .—| *same as* **firik**.

ferik[kı] 4 (.—) فريق A *lrnd.* group of men; army division.
ferikayn (.——) فريقين A *lrnd.* two army divisions.
feriklik[ği] فريقلك the rank of a Divisional General. Divisional General.
ferise (.—.) فريس A *lrnd.* taken as prey; killed.
Ferisî (.——) فريسى A *Bib.* Pharisee.
ferişte فرشته [**firişte**] *rel.* angel.
Fer'iye (.—.) فرعيّه A *lrnd.*, *fem.* of **fer'î** 2. in — **Sarayları** name of a group of palaces between Beşiktaş and Ortaköy on the Bosphorus (today the first part of **Kabataş Lisesi** and **Galatasaray Lisesi**).
feriza (.—.) فريضه A 1. *rel.* sacred duty, sacred obligation. 2. *can. law* obligatory share of an inheritance.
ferkad فرقد A *astr.* either of the two stars β and γ Ursae Minoris. —**an** (..—) A, —**eyn** A the two stars β and Ursae Minoris.
ferkadsay (..—) فرقدساى P *lrnd.* so high as to touch the Farkad stars.
ferle=[r] فرلمك [*based on Arabic*] *slang* to run away.
ferma 1 (.'.) فرما It *sport* a pointing, setting. — **et**= to point, to set.
-**ferma** 2 (.—) P *lrnd.* that commands, compels, *as in* **fermanferma, hükümferma**.
ferman (.—) فرمان P 1. firman, imperial edict. 2. *lrnd.* command, order. —**ı âli** imperial edict. — **çıktı** An imperial command has been uttered. — **dinleme**= to be recalcitrant. — **gemisi** *Ott. hist.* boat for checking the *laissez-passers* of ships going through the Dardanelles. — **ısdar et**= to issue a firman. —**ı ilâhi** Divine command. — **oldu** An imperial order has been given. — **sizin** as you wish.
fermanber (.—.) فرمانبر P *lrnd.* obedient.
fermanberdar فرمانبردار (.—.—) P *lrnd.* obedient, subject. —**î** (.—.——) P obedience.
fermandih (.—.) فرمانده , **fermanferma** (.—.—) فرمانفرما P *lrnd.* who issues edicts.
fermanlı فرمانلى *Ott. hist.* 1. one against whom an edict has been issued, outlaw. 2. having a rank superior to major (army officer).
fermanname (.——.) فرماننامه *lrnd.* 1. imperial written order. 2. your letter (courtesy expression).
fermanrev (.—.) فرمانرو P *lrnd.* a domain where the edicts of a sovereign are current.
fermanreva (.—.—) فرمانروا P *lrnd.* whose orders are obeyed; sovereign.
-**fermay** (.—) فرماى P *same as* **ferma 2**.
fermayende (.—..) فرماينده P *lrnd.* 1. who gives orders. 2. sovereign.

fermayiş 1 (.—.) فرمايش [**fermayiş 2**] *obs.* best quality of Cashmere or Lahore shawls.
fermayiş 2 (.—.) فرمايش P *lrnd.* command, order.
fermejüp فرمژوب F patent-fastener, snap-fastener.
fermele فرمل Gk *same as* **fermene**.
fermend فرمند P *lrnd.* 1. brilliant. 2. man of high position.
fermene فرمنه [**fermele**] *obs.* 1. short braided waistcoat. 2. braid used as trimmings. —**ci** maker or seller of braided clothes or garments.
fermuar فرموار F zipper, zip-fastener.
fermude (.—.) فرموده P *lrnd.* commandment, order.
ferraş (.—) فراش A *lrnd.* 1. mosque sweeper. 2. carpet-layer, servant. —**î** (.——) P, —**lık** the office, functions of a sweeper, etc.
ferruh فرّخ P *lrnd.* lucky, fortunate, auspicious. —**fal** (..—) P auspicious. —**zad** (..—) P born lucky.
-**fersa** (.—) فرسا P *lrnd.* which wears, exhausts, *as in* **tahammülfersa, takatfersa**.
fersah فرسخ A *obs.* parasang (3+ miles). — **fersah** greatly, *e. g.,* **fersah fersah daha iyi** greatly superior, miles better.
ferseng فرسنگ P *obs.* parasang.
fersiz فرسز lusterless, dull, without radiance. —**leş**= to become lusterless. —**lik** lack of luster, dullness.
fersude (.—.) فرسوده P *lrnd.* worn out, old, ragged. — **payı** *print.* surplus amount of paper added to meet the loss by dirtying. —**gî** (.—.—) P, —**lik** state of raggedness; wear, waste.
ferş فرش A *lrnd.* 1. a laying, spreading (carpets). 2. carpets, mats. 3. the face of the earth. — **et**= /ı/ to lay down, spread out (carpets); to carpet (room); to lay (rails).
ferşiyat (..—) فرشيات A the laying (of rails, pipes, etc.).
ferşiye (.—.) فرشيه A *building* the expense for the laying (of tiles, etc.).
fert[di] فرد *var.* of **ferd**. —**çi** *phil.* individualist. —**çilik** *phil.* individualism.
fertik[ği] فرتك G *only in* —**i çek**=, —**i kır**=, —**le**= *slang* to run away, to make off.
fertut (.—) فرتوت P *lrnd.* decrepit. —**âne** (.——.) P decrepitly. —**e** *fem.* —**î** (.——) P, —**iyet** (.——.), —**luk** decrepitude; imbecility of old age.
feruh (.—) فروح A *lrnd.* very cheerful, glad, happy.
ferve فروه A *obs.* fur-lined garment. —**i beyza** white fur worn by the Sheikhul-islam. —**i murabba** garment lined with fox fur.
Ferverdin فرورديس P *name of the first month*

feryad

of the Persian year, and of the genius presiding over it.

feryad (.—) فرياد P 1. cry; cry for help. 2. archaic complaint. **—ı andelib** calendar, name of a storm around the spring equinox. **—ı bas=** to start wailing. **— et=** 1. to cry out, to lament; to call for help. 2. archaic to complain. **— u figan** lrnd. wailing, lamentation. **—a yetiş=** archaic to succor, to go to the rescue (of one in distress)

feryadcı فريادجى archaic messenger sent to submit a complaint.

feryadhan (.——) فريادخان P lrnd. one who calls for help.

feryadname (.———.) فريادنامه P archaic letter of complaint.

feryadres (.—.) فريادرس P lrnd. coming for help; succorer.

feryat[dı] فرياد [feryad] same as **feryad**.

ferz فرز [Persian firz] chess queen.

ferzane (.—.) فرزانه P lrnd. 1. eminent. 2. learned. **—gân** (.—.—) P pl. **—gi** (.—.—) P abstr. n. **—hu** (.—.—) P of lofty, noble habits. **—lik** eminence; erudition.

ferzend فرزند P lrnd. son; child. **—i âb** 1. aquatic animals. 2. bubbles. **—i afitab**, **—i haver** poet. ruby.

ferzendşad, **ferzenşad** (..—) فرزند شاد P lrnd. meditation.

ferzîn (.—) فرزين P lrnd., same as **ferz**.

fes فس fez. **— boyası** the dye madder-root. **—ini havaya at=** to be very happy, to be very cheerful. **— ibiği** crest on top of a fez where the tassel is attached. **— kalıbı** fez-block. **— püskülü** fez tassel. **— rengi** wine red. **— tablası** the flat top of a fez. **— tarağı** fuller's teasel, bot., Dipsacus fullonum.

fesad (.—) فساد A same as **fesat**. **—engiz** (.—.—) P lrnd. intriguing.

fesahat[ti] 1 (.—.) فصاحت A lrnd. purity of speech, eloquence.

fesahat[ti] 2 (.—.) فساحت A lrnd. spaciousness.

fesahatperdaz (.—.—) فصاحت پرداز P lrnd. 1. eloquent. 2. orator.

fesan (.—) فسان P lrnd. whetstone.

fesane (.—.) فسانه P lrnd., same as **efsane**.

fesat[dı] (.—) فساد [fesad] 1. malice, depravity, intrigue, duplicity, mischief. 2. mischievous, intriguer. 3. lrnd. sedition, disorder. **—ı ahlâk** bad morals, demoralization of character. **— başı** main plotter, main intriguer. **— çıkar=** to plot mischief, to conspire. **— et=** obs. to plot mischief. **— karıştır=** to intrigue. **— kazanları kayna=** for mischief to be brewing. **— kumkuması** a great mischief-maker. **— kur=** to conspire, to plot. **— kutusu** mischief-maker. **— ocağı** den of mischief. **— tohumu** seeds of intrigue.

fesatçı فسادجى mischief-maker; intriguer, plotter. **—lık** subversive activity, intrigue.

fesede فسده A lrnd., pl. of **fasid**.

feseka فسقه A lrnd., pl. of **fasik**.

fesh فسخ A abolition, cancellation, dissolution, annulment. **— et=***. **—i ihbar** law notice of termination of a contract.

feshane (.—.) فسخانه fez factory.

feshet=[der] فسخ ايتمك /ı/ to abolish, cancel, annul, rescind.

fesih[shi] 1 فسخ var. of **fesh**.

fesih 2 (.—) فسيح A lrnd. wide, spacious.

fesleğen فسلكن Gk sweet basil, bot., Ocimum basilicum.

festival[li] فستيوال F 1. festival, season of entertainment. 2. colloq. fiasco, utter failure. 3. slang object of ridicule.

fesüphanallah (..—.—) فسبحان الله A (lit. Praise to God!) Oh my God! (said in exasperation).

feşafaş (.——), **feşafeş** (.—.) فشافش فشافش P lrnd. a rustling noise, swish; a whizzing of arrows.

-feşan 1 (.—) فشان P lrnd., same as **-efşan**, as in **ziyafeşan**.

feşan 2 (.—) فشان P Or. mus. a rhythmic pattern.

-feşar (.—) فشار P lrnd., same as **-efşar**.

feşel فشل [Arabic fashil] prov. naughty, good-for-nothing.

fetâ (.—) فتى A lrnd. 1. lad, youth. 2. generous, large-hearted man. 3. servant, page. **La fetâ illâ Ali** There is no one as valiant as Ali.

fetanet (.—.) فطانت A lrnd. intelligence, shrewdness. **—li** intelligent, shrewd. **—siz** unintelligent.

fetava (.——) فتاوى فتاوا A lrnd., pl. of **fetva**. **—yı Alemgîrî** hist. the **fetvas** of Alemgir, emperor of Hindustan, collected as a legal authority.

fetebarek (..—.) فتبارك A rel. May He be blessed! (expression of congratulation).

feteyan (..—) فتيان A lrnd. 1. dual of **feta**. 2. day and night; morning and evening.

feth فتح A lrnd. 1. same as **fetih**. 2. same as **fetha**. **— et=***.

fetha فتحة A 1. Arabic script vowel sign for a, e. 2. anat. opening, orifice.

fethet=[der] فتح ايتمك /ı/ 1. to conquer. 2. lrnd. to open.

fethî (.—) فتحى A lrnd. pertaining to conquest.

fethiye (.—.) فتحية A 1. literature ode of conquest. 2. lrnd. structure built to celebrate a conquest.

fetih[thi] فتح [feth] 1. conquest; victory. 2. lrnd. act of opening; act of commencing; act of solving (a difficulty). 3. *lrnd.* Divine gift. **—i bab** *lrnd.* opening of a door. **— hakkı** *law* right of conquest. **—i meyit, —i meyyit** autopsy, post-mortem examination. **—i müşkilât** *lrnd.* a solving of difficulties.

fetihname (..—.) فَتِحْ نَامَه P 1. Imperial letter announcing a conquest. 2. poem or treatise describing a conquest.

fetil (.—) فَتِيل A *lrnd., same as* **fitil.**

fetir فَطِير |Arabic .—| *prov.* unleavened bread.

fetiş F fetish. **—izm** F fetishism.

fetk[kı] **1** فَتْق A *lrnd.* 1. a tearing, rupture. 2. *same as* **fıtık. —ı batnî** *path.* abdominal hernia. **— ü retk-ı umûr** a settling of affairs.

fetk 2 فَتْك A *lrnd.* a killing someone suddenly.

fetret فَتْرَت A *lrnd., same as* **fitret.**

Fettah (.—) فَتَّاح A *lrnd.* the Opener of All Ways, God.

fettak[kı] (.—) فَتَّاك A *lrnd.* blood-thirsty robber.

fettan (.—) فَتَّان A 1. alluring, seducing; seducer. 2. intriguer. **—lık** mischievousness; intriguing.

fetva (.—) فَتْوَى A, فَتْوَا fatwa, opinion on legal matter, furnished by a mufti on application. **— al=** to obtain a fatwa. **— emini** *Ott. hist.* head of the office dealing out fatwas, under the **Şeyhülislâm. — ver=** 1. to give or pronounce a fatwa. 2. *colloq.* to lay down the law. **—cı** *colloq.* one who makes pronouncements.

fetvahane (.——.) فَتْوَى خَانَه P *Ott. hist.* fatwa department under the **Şeyhulislâm.**

Fetvapenah (..—.—) فَتْوَى پَنَاه P *Ott. hist.*, title of the **Şeyhülislâm. —i** (.—.——) P *Ott. hist.* pertaining to the **Şeyhülislâm.**

fevahir (..—.) فَوَاضِر A *lrnd.* praiseworthy things.

fevahiş (..—.) فَوَاحِش A *lrnd.* 1. gross errors; shameful things. 2. *pl.* of **fahişe.**

fevaid (..—.) فَوَائِد A *lrnd., pl.* of **faide.**

fevaih (..—.) فَوَائِح A *lrnd.* odors, perfumes (of flowers).

fevakih (..—.) فَوَاكِه A *lrnd., pl.* of **fâkihe.**

fevaris (..—.) فَوَارِس A *lrnd., pl.* of **faris.**

fevasıl (..—.) فَوَاصِل A *lrnd., pl.* of **fâsıla.**

fevat (.—) فَوَات A *lrnd.* death, a passing away; sudden death.

fevatih (..—.) فَوَاتِح A *lrnd., pl.* of **Fatiha.**

fevc فَوْج A *lrnd.* troop of men, crowd; body of troops. **—a fevc, — fevc** *same as* **fevç fevç.**

fevç fevç فَوْج فَوْج [fevc] in groups, in troops, in crowds, in streams.

fevehan (..—) فَوَهَان A *lrnd.* 1. diffusion (of perfume). 2. scents, perfumes.

feveran (..—) فَوَرَان A 1. a flaring up (with anger); rage. 2. *lrnd.* a boiling up, effervescence, ebullition. 3. *lrnd.* eruption (of a volcano). **—ı âb** the spurting out of water. **—ı dem** 1. boiling up with anger. 2. spurting out of blood. **— et=** 1. to boil over with anger. 2. *lrnd.* to boil up, to effervesce. 3. *lrnd.* to erupt (volcano). **—ı gazab** an outburst of anger. **—ı zaman** the impetuosity of the present time.

fevha 1 فَوْهَه A *anat.* orifice, aperture.

fevha 2 فَوْحَه A *lrnd.* whiff of perfume.

feviye (.—.) |based on Arabic| *bot.*, Rubiaceae.

fevk[kı, ki] فَوْق A 1. superior. 2. *lrnd.* upper surface; upper part, top. **—ında, —inde** 1. above, *e. g.*, **ufkun fevkinde** above the horizon. 2. superior to, *e. g.*, **yüzbaşının fevkinde olan rütbeler** the ranks superior to captain. **—i işba** *sc.* supersaturation.

fevkalâde (.'. —.) فَوْقَ الْعَادَه A 1. extraordinary; extraordinarily, exceedingly, excessively. 2. excellent; excellently. **—den** by way of exception, by special permission. **— ahval, — haller** exceptional circumstances. **— ikame** *law* appointment of a reversionary heir, fideicommissary substitution. **F— Komiser** High Commissioner. **— murahhas** envoy, ambassador extraordinary. **— murahhas büyük elçi** ambassador extraordinary and plenipotentiary. **— nüsha** special edition. **— olarak** 1. extraordinarily. 2. exceptionally, by way of exception. **—den terfi et=** to get a special promotion. **— vaziyet** state of emergency.

fevkalâdelik[ği] فَوْقَ الْعَادَهْ لِك 1. singularity; a being extraordinary. 2. exceptional state, peculiarity, strangeness. **— göster=** to be very successful, to show extraordinary ability.

fevkalbeşer (.'. ...) فَوْقَ الْبَشَر A 1. superhuman. 2. *phil.* superman.

fevkalgaye (.'.—.) فَوْقَ الْغَايَه A *lrnd.* extremely.

fevkalhad (.'..) فَوْقَ الْحَد A *lrnd.* beyond the limit, extremely, excessively.

fevkalkilye فَوْقَ الْكُلْيِه |based on Arabic| *anat.* suprarenal; suprarenal gland.

fevkalmemul[lü] (.'...—) فَوْقَ الْمَأْمُول A *lrnd.* beyond expectation, unexpected.

fevkani (.——) فَوْقَانِي A *lrnd.* 1. upper, superior. 2. having an upper floor or story. 3. *Arabic script* letter having a dot or dots above.

fevkattabia (...—.) فَوْقَ الطَّبِيعَه A *phil.* supernatural.

fevke mayetasavver (.'. —...) فَوْقَ مَا يَتَصَوَّر A *lrnd.* surpassing the imagination, beyond expectation.

fevr فَوْر A *lrnd.* haste, hurry.

Red 24

fevren (..) فورا A promptly, at once; impulsively.

fevrî (.—) فوري A speedy, sudden; impulsive.

fevt فوت A lrnd. 1. a letting escape (an opportunity). 2. a going by; irreparable loss. 3. death. **— et=** /ı/ to let escape, to lose (opportunity). **— ol=** to die. **— olun=** pass. of fevt et=.

fevvare (.—.) فوّاره A poet. 1. water jet. 2. gushing spring.

fevz فوز A lrnd. success, victory, triumph. **— ü necat** salvation. **— ü nusret** victory.

fevza (.—) فوضى A sociol. anarchy. **—i** (.——) A anarchist. **—vî** (.——) A anarchic, chaotic. **—iyet** (.——.) A anarchism.

fevzi (.—) فوزى A 1. lrnd. pertaining to success. 2. w. cap., man's name.

fey[yı] فى A can. law revenue of the Islamic state from non-Muslim subjects.

feyafi (.——) فيافى A lrnd., pl. of feyfa.

feyezan (..—) فيضان A 1. inundation, overflowing, flood. 2. lrnd. abundance.

feyfa (.—) فيفاء A lrnd. desert.

feyfaneverd فيفا نورد P lrnd. travelling in the desert.

feyha (.—) فيحاء A lrnd. wide, spacious, vast.

feyiz[yzi] فيض var. of feyz.

feylesof فيلسوف |Arabic failasuf| philosopher. **—ane** (...—.) P philosophically; philosophical (attitude).

feysal[li] فيصل A lrnd. 1. separation. 2. decision, judgment.

feyyaz (.—) فيّاض A lrnd. 1. munificent, generous. 2. overflowing, abounding, flourishing. **F—ı Mutlak** the great Distributor of blessings, God.

feyyil فيّل A lrnd. weak of judgment.

feyz فيض A 1. abundance; prosperity; bountifulness, fertility. 2. the spiritual power that emanates from a person and inspires another, enlightenment. 3. bounteous gift. **— al=** /dan/ to be enlightened (by), to learn (from). **— ü bereket** prosperity, abundance. **— bul=** to flourish, prosper, advance. **—i Hak, —i İlâhî, —i Rabbani** Divine blessing. **—aver** (.—.) P, **—bahş** P lrnd. bountiful, generous. **—dar** (.—) P lrnd. prosperous, blessed, successful.

feyzî (.—) فيضى A 1. pertaining to God's blessing and favor. 2. w. cap., man's name.

feyzli فيضلى abundant; prosperous; productive, bountiful; blessed, successful.

feyznak (.—) فيضناك P lrnd. bountiful, prosperous.

feyzresan (..—) فيض رسان P lrnd. creating abundance, productive.

feyzyab (.—) فيضياب P lrnd. prosperous, flourishing.

feza 1 (.—) فضاء A phil., geom., astr. space. **—i namütenahi** infinite space.

-feza 2 (.—) فزا P lrnd. that increases, as in **ferahfeza**.

fezai (.——) فضائى A phil., geom., astr. spatial.

fezaih (.—.) فضائح A lrnd., pl. of faziha.

fezail (.—.) فضائل A lrnd., pl. of fazilet. **—i asliye, —i esasiye** phil. cardinal virtues. **—penah** (.—..—) P virtuous, pious (title applied to jurists).

-fezay (.—) فزاى P var. of -feza 2.

fezayende (.—..) فزاينده P lrnd. that increases.

fezayiş (.—.) فزايش P lrnd. increase.

fezleke فذلكه A lrnd. 1. summary. 2. memorandum. 3. law summary of a cross-examination; police report.

fıçı فيچى Gk 1. barrel, cask. 2. tub. 3. archaic unit of measurement of a ship's capacity. **— balığı** salted fish in barrels. **— birası** draught beer. **— çember** hoop. **— dibi** grounds of a cask of wine. **━ dibinden ayrılma=** to be a regular boozer. **━ gibi** very fat. **— musluğu** barrel tap. **— peyniri** fresh cheese in brine. **— şamandıra** barrel buoy. **— şekeri** sugar in hogsheads. **— tahtası** barrel stave. **— üzümü** grapes marketed in barrels. **—cı** cooper. **—lık** 1. containing so many barrels. 2. barrel wood.

fıdda فضّة A lrnd. 1. silver. 2. silver coin.

fıddî (.—) فضّى A lrnd. pertaining to silver; of silver; silver-white.

fıkar فقر A lrnd., pl. of fıkra.

fıkara (..—) فقراء |fukara| 1. poor; pauper. 2. beggar. **—lık** poverty, pauperism. **—lık maskaralık** proverb Poverty leads to embarrassing situations.

fıkarat (..—) فقرات A lrnd., pl. of fıkra. **—ı acziye** anat. sacral vertebrae. **—ı ânife** the passages quoted above. **—ı katâniye** anat. lumbar vertebrae. **—ı müntehabe** selected anecdotes. **—ı rakabiye, —ı unkiye** anat. cervical vertebrae. **—ı us'usiye** anat. coccygeal vertebrae. **—ı zahriye** anat. dorsal vertebrae.

fıkari (..—) فقرى A 1. anat. vertebral. 2. zool. vertebrate.

fıkariye (..—.) فقريّة A zool. vertebrates, Vertebratae.

fıkdan (.—) فقدان A lrnd. 1. absence, lack. 2. want, need. **—ı akl** lack of intelligence. **—ı dem** path. anemia. **—ı elem** path. analgesia. **—ı hareket** path. apraxia.

—ı **hıfz** *psych.* amnesia. —ı **irade** *psych.* abulia. —ı **nukud** lack of money. —ı **nutuk** *psych.* aphasia.

fıkh فقه A *lrnd.*, same as **fıkıh**. —**î** (.—) A pertaining to canonical jurisprudence, canonical.

fıkıh^{khı} فقه [**fıkh**] Muslim canonical jurisprudence.

fıkırda=^r فقردامق 1. to make a bubbling noise, to bubble. 2. to behave coquettishly; to giggle.

fıkırdak^{ğı} coquettish.

fıkır fıkır فقر فقر فيقير فيقير 1. with a bubbling noise. 2. coquettish. — **kayna=** to boil; to boil with anger, impatience, excess of energy.

fıkırtı فقردى bubbling noise.

fıkra فقره A 1. anecdote; short column (of a columnist). 2. paragraph; passage; *law* paragraph. 3. *zool.* order. 4. *anat.* vertebra. —**cı** columnist. —**gû** (..—) P same as **fıkrahan**.

fıkrahan (..—) فقره خان P *lrnd.* professional teller of anecdotes.

fıldır fıldır فيلدر فيلدر rolling (eyes). — **ara=** /ı/ to hunt (for something) feverishly. — **bak=** to look with rolling eyes.

fındık^{ğı} فندق A 1. hazel-nut, filbert. 2. *archaic* ball, pellet (for crossbow or rifle). — **ağacı** hazel, *bot.*, *Corylus avellana*. — **altını** *Ott. hist.*, name of a gold coin. — **faresi** 1. common house mouse. 2. cunning little child. — **kabuğunu doldurmaz** trifling, unimportant; nonsensical. — **kıran** nutcrackers. — **kurdu** plump and coquettish little woman. — **rubiyesi** *Ott. hist.* quarter of an old gold coin. — **sıçanı** same as **fındık faresi**. —**cı** 1. seller of nuts. 2. woman who uses her charms to get something out of a man. —**î** (..—) nut brown, hazel. —**lı** containing nuts; prepared with hazel nuts. —**lık** nut grove.

fır فر whirr. — **dön=** /etrafında/ to hover (round). — **fır** same as **fırıl fırıl**.

fırak^{ğı} 1 *var. of* **frak**.

fırak^{kı} 2 فرق A *lrnd.*, *pl. of* **fırka**. —**ı dalle** heretics. — **fırak** in groups.

Fırat فرات [*Arabic* **Furat**] the Euphrates.

fırça فرچه فورچه فيرچه Gk brush. — **gibi** hard and coarse (hair).

fırçala=^r فيرچه لمق /ı/ to brush. —**n=** 1. to be brushed. 2. to brush oneself. —**t=** /ı, a/ *caus. of* **fırçala=**.

fırdolayı (.'...) فردولايى all around; round about.

fırdöndü فردوندى 1. swivel. 2. lathe carrier. 3. gambler's top.

fırfırı فرفيرى [**ferferek**] *prov.*, same as **fırıldak**¹⁻³.

fırıldak^{ğı} فرلداق فيرلامه 1. weather-cock. 2. spinning-top; whirligig. 3. windmill (child's toy). 4. intrigue, deception, ruse, trick. — **çevir=** to intrigue, to be up to some mischief. —**çı** trickster.

fırıldan=^{ır} فرلدانمق to spin round; to move around hurriedly and anxiously.

fırıldat=^{ır} فرلداتمق /ı/ to let spin round.

fırıl fırıl فرل فرل in **fırıl fırıl ara=** /ı/ to search high and low (for).

fırın فرون فيرين [*Arabic* **furn**] 1. oven; bakery. 2. kiln. 3. furnace. — **gibi** very hot. — **kapağı** thick-skinned, unruffled. — **kebabı** meat dish baked in the oven.

fırıncı فيرينجى baker. —**lık** baker's trade.

fırınla=^r فرونلامق /ı/ to dry in an oven or kiln, to kiln-dry. —**n=** *pass. of* **fırınla=**. —**nmış** kiln-dried. —**t=** 1. /ı/ *same as* **fırınla=**. 2. /ı, a/ *caus. of* **fırınla=**.

fırınlık^{ğı} فرونلق quantity turned out by an oven.

fırışka (..'.) فريشقه It *naut.* light breeze.

fırka فرقه A 1. *pol.* party. 2. *mil.* division; navy squadron. 3. *lrnd.* group. —**i dâlle** heretics. — **fırka** in groups. —**i naciye** the Believers.

fırkacı فرقه جى *pol.* partisan. —**lık** *pol.* 1. partisanship. 2. party work.

fırla=^r فرلامق 1. to fly out; to leap up. 2. to rush. 3. to soar (price). 4. to protrude, to stick out. 5. *obs.* for a piece to fly off from an edge.

fırlak^{ğı} فرلاق protruding, sticking out.

fırlama فرلامه *slang* bastard; brat.

fırlat=^{ır} فرلاتمق /ı/ 1. to hurl. 2. *caus. of* **fırla=**. —**ıl=** *pass. of* —**t=**.

fırlayış فرلايش *verbal n. of* **fırla=**.

fırsat فرصت [**fursat**] opportunity, chance; occasion. — **ara=**, — **avla=** to seek an opportunity. — **bekle=** to wait for an opportunity. — **budur**, — **bu fırsat** This is my (your, his) chance! — **bul=** to find an opportunity. — **çıktı**, — **düştü** An opportunity opened up. — **düşkünü** one who recklessly takes advantage of every opportunity. —**ı elde et=**, —**ı ele geçir=** to find an opportunity. — **ganimettir** same as **fırsat budur**. —**ı ganimet bil=** to seize the opportunity. — **gözet=** to be on the lookout for an opportunity. —**tan istifade** a taking advantage of an opportunity. —**ı kaçır=** to miss the chance. — **kolla=** to lie in wait for an opportunity. — **ver=** to give an opportunity. — **yoksulu** one who would do evil if he had a chance. —**çı** who is on the lookout for a profitable chance.

fırt fırt فرط فرط 1. continually (going in and out). 2. *name of a card game*.

fırtık^{ğı} *prov.* 1. coquettish. 2. draught, mouthful.

fırtına (..'., ...') فورتونه فرتنه فرطونه

fıs

It storm, tempest, gale. — **çıktı** A storm came up. — **koptu** A storm broke out. — **kuşları** zool., Tubinares. —**ya tutul**= to be caught in a storm. — **yatıştı** The storm calmed down. —**lı** stormy.

fıs فص whispering sound; hiss. — **fıs** 1. whisper. 2. gossip. — **geç**= slang to whisper.

fısfıs فص فص scent spray, perfume spray.

Fısh فصح A Jewish Passover; Christian Easter.

fısılda=ʳ فيصيلدامه /ı/ to whisper. —**n**= pass. —**ş**= to whisper to each other.

fısıl fısıl فصل فصل with a whisper, with a whispering voice.

fısıltı فصلتى whisper.

fısır fısır فصر فصر with a light puffing noise.

fısırtı فصرتى light puffing noise.

fıskᵏⁱ فسق A lrnd. immorality, vice, a sinning. — **u fücur** debauche, vice.

fıskiye فسقيه A fountain, water jet.

fısla=ʳ فصلامه /ı/ 1. to whisper. 2. secretly to impart (information).

fıstıkᵍⁱ فستق [Arabic fustuq] pistachio nut. — **çamı** pine, bot., Pinus pinea. — **gibi** stout, plump and firm. —**çı** vendor of salted pistachios.

fıstıkî (..—) فستقى pistachio green, light green. — **kâğıt** obs. fine thin silk paper, generally buff-colored. — **makam** cf. **ağır ezgi fıstıkî makam**.

fıstıklıkᵍⁱ فستقلى pistachio grove.

fış fış فش فش with a splashing noise.

fışılda=ʳ فشلدامه to make a splashing noise. —**t**= /ı/ caus.

fışıl fışıl فشل فشل same as **fış fış**.

fışıltı فشلتى splashing noise.

fışırda= فشردامه same as **fışılda**=.

fışır fışır فشر فشر same as **fış fış**.

fışırtı فشرتى splashing noise.

fışka (ʹ.) فشقه It naut. the act of fishing the anchor. — **anelesi** fish shackle. — **et**= /ı/ to fish (anchor). — **palangası** fish tackle.

fışkı فشقى Gk horse dung; manure. —**cı** collector of dung for manure. —**la**= 1. /ı/ to manure with dung. 2. to dung (horse). —**lan**= pass. of **fışkıla**=. —**lat**= /ı, a/ caus. of **fışkıla**=. —**lı** strewn with dung. —**lık** dunghill.

fışkın فشقين shoot, sucker.

fışkır=ʳ فشقرمه to gush out, to spurt out, to squirt forth, to jet; to spring up (plant). —**dak** neol., chem. washing-flask. —**ık** squirt, syringe. —**ma** 1. verbal n. of **fışkır**=. 2. neol., astr. protuberance. —**t**= /ı/ caus. of **fışkır**=.

fışla=, **fışna**=, **fışra**= فشدمه فشنامه فشرامه to go sour, to spoil by fermentation. —**t**= /ı/ caus.

fıta 1 فوط var. of **futa 1**.

fıta 2 var. of **futa 2**.

fıtam (.—) فطام A physiol. a weaning.

fıtıkᵍⁱ فتق [fıtk] path. hernia, rupture. — **bağı** med. truss.

fıtırᵗⁿ فطر [fıtr] the ending of a religious fast.

fıtkᵏⁱ فتقى A lrnd., same as **fıtık**. —**ı mağbenî** path. inguinal hernia. —**ı sürrevî** path. umbilical hernia.

fıtnatᵗⁱ فطنت A lrnd. natural intelligence.

fıtr فطر A same as **fıtır**.

fıtratᵗⁱ فطرت A nature, constitution, natural disposition; creation. —**en** (ʹ..) A by nature, naturally; by birth, congenitally.

fıtrî (.—) فطرى congenital, innate, natural. —**ye** phil. nativism.

fi 1 (—) فى A 1. only in **fi tarihinde** long ago, in the days of yore. 2. lrnd. in, on, as in **fimabad**, **fisebilillâh**. — **hududi** about (a certain date). فى امان الله

fi 2 (—) فى [fi 1²] com. price, rate. —**i maktu** fixed price. —**i mîrî** official price, official rate.

fialⁱⁱ (.—) فعال A lrnd., pl. of **fi'l**.

fiatᵗⁱ, ᵗⁱ فيات فأت فئات [based on fi 2] price. —**ından aşağıya sat**= /ı/ to sell under the price. — **biç**= /a/ to estimate a price (for). — **endeksi** econ. price index. — **farkı** price difference. — **haddi** econ. price limit, ceiling price. — **indirme** price reduction. — **kes**= /a/ same as **fiat biç**=. — **kır**= 1. to reduce the price. 2. to cause a drop of prices by undercutting. — **koy**= /a/ to fix the price (of). — **murakabe heyeti** price control commission. — **seviyesi** price level. — **tâyin et**= /a/ com. to set a price (on), to quote the price (of). — **tenezzülü** com. reduction of the price. — **tesbiti** com. fixation of the price. —**lı** expensive.

fiber F mech. washer.

fibrin F biochem. fibrin.

fida (.—) فدا A lrnd., same as **feda**.

fidan فدان Gk 1. sapling, young tree. 2. plant. — **biti** plant louse, zool., Aphis. — **boylu**, — **gibi** tall and slender. —**lık** hort. nursery.

fide فيده Gk seedling. —**le**= /ı/ to plant out seedlings. —**lik** nursery bed.

fidevi (..—), **fidvi** (.—) فدوى P obs. your devoted servant. —**yane** (..——.) P pertaining to your devoted servant.

fidye 1 فديه A 1. ransom. 2. rel. alms given in lieu of ritual fasting. —**i necat** ransom.

fidye 2 فديه Gk prov. young vineyard.

fie فئه A lrnd. group of men, crowd, military force.

fiemanillâh (—.—.—) فى امان الله A rel. in God's protection, in God's hands.

fifre (ʹ.) فيفره F fife.

figan (. —) فغان P cry of distress, wail, lamentation. — **et=** to lament.

-figâr (. —) نگار P lrnd. sore, wounded, afflicted, *as in* **dilfigâr**.

figüran فیغوران F theat. walker-on; *movie extra*.

fiğ فیك [fik] vetch, *bot.*, *Vicia sativa*.

-fih (—) فیه A lrnd. in it (him), into it, about it, *as in* **manahnüfih, mef'ulünfih, münazaünfih**.

-fiha (——) فیها A lrnd. in her (it), into her, about her, *as in* **manahnüfiha**.

fihal[li] (.—) فئال A lrnd., pl. of **fahl**.

fiham (.—) فئام A lrnd., pl. of **fahim** 1.

fihris, fihrist[ti] فهرست A 1. table of contents; index. 2. catalogue, list. — **peşrev ve saz semaisi** *Or. mus.* a musical work that moves in many **makams**; it takes its name according to the movement of the **makam** being used.

fiil[fi'li] فعل [fi'l] 1. act, deed; *law* act. 2. *gram.* verb; predicate. —**den** *neol., gram.* deverbal. —**den ad** *neol., gram.* deverbal noun. —**i asam** *Arabic gram., verbum mediae geminatae*. —**i cevherî** *gram.* substantive verb. —**e çıkar=** /ı/ to carry out, execute. —**i ecvef** *Arabic gram.* hollow verb. —**den fiil** *gram.* deverbal verb. —**i gayrımüteaddi** *gram.* intransitive verb. —**e gel=** to be carried out. —**e getir=** /ı/ to carry out. — **gövdesi** *gram.* verb stem. —**i humasi** *Arabic gram.* quinqueliteral verb. —**i iane** *gram.* auxiliary verb. —**i iktidarî** *Turkish gram.* potential verb, verb in possibilitive mood. —**i iltizami** *Turkish gram.* verb in necessitative mood. —**i inşa** *gram.* inchoative verb. — **ismi** *gram.* verbal noun. —**i istimrari** *gram.* durative verb. —**i kabih** *law* improper act. —**i kıyasi** *gram.* regular verb. —**i lâzım** *gram.* intransitive verb. —**i malûm** *gram.* active verb. —**i meçhul** *gram.* passive verb. —**i mukarebe** *Turkish gram.* approximative verb. —**i mutavaat** *gram.* reflexive verb. —**i mücerred** *Arabic gram.* verb form consisting, when written, of the radicals only. —**i müessir** *law* assault and battery. —**i mün'akis** *physiol.* reflex. —**i müşareket** *Turkish gram.* reciprocative verb. —**i müteaddi** *gram.* transitive verb. —**i nâkıs** *gram.* defective verb. —**i nebi** a voluntary action of a prophet. —**i nâsezâ** unseemly act. —**i rivayet** *Turkish gram.* verb in narrative mood. —**i rubai** *Arabic gram.* quadriliteral verb. —**i selâsi** *Arabic gram.* triliteral verb. —**den sıfat** *gram.* deverbal adjective. —**i şart** *Turkish gram.* verb in conditional mood. —**i şenî** *law* indecent assault. —**i tâcilî** *Turkish gram.* accelerative verb. —**i temenni** *gram.* verb in desiderative mood. — **tümleci** *neol., gram.* complement of verb. —**i vücubi** *Turkish gram.* verb in necessitative mood. — **zamiri** *gram.* pronominal suffix of a verb.

fiilen (—'.) فعلاً [fi'len] actually, really; *law* in act; *pol.* de facto.

fiilî (..—) فعلی [fi'lî] 1. actual, real; de facto; acting. 2. *gram.* verbal. — **hükûmet** *pol.* de facto government. — **şirket** *com.* de facto corporation.

fiilimsi *neol., gram.* non-finite verbal form.

fiiliyat (..——) فعلیات [fi'liyat] acts, deeds. —**ta** in practice.

fiiliye (..—.) فعلیه [based on **fiil**] *phil.* activism.

fiilsi *neol., gram., same as* **fiilimsi**.

fik[ki] Gk *same as* **fiğ**.

-fikâr (. —) فکار *var. of* **-figâr**.

-fiken فکن P lrnd., *same as* **efgen**, *as in* **sayefiken**.

fikende فکنده P lrnd., *same as* **efgende**. —**ser** who has cast down his head; contemplative; ashamed, confounded.

fikir[kri] فکر [fikr] thought; idea; opinion; mind. —**imce** in my opinion. —**iyle** with the idea of, with the intention of, *e. g.*, **öğrenmek fikriyle** with the intention of learning. —**ini aç=** to express one's opinion. —**ini al=** /ın/ to consult, to ask somebody's opinion. — **beyan et=** to give an opinion. —**inde bulun=** *same as* **fikrinde ol=**. —**i dağınık** distracted, absent-minded. —**e dal=** to be plunged in thought. — **edin=** /hakkında/ to have an idea, to form an opinion (about). — **et=***. —**ine gel=** to occur to one's mind. —**ime göre** in my opinion. — **hareketleri** currents of ideas. —**ine koy=** 1. /ı/ to make up one's mind (about). 2. /ı, ın/ to put into the mind (of another). —**inde ol=** to be of the opinion, to have the intention (of), *e. g.*, **kalmak fikrinde olan** he who intends to stay. —**i sabit** fixed idea, fixation. —**ini sor=** /ın/ *same as* **fikrini al=**. —**i takib** sense of sequence, esprit de suite. — **teatisi** exchange of views. —**i teşebbüs** initiative. —**e var=** archaic, *same as* **fikre dal=**. — **ver=** /hakkında/ to give an idea (about). — **yor=** to exert one's mind. — **yürüt=** to put forward an idea, to state one's opinion.

fikr فکر A *cf.* **fikir**.

fikren (.') فکراً A in ideas, in thought.

fikret=[der] 1 فکرت /ı/ lrnd. to think over.

fikret 2 فکرت A lrnd. thought, reflection.

fikrî (.—) فکری A mental, intellectual.

fikriyat (.——) فکریات A *phil.* 1. intellectual aspects (of a matter). 2. ideology.

fikriye (.—.) فکریه [based on **fikr**] *phil.* idealism.

fikriyen (.—´.) تَفَكُّرًا [based on Arabic] mentally, intellectually.
fikstür F sport schedule of games.
fil 1 فيل [Arabic —] 1. elephant. 2. chess bishop. — **burnu***. — **dişi***. — **elması** elephant-apple, wood-apple, bot., Feronia elephantum. — **gibi** huge, enormous. — **gibi ye=** to eat enormously, to have an enormous appetite. — **hastalığı** path. elephantiasis.
fi'l 2 فعل A lrnd., same as **fiil**.
filâdor, filâdur فيلادور It naut. lanyard of a shroud. — **bağı** rose lashing. — **cevizi** double wall knot.
fil'ağleb فى الأغلب A lrnd. more usually, more generally, for the most part.
filâj F only in — **et=** /ı/ card games to run (through one's cards).
filâma (.´.) فيلامه [flama] 1. signal flag; streamer, pennant. 2. measuring stick used by land surveyors. —**cı** pennant-bearer.
filâmur فيلامور Gk prov., same as **ıhlamur**.
filân فلان [Arabic fulan] same as **falan**.
filândra (.´.) فيلاندره It 1. red bandfish, zool., Cepola rubescens. 2. naut. pennant; long, narrow streamer carried at the head of the mainmast.
filândri فيلاندرى water hemlock, bot., Cicuta virosa.
filânistan (.—.—) فلانستان P lrnd. such and such a land; the residence of anyone.
filântrop فيلانترپ F philanthropist. —**i** F philanthropy.
filâr فيلار archaic lightweight slipper.
filâri (.´.) فيلارى It naut. the repeated looping of the end of a rope.
filariz فيلاريز mallet for beating out flax.
filârmonikᵍⁱ فيلارمونيك F only in — **orkestra** mus. philharmonic orchestra.
filâsa (.´.) فيلاسا It naut. rope yarn.
fil'asl فى الأصل A by origin, originally.
filâtor, filâtür F text. spinning-mill; spinning machine.
filâvta (.´.) فيلاوطه var. of **flâvta**.
filbahar, filbahri فل بهر A virgin's-bower, bot., Clematis.
filburnuⁿᵘ فيل بورنى It wild bay tree, bot., Viburnum Tinus.
filcan فلجان var. of **fincan**.
filci فيلجى keeper of an elephant.
filcümle فى الجمله A on the whole.
fildekoz فيلده قوز F text. Lisle thread; Lisle.
fildişiⁿⁱ فيل ديشى ivory. — **siyahı** ivory black.
file 1 فيله F netting; hair-net; net (bag).
file 2 فيله F print., bookbinding fillet.
filefgen (—..) فيل افكن P lrnd. overthrower of elephants, strong.
fi'len (.´.) فعلًا A same as **fiilen**.
filençᶜⁱ E mech. flange.

filenkᵍⁱ var. of **felenk**.
filet It naut. waters with even bottom, shallows.
fileto (.´.) فيلتو It butcher loin (of beef or mutton); club steak.
filez فلز A lrnd., pl. of **filze**.
filfil فلفل A lrnd., var. of **fülfül**.
filgalib (.—.) فى الغالب A lrnd. for the most part, generally.
filhakika (..—.) فى الحقيقة A in truth, truly, in fact.
filhal (.—) فى الحال A at once, instantly.
filhane (.—.) فيلخانه [Persian ——.] elephant stable.
fi'lî 1 (.—) فعلى A same as **fiilî**.
filî 2 (——) فيلى A lrnd. elephantine.
Filibe (.´.) فيبه geog. Philippopolis, Plovdiv.
filibit فيلبيت F phlebitis.
Filifus فيليفس archaic, hist. Philip.
filigran فيليغران F watermark (in paper). —**lı** watermarked.
filikᵍⁱ فيليك finest mohair.
filika (.´.) فلوقه It naut. ship's boat. — **demiri** boat anchor. —**i humayun** Ott. hist. Sultan's state barge.
Filikos فيليقوس var. of **Filifus**.
filmˡᵐⁱ فيلم F film; movie. —**ini al=** /ın/ 1. to film. 2. to x-ray. — **çek=** to film. —**e çek=** /ı/ to film. — **çevir=** 1. to film. 2. slang to show off, swagger. — **kopar=** slang to talk incoherently (when drunk). — **makinası** movie camera. —**cilik** film industry.
filinta (.´.) فلينته Roum carbine, short gun. — **gibi** smart, handsome (person).
Filipin فيليپين Philippine. — **adaları** Philippine Islands. —**li** Filipino.
filiskin فلسكين Gk pennyroyal, bot., Mentha pulegium.
filispit فيليسپيت E slang dead drunk.
Filistin (.´.) فلسطين [Arabic **Falastin**] Palestine. —**li** Palestinian.
filitre (.´.) فيلتره var. of **filtre**.
fi'liyat (.——) فعليات A same as **fiiliyat**.
filiz 1 فلز: فيليز Gk young shoot; bud; tendril. — **gibi** slender. — **kıran fırtınası** calendar cold east wind on May 16th. — **sür=** to shoot, to sprout.
filiz 2 فلز [Arabic **filizz**] min. ore.
filizî (..—) فلزى bright green.
filizle=ʳ فيلزلمك /ı/ to prune the surplus shoots of a plant. —**n=** 1. pass. 2. to shoot, to sprout.
filizli فيلزلو having shoots or tendrils.
filizzat (..—) فلزات A lrnd. ores; metals. —**ı seb'a** the seven metals (gold, silver, mercury, copper, iron, speculum metal, tin or lead).

fillenk fillenk فلنك same as **fellek** fellek.

filmesel فالمثل A obs. for instance. [/filo/ see /flo/.]

filo 1 (´.) فيلو It 1. fleet. 2. squadron.

filo 2 (´.) فيلو It only in — et= /ı/ naut. to round in (sail).

filokᵏᵘ var. of flok.

filoksera (.´..) F zool., phylloxera.

filologᵍᵘ فيلولوغ F philologist.

filoloji فيلولوژى F philology.

filon فيلون F geol. vein, seam, lode.

filorcin فلورجين It same as **flûrcun**.

filori فلورى It hist. florin.

filosof فيلوسوف F obs., same as **filozof**.

filotillâ (...´.) فيلوتيلا It naut. flotilla.

filoz فيلوز Gk fishing float, buoy.

filozof فيلوسوف F 1. philosopher. 2. philosophical (in character). —ça philosophical, philosophically. —luk abstr. n. of filozof. [/filö/ see /flö/.]

filtre (´.) فيلتره P sc., mech. filter. — kâğıdı filter paper.

filûri فلورى var. of **filori**.

filvaki (´—.) فالواقع A in fact, actually.

filze فلذه A lrnd. 1. slice or piece of flesh. 2. metal or mineral.

fimaba'd (——.) فيما بعد A, **fimabait** (——..) hereafter.

fimabeyn (———) فيما بين A lrnd. in what is between.

fimakablˡⁱ (——.) فيما قبل A, **fimatakaddem** (——...) فيما تقدم A law heretofore, in the past.

Fin فين Finn; Finnish.

finalˡⁱ فينال 1. sport final. 2. mus. finale. —e kal= sport to go on to the finals.

finans فينانس F finance. — ataşesi financial attaché.

finansal neol. financial.

finanse F only in — et= /ı/ to finance.

finansman F a financing.

fincan فنجان |Arabic .—| 1. coffee cup, tea cup. 2. elec. porcelain insulator. — böreği kind of round börek. — gibi wide open, bulging (eyes). bir — kahvenin kırk yıl hatırı var proverb Hospitality is remembered for a long time. — oyunu parlor game in which a ring is hidden under one of a trayful of inverted cups. — zarfı metal cup-holder. —cı maker or seller of cups. —cı katırlarını ürküt= to bring unnecessary trouble upon oneself.

finefsil'emr (—...) فى نفس الأمر A lrnd. in essence, essentially, fundamentally.

finet F text. flannelette with fluffy underside.

finfon فن فون colloq., expression describing the sound of French.

fing فنك same as **fink**.

fingirde⁼ʳ فنكرده مك to behave coquettishly.

fingirdekᵍⁱ فنكردك coquettish, frivolous.

fingirdeş⁼ⁱʳ فنكردشمك to flirt.

finkᵍⁱ فنك only in — at=, archaic — ur= 1. to flirt around. 2. to be wild with joy.

Finlândiya (.´..) فنلانديا Finland. —lı Finn.

Finli فنلى Finn.

fino 1 (´.) فينو pet dog, lap dog.

fino 2 (´.) فينو It obs. fine, of good quality. — fes small fez for a lady.

firade firade (—..—.) فراده فراده [fürade] pop. one by one.

firakᵏⁱ (.—) فراق A poet. 1. separation. 2. grief at separation. —iye (.——.) A literature poem expressing sorrow at separation. —lı sad, melancholy (story, poem, song, tune). —zede P lrnd. suffering from separation.

firar (.—) فرار A 1. a running away, flight. 2. mil. desertion. —ı efkâr psych. morbid flight of imagination. — et= 1. to run away, to flee, to take to flight. 2. mil. to desert. —a kadem bas= obs. to run away. — noktası perspective vanishing-point. — teşebbüsü attempt at flight.

firarî (.——) فرارى P 1. fugitive. 2. mil. deserter.

firaset (.—.) فراست A lrnd., same as **feraset**.

firaş (.—) فراش A lrnd. bed; can. law intercourse.

firaşkın, firaşkon فراشقين فراشقون It naut. tackle of two triple blocks.

firavan (.——) فراوان P lrnd. plentiful, abundant; many, numerous. — ol= to abound. —î (.———) P, —lık abundance, plenty.

Fir'avnî (..—) فرعونى A lrnd. Pharaonic.

Firavun فرعون [Arabic Fir'awn] 1. Pharaoh. 2. l. c. haughty, despotical (person). f— faresi ichneumon, zool., Herpestes ichneumon. — inadı extreme obstinacy. — inciri sycamore fig, bot., Ficus sycomorus. — tacı bishop's miter shell, zool., Mitra episcopalis. —luk self-willed craft and obstinacy.

firaz 1 (.—) فراز P var. of **feraz 1**.

-firaz 2 (.—) فراز P var. of **-feraz 2**.

fircarî (.——) فرجارى A lrnd. circular.

firdevs فردوس A lrnd. 1. garden of Paradise. 2. heaven. —aşyan (..——) P who dwells in Paradise, the deceased. F—î (..—) Firdausi (Persian poet). —mekân (...—) P who dwells in Paradise, the deceased.

fire (´.) فره Gk com. loss, decrease, diminution (of weight); wastage; shrinkage.

— ver= to suffer wastage; to diminish; to shrink.
[/fir/ see /fr/.]
Firenc فِرَنْج A *same as* **Efrenc**.
Firense (..'.) فُرَنْسَ It *obs.* Florence.
firez فِيرَز *prov.* stubble.
firfir (.—) فِرْفِير *lrnd.* blossom of the Judas tree. —**î** (.—.—) purple.
-firib (.—) فَرِيب P *lrnd.* deceiving, cheating, *as in* **avamfirib, dilfirib**.
firifte (.—.) فَرِيفْتَه P *lrnd.* deceived; seduced.
firikᵍⁱ فَرِيك |ferik 3| *prov.* roasted unripe wheat.
firistade (..—.) فِرِسْتَادَه P *lrnd.* 1. who has sent. 2. sent; messenger; apostle.
firişte فِرِشْتَه P *lrnd.*, *same as* **ferişte**. —**i merg** Angel of Death. —**gân** (...—) P *pl. of* **firişte**. —**gânî** (...—.—) P angelic.
firkatᵗⁱ فُرْقَت |furkat| *poet.* separation, absence. — **çek=** to suffer separation. — **et=** /dan/ to part, to separate (from).
firkata (..'.) فِرْقَتَه It *hist.* light galley frigate.
firkateyn فِرْقَتَيْن, *obs.* **firkatun** فِرْقَتُن It *hist.* frigate.
firkatzede فِرْقَتْ زَده |firkat+zede| *poet.* suffering separation.
firkete (..'.) فِيرْكَتَه It hairpin.
firma (.'.) فِيرْمَ It *com.* 1. firm. 2. trade name.
firuz (——) فِيروز P *lrnd.* victorious; prosperous, lucky. —**baht** (——.) P victorious, lucky.
firuze (——.) فِيروزَه P 1. turquoise. 2. turquoise blue, azure. 3. *text.* mixed silk material with longitudinal stripes. 4. *poet.* vault of heaven. —**derya** (——..—) P *poet.* sky. —**fam** (——.—) P *poet.* turquoise blue. —**gâh** (——.—) P *poet.* sky. —**reng** (——..) P *poet.* turquoise blue. —**tac** (——.—) P *poet.* the turquoise crown (of the Persian kings). —**taht** (——.—) P *poet.* 1. the turquoise throne. 2. sky.
firuzmend (——.) فِيروزمَنْد P *lrnd.* conqueror. —**î** (——.—) P, —**lik** victory, success; prosperity; auspiciousness.
Fisagòr فِيسَاغور A Pythagoras. — **dâvası** *math.* Pythagorean theorem.
fisebilillâh (—.—.—) A, **fisebilullah** (—.—.—) فِي سَبِيل الله (*lit.*, in the way of God) expecting nothing in return.
fiskᵏⁱ فِسْق A *lrnd.*, *same as* **fısk**.
fiske فِسْكَه Gk 1. flick, flip (with the finger). 2. pinch. 3. pimple. — **dokundurma=** /a/ to protect from the slightest aggression. — **fiske kabar=**, — **fiske ol=** to be covered with small bruises. — **kondurma=** /a/ *same as* **fiske dokundurma=**. — **şamdanı** small candlestick. — **taşı** 1. small pebble to be shot by a flip. 2. *building* gravel (as used on concrete). — **vur=** /a/ to give a flip. —**le=** /ı/ 1. to give a flip. 2. to wound with words. —**len=** to be covered with small bumps (paint, plaster).
fisket فِسْكَت It *naut.* boatswain's pipe; whistle. — **çal=** to pipe (on board ship).
fiskos فِسْقوس whispering; gossip.
fistan فِسْتَان It 1. woman's skirt, dress, petticoat. 2. kilt. 3. *naut.* coat. —**lık** cloth (for making **fistan**).
fistül فِسْتُول F *med.* fistula.
fiş فِيش F 1. counter (games). 2. card (for index). 3. *elec.* plug. 4. form (to be filled).
fişekᵍⁱ فِشَك 1. cartridge. 2. rocket. 3. roll of coins. 4. fireworks. — **kovanı** empty cartridge; rocket case. —**çi** cartridge-maker; pyrotechnist. —**hane** (..—.) cartridge factory. —**lik** cartridge-belt; bandolier; ammunition pouch; cartridge-box.
fişle=ʳ فِشْلَه /ı/ to make a card index (of).
fişne فِشْنَه *var. of* **vişne**.
fit 1 فِيت instigation; incitement. — **sok=**, — **ver=** /e/ to instigate, to excite; to spread discontent.
fit 2 فِيت 1. equivalent gain or loss at a game of chance; quits. 2. *colloq.* ready; consenting. — **ol=** *colloq.* to be quits; to come to an agreement about price.
fit 3 فِيت E *in* **fit-tulumbası** feed-pump.
fiten فِتَن A *lrnd., pl. of* **fitne**.
fitil فِتِيل [fetil] 1. wick. 2. *med.* seton, tent. 3. *mil.* fuse. 4. *tailor.* piping. 5. *slang* drunk. —**i al=** to flare up, to become alarmed. — **gibi** as drunk as a lord. — **ver=** /a/ to make a mischievous suggestion (to). —**ci** trouble-maker. —**le=** /ı/ 1. to light (the fuse of a mine). 2. *colloq.* to incite. —**li** fitted with a wick, fuse, seton, or piping. —**li tüfek** matchlock-gun.
fitle=ʳ فِتْلَه /ı/ to instigate, to excite. —**yici** mischiefmaker, intriguer.
fitne فِتْنَه A 1. instigation; mischiefmaking. 2. *obs.* sedition, disorder, rebellion. —**i âlem** *lrnd.* a beauty who sets the whole world in commotion. — **fücur** mischiefmaker. — **kumkuması** dangerous mischiefmaker. —**âmiz** (..——) P *lrnd.* intriguer. —**biz** (..—) P *lrnd.* intriguing, mischievous. —**ci** intriguer. —**cilik** incitement. —**cu** (..—) P *lrnd.* troublemaker. —**engiz** (...—) P *lrnd.* troublemaker, mischiefmaker. —**kâr** P *lrnd.* troublemaker, intriguer. —**le=** /ı/ to inform (on). —**lik** intrigue, mischief.

fitrâk[kı] (.—) فتراك P lrnd. strap attached to a saddle (for attaching small articles).
fitre فطره A alms given at the close of Ramazan.
fitret فترت [fetret] lrnd. interregnum.
fityan (.—) فتیان A lrnd., pl. of feta.
fiyaka (..'.) فیاقه slang showing off; swagger. —sını boz= /ın/ to ridicule someone's swagger. — yap= to show off. —cı swaggerer. —lı showy; ostentatious.
fiyango (..'.) فیانغو var. of **fiyongo**.
fiyasko (..'.) فیاسقو It failure; washout. — ver= to end in failure.
fiyat[iı] فیات same as **fiat**.
fiyevmina (—..—) فى یومنا A lrnd. today; at the present age.
fiyonga, fiyongo (..'.), **fiyonk**[gu] فیونغا فیونغو فیونك It bow tie; bowknot, bow.
fiyort[du] فیورد F geog. fiord.
fizamanina (—.—.—) فى زماننا A lrnd. at the present time, in our time.
fizik[ği] فیزیك F 1. physics. 2. physical. — ötesi neol., phil. metaphysics. —çi physicist. —î (..—) physical. —sel neol. physical.
fizyolog فیزیولوغ F physiologist.
fizyoloji فیزیولوژى F physiology.
fizyolojik[ği] فیزیولوژیك F physiological.
fizyonomi فیزیونومى F physiognomy.
fizyoterapi فیزیوتراپى F physiotherapy.
flâma (.'.) فلامه It same as **filâma**.
Flâman فلامان F Flemish; Fleming.
flândra (.'..) فلاندره It var. of **filandra**.
flâvta (.'.) فلاوطه It obs. flute. —cı flutist.
flebit فلبیت F med. phlebitis.
flok[ku] فلوك It naut. jibsail.
florin فلورین It florin.
florya (.'.) فلوریه Gk 1. greenfinch, zool., Chloris chloris. 2. w. cap. a suburb of Istanbul on the Marmara.
floş 1 فلوش F text. floss silk.
floş 2 فلوش E card games flush.
flört[tü] فلورت F flirt. — et= to flirt.
flûrcun فلورجین [filorcin] hawfinch, zool., Coccothraustes coccothraustes.
flûrya (.'.) فلوریه var. of **florya**.
flüor F chem. fluorine. — ışı neol., phys. fluorescente. — ışıl neol., phys. fluorescent.
flüoresan F fluorescent (lamp).
flüorin F min. fluorite, fluorspar.
flüt فلوت F flute. —çü flutist.
fob فوب E F.o.b., free on board.
fobi فوبى F, **fobya** (.'.) L psych. phobia.
fodla فودلا A Ott. hist. cake of bread (formerly distributed in the soup-kitchens). —cı one who takes a job as a sinecure.
fodra (.'.) فودرا It lining or padding (of a coat).

fodul فضول [Arabic .—] A vain, presumptuous. —luk vanity, presumption.
foga (.'.) فوغه It obs., naut. Fire! — et= to fire.
fok[ku] فوق F seal. — balığı seal.
fokstrot فوقسترت E foxtrot.
fokur فوقور in **fokur fokur**.
fokurda= فوقورده to boil up, to bubble noisily. —t= /ı/ caus.
fokur fokur فوقور فوقور boiling up, bubbling noisily.
fokurtu فوقورده bubbling noise.
fol فول Gk nest egg. — yok yumurta yok a mere fancy; there's nothing.
folikül F anat., bot. follicle.
folkon فولقون It naut. frame-liner, timber-band (of a wooden ship).
folluk[ğu] فوللوك nesting-box (for hen).
fon فون F law fund, asset.
fonda (.'.) فوندا It naut. Let go the anchor. — et= to let go (the anchor).
fondan فوندان F kind of candy.
fondo (.'.) فوندو It obs., com. stock; bond; funds.
fonetik[ği] فونتیك F 1. phonetics. 2. phonetic.
fonksiyon فونقسیون F 1. law function. 2. physiol. function.
font karter F auto. sump.
fora (.'.) فورا It 1. Out. Open. 2. open, opened up. 3. naut. Unfurl (sails). — et= to take down, open up. — kürek Ship oars. — vele obs., naut. to make sail.
forma (.'.) فورمه It 1. print. sheet (of 16 pages); folio; compositor's form. 2. colors (of a sporting club). 3. school uniform; uniform. — forma in parts (publication).
formalite فورمالیته F 1. formality. 2. red tape.
formül فورمول F 1. formula. 2. law formulary.
formüle فورموله F only in — et= /ı/ to formulate.
formüler فورمولر F formulary.
foroz فوروز Gk catch of fish in one cast of the net. — kayığı small fishing boat.
fors 1 فورس naut. admiral's flag at the main; personal flag flown on a ship.
fors 2 فورس F power; influence. —u ol= to have influence.
forsa 1 (.'.) فورصا It galley-slave.
forsa 2 (.'.) فورصه F print. pressure.
forseps فورسپس F surg. forceps.
forsmajör فورس ماژور F force majeure; compulsion.
foryaz فوریاز Gk archaic for **poyraz**.
fos فوس Gk colloq. false, bad. — çık= same as **fosla**=.
fosfat فوسفات F chem. phosphate.
fosfen F physiol. phosphene.
fosfor فوسفور F chem. phosphorus. — ışıl

fosil

neol., chem. phosphorescent. **—lu** chem. phosphorous; phosphoric.
fosil فوسیل F geol. fossil. **—leşme** fossilization.
fosla=ᵣ فوصدومی to turn up bad or false; to be confused or upset.
fosurdat=ᵗʳ فوصوردائی /ı/ to smoke and puff comfortably.
fosur fosur فوصور فوصور in puffs.
fota فوطه var. of **futa 2**.
foto فوطو F photo.
fotoğraf فوطوغراف F photography; photograph. **— albümü** photograph album. **— atölyesi** photographer's studio. **— çek=** to take a photograph. **— çektir=** to have one's photo taken. **— makinesi** camera. **— malzemesi** photographic materials. **— röportajı** reporting by pictures. **—cı** photographer; cameraman. **—cılık** profession of a photographer. **—hane** (...—.) photographer's studio.
fotoğrafi F, **fotoğrafya** فوطوغرافیا It obs. photography.
fotojenikᵍⁱ فوطوژنیك F photogenic.
fova (ˊ.) فوه It naut. crossjack yard. **— sereni** crossjack yard. **— yelkeni** crossjack.
foya فویا It 1. foil (for setting off a gem). 2. eyewash; fraud. **—sı meydana çık=** to be shown up. **— ver=** to give oneself away.
fötr فوتر F felt. **— şapka** felt hat. **— terlik** felt slipper.
frakᵍⁱ فراك F swallow-tail coat. **—lı** in swallow-tails.
fraktür فراقتور F surg. fracture.
francala (ˊ..) فرانجله فرانیله فرانجلا It fine white bread; roll. **—cı** baker or seller of white bread.
França (ˊ.) فرانچه It archaic France.
frankᵍⁱ فرانك F franc.
frankoporto (ˊ...) فرانقوپورطو It naut. free port.
Fransa (ˊ.) فرانسه It France. **—lı** Frenchman.
Fransevî (..—) فرانسوی archaic French.
Fransız فرانسز It French; Frenchman. **—ca** French language; in French.
frapan فراپان F striking.
frekans فرقانس F phys. frequency.
fren فرن F brake. **— ayarı** brake adjustment. **— balatası** auto. brake lining. **— çubuğu** brake rod. **— kasnağı** brake drum. **— kolu** connecting rod of a brake. **— mili** brake shaft. **— pedalı** brake pedal.
Freng فرنك var. of **Frenk**. **f—i fer** Or. mus. a rhythmic pattern of 28 beats.
frengi 1 فرنگی [frengî 3] 1. syphilis. 2. prov. kind of lock.
frengi 2 فرنگی It only in **— deliği** naut. scupper hole.

frengî 3 (.—) فرنگی P archaic European; Europeanized.
frengili فرنگیلی syphilitic.
Frengistan فرنگستان P archaic the country of Franks; Europe.
Frenkᵍⁱ فرنك P European. **f— altını** debased gold. **f— arpası** pearl barley. **f— eriği** greengage plum. **f— gömleği** shirt; stiff shirt. **f— inciri** prickly pear. **f— lâhanası** Brussels sprouts. **f— maydanozu** chervil. **f— patlıcanı** obs. tomato. **f— salatası** endive; chicory. **f— sicimi** whipcord. **f— sicimiyle asıl=** to hang oneself with good, strong rope. **f— taflanı** Portugal laurel, bot., Cerasus lusitanica. **f— turpu** red radish. **f— üzümü** red currant. **f— yakısı** court plaster. **f— zahmeti** obs. syphilis.
Frenkçe (ˊ.) فرنكچه 1. European language. 2. French.
Frenkçin (.—) فرنكچین P Or. mus. a rhythmic pattern of twelve beats.
frenkhane (.—.) فرنكخانه [based on Persian] obs. large house let out in apartments to Europeans in Turkish towns.
frenkmeşrepᵇⁱ فرنكمشرب [based on Persian] lrnd. who imitates European ways of life.
frenle=ʳ فرنله /ı/ to brake.
freskᵏⁱ فرسك F fresco; wall-painting.
freze فرزه F milling cutter. **— makinesi** milling machine.
fribort فریبورت E naut. freeboard.
frikikᵍⁱ E sport free kick.
friksiyon فریكسیون F hairdressing massage; rubbing (the body with alcohol etc.).
Frikya (ˊ.) فریكیا L hist. Phrygia. **—lı** Phrygian.
frilya (ˊ.) فریلیا greenfinch, zool., Chloris chloris.
frişka (ˊ.) فریشقه It naut. fresh wind.
fuad (.—) فواد A lrnd. 1. heart. 2. mind, intellect. **—ı mide** anat. cardia.
fuar فوار F com. fair, exposition.
fuaye فوایه F 1. phys. focus. 2. theater foyer.
fudalâ (..—) فضلاء A lrnd., pl. of **fadıl**.
fufel (—.) فوفل P lrnd. areca nut.
fuhş فحش A 1. prostitution. 2. immorality, indecency. **—a teşvik et=** law to incite to prostitution.
fuhşiyat (.——) فحشیّات A obscenities, immoralities; prostitution. **—a tahrik et=** law to incite to prostitution.
fuhulˡü (.—) فحول A lrnd. those who excel over others.
fuhuşʰˢᵘ فحش var. of **fuhş**.
fujer فوژر F fern.
fukaha (..—) فقهاء A lrnd., pl. of **fakih**.
fukara (..—) فقراء A 1. same as **fıkara**.

2. *lrnd.* the poor; dervishes. **—perver** P benevolent; charitable.
fulᵘ̈ 1 (—) فول A *lrnd.* broad bean.
fulᵘ̈ 2 فل [*Arabic* **full**] syringa, *bot.*, *Philadelphus coronarius.*
fulâd (— —) فولاد P *lrnd.* tempered steel.
fulya (.'.) فوليه jonquil, *bot.*, *Narcissus Jonquilla.* **— balığı** eagle ray.
fund فوند G pound (German weight).
funda 1 (.'.) فونده *var. of* **fonda**.
funda 2 (.'.) فونده heath, *bot.*, *Erica;* heather, *bot.*, *Calluna*. **— toprağı** humus of heath or heather. **—giller** *neol.*, *bot.*, *Ericaceae.* **—lık** land covered with heath or brushwood.
funya (.'.) فونيه Gk artillery primer.
furgon فورغون F freight-car.
fursat فرصت A *lrnd.*, same as **fırsat**. **—cu** (..—) P opportunist. **—yab** (..—) P who finds an opportunity.
furş فورش F fork of a bicycle.
furya (.'.) فوريه It rush; glut.
fusaha (..—) فصحاء A *lrnd.*, *pl. of* **fasih**.
fusulᵘ̈ (.—) فصول A *lrnd.*, *pl. of* **fasl**. **—ü erbaa** the four seasons.
fusus (.—) فصوص A *lrnd.*, *pl. of* **fas** 3.
futa 1 فوطه [*Arabic* —.] apron, bath wrapper.
futa 2 فوطه Gk 1. skiff. 2. *obs.* long cask for making wine; open cask for carrying grapes.
futbolᵘ̈ فوتبول F soccer, football. **— takımı** soccer team. **—cu** soccer player.
fuzalâ (..—) فضلاء A *lrnd.*, *pl. of* **fazıl**.
fuzulᵘ̈ (.—) فضول A *lrnd.* a being more; excess. **—en** (.—'.) A superfluously; without right; unjustly.
fuzulî (.——) فضولى A meddling; officious; excessive; exceeding his rights; unnecessarily. **— işgal** *law* unlawful occupation of property, squatting. **— tasarruflar** *law* dispositions (contracts) made without authority.
füccar (.—) فجار A *lrnd.*, *pl. of* **facir**.
füc'e فجاة A *lrnd.* a sudden happening.
füc'eten (.'..) فجأة A suddenly (to die). **— vefat et=** to die a sudden death.
fücur (.—) فجور A *lrnd.* debauchery; immorality; incest.
fülân (.—) فلان A *lrnd.*, same as **falan**.
fülfül فلفل A *lrnd.* pepper. **—ü ahmer** red pepper. **—iye** (..—.) *bot.*, *Piperaceae*.
fülkᵏᵘ فلك A *lrnd.* 1. ship; boat. 2. Noah's ark.
füls فلس [*Arabic* **fals**] *lrnd.* small coin, mite.
fülûs (.—) فلوس A *lrnd.* small coins, mites. **—ü ahmere muhtaç ol=** not to have a cent, to be penniless.

fümuar فوموار F smoking room.
fündukᵏᵘ فندق A *lrnd.* inn.
fünun (.—) فنون A *lrnd.*, *pl. of* **fen**. **—u harbiye** military science.
fürade (.—.) فراده P same as **firade**.
fürce فرجه A 1. *anat.* fissure; *lrnd.* breach, gap. 2. *lrnd.* leisure. **—yab ol=** /a/ *lrnd.* to find an opportunity (to).
fürkan (.—) فرقان A 1. *lrnd.* that distinguishes truth from error. 2. *w. cap.* the Quran. **F— Suresi** Name of the 25th sura of the Quran.
Fürs فرس A *lrnd.* Persians.
fürsan (.—) فرسان A *lrnd.*, *pl. of* **faris**¹.
Fürsi (.—) فرسى A *lrnd.* Persian. **—yat** (.——) A Persian literary rules and expressions.
füru- 1 (.—) فرو P *lrnd.* low, as in **fürumaye**.
füruᵘᵘ 2 (.—) فروع A *law* descendants; issue.
furuat (.——) فروعات A *lrnd.* branches (of science, etc.)
fürubürde (.—..) فروبرده P *lrnd.* bent down.
füruc (.—) فروج A *lrnd.*, *pl. of* **ferc**.
füruğ (.—) فروغ P *lrnd.* flame, blaze.
füruht (.—) فروخت P *lrnd.* a selling; sale. **— et=** /ı/ to sell. **— ü harid** sale and purchase; trade.
fürukᵏᵘ (.—) فروق A *lrnd.*, *pl. of* **fark**.
fürumande (.——.) فرومانده P *lrnd.* weak, fatigued, depressed; helpless. **—gî** (.——.—) P. exhaustion.
fürumaye (.——.) فرومايه P *lrnd* ignoble, mean, base, low, vile.
füruset (.—.) فروست A *lrnd.* horsemanship.
-füruş (.—) فروش P *lrnd.* that sells, seller of, as in **malûmatfüruş**.
-füruz (.—) فروز P *lrnd.* that lights; enlightens, as in **dilfüruz**.
füruzan (.——) فروزان P *lrnd.* bright; shining.
füruzende (.—.ر.) فروزنده P *lrnd.* polisher; which illuminates.
füshatᵘ̈ فسحت A *lrnd.* spaciousness; wide space. **—saray** (...—) P spacious palace. **—saray-ı âlem** the wide world.
Füstat (.—) فسطاط A *geog.* Old Cairo.
füsun (.—) فسون P enchantment; charm; fascination. **—kâr** (.——) P enchanting; charming; fascinating. **—lu** enchanting; charming; fascinating.
füsürde فسرده P *lrnd.* congealed; insensible.
fütade (.—.) فتاده P *lrnd.* fallen; in love.
fütuh (.—) فتوح A *lrnd.*, *pl. of* **feth**.
fütuhat (.——) فتوحات A victories; conquests. **—çı** conqueror; imperialist.
fütur (.—) فتور A languor; abatement; a

fütüvvet becoming dispirited. **— et=** to be discouraged. **— getir=** to lose zeal, to show loss of energy. **—suz** 1. indifferent. 2. undeterred.

fütüvvet فتوّت A 1. *hist.* Futuwa (a semi-religious movement in Islamic countries). 2. *lrnd.* youth; prime of life. 3. *lrnd.* generosity; large-heartedness. **—lû** (... —) P *obs.*, *title given to junior officials*. **—mend** P *lrnd.* generous.

füyuz (. —) فيوض A *lrnd.*, *pl. of* **feyz**. **—at** (. — —) *same as* **füyuz**.

füze (ˊ.) فوزه F *artillery* rocket.

füzen فوزن F charcoal pencil (drawing).

füzun (. —) فزون P *lrnd.*, *same as* **efzun**.

G

g, G the eighth letter of the alphabet.

gabardin غبار دين F gabardine.

gabari غابارى F *transport* loading gauge.

gabavet (. —.) غباوت A *lrnd.* stupidity, slowness in the uptake.

gabe (— .) غابه A *lrnd.* forest, thicket, wild beast's haunt.

gabgab غبغب A *lrnd.* double chin. **—simîn** silvery white neck.

gabi (. —) غبى A *lrnd.* stupid, slow in the uptake.

gabin[bni] **1** غبن A *law* fraud, overcharge. **—i fahiş** heavy overcharge. **—i yesir** slight overcharge.

gabin 2 (—.) غابن A *law* cheating on a sale; fraudulent.

gabin 3 غبين Sl *prov.* shepherd's cloak, raincoat.

gabinet (. —.) غبينت A 1. *law* a fraudulently overcharging. 2. *archaic* regret, despair.

gabir (—.) غابر A *lrnd.* 1. remaining. 2. *Arabic gram.* future tense.

gabra (. —) غبرا A *lrnd.* 1. *fem. of* **ağber**. 2. earth, ground, soil.

gabuk[ku] (. —) غبوب A *lrnd.* a drink of milk or wine taken in the evening.

gabya (ˊ.) غابيه It *naut.* pertaining to the topmast. **— çubuğu** topmast. **— grandi** pertaining to the main-topmast. **— patrisası** topmast backstay. **— prova** pertaining to the fore-topsail. **— sereni** topsail yard. **— yelkeni** topsail.

gabyar غابيار It *naut.* sailor assigned to the topmast.

gacı غاجى *prov.* younger sister.

gacır غاجر *only in* **— gucur** producing a continuous creaking noise. **—da=** to creak. **—dat=** /ı/ *caus. of* **gacırda=**. **—tı** continual creaking noise.

gaco غاجو Romany *slang* woman, sweetheart. **— eskisi** English pound (gold coin with the portrait of Queen Victoria).

gad غد A *lrnd.* 1. the next day, the morrow. 2. some future day.

gada (. —) غدا A *lrnd.* morning meal; morning drink.

gadarif (. — —) غضاريف A *lrnd.*, *pl. of* **gudruf**.

gadat (. —) غدات A *lrnd.* early morning between dawn and sunrise.

gaddar (. —) غدّار 1. cruel, tyrannical. 2. *archaic* who asks a prohibitive price. 3. *lrnd.* perfidious. **—ane** (. — —ˊ.) P cruel, tyrannical; in a cruel way.

gaddare (. —.) غدّاره large, heavy, double-edged scimitar.

gaddari (. — —) غدّارى P *lrnd.* **gaddarlık**[ğı] غدّاره لق *abstr. n. of* **gaddar**.

gadebos غاده بوس It *naut.* beam ends at the prow of small sailing vessels, by which they are moored and pulled ashore.

gadir[dri] **1** غدر |**gadr**| 1. wrong, injustice; tyranny. 2. *can. law* perfidy; breach of treaty. **—e uğra=** to be wronged.

gadir 2 (—.) غادر A *lrnd.* deceitful.

gadîr 3 (. —) غدير A *lrnd.* pond, pool. **—î** (. — —) A *biol.*, *geol.* lacustrine. **—iye** (. — —.) A *bot.*, *Lemnaceae*.

gadiye (. —.) غديه A *lrnd.* early morning between dawn and sunrise.

gadr غدر A *same as* **gadir 1**. **—i felek** *lrnd.* tyranny of fortune. **— et=** 1. /a/ to do wrong (to), to treat unjustly, to act unjustly (toward). 2. *can. law* to commit a breach of trust.

|/ga/ *see* /ka/.|

gadrdide (. — .) غَـدَرْدِيدَه P *lrnd.* wronged.
gadruf (. —) غَضْروف *var. of* **gudruf.**
gadur (. —) غَدور A *lrnd.* unjust, unscrupulous.
gaf غاف F faux pas, blunder, gaff. **— yap=** to blunder.
gaferallahu leh (. ́. . — . . ́.) **gaferallahu lehü** (. ́. . . — . . ́.) غَفَرَ اللّٰهُ لَه A *rel. formula* May God forgive him (said about a dead person).
Gaffar (. —) غَفَّار A *lrnd.* the Pardoner, God.
Gaffarülmüznibin (. — . . . —) غَفَّارُ الْمُذْنِبِين A *lrnd.* Pardoner of sinners, God.
Gaffarüzzünub (. — . . —) غَفَّارُ الذُّنُوب A *lrnd.* Pardoner of sins, God.
gafil (— .) غافِل A 1. careless, heedless, unmindful, unwary. 2. /dan/ unaware (of). **— avla=** /ı/ to catch unawares. **— davran=** to act unwarily. **—âne** (— . — .) P, **—ce** unwary, heedless (act); unwarily, heedlessly. **—î** (— . —) P *lrnd.*, **—lik** *abstr. n. of* **gafil.**
gafir 1 (. —) غَفير A *lrnd.* comprehensive, inclusive.
gafir 2 (— .) غافِر A *lrnd.* the Pardoner, God. **G— Suresi** *name of the 40th sura of the Quran.*
Gafirüzzenb (— . . .) غافِرُ الذَّنْب A *lrnd.* the Forgiver of sin, God.
gaflet غَفْلَت A 1. *abstr. n. of* **gafil.** 2. somnolence, sleepiness; sleep. **—le** heedlessly, thoughtlessly. **— bastı** /a/ He was overcome by sleep. **—e düş=, — et=** to act heedlessly, to be careless, to make an absent-minded mistake. **— geldi** /a/ *same as* **gaflet bastı. — göster=** to be heedlessly neglectful. **— uykusu** indolent indifference. **— üzere bulun=** /dan/ to be unaware (of).
gafleten (. ́. .) غَفْلَةً A *lrnd.* inadvertently, unawares, absentmindedly.
gafur (. —) غَفور A all-forgiving (God).
gaga غاغا غاغ غَغَه غغا 1. beak, bill. 2. *naut.* anchor's bill, peak. **— burun** aquiline; hook nose; hook-nosed. **—sından yakala=** /ı/ to catch by the nose. **—la=** /ı/ to peck. **—laş=** 1. to peck one another. 2. to bill and coo. **—lat=** /ı, a/ *caus. of* **gagala=.** **—lı** 1. beaked. 2. *naut.* small sailing vessel with high prow and stern, used on the Black Sea. **—msı** *anat.* coronoid.
Gagauz غاغاوز a Turkish-speaking Christian people in the Balkans.
gâh 1 گاه P *repeated* sometimes, *e. g.*, **gâh uykuda, gâh uyanık** sometimes asleep, sometimes awake; now asleep, now awake.
gâh 2 (—) گاه P *lrnd.* 1. time, moment, instant. 2. place; throne. **— begâh** at times, now and then. **— ü bigâh, — bigâh** well-timed or ill-timed, at all times, at every turn. **— gâh** some time or other.
-gâh 3 (—) گاه P *lrnd.* place of, *as in* **ikametgâh, namazgâh, ordugâh.**
gâhi (— —) گاهی P *lrnd.* sometimes, at times. **—ce** *obs.* sometimes, but rarely.
gâhvare (— — .) گاهواره P *same as* **gehvare.**
gai (— —) غائِيّة [*based on Arabic*] *phil.* 1. final, conclusive. 2. final, pertaining to purpose; teleological.
gaib (— .) غائِب A *cf.* **gaip. —âne** (— . — .) P *lrnd.* in the absence of the person talked about, behind the back.
gaile (— . .) غائِلَه A 1. anxiety, trouble, worry, difficulty. 2. *lrnd.* period of disturbance; war. **—i zailede** *lrnd.* in the last war. **—li** full of trouble; troubled, worried.
gaip[bi] (— . .) غائِب [**gaib**] 1. absent, invisible; *law* absentee, party who does not appear in court. 2. missing, lost; hidden. 3. the invisible world. 4. *gram.* third person. **—ten haber ver=** to foretell, to divine. **—lere karış=** *same as* **kayıplara karış=. —ten ses** a voice from the unknown world. **—ten söyle=** *same as* **gaipten haber ver=. —lik** *law* disappearance. **—lik kararı** *law* a declaring a missing person legally presumed dead.
gait (— .), **gaita** (— . .) غائِط A *physiol.* feces, human excrement.
gaiyat (— — —) غائِيَّات [*based on* **gai**] *phil.* teleology.
gaiye (— — .) غائِيَّة [*based on* **gai**] *phil.* finalism.
gaiyet (— — .) غائِيَّت [*based on* **gai**] *phil.* finality.
gak[kı] غاق caw! (call of a crow). **—la=** 1. to caw. 2. to bring up the wind, burp (an infant).
Gal[li] غال F Wales.
galâ 1 (. ́.) غالا 1. gala, festivity. 2. state dinner. **— gecesi** gala performance where evening dress is obligatory.
galâ 2 (. —) غَلاء A *lrnd.* scarcity, expensiveness.
galân غالان F 1. chivalrous, generous, polite. 2. lady's man, gallant. 3. *gamblers' slang* rich, having plenty of money.
galat غَلَط A 1. error, mistake. 2. barbarism, erroneous expression. 3. /dan/ corrupt version (of); corruption (of a word). **—ı basar** optical error. **—ı elvan** *psych.* faulty color vision, dyschromatopsia; color blindness. **— et=** *obs.* to make a mistake, to commit an error. **—ı fahiş** bad error. **—ı fikir** *psych.* misapprehension. **—ı hilkat** freak of nature, monster. **—ı his** *psych.* illusion. **—ı meşhur** commonly accepted error (in language). **—ı rüyet** distorted vision, optical illusion. **— söyle=** *obs.* to use erroneous expressions in talking. **—ı**

Galata

tercüme faulty translation, wrong translation. **— yaz=** *obs.* to use erroneous expressions in writing.

Galata (..´.) غلط the town of Galata, now part of Istanbul.

galatat (..—) غلطات *A lrnd.* barbarisms, erroneous expressions.

galatgû (..—) غلط گو *P lrnd.* liar. **—yi** (..——) *P* telling of falsehoods.

galatnüvis (...—) غلط نویس *P lrnd.* erroneous writer.

galdır guldur غالدر غولدر with an uneven, heavy, rolling gait.

gale غال *F print.* composing galley.

galebe غلبه *A* 1. victory. 2. supremacy, predominance, prevalence. 3. *archaic* crowd. **— çal=** /a/ to conquer, to overwhelm. **— divanı** *Ott. hist.* special Council of State with more than the ordinary number of members. **— et=** 1. to gain the upper hand. 2. /a/ to overcome, overwhelm. **—lik** *same as* **kalabalık**.

galef غلف *A lrnd.* state of being uncircumcised.

galen غالن *F min.* galena.

galeri غالری *F* 1. art gallery. 2. *min.* gallery, working drift. 3. *theat.* gallery.

galeta (..´.) غالتة *It* small dry bread, biscuit, rusk. **— tozu** bread crumbs (for cooking). **— unu** fine white flour.

galeyan (..—) غلیان *A* 1. rage, agitation, excitement. 2. *phys.* ebullition. **—ı dem** *lrnd.* boiling of the blood. **—ı efkâr** public excitement. **— et=** 1. to boil with rage. 2. *phys.* to boil. **—a gel=** to be agitated, to get worked up. **—a getir=** /ı/ *caus.* **— noktası** *phys.* boiling point.

gali 1 (——) غالی *A lrnd.* 1. expensive, high-priced; exorbitant (price). 2. ebullient, effervescent.

galî 2 (.—) غلی *A same as* **gali 1**¹.

gali 3 غالی *E hist.* galley.

galib (—.) غالب *A cf.* **galip**.

galiba (—.—) غالبا *P* probably, presumably; most probably.

galibane (—.—.) غالبانه *P lrnd.* victoriously.

galibarda (..´.) غالیباردا *It* bright scarlet color.

galiben (—´..) غالباً *lrnd.* 1. victoriously. 2. generally.

galibiyet (—.—.) غالبیت [based on **galib**] victory.

Galiçya (..´.) غالیچیا *It* Galicia (in Poland).

galipᵇⁱ (—.) غالب [**galib**] 1. victorious; victor, vanquisher. 2. dominant, prevailing. **— çık=** /dan/ to come out victorious (from a fight). **— ekseriyet** great majority. **— gel=**

/da/ to win, to be victorious (in a fight). **— ihtimal** probability.

galiya, galiye (—..) غالیا غالیه *A lrnd.* 1. the perfume compound *Galia moschata*. 2. black. **—bar** (—..—) *P* perfumed, fragrant. **—dan** (—..—) *P* scent box. **—fam** (—..—), **—gûn** (—..—) *P* of black color. **—misk**, **—müşk** (—...) *same as* **kalemis**. **—mu** (—..—) *P* 1. with fragrant hair. 2. black-haired. **—say** (—..—) *P* 1. perfumed, fragrant. 2. maker of *Galia moschata*.

galiz (.—) غلیظ *A* 1. foul, dirty, filthy, indecent, obscene. 2. *lrnd.* coarse, thick; unintelligent, obtuse. 3. *lrnd.* dreadful, dire, vehement. **—lik** coarseness; rudeness; thickness.

galle غلّه *A* 1. *can. law* income, rent, yield. 2. *lrnd.* grain, cereal, corn. **—i adem** *lrnd.* grave. **—i vakf** *can. law* income of a pious foundation. **—dan** (..—) *P lrnd.* 1. granary. 2. receptacle for money. **—fürûş** (...—) *P lrnd.* grain dealer. **—zar** (..—) *P lrnd.* sown field.

galon غالون *F com.* 1. gallon. 2. container for gasoline, gas can.

galoş غالوش *F same as* **kaloş**.

galsama, galsame غصمه *A* 1. *biol.* gill, branchia. 2. *lrnd.* larynx.

galsami (..—) غلصمی *A biol.* branchial.

galtan (.—) غلطان *P lrnd.* turning, rolling, revolving. **— piçan** wallowing, rolling and writhing.

galtide (.—.) غلطیده *P lrnd.* rolled. **—i hâk-i mezellet** rolling in the soil of degradation.

galvaniz غالوانیز [**galvanize**] *mech.* galvanization. **— yap=** /ı/ to galvanize.

galvanizasyon غالوانیزاسیون *F med.* galvanization.

galvanize غالوانیزه *F mech.* galvanized. **— et=** /ı/ to galvanize.

galvanizle=ʳ غالوانیزلمك /ı/ *mech.* to galvanize.

galvanizli غالوانیزلی *mech.* galvanized.

galvanizm غالوانیزم *F phys.* galvanism.

galvano غالوانو *F print.* electrotype, electro.

galvanometre (....´.) غالوانومستره *F phys.* galvanometer.

galvanoplâsti غالوانوپلاستی *F* 1. *phys.* galvanoplastics. 2. *print.* electrotype.

galve غلوه *A lrnd.* bowshot.

galyan (.—) غلیان *A same as* **kalyan**.

galyot غالیوت *F hist.* galliot.

gam 1 غم *P* 1. grief, anxiety, worry. 2. gloom. **— çek=** to be oppressed with anxiety, to grieve. **— dağıt=** to drive one's cares away. **— değil** *archaic* It does not matter. **—ı ferda** *poet.* care for the morrow. **— ye=** to grieve, to worry.

gamᵐᵐⁱ **2** غم *A poet., same as* **gam 1**.

gam 3 غام F *mus.* scale, gamut.
gama غاما F gamma. — ışınları, — şuaları *phys.* gamma rays.
gamabad (..—), **gamagin** (.——) غم آباد ,غم اگین P *poet.* full of sadness, tinged with sadness.
gamalı غامالى comprising a gamma. — **haç** swastika; gammadion.
gamalûd (.——) غم آلود P same as **gamabad**.
gamam (.—) غمام A *poet.* clouds.
gaman (.—) غمنات P *poet.* sad, sorrowful.
gamaşam (.——) غم آشام P *poet.* oppressed with sorrows.
gamba 1 (.'.) غامبه It *naut.* kink (in a rope).
gamba 2 (.'.) غامبه It *shoemaking* sides of the upper of a shoe or boot.
gambot غابوط [ganbot] gunboat.
gambrik غابريد [ganbrik] gun brig.
gamd 1 غمد *var.* of **gımd**.
gamd 2 غمد A *lrnd.* 1. a sheathing. 2. a covering, enveloping.
gamdan (.—) غمدان P *poet.* abode of sorrow; the world.
gamdide (.—.) غمديده P *poet.* who has gone through much suffering.
gamedallahu (...—.) غمدالله A *rel. formula* May the mercy of God be upon him! (said of a deceased Muslim).
gamengiz (..—) غم انگيز P *poet.* gloomy.
gamerat (..—) غمرات A *lrnd., pl.* of **gamre**. —ı **cehennem** the overwhelming abysses of hell. —ı **harb** the thick of a fight. —ı **mevt** the agonies of death.
gamet غامت F *biol.* gamete.
gamfersa (..—) غم فرسا P *poet.* driving away sorrow.
gamfersud (..—) غم فرسود P *poet.* careworn.
gamfeza (..—) غم فزا P *poet.* grief-increasing.
gamgama غمغمه A *lrnd.* clamor of warriors.
gamgin (.—) غمگين P *poet.* sorrowful.
gamgüsar (..—) غمگسار P same as **gamküsar**.
gamgüsil غم گسل P *poet.* sorrow-dispersing.
gamhane (.—.) غمخانه P *poet.* house of mourning; the world.
gamhar (.—) غمخوار P *poet.* oppressed with care, dejected. —**i** (.——) P, —**lık** *abstr. n.*
gamız [mzı] **1** غمز *var.* of **gamz**.
gamız 2 (—.) غامض A *lrnd.* obscure, abstruse; profound, hidden.
gamıza (—..) غامضه A *lrnd.* something difficult to understand, mystery.
gamızla= غمزلامق /1, a/ same as **gammazla=**.
gami (.—) غمى , **gamin** (.—) غمين P *poet.* sorrowful, sad.
gamir (—.) غامر A *lrnd.* waste (land).

gamkede غمكده P *poet.* mansion of sorrow; the world.
gamkeş غمكش P *poet.* who endures grief; careworn.
gamküsar (..—) غمگسار P *poet.* 1. friend, companion, confident. 2. dispeller of care. —**âne** (..——.) P care-dispelling, cheering. —**î** (..——) P, —**lık** driving away of melancholy; companionship, friendship.
gamlan= غملنمك to grow sad.
gamlı غملى grieved, sorrowing.
gammaz 1 غمّاز [gammaz 2] 1. tell-tale, informer, sneak. 2. intriguer.
gammaz 2 (.—) غمّاز A *lrnd.,* same as **gammaz 1.** —**âne** (.——.) P *lrnd.* sneakingly. —**î** (.——) P *lrnd., abstr. n.* of **gammaz 1.**
gammazla= غمّازلامق /1, a/ to inform (against), to tell on, to tell tales (about).
gammazlık[ğı] غمّازلق tale-bearing.
gamnak[kı] (.—) غمناك P *poet.* sorrowful, disconsolate, grieved.
gamnisar, gamnişan (..—) غمنثار P *poet.* spreading melancholy.
gamperest غم پرست P *poet.* addicted to grief, given to brooding.
gamperver غم پرور P *poet.* that nourishes a grief.
gamr غمر A *lrnd.* 1. abyss, depth; deep. 2. dark, obscure.
gamre غمره A *lrnd.* 1. depth, abyss. 2. dense and surging crowd.
gamsele غمسله Gk raincoat, mackintosh, oilskin.
gamsız غمسز carefree, lighthearted.
gâmus (—.) گاموس P *lrnd.* buffalo.
gamz غمز A *lrnd.* 1. wink, sign with the eye, glad-eye. 2. tale-telling, denunciation. 3. intrigue. —**ı ayn** blink, wink.
gamze غمزه A 1. dimple. 2. *poet.* twinkle, coquettish glance. —**i ahter** *poet.* twinkling of a star. —**i cellâd** *poet.* ravishing glance. —**i gül** *poet.* opening of a rose.
gamzede غمزده P *poet.* sad, sorrowful. —**gi** (...—) P *abstr. n.*
gamzet=[der] غمز ايتمك /1, a/ to report, denounce, to tell on.
gamzî (.—) غمزى [based on **gamz**] *biol.* nictitating.
gamzida (..—) غمزدا P *poet.* that drives away care, exhilarating. —**î** (..——) P quality or act of driving away care or grief.
-gân 1 (—). گان P *cf.* **-an 8.**
gân 2 (—) گان P *lrnd.* sexual intercourse.
gana (.—) غناء A *lrnd.* 1. wealth, richness. 2. freedom from want, self-sufficiency.
ganaim (.—.) غنائم A *lrnd., pl.* of **ganimet.** —**i bahriye** *law* prize, naval war

ganbot ‏غانبوط‎ E gunboat.
booty. —**i bahriye mahkemesi** *law* prize court. —**i gayri me'lûfe** *can. law* landed property as war booty. —**i harbiye** *law* war booty, spoils of war. — **mahkemesi** *law* prize court. —**i maksume** *can. law* the bulk of distributable war booty (after deduction of the fifth belonging to the state). —**i me'lûfe** *can. law* the bulk of war booty (comprising only movable property).

ganbot ‏غانبوط‎ E gunboat.
ganbrikᵍⁱ ‏غانبريق‎ E gun brig.
ganc ‏غنج‎ P *poet.* amorous gesture.
Gand ‏غاند‎ F *geog.* Ghent.
ganem ‏غنم‎ A *lrnd.* 1. sheep. 2. sheep or goats. —**î** (..—) A ovine. —**î sahreler** *geol.* ice-smoothed rocks.
gang ‏غانك‎ F *mining* gangue.
gangava (..′.) ‏غانگاوه‎ Gk 1. dragnet used in sponge fishing. 2. small craft used in sponge fishing.
gangliyon ‏غانغليون‎ F *anat.* ganglion.
gangren ‏غانغرن‎ F *path.* gangrene. — **ol**= to become gangrenous. —**li** gangrenous.
gangster ‏غانغستر‎ F gangster.
gani 1 (.—) ‏غنى‎ A 1. copious, lavish, abundant. 2. *lrnd.* rich, wealthy; *w. cap.* God, who possesses everything. —**si** /ın/ not being in need (of). — **gani** lavishly, copiously. — **ganimet** abundance of anything to be had for the taking. — **gönüllü** generous-hearted.
gani 2 (——) ‏غانى‎ A *lrnd.* rich, wealthy.
ganilikᵍⁱ (.—.) ‏غنيلك‎ 1. abundance, plenty. 2. wealthiness.
ganim 1 (—.) ‏غانم‎ A 1. *can. law* warrior who has the right to a share in spoil. 2. *lrnd.* who takes spoil; who seizes.
ganim 2 (.—) ‏غنيم‎ A *lrnd.* 1. plunder, spoil. 2. taker of spoil, plunderer; enemy, foe.
ganimen (—′..) ‏غانماً‎ A *lrnd.* taking booty, booty-laden.
ganimet (.—.) ‏غنيمت‎ A 1. spoil, booty, loot. 2. godsend. 3. anything had for the mere taking; very copious, abundant. — **al**= /ı/ to seize, capture. — **bil**= /ı/ to look (upon) as a godsend; to seize (an opportunity). —**lik** suitable for spoil.
ganimîn (—.—) ‏غانمين‎ A *lrnd., pl. of* **ganim 1.**
ganiye (—..) ‏غانيه‎ A *lrnd.* 1. a modest beauty who prefers to go unadorned. 2. female singer.
Ganj ‏غانژ‎ F *geog.* Ganges.
gankᵏⁱ ‏غنك‎ G *obs., mining* vein, lode.
gannac (.—) ‏غنّاج‎ |*based on Arabic*| *poet.* coquettish (person).
gant ‏غانت‎ F *sports* boxing glove.
ganyan ‏غانيان‎ F *horse race* the winner (horse); winning ticket.

ganyot ‏غانيوط‎ [*French* **cagnotte**] *gamblers slang* the rake-off.
gar 1 ‏غار‎ F large railway station.
gar 2 (—) ‏غار‎ A 1. *anat.* cavern, antrum. 2. *lrnd.* cave, cavern; cavity. —**ı şerif** *Isl. hist.* the Sacred Cave (where the Prophet hid from his persecutors).
-**gâr 3** (—) ‏گار‎ P *lrnd.* who makes, *as in* **yadgâr** (**yadigâr**).
garabet (.—.) ‏غرابت‎ A 1. strangeness, curiosity, singularity; outlandishness; strangeness in style. 2. *lrnd.* a being away from home, a finding oneself in a foreign environment. —**i fikir** *psych.* mania. —**cû** (.—.—) P looking for curious things; who likes strange things. —**nüma** (.—..—) P *lrnd.* strange, singular.
garabil (.——) ‏غرابيل‎ A *lrnd.* sieves.
garaib (.—.) ‏غرائب‎ A *lrnd., pl. of* **garibe.**
garaj ‏غاراژ‎ F garage.
garam (.—) ‏غرام‎ A *poet.* passion, love; eager desire, ardent yearning.
garamet 1 (.—.) ‏غرامت‎ |**garamet 2**| *prov.* slander, calumny.
garamet 2 (.—.) ‏غرامت‎ A *law* liability, debt, obligation. —**en** (.—′..) A pro rata. —**en tevzi** pro rata distribution. —**zede** P indebted.
garami (.——) ‏غرامى‎ |*based on* **garam**| *literature* lyrical. —**yat** (.———) A lyricism.
garanti 1 ‏غارانتى‎ F guaranty, guarantee. — **akçesi** *com.* guarantee fund. — **et**= /ı/ to guarantee, to warrant. — **ver**= /a/ to give security, to stand guarantor.
garanti 2 (...′) ‏غارانتى‎ |**garanti 1**| *colloq.* sure, certain; certainly, without doubt.
garantile=ʳ ‏غارانتيلمك‎ /ı/ 1. to guarantee. 2. to make certain, to make sure (of).
garantili ‏غارانتيلى‎ 1. guaranteed. 2. sure, certain.
garaz ‏غرض‎ A 1. /a/ rancor, grudge, resentment, animosity, malice, prejudice (against); prejudiced, hostile. 2. /dan/ *lrnd.* purpose (of); aim, object. — **bağla**= /a/ to cherish a grudge (against). — **u ivazdan âri** disinterested. — **ki** *archaic* The thing is that... **bir** —**a mebni** *lrnd.* 1. for some private end. 2. because of a grudge. — **ol**= /a/ same as **garaz bağla**=. —**ı ol**= /a/ to nourish a spite, to bear a grudge (against). — **tut**= /a/ same as **garaz bağla**=.
garazalûd (..——) ‏غرض آلود‎ P *lrnd.* marked with some selfish motive, tendentious.
garazen (..′.) ‏غرضاً‎ A *lrnd.* for selfish purposes.
garazkâr (..—) ‏غرضكار‎ P *lrnd.* 1. malicious; grudging. 2. prejudiced; biased; selfish,

interested. **—âne** (..——.) P maliciously; selfishly. **—î** (..——) P maliciousness.

garazsız غَرَضْسِزْ unprejudiced, unbiased. **— ivazsız** unprejudiced, impartial, unbiased, disinterested, without ulterior motive.

garb غَرْب A cf. **garp**.

garben (.'.) غَرْبًا A westwards.

garbi (.—) غَرْبِى A 1. western. 2. *archaic* west wind.

Garbiyun (.——) غَرْبِيُّونْ A *lrnd.* 1. Westerners, Europeans. 2. partisans of Westernization.

gardenparti غَارْدَنْ پَارْتِى E garden party.

gardıfren غَارْدِيفْرَنْ F *rail.* brakeman.

gardırop[bu] غَارْدُرُوب F 1. cloakroom. 2. wardrobe.

gardiya غَارْدِيَا It *obs.* European corps of guards; guardsman. **—cı** guard, watchman.

gardiyan غَارْدِيَانْ It 1. prison guard. 2. guard in a lunatic asylum. 3. quarantine guard. **—lık** the occupation of a guard.

gardrop[bu] غَارْدُرُوب F *same as* **gardırop**.

garet (—.) غَارَتْ A *lrnd.* 1. pillage, plundering; sack of a place. 2. booty, plunder. 3. raiding incursion. **— et=** /ı/ to raid, sack, plunder, loot, pillage.

garetger (—..) غَارَتْ گَرْ P *lrnd.* pillaging, plundering. **—gerân** (—..—) P pillagers.

garez غَرَضْ *var. of* **garaz**.

gargara غَرْغَرَه A 1. a gargling. 2. gargle. **— et=** to gargle.

gargari (..'.) غَرْغَرِى It *naut.* downhaul of a staysail.

garık[kı] (—.) غَارِق A *lrnd.* under water, submerged.

garib (.—) غَرِيب A cf. **garip**. **— hicaz** *Or. mus.*, name given to the **hümayun makam**, presently out of use. **— hüzzam** *Or. mus.*, a *makam* supposedly named by *Selânikli Udi Ahmet*, presently out of use. **—ane** (.——.) P pertaining to a stranger, like a stranger.

garibe (.—.) غَرِيبَه A strange thing, strange event, curiosity; freak of nature.

garibî (.——) غَرِيبِى P *lrnd., abstr. n. of* **garib**.

garibnevaz, garibnüvaz (.—.—) غَرِيبْنَوَازْ, **garibperver** (.—..) غَرِيبْپَرْوَرْ P *lrnd.* kind to strangers, hospitable.

garibüddiyar (.—..—) غَرِيبُ الدِّيَارْ A *lrnd.* stranger, foreigner.

garik[kı] (.—.) غَرِيق A *lrnd.* 1. drowned; immersed, submerged. 2. overwhelmed, covered (with favors).

garikun (——.—) غَارِيقُونْ A agaric, *bot.,* *Polyporus officinalis*.

garim (.—) غَرِيم A *lrnd.* 1. creditor; debtor. 2. adversary. 3. fond lover.

garip[bı] (.—) غَرِيب [garib] 1. strange, curious, queer, peculiar. 2. *pop.* stranger, person away from home; poor, needy, destitute, abandoned, lonely; melancholy. **—ine git=** /ın/ to strike as odd, to appear strange (to). **— kuşun yuvasını Allah yapar** *proverb* God builds a nest for the homeless bird. **— yiğit** 1. country bumpkin. 2. poor man. 3. *Ott. hist.* member of a certain cavalry unit. **—lik** *abstr. n. of* **garip**. **bir —lik çöktü** /a/ A sense of loneliness engulfed (someone).

garipse=[r] 1. to feel lonely and homesick. 2. /ı/ to find strange, to deem curious.

gariye (——.) غَارِيَه [based on Arabic] *bot.,* Lauraceae.

garize (.—.) غَرِيزَه A *phys., psych.* nature, natural disposition, instinct.

garizî (.——) غَرِيزِى A *phys., psych.* natural, innate, spontaneous, instinctive. **— hararet** *phys.* normal warmth of a body.

gariziyat غَرِيزِيَّاتْ [based on **garizî**] physiology.

gark[kı] غَرْق A /a/ *lrnd.* 1. a being drowned; a being submerged, immersed; a sinking. 2. a being overwhelmed (with sorrow), a being covered (with favors). **—ı nur ol=** to be flooded with light. **—ı yeis ol=** to be drowned in despair.

garka غَرْقَا P *poet.* drowned. **—yı hun** drowned in blood.

garkab (.—) غَرْقَاب P *poet.* drowned; submerged. **— et=** /ı/ to drown, submerge. **— ol=** /a/ to be drowned, submerged (in).

garket=[der] غَرْق ايتمك /ı, a/ 1. to overwhelm (with favors). 2. *lrnd.* to drown; to submerge.

garkol=[ur] غَرْق اولمق /a/ 1. to be overwhelmed (with). 2. *lrnd.* to be drowned; to be submerged.

garnitür غَارْنِيتُورْ F 1. *cookery* garnish, garniture, trimmings (of a dish). 2. *tailor.* trimmings (of a dress). 3. *print.* fittings.

garnizon غَارْنِيزُونْ F *mil.* garrison; garrison town. **— komutanı, — kumandanı** garrison commander.

garoz غَارُوزْ Gk liver of the horse mackerel.

garp[bı] غَرْب [garb] 1. the west. 2. *w. cap.* the West, Occident. **G— Ocakları** *Ott. hist.* the North African dominions (Tripoli, Tunis, and Algeria). **—çı** westernizer.

Garplı غَرْبْلِى Westerner, Occidental. **—laş=** to become westernized. **—laşma** westernization. **—laştır=** /ı/ to westernize. **—lık** Occidentalism.

garra (.—) غَرَّا A *lrnd.* illustrious, brilliant.

gars غَرْس A *lrnd.* a planting. **—ı yemin** protége. **— et=** /ı/ to plant.

garson غَارْسُونْ F waiter. **—iye** service charge in a restaurant.

garsoniyer غَارْسُونِيرْ F bachelor's establishment.

Garüssevr (—..) غَارُ الثَّوْرْ A *Isl. hist.* the

Red 25

garz Cave in Mount Thawr (where the Prophet took refuge).
garz غَرْز A lrnd. 1. a pricking. 2. insertion.
gasˢˢⁱ غَثّ A lrnd. 1. lean; leanness. 2. poor; poverty. 3. meager; meagerness. **— u semin** 1. fat and thin. 2. rich and poor.
gasb غَصْب A same as **gasıp**.
gasbeanek غَصْب عَنك A lrnd. by force, by violence.
gasben (.'.) غَصْبًا A lrnd. by force (to take).
gasbet=ᵈᵉʳ غَصْبِ اِتمَك /ı/ to seize by violence; to take wrongfully, to usurp, to snatch away.
gaseyan (..—) غَثَيان A 1. a vomiting. 2. lrnd. a being nauseated. **— et=** to vomit.
gasıpᵇⁱ 1 (—.) غاصِب A one who seizes by violence; usurper.
gasıpˢᵇⁱ 2 غَصْب [gasb] 1. seizure by violence, usurpation. 2. law wrongful seizure; unauthorized assumption (of a name), false representation (as to name, title, or office); unlawful wearing (of decorations and uniforms).
gasilˢˡⁱ 1 غسل [gasl] 1. rel. a washing of the dead. 2. lrnd. a washing with water.
gasil 2 (—.) غاسِل A lrnd. washer of the dead.
gaslˡⁱ غسل A same as **gasil** 1. **— et=** /ı/ rel. to wash (the dead).
gaspᵇⁱ غَصْب [gasb] cf. **gasıp** 2.
gassalˡⁱ (.—) غَسّال A rel. washer of the dead. **—e** (.—.) A fem.
gastrit غاسترِيت F path. gastritis.
gasyan غَثَيان vulg., var. of **gaseyan**.
gaşeyan (..—) غَثَيان A lrnd., same as **gaşy**.
gaşiyˢʸⁱ غاشي var. of **gaşy**.
gaşiye (—..) غاشِيه A lrnd. 1. saddlecloth, horsecloth. 2. a covering, curtain, veil. 3. Day of Judgment; calamity. **—i kalb** pericardium. **— berduş** groom; very humble servant.
gaşiyedar (—..—) غاشِيه دار P lrnd. groom.
gaşum (.—) غَشوم A lrnd. willful; impetuous; tyrannical.
gaşyʸⁱ غَشي A lrnd. 1. ecstasy. 2. a fainting, swooning. 3. path. syncope.
gaşyaver (.—.) غشي آور P lrnd. causing to faint.
gaşyet 1 غَشيَت A lrnd. a fainting, swoon. **—i mevt** path. coma before death.
gaşyet=ᵈᵉʳ 2 غَشيَت اِتمَك /ı/ lrnd. 1. to enrapture, to fill with ecstasy. 2. to cause to faint.
gaşyol=ᵘʳ غَشي اولمق pass. of **gaşyet**=.
gats غَطس A lrnd. 1. a plunging. 2. a diving. **—iye** (.—.) A mech. immersion.
gâv (—) گاو P lrnd. 1. ox. 2. bovine beast. **—ı arz** Isl. myth. the bull that supports the globe on his horns. **—ı Samirî** Isl. rel. the Samaritan's ox (i. e. the Golden Calf of the Bible). **—ı zemin** same as **gâvı arz**.

gavail (.—.) غَوائل A · lrnd., pl. of **gaile**.
gavali (.——) غَوالي A lrnd., pl. of **galiye**.
gavamız (.—.) غَوامِض A lrnd., pl. of **gamıza**. **—ına aşina, —ına vâkıf** /ın/ well versed (in), knowing thoroughly.
gavani (.——) غَواني A lrnd., pl. of **ganiye**.
gavaşi (.——) غَواشي A lrnd., pl. of **gaşiye**.
gavaya (.——) غَوايا A lrnd., pl. of **gaviye**.
gavayet (.—.) غَوايَت A lrnd. a straying; error, perdition.
gâvçeşm (—.) گاوچشم P lrnd. 1. large-eyed. 2. oxeyed daisy.
gâvdil (—.) گاودِل P lrnd. ignorant, dull.
gâvdüm (—.) گاودم P lrnd. kind of brass trumpet.
gâvdümbalˡⁱ (—.—) گاودنبال P lrnd. conically tapering.
gâvers (—.) گاورس P lrnd. millet. **—i sim star. —î** (—.—) P path.· miliary.
gavga 1 (.—) غَوغاء P same as **kavga**.
gavga 2 (.—) غَوغاء A lrnd. mob, noisy crowd; tumult.
gavgav غاوغاو Arm slang testicle.
gavi (——), **gavi** (.—) غاوى A lrnd. erring, astray.
gaviye (—..) غاوِيه A lrnd. camel that carries water.
gâvmade (——.) گاوماده P lrnd. cow.
gâvmiş (——) گاوميش P lrnd. buffalo.
gâvpeyker (—..) گاوپيكر P poet. Feridun's ox-headed mace.
gavr غَور A 1. anat., fundus. 2. lrnd. bottom, depth; essential truth (of a matter). **—ına var=** /ın/ to get to the bottom (of a matter).
gâvriş (——) گاوريش P lrnd. fool.
gavs 1 غَوص A lrnd. a diving deep.
gavsˢⁱ 2 غَوث A lrnd. 1. cry for help; help, aid. 2. myst., a title of certain saints.
gâvşir (——) گاوشير P lrnd. opopanax.
gavt غَوط A lrnd. 1. hollow, cavity; deep depression in the ground. 2. a sinking, penetrating into a substance.
gavta 1 غَوط A lrnd. low-lying tract of country. **G—i Şam** the plain of Damascus.
gavta 2 غَوط P. lrnd. a dipping in water. **— ye=** to dip in water, to duck under. **—baz** P (..—) diver. **—gâh** (..—) P diving place. **—har** P (..—) diving, ducking, sinking.
gâvur گاور P, گاوور vulg. 1. giaour, infidel, unbeliever, non-Muslim; Christian. 2. godless, heathen, irreligious; cruel, heartless wretch. **— et=** /ı/ to squander, to waste (money). **— eziyeti** a deliberately making someone's job hard. **— icadı** invention imported from the West. **— inadı** pigheadedness, obstinacy. **—a kızıp oruç ye=** to spoil one's fast to spite an infidel. **— orucu gibi uza=** to be interminable,

to go on endlessly. — **ölüsü gibi** unexpectedly heavy and bulky.

gâvurca (..'.) كاوورجه 1. in the manner of an infidel; heartlessly, cruelly. 2. in a European language.

gâvurluk^gu كاوورلىغى 1. *abstr. n.* of **gâvur**. 2. country or place inhabited by Christians.

gavvas (.—) غوّاص A *lrnd.* 1. diver. 2. thorough student.

gavvase (.—.) غوّاصه |*based on Arabic*| *obs.* a kind of submarine.

gâvzad (—.—) كاوزاد P *lrnd.* godsend, unexpected good fortune.

gayb غيب A *lrnd.* absence, invisibility; the invisible world; absent, invisible, secret, or hidden thing. **— erenleri** *myst.* saints who exist in every period and who communicate with God and each other without words. **—dan haber ver=** *same as* **gaipten haber ver=**. **—dan ses** *same as* **gaipten ses**.

gaybdan (.—) غيبدان P *lrnd.* 1. skillful in discovering hidden things; diviner. 2. omniscient.

gaybet غيبت A *lrnd.* 1. absence; invisibility; loss. 2. a setting (of a heavenly body). 3. *myst.* a being lost to material things. **— et=** to go away. **—i hâfıza** *psych.* loss of memory. **—i munkatıa** prolonged absence with utter silence. **—i şuur** *psych.* loss of consciousness.

gaybî (.—) غيبى A *lrnd.* pertaining to the absent; pertaining to the unknown, invisible, occult.

gaybubet (.—.) غيبوبت A absence. **— et=** /dan/ to absent oneself (from).

gayda (.'.) غايدا Sp bagpipe. **—cı** 1. player of the bagpipe. 2. maker or seller of bagpipes.

gaye (—.) غايه A 1. aim, object, end. 2. *math.* limit; *lrnd.* the utmost, extremity, end. **—siyle** for the purpose of, aiming at, *e. g.*, **muvaffak olmak gayesiyle** with the aim of succeeding. **—sini güt=** /ın/ to aim (at). **—i hayal** *lrnd.* the object of someone's wishes. **—ye ulaş=**, **—ye var=** to attain the aim.

gayet 1 (—.) غايت |**gayet 2**| very, extremely, greatly, **—le** extremely, greatly.

gayet 2 (—.) غايت A *archaic, same as* **gaye**. **—i belâhet** the extreme of stupidity. **—i irtifa** *astr.* meridian height. **—siz** infinite, boundless, endless.

gayetülgaye (—..—.) غاية الغايه A *lrnd.* to the very utmost limit.

gayevî (—.—)· غايوى |*based on* **gaye**| *phil.* teleological; final.

gaygay غاى غاى with a shrill grating sound.

gaym غيم A *lrnd.* 1. clouds covering the whole sky. 2. thirst. 3. hatred, malice.

gayn غ A Arabic script, *name of the letter* (This letter is the nineteenth letter of the Arabic, twenty-second letter of the Ottoman Turkish alphabets, pronounced as the velar g in initial or postconsonantal position or as velar ğ in intervocalic or final position. In chronograms, it has the numerical value of 1000).

gayr^ri غير A *lrnd.* another person or thing; others.

gayrendiş (..—) غيراندىش P *lrnd.* altruistic.

gayret غيرت A 1. energy, effort, perseverance. 2. zeal, ardor. 3. *lrnd.* jealousy. **—!** A little more effort! **—i bâtıla** *lrnd.* misled zeal. **—i cahiliye** *lrnd.* blind fanaticism. **—ini çek=** /ın/ to take the part (of), to side (with). **— dayıya düştü** Uncle has to take care of it (said when work has been left undone and someone else must now do it). **—i diniye** religious zeal. **—ine dokun=** /ın/ to rouse someone's zeal, to stir up. **— et=** /a/ to endeavor, to try hard, to do one's best. **—e gel=** 1. to get into working spirit. 2. to become enthusiastic, to display zeal. **—e getir=** /ı/ to inspirit, encourage. **— göster=** /da/ to do one's best. **—ini güt=** /ın/ *same as* **gayretini çek=**. **—i Hak**, **—i ilâhiye** divine zeal. **—i İslâmiye** zeal inspired by the Islamic religion. **— kuşağı** *myst. orders* girdle worn by dervishes at certain ceremonies. **— kuşağını kuşan=** to bestir oneself; to step in for someone else. **— ver=** /a/ to encourage.

gayretkeş غيرتكش P 1. zealous; zealot. 2. partisan. 3. *lrnd.* jealous.

gayretlen=^ir غيرتلنمك 1. to get into working spirit. 2. to display zeal.

gayretli غيرتلى 1. hard-working, persevering. 2. zealous.

gayretmend غيرتمند P *lrnd.* 1. *same as* **gayretli**. 2. jealous.

gayretullah (...—) غيرة الله A *only in* **—a dokun=** to be offensive to God.

gayrezgüzeşte غيراز گذشته P *archaic, com.* apart from the interest.

gayrı 1 (.'.) غيرى |**gayri 1**| *prov.* 1. now, well then, at length, finally, *e. g.*, **gayrı başlamalı** Now it's time to begin. 2. (not) any more, (no) longer, *e. g.*, **gayrı ümit kalmadı** There is no hope left.

gayrı 2 غيرى *var.* of **gayri 2**.

gayrı 3 غيرى *var.* of **gayri 3**.

gayri 1 (.'.) غيرى |**gayri 2**| *same as* **gayrı 1**.

gayri 2 غيرى |*based on* **gayr**| 1. /dan/ other than, besides, apart from, *e. g.*, **duadan gayri** other than praying. 2. *obs.* other, different. **—si** another, others. **—ye muhtaç ol=** to be in need of another, to be dependent on another person.

gayri 3 (.'.)· غيرى |**gayr**| *before adjectives* un-, non-. **— ahlâkî** immoral. **— ahlâkiye** *phil.* immoralism. **— aklî** *phil.* irrational.

gayri

— **askerî** *intern. law* demilitarized. — **caiz** illicit, improper. — **cebrî aded** *math.* transcendental numbers. — **cismani** *phil.* incorporeal. — **devrî** *phys.* aperiodic. — **ene** *phil.* nonego. — **faal** inactive. — **ihtiyari** involuntary; unintended; involuntarily, instinctively, without wanting to. — **insanî** inhuman, cruel. — **iradî** *psych.* 1. involuntary. 2. nonvoluntary. — **kabil** impossible. — **kabili akis** *sc.* irreversible. — **kabili hal** *phil.* unsolvable. — **kabili hal mesele** *phil.* aporia. — **kabili inkısam** indivisible. — **kabili irca** *sc.* irreducible. — **kabili isbat** unprovable. — **kabili iştial** *chem.* non-flammable. — **kabili itiraz** unobjectionable. — **kabili kabul** unacceptable. — **kabili kabul poliçe** *fin.* bill of trade not requiring confirmation of acceptance. — **kabili kıyas** incomparable. — **kabili nüfuz** *sc.* impermeable. — **kabili red** irrefutable; unrejectable. — **kabili şifa** incurable. — **kabili tahammül** insupportable, unbearable, untenable. — **kabili tahmin** unforeseeable, unpredictable, incalculable. — **kabili tarif** indefinable. — **kabili tefrik** inseparable; indistinguishable. — **kabili telâfi** irrecompensible. — **kabili telif** incompatible. — **kabili temyiz** *phil.* indiscernible. — **kabili tezelzül** unshakable, unswerving. — **kabili vezn** imponderable. — **kâfi** insufficient. — **kanuni** illegal, unlawful. — **kanuni rekabet** *law* unfair competition. — **kıyasi** *gram.* irregular. — **maddî** immaterial, incorporeal. — **maddiye mezhebi** *phil.* immaterialism. — **ma'dud** innumerable. — **mahdut** unlimited. — **mahsus** imperceptible. — **makul** unreasonable. — **malûm** unknown. — **mantıki** illogical. — **matbu** not printed, in manuscript. — **medenî** uncivilized. — **melhuz** improbable; unexpected, unforeseen. — **memnun** dissatisfied, discontented, displeased. — **memul** unexpected, unpredicted. — **menkul** *law* immovable; real estate, immovable property. — **menkul kredi müesseseleri** *fin.* land credit institutions. — **menkul mal** *law* real estate, landed property, *pl.* immovables. — **menkul mükellefiyeti** *law* obligation on landed property. — **me'nus** unfamiliar, strange, unusual. — **mer'i 1** invalid. — **mer'i 2** invisible; microscopic. — **mesbuk** unprecedented. — **meskûn** uninhabited, unpopulated. — **mesul** not responsible. — **meşbu** *chem.* unsaturated. — **meşru** illegitimate, unlawful; illicit (gain); unjust (war). — **meşrut** *phil.* absolute. — **meş'ur** *psych.* unconscious; the unconscious. — **mevkuf olarak** *law* not under arrest. — **mevzun** 1. out of equilibrium, unbalanced. 2. ill-proportioned. — **mezru** uncultivated (land). — **muarref** *math.* indefinite. — **mu-**
ayyen uncertain, indefinite, indeterminate. — **mufarık** inseparable, inherent. — **muharip** 1. *mil.* non-combatant. 2. *intern. law* non-belligerent. — **muhtemel** improbable, unlikely; impossible. — **muktedir** incapable. — **munsarif** *gram.* indeclinable. — **muntak aded** *math.* irrational number. — **muntazam** 1. irregular; irregularly. 2. disorderly. — **muntazar** *lrnd.* unexpected, unforeseen. — **muteber** invalid, not in force. — **mübadil** *intern. law* not subject to exchange (population). — **mümbit** infertile, barren. — **mümkün** impossible. — **münfek** *lrnd.* inseparable, adhering. — **münhal** *chem.* insoluble. — **müntesir** unpublished. — **müntic** *log.* inconsequent. — **müsait** unfavorable; unsuitable, inconvenient, inopportune. — **müsait karşıla=** /ı/ to react unfavorably (to). — **müsavi** unequal. — **müsellâh** unarmed. G— **Müslim** non-Muslim. — **müsmir** *fin.* dead (capital). — **müstamel** *ling.* obsolete. — **müstaid** incapable. — **müştak** not derived. — **müşterekülmikyas** *math.* incommensurable (numbers). — **mütecanis** heterogenous. — **mütecessid** incorporeal; immaterial. — **mütecezzi** *law* indivisible. — **mütemerkiz** decentralized. — **mütenasip** disproportionate. — **mütenazır** asymmetrical. — **nâkil** *phys.* non-conductor. — **öklidî** *geom.* non-Euclidean. — **resmî** unofficial; informal. — **sâfi** *com.* gross. — **sâfi ağırlık** *com.* gross weight. — **sâfi gelir**, — **sâfi hasılât** *fin.* gross income, gross receipt. — **sâfi kâr** *fin.* gross profit. — **samimî** insincere. — **sarih mef'ul** *gram.* indefinite object. — **sarih oran** *statistics* unadjusted ratio. — **şahsi** impersonal. — **şeffaf** *phys.* opaque. — **şuurî** *psych.* unconscious. — **tabiî** unnatural, abnormal, strange. — **tabiî mukarenet** *law* unnatural sexual intercourse. G— **Türk** non-Turkish; non-Turk. — **uzvi** *chem.* inorganic. — **vâki** that did not happen. — **vazıh** imprecise, unclear, vague.

gayriyet (.—.) غَيْرِيَّت A *lrnd.* 1. non-identity. 2. the quality of pertaining to others.

gayrizati (..——) غَيْرِذَاتِىّ A *phil.* extrinsic.

gays غَيْث A *lrnd.* rain. —**i nâfi** 1. useful rain. 2. cloud.

gaytan غَيْطَان Gk *same as* **kaytan**.

gayur (.—) غَيُور A *lrnd.* 1. very zealous, indefatigable, unsparing. 2. public-spirited. 3. jealous. —**ân** (.——) A the very zealous. —**âne** (.——.) P zealously, diligently.

Gayya (.—) غَيَّا [based on *Arabic*] *Isl. rel.*, name of a deep pit in hell. — **kuyusu** 1. the Gayya pit of hell. 2. hopeless impasse.

gayz غَيْظ A *lrnd.* wrath, rage, anger. — **ü gazab** wrath and fury. —**efşan** (.——) P raging with anger.

gaz[z1, zi] 1 غاز F 1. kerosene. 2. *phys.* gas. 3. *prov.* kerosene lamp. **—a bas=** *auto.* to step on the gas, to accelerate. **— bombası** gas bomb. **— geçmez** gastight. **— hali** *chem.* gaseous state. **— haline getir=** /ı/ to gasify. **— ışığı** gaslight. **— ibiği** gas burner. **— kelebeği** *auto.* throttle valve (in carburetor). **—ı kes=** *mech.* to throttle back (gas). **— lâmbası** kerosene lamp. **— maskesi** gas mask. **— memesi** gas burner nipple. **—i mühlik** fatal gas. **—i münir** light-giving gas. **— ocağı** kerosene kitchen stove. **— pedalı** *auto.* accelerator pedal. **— saati** gas meter. **— sayacı** gas meter. **— sobası** kerosene stove. **— şaloması** gas burner. **— şişesi** *prov.* glass chimney of a kerosene lamp. **— tenekesi** kerosene can. **— yağı** kerosene.

gaz 2 غاز F gauze. **— boyaması** dyed cotton gauze.

gaza (.—) غزا A military expedition on behalf of Islam.

gazab غضب A cf. **gazap**. **—ı ilâhi** divine wrath.

gazaban (.'..) غضبا A *lrnd.* in anger.

gazabnâk[ki] (..—) غضبناك P *lrnd.* angry, infuriated; passionate, irritable.

gazal[li] (.—) غزال A *poet.* 1. gazelle, antelope; antelope fawn. 2. young person of fawnlike grace; singer, musician; cup-bearer. **—i Ka'be** Arabic antiquity fawn of the Kaaba (gold figure of a fawn set up as an idol in the temple of Mecca). **—ân** (.—) A antelopes.

gazale (.—.) غزال A *poet.* 1. female gazelle; female fawn. 2. the rising sun.

gazanfer غضنفر A *poet.* 1. lion. 2. brave man. 3. the Caliph Ali. **—i gazûb** 1. infuriated lion. 2. same as **gazanfer**[2, 3]. **—âne** (...—.) P like a lion, bravely.

gazap[bı] غضب |gazab] wrath, anger, rage. **— et=** *archaic*, **—a gel=** to become angry. **—a getir=** /ı/ to put into a passion. **—lan=** to become infuriated. **—landır=** /ı/ *caus.* of **gazaplan=**. **—lı** infuriated, angry; passionate, irritable.

gazat 1 (.—) غزات A *lrnd.*, same as **gaza**.
gazat 2 (——) غازات A *lrnd.*, pl. of **gaz** 1[2].
gazavat (..—) غزوات A pl. of **gazve**. **—name** (..——.) P literature heroic poem of military exploits.

gazavet (.—.) غزاوت P *lrnd.* 1. same as **gaza** 1. 2. abstr. n. of **gazi**.

gazban (.—) غضبان A *lrnd.* 1. angry; choleric, irritable, passionate.

gaze 1 (—.) غازه F gauze.
gaze 2 (—.) غازه P *lrnd.* rouge.
gazeke, gazeki غازکی *prov.* short jacket.
gazel 1 غزل A 1. *pros.* lyric poem of a certain pattern (comprising 4-15 couplets, with the first couplet rhyming, and all the second hemistichs rhyming with the hemistichs of the first couplet). 2. *Or. mus.* extemporaneous vocal **taksim**. **— oku=** 1. *Or. mus.* to give a vocal recital, to sing a solo. 2. to tell lies. **— söyle=** to compose lyric poems of the **gazel** pattern.

gazel 2 غزل [hazan] autumn, leaves. **— mevsimi**, **— vakti** autumn, fall.

gazel 3 غزل [gazal] only in **— boynuzu** bird's-foot trefoil, *bot.*, Lotus corniculatus.

gazelhan (..—) غزل خوان P *lrnd.* singer, giver of a vocal recital, soloist. **—î** (..——) P 1. **gazel**- singing. 2. **gazel**- writing.

gazeliyat (...—) غزليات A lyric poems of the **gazel** pattern.

gazellen=[ir] غزللنمك to dry and fall (leaves of autumn).

gazelsera (...—) غزلسرا , **gazelnüvis** غزلنويس P *lrnd.* writer of **gazels**.

gazep[bi] غضب var. of **gazap**.

gazeta (.'.) غزته It obs., same as **gazete**.

gazete (.'.) غزته [gazeta] newspaper, daily paper. **— bayii** wholesale distributor of newspapers. **— çıkar=** to publish a newspaper. **— idarehanesi** newspaper office. **— ilânı** advertisement. **— kapa=** to close down a newspaper. **— muhabiri** newspaper correspondent. **— muharriri** journalist. **— muhbiri** newspaper reporter. **— müvezzii** newsboy; news vendor. **— toplat=** to seize an issue of a newspaper.

gazeteci غزته جی 1. journalist. 2. seller of newspapers, news vendor; newsboy. 3. owner of a newspaper. **—lik** 1. journalism. 2. abstr. n. of **gazeteci**.

gazetehane (...—.) غزته خانه obs. newspaper office.

gazevat (..—) غزوات A same as **gazavat**.
gazevi 1 (..—) غزوی A same as **kazevi**.
gazevî 2 (..—) غزوی A *lrnd.* pertaining to military expeditions for the cause of Islam.

gazhane (.—.) غازخانه gasworks. **— koku**, **— kömürü** coke.

gazışı *neol., phys.* luminescence.
gazışıl *neol., phys.* luminescent.

gazi 1 (——) غازی A 1. one who fights on behalf of Islam, champion of Islam; *hist.* frontier raider into a non-Muslim country. 2. ghazi (title given to generals for outstanding exploits); *w. cap.* Atatürk. 3. war veteran. 4. *hist.* Ottoman gold coin of 20 piasters.

gazi 2 (——) غازی [based on **gaz** 1] *phys.* gaseous.

Gaziantep[bi] (—...) غازی عينتاب city and **vilâyet** in south-east Turkey, formerly Aintab. **— helvası** sweet confection made of sugar, flour, and butter.

gazino (..'.) غازينو It café, casino, place serving refreshments (usually outdoors).
gazir (.—) غزير A lrnd. copious, abundant; abundantly flowing.
gaziya غازِيَه Gk silver wattle, bot., Acacia dealbata.
gaziyan (———) غازِيان P lrnd., pl. of gazi 1. —ı Hacı Bektaş-ı Veli Ott. hist. Janissaries.
gaziyane (———.) غازِيانه P bravely; brave (act).
gazla=ᵣ, **gazle**=ᵣ غازلامك /ı/ 1. to gas. 2. to smear or sprinkle with kerosene. 3. to accelerate (automobile). —n= pass.
gazlı, gazli غازلى 1. containing gas. 2. containing kerosene. — bez gauze.
Gazne غزنه Ghazna. —li, —vî (..—) A native of Ghazna; Ghaznavid. —viye (..—.) A the Ghaznavid dynasty.
gazoma غازومه Gk shoemaking seam around the edge of a stitched sole.
gazometre (..'.) غازومتره F large gas storage tank.
gazoz غازوز F sweetened carbonated water.
gazölçer neol., phys. gas meter.
gazûb (.—) غضوب A lrnd. irritable, passionate; wrathful. —ane (.——.) P angry; passionately.
gazve غزوه A lrnd., same as gaza.
gazzaz (.—) غزّاز var. of kazzaz.
Gazze غزّه A geog. Gaza.
ge name of the letter g.
gebe گبه pregnant, expectant; /a/ big (with child, events). — bırak=, — et= /ı/ to get with child; to impregnate. — kal=, — ol= /dan/ to become pregnant (by). — zar gamblers' slang loaded die. —lik pregnancy.
geber=ⁱʳ گبرمك to die (used contemptuously); —t= /ı/ to kill off.
gebeş 1 گبش vulg. short and fat, dumpy, squat.
gebeş 2 گبش 1. slang idiot, fool, blockhead. 2. archaic bold, brave. —aki (..—.) fool, idiot. —oğlu bold, brave man.
Gebirᵇʳⁱ گبير var. of Gebr.
Gebr گبر P1. a Zoroastrian. 2. lrnd., same as gâvur. — ü tersa Zoroastrian and Christian.
gebre گبره haircloth glove for grooming horses.
gec 1 cf. geç 1.
gec 2 گچ P lrnd. lime, mortar, plaster; whiting.
gece گجه 1. night; at night; last night; tonight. 2. night entertainment. — balıkçılı night-heron, zool., Nycticorax. — baskını night raid. — bekçisi night watchman. —yi diri dut= archaic, same as geceyi ihya et=. —ler gebedir proverb Nights are pregnant with new events. — gözü kör gözü proverb Fine work needs the light of day. —yi gündüze kat= to work continuously. — gündüz day and night, continuously. — gündüz deme= to take no account of the time of day. —niz hayırlı olsun Good night. —yi ihya et= to pass the night in praying or working. — ile archaic at night. — işçisi 1. workman on the night shift. 2. slang burglar. — kadısı colloq. wife who exerts influence on her husband. — kaim gündüz saim spending the night in religious exercises and the daytime in fasting. — kal= to stay for the night. — kandili night light. — kelebekleri zool. moths. — kondu unauthorized construction set up in one night, squatter's house, shanty. — kuşu 1. owl; prov. bat. 2. night owl, person who goes about by night. — sefa, — sefası 1. morning-glory, bot., Ipomoea purpurea. 2. four-o'clock plant, bot., Mirabilis Jalappa. — silâhlı, gündüz külâhlı leading a double life (like Dr. Jekyll and Mr. Hyde). — vakti at night. — yanığı kind of skin eruption, esp. on face or hands. — yarısı midnight. — yatısı overnight visit.
gececi گجه‌جى working on the nightshift.
gecele=ʳ گجه‌لمك 1. /da/ to spend the night (in a place). 2. for night to fall. —t= /ı/ caus.
geceleyin گجه‌لين by night.
geceli گجه‌لى in — gündüzlü day and night, continuously; continuous.
gecelikᵍⁱ گجه‌لك 1. pertaining to the night; lasting the night. 2. nightdress, nightgown, night shirt. 3. fee for the night. — entari, — entarisi nightgown, nightshirt. — külâhıma anlat colloq. Tell it to my nightshirt and kerchief; you are lying.
gecere گجره prov. yarn-winding apparatus.
gecik=ⁱʳ گجيكمك to be late, to be delayed. —me delay. —sen=, —si=, —sin= /ı/ prov. to consider late. —tir= /ı/ caus. of gecik=.
geçᶜⁱ,ᶜⁱ **1** گچ late, delayed. — işte hayır vardır proverb A delay is sometimes a gain. — kal= to be late. — olsun da güç olmasın Better late than never. — vakit late in the evening.
geç=ᵉʳ **2** گچمك 1. to pass by, to pass through; /dan, or ı/ to pass (by, through, over); /dan, a/ to pass (from, to); to be inherited; to be transmitted, to be caught (disease, by, from). 2. /ı/ to pass, surpass, overpass, leave behind; to exceed; to pass over, omit, not to heed; /dan/ to abandon, to give up, renounce; archaic to pardon, overlook. 3. /dan/ to undergo (examination); /ı/ to pass (examination), to be promoted (in class). 4. to be current (money), to be valid (document); to be

acceptable (word); *com.* to be marketable. 5. /a/ to move (to, into), to get (to); to succeed (to a post), to be appointed (to an office); to penetrate (into). 6. to pass, elapse; to come to an end, pass away, expire, lapse; to be over; to be overripe, to spoil; *prov.* to fade; /dan/ to be over (for someone, age), *e. g.*, **benden geçti artık** It's beyond me now. 7. to occur, to turn up; to occur, come up (in conversation), to be mentioned. 8. /a/ to be contributed (to), *e. g.*, **ona çok hizmetim geçmiştir** I have done him many services. 9. /ı, a/ *colloq.* to report (someone to his superior). 10. /ı/ to sing, play (song, tune); *slang* to tell, relate; /ı, dan/ to learn (a song or tune from someone). 11. *after verbal noun*, *slang* to do, to make, *e. g.*, **alay geç=** same as **alay et=**. **işmar geç=** same as **işmar et=**. **tenbih geç=** same as **tenbih et=**. —!, — **efendim!** *colloq.* Leave it. Don't waste your time on it. It's not worth talking about, *e. g.*, — **başka şeyler konuşalım** Let's leave that alone and talk about other things. —e*. —elim Let us not talk about it. —en*. —er*. —miş*. —tim let alone, *e. g.*, **mektubu geçtim, bir kartpostal olsun yazamıyor mu?** Can't he at least write a postcard, let alone a letter? —ti **Bor'un pazarı, sür eşeğini Niğde'ye!** It is too late to do anything. —**ip git=** 1. to pass by and go on. 2. to go away; to pass away. —**me nâmerd köprüsünden, ko aparsın su seni!** *proverb* Better to die than be obliged to a mean person. —**tim ola**, —**tim olsun** God forbid, *e. g.*, **bir şey olur da, geçtim ola, ödemesi bize düşer!** Something may happen and, God forbid, we may have to pay for it. — **yiğitim geç** Pass by, my brave one (said in giving way to someone of whom one is afraid).

geçe 1 *for indication of time* at... past..., *e. g.*, **saat dokuzu on geçe** at 10 past 9.
geçe 2 *prov.* side.
geçek[si] *prov.* place of passage; ford; narrow wooden bridge.
geçen past, last. —**de**, —**lerde** lately, recently. — **gün** the other day. — **sefer** last time. — **sene**, — **yıl** last year.
geçer current, in circulation, in common use. — **akçe** 1. current coin. 2. something valued by everybody. — **beş** a grade of five given in order to pass a student. — **mal** something valued by everybody. —**lik** a being in demand, a being current.
geçgere *prov.*, *var* of **teskere**.
geçici 1. passing, temporary, transitory. 2. contagious.
geçid *cf.* **geçit**.
geçil=[ir] *pass.* of **geç=** 2. —**miyor** /dan/ There is great abundance (of), *e. g.*, **sokakta arabalardan geçilmiyor**.
geçim 1. a living, livelihood. 2. a getting along with one another, harmony. 3. *hist.* coat of mail. 4. *obs.* current value of a coin, currency. — **derdi** the struggle to make a living. — **dünyası** One has to get along with others. — **masrafı** cost of living. — **vasıtası**, — **yolu** means of subsistence.
geçimli easy to get on with.
geçimsiz difficult, quarrelsome. —**lik** inability to get on with others or with each other; lack of harmony.
geçin=[ir] 1. /la/ to get along (with), to live (on), to subsist (on); /dan/ to live (on someone else), to sponge (on a person). 2. /la/ to get on well (with). 3. to pretend to be, to pass (for). 4. *prov.* to die. —**ip git=** to manage to live. —**meğe gönlüm yok ki** I just don't care. —**dir=** /ı/ *caus.* of **geçin=**. —**im**, —**me** *verbal n.* of **geçin=**; subsistence.
geçir=[ir] 1. /ı, a *or* dan/ *caus.* of **geç=** 2[1-6]; to infect (someone with a disease). 2. /ı, a/ to slip on (cover on a book, case on a quilt), to fit, fix, insert (glass into frame); to enter, register (account), to copy out. 3. /ı/ to pass (time); to undergo (an operation), to get over (a disease); to have (attack). 4. /ı, dan/ to pass (something through something); /ı/ to ponder (over); /ı, a/ to accompany (someone to a place); /ı/ to see off. 5. /ı/ *colloq.* to gossip (about), to criticize. 6. /a/ *slang* to know carnally. 7. /ı/ *archaic* to forgive. —**gen** *neol.*, *sc.* permeable. —**genlik** *neol.*, *sc.* permeability. —**il=** *pass.* of **geçir=**. —**imli** *neol.*, *sc.* permeable. —**imlilik** *neol.*, *sc.* permeability. —**imsiz** *neol.*, *sc.* impermeable. —**imsizlik** *neol.*, *sc.* impermeability.
geçirme 1. *verbal n.* of **geçir=**. 2. fitted on; fittable. 3. *art* tracing.
geçirmez impermeable, tight. —**lik** impermeability.
geçirt=[ir] /ı, a/ 1. *caus.* of **geçir=**. 2. *colloq.*, same as **geçir=**[1, 2].
geçiş 1 *verbal n.* of **geç=** 2; transition. — **üstünlüğü** road traffic right of way. —**li** *neol.*, *gram.* transitive. —**siz** *neol.*, *gram.* intransitive.
geçiş=[ir] 2 *neol.*, *sc.* to be diffused, to intermix. —**me** *phys.* osmosis. —**mel** *phys.* osmotic.
geçiştir=[ir] /ı/ to pass over with little harm, to get rid of quite easily.
geçit[di] 1. passageway, passage; mountain pass; ford; *naut.* narrows, fairway; *anat.* isthmus. 2. a passing, passage; *mil.* parade. — **alayı** procession, parade. — **hakkı**

geçitçi

toll. **— resmi** *mil.* parade. **— töreni** parade. **— ver=** to afford a passage. **— yeri** ford; mountain pass; passage.

geçitçi ‏گچیتجی‎ 1. keeper of, attendant on a ford or ferry; ferryman. 2. guard of a mountain pass.

geçki ‏گچکی‎ *prov.*, weaving a weft thread passed through by hand.

geçkin ‏گچکین‎ 1. elderly, past the prime of youth; overripe (fruit); overmatured (wood). 2. /ı/ past, e. g., **elliyi geçkin** over fifty. 3. *archaic* beyond self-control (from sickness or intoxication). **—ce** somewhat past the prime. **—ci** seller of overripe fruit at cut prices. **—le=** to begin to become overripe. **—lik** the condition of overripeness.

geçlikᵍⁱ ‏گچلك‎ lateness.

geçme ‏گچمه‎ 1. *verbal n. of* **geç=** 2. 2. that fits into or on to something else; dovetailed; telescoped; *carp.* joined by mortise and tenon. 3. *carp.* tenon. **— çubuk** sectioned tobacco pipe. **— kapak** sliding lid. **— rahle** book stand consisting of two interlaced slanting boards. **—ce, —cesine** with the purpose of overtaking. **—lik** *neol.* toll.

geçmiş ‏گچمش‎ 1. past; overripe; passed away, deceased, dead. 2. something between two persons, an incident in the past, e. g., **onunla bir geçmişi var** They are cross with each other because of some old affair. **—i boklu** *vulg.* damned (for a person). **—te gelecek** *gram.* past of intentional (**=ecekti**). **—te geniş zaman** *Turk. gram.* aorist past (**=erdi**). **—i kandilli** *colloq.* damned (for a person). **—lerini karıştır=** /ın/ to abuse the ancestors (of a person). **—i kınalı** *same as* **geçmişi kandilli. —e mazi, yenmişe kuzu derler** Let bygones be bygones. **— ola** 1. Gone forever (said about a missed opportunity). 2. *same as* **geçmiş olsun. — olsun** Too bad! (expression of sympathy for a person who has had or who is having an illness or misfortune). **— olsuna git=** to pay a visit to one who has experienced illness or anything dangerous or disagreeable. **— öncesi** *gram.* pluperfect (**=mişti**). **—ine rahmet** Mercy be upon your (his) dead relatives (formula of blessing). **—i tenekeli, —ine yandığım** *same as* **geçmişi kandilli. — zaman** *gram.* past (**=ti**).

ged=ᵉʳ ‏گدك‎ /ı/ *archaic for* **kert=**.

geda (.—) ‏گدا‎ P *poet.* beggar, poor man. **—çeşm** (.—.) P, **—dil** (.—.) P greedy. **—gazi** (.———) P rope-dancer; public dancer; prostitute. **—i** (.——) P mendicancy, begging. **—yan** (.——) P beggars.

gedekᵍⁱ ‏گدك‎ *prov.* water buffalo calf.

gedeleçᶜⁱ ‏گدلج‎ *prov.* quiver.

gedikᵍⁱ ‏گدیك‎ 1. breach, gap; mountain pass; *archaic* notch; notched, chipped at the edge; with teeth missing. 2. *Ott. hist.* an established place in a household or in the public service held by a kind of feudal tenure; trade monopoly, license, the right to exclusive exercise of a trade in a particular area; place of business in a building held by patent or warrant; kind of leasehold; share in a property belonging to a pious foundation. **— aç=** /da/ to make a breach (in). **— düz=** *archaic* to make good what is lacking. **—ler kalemi** *Ott. adm.* office for the registration of leasehold property. **— kapa=** to fill up the gap; *mil.* to close a gap. **—ten kurtul=** to get out of a difficult situation. **—e takıl=** to be cornered. **—leri tıka=** to stop up the gaps. **—len=** to become notched on the edge.

gedikli ‏گدیکلی‎ 1. regular guest, patron, constant frequenter. 2. *mil.* regular N.C.O. 3. *Ott. hist.* holder of a privilege which is a reward for long service; shares on the basis of a title deed (property). 4. *obs.* breached; gapped; notched, chipped. **— çavuş** 1. *mil.* sergeant; warrant officer. 2. *Ott. hist.* veteran sergeant in the Sultan's service. **— efendi** *Ott. hist.* secretary of the Sultan's treasury. **— er** *mil.* veteran. **— erbaş** *mil.* warrant officer. **— kadın** *Ott. hist.* high-ranking woman of the harem, performing personal services for the Sultan. **— küçük zabiti** *obs.* warrant officer. **— tellâl** *Ott. hist.* broker in the Istanbul bazaar.

gedil 1 ‏گدیل‎ *prov.* sack.

gedil=ⁱʳ 2 ‏گدیلك‎ *pass. of* **ged=**.

gef ‏گف‎ Arabic script, name of the letter ‏گ‎. (The letter is the twenty-sixth letter of the Persian alphabet.)

geğe ‏گگه‎ *prov.* crook; shepherd's staff; gardener's crook for gathering fruit.

geğeçᶜⁱ ‏گگج‎ *prov.* stinging, biting; pecking. **—me, —meç** bill, beak.

geğir=ⁱʳ ‏گگیرمك‎ to belch, eructate. **—iş, —me** a belch. **—t=** /ı/ *caus. of* **geğir=**. **—ti** belch, eructation.

geğrekᵍⁱ ‏گگرك‎ lower rib, false rib. **— altı** pit of the stomach. **— batması** stitch in the side.

geh 1 ‏گه‎ P *lrnd.*, *var. of* **gâh** 1, 2.

-geh 2 ‏گه‎ P *lrnd.*, *var. of* **-gâh** 3.

-gehân (.—) ‏گهان‎ P *lrnd.* time, e. g., **nâgehan** suddenly, **sehergehan** in the early morning.

geh geh ‏گه گه‎ expression used for calling chickens.

gehi (.—) ‏گهی‎ P *same as* **gâhi.**

gehvare (.—.) ‏گهواره‎ P *lrnd.* cradle, cot.

gek=ᵉʳ ‏گکمك‎ /ı/ *prov.* to peck, to pick up. **—me, —meç** bill, beak.

gel=ⁱʳ گلمك 1. /dan, a/ to come (from, to); to arrive; to derive, proceed (from); to occur, befall; to be met (by), e. g., **ahıma geldi** He has found his punishment for the evil he did to me; *archaic* to be related. 2. /a/ to enter a state of, *as in* **kıvama gel=, merhamete gel=**. 3. to arouse (envy, desire etc.), e. g., **sizi göreceğim geldi** I long to see you; **gülesim geldi** I can't (couldn't) help laughing. 4. /a/ to fit, suit; to answer (a purpose); to bear, tolerate, endure. 5. /a/ to seem, appear, e. g., **bana pahalı geldi** I found it too expensive. 6. /a/ to cost, e. g., **size kaça geldi?** How much did it cost you? **bana pahalıya geldi** I had to pay a lot for it. 7. /dan/ to feign, pretend, e. g., **işitmemezlikten geldi** He pretended not to hear. **gel** 1. Come now, e. g., **gel, bu işten vazgeçelim!** Come now, let's leave this. 2. followed by *negative imperative* if you can help it, e. g., **gel, şimdi kızma!** Now, who could keep quiet under this? **—elim** /a/ let us turn (to another subject). **—ince** /a/ as for, e. g., **bana gelince, her zaman sizinleyim** As for me, I am always with you. **—sin** *followed by noun, describes lavishness, an easy, leisurely manner*, e. g., **ondan sonra gelsin kahkahalar, şarkılar...** Then, there was hearty laughing and singing... **— beri et=** /ı/ *slang* to snatch, steal, pilfer. **—ip çat=** to come and be close at hand (time). **—ici geçici, —ip geçici** transient, passing. **— gelelim** but unfortunately, however by ill-chance; but, and yet. **—ip git=** /a/ to come and go, to frequent. **—en gideni aratır, —en gidene rahmet okutur** The newcomer makes one long for his predecessor. **— keyfim gel!** How pleasant. How relaxing! **—eceği varsa göreceği de var!** Let him come and see what is waiting for him; let him try it on! **— zaman git zaman** long, long afterwards.
gelberi گلبری poker, rake (implements).
geldir=ⁱʳ كلدرمك *obs.* /ı/ to cause to come.
gele 1 گل *backgammon* blank throw.
gele 2 گل P same as **gelle**.
gelecekᵍⁱ كلجك coming, next; future. **— zaman** *gram.* the future.
geleğen *neol.; geog.* tributary (river).
gelenekᵍⁱ *neol.* tradition. **—çi** traditionalist.
gelengi گلنكی *prov.* meadow mouse, *zool.*, Arvicola.
gelgeçᶜⁱ گل كج fickle, inconstant. **— hanı** place where people come and go.
gelgel گل گل *prov.* attractiveness. **—li** attractive.
gelgit گل گیت 1. many trips required by a petitioner (because of dilatory office practices). 2. *neol.* the tides.
Gelibolu (..´..) گلیبولی *geog.* Gallipoli.

geliçᶜⁱ گلیچ *prov.* kind of poisonous herb.
gelikᵍⁱ گلك Gk *prov.* kind of sandal.
gelim گلم *verbal n.* of **gel=**.
gelin گلین 1. bride. 2. daughter-in-law; wife of a younger member of the family. **— alayı** bridal procession. **— alıcı** 1. person sent by the bridegroom to fetch the bride. 2. *slang* policeman, cop. **— ata binmiş, ya nasip!** *proverb* The bride is on her way; I hope the wedding takes place. **— böceği** kind of ladybug. **— feneri** winter cherry, *bot.*, Physalis Alkekengi. **— git=** /a/ to marry (into, for the bride). **— hamamı** the bridal bath (joyous gathering in a public bath, a few days before the wedding). **— havası** fine weather. **— kuşağı** *prov.* rainbow. **— odası** bridal chamber. **— odası gibi** attractive and very tidy (room). **— parası** coins showered over the bride's head at the wedding. **— parmağı** *prov.* kind of grape. **— saçı** dodder, *bot.*, Cuscuta. **— teli** silver or gold thread used to decorate a bride's hair. **— yazma** *prov.* ceremony of decorating the bride's face.
gelincikᵍⁱ گلینجك 1. poppy. 2. weasel, *zool.*, Mustela. 3. three-bearded rockling, *zool.*, Gaidropsarus mediterraneus. 4. *pop.* hectic fever; erysipelas; dropsy; hematuria; lymphadenitis; sty. **— balığı** same as **gelincik³**. **— böceği** ladybug. **—giller** *bot.*, Papaveraceae.
gelinlikᵍⁱ گلینلك 1. fit for a bride; marriageable (girl); wedding-dress. 2. the state of a bride. **— et=** to show a daughter-in-law how she is to behave. (In certain circles, the newly married woman is subjected to a set of social rules in her behavior toward the members of her husband's family).
gelinti گلنتی *prov.* newcomer; immigrant.
gelir گلیر income; revenue; rent. **— kaynağı** source of income. **— vergisi** income tax. **—li** having an income.
geliş 1 گلیش 1. *verbal n.* of **gel=**. 2. return. **—i güzel** by chance, at random, haphazard, as it comes.
geliş=ⁱʳ **2** گلیشمك to grow up; to grow healthy, to grow fat; to mature; to make progress, to develop. **—miş kız** grownup girl.
gelişat (..—) گلیشات [pseudo-Arabic pl.] indications of coming ability or success, promise of development. **—lı** promising; physically well developed.
gelişim *neol.*, same as **gelişme**.
gelişme گلیشمه *verbal n.* of **geliş= 2**.
geliştir=ⁱʳ گلیشدیرمك /ı/ 1. *caus.* of **geliş= 2**. 2. *prov.* to make up, to find a way of doing, to improvise (something).
gelle گل P *lrnd.* flock, herd. **—i saili** a

gelme

bevy of beggars. **—ban** (..—) P herdsman, shepherd.
gelme 1. verbal n. of **gel=**; optics incidence. 2. /dan/ originating (from); derived (from).
gelû (.—) P lrnd., var. of **gülû**.
gelûz (.—) P lrnd. nut, filbert; wild almond.
gem 1 1. bit (of a bridle). 2. anat., frenulum. **— al=** to take the bit, to be broken in (horse). **— almaz** uncontrollable, unbridled; unbroken (horse). **—i azıya al=** to get out of control, to take the bit between the teeth, to bolt. **— gev=** to champ the bit. **—ini kıs=** /ın/ to shorten the rein (of someone). **— vur=** /a/ to restrain, curb.
gem 2 prov. threshing.
geme prov., same as **keme 2**.
gemi ship, vessel, boat. **— adamları** crew, ship's company. **— arslanı** 1. figurehead. 2. good-looking but useless person, stuffed dummy. **— beşiği** naut. ship's cradle. **—ye bin=** to embark, to go on board. **— donat=** to rig a ship; to fit out a ship. **—yi duvarda gör=** to have seen nothing of the world. **— enkazı** wreck. **— havuzu** repair docks. **— hocası** archaic 1. purser of a ship. 2. ship's imam. **— imamı** navy ship's imam. **— indir=** to launch a ship. **— kirala=** to charter a ship. **—sini kurtaran kaptan** proverb He who succeeds is acknowledged as an able person. **— leşi** wreck. **— marangozu** ship's carpenter. **— mürettebatı** crew, ship's company. **— müsteciri** com. charterer. **— sahibi** mar. law shipowner. **—si şapa otur=** /ın/ to undergo irreparable loss in business. **—de teslim** com. free on board, f.o.b. **— tezgâhı** stocks, dockyard. **— yatağı** naut. ship's berth, port of shelter. **— zabiti** naut. ship's officer.
gemici sailor, mariner. **— feneri** barn lantern, railroad lantern. **—lik** 1. seamanship. 2. navigation; seafaring.
|/ge/ see /ke/.|
gen 1 G biol. gene.
gen 2 prov. 1. broad, vast, wide, spacious; ample, bountiful, abundant. 2. newly broken ground.
gen=ᵉʳ 3 archaic to widen, amplify, broaden.
genc 1 cf. **genç**.
genc 2 P lrnd. treasure; hidden treasure. **—i arus**, **—i bad**, **—i bar**, **—i dibe**, **—i Efrasyab**, **—i gâv**, **—i gâvan**, **—i gâvmiş**, **—i hadra** poet., names of the treasures of Khosrau Parviz. **—i hakî** 1. Adam. 2. man. **—i hakîm Fatiha** (first Sura of the Quran). **—i ilâhî**, **—i kanaat** contentment. **—i maani** treasure of spiritual things; treasure of poetry. **—i**

nihân hidden treasure. **—i revan** the treasures of Korah (swallowed up by the earth). **—i suhte**, **—i şadaverd**, **—i şaygân** poet., names of the treasures of Khusrau Parviz.
gencar (.—), **gencare** (.—.) P lrnd. rouge.
gencdar (.—) P lrnd. 1. that has a treasure. 2. treasurer.
gencecikᵍⁱ very young.
gencel=ⁱʳ prov., same as **gençleş=**.
gencer, **gencere** P lrnd., same as **gencar**.
Gencevî (..—) A native of Gandj (now Kirovabad).
gencine (.—.) P lrnd. 1. treasure. 2. treasury. **—dar** P treasurer.
gencname (.—.) P lrnd. 1. treasure book. 2. treatise on discovering treasure. 3. written talisman for guarding treasure.
gencver P lrnd. treasurer.
gençᶜⁱ 1. young, in the prime of youth, youthful. 2. young man. **— ay** archaic new moon. **— irisi** tall and robust young person. **G— Kalemler** Turk. literature, name of a journal and a group of writers early in the twentieth century.
gençleş=ⁱʳ to become youthful, to be rejuvenated, to take a new lease on life. **—tir=** /ı/ caus. to rejuvenate.
gençlikᵍⁱ 1. youth, youthfulness. 2. the young, youth, younger generation. **—ine doyama=**, **—ine doyma=** not to enjoy one's youth (said of someone who has died young).
gendüm P lrnd. wheat. **—gûn** P swarthy. **—nümâyı cevfürûş** (lit. One who shows wheat but sells barley.) cheat, deceiver.
gene (.'.) same as **yine**.
genegerçekᵍⁱ [Persian kana, karchak] castor oil plant, bot., Ricinus.
genel 1 neol. general. **— direktör** general director. **— ekonomi** political economy. **— emniyet** public security. **— ev** brothel. **— karargâh** general headquarters. **— konsolos** consul general. **— kurmay** mil. General Staff. **— kurul** general meeting. **— merkez** central office (of an organization). **— müdür** general director. **— olarak** in general. **— seçim** pol. general election. **— seferberlik** mil. general mobilization. **— sekreter** secretary general. **— taarruz** mil. general attack. **— yazman** secretary general.
genel=ⁱʳ **2** prov. to widen, broaden.
geneleme neol., log. tautology, rhet. pleonasm.
genelge neol., adm. circular, notice.
genelle=ʳ /ı/ neol. to generalize. **—me** generalization. **—ş=** to become general, to be generalized; to become common property.
generalⁱⁱ G mil. general.

generator گنراتور G 1. *mech.* gas generator. 2. *elec.* generator, dynamo.

genez 1 گنز *prov.* so it appears.

genez 2 گنز archaic easily, with ease; easy. **—lik** ease, easiness.

Geng گنگ *geog.; lrnd.* Ganges.

geniş گنیش گلگش میکش مکش 1. wide, broad; spacious, extensive, ample, vast. 2. carefree. **— açı** *neol., geom.* obtuse angle. **— fikirli** broad-minded, liberal. **— gönüllü, — kalpli** generous, munificent. **— mezhepli** tolerant, not too scrupulous. **— mikyasta** on a vast scale. **— bir nefes al=** to feel relief. **— ölçüde** on a vast scale. **— tut=** /ı/ to leave a broad margin (in some arrangement); to do something on a broad scale. **— yapraklı** *bot.* broad-leaved. **— yürekli** generous, munificent. **— zaman** *neol., Turk. gram.* aorist.

genişle=ʳ گنیشلمك to widen, broaden; to expand; to ease up (circumstances). **—t=** /ı/ *caus.*

genişlikᵍⁱ گنیشلك wideness, width; extensiveness; openness.

genit=ⁱʳ گنیتمك /ı/ archaic, *caus.* of **gen=** 3.

genizⁿᶻⁱ گكز nasal passages, nasal fossae. **—e kaç=** to go down the wrong way (food). **—den konuş=** to speak through the nose. **— sesi** *phon.* nasal. **—i tıkan=** to have a stuffy nose. **—ini yak=** to stifle, choke on (smoke, or a pungent smell). **—lenme, —leşme** *phon.* nasalization.

genleşme *neol., sc.* dilatation.

genlikᵍⁱ گكلك *prov., abstr. n.* of **gen** 2.

gensoru *neol., pol.* general questioning in parliament (of a minister by members).

genşe=ʳ گكشه مك *prov., same as* **gevşe= 1.**

genzekᵍⁱ گكزك *prov.* who speaks through the nose.

genzel *neol., phon.* nasal.

geometri گیومتری L geometry.

geometrikᵍⁱ گیومتریك L geometrical. **— dizi** *math.* geometrical progression. **— ortalama** *math.* geometric mean. **— toplamı** *math.* geometrical sum. **— yer** *geom.* locus.

ger=ᵉʳ **1** گرمك 1. /ı/ to stretch, tighten. 2. /ı, a/ to spread out and stretch (over).

ger 2 گر P *poet., var.* of **eger.**

-ger 3 گر P *lrnd.* maker, worker of, *as in* **kefşger, kimyager.**

ger 4 گر *prov.* sprinkled with gray; having a white spot in the fur.

gerçekᵍⁱ گرچك real, true, genuine, authentic; reality, truth; really, in truth. **—ten** in fact; actually, really. **— er, — eren** *myst.* sufi who has attained perfection. **—çi** 1. *art, literature* realist; realistic. 2. who always speaks the truth. **—çilik** *phil., art, literature* realism. **—le=** /ı/ 1. to confirm. 2. *neol.,* *phil.* to verify. **—len=** *pass.* of **gerçekle=. —leş=** to become true, to materialize. **—leştir=** /ı/ *caus.* of **gerçekleş=,** to realize, make real. **—li** *neol., gram.* real. **—lik** *abstr. n.* **—siz** *neol., gram.* unreal.

gerçi گرچه P although, though, it is true that.

gerd 1 گرد P *lrnd.* 1. dust, motes; earth. 2. care, sorrow, vexation. 3. a turning, revolving; orbit; celestial globe; sphere; planet. **—i küduret, —i siyah** care, sorrow. **—i zümürrüd** *poet.* sprouting beard.

-gerd 2 گرد P *lrnd.* turning around, wandering over, *e. g.,* **afakgerd** world-wanderer.

gerdalûd (.——), گردآلود **gerdalûde** (.——.) گردآلوده P *lrnd.* dusty.

gerdan 1 گردان [gerden] 1. neck, throat. 2. front of the neck; double chin; dewlap. 3. *butchery* neck, chuck. **— kır=** to make coquettish movements with the head, *esp.,* in dancing; to swing the head in walking (horse). **— kıran** wryneck, *zool., Jynx torquilla.*

-gerdan 2 (.—) گردان P *lrnd.* turning, *as in* **rugerdan, sergerdan.**

gerdane (.—.) گردانه P *mil.* ring for a rifle sling.

gerdaniye (.——.) گردانیه P *Or. mus.* one of the oldest compound **makams. — puselik** a compound **makam** approximately six centuries old.

gerdanlıkᵍⁱ گردانلق 1. necklace, neckband. 2. striped marking round the neck; collar.

gerde 1 گرده P *lrnd.* pounce, charcoal powder for making stenciled patterns.

-gerde 2 گرده *var.* of **kerde.**

gerdekᵍⁱ گردك [Persian **girdak**] nuptial chamber, bridal chamber. **— gecesi** nuptial night. **—e gir=** to enter the nuptial chamber (bridegroom).

gerdel گردل It pail, wooden bucket; leather bucket.

gerden گردن P 1. *lrnd., same as* **gerdan 1**¹,². 2. *prov., same as* **gerdan 1. —bend** *lrnd.* 1. necklace. 2. necktie. 3. dog's collar. **—dade** (..—.) P *lrnd.* submissive, obedient. **—efraz** (...—) P, **—firaz** (...—) P, **—keş** P *lrnd.* 1. proud, arrogant. 2. disobedient, rebellious, obstinate.

gerdide (.—.) گردیده P *lrnd.* 1. that has turned, become. 2. that has circulated, traveled about.

gerdir=ⁱʳ گردیرمك /ı, a/ *caus.* of **ger= 1. —t=** /ı, a/ 1. *caus.* of **gerdir=.** 2. *same as* **gerdir=.**

gerdiş گردش P *lrnd.* 1. revolution, a revolving. 2. a circulating, wandering about. 3. change, turn of fortune. **—i devran, —i eflâk, —i zaman** the revolving of time.

gerdun (.—) گردون P *lrnd.* 1. wheel.

gerdune

2. heaven, celestial sphere. 3. fortune. **—i dûn, —i dunnevaz** fortune that favors the vile.
gerdune (. —.) گردونه P *lrnd.* carriage, chariot. **—i iclâl** royal carriage.
gerdungiray (. —. —)گردون گرای **gerdunhimmet** (. —..) گردون همّت P *lrnd.* who has great aspirations and ambitions.
gerduniktidar (. —.. —) گردون اقتدار P *lrnd.* omnipotent as heaven.
gerdunpaye (. — —.) گردون پایه P *lrnd.* high in dignity as the heavens.
gerdunpenah (. —. —) گردون پناه P *lrnd.* who takes refuge in heaven.
gerdunserir (. —. —) گردون سریر P *lrnd.* whose throne is as exalted as the heavens.
gerdunseyr (. —.) گردون سیر P *lrnd.* 1. as swiftly whirling as the spheres. 2. traveling in the sky.
gerdunsirişt (. —..) گردون سرشت P *lrnd.* fickle as Fortune.
gerdunsiyaset (. —. —.) گردون سیاست P *lrnd.* sphere-ruling.
gerdunsüvar (. —. —) گردون سوار P *lrnd.* traveling in the sky.
gerduntemkin (. —. —) گردون تمکین P *lrnd.* equal to heaven in dignity or power.
gereçᶜⁱ *neol.* material.
gerek 1 گرک repeated, preceding nouns or phrases in parallel position 1. whether... or, e. g., **gerek ben gideyim, gerek siz gidin, gerek o gitsin, farketmez** Whether I go or you or he, it does not make any difference. 2. both... and... e. g., **gerek annesi, gerek babası aynı yerdendirler** Both his mother and his father are from the same place.
gerekᵍⁱ **2** گرک /a/ 1. necessary, needed. **bize çalışacak adam gerek** We need people who work. **beklemek gerek** One has to wait. **bana sen gereksin** (*archaic:* **bana seni gerek**) I need you. 2. fitting, suiting, proper. **—ince** 1. in accordance with, following, e. g., **kanun gereğince** according to the law. 2. *archaic* as required. **—i gibi** as is due, properly. **— ve yeter şart** *math.* necessary and sufficient condition. **—i yok** /a/ not to be necessary (to), e. g., **bunun bize gereği yok** We don't need this.
gerek=ⁱʳ **3** گرکلک /a/ 1. to be necessary, needed, required; to be lacking. 2. to be fitting, suitable, proper.
gerekçe *neol.* 1. *law* statement of reasons, covering memorandum; *pol.* written argument in favor of a bill. 2. *log., math.* corollary.
gerekirci *neol., phil.* determinist, deterministic. **—lik** determinism.
gerekli گرکلی necessary, needed, required.
gereklikᵍⁱ گرکلک *abstr. n.* of **gerek 2**. **— kipi** *gram.* necessitative (**=malı**).

gerekse=ʳ, **gereksin=**ⁱʳ گرکسه، گرکسین /1/ *prov.* to consider necessary, to feel the necessity (of).
gerektir=ⁱʳ گرکتیرمک /1/ *caus.* of **gerek= 3**; to necessitate, require, entail, determine. **—im, —me** *neol., phil.* determination.
gerelti گرلتی *prov.* obstacle obstructing the view.
geren 1 گرن *prov.* clayey soil.
geren 2 گرن *prov.* misty and cloudy weather.
gergedan, gergeden گرگدان |*Persian* kargadan| 1. rhinoceros. 2. rhinoceros horn.
gergef گرگف |kârgâh| embroidery frame. **— işi** embroidery worked on a frame. **— işle=** to embroider with a frame.
gergi گرگی 1. instrument for stretching, stretcher. 2. *arch.* tie-beam (of a roof). 3. *naut.* stretcher of a rowing boat. 4. *prov.* curtain. 5. *archaic* rack (instrument of torture). **—li** 1. furnished with a stretcher. 2. stretched tight.
gergin گرگین stretched, taut, tight; tense; strained (relations). **—leş=** to become taut, to become stretched; to become tense. **—leştir=** /1/ *caus.* of **gerginleş=**. **—lik** tightness, tension.
geri گری 1. back, backward, toward the rear, behind. 2. rear, hinder part; remainder; hinder, posterior. 3. behind in time, slow (clock); backward, undeveloped. 4. *archaic* again; /dan/ after. **—den** from behind, from the rear. **—since** /in/ after him, following him, behind him. **—sinde** /in/ behind, e. g., **evin gerisinde** behind the house. **—ye** back, backward. **— al=, —ye al=** /1/ 1. to take back; to recover, regain, to get back. 2. to take back, withdraw (word, order). 3. to recall, call back (ambassador, troops). **—sini al=** /in/ to complete. **— at=** /1/ *mil.* to repulse, to throw back. **—ye at=** /1/ to postpone. **—si Aydın havası** *joc.* The rest is of no avail. **—den bak=** /a/ to look from a distance (at); to be an onlooker. **— bas=** to back (horse); to reverse the car. **— bırak=** /1, a/ to keep back (for). **—de bırak=** /1/ to leave behind; to pass; to surpass. **—ye bırak=** /1/ to put off, postpone. **— çağır=** /1/ to recall (ambassador). **— çek=** /1/ to draw back. **— çekil=** /dan/ to withdraw (from). **— çekme yayı** *mil.* return spring. **— çevir=** /1/ to turn back, to send back. **— dön=** to come back, to return. **—ye dön!** *mil.* About turn! **— dur=** 1. to hang back, to keep apart. 2. /dan/ to refrain, abstain (from). **— et=** /1/ to move back, to reverse; to put back (clock). **— gel=** to come back. **—sin geriye** backwards. **— geri git=** to draw back (in fear). **— git=** 1. to go back. 2. to decline. 3. to be slow (clock). **— gönder=** /1/ to send back. **— hizmeti** *mil.*

supply service behind the front. — **iste=** /ı/ to demand back, to reclaim. — **kaç=** to flee, recede; to draw back hastily, retreat. — **kademe** *mil.* rear echelon. — **kal=** 1. to stay behind, to remain behind. 2. to be slow (clock). —**de kal=** to remain behind; to be in arrears. — **kalan**, —**ye kalan** remainder, rest; leftovers. — **kalma=** /dan/ 1. not to lag behind, not to hang back (from), to match, equal, not to be less good. 2. not to fail (to do something). — **kalmış** underdeveloped. —**ye kalan tutar** *com.* balance. — **ko=**, — **koy=** /ı/ 1. to put back. 2. to postpone; to leave undone. — **marş!** —**ye marş!** *mil.* To the rear, march! — **öde=** /ı/ to pay back; to reimburse. —**sini sağla=** *mil.* to keep open the way of retreat. — **satın al=** /ı/ *com. law* to buy back, to repurchase. — **tep=** 1. /ı/ to kick back; to push back. 2. *mil.* to recoil. —**si tutma=** not to be able to control one's bowels. — **ver=** /ı/ to give back, return. — **vites** *auto.* reversing gear. —**si yufka** What comes after is not much (food).

gerici 1 *anat.* tensor.

gerici 2 *neol.* reactionary. —**lik** reaction, reactionary attitudes.

geriden F round pedestal table.

geril=ir 1. *pass. of* **ger= 1**. 2. *refl. of* **ger= 1**.

gerile=r 1. to draw back, move backward; to fall to the rear; to recede. 2. to fall behind, to worsen. —**k** *neol., phon., phil.* regressive. —**me** *verbal n. of* **gerile=**; *neol., sc.* retrogression; regression. —**t=** /ı/ *caus. of* **gerile=**.

gerili stretched, tight, taut.

gerilikği *abstr n. of* **geri**; backwardness.

gerilim *neol., phys.* tension.

gerillâ (..'.) F guerrilla. — **harbi** guerrilla warfare.

gerilme *verbal n. of* **geril=**. — **kuvveti** *phys.* tensile strength.

gerim 1. *verbal n. of* **ger= 1**. 2. *prov.* physical force, free play of the limbs. —**le=** *prov.* to stretch the limbs in moving. —**li** *prov.* strong, well developed.

gerin=ir to stretch oneself. —**dir=** /ı/ *caus.* —**iş**, —**me** *verbal n. of* **gerin=**.

geriş *prov.* watershed line, crest line.

gerive (.—.) P *lrnd., var. of* **girive**.

geriz. *var. of* **keriz 1**.

germ P *lrnd.* 1. warm, hot. 2. ardent, fiery, passionate. — **ü serd** things pleasant and unpleasant, prosperity and adversity, ups and downs. —**a** (.—) P heat, warmth; summer. —**abe** (.—.) P hot bath. —**a-germ** (.—.) P piping hot. —**dil** P heart-burning; ardent lover.

germe 1. *verbal n. of* **ger= 1**; *phys.* tension. 2. stretched, stretched out, taut. 3. *prov.* fence.

Germen G *same as* **Cermen**.

germeşikği wild cornel, *bot., Cornus sanguinea*.

germhun (.—) P *lrnd.* hotblooded, affectionate, amorous.

germî (.—) P *lrnd.* 1. warmth, heat; feverishness. 2. ardor, eagerness. — **ver=** to redouble (efforts), to intensify (work).

Germiyan (..—) *hist.* Germian (name of a Turkish principality founded at Kütahya on the break-up of the Seljuk Kingdom). — **oğulları** the Germianids.

germiyet (.—.) [*based on* **germ**] *lrnd.* 1. warmth, heat. 2. ardor, eagerness.

germsir (.—) P *lrnd.* hot lowland.

geşt P *lrnd.* a passing, going by; stroll, walk; promenade. — **ü güzar** a walking or riding about.

geşte P *lrnd.* passed, gone by; reversed.

getir=ir **1** /ı, a/ *caus. of* **gel=**, to bring; to yield, give. —**il=** *pass. of* **getir=**. —**me** 1. *verbal n. of* **getir=**. 2. /dan/ brought (from). —**t=** 1. /ı, a/ *caus. of* **getir=**; to send (for). 2. /ı, dan/ to order, to import (from). —**til=** *pass. of* **getirt=**.

getirtri **2**, **getr** F gaiter.

gev=er **1** /ı/ 1. to mumble; to chew (the cud). 2. to champ (at the bit).

gev 2 *obs., only in* **gev getir=**, *same as* **geviş getir=**.

gevah (.—) P *lrnd.* witness. —**î** witnessing.

gevan (.—) P *lrnd.* heroes.

gevare (.—.) P *lrnd.* 1. herd of oxen. 2. beehive.

gevde *archaic for* **gövde**.

gevden P *lrnd.* stupid, imbecile.

gevder P *lrnd.* 1. calf; fawn. 2. calfskin.

gevele=r /ı/ 1. to mumble, chew. 2. to mumble, hum and haw.

geven gum-tragacanth plant, *bot., Astragalus Tragacantha*.

gever 1 *prov.* small lateral channel for irrigation.

gever=ir **2** /ı, a/ *prov.* to let in, to insert (into).

geveşt *Or. mus.* one of the oldest compound **makams**.

geveze 1. talkative, chattering; babbler. 2. indiscreet, unable to keep a secret.

gevezelikği a babbling, gossip; indiscreet talk. — **et=** 1. to babble, prattle. 2. to be indiscreet, to blab, to let the cat out of the bag.

gevgeçᶜⁱ گوگچ *prov.* with drooping ears (horse, donkey).

gevher گوهر P *poet.* 1. gem, jewel; pearl. 2. substance, essence; root, origin; element. 3. intellect, wisdom; beautiful or witty saying. 4. grain of a sword blade. **—i nasüfte** 1. unbored pearl. 2. virgin. 3. a beautiful and original saying. **—i nimsüfte** 1. half-bored pearl. 2. incomplete saying. **—i süfte** 1. bored, pierced pearl. 2. chaste matron. 3. beautiful saying. **—i şehvar** pearl of great price. **—i ter** tear. **—i yekta** unique, matchless pearl. **—an** (..—) P the four elements. **—bar** (..—) P, **—efşan** (...—) P pearl-showering. **—fürûş** (...—) P jeweller. **—ger** P one who cleans, strings, or embroiders with pearls or precious stones; jeweller. **—i** (..—) P 1. adorned with gems or pearls. 2. jeweller; gem connoisseur. 3. of noble origin. 4. essential; elemental. **—in** (..—) P 1. adorned with gems or pearls. 2. gemlike, pearly. **—nisar** (...—) P gem scattering. **—nişan** (...—) P set with jewels. **—pare** (..—.) P large jewel. **—paş** (..—)P 1. gem-scattering. 2. one who speaks elegantly. **—riz** (..—) P 1. that showers jewels. 2. one who speaks elegantly. **—şinas** (...—) P gem connoisseur. **—zar** (..—) P mine of precious stones.

gevilcen گویلجن *prov.* heat rash.

gevir=ⁱʳ گویرمك /ı/ to chew, to mumble.

geviş 1 گویش a chewing the cud, rumination. **— getir=** 1. to ruminate. 2. to muse, to ponder. **— getirenler** variety of mackerel, *zool., Ruminantia*.

geviş=ⁱʳ **2** گویشمك *obs.* to chew the cud, to ruminate.

Gevr گور P *var. of* Gebr.

gevre=ʳ گورمك 1. *prov.* to become crisp, dry, brittle. 2. *obs.* to suffer from heat or cold. **—ye kal=** *obs.* to become stiff, to die.

gevrekᵍⁱ گورك 1. crisp, brittle, crackly. 2. dry toast; *prov.* ring-shaped roll of bread. **— gevrek gül=** to laugh in an easy and lively way. **—çi** seller of dry toast; *prov.* seller of ring-shaped rolls. **—len=** to become crisp. **—lik** crispness.

gevren=ⁱʳ گورنمك *obs.* to be tortured by impatience.

gevret=ⁱʳ گورتمك /ı/ *caus. of* gevre=.

gevşe=ʳ **1** گوشمك 1. to become loose, slack, lax. 2. to grow feeble, to slacken, to diminish. 3. *prov.* to grow lean, to grow thin.

gevşe=ʳ **2** گوشمك *prov.* to ruminate.

gevşekᵍⁱ گوشك 1. loose, lax, slack. 2. soft, feeble, weak; lacking in zeal, lax. **— ağızlı** blab. **— davran=** to act in a lukewarm manner. **— gevşek gül=** to laugh in a vulgar and rather too free-and-easy manner. **— tut=** /ı/ not to do wholeheartedly, not to be diligent (in doing something). **—le=** to become loose, to slacken. **—let=** /ı/ *caus. of* gevşekle=. **—lik** *abstr. n.*

gevşel=ⁱʳ گوشلك *prov.*, *same as* gevşe= 1. **—t=** /ı/ *caus.*

gevşeme گوشمه *verbal n. of* gevşe= 1.

gevşet=ⁱʳ گوشتمك /ı/ *caus. of* gevşe= 1. **—il=** *pass.*

gevz گوز P *lrnd.* walnut.

gevzine (.—.) گوزینه P *lrnd.* sweet made of walnuts.

gey=ᵉʳ **1** گیمك /ı/ *prov.*, *same as* giy=.

gey 2 گی *archaic* 1. good, proper; /dan/ better. 2. very, strongly; much, very much.

geyesi گیسی *same as* geysi.

geygel گیگل *prov.* itinerant smith.

geyikᵍⁱ گیك 1. deer, stag, hart. 2. *slang* pander. **— derisi** buckskin, deerskin. **— dikeni** buckthorn, *bot., Rhamnus cathartica*. **— dili** hart's tongue fern, *bot., Phyllitis Scolopendrium*. **— etine gir=** to take on the physical appearance of a woman (said of a growing girl). **— göbeği** *bot., Jurinea pinnatisecta*. **— otu** white dittany, *bot., Dictamnus albus*. **— ruhu** hartshorn.

geyim گییم *archaic* 1. *same as* giyim. 2. coat of mail, shirt of mail or thickly padded material.

geyin گیین *prov.* vulva (of ruminants).

geyrekᵍⁱ گیرك *prov.* false rib.

geysi گیسی 1. *prov.* underwear. 2. *archaic* clothes.

geyür=ᵘʳ گیورمك /ı, a/ *archaic, caus. of* gey= 1.

gez=ᵉʳ **1** گزمك 1. to walk about, go about, move about, to rove, stroll, wander; to lounge, loaf about. 2. to go on a spree, to go places, to eat out and spend one's time in places of amusement. 3. /ı/ to travel, traverse; to visit, inspect, to go (over), to see inside; to patrol. **—ip toz=** to saunter about and enjoy oneself.

gez 2 گز 1. notch in an arrow; rear sight (of a gun). 2. *prov.* passage, pass; mountain pass. **— deliği** *mil.* loophole.

gez 3 گز *prov.* time, *e. g.*, üç gez three times.

gez 4 گز [*Persian* gaz] *prov.* shears, scissors; pincers, forceps; tweezers; fork.

gez 5 گز *prov.* young goat.

gez 6 گز P *lrnd.* 1. tamarisk tree; manna tree; manna. 2. arrow shaft; sort of arrow or dart without wing or point (the ends being small and the middle thick). 3. rope with knots at intervals for measuring ground; measure of length (26 or 42 inches); plumbline. **— menni** manna. **—e vur=** to level, to adjust; to measure.

-gez 7 گز , **-geza** (.—) گزا P *lrnd.*

biting, pungent, hurting, *as in* **zebangez, cangeza.**
gezan (.—) غزان P *lrnd.* biting; pungent.
gezdan گزدان *prov.* kid; goat up to two years; barren goat.
gezdir=ⁱʳ گزديرمك /ı/ 1. *caus.* of **gez**= 1. 2. *cookery* to sprinkle, to pour lightly over (as oil on salad). 3. *naut.* to be unable to hold (the ship) on her course.
gezeğen 1. *neol., astr.* planet. 2. *prov.* ever wandering; vagrant.
gezele=ʳ گزه لك *prov.* to wander all the time.
gezem گزم *prov.* young goat.
gezend گزند P *lrnd.* harm, injury, loss.
gezende گزنده P *lrnd.* 1. biting. 2. venomous reptile.
gezengi گزنگی [Persian **gazangu**] *prov.* manna.
gezente, gezenti گزنته گزنتی [**gezende**] *prov.* 1. kind of bug found on vegetables. 2. who wanders about excessively.
gezer 1 *neol.* mobile. — **hasta** outpatient.
gezer 2 گزر P *prov.* carrot.
gezgin گزگین widely traveled. —**ci** that travels much, itinerant; itinerant peddler.
gezi 1 *neol.* 1. excursion, outing. 2. promenade, public walk.
gezi 2 گزی [Persian **gazı**] silk and cotton material.
gezici گزیجی one who habitually goes about, itinerant. — **esnaf** peddler; hawker.
-**gezide** (.—.) گزیده P bitten, stung by, *e. g.*, **margezide** bitten by a snake.
gezil=ⁱʳ گزيلمك *pass.* of **gez**= 1.
gezincimlikᵍⁱ *neol., phil.* the philosophy of the Peripatetics.
gezin=ⁱʳ **1** گزينمك 1. *refl.* of **gez**= 1, to wander about without any definite purpose. 2. *mus.* to run over the notes of a musical instrument; to pass from one key to another, *e. g.*, **makamdan makama gezindi** He wandered from key to key.
gezin 2 گزن *archaic*, time *e. g.*, **bu gezin** this time, **yedi gezin** seven times.
gezinti گزنتی 1. walk, stroll, pleasure trip, outing. 2. floor, corridor; catwalk in a castle. 3. *abstr. n.* of **gezin**=².
gezle=ʳ **1** گزله مك /ı/ 1. to aim (at). 2. *archaic* to notch an arrow.
gezle=ʳ **2** گزله مك /ı/ 1. *archaic* to fit with a shaft (arrow head). 2. *lrnd.* to measure; to adjust, to level.
gezlen=ⁱʳ گزلنمك *archaic, pass.* of **gezle**= 1, 2.
gezli گزلی *archaic* 1. notched (arrow). 2. shafted (arrow head).
gezlikᵍⁱ گزلك *archaic* clasp knife, kind of curved sword, saber.
gezme گزمه 1. *verbal n.* of **gez**= 1. 2. *archaic* patrol, watchman. — **başı** *archaic* chief of a patrol.
gezmen *neol.* traveller.
-**gı 1, -gi 1, -gu, -gü,** *after vowel* -**ğı, -ği,** *after unvoiced consonant* -**kı, -ki 2, -ku, -kü** غی گی قی کی 1. abstract noun, as in **bilgi, sevgi.** 2. object noun, as in **içki, vergi.** 3. name of an instrument, as in **burgu, dağlağı, keski.**
-**gı 2, -gi** غی گی *archaic,* same as -**ki 1.** *e, g.,* **yarıngı** tomorrow's.
gıbᵇᵇⁱ **1** غبّ A *lrnd., path.* attacking every other day (fever), tertian fever.
gıbᵇᵇⁱ **2** غبّ A *lrnd.* after...; end.
gıbban (.'.) غبّا A *lrnd.* at intervals, now and then.
gıbbeddua (...—) غبّ الدعا A *lrnd.* after prayer.
gıbbeşşehade (...—.) غبّ الشهاده A *lrnd.* after testimony.
gıbbettahkik (...—) غبّ التحقيق A *lrnd.* after investigation.
gıbta غبطة A *lrnd.,* same as **gıpta.** —**aver** (..—.) P envy-provoking. —**efza** (...—) P envy-increasing. —**keş** P envious, envying.
gıcıkᵍⁱ **1** غجیق 1. tickling sensation in the throat. 2. suspicion, mistrust. —**ı tut**= to have a tickle in the throat, to wish to cough. — **ver**= /a/ to cause to cough. —**la**= /ı/ 1. to cause to cough. 2. to engender mistrust.
gıcıkᵍⁱ **2** غجیق *prov.* 1. kid. 2. immature goat or sheep; lamb; kind of mutton. 3. man of small stature, dwarf.
gıcık=ⁱʳ **3** غجیقمق to have a tickling sensation, to tickle. —**tır**= /ı/ *caus.*
gıcıla=ʳ غجیلامق 1. to grind the teeth (in rage). 2. to creak, to rustle.
gıcır غجیر 1. gum of sarsaparilla used as masticatory. 2. sound of gum chewing. 3. *slang* new. —**ı bükme** *slang* perfunctory, done in haste; by force. — **gıcır** 1. very clean, 2. brand new. — **otu** sarsaparilla, *bot.*, *Smilax aspera.* —**da**= to creak, rustle; to grind (teeth). —**dat**= /ı/ *caus.* of **gıcırda**=. —**tı** creaking noise, rustling sound.
gıda (.—) غذا [**gıza**] 1. food; nourishment, diet; nutriment. 2. *obs.* dose (of medicine); charge (of a gun). — **maddeleri** victuals. —**î** (.——) *sc.* nutritious; nutrient, alimentary.
gıdakla=ʳ غدا قلامق 1. to cackle. 2. *colloq.* to prattle.
gıdalan=ʳ (.—..) غذالنمق 1. to be fed, nourished; to obtain food. 2. *obs.* to be rationed with a fixed allowance; to be charged (gun). —**dır** /ı/ *caus.* to nourish.
gıdalı (.—.) غذالو غذالى nutritious, nourishing.

gıdasız (. —.) غِذاسِزْ 1. not nutritious. 2. without food. 3. undernourished. **— kal=** 1. to be without food. 2. to be undernourished.

gıdgıd gıdak imitation of the clucking of a hen that has laid an egg.

gıdı غِیدى prov. under part of the chin.

gıdık^{gi} 1 غِدیك 1. a tickling. 2. child language under part of the chin.

gıdık^{gi} 2 غِدیك prov. kid.

gıdıkla=^{r} غِدیقلامق /ı/ 1. to tickle. 2. slang to flatter. **—n=** 1. pass. 2. to feel a tickling.

gıgı, gıgık^{gi} غِغِی، غِغِیك child language, vars. of gıdı, gıdık 1².

gığılama neol., phon. glottal articulation of the letter r.

gık^{kı} غِق، غِیق in **— de=** /dan/ to be sick (of). **— dedirt=** /a/ to cause someone to be sick (of). **— dedirtme=** /a/ to listen to no objections, not to allow another to utter a syllable. **— deme=** not to say a word, not to object. **— gel=** to be fed up.

=gıl 1 غل archaic, amplifier of imperative of 2nd person singular, e. g., **kılgıl** Do. **okumagıl** Do not read.

gıl^{lli} 2 غِلّ A lrnd. malice, envy. **— u gış** intrigue, malice; malicious intent, envy and hatred. **— u gıştan ârî** utterly sincere. **— u gışlı** malicious, untrustworthy. **— u gışsız** free from malice, open, sincere.

gılâ (. —.) غِلا A lrnd., var. of galâ 2.

gılâf (. —.) غِلاف A 1. lrnd. covering, case; membrane. 2. anat. vagina. **—ı adalât sarcolemma. —ı bızır** praeputium clitoridis. **—ı dahilî-i semer** bot. endocarp. **—ı haricî-i semer** bot. exocarp, epicarp. **—ı mutavassıt-ı semer** bot. mesocarp. **—ı veterî** anat. sheath of a tendon, perimysium. **—ı veterî iltihabı** path. inflammation of the sheath of a tendon. **—ı veterî istiskası** path. hygroma of the sheath of a tendon.

gılafülkalb^{bi} (. —..) غِلافُ القلب A lrnd., anat. pericardium.

gılâfülkamer (. —...) غِلافُ القَمَر A lrnd. the case into which the moon is supposed to slip during an eclipse, the earth's shadow on the moon.

gılâl^{lli} (. —) غِلال A lrnd., pl. of galle.

gılâz (. —.) غِلاظ A lrnd., pl. of galiz $^{2-3}$.

gılâzet (. —..) غِلاظت A lrnd. thickness, grossness.

gıldır gıldır غِلدیر غِلدیر with a roaring sound, e. g., **makine gıldır gıldır çalışıyor** The engine is roaring along.

gılgıl غِلغِل prov. jug.

gılman (. —) غِلمان A lrnd. 1. pl. of gulâm. 2. Ott. hist. youths educated for the Sultan's service. **— ü cevari** male and female slaves.

—ı Enderun, —ı hassa Ott. hist. pages in the Sultan's palace.

gılme غِلمه A lrnd., pl. of gulâm.

gılzet غِلظت A lrnd. thickness, grossness. **—i mizac** roughness of temperament. **—i zihn** grossness of mind, lack of education.

gımame (. —.) غِمامه A lrnd. 1. hawk's hood. 2. muzzle.

gımd غِمد A 1. anat., biol. sheath. 2. lrnd. sheath, case.

gına 1 (. —) غِنا A var. of gana. **— geldi** /dan/ I (you, etc.) have had enough (of), I am bored (with). **— getir=** /dan/ to be tired (of), to be fed up (with).

gına 2 (. —) غِناء A lrnd. 1. song, air, tune; a singing through the nose. 2. obs. music. **—î** (. — —) A lyrical.

gındaza (..'.) غِندازه It naut. mast rope.

gıpta غِبطه [gıbta] A envy without malice. **— et=** /a/ to envy.

gır غِر 1. sound of a snarl, snore. 2. slang gossip, talk; lie. **— aç=, — at=** slang to chat, to gossip; to tell lies. **— geç=** slang to be absent-minded. **— gır** with a snarl, with a monotonous voice. **— gır geç=** to mock. **— kaynat=** slang to chat. **— gır söyle=** to harp querulously on something.

gırar (. —) غِرار A lrnd., same as harar.

gırbal^{li} (. —) غِربال A lrnd. sieve, riddle, screen. **—i âbgun** P poet. sky, firmament. **—î** (. — —) A anat. ethmoid.

gırbaliüşşekl (. — —..) غِربالى الشكل A lrnd., anat. cribriform, sievelike.

gırban (. —) غِربان A lrnd., pl. of gurab 1.

gırcı غِرجى slang liar.

gırcıla (..'.) غِرجیله It naut. marline.

gırgır غِرغِر 1. tiresome noise; repeated snoring. 2. dispute, quarrel. 3. small motorboat. 4. large bag-shaped fishing net. 5. zipper.

gırıl غِرِل in **— gırıl** with a creaking or rattling sound. **— gırıl öt=** to creak, to rattle, to clank. **—da=** to creak, to clank, to rattle. **—tı** continued creak, rattle, clank.

gıriv (. —) غِریو P lrnd. scream; cry.

gırivan (. — —) غِریوان P lrnd. screaming; crying.

gırıze (. —.) غِریزه var. of garize.

gırızî (. — —) غِریزى var. of garizî.

gırla 1 (.'.) غِرلا slang abundantly, amply, too much; incessantly, to the utmost. **— gidiyor** It is going with a swing.

gırla=^{r} 2 غِرلامق to creak, to rattle, rumble.

gırlı غِرلى 1. humming, buzzing, noisy; annoying. 2. restless, excited.

gırret غِرّت A lrnd. heedlessness, negligence.

gırt غِرت، غِیرت tearing sound. **— gırt kes=** /ı/ to cut with a tearing sound.

gırtlak^{gi} غِرتلاق، غِیرتلاق larynx, throat. **—ına**

bas= /ın/ to get someone by the throat, to force someone to do something. **—ına düşkün** greedy. **— gırtlağa atıl=, — gırtlağa gel=, — gırtlağa ol=** to fly at one another's throats, to quarrel violently. **—ına kadar borç içinde ol=** to be in debt up to one's neck. **— kapağı** *anat.* epiglottis. **— kapantısı** *neol., phon.* glottal stop. **— kemiği** Adam's apple. **—ından keseme=** to gorge greedily, thus be unable to put aside money for other things. **—ına sarıl=** /ın/ to choke, to throttle (somebody); to dun. **—ını sık=** /ın/ to press, to insist; to dun. **—la=** /ı/ to strangle (someone).

gışˢˢ¹ غِشّ *A lrnd.* 1. deceit, treachery. 2. fraud, adulteration; adulterated coin.

gışa (. —) غِشاء *A* 1. *sc.* membrane. 2. *lrnd.* covering, cover, case, sheath. **—yi bekâret, —yi bikir** *anat.* hymen. **—yi cenb** *anat.* pleura. **—yi haricî** *bot.* exoderm. **—yi kalb** *anat.* pericardium. **—yi muhati** *anat.* mucous membrane. **—yi nevati** *biol.* nuclear membrane. **—yi rakik** *anat., pia mater.* **—yi sulb** *anat., dura mater.* **—yi tabl** *anat.* tympanic membrane. **—î** (. — —) *A sc.* membranous.

gışaiyülcenah (. — — .. —) غشاءُ الجناح *A zool.,* Hymenoptera.

gışave, gışavet, gışayet (. —.) غشاوه غشاوت غشایة *A lrnd.* a covering, cover; cataract (of the eye).

gıta (. —) غطاء *A lrnd.* cover, veil, lid.

gıtas (. —) غطاس *A lrnd.* immersion.

gıyab (. —) غياب *A same as* **gıyap.**

gıyaben (. —.) غِياباً *A lrnd.* 1. by name only, by repute (to know). 2. *law* by default.

gıyabî (. — —) غيابي *A law* defaulting. **— hüküm, — karar** *law* judgment given in default. **— tanışma** a getting acquainted by name only, without meeting.

gıyapᵇⁱ (. —) غياب |gıyab| absence. **—ında** in his absence. **— kararı** *law* judgment given in default.

gıyas (. —) غياث *A lrnd.* 1. help, assistance, 2. helper.

gıybet غيبت *A* slander, calumny, backbiting, defamation. **— et=** /ı/ to slander, backbite. **—çi** backbiter, slanderer.

gıygıy غيغى imitation of the sound of a violin.

gıza (. —) غذاء *A lrnd., same as* **gıda.**

-gi 1 گي *cf.* **-gı 1.**

-gi 2 (—) گي *P lrnd.,* following adjective or noun with final vowel, forms abstract noun (*cf.* **—î** 6), *e. g.,* **bendegi** servitude.

-gi 3 گي *cf.* **-gı 2.**

gibi گيبى 1. like, *e. g.,* **çocuk gibi** like a child. 2. *after predicate* almost, nearly, somewhat, *e. g.,* **bugün ateşim yok gibi** Today I have almost no fever. **bitti gibi** It is as good as finished. **—ler** likes, *e. g.,* **onun gibiler** the likes of him. **—lerden** as if to say, *e. g.,* **iyi ettin gibilerden göz kırptı** He winked as if he wanted to say: You did well. **—sine gel=** to seem, to appear, *e. g.,* **olmaz gibime geliyor** It seems impossible to me. **—sine getir=** /ı/ to insinuate, *e. g.,* **beni evinde istemiyor gibisine getirdi** He insinuated that he did not want me in his house. **—ce** somewhat like.

gibin گيبين *archaic, same as* **gibi.**

gici=ʳ 1 گيجمك *prov.* to itch.

gici 2 گيجى *archaic* slight tickling sensation, irritation.

gicikᵍⁱ گيجيك *prov.* itch, irritation. **— otu** small scabious, *bot.,* Scabiosa Columbaria.

gicimikᵍⁱ گيجيمك *prov.* itch.

giciş=ⁱʳ گيجيشمك *prov.* to itch. **—tir=** /ı/ *caus.*

giciyükᵍᵘ گيجيك *archaic* itch.

gid=ᵉʳ گيد مك *cf.* **git=.**

gider=ⁱʳ 1 گيدر مك /ı/ to remove, make disappear, cause to cease (pain, thirst).

gider 2 *neol.* expenditure, expense.

giderayak گيدر آياق at the last moment, just before leaving.

giderek گيدر ك *prov.* gradually.

gidert=ⁱʳ گيدرتمك /ı, a/ *caus. of* **gider=** 1.

gidi گيدى *P,* گدى 1. *in the exclamations* **hey gidi, seni gidi.** 2. *prov.* pander.

gidimli *neol., log.* discursive.

gidiş 1 گيديش 1. *verbal n. of* **git=.** 2. conduct, manner of living, way of life. 3. *obs.* departure of a high personality on an official journey. **—ini beğenme=** /ın/ to disapprove of (someone's) manner of living; not to like the way something is going. **— dönüş, — geliş** a going and returning, return (ticket), round-trip (ticket). **— memuru, — müdürü** *Ott. hist.* marshal who arranges for horses and coaches when the Sultan goes out. **— o gidiş** That was the last that was seen of him.

gidiş=ⁱʳ 2 گيديشمك to itch.

gidişat (.. —) گيديشات [*pseudo-Arabic pl.*] run, development, course.

gidişken گيديشكن *prov.* nettle.

gidiştir=ⁱʳ گيديشتيرمك /ı/ *caus. of* **gidiş=** 2.

gidon 1 گيدون *F mech.* handlebar (of a bicycle).

gidon 2 گيدون *F naut.* burgee.

-gil 1 گيل *prov.* the family of, *e. g.,* **Hasangil** Hasan's family, Hasan and his family. **amcamgil** my uncle's family, my uncle and his family. **—ler** *neol., bot.* family, *as in* **ebegümecigiller.**

-gil 2 گل *cf.* **-gıl 1.**

gil 3 گل *P lrnd., same as* **kil. —i ermeni** *same as* **Kilermeni. —i horasani** edible clay, terra alba from Khorasan. **—i mahtum, —i**

gilân

nibişte Lemnian earth, *terra lemnia, terra sigillata.* **—i parsi** lake-colored ocher. **—i rumi** red ocher, ruddle. **—i şamusi** Samian earth, *terra sigillata.* **—i zerd** yellow ocher.
gilân (— —) غيلان A *lrnd., pl. of* **gul 1.**
gildaru (— — —) گيلدارو P *lrnd.* a kind of drug.
gile گله P *lrnd.* complaint, lamentation. **—dar** (.. —) P, **—mend** P complaining, lamenting.
gilî (. —) گلى P *lrnd.* clayey, earthen, muddy, ocherous.
giliger (. — .) گلگر P *lrnd.* potter.
gilim (. —) گليم P *lrnd., same as* **kilim.** **G— gûşan** *name of a legendary tribe with ears so large that they rest on one ear and cover themselves with the other.* **—puş** (. — —) P clad in a kersey blanket. **—şuy** (. — —) P 1. fuller. 2. soapwort.
gilnak[ki] (. —) گلناك P *lrnd.* clayey, muddy.
gilşah (. —), **gilşeh** گلشه و گلشاه P *lrnd.* the «man of clay» (Adam, or Kayumarth, the mythical first king of Persia).
gilzar (. —) گلزار P *lrnd.* clayey or muddy place.
gimi گيمى *prov., var. of* **gibi.**
-gin (—) گين P *lrnd.,* forms adjectives, *as in* **gamgin.**
gine 1 (.' .) گنه *same as* **yine.**
Gine 2 گنه F *geog.* Guinea.
gir=[er] **1** گيرمك /a/ 1. to come in, enter, go (in, into), get (into). 2. to join, participate (in). 3. to begin, start (era).
-gir 2 (—) گير P *lrnd.* that takes, seizes, holds, *as in* **âlemgir, cihangir.**
giran (. —) گران P hard, heavy; disagreeable. **— gel=** /a/ to hurt, to pain; to offend. **—baha** (. —. —) P costly, precious. **—bar** (. — —) P *lrnd.* heavily laden; fruit-bearing (tree); pregnant. **—can** (. — —) P *lrnd.* slow, lazy; tiresome, tedious. **—dest** (. —.) P *lrnd.* slow-working. **—hatır** (. — .) P *lrnd.* offended, aggrieved. **—huy** (. — —) P bad-natured. **—î** (. — —) P *lrnd., abstr. n. of* **giran. —kadr** (. — .) P very precious. **—maye** (. — —.) P *lrnd.* precious, heavy and costly; of noble birth. **—saye** (. — —.) P man of high position; commander of an army. **—ser** (. — .) P proud, conceited. **—seyr** (. — .) P walking slowly.
Giray گراى *hist., surname of the family of the Khans of the Crimea.*
gird گرد P *lrnd.* circuit, surroundings. **— a-gird** (. —.) P all around.
girdap[bi] (. —) گرداب P 1. whirlpool. 2. *prov.* mark on a horse's coat. **— ağası** *Ott. hist.* river pilot. **—ı belâ** whirlpool of calamity, great misfortune.

girdar (. —) گردار P *lrnd.* 1. work, business. 2. custom, way, behavior.
girdbad (. —) گرد باد P *same as* **girdibat.**
girde گرده P 1. flat bread. 2. *lrnd.* disk; round flat pillow; round yellow patch sewed on a Jew's garment. **—balin** (.. — —) P, **—baliş** (.. — .) P *lrnd.* round flat pillow. **—ban** (.. —) P *lrnd.* watchman.
girdi گردى *only in* **girdisi çıktısı** 1. the ins and outs of, *e. g.,* **bu işin girdisini çıktısını biliyor** He knows the ins and outs of this matter. 2. close relation, *e. g.,* **onunla girdimiz çıktımız yok** We have nothing to do with him. 3. income and expenditure.
girdibat[di] (.. —) گرديبات [**girdbad**] *geog.* whirlwind.
girdir=[ir] گيردرمك گيردرمك /ı, a/ *caus. of* **gir=** 1. **—t=** /ı, a/ *caus. of* **girdir=.**
girebi گربى *Gk prov.* pruning knife, adze.
giregen گيرگن *archaic* penetrating, entering deeply.
gireği گيرگى *Gk prov.* Sunday. **— ertesi,** Monday.
girek[gi] گيرك *prov.* entrance, entry.
giren گيرن *prov., same as* **geren 2.**
girev گرو P *lrnd.* pawn, pledge; wager, stake; bail, surety.
girgin گيرگين 1. who knows how to ingratiate himself, coaxing, wheedling; pushing, bold. 2. *obs.* who has won one's confidence, favorite. **—lik** ability to win one's way into favor.
giriban (. — —) گريبان P *lrnd.* collar.
Girid گريد *cf.* **Girit. —î** (. — —) *lrnd.* Cretan.
girift گرفت P 1. involved, intricate. 2. *calligraphy* intricate (style). 3. *Or. mus.* a kind of **ney** no longer used. 4. *lrnd.* a taking, seizure, capture; captive, prisoner. 5. *lrnd.* fault, sin, crime. 6. *lrnd.* eclipse.
giriftar (.. —) گرفتار P /a/ *lrnd.* 1. captive (of). 2. afflicted (with), suffering (from), victim (of). **—î** (.. — —) P, **—lık** the condition of one seized or afflicted.
girifte گرفته P *lrnd.* taken, seized, captured. **—dem** P asthmatic. **—gî** (... —) P *abstr. n. of* **girifte. —hatır** (... —.) P offended, hurt. **—leb** P tongue-tied. **—ser** P whose mind is confused. **—zeban** (... —) P tongue-tied, stammering.
giriftzen گرفتزن P *Or. mus.* player of the flageolet (short **ney**).
girih گره P *lrnd.* 1. knot, hitch. 2. Persian measure of length (about 2 $^5/_8$ inches). **—bend** P one who ties a knot. **—bür** P pickpocket. **—gir** (... —) P tangled, knotted. **—küşa** (... —) P untier of knots; solver of difficulties.
girilir گيريلير entrance, way in.

girilmez گیریلمز No entrance.
girinci گیرنجی prov. young camel (three to seven years old).
girinti گیرنده ی گیرینتی 1. recess, indentation. 2. prov. stranger who has found shelter in a household.
girintili گیرینتیلی having recesses, indented. **— çıkıntılı** wavy, zigzag, toothed (border line).
giriş 1 گیریش 1. verbal. n. of **gir= 1**. 2. entry, entrance. 3. literature introduction. **— çıkış** entrance and exit; a going in and out. **— imtihanı** entrance examination. **— subabı** mech. inlet valve.
giriş=ir **2** گیریشمك /a/ 1. to meddle, interfere; to mix up (in). 2. to attempt, undertake; to set about. **—ik** intricate; intermingled; complex. **—ik cümle** neol., gram. complex sentence. **—im** neol., phys. interference.
girişken گیریشكن enterprising, pushing.
girişli گیریشلی in **— çıkışlı** movable, sliding.
Giritdi گریت geog. Crete. **— lâdeni** Cretan rock-rose, bot., Cistus polymorphus. **— lâlesi** ranunculus, crowfoot, buttercup, bot., Ranunculus. **— otu** Cretan dittany, bot., Origanum Dictamnus. **—li** Cretan.
girive (.—.) گریوه P lrnd. 1. rocky hill. 2. steep and difficult pass, ravine; abyss. 3. difficult situation, impasse. **—ye düş=** to get into a great fix.
-giriz (.—) گریز [Persian gurez] lrnd. that flees, escapes, as in **merdümgiriz**.
girizan (.——) گریزان P same as **gürezan**.
girizgâh (..—) گریزگاه [Persian gurezgah] 1. introduction to a subject; poetry proem, prologue. 2. lrnd. place or time of flight; asylum, refuge.
girme گیرمه 1. verbal n. of **gir= 1**; mil. penetration. 2. entered; that enters. **—li çıkmalı** indented, zigzag, toothed (border line).
girü گیرو archaic for **geri**.
girüdar (—.—) گیرودار P lrnd. confusion, uproar, tumult.
girya, giryan (.—) گریا گریان P poet. weeping.
girye گریه P poet. a weeping, tears. **—bar** (..—) P, **—dar** (..—) P tearful. **—engiz** (...—) P causing tears, evoking tears. **—feşan** (...—) P lachrymose. **—hiz** (..—) P bringing up tears. **—künan** (...—) P weeping. **—mend** P, **—nak** (..—) P tearful, lachrymose.
giryende گرینده P poet. weeping.
giryenikab (...—) گریه نقاب P poet. misty with tears.
giryenüma (...—) گریه نما P poet. showing tears, tearful.
giryepaş (..—) گریه پاش P poet. lachrymose.

giryeperverd گریه پرورد P poet. bringing tears; causing to weep.
gisu (——) گیسو P poet. ringlet of hair, forelock, sidelock. **—bend** (——.) P fillet for the hair. **—dar** (———) P with the hair in ringlets.
giş 1 (—) غیش P lrnd. 1. copious, abundant; denseness. 2. sorrow, sadness, troubles.
giş 2 (—) گیش P lrnd. marten; sable.
gişe گیشه F cashier's desk, ticket window, pay desk (hotel), booking office (station), box office (theater).
git=der گیتمك 1. /dan, a/ to go; to lead (road). 2. to go away, depart, leave; to perish, be lost; to die; to fall asleep, to drop off. 3. /a/ to suit, fit, become (color, dress). 4. to last, endure (material); /a/ to be sufficient (for). 5. to go on, to continue. **—erek*. —sin** after imperative in order to bring the matter to an end, e. g., **imzanı atıver gitsin** Sign and let's be done with it. **—ti** after verb in past tense 1. certainly, definitely, it can't be helped, too late, it is out now, e. g., **bunu gördü mü, darıldı gitti** If he sees it, he certainly will get cross. 2. however much one tries, e. g., **anlatamadım gitti** I could not make myself understood, however hard I tried. 3. so be it! e. g., **verdim gitti** You can have it. **—tikçe** gradually, little by little; more and more. **—ene ağam, gelene paşam** An outgoing superior is less honored than his successor. **—er ayak*. —ti bezzaz, geldi kazzaz** A change of person makes no difference; one is as good as another. **—er eteri, gelir beteri** The newcomer is worse than his predecessor. **—ip gel=** 1. /a/ to go and return; to go regularly, to frequent. 2. to go to and fro. **—ti de geldi** He escaped from certain death; he was as good as dead. **— gide, —e gide, — git** gradually, more and more. **—ti gider, —ti gider dahi gider** gone for ever.
giti (——) گیتی P lrnd. 1. world, earth. 2. fortune. **—ara, —aray** (————) P world-adorning. **—ban** (————) P protector of the world, king. **—füruz** (———.—) P world-illuminating. **—neverd** (———..) P 1. world traveler. 2. the sun. **—nüma** (——.—) P world-showing. **—pijuh** (————) P 1. worldly-minded. 2. king. **—sitan** (———.—) P world conquering.
gitme گیتمه verbal n. of **git=**.
giv (—) غیو P lrnd. loud cry, shout.
give (..—) گیوه P lrnd. kind of slipper with a sole of rags, and the upper part of knitted string.
givür=ür گیورمك /1, a/ archaic to put, thrust, drive (into).

giy=ᵉʳ گیمك گیبمك /ı/ 1. to put on, to wear. 2. to listen silently (to abuse).

giyah (.—) گیاه P lrnd. grass, hay. —ı **kayser** melilot. —ı **nemnak** purslane.

giybet غیبت A same as **gıybet**.

giydir=ⁱʳ گیدیرمك 1. /ı, a/ caus. of **giy=**¹. 2. /ı/ to dress, to clothe (someone). 3. /ı/ to abuse, reproach. 4. /ı/ print. to cut the lines along the border (of a picture or ornament). **—il=** pass. of **giydir=**.

giyecekᵍⁱ گییجك clothes, wearing apparel.

giyeh گیه P var. of **giyah**.

giyesi گیسی same as **geysi**.

giyil=ⁱʳ گیلمك pass. of **giy=** 1.

giyim گییم 1. Clothing, dress, attire. 2. a change of clothes, e. g., **iki giyim çamaşırım kaldı** I have only two changes of underclothes left; **bir giyim nal** a set of horseshoes. 3. archaic armor. **— başı** Ott. hist. squire. **— eşyası** clothes, clothing. **— kuşam** dress and finery, garments, attire.

giyimli گییملی 1. dressed. 2. archaic armed. **— kuşamlı** well turned out; smartly dressed.

giyin=ⁱʳ گیینمك 1. to dress oneself. 2. /ı/ to put on (clothes, hat, shoes). 3. /a/ to be angry (at) without showing it. **—ip kuşan=** to dress oneself up, to put on one's best clothes.

giyindi گییندی archaic dress, garment. **—li** dressed.

giyindir=ⁱʳ گییندیرمك caus. of **giyin=**.

giyiniş گیینیش mode of dressing.

giyiş گییش mode of putting on or wearing a garment. **—li** archaic dressed.

giyotin گیوتین F guillotine; printing paper knife.

giyür=ⁱʳ گیورمك archaic, caus. of **giy=**¹.

giz گیز It naut. gaff, spanker gaff. **— cundası** peak of gaff. **— çatalı** jaw of gaff.

gizem neol., phil. mystery. **—ci** mystic. **—cilik** mysticism. **—sel** mystical.

gizil neol. 1. phys. potential, latent. 2. phil. virtual. **— güç** phys. potential.

gizir 1 گیزیر |Persian .—| prov. headman's aide.

gizir 2 گیزیر prov. dwarf, squat (person, animal).

gizle=ʳ گیزلمك /ı, dan/ to hide, conceal. **—me** verbal n.; mil. camouflage. **—n=** refl. **—nce** prov. visiting clothes. **—t=** /ı, a/ caus. of **gizle=**.

gizli گیزلی hidden, concealed; secret, confidential; occult; secretly. **— celse** secret session; law a hearing in camera. **— din taşı=** 1. to have a secret religion. 2. to have secret convictions. **— gizli** secretly. **—den gizliye** secretly, in all secrecy. **— kapaklı** clandestine, obscure, suspicious. **— oturum** same as **gizli celse**. **— oy** secret vote, vote by ballot. **— pençe** shoemaking half sole. **— polis** secret policeman. **— rey** same as **gizli oy**. **— sıtma** 1. dormant malaria. 2. one who acts in a sly and underhand manner. **— tut=** /ı/ to hide, to keep secret.

gizlice (.'..) گیزلیجه secretly.

gizlikᵍⁱ گیزلك var. of **gezlik**.

gizlilikᵍⁱ گیزلیلك secrecy, stealth.

glâse غلاسه F patent leather.

glâsiye غلاسیه F geol. glacier.

glikojen غلیكوژن F biochem. glycogen.

glikojenez غلیكوژنز F biochem. glycogenesis.

glikoz غلیكوز F chem. glucose.

glikozit غلیكوزید F chem. glucoside.

glikozüri غلیكوزوری F path. glucosuria.

glisemi غلیسمی F biochem. glycemia.

gliserin غلیسرین F glycerine, glycerol.

glokom غلوكوم F path. glaucoma.

glokoni غلوكونی F min. glauconite.

glomerül غلومرول F anat. glomerule.

glosit غلوسیت F path. glossitis.

glotis غلوتیس F anat. glottis.

glüten غلوتن F biochem. gluten. **— ekmeği** gluten bread.

goblen غوبلن F Gobelin tapestry. **— işi embroidery** Gobelin stitch, tapestry stitch; petit point.

gocukᵍᵘ غوجوق Sl sheepskin cloak.

gocun=ᵘʳ غوجونمق /dan/ to take offense (at); to be suspicious because of bad conscience.

godoş غودوش Arm slang pimp; pander to his wife.

gofre غوفره F 1. cookery chocolate wafer biscuit. 2. text. puckered (material). **— kâğıt** crepe paper.

golˡᵘ غول F sport goal. **— at=**, **— yap=** 1. to score a goal, to kick a goal. 2. slang to cheat, dupe. **— ye=** 1.to have a goal scored against them, to be down a goal. 2. slang to be duped.

golet غولت F schooner.

golf غرلف F 1. sport golf. 2. same as **golf pantolon**. **— pantolon** plus-fours.

Golfstrim غولفستریم E geog. Gulf Stream.

Golos (.'.) غولوس geog. Volos.

gomalaka (...'.) غوما لاقا, **gomalak**ᵍⁱ غوما لاق It shellac.

gomalâstikᵍⁱ غوما لاستیك obs. rubber, eraser.

gomba, gombar (.'.) غومبه coir rope.

gomena, gomene, gomina (.'.) غومنه It naut. 1. ship's cable. 2. cable, cable's length (a tenth of a nautical mile). **— bağı** cable band. **— bük=** to lay a cable. **— dikişi** cable splice.

gonca غنجه [Persian —.] lrnd. 1. bud. 2. poet. rosebud mouth. **—i ab** poet. bubble.

—i erguvan *poet.* spark of fire. **—i râna** 1. *poet.* tender bud. 2. *Or. mus.* an old makam no longer used. **—dehan, —dehen, —fem** P *poet.* rosebud mouthed, rosebud lipped. **—gül** P *poet.* budding rose. **—leb** P *poet.* rosebud lipped.

gondolˡü عوندول F gondola.
gong, gonkᵍᵘ عونغ F gong.
gonore عونوره F *path.* gonorrhea.
gonyometre (....) عونيومتره F goniometer.
goril, gorilâ (..'.) عوريلا F gorilla.
got عوت *prov.* kind of grain measure.
gotikᵍⁱ عوتيك F 1. Gothic. 2. *print.* black letter type, Gothic type.
goygoycu عويغوجى blind beggar formerly led round to collect provisions on the 10th of Muharrem.
göbekᵍⁱ كوبك 1. navel; umbilical cord; vein, orifice (in lungs, kidney, spleen). 2. paunch, potbelly. 3. central part, center, heart (of town, vegetables); central boss, central ornament. 4. generation, degree in a genealogy. 5. *archery* of an arrowshaft divided into twenty-four sections, the fifth to eleventh sections. 6. *prov.* a kind of edible mushroom. **— adı** name given to a child at the cutting of the umbilical cord (This name is often not used). **— anası** *prov.* midwife. **— at=** 1. to perform a belly dance. 2. *colloq.* to be wild with joy. 3. *print.* to buckle up in the middle (form). **— bağı** 1. infant's belly band. 2. *bot.* funicle. **— bağla=** to have a stomach on one, to be getting paunchy. **—i bağlı, —i beraber kesilmiş, —i bitişik** inseparable friends. **—imiz buraya mı gömülmüş?** What's to hold us? We are not bound to stay here for good. **— burusu** *archaic* stomachache. **— çalka= same as göbek at=**¹. **—i çatla=** to exert oneself to the utmost. **—i düş=** 1. for an infant's umbilical cord to be shed. 2. to develop an umbilical hernia. 3. *pop.* to strain one's umbilical muscles through some trouble, exertion, or fright. 4. *same as* **göbeği çatla=**. **— düşmesi** umbilical hernia. **— fıtığı** *path.* umbilical hernia. **—inden işet=** *slang* to stab, to knife. **—i kay=** *same as* **göbeği düş=**³. **—ini kes=** /ın/ cut the navel string. **— kordonu** *anat.* umbilical cord. **— kürk** fur of the umbilical region. **— mantarı** morel, *bot.*, *Morchella esculenta*. **— salıver=** *same as* **göbek bağla=**. **—i sokakta kesilmiş** person always out and about. **—i sökül=** to use the utmost effort. **— taşı** central massage slab in a Turkish bath. **— tütün** tobacco from the middle part of a bale.
göbeklen=ⁱʳ كوبكلنك 1. to become paunchy, to get a stomach on one. 2. to develop a heart (vegetables).

göbekli كوبكلى naveled; with a central boss; fat-stomached.
göbel كوبل Gk *prov.* street urchin; bastard.
göbelekᵍⁱ كوبلك *prov.* 1. mushroom. 2. *var. of* **kelebek**.
göbelez كوبلز *prov., same as* **gövlez**.
göbet كوبت *prov.* 1. tract of woodland cleared for agricultural use, clearing. 2. pond.
göbez كوبز *prov., same as* **gövlez**.
göce كوجه Gk *prov.* 1. split cereal; pearl wheat. 2. meal made of split cereal. **— tarhanası** preparation of dried curds with pearl wheat.
göcen كوجن *prov.* leveret.
göç=ᵉʳ 1 كوجمك 1. /a/ to migrate, to move off, to move (to); to change one's abode. 2. to migrate seasonally. 3. to fall down, to cave in, to subside (building). 4. to die.
göç 2 كوج 1. migration, change of abode. 2. transhumance. 3. goods and chattels of migrating people. 4. death. **— borusu** trumpet signal for departure. **— çek=** *archaic* to migrate. **— eskisi** *Ott. hist.* chamberlain who accompanied the Sultan to his summer residence. **— eşyası** *same as* **göç** 2³. **— et=** 1. to migrate, to trek; to move. 2. to migrate seasonally. **— evi** *archaic* tent. **—i hümayun** *Ott. hist.* the Sultan's move to his summer residence. **— tut=** to prepare for a journey.
göçebe كوجبه 1. nomad; nomadic. 2. wanderer; wandering. **— takımı** nomads. **—lik** nomadic life; migration, a wandering.
göçer كوجر nomadic, migratory, migrating, wandering. **— el** *archaic* wandering tribe. **— ev** *archaic* nomad tent. **— evli** *archaic* nomad. **— konar** nomad, nomadic, wandering. **— ulus taifesi** *archaic* nomads.
göçkün كوجكون 1. *prov.* nomad, nomadic, wandering. 2. *archaic* nomad's goods. **—cü** *archaic* nomad, nomadic, wandering.
göçme كوجمه *verbal n. of* **göç=** 1.
göçmel كوجمل *prov.* immigrant, settler.
göçmen *neol.* immigrant, settler. **— hücre** *biol.* migratory cell. **—lik** immigration.
göçü *neol.* landslide, landslip.
göçükᵍü كوجوك *prov., same as* **göçü**.
göçün=ᵘʳ كوجونمك *obs.* to die.
göçür=ᵘʳ كوجورمك 1. /ı, a/ *caus. of* **göç=** 1. 2. /ı/ *colloq.* to gobble up. **—ücü** *Ott. hist.* official responsible for the transport of the imperial tent and tuğ during a campaign. **—ül=** *pass. of* **göçür=**.
göde كوده *prov.* fat, paunchy; short, dumpy, squat.
gödekᵍⁱ كودك *prov.* kind of pastry.
göden 1 كودن *prov.* large intestine; rectum; blind gut, caecum. **— bağırsağı, — bağırsak**

same as **göden**; *anat.* rectum. — **bumbarı** fresh sausage of rice and meat.
göden 2 گودن [kevden] *archaic* foolish, stupid.
göğde گوگده *var. of* **gövde**.
göğe گوگه It *hist.* man-of-war with 26 pairs of oars.
göğelâ *same as* **gök elâ**.
göğem گوگم *prov.* 1. blue, bluish; violet. 2. sloe, hawthorn. 3. kind of horsefly. — **eriği** bullace. — **gözlü** sloe-eyed.
göğer=[ir] گوگرمك *same as* **göver**=. —**ti** *prov.* 1. greenish or violet color. 2. meadow.
göğüs[gsü] گوگس 1. chest, breast; bosom. 2. forward part; *naut.* bow, flare of a ship's bow. — **ağrısı** pain in the chest. — **bağır açık** with the shirt open, carelessly dressed; disorderly. — **başı** upper part of the chest. — **çukuru** pit of the stomach. — **darlığı** asthma. — **geçir**= to sigh, to groan. — **ger**= /a/ to face, to stand up (to). —**ünü ger**= to stick out the chest in confidence or determination. — **göğse gel**= to come to hand-to-hand fighting. — **göğse muharebe** hand-to-hand fight, combat at close quarters. — **göğse ver**= to embrace one another. — **göğse vur**= *obs.* to fight hand-to-hand. — **hastalığı** chest disease, tuberculosis. — **içi** *anat.* pectoral cavity, endothorax. — **illeti** *same as* **göğüs hastalığı**. —**ü kabar**= to be proud, to swell with pride. — **kanalı** *anat.* thoracic duct. — **kası** *anat.* pectoral muscle. — **kayışı** horse harness breastband. — **kemiği** *anat.* breastbone, sternum. — **kolanı** horse harness breastband. — **kovuğu** *anat.* thoracic cavity. — **kuşağı** *same as* **göğüs kayışı**. — **paleti** *naut.* breastrope. — **sesi** *mus.* chest voice. — **tahtası** breastbone, sternum. — **ver**= 1. /a/ to press with the breast (against a thing). 2. to develop a breast (girl). — **vur**= to beat the breast in grief or despair. — **yatırması** *naut.* breasthook. — **yüzgeci** *zool.* pectoral fin. — **zarı** *anat.* pleura. — **zırhı** breastplate.
göğüsle=[r] گوگسلمك /1/ to breast, to push with the breast.
göğüsleme گوگسلمه *arch.* strut. — **kemeri** *arch.* flying buttress, arched buttress.
göğüslü گوگسلو 1. broad-chested; full-bosomed. 2. *naut.* having a flared bow.
göğüslük[gü] گوگسلك 1. bib, pinafore (for children); plastron. 2. breast harness, breastplate.
göğüssel *neol., biol.* pectoral, thoracic.
gök[gü, kü] 1 گوك sky, firmament, heaven. —**te ararken yerde bul**= /1/ to obtain in an unexpected manner, to run across someone one has long been looking for. — **cismi** *astr.* celestial body. —**e çık**=, —**lere çık**= *obs.* to get into a towering rage. —**e çıkar**=, —**lere çıkar**= /1/ to praise to the skies. —**e çıkış** *rel.* ascension. — **deldi**, — **delen** skyscraper. —**ün dibi delinmiş** Rain is falling in torrents. —**ün direkleri alın**= 1. for one's world to collapse. 2. *obs.* to open (sky, in a cloudburst). — **ekseni** *astr.* celestial axis. — **gürle**= to thunder. — **gürlemesi**, — **gürültüsü** thunder, a clap of thunder. — **haritası** *astr.* celestial map. — **kubbesi** vault of heaven, celestial vault. — **kuşağı** rainbow. — **kutbu** *astr.* celestial pole. — **mavisi** sky blue. — **mihaniği** *astr.* celestial mechanics. —**ün muslukları açıldı** The heavens opened (strong rain). — **nişanı** carrion flower, *bot.*, *Stapelia.* — **rengi** sky-colored. — **taşı** 1. *astr.* meteor, meteorite, aerolite; bolide. 2. turquoise. — **tüz** *neol., astr.* celestial body. —**lere uçur**= /1/ to praise to the skies. —**le yer arasında asılı kal**= to hang in mid-air, to be in an uncertain position. —**te yıldız ararken yerdeki çukuru görme**= not to see the pit at one's feet because one's eyes are fixed on the stars. **G— yolu** Milky Way. — **yüzü** firmament. —**ten zembille inme**= not to come down ready-made from heaven.
gök[kü] 2 گوك blue, sky blue, azure; green. — **at** *prov.* blue roan horse. **G— dere** *prov.* Milky Way. — **ekin** *archaic* green crops. — **elâ** bluish-gray (eye). — **gözlü** 1. blue-eyed. 2. mischievous, injurious. — **kandil** *archaic* very drunk, dead drunk. — **karga** rook, *zool.*, *Corvus frugilegus.* — **kır** blue roan (horse); blue-gray (hair). — **kubbe** the blue vault (of heaven). — **mavi** sky blue. **G— Türk** Kök Turk, Kök Turkish. — **yakut** 1. sapphire. 2. sapphire blue. — **yemiş** *archaic* green, unripe fruit. — **yeşil** *prov.* kind of large lizard. — **zurna** *archaic, same as* **gök kandil**.
gökçe گوكچه 1. bluish, blue-green, somewhat blue or green. 2. mistletoe, *bot.*, *Loranthus europaeus.* 3. rock-dove, rock pigeon, *zool.*, *Columba livia.* 4. *prov.* pretty, beautiful (person). — **balığı** bleak, *zool.*, *Alburnus Mento.* — **karga** *prov., same as* **gök karga**.
gökçek[gi] گوكجك *archaic* pretty, pleasant.
gökçen گوكجن *prov.* pretty, pleasant.
gökçül گوكجل bluish, tinged with blue.
göklük[gü] گوكلك 1. blueness, blue color. 2. destined for heaven.
gökmen گوكمن *prov.* blue-eyed; blond.
göl[lü] گول lake. — **alası** lake trout, *zool.*, *Salmo lacustris.* — **ayağı** outlet of a lake, stream from a lake. — **başı** head of a lake, stream into a lake, inlet. — **evi** *hist.* lake dwelling, pile dwelling. — **kestanesi** water

caltrop, *bot.*, *Trapa*. — **midyesi** pond mussel, *zool.*, *Anodonta cygnaeus*. — **otu** pond lily, yellow water-lily, *bot.*, *Nymphara lutea*. — **şehri** *hist.* lacustrine village.
gölbeç^cı, **gölbek**^ği گول بيج گول لباك *prov.* pool, puddle.
gölcük^ğü گول جك small lake, pond.
göleç^cı, **gölek**^ği, **gölembeç**^cı گول چ گول لك گول مبج *prov.* pond, puddle.
gölemez گول مز [*Persian* **kûremez**] *prov.* 1. kind of milky meal. 2. beestings.
göler=^ır گول رمك *prov.* 1. for a pond or puddle to form. 2. to wallow in the water (animal).
gölet گولت *prov.* pool, puddle.
gölge گولگه shadow, shade; *art* shading. — **balığı** grayling, *zool.*, *Thymallus thymallus*. —**de bırak**= /ı/ to put in the shade, to surpass. — **et**= /a/ to shade, to cast a shadow (upon). — **etme, başka ihsan istemem** Don't trouble me: that's all I want from you. — **hâdise** *phil.* epiphenomenon. — **ışık** *art* chiaroscuro, light and shade. — **kabine** *pol.* shadow cabinet. —**de kal**= to keep in the background. —**sinden kork**= to be frightened of one's own shadow. — **ol**= /a/ to protect, to take under one's wing. — **olay** *neol.*, *phil.*, same as **gölge hâdise**. — **olaycılık** *neol.*, *phil.* epiphenomenalism. — **resim** *art* silhouette. — **tarafı** *geog.* shady side (of a mountain). — **vur**= /a/ *art* to shade. — **yap**= /a/ same as **gölge et**=. —**de yetişen**, —**cil** *neol.*, *bot.* shade-bearing, liking the shade.
gölgele=^r گول گله مك /ı/ 1. to put in the shade. 2. to overshadow. 3. *art* to shade in.
gölgeleme گول گلمه *art* a shading-in.
gölgelen=^ır گول گلنمك 1. *pass.* of **gölgele**=. 2. to grow shadowy. 3. to sit or lie in the shade. —**dir**= /ı/ to shade, to give shade.
gölgeli گول گلى shadowy, shady; shaded; umbrageous. — **baskı** *print.* blurred copy. — **filigran** shaded watermark. — **resim** *paint.* shaded drawing.
gölgelik^ği گول گلك shady spot; arbor, bower.
gölle گوله Gk *prov.* dish prepared with boiled cereals and sugar.
göllen=^ır گول لنمك to form into a lake, pond or puddle. —**dir**= /ı/ *caus.*
gölsel *neol.*, *geog.* lacustrine.
gölük^ğü گولوك 1. beast of burden (horse, mule, ass). 2. *prov.* herd of horses or asses.
göm=^er 1 گوممك /ı, a/ to bury; to inter; to bury (a weapon, etc.) deep (into); *arch.* to set in (cupboard). —**dür**= /ı, a/ *caus.*
göm 2 گوم only in **kuş gömü***.
gömdür=^ür گومدرمك /ı, a/ *caus.* of **göm**= 1.
gömeç^cı گومج *prov.*, same as **gümeç**.
gömele گومله *prov.* hut, hovel.
gömgök^ğü گومگوك intensely blue, dark blue.

gömlek^ği گوملك 1. shirt, chemise, smock. 2. white coat (as for a doctor); *mil.* jacket (of a projectile). 3. fleece; slough (of a serpent or insect); *biol.* coat, covering, tunic; *anat.* integument. 4. cover, case; file cover, folder; *paint.* layer; *mech.* sleeve; *naut.* sail cover. 5. degree, rank, level, shade (of color); generation. — **değiştir**= 1. to slough, to change one's skin. 2. to change one's opinion; to be a change-coat. — **eskit**= to live a long life, to have a fund of experience. —**inden geçir**=, —**ten geçir**= /ı/ *prov.* to pass (an infant) through one's shirt, as a ceremony of adoption, to adopt. —**ten geçme** *prov.* adopted child. —**i kalın** *colloq.* wealthy, well-to-do, having well-lined pockets. — **sarması** lamb's liver stuffed with rice. —**çek** *prov.* with nothing on but a shirt; in one's shirt sleeves. —**çi** shirt maker; seller of shirts. —**li** wearing a shirt. —**lik** 1. shirting. 2. a shirt-length of material. —**liler** *zool.* tunicates, *Tunicata*.
gömme گومه 1. *verbal n.* of **göm**= 1. 2. buried; embedded; let-in, recessed, inlaid; *arch.* engaged. 3. *print.* inset. 4. *prov.* bread or pie baked in ashes. — **ayak** *arch.* pilaster, engaged pillar. — **banyo** bath with a surround, panelled bath. — **dolap** inset cupboard, closet. — **sütun** engaged column.
gömü گوموى buried treasure. —**cü** 1. burying; *zool.* food-secreting (bird). 2. person searching for hidden treasure.
gömük^ğü گوموك 1. /a/ buried, plunged (into). 2. *prov.* marsh, swamp.
gömül=^ür گومولمك 1. *pass.* of **göm**=. 2. /a/ to sink deeply (into).
gömüldürük^ğü گوموالدوروك 1. *horse harness.* breastband. 2. part of an ox yoke.
gömülü گومولى /a/ 1. buried. 2. sunk (into); grown (into).
gön گون coarse leather. —**cü** saddler, leather-worker. —**cük** *obs.*, *naut.* leather to which cords are fastened which stretch the sail.
gönç^cü گونج *prov.* 1. prosperous, wealthy. 2. gay, happy. 3. dense, luxuriant (foliage).
gönder=^ır گوندرمك 1. /ı, a/ to send, dispatch. 2. /ı/ to send away; to see off. —**en** sender. —**i çık**=, —**i git**= /ı/ *archaic* to see off.
gönder 2 گوندر Gk 1. pole, staff. 2. *naut.* flag staff; punt pole. 3. *hist.* lance, spear. — **ağırşağı** *naut.* flag pole cap. —**li balta** *archaic* poleaxe, halberd.
gönderil=^ır گوندریلمك *pass.* of **gönder**= 1.
gönderiş, **gönderme** گوندریش گوندرمه *verbal n.* of **gönder**= 1.
göndert=^ır گوندرتمك /ı, a/ *caus.* of **gönder**= 1.
göndür=^ür گوندرمك *archaic*, same as **gönder**= 1.
gönel=^ır گونلمك /a/ *prov.* to direct oneself, to turn (toward).

gönen 1 گۄناک *prov.* humid (soil).
gönen=ᶦʳ **2** گۄنالك *prov.* to prosper, to enjoy. **—ç** *neol.* prosperity. **—dir=** /ı/ *caus. of* **gönen= 2.**
gönlekᵍⁱ گۄنلك *archaic, same as* **gömlek.**
gönülⁿˡᵘ, *pop.*ʸⁿᵘ گۄنل 1. heart; mind. 2. inclination, desire, willingness. **—den** heartfelt, most sincerely. **—ünce** to his heart's content. **— acısı** pangs of love. **— aç=** to cheer up, to make happy. **—ü açık** 1. openhearted, frank. 2. free from trouble, carefree. **— açıklığı** cheerfulness, hilarity. **—ü açıl=** to become cheerful. **—ü ak=** /a/ to feel attracted (by). **— al=, —ünü al=** /ın/ to please, to content; to repair a hardship. **—ü alçak** modest, unpretentious. **— alçaklığı** modesty. **— aldır=, —ünü aldır=** /a/ to fall in love (with). **—ü alma=** /ı/ not to have the heart (to eat). **—ünü ara=** /ın/ *archaic* to sound (someone). **— arılığı** *archaic* pureness of heart. **— avcısı** heart hunter. **— avla=** to hunt hearts. **— avut=** 1. to dally with love. 2. /la/ to resign oneself (to a lesser portion), to content oneself (with little). **— bağla=** /a/ to set one's heart (upon). **— belâsı** trouble caused by love. **— birliği** agreement, harmony. **—ü bol** generoushearted. **— budalası** hopelessly in love. **—ü bulan=** 1. to feel sick, nauseated, to have heartburn. 2. to feel suspicious (about). **—ünü bulandır=** /ın/ *caus. of* **gönlü bulan=.** **— bulantısı** 1. nausea. 2. uneasiness; suspicion, qualm. **—ü çek=** /ı/ to desire. **—ünü çel=** /ın/ to charm, to inflame with love. **—den çıkar=, —ünden çıkar=** /ı/ to forget, to cast someone out of one's heart. **—ü çök=** to have a breakdown in morale, to give up. **—üne danış=** to think over, to ponder. **—ü daral=** to become weary, distressed. **— darlığı** foreboding, anxiety. **— değiştir=** to change sweethearts. **— delisi** one who keeps falling in love. **— dilencisi** one who is so madly in love that he undergoes any humiliation provided he can be near his beloved. **—üne doğ=** to have a foreboding. **— döndür=** *archaic* to cause nausea. **—ünün dümeni bozuk** *colloq.* one who is not serious in his love affairs. **— eğlencesi** toy of love; flirt. **— eğlendir=** to amuse oneself. **— eri** tolerant, sensible and manly person. **— et=** /a/ to wish good or evil (for someone). **—ünü et=** /ın/ 1. to obtain the acquiescence (of), to induce (to), to make willing. 2. to please, to conciliate. **—ü gani** 1. generous. 2. contented. **—den geç=** to come to mind, to occur to one. **—ünden geçir=** /ı/ to think (of doing, about doing). **—ü geniş** generous, liberal. **—üne göre** according to one's heart's desire. **— gözü** perception, insight. **—ü gözü açıl=** to be cheered up, to feel revived. **—ü gözü gani** *same as* **gönlü gani. —ünü hoş et=** /ın/ to please, to make contented. **—ünü hoş tut!** Don't worry. **— hoşluğu ile** willingly. **—ü iliş=** /a/ to feel attracted (to someone). **— indir=** to be willing to do some job that is beneath him. **— işi** affair of the heart. **—ü kal=** 1. to feel resentment, to feel hurt. 2. /da/ to long (for). **—ü kan=** to stop worrying. **—ünü kap=** /ın/ to captivate someone's heart. **—ü kara** malevolent, blackhearted. **—ü karar=** to feel disgusted with life. **—ünü kır=** /ın/ to hurt the feelings (of). **— kimi severse güzel odur** Beauty is a matter of taste. **—den kop=, —ünden kop=** to be given gladly. **—ünüzden ne koparsa veriniz** Give what you feel like giving. **— maskarası** one who allows himself to be ridiculed because of some love affair. **— okşa=** to treat someone kindly. **—ü ol=** 1. /a/ to agree (to). 2. /da/ to be in love (with). **—ünü pazara çıkar=** to fall in love with an unworthy person. **— rızası ile** voluntarily, willingly. **—ü takıl=** /a/ to be attracted (by). **—ü tez** impatient, hustler. **—ü tok** contented, satisfied. **— tokluğu** content. **—ü var** 1. /a/ he is willing. 2. /da/ he is in love (with). **— ver=** /a/ to give one's heart (to), to fall in love (with). **—ünü yap=** /ın/ *same as* **gönlünü et=. —ünü yık=** /ı/ to offend, to hurt, to wound to the quick. **—ü yok** 1. /a/ He is unwilling. 2. /da/ He is not in love (with). **—ü yufka** soft-hearted, tender-hearted. **— yufkalığı** soft-heartedness, tender-heartedness.
gönüldeş گۄنلدش *obs.* united in mind and feelings.
gönülle=ʳ گۄنللەمك /ı/ *prov.* to please, to content. **—n=** *prov.* to be hurt, to take something to heart.
gönüllü گۄنللو 1. volunteer. 2. willing. 3. lover. 4. *archaic* courageous. **— ağası** *Ott. hist.* head of volunteers. **— ordu** volunteer army.
gönülsüz گۄنلسز 1. humble, modest. 2. unwilling, disinclined. **— aş ya karın ağrıtır ya baş** *proverb* (*lit.* Food eaten with no appetite gives either a stomachache or headache.) Something done unwillingly will not do good. **— köpek ava gitmez** You can't force an unwilling dog to go hunting. **—lük** 1. modesty. 2. unwillingness, disinclination.
gönye (ˊ.) گۄنيا *Gk* set-square (for drawing, dressmaking, or in masonry). **—sinde ol=** to be at right angles. **— tut=** /a/ to square. **—li** at right angles.
gör=ᵘʳ مك 1. to see. 2. /ı/ to see, to notice, to perceive; to deem, to consider, to regard (as). 3. /ı/ to visit, to call upon; to meet.

4. /ı/ to experience, to pass through, to undergo. 5. /ı/ to do, to perform, to accomplish (a matter); to furnish (expenses). 6. *following verb* + *-a cf.* =agör=; *following verb* + =maya *cf.* =mayagör=. —erek atış *mil.* direct fire. —meyerek atış *mil.* indirect fire. gör= geçir=, —üp geçir= to experience, endure, suffer, to go through; to have seen better days. —müş geçirmiş experienced; gone through many hardships; having seen better days. —eceğim geldi, —esim geldi /ı/ I wish I could see him, I miss him (or her). —üp göreceği rahmet budur This is all he will ever get. —üp gözet= /ı/ to protect, to guard, to keep an eye (on). —eyim seni! Let's see what you can do.

gördek⁶ⁱ گوردک bitterling, *zool.*, Rhodeus amarus.

gördür=ᵘʳ گوردورمك /ı/ *caus. of* gör=⁵.

göre گوره 1. /a/ according to, as to, in respect of. 2. *neol., phil.* relative. —cilik *neol., phil.* relativism. —li *neol., phil.* relative. —lik *neol., phil.* relation. —lilik *neol., phil.* relativity.

göremez گورمز |*Persian* kuramaz| *prov.* sour curds mixed with fresh milk.

görenek⁶ⁱ گورنك 1. custom, usage, use; routine. 2. *prov.* model, example; precedent. —li 1. that has precedent. 2. experienced.

göresek⁶ⁱ گورسك *prov., same as* görenek².

göresi=ʳ گورسى *prov.* /ı/ to desire to see, to yearn (for); to miss.

görev *neol.* duty; function. —e al= /ı/ to nominate, to appoint. —den çıkar= /ı/ to discharge, to dismiss, to sack. —deşlik *physiol.* synergy, synergism. —lendir= /ı, la/ to charge, to entrust (with a task). —li charged, entrusted with a duty, in charge.

görgü گورگو 1. experience. 2. good manners, social education. 3. contentment. 4. *prov.* mirror. — şahidi eyewitness. —cülük *neol., phil.* empiricism. —l *neol., phil.* empiric. —len= to gain experience, to see and learn.

görgülü گورگولى 1. experienced. 2. of good manners.

görgüsüz گورگوسز 1. inexperienced. 2. without manners, unmannerly, ill-bred. —lük 1. inexperience. 2. unmannerliness.

görk⁶ᵘ گورك *archaic* goodly appearance, beauty.

görkem گوركم *archaic* pomp, splendor. —li pompous, splendid, magnificent.

görklü گوركلو *archaic* of good appearance, beautiful.

görme گورمه 1. sight, vision. 2. seen. 3. who has seen. — alanı field of vision. — aygıtı, — cihazı 1. optical apparatus. 2. *biol.* organ of vision, visual organ. — işareti *mil.* visual signal, visible mark.

görmece گورمجه 1. subject to the condition of being seen (sale). 2. by visual estimation, at sight.

görmedik⁶ⁱ گورمديك 1. upstart, parvenu. 2. unmannerly, common.

görmeli گورملى *in* — telgraf *mil.* visual telegraphy.

görmemezlik⁶ⁱ گورممزلك a pretending not to see. —e gel=, —ten gel= /ı/ to pretend not to see.

görmemiş گورممش *same as* görmedik.

görmez گورمز unseeing, blind. —e ur=, —len= *archaic* /ı/ to feign not to see. —lik 1. blindness. 2. *same as* görmemezlikten gel=.

görmüşlük duygusuⁿᵘ *neol., psych.* paramnesia.

görset=ⁱʳ گورستمك /ı, a/ *prov.* to show.

görü *neol.* 1. view. 2. *anat.* vision, eyesight.

görücü گورجى woman sent to find a prospective bride, female go-between. —ye çık= to show oneself to the female go-between (prospective bride). — git=, —lüğe çık= to pay a visit to see a prospective bride.

görül=ᵘʳ گورلمك *pass. of* gör=. —düğünde *fin.* at sight.

görüm گوروم 1. sight, look. 2. *neol.* eyesight.

görümce گورومجه husband's sister, sister-in-law of the wife.

görümlük⁶ᵘ گورملك 1. something worth seeing. 2. *obs.* money or present given when something is displayed; *same as* yüz görümlüğü.

görümsü *neol.* phantom, ghost; apparition.

görün=ᵘʳ گورنمك /a/ 1. to show oneself (to), to appear, to come in sight; to be visible, to be seen. 2. to seem, to create an impression (of). —dü *naut.* Anchor's awash. —en *neol., astr.* apparent. —en köy kılavuz istemez, —en köye kılavuz istemez It is perfectly obvious. —dü Sıvasın bağları *said when something unpleasant begins to happen as feared.* —gü *neol., phil.* phenomenon. —mez invisible, not apparent; unforeseen. —mezden gel= /ı/ *prov.* to pretend not to see. —mez ol= 1. not to have been seen (for a long time). 2. to disappear. —tü 1. phantom, phantasm, specter. 2. *neol., phys.* image. —ü, —üm *neol.* appearance, view. —ü açısı, —üm açısı *astr.* apparent diameter.

görünür گورونور apparent, visible, in sight. —de in appearance; in sight. —de yok, —lerde yok not in sight.

görünüş گورونش appearance, sight, spectacle; external view; aspect. —te apparently, as far as can be seen.

görüş 1 گوروش 1. act or manner of seeing; sight. 2. point of view, opinion;

görüş= conception. — açısı *neol.* angle of vision. — ayrılığı difference of opinion, disparity of views. — birliği agreement of opinion. — farkı *same as* görüş ayrılığı. — tarzı point of view. — zaviyesi *same as* görüş açısı.

görüş=^{ür} 2 گوريشمك 1. /la/ to meet; to converse, to have an interview; to see each other, to have relations (with). 2. /ı/ to discuss, to negotiate. —me interview; discussion, negotiation; meeting. —tür= /ı, la/ to arrange a meeting (for); to introduce someone (to). —ül= *pass. of* görüş= 2².

gösgötürü گوس گوترو *archaic* wholly, entirely, completely.

göster=^{ir} گوسترمك 1. /ı/ to show, to exhibit, to indicate; to point (at, to); to present (movie), to demonstrate, to prove (an assertion). 2. /ı, a/ to expose (to the influence of). 3. to appear, to look, to seem. —ge *neol.*, *phys.* indicator. —i *neol.* demonstration, manifestation, show. —il= *pass. of* göster=.

gösteriş گوستریش گوسترش show, display, ostentation, demonstration; striking appearance. — hareketi *mil.* demonstration. — muharebesi, — savaşı *mil.* mock battle. — taarruzu *mil.* mock attack, sham attack. — yap= 1. to make an ambitious, ostentatious display. 2. to make a demonstration./ —çi one who likes to be ostentatious. —leme *neol.* bombast. —li of striking appearance, imposing, conspicuous. —siz poor-looking, unimposing, inconspicuous.

gösterit *neol.* theater performance.

gösterme گوسترمه *verbal n. of* göster=. — parmağı forefinger, index finger. —lik 1. sample, specimen, showpiece. 2. *shadow theat.* scenery put up before the beginning of the show.

göstert=^{ir} گوسترتمك /ı/ *caus. of* göster=.

göt گوت *vulg.* 1. bottom; buttocks, backside. 2. bottom; breech (of a cannon). 3. courage, audacity. —ü açık wearing patched and seedy clothes, out at the seat. —ten bacak, —ten bacaklı short, having short legs (person). —ün götün backwards. —üne kına yak! Triumph over him now he's down. —ü kırmızı 1. dip-candle with lower end tinged with dye. 2. *prov.* dancing monkey. —e küstü *prov.* short fur jacket reaching to the waist. — tokuştur= /la/ *vulg.* to chum up (with). —ü trampet çal= *slang* to be delighted. — üstü otur= *vulg.* to get into hot water. —ü var He has courage. —ü varıp gel= to be in an agony of fear. —lek passive pederast. —lük back part of the saddle blanket. —süz 1. without bottom; without breech. 2. lacking courage.

götür=^{ür} گوتورمك /ı/ 1. to take away, to carry away, to carry off; to kill (illness). 2. /ı, a/ to lead, to conduct (to); to accompany. 3. to bear, to support, to endure. 4. *archaic* to remove, to put an end (to). —en *neol.*, *anat.* efferent. —ge *prov.* lever. —gen *neol.*, *same as* götüren. —t= /ı, a/ *caus. of* götür=.

götürü 1 گوتورو گوترو in the lump, by the job, by contract; *mining* paid by the load. — al= /ı/ to buy outright, in the lump, as a job lot; to contract at a lump price. — alış wholesale purchase. — bina building put up by contract. — çalış= to do piece-work. — fiat contract-price; flat rate. — iş job-work, piece work; *mining* work paid by the load, task-work. — işçi piece-worker, jobber. — meblâğ lump sum. — pazar, — pàzarlık lump bargain, contract, compact. — sat= to sell outright as a job lot. — satış outright sale. — usul competitive wage system. — ücret piece-rate wages.

götürü 2 گوتورو گوترو *prov.* wedding present.

götürücü گوتوریجی 1. carrying away. 2. *com.* sub-contractor, jobber.

götürül=^{ür} گوترلمك *pass. of* götür=.

götürüm *neol.* endurance. —lü *neol.* enduring, supporting. —süz *neol.* one who is incapable of enduring, supporting.

götürün=^{ür} گوترنمك *archaic, refl. of* götür=.

gövde گوده گوده 1. body, trunk, stem; body (of a musical instrument); case, barrel (of a watch, etc.). 2. meat carcass, *e. g.*, bir gövde koyun a sheep's carcass. 3. *neol.*, *gram.* theme, stem. 4. *print.* size of type. —ye at= /ı/ to gulp down. — bağla= *archaic* to grow fat. — bölmeleri *mil.* sections of an army corps. —sinde canı yok *prov.* He is quite insensitive, apathetic, unexcitable. —sinde bir çiğnem sakız *prov.* an only child. — gösterisi *pól.* demonstration of strength. —ye indir= /ı/ *same as* gövdeye at=. —len= 1. to become corpulent. 2. to develop a trunk (tree).

gövdeli گودلی 1. stout, corpulent, husky. 2. *prov.* pregnant.

gövel گول *prov.* wild duck.

gövelâ گولا *same as* gök elâ.

gövelek^{ği} گولك *prov.* mistletoe.

gövem گوم *prov.*, *var. of* göğem.

göver=^{ir} گورمك to turn green (vegetation); to turn blue. —i *prov.* green vegetables. —t= /ı/ *caus. of* göver=.

göverti گورتی *prov.* 1. *same as* göveri. 2. blue spot on the skin, bruise.

gövlez گولز *prov.* 1. puppy, pup. 2. kitten.

gövün=^{ür} گونمك *prov.*, *same as* göyün=.

göy=^{er} گومك *archaic* to burn, to be on fire.

göya گویا P *var. of* gûya 1.

göyde گویده *archaic, same as* gövde

göydür=ür گویدرمك گوگـمك /ı/ archaic, caus. of **göy**=.
göynü=r گوگنك prov., var. of **göyün**=.
göynükgü گوگنك prov. 1. burned. 2. decayed, putrid, rotten. 3. distress, pain. —**lü** archaic distressing, painful.
göyükgü گویك prov. 1. burned, singed; ripe. 2. fever.
göyün=ür گوینك prov. 1. to be burned, to be scorched, browned by heat. 2. to ripen. 3. to burn with anger, desire. —**dür**= /ı/ caus.
göz گوز 1. eye. 2. evil eye. 3. drawer, pigeonhole. 4. arch (of a bridge); cell (in a honeycomb); eye (of a needle); mesh (in a net); pore (of a sponge); room, section of a house or flat; scale (of a balance); square (in a questionblank etc.). 5. spring (of water); eye, bud. —**de** in favor, much liked, much thought of, in the public eye. —**ü aç** avaricious, insatiable. — **aç**= 1. to open one's eyes, to awake from sleep. 2. to rest. —**lerini aç**=, —**ünü aç**= 1. to wake up, to open one's eyes (after birth). 2. to open one's eyes wide in surprise. 3. /ın/ to open a person's eyes, to undeceive. — **açama**= to have no rest or respite. —**ü açık** wide awake, shrewd; sharp. —**ü açık git**= to die disappointed. — **açıklığı** vigilance; cleverness, shrewdness. —**ü açıl**= to become shrewd. — **açıp kapamadan**, —**ünü açıp kapayıncaya kadar** in the twinkling of an eye, in an instant. — **açma**= to have no rest or peace. — **açtırma**= /a/ to give no respite (to), to give no chance to recover. — **ağrısı** 1. eye-strain. 2. one's old or first love or sweetheart, as in eski göz ağrısı, ilk göz ağrısı. — **ahbaplığı** a knowing someone by sight. —**ü ak**= to be blinded (by accident). — **akı** the white of the eye. —**e ak düş**= 1. to have cataract of the eye. 2. to become very old. — **al**= to dazzle. —**e al**= /ı/ to venture, to risk. —**ün alabildiği kadar**, —**ün alabildiğine** as far as the eye can see. — **alanı** field of vision. — **aldanımı**, — **aldanması** optical illusion. — **alıcı** eye-catching. — **alımı** eyeshot. — **altına al**= /ı/ to place under police supervision. — **altında bulundur**= /ı/ to watch (over), to keep an eye on. — **altı et**= /ı/ same as göz altına al=. —**ü ardında git**=, —**ü arkada kal**= to die or leave having left something undone or a desire unaccomplished; to pass away without obtaining one's desire. — **aşınalığı** same as göz ahbaplığı. — **at**= /a/ to glance (at), to run an eye over. — **atımı** glance, look. —**ün aydın**, —**ünüz aydın** Congratulations! — **aydına git**= /a/ to pay a visit of congratulation. — **ayırma**= /dan/ not to take one's eyes off. — **aynası** med. ophthalmoscope. — **bağ**= obs. to cast a spell. — **bağı** 1. eyeshade, patch. 2. magic, spell, enchantment. — **bağıcı** magician, conjurer; juggler. — **bağla**=, —**ünü bağla**= /ın/ to blindfold; to hoodwink. —**ü bağlı** unconscious, unsuspecting; bewitched. —**üne bak**= /ın/ same as gözünün içine bak=. —**e bat**= /ın/ to be conspicuous, striking. —**leri batkın** whose eyes are sunken. — **baycı**, — **bayıcı** prov., same as göz bağıcı. —**leri bayıl**= to become languid. — **bebeği** 1. pupil of the eye. 2. apple of the eye, darling. — **bebeği gibi sev**= /ı/ to love somebody like the apple of one's eye. —**lerini belert**= prov. to open the eyes wide (in astonishment or anger). — **boncuğu** bead for averting the evil eye. — **boya**= to throw dust in someone's eyes, to mislead, delude. —**ü bozardı** prov. He lost his eyesight. —**ü bulandı** His eyes became opaque. —**leri bulutlandı** His eyes clouded (as if he were going to weep). —**ü büyü**=, —**leri büyü**= 1. to open one's eyes wide (in surprise, with terror, etc.). 2. to become ambitious. —**ünde büyü**= to assume great proportions (to someone). —**ü büyükte ol**=, —**ü büyüklerde ol**= to be full of ambition. —**ünde büyüt**= /ı/ to exaggerate the importance (of). —**leri çakmak çakmak ol**= to be heavy-eyed (from fever). —**e çarp**= to strike or catch the eye; to be conspicuous. —**den çık**= to fall from favor, to fall in estimation. —**den çıkar**= /ı/ to be prepared to pay or sacrifice. —**ünü çıkar**= /ın/ to do great harm; to spoil; to punish ruthlessly. — **çukuru** anat. eye-socket, orbit. —**leri çukura gitmiş** His eyes are sunken. — **dağı** intimidation, fright. — **dağı ver**= /a/ to intimidate, to scare. —**ü dal**= to gaze vacantly, to stare into space. —**ünü daldan budaktan esirgeme**=, —**ünü daldan budaktan sakınma**= to disregard dangers. — **damlası** 1. eye drops, eye lotion. 2. dropper for eye medicine. — **değ**= /a/ to be affected by the evil eye. — **deliği** observation hole; look-out slit; visor. — **demiri** naut. bower anchor. —**lerini devir**= to roll one's eyes. —**ü dışarda** having one's eyes on something else (because of discontent). —**leri dışarı fırlamış**, —**leri dışarı uğramış** He is frightened out of his wits; his eyes have popped out of his head. — **dik**= /a/ to covet; to long to possess. —**lerini dik**=, —**ünü dik**= /a/ to stare, to gaze fixedly (at). — **dikeği** neol. aim, purpose, object. —**e diken ol**= to provoke jealousy. — **dişi** eyetooth, canine tooth. —**üne dizine dursun!** May it choke him! (said about an ungrateful person). — **doktoru** oculist, ophthalmologist. —**leri doldu**, —**ü doldu**, —**leri dolu dolu oldu** His eyes filled

with tears. —**ü doy=** to become satisfied. —**leri dön=** 1. to be furious (with anger, passion). 2. for one's eyeballs to slip back (on the point of death). —**ünü dört aç=** to be all eyes. —**ünü duman bürü=**, —**ü dumanlan=** *slang* to be furious. —**ü dumanlı** whose eyes are clouded with anger. —**den düş=** to fall into disfavor, to fall out of favor. — **erimi** *prov.* eyeshot. — **et=** /a/ to wink (at). — **evi** eye socket. —**ünü fal taşı gibi aç=** to stare in amazement. —**leri fincan gibi ol=** to have eyes as large as saucers. —**den geçir=** /ı/ to scrutinize, to go over, to look over. —**e gel=** *same as* **göz değ=**. — **gezdir=** /a, üzerinde/ to cast an eye (over). —**ü gibi sev=** /ı/ to love (someone) like the apple of one's eye. —**e gir=**, —**üne gir=** /ın/ to ingratiate oneself with someone, to curry favor. —**ü git=** /a/ to see by chance; to catch sight of. —**ü gönlü açıl=** to become cheerful, to cheer up. — **göre,** — **göre göre** openly, publicly; patently; knowingly; with one's eyes open. —**ü görme=** to be blind. —**üm görmesin!** /ı/ I don't want to set eyes on him. —**e görün=** to be visible; to show, to meet the eye. — **göz** all holes, porous; cellular. —**e göz, dişe diş** an eye for an eye, a tooth for a tooth. — **göze gel=** for looks to meet, to catch someone's eye. — **gözü görmüyor** One cannot see one's hand before one (because of mist, fog, smoke, etc.). — **hakkı** small share given to the onlooker to ward off the evil eye. — **hapsine al=** /ı/ to keep under surveillance, observation; to fix one's eyes (on), to watch closely. — **hastalığı** eye complaint. — **hekimi** oculist, ophthalmologist. —**den ırak ol=** to be far away. —**den ırak olan gönülden de ırak olur** Out of sight out of mind. —**üm ısırıyor** /ı/ I seem to know him; I think I have met him before. —**ünün içine bak=** /ın/ 1. to cherish dearly. 2. to be at the beck and call (of), to be at the disposal (of). 3. to look entreatingly (at). —**lerinin içi gül=** for one's eyes to shine with joy. —**lerinin içine kadar kızar=** to blush to the roots of one's hair. —**ü ile bak=** /a/ to consider (as), *as in* **ona evlât gözü ile bakıyor** He regards him as his own son. —**e iliş=** to catch the eye. —**ü iliş=** /a/ to notice, become aware (of). — **iltihabı** inflammation of the eye, ophthalmia, ophthalmitis. —**lerine inanma=** not to believe one's eyes. —**den kaç=** to be overlooked, not to have been noticed. —**lerini kaçır=** not to be able to look some one in the eye. — **kafiyesi** *poet.* visual rhyme. —**ü kal=** /da/ to long for (enviable object). — **kamaştır=** 1. to dazzle. 2. to fascinate. — **kamaştırıcı** brilliant, wonderful. —**ünü kan bürü=** to see red.

—**leri kan çanağına dön=** to have bloodshot eyes. —**ünü kapa=** 1. to shut the eyes (at), to connive (at); to fall asleep. 2. to die. 3. /a/ to pretend not to see. — **kapağı** eyelid. —**ü kapalı** 1. without hesitation, without deliberation, blindly. 2. without knowledge of the world, inexperienced. —**leri kapan=** not to be able to keep one's eyes open, for one's eyelids to become heavy. —**ü kapıda** 1. looking for an opportunity to leave. 2. anxiously expecting someone's arrival, with eyes glued on the door. — **karası** *prov.* pupil of the eye. —**ü karar=** 1. to feel near fainting. 2. to lose self-control, to lose one's temper. — **kararı** judgment at sight, visual estimation, guess, conjecture; by rule of thumb. —**le kaş arasında** *same as* **kaşla göz arasında.** —**ü kay=** 1. /a/ to see by chance, to see out of the corner of one's eye. 2. to squint slightly. —**den kaybet=** /ı/ to lose sight (of). —**den kaybol=** to be lost to sight, to disappear. —**ü kes=** /ı/ 1. to feel oneself capable (of). 2. to take a liking or fancy (to), to like. — **kesil=** to be all eyes. —**ü keskin** sharp-eyed, sharp-sighted. — **keskinliği** keenness of sight. —**üne kestir=** /ı/ 1. to have one's eye on something as a desirable possession. 2. to feel oneself capable (of). — **keşfi** *mil.* reconnaissance (by sight). — **kıp=** *prov.*, — **kırp=** to wink, blink, twinkle; *physiol.* to nictate. — **kırpan zar** *biol.* nictating membrane. — **kırpma** *physiol.* nictation. — **kırpma ıspazmosu** *path.* nictating spasm. —**ünü kırpmadan** without batting an eyelid. —**ü kız=** to breathe fire and fury, to see red. —**ü kızar=** to have red eyes from weeping. — **kliniği** ophthalmic hospital, eye clinic. — **konuğu** 1. reflected image in another's eye. 2. pupil of the eye. —**ü kork=** /dan/ to go in fear. —**ünü korkut=** /ın/ to daunt, to intimidate. — **koy=** /a/ to cast covetous eyes (upon), to want to possess. —**ü kör olası,** —**ü kör olasıca** damned, darned. —**ü kör olsun** Curse it! Hang it! — **kulak kesil=** /a/ to be all eyes and ears. — **kulak ol=** /a/ to keep an eye (on). — **kuyruğu** the corner of the eye. —**ünün kuyruğu ile bak=** /a/ to look out of the corner of one's eye (at). —**leri kuyuda** with deep-set, sunken eyes, hollow-eyed. — **loçası** *naut.* hawsehole for the bower. — **merceği** *anat.* crystalline lens. —**lerine mil çek=** /ın/ to blind with a style or red hot iron. — **nuru** 1. eye-straining work. 2. visual faculty, strength of vision. —**ümün nuru!** light of my eyes, darling!, beloved! — **nuru dök=** to engage in eye-straining work. —**ü ol=** /da/ to desire strongly, to covet. — **otu** eyebright, euphrasy, *bot., Euphrasia officinalis.* —**ünü oy=** /ın/

to try to do the utmost harm (to). **— oynatıcı sinir** *anat.* oculomotor nerve. **— oyuğu** *anat.*, *same as* **göz çukuru**. **— önünde** in front of one's eyes. **— önünde bulundur=** /ı/ 1. to have something before one. 2. *same as* **göz önünde tut=**. **—ünün önüne gel=** to come vividly into one's mind, to be visualized. **—ünün önüne getir=** /ı/ to imagine readily, to envisage. **— önünde tut=** /ı/ to bear in mind, to remember, to realize. **—lerinden öp=** /ın/, **—lerini öp=** /ın/ to kiss the eyes (of a younger person). **—lerinizden öperim** kind regards (concluding greeting in a letter to a junior). **— ü pek** bold, brave, courageous, daredevil. **— pekliği** boldness, courage, daring. **—ü pencerede** *same as* **gözü kapıda. — perdesi** *path.* cataract. **—ü perdeli** heedless and blind. **— pınarı** inner corner of the eye. **— sanısı** *neol.* optical illusion. **— seçimi** range of vision, eyeshot. **— seçimi dışında kal=** to be out of sight. **—ü seğir=** to twitch (eye). **— sevdası** love at sight. **—ünü sevdiğim** my dear. **—ünü seveyim** Be so good (as to), have the kindness (to), please! **—ü sidikli** *vulg.* a blubberer. **— siperi** eye-shade. **—üne sok=** /ı/ to thrust something under someone's eyes by way of reproof or accusation. **—ü sön=** to be blinded (by accident). **—leri sulan=** to become watery (eyes). **—ü sulu** *same as* **gözü sidikli. —den sürmeyi çal=, —den sürmeyi çek=** to be very clever and skillful in persuading people. **— süz=** /a/ to regard coquettishly or amorously, to cast amorous glances (at). **—leri süzül=** for someone's eyes to be half-closed, to be sleepy. **— tabibi** oculist, ophthalmologist. **— tahmini** visual estimation, approximate measure. **—ü takıl=** /a/ for someone's eye to be caught (by). **— taşı** copper sulfate. **—ünde taşı=** /ı/ to take a probability into account. **— tedavi ilmi** ophthalmology. **— titremesi** *path.* nystagmus. **—ü tok** contented, not covetous. **—ü toprağa bak=** to have one foot in the grave. **—ünü toprak doyursun** His greed will never be satisfied. **—ü toprakta ol=** to have one foot in the grave. **—de tut=** /ı/ to hold in favor. **—ü tut=** /ı/ to consider fit, to deem proper, good. **—ünde tüt=** to have an intense longing, an ardent desire (for). **— ucu ile bak=** /a/ to cast a furtive glance (at). **—den uyku ak=** to be very sleepy. **—lerine uyku girme=, —lerine uyku haram ol=, —lerini uyku tutma=** not to be able to sleep. **—den uzak tutma=** /ı/ to keep in sight, to keep in mind, to keep in view. **—den uzaklaş=** to go away, to depart. **—ü üstünde kaşı var deme=** to raise not the slightest objection. **—ü üzerinde ol=** /ın/ to watch (over), to protect.

—leri velfecri oku= to give the impression of being very astute and wide awake. **— verimi** *prov.* horizon. **—üne yandığım** *slang* 1. cursed, damned. 2. priceless, unique. **— yaşı** tear. **—ünün yaşına bakma=** /ın/ to have no pity (on). **— yaşı bezi** *anat.* lachrymal gland. **— yaşı dök=** to shed tears. **— yaşı etçiği** *anat.* lachrymal caruncle. **— yaşı kesesi** *anat.* lachrymal bag. **— yaşı testisi** *archeol.* lachrymatory. **— yaşı yolu** *anat.* lachrymal duct, tear duct. **—ü yaşar=** for the eyes to water, for tears to come into one's eyes. **— yaşartıcı gaz** tear gas. **— yaylası** *neol.* field of vision. **—le ye=** /ı/ 1. to envy, grudge very much. 2. to stare covetously (at). **—ü yeme=** /ı/ not to venture (to), not to dare. **—ü yerinden oyna=** *same as* **gözü dön=. —ü yıl=** /dan/ *same as* **gözü kork=. — yılgınlığı** extreme fear, terror. **—ünde yok** /ın/ He does not care for it. **—ü yolda** waiting for someone to come. **—leri yollarda kal=** to have been waiting for a long time. **— yum=** /a/ to connive (at), to condone, to take no notice (of); to wink at. **—ünü yum=** to shut the eyes. **— yumup açıncıya kadar** in the twinkling of an eye. **— yuvarlağı** eyeball. **—ü yüksekte ol=** to look high, to have high ambitions. **— za'fı** weakness of sight, asthenopia.

gözcü 1. watchman; *mil.* scout, observer. 2. *colloq.* oculist. **— uçağı** *mil.* reconnaisance plane. **— yeri** *mil.* observation post.

gözde favorite (woman).

göze 1 1. *neol., biol.* cell. 2. *prov.* spring, source.

göze 2 [kûze] *prov.* pitcher, jug.

göze= 3 *prov.* /ı/ to patch, to mend; to embroider with double-looped silk thread.

gözek[gi] *prov.* 1. spring source. 2. patched, mended.

gözel 1 *prov., same as* **güzel**.

gözel 2 *var. of* **gözer**.

gözeme *prov.* double-looped embroidery.

gözen=[ir] *prov., pass. of* **göze=** 3.

gözene *prov.* beekeeper's mask.

gözenek[gi] 1. *neol., biol., bot.* stoma; *geol.* pore. 2. *prov.* window. 3. *prov.* hemstitch. **—li** pierced with holes, meshed; *geol.* porous.

gözer [Persian kuzar] *prov.* coarse sieve. **—le=** /ı/ to sift.

gözet=[ir] /ı/ 1. to look after, to take care (of); to guard, to protect. 2. to consider, respect; to observe, regard (law, rule). **—il=** *pass.* **—im** *neol.* supervision; watch, care.

gözetle=[r] /ı/ to observe secretly, to watch secretly, to peep.

gözetleme *mil.* observation. **— aynası** window-mirror. **— postası** *mil.* observation

gözetleyici

post. — **yeri** mil. observation point, lookout. **—li ateş** mil. observed fire, observed shooting. **—siz ateş** mil. unobserved fire, unobserved shooting.

gözetleyici گوزتلیجی mil. observer, lookout.

gözetme گوزتمه a taking care, guarding, protection.

gözettir=ir گوزتدرمك /ı, a/ caus. of **gözet=**.

gözgü گوزگی archaic mirror.

gözle=r گوزلمك /ı/ 1. to watch (for), to wait (for), to keep an eye (on). 2. to prick with holes. **—ği** prov., **—k** neol. observation place, lookout. **—m** neol., astr., phil. observation. **—m evi** neol. observatory.

gözleme گوزلمه 1. an eyeing, a watching (for); observation. 2. fritter, pancake steeped in hot syrup. **— mevzii** mil. observation point. **—ci** maker or seller of fritters, pancakes. **—ç** fritter, pancake. **—n** neol., astr., aero. observer.

gözlen=r گوزلنمك pass. of **gözle=**.

gözlet=ir گوزلتمك /ı, a/ caus. of **gözle=**.

gözleyici گوزلیجی observer.

gözlü گوزلو 1. having eyes; archaic possessed of discernment, sagacious. 2. having drawers or pigeon-holes. **— çıban** pitted abcess. **— dolap** cupboard with drawers or pigeon-holes.

gözlükgü گوزلوك 1. spectacles, eyeglasses, glasses. **— camı** spectacle lens. **— çerçevesi** eyeglass frame. **—ü çıkar=** to take off one's glasses. **— kılıfı, — mahfazası** spectacle case. **— tak=** to wear glasses. **—ü tak=** to put on one's glasses. **—çü** optician, maker or seller of eyeglasses.

gözlüklü گوزلكلو 1. wearing glasses. 2. hooded, spectacled (birds, snake). **— çalı bülbülü** spectacled warbler, zool., Sylvia conspicillata. **— yılan** hooded snake.

gözsüz گوزسز eyeless, blind. **— sıçan** prov. mole. **— tebek** archaic mole. **—lük** blindness.

gözük=ür گوزكمك to appear, to be or become visible, to be seen; to show oneself.

gradin غرادین It naut. boltrope. **— halatı** same as **gradin**.

grado (. .) غرادو It 1. percentage of alcoholic content. 2. colloq. the proper degree; obs. grade, degree.

grafikği غرافیك F 1. graphics, graph; graphic table, diagram. 2. graphic. **— metodu** graphic method. **— olarak** graphically. **— sanatlar** graphic arts. **—çe, —le** graphically.

grafit غرافیت F graphite, black-lead, plumbago. **— tozu** charcoal dust.

grafito (. . .) غرافیتو It archeol. graffito.

grafoloji غرافولوژی F graphology.

grafometre (. . . .) غرافومتره F graphometer. **—li gönye** graphometrical square.

grafometri غرافومتری F graphometrics.

gram غرام F gram. **— santimetre** F phys. gram centimeter.

grama (. .) غراما Gk obs. 1. gram. 2. a writing. **— tezkeresi** obs. permit given to workmen in Istanbul.

gramatikos غراماتیقوس Ott. hist. Greek clerk working at the **Divanı Hümayun**.

gramer غرامر F grammar. **— bakımından, —e göre** grammatically. **—ci** grammarian.

gramofon غرامفون F phonograph. **— iğnesi** phonograph needle. **— plâğı** phonograph record.

grandi (. .) غراندی It naut. mainmast; main. **— babafingo yelkeni** main top-gallant sail. **— çanaklığı** main top. **— direği** main mast. **— gabya çubuğu** main topmast. **— gabya yelkeni** main topsail. **— kuntra yelkeni** main royal.

granduka (. . .) غرانددوقا It grand duke, archduke. **—lık** grand duchy.

grandükkü غرانددوك F same as **granduka**.

grandüşes غرانددوشس F grand duchess.

granit غرانیت F granite. **— mermer** granite marble.

grantkapitalli غرانتقاپیتال F print. large capital.

granül غرانول F anat. granule. **— hücresi** biol. granule cell.

granülasyon F path. granulation.

granüle F sc. granulated.

granüler F sc. granular.

granülit F geol. granulite.

granülom F path. granuloma.

granüloz F chem., physiol. granulose.

gravidite F physiol. gravidity, pregnancy.

gravimetre F phys. gravimeter.

gravitasyon غراویتاسیون F phys. gravitation.

gravür غراوور F engraving. **—cü** engraver.

gravye غراویه F gravel, grit.

gravyer غراویر F Gruyere, Gruyere cheese, Swiss cheese. **— peyniri** same as **gravyer**.

gre غره F geol. sandstone, freestone.

Gregoryen غرگوریان F Gregorian. **— takvimi** Gregorian calendar.

Grekki غرك F Greek, pertaining to Greek language or civilization. **—çe** Greek, the Greek language.

Grekoromen غرکورومن F Greco-Roman. **— güreş** Greco-Roman wrestling.

grena غرنا F geol. garnet.

grenadin غرنادین F text. grenadine.

grepfrut غره پ فروت E same as **greypfrut**.

gres غره س F mech. lubricating grease.

gresör غره سور F, **gresörlük** mech. lubricator, grease cup.

grev غرو F strike. **—i boz=** to break the strike. **— ilân et=** to call a strike. **— kasası** strike funds. **— postaları** pickets. **— ücreti**

strike pay. — **yap=** to strike, to be on strike. **— yasağı** law forbidding strikes. **—ci** striker.
greypfrut غريپفرت E grapefruit, bot., *Citrus aurantium maxima*.
gri غري F gray.
griffon غريفون F *art hist.* griffin, gryphon.
Griniçⁱ (.'.) گرينيچ E Greenwich. **— meridyeni, — nısfınneharı** Greenwich meridian.
grip غريپ F influenza, grippe, flu. **— ol=** to have influenza. **—e tutul=** to go down with flu. **—li** suffering from flu.
griva (.'.) غريوه [gruva] *naut.* cathead. **—ya al=** /ı/ to cat (anchor). **— kaponu** anchor stopper. **— makarası** cat block. **— metaforası** cat davit. **— olmuş** acockbill (anchor). **— paraçolu, — praçolu** cathead knee.
grizu غريزو F firedamp, pit gas. **— patlaması** firedamp explosion.
grog غروغ F toddy, grog.
grogren, gron غروغرن F *text.* coarse-grained material, grosgrain.
gros غروس E *naut.* gross. **— ağırlık** gross weight.
grosa, grossa (.'.) غروسه It *com.* gross (twelve dozen).
groteskᵏⁱ غروتسك F grotesque.
grupᵖᵘ, ᵇᵘ غروپ F group; section. **— ateşi** *mil.* group firing, firing by sections. **— grup** in groups. **— halinde** grouped, in groups. **— halinde eğitim, — halinde talim ve terbiye** *mil.* group drill, group instruction. **— komutanı** *mil.* group commander. **— ol=** to be grouped, to be arranged in a group, to form a group. **— sigortası** *com.* group insurance. **—lan=** 1. to be grouped. 2. to form groups. **—landır=** /ı/ to group.
gruva (.'.) غروا It same as **griva**.
-gu 1 *cf.* **-gı 1**.
gû 2 (—) گو P *lrnd.* a saying, talk, conversation.
-gû 3 (—) گو P *lrnd.* that speaks, says, talks, *as in* **hicagû, rastgû**.
guatr غواتر F *path.* goiter, goitre. **—lı** goitrous.
gubar (.—) غبار A *lrnd.* dust. **—ı tal** *bot.* pollen. **—alûd** (.—.—) P soiled with dust, covered with dust, dusty.
gubarî (.——) غباري A *calligraphy* smallest kind of Arabic writing. **—ye** (.——.) A service tree and its fruit, *bot.*, *Sorbus domestica*.
gube غوه kind of sardine.
gubret غبرت A *lrnd.* dust color.
gucur غوجور *prov.* potato.
gudaf (.—) غداف A *lrnd.* black crow.

gudde غدّه A *anat.* gland. **—i dem'iye** lachrymal gland. **—i derekiye** thyroid. **—i lûabiye** salivary gland. **—i mideviye** gastric gland. **—i nahamiye** pituitary gland. **—i nekfiye** axillary gland. **—i sanavberiye** pineal gland. **—i tahtelfekkiye** maxillary gland. **—i tahtellisan, —i tahtellisaniye** sublingual gland. **—î** (..—) glandular. **—li** having glands. **—vî** (..—) glandular.
guddî (.—) غدّي [based on Arabic] *physiol.* glandular.
gudruf (.—) غضروف A *anat.* cartilage, gristle, chondrus. **—i derakî** thyroid cartilage. **—i halkavî** cricoid cartilage. **—i türsî** thyroid cartilage. **—i vustani** septum of the nose. **—î** (.——) A cartilaginous, gristly.
gudubet (...) غضوبت [based on Arabic] *fam.* ugly, clumsy, overgrown. **— bozuntusu** hideously ugly.
guduvᵛᵛᵘ غدو A *lrnd.* early morning task; early morning.
gudve غدوه A *lrnd.* early morning between dawn and sunrise.
guflᵘ, **guflân** (.—) غفل، غفلان A *lrnd.* heedlessness, carelessness, negligence.
gufran (.—) غفران A *lrnd.* God's pardon, God's mercy. **—penah** (.—.—) P blessed dead.
gufulᵘ (.—) غفول A *lrnd.* heedlessness, inadvertency, inattention.
gufur (.—) غفور A *lrnd.* a pardoning, forgiveness.
gugu (——) غوغو P *lrnd.* 1. pigeon, dove. 2. a cooing.
gugucukᵍᵘ غوغوجك *prov.* dove.
gugukᵍᵘ غوغوك 1. cuckoo, *zool.*, *Cuculus canorus*. 2. cuckoo! (call of the cuckoo; teasing derisory cry of children). **— gibi kal=, — gibi otur=** to be alone, solitary, to live alone. **— kuşu** cuckoo. **— yap=** /a/ to make fun (of), to make merry (with). **—giller** cuckoos, *zool.*, *Cuculidae*. **—lu, —lu saat** cuckoo clock.
gugurikᵍⁱ غوغوريك *colloq.* odd, ridiculous.
gûh گوه P *lrnd.* excrement.
gukᵏᵘ (—) غورك P *lrnd.* frog.
gulᵘ 1 (—) غول A *lrnd.* monster, demon of the wilds, ghoul. **—i beyabanî** demon supposed to decoy and destroy travelers; will o' the wisp.
gûlᵘ 2 (—) گول P *lrnd.* stupid, idiotic.
gulᵘ 3 غل A *lrnd.* ring for the neck and hands of a captive.
gulâle (.—.) غلاله P *lrnd.* tress or lock of hair; side lock, lovelock.
gulâm (.—) غلام A *poet.* boy, lad; archaic male slave. **—e** (.—.) A *lrnd.* girl, female slave. **—î** (.——) P 1. boyhood, youth; slavery. 2. fond of boys; sodomite. **—lık**

boyhood; slavery. **—pare** (.——.) P, **—perest** P active pederast.

gulâne (——.) غولانه [based on gul 1] lrnd. monstrous, gigantic; having extraordinary energy.

gulât (.—) غلات A lrnd. those outrageously bigoted in a sectarian creed, zealots. **—ı şi'a** the most unreasonable of the Shiites, (so called for asserting that Ali was God).

gulâz (.—) غلاظ A lrnd. thick, coarse, rude.

gule 1 (—.) غله P lrnd. granary; till, money box.

gûle 2 (—.) گوله P lrnd. ball. **—endaz** (—..—) P sharpshooter.

gulet غولت var. of **golet**.

gulf غلف A lrnd. sheathed, covered; uncircumcised.

gulfe غلفه A anat. prepuce, foreskin.

gulgullü غلغل P lrnd. clamor, vociferous cry; chirping of birds; noise made by liquor poured from a bottle; echoes of a vault. **— ol=** to resound.

gulgule غلغله P lrnd., same as **gulgul**.

gulgulendaz (...—) غلغل انداز P resounding.

gûlî (——) گولى P lrnd. stupidity, idiocy.

gulu, gulukğu غلو غلون prov. turkey.

gulûllü (.—) غلول A lrnd. fraud, deceit.

gulûle (.—.) غلوله P lrnd. ball of yarn; bullet; tumor.

gulüvvvü غلو A lrnd. 1. speeding (an arrow) with a strong bowshot; flying high (arrow). 2. immoderateness, extreme exaggeration; literature hyperbole. 3. rebellion, insurrection; tumult. **—i âm** general insurrection.

gulyabani (..——) غوليبانى فى قوليبانى |guli beyabanî] ogre, ogress, demon.

gumena (.'.) غومنه var. of **gomena**.

gumer غمر A lrnd. small drinking-bowl, cup.

gumum (.—) غموم A lrnd., pl. of **gam 2**.

gumuz (.—), **gumuzet** (.—.) غموض غموضت A lrnd. incomprehensibility.

gûn 1 (—) گون P lrnd. color, tinge; sort, kind, way, manner.

-gûn 2 (—) گون P lrnd. colored, as in **gülgûn, nilgûn**.

gûna (——) گونا P lrnd. sort, kind, variety; way, manner.

gûnagûn (———) گوناگون P lrnd. various, of various sorts.

gunc غنج A lrnd. coquettishness.

gûne (—.) گونه P lrnd., var. of **gûna**. **— gûne** various; variously.

gungula, gungulu prov. small jar, water-bowl.

gunne غنّه A Quran recitation nasal twang, hum. **—li** sonorous.

gunude (.—.) غنوده P lrnd. gone to sleep, asleep. **—i hâk, —i rahmet** gone to his reward, dead.

gunudgâh (.—) غنودگاه P lrnd. sleeping place, cubicle.

gunum (.—) غنم A lrnd., pl. of **ganem**.

gupilya (.'.) غوبيليا mech. split pin, cotter pin.

gûr 1 (—) گور P lrnd. grave, tomb.

gûr 2 (—) گور P [Persian **gor**] lrnd. wild ass.

gurab 1 (.—) غراب A lrnd. crow; any bird resembling a crow. **—ı ebka, —ı eblak** magpie. **—ı esved** raven. **—ı zemin** night, darkness.

gurab 2 (.—) غراب A lrnd. pirate ship. **G—ı Nuh** Noah's ark.

guraba (..—) غرباء A same as **gureba**.

gurabe (——.) گوربه P lrnd. tomb with cupola.

gurabin (.——) غرابين A lrnd. crows.

gurabiye (.—..) غرابيه A same as **kurabiye**.

gurabülbeyn (.—.—) غراب البين A lrnd. crow that frequents deserted grounds (portending separation).

gurama (..—) غرماء A lrnd. 1. creditors. 2. rivals, enemies. 3. the first rays of light at dawn.

gûrban (——) گوربان P lrnd. guardian of a tomb.

gurbet غربت A a being away from home; foreign travel; exile. **— çek=** to suffer absence from home, to suffer exile. **— diyarı, — eli** place away from home. **—te gez=** to wander about away from home. **—e git=** to take to the road, to go wandering. **—i ihtiyar et=** to become a voluntary exile. **—te ol=** to be away from home, to be abroad. **— uşağı** one obliged to live away from home. **—çi** one who goes away from home.

gurbetzede غربت زده P driven from home, exile.

gûrca (——) گورجا P lrnd. cemetery.

gurcata, gurçata (.'.) غرجاته It naut. top-mast cross-tree.

gure (—.) غوره P lrnd. unripe grapes; unripe dates.

gureba (..—) غرباء A lrnd. strangers, people away from home; the poor and destitute. **— hastanesi** hospital for the poor. **—i Müslimin** destitute Muslims. **—i yemin** Ott. hist. right wing of cavalry. **—i yesar** Ott. hist. left wing of cavalry.

guref غرف A lrnd., pl. of **gurfe**. **G— Suresi** name of the 39th sura of the Quran.

gurema (..—) غرماء A lrnd., pl. of **garim**. **— taksimi** division of credit among creditors.

gurer غرر A lrnd., pl. of **gurre**.

gurfe غرفه A lrnd. upper chamber, hall; belvedere.

gurgur عُرْعُر rumbling sound. — **et**= to rumble.

gûrhane (-̣.—.) گورخانه P lrnd. mausoleum.

gûrhar (—.) گورخر P lrnd. wild ass.

guristan (—.—) گورستان P lrnd. burial ground, cemetery.

gurkᵏᵘ گُرْك [Persian **kurg**] prov. 1. broody (hen). 2. in a state of excitement and strutting (turkey cock). —**la**= 1. to be broody (hen). 2. to be excited (turkey cock).

gûrken (—.) گورکن P lrnd. grave-digger.

gurla=ʳ گُرْلامِش to emit a hollow, rumbling sound. —**t**= /ı/ caus.

gurm گُرْم A lrnd. debt.

gurran (.—) غَرّان P lrnd. roaring, thundering.

gurre غُرّه A lrnd. 1. the first day of a lunar month. 2. first glow of dawn. 3. star of white hairs on the forehead of a beast. 4. noble man; elite. 5. can. law fine for having caused an abortion.

gurrende غَرَنده P lrnd. roaring, furious (lion).

gurub (.—) غُروب A same as **gurup** 1. —**î** (.——) A lrnd. pertaining to sunset. —**î saat** obs. the system of numbering the hours from sunset.

gurufat (..—) غُرَفات A lrnd., pl. of **gurfe**.

gurulda=ʳ گُرُلدامِش to rumble. —**t**= /ı/ caus.

gurultu گُرُلتو rumbling noise.

gurupᵇᵘ 1 (.—) غُروب [**gurub**] sunset; sundown; astr. setting of a heavenly body. — **et**= 1. to set (heavenly body). 2. poet. to vanish.

gurupᵇᵘ 2 غُروب var. of **grup**.

gurur (.—) غُرور A 1. pride, vanity, conceit. 2. Or. mus. an obsolete **makam**. —**i civanî** lrnd. presumptuousness of youth. — **duy**= /dan/ to feel proud (of), to take pride (in). — **et**= obs., same as **gurur göster**=. — **gel**= /a, dan/ to put on airs; to be conceited, proud (of). — **getir**= to become proud. — **göster**= /dan/ to boast (of), to vaunt. — **hisset**= /dan/ same as **gurur duy**=. —**unu okşa**= /ın/ 1. to play on someone's pride, to flatter somebody's pride. 2. to butter someone up. —**lan**= /dan/ to grow proud (of). —**lu** conceited, vain, haughty.

guruş گُروش same as **kuruş**.

gurzuf (.—) غُرْضوف A lrnd., same as **gudruf**.

gusale (.—) غُساله A lrnd. 1. water in which a thing has been washed or is to be washed. 2. dirty washing sediment. 3. liquid extract.

gusas غُصَص A lrnd., pl. of **gussa**. —**ı mevt** death agonies.

gûsfend (—.) گوسفند P lrnd. sheep.

guslˡᵘ غُسْل A lrnd., same as **gusül**. — **et**= 1. to take a ritual bath. 2. /ı/ to wash (the dead).

gusn غُصْن A lrnd. bough, branch.

gusne 1 غُصَينه A lrnd. twig, sprig.

gusne 2 غُصْنه A lrnd. lock, ringlet or tress of hair.

gûspend (—.) گوسپند P [Persian **gospand**] lrnd., var. of **gûsfend**. —**küşan** (—..—) P festival of sacrifice.

gussa غُصّه A poet. grief, anxiety, sorrow, sadness. — **et**= to be oppressed with grief, sorrow. —**lan**= to become troubled, sorrowful, sad. —**lı** careworn. —**nak** (..—) P lrnd. afflicted, grieved. —**sız** carefree.

gusto (.'.) غوستو It taste; gusto, zest. —**lu** having good taste; tasteful, elegant, smart. —**lu giyin**= to dress with good taste, to dress tastefully. —**suz** having no taste, tasteless.

gusun (.—) غُصون A lrnd., pl. of **gusn**.

gusülˢˡᵘ غُسْل [**gusl**] Isl. rel. ritual total ablution of the body (after pollution or coition). — **abdesti** ritual total ablution; — **abdesti al**= to perform total ablution.

gusulhane (..—.) غُسُلخانه P bathroom for ritual washing; small domestic bathroom.

gûş 1 (—) گوش lrnd. 1. ear; hearing faculty. 2. ear-like appendage. —**i can ile** with all ears. — **et**= /ı/ to lend an ear (to), to listen (to). —**i hûş ile** same as **gûş-i can ile**. —**i mahi** marine mollusk shell; cup made of shell.

gûş 2 (—) گوش P lrnd. beech.

guşa (.'.) گوشه Alb goiter.

gûşan (——) گوشان P lrnd. grape juice.

gûşbend (—.) گوشبند P lrnd. car-cover.

gûşçu (—.) گوشچی [Persian **gosechî**] lrnd. spy; eavesdropper.

gûşdar (——) گوشدار P lrnd. 1. eared. 2. one who listens attentively, one who pays attention.

gûşe (—.) گوشه P lrnd., var. of **köşe**. —**i çeşm** corner of the eye. —**i keman** notch for the string at the end of a bow. —**i uzlet** retirement. —**dar** (—.—) P angular, cornered. —**gir** (—.—) P, —**nişin** (—..—) P solitary; hermit, anchorite.

gûşgüzar (—.—) گوشگذار P lrnd. which passes into the ear, heard. — **ol**= to be heard.

gûşmalˡⁱ (——) گوشمال P lrnd. 1. punishing by twisting the ear. 2. rebuke, reproof, reprimand. — **et**= /a/ 1. to punish by twisting the ear. 2. to drop a hint (to).

gûşt (—) گوشت P lrnd. flesh, meat; pulp of fruit. —**abe** (——.) P gravy, broth of meat. —**âgende** (——..) P meat-pie, sausage. —**âhenc** (——.) P 1. flesh-hook. 2. kite (toy). —**âve** (——.) P var. of **gûştâbe**. —**âviz** (———) P butcher's stall, meat-market. —**ber** (—.) P well-fleshed;

corpulent. —**dar** (——) P fleshy, pulpy.
—**har** (——) P flesh-eating, carnivorous.
—**mend** (—.) P fleshy, made of flesh; carnal.
—**nâk** (——) P fleshy, pulpy. —**pare**
(——.) P 1. morsel of meat, meat. 2. lobe-shaped organ; uvula. 3. gland. —**refte** (—..)
P lean, emaciated, skinny, fleshless. — **rüba**
(—.—) P 1. kite (toy). 2. fleshhook.
gûşvar (——) گوشوار P lrnd. 1. earring.
2. a taking as a warning. 3. first couplet of a
gazel or **kaside**.
gûşvare (——.) گوشواره P lrnd., same as
gûşvar. —**i felek** new moon.
gûşzed (—.) گوشزد P lrnd. what has struck
the ear, heard. — **ol**= to have been heard.
gut عزت F path. gout. —**u ol**= to have the
gout.
guta (—.) غوط A lrnd., same as **gavta 1**.
gutalâmba, gutalomba (...'.) غوط لامبا غوط لومبا
It gamboge.
gutlu غوطى F path. gouty.
guvaş F paint. gouache.
guvat (.—) غزوات A lrnd., pl. of **gavi 1**.
gûy 1 (—) گوى P lrnd., var. of **gû 2**.
-**gûy 2** (—) گوى P lrnd., var. of -**gû 3**.
gûy 3 (—) گوى P poet. ball, globe.
—**i müsabakat** ball used in games. —**i sakin**
terrestrial globe. —**i sim** orb of silver (moon).
—**i zer** orb of gold (sun).
gûya 1 (——) گویا P 1. as if, as though,
just as though. 2. supposedly.
gûya 2 (——) گویا P lrnd. speaking,
talking, narrating. —**yı devr** historian. —**yı
gehvare**, —**yı mehd** speaking in the cradle
(Jesus Christ).
-**gûya 3** (——) گویا P lrnd., var. of
-**gû 3**, -**gûy 2**, e. g., **andelibgûya** who discourses like a nightingale.
gûybaz (——) گوى باز P lrnd. ballplayer.
gûyende (—..) گوینده P lrnd. 1. speaker,
orator; singer. 2. tongue; musical instrument.
—**gî** (—..—) P mode of speaking or singing;
dialect.
gûygerdan (—.—) گویگردان P lrnd.
tumbledung, tumblebug.
gûyi (——) گوئى P lrnd. quality or act
of speaking, speech, eloquence.
gûyiş (—.) گویش P lrnd. speech, discourse,
narration.
guyub (.—) غیوب A lrnd., pl. of **gayb**.
guyubet (.—.) غیوبت A lrnd. absence,
invisibility.
guyum (.—) غیوم A lrnd., pl. of **gaym**.
guyyab (.—) غیاب A lrnd., pl. of **gaib**.
Guz^zzu غز A lrnd., var. of **Oğuz**.
guzat (.—) غزات A lrnd., pl. of **gazi 1**.
guze 1 (—..) غزه P lrnd. 1. same as **koza**.
2. ball of silver or gold lace. —**i âb** bubble of
water. —**i nukra** prayer beads.
gûze 2 (—.) گوزه P lrnd., same as **koza**.
guzine (..'.) گوزینه Gk same as **kuzine**.
guzme غذمه A lrnd. portion, share.
guzmet غذمت A lrnd. duskiness, dinginess.
guzuzet (.—.) غضوضت A lrnd. a being
fresh, vigorous.
guzza (.—) غزّاء A lrnd., pl. of
gazi 4.
-**gü** cf. -**gı 1**.
gübel گوبل prov., var. of **göbel**.
gübre گوبره Gk dung, manure, fertilizer,
droppings. — **çukuru** dung hole, dungpit,
compost hole. — **fabrikası** fertilizer factory.
— **şerbeti** liquid manure, dung water. — **ver**=
/a/ to fertilize, to manure, to muck. — **yığını**
dunghill, muck heap, manure heap, compost
heap. —**le**= /ı/ to dung, to manure. —**len**=
pass. of **gübrele**=. —**li** manured, fertilized.
—**lik** dunghill; dung hole.
gübür گوبور Gk prov. 1. sweepings, rubbish.
2. dung. — **kabı** garbage can. — **kaldıran**
mushroom grown under fallen pine needles.
—**len**= to become dirty, to get mucky.
güc 1 گوج strength, force; violence; phys.
power. — **degür**= /a/ archaic to do wrong
(to). — **dök**= /a/ archaic to employ all
one's strength (in). — **götür**= archaic to
endure, to withstand violence. —**ü gücü yetene**
by jungle law. — **ile** with violence, by force.
—**ünü yen**= to suppress one's anger, to be
patient under provocation. —**ü yet**= /a/ to
be strong enough, to be able (to), to have the
force (of); to be powerful enough to harm
(another person). —**ü yettiği kadar** as well as
he can, with all his might.
güc 2 گوج cf. **güç 2**.
gücem گوجم archaic injustice, unfair
treatment. —**le**= /ı/ to force.
gücen=^ir گوجنمك 1. to be offended, to be hurt.
2. /a/ to be angry (with), to have a grudge
(against). —**dir**= /ı/ to offend, hurt, vex,
anger.
gücenik^gi گوجنلك offended, hurt. —**lik** offense,
hurt.
gücenme گوجنمه 1. a being offended. 2. friction,
vexation.
gücü 1 گوجى text. weaver's reed, sley.
gücük^gü گوجك prov. 1. tailless; dock-tailed.
2. February. — **ay** February.
gücümse=^r گوجمسه مك /ı/ to find difficult, to
regard as difficult.
gücün (.'.) گوجین prov. 1. with difficulty.
2. by force.
güç^cü **1** گوج difficult; difficulty.
— **belâ** with great difficulty. — **et**= /a/
archaic to force, to exert strength. — **halle**,

— **hal ile** by dint of great exertion. — **ile** with difficulty, with great trouble. **—e koş=** /ı/ to make difficulties; to take the more difficult course. **—e sar=** to become difficult, hard, serious. **—e uğra=** *archaic* to meet with difficulties; to experience difficulties.

güçᶜᵘ **2** گوچ *same as* **güç 1**. **—üne git=** /ın/ to be offended, to be hurt. **—ü gücüne** with great difficulty.

güçᶜᵘ **3** گوچ *var. of* **güc 1**.

güççükᵍᵘ گوچجك *prov., var. of* **küçük**.

güçle=ʳ گوچله‌مك *archaic* 1. /ı/ to force. 2. to become difficult.

güçlen=ⁱʳ گوچلنمك *obs.* 1. to become difficult. 2. to be strengthened. **—dir=** /ı/ *caus.*

güçleş=ⁱʳ گوچلشمك to grow difficult. **—tir=** /ı/ *caus.*

güçlet=ⁱʳ گوچلتمك /ı/ to cause to be difficult.

güçlü گوچلی 1. strong, powerful. 2. *Or. mus.* hold which usually occurs just before the last note of a melodic line in a **makam** or scale. — **kuvvetli** very strong and healthy.

güçlükᵍᵘ گوچلك difficulty, trouble, pain. **— çek=** to experience difficulties. **— çıkar=**, **— göster=** /a/ to make difficulties (for).

güçsü=ʳ گوچسمك, **güçsün=**ᵘʳ گوچسنمك /ı/ to consider difficult, to find hard.

güçsüz گوچسز weak, feeble. **— kuvvetsiz** strengthless, weak and feeble. **—lük** weakness, feebleness.

güd=ᵉʳ گودمك *cf.* **güt=**.

güdahte (.—.) گداخته P *lrnd.* melted, dissolved.

güdaz 1 (.—) گداز P *lrnd.* a melting, a dissolving.

-güdaz 2 (.—) گداز P *lrnd.* that melts, that causes to melt, *as in* **cangüdaz, takatgüdaz.**

güdazende (.—..) گدازنده P *lrnd.* that melts, causes to melt.

güdaziş (.—.) گدازش P *lrnd.* 1. a melting, a dissolving. 2. a pining away.

güde, güdekᵍⁱ **1** گوده prov., same as **göde**.

güdekᵍⁱ **2** *neol.* aim, purpose.

güdele=ʳ گودله‌مك /ı/ *prov.* to pursue.

güdeleçᶜⁱ, **güdemen** گودمج *prov.* of short stature, dumpy.

güden 1 گودن *prov., var. of* **göden 1**.

güden 2 گودن *prov.* shepherd.

güderi گودری [gevder] chamois leather, deerskin; parchment.

güdü 1 1. *neol.* drive, push; *psych.* incentive, motive. 2. *neol.* aim, purpose; *mil.* objective, target. 3. *prov.* herd, flock. **—ye ver=** /ı/ *prov.* to put out to pasture. **— yeri** *prov.* pasture land.

güdü 2 گودی *prov.* 1. short of stature (person and animal). 2. earthenware cup; small mattock; head of a drumstick.

güdücü گودجی 1. who tends or pastures, shepherd; cattle drover. 2. who follows or aims (at).

güdükᵍᵘ گودك 1. incomplete, deficient; docked; tailless; childless. 2. thick-set, squat, dumpy. 3. *prov.* sleeved waistcoat. 4. *prov.* interest (on capital). **— aylar** the shorter months of the year. **— kal=** to be unfinished, incomplete; without result; to be childless. **— tavuk** 1. a hen without tail feathers. 2. poor, insignificant fellow. **— torno** *naut.* clump block. **—çü** *prov.* moneylender, usurer. **—leme** *neol., pros.* catalexis.

güdül=ᵘʳ **1** گودلمك *pass. of* **güt=**.

güdül 2 گودل *prov., same as* **güdük**¹, ².

güdüm 1. *neol.* a driving, leading, management, guidance, direction. 2. *prov.* shepherd's pay.

güdümlü *neol.* controlled, directed. **— balon** dirigible balloon. **— ekonomi**, **— iktisat** planned economy. **— mermi** guided missile.

güdür گودور *prov.* small-eared sheep or goat.

güft گفت P *lrnd.* spoken word; speech, utterance. **— ü gû** talk, chatter; gossip, tittle-tattle. **— ü gû et=** to talk, chatter; to gossip. **— ü kal** *same as* **güft ü gû**. **— ü şemid** what is said and heard.

güftar 1 (.—) گفتار P *lrnd.* talk, speech, utterance. **—a gel=** to start to talk.

-güftar 2 (.—) گفتار P *lrnd.* who talks, speaks, *e. g.,* **şekergüftar**.

güfte گفته P 1. text for music. 2. *lrnd.* said, spoken, uttered. **—kâri** (..——) P *art* superscribed (vessel, dish, tissue).

güğem گوگم *prov., var. of* **göğem**.

güğer=ⁱʳ گوگرمك *prov., var. of* **göğer=**.

güğül گوگل Gk *prov.* cocoon. **— kurdu** silkworm. **— kuşu** *archaic* silkworm moth.

güğüm گوگم Gk copper jug with handle, spout and lid. **G— başı** *Ott. hist.*, title of an official in personal attendance on the Sultan.

güher گهر P *lrnd., same as* **gevher**.

güherçile گهرچیله [based on Persian] saltpeter, potassium nitrate. **— kaymağı** magnesium oxide. **— tuzu** potassium nitrate.

gül 1 گل P 1. rose, *bot., Rosa.* 2. rose-shaped, roseate ornament; ornament; roundel, rosette; boss; escutcheon of a keyhole; *dervish orders* round badge on a cap. 3. dial (of a compass). 4. *dervish orders* spiked ball of iron. 5. *poet.* flower, blossom; live coal; open wound. 6. *lrnd.* snuff (of a candle); wad of half-burned tobacco from the bottom of a pipe. **—üm** my darling. **— ağacı** rosewood. **—i aşr** *lrnd.* flower-shaped ornament in a Quran, marking the end of a section of ten verses. **—üne bak.**

goncasını al *proverb* Take a look at the mother before marrying the daughter. **— balı** Honey produced from rose gardens. **— bayramı** *Jewish rel.* Feast of Tabernacles. **—i caferî** *lrnd.* 1. African marigold, *bot., Tagetes erecta.* 2. button sewed on the cap of some dervishes. **— çehreli** rosy-cheeked. **—i çerağ** *lrnd.* snuff of the wick of a burning lamp. **— dalına bülbül konmuş** A piece of food has stuck to your beard (polite hint at table). **— defnesi** oleander, *bot., Nerium Oleander.* **— demeti** bunch of roses. **— dikensiz olmaz** *proverb* There is no rose without a thorn. **— elması** rose apple, *bot., Jambosa vulgaris.* **— fidanı** rose bush. **— gibi geçin=** to get along very well. **— goncası** rosebud. **— gülistan** *same as* **güllük gülistanlık. — ıtrı** attar of roses. **—i kahpe** *poet.* double-faced rose, (i. e., rose of two colors). **— kokusu** 1. rose perfume. 2. scent of roses. **— kurusu** dirty pink. **— likörü** rose-flavored liqueur. **— mevsimi** season of roses. **— oya** rose embroidery on the edge of a garment. **— pembe** rose pink. **— rakısı** rose-flavored raki. **—i rânâ** *poet.* yellowish rose with reddish heart. **— reçeli** rose jam. **— rengi** rose-pink. **—i sadberk** *lrnd.* cabbage rose, *bot., Rosa centifolia.* **—ü seven dikenine katlanır** *proverb* If you would have the roses you must put up with the thorns. **— sirkesi** rose vinegar. **—i surh** *lrnd.* red rose. **—i surî** *lrnd.* damask rose. **— suyu** rose water. **— süngeri** sweetbrier-sponge, bedeguar. **—i şem** *lrnd.* snuff of a burning candle. **—ü tarife ne hacet, ne çiçektir biliriz** You need not tell me, I know all about the fellow. **—i tesbih** *lrnd.* head bead into which the two ends of a string of prayer beads are brought and fastened. **—i uşnan** *lrnd.* yellow-flowered soapwort, *bot., Saponaria officinalis.* **— üstüne gül kokla=** to be disloyal to one's sweetheart by loving another person. **— yağı** attar of roses. **— yanaklı** with rosy cheeks. **— yaprağı** rose leaf. **—i yekçeşm** *lrnd.,* glans penis. **— yüzlü** rosy-faced. **—i ziba** *poet., same as* **güli rânâ.**

gül=ᵉʳ 2 گولمك to laugh; /a/ to laugh (at). **—er*. —mekten ağla=** to laugh till one cries. **—eyim bari!** Don't make me laugh! That's enough to make one laugh. **—meden bayıl=, —mekten bayıl=** to faint with laughter. **—meden çatla=, —mekten çatla=** to crack one's sides with laughter. **—e güle!** 1. goodbye (the conventional response to one saying **Allahaısmarladık,** i. e. farewell). 2. Good luck. **—e güle gidin(iz)!** Happy journey. **—e güle giyin(iz)!** May you be happy wearing it (said upon seeing someone in a new garment). **—e güle kirlenin(iz)!** May you get dirty again happily (said in greeting to someone just coming from a bath). **—e güle kullanın(ız)** Be fortunate in its use (said to someone acquiring a new possession). **—meden katıl=, —mekten kırıl=** to be doubled up with laughter. **—me komşuna gelir başına** *proverb* Don't laugh at another's misfortune; it may happen to you one day. **—en kumru** collared turtle dove, *zool., Streptopelia decaocto.* **—üp oyna=** to laugh and be merry.

gülâb (.—) گلاب P *lrnd.* rose water, julep. **—çeşm** *lrnd.* pink-eyed hawk. **—dan** (.——) P rose water flask. **—î** (.——) P 1. rose-colored, pink. 2. rose water flask. 3. kind of blancmange. 4. maker of rose water.
gülabiye (.—..) گلابیه [*Persian* **kulabiya**] *lrnd.* kind of cake.
gülâc گل و آج ، گور و آج P *lrnd., same as* **güllaç.**
gülâle (.—.) گلاله P 1. *lrnd.* shirt, smock, chemise. 2. *poet.* a long ringlet of hair.
gülbahar (..—) گلبهار P 1. *paint.* kind of pink dye. 2. *games* kind of backgammon.
gülbağ (.—) گلباغ P *lrnd.* rose garden.
gülbam (.—) گلبام P *lrnd.* shout.
gülbang (.—) گلبانك P 1. *Isl. rel.* call to prayer; Muslim battle-cry of **Allâhu ekber;** prayer of the Janissary troops; hymn or prayer chanted in unison; collective prayer of the Bektashis. 2. *poet.* song of the nightingale. 3. *lrnd.* loud shout. **— çek=** *Ott. hist.* to recite the prayer before the Janissary troops. **—i Muhammedî** *Isl. rel.* call to prayer. **— taşı** *Ott. hist.* stone in the middle of the Janissary camp, where an officer recited the prayer before the troops.
gülbankᵏı گلبانك *var. of* **gülbang.**
gülbeden گلبدن P *lrnd.* whose body is as beautiful as a rose.
gülbeng گلبنك P *same as* **gülbang.**
gülberkᵏı گلبرك P *lrnd.* rose petal.
gülbeşeker گل به شكر، گل بشكر، گلبشكر P rose jam.
gülbister گلبستر P *poet.* bed of roses.
gülbiz (.—) گلبیز P *poet.* scattering roses.
gülbuse (.—.) گلبوسه P *poet.* a kiss like a rose.
gülbün گلبن P *lrnd.* rosebush, rose tree.
gülçe گلچه P 1. *art* rosette. 2. *lrnd.* little rose, little flower.
gülçehre گلچهره P *poet.* with a face of rosy hue.
gülçeşm گلچشم P *lrnd.* pink-eyed; that has a speck or spot in an eye.
gülçin (.—) گلچین P *lrnd.* who gathers flowers or roses.
güldan (.—) گلدان P *lrnd.* rose-bowl.
güldar (.—) گلدار P *lrnd.* bearing flowers, in flower.

güldehan (..—), **güldehen** گل دهان گل دهن P poet. rose-mouthed.
güldeste گلدسته P lrnd. 1. bunch of flowers, nosegay, bouquet. 2. anthology of poems. 3. *Or. mus.* a compound **makam** only recently named.
gülduzi (.—.—) گل دوزی P lrnd. flower motifs in embroidery.
güldür=ür گولدرمك /ı or ı, a/ *caus.* of **gül=** 2¹. **—ücü** causing laughter. **—ücü kas** *anat.*, Risorius.
güldür güldür گولدر گولدر imitates the sound of steady flowing, burning, or fluent reading.
güleçci گولج smiling, merry.
gülefşan (..—) گل افشان P poet. rose-scattering.
güleğen گولگن *archaic* always smiling.
gülendam (..—) گل اندام P poet. rose-bodied.
gülengübin (...—) گل انگبین P lrnd. rose petals in honey.
gülepçe گولپچه *obs., var.* of **kelepçe**.
gülepe گولپه *obs.* metal disk, coil, or ring.
güler گولر always laughing. **— çehre, — yüz** smiling, cheerful face; friendly look. **— yüz göster=** /a/ to be friendly (to), to act in a friendly manner (towards). **— yüzlü** merry, cheerful, affable.
güleş=ir 1 گولشمك *var.* of **güreş=** 1.
güleş 2 گولش *var.* of **güreş** 2.
gülfam (.—) گلفام P poet. rose-colored, rosy, ruddy.
gülfeşan, gülfişan (..—) گلفشان P poet., same as **gülefşan**.
gülgande گلغنده P lrnd. cotton ready for spinning.
gülgen گولگن *var.* of **gürgen**.
gülgeşt گلگشت P poet. flowery mead, park or garden for pleasant walking.
gülgiller *neol., bot.,* Rosaceae.
gülgonca گلغنچه P lrnd. 1. rosebud, flower bud. 2. rouge for the face.
gülgûn (.—) گلگون P lrnd. rose-colored, rosy.
gülgunde (.—.) گلغنده P lrnd., same as **gülgande**.
gülgûne (.—.) گلگونه P poet. rose-colored; rouge. **—i çarh** afterglow following sunset.
gülgülü گلگلی [gülgûne] *prov.* pink, pink-colored.
gülhan گلخن P lrnd., same as **külhan**.
gülhane (.—.) گلخانه P 1. lrnd. rose-garden. 2. *w. cap.* park of the Great Palace. **G— Hatt-ı Hümayunu** *Ott. hist.* firman read by the Foreign Minister Mustafa Reshid Pasha on Oct. 3, 1839, in Gülhane Park, declaring the political reforms of Sultan Abdulmejid.
gülhanî (..—), **gülhantab** (..—) گلخنی گلخن تاب P lrnd. stoker of a bath.

gülhatmi گلختمی [Persian **gül-i-khitmî**] rose mallow, hollyhock, *bot.*, Althaea rosea.
güihiz (.—) گلخیز P poet. producing roses.
gülibrişim گل ابریشم [Persian **gul-i abrışam**] rose acacia, bristly acacia, *bot.*, Robinia hispida.
gülistan (..—) گلستان P 1. poet. rose garden, flower garden. 2. *Or. mus.* a **makam** no longer used.
gülizar (..—.—) گلعذار P 1. poet. rosy-cheeked. 2. *Or. mus.* a compound **makam** approximately five centuries old.
gülkand گلقند P lrnd. rose-scented sugar candy.
gülkâr (.—) گلکار P lrnd. 1. flower gardener, florist. 2. flower embroiderer; artificial flower maker. **—î** (.—.—) P 1. art or business of a florist. 2. flower-embroidery; artificial flower work. 3. flower garden.
güllâbî (.—.—), **güllâbici** گلابی گلابیجی [gülâbi] 1. warden in a lunatic asylum. 2. flatterer, coaxer. **—lik et=** to flatter, to say nice things.
güllâçcı گلاچ [gülac] 1. starch wafer. 2. sweet made from starch wafers filled with nuts and milky syrup flavored with rose water. 3. *pharm.* capsule.
gülle گله [gülûle] 1. cannon ball, shell. 2. *sports* weight, shot; barbell. **— at=** 1. /a/ to shell, to bombard. 2. *sports* to put the shot. **— gibi** very heavy. **— kaldır=** *sports* to weightlift. **—ci** *sports* shot putter. **—len=** to become a ball; to grow round and puffy.
güllü گللی 1. flowered, in blossom. 2. ornamented with flowers, ornamented (printed fabric).
güllükgü گللک rose garden, rose bed, place full of roses. **— gülistanlık** in a state of peace and concord.
gülme گولمه a laughing, laughter. **— al=** /ı/ to be seized with a fit of laughter. **—den bayıl=** *same as* **gülmekten bayıl=**. **—si tut=** to burst out laughing. **—ce** 1. *neol., literature* farce. 2. *prov.* jest, joke.
gülmez گولمز sullen, sour-faced, severe, unsmiling. **— sultan** sulky person.
gülmıh گلمیخ P lrnd. brass-headed rose nail.
gülnahlli گلنهال P poet. rose bush.
gülnakkı (.—) گلناک P poet. flowery; embellished with roses.
gülnar (.—) گلنار P poet. pomegranate flower; deep red double rose; *art* pomegranate flower motif. **—î** (.—.—) P of the color of the pomegranate flower, flame red.
gülnesrin (..—) گلنسرین P lrnd. dog rose, briar, *bot.*, Rosa canina.

gülnihal

gülnihalⁱⁱ (..—) گلنهال P poet. young rose plant.

gülnikab (..—) گلنقاب P poet. covered with roses.

gülpaş (.—) گلپاش P lrnd. that sprinkles rose water; rose water sprinkler.

gülpuş (.—) گلپوش P poet. adorned with roses or flowers.

gülrenkᵍⁱ گلرنك P poet. rose-colored, pink.

gülriz (.—) گلریز P poet. that scatters flowers, roses; sprinkled over with flowers, roses.

gülru (.—) گلرو P poet. rosy-faced.

gülruh گلرخ P 1. poet. rose-cheeked. 2. Or. mus. a makam no longer used.

gülruhsar (..—) گلرخسار P poet. rose-cheeked.

gülruy (.—) گلروی P poet., var. of **gülru**.

gülşeker گلشکر P poet. rose jam.

gülşen (.—) گلشن P poet. rose garden. **—i kuds** gardens of paradise. **—i vefa** Or. mus. a compound **makam** composed at the beginning of the XXth century, no longer used. **—ara** (..—-) P gardener, horticulturist. **—füruz** (...—) P who plants roses, gardener. **—gâh** (..—) P rose garden. **—saray** (...—) P garden palace. **—tiraz** (...—) P gardener, horticulturist.

gülten گلتن [based on Persian] poet. rose-bodied, fresh and dainty.

gülteraş (..—) گلتراش P lrnd. candle snuffer.

gülû (.—) گلو P lrnd. throat, windpipe, gullet. **—bend** (.—.) P necktie, collar; anything that is bound round the neck, stock. **—bende** (.—..) P slave to his gullet, glutton, gourmand. **—beste** (.—..) P silent. **—gâh** (.——) P, **—geh** (.—.) P seat of the throat, throat. **—gir** (.——) P suffocating; which sticks in the throat (food). **—girifte** (.—...) P seized by the throat, throttled; hoarse.

gülûle (.—.) گلوله P lrnd. 1. ball of yarn. 2. pellet, bullet, cannon ball. 3. lumpy swelling in the body.

gülûsuz (.——) گلوسوز P lrnd. that burns or irritates the throat.

gülûteh (.—.) گلوته P lrnd. pointed cap lined with cotton, and tied under the chin (for children, women).

gülü 1 گولو prov. turkey.

gülü=ʳ 2 گولمك prov. to fetter.

gülücü گولوجی who is always laughing and smiling.

gülücükᵗᵘ گولوجك nursery smile (of an infant). **— yap=** to smile (infant).

gülükᵍᵘ 1 گولوك prov. turkey.

gülük 2 گولوك prov., var. of **gurk**.

gülüm گولوم obs. laugh. **—lü** laughable.

gülümse=ʳ گولومسمك to smile; /a/ to smile (at).

gülümsi=ʳ, **gülümsü**=ʳ, **gülümsün**=ᵘʳ گولومسمك archaic, same as **gülümse**=.

gülün=ᵘʳ گولونمك archaic to laugh to one's self.

gülünçᶜᵘ گولنج ridiculous, laughable; funny. **— yap=** /ı/ to ridicule, to make a laughingstock. **—lü** neol. comical, funny.

gülüş 1 گولوش manner of laughing, laughter.

gülüş=ᵘʳ 2 گولوشمك to laugh together; to laugh at each other. **—ken** archaic who habitually laughs. **—tür** /ı/ caus. of **gülüş**=.

gülzar (.—) گلزار P 1. poet. flower garden, rose garden. 2. Or. mus. an obsolete compound makam.

güm 1 گوم 1. hollow or booming sound. 2. slang lie, fabricated story, made-up story, fable. **— at=** slang to fool someone with lies, to pull a fast one. **—e git=** to be lost in a confusion, to be a victim; for the innocent to suffer with the guilty. **— güm at=** to beat violently (heart, etc.) **— güm öt=** to give out a booming sound.

güm 2 گم P lrnd. 1. lost; stray. 2. erring, in error.

güman (.—) گمان P lrnd. 1. doubt, suspicion. 2. opinion, fancy, supposition.

gümaşte (.—.) گماشته P lrnd. 1. appointed. 2. minister; emissary.

gümbed گنبد P lrnd., same as **kümbet**. **—i âb** bubble. **—i a'zam** the highest heaven, ninth heaven. **—i azrak** vault of heaven. **—i destar** turban. **—i dimağ** palate, roof of the mouth. **—i gül** 1. rosebud. 2. golden goblet. **—i hazra** sky. **—i imame** turban. **—i mail** fourth heaven. **—i muamber** head of the beloved one. **—î** (..—) P conical; dome-shaped.

gümbedek (.'..) گومبدك with a rumbling noise (to fall); suddenly, all of a sudden.

gümbür گومبور a reverberating, booming sound. **— gümbür** a roaring sound, a booming noise. **—de=** 1. to boom, thunder, reverberate. 2. slang to die.

gümbürtü گومبورتو a booming. **—lü** rumbling, roaring, booming.

güme گومه P prov. hut, shed; hunting lodge.

gümeçᶜⁱ گومج honeycomb. **— balı** honey in the comb.

gümele گومله prov. hut, cabin.

gümgeşte گمگشته P lrnd. lost.

gümkerde گمکرده P lrnd. lost.

gümle=ʳ گوملمك 1. to emit a hollow or booming sound. 2. slang to die. **—t=** /ı/ caus.

gümnam (.—) گمنام P lrnd. whose name is lost, forgotten.

gümrah 1 گُمراه ، گُمراه [**gümrah 2**] copious, abundant, dense, luxuriant. **— saçlı** bushy-haired, thick-haired. **— sesli** having a booming voice.

gümrah 2 (.—) گُمراه P *lrnd.* astray; erring, heretical, wicked. **—î** (.— —) P wickedness.

gümrahlık^(gı) گُمراهلِق abundance, luxuriance.

gümreh گُمره P *lrnd.*, *var. of* **gümrah 2**.

gümren=^(lr) گُمرنك *prov.* to murmur (against).

gümrük^(gü) گرك گروك گومروك گومراك Gk 1. custom, duty; tariff. 2. customs house, customs. **— al**= /dan/ to collect duty (on). **— ambarı** bonded warehouse. **— anlaşması** customs treaty. **— antreposu** *same as* **gümrük ambarı**. **— beyanı** customs entry, customs declaration. **— beyannamesi** bill of entry. **— birliği** customs union. **— bölgesi** customs district. **—ten çıkar**= /ı/ to clear through the customs. **— dairesi** custom house. **— deposu** bonded warehouse. **— didebanı** *obs.* coast guard. **— emaneti** *obs.* controllership of the custom house. **— emini** *obs.* customs controller. **— faturası** certified invoice. **—ten geç**= to pass through the customs. **—ten geçir**= /ı/ to clear through the customs. **— harbi** tariff war. **— hattı** customs line. **— ilmühaberi** permit, bill of clearance. **— ittihadı** customs union. **— kaçağı** smuggled (goods). **— kaçakçısı** smuggler. **— kaçakçılığı** smuggling. **— kanunu** customs law. **— kolcusu** customs house watchman; customs guard. **— komisyoncusu** customs broker. **— kontrolü** customs control. **— makbuzu** docket, receipt. **—ten mal kaçırır gibi** hurried and flustered. **— mânifestosu** customs manifest. **— memuru** customs official. **— mıntakası** customs district. **—ten muaf** duty-free. **— muafiyeti** exemption from duty. **— muamelesi** custom house formalities. **— muamelesini yap**= to effect customs clearance. **— muayenesi** customs examination; examination of passenger's luggage. **— muhafaza memuru** guard of the customs. **— muhammini** customs valuer. **— müfettişi** customs officer. **— nâzırı** *obs.* superintendent of the customs. **— resmi** customs charges. **— serbestisi**, **— serbestiyeti** free trade. **—e tâbi** dutiable, liable or subject to duty, custom. **— tahsildarı** collector of customs. **— tarifesi** customs rate list. **G— ve Tekel Bakanlığı** the Ministry of Customs and Monopolies. **— tellalı** customs broker. **— tezkeresi** permit, clearance bill. **— vazifesi** *Ott. hist.* allowance assigned to the poor out of the customs revenue. **— vesikası** customs certificate, custom bond. **—cü** customs officer. **—le**= /ı/ to clear at the customs house. **—leme** payment of the duty, clearing at the custom house. **—süz** duty-free.

gümşüde گُمشُده P *lrnd.* lost.

gümül گُمُل *prov.* half a dozen; bunch, bundle; heap.

gümür گُمُر rumble, grumble, roar.

gümürde=^(r) گُمُردَه to roar; to grumble. **—n**= to roar; to grumble to oneself. **—t**= /ı/ *caus. of* **gümürde**=.

gümürtü گُمُردُو rumbling or booming, roaring sound; roar.

gümüş گُمُش گوموش گموش 1. silver; (of) silver, silvery. 2. *slang* balding. **— ayarı** silver carat. **— balığı** sand-smelt, atherine, *zool.*, *Atherina presbyter*. **— beyazı** silvery-white, silver-colored. **— cevheri** silver ore. **— çubuğu** silver bar. **— damarı** vein of silver. **— gerdan** silver-white neck. **— gibi parılda**= to have a silvery tinge. **— göz** *obs.* money-grasping, money-grubber. **— işi** silver-work; worked in silver; filigree silver. **— kaplama** silver-plated; silver plating. **— kaplı** silver-plated. **— kavak** white poplar, silver poplar, *bot.*, *Populus alba*. **— madeni** 1. silver ore. 2. silver mine. **— para** silver coin. **— para sistemi** silver currency. **— rengi** silver colored. **— selvi** reflection of moonlight on water. **— sırma** silver thread, silver lace. **— suyu** silver bath; silvering. **— sülün** silver pheasant, *zool.*, *Gennaeus mycthemerus*. **— takımı** set of silver. **— taşı** ceramics potter's lead, natural lead sulfide. **— tel** silver wire. **— tilki** silver fox. **— varak** silver foil, silver leaf. **— yaldız** silver bath; silvering. **— yaprak** silver leaf.

gümüşî گُمُشی grey.

gümüşle=^(r) گُمُشلَه /ı/ to silver plate. **—n**= *pass.* **—t**= *caus. of* **gümüşle**=.

gümüşlü گُمُشلُی 1. containing silver. 2. ornamented with silver.

gümüşü گُمُشو silver-gray. **— martı** herring gull, *zool.*, *Larus argentatus*.

gün گُون 1. day; daytime. 2. a lady's at-home day. 3. time; period; age. 4. feast day. 5. happy days, better days. 6. sun; light. **—lerce** for days. **—ünde** in its day. **— ağarması** daybreak. **— ağılı** halo around the sun. **— akşamlıdır** The day has an evening (i. e. Death may come any time). **— âşığı**, **—e âşık** *prov.* sunflower. **— aşırı** every other day. **— atlama**= not to miss out a day. **— aydın!** Good morning! **—e bakan**, **—e bakar** sunflower. **— balı** *prov.* grape juice condensed by exposure to the sun. **— balığı** kind of wrasse, *zool.*, *Julis pavo*. **— batısı** west; west wind. **— batması** sunset, sundown. **— begün** day by day. **— beri** *neol.*, *astr.* perihelion. **—ün birinde** one day, once; some day.

günah

—lerden bir gün once upon a time. —ü birlik*. — bugün Now is the right time; this opportunity will never come again. — çiçeği sunflower. — doğ= (of the sun) to rise, to dawn. — doğmadan neler doğar Before daybreak many things may happen. —e doğrulum neol., bot. heliotropism. — doğrusu, — doğusu east, easterly wind. —ünü doldur= to finish a fixed term; com. to fall due, to be mature. — dön= for the sun to begin to return from the solstice. — döndü prov. sunflower. — dönümü, — durumu solstice. — eğişmesi, — eşiği prov. early afternoon. bir — evvel 1. a day before. 2. at as early a day as possible, as soon as possible. —leri gece ol= /ın/ for one's day to turn to night. — geç= 1. for a day to pass, for the appointed term to be passed. 2. to get sunstroke, as in başına gün geçti. — geçir= 1. to spend the day or time; to live; to while away time; to have a comfortable and untroubled time. —ü geçir= to be late, miss the day. — gibi âşikâr altogether clear, very clear or manifest. — gör= to live prosperously. —ünü gör= 1. to come to a bad end. 2. to have her periods. — görmemiş of no standing, inexperienced. — görmez where the light of day never comes; sunless (place); obscure or secret (place). — görmüş who has seen better days. —ünü görürsün! I'll show you. You'll get your deserts. Retribution will come. — görmez evliyası misanthrope, unsociable person. — göster= /a/ caus. of gün gör=. — gün, —den güne from day to day, gradually. —ü gününe punctually; exactly on the fixed day, to the very day. —ünü gün et= to really be enjoying oneself. —ü gününe uyma= to have a changeable character, to have an inconstant temperament. —ün günü var Wait; the day will come. — in= prov. (of the sun) to set. — kaşı prov. the first light of sunrise. — kavuş= (of the sun) to go down, to set. — koy= /a/ to put aside a day, to assign some time (for), as in bu işe beş gün koydum I have assigned five days for this work. —e küsen, —e küstü prov. marvel-of-Peru; four-o'clock. — merkezli neol., astr. heliocentric. — orta prov. midday, noon. — önü prov. daybreak, dawn. — öte neol., astr. apogee. — pekmezi same as gün balı. —leri sayılı His days are numbered. — sür= to live prosperously. — tutul= to be eclipsed (the sun). — tutulması eclipse of the sun. — tün eşitliği neol., astr. equinox. — ver= /a/ prov. to send to prison, to give one so many days (in prison). — vur= /a/ to cause sunstroke. — yanığı sunburn. —ü yet= to fall due; to have lived one's span. — yılımı prov. early afternoon.

günah (. —) گناه P 1. sin; guilt, crime; fault. 2. Isn't it a pity! Shame! —ını al= /ın/ .to accuse wrongly of. — benden gitti I am telling you; now it is your responsibility; it is no longer my responsibility. —ı boynuna The moral responsibility rests upon him. —ını çek= to suffer or to pay for his sin, guilt, fault. — çıkar= Christ. rel. to confess, to go to confession. — çıkart= Christ. rel. to hear confession. —ına değme= to be worthless. — et= obs., same as günah işle=. —ından geç= /ın/ to pass over someone's sin, to forgive. —a gir= to sin, to commit a sin. —ına gir= /ın/ to accuse wrongly, to wrong. — işle= to commit a sin. —ı kadar sevme= to hate like poison. — olur It would be a pity. —a sok= /ı/ 1. to cause to sin, to tempt. 2. to make one lose patience, to exasperate, to drive to blasphemy. —ı üzerinden at= to get rid of the responsibility (for). —ını vermez He is very stingy.

günahkâr (. — —) گناهکار P sinner, culprit, wrongdoer; culpable, sinful, impious. —âne (. — — .) P sinfully. —lık sinfulness.
günahlı گناهلی sinful.
günahpişe (. — — .) گناه‌پیشه P lrnd. habitual sinner.
günahsız (. — .) گناه‌سز sinless, innocent, faultless. —lık sinlessness, state of grace, innocence.
günc گنج P lrnd. space, room, capacity.
güncar (. —) گنجار P lrnd., same as gencar.
güncayiş (. —) گنجایش P lrnd. a getting in, squeezing in, fitting in; capacity, a holding, containing. — pezir (. — . —) P capable of being held or contained.
güncekᵍⁱ گنجک prov. umbrella.
güncide (. —.) گنجیده P lrnd. pressed or squeezed into.
güncişkᵏⁱ گنجشک P lrnd. sparrow.
gündeleş=ⁱʳ گونده‌لش to become daily.
gündelikᵍⁱ 1 گوندلک 1. daily, everyday. 2. day's wages, daily fee. —le çalış= to work by the day. — çalışma day's work, day labor. — elbise, — esvap everyday clothes. — gazete daily, daily paper. — hizmet duty of the day, day service. — kıyafet everyday dress; lounge suit. — siyaset day-to-day politics, politics of the day. — ücret day's wages, daily wages.
gündelikᵍⁱ 2 گوندلک who works for daily wages; paid by the day.
gündelikçi گوندلکچی day laborer, hired man. — kadın hired woman, charwoman, workwoman. —lik day labor.
gündem neol. agenda. —e al= /ı/ to put on the agenda. —e geç= to pass to the agenda.

gündüz گوندوز daytime; by day, in the daytime, in or by daylight. **—leri** during the day, in the daytime. **— feneri** *joc.* Negro. **— hava akını** *mil.* daylight raid. **— kavsi** *astr.* diurnal arc. **— külâhlı, gece silâhlı** carrying a knife in his boot; worse than he appears. **— sefası** bindweed, *bot.*, *Convulvulus arvensis.* **— uçuşu** daylight flight. **— taarruzu** *mil.* daylight attack. **— vakti** in the daytime, during the day. **—cü** 1. on day duty. 2. day drinker. **—leme** (*lit.* child conceived in the daytime) *slang* brat.

gündüzlü گوندوزلو 1. day student. 2. cf. **geceli gündüzlü.**

gündüzlükᵍᵘ گوندوزلك for everyday (dress etc.).

gündüzün (.'..) گوندوزين during the day, by day.

güneğikᵍⁱ گونیك chicory, *bot.*, *Cichorium intybus.*

güneh گنه P *lrnd.*, *var. of* **günah.**

güneş گونش sun, sunshine. **— aç=** to become sunny. **— al=** to sun oneself. **—in altında** in the direct sun. **—e arzet=** /ı/ to expose to the sun. **— ayı** *astr.* solar month. **— balçıkla sıvanmaz** One can't hide the truth. **— balığı** a kind of rockfish, *zool.*, *Coris julis.* **— banyosu** sun bath, sun bathing. **— bat=** to set, to go down (sun). **— batması** sunset, sundown. **— çarp=** /ı/ to get sunstroke. **— çarpması** sunstroke. **G— Dil teorisi** the theory of the "Sun Language" (a theory concerning the origin of language put forward in Turkey in the early 1930's). **— doğ=** to rise (sun). **— doğması** sunrise. **— geç=** /a/ to cause sun stroke. **— gibi aşikâr** clear as daylight. **— gör=** to be light and sunny. **—e göster=** /ı/ to expose to the sun. **— gözlüğü** sunglasses. **— günü** *astr.* solar day. **— harfleri** *Arabic gram.* sun letters. **— inşia sabiti** *astr.* solar constant. **—e karşı işe=** *vulg.* to be insolent. **— lekesi** *astr.* sunspot. **— manzumesi** *astr.* solar system. **— saati** 1. sundial. 2. *astr.* solar time. **— sabitesi** *astr.* solar constant. **— senesi** *astr.* solar year. **— sistemi** *astr.* solar system. **— şemsiyesi** parasol, sunshade. **— şuaı** sun ray, sunbeam. **— tarafı** sunny side. **— tayfı** *phys.* solar spectrum. **— tutul=** to be eclipsed (sun). **— tutulması** solar eclipse. **— vur=** /a/ 1. to cause sunstroke. 2. to shine (on a place, sun). **— vurması** sunstroke. **— yak=** /ı/ to cause sunstroke. **—te yan=** to be sunburnt, to be tanned. **— yanığı** sunburn, tan. **— yılı** *astr.* solar year. **—len=** 1. to sunbathe. 2. to be spread in the sun to dry. **—let=** /ı/ to leave in the sun to dry, to expose to the sun. **—li** sunny. **—lik** 1. sunny place. 2. sunshade; sun-hat; visor of cap.

güvenikᵍⁱ گونلك *var. of* **güneğik.**

güney 1. *neol.* south; southern. 2. *prov.* sunny side. **— haçı** *astr.* Southern Cross. **— kutbu** South Pole.

güneyikᵍⁱ گنیك *var. of* **güneğik.**

günindi گنندی *prov.* west.

günle=ʳ گونله 1. *obs.* to pass the day, to spend the day. 2. /ı/ *prov.* to fix the day (of).

günlem *neol.* chronicle.

günleme *neol.* date.

günlükᵍᵘ 1 گونلك 1. daily; of the same day; usual. 2. for or since so many days; a quantity sufficient for (given) number of days; so many days old. 3. *neol.* diary. 4. *prov.* umbrella; awning. **— defter** diary; memorandum-book. **— devir** daily sale. **— emir** *mil.* order of the day. **— fiat** current price. **— güneşlik** sunny. **— iş** day's work, routine. **— kur** daily rate of exchange, current rate. **— rapor** daily report, bulletin. **— yumurta** fresh egg.

günlükᵍᵘ 2 گونلك frankincense, incense; myrrh. **— ağacı** liquidambar tree, *bot.*, *Styrax.*

günü گنو *prov.* envy, jealousy.

günübirlikᵍⁱ گونوبرلك confined to the day, not including the night (visit). **—ine git=** to make a day visit.

günücü گنوجی *prov.* jealous, envious.

günüle=ʳ گنوله *prov.* /ı/ to be envious, to be jealous.

günülü گنولو *prov.* envious, jealous.

güpegündüz گوپه گوندوز in broad daylight.

gür 1 گور abundant, dense, thick; rank. **— sesle** with a fine strong voice.

gür 2 گور gurgling or humming sound. **— gür et=** to make a gurgling or humming noise.

gür 3 گور P *prov.* wood, bush, marshy land.

güraz (.—) گراز P *lrnd.* boar; wild boar.

gürbe گربه P *lrnd.* cat.

gürbüz گوربوز P, sturdy, robust, healthy. **—lük** sturdiness, healthiness.

Gürcice (.—.) گرجیجه Georgian language.

Gürcistan (..—) گرجستان P Georgia (in the Caucasus).

Gürcü گرجی P Georgian; Georgians (of the Caucasus). **—ce** *var. of* **Gürcice.**

gürd گرد P *lrnd.* brave warrior, hero.

—gir (.—) P brave champion.

gürdük 1 گردك *prov.* heat (sexual).

gürdük=ᵘʳ 2 گوردك *prov.* to be in heat.

güre 1 گوره *prov.* wild; unbroken; uncouth, raw.

güre 2 گوره [Persian **kurra**] *prov.* colt (up to three years old). **—ci** one who looks after colts.

gürel *neol., phil.* dynamic.

güreli *neol., phil.* energetic.

güreş=ⁱʳ 1 گورشمك to wrestle.

güreş 2 گورش wrestling, wrestling match,

güreşme گُرشمه a wrestling.
güreştir=ir گُرشتیرمك /ı/ caus. of **güreş=** 1.
gürg گرگ P lrnd. wolf. **—i barandide** experienced and astute man. **—beçe** P wolf cub.
gürgen گُرگن 1. hornbeam, horn beech, bot., Carpinus betulus. 2. made of hornbeam. **—giller** neol. Fagaceae.
gürihte (.—.) گریخته P lrnd. that has escaped, absconded.
gürisne گرسنه P lrnd. hungry. **—çeşm** P greedy, covetous, insatiable. **—gî** P hunger.
-güriz گریز P lrnd., var. of **-giriz**.
gürizan (.——) گریزان P lrnd. fleeing, in flight. **— ol=** to flee, to escape.
gürizende (.—..) گریزنده P lrnd. 1. fugitive. 2. quicksilver, mercury.
gürizgâh (.——) گریزگاه P lrnd., var. of **girizgâh**.
gürle=r گُرلمك 1. to make a loud noise; to thunder; to roar. 2. slang to die. **—me** a making a loud thundering noise; loud thundering noise. **—t=** /ı/ caus. of **gürle=**.
gürlükgü گُرلك abundance, luxuriance, fullness.
güruh (.—) گروه P gang, band, group, flock. **—u lâyeflehun** an incorrigible lot.
güruhe (.—.) گروهه P lrnd. ball of yarn.
gürülde=r گُرُلدمك to make a loud, thundering noise.
gürül gürül گُرُل گُرُل bubbling, gurgling; in a loud throaty voice. **— ak=** to flow abundantly or with a gurgling sound. **— oku=** to read in a loud, rich voice.
gürültü گُرُلتی 1. noise, uproar. 2. trouble, confusion. **—ye boğ=** /ı/ deliberately to distract attention from something by clamor or extraneous action. **— çıkar=** to cause trouble or a disturbance. **— et=** to make a noise. **—ye gel=** to be lost in the confusion. **—ye getir=** /ı/ to cause something to be lost in the confusion. **—ye git=** to suffer punishment or loss through no fault of one's own; to perish. **— kopar=** same as **gürültü çıkar=**. **—ye pabuç bırakma=** not to be easily intimidated by mere threats. **—. patırdı** noise, trouble. **— yap=** to make a noise. **—cü** noisy, troublesome (person). **—lü** noisy, tumultuous, clamorous. **—süz** noiseless, quiet.
güryân (.—) گُریان P lrnd. 1. stokehole of a bathhouse. 2. ransom.
gürz گُرز P, گُرز iron club; mace used in battle.

-güsar (.—) گُسار P lrnd. that drinks, consumes, that drives away, as in gamgüsar.
güsiste گسسته P lrnd. broken, parted; broken down. **—âşiyan** (...—.—) P poet. whose nest has been destroyed. **—dem** P lrnd. breathless, exhausted. **—dil** P poet. broken-hearted; grieved.
güstah (.—) گُستاخ P lrnd., same as **küstah**.
-güster گُستر P lrnd., used in compounds, that spreads, diffuses, dispenses, as in **dadgüster, sayegüster**.
güsterde گُسترده P lrnd. spread; extended; diffused.
güt=der گُتمك 1. to drive; to watch over, to pasture; to follow. 2. to aim; to cherish, to nourish.
gütaperka (...'.) F guttapercha. **— ağacı** guttapercha tree.
güva, güvah (.—) گُواه P lrnd. 1. witness. 2. evidence. **—î** (.——) P quality or act of a witness.
-güvar (.—) گُوار P lrnd. which goes down the throat and is digested, as in **hoşgüvar**.
güvarende (.—..) گُوارنده P lrnd. agreeable to the palate and light to digest.
güvariş (.—.) گُوارش P lrnd. electuary to facilitate digestion.
güve گُوه clothes moth, zool., Tinen pellionella. **— yemiş** moth-eaten. **— yeniği** moth hole.
güveçci گُوج 1. earthenware cooking pot. 2. vegetables and meat cooked in an earthenware cooking pot.
güven 1 گُون trust, reliance, confidence. **—i ol=** /a/ to have confidence (in). **— olmaz** /a/ untrustworthy, undependable.
güven=ir **2** گُونمك /a/ to trust (in), to rely (on). **—diği dağlara kar yağdı** He was sorely disappointed; he was let down. **—ç** trust, confidence, reliance. **—dir=** to give one confidence (in). **—iklik** trust, confidence. **—ilir** reliable, safe.
güvenlikği neol. security; public order. **G— Konseyi** Inter. law Security Council.
güvensiz neol. distrustful. **—lik** lack of confidence.
güvercin گُورجین pigeon, rock dove, zool., Columba livia. **—ler** pigeons and doves, zool., Columbidae. **— boynu, — gerdanı** multicolored, shot, dove colored. **— kökü** pharm. columbo, calumba, root of Jateorhiza palmata. **— kümesi** pigeon house, dovecote. **— otu** vervain, bot., Verbena officinalis. **— postası** pigeon post. **—lik** 1. pigeon house, dovecote. 2. round tower.
güverte (.'.) گُورته It deck. **— yolcusu** deck passenger. **—li** with decks.
güvey, güveyi گُوگی bridegroom; son-in-

law. — **feneri** winter cherry, *bot., Physalis alkakengi.* — **gir=** to enter the bridal chamber (bridegroom). — **kılavuzu** woman who goes on the part of a suitor to see and report upon a prospective bride. — **otu** marjoram, *bot., Majorana majorana.* —**lik** 1. condition of a bridegroom. 2. things used or worn by the bridegroom.

güvez گوز dark red or violet.

güz گز autumn, fall. — **çiğdemi** autumn crocus, meadow saffron, *bot., Colchicum autumnale.* — **noktası** *astr.* fall equinox.

güzaf (. —) گزاف P *lrnd.* chitchat, idle talk.

güzar 1 (. —) گذار P *lrnd.* a passing, passage. — **et=** to pass, to go by.

-güzar 2 (. —) گذار P *lrnd.* that performs, carries out, pays, *as in* **işgüzar, maslahatgüzar.**

güzarende (. — ..) گذارنده P *lrnd.* 1. who causes to pass. 2. performer of a duty; payer of a debt. 3. interpreter of a dream.

güzariş (. —.) گزارش P *lrnd.* 1. an act of passing, a passage. 2. performance; payment. 3. interpretation of a dream. **—ger** (. — ..) P 1. performer of a duty; payer of a debt. 2. interpreter of dreams. **—nâme** (. — . —.) P 1. dream-book. 2. marginal note, commentary.

güzaşte (. —.) گذشته P *lrnd.* 1. who has passed, performed (something). 2. passed, performed; past.

güzel گوزل 1. beautiful, pretty, good, nice, fine, graceful; beauty, belle. 2. Well! Good! All right. **—im** 1. Darling. 2. that beautiful (thing or person), *e. g.,* **o güzelim evi harap etmişler** They have spoiled that beautiful house; **o güzelim kızı mahvetmişler** They have ruined that lovely girl. — **avrat otu** deadly nightshade, belladonna, *bot., Atropa belladonna.* —**e göz ağrısı da yaraşır** If she is beautiful, she can get away with anything. — **güzel** calmly. — **hatun otu** *same as* **güzel avrat otu.** — **hava** fine weather. — **sahife** *print.* right-hand page. — **sanatlar** fine arts. **G— Sanatlar Akademisi** The Academy of Fine Arts. — **yakıştı** It suits you (her, him) well (new dress, hat, etc.) **—ce** 1. (...́) pretty fair, of modest beauty. 2. (..́.) thoroughly. **—leme** *literature* kind of folk-song of praise for a special person. **—len=, —leş=** to become beautiful, pretty, good. **—leştir=, —let=** /ı/ to make beautiful or pretty; to embellish, to adorn.

güzellik^{ği} گوزللك beauty, prettiness, fineness; goodness. — **enstitüsü** beauty parlor. — **kıraliçesi** beauty queen. — **müsabakası** beauty contest. **—le** gently, without using force.

güzelsi=^{r}, **güzelsin=**^{lr} گوزلسمك /ı/ *prov.* to deem beautiful, pretty, good.

güzeran (.. —) گذران P *lrnd.* passing, happening; passage. — **et=, — ol=** to pass, to elapse; to happen, to occur.

güzergâh (.. —) گذرگاه P 1. route (of a bus, etc.). 2. *lrnd.* place of passage, ford, ferry.

güzeşt گذشت *lrnd.* an act of passing, passage.

güzeşte گذشته P *lrnd.* 1. that has passed; past. 2. interest (on money). **—gân** (... —) P those who have passed away, the dead.

güzey *neol., geog.,* shady side.

güzide (. — .) گزیده P distinguished, select, outstanding; choice. **—lik** choiceness.

güzin 1 (. —) گزین P *lrnd.* distinguished, select.

-güzin 2 (. —) گزین P *lrnd.* who chooses or elects, *as in* **halvetgüzin.**

güzlük^{ğü} گوزلك autumn-sown (crops).

güzün (.́.) گوزن in the autumn.

Ğ

ğ, Ğ *ninth letter of the alphabet* (pronounced after **e, i, ö, ü,** like y in yellow; between pairs of **a, ı, o, u** it is not audible; between **a, ı, o, u** and a consonant it results in lengthening of the vowel).

-ğı 1 غی *cf.* **-gı 1.**
-ğı 2, -ği کی *ك* *archaic for* **-ki.**
-ği کی *cf.* **-gı 1.**

H

h, H the tenth letter of the alphabet.
ha 1 لا A 1. *in initial position* Oh, I see! Oh, yes. *e. g.,* **ha, anladım** Oh, yes, I understand. 2. *in final position* See! Now! Really! *e. g.,* **amma güzel ha!** Isn't it beautiful! **kazandılar ha?** They have won, haven't they? 3. *in final position* I warn you! *e. g.,* **sakın ha!** Beware! 4. *colloq.* What? What did you say?
ha 2 لا A 1. Well, go on. *e. g.,* **ha göreyim seni** Well, let us see what you can do. 2. *between repeated imperatives* on and on, in a burdensome way, *e. g.,* **çalış ha çalış** Go on working and working. 3. *in initial contraposition* either ... or, *e. g.,* **ha ben ha o!** Either I or he. 4. *preceding past and future forms of a verb resulting in the meaning* to be on the point of, *e. g.,* **ha düştü ha düşecek** He is nearly falling; he may fall any moment. 5. *colloq.* Yes. — **babam!,** — **babam ha!** 1. Push on; on with you; get on. 2. continuously, on and on. — **bire** nonstop, uninterruptedly. — **bugün ha yarın** any time, any day (said of the near future). — **deyince** at a moment's notice, at once. — **hoca Ali ha Ali hoca** It's all the same. — **şöyle** That's better; that's right. — **şunu bileydin** You've said it. That's right.
ha 3 ها A *name of the letter* ح. (This letter is the sixth letter of the Arabic, the eighth letter of the Ottoman alphabet, in Turkish pronouned as **h**. In chronograms, it has the numerical value of 8. In dates, it is the abbreviation for **Cumaziyül'ahir**.) —**yi menkuta,** —**yi mu'cema** the dotted خ. —**yi mühmele** the undotted ح.
-ha 4 (—) لا P *lrnd.*, *plural form* (for inanimate nouns) *e. g.,* **bağha** gardens.
-ha 5 (—) خا P *lrnd.* who chews, nibbler, *as in* **şekerha**, **jajha**.

hab[bbi] **1** حبّ A *same as* **hap.** —**i gar** *pharm.* laurel berries. —**i leziz** *var. of* **habbülaziz.** —**i sevda** *same as* **habbetüssevda.**
hâb 2 (—) خواب P *lrnd.* 1. sleep. 2. dream. 3. death. 4. stupor, lethargy. —**ı gaflet** indolent indifference. —**ı gurur** presumption. —**ı hargûş** (*lit.*, a hare's sleep) feigned sleep, pretended inattention; cheating; swindling.
habab (.—) حباب A *lrnd.* 1. bubbles; bubble. 2. dewdrops; dewdrop.
habab (.—.) حبابه A *lrnd.* 1. bubble 2. dewdrop.
habail (.—.) حبائل A *lrnd.*, *pl. of* **hibale.**
habais (.—.) خبائث A *lrnd.* abominable things.
habak[gi] حبق A pennyroyal, *bot.*, *Mentha pulegium.*
habalûd (———) خواب آلود P *lrnd.* sleepy, drowsy.
habaset (.—.) خباثت A *lrnd.* villainy, infamy, baseness.
habazan خبازان Romany *same as* **abazan.**
habbal[li] (.—) حبّال A *lrnd.* maker or seller of ropes.
habbat (.—) حبّات A *lrnd.*, *pl. of* **habbe.**
habbaz (.—) خبّاز A *lrnd.* baker.
habbaza (..—) حبّذا A *lrnd.* Wonderful; Lovely! Beautiful! How charming.
habbazi (.——) خبّازى P *lrnd.* bakery.
habbazin (.——) خبازين A *lrnd.*, *pl. of* **habbaz.** —**i hasse** *Ott. hist.* bakers in the Sultan's palace.
habbe حبّه A 1. grain, seed, kernel, berry. 2. *microscopy* small air bubble. —**si kalmadı** not a scrap left. —**yi kubbe yap**= to make a dome out of a speck.
habbetüssevda (....—) حبّة السوداء A *pharm.* black cumin, *bot.*, *Nigella sativa.*
habbülarûs (...—) حبّ العروس A *pharm.*

1. cubebs, seeds of *Piper cubeba.* 2. berries of *Physalis Alkekengi.*
habbülâs (..—) حبّ الآس A *pharm.* myrtle berries.
habbül'aziz (...—) حبّ العزيز A *pharm.* 1. seeds of Cassia. 2. seeds of the milk thistle, *bot., Cardinus Marianus.*
habbülban (..—) حبّ البان A *pharm.* 1. benniseed. 2. seeds of the horseradish tree.
habbülbelesan (....—) حبّ البلسان A *pharm.* berries of the balsanî tree, *Carpobalsamum.*
habbülesl حبّ الأثل A *pharm.* berries or galls of *Tamarix mannifera.*
habbülfehm حبّ الفحم A *pharm.* seeds of *Semecarpus anacardium.*
habbülfena (...—) حبّ الفنا A *pharm.* berries of black nightshade, *Solanum nigrum.*
habbülfücl حبّ الفجل A *pharm.* seed of *Raphanus oleiferus.*
habbülgamâm (...—) حبّ الغمام A *poet.* hailstone.
habbülgûl^{lü} (..—) حبّ الغول A *pharm.* fruit of the mastic tree *Pistacia lentiscus.*
habbülgurâb (...—) حبّ الغراب A *pharm.*, *nux vomica.*
habbülhâl^{li} (..—) حبّ الهال A *pharm.*, Cardamoms.
habbülkalb^{bi} حبّ القلب A *pharm.* puccoon, *Lithospermum.*
habbülkar 1 حبّ القرّ A *lrnd.* hailstones.
habbülkar^{rı} **2** حبّ القرع A 1. *pharm.* seeds of gourd or pumpkin. 2. *path.* intestinal worms, *ascarides.*
habbülkılkıl حبّ القلقل A *pharm.* seeds of wild pomegranate; seeds of *Cardiospermum Halicacabum;* seeds of *Cassia tora.*
habbülkilt حبّ القلت A *pharm.* seeds of *Dolichos uniflorus.*
habbülkutn حبّ القطن A *pharm.* cotton seeds.
habbüllehv حبّ اللهو A *pharm.* berries of Chinese lantern plant, *Physalis Alkekengi.*
habbülleziz (...—) حبّ اللذيذ A [**habbülaziz**] *pharm.* earthnut, earth chestnut, *bot., Carum bulbo castanum.*
habbülmisk^{ki} حبّ المسك A *pharm.* seeds of *Abelmoschus moschatus.*
habbülmülük^{kü} (...—) حبّ الملوك A *pharm.* 1. fruits of *Euphorbia nereifolia.* 2. fruit of the Baalbek cherry, *Cerasus Aproniniana.* 3. pine nuts. 4. castor beans, *Ricinus communis.* 5. croton seeds, seeds of *Croton tiglium.*
habbülmüzn حبّ المزن A *lrnd.* hailstones.
habbülyehud (...—) حبّ اليهود A same as **habbüllehv.**
habbürre's حبّ الرأس A *pharm.* seeds of stavesacre, *Delphinium Staphisagria* (used for destroying vermin on the head).

habbürreşad (...—) حبّ الرشاد A *lrnd.* garden cress.
habbüsselâtin (...— —) حبّ السلاطين *cf.* **abdüsselâtin.**
habe 1 (—.) هواء P *lrnd.* sleep, slumber.
habe 2 خابه Romany *slang* bread. —**den** for nothing, without payment, free, gratis. — **et=**, — **kay=**, — **uçlan=** to eat, to gulp down, to gobble up.
habeci خابه‌جي *slang* stupid; fool.
habel حبل A *lrnd.* pregnancy.
haber خبر A 1. news, information, message, tidings, rumor. 2. *gram.* predicate. 3. *lrnd.* anecdote, narrative, legend, story. —**i âhad** report related by a few individuals. — **al=** 1. to receive information; to make an inquiry. 2. to learn (the news). —**ini al=** /ın/ to hear, to learn, to get wind (of). — **alma** *mil.* intelligence; information. — **alma dairesi** *mil.* intelligence department. — **et=**, — **gönder=** /a/ to send news; to send a message. — **güvercini** *mil.* carrier pigeon, homing pigeon. —**i Hızrî** *lrnd.* news guessed at by the public. — **köpeği** *mil.* messenger dog. —**i meşhur** *Isl. rel.* tradition originally reported by only a few companions of the Prophet but thenceforward handed down by many. —**i mutevatir** *lrnd.* 1. well-substantiated information. 2. rumor generally current. 3. *Isl. rel.* a tradition of the Prophet reported by many and therefore undoubted. —**i ol=** /dan/ to be informed (of). —**i sadık** *theol.* true message, authentic tradition. — **sal=** /a/ to send news (to). —**in sıhhatini Lokmandan al=** to get information from the right source. — **sızdırma=** not to let any information leak out. — **sor=** /a/ to ask for news. — **toplama merkezi** *mil.* intelligence center. — **torbası** *mil.* information bag. — **uçur=** /a/ to send an urgent message. —**i vahit** *Isl. rel.* tradition supplied by only one person. —**im var** I know it. **bir — var mı?** Is there any news? Have you heard anything? — **ver=** /ı, a/ to announce (to), to inform (someone of something). — **yetiştir=** /a/ to send information. —**im yok** I know nothing about it. I haven't heard it. —**ci** messenger, herald, forerunner.
haberdar (..—) خبردار P *lrnd.* possessed of information. — **et=** /ı, dan/ to inform (someone of something).
habere خبره A *lrnd.* lady's garment or cloak of silk worn in some Arabian countries.
haberi (..—) خبري A *lrnd.* 1. pertaining to information. 2. *gram.* indicative (sentence); predicative (word, *etc.*). 3. historian.
haberleş=^{ir} خبرلشمك /la/ to correspond, to communicate (with one another). —**me** *verbal*

haberpijuh *n.* —**me sırrı** *law* secrecy of the postal service. —**tir**= /ı/ *caus. of* **haberleş**=.

haberpijuh (...—) مُخبر پژوه P *lrnd.* 1. seeker after information. 2. investigator of historical facts, legends or traditions.

haberşinas (...—) خبرشناس P *lrnd.* well informed in history and tradition.

habes خبث A *lrnd.* 1. filth, dirt, impurity, nastiness. 2. dross (of metal).

habese خبثه A *lrnd., pl. of* **habis 1.**

Habeş حبش A 1. an Abyssinian; *lrnd.* the Abyssinians. 2. *l. c.* dark, olive-colored, swarthy. — **maymunu** baboon. —**e** A *lrnd.* 1. Abyssinia. 2. the Abyssinians. —**î** (..—) A an Abyssinian; *hist.* Abyssinian slave. —**î ağa** *Ott. hist.* black eunuch in the Palace.

Habeşistan (...—) حبشستان P Abyssinia. —**lı** an Abyssinian.

habgâh (——) خوابگاه P *lrnd.* 1. bed. 2. bedroom.

habib (.—) حبيب A *lrnd.* friend, lover, beloved.

habibe (.—.) حبيبه A *lrnd.* beloved woman.

habibullah (.—.—) حبيب الله A the beloved of God, Muhammad.

habide (——.) خوابيده P *lrnd.* asleep. —**gân** (——.—) P sleepers.

habie (.—.) خبيئه A *lrnd.* hidden; hidden or unseen thing.

habike (.—.) حبيكه A *lrnd.* 1. streak, line. 2. the Milky Way.

Habil 1 (——) هابيل A *Bib.* Abel.

habil[bli] **2** حبل *var. of* **habl.**

habil 3 حبل A *lrnd.* 1. snared, tied. 2. brave, courageous, firm.

habil 4 (—.) هابل A *lrnd.* sorcerer.

habile (—..) هابله A *lrnd.* pregnant.

habir (.—) خبير A *lrnd.* 1. informed, aware. 2. learned, erudite. 3. *w. cap.* God omniscient. —**âne** (.——.) P learnedly, in an erudite manner.

habis 1 (.—) خبيث A 1. abominable, wicked, vicious; scoundrel. 2. *path.* malignant (tumor).

habis 2 (.—) حبس A *law* dedicated in mortmain to pious uses.

habis 3 (—.) حابس A *lrnd.* 1. that restrains or imprisons. 2. *law.* who dedicates in mortmain to pious uses.

Habisülfil (—..—) حابس الفيل A (*lit.* He who restrained the elephant) *Isl. Rel.* 1. God. 2. the Angel Gabriel who stopped the elephant of Abraha advancing against Mecca in the year the Prophet Muhammad was born.

hâbıt (—.) هابط *Or. mus., obs.* flat.

habl[li] حبل A *lrnd.* rope, cord; cable. —**i metin** *rel.* Islam. —**i sürrevi** *anat.* umbilical cord. —**i tabl** *anat., chorda tympani,* tympanichord.

Hablullah (..—) حبل الله A *Isl. rel.* (*lit.* the covenant of God) the Quran.

hablülverid (...—) حبل الوريد A *anat.* carotid artery.

habnak[ki] (——) خوابناك P *lrnd.* sleepy.

habr حبر A *lrnd.* 1. man of learning, scholar. 2. pious man. 3. Jewish rabbi. 4. bruise, scar.

habs حبس A *lrnd., same as* **hapis 1.** —**i bevl** *path.* retention of urine. —**i dem,** —**i nefes** retention of the breath as a spiritual exercise.

habt 1 حبط A *lrnd.* a silencing (somebody) in a discussion.

habt 2 ضبط A *lrnd.* mistake, error. —**ı dimağ** insanity. — **ü hata,** — **ü halel** blundering, mistake.

habtet=[der] ضبط ايتمك /ı/ to silence.

hac[cci] **1** حج pilgrimage to Mecca. —**ı asgar** the "lesser pilgrimage" (made in any year). —**ı ekber** the "greater pilgrimage" (in a year when the 9th of the month **Zilhicce** falls on a Friday). — **et**=*. —**a git**= to go on a pilgrimage to Mecca. —**ı İslâm** the pilgrimage to Mecca, the theoretical duty of every Muslim.

hâc[cci] **2** (—) حاج A *lrnd., same as* **hacı.**

hacalet (.—.) حجالت A shame, mortification.

hacamat حجامات |*Arabic* hacama| 1. a cupping. 2. *slang* slight wound. — **baltası** lancet for cupping. — **boynuzu** horn used instead of a cupping glass. — **et**= /ı/ 1. to cup. 2. *slang* to wound slightly. — **şişesi** cupping glass. — **zembereği** cupper's spring lancet-box. —**çı** cupper. —**la**= /ı/ *slang* to wound slightly.

hacat (——) حاجات A *lrnd., pl. of* **hacet.**

hacb حجب A *lrnd.* 1. a veiling, hiding, protecting. 2. a preventing, hindering; *law* a cutting off an heir from his portion.

Haccac (.—) حجاج A *name of a famous governor of Iraq known for his cruelty.*

haccam (.—) حجام A *lrnd.* bleeder, cupper, scarifier.

hacce (—.) حاجه A a woman pilgrim.

haccet=[der] حج ايتمك to go on pilgrimage.

hace (—.) خواجه P *lrnd.* 1. master of a household. 2. elder, superior, teacher. 3. ruler, magistrate. 4. *Ott. hist.* senior clerk of the government service. —**i âlem,** —**i dü serâ,** —**i kâinat** the Prophet Muhammad.

hacegân (—.—) خواجگان P *lrnd., pl. of* **hace.** —**ı Divan-ı Hümayûn** *Ott. hist., title given to the department chief of the Imperial chancery of State.*

hacegi (—.—) خواجگی P 1. *lrnd.* rank of a **hace.** 2. *archaic* wealthy merchant.

hacel حجل A *lrnd.* shame, a feeling of shame.

hacelik[ği] (—..) حاجملك *lrnd., abstr. noun of* **hace.**

hacer¹ حَجَر A *lrnd.* stone, rock, boulder. **—i ahmer** ruby. **—i billûr** rock crystal. **—i bürkâni** volcanic stone. **—i cahim** silver nitrate. **—i ebyaz** white stone, *lapis galactitis*. **—i Ermeni** lapis lazuli, *lapis armeniacus*. **—i esved** 1. the sacred black stone built into the southeastern corner of the Kaaba in Mecca. 2. *myst.* the nobility of human nature, soiled by human frailties. **—i fitile** asbestos. **—i kilye** renal calculus, nephritic stone. **—i mesane** bladder stone. **—i miknatisi** lodestone. **—i şem** stone used to detect poison. **—i semavi** meteorite. **— şecer makulesi** worthless things; the rabble. **—i şeceri** branched coral. **—i Yehud** lapis judaicus.
Hacer 2 (—.) حاجر A *Bib. and Isl. rel.* Hagar.
hacere حجره A *lrnd.* a single stone, rock.
haceri (..—) حجرى A *lrnd.* pertaining to stone, like stone. **—yet** (..—.) A quality of stone; stoniness.
haceröddem حجرالدم A *lrnd.* bloodstone.
hacerülbakar حجرالبقر A *zool.* a stone found in the gallbladder of an ox.
hacet (—.) حاجت A 1. need, requirement, necessity; a want of nature. 2. affair, business, matter. **— bağı** piece of cloth tied to the grating of the window of a saint's tomb for the fulfillment of a wish. **— dile=** to ask in prayer what is in one's heart. **— gör=** 1. to answer a need. 2. to relieve nature. **— kapısı, — penceresi** door or window of a saint's tomb where people pray for the fulfillment of wishes. **— yok** There is no need.
hacetmend (—..) حاجتمند P *lrnd.* in want, needy, necessitous. **—âne** (—..—.) P pertaining to one in need or poor. **—î** (—..—) P, **—lik** want, need, poverty.
hacı حاجى [hâc 2] 1. one who has performed the rites of the pilgrimage at Mecca, pilgrim, hadji. 2. Christian pilgrim to Jerusalem. 3. *title of respect sometimes used in addressing strangers.* **—m** my dear fellow. **— ağa** 1. a provincial nouveau-riche. 2. ostentatious squanderer. **— ağalık et=** to squander ostentatiously. **— baba** 1. an aged pilgrim. 2. a venerable old man. **— bayramı** celebration of a pilgrim's return from Mecca. **— bekler gibi bekle=** /i/ to wait impatiently (for someone). **H— Bektaş Oğulları** *Ott. hist.* the Janissaries. **H— Bektaş taşı** a kind of meerschaum. **H— Bektaş tuzu** kind of very fine salt; rock salt. **H— Bektaş-ı Veli** name of the founder of the Bektaşi order of dervishes, the patron of the Janissary Corps. **H— bey** *slang* an old absent-minded gentleman. **— fışfış** *a nickname for Arabs.* **— gözü** innocent eye, *as in* **bende o hacı gözü yok** I won't be taken in; you cannot cheat me. **— hanım** 1. Muslim woman who has performed the pilgrimage. 2. an elderly lady. **—sı hocası** all members of the Muslim clergy. **— kadın** *same as* **hacı hanım. — lokumu** Turkish delight offered at the celebration of a pilgrim's return. **— otu** mandrake, *bot., Mandragora officinarum.* **H— Pintoros'a kavuş=** *slang* to be beaten. **— tehniyesi** *same as* **hacı bayramı. — yağı** kind of heavy perfume. **—lar yolu** the Milky Way.
hacimᶜᵐ¹ حجم [hacm] 1. volume, bulk, size. 2. *naut.* tonnage.
hacıyatmaz حاجى يتماز 1. tumbler (toy). 2. restless, mischievous urchin. 3. resilient (person).
hacib (—.) حاجب A 1. *hist.* doorkeeper; usher; chamberlain to a prince, a mayor of the palace. 2. *poet.* eyebrow. 3. *anat.* separating or enclosing membrane. **H—i bar** the Archangel Gabriel. **—eyn** (—.—) A the two eyebrows.
hacif (.—) حجيف A *lrnd.* rumbling in the bowels.
hacil حجل A *lrnd.* confused with shame, ashamed, mortified.
hacim حجم [hacm] *same as* **hacım**.
hacir 1 (—.) حاجر A *lrnd.* 1. who emigrates, emigrant. 2. superior, excellent.
hacir 2 (—.) حاجر A *lrnd.* 1. a high bank of a river or valley. 2. a wall between houses.
hacirᶜʳⁱ **3** حجر *var. of* **hacr.**
hacis (—.), **hacise** (—..) حاجس حاجسه A *lrnd.* that occurs to the mind (thought).
Hacivat (.—.) حاجيوات one of the main characters of the Karagöz shadow play.
hacizᶜᶻⁱ **1** حجز [hacz] *law* distraint, sequestration, seizure. **— altına al=** /i/ to sequestrate. **—i caiz olmıyan mallar** non-distrainable chattels. **— kararı** warrant of distraint.
haciz 2 (—.) حاجز A 1. *law* distrainer. 2. *lrnd.* that intervenes and separates.
hacle حجله A *lrnd.* bridal chamber. **—gâh** (..—) P bridal chamber.
haclet حجلت A *lrnd.*, *same as* **hacalet.**
hacm حجم A *same as* **hacım. —en** (.'.) A in size or volume.
hacr حجر A *law* a putting under restraint (legally incompetent person). **— et=** /i/ to place under the care of a guardian. **—en** (.'.) A by putting under restraint.
hâcülharemeyn (—...—) حاج الحرمين A *rel.* pilgrim who has visited both Mecca and Medina.
haczᶻⁱ حجز A *same as* **haciz 1.**
haçᶜⁱ حاچ خاچ *Christ. rel.* the Cross. **— çıkar=** to make the sign of the cross, to cross oneself. **—a ger=** /i/ to crucify. **—ı suya atma yortusu** Epiphany (the feast of casting the cross into the water, Jan. 6th).

haçan هچان archaic, var. of **kaçan**.
haçla=ʳ خاچلامق /ı/ to crucify.
haçlı خاچلی 1. having a cross. 2. crusader. **— seferi** Crusade.
haçvari (. — —) خاچواری cross-shaped, crosswise.
hadᵈᵈⁱ **1** حدّ A 1. limit, boundary; limit of moderation; end, extremity, point, margin, degree. 2. hindrance, obstacle. 3. *math.* term. 4. *can. law* punishment. **—im mi?** Dare I? I don't dare. **— ve addi yok, — ve adedi yok** There is no limit to it. **—i asgar** *log.* the minor term of a syllogism. **—i asgari tesir** *psych.* minimum sensible. **—ini aş=** to go too far, to overstep the limit. **—den aşırı** excessive, exaggerated. **—ini bil=** to know one's place. **—ini bildir=** /a/ to put (someone) in his place. **—ini bilme=** to presume. **—ini bilmez** presumptuous, impertinent. **—i bülûğ** age of puberty. **— çiz=** /a/ to set a limit (to). **—im değil** I wouldn't dare; it isn't for me to say. **—ine mi düşmüş?** He wouldn't dare. **—den efzun** excessive. **—i ekber** *log.* major term of a syllogism. **—ine er=, —ine eriş=** to reach its utmost limit of growth or perfection. **—i evsat** *log.* middle term of a syllogism. **—i fâsıl** *lrnd.* boundary. **—inden fazla** excessive. **—i hakiki** *log.* essential definition of a term. **— ve hudut bilmez** knowing no bounds, immoderate. **—i imkân** the measure of possibility. **—i istiabî** capacity, limit of capacity. **—i itidalde** moderate, reasonable. **bir —e kadar** to a certain extent. **—i kifayeyi bul=** to be sufficient. **—i lafzî** *log.* nominal definition. **—i mâruf** proper limit, the usual limit. **—i müşterek** the common border of two adjacent things. **—den mütecaviz** *obs.* beyond all bounds, excessive. **—im olmıyarak** if I may say so. **—i tâbir** the power of expression and description. **—ini tecavüz et=** to go too far, to be impudent. **—i teklif** *law* the limit or time when a minor or madman becomes responsible for his actions. **—i varsa** if he dares. **— vur=** *can. law* to inflict punishment; to flog. **—im yok** I have no right, I don't dare. **—i zatında** really, essentially, in point of fact, in itself. **—den ziyade** excessively, beyond the limit.
hâdᵈᵈⁱ **2** (—) حادّ A 1. *med.* acute; *geom.* acute (angle). 2. *Or. mus.* the highest string of a stringed instrument.
hadᵈᵈⁱ **3** (—) خدّ A *poet.* cheek.
hadaa خدعه A *lrnd., pl. of* **hadi 3**.
hadaikᵏⁱ (. — .) حدائق A *lrnd., pl. of* **hadika**.
hadaka حدقه A *same as* **hadeka**.
hadaki حدقی A *same as* **hadekî**. **—i hâssa** *Ott. hist.* the imperial gardens.

hadaret 1 (.—.) حضارت A *lrnd.* modesty; a woman's keeping herself veiled.
hadaret 2 (.—.) حضارت A *lrnd.* greenness.
hadaset (.—.) حداثت A *lrnd.* youth, newness. **—i sin** youth.
hadbe حدبه A *anat.* protuberance.
haddaᵃ¹ (.—) خدّاع A *lrnd.* cheat, impostor.
haddad (.—) حدّاد A *lrnd.* 1. blacksmith. 2. doorkeeper. 3. jailor.
haddam (.—) خدّام A *lrnd.* servant.
haddan (.—) حدّان P *poet., dual of* **had 3**, cheeks.
haddas (.—) حدّاس A *lrnd.* who conjectures much or habitually.
hadde حدّه [*Arabic* **hadida**] 1. rolling mill. 2. wire-drawer's plate. **—den çek=** /ı/ to examine carefully. **—den geçir=** 1. to roll (metals). 2. to examine minutely. **—i tetkikten geçir=** /ı/ to examine minutely. **—hâne** (..—.) rolling-mill.
hadeb 1 حدب A *lrnd.* 1. tallness and stupidity. 2. presumption.
hadeb 2 حدب A *lrnd.* 1. hump. 2. mound, ridge, protuberance. 3. tumor, swelling (from a blow). **—at** (..—) A *astr.* protuberances.
hadebe حدبه A *lrnd.* 1. hump on the back. 2. slope of land, ridge. 3. curvature of the spine.
hadebiyet (..—.) حدبیت A *lrnd.* hunchbackedness.
hadec حدج A *lrnd.* colocynth, bitter apple, *bot., Citrullus colocynthis*.
haded حدد A *lrnd.* hindrance, obstacle, prohibition.
hadeka حدقه A 1. *anat.* pupil. 2. *lrnd.* dark part of the eye; eye; eyeball.
hadekî (..—) حدقی A *anat.* pupillary.
hadem خدم A *lrnd., pl. of* **hâdim 1**. **— ü haşem** servants and attendants, retinue.
hademe خدمه A servant (in government offices, schools, etc.) **—i hassa** *Ott. hist.* officials of the Sultan's palace. **—i hayrat** *adm.* personnel of religious institutions. **—i şahane** *Ott. hist.* officials of the Sultan's palace.
hadeng خدنگ P *poet.* arrow.
hader 1 خدر A *lrnd.* numbness, torpidity; sluggishness.
hader 2 حدر A *lrnd.* a squinting; an eye's running with tears.
hades 1 حدث A *lrnd.* 1. novelty. 2. religious innovation. 3. accident. 4. physical accident that causes canonical impurity, as the issue of any impure substance from the body.
hades 2 حدث A *lrnd.* young, youthful.
hadesan (.—) حدثان A *lrnd.* misfortune, accident, casualty, disaster.
hadesat (...—) حدثات A *lrnd., pl. of* **hades 1**.
hadım خادم [**hadim**] eunuch. **— ağası** *Ott.*

hist. chief eunuch in the Sultan's palace. — et≡, —laştır≡ /ı/ to castrate.

hadımlaştırma خادملشدیرمه‌سی *law* castration.

hadi 1 (..ˊ) قادی same as **haydi**. — **hadi!** Enough! Stop it! — **ordan** Off with you.

hadi 2 (— —) هادی A *lrnd*. 1. one who shows the right way, God. 2. beginning. 3. head of a spear. **H—i Sebil** the Prophet Muhammad.

hadi⁽ⁱⁱ⁾ 3 (—.) خادع A *lrnd*. 1. deceiver, cheat. 2. bad, foul.

hadi 4 (— —) حادی A *lrnd*. 1. camel driver. 2. person or thing that drives or excites to action.

hadi 5 (—.) حادی A *in compound numbers, lrnd.* first. — **aşer** eleventh.

hadia (— ..) خادعه A *lrnd*. trick, cheat, deceit, fraud.

Hadice (. —.) خدیجه A Khadija (the Prophet Muhammad's first wife).

hadid 1 (. —) حدید A *lrnd*. 1. violent, irascible. 2. sharp, keen, sharp-pointed. 3. shrewd, intelligent, piercing, penetrating.

hadid 2 (. —) حدید A *lrnd*. iron; steel. **H— Suresi** *name of the fifty-ninth sura of the Quran.*

hadid 3 (. —) حضیض A same as **haziz**.

hadidî (. — —) حدیدی, **hadidiye** (. — — .) حدیدیه A *lrnd*. of iron; made of iron.

hadidülbasar (. — ...) حدیدالبصر A *lrnd*. keen, sharp-sighted.

hadidülmizac (. — .. —) حدیدالمزاج A *lrnd*. irascible, irritable, excitable.

hadife (—..) خادفه A *lrnd*. body of people, crowd.

hadika (. —.) حدیقه A *poet*. garden, park, orchard.

Hadikatül'ervah (. — ...—) حدیقةالارواح A "garden of spirits" (mausoleums in Konya).

hadil (—.) هادل A *lrnd*. hanging, suspended.

hadim 1 (—.) خادم A *lrnd*. 1. manservant. 2. /a/ serving.

hadim 2 (—.) هادم A *lrnd*. destroying, demolishing, ruining.

hadimüllezzat (— ...—) هادم اللذات A *lrnd*. death, angel of death.

hadin (. —) ضین A *lrnd*. friend, companion.

hadis 1 (. —) حدیث A *Isl. rel.* 1. record of a saying or action of the Prophet Muhammad, handed down by his companions, tradition; the study of the tradition of the words and deeds of the Prophet. 2. *lrnd*. story, narrative, anecdote. 3. *lrnd*. new, fresh, recent, modern, young, innovated, invented. **—i alil** a tradition apparently genuine but having some obscurity in the text or in the chain of authorities. **—i aziz** a tradition reported by only two or three. **—i ferd**, **—i garib** tradition reported at some length by only one person. **—i hasen** a probable tradition not sufficiently authenticated. **—i ilâhi** an extra-quranic tradition related by the Prophet Muhammad as communicated by God. **—i makbul** a tradition received and accepted by the learned as geniune. **—i maklûb** a tradition in the text of which a permutation of letters has been made, or where the text is assigned to a wrong chain of reporters. **—i maktu** a tradition regarding a saying or action of one of the second generation after the Prophet Muhammad. **—i mâlûl** *same as* **hadisi alil**. **—i maruf** a weak tradition that conflicts with another still weaker called **münker**. **—i merfu** a tradition that directly attributes to the Prophet a saying or act. **—i meşhur** a tradition reported by three or more reliable authorities; a tradition unanimously received of old by the learned. **—i mevkûf** a tradition that relates a statement or action of a companion. **—i mevkûf ve mukayyed** a tradition that relates what a reporter later than the second generation after the Prophet Muhammad attributed to a companion. **—i mevsul** *same as* **hadisi muttasıl**. **—i mevzu** fabricated tradition. **—i muallâk** a tradition with no chain of authorities. **—i muallel** *same as* **hadisi alil**. **—i muan'an** a tradition in which the relater gives the name of the authority without stating whether he received it from him personally. **—i mu'del** a tradition in which two or more links in the chain of reporters are wanting. **—i muharref** a tradition in which a letter of different shape or a case vowel has been substituted. **—i munkati** a tradition in which there is a hiatus in the chain of evidence. **—i musahhaf** a tradition in which a dot or dots are incorrectly added or omitted. **—i mutel** *same as* **hadisi alil**. **—i muttasıl** a tradition with a complete chain of transmitters. **—i muztarib** a tradition reported with a variation by perfectly equal authorities. **—i müdelles** a tradition where a reporter tries by subterfuge to strengthen a chain of evidence. **—i müdrec** a tradition into which something has been interpolated. **—i münkalib** *same as* **hadisi maklub**. **—i münker** a tradition at variance with another weak but preferable tradition. **—i mürsel** a tradition originating with a reporter of the second generation without mention of the companion from whom it was received. **—i müselsel** a tradition reported without variation by every reporter. **—i müsned** a tradition with complete chain of trustworthy transmitters. **—i müstefiz** a tradition universally reported from the earliest times. **—i mütevatir** a tradition of wide circulation. **—i nebevî** a tradition attributed

hadis

to the Prophet without his having said it was of divine origin. **—i sahih** authentic tradition. **—i saz** a tradition that conflicts with what is authenticated. **—i zaidüssikka** a tradition with a word or so more than is fully authenticated. **—i zaif** defectively transmitted tradition.

hadis 2 (—.) حادث A *lrnd*. 1. new, fresh, recent. 2. newly coming into existence. 3. not eternal as to past. **— dâva** *law* incidental claim. **— ol=** to come into existence, to occur, to spring up.

hâdisat (—.—) حادثات A *lrnd.*, pl. of **hâdise**, *phil.* phenomena.

hâdise (—..) حادثه A 1. event, incident, occurrence. 2. accident, mishap. 3. *phil.* phenomenon. **— çıkar=** to provoke an incident. **—cilik** *phil.* phenomenalism. **—vî** (—..—) A *phil.* phenomenal.

hadisül'ahd (.—..) حديث العهد A *lrnd.* of recent date.

hadnaşinas (.—.—) حدناشناس P *lrnd.* who does not know his place, impudent.

hadra (.—) حضرا A 1. *same as* **hazra**. 2. *Or. mus.* an extinct makam.

Hadramut حضرموت *geog.* Hadhramaut (middle region of South Arabia).

hadsˢⁱ حدس A *phil.* intuition. **—çilik** *phil.* intuitionism.

hadsî (.—) حدسی A *phil.* intuitive. **—yat** (.——) A things known by intuition.

hadsiz حدسز unlimited, unbounded. **— hesapsız** innumerable, countless.

hadşe حدشه A *lrnd.* 1. scratch. 2. disquietude (of mind). **—i derûn**, **—i hatır** anxiety, suspicion.

haf حاف E *sports* half-back.

hafa (.—) خفاء A *lrnd.* concealment, secrecy.

hafair (.—.) خفائر A pl. of **hafire 1**.

hafakan (..—) خفقان A palpitation. **—lar basıyor**, **—lar boğuyor** (I, he, etc.) feel exasperated.

hafaya (.——) خفایا A *lrnd.*, pl. of **hafî 1**. **—yı umur** the secret side of events.

hafaza حفظه A *lrnd.*, pl. of **hâfız 1**.

hafazanallah (....—) حفظنا الله A May God protect us (used when talking about a misfortune).

hafe (—.) حافه A *lrnd.* seashore, bank; border, edge. **—i nehr** river bank. **—i tarik** wayside.

haffaf (.—) حفاف A *lrnd.*, same as **kavaf**.

hafıkᵏⁱ **1** (.—) خافی A quivering, fluttering, vibrating.

hafıkᵏⁱ **2**. (.—) خافی A *lrnd.* 1. place of sunset or sunrise. 2. one of the four cardinal points of the horizon.

hafıkeyn (—..) خافقین A *lrnd.* Orient and Occident.

hâfız (—.) حافظ A 1. one who knows the whole Quran by heart. 2. *slang* simpleton, fool. 3. *lrnd.* one who commits to memory. 4. *lrnd.* keeper, protector, guardian, God. **H—ı hakiki** God; the true preserver. **—ı kütüp** librarian. **—ı Mesnevi** one who knows the Mesnevi by heart. **H—ı Mutlak** God. **H— Paşa topu** locally manufactured gun invented by Hafız Pasha during the Crimean War (1854). **H—ı Şirazî** the Persian poet Hafiz of Shiraz.

hâfıza (—..) حافظه A 1. memory. 2. *lrnd.* woman who knows the whole Quran by heart. **—vî** (—..—) mnemonic.

hafızapîra (—..——) حافظه پیرا P *lrnd.* 1. adorning the memory. 2. learned by heart for pleasure.

hafî 1 (.—) خفی A *lrnd.* secret; hidden; private; unknown; undiscovered. **— ve celî** secret and open; hidden and discovered. **— celse** *law* secret session.

hafî 2 (——) حافی A *lrnd.* 1. who shows joy at meeting another. 2. who goes barefooted.

hafîd (.—) حفید A *lrnd.* grandson. **—e** (.—.) A granddaughter.

hafif 1 (.—) خفیف A 1.*lrnd.*, same as **hafif 2**. 2. *pros.* meter which changes from trochee to iamb (most commonly : —.——/.—.—/..—) 3. *Or. mus.* a rhythmic pattern of 32 beats.

hafif 2 خفیف [hafif 1] 1. light in weight. 2. light in degree; slight. 3. flighty, amoral, light-headed. 4. *slang* penniless, pauper. **—ten al=** /ı/ *slang* to take (things) lightly. **— birlik** *mil.* light unit. **— donanma** same as **ince donanma**. **— hapis** *law* imprisonment without hard labor. **— para cezası** *law* fine, penalty. **— tertip** lightly, slightly.

hafifle=ʳ خفیفلمك 1. to diminish; to lose weight. 2. to become relieved. **—n=**, **—ş=** 1. to become lighter, to diminish. 2. to become flighty, to become light-headed. **—ştir=**, **—t=** /ı/ to lighten.

hafiflikᵍⁱ خفیفلك 1. lightness, slightness, mildness. 2. relief, ease of mind. 3. flightiness.

hafifmeşrepᵇⁱ خفیف مشرب P flighty, frivolous.

hafifse=ʳ خفیفسمك /ı/ 1. to take lightly (things). 2. to consider unimportant.

hâfir 1 (—.) حافر A *lrnd.* 1. excavator. 2. uncloven hoof.

hafir 2 (.—) حفیر A *lrnd.* 1. wide pit; hollow, cavity, ditch. 2. grave.

hafirᶠʳⁱ **3** حفر *var.* of **hafr**.

hafire 1 (.—.) حفیره A *lrnd.*, same as **hafir 2**.

hâfire 2 (—..) حافره A *lrnd.* 1. woman excavator. 2. the first moment of a meeting.

hafiyat (.—-—) هفيات A *lrnd.* secret things. **—ı umur** the secret side of affairs.
hafiye هفيه A detective, secret agent.
hafiyeten (.—´..), **hafiyyen** (.—´.) هفية A *lrnd.* secretly, stealthily; privately.
hafîz (.—) هفيظ A *lrnd.* protector, keeper, God. **— Allah** God forbid!
hafr حفر A *lrnd.* a digging, excavation. **— et=** /ı/ to dig, to excavate.
hafriyat (..—) حفريات A excavation, excavations.
hafta هفته P week. **—larca** for weeks. **—sına** a week from today. **—ya** in a week's time, next week. **— arasında** during the week. **— başı** the first day of the week. **—da bir** once a week, weekly. **— günü** weekday. **— içinde** during the week. **—sına kalmaz** within a week. **— sekiz gün dokuz** very frequently. **— sonu, — tatili** week end.
haftalık[gı] 1. weekly; per week. 2. weekly wages. 3. weekly paper, a weekly. **—çı, —lı** workman paid by the week.
haftan (.—) هفتان P *lrnd.,* same as **kaftan.**
haftaym هافتايم E *sports* half time.
hah 1 هه There! Now! exactly.
hah 2 (—) خواه P *lrnd.* who wishes; e. g., **bedhah, hayırhah.**
haham خاخام Heb Jewish rabbi. **— başı** the chief Rabbi (of Istanbul). **—lık** rabbinate.
hâhân (——) خواهان *lrnd.* desirous, willing.
hâhende (—..) خواهنده P *lrnd.* desirous.
hâher (—.) خواهر P *lrnd.* sister. **— zâde** (—.—.) P sister's son, nephew.
hahha, hahhah (.—) هاها هاها Ha! Haha! **— güleyim bari** What a joke!
hâhiş (—.) خواهش P *lrnd.* wish, desire, will, inclination. **—ger** P desirous. **—geri** (—..—) P desire, willingness. **—mend** (—..) P desirous.
hâhnâhâh (———) خواه نا خواه P *lrnd.* unwillingly, like it or not, will-nilly.
hâib 1 (—.) خائب A *lrnd.* disappointed, frustrated; unsuccessful. **— u hâsır** frustrated and confounded, disappointed.
hâib 2 (—.) خائب A *lrnd.* fearful, timid.
hâiben (—´..) خائباً A *lrnd.* disappointedly; unsuccessfully.
haic (—.) خائج A *lrnd.* excited, furious, raging.
haif 1 (—.) خائف A *lrnd.* fearing, anxious.
haif 2 (—.) حائف A *lrnd.* unjust, cruel, tyrannical.
hail 1 (—.) حائل A 1. *phys.* curtain, screen. 2. *law* enclosure. 3. *lrnd.* obstacle, hindrance; obstruction, barrier. **— ol=** /a/ to intervene, to interpose; to block the way.
hail 2 (—.) هائل A *lrnd.* fearful, frightful.
haile (—..) هائلة [*based on Arabic*] *lrnd.,* *theat.* tragedy, drama. **—nüvis** (—...—) P tragedian.
haim (—.) هائم A *lrnd.* 1. astonished, confused, distracted. 2. distracted with love.
hain (—.) خائن A 1. treacherous, traitor. 2. deceitful. 3. ungrateful. 4. mischievous. **—i nân u nemek** *lrnd.* ungrateful to his host or master. **—âne** (—.—.) P, **—ce, —cesine** treacherously, ungratefully.
hainleş=[ir] خائنلشمك to become treacherous.
hainlik[ği] خائنلك treachery, perfidy.
hair (—.) حائر A *lrnd.* confused, confounded; bewildered. **— bair, — ü bair** confused and bewildered, astonished, stupified.
hait (—.) حائط A *lrnd.* wall; fence; railing.
haiz (—.) حائز A /ı/ 1. containing, obtaining, possessing. 2. provided (with). **—i ehemmiyet** of importance. **— ol=** /a/ to possess.
hak[kkı] 1 حق A 1. the right; justice, equity, law; right, just. 2. a right; due, share; remuneration, fee. 3. truth; true. 4. *w. cap.* God. **—ında*. —ını al=** to get one's due; to take one's share. **—ını ara=** to insist on one's due. **H— âşığı** lover of God, righteous (person). **— bu ki** The rights of the matter are, in fact. **H— celle celâlühü** God, whose majesty be exalted. **—ı civar** neighbor's right. **H— dini** Islam, the true religion. **— et=*. — erenler** men of God, devout and fair-minded people. **—ından gel=** /ın/ 1. to manage successfully. 2. to pay somebody back, to punish. **— getire** There isn't any, e. g., **onda akıl hak getire** He doesn't have any brains at all. **—ı haket=** to do justice, to render justice. **—ı hayat** the right to live. **—ımı helal ettim** I have given it to you whole-heartedly; I wish you good luck with it; may you enjoy what I've given you. **—ı hiyar** *law* benefit of option. **—ı huzur** daily attendance allowance. **—ı ibâd** *lrnd.* a right due from man to man. **—ı için** *formula of adjuration* for the sake of, e. g., **Allah hakkı için** for God's sake. **—ı intifa** *law* the right of using, usufruct. **—ı kadem** pay for travelling, house call fee. **— kazan=** /a/ 1. to deserve, to earn, to have the right (of). 2. to prove right, to be justified. **— kuran** same as **hakuran. — kuşu** hoopoe, *zool., Upupa epops.* **—ı mürûr** *law* right of way. **—ı nân u nemek** loyalty, gratitude. **—ı nâr** *law* remedy, tolerance, allowance of weight of fineness (coinage). **—ı nefs** anything necessary for the preservation of life. **—ı ödenmez** Nothing can repay him. **H—ın rahmetine kavuş=, H—ın rahmetine yürü=** to die. **—ı rüçhan** *law* right of priority. **— sahibi** *law* holder of a right. **— sever** just; truth-loving. **— söz acıdır** Truth is bitter. **—ı sükût** hush money. **H— süpha-**

hâk

nehü ve taalâ God whose praises I recite, the Exalted. **H— Taalâ** God Almighty. **—ı takdim** *law* right of priority. **—ı talep** *law* right of claim. **— tanır** just, rightful; righteous. **—ı tapu** *Ott. hist.* the rights by which crown land is held by a proprietor. **—ı tarik** *law* public right of way. **H— tebâreke ve taalâ** God, may he be hallowed and exalted. **—ı telif** *law* copyright. **—ını teslim et=** /ın/ to concede that (someone) is right. **— üzere, — üzre** rightfully, justly. **—ı var** /ın/ He is right. **— vere!** *same as* **Hak getire. — ver=** /a/ to acknowledge (somebody) to be right. **—ını ver=** /ın/ 1. to give one one's due. 2. *slang* to give (one) a beating. **H—ı yakin** God. **— ye=** to be unjust. **—ını ye=** /ın/ to cheat, to do an injustice (to). **— yerini bulur** The truth will out; justice will prevail. **— yerde kalmaz** Justice will always prevail. **— yolu** the way of right, justice. **H— yolu** the spiritual way, the path of God. **H— yoluna** for God.

hâk[ki] **2** (—) خاك P *lrnd.* 1. earth; soil; dust. 2. world. 3. grave, tomb. **— ü âb** *poet.* the human body. **— berleb** 1. dead; silent. 2. dim (light); humble. **— berser** grieved and mourning. **—i helâke ser=** to spread on the ground (in death). **— ile yeksan et=** to raze to the ground. **—i kadem, —i pay** the dust under foot. **—i payiniz** your presence; you. **—i paye gel=** to come (into the presence of the person addressed). **—i paye yüz sür=** to pay one's respects (to a superior). **—i rengin** *poet.* 1. gold, silver. 2. bed of flowers. 3. man. **—i siyah** *poet.* the black earth (of the grave). **—i sürme** native ore of antimony. **—i teng** *poet.* grave, tomb. **—i tîre** *poet.* 1. the black earth (of the grave). 2. the world. **—i zaif** *poet.* man.

hak[kki] **3** خلّ A 1. an engraving, incising. 2. an erasing. **— et=***.

hakaik[ki] (. — .) خقائن A *lrnd., pl. of* **hakikat.**

hakalûd (———) خاك آلود P *poet.* soiled, dirtied, begrimed.

hakan (——) خاقان P khan, Sultan; emperor. **—ı berreyn u bahreyn** Ruler of two continents and two seas (a title of the Ottoman Sultan).

hakanî (———) خاقانى P imperial. **— helvası** homemade milk pudding. **— kös** a kind of drum. **—yân** (————) P *lrnd.* sovereigns.

hakanlık[ğı] خاقانلق emperorship.

hakaret (. — .) خقارت A insult, contempt. **—âmiz** insulting, scornful. **— et=** /a/ to insult. **— gör=** /dan/ to be insulted (by a person).

hakâşina (. — . —) خاك آشنا P *lrnd.* he who recognizes right and truth.

hakbin (.—) حق بين P *lrnd.* seeing God, perceiving the Almighty. **—âne** (. — — .) P justly, rightfully. **—lik** *abstr. n.*

hâkbiz (— —) خاك بيز P *lrnd.* 1. sifter of dust. 2. diligent inquirer.

hâkbûs (— —) خاك بوس P *lrnd.* kissing the feet (in respect of entreaty).

hakcû (.—) حق جو P *lrnd.* 1. who seeks after right, just. 2. truth-seeking.

hakça حقجه rightly. **—sı** the truth of it.

hâkdân (— —) خاكدان P *lrnd.* 1. dust hole; dust heap. 2. the world. **—ı dev, —ı fena, —ı gurûr** the world.

hakdâr (.—) حق دار P *lrnd.* 1. who has the right in a dispute. 2. who has a claim to a thing.

hakdil (— .) خاكدل P *lrnd.* worldly minded.

hakem حكم A referee; umpire, arbitrator. **— encümeni** *law* arbitration committee. **— kararı** *law* arbitral award, arbitration. **— mahkemesi** *law* court of arbitration. **—lik** state of being a referee.

hâkeza (— . —) هكذا A *lrnd.* also, likewise.

hakgû (.—) حق گو P *lrnd.* speaking the truth, plain-spoken.

hakgüzâr (. . —) حق گزار P *lrnd.* administering justice, loyal to the right.

hâki 1 (— —) خاكى P 1. khaki. 2. *lrnd.* earthy, terrestrial.

hâki 2 (— —) حاكى 'A *lrnd.* storyteller, narrator; narrating.

hakibe (. — .) حقيبه A *lrnd., same as* **heybe.**

hakik[kı] **1** (.—) عقيق *var. of* **akik 1.**

hakik[kı] **2** (.—) حقيق A *lrnd.* 1. deserving, worthy, competent. 2. rightful, right.

hakikat[ti] (. — .) حقيقت A 1. truth; reality, fact; true statement, true; real; truly, really. 2. sincerity, loyalty. 3. *myst.* spritual vision of God by a believer; belief and confession of God's unity. **—i akliye** *lrnd.* the literal sense of an expression. **—i âlem** *myst.* a qualified entity, world, universe. **—i ehadiye** *myst.* God, the sole entity. **— ehli** *myst.* a mystic. **—i eşya** *phil.* noumenon. **—i hal** *lrnd.* the truth of the matter, the true state of the case. **—i halde** as a matter of fact. **— hükmü** *phil.* judgment of reality. **—i ilâhiye** the reality of God. **—i kasıra** *rhet.* a figurative expression susceptible of more meanings than one. **—i lûgaviye** *same as* **hakikati akliye. —i Muhammediye** the true essence of Islam. **—i mukayyide** *myst.* a qualified entity, world, universe. **—i mutlaka** *myst.* God, the unqualified entity. **—i örfiye** *rhet.* an expression whose figurative meaning is conventionally accepted as literal. **—i şer'iye** *law* a word or thing canonically defined.

hakikatbin (.—.—) مققتبين P lrnd. right, true, just.
hakikaten (.—..) مققتة A really, truly.
hakikatgû (.—.—) مققتگو P lrnd. right, true, just.
hakikatli (.—..) مققتى faithful, true; sincere and constant, loyal.
hakikatniyuş (.—..—) مققت نيوش P lrnd. listening to the truth.
hakikatperest (.—...) مققت پرست P lrnd. lover of justice, standing for the truth and right.
hakikatsiz (.—..) مققتسز unfaithful, inconstant, disloyal, false in friendship. —**lik** unfaithfulness, disloyalty.
hakikatşinas (.—..—) مققت شناس P lrnd. knowing the truth. —**âne** (.—..——.) P intelligently, in a manner of knowing the truth. —**î** (.—.——) P, —**lık** recognition of truth.
hakikatülemr (.—...) مققت الامر A lrnd. the truth of the matter.
hakikatülhakaik (.—...—.) مققت الحقائق A lrnd. 1. God, the essence of essences. 2. *myst.* the annihilation of the consciousness of all things, including God.
hakiki (.——) مققى A 1. true, real; genuine; sincere, unfeigned. 2. essential; concrete. 3. *log.* objective (proposition); alternative (disjunctive hypothetical proposition). — **adet** *math.* real number. — **itidal** *astr.* true equinox. — **şahıs** *law* natural person.
hakikiye (.——.) مققيه [based on Arabic] *phil.* realism.
hakikiyun (.———) مققيون [based on Arabic] *phil.* realists.
hâkim 1 (—.) حاكم A 1. ruler, governor; /a/ dominating, ruling (over). 2. judge, magistrate. 3. /a/ overlooking. —**i hakiki** God. —**ler heyeti** *law* bench of justices. — **kıl=** /ı, a/ to cause to dominate. H—**i lemyezel** *rel.* the eternal God. — **muavini** assessor, assistant judge. H—**i mutlak** God almighty, the absolute judge of all. —**i münferit** *law* single judge. — **namzedi** judicial assistant, prospective judge. — **ol=** /a/ to dominate, to rule (over), to be master (of), to prevail. —**in reddi** *law* recusation, rejection of a judge. —**i şer'** judge of the canon law of Islam. —**i vakt** *lrnd.* ruler of the time. — **vasıf** dominant character.
hakîm 2 (.—) حكيم A *lrnd.* 1. sage, of great wisdom; philosopher. 2. God. 3. physician, doctor of medicine. —**i mutlak** the Absolutely-Wise God.
hâkimane 1 (—.—.) حاكمانه P as befits a ruler, lordly.
hakimane 2 (.——.) حكيمانه P wise, philosophical (word, act); wisely, philosophically.
hâkimiyet (—...) حاكميت A sovereignty; domination, rule. —**i milliye** sovereignty of the nation. — **muamelesi** *law* act of state, act of sovereignty. —**in tahdidi** limitations on sovereignty.
hâkimlikᵍⁱ (—..) حاكملك 1. judgeship; rulership. 2. domination.
hâkimüşşer (—...) حاكم الشرع A *can. law* judge of the canon law of Islam.
hakinihad (——.—) خاك نهاد P lrnd. lowly by nature, humble.
hakir (.—) حقير A 1. insignificant, small, trifling; of no account. 2. mean, low, despicable. 3. your humble servant. — **gör=** /ı/ to despise, to hold in contempt. — **ü nakir** *lrnd.* a nothing, a nobody. —**âne** (.——.) P humbly.
hakister (—.—) خاكستر P lrnd. ashes.
hakiyan 1 (—.—) خاكيان P lrnd., pl. of **hâki 1²**.
hakiyan 2 (—.—) حاكيان P lrnd., pl. of **hâki 2**.
hakka 1 (.—) حقا A *lrnd.* in truth.
hakka 2 (—.) حاقه A *lrnd.* 1. true, real. 2. real calamity. 3. the Resurrection and Last Judgment. H— **Suresi** *the 69th sura of the Quran.*
hakkakᵏⁱ (.—) حكاك A engraver. — **kalemi** seal-engraver's tool. —**lık** art of engraving.
hakkalinsaf (...—) حق الانصاف A *lrnd.* in a fair and just manner.
hakkan ('.) حقا A *lrnd.* by right, as a right.
hakkani (.——) حقانى A *lrnd.* 1. just, equitable. 2. regarding God.
hakkaniyet (.—..) حقانيت A 1. justice, equity. 2. *lrnd.* man's love for God. —**li** just, fair. —**siz** unjust. —**sizlik** injustice.
hakket=ᵈᵉʳ **1** حق ايتمك /ı/ to deserve.
hakket=ᵈᵉʳ **2** حك ايتمك /ı/ 1. to engrave, incise. 2. to erase.
hakkında حقنده about, for, concerning, regarding, e. g., **bu kanun hakkında** about this law, concerning this law.
hakkiyle (..'.) حقيله properly, rightfully; thoroughly.
hakla=ʳ حقلامق /ı/ 1. to beat, to overcome, to crush, to suppress. 2. to eat up.
haklaş=ˡʳ حقلاشمق /la/ to settle mutual rights or claims; to be quits. —**tır=** /ı/ *caus.*
haklı حقلى right, just; who has right on his side.
haknaşinas (.—.—) حق ناشناس P lrnd. 1. ungrateful. 2. unjust, unappreciative.
haknişin (.—.—) خاك نشين P lrnd. poor, abject, humble, lowly.

hakperest مو پرست P *lrnd.* right, just, fair-minded.
hâkrub (— —) خاکروب P *lrnd.* broom; sweeper.
hâksar (— —) خاکسار P *lrnd.* 1. dustlike, of the earth. 2. humble, miserable, base. **—i** (— — —) P humility, lowliness, humiliation.
haksız حقسز unjust, unjustifiable, wrong. **— çık=** to turn out to be in the wrong, to lose (a claim). **— çıkar=** /ı/ to prove to be wrong. **— fiili** *law* a wrong. **— iktisap** *law* usurpation, assumption. **— rekabet** *law* unfair competition. **— yere** unjustly, without justification.
haksızlık[1] حقسزلق injustice, wrongfulness. **— et=** to act unjustly; /a/ to do injustice (to).
hakşinas (. . —) حقشناس P *lrnd.* just, rightful, fair. **—âne** (. . — —.) P justly, fairly. **—î** (. . — —) P, **—lık** sense of justice.
hakud (. —) حقود A *lrnd.* filled with hate, malicious.
hakuran, hakvuran حقوران a variety of dove. **— kafesi gibi** tumbledown (house).
hal[li] 1 (—) حال 1. state, condition, situation; state of affairs. 2. strength, energy. 3. quality; behavior. 4. bad situation, trouble. 5. *gram.* present tense (=ıyor). 6. *gram.* case. 7. *myst.* mental state such as joy, grief etc; trance, ecstasy, ecstatic love towards God. **—iyle** naturally, as a matter of fact; consequently. **—den anla=** to sympathize, to be sensitive and understanding. **—e bak!** How terrible! How strange! **—ine bak** /ın/ Just look at him! Poor dear! **—ine bakmadan** forgetting his weakness. **— böyle iken** and yet, nevertheless; although. **— buki*. — buysa*. —i dil** *lrnd.* the state of one's heart, love. **—i dumandır** /ın/ He is in a mess; he is in danger. **— duygusu** *phil.* coenesthesia. **—den düş=** to fail in health, to get weak. **—ini gör=** *obs.* to suffer for one's deeds. **—ini göster=** /ın/ *obs.* to chastise. **—den hale gir=** to change greatly for the worse, to go from bad to worse. **—i haraptır** /ın/ He is done for. **—i harb** *pol.* state of war. **— hatır sor=** to inquire after somebody's health. **—i hâzır** 1. the present time. 2. *gram.* present tense. **—i hâzırda** nowadays, at present. **—i ihtizarda** at the point of death, in mortal agony. **—i intizar** expectation. **—i işbaa gel=** to be saturated. **—den kal=** *prov., same as* **halden düş=. —i kalma=** to be exhausted. **— karakteristikleri** *astr.* physical parameters. **—ine koy=** /ı/ to let (somebody) alone. **—ine köpekler güler** He will be a laughingstock. **—i mâzi** *gram.* past continuous, imperfect tense. **—i medeni** *law* civil status. **—i müstakbel** *gram.* future tense. **—in nedir diyen olmadı** Nobody took

any interest in me (him, her). **—i neye varacak** /ın/ What is to become of him? How will he end up? **— ol=** to be exhausted. **—i olma=** not to have enough strength. **bir — olmuş!** /a/ What's wrong with him?, How he has changed! **bir — olursa** /a/ If anything should happen (to one); if one should die. **—i perişan, —i pürmelal** a very sorry state. **—i sâbıka irca** entire restitution, reinstatement. **—i sahv** *law* lucid interval. **—ini sor=** /ın/ to inquire after one's health. **—imi sorma!** You'd better not ask! (I am in a terrible state.) **—i tavrı yerinde** worthy, well-behaved. **— tercümesi** biography, short autobiography. **—i tevellüdî** *chem.* nascent state. **—i vakti yerinde** well off, rich. **—im yok** I am not feeling well. **—e yola koy=** /ı/ to put in order, to arrange. **—i zihnî** *psych.* mental attitude.
hal[lı] 2 خلع A *lrnd.* 1. dethronement. 2. taking off (clothes or shoes). **—' et=*.**
hâl[li] 3 (—) خال *poet.* mole (on the body). **—i müşkin** beauty spot.
hal[lıı] 4 حل A 1. solution, a solving (a problem). 2. *sc.* a melting, dissolving, liquefaction. 3. *lrnd.* an untying, undoing (knot, tangle); a removing an impediment. **— ü akd** *lrnd.* a settling and deciding; an administering. **— et=*. — ü faslet=** /ı/ to settle (finally). **— ü hamur ol=** /la/ to be part and parcel (of), to be one (with somebody). **— olun=*.**
hal[lı] 5 هال F covered fruit-and-vegetable market.
hal[lıı] 6 خل A *lrnd.* vinegar.
hala 1 خالة [**hale** 2] paternal aunt, father's sister.
hâlâ 2 (— —) حالا [**hâlen**] 1. yet, still. 2. *lrnd.* at the present time. **— mı?** Still going on?
halâ 3 (. —) خلا A 1. *phys.* void, vacuum, vacant place. 2. *same as* **helâ.**
halahil (. — —) حلاحيل A *lrnd., pl. of* **halhal 1.**
halaik[kı] (. — .) خلائق A *lrnd.* creatures, men, peoples.
halaiyyun (. — — —) خلائيون A *phil.* vacuists.
halak[kı] خلق A *lrnd.* ragged, tattered; rag, ragged cloth or garment.
halal حلال A *prov., var. of* **helâl.**
halalım حلالم gambler's slang dupe, sucker.
halâs (. —) خلاص A *lrnd.* salvation, deliverance. **— bul=, — ol=** /dan/ to be saved; to escape (from danger); to get rid (of).
halaskâr (. — —) خلاصكار P savior, deliverer.
halâşina (— — . —) حلاآشنا P *lrnd.* sympathetic, understanding.
halat 1 خلط Gk *naut.* rope, hawser, cord.

halid

— **çekme** sport tug of war. —ı **çeliğe volta et=** to belay a rope. — **kasnağı** cable drum. — **matafyon** rope eyelet, cringle. — **nete et=** to clear a rope. — **ör=** to strand, to splice a rope, to make a rope by twisting together strands. — **simidi** grommet. — **süngeri** swab, rope mop.

hâlât 2 (— —) حالات A lrnd., pl. of hâlet 2.

halâvet (. —.) حلاوت A lrnd. sweetness; agreeableness. —**bahş** P giving sweetness, sweetening. —**li** sweet, pleasant, agreeable. —**siz** lacking sweetness, insipid.

halay حالاى [alay] prov. kind of folk dance performed in a circle holding hands (accompanied by drum and pipe). — **çek=**, — **tep=** to dance the **halay**.

halayık[t] حلايق [halaik] female slave, female servant.

halazade (.. —.) خاله زاده paternal aunt's son or daughter, cousin.

halbe حلبه A lrnd. race meeting, racecourse.

halbuki (.'. .) حالبوكه whereas; however, nevertheless.

halbuysa (.'. .) حالبويسه prov., same as halbuki.

hâldâr (— —) حالدار P poet. adorned with moles.

haldaş (— —) حالداش sympathetic friend.

hâle 1 (—.) هاله A 1. halo (round the moon). 2. art. nimbus. 3. anat. areola.

hâle 2 (—.) خاله A lrnd., same as hala 1.

Halebî (.. —) حلبى A 1. obs. cloth measure of 20-30 inches. 2. lrnd. native of Aleppo.

halecan (.. —) خلجان A lrnd. 1. agitation, excitement, anxiety. 2. palpitation (of the heart). — **çek=**, — **içinde ol=** to be in a state of excitement, to be agitated. —**a uğra=** same as halecanlan=.

halecanlan=[ır] خلجانلنمق to become excited.

hâledâr (— . —) هاله دار P lrnd. having a halo or nimbus.

halef خلف A successor; descendant, son. — **ve selef** successor and predecessor. — **selef ol=** to be successor and predecessor in the holding of an office, etc.

halefen (.'.) خلفاً A lrnd. as a successor. — **ba'de halef** successor after successor.

halefiyet خلفيت [based on Arabic] lrnd. 1. succession. 2. law subrogation, transfer of rights.

halel خلل A 1. injury, defect, damage, harm. 2. path. weakness, disorder, decay. 3. lrnd. interval, opening, gap. —**i dimağî** path. mental disorder. — **gel=** /a/ to be harmed, to be injured; to get spoiled. — **getir=**, — **ver=** /a/ to injure, to damage; to spoil.

haleldâr (.. —) خللدار P injured, defaced, damaged, harmed.

halelpezîr (... —) خللپذير P lrnd. harmed, injured.

halemi (.. —) حلمى A anat. mastoid.

hâlen (—'.) حالاً A now, at the present time.

halenciye (.. —.) خلنجيه A bot., Ericaceae.

Halep[bi] حلب A geog. Aleppo. — **çamı** Aleppo pine, Jerusalem pine, bot., Pinus Halepensis. — **çıbanı** Aleppo boil, Aleppo button. — **orada ise arşın burada!** Try and see; well, prove it.

hal'et=[der] 1 خلع ايتمك /ı/ to dethrone (a sultan).

hâlet 2 (— .) حالت A lrnd. 1. situation, condition, aspect. 2. fact, act. —**i mâraziye-i ruhiye** psych. psychopathy. —**i nezi** path. death agony. —**i ruhiye** state of mind, mental attitude.

hâlevâr (— . —) هاله وار P lrnd. circularly (like a halo).

halezon حلزون A same as **helezon**.

half 1 حلف A lrnd. oath. —**i meçhul** can. law an oath left undefined as to duration of obligation.

half 2 خلف A lrnd. back; anat. posterior.

halfa (.'.) حلفا G esparto grass, bot., Stipa tenacissima.

halfî (. —) خلفى A anat. posterior.

halhal[li] خلخال A lrnd. anklet, bangle.

halı خالى [kali 1] carpet. — **döşe=** to lay a carpet. — **süpürgesi** fine broom. —**cı** carpet maker.

hâli 1 (— —) خالى A lrnd. 1. empty, vacant; unoccupied, uninhabited; unowned; deserted. 2. /dan/ void, clear, destitute (of), lacking, free (from).

hâli 2 (— —) حالى A lrnd. pertaining to the present; present, actual, current.

hali[ri] **3** خلع var. of **hal' 2**.

hali[ii] **4** (. —) خليع A lrnd. 1. taken off, cast-off (garment). 2. discarded, disowned as incorrigible or worthless (man), outcast. 3. one who has broken with decent society.

halib 1 (— .) حالب A 1. anat. ureter. 2. lrnd. who milks a beast.

halib 2 (. —) حليب A lrnd. milk.

halib 3 (. —) خالب A lrnd. deceiving, deceitful; deceiver.

halic 1 (. —) خليج A lrnd. bay, gulf. **H—i Bahri Sefid** the Dardanelles. **H—i Bahri Siyah** the Bosphorus. **H—i Dersaadet** the Golden Horn.

halic 2 (— .) حالج A lrnd. cotton carder and beater.

halic 3 (— .) خالج A lrnd. shaking, pulling, agitating.

halice (— . .) خالجه A lrnd. perplexing matter.

Haliç[ci] (. —) خليج [halic 1] the Golden Horn.

halid (— .) خالد A lrnd. eternal, perpetual.

halide 1 (–́..) خالدﻩ A 1. *lrnd.* eternal, perpetual. 2. *w. cap.* woman's name.
halide 2 (.—.) خَنيدﻩ P *lrnd.* pierced, stabbed; stung; pricked.
halif 1 (—.) حالف A *lrnd.* who swears, who takes an oath.
halif 2 (.—) حليف A *lrnd.* loyal friend, companion.
halif 3 (—.) خالف A *lrnd.* 1. following, remaining behind. 2. substitute, successor. 3. who retreats, backslides. 4. corrupt, wicked, perverse.
halif 4 (.—) خليف A *lrnd.* successor, substitute.
halife (.—.) خليفه A 1. Caliph. 2. *myst. orders* officially ordained assistant to a sheikh. 3. *lrnd.* assistant, substitute, successor. 4. *obs.* junior clerk in a public office; *same as* kalfa. H—i Müslimin, H—i ruyi zemin Caliph.
Halifetullah fil'arz (.—..—..) خليفة الله في الأرض A *Isl. rel.* 1. God's substitute on earth, the caliph. 2. Adam; man.
halik^kı 1 (—.) خالق A *lrnd.* the Creator, God.
halik^kı 2 (—.) هالك A *lrnd.* perishing, perished, dead; perishable.
halik^kı 3 (.—) حليق A *lrnd.* shaved, shaven.
halik^kı 4 (—.) حالق A *lrnd.* 1. shaving; destroying. 2. barber.
halika 1 (—.) خليقة A *lrnd.* creation, mankind; nature.
halika 2 (—..) حالقة A *lrnd.* 1. barber (woman). 2. year of drought, famine and death. 3. disunion, discord.
halikatullah (.—..—) خليفة الله A *lrnd.* God's creation.
halikiyet (.—.) خالقيّت A *lrnd.* creative power.
Halikülberaya (—...——) خالق البرايا A *lrnd.* the Creator of men and all beings.
halil 1 (.—) خليل A *lrnd.* 1. sincere and intimate friend. 2. *w. cap.*, man's name.
halil 2 (.—) حليل A *lrnd.* canonically lawful; spouse.
halile 1 (.—.) حليله *var. of* helile.
halile 2 (.—.) حليله A *lrnd.* canonically lawful wife.
halile 3 (.—.) حليله largish cymbals held in the hands and played by beating them together; they are used in religious music and especially during the Mevlevi **âyin** music.
Halilullah (.—.—) خليل الله A *rel.* God's friend (*i. e.,* Abraham).
halim (.—) حليم A 1. mild, gentle, patient. 2. *w. cap., rel.* God, the Clement. **— selim** gentle and good-tempered. **—len=, —leş=** to become gentle, to soften.
halis (—.) خالص A 1. pure, unmixed; genuine, true, choice. 2. sincere. **— muhlis** authentic, true, real; typical.
halisâne (—.—.) خالصانه sincere; sincerely; without ulterior motive.
halisiyet (—.—.) خالصيّت A *lrnd.* sincerity; pureness, genuineness.
halisuddem (—...) خالص الدّم A *lrnd.* thoroughbred, pure-blooded.
halita (.—.) خليطة A *lrnd.* mixed substance, mixture; alloy; combination; medley.
haliül'izar (.—..—) خليع العذار A *lrnd.* 1. that has slipped the halter. 2. one who has cast off all restraint, vagabond.
hâliyâ (—.—) حاليا [*based on Arabic*] *lrnd.* at the present time, now.
Haliye (——.) حاليّه A *myst. orders* a Muslim sect who become ecstatically entranced by singing, bodily movement, shouting, and clapping of the hands.
haliyen (—'..) حاليًا A *lrnd.* vacantly.
halk^kı 1 خلق A 1. the common people, folk; people, nation; population; crowd. 2. *lrnd.* creation; mankind, a creating; invention. **— ağzı** 1. gossip. 2. vernacular, language of the people. **—ın ağzına düş=** to be subject of gossip or scandal. **. —ın ağzı torba değil ki büzesin** You cannot keep people from gossiping. **—ı âlem** *lrnd.* mankind. **— bilgisi** study of folklore. **— dili** *same as* halk ağzı. **— edebiyatı** folk literature. **— hâkimiyeti** democracy. **— matinesi** cheap afternoon performance (cinema, theater, etc.) **— musikisi** music of the uneducated people having many special characteristics but the same system and technique as Turkish art music. **—ın reyine müracaat** *law* plebiscite, referendum. **— sandığı** local savings bank. **—ın sesi Hakkın sesidir** *proverb* The voice of the people is the voice of God.
halk^kı 2 حلق A *lrnd.* throat.
halka حلقه A 1. ring; hoop; circle; link; *mech.* flange. 2. ring-shaped plain biscuit (made of flour, butter and salt). **—i âbgûn** *poet.* sky. **—i âşıkan** *myst. orders* circle of dervishes. **—yı burnuna tak=** /ın/ to bring into submission. **—i der** *lrnd.* ring-shaped door knocker. **—i dervişân** *myst. orders* circle of dervishes. **—i destbend** *lrnd.* 1. handcuff. 2. bracelet. **— dizilişli yapraklar** *bot.* verticillate leaves. **—i gudrufiye** *anat.* cartilaginous ring. **— halka** in rings, in links, in circles. **—i nûş** *poet.* beloved's lips. **— ol=** to form a circle. **— oyunu** round dance. **—i rindan** *myst. orders* circle of dervishes. **—i sîmîn** *poet.* 1. silver ring. 2. full moon. **—i şiven** *lrnd.* circle of wailing women. **—i tesbih** *lrnd.* 1. prayer beads. 2. circle of people reciting prayers of praise. **—i teslim** *myst.*

orders 1. circle of dervishes. 2. stone worn by dervishes as a sign of submission. 3. submission. **— teşkil et=** 1. to form a ring or circle. 2. to have a gathering of intimate friends. **—i tevhid, —i zikr** *myst. orders* a circle of devotees assembled to perform the **zikr. —i zülf** *poet.* ringlet of the beloved's hair, lovelock.

halkabegûş (...—) خلقه بگوش P *lrnd.* having a ring in the ear; slave. **—ân** (...——) P *lrnd.* slaves.

halkabend حلقه بند P *lrnd.* grouped in a circle (people).

halkacı حلقه جی maker or seller of rings.

halkala=ʳ حلقه لامق /ı/ to furnish with rings; to encircle; to fasten with a ring. **—n=** 1. *pass.* 2. to curl in ringlets. 3. to form a circle. **—ndır=** *caus. of* **halkalan=²,³. —t=** /ı, a/ *caus. of* **halkala=**.

halkalı حلقه لی furnished with rings, ringed, linked in coils. **—lar** *zool.,* Annelida; *bot.,* Oenothera. **— damar** *bot.* annular tube. **— mapa** *naut.* ringbolt.

halkâri (.——) حلقه کاری P 1. chrysography, gilding. 2. robe embroidered with gold.

halkavar (..—), **halkavari** (..——) حلقه وار, حلقه واری P *lrnd.* ring-shaped, circular.

halkavi (..—) حلقوی A 1. *zool.* annulated; *bot.* whorled, verticillate. 2. *lrnd.* circular, ring-shaped. **— küsûf, — örtme** *astr.* annular eclipse. **—ye** *same as* **halkalılar.**

halkçı حلقجی 1. one who stands for the rights of the people, democrat, populist. 2. partisan of the Turkish Republican People's Party. **—lık** populism.

halken (.'.) خلقا A *lrnd.* in appearance or features.

halket=ᵈᵉʳ خلق ایتمک *lrnd.* /ı/ to create, to give existence to; to give life to.

halkî (.—) حلقی A *lrnd.* 1. pharyngeal. 2. guttural (letter). **—yet** guttural quality of a letter.

halkullah (..—) خلق الله A *lrnd.* God's creatures, creation.

hallâb (.—) خلّاب A *lrnd.* deceiver; deceitful; liar.

hallâc (.—) حلّاج A *lrnd., same as* **hallaç. H—ı Mansûr** name of a famous Muslim mystic. **H—iye** name of a mystical order.

hallaç حلاج [hallâc] cotton or wool fluffer who works with bow and mallet. **— pamuğu gibi at=** /ı/ to scatter about.

hallaçla=ʳ حلاجلامق /ı/ to fluff (cotton or wool). **—n=** *pass.* **—t=** *caus. of* **hallaçla=.**

hallaçlıkᵍ¹ حلاجلق cotton-fluffing, profession of a cotton-fluffer.

hallade (.'..) حلّد A *lrnd.* May God make perpetual (said in prayer).

hallâf 1 (.—) حلّاف A *lrnd.* one who swears much, one who is free in taking oaths.

hallaf 2 (.—) خلّاف A *lrnd.* 1. who goes back on his word. 2. quarrelsome, contentious.

hallâkᵏ¹ 1 (.—) خلّاق A *lrnd.* Creator, God. **H—ı Âlem** Creator of the universe, God.

hallakᵏ¹ 2 (.—) حلّاق A *lrnd.* one who shaves, barber.

hallâlˡⁱ (.—) حلّال A *lrnd.* one who loosens, solver. **—i müşkilât** solver of difficulties.

hallât (.—) خلّاط A *lrnd.* mischief-maker; double dealer, telltale.

halle حلّه A *prov.* very large metal pan.

hallen=ⁱʳ حالّنمك 1. to acquire a new form or condition. 2. to recover strength. 3. to go into ecstasy. 4. /a/ *slang* to desire, to covet. **—ip küllen=** to get along on one's own resources, to live moderately. **—dir=** /ı/ *caus. of* **hallen=**.

halleş=ⁱʳ حاللشمك to have a heart-to-heart talk, to confide in one another. **—tir=** /ı/ *caus.*

hallet=ᵈᵉʳ حلّ ایتمك /ı/ 1. to solve (a problem); to settle; to decipher; to explain; to analyse. 2. to dissolve, to melt.

hallî 1 (.—) حلّی A *lrnd.* analytic.

hallî 2 (.—) خلّی A *chem.* acetic.

hallice حاليجه pretty well off; /dan/ somewhat better (than).

halliyet حلّيت A *chem.* acetate.

hallolun=ᵘʳ حلّ اولنمك *pass. of* **hallet=**.

halsiz حالسز weak, exhausted. **—lik** weakness.

halt خلط A 1. *colloq.* improper act; stupid utterance; dirt; filth. 2. *lrnd.* a mixing, mixture; confusion. **— et=***. **— etme!** Shut up! **— karıştır=, — ye=** to make a great blunder.

halta خلطا، خالتا A *archaic* dog collar. **—lı** wearing a dog collar.

halter هالتر F *sport* dumbbell, barbell.

haltet=ᵈᵉʳ خلط ایتمك to say something improper or provoking, to utter nonsense.

haltıyat (..—) خلطيات [*based on* **halt**] *archaic* improper speech, nonsense.

halukᵏᵘ (.—) خلوق A *lrnd.* good natured, of good character, well-disposed, decent.

halva حلوا A *prov. for* **helva.**

halvet خلوت A 1. solitude, loneliness; retirement, privacy; *myst.* retirement for devotion. 2. retired place; cell for religious exercises. 3. single room in a public bath; very hot place. **—e çekil=** to withdraw into seclusion. **—e dön=** to become very hot and close (room). **— et=** /ı/ 1. to make (a room) private by emptying it of other people. 2. *hist.* to organize as a private council. **— gibi** very hot. **—e gir=** to retire to a private room. **—i hümayun sokakları** *Ott. hist.* canvas walls

halvetgâh 442

stretched along a street to provide a private passage for the Sultan and his retinue. **— iste=** *Ott. hist.* to ask for a private audience. **— odası** private room, retiring room. **— ol=** to meet in private.

halvetgâh (..—), **halvetgeh** خلوتگاه ، خلوتگه P *lrnd.* solitary place, place for retirement and seclusion.

halvetgüzin (...—) خلوت گزین P *lrnd.* one who chooses retirement, recluse, hermit.

halvethane (..—.) خلوتخانه P *lrnd.* private room, private apartment.

Halveti (..—) خلوتی A member of the **Halvetiye** order of dervishes.

Halvetiye (..—.) خلوتیه A *name of an order of dervishes who practise religious seclusion.*

halvetnişin (...—) خلوت نشین P *lrnd.* living in seclusion; recluse, hermit.

halvetsaray خلوت سرای P *lrnd.* private pavilion of a sovereign.

ham 1 خام P 1. unripe, immature, green. 2. raw, crude, unrefined; inexperienced, tyro; untrained; unaccustomed to work, out of training. 3. unreasonable, vain, useless. **— adam** inconsiderate person, tactless man. **— arazi** *same as* **ham toprak.** **— avla=** to dupe. **— bakır** raw copper. **— besi suyu** *neol., bot.* crude sap. **— çelik** crude steel. **— demir** pig iron. **— deri** crude leather. **— ervah** crude, insensitive, unrefined; rude. **— fikir** ridiculous idea, absurdity. **— halat*.** **— hayal** 1. vain illusion. 2. crudely ambitious. **— ipek** raw silk. **— keyif** moody and drowsy. **— madde** raw material. **— maden** crude metal. **— mahsuller** raw products. **— mamulat** raw produce. **— meyva** unripe fruit. **— pamuk** raw cotton. **— petrol** crude oil. **— şeker** raw, unrefined sugar, brown sugar. **— toprak** uncultivated land, hard earth. **— tuğla** slackly-baked brick. **— usare** *bot.* raw sap. **— ümit** unrealizable hope. **— vücut** body out of training; languid body. **— yağ** crude oil.

ham 2 خم P *lrnd.* 1. bent, curved, curled; curl, ringlet. 2. ridged roof; sky. **— beham, — ender ham** curling (locks), twist upon twist. **— gisu, — zülf** locks, ringlets.

hamaid (.—.) حمائد A *lrnd.* praiseworthy acts or qualities.

hamail (.—.) حمائل A *lrnd.* 1. baldric, cross-shoulder strap for a sword; ribbon of an order. 2. *lrnd., same as* **hamaylı.** **— çıkar=** *Ott. hist.* to split an enemy's body with one blow of the sword diagonally from one shoulder to the other hip. **—i felek** the ecliptic, zodiac. **—î** (.—.—) A 1. hung from a shoulder to the opposite hip; resembling a baldric. 2. *astr.* oblique (revolution of the sphere).

hamaim (.—.) حمائم A *lrnd., pl. of* **hamame.**

hamak[1] حماك E hammock.

hamakat[ü] (.—.) حماقت A stupidity, folly.

hamal حمال [**hammal**] 1. porter, carrier; stevedore; unskilled laborer; day laborer. 2. common, coarse fellow. **— camal** rabble, mob, street gang. **—iye** porterage.

hamallık[1] حمالّى 1. profession of a porter. 2. porterage. 3. hard work, toiling and slaving; unnecessary burden. **—ını et=** /ın/ to do the heavy work.

hamam 1 حمام [**hammam**] 1. bath; bathroom; bathhouse; public bath; Turkish bath; very hot room. 2. *School slang* disciplinary committee. **— anası** 1. manageress or attendant in the outer rooms of a public bath for women. 2. huge woman. 3. hard-hearted, rough-mannered mother. **— böceği** cockroach, *zool.*, *Blatta orientalis.* **— deliye kaldı** *prov.* The place is left in incompetent hands. **—da deli var** There is a madman in the bath (used to describe a sudden commotion). **— gibi** very hot. **—a giren terler** He who enters a business must bear all the difficulties. **— kesesi** rough washing-glove for rubbing the body in the bath. **— nalını suratlı** very ugly, monstrous (woman). **—ın namusunu kurtar=** to try to give some semblance of honesty in a questionable situation. **— natırı** woman serving in a public bath. **— odası** dressing room in the bath quarters of a large house. **— otu** depilatory. **— takımı** set of supplies for the Turkish bath. **— tası** metal bowl (used in a Turkish bath). **— ustası** attendant in a women's bath.

hamam 2 (.—) حمام A *lrnd.* wood pigeon; dove.

hamamcı حمامجی 1. proprietor or keeper of a public bath. 2. canonically unclean and in need of a ritual bath. 3. *same as* **hamamcı ustası.** **— başı** *Ott. hist.* Chief of the bath keepers in the Sultan's palace. **— derzi** *arch.* watertight joint of a wall (the mortar being mixed with oakum). **— ustası** *obs.* bricklayer or stonemason skilled in the construction of watertight walls for bathhouses, cisterns, etc. **—lık** profession of the proprietor of a public bath.

hamame (.—.) حمامه A *lrnd.* 1. wood pigeon, ringdove. 2. beautiful woman.

hamamülbitaka (.—..—.) حمام البطاقة A *lrnd.* carrier pigeon.

Haman (——) هامان A *a name associated with Pharaoh in the Quran.*

hamarat حمارت [*based on Arabic*] hard-working, industrious (woman).

hamas حماس *prov., same as* **gammaz.**[1]

hamaset (.—.) حماست A literature valor, heroism.

hamasi (.——) حماسی A literature heroic; epic.

hamasiyat (.———) حماسیات A literature epic poems, heroic poems.

hamaylı حمایلی [hamail] 1. amulet; charm. 2. naut. bunt; buntline.

Hambelî (..—) حنبلی A Isl. rel. Hanbali, pertaining to the school of canonical law of Ibn Hanbal; follower of the Hanbali school.

hamd حمد A giving praise and glory to God; grateful praise. — **et**=*. — **olsun**!* —**en lillâh** (.'. .—') A as an act of praise to God. —**en sümme hamden** (.'. .'. .'.) A glory; Glory to God! **H— Suresi** a name of the first sura of the Quran.

hamdele حمدله A rel. 1. a pronouncing the formula **Elhamdülillâh.** 2. the formula **Elhamdülillâh.**

hamdet=ᵈᵉʳ حمد ایتمك /a/ to praise (God).

hamdolsun حمد اولسون Praise be to God! Thank God.

hame 1 (—.) خامه P lrnd. 1. reed pen, pen. 2. reed. —**i edeb** literary pen. —**i ezel** God's everlasting ordinance. —**i gevhernisar** a flowery pen. — **vü şemşir** the pen and the sword.

hame 2 (—.) خامه A lrnd. 1. top of the head. 2. head of any animal. 3. chieftain.

hamecümban (—..—) خامه جنبان P lrnd. writer, scribe.

hamedan (—.—) خامه دان P lrnd. pen case.

hamegüzar (—..—) خامه گذار P lrnd. a writing.

hamekeş (—..) خامه کش P lrnd. 1. who writes. 2. who erases, who cancels.

Hamel حمل A 1. astr., Aries. 2. l. c., lrnd. lamb.

hamelat (..—) حملات A lrnd., pl. of **hamle.**

hamele حمله A lrnd., pl. of **hamil 1.** —**i arş** the angels who bear up the throne of God. —**i hüccet** the recording angels. —**i Kur'an** those who know the Quran by heart.

hamepira (—.——) خامه پیرا P lrnd. adorning the head.

hameran (—.—) خامه ران P lrnd. writer.

hamezen (—..) خامه زن P lrnd. 1. one who nibs a reed pen. 2. small disk on which reed pens are nibbed.

hamfendi (.'..) خانم افندی var. of **hanım efendi.**

hamgeşte حم گشته P lrnd. that has become bent, curved, or crooked.

hamhalat حم حالات colloq. clumsy, boorish, rough.

hamhame حمحمه A lrnd. a speaking through the nose, nasal sound; a muttering.

hamhum حم هوم hemming and hawing. — **et=** 1. to hem and haw. 2. to use empty words in order to get rid of someone. — **şaralop** empty words; swindle.

hâmız (—.) حامض A chem. acid; lrnd. sour. —**ı azot** nitric acid. —**ı fahm,** —**ı fahmî** carbonic acid. —**ı hadid** ferric acid. —**ı hummaz** oxalic acid. —**ı kibrit** sulfuric acid. —**ı kiyanus** cyanic acid. —**ı neml** formic acid. —**ı tırtır** tartaric acid. —**iyet** (—.—.) A acidity.

hâmızülfuad (—...—) حامض الفؤاد A lrnd. sour-tempered, ill-humored.

hami 1 (——) حامی A protector, defender; patron.

Hami 2 (——) حامی A Hamite; Hamitic.

hami 3 (.—) حمی A lrnd. 1. protected, defended; guarded. 2. sensitive.

hâmid 1 (—.) حامد A lrnd. who praises; one who gives thanks unto God.

hamîd 2 (.—) حمید A lrnd. 1. praised, praiseworthy. 2. God, the Praiseworthy.

hamide 1 (..—.) حمیده A lrnd. 1. praised, worthy. 2. w. cap., woman's name.

hamide 2 (..—.) خمیده P lrnd. bent, crooked, curved. — **kamet** (.—.—.) P bent double (with age). —**gi** (.—.—) P crookedness.

Hamîdeli حمید ایلی obs., name of a province in Southwest Anatolia.

hamidiye (.——.) حمیدیه Kind of fez worn during the reign of Sultan Abdulhamid II.

hâmil 1 (—.) حامل A 1. /ı/ bearing, supporting, carrying; wearing; bearer, carrier; fin. holder. 2. lrnd. pregnant; in fruit (tree). —**i bâr-ı girân** poet. heavily laden, greatly burdened. —**i esfâr** lrnd. 1. ass. 2. ignorant; one who simply mouths words. —**i eş'ar** bot. piliferous. —**i Kur'an** lrnd. who knows the Quran by heart. —**i mektup** the bearer of the letter. —**i mevkuf** pros. distich in which the sense remains incomplete, being completed in the following distich. —**e muharrer senetler** fin. bearer securities, obligations to bearer. —**i müştiye** zool., Etenophora. —**i nişan** bearer of an order. — **ol=** /ı/ lrnd. to bear, to carry; fin. to hold. —**i tedvîr** astr. deferent of a planet. —**i vahy** Isl. rel. the conveyor of revelation, the archangel Gabriel. —**i varaka** the bearer of the document or letter.

hâmil 2 (—.) خامل A lrnd. of no repute; unheard of, obscure.

hâmile (—..) حامله A pregnant (woman). — **kal=** to become pregnant; /dan/ to be with child (by somebody). — **ol=** to become pregnant; to be with child.

hâmilen 1 (—'..) حاملاً A carrying, bearing.

hâmilen 2 (—'..) خاملاً A lrnd. without caring for fame, modestly.

hamim 1 (.—) حمیم A lrnd. 1. hot water. 2. close relation or friend.

hâ mim 2 (— —) حاميم A *Isl. rel.* the two letters ح and م at the beginning of each of seven suras of the Quran; any one of the suras from the fortieth to the forty-sixth of the Quran. **— ayn sin kaf, — sin kaf** *the forty-second sura of the Quran.*

haminne (..'.) حا مِنَّه *var. of* **hanım nine.**

haminto (..'.) حا مِنتُو *slang* illicit gain, improper gain.

hamîr 1 (.—) حمير A *lrnd.* leaven; leavened, fermented; leavened bread, fermented dough.

hamîr 2 (.—) حمير A *lrnd., pl. of* **himar.**

hamirmaye (.——.) حميرمايه P *lrnd.* 1. leaven. 2. nature, substance.

hamis 1 (—.) خامس A *lrnd.* fifth.

hamîs 2 (—.) حميس A *lrnd.* 1. Thursday. 2. army (as composed of five parts: the van, center, right and left wings, and rear guard or reserve).

hamise (—..) خامسه A *Ott. hist.* lowest grade of the Civil Service.

hamisen (—'..) خامساً A *lrnd.* in the fifth place, fifthly.

hamiş (—.) حامش A *lrnd.* 1. marginal note. 2. postscript.

hamiyet حميت A patriotism, public spirit. **—i cahiliye** *lrnd.* mistaken zeal, fanaticism. **—i İslamiye** *lrnd.* Islamic zeal.

hamiyetli حميتلى zealous, patriotic, public-spirited.

hamiyetlû (...—) حميتلو *archaic* honorable, *title applied to line officers or lower officials.*

hamiyetmend حميتمند P *lrnd., same as* **hamiyetli. —ane** (....—.) P *lrnd.* zealously.

hamiyetsiz حميتسز without sense of honor, unpatriotic; selfishly negligent of others. **—lik** lack of all sense of honor.

hamka (.—) حمقا A *lrnd., fem. of* **ahmak.**

hamkâr (——) حامكار P *lrnd.* inexperienced, unreasonable.

hamlⁱⁱ حمل A *lrnd.* 1. load, burden; a loading upon. 2. *Ott. hist.* 100.000 aspers. 3. attribution, a charging an offense. 4. a predicating, an affirming, assertion. 5. fetus (in the womb); pregnancy. **— et=*.**

hamla 1 حمله [**hamle**] single stroke of an oar.

hamla=ʳ **2** حاملا to get out of condition or out of practice; to become soft from lack of work.

hamlacı حمله‌جى 1. rower in a big boat. 2. *Ott. hist., title of the Palace boatmen.* **— başı** *Ott. hist.* 1. chief rower in the Sultan's boat. 2. chief of the boathouse department of the corps of the Imperial Guards.

hamlaç حملاچ [*Arabic* **himlac**] *chem.* blowpipe.

hamlaş=ⁱⁱ حاملاشمك *same as* **hamla= 2.**

hamle حمله A 1. attack, onslaught, assault. 2. effort; dash. 3. turn (at chess, checkers, etc.). **— et=** 1. to make an attack. 2. to make a great effort. **—i hayat** vital impulse.

hamlet=ᵈᵉʳ حمل ايتمك /ı, a/ 1. to attribute, to ascribe, to impute (to). 2. to load.

hamlıkᵍⁱ حاملق 1. unripeness, greenness, immaturity, crudeness. 2. rawness, lack of experience or of training. 3. unreasonableness.

hamlî (.—) حملى A *lrnd.* categorical (proposition).

hammalⁱⁱ (.—) حمّال A *same as* **hamal.**

hammaletülhatab (.—....) حمالة الحطب A *lrnd.* 1. woman who carries firewood; *w. cap.,* the wife of Abu-Jahl, who carried fuel to his fire in hell. 2. talebearer.

hammam (.—) حمام A *lrnd., same as* **hamam 1. —î** (.——) A *same as* **hamamcı.**

hammamiye (.——.) حماميه A *literature* poem about public baths.

hammar (.—) حمّار A *lrnd.* vintner, wine merchant.

hamme (—.) حامّه A *lrnd.* insect.

hampa (.—) حمپا P *vulg., same as* **hempa.**

Hamparsum notası حامپارسوم نوطه‌سى *Turkish mus.* a kind of music notation using certain letters invented by Hamparsum Limonjiyan (1768-1839).

hamr حمر A *lrnd.* wine.

hamra (.—) حمرا A *lrnd.* red; white; fair (woman).

hamrî (.—) حمرى A *lrnd.* pertaining to wine.

hamriş (——) حامريش P *lrnd.* immaturely bearded; callow, buffoon.

hamriye (.—.) حمريه A *literature* poem in praise of wine.

hamse حمسه A 1. *literature* set of a poet's five works in the mesnevi form. 2. *lrnd.* five. **—i hâzıma** *lrnd.* five cups of wine recommended for digestion.

hamsenüvis (...—) حمسه‌نويس P *lrnd.* poet who writes a set of five works in the Mesnevi form.

hamsi حمسى Gk anchovy (fish), *zool., Engraulis encrasicholus.*

hamsîn (.—) حمسين A 1. the period of fifty days following the forty days of most severe winter, ending at the vernal equinox. 2. *lrnd.* fifty. **H— bayramı** the Christian feast of Pentecost.

hamu حمو *archaic, same as* **kamu.**

hamulⁱⁱ (.—) حمول A *lrnd.* patient, long-suffering, forbearing.

hamule (.—.) حموله A load, burden; cargo; *elec.* charge.

hâmun (——) حامون P *lrnd.* wild, uninhabited plain or steppe.

hâmunneverd (— —..) هامون نورد P lrnd. a desert traveler.

hamur خامیر [hamîr 1] 1. dough, leavened dough, paste; anything of the consistency of dough. 2. half-cooked (bread or cake). 3. paper pulp; quality (of paper). 4. essence, nature; material, stuff; structure; *archeol.* clay (of a pot). **— aç=** to roll out dough. **— dök=** to pour out a thin fluid paste (for a sweet). **— et=** to prepare dough by kneading. **bir — et=** /ı/ to combine into one mass. **— gibi** doughlike, soft; limp, flabby. **— işi** pastry. **— işine karış=** to meddle in a delicate or disagreeable matter. **— ol=** to become soft and flabby like dough; to lose energy. **bir — ol=** to be combined into one mass. **— tahtası** pastry board. **— teknesi** kneading trough. **— tut=, — yap=, — yoğur=** to prepare dough by kneading. **—cu** same as **hamurkâr**.

hamurkâr (..—) خامورکار dough kneader (in a bakery).

hamurla=ᵣ خامورلامق /ı/ to cover or soil with dough; to cover the edges with dough (of a covered pot); to lute (a vessel, with clay-paste). **—n=** pass. of **hamurla=**. **—ş=** 1. to become soggy. 2. to become flabby. **—ştır=** /ı/ caus. of **hamurlaş=**.

hamursuz خامورسز unleavened; unleavened bread. **— ekmek** unleavened bread. **H— Bayramı** the Jewish feast of Passover.

hâmuş (— —) خاموش P lrnd. silent, dumb. **—ân** (— — — —) P 1. the silent; the dead. 2. cemetery; burial ground for dervishes who hold that death is merely sleep. **—âne** (— — — —.) P silently. **—î** (— — — —) P 1. silence. 2. death.

hamut خاموت حمود خاموت Sl a draft-horse collar; *mil.* rolled overcoat of an infantryman slung over the shoulder and under the arm.

hamyâze (.—., — —.) خامیازه P lrnd. 1. gape, yawn; a gaping, yawning. 2. weariness, fatigue. **—sini çek=** /ın/ 1. to suffer the fatigue of a trying, tedious matter. 2. to put up with someone's inconsiderate manner.

hamyazekeş (— —..) خامیازه کش P lrnd. one who yawns or stretches himself.

hamz حمض A lrnd., same as **humz**.

Hamza حمزه A man's name. **— geldi** *colloq.* The sandman has come; one feels sleepy.

Hamzaname (..—.) حمزه نامه P 1. name of a legendary history of Hamza, uncle of the Prophet. 2. *l. c.* any tale of fabulous exploits.

han 1 خان P 1. caravansary, khan; inn. 2. large commercial building. **—a çek=** /ı/ to bring into the inn. **— gibi** vast. **— hamam sahibi** a man of property, rich.

han 2 خان sovereign, ruler; khan; *w. cap.*, after name, a title of the Ottoman Sultan.

han 3 (—) خوان P lrnd. 1. dining table; large tray. 2. food; meal. **—i yağma** food distributed to the poor.

hân 4 (—) خوان P lrnd. who reads, recites or chants, e. g., **duahan, mesnevihan**.

Hanabile (.—..) حنابله A lrnd., pl. of **Hanbeli**.

hanacir 1 (.—.) حناجر A lrnd., pl. of **hancere**.

hanacir 2 (.—.) حناجر A lrnd., pl. of **hancer**.

hanadıkᵏᴵ (.—.) حنادک A lrnd., pl. of **handek**.

hanakᵏᴵ حنك A lrnd. anger, rage, wrath; malice; a bearing malice.

hanân (.—) حنان A lrnd. mercy, compassion, pity; kindness.

hanat (— —) حانات A lrnd. 1. shop. 2. wineshop.

hanay حاناى Gk prov. 1. hall; large room. 2. house with one or more stories.

hanazir (.— —) خنازیر A lrnd., pl. of **hınzır**.

Hanbalıkᶠᴵ خان بالیق hist. Peking. **— kâğıdı** best Chinese silk writing paper.

Hanbeli (..—) حنبلى A same as **Hambeli**.

hancer خنجر A lrnd. 1. same as **hançer**. 2. ray of light. **—i elmas** poet. 1. diamond-hilted dagger. 2. blade of a plant just peeping through the soil. **—i felek** poet. morning ray, sunrise. **—i İmam** 1. dagger by which the **İmam Hüseyin** was killed, which could not be withdrawn. 2. thorn in the flesh; pestilent fellow that cannot be got rid of. **—i sîm** poet. morning beam. **—i subh** poet. beam of sunrise. **—i zer** poet. sun; beam of sunrise.

hancere حنجره A lrnd., same as **hançere**.

hancerî (..—) حنجرى A anat. laryngeal.

hancı خانجى innkeeper.

hânçe (—.) خوانچه P lrnd. small tray, salver. **—i zer** poet. the sun.

hançer خنجر [hancer] short, curved dagger, khanjar.

hançere خنجره [hancere] anat. larynx.

handa خنده archaic, same as **kanda**.

handâhand (.—.) خند اخند P lrnd. prolonged guffaws of laughter.

handan (.—) خندان P poet. 1. laughing, smiling; cheerful, happy. 2. gleaming, flashing. 3. blooming, blossoming; bloom, blossom. **—dil** (.—.) P merry-hearted.

handavallı خاندا والى slang, same as **andavallı**.

hande 1 خنده P poet. 1. laugh, laughter; smile. 2. flash, gleam. **—i âfitab** sunrise. **—i berk** flash of lightning. **— berleb** with smiling lips. **—i câm** the glistening and coloring of the glass when wine is poured. **—i gül** the

hande opening of a rosebud. **—i zemin** *poet.* green and flowers (of spring). **—bahş** P, **—bahşa** (...—) P bringing a smile, causing laughter. **—bar** (..—) P, **—ferma** (...—) P causing laughter, amusing; ludicrous. **—feşan** (...—) P scattering laughter. **—feza** (...—) P rousing laughter, amusing.
hande 2 خنده *poet.*, same as **kanda**. **— ise** same as **handiyse**.
handek[ki] خندك A *lrnd.*, same as **hendek**.
handekünân (...—) خنده كنان P *lrnd.* laughing.
handemeşhun (...—) خنده مشحون P *lrnd.* full of laughter.
handemutad (...—) خنده معتاد P *lrnd.* gay, joyful, merry, always laughing.
handenüma (...—) خنده نما P *lrnd.* laughing happily.
handerili خندريكى Gk gum succory, *bot.*, *Chondrilla juncea*.
handeris (..—) خنده ريس A *lrnd.* wine, old wine.
handeriş (..—) خنده ريش P *lrnd.* 1. jest, jeer. 2. laughingstock.
handerû (..—) خنده رو P *lrnd.* smiling (person).
handezen خنده زن P *lrnd.* smiling sweetly, smiling.
handiyse ('..) خانديس *colloq.* any moment, now, soon.
hane 1 (—.) خانه P 1. house; building; dwelling. 2. compartment, chamber, closet; cell. 3. subdivision in a scheme or table; square (of a chess-board); rubric. 4. *arith.* place of a digit (in the decimal system); *ancient astr.* sign of the Zodiac. 5. *mus.* section of an instrumental composition; note. **—i ankebût** *lrnd.* 1. spider's web. 2. modest house. **—i çeşm** *lrnd.* eye socket. **—i ferda** *lrnd.* the future world. **—i gül** *lrnd.* this world. **— hane** 1. separate houses or buildings; separate compartments; in separate compartments or columns; cellular. 2. from house to house. **—i hâs** *Ott. hist.*, same as **has oda**. **—i Hassa** *Ott. hist.* department in the Sultan's Palace where the sacred relics were kept. **—i Hüda** *lrnd.* the House of God, the Kaaba. **—i kalem** *lrnd.* the tip of a reed pen. **—i keman** *lrnd.* 1. the curved part of each arm of an archery bow. 2. the span of an archery bow. **—i kilk** *lrnd.* tip of a reed pen. **—i nühder** *lrnd.* (lit., house with nine doors.) 1. the earth. 2. the human body. **—i sagîr** *Ott. hist.* the immediate household of the Sultan; the officers of the middle court of the Palace. **— sahibi** 1. householder, landlord. 2. host; hospitable person. **—i seferlû** *Ott. hist.* the traveling establishment of the Sultan. **—i satranç** *lrnd.* square on a chess board. **—i şeşder** *lrnd.* the world, with its six points of direction: right, left, front, back, up, down. **—i tanbûr** *mus.* body of a guitar. **—i zer** *lrnd.* 1. sun. 2. the fourth heaven. 3. the sign Leo. **—i zerrin** *lrnd.* 1. sun. 2. stars. 3. the eighth heaven. **—i zîn** *lrnd.* the seat of a saddle.
-hane 2 (—.) خانه P house, as in **çilehane, hastahane**.
hane 3 (—.) خانه A *lrnd.* shop; wine shop, tavern.
haneâbâd (—.—) خانه آباد P *lrnd.* in prosperous circumstances; whose house is frequented.
haneb حنب A *lrnd.* ankle joint (horse), curvature of the hind shank.
hanebaf (—.—) خانه باف P *lrnd.* home woven (cloth).
hanebâz (—.—) خانه باز P *lrnd.* one who stakes his all (in gambling). **—i** (—.—) P, **—lık** gambling desperately.
hanebeduş, haneberduş (—..—) خانه بدوش . خانه بردوش P *lrnd.* vagrant; vagabond; nomad; homeless.
haneberendâz (—...—) خانه براندار P *lrnd.* one who ruins his house, spendthrift, prodigal, squanderer. **—i** (—...——) P, **—lık** prodigality.
hanedan (—.—) خاندان P 1. dynasty; noble family. 2. of illustrious descent, noble; courteous, hospitable. **H—ı Nübüvvet** the family of the Prophet. **H—ı Âl-i Osman, H—ı Osmanî** the Ottoman Dynasty.
hanedanlık[kı] خاندانلك 1. nobility. 2. the courteous hospitality of a gentleman.
hanedâr (—.—) خانه دار P *lrnd.* 1. master of a house. 2. steward, housekeeper.
Hanefî (..—) حنفى A *Isl. rel.* Hanafi, pertaining to the school of canonical law of Abu Hanifa; follower of the Hanafi school.
Hanefîye (..—.) حنفيه A *Isl. rel.* the Hanafi school of canonical law.
hanefürûş (—..—) خانه فروش P *lrnd.* 1. renouncing the world, hermit. 2. vagabond.
hanegâh (—.—) خانه گاه P *lrnd.* dervish monastery.
hanegî (—.—) خانگى P *lrnd.* 1. belonging to the house, domestic, domesticated. 2. homemade. 3. shut in the house (ignorant of the outside world); inexperienced.
hanegîr (—.—) خانه گير P *lrnd.* 1. one who takes or sets up a house. 2. a variant of the game backgammon.
haneharab (—..—) خانه خراب P *lrnd.* 1. one whose house is ruined, ruined. 2. good-for-nothing, scamp. **—î** (—..——) P, **—lık** 1. ruinedness. 2. rascality.
hanehüda (—..—) خانه خدا P *lrnd.* master of a house, host.

hanekᵏⁱ حنك A 1. *anat.* palate. 2. *prov.* talk. 3. *lrnd.* bird's beak. **— et=** *prov.* to talk, to chatter.

hanekah (—.—) خانقاه A *lrnd.* dervish monastery. **—ı bâlâ** heaven; the spheres; the angels.

haneken (—..) خانه‌کن P *lrnd.* spendthrift.

hanende (—..) خواننده P *Or. mus.* singer. **—gî** (—..—) P *lrnd.*, same as **hanendelik**.

hanendelikᵍⁱ خوانندلك 1. singing. 2. profession of a singer.

hanenişîn (—..—) خانه‌نشین P *lrnd.* stay-at-home.

haneperdâz (—..—) خانه‌پرداز P *lrnd.* 1. one who keeps a house clean. 2. spendthrift, squanderer.

haneperver (—...) خانه‌پرور P *lrnd.* brought up at home.

haneperverd (—...) خانه‌پرورد P *lrnd.* born and bred in the house, inexperienced (youth); cosset. **—î** (—...—) P, **—lik** inexperience, rawness.

hanesiyah (—..—) خانه‌سیاه P *lrnd.*, same as **haneharab**.

hanesûz (—.—) خانه‌سوز P *lrnd.* disgracing one's family.

haneşiye (..—.) خنشیه A *zool.*, Ophidia.

hanezâd (—.—) خانه‌زاد P *lrnd.* the child of a slave born in the master's house.

hangar خانگار F hangar.

hangi (.'.) خانگی which; whichever. **—niz** which of you. **—si, — biri** which one. **— cehennemin dibinden geldin?** Where on earth did you come from? **— dağda kurt öldü?** What a miracle! How did it happen? **— peygambere kulluk edeceğimi şaşırdım** I am at a loss and don't know whom to please. **— rüzgâr attı?** What brought you here? **— taşı kaldırsan altından çıkar** You will find him under any stone you lift. He has a finger in every pie. **— taş pekse başını ona vur** It is too late; nothing can be done and you yourself are to blame.

hânıkᵏⁱ (—.) خانق A *lrnd.* choking, strangling, suffocating; *path.* choked with tonsillitis.

hanıkülkelb (—...) خانق‌الکلب A *lrnd.* dogsbane *bot.*, Aponogeton erectum.

hanıkülmelikᵏⁱ (—....) خانق‌الملک A bot. gall, oak apple.

hanıkünnemr (—...) خانق‌النمر A *lrnd.* wolfsbane, *bot.*, Aconitum lycoctonum.

hanıküzzi'b (—...) خانق‌الذئب A *lrnd.* wolfsbane, *bot.*, Aconitum napellus.

hanım خانم 1. lady; woman; *after name* Mrs., Miss. 2. ladylike. 3. wife. 4. mistress (of a household). **— abla** elder sister; sister (said as a term of respect in addressing a lady, stranger or acquaintance). **— böceği** ladybug, *zool.*, Coccinella. **— efendi*. — eli** honeysuckle, *bot.*, Lonicera Caprifolium. **— eligiller** *bot.*, Caprifoliaceae. **— evlâdı** *colloq.* mollycoddle, milksop, mother's boy. **— göbeği** same as **kadın göbeği**. **— hanımcık** perfect housewife; quiet and well-behaved girl or woman. **— iğnesi** 1. elegant and fine-built long rowing-boat. 2. *School slang* effeminate, dandy. **— kadın** good housewife. **— kırarsa kaza, halayık kırarsa suç olur** When the mistress breaks something it is an accident; but when the servant does the same it is a crime. **— kız** young lady, young maiden; well-behaved young lady. **— nine** grandmother, good old lady. **— ördeği** sheldrake. **— parmağı** kind of long grape. **H— Sultan** *Ott. hist.* daughter of a princess and a commoner. **— teyze** aunt.

hanımcağız خانمجغز 1. modest woman, woman. 2. poor woman.

hanımcıkᵍⁱ خانمجك little lady, little woman.

hanımefendi خانم‌افندی 1. lady. 2. madam, my lady. **—ciğim** My dear lady.

hanımlıkᵍⁱ خانملق quality and acts of a lady.

hani 1 (.'.) خانی 1. Where? Where is it, then? 2. Well? You know! *e. g.*, **hani geleceektin?** Well, you said you would come; why didn't you? 3. Well, what about it? 4. After all, well, really. **—dir** for a long time. **— bana?** What about me? Where is my share? **— o günler!** 1. Ah, those good old days are over. 2. I only wish we could; out of the question. **— ya!** How about it? Well, where is it? **— yok mu?** 1. What about it? 2. Don't you have any? 3. You know what I mean.

hani 2 خانی Gk kind of bass, *zool.*, Serranus Cabrilla.

hanif 1 (.—) حنیف A *lrnd.* 1. orthodox Muslim; sincere and steadfast in the faith. 2. devout, pious; God-seeker (in pre-Islamic Arabia).

hanif 2 (—.) حانف A *lrnd.* 1. angry, cross. 2. proud.

hanifiyet (.—.) حنیفیت A *lrnd.* orthodoxy.

hanîn (.—) حنین A *lrnd.* 1. a yearning, the yearning for affection or pity. 2. emotion; gentle cry or sound expressive of tender emotion. 3. twang (of a bowstring or of a cord).

hanis (—.) حانث A *lrnd.* one who breaks his oath, false swearer, perjurer.

hankᵏⁱ حنق A *lrnd.* a choking, strangling, drowning, suffocation.

hankah (——) خانقاه var. of **hanekah**.

hankan (.'.) حنقاً A *lrnd.* by strangling, choking, drowning.

hanlıkᵍⁱ خانلق 1. sovereignty, rulership. 2. khanate.

hannak

hannak^{kı} (.—) حنّاك A *lrnd.* professional strangler, executioner.
hannân (.—) حنّان A *Isl. rel.* most compassionate (one of the attributes of God).
hannâs (.—) حنّاس A *lrnd.* 1. satan, devil. 2. wicked man, sneak. —**î** (.——) A devilish, diabolical, satanic.
hannûr (.—) حنّور A *lrnd.* 1. reed of which arrows are made. 2. worldly comfort, luxury.
hanot حانوت [**hanut 1**] *shopkeeper's slang* commission given to a person who introduces a new customer. —**çu** person who lives on such commissions.
hânsalâr (————) خوانسالار P *lrnd.* butler.
hansi هانسی *archaic, same as* **hangi**.
hantal هنطال حنطال منطال 1. clumsy, coarse. 2. unnecessarily large, huge, coarsely made. 3. clownish, boorish.
hantallaş=^{ır} هنطالّشمق to become clumsy, coarse or clownish. —**tır**= /ı/ *caus. of* **hantallaş**=.
hantallık^{ğı} هنطالّلق clumsiness, coarseness, clownishness.
Hanuh (.—) حنوخ *Heb. Bib.* Enoch.
hanut 1 (——) حانوت A *lrnd.* shop; wineshop, tavern.
hanut 2 (.—) حنوط A *lrnd.* a mixture of camphor, sandalwood, etc., used for sprinkling over corpses.
hanümân (—.—) خانمان P *lrnd.* home, family. —**ı sön**= to be ruined, to lose one's home and family. —**ber endaz** one who ruins homes. —**suz** (—.——) P destroyer of homes.
Hanya (.'.) هانیه *geog.* Khania (in Crete). —**yı Konya'yı anla**= to learn by bitter experience. —**yı Konya'yı göster**= /a/ to teach one a lesson (said as a threat); to punish.
hanzal^{li} حنظال A colocynth, bitter apple, bitter gourd, *bot.*, *Citrullus colocynthis*.
hap 1 حبّ [**hab 1**] 1. pill. 2. *slang* dope. —**ı yut**= to be done for, to be in trouble.
hap 2 هاب sound of snapping; snap. — **et**= /ı/ *child's talk* to snap; to swallow.
hapaz هاپاز [**apaz**] 1. *var. of* **apaz**. 2. *slang* pickings; food.
haphap هپهپ [**kabkab**] *prov.* high wooden clog.
hapır hapır, **hapır-hupur** *colloq.*, *only in* — **ye**= /ı/ to gulp down (food).
hapis^{psi} حبس [**habs**] 1. confinement, imprisonment. 2. *vulg.* prison. 3. *vulg.* prisoner; imprisoned. —**e at**= /ı/ to cast into prison. — **giy**= to be sentenced to prison. — **hakkı** *law* right of retention. — **kaçır**= *vulg.* to break wind. — **olun**= to be imprisoned. —**e tık**= /ı/ to cast into prison. — **yat**= to be in prison. —**ane** *same as* **hapishane**.

hapishane (..—.) حبسخانه P prison, jail. —**yi boyla**= to go straight to prison, to find oneself in jail. — **kaçkını** worthy of prison; scoundrel.
haps^{si} حبس *cf.* **hapis**.
hapsen (.'.) حبساً A *lrnd.* under arrest. — **tazyik** *law* arrest for debt, attachment.
hapset=^{der} حبستمك /ı/ 1. to imprison, confine, cast into prison. 2. to detain, retain.
hapşır=^{ır} هاپشرمق to sneeze.
hapşu (.—) هاپشو atch-choo!
haptet=^{der} ضبط ایتمك *var. of* **habtet**=.
har 1 هار *in* —**ı başına vur**= to go wild, to let oneself get out of control. —**ı geç**= to cool down (fury etc.), cool off (zest).
har 2 هار *only in* — **vurup harman savur**= to squander.
har 3 (—) خار P *lrnd.* thorn. — **ü has** rubbish, sweepings.
har 4 خر P *lrnd.* 1. donkey. 2. stupid fellow. 3. bridge of a stringed instrument. —**ı ba teşdid** very stupid man. —**ı büksisteinan** an ass let loose, an utter ass. —**ı deştî** wild ass. —**ı dupa** two-footed ass, an ass-like person. —**ı Hüda** wood louse. —**i İsa** the ass on which Jesus rode (on Palm Sunday). —**ı müşedded** *same as* **harı ba teşdid**.
hâr^{rı} **5** (—) هار A *lrnd.* 1. hot, warm. 2. sharp, pungent, hot. — **u yâr** hot and sultry.
har^{rı} **6** حرّ A *lrnd.* 1. hot, warm, sultry. 2. heat, warmth, sultriness; feverishness.
har 7 (—) خار P *lrnd.* that pricks, scratches, irritates, annoys, *as in* **dilhâr**.
har 8 (—) خوار P *lrnd.* 1. mean, vile, miserable, contemptible. 2. poor, abandoned, wretched. 3. little, few; easy. — **u zar** abased and miserable.
har 9 (—) خوار P *lrnd.* food; victuals.
har 10 (—) خوار P *lrnd.* eating, drinking, *as in* **hunhar**, **merdümhâr**.
hara 1 (.'.) هارا F stud farm, stock farm.
hara 2 (——) هارا P *lrnd.*, *same as* **hare 1**.
harab (.—) خراب A *lrnd.* 1. *same as* **harap**. 2. a ruining, destruction. — **u yebâb** marred and spoiled. —**abad** (.———) P place of ruins; the world.
harabat (.——) خرابات A *lrnd.* 1. *pl. of* **harabe**. 2. *poet.* wine shop, tavern; brothel. 3. *myst.* house of contemplation where a novice is indoctrinated; state of trance through a manifestation of the divine glory; absorption and annihilation of human faculties and existence in God's glory, when the saint becomes united with God.
harabatî (.———) خراباتی P *lrnd.* 1. careless about his dress and unconventional in his habits; bohemian; dissolute vagabond; confirmed

drunkard. 2. *myst.* saint who has received power to perform miracles and is under God's guidance.

harabatilikᵍⁱ ضرابا تيلك dissoluteness, bohemianism. **—e vur=** to let oneself go in desperation.

harabatiyane (.—————.) خرابا تیانه P in a ruined state, drunkenly.

harabe (.—.) خرابه A a ruin; tumbledown houses or town. **—nişin** (.—..—) P *lrnd.* who dwells in a ruin.

haraben türâbâ (.—´. .——) خرابا ترابا A *lrnd.* tumble-down, utterly ruined.

harabet=ᵈᵉʳ (.—..) خراب ایتمك /ı/ to ruin, destroy.

harabezar (.—.—) خرابه زار P *lrnd.* full of ruins.

harabi (.——) خرابى P *lrnd.* ruin; poverty, misery.

harabiyet (.——.) خرابیت [based on **harab**] *sc.* damage, destruction.

harac (.—) خرج A *lrnd.*, same as **haraç**.

haracgüzar (..—.—) خراج گذار P *lrnd.* tributary, who pays tribute.

haraçᶜⁱ خراج [harac] tax, tribute; *can. law* land tax paid by non-Muslims. **—ı arz** *Ott. hist.* land tax. **—a bağla=** /ı/ *Ott. hist.* to levy a tribute (on). **—a çıkar=** to put up for auction. **—, haraç!** Going! Going! (at an auction). **—a kes=** /ı/ to extort heavy taxes, to oppress. **— mezat sat=** to auction. **—ı Mısır** 1. *Ott. hist.* the tribute of Egypt. 2. an immense sum of money. 3. a sweetheart's kiss. **—ı mukaseme** *Ott. hist.* tribute calculated as a fraction of the produce. **—ı muvazzaf** *Ott. hist.* yearly tax. **—ı re's, —ı ser** *Ott. hist.* poll tax. **—ı vazife** same as **haracı muvazzaf**. **— ye=** *slang* to live on someone else, to sponge on another. **—çı** collector of tribute.

harahir (.—.) خراحر A *lrnd.*, *pl.* of **harhara**.
haraid (.—.) خرائد A *lrnd.*, *pl.* of **haride 1**.
harakif (.—.) خرائف A *lrnd.*, *pl.* of **harkafe**.
harakiri خراكيرى F harakiri.
haram (.—) حرام A 1. forbidden by religion; unlawful, illegitimate, wrong. 2. *Isl. rel.* in the state of canonical interdict attaching to the pilgrimage rites at Mecca. 3. *lrnd.* sacred, inviolable (place). **— et=** /ı, a/ 1. to spoil (somebody's enjoyment of something). 2. to make unlawful, to forbid the use (of something). **— işle=** to commit an illicit act. **— mal** property unlawfully acquired; ill-gotten gains. **— ol** /a/ 1. to be spoiled (pleasure, enjoyment). 2. to be unlawful, illicit, prohibited. **— olsun!** May you get no benefit from it. **— para** money illegitimately acquired. **—a uçkur çöz=** to commit adultery. **— ye=** to acquire property in an unlawful manner.

harami (.——) حرامى A a robber. **—lik** robbery.

haramkâr (.——) حرامكار P *lrnd.* who commits an unlawful act; sinner.

harammağz (.—.) حرام مغز P *lrnd.* spinal marrow.

haramnemek (.—..) حرام نمك P *lrnd.* not worth his salt; lazy; treacherous.

haramzade (.——.) حرامزاده حرام زاده) P 1. bastard. 2. villain, knave; rogue; trickster. **—gî** (.——.—) P *lrnd.* bastardy, illegitimacy.

harapᵇⁱ (.—) خراب [harab] 1. ruined, in ruins. 2. desolated, devastated; uninhabited, desolate. 3. marred, spoiled. 4. desperate; mad with love. **—lık** desolation; ruin.

harar خرار [gırar] large haircloth sack. **— gibi** very large, huge.

hararet (.—.) حرارت A 1. heat, warmth. 2. *med.* fever, temperature, feverishness. 3. thirst. 4. vehemence, fervor, exaltation. **— bas=** /a/ to feel very thirsty. **— derecesi** degree of temperature. **—i gariziye** *biol.* animal heat. **—e gel=** to get warm, to become excited. **—i mahsusa** *phys.* specific heat. **— motorü** *phys.* thermic motor. **— söndür=** to quench thirst. **— ver=** /a/ to make thirsty; to animate. **—bîn** (.—.—) P *obs.*, *phys.* pyroscope, thermoscope.

hararetlen=ⁱʳ حرارتلنمك to become warm, feverish, thirsty, excited. **—dir=** /ı/ *caus.*

hararetli حرارتلى 1. thirsty. 2. feverish; fiery. 3. vehement, intense; enthusiastic. **— hararetli** with great enthusiasm, excitement or vehemence.

hararetnüvis (.—..—) حرارت نویس P *obs.*, *phys.* recording thermometer.

haras (.—) خراس P *lrnd.* mill turned by a donkey, donkey mill. **—i harâb, —i hasisân** the world; the firmament.

haraşo 1 (..´.) خاراشو knitting plain knitting, stocking stitch.

haraşo 2 خاراشو Russ *slang* Russian woman.

haraza 1 خارازا *slang* quarrel, row. **— çıkar=** to quarrel, to cause trouble.

haraza 2 خرزه A *prov.* 1. gallstone of an ox. 2. ring-shaped stone forming the mouth of a well.

harbᵇⁱ حرب A war; battle, fight; combat. **— aç=** to start a war, to fight. **H— Akademisi** War Academy. **— ceridesi** war news bulletin, war diary. **— darp** war, war and confusion. **— dışı** 1. non-belligerent, neutral. 2. disabled. **— esiri** prisoner of war. **— fenni** art of warfare. **— filosu** war fleet. **— gemisi** warship. **— hali** state of war. **— hilesi** stratagem. **— hukuku** law of war. **— ilâhı** god of war. **— ilânı** declaration of war. **— kaçağı** contraband of war. **— malûlü** war

harbak

casualty, invalid, disabled soldier. **— meydanı** battlefield. **—e müracaat et=** to have recourse to war. **— nârası** battle cry. **— nevrozu** war neurosis. **— okulu** military college. **— oyunu** kriegspiel. **— sahası** theater of war. **— sebebi** *casus belli.* **—in sevk ve idaresi** conduct of the war. **— sınıfı** executive (class of soldiers and officers). **— sonu** postwar. **H— Şûrası** Supreme War Council. **— tazminatı** war indemnity. **— techizatı** military equipment, munitions. **— usulü** system of war. **— zararları** war damages. **— zengini** war profiteer.

harbakᵍⁱ ضربی A hellebore, *bot., Veratrum.*
harban (.—) ضربان P *lrnd.* donkey driver.
harbcı ضربجی bellicose, warlike.
harbcu (.—) ضربجو P *lrnd.* warlike; warmonger.
harbe ضربه A *archaic* javelin; pike, halberd. **—ci** *Ott. hist.* halberdier; guardsman.
harben (.'.) ضرباً A *lrnd.* by force of arms, by war.
harbende ضربنده P 1. *lrnd.* donkey-driver; muleteer. 2. *Ott. hist.* muleteer in the Sultan's palace. **— başı** chief muleteer in the Palace.
harbgâh (.—) ضربگاه P *lrnd.* battlefield.
harbi 1 (.—) ضربی A *lrnd.* 1. pertaining to war, military. 2. enemy; non-Muslim; not under truce or safe-conduct.
harbi 2 ضربی |harbe| 1. *artillery* ramrod. 2. *slang* correct, straight. **— konuş=** *slang* to speak the truth. **— zar** *slang* straight, true dice.
Harbiye ضربیه A *Ott. hist.* Military College; Ministry of War. **— mektebi** War Academy. **— Nâzırı** Minister of War. **— Nezareti** Ministry of War, War Office. **—li** student of the War Academy.
harbüz, harbüze خربزه P *lrnd.* watermelon.
harc ضرع A *same as* **harç 2. —ı âlem*. —ı rah*.**
harca=ʳ ضرع ماس /ı/ 1. to spend; to expend; to use. 2. to waste (person); to get rid (of), to dispense (with). 3. *slang* to kill. **—n=** pass.
harcıalem (..—.) ضرع عالم P common, ordinary, used by everybody.
harcırah (..—) ضرع راه P travel allowance.
harcî (.—) ضرجی |based on **harc**| *obs.* for everyday use, ordinary.
harçᶜⁱ **1** ضرع [harç 2] 1. mortar; plaster. 2. ingredients; raw material. 3. trimming (of a garment). 4. *gardening* soil mixture, compost.
harçᶜⁱ **2** ضرع [harc] 1. expenditure, outlay, expenses, debit. 2. customs duties. **—ım değil** It is not for me: it is beyond my means. **—ı**

ferağ *obs.* fee for transfer of property. **—ını gör=** /ın/ to defray the expense (of). **—ı ol=** to be within one's power or means. **— tarifesi** customs rate list. **—ını ver=** /ın/ *slang* to scold.

harçenkᵍⁱ خرچنگ P *lrnd.* crab; *astr.* Cancer.
harçlı خرجلی 1. containing mortar or plaster. 2. of expensive material. 3. decorated, trimmed (dress).
harçlıkᵍⁱ خرجلی allowance; pocket money.
hardal خردال A mustard. **— lâpası** mustard poultice. **— tanesi** 1. grain of mustard seed. 2. very small thing. **— yakısı** mustard plaster. **—iye** grapejuice flavored with mustard.
hardar (——) خاردار P *lrnd.* 1. thorny, prickly. 2. that gives anxiety.
hare 1 (—.) خاره P 1. watermarking (of silk, etc.); kind of watered silk. 2. *lrnd.* very hard rock or stone. **— hare** *poet.* beautifully moired.
hare 2 (—.) ضواره P *lrnd.* food.
harekât (..—) حركات A *lrnd., pl. of* **hareket**. **—ı amibiye** *phys.* amoeboid movements. **—ı harbiye** *mil.* war operations. **— mıntakası** *mil.* operation zone. **— sahası** *mil.* field of operations. **— ve sekenât** behavior, conduct, manner, way. **—ı tecavüziye** *mil.* offensive operations. **— üssü** *mil.* operation base. **—ı zaruriye** necessary operations.
hareke حركه A *Arabic gram.* 1. vowel point. 2. vowel sound.
harekele=ʳ حركله to add the vowel points. **—n=** to take a vowel point; to be read with a vowel sound. **—ndir=** /ı/· *caus. of* **harekelen=**.
harekeli حركلی having a vowel point; with the vowel points added.
hareket حركت A 1. movement, motion. 2. act, deed, move; proceeding; conduct, behavior; action; activity. 3. departure, act of starting. 4. excitement; agitation. 5. earthquake. 6. *mil.* operation. 7. *mus.* movement. 8. *myst.* progress on the path to God. 9. *Ott. hist.* medrese diploma; senior class of a medrese. **—i altmışlı** *Ott. hist.*, *title given to senior medrese teachers.* **—i arz** earthquake. **—i arz |arz 3|** *astr.* eccentric motion of a planet. **—i batiye** *astr.* direct motion of a planet. **— bereket** Movement is a blessing. **— cetveli** *rail.* timetable. **—i dahil** *Ott. hist.*, *title given to senior medrese teachers.* **H— Dairesi** 1. rail transport control office. 2. *mil.* office controlling operations. **—i devriye** *phys.* circular motion; rotatory motion, revolution. **— et=** 1. to move, stir, act. 2. to act, to behave. 3. set out, start; to depart; /a/ to leave (for). **—i garbiye** *astr.* direct motion of a planet. **—e geç=** 1. to start action, to begin,

harf

start. 2. to start, to set out on one's way. **—e gel=** 1. to begin to move or act; to take steps. 2. to become animated. **—e getir=** /ı/ 1. to set in motion. 2. to stir up, to animate. **— harbi** *mil.* moving warfare. **—i hariç** *Ott. hist.*, *title given to certain medresse teachers*. **— kolu** *mech.* starting handle. **H— Ordusu** *Ott. hist.*, *name of the army which came to Istanbul from Thrace in 1909 to subdue the anti-constitutional rebellion, known as the affair of March 31*. **—i taklidî** *psych.*, echopraxia. **—i ulâ** *phil.* motion of the *primum mobile*.

hareketlen=ir مرکتنمك to get into motion or action, to start. **—dir=** /ı/ *caus.*

hareketli مرکتلی moving, active; vivacious, animated.

hareketsiz مرکتسز motionless, inactive; inanimate, dull, stiff. **—lik** immobility.

harekî (..—) مركى A pertaining to motion; *phys.* kinetic; *physiol.* motor (nerve). **—yat** (..——) *phys.* kinematics.

harelen=ir (—...) غاره لنمك to be rippled, watermarked, moire. **—dir=** /ı/ *caus.*

hareli (—..) غاره لى moiré, wavy, waved. **— ipek** watered silk, moiré.

harem حرم A 1. women's apartments, harem. 2. wife; female members of a man's family. 3. *Isl. rel.* sacred territory, especially that of Mecca or Medina. 4. *lrnd.* a reserved place, privacy. **— ağası** 1. *Ott. hist.* black eunuch of the Sultan's Palace. 2. effeminate man. **— bahçesi** garden of the harem. **— dairesi** women's department, harem. **H—i Hümayûn** *Ott. hist.* the Sultan's Harem. **— kâhyası** housekeeper of the harem. **H—i Nebevî, H—i Resulullah** the territory of the mosque or mausoleum of the Prophet; the city of Medina. **— selamlık** women's and men's apartments in a Muslim palace or house. **— selamlık olmasın** Let us not divide into a men's group and a women's group. **H—i Şerif** the Prophet's mausoleum in Medina.

haremeyn (..—) حرمین A *Isl. rel.* the sacred cities and territories of Mecca and Medina. **— aşiretleri** *Ott. hist.*, *name of certain tribes inhabiting the region of Karasi (in Anatolia)*. **— dolabı** *Ott. hist.* department at the Palace where the treasury of the *Haremeyn* was kept. **H— Nezareti** Department of the **Haremeyn** estates in mortmain, founded in 1836. **— payesi** *Ott. hist.* grade of a judge of Mecca and Medina. **H—i Şerifeyn** the sacred cities, Mecca and Medina.

haremlikği حرملك *only in* **— selâmlık olma=** *same as* **harem selâmlık olma=**.

haremsaray (...—) حرمسرای P *lrnd.* 1. the Harem (in the Palace). 2. inner part of a mosque.

hares حرس A *lrnd.* dumbness.

harffi حرف A 1. letter (of the alphabet). 2. *print.* type. 3. *gram.* particle. 4. *literature* allusion, witticism. 5. *lrnd.* word; speech; language. 6. *myst.* medium through which the word is made known. **—i âbdâr** *poet.* witty or pregnant saying. **—i âbî** *onom.* any one of the letters ج.خ.ز.س.ع.ك **—i âlâ** *onom.* any one of the letters ق.ك.ل.م.ص.س.ر.ح ن.ه.ى.ط.ع.ر**—i arzî** *onom.* any one of the letters ج.د.ذ.ش.ف.ل. **—i aslî** *Arabic gram.* radical. **— at=** /a/ 1. to make insulting remarks (to women) in the street. 2. to try to attract someone's attention by irrelevant words, to interrupt. 3. *archaic* to criticize, to insult. **—i âteşî** *onom.* any one of the letters ت.ص.ض.ط.م.لا **—i atf** *gram.* conjunction. **—i bimağz** *lrnd.* a foolish saying, stupidity. **—i cer** *gram.* preposition. **—i cevab** *gram.* consecutive conjunction. **—i edna** *onom.* any one of the letters ب.ت.د.ذ ض.ع.و**—i gülûsuz** *lrnd.* 1. an offensive expression. 2. the keen edge of a sword. **—i hâkî** *same as* **harfi arzî**. **—i halk** *same as* **harfi edna**. **—i harfine** to the very letter, word for word. **—i hatırrenc** *lrnd.* a hurtful remark. **—i havi** *Arabic gram.* the letter ا when standing for a long **a**. **—i heca** a letter of the alphabet. **—i hevai** *onom.* any one of the letters ب.ث.ظ.ق.ن.و.ى **—i Hindî** an Arabic numeral (١ , ٢ , ٣, *etc.*). **—i huşk** *lrnd.* inexpressive, inelegant word. **—i illet** *gram.* any of the letters ا , و , ى, when designating a long vowel. **—i inhiraf** *Arabic gram.* a liquid consonant (ل or ر). **— inkılabı** reform of the alphabet *esp.*, the Latinization of the alphabet in Turkey in 1928. **—i istidrak** *gram.* disjunctive conjunction. **—i istifham** *gram.* interrogative particle. **—i istisna** *gram.* concessive conjunction. **—i istitale** the letter ض. **—i kalb** *onom.* middle letter of a pattern. **—i kalkale** *art of Quran recitation* a tremolo letter (ك.ق.ط.د.ب). **—i kasr** *Arabic gram.* a final ى or ا pronounced as a short **a**. **—i laklaka** *same as* **harfi kalkale**. **—i magzdan** *lrnd.* a weighty saying. **—i mai** *same as* **harfi âbî**. **—i maksur** *same as* **harfi kasr**. **—i mâna** *Arabic gram.* a particle; any word not a noun or a verb. **—i maruf** *Persian gram.* either a vowel و pronounced as a long **u** or a vowel ى pronounced as a long **i**. **—i mechul** *Persian gram.* either a vowel و pronounced as **o** or a vowel ى pronounced as **e**. **—i meczum** 1. *Arabic gram.* a final quiescent consonant. 2. *same as* **harfi sakin**. **—i med** *Arabic gram.*

a long vowel (ی or و ، ا). **—i mehmus** *onom.* any one of the letters ف ص ش س خ ح ث ت ك ، ه. **—i mektubi, —i melbubî** *onom.* any one of the letters و ، ن ، م. **—i melfuzi** *onom.* any one of the thirteen letters the names of which are written with three letters each, no letter being repeated in any one name. **—i menkut** *Arabic script* dotted letter. **—i merfu** 1. *Arabic gram.* a final consonant in the nominative case. 2. *onom.*, same as **harfi ateşî. —i mesruk** *Persian pros.* a letter written but not pronounced; the second of two consecutive quiescent consonants at the end of a syllable in poetry and not counted for meter. **—i mesruri** *onom.* a letter whose name is written with two letters; any one of the letters و ن م. **—i mu'cem** *Arabic script* 1. letter of the alphabet. 2. dotted letter. **—i mukatta** *Arabic script* a letter written in its isolated form. **—i musavvat** *Arabic gram.* letter designating a vowel. **—i mutbak** *art of Quran recitation* a letter in pronouncing which the middle of the tongue is applied to the palate (ظ ط ض ص). **—i mücerret** *Arabic script* undotted letter. **—i mücevher** same as **harfi mucem. —i müfred** *Arabic gram.* a letter that is unlike any other in form as ا / م و ه etc.; any letter of the alphabet when written by itself. **—i mühmel** same as **harfi mücerred. —i münfetih** *art of Quran recitation* any letter excepting ظ ط ض ص. **—i müselsel** *lrnd.* a discourse on a connected chain of ideas. **—i müstakil** *art of Quran recitation* any letter that is not a **harfi müstali. —i müstali** *art of Quran recitation* a letter for the pronunciation of which the tongue is raised (خ ص ض ط ظ ع غ ق). **—i müşkilâlûd** *lrnd.* a difficult saying or discourse. **—i mütecanis** *art of Quran recitation* a letter of the same class with another as ت and ط، ظ and ث. **—i mütekarib** *art of Quran recitation* a letter similar in pronunciation to another as ذ with ض etc. **—i müteşabih, —i mütezaviç** *Arabic script* a letter that is distinguished by means of dots (ب ت ث etc.). **—i nefy** *gram.* negative adverb. **—i nida** *gram.* vocative interjection. **—i nurani** same as **harfi âlâ. —i pehludar** *lrnd.* innuendo. **—i revi** 1. *Arabic pros.* fundamental consonant of a rhyme. 2. *Persian pros.* last letter of a rhyme. **—i safir** *gram.* sibilant (ص س ز). **—i sahih** *Arabic gram.* any letter of the alphabet except ا ، و and ی (which are subject to grammatical permutations). **—i sâit** *gram.* vowel. **—i sâkin** *Arabic gram.* letter that is quiescent by nature or position. **—i sâmit** *gram.* consonant, inclusive of أ و ی when consonants. **—i sebk, —i sehl** *lrnd.* thought-less word. **—i serd** *lrnd.* an expression that offends. **—i şedid** *art of Quran recitation* letter the sound of which is not prolonged when it terminates a syllable (أب ت ج د ط ق ك). **—i şefehi, —i şefevi** *gram.* labial. **—i şemsî** *Arabic gram.* letter that assimilates the ا of the article (ت ث د ذ ر ز س ش ص ض ط ظ ل ن). **—i taksir** *Arabic gram.*, same as **harfi kasr. —i tarif** *gram.* article. **—i tarifi gayri muayyen** *gram.* indefinite article. **—i tarifi muayyen** *gram.* definite article. **—i tenkir** *Arabic gram.* indefinite article. **—i vâhi** *lrnd.* frivolous remark. **—i vâhid** followed by negative verb not a single word. **—i varakgîr** *calligraphy* a letter lengthened to fill a space. **—i veted** *onom.* the first, fourth, seventh and tenth letters of a line. **—i zâid** *Arabic gram.* grammatical augment in a word, especially ا و or ی when letters of prolongation. **—i zamanî** *art of Quran recitation* a letter that may be prolonged in pronunciation (ا و ی) when long vowels and س ش ف ق). **—i zulmanî** same as **harf-i edna. —i zumuht** *lrnd.* bitter expression.

harfâferin (.—.—) حرفآفرین P *lrnd.* 1. God, the creator of speech. 2. poet, writer, orator.
harfakan حرفقان [*Persian* **harfgan**] drug. commercial arsenic.
harfâşinâ (.—.—) حرفآشنا P *lrnd.* acquainted with the niceties of speech.
harfbeharf (.'..) حرفبحرف P word by word, to the very letter.
harfçin (.—) حرفچین P *lrnd.* 1. busybody. 2. talebearer.
harfendaz (..—) حرفانداز P 1. one who makes insulting remarks to women in the street. 2. *lrnd.* one who criticizes or blames. **—î** (..——) P *lrnd.*, same as **harfendazlık.**
harfendazlık[k1] حرفاندازلق act of one who annoys women with impertinent remarks. **—ta bulun=** to molest a woman.
harfgîr (.—) حرفگیر P *lrnd.* censor, caviler, critic. **—î** (.——) P, **—lik** criticism, cavil, censure.
harfi (.—) حرفی A *lrnd.* literal; pertaining to letters. **—yen** (.—'.) A word for word, exactly.
harfkeş حرفکش P *lrnd.* 1. scribe. 2. dull talker.
harfpeyma (..—) حرفپیما P *lrnd.* fluent talker.
hargâh (.—), **hargeh** هرگاه P *lrnd.* 1. marquee, pavilion. 2. sky. **—ı ezrak, —ı gâvpuşt** sky. **—ı kamer** halo around the moon.
hargûş (.—) هرگوش P *lrnd.* hare. **—ek** baby rabbit.
hargür هاگور noise, tumult.

harhar 1 خار خار 1. continued snarling noise; continuous or repeated harsh noise. 2. *same as* **harıl harıl.**

hârhâr 2 (— —) خار خار P *lrnd.* 1. scratching, itch. 2. desire, yearning, longing. 3. affliction, anguish.

harhara هرهره A *lrnd.* continuous snoring; death-rattle.

harharyas خارخاریاس Gk porbeagle, mackerel shark, *zool.*, *Lamna nasus*.

harhur خارخور noise; confusion and misunderstanding.

harılda=ʳ خارلدا to make a gurgling noise.

harıl harıl خارل خارل continuously, with great effort; incessantly. — **çalışıyor** He works like mad. — **yanıyor** It is burning furiously.

harıltı خارلتی loud and continuous noise.

harın خارین [harun] 1. intractable (beast). 2. obstinate, bad-tempered. —**la=** 1. to become intractable. 2. to be obstinate or bad-tempered.

hari (. —) حری A *lrnd.* worthy, fit, suited.

harib 1 (—.) هارب A *lrnd.* fugitive.

harib 2 (—.) خارب A *lrnd.* devastating, destroying.

harib 3 (. —) حریب A *lrnd.* robbed, plundered.

haribe (. —.) حریبه A *lrnd.* 1. property of which one has been despoiled. 2. effects on which one subsists.

haric (—.) خارج A 1. the outside surface or part of a thing, outside, exterior; external (surface or appearance). 2. excluded. 3. abroad, foreign countries. 4. *astr.* a star that is not included in the figure of a constellation. — **anilmerkez** eccentric. — **et=** /ı/ to exclude, to leave outside. — **ez defter** 1. out of the list, out of consideration. 2. surplus of persons; surplus of land compared with the former land registry when a new one is made. — **ez kanun** *law* extralegal. — **ez memleket** *lrnd.* exterritorial. —**i kısmet** 1. *arith.* quotient. 2. outside of the allotment; dead. — **medresesi** *Ott. hist.* the primary school of the medresse. — **ol=** to be excluded.

haricen (—´..) خارجاً A outwardly, externally.

harici (—.—) خارجی A 1. external, exterior. 2. foreign. 3. *Isl. rel.* heretic, pertaining to the Khawarij sect. 4. *obs.* day student. 5. *phil.* exoteric, extrinsic. — **karakol** *mil.* exterior guard.

hariciye (—...) خارجیه A 1. foreign affairs. 2. external diseases. — **dairesi** *Ott. hist.* department of the Ministry of Foreign Affairs. — **kâtibi** *Ott. hist.* private secretary of the Department of Foreign Affairs. — **memuru** Foreign Office official. — **Müsteşarı** undersecretary for Foreign Affairs. **H— Nazırı** 1. *Ott. hist.* Minister of Foreign Affairs. 2. Foreign Minister. **H— Nezareti** *Ott. hist.* Ministry of Foreign Affairs. **H— Teşrifatçısı** *Ott. hist.* Master of ceremonies. **H— Vekâleti** Ministry of Foreign Affairs. **H— Vekili** Minister of Foreign Affairs.

hariciyeci خارجیه جی 1. member of the Foreign Service. 2. specialist in external diseases.

hariçᶜⁱ (—.) خارج *var. of* **haric.**

harid 1 (.—) خرید P *lrnd.* purchase. — **ü füruş** buying and selling, trade.

-harid 2 (.—) خرید P *lrnd.* bought, purchased, *e. g.*, **zerharid.**

harid 3 (.—) حرید A *same as* **haride 1.**

haridar (.— —) خریدار P *lrnd.* 1. purchaser, customer. 2. bidder, inquirer. 3. candidate.

haride 1 (.—.) حریده A *lrnd.* 1. unpierced pearl. 2. virgin.

haride 2 (.—.) خریده P *lrnd.* bought, purchased.

harif 1 (.—) حریف A *lrnd.* autumn.

harif 2 (.—) حریف A *lrnd.* colleague, companion. —**ane** (.—.) P *same as* **arifane 2.**

harikᵏⁱ **1** (.—) حریق A *lrnd.* 1. a burning, combustion. 2. fire, conflagration. 3. burnt; suffering; victim (of a fire, etc.).

harikᵏⁱ **2** (—.) هارق A *lrnd.* burning, that burns a thing.

harikᵏⁱ **3** (—.) خارق A *lrnd.* splitting, rending, bursting, tearing.

harikᵏⁱ **4** (.—) حریك A *lrnd.* 1. sexually impotent. 2. weak in the waist.

harika 1 (—..) هارقه A *lrnd.* fire.

harika 2 (.—.) حریقه A *lrnd.* 1. burning sensation, smart. 2. anguish.

harika 3 (—..) خارقه A *lrnd.* wonder, miracle; marvelous, extraordinary.

harikavî (—..—) خارقوی P *lrnd.* wondrous, miraculous.

harikulâde (—..—.) خارق العاده A *lrnd.* extraordinary, unusual, wonderful.

harikzede (.—..) حریق زده P *lrnd.* injured by fire; rendered homeless by a fire. —**gân** (.—..—) *pl. of* **harikzede.**

harim (.—) حریم A *lrnd.* 1. most intimate and private place or part. 2. anything which a man is bound to protect and defend. 3. sacred and inviolable; innermost place or part, sanctuary. 4. women's apartment in a house. 5. very intimate friend. —**i ismet** innermost shrine, the very heart.

harir 1 (.—) حریر A *lrnd.* 1. hot, warm, fiery; sultry. 2. hot with anger, burning with rage, furious.

harir 2 (.—) حریر A *lrnd.* 1. silk. 2. silk paper. —**i Hindî** a kind of silk paper (made in India).

hariri (.——) حَرِيرِي A *lrnd.* made of silk, soft as silk.

Haririye (.—..) حَرِيرِيَه A order of dervishes founded by Ahmed-ür-Rufaî.

haris 1 (.—) حَرِيص A 1. inordinately greedy and covetous; avaricious, ambitious. 2. ambitiously desirous, very particular.

hâris 2 (—.) حَارِث A *lrnd.* husbandman, yeoman, plowman, farmer.

hâris 3 (—.) حَارِس A *lrnd.* guard, watchman; keeper.

haristân (—.—) خَارِسْتَان P *lrnd.* thorny place, "the bush".

hâriş (—.) خَارِش P *lrnd.* 1. an itching; a scatching. 2. annoyance, irritation.

harita 1 (.ʹ.) خَرِيطَة Gk geographic map, topographic plan. —**sını al**= /ın/ to make a topographical survey (of), to survey. —**i âlem** world map, the world. — **çantası** map case, map holder. — **dairesi** survey department. **H— Umum Müdürlüğü** Ordnance Survey Department. —**da yoktur** It's altogether unexpected, unforeseen (of difficulties).

harita 2 (.—.) خَرِيطَة A *lrnd.* bag, pouch; wallet.

haritacı (..ʹ..) خَرِيطَجِي surveyor; cartographer. —**lık** surveying.

harkᵏ¹ **1** حَرْك *lrnd.*, same as **ark 1.**

harkᵏ¹ **2** حَرْك A *lrnd.* a tearing, bursting, splitting.

harkᵏ¹ **3** حَرْك A *lrnd.* a burning; combustion.

harka حَرْقَة A *lrnd.* 1. burning or smarting sensation; mental anguish. 2. ardor, heat; burn, scald. —**i bevl** *path.* painful micturation, gonorrhea.

harkafa, harkafe مَرْقَفَى A *anat.* hipbone, *ilium.*

harkafî (..—) مَرْقَفِي A *anat.* iliac.

harkatᵗⁱ حَرْقَت A same as **harka.**

harkürre حَرْكُرَّه P *lrnd.* donkey colt.

harla=ʳ خَارْلَامَق 1. to burn furiously, to be in flames, to flare. 2. to get suddenly angry, to flare up. —**t**= /ı/ *caus.*

harlı خَارْلِى 1. burning in flames. 2. hot-tempered.

harman خَرْمَن خَرْمَان خَرْمَن [**hirmen**] 1. heap of grain for threshing; heap, mass. 2. operation of threshing. 3. harvest. 4. blend (of tea, tobacco, etc.); mixture. 5. *print.* gathering. 6. *min.* waste heap (coal), dump. 7. *slang* feeling low for want of narcotics. — **çorman** *slang* in utter disorder. — **dolabı** threshing machine. — **döv**= to thresh. — **döveni** threshing sledge. — **et**= /ı/ 1. to blend; to sort and arrange. 2. *prov.* to arrange for threshing, to thresh. — **gibi** in a great heap. —**da hesaplaş**= 1. to settle one's account at the end of the harvest. 2. to settle one's

grudges when the time comes. — **kaya** shelf, level rocks at the bottom of the sea. — **kilesi** a large grain measure (a kind of bushel). — **makinası** threshing machine, thresher. — **savur**= to winnow grain. — **sonu** 1. end of the threshing season; after the harvest. 2. residue of grain (mixed with stones and dust left after threshing), gleanings. 3. remnants of a fortune or business. — **sonu dervişlerin** *proverb* Patience is always rewarded. — **tozluğu** 1. grain mixed with dust and earth after winnowing. 2. an allowance of clean grain claimed as compensation for dirt found mixed with grain. — **yeri** threshing floor, threshing field.

harmancı خَرْمَانْجِى 1. thresher. 2. blender (of tobacco, etc.).

harmandalı خَرْمَانْدَالِى a kind of folk dance (in Izmir and vicinity).

harmani (.——) خَرْمَانِى , **harmaniye** (.——.) خَرْمَانِيَه a kind of long cape.

harmanla=ʳ خَرْمَانْلَامَق /ı/ 1. to blend (tobacco etc.). 2. to go all around; to run in a circle (horse). 3. *naut.* to go all around (ship). —**n**= to be encircled by a halo.

harmeniş خَرْمَنِش P *lrnd.* mulish, obstinate, pigheaded.

harmoni خَارْمُنِى F *mus.* harmony.

harmonikᵍⁱ خَارْمُنِيك F *mus.* harmonic.

harmonium خَارْمُنِيُوم F harmonium, small organ.

harmuş (.—) خَرْمُوش P *lrnd.* rat, large mouse.

harmühre خَرْمُهْرَه P *lrnd.* 1. large bead of colored glass (used as a charm or ornament). 2. large conch shell used as a horn by dervishes.

harnakᵏⁱ (——) خَارْنَاك P *lrnd.* thorny, prickly.

harnupᵇᵘ خَرْنُوب [A .—] carob; carob tree, *bot., Ceratonia siliqua.*

harpᵖ¹, **harpa** (.ʹ.) خَارْپَا F *mus.* harp.

harpuşta, harpüşte خَرْپُشْتَه P *arch.* ridged (roof), donkeyback. — **köprü** one-arched ridged bridge.

harraka (.—.) حَرَّاقَة A *hist.* fire ship, flame-thrower.

harran حَرَّان *Or. mus.* an extinct **makam.**

harrangürra (.———) حَرَّانْگُرَّه *colloq.* in a disorderly and noisy manner.

harras (.—) حَرَّاث A *lrnd.* husbandman, farmer, yeoman.

harrât¹ (.—) خَرَّاط A *lrnd.* lathe operator, one who pares off outer surfaces.

harrengurra same as **harrangürra.**

harsˢⁱ حَرْث A 1. culture. 2. *lrnd.* cultivation, a plowing. 3. *lrnd.* arable land; piece of land prepared for sowing. —**î** (.—) 1. cultural. 2. *lrnd.* agricultural.

harşef حَرْشَف A *lrnd.* 1. fish scale. 2. artichoke,

bot., *Cynara scolymus;* cardoon, bot., *Cynara cardunculus.* —**iye** (..—.) A bot., *Cynara.*
harşefiyülcenah (..—..—) مرشغی لجناح A zool., *Lepidoptera.*
harta (´.) مَرْطِهٔ var. of **harita 1.**
hartadak خارطه دن very suddenly (to seize upon; to snap at, to bite), e. g., — **elimi ısırdı** He suddenly bit my hand.
hartama خارتاما prov. shingle.
hart hart خارت خارت scratch, scratch.
hart hurt خارت خورت noise of impolite or beastly eating.
hartuçᶜᵘ خرتوچ مرطوج مارطوج [kartuç] Gk artillery cartridge. —**çu** cartridge boy, powder monkey.
harukᵏᵘ (.—) حروقه A lrnd. tinder.
Harun 1 (——) هارون A *man's name;* Aaron.
harun 2 (.—) حرون A same as **harın.**
harupᵇᵘ خروب A same as **harnup.**
harur (.—) حرور A 1. obs., phys. heat. 2. lrnd. hot wind; hot night wind. —**î** (.——) A phys. caloric.
Harût (——) هاروت A Isl. rel., name of a fallen angel confined in a pit at Babylon with his companion Marut. —**fen** (——.) P skillful magician.
Harûtî (———) هاروتی P Isl. rel. 1. disciple of Harut. 2. magician, sorcerer; magic.
harvar 1 (——) خاروار P lrnd. thorny, pointed like a thorn.
harvar 2 (.—) خروار P lrnd. a donkey-load.
harveş خروش P lrnd. like an ass, asinine.
harz حرز A lrnd. a guarding, a preserving.
harzar (——) خارزار P lrnd. thorny place.
hasˢˢ¹ **1** خاص [has 2] 1. special, particular; private, individual; privy, belonging to the person of the sovereign; /a/ peculiar (to). 2. pure, unmixed, unadulterated. — **ahır** hist. Sultan's stable. — **bahçe** hist. private garden of the Sultan. — **boya** fast dye; natural color. — **dur!** obs. mil. Shoulder arms! — **ekmek** fine white bread. — **kefal** common gray mullet, zool., *Mugil cephalus.* — **kullar** Ott. hist., title of the corps of Bostancıs. — **oda** Ott. hist. the royal ward of the Sultan's palace. — **un** fine white flour.
hasˢˢ¹ **2** خاص A 1. Ott. hist. royal domain; fief with a yearly income of over 100,000 aspers. 2. archaic the upper class. —**u âm,** — **ve âm** the elite and the common people, the high and the low. —**lar mukataası** Royal Domain Office (a department of the Ministry of Finance).
has 3 خس P lrnd. 1. straw, chip of wood; rubbish. 2. weed. 3. nobody. — **u hâşâk** 1. sticks and straws; rubbish. 2. the rabble.
hasa حسه calico.
hasad (.—) حصاد A lrnd., same as **hasat.**

hasafet (.—.) مصافت A lrnd. a being endowed with sound judgment.
hasaid (.—.) حصائد A lrnd. harvests. —**i elsine** reputations demolished by evil tongues.
hasail (.—.) خصائل A lrnd., pl. of **haslet.**
hasais (.—.) خصائص A lrnd., pl. of **hasiyet.**
hasanet (.—.) حصانت A lrnd. 1. a place's being impregnable; impregnability, strength. 2. chastity.
hasar (.—) خسار A damage, loss; injury; risk. —**a uğra=** to suffer damage.
hasarat (.——) خسارات A pl. of **hasaret.** —**ı bahriye** com. average.
hasaret (.—.) خسارت A same as **hasar.** —**dide** (.—.—.) P lrnd. devastated, ruined.
hasaset (.—.) خساست A lrnd. stinginess, miserliness, avarice.
hasatᵈⁱ حصاد [hasad] 1. a reaping. 2. harvest.
hasb حسب A lrnd. according to, because of. —**ı hal*.**
hasbe حصبه A lrnd., med. measles. —**i muhtelite** complex measles. —**i muzaafa** confluent measles.
hasbelbeşeriye (....—.) حسب البشریة A. lrnd. because of being human.
hasbelicab (..——) حسب الایجاب A lrnd. according to need.
hasbel'iktiza (....—) حسب الاقتضا A lrnd. according to the requirements of the case.
hasbel'imkân (...—) حسب الامکان A lrnd. as far as possible, as much as possible.
hasbellüzum (...—) حسب اللزوم A lrnd. according to need.
hasbelmakdûr (...—) حسب المقدور A lrnd. to the utmost of one's power.
hasbelmeram (...—) حسب المرام A lrnd. as was intended.
hasbelvazife (...—.) حسب الوظیفه A lrnd. as required by duty, for duty's sake.
hasbennezake (...—.) حسب النزاکه [based on Arabic] lrnd. out of politeness.
hasbetenlillah (.´...—´) حسبةً لله A lrnd. for love of God; disinterestedly; without expecting anything in return.
hasbıhalˡⁱ (..—) حسب حال A friendly chat. — **et=** to have a friendly chat; to exchange confidences.
hasbî 1 (.—) حسبی A for the love of God; gratuitous; disinterested.
hasbi 2 حسبی [hasbî 1] in — **geç=** slang not to care at all.
hasbinallah حسبنا الله A Good God!
hase (—.) خاصه same as **hasa.**
haseb حسب A lrnd. personal qualities, merits. —**iyle** because of; by reason of; since. — **u neseb** personal merits and ancestral distinction. —**î** (..—) A pertaining to personal distinction and honor.

hased حسد A same as **haset**.
hasede حسده A lrnd., pl. of **hasid**.
hasedpişe (..—.) حسدپيشه P lrnd. habitually jealous and envious.
haseki خاصگى [Persian khasağı] Ott. hist. 1. sergeant at arms in the bodyguard of the Sultan. 2. the Sultan's favorite wife. — **ağa** lieutenant of the **Bostancıbaşı**. — **baratası** same as **haseki küpesi**. **H— Başı** the Receiver-General of the estates of the sacred places of Mecca and Medina, fourth officer of the corps of the **Baltacı**. **H— Başkâtibi** the Chief Clerk under the **Haseki Başı** and fifth officer of the **Baltacı** corps. **H— Kadın** Sultan's wife who has borne him a daughter. — **küpesi** 1. common columbine, bot., Aquilegia vulgaris. 2. columbine-shaped ornament. **H— Sultan** Sultan's wife who has borne him a son.
hasele حَضَلْ A obs., anat. abdominal region; hypogastrium.
haselî (..—) حَضَلى A obs., anat. abdominal, hypogastric.
hasen حسن A lrnd. good, fair and comely, beautiful, pleasant, agreeable. — **besen** beautiful, elegant.
hasenât (..—) حسنات A lrnd., pl. of **hasene**.
hasene حسنة A lrnd. 1. good work, pious deed. 2. good, pleasant, agreeable. 3. beautiful woman. 4. an old gold coin.
Haseneyn (..—) حسنين A Isl. hist. Hasan and Husain, the two sons of Ali, both murdered and considered as martyrs.
hasep[bl] حسب var. of **haseb**.
haset[dl] حسد [hased] envy, jealousy; an envying; colloq. envious, jealous. —**ten çatla=** to be consumed with jealousy. — **et=** /a/ to envy. —**çi** habitually envious and jealous.
hâsib (—.) حاصب A lrnd. scattering gravel or flakes of snow (wind); discharging snow or hail (cloud); violent wind that drives pebbles along.
hâsid (—.) حاصد A lrnd. reaper, harvester.
hâsıl 1 (—.) حاصل A 1. resulting; result, effect, produced, growing; produce; profit; gain; math. result. 2. lrnd. occurring, befalling; existing. —**ı** in short, in brief; to sum up. — **et=** /ı/ 1. to produce. 2. to acquire, to gain. —**ı kelâm** in short, in a word; the long and short of it is. —**ı mastar** gram. verbal noun. — **ol=** to result, accrue; to be produced, to be attained, obtained, acquired; to happen, to occur, to come into existence, to remain over. —**ı tahsil et=** to produce what has already been produced, to waste one's time and energy. —**ı zarp** math. product.
hasıl 2 حاصل [Arabic —.] green barley for use as fodder.

hasılât (—.—) حاصلات A 1. produce; products. 2. revenue, returns; profit, proceeds. —**ı gayri safiye** gross profit. —**ı safiye** net profit, net proceeds. —**lı** productive; profitable.
hasıllan=[ır] حاصللن 1. to produce green ears (barley). 2. to grow up.
hâsılsız (—..) حاصلسز 1. non-productive, producing or yielding nothing. 2. unprofitable, useless.
hâsılülemr (—...) حاصل الامر A lrnd. the sum and substance of a matter.
hasım[smı] حصم [hasm 1] adversary, antagonist, enemy. —**lık** enmity, antagonism.
hâsına (—..) حاصنة A lrnd. chaste, virtuous, modest (woman).
hasır 1 حصير [hasir 3] rush mat; matting. — **altı et=** /ı/ 1. to shelve a matter; to leave unanswered (request). 2. to hide, to hush up. — **altına git=** to be shelved and forgotten. — **biçimi yelken** lugsail. — **döşe=** /a/ to lay mats, matting (in a room). — **eskileri** remains of old mats (jokingly used instead of **hazretleri**). — **gibi seril=** to abound, to be in great quantities; to be spread like a carpet. — **iskemle** wicker chair. — **işi** wicker work. — **kapla=** /a/ to cover with wicker or matting. — **koltuk** wicker chair. — **ol=** slang to be floored, to be beaten (in games). — **otu** rush, bot., Juncus arabicus. — **örgü** mat, matting. — **sandalye** wicker chair. — **sazı** bulrush, bot., Scirpus cernuus. — **şapka** straw hat.
hasır 2 (—.) حاصر A lrnd. 1. who detains, that restrains. 2. that hems in, shuts in, besieges, besets.
hasır[srı] **3** حصر var. of **hasr**.
hasıra (—..) حاصره A lrnd. flank, side.
hasırcı حصيرجى mat maker; dealer in mats.
hasırcıyan (...—) حصيرجيان lrnd. mat makers. —**ı hasse** Ott. hist. the Palace mat makers.
hasırla=[r] حصيرله /ı/ to cover with matting. —**n=** pass. —**t=** /ı, a/ caus. of **hasırla=**.
hasırlı حصيرلى 1. covered with matting. 2. made of wicker work. 3. large bottle covered in wicker work.
hasi (.—) خصى A lrnd. castrated; eunuch.
hasib (.—) حسيب A lrnd. 1. estimated, esteemed, valued. 2. God, as the Great Reckoner, and also the All-sufficient.
hasid (—.) حاسد A lrnd. envious, jealous.
hasif (—.) خاسف A lrnd. engulfed, sunken; eclipsed (sun or moon).
hasim (—.) حاسم A lrnd. 1. that cuts through or off. 2. that arbitrates who ends disputes.

hasin (.—) حصين A *lrnd.* strong, guarded, fortified.

hasir 1 (—.) خاسر A *lrnd.* disappointed, frustrated, confounded; loser.

hasir 2 (—.) حاسر A *lrnd.* grieving for a loss, absence or want; deprived; destitute.

hasir 3 (.—) حسير A *lrnd.*, same as **hasır 1**.

hasis 1 (.—) خسيس A 1. miser, mean, petty; miserly, stingy, vile. 2. *lrnd.* insignificant.

hasis 2 (.—) حثيث A *lrnd.* 1. inciting, instigating; incited, instigated. 2. prompt, quick, rapid.

hasislikᵍⁱ خسيسلك stinginess, avarice, parsimony.

hasisüsseyr (.—..) حثيث السير A *lrnd.* swift of foot.

hasiyet (—..) خاصيت [*Arabic* **khassıya**] *lrnd.* 1. special quality, special virtue. 2. usefulness; utility (of food, etc.). —**li** 1. having a special quality. 2. useful to the health. 3. savoury.

haslet خصلت A *lrnd.* virtue; merit.

hasm 1 خصم A *lrnd.*, same as **hasım**. —ı **can** deadly enemy, mortal foe.

hasm 2 حسم A *lrnd.* a cutting through or off; a forbidding, hindrance.

hasmane (.—.) خصمانه P *lrnd.* hostile (attitude, etc.). — **hareket** *law* hostile act.

hasmeyn (.—) خصمين A *law* the two parties to a law suit (*i. e.*, plaintiff and defendant).

hasna (.—) حسناء A *lrnd.* 1. very beautiful (woman). 2. good and pleasant (woman). —**yi müstesna** an exceptional beauty.

haspa حسبه [**hasbe**] minx; rascal (used affectionately of a girl or woman); hussy.

hasr حصر A *lrnd.* 1. a restraining; restriction; a confining. 2. a devoting or consecrating to one purpose. —ı **cali** arbitrary restriction.

hasret=ᵈᵉʳ **1** حصرتمك 1. to confine, to limit, to restrict. 2. /ı, a/ to appropriate, to devote, consecrate (to).

hasret 2 حسرت A 1. a longing, yearning, nostalgia, homesickness; ardent desire. 2. regret (for something lost); feeling a loss. — **çek**= /a/ to long, to pine, to yearn (for). —**ini çek**= /in/ 1. to long to see again (person or thing). 2. to miss, to suffer from the lack of. — **git**= /a/ to die disappointed, with a great longing. —**ten hasrete koşuyor** He goes from one longing to another. — **kal**= /a/ to feel the loss or absence of, to miss greatly.

hasretdide (..—.) حسرت ديده P *lrnd.* that suffers the pang of separation.

hasrethane (..—.) حسرتخانه P *poet.* house of the disappointed; prison.

hasretkeş حسرتكش P *lrnd.* disappointed; suffering the pangs of separation.

hasretname (..—.) حسرتنامه P *lrnd.* a letter complaining of separation and longing.

hasretzede (..—.) حسرتزده P *lrnd.* disappointed; woebegone, sad.

hassa 1 (—.) خاصّه A 1. quality; property; peculiarity. 2. *lrnd.*, *fem. of* **has 1**.

hassa 2 خاصّه [**hassa 1**] 1. *Ott. hist.* Sultan's bodyguard. 2. private domain, given as a fief to a servant of the state. — **ve âmme** 1. state servants and the public. 2. the upper and lower classes (of people). — **askeri** guardsman. **H— Müşiri** field marshal commanding the guards. **H— Ordusu** imperial guard regiments. — **piyadesi** infantry of the guards. — **süvarisi** cavalry guards.

hassâd (.—) حصّاد A *lrnd.* reaper.

Hassan (.—) حسّان A *name of an Arabic poet, companion and eulogist of the Prophet.*

hassas (.—) حسّاس A 1. sensitive, responsive; delicate in feeling; scrupulous, conscientious. 2. touchy, over-sensitive, susceptible. — **mekanik** fine mechanics; precision-tool manufacturer.

hassasiyet (.——.) حسّاسيت A 1. sensitiveness, sensitivity. 2. touchiness, susceptibility.

hassaten (.'..) خاصّةً [*Arabic* —..] A *lrnd.* especially, particularly, most particularly.

hasse (—.) حاسّه A *physiol.* sense, each of the five senses. —**i selime** common sense.

hassiyet 1 (——.) خاصّيت A *lrnd.* 1. peculiarity, speciality; selectness; purity, goodness. 2. peculiar virtue, power, effect, quality; habit.

hassiyet 2 (——.) حاسّيت A *lrnd.* sense, sensitivity.

hassülhas (—.—) خاصّ الخاصّ A *lrnd.* the very best, the most excellent.

hasta خسته P 1. sick, ill; invalid, unwell; patient. 2. worn out, not in good condition, out of order; *slang* penniless; *school slang* lazy; *gambler's slang* losing (card). **H— Adam** *Ott. hist.* Sick Man of Europe. — **arabası** ambulance. —**ya bak**= to nurse a patient; to treat a patient; to examine a patient. — **bakıcı** trained nurse; hospital attendant. — **bakıcılık** sick-nursing. — **çorbası** tasteless and insipid thing. —**ya çorba sorulur mu?** (*lit.* Why ask a sick man if he wants soup?) Why hesitate, go on and do it. Of course I want it. — **düş**= to fall sick. — **et**= /ı/ to make ill. — **ne sahanda kor ne tasta!** He eats too heartily to be truly sick. — **ol**= to get sick, to be ill. —**sı ol**= /ın/ to be an addict, to be a slave (to). — **teskeresi** stretcher. — **yatağı** sickbed.

hastabend حسته بند P *lrnd.* 1. bandage, roller-bandage for fractured limbs. 2. one who binds up broken bones, bonesetter.

hastaciger حسته جگر P *poet.* 1. sick at heart; sorrowful. 2. pining with love.

hastadil حسته دل P *lrnd.* sick at heart; disappointed, sorrowful.

hastahal (..—) خسته مآل P *lrnd.* 1. unwell. 2. in a sad way.

hastahane (..—.) خسته خانه *same as* **hastane**.

hastalan=ᵊ خسته لانمن to become ill. **—dır**= /¹/ *caus.*

hastalıkᵏ¹ خسته لوک 1. sickness, illness; ill health. 2. disease; morbid condition; epidemic. 3. addiction. **— al**= to catch an infection. **— geçir**= to be ill, to have an illness. **— kap**= *same as* **hastalık al**=. **—a yakalan**= to fall sick, to be taken ill. **—lı** 1. in bad health, sickly, ailing. 2. unhealthful; disease-laden.

hastamizac (...—) خسته مزاج P *lrnd.* 1. weak, sickly, unhealthy; delicate. 2. chronic invalid.

hastane (.—.) خسته خانه [**hastahane**] hospital, infirmary; *naut.* sickbay.

haste 1 خسته P *lrnd.*, *same as* **hasta**.

hâste 2 (—.) خاسته P *lrnd.* 1. risen, raised. 2. grown (sown seed). 3. occurring.

haste 3 (—.) خواسته P *lrnd.* 1. desired, wished (for), willed, wanted. 2. wealth, money, possessions.

hastegân (..—) خستگان P *lrnd.* the sick.

hàstegi (..—) خستگی P *lrnd.* sickness; fatigue; hurt, wound.

hâstgâr, hastkâr (——) خواستگار P *lrnd.* 1. desiring, asking for. 2. applicant, supplicant. **—î** (———) P, **—lık** request; wish.

hasud (.—) حسود A very envious, jealous. **—âne** (.——.) P *lrnd.* enviously, jealously.

hasutᵈᵘ (.—) حسود [**hasud**] jealous.

hasve حسوه A *lrnd.* a sip, sipping.

hâş (—) خاش P *lrnd.* 1. rubbish, chips, parings; odds and ends. 2. impetuosity, vehemence; war, battle. **— u heş** 1. rubbish, trash. 2. the rabble.

hâşa 1 (—'.) حاشا A God forbid! *e. g.*, Hâşa, siz kabalık etmezsiniz! God forbid, you wouldn't be rude. **— huzurdan**, **— minelhuzur** with all due respect; excuse the expression. **— sümme hâşa** I greatly regret the expression.

haşa 2 حاشا خاشه [**gaşiye**] saddlecloth, saddle housing.

haşa 3 (.—) حشا A 1. *anat.* the whole contents of the abdomen. 2. *lrnd.* side, border, tract.

haşacı خاشاجی maker or seller of horsecloths.

haşahiş (.——) مناقيش A *lrnd.*, *pl. of* **haşhaş**.

haşaiş (.—.) حشائش A *lrnd.*, *pl. of* **haşiş**.

hâşâkᵏ¹ (——) خاشاک P *lrnd.* 1. straw, a bit of stick; chips, leaves, shavings. 2. rubbish, siftings.

haşarat (..—) حشرات A 1. insects, vermin. 2. mob, rabble. **— takımı** the rabble.

haşarı حشری [*Arabic* haşarı] 1. out of hand, disorderly, naughty, mischievous. 2. wild, dissolute. **—lık** unruly behavior, wild prank.

haşat حاشات *chauffeur's slang* worn out (automobile).

haşeb خشب A *lrnd.* wood, timber.

haşebe خشبه A *lrnd.* piece of wood.

haşebî (..—) خشبی A 1. *sc.* wooden, ligneous. 2. *obs.* kind of ligneous paper. **—yet** A *sc.* lignosity, woodiness.

haşefe خشفه A 1. *anat., can. law* tip of the penis. 2. *lrnd.* stubble; rock jutting out of water.

haşelillah (—..—) حاشلله A *lrnd.* God forbid!

haşem حشم A *lrnd.* retinue, suite, following, staff, domestics.

haşerat (..—) حشرات A *same as* **haşarat**.

haşere حشره A creeping thing, insect.

haşergâh (..—) حشرگاه P *Isl. rel.* 1. a place where people collect, especially for the last judgment. 2. place where men collect to weep for the martyrs, Hasan and Husain.

haşevi (..—) حشوی A *anat.* splanchnic, visceral, intestinal.

haşhaş خشخاش A poppy, *bot.*, *Papaver somniferum*.

haşhaşiye (.—..) خشخاشیه A *bot.*, *Papaveraceae*.

haşıl حشیل *text.* sizing, starch. **—la**= /¹/ to dress with size or starch. **—lan**= *pass. of* **haşılla**=.

haşır خاشر *in* **— haşır**, **— huşur** crunch, crash.

haşırda=ʳ خاشیردامن to make a crashing sound. **—t**= *caus.*

haşırtı خاشیردی harsh crashing sound.

hâşi 1 (——) خاشی A *lrnd.* fearful, fearing, apprehensive, timid.

hâşiⁱⁱ **2** (—.) خاشع A *lrnd.* who bows the head and speaks in a low tone, especially in worship; humble. **—en** (—'..) A humbly.

haşiîn (—.—) خاشعین A *pl.* **— ve haşiât** reverently submissive people.

Haşimî (—.—) هاشمی A 1. *Isl. hist.* Hashimid (member of a notable family in Mecca). 2. Hashimite (Arabic dynasty).

haşin (.—) خشین A bad-tempered, harsh, rude. **—lik** bad temper, harshness, rudeness.

haşir 1 حشر *var. of* **haşr**. **— neşir ol**= /la/ to be cheek by jowl, to be hand in glove with, to be in close contact (with).

hâşir 2 (—.) حاشر A *lrnd.* who assembles people together; God, who will assemble the dead for judgment; Muhammad, who gathers mankind to his faith.

haşiş (.—) حشیش A 1. hashish. 2. *lrnd.* dry herbage. **—e** (.—.) A stalk or blade of hay, one herb.

haşişetüssüalⁱⁱ (.—...—) مشیئة السعال coltsfoot, *bot.*, *Tussilago farfara*.

haşişî (. — —) حَشيشى A *sc.* herbaceous. **— nebatlar** herbaceous vegetation.
haşiv^{svi} حَشو *var. of* **haşv**.
haşiye (— ..) حاشِيَه A 1. marginal note; footnote, gloss. 2. commentary. 3. *lrnd.* edge, margin. **—li** annotated. **—nüvis** (— ... —) P *lrnd.* annotator.
haşla=^{r} حَشلامَن خَنْدَمَن خاشلى /ı/ 1. to boil, to cook in boiling water. 2. to scald. 3. to nip (frost). 4. to sting all over (insect). 5. to scold. **—ma** 1. *verbal n.* 2. boiled; boiled meat. **—n=** *pass. of* **haşla=**. **—t=** *caus. of* **haşla=**.
haşlamalılar *neol., zool.* Infusoria.
haşmet حَشمَت A majesty, pomp, grandeur. **—li** 1. majestic, grand. 2. *same as* **haşmetlû**. **—lû** (.. —), **—meab** (... —) P His Majesty (titles given to European sovereigns).
haşr حَشر A *lrnd.* 1. a collecting people together. 2. God's causing the dead to arise and assemble for judgment; resurrection and assembling for judgment; Day of Resurrection, Judgment Day. **—e dek** until Doomsday. **— enderhaşır** a big crowd, a host of people. **— et=** /ı/ to assemble (people). **— ü neşr** 1. resurrection and assembling for judgment. 2. *same as* **haşır neşir**.
haşşaş (. —) حَشّاش A *prov.* drunkard; scoundrel; *lrnd.* hashish addict.
haştek^{gi} حَشتَك *prov. clothing* underarm gusset.
haşv^{vi} حَشو A *rhet.* 1. expletive, redundant word; parenthesis; digression. 2. *lrnd.* stuffing, padding. 3. *lrnd.* small folk, people of small account. **—i gayri müfsid** a redundant word not injurious to the sense. **—i kabih** a redundancy to excise which would improve a clause. **—i melih** parenthetical clause adding beauty to a sentence. **—i mutevassıt** redundancy that neither embellishes nor injures a clause. **—i müfsid** redundancy injurious to clearness or beauty.
haşviyât (.. —) حَشويات A *lrnd.* redundant words or phrases, verbiage, padding.
haşye, haşyet خَشيَت A *lrnd.* fear, awe.
haşyeten (.'..) خَشيَةً A *lrnd.* with awe, awesomely. **— min-Allah** in the fear of God.
haşyetullâh خَشيَةُ الله A *lrnd.* fear of God.
hat^{ttı} خَط A 1. line; stroke, dash; stripe; scratch, long mark. 2. line (of ship, railway, telephone, etc.) 3. *pl.* facial characteristic, features. 4. writing; handwriting, calligraphy; *Ott. hist.* decree, imperial mandate written or signed by the Sultan's own hand. 5. *obs.* twelfth part of a Turkish inch (lineal measure). 6. *poet.* youthful beginnings of a beard. 7. *myst.* the real; the world of apparent and hidden things; the nearest approach to God's essence. **—ı âb** *lrnd.* evanescent or invisible writing. **— aç=** *mil.* to draw up in battle formation. **—ı âfitabî** *Arabic calligraphy* mode of handwriting with flourishes on the tailed letters. **—ı âteşhan** *Arabic calligraphy* writing made legible by holding to the fire. **—ı ayâğ** *poet.* 1. rim of a cup or goblet. 2. line of poetry inscribed on the cup of Jamshid. **—ı âzâdi** *lrnd.* letter of manumission. **—ı Bağdad** *poet.* the second line of writing inscribed on the cup of Jamshid. **—ı bâlâ** *geog.* crest-line, watershed. **—ı Basra** *poet.* third line on the cup of Jamshid. **—ı batıl** *lrnd.* line of cancellation. **— bekçisi** *rail.* linesman. **—ı bendegî** *lrnd.* certificate of ownership of a slave. **—ı beyzavî** *Arabic calligraphy* mode of handwriting with oval curves on the tailed letters. **—ı butlân** *lrnd.* line of cancellation. **—ı câm** *poet.* line on Jamshid's cup. **—ı celi** *Arabic calligraphy* peculiar kind of large text hand used in state documents. **—î cevr** *poet.* the first line on Jamshid's cup. **— çek=** to install a line (telephone, telegraph). **—ı çeşm-i murî** *Arabic calligraphy* microscopic writing. **—ı dest** 1. *hist.* document handwritten by an important person. 2. *lrnd.* one's own handwriting. **—ı divanî** *Arabic calligraphy* large style of writing used especially in state documents. **—ı emân** *lrnd.* safeconduct; pardon. **—ı esas** *geom.* base-line. **—ı eşk** *poet.* the fifth line of poetry on the cup of Jamshid. **—ı evvel** *lrnd.* 1. God's eternal decrees. 2. the throne of God; Mecca. 3. the letter ا (elif). **—ı fâsıl** dividing line; boundary line. **—ı gubarî** *Arabic calligraphy* a style of writing. **—ı gülzar** *Arabic calligraphy* ornamental writing with flowers traced round the letters. **—ı harb** *mil.* line of battle. **—ı hareket** line of conduct, method of procedure. **—ı hata** *lrnd.* line of cancellation. **— ve hâtim** *lrnd.* the hand and seal of a person. **—ı havai** ropeway; cableway. **—ı hisar** *lrnd.* magic circle. **—ı hudud** *lrnd.* border line. **—ı hümayun** *Ott. hist.* mandate of the Sultan sent to the Grand Vizier for execution; Imperial decree. **—ı hun** *lrnd.* sentence of death by beheading. **—ı icazet** *Ott. calligraphy* Style of writing between **sülüs** and **nesih**. **—ı içtimaı miyah** *geog.* thalweg. **—ı istiva** *same as* **hattı üstüva**. **—ı itidal** *astr.* 1. equinoctial line. 2. the east-and-west line on a dial. **—ı kaime** *geom.* perpendicular. **—ı katı** *geom.* secant. **—ı kebir** *rail.* main line. **—ı kebk** *lrnd.* bar or mark on the plumage of a partridge. **—ı kerdar** *lrnd.* the angelic record of one's actions; register of divine decrees. **—ı kûfi** *Arabic calligraphy* cufic writing. **—ı leb** *poet.* down on the lip of a youth. **—ı mendel** *lrnd.* magic circle. **—ı mihî**, **—ı mismari** cuneiform

writing. —ı **muaddilünnehar** *astr.* equinoctial line. —ı **muvazi** *geom.* parallel line. —ı **mücanib** *geom.* asymptote. —ı **müdafaa** *mil.* line of defense. —ı **mümas** *geom.* tangent. —ı **münhani** *geom.* curved line. —ı **münkesir** *geom.* broken line. —ı **müstakim** *geom.* straight line. —ı **müstedir** *geom.* circular line. —ı **müşkin** *poet.* a mole on the cheek. —ı **nâzım** *geom.* normal line. —ı **nesih** *Arabic calligraphy* the text-hand in which the Quran is generally written. —ı **nestâlik** *Arabic calligraphy* a kind of **hattı talik**. —ı **nev**, —ı **nevhiz**, —ı **nevin** *poet.* down on the cheeks of a youth. —ı **nısfülleyl** *astr.* midnight line. —ı **nısfünnehar** *astr.* meridian line. —ı **nil** *lrnd.* mark made on a child's forehead as a charm against the evil eye. —ı **nisyan** *poet.* oblivion. —ı **nişeste** *lrnd.* handwriting developed by practice. —ı **pây-ı kelâğ**, —ı **pençei gürbe** *lrnd.* illegible writing. —ı **pergâr** *geom.* circular line. —ı **pişâni** *lrnd.* the writing on one's forehead, destiny. —ı **puhte** *lrnd.* well-developed handwriting. —ı **rah** 1. *mil.* route. 2. *obs.* road pass, passport. — **reyhâni** *Arabic calligraphy* ornamental text with flowers and flourishes, arabesques, etc. —ı **rik'a** *Arabic calligraphy* ordinary cursive writing. —ı **sâk** *geom.* leg of a triangle. —ı **semt** *astr.* azimuth line. — **semti kıble** *lrnd.* the direction of the Kaaba of Mecca. —ı **sebz** *lrnd.* 1. fresh-sprouting verdure. 2. fresh down on a boy's cheek. 3. *myst.* the invisible world interposed between time and eternity. —ı **siyah** *poet.* the fourth line of poetry on the cup of Jamshid. —ı **siyakat** *Ott. calligraphy* script used in financial documents. —ı **sülüs** *Arabic calligraphy* large text handwriting. —ı **şafak u fecir** *astr.* line of dawn and twilight on an astrolabe. —ı **şakuli** *geom.* perpendicular line. —ı **şeb** *same as* **hattı siyah**. —ı **şeceri** *Arabic calligraphy* kind of ornamented writing. —ı **şehriyarî** *Ott. hist.* document signed or annotated by the Sultan. —ı **şerif** *same as* **hattı hümayûn**. —ı **şikeste** *Arabic calligraphy* the ordinary cursive writing of Persia and India. —ı **taksim**, —ı **taksim-i miyah** *geog.* watershed line. —ı **talik** *Arabic calligraphy* a Persian mode of writing. —ı **taziyane** *lrnd.* weal from a blow with a whip. —ı **tertip** 1. *geom.* ordinate. 2. *astr.* the edge of the index of an astrolabe. —ı **tevemân** *lrnd.* writing so placed on two sheets of paper that it cannot be read until both are put together. —ı **ufk** *lrnd.* horizon. —ı **ufki** *lrnd.* horizontal line. —ı **üstüva** 1. equator. 2. *astr.* prime vertical. —ı **üstüva âleti** *astr.* equatorial instrument, equatorial. —ı **vasatüssema** *same as* **hattı nısfınnehar**. —ı **vâsıt** *lrnd.* median line. —ı **vetedülarz** *lrnd.* line on an astrolabe showing the degree of the ecliptic on the meridian below the earth. —ı **veter** 1. *geom.* chord; diagonal line; hypotenuse. 2. *anat.* sinew, tendon. — **zaviyesi** *geom.* limit angle. —ı **zemîn** *same as* **hattı esas**. —ı **zerendûd** *art* kind of writing ornamented with gold, chrysography. —ı **zeval** *astr.* meridian line on an astrolabe.

hata 1 (. —) خطاء A 1. mistake, error, fault, blunder; offense. 2. wrong action, sin, crime. 3. a miss (in shooting or throwing). — **benden atâ senden!** The offense is mine, forgiveness yours! *(said in asking pardon for an offense)*. —**ya düş**= to make a mistake; to fall into error. — **et**=, — **eyle**= 1. to make a mistake, to blunder; to do wrong. 2. to miss in shooting or throwing. — **fonksiyonu** *sc.* law of error. — **ve hatar** *lrnd.* a sin and its consequences. — **hududu** margin of error, tolerance. — **işle**= to do wrong, to commit an error or sin. — **ve nisyan müstesna** *com.* error or omission excepted. — **savab cetveli** errata, list of errors. — **tevzini** *astr.* law of compensation for error. — **yap**= to make a mistake.

Hata 2 (. —) خطا hist. Cathay, northern China.

hatab مطب A *lrnd.* 1. firewood, fuel. 2. blockhead. —**ullahı ormanî zırtullahı kermanî** addleheaded, blockhead.

hatabahş (. —.) خطا بخش P *lrnd.* 1. forgiver of offenses or sins, pardoner. 2. tolerant. —**âne** (. —. —.) P forgivingly; toleratingly. —**î** (. —. —) P habitual forgiveness.

hataen (. —´.) خطأ A *lrnd.* by mistake; wrongly.

hataiyat (. — — —) خطائیات [based on **hata** 1] *lrnd.* errors, mistakes; falling into error.

hatakâr (. — —) خطا کار P *lrnd.* who makes mistakes; sinner, offender. —**î** (. — — —) P, —**lık** act of offending, sinfulness.

hatapuş (. — —) خطا پوش P *lrnd.* merciful.

hatar خطر A *lrnd.* 1. danger, peril, hazard; insecurity. 2. risk; fear. —**gâh** (. . —) P dangerous place; place of danger. —**mend** P, —**nak** (. . —) P dangerous, perilous; insecure, unsafe.

hatatif (. — —) خطاطیف A *lrnd.*, *pl. of* **huttâf**.

hatavat (. . —) خطوات A *lrnd.*, *pl. of* **hatve**.

hataver (. —.) خط آور P *poet.* who has down on his cheek (youth).

Hatay 1 (. —) خطای *geog.* Hatay (the Province of Antakya).

Hatay 2 (. —) خطای *lrnd.*, *hist.*, *same as* **Hata** 2.

hataya (. — —) خطایا A *lrnd.*, *pl. of* **hatie**.

hatem 1 (—.) خاتم A *lrnd.* 1. seal, seal ring; ring, finger ring. 2. end, conclusion; the last. **H—i Cem, H—i Cemşid** *lrnd.* 1. the seal of Jamshid. 2. Solomon's seal. **— çiçeği** *same as* **hatmi. H—i Enbiya** *lrnd., same as* **Hatemülenbiya. —i gûya** *poet.* mouth or lips of a beauty. **—i sadaret** *Ott. hist.* the seal of the Sultan entrusted to the Grand Vizier. **H—i Süleyman** *lrnd.* Solomon's seal. **—i şerif, —i vekâlet** *same as* **hatemi sadaret.**

Hatem 2 (—.) خاتم [**Hâtim 3**] *Arabian hist.* Hatim (proverbial for his generosity). **—âne** (—.—.) P *lrnd.* most generously.

hatemallah (...—) ضمّ الله A *lrnd.* May God conclude! **— avakibahu bilhayr** May God end his days with good (i. e., May God bring him to adopt the faith of Islam.)

hatemat (..—) ختمات A *lrnd., pl. of* **hatme.**

hatembend (—..) خاتم بند P *lrnd.* seal engraver.

hatemî (—.—) خاتمى A *lrnd.* 1. pertaining to a seal or signet ring. 2. maker or seller of seals or rings.

hatemkâri (—.——) خاتمكارى P *art* glyptics.

hatemşinasî (—..——) خاتم شناس P *lrnd.* sigillography.

Hatemül'enbiya (—....—) خاتم الانبياء A *lrnd.* the seal of the prophets, Muhammad, the last of the prophets.

hatemülmülk (—...) خاتم الملك A *lrnd.* 1. a sovereign's seal; the great seal of the realm. 2. a kind of Indian gum for ink.

hatemülvahy (—...) خاتم الوحى A *Isl. rel.* the Seal of Revelation, Muhammad.

hatemünnebiyin (—....—) خاتم النبيين A *Isl. rel.* the last of the prophets, Muhammad.

hatemünnübüvvet (—.....) خاتم النبوّت A *lrnd.* the mark of prophethood (a birthmark between Muhammad's shoulders).

hatene ختنه A *lrnd.* mother-in-law.

hatf[fi] **1** حتف A *lrnd.* death. **—e enfihi** of a natural death.

hatf 2 خطف A *lrnd.* 1. a seizing and carrying off. 2. a being dazzled by lightning.

hatıb (—.) خاطب A *lrnd.* who collects firewood. **—ı leyl** 1. one who collects wood in the night. 2. great talker mixing good and evil in his speech.

hatıf (—.) خاطف A *lrnd.* 1. seizer, snatcher. 2. that takes away the sight (lightning); blinding, dazzling.

hatıl 1 خطيل خاطل خاطل خطل مطل *arch.* 1. crosstimber, horizontal beam. 2. course of tiles in a stone wall. **— vur=** to lay a beam in a wall.

hâtıl[li] **2** (—.) خاطل A *lrnd.* falling in showers (rain); incessant fine (rain).

hatılla=[r] خطلمه /ı/ to strengthen with horizontal timber-ties (wall).

hatın خاتون *prov., var. of* **hatun.**

hatır 1 خاطر [**hâtır 2**] 1. influence, consideration, weight, the consideration that one person expects from another. 2. memory, mind; thought, idea. 3. one's feelings, frame of mind, health. **—ını al=** /ın/ to have a kindly thought (for somebody); to content (someone). **—ına bir şey gelmesin!** Don't misunderstand me. **—dan çıkar=** /ı/ to forget. **—ından çıkarma=** /ın/ not to refuse something for somebody's sake. **—dan geç=** to pass through the mind, to be thought of. **—a gel=** to occur, to come to mind. **—a getir=** /ı/ to remember, to think of, to call to mind. **—ına getir=** /ın, ı/ to remind (someone of something.). **— gönül** personal consideration. **—a gönüle bakma=** to be impartial, to set aside all personal considerations. **— gönül bilme=** not to take other people's feelings into account, not to consider others. **— gönül kalmasın** Nobody should be offended; I am telling you openly, I am warning you. **— gözet=** to have consideration for friendship; to act partially, to favor someone. **—a hayale gelme=** not even to occur to one (possibility). **—ını hoş et=** /ın/ to please (somebody). **—ını hoş tut=** 1. to remain easy in one's mind about something. 2. /ın/ to keep (another) pleased and satisfied. **—ım için** for my sake. **— için çiğ tavuk bile yenir** *prov.* One can even eat raw chicken out of friendship. **—da kal=** to be remembered. **—ı kal=** to feel hurt or offended, to take offense (at). **—ını kır=** /ın/ to disappoint, to offend. **—a riayet et=, — say=** to pay respect to feelings, rank or position. **—ı sayıl=** /ın/ 1. to have influence and weight. 2. to have one's feelings respected. **—ı sayılır** 1. considerable. 2. respected. **— senedi** *com.* accommodation bill. **— sor=** to enquire after one's welfare. **—da tut=** /ı/ to remember, to keep in mind. **—ını yap=** /ın/ to make amends (to somebody). **— yık=** to offend. **—ım yok mu?** Don't I count for anything? Have I no weight or influence?

hâtır 2 (—.) خاطر A *lrnd.* 1. *same as* **hatır 1.** 2. *myst.* inspiration, inner thought; affection, love. **—ı âtır** the esteemed welfare (of a friend, usually used in a letter). **—ı fâtir** languid mind. **—a hutur et=** to occur to the mind. **—ı melekî** *myst.* otherworldliness. **—ı nefsanî** *myst.* love of the carnal world. **—ı Rabbanî** *myst.* thought inspired by God. **—ı Rahmanî** *myst.* love of God; peace found in the communion with God. **—ı şeytanî** *myst.* lust and sin inspired by Satan.

hâtıra (—..) خاطره A 1. recollection, memory, remembrance; memoirs. 2. souvenir, memento, relic. 3. *obs.* sudden thought.

— defteri diary. **— olarak** as a souvenir. **—sı olarak** /ın/ in memory of.

hâtırâsâ (—.——) خاطر آسا P lrnd. tranquil in mind, mentally at ease.

hâtıraşüfte (—.—..) خاطر آشفته P lrnd. put out, angry.

hâtırat (—.—) خاطرات A lrnd. memories; memoirs.

hâtırazâde (—.——.) خاطر آزاده P lrnd. having peace of mind; free from worry.

hâtırazar (—.——) خاطر آزار P lrnd. who vexes, annoys.

hâtırâzürde (—.—..) خاطر آزرده P lrnd. hurt, offended, vexed, sad.

hâtırcem[mʹi] (—..) خاطر جمع P lrnd. collected, composed in mind; contented, tranquil, at ease.

hâtırcû (—.—) خاطر جو P lrnd. affable, courteous, charming.

hâtırfirib (—..—) خاطر فریب P lrnd. heart-stealing, alluring, captivating.

hâtırgirifte (—....) خاطر گرفته P lrnd. vexed, displeased, ruffled.

hâtırhâh (—.—) خاطر خواه P lrnd. falling in with one's wishes.

hatır hatır خاطر خاطر same as **hatır hutur**.

hâtırhıraş (—..—) خاطر خراش P lrnd. hurting, vexing, greatly disappointing.

hatır hutur خاطر خطور 1. crisp, crunching. 2. raw, crude, gawky, awkward.

hatırküşa (—..—) خاطر کشا P lrnd. 1. heart-rejoicing. 2. conquering the heart. 3. outraging the feelings.

hatırla=[r] خاطرلامك /ı/ to remember, to recall, to recollect. **—n=** to be remembered. **—t=** /ı, a/ to remind, to call attention (to); to warn.

hatırlı خاطرلی influential, esteemed, person of consequence.

hâtırmanda, hâtırmande (—.—.) خاطر مانده P lrnd. offended, hurt.

hâtırnaz (—.—) خاطر ناز [hatırnüvaz] colloq. polite, considerate of other peoples' feelings.

hâtırnevaz (—..—) خاطر نواز P lrnd., same as **hâtırnüvaz**. **—î** (—..——) P abstr. n.

hâtırnişan (—..—) خاطر نشان P lrnd. remembrance; impressed on the mind, not forgotten.

hâtırnüvaz (—..—) خاطر نواز P lrnd. affable, gracious, polite; charming, agreeable. **—î** (—..——) P, **—lık** affability, graciousness.

hâtırpesend (—...) خاطر پسند P lrnd. agreeable, liked.

hâtırpezir (—..—) خاطر پذیر P lrnd. agreeable, commendable.

hâtırpürs (—..) خاطر پرس P lrnd. who inquires after the health and happiness of another. **—î** (—..—) P abstr. n.

hâtırşiken (—...) خاطر شکن P lrnd. offending,

hurting; inconsiderate of other peoples' feelings.

hâtırşinas (—..—) خاطر شناس P lrnd. obliging, pleasant. **—âne** (—..——.) P obligingly, pleasantly. **—î** (—..——) P, **—lık** the act of obliging.

hâtırzad (—.—) خاطر زاد P lrnd. coming to mind; remembered.

hatib (.—) خطیب A lrnd., same as **hatip**. **—i felek** poet. Jupiter. **—âne** (.——.) P oratorically. **—î** (.——) P oratory; a preaching, sermonizing.

hatibül'enbiya (.—...—) خطیب الانبیاء A Isl. rel. "Preacher to the Prophets" (surname of Shiaib, father-in-law of Moses).

hatie (.—.) خطیئة A lrnd. 1. sin, iniquity. 2. fault, mistake.

hâtif (—.) هاتف A lrnd. voice from heaven, voice of an invisible power, mysterious voice. **—i gaib** lrnd. invisible speaker, the inner voice, the conscience. **—âne** (—.—.) P lrnd. in the manner of a mysterious voice. **—î** (—.—) P lrnd. pertaining to a mysterious voice.

hatim[tmi] **1** ختم [hatm] 1. recitation of the Quran from beginning to end. 2. lrnd. completion, conclusion. **— duası** prayer after repetition of the whole Quran. **— indir=** to finish repeating the whole Quran. **—i kelâm et=** lrnd. to finish speaking.

hâtim 2 (—.) خاتم A same as **hatem 1**.
Hâtim 3 (—.) هاتم A same as **Hatem 2**.

hatime (—..) خاتمه A lrnd. 1. end, last part of a thing, conclusion. 2. epilogue; peroration. **— çek=** /a/ to come to an end, to conclude, to accomplish, to finish up. **—keş** (—...) one who concludes, terminates.

hatip[bi] (.—) خطیب [hatib] 1. public speaker, orator; a good speaker. 2. preacher. **—lik** 1. oratory, power of elocution. 2. preacher's job.

hatm ختم A lrnd., same as **hatim 1**.

hatme ختمه A a single recitation of the whole Quran.

hatmet=[der] ختمتمك /ı/ 1. to conclude, to complete. 2. to recite the Quran from beginning to end. 3. to learn by rote.

hatmi ختمی [Arabic .—] A 1. marsh mallow, bot., Althea officinalis. 2. hollyhock, bot., Althea rosa.

hats حدث var. of **hads**.

hatşinas (..—) خط شناس P lrnd. calligrapher.

hattâ (.—) حتی A even; so much so that.

hattab (.—) حطاب A lrnd. collector or seller of firewood.

hattaf (.—) خطاف A lrnd. 1. one who seizes, carries off, ravishes. 2. eavesdropper; Satan.

hattan (. —) ختّان A *lrnd.* professional circumciser.

hattat (. —) خطّاط A calligrapher. **—lık** profession of a calligrapher; calligraphy.

hattî (. —) خطّى A *lrnd.* lineal, linear.

hatun 1 (— .) خاتون |**hatun 2**| 1. lady. 2. woman; wife. **— gerek bey doğura** *proverb* You need a lady to give birth to a gentleman. **— kişi** woman.

hatun 2 (— —) خاتون P *lrnd., same as* **hatun 1**. **H—i Arab** Mecca. **H—i Cennet** queen of Paradise (title given to Fatima, daughter of the Prophet Muhammad). **—i cihan, —i felek** the sun. **—i hum** wine. **H—i Kainat** Mecca. **—i yağma** the sun.

hatuncukᵍᵘ (— ..) خاتونجه 1. little lady, young lady. 2. middle-class woman.

hatve خطوه A *lrnd.* 1. step in walking. 2. pace as a measure of length. **— at=** to go forward.

hav هاو P nap, pile of cloth; down, soft hair.

hava 1 هوا |*Arabic* .—| 1. air, atmosphere; current of opinion; *colloq.* nothing. 2. weather; light wind, breeze; climate. 3. musical tune, melody, air. 4. *law* the right to add stories to a building. **—dan** 1. for nothing; without any effort; as a windfall, out of the blue. 2. worthless. **—ya** for nothing, in vain. **— açtı, — açıldı** The weather has cleared up, has become fine. **— akını** *mil.* air raid, air attack. **— al=** 1. to air, to be exposed to fresh air; to go for a walk in the fresh air, to have an airing. 2. *slang* to be left empty-handed, to be dismissed. **— altı** *geol.* subarial. **—dan at=** *slang* to tell lies. **— birliği** *mil.* air formation. **— boşluğu** atmospheric vacuum. **—sını bul=** /ın/ to get someone's measure. **— ceketi** *mech.* air jacket. **— cereyanı** draft, current of air, breeze. **— cıva*. — cüz i tammı** *same as* **hava birliği. — çarp=** 1. to be affected by being exposed to air or wind. 2. *prov.* to catch malaria. **— çekici** *mech.* pneumatic hammer. **— def ü tardı** *mil.* antiaircraft (defense), air defense. **— değişikliği** change of air. **— deliği** 1. ventilating hole. 2. *aero.* air pocket. **— filosu** air fleet. **— fişeği** rocket. **— freni** airbrake, pneumatic brake. **— gazı*. — geçmez** airtight, hermetically sealed. **— gemisi** airship, dirigible. **—ya git=** to be in vain, to be wasted. **—nın gözü yaşlı** It looks like rain. **— haznesi** air compartment. **— hukuku** *law* law of the air and air transportation. **— kabarcığı** bubble. **— kapandı** The sky has become overcast. **— karardı** The sky has darkened. **— kesesi** *zool.* air bladder. **— keşfi** *mil.* air reconnaissance. **— korunması** *mil.* air defense, air raid protection. **— kuvvetleri** *mil.* air forces. **— meydanı** airport.

— oyunu shady speculation on the stock exchange. **—ya pala salla=** to waste one's energy and effort in vain. **— parası** lump sum required by a landlord because the legal rent is low. **— payı** margin of safety. **— postası** airmail. **— raporu** weather report. **—ya savur=** /ı/ 1. to scatter about. 2. to spend thoughtlessly (money). **— süzgeci** *mech.* air filter. **— taşı** aerolite. **— tazyiki** air pressure, atmospheric pressure. **— tebdili** change of air. **— tehlikesi işareti** air raid alarm. **— tulumbası** air pump. **—ya uçur=** /ı/ to blow up. **—sına uy=** /ın/ to adapt oneself (to), to fit in (with). **— üssü** *mil.* air base. **— ver=** /a/ 1. to give air, to fill with air. 2. *med.* to aerate (the lungs). **— yeri** *archery* the place where the arrow falls. **— yolları** air lines. **— zabıtası** air police.

hava 2 (. —) هوا *same as* **heva**.

havacı هواجى 1. airman, pilot. 2. *Ott. hist.* referee who watched the place where the arrow fell, in archery. **—lık** aviation.

havacıva هواجيوا هواجيوا هواجيوا هواجيوا 1. alkanet, *bot.*, *Alkanna tinctoria, Anchusa tinctoria.* 2. *colloq.* trifles, worthless words; nonsense. **— merhemi** ointment of alkanet.

havacib (. — .) هواجب A *lrnd., pl. of* **hacib 2**.

havadar هوادار |*Persian* ..—| airy, having plenty of air. **—lık** airiness.

havadis (. —.) هوادث A 1. news, rumors. 2. *lrnd.* events, occurrences. **— kumkuması** tale-bearer.

havagazıⁿⁱ هواغازى coal gas, water gas, public utility gas.

havai (. — —) هوائى A 1. aerial, pertaining to the air. 2. fanciful, unreasonable, flighty; inconstant, idle. 3. light sky-blue. 4. *slang* loaded dice. **— fişek** rocket. **— hat** overhead railway, funicular. **— mania** *mil.* air barrage. **— mavi** sky-blue. **— sözler** idle talk; gossip.

havaic (. —.) هوائج A *same as* **havayic**.

havailikᵍⁱ (. — — .) هوائيلك flightiness, inconstancy.

havaimeşreb (. — — ..) هوائى مشرب P flighty; inconstant.

havaiyat (. — . —) هوائيات A trifles, futilities.

havak=ⁱʳ هواقمى *prov.* to become angry (wound).

havakin (. — —) هواقين A *lrnd., pl. of* **hakan**.

havalan=ⁱʳ هوالانمى 1. to be aired, to take in air; to be ventilated. 2. to take to the air, to fly, to be airborne, to rise (in the air), to take off (airplane). 3. to become flighty and frivolous. **—dır=** /ı/ *caus.* **—ma** *verbal n. of* **havalan=**.

havale (. —.) هواله A 1. assignment (of an affair); the referring or transfer of a matter; a

havalegâh

confiding to the charge of another. 2. money order; bill of exchange; letter of credit; transfer. 3. fence of planks, boarding. 4. towering height. 5. *path.* infantile convulsions; eclampsia. 6. *lrnd.* a striking, a giving a blow; an aiming, pointing (a thing). 7. *Ott. hist.* official who collects arrears of state revenue; official who collects dues belonging to Imperial property. — **çek=** 1. to draw a money order (from bank or post-office). 2. to suffer from infantile convulsions. 3. /a/ to fence off; to enclose (land). — **et=** /ı, a/ 1. to assign, to transfer; to endorse. 2. to refer (a matter to another person or department). 3. to point or aim towards (weapon); to brandish over another (sword, spear, etc.). — **gönder=** to send a money order.

havalegâh (. — . —) حواله گاه P *lrnd.* 1. place to which one has recourse when in difficulty. 2. place to which people flock for pleasure; esplanade.

havaleli حواله لى 1. high and somewhat overhanging, unusually high (load); bulky, top-heavy, unwieldy; with a high superstructure (ship). 2. surrounded, enclosed, fenced. 3. *path.* given to convulsions, eclamptic.

havalenâme (. — . — .) حواله نامه P money order, order for payment.

havaleten (. — . .) حوالةً A *adm.* being referred or transferred (to somebody).

havalı حوالى airy; exposed to the air; breezy.

havali (. — —) حوالى A 1. neighborhood, vicinity, surrounding; environs; suburbs. 2. regions, districts.

havan حاوان |Persian — . | 1. mortar (for pounding). 2. *mil.* mortar (gun). 3. tobacco-cutting machine. — **bataryası** *mil.* mortar battery. — **dövücünün hık deyicisi** one who, to curry favor, agrees with all that another says. — **eli** pestle. — **kundağı** *mil.* bed of a mortar. —**da su döv=** to engage in useless discussion or fruitless work. — **topu** *mil.* mortar, howitzer.

havanık[kı] (. — .) حوانك A *lrnd., pl. of* **hankah**.

havanik[kı] (. — —) حوانين A *lrnd., pl. of* **hunuk**.

havara حواره |Arabic . — . | *prov.* 1. kind of soft building stone. 2. whitewash.

havarık[kı] (. — .) حوارق A *lrnd., pl. of* **harık** 3, **harika** 3. —**ı âde** prodigies.

havari (. — —) حوارى A disciple (of a prophet), apostle.

havaric (. — .) حوارج A *lrnd.* 1. *pl. of* **haric**. 2. a sect of Muslims who broke their allegiance to the caliph Ali.

havariyun (. — — —) حواريّون A *pl. of* havari. **H— Suresi** *name of the 61st sura of the Quran.*

havas[ssı] 1 (. —) حواصّ A *pl. of* **has** 2. — **ve avam** the high and the low. **H—ı refia** *Ott. hist., title given to the Kadi of the Eyüp district in Istanbul until 1908.*

havas[ssı] 2 (. —) حواسّ A *pl. of* **hasse**. —**ı hamse** the five senses.

havasız حواسز airless, stuffy, badly ventilated.

havaşi (. — —) حواشى A *lrnd., pl. of* **haşiye**.

havatır (. — .) حواطر A *lrnd., pl. of* **hâtıra**. —**ı nefsaniye** carnal promptings of the passions. —**ı rabbaniye** divinely inspired ideas. —**ı şeytaniye** devilish suggestions.

havatim (. — .) حواتم A *lrnd., pl. of* **hâtim** 2.

havatin (. — —) حواتين A *lrnd., pl. of* **hatun**.

havayic (. — .) حوايج A *lrnd.* necessities; provisions. —**i zaruriye** indispensable needs, necessities (of life).

havel حول A *path.* a squinting; strabismus.

havelân (. . —) حولان A *lrnd.* a going round, turning, changing.

havend (—.) حاوند P *lrnd.* lord, master.

havendgâr (—. —) حاوندگار *lrnd., same as* **hudavendgâr**.

havendi (. — . —) حاوندى P mastery, dominion, overlordship.

havene حونه A *lrnd., pl. of* **hain**.

haver 1 حاور Heb *slang* partner.

haver 2 (—.) حاور P *lrnd.* west; east. **H—i Huda** Lord of the West (title of the eldest son of Feridun). —**an** (—. —) the East and the West. —**î** (—. —) west, western; east, eastern.

haves حوس A *prov., same as* **heves**.

havf[fı] حوف A *lrnd.* fear, fright, terror. —**i füşhat**, —**i meydan** *psych.* agorafobia. —**i teceddüd** *psych.* misoneism.

havfen (.'.) حوفاً A *lrnd.* for fear, being afraid.

havfnâk[kı] (. —) حوفناك P *lrnd.* 1. afraid. 2. fearful, frightening.

havhav حاوحاو 1. a barking, baying. 2. *children's language* bow-wow.

havi 1 (— —) حاوى A /ı/ containing, including.

havî 2 (— —) حاوى *Or. mus.* a medium-fast pattern of 64 beats.

haviye (— . .) حاويه A *lrnd.* 1. deep pit, abyss. 2. hell, the deepest hell.

havkale حوقل A *lrnd.* the formula **Lâ havle ve lâ kuvvete illâ billâh**; an exclaiming this formula. —**gû** (. . . —) P who pronounces the **havkale** formula.

havl[li] 1 حول A *lrnd.* 1. surrounding, vicinity; a going round; a turning round. 2. a changing of state. 3. the whole annual cycle, year. 4. power, ability, force.

havl[li] 2 حول A *lrnd., same as* **hevl**.

havla=[r] حاولامق حاولاسمق to bark, to bay.

havla=ʳ هاولامق ،هاولامهٔ هاولامق to bark, to bay.
havlaka هوالقه A *same as* **havkale**.
havlı هاولو هاولى 1. having a nap or pile; downy. 2. *same as* **havlu 1**.
havlican, havlincan هاولنجان خولنجان P galingale (an aromatic root).
havlu 1 هاولو هاولى towel, Turkish towel.
havlu 2 هولى *var. of* **avlu**.
havra هاوره هورا هاوره هاوره 1. Jewish synagogue. 2. noisy place of assembly; bedlam.
havruz هاوروز هورروز |âbriz| *vulg.* urinal, chamber pot.
havsala هوصله A 1. intelligence, comprehension. 2. *anat.* pelvis. 3. *lrnd.* hypogastric region in man or beast; gizzard. **— almaz** beyond comprehension. **—sı dar** 1. whose comprehension is narrow. 2. intolerant. **—ya sığmaz** incomprehensible.
havsalasuz (...—) هوصله سوز P *lrnd.* insufferable, unbearable.
havsalî (..—) هوصلى |based on **havsala**| *anat.* pelvic.
havşa هوشه 1. countersink; gimlet. 2. chamfered hole made with a gouge. **— aç=** /a/ to chamfer, to countersink, to counterbore. **—lı perçin** countersunk rivet.
havuçᶜᵘ هاوج هاووج هاويج carrot, *bot.*, Daucus carota.
havut هاوت هاويد هووت هاوود camel's packsaddle.
havuz هوض |havz| 1. artificial basin; pond. 2. *naut.* dock, drydock, floating dock. **— balığı** crucian carp, *zool.*, Carassius carassius. **—a çek=** /ı/ *naut.* to dock (a ship). **—a gir=** *naut.* to be docked (ship). **— kapakları** dock gates. **—cuk** pondlet, *anat.* calyx. **—la=** /ı/ *naut.* to dock, to place in a dock. **—lan=** *pass. of* **havuzla=**. **—landır=** /ı/ *caus. of* **havuzlan=**. **—lu** furnished with a pond.
Havva (.—) حوّاء A *Bib.* Eve (wife of Adam).
havya هاويه havya soldering iron.
havyar هاويار- هاوياره Gk caviar. **— kes=** *slang* to idle around, to moon around.
havz هوض A *lrnd.*, *same as* **havuz**. **—ı hayal** *poet.* reverie, world of imagination. **—ı kevser** *Isl. rel.*, *name of a pond in Paradise.* **—ı mahî** 1. fish pond. 2. *astr.* Pisces. **—ı mevt** death, the waters of Lethe. **H—ı Resûl** *name for the pond in Paradise from which all the blessed will drink on the Day of Judgment.* **—ı tersa** vessel in which wine is fermented.
havza هوضه A *geog.* 1. river basin, catchment area. 2. region, district, territory, site.
havze هوزه A *lrnd.* 1. territory, dominions of a state or people. 2. site, region, district. **—i tasarrufuna geçir=** /ı/ to bring into one's domain, to take possession (of), to annex.

hay 1 هاى Hallo! Hey! Alas! Oh! **— anasını!** *slang* What a pity! **—dan gelen huya gider** Easy come easy go (money). **— hay** By all means, certainly, yes.
hayʸʸⁱ **2** حىّ A *lrnd.* alive, living; the Everliving God.
hayâ 1 (.—) حياء A shame; modesty, bashfulness. **— et=** 1. to feel ashamed; to be restrained by shame. 2. to be modest or bashful.
hayâ 2 خايه |hâye| testicle.
hayahay (———) هاى هاى P *lrnd.* cries of mourning, lamentations, wailing.
hayahûy (———) هاى هوى P *lrnd.* shout of joy and festivity.
hayalˡⁱ (.—) خيال A 1. imagination, fancy; image; idea; illusion. 2. specter; ghost, apparition, phantom. 3. *phys.* image. 4. *myst.* the phenomenal universe. **—i dilâvız** *lrnd.* a witty pun. **— et=** /ı/ to imagine. **—i fener** 1. very thin, skinny. 2. *obs.* kind of magic lantern. **—i hâb** *lrnd.* dream. **—i ham** ridiculous idea; utopia. **— inkisarı** disappointment. **— inkisarına uğra=** to be disappointed. **—e kapıl=** to be given to fancy; to build high hopes. **— kırıklığı** disappointment. **— kur=** to dream unrealistically of one's future. **— meyal** hardly perceptible, evanescent. **— oyunu** shadow show, shadow play. **— perdesi** shadow-show screen. **—i zıl** shadow show.
hayalat (.——) خيالات A *lrnd.* empty imaginings, illusions. **—a kapıl=** to feed on illusions.
hayalbaz (.——) خيالباز P *lrnd.*, *same as* **hayali** ².
hayalci (.—.) خيالجى 1. *same as* **hayalî** ². 2. daydreamer, visionary.
hayalen (.—.) خيالاً A in imagination.
hayalet (.—.) خيالت A ghost, specter, apparition; shadow, phantom.
hayalhane (.——.) خيالخانه realm of imagination, mind, phantasy, fancy.
hayalî (.——) خيالى A 1. imaginary, fantastic; utopian. 2. shadow theater player.
hayalistân (.—.—) خيالستان P *lrnd.* the land of fancies, fantastic mind.
hayaliyat (.———) خيالیات A *lrnd.* fantasies, imaginings.
hayaliye (.——.) خيالیه A *zool.*, Lemuridae.
hayaliyun (.———) خيالیّون A *literature* the romantics, romanticists.
hayalkede (.—..) خيالکده P *lrnd.* a place haunted by phantoms; the world.
hayalperest (.—..) خيالپرست P given to imagination; visionary, day-dreamer. **—î** (.—..—) P *lrnd.*, **—lik** imagination, day-dreaming.
hayalperver (.—..) خيالپرور P *lrnd.* fed on illusions; fond of imagining things.

hayasız (.—.) حَيَاسِزْ shameless, impudent. **—lık** shamelessness, impudence.

hayat 1 (.—) حَيَات A 1. life; living; existence. 2. liveliness, movement. **—ım** My love. My darling. **—ta** living, alive. **— ağacı** 1. *bot.*, *arbor vitae*. 2. *art* Tree of Life. **—ın baharı** the prime of life. **—ı cavidân, —ı cavidanî** *lrnd.* eternal life. **—ını kazan=** to earn one's living. **—ı mâneviye** *lrnd.* spiritual life. **— memat meselesi** matter of life and death, vital question. **—ı müstear** *lrnd.* borrowed life, transitory life. **—ı müştereke** *biol.* symbiosis. **—ı nebatiye mahrutu** cone of vegetation. **— pahalılığı** high cost of living. **— sahası** living space; sphere of existence. **— sigortası** life insurance. **—ı uhreviye** *lrnd.* future life, eternal life.

hayat 2 حَيَاط A *prov.* courtyard; covered court.

hayatbahş (.—.) حَيَاتْبَخْشْ P *lrnd.* lifegiving.

hayatî (.——) حَيَاتِى A vital, pertaining to life.

hayatiyat (.—.—) حَيَاتِيَات A biology.

hayatiye (.—.., .——.) حَيَاتِيَه A *phil.*, *biol.* vitalism.

hayatiyet (.—..) حَيَاتِيَت A vitality; liveliness, vigor.

hayatiyun (.———) حَيَاتِيُّونْ A *phil.* vitalists.

haybeci حَايْبَهْجِى *slang* sucker, person singled out to be robbed (by swindlers).

haybeden حَايْبَهْدَنْ *slang* free, gratis, for nothing.

haybet حَيْبَت A *lrnd.* disappointment, frustration, despair. **—zede** P disappointed, frustrated, desperate.

hayda=ʳ, haydala=ʳ حَايْدَه لَامَهْ، حَايْدَامَهْ حَايْدَالَامَهْ /ı/ 1. to drive on (animals with loud shouts). 2. *slang* to fire.

haydamakᵍⁱ حَايْدَامَهْ *archaic* cattle-rustler, marauder, vagabond. **— kazağı** cossack freebooter.

Haydar حَيْدَر *a surname of the Caliph Ali.*

haydarî (..—), **haydariye** (..—.) حَيْدَرِى حَيْدَرِيَه *same as* **hayderî, hayderiye**.

hayder حَيْدَر A *lrnd.* 1. lion; very brave, valiant. 2. *w. cap.*, *same as* **Haydar. —âne** (..—.) P 1. pertaining to a lion. 2. bravely, valiantly.

hayderî (..—), **hayderiye** (..—.) حَيْدَرِى حَيْدَرِيَه A sleeveless jacket (usually worn by dervishes).

haydi (.'.) حَايْدِى حَايْدِى 1. Hurry up. Now then. Go on. 2. All right. Very well. **—n, —yin!** Come along, all of you. **—ndi** Now then. Let's see. **—sene!** Come along. **— bakalım** Come on then. Hurry up. **— gidelim** Come along, let's go. **— git!** Go away! **— haydi** 1. easily, amply. 2. at the most. 3. all the more; *phil.* a fortiori.

haydutᵈᵘ حَيْدُودْ Hung 1. bandit, brigand, robber. 2. naughty, mischievous. **— gibi** huge and bulky (person). **— yatağı** den of thieves. **—luk** 1. brigandage. 2. mischief.

hâye (—.) حَايَه P *lrnd.* 1. *same as* **haya 2.** 2. egg. **—i iblis** eagle-stone. **—i zer** *poet.* the sun.

hayevî 1 (..—) حَيَوِى A *phil.* vital; pertaining to vitalism.

hayevî 2 (..—) حَيَوِى A *lrnd.* pertaining to a snake, serpentine.

hayeviye (..—.) حَيَوِيَه A *phil.* vitalism.

hayf 1 حَيْف A *lrnd.* 1. *same as* **hayıf**. 2. injustice, violence, oppression.

hayf 2 حَيْف A *lrnd.* 1. region, quarter, side. 2. talus. 3. patch of land (of a different color from what surrounds it).

Hayfa 1 (.'.) حَيْفَا *geog.* Jaffa, ancient Joppa.

hayfa 2 (.—') حَيْفَا P *lrnd.* Alas. **— ki** P Alas!

hayhuy (——) حَاىْ هُوى P loud and continued noise, tumult; confusion.

hayıf حَيْف [hayf 1] What a pity! **— al=** /dan/ *prov.* to take revenge, to revenge. **—lan=** 1. to lament, to moan. 2. to regret.

hayın حَايِن *var. of* **hain**.

hayır 1 (.'.) حَيْر غَايِر [hayr] 1. no. 2. on the contrary.

hayırʸʳⁱ **2** خَيْر [hayr] 1. good, goodness; prosperity, health; excellence. 2. profit, advantage; advantageous, auspicious. 3. charity, philanthropy. **—ı dokun=** to serve a useful purpose; to be of use. **— dua** blessing, benediction. **— etme=** to be of no use; to do no good. **—ını gör=** /ın/ to enjoy the advantage or profits (of). **—ını gör!** 1. May it bring you luck. 2. *iron.* Well, I wish you luck with it. **— haber** good news. **— hasenat** good works; charity and benevolence. **—dır inşallah!** I hope all is well; I hope there is nothing wrong. **— işle=** to do good, to be charitable. **— işleri** charities, philanthropy. **— kalma=** /da/ to be of no more use. **— müessesesi** philanthropic institution, charitable foundation. **— ola!** What's the matter? All is well, I hope? **— sahibi** philanthropist. **— san=** /a/ *archaic* to wish someone well. **— yok!** /dan/ *colloq.* 1. He's of no use. 2. He is done for. **—ı yok** /ın, a/ to be of no use (to somebody). **—a yor=** to interpret favorably, to regard as auspicious (dream, omen).

hayır 3 خَيْر *prov. fig.*

hayırhâh (..—) خَيْرْخَواه P wellwisher, benevolent; kind. **—âne** (..——.) P *lrnd.* benevolently; kindly. **—î** (..——) P *lrnd.* **—lık** benevolence, goodwill.

hayırlaş= ⁱʳ خیرلاشمی to exchange good wishes after having come to terms in a bargain. **—tır=** /ı/ *caus.*

hayırlı خیرلی 1. good, advantageous. 2. auspicious; beneficial; blessed. 3. happy, lucky. **—sı!** Let's hope for the best. **—sı Allahtan!** May God help. **— evlât** filial son or daughter. **— olsun!** Good luck! Congratulations! **—sı olsun!** Let's hope for the best. **— yolculuk!** Bon voyage!

hayırsever خیرسور *neol.* philanthropist; charitable.

hayırsız خیرسز 1. good for nothing, useless. 2. unproductive, waste (land). 3. ill-omened. **H— Ada** Oxia (one of the small islands near Istanbul). **— evlât** a good-for-nothing son or daughter. **—lık** uselessness; unproductiveness.

hayıtᵈⁱ حایط *same as* **ayıt** 1.

hayızʸᶻ¹ حیض [hayz 1] menstruation, period. **— gör=** to menstruate. **—dan nifastan kesil=** to reach menopause.

hayide (— —.) حاییده P *lrnd.* 1. chewed, gnawed. 2. hackneyed (words), stale (joke). **—gû** (— — . —) P commonplace writer or poet.

haykır= ⁱʳ حایقرمق to cry out, shout, scream. **—ış** cry, shouting. **—ış=** /la/ to scold each other noisily. **—t=** /ı/ *caus. of* **haykır=**.

hayl خیل A *lrnd.* 1. herd of horses. 2. horsemen; cavalry. 3. tribe, multitude.

hayla= ⁱʳ حایلامق خیلامق 1. to urge on with cries (carriage animals). 2. /ı/ *prov.* to consider, to care (for). **—ma=** /ı/ *colloq.* not to care, not to consider.

haylaz حایلاز غیلاز 1. vagabond; idler, loafer, bum. 2. lazy, idle, lazybones. **—lan=** to become lazy. **—lık** lazy idleness.

hayli (ˊ.) خیلی P many, much, very, a good deal. **—den hayliye** a good deal, considerably. **—ce** somewhat, much, considerably.

haylûlet (. — .) حیلولت A *lrnd.* 1. intervention, interposition. 2. arrival.

haymana حایمانه prairie grazing land. **— beygiri gibi dolaş=** to wander about aimlessly. **— öküzü, — sığırı** good-for-nothing idler.

haymatloz حایماتلوز G *inter. law* stateless.

hayme خیمه A *lrnd.* tent; shelter. **—i ezrak** sky. **—berduş** (. . . —) P nomad, migratory; poor, vagabond. **—duz** (. . —) P tentmaker. **—gâh** (. . —) P camping ground, camp. **—nişin** (. . . —) P tentdweller. **—saray** (. . . —) P 1. royal marquee. 2. sky. **—zen** P tent-pitcher.

hayr خیر A *lrnd.*, *same as* **hayır** 2. **—i âlâ** sovereign good. **—i mutlak** absolute good. **— ola!** What's the matter? All is well, I hope?

hayran (. —) حیران A 1. bewildered, amazed; filled with admiration; admirer, lover, adorer. 2. *lrnd.* perplexed, confounded. **— kal=** 1. to be astounded and petrified with wonder. 2. /a/ to admire. **— ol=** 1. to be perplexed, bewildered or amazed. 2. /a/ to admire.

hayranlıkᶠⁱ حیرانلغی amazement; admiration, appreciation, praise; rapture, love, adoration.

hayrat (. —) خیرات A 1. pious foundation. 2. pious deeds, good actions; charities. **— ve hasenat** *lrnd.* pious foundations.

hayrendiş (. . —) خیراندیش P *lrnd.* well-wisher. **—ane** (. . — — .) P well-wishing. **—î** (. . — —) P, **—lik** well-wishing.

hayret حیرت A 1. amazement, astonishment, surprise. 2. How surprising! **—te bırak=** /ı/ to astound. **— ender hayret** How amazing! Most astonishing! **— et=** /a/ to be perplexed, bewildered, astonished, surprised (at). **—te kal=** to be lost in amazement, to be amazed. **— ver=** /a/ to cause amazement (to).

hayretbahş حیرتبخش P *lrnd.* amazing.

hayretefza (. . . —) حیرتافزا P *lrnd.* most amazing.

hayretengiz (. . . —) حیرتانگیز P *lrnd.* amazing, astounding.

hayretkede حیرتکده P *poet.* abode of amazement, the world.

hayretnigâh (. . . —) حیرتنگاه P *lrnd.* who stares in amazement.

hayretzede حیرتزده P *lrnd.* bewildered, amazed, astonished.

hayri (. —) خیری A *lrnd.* pertaining to what is good and beneficial.

hayriye (. — .) خیریه A *lrnd., fem. of* **hayri.** **— altını** gold coin issued in 1830 and 1831 on the occasion of the anniversaries of Sultan Mehmet II's accession to the throne.

hayrülbeşer خیرالبشر A *rel.* the Prophet Muhammad.

hayrülhalef خیرالخلف A worthy successor.

haysiyet حیثیت A personal dignity, honor; *colloq.* worth, value. **— divanı** *law* court of honor. **—iyle** because of. **—li** dignified, self-respecting.

haysiyetsiz حیثیتسز undignified, having no sense of honor. **—lik** 1. dishonor, demerit. 2. insignificance.

haysiyetşiken حیثیتشکن P *lrnd.* that hurts one's self-respect, humiliating.

hayşum (. —) حیشوم A *lrnd.* the nasal passage; nose. **—i** (. — —) A nasal.

hayt خیط A 1. *bot., anat.* string, cord, filament. 2. *lrnd.* streak of light or shadow. **—ı batıl** *lrnd.* 1. threads of floating gossamer. 2. beam of light with shining motes. 3. tall but dull minded person. **—ı ebyaz** *poet.* daybreak. **—ı esfel** *lrnd.* the dim conical column of the false dawn; the first appearance or morning light. **—ı mülevven** *bot.* 1. chromatic

hayta

fiber. 2. chromatin. **—ı rakabî** *anat.* cervical cord.

hayta 1 هايطة 1. mischievous young hooligan. 2. *Ott. hist.* armed and mounted guard who escorted a caravan; armed and mounted brigand.

hayta 2 هيط A *lrnd.* 1. thread, string, cord. 2. tent rope; tent stake. **—i hayme** same as **hayta 2**.

haytiye (.—.) هيطية A *zool.*, Nematoda.

hayva هايوا *colloq.*, same as **ayva**.

hayuhuy (—.—) هاى و هوى P the humdrum of everyday life; worries and troubles.

hayvan 1 حيوان [hayvan 2] 1. animal, living creature; beast of burden; horse. 2. fool, idiot. **—ın alacası dışında insanın alacası içinde** Judge a horse by its form but a man by his character. **— alım satımı** livestock market. **— bakışlı** stupid looking. **— borsası** cattle market. **— gibi** asinine, stupid. **— hırsızı** cattle-thief, rustler. **— hırsızlığı** cattle rustling. **— kliniği** veterinary clinic. **— kömürü** animal charcoal, charred bones. **— kuvveti var** He is as strong as an ox. **— panayırı** cattle fair, stock fair. **— vagonu** stock car (on a train). **— yulardan yiğit ikrardan tutulur** Animals are caught by their halters, men by their words.

hayvan 2 (.—) حيوان [*Persian, from Arabic* hayawan] *lrnd.* 1. same as **hayvan 1**. 2. life. **—ı gayri-nâtık** beast, brute. **—ı nâtık** 1. man, human being. 2. fool.

hayvanat (.——) حيوانات [*Persian, from Arabic* hayawanat] 1. *pl. of* **hayvan**. 2. zoology. **— bahçesi** zoological garden, zoo. **—ı hamse** *Isl. rel.* the five beasts killing of which is canonically lawful (rat or mouse, biting dog, snake, crow or kite, scorpion). **—ı iptidaiye** *zool.*, Protozoa. **—ı nebatiye** *zool.*, Holothurioidea. **—ı şibh-i nebatiye** *zool.*, Phytozoaria. **—ı taliye** *zool.*, Metazoa.

hayvanca (..'.) حيوانجه bestially, rudely; stupidly. **—sına** like an animal, bestially; stupidly.

hayvancıkᵍ¹ حيوانجق *biol.* animalcule.

hayvancılıkᵍ¹ حيوانجيلق 1. stock-breeding. 2. cattle-dealing.

hayvani (.——) حيواني A 1. animal-like, bestial, animal. 2. sensual, carnal. **—yet** *abstr. n.*

hayvanlaş=ᵗʳ حيوانلشمك to become like an animal or beast; to be brutalized; to become sensual. **—tır**= /ı/ *caus.*

hayvanlıkᵍ¹ حيوانلق 1. quality of an animal, bestiality. 2. stupidity; brutality; brutal action. **— et**= to act stupidly or brutally.

hayvansal *neol.*, *biol.* pertaining to an animal, animal.

hayyâkᵏ¹ (.—) حياك A *lrnd.* weaver.

hayyâkallah (.—.—) حياك الله A *lrnd.* May you live long.

hayyâlⁱⁱ (.—) حيال A *lrnd.* horseman, cavalier.

hayyam (.—) حيام A *lrnd.* tent maker.

hayyat 1 (.—) حياط A *lrnd.*, *pl. of* **hayye**.

hayyat 2 (.—) حياط A *lrnd.* tailor. **—in-i hassa** *Ott. hist.* court tailors.

hayye حيّه A *lrnd.* snake, serpent.

hayyealelfelâh (.....—) حي على الفلاح A *rel.* Up! To happiness! (one of the formulas of the call to prayer.)

hayyealessalâ (.....—) حي على الصلاة A 1. *rel.* Hasten to divine worship! (one of the formulas of the call to prayer.) 2. *colloq.* I'll get even (a threat); it is no use, it is finished.

hayyen ('.) حيّا A *lrnd.* alive, living. **— meyyiten** alive or dead.

hayyir خيّر A *lrnd.* habitually good, beneficient.

hayyiz حيّز A *phil.* space.

hayyülkayyum (...—) حي القيوم A *lrnd.* the Eternal Being, God.

hayz 1 حيض A same as **hayız**. **—i duhter-i rez** *poet.* wine, red wine.

hayz 2 حيز A *lrnd.*, same as **hayyiz**.

hayzuran (..—) حيزران A *lrnd.*, same as **hazaren**.

hazᶻᶻ¹ **1** حظ A pleasure, delight, enjoyment. **— duy**= to be delighted, to enjoy. **— et** /dan/ same as **hazzet**=. **—ı nefs** 1. sensual pleasure. 2. luxury.

hazᶻ¹ **2** حز A *lrnd.* a cutting, cutting off, cutting through. **—ı batn** *surg.* abdominal operation; gastrostomy.

hâzâ (——) هذا A *colloq.* perfect, complete, out-and-out, e. g., **hâzâ sersem** an out-and-out idiot; **hâzâ şehzade** a perfect prince.

hazain (.—.) خزائن A *lrnd.*, *pl. of* **hazine**.

hazair (.—.) حظائر A *lrnd.*, *pl. of* **hazire**.

hazaka (.—.) حذاقة A *lrnd.* group, mass; multitude.

hazakat (.——) حذاقت A skill, skillfulness, ability (especially in medicine). **—li** skilled, skillful; capable.

hazamet (.——) حزامت A *lrnd.* prudence; intelligence, judgment.

hazan (.—) خزان P *poet.* autumn, fall. **— yaprağı gibi titre**= to tremble like an aspen leaf.

hazandide (.——.) خزانديده P *lrnd.* 1. who has experienced the cold of autumn. 2. smitten by adversity or death.

hazane (.—.) خزانه *var. of* **hızane**.

hazani (.——) خزاني P *poet.* autumnal.

hazanistan (.—.—) خزانستان P *poet.* place of sorrow, dismal place; transitory world.

hazanlika (.—.—) خزان لقاء P poet. pale, withered.

hazannüma (.—.—) خزان نما P poet. dismal-looking, pale.

hazanreside (.—.—.) خزان رسیده P lrnd., same as **hazandide**.

hazar 1 حضر A 1. mil. peace, peace time. 2. lrnd. residence at home. 3. lrnd. settled region. —**a geçiş** mil. demobilization. — **hali** mil. peace time, state of peace. — **kadrosu** mil. peacetime establishment. — **kuvvesi** mil. peacetime strength. — **ve sefer** 1. peace and war. 2. residence and travel.

hazar 2 حزار same as **hizar**.

Hazar 3 خزر A hist. Khazar. — **Denizi** geog. Caspian Sea.

hazarî (..—) حضری A mil. 1. peacetime establishment. 2. lrnd. home life, domestic. 3. lrnd. urban dweller.

hazariye (..—.) حضریة A 1. fem. of **hazarî**. 2. Ott. hist. real or cash aid given by imperial edict to meet the food expenses of tekkes.

hazcılık[fi] neol., phil. hedonism.

hazef خزف A lrnd. pottery, earthenware. —**iye** (..—.) A ceramic. —**pâre** (..—.) P, —**rize** (..—.) P fragment of pottery, shard.

hazelât (..—) خزلات [based on **hazele**] lrnd., same as **hazele**.

hazele خزلة A lrnd. deserters; rogues, villains. — **bezele** hooligans.

hazen 1 حزن A lrnd. grief, sadness, affliction, sorrow.

hazen 2 (—.), **hazene** (—..) خانه خاتنه P lrnd. wife's sister, sister-in-law.

hazer حذر A lrnd. care, caution; precaution. — **et**=, — **üzre bulun**= /dan/ to be on the alert.

hazerat (..—) حضرات A lrnd., pl. of **hazret**. —**ı hamse** myst. the five degrees of God's manifestation.

hazf[fi] حذف A 1. omission; elision. 2. pros. suppression of the final syllable of a foot. — **et**= /ı/ to omit, to elide, to suppress.

hazık[kı] (—.) حاذق A 1. skillful, skilled; expert (doctor). 2. lrnd. sharp, keen. — **bazık** lrnd. quickly; shrewd, sagacious. —**âne** (—.—.) P skillfully. —**ıyet** (—.—.), —**lık** skillfulness, skill.

hazım[mı] 1 هضم [hazm 1] digestion. — **cihazı** physiol. digestive system.

hâzım 2 (—.) حازم A lrnd. 1. digestive. 2. patient; patiently bearing an insult.

hazımlı patient person.

hazımsız 1. having a poor digestion; indigestible. 2. irritable, touchy. —**lık** indigestion. 2. inability to stomach an insult. 3. irritability, touchiness.

hâzına (—..) حاضنة A lrnd. child's nurse; child's foster-mother.

hazır 1 حاضر [hâzır 2] 1. ready, prepared; ready-made. 2. present, not absent; present time. 3. since, as; now that, e. g., **hazır gelmişken bu işi de bitirelim** Let's finish this too, now we're here. — **bulun**= to be present. — **cevap***. — **ekmek ye**= to live without working. — **elbise** ready-made clothing. — **et**= /ı/ to prepare, to get ready. —**a kon**= to settle down to enjoy what is already prepared; to enjoy the fruits of others' labors. — **lop***. — **mezarın ölüsü** Things just drop into his lap. — **ol** 1. Be prepared; make ready. 2. mil. Attention! — **para** ready money, cash. —**dan ye**= to live on one's capital. — **yemek** food already prepared (such as canned soups, vegetables, etc.). — **yiyici** 1. one who lives on his capital. 2. one who lives on other people; lazy and good-for-nothing person.

hâzır 2 (—.) حاضر A lrnd., same as **hazır 1**. — **âmâde** ready and prepared. — **bilmeclis** present at a meeting or assembly. — **ve müheyya** ready and prepared. — **ve nâzır** omnipresent and all-seeing, God.

hâzıra (—..) حاضرة A lrnd. 1. a tribe or assembly of people resident or encamped (especially near water). 2. a region or district of towns, villages or inhabited houses; a settled country.

hâzıran (—.—) حاضران P lrnd. those present.

hâzırat (—.—) حاضرات A lrnd. 1. those present. 2. angels, demons or spirits invoked by spells in a flame or mirror by a conjuror; the displaying of such spirits. —**çı** juggler who exhibits persons, things or events in a flame, mirror, crystal, etc.

hazırcevap[bı] (...—) حاضرجواب [Persian —..—] quick at repartee, witty. —**lık** wittiness.

hazırcı حاضرجی 1. seller of ready-made clothes. 2. one who likes to find everything ready.

hâzırîn (—.—) حاضرین A lrnd., pl. of **hâzır 2**.

hazırla=[r] حاضرلامق to prepare, to make ready. —**ma** preparation. —**n**= 1. pass. of **hazırla**=. 2. to prepare, to get ready. —**t**= /ı, a/ caus. of **hazırla**=.

hazırlık[ğı] حاضرلق readiness; preparedness; preparation. — **gör**= to make preparations. — **tahkikatı** law preliminary criminal proceeding, preliminary investigations. —**lı** prepared, well prepared.

hazırlop حاضرلوب 1. hard boiled (egg). 2. ready-made, without trouble.

hâzırun (—.—) حاضرون A lrnd. persons present.

hazif 1 (—.) حاذف A lrnd. who elides (in pronunciation).

hazifⁿ 2 عذف var. of **hazf**.
hazifüttekbir (—...—) ما ذف التكبير A lrnd. who utters the cry **Allahu ekber** without fully articulating all its letters.
hazikᵏⁱ (—.) ماذق A same as **hazık**.
hazim 1 (—.) حازم A lrnd. prudent, discreet, circumspect.
hazim 2 (—.) هاذم A lrnd. 1. that bruises, crushing. 2. who defeats, routing.
hazin 1 (.—) حزين A 1. sad, sorrowful, touching, tragic. 2. pathetic, melancholic.
hâzin 2 (—.) خازن A lrnd. 1. treasurer. 2. guardian, guard. **H—i bâb-i Hümayun** Ott. hist. Imperial treasurer.
hazine (.—.) خزينة A 1. treasure. 2. public treasury, exchequer; treasury. 3. Ott. hist. a sum of 36.000 kese. 4. same as **hazne**. **— ağası** treasurer of a great household; Ott. hist., title of an officer of the Janissary corps. **—i âmire** Ott. hist. the Exchequer. **— avukatı** official lawyer of the Ministry of Finance. **—i bîrûn** Ott. hist. public treasury. **— bonosu** fin. treasury bill. **—i emiriye** Ott. hist. Finance Department. **—i enderûn** Ott. hist. private treasury of the Palace. **—i evrak** state archives. **—i hassa** Ott. hist. the Sultan's privy purse. **—i hümayun** Ott. hist. Imperial Treasury. **— kethüdası** Ott. hist. superintendent of the Treasury. **— odası** Ott. hist. chamber of accounts of the Sultan's Treasury. **—i padişahî** Ott. hist. Imperial Treasury. **—i raht** Ott. hist. treasury of the Imperial stables. **— tahvilatı** fin. treasury bonds. **— vekili** Ott. hist., title of the fifth in rank of the black eunuchs of the Palace.
hazinedar (.—.—.) خزينه دار P hist. treasurer. **— ağa** Ott. hist. 1. title of the second black eunuch of the Imperial household. 2. treasurer of a large household. **— başı** Ott. hist. 1. title of the second assistant to the chief of the black eunuchs. 2. title of the fourth officer of the white eunuchs. **— usta** Ott. hist., title of the second woman supervisor of the Harem. **—î** (.—.——) P, **—lık** office and occupation of the treasurer.
hazinemande (.—.—.) خزينه مانده P lrnd. lapsed to the treasury, reverted to the crown.
Haziran (.—.) حزيران [Arabic .——] calendar June.
hazîre (.—.) حظيره A 1. arch. enclosed graveyard, especially in the grounds of a mosque. 2. lrnd. cattle pen, cattle fold. **H—i Kuds** lrnd. Paradise.
haziz (.—) حضيض A astr. perihelion.
hazm 1 هضم A same as **hazım 1. — et=**. **—ı nefs** a bearing patiently and curbing one's own passions.

hazm 2 حزم A lrnd. prudence, circumspection; intelligence, ability, tact.
hazmet=ᵈᵉʳ هضم ايتمك /ı/ 1. to digest. 2. to stomach (an insult).
hazmî (.—) هضمى A lrnd. digestive.
hazne خزنه [**hazine**] 1. same as **hazine**. 2. reservoir; store-room; chamber (of a gun). 3. womb; vagina. 4. segment of a tent, tarpaulin. **—dar** (..—) var. of **hazinedar**. **—li mermi** mil. hollow projectile. **—li tüfek** mil. magazine rifle.
hazra (.—) خضراء A lrnd. 1. green; vegetation, verdure; fresh; tender (shoot, sapling). 2. sky. 3. Or. mus., same as **hadra**.
Hazremevt حضرموت A same as **Hadramut**.
Hazremi (..—) حضرمى A of or belonging to Hadhramaut; native of Hadhramaut.
hazret حضرت A 1. fam. old man, old fellow (when addressing a comrade). 2. lrnd. presence; dignity. **—i** before name; title of an exalted personage. **—leri** (used after a title) His excellency. **—i Allah** God, the Lord God. **—i fetvapenahi** Ott. hist. the Sheikh-ul-Islam. **—i İsa** Jesus Christ. **—i Mesih** the Messiah, Jesus Christ. **—i Nuhtan kalma** very old, ancient. **—i Peygamber** the Prophet Muhammad.
hazur (.—) حذور A lrnd. very prudent, extremely cautious.
hazzet=ᵈᵉʳ حظ ايتمك to like, to be pleased (with).
he 1 1. name of the letter **h**. 2. Arabic script, name of the letter ه (This is the 27th letter of the Arabic, 30th letter of the Ottoman alphabet, pronounced as **h**. In chronograms, it has the numerical value of 5.)
he 2 هه prov. Well, very well; yes. **— de=** to agree, to accept; to say yes. **— mi?** Isn't it?
heba (.—) هباء A 1. waste, loss. 2. lrnd. dust, especially the finer particles which fly about and are only conspicuous in the sun's rays. **— et=** /ı/ 1. to waste, to spoil. 2. lrnd. to reduce to a powder. **—ya git=**, **— ol=**, to be wasted, to go for nothing, to come to naught.
hebenneka هبنّقة A 1. idiot, fool. 2. w. cap., surname of a celebrated imbecile in Arabic stories.
heca (.—) هجاء [**hica**] obs., same as **hece**.
heccav (.—) هجّاو A satirist.
hece هجه [**heca**] syllable. **— oku=** to read syllable by syllable. **— taşı** tombstone. **— vezni** syllabic meter.
hecele=ʳ هجه لمك /ı/ to spell out by syllables.
hecemat (..—) هجمات A lrnd. assaults, attacks.
hecin (.—) هجين A a swift dromedary of great endurance. **— süvar** (.—.—) P lrnd. camel rider.
hecr هجر A same as **hicr**.

hecv صبو A *same as* **hicv**.
heç هيچ *prov., var. of* **hiç**.
hedaik[kı] (.—.) حدائق A *lrnd., pl. of* **hadika**. —**i hasse** *Ott. hist.* royal gardens in Istanbul and its suburbs.
hedaya (.——) هدايا A *lrnd., pl. of* **hediye**.
hedde هدّه A *lrnd.* noise of a falling building, crash!
hedef هدف A target, mark; object, aim. —**e isabet et=** 1. to hit the target. 2. to obtain one's object.
heder هدر A 1. waste, loss. 2. *lrnd.* a being shed or allowed to be shed unrevenged (blood). — **et=** /ı/ to waste. — **ol=** to be wasted; to be sacrificed uselessly.
hedhede هدهده A *lrnd.* 1. birds' cooing or singing. 2. camels' bellowing.
hedik[ği] هديك *Arm prov.* boiled wheat.
hedim هدم *var. of* **hedm**.
hediye هديه [*Arabic* .—.] A 1. gift, present. 2. price. — **et=** to make a present (of); to give as a gift.
hediyelik[ği] هديه لك fit for a present; choice thing.
hediyeten (.—'..) هديةً A as a gift.
hedm هدم A *lrnd.* a pulling down, a demolishing. — **et=** to pull down, to demolish.
hefevat (..—) هفوات A *lrnd., pl. of* **hefve**.
heft هفت P *lrnd.* seven. — **âbâ** the seven spheres. — **ahter** the seven planets. — **âsiye** the orbits of the seven planets. — **âsuman** the seven heavens. — **âyine**, — **bânû** the seven planets. — **cûş** an extremely hard kind of bronze. — **dâne** the seven kinds of grain used in preparing the pudding called **aşure**. — **derya** the seven seas. — **devr** the seven cycles of time from the creation to the day of judgment. — **ecrâm**, — **ejdehâ** the seven planets. — **elvân** 1. seven kinds of food sent down to Jesus from heaven. 2. dish of meat with various kinds of vegetables. — **endâm** 1. the seven members of the body. 2. aorta. — **evrenk** 1. the Big Dipper. 2. the seven heavens. — **hum** the seven heavens. — **hun** the seven pits of hell. — **iklim** the seven climes, the habitable world. — **kalem** *calligraphy* the seven styles of writing. — **kişver** the seven climes. — **merd**, — **merdân** 1. the Seven Sleepers. 2. the seven orders of saints on earth. — **meyve** the seven fruits most frequently dried. — **muhit** the seven oceans. — **peyker** the seven planets; the seven heavens. — **pîr** the seven masters in reading the Quran. — **reng** the seven colors which are associated with the seven planets. — **ten** the seven planets. — **tenân** *same as* **heft merdan**.
heftad (.—). هفتاد P *lrnd.* seventy. — **u dü şâh** 1. the seventy-two branches of the human race. 2. the seventy-two religious sects of Islam.
heftadüm (.—.) هفتادم P *lrnd.* seventieth.
heftdeh هفتده P *lrnd.* seventeen. —**üm** P seventeenth.
heftgâh (.—) هفتگاه P *lrnd., Or. mus.* a **şed** compound **makam**.
hefte هفته P *lrnd., same as* **hafta**.
heftgâne (.—.) هفتگانه P *lrnd.* composed of seven elements; in sevens, sevenfold.
heftsad هفتصد P *lrnd.* seven hundred.
heftüm, heftümin (..—) هفتم P *lrnd.* seventh.
hefve هفوه A *lrnd.* slipping of the foot; mistake, error.
hegemonya (...'.) Gk hegemony.
hejdeh هژده P *lrnd.* eighteen. —**üm** P eighteenth.
hekim حكيم [hakim 2] physician, doctor of medicine. — **başı** *Ott. hist.* Sultan's chief physician. —**lik** 1. profession of a doctor. 2. medical science, medicine.
hektar هكتار F hectare.
hekto هكتو F hecto. —**gram** F hectogram. —**litre** F hectoliter. —**metre** F hectometer. —**metre kare** square hectometer. —**metreküp** F cubic hectometer.
helâ (.—) خلا [halâ 3] toilet, water closet.
helâhil (.—.) هلاهل P *lrnd.* instantaneously mortal; deadly poison. —**rîz** (.—.—) P scattering poison or venom.
helâk[kı] (.—) هلاك A destruction, death, perishing; exhaustion. — **et=** /ı/ 1. to destroy, to kill. 2. to wear out with fatigue. — **ol=** 1. to perish. 2. to be utterly done in.
helâl[lı] (.—) حلال A canonically lawful, legitimate; lawful spouse. —**inden** legitimately, honestly, lawfully earned. — **et=** /ı, a/ to give up a legitimate claim to another; not to begrudge (something given). —**i hoş olsun!** Let it be yours to have and enjoy. — **olsun!** I give it to you freely; I give up all claim. — **süt emmiş** entirely trustworthy.
helâli (.—.) حلالى A 1. *text.* a cloth of silk warp and cotton, flaxen, or woolen woof (canonically lawful to be worn); shirt made of such material. 2. pinchbeck.
helâllaş=[ır] حلاللشمك mutually to give or forgive all that has been or may have been unjustly taken or done (usually performed on death beds, before battles, or long separations). —**tır=** /ı/ *caus.*
helâllik[ği] حلاللق 1. legitimate spouse. 2. a forgiving an unlawful act; being canonically lawful. —**a al=** /ı/ to take as one's lawful wife; to marry. — **dile=** /dan/ to ask forgiveness for an unlawful act.
helâlli حلاللى legitimate spouse.

helâlnemekᵏⁱ (. — ..) حلال نمك P lrnd. faithful, true.

helâlûş (. — —) حلالوش P lrnd. riot, clamor, tumult, uproar.

helalzade (. — — .) حلالزاده P 1. legitimate offspring. 2. honest man. **—lik** legitimacy of birth.

helâvet (. — .) حلاوت A same as **halavet**.

helbet (.'.) هلبت A prov. of course, most certainly.

hele (.'.) هله P 1. above all, especially. 2. at least. 3. At last! 4. Now then! Well! Listen to me! e. g., **— bak neler söylüyor** Just listen to him. **— hele** Now tell me the truth.

helecan طپلان A same as **halecan**.

heleke هلكه prov., var. of **helke**.

helezon حلزون A 1. spiral, helix; helicoid. 2. propeller. 3. snail, snail shell. 4. anat. cochlea. **—î** (. . — —) A helical, spiral; helicoidal. **—î merdiven** spiral stairs.

helikᵏⁱ هليك Gk prov. pebble.

helile (. — .) هليله P myrobalan, bot., Phyllanthus emblica. **—i Kâbülî** chebulic myrobalan, bot., Terminalia chebula.

helim (. —) هليم A lrnd. sticking, adhering, sticky.

helke هلكه Gk prov. pail, bucket.

helme هلمه [**helime**] gelatinous fluid from boiled rice or dried beans. **— dök=** same as **helmelen=**.

helmelen=ⁱʳ هلملنمك to develop much gelatinous fluid (rice, beans).

helmeli هلملى prepared with a large quantity of liquid, sloppy.

helümme (.'.)ʹ هلمّ A lrnd. Come on! Now then! Hurry up!

helva حلوا [Arabic .—] a sweet prepared in many varieties with sesame oil, various cereals, and syrup or honey. **— sohbeti** social feast at which **helva** is the chief dish.

helvacı حلواجى maker or seller of **helva**. **— çöveni** soapwort, bot., Saponaria officinalis. **— kabağı** Spanish gourd, winter squash. **— kâğıdı** 1. thick coarse wrapping paper. 2. worthless papers. **—lık** the trade of making or selling helva.

helvager (. — .) حلواگر P lrnd., same as **helvacı**.

helvaciyan-ı hassa (... —. —.) حلواجيان خاصّه Ott. hist. sweet-makers in the Sultan's Palace.

helvahane (.. — .) حلواخانه 1. large copper cauldron for making helva. 2. Ott. hist. special kitchen in the Palace for making sweets.

helvalıkᵏⁱ حلوالق child's pocket money.

Helveçya (.'.) هلوچيا L archaic Helvetia, Switzerland.

hem 1 هم P 1. repeated symmetrically both... and, and also, as well as, e. g., **hem ben hem sen** both you and I. 2. in initial position and, too, and yet, e. g., **hem biliyor musunuz, ben onu zaten anlamıştım** And you know, I knew that beforehand. **— ağlarım hem giderim** I'll cry but I'll go all the same (said of a person who pretends to be reluctant). **— çalar hem oynar** noisy and exuberant. **— de** moreover, and also, and besides. **— İsayı hem Musayı memnun et=** to try to please everyone. **— kaç=, hem davul çal=** to want a thing eagerly while pretending not to want it. **— karnım doysun, hem çörek bütün kalsın** One can't eat one's cake and have it. **— kel hem fodul** in the wrong, but presumptuous. **— nalına hem mıhına vur=** 1. to hammer both horseshoe and nail. 2. to hit out right and left regardless of person. **— sağır hem sığır** same as **hem kel hem fodul**. **—. suçlu hem güçlü, — uyuz hem yavuz** offensive though at fault. **— yardan hem serden ol=** to lose everything precious one has. **— ziyaret hem ticaret** combining business with pleasure.

hem- 2 هم P mutual, in common. co-, -con; of the same, fellow- as in **hemasr, hemcins, hemhudut**.

hemᵐᵐⁱ **3** هم A lrnd. care, thought; anxiety; trouble.

hemagûş (. — —) هم آغوش P lrnd. locked in each other's arms.

hemâhenkᵏⁱ (. — .) هم آهنك P harmonious; concordant.

hemahim (. — .) هم A lrnd. cares, anxieties; troubles.

hemalⁱⁱ (. —) همال P lrnd. alike, equal, peer.

hemân (. —) همان P lrnd., same as **hemen**.

hemanâ (. — —) همانا P lrnd. 1. apparently; as if. 2. exactly, certainly, surely.

hemandem (. — .) همان دم P lrnd., same as **hemangâh**.

hemangâh (. — —) همان گاه P lrnd. as soon as, very soon.

hemâra (. — —) همارا P lrnd. always, constantly.

hemâramiş (. — —.) هم آرامش P lrnd. a resting together.

hemâre (. — .) همّاره P lrnd., same as **hemâra**.

hemaslⁱⁱ هم اصل P lrnd. of the same origin.

hemasr هم عصر P lrnd. contemporary.

hemaşiyan (. — . —) هم آشيان P lrnd. of the same nest; living together.

hematit هماتيت F geol. hematite.

hemâvâz (. — —) هم آواز P lrnd. 1. singing in unison; speaking in the same tone of voice. 2. harmonious; congenial friend, companion.

hemâver (. — .) هم آور P lrnd. 1. companion. 2. equal, alike.

hemâverd (.—.) هماورد P *lrnd.* rival, antagonist.

hemayar (..—) هميا - هم عيار P *lrnd.* equal; of the same degree or rank.

hembâr (.—) همبار P *lrnd.* carrying the same burden; companion in oppression, labor or affliction.

hembâz (.—) همباز P *lrnd.* playmate; companion.

hember همبر P *lrnd.* bosom friend, companion.

hembezm همبزم P associate, convivial companion; one who sits with others at a feast.

hembûy (.—) همبوى P *lrnd.* of the same nature.

hemcây (.—) همجاى P *lrnd.* fellow citizen, countryman.

hemcenah (..—) هم جناح P *lrnd.* having similar wings, of the same nature; equal; companion.

hemcenb هم جنب P *lrnd.* sitting together; friend.

hemcins همجنس P fellow-man; of the same kind. —î (..—) P, —lik homogeneity.

hemcivar (..—) همجوار P neighboring, adjacent, bordering. —î (..——) P, —lık neighborhood, state of being neighbors.

hemçu, hemçûn (.—) همچو همچون P *lrnd.* as; like; as if.

hemçunan, hemçunin (..—) همچنان همچنين P *lrnd.* in the same way, thus.

hemdâmân (.——) همدامان P *lrnd.* husband of wife's sister.

hemdâstân (.——) همداستان P *lrnd.* 1. intimate friend, inseparable companion. 2. confidant, secretary.

hemdâstani (.———) همداستانى P *lrnd.* taxes, tribute.

hemdem همدم P *lrnd.* intimate friend, constant companion. —î (..—) P, —lik intimacy, close friendship.

hemdert[di] همدرد P fellow sufferer.

hemdest همدست P *lrnd.* 1. partner, companion; accomplice. 2. equal, match.

hemdestan (..—) همدستان P *lrnd.* 1. hand in hand. 2. pl. of **hemdest**.

hemdiger (.—.) همديگر P *lrnd.* one another, each, each other.

hemdih همده P *lrnd.* of the same village.

hemdil همدل P *lrnd.* of the same opinion, cordial friend.

hemdûş (.—) همدوش P *lrnd.* equal, companion.

heme هم P *lrnd.* all.

hemen (.'.) همان [hemân] 1. at once, instantly; right now, just. 2. nearly, almost, about. 3. *lrnd.* only. — **hemen** almost, very nearly. — **şimdi** at once. —**cecik**, —**cek** at once.

hemfiil[fi'il] همفعل P *law* accomplice.

hemfikir[kri] همفكر P of the same opinion, like-minded.

hemfiraş (..—) همفراش P *lrnd.* bedfellow.

hemger همگر P *lrnd.* weaver.

hemginân (..—) همگنان P *lrnd.* all, all men; the whole world.

hemhâb (.—), **hemhâbe** (.—.) همخواب همخوابه P *lrnd.* bedfellow; spouse.

hemhâh (.—) همخواه P *lrnd.* desiring the same thing.

hemhâl[li] (.—) همحال P in the same state or condition; fellow-sufferer.

hemhâlet (.—.) همحالت P *lrnd.*, same as **hemhâl**.

hemhâne (.—.) همخانه P *lrnd.* cohabiting; companion, partner, spouse.

hemhudut[du] (..—) همحدود P contiguous.

hemhuy (.—) همخوى P *lrnd.* of the same character or habit.

hemialji هميالژى F *path.* hemialgia.

hemicik[ği] هميجك *colloq.* country bumpkin.

hemîn (.—) همين P *lrnd.* 1. only, solely. 2. in the same way, likewise, too.

hem'inân (..—) همعنان P *lrnd.* 1. riding side by side. 2. equal, friend, peer.

hemipleji هميپلژى F *path.* hemiplegia.

hemişe (.—.) هميشه P *lrnd.* always. — **cevan** P evergreen, always young.

hemk[ki] همك A *lrnd.* a plunging headlong into any matter.

hemkad[ddi] همقد P *lrnd.* of the same stature.

hemkadeh همقدح P *lrnd.* tippling companion, boon companion.

hemkadem همقدم P *lrnd.* equal in rank and power.

hemkadr[ri] همقدر P *lrnd.* equal in worth or dignity.

hemkâr (.—) همكار P *lrnd.* of the same occupation; fellow workman.

hemkâse (.—.) همكاسه P *lrnd.* pot companion; friend.

hemken همكن P *lrnd.* fellow workman.

hemkıran (..—) همقران P *lrnd.* 1. of the same age or generation. 2. equal in power.

hemkîş (.—) همكيش P *lrnd.* coreligionist.

hemkitab (..—) همكتاب P *lrnd.* 1. fellow student. 2. coreligionist.

hemkün همكن P *lrnd.*, same as **hemken**.

hemmânâ (.——) همعنا هم معنى P *lrnd.* synonymous.

hemmeşreb هممشرب P *lrnd.* like-tempered; alike in character.

hemmezheb همذهب هم مذهب P *lrnd.* coreligionist.

hemnâm (.—) همنام P *lrnd.* namesake.

hemneberd همنبرد P *lrnd.* fellow combatant; antagonist.

hemnefes همنفس P *lrnd.* friend, intimate companion.

hemnesl همنسل P *lrnd.* of the same generation, family or race.
hemnişin (..—) همنشین P *lrnd.* living together; close friend.
hemoglobin هموغلوبین F *biol.* hemoglobin.
hemoptizi هموپتزی F *path.* hemoptysis.
hempâ (.—) همپا P *lrnd.* 1. companion, confederate. 2. evil companion, accomplice.
hempâye (.—.) همپایه P *lrnd.* of equal dignity or rank.
hempîşe (.—.) همپیشه P *lrnd.* fellow craftsman.
hemrâh (.—) همراه P *lrnd.* fellow traveler, companion. —î (.——) P, —lık a traveling together.
hemrâz (.—) همراز P *lrnd.* bosom friend, close companion. —î (.——) P close friendship.
hemreh همره P *lrnd.*, same as **hemrâh.**
hemreng همرنگ P *lrnd.* 1. of the same color. 2. of the same character.
hemrev همرو P *lrnd.* 1. fellow traveler; going together, going at the same pace. 2. equal.
hemrey همرای P *lrnd.* of the same opinion.
hemrikâb (..—) همرکاب P *lrnd.* riding side by side.
hemrîş (.—) همریش P *lrnd.*, same as **hemdâmân.**
hemrütbe همرتبه P *lrnd.* having the same rank or position, equal.
hemrûzgâr (.——) همروزگار P *lrnd.* 1. contemporary. 2. companion, friend.
hems همس A *lrnd.* slight sound.
hemsâl[lı] (.—) همسال P *lrnd.* of the same year or age.
hemsâye (.—.) همسایه P *lrnd.* neighbor. —i Mesih the sun (whose seat is the fourth heaven). —gî (.—.—) P neighborliness; neighborhood.
hemsâz (.—) همساز P *lrnd.* 1. unanimous. 2. friend, companion.
hemsebak[kı] همسبق P *lrnd.* school fellow, classmate.
hemsefer همسفر P *lrnd.* fellow traveler, traveling companion.
hemseferân (...—) همسفران P *lrnd.*, pl. of **hemsefer.** —ı cahil the ignorant fellow travelers, i. e. the soul and the body.
hemseng همسنگ P *lrnd.* of the same weight, equal.
hemser همسر P *lrnd.* 1. equal. 2. spouse. —î (..—) P, —lik equality.
hemsıfat همصفت P *lrnd.* equally gifted, having attributes in common.
hemsin[nni] همسن P *lrnd.* of the same age.
hemsofra همسفره P *lrnd.* table companion.
hemsohbet همصحبت P *lrnd.* social companion, associate.

hemsüvar (..—) همسوار P *lrnd.* fellow rider.
hemşehri (..—) همشهری P same as **hemşeri.**
hemşekl همشکل P *lrnd.* like, resembling.
hemşeri همشری [**hemşehri**] fellow countryman, fellow citizen, compatriot. —lik citizenship.
hemşevher همشوهر P *lrnd.* fellow wife in a polygamous household.
hemşikem همشکم P *lrnd.* uterine (brother); twin.
hemşire (.—.) همشیره P 1. sister. 2. nurse, being a sister.
hemşirezade (.—.—.) همشیره‌زاده P sister's child, nephew, niece.
hemşûy (.—) همشوی P *lrnd.*, same as **hemşevher.**
hemta (.—) همتا P *lrnd.* equal, of the same grade, fellow.
hemvar (.—) هموار P *lrnd.* 1. level, smooth. 2. equal, uniform, even. — et= /ı/ to level. — ol= pass.
hemvare (.—.) همواره P *lrnd.* always, continually, constantly.
hemvarî (.——) همواری P *lrnd.* levelness, smoothness.
hemz همز A *lrnd.* 1. a squeezing, pressing; a squeeze with the hand. 2. a piercing, pricking, biting. 3. a breaking, dashing upon the ground.
hemzad (.—) همزاد P *lrnd.* born together, twin; of equal age.
hemzanu (.——) همزانو P *lrnd.* sitting with another; knee to knee.
hemze همزه A *Arabic script* hamza (the sign marking the hiatus). —i katı' *Arabic gram.* initial hamza not connected in pronunciation with the preceding word. —i sakine *Arabic gram.* hamza at the end of a syllable, not followed by a vowel. —i vasıl *Arabic gram.* initial hamza (آ) in post-pausal position, which, when preceded by another word, is replaced by آ and not pronounced.
hemzeban (..—) همزبان P *lrnd.* 1. of the same language. 2. unanimous in expression, agreed.
hemzemin (..—) همزمین P *lrnd.* on the same level. — geçit level crossing.
hencar (.—) هنجار P *lrnd.* 1. the right and proper way of acting. 2. way, road; rule, law; habit, custom, conduct. 3. color.
hendek[ği] هندک A ditch, trench, gutter, moat. H— gazvesi *Isl. hist.* the expedition in defense of the trench of Medina.
hendese هندسه A geometry; mathematics. —i küreviye spherical geometry. —hane (...—.) *Ott. hist.* mathematical college. —li geometrical.
hendesî (..—) هندسی A geometrical, mathematical.
henek[ği] هنک A *prov.* 1. talk. 2. joke. — et= 1. to talk. 2. to joke.

nengâm (.—) هنگام P lrnd. time, season, period.
hengâme (.—.) هنگامه P crowd, throng; uproar, tumult. **—gir** (.—.—) P lrnd. tumultuous, uproarious.
heni (.—) هنی A lrnd. easily digestible.
henüz 1 (.'.) هنوز P just now, a minute or so ago, only just.
henüz 2 هنوز P *in negative sentence* yet.
hep هپ 1. all; the whole, wholly, entirely. 2. always. **—imiz** all of us. **—si** all of it; all of them. **—ten** entirely. **— beraber** all together. **— bir ağızdan** in unison, with one voice. **— bir koyun aşığıyız** *colloq.* We are all equal. **— ile hiç ilkesi** the principle of all or nothing. **— yek** *dice* double one. **—sinden ziyade** above all.
her 1 هر P every, each. **— an** at any moment, always. **— aşın kaşığı** meddler, interloper. **— bakımdan** in every respect. **— bapta** in every respect, on every subject. **— bir** each, every single. **— biri** /ın/ each one, every one (of). **— boyadan boyadı, fıstıkisi kaldı** He never seems to be able to succeed at anything. **— daim** always. **— defa**, **— defasında** /da/ each time. **— derde deva** cure-all, panacea. **— Firavunun bir Musası var** *prov.* There is a Moses for every Pharaoh. **— gün** every day; always; daily. **— günlük** for every day; everyday clothes. **— gün papaz pilav yemez** *proverb* Good things don't happen every day. **— halde** 1. in every case, under any circumstances, whatever happens. 2. for sure. 3. apparently, probably. **— hal ü kârda** *lrnd.* in any case, under any circumstances. **— hangi** whichever, whatever; *in negative sentence* any, whatsoever. **— havadan çal=** same as **her telden çal=**. **— horoz kendi çöplüğünde öter** *proverb* Every cock crows on his own dunghill. **— hususta** in all respects, from all points of view, in every way. **— ihtimale karşı** just in case. **— işe burnunu sok=** to poke one's nose into everything. **— kaça olursa olsun** *colloq.* at whatever price. **— kaçan ki** *archaic* whenever, when. **— kafadan bir ses çıkıyor.** 1. Everyone is shouting his opinion. 2. What a tumult! **— kande** *archaic* wherever. **— kes***, **— kim**, **— kim ki** whoever. **— kim olursa olsun** no matter who it is, whoever it may be. **— koyun kendi bacağından asılır** *proverb* Every mutton is hung by its own legs. He is responsible for himself. **— kuşun eti yenmez** *proverb* Not every bird is edible. Not every person will bend to your will. **— makamdan söyle=** to talk on all kinds of subjects. **— nasıl** in whatever way. **— nasılsa** somehow or other. **— ne** whatever. **— nedense** somehow; for some reason or other;

I don't know why. **— ne hal ise** anyhow, anyway. **— ne kadar** although, notwithstanding that, in spite of; however much. **— ne pahasına olursa olsun** at whatever cost. **— nerede** wherever. **— ne vakit** whenever. **— neyse** anyhow, anyway. **— ne zaman** whenever. **— nice** *archaic* 1. although. 2. whichever. **— sakallıyı baban mı sanırsın?** You mustn't expect everyone to be your friend. **— suretle** in every regard. **— şey** everything. **— tarafta** all around, everywhere, on all sides. **— taraftan** from everywhere. **— tarakta bezi var** He has a finger in every pie. **— tel başka hava çalıyor** Everyone is playing a different tune. **— telden çal=** to be versatile; to know a bit of everything. **— vadiden** on every subject. **— vakit** always. **— yerde** everywhere. **— yerdelik** *neol., phil.* ubiquity, omnipresence. **— yiğidin bir yoğurt yiyişi var** *proverb* Everyone has his own way of doing things. **— yiğidin gönlünde bir arslan yatar** *proverb* Everyone has an ambition. **— zaman** every time, always.
her 2 هر *var. of* **har 4**.
heragil (.—.) هراگل A lrnd., pl. of **hergele**.
herahad (.—.) هراحد P lrnd. every one.
heranci (.—'.) هرانچ P lrnd. everything that.
heranki (.—'.) هرانکه P lrnd. everyone who.
herayine (.—..) هرآیینه P lrnd. always, in any case, at all events.
herbar (.—) هربار P lrnd. every time, always.
herc هرج A lrnd. confusion, turmoil. **— ü merc***.
herca (.—) هرجا P lrnd. everywhere; always.
hercai, hercayi (.——) هرجائی P 1. inconstant, unsettled. 2. lrnd. ubiquitous, roving. **— menekşe** pansy, *bot.*, *Viola tricolor*. **—lik** inconstancy.
hercümerc هرج و مرج P tumult, confusion.
herçendki (.'.) هرچندکه P lrnd. although, notwithstanding.
herçi (.'.) هرچه P lrnd. whatsoever.
herçibadabad (..——) هرچه بادا باد P lrnd. whatever may happen; whatever the consequence.
herdemtaze (..—.) هردم تازه 1. evergreen; always fresh, young. 2. ageless. 3. trumpet honeysuckle, *bot.*, *Lonicera sempervirens*; livelong, *bot.*, *Sedum Telephium*.
hereb هرب A lrnd. a running away in fright; flight.
herek[gi] **1** هرك Gk 1. prop, pole, stick (for grapevine, beans, young trees). 2. *prov.* temporary platform used for drying raisins, tobacco, etc. 3. *obs.* bridge (of a lute).

herek⁹¹ 2 هرك *prov.* small variety of fat-tailed sheep.
herekle=ᵣ هركلك /ı/ 1. to prop (vine, etc.). 2. to spread on a temporary platfrom to dry (grapes, etc.). 3. to bridge (lute).
herem هرم A *lrnd.* 1. senility, decrepitude; old age. 2. pyramid. **—ân** (..—) A the two great pyramids on the Nile. **—î** (..—) A pyramidal, pyramid-like. **—reside** (...—.) P aged.
hereni هرنى *prov.* 1. large cooking pot. 2. double-handled small cauldron, boiler.
herfene هرفنه *var. of* **herifane**.
hergâh (.—) هرگاه P *lrnd.* always, constantly; whenever, wherever.
hergele هرگلى P 1. vulgar and unscrupulous fellow; a lot of roughs. 2. herd; herds and flocks of a village; breeding herd of mares and colts; unbroken horse. **—ci** 1. village herdsman. 2. rough fellow.
hergiz هرگز P *lrnd.* always, ever; *in negative sentences* never.
herheft هرهفت P *lrnd.* cosmetics.
herif هريف [harif 2] 1. fellow (always derogatory). 2. *prov.* husband; male, man. **— cicoz** *slang* The fellow is gone; he is dead. **—çi oğlu** *slang* the fellow.
herifane (.——.) هريفانه P *lrnd., same as* **arifane**.
herim هرم A *lrnd.* very old and feeble.
herir (.—) هرير A *lrnd.* a dog's whine, whining (as a dog from the cold.)
herise (.—.) هريسه A *lrnd., same as* **herse**.
herkᵏⁱ هرك P *prov.* a fallowing.
herkâre (.—.) هركاره P *lrnd.* jack of all trades.
herkele هركله A *lrnd.* graceful (woman); graceful gait.
herkes (.ˊ.) هركس P everybody, everyone. **—ler** everybody. **— bir hava çalıyor** Everyone expresses a different opinion.
herkil هركيل *prov.* big barn made of mud or wood.
hernekadar (.ˊ..) هرنه قدر although.
hernice (..ˊ.) هرنيجه archaic although.
hers هرس P *lrnd.* board or shingle used in covering a roof.
herse هرسه [herise] *prov.* pudding of boiled wheat.
Hersek⁹¹ هرسك *geog.* Herzegovina.
herseme هرسمه A *lrnd.* 1. tip of the nose. 2. lion.
hervele هروله A *lrnd.* a going along at a jog-trot, an ambling; jog-trot.
herze هرزه P nonsense. **— ye=** to talk nonsense. **—çâne** (..—.) P, **—deray** (...—) P, **—gû** (..—) P *lrnd.* idle talker; babbler; prattler. **—ha** (..—) P *lrnd.* prattler. **—hand** P *lrnd.* silly giggler. **—hâr** (..—) P, **—hây** (..—) P *lrnd.* prattling fellow. **—kâr** (..—) P *lrnd.* trifler, one who does silly things. **—lây** (..—) P *same as* **herzegû**. **—rev** P *lrnd.* one who runs about in a foolish way. **—vat** (..—) P trifles, falsehoods.
herzevekil (...—) هرزه وكيل P 1. busybody. 2. prattler, babbler.
hesab (.—) حساب [hisab] *cf.* **hesap**. **— et=** /ı/ 1. to calculate, to reckon; to work out a problem. 2. to count. 3. to plan, to think out. **—ı asgarı nâmütenahî** infinitesimal calculus. **—ı âşarî** decimal calculation. **—ı câmid** *naut.* dead-reckoning. **—ı carî** *com.* current account, open account. **—ı cümel** *lrnd.* calculation by the numerical values of Arabic letters. **—ı havaî** mental arithmetic. **—ı ihtimalî** *math.* calculus of probabilities. **—ı tamamî** *math.* integral calculus. **—ı tefazulî** *math.* differential calculus. **—ı zihnî** mental arithmetic.
hesabî (.——) حسابى [based on **hesab**] economical, thrifty; calculating; stingy.
hesapᵇⁱ حساب [hesab] 1. a reckoning, counting, numbering, computation; calculation; arithmetic. 2. account; bill. 3. a considering, comparing, weighing; plan, scheme. **—ı** as one would say, as in the case of (referring to a saying or to a known story), *e. g.*, **körlerle fil hesabı** as in the story of the elephant and the blind men. **— aç=** *com.* to open an account. **—a al=** /ı/ *same as* **hesaba kat=**. **—ını Allah bilir** /ın/ God knows how many. **—a bak=** to examine the accounts. **— bakiyesi** balance (of an account), arrears. **—ını bil=** to be economical and careful, to be cautious. **— cetveli** slide rule. **— cüzdanı** bank book, pass book. **—a çek=** /ı/ to call to account, to hold responsible. **— çıkar=** to make out the accounts. **— devresi** *fin.* accounting period. **— dökümü** settlement of account; presenting of accounts. **—tan düş=** /ı/ to deduct. **—a geçir=** /ı/ to put on to an account. **—ına gel=** /ın/ to suit one's calculations, to fit one's views or interest. **—a gelmez** incalculable, countless, unbounded, unaccountable. **— gör=** 1. to pay the bill. 2. to settle accounts. **—ını gör=** /ın/ 1. to settle somebody's account. 2. to eliminate (someone who is a nuisance), to do away (with). **— hülâsası** presenting of accounts, statement of account. **— iste=** /dan/ 1. to ask for the account or the bill. 2. to reckon (with); to hold responsible. **— işi** embroidery made by counting the threads. **—ı kapa=, —ı kapat=** to close the acount; to settle the accounts. **—a kat=** /ı/ to take into account. **—ı kes=** 1. to settle an account. 2. to cut all relations (with somebody). **— kesimi** closing of

heyakil

accounts. **— kitap** after full consideration. **—a kitaba sığmaz** 1. incalculable. 2. imponderable. 3. inconsistent. **—ı kitabı yok** uncontrolled, unlimited; extravagant. **— memuru** 1. accountant. 2. *mil.* paymaster, *navy* purser. **— meydanda** It's quite obvious. **— müfettişi** auditor. **— senesi** *law* financial year. **—ını temizle=** to clear one's account. **— tut=** to keep an account, to do bookkeeping. **— uzmanı** trained accountant. **— ver=** to render account (of), to account (for), to explain. **—ta yok** 1. not included in the account. 2. unthought of, unexpected.

hesapça صابجه 1. according to calculation. 2. normally, properly speaking.

hesapçı صابجى calculating, careful, miserly.

hesapla=ʳ صابلامق /ı/ 1. to reckon, to calculate; to estimate. 2. to take into consideration 3. to plan. **—ş=** to settle accounts mutually; to settle up (a matter). **—ştır=** /ı/ *caus.* of **hesaplaş=**.

hesaplı صابلى 1. well-calculated, measured, planned; well considered. 2. well-balanced, economical.

hesapsız صابسز 1. innumerable; incalculable. 2. not duly considered; imprudent; without reflection, unplanned. **— kitapsız** 1. uncontrolled (expenses). 2. thoughtlessly, at random, casual. **—lık** 1. innumerability. 2. unplannedness. 3. inconsiderateness.

hestî (.—) هستى P *lrnd.* existence, being.

heşt هشت P *lrnd.* eight. **H— Bihişt** the eight Paradises mentioned in the Quran. **— genc, — genc-i Husrevî** the eight treasures of Husrev Perviz. **H— Heykel-i Rıdvan** *same as* **Heşt Bihişt.**

heştad (.—) هشتاد P *lrnd.* eighty.

heştgâh (.—) هشتگاه P *Or. mus.* the note g″.

heştüm, heştümin (..—) هشتم هشتمين P *lrnd.* eighth.

hetepete ہتہ پتہ *obs.* with a stammer, stuttering.

heterogen ہتروژن G *phys.* heterogeneous.

heteropati ہتروپاتى F *psych.* heteropathy.

hetf هتف A *lrnd.* 1. dove's cooing; calling. 2. a eulogizing.

het hüt ہت ہوت *only in* **het hüt et=** to behave in a bullying manner, to talk loudly and menacingly.

hetkᵏⁱ هتك A *lrnd.* 1. a rending, tearing open. 2. a violating one's honor, ravishing. **—i hisab-ı ismet et=, —i perde-i ırz et=** to outrage, to violate, to defame; to rape.

hetman ہتمان Pol. *hist.* hetman, Cossack headman.

hettakᵏⁱ (.—) هتاك A *lrnd.* violator, ravisher; profaner.

heva (.—) هوا A *lrnd.* affection, favor, love, desire; fancy, whim. **— ve heves** lust, luxury; carnal passions, sensuality. **—sına tâbi ol=** to follow one's own fancies.

hevacû (.——) هواجو P *lrnd.* lover.

hevadar (.——) هوادار P *lrnd.* desirous; lover.

hevahâh (.——) هواخواه P *lrnd.* 1. beloved, friend. 2. vain, ambitious.

hevaî (.——) هوائى P idle, vain.

hevamᵐᵐⁱ (.—) هوام A *lrnd.* insects; creeping, crawling animals; reptiles. **—ı cerebî** *zool.*, Arachnida.

hevan (.—) هوان A *lrnd.* a being or becoming of no account; contempt, scorn.

hevaperest (.—..) هواپرست P *lrnd.* a slave to fancy and passion.

hevdec هودع A *lrnd.* canopied camel-litter (for women), howdah.

hevenkᵍⁱ هونك P bunch of grapes or other fruit hung up.

heves هوس A strong desire; inclination; zeal, mania. **—ini al=** /dan/ to satisfy one's whim. **— et=** /a/ to have a strong desire, to have a fancy (for).

hevesât (..—) هوسات A *lrnd., pl. of* **heves.**

hevesbaz (..—) هوسباز P *lrnd.* one who follows zealously any desire.

hevesdar (..—) هوسدار P *lrnd.* desirous, inclined.

heveskâr (..—) هوسكار P 1. desirous, inclined. 2. amateur; having a hobby. **—âne** (..——.) P desirously. **—lık** passing desire; longing; hobby, amateurship.

heveslen=ⁱʳ هوسلنمك /a/ to desire, to long (for). **—dir=** /ı/ *caus.*

hevesli هوسلى desirous, eager; having aspirations; dilettante.

hevesnâkᵏⁱ (..—) هوسناك P *lrnd., same as* **hevesli.**

hevesperver هوس پرور P *lrnd.* desirous.

hevessiz هوسسز disinclined, having no ambition.

hevilᵛⁱⁱ هول *var. of* **hevl.**

hevl هول A *lrnd.* horror, terror, fright. **—âver** (.—.) P, **—engiz** (..—) P, **—nâk** (.—) P *lrnd.* horrible, awful, frightful, terrific.

hevn هون A *lrnd.* 1. easiness, facility. 2. a being slow and leisurely.

hey هى 1. hello; look here; see. 2. *in exclamations of reproach or regret* O...! *e. g.,* **hey talih!** O Fate! **— gidi** *in nostalgic reference to the past, e. g.,* **hey gidi gençlik!** Oh for the days of youth! **— gidi hey!** O those times!

heyadid (.——) هياديد [*based on* **haydut**] *lrnd.* bandits, robbers.

heyahu (.——) هياهو P *lrnd.* clamor, shouts in battle.

heyakil (.—.) هياكل A *lrnd., pl. of* **heykel.**

heyamola (...'.) حيامولا It Heave, ho! Pull away, boys! — **ile** with great difficulty.

hey'at (.—) هيآت A *lrnd.*, *pl.* of **heyet**.

heyban (.—) هيبان A *lrnd.* 1. very timid. 2. formidable, frightening.

heybe هيبه [hakîbe] saddle-bag. —**ci** maker of saddle-bags.

Heybeliada هيبلى آطه one of the islands near Istanbul (ancient Khalki).

heybet هيبت A 1. awe and dread. 2. grandeur, majesty; imposing air. —**li** awesome, awe-inspiring; imposing, grand, majestic. —**var** (..—) P *lrnd.*, same as **heybetli**.

heyca (.—) هيجا A *lrnd.* excitement; tumult; battle. —**zar** (.——) P field of battle.

heye هَيَه *prov.* yes.

heyecan (..—) هيجان A excitement; enthusiasm, emotion. — **çarpısı**, — **çarpması** *path.* emotive ictus. —**a gel=** to get excited.

heyecanlan= هيجانلانمق to get excited; to be moved. —**dır=** /ı/ *caus.*

heyecanlı هيجانلى 1. exciting, thrilling. 2. excited, thrilled, enthusiastic. 3. *psych.* emotive. —**lık** *psych.* emotivity.

heyecansız هيجانسز unemotional, unexciting; calmly.

heyelân (..—) هيلان A landslide.

heyeman (..—) هيمان A *lrnd.* love, a being in love.

heyet هيئت A 1. committee; delegation; board. 2. astronomy. 3. *lrnd.* shape, form; state, condition, aspect; constitution, system. —**iyle** as it is, as a whole. —**i adûl** *law* jury. —**i asliye** original form. —**i âyan** *Ott. hist.* Senate. —**i bahriye** nautical astronomy. —**i içtimaiye** *lrnd.* mankind, society. —**i idare** executive board, board of directors. —**i ihtiyariye** elders of a community. — **ilmi** astronomy; cosmography. —**i ittihamiye** *law* grand jury; chamber of accusation. —**i mebusan** *Ott. hist.* Assembly of Deputies. —**i mecmuası itibarile** taken as a whole. —**i sefiriye** expedition; military expedition. —**i teşriiye** legislative assembly. —**i umumiye** the whole; the general assembly. —**i umumiyesiyle** taken as a whole. —**i vekile**, —**i vükelâ** cabinet of ministers.

heyetşinas (...—) هيئتشناس P *lrnd.* astronomer; cosmographer.

heyhat (.—) هيهات A Alas!

heyhey 1 هَى هَى P 1. *lrnd.* a large goblet filled with wine which is drunk off at the end of a repast. 2. orgy; carousal; song.

heyhey 2 هَى هَى used in —**ler geçir=** to have a fit of nerves; to be very agitated. —**leri tut=** to have a fit of nerves. —**leri üstünde** /ın/ in a black mood.

hey'i (.—) هيئى A *lrnd.* astronomical.

heykel هيكل A 1. statue. 2. *lrnd.* temple, huge building. 3. *lrnd.* gigantic form. 4. inanimate, stony, unemotional.

heykeltraş (..—) هيكلتراش [based on Persian] sculptor. —**î** (..——) P, —**lık** sculpture.

heyn هين A *lrnd.* easy; easygoing, quiet.

Heytalli هيطل A *hist.* White Huns (5th Century).

heyulâ (.——) هيولا A 1. bogey, apparition, spook. 2. *phil.* matter; chaos. — **gibi** huge and nightmarish.

heyulâî (.———) هيولائى A 1. *phil.* material. 2. ghostlike; gigantic.

heyulânî (.———) هيولانى A *phil.* 1. pertaining to matter, material. 2. materialist. —**yun** (.————) A materialists.

heyzüm هيزم *var.* of **hizem**.

hezzı هَزّ A *lrnd.* sneer, scoff.

hezar 1 (.—) هزار P *poet.* nightingale.

hezar 2 (.—) هزار P *lrnd.* 1. thousand. 2. very many. — **bar** (.——) P a thousand times. — **pare** (.———.) P in many pieces, in a thousand bits.

hezaran 1 (.——) هزاران [hayzuran] same as **hezaren**.

hezaran 2 (.——) هزاران P *lrnd.* 1. *pl.* of **hezar**; thousands. 2. nightingale.

hezaraşina (.——.—) هزارآشنا P *lrnd.* who has many friends.

hezarava (.———), **hezaravaz** (.————) هزارآوا هزارآواز P *poet.* nightingale.

hezarçeşme (.—..) هزارچشمه P *lrnd.* cancer.

hezardastan (.———) هزارداستان P *poet.* nightingale.

hezaren (.—.) هزارن [hezaran 1] 1. cane, rattan cane, *bot.*, *Calamus rotang.* 2. larkspur, *bot.*, *Delphinium.* — **baston** cane, walking stick. — **sandalye** cane-bottomed chair, rattan chair.

hezarfennnî (.—.) هزارفن P *lrnd.* versatile.

hezarmih (.——) هزارميخ P *lrnd.* 1. the starry firmament. 2. much-patched garment.

hezarpa (.——) هزارپا P *lrnd.* scolopendrid, centipede.

hezarreng (.—.) هزاررنگ P *lrnd.* variegated, of a thousand colors.

hezarrenkgî (.—.) هزاررنك *var.* of **hezarreng**.

hezec هَزَج A 1. *pros.* meter characterized by the iambic beginning of each tetrasyllabic foot (most commonly: .——/.——/.—— —/.——). 2. *lrnd.* lively song, ballad tune.

hezeliyat (...—) هزليات literature jests, pleasantries; satires.

hezen هَزَن *prov.* wooden beam, tie-beam.

hezeyan (..—) هزيان A a talking nonsense; nonsense; *path.* delirium, raving. —**ı itisafî** *path.* persecutional mania, obsession. —**ı**

mürtaiş *path.* delirium tremens. —at (. . — —) A *lrnd., pl. of* **hezeyan.**

hezimet (. — .) نَزِيمَت A crushing defeat, rout; complete failure. **—e uğra=** to be completely defeated; to fail completely. **—e uğrat=** /ı/ to defeat, to rout.

hezl هَزْل A *lrnd.* jest, joke; comic tale; satirical poem. **—âmiz** (. — —) P spiced with jest. **—gû** (. —) P 1. joker, jester; satirist. 2. idle talker. **—î** (. —) A jocular. **—iyat** (. — —) A *same as* **hezeliyat.**

hezm هَزْم A *lrnd.* 1. a routing, defeat. 2. a depressing, a crushing.

hı 1 ح A *Arabic script, name of the letter* ح (This is the 7th letter of the Arabic, 9th of the Ottoman alphabet, pronounced as **h**; in chronograms it represents the number 600).

hı 2 حِی *colloq.* yes.

hıba (. —) ضِبا A *lrnd.* 1. tent. 2. *astr.*, *name of the two lunar mansions.* **—yı yemanî** the constellation Corvus.

hıbazet (. — .) خِبازَت A *lrnd.* business of a baker, baking.

hıçkır=ᴵʳ 1. to hiccup. 2. to sob.

hıçkırıkᵍᴵ 1. hiccup. 2. sob. **—larla ağla=** to sob. **— tut=** to have the hiccups.

hıdad (. —) حِداد A *can. law* a widow's abstaining from perfumes and ornaments as a sign of mourning.

hıdatᵈᴵ خِطاط [*Arabic* **hadad**] *prov.* cosmetic used for blackening the eyebrows.

Hıdır خِضِر *same as* **Hızır.**

Hıdırellez خِضِر الياس *var. of* **Hıdrellez.**

hıdiv (. —) خِدِيو P khedive. **—âne** (. — — .) P khedive-like. **—î** (. — —) P khedivial. **—iyet** (. — — .) A, **—lik** khediviate.

hıdn خِدْن A *lrnd.* 1. friend, companion, associate, 2. lover; mistress.

Hıdrellez خِضِر الياس [**Hıdır**, **İlyas**] the 40th day after the spring equinox (May 6th, popularly considered as the beginning of summer).

hıfızᶠᶻᴵ خِفْظ *var. of* **hıfz.**

hıfz خِفْظ A 1. a guarding, protecting, preserving, protection. 2. a keeping, a keeping hold of. 3. a committing to memory; a committing the Quran to memory; a bearing in mind, a remembering. **—a çalış=** to be trained in learning the Quran by heart. **— et=** /ı/ 1. to keep, to hold; to guard, to protect, to preserve. 2. to commit to memory. 3. to bear in mind, to remember.

hıfzıssıhha حِفْظ الصِحَّة A *lrnd.* hygiene.

hık حِیق *as in* **— demiş burnundan düşmüş** He is the very image of him. **— da dese mık da dese bu iş olacak** This is going to be done no matter what he says. **— mık et=** to hem and haw, to hesitate. **—ı mıkı yok** There is no question about it.

hıkd حِقْد A *lrnd.* hatred, malice, rancor.

hıl'atᵗᴵ خِلْعَت A *same as* **hil'at.**

hılt خِلْط A 1. *anat.* humor, fluid of the body. 2. *prov.* chilblains. 3. *lrnd.* ingredient in a mixture; compound. **—ı mahmud** *anat.* healthy, natural humor of the body. **—ı redî** *folk med.* morbid humor of the body. **—î** (. —) A pertaining to the fluid of the body. **—iyûn** (. — —) A *phil.* humoralists.

hım حِم *colloq.* Oh, yes. Is that so? Oh.

hımbıl حِمْبِل *colloq.* stupid, imbecile; slow; slack; idle.

hımhım حِمْحِم 1. a speaking through the nose. 2. one who speaks through his nose. **biri — biri burunsuz, birbirinden uğursuz** One is as bad as the other. **— et=**, **— söyle=** to speak through the nose; to have a nasal twang.

hımhımla=ʳ to speak through the nose.

hımhımlıkᵍᴵ speaking through the nose.

hımış حِمِش *arch.* timber construction with brick filling.

hımsı=ʳ *prov.* to get spoiled, go bad (food).

hına (. —) حِنا [**hınna**] *lrnd.* henna; plant. **—i girye** *poet.* bitter tears. **—i kadeh** *poet.* red wine.

hınat حِنَط A *lrnd., pl. of* **hınta.**

hıncahınçᶜᴵ (. ´. . .) ضِنْج jammed, crammed, greatly crowded.

hınçᶜᴵ حِنْج 1. hatred, rancor, grudge. 2. revenge. **— al=**, **—ını al=** to revenge. **—ını çıkar=** to take revenge (on), to vent one's spleen (on).

hınçkır=ᴵʳ *same as* **hıçkır=.**

hındım حِنْدِم *slang* orgy; carousal. **—la=** /ı/ to attack and overwhelm, to fall (upon).

hınk حِنْك 1. *same as* **hık.** 2. *sound made when expending effort in hard manual labor.*

hınna (. —) حِنّاء A *lrnd., same as* **hına.** **—î** (. — —) A seller of henna.

hınsır حِنْصِر A *lrnd.* the little finger or toe.

hınsîr (. —) حِنْصِير A *lrnd.* worthless, base, vile.

hınt حِنْط *Arm slang* crazy, mad.

hınta حِنْطَة A *lrnd.* 1. wheat. 2. *anat.* tragus.

hınzır حِنْزِير [**hınzir**] 1. swine, pig, hog. 2. brutal, despicable fellow. 3. *colloq.* swinish (sometimes used in joking admiration). **— ekmeği** truffle. **—lık** swinish behavior; a dirty trick.

hınzir (. —) حِنْزِير A *lrnd., same as* **hınzır.** **—e** (. — .) A 1. sow; wild sow. 2. hussy. **—î** (. — —) A swinish.

hır خِر 1. snarling sound. 2. *slang* row, quarrel. **— çıkar=** *slang* to start a quarrel; to cause a row. **— dediğin bundan çıkar** This is the very thing to cause a quarrel

hıra *prov.* thin and weak. — **cura** puny, thin and weak.

hırbo (.'.) *vulg.* booby, lout; clumsy, boorish fellow.

hırçın ill-tempered, cross; peevish; obstinate; wicked (horse); angry (sea).

hırçınlan=ᵣ, hırçınlaş=ᵢᵣ to become cross or obstinate.

hırçınlıkᵍⁱ bad temper, violence of temper, obstinacy, irritability.

hırdavat [hurdavat] 1. small pieces, scraps; trash, rubbish. 2. scrap iron, small wares; gewgaws; hardware.

hırdavatçı peddler, seller of small wares; hardware seller. —**lık** the hardware business.

hıred P *lrnd.* understanding, intellect, sense, reason, wisdom, judgment. —**âmûz** (..——) P teaching, instructive; instructor. —**âşub** (..——) P disturbing the mind. —**efruz** (...—) P which brightens the intellect. —**fersa** (...—) P tiring to the mind, very difficult. —**mend** P wise, sensible, understanding. —**meniş** P wise. —**perver** P fostering wisdom. —**pesend** P commendable; reasonable. —**pîşe** (..—.) P wise, practicing wisdom. —**sûz** (..—) P maddening, distracting; consuming the understanding. —**ver** P wise, sensible; reasonable.

hırgür *colloq.* noisy quarrel, squabble.

hırhır 1. continuous snarling. 2. continuous quarreling.

hırhıryas *var. of* **harharyas**.

hırılda=ᵣ to snarl, to snore continuously; to growl; to have a rattle in the chest. —**n=** to snarl continuously to oneself; to growl. —**ş=** /la/ to snarl continuously at each other; to quarrel (without reason).

hırılhırıl repeated snort. — **et=** to make a gurgling sound.

hırıltı 1. sound of snoring or snarling, growling. 2. quarrel, squabble. 3. death-rattle; râle. —**cı** quarrelsome. —**lı** having a rattling noise.

hırızma (.'.) nose-ring. —**sı çıkmış** 1. all skin and bone. 2. gone to tatters, rotten.

Hıristiyan Gk Christian. —**î** (...——) P Christian, pertaining to Christianity.

Hıristiyanlıkᵍⁱ Christianity, Christendom.

Hıristos (...') Gk Christ.

hırka A 1. woolen jacket; wadded and quilted jacket. 2. dervish's cloak. —**yı başına çek=** to withdraw from the world, to live in seclusion. — **giy=** *dervish orders* to be invested with a cloak. —**i hezarpare** *lrnd.* patched cloak of a dervish. —**i murakkaa** *same as* **hırkai hezarpare**. H—**i Saadet** *same as* **Hırkai Şerif**. —**i sofiye** *lrnd.* dervish's cloak. H—**i Şerif** mantle of the Prophet, kept as a relic. —**i tarikat** *myst. orders* dervish cloak.

hırkaberendaş (....—) P *lrnd.* lost in ecstasy.

hırkapuş (..—) P *lrnd.* wearing a dervish's cloak; dervish.

hırla=ᵣ to snarl, to growl (dog). —**n=** to grumble, to snarl aggressively. —**ş=** *slang* to snarl or growl at each other, to quarrel with each other; to squabble noisily.

hırlı *colloq.* good, auspicious, lucky. — **ayakkabı değil** He is not a good man. — **mı hırsız mı bilmiyorum** I don't know whether he is honest or evil.

hırman (.—) A *lrnd.* frustration, disappointment; hopelessness.

hırpadak *prov.* 1. suddenly, all of a sudden (to stop). 2. exactly (to fit).

hırpala=ᵣ /ı/ to ill-treat; to misuse. —**n=** *pass.* —**t=** /ı, a/ *caus. of* **hırpala=**.

hırpani (.——) *colloq.* in tatters.

hırs 1 A 1. greed; blind ambition; furious exertion; passion. 2. hate, anger, rage. —**ını alama=** to be unable to vent one's anger. —**ından boğul=** to be helplessly mad with anger. —**i câh** *lrnd.* inordinate ambition. —**ından çatla=** to be ready to burst with anger. —**ını çıkar=** /dan/ to vent one's spleen (on). —**i şan** inordinate ambition for fame.

hırs 2 P *lrnd.* 1. bear. 2. rough fellow, clown, boor. —**ban** (.—) P bear-keeper. —**baz** (.—) P bear-dancer.

hırsız thief, burglar; robber; dishonest; trickster; embezzler. — **anahtarı** skeleton key. — **çekmecesi** secret drawer in a desk. — **çetesi** gang of thieves. — **feneri** dark-lantern. — **gibi** stealthily. — **malı** stolen goods. — **yatağı** 1. thieves' den. 2. receiver of stolen goods. —**a yol göster=** to help a wrongdoer inadvertently; to be very incautious.

hırsızlama 1. like a thief, stealing. 2. stealthily, surreptitiously.

hırsızlıkᵍⁱ theft, burglary; robbery, embezzlement; *law* larceny. — **et=** to steal, to rob, to embezzle, to swindle.

hırslan=ᵢᵣ 1. to become furious with envy, hate or rage; to get angry. 2. to become inordinately greedy. —**dır=** /ı/ *caus.*

hırslı 1. angry; furious. 2. greedy; ambitious; avaricious.

hırt *slang* coarse and vulgar yet conceited; fool, stupid.

hırtapoz *slang* fool, stupid.

hırtavi *Ott. hist.* kind of felt helmet worn by the Sipahi cavalry.

hırtıpırtı مرق برق trifles, rubbish; old clothes.
hırtlakˢˡ مرطلاق prov., same as **gırtlak**.
hırtlamba مرطلامبه colloq. 1. poorly and untidily clothed. 2. continually coughing and spitting; sickly person. **—sı çık=** 1. to be weak and sickly. 2. to be in rags and tatters. **— gibi giyin=** to be untidily dressed with an excess of clothing.
hırvaᵃˡ مروع A lrnd. castor-oil plant, bot., Ricinus.
Hırvat مروات 1. Croat, Croatian. 2. great big man. **—ca** Croatian, the Croat language. **—istan** (...—) Croatia.
hırz مرز A lrnd. 1. stronghold, fortification, castle; asylum. 2. amulet, talisman. 3. law place of safe-keeping, chest, cupboard. **—i can** thing kept and preserved like one's very life. **—i Yemani** prayer said to have been taught to Ali by the Prophet Muhammad.
hısa (.—) حصاء A lrnd. a castrating, orchiectomy.
hısam (.—) حصام A lrnd. contention, quarrel.
hısan (.—) حصان A lrnd. highbred (horse); stallion kept for serving mares, stallion.
hısas حصص A lrnd., pl. of **hisse**.
hısb حصب A lrnd. rich vegetation; abundance of life; fruitfulness, plenty; cheapness of living.
hısım حصم relative, kin. **— akraba** kith and kin. **—lık** relationship, kinship.
hısn حصن A lrnd. castle, fortification, stronghold, fortress.
hış هيش Hey! Hi! Look here.
hışf خشف A lrnd. female of the red deer, hind, doe.
hışhış خش خش a repeated rustling sound of friction or tearing. **— et=** to rustle.
hışılda=ʳ خشلدا to make a repeated rustling or wheezing noise. **—t=** /ı/ caus.
hışılhışıl خشل خشل with a rustling or wheezing noise. **— et=** to make a rustling or wheezing noise.
hışıltı خشلتى خشلدى repeated wheezing or rustling noise.
hışımˢᵐˡ خشم [hışm] anger, indignation, rage, fury. **—a gel=** to get into a rage. **—ına uğra=** /ın/ to be the object of somebody's rage.
hışımlan=ˡʳ خشملنور to become angry or furious. **—dır=** /ı/ to enrage.
hışımlı خشملى furious; haughty; arrogant.
hışır 1 خشر [kışr] 1. unripe (melon). 2. rind of a melon. 3. slang stupid, idiot, imbecile, simpleton; rude and awkward.
hışır 2 خشر prov. 1. necklace. 2. straw cushion.
hışırda=ʳ خشرداس to make a continuous rustling noise (dry leaves, paper, silk). **—t=** /ı/ caus.

hışırhışır خشر خشر harsh grating noise.
hışırtı خشرتى a rustling, grating.
hışla=ʳ خشلامز same as **hışılda=**. **—t=** /ı/ caus.
hışm خشم P lrnd., same as **hışım**. **—alûd** (.—‐) P, **—gîn** (.—) P, **—nâk** (.—) P passionate, furious, enraged.
Hıta 1 (.—) خطا same as **Hata 2**.
hıta 2 خطا [Arabic gıtha] prov. snake cucumber, bot., Cucumis sativus flexuosus.
hıtam (.—) خطام A lrnd. halter, bridle.
hıtbe خطبه A can. law a request that a girl be given in marriage (for a son).
hıtta خطه A lrnd. country; region; district; plot of land.
hıyanet (.—.) خيانت A 1. treachery; ingratitude; perfidy; law treason. 2. colloq. perfidious, treacherous, basely ungrateful. **—i vataniye** law high treason, felonious treason.
hıyanetkâr (.—.—) خيانتكار P treacherous, perfidious. **—ane** (.—.——.) P treacherously, perfidiously.
hıyanetlikˢˡ خيانتلك colloq. treachery, malicious act.
hıyar 1 خيار A 1. cucumber, bot., Cucumis sativus. 2. slang dolt, blockhead; uncouth and stupid.
hıyar 2 (.—) خيار A law option.
hıyar 3 (.—) خيار A lrnd., pl. of **hayr**.
hıyarat (.—.—) خيارات A lrnd., pl. of **hıyar 2**.
hıyarcıkˢˡ خيارجيق path. glandular tumor, bubo, adenoma. **— burunlu** colloq. having a huge nose.
hıyarşembe, hıyarşember خيارشنبه خيارشنبر [Arabic, Persian hiyarsanbar] cassia, bot., Cassia Fistula.
hıyat (.—) خياط A lrnd. 1. thread, silk thread. 2. needle.
hıyatet (.—.) خياطت A 1. surg. seam, suture, catgut. 2. lrnd. tailoring. **—hane** (.—.—.) P lrnd. tailor's shop.
hıyaz (.—) خياض A lrnd., pl. of **havz**.
hıyem خيم A lrnd., pl. of **hayme**.
hıyere خيره A lrnd. 1. choice, preference. 2. chosen, elite. **—i nâs** the elite.
hız خيز speed, velocity; rush, impetus, dash, elan. **— al=** to get up speed; to be accelerated. **—ını al=** to slow down, to restrain the impetus. **—ını alama=** to be unable to slow down. **— ver=** /a/ to increase the speed (of); to accelerate. **—ını yeneme=** same as **hızını alama=**.
hızane (.—.) خزانه A lrnd. 1. treasury; storehouse; cupboard. 2. reservoir. 3. heart, soul. **—dar** (.—.—) P treasurer. **—gâh** (.—.—) P treasure-house, storehouse.
hızanet 1 (.—.) خزانت A lrnd. office of treasurer, keeper or custodian.
hızanet 2 (.—.) خضانت A lrnd. a nursing,

hızar

carrying about in arms. — **hakkı** *law* a divorced wife's right to keep her child.

hızar فزار *same as* **hizar.**

Hızır خضر [hızr] *Isl. rel.* legendary person who attained immortality by drinking from the water of Life. — **gibi yetiş=** to come as a godsend; to come to the rescue at the right moment. — **İlyas** *prov.*, *same as* **Hıdrellez.**

hızlan= خیزلانمق to gain speed or momentum, to be accelerated. —**dır=** /ı/ *caus.*

hızlı خیزلو 1. swift, rapid, speedy, quick. 2. strong (blow). 3. loud.

Hızr خضر A *same as* **Hızır.** —**ı râh** *lrnd.* road-guide who suddenly turns up when one is puzzled.

hızy خزی A *lrnd.* a being despicable.

hibᵇᵇⁱ حبّ A *lrnd.* 1. love, affection. 2. beloved one; lover.

hibalⁱⁱ (.—) حبال A *lrnd.*, *pl. of* **habl.**

hibale (.—.) حباله A *lrnd.* noose, snare, net. —**i izdivaç** bond of marriage. —**i telbisat** concealed conspiracy.

hibat (.—) حبات A *lrnd.*, *pl. of* **hibe.**

hibban (.—) حبّان A *lrnd.*, *pl. of* **hib.**

hibe حبه A *law* gift, present, donation.

hibr 1 حبر A *lrnd.* ink.

hibr 2 حبر A *lrnd.* learned man, teacher.

hibre, hibret خبره، خبرت A *lrnd.* 1. knowledge, information, expertness. 2. experience; experiment.

hica (.—) هجا A *lrnd.* 1. *same as* **hece.** 2. a satirizing, ridiculing, satire.

hicab (.—) حجاب A 1. *same as* **hicap.** 2. *anat.* septum. 3. *lrnd.* a veiling, covering, concealing or protecting; screen, curtain; barrier, obstacle; *myst.* anything standing as a barrier between man and God. — **duy=** to feel ashamed, to be embarrassed. — **et=** to feel ashamed. —**ı hâciz** *anat.* diaphragm. —**ı kühlî** *poet.* darkness; black cloud; cloud of dust; sky. —**ı meşimî** *anat.* chorion. —**ı müstabtın** *anat.* pleura. —**ı zulmanî** *poet.* the somber veil of night.

hicabet (.—.) حجابت A *hist.* office of a doorkeeper, usher, or chamberlain.

hicac (.—) حجاج A *anat.* orbit.

hicagû (.——) هجاگو P *lrnd.* satirist.

hicalⁱⁱ (.—) حجال A *lrnd.*, *pl. of* **hacle.**

hicamet (.—.) حجامت A *lrnd.*, *same as* **hacamat.**

hicapᵇⁱ (.—) حجاب [hicab] shame; bashfulness; modesty. —**lı** 1. modest, bashful. 2. screened, veiled. —**sız** 1. shameless, brazenfaced. 2. unveiled.

Hicaz (.—) حجاز A 1. *geog.* the Hejaz. 2. *l. c.* P *Or. mus.* one of the most-used makams. — **aşiran** *Or. mus.* another name for the makam "rahatfeza." — **büzürk** *Or. mus.* makam used about six centuries ago. — **hümayun** *Or. mus.* one of the hicaz varieties of makam. —**ı ırak** *Or. mus.* a makam. — **puselik** *Or. mus.* a compound makam. — **zemzeme** *Or. mus.* a makam. — **zirgüle** *Or. mus.* one of the makams of the hicaz.

hicazeyn (.—.) حجازین *Or. mus.* a compound makam used by Sultan Selim III.

Hicazkâr (.——) حجازکار P *Or. mus.* one of the şed makams. —**ı kürdî** *same as* **kürdili hicazkâr.**

hicce حجّ A *lrnd.* pilgrimage to Mecca.

hiccetülvedaᵃⁱ حجّة الوداع A *Isl. rel.* the last pilgrimage of the Prophet to Mecca.

Hicivᵉᵛⁱ هجو *var. of* **hicv.** —**ci** satirist.

hicr هجر [hecr] *lrnd.* 1. separation. 2. a forsaking, abandoning. 3. abstention. 4. delirium, a raving.

hicran 1 (.—) هجران A 1. separation. 2. bitterness of heart, mental pain. — **ol=** /a/ to cause a pang of separation, to cause deep pain (to).

hicran 2 هجران [hicran 1] *prov.* pus, suppuration.

hicret هجرت A 1. emigration. 2. *Isl. hist.* the emigration of the Prophet Muhammad from Mecca to Medina, the Hegira.

hicretân (..—) هجرتان A *Isl. hist.* the two emigrations of Muslims from Mecca to Abyssinia, and then to Medina.

hicrî (.—) هجری A pertaining to the Hegira, of the Hegira. — **sene** the date in the Muslim Calendar.

hicv هجو [hecv] a satirizing, lampooning; satire. — **et=** /ı/ to satirize. —**i melih** *lrnd.* irony. —**î** (.—) A satirical.

hicviyât (.——) هجویات A *literature* satirical poem, satires.

hicviye (.—.) هجویّه *literature* satirical poem.

hiç 1 هیچ [hiç 2] 1. nothing, a mere trifle. 2. *in negative sentence* no, none whatever, none at all; never, never at all, not the least. 3. *in interrogative sentence* ever. 4. *math.* null, zero. —**ten** 1. out of nothing. 2. a nobody, worthless; sprung from nothing, parvenu. — **biri** not one of them, none. — **bir kimse** nobody, no one. —**ten bir sebep** a trifling reason, a mere pretext. — **bir surette** by no means, in no way; never. — **bir şey** nothing, nothing at all. — **bir vakit** never; not at all. — **bir veçhile** in no way, by no means, never. — **bir yerde** nowhere. — **bir zaman** never; not at all. — **değil** no, not at all, not so. — **değilse** at least. —**e git=** to be wasted. —**lere karış=** to disappear, to vanish. — **mi hiç** absolutely nothing. —**ten ne çıkar?** What can you get out of nothing? — **ol=** 1. to become nothing. 2. to perish, to vanish. **— olmazsa** at least. **— olur mu?** Is it possible? It won't do. **— te öyle değil!** It's not as you think. Not a bit so. **— sallama=** /ı/ not to care at all (for); to pay no attention (to). **—e say=** /ı/ to hold as of no account; to disregard. **— yoksa** at least. **— yoktan** for no reason; out of nothing; suddenly, unexpectedly. **— yoktan iyi** better than nothing. **— yoktan torlak yeydir** An unbroken colt is better than nothing. **— yüzünden** for no reason at all.

hiç 2 (—) چیچ P *lrnd.* nothing, a mere trifle. **—a hiç** (— — — —) P absolutely nothing. **—î** (— —) P nothingness, nullity; utter insignificance. **—istan** (—.—) P land of nothingness. **—kâre** (— —.) P 1. idle, indolent. 2. incapable, fit for nothing. **—kes** (—.) P nobody; low, vile.

hiçlikᵍⁱ چیچلك nothingness, nullity; utter insignificance.

hiçmedan (—.—) چیچمدان P *lrnd.* perfectly ignorant.

hidayet (.—.) هدایت A *rel.* 1. the right way, the way to Islam; spiritual guidance. 2. a searching for the right way. 3. *w. cap.*, personal name. **— bul=** to be guided into the true faith. **—e gel=** to embrace the faith of Islam.

hiddet حدّت A 1. anger, rage, fury; violence; sharpness of temper, irascibility. 2. *lrnd.* vigor, energy, strength of intellect; sharpness; acuteness, keenness. **—i basar** *psych.* sharpness of sight. **— et=** to get angry. **—e gel=** to get into a passion, to flare up, to be furious. **—i havas** *psych.* keenness of senses.

hiddetlen=ⁱʳ حدّتلنمك to fly into a passion, to become furious; /a/ to be angry (with). **—dir=** /ı/ *caus.*

hiddetli حدّتلی passionate, irritable, irascible; angry, violent.

hidem هدم A *lrnd., pl. of* **hidmet.**

hidemat (..—) هدمات A *lrnd., pl. of* **hidmet.** **—ı âmme** *law* public offices. **—ı şakka** *law* forced labor, penal servitude.

hidiv (.—) هدیو P *same as* **hıdiv.**

hidmet هدمت A *lrnd., same as* **hizmet.**

hidrasitᵈⁱ هیدراسید F *chem.* hydracid.

hidrat هیدرات F *chem.* hydrate.

hidrofil هیدروفیل F *chem.* absorbent.

hidrografi هیدروغرافی F hydrography.

hidrojen هیدروژن F *chem.* hydrogen. **— bombası** hydrogen bomb.

hidrokarbon هیدروکاربون F *chem.* hydrocarbon.

hidroksil هیدروکسیل F *chem.* hydroxyl.

hidroksitᵈⁱ هیدروکسید F *chem.* hydroxide.

hidrolikᵍⁱ هیدرولیك F *mech.* hydraulic. **— baskı** hydraulic press. **— fren** hydraulic brake.

hidroliz هیدرولیز F *chem.* hydrolysis.

hidroloji هیدرولوژی F *geol.* hydrology.

hidromekanikᵍⁱ هیدرومکانیك G *phys.* hydromechanics; hydromechanical.

hidrometre (...'.) هیدرومتر F *phys.* hydrometer.

hidrosfer هیدروسفر F *geog.* hydrosphere.

hidroskopi هیدروسکوپی F *geol.* a water-divining, search for subterranean water.

hidrostatikᵍⁱ هیدروستاتیك F *phys.* hydrostatics; hydrostatic.

hidroterapi هیدروتراپی F *med.* hydrotherapy.

hidrozolᵘⁱ هیدروزول F *chem.* hydrosol.

hiffet خفّت A 1. levity, frivolity. 2. *lrnd.* lightness (of weight). **—i mizac** *lrnd.* levity; inconsiderateness. **—i yed** *lrnd.* lightness of hand; dexterity.

higrometre (...'.) هیگرومتر F *phys.* hygrometer.

higroskop هیگروسکوپ F *phys.* hygroscope.

hîkᵏⁱ (—) خیك P *lrnd.* waterskin, leather bottle.

hikâyat (.——) حکایات A *lrnd., pl. of* **hikâye, hikâyet.**

hikâye (.—.) حکایه A 1. story, tale, yarn; *literature* short story. 2. *gram.* compound imperfect (**=ıyordu**). **— et=** /ı/ to tell, narrate, relate. **—i hal, —i hal filmazi** *gram.* past continuous, imperfect tense. **—i istikbal** *gram.* future continuous.

hikâyeci (.—..) حکایه‌جی short story writer; narrator, storyteller. **—lik** the art of storytelling; short story writing.

hikâyenüvis (.—..—) حکایه‌نویس P *lrnd.* novelist, story writer.

hikâyeperdaz (.—..—) حکایه‌پرداز P *lrnd.* story teller, narrator.

hikâyet (.—.) حکایت A archaic, same as **hikâye.**

hikem حکم A *lrnd., pl. of* **hikmet.**

hikemî (..—) حکمی A *lrnd.* 1. rational, reasonable; philosophical. 2. physical. **—yat** (..——) A philosophical words or sayings, wise sayings.

hikke حکّه A *lrnd.* 1. an itching; scab or any similar itching disease. 2. doubt, suspicion.

hikmet حکمت A 1. wisdom; philosophy; wise saying; Divine Wisdom. 2. inner meaning, intrinsic object; cause, reason, motive. 3. *lrnd.* physics; science. **—!** Strange! Wonderful! **—i ameliye** *lrnd.* practical philosophy; science of human action. **—i hulkiye** *lrnd.* moral philosophy, ethics. **—i Hüda** 1. divine wisdom, 2. Heaven knows why; strangely enough; for some mysterious reason. **—i hükûmet** governmental wisdom; high political reason. **—i İlâhiye** 1. divine reason for the existence of all creation; *phil.* providence. 2. metaphysics. **—i Lokman'dan haber al=** to get knowledge from the most reliable sources. **—i mechule** *myst.* mysterious dispensations of God's

hikmetamiz

providence. **—i nazariye** *lrnd.* the theoretical sciences (metaphysics, mathematics and physics). **—i nedir?** What is the motive or intention? **—i riyaziye** *lrnd.* mathematics. **—i siyasiye** *lrnd.* political economy, political philosophy. **—inden sual olunmaz** Heaven only knows why; it is a mystery. **—i tabiiye** *lrnd.* physical science, physics. **—i vücud** 1. the real reason. 2. reason or justification for existence.

hikmetamiz (..——) حكمت آميز P *lrnd.* mingled with wise sayings.

hikmetamuz (..——) حكمت آموز P *lrnd.* teaching wisdom, wise.

hikmetfüruş (...—) حكمت فروش P *lrnd.* scattering wisdom, showing wisdom; one who thinks that he can utter wise words.

hikmetli حكمتلى wise, full of wisdom.

hikmetperest حكمت پرست P *lrnd.* who obeys philosophy, philosopher.

hikmetşinas (...—) حكمت شناس P *lrnd.* 1. sage. 2. physicist; worker in the natural sciences.

hilâf 1 (.—) خلاف A 1. contrary, opposite; contradiction, contravention, difference, opposition. 2. lie; untrue, false. **—ına** /ın/ contrary to, against, in opposition to, in contravention to. **—ınca** *obs.,* same as **hilâfına**. **—ı âde**, **—ı âdet** *lrnd.* contrary to ordinary practice, unusual. **—ı hakikat** contrary to the truth, untrue. **— olmasın** *colloq.* If I'm not mistaken. **— söyle=** to tell a lie, to speak falsely. **—ı tabiat** contrary to nature, unnatural. **—ım varsa** If I lie...

hilâf 2 (.—) خلاف A *lrnd.* willow. **—ı Belhî** weeping willow.

hilâfen (.—'.) خلافاً A *lrnd.* /a/ contrarily, in contradiction to.

hilâfet (.—.) خلافت A 1. Caliphate. 2. *myst. orders* office of the officially ordained assistant to a sheikh. 3. *lrnd.* substitution, succession.

hilâfetname (.—.—.) خلافتنامه P *myst. orders* certificate given by a sheikh to a senior dervish authorizing him to instruct others.

Hilâfetpenah (.—..—) خلافت پناه P *Ott. hist.* "shelter of the Caliphate" (title of the Ottoman Sultan); Caliph. **—î** (.—..——) P, **—lık** pertaining to the Caliph.

hilâfgîr (.——) خلافگير P *lrnd.* opposing, contrary, contradictory; adversary, **—î** (.———) P, **—lik** opposition; contradictoriness; adversity.

hilâfi (.——) خلافى [based on **Arabic**] *lrnd.* 1. controversial. 2. controversialist, polemist. **—yat** (.———) A 1. controversial rules, matters or questions. 2. polemics.

hilâlⁱⁱ **1** ?.—) هلال A 1. new moon, crescent. 2. lunule (on the fingernail). 3. *poet.* arched eyebrow. **H—i Ahmer** *obs.* the Red Crescent (Turkish society corresponding to the Red Cross; its name is now **Kızılay**). **H—i Ahmere lâf konuş=** *slang* to speak nonsense to irritate somebody. **H—i Ahzar** *obs.* the Green Crescent (anti-alcoholic Society, now called **Yeşilay**).

hilâlⁱⁱ **2** (.—) هلال A 1. toothpick (of bone or ivory); earpick. 2. pointer (formerly used in reading lessons). 3. *lrnd.* interval, gap, crevice; interval of time. **—inde** *lrnd.* during, at the time of, in *e. g.*, **Ramazan hilâlinde** or **hilâli Ramazanda** during Ramadan. **— otu** caltrop, *bot., Tribulus terrestris.*

hilâldan (.——) هلالدان P *lrnd.* toothpick case.

hilâle (.—.) هلاله A *lrnd.* halo, nimbus.

hilâlebru (.—.—) هلال ابرو P *lrnd.* with eyebrows arched like the new moon.

hilâli 1 (.——) هلالى A 1. pertaining to a crescent; crescent shaped, lunate. 2. same as **helâli 2.**

hilâli 2 (.——) هلالى A *anat.* interstitial.

hilâliye (.—..) هلاليه [based on Arabic] celandine, *bot., Chelidonium majus.*

hilâlvari (.———) هلالوارى P crescent-shaped, crescentlike. هلال وارى

hil'atⁱⁱ خلعت A 1. *hist.* robe of honor, Killut, Khelaut. 2. *Ott. calligraphy* arch-shaped mark made by the teacher over or around a well-formed letter of a pupil. **—i fâhire** very precious robe of honor, royal robe. **— giydir=** /a/ to reward with a robe of honor.

hil'atduz (..—) خلعت دوز P *lrnd.* tailor who makes robes of honor.

hilb حلب A *lrnd.* finger or toe nail; claw; talon.

hile (—.) حيله A trick, cheating, wile, stratagem, fraud. **— et=** same as **hile yap=**. **— hurda bilmez** There is no guile in him. **—i şer'iye** canonical device for compassing an apparently illegal purpose; a way of getting around the law. **— yap=** to swindle, cheat. **—baz** (..—) P, **—ci** same as **hilekâr**.

hilekâr (—.—) حيله كار P trickster; cheat, deceiver; tricky.

hileli حيله لى 1. tricky; dishonest; false. 2. adulterated, impure; spurious. *law* fraudulent. **— iflâs** *law* fraudulent bankruptcy.

hileperdaz (—..—) حيله پرداز, **hilesaz** (—.—) حيله ساز P *lrnd.* trickster, cheat.

hilesiz حيله سز 1. honest, true. 2. genuine, pure, unadulterated.

hilf 1 حلف A *lrnd.* a swearing, attestation.

hilf 2 حلف A *lrnd.* 1. confederacy, league, compact. 2. confederate, ally.

hilim حلم *var.* of **hilm**.

hilkatⁱⁱ خلقت A 1. creation. 2. natural disposition; natural constitution, nature.

hilkaten (..'.) خِلْقَةً A *lrnd.* by nature, innate.
hilkatî (..—) خِلْقَتِي A *lrnd.* 1. natural, inborn, congenital. 2. pertaining to creation. **—yat** (..— —) *lrnd.* characteristics of creation; natural qualities. **—yet** (..—.) *lrnd.* innateness, congenitalness.
hilm حِلْم A *lrnd.* mildness, gentleness; patience, forebearance; quietness; sedateness. **—i** (.—) A mild, gentle. **—iyet** (.—.) A mildness, placidity, sedateness.
hilozoizm هيلوزويزم F *phil.* hylozoism.
hilye حِلْيَة A *lrnd.* 1. external personal appearance, form and features, description of the personal virtues and the qualities of the Prophet. 2. jewel, ornament.
him هيم Arm *prov.* foundation, base.
himar (.—) حِمار A *lrnd.* 1. ass, donkey. 2. fool. **—i** (.— —) A pertaining to an ass; asinine. **—iyet** (.— —.) 1. quality of a donkey. 2. asininity; foolishness.
himaye (.—.) حِماية A 1. protection, defense; support. 2. protection, patronage. 3. *law* protectorate. **—sinde** /ın/ under the protection of, under the patronage of. **—sine al=** /ı/ to take under one's protection, to patronize. **— et=** /ı/ 1. to protect, to defend; to give political protection (to). 2. to patronize, favor. **— usulü**, **—cilik** *econ.* protectionism.
himayekâr (.—.—) حِمايه كار P *lrnd.* 1. protective. 2. patronizing, favoring, partial.
himayeli حِمايه لی under protection; escorted (convoy). **— kafile** escorted convoy.
himayesiz حِمايه سِز unprotected; undefended; left alone, helpless; unescorted (convoy).
himayet (.—.) حِمايت A *lrnd.*, same as **himaye**. **—ger** (.—..) P defender, protector.
hime (—.) هيمه P *lrnd.* firewood, fuel.
himem هِمَم A *lrnd.*, *pl. of* **himmet**. **—at** (..—) A same as **himem**.
himen هيمن F *anat.* hymen.
himl حِمْل A *lrnd.* load, burden.
himmet هِمّت A 1. endeavor, zeal, effort. 2. influence, auspices, grace, favor; moral support; help. 3. *myst.* miraculous influence or support exerted by a saint. **—inizle** thanks to you, by your help or influence. **— et=** to take the trouble, to exert oneself; to help. **—i hazır olsun** May his blessing help us (speaking of a saintly person).
himye حِمْيه A *med.* diet, abstinence.
Himyeri (..—) حِمْيَری A *hist.* Himyarite, Himyaritic.
himyevî (..—) حِمْيَوی A *lrnd.* dietetic.
hin 1 هين [heyn] only in **hinoğlu, hinoğlu hin** *colloq.* son of the devil, scoundrel; very crafty fellow.

hîn 2 (—) حين A *lrnd.* time, space of time, moment; special or appointed time. **—i hacette** when needed, in case of necessity. **—i vürutta** at the time of arrival.
hinas (.—) حِناث A *lrnd.*, *pl. of* **hünsa**.
Hind هند A same as **Hint**. **—i Çini*. —i Garbî** *geog.* West Indies.
hindi 1 هندی [**Hindî 2**] turkey, *zool.*, *Meleagris gallopavo*. **— gibi kabar=** to get puffed up like a turkey.
Hindî 2 (.—) هندی A 1. *lrnd.* pertaining to India, Indian. 2. *l. c.*, India paper.
hindiba (..—) هِندبا A wild chicory, succory, *bot.*, *Cichorium intybus*.
Hindiçini (..— —) هندیچینی Indochina.
Hindistan (..—) هندستان [**Hindustan**] India. **— cevizi** 1. coconut; coconut palm, *bot.*, *Cocos nucifera*. 2. nutmeg, nutmeg tree, *bot.*, *Mystica fragrans*. **— hıyarı** fruit of Indian bel, Bengal quince, *bot.*, *Aegle Marmelos*. **—î** (..— —) A 1. the Hindustani language. 2. *lrnd.* pertaining to India.
Hindu (.—) هندو P 1. Hindu; *lrnd.* East Indian; very dark-colored, black man. 2. *poet.* mole on a woman's cheek.
Hindustan (.— —) هندوستان P *lrnd.* India.
hing هنگ P *lrnd.* white or gray horse. **—i şebâheng** 1. *poet.* the moon; break of day. 2. the steed Buraq that carried Muhammad on his visit to paradise.
hins حِنث A *lrnd.* sin, crime; a swearing falsely, perjury.
Hint^dı هند [**Hind**] India. **— âbadisi** India paper. **— Adaları** the East Indies, Malay Archipelago. **— ayvası** Indian bel, *bot.*, *Aegle Marmelos*. **— baklası** tonka bean, *bot.*, *Dipteryx odarata*. **— bamyası** ambary hemp, *bot.*, *Hibiscus cannabinus*. **— domuzu** *obs.* guinea pig, cavy, *zool.*, *Cavia cobaya*. **— fakiri** fakir. **— fasulyesi** 1. same as **Hint baklası**. 2. Indian basil, ocyme, *bot.*, *Ocimum*. **— helvası** catechu, *bot.*, *Acacia catechu*. **— Irmağı** *obs.* the River Indus. **— inciri** banyan tree, Bengal fig, *bot.*, *Ficus bengalensis*. **— kâğıdı** 1. India paper. 2. catechu. **— keneviri** Indian hemp, *bot.*, *Cannabis sativa*. **— kitabisi** Indian striped muslin. **— kumaşı** 1. Indian silk. 2. very rare and precious thing. **— Okyanusu** Indian Ocean. **— sevayisi** kind of oriental silk cloth. **— tavuğu** *obs.* turkey hen. **— tesbih ağacı** margosa tree, *bot.*, *Melia azadirachta*. **— yağı** castor oil.
hinterland هنترلاند G hinterland.
Hintli هندلی an Indian.
hinto هنتو Hung *obs.* coach, carriage. **—cu** coachman.
hiperbol^lü هيپربول F *geom.* hyperbola.

hipermetrop حیپرمتروپ F *path.* far-sighted, hypermetropic.
hipermetropi حیپرمتروپی F *path.* hypermetropia.
hipertansiyon حیپرتانسیون F *path.* hypertension.
hipnotizm حیپنوتیزم F hypnotism.
hipnoz حیپنوز F hypnosis.
hipodrom حیپودروم F hippodrome, race track.
hipokondri حیپوکندری F psychiatry hypochondria.
hipokondriak[1] حیپوکندریاك F psychiatry hypochondriac.
hipoplazi حیپوپلازی F *path.* hypoplasia.
hipostaz حیپوستاز F *phil.* hypostasis.
hipotansiyon حیپوتانسیون F *path.* hypotension.
hipotenüs حیپوتنوس F *geom.* hypotenuse.
hipotez حیپوتز F hypothesis.
hipotoni حیپوتونی F *Physiol.* hypotonicity.
hipsometri حیپسومتری F *geodesy* hypsometry.
hipsometrik[1] حیپسومتریك F *geodesy* hypsometric. — **münhaniler** contour lines.
hiram (.—) خرام P *lrnd.* strut; proud or elegant gait.
hiraman (.——) خرامان P *lrnd.* walking elegantly.
hiramende (.—..) خرامنده P *lrnd.* who goes along gracefully; elegant walker.
hiras (.—) هراس P *lrnd.* fear, fright, terror. **—an** (.——) P frightened, fearing; timid.
hiraset 1 (.—.) حراثت A *lrnd.* a plowing; agriculture.
hiraset 2 (.—.) حراست A *lrnd.* a keeping, guarding, defending; protection, defense.
-hiraş (.—) خراش P *lrnd.* piercing, scratching; tearing, *e. g.*, **dilhiraş, hatırhiraş**.
hirave (.—.) هراوه A *lrnd.* walking-stick, staff.
Hirażgrad هرازغراد *geog.* Razgrad in Bulgaria.
hirba (.—) حرباء A *lrnd.* chameleon.
hirbed (—.) هربد *var. of* **hirbüd**.
hirbüd (—.) هیربد P *lrnd.* Zoroastrian priest.
hire (—.) خیره P *lrnd.* 1. dazzled; perplexed, bewildered, amazed. 2. vain, purposeless; useless. 3. bold, careless, daring. 4. impudent, shameless. **—çeşm** (—..) P 1. weak-eyed. 2. saucy-looking; impudent. **—dest** (—..) P unskillful, clumsy. **—gî** (—.—) P 1. perplexity, bewilderment, amazement. 2. vanity, uselessness, absurdity. 3. obscurity, dimness. **—küş** (—..) P 1. tyrannical, oppressive. 2. fearless. **—rey** (—..) P of mean intelligence, confused. **—lik** *same as* **hiregi**. **—ser** (—..) P stupid, blundering, silly.
hirfet حرفت A *lrnd.* trade, handicraft, business.
hirmen هرمن P *lrnd., same as* **harman**. **—i mah** 1. halo around the moon. 2. mole on the cheek.

hirmend (—.) هیرمند P *lrnd.* 1. devout, pious. 2. priest of the Magi.
hirmengâh (..—) هرمنکاه P *lrnd.* threshing floor.
hirre حرة A *lrnd.* she-cat.
his[ssi] حس A 1. sense, perception, faculty. 2. feeling, sensation, sentiment. **—i bâtın, —i derûnî** *lrnd.* inner perception, interior sense. **—i hal** *psych.* coenesthesis. **—i hareket** *psych.* kinesthesia. **—i hayalî** *psych.* hallucination. **—i kablelvuku** ' presentiment, premonition. **—lerine kapıl=** to be carried away by one's feelings. **—i müşterek** *Aristotelian phil.* the 'common sense' (in which are received all impressions of the external senses). **—i selim** common sense. **—i zâhir** *psych.* exterior sense.
hisa (.'.) حصا It *naut.* Hoist away. **— et=** /I/ to hoist, to raise by a rope; to hoist away. **— punya** Clew up the mainsail.
hisab (.—) حساب A *lrnd., same as* **hesap**.
hisal[li] (.—) حصال A *lrnd., pl. of* **haslet**.
hisar 1 حصار [**hisar 2**] castle, fort.
hisar 2 (.—) حصار A *lrnd.* 1. *same as* **hisar 1**. 2. P *Or. mus.* an ancient compound **makam**. 3. siege, blockade. **—ı berin** the ninth heaven. **— buselik** a compound **makam** about two or three centuries old. **— eri, — erenleri** *Ott. hist.* guards of a fort. **—ı firuze** the azure vault of heaven, the sky. **— gediği** *Ott. hist.* place of the guards of the fort. **—ı hezarmihî** star-covered sky. **—ı muallak** vault of heaven. **— perdesi** *Or. mus.* a mode mostly based on **d** sharp but partly on **e** flat.
hisarbeçe (.—..) حصاربچه P barbican, outwork.
hisarcı حصارجی *Ott. hist.* 1. peasant bound to work at repairs of a fortress. 2. feudal retainer who holds land on condition of defending a fortress.
hisarî (.——) حصاری P *lrnd.* 1. man living in a fortress. 2. soldier in a garrison.
hisarlı حصارلی 1. castle dweller; *w. cap.*, inhabitant of Anadolu Hisarı or Rumeli Hisarı on the Bosphorus. 2. *Ott. hist., same as* **hisarcı**[2].
hisli حسلی sensitive, sentimental.
hisse حصه A 1. share; allotted portion; part, lot. 2. lesson, warning. **—i ibret** *lrnd.* warning, example, lesson. **—i iştirak** *com.* contribution. **— kap=** /dan/ to learn a lesson (from). **—i menfaat** *fin.* interest. **— senedi** *fin.* share. **—i şayia** *law* co-ownership.
hissedar (..—) حصه دار P 1. *com.* shareholder. 2. *lrnd.* participator, partaker. **—lık** partnership; a being a shareholder; participancy.
hisseli حصه لی having shares; divided into shares; belonging to various people.
hissemend حصه مند P *lrnd.* having a share; having an interest; who profits.

hissen (.'.) حِسّاً A *lrnd.* as far as one's feelings are concerned.
hisset=[der] **1** صَلْ بَتْمَكْ to feel, to perceive; to understand; to notice.
hisset 2 خِسَّتْ A *lrnd.* meanness, stinginess, miserliness, avarice.
hissettir=[ir] صِلْ بَتْدِرِمَكْ *caus. of* **hisset= 1**.
hisseyab (..—) حِصّه ياب P *lrnd.* having a share. **— ol=** /dan/ to have a share (in).
hissî (.—) حِسِّى A 1. sentimental. 2. *physiol.* pertaining to sense, sensible; sensorial; sensory.
hissiyat (..—) حِسِّيَّاتْ A sensations, feelings; sentiment. **—a kapıl=**' to be biased; to be driven by sentiment.
hissiyet (.—.) حِسِّيَّتْ A *lrnd.* sensibility. **—i adaliye** *psych.* muscular sense.
hissiz حِسْسِزْ 1. insensitive, callous, unfeeling. 2. insensible, without sensation. **—lik** insensibility.
histeri هِسْتَرِى F *var. of* **isteri**.
histoloji هِسْتُولُوژِى F histology.
hiş 1 هِيشْ Hey! Look here! **— piş et=** to call out "Hist!"
'hîş 2 (—) خُوِيشْ P *lrnd.* 1. kinsman, relative. 2. self, oneself. **—avend** (——.) P kinsman, relative. **—avendî** (——.—) P, **—î** (——) P kinship, kindred, relationship.
hişt 1 هِشْتْ Hist! Look here!
hişt 2 خِشْتْ P *lrnd.* 1. mud brick; brick, tile. 2. dart, javelin; spear. **—i ham** mud brick, unbaked brick. **—i puhte** brick, burnt brick. **—i zer** *poet.* the sun.
hiştek[ki] خِشْتَكْ P *lrnd.* 1. small brick. 2. gusset in a garment.
hişttabe (.—.) خِشْت تابَه P *lrnd.* brick kiln.
hişttzen خِشْتْ زَنْ P *lrnd.* 1. brick-maker. 2. dart-thrower, lancer.
hitab (.—) خِطَابْ A 1. an addressing (a person). 2. *lrnd.* address, discourse. **— et=** 1. /a/ to address (a person). 2. *lrnd.* to deliver a speech. **—ı izzet** the word of God.
hitabe (.—.) خِطَابَه A speech, address. **—de bulun=** to deliver a speech.
hitaben (.—'.) خِطَابَاً A /a/ addressing, as an address (to).
hitabet (.—.) خِطَابَتْ A 1. command of words, powers of oratory; rhetoric. 2. *lrnd.* office of a preacher.
hitabî (.——) خِطَابِى A *lrnd.* pertaining to elocution; verbal, by speech.
hitam (.—) خِتَامْ A 1. end, close, conclusion; completion. 2. *myst.* the utmost grade attained by a saint, with the power of working miracles. **— bul=**, **—a er=** to come to a conclusion; to be completed. **—pezir** (.—.—) P *lrnd.* completed; finished.
hitan 1 (.—) خِتَانْ A *lrnd.* circumcision. **— cemiyeti** circumcision feast.

hitan 2 (——) خِيطَانْ A *lrnd.*, *pl. of* **hait**.
hitanet (.—.) خِتَانَتْ A *lrnd.* 1. circumcision. 2. profession of a circumciser.
hitap[bı] (.—) خِطَابْ *var. of* **hitab**.
hiyab (.—) خِيَابْ A *lrnd.* 1. a sinning; sin. 2. want, poverty, distress.
hiyaban (.——) خِيَابَانْ P *lrnd.* avenue, boulevard.
hiyabet (.—.) خِيَابَتْ A *lrnd.*, *same as* **hiyab**.
hiyac (.—) هِيَاجْ A *lrnd.* 1. a being excited, a being in a rage, excitement. 2. a rising in the air (dust). 3. a withering (plant). 4. battle.
hiyaket (.—.) حِيَاكَتْ A *lrnd.* art of weaving.
hiyam (.—) خِيَامْ A *lrnd.*, *pl. of* **hayme**.
hiyat 1 (.—) خِيَاطْ A *lrnd.*, *pl. of* **hait**.
hiyat 2 (.—), **hiyatet** (.—.) خِيَاطَتْ حِيَاطْ A *lrnd.* 1. a surrounding, enclosing. 2. protection.
hiyel حِيَلْ A *lrnd.*, *pl. of* **hile**.
hiyelâ (..—) حِيَلَا A *lrnd.* pride, conceit.
hiyerarşi هِيَرَارْشِى F hierarchy.
hiyeroglif هِيَرُوغْلِيفْ F hieroglyph.
hiz 1 (—) هِيزْ P *lrnd.* 1. a springing, leaping, rising. 2. wave (of the sea). 3. ecstasy, delirium of delight or passion.
hiz 2 (—) هِيزْ P *lrnd.* catamite.
hiza (.—) حِذَا A line, level (to which something may be adjusted). **bir —da** in one line, on one level. **—sını al=** /ın/ to take the bearing or level. **—ya gel=** to get into line. **— sına kadar** /ın/ up to level (of).
hizab (——) خِضَابْ P *lrnd.* wave, surge.
hizan (——) خِيزَانْ P *lrnd.* rising, rising up.
hizar حِزَارْ large saw, pit saw. **— tahtası** thick plank. **—cı** pit sawyer.
hizb حِزْبْ A 1. *same as* **hizip**. 2. portion of the Quran.
hizebr هِزَبْرْ A *lrnd.* 1. lion. 2. brave man. **—ane** (..—.) P lion-like (act).
hizem حِيزَمْ P *lrnd.* firewood.
hizip[zbı] حِزْبْ [**hizb**] *pol.* clique, coterie. **—çilik** cliquishness.
hizlân (.—) خِذْلَانْ A *lrnd.* 1. helpless abandonment in an hour of need.
hizmet خِدْمَتْ [**hidmet**] 1. service, utility. 2. duty; work; care; function. 3. employment. 4. *lrnd.* gift offered to a superior. **— akdi** *law* contract of service. **— bölükleri** *mil.* service troops. **—inde bulun=** /ın/ to be in the service (of). **bir —te bulun=** to render a service. **—ten çekil=** to retire from service. **—ten çıkar=** to dismiss from service. **— eri** *mil.* orderly. **— et=** /a/ to serve, to render service. **— gör=** to serve; to render service. **—ini gör=** /ın/ to serve (for); take the place (of).
hizmetçi خِدْمَتْچِى servant. **—lik** position and duties of a servant.

hizmetkâr (..—) خدمتكار P servant. **—lık** same as **hizmetçilik**.

hoca خواجه خوجه [hace] 1. teacher. 2. hodja, Muslim teacher. **— çık=** to become a teacher. **— önünde diz çök=** to receive instruction from a teacher. **—lık** 1. teacher's job; a teaching. 2. hodja's profession.

hod خود P lrnd. 1. self, one's self. 2. own. **— kendim** I myself. **— malı** /ın/ his own property.

hodan خودان common borrage, bot., Borago officinalis.

hodara (.—-) خودآرا P lrnd. proud, arrogant.

hodbehod خودبخود P of one's own accord.

hodbin 1 خودبين [hodbin 2] selfish, egotistical. **—lik** selfishness.

hodbin 2 (.—) خودبين P lrnd. 1. same as **hodbin 1**. 2. lrnd. proud, conceited. **—î** (.——) P abstr. n.

hoddar (.—) خوددار P lrnd. self-possessed, master of one's self.

hodfiken خودفكن P lrnd. who plunges voluntarily into danger.

hodfüruş (..—) خودفروش P lrnd. boasting, vaunting; vainglorious; braggart.

hodgâm (.—) خودگام var. of **hodkâm**.

hodgeşte خودگشته P lrnd. careless of self.

hodî (.—) خودى P lrnd. selfishness, conceit.

hodkâm (..—) خودكام P 1. selfish, egotistical. 2. arrogant; willful, obstinate.

hodkerde خودكرده P lrnd. self-inflicted.

hodküş خودكش P lrnd. who kills himself.

hodnüma (..—) خودنما P lrnd. vainglorious.

hodpend خودپند P lrnd. who follows his own council, rash.

hodperest خودپرست P lrnd. egotistical, selfish.

hodpesend خودپسند P lrnd. self-satisfied, conceited.

hodreng خودرنك P lrnd. of its natural color (not dyed).

hodreste خودرسته P lrnd. self-grown, wild (plant).

hodrev خودرو P lrnd. who follows his own inclination.

hodrey خودراى P lrnd. opinionated, capricious.

hodri خودرى only in **— meydan** colloq. Come and try! (a challenge).

hodru, hodruy (.—) خودرو خودروى P lrnd. growing of itself, wild (plant).

hodser خودسر P lrnd. willful, obstinate, capricious.

hodsita, hodsitay (..—) خودستا خودستاى P lrnd. self-lauding, boaster.

hodsüvar (..—) خودسوار P lrnd. who rides a hobby.

hodşinas (..—) خودشناس P lrnd. who knows his own value or weakness; who knows his own place.

hohla=[r] هوهله /a/ to breathe (upon).

hokey هوكى F sports hockey.

hokka حقه A 1. inkstand, inkpot. 2. cup, pot. **—nın altına git=** colloq., same as **okkanın altına git=**. **— ağız** small round mouth. **—i bimağz** brainless, senseless, heartless person. **—i dehen** small, round mouth. **— gibi** small and round (mouth). **— gibi otur=** to fit (clothes). **—i mina** poet. the sky.

hokkabaz (..—) حقه‌باز P 1. juggler, conjurer. 2. clown; cheat, knave. **—lık** jugglery; trickery; clownery.

hokna حقنه A injection; enema.

hol[iü] هول F entrance, hall, vestibule, corridor.

Holânda (.'.) هولاندا Holland, the Netherlands. **— tipi peynir** Edam cheese. **—lı** Dutchman.

homurdan=[ır] هومورداتمق to mutter to oneself; to grumble.

homur homur هومور هومور only in **— söylen=** to grumble, to mutter to oneself.

homurtu هومورتو a muttering, grumbling.

hond خوند P lrnd. lord, owner, ruler, king.

hop هوپ Now then! Up! Jump! Then. **— dedik!** colloq. Look out! Watch out! **— hop sıçra=** to jump and play for joy; to jump up and down, to hop. **— oturup hop kalk=** to keep on jumping up and down with excitement; to be agitated or shaken about.

hoparlör هوپارلور F loudspeaker.

hopla=[r] هوپلامق 1. to hop and jump about. 2. to palpitate; to get excited. **—t=** /ı/ caus.

hoppa (..) هوپپا flippant, flighty; fop, foppish.

hoppala (.'..) هوپپالا 1. Now then, jump! 2. Here we go up. 3. How strange! What an idea! 4. baby's play-chair hung by a spring. **— bebek, — paşa** a young man who still behaves like a child.

hoppalık[ğı] هوپپالق levity, flightiness.

hopurdat=[ır] هوپوردتمق /ı/ same as **höpürdet=**.

hor 1 خور P 1. despicable, contemptible, abject. **— bak=** /a/, **— gör=** /ı/ to look down (upon), to treat as of no account. **— kullan=** /ı/ to misuse, to use for the commonest purposes. **— tut=** /ı/ to hold as of no account, to illtreat, to use roughly.

hor 2 خور P lrnd. the sun; light, splendor, brilliance.

hor 3 خور P lrnd. eating, consuming as in **merdümhor, mirashor**.

hora (.'.) هورا خوره Gk 1. a kind of round dance. 2. noisy party. **— havası** a folk dance tune. **— tep=** 1. to dance hora. 2. to make a terrible noise.

horasan 1 خراسان [Horasan 2] mortar made of brickdust and lime.

Horasan 2 (.——) خراسان P geog. Khorasan. **—î** (.———) P 1. native of Khorasan;

pertaining to Khorasan. 2. *l. c.* holy wormwood, *bot.*, *Artemisia santonica*. 3. *l. c.*, *obs.* government clerk's turban, in which the cap projected above the muslin.

horata خراط Gk *archaic* joke, a jesting; loud noise. **—cı** boisterous fellow.

hord خرد P *lrnd.* food.

horde خرده P *lrnd.* eaten; drunk; affected by, as in **derdhorde, salhorde, şarabhorde**.

hordeni (..—) خردنی P *lrnd.* fit to be eaten, edible; food.

horende خرنده P *lrnd.* eater; family; domestics; household.

horla=ʳ 1 خورلامق to snore.

horla=ʳ 2 خورلامق /ı/ to insult; to ill-treat; to look down upon. **—n**= to be insulted or looked down upon. **—t**= /ı, a/ *caus.* of **horla**=.

horlukᵍᵘ خورلوق 1. meanness, vileness, shame. 2. insult, contempt, disdain.

hormon هرمون F *physiol.* hormone.

horon هورون Gk *prov.* a folk-dance of the eastern Black Sea district.

horoz خروز [**horus**] 1. cock, rooster. 2. hammer of a gun, cock. 3. bridge of a lock. **— akıllı** *colloq.* hare-brained; vain, presumptuous. **— ayağı** corkscrew; cartridge extractor. **—u başına bağla**= to go out very early in the morning. **—u bile yumurtlar** Even his cock lays eggs; he is very fortunate. **—u çok olan köyde sabah geç olur** In a village with too many cocks, morning comes late. **— döğüşü** cockfight. **— fasulyası** a kind of bean. **— gibi** fond of fighting, quarrelsome. **— gözü** oxeye, field camomile, *bot.*, *Buphtalmum*. **— ibiği***. **— işi** badly made. **—dan kaç**= ostentatiously to avoid all contact with men (woman). **— kafalı** harebrained. **— mantarı** chanterelle, *bot.*, *Cantharellus cibarius*. **— oğlu** *colloq.* scamp, rascal. **— oğlu işi** *colloq.* coarse material or craftsmanship; sham work. **— ölür gözü çöplükte kalır** (*lit.* The cock dies but his eyes remain on the dung-heap) Even in very bad circumstances people still hold on to their ambitious desires. **— ötmeden** at daybreak. **—lar öttü** The cocks have crowed; morning has come. **— şekeri** lollipop in the shape of a rooster. **— taşı** small smooth stone found in the cock's stomach (believed to quench thirst). **— yumurtası** pullet's egg, very small egg.

horozbina (...) خروزبینا blenny, *zool.*, *Blenniidae*.

horozibiği خروزایبیگی cockscomb, *bot.*, *Celeria cristata, Rhinanthus Crista-galli*. **—giller** *neol.*, *bot.*, *Amaranthaceae*.

horozlan=ⁱʳ خروزلانمق to strut about; to give oneself airs.

horradakᵍⁱ خرداق slang with speed and noise.

horsun=ᵘʳ خرسونمق /ı/ to look down (upon), to disdain.

hortla=ʳ 1 خورتلامق 1. to rise from the grave and haunt people; to become a ghost. 2. to arise again (troublesome question).

hortla=ʳ 2 خورتلامق *archaic* to snort or grunt.

hortlakᵍⁱ خورتلاق specter, ghost of a dead person.

hortum خرطوم [*Arabic* .—] 1. trunk, proboscis. 2. hose-pipe, garden hose. 3. waterspout; vortex. **— kayası** rock goby, *zool.*, *Gobius paganellus*. **— sık**= /a/ to use a fire hose. **—lular** *zool.* proboscidians.

hortzort خرت زورت same as **het hüt**.

horulda=ʳ خورولدامق to snore, gurgle.

horul horul خرل خرل snoring, with a snoring sound.

horultu خورلتی snore, a snoring.

horyat خوریات Gk *archaic*, same as **hoyrat**.

hoş خوش P 1. pleasant, pleasing, agreeable, nice. 2. good, charming. 3. queer, laughable, quaint, strange. 4. well; even, nevertheless; anyway. **— beş***. **— bulduk** I am pleased to see you, thank you (in response to a welcoming host who greets one saying **hoş geldiniz**). **— dirlik** *archaic* comfortable life, comfort, luxury. **— geç**= *archaic* to have a pleasant time, to enjoy oneself. **— geçin**= /la/ to get on well (with). **— geldiniz** Welcome! I am pleased to see you (said by a host to welcome a guest). **—a git**=, **—una git**= /ın/ to please, to be agreeable (to). **— gör**= /ı/ to tolerate, to overlook. **— görü***. **— imdi** *archaic* very well, then. **— kullan**= /ı/ to use with care. **bir hoş ol**= 1. to feel embarrassed, to be disconcerted, to be put off. 2. to feel faint. **— tut**= /ı/ to treat well (person), to be kind to.

hoşâ (.—) خوشا P *lrnd.* How nice! How lovely! How happy!

hoşab (.—) خوشاب P 1. *lrnd.*, same as **hoşaf**. 2. pearl, jewel. 3. clear, pellucid, brilliant.

hoşaf خوشاف [**hoşab**] cold drink of stewed fruit with an abundance of juice. **—ına git**= /ın/ slang to please. **—ın yağı kesil**= /da/ to be dumbfounded, confused, upset.

hoşaheng (.—.) خوش آهنگ P *lrnd.* melodious, harmonious.

hoşamed (.—.) خوش آمد P *lrnd.* Welcome! a welcoming. **—gû** (.—.—) P 1. welcomer. 2. flatterer. **—î** (.—.—) P a welcoming.

hoşavaz (.——) خوش آواز P *lrnd.* having a sweet voice.

hoşayende (.—..) خوش آینده P *lrnd.* amiable, agreeable to all; elegant.

hoşbeş خوش بش [*Persian* **khush bash**] friendly chat, friendly greeting. **— et**= /la/ to have a

hoşbu

friendly chat (with). **—i olma=** /la/ not to have friendly relations with.

hoşbu, hoşbuy (.—) خوشبوی خوشبو P lrnd. pleasantly scented, perfumed.

hoşça (.ˈ.) خوشچه pretty well, somewhat pleasant. **— kal** goodby.

hoşdem خوشدم P lrnd. congenial companion, friend.

hoşdil خوشدل P lrnd. cheerful, gay; contented.

hoşeda (..—) خوشأدا P lrnd. of charming manners, voice or bearing; charming, graceful.

hoşelhan (..—) خوش الحان P lrnd. chanting with a sweet voice.

hoşendam (..—) خوش اندام P lrnd. having a lovely figure.

hoşengüşt خوش انگشت P lrnd. who has a fine touch in music.

hoşgörü neol. tolerance. **—cü** tolerant.

hoşgû (.—) خوشگو P lrnd. gentle, soft-spoken; melodious; eloquent. **—yî** (.——) P pleasant and eloquent speech.

hoşgüftar (..—) خوش گفتار P lrnd. of pleasant speech; eloquent. **—î** (..——) P eloquence.

hoşgüvar (..—) خوشگوار P lrnd. pleasant to swallow and easy to digest.

hoşgüzeşte خوشگذشته P lrnd. pleasantly lived (past time).

hoşhal[li] (..—) خوشحال P lrnd. in pleasant circumstances, happy, fortunate.

hoşhayalnüma خوشخيالنما P lrnd. kaleidoscope.

hoşhiram (..—) خوشخرام P lrnd. who walks elegantly.

hoşhuy (..—) خوشخوی P lrnd. good-natured.

hoşî (.—) خوشی P lrnd. pleasantness; happiness; comfort.

hoşkadem خوشقدم P lrnd. bringing good luck (person).

hoşkalem خوشقلم P lrnd. 1. a good penman, an elegant writer. 2. good paper for writing on. 3. forger.

hoşkâm (.—) خوشکام P lrnd. whose wishes are satisfied; happy.

hoşlan=[ır] خوشلنمق /dan/ to like, to be pleased (with); to enjoy. **—dır=** /ı, dan/ caus.

hoşlaş=[ır] خوشلاشمق 1. to like one another, to become friendly with one another. 2. to become pleasant and agreeable.

hoşluk[ğu] خوشلوق 1. pleasantness; comfortableness; comfort. 2. health, beauty, happiness. 3. queerness, quaintness. **bir —um var** I am feeling rather queer.

hoşmanzar خوشمنظر P lrnd. of a goodly aspect; pretty to look at.

hoşmeniş خوشمنش P lrnd. having a good heart or excellent spirits.

hoşmerim خوشمریم prov. sweet made with unsalted fresh cheese mixed with flour and sugar or honey.

hoşmeşreb خوش مشرب P lrnd. good-natured; pleasant, agreeable.

hoşmeze خوشمزه P lrnd. having a pleasant taste, delicious, well-flavored.

hoşnemek[ki] خوشنمك P lrnd. 1. nicely salted. 2. witty; charming.

hoşneva (..—) خوشنوا P lrnd. sweet-voiced, melodious.

hoşnihad (..—) خوشنهاد P lrnd. good-natured, of a pleasant disposition.

hoşnişin (..—) خوشنشین P lrnd. 1. comfortably housed. 2. nomadic.

hoşnud (.—) خوشنود P same as **hoşnut**. **—î** (.——) P, **—iyet** (.——.) lrnd. satisfaction, contentment, pleasure.

hoşnut[du] خوشنود [hoşnud] /dan/ satisfied, pleased, contented (with). **—luk** satisfaction, contentment, pleasure.

hoşnutsuz خوشنودسز discontented, displeased. **—luk** dissatisfaction, discontent.

hoşnüma (..—) خوشنما P lrnd. pleasant-looking, charming; elegant, neat.

hoşnüvis (..—) خوشنویس P lrnd. calligraphist.

hoşor خوشور Arm slang plump and pretty (woman).

hoşreftar (..—) خوش رفتار P lrnd. graceful in walking.

hoşruy (..—) خوشروی P lrnd. having a beautiful face.

hoşsohbet خوش صحبت P pleasant, agreeable; good company; conversationalist.

hoşt خوشت noise made to frighten away a dog.

hoştab[b'ı] خوشطبع P lrnd. good-natured, pleasant.

hoşter خوشتر P lrnd. sweeter, more pleasant. **—in** (..—) P most pleasant.

hoşvakt[ti] خوشوقت P lrnd. in happy circumstances, comfortable, happy, pleased.

hotaz خوتاز ∙ خوطاس archaic, same as **hotoz**.

hotkâm (.—) خودکام same as **hodkâm**.

hotoz خوتوز [kotas] 1. kind of headgear for women; hair done in a knot or bun. 2. crest, plume, aigrette. 3. arch. crown.

hovarda خواره 1. spendthrift, prodigal; generous; pleasure-loving; rake, scapegrace. 2. rich lover of a prostitute. **—lık** dissoluteness; rakishness; being free with money.

hoyrat خویرات [horyat] rough; boorish, boor; coarse and clumsy (person). **— şakası** rough skylarking. **—lık** clumsiness, boorishness.

höcre حجره A same as **hücre**.

hödük[ğü] هودوك boor; lout, clumsy, bumpkin. **—lük** boorishness, clumsiness.

hökelek[ği] هوكلك prov. conceit, show ostentation. **—li** conceited.

höl هول *prov., var. of* **öl**.
höllükᵍᵘ هوللك *prov.* porous red earth warmed and used in babies' diapers to keep them dry.
höpürdetⁱʳ هوپورد تمك /ı/ to sip noisily.
hörgüçᶜᵘ هورگوج camel's hump. —**lü** humped. —**lük** 1. humpiness, protuberance. 2. cloth for a camel's hump.
hörmet حرمت *var. of* **hürmet**.
hörü هورى *prov., var. of* **huri**.
hös=ᵉʳ اهوسمك *prov.* to be silent.
höşmerim هوشمریم *prov., same as* **hoşmerim**.
höykür=ᵘʳ هويكورمك *prov.* to chant a religious formula.
höyükᵍᵘ هويوك artificial mound or hill, tumulus.
hu 1 (—) هو A 1. Hey, there. 2. *myst. orders, greeting formula*. 3. He (*i. e.*, God). —**çek**= 1. to chant «Hu!» repeatedly. 2. to coo (pigeons).
hu 2 هُو |hu 3| *only in* **huyu husu** (*see* **huy 1**).
hu 3 (—) هو P *lrnd., same as* **huy**.
hubᵇᵇᵘ **1** حبّ A *lrnd.* love, affection. —**i câh** love of high position. —**i gayr** altruism. —**i nefs** selfishness, egotism.
hub 2 (—) هوب P *lrnd.* good, excellent, beautiful, elegant, graceful.
huban (— —) هوبان P beauties, the fair ones. —**name** (— — —.) P book about beauties.
hubbaz (. —) خبّاز A *lrnd.* mallow, marsh mallow.
hubesa (..—) خبثاء A *lrnd., pl. of* **habis 1**.
hubeyb حبیب A *sc.* granule. —**î** (..—) A granular.
hubi (— —) هوبى P *lrnd.* beauty; goodness.
hublâ (. —) حبلى A *lrnd.* pregnant.
hublika (—.—) حبلقا P *lrnd.* lovely-faced.
hubru (— —) هوبرو P *lrnd.* lovely-faced.
hubsˢⁱ حبث A *lrnd.* 1. badness, wickedness. 2. adultery, fornication. 3. impurity.
hubter (—.) هوبتر P *lrnd.* better; more beautiful.
hubub (.—) حبوب A *lrnd., pl. of* **hab 1**.
hububat (.— —) حبوبات A cereal grains.
hubulˡᵘ (.—) حبول A *lrnd., pl. of* **habl**.
hubur 1 (.—) حبور A *lrnd., pl. of* **hıbr 1, 2**.
hubur 2 (.—) حبور A *lrnd.* happiness, delight, comfort.
hubut (.—) هبوط *same as* **hübut**.
hubz خبز A *lrnd.* bread.
huccab (.—) حجّاب *lrnd., pl. of* **hacib**.
huccac (.—) حجّاج *same as* **hüccac**.
hucec حجج A *lrnd., pl. of* **hüccet**.
hucerat (..—) حجرات A *lrnd., pl. of* **hücre**.
huceste حجسته P *lrnd.* auspicious, fortunate, happy. —**ahter** P born under a lucky star. —**fal** (...—) P lucky. —**mâna** (...— —) P auspicious in meaning. —**rey** whose thought is auspicious. —**sıfat** (....—) P of auspicious qualities. —**tali** (...—.) P lucky, fortunate.
hucr حجر A *lrnd.* breast, bosom.
hucüb حجب A *lrnd., pl. of* **hicab**.
hud (—) خود P *lrnd.* helmet. —**i hurûs** cock's comb.
Huda 1 (.—) خدا P *lrnd., same as* **Hüda 2**.
hud'a 2 خدعه A *lrnd.* wile, trick, stratagem; fraud, deceit. —**ger** P, —**kâr** (..—) P trickster, deceiver, fraud.
huddam (.—) خدّام A 1. spirits in the service of a person. 2. *lrnd., pl. of* **hadim 1**. —**lı hoca** hodja with powers to control spirits.
hudret حضرت A *same as* **huzret**.
hudud (.—) حدود A 1. *same as* **hudut**. 2. *lrnd., pl. of* **had 1**.
hudus (.—) حدوث A *lrnd.* 1. a beginning, originating; a happening, occurring. 2. a reappearing, emerging. 3. novelty.
hudutᵈᵘ (.—) حدود [hudud] frontier; border, boundary; limit, end. —**harici et**= /ı/ to expel from the country. —**işareti** boundary-stone. —**name** (.— —.) P document demarcating a boundary. —**suz** unlimited, boundless; endless.
hufᶠᶠᵘ خفّ A *lrnd.* light shoe. —**u hâfir** camels and horses.
huffaş (.—) خفّاش A *lrnd.* bat (flying rodent).
huffaz (.—) حفّاظ A *lrnd., pl. of* **hâfız**.
hufre حفره A *lrnd.* pit, ditch; trench; chasm.
hufte خفته P *lrnd.* lying down; asleep; torpid. —**gân** (..—) P those who are asleep. —**gî** (..—) P a lying down; torpidity.
huftuhîz (..—) خفت وخیز P *lrnd.* 1. slowness. 2. agitation, commotion; restlessness, inconstancy.
huğ هوغ A *prov.* hut, booth.
Huht (—) خوحت P *lrnd.* Jerusalem; the Temple at Jerusalem.
hukᵏᵘ (—) خوك P *lrnd.* hog, swine. —**i mahî** porpoise. —**ban** (— —) P swineherd.
hukukᵏᵘ (.—) حقوق A 1. law, jurisprudence. 2. friendly relationship, friendship; good relations. 3. *pl. of* **hak 1**. —**i âdiye** *law* common law. —**i âmme** *law* public law. —**a bağlı** *law* law-abiding. —**i beşer** law of man. —**i cezaiye** *law* criminal law. —**dâvası** lawsuit. —**divanı** court of justice for civil rights. **H— Doktoru** Doctor of Law. —**i düvel** *law* international law. —**i esasiye** *law* constitutional law. **H— Fakültesi** Law Faculty; Law School. —**felsefesi** philosophy of law; jurisprudence. —**i hususiye-i düvel** *law* international private law. —**i ibad** *can. law* private law. —**i idare** *law* administrative law. —**i ilâhiye** *can. law* public law. —**ilmi** jurispru-

hukukî

dence. **— mahkemesi** civil court. **—i medeniye** *law* civil law; civil rights. **—i mevzua** *law* statutory law. **— mezunu** Bachelor of Law. **—i milel** *law* international law, law of nations. **—a mugayeret** *law* illegality. **— muhakemeleri usulü** *law* civil procedure. **—i müktesebe** acquired rights; tacitly recognized rights. **— müşaviri** legal adviser. **—i siyasiye** *law* political rights. **—i tabiiye** natural law. **—i ticaret** *law* commercial law. **—i umumiye** *obs., law* public law. **—umuz var** /la/ We are old friends. **—undan vazgeç=** to give up one's rights. **—çu** jurist.

hukukî (.— —) مُعْرَقِي A legal, juridical. **— hata** error of law. **— muamele** act at law.

hukukiyat (.— — —) مَعْرُقِيَّات A *obs.* jurisprudence.

hul[lü] خُلْع A *can. law* 1. divorce by a husband of his wife at her request. 2. a wife's request for divorce.

hulan=[ır] خُرِلْنَمَق *archaic* to form a habit.

hulâsa 1 (.—.) خُلَاصَة A 1. summary, resume. 2. extract (of a substance). **—sını al=, —sını çıkar=** /ın/ 1. to sum up. 2. to get the extract (of). **— et=** /ı/ to summarize, to sum up. **—i hesabiye** *lrnd.* statement of account. **—i kelâm** the sum and substance of what has been said; in short.

hulâsa 2 (.—´.) خُلَاصَة [hulâsa 1] in short, summing up.

hulâsaten (.—´..) خُلَاصَةً A in short, summing up, briefly.

hulâsatülhulâsa (.— —...—.) خُلَاصَة الخُلَاصَة A *lrnd.* the very essence; in one word.

huld خُلْد A *lrnd.* 1. permanency, perpetual existence, eternal duration. 2. paradise, heaven; eternity. **—i berin** paradise the sublime. **—zar** (.—) P paradise.

hulefa (..—) خُلَفَاء A *lrnd., pl. of* halife. **H—i Raşidin** *Isl. hist.* the first four caliphs.

hulel حُلَل A *lrnd., pl. of* hulle.

hulema (..—) حُلَمَاء A *lrnd., pl. of* halib.

huleyme حُلَيْمَة [based on Arabic] *anat.* papilla, nipple.

hulf خُلْف A *lrnd.* false promise, breach of promise. **—i va'd et=** to break a promise. **—i yemin et=** to violate an oath.

hulk[ku] خُلْق A *lrnd.* moral quality, nature, character habit. **—u dar** *archaic* quick-tempered. **—an** (.´.) A by nature.

hulklan=[ır] خُلْقْلَنْمَق *prov.* to be cross, to get angry. **—dır=** /ı/ *caus.*

hulkum (.—) حُلْقُوم A *anat.* pharynx. **—î** (.— —) A guttural.

hulle حُلَّة A 1. *same as* hülle. 2. *lrnd.* suit of clothing, raiment; celestial garment. **—i Âdem** Adam's garment of fig leaves.

hullebaf (..—) حُلَّه‌باف P *lrnd.* tailor.

hullet خُلَّت A *lrnd.* sincere friendship; *myst.* pure love for God.

hulliyat (.— —) حُلِّيَّات [based on Arabic] *lrnd.* ornaments, jewelry.

hulm حُلْم A *lrnd.* 1. dream; a dreaming. 2. a having an emission of semen.

hulûd (.—) خُلُود A *lrnd.* permanency, perpetuality.

hulûl[lü] (.—) حُلُول A 1. an entering; penetration, infiltration. 2. a coming, occurring; a beginning (of a season). 3. *sc.* osmosis. 4. *myst.* incarnation of God; *phil.* reincarnation; metempsychosis, transmigration of souls. **— et=** /a/ 1. to enter, penetrate, infiltrate. 2. to come, begin. **—î** (.— —) *sc.* osmotic. **—iye** (.— —.) A *phil.* belief in reincarnation.

hulûs (.—) خُلُوص A 1. sincerity, devotion; purity of heart. 2. a toadying. **— çak=** /a/ *colloq.* to toady, to flatter. **—î** (.— —) *lrnd.* sincere.

huluskâr (.— —) خُلُوصْكار 1. sincere, sincere friend. 2. hypocritical; sycophant, flatterer. **—âne** (.— — —.) P 1. sincerely, in a friendly manner. 2. hypocritically. **—î** (.— — — —) P, **—lık** 1. sincerity. 2. flattery.

hulüvv[vü] خُلُوّ A *lrnd.* emptiness, vacancy.

hulv حُلْو A *lrnd.* 1. sweet. 2. pleasant, agreeable, charming. **—iyat** (.— —) A 1. sweet dishes. 2. agreeable things.

hulya (.—) خُلْيَا Gk fancy, daydream. **— kur=** to fancy, to daydream. **—âmiz** (.— — —) P evoking fancy. **—lı** dreamy, romantic; fanciful.

hum خُم P *lrnd.* 1. large jar, pithos. 2. kettledrum. 3. sky.

humaka (..—) حُمَقَاء A *lrnd.* fools.

humar (.—) خُمَار A 1. hangover, drunken headache; *lrnd.* stupor arising from excess or suffering. 2. *poet.* languishing look. **—alûd** (.— — —) P *lrnd.* 1. having a hangover. 2. stupefied. 3. languishing (eyes).

humasî (.— —) حُمَاسِي A 1. *Arabic gram.* having five root letters, quinqueliteral. 2. *bot.* fivefold, five-leaved, five-cornered.

humayun (.— —) حُمَايُون P *var. of* hümayun.

humbara حُمْبَرَه P *archaic, same as* kumbara.

humçe خُمْچَه P *lrnd.* small jar. **humhane** (.—.), **humistan** (..—) خُمْخَانَه P *lrnd.* wine vault, wine cellar; wineshop; tavern.

humk[ku] حُمْق A *lrnd.* stupidity.

humma حُمَّى A *path.* fever. **—i balgamiye** lymphatic fever. **—i cemreviye** splenic fever, anthrax. **—i cerhiye** traumatic fever. **—i daire** recurrent fever, relapsing fever. **—i dık, —i dıkkiye** hectic fever. **—i gıb** tertian fever. **—i kulâi** *vet.* foot-and-mouth disease. **—i**

merzagiye swamp-fever. **—i müsellese** tertian fever. **—i mütereddide** remittent fever. **—i nehariye** daytime fever. **—i nifasiye** childbed fever. **—i racia** relapsing fever, remittent fever. **—i rub'** quartan fever. **—i ruh** lrnd. bore, wearisome person. **—i safra** yellow fever. **—i safraviye** bilious fever. **—i sevdaviye** splenetic fever. **—i vebaiye** epidemic fever.

hummalı حمّالى 1. having fever, feverish. 2. feverishly, intensively; continual and intense (efforts etc.).

hummaz (.—) حمّاض A 1. sorrel, bot., Rumex. 2. red-colored sugar used in preparing a hot drink offered to visitors after a baby is born. **—iye** bot., Oxalidaceae.

hummus حمّص A lrnd. chickpea.

humret حمرت A lrnd. redness, ruddiness.

hums خمس A lrnd. one fifth.

humud (.—) حمود A lrnd. 1. a going out (flame or fire). 2. a fever's abating.

humul[lü] 1 (.—) حمول A lrnd., pl. of **haml**.

humul[lü] 2 (.—) حمول A lrnd. 1. a disappearing; obliteration; oblivion. 2. a being unknown to fame, obscurity; contempt.

humus 1 (.'.) هوموس G geol., forestry humus.

humus 2 حمّص [hummus] mashed chickpeas.

humus[msu] 3 حمس var. of **hums**.

humuzet (.—) حموضت A lrnd. sourness, acid.

humz حمض A chem. oxide.

hun (—) خون P lrnd. 1. blood. 2. blood-guiltiness; murder. 3. vengeance for blood shed; blood feud. **—i cam** poet. red wine. **—i ciger, —i dil** poet. 1. bitter tears. 2. grief; anxiety; deep affliction. **—i helâl** blood that may be shed lawfully. **—i kebuter** poet. wine. **—i mürde** extravasated blood of a bruise. **—i siyavuş, —i siyavuşan** poet. 1. wine. 2. the rosy dawn. **—i şişe** poet. wine. **—âb** (——), **—âbe** (——.) P poet. bitter tears of blood. **—âlûd** (———) P bloodstained. **—âşam** (———) P bloodthirsty, ferocious, cruel. **—bâr** (——) P shedding blood (generally said of the eyes of a lover). **—beha** (—.—) P blood price. **—çegân** (—.—) P dripping blood, blood-shedding. **—dâr** (——) P 1. blood-guilty. 2. avenger of blood. **—efşan** (—.—) P, **—feşan** (—.—) P 1. shedding blood, bleeding. 2. shedding tears; weeping.

hunhah (——) خونخواه P lrnd. 1. one who seeks another's blood. 2. avenger of blood.

hunhar (.—) خونخوار P bloodthirsty. **—âne** (.——.) P in a cruel way. **—lık** bloodthirstiness, cruelty.

huni 1 خونى Gk funnel for pouring liquids.

huni 2 (——) خونى P lrnd. bloody; blood-guilty; cruel.

hunin (—.—) خونين P lrnd. of blood; bloody.

hunkâr (.—) خنكار P same as **hünkâr**. **—î** (.——) P fit for a sultan.

hunnak[kı, ğı] (.—) خنّاق A path. 1. quinsy, inflammation of the throat. 2. diphtheria.

hunpaş (——), **hunriz** (——) خونپاش خونريز P lrnd. blood-shedding, bloodthirsty.

hur (—) حور A lrnd. virgin or virgins of paradise, houri. **—i ayn** dark-eyed (virgins); the houris. **—i bihiştî** houris.

hurac (.—) خراج A path eruptions of the skin, boils, pustules.

hurada خرابا [based on Arabic] worn-out.

hurafat (.——) خرافات A pl. of **hurafe**.

hurafe (.—.) خرافة A 1. superstition. 2. legend, myth; silly tale.

huran (——) حوران P lrnd., pl. of **hur**.

huraşe (.—.) خراشه A lrnd. scrapings, filings.

hurc[cu] خرج A large leather saddle-bag.

hurçun خرجون [Persian **khurjin**] prov. saddle-bags.

hurd خرد P 1. lrnd. small, little; petty, insignificant. 2. lrnd. broken, small. **— u haş** crushed, broken to pieces. **— ü mürd** lrnd. trifles, insignificant things.

hurda 1 خرده P 1. old (iron), scrap (metal). 2. small, fine. 3. slang hashish. **—sı çıkmış** old and worn out. **— demir** scrap iron. **— fiatına** at scrap price; for the value of the materials.

hurda 2 خرده [hud'a 2] only in **hile hurda**.

hurdacı خرده‌جى scrap dealer.

Hurdad (.—) خرداد P lrnd. 1. name of the third Persian month; name of the sixth day of the month. 2. name of the patron angel of rivers and trees.

hurdalaş[ır] خرده‌لاشمك to be worn out; to become too old.

hurdavat خرده‌وات [Persian ..—] same as **hırdavat**.

hurde خرده P lrnd. 1. small bit, trifle; particle. 2. fine point, nicety. 3. small, trifling, minute; unimportant. **—i dest** wrist. **—i elmas** small particles of diamond. **—i kâfur** 1. small particles of camphor. 2. poet. stars. **—i kalem** 1. cuttings from reed pens. 2. slip of the pen. **—i kündür** particles of frankincense. **—i mina** 1. particles of enamel. 2. poet. wine, red wine. **—i zer** 1. gold dust. 2. pollen of flowers.

hurdebin 1 (..—) خرده‌بين [hurdebin 2] obs. microscope.

hurdebin 2 (..—) خرده‌بين P lrnd. 1. having acute perception or observation. 2. censorious, hypercritical.

hurdebinî (..——) خرده‌بينى obs. microscopic.

hurdeçin (..—) خرده‌چين P lrnd. gathering crumbs; beggar.

hurdedan (..—) خرده‌دان P lrnd. capable of

hurdefürus

understanding fine points and witty sayings; sagacious; a critic.
hurdefüruş (...—) خرده فروش P *lrnd.* 1. vendor of small wares. 2. ignorant person who likes to brag.
hurdegîr (..—) خرده گیر P *lrnd.* faultfinder, censorious person.
hurdehaş (..—) خرده خاش P *var. of* **hurd u haş.**
hurdekâr (..—) خرده کار P *lrnd.* worker in filigree or other delicate work. —**î** (..——) P filigree; tessellated work.
hurdemürde خرده مرده P *lrnd.* small things; trifles.
hurdeşinas (...—) خرده شناس P *lrnd., same as* **hurdedan.**
hurdî (.—) خردی P *lrnd.* smallness, minuteness.
hurdsal[u] (.—) خردسال P *lrnd.* youth of tender years.
huri (——) حوری P houri. — **gibi** very beautiful (girl).
hurka حرق A *lrnd., same as* **harka.**
hurlika (—.—) حورلقا P *lrnd.* angel-faced, very beautiful.
hurma خرما [*Persian* .—] date. — **ağacı** date palm, *bot.,* Phoenix dactylifera. — **dorusu** brown, bay-colored (horse). — **gözlü** gazelle-eyed. — **koruğu** unripe date. — **revendi** dish made with dates, butter and eggs. — **sıçanı** kind of squirrel. — **tatlısı** sweet made of dough cut into date-shaped pieces, fried and soaked in syrup.
hurmalık[ʳ] خرمالی date grove.
hurpeyker (—..) حورپیکر P *lrnd.* houri-faced.
hurras (.—) حراس A *lrnd., pl. of* **hâris 3.**
hurrem خرم P *lrnd.* 1. joyful; happy; smiling; glad. 2. fresh, blooming, green, luxuriant. 3. agreeable, pleasant. —**î** (..—) P happiness, joyfulness; freshness, greenness.
hurremrû (..—) خرم رو P *lrnd.* happy faced, beautiful-faced.
hurremrûz (..—) خرم روز P *lrnd.,* Zoroastrian *calendar* the eighth day of a month.
hursend, hursende خرسنده P *lrnd.* contented, satisfied, pleased, grateful.
hursendi (..—) خرسندی P *lrnd.* content, satisfaction, pleasure, gratitude.
hurşid (.—) خورشید P *lrnd.* 1. sun. 2. soul. —**i cihantâb** the world-illuminating sun. —**i iştihar** the sun of fame. —**i leb-i bâm** 1. sunset. 2. the termination of life. —**i ser-i divan** *same as* **hurşidi leb-i bâm.** —**i surahi** wine. —**fürug** (.—.—) P, — **lemaan** (.—..—) P beaming, resplendent as the sun. —**perestan** P sun-worshippers. —**süvaran** (.—.——) P 1. early risers. 2. Christian monks. 3. angels. —**tal'at** (.—..) P whose first appearance is like sunrise.

hurub (.—) حروب A *lrnd., pl. of* **harb.**
huruc (.—) خروج A, **huruç**[cu] (.—)
1. *mil.* sortie, sally. 2. *lrnd.* a coming or going out; a proceeding; start, origin. (of a new movement), exodus; a migrating. 3. *lrnd.* rebellion. — **et=** 1. *mil.* to sally, to burst forth. 2. *lrnd.* to come out; to start.
huruf (.—) حروف A *lrnd., pl. of* **harf.** —**i âliyat** *myst.* matters yet concealed in the mystery of the Divine purpose. —**i âniye** Arabic *Phon.* explosive letters which are not prolonged in their pronunciation. —**i bedel** Arabic *gram.* letters which are substituted for weak radicals. —**i hanceriye** Arabic *phon.* guttural letters. —**i hica** Arabic *gram.* consonants. —**i imlâ** Arabic *gram.* vowels. —**i kalkale** Quran *recitation* the letters ق,ط,د,ج,ب—**i kameriye** Arabic *gram.* letters which do not assimilate the article. —**i lisevî** Arabic *phon.* gingival letters. —**i mechure** Arabic *phon.* emphatic letters. —**i munfasıla** Arabic *script* letters not joined to a following letter. —**i nâriye** *onom.* the letters ت,ض,—**i nıt'iye** Arabic *phon.* palatal letters. —**i rahve** Arabic *phon.* soft letters. —**i safir** Arabic *phon.* sibilants. —**i şefeviye** Arabic *phon.* labials. —**i şemsiye** Arabic *gram.* letters which assimilate the article. —**i tehecci** Arabic *gram.* letters of the alphabet. —**i vasliye** Arabic *script* letters which are joined to a following letter. —**i zevlâkiye** Arabic *phon.* labiolinguals. —**i zulmaniye** *onom.* letters not found superscribed at the head of any chapter of the Quran.
hurufat (.——) حروفات A *print.* type. — **dök=** to cast type. — **dökmecisi** type founder. — **kasası** type case.
Hurufî (.——) حروفی A 1. follower of the Islamic Hurufî sect. 2. *l. c.* who draws conclusions from combinations of letters; one who uses onomancy. —**lik** the Hurufî sect.
hurus (.—) خروس P *lrnd., same as* **horoz.** —**i arş** *Isl. myth.* heavenly cock whose crowing starts the dawn cock crowing. —**i bimahal** person who speaks out of season or place. —**i hindî** turkey cock. —**i sahraî** pheasant.
huruş (.—) خروش P *lrnd.* loud cry, shout; lamentation; clamor.
huruşan (.——) خروشان P *lrnd.* calling out, shouting, lamenting; clamorous.
hurzad (——) حورزاد P *lrnd.* born of a celestial nymph; beautiful.
husema (..—) حصما A *lrnd., pl. of* **hasm 1.**
husr حصر A *med.* 1. constipation. 2. retention of the urine.
husran (.—) خسران A *same as* **hüsran.**

Husrev خسرو *lrnd.* 1. Cyrus. 2. *l. c.* monarch, sovereign. **—âne** (..—.) P royal, kingly. **—anî** (..——) P royal, imperial; grand, elegant, regal. **—î** (..—) P belonging to a king, royal; sovereignty. **—perest** P faithful to his sovereign.

hussad (.—) عُسّاد A *lrnd., pl. of* hâsid.

husuf (.—) خسوف A *astr.* eclipse of the moon. **—i cüz'i** partial eclipse of the moon. **—i küllî** total eclipse of the moon.

husul[lu] (.—) حصول A 1. an occurring, coming to pass. 2. an appearing, being produced. 3. attainment, acquisition. **— bul=** to succeed (desire, endeavor). **—e gel=** to come into being, to come to pass, originate, form, develop. **—e getir=** /ı/ to accomplish, to bring to pass, to bring about.

husulpezir (.—.—) حصولپذیر P *lrnd.* resulting, attained, accomplished. **— ol=** *lrnd.* to result, to be attained, accomplished.

husum (.—) حصوم A *lrnd., pl. of* hasm 1.

husumet (.—.) حصومت A enmity, spite, hostility; antagonism, opposition.

husun (.—) حصون A *lrnd., pl. of* hısn.

husus (.—) خصوص A 1. matter, subject, question; case. 2. a particular, point; relation, respect, connection; peculiarity, particularity. **—iyle** particularly, especially. **—unda** with reference to; regarding.

hususa (.—ʹ—) خصوصا A *lrnd.* especially, particularly, above all.

hususat (.—.—) خصوصات A *lrnd., pl. of* husus.

hususen (.—ʹ.) خصوصا A *lrnd., same as* hususa.

hususi (.——) خصوصى A 1. special, particular; exceptional characteristic, distinctive. 2. private, personal; reserved (seat). **— ders** private lesson. **— hukuk** private law. **— kalem müdürü** private secretary (of a minister). **—lik** peculiarity, peculiar feature.

hususiyat (.—.—) خصوصیات A *lrnd.* private affairs.

hususiyet (.—..) خصوصیت A 1. peculiarity, special feature; characteristics. 2. intimacy, close relations. **—i ol=** 1. /la/ to be intimate (with). 2. to have a special character or feature.

husye خصیه A *anat.* testicle.

huş 1 خوش birch, *bot.*, Betula alba.

huş 2 (—) خوش P *lrnd.* intellect, sense; reason.

huşe (—.) خوشه P *lrnd.* 1. bunch, cluster of fruit. 2. ear of grain. **—i çerh, —i felek** the constellation Virgo.

huşeçin (—.—) خوشه‌چین P *lrnd.* 1. gleaner. 2. plagiarizer. **—î** (—.——) P 1. gleaning. 2. plagiarism.

huşfersa (—.—) هوشفرسا P *lrnd.* perplexing.

huşk[ü] خشک P *lrnd.* 1. dry; dried; withered. 2. hard, harsh to the touch; rough, rude, coarse. 3. bare, simple; unalloyed, unadulterated, pure. 4. unprofitable; unavailing, stingy, miserly. **— ü ter** 1. dry and moist; dried and fresh. 2. bread and water. 3. bad and good; frowns and smiles of fortune. 4. land and sea. **—ahur** (.——) P year of scarcity, barren year. **—can** (.—) P 1. ignorant, unskillful; stupid, stolid. 2. devoid of affection. **—î** (.—) P dryness; scarcity occasioned by drought. **—mağz** (.—) P fool, blockhead. **—nihad** (..—) P useless person. **—pey** P ill-omened, inauspicious. **—sal** (.—) P *lrnd.* year of drought and famine; scarcity. **—ser** P addle-pated. **—şane** (—.) P pride, arrogance; proud, haughty. **—tıynet** (—.—) P useless person.

huşmend (—.) هوشمند P *lrnd.* reasonable, sober-minded; prudent, wise. **—î** (—.—) P understanding, prudence.

huşu[uu] (.—) خشوع A *lrnd.* pious reverence.

huşunet (—.—) خشونت A *lrnd.* harshness; roughness; coarseness.

huşyar (——) هوشیار *lrnd.* sober-minded, reasonable; prudent; wise. **—î** (———) P, **—lık** sober-mindedness, prudence.

hut (—) حوت A *astr.,* Pisces. **—i cenubî** Piscis Australis. **—i gerdun** Pisces. **—i şimalî** Piscis Septentrionis.

hutab خطب A *lrnd., pl. of* hutbe.

hutaba (..—) خطباء A *lrnd., pl. of* hatib.

hutam (.—) حطام A *lrnd.* 1. fragments, shreds. 2. rubbish, trash. **—ı dünya** the vanities of this world.

hutbe خطبه A sermon delivered after the Friday prayer; sermon, oration.

huttaf (.—) خطاف A *lrnd.* swallow, *zool.,* hirundo.

hutur (.—) خطور A *lrnd.* an occurring to the mind.

hutut (.—) خطوط A *lrnd., pl. of* hat.

huval حوال upper piece of the instep of a shoemaker's last, wedge for stretching a boot.

huveynat (.—.—) حوینات A *same as* hüveynat.

huveysal[lu] حویصل A *anat.* vesicle, vesicula.

huy 1 خوی [Persian —] 1. habit, temper, disposition. 2. bad habit; obstinacy. **— canın altındadır** You can't eradicate what is innate. **—una çek** /ın/ to take after someone's habit. **— edin=, — et=** /ı/ to form the habit (of); to make (something) one's bad habit. **—unu husunu bilme=** not to know someone's temperament or character. **—u huyuna, suyu suyuna pek uygun** They get on very well together; they are of the same disposition.

— **kap**= /dan/ to contract bad habits (from). —**una suyuna git**= /ın/ to humor.

-huy 2 (—) خوى P lrnd. tempered, natured, as in **bedhuy, hoşhuy**.

huykerde (—..) خوى كرده P lrnd. accustomed, used to.

huylan=ır خوىلنمق 1. to get nervous, to be irritated; to get excited (sensually). 2. to feel suspicious. 3. to become obstinate (animal). —**dır**= /ı/ caus.

huylu خوىلو 1. bad-tempered; suspicious, touchy. 2. obstinate (animal).

huysuz خوىسز bad-tempered, obstinate. —**lan**= to show bad temper, to become obstinate.

huysuzlukğu خوىسزلق bad temper, obstinacy. —**u tut**= /ın/ to have a fit of bad temper.

huyullü (.—) خيول A lrnd., pl. of **hayl**.

huyut (.—) خيوط A lrnd., pl. of **hayt**.

huzemat (..—) حزمات A lrnd., pl. of **huzme**.

huzî حزى A Or. mus. a compound makam about six centuries old, no longer used.

huzme حزمه A 1. bundle, bunch; rays, beams. 2. geom., opt. pencil of rays.

huzret حضرت A lrnd. greenness. —**i evrak** sc. chlorophyl.

huzuuu (.—) خضوع A lrnd. humility; submission; respect, veneration. — **ve huşu ile** with deep humility and veneration.

huzur (.—) حضور A 1. presence. 2. peace of mind; freedom from anxiety, repose, quiet, ease. 3. audience (of a sovereign). —**da** in audience (with a sovereign). —**iyle**, —**unda** /ın/ in the presence of. —**i âli** the esteemed presence (said about a superior). — **ve asayiş** peace and security. —**a çık**= to have an audience, to enter the presence (of a sovereign). — **dersi** Ott. hist. lecture in the Sultan's presence, in a mosque or in the Palace on certain days in Ramazan. — **divanı** a council convened under the presidency of the Sheikhu'l-Islam to decide some important legal question of state. — **hakkı** daily attendance allowance. —**a kabûl olun**= to be admitted to audience by a sovereign. —**i kalb** peace of mind. —**i küllî** omnipresence, —**i meymenetmevfur** the presence, abounding in auspiciousness (of the sovereign). —**lu** at ease, in peace.

huzursuz حضورسز uneasy, troubled. —**luk** uneasiness; trouble, disorder; want of peace and tranquillity.

huzuz (.—), **huzuzat** (.——) حظوظ حظوظات A lrnd., pl. of **haz 1**.

huzzakkı (.—) حذاق A lrnd., pl. of **hazık**.

huzzar (.—) حضار A lrnd., pl. of **hazır 2**.

hübub (.—) هبوب A lrnd. blowing of the wind.

hübut (.—) هبوط A lrnd. a falling, fall; a descending, descent. —**i Âdem** Adam's fall.

— **et**= to fall, to descend. —**i kuva** prostration of forces.

hüccac (.—) حجاج A lrnd., pl. of **hâc 2**.

hüccet حجت A 1. argument; proof. 2. document, voucher; title-deed.

Hüccetülislâm (....—) حجة الاسلام A lrnd. proof of Islam (honorific title of al Ghazali).

hücerat (..—) حجرات A lrnd., pl. of **hücre**. **H— Suresi** name of the 49th sura of the Quran.

hüceste حجسته P same as **huceste**.

hüceyrat (..—) حجيرات A lrnd., pl. of **hüceyre**.

hüceyre حجيره A anat. cellule.

hücnet حجنت lrnd. 1. meanness, stinginess. 2. impropriety in language. —**i kelâm** impropriety of language.

hücra (.—) حجرا remote, solitary place.

hücre حجره A 1. cell, room, chamber; alcove, niche. 2. biol. cell. — **hapsi sistemi** law cell system. — **özsuyu** bot. cellulary sap. —**lerarası** biol. intercellular.

hücrevi (..—) حجروى A biol. cellular.

hücuuu (.—) حجوع A lrnd. sleep.

hücud (.—) حجود A lrnd. sleep.

hücum (.—) حجوم A attack, assault; onset, charge; a storming. — **botu** assault boat. —**i dem** rush of blood. — **et**= /a/ to break in suddenly (on one), to attack, to make an assault (upon). — **kıt'aları** mil. storm troops. —**a uğra**= to be attacked.

hüda 1 (.—) هدى A lrnd. 1. guidance. 2. right road, the way of salvation; the Islamic faith.

Hüda 2 (.—) خدا P lrnd. God. — **hafız** goodby. —**yı müteal** the most high and supreme God. —**bende** (.—..) P God-serving. —**dad** (.——) P gift of God, given by God. —**dan** (.——) P who knows God. —**dur** (.——) P distant, estranged from God. —**fürus** (.—.—) P hypocrite. —**gir** (.——) P visited by divine judgment. —**han** (.——) P 1. that calls on God. 2. the four fingers of the right hand raised as an attestation of God's unity. —**meşreb** (.—..) P pious, godly. —**naters** (.——.) P who does not fear God. —**nekerde** (.—...) P God forbid! —**perest** (.—..) P God-worshipper. —**pesend** (.—..) P pleasing to God. —**râ** (.——) P for God's sake. —**şinas** (.—.—) P God-knowing. —**ters** (.—.) P God-fearing, godly.

hüdavend (.—.) خداوند P lrnd. 1. God. 2. Lord, master; king. —**î** (.—.—) P lordship; deity; dominion.

hüdavendigâr (.—..—) خداوندگار P 1. creator of the world, God. 2. the sultan; title given to Sultan Murad I. **H— vilâyeti** Ott. hist., name of a province comprising a large part of northwestern Anatolia. —**ane** (.—..——.)

P, —î (.—..——) P 1. divine. 2. royal, princely.
Hüdaya (.——) خدایا P lrnd. O God.
hüdayi (.——) خدائی P lrnd. 1. divine; created by God, natural. 2. Godhood, divinity. — küpe sheep's ear naturally split with one part hanging down. — sille a strong blow on the face.
hüdayigân (.—.—) خدایگان P lrnd. 1. great lord; great king. 2. God. —î (.—.——) P lordship; sovereignty; lordly, sovereign.
hüdayinabit (.—.—.) خدای نابت P 1. wild-growing; of spontaneous growth; running wild (child). 2. untaught, amateur.
hüdeybe حدیبه A anat. tubercle.
hüdhüd هدهد A lrnd. hoopoe.
hüdne هدنه A lrnd. 1. peace concluded. 2. peace, tranquillity.
hüdüb هدب A 1. bot. stipule. 2. lrnd. eyelash.
hükema (..—) حکما A lrnd., pl. of hakîm 2. —i âfâk the wise men of the age.
hükkâm (.—) حکام A lrnd., pl. of hakîm 1.
hükm حکم A lrnd., same as hüküm. — et=*.
hükmen (.'.) حکماً A 1. in accordance with rules or regulations; legally. 2. sports with the decision of the referee.
hükmet=der حکم اتمک /a/ 1. to rule, to dominate, to command, to govern, to exert influence (upon). 2. to sentence, to decide (on), to judge. 3. to consider, to think; to believe; to assume.
hükmî (.—) حکمی A 1. legal, judicial; done in accordance with rules. 2. nominal. — şahıs law artificial person, legal person.
hükûmat (.——) حکومات A lrnd., pl. of hükûmet.
hükûmet (.—.) حکومت A 1. government; state; administration; sovereignty, rule, dominion. 2. authority; jurisdiction, power. 3. government office. 4. slang prison warden. —i ağniya pol. plutocracy. —i âmme pol. democracy. — darbesi pol. coup d'état. — et= same as hükûmet sür=. — gibi karı vulg. a woman well versed in managing her own affairs. — kapısına düş= to have dealings with the authorities. — konağı government office (in a town). — merkezi capital, seat of government. —i meşruta pol. constitutional government. —i mutlaka pol. absolute government, monarchy. —i ruhaniye, —i ruhbaniye pol. theocracy. — sür= to rule, to reign; to govern; to dominate. —i zâdegân pol. oligarchy.
hükûmetgâh (.—.—) حکومتگاه P lrnd. seat of government, government house; court.
hüküm^{kmü} حکم [hükm] 1. sentence, decree, judicial decision; judicial authority, jurisdiction. 2. rule, dominion, authority, government.
3. command, edict. 4. law statute; divine ordinance; judgment. 5. effect, influence, importance. 6. assumption, thought, belief; opinion. 7. requirement (of a matter). 8. the value, effect or tenor of a law or document. —ünce according to the tenor of. —ünde equivalent to, in lieu of. —i aklî psych. intellectual perception, judgment, assertion. —i beyazî hist. royal mandate issued with secrecy and dispatch. —den düş= to be no longer valid. —i gayrı şer'i can. law extra-canonical judgment. —ü geç= 1. to expire (validity), to be over with. 2. /a/ to have authority (over), to carry weight. —ünü geçir= /a/ to assert one's authority. — giy= law to lose one's case; to be condemned. — giydir= /a/ to pass sentence (upon). — günü judgment day. —i hümayun imperial edict, firman. —i kader decree of fate. —i karakuşi despotic, arbitrary judgment. —i kaza decree of fate. —ü ol= 1. to command, to rule. 2. to be in force, valid. —ünde ol= /ın/ 1. to be considered (as); to be of the same effect (as). 2. to be under the authority (of). — sür= to rule, to reign; to prevail. —i şer'i can. law canonical ordinance. —i şerif firman. —i şifahî oral command. —i ümmehat sociol. matriarchate. — ver= 1. to issue a sentence, decision, judgment. 2. to assume; to judge; to think.
hükümdar (..—) حکمدار P ruler, monarch, sovereign. —âne (..——.) lrnd. royal, imperial, sovereign. —î (..——) lrnd., —lık sovereignty; kingdom, empire.
hükümet حکومت colloq., var. of hükûmet.
hükümferma (...—) حکمفرما P lrnd. ruling, prevailing.
hükümlü حکملی 1. sentenced, condemned; convict. 2. decisive.
hükümnâme (..—.) حکمنامه P lrnd. 1. judgment, decree, order. 2. letter from a superior.
hükümrân (..—) حکمران P ruling, reigning; ruler, sovereign. —î (..——) lrnd., —lık sovereign, sovereignty.
hükümsüz حکمسز no longer in force, null; abolished. —lük nullity.
hülâm (.—) حلام A veal jelly; gelatine. —î (.——) gelatinous; albuminous.
hülâsa (.—.) خلاصه A var. of hulâsa 1, 2.
hülle حله A can. law interim marriage necessary before a divorced couple can remarry.
hülleci حله جی man who marries a divorced woman on condition of divorcing her in a very short time so that she can remarry her previous husband.
hülya (.—) خلیا var. of hulya.
hüma (.—) هما P myth. mythical bird;

hümam

bird of paradise. **—yi beyza-i din** *lrnd.* the Prophet Muhammad. **—yi lâmekân** *lrnd.* God who dwells in no place.

hümam (.—) همام . A *lrnd.* great and generous prince; liberal, munificent man.

hümanist هماّنست F *phil.* humanist.

hümanizm همانيزم F *phil.* humanism.

hümapaye (.——.) همايه P *lrnd.* most illustrious, most exalted.

hümapervaz (.—.—) همايه واز P *lrnd.* ambitious, arrogant.

hümayun (.——) همايون P 1. *Ott. hist.* royal, imperial, as in **Bab-ı Hümayun, divan-ı hümayun, hatt-ı hümayun, Saray-ı Hümayun.** 2. *Or. mus.* one of the **makams** of the **hicaz** group.

hümayunbaht (.——.) همايون بخت P *lrnd.* very fortunate.

hümayungâh (.———) همايونگاه P *lrnd.* imperial palace.

hümud (.—) همود A *lrnd.* 1. extinction, a being extinguished (fire). 2. death, a dying.

hümum (.—) هموم A *lrnd.*, *pl. of* **hem 3.**

hüner هنر P 1. skill, dexterity; ability; art; talent. 2. accomplishment; merit. 3. object of art; work of dexterity. **— göster=** to exhibit skill, talent, cleverness. **— sat=** to pretend to be clever. **—bend** P *lrnd.* skillful performer. **—dar** (..—) P *lrnd.* skillful, talented. **—füruş** (...—) P *lrnd.* who pretends to be clever. **—li** talented, skillful. **—mend** P *lrnd.* excellent, skillful, industrious, **—perver** P *lrnd.* lover, cultivator, encourager of science or talent. **—ver** P *lrnd.* skillful, clever.

hüngürde=ʳ هنگورده مك to sob violently.

hüngür hüngür هنگر هنگر هنگر هنگر *only in* **hüngür hüngür ağla=** to sob violently, bitterly.

hünkâr (.—) هنكار P sovereign, sultan. **— beğendi** dish of pureéd eggplant. **—a çat=** to encounter the Sultan in the **Harem** (a word). **— imamı** the imam whose duty is to lead the **namaz** when the Sultan is present. **— namı gibi** with an air of great importance. **— mahfili** *Ott. hist.* special place in a mosque where the Sultan performs the **namaz.** **— müezzini** *Ott. hist.* muezzin in the palace mosque who also calls the ezan on Fridays and festal occasions when the Sultan goes to other mosques for prayer.

hünnapᵇⁱ عناب [*Arabic* **ünnâb**] jujube, *bot., Ziziphus sativa.* **—giller** *bot., Rhamnaceae.*

hünsa (.—) خنثى A hermaphrodite. **—iyet** (.——.) hermaphroditism.

Hünud (.—) هنود A *lrnd., pl. of* **Hind, Hindî 2.**

hürʳʳü حر A 1. free, free-born; well-born; freeman. 2. independent; at liberty.

hürle حورل a species of grain.

hürmet حرمت A 1. respect; reverence; veneration; regard. 2. honor; dignity; commanding respect. 3. *lrnd.* sacredness and inviolability; illegal. **—lerimle** with my respects; respectfully yours. **— et=** to respect, to honor. **—i mümâlâha** *lrnd.* the sacred bond arising from eating salt together.

hürmeten (.´..) حرمة A out of respect; /a/ in respectful consideration (of).

hürmetkâr (..—) حرمتكار P respectful. **—âne** (..——.) P respectfully. **—lık** respect.

hürmetli حرمتلو 1. reverend, venerable, worthy of respect, respectable. 2. *colloq.* big, large, huge; considerable. **—ce** *colloq.* rather large, biggish.

hürmetsiz حرمتسز disrespectful, irreverent.

hürmetsizlikᵍⁱ حرمتسزلك disrespect, irreverence. **— et=, — göster=** /a/ to act disrespectfully (toward), to be disrespectful (to).

Hürmüz هرمز P 1. *geog.* Ormuz. 2. *lrnd.* Ormazd, Ahura-Mazda; God; *name of the first day of the Persian solar month; the planet Jupiter; name of an angel.*

hürre حرة A *lrnd.* free woman, freeborn or noble woman.

hürriyet حريت A freedom, liberty; independence. **—i âmme** *myst.* freedom from cupidity. **—i bağlıyan cezalar** *law* penalties restricting liberty. **—i hâssa** *myst.* freedom from selfwill. **—i hassatülhâssa** *myst.* freedom from the observation of rules and ordinances.

hürriyetperver حريت پرور P lover of freedom, liberal. **—âne** (.....—.) P as becomes a lover of freedom.

hürya (.´.) حوريا in a rush, in a sudden burst (of a crowd, etc.).

hüsam (.—) حسام A *lrnd.* sharp sword; sharp edge.

hüsame (.—.) حسامة [*Arabic* **huzama**] true lavender, *bot., Lavandula vera.*

hüseynî (..—) حسينى A 1. P. *Or. mus.* a simple **makam.** 2. *obs.* cord or fringe used to decorate women's garments. 3. *w. cap., lrnd.* relating to Husain. **— aşîrân** *Or. mus.* one of the oldest compound **makams. — zemzeme** a compound **makam** about five centuries old.

hüsn حسن A 1. beauty, comeliness. 2. grace, charm, elegance. 3. goodness, pleasantness; agreeableness. **—i âdâb** good manners; politeness. **—i ahlâk** good chracter; decency. **— ü ân** *poet.* beauty and grace. **—i beyan** *rhet.* beauty of expression. **—i cîret** good neighborliness. **—i hal*. —i hareket** good behavior. **—i hat*. —i hitam** full completion, good ending. **—i hulk** 1. goodness of character; good disposition. 2. good point of character. **—i idare** good management, good administration. —i ihtiyar free will. —i imtizac a getting on well with others. —i insicam flowing style in prose or verse. —i intizam good management, good discipline. —i ittifak 1. happy accord. 2. fortunate combination, coincidence. —i kabul*. —i kıyas rhet. graceful use of a word in consecutive clauses with a different significance in each. —ü kuruntu*. —i makta poet. the next to the last couplet of a poem. —i matlab graceful preface to a request. —i muamele good treatment. —i muaşeret good behavior. —i nazar esteem and consideration. —ü nesak artistic disposition of clauses. —i netice good result. —i niyet*. —i rey sound opinion, judgment, advice. —i semt goodness, virtue; piety. —i suret beauty of countenance. —i sülûk upright conduct. —i tabiat good taste. —i tabir euphemism. —i tahallûs rhet. natural and graceful transition; elegance of transition from preface to subject. —i takvim the most perfect and correct order or form (i. e. the human form). —i tâlil rhet. witty assignment in an eulogium of a supposititious reason for some event connected with a quality of the person eulogized. —i tedbir thoughtful management. —i tefsir favorable interpretation. —i telâkki favorably biased interpretation. —i tesadüf happy coincidence. —i tesir good impression. —i teveccüh kindly treatment; good will. —i Yusuf*. —i zan good opinion (respecting a person).

hüsna (.—) حسنى A lrnd. 1. better; best. 2. more beautiful, most agreeable. 3. beneficent act, good character.

hüsnaver (.—.) حسناور P lrnd. beautiful.

hüsnî (.—) حسنى A lrnd. pertaining to goodness and beauty. —yat (.——) A beautiful and good qualities; embellishments; good effects.

hüsnühal^li (..—) حسن حال P good conduct. — kâğıdı, — varakası certificate of good conduct.

hüsnühat^tı حسن خط P calligraphy; fine penmanship.

hüsnükabul^lü (...—) حسن قبول P friendly reception. — göster= /a/ to receive with a friendly welcome; to behave politely (toward).

hüsnükuruntu حسن قورونتو colloq. wishful thinking; fond imagination.

hüsnüniyet حسن نيت P good will, good intention; good faith.

hüsnüyusuf (..—.) حسن يوسف P sweet william, bot., Dianthus barbatus.

hüsran (.—) خسران A 1. disappointment. 2. frustration. —a uğra= to be greatly disappointed.

Hüsrev خسرو var. of Husrev.
hüsün^snü حسنى var. of hüsn.
Hüt هوت only in Hüt dağı gibi very swollen (stomach, belly).

hütaf (.—) هتاف A lrnd. a calling out, an exclaiming.

hüthüt هدهد var. of hüdhüd.
Hüve هو A lrnd. God. h—si hüvesine*.
hüvelbaki (..——) هوالباقى A rel. formula written on tombstones God is the only eternal one.

hüvesi hüvesine هوسى هوسنه [hüve] colloq. exactly alike.

hüveyda (..—) هويدا P lrnd. evident, clear, manifest; conspicuous.

hüveynat (..—) هوينات A lrnd. microorganisms. —ı meneviye spermatozoa.

hüviyet هويت [Arabic .—.] •1. identity; character, essence. 2. colloq., same as hüviyet cüzdanı. 3. lrnd. divinity. — cüzdanı identity card, birth certificate. —ini ispat et= to prove one's identity. — varakası same as hüviyet cüzdanı.

hüyam (.—) هيام A lrnd. madness from love. —i rahm psych. nymphomania.

hüyük^gü هيوك A var. of höyük.
hüyyam (.—) هيام lrnd., pl. of haim.
hüzal^li (.—) هزال A lrnd. emaciation leanness. —i âsâb obs., path. neurasthenia.

hüzn حزن A lrnd., same as hüzün. —âmiz (.——) P, —âver (.—.) P, —efza (..—) P, —engiz (:.—) P sorrowful, sad.

hüzün^znü حزن [hüzn] sadness, sorrow, grief; melancholy. —len= to feel sad, to be grieved. —lü sad, gloomy; melancholic.

hüzzam (.—) هزام P Or. mus. one of the popular compound makams.

I

ı, I 1 *the eleventh letter of the alphabet.*
-ı 2, -i, -u, -ü, *after vowels* -yı, -yi, -yu, -yü *definite accusative, e. g.,* **adamı gördüm** *I saw the man. (Wherever the form is irregular, it is indicated in the dictionary.)*
-ı⁽ⁿⁱ⁾ 3 *etc., after vowels* -sı⁽ⁿⁱ⁾, *etc. (irregular:* **suyu**⁽ⁿᵘ⁾*) 3rd person possessive his, its, her, their, e. g.,* **kızı** *her daughter.*
-ı 4, *etc. archaic for* -a 9.
ıblık⁽ᵗⁱ⁾ ابرىق *archaic for* ımlık.
ıbt ابط *A lrnd.* armpit.
ıbtî (.—) ابطى *A anat.* axillary.
=ıcak, =icek, *after vowels* =yıcak, =yicek *archaic when, e. g.,* **varıcak** *when ... arrived, on arriving.*
=ıcı *etc. noun or adjective of agent, e. g.,* **kesici** *who cuts, that cuts,* **süpürücü** *who sweeps,* **yıkayıcı** *who washes.*
ıcık⁽ᵗⁱ⁾ cıcık⁽ᵗⁱ⁾ ايجيق جيجيق *colloq., only in* ıcığını cıcığını anla=, çıkar=, öğren= /ın/ *to get to the root (of a thing), to probe (a question).*
ıçkı ايچقى *same as* ışkı.
ıçkır=⁽ⁱʳ⁾ ايچقريمك *var. of* hıçkır=.
ıdhak⁽ᵏⁱ⁾ (.—) اضحاك *A lrnd.* a causing laughter.
ıdlâl⁽ˡⁱ⁾ (.—) اضلال *A lrnd.* a misleading, a leading astray; perversion. — et= /ı/ *to lead astray, to pervert.*
ığıl ığıl ايغل ايغل *gurgling softly, flowing gently.*
ığrıp⁽ᵇⁱ⁾ 1 ايغرب *Gk* large fishing net, trawl, seine. — kayığı *seine boat, trawler.*
ığrıp⁽ᵇⁱ⁾ 2 ايغرب *Gk prov.* way, manner; trick. — çevir= *to play a trick.*
ıh=⁽ᵃʳ⁾ 1 ايخمق *prov.* to kneel down (camel).

ıh 2 اخ *onomatop. for a sigh, heavy breathing from exhaustion* ah! —la= pıhla= *to breathe heavily, to groan.*
ıhlamur اخلامور *Gk* 1. linden tree, *bot.,* Tilia europaea. 2. tea made of dried linden blossoms. —giller *bot.,* Tiliaceae.
ıhlat=⁽ⁱʳ⁾ اخلاتمق *caus. of* ıhla=.
ıhtır=⁽ⁱʳ⁾ اخترمق /ı/ *caus. of* ıh= 1.
-ık 1 *etc., prov. for* -ız *etc., we are.*
=ık 2 يق *cf.* =k 2.
ıkab (.—) عقاب *A lrnd.* punishment; reward.
ıkar (.—) عقار *A lrnd., var. of* akar 4.
ıkaret (.—.) عقارت *A lrnd., var. of* akaret 2.
ıkd عقد *A lrnd.* necklace, string of beads or pearls. —i mufassal *necklace in which each bead or section is separated from the next by something of a different kind.* —i pervin *the Pleiades.* —i şebefruz *stars.* —i şeb ü rûz *time, the world, fortune.*
ıkıl ıkıl ايقل ايقل *only in* ıkıl ıkıl nefes al= *to gasp for breath.*
ıkın=⁽ⁱʳ⁾ ايقنمق *to grunt when making a great physical effort; to moan when constipated or in childbirth.* —a sıkına *grunting and moaning; with great effort.* —tı *great effort; a moaning, a sobbing.*
ıkla=⁽ʳ⁾ ايقلامق *to breathe with difficulty; to sigh, groan.* —ya sıklaya *with the greatest effort.*
ıklık⁽ᵗⁱ⁾ ايقليق *prov.* kind of three-stringed violin used in classical music.
ıklım tıklım ايقليم طيقليم *brimful, filled to overflowing.*
ıklim (.—) اقليم *var. of* iklim.

ıktifa (..—) اِقْتِفا lrnd. a going after, a following. — et= /a/ to follow. —en (..—́.) A /a/ following, in compliance (with).
=ıl= etc., after vowels =yıl= etc. 1. passive, e. g., kırıl= to be broken, yazıl= to be written. 2. reflexive, e. g., kırıl= to break (intr.), yazıl= to register (intr.). 3. impersonal verb form, e. g., oturuldu One sat down; people sat down; everybody sat down.
ıldırgıç prov. pretext; deceit, swindle.
ıldırım archaic for yıldırım.
ıldız prov., var. of yıldız.
ılga= prov. to gallop.
ılgar 1 1. prov. swift gallop. 2. archaic cavalry raid, incursion, foray. — et= archaic to make a raid.
ılgar= 2 prov. to germinate, sprout; to rise (sun, etc.).
ılgarcı archaic raider.
ılgıdır prov. reel or winder for skeining yarn.
ılgım prov. mirage.
ılgın 1 tamarisk, bot., Tamarix.
ılgın 2 prov., var. of ılgım.
ılgıt ılgıt prov. slowly, gently.
ılgız prov. reel for winding yarn.
ılı 1 prov., same as ılık. — su archaic bath.
ılı= 2 to grow lukewarm.
-ılı 3 cf. -lı 2.
ılıca 1 hot spring, health resort.
ılıca 2, ılıcak tepid, lukewarm.
ılık tepid, lukewarm. —ça slightly warm. —landır= /ı/ to make lukewarm. —laş= to become lukewarm. —laştır=, —lat= /ı/ to make lukewarm.
ılım neol., psych. temperance, moderation.
ılıman prov. 1. lukewarm water; warm spring or source. 2. mild (weather).
ılımlı neol., psych. temperate, moderate.
ılın= to grow lukewarm. —dır= /ı/ caus.
ılıştır=, ılıt= /ı/ to make tepid or lukewarm.
ılkı prov., var. of yılkı.
ılkıdır prov., var. of ılgıdır.
ılkıt ılkıt prov., var. of ılgıt ılgıt.
ılmık prov. newly growing crops.
-ım 1 cf. -m 1.
-ım 2 cf. -m 2.
-ım 3, etc., I am, e. g., hastayım I am sick. Osmanım I am Osman.
=ıma=, =ime=, =uma= 1, =üme=, after vowels, =yıma=, etc., archaic for =ama= 3.
-ımdır, etc. [-ım 3 + -dır] I am indeed, e. g., babanımdır I am indeed your father.
ımık prov. 1. mild weather. 2. place sheltered from the wind. 3. tepid water.
ımıl ımıl prov. slowly, gently.
-ımız cf. -mız (poss.).
ımızga= prov. to doze, to be half asleep. —n= 1. same as ımızga=. 2. prov. to be almost out (fire). —ndır= /ı/ caus. —nma halleri neol., psych. semi-hypnotic state.
ımızka= prov., var. of ımızga=.
ımlık prov. castrated, gelded (animal, man). — et=, —la= /ı/ to castrate. —lan= pass. —lat= /ı/ caus. of ımlıkla=.
-ımsı cf. -msı.
ımsık prov., var. of ımzık.
-ımtrak cf. -mtrak.
ımzık 1 prov. 1. sluggish, slovenly; shy. 2. spoiled, gone (food).
ımzık= 2 prov. to get spoiled (food).
-ın 1 cf. -n 4.
=ın 2 cf. =n 2.
-ın 3 etc., after vowels -nın etc. (exceptions: neyin, suyun) genitive, e. g., babamın my father's, of my father.
=ın 4 etc., after vowels =yın etc., imperative 2nd pers. pl., e. g., Selâmlaşın Greet each other.
-ın 5, after vowels -yın, etc., adverbial case, e. g., kışın in the winter, güzün in the autumn, dönüşün upon returning, ikindiyin in the afternoon.
-ın 6, after vowels -sın, etc., archaic for -ını (poss. 3rd pers. + accus.)
ınak archaic trustworthy, confidential (person).
=ınca, etc., after vowels =yınca, etc. when, as soon as; archaic until.
=ıncak, etc., after vowels =yıncak, etc., prov. for =ınca.
ıncalız wild bulb (used for pickles).
=ıncayadek, =inceyedek, =uncayadek, =ünceyedek, after vowels =yıncayadek, etc., archaic for =ıncaya kadar.
=ıncaya kadar, =inceye kadar, etc., after vowels =yıncaya kadar, etc. until.
=ıncaz, =incez, etc., after vowels =yıncaz, etc., prov. for =ınca.
-ıncı cf. -ncı.
ıncık prov. hard to please; extremely careful.
=ıncıya kadar var. of =ıncaya kadar.
ınçkır= archaic to hiccup, to sob.
-ındı 1 cf. -ndı.
=ındı 2, etc., prov. imperative 2nd pers. sing., e. g., bakındı Do look rarely after non-verbal stems, haydindi Hurry up.
ıngılda= prov. to move, stir.

ını اِنِى' cf. -ı 3.
ınık=ᵘʳ يِڭْشِر' /ı/ prov. to acquire a habit.
ınır=ᶦʳ ايكْرمه' prov. to bellow (camel).
ınız 1 ايكْز' cf. -nız.
=ınız 2, =iniz 2, etc., after vowels =yınız, etc., imperative 2nd pers. pl., e. g., Kalkınız Get up. Rise up.
ınnin (. —) ينّى A var. of innîn.
ınra=ʳ ايڭره' archaic to low, bellow.
-ıntı ىنتى cf. -ntı.
=ıp, etc., after vowels =yıp, etc., gerund of temporal succession, e. g., yırtıp attı Having torn it up he threw it away. He tore it up and threw it away.
ıpar ايپر' archaic musk.
ıpıla=ʳ, ıpılda=ʳ ايپيلدامق' prov. to gleam, glitter, twinkle.
ıpılık ايپيلڭ' lukewarm.
ıpıslak ايپصلاڭ' all wet.
ıpıssız ايپصز'quite deserted, desolate, entirely uninhabited.
=ır 1 cf. =r 2.
=ır=ᶦʳ 2, =ir=ᶦʳ, =ur=ᵘʳ, =ür=ᵘʳ, caus., e. g., kaçır= to let escape, bitir= to finish, doyur= to satiate, düşür= to cause to fall.
ır 3 اير' prov. song, tune.
ır=ᵃʳ 4 ايرمق' prov., same as ayır=.
ıra=ʳ ايرامق' prov. /dan/ to retire, to draw away (from).
ırak 1 ايراق' far, distant, remote; distance, remoteness.
Irak 2 عراق [Irak 3] Iraq. — çıbanı path. Baghdad boil, Aleppo button.
Irak 3 (. —) عراقى A lrnd. 1. same as Irak 2. 2. l. c., Or. mus. a very old compound makam. —ı Acem Persian Iraq, Media. —ı Arab Arabian Iraq, Babylonia, Chaldea.
Irakan (. — —), Irakeyn (. —.) عراقان A 1. the two countries of Iraq, e. g., Media and Babylonia. 2. early Isl. hist. Basra and Kufa.
Irakî (. — —) عراقى A pertaining to Iraq, Iraqi.
ıraklama neol. literature digression.
ıraklaş=ᶦʳ ايراقلشمق' /dan/ to become remote, to recede to a distance (from).
Iraklı عراقلى Iraqi.
ıraksak neol., math., phys. divergent.
ıraksama neol., math., phys. divergence.
=ırdı cf. =rdı.
ırgadiye ايرغاديه' obligation for a few days work; fee paid for such work.
ırgala=ʳ ايرغالامق' /ı/ to shake, move. —n= pass. —t= /ı/ caus. of ırgala=.
ırgan=ᶦʳ ايرغانمق'prov., same as ırgalan=.
ırgat¹, ᵈ¹ 1 ايرغات ارغاد' Gk day-laborer, workman. — başı foreman. — pazarı labor market, place where laborers collect to be hired.

ırgat¹, ᵈ¹ 2 ايرغات' Gk naut. capstan. — başı capstan head. — bedeni barrel. — tablası pawl rim.
ırgatlık ايرغاتلق' day labor; a day's wages.
ırgın ايرغين' prov. dropsical, weak; tired.
ırıl=ᶦʳ ايريلمق' prov., same as ayrıl=.
ırıp 1 ايريب' var. of ığrıp 1.
ırıp 2 ايريب' var. of ığrıp 2.
ırk عرق A 1. race. 2. lrnd. root; vein, artery; temperament, emotion. —ı ahmer American Indian. —ı asfer yellow race. —ı ebyaz white race. —ı esved black race. —ı gayret lrnd. a fit of zeal or jealousy. — kavgası race riot. —ı lifî lrnd. capillary vessel, capillary. —ı medenî med. Guinea-worm, zool., Filaria medinensis. —ı nâbız lrnd. artery. —ı sübatî lrnd. carotid artery. —ı übüvvet lrnd. fatherly affection. —an (..) A by race, racially. —bilim neol. the study of races.
ırkçı عرقچى racist. —lık racialism.
=ırken ايركن' cf. =rken.
ırkî (. —) عرقى racial.
ırkiyat (. .—) عرقيات A lrnd. the study of races.
ırkunnesa (. . . —) عرق النسا A lrnd. femoral artery; sciatica.
ırla=ʳ ايرلامق ايرلامه' prov. to sing. —ma song. —yıcı singer.
ırmak ايرماق ارماق' river. — ardıcı great reed warbler, zool., Acrocephalus arundinaceus. — çatalı phys. geog. fork of a river.
ırmık ايرميق' It naut. towrope.
=ırmış ايرمش' cf. =rmış.
=ırmışçasına ايرمشجسنه' cf. =rmışçasına.
=ırmış gibi ايرمش گبى' cf. =rmış gibi.
=ırsa ايرسه' cf. =rsa.
ırvasa ايروسه' prov., same as urasa.
ırz عرض A chastity, purity, honor. —ını boz= /ın/ to dishonor, to deflower (virgin). —ına dokun= /ın/ to touch the honor (of), to dishonor (woman). — düşmanı rapist. — ehli honest, virtuous; chaste (woman). —ına geç= /ın/ to violate, ravish, dishonor (woman). — gözet= to be careful of one's honor. —a tecavüz law violation, a dishonoring. —ına tecavüz et= /ın/ same as ırzına geç=.
ırza (. —) عرضا A same as irza.
ırzan (. .) عرضا A in regard to honor and chastity.
ırzlı عرضلى honest, virtuous; chaste.
ıs اس ايص' archaic, same as is 2.
ıs'ab (. —) اصعاب A lrnd. a making difficult.
ısabe (. .—) عصابه' var. of isabe.
ıs'ad (. —) اصعاد A lrnd. a causing to mount or ascend; an ascending.

=ısar, =iser, *after vowels* =yısar, =yiser *archaic, future* (he) will.

ısbı" اصبع [*Arabic* **asba**] *obs.* an old linear measure of about one inch.

ısda (.—) اصدا A *lrnd.* echo.

ısdar (.—) اصدار A *lrnd.* an issuing. — **et**= /ı/ to issue.

ısfa (.—) اصفا A *lrnd.* 1. a choosing, a selecting. 2. a being or becoming destitute.

ısfaf (.—) اصفاف A *lrnd.* a ranging in line or in series.

Isfahan (..—) اصفهان 1. *geog.* Isfahan. 2. P *Or. mus.* a very old compound **makam**.

Isfahanek[ki] (..—.) اصفهانك P *Or. mus.* a compound **makam** six centuries old.

ısfirar (..—) اصفرار A *lrnd.* a being or becoming yellow.

ısga اصغا A *lrnd.* 1. a listening. 2. an obeying. — **et**= /ı/ 1. to listen (to); to auscultate. 2. to obey.

ısgar (.—) اصغار A *lrnd.* a making small or contemptible.

ısgara (..'.) اصغارا [**ıskara**] *same as* **ızgara**.

ıshar (.—) اصهار A *lrnd.* a being or becoming related by marriage, generally as son-in-law or brother-in-law.

ısı *neol., phys.* heat; thermal; *geog.* hot, torrid. —**alan** *neol., chem.* endothermic, endothermal.

ısıcak[gı] اصيجان ايصيجان prov., var. of **sıcak**.

ısıl *neol., phys.* calorific, thermal. — **duyu** *physiol.* thermic sense.

ısıla=[r] ايصيلامق *prov.* /ı/ to warm, to heat.

ısın=[r] ايصينمق 1. to grow warm. 2. to warm oneself. 3. /a/ to become fond (of), to get accustomed (to). —**dır**= /ı, a/ *caus. of* **ısın**= 3. —**ma ısısı** *neol., phys.* specific heat.

ısıölçer *neol., phys.* calorimeter.

ısır=[ır] ايصيرمق اصرمه /ı/ to bite.

ısıran ايصيران *prov.* instrument to scrape dough out of a baker's trough.

ısırgan ايصرغان 1. stinging nettle. 2. which bites habitually, biter, snappy (animal). — **balığı** garfish, needle-fish. — **otu** stinging nettle, *bot.*, Urtica urens. —**giller** *neol., bot.*, Urticaceae.

ısırgı ايصيرغى *archaic* erysipelas.

ısırgın ايصيرغين *archaic* pimple, rash.

ısırıcı ايصيريجى who or which bites; biter; snappish.

ısırık[ğı] ايصيريك bite; sting.

ısırıl=[ır] ايصيريلمق *pass. of* **ısır**=.

ısırt=[ır] ايصيرتمق *caus. of* **ısır**=.

ısıt=[ır] ايصيتمق ايصتمق ايستمق to warm, to heat. —**ıl**= *pass.* —**ım** *neol.* a heating.

ısıtma ايصيتمه 1. a warming, a heating. 2. *prov.*, *same as* **sıtma**. —**lı** *prov.*, *same as* **sıtmalı**.

ısıttır=[ır] ايصيتديرمق /a, ı/ *caus. of* **ısıt**=.

ısıveren *neol., chem.* exothermic.

ıska اسقا *slang, only in* **ıska geç**= /ı/ to miss (aim); to ignore, to pay no attention (to).

ıskaça (.'.) اسقاجه It *naut.* step (of a mast). —**ya oturt**= /ı/ to step (a mast).

ıskala (.'.) اسقالا It *mus.* scale, gamut. — **yap**= to practise scales.

ıskalara, ıskalarya (...'.) اسقالاريه It *naut.* ratline, ratlin; port gangway of a man-of-war.

ıskanca (.'.) اسقانجه It *naut., only in* — **et**= /ı/ to relieve (from duty). — **vardiya et**= to relieve the watch.

ıskaparma (...'.) اسقاپارمه It *naut.* charter party.

ıskara (.'.) اسقارا Gk *same as* **ızgara**.

ıskarça (.'.) اسقارجه It *naut. and colloq.* crowded, packed.

ıskarlat اسقارلت It *obs.* scarlet cloth.

ıskarmoz اسقارموز Gk 1. *naut.* oarlock, thole, thole pin. 2. rib of a ship. 3. barracuda, *zool.*, Sphyraena sphyraena.

ıskarpa (.'.) اسقارپه It scarp; *mil.* escarpment.

ıskarpelâ (...'.) اسقارپله It *same as* **iskarpelâ**.

ıskarsa, ıskarso اسقارصه It *naut., same as* **ıskarça**.

ıskarta (.'.) اسقارطه It 1. *com.* waste. 2. discarded; discard (in card-playing). —**ya çıkar**= /ı/, — **et**= /ı/ to discard. — **mal** waste matter.

ıskat (.—) اسقاط A 1. alms given on behalf of the dead as compensation for their neglected religious duties. 2. *lrnd.* a throwing down, a dropping; a casting out; annulment; rejection, a dismissing. —**ı cenin** *med. or law* abortion. — **et**= *lrnd.* /ı/ to throw down, to drop; to cast out; to annul; to reject, to dismiss. — **parası** money or alms given on behalf of the dead.

ıskatçı اسقاطجى priest or beggar receiving alms given on behalf of the dead.

ıskona (.'.) اسقونه It *naut., same as* **uskuna**.

ıskonto (.'.) اسقونطو *var. of* **iskonto**.

ıskota (.'.) اسقوطه It *naut., same as* **uskuta**.

ısla=[r] اصلامق *prov., same as* **ıslat**=. —**dıl**= *same as* **ıslatıl**=.

ıslah (.—) اصلاح A 1. amelioration, betterment, correction; improvement, a redressing; reformation. 2. *math.* elimination. 3. *prov.* good; beautiful, nice. —**ı beyn et**= /ı/ *lrnd.* to reconcile. — **et**= /ı/ 1. to ameliorate, to better, to correct; to improve, to redress; to reform. 2. *math.* to eliminate. — **evi** reformatory. —**ı hal et**= to improve one's conduct. — **olmaz** incorrigible. —**ı zatülbeyn** *lrnd.* a reconciling two persons.

ıslahane (.—.) اصلاحخانه [**ıslahhane**] reformatory.

ıslahat (.—) اصلاحات A reform; improve

ment, betterment. — **fermanları** *Ott. hist.* imperial reform edicts. — **yap**= to make reforms.

ıslahatçı اصلاحاتچی reformer, renovator.

ıslahatperver (.——..) اصلاحات پرور P *lrnd.* pro-reform.

ıslahhane (.——.) اصلاح خانه P *lrnd.*, same as **ıslahane**.

ıslahî (.——) اصلاحی A *lrnd.* reformative; ameliorative.

ıslahpezir (.—.—) اصلاح پذیر P *lrnd.* admitting of improvement.

ıslak[¹] ایصلاق wet. — **karga** soaked to the skin; *slang* frightened, timid fellow. — **kargaya dön**= to get wet through; to become timid. —**lık** wetness, humidity, moisture.

ıslan=[ir] ایصلانمق to get wet, to be wetted.

ıslat=[ir] ایصلاتمق /ı/ 1. to wet; to soak (in water), to damp down (dry linen). 2. *colloq.* to cudgel, beat. —**ıl**= *pass.* —**tır**= /ı, a/ *caus. of* **ıslat**=.

ıslık[ġı] ایصلیق اصلی ایصلو اسلیو whistle, whistling sound. — **çal**= 1. to whistle; to hiss (snake, goose). 2. /a/ to hiss, to hoot (at), to give the bird (to). — **la çal** /ı/ to whistle (a tune). — **la**= /ı/ *same as* **ıslık çal**=². —**lı** *neol., phon.* sibilant.

ısmarla=[ir] ایسمارلامق /a, ı/ 1. to order (from); to book, to engage (seat, room). 2. to commend (to or to someone's care), to recommend (to). 3. to tell to do.

ısmarlama ایسمارلامه 1. ordered, made to order; *tailor., shoemaking* made to measure, custom made. 2. *verbal n.* — **elbise** custom-made suit.

ısmarlan=[ir] ایسمارلانمق *pass. of* **ısmarla**=.

ısmarlat=[ir] ایسمارلاتمق /ı, a/ *caus. of* **ısmarla**=.

ısmık[ġı] یصمیق *var. of* **ımsık**, **ımzık**¹.

ıspagula (.'...) اسپاغول *same as* **ıspavli**.

ıspanak[ġı] اسپاناق اسپنا اسپانه Gk 1. spinach, *bot.*, *Spinacia cleracea*. 2. *slang* imbecile, stupid. —**giller** *neol., bot., Chenopodiaceae*.

ısparçana, **ısparçına** (.'..) اسپارچینه اسپارچنه [**ısparçina**] *naut.* marline. — **bükümü** hawser-laid (rope). — **et**= /ı/ to serve (a rope) with marline. — **halatı** hawser-laid rope.

ısparmaça (...'.) اسپارماچه It *naut.* entanglement of several chains (in the sea).

ısparoz اسپاروز *same as* **ıspari**.

ıspati (.'.) اسپاتی *same as* **ıspati**.

ıspatulâ (..'.) اسپاتولا spatula, palette knife.

ıspavli (.'.) اسپاولی [**ıspagula**] *naut.* twine, kind of strong string.

ıspazmoz اسپازموز Gk spasm, convulsion.

ısplâta (.'.) اسپلاته Sl kind of river barge.

ısrar (.—) اصرار A insistence, persistence. — **et**= /da *or* üzerinde/ to insist (upon or on), to persist (in). —**la**= insistingly, persistently, emphatically, with emphasis.

ıssı اسی *prov.* warm, hot. — **dam** Turkish bath. — **sovuk** *archaic* good and bad days. — **vur**= /a/ to shine on (sun). —**lık** warmth, heat.

ıssız ایسیز اسن ابسز سوز lonely, desolate (place), uninhabited. —**lık** loneliness, desolation.

ıstabl[lı] اسطبل A *lrnd.* stable. —**i âmire** *Ott. hist.* the Imperial stables. —**i âmire müdiri** *Ott. hist.* the Grand Equerry. —**i âmire payesi** the rank of an Imperial equerry.

ıstağfurullah (.—...) استغفرالله *colloq.*, *var. of* **estağfurullah**.

Istahr اصطخر P *lrnd.* Persepolis.

ıstaka (.'..) استاقا [**isteka**] 1. billiard cue. 2. *bookbinding* folding-stick, folder.

ıstakoz استاقوز Gk lobster, *zool.*, *Homarus vulgaris*.

ıstampa (.'.) استامپه It 1. inkpad. 2. stamp, mark. — **resim** *fine arts* engraving, print.

ıstampaj استامپاج F *obs., var. of* **estampaj**.

ıstar استار Gk *prov.* loom.

ıstavroz استاورز استاوروس Gk 1. cross; crucifix. 2. sign of the cross. 3. *naut.* bunt gasket. — **çıkar**= to make the sign of the cross, to cross oneself. — **kemer** *arch.* cloister arch. — **mili** *auto.* differential pivot.

ıstıbah (..—) اصطباح A *poet.* a taking a morning drink.

ıstıbar (..—) اصطبار A *lrnd.* a being patient, an enduring.

ıstıca[aı] (..—) اضطجاع A *lrnd.* 1. a lying on one side. 2. a putting the breast to the ground in worship.

ıstıfa (..—) اصطفا A 1. natural selection. 2. *lrnd.* a choosing, a selecting. — **et**= /ı/ *lrnd.* to choose, to select. — **nazariyesi** theory of natural selection.

ıstıfaf (..——) اصطفاف A *lrnd.* getting lined up.

ıstıfaî (..——) اصطفائی A *psych.* elective.

ıstılah (..—) اصطلاح A 1. term, technical term; idiom. 2. pompous expression. — **parala**= to use precious expressions. —**at** (..——) A technical terms; terminology; expressions.

ıstılahî (..——) اصطلاحی A terminological.

ıstılahperdaz (..—.—) اصطلاح پرداز P *lrnd.* who uses pompous and precious language.

ıstına[aı] (..—) اصطناع A *lrnd.* 1. a selecting, a choosing. 2. a rearing, preparing, educating, bringing up.

ıstırap[bı] (..—) اضطراب [**ıztırab**] A suffering, affliction, pain, distress. — **çek**= to suffer. — **ver**= /a/ to cause pain (to), to hurt. —**lı** full of suffering, full of anguish; painful.

ıstırar (..—) اضطرار [**ıztırar**] compulsion, constraint; need. — **hali** case of necessity.

—ında kal= to have to, to be forced to; to have no alternative. —î (..— —) A necessary, compulsory.

ıstırlap^(bı) اطرلاب var. of usturlâb.

ıstiyad (..—) اصطياد A lrnd. a hunting.

ıstok^(ku) استوك E com. stock. — mal shopworn goods.

ıstor استور F roller blind, window shade. —lu yazıhane roll-top desk.

ısvad (.—) اصواد A lrnd. 1. tangle, maze. 2. mob.

=ış 1, etc., after vowels =yış, etc., verbal noun, e. g., geliş a coming.

=ış 2 cf. =ş=.

ışı=^r ايشيمق to grow light (dawn); to glow.

ışık^(ğı) ايشق 1. light; source of light. 2. archaic helmet. 3. archaic dervish. — al= phot. to be light-struck (film exposure). — aynası reflecting mirror, reflector; searchlight. — bacası arch. lantern. — bilgisi phys. optics, science of light. —a doğrulum neol., bot. phototropism. — göster= /a/ to show the way (to), to direct, to cast light on a subject. —a göster= /ı/ to hold up to the light. — işareti lighted signal. — karartma blackout. — oyunu luminous effect. — reklâmı lighted advertising, sky sign, electric sign. — saç= to emit, give out rays, to radiate, to shine. — serp= /a/ to diffuse light (over), to throw or shed light (upon). — tut= /a/ to show the way (to), to direct. —a tut= /ı/ to hold up to the light. — yılı light year. —göçüm neol., bot. phototaxy. —küre neol., astr. photosphere.

ışıklandır=^r ايشيقلندرمق /ı/ to illuminate, to light up.

ışıklı ايشيقلى illuminated, lighted up, bright. — reklâm lighted advertising, sky sign, electric sign.

ışıklık^(ğı) ايشيقلق arch. inner court, glass-roofed court.

ışıkölçer neol. photometer, light meter.

ışıksız ايشيقسز without light, unlit, dark.

ışıla=^r ايشيلامق 1. to shine, to sparkle, to flash, flare. 2. prov. to dawn.

ışılak^(ğı) ايشيلاق prov. bright, sparkling.

ışılda=^r ايشيلدامق to shine, gleam, sparkle, twinkle.

ışıldak^(ğı) 1. neol. searchlight, projector, spotlight. 2. prov. bright, sparkling.

ışıl ışıl ايشيل ايشيل sparkling; shining brightly.

ışıltı ايشيلتى brightness, flash, twinkle.

ışıma neol., phys. radiation. — ısısı radiant heat. — kuvveti emissivity.

ışın 1 neol., phys. ray; math. radius. — kırılması refraction.

ışın=^r 2 neol. to radiate, beam.

ışınım neol., phys. radiation.

ışınlı neol. radiant; radiate. —lar radiolarians, zool., Radiolaria.

ışk^(kı) عشق A lrnd., same as aşk. —baz (.—) P same as aşkbaz. —bazi (.— —) P same as aşkbazi.

ışkı ايشقى prov. curved paring knife with two handles.

ışkın ايشقين prov. tendril.

ışkır=^ır 1 ايشقيرمق obs. to whistle.

ışkır=^ır 2 ايشقيرمق obs., same as hıçkır=.

ışkırık^(ğı) ايشقيريق obs. earthen water whistle.

ışkırlak^(ğı) اشقرلاق 1. shadow-play pointed cap worn by Karagöz. 2. prov. hat, cap (for men). — kavuğu, — kavuk same as ışkırlak^1.

ışkî (.—) عشقى A lrnd., same as aşkî.

=ıt= cf. =t= 2.

ıtaret (.—.) عطارت A lrnd. business of a perfumer; perfumery.

ıtbak^(kı) (.—) اطباق A lrnd. a covering; a closing, a shutting.

ıtfe عطف A lrnd., var. of atfe.

ıtık^(tkı) عتق [ıtk] law manumission. —name (..—.) certificate of manumission.

ıtır^(trı) عطر [ıtr] 1. perfume, aroma, fragrance. 2. pelargonium. — çiçeği rose-geranium; pelargonium. —ı şah lrnd., — şahi sweet pea, bot., Lathyrus odoratus. — yağı attar of roses. — yaprağı an ornamental motif in Turkish decorative art. —cı perfumer. —lı aromatic, perfumed.

ıtk^(kı) عتق A cf. ıtık.

ıtla 1 (.—) اطلاء A lrnd. a smearing; an applying.

ıtla^aı 2 (.—) اطلاع A lrnd. an informing, information, notification.

ıtlak^(kı) اطلاق A lrnd. a setting free, liberation. — et= /ı/ 1. to set free. 2. to divorce, repudiate. 3. to call, to refer (to) as. — olun= pass.

ıtma^aı (.—) اطماع A lrnd. 1. temptation, a tempting. 2. incitement. 3. a satisfying — et= to tempt; to incite; to satisfy. —iyat (.— — —) A inciting speech.

ıtnab (.—) اطناب A literature prolixity, verbosity. — et= to be verbose. —lı prolix, verbose.

ıtnabe (.—.) اطنابه A lrnd. awning; shade tent.

ıtr عطر A lrnd., same as ıtır. —nâk (.—) P, —sa (.—) P lrnd. fragrant, perfumed.

ıtra (.—) اطراء A lrnd. a praising extravagantly, eulogy, panegyric. — et= /ı/ to eulogize.

ıtrab (.—) اطراب A lrnd. a gladdening, a rejoicing.

ıtrad (.—) اطراد A lrnd. expulsion, banishment. — et= /ı/ to expel, to banish.

ıtrah (. —) اطراح A *physiol.* excretion, elimination. — et= /ı/ to excrete, to eliminate.
ıtret عترت A *lrnd.* race, family, house, line.
ıtretünnebi (....—), ıtretüttahirin (... —. —) عترة النبى عترة الطاهرين A *lrnd.* the family of the Prophet Muhammad.
ıtrî 1 (. —) عترى A *lrnd.* pertaining to a stock or family, of the line of.
ıtrî 2 (. —) عطرى A *lrnd.* perfumed, aromatic, fragrant.
ıtriyat (. — —) عطريات A perfumes, perfumery. —çı perfumer.
ıtriyet (. —.) عطريت A *lrnd.* fragrance.
ıttıba (.. —) اقتبا A *lrnd.* a calling, invitation.
ıttılâ᷾ (.. —) اطلاع A *lrnd.* cognizance, information, knowledge. — hâsıl et= to get information. — husulü için for information. — kesbet= to obtain information.
ıttımal᷾ (.. —) اضمحلال A *lrnd.* a ceasing to exist, a disappearing.
ıtval᷾ (. —) ' اطوال A *lrnd.* prolongation.
ıvıl ıvıl ايول ايول *var. of* ığıl ığıl.
ıvır zıvır ايوير زيوير *colloq.* trifling, unimportant, nonsensical; trifles, nonsense.
=ıyor يور *cf.* =yor 3.
=ıyordu يوردى *cf.* =yordu.
=ıyorken يوركى *cf.* =yorken.
=ıyormuş يورمش *cf.* =yormuş.
=ıyormuşçasına يورمشجسينه *cf.* =yormuşçasına.
=ıyormuş gibi يورمش كبى *cf.* =yormuş gibi.
=ıyorsa يورسه *cf.* =yorsa.

-ız, *etc., after vowels* -yız, *etc., pl. of* -ım 3 we are, *e. g.*, buradayız We are here.
ızbandut^du ازبانذود It 1. huge and terrifying man. 2. *obs.* bandit, brigand. — gibi very strong and tall, giantlike. —luk *obs.* brigandage.
ızbarçına (..´.) ازبارچينه *var. of* ısparçana.
ızbarço (..´.) ازبارجو It *naut.* bowline hitch. — iskele bosun's chair.
ızd عضد A *lrnd., var. of* adud.
=ızdır, =izdir, =uzdur, =üzdür, *after vowels* =yızdır, *etc.* [-ız + dır, *pl. of* -ımdır] we are indeed, *e. g.*, memnunuzdur We are indeed glad.
ızdırap^bı (.. —) اضطراب *var. of* ıztırap.
ızgar ازغار *prov.* 1. stingy, greedy. 2. lazy.
ızgara (..´.) ازغاره [ıskara] 1. gridiron; grate; lattice, trellis; *naut.* ways. 2. grilled (meat, fish). —ya çek= /ı/ *naut.* to haul up on the ways (a ship). — çubukları the bars of a grating. — et= /ı/ *obs.* to grill. — işi grilled (meat or fish). — köfte, — köftesi grilled meat balls. — yap= /ı/, —sını yap= /ın/ to grill.
ızlâl᷾ (. —) اضلال A *lrnd., var. of* ıdlâl.
ızmam (. —) اضمام A *lrnd.* an adding, addition.
ızmar (. —) اضمار A *lrnd.* dissimulation. — et= /ı/ to cover up (one's feelings).
ızrar (. —) اضرار A *lrnd.* a harming. — et= /ı/ to harm, injure.
ıztırap^bı (.. —) اضطراب A *same as* ıstırap.
ıztırar (.. —) اضطرار A *same as* ıstırar

İ

i, İ 1 the twelfth letter of the alphabet.
-i 2 cf. **-ı 2**.
-i^ni 3 cf. **-ı 3**.
-i 4 cf. **-ı 4**.
-i 5 (—) ى P -colored, as in **filizî, gümüşî, nohudî**.
-î 6 (—) ى P lrnd., added to adjective to form abstract noun, as in, **serbestî**.
-î 7 (—) ى A lrnd. 1. after place names native of, e. g., **Irakî**. 2. after name of person descendant of, e. g., **Abbasî**. 3. after nouns, forms adjectives, as in **askerî**.
i= 8 only in **idi, imiş, ise**, and derived forms, **iken**, and, archaic, **idüği, idiği** to be.
i 9 ا archaic O!
iade (. —.) اعاده A 1. restoration, restitution; a returning, giving back; newspaper trade unsold copy returned to the publisher. 2. lrnd. repetition, a reiterating. **— et=** 1. /ı, a/ to give back, restore, return (to). 2. /ı/ lrnd. to repeat, reiterate. **—i hayat** med. revival. **—i itibar** law rehabilitation; restoration of one's credit. **—i muhakeme** law reopening of a case; revision of a judgment. **—i mücrimin** law extradition of criminals. **—i münasebet** dipl. reestablishment of relations. **—i sıhhat** recuperation, recovery. **—i sulh** reestablishment of peace. **—i ziyaret** a returning a visit.
iadeli اعاده لى reply paid (letter, etc.). **— taahhütlü** registered and reply paid (letter).
iane (. —.) اعانه A donation; lrnd. help, aid, assistance. **—i cihadiye** Ott. hist. supplementary tax imposed by the government in times of war. **— defteri** list of subscriptions or contributions. **— topla=** to collect contributions. **—i umumiye** Ott. hist. an extra tax imposed on government officials and merchants in 1852 in the effort to abolish paper money.
ianeten (. —'..) اعانةً A as a donation or help.
iare (. —.) اعاره A loan; law loan for use; a lending.
iaşe (. —.) اعاشه A a feeding; maintenance; civil or mil. adm. food supplies, commissariat. **— âmirliği**, **— dairesi** mil. commissariat department. **— et=** /ı/ to sustain, feed. **— ve ibate** board and lodging. **— kolu** mil. supply column. **— subayı** mil. mess officer.
iba (. —) ابا A lrnd. a refusing or neglecting to fulfill a command; refusal, noncompliance.
ibad 1 (. —) عباد A lrnd. 1. servants; servants of God; men. 2. worshippers.
ib'ad 2 (. —) ابعاد A lrnd. a removing to a distance, a driving away; an alienating.
ibadat (. — —) عبادات A lrnd., pl. of **ibadet**.
ibadet (. —.) عبادت A rel. worship, prayers, piety; act of worship, divine service.
ibadetgâh (. —.—) عبادتگاه P place of worship, sanctuary.
ibadethane (. —.—.) عبادتخانه P building consecrated to worship, sanctuary, temple, house of God.
ibadetkâr (. —.—) عبادتكار P lrnd. religious, devout. **—ane** (. —. — —.) P lrnd. devoutly. **—î** (. —. — —) P lrnd. piety; devotion.
ibadullah (. —..) عبادالله [Arabic . —.—] 1. servants of God; men. 2. colloq. a lot, a great many.
ibahat^ti, ibahe (. —.) اباحت A can. law 1. a rendering lawful. 2. religious libertinism.
ibahi (. — —) اباحى A lrnd. one who

believes in making prohibited things lawful.

ibakᵏı (. —) اِباق A *law* a running away, absconding (of a slave).

ibarat (. — —) عِبارات A *lrnd.*, *pl. of* **ibare**.

ibare (. —.) عِباره A passage, paragraph; formulation.

ibaret (. —.) عِبارت A /dan/ consisting (of), composed (of).

ibate (. —.) اِباته A *law* accommodation, lodging, housing; *mil.* billeting, quarters.

ibcalˡı (. —) اِبجال A *lrnd.* an honoring, a respecting.

ibda 1 (. —) اِبدا A *lrnd.* a producing, causing to begin.

ibdaᵃı **2** (. —) اِبداع A *lrnd.* invention, innovation. **—î** (. — —) A creative.

ibdalˡı (. —) اِبدال A *lrnd.* 1. change; conversion. 2. substitution.

iber 1 عِبر A *lrnd.*, *pl. of* **ibret**.

iber 2 عِبر A *lrnd.*, *pl. of* **ibre**.

ibgaz (. —) اِبغاض A *lrnd.* a hating, a loathing, a bearing hatred.

ibhac (. —) اِبهاج A *lrnd.* 1. a making joyful; exhilaration. 2. a being or becoming verdant (earth).

ibham 1 (. —) اِبهام A *lrnd.* thumb; big toe.

ibham 2 (. —) اِبهام A *rhet.* intended obscurity of expression, ambiguity. **—ı zihnî** *psych.* mental confusion.

ibibikᵇı ابيبيك *prov.* hoopoe.

ibikᵏı ابيك 1. comb (on a fowl's head); crest. 2. *anat.* crest, *crista*. 3. *archaic* hoopoe. **—ini kaldır=** *slang* to act defiantly. **—i yere dik=** to knuckle down. **—li** crested (bird).

ibinᵇnı اِبن *var. of* **ibn**.

İbiş اِبيش [*short for* **İbrahim**] 1. *name of the foolish servant in the* **Orta Oyunu** *theater*. 2. *l. c., colloq.* fool, idiot.

ibka 1 (. —) اِبقا A 1. a keeping, preserving, maintaining, retaining. 2. a pupil's failing to be promoted in his class. **— et=** /ı/ 1. to keep, preserve; to make permanent. 2. to maintain, retain (in its place); to confirm in his post (an official); not to promote (a pupil). **— fermanı** *Ott. hist.* Imperial edict (issued on the occasion of the anniversary of the Sultan's accession to the throne) that extended the terms of government officials. **— hil'ati** *Ott. hist.* robe of honor awarded every year to officials who maintained their positions.

ibkâ 2 (. —) اِبكا A *lrnd.* a making one weep.

ibkaen (. —.) اِبقاءً A *lrnd.* making permanent; maintaining; by way of permanency. **— intihab et=** /ı/ to reelect. **— nasbet=**, **— tayin et=** /ı/ to confirm in his former position (an official).

iblâğ (. —) اِبلاغ A a sending, communicating. **— et=** /ı, a/ 1. to send, deliver; to communicate (message). 2. to increase, raise, bring (a number, to).

iblis (. —) اِبليس A 1. *w. cap.* Satan, the Devil. 2. devil, demon, imp. 3. devilish, crafty man. **— tırnağı** (*lit.*, Satan's claw) onycha (an incense). **—âne** (. — —.) P devilish.

ibliskârane (. — — —.) اِبليسكارانه P *lrnd.* devilish, crafty.

ibn اِبن A *lrnd.* son. **—i amm** son of a paternal uncle, cousin. **—i arz** stranger; traveler. **—i haram** bastard. **—i harb** man of war, veteran, warrior. **—i helâl** legitimate son. **—i hürre** upright and decent man. **—i irs** weasel. **—i leyl** thief. **—i müzne** the moon peeping through a cloud. **—i sebil** traveler. **—i tarik** 1. traveler. 2. *myst. orders* dervish. 3. robber, highwayman. **—i tıyn** Adam. **—i üsbueyn** 1. the full moon. 2. moonfaced beauty. **—i vakt** timeserver; opportunist; sycophant. **—i yevm** one who has no care for the morrow; improvident; thoughtless.

ibne اِبنه A 1. catamite. 2. *lrnd.* daughter.

ibnetor اِبنه تور *slang* catamite.

ibnetülcebel اِبنة الجبل A *lrnd.* (*lit.* daughter of the mountain) echo.

ibra (. —) اِبرا A an acquitting, absolving. **— et=** /ı/ 1. to declare free from obligation, to discharge (a debt); to pass (accounts). 2. *lrnd.* to restore to health. **— kâğıdı** certificate of discharge, receipt. **—i zimmet** the discharge of a debt or obligation.

ibrad (. —) اِبراد A *lrnd.* a cooling.

İbrahim (. — —.) اِبراهيم [*Arabic* . — —] A Abraham. **— dikeni** field eryngo, *bot., Eryngium campestre;* sea eryngo, sea holly, *bot., Eryngium maritimum.*

İbrail اِبرائيل *geog.* Braila.

ibram (. —) اِبرام A a dwelling insistently upon (a request or command). **— et=** *lrnd.* to insist, to be overpersistent.

ibraname (. — —.) اِبرانامه P same as **ibra kâğıdı**.

İbranî (. — —) عِبرانى A Hebrew. **—ce** the Hebrew language; in Hebrew.

ibraz (. —) اِبراز A a showing, presentation. **— et=** /ı/ to show; to present (bill, account book, document, identification card).

ibre اِبره A 1. needle of an instrument, pointer; magnetic needle; *lrnd.* needle. 2. *bot.* style. 3. *lrnd.* sting (of a bee or scorpion); slander, calumny. **—i havam** *lrnd.* sting of a bee or scorpion, etc. **—nin inhitatı** dip of the needle (of a compass). **—i mıknatısiye** magnetic needle.

ibret عِبرت A 1. warning, example, admonition. 2. strange, ridiculous. **bir —!** Ridiculous!

— al= to take warning. —i âlem için so that it may be a warning to others. — gözü ile bak= to take something as a warning or a lesson. —in kudreti horrible and hideous. — ol= /a/ to be a lesson or an example to. —âmiz (.. ——) P lrnd. exemplary, offering a warning. —bahş P lrnd. exemplary. —bin (.. —) P lrnd. susceptible to a warning, impressed by an example.

ibreten (.'..) عِبْرَة lrnd. as an example that deters. — lissairin lrnd. as a deterrent to others.

ibretenduz (... —) عبرتاندوز P lrnd. 1. exemplary. 2. wonderful.

ibretnüma (... —) عبرتنما P lrnd. exemplary.

ibretpezir (... —) عبرت پذیر P lrnd. taking warning or example; warned, admonished.

ibrevî (.. —) اِبْرَوِي A anat. styloid. —ye (.. —.) bot., Geraniaceae.

ibri 1 (. —) اِبْرِي A bot. styloid.

İbri 2 (. —) عِبْرِي A lrnd. Hebrew, Hebraic.

ibrik^ği 1 اِبْرِيق [Arabic .—] water ewer with handle and long spout, used for ablutions, etc.; ewer, teapot, kettle.

ibrik^ği 2 اِبْرِيق It naut. brig, brigantine.

ibrikdar (. ——) اِبْرِيقدار P Ott. hist. official whose duty was to superintend the Sultan's ablutions.

ibriksi neol., anat. arytenoid.

ibrişim اِبْرِيشم [ebrişem] silk thread. — kurdu obs. silkworm. —ci maker or seller of silk thread.

ibriz (. —) اِبْرِيز A lrnd. pure gold. —î (. ——) A quite pure, fine (gold).

ibsar (. —) اِبْصَار A lrnd. a looking; a seeing, perceiving.

ibşar (. —) اِبْشَار A lrnd. 1. a causing joy, giving joy. 2. a rejoicing at good news.

ibta (. —) اِبْطَاء lrnd. 1. a delaying. 2. slowness, tardiness, lateness.

ibtal^lı (. —) اِبْطَال A same as iptal.

ibtar (. —) اِبْتَار A lrnd. 1. cutting off, severing. 2. docking (tail). 3. rendering childless (man). 4. deciding; cutting short (matter). 5. performing one's devotions when the sun is just above the eastern horizon.

ibtat (. —) اِبْتَات A lrnd. 1. a cutting off or through, severing, lopping. 2. a making final and definitive (act).

ibtida^aı 1 (.. —) اِبْتِدَاء A lrnd. 1. invention, creation. 2. innovation.

ibtida 2 (.. —) اِبْتِدَا A same as iptida. —i dâhil Ott. hist. third grade in the medresse system. —i haric Ott. hist. lowest grade in the medresse system. —i semt astr. the east or west point of the horizon; the prime vertical; the north or south point of the horizon; the meridian. —i zuhur lrnd. the beginning, the first appearance of a thing.

ibtidai (.. ——) اِبْتِدَائِي A same as iptidai. —yat (.. ————) A lrnd. the beginnings.

ibtidar (.. —) اِبْتِدَار A lrnd. a setting to work (on something).

ibtiga (.. —) اِبْتِغَاء A lrnd. a longing and seeking for (a thing).

ibtihac (.. —) اِبْتِهَاج A lrnd. a being joyful; joy, gladness, exaltation.

ibtihal^lı (.. —) اِبْتِهَال A lrnd. a humbling oneself in prayer, a supplicating.

ibtihas (.. —) اِبْتِهَاس A lrnd. a search, investigation.

ibtikâ (.. —) اِبْتِكَاء A lrnd. a weeping.

ibtikâr (.. —) اِبْتِكَار A lrnd. 1. a rising early; an arriving in the morning. 2. a coming to public worship in time. 3. a taking the first fruits. 4. defloration. 5. primiparity.

ibtilâ 1 (.. —) اِبْتِلَاء A same as iptilâ.

ibtilâ^aı 2 (.. —) اِبْتِلَاع A lrnd. a swallowing.

ibtilâl^lı (.. —) اِبْتِلَال A lrnd. 1. a being moistened; a becoming damp. 2. a becoming strong and vigorous, recovering health.

ibtina (.. —) اِبْتِنَاء A lrnd. a building, constructing; construction.

ibtinaen (.. —.) اِبْتِنَاءً A /a/ depending (on), by reason (of), e. g., buna ibtinaen consequently.

ibtisam (.. —) اِبْتِسَام A lrnd. a smiling.

ibtisar (.. —) اِبْتِصَار A lrnd. a perceiving, having insight into.

ibtiya^aı (.. —) اِبْتِيَاع A lrnd. a purchasing, buying; purchase.

ibtizal^lı (.. —) اِبْتِذَال A same as iptizal.

İbtülcevza (... —) اِبْط الجوزاء A astr. Betelgeuze.

ibzal^lı (. —) اِبْذَال A lrnd. a giving lavishly and freely, openhandedness. — et= to give without stint.

ica^aı (——) اِيجَاع A lrnd. a causing pain; a hurting; a tormenting.

i'cab 1 (. —) اِعْجَاب A lrnd. a causing surprise.

icab 2 (——) اِيجَاب A same as icap. — et= 1. to be necessary. 2. /ı/ to necessitate, require. — ettir= /ı/ to necessitate, require.

icabat (———) اِيجَابَات A lrnd. requirements, exigencies.

icaben (———.) اِيجَابًا A lrnd. necessarily.

icabet (. —.) اِجَابَت A 1. an answering favorably, accepting (prayer, request, etc.), acceptance. 2. an answering (question, etc.), reply. — et= /a/ 1. to accept (invitation). 2. accede (to a request). —i mekrun lrnd. accepted, acceptable (prayer).

icabî (———) اِيجَابِي A lrnd. affirmative (proposition).

icabiye (— — —.) اِيجابِيّه A obs., phil. determinism.

icad (— —) اِيجاد A a creating; an inventing; creation; production; invention; innovation. **— çıkar=** to start innovations, to abandon a good habit. **— et=** /ı/ 1. to invent; to produce, to create. 2. to trump up, to fabricate. **—î** (— — —) A phil. heuristic.

icadkerde (— — ..) اِيجادكرده P lrnd. invention.

i'cal^{li} (. —) A, **ical**^{li} (— —) اِعجال A lrnd. a hurrying, hastening.

icale (. —.) اِجاله A lrnd. a causing to turn round, circle, revolve. **— et=** to set in circular motion, to make go round. **—i fikir** a pondering over (a thing).

icalet (. —.) عجالت A lrnd. 1. a thing done in haste. 2. manual, handbook. **—en** (. —´..) A in haste; instantly.

i'cam 1 (. —) اِعجام A lrnd. 1. a dotting a letter of the Arabic alphabet. 2. a being unidiomatic or ungrammatical.

İcâm 2 (. —) اِعجام A lrnd., var. of **Acâm**.

icap^{bı} (— —) اِيجاب [icab 2] 1. a rendering necessary; a necessitating; a requiring; demand. 2. log. an affirming, affirmation. 3. law a making a first offer concerning a contract. 4. theol. an acting so as to deserve (heaven or hell). **—ında** in case of necessity; when required. **—ına bak=** /ın/ 1. to do what is necessary. 2. colloq. to do away with (him). **— ve kabul** law offer and acceptance. **—ı maslahat** as fits the requirements, in accordance with circumstances. **—ı var** It is needed, wanted, necessary.

icar (— —) اِيجار A law rent; a letting; a hiring. **— et=** /ı/ to let out; to hire, to lease. **— ve iare kanunu** int. law Lend-Lease Act. **—a ver=** /ı/ to lease.

icarat (. — —) اِجارات A lrnd., pl. of **icare**.

icare, icaret (. —.) اِجاره A lrnd. 1. rent, hire. 2. rent paid to the Vakf or the Government.

icat^{dı} (. —) اِيجاد var. of **icad**.

icaz 1 (— —) اِيجاز A lrnd. an abridging, abridgement; conciseness, terseness; brevity. **—ı hasr** saying a great deal in a few words. **—ı muhil** abbreviating something to obscure the meaning. **— yoluyla** in brief.

i'caz 2 (. —) A, **icaz** (— —) اِعجاز lrnd. 1. a rendering weak; a baffling; a frustrating. 2. a being baffled or frustrated; impotence; incapacity. 3. miracle, marvel.

icâzâne (— — —.) اِيجازانه P lrnd. brief, terse; laconic.

icazet (. — .) اِجازت A 1. a giving permission; authorizing, legalizing; authorization; certificate, diploma. 2. permission; law ratification. **— al=** /dan/ archaic 1. to acquire a diploma. 2. to ask for permission. **— ver=** /a/ archaic 1. to give a certificate or diploma (to). 2. to grant permission. **— ruusu, — tezkeresi** Ott. hist. certificate or diploma granted by a medresse to a graduate to teach or act as a teacher. **— ver=** /a/ archaic 1. to give a certificate or diploma (to).

icazetname (. — . — .) اِجازتنامه P Ott. hist. diploma (given by a medresse; authorization to teach.

i'cazkâr (. — —) اِعجازكار P lrnd. awe-inspiring work, miraculous act; wonderworker. **—âne** (. — — —.) P wonderously, miraculously. **—î** (. — — —) P miraculousness.

i'caznüma (. — . —) اِعجازنما P lrnd. wonderworker.

icbar (. —) اِجبار A a compelling, constraining, forcing; pressure, compulsion. **— et=** /ı/ to compel, to force (one to do something).

iccas (. —) اِجّاص A lrnd. plums, plum, bot., prunus.

=icek ـيجك cf. **=ıcak**.

ichar (. —) اِجهار A lrnd. 1. a showing, a manifesting openly (a thing), a revealing. 2. a speaking clearly, publishing. 3. a making audible (voice, word or letter); recitation. **— et=** /ı/ 1. to show, manifest openly. 2. to say out loud.

=ici ـيجى cf. **=ıcı**.

-icik^{ği} **cicik**^{ği} ـيجيك جيجيك var. of **ıcık cıcık**.

icl اِجل A obs., med. wryneck, torticollis; stiff neck.

iclâ (. —) اِجلاء A lrnd. 1. a banishing, an exiling (person). 2. a cleaning, polishing, furbishing up (a thing). **—i vatan** expatriation, exile from home.

iclâl^{li} (. —) اِجلال A lrnd. 1. an honoring, magnifying, exalting. 2. a feeling and showing the greatest awe and veneration (for), reverence. 3. magnificence, greatness; glory. **—î** (. — —) A 1. pertaining to magnificence, magnificent, glorious. 2. precious, worthy.

iclâs (. —) اِجلاس A lrnd. 1. an enthroning, enthronment. 2. a making (one) sit down. **— et=** /ı/ 1. to enthrone (a king). 2. to seat (person).

icma'^{aı} (. —) اِجماع A lrnd. 1. a collecting, putting together (things). 2. a putting in order, setting straight, arranging (a matter). 3. an agreeing (on a matter); concurrence; agreement. 4. meeting, concord, convocation. **—i ümmet** can. law the general concurrence and agreement in opinion and decision of the legalists.

icmaen (. —´.) اِجماعاً can. law as a consensus (on religious matters).

ıcmal[ii] (. —) اِجْمَالٍ A 1. a summing up, summary, resumé, précis, synopsis; an adding up (accounts). 2. *lrnd., math*. addition. **— et=** /ı/ to summarize; to sum up. **—en** (. —´.) A briefly, as a summary. **—î** (. — —) A *lrnd*. summarized.

icra (. —) اِجْرَاء ,اِجْرَا A 1. a doing, performing (a thing). 2. an executing; execution; a carrying out; a practicing. 3. *art* performance; a playing (musical instrument). 4. a making or letting take its course (event). 5. *lrnd*. a making or allowing to flow freely (water, etc.). **— başlangıcı** *law* commencement of execution. **— dairesi** Court-bailiff's office. **— emri** *law* execution warrant, enforcement order. **— et=** /ı/ 1. to execute, carry out; practice; to do, perform; to work, to act. 2. to play (musical instrument). 3. *lrnd*. to make flow or run. **— hâkimi** court bailiff; executive judge. **— heyeti** 1. executive board, executive committee. 2. *mus.* performers. **— kuvveti** executive power. **— memuru** bailiff. **İ— Vekilleri Heyeti** *pol*. the Cabinet. **—ya ver=** /ı/ to refer to the court bailiff.

icraat (. — —) اِجْرَاآت A 1. activities; achievements; acts. 2. operations, performances. 3. judicial acts. 4. affairs, deeds.

icraî (. — —) اِجْرَائِي A executive. **— haciz** *law* attachment, seizure, distraint. **— karar** *law* executive decision.

ictiba (. . —) اِجْتِبَاء A *lrnd*. 1. a choosing, electing, selecting. 2. a collecting (money).

ictihad (. . —) اِجْتِهَاد A 1. *law* jurisprudence; doctrine. 2. *lrnd*. a striving, exerting oneself, doing one's utmost, using one's best endeavors. 3. interpretation; opinion, conviction. **— kapısı kapandı** There is no longer any room for innovation (in establishing a religious precedent). **—at** (. . — —) A *pl*.

ictima[aı] (. . —) اِجْتِمَاع A 1. *same as* **içtima**. 2. *astr*. conjunction. **—i süflâ** *astr*. inferior conjunction. **—i ülya** *astr*. superior conjunction. **—at** (. . — —) A *pl. of* **ictima**.

ictimaî (. . — —) اِجْتِمَاعِي A *same as* **içtimaî**.

ictina (. . —) اِجْتِنَاء A *lrnd*. 1. a gathering, picking (fruit), plucking. 2. an obtaining.

ictinab (. . —) اِجْتِنَاب A *lrnd., same as* **içtinap**.

ictira (. . —) اِجْتِرَاء A *lrnd*. a venturing, daring; a bold, audacious act.

ictisar (. . —) اِجْتِسَار A *lrnd*. a daring, venturing. **— et=** to take the liberty (of); to dare (to).

ictizab (. . —) اِجْتِذَاب A *lrnd*. 1. a being attracted to. 2. a gathering around (someone).

iç 1 اِچ 1. the inside of anything, interior; inner substance, lining. 2. heart, mind. 3. in... ...ner 4. kernel, pulp. 5. the inside story (of a matter). 6. the internal parts, guts, intestines, stomach, offal. **—imde** within me. **—inden** from within you, him, her, it. **—ine** into him, her, it, you. **—ler** 1. the inner parts. 2. heart; soul. **—ler acısı** tragic, heart-rending. **—ten*.** **— aç=** to set at ease, to cheer up. **— açı** *neol., geom*. interior angle. **— açıcı** pleasant, heart-warming. **— açıl=** to feel relieved, to be cheered up. **— ağası** *Ott. hist*. a valet that serves in the reception room. **—ine al=** /ı/ to include, to contain, encompass. **—i alma=** /ı/ not to feel like eating. **—ine at=** /ı/ to endure in silence, to stomach. **— bağla=** to fill out pulp or kernel (fruit, etc.). **—e bakış** *neol., psych*. introspection. **— bakla** shelled broad beans. **— başkalaşım** *neol., geol*. endomorphism. **—i bayıl=** to feel faint (with hunger, etc.). **—ini bayılt=** /ın/ to make one feel sick (oversweet food). **—i beni yakar dışı eli yakar** He is not all that he appears to be. He looks attractive to those who do not know him personally. **— bezelye** shelled peas. **—ini boşalt=** to make a clean breast of it. **—i bulan=** to feel nauseated. **— bulantısı** nausea. **— bükey** *neol., geom*. concave. **—ine çakıl kaçmış** worried, restless. **— çamaşırı** underclothing. **— çek=** 1. to sigh. 2. to sob. **—i çek=** /ı/ to have a longing for, to desire. **—ini çek=** to sigh. **—i çıfıt çarşısı** evil-minded. **—inden çık=** /ın/ to accomplish, to be able to do. **—inden çıkama=** /ın/ to be unable to settle (something). **—i çürük** suspicious. **— daire** *neol., geom*. inscribed circle. **—i dar** impatient, restless (person). **— deniz** inland sea. **—ine dert ol=** to have a troubled feeling (about something). **— deri** *neol., biol*. endoderm. **—i dışı bir** sincere, open-hearted. **—inden doğ=** to have a sudden impulse (to do something). **—ine doğ=** to have a presentiment. **— donu** men's underpants. **—ini dök=** to unburden oneself, to pour out one's troubles; to make a clean breast of it. **—i dön=** to be nauseated. **—e dönük** *neol., psych*. introvert. **—e dönüş** *neol., psych*. introversion. **— edik** *archaic* soft slippers worn inside shoes. **— ek** *neol., gram*. infix. **—i eri=** to be greatly worried. **— et=** /ı/ *colloq*. to keep for one's own use without the knowledge of the owner. **—ine et=** /ın/ *vulg*. to soil, to spoil. **— etkinlik duyumu** *neol., psych*. kinesthesia. **— ezan** repetition of the call to prayer inside the mosque at the Friday noon prayer. **—i ezil=** to feel hungry. **—i fesat** who always takes things the wrong way. **— fesi** *obs*. an underfez. **—i geç=** to doze. **—inden geç=** 1. /ın/ to pass (through). 2. to occur to one. **— geçir=** to sigh. **—inden geçir=** /ı/ to occur to one to think (about something). **—i geçmiş** 1. worn out (with age). 2. overripe (fruit). **—ten gelme** heartfelt, sincere. **—i geniş** easygoing, unworried. **—e git=** to lose (money, game, etc.). **—i git=** to desire strongly, to be very anxious to have. **— göbek** *neol., biol.* chalaza. **— gömleği** undershirt. **—i götürme=** to be unable to bear. **—i göyün=** *archaic* to feel troubled, to suffer. **— güdü** *neol., psych.* instinct. **—i gül=** to rejoice inwardly, to smile secretly. **—inden gül=** to mock somebody inwardly. **— güvey, — güveyisi** man who lives with his wife's parents. **— güveyisinden hallice** (*lit.* little better off than a man living with his wife's parents) not too well, so so. **— halkı** *Ott. hist.* the service staff of the Sultan's palace. **— hizmet** *mil.* home service. **— içe** one within the other; one opening into another (room); one inside the other; *geom.* concentric. **—ten içe** 1. secretly, underhandedly. 2. to the innermost recesses. **—i içine bat=** to be sorry (about something). **—i içine sığma=** to be bubbling over with excitement; to feel very restless or impatient. **—i içini ye=** to feel worried (about being unable to do something). **—ine işle=** 1. to feel deeply (words, etc.). 2. to get thoroughly soaked (rain). **İ— İşleri** Home Affairs, Internal Affairs. **—i kabar=** 1. to feel nauseated. 2. to be moved. **—i kabul etme=** not to feel like eating. **— kale** citadel. **—i kalk=** 1. to have a feeling of nausea. 2. to be moved. **—i kan ağla=**, **—inden kan git=** to be deeply grieved, to be in great sorrow. **—i kapan=** /ın/ to feel depressed. **—e kapanık** *neol., psychol.* introvert. **—e kapanış** *neol., psychol.* autism. **—i kara** hard-hearted; evil-minded, blackhearted. **— karakol** *mil.* security force. **—i karar=** to be dismayed, to feel hopeless. **— karinası** *naut.* keelson. **—i kazın=** to feel very hungry. **—ini kemir=** to be consumed with anxiety, etc. **—ine kurt düş=** to have a gnawing suspicion; to suspect. **—ini kurt ye=** to be in a continual state of anxiety. **— lâstik** *auto.* inner tube. **— lenf** *anat.* endolymph. **— mehteri** *Ott. hist.* indoor servant or chamberlain at the Sultan's palace. **— merkez** *biol.* hypocentrum, intercentrum. **— muhacim** *football* inside forward, inner. **— oğlanı** *Ott. hist.* 1. page in the Sultan's palace. 2. youth educated for service at court. **—inden oku=** 1. to read to oneself. 2. *slang* to swear under one's breath (at somebody). **— organlar** *anat.* internal organs, viscera. **—e oyna=** *slang* to be lost. **—ime öyle geliyor ki** I feel as though, I have a presentiment (something is going to happen). **—i paralan=**, **—i parçalan=** to be greatly moved (by someone's suffering). **—inden pazarlıklı** hypocritical, two-faced. **— pilâv** pilaf prepared with liver, butter, currants, and nuts. **— piyasa** *com.* home market. **— plazma** *biol.* endoplasm. **—ine sıç=** /ın/ *vulg.* to spoil utterly. **— sık=** to annoy; to be tedious or dull. **— sıkıcı** wearisome; boring; dull, tedious. **—i sıkıl=** to feel bored. **— sıkıntısı** boredom. **—ine sin=** 1. to feel at ease or happy. 2. /ın/ to permeate, seep into (smell, etc.). **— sular** inland rivers and lakes. **—i sür=** to have diarrhea. **— tepi** *neol., psych.* impulsion. **—i tez** energetic; hustler; impatient. **— ticareti** home trade. **—i titre=** 1. to set one's heart on. 2. to be very concerned (about somebody's health, etc.). **—ine tükür=** /ın/ *slang* to spoil (a matter, etc.). **— tüzük** *neol.* standing orders (parliament), house regulations, rules. **—i vık vık et=** *colloq.* to be very impatient. **— yağı** suet. **—i yağ bağla=** to feel happy. **—inin yağı eri=** to pine away with anxiety or sorrow. **—i yan=** 1. to be deeply grieved (with pity or anxiety). 2. to be very thirsty. **— yarıçap** *geom.* apothem. **— yürek zarı** *neol., anat.* endocardium. **— yüz** the inside story, the real truth; the inner meaning. **— zar** *bot.* intine.

iç=[er] 2 بَحْلَك ' 1. to drink. 2. to smoke. 3. to absorb, imbibe (fluid). 4. to drink (alcohol habitually). **—tikleri su ayrı gitmez** They are very close friends.

içecek[ği] بَحْلَك اِيَجَك ' beverage, drink; drinkable. **— su** fresh water, drinking water.

içegü يَجَكو ' *archaic* internal organs (of the body).

içer=[ir] 1 بَحْلَك ' /ı/ *slang* to beat, to thrash.

içer=[ir] 2 *neol., log.* /ı/ to imply.

içerde ايْچَرده ' *var.* of **içeride**.

içerden ايْچَرده ن ' *var.* of **içeriden**.

içeri ايَجَرو ايَجَرى ' 1. inside; interior, inner part. 2. heart; conscience; mind. **—de** 1. inside, within. 2. in prison. 3. losing; in debt. **—den** from within, from the inside. **—si** the interior of. **—ye** to the inside. **— buyurun**, **—ye buyurun** Walk in; please come in. **— daire** inner circle. **— dal=** to walk right in; to plunge in. **— düş=** 1. to fall in. 2. *slang* to go to jail. **— gir=** 1. to go in, to enter. 2. to go to prison. 3. to lose (in trade); to be losing (in a game). **—de ol=** to lose (in trade). **— tep=**, **— vur=** to go deep (disease).

içerik[ği] *neol., log.* implicit.

içerle=[r] يَجَرْلَه ' /a/ to be annoyed (with), to resent.

içerlek[ği] يَجَرْلَك ' set back (house); secluded.

içerme · *neol., log.* implication.

içersi يَجَرْسى ' *var.* of **içerisi**.

içgil يَجْگِل ' *archaic* malice, secret hate.

içil=ᶦʳ ايچيلمك pass. of iç= 2.
içim ايچيم 1. the quantity drunk down at a gulp; mouthful. 2. taste. bir — su very beautiful, lovely (woman). bir — suya git= to go for next to nothing.
içimli ايچيملى pleasant to drink; agreeable to the taste.
için ايچون 1. for; on account of; by reason of; out of consideration for, e. g., bunun için for this reason, senin için geldim I came for you, onun için for his sake, on account of him. 2. in order to, e. g., bu işi yapmak için gece gündüz çalıştım I worked day and night to get this done. 3. so that, e. g., mes'ut olmanız için so that you may be happy.
içindeleme neol., log. inclusion.
içindelik⁽ᵍⁱ⁾ neol. phil. spontaneity.
için için ايچين ايچين 1. secretly; imperceptibly. 2. internally. — ağla= to weep inwardly.
içir=ᶦʳ ايچيرمك /1, a/ caus. of iç= 2.
içiş ايچيش verbal n. of iç= 2.
içitim neol., med. injection.
içki ايچكى intoxicating drink, liquor; drink. —ye düşkün addicted to drink. — iç=, — kullan= to drink (habitually). — yasağı prohibition of alcoholic beverages.
içkili ايچكيلى 1. offering alcoholic beverages (restaurant). 2. intoxicated.
içkin neol., phil. immanent.
içlem neol., log. comprehension.
içlen=ᶦʳ ايچلنمك to be emotionally affected; to take to heart.
içli ايچلى 1. having an inside, kernel, pulp, etc. 2. sensitive; touchy. 3. emotional; sad, hurt. — dışlı intimate, familiar.
içlik⁽ᵍⁱ⁾ ايچليك 1. pertaining to the inside, interior. 2. prov. undershirt; shirt, blouse.
içme ايچمه 1. verbal n. of iç= 2. 2. usu. pl. mineral spring. — suyu fresh water, drinking water.
içre ايچره archaic 1. in, within; interior. 2. among, amongst.
içrek⁽ᵍⁱ⁾ neol., phil. esoteric.
içsel neol., psych. internal.
içten ايچدن 1. from within. 2. sincere, friendly, from the heart, intimate. — konuşma psych. inner (speech). —lik sincerity.
içtihad (..—) var. of ictihad.
ictimaᵃⁱ (..—) اجتماع [ictima] a gathering, meeting, coming together; assembly, general meeting. — hürriyeti law right of public assembly; freedom of meeting.
ictimaî (..——) اجتماعى [ictimaî] social. — devir astr. revolution. (Other astr. meanings under ictima). — ilimler social sciences. — kesafet social density.

ictimaileş=ᶦʳ اجتماعيلشمك to become social, to adapt oneself to community life.
ictimaiyat (..———) اجتماعيات A sociology, social sciences.
ictimaiyun (..———) اجتماعيون A sociologists.
ictinapᵇⁱ (..—) اجتناب [ictinab] a refraining, abstaining; abstention. — et= /dan/ to refrain (from), abstain (from).
içün ايچون archaic, same as için.
îd (—) عيد A lrnd. festival, religious festival. İ—i Adha Isl. rel. the festival of Kurban Bayramı. İ—i Beşaret Christ. rel. the Feast of the Annunciation. İ—i Fıtr Isl. rel. the festival of Şeker Bayramı (ending the Ramazan fast). İ—i Hamsin Christ. rel. the Feast of Pentecost. İ—i Kebir, İ—i Kurban Isl. rel., same as İd-i Adha. İ—i Mevlid Isl. rel. the festival of the birth of the Prophet Muhammad (the twelfth of Rebiülevvel). İ—i Sagir Isl. rel., same as İd-i Fıtr. İ—i Tecelli Christ. rel. the Feast of the Transfiguration.
idaᵃⁱ (——) ايداع A lrnd. 1. a giving, delivering, committing for safe keeping. 2. law deposit, bail. —i ruh a giving up the ghost; a dying.
i'dad 1 (.—) اعداد A lrnd. a making ready, preparing; preparation.
idad 2 (.—) اعداد A lrnd. 1. recurrence; anniversary. 2. the appointed time of death. 3. number; total. 4. lot, portion.
i'dadî (.——) اعدادى A Ott. hist. preparatory (school). —ye, —ye mektebi preparatory school (roughly corresponding to senior high school).
idale (.—.) ادالە A lrnd. a handing from one to another; taking turns; circulation (money).
i'dam 1 (.—) A, idam (——) اعدام capital punishment, execution.
idâm 2 (.—) ادام A lrnd. any condiment eaten to make bread savory.
idame (.—.) ادامه A extension, prolongation. — et= /ı/ to prolong, extend; to preserve, perpetuate.
idane (.—.) ادانە A lrnd. 1. a lending (money). 2. a declaring one a debtor. 3. a running into debt.
idaneten (.—´..) ادانة A lrnd. as a loan.
idare (.—.) اداره A 1. a managing, directing, conducting, superintending, management, direction, superintendence; the administration. 2. a ruling, governing. 3. government office, bureau; board of directors. 4. an economizing, a being economical, economy; a saving, putting by; a sufficing, being enough. 5. an operating, a driving (car). 6. night light. 7. lrnd. a making or letting a thing go round, circle, circulate or revolve. —i akdah lrnd. a circling of the cups.

— **âmiri** chief, administrator. **İ—i Aziziye** same as **İ—i Mahsusa.** **—i beytiye** *lrnd.* domestic economy, home economics. **— bezi** a kind of cheap and coarse cloth. **—sini bil=** to live economically. **— et=** /ı/ 1. to manage (a business etc.), to administer; to control; to govern; to conduct, to direct, to lead. 2. to economize, make ends meet; to manage somehow; to suffice, to be enough. 3. to drive, to use (car). 4. *colloq.* /ı/ to tolerate, put up with; to handle carefully (someone because he is easily upset etc.). **— etmez** It doesn't pay. **— fitili** wick for a night light. **—yle geçin=** to live economically. **— heyeti** administrative committee; board of directors. **— hukuku** administrative law. **—i hususiye** local government. **— kandili** night light. **—i kelâm et=** to talk diplomatically. **— lâmbası** night light. **İ—i Mahsusa** *Ott. hist., former name of the* **Seyri Sefain,** *the present* **Türk Deniz Yolları** (National Maritime Line). *Cf. also* **İ—i Aziziye.** **— makamları** the authorities. **—i maslahat** makeshift. **—i maslahat et=** 1. to manage somehow or other; to make the best of a matter. 2. to cope successfully with difficult situations. **—i maslahat siyaseti** policy of appeasement. **— meclisi** board of directors (of a business). **—i meşruta** *lrnd.* constitutional monarchy. **—i mutlaka** *lrnd.* absolute monarchy. **—i örfiye** martial law. **—i umur** *lrnd.* administration, management of affairs. **— yılı** scarcity; poverty, lean year.

idareci اداره جی 1. manager, administrator, organizer. 2. economical person, good manager. 3. economist. 4. specialist in administrative law. 5. tactful person. **—lik** administration.

idarehane (.—.—.) اداره خانه P office, bureau; administration.

idareli اداره لی 1. economical. 2. efficient, good at managing.

idaresiz اداره سز 1. unable to manage, incompetent, inefficient. 2. lacking management. 3. wasteful, uneconomical. **—lik** incompetence, lack of management.

idareten (.—´..) اداره ة A 1. as a makeshift, as a temporary measure; temporarily, for the time being. 2. tactfully. 3. administratively; by way of administration.

idarî (.——) اداری A administrative; departmental. **— dâva** *law* law suit against the administration. **— irtifak** *law* administrative easement, public purposes easement. **— mahkemeleri** administrative courts. **— muamele** administrative act. **— murakabe** administrative control, supervision. **— tahsis** *law* appropriation for administrative purposes. **— tasarruf** *law* disposition, disposal. **— teamül** *law* administrative custom. **— vesayet** *law* administrative supervision. **— zabıta** municipal police.

idbar (.—) ادبار A *lrnd.* adversity, misfortune; a falling into disgrace.

iddet عدّت A 1. *can. law* the space of time within which a woman may not remarry. 2. *lrnd.* number, multitude.

iddia (..—) ادّعا A 1. a claiming, claim. 2. pretention, assertion, allegation. 3. obstinacy, presumption. **— et=** /ı/ 1. to claim; to urge; to assert. 2. to pretend. 3. to insist. 4. to wager. **—ya giriş=** to lay a wager. **İ— Makamı** *law* the Public Prosecutor. **— olunan şey** *law* question at issue. **—ya tutuş=** to lay a wager.

iddiacı ادعاجی obstinate, persistent; assertive.

iddiaî (..——) ادّعائی A *lrnd.* 1. pretentious; without proof. 2. arbitrary; capricious. **—yat** (..———) A 1. pretentions. 2. arbitrary things.

iddialı ادعالی 1. pretentious; arrogant. 2. disputed (matter).

iddianame (..———.) ادعانامه P *law* indictment.

iddiasız ادعاسز unpretentious; simple; modest.

iddihar (..—) ادّخار A *lrnd.* 1. a storing, a laying up in store. 2. a hoarding, accumulating.

idea *Gk neol., phil.* idea. **—cılık** idealism.

ideal[ii] ایده آل F *phil.* ideal. **—ist** idealist; idealistic. **—izm** idealism.

identik[gi] F *neol., math.* identical. **—le=** /ı/ to identify. **—lik** identity.

ideografi ایده وغرافی F ideography.

ideogram ایده وغرام F ideogram.

ideolog ایده ولوغ F *phil.* ideologist.

ideoloji ایده ولوژی F *phil.* ideology.

ideolojik[gi] ایده ولوژیك F *phil.* ideological.

îdgâh (——) عیدگاه P *poet.* place of solemn festivities; fair grounds.

idgam (.—) ادغام A *Arabic gram.* an inserting one letter in place of another of the same class in pronunciation or writing; coalescence. **—lı konuş=** to speak too accurately, to be pedantic in one's speech.

idhal[ii] (.—) ادخال A *same as* **ithal.**

idhalat (.——) ادخالات *com.* imported things; importation.

îdî 1 (——) عیدی A *lrnd.* pertaining to a religious festival.

idi 2 ایدی (he, she, it) was. **—ler** (they) were.

idiği[ni] ایدوگی *same as* **idüğü.**

idik[gi] ایدك we were.

İdil 1 ایدل *hist.* Volga River.

idil 2 ایدل F *poet.* idyll.

idim ایدم I was.

idin ایدك you were (sing.).

idiniz ایدکز you were (pl. or polite address).

idiş ایکدیش *var. of* **iğdiş.**

i'diye (— —.) عِیدِیَّه A 1. given on the occasion of a festival (present etc.). 2. poem recited on the Feast of Sacrifice.

idmac (.—) ادماج A *rhet.* alluding to one or more occult matters in a verse, besides its plain grammatical sense.

idman ادمان [*Arabic* .—] 1. gymnastics, physical exercise; training. 2. endurance; practice. **—cı** athlete in training. **—lı** in good training; well trained.

idrâkᵏⁱ (.—) ادراك A 1. a perceiving, a comprehending; perception, comprehension, understanding, sense, mental ability or quickness. 2. a reaching maturity, becoming ripe. 3. a reaching, an attaining. **— et**= /ı/ 1. to perceive, understand, apprehend. 2. to reach, attain. 3. *law* to take possession of (revenues, rents, *etc.*).

idrakî (.— —) ادراكى A *psych.* perceptual. **—ye** (.— —.) A *psych.* perceptionism.

idrakli ادراكلى perceptive, intelligent, understanding.

idraksiz ادراكسز unintelligent, dense, dull-witted.

idrar ادرار [*Arabic* .—] urine. **—da şeker** *path.* glycosuria. **— torbası** *anat.* urinary bladder. **— yolu** urethra. **— zorluğu** dysuria.

İdris (.—) ادریس A *Isl. rel., Quranic name sometimes equated with Enoch*. **— ağacı** perfumed cherry, St. Lucy cherry; *bot.*, *Prunus Mahaleb*. **— otu** *bot.*, *Andropogon*.

idüğüⁿᵘ ایدوگی *archaic, only in* **ne idüğü** what it is.

ifa (— —) ایفا A 1. a paying, delivering, rendering; payment. 2. a fulfilling, performing (promise, duty, etc.). **—yi bendegi et**= *lrnd.* to do one's duty towards a superior. **— et**= /ı/ to fulfill, perform, execute, pay. **— ve istifa** *law* complete payment and receipt of a debt. **— karinesi** *law* presumption of performance. **—yi vazife et**= to perform one's duty. **— yeri** *law* place of performance. **— yerini tutan eda** *law* substitution in lieu of the promised performance. **— zamanı** *law* time of performance.

ifad (— —) ایفاد A *lrnd.* a sending an ambassador.

ifade (.—.) افاده A 1. expression; statement, an expounding. 2. evidence; deposition. 3. *slang* affair, business. **—sini al**= 1. *law* to receive (and record) a person's statement. 2. *slang* to listen to someone's troubles. **— vü istifade** teaching and learning. **—i meram** 1. expression of one's thoughts. 2. *obs.* preface. **—i meram et**= to express one's thoughts, to convey one's idea, to express oneself. **—si tamam ol**= *slang* to be done for. **— ver**= *law* to give evidence.

ifakatᵗⁱ (.— .) افاقت A *lrnd.* recovery of health. **— bul**= to get well.

ifakatyab (.— . —) افاقتیاب P recovered from illness. **— ol**= to get well.

if'alˡⁱ (.—) افعال A *only in* **— babı** *Arabic gram.* the fourth form of the verb. **— babına çek**= /ı/ *colloq.* to rape (woman).

ifate (.—.) افاته A *lrnd.* 1. a missing; a letting slip (an opportunity). 2. loss, waste (of time). **—i fırsat** letting an opportunity go by. **—i vakt** losing the time uselessly.

ifaza (.—.) افاضه A *lrnd.* 1. a pouring out; showering down; a rushing along in a stream; an overflowing. 2. an enlightening; a filling with knowledge (mind).

iffet عفّت A chastity, innocence; honesty, uprightness. **—fürus** (. . .—) P *lrnd.* who pretends to be innocent or honest. **—li** chaste; innocent; virtuous; upright; honest.

iffetlû (. .—) عفّتلو *archaic* honorable, virtuous (an honorific in addressing a lady).

iffetsiz عفّتسز dishonest; unchaste. **—lik** misconduct; dishonesty.

ifham 1 (.—) افهام A *lrnd.* a giving to understand; an explaining.

ifham 2 (.—) افحام A *lrnd.* a silencing, an overcoming in argument.

ifhar (.—) افخار A *lrnd.* a regarding one as finer and more glorious than another; a preferring, promoting.

ifkᵏⁱ افك A *lrnd.* 1. lie, falsehood, untruth. 2. calumny; slander. **—i mübin** flagrant lie, calumny.

iflâh (.—) افلاح A a being in security, prosperity, comfort or happiness. **—ı kesil**= *colloq.* to be exhausted, to be done for. **— olmaz** incorrigible, hopeless (person).

iflâs (.—) افلاس A 1. bankruptcy, insolvency. 2. great failure. **—ın açılması** *law* bankruptcy proceedings. **— borusu çaldı** *colloq.* finished, spoiled; gone to pieces. **— bürosu** *law* committee of inspection, board of bankruptcy. **— dairesi** *law* bankruptcy office. **— et**= to go bankrupt. **— hukuku** law of bankruptcy. **— idaresi** administration of bankruptcy assets), trustee in bankruptcy. **—ın kapanması** *law* closing of the bankruptcy. **— kararı** *law* declaration or adjudication of insolvency, adjudication order. **— masası** *law* bankrupt's estate, assets.

ifna (.—) افناء A *lrnd.* a destroying, destruction, annihilation.

ifrad (.—) افراد A *lrnd.* 1. a making solitary or alone, isolating. 2. a performing the pilgrimage alone. 3. a putting into the singular number.

ifrağ (.—) افراغ A *lrnd.* 1. a pouring out; an emptying. 2. a casting, molding, shaping. 3. *biol.* excretion.

ifrah (.—) اِفْراح A *lrnd.* a gladdening, cheering.

ifrat (.—) اِفْراط A 1. a going to excess, an overdoing; excess. 2. exaggeration. **—la** excessively; exaggeratedly. **—ı his** *psych.* oversensitiveness, hyperaesthesia. **—a kaç=** to overdo, to carry too far; to exaggerate. **— ve tefrit** excess in one direction and in the other. **—a vardır=** /ı/ to carry to excess (a thing), to overdo; to exaggerate.

ifratkâr (.—.—) اِفْراطكار P *lrnd.* exaggerating, exaggerator.

ifraz (.—) اِفْراز A 1. a separating, separation. 2. *law* allotment, parcelling out. 3. *physiol.* secretion.

ifrazat (.—.—) اِفْرازات A *physiol.* secretion. **—ı dahiliye guddeleri** *anat.* endocrine glands.

ifrazciyan (.—.—) اِفْرازجيان P *Ott. hist.* sorters of metal in the imperial mint; makers of coins.

ifrit 1 عفريت اِفريت [ifrit 2] *only in* **— kesil=**, **— ol=** to be mad with fury.

ifrit 2 (.—) عفريت A *Isl. myth.* demon of the most malicious kind.

ifsad (.—) A, **ifsat**^dı (.—) اِفساد 1. a spoiling, corruption. 2. a seducing; an inciting (to treachery or rebellion); subversion. **— et=** /ı/ 1. to spoil; to corrupt. 2. to upset the stomach. 3. to seduce; incite (to revolt). **—at** (.—.—) A *lrnd.*, *pl. of* **ifsad**, corruptions; incitements. **—cı** political inciter.

ifşa (.—) اِفشا A a disclosing a secret, revealing, divulging. **— et=** /ı/ to disclose, reveal, expose, divulge; to betray a secret. **—at** (.—.—) A revelations.

ifta (.—) اِفتا A *can. law* a mufti's giving a legal opinion or decision.

iftar اِفطار [*Arabic* .—] 1. a breaking one's fast. 2. the meal taken at sundown (during the fast of Ramazan). **— et=** to break one's fast. **— topu** gun fired at sunset during Ramazan as a signal for breaking the fast.

iftariye (.—..) اِفطاريه 1. light food suitable for breaking the fast. 2. present made to guests at the **iftar**.

iftarlık^ğı اِفطارلق suitable for breaking the fast; hors-d'oeuvres eaten at the **iftar**. **— reçel** very little.

iftihar (..—) اِفتخار A a feeling proud, laudable pride. **— et=** /la/ to take pride (in), to be proud (of). **— listesi** honor roll (in school).

iftikad (..—) اِفتقاد A *lrnd.* 1. a losing, missing. 2. a searching for a thing lost; search.

iftikâk^kı (..—) اِفتكاك A *lrnd.* a redeeming, releasing (pledge or pawn).

iftikar (..—) اِفتقار A *lrnd.* 1. a being needy, becoming poor; necessity, want, destitu-tion. 2. a needing, a being in want of, poverty. 3. a humbling oneself.

iftikâri (..—.—) اِفتكارى A *lrnd.* ideal. **—ye** (..—.—.) Á *sc.* idealism. **—yet** (..—.—.) A idealism.

iftira (..—) اِفترا A 1. slander, a calumniating; calumny. 2. forgery, fabrication. **— at=**, **— et=** /a/ to calumniate, to slander. **—cı** slanderer, calumniator.

iftirak^kı (..—) اِفتراق A *lrnd.* 1. separation, absence. 2. a dispersing; a parting; a splitting into two or more parts.

iftiras (..—) اِفتراس A *lrnd.* a seizing prey by the neck; a tearing. **— et=** to seize prey.

iftisad (..—) اِفتصاد A *lrnd.* 1. an opening a vein, bleeding. 2. a being bled.

iftisal^li (..—) اِفتصال A *lrnd.* 1. a weaning a child. 2. a transplanting.

iftitah (..—) اِفتتاح A *lrnd.* 1. an opening. 2. a beginning; a formally opening worship by chanting the words «**Allahü ekber**».

iftitahî (..—.—) اِفتتاحى A *lrnd.* opening (speech, etc.), inauguration.

iftitan (..—) اِفتتان A *lrnd.* a being tempted, seduced; a falling into temptation.

iftizaz (..—) اِفتضاض A *lrnd.* 1. a deflowering. 2. a formal breaking of legal mourning at its completion (widow).

ifzal^li (.—) اِفضال A *lrnd.* a conferring a favor, benefit or grace (upon).

igare (.—.) اِغاره A *lrnd.* a raiding.

igase (.—.) اِغاثه A *lrnd.* a helping, assisting; succoring.

igrek^ki اِغرك F *algebra* the letter y.

iğ 1 ایك 1. spindle. 2. pivot, axis, axle. **— ağacı** prickwood, spindle tree, *bot.*, *Evonymus latifolius.* **— biçim** *neol., sc.* fusiform. **— taşı** the upper of two millstones.

iğ 2 ایك *obs.* pulmonary tuberculosis.

iğ=^er **3** ایكمك /ı/ 1. to bend, to curve. 2. to bow. 3. to incline, to persuade.

iğbirar (..—) اِغبرار A *lrnd.* annoyance; disappointment; vexation. **—ı hâtır** annoyance, disappointment.

iğde اِگده oleaster, *bot., Elaeagnus angustifolia,* **—giller** *bot., Elaeagnaceae.*

iğdic, iğdiç^ci اِگديج same as **iğdiş**.

iğdin اِگدين *archaic* rotten; addled; bad (egg). **— ol=** to rot; to stink.

iğdir=^ir اِگدیرمك *caus. of* **iğ= 3**.

iğdiş اِگديش 1. gelding. 2. castrated, emasculated. 3. *obs.* common packhorse. **— et=** /ı/ to geld, to castrate.

iğfal^li (.—) اِغفال A seduction, deception; rape. **— et=** /ı/ to seduce, to deceive, to cheat, to delude; to rape; to take advantage of another's negligence. **—ât** (.—.—) A *pl.*

—iyat (. — . —) A alluring or seducing words.
iğik[ği] اِبْگِيلَك 1. bent down. 2. inclined, sloping down, slant.
iğil=[ir] اِبْگِيلَمَك الْگِيلَمَك 1. to bend; to curve; to warp. 2. to bow; to bow down. 3. to stoop. 4. to incline.
iğiliç[ci] اِبْگِيلِيج dodder, *bot., Cuscuta.*
iğim *neol., sc.* slope. **— ölçeği** *geom.* slope of a line.
iğinik[ği] اِگِنِك *prov.* dysentery.
iğirmi اِگِيرمِي *archaic for* **yirmi**.
iğit[di] اِگِت *archaic for* **yiğit**.
iğlâ (. —) اِغْلَا A *lrnd.* 1. a making costly. 2. a demanding or receiving an excessive price.
iğlâk[kı] (. —) اِغْلَاق A *lrnd.* an obscuring; complicating; confusion (in writing).
iğlât (. —) اِغْلَاط A *lrnd.* a leading one into a mistake or error of speech.
iğlâz (. —) اِغْلَاظ A *lrnd.* 1. a using coarse language. 2. a vowing a strong oath. **—ât** (. — —) A coarse words.
iğma (. —) اِغْمَا A *lrnd.* a swooning; faintness, swoon.
iğmad (. —) اِغْمَاد A *lrnd.* a sheathing, putting into a sheath. **—ı seyf** 1. putting a sword into its sheath. 2. tucking many things in together.
iğmam (. —) اِغْمَام A *lrnd.* 1. a clouding over. 2. a saddening; gloominess.
iğmaz (. —) اِغْمَاض A *lrnd.* 1. a closing the eyes; a winking. 2. connivance; a neglecting. **—ı ayn et=** 1. to shut one's eyes; to wink. 2. /ı/ to connive (at); to pretend not to see; to take no notice (of). **—dan gel=** to be indifferent (to something).
iğme اِگمَه *verbal n. of* **iğ=** 3.
iğna (. —) اِغْنَا A *lrnd.* a making rich, independent, or satisfied. **— et=** /ı/ to enrich.
iğne اِگنَه 1. needle, pin. 2. ornamental pin, brooch. 3. thorn, prickle; sting. 4. fish-hook. 5. indicator, pointer; style; gnomon of a sundial. 6. *med.* injection; hypodermic needle or syringe. 7. pinprick; biting word. **— ardı** needlework backstitch. **— atsan yere düşmez** extremely crowded place. **— batır=** /a/ 1. to stick a needle into. 2. to harass, to annoy, goad. **— deliği** the eye of a needle. **— deliğinden Hindistanı seyret=** to be able to discover great meanings from a small event; to be very wise and clever. **— deliğine kaç=** to want to hide oneself in confusion. **— gözü** the eye of a needle. **— ile kuyu kaz=** 1. to do a hard job patiently and elaborately. 2. to do something very slowly and inefficiently. **— iplik** very thin, skin and bones. **— ipliğe dön=** to become skin and bones. **—ye iplik geçir=** to thread a needle. **—den ipliğe kadar** down to the last detail; absolutely everything. **— işi** needlework. **— kaldı** almost; a close scrape, *e. g.,* **çiğnenmesine iğne kaldı.** He escaped being run over by a hair's breadth. **— kalem** sharp-pointed engraver's pen. **— kulağı** *obs.* eye of a needle. **—yi önce kendine batır, sonra çuvaldızı ele** Prick yourself with a needle before you stick a darning needle into others. **— perdahı** *art* ornamental dots on gilding made with a blunt needle. **—den sürmeye kadar** *same as* **iğneden ipliğe kadar.** **— topu, — topuzu** pinhead. **— üstünde otur=** to be on pins and needles, on tenterhooks. **— vur=, — yap=** /a/ *med.* to give an injection. **— yapraklılar** *neol., bot. Coniferae, Pinales,* pine trees (etc.). **— yastığı** pin-cushion. **— ye= **med.* to have an injection. **— yurdusu** *archaic* eye of a needle. **— yutmuş köpeğe dön=** to be thoroughly exhausted.
iğneci اِگنَه جِي 1. maker or seller of needles. 2. *med.* person who gives injections.
iğnecik[ği] اِگنَه جِك 1. a small needle or pin. 2. pintle or bolt of a rudder.
iğnedan (. . —) اِگنَه دَان P needle case; pin-cushion. **—lık** needle case.
iğnedenlik[ği] اِگنَه دَنلِك *same as* **iğnedanlık.**
iğnele=[r] اِگنَه لَه مَك 1. to fix with a pin or needle; to pin. 2. to prick with pins or needles. 3. to hurt with words. **—n=** *pass.* **—yici** pricking; stinging; biting.
iğneli اِگنَه لِي 1. having a needle, pin, thorn, sting. 2. biting, hurting, caustic (words). **— beşik, — fıçı** 1. barrel set with needle-points, in which people are said to have been tortured. 2. very troublesome situation. **— karınca** stinging ant. **— söz** biting word. **— tüfek** needle gun.
iğnelik[ği] اِگنَه لِك needle case; pincushion.
iğnemsi *neol., anat.* styloid.
iğra (. —) اِغْرَا A *lrnd.* an inciting; a stimulating, exciting, instigating.
iğrak[kı] (. —) اِغْرَاق A *lrnd.* 1. a submerging; a sinking, a drowning. 2. an overwhelming, engulfing. 3. a being excessive; an immoderate praising or blaming. **—at** (. — —) A immoderate praise or blame, exaggerations. **—iyat** (. — — —) A words of great exaggeration, hyperbole.
iğras (. —) اِغْرَاس A *lrnd.* a setting out; a planting.
iğrelti اِگرَلتِي *same as* **eğrelti.**
iğren=[ir] اِگرَن مَك /dan/ 1. to feel disgust, horror, loathing; to be disgusted. 2. to hate, to feel an aversion (for).
iğrenç[ci] اِگرَنج hateful; loathsome, disgusting; disgust. **— getir=** to be disgusted. **—lik** loathsomeness.

iğrendir=ᵢᵣ ايگرندرمك اگرنديرمك /ı/ caus. of **iğren=**.
iğrenecekᵍⁱ ايگرنه جك disgusting; hateful.
iğrengeçᶜⁱ ايگرنگچ prov. one who is habitually disgusted.
iğrengen ايگرنگن archaic, same as **iğrengeç**.
iğreniş, iğrenme ايگرنش ايگرنمه verbal n. of **iğren=**.
iğrenti ايگرنتى disgust.
iğreti ايگرتى اگرتى [eğreti] 1. temporary; makeshift; provisional. 2. borrowed. 3. false, artificial. —**den** temporarily; superficial; careless. — **al=** /ı/ to borrow (for temporary use). — **ye al=** to prop up temporarily. — **ata binen tez iner** proverb He who rides a borrowed horse must soon dismount. — **ver=** /ı, a/ to lend. —**lik** temporariness.
iğri اگرى [eğri] 1. crooked. 2. bent, curved; bend, curve, angle; neol., geom. curved line. 3. inclined, awry, askew. 4. perverse, wrong; unjust; untrue. 5. naut. top-timber in a ship's frame. 6. prov. hook; hook for collecting honey. — **bacak** bowlegged. — **bak=** 1. to look at something slantwise. 2. to look at one angrily or enviously; to look at one with evil intention. — **boyun** 1. wry-necked. 2. snowdrop, bot., Galanthus nivalis. — **büğrü** bent and crooked, contorted, twisted, gnarled, devious. — **çehre** sourface, cross look. — **çizgi** geom. curved line. — **git=** to deviate, to go wrong. — **kalem** chisel. — **otur=** 1. to sit informally. 2. to be coarse or ill-mannered. — **söz** malicious words. — **yüzey** neol. curved surface.
iğrice اگرجه 1. somewhat crooked, bent, curved, inclined. 2. anat. Achilles tendon. 3. zool. a kind of gadfly.
iğril=ⁱʳ اگريلمك to become bent; to incline, to lean, to warp. —**ip büğrül=** to bend, curve, twist, warp.
iğrili neol., geom. curvilinear.
iğrilikᵍⁱ اگريلك 1. crookedness, curvature. 2. dishonesty. — **büğrülük** crookedness, contortedness.
iğrilt=ⁱʳ اگرتمك /ı/ to bend, twist. —**ip büğrült=** to make crooked.
iğrit=ⁱʳ اگرتمك same as **iğrilt=**.
iğşa (.—) اغشاء A lrnd. 1. a causing or allowing to be covered; a covering, a spreading a veil. 2. God's veiling the understanding or senses. 3. a being or becoming dark.
iğtimam (..—) اغتمام A lrnd. a being sad or gloomy; sadness, gloom.
iğtinam (..—) اغتنام A lrnd. a getting spoil or plunder; a seizing. — **et=** /ı/ to seize; to take as booty. —**ı fursat et=** to seize an opportunity.
iğtirab (..—) اغتراب A lrnd. 1. a going to or being in a strange land; a going abroad. 2. a marrying a foreign wife.

iğtirakᵏⁱ (..—) اغتراق A lrnd. a being drowned; a being submerged in water.
iğtirar (..—) اغترار A lrnd. a being presumptuous, forward; a being overconfident; presumption, foolhardiness, self-deception.
iğtisab (..—) اغتصاب A lrnd. 1. a wrongful seizing; a ravishing. 2. a compelling. — **et=** /ı/ to take by force.
iğtisalˡⁱ (..—) اغتسال A lrnd. 1. a washing oneself, ablution. 2. a sweating all over.
iğtişaş (..—) اغتشاش A riot, disturbance, insurrection, uproar. —**ât** (..——) A pl.
iğtiyab (..—) اغتياب A lrnd. a backbiting, a talking behind someone's back.
iğtiyalˡⁱ (..—) اغتيال A lrnd. a killing or attempting to kill treacherously.
iğtiyar (..—) اغتيار A lrnd. 1. an obtaining, a providing. 2. a deriving profit or advantage. 3. phil. heteronomy.
iğtiyaz (..—) اغتياظ A lrnd. a being angry, enraged.
iğtizab (..—) اغتضاب A lrnd. a being angry; a flying into a passion.
iğva (.—) اغواء A a seducing, leading astray, a tempting to sin; temptation, seduction. — **et=** /ı/ to tempt, to lead astray.
iğzab (.—) اغضاب A lrnd. a provoking, enraging, angering. — **et=** /ı/ to enrage, to provoke.
ihafe (.—.) اخافه A lrnd. 1. a frightening; intimidation. 2. a threatening, menacing. — **et=** /ı/ to frighten, to threaten.
ihale (.—.) احاله A 1. adjudication, the practice of awarding a contract to the lowest bidder. 2. a referring; a transferring. — **et=** /ı/ 1. to award the contract (for a public construction project). 2. to transfer, refer (to). — **müddeti** adjudication time-limit.
ihaleten (.—'..) احالةً A lrnd. by adjudication, by award.
i haliⁿⁱ neol., gram. accusative.
iham (——) ايهام A 1. rhet. ambiguity, amphibology. 2. lrnd. a causing to be doubtful and puzzled; an exciting suspicion. —**ı kabih** a using an impolite expression well knowing its improper implications. —**ı mücerred** rhet. a simple amphibology. —**ı müreşşeh** rhet. a complex amphibology.
ihanet 1 (.—.) اهانت A lrnd. a treating with contempt, insulting.
ihanet 2 (.—.) اخانت A a betraying, treachery. — **et=** /a/ to betray; to deceive; to disclose.
ihata, ihate (.—.) احاطه 1. a surrounding, embracing. 2. a comprehending, understanding; comprehension, encompassing. 3. erudition, comprehensive knowledge. — **et=** /ı/ 1. to surround; to embrace. 2. to comprehend, under-

stand, fathom; to encompass. **—lı** 1. erudite, widely read. 2. vast.

ihbar (.—) اخبار A 1. denunciation. 2. notice, warning, demand, note. 3. a communicating, informing; notification. **— et=** 1. to denounce, to report; to warn. 2. *lrnd.* to inform, to communicate; to convey (information, news). **— hücceti** declaration, declaratory document (given by a court of justice). **— tasrifi** *gram.* indicative.

ihbarî (.— —) اخباری A 1. relating to information, informative. 2. *gram.* indicative.

ihbariye (.— —.) اخباریّة A 1. reward for giving information or denouncing a person. 2. official notice.

ihbarname (.— —.) اخبارنامه notice, warning, demand, note; notification, declaration.

ihcalli (.—) اخجال A *lrnd.* a covering with shame and confusion.

ihda (.—) اهداء A *lrnd.* 1. a giving a gift, presenting. 2. a guiding, a putting one in the right direction. **— et=** 1. to present (with). 2. to direct, to guide.

ihdas (.—) احداث A a producing, creating, inventing; an introducing (a new thing). **— et=** /ı/ to produce, create, invent, introduce (a new thing).

ihdaskerde (.—..) احداث کرده P *lrnd.* produced, created, invented, introduced (thing); production; invention.

ihfa (.—) اخفاء A *lrnd.* a hiding, concealing (a thing). **— et=** /ı/ to hide, conceal.

ihkakkı (.—) احقاق A a fully establishing a right. **— et=** /ı/ to establish a right fully, to do justice. **—ı hak et=** to establish justice, to administer justice. **—ı haktan imtina** *law* a withholding justice (from).

ihlâ 1 (.—) احلاء A *lrnd.* a sweetening (food etc.).

ihlâ 2 (.—) اخلاء A *lrnd.* an emptying; vacant, void.

ihlâf (.—) احلاف A *lrnd.* a making one take an oath. **— et=** /ı/ to swear in.

ihlâkki (.—) اهلاک A *lrnd.* a killing, destroying. **— et=** /ı/ to destroy.

ihlâlli **1** (.—) اخلال A 1. *law* a breaking, disobeying (law); infringement (of a law or treaty). 2. *lrnd.* a spoiling, corrupting (a thing). **— et=** /ı/ *law* to break (law, treaty), to infringe (upon).

ihlâlli **2** (.—) احلال A 1. *psych.* locality. 2. *lrnd.* a making a thing or act lawful.

ihlâs (.—) اخلاص A *lrnd.* 1. a being sincere; pure sincerity of heart; sincere worship or belief. 2. *short for* **Sure-i İhlâs. İ— Suresi** the 112th sura of the Quran. **—kâr** (.— —) P sincere, friendly.

ihlâsmend (.—.) اخلاصمند P *lrnd.* sincerely devoted (person); friendly. **—âne** (.—.—.) P in a sincere manner; sincere (act, feeling). **—î** (.—.—) P, **—lik** sincerity, devotedness.

ihlâsperver (.—..) اخلاصپرور P sincere, friendly. **—âne** (.—..—.) P sincerely, devotedly. **—î** (.—..—) P, **—lik** sincerity, devotedness.

ihlâsverz (.—.) اخلاصورز P *lrnd.* who practises sincerity.

ihlil (.—) احليل A *anat.* urethra.

ihmad (.—) اخماد A *lrnd.* 1. a lowering or putting out (fire, lamp); an allaying (fire). 2. a being quiet, a subsiding into silence.

ihmal (.—) اهمال A 1. a neglecting; neglect, negligence; carelessness. 2. *Arabic gram.* omission of the dot of a dotted letter. **— et=** /ı/ to neglect; to act negligently; to be careless.

ihmalci اهمالجی neglectful, negligent; careless. **—lik** carelessness; neglect.

ihmalkâr (.— —) اهمالکار P negligent; careless. **—lık** neglect, carelessness.

ihmirar (..—) احمرار A 1. *med.* erythema. 2. *lrnd.* a reddening.

ihrac (.—) اخراج A *cf.* **ihraç**.

ihracat (.— —) اخراجات A 1. *com.* exports. 2. *physiol.* excretion. 3. *lrnd.* expenses, disbursements, debits. **— ve ithalât** exports and imports. **— primi** bounty for export, premium on exportation. **—çı** *com.* exporter.

ihraçcı (.—) اخراج [ihrac] 1. an exporting; exportation. 2. an extracting; extraction. 3. a driving out; a putting out; expulsion; discharge; deportation. 4. *mil.* disembarkation, a landing. 5. an obtaining (something out of a thing); a producing. **— bankası** bank of issue. **— et=** /ı/ 1. to export. 2. to extract. 3. to expel. 4. to disembark. 5. to produce. **— hareketı** *mil.* landing operations. **—ı meyt** exhumation.

ihrakkı **1** (.—) احراق A *lrnd.* 1. a burning. 2. a causing one to suffer pain or grief. **— binnar** a burning with fire, incineration.

ihrakkı **2** (.—) اهراق A *lrnd.* a pouring out (water); a shedding (blood).

ihrakan (.—.) احراقاً A *lrnd.* by burning (with fire.).

ihrakıye (.—..) احراقیّه fuel; fuel allowance.

ihram (.—) احرام A 1. seamless garment worn by pilgrims in Mecca. 2. a Bedouin cloak. 3. cover for a sofa etc. **—dan çık=** to take off the pilgrim's garb. **—a gir=** to put on the pilgrim's garb.

ihraz (.—) احراز A *lrnd.* 1. a getting, obtaining, acquiring. 2. a holding, possessing, having; attainment. **— et=** /ı/ to obtain, acquire; to possess.

ihsa (.—) احصاء A *lrnd.* a counting, an enumerating (things); enumeration; an applying statistical methods. —î (. — —) A statistical. —iyat (. , — — —) statistics.

ihsan 1 (. —) احسان A 1. favor, benevolence; kindness. 2. gift (granted by a superior); endowment. — **alel ihsan** lrnd. favor upon favor. — **et=** /ı/ to grant, to endow with; to bestow (a favor); to do a kindness. —ı **şahane** Ott. hist. gift made by the Sultan on special occasions.

ihsan 2 (. —) احصان A lrnd. 1. a fortifying, defending; a protecting. 2. a keeping a wife very much secluded. 3. a restraining, keeping clear from sin or impropriety.

ihsanat (. — —) احسانات A lrnd., pl. of **ihsan 1**.

ihsandide (. — — .) احسانديده P lrnd. who has received a kindness or favor. —**gân** (. — — . —) P pl.

ihsas (. —) احساس A 1. a being or becoming sensible of (an object), a perceiving; psych. sensation. 2. a causing to feel or understand. — **et=** 1. to make aware (of); to hint, insinuate. 2. to feel, to perceive. —**ât** (. — —) pl. of **ihsas**. —î (. — —) A physiol. sensorial. —**iye** (. — —.) A phil. sensualism.

ihta (. —) اخطاء A lrnd. 1. a causing to err. 2. a missing (the mark in shooting); a failing. 3. a making a mistake. 4. a doing wrong, sinning. — **et=** /ı/ to cause to err.

ihtar (. —) اخطار A 1. a warning. 2. a reminding; a suggesting. —**da bulun=** /a/ to warn (one), to remind (one). — **cezası** admonition, reprimand. — **et=** /ı/ to warn, to remind; to call attention (to).

ihtarname (. — —.) اخطارنامه P law official warning; protest.

ihtısas (. —) اختصاص A 1. a specializing, speciality, specialization. 2. skill, expert knowledge. 3. lrnd. special attachment, exclusive devotion (to a person). — **kazan=**, — **kesbet=** /da/ 1. to specialize. 2. to gain skill (in). — **mahkemesi** formerly court for the trial of smuggling cases. — **yap=** /da/ to specialize (in), to take up special training (in a field).

ihtısasî (. . — —) اختصاصى A pertaining to a specialty. —**yun** (. . — — —) A specialists.

ihtibar (. . —) اختبار A lrnd. 1. a seeking for information. 2. a being or becoming informed; information, knowledge. 3. medico-legal investigation.

ihtibarî (. . — —) اختبارى A log. empirical. —**ye** (. . : — — —) A phil. empiricism.

ihtibas (. . —) احتباس A 1. path. ischury. 2. psych. repression. 3. lrnd. a restraining, confining, imprisoning; a being detained, imprisonment.

ihticab (. . —) احتجاب A lrnd. 1. a being veiled, concealed (by a curtain); concealment. 2. a being clouded over (sun). 3. a being secluded, a being hindered.

ihticac (. . —) احتجاج A lrnd. a proving, a giving reason, proof, evidence; carrying on litigation; disputing. —**a salih** law valid as evidence; authentic.

ihticam (. . —) احتجام A lrnd. a being cupped or bled; cupping.

ihtida 1 (. . —) اهتداء A 1. conversion to Islam. 2. lrnd. a finding the right road (in travel, conduct, or faith). — **et=** to be converted to Islam.

ihtida^{aı} 2 (. . —) اختداع A lrnd. a deceiving, cheating; deceit.

ihtidad (. . —) احتداد A lrnd. 1. a being or becoming sharp, pointed, acute. 2. a being or growing angry.

ihtifa (. . —) اختفاء A lrnd. a being or becoming concealed; concealment. — **et=** to hide oneself.

ihtifagâh (. . — —) اختفاگاه P lrnd. hiding place.

ihtifal^{li} (. . —) احتفال A commemorative session, jubilee performance, memorial service.

ihtikan (. . —) احتقان A med. 1. administration of an enema. 2. congestion (of blood). — **âleti** enema syringe.

ihtikâr 1 (. . —) احتكار A a profiteering; a hoarding. — **ve istismar** a profiteering and exploiting.

ihtikar 2 (. . —) احتقار A lrnd. a despising, a treating with contempt.

ihtikârcı احتكارجى profiteer.

ihtilâ (. . —) اختلاع A lrnd. a wife's being divorced at her own wish against a compensation given by her to her husband.

ihtilâc (. . —) اختلاج A 1. physiol. convulsion. 2. lrnd. agitation.

ihtilâf (. . —) اختلاف A 1. conflict; dispute; quarrel. 2. a differing; difference; disagreement. —**ı manzara** astr. parallax. —**ı sâni** astr. evection. —**ât** (. . — —) A pl. of **ihtilâf**. —**lı** controversial; conflicting.

ihtilâk^{kı} 1 (. . —) احتلاك A lrnd. a shaving off the hair.

ihtilak^{kı} 2 (. . —) اختلاق A lrnd. 1. a forging, fabricating, inventing (lie, speech, etc.). 2. a having or acquiring some moral habit.

ihtilâl^{li} (. . —) اختلال A 1. revolution, rebellion, riot; disturbance of the public peace. 2. lrnd. a being or becoming mentally defective, unsound, crazy. — **çıkar=** to raise a rebellion. —**i heyecanî** emotional disturbance. —**i nutuk** psych. paraphasia. —**i şuur** psych. paranoia; mental disturbance.

ihtilâlci اختلالجى revolutionary; rebel.

ihtilâm (..—) اِحتِلام A *physiol.* nocturnal emission.

ihtilâs (..—) اِختِلاس A embezzlement; malversation.

ihtilât اِختِلاط A 1. *law* social intercourse; intermingling; relations. 2. *path.* complication. 3. *lrnd.* confusion. — **et=** /la/ 1. to mix, mingle; to have social intercourse (with others) —**tan kesil=** to stop having relations with. —**tan men'et=** /ı/ *law* to isolate. — **yap=** *path.* to lead to a complication.

ihtima (..—) اِحتِما A *lrnd.* an abstaining (from food, etc. as a curative or prophylactic measure).

ihtimalˡⁱ (..—) اِحتِمال A 1. probability. 2. possibility. 3. probably. 4. *lrnd.* a taking up, receiving or bearing (load, burden); an assuming a responsibility. 5. *lrnd.* a being patient, a tolerating. — **ki** It is very likely that. — **ver=** /a/ to regard as possible, to deem likely.

ihtimalât (..——) اِحتِمالات A *lrnd.* probabilities. — **kaidesi** the law of probabilities.

ihtimalî (..——) اِحتِمالى A *lrnd.* 1. probable. 2. problematic. — **hüküm** *log.* problematic proposition or judgment. —**ye** (..——.) A *phil.* probabilism. —**yet** (..——.) A *math.* probability.

ihtimam (..—) اِهتِمام A 1. a taking pains, care; a paying attention; carefulness. 2. *lrnd.* solicitude, anxiety. — **et=** /a/ to take pains, to take great care; to pay attention (to). — **ve takayyüt** diligence, care. —**kâr** (..——) P, —**lı** very careful, attentive; scrupulous; elaborate. —**sız** careless; carelessly made.

ihtimar (..—) اِختِمار A *lrnd.* a fermenting; fermentation.

ihtinakᵏⁱ (..—) اِختِناق A *lrnd.* a being strangled, suffocated, throttled; suffocation. —**ı rahm** hysteria.

ihtira (..—) اِختِراع A an inventing, invention. — **beratı** patent, patent right. — **et=** /ı/ to invent. —**ât** (..——) A *lrnd.* inventions, new inventions. —**î** (..——) A *lrnd.* inventive.

ihtirakᵏⁱ (..—) اِحتِراق A 1. *lrnd.* combustion; burning. 2. *astr.* approach of a planet to the sun; a being lost in the sun's rays. — **et=** to get burned. — **kabiliyeti** combustibility. — **noktası** burning point, focus.

ihtirakerde (..—..) اِحتِراق كرده P *lrnd.* invented; invention.

ihtiram (..—) اِحتِرام A a treating with respect; veneration, reverence, regard, deference. — **duruşu** a standing at attention. — **et=** /a/ to honor, respect; to show consideration. — **kıt'ası** guard of honor.

ihtiramat (..——) اِحتِرامات A *pl. of* **ihtiram**. —**ı faika** *lrnd.* deep respect.

ihtiras 1 (..—) اِحتِراص A passion, ambition, greed.

ihtiras 2 (..—) اِحتِراس A *lrnd.* a preserving oneself (against a foe, etc.).

ihtiraslı اِحتِراصلى passionate, ambitious.

ihtiraz (..—) اِحتِراز A 1. a guarding oneself (against something); precaution. 2. abstention, avoidance. — **et=** /dan/ to guard against, to take precautions against, to avoid. — **kaydı** reservation. —**î** (..——) A precautionary.

ihtisab (..—) اِحتِساب A 1. *Isl. hist.* office of the censor of morals; *Ott. hist.* office of the superintendent of guilds and markets. 2. *lrnd.* a calling to account, a questioning; responsibility. — **ağası** *Ott. hist.* the director or superintendent of guilds and markets. —**iye** tax imposed on a **muhtesib**.

ihtisar (..—) اِختِصار A *lrnd.* a speaking or writing briefly; abbreviation; reduction of a fraction. — **et=** /ı/ to shorten, summarize, abridge.

ihtisaren (..—.) اِختِصاراً A *lrnd.* in brief, briefly.

ihtisas 1 (..—) اِختِصاص A *var. of* **ihtısas**.

ihtısasˢⁱ **2** (..—) اِحتِساس A 1. sentiment. 2. sensation. 3. impression. 4. *psych.* affection. —**at** (..——) A *lrnd.*, *pl.* —**î** (..——) A *psych.* affective.

ihtişa (..—) اِحتِشا A *obs.*, *path.* infarct.

ihtişad (..—) اِحتِشاد A *lrnd.* a congregating, flocking together (for mutual assistance); an assembling.

ihtişam (..—) اِحتِشام A magnificence, grandeur; splendor, pomp and circumstance.

ihtitab 1 (..—) اِحتِطاب A *lrnd.* a collecting firewood. — **hakkı** *law* right to cut or collect wood, *law* housbote, firebote.

ihtitab 2 (..—) اِختِطاب A *lrnd.* 1. a betrothing a maiden. 2. a making anyone marry.

ihtitaf (..—) اِختِطاف A *lrnd.* a seizing, carrying off by force, snatching. —**ı basar** a dazzling the eye.

ihtitam (..—) اِختِتام A *lrnd.* a finishing, completing.

ihtitan (..—) اِختِتان A *lrnd.* a being circumcised, undergoing circumcision.

ihtiva (..—) اِحتِواء A a holding, taking, containing; an including. — **et=** /ı/ to contain, hold; to include, to comprise.

ihtiya (..—) اِحتِياع A *cf.* **ihtiyaç**. —**at** (..——) A *pl.*

ihtiyaçᶜⁱ (..—) اِحتِياج [ihtiyac] A 1. necessity, need, want. 2. poverty. — **içinde kıvran=** 1. to be in great need. 2. to suffer poverty. —**ı ol=** /a/ to be in need of.

ihtiyal (..—) اِمتیال A *lrnd.* 1. a using a device, trick, wile or fraud. 2. a using one's wits; contrivance. —**at** (..— —) A *pl.*

ihtiyar 1 اِختیار [ihtiyar 2] 1. aged, old; old man. 2. elder, chief. **İ— Heyeti** council of elders, village council.

ihtiyar 2 (..—) اِختیار A 1. a choosing, preferring; choice, selection. 2. option, preference; choice. 3. free will; free agency; freedom. —**ı elden git=** to lose one's self-control; to be overcome by emotion. —**ı elden bırak=** to put all considerations aside; to give up one's self-control. — **et=** /ı/ 1. to choose, to prefer; to select. 2. to shoulder (expense, trouble). —**ı sükût et=** to prefer to say nothing. —**ı zahmet et=** to take the trouble.

ihtiyarane (..— —.) اِختیارانه [ihtiyar 1, -ane] *lrnd.* peculiar to an old man.

ihtiyarat (..— —) اِختیارات A *lrnd.* 1. *pl.* of ihtiyar 2. 2. superstitious observances for foretelling inauspicious days and hours for doing things.

ihtiyaren (..—.) اِختیاراً A *lrnd.* of one's own choice; voluntarily.

ihtiyarî (..— —) اِختیاری A optional, facultative. — **durak** request stop, flag stop.

ihtiyariyat (..— — —) اِختیاریات A *lrnd.* things done of one's own choice.

ihtiyarla= اِختیارلامق to grow old, to age. —**t=** /ı/ to turn someone into an old man, e. g., **beni ihtiyarlattı** It took years off my life.

ihtiyarlık اِختیارلق old age. — **sigortası** social security.

ihtiyarsız اِختیارسز without choice, optionless; involuntarily, instinctively, automatically.

ihtiyat (..—) اِحتیاط A 1. precaution; prudence. 2. reserve; *mil.* reserves. — **akçesi** reserve fund. — **kaydiyle** with reservation. — **kuvvetleri** *mil.* reserve forces. —**lık hizmeti** *mil.* reserve service. — **parçası** *mech.* spare part. — **zabiti** *mil.* reserve officer.

ihtiyaten (..—´.) اِحتیاطاً A as a reserve; by way of precaution; with reserve.

ihtiyatî (..— —) اِحتیاطی A precautionary. — **haciz** *law* provisional distraint. — **tedbirler** precautionary measures; measures of conservation.

ihtiyatkâr (..— —) اِحتیاطکار P 1. cautious, prudent. 2. reserved (person), cautious. —**âne** (..— — —.) P cautiously. —**lık** 1. prudence, caution. 2. reservedness, cautiousness.

ihtiyatlı اِحتیاطلی prudent, cautious. — **bulun=** 1. to be ready for unexpected events. 2. to be cautious. — **davran=** to act prudently; to take precautions.

ihtiyatsız اِحتیاطسز imprudent; rash; improvident. —**lık** imprudence; improvidence. —**lık et=**, —**lık göster=** to be imprudent; to act imprudently.

ihtiyol اِختیول F *pharm.* ichthyol.

ihtizar (..—) اِحتضار A *lrnd.* a being at the point of death; death agony. — **halinde bulun=** to be at the point of death, to be in a state of agony.

ihtizaz (..—) اِهتزاز A a trembling, vibrating; vibration; tremor; agitation; commotion. —**at** (..— —) A *pl.* —**î** (..— —) A pertaining to vibration; vibrating. —**lı** vibrating, tremulous.

ihvan (.—) اِخوان A 1. brothers, brethren. 2. friends. —**ı basefa** brethren in the Mevlevi order. —**ı din** coreligionists. —**ı vatan** fellow countrymen. —**lık** brotherhood; friendship.

ihvaniyat (.— .—) اِخوانیات A *lrnd.* letters written by friends.

İhvanüssafa (.— ..—) اِخوان الصفا A *lrnd.* Brother Devotees (a religious and political association of the tenth century).

ihve اِخوه A *lrnd.* brothers.

ihya (.—) اِحیا A 1. a bringing to life, a giving life, animating. 2. a raising from the dead, reviving. 3. a giving new life, vigor, hope or prosperity. 4. an enlivening (the night) with active religious exercises. — **et=** /ı/ 1. to animate. 2. to reanimate. 3. to restore, reinvigorate. 4. to load with favors (person). 5. to enliven with active occupation or religious exercises (night). — **gecesi** the night preceeding Friday or Monday (usually spent in religious exercises). —**yi leyl**, —**yi leyâl**, —**yi leyâlî** spending the night or nights in prayer. —**yi mevât** *lrnd.* a bringing waste land into cultivation.

ihyakerde (.—..) اِحیاکرده P *lrnd.* 1. renewed, restored. 2. favored; benefited.

ihzar (.—) اِحضار A 1. a preparing; preparation. 2. a bringing into the presence (of); sending for; calling, summoning; requiring to appear (person). 3. *psych.* presentation. 4. *biol., psych.* reproduction. — **et=** /ı/ 1. to prepare; to arrange. 2. to produce, present. 3. to call, summon, send for. — **müzekkeresi** *law* summons to appear (witness or offender). —**at** (.— —) A *lrnd., pl.*

ihzaren (.—´.) اِحضاراً A *lrnd.* by way of summoning. — **celb** police summons to appear before the court.

ihzarî (.— —) اِحضاری A preparatory.

ihzariye (.— —.) اِحضاریه A fee, expense of citation or summons.

=ik *cf.* **=k 2**.

ikaʿ (—.) اِیقاع A *lrnd.* 1. a bringing about; a causing; a committing. 2. a stirring up, an exciting, motivating. 3. *Or. mus.* rhythm, rhythmic pattern. — **et=** /ı/ to cause, to bring about, to commit.

i'kab (. —) اعقاب A *lrnd.* a punishing, punishment.

ik'ad 1 (. —) اقعاد A *lrnd.* 1. a causing to sit, compelling one to sit. 2. a placing one in office, an installing. 3. a being paralyzed in the legs.

ikad 2 (— —) ایقاد A *lrnd.* 1. a lighting, kindling. 2. a kindling men to strife. — **et=** /ı/ to light, set fire to.

ikaf (— —) ایقاف A *lrnd.* 1. a making stop, stopping. 2. a giving into trust in mortmain.

ikale (. —.) اقاله A *lrnd.* a recalling a bargain, a withdrawing from an agreement.

ikame (. —.) اقامه A 1. a setting up or establishing. 2. a substituting, substitution. 3. a placing; an appointing to a place. 4. a bringing about, a causing. 5. *law* appointment of a substitute or reversionary heir. **—i dâva et=** *law* to bring an action (against someone). **— prensibi** *law* subrogation, transfer of rights. **—i salât** *Isl. rel.* a commencing the performance of the **namaz** . **—i şer'i şerif** *Isl. rel.* an enforcing the canon law.

ikamet (. —.) اقامت A a remaining; a residing; residence, a dwelling, staying at a place, living. **— beyannamesi** declaration of residence. **— et=** to dwell, to stay. **— mahalli** place of residence. **—e memur** ordered to reside (in a certain place). **— tezkeresi** residence permit. **— yevmiyesi** daily allowance (during official travel).

ikametgâh (. —. —) اقامتگاه P 1. place of residence, legal domicile. 2. house, home, residence.

ikan (— —) ایقان A *lrnd.* a being or growing perfectly sure of, a learning or believing without doubt; certainty, assurance. **—î** (— — —) A *obs., phil.* dogmatic. **—iye** (— — —.) A *obs., phil.* dogmatism.

ik'ansese اقعنسس A *lrnd., joc.* hunchback.

ikaz (— —) ایقاظ A 1. a waking up, arousing. 2. putting one on his guard, warning. 3. a stirring up. **— et=** /ı/ 1. to awake, to awaken. 2. to caution, to warn. 3. to stir up, to arouse.

ikbab (. —) اکباب A *lrnd.* 1. a falling on one's face. 2. a bending over to look. 3. a being assiduous; perseverance.

ikbah (. —) اقباح A *lrnd.* an acting in an unseemly way; a committing a fault.

ikbalⁱⁱ (. —) اقبال A 1. good fortune; prosperity, felicity, success. 2. *Ott. hist.* the Sultan's favorite female slave. 3. *lrnd.* a desiring; accepting. 4. *lrnd.* a facing towards; a turning one's attention (to). 5. *lrnd.* an approaching arrival. **— buyurmaz mısınız?** Will you have some? (said while offering food or drink at table.) **— et=** *lrnd.* to be on the point of arriving; to come, to arrive.

ikbalcu (. — —) اقبالجو P *lrnd.* seeking success and prosperity.

ikballı اقبالی fortunate, lucky; prosperous.

ikbalmend (. — .) اقبالمند P *lrnd.* fortunate, prosperous.

ikbalperest (. — ..) اقبالپرست P very ambitious; high-flying. **—î** (. — .. —) P, **—lik** great ambitions for success and prosperity.

ikbalsiz اقبالسز unfortunate, unlucky; unhappy.

ikbar (. —) اکبار A *lrnd.* a considering anything great; a treasuring something.

ikdam (. —) اقدام A *lrnd.* 1. perseverance. 2. effort, great effort. 3. a going forward, an advancing. **— et=** to persevere. **—lı** persevering.

ikdamsız اقدامسز lacking in perseverance. **—lık** lack in perseverance.

ikdar (. —) اقدار A *lrnd.* 1. an enabling, a giving power. 2. a securing the means for one's maintenance. **— et=** /ı/ 1. to enable. 2. to support.

iken ایکن 1. while, during, while being; when, *e. g.,* **ben orada iken** when I was there; **tam yazacak iken** while on the point of writing. 2. though, although, *e. g.,* **hal böyle iken** while this is true, although this is true.

ikfa (. —) اقفا A *lrnd.* 1. a reversing, an inverting. 2. an employing a false or imperfect rhyme.

ikfar (. —) اکفار A *lrnd.* a deeming one a misbeliever, a calling someone a **kâfir**.

iki ایکی two; a couple of, double. **—dir** for the second time already. **—miz** two of us; we two. **—miz de** both of us. **—si** two of them; **—si de** both of them. **— ağızlı** 1. two-edged. 2. *colloq.* doublecrossing; doubledealing; two-faced. 3. double-barreled (gun). **— ahbap çavuşlar** two chums. **— analı kuzu** *colloq.* person who benefits from two sources. **—si arası** neither this nor that, average, so so. **— arada bir derede kal=** to be in strait circumstances. **— arada kal=** to be harassed between two difficult situations, between two fires. **— ateş arasında kal=** to be in a very difficult situation. **— ayağını bir pabuca koy=**, **— ayağını bir pabuca sok=** /ın/ to put one into a flurry, to hustle. **— ayağı çukurda** very old (person), on the edge of the grave. **— ayaklı eşek** *colloq.* a walking ass, idiot; very stupid person. **— başlı** 1. two-headed; *anat.* biceps. 2. mutual. **— başlı ejder** (*lit.,* double-headed dragon) great calamity. **— başlı tut=** /ı/ to conduct a matter prudently. **— baştan ol=** to be possible only if both parties show good will. **—de bir, —de birde** every

iki now and then, all the time. **—si bir** The two are alike, just the same. **—sini bir kazana koysanız kaynamazlar** (*lit.* Even if you put them into the same cauldron they would not boil together.) They just can't get along together. **— büklüm** 1. bent double with age. 2. two-stranded, two-ply (thread, etc.). **— bükülü** two-stranded (thread, etc.). **— cami arasında kalmış beynamaz gibi** confused, perplexed; not knowing what to do. **— canlı** pregnant (woman). **— cihanda** in this world and the next. **— cinslik** *neol.*, *biol.*, *psych.* bisexuality. **— cisim meselesi** *astr.* problem of two bodies. **— çenekliler** *neol.*, *bot.* dicotyledones. **— çenetli** *neol.*, *bot.* bivalve, bivalvular. **— çıplak bir hamamda yakışır** *colloq.* Two poor people cannot make a happy marriage. **— çift lâf**, **— çift söz** a word or two, a few words, a couple of words. **— çifte**, **— çifte kayık**, **— çifteli** rowboat with two pairs of oars. **— dereceli intihap** indirect suffrage. **— dinden avare** *colloq.* He is neither one nor the other; he has no stable principles. **— dirhem bir çekirdek** dressed up. **— düzlemli** *geom.* dihedral angle. **— el bir baş için** *proverb* (*lit.* Two hands are for one head.) Each one has to take care of himself. **— eli böğründe kal=** to be in a desperate situation; to be helpless. **— eli kanda olsa** no matter how pressed he is. **— eli on parmağı karada** evilminded; calumniator; slanderer. **— elle sarıl=** /a/ to cling (to), to depend greatly (upon), to be faithful (to). **— eli on parmağı yakasında ol=**, **— eli yakasında ol=** /ın/ to insist on one's claim upon another. **— elim yanıma gelecek** Why should I be lying? After all we all come to Judgment Day. **— el yeteneği** *neol.* ambidexterity. **— evcikli** *neol.*, *bot.* dioecious. **— evli** having two wives and two households. **— fazlı** *neol.*, *phys.* diphase. **— geçeli** on both sides. **— gönül bir olunca samanlık seyran olur** It is love that matters; one overcomes all difficulties for love's sake. **— gözüm!** my dear! **— göz arasında** *colloq.* in an instant; in the twinkling of an eye. **— gözle görme** *optics* binocular vision. **— gözü iki çeşme** shedding bitter tears. **— gözüm önüme aksın ki yalanım yoktur** If I am not telling the truth, may my eyes drop out. **— günde bir** every other day; frequently, quite often. **— güverteli** two-decker (ship). **— hadli** *math.* binomial. **— hırtı bir pırtı** very poor (person). **— iki** two by two. **— ilmekli düğüm** double bow; double-bowed knot. **— kardeş** two bright stars, β, γ in the Little Dipper (Ursa Minor). **— kardeş kanı** red showy broom rape, *bot.*, *Phelypaea coccinea*; dragon's-blood tree, *bot.*, *Dracaena Draco*. **— karınlı** *neol.*, *anat.* biventral, digastric. **— karpuz bir koltuğa sığmaz** You cannot do two things at once. **— kat** 1. double (of any number or quantity); twofold; twice. 2. doubled, folded. 3. bent double. **— kat kareli denklem—** *neol.*, *alg.* biquadratic equation. **— kat kök** *neol.*, *alg.* double root. **— katlı** 1. two-storied. 2. two-layered. **— kavrulmuş** same as **çifte kavrulmuş**. **— keçeli** same as **iki geçeli**. **— kere** twice; doubly. **— kere iki dört eder gibi** as sure as two and two is four. **— kılıç altında** under two flags. **— kulak bir dil için** Listen rather than talk. **— kuyruklu** *slang* faulty; defective. **— makaralı palanga** *naut.* tackle with two blocks. **— misli** twofold, twice as much, as much again. **—si ortası** in between the two. **—si ortası olmaz** There is no middle course. **— otuzunda** She is sixty years old. **— paralık et=** /ı/ to discredit, to degrade. **— patlar**, **— patlar top** howitzer (the shell making the second explosion). **— payda bir pay** one half. **— rahmetin biri**, **— rahmetten biri** one of the two mercies, *e. g.*, either death or recovery (said of a very ill person). **— satır dertleş=**, **— satır konuş=** to have a friendly chat. **— seksen uzan=** *slang* to feel glad, to feel contented. **— sözü bir araya getiremez** He can't put two words together. **— söz bir pazar** without bargaining. **— şekilli** *chem.* dimorph. **— şıktan biri** one of two alternatives. **— takdirde** *archaic* in either case. **— taraf ol=** to divide into two controversial groups. **— telli** kind of two-stringed instrument. **— terimli** *neol.*, *math.* binomial. **— tuğlu paşa** *Ott. hist.* pasha of the second grade called **mir-i miran**. **— ucunu bir araya getireme=** not to be able to make two ends meet. **— ucu boklu değnek** *colloq.* distasteful which ever way one turns it, bad through and through. **— üç** two or three, a few. **— voltalı** *naut.* third foot-hook of a ship's timbers. **— yakası bir araya gelme=** not to be able to make two ends meet. **— yaşayışlı** *biol.* amphibious, amphibian. **— yeminden bir emin** *archaic* A concrete proof is better than a theoretical claim; actions speak louder than words. **— yüzlü** two-faced, hypocritical; hypocrite. **— yüzlülük** hypocrisy. **—ci** *neol.*, *phil.* **dualist.**

ikicik only two.

ikile=ʳ ايكيلمك /ı/ to make two, to make a pair.

ikilem *neol.*, *log.* dilemma.

ikilen=ⁱʳ, **ikileş=**ⁱʳ ايكيلشمك to become two, to be doubled.

ikileyin ايكيلين *archaic* for the second time, secondly.

ikili ايكيلى 1. having two parts. 2. *cards* two. **— bölü** *neol.*, *phil.* dichotomy. **— kapacık**

anat. bicuspid.
ikilik[gi] اِكِيلِك 1. consisting of two. 2. division, disunion, difference, duality. 3. *mus.* half note. 4. *archaic* two-piaster coin.
ikinci يَكِنجِى second. **— derece muadelesi** *math.* quadratic equation. **— hamur kâğıt** a lightly glazed book-paper. **— yapı** *bot.* secondary structure. **— zaman** *geol.* Mesozoic. **— zar** *bot.* secundine.
ikincil *neol., phil.* secondary.
ikinç[ci] يَكِنْجِ *archaic* second, for the second time.
ikindi اِيكِنْدِى *Isl. rel.* time of the afternoon prayer. **İ— Divanı** *Ott. hist.* Council of State assembled in the late afternoon in the grand vizier's house. **— ezanı** the call to afternoon prayer. **— güneşi** of short duration. **— kahvaltısı** afternoon tea, snack. **— namazı** the afternoon worship. **—den sonra dükkân aç=** 1. to open shop late in the day. 2. to undertake something rather late in life. **— üstü**, **—yin** in the afternoon.
ikircik[gi] اِيكِرجِك *prov.* doubt, hesitance. **—len=** to hesitate. **—li** hesitant.
ikircil *neol., phil.* equivocal. **— cümle** *gram.* disjunctive proposition.
ikircin اِيكِرجِين *prov.* undecided, hesitant, vacillating. **—lik** indecision.
ikişer اِيكِشَر two each; two at a time. **— ikişer** two by two, in twos.
ikiz اِيكِز 1. twins. 2. each one of a pair of twins. **—ler**[i] *astr.* the twins, Gemini. **— doğ=** to be born twins. **— doğur=** *slang* to be in great pain; to suffer greatly. **— anlam** *neol., log.* amphibology. **—kenar üçgen** *geom.* isosceles triangle. **—kenar yamuk** *geom.* isosceles trapezoid. **—leme** having a twin, geminate; double.
ikizli اِيكِزلى 1. having a twin, geminate; double; having two handles. 2. *log.* ambiguous. **—lik** *log.* ambiguity.
iklil (.—) اِكليل *A lrnd.* 1. crown, diadem, coronal. 2. *bot.* coronet; *astr.* Corona. 3. the border of skin around the nail.
iklilî (.—.—) اِكليلى *A* 1. *anat.* coronary. 2. *lrnd.* crownlike, coronal.
iklim (.—) اِقليم *A* 1. climate. 2. clime, region; country. **—î** (.—.—) *A* climatic.
ikmal[li] (.—) اِكمال *A* 1. a completing, finishing; completion. 2. *mech.* feeding. 3. *mil.* reinforcement; supply. 4. makeup (examination). **— et=** /ı/ to complete, to finish. **— efradı** *mil.* drafts, replacements. **— hatları** *mil.* lines of communication. **— imtihanı** condition, repeat (examination). **—e kal=** to be conditioned (in an examination). **— kolları** *mil.* supply columns. **— kuvvetleri** *mil.* reinforcements. **— nakliyatı** *mil.* supply transport. **— üssü** *mil.* supply base. **—i tahsil et=** to complete one's education. **—ci** student who is on probation.
ikna[aı] (.—) اِقناع *A* a convincing (in argument); satisfaction; persuasion. **— et=** /ı, a/ to convince, to satisfy. **— ol=** /a/ to be convinced, to be satisfied.
ikrah (.—) اِكراه *A* 1. a loathing; disgust. 2. *lrnd.* a forcing, constraining. **— ve tehdit** *law* threats, duress.
ikrahen (.—′.) اِكراهاً *A lrnd.* much against one's will, by force.
ikram (.—) اِكرام *A* 1. a showing honor, honor; courtesy; kindness; gift. 2. discount, abatement on price. **— et=** 1. /a/ to show honor (to). 2. /ı, a/ to give a present; to offer (tea, cigarette, etc.). 3. /ı, a/ to make a reduction in price.
ikramen (.—′.) اِكراماً *A lrnd.* as an honor or out of respect.
ikramiye (.——.) اِكراميّة *A* bonus, gratuity, indemnity; prize in a lottery. **—li** with a premium; with a prize.
ikrar (.—) اِقرار *A* 1. declaring, confessing, admitting; an acknowledging; an avowing; confession; declaration. 2. *lrnd.* an appointing, establishing, confirming; confirmation. **—dan dön=** to retract one's confession. **—a gel=** to change from denial to confession. **—ı marîz** declaration made at deathbed. **—ı mülk** declaration of ownership. **—ı müphem** *lrnd.* dubious declaration. **—ı sarih** explicit declaration.
ikraz (.—) اِقراض *A* a lending money; *law* **— et=** /ı/ to lend (money). **— ve istikraz** *law* lending and borrowing. **— müesseseleri** credit institutions.
iks اِكس *alg.* the letter **X**.
iksa 1 (.—) اِكساء *A lrnd.* a clothing, dressing; a supplying clothes. **— et=** /ı/ to enrobe, clothe.
iksa 2 اِكساء *A lrnd.* a depressing, causing to be depressed. **—yi kalb** depression.
iksar (.—) اِكثار *A lrnd.* a making abundant; an increasing, multiplying. **—ı kelâm et=** to talk too much, to prolong a subject.
iksir (.—) اِكسير *A* 1. elixir. 2. philosopher's stone. 3. any magic substance that produces a wonderful effect. 4. a cordial; liquor. **—i âzam** philosopher's stone. **—i hayat** elixir of life.
ikta (.—) اِقطاع *A* 1. *Isl. hist.* an assigning lands to a functionary for his maintenance; fief. 2. *lrnd.* a silencing in argument.
iktibas (..—) اِقتباس *A* 1. a quoting; quotation. 2. adaptation of a novel, etc. 3. *lrnd.* a borrowing, deriving or receiving light. 4. *lrnd.* a receiving instruction. **— et=** /ı/ to

take or receive at second hand, to borrow; to use as a quotation.

iktibasen (..—'.) اقتباساً A *lrnd.* quoting; as a quotation.

iktida (..—) اقتداء A *lrnd.* a following a teacher or leader and adopting his guidance; emulation. — **et=** /a/ to follow, to be guided by; to emulate.

iktidaen (..—'.) اقتداءً A *lrnd.* by following; imitating.

iktidar (..—) اقتدار A 1. power, ability, capacity. 2. power, government; the ruling party. —**da ol=** to be in power (political party). —**ı ol=** to be able to, to be capable of; to have power or influence. — **partisi** party in power. —**î** (..— —) A potential. —**lı** powerful; capable. —**sız** incapable, inefficient. —**sızlık** impotence.

iktifa (..—) اكتفا A 1. a deeming sufficient; a contenting oneself with; a restricting oneself to. 2. a being sufficient; a sufficing. — **et=** /la/ to be content with.

iktiham (..—) اقتحام A *lrnd.* 1. a precipitating heedlessly (into). 2. a surmounting; an overcoming, enduring.

iktirab (..—) اكتراب A *lrnd.* a being or becoming sorrowful; grief, sorrow.

iktirah (..—) اقتراح A *lrnd.* 1. a speaking extempore; an improvising. 2. an inventing; a discovering.

iktiran (..—) اقتران A *lrnd.* 1. a being associated, joined, united. 2. conjunction of two planets. — **et=** /a/ to meet with (approval, etc.). —**ı sa'deyn** *astrol.* a lucky conjunction in astrology as of Venus and Jupiter.

iktisa (..—) اكتساء A *lrnd.* a wearing a garment, an arraying. — **et=** 1. to wear. 2. to put on a garment.

iktisab (..—) اكتساب A same as **iktisap**. — **et=** /ı/ to acquire. —**î** (..— —) A acquired, gained, earned.

iktisad (..—) اقتصاد A same as **iktisat**. —**en** (..—'.) A economically.

iktisadî (..— —) اقتصادى A pertaining to economics; economic. — **harb** economic warfare. — **yeterlik** autarchy.

iktisadiyat (..— .—) اقتصاديات economics.

iktisadiyun (..— — —) اقتصاديون A *lrnd.* economists.

iktisam (..—) اقتسام A *lrnd.* a mutually dividing and sharing. — **et=** to divide.

iktisap[bı] (..—) اكتساب [iktisab] *law* a gaining; an earning; an acquiring; acquisition, gain.

iktisat[dı] (..—) اقتصاد [iktisad] 1. economy, management of affairs. 2. frugality, economy, thrift, saving. 3. *lrnd.* an acting with moderation; keeping to the middle road. **İ— Fakültesi** School of Economics (in a university). — **ilmi** economics. **İ— Vekâleti** Ministry of Economy. — **yap=** to cut down expenses, to make savings. —**çı** economist.

iktitaf (..—) اقتطاف A *lrnd.* 1. a gathering, a plucking. 2. compilation. —**iye** (..— —.) A *phil.* eclecticism.

iktiza (..—) اقتضاء A a requiring, demanding; requirement; necessity; need, requisite. —**sınca** according to the requirements (of), as being necessary (for). — **et=** to be necessary, to be required. —**sına göre** as may be necessary, as occasion requires. —**i hal** as circumstances require; necessity of circumstances. —**sı ol=** to be necessary.

il 1 ال 1. same as **el 2**. 2. *neol.* administrative province. — **yazıcısı** *Ott. hist.* land registry official.

=il= 2 *cf.* **=ıl=** 1.

il=[er] 3 ايلمك 1. /ı/ *needlework* to baste; to sew slightly. 2. to fasten or tie with a loop. 3. *archaic* to meet (by chance), to come across. 4. *archaic* to be caught (at something); to go through; to penetrate. 5. *prov.* to hit. —**er tutar yeri kalmadı, —er tutar yeri yok** He is done for completely; it is completely destroyed.

ilâ 1 (.—) الى A to, up to; until. — **âhirihi** *lrnd.* and so on until the end, etcetera. — **âhirizzaman** *lrnd.* to the end of time. — **gayrinnihaye** *lrnd.* infinitely; endlessly; ad infinitum. — **hazelyevm** *lrnd.* to this day, up till now. — **inkırazizzaman** *lrnd.* to the end of time. — **maşallah** 1. God only knows until when. 2. same as **maşallah**. — **meta** *lrnd.* until when. — **nihaye** to the end. — **yevmilkıyam** *lrnd.* until the Day of Judgment, until the end of time.

i'lâ 2 (.—) اعلاء A *lrnd.* a raising, an exalting; a magnifying; glorification. —**i kelimetullah** (*lit.*, exalting the word of God.) proclaiming the true religion to unbelievers.

i'lâ[ai] 3 (.—) A, **ilâ**[ai] (— —) اعلاء *lrnd.* 1. a taking an oath; a vowing, swearing. 2. a man's vowing not to have connection with his wife or concubine for a definite period of time.

ilâc 1 (.—) علاج A see **ilâç**.

ilâc 2 (——) ايلمج A *lrnd.* a causing to enter, introducing, inserting.

ilâç[cı] علاج [ilâc 1] 1. medicine; drug, medicinal substance; chemical substance. 2. remedy, cure. 3. means, device. — **et=** /ı/ *archaic* to treat medically; to find a cure. — **iç=** to take medicine. — **için dahi yok** utterly unobtainable.

ilâçla=[r] علاجلمق 1. to spray with a chemical substance (seeds, etc.); to medicate. 2. to disinfect.

ilâçlı عتجي medicated; disinfected. **— pamuk** sterilized cotton.

ilâçsız عدجبر incurable, irremediable.

ilâd (———) ايلاد A *lrnd.* a giving birth to, a bringing forth.

i'lâf 1 (. —) A, **ilâf** (——) ائلاف *lrnd.* a making tame, a causing to become sociable, familiar or accustomed (to); an accustoming.

ilâf 2 (. —) اعلاف A *lrnd.* a giving animals fodder.

ilâh 1 (. —) الٰه A god, deity.

ilâh. 2 (. —) الٰخ A short for **ilâ âhirihi**, *cf.* **ilâ 1**.

ilâhare (. — . .) الى اخره A short for **ilâ âhirihi**.

ilâhe (. —.) الٰاهه A goddess.

ilâhî 1 (. ——) الٰهى A divine; heavenly. **— hukuk** religious law.

ilâhi 2 (. ——) الٰهى [**ilâhî 1**] hymn. **— oku=** to sing a hymn. **—ci** 1. singer of hymns. 2. singer of chants (generally a beggar).

ilâhî 3 (. ——) الٰهى A O God! My God!

ilâhî 4 (. —.) [**ilâhî 3**] priceless; bless you, *as in*, **ilâhî teyze bu işe nasıl inandın?** Bless you, aunt, how could you believe such a thing?

ilâhileş=ⁱʳ (. ——..) الٰهيلشمك to become divine. **—tir=** /ı/ to deify.

ilâhiri الى اخره [**ilâ âhirihi**] etcetera.

ilâhiyat (. — . —) الٰهيات [*Arabic* . ——] theology. **İ— Fakültesi** School of Theology. **—çı** theologian.

ilâhiye (. —..) الٰهيه A *phil.* theism; deism.

ilâhiyet (. —..) الٰهيات [*Arabic* . ——.] *lrnd.* the quality of deity; godhead.

ilâhiyun (. ———) الٰهيون A *lrnd.* theologians.

i'lâlⁿ (. —) اعلال A 1. *Arabic gram.* a modifying in declination or conjugation the letter ا و ى 2. *phil.* causation.

i'lâm (. —) A, **ilâm** (——) اعلام A 1. *law* sentence, judicial decree in writing; copy of the judgment, engrossement. 2. *lrnd.* a making known; a communicating in detail. **— et=** /ı, a/ to notify a fact or sentence (to). **—ı şer'î**, **—ı şer'i şerif** *can. law* written judgment by a judge of a canonical court.

ilan 1 ايلان *prov.*, same as **yılan**.

i'lân (. —) A, **ilân 2** (——) اعلان 1. notice; announcement; declaration; a proclaiming, proclamation. 2. advertisement; publication. **—ı aşk** declaration of love. **— et=** /ı/ 1. to declare, to announce, to proclaim; to spread. 2. to publish, to advertise. **—ı harb** declaration of war. **— pulu** advertisement tax stamp. **— suretiyle yapılan vaitler** public promise of reward. **— ve tasdik** promulgation.

ilânat (———) اعلانات A *lrnd.* advertisements.

ilâncılıkᴱⁱ اعلانجيلك publicity, advertising.

i'lânen (. —'.) A, **ilânen** (——'.) اعلانا *lrnd.* by way of advertisement.

ilânname (———.) اعلاننامه P *lrnd.* proclamation; advertisement.

ilârya (..'.) ايلاريا a kind of mullet, *zool.*, *Mugil*.

ilâvat (.——) علاوات A *lrnd.*, *pl.* of **ilâve**.

ilâve (.—.) علاوه A 1. addition, increase. 2. supplement. 3. exaggeration. 4. postscript. **— et=** /ı, a/ 1. to add (to). 2. to exaggerate, to magnify.

ilâveli علاوه لى having a supplement or addition.

ilâveten (.—'..) علاوةً A in addition; as an addition.

ilbas (. —) الباس A *lrnd.* a putting a garment on a person; a supplying clothes.

ilca (. —) الجا A *lrnd.* a forcing, compelling, constraining; constraint, compulsion.

ilcaat (.——) الجاآت A *lrnd.* compulsion; necessities.

ilcam (. —) الجام A *lrnd.* a bridling or bitting a horse.

ilçe *neol.* administrative district, county.

ildir=ⁱʳ ايلديرمك *archaic* 1. /ı/ to loop, hook, button. 2. to touch.

ile 1 ايله 1. with, together with. 2. and. 3. through; by means of; by.

-ile 2 (—.) ايله *var. of* **-iyle**.

ileł علل A *lrnd.*, *pl* of **illet**. **—i âdiye felsefesi** *phil.* occasional ... **—i sâriye** epidemic, contagious diseases.

ilelebed الى الابد A forever.

ilelmerkez الى المركز A *phys.* centripetal.

ilen 1 ايلن *prov.*, same as **ile 1**.

ilen=ⁱʳ **2** ايلنمك /a/ *prov.* to curse; to utter imprecations. **—ç** *archaic* curse, imprecation. **—dir=** *caus of* **ilen= 2**.

ilerde ايلرده *same as* **ileride**.

ileri ايلرى 1. further on, forward, further forward; further. 2. the forward part; front; future. 3. advanced, in advance, higher in grade or degree. 4. fast (clock). **—de** 1. in the future, later on. 2. further on; ahead. 3. in front. **—deki** 1. the one that is ahead. 2. that is in the future. **—den** 1. from farther on, from a distance. 2. in advance, beforehand. **—si** 1. the future. 2. farther on, the farther part. 3. beyond, farther. **—ye** forward. **— al=** /ı/ 1. to take forward, to bring forward. 2. to advance (person). 3. to put forward (clock). **— atıl=** 1. to spring forward; to rush forward. 2. to have the courage to go into difficult things. **—den beri** from of old. **— çek=** /ı/ 1. to

ileriki

draw forward. 2. *archaic* to advance (person). — **çık=** 1. to go out forwards. 2. *archaic* to go forth to meet (somebody). — **doğru** further forward, ahead. — **geç=** 1. to go to the front. 2. to pass to a higher position. 3. to overtake. — **gel=** 1. to come on further in advance; to come forward. 2. to make progress; to advance in rank. 3. /dan/ to surpass. 4. /dan/ to be due to; to result (from); to arise (from). — **gelenler** notables, important personages. — **geri** 1. forwards and backwards. 2. unsuitable (words). —**sini gerisini düşünme=** not to be prudent; not to weigh all considerations. **bir — bir geri git=** to hesitate. — **geri söyle=** to talk aggressively; to talk in an inappropriate way. — **git=** 1. to go forward, to advance; to precede. 2. to be running fast (clock). 3. to go too far; to be rude. — **hat** *mil.* front line. — **karakol** *mil.* advance outpost, outlying picket. — **karakollar ikame et=** *mil.* to send out pickets. — **kol** *mil.* vanguard. — **sür=** /ı/ 1. to drive forward. 2. to advance (reason, argument); to put before; to submit. 3. *mil.* to send out (pickets, etc.). — **sürme** *neol., log.* assertion. — **var=** to go too far. — **yürüyüş** *mil.* onward march. — **zamanda** *archaic* in old times; once upon a time.

ileriki اِيْلَرِكِى *archaic* the former, the old one.
ilerile=ᵘʳ اِيْلَرِلَمَك *archaic, same as* **ilerle=**.
ilerle=ᵘʳ اِيْلَرلَمَك 1. to advance, to go forward; to progress; to improve. 2. to be fast (clock). 3. to pass away (time); to grow late. —**me** *verbal n.* —**t=** /ı/ *caus. of* **ilerle=**. —**yiş** *verbal n.*
ilerü اِيْلَرُو *archaic, same as* **ileri**.
ilet=ᵘʳ اِيْلَتْمَك *prov.* /ı/ 1. to send; to take or carry away. 2. to carry off, make off with. 3. *elec.* to conduct. —**il=** *pass.* —**ken** *neol., elec.* conductor. —**ken damarlar** *bot.* conductor ducts. —**kenlik** *neol.* conductivity.
iletki *neol., math.* protractor.
iley اِلَى اِلَرِى *archaic* space before something, front. —**inde** before him. —**ini kes=** /ın/ to stop someone by standing in his way.
ileyh اِلَيْهِ A *lrnd.* to him, to it. —**a** (..—) A to her. —**im** A, —**ima** (...—) A to them.
ilga (.—) اِلْغَا A an abolishing; abolition; an annulling; nullification; *law* repeal; abrogation, annulment. — **et=** /ı/ to annul, to abolish; to cancel.
ilgaz (.—) اِلْغَاز A *lrnd.* an expressing oneself enigmatically; a making a riddle. —**la konuş=** to speak enigmatically.
ilgi *neol.* 1. relation, connection; attachment. 2. interest. 3. *chem.* affinity. 4. *gram.* relative case. — **cümlesi** *gram.* relative proposition.

— **göster=** /a/ to be interested; to take interest (in). — **zamiri** *gram.* relative pronoun.
ilgilen=ᵘʳ /la/ 1. to be interested; to pay attention (to). 2. to become interested; to show interest. —**dir=** /ı/ 1. to be of interest (to), to concern. 2. to arouse (someone's) interest.
ilgili 1. interested; connected with. 2. concerning.
ilgisiz indifferent. —**lik** disinterestedness; indifference.
ilh. الخ *abbreviation for* **ilâ âhirihi**, *cf.* **ilâ 1**.
ilhad (.—) اِلْحَاد A *lrnd.* 1. a deviating from the right way. 2. heresy; *phil.* atheism.
ilhah (.—) اِلْحَاح A *lrnd.* a being importunate; importunity.
ilhakᵏⁱ (.—) اِلْحَاق A 1. a joining, an adding. 2. annexation. — **et=** /ı/ to annex; to join on, to add on.
ilham (.—) اِلْهَام A inspiration, divine revelation. — **et=** /ı, a/ to inspire (with); to give the inspiration (for). — **perisi** *poet.* muse. —**i ilâhî**, —**i rabbanî** the inspiration of God. —**î** (.——) A *lrnd.* inspiration-giving.
ilhan (.—) اِلْخَان *archaic* prince; commander; tribal chief. **İ—lı** *hist.* Ilkhanid.
-**ili** لى *cf.* -**lı 2**.
ilikᵍⁱ 1 اِيْلِك 1. marrow. 2. delicious. — **balığı** bitterling, *zool., Rhodeus amarus.* — **beyin** *anat.* myelencephalon, afterbrain. —**ine geç=** /in/ 1. to penetrate to the marrow (cold, etc.); to be drenched. 2. to affect deeply, to touch to the quick. — **gibi** 1. delicious, appetizing. 2. *slang* very pretty (girl). —**ine işle=** *same as* **iliğine geç=**. —**ini kemir=** to affect deeply (pain, etc.). —**ini kurut=** /ın/ to harass greatly, to wear out (a person). —**i sızla=** to feel deeply (pain etc.). — **yağı** suet.
ilikᵍⁱ 2 اِيْلِك loop for a button, hook on clothing; buttonhole. — **düğme** loops and buttons.
ilikle=ᵘʳ اِيْلِكْلَمَك /ı/ to button up; to hook; to fasten with a hook and eye. —**n=** *pass.* —**t=** /ı, a/ *caus.* of **ilikle=**.
ilikli 1 اِيْلِكْلِى buttoned up; fastened up by loops.
ilikli 2 اِيْلِكْلِى containing marrow.
ilikmen اِيْلِكْمَن *Gk prov.* night light.
ilimˡᵐⁱ عِلْم [**ilm**] 1. science. 2. knowledge, learning; theoretical knowledge. 3. dexterity, skillfulness. —**i ahadis**, —**i ahbar** *lrnd.* the science of tradition concerning the acts or words of the Prophet Mohammad and of his personal disciples. —**i ahlâk** *lrnd.* ethics; moral philosophy. —**i ahval-i cev** *lrnd.* meteorology. —**i ahval-i ruh** *lrnd.* psychology. —**i akaid** *lrnd.* theology, catechism. —**i akvam..**

—i akvam-ı beşer *lrnd.* ethnography, ethnology. —i alaim-i cevviye *archaic* meteorology. — ve amel *lrnd.* theory and practice. —i aruz *lrnd.* prosody. —i arz *lrnd.* geology. —i âsâr *lrnd.*, *same as* ilm-i ahadis. —i bâtın *lrnd.* inspired knowledge, speculative science. —i bedayi *lrnd.* esthetics. —i beden *lrnd.* medical science. —i bedi *lrnd.* rhetoric. —i bedihi *lrnd.* intuitive knowledge. —i belâgat *lrnd.* rhetoric, oratory, eloquence. —i beyan *lrnd.* science of rhetorical style. —i cebir *lrnd.* algebra. —i cerri eskal *lrnd.* mechanics, science of dynamics. —i edeb *lrnd.* 1. Arabic philology. 2. ethics, morals. —i edvar *lrnd.* the art of musical composition, music. —i ektaf *lrnd.* science of divining by the shoulderblades of sheep. —i elsine *lrnd.* linguistics, philology. —i emrâz *lrnd.* pathology. —i ensab *lrnd.* genealogy. —i ensac *lrnd.* histology. —i enva *lrnd.* science of computing the times of the lunar mansions. —i esma *Isl. rel.* science of the names and attributes of God, *i. e.*, the names, their meanings, virtues etc. —i ezelî *lrnd.* prescience. —i feraiz *can. law* science of division of inheritances. —i feraset *lrnd.* physiognomy. —i fetva *lrnd.* science of canonical opinions or decisions in Islam. —i fıkh *lrnd.* science of canonical law in Islam. —i gaybî *lrnd.* 1. occult sciences. 2. foreknowledge; divination. — ü haber*. —i hadis science of the traditions of the words and deeds of the Prophet Muhammad. —i hal*. —i hat *lrnd.* geomancy. —i hayvanat *lrnd.* zoology. —i hendese *lrnd.* geometry. —i hesab *lrnd.* arithmetic. —i heyet *lrnd.* astronomy. —i hikmet *lrnd.* 1. philosophy. 2. physics. —i hilâf ü cedel *lrnd.* science of disputation (as a branch of jurisprudence). —i hiyel *lrnd.* mechanics. —i hukuk *lrnd.* science of law; jurisprudence. —i huruf *lrnd.* onomancy. —i ictimai *lrnd.* sociology. —i ihfa *lrnd.* art of rendering oneself invisible. —i iktisad *lrnd.* economics. —i ilâhî *lrnd.* 1. theology. 2. theodicy. —i imlâ *lrnd.* orthography. —i inbat-ı miyah *lrnd.* hydraulics (for wells). —i inşa *lrnd.* the art of prose writing, epistolography. —i i'rab *lrnd.* Arabic syntax. — ve irfan *lrnd.* knowledge and learning. —i isnad *Isl. rel.* science of attribution of traditions to the persons who first said them. —i iştikak *lrnd.* etymology. —i kablettarih *lrnd.* prehistory. —i kafiye *lrnd.* science of rhyme; art of rhyming. —i kef *lrnd.* palmistry, chiromancy. —i kelâm *lrnd.* science of the Quran and of Biblical theology. —i kelâm ve akaid *lrnd.* 1. scholastic theology. 2. metaphysics. —i kıhf *phil.* phrenology. —i kıraat *lrnd.* the art of reading and reciting the Quran as taught by one of the seven original masters. —i kıyafet *lrnd.* physiognomy. —i kimya *lrnd.* 1. chemistry. 2. alchemy. —i kitab *lrnd.* science of exegesis. —i kitabet *lrnd.* art of literary composition. —i ledün *lrnd.* knowledge of Divine Providence. —i lûgat *lrnd.* lexicology. —i maad *lrnd.* 1. eschatology. 2. science of the names and perfections of God. —i mabadelhendese *lrnd.* metageometry. —i mabadüttabia *lrnd.* metaphysics. —i madeniyat *lrnd.* mineralogy. —i mâna *lrnd.* rhetoric. —i mânevi *lrnd.* spiritual knowledge; speculative science. —i mantık *lrnd.* logic. —i meani *lrnd.* etymology, semantics. —i menahic *lrnd.* methodology. —i menazır *lrnd.* science of perspective. —i menşei akvam *lrnd.* ethnology. —i merakizüleskal *lrnd.* the science of the finding of centers of gravity. —i meraya *lrnd.* study of perspective. —i merayayı muhrika *lrnd.* science of burning-mirrors. —i mesaha *lrnd.* geometry; mensuration. —i mevakit *lrnd.* science of chronological or astronomical times (for calculating ephemerides). —i mevcudat *lrnd.* knowledge of natural phenomena. —i muamele *lrnd.* knowledge of the duties of a believer towards God and man. —i musiki *lrnd.* musicology. —i müstahasat *lrnd.* paleontology. —i nahv *lrnd.* grammar, syntax. —i nebatat *lrnd.* botany. —i nücum *lrnd.* astronomy; astrology. —i pişani *lrnd.* science of reading character or fortune from the forehead. —i rakam *lrnd.* arithmetic, science of numbers. —i remil *lrnd.* geomancy. —i rivayet *lrnd.* the science of tradition. —i riyazet *lrnd.* mystical science of ascetism. —i ruh *lrnd.* psychology. —i rümuz *lrnd.* algorism, algorithm. —i rüşeym *lrnd.* embryology. —i saadet *lrnd.* eudaemonism. —i sarf *lrnd.* grammar. —i savt *lrnd.* acoustics. —i secaya *lrnd.* a study of human character, ethology. —i servet *lrnd.* political economy; economics. —i sihr *lrnd.* magic; witchcraft. —i simya *lrnd.* 1. alchemy. 2. palmistry, chiromancy. —i siyak, —i siyakat *lrnd.* the science of public finance arithmetic. —i siyaset *lrnd.* science of law and government. —i suri *lrnd.* acquired knowledge. —i sülûk *lrnd.* art of a saintly life. —i şerayi' ve ahkâm *lrnd.* the applied science of canonical law. —i şerif *lrnd.* the noble science (of the stars). —i tabakatülarz *lrnd.* geology. —i tabii *lrnd.* natural science. —i tarih *lrnd.* historiology. —i tasavvuf *lrnd.* mysticism, sufism. —i tedbir-i menzil *lrnd.* science of domestic economy. —i tedkik-i hutût *lrnd.* paleography. —i tefazüli *lrnd.* differential calculus. —i teksir *lrnd.* onomancy. —i te'lif *lrnd.* the art of musical composition. —i

temamî ve tefazülî *lrnd.* integral and differential calculus. **—i tencim** *lrnd.* astrology. **—i terbiyei etfâl** *lrnd.* pedagogy. **—i tevhid** *lrnd.* science of the unity of God. **—i te'vil** *lrnd.* science of exegesis. **—i tevlid** *lrnd.* 1. science of horticulture. 2. stock-breeding. **—i tıb** *lrnd.* medical science. **—i tılsımat** *lrnd.* art of talismans. **—i vezaif** *lrnd.* deontology, ethics. **—i yakin** *lrnd.* 1. certain knowledge, demonstration. 2. religious life.
iliman ایلمان *archaic, same as* **liman**.
ilimcilikği *neol.* scientism.
ilimhân (..—) علمخوان P *lrnd.* 1. studious. 2. student.
ilin=ir ایلنمك *archaic* /a/ 1. to touch. 2. to be caught by; to be stuck. 3. to be tacked, to be tied in a loop.
ilinekği *neol., log.* accident. **—li** accidental.
ilinti ایلنتی 1. rough sewing together, tacking. 2. *prov.* connection; relation.
ilistir ایلستیر Gk *prov.* perforated skimmer.
iliş=ir ایلشمك /a/ 1. to touch lightly; to touch. 2. to hold on lightly, to be caught at; to be fastened to; to catch. 3. to interfere. 4. to sit modestly (on the edge of something); to remain for a short time. 5. to have a slight quarrel or controversy (with); to molest. 6. to object; to disapprove.
ilişikği ایلشیك 1. attached; enclosed herewith. 2. connected, relating to; related. 3. relation, connection; interest. 4. impediment, hitch. 5. liability, obligation. **—i kalma=** /ın, la/ to have no more relations with; to have no further interest; to be settled up. **—ini kes=** /ın, la/ 1. to sever one's connection with. 2. to dismiss, to discharge. 3. to settle (account). **—li** connected, interested; concerned, related. **—siz** 1. free; unattached; disinterested. 2. settled up.
ilişki *neol., phil.* relation, connection.
ilişkin *neol.* relating to, concerning, regarding.
iliştir=ir ایلشدرمك ایلیشدیرمك /ı, a/ 1. to fasten slightly; to attach. 2. to tack up. 3. to hang up. **—il=** *pass.*
İliya ایلیا [*Arabic* —.—] 1. *Bib.* Elijah. 2. *hist.* Jerusalem.
ilkki ایلك 1. the first, first. 2. initial; beginning. 3. primary. 4. original. **— adım** first step; the beginning. **— ağızda** at the first time; at the first attempt, upon the first occasion. **— ağızdan** in the very beginning. **— akşamdan** *prov.* with nightfall. **— bahar***. **— bahtım altın tahtım** One's first chance is usually the best (often in marriage). **— çağ***. **— defa** for the first time; first. **— eğitim** *neol.* primary education. **— elden** 1. first; from the beginning. 2. direct (sale). **— evvel** first of all, to begin with. **— fırsatta** at the first opportunity. **— görünüş** *neol., psych.* 'presentation. **— görüşte** at first sight. **— göz ağrısı** one's first love. **— hareket kolu** *auto.* starting handle. **— harf** initial, first letter. **— hız** initial speed (of a projectile), muzzle velocity. **— insan** primitive man. **— ipsiler** *neol., zool.* protochordates. **— iptida** *colloq.* first of all, in the first place, to begin with. **— kalemde** first, first of all. **— Kânun***. **— mektep** primary school. **— okul***. **— öğretim** *neol.* primary education. **— önce** first of all, first. **— örnek** archetype. **— partide** first, with the first (shipment, etc.). **— peşin** *colloq.* first of all. **— pişim** *ceramics* first baking. **— proje** preliminary plan, rough draft. **— sezi** *neol., psych.* apprehension. **— söz** foreword, preface. **— tahkikat** *law* preliminary inquiry. **— tedrisat** primary education. **— Teşrin***. **— yaz** *archaic* spring. **— zaman** *geol.* primary age.
ilka (.—) الفاء A *lrnd.* 1. a throwing or dropping into; flinging. 2. a suggesting; suggestion; an imparting; an inspiring. 3. an imputing some offense to a person. **—i asâ** (*lit.*, a throwing down the staff) a ceasing from travel. **— et=** /ı/ 1. to throw in. 2. to suggest; to inspire. **—i hiras et=** to arouse terror.
ilkaat (.——) الفاءات A *lrnd.* a leading astray with seductive words; seductive words; delusions. **— et=** /ı/ to lead astray.
ilkah (.—) القاح A 1. a fecundating, fecundation; fertilization; insemination. 2. *archaic* a vaccinating, vaccination. **— et=** to fecundate; to impregnate.
ilkbahar ایلك بهار 1. spring. 2. vernal. **— çiçeği** daisy, marguerite, *bot., Bellis perennis*; common primrose, *bot., Primula acaulis*. **— noktası** *astr.* vernal equinox.
ilkçağ ایلك چاغ *hist.* Antiquity.
ilke *neol.* element; principle; basis.
ilkel *neol.* elementary; primary; fundamental; primitive. **— fonksiyon** *math.* primitive function.
ilkin (.'.) ایلكین first, firstly; in the first place; at first.
İlkkânun (.——) ایلك كانون December.
ilklikği ایلكلك 1. priority. 2. primariness.
ilksizlikği *neol.* eternity.
İlkteşrin ایلك تشرین October.
illâ (.—) الّا A 1. except; excepting; save; but. 2. unless; or else. 3. whatever happens; without fail; by all means. **— ki** without fail, for sure. **— ve lâkin** *colloq.* but on the other hand.
illallâh (..—) الله الّا *colloq.*, expresses disgust or annoyance; I am fed up. I have had enough of it. **—i ve Resulihi** I'm sick to death of it.

ille (.'.) الا [illâ] 1. without fail, by all means, absolutely. 2. just; especially, particularly.

illet علّت A 1. disease, chronic disease, malady; defect. 2. a suffering; misfortune. 3. *phil.* cause, reason. **—i âdiye** *phil.* occasional cause. **— edin=** /ı/ to pick up a nervous habit. **—i faile** *phil.* efficient cause. **—i failiye** *phil.* direct producing cause. **—i gaiye** *phil.* ultimate cause. **— kazan=** to contract a disease. **—i maddiye** *phil.* material or secondary cause. **—i sûriye** *phil.* outward, formal, secondary cause.

illetli علّتلی 1. diseased; sickly; defective. 2. having some annoying habit. 3. *phil.* having a cause. **—lik** diseasedness, defectiveness.

illetsiz علّتسز 1. free from disease, sound. 2. *phil.* self-existing; spontaneous. **— iktisab** *law* unjustifiable enrichment. **—lik** freedom from disease.

illî (.—) علّی A *lrnd.* causal. **—yet** (.—.) A causality.

illiyîn, illiyun (..—) علیّین A *Isl. rel.* the highest of the eight Paradises mentioned in the Quran.

ilm علم A *cf.* ilim.

ilma' (.—) الماع A *lrnd.* 1. a shining, making a brilliant appearance. 2. a showing suddenly like a flash.

ilmam (.—) الما م A *lrnd.* 1. a committing a slight offense or venial sin. 2. a being or becoming near, approaching.

ilmek^{ği} الملک 1. loop; noose. 2. bow-knot, slipknot.

ilmekle=^r الملکلک /ı/ 1. to tie loosely. 2. to make a loop.

ilmekli الملکلی lightly tied; in a bow; looped. **— düğüm** 1. slipknot. 2. single-looped bow, single bow.

ilmen (.'.) علماً A *lrnd.* scientifically; in a scholarly way; by means of science.

ilmî (.—) علمی A scientific; scholarly; pertaining to knowledge.

ilmihal (..—) علم حال catechism.

ilmik^{ği} الملک *var. of* ilmek.

ilmiyat (..—) علمیات A *obs.* epistemology.

ilmiye (..—.) علمیه A *Isl. rel.* the Ulema class.

ilmühaber علم خبر A 1. identity papers; certificate. 2. receipt; voucher.

ilmülbeyan (...—) علم البیان A *lrnd.* art of style in speech.

ilmülmeftuhat (...——) علم المفتوحات A *lrnd.* science of known quantities, common arithmetic.

ilmülmükâşefe (...—..) علم المکاشف A *lrnd.* knowledge of God given by Himself to a saint.

ilmülyakin (...—) علم الیقین A *lrnd.* 1. sure knowledge; sure belief. 2. firm religious knowledge based upon revelation.

ilmünnefs علم النفس A *lrnd.* psychology.

ilsak^{kı} (.—) الصاق A *lrnd.* a joining on, an attaching, a linking.

ilt=^{er, ür} ایلتک *archaic, same as* **ilet=**.

iltibas (..—) التباس A 1. *log.* a being or becoming obscure or confused. 2. *log.* ambiguity. **—a mahal kalmamak için** to avoid any ambiguity. **—lı** ambiguous.

iltica (..—) التجاء A 1. a taking shelter or refuge. 2. *lrnd.* an asking for quarter. **— et=** /a/ 1. to take shelter (with). 2. to take refuge (with). **—gâh** (..——) P place of refuge.

iltifat (..—) التفات A 1. a treating with courtesy or kindness; courteous or kind treatment; favor. 2. a taking notice of, a paying attention (to). 3. *rhet.* a shift from third to second person, apostrophe. 4. *lrnd.* a turning towards, a turning around to look at. **— bul=** /dan/ to find favor (with). **— et=** /a/ to take notice (of), to treat with favor; to show courtesy. **— gör=** /dan/ to find kindness (with). **— göster=** /a/ to treat with kindness, to show favor to.

iltifatkâr (..——) التفاتکار P kind; kind, affable person. **—âne** (..———.) P courteous (words); in an affable manner.

iltifatlı التفاتلی containing kind words.

iltihab (..—) التهاب A *cf.* iltihap. **—î** (..——) *path.* inflammatory.

iltihak^{kı} (..—) التحاق A 1. a joining or attaching oneself (to); adherence. 2. *law* accession. **— et=** /a/ to join, to adhere to, to connect oneself (with).

iltihap^{bı} (..—) التهاب [iltihab] 1. *path.* inflammation. 2. *path.* infection. 3. *lrnd.* a flaming.

iltihaplan=^{ır} التهابلن to become inflamed.

iltika (..—) التقاء A *lrnd.* an encountering; a joining; a meeting; junction, encounter.

iltikam (..—) التقام A *lrnd.* a swallowing at one gulp.

iltikat (..—) التقاط A *lrnd.* 1. a picking up, gleaning. 2. compilation. 3. *law* a taking of an abandoned child.

iltima' (..—) التماع A *lrnd.* a flash like lightning.

iltimas (..—) التماس A 1. preferential treatment, protection, patronage. 2. *lrnd.* request. **— et=** /ı/ *lrnd.* to request. **— gör=** /dan/ to be favored, protected. **— göster=** /a/ to favor, to show special favor to. **— yap=** /a/ to favor, to treat preferentially (person).

iltimasçı التماسچی one who asks for, or grants favors. **—lık** favoritism, partiality.

iltimaslı التماسلی favored, privileged.

iltisakᵏⁱ (..—) الإلتصاق 1. *path.* adhesion. 2. *lrnd.* contiguity, junction; adherence. **— borusu** *mech.* pipe union. **— hattı** *railway* junction, branch line. **— noktası** junction. **—î** (..— —) A *ling.* agglutinative.

iltiva (..—) الإلتواء A 1. *lrnd.* sinuosity; bend, turn (of a road); coil; entanglement. 2. *geol.* plication; meandering (of a river). 3. *anat.* lateral curvature of the spine; supination of the arm.

iltiyam (..—) الإلتيام A *lrnd.* a being healed, mended or put to rights; cicatrisation. **— bul=** to be healed.

iltiyampezir (..—.—) الإلتيام پذير P *lrnd.* cured, healed; mended. **— ol=** to heal up, to be cured.

iltizam (..—) الإلتزام A 1. a favoring; preference. 2. a taking upon oneself. 3. *hist.* a farming of a branch of the public revenue. **— et=** /ı/ 1. to take the part of, to favor. 2. to take upon oneself. 3. *hist.* to farm a branch of the revenue. **—ı mâlâyelzem** *lrnd.* a taking needless trouble. **—ı sükût et=** to prefer silence. **—a ver=** /ı/ *hist.* to farm (a revenue). **—cı** *hist.* farmer of public revenue.

iltizamen (..—'.) الإلتزاماً 1. by preference. 2. as a voluntary undertaking. 3. *hist.* on lease; by farming out.

iltizamî (..— —) الإلتزامى A 1. done on purpose. 2. partial, showing favor. 3. *gram.* optative. **— muamele** *law* act of disposal.

İlyada (..'.) ايلياده Gk the Iliad.

İlyas (.—) الياس A *Bib.* Elijah.

ilzam (.—) الإلزام A 1. a silencing or convincing in argument. 2. *hist.* a farming out public revenue. **— et=** /ı/ to silence by argument. **— ve iltizam** *hist.* a giving and taking a branch of revenue in farm.

-im 1 *cf.* **-m 2.**
-im 2 *cf.* **-m 3.**
-im 3 *cf.* **-ım 3.**

im 4 1. *neol.*, *phil.* sign. 2. *prov.* signal, sign. **— et=** *prov.* to signal; to beckon. **—i timi yok** *prov.* completely absent.

im 5 ام اِم archaic pair of knickers.

ima 1 (— —) ايما A allusion, innuendo, hint. **— et=** /a/ to make an allusion (to), to hint (at).

ima 2 (.—) اما A *lrnd.* female slaves.

imad (.—) عماد A *lrnd.* 1. pillar, pole, column. 2. prop, stay, support, buttress. 3. confidence, reliance, trust.

imadüddin (.—.—) عمادالدين A *lrnd.* 1. the pillar of religion, *i. e.*, the Quran. 2. *w. cap.*, *man's name.*

i'malⁱⁱ (.—), **imal**ⁱⁱ (— —) اعمال 1. manufacture. 2. *lrnd.* a working, acting, operating. **— et=** /ı/ to manufacture, make, produce, prepare. **—i fikr et=** to think out a matter in detail; to consider thoroughly.

imalât 1 (.— —) اعمالات A manufactured goods, products; production.

imalât 2 (.— —) اعمالات A *lrnd.*, pl. of **imale.**

imalâthane (.— — —.) اعمالتخانه P workshop, factory.

imale (.—.) اماله A 1. *pros.* pronunciation of a short vowel as a long one. 2. *lrnd.* a bending, inclining; persuading, convincing. **—i beyneben** *pros.* (lit., a medium vocal inflection) a slight shortening of the long a. **— et=** /ı/ *lrnd.* 1. to cause to incline. 2. to persuade, to convince. **—i nazar et=** /a/ *lrnd.* to examine, investigate (something).

imalı (— —.) اعمالى containing a hint or implication; allusive; alluding to.

imaliye (.— —.) اعماليه A 1. cost of labor. 2. *colloq.* workmanship.

imam 1 امام [imam 2] *Isl. rel.* 1. imam, prayer leader. 2. successor to the Prophet, Caliph (according to Shiite doctrine). 3. religious leader; chief of a sect; guide, exemplar; the Prophet Muhammad; the Quran. **— bayıldı*.** **—ın dört çiftesine bin=** *slang* to die. **— evi** *obs.* women's prison. **— evinden aş, ölü gözünden yaş çıkmaz** No food is likely to come out of an Imam's house and no tears from a corpse *expression used for a very stingy person.* **— feneri** *obs.* lantern used by district imams while going to the mosque at night. **— kayığı** *slang* coffin. **— kırkı** *colloq.* the first of the forty days of severe winter (December 21st).

imam 2 (.—) امام A *lrnd.*, same as **imam 1. İ—ı A'zam** title of Abu-Hanifa, the founder of the Hanifite school of orthodoxy. **İ—ı Muntazar** the Imam Mahdi who will reappear to judge the world. **—ı mübin** the Quran. **— suyu** *slang* raki. **İ—ı Şafii** title of Muhammad, son of İdris, founder of the Shafiites.

imambayıldı امام بايلدى dish prepared with eggplant and olive oil.

imame 1 (.—.) امامه [imame 2] *lrnd.* 1. stem or junction bead of a string of prayer beads. 2. mouthpiece generally of amber of a tobacco pipe. **— etekliği** the lower piece of amber, etc. in the mouthpiece of a Turkish pipe.

imame 2 (.—.) عمامه A *lrnd.* turban.

imameci (.—..) امامه جى maker or seller of amber mouthpieces for pipes.

imamele=ʳ امامه لمك /ı/ 1. to supply with a junction bead (prayer beads). 2. to supply with a mouthpiece (pipe).

imamet (.—.) امامت A *lrnd.* the quality or

office of an imam, imamate. — et= to perform the office of an imam; to lead in worship.

imamiye (.——.) امامية A *Isl. rel.* the Imamites.

imamlık[tı] اماملق imamate. — et= to be the imam, to serve as an imam.

İmamülmüslimin (.—...—) امام المسلمين A *Isl. rel.* 1. the Prophet Muhammad. 2. the Quran. 3. the Caliph.

imamzade (.——.) امام زاده P *lrnd.* son of an imam.

iman 1 (——) ایمان A 1. faith, belief; a believing. 2. a believing in the faith of Islam. 3. religion. 4. absolute conviction; confidence. —ı bütün a true believer. — et= /a/ 1. to have faith in God. 2. to have great confidence (in). —a gel= 1. to be converted to the true faith, i. e., the faith of Islam. 2. to see reason; to be convinced. — getir= /a/ to have faith in God, to believe in a dogma, etc. —a getir= /ı/ 1. to convert a person to Islam. 2. to get someone to see reason; to subdue. —ı makbul *lrnd.* the true religion. —ı masum *lrnd.* the faith of the prophets. —ı matbu *lrnd.* faith of the angels. —ı merdud *lrnd.* faith of the hypocrite. —ı mevkuf *lrnd.* the faith of those who follow religious innovations. — sahibi a man of faith, a believer. — tahtası *colloq.* breastbone, sternum. —ı taklidî *lrnd.* the lip service of those who have no solid convictions. —ı yeis *lrnd.* a faith in time of adversity or despair. —ı yok *slang* rascal.

iman 2 ایمان [iman 1] *used only in the following expressions* —ım! *slang, expression of emphasis or address.* —ı ağla= /ın/ *slang* to undergo hardship, to have a terrible time. —ı gevre= /ın/ *slang* to have great trouble; to get exhausted. —ına kadar *colloq.* up to the brim; to the utmost degree. —a tak de= *slang* to be exhausted; to be fed up with. —ına yandığım *slang* damned, cursed.

im'an 3 (.—) امعان A *lrnd.* a scrutinizing; an investigating; scrutiny. —ı nazar et= /a/ to peer into, to scrutinize; to fix one's eyes or attention (on).

imandar (———) ایماندار P *lrnd.* believing; having true belief in God; believer, faithful. —î (————) P faith, belief.

imaniye (————.) ایمانیه A *phil.* fideism.
imanlı (.—.) ایمانلی having faith; religious (person).

imansız (——.) ایمانسز 1. unbelieving; without faith, atheist. 2. wicked, unjust, cruel. — git= *colloq.* to die as an unbeliever. — peynir skim cheese. —ca cruelly; —lık lack of faith; atheism.

imanülbey'a (——...) ایمان البیع A *feudal law* oaths of fealty.

imar (——) اعمار A an improving a place by construction of roads and public buildings; public improvements. İ— Bakanı Minister of public improvements. İ— Bakanlığı Ministry of public improvements. — durumu zoning statement, document from the department establishing the zoning limitation on a piece of property. — et= /ı/ *lrnd.* to construct; to improve; to render prosperous. — plânı zoning and construction plan.

imaret (.—.) عمارت A 1. *Ott. hist.* soup-kitchen for the poor. 2. *lrnd.* prosperous condition; wellbeing; cultivation. — çorbası 1. soup from a public kitchen. 2. something got for nothing. — et= /ı/ *lrnd.* to make prosperous. —çi person in charge of a public kitchen.

imate (.—.) اماتة A *lrnd.* a causing to die; a putting to death. — et= /ı/ to put to death.
imbar (.—) امبار P *lrnd.,* same as **inbar**.
imbat امبات It the steady summer south wind.
imbik[ği] انبیق [inbik] still, retort. —ten çek=, — et= /ı/ to distil.
imbisat (..—) انبساط *var. of* **inbisat**.

imdad, imdat[dı] (.—) امداد A 1. a helping, aiding, succoring; help, aid, assistance. 2. *mil.* reinforcement. 3. Help! — et= /a/ to come to the rescue (of); to help, to assist. — gönder= /a/ to send assistance or reinforcements (to). — iste= /dan/ 1. *mil.* to ask for reinforcements. 2. to send an S.O.S. — işareti S.O.S. signal. — kuvvetleri *mil.* auxiliary forces, reinforcements. —ı sıhhî ambulance. —a yetiş= 1. to come to the assistance (of). 2. *mil.* to bring up reinforcements. —çı 1. one who comes to another's help; helper. 2. reinforcement. —î (.——) A *lrnd.* auxiliary. —iye (.——.) *obs.* special emergency tax.

imdi ایمدی 1. therefore; now; thus; and so. 2. *archaic, same as* şimdi.
-imdir ایمدیر *cf.* -ımdır.
ime 1 ایمه *prov.* ibex.
=ime= 2 *cf.* =ıma=.
imece ایمجه Gk work done for the community by the whole village; by the united efforts of the community.
imge *neol., phil.* image. —lem, —leme imagination.
imha (.—) امحا A destruction; effacement; annihilation. — ateşi *mil.* annihilating fire. — et= /ı/ to destroy, obliterate, annihilate. — harbi, — muharebesi *mil.* internecine war, war of extermination.
imhal[li] (.—) امهال A *lrnd.* 1. an extending the time limit within which something has to be done. 2. a postponing; a delaying; a putting off, postponement, procrastination. — et= /ı/ 1. to prolong (a term). 2. to postpone;

delay, procrastinate. **— ve ihmal** delay and neglect.

imikᵍⁱ اِمِك 1. *prov.* throat. 2. *archaic* fontanel of an infant's skull.

imiş اِمِش 1. is said to be, is allegedly. 2. was said to be, is said to have been, was allegedly.

-imiz اِمِز *cf.* **-ımız**.

imizgen⁼ⁱʳ اِمِزغانى *prov.*, same as **ımızgan**⁼.

imkân (. —) اِمكان A 1. possibility; feasibility; probability. 2. *phil.* contingency. **— dahilinde** as far as possible; feasible; practicable. **—ı yok** It is impossible. Absolutely not. **—sız** impossible. **—sızlık** impossibility.

imlâ (. —) اِملاء A 1. orthography; spelling; a dictating; dictation. 2. *lrnd.* a filling; *elec.* a charging; a filling up or heaping up (earth); a charging, loading (gun). **—sı bozuk** 1. having faulty orthography. 2. misspelled. **— et⁼** /ı/ 1. to dictate. 2. to fill. **—i fâsid** *lrnd.* faulty orthography. **—ya gelme⁼** to be incorrigible. **—i sahih** *lrnd.* correct spelling. **—sı yerinde** 1. having a correct orthography. 2. correctly spelled. **—sı yok** He can't write correctly.

imlâen (. —'.) اِملاءً A *lrnd.* orthographically.

imlâhane (. — —.) اِملاءخانه P *lrnd.* cartridge-filling workshop.

imlâkᵏⁱ 1 (. —) اِملاك A *lrnd.* a putting in possession of a thing.

imlakᵏⁱ 2 (. —) اِملاق A *lrnd.* a becoming poor, a being reduced to poverty; want, destitution.

imlâlˡⁱ (. —) اِملال A *lrnd.* a causing to become depressed, worried or vexed; a boring, wearying.

imlâsız (. —.) اِملاسز 1. wrongly spelled. 2. ignorant of orthography. **—lık** lack of orthographical knowledge.

imleçᶜⁱ *neol.*, *phys.* register.

imparator اِمپراطور L emperor. **—î** (. . . . —) *lrnd.* imperial. **—içe** (. . . . .'.) empress. **—luk** empire; emperorship.

imrahor اِمراخور same as **mirahor**.

İmran (. —) عمران A 1. Eastern tradition, name of the father of Moses. 2. Eastern tradition, name of the Virgin Mary's father. 3. Muslim tradition, name of the father of Abu Talib. **—î** (. — —) A pertaining to the family and people of Imran or to the Jews.

imrar 1 (. —) اِمرار A *lrnd.* a letting pass. **—ı hayat eyle⁼** to pass a lifetime, to live. **—ı vakt et⁼** to pass the time.

imrar 2 (. —) اِمرار A *lrnd.* 1. a making bitter or unpleasant; an embittering; a being bitter. 2. a saying bitter things, a speaking bitter words.

imren⁼ⁱʳ اِمرنلك /a/ 1. to long for, to feel an appetite (for); to desire. 2. to covet (a thing possessed by someone else); to envy (a person for some good fortune). **—dir⁼** /ı, a/ *caus.* to arouse someone's appetite (for); to arouse someone's envy.

imruz (. —) اِمروز P *lrnd.* 1. today. 2. in this life.

imsakᵏⁱ (. —) اِمساك A 1. an abstaining; abstinence; continence; a fasting. 2. the hour at which the Ramazan fast begins each day. 3. temperance; self-denial; a dieting. 4. *lrnd.* an abstaining from speech; silence. 5. *lrnd.* a being miserly, avaricious; avarice, parsimony. **— et⁼** /dan/ *lrnd.* to abstain, refrain; to fast.

imsakiye (. — —.) اِمساكيه A timetable giving the hour when the fast begins.

imsal (. —) اِمسال P *lrnd.* this year, the current year.

imsas (. —) اِمصاص A *lrnd.* a causing to be sucked.

-imsi اِمسى *cf.* **-msı**.

imşa (. —) اِمشاء A 1. *lrnd.* a causing to walk; a driving away; a purging, purge. 2. *obs.*, *slang* a dealing out shares (in gain).

imşeb اِمشب P *lrnd.* tonight.

imtidad (. . —) اِمتداد A 1. *lrnd.* prolongation; extension; duration. 2. *phil.* continuity. **—ınca** all along, throughout its length. **—lı** *phil.* extensive.

imtihan (. . —) اِمتحان A 1. examination, an examining; trial; test. 2. ordeal. **—ını al⁼** /ı/ to give someone a test; to examine (a student). **—a çek⁼** /ı/ 1. to examine thoroughly (pupil). 2. to cross-question, to harass with questions. **— et⁼** /ı/ to examine; to test. **— ol⁼** to take an examination. **—ı sav⁼** to pass an examination and get it over. **—a sok⁼** /ı/ to put (someone) to an examination. **İ— Suresi** name of the sixtieth sura of the Quran. **— ver⁼** 1. to take an examination. 2. to pass an examination.

imtilâ (. . —) اِمتلاء A *lrnd.* 1. a being or becoming full (vessel). 2. a being in a state of repletion from overeating; indigestion. 3. congestion. **— ol⁼** 1. to be distended through overeating. 2. to have indigestion.

imtinaᵃⁱ (. . —) اِمتناع A 1. an avoiding; a refusing to do something; refusal, avoidance. 2. a being refractory. 3. a being impregnable. **— et⁼** /dan/ to refuse, to avoid.

imtinan (. . —) اِمتنان A *lrnd.* 1. a continually reminding someone of his obligation for a favor conferred. 2. a conferring a favor.

imtisalˡⁱ (. . —) اِمتثال A 1. a conforming to rule, precept or example. 2. *phil.* imitation; a following r. **— et⁼** /a/ to conform (to).

imtisalen (. . '.) اِمتثالاً A /a/ *lrnd.* 1. in complia (with), following the example (of) 2. conlo bly.

imtisas (..—) اﻣﺘﺼﺎص A *lrnd.* suction, absorption.
imtiyaz (..—) اﻣﺘﯿﺎز A 1. privilege; concession; patent; *Ott. hist.* special privilege of any kind accorded by the Sultan; autonomy to some provinces; *Ott. hist.* a certificate of honor (given to a school pupil). 2. *lrnd.* a being separated or singled out from others; distinction; discrimination; preeminence. **— beratı** a patent of special privilege; license. **— sahibi** 1. privileged person, concessionaire. 2. patentee. 3. licensee.
imtiyazat (..——) اﻣﺘﯿﺎزات A *lrnd.* privileges; concessions. **—ı ecnebiye** *Ott. hist.* capitulations.
imtiyazlı اﻣﺘﯿﺎزﻟﻰ 1. specially privileged. 2. patented.
imtiyazsız اﻣﺘﯿﺎزﺳﺰ underprivileged.
imtizac A, **imtizaç**[c1] (..—) اﻣﺘﺰاج 1. a blending (with something); a mixing; a being mixed. 2. a getting on well with another; harmony; a living harmoniously. 3. an agreeing (with something). **— et=** /la/ 1. to blend with something. 2. to get on well together.
imtizaçsızlık[ğı] اﻣﺘﺰاﺟﺴﺰﻟﻰ 1. incompatibility of temperament, not getting on well together. 2. *law* incompatibility in marriage.
-imtrak اﻣﺘﺮاك *cf.* **-mtrak**.
imza (..—) اﻣﻀﺎء A 1. a signing (a document etc.); signature; subscription. 2. author, writer. **— at=** /a/ to sign. **— çak=** /a/ *colloq.* to sign. **— et=** /ı/ to sign. **— koy=** /a/ to put one's signature (to). **— sahibi** signatory, the undersigned.
imzala=[r] اﻣﻀﺎﻻﻣﻖ /ı/ to sign. **—n=** *pass.* **—t=**, **—ttır=** /ı, a/ *caus.* of **imzala=**.
in=[er] 1 اﯾﻨﻤﻚ 1. to descend, to come down, to step down; to fall down; to land (airplane); to be launched (ship). 2. to alight; to dismount; to get off; to put up (at a hotel), to stay. 3. to go down; to get down. 4. to subside, abate, diminish; to decrease, to die down. 5. to fall (prices). 6. *med.* to attack, strike down (apoplexy). 7. /a/ *slang* to strike, to hit (blow).
=in 2 *cf.* **n** 3.
=in= 3 *cf.* **=n=** 2.
-in 4 *cf.* **-ın 4**.
-in 5 *cf.* **-ın 4**.
=in 6 *cf.* **=ın 5**.
-in 7 *cf.* **-ın 6**.
-in 8 *cf.* **-ın 7**.
in 9 اﯾﻦ 1. wild beast's den, lair. 2. a hiding place; haunt.
in 10 (—) اﻧﺲ [ins] human being *only used in conjunction with* **cin**. **— misin, cin misin?** Are you a human being or a spirit? **— cin top oynuyor** a very desolate place. **— cin yok** completely deserted (place).
în 11 (—) اﯾﻦ P *lrnd.* 1. this; these. 2. the present. **— ü ân** 1. this and that. 2. the present life and the future. 3. so and so, such and such. **— cihan** this world; the present life.
ina (.—) اﻧﺎء A *lrnd.* vessel, pot, dish of any kind.
inabe, inabet (.—.) اﻧﺎﺑﻪ ، اﻧﺎﺑﺖ *lrnd.* 1. an appointing a substitute or deputy. 2. repentance, penitance; conversion (religion). 3. a formally renouncing the world and entering a dervish order. **— al=** to receive the full degree of a dervish in a religious order. **— ver=** to give the full degree of a dervish in a religious order.
inad (.—) ﻋﻨﺎد A *cf.* **inat**. **—î** (.——) A *lrnd.* obstinate. **—iye** (.——.) A *phil.* Pyrrhonism.
inaha (.—.) اﻧﺎﺧﻪ A *lrnd.* a making or letting a camel crouch down.
inak[ğı] اﯾﻨﺎك ، اﯾﻨﺎغ 1. *archaic* trusted in, confided in; confident. 2. *neol., phil.* dogma. **—çılık** *neol., phil.* dogmatism. **—sal** *neol., phil.* dogmatic.
inam 1 اﯾﻨﺎم *archaic* 1. trusted; confidant, confided in. 2. confidence, trust.
in'am 2 (.—) اﻧﻌﺎم A *lrnd.* a bestowing abundantly, conferring a favor; donation, gift; benefaction. **— et=** /ı, a/ to give as a favor (to an inferior). **—at** (.——) A *pl.*
inan 1 اﯾﻨﺎن 1. belief. 2. faith, trust, confidence. **— olsun** *colloq.* Believe me. I assure you.
inan=[ır] 2 اﯾﻨﺎﻧﻤﻖ 1. /a/ to believe; to hold to be true. 2. to believe in the existence of God. 3. /ı, a/ *archaic* to entrust (to).
inan 3 (.—) ﻋﻨﺎن A *lrnd.* 1. rein, the reins of a bridle. 2. control, management, the reins. **—i azimet** the act of proceeding on a journey. **— ber inan** equality.
inanç[cı] اﯾﻨﺎﻧﺞ 1. confidence, trust. 2. *neol.* belief.
inandır=[ır] اﯾﻨﺎﻧﺪﯾﺮﻣﻖ /ı, a/ *caus.* of **inan=** 2.
inanıl=[ır] اﯾﻨﺎﻧﯿﻠﻤﻖ *pass.* of **inan=** 2. **—acak**, **—ılır** credible; believable. **—maz** incredible; unbelievable.
inanış اﯾﻨﺎﻧﯿﺶ belief; faith.
inankeş (.—.) ﻋﻨﺎﻧﻜﺶ P *lrnd.* cautious; calculating.
inare (.—.) اﻧﺎره A *lrnd.* 1. a lighting, illuminating. 2. an enlightening the mind.
inas (.—) اﻧﺎث A *lrnd.* females; women and girls. **— mektebi** *obs.* school for girls.
inat[dı] (.—) ﻋﻨﺎد [inad] 1. obstinacy, a being obstinate, stubbornness. 2. persistence; endurance. 3. obstinate (person); pig-headed. 4. /a/ in order to thwart (someone), out of spite (for). **—ına** (.—..) 1. out of sheer obstinacy; just out of spite. 2. contrarily, just the opposite.

inatçı

— et= 1. to be obstinate. 2./da/ to persist (in). —ı inat very obstinate, stubborn. —ı tut= to have a fit of obstinacy.

inatçı عنادجى obstinate (person). —lık obstinacy, stubbornness. —lık et= to act stubbornly.

inatlaş=ᶦʳ عنادلاشمق to reach a stalemate in an argument.

inayatᵗⁱ (. — —) عناياتA lrnd., pl. of **inayet**.

inayet (. —.) عنايت A 1. grace; favor; kindness. 2. lrnd. care; effort. —te bulun= 1. to do a favor. 2. to exert oneself, to take trouble. — buyurun Be so good; do me the favor. — et= /a/ 1. to give as a favor. 2. to do as an act of grace. —i ilâhî divine favor, grace. —i kerametpenahi lrnd. a generous kindness. — ola! May God help you (said to a beggar when refusing to give alms). —i Rabbaniye phil. divine providence. —i Rabbaniye mesleği phil. providentialism.

inayeten (. —ʹ. .) عنايةً A lrnd. as a favor.

inayetkâr (. —. —) عنايتكار P lrnd. kind, gracious, obliging. —âne (. —. — —.) P kind, gracious; graciously. —î (. —. — —) P graciousness; graciously.

inayetli (. —. .) عنايتلى kind, gracious.

inba (. —) انبا A lrnd. a communicating; communication.

inbəh (. —) انباه A lrnd. 1. an awaking, rousing from sleep. 2. psych. stimulus.

inbar (— — —) انبار P lrnd. 1. this time; on this occasion. 2. latterly, recently.

inbat 1 انبات var. of **imbat**.

inbat 2 (. —) انبات A lrnd. 1. a making a plant grow; a causing to vegetate. 2. a putting forth vegetation (ground). 3. a growing, sprouting (herbage). —î (. — —) A vegetative.

inbias (. . —) انبعاث A lrnd. a being caused by; a proceeding from.

inbikᵍⁱ **1** انبيق [inbik 2] same as **imbik**.

inbikᵏⁱ **2** (. —) انبيق A lrnd., same as **imbik**.

inbisat (. . —) انبساط A 1. a being or becoming spread out; a being extended, extension. 2. a being joyful; gladness, cheerfulness, delight.

inca 1 (. —) انجا A lrnd. a delivering; a liberating.

inca 2 (— —) اينجا P lrnd. 1. here. 2. to this place.

incah (. —) انجاح A lrnd. 1. a causing one to succeed; a granting success. 2. a being successful, prospering; success. — et= /ı/ to accomplish.

incaz (. —) انجاز A lrnd. 1. a carrying out the request of another. 2. a fulfilling a promise, consummating; accomplishing. — et= /ı/ to perform; to fulfill. —ı va'd et= to fulfill a promise.

ince 1 اينجه 1. slender; thin; fine; delicate; naut. thin hawser; 2. colloq. Lesbian. 3. high pitched (voice); ling. front, articulated in the forward part of the mouth (vowel). 4. refined, subtle (thought, expression); sensitive; shrewd. — ağrı colloq. tuberculosis. — barsak small intestine. — barsak askısı anat. mesentery. — bel slender waisted, slim waisted. — boya art thin coating (of paint). — bölme partition, division (in a room). — cevherli fine grained, finely veined. — dal twig, small shoot. — donanma 1. a squadron. 2. mosquito fleet (of light craft). — ele= /ı/ to sift fine, to pass through a fine sieve. — eleyip sık doku= to be too particular, to be very meticulous, to be over-fussy. — fikir 1. subtle intellect. 2. intricate line of thought; intrigue. — hastalık tuberculosis. — ince very fine, imperceptible. —den inceye in a subtle manner; minutely. —sini ipe kalınını çöpe diz= to be too particular, to go into great detail. — iş fine work, fine workmanship. — işle= art to work with fine detail. — kalem 1. fine pen, fine-nibbed pen. 2. finely written. 3. finely worked engraving or carving. — karakol obs. 1. a small patrol party. 2. an advanced guard, body of scouts. — kas anat. gracilis. — kat et= obs. to make a fine nib on a pen. — kesim a spare figure; slim, thin. — kıyımlı tütün finely cut tobacco. — kıyma 1. finely chopped. 2. finely sliced. — kiler larder for small supplies. — marangozluk 1. cabinetmaking. 2. cabinetwork. — rende fine-grain snuff. — saz*. — ses 1. a thin voice. 2. shrill or treble voice. — sesli 1. feeble voiced. 2. soft and treble voiced. 3. squeaking, creaking. 4. gram. palatal (vowel). — sıtma 1. masked fever. 2. bore, nuisance (person). — yağ refined oil. — yonma kalem obs. a fine-nibbed pen. — zanaat slang a keeping a brothel. — zar anat., pia mater.

=ince 2 جه cf. =ınca.

incecikᵍⁱ (.ʹ. .) اينجه جك very slender, slim, thin, fine.

=incek cf. =ıncak.

incel=ᶦʳ اينجه لمك 1. to become slim, slender, thin or fine. 2. to be refined, or delicate. 3. to be too subtle.

incele=ʳ neol. /ı/ to examine carefully, minutely; to go into a matter carefully, to go over something carefully. —me 1. verbal. n. 2. study. —n= pass. of incele=. —t= /ı, a/ caus. of incele=.

incelikᵍⁱ اينجه لك 1. slenderness, slimness, thinness. 2. fineness, finesse; refinement, delicacy, subtlety of thought.

inceliş اینجلیش *verbal n. of* **incel=**.
incelt=[ir] اینجلتمك /1/ *caus. of* **incel=**.
—il= *pass.* **—iş** *verbal n. of* **incelt=**.
incerek[gi] اینجرك *somewhat slender or thin; rather fine.*
incesaz اینجه ساز *Or. mus.* another name given to the band playing **fasıl** music.
=**inceyedek** اینجه یدك *cf.* =**ıncayadak**.
=**inceyekadar** اینجه قدار *cf.* =**ıncayakadar**.
=**incez** اینجز *cf.* =**ıncaz**.
inci 1 اینجی *pearl.* **— avı** pearl fishing. **— avcısı** pearl fisher, pearl diver. **— balığı** pearl fish, *zool., Fierasfer.* **— çiçeği** daisy, marguerite, *bot., Bellis perennis;* lily of the valley, May lily, *bot., Convallaria majalis.* **— dizisi** a string of pearls. **— gibi** pearl-like; very white (teeth); fine and pretty (girl). **— tanesi** 1. a single pearl. 2. sweet little child. 3. *poet.* a single tear. **— taşı** *geol.* perlite, pearlstone.
-inci 2 اینجی *cf.* **-ncı**.
inci=[ir] **3** اینجیمك *to be sprained (limb).*
incik[gi] **1** اینجك *sprain; bruise.*
incik[gi] **2** اینجك *front of the shank, shin; shinbone.* **— kalemi, — kemiği** shinbone, *anat., tibia.* **— yahnisi** stew of sheep's shanks.
incik[gi] **3** اینجك *only in* **— boncuk** *prov.* cheap tawdry jewelry and such like.
İncil انجیل *[Arabic .—]* the Gospel; the New Testament. **— ehli** Christian.
incilâ (..—) انجلاء *A lrnd.* 1. an appearing clear, bright and manifest; manifestation; freedom from cloud or dullness; brightness. 2. a being wiped away or removed (grief).
incili 1 اینجیلی *set with pearls, ornamented or embroidered with pearls, pearled.*
İncilî 2 (.——) انجیلی *A lrnd.* 1. pertaining to the Gospel; evangelical. 2. who believes in the Gospel, Christian.
inciliye (.——.) انجیلیه *A lrnd.* the herb angelica, *bot., Archangelica officinalis.*
incimad (..—) انجماد *A lrnd.* 1. a being or becoming frozen; a freezing. 2. a being or becoming solidified. **— et=** to be frozen or congealed. **— noktası** *phys.* freezing point; point of congelation.
incin=[ir] اینجینمك 1. to be hurt, to be injured. 2. to be offended. **—iş, —me** *verbal n.*
incir اینجیر *[encir]* 1. fig; fig tree. 2. *prov.* vulva. **—i Adem** *lrnd.* sycamore fig, *bot., Ficus Sycomorus;* prickly pear, *bot., Cactus Opuntia, Opuntia vulgaris.* **— ağacı** fig tree, *bot., Ficus Carica.* **— çekirdeğini doldurmaz** trifling; a mere nothing. **— delen, — kuşu** tree pipit, figpecker, beccafico, *zool., Anthus trivialis.*
incirar (..—) انجرار *A lrnd.* 1. a being drawn or dragged along; a being drawn out, extended or prolonged. 2. a tending to or resulting in. 3. *Arabic gram.* a being in the genitive case (noun). **—ı kelâm** in the course of conversation.
incit=[ir] اینجیتمك /1/ 1. to hurt, to injure; to sprain. 2. to offend, to vex; to touch.
incitme اینجیتمه *verbal n. of* **incit=**. **— beni** *prov.* cancer.
=**inciye kadar** اینجیه قدار *var. of* =**inceye kadar**.
incizab (..—) انجذاب *A lrnd.* 1. a being attracted; attraction. 2. gravitation.
incizam (..—) انجزام *A lrnd.* 1. a being broken through. 2. a being cut through or off, a being truncated. 3. *Arabic gram.* a word's ending in a consonant.
inç اینچ *E* inch.
inçünin (—.—) اینچونین *P lrnd.* 1. such. 2. so, thus.
ind عند *A lrnd., with possessive and locative suffix* 1. at the side. 2. in the opinion of; according to. 3. with, before; near. **—imde** in my opinion. **—inde** in his opinion.
indab (.—) اندآب *A lrnd.* 1. a becoming covered with a scab (wound); cicatrization. 2. a healing up (wound).
indallah (..—) عندالله *A lrnd.* before God, in the sight of God.
indeks اندكس *L neol.* 1. index. 2. index finger.
indelba'z عندالبعض *A lrnd.* in the opinion of some.
indelhace (..—.) عندالحاجه *A lrnd.* in case of need.
indelicab (..——) عندالایجاب *A lrnd.* in case of necessity.
indeliktiza (....—), **indellüzum** (...—) عندالاقتضاء ، عندالازوم *A lrnd.* when necessary.
indennas (..—) عندالناس *A lrnd.* in man's sight; in people's opinion.
indettahkik[ki] (...—) عندالتحقیق *A lrnd.* after investigation.
indî 1 (..—) عندی *A* 1. of personal opinion (matter); personal. 2. subjective; arbitrary.
indi 2 اندی *archaic for* **imdi**.
-indi 3 ندی *cf.* **-ndi**.
=**indi 4** اندی *cf.* =**ındı 2**.
indifa[aı] (..—) اندفاع *A lrnd.* 1. eruption (volcanic); volcano. 2. *path.* cutaneous eruption. 3. *lrnd.* a being driven out, pushed away or expelled. **— et=** to erupt; to break out. **—at** (..——) *A lrnd., pl.*
indifaî (..——) اندفاعی *A geol.* eruptive, volcanic. **— sahra** *obs., geol.* volcanic rock.
indihaş (..—) اندهاش *A lrnd.* a being terror-stricken.
indimac (..—) اندماج *A lrnd.* an entering or being entirely within a thing; an adhering fast, cleaving to another; a being entangled. **—î** (..——) *A phil.* imminent.

indimal

indimalⁱⁱ (..—) اندمال A *lrnd.* a healing up (wound), cicatrization.
indir=ⁱʳ اینديرمك اند رمك اندرمك /ı/ to cause to descend; to lower; to calm; to give (a blow).
indirac (..—) اندراج A *lrnd.* 1. a being contained within something else; a being inserted. 2. *log.* subsumption.
indiras (..—) اندراس A *lrnd.* a being utterly obliterated or ruined; obliteration.
indirge=ʳ *neol., math., chem.* /ı/ to reduce. **—me** reduction. **—n** reducing, agent. **—nir** reducible. **—nmez** irreducible.
indiril=ⁱʳ اندرلمك *pass. of* **indir**=.
indirme اینديرمه اند رمه 1. *verbal n. of* **indir**=. 2. *mil.* landing of troops from the air. 3. *obs.* trapdoor. **— kapı** *arch.* spiked portcullis.
indirt=ⁱʳ اندرتمك اینديرتمك /ı, a/ *caus. of* **indir**=.
indiyat (..—) عنديات A *lrnd.* assertions founded upon only private or subjective opinion; arbitrary assertions.
indükle=ʳ [**indüksiyon**] *neol., phys.* to induce. **—ç** inductor. **—me** induction.
indüksiyon ایندوكسیون F *phys.* induction.
ineb عنب A *lrnd.* grapes. **—e** A 1. a single grape. 2. boil, pustule, pimple. **—î** (..—) A grape-shaped.
İnebahtı اینه بختی Gk *geog.* Lepanto.
inebüssa'leb عنب الثعلب A *lrnd.* black nightshade, *bot.*, *Solanum nigrum;* fox grape, *bot.*, *Paris incompleta.*
ineçᶜⁱ *neol., geol.* synclinal.
inek 1 (—.) اینك P *lrnd.* Look here. **— terazû!** Here are the scales; weigh, and check for yourself.
inekᵍⁱ **2** اینك 1. cow. 2. *hunter's term* hind, female deer. 3. *slang* loose woman; catamite. 4. *slang* stupid person, dunce; *school slang* studious and good pupil. **— ağacı** cow tree of Para, Brazilian milk tree, *bot.*, *Mimusops elata.* **— aşısı** *obs.* vaccination. **—çi** cowman, cowherd. **—le**= *school slang* to study hard. **—lik** 1. cowshed. 2. stupidity, imbecility.
inen اینن descending. **— kalın barsak, — kolon** *anat.* descending colon.
ineze اینزه *prov.* feeble, weak.
infakᵏⁱ (.—) انفاق A *lrnd.* a maintaining. **— et**= /ı/ to maintain, to keep other people.
infar (.—) انفار A *lrnd.* a frightening away; a putting to flight.
infaz (.—) انفاذ A an executing, a carrying out. **— et**= /ı/ to execute, to carry out.
infialⁱⁱ (..—) انفعال A indignation; anger; annoyance. **— uyandır**= to arouse indignation.
infialât (..——) انفعالات A *lrnd.* resentments, indignation. **—ı nefsaniye** spiteful resentment, malicious anger.
infialî (..——) انفعالى A *psych.* affective.

inficar (..—) انفجار A *lrnd.* 1. bursting forth; breaking (dawn). 2. *biol.* hatching out (caterpillars). 3. *bot.* dehiscence.
infiham (..—) انفهام A *lrnd.* a being understood.
infikâkᵏⁱ (..—) انفكاك A *law* separation. **— et**= /dan/ to leave one's post (an official, etc.). **— müzekkeresi** warrant of separation. **İ— Suresi** the ninety-eighth sura of the Quran.
infilâkᵏⁱ (..—) انفلاق A explosion. **— et**= to burst, to explode. **—î** (..——) A *lrnd.* explosive.
infirad (..—) انفراد A *lrnd.* isolation. **— et**= to be isolated.
infirakᵏⁱ (..—) انفراق A *lrnd.* separation.
infiratᵈⁱ (..—) انفراد *same as* **infirad**. **—çı** *pol.* isolationist.
infisad (..—) انفساد A *lrnd.* a becoming corrupt or spoiled.
infisah 1 (..—) انفساخ A *lrnd.* disintegration; dissolution; cancellation. **— et**= to be dissolved (assembly).
infisah 2 (..—) انفساح A *lrnd.* a widening.
infisahî (..——) انفساخى A *law* leading to nullification; causing cancellation. **— şart** *law* condition which causes nullification (of a contract).
infisalⁱⁱ (..—) انفصال A *lrnd.* separation; resignation (from a post). **— et**= /dan/ to be separated; to be removed or to retire (from a post); to go away.
infisam (..—) انفصام A *lrnd.* a being broken.
infitah (..—) انفتاح A *lrnd.* a being or becoming open; opening. **—ı ebvâb** the opening of doors.
infitam (..—) انفطام A *lrnd.* a being weaned.
infitar (..—) انفطار A *lrnd.* a cracking, a splitting. **İ— Suresi** the eighty-second sura of the Quran.
İngiliz انكليز It 1. English. 2. Englishman; English woman. 3. pound sterling. **— altını** English gold coin, sovereign. **— anahtarı** wrench. **— arması** *slang* scolding. **— lirası** pound sterling, £. **İ— Milletler Camiası** the British Commonwealth. **— tuzu** Epsom salts.
İngilizce انكليزجه the English language; in English; after the English fashion.
İngiltere (...'.) انكلتره It England; Great Britain. **—li** English, born in England.
inha (.—) انها A 1. official memorandum to a superior department recommending the appointment or promotion of an official. 2. *lrnd.* a sending, bringing or communicating.
inhaf (.—) انحاف A *lrnd.* a making thin or lean, a thinning down, an emaciating.
-in haliⁿⁱ *neol., gram.* genitive.

inhidab (..—) انحداب A *lrnd.* a being or becoming hunchbacked.

inhidad (..—) انحداد A *lrnd.* a being or becoming slender, sharp or pointed; sharpness; slenderness; pointedness; acuteness.

inhidam (..—) انهدام A *lrnd.* a falling down, a being pulled down (building); destruction, demolition, ruin, overthrow; subsidence (of earth).

inhidar (..—) انحدار A 1. *lrnd.* a descending a decline; a being precipitous. 2. *med.* a swelling from an obstruction.

inhidaş (..—) انحداش A *lrnd.* a setting upon or flying at another (dog).

inhifaz (..—) انحفاض A *lrnd.* a being low, depressed, abased; depression, abasement; subsidence.

inhilâlⁱⁱ (..—) انحلال A 1. a being or becoming liquified, melted or dissolved; a melting away; dissolution. 2. a being or becoming disintegrated; a going to pieces; a breaking up; disaggregation; dispersion. 3. *psych.* dissociation. 4. a being vacant, vacancy (job, position). — **et**= 1. to be dissolved, disintegrated, dispersed. 2. to become vacant. — **kabiliyeti** solubility, dissolubility.

inhilâlpezir (..—.—) انحلال پذیر P soluble, dissoluble.

inhimakᵏⁱ (..—) انهماك A *lrnd.* a giving oneself fully to any occupation; addiction; indulgence. — **et**= /a/ to give oneself up entirely to something; to have a weakness for something, to be addicted (to).

inhina (..—) انحنا A 1. a being or becoming bent, curved or crooked; a bending, a curving. 2. a stooping or bowing. 3. bend; curvature. — **merkezi** *math.* radius, center of curvature.

inhinakᵏⁱ (..—) انحناق A *lrnd.* a being suffocated or asphyxiated.

inhinalı (..—.) انحنالی curved; bent; crooked.

inhiraf (..—) انحراف A 1. a turning to one side; a deviating; deviation. 2. *phys.* deflection; *astr.* declination. 3. *psych.* aberration, inversion; deflection. —ı **ârızî** *naut.* deviation. — **et**= /dan/ 1. to turn, to incline (to one side). 2. to deviate, to deflect. 3. to be altered. —ı **hâtır** *lrnd.* displeasure; a feeling hurt or offended. —ı **mafsal** *med.* dislocation of a joint. —ı **manzar** *astr.* parallax. —ı **mizac** *lrnd.* indisposition; illness. —ı **pusula** *lrnd.* deviation of the compass. —ı **rahm** *med.* displacement of the uterus. —ı **semt-i kıble** *lrnd.* azimuth of the direction of Mecca at any place. —ı **süfliyeyn** *obs., astr.* reflection of the epicycle in the two inferior planets. —ı **tabiî** *naut.* variation. — **zaviyesi** angle of deviation. —**at** (..—.—) A *lrnd., pl.*

inhirat (..—) انحراط A *lrnd.* 1. a being thin and lean. 2. a being pierced and strung (beads, pearls). 3. a doing anything in an ignorant, headstrong manner.

inhisaf (..—) انخساف A *lrnd.* 1. eclipse of the moon. 2. a sinking into the earth; a being swallowed up. 3. a losing popularity, a being eclipsed. —**i ayn** 1. *med.* blindness. 2. *geol.* a sinking into the earth. 3. eclipse of the moon.

inhisar (..—) انحصار 1. a being restricted or limited; restraint; limitation; restriction. 2. monopoly. — **altına al**= /ı/ to monopolize. — **et**= /a/ 1. to be restricted or limited (to). 2. to consist only (of). — **maddeleri** monopoly products.

inhisarcı (..—.) انحصارجی monopolist. —**lık** monopolism.

inhitat (..—) انحطاط A 1. a descending; descent; a sinking. 2. a being lowered, diminished or degraded; decline; degradation, fall; diminution. 3. a becoming weak (with age); *psych.* depression. 4. *astr.* dip. 5. *med.* a remitting and diminishing (disease). —ı **cüz'î** *obs., med.* partial remission of a disease. — **devri** period of decline. —ı **küllî** *obs., med.* total remission or final termination of a disease. —ı **ufuk** *lrnd.* dip of the horizon. —**î** (..—.—) A *psych.* depressive.

inhizam (..—) انهزام A a being routed; defeat, rout. —**a uğra**= 1. to be defeated; to collapse. 2. to fail utterly.

ini 1 ینی 1. *prov.* brother-in-law; brother. 2. *archaic* younger brother.

-ini 2 ینی *cf.* -**ı** 2.

in'idam (..—) انعدام A *lrnd.* a being annihilated, annihilation.

inikᵍⁱ 1 اینك 1. pulled down (blind, etc.); lowered. 2. *arch.* depressed, segmental (arch, vault).

inikᵍⁱ 2 اینك *same as* **enik** 1.

in'ikad (..—) انعقاد A *lrnd.* 1. a setting up (of an assembly, etc.); a meeting, an assembling; a sitting. 2. a concluding (agreement); conclusion. 3. a being or becoming tied (knot). — **et**= 1. to assemble, to meet. 2. to be concluded (treaty). —**at** (..—.—) A *pl.*

in'ikâs (..—) انعكاس A 1. a being reflected; reflection. 2. a being inverted; inversion. 3. *psych.* reflex. — **et**= to be reflected; to be inverted. —**i seda** *lrnd.* echo, reverberation. —**i ziya bahsi** *phys.* catoptrics.

inilde=ʳ اینلده مك 1. to moan continuously; to make a moaning noise. 2. to resound. —**t**= /ı/ *caus.*

inile=ʳ اینله مك *archaic for* **inle**=.

inilti اینلتی moan, a moaning; a groaning.

iniltili اینلتیلی 1. moaning, groaning. 2. resounding.

inim inim اینم اینم *only in* — **inle=** to moan and groan bitterly.

in'isâb (..—) انعصاب A *lrnd.* a being or becoming hard, firm or obstinate; obdurate; *physiol.* innervation.

inisyal[li] ايـنـيـسيال F initial.

inisyatif اينيسياتيف F initiative.

iniş اينيش 1. *verbal n. of* **in=** 1. 2. descent, landing (airplane). 3. slope, way down. — **aşağı** downwards; downhill. — **çıkış** 1. descent and ascent. 2. *fin.* fall and rise; fluctuation. — **yokuş** a rising and falling, undulation (of the ground).

inişli اينشلی sloping downwards; having declivities. — **çıkışlı,** — **yokuşlu** undulating, uneven (ground); uphill and downhill.

in'itaf (..—) انعطاف A *lrnd.* a being bent, inclined, deflected, turned in a different direction; deflection; refraction; flexure. — **noktası** *math.* point of inflection. —**ı şua** *phys.* refraction of light. —**at** (..— —) A *pl.*

-iniz 1 ڭز *cf.* **-nız.**

=iniz 2 ڭز *cf.* **=nız 2.**

in'izal[li] (..—) انعزال A *lrnd.* 1. a being removed or dismissed from office. 2. a retiring; a going or being apart from the world.

inkâr (.—) انكار A 1. a denying; a repudiating; an ignoring; denial; refusal. 2. *law* contest, contestation, joinder of issue. — **et=** /ı/ to deny, to refute, to repudiate; *law* to plead not guilty. —**ı uluhiyet** *phil.* atheism.

inkârî (.— —) انكاری A *lrnd.* 1. pertaining to denial; repudiative. 2. negative.

inkas (.—) انقاص A *lrnd.* a lessening, diminishing; diminution.

inkaz (.—) انقاذ A *lrnd.* a saving; deliverance (from evil or fear).

inkıbaz انقباض A 1. a being constipated; constipation. 2. *lrnd.* a being or becoming contracted or retracted; a being grasped and held. 3. *lrnd.* a being cast down (from anger, fear, shame, etc.). — **ol=** to be constipated.

inkıhal[li] (..—) انقحال A *lrnd.* a falling down from weakness.

inkıla'[ı] (..—) انقلاع A *lrnd.* a being forcibly torn from its place, a being pulled up, uprooted.

inkılâb A, **inkılâp**[bı] (..—) انقلاب 1. radical change; revolution. 2. evolution; renovation; innovation; transformation. 3. a changing; inversion. — **et=** /a/ to take the form (of); to be transformed (into); to be changed. —**ı sayfî** *obs., astr.* summer solstice. —**ı şetevî** *obs., astr.* winter solstice.

inkılâpçı انقلابجی 1. revolutionary. 2. innovator. —**lık** revolutionary spirit.

inkıraz (..—) انقراض A 1. a declining, a becoming extinct; decline; extinction. 2. a coming to an end; a ceasing. 3. a leaving no issue, a disappearing without leaving a trace. — **bul=** 1. to become extinct, to decline, to fall. 2. to come to an end.

inkısam (..—) انقسام A *lrnd.* 1. a being divided into parts; division; dismemberment. 2. separation; partition. —**at** (..— —) A *pl.*

inkışar (..—) انقشار A *lrnd.* a being barked, peeled.

inkıta'[ı] (..—) انقطاع A 1. a ceasing, a being interrupted; cessation; interruption. 2. *lrnd.* a being cut off or through. —**i tams** 1. *biol.* menopause. 2. a becoming attached to one person and abandoning all others. —**i teneffüs** suffocation, asphyxia. —**a uğra=** to be interrupted; to cease. —**a uğrat=** /ı/ to interrupt. —**i ziya** *phys.* diffraction.

inkıyad (..—) انقياد A *lrnd.* a being or becoming tractable or obedient; submission; obedience. — **et=** /a/ 1. to submit. 2. to be obedient, to obey.

inkıyaden (..—.) انقياداً A *lrnd.* /a/ obeying; in submission to.

inkıza (..—) انقضاء A *lrnd.* a coming to an end, a finishing, terminating, expiring; end, termination, expiration. —**yı müddet** termination of a period.

inkızaz (..—) انقضاض A *lrnd.* 1. a being cracked and ruined (wall); a falling down in ruins. 2. a swooping down to alight (bird).

inkisaf (..—) انكساف A *lrnd.* a being eclipsed, eclipse (sun).

inkisar (..—) انكسار A 1. curse, malediction. 2. *lrnd.* a being or becoming broken. 3. *lrnd.* a feeling hurt, annoyed, vexed; vexation, annoyance; disappointment. 4. *phys.* refraction. — **et=** 1. /a/ to curse. 2. to feel hurt or vexed. 3. *phys.* to refract. —**i hayal** disappointment; disillusion.

inkişaf (..—) انكشاف A 1. a developing, development; growth, flourishing. 2. evolution. 3. a being or becoming uncovered or clear. — **et=** to develop; to grow; to improve.

inle=' ايكله بكلك اينرمك to moan, to groan, to whine. —**t=** /ı/ *caus.* —**yiş** *verbal n. of* **inle=.**

inme انمه 1. *verbal n. of* **in=** 1. 2. apoplexy, stroke, paralysis. — **in=** /a/ to have a stroke.

inmeli انمه لی paralyzed, struck by apoplexy; apoplectic.

innalillâh (.—..—) انا لله A *colloq.* death. — **ve inna ileyhi raciûn** Verily we belong to God and verily we shall return to him (Quran II: 151).

innallâha maassabirîn (..—. ..—.—) ان الله مع الصابرين A *lrnd.* (*lit.* God is with those who are patient.) O my God! (used to indicate impatience.)

innîn (. —) عنّين A *lrnd.* sexually impotent. **—iyet** (. — —.) A impotency.

inniyet (. —.) إنّيّت A *phil.* nature or quality of an *a posteriori* categorical proposition.

inorganik اينورغانيك L *chem., biol.* inorganic.

inre= ابكره بلك ، اينره بلك *archaic* to make a whining kind of cry; to bellow.

ins انس A *lrnd.* mankind, man, human being.

insa (. —) انسا A *lrnd.* a causing to forget.

insaf (. —) انصاف A 1. a doing justice to; justice; moderation. 2. conscience; fairness. —! Be fair. Be reasonable. — **et=** 1. to have a sense of justice; to act with equity; to have pity. 2. to be moderate and equitable. **—a gel=** 1. to be fair, to show pity. 2. to come around to reason. **—ına kalmış artık** It all depends on his sense of justice. It is at his discretion.

insafkâr (. — —) انصافكار P *lrnd.*, same as **insaflı**. **—lık** reasonableness, justness.

insaflı انصافلى just, equable, equitable, reasonable; conscientious; fair. **—lık** justness, equity, reasonableness; fairness.

insafsız انصافسز unjust, unfair; cruel; inhuman. **—ca** unfairly, unjustly. **—lık** unfairness, inhumanity; cruelty.

insak[kı] (. —) انساك A *lrnd.* a speaking in rhyme. **—ı kelâm, —ı suhan** rhymed prose. **—at** (. — —) A *pl.*

insal[lı] (. —) انسال A *lrnd.* a begetting children; a having issue. **—ât** (. — —) A *pl.*

insan 1 انسان [insan 2] 1. human being, man, mankind. 2. good and just person; humane. 3. one, oneself. **—lar** 1. man, mankind. 2. *zool.*, *Homo sapiens*. **— adam** fair and decent person; good and kind man. **— biçimi** *neol., phil.* anthropomorphic. **— biçimcilik** *neol., phil.* anthropomorphism. **— bilim** *neol.* anthropology. **— çiğ süt emmiştir** Man is not infallible; human beings cannot be wholly trusted. **— eti ağırdır** *proverb* A human burden is difficult to carry (said of a person bedridden either from old age or long illness). **— eti ye=** *colloq.* to backbite, to slander a person. **— evlâdı** good and noble person. **— gibi** like a human being; honestly, decently; properly. **— hakları** *law* human rights. **— hali** 1. human nature. 2. It is only human. **— içine çık=** to go out in public; to mix with people. **— içincilik** *neol., phil.* anthropocentrism. **— kıtlığı** scarcity of great souls. **— kıtlığında** As there is no one better... **— kurusu** human skeleton; just skin and bones. **— oğlu*. — ol=** to be human; to become a decent person. **— sarrafı** a clever discriminator of character, a good judge of men.

insan 2 (. —) انسان A *lrnd.* 1. human being. 2. pupil of the eye. **—ı kâmil** *Isl. myst.* the perfect man. **—ı kebir** *Isl. myst.* the all-embracing Universe. **—ı sağir** *Isl. myst.* mankind.

insanca (. .́.) انسانجه 1. human; humane. 2. properly, decently; fairly; kindly.

insanımsı انسانمسى 1. somewhat human. 2. *neol.* anthropoid. **—lar** *neol.* the anthropoids.

insanî (. — —) انسانى A 1. human; humanly. 2. humane; humanely; kindly.

insaniye (. — — .) انسانيّه A *zool., hominidae.*

insaniyet (. — . .) انسانيّت A 1. humanity, mankind, human kind; human nature. 2. humaneness; kindness.

insaniyetkâr (. — . . —) انسانيّتكار P *lrnd.* humane; kind; benevolent. **—âne** (. — . . — — .) P humanely. **—î** (. — . . — —) P, **—lık** humaneness.

insaniyetli انسانيّتلى humane; kind, benevolent.

insaniyetperest (. — . . . .) انسانيّتپرست P humanist. **—lik** *phil.* humanism.

insaniyetsiz انسانيّتسز inhuman; cruel. **—lik** inhumanity.

insanlık[ğı] انسانلق 1. humanity; human kind. 2. humaneness; kindness, benevolence. **—tan çık=** 1. to be disfigured. 2. to become beastly.

insanoğlu انسان اوغلى man, human being.

insanülayn (. — . .) انسان العين A *lrnd.* pupil of the eye.

insanüstü انسان اوستى superhuman.

insıbab (. . —) انصباب A *lrnd.* 1. a being poured out; a being shed or spilled; a flowing (stream). 2. *path.* extravasation; effusion (of blood, etc.).

insıbağ (. . —) انصباغ A *lrnd.* 1. a being dyed. 2. *Isl. myst.* to be endowed with divine manifestations.

insıraf (. . —) انصراف A *lrnd.* 1. a returning; a departing; return; departure. 2. *Arabic gram.* a being declinable. 3. *med.* revulsion.

insıram (. . —) انصرام A *lrnd.* 1. a being cut through or broken. 2. a being terminated (season).

insicam (. . —) انسجام A 1. coherence (in speech or writing), harmony; regularity. 2. a flowing along, a running smoothly.

insicamlı انسجاملى coherent; consistent; regular. **—lık** coherency.

insicamsız انسجامسز incoherent; irregular. **—lık** incoherency.

insidad (. . —) انسداد A 1. *med.* occlusion. 2. *lrnd.* a being or becoming closed, blocked up or obstructed.

insidal[lı] (. . —) انسدال A 1. *med.* prolapsus. 2. *lrnd.* a being let down (woman's veil, garments or hair).

insihak[kı] (. . —) انسحاك A *lrnd.* a being rubbed and pulverized; a being pounded to powder.

insilâb (..—) انسلاب A *lrnd.* a being taken away; a being spoiled.
insilâh (..—) انسلاخ A *lrnd.* a being flayed, cast off, sloughed off (skin).
insilâkᵏᶦ (..—) انسلاك A *lrnd.* a taking and following a way or order.
insilâlˡⁱ (..—) انسلال A *lrnd.* 1. a slipping out, a being drawn out (sword). 2. a slipping away quietly from a place.
insiyakᵏᶦ (..—) انسياب A 1. *psych.* instinct, automatism. 2. *lrnd.* a being led or driven along. —**î** (..— —) A instinctive.
inşa (.—) انشاء A 1. a building, constructing; construction. 2. *lrnd.* a composing, writing; literary composition; elegance of style especially in letter writing; belles lettres; art of letter writing; book giving models for letter writing. — **et**= /ı/ to build, construct. — **defteri** *obs.* book of models of letters, petitions, etc. — **mektebi** *obs.* school of architecture and construction, especially a school of naval architecture.
inşaallah (...—) انشاءالله A *same as* **inşallah**.
inşaat (.— —) انشاآت A 1. building in the process of construction; act of building, construction. 2. buildings, constructions, works.
inşaatçı انشاآتجى (building) contractor; builder. —**lık** profession of contracting, constructorship.
inşad (.—) انشاد A *lrnd.* a reciting (poetry); recitation. — **et**= /ı/ to recite. —**at** (.— —) A *pl.*
inşaî (.— —) انشائى A *lrnd.* 1. relating to building, construction or shipbuilding; constructive. 2. relating to elegance of style. 3. *gram.* optative, imperative (word or sentence).
inşaîye (.— —.) انشائيه A *lrnd.* 1. naval architecture. 2. engineering staff in shipbuilding. — **mektebi** *same as* **inşa mektebi**.
inşakᵏᶦ (.—) انشاق A 1. *med.* an inhaling. 2. *lrnd.* a snuffing up or causing to snuff up into one's nostrils.
inşallah (..—) انشاءالله [inşaallah] 1. God willing; if God wills. 2. I hope so; all being well.
inşaperdaz (.—.—) انشاء پرداز P *lrnd.* having an elegant style (in literature).
inşatᵈⁱ 1 انشاد *var. of* **inşad**.
inşat 2 (.—) انشاط A *lrnd.* a making brisk and cheerful, a cheering up.
inşiaᵃⁱ (..—) انشعاع A *phys.* radiation. — **muvazeneti** radiative equilibrium. — **sahası** field of radiation. — **tazyiki** pressure of radiation.
inşiab (..—) انشعاب A *lrnd.* a branching out into subdivisions; subdivision; ramification.
inşialˡⁱ (..—) انشعال A *lrnd.* a flaming, a blazing.

inşikakᵏᶦ (..—) انشقاق A *lrnd.* a being or becoming split up, cracked, fissured or divided; *chem.* decomposition. —**ı asa** a split taking place in any matter; disunion; discord. —**ı fecr** break of dawn. —**ı kamer** the splitting in two of the moon (one of the Prophet's miracles). **İ— Suresi** *name of the eighty-fourth sura of the Quran*.
inşimas (..—) انشماس A *lrnd.* insulation.
inşirah (..—) انشراح A 1. a being cheered; gladness; cheerfulness; exhilaration. 2. a being at ease; a breathing freely; relief. — **bul**= to be cheered up; to feel relieved. —**ı derun**, —**ı sadr** joy, ease of mind.
intac (.—) انتاج A 1. a resulting; a producing (a consequence). 2. a bringing to a conclusion. — **et**= /ı/ 1. to result (in); to lead (to). 2. to settle (up), to conclude.
intakᵏᶦ (..—) انطاق A *lrnd.* 1. a causing or enabling to speak. 2. God's endowing man with speech. —**ı Hak** speech as coming from God. —**ı Hak ol**= to be condemned out of his own mouth.
intan (.—) انتان A 1. *pathol.* internal microbic infection. 2. *lrnd.* a stinking, a being fetid.
intanî (.— —) انتانى A *path.* infectious. —**ye** (.— —.) section dealing with infectious diseases.
intaş (.—) انتاش A *biol.* germination.
intelekt انتلكت F *neol., psych.* intellect.
interpolasyon انترپولاسيون F *sc.* interpolation.
intibaᵃⁱ (..—) انطباع A 1. impression; feeling. 2. *lrnd.* a being stamped, impressed or imprinted. — **bırak**= /da/ to make an impression (on). —**at** (..— —) A *pl.*
intibah (..—) انطباخ A *lrnd.* a being cooked. —**ı taam** the cooking of food.
intibakᵏᶦ (..—) انطباق A 1. adjustment; adaptation. 2. accommodation; conformation. 3. *lrnd.* a coinciding; an exactly fitting over in shape and size. 4. *math.* coincidence. — **et**= /a/ to adjust oneself (to); to conform (to). —**ı hayatî** *biol.* vital consensus.
intifa (..—) انطفاء A *lrnd.* a dying down, a being quenched; extinction. —**pezir** (..—.—) P extinguished.
intiva (..—) انطواء A *lrnd.* a being folded or rolled up.
=**inti** *cf.* =**ntı**.
intiaş (..—) انتعاش A *lrnd.* 1. a recovering health. 2. a regaining one's legs after stumbling.
intiaz (..—) انتعاظ A *physiol.* erection.
intibac (..—) انتباج A *path.* a swelling (of a joint).
intibah (..—) انتباه A *lrnd.* 1. a waking from sleep; a being on one's guard. 2. vigilance; caution; circumspection. 3. a taking a lesson

(from). 4. *med.* incitation. — **devri** the Renaissance.

intifaᵃ¹ 1 (..—) انتفاع A *lrnd.* a being benefited; benefit, advantage, gain. — **et=** /dan/ to profit (from). — **hakkı** *law* usufruct. —**ı istihlâke bağlı olan ve olmıyan mallar** *com.* consumable and non-consumable goods. — **senedi** dividend share. — **senetleri** *com.* redeemable shares.

intifa 2 (..—) انتفا lrnd. a being removed, banished.

intifah انتفاخ A *lrnd.* 1. a being inflated and swollen; a being puffed up. —**ı mesâhır** 1. great fright. 2. conceited insolence.

intifaî (..——) انتفاعي A *phil.* utilitarian. —**ye** (..———.) utilitarianism.

intiha (..—) انتها A 1. a finishing, a coming to an end; end. 2. extremity; limit. — **bul=** to come to an end.

intihab 1 (..—) انتخاب A *same as* **intihap.**
intihab 2 (..—) انتهاب A *lrnd.* a carrying away plunder. — **et=** to carry off as spoil.
intihabat (..——) انتخابات A *lrnd.* elections.
intihabi (..——) انتخابي A *psych.* elective.
intihac (..—) انتهاج A *lrnd.* a finding or taking a path.
intihaî (..——) انتهائي A *lrnd.* final, concluding; extreme.
intihalˡⁱ (..—) انتحال A plagiarism. — **et=** /ı/ to plagiarize.
intihapᵇ¹ (..—) انتخاب [**intihab**] a choosing, selecting, electing; selection, choice, election; preference. — **dairesi** electoral district, parliamentary constituency. — **devresi** electoral period, life of a parliament. — **ehliyeti** eligibility for suffrage. — **et=** /ı/ to choose, to select, to ballot (for); to elect, to prefer. — **hakkı** suffrage, right to vote. — **mazbataları** electoral records. — **sandığı** ballot box.
intihapezir (..—.—) انتهاپذير P *lrnd.* that ends, finishes. — **ol=** to come to an end.
intihar (..—) انتحار A suicide. — **et=** to commit suicide.
intihaz 1 (..—) انتهاز A *lrnd.* a seizing (an opportunity).
intihaz 2 (..—) انتهاض A *lrnd.* 1. a rising to one's feet. 2. a setting out, a starting.
intikad (..—) انتقاد A *lrnd.* a criticizing; literary criticism. —**iye** (..——.) *phil.* criticism.
intikah (..—) انتقاه A *lrnd.* 1. a recovering from sickness; recovery. 2. a becoming satisfied in understanding a matter; perfect conviction.
intikalˡⁱ (..—) انتقال A 1. a moving, a being moved; transition, progress; transmission. 2. a passing from one place to another; migration. 3. a passing away; death. 4. perception, understanding, mentally grasping; inference. 5. transfer of property by sale or inheritance. —**i darı baka** death. — **devresi** transition period. — **et=** 1. to pass to another place. 2. to pass away (die). 3. to change to another subject (conversation). 4. /ı/ to perceive. —**î** (..——) A transitory.

intikam (..—) انتقام A revenge, vengeance. — **al=** /dan/ to take vengeance, to revenge oneself (on). —**cı** revenger.

intikamcu (..——) انتقامجو P *lrnd.* revengeful, vindictive.

intikaz (..—) انتقاض A *lrnd.* a falling to pieces; a being pulled to pieces; demolition, disintegration. —**pezîr** (..—.—) P disintegrated.

intima (..—) انتما A *lrnd.* a being related to; relation, relationship.

intisab 1 (..—) انتساب *same as* **intisap.**
intisab 2 (..—) انتصاب A *lrnd.* a standing erect; a standing bolt upright before someone.
intisac (..—) انتساج A *lrnd.* a being or becoming woven or interwoven.
intisaf (..—) انتصاف A *lrnd.* 1. a being divided into two equal parts. 2. a being midday. 3. an obtaining full justice, a payment.
intisah (..—) انتساخ A *lrnd.* a copying out, a writing, transcribing.
intisakᵏ¹ (..—) انتساق A *lrnd.* a being regularly adjusted.
intisapᵇ¹ (..—) انتساب [**intisab** 1] a becoming attached to, adherence; a joining (a group, school, order); a marrying (into a family). — **et=** /a/ 1. to be connected (with) or related (to). 2. to join (group, party, etc.). 3. to enter (upon a career).
intisar 1 (..—) انتشار A *lrnd.* a being scattered about; diffusion.
intisar 2 (..—) انتصار A *lrnd.* 1. a conquering, overcoming. 2. a taking revenge; vengeance.
intişab (..—) انتشاب A *lrnd.* 1. a heaping together; accumulating. 2. a cleaving, clinging, sticking fast (to).
intişar (..—) انتشار A 1. a being or becoming spread open; a being expended; extension; radiation. 2. a being published or disseminated; publication, dissemination. 3. a being dispersed or diffused; diffusion. — **et=**, — **bul=** to spread, to be spread (out).
intizaᵃ¹ (..—) انتزاع A 1. *chem.* dissociation; *psych.* abstraction, dissociation. 2. *lrnd.* a tearing (out), a plucking (up), a forcibly removing.
intizah (..—) انتزاه A *lrnd.* a being completely blameless.
intizam (..—) انتظام A a being regular; order, in time, orderliness, arrangement; tidiness. —**i âmme** public order. — **bul=** to get

into order, to become well arranged. **— üzere** in -good order. **—lı** orderly, regular, tidy. **—perver** (..—..) P *lrnd.* orderly, regular, tidy. **—sız** irregular, disorderly, untidy.

intizar (..—) اِنْتِظار A 1. a waiting; expectation. 2. *colloq.* curse, abuse. **— üzre ol=** to be on the lookout for, expecting (something). **—en** (..—'.) A pending, awaiting.

inzal[li] (.—) اِنْزال A *lrnd.* 1. a making or letting descend. 2. a coming down from heaven (divine revelation, rain, etc.). 3. *physiol.* seminal emission. **— et=** /ı/ to make or let descend. **— ol=** to emit semen.

inzar (.—) اِنْذار A *lrnd.* a warning, cautioning; threatening; a dissuading.

inzıbat (..—) اِنْضِباط A discipline. **— memuru** military policeman. **—î** (..——) A disciplinary. **—sız** undisciplined, uncontrolled.

inzımam (..—) اِنْضِمام A *lrnd.* a being added or joined (to); addition. **— et=** /a/ to be added (to). **—ı rey** concurrence, consent.

inziac (..—) اِنْزِعاج A *lrnd.* a being disturbed and moved from its place; expulsion.

inziva (..—) اِنْزِوا A seclusion, retirement. **—ya çekil=** to retire into seclusion.

ip 1 اِيپ 1. rope; cord; string. 2. *prov.* thread. 3. halter, the "rope", gallows. **— atla=** to jump rope. **—ine basan** *slang* stupid, fool. **—ini boya=** *slang* to carry out something skillfully; to be clever in managing one's business. **— cambazı** rope dancer, tightrope walker. **—e çek=** /ı/ to hang (a criminal). **—ini çek=** /ın/ to keep under control. **—le çek=** /ı/ to be anxiously waiting (for); looking forward to. **—i çöz=** to sever one's connection (with). **—i çürük** undependable. **—e diz=** /ı/ 1. to put in order. 2. to count. **—e gel=** to be brought to the gallows, to be hanged. **—e ger=** to hang (laundry). **— hamalı** porter who carries things by tying a rope around them. **— kaçkını** jailbird, gallows bird. **—ten kazıktan kurtulmuş** (*lit.*, who has escaped the rope and the stake) gallows bird. **—e kazığa vur=** /ı/ to execute by hanging or by impaling. **—ini kes=** /dan/ *slang* to run away, to flee. **—i kır=** *slang* to run away, to flee. **—ini kır=** *colloq.* to get out of hand, to become unmanageable. **—i kırık** *colloq.* vagabond. **—ini kırmış** unbridled, rebellious. **—inin kıvrağı çözül=** /ın/ *slang* to go wrong (business). **—i kopar=** to break the link (with something). **—ini kopar=** to make off. **—ten kuşak** poverty, misery. **—ten kuşak kuşan=** to be poverty-stricken. **—iyle kuyuya inilmez** /ın/ You can't depend on him. **— merdiven** rope ladder. **— parası ver=** /a/ *colloq.* to give one something in order to get rid of him. **—e sapa gelmez** 1. vagabond. 2. irrelevant; incoherent. **—i sapı yok** /ın/ 1. irresponsible. 2. incoherent, without rhyme or reason. **—ini sürü=** to lead a life of crime and deserve to be hanged. **— tak=** /a/ to backbite; to try to harm someone behind his back. **— takma=** /a/ *slang* not to give a damn (for). **—. ucu*. —in ucunu kaçır=** to lose the thread of something, to lose control of something. **—e un ser=** to make vain excuses; to be lazy. **—ini üstüne at=** /ın/ to give somebody his head; to leave someone to his own devices. **—i yok sapı yok** nonsense, nonsensical.

=ip 2 اِيپ cf. **=ıp.**

ipçik[ği] *neol., bot.* string.

ipek[ği] اِيپك 1. silk. 2. silken, made of silk, silky. **— böceği** silkworm. **— çiçeği** the portulaca and mesembryanthemum class of flowering plants. **— fidanı** silk vine, *bot.*, *Periploca graeca.* **— gibi** like silk, silky, soft, fine and smooth. **— kozası** silk cocoon. **— kurdu** silkworm. **— kuşu** hoopoe, *zool.*, *Upupa epops.* **— sobası** a room for rearing silkworms. **— şarabı** mulberry wine. **— şurubu** mulberry syrup. **— tefesi** a hank of wound raw silk, a skein of silk thread. **— teli** silk thread.

ipeka (..'.) اِيپكا F ipecacuanha, *bot.*, *Psychotria ipecacuanha.*

ipekçi اِيپكجی silk merchant; silk manufacturer. **—lik** silk industry.

ipekhane (..—.) اِيپكخانه silk factory.

ipekli اِيپكلی of silk, silken; silk cloth, silk goods.

ipham (.—) اِبهام *var. of* **ibham 2.**

ipince ('..) اِيپنجه very thin.

ipipullah اِيپی پُلّه *colloq., only in* **— sivri külâh** completely destitute, stone broke.

ipka (.—) اِبقا *var. of* **ibka 1.**

iple=[r] اِيپله /ı/ 1. to bind with a rope. 2. *slang* to consider, to respect, to pay attention to.

iplik[ği] اِيپلك 1. thread; yarn; sewing cotton. 2. fiber. 3. *obs.* made of linen, linen. **— bez** *obs.* linen cloth. **— bük=** to spin. **— çek=** to draw threads; to do drawn thread work. **— eğir=** to spin yarn (on a wheel). **— iplik** 1. in fibers. 2. thread by thread, separately. **— iplik ol=** to become threadbare. **—ği pazara çık=** to become known (a person's bad character); to be caught out (in secret dealings); to come to light. **— peyniri** *prov.* kind of cheese marked with the threads of the cheesecloth. **— sar=** /a/ to wind thread (on). **— yumağı** ball of yarn. **—çi** dealer in yarns.

iplikçik[ği] اِيپلكجك a threadlike worm.

iplikhane (..—.) اِيپلكخانه 1. spinning mill. 2. *Ott. hist.* labor prison; penitentiary.

ipliklen=ⁱʳ ابيلكلنمك 1. to separate into fibers. 2. to become fibrous. 3. to become threadbare. **—dir=** /ı/ caus.

ipnotizma (...'.) ايپنوتيزما It hypnotism.

ipnoz ايپنوز F same as **hipnoz**.

ipotekᵍⁱ ايپوتك F mortgage. **—li** mortgaged.

ipotetikᵍⁱ ايپوتتيك F sc. hypothetical.

ipotez ايپوتز F sc. hypothesis.

ipsiler neol. parasitic worms, zool., nematoda.

ipsitᵈⁱ ايپست Gk felloe, felly rim (of a coach or cart wheel).

ipsiz ايپسز 1. ropeless; halterless. 2. vagabond, having no connections. **— sapsız** 1. irrelevant; nonsense. 2. without house or home.

iptalˡⁱ (.—) ابطال A a rendering null and void; annulment, cancelling, declaration of nullity. **— davası** law action for nullity; action for avoidance. **— et=** /ı/ to annul; to cancel.

iptida (..—) ابتدا A 1. a beginning; commencement. 2. first; at first.

iptidaî (..——) ابتدائی A 1. primary, preliminary. 2. primitive. **— madde** raw material. **— mektep** primary school.

iptilâ (..—) ابتلا A 1. a being or becoming addicted (to a person or thing), addiction. 2. passion.

iptizalˡⁱ (..—) ابتذال A excess, superabundance. **—e düş=**, **—e uğra=** to become commonplace, to be vulgarized.

ipucuⁿᵘ ايپوجى clue; indication; hint. **— ver=** to give a clue.

=ir 1 ـىر cf. **=r**.

=ir= 2 ـىر cf. **=ır=** 2.

i'rab (.—) اعراب A Arabic gram. pronunciation of the case endings.

irad (——) ايراد A 1. same as **irat**. 2. a putting forward, adducing; delivering (speech). **— et=** /ı/ 1. to deliver (speech). 2. to adduce proof. **—ı kelâm et=** lrnd. to deliver a speech. **—ı ma'tufat** lrnd. a series of words linked by conjunctions. **—ı mesel** lrnd. quotation of a proverb.

iradât (.——) ايرادات A lrnd., pl. of **irade**.

irade (.—.) اراده A 1. will-power; a willing, wishing; will. 2. command; decree. 3. lrnd. a loving, liking; a seeking for, striving after. **—i âliye** Ott. hist. command given by the grand vizier. **— beyanı** law declaration of intention. **—i cüz'iye** phil. man's individual will, free will. **— dışı** psychol. non-voluntary, involuntary. **—si elden git=** to lose one's self-control. **— fesadı** law lack of mutual assent, defective intention. **—i ilâhiye** the will of God. **— izharı** law declaration of intention. **—i külliye** God's absolute will. **—i milliye** the will of the nation. **—nin muhtariyeti** freedom of the will. **—i seniye**, **—i şahane** Ott. hist. imperial rescript. **— yitimi** neol., psych. abulia. **—i zaife** psych. velleity, incomplete volition. **—cilik** neol., phil. voluntarism.

iradeli (.—..) اراده لى 1. strong-willed, resolute, forceful. 2. voluntary.

iradesiz (.—..) اراده سز 1. weak; irresolute. 2. involuntary.

iradet (.—.) ارادت A lrnd., same as **irade**.

iradî (.——) ارادى A lrnd. voluntary; by free will. **— şart** law conditional clause, proviso. **—ye** (.——.) phil. voluntarism.

irae (.—.) اراءة A lrnd. a showing, manifesting; a pointing out. **— et=** /ı/ to show, manifest, indicate. **—i tarik** a showing the way, a guiding.

irahe (.—.) اراحة A lrnd. 1. a making or letting one rest, breathe, and refresh oneself. 2. God's granting heavenly mercy in death. 3. a reposing, breathing and refreshing oneself; a becoming rested, refreshed and revived. **—i fikr** a refreshing one's mind. **—i ruh** a resting one's soul (in death).

irakᵍⁱ اراك same as **ırak** 1.

iraka (.—.) اراقة A lrnd. a spilling, shedding, pouring forth. **—i dem** bloodshed; slaughter.

İran (——) ايران P geog. Persia, Iran. **—î** (———), **—lı** Persian, Iranian.

İranzemin (——.—) ايران زمين P Persia.

iras (——) ايراث A lrnd. 1. a causing; a giving. 2. a leaving an inheritance, a bequeathing. **— et=** /ı/ to cause, to give. **—ı mazarrat** a causing damage.

iratᵈⁱ (——) ايراد [irad] income, revenue. **İ—ı Cedid** Ott. hist. fund introduced to meet the expenses of the **Nizam-ı Cedid** during the reign of Sultan Selim III (1789-1807). **— getir=** to bring in revenue. **— ve masraf** income and expenditure. **— senedi** annuity charge bond. **— vergisi** income tax.

i'raz (.—) اعراض A lrnd. a turning away (from a thing); a declining, shunning, avoiding.

irb ارب A lrnd. 1. member or part of the human body. 2. intelligence, shrewdness, sagacity. 3. want, need.

irba (.—) اربا A lrnd. 1. an increasing, adding (to a thing); an augmenting, multiplying. 2. a practising usury (on a loan), taking more than was lent.

ircaᵃⁱ (.—) ارجاع A a causing to return; a sending back. **— et=** /ı, a/ 1. to reduce (to). 2. lrnd. to send back; to refer, ascribe (to). **—i inân** lrnd. to turn the reins; to change one's direction. **—i kelâm** lrnd. a coming back to the main subject. **— kısmı** artillery recuperator. **—i nazar** lrnd. a looking back; a going over a thing again.

Red 35.

irdaᵃⁱ (.—) ارضاع A *lrnd., same as* **irza 2**.
irdaf (.—) ارداف A *lrnd.* 1. a being, coming or going behind (another), a following. 2. *rhet.* a using a metaphor or metonymy.
irdele=ʳ ايردهلك *prov.* to examine, inspect, scrutinize. **—me** *neol., sc.* examination, discussion.
=**irdi** ايردى *cf.* =**rdı**.
İrem ارم A *Isl. rel.* the mythical gardens said to have been devised by Shaddad bin Ad in emulation of the garden of Paradise. **— bağı** *same as* **İrem**.
irfah (.—) ارفاه A *lrnd.* a making or being comfortable; accommodating.
irfan (.—) عرفان A 1. culture. 2. *lrnd.* knowledge; spiritual knowledge.
irgab (.—) ارغاب A *lrnd.* a stimulating, making one wish for.
irgam (.—) ارغام A *lrnd.* 1. a rubbing in the dirt (a person's nose). 2. a humbling, abasing, humiliating (a person).
irha (.—) ارخاء A *lrnd.* 1. a making loose, slack. 2. a giving the reins, relaxing. **—i iname** carefreeness. **—i inân** a slackening of the reins; giving a horse his head. **—i lisan** a giving vent to one's tongue; a speaking unreservedly.
irhab (.—) ارهاب A *lrnd.* a frightening, terrifying, threatening, menacing.
irhakᵏⁱ (.—) ارهاق A 1. *lrnd.* an embarrassing or distressing by acts contrary to duty or obedience. 2. *Isl. rel.* a deferring those prayers which ought to be said at one hour till the next time of prayer.
irhan (.—) ارهان A *lrnd.* a depositing a thing in pawn as a permanent pledge. **— et=** /ı/ to pledge, deposit, deliver as a hostage or security; to pawn.
irhas 1 (.—) ارخاص A *lrnd.* a cheapening; a being cheapened.
irhas 2 (.—) ارخاص A *lrnd.* a laying a foundation of large stones for a wall.
irhasat (.— —) ارهاصات A *Isl. rel.* a preparatory sign or miracle giving indications of a future prophet. **—ı nebeviye** the signs that forewarned men that Muhammad was to be a prophet.
iri ايرى 1. large; huge; voluminous; big. 2. coarse, coarse-grained (powder, etc.). 3. *archaic* rough, harsh. **— baş** tadpole. **— boy** large-size, well built. **— cevherli** coarse-grained, coarsely veined. **— cüsseli** big-bodied. **— dişli eğe** coarse file, rough file. **— kesim** *prov.* huge. **— kıyım** 1. large-grained. 2. huge. 3. coarse, impudent. **— kum** gravel. **—sini rafa ufağını çöpe diz=** to tell in detail. **— söyle=** *archaic* to talk big, to boast. **— sözlü** *archaic* slanderer. **— taneli** 1. large-grained, large berried. 2. coarse-grained. **— yarı***. **—ce** largish, sizeable, somewhat coarse.
irigatör ايريغاتور F *med.* enema.
irik=ⁱʳ ايريك *prov., same as* **irk=**.
irileş=ⁱʳ ايريلشمك 1. to grow gradually large. 2. to act or talk harshly. **—me** 1. *verbal n.* 2. *biol.* hypertrophy. **—tir=** /ı/ *caus. of* **irileş=**.
irili ايريلى *only in* **irili ufaklı** big and little, great and small.
irilikᵍⁱ ايريلك 1. largeness; greatness; bigness; coarseness. 2. size; dimension.
irin ايرين pus, matter (of wounds). **— topla=** to suppurate.
irinlen=ⁱʳ ايرينلنمك to suppurate, to fester, to run.
irinli ايرينلى purulent; containing matter; soiled with pus.
iris ايريس F *anat.* iris.
iriş ايريش *var. of* **arış 1, 2**.
iriyarı ايرى يارى powerfully built, big, huge.
irk=ᵉʳ ايرمك *prov.* 1. to collect, to come together. 2. to stop. 3. to form into a stagnant pool. **—me havzası** *neol., geog.* reception basin.
irkâb (.—) اركاب A *lrnd.* a causing to ride; a mounting; embarkation. **— et=** /ı/ to cause to ride; to mount; to embark.
irkaben (.—'.) اركابا۠ /ı, a/ mounting; embarking.
=**irken** كن *cf.* =**rken**.
irkil=ⁱʳ ايركلمك 1. to be startled, draw back in doubt or fear. 2. *archaic* to collect, become stagnant (water). 3. *med.* to become inflamed. **—me** *med.* irritation. **—t=** /ı/ *caus. of* **irkil=**. **—ten** *med.* irritant.
irkinti ايركنتى ايركنتى *archaic* stagnant water; a stagnant mass.
İrlânda (..'.) ايرلاندا It *geog.* Ireland, Eire. **—lı** Irish.
irman (— —) ايرمان P *lrnd.* intruder; uninvited guest; parasite.
irmansaray (— —.—) ايرمان سراى P *lrnd.* 1. a house where one is entertained; rented house. 2. the world, man's temporary abode.
irmikᵍⁱ ايرمك semolina. **— helvası** sweet made of semolina.
=**irmiş** ايرمش *cf.* =**rmiş**.
=**irmişçesine** ايرمشجسنه *cf.* =**rmışçasına**.
=**irmiş gibi** ايرمش كبى *cf.* =**rmış gibi**.
İrmiya (..—) ارميا A *Bib.* Jeremiah.
ironi ايرونى F *phil.* irony.
irs ارث A an inheriting; inheritance; heritage; hereditary quality.
irsa (.—) ارساء A *lrnd.* 1. an anchoring, mooring (ship). 2. a fixing, making firm and

immovable; firmness. **—i lenger et=** to cast anchor.
irsalⁱⁱ (. —) ارسال A a sending, dispatching; a forwarding. **— et=** /ı/ to send, to dispatch. **—i lihye** *lrnd.* to grow a beard. **—iye mektubu** letter of carriage; waybill. **—i mesel** *lrnd.* a giving a single parable and its application in one distich of poetry. **—i meseleyn** *lrnd.* a giving two comparisons in a single distich to exemplify one's meaning.
irsalât (. — —) ارسالات A forwarding, sending out; shipment, goods sent. **— akçesi, — hazinesi** *Ott. hist.* fund received from Egypt every year for the Sultan's private purse. **—çı** sender, remitter, shipper.
irsan (. —) ارصان A *lrnd.* a making firm and strong (thing).
=irse ـرـ' *cf.* **=rsa.**
irsen (´.) ارثاً A by inheritance, hereditarily.
irsî (. —) ارثى A hereditary; inherited. **—yet** (. — .) A *biol.* heredity.
irşa (. —) ارشاء A *lrnd.* a corrupting with a bribe; a bribing.
irşad (. —) ارشاد A 1. a putting on the right way, showing or explaining the road, directing. 2. a teaching one how to act; a guiding, directing (one); enlightenment; initiation. **— et=** /ı/ to direct, guide, teach the right way; to initiate (a novice).
irşadât (. — —) ارشادات A guiding, teaching. **—ta bulun=** to give advice, to guide, to direct.
irşatᵈⁱ (. —) ارشاد [irşad] *same as* **irşad.**
irtiab (. . —) ارتئاب A *lrnd.* a being or becoming frightened, terrified.
irtiad (. . —) ارتعاد A *lrnd., same as* **irtiaş.**
irtiaş (. ! —) ارتعاش A *lrnd.* a trembling or shaking from cold or fever; a quaking with fear.
irtibat (. . —) ارتباط A 1. a being or becoming attached; attachment, connection; tie. 2. *mil.* communication; liaison. **— hatları** *mil.* lines of communication. **— subayı** *mil.* liaison officer.
irticaⁿ 1 (. . —) ارتجاع A a going back; political reaction.
irtica 2 (. . —) ارتجاء A *lrnd.* a hoping, wishing, expecting; hope, wish, expectation.
irticac (. . —) ارتجاج A 1. *lrnd.* a being in commotion, agitation or convulsion, a quivering. 2. *phys.* libration. **—i adalî** *biol.* muscular shock, contraction. **—i derya** the ocean's getting rough. **—i ecram** the glittering of the stars.
irticaf (. . —) ارتجاف A 1. *lrnd.* a being or becoming violently agitated; agitation, commotion. 2. *med.* disturbance; breakdown.
irticaî (. . — —) ارتجاعى A reactionary.

irtical (. . —) ارتجال A a speaking extempore; improvisation.
irticalen (. . —´.) ارتجالاً A extempore; improvisatory.
irticalî (. . — —) ارتجالى A extemporarily.
irtida (. . —) ارتداء A *lrnd.* a putting on a mantle.
irtidad (. . —) ارتداد A *lrnd.* an apostatizing (especially from Islam); apostasy.
irtidaf (. . —) ارتداف A *lrnd.* a following; a riding behind another on the same horse.
irtidatᵈⁱ (. . —) ارتداد A *lrnd., same as* **irtidad.**
irtifaⁿⁱ (. . —) ارتفاع A *lrnd.* a growing tall, a becoming high in station; altitude; height; elevation. **— al=** *astr.* to measure the altitude (of a star, etc.). **— bul=** to rise up high in altitude. **—ı kutb** altitude of the pole. **—ı mahsul** bringing in the harvest from the fields. **—ı mersud** *astr.* apparent altitude. **— tahtası** quadrant, wooden astrolabe. **—ı töhmet** a wiping out all suspicion. **— zaviyesi** angle of altitude.
irtifaât (. . — —) ارتفاعات A *lrnd., pl. of* **irtifa. —ı mütevafika** *astr.* corresponding altitudes.
irtifaen (. . —´.) ارتفاعاً A *lrnd.* in altitude.
irtifakᵏⁱ (. . —) ارتفاق A *lrnd.* 1. a leaning on the elbow or on a cushion. 2. an associating with, becoming a companion (to). 3. *anat.* symphysis, coalescence. **— hakkı** *law* servitude; easement, the rights of another modifying the owner's title.
irtigab (. . —) ارتغاب A *lrnd.* a desiring, wishing; wish, desire.
irtihalⁱⁱ (. . —) ارتحال A a passing away; death. **—i dâr-ı beka** a dying, death.
irtihan (. . —) ارتهان A *lrnd.* a taking a pawn, a receiving a pledge.
irtihas (. . —) ارتخاص A *lrnd.* a being cheap, a being bought at a low price; a being valueless.
irtihaz (. . —) ارتخاض A *lrnd.* a being shamed; shame.
irtika (. . —) ارتقاء A *lrnd.* an ascending; a rising; advancement. **— et=** to ascend; to rise; to increase.
irtikab 1 (. . —) ارتقاب A *lrnd.* a looking for, an expecting, awaiting.
irtikâb 2 (. . —) ارتكاب A *same as* **irtikâp.**
irtikâkᵏⁱ (. . —) ارتكاك A *lrnd.* a stammering in the heat of an argument.
irtikâpᵇⁱ (. . —) ارتكاب [irtikâb] 1. bribery, corruption, subornation, dishonesty. 2. a saying or doing (any bad thing), committing a dishonest act. **— et=** 1. to do wrong, act dishonestly, steal, to accept bribes. 2. to say or do, commit, perpetrate.
irtikâz (. . —) ارتكاز A *lrnd.* 1. a quivering

(muscle, etc.), palpitating. 2. a becoming or being stuck firmly (into the ground, etc.).

irtisam (..—) ارتسام A *lrnd.* 1. a being pictured or delineated (on a thing); projection (pictures, etc.). 2. a reciting the praises of God; prayer, invocation. — **âleti** projector. — **et=** to be projected upon. —**î** (..——) A *math.* of projection.

irtişa (..—) ارتشاء A *lrnd.* an accepting a bribe; bribery; corruption.

irtişah (..—) ارتشاح A *med.* infiltration.

irtiyab (..—) ارتياب A *lrnd.* a doubting; doubt; suspicion.

irtiyad (..—) ارتياد A 1. *lrnd.* a seeking, endeavoring to find; endeavor. 2. *phil.* volition.

irtiyah (..—) ارتياح A *lrnd.* 1. a resting, reposing, taking one's ease. 2. God's mercy, compassion.

irtiza 1 (..—) ارتضاء A *lrnd.* a choosing, preferring, selecting; choice, preference, approval.

irtizaᵃⁱ **2** (..—) ارتضاع A *lrnd.* a sucking milk from the breast (baby).

irtizakᵏⁱ (..—) ارتزاق A *lrnd.* 1. a getting or having means of subsistence, living, maintaining oneself. 2. a receiving pay or rations for subsistence.

irva (.—) ارواء A *lrnd.* 1. a satisfying with drink. 2. a watering, irrigating plentifully. — **ve iska** irrigating.

iryale (.—.) اريال *same as* **riyale**.

irza 1 (.—) ارضاء A *lrnd.* a satisfying, contenting, pleasing.

irzaᵃⁱ **2** (.—) ارضاع A *lrnd.* a suckling (a child).

is 1 ايس 1. soot, lampblack, smut. 2. *prov.* freckles.

isˢˢⁱ **2** *archaic* owner, master.

İsa 1 (——) عيسى A Jesus.

isa 2 (——) ايصا A *lrnd.* 1. an appointing to act as representative in absence or as executor after death; a bequeathing. 2. a commanding, a recommending to be done.

isabe (.—.) عصابة A *lrnd.* 1. band, bandage. 2. fillet or kerchief bound round the head; turban. 3. body of men. —**li** with a fillet or turban.

isabet (.—.) اصابت A 1. a hitting the mark; an attaining, a reaching. 2. a thing said or done just right; insight. —! Well done! —**i ayn** *lrnd.* the evil eye. — **et=** 1. to hit the mark, to strike. 2. to say or do just the right thing; to guess rightly. — **oldu** It was a good thing; it worked out well. —**i rey** an appropriate thought, a sound opinion.

isabetkâr (.—.—) اصابتكار P *lrnd.* hitting the right mark.

isabetkarin (.—..—) اصابتقرين P, **isabetmedar** (.—..—) اصابت مدار P successful; right-minded.

is'ad (.—) اسعاد A *lrnd.* 1. a making happy, fortunate, or prosperous. 2. a helping, supporting, aiding.

İsadem (——.) عيسى دم P *lrnd.* having breath like that of Jesus by which to perform miracles (said of clever physicians).

isaet (.—.) اساءت A *lrnd.* 1. a corrupting, spoiling (a thing). 2. a doing ill or wrong; offence, crime, sin.

is'af (.—) اسعاف A *lrnd.* a granting, compliance (with a request). — **et=** to grant (a request).

isaga (.—.) اصاغ A *lrnd.* a casting metal.

isah (——) ايصاح A *lrnd.* a soiling, defiling.

isalˡⁱ (——) ايصال A *lrnd.* a causing to attain. — **et=** /a/ to bring or send to. —**i mazarrat et=** to inflict injuries, to harm.

isale (.—.) اسالة A *lrnd.* a making or allowing to flow, run (water). — **et=** to bring or divert (water).

İsanefes (——..) عيسى نفس P *lrnd.*, *same as* **İsadem**.

isar 1 (.—) اسار A *lrnd.* 1. a binding with a bond; bond, chain. 2. a making a captive, a taking prisoner or slave. —**i esaret** chain of slavery. — **et=** 1. to bind. 2. to make captive.

is'ar 2 (.—) اسعار A *lrnd.* a fixing the price.

isar 3 (——) ايثار A *lrnd.* 1. a giving lavishly; an honoring. 2. a preferring; preference. — **et=** to give lavishly, to bestow.

isar 4 (——) ايسار A *lrnd.* a being or becoming wealthy; wealth.

i'sar 5 اعصار A *lrnd.* whirlwind; waterspout.

isarbahş (——.) ايثار بخش P *lrnd.* who bestows gifts abundantly.

isbah (.—) اصباح A *lrnd.* 1. an ushering in the dawn; entering on the morning; morning, dawn.

İsbahan (..—) اصبهان P *same as* **Isfahan**.

isbal (.—) اسبال A *lrnd.* 1. a sending, dispatching (by messenger). 2. a falling down, hanging down.

isbat (.—) اثبات A *var. of* **ispat**. —**iye** (.——.) *phil.* positivism.

ise ايسه although; however; as for; if. — **de** even if, although.

=iser ايسر *cf.* **=ısar**.

İsevî (—.—) عيسوى A *lrnd.* Christian; pertaining to Jesus. —**lik** Christianity. —**ye** (—.—.) A *Isl. rel.*, name of a branch of the Kadiri order. —**yet** (—.—.) Christianity.

isfar (.—) اسفار A *lrnd.* 1. a breaking up of cloud or darkness; a shining. 2. unfolding of the dawn. — **vakti** the dawn.

isfehsalar (..——) اسفهسالار P *lrnd.* commander of an army.
isfenac (..—) اسفناج P *lrnd.* spinach.
isfenahiye (..—..) اسفنا ناغىه P *obs., bot.,* Chenopodiaceae.
isfenc اسفنج P *lrnd.* sponge. —**î** (..—) P spongy. —**iye** (..—.) *zool.,* Spongiae.
isfend 1 اسفند P harmel, Syrian rue, *bot.,* Peganum harmala. —**i sefid** white mustard, *bot.,* Sinapis alba.
isfend 2 اسفند A *lrnd.* wine.
isfendan (..—) اسفندان P 1. *lrnd.* white mustard seed. 2. maple tree, bird's-eye maple, *bot., Acer campestre.* —**iye** (..———.) *bot.,* Aceraceae.
isfendilyon اسفنديليون A meadow parsnip, cow parsnip, *bot., Heracleum sphondylium.*
İsfendiyar (...—), **İsfendyar** (..—) اسفنديار P a mythical Persian hero, son of Gushtasp, slain by Rustem.
isfenks اسفينقس Gk sphinx.
isfidac (.——) اسفيداج P *lrnd.* white lead, ceruse.
İshak[kı] اسحاق A *Bib.* Isaac. — **kuşu** horned owl, *zool., Asio flammens.*
ishal[li] (.—) اسهال A a purging; diarrhea. — **ol**= to have diarrhea.
ishan (.—) اسخان A *lrnd.* a warming or being warmed. —**ı ayn** a causing to weep.
ishat (.—) اسخاط A *lrnd.* a displeasing, vexing, irritating.
isilik[ği] اسيلك *colloq.* heat spots, rash. — **ol**= to have heat spots.
isim[mi] اسم [**ism 1**] 1. name, title (books, etc.). 2. noun. —**i aded** *Arabic gram.* cardinal number. —**i âlet,** —**i âm** *Arabic gram.* common noun. —**i ayn** *Arabic gram.* a noun of substance as compared with the abstract. **İ—i Azam** *lrnd.* 1. the great and secret name of God. 2. Allah. —**i cami** *Arabic gram.* collective noun. —**i camid** *Arabic gram.* a noun which is itself a simple root. **İ—i Celâl** *lrnd.* the great name of God. —**i cem'** *Arabic gram.* collective noun. —**i cins** *Arabic gram.* common noun. —**ini cismini bilmiyorum** I don't know a thing about him; he is a complete and utter stranger to me. — **cümlesi** *gram.* noun clause. —**i fail** *gram.* active participle. — **fiil** *gram.* infinitive. —**i geçen** aforementioned, aforesaid, mentioned above. — **hali** *gram.* objective case. —**i has** *gram.* proper noun. —**i işaret** *gram.* demonstrative pronoun. —**i mânâ** *gram.* abstract noun. —**i masdar** *gram.* verbal noun. —**i mef'ul** *gram.* passive participle. —**i mekân** *Arabic gram.,* name of the place where an action occurs or where a thing abounds (in the form of **mef'el**). —**i mensub** *gram.* a kind of adjective which attributes something to a person, place or thing (It ends with **i** in Arabic and Persian, in **lı** or **cı** in Turkish), *e. g.,* **Rumi, partili.** —**i musaggar** *gram.* diminutive noun. —**i muzaf** *gram.* noun annexed to another in the genitive case. —**i muzafünileyh** *gram.* the noun in the genitive to which another is annexed. —**i muzmer** *gram.* pronoun. —**i mübhem** *gram.* demonstrative pronoun. —**i mürekkeb** *gram.* compound noun. —**i müştak** *gram.* derived noun, derivative. —**i nisbet** *gram.* relative adjective. —**i resmi ile** in full detail. —**i sıfat** *gram.* adjectival noun designating a thing by a quality (*e. g.,* the Merciful, for God). —**i tafdil** *gram.* an adjective in the comparative or superlative degree. —**i tahkir** a diminutive noun of contempt. — **tak**= to give a name (to); to nickname. — **takımı** *gram.* genitive or possessive case. —**i tam** *Arabic gram.* an indefinite noun rendered complete either by its own indefinite case ending or by its relation to another noun in the genitive. —**i tasgir** *gram.* diminutive noun, a term of diminution, endearment or contempt. —**i var cismi yok** much heard of but not in sight. —**i vasf** *gram.* adjective. — **ver**= to give a name, to name. —**i vi'â** *gram.* a derivative noun indicating a container especially for something. —**i zaman ve mekân** *Arabic gram.* noun of time and place. —**i zat** the name of the essence of a thing, especially the proper name of God as distinguished from the names of His attributes.
iska (.—) استقاء A *lrnd.* a watering, irrigating; a giving to drink.
iskaça استقاجى *same as* **ıskaça.**
iskambil استانبيل It 1. playing card. 2. kind of card game. — **kâğıdı** playing cards. — **kâğıdı gibi dağıt**= to scatter (something) in all directions. — **oyna**= *colloq.* to play at cards.
iskân (.—) اسكان A a causing to inhabit or settle; a settling in, a dwelling in; inhabiting. — **et**= to cause to dwell; to furnish dwellings (for).
iskandil اسكنديل It 1. *naut.* sounding-lead, fathometer. 2. probe; a sounding. — **at**= to cast the lead. — **et**= 1. to sound; to probe. 2. to sound a man's thoughts or intentions. 3. *slang* to spy upon. — **savlosu** *naut.* sounding line.
iskandille=[r] اسكنديللمك /ı/ to sound, to examine.
iskâr (.—) اسكار A *lrnd.* a making drunk, an intoxicating.
iskarça (..′.) اسقارجه It *same as* **ıskarça.**
iskarmoz اسقارموز Gk *same as* **ıskarmoz.**
iskarpelâ (...′.) اسقارپلا It carpenter's chisel.
iskarpin اسقارپن It woman's shoe.
iskat 1 (.—) اسقاط A *same as* **ıskat.**

iskât

iskâtᵗⁱ 2 (.—) اسكات A *lrnd.* 1. a silencing a person; a convincing in argument. 2. an appeasing; a calming anger. **— et**= /ı/ 1. to silence. 2. to quieten, to appease.
iskele اسكله Gk 1. landing place; wharf; quay. 2. port of call; seaport town. 3. ship's ladder; gangway. 4. a builder's scaffolding. 5. port side of a ship. **— al**= /a/ *slang* to pester a woman with improper advances. **— babası** 1. *naut.* bollard. 2. father who has no authority over his family. **— başı** *naut.* gangway. **— direği** scaffolding pole. **— kethüdası** *obs.* warden of a landing place with authority over the boats plying there, harbormaster. **—yi kokut**= to make a place uncomfortable for a person. **— kur**= to erect scaffolding. **— kuşu** kind of kingfisher, *zool.*, *Alcedo atthis.* **— maddesi** *colloq.* exciting but unfounded things. **—yi tut**= *naut.* to come up (wharf or landing-place); to touch. **— vardavelâsı** *naut.* ladder-handrail, manrope. **— ver**= to let down a gangway (for a ship). **—ye yanaş**= to come alongside (boat).
iskelet اسكلت F 1. skeleton. 2. framework; outline. **—i çık**= to become very thin. **— gibi** like a skeleton; a bag of bones.
iskemle (..´.) اسكمله F chair; stool. **— tekaüdlüğü** *obs.* old age pension.
İskender اسكندر P Alexander the Great. **—i Kebir**, **—i Rumî** Alexander the Great. **—i zulkarneyn** Alexander the Great.
İskenderiye (...—.) اسكندريه A *geog.* Alexandria.
İskendersatvet اسكندرصطوت P *lrnd.* mighty as Alexander.
İskenderun (...—) اسكندرون *geog.* Iskenderun (*formerly* Alexandretta).
iskete (..´.) اسكته coal titmouse, *zool., Parus ater.*
iskil (.—) اسقيل A sea onion, squill, *bot., Scilla maritima, Urginea scilla.*
İskoç اسقوچ Scotch.
İskoçya (..´.) اسقوچيا It *geog.* Scotland. **—lı** Scottish, Scotsman.
iskolâstikᵍⁱ اسقولاستيك F *phil.* scholastic, scholasticism.
iskolofendariyun (....—..) اسقولوفندريون hart's-tongue fern, horse-tongue, *bot., Scolopendrium officinarum.*
iskona (..´.) اسقونه It *same as* **iskuna**.
iskonto (..´.) اسقونطو It discount. **— et**= to discount (a bill).
iskopamar, **iskopomar** اسقوپامار—اسقوپومار It *naut.* ship's lower studding sail. **— sereni** lower studding sail boom.
iskorbüt اسقوربوت F *med.* scurvy.
iskorçilâ (...´.) اسقورچيلا kind of large fishing net.

iskorçina (...´.) اسقورچينا salsify, oyster plant, *bot., Tragopogon orientalis.*
iskordiyun (.—.—) اسقورديون A water germander, scordium, *bot., Teucrium Scordium.*
iskorpit اسقورپيت Gk scorpion fish, *zool., Scorpaena.*
iskota (..´.) اسقوطا It *cf.* **uskuta**.
iskrim اسكريم F fencing.
iskuna (..´.) اسقونه [**iskona**] schooner.
islâkᵏⁱ (.—) اسلاك A *lrnd.* 1. a causing to travel by a road; a guiding towards. 2. an inserting; an introducing; a passing into.
İslâm (.—) اسلام A 1. Islam. 2. Muslim. 3. *lrnd., l. c.* a resigning oneself to God and to his will. **—a gel**= to become a Muslim. **— hukuku** Muslim law.
İslâmbol اسلامبول *Ott. hist.* Istanbul.
İslâmî (.——) اسلامى A Islamic.
İslamiyan (.———) اسلاميان P the Muslims.
İslâmiyet (.—..) اسلاميت A Islamic religion; the Muslim world.
İslânda اسلاندا It *geog.* Iceland.
İslav اسلاو Slav, Slavic, Slavonic.
isle=ʳ ايلمك /ı/ 1. to blacken with soot. 2. to smoke (fish, etc.). 3. to burn slightly (milk pudding, etc.). **—n**= *pass.* **—t**= /ı, a/ *caus. of* **isle**=.
isli ايسلى sooty, begrimed with soot; smoked. **— balık** smoked fish. **— kâğıt** carbon paper.
islim اسليم [**istim**] steam. **— arkadan gelsin** Let the steam come ! *said of enterprises started without considering basic essentials.* **— üzerinde** with steam on.
islimî (.——) اسليمى P having a special kind of ornamentation in curved lines, similar to Chinese forms.
ism 1 اسم A *cf.* **isim**.
ism 2 اثم A *lrnd.* sin; crime; fault.
ismaᵃⁱ (.—) اسماع A *lrnd.* a causing to be heard.
İsmail (.—.) اسماعيل A Ishmael.
İsmailiye (.—.—.) اسماعيليه A name of an Islamic religious sect.
ismen (.´.) اسما A by name.
ismet عصمت A chastity, purity; honor, innocence. **—i me'nus** *lrnd.* always chaste. **—li** chaste, virtuous. **—lû** *obs.* chaste, virtuous (used as an honorific when writing to a lady). **—meab** (...—) P *lrnd.* honorable, virtuous. **—penâh** (...—) P *lrnd.* chaste, honorable.
ismî (.—) اسمى A *lrnd.* pertaining to a name or noun; nominal.
ismirar (..—) اسمرار A *lrnd.* a becoming swarthy; a becoming dusky.
ismiye اسميه A *phil.* nominalism.

ismıyet (.—.) اِسْمِيَّت A *gram.* quality peculiar to nouns or names.
ismiyun (..—) اِسْمِيُّون A *phil.* nominalists. **— mezhebi** nominalism.
isnaaşer (.—..) اِثْنا عَشَر A *lrnd.* twelve. **—e** twelve. **İ—iye** *Isl. rel.* the mystical order of the Twelve Imams.
isnad (.–) اِسْناد A 1. an ascribing, imputing, attributing; imputation; ascription to proof or testimony. 2. *gram.* relation between subject and object. **— et=** /ı, a/ to ascribe, to impute.
isnadat (.——) اِسْنادات A 1. imputations. 2. wrong accusations.
isnadî (.——) اِسْنادى A *lrnd.* pertaining to ascription or imputation; imputative. **—yat** (.———) A 1. wrongful accusations. 2. imputations.
isnan (.—) اِسْنان A *lrnd.* 1. a teething. 2. a being advanced in years; an aging.
isnat[dı] (.—) اِسْناد A *var. of* **isnad**.
isneyn اِثْنَين A *lrnd.* 1. two. 2. Monday. **—iyet** (..—.) A *obs., phil.* duality.
ispalya (..'.) اِسْپالْيا F *hort.* espalier.
İspanya 1 (..'.) اِسْپانْيا It *geog.* Spain.
ispanya 2 (..'.) اِسْپانْيا *obs.* kind of chalk powder used in dying; fuller's earth.
İspanyol اِسْپانْيول F 1. Spaniard. 2. Spanish. **—ca** (...'.) the Spanish language; in Spanish.
ispanyolet اِسْپانْيولِت F espagnolette, window latch.
isparçina (...'.) اِسْپارْچينا It *same as* **ısparçana**.
ispari, isparya اِسْپارى، اِسْپارْيا kind of sea bream, *zool., Sargus annularis*.
ispat (.—) اِثْبات A 1. a proving, affirming; proof; evidence. 2. confirmation. 3. probation. 4. *lrnd.* a making a thing firm, a consolidating. 5. *lrnd.* demonstration. 6. *prov.* witness. **— et=** /ı/ to prove; to affirm; to confirm. **— hakkı** *law* right to prove (one's accusation). **— kudreti** *law* conclusive force. **— külfeti** *law* burden of proof. **—ı vücut et=** 1. to appear in person. 2. to put in an appearance.
ispati (..'.) اِسْپاتى Gk *cards* clubs.
ispatla=[r] *neol., math.* /ı/ to demonstrate.
ispavlo (..'.) اِسْپاوْلو [ıspagula] *same as* **ıspavli**.
ispenc اِسْپَنْج *Ott. hist.* pasturage tax on pigs.
ispence, ispencik[ği] اِسْپَنْجه، اِسْپَنْجِك *Ott. hist.* 1. poll tax on slaves when first brought to market from abroad, as the fiscal fifth due to the Treasury on prisoners of war. 2. small tax imposed on people from the provinces when they came to Istanbul to work or trade.
ispenciyar اِسْپَنْجيار It *lrnd.* apothecary; pharmacist; chemist. **—î** (...——) pharmaceutical. **—iye** (...——.) pharmaceutics.
ispenç[ci] اِسْپَنْچ bantam. **— horozu gibi** cocky.

ispendik[ği] اِسْپَنْدِك small bass, *zool., Labrax lupus*.
isper اِسْپَر *var. of* **siper**.
ispermeçet اِسْپَرْماچِت It spermaceti. **— mumu** stearin candle, sperm candle. **— yağı** sperm oil; sperm.
ispinoz اِسْپينوز Gk 1. chaffinch, *zool., Fringilla coelebs*. 2. *slang* chatterer, gossiping.
ispir اِسْپير It *obs.* groom.
ispiralya (...'.) اِسْپيرالْيا It *naut.* cabin skylight; porthole.
ispiritizma (...'.) اِسْپيريتيزْما It spiritualism, spiritism.
ispirto (..'.) اِسْپيرْتو It alcohol; spirits. **— lâmbası** alcohol lamp.
ispit[di] اِسْپيت *var. of* **ipsit**.
ispitalya (...'.) اِسْپيتالْيا It *obs.* hospital.
ispiyon اِسْپييون It *slang* 1. spy. 2. sneak. **—la=** to spy; to sneak. **—luk** spying.
ispontane F *neol., phil.* spontaneous.
ispor اِسْپور F sport. **—cu** sportsman.
isr اِثْر A *lrnd.* 1. trace; track. 2. path, way; course.
isra[aı] **1** اِسْرا A *lrnd.* a traveling or sending one to travel by night.
isra[aı] **2** (.—) اِسْراع A *lrnd.* a hastening; an accelerating. **— et=** /ı/ to quicken, to hasten.
israf (.—) اِسْراف A a squandering, prodigality; wasteful expenditure. **— et=** /ı/ to waste, to squander; to spend unreasonably.
İsrafil (.—.) اِسْرافيل A angel of death who will blow the last trumpet.
İsrail (.—.) اِسْرائيل A Israel. **—î** (.—.—) A Israelite; Israeli. **—iyat** (.—.——) A *lrnd.* false beliefs, superstitions.
israr (.—) اِسْرار A *lrnd.* a concealing, hiding, secreting.
issi اِسّى *cf.* **is 2**.
istade (.—.) اِسْتاده P *lrnd.* standing, on foot, erect; set up.
istakoz اِسْتاقوز *var. of* **ıstakoz**.
istalâgmit اِسْتالاگْميت F *geol.* stalagmite.
istalâktit اِسْتالاكْتيت F *geol.* stalactite.
istalya (..'.) اِسْتالْيا It *naut.* demurrage.
-istan (.—) اِسْتان P country, region, *as in*, Hindistan, Arabistan; sengistan.
İstanbul (..'.) اِسْتانْبول، اِسْطَنْبول Gk Istanbul. **— Ağası** *Ott. hist.* the Janissary Commandant of Istanbul proper. **— çocuğu** *colloq.* tenderfoot. **— efendisi** real gentleman. **— Efendisi, — Kadısı** *Ott. hist.* canon law judge of Istanbul proper. **— kaldırımı çiğnemiş** who has walked the streets of Istanbul, experienced, knowing. **— kazan ben kepçe** I left no stone unturned in Istanbul. **— Tekfuru** *Ott. hist.* the Roman or Byzantine Emperor of Constantinople. **— zer-i mahbubu** *Ott hist.* small gold coin.

istanbulin ستابولين F *obs.* stambouline, a kind of frock coat.
İstanbullu ستابوللى native of Istanbul.
istandard ستاندارد F standard.
İstanköy (.'.) استانکوى ا Gk *geog.* the Island of Cos, Stanco.
istar ستار Gk *obs.* a weight of 6 1/2 drams.
istasyon استاسيون F station; railway station; stop (bus, etc.).
istatikᵍⁱ استاتيك F 1. static. 2. station.
istatistikᵍⁱ استاتستيك F statistics.
istatüko (..'.) استاتوقو F status quo.
istavritᵈⁱ استاوريت Gk horse mackerel, scad, ~*zool.*, *Trachurus trachurus*. — **azmanı** blue fin tuna, *zool.*, *Orcynus thynnus*.
istavroz استاوروز *var. of* **istavroz**.
iste=ʳ ايستمك استمك استيمك
1. to want; to require; to need. 2. /dan, ı/ to ask for. 3. /ı/ to wish for, to desire; to long for. 4. /ı/ *archaic* to look for. —**mez** I don't want it. It is not required. —**r** is required, needed, desired. —**yerek** willingly, gladly; by one's own wish. —**diği gibi at oynatıyor** He acts in the way he likes (with no one interfering); he just pleases himself. —**r istemez** willingly or unwillingly; like it or not. —**r**... **ister**... whether... or..., *e. g.*, **ister gelsin ister gelmesin** It does not matter whether he comes or not.
istearik F *neol., chem.* stearic.
istearin F *neol., chem.* stearine.
istebrakᵏⁱ استبرق A *lrnd.* kind of thick satin; gold embroidered satin.
istekᵍⁱ استك ايستك wish, desire; inclination; appetite. — **kipi** *gram.* subjunctive, optative (mood).
isteka (.'.) استقا It billiard cue.
isteklen=ⁱʳ ايستكلنمك to become desirous. —**lendir**= /ı, a/ *caus.*
istekli ايستكلى 1. desirous; willing; keen. 2. bidder (at an auction).
isteksiz ايستكسز 1. disinclined, unwilling, without wanting to; reluctant; indifferent; apathetic. 2. having no appetite. —**lik** disinclination, reluctance.
istem *neol., psych.* volition. —**li** *biol.* voluntary. —**seme** *psych.* velleity, low degree of volition. —**siz** *biol.* involuntary.
isten=ⁱʳ ايستنمك استنمك 1. *pass. of* **iste**=. 2. *prov.* to ask for (trouble).
İstendil استنديل *obs., geog.* the Island of Tinos.
isteno استنو F stenographer.
istenograf استنوغراف F stenographer. —**i**, —**ya** stenography, shorthand.
istenotip استنوتيپ F stenotype.
istepᵇˡ‧ᵖⁱ استپ F steppe.
istepne (.'.) ستپنى *auto.* spare tire.
istereografi استره وغرافى F stereography.

istereoskop استره وسقوپ F stereoscope.
istereotip استره وتيپ F stereotype. —**i** stereotypy.
isteri استرى F *psychiatry* hysteria, hysterics.
isterikᵍⁱ استريك F hysterical.
isterilize استريليزه F sterilized. — **et**= /ı/ to sterilize.
isterlin استرلين E pound sterling.
isterya (.'.) ايستريا Gk *same as* **isteri**.
isteş=ⁱʳ استشمك *archaic* to look for one another.
istet=ⁱʳ ايستتمك استتمك /ı, a/ *caus. of* **iste**=.
isteyiş ايستيش verbal n. of **iste**=.
istıktab (..—) استقطاب A *phys.* polarization; *lrnd.* polarity.
istıtlaᵃⁱ (..—) استطلاع A *lrnd.* an asking for information, inquiring. —**at** (..——) A *pl.*
istiab (..—) استيعاب A *lrnd.* 1. a containing, capacity. 2. an occupying or filling a given space. — **haddi** 1. maximum capacity. 2. *naut.* tonnage.
istiade (..—.) استعاده A 1. *lrnd.* asking, desiring, commanding to come back or return. 2. *phil.* reviviscence.
istiane (..—.) استعانة A *lrnd.* an asking or seeking for help and assistance. — **et**= /dan/ to ask for help (from someone).
istiapᵇⁱ (..—) استيعاب *var. of* **istiab**.
istiare (..—.) استعارة A 1. *law* an asking for a loan of something, a borrowing a thing. 2. *rhet.* a using a word metaphorically, metaphor. —**i inadiye** *obs.* paradox. —**i tahyiliye** *rhet.* a metaphor where the object used for comparison is suggested, not named. —**i telmihiye** *rhet.* an allusive metaphor.
istiaza (..—.) استعاضة A *lrnd.* an asking or seeking for a substitute, exchange or compensation (for something).
istiaze (..—.) استعاذة A 1. *lrnd.* a seeking shelter and protection, taking refuge. 2. *Isl. rel.* a pronouncing as an ejaculation or prayer the words **euzi billah**, etc.
istib'ad 1 (..—) استبعاد A *lrnd.* 1. a considering to be removed, far off (person or thing); a being or becoming removed. 2. a considering improbable. — **et**= /ı/ to deem unlikely.
isti'bad 2 (..—) استعباد A *lrnd.* a reducing to slavery, bondage; a treating as a servant or slave.
istibaha (..—.) استباحة A *lrnd.* a deeming lawful; a making lawful.
istibakᵏⁱ (..—) استباق A *lrnd.* a contending for superiority in a race, a competing in a race.
istibane (..—.) استبانة A *lrnd.* 1. a making plain, clear or known; a clarifying, a becoming manifest. 2. a knowing, understanding, having a distinct perception.

isti'bar (..—) استعبار A *lrnd.* an asking the interpretation of a dream.
istibdaᵃ¹ (..—) استبداع A *lrnd.* an esteeming as novel or strange; a producing something new.
istibdad (..—) استبداد A *cf.* **istibdat**.
istibdalˡⁱ (..—) استبدال A *lrnd.* a taking in exchange and exchanging; exchange; replacement; replacement of conscripts by new recruits. — **et=** /ı/ to exchange, to release or disband (conscripts).
istibdatᵈ¹ (..—) استبداد |istibdad| A despotism, absolute rule.
istibka (..—) استبقا A *lrnd.* 1. a causing to remain or endure; a reserving. 2. a reserving for the future.
istibra (..—) استبرا A *can. law* 1. a cleaning oneself from all remains of urine. 2. an abstaining from intercourse with a newly obtained slave girl until after her menstruation, so that, if she proves to be pregnant, this may not be attributed to the new owner.
istibsar (..—) استبصار A *lrnd.* a considering with attention, examining, scrutinizing.
istibşar (..—) استبشار A *lrnd.* a rejoicing at, or announcing good news.
istibtan (..—) استبطان A *lrnd.* a becoming acquainted with the esoteric or internal part of a thing, a being initiated, or being of the initiate.
isti'cab 1 (..—) استعجاب A *lrnd.* a being struck with astonishment; amazement.
isticab 2 (.——) استيجاب A *lrnd.* a requiring something as a necessary consequence.
isticabe, isticabet (..—.) استجابت A *lrnd.* an answering, accepting, granting, a turning a favorable ear to (a person or request). — **et=** to answer (a prayer).
isticade (..—.) استجاده A *lrnd.* 1. a considering generous or excellent; a liking, approval. 2. a beseeching one to be good and generous, kind and liberal.
isti'calˡⁱ (..—) A, **istical**ˡⁱ (.——) استعجال *lrnd.* a hastening, hurrying; haste, hurry.
isticar (.——) استيجار A a hiring. — **et=** to hire, to take on hire.
isticare (..—.) استجاره A *lrnd.* an imploring aid or protection; a taking refuge. — **et=** /a/ to flee for shelter and refuge (to someone).
isticaze (..—.) استجازه A *lrnd.* 1. an asking permission. 2. an asking a reward (for a poem).
isticbar (..—) استجبار A *lrnd.* a striving to constrain and force (someone to do something).
istichalˡⁱ (..—) استجهال A *lrnd.* a considering as ignorant and illiterate; a calling one ignorant.
isticlâb (..—) استجلاب A 1. *lrnd.* a desiring something to be brought; a drawing near (somebody). 2. *psych.* evocation. —**i sena-i enâm** *lrnd.* a drawing down upon oneself the praises of mankind.
isticvab A, **isticvap**ᵇ¹ (..—) استجواب a questioning; *law* interrogation, examination.
istida 1 (..—) استدعا A 1. petition; official request. 2. *lrnd.* request. — **et=** /ı/ *lrnd.* to request, make a formal demand. — **hakkı** *law* right of petition. — **sahibi** petitioner. — **ver=** /a/ to petition.
istida 2 (.——) استيداع A *lrnd.* a depositing for safekeeping; a committing, commanding.
isti'dad (..—) استعداد A *lrnd., same as* **istidat**.
istidame (..—.) استدامه A *lrnd.* 1. a begging, supplicating for a long or perpetual continuance (of something); a lasting long or forever, being perpetual; permanency. 2. soaring in a circle (bird).
istidaname (..——.) استدعانامه P petition, formal written petition.
istidane (..—.) استدانه A *lrnd.* 1. an asking for a loan or credit. 2. borrowing, getting into debt.
istidare (..—.) استداره A 1. *lrnd.* a going round, circling, revolving. 2. *lrnd.* a being or becoming round, circular, globular. 3. *physiol.* peristalsis.
istidarî (..——) استدارى A *physiol.* peristaltic.
istidatᵈ¹ (.——) استعداد |isti'dad| 1. a natural readiness, quickness, aptitude, capacity to learn; skill, talent. 2. capacity to yield to some influence or action. 3. disposition, predisposition. —**ı zâtî** *psych.* idiosyncrasy. —**lı** talented, promising; capable. —**sız** having no talent, unpromising, incapable.
istidbar (..—) استدبار A *lrnd.* a turning one's back (on a thing), rejection.
istidlâlˡⁱ (..—) استدلال A 1. *lrnd.* an inferring, deducing; deduction, inference. 2. *phil.* reasoning. — **et=** /ı, dan/ to infer, deduce. —**ât** (..——) A *lrnd., pl.* inferences. —**en** (..—'.) A by deduction. —**î** (..——) A *lrnd.* inferential.
istidrac (..—) استدراج A *lrnd.* 1. an asking, inviting, inciting, causing to move step by step, degree by degree; a withdrawing or advancing gradually. 2. God's inciting a sinner to perdition little by little by granting success at the beginning of his sin.
istidrakᵏⁱ (..—) استدراك A *lrnd.* a wishing, endeavoring to comprehend.
istif استيف It 1. storage; hoarding, storing. 2. arrangement of goods when laid up in order; a stacking, piling. —**inden başla=** /ın/ *slang* to begin to swear. —**ini boz=** *colloq.* to disconcert, disturb, perturb. —**ini bozma=** *colloq.* to remain undisturbed, imperturbed; not to care.
isti'fa 1 (..—) A, **istifa 1** (.——) استعفا

istifa 1. a resigning; resignation. 2. *lrnd.* an asking forgiveness. — **et=** /dan/ to resign. —**sını ver=** to give one's resignation.

istifa 2 (. — —) اِسْتِيفاء A *lrnd.* a receiving a debt; a demanding and receiving payment in full. —**et=** /i/ 1. to receive the whole. 2. to demand a debt. —**i huzûz** an obtaining full gratification. —**i intikam** a satisfying a revenge.

istifade (.. — .) اِسْتِفاده A a profiting, gaining, benefitting; profit, gain; benefit. — **et=** /dan/ to gain, benefit, profit. —**li** advantageous, profitable; useful.

isti'faf (.. —) اِسْتِعْفاف A *lrnd.* an abstaining from what is forbidden; a keeping oneself pure and free from all sin and improper conduct.

istif'al[li] (.. —) اِسْتِفْعال A *lrnd.* a desiring or requesting one to do something. — **bâbı** *Arabic gram.* conjugation on istif'al.

istifaname (. — — .) اِسْتِعْفانامه P letter of resignation.

istifaza (.. — .) اِسْتِفاضه A *lrnd.* a profiting abundantly (in spiritual matters).

istifçi اِسْتِفْجى 1. hoarder. 2. *naut.* stevedore, packer. —**lik** 1. hoarding for profit. 2. *naut.* stowage.

istifham (.. —) اِسْتِفْهام A 1. *gram.* interrogation. 2. *lrnd.* an asking for explanation. — **işareti** question mark.

istifhamat (.. — —) اِسْتِفْهامات A *lrnd.* questions.

istifhamî (.. — —) اِسْتِفْهامى A *gram.* interrogative.

istifkad (.. —) اِسْتِفْقاد A *lrnd.* search (for something).

istifle=ʳ اِسْتِفْلَهْك ايستِفْلَرْ مك /i/ 1. to store or pack things away; to stack. 2. to hoard. —**n=** pass.

istifrağ (.. —) اِسْتِفْراغ A 1. a vomiting. 2. *lrnd.* a drawing or taking out. — **et=** to vomit, to throw up.

istifraş (.. —) اِسْتِفْراش A *lrnd.* concubinage. — **et=** /i/ to take as a concubine.

istifsar (.. —) اِسْتِفْسار A *lrnd.* 1. an asking for explanation or information. 2. an inquiring after a person. —**ı hatır eyle=** to inquire after someone's health. —**at** (.. — —) A inquiries.

istifta[aı] (.. —) اِسْتِفْتاء A *lrnd.* a consulting a mufti or lawyer, asking for a *fetva.*

istiftah (.. —) اِسْتِفْتاح A *lrnd.* 1. an opening; a causing to be opened. 2. a commencing of business by a first sale, or by first exercising a new function; the opening sale or transaction; the money taken in a first transaction. — **et=** to make a beginning in business.

istigase (.. — .) اِسْتِغاثه A *lrnd.* an asking for aid, help, assistance, succor. — **et=** /dan/ to ask for help.

istiğbar (.. —) اِسْتِغْبار A *bot.* pollination.

istiğfar (.. —) اِسْتِغْفار A *lrnd.* an asking for God's pardon and forgiveness. — **et=** to ask forgiveness from God.

istiğlâl[li] (.. —) اِسْتِغْلال A *lrnd.* a mortgaging an estate or house so that the creditor receives the rent thereof until the mortgage is redeemed.

istiğmat اِسْتِغْمات F *bot.* stigma.

istiğna (.. —) اِسْتِغْناء A *lrnd.* 1. a being able to do without; content, contentedness. 2. independence; disdain. — **göster=** 1. to be disinterested. 2. to show that one has no need of a thing.

istiğrab (.. —) اِسْتِغْراب A *lrnd.* a considering something strange and unusual; a wondering, a being surprised. — **et=** /i/ to be astonished (at).

istiğrak[ı] (.. —) اِسْتِغْراق A *lrnd.* a being totally plunged and immersed (in a thing); a being totally immersed in ecstatic contemplation and beatitude (mystic); entranced ecstasy, transport, rapture.

istihab (. — —) اِسْتِهاب A *lrnd.* a requesting a gift.

istihal[li] (.. —) اِسْتِحال A *lrnd.* a being worthy, deserving; a fitting.

istihale (.. — .) اِسْتِحاله A 1. an altering, change in state; transformation. 2. *zool.* metamorphosis.

istihaliye (.. — —) اِسْتِحاليه A *phil.* transformism.

istihane (.. — .) اِسْتِهانه A *lrnd.* an esteeming contemptible, a despising.

istihare (.. — .) اِسْتِخاره A an asking God to select and decide between two or more courses by a dream or omen. —**ye yat=** to lie down to sleep (after performing duties of worship) in the hope that God will decide for the best by a dream.

istihase (.. — .) اِسْتِحاثه |based on Arabic| *lrnd.* fossilization.

istihbab (.. —) اِسْتِحْباب A *lrnd.* a loving, liking, choosing as a beloved friend.

istihbar (.. —) اِسْتِخْبار A *lrnd.* an asking for information; an obtaining information. — **et=** 1. to obtain information. 2. to inquire (about a matter).

istihbarat (.. — —) اِسْتِخْبارات A news, information; intelligence. — **bürosu** information bureau, inquiry office. **İ— Dairesi** *mil.* Intelligence Department. — **hizmeti** intelligence service.

istihcan (.. —) اِسْتِحْجان A *lrnd.* a regarding as base and shameful; a condemning, a disapproving (of).

istihda (.. —) اِسْتِهْداء A *lrnd.* a seeking for guidance.

istihdaf (.. —) اِسْتِهْداف A *lrnd.* an aiming at

a having an object. — **et=** /ı/ to aim at, to pursue (an object).

istihdam (..—) اِسْتِخْدام A an employing, a taking into service, employment. — **et=** /ı/ to take into service, to employ.

istihfa (..—) اِسْتِخْفا A *lrnd.* a being or becoming concealed, invisible or imperceptible; a hiding, concealing.

istihfaf (..—) اِسْتِخْفاف A a holding in slight esteem; a making light of, a despising; contempt. — **et=** /ı/ to treat lightly, to despise.

istihfafkâr (..——) اِسْتِخْفافكار P contemptuous. —**âne** (..———.) P contemptuously, in a slighting manner.

istihkak[kı] (..—) اِسْتِحْقاق A *lrnd.* 1. a meriting, deserving (a thing); merit, desert. 2. that which is due; fee, remuneration; ration. — **dâvası** *law* action for recovery or restitution of property. — **kazan=**, — **kesbet=** to earn in due form; to become worthy.

istihkâm (..—) اِسْتِحْكام A 1. *mil.* fortification; stronghold. 2. military engineering. 3. *lrnd.* a being or becoming firm, strong, stable, solid, sure. — **bul=** *lrnd.* to be consolidated. — **subayı** engineer officer.

istihkâmat (..——) اِسْتِحْكامات A *lrnd.* fortifications, lines, works (around a camp or town). —**ı mücesseme** *lrnd.* permanent fortifications.

istihkar (..—) اِسْتِحْقار A a scorning, a treating with contempt, a despising. — **et=** /ı/ to treat with contempt.

istihlâb (..—) اِسْتِحْلاب A *lrnd.* a milking, sucking.

istihlâf 1 (..—) اِسْتِخْلاف A *lrnd.* 1. an appointing, leaving as successor. 2. a succeeding, a coming after.

istihlâf 2 (..—) اِسْتِحْلاف A *lrnd.* an asking, requiring, inviting to take an oath and swear; adjuration.

istihlâk[kı] (..—) اِسْتِهْلاك A a consuming; a using up; consumption. — **et=** /ı/ to consume. — **vergisi** *law* excise. —**ât** (..——) A *lrnd.* consumption.

istihlâl[li] **1** (..—) اِسْتِحْلال A *lrnd.* 1. a deeming lawful. 2. an asking someone to consider something lawful and legitimate.

istihlâl[li] **2** (..—) اِسْتِهْلال A *lrnd.* 1. first appearance of the new moon. 2. a seeing of the new moon. 3. a giving the first cry (infant). 4. a foreshadowing, in the exordium, of the matter of a discourse.

istihlâs (..—) اِسْتِخْلاص A *lrnd.* 1. a saving, recovering (a thing from any disaster), rescue. 2. an appropriating something for oneself; a making special and private.

istihmal[li] (..—) اِسْتِحْمال A *lrnd.* 1. an asking to carry. 2. an entrusting (one's affairs to another).

istihmam (..—) اِسْتِحْمام A *lrnd.* a taking a hot bath. — **et=** to take a bath.

istihrac (..—), A **istihraç**[cı] (..—) اِسْتِخْراج *lrnd.* 1. an extracting, drawing out with effort. 2. a deducing; deduction, inference. — **et=** /ı/ to try to get the meaning (of), to deduce. —**ât** (..——) A deduction, interpretations.

istihsal[li] (..—) اِسْتِحْصال A 1. a procuring, obtaining, acquiring, getting (a thing); acquisition. 2. production. — **et=** /ı/ to procure, obtain, get, produce. —**ât** (..——) A production.

istihsan 1 (..—) اِسْتِحْسان A *lrnd.* a regarding as good or beautiful; approval, commendation. — **et=** /ı/ to approve, commend. —**en** (..—ʹ.) A admiringly; approvingly.

istihsan 2 (..—) اِسْتِحْصان A *lrnd.* 1. a being strong, secure, unassailable (place); strength. 2. a taking refuge in a stronghold.

istihya (..—) اِسْتِحْياء A 1. *lrnd.* a feeling or being ashamed, a blushing. 2. *lrnd.* a sparing one's life. 3. *anat.* pudendum. 4. *obs., law* a taking as a slave.

istihza (..—) اِسْتِهْزاء A 1. ridiculing, mocking, jeering, sneering; ridicule, mockery; *rhet.* irony, sarcasm. — **et=** /la/ to mock, to ridicule.

istihzar (..—) اِسْتِحْضار A 1. *lrnd.* a summoning before; an inviting or sending for (a person). 2. *lrnd.* a calling to mind, remembering. 3. *phil.* representation. 4. *phil.* representative.

istika (..ʹ.) اِسْتِيقا It shoemaking sleeker.

istikad (..—) اِسْتِيقاد A *lrnd.* a kindling, lighting.

istikamet (..—.) اِسْتِقامت A 1. direction. 2. straightness, uprightness, integrity. 4. a being moderate; moderation. — **göster=** to act honestly.

istikan (..——) اِسْتِيقان A *lrnd.* a knowing for sure; an ascertaining.

istikâne, istikânet (..—.) اِسْتِكانت A *lrnd.* a humbling oneself, a being submissive; meekness, humility, submissiveness.

istikaz (..——) اِسْتِيقاظ A *lrnd.* a waking, an awakening; a rousing; a becoming alive or active.

istikbah (..—) اِسْتِقباح A *lrnd.* a finding ugly or detestable, an abhorring.

istikbal[li] (..—) اِسْتِقبال A 1. future; *gram.* future tense. 2. a going to meet (someone). 3. *astr.* opposition. —**e çık=** /ı/ to go forth to meet. —**en** (..—ʹ.) A in the future.

istikbalî (..——) اِسْتِقبالي A *lrnd.* 1. pertaining to the future. 2. pertaining to going out to meet. —**ye** (..——.) honorific poem written

on the occasion of welcoming a great personage.
istikbar (..—) اِسْتِكْبار A *lrnd.* a becoming proud, pride.
istikdam (..—) اِسْتِقْدام A *lrnd.* 1. a going before, a preceding. 2. a surpassing in boldness or strength of mind.
istikfal[li] (..—) اِسْتِكْفال A *lrnd.* a standing surety (for someone).
istiklâl[li] (..—) اِسْتِقْلال A independence, a being independent. **İ— Harbi** Turkish War of Independence (1919-1922). **— madalyası** medal of the Turkish War of Independence. **İ— Mahkemesi** the Supreme Court during the Turkish War of Independence. **İ— Marşı** the Turkish National Anthem.
istiklâlî (..— —) اِسْتِقْلالى A pertaining to independence. **—yet** (..— —.) state of being independent; absolute independence or sovereignty.
istikmal[li] (..—) اِسْتِكْمال A *lrnd.* 1. a completing, perfecting; completion. 2. an asking for or recommending completion. **— et=** /ı/ to complete (a thing).
istiknah (..—) اِسْتِكْناه A *lrnd.* a seeking to investigate a matter to the very bottom; a going deeply into something; investigation.
istiknan (..—) اِسْتِكْنان A *lrnd.* 1. an asking or seeking for shelter. 2. a concealing oneself.
istikra 1 (..—) اِسْتِقْراء A *log.* induction, inductive reasoning.
istikra 2 (..—) اِسْتِكْراء A *lrnd.* a hiring, renting; a taking on hire.
istikrah (..—) اِسْتِكْراه A a loathing; aversion. **— et=** /dan/ to loath; to hate.
istikraî (..— —) اِسْتِقْرائى A *log.* inductive. **— istidlâl** *log.* induction.
istikrar (..—) اِسْتِقْرار A a becoming established, a settling; stability, stabilization. **— bul=** to become established. **—lı** established, stable, stabilized, settled; steady.
istikrarsız اِسْتِقْرارسز unstable, unsteady, unsettled; inconsistent. **—lık** unsteadiness, instability.
istikraz (..—) اِسْتِقْراض A a borrowing (money); loan. **— et=** /ı, dan/ to borrow (money).
istiksa[ai] (..—) اِسْتِقْصاء A *lrnd.* a striving to get to the bottom of a matter; strict inquiry.
istiksar (..—) اِسْتِكْثار A *lrnd.* 1. a deeming excessive. 2. overestimation. **— et=** /ı/ to deem excessive.
istiksas (..—) اِسْتِقْصاص A a wishing to retaliate.
istikşaf (..—)اِسْتِكْشاف A 1. *lrnd.* a requesting anything to be laid open or revealed. 2. *lrnd.* an exploring, exploration. 3. *mil.* reconnaissance. **— et=** /ı/ *mil.* 1. to explore. 2. to reconnoiter.
istiktab (..—) اِسْتِكْتاب A *lrnd.* 1. an asking or ordering one to write; an asking to be written out; a dictating. 2. a writing out or copying.
istiktal[li] (..—) اِسْتِقْتال A *lrnd.* a seeking to be killed in battle.
istiktar (..—) اِسْتِقْطار A *lrnd.* a distilling, distillation.
istilâ 1 (.— —) اِسْتيلاء A 1. invasion; occupation. 2. an overcoming, conquering. 3. a covering completely; a filling up, a spreading over. **— et=** /ı/ to invade; to flood.
isti'la 2 (..—) اِسْتِعْلاء A *lrnd.* 1. a being or becoming high, lofty, elevated; loftiness, elevation. 2. a mastering or dominating, a getting the upper hand.
istilâb (..—) اِسْتِلاب A *lrnd.* a seeking and carrying off by force.
istilâcı (.— —.) اِسْتيلاجى invasionist.
istilâd (.— —) اِسْتيلاد A 1. *obs.*, *law* a begetting and acknowledging offspring from a female slave. 2. *phil.* maieutics. **—î** (.— — —) A *phil.* maieutic.
istilâî (.— — —) اِسْتيلائى A *lrnd.* 1. invading. 2. epidemic.
istilâl[li] (..—) اِسْتِلال A *lrnd.* an unsheathing (sword).
isti'lâm 1 (..—) اِسْتِعْلام A *lrnd.* an officially asking for information; note despatched to ask for such information.
istilâm 2 (..—) اِسْتِلام A *lrnd.* a rubbing the forehead against the Black Stone at Mecca.
isti'lâmname (..— —.) اِسْتِعْلامنامه P *lrnd.* an official note of inquiry for information.
istilka (..—) اِسْتِلْقاء A *lrnd.* a lying on one's back, supination.
istilo اِسْتيلو F fountain pen.
istilyoz اِسْتيليوز Gk *naut.* awning, stanchion.
istilzam (..—) اِسْتِلْزام A 1. *lrnd.* a considering a thing necessary. 2. *log.* implication. **— et=** /ı/ to render necessary; to involve, entail.
istilzaz (..—) اِسْتِلْذاذ A *lrnd.* a considering a thing delicious, elegant or agreeable; a delighting in a thing. **—iye** (..— —.) *phil.* hedonism.
istim اِسْتيم E 1. steam. 2. *slang* alcoholic drink. **—ini tut=** 1. to have steam up. 2. *slang* to be boiling with rage etc. 3. *slang* to be drunk.
istima[ai] (..—) اِسْتِماع A 1. *lrnd.* a hearing, listening; a hearing and obeying advice or commands. 2. *law* a hearing.
isti'mal[li] (..—) A, **istimal**[li] (.— —) اِسْتِعْمال a using, employing, making use of a thing. **— et=** /ı/ to use, to employ, make use of a thing.
istimalât (.— — —)اِسْتِعْمالات A *lrnd.* applications, employments.

istimale (..—.) اسْتِمَال A *lrnd.* a trying to persuade; a gaining goodwill, a coaxing.

istiman (.——) اسْتِيمَان A 1. *lrnd.* a begging protection, taking refuge. 2. *Isl. hist.* an asking for quarter, especially an alien's asking for safety of life and limb from a Muslim power.

istimar (.——) اسْتِعْمَار A *lrnd.* 1. an endeavoring to make prosperous with inhabitants and their industry (place); an endeavoring to develop a region. 2. colonization.

istimara (...'.) اسْتِيمَاره It *obs.* act of valuing and appraising. **—cı** valuer; appraiser at the customs house, official valuer.

istimator اسْتِيمَاتور It *obs.* appraiser at the customs house.

istimbot اسْتِمْبوط E small steamboat.

istimdad (..—) A, **istimdat**[dı] (..—) اسْتِمْداد *lrnd.* an asking for help. **— et=** /dan/ to ask for assistance.

istimhal[li] (..—) اسْتِمْهَال A *lrnd.* a requesting a delay; an asking for a period of grace.

istimlâ (..—) اسْتِمْلا A *lrnd.* an asking another to write; a dictating.

istimlâk[ki] (..—) اسْتِمْلاك A legal expropriation.

istimna (..—) اسْتِمْنا A *lrnd.* masturbation. **— bilyed** masturbation by hand.

istimrar (..—) اسْتِمْرار A *lrnd.* a passing without interruption, a being continual or uninterrupted. **—en** (..—'.) A continuously. **—î** (..——) A *gram.* continuative.

istimsal[li] (..—) اسْتِمْثَال A *biol.* assimilation.

istimta (..—) اسْتِمْتاع A *lrnd.* 1. a getting the use of a thing; enjoyment. 2. performance of the lesser pilgrimage at Mecca.

istimval[li] (..—) اسْتِمْوال A *law* requisition.

istimzac (..—) اسْتِمْزاج A *lrnd.* 1. a making polite inquiries about someone's well-being. 2. an inquiring whether a person is *persona grata* to another Government.

istinabe (..—.) اسْتِنابَ A 1. *law* a taking evidence of an absent witness, rogatory commission. 2. *lrnd.* appointment of a proxy. **— suretiyle** by proxy.

istinad (..—) اسْتِناد A *cf.* istinat. **— et=** /a/ to lean (against); to rely (upon).

istinaden (..—.) اسْتِنادًا A *lrnd.* /a/ based on, supported by.

istinadgâh (..——) اسْتِنادگاه P *lrnd.* point of support.

istinaf (.——) اسْتِيناف A 1. *law* a making an appeal, an asking for a new trial; appeal. 2. *lrnd.* a commencing; a making a new beginning. **— mahkemesi** court of appeal. **—en** (.——'.) A on appeal. **—î** (.———) A pertaining to appeal.

istiname (..—.) اسْتِنامَ A *lrnd.* 1. a pretending to be asleep. 2. a sleeping in security.

istinare (..—.) اسْتِناره A *lrnd.* 1. a seeking for light or fire. 2. a being or becoming brilliant and luminous.

istinas (.——) اسْتِيناس A *lrnd.* a being or becoming friendly with a person.

istinat[dı] (..—) اسْتِناد [istinad] a leaning or relying upon. **— duvarı** *arch.* retaining wall, supporting wall. **— noktası** point of support; fulcrum.

istinba (..—) اسْتِنْبا A *lrnd.* an asking for news or information.

istinbat (..—) اسْتِنْباط A *lrnd.* 1. a bringing to light a hidden matter. 2. a deducing, inferring.

istinfar (..—) اسْتِنْفار A *lrnd.* 1. a taking fright and running away. 2. a taking an aversion to and shunning a person.

istinga (..'.) اسْتِنْغا It 1. *naut.* brail. 2. *slang* a stripping off one's pants.

istinkâf (..—) اسْتِنْكاف A *lrnd.* a rejecting, a refusing; rejection, refusal; abstention. **— et=** /dan/ to abstain (from), to draw back, to refuse to do a thing.

istinkâh (..—) اسْتِنْكاح A *lrnd.* a taking a wife, marrying.

istinkas (..—) اسْتِنْقاص A *lrnd.* an asking for a discount; a bargaining.

istinsab (..—) اسْتِنْساب A *lrnd.* 1. a tracing one's geneaology. 2. a seeking to be attached to the service or family of another. 3. a claiming relationship with another.

istinsah 1 (..—) اسْتِنْساخ A a copying in writing. **— et=** /ı/ to copy, to copy out.

istinsah 2 (..—) اسْتِنْصاح A *lrnd.* 1. an asking advice; a receiving and acting on advice. 2. an urging prudence.

istinsar (..—) اسْتِنْصار A *lrnd.* an asking for help or aid. **—en** (..—'.) A expecting help; supporting.

istinşad (..—) اسْتِنْشاد A *lrnd.* an asking another to recite a poem.

istinşak[kı] (..—) اسْتِنْشاق A *lrnd.* 1. a snuffing up water through the nostrils; especially a snuffing up water in ablutions. 2. snuffing up the air.

istintac (..—) A, **istintaç**[cı] (..—) اسْتِنْتاج *lrnd.* a deducing, an inferring; inference, deduction. **— et=** /ı, dan/ to deduce, infer, conclude. **—ât** (..——) A deduction.

istintak[kı] (..—) اسْتِنْطاق A 1. an interrogating, questioning. 2. *law* interrogation, cross-examination. **— et=** /ı/ to interrogate, to cross-examine. **—î** (..——) A interrogative.

istintakname (..——.) اسْتِنْطاقنامه P official record of evidence taken by examining magistrates from an accused person.

istirahat^{ti} (..—.) استراحت A a reposing, resting; repose, rest, ease; relaxation. — et= to rest, repose; to make oneself comfortable.

istirak^{kı} (..—) استراق A *lrnd.* a stealing, carrying off by stealth.

istirbah (..—) استرباح A *lrnd.* an asking or borrowing money on interest.

istirca 1 (..—) استرجاء A *lrnd.* a begging, praying, supplicating with insistance and hope.

istircâ^{aı} **2** (..—) استرجاع A *lrnd.* 1. an asking or taking back the whole or part of anything once given. 2. a pronouncing the pious formula from the Quran (II, 151), **inna lillah** *etc.* in time of affliction.

istirdad (..—) A, **istirdat**^{dı} (..—) استرداد *lrnd.* 1. an asking, demanding to have given back and restored. 2. a recovering (a thing); restitution. — **dâvası** *law* action for restitution, action for claiming back. — **et=** /ı/ to retake, to recover.

istirfa^{aı} (..—) استرفاع A *lrnd.* an asking for a thing to be raised or removed.

istirfah (..—) استرفاه A *lrnd.* a finding rest, repose and ease.

istirha (..—) استرخاء A 1. *biol.* diastole. 2. *lrnd.* a being or becoming loose, a being relaxed and flaccid; relaxation.

istirhab (..—) استرهاب A *lrnd.* a frightening; a being afraid.

istirham (..—) استرحام A 1. an asking for mercy, pity, grace, favor. 2. an imploring, a requesting. — **et=** /dan, ı/ 1. to beg, to plead, to request; to implore. 2. to petition. **—ât** (..——) A *pl.*

istirhamname (..——.) استرحامنامه P written petition.

istirhan (..—) استرهان A *lrnd.* 1. a demanding as a pledge or hostage. 2. an offering or giving as a pledge or hostage.

istirhas (..—) استرخاص A *lrnd.* a deeming cheap.

istiridye (...'.) , استريديه استريديه [**istridye**] oyster, *zool.*, *Ostrea edulis.* **—ci** oyster seller.

istirkab (..—) استرقاب [*based on Arabic*] *lrnd.* a being jealous of, a considering as a rival.

istirkak^{kı} (..—) استرقاق A *lrnd.* 1. a making, keeping or possessing as a slave. 2. a becoming a slave.

istirşa (..—) استرشاء A *lrnd.* an asking, demanding a bribe.

istirşad (..—) استرشاد A *lrnd.* 1. an asking to be directed in the right way. 2. a being on the right way; a being orthodox.

istirvah (..—) استرواح A *lrnd.* a seeking or finding rest; rest, repose, ease.

istirza (..—) استرضاء A *lrnd.* an endeavoring or wishing to please and satisfy, a being anxious to please.

istirzak^{kı} (..—) استرزاق A *lrnd.* an asking for the means of subsistence; pay, allowance.

istirzal^{li} (..—) استرذال A *lrnd.* a holding in contempt; a despising, contemning.

istis'ab (..—) استصعاب A *lrnd.* 1. a considering, finding or discovering to be difficult. 2. a being difficult, perverse, intractable.

istis'ad (..—) استسعاد A *lrnd.* 1. a deeming auspicious, lucky, fortunate, of good omen. 2. a finding luck, being fortunate. **—iye** (..——.) *phil.* eudaemonism.

istis'al^{li} **1** (..—) استسؤال A *lrnd.* an asking (question), a begging (alms).

istisal^{li} **2** (.——) استئصال A 1. *med.* extirpation. 2. *lrnd.* an uprooting; *lrnd.* an exterminating.

istisar (.——) استئثار A *lrnd.* 1. an appropriating; a choosing, singling out for oneself only. 2. God's taking the righteous unto himself.

istisare (..—.) استثاره A *lrnd.* 1. a rousing, stirring up, inciting, exciting. 2. a raising (dust, smoke, etc.).

istisfa (..—) استصفاء A *lrnd.* a choosing, selecting, taking the best and purest part (of a thing).

istisgar (..—) استصغار A *lrnd.* 1. a deeming little, small, insignificant. 2. a considering low; a viewing with contempt, a belittling. — **et=** /ı/ to regard as insignificant; to underestimate; to despise.

istishab (..—) استصحاب A *lrnd.* 1. a wishing for or inviting the company of any person; an associating with, becoming sociable. 2. an acquiring as one's property.

istishal^{li} (..—) استسهال A *lrnd.* a finding easy; a rendering easy.

istishar (..—) استسخار A *lrnd.* a considering ridiculous, a mocking, making a laughing-stock of.

istiska (..—) استسقاء A *lrnd.* 1. dropsy. 2. *lrnd.* tympanitis. 3. *lrnd.* an asking for drink. 4. *lrnd.* a praying to God for rain. **—ya çık=** to go out into the open country to offer prayers for rain. — **duası** prayer for rain. **—i lahmî** *path.* dropsy of the flesh, anarca. **— ol=** to have dropsy; to be dropsical. **—i tablî** *path.* drum-belly, tympanites. **—i zıpkî** *path.* dropsy of the abdomen, *ascites abdominalis.*

istiskal^{li} (..—) استثقال A *lrnd.* a finding a person disagreeable and unbearable; a being bored by someone. — **et=** /ı/ to give someone a cool reception; to show someone that he is not welcome; to be disagreeable.

istislâf (..—) استسلاف A *lrnd.* a paying in

advance, a requesting and receiving advance payment for goods.

istislâm (..—) اسلام A *lrnd.* 1. a being or becoming resigned, resigning oneself. 2. a being or becoming a Muslim.

istismar (..—) استثمار [*based on Arabic*] an exploiting; exploitation. — **et=** to exploit, to profit by. —**cı** exploiter.

istisna (..—) استثناء A exception. —**ât** (..— —) A *lrnd., pl.*

istisnaî (..— —) استثنائى A *lrnd.* exceptional. — **mahkemeler** *law* special courts.

istisnad (..—) استناد A *lrnd.* a leaning against; a supporting oneself.

istisnasız (..—.) استناسز without exception, unexceptionally.

istisvab (..—) استصواب A *lrnd.* a deeming right and proper; approval.

istisvabkerde (..— ..) استصوابكرده P *lrnd.* approved, allowed.

istiş'ar (..—) استشعار A *lrnd.* an asking for an indication or information.

istişare (..—.) استشاره A a consulting, asking for advice and counsel; consultation. — **et=** /la/ to hold a consultation (with).

istişarî (..— —) استشارى A consultative, advisory.

istişfa 1 (..—) استشفاء A *lrnd.* a seeking a cure and recovery from disease; recovery. —**en** (..—.) A as a cure.

istişfa[a] **2** (..—) استشفاع A *lrnd.* an imploring one to intercede, an asking one to act as intercessor.

istişhad (..—) استشهاد A *lrnd.* 1. an asking to be a witness, a calling to witness (person). 2. a citing as proof (passage, book, etc.). 3. a dying a martyr in God's cause.

istişhadât (..— —) استشهادات A *lrnd.* a holding as a witness.

istişhaden (..—'.) استشهاداً A *lrnd.* as a witness or proof.

istişmam (..—) استشمام A *lrnd.* 1. a smelling out. 2. getting an inkling (of a matter). 3. a deducing from clues.

istitaat[u] (..—.) استطاعت A *lrnd.* a being able, having the power or ability (to do or bear something); power, ability, capacity.

istitabe 1 (..—.) استتابه A *lrnd.* an asking to repent, an asking to relent.

istitabe 2 (..—.) استطابه A *lrnd.* a thinking pleasant, a finding agreeable; approval.

isti'taf (..—) استعطاف A *lrnd.* a begging one to become favorably inclined; a seeking the favor or kindness of another.

istitale (..—.) استطاله A *lrnd.* a being or becoming long or tall; elongation, projection.

istit'am (..—) استطعام A *lrnd.* 1. an asking for food. 2. an asking for instruction in reading.

istitar (..—) استتار A *lrnd.* a being or becoming veiled, covered, concealed.

istitbab (..—) استطباب A 1. *med.* indication. 2. *lrnd.* an asking for medical advice, demanding medicine.

istitmam (..—) استتمام A *lrnd.* 1. a desiring, asking that a thing might be completed. 2. a completing, finishing, ending fully.

istitrad (..—) استطراد A *rhet.* a making a digression; digressing. —**en** (..—'.) A by way of digression. —**î** (..— —) A digressive, parenthetical.

istitraf (..—) استطراف A *lrnd.* 1. an esteeming as new (thing). 2. an acquiring a thing as a new possession.

istiva[ai] (..—) استواء A *lrnd.* a being equable, level, straight; uniformity, equableness. — **hattı** the Equator. —**î** (..— —) A equatorial.

istizaa (..—.) استضاءة A *lrnd.* 1. a making bright. 2. an asking for enlightenment.

istizade (..—.) استزاده A *lrnd.* an asking for an increase; a desiring an augmentation.

istiz'af (..—) استضعاف A *lrnd.* a considering weak, poor, powerless; a despising a person for being weak.

istizah (..— —) استيضاح A *pol.* an asking for an explanation; interpellation. — **et=** /ı/ to ask for an explanation; to question a Minister (in Parliament); to interpellate. —**en** (.— —'.) A by way of interpellation.

isti'zam (..—) استعظام A *lrnd.* 1. a deeming to be great or large (thing). 2. a considering with respect, reverence or awe. 3. a thinking oneself great; conceit.

istizan (.— —) استئذان A *lrnd.* 1. an asking for permission. 2. an asking for leave or authorization.

isti'zar (..—) استعذار A *lrnd.* an asking to be excused, an apologizing.

istizare (..—.) استزاره A *lrnd.* an inviting someone for a visit.

istizhar (..—) استظهار A *lrnd.* a seeking or asking for aid and support; imploring assistance or protection.

istizkâr (..—) استذكار A *lrnd.* 1. a calling to mind, remembering. 2. a studying, committing to memory. 3. mnemotechny, mnemonics.

istizlâl[i] **1** (..—) استذلال A *lrnd.* a holding in contempt, despising.

istizlâl[ii] **2** (..—) استظلال A *lrnd.* 1. a sitting in or longing for the shade. 2. a seeking shelter and protection (from a powerful friend).

istoa استوا Gk *phil.* stoa. —**cı** stoic. —**cılık** stoicism.

istofa (.´..) اِستوف It brocade, kind of silk material.
istok اِستوك E same as **ıstok**.
İstokholm اِستوقهولم geog. Stockholm.
istop اِستوپ E stop. — **et=** to stop.
istor اِستور same as **ıstor**.
istralya (..´.) اِسترالیا It naut. stay (of a mast).
istridye (..´.) اِستریدیه Gk same as **istiridye**.
istromaça اِستروماچه It naut. coiled ropes used as a fender.
istrongilos (..´..) اِسترونغیلوس Gk kind of sea bream; zool., Smaris vulgaris.
İsu (— —) عیسو A Bib. Esau, son of Isaac.
İsveç اِسوچ It geog. Sweden. —**çe** the Swedish language, Swedish. —**li** Swede, Swedish.
İsviçre (..´.) اِسویچره It geog. Switzerland. —**li** Swiss.
isvidad (.. —) اِسوداد A lrnd. a being black, a becoming black; blackness.
isyan (. —) عصیان A rioting; rebellion, insurrection, riot, revolt. — **et=** /a/ to rebel (against).
isyankâr (. — —) عصیانکار P rebellious; refractory. —**lık** rebelliousness.
iş 1 ایش 1. work; service; labor; action. 2. business, occupation, profession, job. 3. affair, matter, thing; interest. 4. duty, mission. 5. state of affairs, condition. 6. use, benefit, profit. 7. slang trick, device. — **aç=** to cause trouble; to make a fuss. — **adamı** business man, successful business man. — **akdi** law labor contract. —**in alayında ol=** not to take a thing seriously, to look upon something as a joke. —**i Allaha kalmış** /ın/ He's done for. —**i altın** He is flourishing. —**ten anla=** to be an expert. — **ardından koş=** 1. to go about looking for a job. 2. to follow some business. —**ten artmaz dişten artar** proverb Saving depends on economical living. —**i azıt=** to go too far; to overdo, to overstep the mark. —**e bak=** to attend to business, to occupy oneself with work. —**ine bak** 1. Mind your own business. 2. Have it your own way. —**e balta ile giriş=** to begin work in a rough manner. — **başı** 1. foreman, overseer. 2. hour of beginning work. —**in başı** 1. the main reason, the source. 2. firebrand. — **başında** on the job; during work time. — **başındakiler** the leaders. —**i başından aş=** to be extremely busy. — **başında bulun=** to be personally present at one's post. — **başa düştü** I have to do it personally. — **başı elbisesi** overalls, working clothes. — **başına geç=** 1. to get to work. 2. to take the lead; to come to power. — **başı yap=** to begin work. — **bil=** to be clever at work. 2. to have a head for business. —**ini bil=** to know how to profit from things. —**ten bile değil!** How easy! — **bilenin kılıç kuşananın** (lit. He who is clever will do the job; he who knows how to wear the sword will have it.) Those who are clever and who know how to take advantage of opportunities will succeed. — **birliği** cooperation. — **bit=** 1. to be settled. 2. /dan/ to depend upon somebody (job). —**i bit=** 1. to have one's business settled. 2. to be ruined, to be done for. —**ini bitir=** 1. to finish one's work. 2. /ın/ to settle an affair for someone. 3. to kill, to destroy. —**imiz boru** We are in an awful state. — **bölümü** division of labor. — **buyur=** /a/ 1. to order one about. 2. to tell someone to do a job. — **çığırından çıktı** Things have gone too far. — **çık=** 1. to come out (job), to turn out well. 2. /a/ to arise (trouble, question). — **çıkar=** 1. to do a certain amount of work. 2. to give a person something disagreeable to do. 3. to cause trouble; to raise unnecessary difficulties. — **dayıya düştü** I have to do it personally. — **değil, —ten değil** It is a mere nothing; it is as easy as can be. —**im dokuzdan** slang My business is going well; I am all right. —**i duman** /ın/ slang He is in a bad way. —**i düş=** 1. to have to go somewhere or to someone for business. 2. /a/ to apply to someone for advice or help. — **edin=** /ı/ 1. to be occupied with work. 2. to undertake to follow up something. —**ten el çektir=** /a/ to remove a person from office. — **eri** a skilled business man. —**ine gel=** to suit one's interests, to come just right. —**in gelişi** as it may occur. — **gör=** 1. to perform a service; to work, to do a job. 2. to be useful. —**ine göre** it all depends, as it may happen. — **güç*.** —**ine gücüne bak=** to attend to one's own business. —**ten güçten kal=** to be unable to work, to be disabled. —**i gücü yok** He has nothing to do; he is idle. — **günü** weekday, working day. —**in içinden çıkamadı** He couldn't figure it out; he couldn't make head or tail of it. — **içinde iş** wheels within wheels. —**in içinde iş var** There is something behind all this. — **hukuku** labor legislation. — **ihtilâfı** law labor dispute. — **inada bindi** Each one insisted on his standpoint; they became obstinate. —**imiz iş!** We are lucky (sometimes ironically). — **ve işçi bulma kurumu** labor exchange, employment bureau. — **işle=** 1. to work. 2. to embroider. — **işten geçti** It's too late. It's all over. — **kabart=** archaic to take a matter seriously. — **kaçkını** lazy, always getting out of work. —**inden kal=** to be prevented from doing work, to be interrupted. —**ten kal=** to be unable to work. —**e kapak vur=** slang to cover up something. — **karış-**

tır=, — **kaynat**= to plot mischief. — **kıvamına geldi** The matter is just ripe; things are just right. —**e koş**= /ı/ to put someone to work. — **mükellefiyeti** *law* compulsory service. **İ— Odaları** Chambers of Labor. —**i ol**= /ın/ 1. to have work. 2. to be settled (affair). —**inden ol**= to lose one's job. — **ola** *same as* **iş olsun diye**. —**i oluruna bırak**= to let matters take their natural course. — **olsun diye** just for the sake of doing something (said of one who does something only for show or as eyewash). — **olacağına varır** What will be, will be. — **pişir**= 1. to plot, to contrive. 2. *colloq.* to start a secret love affair. —**i rast git**= 1. to prosper, to go well (one's affairs). 2. to be in luck. —**i resmiyete dök**= to adopt an official course. —**i sağlama bağla**=, —**i sağlam kazığa bağla**= to make a matter safe or sure. — **sahibi** 1. employer, master. 2. *same as* **eshabı mesalih**. — **sarpa sardı** Things have become complicated. — **sendikası** trade union. —**i tıkırında gidiyor** His business is flourishing; he is doing very well. — **tut**= 1. to work. 2. /ı/ to occupy oneself (with). — **ucu** *archaic* result. —**in ucu bana dokunuyor** It's I who'll suffer because of it. —**imiz uygun** Our business is in good trim; everything seems to be going along nicely. —**imiz üç nalla bir ata kaldı** (*lit.* We only need three more horseshoes and a horse to complete our work.) We are only at the beginning of the work with many things lacking. —**im var** 1. I am busy. 2. /la/ I have some business (with). 3. /la/ I am having trouble (with). — **yap**= to do business. — **yaptın** *ironical* you have spoiled it all. —**e yara**= to be useful, to be of use, to come in handy. — **yok** *slang* 1. It won't do. 2. /da/ No use! You can't get anything (out of that person). —**in mi yok**? What an idea! What an absurd suggestion! —**i yolunda** He is well off; he is lucky; he's sitting pretty. —**i yüzüne gözüne bulaştırdı** He has made a mess of it.
=**iş 2** ايش *cf.* =**ış 1**.
=**iş**= **3** ايشلك *cf.* =**ş**= **2**.
iş 4 (—) عيش [ayş] *A lrnd., only in* — **ü nuş***.
işa (. —) عشا *A lrnd.* 1. nightfall. 2. the prayer at nightfall.
işaa, işaatⁱⁱ (. —.) اشاء ، اشاعة *A lrnd.* a spreading; a publishing, a disclosing. — **et**= /ı/ to spread abroad.
iş'alⁱⁱ (. —) اشعال *A lrnd.* 1. a lighting, kindling; a setting on fire. 2. a stirring up anger.
işallah (.′. —) انشالله *colloq., var. of* **inşallah**.
iş'ar (. —) اشعار *A lrnd.* a communicating, making known; communication. —**i ahire değin** until further notice. — **et**= /ı, a/ to communicate, to let know.
iş'arat 1 (. — —) اشارات *A lrnd., pl. of* **iş'ar**.
işarat 2 (. — —) اشارات *A lrnd., pl. of* **işaret**.
işaret (. —.) اشارت *A* 1. sign, mark; a signing to, a pointing out. 2. signal; a signaling. 3. *gram.* demonstrative. 4. *lrnd.* an advising, giving an opinion; *hist.* an order or opinion of the Şeyhülislâm. —**i aliye** *Ott. hist.* order given by the Şeyhülislâm. — **borusu** *mil.* bugle. — **çek**= *naut.* to hoist a signal. —**defteri** *naut.* signal book. — **değneği** traffic indicator. — **et**= /a/ 1. to make a sign; to beckon. 2. to make a mark. 3. to point out, to indicate. — **fişeği** rocket signal; signal shot. — **flâması** *mil.* signal flag. — **gönderi** *naut.* signal post. —**i ilâhiye** *lrnd.* divine inspiration of saints. — **kolu** traffic indicator. — **kulesi** signal tower. — **memuru** traffic policeman. — **parmağı** index finger, forefinger. — **sıfatı** *gram.* demonstrative adjective. —**le söyle**= to speak by signs. — **tabancası** *mil.* signal pistol. — **talimatnamesi** signal code, signal manual. — **ver**= to hoist a signal, to signal. — **zamiri** *gram.* demonstrative pronoun.
işaretçi اشارتجى traffic policeman.
işaretle=ʳ اشارتلمك 1. to mark. 2. *log.* to denote. —**n**= *pass.* —**ş**= to make signs to one another.
işarî 1 (. — —) اشارى *A* 1. *lrnd.* conveyed by a signal, indicated. 2. *gram.* demonstrative.
iş'arî 2 (. . —) اشعارى *A* 1. *lrnd.* as information. 2. *mech.* indicated.
İşaya (. . —) اشعيا *A Bib.* Isaiah.
işbaᵘⁱ (. —) اشباع *A* 1. a satiating; *chem.* saturating; saturation. 2. *Arabic pros.* a prolonging of a vowel sound. — **et**= /ı/ to saturate, to satiate, to fill up. — **halinde** 1. saturated. 2. filled to excess.
işbu (.′.) اوشبو this; the present; the said. —**nlar** *pl.*
işcar (. —) اشجار *A lrnd.* afforestation.
işçi ايشجى 1. workman, laborer; worker; woman worker; *obs.* seamstress. 2. *slang* trickster, gambler. — **kadın** woman worker, charwoman. — **karnesi** employment book, workbook. — **kız** workgirl, working girl. **İ— Partisi** Labor Party. — **sınıfı** working class. — **sigortası** worker's insurance. — **ücreti** wages, worker's pay. —**lik** 1. the quality, occupation, or pay of a worker. 2. workmanship.
işe=ʳ ايشمك ، ايشەمك to urinate, make water. —**gen** *archaic* who habitually passes urine involuntarily. —**t**= /ı/. *caus. of* **işe**=. —**tici** *med.* diuretic.
işgalⁱⁱ (. —) اشغال *A* a causing to be occupied, an occupying; busying; occupation. — **altında**

işgüç under military occupation; occupied. — **et**= /ı/ 1. to keep busy; to engage the attention of a person; to keep somebody from his work. 2. *mil.* to occupy. — **kuvvetleri** *mil.* occupation forces. —**iye** parking fee.

işgüçᶜü اِیشْ گُوچ business, work, occupation, employment. — **et**= /ı/ to occupy oneself (with). — **sahibi** occupied with work; busy.

işgüder *neol.* chargé d'affaires.

işgüzar (..—) ایشْگُزار P 1. efficient, active, diligent. 2. officious. —**lık** officiousness.

işhad (.—) اِشْهاد A *lrnd.* a bringing one to witness; a citing proofs.

işid=ⁱʳ ایشِدمك *archaic*, same as **işit**=.

işidim *neol.* the sense of hearing.

işit=ⁱʳ ایشِتْنَك ایشِدْنَك /ı/ 1. to hear; to listen. 2. to learn (of).

işitgen ایشِتْگَن *archaic* good hearer.

işitici ایشِدِجى hearer.

işitil=ⁱʳ ایشِدِلْنَك ایشِدِلْنَك *pass.* of **işit**=.

işitme ایشِتْمَه *verbal n.* of **işit**=. — **âleti** hearing aid. — **beneği** *biol.* acoustic spot. — **kesesi** *anat.* otocyst. — **taşı** *anat.* otolite, otolith, ear stone. —**lik** *neol.* acoustics.

işitmemezlikǥⁱ (..´...) ایشِتْمَمَزْلِك a not hearing; a pretending not to hear. —**ten gel**= to pretend not to hear, to feign deafness.

işitmez ایشِتْمَز one who does not hear, hard of hearing. —**den gel**= *prov.* to pretend not to hear. —**len**= *archaic* to pretend not to hear. —**lik** *same as* **işitmemezlik**.

işitsel *neol.*, *biol.* auditory.

işittir=ⁱʳ ایشِدِرْنَك اِشْدِرْمَك /ı, a/ *caus.* of **işit**=.

işkâllⁱ (.—) اِشْكال A *lrnd.* a rendering difficult. — **et**= /ı/ to hinder, make difficult, to impede.

işkampaviye (...´..) اِشْكامپاویه It *naut.* long boat; pinnace, launch.

işkembe اِشْكَمْبَه P tripe, paunch. —**den at**= *slang* to invent a story, to exaggerate; to embroider a tale. — **çorbası** tripe soup. — **çorbası hikâyesi** *colloq.* One must not expect too much of an inferior person or article. —**sini düşün**= to think only of one's stomach; to be very selfish. — **feneri** a lantern made of membrane. —**i kübradan at**=, —**i kübradan söyle**= *joc.*, same as **işkembeden at**=. — **suratlı** *slang* puckered faced; very ugly. —**sini şişir**= *colloq.* to fill one's belly, to eat one's fill.

işkembeci اِشْكَمْبَه‌جى 1. dealer in tripe. 2. owner of a tripe restaurant. —**lik** trade of a tripe dresser.

işkembeli اِشْكَمْبَه‌لى pot-bellied.

işkenbe اِشْكَنْبَه P *var.* of **işkembe**.

işkence اِشْكَنْجَه P 1. torture, torment.

2. carpenter's clamp. — **et**=, — **yap**= /a/ to torture, torment.

işkil اِشْكِل ایشْكِل *prov.* doubt, suspicion. —**len**= /dan/ to be suspicious, to suspect; to mistrust. —**lendir**= /ı, dan/ *caus.* of **işkillen**=. —**li** suspicious, anxiously doubtful. —**lik** dubiousness, mistrust.

işkine (..´.) اِشْكِنَه Gk brown maigre, *zool.*, *Corvina nigra*.

İşkodra (..´.) اِشْكودرا *geog.* Scutari (in Albania).

işle=ʳ ایشْلَمَك ایشْلَه‌مَك 1. /ı/ to work up (material), to process; to perform, to do; to manipulate; to embroider; to carve, engrave; to incise; to cultivate (land); to treat (of), to investigate thoroughly (subject); *archaic* to manufacture, to make. 2. to work; to labor; to do work; to function, to operate, to act (instrument); to ply (vehicle); to sail (boat). 3. /a/ to penetrate, to take effect. 4. to fester, to discharge purulent matter; to suppurate. 5. to be open or much used (road); to be frequented (shop). 6. /ı/ *slang* to steal, to pinch. 7. /ı/ *slang* to make fun (of).

işlekǥⁱ ایشْلَك 1. much used, busy (street). 2. much frequented (shop). 3. flowing, cursive (handwriting). 4. *neol.*, *gram.* productive.

işlem *neol.* 1. *adm.* procedure. 2. *math.* operation. 3. *chem.* influence, effect.

işleme ایشْلَمَه 1. *verbal n.* of **işle**=. 2. handwork, embroidery. —**ci** embroiderer, embroideress.

işlemeli ایشْلَمَه‌لى embroidered; ornamented.

işlen=ⁱʳ ایشْلَنْمَك *pass.* of **işle**=. —**iş**, —**me** *verbal n.*

işlet=ⁱʳ ایشْلَتْمَك /ı/ 1. *caus.* of **işle**=, to run, operate, make work. 2. *slang* to deceive by inventing a story; to make fun of, to hoodwink. —**ici** 1. operator (of apparatus). 2. *law* holder. —**il**= *pass.* of **işlet**=.

işletme ایشْلَتْمَه 1. *verbal n.* of **işlet**=. 2. undertaking; administration; management. — **dairesi** traffic control department (railway). — **malzemesi** rolling stock.

işlettir=ⁱʳ ایشْلَتْدِرْمَك ایشْلَتْدِرْمَك /ı, a/ *caus.* of —**işlet**=. —**il**= *pass.*

işlev *neol.*, *phil.* function. — **yitimi** *psych.* apraxia.

işleyiş ایشْلَیش *verbal n.* of **işle**=.

işli ایشْلى ایشْلو 1. at work, employed, occupied. 2. worked; embroidered; ornamented. — **güçlü** 1. having business. 2. very busy.

işlikǥⁱ 1 *neol.* workshop; atelier, studio.

işlikǥⁱ 2 ایشْلِك *prov.*, *var.* of **içlik**.

işmam (.—) اِشْمام A 1. *Arabic gram.* a giving a consonant a slight vowel sound after it. 2. *lrnd.* a causing to be smelled. 3. *lrnd.* to give an inkling of.

işmar اِشْمار sign; nod, wink. **— et=** /a/ to make signs; to wink.

işmizaz (..—) اِشْمِئْزاز A 1. grimace; look of disgust. 2. *lrnd.* an abhorring, detesting; a feeling horror, being horrified. 3. *lrnd.* mental depression.

işporta (..'.) اِشْپورطه It wide, shallow, open basket or wooden tray (used by peddlers). **—ya düş=** to lose value (goods). **— malı** shoddy goods. **—cı** peddler.

işrab (.—) اِشْراب A *lrnd.* 1. an insinuating; insinuation, imputation. 2. a causing to drink. **— et=** /ı/ to insinuate.

işraf (.—) اِشْراف A *lrnd.* 1. a mounting, an ascending, a being elevated. 2. an overlooking, overtopping.

işrak[kı] **1** (.—) اِشْراق A *lrnd.* 1. the rising and shining of sun, moon or star. 2. a being illuminated; illumination.

işrak[kı] **2** (.—) اِشْراك A *lrnd.* 1. a making a person a partner. 2. an asserting that the Deity exists in more than one person.

işrakiye (.——.) اِشْراقِیه *phil.* Pythagoreanism.
işrakiyûn (.———) اِشْراقِیّون *phil.* Pythagoreans.

işret عِشْرت A a drinking, carousing. **— âlemi** drinking party; revelry. **— erbabı** toper; topers, old soaks. **— et=** to drink (wine, etc.), to make merry.

işrîn, işrûn (.—) عِشْرین عِشْرون A *lrnd.* twenty.

işsiz اِيشْسِز 1. having no work, unemployed, out of work. 2. unoccupied, idle, good-for-nothing, loafer. 3. unembroidered. **— güçsüz** idle, doing nothing. **—lik** unemployment.

iştah اِشْتاه [iştiha] appetite; desire. **— aç=** to whet the appetite. **— açıcı** appetizing. **—ı açıldı** His appetite is sharpened; he feels like eating now. **—ı kesildi** He has lost his appetite. **—ım yok** I have no appetite.

iştahlan=[ır] اِشْتاهْلانْمَق /a/ to crave, to have a desire for. **—ma** verbal n. of **iştahlan=**; *psych.* appetite.

iştahlı اِشْتاهْلى 1. having an appetite; hungry. 2. desirous.

iştahsız اِشْتاهْسِز having no appetite; without desire. **—lık** lack of appetite.

işte اِشْته look; here; there; now; thus; oh, well, like that. **— böyle** so; such is the matter. Life is like that.

iştial[li] (..—) اِشْتِعال A *lrnd.* 1. a being kindled, a blazing up; a taking fire. 2. a becoming angry. **— et=** to take fire; to burst into flames. **—ât** (..——) A conflagrations.

iştibah (..—) اِشْتِباه A *lrnd.* a doubting; doubt. **—ât** (..——) A *pl.*

iştidad (..—) اِشْتِداد A *lrnd.* a becoming severe, hard or strong; an increasing. **—i hâfıza** *psych.* hypermnesia. **—î** (..——) A *med.* paroxysmal.

iştigal[li] (..—) اِشْتِغال A an occupying oneself; occupation; work. **— et=** /la/ to occupy oneself with, to be busy with.

iştiha (..—) اِشْتِها A *lrnd.*, same as **iştah**. **—aver** (..——.) P appetizing.

iştihar (..—) اِشْتِهار A *lrnd.* a becoming famous or notorious; fame, notoriety. **— bul=**, **— et=** to acquire fame, to be celebrated.

iştikâ (..—) اِشْتِكاء A *lrnd.* a complaining, complaint.

iştikak[kı] (..—) اِشْتِقاق A 1. *gram., ling.* derivation, etymology. 2. *lrnd.* a dividing into branches; a branching. **— et=** /dan/ to be derived from. **—at** (..——) A *lrnd.* etymologies. **—î** (..——) A etymological.

iştimal[li] (..—) اِشْتِمال A *lrnd.* a comprising, comprehending, containing; an enfolding.

iştimam (..—) اِشْتِمام A *lrnd.* a smelling; a sniffing.

iştira (..—) اِشْتِراء A *lrnd.* a buying; purchase. **— et=** /ı/ to buy. **— hakkı** *law* right of redemption. **— kudreti** *econ.* purchasing power.

iştirak[kı] (..—) اِشْتِراك A a participating; participation. **— et=** /a/ to share; to participate (in). **— hakkı** *law* right of participation. **— halinde mülkiyet** *law* joint tenancy, collective property. **— hissesi** *com.* share, part, contribution. **—i ol=** 1. /da/ to have a share in; to be involved. 2. /la/ to be associated (with). 3. /la/ to be interested (in). **— taahhüdü** *com.* subscription. **— üzre** in participation; jointly.

iştirakî (..——) اِشْتِراكى A participating, cooperative. **—ye** (..——.) *sociol.* collectivism; socialism. **—yûn** the communists.

iştirat (..—) اِشْتِراط A *lrnd.* a stipulating; an imposing conditions.

iştitat (..—) اِشْتِطاط A *lrnd.* a being oppressive and tyrannical in sentencing a prisoner.

iştiyak[kı] (..—) اِشْتِياق A 1. a yearning, longing; ardent desire. 2. *phil.* appetite. **— çek=** to long for.

iştiyakname (..——.) اِشْتِياقنامه P *lrnd.* an ardent love letter.

işünuş (..—) عيش و نوش [ayş u nuş] *lrnd.* carousal; revelry; orgy, bacchanal.

işve عِشْوه A 1. amorous glance or gesture, coquettishness, coquetry. 2. *myst.* slight token of divine favor. **—baz** (..—) P, **—kâr** (..—) P *lrnd.* coquettish. **—li** coquettish, flirtatious. **—sâz** (..—) P, **—zen** P coquettish; coquette, flirt.

işyar *neol.* employee, official.

işyazar *neol., physiol.* ergograph.

it 1 اِیْت ، اِتْ 1. dog. 2. vile man, swine, cur. **—e atsan yemez** not fit even for a dog to eat, very nasty. **— boğan** 1. dogchoke, dogbane, *bot., Apocynum erectum.* 2. meadow saffron, *bot., Colchicum.* **—e bulaşmaktansa çalıyı dolaş=** to go out of one's way to avoid trouble. **— burnu** 1. hip of wild rose, *Cynorrhodon.* 2. dog rose, *bot., Rosa canina.* **— canlı** tough and strong. **—le çuvala girilmez** It is better to avoid trouble with a nasty person. **— damarı tuttu** He is just being doggedly obstinate. **— derneği** 1. a riotous gathering. 2. den of thieves. **— dirliği** inharmonious, quarrelsome life, dog's life. **— dirseği** sty on the eyelid. **— dişi domuz derisi** (*lit.* A dog's tooth and a pig's hide.) It is good to see enemies at each other's throats. **— elli** knockkneed and splayfooted. **— hıyarı** 1. bitter apple, colocynth, *bot., Citrullus colocynthis.* 2. squirting cucumber, *bot., Icballium elaterium.* **— ite it de kuyruğuna** A dog asked another to do something; the other dog asked his tail *said when one asks somebody to do an errand and that person asks another and yet another to do the job.* **— itin kuyruğunu bırakmaz** Birds of a feather flock together. **— izi at izine karışmış** The matter is very complicated; it is all in a mess. **— kadar** very many. **— keseri** 1. earth chestnut, pignut, *bot., Carum Bulbocastanum.* 2. grape hyacinth, *bot., Muscari botryoides.* **—in kıçına sok=** *vulgar* to disgrace utterly. **— menekşesi** dog violet, *bot., Viola canina.* **— nişanı** long horny excrescence on the inside of each leg of a horse, ergot of the skin of the fetlock. **— oğlu** *vulgar* son of a dog. **— oğlu it** *colloq.* 1. cur, foul brute. 2. sharp, shrewd man. **—i öldürene sürütürler** *colloq.* Let him finish his own dirty work. **— sidiği** common white horehound, *bot., Marrubium vulgare.* **— sürüsü** 1. pack of dogs. 2. mob of scoundrels, rabble. **— sürüsü kadar** *colloq.* as many as a pack of hounds, like a crowd of rascals. **— taşlıyan** *colloq.* loafer, idle. **— ürür kervan yürür** *proverb* (*lit.* Dogs bark but the caravan continues on its way.) Do what you think is right, no matter what others say. **— üzümü** black nightshade, *bot., Solanum nigrum.* **— yatağı** thieves' kitchen. **— yılı** *hist.* dog-year, the eleventh year of the old Turkish twelve-year cycle.

it=ᵉʳ **2** اِتْمَكْ to push.
it=ᵉʳ **3** اِتْمَكْ *archaic, same as* **yit= 1.**
=it= 4 اِتْمَكْ *cf.* **=t= 2.**

i'ta 1 (. —) اِعْطاء A *lrnd.* 1. a giving, an offering, a delivering to. 2. a paying; a settling a debt. **— âmiri** official authorized to pass accounts. **— emri** order to pay, order for payment of government money. **— et=** /ı/ 1. to give, to transfer; to make over. 2. to pay.

ita 2 (— —) اِتاء A *lrnd.* 1. a giving, delivering. 2. a bringing, a causing to come.

itaatᵗⁱ (. —.) اِطاعت A 1. an obeying; obedience. 2. submission. **—i altına al=** /ı/ to subdue. **— et=** /a/ to obey; to submit oneself to. **—kâr** (. —. —) P, **—li** obedient; submissive; dutiful.

itaatsiz اِطاعتسز disobedient, insubordinate. **—lik** disobedience.

itab 1 (. —) عِتاب A *lrnd.* a reproving, reprimanding, reproaching; reproof, reprimand, reproach. **— et=** /a/ to reprove, to reproach.

it'ab 2 (. —) اِتعاب A *lrnd.* a fatiguing, wearying, troubling. **— et=** /ı/ to fatigue, tire, weary; to trouble, annoy; to wear out.

itabâmiz (. — — —) عِتاب آمیز P *lrnd.* expressing reproof or reproach; reproachful.

i'takᵏⁱ (. —) اِعتاق A *law* a liberating, emancipating; liberation, emancipation.

itale (. —.) اِطالة A *lrnd.* an extending; a lengthening. **—i lisan** a presumptuously criticizing; an insulting. **—i yed** a laying hands on, an injuring; a meddling.

italikᵍⁱ ایتالیك F 1. *print.* italic (type). 2. *w. cap.* Italic.

İtalya (. .'. .) ایتالیا ، ایطالیا *geog.* Italy. **—lı** Italian.

İtalyan ایتالیان It Italian. **—ca** (. . .'. .) the Italian language, in Italian.

it'am 1 (. —) اِطعام A *lrnd.* a feeding; a giving food.

itam 2 (. —) اِطام A *path.* stricture of bowels or urethra; strangury.

it'amiye (. — . .) اِطعامیه *Ott. hist.* appropriation of food for distribution for the poor.

itapᵇⁱ (. —) عِتاب *var. of* **itab 1.**

itare (. —.) اِطارة A *lrnd.* 1. a causing to fly away; a fleeing. 2. a causing to move rapidly; a sending hastily.

itbaᵃⁱ (. —) اِتباع A 1. *gram.* a semi-alliterative sequence of two words similar to the English 'hurly burly', *e. g.,* **at mat, paşa maşa.** 2. *lrnd.* a following, overtaking; a causing to follow.

itekle=ʳ اِتكلمك /ı/ *prov.* to push roughly; to manhandle, to handle roughly.

itele=ʳ اِتلمك /ı/ 1. to keep on pushing; to force on; to nudge. 2. *phys.* to repulse.

itfa (. —) اِطفاء A 1. *fin.,* com. redemption, amortization. 2. *lrnd.* an extinguishing; a quenching; a smothering. **— akçesi, — bedeli** *com.* sinking fund. **—i düyun** *com.* amortization. **— et=** /ı/ 1. to extinguish (fire). 2. to pay off, redeem (debt).

itfaiye (. — . .) اِطفائیه A fire brigade. **— eri, — neferi** fireman. **—ci** fireman.

ithaf (. —) اِتحاف A 1. a presenting; presentation. 2. a dedicating; dedication. **— et=**

/1, a/ 1. to dedicate (book, etc.). 2. to present something rare. —iye (. ——.) dedication (of a book).

ithafname (. ——.) اتحافنامه P dedicational foreword; dedication.

ithal^(ii) (. —) ادخال A 1. importation. 2. insertion, introduction. 3. inclusion. — et= /1, a/ 1. to import. 2. to insert; to introduce, to let in. — malı imported goods. — resmi com. octroi. — valfı mech. admission valve, inlet valve.

ithalât (. ——) ادخالات A imports; foreign merchandise. — rüsumu import duty.

ithalâtçı ادخالاتچى importer. —lık import business.

itham (. —) اتهام A accusation, imputation. — et= /1, la/ to accuse; to charge, to indict.

ithamname (. ——.) اتهامنامه P indictment.

iti 1 ايتى آن archaic 1. sharp, keen (sword, etc.), whetted. 2. strong, severe; acrimonious.

iti=^r 2 ايتيلمك archaic 1. to be or become sharp. 2. to be acrimonious, to be bitter.

i'tibar (. . —) A, itibar (—. —) اعتبار 1. a regarding; a paying attention to; a considering; esteem; consideration, regard; honor; reverence, influence. 2. com. credit. 3. nominal value. 4. hypothesis. 5. lrnd. a taking an example or warning and profiting by it. —a al= /1/ to consider. —ı bozul= to lose one's credit. —dan düş= to be discredited; to fall from esteem. — emri com. order of credit. — et= /a/ 1. to show consideration and respect. 2. lrnd. to take warning. — gör= to be respected; to be in demand. —ı malî financial credit. — mektubu com. letter of credit. —ı ol= to be held in esteem; to have credit. —ı surat paying attention to the appearances. —ın yerine gelmesi com. rehabilitation. —ât (. . ——) A lrnd. hypotheses.

i'tibaren (. . —'.) A, itibaren (—. —'.) اعتباراً /dan/ from, dating from, as from, e. g., yarından itibaren as from tomorrow.

i'tibari (. . ——) A, itibarî (—. ——) اعتبارى 1. theoretical, conventional; speculative. 2. com. nominal. 3. psych. fictive, imaginary. — kıymet nominal value. — olarak 1. assumedly, supposedly. 2. nominally.

itibariyle اعتباريله as regards: in view of; taking into consideration, . e. g., beş sene itibariyle considering it to be five years.

itibarlı (—. —.) اعتبارلى esteemed; valued; trusted; influential.

itibarsız (—. —.) اعتبارسز discredited; not held in esteem; not influential. —lık discredit; lack of esteem.

i'tidal^(ii) (. . —) A, itidal^(ii) (—. —) اعتدال 1. moderation; temperance; equilibrium. 2. mildness, sobriety, composure; equanimity. 3. astr. equinox. — bul= to become moderate, to calm down. —i dem lrnd. sang-froid, calm; composure. —i harifî astr. autumnal equinox. —ini kaybet= 1. to lose one's temper, to become agitated. 2. to overdo. —i leyl ü nehar astr., obs. equinox. —i mizac psych. temperateness. —i rebiî noktası astr. vernal equinox. — sahibi calm; self-possessed, composed, moderate. —li moderate, temperate, calm, unagitated.

itidalsiz اعتدالسز immoderate, extreme. —lik immoderateness; extremeness.

i'tikad (. . —) A, itikad (—. —) اعتقاد same as itikat. —ı batıl lrnd. superstition. — et= /a/ to believe (in).

itikadat (. . ——) اعتقادات A lrnd. beliefs, convictions, tenets.

itikadî (. . ——) اعتقادى A lrnd. pertaining to belief. —yat (. . ———) A lrnd. matters concerning belief.

i'tikâf (. . —) A, itikaf (—. —) اعتكاف lrnd. a going into retreat for a definite time. —a çekil= to go into retreat or retirement.

i'tikâl^(ii) (. . —) A, itikâl^(ii) اعتكال geol. a being corroded, erosion.

itikat^(dı) (—. —) اعتقاد [itikad] 1. a firmly believing; belief, conviction. 2. creed, faith. —lı who has faith.

itikatsız اعتقادسز unbelieving, doubting; sceptical. —lık scepticism.

itil=^(ir) ايتلمك pass. of it= 2, 3.

i'tilâ (. . —) A, itilâ (—. —) اعتلا lrnd. an ascending, a being elevated; exaltation; progress to a higher standard. — devri hist. period of ascension. — et= to progress.

i'tilâf (. . —) A, itilâf (—. —) ائتلاف 1. pol. entente. 2. lrnd. an agreeing together; agreement. 3. lrnd. harmony; understanding; friendship. İ— Devletleri hist. the Allied Powers (of the first World War), Entente Powers. — et= to come to an agreement; to agree, to harmonize. —ı mukadder phil. preestablished harmony. —ı müselles hist. Triple Entente.

itile=^r ايتيلمك /1/ archaic to sharpen; to whet.

itilme ايتلمه 1. verbal n. of itil=. 2. neol., psych. repression.

i'timad (. . —) A, itimat^(dı) (—. —) اعتماد reliance, trust, confidence, belief. — et= /a/ to rely upon, to trust. —a müstenid hukukî muamele law fiduciary acts. —ı nefs lrnd. self-reliance, self-confidence. — telkin et= to inspire confidence. —en (—. —'.) A lrnd. /a/ relying (upon).

itimatname (—. ——.) اعتمادنامه pol. letter of credence, credentials.

i'tina (. . —) A, itina (—. —) اعتنا care, attention. — et=, — göster= /a/ to give

itinasız

serious attention (to). **— ile** carefully. **—lı** careful, attentive; painstaking.

itinasız اعتناسز careless, inattentive. **—lık** carelessness, inattentiveness.

itinerer ايتينرر F itinerary.

itir=ir ايترمك archaic, same as **yitir=**.

i'tiraf (..—) A, **itiraf** (—.—) اعتراف confession, admission. **— et=** /ı/ to confess (to), to admit. **—ât** (..——) A lrnd. confessions.

i'tiraz (..—) A, **itiraz** (—.—) اعتراض 1. objection; disapproval. 2. law protest. **— et=** /a/ to object (to), to raise an objection (against). **—ât** (..——) A lrnd. objections. **—sız** without any objection; readily.

i'tisaf (..—) A, **itisaf** (—.—) اعتساف lrnd. injustice, oppression, tyranny; persecution. **— cinneti** psychiatry persecution mania. **—ât** (..——) A injustices, oppressive acts.

i'tisam (..—) A, **itisam** (—.—) اعتصام lrnd. 1. a clinging to. 2. a seeking refuge and protection. 3. a preserving oneself from sin.

itiş=ir 1 ايتشمك to push one another; to quarrel together; to brawl. **—ip kakış=** to push and shove one another.

itiş 2 ايتش 1. verbal n. of **it=** 2. 2. verbal n. of **itiş= 1**.

itişme ايتشمه verbal n. of **itiş= 1**.

itiştir=ir ايتشديرمك 1. /ı, la/ caus. of **itiş= 1**. 2. /ı/ to push slightly and continuously.

i'tiyad (..—) اعتياد A lrnd., same as **itiyat**.

i'tiyadat (—.——) اعتيادات A lrnd. habits.

i'tiyadî (—.—ī) اعتيادى A lrnd. habitual, customary. **— suçlar** law habitual offenses.

itiyatdı (..—) اعتياد [i'tiyad] habit, custom. **— edin=**, **— et=** /ı/ to make a habit (of), to accustom oneself (to). **— üzere** habitually, as usual.

i'tizad (..—) A, **itizad** (—.—) اعتضاد lrnd. 1. a taking or putting under the arm. 2. a leaning upon; a begging assistance.

i'tizalli (..—) A, **itizal**li (—.—) اعتزال 1. lrnd. a separating oneself from the rest; a renouncing. 2. Isl. rel. a being or becoming of the sect of **Mutezile**.

i'tizam (..—) A, **itizam** (—.—) اعتزام lrnd. a going (toward), a departing.

i'tizar (..—) A, **itizar** (—.—) اعتذار an offering an excuse; an apologizing. **— et=** to excuse oneself, to apologize.

itkan (.—) اتقان A lrnd. 1. a making solid and sure. 2. a doing anything firmly, properly and well.

itlâf (.—). اتلاف A a causing to perish; a destroying; destruction; waste. **— et=** /ı/ to destroy, to waste.

itlikgi اتلك 1. doggishness. 2. villainy.

itmam اتمام A 1. a completing, perfecting, finishing. 2. math. integration. **— et=** /ı/ to complete, perfect; to finish.

itme ايتمه verbal n. of **it= 2**.

itminan (..—) اطمئنان A lrnd. a being or becoming tranquil in mind, a feeling certain; confidence; relief. **—ı hâtır, —ı kalb** tranquillity of mind, peacefulness.

ıttırad (..—) A, **ıttırat**dı (..—) اطراد a being regular; a proceeding or flowing equally and uninterruptedly; regularity; continuity; monotonous rythm. **—lı** regular; continuous.

ıttıratsız اطرادسز irregular; discontinuous. **—lık** irregularity; discontinuity.

ittiaz (..—) اتعاظ A lrnd. an accepting admonition; an improving from advice or correction.

ittibaaı (..—) اتباع A lrnd. a following upon; a conforming, obeying, imitating, copying. **— et=** /a/ to follow, obey, copy.

ittibaen (..—́.) اتباعا A lrnd. /a/ in conformity (with); following.

itticah (..—) اتجاه A 1. lrnd. a turning toward (direction). 2. phil. orientation.

ittifakkı (..—) اتفاق A 1. a mutually conforming together; accord, concord; harmony. 2. an agreeing, consenting; agreement, alliance. 3. lrnd. a coinciding, happening; coincidence, chance. **— akdet=** 1. to make an agreement. 2. to conclude an alliance. **—i ârâ** lrnd. unanimity; unanimity of opinion. **— et=** to agree, to be unanimous; to be allied. **İ—i Müselles** hist. Triple Alliance.

ittifaka (..——), **ittifakan** (..—́.) اتفاقا A lrnd. 1. by chance, accidentally. 2. by consent and understanding.

ittifakat (..——) اتفاقات A lrnd. alliances. **—i dehr** the chance events of time or fortune.

ittifakî (..——) اتفاقى A lrnd. 1. accidental, casual. 2. agreeing, consenting; pertaining to agreement. **—yat** (..———) accidental matters. **—ye** (..—̄.) phil. occasionalism.

ittihad (..—) اتحاد A lrnd., same as **ittihat**. **—î** (..——) A pertaining to union.

ittiham (..—) اتهام [itham] accusation, imputation.

ittihatdı (..—) اتحاد [ittihad] 1. a becoming united; an agreeing, being unanimous; union. 2. myst. the spiritual union of a saint's soul with God. 3. phil. identity. **İ— ve Terakki Cemiyeti** Ott. hist. Committee of Union and Progress (political party in power after the revolution of 1908).

ittihaz (..—) اتخاذ A lrnd. a taking, procuring for oneself. **— et=** /ı/ to take, to procure, to adopt (a proposal, etc.).

ittika 1 (..—) اتقاء A lrnd. 1. a fearing

(God); piety. 2. a taking care, taking precaution.

ittikâ 2 (..—) اِتِّكَا A *lrnd.* 1. a leaning against; a reclining upon one side. 2. a leaning for support; a depending upon.

ittikâl[li] (..—) اِتِّكَال A *lrnd.* a trusting, relying upon (God), a putting all one's trust (in God).

ittikan (..—) اِتِّقَان A *lrnd.* a knowing something very well; a being sure (of).

ittir=[ir] اِتديرمك /1, a/ *caus. of* **it**= 2.

ittisa[aı] (..—) اِتِّسَاع A *lrnd.* a being or becoming ample, extended, diffused; ampleness; extension. —**iyet** (..——.) extensiveness.

ittisaf (..—) اِتِّصَاف A *lrnd.* a having a quality; description, qualification.

ittisak[kı] (..—) اِتِّسَاق A *lrnd.* a being or becoming arranged in a row, series or border.

ittisal[li] (..—) اِتِّصَال A *lrnd.* contiguity, communication, liaison. —**ât** (..——) A lines of communication.

ittisam (..—) اِتِّسَام A *lrnd.* a having some distinguishing mark.

ittizah (..—) اِتِّضَاح A *lrnd.* a being clear, evident and manifest; clearness, evidence.

ityan (.—) اِتيَان A *lrnd.* a bringing forward, laying down, mentioning (a matter).

iv=[er] ايومك *archaic* to make haste, to be in a hurry.

îva (——) اِيوَا A *lrnd.* a setting a person in some place as a permanent abode.

ivar (——) ايوار P *lrnd.* the late afternoon; time of afternoon worship. — **ü şebgîr** evening and morning; afternoon and early dawn.

ivaz عِوَض A 1. *law* consideration, valuable consideration, equivalent. 2. *lrnd.* a substituting or giving in exchange; substitution; exchange. 3. *lrnd.* thing given in exchange, substitute.

ivazan (..´.) عِوَضًا A *lrnd.* /a/ in substitution, in exchange (for).

ivazsız عِوَض gratuitously, gratis; without anything being given in return.

ivdir=[ir] ايودرمك /1/ *archaic, caus. of* **iv**=.

ivedi ايودى *prov.* haste, hurry; hasty. —**lik** haste. —**likle** in haste, promptly, hurriedly.

ivegen ايوگن *archaic* hurrying; impatient.

ivez ايوز *prov., same as* **üvez** 2.

ivgi ايوگى *prov.* small hatchet.

ivi ايوى *archaic* haste, hurry. —**ci** hasty, hurrying.

i'vicac (..—) A, **ivicaç**[cı] (—.—) اعوجاج 1. crooked; crookedness. 2. curvature. —**lı** curved.

ivik[gi] ايوك *archaic* kind of ski or snowshoe.

ivir=[ir] ايورمك /1/ *archaic, caus. of* **iv**=.

ivme ايومه 1. *verbal n. of* **iv**=. 2. *neol., phys.* acceleration.

iyab (.—) اِياب A *lrnd.* 1. a returning; return. 2. a repenting; repentance.

iyad (.—) عِياد A *lrnd.* a repeating; repetition.

iyadet (.—.) عِيادت A *lrnd.* a visiting (the sick).

iyal[li] (..—) عِيال A *lrnd., same as* **ayal**.

iyan (.—) عِيان A *same as* **ayan** 3.

iyanet (.—.) عِيانت A *lrnd.* 1: an acting as a lookout or spy. 2. spy.

iyar (.—) عِيار A *lrnd., same as* **ayar** 4.

-**iyat** (.—) يات [*Arabic* ——] words of..., work containing..., science dealing with..., as in **gazeliyat, iğrakiyat, şarkiyat**.

iyaz (.—) عِياذ A *lrnd.* a taking refuge; refuge; asylum. —**en billâh!** Heaven forfend! God forbid!

iye 1 اِيه *same as* **eğe** 3.

-**iye 2** (—.) يه A 1. *fem. of* -**î 6**. 2. *phil.* school of, *e. g.*, **ittifakiye, reybiye**; order of (dervishes), *e. g.*, **Kadiriye, Şabaniye**.

-**iye 3** يه [-**iye 2**] fee of, *e. g.*, **duhuliye, kaydiye**.

iyelik[ği] *neol.* possession. — **eki** *gram.* possessive suffix. — **zamiri** *gram.* possessive pronoun.

-**iyet** (—.) يت A added to adjectives to form abstract nouns, as in **cumhuriyet, merbutiyet, muhtariyet**.

iyham (.—) اِيهَام A 1. *rhet.* a using the rarer meaning of an amphibolous word, quibbling. 2. *lrnd.* a misleading; an exciting suspicion.

iyi ايو 1. good; well. 2. in good health. 3. kind; beneficial. —**ye çek**= /1/ 1. to put a good interpretation upon. 2. to consider of good omen. — **et**= /1/ 1. to cure, to heal. 2. to do well. 3. *slang* /1/ to rob. — **gel**= /a/ 1. to suit, to fit. 2. to do good; to help. — **git**= 1. to go well. 2. /a/ to suit. — **gözle bakma**= /a/ to have a bad opinion of. — **gün** prosperity. — **gün dostu** fair weather friend. — **gün görmüş** who has seen better days. — **hal kâğıdı** certificate of good conduct. — **hoş amma** That's all very well but... —**siniz inşallah** I hope you are well. — **iş doğrusu!** What a queer thing! —**den iyi**, —**den iyiye** thoroughly, completely. — **kötü** somehow; in some way or other. —**si mi** The best thing to do is... — **ol**= 1. to recover. 2. to be good, to be in order. — **oldu da**, — **oldu ki** fortunately. — **saatte olsunlar** the djinns. — **var**= *archaic* to act properly; to do the right thing.

iyice 1 (...´) اييجه pretty good. rather well, fairly good.

iyice 2 (..´.) · ايیجه thoroughly, completely, carefully.
iyicene (..´..) ايیجنه colloq. thoroughly.
-iyle ايله cf. **-ile 2**. after vowels **-siyle** with his, with its.
iyilen=ir ايولنمك prov., same as **iyileş**=.
iyileş=ir ايولشمك 1. to get better; to improve. 2. to recover (from illness). —**tir**= /ı/ caus.
iyilikgi ايولك 1. goodness; kindness; favor. 2. good health. 3. good part, good side. —**le** in a friendly way; kindly, softly. — **bil**= to be grateful, to appreciate kindness. — **et**= /a/ to do a kindness (to). — **gör**= /dan/ to experience kindness or favor (from). — **yap**= /a/ 1. to do a kindness (to). 2. slang to report to the police. — **sağlık** All is well, all quiet. —**çi** good, kind, beneficient.
iyimser neol. optimist; optimistic. —**lik** optimism.
iyinikgi ايینك same as **iğinik**.
iyod ايود F chem. iodine.
iyon ايون F chem. ion. —**lanma** ionization. —**lanma enerjisi** energy of ionization. —**lanma potansiyeli** ionization potential.
İyoniya (..´..) ايونيا Gk geog. Ionia. —**lı** Ionian.
=**iyor** ايور cf. =**yor 3**.
=**iyordu** (..´.) ايوردى cf. =**yordu**.
=**iyorken** ايوركن cf. =**yorken**.
=**iyormuş** ايورمش cf. =**yormuş**.
=**iyormuşçasına** ايورمشجسنه cf. =**yormuşçasına**.
=**iyormuş gibi** ايورمش كبى cf. =**yormuş gibi**.
=**iyorsa** ايورسه cf. =**yorsa**.
-iyun (— —) يون [pl. of **-î 6**.] lrnd. adherents of a philosophical school, as in **ittifakiyun, reybiyun**.
iz 1 ايز 1. footmark, footprint. 2. trace, track, trail. —**ini ara**= /ın/ 1. to look for footprints or traces (of). 2. to try to discover (a clue). — **bas**=, —**ine bas**= archaic /ın/ to follow someone's footsteps; to track. —**ine basarak gel**= /ın/ to follow; to imitate. —**i belirsiz** completely disappeared, lost, no trace left. —**ine dön**= to retrace one's steps. —**ine düş**= /ın/ to follow up, to trace. — **genişliği artillery** track. —**ini kaybet**= /ın/ 1. to lose track (of). 2. to bury one's tracks, to go into hiding. —**ine kurşun at**= · /ın/ to hate bitterly. — **mermisi** mil. tracer ammunition. — **müş'iri** artillery tracer. —**i silin**= to disappear completely; to be thoroughly forgotten. — **sür**= /ın/ to follow the traces (of), to trace. —**i tozu kalmadı** It has completely disappeared; there is not the slightest vestige left. —**ine uy**= /ın/ to follow in the footsteps (of). —**inde yürü**=, —**inden yürü**= /ın/ to follow in the footsteps (of); to follow faithfully.
izzzi **2** عز A lrnd. 1. power; glory. 2. value; honor; estimation. — **ü ikbal**, — **ü şeref** worth and honor.
=**iz 3** ايز cf. =**ız**.
iza 1 (— —) ايذا A lrnd. a hurting; an afflicting; a tormenting, an annoying.
izaaı **2** (. —) ايذا A lrnd. whatever is opposite to and corresponding with a thing.
izaa 1 (. —.) · اذاعه A lrnd. a divulging, openly mentioning, or proclaiming (a secret).
izaa 2 (. —.) اضاعه A lrnd. a destroying; a wasting; a losing; waste, loss.
izabe (. —.) اذابه A lrnd. a melting, fusing, liquifying (a thing); fusion. — **fırını** blast furnace. — **noktası** phys. melting point.
iz'ac A, **iz'aç**cı (. —.) ازعاج an annoying, disturbing, worrying; vexation, worry. — **ateşi** mil. harassing fire. — **et**= /ı/ to trouble, annoy, harass.
izae (. —.) اضائه A lrnd. 1. an illuminating, a lighting up. 2. a shining; a causing to shine.
iz'af (. —) اضعاف A lrnd. 1. a multiplying; an increasing. 2. a weakening, an enfeebling.
izafat (. — —) اضافات A lrnd. 1. pl. of **izafet**. 2. worldly interests, worldliness.
izafe (. —.) اضافه A lrnd. an attributing; attaching; an adding; annexation. — **et**= /ı, a/ 1. to attach, to attribute (to). 2. to join words in construction.
izafet (. —.) اضافت A 1. gram. nominal compound, e. g., **Ahmedin kitabı** Ahmed's book, **Bab-ı Âli** Sublime Porte, **masa örtüsü** tablecloth, **demir kapı** iron gate. 2. lrnd. a subsequent annexation, an accidental annexation. 3. phil. relativity. — **terkibi** gram. nominal compound.
izafî (. — —) اضافى A 1. relative. 2. phil. nominal. — **sıklet** phys. specific gravity. —**ye** (. — — .) phil. relativism.
izafiyet (. — — .) اضافيت A phil. relativity. — **nazariyesi** astr. theory of relativity.
izah (. —) ايضاح A explanation; elucidation. — **et**= /ı, a/ to explain (something to someone).
izahat (. — —) ايضاحات A explanations.
izahen (. —´.) ايضاحاً A lrnd. /ın/ in explanation, by way of elucidation (of).
izahname (. — — .) ايضاحنامه P lrnd. written explanation; manifesto.
izaka (. —.) اذاقه A lrnd. a giving one to taste; a tasting, an experiencing a taste.
izale (. —.) ازاله A a removing; a causing to disappear. —**i bikr** defloration. — **et**= /ı/ to remove; to cause to disappear. —**i şuyu** law dividing up of an undivided property.
i'zam 1 A, **izam 1** (— —) اعظام 1. exaggeration. 2. lrnd. enlargement.
i'zam 2 (. —) A, **izam 2** (— —) اعزام lrnd. a sending (a person).

izam 3 (.—) عِظام A *pl. of* **azm 2**, *lrnd.* bones.
izam 4 (.—) عِظام A *lrnd., pl. of* **azîm 4**.
iz'an 1 (.—) اِذعان A 1. a being quick of understanding. 2. consideration for others.
izan 2 (— —) اِذعان A *lrnd.* a communicating (information).
iz'anlı اِذعانلى 1. quick on the uptake, intelligent. 2. considerate, polite.
iz'ansız اِذعانسز inconsiderate, impolite. —**lık** impoliteness, lack of consideration.
izar 1 (.—) اِعتذار A *lrnd.* 1. an excusing; an accepting an excuse. 2. a being justified or excusable.
izar 2 (.—) عِذار A *lrnd.* cheek.
izar 3 (.—) اِزار A *lrnd.* 1. a waist-wrapper, extending, like a petticoat, all round the body. 2. a wrapper covering the body below the waist.
i'zaz A, **izaz** (— —) اِعزاز an honoring, a treating with respect; entertainment. — **et**= /ı/ to honor, treat with respect; entertain. — **ve ikram** an honoring, entertaining.
i'zazen (.—'.) اِعزازاً A *lrnd.* as an honor.
izbandit, izbandut اِزبانديت اِزبانـدود It *same as* **ızbandut**.
izbar (.—) اِزبار A *lrnd.* a writing, inscribing, recording; a causing to be written.
izbe اِزبه Sl 1. den; hut, hovel; basement. 2. dark and dirty.
izbiro (..'.) اِزبيرو It *naut.* sling (for lifting bulky goods), can hook.
izci اِزجى 1. boy scout. 2. tracker. —**lik** scouting.
izdicar (..—) اِزدجار A *lrnd.* 1. a chiding, driving away, prohibiting. 2. a listening and conforming to a chiding voice; a refraining.
izdiham (..—) اِزدحام A a crowding, pressing together; crowd.
=**izdir** اِزدر *cf.* =**ızdır**.
izdiraai (..—) اِزدراء A *lrnd.* 1. a blaming, reproving; blame. 2. a despising, scorning; scorn, disdain.
izdivac A, **izdivaç**cı (..—) اِزدواج a marrying; marriage, matrimony. — **teklifi** marriage proposal.
izdiyad (..—) اِزدياد A *lrnd.* an increasing, augmenting; augmentation, increase. — **bul**= to increase, grow, augment.
izdüşüm *neol., math.* projection.
izdüşür=ür *neol., math.* /ı/ to project.
İzed, İzid (—.) اِيزد P *lrnd.* God. —**î** (—.—) P pertaining to God, divine.
izfaf (.—) اِزفاف A *lrnd.* a conducting a bride home to her husband in state.
izhab (.—) اِذهاب A *lrnd.* 1. a causing one to depart; a removing. 2. a gilding.
izhar (.—) اِظهار A a showing, manifesting,

displaying. — **et**= /ı/ to show, to manifest.
izinzni اِذن [**izn**] A 1. leave, permission; consent; permit. 2. dismissal, discharge. — **al**= /dan/ to get permission, to obtain leave (from). —**ini kullan**= to take one's vacation. —**i sefine fermanı** *Ott. hist.* Imperial firman granting permission to a ship to pass through the Straits. — **ver**= /a/ 1. to grant permission, to give leave. 2. to dismiss, discharge, turn out, send away.
izinli اِذنلى with permission; on vacation, on leave.
izinname (..—.) اِذننامه P 1. a letter of leave or discharge. 2. permit, license. 3. *can. law* marriage license.
izinsiz اِذنسز 1. without permission, unauthorized. 2. 'kept in' (school children).
izkâm (.—) اِزكام A *lrnd.* an afflicting one with a cold in the head. — **et**= /ı/ to give one a cold.
izkâr (.—) اِذكار A *lrnd.* a bringing to mind, a recalling; a causing to remember.
izlâlli 1 (.—) اِضلال A *lrnd., same as* **ıdlâl**.
izlâlli 2 (.—) اِظلال A *lrnd.* a shading, a casting a shadow; an overshadowing.
izlâlli 3 (.—) اِذلال A *lrnd.* a rendering abject; an abasing; a humbling, humiliating; humiliation.
izlâm (.—) اِظلام A *lrnd.* a rendering or becoming dark or gloomy.
İzlanda (..'.) اِزلاندا It *geog.* Iceland. — **dili** Icelandic. — **likeni** Iceland moss, Iceland lichen, *bot., Cetravia islandica.* —**lı** Icelander.
izle=r اِزلمك /ı/ 1. to track by the footmarks; to trace. 2. *archaic* to follow after. —**n**= *pass.* —**ndir**= /ı, a/ *caus. of* **izle**=.
izlenim *neol., psych.* impression.
izmaritdi, ti اِزمارِيت Gk 1. sea bream, *zool., Smaris alcedo.* 2. cigarette butt.
izmavla (..'.) اِزماولا red raspberry, raspberry, *bot., Rubus idaeus.*
izmihlâlli (..—)اِضمحلال A *lrnd.* a disappearing, dispersing; a coming to naught; disappearance, annihilation.
izn اِذن A *lrnd., same as* **izin**.
İznikği اِزنيك *geog.* Iznik (the ancient Nicea).
izobar اِزوبار F *meteor.* isobar.
izolasyon اِزولاسيون F *phys.* isolation.
izoterm اِزوترم F *geog.* isotherm.
izotop اِزوتوپ F *chem.* isotope.
izraf (.—) اِطراف A *lrnd.* a covering, an enveloping, an encasing.
izzet عِزّت A a being glorious; glory, greatness; excellence; honor, dignity, might. —**i nefis,** —**i nefs** self-respect.
izzetfüruş (...—) عِزّت‌فروش P *lrnd.* who assumes himself to be in high esteem, pretentious, very pleased with himself.

izzetle= عزّتلك /ı/ to treat with respect, to honor. **—n=** *pass.*
izzetli, izzetlû عزّتلى *archaic* honorable, excellent, respectable (title given to officers and officials of a certain rank).
izzetmend عزّتمند P *lrnd.* great, excellent. **—âne** (...—.) P pertaining to the great or excellent.

J

j, J ژ P *the thirteenth letter of the Turkish alphabet.*
jaj (—) ژاژ P *lrnd.* 1. any tough, insipid, or bitter plant that a beast munches or rejects. 2. nonsense; insipid speech. **—ha, —hay** (— —) P 1. trifler. 2. one who speaks obscenely.
jakar ژاقار F *text.* jacquard loom.
jaketatay ژاكت آتاى F morning coat.
jale (—.) ژال P *poet.* 1. dew; hoar frost. 2. tears. **—dar** (—.—) P covered with dew.
jalon ژالون F surveyor's staff, range rod.
jaluzi ژالوزى F Venetian blind.
jambon ژامبون F ham.
jandarma (..'.) ژاندارما F police soldier, gendarme.
jant ژانت F *mech.* rim (of a wheel).
Japon ژاپون F 1. Japanese. 2. Japan. **— gülü** guilder rose, *bot., Hortensia.* **—ca** (..'.) the Japanese language.
Japonya (..'.) ژاپونيا [*based on Italian*] Japan.
jardiniyer ('...) ژاردينيه F jardiniére, flower stand.
jarse ژارسه F *same as* **jerse.**
jartiyer ژارتيه F garter.
jelâtin ژلاتن F gelatine, jelly. **—li** gelatinous; jellylike, jellied.
jend ژند P *lrnd.* rag, tatter; tattered garment. **— jend** in rags and tatters.
jende ژنده P *lrnd.* ragged, tattered; tattered garment. **—pûş** (..—) P clothed in rags, tatterdemalion, ragged tramp.
jeng ژنگ P *lrnd.* 1. rust. 2. film of dirt. 3. gum of the eyes. 4. wrinkle. **—âlûd** (.——) P rusty.
jengâr (.—) ژنگار P verdigris; rust. **—î** (.——) P of a bright green color; sea green.

jeodozi ژئودوزى F geodesy.
jeolog ژئولوگ F geologist.
jeoloji ژئولوژى F geology.
jerf ژرف P *lrnd.* deep; profound; far reaching. **—bin** (.—) P penetrating, perspicacious. **—î** (.—) P depth; profundity.
jerse ژرسه F *text.* jersey cloth.
jest ژست F gesture.
jesvit ژسويت F *same as* **cizvit.**
jigle ژگله F *mech.* choke. **— düğmesi** choke. **— kelebeği** throttle valve.
jigolo ژگولو F gigolo.
jile ژله F sleeveless blouse.
jilet ژلت F safety razor. **— bıçağı** razor blade.
jimnastik[gi] ژمناستيك F gymnastics.
jinekolog ژنكولوگ F *med.* gynecologist.
jinekoloji ژنكولوژى F *med.* gynecology.
jive (—.) ژيوه P *lrnd.* quicksilver, mercury.
jiyan (.—) ژيان P *lrnd.* furious, savage, ferocious; rapacious; formidable; fierce; angry.
jul[ü] ژول F *phys.* joule.
julide (— —.) ژوليده P *lrnd.* disordered, disheveled (hair, etc.); untidy.
jura ژورا F *geol.* jurassic.
jurnal[li] ژورنال F 1. report of an informer. 2. diary. **— et=** /ı/ to denounce, report. **—cı** denouncer, delator, informer.
jübile ژوبيله F jubilee.
jujkomiser ژوژكوميسر F *law* bankruptcy commissioner; official receiver in bankruptcy.
jüp[bü] **1** ژوپ |**jüp 2**|. long jacket of a lady's suit.
jüp[bü] **2** ژوپ F tailor. skirt, petticoat.
Jüpiter ژوپيتر F *myth., astron.* Jupiter.
jüpon ژوپون underskirt, slip.
jüri ژورى F jury.
jüt ژوت F jute.

K

k 1, K the fourteenth letter of the alphabet.
=k 2 ك ، after vowels **=ık, =ik, =uk, =ük,** deverbal adjective, as in **parlak, patlak, alışık, kırık, eğik, yenik, uyuşuk, yoluk, bükük, düşük.**
kaa (—.) قاع A lrnd. 1. courtyard. 2. parlor.
kaan (— —) قاآن P lrnd. khan, emperor. **—i Çin** emperor of China. **—î** (— — —) P imperial.
kab 1 قاب 1. receptacle; cover; envelope. 2. vessel; pot; course (of food). **—ı dar** archaic irritable. **— geçir=** /a/ to put a case (on a pillow etc.); to bind (book). **— kacak** same as **kapkacak. bir —a kotarama=** /ı/ to be unable to find a solution (to a problem, etc.). **—ına sığma=** to be uncontrollably impatient or ambitious; to be very energetic. **bir — yemek** one-course dinner. **— yok kacak yok** bare of the simplest necessities.
kâ'b 2 كعب A lrnd. 1. ankle, anklebone; 2. cube number or quantity. 3. dice. **—ında olma=** /ın/ not to reach the standard of. **—ına var=** /ın/ to be or become as able (as), to reach someone's standard. **—ına varılmaz** unrivalled, peerless.
kab 3 (—) قاب A lrnd. space; distance. **—ı kavseyn** distance of two bow lengths.
kaba 1 قابا 1. rough, coarse. 2. common, vulgar, rude, boorish. 3. rough (calculation, guess, etc.). 4. puffy, puffed up; thick (carpet, etc.). 5. archaic mighty, huge (tree). **—sını al=** /ın/ to tidy up roughly, clean up quickly; to trim roughly, to roughhew. **— cevherli** coarse-grained. **— burun** kind of small fish, zool., Chondrostoma nasus. **— çargâh** Or. mus. middle c. **— diken** bramble, bot., Rubus edeus; Christ's-thorn, bot., Rhamnus paliurus. **— döşek** soft downy mattress. **— duvar** rubble masonry, rough masonry. **— et** buttocks. **— hicaz** Or. mus. c **— iş** rough work. **— kafa** uncultured mind. **— kâğıt** 1. coarse paper. 2. blotting paper. **— kalem** 1. ordinary softish reed or pen. 2. ordinary writing. **— kalker** geol. calcareous limestone. **— koz** 1. large, coarse walnut. 2. bungler. **— kumpas** 1. colloq. rough draft. 2. naut. dead reckoning. **— kuşluk** time of morning when the sun is well up; late morning. **— kuyruk** 1. bushy-tailed. 2. term of vituperation dog. **— lâf** vulgar expression. **— post** unshorn sheep skin, rough sheepskin. **— saba*. — sabâ** Or. mus. the note d^b. **— sakal*. — ses** gruff voice; deep, baritone voice. **— sofu** intolerant bigot. **— soğan** of important appearance, but weak and worthless (person). **— su** running pattern of chain-stitch. **— şiş** same as **kabakulak. — şûrî** Or. mus. the note e^b. **— taslak*. — taş** soft stone. **— toprak** freshly dug soil; common earth. **— Türkçe** "vulgar Turkish"; simple Turkish (as opposed to the flowery written language of the last century). **— un** coarse grain flour. **— üstübeç** whiting, prepared chalk. **— yonca** alfalfa, lucern, bot., Medicago sativa. **— zurna** bass oboe.
kaba 2 (.—) قباء A lrnd. cloak; coat, mantle. **—yi âhenîn** armor. **—yi kühlî** sky.
kabaca 1 (...́) قاباجه somewhat grown up; biggish.
kabaca 2 (..́.) قاباجه in a rude way, grossly.
kabaçe (.—.) قباچه P lrnd. short jacket or cloak.
kabadayı قبا داىى 1. rough fellow, swashbuckler.

kabadayılık

bully. 2. the best of anything. 3. manly, brave person.

kabadayılıkᵍⁱ قبادايلق bravado. — **et**= to act with bravado.

kabahatᵘ قباحت [Arabic .—.] fault, offense; guilt, sin; *law* misdemeanor. — **at**= /a/ to accuse (of), to charge (with). — **bende** It is my fault. **bir —te bulun**=, — **et**=, — **işle**=, — **yap**= to commit a fault, to do wrong. —**i yükle**= /a/ to impute a fault (to); to blame.

kabahatli قباحتلی guilty; culpable. — **çık**= to be found in the wrong, guilty. — **çıkar**= /ı/ to blame; to find guilty. —**lik** faultiness; wrongness.

kabahatsiz قباحتسز faultless, innocent; blameless. —**lik** faultlessness, innocence.

kabaih (.—.) قبائح A *lrnd.*, *pl. of* **kabiha**.

kabail (.—.) قبائل A *lrnd.*, *pl. of* **kabile 1**.

kabakᵍⁱ **1** قباق قبانه 1. pumpkin, *bot.*, Cucurbita pepo; vegetable marrow, gourd, squash. 2. gourd-shaped guitar. 3. hashish pipe; *archaic* drinking glass, wine cup. 4. tasteless, unripe (melon); *slang* lout; awkward and stupid. 5. *prov.* cereal measure of 24 okkas (= 67.2 lb.). — **bastısı** stewed vegetable marrow. — **başına patla**= /ın/ *colloq.* to suffer a disaster. — **çek**= to smoke hashish. — **çekirdeği** pumpkin seed. — **çevir**= to pass around the hashish-pipe. — **çık**= to turn out unripe and tasteless (melon, watermelon). — **çiçeği gibi açıl**= *colloq.* to be too familiar and at ease (a newcomer); suddenly to become too free and easy. — **dolması** stuffed squash. — **gibi** 1. hairless, bare. 2. tasteless. — **kalyası**, — **kalyesi** pumpkin stew. — **meltemi** a May wind. — **tadı ver**= to become a bore, to weary, disgust. — **tatlısı** sweet dish prepared with boiled winter squash, walnuts and sugar. — **terazi** *obs.* 1. bulb for weighing or testing a fluid. 2. ball cock of a cistern. — **yavruları** a cat's second litter of the year.

kabakᵍⁱ **2** قباق قبانه 1. *colloq.* bald; closeshaven (head). 2. *prov.* honorless. 3. *prov.* front; space in front of someone or something. —**ına gel**= /ın/ *prov.* to come before, come (of). — **kafa** bald, bareheaded.

kabakçı قباقچی 1. man serving hashish. 2. player of the gourd-shaped guitar. — **Arap** *comic* Negro **kabak**-player.

kabakla=ʳ قباقله prov. 1. to prune radically. 2. to graft (plants, etc.).

kabakulakᵍⁱ قباقولاق *path.* mumps.

kabal قبال [**kabale**] *prov.* wholesale. —**a al**= /ı/ to buy wholesale. —**a ver**= /ı/ to sell wholesale.

kabalakᵍⁱ قبالاق 1. military headgear worn by the Ottoman soldiers in World War I. 2. *prov.* kind of headgear.

kabalaş=ʳ قبالاشمق 1. to grow rough and rude; to become vulgar or impolite. 2. to grow puffy, to puff up. —**tır**= /ı/ *caus.*

kabalcı قبالجی *prov.* 1. farm laborer. 2. contractor at a lump sum, jobber.

kabale (.—.) قباله A *lrnd.* 1. document, title deed; receipt; 2. assessment of Jews by their own community.

kabalıkᵍⁱ قبالق قبالوق 1. coarseness, boorishness, vulgarity. 2. sponginess, porousness, puffiness. — **et**= to behave impolitely or rudely.

kaballa=ʳ قبالمق *prov.* /ı/ 1. to sell in lump. 2. to grab, to seize.

kaban 1 قبان Sl *prov.* wild boar.

kaban 2 قبان *prov.* 1. steep mountain road; field path; hill, hillock. 2. stone.

kabaniçe قبانچه *Ott. hist.* special kind of fur coat worn by the Sultan.

kabanlıkᵍⁱ قبانلق uncultivated stony ground.

kabar=ʳ قبارمق 1. to swell, to be puffed up; to rise (when boiling); to increase; to become fluffy. 2. to assume airs of importance, to swagger; /a/ to act the bully. 3. to become rough (sea).

kabara (..́.) قباره 1. hobnail; boss; ornamental brass-headed nail. 2. *prov.* bracelet. —**lı** ornamented with bosses; having hobnails.

kabarcıkᵍⁱ قبارجق 1. small bubble; blister. *med.*, bulla. 2. pimple; pustule. 3. *prov.* kind of grapes. —**lan**= to become affected with a blister, etc. —**lı** bubbly; blistered, pimply. —**lı düzeç** *neol., phys.* air level, spirit level.

kabarıkᵍⁱ قبارق قبارين 1. swollen, puffy; blistered. 2. a swelling; blister. — **deniz** high tide, high water.

kabar kabar قبار قبار swelled, puffed up. — **kabar**=, — **ol**= 1. to swell up all over. 2. to be greatly puffed up.

kabarma قبارمه 1. *verbal n. of* **kabar**=. 2. *geog.* high tide.

kabart=ʳ قبارتمق /ı/ *caus. of* **kabar**=.

kabartı قبارتی a swelling, a bulging, puffiness.

kabartıl=ʳ قبارتلمق *pass. of* **kabart**=.

kabartma قبارتمه 1. *verbal n. of* **kabart**=. 2. *sculp.* relief; raised, embossed, in relief. — **deri** embossed leather. — **harita** relief map, raised map.

kabartmalı قبارتملی ornamented with a raised design or relief.

kabasaba قباصبا coarse, rough; common; vulgar.

kabasakal قباصقال having a full, bushy beard.

kabaset (.—.) قباست A *lrnd.* male's sexual fecundity.

kabasın=ʳ قباسنمق *archaic* to deem coarse.

kabasorta, kabasorto (..́.) قباصورتو It *naut.* fullrigged, squarerigged.

kabaş قباش *prov.* hornless; bald.
kabataslak[ğı] قبا طا سلوه rough draft; roughly drawn; in outline, without details.
kabayih (.—.) قبايح A *lrnd., var. of* **kabaih**.
kabban (.—) قبّان A *lrnd., same as* **kapan 4**.
Kâbe كعبه [*Arabic* —.] the Kaaba at Mecca. **— belesanı** balm of Gilead. **—i can** *lrnd.* 1. aim or object of one's life. 2. God. **—i cihangerd** *poet.* the sun. **—i ikbal** *lrnd.* place to which one looks for happiness. **—i muazzama** the Kaaba at Mecca. **— örtüsü** the black curtain covering the Kaaba at Mecca. **— pelesengi** balm of Gilead. **— samanı** vetiver, khuskhus grass, *bot., Andropogon muricatum.* **— toprağı** earth taken by pilgrims from Mecca.
Kâberev كعبه رو P *lrnd.* visitor to the Kaaba.
Kâbetan (..—), **Kâbeteyn** كعبتين A *lrnd.* the two temples of Mecca and Jerusalem.
Kâbetüluşşak (....—) كعبة العشّاق A Mevlana Jalaluddin's mausoleum in Konya.
kabış قبش *prov.* maid, female servant.
kabız 1 قبض [*kabz*] constipation; constipated. **— çek=** to suffer from constipation. **— ol=** 1. to be constipated. 2. *slang* to be unemployed. 3. *slang* to be nonplussed.
kabız 2 (—.) قابض A *lrnd.* 1. astringent, styptic. 2. grasping, receiving. **—ı ervah** the angel of death. **—a** (—..) A *anat.* flexor muscle. **—iyet** (—.—.) *same as* **kabızlık 2**.
kabızlık[ğı] **1** قبضلى constipation. **— çek=** to suffer from constipation.
kabızlık[ğı] **2** (—..) قابضلق [*kabız 2*] astringency.
kabih (.—) قبيح A *lrnd.* 1. ugly, hideous. 2. unseemly, improper.
kabiha (.—.) قبيحه A *lrnd.* shameful deed.
kabil 1 (—.) قابل A possible, feasible, practicable. **—i af** pardonable. **—i aks** *phil.* convertible. **—i ekl** *lrnd.* edible. **—i haml** *log.* predicable. **—i hazf** *gram.* elidible. **—i hitab** one with whom one can discourse, one who is capable of understanding. **—i icra** executable. **—i idrak** perceptible. **—i inhilâl** *lrnd., chem.* soluble. **—i inkısam** *lrnd.* divisible. **—i intikal** transferable. **—i irca** *chem., math.* reducible. **—i istifade** serviceable, usable, useful, suitable (for use); efficient (person). **—i iştikak** *math.* differentiable. **—i itiraz** objectionable. **—i kısmet** *lrnd., law* divisible; shareable. **—i nüfuz** *lrnd., phys.* permeable, penetrable. **— olanı yap=** to do one's utmost, to do one's best. **—i rücu** *log.* reversible. **—i seyrüsefer** navigable. **—i sükna** *lrnd.* habitable. **—i taakkul** *psych.* intelligible. **—i tahakkuk** *log.* realizable. **—i tahallül** *chem.* decomposable. **—i tahammuz** *chem.* oxidizable. **—i tahammül** tolerable; bearable. **—i tahayyül** imaginable. **—i taksim** divisible. **—i tatbik** practicable. **—i telif** compatible. **—i temyiz** *phil.* discernible. **—i tenbih** *biol.* excitable.
kabîl 2 (.—) قبيل A sort, kind, category. **bu —, bu —den** of this sort, such, of such a kind. **—inden** of the sort of, something like...
Kâbil 3 (—.) كابل *geog.* Kabul.
Kabil 4 (——) قابيل A *Isl. rel.* Cain.
kabile 1 (.—.) قبيله A tribe. **— reisi** tribal chieftain. **— sistemi** tribal system.
kabile 2 (—..) قابله A *lrnd.* midwife.
kabilevî (.—.—) قبيلوى A tribal.
kabilî (—.—) قابلى A *lrnd.* capable, susceptible (of).
kabiliyat (—.——) قابليات A *lrnd., pl. of* **kabiliyet**.
kabiliyet (—...) قابليت A 1. ability, capability, capacity. 2. faculty; efficiency. 3. *lrnd.* possibility. **—i ahz** *lrnd.* receptivity. **—i aksiye** *lrnd., phil.* convertibility. **—i harbiye** *lrnd.* fighting efficiency. **—i icraiye** *lrnd.* practicability, feasibility, workability. **—i inhilâliye** *lrnd., chem.* solubility. **—i intikal** *lrnd.* transferability. **—i isnad** *lrnd.* imputability. **—i istiabiye** *lrnd.* capacity (of a ship etc.). **—inde ol=** /ın/ to be able, to be capable (of). **— sahibi** capable, talented person. **—i taharrüş** *lrnd., physiol.* irritability. **—i taksim** *lrnd., law* divisibility. **—i teheyyüc** *lrnd., psych.* emotivity. **—i telkin** *lrnd.* power of suggestion.
kabiliyetli قابليتلى 1. talented, gifted. 2. intelligent, skillful.
kabiliyetsiz قابليتسز untalented; incapable. **—lik** incapability, incapacity, inability.
kabilsiz (—..) قابلسز *colloq.* impossible.
kâbin (——) كابين P *can. law* marriage portion contracted to be paid by the husband to his wife if he divorces her without sufficient cause.
kabine قابينه F 1. cabinet, administration. 2. small room, consulting room (of a doctor), office. 3. toilet. **— âzası** member of the cabinet. **— buhranı** ministerial crisis. **— reisi** Prime Minister. **— toplantısı** cabinet meeting.
kabir[bri] **1** قبر [*kabr*] grave, tomb. **— azabı çek=** to be in an agony; to be in great difficulties. **— suali** endless questioning.
kâbir 2 (—.) كابر A *lrnd.* great, old; ancestor; an elder.
kâbiren (—'..) كابراً A *lrnd.* from an ancestor. **— an kâbir** from ancestor to ancestor.
kabl- قبل A *lrnd.* before, *as in* **kablelmilâd**.
kablelmantık[ğı] قبل المنطق A *lrnd., phil.* prelogical.

kablelmilâd (..——) قبل الميلاد A *lrnd.* before Christ (B.C.).
kablelvukuᵘᵘ (...—) قبل الوقوع A *lrnd.* before the event.
kablelvürud (...—) قبل الورود A *lrnd.* before the arrival.
kablen (.'.) قبلاً *lrnd.* anteriorly, before.
kableşşüru (...—) قبل الشروع A *lrnd.* before beginning.
kablettaam (...—) قبل الطعام A *lrnd.* before dinner.
kablettarih (..——) قبل التاريخ A *lrnd.* prehistory —**î** (..———) A prehistoric.
kablettecrübe قبل التجربه A *lrnd.* preempirical.
kablettufan (..——) قبل الطوفان A *lrnd.* antediluvian.
kablezzevalˡⁱ (...—) قبل الزوال A *lrnd.* before noon.
kablezzuhr قبل الظهر A *lrnd.* before noon.
kablî (.—) قبلی A *phil.* a priori.
kablo (.'.) قابلو F cable. — **çek=**, — **döşe=** to lay a cable. — **gemisi** cable ship. — **işareti** cable sign.
kabotaj قابوتاژ F *naut.* cabotage, coasting trade; coast navigation. — **gemisi** coasting vessel. — **hakkı** right of coast trading. — **yap=** to coast.
kabr قبر A *lrnd.*, same as **kabir 1**.
kabran 1 قابران *prov.* 1. measure of capacity (for cereals). 2. manger; basket; beehive. 3. hollow trunk of a tree.
kabran 2 قابران *prov.* without energy, slow, lazy. —**lık** lack of energy.
kabrî (.—) قبری A *lrnd.* sepulchral.
kabristan قبرستان P cemetery, graveyard.
kabucakᵏⁱ قابوجاغه little cover, little shell.
kabukᵍᵘ قابوغه 1. outer covering of anything; bark, rind; peel, skin (of fruit). 2. shell; crust; scab (of a wound). — **bağla=** to form a crust or scab; to heal over. —**una çekil=** to creep into one's own skin. — **kabuk ol=** to be broken up (earth, skin). — **kopar=** *colloq.* to give rise to bad consequences. —**unu soy=** to peel, to strip, to skin.
kabuklan=ⁱʳ قابوقلانمق to grow bark, to form rind; to form a skin.
kabuklu قابوقلی 1. having a shell, skin, bark, etc. 2. *slang* uncircumcised. —**lar** *zool., Crustacea*.
kabuksal *neol., anat.* cortical.
kabuksuz قابوقسز 1. without bark; rindless; shelled. 2. *slang* circumcised. — **yumurtlat=** /ı/ to hurry somebody and cause him to do a thing incompletely.
kabulˡᵘ (.—) قبول A 1. acceptance, admission, reception, assent, agreement. 2. All right, I accept it. I agree. —**ümdür** I accept; •I agree. —**i âmme** P *lrnd.* universal consent. — **eden** *com.* acceptor. — **edil=** to be

accepted, to be admitted. — **edilir**˙ *com.* acceptable, admissible. — **et=** /ı/ to accept, to agree (to); to assent, to approve, to admit; to receive. — **ettir=** /ı, a/ to procure acceptance. — **günü** reception day; visitor's day. — **halinde** *com.* on receipt. — **havzası** *geog.* catchment basin. — **kredisi** *com.* blank credit. —**ü mümkün** acceptable. — **odası** reception room, parlor. — **olunamaz** unacceptable; inadmissible. — **salonu** reception-room. — **ve tasdik et=** /ı/ to approve, to ratify. —**i zimmet** *Ott. hist.* an accepting the status of a non-Muslim subject.
kabulgâh (.——) قبول گاه P *lrnd.* reception place, reception room.
kabullen=ⁱʳ قبوللنمك /ı/ 1. to accept. 2. to seize (for oneself), to appropriate. —**me** appropriation.
kaburga (.'.) قابورغه قابرغه 1. rib; ribs. 2. *naut.* frame timber. —**lar arası** *anat.* intercostal. —**ları çık=** to be skinny; to be nothing but skin and bone. — **dolması** stuffed breast of lamb. — **kaldıran kas** *anat.* scalene muscle. — **kebabı** roast ribs (of mutton). — **kemiği** rib bone, costal bone. —**ları sayılıyor** You can count every rib in his body; you can see his ribs.
kâbus (——) كابوس A nightmare, incubus. — **bas=**, — **çök=** /a/ to have a nightmare. —**lu** nightmarish; dreadful.
Kabuşan (.——) قبوشان 1. *hist.* town in the north of Khorasan (Eastern Persia). 2. *l. c.* cabochon. K— **zümrüdü** uncut emerald from Qabushan.
kabz قبض A *lrnd.* 1. a grasping, a seizing, a taking into possession. 2. a bending a joint; flection. — **ü bast** closure and distension. — **et=***.
kabza قبضه A 1. handle, butt (of sword, knife, rifle, bow). 2. piece, a single one (sword). 3. *slang* a handful of hashish. 4. *obs.* length or thickness of four fingers. 5. *lrnd.* grasp of the hand, possession. — **emniyet mandalı** safety catch (of a gun). — **siperi** hilt guard. —**yi tasarrufa al=** /ı/ to take possession (of). —**i tığ** 1. handle of a sword. 2. a handful. 3. paw.
kabzet=ᵈᵉʳ قبضتمك *lrnd.* /ı/ to grasp, to seize, to take into (one's possession).
kabzımal قبضه مال 1. middleman in fruit, vegetables, fish. 2. *obs.* income collector.
kabzolun=ᵘʳ قبض اولنمق *lrnd.* to be grasped, seized, taken into possession.
kâc (—) كاج P *lrnd.* fir tree, larch.
Kacar 1 (.——) قاجار Kajar (name of a tribe and dynasty in Iran).
kacar 2, kacer قاجار - قاجر *prov.* thin and weak.

kaç 1 قاچ How many? How much? **—a** What is the price? How much (is it)? **—a kaçsınız?** What's the score? How does the game stand? **—ın kur'ası** an old hand smart, experienced. **— kuruşluk (adam, şey) ki?** *colloq.* He (it) is of no value. **—a mal oldu?** How much did it cost? **— para eder?** What's it worth? What's the use? **— paralık (adam, şey) ki?** *colloq.*, same as **kaç kuruşluk (adam, şey) ki? — parça olayım?** *colloq.* I can't cope with everything. **— tane?** How many? **— tarihinde?** At what date? When? **— yaşında?** How old (is he)?

kaç=ᵃʳ **2** قاچمق 1. /dan/ to flee, run away, (from); to escape; to desert; to veil herself before men, as in **erkekten kaçıyor.** 2. to go away inadvertently; to run swiftly; *colloq.* to go (away), to leave. 3. /a/ to slip into, to get into, to penetrate (water, dust, insect, etc. into the eye, ear, room); to have a tint (of red, etc.); to slip, slide down (letter). 4. to seem (rude, inopportune, etc.); to eventuate, to turn out (well, badly). 5. to run (stocking). 6. to leak out. **—anın anası ağlamamış** *proverb* Safety is in being cautious. **— göç*. —maktan kovalamağa vakit olma=** to have no time for primarily important work because of secondary tasks.

kâç 3 (—) كاچ P *lrnd.* varnish (for earthen vessels).

kaçaburukᵍᵘ قاچابوروه It *prov.* bradawl, shoemaker's awl.

kaçağan قاچاغان *archaic* much given to running or to running away.

kaçakᵍⁱ قاچاق 1. fugitive, deserter, runaway. 2. contraband, smuggled; illicit. 3. leakage. **— av** poaching. **— avcı** poacher. **— avla=** to poach. **— dinle=** to tap (radio, telephone). **— dinleyici** unlicensed (radio). **— eşya** smuggled goods. **— inşaat** unlicensed construction. **— kesim** unlicensed killing (of cattle). **— mal** smuggled goods, contraband goods. **— yap=** to leak (fluid, gas).

kaçakçı قاچاقچى smuggler. **— gemisi** smuggler's ship. **—lık** smuggling; illegal trafficking. **—lık et=** to smuggle, to traffic in contraband goods.

kaçaklıkᵍⁱ قاچاقلق desertion.

kaçamakᵍⁱ قاچامق قاچاماق 1. subterfuge; pretext, evasion. 2. escape, opportunity. 3. *obs.* shelter, refuge. 4. *fort.* postern. 5. quickly made pudding of corn flour. **— göster=, — ver=** *archaic, mil.* to feign flight. **— yap=** to try to avoid, to escape. **— yol** excuse or subterfuge for getting out of doing something.

kaçamaklı قاچاملى *evasive, elusive, vague, noncommittal, nebulous. **— cevap** elusive or vague reply, evasion. **— bir surette** evasively, elusively.

kaçan قاجان قان قى *prov.* when, at what time?

kaçar قاجار - how many each?, how much each? **—a?** How much does each cost? How much apiece?

kaçarlan=ᵣ قرلنس *archaic* to pretend to run away.

kaçarula (..´.) قاچارولا It casserole.

kaçgöç قاچ گوچ the practice of women covering their faces in the presence of men.

kaçıkᵍⁱ قاچمق قاچيق 1. crazy, mad; eccentric, abnormal. 2. a run (in a stocking). 3. warped, crooked. **—ça** (..´.) crazily, madly. **—ça** (...´) somewhat crazy or eccentric. **—lık** 1. craziness. 2. crookedness.

kaçıl=ᵣ قاچيلمق *colloq.* to get out of the way.

kaçın=ᵣ قاچينمق /dan/ to abstain (from), to be reluctant; to avoid, to keep away (from).

kaçıncı قاچنجى after how many? (in a series.) **— defa** after how many times?

kaçıngan قاچنغان *prov.* shy, unsociable.

kaçınıl=ᵣ قاچينلمق /dan/ *pass.* of **kaçın=**. **—ması mümkün olmıyan, —maz** inevitable, unavoidable.

kaçınsa=ʳ *neol.* /dan/ to seek a pretext or excuse for avoiding.

kaçır=ᵣ قاچيرمه 1. /ı/ to make or let escape; to let slip, to drive away; to leak (steam, electricity). 2. /ı/ to miss (train, chance), to lose (opportunity). 3. /ı/ to smuggle (goods, currency); to hide (possessions, etc. from a tax-gatherer). 4. /ı/ to kidnap; to abduct; to elope (with). 5. to go off one's head, to go mad. **—ıl=** *pass.*

kaçırma قاچيرمه *law* abduction; kidnapping. **—cı** *obs.* smuggler.

kaçış 1 قاچيش *verbal n. of* **kaç= 2**.

kaçış=ʳ **2** قاچيشمق to flee in confusion; to disperse.

kaçkın قاچقين 1. deserter, fugitive. 2. crazy. **—cı** *archaic, same as* **kaçkın 1**.

kaçlı قاچلى Having how many? Of what number? Of what value (cards)? Of which year? What is his year of birth? **—sınız?** What is your year of birth? To which class do you belong for the military call up?

kaçlıkᵍⁱ قاچلى Worth how many liras? At what price? Enough for how many? How old?

kaçma قاچمه *verbal n. of* **kaç= 2** ; *law* desertion; flight.

kadᵈᵈⁱ قد A *poet.* stature, figure, form. **—i bâlâ** *poet.* tall figure. **— çek=** *lrnd.* to grow in stature. **— ü kamet** *poet.* stature and figure.

kada 1 قادا *prov.* brother; sister.

kada=ʳ **2** قادامو *prov.* /ı/ 1. to nail. 2. to sew coarsely, to tack.

kadakᵍⁱ قاداو *prov.* 1. nail. 2. hook-and-eye. 3. a coarse sewing, a tacking.

kadan=ᵉʳ قالانمق *prov.* 1. to be stuck (in); to be nailed. 2. to be exhausted, to get very tired.

kadana 1 (..′.) قطنه Hung 1. artillery horse. 2. *slang* huge woman.

kadana 2 قالانه It *obs.* fetters (of a prisoner).

kadar قدر قالار [**kadr**] 1. as much as, as many as, as ... as, up to, *e. g.*, **bu kadar** this much; **onun kadar bilgili** as learned as he; **bildiğim kadar** as far as I know; **beşe kadar** up to five; **yetişecek kadar** enough to do it. 2. about, approximately, *e. g.*, **bin kadar** about a thousand. 3. /a/ till, up to, until, *e. g.*, **bugüne kadar** till today; **gelinceye kadar** until he comes; **köprüye kadar** up to the bridge.

kadastro (..′.) قاداسترو It cadastre; land registry. — **çalışmaları** surveying. **—sunu çıkar=** /ın/ to establish the cadastral plan (of a piece of ground). — **dairesi** land-register office. — **haritası** cadastral map. — **krokisi** cadastral sketch. — **memuru** 1. land surveyor and valuer. 2. official in a land-registry office. — **planı** cadastral plan.

kadastrola=ʳ قاداسترولامق /ı/ 1. to survey and value (a piece of ground). 2. to register (property) in the cadastre.

kadavra (..′.) قاداورا It corpse; carcass.

kadayıf قدايف [**kataif**] any of various kinds of sweet pastry; materials of which such pastries are made. **—cı** maker or seller of **kadayıf.**

kaddah (.—) قدّاح A *lrnd.* 1. maker of cups. 2. *same as* **kaddahe.**

kaddahe (.—.) قدّاحه A *lrnd.* flint for striking fire.

kaddam (.—) قدّام A *lrnd.* king, prince; leader.

kaddaver (.—.) قدّاور P *poet.* tall.

kaddes Allahu sırrahu (.′..—.′...), **kaddese sırrahu** قدّس الله سرّه A *Isl. rel.* may God sanctify him (said of a Muslim saint).

kaddus (.—) قدّوس A *Isl. rel.* most holy, all-holy (God).

ka'de قعده A *Isl. rel.* sitting posture in the performance of the **namaz.** **—i ahîre** the last sitting posture in the performance of the **namaz.**

kadeh قدح A 1. drinking glass, tumbler, goblet; wine glass. 2. *bot.* calyx. — **arkadaşı** drinking companion. — **dolusu** glassful, cupful. — **kaldır=** to propose a toast. **—i lâciverdî** the sky. — **tokuştur=** to hobnob, to clink glasses.

kadehçe قدحچه P 1. *lrnd.* small drinking glass. 2. *bot.* calyx.

kadehçikᵍⁱ قدحجك *bot.* cupule.

kadehkâr (..—) قدح كار P *poet.* cup-bearer.

kadem قدم A 1. foot (measure); length of about 15 inches. 2. good luck. 3. *lrnd.* human foot; step. — **bas=** /a/ 1. to set foot (in), enter. 2. *archaic* to take up resolutely. — **getir=** /a/ to bring good luck (to). — **kadem** *lrnd.* step by step. **—i mübarek, —i şerif** footmark of the Prophet Muhammad on a stone. — **ur=** /a/ *archaic* to set about (doing), to undertake. **—i yara=** /a/ to bring good luck (to).

kadembusî (..——) قدم بوسى P *Ott. hist.* a kissing of the foot.

kademe قدمه A 1. degree. 2. *mil.* echelon. 3. *arch.* tier, gradin; *lrnd.* step, stair; rung of a ladder. — **birliği** *mil.* unit in an echelon. — **kademe** in steps, *mil.* in echelons. — **nizamı** *mil.* echelon. **—i ûlâda** *lrnd.* first and foremost.

kademele=ʳ قدمله‌مك /ı/ *mil.* to draw up (troops) in echelon or in depth, to echelon.

kademeli قدمه‌لى 1. *mil.* by or in echelons. 2. *arch.* stepped. — **nişangâh** *mil.* graduated sight.

kademhane (..—.) قدمخانه P *archaic* privy, latrine.

kademî (..—) قدمى A *lrnd.* pertaining to the foot.

kademiye قدميه A *lrnd.* fee for a doctor's home call.

kademkeş قدمكش P *lrnd.* one who gives up going somewhere.

kademli قدملى lucky, auspicious. — **gel=** to come auspiciously, to bring good tidings.

kademnih قدم نه P *lrnd.* one who puts his foot down (on).

kademnihade (...—.) قدم نهاده P *lrnd.* one who has just come.

kademran (..—) قدم ران P *lrnd.* one who walks, goes on.

kademsiz قدمسز unlucky, inauspicious, bringing bad luck, ill omened. **—lik** inauspiciousness, ill omen.

kader قدر A destiny, fate, eternal preordinance; *phil.* fatality. — **böyle imiş** That was preordained (by God). Too bad! **—i ilâhî** divine providence. **—ine küs=** to curse one's bad luck. **—de varmış** It was fated thus. Bad luck! **—cilik** *phil.* fatalism.

kaderî (..—) قدرى A 1. *lrnd., phil.* pertaining to destiny, providential, destined. 2. *Isl. rel.* believer in free will. **—ye** (..—.) A 1. *lrnd., phil.* fatalism. 2. *Isl. rel.* school which holds the doctrine of free will. **—yun** (..——) A 1. *phil.* the fatalists. 2. *Isl. rel.* followers of the doctrine of free will.

kaderle=ʳ قدرله‌مك /ı/ *archaic* to predestine.

kadh قدح A *lrnd.* vituperation; slander, reproach. — **et=** /ı/ to vituperate.

kadı 1 قاضى [**kazi**] Cadi (judge of Islamic canon law, and, in Ottoman history, governor of a kaza). — **asker** same as **kazasker**. — **bitisi** archaic judicial decree. —**lar helvası** manna. — **külâhı** judge's mitre. — **otu** archaic chicoria. — **sicili** Ott. hist. records of a Cadi's office (local magistrate and judge). — **yoran** obstinate, stubborn.

kadı 2 قادە Gk prov. cask; a liquid or dry measure

Kadıköy قاضیکوی name of a section of Istanbul, the ancient Chalcedon. — **taşı** geol. chalcedony.

kadılaş= قاضیلشمر archaic to go to the judge, to go to court (with someone).

kadılık قاضیلق quality, rank, functions or district of a Cadi.

kadın قادین 1. woman, matron; lady; feminine, female. 2. title for women, as in **Ayşe kadın**. — **ağızlı** gossiper like a woman, gossip. — **ana** prov. mother-in-law. — **aşçı** woman cook, cook-maid. — **avcısı** womanizer, ladykiller, wolf. — **budu** meat-ball with eggs and rice. — **çamaşırı** lingerie. — **doktoru** gynecologist. — **düşkünü** man who runs after every girl, woman chaser. — **düşmanı** woman-hater, misogynist. **K— Efendi** Ott. hist. wife of the Sultan. —**ın fendi erkeği yendi** A woman is more cunning than a màn. — **göbeği** 1. sweet dish made with flour and eggs. 2. prov. kind of mushroom. — **gömleği** slip. —**lar hamamı** women's bathhouse; colloq. noisy place. — **hastalıkları** women's diseases. — **kadıncık** quiet, domestic-minded woman; decent woman. — **kısmı** womankind, women. — **milleti** colloq. women, the ladies. — **nine** grandma, grandmother. — **parmağı** 'ladies fingers', a kind of grapes. —**lar saltanatı** petticoat-government. — **terzihanesi** dressmaker's shop. — **terzisi** dressmaker. — **ticareti** white slave trade. — **tuzluğu** barberry, bot., Berberis vulgaris. — **tüccarı** pimp. —**ca** womanly, womanlike, feminine. —**cağız** poor woman; poor thing. —**cık** 1. poor woman. 2. prov. husband's sister. —**cıl** womanizer. —**lı erkekli toplantı** mixed company.

kadınlık قادینلق womanhood; ladyship. — **âlemi** female world, the women. — **gururu** womanly pride, feminine dignity.

kadınsı قادینسی womanish, womanlike, effeminate.

kadırga قدرغه Gk 1. galley. 2. same as **kadırga balığı**. — **balığı** sperm whale, cachalot, zool., Physeter or Catodon.

kadız قادوس Gk prov. large barrel or cask.

kadib (.—) قضیب A lrnd. 1. twig, rod. 2. penis.

kadid (.—) قدید A same as **kadit**.

kadife قطیفه [katife] velvet. — **çiçeği** 1. white coxcomb, tumbleweed, bot., Amaranthus albus. 2. amaranth, Joseph's coat, bot., Amaranthus tricolor. 3. lion's paw, cudweed,

bot., Gnaphalium leontopodium. — **gibi** velvety. — **kalpak** velvet cap (formerly worn by sappers and miners, and junior students of the academy of military engineers). — **otu** velvet grass, soft meadow grass, bot., Notholcus lanatus. —**ci** velvet maker; velvet seller. —**cilik** velvet industry; trade in velvet. —**li** trimmed or lined with velvet.

kadih (—.) قادع A lrnd. who reproaches or blames.

kadilasker (—...) قاضی العسكر A lrnd., same as **kazasker**.

kadilhacat (—.——) قاضی الحاجات A lrnd. God, the judge of the needs (of mankind).

kadilkuzat (—..—) قاضی القضاة A lrnd. judge of judges, chief judge.

kadim 1 (.—) قدیم A 1. old, ancient, olden time, bygone days, yore. 2. archaic antique. 3. lrnd. eternal, God. —**den beri** since days of yore.

kadim 2 (—.) قادم A lrnd. that arrives, advances; newcomer. — **ol=** to go, to come, to advance, to arrive (at a place).

kadime (—..) قادمه A lrnd. 1. van of an army. 2. the longest front pinions of a bird's wing.

kadimen (.—'.) قدیماً A lrnd. in olden times, anciently; from the beginning of time.

kadimî (.——) قدیمی A P lrnd. very ancient, from time immemorial.

kadimiye (—.—.) قادمیة A lrnd. yew family, bot., Taxaceae.

kadinne قادنه [kadın nine] grandmother, old woman.

kadir 1 قدر [kadr] 1. worth, value, rank; dignity. 2. the 27th night of Ramazan. 3. obs. power. 4. astr. magnitude. —**ini bil=** /ın/ to appreciate, to value. **K— Gecesi** Night of Power (the 27th of Ramazan, when the Quran was revealed). **K— Gecesi doğmuş** very lucky; born lucky.

kadir 2 (—.) قادر A 1. mighty, powerful, strong. 2. /a/ capable (of). 3. w. cap. Almighty (God), All-Powerful (God). **K—i Mutlak** lrnd. the Almighty. — **ol=** /a/ to be able (to), to have the power (of), to be capable (of).

kadir 3 (.—) قدیر A lrnd. Almighty, All-Powerful (God).

kadirbahş قدربخش [Persian qadrbakhş] lrnd. who gives dignity and value.

kadirbilir قدربیلیر who appreciates, who values.

kadirdan (..—) قدردان [Persian qadrdan] lrnd. who appreciates, who values. —**î** (..——) P appreciation.

Kadirî (—.—) قادری A Isl. rel. dervish of the **Kadiriye** order.

Kadiriye (—.—.) قادریّه A *Isl. rel.* dervish order established by Abdülkadir Geylânî.

kadirnaşinas (. .—. —) قدرناشناس P *lrnd.* who does not appreciate; ungrateful.

kadirşinas (...—) قدرشناس P *lrnd.* who appreciates, who values. —î (...——)P, —lık appreciation.

kâdis (—.) کادس A *lrnd.* evil, inauspicious.

kadit[di] (.—) قدید [**kadid**] 1. skin and bone, a mere skeleton. 2. *lrnd.* jerked meat in strips. —i çık= to be all skin and bones.

kâdiye (—..) کادیه A *lrnd.* hardship, trouble.

kadr قدر A *lrnd.*, same as **kadir** 1. — ü kıymet worth and value. —i kifaye 1. sufficient quantity. 2. sufficiently, enough.

kadran 1 قادران F face, dial (of clock, barometer, etc.). — dişlisi quadrant gear. —lı nişangâh *mil.* dial sight.

kadran 2 قادران *var. of* **kardan 1.**

kadraşina (.—.—) قدرآشنا P *lrnd.* appreciative.

kadril قدریل F quadrille. — oyna= to dance a quadrille.

kadripleji قادریپلژی F *path.* quadriplegia.

kadro (.'.) قادرو It 1. list of government officials; staff, roll; *mil.* establishment, cadre, skeleton staff. 2. framework; frame (of a bicycle). —ya dahil on the permanent staff. —ya dahil birlik *mil.* organic unit. —ya dahil olmıyan birlik *mil.* nonorganic unit. — dışı not on the permanent staff. —ya gir= to be taken on to the permanent staff. — halinde birlik *mil.* cadre unit. — halindeki teşkilât *mil.* lower establishment. — harici same as kadro dışı. — harici subay *mil.* non-regimental officer. — manevrası *mil.* cadre menoeuvre.

kadron قادرون squared timber.

kaf 1 (—) قاف A *Arabic script, name of the letter* ق (This letter is the 21st letter of the Arabic, the 24th letter of the Ottoman alphabet, in Turkish pronounced as **k**. In chronograms, it has the numerical value of 100. It is the abbreviaton for Quran).

Kaf 2 (—) قاف A 1. mythical mountain, thought to surround the world, and to bind the horizon on all sides; dreary, lonely and inaccessible place. 2. *obs.* Caucasus. — dağı same as **Kaf 2**. — dağının arkasında in a lonely and inaccessible place. — dağına kadar to the ends of the earth. —tan Kaf'a from one end of the world to the other.

kâf 3 (—) کاف A *lrnd.*, same as **kef 1**. —i Acemi the Persian ك or گ, pronounced as g. —i Arabî the Arabic ك, pronounced as k. —i Farisî same as **kâf-i Acemî**. K—i levlâke the Prophet Muhammad (*lit.* the letter **k**, *i. e.*, 'thee', in the Quranic phrase **levlâke** "If it had not been for thee.") — ü nun the Arabic word كن **kun** "be thou", with which God creates; two suras of the Quran so called. —i tâzî same as **kâf-i Arabî**.

kafa 1 قفا [**kafa 2**] 1. head, skull; mind, intelligence; mentality. 2. *child's toy* large marble. —sı alma= /ı/ not to be able to understand, not to be able to take it in. —dan at= to talk without having any knowledge. —sı boş empty-headed, stupid. — boşluğu *anat.*, *cavum cranii*. —yı bul= to become drunk to one's heart's content. —sı bulan= to have a confused mind. —sı çalışmaz stupid. — çanağı *archaic* skull, cranium. —yı çek= to drink heavily, to get drunk. —sından çıkar= /ı/ to put (an idea) out of one's head, to give up, to banish (something) from his thoughts. —sına dank de=, —sına dank et= to dawn on one; to learn one's lesson. — dengi a man of one's own sort, a kindred spirit. —sının dikine git= to have a head or mind of his own, to be stubborn or self-willed, to insist on having one's own way. —sı dinç ol= to be at ease, to have no worries. —sı dön= to get very angry. —sı dumanlı tipsy. —sı dur= to be too tired to think. —sı gaileli ol= to have things enough to think about, to be worried. —dan gayri müsellâh ol= to be over-enthusiastic. —sına girme= 1. not to be understood. 2. to be dim. — göz çıkar=, — göz kır=, — göz yar= 1. to quarrel. 2. to ruin something. 3. to be very tactless. — ile vur= /a/ *sports* to head. — işçisi mental worker. —sı işle= to be intelligent, to have a quick mind. — kafaya ver= to put their heads together. — kafaya vur= to butt. — kâğıdı *colloq.* identity card. —sı kalın thick-headed, stupid. —sı karış= to become muddle-headed, to get all muddled. —sını kaşıyama= to be very busy, not to have time to turn round. —sı kazana dön=, —sı kazan ol= to have a buzzing in the head (because of noise). — kemiği skull. —m kesilecek değil ya! They won't bite my head off. I am not frightened. —sı kız= to get angry suddenly. —sını kızdır= /ın/ to make a person's blood boil. — koçanı *prov.* identity card. —sına koy= /ı/ to put into one's head; to get hold of some idea; to decide to do something. — patlat= to do a lot of hard mental work. — salla= to approve everything, to be a 'yes-man'. — sathı *fort.* berm of an earthwork. —sına söz girmez 1. He is just plain stupid. 2. He is obstinate. —sı şiş= to feel dizzy with boredom. — şişir= to bore, to tire out (with much talk and noise). —sına takılıp kal= to have a fixed idea.

— tası skull, cranium. —sı taşa çarp= to suffer for one's mistake. —sını taştan taşa çarp= to repent bitterly. — tut= /a/ to be defiant, to oppose obstinately, to talk back arrogantly. —sında tut= /ı/ to bear in mind, to keep in mind. —yı tütsüle= *colloq.*, same as —yı çek=; *slang* to flatten someone out with constant talk; to bore someone stiff. —sına vur= to go to one's head (wine, etc.); to affect one's head. —sını vur= /ın/ to strike one's head off, to behead. —sına vura vura by force. — vuruşu *sports* heading (football). — yağı *slang* sperm, semen. —sı yerinde ol= to keep one's head. —sı yerinde olma= to lose one's head. —yı yere vur= to take to one's bed, to be laid low, to be laid up in bed. —dan yetiş= /a/ *obs.* to catch up from behind, to overtake. — yor= to ponder, to think hard. — yorucu mentally tiring. —yı yükselt= *slang* to get tipsy. —dan bacaklılar *neol., zool.*, Cephalopoda.

kafa 2 (. —) قفا A *lrnd.* 1. *anat.* back of the head, occiput, nape. 2. a man's back, the space immediately behind him. —sından ayrılma= /ın/ *obs.* to follow someone wherever he goes.

kafadar قفادار [*Persian* . — —] intimate friend; like-minded. —lık intimate friendship.

kafagâh (. — —) قفاگاه P *lrnd.* back part, rear.

kafalı قفالى having a head on one's shoulders; intelligent, having brains; headed.

kafasız قفاسز unintelligent, stupid; headless.

kafes قفس A, 1. cage; coop, pen. 2. lattice, latticework; wooden latticework over windows, in old style Muslim houses. 3. *arch.* cage framework (of a building); skeleton (of a ship, building). 4. *slang* prison, jail. 5. *slang* double-cross, bunco (in gambling). 6. *obs.* meeting place for women behind a latticed screen (in a mosque). 7. *Ott. hist.* apartment in which a prince was brought up in seclusion. —e al= /ı/ *slang* to annoy with a lot of talk. — arkasında otur= to live in isolation. — çit trellis-work fence. — et= /ı/ *obs.* to strip a wooden house for repairs. — gibi 1. a mere skeleton. 2. loosely woven. —e gir= to be duped. — kafes full of holes. —e koy= /ı/ to deceive, to make a dupe (of), to take, let in. — küre *astr.* armillary sphere. — oyma *arch.* reticulated engraving. — sandık openwork crate. — tamiri extensive repairs to a building.

kafesçi قفسجى 1. maker or seller of cages, latticework. 2. *slang* deceiver.

kafesî (. —) قفسى A *lrnd.* 1. lattice-shaped, reticulated. 2. *obs.* turban with numerous narrow folds. — destar same as kafesî².

kafesle=ʳ تفسلك /ı/ 1. to lattice, to enclose with a lattice. 2. *slang* to deceive, to cheat. —me latticed, reticulated.

kafesli قفسلى latticed.

kafevi (. . —) قفوى A *lrnd., anat.* occipital.

kaffalˡⁱ (. —) قفّال A *lrnd.* locksmith.

kaffas (. —) قفّاص A *lrnd.* maker or seller of cages.

kâffe (—.) كافّه A *lrnd.* the whole, all, every one. —si the whole of, all of.

kâffeten (—ʹ. .) كافّةً A *lrnd.* wholly, entirely.

kâfi (— —) كافى A 1. sufficient, enough. 2. *lrnd.* the All-Sufficing, God. — derecede sufficiently. — gel= to be sufficient, to be enough, to suffice. — miktarda in sufficient quantity. — ve vâfi *lrnd.* ample, sufficient, enough.

kâfilˡⁱ **1** (—.) كافل A *lrnd.* 1. sponsor, guarantor. 2. who undertakes to feed another. — ol= /ı/ to assure, to cover.

kafilˡⁱ **2** (—.) قافل A *lrnd.* who returns from a journey.

kafile (—. .) قافله A caravan; convoy. — başı chief of a caravan. — halinde as a convoy; in flocks. —yi himaye eden kuvvet *mil.* escort force. — memuru *mil.* officer in charge of a convoy, convoying officer.

kafilesâlâr (—. . — —) قافله سالار P *lrnd.* leader of a caravan.

kâfir (—.) كافر A 1. infidel, unbeliever; misbeliever, heretic; non-Muslim. 2. *joc.* wretch; scamp. 3. *geog.* Kaffir. 4. *lrnd.* who denies, denier. —i nimet *lrnd.* ungrateful. K—ler Suresi the 109th sura of the Quran. —âne (—. —.) P *lrnd.* in the manner of an infidel.

Kâfiristan (—. . —) كافرستان P *lrnd.* country of the infidels; Europe.

kâfirkiş (—. —) كافركش P *lrnd.* 1. of a misbelieving mind. 2. cruel, unrelenting (a loved one).

kâfirlik كافرلك 1. unbelief, irreligion, infidelity. 2. maliciousness; cruelty. — et= to act maliciously.

kâfiye 1 (—. .) كافيه in K— Suresi name of the first sura of the Quran.

kafiye 2 (—. .) قافيه A rhyme. —i asliye *lrnd.* main rhyme. — düşür= to find a suitable rhyme. —i mûkayyede *lrnd.* rhyme which ends with two consonants, as bezm / rezm. —i mutlaka *lrnd.* pure rhyme. —i mülhaka *lrnd.* secondary rhyme. — sözlüğü rhyming dictionary.

kafiyeci قافيه جى rhymer, rhymester, versifier.

kafiyeli قافيه لى rhyming, rhymed.

kafiyeperdaz (—. . . —) قافيه پرداز P *lrnd.* composer of rhymes, versifier.

kafiyesenc (—...) تافيه‌سنجى P *lrnd.* weigher of rhymes, versifier. —î (—...—) P *lrnd.* versification.

kafiyesiz تافيه‌سز rhymeless, not rhyming.

kafiz (.—) قفيز A *lrnd.* dry measure of about 250 pounds; linear measure of about 200 feet. **—i dol=** to have lived one's term, to be on the point of death.

Kafkasya (..'.) قفقاسيا 1. *geog.* Caucasia. 2. dark variety of walnut wood. **—lı** Caucasian.

kafr قفر A *lrnd.* desert. **—ı Yahud** bitumen.

kaftan قفتان 1. outer gown or robe with long skirts and sleeves; robe of honor, caftan. 2. all-round illumination of a minaret. **— ağası** *Ott. hist.* keeper of the Imperial State Wardrobe. **— böceği** *prov.* ladybug, *zool.*, *Coccinella.* **— giy=** *Ott. hist.* to receive a robe of honor. **— giydir=**/a/ 1. *Ott. hist.* to invest with a robe of honor. 2. to decorate with lights (a minaret). **— giydirme merasimi** *Ott. hist.* investiture ceremony. **— giyenin, kılıç kuşananın** The gown is his that wears it, and the world is his that enjoys it. **— kalıbı** *obs.* empty-headed man.

kaftancı قفتانجى *Ott. hist.* keeper of the wardrobe. **— başı** *Ott. hist.* head keeper of the wardrobe.

kaftanî (.——) قفتانى A *Ott. hist.*, same as **kaftancı.**

kaftanlı قفتانلى *Ott. hist.* caftan-clad (*name given to* İçoğlans *who used to wear* kaftans).

kâfte (—.) كافته P *lrnd.* 1. cleft, riven. 2. searched, examined.

kâfur (——) كافور A 1. camphor. 2. camphor-white; anything as white as camphor. 3. nickname given in derision to a black male slave. **—i aslî** native camphor. **—i cevdane** *lrnd.* best native camphor, a very fragrant sort of camphor. **—i nunî** *lrnd.* inferior camphor obtained from the wood or the leaves of the tree by boiling. **— otu** southernwood. **— ruhu** spirits of camphor.

kâfurî (———) كافورى P *lrnd.* 1. camphoric, camphoraceous. 2. camphor tree. 3. camphor-white. **—ye** (———.) *lrnd.* southernwood, *bot.*, *Artemisia arborea.*

kâfurlu كافورلى camphored, camphorated.

kâfuru (—..) كافورى [kâfuri] 1. camphor. 2. spirits of camphor.

kâgir (—.) كاگير [kârgir] built of stone or bricks. **— bina** stone building.

kağan 1 تاغان *archaic* roaring. **— arslan** roaring lion, angry lion.

kağan 2 تاغان *archaic* monarch, king, ruler, khan. **—lık** khanate.

kağıf تاغيف *prov.* grain; grai. like earth or dung.

kağır=" 1 تاغرمن *prov.*, *var of* **kığır=**.

kağır=" 2 تاغرمن *prov.*, *var. of* **kanır=**.

kağıştı كاغشتى *archaic* rattling or clattering noise.

kâğıtᵈ¹ كاغد [kâğız] 1. paper; of paper. 2. letter, note, document. 3. playing card. 4. *slang* a lira. **— ağacı** *same as* **kâğıt dutu. — balığı** ribbon fish, *zool.* the species *Trachypterus.* **— bıçağı** paper knife, paper cutter. **— biti** paper moth. **— dağıt=** to deal cards. **—a dök=** /ı/ to put on paper, to write down. **— dutu** paper mulberry, *bot.*, *Papyrius papyrifera.* **— ezmesi** papier mâché. **— fabrikası** paper mill. **— fener** paper lantern, Chinese lantern. **— gibi ol=** to look very pale. **— hamuru** paper pulp; wood pulp. **— helva** — **helvası** kind of pastry in thin layers, pastry wafers. **— kapla=** /a/ to paper, to cover with paper. **— kavafı** *obs.* pettifogging scribe. **— kebabı** pieces of meat cooked in paper. **— kurdu** bookworm, *zool.*, *Ptirida.* **— makası** paper scissors. **— oyna=** to play cards. **— oyunu** game of cards; card-playing. **— para** paper money; note, bill. **— sepeti** wastepaper basket. **— üzerine koy=** /ı/ to put down in writing. **— ver=** to deal cards.

kâğıtçı كاغدجى stationer, paper-dealer. **— başı** *Ott. hist.* official who is in charge of the government's stationery supply. **—lık** paper trade.

kâğıthane (..—.) كاغدخانه 1. *obs.* paper mill, paper factory. 2. *w. cap.* valley of the Sweet Waters of Europe (at the tip of the Golden Horn).

kâğıtlı كاغدلى papered.

kâğıtlıkᵗ¹ كاغدلق stationery-case, writing-case.

kâğız (—.) كاغذ P *lrnd., var of* **kâğıt.**

kağnı تاغنى ox-cart with two solid wooden wheels. **— gibi git=** to go at a snail's pace.

kağşa=ʳ تاغشامن *prov.* to crack with dryness; to become old and wizened; to be on the verge of collapse.

kağşakᵗ¹ تاغشاق dry and crackling, about to collapse.

kâh 1 (—) كاه [gâh 1] at one time; sometimes; now; then. **— kâh** *lrnd.* at times, now and then. **— konuşur kâh konuşmaz** Sometimes he talks; sometimes he doesn't. **— şöyle kâh böyle** now this way then that; always changeable.

kâh 2 (—) كاه P *lrnd.* hay, straw; cut straw and chaff.

kâh 3 (—) كاخ P *lrnd.* 1. pavilion, villa. 2. sign of the Zodiac. 3. heaven, sphere. **—i düvazdeh küngüre** zodiac. **—i mâh** 1. the sign Scorpio. 2. first heaven, lunar sphere. **—i müşteri** 1. the sign Sagittarius; the sign Pisces. 2. sixth heaven, sphere of Jupiter.

-kâh 4 (—) كاه P *lrnd.* that lessens, as in **cankâh.**

kaha كا غا [kaa] *prov.* 1. fold, pen for cattle. 2. courtyard.
kaham كاغام [kavim] *prov.* relative.
kahamet (.—.) كاغامت A *lrnd.* great age, senility.
kâhban (——) كاهبان P *lrnd.* guardian of gathered crops.
kahbe قبه A *lrnd.*, same as **kahpe**. —**gân** (..—) P *pl.* harlots. —**gi** (..—) P harlotry, whoredom.
kâhbun (—.) كاهبن P *lrnd.* stubble, stubble field.
kâhgil (—.) كاهكل P *lrnd.* sun-dried brick made with chopped straw.
kâhhane (——.) كاهخانه P *lrnd.* straw bin, hayloft.
kahhar (.—) قهّار A *lrnd.* 1. overwhelming, crushing (majority). 2. irresistible (God); one of the names of God. —**âne** (.——.) P overpoweringly. —**î** (.——) A pertaining to God as the All-compeller, divine.
kahır[hrı] قهر [kahr] 1. anxiety, distress; deep sorrow. 2. *lrnd.* an overpowering, subduing, subjugation. —**ını çek**= /ın/ to have to put up with someone. —**ından öl**= to die of grief. —**ına uğra**= /ın/ to incur someone's wrath; to be a victim of someone's wrath. — **yüzünden lûtuf** good from evil.
kahırlan=[ır] قهرلنمق to be grieved, distressed.
kâhi 1 (——) كاهى P *archaic* a kind of three-cornered pastry puff.
kâhi 2 (——) كاهى *var. of* **gâhi**.
kâhil (—.) كاهل A 1. adult, mature, middle-aged. 2. *lrnd.* idle, lazy, indolent. —**i pay-i mürud** *lrnd.* one who lies all day long at the foot of a pear tree; doing nothing, lazybones.
kâhilâne (—.—.) كاهلانه P *lrnd.* slowly, lazily.
kâhilî (—.—) كاهلى P *lrnd.* languor, indolence, laziness.
kâhilkadem (—...) كاهل قدم P *lrnd.* slow-walking.
kâhilmizac (—..—) كاهل مزاج P *lrnd.* of an indolent nature; lazy.
kâhilten (—..) كاهلتن P *lrnd.* indolent, sluggish.
kâhilvücud (—..—) كاهل وجود same as **kâhilten**.
kâhin (—.) كاهن A 1. soothsayer, seer, diviner. 2. priest.
kâhinâne (—.—.) كاهنانه P as a soothsayer, like a diviner.
kâhine (—..) كاهنه A 1. woman soothsayer. 2. priestess.
kâhingân (—.—) كاهنكان P *lrnd.* Milky Way.
kâhinî (—.—) كاهنى P *lrnd.*, same as **kâhinlik**.

kâhinlik[ği] كاهنلك 1. soothsaying, prophetic gift. 2. priesthood.
kahir (—.) قاهر A 1. overpowering, crushing, overwhelming. 2. *lrnd.* the Compeller (God).
Kahire (—..) قاهره A *geog.* Cairo.
kâhiste (—..) كاهسته P *lrnd.* diminished.
kâhiş (—.) كاهش P *lrnd.* diminution.
kahit (.—) قحط A *lrnd.* very barren, lean (year); very severe, violent (blow).
kahkaha قهقهه A 1. loud laughter, a laughing out loud, chuckle. 2. same as **kahkaha çiçeği**. — **at**=, —**yı bas**= to burst into laughter, to burst out laughing. — **çiçeği** bindweed, *bot.*, *Convolvulus*. — **ile gül**= to laugh loudly. — **kopar**=, —**salıver**= to burst out laughing.
kahkara (..—) قهقرا A *lrnd.* precipitate retreat.
kahkarî (..—) قهقرى |**kahkara**| *lrnd.* devastating (defeat). — **bir hezimet** utter defeat. — **bir ric'at** shameful retreat.
kâhkeşan (—.—) كاهكشان P *lrnd.* Milky Way.
kâhkül (—.) كاهكل *var. of* **kakül**.
kahpe قبه [kahbe] 1. harlot, prostitute. 2. deceitful, perfidious. —**nin dölü** *vulg.* son of a bitch. — **düşman** perfidious enemy. — **oğlu** *vulg.* son of a bitch.
kahpelik[ği] قبه لك 1. harlotry; fornication. 2. villainy; treachery. — **et**= 1. to be a prostitute. 2. to behave villainously.
kahr قهر A *lrnd.*, same as **kahır**.
kahraman 1 قهرمان [kahraman 2] 1. hero, brave; heroic. 2. hero, heroine (of a novel, etc.).
kahraman 2 (..—) قهرمان P *lrnd.*, same as **kahraman 1**. —**âne** (..——.) P heroically.
kahramanca قهرمانجه heroic; heroically.
kahramanî (..——) قهرمانى P 1. heroism. 2. heroic.
kahramanlık[ğı] قهرمانلق heroism, heroic acts. — **destanı** epic, heroic poems, heroic deeds. — **dramı** heroic drama. — **epopesi** epic poem. — **göster**= to show heroic courage; to behave as a hero.
kahren (.'.) قهراً A *lrnd.* by irresistible force, violently.
kahret=[der] قهر ايتمك 1. /ı/ to oppress, to crush, to annihilate. 2. to feel great sorrow, to be depressed.
kahrol=[ur] قهر اولمق to be depressed; to feel greatly annoyed or distressed. —**sun!** Damn him! To hell with him!
kâhrüba (—.—) كاهربا P *lrnd.*, *var. of* **kehribar**.
kaht قحط A *lrnd.* draught; penury; famine. — **ü galâ** dearth and famine. —**i rical** dearth

of able men. **—lık** state of drought; famine. **—sal** (.—) P year of dearth, lean year. **—zede** P famine-stricken; famished.
kahvaltı قهوه آلتی 1. breakfast. 2. light refreshment. **— et=** to breakfast, to take light refreshment. **— takımı** breakfast set.
kahve قهوه A 1. coffee. 2. coffee house, coffee shop, café. **— ağacı** coffee tree, coffee shrub. **— çek=** to grind coffee. **— çekirdeği** coffee bean. **— değirmeni** coffee mill; coffee grinder. **— dolabı** cylindrical coffee roaster. **— döv=** to pound coffee. **— dövücünün hık deyicisi** one who pretends to be helping someone in his work. **— fincanı** coffee cup, demitasse. **— ibriği** coffee pot. **— kaşığı** coffee spoon. **— kavur=** to roast coffee. **— ocağı** small stove where coffee is made. **— parası** tip. **— pişir=** to prepare coffee, to make coffee. **— şerbeti** hot coffee-stock kept ready for making coffee. **— tabağı** coffee saucer. **— telvesi** coffee grounds. **— tepsisi** coffee tray.
kahveci قهوه جی keeper of a coffee shop. **— başı** *Ott. hist.* person whose job was to prepare the Sultan's coffee. **— çırağı** boy in a coffee shop. **—lik** coffee trade and service. **—lik et=** 1. to keep a coffee shop. 2. to deal in coffee.
kahvehane (. —.) قهوه خانه coffee shop, café.
kahverengi قهوه رنگی brown.
kâhya كهيا كيا [kethüda] 1. steward; majordomo. 2. warden of a trade guild. 3. caretaker in a car park. 4. an officious meddler. **— bey** *Ott. hist., same as* **kethüda bey**. **— kadın** housekeeper. **— kâtibi** *same as* **kethüda kâtibi**. **— kesil=** to take too much on oneself; to interfere in other people's affairs; to presume too much. **—sı yok** He can do as he likes.
kâhyalık^gi كهيالوغى 1. stewardship. 2. guild wardenry. **— et=** to meddle in someone's affairs.
kaır^ka'rı قعر *var. of* **ka'r** 5.
kâib (—.) كاعب A *lrnd.* 1. full, swelling (breast). 2. full-breasted.
kaid 1 (—.) قائد A *lrnd.* 1. who leads. 2. captain, commander.
kaid 2 (—.) قاعد A *lrnd.* 1. who sits. 2. chief, ruler.
kaid 3 (.—) قعيد A *lrnd.* one who sits with another; companion; guardian angel.
kaide (—..) قاعده A *lrnd.* 1. rule, regulation; custom. 2. base; pedestal; *geom.* base. **—i belde** *lrnd.* the law of the land. **—ye göre** according to rule. **—i külliye** *lrnd., phil.* aphorism.
kaiden (—'..) قاعدةً A *lrnd.* while sitting, in a sitting position.
kaidesiz (—...) قاعده سز irregular.

kaideşiken (—....) قاعده شكن P *lrnd.* rule breaker, wrongdoer.
kaideten (—'...) قاعدةً A according to rule, in principle.
kaidetülbatiye (—...—..) قاعدة الباطية A *lrnd.* the star ∝ Crateris.
kaidetülmülk^kü (—....) قاعدة الملك A *lrnd.* capital of a realm.
kaidevî (—..—) قاعدوى A *lrnd.* in accordance with the rules, regular.
kail (—.) قائل A *lrnd.* 1. consenting, agreeing. 2. speaker. **— ol=** /a/ to consent, to agree to.
kaim (—.) قائم A 1. taking the place of, in lieu of, substituting; acting for. 2. *lrnd.* standing, lasting. 3. *lrnd., geom.* perpendicular; right. 4. *lrnd.* that exists permanently, especially God the Existing One. **— bizzat** *phil.* self-existing, self-existent (God). **— ve daim** existent or acting and persistent or persevering. **— ol=** /la/ to exist thanks to..., to be dependent on. **— zaviye** right angle.
kaime (—..) قائمة A 1. banknote; bill, account. 2. *lrnd., geom.* right angle. **—i mutebere-i Osmaniye** *Ott. hist.* the first paper money issued in the Ottoman Empire by Sultan Abdulmejid in 1841.
kaimelik^gi قائملك *obs.* 1. a foolscap-sized sheet of writing paper. 2. a portfolio for banknotes.
kaimen (—'..) قائماً A *lrnd.* standing, perpendicularly. **— kıymet** standing value (of a building).
kaimmakam (—..—) قائم مقام A 1. *same as* **kaymakam**. 2. *lrnd.* lieutenant, representative, substitute.
kaimüzzaviye (—..—..) قائم الزاوية A *lrnd., geom.* right-angled (triangle).
kaimüzzevaya (—...——) قائم الزوايا A *lrnd., geom.* rectangular (parallelogram).
kâin (—.) كائن A *lrnd.* 1. situated, lying, located. 2. being, existent, that is, was, or will be. **—i mutlak** the Absolute Being, God. **— ol=** 1. to be situated. 2. to exist, to be.
kâinat (—.—) كائنات A cosmos, the universe; all creation.
kair (.—) قعير A *lrnd.* profound, deep.
kais قعس A *lrnd.* pigeon-breasted, one who has a protuberant breast.
kak=^ar 1 قاقمق /ı, a/ 1. to push, to give a push (to). 2. to drive a nail in. 3. to encrust, to inlay.
kak^kı 2 قاق *prov.* 1. dried fruit. 2. jam. 3. meal made of flour, butter and eggs.
kak^kı 3 قاق *prov.* cavity in a rock where water collects.
kâk^ki 4 كاك P *lrnd.* biscuit, dry bread. **— lokması** *obs.* kind of sweet fritter prepared in the Imperial kitchen.

kaka 1 قا قا *nursery* 1. child's excrement. 2. nasty, dirty. — **bebek** naughty baby. — **el** left hand. — **et**=, — **yap**= to defecate (child).
kaka 2 قا قا *prov.* elder brother; foster brother.
ka'kaa تعقعُ A *lrnd.* clang of arms.
kakaçᶜⁱ قا قا ۽ *prov.* 1. dried meat; salted and dried fish. 2. thin and weak, mere skin and bone. 3. dried rose petal. 4. woodpecker. 5. beak, bill.
kakala 1 قا قا لا *prov.* kind of round bread with a hollow center.
kakala=ʳ **2** قا قا لاموى /ı/ to keep giving pushes.
kakala=ʳ **3** قا قا لموى 1. to have a stool (baby). 2. /ı/ to speak ill (of), to slander. —**ş**= to become bad.
kakanos قا قا نوس *slang* ugly; quarrelsome.
kakao (..'.) قا قا ئو F 1. cacao, cocoa, *bot.*, Theobroma cacao. 2. cocoa (beverage). — **ağacı** cacao tree. — **çekirdeği** cacao seed, cacao bean. — **yağı** cacao butter.
kakavan قا قا وان *slang* old and peevish; ugly (person).
kakı=ʳ قا قى *archaic* /a/ to rail (at), to reproach; to be angry (with).
kakıçᶜⁱ **1** قا قج *prov.* reproach.
kakıçᶜⁱ **2** قا قج fisherman's gaff.
kakıl=ⁱʳ قا قل *pass.* of **kak**= 1.
kakılı قا قلى nailed, driven in.
kakım 1 قا قم [kakum] ermine, stoat. — **kürk** ermine fur.
kakım 2 قا قم push; kick.
kakım 3 قا قم *prov.* a scolding, railing.
kakın=ⁱʳ قا قنى *archaic* to become a victim to someone's anger.
kakınçᶜⁱ قا قنج anger; reproach.
kakır قا قر *archaic* dry and rustling, crackling.
kakırca قا قرجه dormouse, *zool.*, Muscardinus avellanarius.
kakırda=ʳ قا قرداموق 1. to rattle, rustle, crackle, to make a harsh sound. 2. to become dry and rattling. 3. *slang* to die (old people).
kakırdakᵍⁱ قا قرداق crackling, greaves.
kakırdat=ⁱʳ قا قردامق *caus.* of **kakırda**=.
kakış=ⁱʳ قا قشمو 1. to keep nudging. 2. *prov.* to dispute. —**tır**= /ı/ to keep pushing slightly.
kakla=ʳ قا قلاموق *prov.* /ı/ to dry (fruit).
kaklıkᵍⁱ قا قلى *prov.* drying place for fruit.
kakma قا قمه 1. work in relief, repoussé work. 2. a pushing, tapping, driving.
kakmacı قا قمجى maker of repoussé work. —**lık** repoussage, a damascening, ornamental inlaying or encrustation.
kakmalı قا قملى with a decoration in relief, inlaid, encrusted (with jewels, silver, etc.).
kakmıkᵍⁱ قا قمق *prov.* banquet given by the bridegroom to his friends on the wedding night.
kakmukᵍᵘ قا قموق *prov.* blow with the fist.
kakmukla=ʳ قا قمولامق /ı/ to hit with the fist.
kaknem قا قنم 1. *slang* very ugly (woman). 2. *prov.* dropsical; thin and weak.
kaknus قا قنس [kuknus] *lrnd.* mythical bird, phoenix.
kaksı=ʳ قا قيمق *prov.* to decay, rot, to turn rancid.
kaksıkᵍⁱ قا قيق rotten, rancid, rank (butter, etc.).
kaktır=ⁱʳ قا قدرمق *caus.* of **kak**= 1.
kâkû (— —) كاكو P *lrnd.* maternal uncle.
kakule 1 قا قوله [Arabic qaqulla] cardamom, *bot.*, Amomum cardamomum.
kakule 2 قا قوله F mule litter.
kakum (—.) قا قم P *lrnd.*, *same as* **kakım 1**.
kakumendam (—..—) قا قم اندام P *lrnd.* white-limbed, fair mistress.
kâkül (—,) كاكل P lock of hair, side lock. —**lü** having pendant locks. —**lü belâ** damned nuisance.
kal=ⁱʳ **1** قالمق 1. to remain, stay, dwell, stop, be kept; to remain behind, be left over; to hold (on). 2. to cease, leave off, drop, die away (rain, wind); to be abandoned, cancelled. 3. to fail to get a promotion, to stay back. 4. /a/ to be postponed (until). 5. /a, dan/ to fall to one's bid; to be left an inheritance (from). 6. /dan/ to be kept, detained, prevented (from). 7. *after* =**a**, =**e**, *and* =**ıp**, *etc.* to remain ...ing, to become ...ed, *e. g.*, **donakal**= to be petrified (with horror or fear), **şaşıp kal**= to be stupefied. —**a***. —**an***. —**dı ki** There remains the fact that..., and moreover; besides. —**sın** Leave it! It doesn't matter; you may keep it.
kalʰ **2** قال a smelting; a refining (of metals), cupellation. —**a dayan**= to resist smelting; to stand intense heat. — **et**=*. — **ocağı** smelting furnace; refining furnace. — **potası** cupel, refiner's crucible. — **usulü** cupellation.
kalʰ **3** (—) قال A *lrnd.* word, talk, speech. —**e al**= /ı/ to take into consideration. —**e alınmaz** insignificant, negligible. —**e alma**= /ı/ not to take into account, to leave out of account. —**e gel**= to be mentioned, discussed.
kalʰⁱ **4** قلع A *lrnd.* a pulling up by the roots, eradicating. —**i esnan** tooth extraction. — **et**=*. — **ü kam' et**= /ı/ to put down (a reprehensible thing).
kala 1 قالا [kal= 1] remaining, *in expressions as* **dörde beş kala** five minutes to four, **gelmesine on gün kala** ten days before his arrival. — **kal**= suddenly to find oneself in a difficult situation; to remain rooted to the spot. — **kala** there only remains; all that is left.
kala=ʳ **2** قالاموق *prov.* to pile up wood for fire.
kal'a 3 قلعه A *lrnd.*, *var. of* **kale 1**.

kâlâ 4 (— —) كالا P *lrnd.* 1. cloth, silk cloth. 2. things, goods; household furniture.
kalaba قالبا [**galebe**] *prov.* 1. sheep with thick wool. 2. crowd, mass, multitude.
kalabalık[1] قالبالق غلبه لك [**galebelik**] crowd, confused mass, throng; crowded, thronged, thickly peopled; overpopulated. — **bas**= /ı/ to become overcrowded. — **et**= 1. to be in the way, to be superfluous. 2. to assemble as a crowd; to crowd. —**ı kaldır**= to tidy up. — **yap**= *same as* **kalabalık et**=.
kalâçuri (. — — —) قلمچورى P *poet.* glittering sword; a kind of long sword.
kalafat قالافات قالفات قدفات قلفات قلفت Gk 1. a caulking. 2. *prov.* caulker. 3. *Ott. hist.* kind of headgear worn by high officials and officers. —**ı at**= /ın/ to fall out (caulking). —**a bastır**= /ı/ to heave down (for caulking). —**a çek**= /ı/ to draw (a ship) to careenage. — **et**= /ı/ 1. to caulk, careen, grave. 2. to repair superficially, to embellish externally only. — **keskisi** caulking iron. — **tokmağı** caulking hammer, caulking mallet. — **yap**= /ı/ *same as* **kalafat et**=. — **yeri** careening ground, caulking wharf.
kalafatçı قلمفاجى caulker. — **köpeği** *slang, abusive term.*
kalafatla= قلمفاتلمك /ı/ *same as* **kalafat et**=.
kalafatsız قلمفاتسز uncaulked. — **halat** untarred rope.
kalâid (. — .) قلائد A *lrnd.,* pl. of **kılâde.**
kalâil (. — .) قلائل A *lrnd.,* pl. of **kalil, kalile.**
kalak[1] **1** قالاق *prov.* 1. nostril (of a beast). 2. horn. 3. bridal garland; woman's ornamented headgear.
kalak[kı] **2** قلق A *lrnd.* restlessness, disquietude, anxiety; commotion.
kalakla= قلمدلمك *prov.* 1. to get excited. 2. to totter, stagger.
kalaklı قلمقلى *prov.* proud, presumptuous.
kalamar قلامار ـ قالامار Gk squid, *zool., Loligo vulgaris.*
kalamış قلمش Gk reed bed, marsh (on the sea-shore).
kalan قالان [**kal**= **1**] remaining; remainder.
kalantor قالانطور It *colloq.* fat man having a well-to-do and important appearance.
kalas قلاص beam; joist (of a ceiling); rafter (of a roof). — **köprü** girder-bridge. —**lı tavan** trabeated ceiling.
kalastra (. ′.) قالاستره It boat chock.
kalavra (. ′.) قالاوره ـ قلاوره *obs.* 1. rough leather shoe; patched shoe. 2. leather goods.
kalavrahane (. . . —.) قالاوره خانه 1. *Ott. hist.* factory for leather goods. 2. *obs.* cobbler's workshop.

kalay قلاى ـ قالاى [*Arabic* **qala**] 1. tin; tinfoil. 2. *colloq.* a scolding, rating. — **asidi** stannic acid. —**ı at**= /ı/ to give a good scolding (to). —**ı bas**= /a/ to scold. — **cevheri** tin ore. — **kapla**= /a/ to cover with tin, to tin. — **muhtevalı** stanniferous. — **oksid** stannic oxide. — **sac** tin plate. — **tuzu** salt of tin. — **ver**= /a/ to scold. — **yaprağı** tinfoil.
kalaycı قالايجى 1. tinner, tinsmith. 2. impostor, whitewasher, deceiver. —**lık** 1. profession of a tinner. 2. imposture.
kalayhane (. . —.) قالاى خانه *obs.* tinning workshop.
kalayla= قالايلمك /ı/ 1. to tin. 2. *colloq.* to scold. 3. to cover up the faults (of).
kalaylı قالايلى 1. tinned; containing tin, mixed with tin. 2. false, varnished, deceptive. — **kaptan su iç**= to marry a female relative (on the assumption that it is safer to marry a girl one knows everything about).
kalaysız قالايسز untinned.
kalb[bı] **1** قلب A 1. heart. 2. center, innermost part; core, kernel. —**den** cordially, sincerely, affectionately. — **acısı** deep sorrow. —**ini aç**= /a/ to pour out, to open one's heart (to). — **adalesi** *anat.* myocardium. — **adalesi iltihabı** *path.* myocarditis. — **ağrısı** heartache, grief. —**i at**= for one's heart to beat, to pulsate. — **atması** palpitation. — **biçiminde** heart-shaped, cordiform, *bot.* cordate (leaves). — **bilgisi** cardiology. —**i bozuk** 1. evil-minded, malignant, malicious. 2. *path.* weak-hearted, suffering from heart disease. — **bölgesi** *anat.* cardiac region. —**i bütün** noble-minded, good-hearted, honest. — **büyü**= *path.* to suffer from a dilated heart. — **büyümesi** *path.* cardiac dilatation, hypertrophy of the heart. —**ini çal**= *poet.* to steal the heart (of). —**i çarp**= for one's heart to palpitate, throb; to beat fast. — **çarpıntısı** *path.* tachycardia, palpitation. — **dış zarı** *anat.* pericardium. — **dış zarı iltihabı** *path.* pericarditis. —**ine doğ**= to have a presentiment. —**ine dokun**= /ın/ 1. to affect the heart (of). 2. to hurt the feelings (of). — **durması** *path.* apoplexy of the heart. —**inin en gizli köşesinde** in the innermost recesses of his heart. — **felci** *path.* cardiac paralysis. —**i fesat** envious, grudging. —**den gelen** cordial, sincere, heartfelt. —**i geniş** carefree, easy-going. —**ine gir**= /ın/ to win one's way to the heart (of). —**ine göre** after his own heart. — **hastası** heart patient. — **hastalığı** heart disease. — **hırıltısı** *path.* cardiac murmurs. — **iç zarı** *anat.* endocardium. — **iç zarı iltihabı** *path.* endocarditis. —**ine işle**= /ın/ to go to the heart (of), to stir the heart (of), to strike a person to the quick. — **kalbe karşıdır** Friendship is mutual. —**i**

kana= /ın/ for one's heart to bleed. **—i kanayarak** with a bleeding heart. **— kapağı** *anat.* cardiac valve. **—i karar=** /ın/ to lose one's religious belief. **— karıncığı** *anat.* ventricle. **—ini kazan=** /ın/ to win the heart (of). **—ini kır=** /ın/ to hurt someone's feelings. **—i kırık** heart-broken; hurt. **— kifayetsizliği** *path.* cardiac insufficiency. **— kireçlenmesi** *path.* calcification of the heart. **—inden kop=** to be given gladly. **— kulakçığı** *anat.* auricle. **—i mahzun** heavy hearted. **— münebbihi** heart stimulant. **— mütehassısı** heart specialist, cardiologist. **—i ol=** to have a weak heart, to suffer from heart trouble. **—i parça parça ol=** to have great pity. **—i rahat** relieved, calm. **—inden rahatsız** suffering from heart disease. **—i sağ** true and honest. **— sektesi** heart attack. **— sesleri** *med.* heart sounds. **—i sıcak** warmhearted. **—i sızla=** /a/ to be deeply afflicted (with). **— tepesi, — ucu** *anat.* apex of the heart. **—ini ver=** /a/ to give one's heart (to). **— vuruşu** palpitation of the heart. **—in yağ bağlaması** *path.* fatty degeneration of the heart. **— yetersizliği** *neol.,* same as **kalb kifayetsizliği**.

kalb[bi] 2 قلب A *lrnd.* change, transmutation, conversion, inversion, transposition; anagram. **—i ba'z** partial transposition of letters in an anagram, as in بهمال ihmal. امهال imhal. **—i kül, —i tam** total inversion of letters in an anagram, as in كلف kelef فلك felek.

kalben (.'.) قلبا A cordially, heartily, from the heart; heartfelt.

kalbet=[der] قلب ايتمك 1. /ı, a/ to change (into). 2. /ı/ to invert, reverse, transpose.

kalbgâh (.—) قلبگاه P 1. center; *mil.* center of the army. 2. *lrnd.* innermost part of the heart. **—ından vurul=** to receive a vital blow; to be struck dead.

kalbî (.—) قلبى A 1. cordial. 2. silent, silently (prayer, etc.).

kalbsiz قلب... heartless; cruel.

kalbur قلبور [gırbal] 1. rimmed sieve with coarse meshes. 2. *obs.* a grain measure. **— altı** siftings (of grain, etc.), screenings (of coal, sand, etc.). **—a çevir=** /ı/ to riddle with holes. **— çıbanı** archaic cancer (disease). **— damarlar** *bot.,* cribriform tubes. **—a dön=** to be riddled with holes. **—dan geçir=** /ı/ to sift, screen. **— gibi** riddled, full of holes. **— kemik, — kemiği** *anat.* ethmoid bone. **— makinesi** screening machine, bolting machine. **—la su taşı=** to make futile efforts. **— üstü** the best, the choicest.

kalburcu قلبورجى 1. maker or seller of sieves or screens. 2. sifter, screener.

kalburla=[r] قلبورلامق /ı/ to sift, screen.

kalbursu *neol., anat.* sieve-like, cribriform.

kalbüd (—.) كالبد P *lrnd.* body of a man; form; carcass.

kalbülakreb قلب العقرب A *lrnd.* the star α Scorpionis.

kalbülceyş قلب الجيش A *lrnd.* main body of an army.

kalbülesed قلب الاسد A *lrnd.* the star α Leonis.

kalbzen قلبزن P *lrnd.* 1. same as **kalpazan.** 2. cheat, liar, hypocrite.

kalcı 1 قالجى 1. maker or seller of shields. 2. fencer with sword and shield.

kalcı 2 قالجى smelter of ores, refiner of metals.

kalça قالچه hip. **— başı** ridge of the hipbone. **— kemiği** hipbone.

kalçak[gı] قالچاق archaic, same as **kalça.**

kalçalı قالچه لى hipped, haunched.

kalçete (..'.) قالچته It *naut.* gasket. **— halatı** gasket rope, gasket line.

kalçın قالچين قالچينلر It long felt hose, long felt boot. **— çizme** long boot. **—cı** maker or seller of long felt hose or boots.

kaldır=[ır] قالديرمق /ı/ 1. to rouse, raise, elevate, lift, remove, take away. 2. to bear, endure, tolerate, support. 3. to abolish, abrogate, annul. 4. *slang* to steal. 5. to startle.

kaldıraç[cı] *neol., mech.* crank.

kaldırak[ğı] *neol.* crane, winch.

kaldırım قالديريم 1. sidewalk, footway, causeway. 2. pavement. 3. submarine rock shelf. **— aşındır=** to loaf in the streets. **— çiçeği** *colloq.* streetwalker. **— çiğne=** to increase one's experiences by living in town; to become a man about town. **— döşe=** to lay down a pavement. **— kargası** *slang* street waif. **— kenarı** curb, edge of the pavement. **— mühendisi** *colloq.* loafer, idler. **— süpürgesi** *colloq.* sauntering woman. **— taşı** paving stone. **— üstünde sürün=** to lead a vagabond life of poverty. **— yaması** *colloq.* loose woman.

kaldırımcı قالديريمجى 1. paver. 2. *slang* swindler; pickpocket, purse-snatcher. **— çekici** paver's pick. **— tokmağı** paver's rammer, paving-beatle. **—lık** 1. profession of a paver. 2. picking pockets.

kaldırımlı قالديريملى paved.

kaldırımsı *neol., anat.* rotular. **— doku** *neol., anat.* pavement tissue, rotular tissue.

kaldırt=[ır] قالديرتمق /ı, a/ *caus.* of **kaldır=.**

kale 1 قلعه [kal'a 3] 1. fortress, castle, wall round a fortress. 2. *sports* goal post. 3. stronghold, citadel. 4. *chess* castle, rook. **— ağası** castellan. **— bedeni** main wall of a castle; battlement of a castle wall. **— beyi** lord of a castle. **— burcu** wall tower of a castle. **— dizdarı** castellan, warden of a castle. **— gibi** 1. as firm as a castle. 2. dependable, firm person. 3. one who is financially secure.

kâle

— **gözetleme kulesi** watchtower, lookout turret of a castle. — **harbi** siege operations. — **hendeği** castle moat, fosse. — **hizmeti** *Ott. hist.* service pertaining to a fortress. — **içi** 1. inner part of a castle, inner bailey, inner ward. 2. part of city located within city walls. **—yi içinden fethet=** to have someone in the opposite camp. — **kalkanı** parapet of a fortress. — **kapısı** sally port. — **kapısı trabzanı** portcullis. — **nizamı** block formation of troops. — **ol=** for troops to form or be formed into a square. — **siperi** parapet of a fortress. **K—i Sultaniye** old name of **Çanakkale**. — **topçusu** siege-artilleryman.

kâle 2 (—.) كال P *lrnd.* unripe melon or gourd.

kâle 3 (—.) كالە P *lrnd., var. of* **kâlâ 4**.

kale 4 (—.) قال A *lrnd., var. of* **kal 3**.

kâlek[ki] (—.) كالك P *lrnd., same as* **kelek**.

kalebend قلعه بند P confined in a fortress, state prisoner. — **edil=**, — **ol=** to be confined in a fortress. —**lik** confinement in a fortress.

kaleci قلعه جى *sports* goal-keeper.

kal'eken قلعه كن P *lrnd.* demolisher of castles.

kalem قلم A 1. pencil, pen; reed (for Arabic script); style (for waxed tablets); quill (-pen). 2. chisel; gouge. 3. pencil or brush for fine painting. 4. clerical office. 5. item, entry (in a register, account); sort, *e. g.*, **beş kalem erzak** five sorts of provisions. 6. slip for grafting, scion. 7. bobbin of a shuttle. 8. vaccine container. 9. shaft (of an arrow). 10. *lrnd.* God's power and act of decreeing. — **aç=** 1. to sharpen a pencil. 2. to cut a reed or quill and make it into a pen. — **ağzı** point of a pen, reed, etc. —**e al=** /ı/ to draw up, to compose; to write out. — **aşısı** graft, gardner's graft. — **at=** /a/ *prov.* to graft. — **çal=** *prov.* to write. — **çek=** /a/ to draw a stroke (through), to cancel. **—inden çıkma** /ın/ written by. — **darbesi** stroke or dash of the pen. — **efendisi** *obs.* clerk in a government office. — **ehli**, — **erbabı** penmen, literati. — **eri** 1. good penman. 2. *obs.* clerk in a goverment office. **—e gelmez** 1. indescribable. 2. nonsensical, absurd (speech). **—e getir=** /ı/ to put on paper. — **gezdir=** /üzerinde/ to retouch slightly (a manuscript). — **işi** a writing or engraving done with a pen or graver. — **işli** ornamented with a pen, graver, etc. — **kalem** striped. **—inden kan damla=** to have a brilliant style; to be a master of words. — **kaş** long, narrow eyebrow. — **kat'et=**, — **kes=** to nib a pen. — **kömürü** charcoal of high quality. — **kulak** small, pointed ear (of a horse). — **kutusu** pencase, pencil box. —**i kuvvetli** good penman. —**i mahsus** private secretariat of a Minister.

— **odası** secretary's office. — **oyma** a chiseling. — **oynat=** 1. to write. 2. /da/ to correct. 3. to spoil by altering. — **parmak** long, slim, tapering finger. — **perdaht et=** *obs.* to finish a reed pen off carefully. — **sahibi** man of letters; a good writer. — **sapı** penholder. **—e sarıl=** to take pen in hand, to take up one's pen. — **savaşı** war of (written) words. — **silecek** penwiper. — **ucu** nib. — **yont=** to sharpen a pencil. — **yürüt=** to write, draw up.

kalembek[gi] قلمبك P calambac agalloch (a kind of fragrant wood).

kalemci قلمجى seller of pencils and pens; *obs.* seller of reeds for pens.

kalemdan (..—) قلمدان P *lrnd.* pen case. —**lık** *colloq., same as* **kalemdan**.

kalemen ('..) قلماً A *lrnd.* 1. in writing, written. 2. by items, by entries.

kalemgir (..—) قلمگیر P *lrnd.* which is easy to write on (paper).

kalemî (..—) قلمى A *lrnd.* 1. pertaining to or shaped like a reed, pen, pencil, etc.; pertaining to an office. 2. seller of reeds for pens. 3. worker with pen, etc.

kalemis, kalemisk[ki] قالامسك [**galiye misk**] *obs.* galia moschata (a kind of compound perfume).

kalemiye قلمیه *obs.* office fees.

kalemkâr (..—) قلمكار P *lrnd.* 1. painter of designs on muslin, etc.; engraver on gold or silver; wall-decorator. 2. painting, engraving, ornamental handwork, painted muslin handkerchief. — **işi** artist's work done with a pen, etc.

kalemkârî (..——) قلمكارى P 1. a writing; engraving art; a painting. 2. painted or engraved by hand.

kalemkârlık[gi] قلمكارلق 1. profession or work of a decorator. 2. decorations.

kalemkeş قلمكش P *lrnd.* 1. writer, calligrapher. 2. one who cancels, canceler.

kalemleme قلملمه 1. chiseled, engraved, tooled. 2. a chiseling, engraving, tooling.

kalemli قلملى 1. having a pen. 2. striped. 3. *Ott. hist.* kind of jerid game. — **futa** large striped bath towel.

kalemlik[gi] قلملك 1. lathe tool post. 2. rack for pens and pencils. 3. *archaic* reed bed.

kalemrev قلمرو P *lrnd.* country in which the written mandates of a sovereign are current as law, empire, dominion, sovereignty.

kalemşor قلمشور P *ironic* penpusher.

kalemtıraş, kalemtraş قلمتراش [Persian ...—] 1. pencil sharpener. 2. *obs.* knife for cutting reed pens; knife for making or mending quill pens. —**çı** *obs.* maker or seller of reed pen knives.

kalemzede قلمزده P lrnd. written, committed to writing.
kalemzen قلمزن P lrnd. one who writes.
kalen (—́.) قالاً A lrnd. orally.
kalender قلندر P 1. unconventional person, bohemian. 2. wandering mendicant dervish. — **yurdu** obs. hospice for wandering dervishes. **—ane** (...—.) P, **—ce** unconventional, free and easy, bohemian.
kalenderhane (...—.) قلندرخانه P same as **kalender yurdu**.
kalenderî (...—) قلندرى P 1. mystical poem sung to the accompaniment of **saz** music. 2. lrnd. small shelter tent.
Kalenderiye (...——) قلندريّه the **Kalender** order of dervishes.
kalenderlikᵍⁱ قلندرلك unconventionality, free-and-easiness, bohemian existence. **—e vur**= /ı/ to take philosophically.
kalendermeşreb قلندرمشرب P carefree and good-natured, easygoing.
kalensöve قلنسوه A 1. obs. peaked cap. 2. bot. calyptra.
kalerya (.´.) قالريه It deck of a ship of the line.
kaleska (.´.) قالسقه It light open carriage.
kal'et=ᵈᵉʳ 1 قلع اتمك lrnd. /ı/ to pull up or out by the roots, to eradicate; to extirpate.
kalet=ᵈᵉʳ 2 قال اتمك to refine (metals); to smelt.
kaleta (.´.) قالته It var. of **galeta**.
kalevele قالوله same as **kalevle**.
kalevi (..—) قلوى A chem. alkali, alkaline. **—ler** alkalies.
kalevileş=ⁱʳ قلوىلشمك to become alkaline, alkalescent; to be alkalized. **—me** alkalescency. **—tir**= /ı/ to alkalize. **—tirme** alkalization.
kalevle, kalevre قالوله قالوره Gk prov., same as **kalavra** 1.
kalfa (.´.) قالفا خلفه [Arabic halife] 1. assistant master (in a workshop). 2. master builder; qualified workman; supervisor of workmen, overseer. 3. title for persons of inferior position, as in **Emine kalfa, Osman kalfa**. 4. obs. stewardess, senior negro maid. 5. obs. usher or monitor in a primary school. — **kadın** elderly domestic servant.
kalfalıkᵍⁱ قالفالق quality, rank and functions of a kalfa.
kalgay 1 قالغاى Ott. hist., title given to the heir to the throne of the Crimean Khans.
kalgay 2 neol. boy scout captain.
kalgı=ⁱʳ قالغيمق archaic to give a slight jump, start; to start, to prance.
kalgın قالغين prov. left on the shelf (girl); wallflower.
kalgıt=ⁱʳ قالغتمق caus. of **kalgı**=.
kalgıyan قالغيان prov. grasshopper.

kalhane (.—.) قالخانه smelting house; metal refinery.
kalıb قالب [kalib] same as **kalıp**.
kalıcı قاليجى [kal= 1] permanent, lasting
kalıçᵍⁱ قاليج prov. sickle.
kalıkᵍⁱ قالوق قاليق prov. 1. remaining, left; left on the shelf (girl), wallflower. 2. defective; incomplete. **—lık** defectiveness, incompleteness.
kalım قاليم قالم only in **ölüm kalım**. **—lı** neol. permanent, lasting. **—sız** neol. transient, transitory; fleeting, frail.
kalın 1 قالين قالى 1. thick, stout, coarse. 2. slang rich, wealthy. 3. phonetics velar. 4. archaic crowded, dense. — **bağırsak** large intestine. — **başlı**, — **beyinli**, — **kafa**, — **kafalı** thick-headed, stupid. — **kalem** 1. broad-nibbed pen. 2. large and thick writing. — **ses** 1. deep voice. 2. phonetics velar sound. — **yağ** heavy oil.
kalın 2 قالق قاليں prov. 1. present or settlement given by the bridegroom to the bride. 2. bridal trousseau.
kalın=ⁱʳ 3 قالينمق 1. to stay, to stop, to rest. 2. prov. to pass the night.
kalınır=ⁱʳ قالينير archaic to become thick, coarse.
kalınlaş=ⁱʳ قالينلشمق to become thick; to thicken. **—ma** verbal n. **—tır**= /ı/ caus. of **kalınlaş**=.
kalınlat=ⁱʳ قالينلتمق to render thick; to thicken.
kalınlıkᵍⁱ قالينلق 1. thickness; coarseness. 2. stupidity.
kalıntı قالنتى 1. remnant, remainder, leftovers. 2. trace, mark, indication. 3. prov. lagging behind the herd; straggler.
kalıpᵇⁱ قالب [kalib] A 1. that on or to which anything is formed, mold, form, block, hatter's block; last. 2. matrix, casting-mold. 3. modelled form, bar, cake, piece, e. g., **bir kalıp sabun** a cake of soap. 4. shape, form; external corporeal form, mold. 5. pattern, model. 6. trick, fraud. **—ının adamı değil** He is not the man he looks. — **al**= to mold, to make a mold of. **—ını al**= /ın/ to form a mold (of). **—ını bas**= /a, or için/ slang to guarantee, to take the entire responsibility (for). — **çakma** stamping, embossing (of silver, leather, etc.), impressing (of a pattern on clay). **—a çek**= /ı/ to give proper form or figure (to), to shape, to mold. — **çıkar**= same as **kalıp al**=. **—ını çıkar**= /ın/ same as **kalıbını al**=. **—ı değiştir**=, **—ı dinlendir**= slang to die. **—a dök**= /ı/ to pour into a mold, to cast. — **et**= to play a trick, to practice a deception. **—a geçir**= /ı/ to put upon the block or last. — **gibi seril**= to lie stretched out like a log. — **gibi uyu**= to sleep like a log. — **gibi yat**= to lie still (tiredly or lazily). — **işi** cast work.

— **kâğıdı** paper marked with parallel lines or watermarks, as if ribbed from parallel wires, laid paper. **—ı kalıbına** exactly fitting. **—tan kalıba al=** /ı/ to cast a mold from an existing plate. **—tan kalıba gir=** *colloq.* to change incessantly, to be fickle or inconstant. **— kesil=** to be petrified. **— kıyafet** external form, stature. **—a koy=** /ı/ to put on a last or tree. **— mumu** molding wax. **—a vur=** /ı/ same as **kalıba geçir=**.

kalıpçı قالبجى 1. maker or seller of molds, forms, matrices, etc. 2. *obs.* reblocker of fezzes. 3. trickster, knave.

kalıpla=ᵣ قالبلمك /ı/ 1. to make into a mold, form. 2. to clean and reblock (hat, fez). **—n=** *pass.* of **kalıpla=**. **—t=** /ı/ *caus.* of **kalıpla=**.

kalıplı قالبلى made or shaped by molds, etc.

kalıpsız قالبسز *obs.* out of shape (fez).

kalıt *neol.* inheritance.

kalıtım *neol.* 1. inheritance. 2. *biol., psychol.* heritage, genetic heritage.

kali 1 (— —) قالى P *lrnd.* carpet.

kaliⁱⁱ 2 (—.) قالع A *lrnd.* that plucks out.

kalib (—.) قالب A *lrnd.* form, mold. **—i bîcan** 1. languid, feeble person. 2. lifeless corpse.

kalibre (.´.) قاليبره F caliber.

kaliçe (— — .) قاليچه P *lrnd.* small carpet, rug.

kâlide (— — .) كاليده P *lrnd.* disordered, in confusion.

kâlih (—.) كالح A *lrnd.* sour-visaged, morose.

kalikut قاليقوت E calico.

kalil (.—) قليل A *lrnd.* little, few, small; short; rare.

kalila (.— —) قليلا A same as **kalilen**.

kalilen (.—´.) قليلا A in small quantity or number; seldom. **— kalilen** little by little, by degrees.

kalilüladed (.—...) قليل العدد A *lrnd.* few in number.

kalilülbizaa (.—..—.) قليل البضاعه A *lrnd.* 1. with a small capital. 2. without much store of learning.

kalilülhaya (.—..—) قليل الحياء A *lrnd.* shameless.

kalilülhürmet (.—...) قليل الحرمت A *lrnd.* profane, unworthy of veneration.

kalilülitibar (.—.—.—) قليل الاعتبار A *lrnd.* of small estimation, little esteemed.

kalinis قالينيس Gk dotterel plover, *zool., Eudromias morinellus.*

kalinos قالينوس Gk European perch, *zool., Perca fluviatilis.*

kalite قاليته F quality. **—si bozuk** *slang* degenerate, base, dishonest.

kaliye قليه A *lrnd.* meat stewed with vegetables. **—i suğdî** dish of meat, eggs, onions, almonds, etc.

kaliyehar (...—) قليه خوار P *lrnd.* mediator between lovers; pander.

kalk=ᵃʳ قالقمق 1. to get up, stand up, rise; to become erect. 2. to be lifted, to be taken away. 3. to start, to set out (on a journey). 4. /a/ to start (to do), to take into one's head (to do). 5. to be annulled, cancelled, removed, abandoned, abolished, to fall into disuse. 6. to become unstuck, unglued; to peel off (skin). 7. to rise in rebellion. **— borusu** *mil.* reveille. **— borusu çal=** *mil.* to sound the reveille. **— gidelim et=** /ı/ to steal, to pinch, pilfer. **— işareti** starting signal. **—ıp kalkıp otur=** to be greatly agitated, terribly upset. **—ar köprü** drawbridge, bascule bridge.

kalkala قلقله A *lrnd.* 1. a moving, disturbing, shaking, agitating. 2. a making a noise, a producing a sound.

kalkan قالقان 1. shield, buckler. 2. turbot. 3. *arch.* gable. **— balığı** turbot, *zool., Rhombus maximus.* **— bezi** *anat.* thyroid (gland). **— dikeni** blessed or holy thistle, *bot., Carduus benedictus.* **—ların havaya kaldırılması** armed rising, insurrection. **— otu** same as **kalkan dikeni.** **— tavası** fried turbot. **— yapın=** *archaic* to shield oneself.

kalkancı قالقانجى 1. maker or seller of shields. 2. fencer with sword and shield.

kalkanlı قالقانلى armed with a shield, bearing a shield. **— batarya** *mil.* shield battery.

kalker قالقر F limestone; chalky stone; calcareous. **— tüfü** travertine, calcareous tufa. **—li** calcareous.

kalkı=ᵣ قالقيمق *archaic, var. of* **kalgı=**.

kalkıkᵉⁱ قالقيق risen, raised; erect; standing on end (hair). **— burunlu** snub nosed. **— kaş** high arched eyebrow. **— kuyruk** cocktail rove-beetle, *zool., Ocypus olens.*

kalkım قالقم *prov.* precipice, crevasse, cliff.

kalkın=ᵢᵣ قالقينمق 1. to make a material recovery; to make progress, to develop. 2. to pick up (after sickness). **—dır=** *caus.*

kalkınma قالقينمه recovery; progress; development. **K— Bakanlığı** Ministry of Development. **— programı** development program.

kalkış=ᵢʳ 1 قالقيشمق to try or pretend (to do something beyond one's ability or competence).

kalkış 2 قالقيش 1. a rising, a getting up; venture. 2. departure.

kalkıt=ᵢʳ قالقيتمق /ı/ *archaic, caus.* of **kalkı=**.

kalkma قالقمه *verbal n.* of **kalk=**.

kalkopirit قالقوپيريت F *geol.* chalcopyrite, copper sulfide.

kallâb (.—) قلّاب A *lrnd.* forger of coins.

kallâş (.—) قَمّاش A lrnd., same as **kalleş**.
kallâvi قَلّاوی A 1. Ott. hist. ceremonial turban worn by ministers. 2. large coffee cup. 3. colloq. large, huge; weighty. — **sarık** same as **kallâvi**¹.
kalleş قَلّش [**kallâş**] colloq. untrustworthy, unreliable, treacherous; base fellow.
kalleşlikᵍⁱ قَلّشلك deceit, dishonesty; a dirty trick. — **et**= to behave untrustworthily, to break one's promise.
kallı قَلّى armed with a shield, bearing a shield. — **batarya** mil. shield battery.
kalma قَلمَه 1. verbal n. of **kal**= 1. 2. /dan/ that has remained, left behind; dating (from); handed down, inherited, as in **babadan kalma**. 3. neol., psych. conservation.
kalmar قَلمار var. of **kalamar**.
kalmaş قَلمَاش P prov. vain, futile, frivolous.
Kalmukᵍᵘ قَلموق Kalmuck. —**ça** Kalmuck language.
kaloma (.'.) قَلومَه It naut. slack (of a rope), a paying out (a rope). — **et**= /ı/ to pay out, to slacken, to leave loose (a rope, chain). — **ver**= /a/ same as **kaloma et**=.
kalori قَلورى F phys. calory. — **ünitesi** caloric unit, heat unit.
kalorifer قَلوريفر F central heating, radiator. — **borusu** heating pipe. — **kazanı** central heating boiler, furnace. —**ci** 1. installer of central heating. 2. stoker of the boiler for central heating. —**li** furnished with central heating. —**siz** without central heating.
kalorikᵍⁱ قَلوريك F caloric.
kalorimetre قَلوريمتره F calorimeter.
kalorimetri قَلوريمترى F calorimetry.
kaloş قَلوش F galosh.
kalpᵇⁱ 1 قَلب var. of **kalb** 1.
kalpᵇⁱ 2 قَلب A 1. false, forged; spurious, unreliable. 2. false coin. 3. good for nothing. — **adam** false fellow, unreliable man. — **akçe** false coin, forged money. — **akçe sahibine döner** proverb False money comes back. — **beşlik gibi boz**= /ı/ to bring someone to the utmost shame. — **herif** slang false fellow. — **para** false money, counterfeit coin.
kalpakᵍⁱ قَلپاق fur cap. —**çı** maker or seller of fur caps. —**lı** 1. wearing a fur cap. 2. archaic policeman. —**lık** fur (for making fur caps).
kalpazan قَلپازان [**kalbzen**] 1. maker of false coins, counterfeiter. 2. liar, cheat; hypocrite. —**lık** 1. counterfeiting. 2. cheating, trickery; deceit.
kalplıkᵍⁱ قَلبلك 1. falseness, baseness (of a coin), spuriousness. 2. a being good for nothing.
kalseduan قَلسدوان F geol. chalcedony.
kalsifikasyon قَلسيفيكاسيون F path. calcification.

kalsit قَلسيت F geol. calcite.
kalsiyum (.'..) قَلسيوم F · chem. calcium. — **ziyası** limelight, calcium light.
kaltaban قَلتابان P slang pander, pimp; dishonest or mean person. —**lık** pandering; meanness. —**lık et**= to pander, to pimp.
kaltakᵍⁱ قَلتاق 1. strumpet, harlot, whore. 2. saddletree, Eastern saddle. — **kaşı** pommel or cantle of a saddle, raised part in front and back of an Eastern saddle. — **şiltesi** saddle bolster.
kaltaklıkᵍⁱ قَلتاقلق 1. harlotry. 2. baseness, mean behavior (of a woman).
kalûbelâ (——.—) قالوبلا A lrnd. creation of the world, past eternity. —**dan beri** from time immemorial, ever since.
kaluçᶜᵘ قَلوج prov., var. of **kalıç**.
kaluğan قَلوغان prov. thistle.
kâlûs (——) كالوس P lrnd. foolish, stupid, idiot.
kâlüfte (—..) كالفته P lrnd. mentally agitated.
kalya 1 قَليه A stewed marrow.
kalya 2 قَليه [Arabic **kıla**] potash. — **otu** saltwort, glasswort, bot., Salsola kali. — **taşı** pearlash, crude potash. — **tozu** potassium carbonate.
kalya 3 قَليه [**galiye**] var. of **galiye**.
kalyan قليان P hookah, waterpipe, narghile; hubble-bubble.
kalye قَليه var. of **kalya** 1.
kalyon قَليون It galleon. —**lar kâtibi** Ott. hist. galleon clerk who provided the ships supplies and kept the accounts. — **defterdarı** Ott. hist. bookkeeper attached to the galleon clerk.
kalyoncu قَليونجى 1. slang old seadog, seawolf. 2. obs. sailor. — **kulluğu** Ott. hist. military service in the navy. — **tüfekçisi** Ott. hist. marine (soldier).
kâm 1 (—) كام P lrnd. wish, desire; pleasure. — **al**= /dan/ to enjoy to the full. — **u nâkâm** like it or not; surely.
kam 2 قام rel. shaman.
kamᵐⁱ 3 قمع A lrnd. 1. a striking on the head with a mace. 2. a subjugating, a putting down.
kam 4 قام E mech. cam.
kama قَما قَامَه قَامَا 1. dagger, poniard; dirk. 2. wedge. 3. artillery breech-block. 4. mark used for games won, scoring marks. 5. mil. slot for key. — **bas**= to win a game; to score, to chalk up or have success in a game. —**yı çek**= to draw a dagger. — **darbesi** dagger stab, thrust with a dagger. — **kamaya gel**= to come to knives, to be at daggers drawn. — **kuyruk** a crossbreed of sheep. — **nizamı** mil. spearhead, arrowhead, coign. — **sür**=

kama= /a/ to drive a wedge (into). — **tertibatı** *artillery* breech-block mechanism. — **vur=** *same as* **kama sür=**. — **vuruşu** *same as* **kama darbesi**.

kama=ᵣ قامه *prov.* 1. to nail; to make fast. 2. to shut (door, window, etc.).

kamacı قامجى *artillery* artificer.

kamala=ᵣ قامه لامه /ı/ 1. to dirk, to poniard, to stab. 2. to split or fix with a wedge.

kamalakᵏⁱ قالانه *prov.* exhausted. —**la=** *archaic* /ı/ to besiege.

kamalı قامالى قالى having a dagger. — **mil** *auto.* countershaft.

kamanço (..´.) قامانجو [kavanca] *slang* a turning over. — **et=** /ı/ to turn over; to hand over.

kamara (´..) قامره قاره It 1. ship's cabin. 2. House or Chamber of Parliament, *as in* **Avam Kamarası, Lordlar Kamarası**. — **iskelesi** companion ladder. — **yolcusu** cabin passenger.

kamarilla (...´.) قامريلا Sp camarilla.

kamarot قامارت *It* ship's steward.

kamaş=ᵣ قاماشمه 1. to be dazzled (eyes). 2. to be set on edge (teeth).

kamaşıkᵏⁱ قاماشيق 1. dazzled (eyes). 2. set on edge (teeth).

kamaştır=ᵣ قاماشديرمه /ı/ *caus. of* **kamaş=**.

kamaz قاز *prov.* whirlwind, storm.

kâmbahş (—.) كامبخش P *lrnd.* desire-fulfilling.

kambakᵏⁱ قاماب *prov.* 1. hornless sheep, goat, ox. 2. bald.

kambel قنبل *obs.* curved spine, hunched, curved back. —**i çıkmış** doubled up with age.

kamber قنبر A 1. *w. cap., man's name;* name of a freedman of the Caliph Ali. 2. *obs.* faithful servant; inseparable companion. —**siz düğün olmaz** Of course, he (she) cannot be left out or passed over.

kamberiye (..—.) قنبريه Bektashi Order belt worn in memory of Kamber, freedman of the Caliph Ali.

kâmbin (——) كامبين P *lrnd.* fortunate, happy, successful.

kambiyalⁱⁱ قامبيال It bill of exchange.

kambiyo (´..) قامبيو It 1. foreign exchange; rate of exchange. 2. *same as* **kambiyo müdürlüğü**. — **gişesi** exchange office. — **hukuku** law of exchange. — **kuru** exchange rate. — **masrafları** exchange charges. — **mevzuatı** foreign exchange regulations. — **müdürlüğü** foreign exchange department. — **piyasası** foreign exchange market.

kambiyocu قامبيوجى money changer. —**luk** business in foreign exchange.

kambrikᵏⁱ قامبريك E cambric. — **sargı** cambric bandage.

kambur قامبور قنبور 1. hump, hunch. 2. humpback, hunchback; humpbacked, hunchbacked, humped; crooked, bulged, warped. —**u çık=** 1. to become bulged or warped. 2. to grow hunchbacked. —**unu çıkar=** to arch one's back (person, cat, etc.). — **felek** cruel fate. — **makinası** *bookbinding, same as* **kambura**. — **üstüne kambur** one trouble on top of another. — **zambur** bumpy, uneven.

kambura (..´.) قامبوره *bookbinding* machine backer.

kamburlan=ᵣ قنبورلنمه *same as* **kamburlaş=**.

kamburlaş=ᵣ قنبورلاشمه to become hunchbacked, bulged. —**tır=** /ı/ *caus.*

kamburlukᵏᵘ قنبورلوق 1. hunch, prominence. 2. state of being hunchbacked, bulged.

kâmcu (——) كامجو P *lrnd.* seeking enjoyment, ambitious.

kamçı قامجى 1. whip; a whipping. 2. *naut.* pendant, tail. — **bağı** *naut.* pendant bend, rolling hitch. — **başı** coarse cotton net. — **çal=** *prov.* /a/ to give a blow or blows with a whip. — **darbesi** stroke with a whip, lash. — **ipi** whipcord, lash. — **kayışı** thong of a whip. — **kılıç** narrow bladed saber, curved sword. — **kuyruk** hairless tail (esp. of a horse). — **şaklaması** crack of a whip. — **şaklat=** to crack a whip. — **sapı** whip handle. — **ucu** whip end. — **vur=** /a/ to give a blow with a whip. — **ye=** to be whipped.

kamçıla=ᵣ قامجيلامه /ı/ 1. to whip, to flog, to flagellate. 2. to stimulate, to whip up. —**n=** *pass.* —**t=** /ı/ *caus. of* **kamçıla=**.

kamçılı قامجيلى 1. having a whip or lash; *sc.* flagellate, flagellated, flagelliforous. 2. oppressing, tyrant. — **palanga** *naut.* tail tackle, handy billy, jigger. — **torna** *naut.* tail block. —**lar** *neol.* flagellates, *zool., bot., Flagellata*.

kameleon قامليون F *text.* shot silk.

kamelya (..´.) قاميليا F camelia, *bot., Thea japonica*.

kamer قمر A *lrnd.* moon. — **ayı** *neol.* lunar month. **K—i Ken'an** *poet.* Joseph (son of Jacob). **K— Suresi** name of the fifty-fourth sura of the Quran. — **yılı** *neol.* lunar year.

kamerî (..—) قمرى A lunar. — **ay** lunar month. — **harfler** the letters ج ح خ ك ق ف غ ع ى و ه م in the Arabic alphabet. — **sene** lunar year.

kameriye قمريه It 1. arbor, bower; summer house. 2. *same as* **kamerî**.

kamet 1 (—.) قامت A *lrnd.* 1. stature. 2. fathom. —**i arttır=** *same as* —**i uzat=**. —**i bâlâ** stature. —**i dilcû** attractive stature. —**i mevzûn** balanced and beautiful stature. —**i ömr** throughout a whole life. —**i şimşid** straight and lovely stature. — **ver=** to raise hell. **—i uzat=** *colloq.* to become more and more insistent, to clamor.

kamet 2 (—.) قامت A muezzin's call signaling the beginning of the **namaz**. **— getir=** to announce the beginning of the **namaz**.

kamga قامغه *prov.* chip (of wood).

kâmgâr (——) كاگار P *lrnd.* successful, happy.

kâmgüzar (—.—) كامگذار P *lrnd.* one who has the means of gratifying all his desires.

kamış قامش 1. reed, common reed, *bot.*, *Trichoon phragmites;* made of reed. 2. bamboo, *bot.*, *Bambusa arundinacea*. 3. fishing rod. 4. *anat.* penis. 5. mollusk, shellfish, *zool.*, *Mollusca*. 6. *prov.* pitcher. **K— bayramı** Jewish Feast of Tabernacles. **— boğumu** node, articulation, internode of a reed. **— böceği** reed beetle, *zool.*, *Donanica*. **— kalem** reed pen. **—ı kır=** *slang* to have a chill. **— koy=** /a/ *slang* to play a trick (on). **— kulak** 1. long and upright ear (of a horse). 2. same as **kamış kulaklı**. **— kulaklı** long-eared (horse). **— örgüsü** cane work, cane plaiting. **—a su yürü=** *slang* to reach the age of puberty (boy). **— şekeri** cane sugar.

kamışçık[ğı] قامشجق nozzle of a bellows; blowpipe.

kamışlı قامشلى reedy; furnished with a reed or spout; large-stemmed (pipe).

kamışlık[ğı] قامشلق place overgrown with reeds, reed bed.

kâmil (—.) كامل A 1. perfect; complete; mature, of mature age; well-conducted. 2. *pros.* meter characterized by the anapestic beginning of its feet (..—.—/.——.—/..—.—). 3. *w. cap.*, man's name. **K— efendi** *colloq.* wife; woman. **—ce** (—'..) in a quiet, well-behaved fashion.

kâmilen كاملاً A perfectly, completely, entirely, fully.

kâmilî (—.—) كاملى A *lrnd.* pertaining to a perfect one: pertaining to a man called Kâmil.

Kâmiliye (—.—.) كاملية A a Shi'i sect (followers of Ebu Kâmil).

kâmillen=[ir] كاملنمك to become mature in conduct.

kâmillik[ği] كاملك perfection; fullness, completeness.

kâmin (—.) كامن A 1. *lrnd.* concealed, hidden. 2. *phys.* latent, potential.

kamineto (..'.) قامينتو It alcohol lamp.

kamir (.—) قمير A *lrnd.* gambler's adversary at play.

'kamis (.—) قميص A *lrnd.* shirt, shift, chemise; slip; *anat.* tunic; *bot.* tunic, film. **—i Yusuf** Joseph's shirt sent by him from Egypt to his father Jacob.

kamisiye (.——.) قميصية A *lrnd.*, *zool.*, *Tunicata*.

kâmkâr (——) كامكار P *lrnd.*, var. of **kâmgâr**.

kaml قمل A *lrnd.* lice.

kamlet قاملت It *obs.* camlet (cloth).

kamp قامپ F camp; encampment. **—ı boz=** to break camp. **—a çık=** to go camping. **—a gir=** to withdraw into camp (for sport training). **— hastahanesi** field hospital. **— hizmeti** camp duty. **— kur=** to pitch camp. **— yeri** camping site, camping ground. **—a yerleştir=** /ı/ to encamp (troops), to put (troops) under canvas.

kampana (..'.) قامپانه It 1. bell. 2. *auto.* brake drum. **— çal=** to ring a bell.

kampanacı قامپانه‌جى *slang* charlatan, quack, mountebank.

kampanya (..'.) قامپانيا It 1. campaign. 2. cropping season (esp. of sugar beet).

kâmran (——) كامران P *lrnd.* successful; fortunate, happy, blessed. **—î** (———) P, **—lık** happiness, fortune, prosperity.

kâmreva (—.—) كامروا P *lrnd.* enjoying, gratified.

kamu قامو 1. *archaic* all, the whole; everybody. 2. *neol.* the public. **— hakları** *neol.* public rights. **— hizmeti** *neol.* public service. **— hukuku** *neol.* civil law. **— oyu** *neol.* public opinion. **—laştır=** *neol.* /ı/ to nationalize.

kamus (——) قاموس A 1. lexicon, large dictionary. 2. *lrnd.* ocean.

kamutanrıcı *neol.* pantheist. **—lık** pantheism.

Kamutay *neol.* National Assembly, Parliament.

kâmver (—.) كامور P *lrnd.* successful, as one wished.

kâmyab (——) كامياب P *lrnd.* one who obtains what he desires; prosperous, successful.

kamyon قاميون F 1. truck, lorry. 2. *slang* harlot. **—a bindirme yeri** *mil.* transport point. **—dan indirme merkezi** *mil.* truckhead, detrucking point. **— kolu** *mil.* mechanical transport column. **— nakliye bölüğü** *mil.* truck company.

kamyoncu قاميونجى 1. truck owner. 2. truck driver. **—luk** trucking.

kamyonet قاميونت F small truck.

kan قان 1. blood. 2. descent, lineage, family. 3. bloodshed, murder. 4. blood revenge, blood feud, vendetta. **—ı ağır** slow in action and motion, dull. **— ağla=** to shed tears of blood, to be in deep distress. **— ak=** 1. to be shed (blood). 2. to flow (blood). **— akçası** blood money (for murder or wrongdoing). **— akımı** blood stream. **— akıt=** to shed blood. **—ını akıt=** to give, to shed one's blood (for). **— akmaksızın** without bloodshed. **— akması** *path.* extravasation of blood, hematoma. **— akrabalığı** blood relationship, consanguinity.

kan

— **aktar=** /a/ to give a blood transfusion (to). — **aktarması** transfusion of blood, blood transfusion. — **al=** /dan/ to take blood (from), to bleed, to cup. — **alıcı** *prov.* cupper, scarifier. — **ara=** to be out for (someone's blood). — **bağları** ties of blood. — **bankası** blood bank. — **baskısı** blood pressure. — **başına sıçra=**, — **beynine çık=**, — **beynine vur=** to rush to the head (blood); to become infuriated, to see red. — **boğ=** /ı/ to die of cerebral hemorrhage. —**a boya=** /a/ to stain or smear with blood; to shed blood, to slaughter. —**a boyan=** to be bloodstained. —**ı bozuk** with bad blood in his veins, degenerate. —**a bula=** /ı/ 1. to turn into a blood bath, to cause a general massacre. 2. to stain with blood. — **cisimciği** *anat.* blood corpuscle. — **çıbanı** furuncle. — **çıkar** Blood will flow. There will be a big fight. — **dalgası** a rush of blood to the head, blush. — **damarı** blood vessel. — **damlası** drop of blood. — **dâvası** blood feud, vendetta. — **deveranı** circulation of the blood. —**ı dindir=** to stanch blood. —**ına dokun=** /ın/ to make one's blood boil. — **dolaşımı** *same as* **kan deveranı**. —**ı don=** to turn to water, to turn cold with horror (one's blood); to be shocked, petrified (with horror or fear). — **dök=** to shed blood. —**ına ekmek doğra=** /ın/ to torture mentally. —**ını em=** /ın/ to blood-suck (person); to exhaust, drain (land). — **et=** *archaic* to kill. — **fındığı** blood hazel nut. — **formülü** blood count. — **gel=** for the blood to run. — **gider** *same as* **kan çıkar**. —**ına gir=** /ın/ to have someone's blood on one's hands. — **git=** to bleed strongly (esp. at menstruation and defecation). — **gövdeyi götür=** to go on, continue (horrible bloodshed). — **grupu** blood group. — **güt=** to continue a vendetta, to cherish revenge. — **hararetı** blood heat. — **hısımı** blood relative, consanguine. — **hücresi** blood cell. — **ısısı** *same as* **kan hararetı**. —**ını iç=** /ın/ to wreak vengeance (on). —**ını içine akıt=** to hide one's sorrows. — **iğnesi** phlebotomy needle. — **iste=** to demand the death (of). — **işeme** *path.* hematuria. — **izi** bloodstain, blood mark. —**a kan** Blood for blood; death for the murderer! —**a kan=** to shed blood endlessly. —**ı kanla yıka=** to wash blood with blood. — **karabeti** blood relationship. — **kardeşi** blood brother. — **kaybı** loss of blood. —**ı kayna=** 1. to be hotblooded, restless or enthusiastic. 2. /a/ to get to like, to become attached (to), to grow fond (of). —**ları kaynaş=** to come to like each other, to become good friends. — **kesici** blood-stanching, styptic. — **kesme ilâcı** hemostatic, styptic. — **kırmızı** blood red, dark crimson, sanguine.

—**ı kuru=** to be beside oneself with anxiety or suffering. —**ını kurut=** /ın/ to torture, to exasperate. — **kurutan otu** mandrake, *bot.*, *Mandragora officinalis*. — **kus=** 1. to vomit blood. 2. to be extremely pained or grieved. — **kusup kızılcık şerbeti içtim de=** to laugh bravely at one's own grief. — **kustur=** /a/ to oppress ruthlessly, to act most cruelly (towards). — **kürecikleri**, — **küreyvatı** blood cells. — **lekesi** blood stain, spot of blood. — **muayenesi** blood examination. —**ında ol=** /ın/ to run in the blood (of), to be in one's blood. — **oturması** /a/ rush of blood (to), congestion. —**iyle öde=** /ı/ to pay with one's life (for). — **pahası** blood-money, talion. —**ı pahasına** at the cost of one's life. — **pıhtılaşması** blood coagulation. — **portakalı** blood orange. — **revan içinde** bleeding freely, blood-bespattered, covered in blood. —**ı sıcak** sympathetic, sociable. —**ı soğuk** unsociable, reserved, cold. — **sulanması** *path.* anemia. —**a susa=** to be thirsting for vengeance. —**ına susa=** 1. to risk one's own life blindly. 2. /ın/ to seek another's death. — **suyu** lymph, serum. — **şekeri** blood-sugar. — **tahlili** blood-analysis. — **taşı** *min.* bloodstone, hematite. — **tepeye sıçra=** (*lit.*, for the blood to rush to one's crown) to boil with rage. — **tere bat=** to be bathed in sweat. — **ter içinde** streaming with perspiration. — **terle=** to sweat blood and tears, to be streaming with perspiration. — **testi** blood test. — **toplanması** blood blister. — **tut=** /ı/ 1. to faint at the sight of blood. 2. to be haunted by a murdered man (murderer). — **tükür=** to spit blood. — **tükürme** *path.* spitting of blood, hemoptysis. — **verici** blood donor. — **verme** blood transfusion. — **yalaş=** *obs.* to lick each other's blood in order to become blood brothers. — **yut=** to pine away from grief. — **yuttur=** /a/ to torture. — **yürümesi** hyperemia. — **yüzüne çıktı** The blood rushed to his face. — **zehirlenmesi** blood poisoning, pyemia, sepsis, toxaemia. — **zıyaı** *same as* **kan kaybı**.

kan=ar 2 قانع 1. /a/ to believe; to be persuaded. 2. to be misled, deceived, duped. 3. /a/ to be satiated (with drink). 4. /la/ to be contented (with). —**a kana iç=** to drink to repletion.

kân 3 (—) كان P *lrnd.* mine, quarry. —**ı kerem**, —**ı merhamet** the mine of mercy and generosity, God.

kana=r 1 قانه to bleed.

kana 2 (. .) قانه It waterline marks (on the stem and stern of a ship).

kanaatti (. — .) قناعت A 1. conviction, opinion. 2. contentment, satisfaction. —**imce** in my opinion. — **et=** /la/ to be satisfied, contented (with). — **getir=** /a/, — **hâsıl**

et= to come to the conclusion, opinion (that). — **notu,** — **numarası** mark based on the observation of the teacher. —**i ol**= to have his opinion, conviction. —**inde ol**= ˒ to be of the opinion (that), *e. g.,* **bu işin doğru olduğu kanaatindeyim** I am of the opinion that this matter is right. — **sahibi** contented, satisfied with little. **bir** —**e sahip ol**= to have an opinion. — **uyandır**= to create the impression.
kanaatbahş (.—..) قناعتبخش P *lrnd.* convincing.
kanaatkâr (.—.—) قناعتكار P contented, satisfied with little; unassuming. —**âne** (.—.——.) P *lrnd.* contentedly, without pretention, modestly. —**lık** contentedness, modesty.
kanaatli قناعتلى *same as* **kanaatkâr.**
kanad قناد *same as* **kanat 1.**
Kanada (.´..) قانادا *geog.* Canada; Canadian. — **merhemi** Canada balsam. —**lı** a Canadian.
kanadil (.——) قناديل A *lrnd.*, *pl. of* **kandil.** —**i çarh** *poet.* stars.
kanağan *neol., phil.* credulous. —**lık** credulity.
kanal قنال F canal, waterway; channel; *naut.* lane; *anat.* canal, duct. —**iyle** by way (of), by means (of), through. — **aç**= to open a canal. — **başı** the very edge of an eddy, where it meets the main current. — **eklüzü,** — **havuzu** canal lock. — **köprüsü** canal bridge. — **resmi,** — **rüsumu** canal dues. —**cık** *anat.* canaliculus.
kanalizasyon قناليزاسيون F sewerage, drainage. — **tertibatı** system of sewers, sewerage. —**unu yap**= /ın/ to drain a street by means of sewers, to sewer (a city).
kanama قناما a bleeding, hemorrhage.
kanape 1 (.´.) قناپه F sofa, couch, settee; bench.
kanape 2 قناپه F canapé.
kanara 1 قناره [kınnare] *obs.* slaughterhouse.
kanara 2 قناره *prov.* glutton, gluttonous; covetous, eager.
kanarya (.´.) قنارية It canary, *zool., Serinus canarius.* **K— adaları** Canary Islands. — **çiçeği** canary flower, *bot., Tropaeolum peregrinum.* — **otu** canary grass, *bot., Phalaris canariensis.* — **sarısı** canary yellow. — **yemi** canary seed, seed of canary grass. —**lık** canary breeding place.
kanat[1] **1** قنات قانات 1. wing (of a bird, airplane, etc.); fin (of a fish). 2. wing, leaf (of a door, window), shutter, blind (of a window), wing (of a building). 3. sail, vane (of a windmill), paddle, spur (of a watermill); blade, vane (of a propeller), fan (of a propeller screw); wing, feather (of a valve). 4. wing (of an army, party). — **açısı** *neol., math.,*
aero. dihedral angle. —**ı altında** under one's wing, under one's protection. —**ı altına al**= /ı/ to take under one's wing. —**ı altına sığın**= /ın/ to seek shelter under the protection (of). — **derinliği** *aero.* wing depth. — **kirişi** *aero.* wing spar. — **taarruzu** *mil.* flank attack. — **uzunluğu** wing span. — **vuruşu** wingbeat, wing stroke.
kanat[r] **2** قاناتمق /ı/ *caus. of* **kana 1**; to bleed.
kanat 3 (.—) قنات A *lrnd.* 1. *anat.* canal. 2. pipe for a subterranean water conduit. —**ı dâfika** *anat.* ejaculatory canal. —**ı sadrî** *anat.* thoracic canal. —**ı safraî** *anat.* bile duct, gall duct.
kanata (.´.) قناتة It *prov.* goblet.
kanatçık[1] قناتجق 1. *aero.* aileron. 2. *zool.* winglet.
kanatıl[r] قاناتلمق *pass. of* **kanat**= 2.
kanatır (.—.) قناطر A *lrnd., pl. of* **kantara.**
kanatir (.——) قناطير A *lrnd., pl. of* **kantar.**
kanatlan[r] قناتلانمق 1. to grow wings. 2. to take wing and fly away.
kanatlı قناتلى winged, finned. — **at** winged horse, Pegasus. — **bomba** finned bomb. — **karınca** flying ant, termite. — **supap** butterfly valve. — **tekerlek** vane wheel. — **tohum** winged seed.
kanatsı *neol.* winglike.
kanatsız قناتسز wingless, *biol.* apterous. —**lar** apterous insects, *zool., Apterygota.*
kanava (.´.) قناوا F canvas for embroidering. — **işi** needlepoint.
kanaviçe (...´.) قناويچه It canvas for embroidering. — **işle**= to embroider on canvas. — **işlemesi,** — **nakşı** embroidery on canvas.
kanayak[1], **kanayaklı** قان آياق قان آياقلى *prov.* woman.
kanbele قنبل A *lrnd.* group of men or horses.
kanber قنبر A *var. of* **kamber.**
kanca 1 (.´.) قانجه It hook. — **at**=, —**yı at**= /a/ to tackle or grapple. — **baş**. *obs.* barge with high and recurved cutwater. — **çengeli** iron hook of a boat hook. —**yı tak**= /a/ to get one's claws into, to keep looking for a reason to quarrel.
kanca 2 قانجه قنجه *archaic* whither? where?
kancala[r] قانجه لمق /ı/ to grapple with a hook, to put on a hook.
kancalı قانجه لى provided with a hook, hooked. — **çivi** hooked nail, clasp nail. — **iğne** safety pin. — **kurt** hookworm, *zool., Ancylostoma.* — **kurt hastalığı** hookworm disease, tunnel disease, *ancylostomiasis.*
kancaru قنجارو *archaic* in or toward what place?, in what direction?

kancı تا بجی 1. bloodletter, phlebotomist. 2. bloody tyrant. — **mengenesi** spring cupping instrument.

kancığa تا بُجْغَه تا بُجْغَ تا بُجْغَه archaic breast strap at the front of a saddle.

kancıkᵍ¹ **1** تا بجی تا بجی 1. mean and treacherous person. 2. bitch; female donkey. 3. prov. woman.

kancık⁼ⁱʳ **2** تا بجغمی archaic to become congested.

kancıklıkᵍ¹ تا بجاغی treachery, meanness, deceit. — **et**⁼, — **yap**⁼ to behave treacherously, to be deceitful.

kançılâr تا نجیلاد ـ تا نجیلد ـ It head of the registry office of a consulate.

kançılarya (...ʼ.) تا نجیلد یا It registry office of a consulate.

kandᵈⁱ قَنْد A lrnd. sugar, candy, sweets. —**i dübare** P twice refined sugar. —**i ham** rough sugar. —**i mükerrer** 1. refined sugar. 2. poet. lips of a beloved.

kanda تا نده قَنْدَه archaic where?

kandab (.—) قَنْدْآب P lrnd. sweet drink; wine.

kandakᵍ¹ تا نداق A prov. 1. ditch, fosse, ravine. 2. puddle, pool.

kandan تا نده ن قَنْدَ ن archaic whence, from where?

kandaş تا نداش cognate. —**lık** cognation.

kande قَنْدَه P same as **kanda**.

kandelisa (...ʼ.) قَنْدلیسا It same as **kandilisa**.

kandır⁼ⁱʳ تا ندیرمق /ı/ 1. to persuade, to convince; to seduce, to mislead. 2. to satisfy, satiate (with drink); to saturate. —**ıcı** convincing; satisfying. —**ıl**⁼ pass. of **kandır**⁼. —**ış**, —**ma** a persuading, a convincing; seduction, a misleading.

kandil قَنْدیل [Arabic kındıl] 1. old-fashioned oil lamp; electric lamp in the shape of an oil lamp used in the mosque. 2. Isl. rel., w. cap. one of the four night feasts with illumination of the minarets. 3. slang very drunk. — **böceği** glowworm, zool., Lampyris noctiluca. —**i çarh** poet. 1. the sun. 2. the moon. — **çiçeği** milfoil, yarrow, bot., Achillea millefolium. — **çöreği** cakes eaten at a **kandil** feast. — **donanması** festive illumination of the minarets. **K— Gecesi** Isl. rel. one of the four feasts when the minarets are illuminated: the Prophet Muhammad's birthday, his conception, his night ascent, and the Night of Power. **K— Günü** Isl. rel. day preceding the **Kandil Gecesi**. —**i İsa** sphere of the sun in which Jesus is said to dwell. — **simidi** same as **kandil çöreği**. — **topu** globe or glass shade for an oil lamp. —**uçur**⁼ obs. 1. to float a soap bubble in the air. 2. to float a firework star in the air. — **üfle**⁼ obs. to blow soap bubbles. — **yağı** poor quality olive oil. —**in yağı tüken**⁼ to die.

kandilci قَنْدیلجی obs. 1. maker or seller of oil lamps. 2. tender of oil lamps in a mosque.

kandilisa (...ʼ.) قَنْدیلیسا It naut. halyard.

kandilleş⁼ⁱʳ قَنْدیلَلْشْمك to greet one another on a Kandil feast.

kandilli قَنْدیلّی 1. illuminated by an oil lamp. 2. slang very drunk. 3. w. cap., name of a suburb of Istanbul on the Asiatic shore of the Bosphorus. — **kalemkârı** obs. painted muslin handkerchief of Kandilli. — **küfür** rough swearing. — **selâm**, — **temenna** old-fashioned very polite salutation, raising the hand from the ground in several movements.

kandillikᵍ¹ قَنْدیلّك 1. stand for an oil lamp. 2. pertaining to, related to a **kandil** feast.

Kandiye قَنْدیه geog. Candia. — **sabunu** obs. hard olive oil soap.

kandleb قَنْدلب P lrnd. with lips sweet as sugar candy, sweet-spoken.

kandriz (.—) قَنْدریز P lrnd. 1. that pours out sugar. 2. that pours out smiles or kisses.

kanemi ol⁼ᵘʳ تا نِمی اولمق slang to blush, to flush.

kanepe تا نپه F var. of **kanape**.

kanfese قَنْفسه A lrnd. wood louse.

kangal تا نغال تنغال قنغل 1. coil; skein. 2. anat. ansa. — **et**⁼ /ı/ to coil, to wind in a skein. — **halinde** in coils, coiled (up). — **ol**⁼ to become a coil; to coil up (serpent). — **yap**⁼ same as **kangal et**⁼.

kangalla⁼ʳ تا نغالّمق /ı/ to coil, to make a coil or ring.

kangı تا نغی archaic, same as **hangi**.

kangren تا نغرن F gangrene.

kanguru تا نغرو F kangaroo.

kanı 1 neol. conviction, opinion.

kanı 2 تا نی archaic, same as **hani 1**.

kanık⁼ⁱʳ **1** تا نقمق 1. prov. /a/ to become satiated. 2. archaic to thirst for blood.

kanıkᵍ¹ **2** تا نق prov. 1. satisfied, content. 2. deceived. —**la**⁼ /la/ to be satisfied, contented (with). —**lık** satisfaction, contentedness.

kanıksa⁼ʳ, **kanıksı**⁼ʳ تا نقسامق تا نقسیمق /a/ to become indifferent after having had too much of something, to lose the sensitiveness of reaction (against something).

kanım neol., phil. conviction.

kanır⁼ⁱʳ تا کرمق /ı/ to pull aside, to twist, to bend, to deflect. —**ma** verbal n. —**ma kolu** lever, crank. —**t**⁼ /ı/ same as **kanır**⁼.

kanırtmaçᶜ¹ تا کرتماج prov. 1. lever, crank. 2. hort. a cutting.

kanış 1 تا نش a persuading, persuasion; seduction.

kanış=ᴵʳ 2 قا نیشمی‎ *prov.* to come to an understanding.
kanıt 1 (—.) قا نط‎ A *lrnd.* despairing, desperate.
kanıt 2 *neol., log.* argument. —**lı** supported by evidence. —**sa**= /ı/ to take as evidence (of) or proof (of, for).
kaniⁱⁱ 1 (—.) قا نع‎ A convinced. — **ol**= /a/ to be convinced (of); to be satisfied, relieved.
kâni 2 (— —) كا نی‎ P *lrnd.* found in a mine, mineral.
kâni 3 (— —) كا نی‎ A *lrnd.* one who uses words with an allusive meaning.
kani 4 قنی‎ *archaic, var of* **kanı** 2.
kânken (—.) كا نکنی‎ P *lrnd.* miner. —**î** (— . —) P working in a mine.
kanla=ʳ قا نلامه‎ /ı/ to stain with blood. —**n**= 1. to gain new blood, to become healthy. 2. to be bloodstained. —**ş**= to turn to blood. —**t**= /ı/ *caus. of* **kanla**=.
kanlı 1 قا نلو قا نلی‎ 1. bloody, blood-covered, bloodstained. 2. bleeding. 3. sanguinary, bloody. 4. bloodthirsty, murderous. 5. full-blooded; plethoric, plethorus. 6. *archaic* murderer. — **basur** dysentery. — **bıçaklı** mortal or deadly enemy, sworn enemy. — **canlı** full of health. — **gömleğini giy**= /ın/ to be out for someone's blood. — **katil** bloodthirsty criminal, notorious murderer. — **kavga** bloody brawl. — **kuyu** 1. sink or cesspool of a slaughter house. 2. pit in a dungeon into which murdered victims were thrown. — **pirzola** underdone chop or cutlet. — **savaş** bloody battle.
kanlı 2 قا نلكی‎ *archaic, same as* **kağnı**.
kanmaz قا نماز‎ never satisfied; always discontented.
kansa قانسا‎ *archaic, same as* **konsu**.
kanser قا نسر‎ F cancer. — **ilâcı** *slang* clumsy, boorish; stupid fellow. — **ol**= to become cancerous. —**li** cancerous.
kansı قا نسی‎ *archaic* which?, whichever?
kansız قا نسز‎ anemic, bloodless. —**lık** deficiency of blood, bloodlessness, anemia.
kantar 1 قنطار‎ [*Arabic* **kıntar**] 1. steelyard for weighing. 2. *obs.* a weight of about 120 pounds. — **ağası** *obs.* public controller of weights. —**ı belinde** *colloq.* attentive to his trade. —**a çek**= /ı/ 1. to weigh with a steelyard. 2. to weigh in one's mind. —**a gel**= to be weighable. — **kabağı** very large kind of pumpkin. — **kavunu** large kind of muskmelon. — **kefesi** scale of a steelyard. — **kertesi** notch on the arm of a steelyard. — **kolu** arm of a steelyard. — **parası**, — **resmi** weighing fee. — **topu** ball of a steelyard. —**ın topunu kaçır**= to overstep the limit, to go to extremes. —**a vur**= /ı/ *same as* **kantara çek**=.

kantar=ᴵʳ 2 قا نتارمه قنتارمه قا کنارمه‎ /ı/ to pull up (a horse).
kantara قنطره‎ A *lrnd.* 1. stone bridge. 2. arched building. —**i Varol** *anat.* pons Varolii.
kantarcı قنطارجی‎ 1. maker or seller of steelyards. 2. weigher; public weigher, weighmaster.
kantariye قنطاریه‎ A weighing fee.
kantarla=ʳ قنطارلامه‎ *prov.* /ı/ to test, to examine.
kantarlı قنطارلو‎ *slang* 1. heavy, severe *as in* **kantarlı küfür**. 2. a cursing and swearing, abusive language. — **at**= to curse and swear. — **küfür** violent abuse, vituperation.
kantarlıkᵍⁱ قنطارلق‎ 1. rack or cupboard for keeping the steelyard. 2. weighing so many **kantars**, e. g., **bir kantarlık kömür** coal weighing one kantar.
kantarma قا نتارمه قنطارمه قا کنارمه‎ spurred bit for a horse.
kantaron قا نتارون‎ Gk centaury, *bot., Centaurea acaulis.* — **yağı** centaury oil. —**giller** *neol., bot., Centaureae.*
kantaryon قنطاریون قا نتاریون‎ Gk *var. of* **kantaron**.
kantin قا نتین‎ F 1. canteen. 2. *slang* lie, story, fib. — **at**= *slang* to tell lies or exaggerated stories, to tell a fib.
kanto (.′.) قا نتو‎ It song (in cabaret or theater). —**cu** singer in a cabaret or theater.
kanuᵘᵘ (. —) قنوع‎ A *lrnd.* contented with little; humble, suppliant.
kanun 1 (— —) قا نون‎ A 1. law, statute, act; code (of laws); rule. 2. *obs.* military policeman. —**a aykırı** unlawful, illegal. —**a aykırı olarak** against the law. —**da boşluk** loophole in the law. —**u boz**= to break the law. —**la çatış**= to fall foul of the law. —**a dayan**= to be based on the law. — **dışı** outlaw. —**ı dua** *Ott. hist.* prayer ceremony performed every evening while the army is in enemy territory. —**ı esasî** constitution, charter. — **günü** legal force, legal power. —**un harfi** letter of the law. — **harici** *same as* **kanun dışı**. — **hukuku** statute law. — **hükmünde ol**= to have the force of law, to be as good as a law. —**a hürmet et**= to be law-abiding; to respect the law. —**a itaatkâr ol**= to obey the law. —**u kabul et**= to pass a law. — **kitabı** law book, code (of laws). — **kuvveti** *same as* **kanun gücü** — **külliyatı** body of laws, statute book. —**ı külliyet** *psych.* law of redintegration. — **lâyıhası** bill of law. — **maddesi** article of the law. — **mecmuası** *same as* **kanun külliyatı**. —**ı medenî** civil law. —**a muhalif** *same as* **kanuna aykırı**. — **müvacehesinde** in the eye of the law. — **nazarında** *same as* **kanun müvacehesinde**. —**ı nev Müslim** *Ott. hist.* ceremony in which a donation of money was

kanun

made to new converts to the Muslim religion. **—ı örfî** martial law. **—a riayet et=** to comply with the law, to observe or to respect the law. **—a riayet etme=** to break the law, to infringe the law. **—un ruhu** spirit of the law. **—a sığın=** to appeal to the law. **— tanımıyan** infringer of the law. **— tasarısı** bill, draft of a law. **— tasarısını kabul et=** to pass a bill. **— tasarısını reddet=** to throw out a bill. **—ı teferrüd** *lrnd., phil.* principle of individuation. **— tefsiri** interpretation of the law. **—ı tekevvün** *lrnd., biol.* biogenetic law. **— teklifi** bill (of a law). **—a uygun** conformable to law, lawful. **—vaz'et=** to enact a law, to make a law. **— vaz'ı** legislation. **— vâzı'ı** legislator, lawgiver. **— yap=** same as kanun vaz'et=. **—u yapan** same as kanun vâzıı. **— yolu ile** legally, by law. **— yürürlüğe girdi** The law has come into force. **—u yürürlüğe koy=** to put a law into force. **— yürürlüktedir** The law is in effect. **— zabiti** *obs.* regimental police officer.

kanun 2 (——) قانون A a zither-like musical instrument with 72 strings.

kânun 3 (——) كانون A 1. *lrnd.* hearth or furnace; chafing-dish. 2. the first two months of the winter. **—ı evvel** December. **—ı sâni** January.

kanuncu (——.) قانونجى player on the zither; maker or seller of zithers.

kanunçe (——.) قانونچه P *lrnd.* small zither.

kanunen (——.) قانونا A by law, according to law, legally.

kanunî 1 (———) قانونى A 1. lawful, legal, legitimate, statutory. 2. lawgiver. 3. *w. cap.*, name given to Suleiman the Magnificent. **— borç** legal liability. **— faiz** legal interest. **— gün** legal day. **— ihtiyatlar** *econ.* legal reserves. **— karşılıklar nispeti** *econ.* reserve ratio. **— kıymet** *econ.* legal asset. **— muadeleler** *astr.* canonical equations. **— para** *econ.* lawful money, legal tender. **— sermaye** legal capital. **— unsurlar** *astr.* canonical elements. **— vaziyetler** *astr.* canonical coordinates. **— yola baş vur=** to go to law, to appeal to the law.

kanunî 2 (———) قانونى A player of the zither.

kanunilikᵍⁱ (———.) قانونيلك legitimacy, lawfulness.

kanuniyet (———.) قانونيت A legal force, legal power, legality. **— kesbet=** to become a law, to come into legal force.

kanunlaş=ⁱʳ (—...) قانونلاشمك to become a law, to pass into law.

kanunlu (—..) قانونلو lawful, legal, legitimate. **—luk** lawfulness, legality, legitimacy.

kanunname (———.) قانوننامه P *lrnd.* code of laws, lawbook, statute book.

kanunsuz (—..) قانونسز lawless, unlawful, anarchic. **—luk** lawlessness, unlawfulness, anarchy.

kanunşinas (———.—) قانون شناس P *lrnd.* jurist, jurisconsult.

kanül قانول F *anat.* cannula.

kanyakᵍⁱ *neol.* cognac, French brandy.

kanyon قانيون Sp *geol.* canyon.

kanyot قانيوت F pool, pot (in gambling).

kanzaa قنزعه A *lrnd.* cock's comb, crest.

kaolin قاولين F *geol.* kaolin. **—leş=** to be kaolinized. **—leştir=** /ı/ to kaolinize. **—leştirme** kaolinization.

kaos قاوس Gk chaos.

kapᵇⁱ 1 قاب same as **kab** 1.

kap=ᵃʳ 2 قاپمق /ı/ 1. to snatch, seize, catch, grasp, snap (up). 2. to carry off, to catch, *e. g.*, **makina parmağını kapmış** The machine caught his finger. 3. to learn quickly, to pick up, *e. g.*, **ağızdan kap=** to learn by listening. 4. to manage to win (a desirable thing), to get (with suggestion of fraud or cunning), as in **post kap=**. 5. to catch (a disease), as in **hastalık kap=**; to fester, *e. g.*, **su kaptı** A blister has formed. **— kaç*. kendini —ıp salıver=** to neglect himself, to let himself go.

kap 3 قاب F cape, mantle.

Kap 4 قاب F *geog.* Cape (of Good Hope). **— Müstemlekesi, — Sömürgesi** Cape Colony.

kapa=ʳ قاپامق /ı/ 1. to shut, close (door, eyes, book); to shut up (space); to glue or paste up (envelope). 2. to stop up, to fill up (opening). 3. to cover up (face), to draw (curtain). 4. to cut off (panorama). 5. to hush up (a matter). 6. to shut, to turn off (tap); to occlude (street, pipe), to obstruct, to stop (traffic), to close (frontier), to blockade, to block (port). 7. to close, settle (account, balance, dispute), to conclude (speech, proceedings, transaction). 8. to shut up, to confine, to imprison. 9. to hide, to hoard. 10. *print.* to leave less space.

kapacıkᵍⁱ *neol., anat.* valvule, valvula.

kapakᵍⁱ قاپاق 1. lid, cover; cover (of a book); stopper. 2. *geom.* segment. 3. *anat.* valvula. 3. *gambling* kind of cheating (especially in poker). **—ı at=** /a/ to take refuge (in); to succeed in getting (into). **—ı dar at=** /a/ succeed in getting hurriedly (to a place). **— halkası** artillery locking ring. **— pencere** hinged skylight. **— süslemesi** decorative frontispiece, cover (of a book etc.). **— süvarisi** *obs.* post captain in the navy. **— taşı** flat stone (as cover to a conduit). **— vur=** /a/ to hush a matter up, to cover over.

kapaklan= قاپاقلنمق to stumble and fall on one's face; to capsize, overturn.
kapaklı قاپاقلی 1. provided with a lid or cover. 2. clandestine, concealed; hushed up.
kapaksız قاپاقسز without a lid.
kapalı قپالی قاپالو 1. shut, closed, covered. 2. secluded; reserved. 3. overcast. (sky). 4. obscure. — **avlu** covered courtyard. — **celse** closed session. — **çarşı** covered market, bazaar. — **geç=** /ı/ to pass over a point without mention. — **hava** overcast sky. — **hece** closed syllable. — **kutu** inscrutable (person); secret. — **sözler** mysterious words; obscure words; ambiguous words. — **tohumlular** neol., bot., Angiospermae. — **yer korkusu** psych. claustrophobia. — **zarf usulü ile** by sealed tender.
kapama قپامه قاپامه 1. verbal n. of **kapa=**. 2. lamb and onion stew. 3. prov. kind of coat or cloak fastening in front; complete suit of ready-made clothes.
kapamacı قاپاجی dealer in ready-made clothing.
kapan=‫ 1 قپانمق قاپانمق 1. pass. of **kapa=**. 2. to shut, close of itself (door, window etc.). 3. to veil herself before men (woman). 4. to shut down (factory). 5. to heal up (wound). 6. same as **kapaklan=**.
kapan 2 قپان قاپان trap. — **a gir=** to be entrapped, to fall into a trap. — **a kısıl=** to be caught in a trap. — **kur=** to set a trap. — **a tutul=** same as **kapana kısıl=**.
kapan 3 قپان قاپان [kap= 2] that snatches, seizes, grabs. — **ın elinde kal=** to be in great demand. — **kapana** a general scramble.
kapan 4 قپان قاپان [kabban] obs. 1. large public weighing machine. 2. an office where there is a public weighing machine for wholesale commodities. 3. prov. market-place. — **hakkı** Ott. hist. fee received for using the public weighing machine. — **cı** public weighing official.
kapanca 1 قپانجه قاپانجه prov. washing basket, laundry basket.
kapanca 2 قپانجه قاپانجه small trap for birds.
kapandır=‫ قاپاندرمق قاپانديرمق /ı/ 1. to cause to stumble. 2. naut. to make a ship broach to.
kapanık‫ قاپانق قاپانیق 1. shut in, confined; gloomy (place). 2. cloudy, overcast. 3. shy, unsociable. — **mizaclı** of reserved nature; secluded, restrained.
kapanıklık‫ قاپانقلق 1. closeness, confinedness. 2. cloudiness, darkness; dullness; gloominess. 3. reservedness.
kapanış قاپانش قاپانیش verbal n. of **kapan=** 1. — **borsa cetveli** com. closing quotation. — **fiatları** com. closing prices. — **hesapları** com. closing entries. — **kuru** com. closing rate.

kapaniçe (..´.) قپانیجه Sl archaic a kind of fur cloak (worn by high state officials).
kaparo (..´.) قاپارو It earnest money.
kaparoz قاپاروز slang illicit gain; bribe. — **et=** to grasp, to seize, to plunder. — **da gez=** to be on the lookout for pickings. — **cu** one who picks up what he can, who lives on his wits; plunderer. — **la=** to grasp, to seize, to plunder.
kapat=‫ قپاتمق قاپاتمق /ı/ 1. caus. of **kapa=**. 2. to acquire by a trick or maneuver; to get something very cheap. 3. to keep (a mistress). — **ıl=** pass.
kapatma قاپاتمه 1. verbal n. of **kapat=**. 2. kept mistress.
kapçak‫ قاپچاق large hook with a long handle.
kapçık‫ قاپچیق bot. bud; husk. — **meyva** neol. achene.
kapela (..´.) قاپله قاپیله قاپیلا It 1. cap; casque. 2. naut. truck.
kapı قاپی قپو قاپو 1. door, gate. 2. employment; place of employment. 3. possibility, e. g., **bütün kapılar kapandı** There is no way out. 4. prov. government house in a province. 5. Ott. hist. central office of the Government at Istanbul. 6. a point in backgammon. — **sında** close, near; in the household of, e. g., **kapısında büyü=**, **kapısında çalış=** to grow up in the household of, to serve in the house of (some dignitary). — **aç=** 1. to open a door. 2. /a/ to prepare the ground (for); to make overtures (to), to hint (at), to be the inaugurator of..., to be the first to... — **sı açık** generous, hospitable. — **ağası** Ott. hist. chief white eunuch in the Imperial palace. — **ının ağzında** by the door. — **altı** 1. Ott. hist. police station and prison. 2. prov. country police station. — **sını aşındır=** /ın/ to pester with frequent visits. — **dan atsalar bacadan girer** persistent bore. — **aralığı** slight opening of the door. — **baca açık** unguarded, open (place). — **sı bacası yok** tumbledown or jerry-built. — **basarığı** archaic a bar across the door with which it is kept closed. — **yı büyük aç=** to start an expensive undertaking, to spend money prodigally. — **çal=** to knock or ring at the door. — **çalınıyor** Somebody is knocking; somebody is ringing the doorbell. — **çavuşu** 1. Ott. hist. an agent of certain Janissary regiments at the office of the Agha. 2. special messenger to the Government House from the chief of the Emirs. — **yı çek=** to shut the door. — **çerçevesi** door frame. **bir** — **ya çıkar** It's all the same; it boils down to the same thing. — **çuhadarı** Ott. hist. messenger between a provincial agent and the central Government office. — **dayağı** piece of timber put behind a door to keep it shut. — **dışarı et=** /ı/ to show the door (to), to turn out of doors; to sack, to dismiss.

— duvar No one opened the door; there was no answer (to a knock or ring). **— gibi** well built (man). **bir —ya gir=** to find a job in a house as a servant. **— halkı** 1. the household of a great house. 2. *Ott. hist.* the officials of the Sublime Porte. 3. household guards of a sovereign or grandee. **— hasekisi** *Ott. hist.* accredited agent or messenger of the chief of the Eunuchs for business at Government-House. **— kapamaca, — kapamacasına** everyone in the house; the whole household. **— kapı dolaş=** to go from door to door; to knock at every door. **— kethüdası** *Ott. hist.* official representative of a provincial governor (in Istanbul). **—dan koğsan bacadan düşer** an insufferable bore. **— kolu** door latch; door handle. **— komşusu** next-door neighbor. **— kulu** *Ott. hist.* Janissary guard; palace servant. **— kuzusu** wicket in a large door or gate. **— mandalı** 1. door latch. 2. unimportant person. **— odunu** wooden bar for fastening a door. **—yı odun et=** to be driven to the greatest straits by poverty. **— oğlanı** *Ott. hist.* official assistant, messenger; messenger employed at embassies. **—dan ol=** to lose one's job. **—sı ol=** /ın/ to require so much money, *e. g.*, **bu, on liranın kapısıdır** This is a matter of ten liras. **— plâkası** door plate. **— resmi** *Ott. hist.* tax collected on goods brought through the fortress gate. **— somunu** door post, jamb to which a door is hinged. **— tokmağı** knocker, door handle. **— toplar damarı** *neol., biol.* portal vein. **— topuzu** doorknob. **— tut=** to engage oneself in service. **—yı vur=** to knock at the door. **— yap=** 1. to prepare the way for something one is going to say. 2. *backgammon* to cover a blot. **— yavrusu** same as **kapı kuzusu. — yoldaşı** fellowservant. **— zinciri** door chain.

kapıcı 1 قپوجى door keeper, porter, janitor. **—lar kethüdası** *Ott. hist.* 1. Superintendent of the Ushers, *title of a high functionary of state who took petitions to the Sultan as they were offered in public*. 2. the Controller of the Warders.

kapıcı 2 قاپيجى [**kap=** 2] one who seizes, snatches. **— kuş** bird of prey.

kapıcıbaşı قپوجى باشى *Ott. hist.* head of the palace doorkeepers (a high office).

kapıcılık[g1] قپوجيلق the occupation and duty of a doorkeeper.

kapıl=[ır] قاپلمق 1. *pass.* of **kap=** 2. 2. /a/ to be carried away (by some idea, current, etc.).

kapılan=[ır] قپولانمق /a/ to get a job or situation, to find a livelihood. **—dır=** /ı/ to find a job (for).

kapılgan قاپلغان easily misled, easily carried away (by emotion, etc.).

kapılı قپولو قاپولى 1. having a door. 2. in service (person); belonging to a government office (person). 3. who has made a point (at backgammon); covered and secured (a piece or point at backgammon). **— bacalı ol=** *colloq.* to fall out, to get into a dispute. **— Yeniçeri** *Ott. hist.* Janissary who does not join military campaigns but is in the service of high government officials.

kapısız قاپوسز 1. without a door or gate, doorless, gateless. 2. without a job, unemployed. **— kal=** to lose one's job, to become unemployed.

kapış=[ır] **1** قاپيشمق 1. /ı/ to snatch (for), to scramble (for) together; to buy eagerly, to rush to purchase. 2. /la/ to scramble, to snatch from one another; to get to grips (with). 3. *slang* to kiss each other.

kapış 2 قاپيش 1. *verbal n.* of **kapış=** 1. 2. *verbal n.* of **kap=** 2. 3. scramble. **— kap=** /ı/ to seize violently. **— kapış** grabbingly, as a continued scramble. **— kapış git=** to sell, be sold like hot cakes. **— kapış kapış=** /ı/ to buy eagerly. **— kapış ye=** /ı/ to eat greedily.

kapıştır=[ır] قاپيشدرمق /ı/ *caus.* of **kapış= 1.**

kapik[g1] قاپيك Russ kopek.

kapital[li] قاپيتال F 1. *econ.* capital, funds. 2. *print.* capital, capital letter. **— devri** stock turnover. **— hesabı** capital account; stock account. **— yatırımı** investment of capital.

kapitalist قاپيتاليست F capitalist.

kapitalizm قاپيتاليزم F capitalism.

kapiton قاپيتون F cushioned back (of a seat). **—e, —lu** padded, upholstered; quilted.

kapitülâsyon قاپيتولاسيون F capitulation. **K—lar** *Ott. hist.* Capitulations, conventions granting certain rights to foreigners.

kapkacak[g1] قاپ قاجاق pots and pans.

kapkaç قاپ قاچ a stealing by snatching.

kapkara (´..) قاپ قره entirely black, pitch-dark, pitch-black.

kapla=[r] قاپلامق /ı/ 1. to cover over; to cover (with). 2. to overlay (with), to plate (with); to cover with a protecting paper (book). 3. to sheathe (a ship). 4. to surround, to invade. **—m** *neol., phil.* extension, extent.

kaplama قاپلامه 1. *verbal n.* of **kapla=**. 2. cover, coverlet, coating, plate; crown (of a tooth), veneer. 3. *naut.* planking, planks, side piece. 4. covered, coated, lined, faced, plated; crowned (tooth). 5. *prov.* kind of jacket. **— başı** *naut.* quarter. **— diş** crowned tooth. **— saat** rolled gold or silver-plated watch. **— süsü** garnish, garnishing. **—cı** plater; veneerer; garnisher. **—lık** (material) for covering, plating, etc.

kaplan 1 قاپلان 1. tiger, *zool.*, *Panthera tigris*. 2. *prov.* panther. **— boğan** aconite bot., *Aconitum napellus*. — **postu** tiger lily, bot., *Lilium tigrinum*.

kaplan=ⁱʳ 2 قاپلانى قيدڭى *pass. of* **kapla**=.

kaplat=ⁱʳ قاپلاتمه قيدڭه /ı, a/ *caus. of* **kapla**=.

kaplayı قيدڭى *archaic* completely covering; covered over completely.

kaplayıcı قيدڭيجى 1. covering, surrounding. 2. plater; garnisher.

kaplı قاپلو قاپلى covered, coated, plated; with a paper jacket (book). — **kaya** considerable extent of solid rock.

kaplıca 1 قاپلوجه قاپليجى hot spring.

kaplıca 2 قاپلوجه قاپليجى wild oats growing among grain, bot., *Avena fatua*. — **buğday** spelt, German wheat, bot., *Triticum sativum spelta*.

kaplıkᵍⁱ قاپلق for covering. — **kâğıt** paper for covering books.

kaplubağa قاپلوباغا قاپلوبغ *archaic*, *same as* **kaplumbağa**.

kaplumbağa قاپلومباغ 1. tortoise, turtle, *zool.*, *Testudo graeca*. 2. *naut.* compressor; controller. —**lar** *zool.* turtles and tortoises, Chelonia. —**ya bin**= to be slow as a tortoise, to go at a snail's pace. — **gibi** slow as a tortoise. — **yürüyüşü** snail's pace.

kapma قاپمه 1. *verbal n. of* **kap**= 2. 2. snatched, seized; got by a trick.

kapmaca قاپمجه puss in the corner (children's game).

kapon قاپون *It naut.* cat tackle for the anchor. — **çengeli** cat hook. — **çıması** cat tackle fall. — **makarası** cat block. — **palangası** cat tackle. — **tetiği** cat trigger.

kaport, kaporta (.´.—) قاپورته *It naut.* 1. companion hatchway. 2. companion hatch over companionway. — **ağzı** companion. — **iskelesi** companion ladder. — **tüfeği** *mil.* fixed gun.

kapot قاپوت *It same as* **kaput**.

kapris قاپريس F caprice, fancy. —**li** capricious; fanciful.

kapsa=ʳ 1 *neol.* to comprise, contain.

kapsa 2, kapsakᵍⁱ, **kapsalak**ᵍⁱ, **kapsalık**ᵍⁱ قاپسه قاپسالاه قاپساليه *prov.* garden door.

kapsız قاپسز uncovered, without a cover or envelope, loose.

kapsolˡⁱ, **kapsül** قاپسول F 1. medicinal capsule. 2. *artillery* percussion cap, primer. 3. *anat.*, *bot.* capsule. — **barutu** *artillery* priming charge. — **yüksüğü** *artillery* fuse cup, cap chamber (of fuse), primer holder. —**lü** 1. enclosed in a (medicinal) capsule. 2. furnished with a percussion cap. 3. capsulate.

kaptan قپودان قبتان *It* 1. *naut.* captan; shipmaster; skipper, mate. 2. *sports* captain. — **köprüsü**, — **köşkü** *naut.* conning bridge.

— **kulesi** *naut.* conning tower. — **oyna**= to play marbles. **K— Paşa** *Ott. hist.* admiral.

kaptanlık قبتانلى captainship. — **et**=, — **yap**= /a/ to captain.

kaptıkaçtı قاپديقاچدى 1. small motorbus, minibus. 2. kind of card game. 3. stealing by snatching.

kaptır=ⁱʳ قاپديرمه /ı, a/ *caus. of* **kap**= 2. —**ma** 1. *verbal n.* 2. handsaw; whipsaw.

kapu قاپو *var. of* **kapı**.

kapudan (..—) قپودان *It Ott. hist.* captain or commander in the navy. **K—ı Derya, K— Paşa** High Admiral and Minister of Marine.

kapudane (..—.) قپودانه *It Ott. hist.* 1. full admiral. 2. full admiral's flagship. **K— Bey** title of the full admiral. — **gemisi** flagship of the fleet. **K— Paşa** admiral of the fleet.

kapurta (.´.) قپورطه *It var. of* **kaporta**.

kapuska (.´.) قاپوسقه Sl cabbage stew.

kaput قاپوت F 1. military cloak; capote. 2. condom, contraceptive. 3. a winning all the tricks in a card game. — **bezi** coarse white calico. — **et**= /ı/ to beat completely (one's adversary at cards). — **git**= *school slang* to fail all of the exams. — **ol**= to be completely beaten (at cards).

kapuz قاپوز قاپوز *prov.* defile, mountain pass, gorge.

kar 1 قار snow, snowfall. —**dan adam** snowman. — **alaca oldu** Snow is melting and changing; winter is approaching its end. — **bas**= 1. /ı/ to cover up, to overwhelm (snow). 2. /a/ to store snow for summer use. — **çığırı** tracks in the snow. — **çiçeği** white hellebore, bot., *Helleborus vernalis*. — **delen** snowdrop, bot., *Galanthus nivalis*. — **dişi** icicle. — **düş**= /a/ to fall (snow), to snow. — **fırtınası** snowstorm, blizzard. —**da gezer izini belli etmez** He walks on snow without leaving footmarks *said of a very cunning or adroit person*. — **gibi**, — **gibi beyaz** snow-like, snow-white. — **gözlüğü** snow-goggles. — **helvası** snow mixed with honey or molasses. — **körü** snow-blind. — **kurdu** snowworm. — **kuşu** snow-bunting, *zool.*, *Plectrophenax nivalis*. — **kuyusu** pit for preserving snow for summer use. — **küreme makinası** revolving snowplow. — **lâpası** large snowflake. —**la örtülü** snowcapped. — **parçası** snow-white (object). —**a saplan**= to be snowed in. — **sınırı** *geog.* snowline. — **tanesi** snowflake. — **temizleme pulluğu** snowplow. — **topu** 1. snowball. 2. snowball, Guelder rose, bot., *Viburnum opulus*. — **topu oyna**= to play snowball. — **tut**= to stick (snow). — **yağ**= to snow, to fall (snow). — **yağdı** pepper-and-salt color. — **yağdılı** speckled, spotted (white and black), pepper-and-salt colored. — **yalağı** *geol.* firn, névé. — **yığıntısı** snowdrift.

kâr 2 (—) ⸺ P 1. profit, gain. 2. deed, act. 3. work; effect; operation. **—ı âb** *lrnd.* drinking bout, excessive drinking. **—ı âkıl** *lrnd.* reasonable act. — **ü bar** *lrnd.* burden of business; work and care. — **bırak**= to leave or yield a profit. — **çıkar**= /dan/ to profit (by), to derive profit (from). — **et**=*. — **gayesi gütmeyen şirket** nonprofit concern, corporation. — **getir**= to yield or bring profit. — **haddi** profit limit. — **hesabı** profit account. — **hissesi** share of profit, share in the profits. **—ın hisse senedi şeklinde tevzii** stock dividend. **—a iştirak** profit sharing. **—ı kadîm** *lrnd.* old-fashioned, of an old type. — **kal**= to remain as profit. — **nispeti** rate of profit. **—ı olma**= not to be able to do, *e. g.*, **bu benim kârım değildir** I am not able to do it. **—ına sat**=, **—la sat**= /ı/ to sell at a profit. **—ını tamam et**= *colloq.* to commit murder. — **tevzii** distribution of profits. — **ve zarar**, — **zarar** gain and loss, profit and loss. **—dan zarar** not to get all one hoped, but still to get something. — **zarar cetveli** profit and loss statement, income statement.

kar=ᵃʳ **3** ⸺ 1. to make a mash of; to knead. 2. to mix (cement etc., with water). 3. to shuffle (cards). 4. /a/ to thrust into.

kâr 4 (—) ⸺ P *Or. mus.* a form; the first piece sung after the "peşrev" in a classical "fasıl." **—ı nâtık** secular vocal composition which runs through several makams and or rhythmic patterns.

-kâr 5 (—) ⸺ P *lrnd.* 1. who acts, does, attends, *e. g.*, **cefakâr**, **hilekâr**. 2. worked, wrought, *e. g.*, **derkâr**.

ka'r 6 ⸺ A *lrnd.* bottom, deepest part of a sea or of a matter. **—ı nâyâb** (..⸺) P abyss.

karʳ¹ **7** ⸺ A 1. *lrnd.* a knocking. 2. *med.* percussion.

karʳ¹ **8** ⸺ A *lrnd.* gourds, pumpkins.

kar 9 (—) ⸺ A *lrnd.* pitch.

karʳ¹ **10** ⸺ A *lrnd.* 1. a settling down, becoming fixed. 2. a quieting down.

kara 1 ⸺ 1. black; dark, obscure; blackness. 2. unlucky; gloomy. — **ağaç***. — **ağaca kandil as**= to get a black mark. — **ağrı** *prov.*, *same as* **kara humma**. — **amber** jet. **K— Amid** former name of Diyarbakır. — **Arap** Negro. — **ardıç** black juniper, *bot.*, *Juniperus sabina*. — **asma** kind of bryony. — **ayit** agnus castus, *bot.*, *Vitex agnus castus*. — **bağa** *same as* **kara kurbağa**. — **baht** sad lot. — **balık** tench, *zool.*, *Tinca tinca*. — **basan** nightmare. — **baş***. — **baş martı** black-headed gull, laughing gull, *zool.*, *Xema ridibundus*. — **başak** *prov.* rye. — **başlı iskete** siskin, *zool.*, *Carduelis Spinus*. — **başlı martı** *same as* **kara baş martı**. — **başlı ötleğen** blackcap, *zool.*, *Sylvia atricapilla*. — **bayram** mourning. — **belâ** great trouble. — **beniz**, — **benizli** dark skinned. — **borsa** black market. — **borsacı** black marketer. — **borsacılık** illicit trade. — **böce** *archaic* pill beetle. — **böcü** *prov.* pig, wild boar. — **buhur** styrax tree, *bot.*, *Styrax officinale*. — **bulut** dark cloud, rain cloud, nimbus. — **buran** sandstorm. — **cahil** utterly ignorant. — **cehennem** morose. — **cümle** *colloq.* simple arithmetic. — **cümlesi eksik**, — **cümlesi zayıf** *colloq.* His arithmetic is weak; he does not know much about accounts. — **çal**= *prov.*, *same as* **kara sür**=. — **çam** larch, *bot.*, *Larix europaea*. — **çanaklı** poor, destitute, miserable. — **çepiş** *prov.* blind man's buff. **—ları çıkar**= to come out of mourning. — **çöpleme** black hellebore, *bot.*, *Helleborus officinalis*. — **damar** *anat.* vein. — **davar** black cattle, neat cattle. — **demir** wrought iron. — **duman** *prov.* fog. — **dut** black mulberry, *bot.*, *Morus niger*. — **düş** *archaic* nightmare. — **düzen** *archaic* kind of three or four-stringed guitar. **K— Eflâk** *Ott. hist.* Moldavia. **—sı elinde** slanderer, calumniator. — **elmas** 1. black diamonds, coal. 2. carbonado; carbon diamond. **K— erik fırtınası** storm occurring during the last week of July. — **et** lean and sinewy meat. — **ev** *archaic* large tent of black goat's hair. **—lara gir**=, **—lar giy**= 1. to go into mourning. 2. to wear mourning clothes. **K— Gömlekli** *hist.* Black-shirts (in Italy). — **gönüllü** *archaic* ignorant. — **gün** time of distress or need, misfortune. — **gün dostu** helper in need or distress, foul-weather friend. — **günlü** unfortunate, unlucky. — **günlük** storax-bark, after the liquid storax has been extracted from it. — **günlük yağı** liquid storax. — **gürgen** common beech, *bot.*, *Fagus sylvatica*. — **haber** news of a death or disaster. — **haberci** bringer of bad news. — **halk** *archaic* common people; mob. — **haspa** *archaic* boil on the body (sometimes fatal). — **hindiba** dandelion, *bot.*, *Taraxacum officinale*. — **horasan** finest Damascus steel. — **humma** a kind of typhus. — **iğne** 1. compass needle. 2. *prov.* stinging ant. — **kabarcık** anthrax. — **kabuk midyesi** (edible) mussel, *zool.*, *Mytilus edulis*. — **kaplı kitap** orthodox, formal, traditional way; the law. — **karaman** fat-tailed sheep of inferior quality. — **karga** common raven, *zool.*, *Corvus corax*. — **karınca** small black ant. — **kavak** black poplar, *bot.*, *Populus nigra*. — **kavza** root of parsnip. — **kaya balığı** black goby, *zool.*, *Gobius niger*. — **kayağan**-

slate, black oilstone. — **kaza** great disaster. — **kedi geç=** only in **aramızdan (aranızdan,** etc.) **kara kedi geçti** (*lit.* A black cat has passed between us.) We (you etc.) are vexed with each other. — **kehribar** pitch coal. — **keş** whey of sour curds dried into a mass. — **kış***. — **kimyon** black cumin. — **koca** *prov.* old man whose hair has not turned gray. — **kurbağa** toad, *zool., Bufo bufo.* — **kuru** swarthy and skinny; ugly. — **kuruş** *archaic* Spanish dollar. — **kurut** kind of cheese made from whey. — **kuvvet** the force of religious fanaticism. — **lâhana** dark-colored Scotch kale, red cabbage. — **leylek** black stork, episcopal stork, *zool., Ciconia nigra.* — **liste** *pol.* black list. — **listeye al=** /ı/ to blacklist. — **maça** *playing cards* spade. — **mermer** basalt. — **mersin** 1. black myrtle. 2. black (red, lake, river, stone, rock) sturgeon, *zool., Acipenser rubicundus.* — **mika** black mica, biotite. — **mum** propolis. — **mut** *archaic* ill luck. — **namlu** old fashioned rifle. — **oğlan** 1. dark youth. 2. gipsy, Bohemian. — **patlıcan** *prov., same as* **patlıcan**. — **pazı** orach, *bot., Atriplex hortensis.* — **pelin** southernwood, abrotanum, *bot., Artemisia abrotanum.* — **pus** 1. black fog. 2. *archaic* anxiety. — **saban** primitive plow. — **sakız** pitch; rosin. — **salgun** *Ott. hist.* tax levied on farmers during harvest time (in Eastern Anatolia). — **sandık** *Ott. hist.* cash department where money received from sales of deceased Janissaries' properties was deposited. — **sevda** *psych.* melancholy. — **sığır** 1. buffalo, *zool., Bos bubalus.* 2. black cattle, neat cattle. — **sinek** common housefly. — **söğüt** black willow, *bot., Salix nigra.* — **su** deep and quiet running stream. — **sungur** 1. black-winged kite, *zool., Elanus caeruleus.* 2. goshawk, *zool., Astur palumbarius.* — **sür=** /a/ to blacken, to calumniate. — **tahın** *prov.* anthrax of sheep. — **tahta** blackboard. — **talih** misfortune, sad lot. — **tamga** *Ott. hist.* custom tax. — **taş** slate. — **toprak** black earth, black soil. — **turp** horseradish, *bot., Armoracia lapathifolia.* — **uğrusu** *archaic* night thief. — **yağız** very dark-skinned; swarthy and sturdy boy. — **yakmaca** *prov.* anthrax of sheep. — **yandık** camel's thorn, *bot., Alhagi Maurorum.* — **yanı** *archaic* painful subcutaneous tumor. — **yanık** *vet.* anthrax of sheep. — **yas** deep mourning. — **yazı***. — **yel***. — **yer** 1. *colloq.* grave. 2. *archaic* earth, soil. — **yer prasası** black horehound, *bot., Ballota nigra.* — **yılan** ringed snake, grass snake, *zool., Tropidonotus natrix.* — **yoksul** *archaic* very poor, miserable. — **yonca** black medick, *bot., Medicago lupulina.* — **yosunlar** *bot., Bryophyta.* — **yurt** *archaic* arid tract of land.

— **yüz** dishonor, disgrace, ignominy. — **yüzlü** dishonored, disgraced, who is shamed by some bad act.

kara 2 قَارَه قَرَه [*Arabic* **garra**] 1. land, dry land; mainland, continent; shore. 2. ground, land; territorial, terrestrial. —**da** on land, ashore, on shore. —**dan** by land. — **askeri** land soldier. —**ya at=** /ı/ to bring to shore, to put on land, to strand. — **ataşesi** military attaché. —**ya ayak bas=** to go ashore, to disembark. — **bölgesi** land sector. —**ya çek=** /ı/ to haul up on the shore, to beach. —**ya çık=** to land, to disembark, to go ashore. —**ya çıkar=** /ı/ to land, disembark; to discharge. —**ya çıkma izni** *naut.* free gangway. —**da ve denizde müdafaa** amphibious defense. — **ve deniz uçağı** amphibian (airplane). —**ya düş=** 1. to be beached, to be stranded, to strand, to be driven ashore. 2. *slang* to fall or walk into a trap, to be trapped, duped. —**ya düşür=** /ı/ *slang* to ruin. —**dan git=** *same as* **karaya düş=**[1]. — **gümrüğü**, — **gümrük** custom house for inland merchandise. — **harbi** land warfare, territorial war. — **harb kuvvetleri** territorial forces. — **hedefi** *mil.* ground target. — **hizmeti** *naut.* service ashore. —**ya in=** 1. *aero.* to alight, to land. 2. to go ashore, to land. — **kaplumbağası** tortoise. — **kesimi** *neol.* land sector. — **keşfi** *mil.* ground reconnaissance. — **kıt'aları** *mil.* land troops. —**sı kurası** *colloq.* its land and appurtenances. — **kuvvetleri** *mil.* land forces, territorial forces. — **ordusu** land army, the army. —**ya otur=** *naut.* to run aground, to be stranded. — **postası** overland post. — **resmi** *Ott. hist.* a sheep tax. — **seyahati**, —**da seyahat** journey by land, overland journey. — **suları** territorial waters. —**da ve suda işler** amphibious, running both on land and water. — **tayyaresi** land plane. — **ticareti** overland trade. — **torpili** subterranean mine. — **üssü** *aero.* land base; *naut.* shore base. — **vapuru** *colloq.* train. —**ya vur=** to run or be driven ashore (fish). —**da yaşar** terrestrial, inhabiting the land. — **yolu** overland route. — **yosunları** mosses, *bot., Musci.*

kara=[3] قَالَامَق prov. /ı/ 1. to slander. 2. to blame.

kar'a 4 قَرَع A *lrnd.* gourd, pumpkin, squash.

karaağaç[1] قَارَه آغَاج elm, *bot., Ulmus.* —**giller** *neol.* elm family, *bot., Ulmaceae.*

karabaldır قَرَه بَالدِر maidenhair, *bot., Adiantum capillus Veneris.*

karabaş قَارَه بَاش 1. Anatolian sheep dog. 2. French lavender, *bot., Lavendula stoechas.* 3. buckwheat, *bot., Fagopyrum.* 4. *archaic* monk; *prov.* old bachelor. 5. *archaic* female slave.

karabatak¹ قره بتاق غاره باناوه 1. cormorant, zool., *Phalacrocorax carbo*. 2. *Or. mus.* the playing alternately of the bowed instruments and those played with a plectrum in a musical performance. — **gibi** person who is frequently in and out of sight. — **peşrev** a kind of **peşrev** with solo and chorus sections.

karabet (. — .) قرابت A 1. relationship, kinship, affinity. 2. nearness, proximity. —**i eb** *lrnd.* agnation. —**i gayrivilâd** *law* consanguinity excluding father or mother and children. —**i sıhriye** *lrnd.* relationship by marriage. —**i vilâd** *lrnd.* consanguinity between parents and children or grandparents and grandchildren.

karabiber قره بيبر غاره بيبر pepper, *bot.*, *Piper nigrum*. —**giller** *neol.* pepper family, *bot.*, *Piperaceae*.

karabin (. — —) قرا بين A *lrnd.*, *pl.* of **kurban 1.**

karabina (. . . . .) قره بينه قرا بينه It carbine; blunderbuss. —**lı** carabineer.

karabinyer قره بينيه قالا بينيه It Italian gendarme.

karaboğa قره بوغا قالا بوغا bull buffalo.

karaboğaz قره بوغاز قالا بوغاز male sparrow.

karaboya قره بويا قالا بويا sulphuric acid.

karabuğday قره بغداى قالا بوغداى buckwheat, *bot.*, *Fagopyrum*. —**giller** *neol.*, *bot.*, *Polygonaceae*.

karaburçak¹ قره بورجاق قالا بورجاق bitter vetch, *bot.*, *Vicia ervilia*.

karaca 1 قره جه roe, roe deer, *zool.*, *Capreolus capreolus*. — **derisi** doeskin.

karaca 2 (. . .') قره جه somewhat black or dark. — **balığı** kind of sturgeon, *zool.*, *Acipenser guldenstadtii*. — **ot** black hellebore, Christmas rose, *bot.*, *Helleborus niger*. — **ördek** black duck. — **renkli** fallow, fawn (colored).

karaca 3 قره جه biceps and triceps muscle; upper arm. — **et** muscle of the upper arm. — **kemiği** *anat.* humerus, bone of the brachium.

karaca 4 قره جه قارا جه *prov.* onion seed; nigella seed.

karacı 1 قره جى قالا جى backbiter.

karacı 2 قره جى 1. gipsy. 2. brigand, highwayman. 3. *prov.* trickster.

karaciğer قره جكر قالا جكر liver; *med.* hepatic, hepato-. — **hastalığı** disease of the liver. — **iltihabı** hepatitis. — **kanaması** bleeding of the liver. — **sirozu** hepatocirrhosis.

karaçalı قره چالى 1. furze, gorse, *bot.*, *Ulex europaeus*. 2. unpleasant person in the company. —**sı elinde** habitual backbiter.

karaçav قره چاو [karoça] *prov.* removable side of an oxcart.

karaçayır قره چاير قالا چاير rye grass, meadow grass, darnel, *bot.*, *Lolium*.

karaçuri (. — —) قراچورى P *lrnd.* kind of long sword.

Karadağ قره طاغ *geog.* Montenegro.

karadamak¹ قره داماق *prov.* obstinate.

karadamla قره دامله *prov.* apoplexy, paralysis.

Karadeniz قره دكز قالا دكز *geog.* Black Sea. — **boğazı** the Bosphorus.

karadiken قره ديكن blackthorn.

karadoğu قره دوغى *prov.* spurred rye, ergot of rye.

karafatma قره فاطمه black beetle, cockroach, *zool.*, *Blatta orientalis*.

kâragâh (— — —) كاراگاه P *lrnd.* acquainted with the truth of any affair; sagacious, experienced. —**î** (— — — —) P knowledge of the matter.

karagöt قره گوت gadwall, *zool.*, *Anas strepera*.

karagöz قره گوز 1. Turkish shadow show. 2. *w. cap.* main figure of the Turkish shadow show. 3. *colloq.* funny fellow. 4. black spectacled animal; breed of sheep of the Black Sea region of Anatolia. 5. same as **karagöz balığı**. 6. *slang* small dice. 7. *prov.* kidney bean. — **balığı** sea bream, *zool.*, *Sargus*. — **istavrit balığı** Mediterranean scad, saurel, *zool.*, *Trachurus Mediterraneus*. — **oynat**= to perform the shadow show. — **oyunu** Turkish shadow show. — **tirsi** Pontic herring, *zool.*, *Clupea Pontica*.

karagözcü قره گوزجى shadow show operator, Karagöz player. —**lük** profession of a **karagöz** showman.

karagözle=ʳ قره گوزله /1/ to prune down to a mere stump.

karagözlükᵍᵘ قره گوزلك buffoonery. — **et**= to play the fool.

karagül قره گول breed of sheep from whose lambs astrakhan is obtained.

karagat قراغات archaic galingale.

karağı قراغى *prov.* 1. crooked stick; polo stick; fire-rake; crook. 2. nightblindness.

karağul قراغول archaic, same as **karavul.**

karah (. —) قراه A *lrnd.* 1. good soil. 2. field ready plowed for sowing.

karahalile قره هليله black myrobalan.

karaiğne قره ايگنه stinging ant.

karain (. — .) قراين A *lrnd.*, *pl.* of **karine**.

karak=ʳ 1 قراق *prov.* to become hoarse (voice).

karakᵍⁱ 2 قراق archaic 1. look, sight; eye. 2. a marauding attack, raid.

karakaçan قره قاچان breed of sheep in Thrace and Bulgaria.

karakafes قره قفس 1. Montpellier coris, *bot.*, *Coris Monspelientis*. 2. comfrey, *bot.*, *Symphytum*.

karakalem قره قلم pencil or charcoal drawing; having a black design. — **kâğıdı** drawing paper.

karakavukᵍᵘ قره قاوق *prov.* chicory.

karakçı قَرَا فْجی archaic marauder, plunderer.

karakeçi قَرَه كچی barbel, zool., *Barbus fluviatilis*.

karakılçık[gı] قره قیلجی *prov.* kind of wheat or barley.

karakış قره قیش severe winter, depth of winter. — **fırtınası** storm occurring about the 13th of December.

karakla=[r] قَرَا قَدَمَه archaic to maraud, to make a raid for plunder.

karakol قَرَا قول قره قول قره غول قراول 1. police station, station house; *mil.* outpost; guard. 2. patrol. — **binası** station house. —**a celbet=** /ı/ to summon to the police station. — **efradı**, — **eratı** men in a police station or at an outpost. — **filikası** guard boat, patrol boat. — **gemisi** guard ship, patrol vessel. — **gez=** to patrol the beat, to go the rounds. — **hattı**, —**lar hattı** line of outposts. — **hizmeti** patrol service. — **kumandanı** commander on guard, *naut.* officer of the watch. — **müfrezesi** patrol detachment. — **nöbetçisi** sentry, post, guard, picket, *naut.* lookout. — **vazifesi** patrol duty, *naut.* watch duty. — **vazifesi yap=** to be on the beat, to be on guard duty.

karakolhane (...—.) قره قول خانه archaic police station, station house.

karakolluk ol=[ur] قره قوللیا وله to be taken to the police station.

karakoncolos قَرَا قونجُولُوس قره قونجُلوس Gk black bogey, demon invoked for frightening naughty children; very ugly person.

karakter قَالَ قتَر F character. — **aktörü** character actor. — **eğitimi** character training. — **komedisi** character comedy, comedy of manners. — **piyesi** character play. — **rolü** character part. —**i sağlam** of upright character. — **sağlamlığı**, — **salâbeti** firmness or strength of character. — **teşekkülü**, — **teşkili** formation of character.

karakteristik[gı] قَالَ كتَریستیك F 1. characterization, characteristics, characteristic, distinctive. 2. *math.* characteristic. — **alâmet** characteristic strain. — **hususiyet** a characteristic. — **bir şekilde** characteristically. — **vasıf** distinctiveness, characteristic.

karaktersiz قَالَ كتَرسز characterless, unprincipled, fickle. —**lik** want of character.

karakulak[gı] قَرَه قُولَقْ 1. w. cap., a noted spring of water near Istanbul. 2. bobcat, lynx, zool., *Caracal melanotis*. 3. *prov.* a kind of dagger. 4. *Ott. hist.* confidential messenger of the Grand Vizier; detective. **K— suyu gibi hafif** easily digested.

karakullukçu قره قوللقجی *Ott. hist.* orderly of a Janissary officer.

karakus قَرَا قوش 1. eagle, zool., *aquila*.

2. *prov.* morbid enlargement on the crus of hoofed animal.

karakuşi (..—–) قره قوشی P despotic, arbitrary, high-handed (from the name of a despotic ruler), *only in* **hükm-i karakuşî** arbitrary decision.

karala=[r] قَرَالامَه قَالَ لا مَق /ı/ 1. to blacken, to make black; to blot out; to scribble; to write hastily. 2. to blacken, to calumniate, to slander.

karalama قَالَ لامَه 1. *verbal n.* of **karala=**[1, 2]. 2. calligraphic exercise. — **kâğıdı** 1. draft-paper, scratch paper. 2. *obs.* paper, very highly glazed, so that the writing can be washed out, used for calligraphic exercises. — **yaz=** to practise handwriting by scribbling, to write calligraphic exercises.

karalaş=[ır] قَره لاشمَق to become black gradually.

karalat=[ır] قره لاتمَق /ı/ *caus.* of **karala=**.

karalı قَرَه لى having black spots, mixed or spotted with black.

karalık[gı] قَره لیق blackness, darkness.

karaltı قَالَ لْتى قَرَالْتى 1. indistinct figure, blackness. 2. *prov.* household gear; mass.

Karaman 1 قَرَامَان 1. Caraman (former principality in Asia Minor). 2. town in the vilayet of Konya. 3. *l. c.* fat-tailed sheep of inferior quality. — **kimyonu** caraway seed. — **koyunu** *same as* **karaman**[3]. —**ın koyunu, sonra çıkar oyunu** *colloq.* You'll see later how cunning he was.

karaman 2 قَرَامَان very dark (person).

karaman 3 قَرَامَان *naut.* drop hammer. — **halatı** drag rope, tow rope, used for floating a ship. — **kancası** hook for a drag rope. — **vur=** *same as* **karamanla=**.

karamandola (...´..) قَرَا مَاندُولَه قَرَامَاندُولَه *text.* prunella, prunello; satin jean.

karamanla=[r] قَرَامَانْلامَق to flap wildly about (sail).

Karamanlı قَالَ مَانْلى قَرَه مَانلى 1. person from Karaman. 2. Caramanian, Turkish-speaking Greek Orthodox of the Karaman region. —**ca** Turkish dialect spoken by the Caramanians and written in Greek characters.

Karamanoğulları قَرَامَان أوغُلَّرى *hist.* the Karamanids (a fourteenth-century dynasty in Konya).

karambol قَالَ مبُول F 1. *colloq.* collision (of vehicles). 2. cannon, carom (billiards). — **yap=** 1. to collide, to come into collision. 2. to kiss (billiards).

karamela (...´.) قَالَ مِلا It caramel, burnt sugar. —**lı** mixed or sweetened with caramel.

karamık[gı] قَرَامیق قره میق *var. of* **karamuk**.

karamsar *neol.* pessimistic.

karamsı=[r] 1 *neol.* to be pessimistic.

karamsı 2 قَره مسى blackish. —**lık** black spots on the face.

karamtık, karamtırak, karamtul قَرامْتیق قَرَامتراق قَرَامْترل archaic blackish, dark-colored

karamuk

karamukᵍᵘ قاراموق قره موه 1. corn cockle, *bot.*, *Agrostemma githago*. 2. *prov.* blackberry.
karamusal قره موصال It *naut.* mooring swivel. **—a vur** /ı/ to connect the chains of a vessel lying on two anchors by means of a mooring swivel, to moor.
kâramuz (— — —) كارآموز P *lrnd.* skillful, expert.
Karamürsel 1 قره مرسل 1. *a town on the Gulf of Izmit.* 2. *l. c., hist.* small craft carrying cargo. **— sepeti san** *slang* /ı/ to underestimate.
karamürsel 2 قره مرسل *var. of* **karamusal**.
karan=ʳ قرانمق *archaic* to curse; to damn.
karanfil 1 قرنفل A 1. garden pink, carnation, *bot.*, *Dianthus plumarius*. 2. clove, clove pink, gillyflower, *bot.*, *Dianthus caryophyllus*. 3. clove tree, *bot.*, *Caryophyllus aromaticus*. 4. *slang* arse. **— ağacı** *same as* **karanfil³**. **— çiçeği** 1. clove blossom. 2. *same as* **karanfil²**. **— kabuğu** Indian clove bark, bark of *Cinnamonum culilawan*. **— kokusu** carnation scent. **— kökü** bennet, root of common avens. **—i merşuş** *lrnd.* picotee. **— otu** herb bennet, avens, *bot.*, *Geum urbanum*. **—i sık**= *slang* to endure, to hold out. **— yağı** oil of cloves. **— yarpuzu** clove balm. **— yatağı** flowering bed of pinks.
karanfil 2 قرنفل قرنفيل It *naut.* Spanish burton, garnet; guy. **— palangası** guy tackle, span.
karanfilgiller *neol., same as* **karanfiliye**.
karanfiliye (...—.) قرنفليّة *bot.*, *Caryophyllaceae*.
karaniya (.—.—) قرانيا A cornel, *bot.*, *Cornus*.
karanlıkᵍⁱ قرانلق darkness, obscurity; dark place; dark, obscure; blackness, gloom. **—ta** in the dark, in the darkness. **— bas**= to grow dark, to become dusk; to fall (night). **— basarken** at dusk. **— basmadan** before dusk. **—a çık**= to go out into the dark. **K— Denizi** *obs.* Arctic Ocean. **— düşünce** dark thought. **— et**= /ı/ to cause darkness, to render dark or obscure, to darken. **—ta göz kırp**= to wink in the dark *said of a wasted effort to communicate*. **— hücre** dark cell. **—a kal**= to be benighted. **K— Kıta** Dark Continent. **— maksad**, **— niyet** sinister intention. **— oda** *phys.* camera obscura; *phot.* darkroom. **— ol**= to become dark, to fall (night). **—ta yürü**= to grope about in the dark; *fig.* to do something without understanding the situation.
karantina (..´..) قرانتينه قرانتنه قرننه It quarantine. **— bayrağı** quarantine flag, yellow flag. **— bekle**= to be in quarantine. **— dairesi** quarantine office. **— et**= to quarantine. **—dan geç**= to go through quarantine. **— kordon** quarantine or sanitary cordon. **— koy**= /a/ to quarantine, to put in quarantine. **— memuru** quarantine officer. **—ya tâbi ol**= to be subject to quarantine. **—da yat**= to be in quarantine (ship, etc.).
karantinahane (....—.) قرانتينه خانه 1. quarantine hospital, lazaretto. 2. quarantine office.
karantinhane (...—.) قرانتنخانه *same as* **karantinahane**.
karanu قرانو قره نو *archaic* dark, obscure; darkness, obscurity. **—luk** darkness, obscurity.
karar 1 قرار [karar 2] A 1. decision, resolution, resolve, determination; *jur.* decree. 2. stability, firmness. 3. right quantity, reasonable degree. 4. *Or. mus.* pause. **bir —da** in an unvarying degree, in a uniform manner. **—ınca** as much as necessary, as usual. **—ında** just in the right quantity, degree or quality, normal. **—ında ol**= *with the infinitive* to be determined, resolved, decided, to have made up one's mind (to do), to be bent (on doing), *e. g.*, **gitmek kararındayım** I am determined to go. **—larında** about, around (time), *e. g.*, **saat sekiz kararlarında** about eight o'clock. **— al**= /üzerinde, hakkında/ to take a decision (on), to make a resolution (about). **— altına al**= /ı/ to decide, determine, resolve (on). **—a bağla**= /ı/ to arrive at a decision, to bring to a conclusion. **— başı** *jur.* preamble. **— birisinin lehine tecelli et**= to be in someone's favor (decision). **— bul**= to become settled or stable, to acquire stability, to settle down. **—ını bul**= to come to a fixed condition. **—ı firara tebdil et**= to cease resistance and flee. **—ı kadar** *same as* **kararınca**. **—a kaldı** *jud.* completed except for the final decision. **— kıl**= /da/ 1. to abide by a decision. 2. to settle down (to). **— nisabı** quorum. **bir — üzre** *same as* **bir kararda**. **—a var**= to arrive at a decision, to come to a resolution, to reach a decision. **— ver**= /a/ to decide (to), to make up one's mind (to); /hakkında, üzerinde/ to decide upon, *jud.* to give a ruling (on).
karar 2 (.—) قرار A *lrnd., same as* **karar 1**. **—ı idad** *lrnd., jur.* preparatory decision. **— kararı sâbık** *lrnd.* The previous decision stands. **—ı karine** *lrnd., jud.* conjectural decree. **—ı kat'î** *lrnd.* decisive or peremptory resolution, decree. **—ı muvakkat** *lrnd.* temporary resolution, agreement, state or decision.
karar=ʳ 3 تارامه قرارمه 1. to become black, dark or obscure; to become overclouded or overcast (sky); to darken. 2. *archaic* to become sorrowful, to be grieved.

karardad (.——) قرارداد P lrnd. established, confirmed, ratified.

karardade (.——.) قراردادە P lrnd. decided on; agreement, decision. **—sini çek=** /ın/ to draw up the agreement or decision about it.

karardar (.——) قراردار P lrnd. fixed, consolidated, permanent.

karargâh 1 (..—) قرارگاه [**karargâh 2**] headquarters. **— erkânı** mil. staff party. **— heyeti** mil. staff. **— kur=** to set up headquarters. **— subayı** staff officer. **—ı umumi** mil. general headquarters.

karargâh 2 (.——) قرارگاه P lrnd. 1. same as **karargâh 1**. 2. mansion, residence.

karargir (.——) قرارگیر P lrnd. fixed, settled, decided. **—î** (.———) P quiet, peace, security.

kararî (.——) قراری A lrnd. sedentary.

kararla= قرارلامق /ı/ to estimate by eye, by sight. **—ma** estimated by guess. **—madan** at a guess. **—ş=** to be decided. **—ştır=** /ı/ to decide, to agree (upon).

kararlı قرارلی 1. /da/ decided (to, upon). 2. stable, constant, fixed. 3. phys. stationary (waves). **— denge** phys. stable equilibrium.

kararname (..—.) قرارنامە [Persian .——.] P written decree, decision or agreement.

kararsız قرارسز 1. undecided, irresolute, undetermined; perplexed, puzzled. 2. changeable, unstable (weather, market, etc.). **— denge** phys. unstable equilibrium. **— ol=** /da/ to hesitate, waver, to be of two minds (about).

kararsızlık قرارسزلق 1. indecision, irresoluteness, wavering. 2. instability. **— içinde ol=** to be hesitant, to be vacillating; to be wavering or in a state of indecision.

karart= قرارتمق /ı/ 1. to make dark or obscure, to blacken, to darken. 2. to shade, to make shadows. **—ı** same as **karaltı¹**. **—ıl=** pass. of **karart=**. **—ma** 1. verbal n. 2. blackout.

karasağı قراصغی archaic blackish.

karasal neol. continental. **—lar** terrestrial, zool., Territelae. **— kumul** geol. continental dune. **— oluşuk** geol. continental formation.

Karası قرەسی var. of **Karesi**.

karasör قراسور var. of **karoseri**.

karasu قرەصو 1. path. glaucoma. 2. disease in the legs of cattle. **— humması** path. black water fever.

karaşat قراشت A lrnd. the sixth mnemonic formula of Arabic letters according to their numerical value (ق = 100, ر = 200, ش =300, ت = 400).

karaşın قراشین prov. brown, dark-skinned, brunet.

kârașina (——.—) كاراشنا P lrnd. sagacious; experienced, skillful.

karat= قراتمه archaic, caus. of **kara=** 3.

karatavuk قاراطاووق blackbird, zool., Turdus merula.

karatis (.——) قراطیس A lrnd., pl. of **kırtas**.

karavana (..´..) قروانه 1. copper dish used as a mess tin by soldiers and sailors. 2. soldiers' and sailors' meal. 3. flattish diamond. 4. miss in target shooting. **— borusu** mil. trumpet signal for mess. **—i kebir** large platter. **—dan ye=** colloq. 1. to eat out of a platter, to mess together. 2. to lead a simple existence, to live simply.

karavanacı قروانه جی mil. 1. mess carrier. 2. soldier who misses in target shooting.

karavaş قراواش archaic female slave, servant, maid.

karavela, karaveli (...´.) قاراولا قرەولە It 1. archaic ship of war, caravel. 2. prov. shoe, summer shoe.

karavi (.´.) قراوی Gk large sailing boat.

karavide (...´.) قراویده Gk freshwater crayfish, zool., Cambarus, Astacus.

karavul قراول archaic sentry, guard, watchman; outpost. **—hane** (...—.) guardhouse, sentry or outpost station.

karayaka قرەیقە prov. breed of sheep of the Black Sea region of Anatolia.

karayazı قرەیازی black decree of Providence, evil fate.

karayel قرەیل northwest wind; north west.

kârazma (———), **kârazmude** (———.) كارآزما كارآزمودە P lrnd. skillful, expert, intelligent, practised.

karban 1 قاربان prov. basket; box; wooden bucket.

kârban 2 (——) كاربان P lrnd., same as **kervan**.

karbanseray (——.—) كاربانسرای same as **kervansaray**.

karbit قاربیت F same as **karpit**.

karboksil قاربوكسیل F chem. carboxyl.

karbol قاربول F chem. carbolic acid.

karbon قاربون F chem. carbon, geol. carboniferous formation. **— baskısı** carbon print. **— devri** carboniferous age. **— dioksid** carbon dioxide. **— gazı** coal gas. **— kâğıdı** 1. carbon paper. 2. phot. carbon paper, carbon tissue. **— monoksid** chem. carbon monoxide. **— oksid** carbon dioxide. **— oksid gazı** carbon dioxide gas. **— tozlu mikrofon** carbon granule microphone.

karbonad قاربونا د F washing soda.

karbonat قاربونات F chem. carbonate (salt). **—la=** /ı/ to carbonate, to impregnate with carbonic acid. **—lama** a carbonating.

karbonik قاربونیك F chem. carbonic. **— asit** carbonic acid.

karbonlaş=ᵗʳ قاربونلاشمق to become carbonized, charred. —**mış çelik** blister steel, converted steel. —**tır**= /ı/ to carbonize, to char.
karbonlu قاربونلی carbonaceous, carboniferous.
karbüratör قاربوراتور F carburetor. — **ayarı** carburetor adjustment. — **kolu** carburetor lever. — **memesi** carburetor nozzle. — **pistonu** carburetor piston. — **şamandırası** carburetor float. — **valfı** carburetor valve.
karcaş=ᵗʳ قارجشمق prov. to become disordered, confused, tangled.
karcaşıkᵍⁱ قارجشق prov. mixed, confused, tangled. — **yel** archaic tempest. —**lık** disorder, confusion.
karcı قارجی seller of snow.
Karcığar قارجغار Or. mus. a simple makam about five centuries old.
karcık=ᵗʳ قارجقمق prov. to become hoarse (voice).
karcış=ᵗʳ قارجشمق archaic, var. of **karcaş**=. —**tır**= /ı/ to confuse.
kârçe (—.) كارچه P Or. mus. small kâr.
karçıllan=ᵗʳ قارچللنمق archaic to be covered with a thin fall of snow.
karçuğa قارچوغا archaic species of hawk.
kârd (—) كارد P lrnd. sheath knife.
kardamana (..—.) قردمانا A cardamom.
kardamina قاردامینه It cardamine, bot., Cardamina amara.
kardan 1 قاردان F mech. cardan. — **contası** Cardan joint. — **mafsalı** auto. universal joint, Hooke's coupling. — **sisteminde asma** cardanic suspension.
kârdan 2 (——) كاردان P lrnd. experienced, skillful. —**î** (———) P, —**lık** experience, skill.
kârdar (——) كاردار P lrnd. who manages affairs.
kârdaran (———) كارداران P managers of affairs. —**ı felek** planets.
kardaş قارداش prov., var. of **kardeş**. — **okuş**=, —**laş**= archaic to declare each other adoptive brothers.
kardeş قارداش brother or sister, brother(s) and sister(s); fraternal. — **harbi** fratricidal war, civil war. —**ten ileri ol**= to be bosom friends. — **kardeş** brotherly, sisterly; fraternally. — **katili** fratricide, brother's or sister's murderer. — **katli** fratricide, brother's or sister's murder. — **kavgası** fratricidal quarrel. — **okun**= obs. to be publicly adopted as a brother or sister. — **payı** equal share. — **payı yap**= /ı/ to divide equally, to go halves. — **savaşı** fratricidal strife or war.
kardeşçe قارداشجه brotherly, sisterly, fraternal; in a brotherly or sisterly manner.
kardeşkanı قارداش قانی dragon's blood. — **ağacı** dragon gum tree, bot., Pterocarpus Draco.

kardeşle=ᵗʳ قارداشلمك archaic to push out shoots.
kardeşlikᵍⁱ قارداشلق 1. brotherhood, sisterhood, fraternity. 2. adoptive brother or sister.
kârdger (—.) كاردگر P Ott. hist. imperial cutler.
kârdide (———.) كاردیده P lrnd. experienced, veteran.
kardinalⁱⁱ قاردینال F cardinal (of the Catholic church). **K—ler Heyeti** College of Cardinals. — **şapkası** cardinal's hat. —**lik** cardinalate.
kare قاره F 1. math. square; geom. quadrat. 2. party of four players (cards). —**sini al**= math. /ın/ same as **kareye yükselt**=. — **kök** neol., math. square root. — **kökünü al**= neol., math. /ın/ to extract the square root (of). — **şeklinde** quadratic. —**ye yükselt**= neol., math. /ı/ to square. —**leme** neol., math. quadrature.
kareli قاره لی 1. checkered, cross-lined. 2. math. quadratic; square, squared.
Karesi قره سی Ott. hist. Province of Balıkesir (ancient Mysia).
kâret=ᵈᵉʳ كارتمك 1. to win; to profit. 2. to produce an effect, tell. —**mez** no use.
karevele (...'.) قره وله Gk var. of **karavela**.
karevle قره وله prov. low shoe, outdoor slipper.
kârferma (—.—) كارفرما P lrnd. who commands in affairs of state; sovereign, minister, governor.
karfiçe (..'.) قارفیچه Gk small-headed nail; pin.
karga 1 قارغا 1. crow, zool., Corvus. —**lar** zool., Corvidae. — **bardağı** prov. aristolochia, birthwort. — **beyin**, — **beyni** prov. meal prepared with yogurt and grape syrup. — **bok yemeden** vulg. very early in the morning. — **burnu** same as **karga burun 2**. — **burun** 1. person with a prominent nose. 2. round or flat pliers. 3. doorlatch. — **burun çıkıntısı** anat. caracoid. — **büken** nux vomica. —**yı bülbül diye sat**= colloq. to swindle. — **derneği** crowd of roughs. — **düğleği**, — **düleği**, — **düvleği** prov. colocynth. — **gibi** swarthy and skinny. — **karganın gözünü oymaz** A crow won't peck a crow; there's honor among thieves. — **sekmez** desolate place. — **taşla**= slang to molest or beset a girl or woman.
karga 2 (.'.) قارغا غا قارغا It naut. Haul down. Upside down. Topped. — **et**= /ı/ to top. — **ol**= to be topped.
karga 3 (.'.) قرغا It naut. brail.
karga 4 (.'.) قارغا It only in — **et**= /ı/ naut. to fetch (the pump). — **tulumba et**= /ı/ to carry off someone by their arms and legs.
karga=ᵗʳ 5 قارغامق prov. /ı/ to curse, to damn.

kargabaso (..´..) قارغاباصو It *naut.* lowering a sail.
kargabaşı, kargabaşo (...´.) قارغاباشى قارغاباشو It *naut., var. of* **kargabaso**.
kargaborina, kargaburina (....´.) قارغابورينه قارغابورينه It *naut.* 1. leech line. 2. snatch block. 3. external shape of timbers or frames of a ship.
kargacık[¹] قارغهجى 1. little or pet crow. 2. flourish in calligraphic Arabic script. — **burgacık** 1. scrawl (writing). 2. irregular or ill-shaped thing. — **burgacık yaz=** to scrawl, to scribble.
kargacunda (...´.) قارغاجونده It *naut.* topping of yards. — **et=** /ı/ to top (a yard), to cockbill (the yards).
kargadelen قارغادلن soft-shelled almond.
kargafunda, kargafundo (...´.) قارغافونده قارغافوندو It *naut.* buntline of a sail. — **et=** /ı/ to haul up with a buntline.
kârgâh (— —) كارگاه P *lrnd.* 1. workshop, place of business. 2. the world.
kargamsı *neol., anat.* coracoid. — **çıkıntı** coracoid process.
kargapunta (...´.) قارغابونط It *naut.* clew line.
kargaşa, kargaşalık[¹] قارغاشا قرغش confusion, confused cries; dispute, quarrel, disorder, agitation.
kârgeh (—.) كارگ P *lrnd., var. of* **kârgâh**.
kârger (—.) كارگر P *lrnd.* 1. workman, man of business. 2. God, the Maker of all.
kargı 1 قارغى 1. *archaic* pike; javelin; lance. 2. *prov.* cane.
kargı=[ʳ] 2 قارغى *prov., var. of* **karga=** 5.
kargın 1 قارغين large carpenter's plane.
kargın 2 قارغين *prov.* flood.
kargın 3 قارغين *archaic* calfskin leather.
kargış قارغش *prov.* curse, malediction. — **dök=** /a/ to curse, to damn. — **la=** /ı/ *same as* **kargış dök=**.
kârgir (—.) كارگير [*Persian* — —] *same as* **kâgir**.
kârgüzar (—.—) كارگزار P *lrnd.* skillful, discharging one's duty.
karh قرح A *lrnd.* a wounding; sore, wound.
karha قرحه A *lrnd.* sore, wound; spot; boil.
karhane 1 (.—.) قارخانه house or place for storing snow.
kârhane 2 (— —.) كارخانه P 1. *archaic* factory, workshop. 2. *var. of* **kerhane**. —**i cameşuy** *Ott. hist.* washhouse in the Janissary barracks. —**i hassa** *Ott. hist.* imperial factory.
kârhaneli كارخانه لى *Ott. hist.* worker of a Janissary factory.
kârı 1 قارى قارو قرى 1. woman, old woman (derogatory). 2. wife, spouse; *law* married woman. 3. *prov.* aged woman. — **ağızlı** womanish. —**sı ağızlı** who chimes in with his wife. — **al=** /ı/ to marry. — **çekiştirmesi, — dedikodusu** women's gossip. — **düzeni, — fendi** woman's wiles or artfulness. — **hâkimiyeti** petticoat government. —**lar hamamı** very noisy place. — **kısmı** womankind. — **kızan** *prov.* the whole household, wife and children. — **koca** wife and husband, married couple. — **koca hayatı** conjugal life, married life. — **koca kavgası** family quarrel. — **koca ocağı** conjugal family. —**sı kurusu** his wife and his household. — **lâkırdısı** old wives' tale. — **milleti** womenfolk. — **pazarı** assembly of clamorous people.
karı=[ʳ] 2 قارىمق *prov.* to grow old, to become old.
karık[¹] 1 قاريه snowblindness; snowblind.
karık[¹] 2 قاريو *prov.* furrow.
karık[¹] 3 قاريو *prov.* raucous, husky (voice).
karık=[ʳ] 4 قاريقمق *prov.* 1. to become raucous, husky (voice). 2. to be dazzled (eyes).
karıl=[ʳ] قاريلمق *prov.* 1. to be mixed, mingled; to pair, mate (animals). 2. to become raucous, husky (voice).
karılı قارىلى having a wife, married.
karılık[¹] قاريليق womanhood, wifehood; quality and functions of a wife. — **et=** 1. /a/ to be the wife (of). 2. to do the duties of a wife. 3. to play a dirty trick.
karımsı 1 قاريمسى 1. snowlike, sleety. 2. hoarfrost, rime.
karımsı 2 قاريمسى womanlike, womanish.
karın[ʳᵐ] 1 قارين قارن 1. *anat.* abdomen, belly; abdominal, ventral. 2. stomach; womb. 3. swelling, protuberant part; bulge, bilge of a vessel. 4. inside (of anything). —**ı acık=** to be hungry. —**ı aç** hungry. — **adalesi** abdominal muscle. —**ı ağrı=** to have a stomach ache. — **ağrısı** 1. stomach ache, colic. 2. *colloq.* tiresome person. — **ağrısına uğra=** to have a grievance, worries. — **altı** hypogastric region. —**dan bacaklılar** *neol.* gastropodes, *zool., Gastropoda.* — **bağı** belly band, abdominal bandage. — **biçiminde** belly-shaped, bulging. — **boşluğu** abdominal cavity. — **bölgesi** abdominal regions. —**ı burnunda** pregnant. — **cidarı** abdominal wall. — **cidarı çatlaması** interstitial hernia. — **çatlağı** abdominal rupture. —**ını deş=** /ın/ to disembowel, to eviscerate. —**ı doy=** to be satisfied (with food). —**ını doyur=** to eat one's fill. —**ı dümbelek çal=** *same as* **karnı zil çal=**. — **fıtığı** hernia. — **gebeliği** abdominal pregnancy, extrauterine pregnancy. —**ından geç=** *prov.* /ın/ to come into one's mind. —**ı geniş** easygoing, tolerant. —**ı kara** *prov.* kidney

bean. —ı karnına geçmiş very thin. — karındaştan yakın *colloq.* One's own interests come first. —ından konuş= 1. to ventriloquize. 2. *prov.* to muse, to meditate, to reflect. —ından konuşan (adam) ventriloquist. —ından konuşma ventriloquism. — kovuğu abdominal cavity. — kuşağı belt. — salya bezi pancreas. —ından söyle= *colloq.* to contrive, to invent. —ın su toplaması dropsy in the abdomen, ascites. —ı tok not hungry, full up. —ım tok (bu sözlere) *colloq.* I won't be taken in by such words. —ı tok, sırtı pek well fed and well clothed. — üstüne iniş *aero.* pancake-landing. —ını yar= /ın/ same as karnını deş=. —ı yarık 1. dish of split eggplant stuffed with chopped meat. 2. fleawort, *bot., Plantago psyllium.* 3. fleabane, *bot., Pulicaria dysenterica.* 4. *naut.,* same as karnı yarık makara. —ı yarık makara *naut.* snatch block. — yüzgeci ventral fin, abdominal fin. — zarı peritoneum. — zarı iltihabı peritonitis. — zarı kovuğu peritoneal cavity. —ı zil çal= to rumble (stomach); to be very hungry.

karın=" 2 قارِنٌ *prov.* 1. to pair, to copulate. 2. same as karış= 2.

karınca (..'.) قارِنجَه قارنج قرنجه 1. ant, *zool., Formica.* 2. blowhole (in cast iron). — ağzı very small opening. — asidi *chem.* formic acid. — belli small waisted. — beyi myrmeleon, antlion. —ya bin= to go at a snail's pace. — duası 1. kind of written charm for keeping ants away. 2. very illegible writing. — gibi kayna=, — gibi kaynaş= to swarm like ants. —yı incitme= not to hurt an ant, to be very tender hearted. — kaderince in all modesty, as much as one could do or offer, every one according to his means. —ya kanadı zarardır *proverb* Modesty is safety. — kararınca same as karınca kaderince. — sürüsü swarm of ants. — yağı chloroform. — yuvası ant's nest; ant hill, formicary. — yuvası gibi kayna=, — yuvası gibi kaynaş= to be very crowded, to be teeming.

karıncalan=" قارِنجَه‌لَنْ 1. to have the feeling of formication, to have pins and needles, to feel benumbed. 2. to become blowholed, honeycombed (cast iron).

karıncalaş=" قارِنجَه‌لَشْ same as karıncalan=".

karıncalı قارِنجَه‌لى blowholed, honeycombed, eaten into with rust (cast iron).

karıncık⁶¹ قارِنجِق *anat.* ventricle.

karındaş قارِنداش *archaic,* same as kardeş.

karınla=" قارِنلَه *naut.* /a/ to strike or press with its hull, to touch alongside; to board (ship). —ma kancası grappling iron. —şma bulge, a bulging, a swelling.

karınlı قارِنلى pot bellied, having a large belly; corpulent, fat.

karınsa قارِنسَه قارِنْسْ molting (birds). —ya gir= to begin to molt.

karıntı قارِنتى قارِنْتى vortex (in water), eddy (of water).

karış 1 قارِش span (space). bir — boy very short of stature. bir — boyun mu uzayacak? What does it profit you? What is the use of it? bir — dil uzat= to behave impertinently, to answer back rudely. — karış every inch (of), inch by inch, closely, carefully.

karış=" 2 قارِش 1. /la/ to be mingled, commingled, mixed; to commingle, mix (with), e. g., su ile yağ karışmaz Water will not mix with oil. 2. to become confused, to be mixed up; to become changeable, fickle, capricious (weather). 3. /a/ to meddle (with, in), interfere (in, with), mingle (in), e. g., başkasının işine karış= to interfere with other people's business; to fall, flow (into), e. g., Tuna Karadenize karışır The Danube flows into the Black Sea. 4. /a/ to deal (with), to be in charge (of), to exercise control (over). —ma Mind your own business. Don't interfere. —mam It is not my business. I don't want to have anything to do with it. Well, don't blame me if things go wrong. —anı görüşeni olma= to be free from interference, to be able to act independently.

karış 3 قارِش *archaic* confusion, turmoil. — karış et= /ı/ to throw into utter confusion. — katış, — muruş all mixed up, in utter disorder.

karış 4 قارِش *prov.* malediction, curse. — götür= to be cursed, execrated. — kar=, — ver= /a/ to curse, execrate.

karışık⁶¹ قارِشيق 1. mixed; adulterated, not pure. 2. confused, in disorder; complicated; complex. — bir adam man about whom one has doubts. — devirli ondalık kesir *neol., math.* mixed periodical decimal fraction. — dil hybrid language. — hisler mixed feelings. — ırk crossbreed. — ism-i fail *colloq.* complicated matter. — bir iş complicated matter. — konuş= to speak incoherently or contradictorily. — mal miscellaneous goods.

karışıklık⁶¹ قارِشيقلق confusion, tumult; troubles, disorders, agitations. — çık= to arise (troubles, disorders, agitation). — çıkar= to cause troubles, disorders, agitations. — ol= same as karışıklık çık=.

karışıl=" قارِشيل /a/ to be interfered (with).

karışım *neol.* mix, mixture, medley.

karışkanlık⁶¹ قارِشقانلق *archaic,* same as karışıklık.

karışla=" قارِشله /ı/ to measure by the span. —n= to become a span in length; to be measured by the span. —t= /ı, a/ *caus.* of karışla=.

karışma قاريشر *verbal n. of* **karış**= 2.
karışmaz قرشمز قاريشماز *archaic* blacksmith's cutting chisel.
karıştır=ᵘʳ قاريشديرمه قاريشديرمي /ı/ 1. *caus. of* **karış**= 2. 2. to examine (as if turning things over), *as in* **cepleri, dolabı, sahifeleri karıştır**=. 3. to pick (teeth, ear, nose). —**acak** instrument for mixing, picking, turning over, *e. g.*, **ateş karıştıracak** fire poker.
karıştırıcı قاريشديريجى 1. mixer, mixing, picking; confusing, complicating, misleading. 2. troublemaker, gossiper. — **devre** *radio* mixer stage. — **lâmba** mixer tube. — **unsurlar** disturbing, agitating elements.
karıştırıl=ᵘʳ قاريشديريلمى *pass. of* **karıştır**=.
karıştırma قاريشديرمه *verbal n. of* **karıştır**=. — **kabı** mixing vessel. — **makinesi** mixing machine. — **musluğu** mixing valve.
kari 1 (—.) قارى A *lrnd.* 1. reader. 2. professional reader of the Quran.
kârî 2 (——) كارى P *lrnd.* effective, effectual.
-kârî 3 (——) كارى P in the style of, worked in, work of, *as in* **Arapkârî süs, telkârî**.
karia (—..) قارعه A *lrnd.* 1. misfortune; last judgment, doom. 2. word that offends. 3. verse of the Quran recited to repel evil. **K—Suresi** the hundred and first sura of the Quran.
karib (.—) قريب A *lrnd.* near, nigh; near relation, kinsman. — **ol**= /a/ to be near. —**en** (.—'.) A soon, in a short time. —**lik** nearness, proximity.
karides (.'.) قاريده س Gk shrimp, prawn. — **avla**=, — **tut**= to shrimp, to go shrimping.
karih (.—) قريح A *lrnd.* wounded, sore.
kariha (.—.) قريحه A *lrnd.* fertile mind, imaginative power. —**dan** as an inspiration, improvised, extempore. —**dan at**= /ı/ to contrive, to invent. —**sı geniş** having a fertile, resourceful mind. —**dan konuş**=, —**dan söyle**= to extemporize, to improvise, to speak off the cuff.
karihazad (.—.—) قريحه زاد P *lrnd.* sudden inspiration, improvisation.
karikatür قاريقاتور F 1. cartoon. 2. caricature. — **serisi** comic strip. —**ünü yap**= /ın/ to make a caricature, a cartoon (of). —**cü** caricaturist; cartoonist.
karikatürist قاريقاتوريست F caricaturist, cartoonist.
karikatürleştir=ᵘʳ قاريقاتورلشديرمك /ı/ to caricature (a picture), to make a caricature (of).
karin 1 (.—) قرين A *lrnd.* near; associated; companion. — **et**= /ı/ to approximate, to associate. —**i kabul** accepted. — **ol**= /a/ to be near (to), to be associated (with). —**i tahsin** admired, approved.
karinʳⁿⁱ **2** قرن A *var. of* **karn**.

karina (..'.) قارينه قارينه It *naut.* 1. bottom of a ship or boat. 2. keel. 3. a careening, careen. —**ya bas**=, — **et**= /ı/ to careen, to heave down (a ship). — **fırçası** hog. —**yı yak**= to bream. — **zinciri** careen chain.
karine (.—.) قرينه A 1. conjecture, deduction from an accompanying circumstance. 2. *phys.* index (of refraction). — **ile anla**= /ı/ to infer, to conjecture, to deduce from an accompanying circumstance. —**i inkisar** *phys.* index of refraction.
karir (.—) قرير A *lrnd.* cold, cool.
karirülayn (.—..) قريرالعين A *lrnd.* whose eyes are sparkling, who is happy.
kariyer قاريير F career. — **yap**= to get on (in life), to work one's way up. —**ci** careerist.
kâriz (——) كاريز P *lrnd., same as* **keriz 1**.
karkador قارقه دور It *archaic* poor landing place without a harbor, roadstead.
karkar (.—) قرقار P *lrnd.* carrier pigeon, homing pigeon.
karkara قرقره A *lrnd.* crowned crane, heron.
karkas قارقاس F cadaver (used in anatomical study).
karkaşa قرقشه *archaic, var. of* **kargaşa**.
karkaşanlıkᵍⁱ قرقشانلق *archaic, var. of* **kargaşalık**.
karkırt=ᵘʳ قرقرتمى *archaic* /ı/ to blacken.
kârkün (—.) كاركن P *lrnd.* workman, maker.
karla=ʳ قارلامه to snow, to begin to fall (snow), *as in* **hava karladı**.
karlağuçᶜᵘ قرلغوج *archaic, same as* **kırlangıç**.
karlamaçᶜⁱ, **karlambaç**ᶜⁱ قارلاماج *prov.* snow mixed with molasses.
karlı 1 قارلى snowy, snowclad, covered with snow. — **dağlar** snowclad mountains, snow-capped mountains. — **hava** snowy weather. — **yıl kârlı yıl** a snow year and a rich year.
kârlı 2 (—.) كارلى profitable, advantageous. — **çık**= to come out ahead; to turn out profitable (business).
karlıkᵍⁱ قارلق 1. glass vessel of two compartments, one of which is filled with snow or ice for cooling liquids, cooling vessel. 2. pit for storing snow or ice.
kârlılıkᵍⁱ (—..) كارليلك lucrativeness, profitableness.
karma قارمه 1. *verbal n. of* **kar**= 3. 2. *neol.* mixed. — **karış**, — **karışık** in utter disorder, in complete confusion. — **komisyon** joint committee. — **okul** coeducational school. — **öğretim** coeducation. — **takım** sports mixed team.
karmaçᶜⁱ 1. *neol., chem.* agitator. 2. *prov.* loam mud mixed with straw for filling up gaps.

karman çorman قارمان چورمان in utter confusion or disorder.
karmanyola (...´.) قارمانیولا It robbery, onslaught. **—ya al=** slang /ı/ to render immobile. **— et=** /ı/ to rob. **—cı** robber.
karmaş=ᴵʳ قارماشمق archaic to be in utter confusion. **—ık** neol., log., chem. complex. **—ık sayı** neol. complex number.
karmen قارمن F carmine. **— kırmızısı** carmine red. **— lâkesi** cochineal lac, carmine lake. **— mavisi** indigo carmine. **— renkli şakrak kuşu** scarlet grosbeak, zool., Carpodacus erythrinus.
karmıkᵍⁱ قارمیق fishing weir (at a river's mouth).
karmukᵍᵘ قارموق grappling iron, hook.
karn قرن A lrnd. 1. century; age, period. 2. generation. 3. horn.
kârna (.´.) كارنه It square net.
karnabahar قرنبهار cauliflower.
karnabit قارنابیت same as **karnabahar**.
karnaksı قارناقسی colloq. tiresome person, nuisance, pest.
karnal 1 قارنال prov. hand basket.
karnal 2 قارنال obs. pander to his own wife.
kârname 1 (— —.) كارنامه P lrnd. biography.
kârname 2 (— —.) كارنامه [**kârnüma**] archaic specimen of work prepared by an apprentice who wishes to be admitted as a master workman.
karnapa قارناپا prov. glutton, gluttonous; obese.
karnavalˡⁱ قارناوال F 1. carnival. 2. colloq. figure of fun.
karne قارنه F 1. book of tickets; ration card. 2. pupil's report card.
karni قارنی F chem. retort.
karniye (.— .) قرنیه A anat. cornea; corneal. **— tabakası** 1. horny layer (of the epidermis). 2. cornea.
kârnüma (— .—) كارنما P lrnd., same as **kârname 2**.
Karnüssevrülcenubî (.....— —) قرن الثور الجنوبي A lrnd. the star ξ Tauri.
Karnüssevrülşimalî (.:....— —) قرن الثور الشمالي A lrnd. the Star υ Tauri.
karo (.´.) قارو F 1. card games diamonds. 2. small square. **— beykozu** colloq. ace of diamonds.
karoça (.´.) قاروچه It coach, carriage.
karoseri قاروسری F body (of a car or carriage). **— sacı** body sheet. **—ci** maker of car bodies.
karotis قاروتیس L anat. carotid artery. **— ana arteri** primitive carotid artery.
kârperdaz (—.—) كارپرداز P lrnd. transactor of business, manager.
karpit قارپیت [**karbid**] carbide, calcium carbide. **— lâmbası** carbide lamp, acetylene lamp.
karpuz قارپوز [**harbuz**] 1. watermelon, bot.,

Citrullus vulgaris. 2. anything globular; globe (of a lamp). **— araba** round-bodied coach. **— balığı** sea urchin. **— fener** globular (paper) lantern. **— göbeği** heart of a watermelon. **— kıçlı** naut. round-pooped. **—cu** watermelon seller.
karra (. —) قرئ A lrnd. professional Quran reader.
kârreva (—.—) كاروا P lrnd. efficient.
karsakᵍⁱ قارصاق قارصه corsac, Tartar fox.
karsala=ʳ قارسالامق prov. to be frostbitten.
karsamba قارسامبا prov. crowd; jumble of furniture.
karsambaçᶜⁱ قارسامباج prov. yogurt mixed with snow; fruit juice cooled with snow.
kârsaz (— —) كارساز P lrnd. dexterous, skillful, clever. **—î** (— — —) P dexterity, skillfulness.
kârsız (—.) كارسز 1. without profit or gain. 2. lrnd. without work, idle.
karsinom قارسینوم F path. carcinoma.
karşı قارشی قرشو 1. opposite, opposite side or direction. 2. contrary, opposed. 3. /a/ against, e. g., **düşmana karşı** against the enemy; contrary (to), e. g., **anlaşmaya karşı hareket** action contrary to the agreement; towards, a little before, e. g., **sabaha karşı** towards morning; for, e. g., **nezleye karşı ilâç** medicine for a cold; in return for, e. g., **senede karşı borç** a loan in return for a voucher. **—da** on the opposite side, across. **—sında** over against, opposite, e. g., **camiin karşısında** opposite the mosque; in the presence of, e. g., **müdürün karşısında** in the presence of the director; upon, in view (of), e. g., **hâdiseler karşısında** in view of the events. **—dan bak=** /a/ to watch idly. **—dan baktır=** /ı/ to tantalize. **— çık=** /a/ 1. to go to meet. 2. to come out opposite (in argument, etc.). **—sına çık=** /ın/ to appear suddenly in front of one. **— dur=** /a/ to resist, to oppose. **—ya geç=** to pass over to the opposite side, to cross over. **— gel=** /a/ to oppose, to disobey; to answer back impertinently. **— gelim** biol., neol. antagonism. **— git=** /a/ to go out to meet. **— hareket** countermovement. **— hücum** counterattack, counterassault. **— hücuma geç=** to start a counterattack. **— itham** countercharge. **— ithamda bulun=** /a/ to countercharge. **— karşıya** face to face. **—dan karşıya** from one side to another, across. **— ko=**, **— koy=** /a/ to oppose, resist, to make a stand (against). **— koyma** resistance. **— ol=** to be against. **— olma**, **— olum** neol., log. opposition. **— rüzgâr** counterwind. **— sav** neol., log. antithesis. **— söyle=** /a/ to speak against, to oppose, to speak in contradiction (to). **— taarruz** counteroffensive. **— taarruza**

geç= to start a counteroffensive. — **takım** opposite team. — **taraf** opposite side. — **teklif** counteroffer. — **var**= /a/ *archaic* to go out to meet. — **yaka** opposite shore. — **yürü**= /a/ *archaic*, same as **karşı var**=.

karşıcı نار شیجی *prov.* person who goes out to meet a visitor, welcomer.

karşıki نار شیكی facing, opposite.

karşıla=ᵣ نار شیلامق قرشولامق /ı/ 1. to go to meet, to receive, to welcome. 2. to receive (with), to greet (with), *e. g.*, **dehşetle karşıla**= to receive with horror, **hayal kırıklığı ile karşıla**= to greet with disappointment, **iyi karşıla**= to approve. 3. to cover, to reimburse, to meet, *e. g.*, **masrafları karşıla**= to cover expenses, **arz talebi karşılamıyor** The supply does not meet the demand; to defray, *e. g.*, **hükûmet masrafı karşılayacaktır** The government will defray the expenses. 4. /ı, la/ to reciprocate with, to return (for), *e. g.*, **iyiliği kötülükle karşıla**= to return bad for good. 5. /ı/ to prevent, *e. g.*, **ilâç hastalığı karşıladı** The medicine prevented the disease. 6. /ı/ *naut.* to counterbalance.

karşılama نار شیلامه 1. *verbal n.* a meeting, greeting, reception, welcome. 2. Turkish folk music played or sung when meeting a bridal procession, etc. — **töreni** welcoming ceremony.

karşılan=ᵣᵣ نار شیلانمه *pass.* of **karşıla**=.

karşılaş=ᵣᵣ نار شیلاشمق 1. to meet (one another); to meet (with), to encounter, to be faced (with), to be confronted (with); to be up (against), *e. g.*, **müşkilâtla karşılaş**= to meet with difficulties. 2. to cross, to meet and pass, *e. g.*, **mektuplarımız karşılaşmış** Our letters crossed. 3. to clash (times, dates). —**ma** *verbal n.* of **karşılaş**= sports game. —**tır**= /ı/ 1. *caus.* of **karşılaş**=. 2. to compare. —**tırıl**= *pass.* of **karşılaştır**=.

karşılaştırma نار شیلاشدیرمه 1. *verbal n.* of **karşılaştır**=. 2. *jur.* confrontation. — **düzlemi** *neol., geom.* plane of comparison. —**lı** *neol.* comparative. —**lı dil bilgisi** *neol.* comparative linguistics.

karşılıkᵍ¹ نار شیلیق قارشولوق قرشولوق 1. return, recompense; requital, retaliation. 2. answer, reply. 3. equivalent, *e. g.*, **doların Türk parasiyle karşılığı** the equivalent of the dollar in Turkish money. 4. *fin.* cover, reserve, provision. — **hücumu** reprisal attack, spite raid. — **istemez** No backchat. No answering back. —**ın kifayeti** *fin.* reserve coverage. — **lağım** countermine. — **olarak** 1. in return. 2. in reply (to). — **ver**= /a/ 1. to talk back, to chat back, to answer back. 2. to respond, be responsive. —**ını yap**= /ın/ to return, to reciprocate, to retort.

karşılıklı نار شیلیقلی 1. opposite, facing one another.

2. mutual, reciprocal; *math.* corresponding; mutually, reciprocally. — **dâva** *jur.* countercharge. — **hülûl ve nüfuz** interpenetration. — **münasebet** interrelation. — **münasebette bulun**= /la/ to correlate (to, with). — **sigorta** mutual insurance. — **taahhüt** mutual liability. — **tesir** interaction, interplay. — **yapraklar** *bot.* opposite leaves. — **yardım** mutual assistance. — **yükseklikler** *astr.* opposite altitudes.

karşılıksız نار شیلیقسز 1. *fin.* uncovered, not secured; without provision. 2. unreturned, unrequited, not reciprocated, unanswered. — **emre muharrer sened** bill of credit. — **kabul** *fin.* acceptance in blank, blank or uncovered acceptance. — **kâğıt para çıkarma** fiduciary note issue. — **kredi** blank credit. — **satış** short sale. — **satış yap**= to sell short.

karşılılıkᵍ¹ *neol.* reciprocity.

karşıma *neol., astr.* opposition.

karşıtᵈ¹ *neol.* contrary; counter, anti-. — **anlamlı** antonymous. — **basınç** counterpressure. — **duygu** antipathy. — **imparator** antiemperor. — **kas** *anat.* opponens. — **olarak** contrarily. — **papa** antipope. — **peygamber** antiprophet. — **reform**, — **reformasyon** *rel.* counterreformation.

karşıtlama *neol., rhet.* antithesis. —**lı** *rhet.* antithetic, antithetical. —**lı olarak** *rhet.* antithetically.

karşıtlı *neol., gram.* adversative. — **bağlaç** *gram.* adversative conjunction. — **cümle** *gram.* adversative proposition.

karşıtlık *neol., psych.* contrast. —**la çağrışım** *psych.* association by contrast.

kârşinas (— . —) كارشناس P *lrnd.* skillful in business.

kart 1 قارت 1. tough, hard; not fresh or tender. 2. *colloq.* past its prime. — **kız** *colloq.* old maid.

kart 2 قارت F card; postcard; visiting card. — **bırak**=, —**ını bırak**= to leave a card.

karta (.ˊ.) قارتا It *archaic* sea chart.

Kartaca (..ˊ.) قرطاجه *hist.* Carthage. —**lı** Carthaginian.

kartadak قارتداق *same as* **hartadak**.

kartal 1 قارتال eagle, *zool., Aquila.* — **ağacı** 1. eaglewood tree, aloeswood, *bot., Aquilaria agalloscha.* 2. mezereon, *bot., Daphne mezereum.* — **burun** aquiline nose. — **gözlü** eagle-eyed, keen-sighted. — **kayası** *geol.* geode, druse. — **taşı** *geol.* eaglestone. — **tüyü** eagle feather. — **yavrusu** eaglet.

kartal=ᵣᵣ 2 قارتالمق *prov.* to become old.

Kartal 3 قارتال name of a small town on the sea of Marmara. —**a kaç**=, —**a var**= *joc.* to grow old, become senile.

kartalaçᶜ¹ قارتالاچ *prov.* kind of flat bread.

kartalakᵍⁱ قارتالاق *prov.* uneven and lumpy.
kartaloz قارتالوز *slang* old, aged.
kartamsa=ʳ قارتامساـ *prov.* to begin to decay.
karte قارته *Ott. hist.* weight measure used in Egypt.
kartel 1 قارتل F *econ.* cartel.
kartel 2 قارتل It *naut.* small scuttle, water cask in a boat.
karter قارتر F *auto.* oil sump, sump.
karti قارتى Gk 1. *archaic* sea chart. 2. *prov.* ship compass.
kartlan=ʳ, **kartlaş=**ʳ قارتلانمق to grow old, to lose its freshness.
kartlıkᵍⁱ قارتلق senility, oldness; lack of freshness.
kartograf قارتوغراف F cartographer, map maker.
kartografi قارتوغرافى F cartography.
kartografya (...) قارتوغرافيا cartography, map-making. — **bölümü**, — **şubesi** map department. —**cı** *same as* **kartograf**.
kartoloz قارتولوز *var. of* **kartaloz**.
karton قارتون F 1. cardboard, pasteboard. 2. *painting* cartoon. — **cilt** cardboard covered (book). — **ciltli** having cardboard covers (book). — **dolabı** filing cabinet. — **kapak** cardboard cover (of a book). — **kapla=** /ı/ to bind in a stiff cover. — **kaplama** 1. a binding in cardboard. 2. bound in cardboard. —**la=** /ı/ *same as* **karton kapla=**. —**luk** *same as* **karton dolabı**.
kartonpat, karton piyer قارتون پيير F 1. papier-mâché. 2. ceiling decoration of pasteboard.
kartotekᵍⁱ قارتوتك F card register, card index, card catalogue. — **fişi** index card. — **kartonu** index cardboard. — **kutusu** card index box.
kartpostalˡⁱ قارتپوستال F postcard.
kartuçᶜᵘ قارتوچ It *obs., same as* **hartuç**.
kartukᵍᵘ قارتوق *obs.* large rake.
kartvizit قارتويزيت F calling card. — **bırak=** 1. to leave a card. 2. *slang* to retch, to vomit.
karula (.'..) قارولا It *naut.* tack of a spanker or trysail, sail gasket. — **halatı** tripping line. — **kandilisası** tack tie. — **palangası** tack tackle. — **yakası** corner of a tack.
Karun (——) قارون A 1. name of a rich man in the Quran. 2. very rich person, a Croesus. — **malı** the wealth of Croesus. **k—laş=** to become very rich.
karure (——.) قاروره A *lrnd.* gourd shaped bottle, flank; bottle shaped urinal.
karva=ʳ قارواميق *archaic, same as* **kavra=**.
kârvan (——) كاروان P *lrnd., same as* **kervan**. —**î** (———) P member of a caravan.
kârvansaray (——.—) كاروانسراى P *same as* **kervansaray**.
karye قريه A *lrnd.* village.

karyokinez قاريوكينز F *biol.* karyokinesis.
karyola (.'..) قاريولا It bedstead, bed.
karz قرض A *lrnd.* 1. loan, a lending. 2. a cutting or clipping with scissors. 3. reciting or composing (verse). — **al=** /ı/ to borrow (money). — **et=** /ı/ to lend (money). —**ı hasen** a lending without interest. —**ı şiir** recitation of poetry. — **ver=** /ı/ to lend money. —**an** (.'.) A as a loan, borrowed.
kârzar (——) كارزار P *lrnd.* battle, combat; field of battle. —**gâh** (———) P field of battle.
karzdar (.—) قرضدار P *lrnd.* 1. debtor. 2. borrower.
karzhah (.—) قرضخواه P *lrnd.* 1. one who asks for a loan. 2. one who wishes for repayment of a loan.
karzî (.—) قرضى A *lrnd.* 1. borrowed, on credit. 2. debtor, borrower. —**ye** (.—.) loan. —**yet** (.—.) quality of a money loan.
kas=ᵃʳ **1** قاصمق /ı/ to stretch tight, to tighten; to take in (a garment); to curtail. —**ıp kavur=** /ı/ to tyrannize, to oppress, to terrorize.
kas 2 *neol.* muscle; muscular. — **ağrısı** myalgia. — **doku** muscular tissue. — **teli** muscular fiber. — **zarı** muscular membrane, sarcolemma.
kasˢˢⁱ **3** قصّ A *lrnd.* breast.
kasa 1 (.'.) قاصه It 1. cash box, strong box, chest, safe. 2. till; cashier's office; box office; cash register. 3. case (for bottles); type case, letter case. 4. window frame, door frame; framework of body (of a car). — **açığı** deficit of money. — **ayağı** *print.* case stand. — **bakiyesi** remainder of cash balance. — **bilânçosu** balance sheet. — **bilânçosu yap=** to balance the cash. — **dairesi** safe deposit, strong room. — **defteri** cash book. — **fazlası** cash over. — **fişi** cash coupon, coupon. — **gözü** *print.* case box. — **hesabı** cash account. — **hırsızı** safebreaker. — **iskontosu** cash discount. — **kontrolü** cash auditing, audit. — **makinası** cash register. — **mevcudu** cash or balance in hand, cash balance, balance in cash, cash ratio. — **müfettişi** official auditor, auditor. — **soy=** to break a safe. — **vaziyeti** cash statement. — **yevmiyesi** daily cash book.
kasa 2 (.'.) قاصا It *naut.* spliced loop or eye of a rope. — **çeliği** toggle. — **dikişi** eye, splice. — **piyanı** eye seizing. —**lı izbiro** frapped sling, buttend sling.
kasa 3 (.'.) قاصا It *naut.* Frap. Haul out. — **et=** /ı/ to frap, to haul, to set a fore-and-aft-sail. — **iskota** Sheet home. — **iskota et=** to sheet home. — **iskota randa** Haul out the spanker sheet. — **randa** Sheet home the spanker. Haul out the spanker. — **randa et=** to set the spanker.
kas'a 4 قصعة A *lrnd.* bowl, basin.

kasab 1 قصاب [kassab] *same as* **kasap.**
kasab 2 قصب A *lrnd.* 1. reed; culm. 2. windpipe. 3. fine linen cloth, muslin. **—ı Mısrî** fine linen of Egypt. **—ı sükker** sugar cane.
kasaba قصبه A 1. small town, borough. 2. *lrnd.* reed, cane; windpipe. **— ahalisi** townspeople.
kasabat (..—) قصبات A *lrnd.* bronchial tubes.
kasabî (..—ﻰ) قصبى A *lrnd.* 1. reed-like, culm-like. 2. bronchial.
kasabülhabib (....—) قصبالطبيب A *lrnd.* friendly pen; sugar cane.
kasabülhind قصبالهند A *lrnd.* fine linen of India.
kasabüssabakᵏı قصبالسبق A *lrnd.* person superior in quality to his contemporaries or peers.
kasabüssükker قصبالسكر A *lrnd.* sugar cane.
kasabüzzerire (....—.) قصبالذريره A *lrnd.* chiretta root.
kasadar (..—) قاصدار 1. cashier, teller. 2. treasurer. **—lık** occupation of a cashier. **—lık et=** to act as cashier, to be cashier.
kasaid (.—.) قصائد A *lrnd., pl. of* **kaside.**
kasal=ᵢʳ قصالو *prov.* to vaunt, to boast. **—ak** boastful. **—t=** /ı/ to flatter.
kasame, kasamet (.—.) قسام A *lrnd., can. law* oath of accusation taken by fifty persons in a case of murder where the murderer is not identified.
kasan 1 قاصان grip of an archery bow.
kasan 2 قاصان *prov.* sediment (left by inundation).
kasapᵇı قصاب [kassab] butcher. **— akçesi** *Ott. hist.* tax levied on animals brought to Istanbul landing-places. **— başı** *Ott. hist.* chief butcher, superintendent of the butcher's guild and director of the sheep tax. **— bıçağı** butcher's knife, slaughtering knife. **— çırağı** butcher's boy. **— dükkânı** butcher's shop, the butcher's. **— havası** melody of a folk dance. **— merhemi** *prov.* basilicon ointment composed of oil, suet, resin and other ingredients. **— satırı** butcher's cleaver. **— süngeri** very nasty thing. **— süngeri ile silinmiş** half washed or dirtier than if not washed at all, disgusting, nasty dirt; most unabashed. **— yamağı** butcher's boy. **—hane** slaughterhouse.
kasaplıkᵍı قصابلق 1. butchery, butcher's trade or business, a butchering. 2. beasts for slaughter. **— et=** to be a butcher. **— hayvan** fattened beasts. **— koyun** sheep for slaughter. **— öküz** stalled ox.
kasar 1 قصا [kassar] *prov., same as* **kastar 1.**

kasar 2 قصا *prov.* grain remaining in the ear after threshing.
kasara (.´..) قاصره قصاره It *naut.* castle, deck cabin; *also in* **baş kasara, baş kasarası** forecastle, **kıç kasara, kıç kasarası** poop deck, quarter deck, **orta kasara** upper half deck in the center. **— altı** steerage. **— altı yolcusu** steerage passenger. **— güvertesi** poop deck. **— kamarası** steerage cabin. **— üstü** poop deck. **—lı gemi** ship with quarterdeck and forecastle.
kasaret (.—.) قصارت A *lrnd.* shortness, brevity.
kâsat (——) كاسات A *lrnd., pl. of* **ke's 2.**
kasatura (...´.) قاصاتوره قاصانوره sidearm; bayonet.
kasavele (...´.) قاصاوله قاصاوله It *naut.* clothesline; heavy tackle. **— donat=** to rig the clothesline. **— palangası** clothesline tackle.
kasavet (.—.) قساوت A anxiety, sorrow, pain. **— çek=** to labor under care or sorrow. **— et=** *archaic* to be anxious or sorry. **—len=** /a/ to be anxious (about), to become sorrowful (at, over).
kasavetli قساوتلى anxious, sorrowful.
kasbilim *neol., anat.* myology.
kasd قصد A *same as* **kasıt.**
kasden (.´.) قصداً A 1. intentionally, deliberately. 2. *jud.* with malice aforethought.
kasdet=ᵈᵉʳ قصد ایتمك 1. to purpose, to intend. 2. /a/ to have a design against. 3. /ı/ to mean, to understand (by).
kasdî (.—) قصدى A premeditated, deliberate.
kâse (—.) كاسه P 1. bowl, basin. 2. *slang* arse. **K—i dervişan** *lrnd.* constellation of Northern Crown, Corona Borealis. **—i ser** *lrnd.* skull. **K—i şikeste** *lrnd.* the constellation Corona Borealis. **—i tambur** *lrnd.* body of a lute. **K—i yetiman** *lrnd., same as* **Kâse-i şikeste.**
kâselis (—.—) كاسليس P *lrnd.* sponger, parasite, toady, sycophant. **—ane** (—.——.) P toadying, sycophantic. **—î** (—.——) P toadyism, sycophancy.
kasem قسم A *lrnd.* oath. **— billâh et=** to swear by God.
kâsepüşt (—..) كاسپشت P *lrnd.* 1. tortoise, turtle. 2. sky.
kâseşuy (—.—.) كاسشوى P *lrnd.* dishwasher.
kasıd (—.) قاصد A *lrnd.* 1. messenger, courier. 2. who has an intention, is aiming (at). **—ı çarh** the sun; moon.
kasıf (—.) قاصف A *lrnd.* that breaks; crashing (thunder). **—a** (—.—) A violent wind.
kasıkᵍı 1 قاصيق قاصوق groin; inguinal. **— altı bölgesi** *anat.* subinguinal region. **— bağı** truss for hernia. **— bağıcı** truss maker. **— bezi**

inguinal gland. — **biti** crab louse. — **bölgesi** *anat.* inguinal region. —ı **çatla=** to get a hernia. —**ları çatla=** /dan/ to burst (with). — **çatlağı** hernia. — **çatlaması** inguinal rupture, rupture in the groins. — **kanalı** inguinal canal. — **kemiği** pubis, *os pubis.* — **kılı** hair of the pubis. — **otu** agrimony, *bot., Agrimonia.* — **yarığı** hernia.
kasıkᵍ¹ 2 ناصين stretched tight.
kasıl=ⁱʳ 1 ناصلوا ناصلي 1. to be stretched tight, contracted, to be shortened, tightened. 2. to pose, to attitudinize, to strike an attitude.
kasıl 2 *neol.* muscular. — **duyum** muscular sense. — **sarsılma** muscular convulsion.
Kasım 1 ناڪم [kasım 2] 1. *neol.* November. 2. the 8th of November, popularly reckoned the beginning of the winter period ending on the 5th of May. — **fırtınası** storm about the beginning of the winter period. — **günü** *same as* **Kasım**².
kasım 2 (—.) ناڪم A 1. *lrnd.* dividing, divider; *math.* factor, submultiple. 2. *w. cap.,* man's name. —ı **müşterek** common factor. —ı **müşterek-i a'zam** greatest common factor.
kasıma (—..) ناڪم A *lrnd., math.* discriminant.
kasımpatıⁿⁱ ناڪمپاتى chrysanthemum.
kasın=ⁱʳ 1 ناڪمنى to curtail, to pinch (expenses), to be frugal.
kasın 2 ناڪصين *prov.* sediment (result of inundation).
kasınçᶜⁱ ناڪصينج ناڪصينج tightness, tension, contraction.
kasıntı ناڪمنتى ناڪصنتى 1. a tightening, a taking in (a dress). 2. *same as* **kasınç**. 3. *colloq.* posing attitude. — **kastır=** to have the waist of a dress taken in.
kasırˢʳᵗ 1 قصر [kasr 1] summer palace, mansion. —ı **düvazdeh derî** *lrnd.* sky with the twelve signs of the zodiac. —ı **hümayun** *lrnd.* imperial pavilion. —ı **mina** *lrnd.* sky. —ı **vücud** *lrnd.* 1. human body. 2. world.
kasır 2 (—.) ناصر A 1. *lrnd.* short; deficient, defective. 2. *law* pupil, minor. —**âne** (—.—.) P humbly.
kasırga ناصرغ 1. whirlwind, cyclone. 2. waterspout.
kasırlıkᵍ¹ ناصرلق *law* pupilage.
kasırülbeyan (—...—) ناصرالبيان A *lrnd.* inadequate explanation.
kasırülyed (—...) ناصراليد A *lrnd.* poor; powerless.
kasıtˢᵈ¹ قصد [kasd] A intention, endeavor, aim, purpose; premeditation; evil intent; attempt on someone's life. —**iyle** with the intention (of), aiming (at), in order (to), *e. g.,* **katil kasdiyle** with the intention of murdering. —**a makrun** *lrnd.* intentional, intentionally,

purposely. —ı **ol=** /a/ to have evil intentions (against).
kasıtlı قصدلى 1. who has a design (against). 2. purposeful; having a hidden meaning.
kasi 1 (—.) ناسى A *lrnd.* hard; unyielding, unfeeling.
kasi 2 (—.) ناصى A *lrnd.* far off, remote; old.
kasî 3 (.—) قسى A *lrnd.* very hard.
kasî 4 (.—) قصى A *lrnd.* very far, very remote.
kâsib (—.) كاسب A *lrnd.* who earns, gains; merchant.
kasid 1 (.—) قصيد A *lrnd.* 1. well weighed, polished (poem). 2. *same as* **kaside**.
kâsid 2 (—.) كاسد A *lrnd.* not in demand, dull (market).
kaside (.—.) قصيده A 1. poem of more than fifteen rhyming distichs in which a person is praised. 2. eulogy or commemorative poem put to music and considered as religious music. **K—i Bürde** *lrnd.* Ode of the Mantle (a celebrated Arabic poem, composed and recited by Ka'b in praise of the Prophet Muhammad, when he embraced Islam; as a recompense, Muhammad placed his own mantle over the shoulders of the poet). —**i mimiye** *lrnd.* **kaside** ending in م (mim) in each distich. —**i sulhiye** *lrnd.* **kaside** written on the occasion of the establishment of peace. —**i suriye** *lrnd.* epithalamium. —**i taiye** *lrnd.* **kaside** rhyming with the letter ت (tâ). —**ci** 1. the poet of a **kaside**. 2. *colloq.* hypocrite. —**gû** (.—.—) P, —**perdaz** (.—..—) P, —**sera** (.—..—) P *lrnd.* the poet of a **kaside**.
kâsif (—.) كاسف A *lrnd.* eclipsed, hidden; unfortunate; unpropitious.
kasil قصيل [*Arabic* .—] *prov.* grain cut green for fodder.
kasir 1 (—.) ناسر A *lrnd.* compelling, constraining.
kasir 2 (.—) قصير A *lrnd.* short.
kâsir 3 (—.) كاسر A *lrnd.* breaking, refractive.
kâsir 4 (—.) كاثر A *lrnd.* much, many, copious.
kasirâne (.——.) قصيرانه P *lrnd.* humbly.
kasire (.—.) قصيره A *lrnd.* 1. *fem. of* **kasir** 2. 2. woman kept strictly secluded at home.
kasirülakl (.—..) قصيرالعقل A *lrnd.* short minded, possessed of little intellect.
kasirülbaᵃ¹ (.—.—) قصيرالباع A *lrnd.* 1. short of stature. 2. possessed of little power or ability. 3. niggardly, miserly.
kasirülbasar (.—...) قصيرالبصر A *lrnd.* myopic, shortsighted.

kâsirülesnam (—...—) كاسرالاصنام A *lrnd.* idol breaker.
kâsirülhacer (—....) كاسرالحجر A *lrnd.* saxifrage.
kasirül'inan (.—..—) قصيرالعنان A *lrnd.* 1. short necked (horse). 2. stingy, close fisted.
kasirülkame (.—.—.) قصيرالقامه A *lrnd.* short in stature.
kasirürre's (.—..) قصيرالرأس A *lrnd.* brachycephalic.
kasis (.—) قسيس A *lrnd.* Christian priest.
kasiülkalb (—...) قاسىالقلب A *lrnd.* hardhearted.
kasiyer قاسيير F cashier, teller, treasurer.
kaska قاصفه It *naut.*, only in **kaska et**= /1/ to make fast, to hold fast.
kaskatı قاصقاق very hard, as hard as stone. **— kal**= 1. to remain quite hard or rigid. 2. /dan/ to become petrified (with).
kasket قاسكت F cap; peaked cap. **— siperi** peak of a cap. **—çi** capmaker; capseller. **—li** wearing a cap.
kasnak[ˢ¹] قاصناق 1. embroidery frame, embroiderer's hoop. 2. hoop or rim of a sieve, tambourine etc. 3. *arch.* tambour or drum (of a cupola); trimmer beam. 4. belt pulley. 5. deep hem on a wrestler's garment. 6. kind of folk dance. **— boyunduruğu** *arch.* trimmer. **— çemberi** hoop (of drum, embroidery frame). **— dişlisi** pinion gear. **— iğnesi** embroidery needle, crewel needle. **— işi** tambour work, embroidery. **— işle**= to tambour. **— kayışı** *mech.* belt. **— nakışı** *same as* **kasnak işi**. **— tığı** crochet needle.
kasnı قاصنى *archaic* galbanum, gum of *Galbanum officinale*.
kaspanak, kaspannek, kaspeannek غصبأ ناك [*Arabic* **gasbenannek**] *slang* by force, willy-nilly; like it or not.
kasr 1 قصر A *same as* **kasır 1**.
kasr 2 قصر A *lrnd.* a shortening; a being short, shortness; *literature* reduction of a foot. **—ı basar** myopia, short-sightedness. **—ı yed** renunciation, resignation, abandonment. **—ı yed et**= /dan/ to renounce, to resign, to abandon.
kasr 3 قسر A *lrnd.* a forcing, constraining to act against the will; force, constraint.
kasret=ᵈᵉʳ قصرتمك /1/ to shorten, to reduce.
kasrî (.—) قصرى A *lrnd.* compulsory, obligatory. **—iyet** (.—.) compulsoriness.
kassab (.—) قصاب A *lrnd., same as* **kasap**.
kassam (.—) قسام A 1. *can. law* law official who fixes inheritance shares. 2. *lrnd.* distributor, divider. **—iye** (.——.), **—lık** fee payable to the legal distributor of inheritance shares.
kassar (.—) قصار A *lrnd.* bleacher, fuller.

—la= *same as* **kastarla**=. **—lık** *same as* **kastarlık**.
kassas (.—) قصاص A *obs.* executor of the law of talion; executioner by the law of talion.
kassî 1 قصى A *lrnd.* pectoral.
kassî 2 قسى A *lrnd.* cloth made of a silk and flax mixture.
kast 1 قاست F caste.
kâst 2 (—) كاست P *lrnd.* diminution; defect, deficiency, *as in* **bi-kem ü kâst** without lack or deficiency.
kastal 1 (.—) قطال A *lrnd.* dust.
kastal 2 قصطل A *prov.* watering place for cattle; fountain.
kastanyet قاستانيت F castanet, castanets.
kastanyola (...'.) قاستانيولا It *naut.* cleat, pawl (of a capstan). **— palangası** cleat tackle, sail tackle. **— yuvası** pawl's rack.
kastar 1 قطار A *lrnd.* shrewd, clever.
kastar 2 قصار [**kassar**] a bleaching, fulling (cloth). **— et**= /1/ to bleach, to full. **—cı** bleacher. **—la**= /1/ *same as* **kastar et**=. **—lat**= *caus. of* **kastarla**=. **—lı** bleached, fulled. **—lık** occupation of a bleacher or fuller.
kâste (—.) كاسته P *lrnd.* diminished, lessened.
kastel 1 قصطل It *obs.* castle, fort.
kastel 2 قصطل A *lrnd., var. of* **kastal 1**.
kastır=ᶦʳ قاصدرمق /1, a/ to make or let be stretched tight.
kastor قاستور F beaver, castor (fur). **— kürk** beaver fur.
kasvet قسوت A 1. depression, sadness; gloom. 2. *lrnd.* a being hard as stone; hardness, stoniness; cruelty. **— bas**= /a/ to become dejected, low spirited or gloomy. **— çek**= to be anxious or distressed. **—i kalb** *lrnd.* hardness of heart, resistance to God.
kasvetefza (...—) قسوتافزا P *lrnd.* increasing depression, promoting sadness.
kasvetengiz (...—) قسوتانگيز P *lrnd.* causing depression, gloomy.
kasvetli قسوتلى oppressing, gloomy.
kaş 1 قاش 1. eyebrow. 2. curved or projecting, salient thing, *e. g.*, **eyer kaşı** pommel of a saddle, **kılıç kaşı** sword guard, **yüzük kaşı** collet of a ring. 3. *arch.* Moorish arch. 4. *mus.* brace, bracket, accolade. 5. spotless white stone. 6. *prov.* ridge line. 7. *prov.* fence, wall. 8. *archaic* front part, *e. g.*, **kaşında** in front (of). **— arası** *anat.* glabella. **— at**= /a/ to make a signal with the eyebrow. **— bastı** *archaic* fillet around the forehead. **— burtur**= *archaic*, **— çat**=, **—ın çin bırak**= *archaic* to knit the eyebrows, to frown. **— et**= /a/ to give a sign with the eyebrows (to). **— göz et**= /a/ to wink (at), to make a sign with

the eye and eyebrow. — **ile göz arasında** in the twinkling of an eye, in a trice. — **ile göz kalanı söz** very nice, handsome woman. — **kantar=**, — **karak çat=** *archaic*, same as **kaş çat=**. — **karar=** *archaic* to be getting dark. — **kaş** *prov.* in rows. —**tan kaşa** *archaic* from one end to the other. — **kemiği** upper bone of the eye socket. —**ının üstünde gözün var deme=** not to raise the slightest objection. — **yapayım derken göz çıkar=** to make a greater blunder, to make matters worse.

kâş 2 (—) كاشْ P *lrnd.*, same as **keşke**.
kaş= 3 قاشمی *prov.* to clap hands.
kaşa= 1 قاشامق *archaic* /ı/ to curry, to groom.
kaşa 2 قاشا Bulg *prov.* gruel made of rice or corn meal.
kaşağı قاشاغو قاشاغی 1. currycomb. 2. back scratcher. — **rendesi** very fine polishing plane. —**la=** /ı/ to curry, to groom.
kaşak[1] 1 قاشاك back scratcher.
kaşak[2] 2 قاشاك *prov.* fold, pen (for cattle).
kaşalot قاشالوت *slang* imbecile, idiot, stupid fellow. —**zade** son of an idiot, utterly stupid.
kaşan 1 قاشان قاشان urine (of horse, donkey, etc.), stale. —**ı gel=** to wish to stale.
Kaşan 2 (——) كاشان Kashan, a city in Iran famous for its glazed tiles.
kaşan= 3 قاشانمی 1. to be curried, groomed. 2. to scratch one's own back with a back scratcher.
kaşan= 4 قاشانمق to stale.
kâşane (——.) كاشانه P luxurious dwelling, mansion.
kaşar 1 قاشار ـ قشر 1. sheep cheese (prepared especially in Thrace). 2. *slang* deceitful, sly (in gambling). — **peyniri** same as **kaşar**.
kaşar= 2 قاشارمہ *prov.* to be taciturn.
kaşarlan= قاشارلانمہ to become callous (about), to become hardened or insensitive (to).
kaşarlanmış قاشارلانمش callous, insensible; experienced, cunning.
kaşarlı قاشارلی same as **kaşarlanmış**.
kaşat= قاشاتمہ same as **kaşandır=**.
kaşave قشاوه *archaic*, same as **kaşağı**.
kaşe قاشه F 1. capsule, cachet. 2. mark, trademark.
kaşer 1 قاشر var. of **kaşar 1**.
kaşer= 2 قاشرمك var. of **kaşarlan=**.
kaşevi قاشه وی *prov.*, same as **kaşağı**.
kaşı= قاشیمق /ı/ to scratch with the nails.
kaşık[1] قاشق 1. spoon. 2. spoonful. 3. stoneworker's spoon-shaped crowbar. 4. *Ott. hist.* spoon-shaped epaulette. 5. wooden spoons used in Turkish folk music as rhythmic instruments by dancers, and by players of dance music. — **ağırlığı** *archaic* case for carrying a spoon. — **at=**, — **çal=** to eat

heartily. — **çalımı** *prov.* time of evening prayer. — **düşmanı** *colloq.* one's wife. — **gaga** shoveler duck, *zool.*, Spatula clypeata. — **kadar** emaciated, e. g., **yüzü kaşık kadar kalmış** He has grown very thin in the face. — **kaşı=** to hollow out a spoon. — **kaşık by spoonful**, by ladlefuls. — **kepçesi** bowl of a spoon. — **makabı** shell auger, wimble. — **otu** spoonwort, scurvy grass, *bot.*, Cochlearia officinalis. — **oyunu** folk dance performed with wooden spoons. — **sapı** spoonhandle. **bir — suda boğ=**/ı/ to hate like poison, to be a bitter enemy (of). —**la yedirip sapıyla gözünü çıkar=** (*lit.*, to feed someone with one's spoon and knock his eye out with its handle) to spoil a good deed by a bad one.

kaşıkçı قاشقچی spoonmaker, spoon seller. — **avurdu** *obs.* grimace of disappointment (such as the spoonmaker may be supposed to have made when his diamond was seized by the crown). — **elması** largest diamond in the Ottoman regalia (found by a poor woman, and sold by her to a spoonmaker for a dozen spoons). — **kuşları** pelicans, *zool.*, Pelecanidae. — **kuşu** pelican, *zool.*, Pelecanus onocrotalus.
kaşıkçın قاشقچین spoonbill, *zool.*, Platalea lencordodia.
kaşıkla= قاشقلامہ /ı/ to eat with a spoon, to spoon out, to ladle out.
kaşıklağı قاشقلاغی *prov.* spoon rack.
kaşıklı قاشقلی having a spoon. — **balıkçıl** spoonbill, *zool.*, Platalea leucorodia. — **balıkçıllar** spoonbills, ibises, *zool.*, Threshkiornithidea.
kaşıklık[1] قاشقلق 1. spoon rack. 2. *Ott. hist.* metal piece in the front part of the Janissary cap into which a feather is fixed.
kaşın= قاشینمہ 1. to itch. 2. to scratch oneself. 3. *colloq.* to ask for a beating or scolding. —**dır=** /ı/ *caus. of* **kaşın=**. —**ma** *verbal n. of* **kaşın=**.
kaşıntı قاشینتی an itching, pruriency.
kaşıt= قاشیتمہ /ı, a/ *caus. of* **kaşı=**.
kaşıyacak[1] قاشییجك *obs.* back scratcher.
kâşî (——) كاشی P *lrnd.* painted and glazed tile (originally made in Kashan).
kâşif (——.) كاشف A 1. discoverer, explorer. 2. *Ott. hist.* administrator of land affairs in Egypt.
kâşiger (——.) كاشیگر P *lrnd.* maker of glazed tiles.
kaşka قاشقا 1. blaze on the forehead of an animal, *esp.* a horse. 2. having a blaze on the forehead.
kaşkariko (...'.) قاشقاریقو *slang* trick, deceit. — **yap=** to trick, to cheat. —**cu** trickster, deceiver.

kaşkaval 1 قاشقوال It 1. sheep cheese. 2. *slang* simpleton. — **peyniri** *same as* **kaşkaval** [1].
kaşkaval 2 قاشقوال تمشقوال It *naut.* fid. — **deliği**, — **yuvası** fid hole.
kâşki (—.) كاشكِ P *lrnd., same as* **keşke**.
kaşkol قاشقول F scarf, neckerchief.
kaşkorse قاشقورسه F under-bodice, camisole.
kaşlı قاشلى 1. having eyebrows. 2. having a collet or stone (ring). — **gözlü** perfect; pretty.
kaşmer قاشمر *قشر* buffoon, tomfool. —**dikoz** *slang* odd sort of chap, screwball. —**lik** buffoonery, tomfoolery; *neol.* burlesque.
kaşmir قاشمير F cashmere.
kaştar=ir قاشتاريمه *prov.* /ı/ to protect.
kat 1 قات 1. story (of a building), floor. 2. layer, stratum; fold. 3. set (of clothes). 4. *neol., math.* multiple. 5. *archaic* presence, side, near, *e. g.,* **padişahın katında** in the presence of the sovereign, **katımda** beside me. — **çık**= /a/ to add a story (to a building). **bir** — **daha** twice as much. — **ender kat** a great deal more. — **et**= /ı/ to fold, to pile in layers or tiers. — **kat** 1. in layers; in several stories. 2. many times more, much more. — **kat et**= /ı/ to fold or stow in layers or tiers. — **kat koy**= to put layer on layer. — **mülkiyeti** ownership of a flat in an apartment house. — **yeri** crease (line made by folding).
kat=ar 2 قاتمى 1. /a/ to add (to), to join (to). 2. /a/ to mix (to, into). 3. /ı, a/ to let pair (with), to let cover (animals), *as in* **keçiyi tekeye kat**=, **kısrağı aygıra kat**=. 4. /ı/ to drive in front of one *as in* **önüne kat**=.
kat'ı 3 قطع A *lrnd.* a cutting, interrupting, intersecting, clipping, a reducing a verse foot. —**ı alâka et**= /la/ to discontinue relations, to cut relations with. —**ı amudî** perpendicular section. —**ı cevab et**= to cease replying. —**ı daire** segment of a circle. — **et**=*. —**ı hayat** ending of life, death. —**ı kâmil** folio size. —**ı kelâm** interruption of a speech. —**ı mail** oblique section. —**ı merahil et**= to travel, to make a journey. —**ı meratib** promotion to higher ranks. —**ı mesafe** travel, journey. —**ı muhabere et**= to cease correspondence. —**ı mükâfi** *geom.* parabola. —**ı mükâfi-i mücessem** *geom.* paraboloid. —**ı münasebet** interruption of relations. —**ı müsnim** transverse section. —**ı nâkıs** ellipse. —**ı nâkısî** elliptic. —**ı nâkıs-ı mücessem** ellipsoid. —**ı nazar** 1. a leaving out of consideration. 2. /dan/ besides, apart from. —**ı nazar et**= /dan/ to leave out of consideration. —**ı niza et**= to decide a lawsuit. —**ı rah et**= to travel, to go along. —**ı rahm et**= to break off all connection with relations. —**ı tarîk** 1. a barring or blocking the road. 2. highway robbery. —**ı ufkî** horizontal section. —**ı uzuv** a cutting off a limb, amputation. —**ı ümid et**= to give up all hope, to despair. —**ı vazife et**= /ı/ to cut off the allowance (of). —**ı zaid** hyperbola. —**ı zaidî** hyperbolic. —**ı zaid-i mücessem** hyperboloid.
kat 4 قات *archaic, in* — **kal**= 1. to be petrified (with emotion, etc.). 2. to be immovable.
kat'a (.—) قطعا A *lrnd.* absolutely (not), in no way.
kataif (.—.) قطائف A *lrnd., pl. of* **katife**.
katakla=r قاتاقلامه *prov.* to chase.
katakofti 1 (...'.) قاتاقوفتى Gk *slang* swagger.
katakofti 2 (...'.) قاتاقوفتى *Or. mus., same as* **müsemmen**.
katakulli (...'.) قاتاقوللى *slang* cheat, trick, swindle. —**ye gel**= to be taken in. — **oyna**=, — **yap**= /a/ to cheat, to swindle.
katalavis (...'.) قاتالاويس Gk *slang* Do you understand?
katalepsi قاتالپسى F catalepsy.
kataloggu قاتالوغ F catalogue.
katalpa (..'.) قاتالپا F catalpa, *bot., Catalpa syringaefolia*.
kat'an 1 قطعا A *lrnd., same as* **kat'a**. — **ve katıbeten** absolutely (not), in no way.
katan 2 قطن A *lrnd.* loin, lumbar, spine. —**î** lumbar.
katar قطار A 1. railway train. 2. string, file or train (of animals, carts etc.); string (of dried fruits, pearls etc.). — **ağaları** *Ott. hist.* commanders-in-chief of the Janissaries. — **katar** in rows, in files. — **kılavuzu** 1. donkey at the head of a file of camels. 2. pilot engine. — **şeyhleri** *archaic* body of preachers of the great mosques. — **tut**= *archaic* to form a file or train.
katarakt قاتاراقت F *path.* cataract. — **ol**= to have a cataract, to suffer from cataract.
katarat (..—) قطرات A *lrnd., pl. of* **katre**.
katarcı قطارجى *archaic* driver of a train of animals.
katarla=r قطارلامه /ı/ to arrange in a file. —**n**= *pass.*
katarsis (..'.) قاتارسيس Gk 1. *med.* purgation (of the body), catharsis. 2. *psych., phil.* catharsis. —**li** *neol., med., same as* **katartik**.
katartikgi قاتارتيك F *med.* purgative, cathartic.
katat قطط A *lrnd.* 1. short, crisp and curly (hair). 2. short, crisp and curly headed.
katatüşşa'r قطط الشعر A *lrnd.* short, crisp, and curly headed.
katavaşya (...'.) قاتاواشيه Gk winter migration of fish from the Black Sea into the Mediterranean.
katavaz قاتاواز *prov.* stubborn, obstinate.

kated قتد A *lrnd.* wooden frame of a camel's saddle.
katedralⁱⁱ قاتدرال F cathedral.
kategori قاتغورى F category.
kat'et=ᵈᵉʳ قطع إملاك 1. /ı/ to cut, to cut off or through; to clip; to interrupt. 2. /ı/ to intersect. 3. to travel over, to traverse.
katgütᵗⁱⁱ قتگوت F catgut.
katı 1 قاتى 1. hard, stiff; *phys.* solid. 2. gizzard, maw, crop. 3. *archaic* very, much; violent, vehement. — **ekmek** dry hard bread. — **gönüllü** *archaic, same as* **katı yürekli**. — **mum** *obs.* sealing wax. — **ol**= to become hard, to be hardened, to harden. — **söz** harsh word. — **taş** 1. hard stone (hard kind of stone). 2. *archaic* marble. — **tut**= /ı/ *archaic* to be hard (on a person), to be severe or strict (with a person). — **yağ** grease, fat; solidified oil. — **yumurta** hard boiled egg. — **yürek** hard of heart. — **yürekli** hardhearted, heartless. — **yüzlü** *archaic* shameless, importunate.
katıⁱⁱ 2 (—.) قاطع A *lrnd.* 1. cutting, incisive; sharp; interrupting. 2. decisive, definitive. 3. *geom.* secant. —**ı tarik** highwayman.
katıᵗⁱ¹ 3 قطع A *var. of* **kat 3**.
katı=ʳ 4 قاتمى *archaic, same as* **katılaş**=.
katıa (—..) قاطعه A 1. *elec.* cutout, circuit breaker. 2. *anat.* incisor (tooth). 3. *calligraphy* ornamental page produced with writing cut out and pasted on. —**t** (—.—) A *pl.*
katıatüddem (—.—..) قاطعات الدم A *lrnd.* styptic medicines.
katıbe (—..) قاطبه A *lrnd.* the whole, totality, all. —**i ahvalde** in all circumstances. —**i nâs** all the people, everyone.
katıbeten (—ʹ...) قاطبة A *lrnd.* not at all, in no wise.
katıcakᵍⁱ قاتيجاق *archaic* a little food.
katıkᵍⁱ قاتيق 1. anything eaten with bread. 2. *prov.* yogurt; buttermilk. — **et**= /ı, a/ to eat with bread.
katıkla=ʳ قاتقله *prov.* /ı/ to exaggerate.
katıklı قاتقلى *prov.* adulterated, mixed (with baser substances). — **aş** *prov.* soup of cracked wheat with yogurt.
katıksız قاتقسز unadulterated, unmixed; eaten with nothing else (bread). — **hapis** *mil.* detention on bread and water.
katıl=ʳ 1 قاتيلمق /a/ 1. to be added (to), to be mixed (with); to join, participate.
katıl=ʳ 2 قاتيلمق 1. to be out of breath (from laughing or weeping). 2. *same as* **katılaş**=. —**a katıla ağla**= to choke with tears. —**a katıla gül**= to split one's sides with laughter.

katılan=ⁱʳ قاتيلان *same as* **katılaş**=. —**dır**= /ı/ *caus.*
katılaş=ⁱʳ قاتيلاشمق to become hard, dry, stiff or solid, to be solidified, to solidify; to coagulate.
katılaşma قاتيلاشمه 1. *verbal n.* of **katılaş**=. 2. *neol., sc.* solidification.
katılgan *neol.* additional; conjunctive. — **doku** *biol.* conjunctive tissue. — **harfler** servile or redundant letters (in the Semitic alphabets).
katılıkᵍⁱ قاتيلق 1. hardness, stiffness, rigidness, solidity. 2. *archaic* hardship, suffering; difficulty.
katım قاتم an adding, a mixing, a joining. —**lık** quantity to be added, mixed in.
katıntı قاتنتى 1. mixture. 2. added, mixed.
katır قاطر 1. mule. 2. stubborn person, mule; ungrateful or malicious person. 3. *prov., same as* **katır yemeni**. — **boncuğu** 1. large blue bead (often hung round animals' necks). 2. cowrie-shell. — **kuyruğu** stinking wood, *bot., Anagyris foetida*. — **tırnağı** broom, genista, *bot., Genista scoparia*. — **yemeni** *prov.* a coarse kind of shoe with heels tipped with iron (commonly worn by children). — **yılanı** *prov.* a kind of adder or viper. —**cı** muleteer.
katır kutur قاتر قوتر crackling sound, *e. g.*, **elmayı** — **ye**= to eat an apple noisily. — **adam** insensitive, apathetic man.
katış=ⁱʳ قاتشمق /a/ to join in and mix (with). —**ık** 1. mixed. 2. *neol., gram.* complex. —**maç** *neol., phil.* aggregate. —**tır**= /ı/ to add.
katıürrahm (—...) قاطع الرحم A *lrnd.* who breaks off relations with his relatives.
katıüttarikᵏⁱ (—...—) قاطع الطريق A *lrnd.* highway robber.
kat'î 1 قطعى A decisive, definitive, final; definite; categorical, absolute. — **cevap** categorical reply, definite answer. — **darbe** decisive blow, *sport* knockout blow. — **ferağ** *law* absolute transfer of property. — **karar** final decision. — **nizam** final balance. — **muamele** *com.* business on fixed terms. — **muharebe** decisive battle. — **netice** final result. — **olarak** *same as* **kat'î bir şekilde**. — **sat**= /ı/ *com.* to sell firm. — **satın al**= /ı/ *com.* to buy firm. — **savaş** decisive battle. — **bir şekilde** decisively, definitively, finally; definitely; categorically, absolutely. — **taarruz** decisive attack.
katiᵗⁱ¹ 2 (.—) قطيع A *lrnd.* detached portion of a flock.
kâtib (—.) كاتب A *same as* **kâtip**.
kâtibâne (—.—.) كاتبانه P *lrnd.* in a literary style.
kâtibe (—..) كاتبه A lady clerk, secretary.

kâtibî (—.—) كاتبى A *lrnd.* pertaining to a clerk or secretary.
katife قطيفة A *lrnd.*, same as **kadife**.
katikofti (..´.) قا تيقفرمقتى *Or. mus.* a fast rhythmic pattern of eight beats. (*cf.* **katakofti 2**).
katil 1 (—.) قاتل A murderer, assassin, killer. **—i ahih** *lrnd.*, *bot.* frog orchis. **—i ebih** *lrnd.* austere strawberry tree. **—i nefsih** *lrnd.*, *bot.* spurge, euphorbia.
katil[III] **2** قتل A a killing, assassination, murder. **—i âm** massacre. **—i amd** *lrnd.* premeditated murder. **—i nefs** *lrnd.* homicide, manslaughter.
katîl 3 (.—) قتيل A *lrnd.* killed, slain.
katilî (—.—) قاتلى A *lrnd.* pertaining to a murderer.
katillik[ği] قاتللك a being a murderer; murder.
kâtim (—.) كاتم A *lrnd.* who keeps a secret.
kâtip[bi] (—.) كاتب [**kâtib**] clerk, scribe; secretary; writer. **— adam** good literary composer, good writer. **—i adil** notary public. **— ağzı** well-worded (speech), well-chosen (words). **—i beytülmal** *Ott. hist.* officer of the bureau of inheritances. **—i divan** *Ott. hist.* secretary of the Council of State. **K—i ezeli** *poet.* God. **K—i felek** *poet.* Mercury (planet). **—i huruf** *lrnd.* the undersigned. **—i hususî** *lrnd.* private secretary. **— kavuğu** *Ott. hist.* cylindrical head covering about eight inches high, quilted, with perpendicular pleats all around. **—i maiyet** *lrnd.* functionary official. **—i mizan** *Ott. hist.* official weigher. **—i umumî** *lrnd.* secretary general. **—i vahy** *lrnd.* amanuensis of the revelation (a title of the Caliph Othman).
kâtiplik[ği] كاتبلك quality or profession of a clerk or secretary, clerkship, secretaryship.
kat'iyen (..´.) قطعيا A 1. by no means, never. 2. categorically, absolutely, definitely, finally.
kat'iyet قطعيت A definiteness, decisiveness, irrevocability. **— kesbet=** to become definite.
katkı 1. *neol.* addition, supplement, annex. 2. *prov.* wedding gift.
katla=[r] **1** قاتلامق /ı/ 1. to fold, to pleat. 2. *archaic* to repeat.
katla 2 قاتلا *archaic* time, times (after numerals), *e. g.*, **bir katla, yüz katla, bu katla** once, a hundred times, this time.
katla 3 تقتل A *lrnd.*, *pl.* of **katîl 3**.
katlaç[cı] قاتلاج *prov.* thin wafer (of bread).
katlak[ği] قاتلق *archaic* unleavened bread baked in thin cakes on sheets of iron.
katlama قاتلامه 1. *verbal n.* of **katla=**. 2. folded, pleated, doubled. 3. *prov.*, same as **katlak. — kapı** folding door. **— makinesi** folding or pleating machine.

katlamaç[cı] قاتلاماج *prov.* unleavened corn bread.
katlan=[ır] قاتلانمق 1. /a/ to bear, tolerate, connive, endure. 2. *pass. of* **katla= 1. —dır=** /ı, a/ *caus of.* **katlan=**.
katlanır قاتلانير folding, collapsible. **— iskemle** folding chair, folding stool, camp stool; **— kayık** folding boat, collapsible boat. **— metre, — mezura** folding rule. **— sehpa** collapsible tripod. **— yelpaze** folding fan.
katlat=[ır] قاتلاتمق /ı, a/ *caus. of* **katla= 1**.
katlet=[der] قتل ايتمك /ı/ to kill, murder, assassinate.
katlı قاتلى 1. storied. 2. folded, pleated.
katma قاتمه 1. *verbal n. of* **kat= 2**. 2. addition, appendage; *chem.* addition. 3. *prov.* string. **— bütçe** *neol.* subsidiary or supplementary budget.
katman *neol., geol.* stratum, layer, bed. **— bulut** *meteor.* stratus. **—laş=** *meteor.* to be arranged or formed in strata, to stratify. **—laşma** *meteor.* stratification.
katmer قاتمر 1. flaky pastry. 2. double (flower). **— kaldır=** *prov.* to cause troubles or disorder. **— katmer** in layers; double (flower), many-petaled. **—ci** maker and seller of flaky pastry.
katmerlen=[ir], **katmerleş=**[ir] قاتمرلنمك to become double, redoubled or many petaled.
katmerli قاتمرلى manifold; multiplied; double, many petaled. **— akıllı** *colloq.* very sly, very cunning. **— gelincik** red double garden poppy. **— gül** double rose. **— menekşe** double violet. **— tütün** double-flowered tobacco. **— zakkum** double-flowered oleander.
katoki (.´.) قاتوكى Gk shoemaker's stirrup.
Katolik[ği] قاتوليك F Catholic. **— Kilisesi** Catholic Church. **— ol=** to become Catholic. **— yap=** to make Catholic, to Catholicize. **—lik** Catholicism.
katot[du] قاتود E *elec.* cathode.
katra قطره A a drop. **— katra** drop by drop, by drops.
katran قطران [*Arabic* .—] tar. **— ağacı** cedar of Lebanon, *bot., Cedrus Libani;* Chian turpentine tree, *bot., Pistacia terebinthinus.* **— arabası** tar wagon. **— çamı** wild pine, Scotch fir, *bot., Pinus sylvestris.* **— fırçası** tar brush. **— fırını** tar kiln. **— gibi yapışkan** clinging bore. **— köpüğü** agaric, *bot., Polyporus igniarius.* **— kuyusu** bitumen or naphtha well. **— mantarı** white agaric of larch. **— püskürtme** infusion of tar. **— ruhu** creosote. **— taşı** *geol.* bitumen. **— tulumu** skin vessel for holding tar. **— yağı** tar oil. **—cı** tar maker.
katranla=[r] قطرانلامق /ı/ to tar, to smear with tar.
katranlı قطرانلى tarred, tarry. **— halat** tarred

katrat

rope. — **kâğıt** tar paper. — **mukavva** tar board. — **muşamba** tarpaulin. — **sabun** tar soap. — **üstüpü** black oakum. — **yol** tarred road.

katrat تا ئرات F *print*. quadrat.
katre قطرە A *lrnd.*, *same as* **katra**.
katredüzd قطرەدزد P *poet.* cloud, clouds.
katrezen قطرەزن P *poet.* fast runner.
katrilyon قاترىليون F *quadrillion* (10¹⁵ French and U.S.A.; 10³⁰ English and German).
katsayı *neol., math.* coefficient.
kattalⁱⁱ (.—) قتّال A *lrnd.* killer, slayer, murderer.
katuna قاتونا *Ott. hist.* Gipsy nomads.
katzen قطزن P *lrnd.* flat bone or ivory on which reed pens are nibbed.
kauçukᵍᵘ قاوچوق F India rubber; hard rubber. — **ağacı** rubber tree.
kaur (.—) قعور A *lrnd.* very deep.
kav 1 قاو tinder, punk. — **çakmak** tinder and flint. — **gibi** 1. easily burned, very inflammable. 2. soft, very light. — **göbeği** the very best punk. — **mantarı** punk, German tinder, amadou.
kav 2 قاو *prov.* clay.
kav 3 قاو *prov.* the shed skin of a snake.
kav 4 قاو F card game pool.
kavabil (.—.) قوابل A *lrnd.*, *pl. of* **kabil 1, kabile 2**.
kavadim (.—.) قوادم A *lrnd.*, *pl. of* **kadime**.
kavaf قواف [*haffaf*] maker or seller of cheap shoes. — **işi** coarsely made. — **malı** shoddy goods.
kavafhane (..—.) قوافخا *obs.* shoe workshop.
kavafi (.——) قوافى A *lrnd.*, *pl. of* **kafiye**.
kavafil (.—.) قوافل A *lrnd.*, *pl. of* **kafile**.
kavafiye قوافيه A 1. ready-made shoe shop. 2. stock in a ready-made shoe shop.
kavaflıkᵍⁱ قوافلق the cheap shoe trade.
kavaid (.—.) قواعد A *lrnd.*, *pl. of* **kaide**. —**i diniye** religious rules and precepts. —**i külliye** general canonical rules.
kavaim (.—.) قوائم A *lrnd.*, *pl. of* **kaime**.
kavakᵍⁱ قاواق *poplar, bot., Populus*; of poplar wood. — **ağacı** poplar tree. — **at=** *prov.* to throw (in wrestling). — **inciri** purple fig.
kavakla=ʳ قاواقلامە *prov.* to go to seed.
kavaklıkᵍⁱ قاواقلغى poplar grove.
kaval قاوال 1. shepherd's pipe, flageolet. 2. smooth-bore gun barrel. 3. *arch.* torus\ — **burunlu** straight-nosed. — **çal=** to play the pipe or flageolet. — **çubuk** *arch.* astragal, baguette. — **kemiği**, — **kemik** *anat.* fibula. — **namlu** *same as* **kaval²**. — **topu** muzzle loader. — **tüfeği**, — **tüfek** smooth bore gun. —**cı** pipe player, flageolet player.

kavalib (.—.) قوالب A *lrnd., pl. of* **kalıp**.
kavallan=ʳ قواللانمە *slang* /ı/ to bother, to annoy.
kavalye (.ˊ.) قواليه F a lady's escort. —**lik et=** /a/ to escort or accompany a lady.
kavanca (.ˊ.) قوانجه It *naut.* Shift. — **et=** /ı/ to shift. — **gardiya** *same as* **kavanca vardiya**. — **halatı** shifting rope. — **iskota** Shift the sheets. — **iskota flok** Shift over and set the jibs. — **ol=** to come over. — **palanga** Fleet ho! — **uskuta grandi** Shift the main-sheets. — **vardiya** change of watch (on deck).
kavança, kavanço (.ˊ.) قوانجه It *naut.* 1. *var. of* **kavanca**. 2. transshipment (of goods), transfer, handing over. — **et=** *slang* 1. /ı, a/ to transfer a work to another. 2. /ı, la/ to exchange (with).
kavanin (.——) قوانين A *lrnd., pl. of* **kanun 1**.
kavanla=ʳ قوانلامە *prov.* /ı/ 1. to protect. 2. to watch.
kavanoz قوانوز Gk glass, earthenware or wooden jar, pot.
kavara 1 قوارە 1. *archaic* a fart, a breaking wind. 2. *slang* idle talk, mere noise.
kavara 2 قوارە [Arabic **kavvara**] emptied honeycomb.
kavaracı قوارەجى *slang* swaggerer, liar.
kavariⁱⁱ (.—.) قوارع A *lrnd., pl. of* **karia**.
kavas قواس [Arabic **kavvas**] 1. messenger of an embassy or consulate; doorkeeper of a big establishment. 2. *obs.* guard in attendance on a dignitary.
kavasıf (.—.) قواصف A *lrnd., pl. of* **kasıfa**.
kavasya (.ˊ.) قواسيا F bitterwood, quassia, *bot., Quassia amara*.
kavat 1 قواط Gk *prov.* wooden bowl.
kavat 2 قواط [**kavvad**] coward.
kavata 1 قواطه *prov.* round wooden bowl.
kavata 2 (.ˊ.) قواطه Arm sour green tomato (for pickling).
kavazakᵍⁱ, **kavazan** قوازاق Arm *prov.* babbler, chatterbox.
kavcakla=ʳ قواجاقلامە *prov.* /ı/ to grasp, to seize, to snap.
kavcar قواجار *prov.* shell, bark; wood shavings.
kavcı قواجى maker or seller of punk.
kaved قود A *lrnd.* execution of the law of talion.
kavelâ (.ˊ.), **kavele** (.ˊ.) قاولا It *naut.* 1. treenail. 2. a whipping. — **bağı** marline spike hitch. — **et=** /ı/ to whip a rope, to work the end of a rope into a tapering form, to point. — **ör=** to whip a rope. — **vur=** /a/ to drive a fid into a rope in order

to open the strands in splicing. — **yap=** same as **kaṿala et=**.

kaveleta, kavelete (...˙.) قواله قوه لتا ناوه ل ته It trestle; *naut.* trestle for winding rope. — **halatı** *naut.* messenger.

kavelya, kavelye (.˙.) ناويليا ناويليه It *var. of* **kavela, kavele**.

kavga ناوغا قوغا غوغا غاوغا [**gavga**] quarrel, row, brawl; fight, battle. — **ara=** /la/ to pick a quarrel. — **bizim yorganın başında imiş** The whole fight was in order to get hold of our quilt *said by the person whose loss, sacrifice or giving way to others puts an end to a quarrel*. — **çıkar=** to provoke a quarrel. — **et=** /la/ to quarrel (with), to fight. —**ya giriş=** /la/ to take up a quarrel (with). — **kaşağısı** frivolous pretext for a quarrel. —**ya kaşın=** to keep doing things likely to lead to a quarrel. —**ya tutuş=** same as **kavgaya giriş=**.

kavgacı ناوغاجى quarrelsome, brawling; quarreler.

kavgalaş=[ir] ناوغالشمك to quarrel, bicker, wrangle.

kavgalı ناوغالى 1. quarrelled, disputed (about). 2. quarrelling, angry.

kavgasız ناوغاسز without quarrelling, dispute or fight; peacefully, amicably.

kavgır=[ir] ناوغيرمه prov. 1. to hop or jump about. 2. to hurry.

kâvgir كاوگير *var. of* **kârgir**.

kavız قوز *prov.* husk (of grains).

kavi 1 (.—) قوى A *lrnd.* strong, solid, robust.

kâvi 2 (——) كاوى A *lrnd., chem.* caustic.

kavibaht (.—.) قوى بخت P *lrnd.* whose fortune is sure.

kavil[vll] قول [**kavl**] 1. agreement, accord. 2. *lrnd.* word, assertion. —**ince** according to him, according to his assertion. — **ve fiil** word and deed, profession and practice. —**i ile** with this condition or understanding. — **ve karar** mutual agreement, final understanding. —**i mâruf** *lrnd.* kind word (in refusal or reproof). —**i mücerred** unwarranted assertion, mere words. —**i mücerredde kal=** to be only in words (with no action). —**i nebi** *lrnd.* words of the Prophet. — **yeri** place appointed for a meeting, rendezvous. —**i zaif** *lrnd.* assertion of little or no authority.

kavilen=[ir] قويلنمك *same as* **kavileş=**.

kavileş=[ir] قويلشمك to become strong, solid or robust. —**tir=** *caus.*

kavilleş=[ir] قوللشمك to agree, to decide mutually. —**il=** *pass.*

kavilli قوللى agreed.

kavilname (..—.) قوللنامه P written agreement.

kavilya (.˙.) ناويليه It *var. of* **kavela, kavele**.

kavim[vml] **1** قوم [**kavm**] people, nation; tribe, family; sect. —**i fil** *Isl. hist.* followers of King Abraha on his expedition against Mecca. —**i gayri mahsur** *can. law* group consisting of a hundred or more persons. —**i Hûd** *lrnd.* the pre-Semitic people of Ad. —**i İsa** *lrnd.* 1. the Jews of the time of Jesus. 2. the disciples of Jesus. — **kabile** kith and kin. —**i Lût** *lrnd.* people of Lot, inhabitants of Sodom. —**i mahsur** *can. law* a group consisting of less than a hundred persons. —**i Musa** *lrnd.* people of Moses, Israelites. —**i müneccimin** *lrnd.* the astrologers.

kavîm 2 (.—) قويم A *lrnd.* straight; right, correct.

kavis[vsi] قوس [**kavs**] 1. bend, bow, curved line. 2. *geom.* arc (of circle); *arch.* 3. bracket, parenthesis. 4. *astr.* Sagittarius. 5. *naut.* sheer (curvature of the deck). —**i asabî** *lrnd.* neural arch. —**i azmî** *lrnd.* osseous arch. — **burcu** *astr.* the sign or constellation of Sagittarius. — **çiz=** to describe a curve. —**i elektrikî** *lrnd.* electric arc. —**i galsamî** *lrnd.* branchial arch. — **ışığı** *elec.* arc light. — **içine al=** /ı/ to parenthesize. —**i irtifa** *lrnd.* arc of altitude (of an astrolabe or projection). —**i kudret** *poet.*, —**i kuzah** rainbow. — **lâmbası** *elec.* arc lamp. —**i leyl**, —**i leylî** *lrnd.* nocturnal arc (of an astrolabe or projection). —**i münakkah** *geom.* arc of which the supplement has been calculated. —**i nehar**, —**i neharî** *lrnd.* diurnal arc (of an astrolabe or projection). —**i nüzul** *Isl. myst.* arc of descent (transformation of the divine light into the four elements). —**i rahî** *anat.* palmar arch. — **şeklinde** bent, curved, arched, arch shaped; in a curve. — **tulü** *geom.* length of arc. —**i uruc** *Isl. myst.* arc of ascent (return of the divine light to God after having passed through the four elements).

kavisname (..—.) قوسنامه P *lrnd.* archery book.

kâviş (—.) كاوش P *lrnd.* a digging, excavating; a scrutinizing, investigation. —**ger** (—..) P digger.

kâviyet (—..) كاويت A *lrnd., chem.* causticity.

kaviyülbünye قوى البنيه A *lrnd.* of strong physical constitution.

kaviyyen (..˙.) قويا A *lrnd.* strongly.

kavkaa قوقع A *anat.* cochlea.

kavkaî قوقعى A shelly, conchoidal. — **kalker** *geol.* shell lime.

kavkas, kavkaz قوقناز 1. horehound, *bot., Marrubium vulgare.* 2. *prov.* brushwood.

kavkı *neol.* shell; *anat., cochlea.*

kavl قول A *same as* **kavil**.

kavla=[r] قولامق to peel off, scale off; to rise in

kavlak

blisters and fall off (skin, bark, etc.); to chip off (painting, pottery, etc.).

kavlakᵍ¹ قوللوه 1. peeled off, risen in blisters (skin, bark, etc.), barkless. 2. *prov.* beardless, unbearded. 3. *prov.* simpleton, idiot. — **yağı** *prov.* cream.

kavlen (.'.) قولًا A *lrnd.* by word, by agreement. — **ve fi'len** by word and deed.

kavlet=ᵈᵉʳ قوللاتمك to agree mutually.

kavlıçᶜ¹ قولیج ruptured; suffering from hernia.

kavlıkᵍ¹ قاولوه *prov.* tinder and touchwood pouch.

kavlî (. —) قولی A *lrnd.* verbal, promised, asserted.

kavliyat (. — —) قولیات A *lrnd.* mere words, verbal statements or assertions.

kavlu قاولو furnished with tinder or punk.

kavm قوم A same as **kavim 1**.

kavmî (. —) قومی A ethnical. —**yat** (. — —) A *lrnd.* ethnography. —**yet** (. — .) A *lrnd.* ethnical character, nationality.

kavra=ʳ قاورامه /ı/ 1. to comprehend, to conceive. 2. to seize, to grasp, to grab. 3. *prov.* to reap with a sickle.

kavrak قاوراه *prov.* dry leaves or brushwood for lighting a fire.

kavrala=ʳ قاورالامه *prov.* /ı/ to try to seize or grasp.

kavram 1. *neol.* concept, idea, notion. 2. *prov.* handful (of). 3. *anat.* peritoneum. — **bilgisi** *phil.* ideology. — **yağı** intestinal fat.

kavrama قاورامه 1. verbal *n.* of **kavra**=. 2. *mech.* coupling; *auto.* clutch, cone clutch. 3. *building* crosspiece, binding piece, tie beam. — **çatalı** *mech.* coupling fork. — **diski** *mech.* coupling disc. — **işareti** *print.* brace. — **kabiliyeti** comprehension, intellect. — **kapağı** *mech.* clutch housing. — **kasnağı** *mech.*, same as **kavrama diski**. — **kutusu** *mech.* clutch box. — **manivelâsı** *mech.* coupling lever. — **mili** *auto.* clutch shaft. — **pedalı** *auto.* clutch pedal. — **yayı** *mech.* coupling spring.

kavramcı *neol., phil.* conceptualist; conceptualistic. —**lık** *neol., phil.* conceptualism.

kavramlı *neol.* exhaustive, comprehensive.

kavran 1 قاوران *prov.* 1. box; wooden receptacle. 2. empty honeycomb.

kavran=ʳ **2** قاورانمه 1. pass. of **kavra**=. 2. *prov.* /ı/ to seek eagerly. —**ıl**= same as **kavran**=¹. —**ılmaz** inconceivable.

kavrat=ʳ قاوراتمه /ı/ caus. of **kavra**=. —**ma** *pottery* cementation.

kavrayış قاورایش conception, comprehension. — **birliği** unity of conception. —**lı** quick at understanding.

kavrukᵍᵘ قاوروه 1. stunted, dried up. 2. scorched.

kavrul=ᵘʳ قاورولمه to be roasted; to roast.

kavrulmuş قاورولش roasted. — **kahve** roasted coffee.

kavs قوس A same as **kavis**.

kavsara قوصره A *prov.* basket or box made of matting. —**sı dar** easily vexed, irritable.

kavsî (. —) قوسی [based on **kavs**] curved; arched.

kavsülleyl قوس الليل A *lrnd.* nocturnal arc on an astrolobe.

kavşa=ʳ قاوشامه *prov., var.* of **kağşa**=.

kavşakᵍ¹ **1** قاوشانه crossing point, junction, crossroads. — **noktası** crossing point.

kavşakᵍ¹ **2** قاوشانه *prov.* dry and crackling, about to collapse.

kavşır=ᵘʳ قاوشيرمه /ı/ *prov.* 1. same as **kavuştur**=. 2. to surround.

kavşıt قاوشيت *prov.* 1. joining point. 2. horizon.

kavşur=ᵘʳ قاوشورمه archaic, same as **kavuştur**=.

kavukᵍᵘ قاووه قاغوه 1. quilted turban. 2. *prov.* urinary bladder (animals). 3. *archaic* hollow. — **u büyük, kendi küçük şalgam efendi** Little master turnip who has a big turban but is small himself *term of derision applied to any insignificant but pretentious man*. — **uma dinlet sen onu!** same as **külâhıma anlat**. — **fitili** piping in the seam of a wadded turban. — **giydir**= /a/ to hoax. — **salla**= /a/ to fawn on, to act the sycophant. — **sarığı** turban cloth.

kavukçu قاووقچی 1. toady, sycophant, flatterer. 2. maker or seller of quilted turbans.

kavuklu قاووقلی 1. wearing a quilted turban; *w. cap.,* name of one of the two staple characters in the old Turkish theater (**Orta Oyunu**). 2. *archaic* cavernous.

kavuklukᵍᵘ قاووقلغی wooden stand for a quilted turban.

kavun قاوون muskmelon, melon, *bot., Cucumis melo*. — **ağacı** papaya tree, papaya, melon tree, *bot., Carica papaya*. — **içi** light yellow color (peculiar to the flesh of the muskmelon). — **portakalı** shaddock, *bot., Citrus grandis*.

kavunlukᵍᵘ قاوونلغی bed of muskmelons; place where muskmelons are stored.

kavur=ᵘʳ قاوورمه قاورمه /ı/ to fry, to roast, to dry.

kavurga قاورغه *prov.* dried or roasted wheat, corn or chickpeas.

kavurma قاورمه 1. verbal *n.* 2. fried meat, preserve of fried meat. 2. a frying, roasting, drying.

kavurmaçᶜ¹ قاورماج *prov.* roasted wheat.

kavuş=ᵘʳ قاووشمه /ı/ 1. to meet, to come together, to meet again after a long absence. 2. to obtain, to attain, to touch.

kavuşakᵍⁱ قاوشانه قاوشانه *same as* **kavşak 1.**
kavuşkan قاوشغان *archaic* importunate.
kavuşma قاوشم 1. *verbal n. of* **kavuş=**. 2. *bot.* conjugation. 3. *astr.* synodic. **— devri** *astr.* synodic revolution.
kavuştur=ᵘʳ قاوشديرمق *caus. of* **kavuş=**. **—malık** join, joining, juncture (in a building), joint, coupling, junction (of pipes).
kavuşukᵍᵘ قاوشيق joined, touched. **—luk** contiguity.
kavuşum *neol., astr.* conjunction. **— devri** *astr.* period of conjunction, synodic period.
kavuşur=ᵘʳ قاوشورمق /1, a/ *archaic, same as* **kavuştur=**.
kavut قاوت *prov.* roasted wheat ground to flour; gruel made of such flour.
kavuz قاوز 1. *neol., bot.* glume. 2. *same as* **kavız**. **—lu** *neol.* glumaceous, glumiferous. **—lular** *neol., bot.*, Glumiferae.
kavvad (. —) قوّاد A *lrnd.* pander, pimp.
kavvalˡⁱ (. —) قوّال A *lrnd.* babbler, tattler, chatterbox; one who speaks fluently, eloquent.
kavvale (. — .) قوّاله A *lrnd.* extremely eloquent.
kavza=ʳ 1 قاوزامق *prov.* /1/ to guard, to protect; to hold firmly.
kavza 2 قاوزه parsnip, *bot., Pastinaca sativa.*
kay=ᵃʳ 1 قايمق 1. to glide, to slide, to slip. 2. to blink, to squint.
kayʸⁱ 2 قئ A a vomiting. **— et=** to vomit.
kay 3 قاى *archaic* fine rain.
kaya قايا rock. **— balığı** goby, black goby. **— balıkları** gobies, *zool., Gobiidae.* **— başı** 1. rural ballad, shepherd's song. 2. top of a rocky cliff. **—ya bindir=** to run aground on rocks (ship). **— boncuğu** bead of rock crystal. **— döküntüsü** reef of rocks. **— güvercini** rock dove, *zool., Columba livia.* **— horozu** cock of the rock, *zool., Rupicola crocea.* **— kartalı** golden eagle, *zool., Aquila chrysaetos.* **— kekiği** winter savory, *bot., Satureia montana.* **— keleri** chameleon, *zool., Chameleo vulgaris.* **— kınası** *obs.* orcella and cudbear weed, used as dyes. **— koruğu** stone crop, *bot., Sedum sempervivum.* **— kuşu** sand grouse, *zool., Pterocles arenarius.* **— lifi** *obs.* asbestos. **— meşesi** British oak, English oak, *bot., Quercus robur.* **— mezar** rock tomb. **— pirinci** kind of rice growing on dry soil. **— sıvacı kuşu** rock nuthatch, *zool., Sitta neumayer.* **— sirkesi** *same as* **kaya koruğu.** **— suyu** rock spring. **— tuzu** rock salt.
kayacıkᵍⁱ قايجق small rock.
kayağan قاياغان slate; schist. **— taşı** slaty stone, schist.
kayakᵍⁱ قاياق 1. ski. 2. *prov.* sledge. 3. *prov.* ravine. 4. *prov.* inconstant, fickle. **— değnekleri** ski poles, ski sticks, snow sticks. **— kay=** to ski, to go skiing. **— yolu** ski run. **—cı** skier.
kayalakᵍⁱ قايالق *prov., same as* **kayalık 2.**
kayalıkᵍⁱ 1 قايالق rocky; rocky place. **— ada** rocky island. **— serçesi** rock sparrow, *zool., Petronia petronia.*
kayalıkᵍⁱ 2 قايالق *prov.* prolific female camel.
kayan قايان *prov.* temporary mountain torrent.
kayanakᵍⁱ قايانق *prov., same as* **kayağan.**
kayar قايار A *prov.* rough or hooked horseshoe (for walking on ice). **— et=** /1/ to shoe with a roughed or hooked horseshoes.
kayarla=ʳ قايارلامق *prov.* /1/ to scold, to rebuke.
kayarlı قايارلو *prov.* with a hoof worn or broken from passing over rocky country.
kayarto (.´.) قايارتو *slang* immoral, wicked, corrupt person.
kayasa قاياسا 1. breast strap (at the front of a saddle). 2. *prov.* camel-hair rope.
kayasire (. — ..) قياصره A *lrnd., pl. of* **kayser.**
kaybana قايبانه *prov.* property left (at death).
kaybedil=ⁱʳ غايب ايدلمك *pass. of* **kaybet=**.
kaybet=ᵈᵉʳ غايب ايتمك /1/ to lose. **—tir=** /1, a/ *caus.*
kaybol=ᵘʳ غايب اولمق to be lost; to disappear from sight.
kayd قيد A *same as* **kayıt 1. — ü bend** *lrnd.* a binding. **— ü şart** *lrnd.* proviso, restrictions.
kayda قايده *archaic* Where?
kaydet=ᵉʳ قيد ايتمك /1/ 1. to enroll, to register; to note down. 2. to take notice (of).
kaydır=ⁱʳ قايديرمق 1. /1/ *caus. of* **kay= 1.** 2. *mil.* to remove.
kaydırakᵍⁱ قايديراق 1. flat circular stone (used in a game resembling quoits). 2. hopscotch. 3. *neol., geol.* flat shingle or pebble.
kaydırıl=ⁱʳ قايديرلمق *pass. of* **kaydır=**.
kaydiye قيديه A registration fee.
kaygan قايغان 1. slippery; polished. 2. fickle, mercurial. **— taş, — taşı** slate.
kaygana قايغنه [kaygına] omelet with cheese or chopped meat; sweet dessert made of eggs.
kaygı قايغى anxiety, grief; care. **— çek=** /dan/ to worry or grieve (about). **—sına düş=** /ın/ to be anxious (for).
kaygılan=ⁱʳ قايغلانمق to worry, to grieve.
kaygılı قايغلى anxious, worried; causing anxiety.
kaygın قايغين 1. polished; slippery. 2. *prov.* pregnant (animal).
kaygına قايغنه [*Persian* khayagına] *prov., same as* **kaygana.**
kaygısız قايغيسز without care or anxiety,

kaygu

carefree. **—lık** carefreeness, freedom from care or anxiety.
kaygu تاىغو تيغو *archaic, var. of* **kaygı**.
— ye= to trouble oneself, to be anxious.
kayı تاىى *archaic, var. of* **kaygu**.
kayık[g1] **1** تاىىه 1. boat, rowboat, caique. 2. *prov.* sledge. **— astarı** side lining boards of a rowboat. **— biçimi** *prov.* kind of lady's shoe. **— boynası** steering paddle. **— hotoz** *obs.* boat-shaped headdress. **— iskarmozu** thole pin. **— kızağı** cradle on which a boat is drawn up on the land. **— pervazı** inner gunwale of a boat. **— sahan** oval copper dish. **— tabak** oval dish. **— yarışı** boat race.
kayık=[ır] **2** تيضى *archaic* to deviate; to incline.
kayık=[ır] **3** تيضى *archaic* 1. to worry, to grieve. 2. to hesitate.
kayıkçı تاىىجى boatman.
kayıkhane (..—.) تاىغزا:ه boathouse.
kayın[yn1] **1** تاىن brother-in-law. **— ana** *same as* **kaynana**. **— ata** *same as* **kaynata**. **— baba** father-in-law. **— birader** brother-in-law. **— hısımlığı** relationship by marriage. **— peder** father-in-law. **— valide** mother-in-law.
kayın 2 تاىن beech, *bot., Fagus sylvatica.* **— ağacı** beech tree. **— kozalağı** beech nut, beech mast. **— ormanı** beech wood. **— yağı** beech oil. **—giller** *neol., bot., Fagaceae.*
kayıntı تاىنتى *slang* food. **— yap=** to have a meal.
kayıp[yb1] تاىب غيب [gayb] loss; *mil.* casualties. **—lara karış=** to disappear, to abscond. **— listesi** *mil.* casualty list, casualties.
kayır=[ır] **1** تاىرمه /ı/ to protect, to back, to support; to look after, to care (for).
kayır 2 تاىر shifting sandbank in a stream.
kayırıcı تاىرجى protector, supporter; who looks after.
kayırıl=[ır] تاىرىله *pass. of* **kayır=** 1.
kayırmaz تاىرماز *prov.* It doesn't matter.
kayırt=[ır] تاىرتنه /ı, a/ *caus. of* **kayır=** 1.
kayısı تاىسى قىسى apricot, *bot., Prunus armeniaca.* **— ağacı** apricot tree. **— gibi** with the yolk still liquid (of a boiled egg). **— gülü** a variety of rose (small and yellow).
kayış تاىش strap, thong; belt. **— avarası** *mech.* belt shifter. **— bağlantısı** belt buckle. **— balığı** cusk eel, *zool., Ophidium barbatum.* **— çatalı** *mech.* belt fork. **—a çek=** /ı/ 1. *colloq.* to make a dupe (of). 2. to strop. **—ı çık=** to bear the main burden. **— dili** 1. coarse manner of speaking. 2. thieves' slang. **— gibi** 1. hard as leather (meat). 2. well-knit, strong. 3. very brown (skin). **— kanat** *prov.* bat. **— kancası** *mech.* belt fastener. **— kasnağı** *mech.* belt pulley. **— kılavuzu** *mech.* belt guide. **— kıran** rest harrow, *bot., Ononis arvensis.* **— mengenesi** *mech.* belt stretcher.

— tertibatı *mech.* belt gear. **— testeresi** whipsaw, handsaw. **— vidası** *mech.* belt screw. **—a vur=** /ı/ to strop (razor).
kayışçı تاىشجى 1. strap maker, strap cutter, belt maker, strap seller, belt seller. 2. *slang* thief, pilferer.
kayışlı تاىشلى having a strap or belt. **— transmisyon** *mech.* belt drive. **— transportör sistemi** *mech.* belt system.
kayıt[yd1] **1** قىد [kayd] 1. a registering, record, enrollment, enlistment; *fin.* quotation. 2. restriction, reservation; fetter. 3. a caring, a paying attention. **— altında** restricted. **— altına gir=** to be bound by restrictions. **— defteri** register (book). **—a değer** worthy of note. **—ım değil** *archaic* I don't care about... **—ına düş=** /ın/ to be concerned (with). **—tan düş=** /ı/ to cancel an entry in a register. **— evrakı** registration records. **—a geçir=** /ı/ to register, to enter in the register. **—ını gör=** *archaic* /ın/ to destroy, to ruin, to wreck; to do for. **—i hayat şartiyle** for life, during life. **—i ihtirazî** *lrnd.* reservation, proviso. **—i ihtiyat** *same as* **kaydi ihtirazî**. **— kuyut** restrictions. **— kuyut tanıma=** to pay no attention to restrictions. **— muamelesi** formalities of registration or enrollment. **—ları naklet=** bookkeeping to post, to transfer an entry. **—ların sıhhatini kontrol** bookkeeping test check. **—ını sil=** /ın/ to delete the record (of). **—ını terkin et=** *same as* **kaydını sil=**. **— ücreti** registration fee. **—ını ye=** *archaic* to be anxious (for).
kayıt=[ır] **2** قىتنه *archaic* to return. **—ım** *neol., phil.* recurrence.
kayıtla=[r] *neol.* to restrict, to limit.
kayıtlı قىدلى registered, recorded, enlisted; inscribed.
kayıtsız قىدسز 1. indifferent, carefree; careless; without any condition or restriction. 2. unregistered, uninscribed. **— kal=** /a/ to be indifferent (to, towards). **— şartsız** unconditional, without any condition or reservation. **— şartsız mülk** *law* fee simple. **— şartsız teslim** unconditional surrender.
kayıtsızlık[g1] قىدسزلوه indifference, unconcern; carelessness, nonchalance.
kaykı تاىغى *prov.* 1. oblique, slanting, inclined, sloping. 2. cross, peevish; obstinate, headstrong. 3. sledge.
kaykıl=[ır] تاىغىله 1. to slant, to slope. 2. to lean (against), to rest. 3. *prov.* to die.
kayl قىل A *lrnd., a title of the ancient Himyarite kings of Arabia.*
kaylan 1 تاىلان *prov.* stony and loamy soil.
kaylan=[ır] **2** تاىلانه *prov.* to become crusted (soil, after rain).
kaylık[g1] تاىلىه *prov.* 1. overcoat, furred coat;

shepherd's coat. 2. quilt, blanket. 3. hut; cart house.

kaylule (. — .) قَيْلُولَه A *lrnd.* sleep in the forenoon; siesta.

kayma قَايْمَه 1. *verbal n. of* **kay=** 1. 2. *geol.* landslide. — **açısı** gliding angle. — **düzeyi** *neol.* gliding surface, guide surface. — **rayı** guide rail; *naut.* shipway, sliding ways. — **sathı** *same as* **kayma düzeyi**. — **yolu** sliding ways, chute. — **yüzeyi** *same as* **kayma düzeyi**.

kaymaçᶜᶦ قَايْمَاچ with the outer corner sloping upwards (eye). — **göz** eye with an upward-sloping outer corner.

kaymakᵍᶦ قَايْمَاق 1. cream, clotted cream; dish of sweetened clotted cream. 2. hard crust (left on the soil after rain or flooding). 3. essence. 4. very soft and white. — **ağzı** surface of clotted cream. —**ını al=** /ın/ to skim. — **altı** skim milk. — **bağla=** to form cream. — **gibi** 1. very white and smooth. 2. delicious, attractive. — **kâğıdı**, — **kâğıt** surface-coated paper, baryta paper, art paper. — **melhemi**, — **merhemi** cold cream. — **mermeri** *same as* **kaymak taşı**. — **taşı** alabaster. — **tut=** *same as* **kaymak bağla=**. — **üstü** skin on the surface of clotted cream. — **yağı** fresh butter.

kaymakam قَايْمَقَام A 1. head official of a district. 2. *formerly* lieutenant colonel. —**lık** office, rank or district of a **kaymakam**.

kaymakçı قَايْمَاقْچِى maker or seller of clotted cream.

kaymaklan=ᴵʳ قَايْمَاقْلَانْمَق to form cream.

kaymaklı قَايْمَاقْلِى 1. creamy, made with cream. 2. coated with cream. — **dondurma** ice cream. — **kadaif** dish prepared with **tel kadaifi** in two layers, with clotted cream, almonds, and pistachios between.

kayna=ʳ قَايْنَامَق 1. to boil; to be boiled; to be hot (weather). 2. to ferment, to effervesce; to burn, to sour (stomach). 3. /dan/ to gush forth, to well up out (of). 4. to teem with, to be full (of), *e. g.,* **sokakta insanlar kaynıyor** The streets are teaming with people. 5. to be perpetually moving; to be in agitation. 6. *tech.* to weld, to be welded; to heal up; to knit (bone). 7. to be lost in the midst of confusion, to be forgotten, abandoned, *e. g.,* **bizim seyahat kaynadı gitti** We abandoned our plan for taking a trip; *slang* to be stolen.

kaynaçᶜᶦ *neol., geol.* geyser. — **taşı** geyserite.

kaynakᵍᶦ قَايْنَاق 1. spring, fountain, source. 2. *tech.* weld, a welding. 3. *colloq.* the buttocks. 4. *slang* a kind of hashish. 5. *prov.* sympathetic, congenial. — **tozu** welding powder, flux. — **yap=** /ı/ to weld (together); to patch (a tire). —**çı** welder. —**la=** /ı/

same as **kaynak yap=**. —**lı** welded; *prov.* congenial.

kaynama قَايْنَامَه 1. *verbal n. of* **kayna=** 1. 2. boiled. — **ısısı** boiling heat, boiling temperature. — **noktası** boiling point. — **sıcaklığı** *same as* **kaynama ısısı**.

kaynana قَايْنَانَا mother-in-law. — **dili** *pop.* cactus. — **zırıltısı** rattle (toy). —**lık et=** /a/ *colloq.* to interfere.

kaynar قَايْنَار 1. boiling, ebullient, bubbling. 2. *prov.* spring, source. 3. *prov.* drink offered to guests visiting a woman who has just given birth to a child. 4. *slang* hashish.

kaynarca قَايْنَارْجَه hot spring, thermal spring.

kaynaş=ᴵʳ قَايْنَاشْمَق 1. to weld; /la/ to coalesce (with). 2. to move restlessly, to become agitated; to swarm, to be full. 3. /la/ to become good friends; to get on well with each other. —**tır=** *caus.*

kaynat=ᴵʳ قَايْنَاتْمَق 1. /ı/ to boil; to ferment; to burn (stomach); to weld; to heal up, to knit (bones). 2. *colloq.* to chat, to have a friendly chat. 3. to plot; to gossip. 4. *slang* /ı/ to pilfer, to steal.

kaynata قَايْنَاتَا father-in-law.

kaynatıl=ᴵʳ قَايْنَاتِيلْمَق *pass. of* **kaynat=**.

kaynattır=ᴵʳ قَايْنَاتْدِيرْمَق /ı, a/ *caus. of* **kaynat=**.

kaypa=ʳ قَايْپَامَق *prov.* to slip, to get away by slipping off; to slide; to disappear.

kaypakᵍᶦ قَايْپَاق 1. unreliable, slippery, fickle. 2. slippery; *neol., chem.* unctuous, oily, fat. 3. *colloq.* stolen; thievish. 4. *prov.* a kind of stuffed pastry. — **gözlü** whose eye blinks continually. — **mal** stolen or smuggled goods. — **semender** smooth newt, *zool.,* Triton (Lissotriton) punctatus.

kaypakçı قَايْپَاقْچِى thief; smuggler; receiver of stolen goods.

kaypan=ᴵʳ قَايْپَانْمَق to flinch or jump on one side, to dodge.

kaypanç قَايْپَانْچ *prov.* slippery.

kaypı=ʳ قَايْپِيمَق *archaic, same as* **kaypa=**.

kaypın=ᴵʳ قَايْپِينْمَق *archaic* /dan/ to beware (of); to refrain from.

kayracılıkᵍᶦ *neol., phil.* providentialism.

kayrakᵍᶦ قَايْرَاق 1. shifting, sandy (soil), slippery (earth). 2. *neol.* sliding place. 3. flat round stone (used as a quoit). 4. *prov.* whetstone. — **at=** to throw a flat stone (like a quoit). — **kum** quicksand, shifting sand.

kayral=ᴵʳ قَايْرَالْمَق to become choked with sand (stream, etc.).

kayran قَايْرَان 1. clearing in a forest. 2. stony, sandy soil; slippery soil.

Kayrevan (. . —) قَيْرَوَان A *geog.* Kairouan. —**iye** *phil.* Cyrenaic school.

kayrıl=ᴵʳ قَايْرِيلْمَق *var. of* **kayırıl=**.

Kays قَيْس A *literature,* Arabic poet under

the name of **Mecnun** famous for his love of Leylâ.

kaysa, kaysakᵍⁱ نايساك ، نايسه prov. crust.

kaysaklan=ⁱʳ نايساقمو prov. to form a crust.

kayser قيصر A emperor, caesar.

Kayseri (...); **Kayseriye** قيصريه، قيصرى geog. Kayseri, ancient Caesarea.

kaysı نايسى same as **kayısı**.

kayşa 1 neol., geol. landslip, landslide.

kayşa=ʳ 2 neol., geol. to slip, to slide (land).

kayşakᵍⁱ نايشاك prov. tending to give way (soil).

kayşan=ⁱʳ neol., geol. to sink (land).

kayşat neol., geol. debris.

kaytan قيطان نايتان 1. cotton or silk cord, braid. 2. naut. gasket. — **bıyık, — bıyıklı** having a thin curling moustache. — **halka** arch. amulet. — **iskele** rope ladder. — **işi** braid trimming. — **yakısı** surgery seton.

kaytanlı نايتانلى having a cord, braided. — **oluk, — yiv** arch. cabling.

kaytar=ⁱʳ نايتارمه 1. /dan/ to get out of (doing), to dodge (doing). 2. prov. /ı/ to let return, to recall.

kaytas (.—) قيطاس A lrnd. whale.

kaytasî (.——) قيطاسى A lrnd. cetaceous. —**ye** (.——.) zool. 1. Cetacea. 2. cetacean.

kaytaz 1 نايتاز archaic crest (of a bird), pennon or ornament (horse-hair); bonnet or turban for women.

kaytaz 2 نايتاز prov. negligent, careless; cunning fellow; thief.

kaytus قيطس A astr. the constellation Cetus.

kayu نيمر archaic anxiety. — **et**=, —**lan**= to grieve.

kayyam (.—) قيّام A lrnd. eternally self-existent.

kayyım, kayyim قيّم var. of **kayyum** 1.

kayyum 1 قيّوم [kayyum 2] 1. caretaker of a mosque. 2. law person appointed by court to administer an estate.

kayyum 2 (.—) قيّوم A lrnd. ever self-existent; eternal God. —**iyet** phil. aseity, self-existence of God.

kayz قيظ A lrnd. hottest part of the summer.

kaz 1 قاز 1. goose, zool., Anser. 2. silly, simpleton. — **adımı** mil. goosestep. — **ayağı***. —**ın ayağı öyle değil** (lit. The goose's foot is not like that.) The fact of the matter is really quite otherwise; the thing is altogether different. — **beyinli** colloq. simple, gullible. — **boku** ugly pale green color. — **boynu** gooseneck, curved tube or pipe resembling the neck of a goose. — **ciğeri** pâte de foie gras, goose-liver sausage. — **gibi** stupidly. — **göğsü** chamfer, chamfered edge, bevelled edge. — **göğsü başlık** Turk. arch. chamfered capital. — **göğsü yap**= /ı/ to chamfer, to bevel. — **kafalı** same as **kaz beyinli**. — **kanadı**

1. Turk. wrestling joining of hands at the back of the opponent. 2. a goose-wing used as a duster. — **kanadına al**= /ı/ Turk. wrestling to join hands at the back of the opponent. — **karabatağı** snakebird, darter, zool., Anhinga rufa. —**ı koz anla**= to misunderstand out of ignorance. — **palazı** gosling, young goose. — **tüyü** quill (for writing).

kaz=ᵃʳ 2 نازمه /ı/ 1. to dig, to excavate, to trench. 2. same as **kazı**= 1. —**ma kuyuyu kazarlar kuyunu** (lit. Don't dig the trap; others will dig a trap for you.) A wicked deed can lead to your own misfortune.

kazᶻᶻⁱ 3 قزّ A lrnd. raw silk.

kâz 4 (—) كاز P lrnd. pruning knife.

kaza 1 (.—) قضا A 1. accident, mishap; mischance, misfortune. 2. God's decree, chance, fate, hazard. 3. Isl. rel. late performance of an act of worship omitted at the proper time. 4. lrnd. performance of an act, payment of a debt. —**i hacet** lrnd. 1. performance of any necessary act. 2. a going to the toilet. —**i hacet et**= lrnd. to accomplish one's wish; to go to the toilet; to have sexual intercourse. — **ile** by chance, by accident. — **ve kader** destiny, fate, predestination. — **kurşunu** stray bullet. —**i mübrem** lrnd. inexorable decree of Providence. —**i nagehanî** lrnd. sudden accident. — **oku** a stroke of destiny that strikes one down. —**ya rıza** submission to one's fate. — **sigortası** accident insurance, casualty insurance. — **tazminatı** workmen's compensation insurance. —**ya uğra**= to meet with an accident, to suffer a mishap.

kaza 2 (.—) قضا A 1. district of a **vilâyet**, township governed by a **kaymakam**; Ott. hist. administrative and juridical district of a Cadi. 2. lrnd. office and functions of a Cadi; law jurisdiction. — **hakkı** law justice, jurisdiction. —**i kavlî** can. law a judge's oral decision. — **kuvveti** judicial power. — **merkezi** administrative center of a district.

kazaen (.—'.) قضاءً A by accident, by chance. — **takdir** a fixing by judicial or legal decision.

kazaî (.——) قضائى A 1. law juridical. 2. lrnd. accidental. — **içtihad** juridical opinion. — **muamele** judicial proceeding, legal procedure. — **rüşd** declaration of majority. — **salâhiyet** judicial competence. — **temlik** transfer by judgment.

Kazakᵍⁱ 1 قازاق 1. Cossack, the Cossacks. 2. despotic husband. — **köle** obs. aged male slave. — **mersini** smoked sturgeon.

kazakᵍⁱ 2 قازاق F jersey; pullover.

kazakᵍⁱ 3 قازاق prov. 1. scraper, knife for scraping. 2. thresher's shovel.

kazalı (.—.) قضالو dangerous, unsafe,

causing accidents. — **işler** risky adventures, ventures.

kazamat قاناماتF *var. of* **kazemat**.

kazan 1 قزغان تاناتی قزان cauldron, large kettle, boiler. — **astarı** boiler covering. — **ayağı** boiler emplacement. — **basıncı** boiler pressure. — **borusu** boiler tube, boiler pipe. — **cidarı** boiler wall, boiler shell. — **dairesi** boiler room, boiler house; *naut.* stokehold. — **deposu** boiler drum. — **desteği** boiler stays. — **devir=** *same as* **kazan kaldır=**. — **dibi** 1. slightly burned milk pudding. 2. boiler bottom. — **kaldır=** to overturn the kettle *a sign of mutiny among the Janissaries*, to mutiny. —**ı kapalı kayna=** /ın/ not to allow others to know about his affairs. — **kaplaması** boiler covering. **bir —da kayna=** to be in complete agreement. — **kaynamıyan yerde maymun oynamaz** (*lit.* The monkey won't dance where there is no pot boiling.) People won't work without proper recompense. — **mahfazası** boiler casing. — **mevcudu** *mil.* all present. — **önü** *naut.* boiler room. — **sacı** boilerplate. — **tertibatı** boiler fittings. — **tuzu** boiler scale. — **yatağı** boiler emplacement, boiler stays. — **yeri** *same as* **kazan dairesi**. — **zarfı** boiler wall.

kazan=[r] **2** تانانم قزانم /ı/ to win, to gain, to acquire, to earn, to make a profit, to make money. —**an numara** winning number (in a lottery).

kazancı تانا نجی 1. cauldron maker, boiler or kettle maker; cauldron or kettle seller. 2. stoker, fireman. —**lık** 1. cauldron making. 2. coppersmith's or brazier's work.

kazanç[cı] قزانج تانانج 1. gain, profit, earnings, winnings. 2. advantage, benefit. — **et=** *archaic* to make a profit. — **vergisi** profits tax. — **yolu yap=** /ı/ to make a trade (of).

kazandır=[r] تانانديرمه قزانديرمه /ı, a/ *caus. of* **kazan= 2**. —**ıl=** *pass.*

kazanıl=[r] تانانلی قزانلمی *pass. of* **kazan= 2**. —**mış** earned; acquired.

kazârâ (.——) قضايا P by chance, by accident.

kazasker تاضيعسكر [**kadilasker**] *Ott. hist.* 1. chief military judge. 2. high official in the hierarchy of the Muslim Judiciary. — **divanı** the Divan held on Fridays to discuss legal matters. — **payesi** titular rank of a **kazasker**. —**lik** rank and functions of a **kazasker**.

kazatüvan (.—.—) تضانوان P *lrnd.* powerful as the divine decree, irresistible.

kazaya (.——) قضايا A *lrnd., pl. of* **kaziye**. —**yi mütedahile** *log.* subaltern propositions.

kazayağı[nı] تاناآغی 1. pigweed, goosefoot, *bot.*, *Chenopodium*. 2. hook with several prongs. 3. *naut.* branching lanyard, three-ended rope, crowfoot. 4. crossroads. 5. shear-legs (crane). 6. *anat.* goosefoot, *pes anserinus*.

kazaz قزاز [**kazzaz**] silk manufacturer.

kazazede (.—..) قضازده P who has had an accident; wrecked; shipwrecked.

kazdır=[r] تانادرمه قزاندرمه /a, ı/ *caus. of* **kaz= 2**.

kazel قزل *var. of* **gazel 2**.

kazemat قزامات F casemate.

kazevi تاذوی قزوی [**gazevi**] a reed or palm-leaf basket.

kazf قذف A *lrnd.* 1. a throwing (a missile, etc.). 2. an accusing of incontinence (a virtuous woman). 3. a vomiting. — **bilgayb** an accusing one on a mere surmise.

kazgan قزغان *archaic, same as* **kazan 1**.

kazı=[r] **1** تانایحمی /ı/ 1. to erase by scraping, to scratch. 2. to extirpate, to eradicate, to destroy. 3. to shave off (a beard, hair).

kazı 2 *neol.* 1. excavation (of ruins). 2. an engraving. — **kalemi** graver, graving tool, etcher's needle, burin. — **makinesi** engraving machine. — **resim** *neol.* engraving (picture). —**lar yap=** *archeol.* to make excavations. —**cı** engraver.

kazık[ğı] تانایه 1. pale, stake, pile. 2. *slang* deceit, trick, swindle; very expensive. 3. *Turk. wrestling* a putting one hand deep into the opponent's shorts. 4. *hist.* impalement. — **at=** /a/ *slang* to cheat, to play a trick (on). — **ayaklı köprü** pile bridge. — **bağı** *naut.* clove hitch. —**a bağla=** /ı/ to impale. — **çak=** /a/ 1. to drive in piles. 2. to remain permanently, *e. g.*, **dünyaya kazık çakacak değiliz ya** (*lit.* We won't drive a stake into the world.) We won't stay on the earth forever. —**larla çevir=** /ı/ to fence with stakes. — **çit** palisade, paling. — **gibi** straight as a mast. — **hattı** *mil.* pile line, palisade. — **humması** tetanus. — **kadar** *colloq.* big (boy or girl). — **kak=** /a/ *same as* **kazık çak=**[1]. — **kesil=** to be as if petrified. —**ını kopar=** to make one's escape; to get loose (animal). — **kök** *bot.* taproot. — **köprü** pile bridge. — **kuyruk balığı** butterfly ray (fish), *zool., Pteroplatea altavela*. — **kuyruk balıkları** *zool., Pteroplateas*. — **mania** pile barricade. — **marka** *colloq.* very expensive. —**a oturt=** /ı/ to impale. — **resmi** *Ott. hist.* tax imposed per dönüm on newly planted vineyards. — **sırası** *same as* **kazık hattı**. — **sok=** /a/ *same as* **kazık at=**. — **tokmağı** pile driver. —**a vur=** /ı/ *same as* **kazığa oturt=**. — **ye=** to be duped, cheated. — **yutmuş gibi** very stiff (person).

kazıkçı تانایقجی trickster, swindler.

kazıkla=[r] تانایقلامی /ı/ *same as* **kazık at=**. —**n=** *same as* **kazık ye=**.

kazıklı تانایقلی furnished with, or supported by

stakes, pales or piles. **— humma** tetanus. **— tahkimat** *mil.* stockade, palisade.
kazıl=ᵣ 1 قازيلو *pass. of* **kaz= 2.**
kazıl 2 قزل [*Arabic* **gazl**] *prov.* thread of goat hair.
kazılı 1 قازيلو dug, dug up, excavated.
kazılı 2 قازيلو engraved; scratched, scraped.
kâzım (—.) كاظم A 1. *lrnd.* who suppresses or controls anger. 2. *w. cap.*, *man's name*.
kazıma قازيمه 1. *verbal n. of* **kazı= 1.** 2. *neol.*, *surg.* curetting, curettage. **— yap=** *surg.* to perform an abortion.
kazımıkᵏⁱ قازيموق *prov.* scrapings, scraped off matter.
kazın=ʳ قازينمق 1. to scratch oneself. 2. to be scraped out. **—dır=** /ı, a/ *caus.*
kazıntı قازينتى قازينده 1. scrapings, scraped off matter. 2. erasure. **—lı** with an erasure; erased.
kazıt=ᵗʳ قازيتمق /ı, a/ *caus. of* **kazı= 1.**
kazıyacakᵏⁱ قازياجق scraper (instrument).
kazıyıcı قازيجى 1. scraper (instrument). 2. one who scrapes, scraper.
kazi (——) قاضى A *lrnd.*, *same as* **kadı 1.**
kâzib 1 (—.) كاذب A *lrnd.* 1. false; liar. 2. pseudo-. **— asabiyülcenah** *zool.*, *Pseudoneuroptera.* **— hâfıza** pseudomnesia.
kazib 2 (.—) قضيب A *lrnd.*, *var. of* **kadib.**
kazif (—.) قاذف A *lrnd.* one who accuses another of adultery.
kazil قزيل *prov., var. of* **kazıl 3.**
Kazilkuzat (—..—) قاضى القضاة A *Isl. hist.* the Chief Judge.
kaziye قضيه A *lrnd.* 1. question, affair, matter. 2. *law* sentence, decision. 3. *log.* premise; *log., math.* proposition, thesis; *math.* theorem; assertion, statement requiring proof. 4. *gram.* clause. **—i asliye** *gram.* principal clause. **—i beyaniye** *log.* assertory proposition. **—i cüz'iye** *log.* particular proposition. **—i hükmiye** judicial matter. **—i külliye** *log.* universal proposition. **—i mucibe-i cüz'iye** *log.* particular affirmative proposition. **—i mucibe-i külliye** *log.* universal affirmative proposition. **—i muhkeme** *law* decided matter, *res judicata*. **—i münfasıla** *log.* disjunctive proposition; *gram.* disjunctive clause. **—i mütemmime** *gram.* subordinate clause. **—i sâlibe-i cüz'iye** *log.* particular negative proposition. **—i sâlibe-i külliye** *log.* universal negative proposition. **—i şartiye** *log.* conditional proposition; *gram.* conditional clause. **—i zaruriye** *log.* necessary proposition. **—i zihniye** *log.* mental proposition.
kaziyülhacat (—..——) قاضى الحاجات A *lrnd.* who satisfies the wants of all (God).
kazma قازمه 1. *verbal n. of* **kaz= 2.** 2. pickaxe, mattock. 3. dug, trenched, excavated. **— ame-liyatı** *mil.* a sapping. **— kürek** digging implements, pickaxe and shovel. **— resim** engraving (picture). **— yazı** incised script.
kazmacı قازمجى *mil.* sapper, pioneer.
kazmir قازمير F cassimere. **—ci** cassimere merchant.
kazulet قازولت [**kazurat**] *colloq.* ugly and coarse fellow.
kazurat (.——) قازورات A feces.
kazzaz (.—) قزّاز A *lrnd.*, *same as* **kazaz.**
ke 1 كه *name of the letter* **k.**
ke- 2 كه A *lrnd.*, *as, like, as in* **kel'evvel.**
kebab (.—) كباب A *lrnd.*, *same as* **kebap.**
kebabe (.—.) كبابه A *lrnd.* cubeb, *bot.*, *Piper cubeba.*
kebabiye (.—..) كبابيه [*based on* **kebab**] *slang* cigarette stub; pipe residue, dottle.
kebade (.—.) كباده P *lrnd.* junior-sized bow for archery beginners.
kebair (.—.) كبائر A *lrnd., pl. of* **kebire.**
kebapᵇⁱ كباب [**kebab**] A 1. roast, broiled flesh or meat. 2. roasted (chestnuts, corn). **— et=** /ı/ *same as* **kebap yap=.** **— fındık** roasted hazelnuts. **— kestane** roast chestnuts. **— ol=** 1. to be roasted, broiled. 2. to suffer from intense heat. **— yap=** /ı/ to roast, to broil. **—ını yap=** /ın/ to make roast meat (of).
kebapçı كبابجى cook and seller of roast meat. **— kedisi gibi yutkun=** (*lit.*, to swallow one's saliva like a cookshop cat) to desire in vain. **—lık** profession of a roast meat cook.
kebbastı كبّاصدى Gk large net (used at fishing stations).
kebd كبد A *lrnd.*, *same as* **kebed.**
kebe كبه a very thick kind of felt; short felt jacket; blanket made of such felt.
kebebe كببه *var. of* **kebabe.**
kebed كبد [**kebd**] *lrnd.* liver. **—î** (..—) A hepatic. **—iye** (..—.) A liverwort, *bot.*, *Hepatica hepatica.*
keber كبر A *lrnd., pl. of* **kebere.** **— fidanı** caper bush.
kebere كبره A caper, *bot.*, *Capparis spinosa*. **—ler** capers, *bot.*, *Capparidaceae*.
kebikeç (.—.) كبيكج *lrnd., myth.* king of the moths (in the form of **ya kebikeç** frequently inscribed on the pages of a manuscript, under the belief that, out of respect for the name of their king, the moths will spare it).
kebin كبين [**kâbin**] *prov.* bride-money.
kebir (.—) كبير A *lrnd.* 1. great, grand. 2. old (person).
kebire (.—.) كبيره A *rel.* heinous or deadly sin.
kebise (.—.) كبيسه A *lrnd.* leapyear.
kebk كبك P *lrnd.* partridge.
kebs كبس A *lrnd.* a filling and leveling a pit,

well, etc. with earth. — **et=** /ı/ to fill up and level with earth.

kebş کبش A *lrnd.* ram.

kebud (.—) کبود P *lrnd.* blue, azure. **— güvercin** Nicobar pigeon, *zool., Caloenas nicobarica.* **—fam** (.——) P blue.

kebudî (.——) کبودی P *lrnd.* blue. **— kebud** deep blue.

kebuter (.—.) کبوتر P *lrnd.* pigeon. **—i çarhî** tumbler pigeon. **—i dübame, —i dübürcî** inconstant, turncoat. **—i harem** 1. Mecca pigeon held secure from harm. 2. lady whose hand it is difficult to obtain. **—i nâmeber** carrier pigeon. **—i şalvarî** pigeon with plumage to its toes. **—i terazu** pivot on which the beam of a balance swings. **—i tizper** racing pigeon. **—i yahu** loudly cooing pigeon.

kebuterban (.—.—) کبوتربان P *lrnd.* breeder or trainer of pigeons, pigeon fancier.

kebuterbaz (.—.—) کبوترباز P *lrnd.* gambler on the flight of pigeons.

kebuterhane (.—.—.) کبوترخانه P *lrnd.* pigeon cote.

kebze کبزه 1. shoulder blade, omoplate, scapula. 2. soothsaying by inspection of shoulder blades, omoplastoscopy, scapulimancy.

kebzeci کبزه‌جی soothsayer, foreteller of events by inspecting the shoulder blades of sheep.

kec کج P *lrnd.* crooked, bent, distorted; slanting, oblique; treacherous. **— bak=** to look askance. **— mec, — ü mec** crooked, perverse, queer. **— otur=** to sit with body bent.

kecabe (.—.) کجابه P *lrnd.* camel litter for women. **—nişin** (.—..—) P seated in a camel litter.

kecagend (.—.) کج آغند P *lrnd.*, *var. of* **kejagend.**

kecave (.—.) کجاوه P *var. of* **kecabe.**

kecbahs کج‌بحث P *lrnd.* who reasons perversely, absurd reasoner.

kecbaz (.—) کج‌باز P *lrnd.* unfair player; fraudulent.

kecbeyʸ¹ کج‌بیع P *lrnd.* who cheats, defrauds in selling.

kecbekec کج‌بکج P *lrnd.* very crooked.

kecbin (.—) کج‌بین P *lrnd.* 1. squint-eyed; looking askance, crosseyed. 2. who sees matters in a wrong light.

kecdüm کج‌دم P *lrnd., var. of* **kejdüm.**

kece کجه P *lrnd.* crook; hook.

kecefe, kecele, kecere کفه کله کره *prov.* reel, winding apparatus (for making yarn into skeins).

kecefehm کج‌فهم P *lrnd.* misunderstanding; perverting a meaning.

kechah (.—) کجاه P *lrnd.* ill-wishing, deceitful. **—î** (.——) P deceitfulness.

kechulkᵏᵘ کج‌خلق P *lrnd.* ill-tempered, crossgrained.

keci 1 کجی [*Persian* .—] *prov.* silk: silkworm; silk cocoon.

kecî 2 (.—) کجی P *lrnd.* crookedness; wryness, distortion; treachery.

kecim کجیم *prov.* coarse flax fiber.

keckülâh (..—) کج‌کلاه P *lrnd.* 1. who wears his hat on one side of the head. 2. affected dandy.

kecle کجله P *lrnd.* magpie.

keclikᵍⁱ کجلک *archaic* crookedness; obliquity.

kecmizac (..—) کج‌مزاج P *lrnd.* peevish, ill humored, ill tempered.

kecnazar کج‌نظر P *lrnd.* envious, malignant.

kecnigâh (..—) کج‌نگاه P *lrnd.* squinteyed; malignant.

kecnihad (..—) کج‌نهاد P *lrnd.* crooked-minded; ill natured.

kecreftar (..—) کج‌رفتار P *lrnd.* going awry, crooked; wavering.

kecrev کج‌رو P *lrnd.* ill-conducted; sidling, shying (beast).

kecrey کج‌رای P *lrnd.* wrongheaded; of crooked policy.

kectabᵇ¹ کج‌طبع P *lrnd.* crossgrained, cross tempered.

keçe 1 کچه felt; carpet, mat; made of felt. **— baş** *prov.* goat or sheep tuberculosis. **— çizme** felt boots. **— delen, — geçiren** *prov.* light rain. **— gibi** matted. **— külâh** felt cap. **—den minare** *joc.* false, unreal, sham. **— rondela** *tech.* felt washer. **—sini sudan çıkar=** to back out cleverly, to retreat cleverly from a difficulty; to manage dexterously. **— şapka** felt hat. **— terlik** felt slippers.

keçe 2 کچه *prov.* sides.

keçeci کچه‌جی felt maker; felt seller.

keçel کچل *prov.* bald.

keçelen=ⁱʳ کچه‌لنمك 1. to become numb, to be benumbed. 2. to become felt. **—dir=** /ı/ *caus.*

keçeleş=ⁱʳ کچه‌لشمك to become numb; to become gradually felted or matted. **—tir=** /ı/ *caus.*

keçeli 1 کچه‌لی felted over; made of felt.

keçeli 2 کچه‌لی having sides, sided, e. g., **iki keçeli** on both sides.

keçi کچی 1. she-goat, goat, *zool., Capra hircus.* 2. obstinate, stubborn. 3. *slang* passive pederast. **— ağızlı** *colloq.* glutton, gluttonous; gourmand. **— boynuzu** carob (bean), St. John's bread, carob fruit. **— boynuzu ağacı** carob tree, *bot., Ceratonia Siliqua.* **— çobanı** goatherd. **— derisi** goatskin; kid leather. **— emciği** *prov.* a kind of black fig. **— kafalı** *colloq.* obstinate, stubborn. **— kılı** goat's hair. **— kulağı** wild rhubarb. **— mantarı** common mushroom, *bot., Agaricus campestris.* **— mayasıl otu** goat-scented Saint John's wort, *bot.*,

keçileş

Hypericum hircinum. — **memesi** *prov*. a kind of grape. — **peyniri** goat cheese. — **pöstekisi** goat's skin with the hair on it. — **sağan** goatsucker, nightjar, *zool*., *Caprimulgus europaeus*. — **sakal** French beard, goatee. — **sakalı** 1. goatsbeard, *bot*., *Aruncus sylvester*. 2. goatsbeard, steepleweed, *bot*., *Spiraea aruncus*. 3. rockrose, *bot*., *Cistus creticus*. 4. sea holly, sea eringo, *bot*., *Eryngium maritimum*. 5. *same as* **keçi sedefi**. — **sedefi** common goat's-rue, *bot*., *Galega officinalis*. — **söğüt ağacı** goat willow, sallow, *bot*., *Salix caprea*. — **sütü** goat's milk. — **yavrusu** kid. — **yemişi** whortleberry, *bot*., *Vaccinium myrtillus*. — **yolu** goat trail, footpath (on the hills, etc.), narrow path, byway.

keçileş=ⁱʳ *colloq*. to get headstrong, to become pigheaded.

keçili *slang* hundred-lira piece.

keçikᵍⁱ *prov*. kerchief, veil.

keçkül P *lrnd*., *var. of* **keşkül**.

kedᵈᵈⁱ A *lrnd*. an exerting oneself in manual labor; diligent labor. —**i yed**, —**i yemin** manual labor; fruit of labor.

kedaret (. — .) A *lrnd*. grief, annoyance; turbidity.

kedbanu (. — —) P *lrnd*. mistress of a household; housekeeper.

-kede P *lrnd*. house, temple, *as in* **ateşkede, bütkede, meykede**.

kedene A *prov*. horse collar.

keder A 1. care, grief, affliction. 2. *lrnd*. a being turbid; turbidity; murkiness. — **çek**= to suffer from grief. — **et**= /a/ 1. to deplore, to lament (for, over). 2. to be troubled or grieved (at). — **iras et**= /a/ *lrnd*. to cause sorrow (to). —**ine iştirak et**= /ın/ to share another person's sorrow; to express one's sympathy (with a person in a loss). — **ver**= /a/ 1. to give sorrow (to). 2. *lrnd*. to disturb, *e. g*., **sulha keder ver**= to disturb the peace.

kederlen=ⁱʳ /a/ to become sorrowful, to be grieved.

kederli sorrowful, grieved, grievous.

kedernâkᵏⁱ (. . —) P *lrnd*., *same as* **kederli**.

kedersiz 1. free from grief. 2. *lrnd*. free from injury or loss.

kedhüda (. . —) P *lrnd*., *var. of* **kethüda**.

kedi cat, *zool*., *Felis domesticus*. — **ayağı** cat's-foot, *bot*., *Antennaria diocia*. — **ayası** small or lesser celandine, *bot*., *Ficaria ficaria*. — **balı** gum of plum tree or apricot tree. — **balığı** spotted dogfish, *zool*., *Scyllium canicula*. — **balıkları** selachians, *zool*., *Selachii*. — **başı** hemp nettle, holy hemp, *bot*., *Galeopsis*. —**lerin bulunmadığı yerde fareler cirit oynar** Where there are no cats the mice play games. — **ciğere bakar gibi bak**= to stare covetously. —**ye ciğer emanet et**=, —**ye ciğer ısmarla**= to entrust something to an untrustworthy person. — **çınağı** everlasting pea, *bot*., *Lathyrus latifolius*. — **dutu** *prov*. blackberry. —**nin fare ile oynaması gibi** playing cat-and-mouse (with). — **gibi** catlike, like a cat. — **gibi dört ayak üstüne düş**= (*lit*., to fall on all four feet like a cat) to be always safe and sound. — **gözü** *auto*. rear light of a certain shape. — **gözlü** having eyes like a cat. — **ile köpek gibi ol**= to lead a cat-and-dog's life. — **köpek** cat-and-dog, always quarrelling. — **kürkü** cat fur. — **nanesi** catnip, *bot*., *Nepeta Cataria*. — **ne, budu ne?** What can you expect from such a poor creature? — **olalı bir fare tuttu** (*lit*. Since he became a cat he has caught one mouse.) At last he has done something worth-while. — **otu** valerian, *bot*., *Valeriana officinalis*. —**ye peynir emanet et**=, **kediye peynir tulumu emanet et**= *same as* **kediye ciğer emanet et**=. — **taşağı** *prov*. tumor in the armpit. — **uzanamadığı ciğere pis dermiş** The cat could not reach the liver so he said it was dirty. — **yaygarası** caterwauling, mewing of cats.

kedime Gk *prov*. lacework.

kedme A *lrnd*. mark, scar.

kedu (. —) P *lrnd*. pumpkin, gourd, vegetable marrow. —**i haccam** cupper's gourd or glass. —**i nergis** gourd containing water, and used to grow bulbs in. —**i telh** colocynth.

kedudane (. — —.) P 1. gourd or pumpkin seed. 2. intestinal worm.

keduret (. — .) A *lrnd*., *var. of* **küduret**.

keenlemyekün A *lrnd*. as though it had never existed. — **hükmüne konul**= to be considered as nonexistent, to be ignored.

keenne (. ′ .) A *lrnd*. as if, as though, quasi.

kef 1 [kâf 3] Arabic script, name of the letter ك (This is the twenty-second letter of the Arabic, the twenty-fifth letter of the Ottoman alphabet, in Turkish pronounced as **k**, in the older language also as **ng**, in the latter case mostly written ڭ. In chronograms, it has the numerical value of 20). [*cf*. **gef**] —**in kolu** dash of the letter ك in its initial and medial forms.

kefᶠᶠⁱ **2** A *lrnd*. palm of the hand; sole of the foot. —**i ayşe** root of *Digitus citrinus*. —**i beyza** 1. white (*i. e*., miracle-working) hand of Moses. 2. masterhand in any art. —**i cezma** Star α Ceti; the five stars α, δ, λ μ, ζ Ceti. —**i dest** palm of the hand. —**i esed** sowbread, cyclamen. —**i hazib** star β Cassiopeae. —**i kifâyet** able hand, *i. e*., ability (of a talented person). —i **mercan** coral branch. —i **Meryem** St. Mary's flower; rose of Jericho, *bot.*, *Anastatica hierochuntica;* throatwort, blue foxglove, *bot.*, *Campanula trachelium.* —i **müselsele** star *k* Andromedae. —i **Musa** the wonderworking hand of Moses. —i **pa** sole of the foot. —i **sefid** *same as* **keff-i beyza.**

kef[ffi] **3** كفّ A 1. *lrnd.* a withdrawing, a drawing back one's hand. 2. *pros.* a dropping the last consonant of the feet **fâilâtün** (—.——) and **mefâ'îlün** (.———), which become **fâ'ilâtü** (—.—.) and **mefâ'ilü** (.——.). —i **nefs et**= to suppress one's passions. —i **yed** withdrawal, renunciation. —i **yed et**= /dan/ to withdraw (from), to renounce.

kef 4 كف P 1. *lrnd.* froth, foam, scum. 2. *prov.* sediment, foam. —i **derya** *lrnd.* 1. froth of the sea. 2. pumice stone; madrepore coral.

kef 5 كف [**kef 2**] *prov.* harvester's leather glove.

kefa (.—) كفا A *lrnd.* equality of man with man.

kefaet (.—.) كفاءت A *lrnd.* equality in social or legal estimation.

kefaf (.—) كفاف A *lrnd.* sufficiency of the means of subsistence. —i **nefs** enough to supply the wants of life. —i **nefs et**= /la/ to be contented (with frugal nourishment).

kefal كفال Gk 1. gray mullet, *zool.*, *Mugil cephalus.* 2. *slang* a grade of five (in Turkish schools, just enough to pass the class). — **azmanı** overgrown gray mullet; monster fish. — **balığı** *same as* **kefal**[1]. — **tut**= *slang* to obtain the grade of five.

kefalet كفالت A 1. *civil law*, *com.* guarantee, guaranty, security. 2. *penal law* bail, surety. — **akçesi** *com.* caution money. — **akdi** contract of guarantee, contract of surety. —**e bağla**= /ı/ to take bail or security (for). — **et**= /a/ to go bail (for), to stand surety (for). —**e mukabil avans** *com.* advance on a guarantee. —i **müştereke** *lrnd.* joint guarantee. —i **nakdiye** *lrnd.* money bail. —i **nefs**, —i **nefsiye** *lrnd.* a being bail or security for the person of another. —**e raptet**= /ı/ *same as* **kefalete bağla**=.

kefaleten (.—'..) كفالةً A as bail, as security.

kefaletle كفالتله on bail.

kefaletname (.—.—.) كفالتنامه P bail bond, letter of guarantee.

kefalik[g1] كفاليك L *anat.* cephalic. — **endeks** cephalic index.

kefaret (.—.) كفارت [**keffaret**] atonement (for a sin), expiation. —**ini öde**= /ın/ to expiate, to atone (for). —i **yemin** *lrnd.* expiation for a broken oath. —i **zünub** *lrnd.* expiation of sins.

kefçe كفچه P *lrnd.*, *same as* **kepçe.**

kefçegir (..—) كفچه گير P *lrnd.*, *Ott. hist.* worker whose job was to stir the melted iron for making guns in the state foundry.

kefe 1 كفه [**keffe**] scale of a balance.

kefe 2 كفه hair-cloth bag used for grooming horses.

kefeki كفكى tartar (on teeth). —**ye dön**= to be all in holes. — **taşı** coarse sandstone; softish sandstone grit that withstands fire well.

kefele=[r] كفه لك 1. /ı/ to rub (a horse) down with a hair-cloth bag. 2. *prov.* to wrestle.

kefeli كفه لو rubbed down (horse).

kefen كفن A 1. shroud, winding sheet. 2. *obs.* paper for cooking things in. —**e sar**= /ı/ 1. to wind in a shroud (corpse). 2. *obs.* to wrap in cooking paper (a roast). —i **yırt**= to recover from a serious illness, to cheat death.

kefenci كفنجى 1. shroud maker; shroud seller. 2. thief of grave clothes. 3. *slang* extortioner.

kefendüzd كفن دزد P *lrnd.* thief of grave clothes.

kefenle=[r] كفنله مك /ı/ 1. to shroud (a corpse). 2. to cover in batter before roasting (a fowl, etc.).

kefenli كفنلى 1. wrapped in a shroud. 2. covered with batter. — **kebap** roast cooked in a wrapping of bread, etc.

kefere كفره A unbelievers.

keffaret, (.—.) كفّارت A *lrnd.*, *same as* **kefaret.**

keffe كفّه A *lrnd.*, *same as* **kefe 1.**

keffüleczem كفّ الجذم A *lrnd.* 1. hyacinth root. 2. salep root.

keffülesed كفّ الأسد A *lrnd.* sowbread, cyclamen.

keffülkelb كفّ الكلب A *lrnd.* horehound, *bot.*, *Marrubium vulgare.*

kefgir (.—) كفگير P *lrnd.*, *same as* **kevgir.**

kefil (.—) كفيل A guarantor, sponsor; bail, security, surety. —i **bilmal** *lrnd.* guarantor for the value of a thing. —i **binnefs** *lrnd.* bail, security for the person of another. —i **bittesliğm** *lrnd.* guarantor, bail, security for the delivery of a thing. — **göster**= /ı/ to appoint a guarantor. —**e kefalet** secondary guarantee. —**e kefil**, —**in kefili** secondary guarantor, after-bail. —i **muteber** *lrnd.* good and sufficient surety. — **ol**= /a/ to go bail, to stand surety (for); to be the guarantor (of).

kefillik[g1] كفيلّيك guarantee, security.

kefin كفن *var. of* **kefen.**

kefiye كفيه A light shawl (worn as headdress by Arabs).

kefle=[r] كفله مك *prov.* to put powder, etc. from the hollow of the hand into the mouth.

kefne کفنه sailmaker's gauntlet.
kefş کفش P lrnd. shoe, slipper.
kefşe کفشه obs. money changer's balance for weighing single coins.
kefşger کفشگر P lrnd. shoemaker.
kefte کفته P lrnd. 1. split, cleft, fissured. 2. fissure. **—ser** 1. broken headed. 2. forked or split at the end. **—süm** cloven hoofed.
kefur (.—) کفور A lrnd. exceedingly ungrateful or misbelieving.
kefyar (.—) کفیار P lrnd. diligent, industrious, painstaking.
keh 1 که prov. 1. edge, border, corner. 2. hill, mound. 3. slope; precipice.
keh 2 که P lrnd., var of **kâh 1**.
keh 3 که P lrnd., var. of **kâh 2**.
kehanet (.—.) کهانت A a soothsaying, augury, presage; oracle. **—te bulun=**, **—et=** to foretell, to predict the future.
kehel کهل [kâhil] prov. 1. lazy, indolent. 2. light; slow, sluggish.
kehene کهنه A lrnd., pl. of **kâhin**.
keher کهر P 1. lrnd. dark bay (horse). 2. prov. bay horse.
kehf کهف A lrnd. cave, cavern; anat. cavern. **K— Suresi** name of the eighteenth sura of the Quran. **—î** (.—) A cavernous.
kehhal[li] (.—) کحال A lrnd. 1. maker or dealer in antimony for the eyes. 2. eye-doctor; oculist. **K—i Şeri'at** the Prophet Muhammad. **—başı** Ott. hist. chief oculist in the Palace. **—lik** abstr. n.
kehif[hfi] کهیف var. of. **kehf**.
kehil 1 کهل [kâhil] prov., same as **kehel**.
kehîl 2 (.—) کهیل A lrnd. tinged with antimony (eye).
kehilde=[r] کهلده ماک to pant heavily, violently.
kehil kehil کهل کهل prov. with the sound of violent panting. **— et=**, **— solu=** to pant hoarsely.
kehillen=[ir] کهللنک prov. to become lazy, indolent.
kehkeşan (..—) کهکشان P lrnd. Milky Way.
kehl کهل A lrnd. of full age (from thirty to fifty).
kehle=[r] کهله ماک prov. to pant.
kehle 2 کهله louse. **—len=** 1. to become infested with lice. 2. to delouse oneself. **—li** lousy.
kehlibar, kehribar کهلیبار-کهریبا [kehrüba] amber, yellow amber. **— balı** clear yellow honey. **— sarısı** amber yellow. **— yağı** copal varnish
kehriz کهریز var. of **keriz 1**.
kehrüba (..—) کهربا P lrnd., same as **kehlibar**. **—î** (..—.—) P electricity.
kehvar (.—.) کهوار P lrnd. cradle. **—i fena** (lit. cradle of corruption) the world. **—gî** (.—.—) P infant in the cradle.
kehya کهیا var. of **kâhya**.
keis[ke'si] کأس A lrnd. 1. bot. calyx. 2. cup, goblet; glass of wine.
kej کژ P lrnd., var. of **kec**.
kejabe (.—.) کژابه P lrnd., var. of **kecabe**.
kejagend (.—.) کژاگند P lrnd. thickly padded battle coat.
kejave (.—.) کژاوه P lrnd., var. of **kecave**.
kejdüm کژدم P lrnd. scorpion. **—i bahri** sea-scorpion. **—i felek** the constellation Scorpio, the sign Scorpio.
keje کژه P lrnd., var. of **kece**.
kejî (.—) کژی P lrnd., var. of **kecî 2**.
kek 1 کک E cake, tea cake.
kek=[er] **2** ککمک prov. to peck with the beak.
kek=[er] **3** ککمک prov. to miss the mark or goal.
kekâ, kekâh (.—') ککا colloq. expression of a feeling of comfort, e. g., **orada müdürlük kekâ** A director there? How fine!
keke 1 ککه stammering; stutterer.
keke=[r] **2** ککه ماک prov., same as **kekele=**.
kekeç[ci] ککج prov. stuttering, stammering; stutterer.
kekele=[r] ککله ماک to stutter, to stammer; to falter.
kekeme ککمه having a stammer; stammerer. **—lik** a stuttering; stammer.
kekeyi ککیی archaic stutterer.
kekez ککز prov. passive pederast.
kekik[gi] ککیک garden thyme, bot., Thymus vulgaris. **— az=** archaic to suffer from indigestion. **— otu** same as **kekik**. **— yağı** oil of thyme. **—li** seasoned with thyme.
keklik[gi] ککلیک partridge, zool., Perdix perdix. **— çiğdemi** gladiolus, bot., Gladiolus byzantinus. **— otu** 1. wild marjoram, origan, bot., Origanum vulgare. 2. same as **kekik**, **kekik otu**. **— palazı** young partridge.
kekme, kekmek[gi], **kekmik**[gi], **kekmük**[gü] ککمه ککمک ککمیک ککموک prov. bill, beak.
kekre 1 ککره acrid, harsh, sharp (in taste). **— şarap** rough wine.
kekre=[r] **2** ککره ماک to become acrid (milk, wine, etc.).
kekre 3 ککره prov. garden thyme.
kekremsi ککرمسی somewhat acrid.
kekremti ککرمتی archaic, same as **kekremsi**.
kel کل 1. ringwormy; scabby; scabby-headed; bald; ringworm, baldness. 2. bare of vegetation. 3. prov. parasitic plant fungus. **— açıl=** same as **keli görün=**. **— başa şimşir tarak** out of place luxury. **—i görün=** /ın/ to become evident (defect). **— hastalığı** ringworm disease, fovus. **— kâhya** busybody. **—i kız=** /ın/ to lose one's temper (of one not easily angered). **—i körü topla=** to fill with incompetent people (an office, etc.). **—den köşeye**

yardım The blind leading the blind. **—in merhemi olsa kendi başına sürer** Do not expect help from a weak or poor person. **— oğlan*. — ol=** to be or to become baldheaded. **— tavuk kel horozla** The bald hen prefers a bald rooster. **—in tırnağı olsa kendi başını kaşır** If it were possible, I would have done it for myself.

kelâ (. —) کلا A lrnd. green vegetation.

kelâb (. —) کلب A lrnd. rabies, hydrophobia.

kelâğ (. —) کلاغ P lrnd. raven. **—i eblak** magpie.

kelâl[li] (. —) کلال A lrnd. lassitude, weariness, exhaustion. **— gel=** /a/ to become weary. **— ver=** /a/ to tire.

kelalâver (. — —.) کلالآور P lrnd. fatiguing, tiring, dragging.

kelâlet (. —.) کلالت A lrnd., same as **kelâl**.

kelâm (. —) کلام A lrnd. word, a saying, speech; the words of the Scriptures; conversation, talk; sentence; language. **—ı Arab** the Arabic language. **—ı derunî** psych. interior word. **— ilmi** study of the Quran, theology. **K—ı kadîm** eternally preexistent word of God, the Quran. **—ı kibar** a saying of the sages, apothegm. **—ı makûs** inverted sentence. **—ı manzûm** verse. **—ı mensûr** prose. **—ı nefsî** endophasy. **—ı Resûl** a saying spoken by the Prophet Muhammad.

kelâmcı کلامجی versed in the knowledge of the Quran.

kelâmî (. — —) کلامی A lrnd. 1. pertaining to a word, speech, or to the Quran; verbal. 2. scholastic theologian, Scholastic. 3. member of the Kelâmiye sect. **K—ye** (. — — .) Isl. rel. sect of the Kelamians. **—yun** (. — — —) scholastic theologians.

Kelâmullâh (. —. —) کلام الله A word of God, the Quran.

kelân (. —) کلان P lrnd. large, great; important; chief. **K—ı ravza** the Prophet Muhammad. **—sal** (. — —) P great in years, old. **—ter** (. —.) P larger, greater, more important; chief man, mayor.

kelb کلب A lrnd. dog. **—i muallem** trained dog. **—i mütekaddem** the constellation Canis minor.

kelbetan (.. —), **kelbeteyn** کلبتین A lrnd., same as **kerpeten**.

kelbeyn کلبین A lrnd. the two constellations Canis Major and Canis Minor.

kelbî (. —) کلبی A 1. lrnd. canine. 2. phil. Cynic, cynical. **—ye** (. —.) 1. zool., Canidae. 2. phil. cynicism. **—yun** (. — —) the Cynics.

kelbülasgar کلب الاصغر A astr. Canis Minor.

kelbülcebbar (... —) کلب الجبار A astr. the star ∝ Canis Majoris.

kelbülekber کلب الاکبر A astr. Canis Major.

kelbürraî (.. — —) کلب الراعی A astr. 1. the star ρ Cephei. 2. the star β Ophiuchi.

kele 1 کله prov. O you; hey.

kele 2 کله prov. bull, young bull.

kelebe کلبه [Persian **kelâbe**] prov., var. of **kelefe**.

kelebek[gi] کلبک 1. butterfly; moth. 2. liver disease of sheep, staggers of sheep. 3. tech. throttle, throttle valve; auto. disc throttle. 4. window catch. **— gözlük** pince-nez. **— hastalığı** same as **kelebek**[2]. **— kravat** bow tie. **— kurbağalama** swimming butterfly stroke. **— mili** auto. throttle spindle. **— otu** black medic, bot., Medicago lupulina. **— somun** mech. butterfly nut, wing nut. **— vida** thumb-screw. **—li somun** same as **kelebek somun**.

keleci کله جی archaic talk, speech. **— et=, — eyle=, — kıl=** to talk, to chat.

kelef کلف P freckle.

kelefe کلفه P prov. 1. spindle; bobbin. 2. skein (of spun cotton or silk).

kelek[gi] کلک [**kalek**] 1. unripe melon. 2. raft or float constructed of inflated skins. 3. partly bald, little ringworm, tetter (patch).

kelem کلم P prov. cabbage.

keleme کلمه prov. fallow field, fallow.

kelemen کلمن A lrnd. the fourth mnemonic formula of Arabic letters according to their numerical value (ك = 20, ل = 30, م = 40, ن = 50).

kelemle, kelemne کلمنه prov., var. of **keleme**.

kelengi, keleni کلنگی prov. field vole, harvest mouse.

kelep[bi] کلپ prov., var. of **kelebe, kelefe**.

kelepçe کلپچه P 1. manacle, handcuff. 2. tech. pipe clip. 3. prov., var. of **kelefe**. **— tak=, — vur=** /a/ to put handcuffs (on). **—le=** /ı/ to handcuff. **—li** handcuffed, with handcuffs.

kelepir 1 کلپیر Gk colloq. 1. chance bargain, golden opportunity; worth its price, very cheap. 2. stepchild. **—e kon=, — yakala=** to get a prize or bargain.

kelepir 2 کلپیر prov. stake or pole to support a vine, etc.

kelepirci کلپیرجی bargain hunter, habitual buyer of bargain goods.

keler 1 کلر 1. reptile of the lizard family. 2. sharkskin (used as sandpaper), shagreen. **—ler** neol., Sauria. **— balığı** angel shark, monkfish, squat, zool., Squatina squatina. **— derisi** same as **keler**[2].

keler 2 کلر Gk prov. rock cavern.

keler=[lr] 3 کلرمك prov. to put on airs.

keleş 1 کلش 1. ringwormy, bald. 2. idiot.

keleş 2 کلش [Arabic kelec] prov. handsome; generous, brave.

kelete کلته A prov. 1. small amount of ground cereals. 2. measure for cereals; sack, bag.

keleter, keletir کلتر Gk prov. tray, flat basket. — **kafalı** idiot, stupid.

keleve کلوه prov., var. of **kelefe**.

kelevvel کالاول A lrnd. as at the first, like the first, as before.

kelez کلز prov. lean, meager, emaciated; sickly. —**i=** to become lean, thin, to weaken.

keli کلی prov. ridge between two fields, balk.

kelif کلیف Gk prov. hut.

kelik^gi کلیك prov. 1. old shoe or slipper; child's shoe. 2. woman always walking the streets.

kelil (.—) کلیل A lrnd. 1. dull (organ or faculty); dim (sight); blunt (sword). 2. tired, fatigued.

Kelile (.—.) کلیله A name of a jackal in the book called **Kelile ve Dimne**, adapted from the Fables of Bidpay.

kelim (.—) کلیم A lrnd. interlocutor; a title of Moses.

kelimat (..—) کلمات A lrnd., pl. of **kelime**. **K—ı Aşere, K—ı Aşr** Bib. the Ten Commandments, Decalogue. —**ı ilâhiye** Isl. myst. divine words.

kelimdest (.—.) کلیمدست P lrnd. dexterous, successful (as though having the hand of Moses).

kelime کلمه A 1. word, vocable; a saying. 2. lrnd. precept, command. — **arası** print. spacing. **K—i Bakiye** lrnd., same as **Kelime-i Tevhid**. — **bekelime** word for word, literally. — **karışıklığı** path. paraphasy. — **kelime** word by word; word for word. —**i mukattaa** lrnd. written word in the Arabic alphabet, none of whose letters join. —**i müvellede** lrnd. newly constructed word. — **oyunu** pun, quibble. **K—i Şehadet** Isl. rel. the confession of faith (اشهد ان لا اله الا الله) (و اشهد ان محمداً رسول الله) **K—i Şehadet getir=** to confess one's faith by pronouncing the **Kelime-i Şehadet. K—i tayyibe** lrnd. the declaration that there is no god but God (لا اله الا الله). — **teşevvüşü** same as **kelime karışıklığı. K—i Tevhid** Isl. rel. the declaration of God's unity (لا اله الا الله).

kelimetan (...—), **kelimeteyn** (...—) کلمتان A lrnd. the two propositions of the Moslem confession of faith, i. e. There is no god but God and Muhammad is the apostle of God.

Kelimetullâh کلمة الله A lrnd. 1. same as **Kelime-i Tevhid**. 2. the Word of God, Jesus Christ.

kelimetülfasl^li کلمة الفصل A Isl. rel. the sentence to be passed by God at the Last Judgment on each man.

Kelimullah (.—.—) کلیم الله A lrnd. one who speaks to God; a title of Moses.

Kelkete (.'..) کلکته lrnd., geog. Calcutta.

kellâ (.—) کلا A lrnd. certainly not; by no means.

kelle کله P 1. head; sheep's head. 2. loaf (of sugar); cake (of cheese). 3. ear or head of grain. — **götürür gibi** with unnecessary haste and fuss. —**sini koltuğuna al=**, —**si koltuğunda ol=** to take a great risk. — **kulak yerinde** strongly built and big (man). — **peyniri** cheese in cakes. — **şekeri** loaf sugar. —**sini uçur=** /ın/ to behead; to execute. —**yi ver=** to be beheaded, to be executed.

kellehuşk کله خشك P lrnd. mad, crazy.

kellepuş (..—) کله پوش P lrnd. headdress, head covering.

kelli 1 کلی prov. /dan/ after, since, because, as.

kelli 2 کلی prov. affected with ringworm.

kelli felli کلی فلی colloq. 1. well dressed, showy. 2. serious, dignified.

kellik^gi کللك 1. ringworm; tetter; baldness. 2. bare waste land.

keloğlan کل اوغلان a popular hero of Turkish folk tales, who starts as an unknown and poor boy but thanks to his talents, eventually achieves success (used sometimes affectionately for a poor child adopted by a family or taken as an apprentice).

kelp^bi کلب A same as **kelb**.

kelpe کلپه vine prop.

kelpeten کلپتن [kelbetan] same as **kerpeten**.

Kelt کلت Celt, Kelt.

kelte کلته P prov. 1. helpless; awkward, clumsy. 2. stranger; who does not belong to an order.

keltekele, keltekeler, keltenkele کلته کله archaic, vars. of **kertenkele**.

kem 1 کم P 1. bad, evil, malicious; deficient. 2. lrnd. little, few. — **değil** Well said. Not bad. — **göz** evil eye; malicious regard. — **san=** archaic to wish one ill. — **söz** malicious remark, calumny.

kem 2 کم A lrnd. How much? How many?

kem^mmi **3** کم A lrnd. quantity.

kema (.—) کما A lrnd. as, like.

kemabiş (.—) کما بیش P lrnd. more or less.

kemafilevvel (.'—...) کما فی الاول A lrnd. as at the first, as formerly.

kemafissabık (.'—.—.) کما فی السابق A lrnd. as formerly, as in the past.

kemahiye (.'—..) کما هی A lrnd. as it is; true state.

kemahu (. — ·̇ —), **kemahüve** (.· — ..) كما هو A *lrnd.* as he is, as it is.
kemahüvelmu'tad (. — ... —) كما هو المعتاد A *lrnd.* as usual.
kemahüvelvaki كما هو الواقع A *lrnd.* as it actually is.
kemakân (.· — —) كما كان A *lrnd.* as he was, as it used to be.
kemâl (.ـَـ) كمال A 1. perfection, maturity; cultural attainment. 2. moral quality; the most that can be said of a person or thing. 3. value, price, e. g., **—i beş lira** Its value is only five liras after all. **—ini bul=** to attain to its perfection or maturity. **—i bülûğ** *lrnd.* prime of manhood. **—i ciddiyetle** in good earnest, quite seriously. **— derecesinde** to perfection. **— ehli** possessed of every excellence, sage. **—e er=** to reach perfection, to arrive at maturity. **—i evvel** *lrnd., phil.* entelechy. **—e gel=** same as **kemale er=**. **—i ihtiramla** with utmost consideration, most respectfully. **—i muhabbetle** with full affection. **—i ne?, —i nedir ki?** It is a trifle; it has no value whatsoever.
kemalât (. — —) كمالات A *lrnd.* all perfections, virtues, acquirements. **—ı bâhire** accomplishments and talents.
kemalî (. — —) كمالى A *lrnd.* pertaining to perfection.
Kemalist كماليست Kemalist, adherent of the doctrine of Kemalism.
Kemalizm كماليزم Kemalism, the political doctrine developed in Turkey in the 1930's (named for Kemal Atatürk).
keman 1 كمان |keman 2| violin. **— anahtarı** *mus.* treble clef, violin clef. **— çal=** to play the violin. **— köprüsü** violin bridge. **— oku** violin box. **— teli** violin string. **— yayı** violin bow.
keman 2 (. —) كمان P *lrnd.* 1. archery bow; arched like a bow. 2. sign and constellation of Sagittarius. **—i âsûman** 1. Sagittarius. 2. rainbow. **—i behmen** rainbow. **—i çarh** same as **keman-i asuman**. **—ı çeşni et=** *archaic* to try a bow. **—a çile geçir=** to string a bow. **— et=** /ı/ to bend into the shape of a bow. **—i felek** *lrnd.*, same as **keman-i asuman**. **—i fulâd** steel bow, used for practicing the muscles. **—i gerdun** 1. rainbow. 2. Sagittarius. **—i halka** unstrung bow curled reversely into a complete circle; a bow not drawn. **—i hallâcî** cotton-carder's bow. **—i hikmet** ballista for throwing stones or arrows. **— kaş** 1. arched eyebrow. 2. who has arched eyebrows. **—i mühre** crossbow. **— ol=** to become bent (into the shape of a bow). **—i resm** rainbow. **—i sade** the sun; sunshine; moonlight. **—i sadmen, —i sadmenî** strong and heavy bow. **—i sam, —i şeytan** *poet.* rainbow. **—i zenburî** musket, firelock.

kemanbend (. — .) كمان بند P *lrnd.* apparatus for stringing a bow.
kemancule (. — — .) كمان جوله P *lrnd.* archer's bowcase.
kemançe (. — .) كمانچه 1. same as **kemençe**. 2. *Ott. hist.* long curved flourish to an official signature. **—i hallâcî** *lrnd.* small wool-carder's bow.
kemandan (. — —) كماندان P *lrnd.* bow case.
kemandar (. — —) كماندار P *lrnd.* archer, bowman. **—î** (. — — —) P archery.
kemane (. — .) كمانه P 1. violin with five strings. 2. *lrnd.* bow for archery, for a violin or for turning a small wood lathe. 3. *Turk. wrestling* a locking the hands on the breast or stomach of the opponent. 4. *naut.* head sails. **— çal=** to fiddle. **— çek=** *Turk. wrestling* to press on the breast or stomach of the opponent by moving the locked hands. **— yayı** *naut.* headboards.
kemanebru (. — ..) كمان ابرو P *poet.* with well arched eyebrows.
kemanger (. — .) كمانگر P *lrnd.* maker of bows or of violins.
kemangir (. — —) كمانگیر P *lrnd.* expert archer.
kemanî (. — —) كمانى P 1. violinist who plays Turkish music. 2. *lrnd.* violin maker.
kemankeş (. — .) كمانكش P 1. bowman, archer. 2. *Ott. hist.* member of a fraternity. **— sırrı** mere humbug.
kemanpüşt (. — .) كمان پشت P *lrnd.* with a crooked back.
kemansaz (. — —) كمان ساز P *lrnd.* bow maker, archer; violin maker.
kemasl كم اصل P *lrnd.* of mean origin, lowborn.
kemayar (.. —) كم عیار P *lrnd.* below standard; of base alloy.
kemayenbaği (.· — ..—) كماینبغی A *lrnd.* as it should be, as is proper.
kemazar (. — —) كم آزار P *lrnd.* noninjurious, not cruel.
kemazükir, kemazükire كما ذكر A *lrnd.* as has been stated.
kembaha (.. —) كم بها P *lrnd.* cheap; of little value.
kembaht كم بخت P *lrnd.* unlucky; wretched.
kembıza'a (.. — .), **kembızaat** (.. — .) كم بضاعه ، كم بضاعت P *lrnd.* having little ability, having small capital.
kemcevab (.. —) كم جواب P *lrnd.* who answers little or nothing, reticent.
kemdil كم دل P *lrnd.* chicken hearted.
keme 1 كمه A truffle, *bot., Tuber Micheli*: winter truffle, *bot., Tuber brumale*.

keme 2 پروو. rat. — sıçanı brown rat, zool., Mus decumanus.

kemençe (...) كمانچه [kemançe] 1. small violin with three strings, played like a cello. 2. instrument for spreading artificial fertilizer. —**ci** player or seller of **kemençes**.

kemend P, **kement**di كمند 1. lasso; oiled noose used for executions. 2. poet. dangling curls, tress (of hair). — **at**= /a/, — **geçir**= /a/ to throw a lasso (at). —**i vahdet** Isl. myst. pious meditation when a devotee ties a rope round his waist that prevents his lying down.

kemendendaz (...—) كمندانداز P lrnd. lasso thrower.

kementle=ᵣ كنت ملك slang /ı/ to swindle money out (of).

kemer كمر P 1. belt, girdle. 2. arch, vault. 3. aqueduct. —**ler** arcade. — **altı** 1. vaulted bazaar. 2. solo folk dance. — **ayağı** pier of an arch. — **burun** Roman nose. — **çaprazı** large ornamental clasp for a girdle. — **çatalı** meeting-angle of a groin arch. — **gözü** bay of an arch. — **kayışı** waist belt. — **kilidi** keystone. — **köprü** arched bridge. — **patlıcan** large round eggplant. — **pencere** arched window. —**ini sık**= to tighten one's belt. — **taşı** keystone of an arch. — **tokası** belt buckle. — **üzengisi**, — **yatağı** arch. impost.

kemerbend كمربند P 1. arch. archivolt. 2. lrnd. ready for service.

kemerbest كمربست P lrnd. bravery. —**e** P lrnd. 1. girded. 2. ready, prepared.

kemere كمره Gk naut. beam under the deck. — **astarı** clamp of an under-deck beam. — **çeliği** carling. — **istikametinde** abeam. — **puntalı** deck stanchion.

kemerli كمرلو 1. girdled. 2. arched, arch shaped; vaulted. — **payanda** flying buttress.

kemerlikği كمرلك leather belt used by lemonade sellers for holding glasses.

kemeviyüşşekl كمروىالشكل A anat., obs. fungiform.

kemgû (.—), **kemgüftar** (..—) كمگو كمگفتار P lrnd. silent; reticent.

kemha (.—) كمخا P archaic brocade; silk velvet.

kemhab (.—) كمخواب P 1. var. of **kemha**. 2. lrnd. one who sleeps little.

kemhacı كمخاجى maker or seller of brocade.

kemhav (.—) كمخواو same as **kemhab**.

kemhavsala كمحوصله P lrnd. 1. of small capacity; poor spirited. 2. unaspiring, unambitious.

kemhired كمخرد P lrnd. of little wisdom or intelligence, foolish, ignorant (person).

kemhimmet كمهمت P lrnd. unenterprising; poor spirited.

kemhuy كمخوى P lrnd. of evil disposition; having bad habits.

kemî 1 (.—) كمى P lrnd. 1. badness. 2. deficiency.

kemi 2 (.—) كمى A lrnd. mailed warrior; champion, hero.

kemikği كميك bone; anat. osseous. — **ağrısı** bone-ache. — **arası** anat. interosseous. — **at**= /a/ 1. to throw a bone (to. a dog). 2. to appease by a favor. — **bilim** neol. osteology. — **burkul**= to be sprained at a joint (bone). — **cilâsı** bone varnish. — **çık**= to be dislocated (bone). — **çıkıntısı**. anat. process of a bone, projection. — **desteresi** surg. bone saw. — **dış zarı** anat. periosteum. — **dikişi** anat. suture. — **doku** neol., anat. bone tissue. — **gibi** as hard as a bone. — **gövdesi** anat. diaphysis. — **gübresi** bone manure, bone dust. — **iliği** bone marrow. — **iltihabı** bone inflammation, ostitis. —**e kadar işle**= to penetrate to the very marrow. — **kırığı** fracture. — **kıymığı** splinter or sliver of bone. — **kömürü** chem. bone charcoal, animal charcoal, bone black. — **külü** bone ash. — **levhacığı** anat. osseous lamella. — **pensi** surg. bone nippers. — **sistemi** anat. bone system. — **şişi** path. exostosis. — **törpüsü** surg. bone file, raspatory. — **tutkalı** bone glue. — **ucu** anat. epiphysis. — **unu** bone dust. — **veremi** tuberculosis of the bones. — **yağı** bone oil, neatsfoot oil. — **yalayıcı** toady, sycophant, bootlicker. — **yapan** bone-forming, osteoplastic. — **yaylar** osseous arches. — **yumuşaması** path. softening of the bones, osteomalacia. — **zarı** anat. periosteum. — **zarı iltihabı** path. periostitis.

kemikçikği كميكجك ossicle.

kemikleş=ir كميكلشمك to ossify, to become bone. —**me** ossification. —**tir**= /ı/ to ossify.

kemikli كميكلى 1. having bones. 2. bony, large boned. — **balıklar** the bony fishes, zool., Teleostomi.

kemin 1 (.—) كمين P lrnd. very little, very small, very few.

kemin 2 (.—) كمين A lrnd. ambush; those who lie in ambush. —**dar** (.——) P one lying in ambush. —**gâh** (.——), —**geh** (.—.) P place of ambush. —**saz** (.——) P ambusher.

kemir=ir كميرمك /ı/ to gnaw, to nibble; to corrode.

kemircikği كميرجك anat. cartilage, gristle (of nose, ear).

kemirdekği كميردك archaic cartilage; gristly part of a tail bone.

kemirgen neol. rodent. —**ler** zool., Rodentia.

kemirici . كميرجى gnawing, rodent; corrosive.

— **memeliler**, **—ler** gnawing or rodent mammals, *zool.*, Rodentia.

kemiril=ᴵʳ كمريلمك to be gnawed, nibbled; corroded.

kemirt=ᴵʳ كميرتمك /ı, a/ *caus. of* **kemir=**. **—il=** *pass.*

kemirtlekᵍⁱ كميرتلك *archaic, var. of* **kemirdek**.

ķemiş=ᴵʳ كمشمك *archaic* to throw; to abandon.

kemiyat (. — —) كميّات *A lrnd., pl. of* **kemiyet**. **—ı vaz'iye** *math.* coordinates.

kemiyet كميّة *A* quantity. **— itibariyle** quantitatively, in quantity or number. **— ve keyfiyet** quantity and quality. **—i munfasıla** *lrnd., math.* discontinuous quantity.

kemiyeten (..´.) كميّةً *A lrnd.* quantitatively.

kemkâr (. —) كم كار *P lrnd.* not much occupied; not very efficient.

kemkâse (. — .) كم كاسه *P lrnd.* mean (hospitality); poor (capacity).

kemküm كم كوم hesitatingly; confusedly (said of speech). **— et=** to hem and haw, to talk falteringly.

kemlikᵍⁱ كملك badness, evil, ill will; malicious act. **— et=** to do evil, to act in a malicious manner.

kemmaye (. — .) كمّايه *P lrnd.* 1. of little value. 2. possessing little ability or talent; ill-provided or stocked. 3. evil disposition; evilly disposed.

kemmî (. —) كمّى *A lrnd.* quantitative.

kemmiyet كمّية *A lrnd., var. of* **kemiyet**.

kemmun (. —) كمّون *A lrnd.* cummin. **—i esved** wild cummin. **—î** flavored with cummin.

kemnam (. —) كمنام *P lrnd.* of little repute; unknown.

kemnazar كم نظر *P* 1. evil eye. 2. *lrnd.* who sees or foresees but little.

kemne كمنه *A lrnd., path.* amaurosis.

kemniyet كم نيّت *P* 1. evil intention, malicious design. 2. evil intentioned.

kempay (. —) كم پاى *P lrnd.* of small endurance; transient.

kemrah (. —) كمراه *P lrnd.* slow-paced (beast).

kemre 1 كمره *P prov.* dung, manure.

kemre 2 كمره scab. **—len=** to scab (wound).

kemsalⁱⁱ (. —) كم سال *P lrnd.* young, juvenile.

kemşerm كم شرم *P lrnd.* shameless, immodest.

kemtabiatᵗⁱ (. — . —) كم طبيعت *P lrnd.* of little taste, lacking in taste.

kemter كمتر *P lrnd.* less, inferior, worse; **—leri** your humble servant, *i. e.* I. **—âne** (.. — .) *P* humbly. **—î** (.. —) *P same as* **kemterleri**. **—în** (.. —) *P* most inferior, most humble.

kemyab (. —) كمياب *P lrnd.* rare, difficult to find.

kemzihn كم ذهن *P lrnd.* 1. with little mind, stupid. 2. forgetful.

-ken 1 كن [iken] *after vowels* **—yken**, while, *as in* **gençken, çalışırken**.

-ken 2 كن *P lrnd.* one who digs, tears out, eradicates, *as in* **kal'aken, kûhken**.

ken 3 كن *prov.* edge, border, side.

kena'is (. — .) كنائس *A lrnd., pl. of* **kenise**.

Ken'an (. —) كنعان *A Bib.* Canaan. **—î** (. — —) *A* Canaanite.

kenar 1 كنار [kenar 2] 1. edge, border, brink; margin; cant (of a building). 2. marginal (note); postscript. 3. retired place, nook, corner. 4. out of the way, remote; suburb. **—a at=** /ı/ to put aside. **— baskısı** hem (of cloth). **— çek=** /a/ to hem, to border, to edge. **—a çekil=**, **bir —a çekil=** to get out of the way, to retire apart. **— devletler** border states. **—ın dilberi** girl or woman lacking in refinement. **—da dur=** to stand aside. **—da kal=** to remain aside. **— karaltısı** *astr.* darkness towards the limb. **— kıvır=** /a/ *same as* **kenar çek=**. **—da köşede** in nooks and corners. **— mahalle** poor quarter near the edge of town. **— ol=** *obs.* 1. to get out of the way. 2. to get to the shore. **— ortay** *neol., math.* median. **—da otur=** to sit apart, away from the chiefs of an assembly. **— pervazı**, **— suyu** border, rim, edging. **— tezyinatı** *arch.* ornamental border. **— yap=** *same as* **kenar çek=**. **— yazısı** marginal inscription, legend (on coins). **— yer** retired place, place out of the way.

kenar 2 (. —) كنار *P lrnd.* 1. *same as* **kenar 1**. 2. embrace. **—a al=** /ı/ to embrace. **— ü bus** embracing and kissing. **—a çek=** /ı/ to embrace.

kenarbend (. — .) كنار بند *P lrnd.* ornamental border of a book cover.

kenare (. — .) كناره *P lrnd.* edge, margin. **—gir** (. — . —) *P same as* **kenargir**.

kenargir (. — —) كنار گير *P lrnd.* 1. who withdraws from a crowd, business or from the world. 2. coaster (ship).

kenargirifte (. — . . .) كنار گرفته *P lrnd.* one who has taken a post in a retired place.

kenarla=ʳ كنارلامق /ı/ 1. to hem, to border, to edge. 2. to align two maps by means of grid lines.

kenarlı كنارلو having an edge, border or margin.

kenarlıkᵍⁱ كنارلق edging, border of a flower bed.

kend كند *archaic, var. of* **kent 1**.

kende كنده *P lrnd.* 1. ditch, trench, moat. 2. dug, excavated; engraved, carved.

kendeger كنده گر *P lrnd. same as* **kendekâr**.

kendekâr (..—) کنده کار P *lrnd.* engraver, carver, sculptor.

kendi کندی oneself; self, own, *e. g.,* **kendi evim** my own house. **—leri** themselves. **—m** myself. **—minki** mine. **—miz** ourselves. **—nden** 1. by itself. 2. *phil.,* same as **kendiliğinden**. **—si** himself, herself. **— ağzı ile tutul=** to be given away by his own words. **— âleminde ol=** to live in his own world. **— başına** independent, of his own accord. **—ini beğenmiş** conceited, arrogant, haughty. **— beslek** *neol., biol.* self-feeding, autotrophe. **—ni bil** Know thyself. *colloq.* Mind your manners. **—ni bilen, —ni bilir** reasonable and decent (person). **—ni bilmez** assuming, impertinent. **—ni bilmeze vur=** to feign ignorance. **—ni bir şey san=** to think himself important. **—ni bul=** to recover, to regain a former good state. **—ne çeki düzen ver=** to tidy oneself up. **— çıkarı için** for his own interest. **—ni dar at=** /a/ to manage to take refuge. **— derdine düş=** to be completely preoccupied with his own troubles. **—ni dev aynasında gör=** to overrate oneself enormously, to think a great deal of oneself. **—ni dirhem dirhem sat=** to give oneself airs; to act in a very self-important way. **— düşen ağlamaz** One has to bear the consequence of his own acts. **— eliyle** 1. with one's own hand. 2. personal. **— eliyle teslim** personal delivery. **—ne et=** to harm oneself. **—ni fasulya gibi nimetten say=** to overrate oneself ridiculously, to think oneself very important. **—nden geç=**, **—sinden geç=** to be in ecstasy, to be enraptured, enravished. **—ne gel=, —sine gel=** to come to oneself again, to pull oneself together. **— gelen** godsend. **— göbeğini kendi kes=** *colloq.* to rely only on oneself in everything. **—ni göster=** to prove one's worth. **—ne güvenme** self confidence, self reliance. **— halinde** quiet; inoffensive, harmless (person). **— haline bırak=** /ı/ to leave to himself or to his fate, to let (a thing) take care of itself. **—ne has** individual, particular, special. **— havasına git=, — havasında ol=** to follow one's own fancies. **—ni hissettir=** to make itself felt. **— hodum** *archaic* I myself. **— işler** *neol.* automatic. **—ni kapıp koyver=** to cease to take an interest in oneself, to let oneself go. **—ni kaptır=** /a/ to give oneself up or over (to), to be an addict (to). **—ni kaybet=** to become unconscious; to be enraged. **— kendime** by myself, for myself. **— kendine gelin güvey ol=** to dream of impossible things, to have illusions. **— kendini idare** self-government, autonomy. **— kendine telkin** autosuggestion. **— kendini tenkid** self-criticism. **— kendini ye=** same as **kendini ye=**. **— kendine yet=** to be self-sufficient or self-supporting. **— kendine yeterlik** self-sufficiency. **— kuyusunu kendi kaz=** to dig one's own pit, to be caught in one's own trap. **—ne malik olma=** to have lost all self-control, to be beside oneself. **— miktarını bil=** to know one's place. **—ni müdafaa** self-defense. **— namına hutbe okut=** *Isl. hist.* to have the Friday sermon preached with his own name (as a sign of independence); to announce one's independence. **—ni naza çek=** to show affected reluctance. **— nefsi için** for his own self. **—nde olma=** *same as* **kendine malik olma=**. **—ni pabucu büyüğe okut** You must be crazy (to do such a thing). **— payıma** for my part, as to me. **—ni sat=** to display one's own abilities. **—ni tart=** to weigh up one's own abilities. **—ni toparla=** to pull oneself together, to brace oneself. **—ni tut=** to keep one's countenance, to keep calm. **—ni ver=** /a/ to devote oneself (to). **— yağı ile kavrul=** to get along by oneself, to carry on by one's own means; to live or subsist modestly. **—den yana yont=** to care for oneself only; to turn to one's own advantage. **—ni ye=** to worry or torment oneself to death. **—ne yedireme=** /ı/ to be unable to bring oneself to do. **—ne yont=** same as **kendinden yana yont=**.

kendilik[gi] *neol., phil.* entity. **—inden** by oneself, by himself; automatically, spontaneously. **—inden türeme** *neol., biol.* spontaneous generation, abiogenesis.

kendir کندیر ـ کندر 1. hemp, *bot., Cannabis sativa.* 2. *prov.* rope, hawser. **— bezi** hempen cloth. **— halat** hemp, rope, cord. **— iplik** hemp thread. **— lifi** hemp fiber. **— tohumu** hempseed. **— yağı** hemp oil. **—giller** *neol.,* **—iye** *lrnd., bot., Cannabinaceae.*

kendu (.—) کندو P *lrnd.* clay vessel for keeping grain.

kendure (.—.) کندوره P *lrnd.* linen or leather cover spread on the ground and used in place of a table; tablecloth.

kendü کندو *archaic, same as* **kendi**.

kendüzi کندوزی *archaic, same as* **kendi, kendisi**.

kene کنه P 1. tick. 2. castor bean. **— biberi** malaguetta pepper; grain of paradise. **— gibi yapış=** to stick like a bur, to be a bore. **— göz** very small eye; small-eyed. **— otu** castor oil plant.

kenef 1 کنف |kenif| *vulg.* 1. toilet. 2. very dirty; very ugly. **— sazlığı, — süpürgesi** *vulg.* man with a sparse mustache.

kenef 2 کنف A *lrnd.* 1. side, edge, margin; coast, shore. 2. region, district. 3. shadow; protection.

kenet[di] کنت ـ کینت metal clamp (for

strengthening a joint in masonry, etc.), cramp iron. — **taşı** arch. keystone.
kenetle=ʳ كنتلمك /ı/ 1. to clamp, to join by clamps. 2. to bind tightly; to clasp (hands). **—n=** pass. of **kenetle=**.
kenetli كنتلى clamped together, closely united.
kenevir كنوير - كنویر hemp, hemp plant.
kenger كنكر P 1. cardoon, bot., Cynara cardunculus. 2. artichoke, bot., Cynara scolymus. — **sakızı** boiled-down juice of the milk thistle. — **yaprağı** arch. acanthus, acanthus leaf. **—zed** P lrnd., same as **kenger sakızı**.
kengi كنگى prov. 1. syphilis. 2. rheumatism. 3. common cold.
kenif (.—) كنيف A lrnd. toilet, privy.
kenisa, kenise (.—.) كنيسا A lrnd. church.
keniz (.—) كنيز P lrnd. 1. slave girl. 2. maid, girl. **—beçe** (.—..) P son of a slave woman..
kenizekᵏⁱ (.—.) كنيزك P lrnd. 1. slave girl. 2. little girl.
kennas (.—) كناس A lrnd. sweeper.
kent 1 كنت 1. town, city. 2. prov. village.
kent=ᵉʳ **2** كنتمك to notch, cut, serrate.
kentalˡⁱ كنتال F weight of one hundred kilos.
kentikᵍⁱ كنتك notch.
kenud (.—) كنود A lrnd. unthankful, ungrateful.
kenz كنز A lrnd. 1. buried treasure. 2. treasury. **—i mahfi** Isl. myst. hidden treasure, i. e., absolute unity of God before the creation of the world. **K— Suresi** a name of the first sura of the Quran.
kep كپ E ceremonial cap, mortarboard.
kepade (.—.) كپاده P lrnd. training arrow. **—keş** (.—..) P a novice in archery.
kepaze 1 (.—.) كپازه vile, contemptible, shameless; ridiculous or contemptible person. — **et=** /ı/ to scoff (at), to treat with scorn; to disgrace. — **ol=** to be a laughingstock, to be shamed, humiliated.
kepaze 2 (.—.) كپازه P lrnd., var. of **kepade**.
kepazele=ʳ (.—...) كپازه لمك /ı/ to render vile or contemptible; to cause to be worthless; to cheapen. **—n=** pass.
kepazelikᵍⁱ (.—..) كپازه لك 1. dishonor, degradation; vileness; ignominy. 2. shame, scandal.
kepbastı كپباصدى Gk var. of **kebbastı**.
kepçe كپچه P 1. ladle, skimmer, scoop. 2. scoop net, butterfly net. 3. naut. buttock. 4. Turk. wrestling a passing one hand from behind through the legs of the opponent. — **kepçe** ladlefuls (of), scoops (of). — **kulak** having large, prominent ears. — **kuyruk** slang sponger. — **surat** having a small face.

kepçecikᵍⁱ كپچه جك prov. children's prayer for rain.
kepekᵍⁱ كپك 1. bran. 2. dandruff, scurf. 3. prov. necessities of livelihood. — **unu** bran, pollard, grit.
kepeklen=ⁱʳ كپكلنمك to become scurfy.
kepekli كپكلى 1. branny, mixed with bran, containing bran. 2. scurfy, covered with scurf.
kepenekᵍⁱ **1** كپه نك coarse cape or cloak worn by shepherds.
kepenekᵍⁱ **2** كپه نك prov. 1. butterfly, moth. 2. liver disease of sheep, staggers of sheep.
kepenkᵍⁱ كپنك large pull-down shutter; trapdoor; wooden cover.
kepez كپز prov. 1. rock on shore, cliff; hill; barren soil. 2. headdress, headgear of a bride; bride's veil. 3. crest (of a bird), cock's comb.
kepi كپى prov. piece of leather or rag.
kepici كپجى prov. greedy, stingy.
kepir كپير prov. marshy, barren soil.
keprem كپرم prov. awkward, clumsy; foolish, idiot; incapable, invalid. — **et=** /ı/ to speak ill (of).
ker 1 كر P lrnd. pomp. — **ü fer***.
ker 2 كر P lrnd. deaf; deaf man.
kerʳʳⁱ **3** كر A lrnd. an attacking and renewing an attack. — **ü fer** attack and retreat.
kerahatᵗⁱ (.—.) كراهت A 1. a being abominable. 2. lrnd. dislike, aversion, repugnance. 3. a lawful but blameworthy act. — **et=**, — **getir=** /dan/ to have a dislike, aversion (for), to detest. — **vakti** joc. drinking time.
kerahaten (.—'..) كراهةً A lrnd. with aversion, repugnantly.
kerahatli كراهتلى abominable, detestable, nasty.
kerahiyet (.—..) كراهيت A lrnd., same as **kerahat**.
kerake (.—.) كراكه var. of **kerrake**.
keramat (.——) كرامات A lrnd., pl. of **keramet**. — **erbabı** workers of miracles.
keramet (.—.) كرامت A 1. miracle worked through the agency of a saint; power of sanctity by which miracles are worked; wonder, marvel. 2. opportune word, hint. 3. lrnd. generosity, munificence, excellence. **—te bulun=** to work miracles. — **buyurdunuz** Your words are wonderful. — **göster=** same as **keramette bulun=**. **—i kevniye** lrnd. wonder of creation. — **sahibi** miracle worker. **—im yok ya** I am no prophet. How would I know?
kerametli كرامتلى 1. holy (as a medium of miracles). 2. lrnd. generous, noble.
kerametmedar (.—..—) كرامت مدار P lrnd. 1. man of sanctity manifested by miracles. 2. kind, good man.
keramikᵍⁱ كراميك Gk ceramics.
keran (.—) كران P lrnd. 1. edge, margin,

kerata side; shore. 2. end; limit. **— tâ keran** from end to end.

kerata كراته Gk 1. pander, pimp; cuckold. 2. scoundrel, rascal (also used affectionately). 3. shoehorn. **—ya bak hele** Look at the little rascal.

keratit كراتيت Gk *path.* keratitis, inflammation of the cornea.

keratoz كراتوز Gk *path.* keratosis.

keraviya (.—..) كراويه P *lrnd.* common caraway, *bot., Carum carvi*.

kerb كرب A. *lrnd.* care, anxiety; grief.

Kerbelâ (..—) كربلا A *name of a place in Iraq, noted for the murder of Husain, son of Ali*. **—î** pertaining to Kerbela, from Kerbela.

kerç[çi] كرچ *prov.* 1. mockery, a teasing; derision. 2. grudge, spite. 3. reproach, complaint. **— et=** /ı/ to make fun of.

-kerde كرده P *used in compounds* made, done; performed, *as in* **huykerde, tasmimkerde**.

kerdeme كردمه Gk *bot.* cress; winter cress; yellow rocket, etc.

kere 1 كره [**kerre**] A 1. time, times. 2. bracket, parenthesis. **bir —** 1. once; just. 2. Let it be said that...; for one thing...; to begin with. **— içine al='** /ı/ to bracket, to place within brackets or parentheses.

kere 2 كره P *prov.* cream; butter. **— peyniri** cream cheese. **— yağı** *same as* **tere yağı**.

kerecik[ği] كره جك diminutive of **kere 1**, *e. g.*, **bir —** just once, only just once.

kerefs كرفس A *lrnd.* celery.

kerem كرم A 1. kindness, goodness, benevolence, favor. 2. beneficence, munificence. **— buyurunuz, — eyleyiniz** Please, I beg you. **— et=** 1. to have the kindness to (so and so). 2. to be kind. **— sahibi** generous, munificent, magnanimous.

keremen (.'..) كرمًا A *lrnd.* out of kindness, as a favor.

keremgüster كرمگستر P *lrnd.* gracious. **—âne** (....—.) P graciously, generously. **—î** (،...—) P graciousness, generosity.

keremkâr (..—) كرمكار P *lrnd.* generous, gracious, beneficent. **—âne** (..——.) P *lrnd.* 1. generous, benevolent (act). 2. generously, benevolently. **—î** (..——) P *lrnd.*, **—lık** kindness, generosity, munificence.

kerempe كرمپه rocky promontory.

keremperver كرمپرور P *lrnd.* generous, munificent. **—âne** (....—.) P generously. **—î** (....—) P generousness.

kerempişe (..—.) كرمپيشه P *lrnd.* kind, of generous habit, liberal.

kerenb كرنب P *lrnd.* cabbage.

keres كرس large bowl, vessel.

kereste كرسته P 1. timber, lumber. 2. *slang* fool, simpleton, idiot. **—si kavi** strongly built (perşon). **—ci** timber merchant. **—li** strongly built (person).

keret كرت *archaic, var. of* **kere 1**.

kerevet 1 كروت Gk 1. wooden bedstead, wooden divan. 2. trellis for a vine.

kerevet 2 كروت F prawn, *zool., Palemon serratus*.

kerevid, kerevides, kerevit[di] كرويس Gk crawfish, *zool., Astacus fluviatilis*.

kereviz كرويز [**kerefs**] celery, *bot., Apium graveolens*.

kerez كرز *slang* coffee, drink, food, etc., offered to a guest.

kerg كرگ P *lrnd.* rhinoceros.

kerh كره A aversion, detestation, abhorrence, repugnance.

kerhane (.—.) كرهانه [**kârhane 2**] brothel. **—ci** brothel keeper.

kerhen (.'.) كرهًا A reluctantly, with aversion or repugnance, unwillingly.

kerih (.—) كريه A disgusting, detestable, abominable.

kerihe (.—.) كريهه A *lrnd.* disgusting, abominable thing.

kerihülmanzar (.—...) كريه المنظر A *lrnd.* of repulsive aspect.

kerihünnefes (.—...) كريه النفس A *lrnd.* having foul breath.

kerihüssavt (.—..) كريه الصوت A *lrnd.* bad-toned, unmelodious; having an unpleasant voice.

kerim (.—) كريم A 1. kind, generous, munificent, gracious. 2. *lrnd.* noble, honorable. **—âne** (.——.) P *lrnd.* kindly, in a generous manner.

kerime (.—.) كريمه A 1. daughter. 2. *lrnd.* verse of the Quran.

kerimülahlâk[kı] (.—..—) كريم الاخلاق A *lrnd.* most generous and noble.

kerimülfaâl[li] (.—..—) كريم الفعال A *lrnd.* generous, gracious.

kerimülhucze (.—...) كريم الحجزه A *lrnd.* decorous and chaste in conduct.

kerimülkışb (.—..) كريم القشب A *lrnd.* of a noble and generous disposition.

kerimülmahser (.—...) كريم المحشر A *lrnd.* of a generous disposition.

kerimülma'sar (.—...) كريم المعصر A *lrnd.* generous as yielding abundantly when importuned.

kerimülmefariş (.—..—.) كريم المفارش A *lrnd.* who has noble wives.

kerimülmu'tasar (.—....) كريم المعتصر A *lrnd.* generous when applied to.

kerimunnakibe (.—..—.) كريم النقيبه A *lrnd.* noble minded, of kind disposition.

kerimunnakir (.—..—) كريم النقير A *lrnd.* of a noble origin.

kerimünnefs (.—..) كَرِيمُ النَّفْس A lrnd. noble minded, of a generous soul.

kerimüşşiyem (.—...) كَرِيمُ الشِّيَم A lrnd. with noble and generous qualities.

keriş كرش A lrnd. first stomach of a ruminant.

keriz 1 كَرِيز [kariz] sewer, drain.

keriz 2 كَرِيز slang 1. gambling. 2. credulous, easy to be duped. 3. amusement. **— alayı** troop of Gipsy musicians. **—e bayıl=** /ı/ to lose in gambling. **—e et=** to be a cardsharp.

kerizci كَرِيزجى 1. musician. 2. cheating gamester, sharper.

kerizle=[r] كَرِيزلَمَك to play music.

kerkem كَرْكَم P lrnd. rainbow.

kerkenez كَرْكَنَز kestrel, zool., Falco tinnunculus.

kerkes كَرْكَس P lrnd. 1. vulture. 2. a sort of arrow. **—i felek** 1. the constellation Aquila. 2. the constellation Lyra. **— taşı** eaglestone, aetites. **—i terkeş** arrow left in the quiver.

kerki 1 كَرْكِى large ax.

kerki=[r] **2** كَرْكِمَك archaic /ı/ to clutch violently and hold down or force downwards.

kerkin=[ir] كَرْكِنمَك prov. to mount upon a person or thing in a violent manner; clinging as by use of the claws.

kerli ferli كَرْلى فَرْلى same as **kelli felli**.

kerm كَرْم A lrnd. 1. grapevine. 2. vineyard.

kerme كَرْمَه prov., var. of **kemre 1**.

kermen كَرْمَن prov., same as **kirmen**.

kermes كَرْمَس F local outdoor festival, fair, kermis.

kermuş (.—) كَرْمُوش P lrnd. mole, zool., Talpa; muskrat.

kerpeten كَرْپَتَن [kelbetan] pair of forceps, pincers.

kerpiç[ci] كَرْپِيچ 1. sundried brick, adobe. 2. made of sundried bricks; hard; dry. **— gibi** very hard and dry, petrified. **— kalıbı** mold for sundried bricks. **— kes=** to cut out sundried bricks. **— kesil=** 1. to become very hard or tough. 2. to become petrified or stupefied with shame. **—çi** maker or cutter of sundried bricks.

kerrake (.—.) كَرَّاكَه a former kind of light cloak, used in expressions like **anlaşıldı Vehbi'nin kerrakesi** Now all is clear.

kerrar (.—) كَرَّار A lrnd. impetuous attacker.

kerrat (.—) كَرَّات A lrnd., pl. of **kere 1**[1]. **—la** repeatedly, several times. **— cetveli** multiplication table. **— ve merrat ile** lrnd. time after time, over and over again.

kerre كَرَّه A same as **kere 1**.

kerrenay (..—) كَرَّناى P Ott. hist. large brass trumpet used in the army.

kerretan (..—) كَرَّتان A lrnd. twice; in the morning and evening.

kerreten (.'..) كَرَّةً A lrnd. at one time, at another time; sometimes.

kerrubî (.——) كَرُّوبى var. of **kerubî**.

kersen كَرْسَن P prov. wooden trough; earthen milk or yogurt bowl.

kert=[er] كَرْتمَك /ı/ to notch, cut; to scrape against.

kerte 1 كَرْتَه Gk 1. naut. rhumb of the mariner's compass; each of the sixteen smallest points of the compass. 2. degree; bearing. 3. best state or quality, right moment. **—sini al=** /ın/ to take the bearing or elevation (of). **—sini geç=** /ın/ to pass, the exact point; to be overdone. **—sine gel=** to reach just the right point, degree or moment. **—sine getir=** /ı/ to bring to the right point; to choose the very best time.

kerte 2 كَرْتَه var. of **kerti 1**.

kerte 3 كَرْتَه P furrow for drainage in a field.

kerte 4 كَرْتَه It archaic, var. of **karta 1**.

kerteleme neol. graduation, gradualness.

kerteles كَرْتَلَس a kind of camel of mixed breeds.

kertenkele كَرْتَنْكَلَه ordinary lizard, zool., Ophisops elegans. **—giller** zool. lizards belonging to the order Lacertilia.

kertenkeler كَرْتَنْكَلَر archaic, var. of **kertenkele**.

kerteriz كَرْتَرِيز Gk naut. bearing. **— al=**, **— et=** naut. to take a bearing. **— hattı** line of bearing. **— noktası** point of bearing.

kerti 1 كَرْتى incised mark, notch.

kerti 2 كَرْتى prov. stale, not fresh.

kertik[ği] كَرْتِك 1. notch, cut, score, incision, gash; tally. 2. notched, gashed, cut, tallied. 3. fraction (of a pound, etc.). **—ine koy=** /ı/ carpentry to join by a notch or scarf-joint (timbers).

kertikli كَرْتِكلى 1. notched; crenate. 2. giving fractions (i. e., the exact sum, not just a round figure).

kertil=[ir] **1** كَرْتِلمَك to be notched, incised, gashed.

kertil 2 كَرْتِل prov. narrow mountain road.

kertin=[ir] كَرْتِنمَك to become notched, incised, gashed.

kertme كَرْتمَه 1. a notching, gashing, tallying. 2. notched, gashed, tallied.

kerubî (.——) كَرُوبى A cherub. **—yan** (.———) P, **—yun** (.———) A lrnd. cherubim.

keruker (.—.) كَرُوكَر P lrnd. the Almighty Creator, God.

kerüfer كَرُوفَر P lrnd. magnificence and display; pomp.

kervan كَرْوان [Persian .—] caravan. **— başı** 1. leader, commander of a caravan. 2. front of a caravan. **— çulluğu** curlew, zool., Numenius arquata, slender billed curlew, zool., Numenius tenuirostris. **—a katıl=** to go with the rest,

kervansaray

to join in. **K— kıran, K— kıran yıldızı** the planet Venus when it rises before daylight. **— kuşu** obs. screaming bustard. **—cı** same as **kervan başı.**

kervansaray [Persian .—.—] caravanserai, inn with a large courtyard.

kerye 1 a kind of godfather who holds a boy during his circumcision; also a companion who keeps at the side of the boy during circumcision ceremonies.

kerye 2 iron hoop (tightened by bolts); connecting part of a handcuff.

kes=[er] **1** 1. /ı/ to cut (through, down or off); to slaughter, butcher (animals); to cut the throat of, kill. 2. prov. to slander. 3. /ı/ to interrupt, intercept, block, break off; to discontinue, stop; to break (circuit); to give up, abandon. 4. to take or knock off (a sum from), to deduct (from wages). 5. to punch (a ticket in a bus). 6. to cut (cards). 7. slang to talk boringly. 8. to define, determine, decide; to agree upon. 9. to coin. 10. to cut well, be sharp. **—ip at=** /ı/ 1. to settle offhand, settle once and for all. 2. to destroy root and branch. **—ip biç=** /ı/ to consider and decide. **—tiği tırnak olma=** /ın/ colloq. to be of very little value.

ke's 2 A 1. calyx (of a flower). 2. lrnd. cup, goblet with a beverage in it; cupful of wine. 3. lrnd. the constellation Crater.

-kes 3 P lrnd. person, as in **bikes, herkes, nakes.**

kes 4 archaic dumbfounded, confused. **— dön=** to become dumbfounded with shame. **— düşür=** to render dumbfounded with shame.

kesad (.—) A same as **kesat.**

kesafet 1 (.—.) A density, thickness; compactness. **—i cereyan** elec. current density. **— fonksiyonu** astr. density function. **—i mıknatisiye** phys. magnetic density.

kesafet 2 (.—.) A lrnd. obscurity, dullness; eclipse.

kesalet (.—.) A lrnd. indolence, heaviness, slowness.

kesan (.—) P lrnd., pl. of **kes 3**, persons, people.

kesane (.—.) P lrnd. human, manly; noble (acts, etc.).

kesaset (.—.) A lrnd. a being thick, dense, bushy; density, thickness.

kesat[dı] [kesad] 1. dull, flat, lifeless. 2. com. stagnant (market, trade); slack (season); scarcity.

kesatlık[ğı] dullness, flatness, slackness, stagnancy, stagnation; time of scarcity or unemployment.

kesb A lrnd. an earning, gaining, acquiring, acquisition. **—i fezail** acquisition of excellencies. **—i haram** illegal gain. **—i helâl** lawful gain. **—i ıttılâ eyle=** to acquire information. **—i istihkak et=** /a/ to acquire the right (of), to deserve. **—i itidal et=** to keep within bounds. **— ü kâr** business. **—i maaş et=** to gain one's livelihood. **—i mümareset et=** /da/ to acquire dexterity by practice (in). **—i sükûnet et=** to be calmed, appeased. **—i şeref eyle=** /la/ to have the honor (of). **—i tahayyüz eyle=** to acquire distinction. **—i takarrub eyle=** /a/ to be favored with free access (to the presence of a great person). **—i vukuf eyle=** /da, hakkında/ to obtain information, to become aware (of).

kesbet=[der] /ı/ to earn, gain, acquire.

kese 1 [kise] 1. purse; small bag, case; pouch. 2. coarse cloth bath glove (for rubbing the body in a Turkish bath). 3. pocket, purse; wealth. 4. path. cyst; anat. sac. 5. Ott. hist. a varying sum of money, in later centuries 500 kurush. **—nin ağzını aç=** to loosen the purse strings. **bir — altın** 1. one purse of gold. 2. Ott. hist. ten thousand pieces of gold. **— cebi** pocket for a money bag. **—nin dibi görün=** to run out of money. **—den ekle=** /ı/ to add from one's own pocket. **—sine güven=** to be able to afford. **— kâğıdı, — kâğıt** paper bag. **— kurt** obs. tapeworm, zool., Taenia. **— sür=** /a/ to rub down with a bath glove (in a Turkish bath).

kese 2 prov. shortcut. **— yol** shortcut. **— yoldan git=** to take a shortcut.

kesecik[ği] 1. small purse. 2. neol., anat. saccule, sacculus.

kesedar (..—) [kisedar] Ott. hist. keeper of the purse, treasurer. **— efendi razı olmaz** (lit. Mr. Purse-bearer will not consent.) I cannot afford it.

keseğen prov. cockchafer.

kesek[ği] 1. clod, lump of earth; cloddy, lumpy. 2. lump of manure dried for fuel; peat.

keseklen=[ir] to become a clod, to become cloddy.

kesekli[ği] peaty; cloddy, lumpy.

keseklik[ği] peat bog, peat moss.

kesel A lrnd. slackness, indolence, languor. **— gel=** /a/ to become tired, wearied, sluggish, indolent.

keselân (..—) A same as **kesel.**

kesele=[r] /ı/ to rub with a bath glove. **—n=** pass. and refl.

keseli having a bag, purse, case or pouch. **—ler** marsupials, zool., Marsupialia. **— kurt** cysticercus.

keselnak[kı] (..—) P lrnd. indolent, sluggish.

kesen [kes= 1] 1. that cuts, cuts off. 2. neol., geom. secant.

kesenkes كسكس decisive, categorical; decisively, categorically.
keser كسر adze.
kesf كسف A 1. *lrnd.* an eclipsing (sun, moon); obliteration. 2. *pros.* an abbreviating the foot **mef'ûlâtü** into **mef'ûlâ.**
kesi 1 كسى *archaic* 1. cut out garments, especially, linen underclothing. 2. charge measure at the mouth of a powder flask. — **taşı** flat stone in a brook or fountain on which clothes are beaten.
ke'sî 2 كأسى A *lrnd., bot.* calycinal, calycine.
kesici كسيجى 1. cutter (agent or instrument). 2. cutting, sharp, incisive. 3. *auto.* interruptor. — **diş** incisor, cutting tooth.
kesif (.—) كثيف A dense; thick (foliage, forest). — **nüfus** dense population.
kesik[gi] كسيك 1. cut (through or off), broken (off); a cut; interrupted; *geom.* truncated. 2. curdled, coagulated. 3. weary. 4. *prov.* trench, ditch; fence, enclosure. 5. *prov.* skim milk, cheese. 6. *slang* bad. — **alınlık** *arch.* broken pediment. — **altın** clipped gold coin. — **arazi** *mil.* broken ground, cut-up ground. — **çizgi** intersecting line, secant. — **kal=** to remain cut, interrupted, or abruptly ended. — **kesik** disjointed, chopped; interrupted; brokenly. — **korniş** *arch.* truncated cornice. — **kristal** *min.* truncated crystal. — **nefes** spasmodic breathing. — **otu** *prov.* a kind of blood-staunching plant. — **söz** interrupted words; abruptly ended discourse. — **sulama** system of supplying irrigation for certain periods only. — **süt** curdled sour milk. — **sütun** *arch.* truncated column. — **un** damaged flour.
kesikli كسيكلى discontinued, interrupted; *phil.* discontinuous; *geog.* intermittent. — **akım** *neol.* alternating current. — **nicelik** *neol., math.* discontinuous quantity. — **tayf** *neol., phys.* discontinuous spectrum.
kesiklik[gi] كسيكلك 1. weakness, languor, lassitude. 2. state of being cut or broken.
kesiksiz كسيكسز continued, continuous. — **akım** *neol.* direct current. — **kesir** *neol., math.* continued fraction. — **tayf** *neol., phys.* continuous spectrum. —**lik** continuity.
kesil=[ir] كسيلمك 1. *pass.* of **kes=** 1 [1-3]. 2. to end, cease, come to an end; to calm down, settle down, abate (wind, etc.), to subside (excitement, fear, pain), to quiet down (noise, motion). 3. to be exhausted, tired out; /dan/ to cease (from doing), to be unable to do any longer. 4. to become like, *as in* **taş kesil=**. 5. to become curdled, coagulated, clotted (milk). —**miş baş bir daha bitmez** (*lit.* A head cut off does not grow again.) What is done cannot be undone. —**me noktası** cut-off point.

kesim كسيم 1. act of cutting, slaughtering, slaughter (of animals). 2. *tailor.* cut, make, shape; build (of a coat); *prov.* stature, figure. 3. time of cutting, reaping, slaughtering, ending. 4. *neol.* section, zone, sector. 5. *prov.* fixed or agreed price; agreement; *archaic* ransom; *Ott. hist.* a kind of tax paid instead of **öşür.** 6. abstention; vacation. 7. *prov.* land of four **dönüms.** — **akçesi** *prov.* dower agreed to be paid to a wife in the event of her being divorced. —**e bağla=** /ı/ *archaic* to hold (a captive) for ransom; *prov.* to agree on installments. — **kes=** *prov.* to agree upon. —**e kes=** /ı/ *prov.* to agree on installments. — **noktası** cut-off-point. — **parası** *archaic* ransom money; *prov.* money to be paid by agreement. — **vakti** *prov.* agreed time of payment. —**e ver=** /ı/ *prov.* to put up for rent.
kesimci كسيمجى *archaic* contractor who undertakes to farm a branch of revenue.
kesimle=[r] كسيملمك /ı/ *prov.* to fix (price).
kesimli كسيملى *prov.* 1. shapely, well-formed. 2. fixed, rationed.
kesin=[ir] **1** كسينمك *archaic* to cut out for oneself (clothes).
kesin 2 *neol.* decisive, categorical, definitive, final; definite, certain. — **bilgi** *phil.* certitude. — **hesap** final account. — **hüküm** final judgment. — **olarak** for certain, certainly, categorically.
kesinle=[r] *neol.* /ı/ to specify, to state precisely. —**ş=** to become final, decisive. —**ştir=** /ı/ to make final, decisive, definitive.
kesinlik[gi] *neol.* decisiveness, definitiveness.
kesinliksiz *neol.* indecisive, indefinite, uncertain, not final. —**lik** indecisiveness, indefiniteness, uncertainty.
kesinti كسنتى 1. deduction (from a sum or wages). 2. cuttings, clippings; cuts, curtailment. 3. *neol.* interruption. —**ye al=** /ı/ *slang* to make fun of someone secretly. —**li** liable to deduction. —**siz** clear, without deduction, net.
kesir[sri] **1** كسر [kesr] 1. *math.* fraction. 2. *lrnd.* a breaking, fracture; a harming, damaging (a person's prestige, honor, etc.); a mortifying or subduing one's passions, flesh, etc. 3. *Arabic gram.* a marking a letter with **kesre.** —**i âdi** P *math.* fraction. —**i aşari** P *math.* decimal fraction. —**i basit** *math.* proper fraction. —**i gayri vacib** *math.* improper fraction. —**i kal** *lrnd.* diminution caused by refining. —**i müfred** *math.* simple fraction. —**i mükerrer** *lrnd.* fraction expressed by the Arabic dual. —**i mültef** *math.* complex fraction. —**i mürekkeb** *math.* compound fraction. —**i mütevali** *lrnd.* continued fraction.

kesir

—i müzaf lrnd., same as kesr-i mürekkeb. —i nefs et= lrnd. to mortify the flesh, to humble oneself. —i vacib math. proper fraction.

kesîr 2 (. —) كثير A lrnd. 1. many, much, copious, numerous. 2. frequent. — ü kalîl much or little.

kesîren (. —́ .) كثيراً A lrnd. frequently, often; in great numbers.

kesirli كسرلى fractional. — aded fractional number.

kesirüladlâⁿ (. — .. —) كثيرالاضلاع A math. polygon.

kesirülcihad (. — .. —) كثيرالجهاد A lrnd. warlike, heroic.

kesirüleşkâlⁿ (. — .. —) كثيرالاشكال A lrnd. polymorphous, multiform.

kesirülevlâd (. — .. —) كثيرالاولاد A lrnd. having many children.

kesirülhücre (. — ...) كثيرالحجرة A lrnd. multicellular.

kesirülihsan (. — .. —) كثيرالاحسان A lrnd. most beneficent, munificent.

kesirüliyal (. — . —) كثيرالعيال A lrnd. having a numerous family.

kesirülma'na (. — .. —) كثيرالمعنى A lrnd. of many meanings.

kesirülvukuᵘᵘ (. — .. —) كثيرالوقوع A lrnd. of frequent occurrence.

kesirülvücuh (. — .. —) كثيرالوجوه A lrnd., geom. polyhedron.

kesirünnefʳⁱ (. — ..) كثيرالنفع A lrnd. very beneficial, very useful.

kesirünnevalⁱⁱ (. — .. —) كثيرالنوال A lrnd. most beneficent.

kesirüzzarar (. — ...) كثيرالضرر A lrnd. most noxious, injurious or harmful.

kesiş=ⁱʳ كشرك 1. to cut across, cut each other, to intersect. 2. to decide, to come to an agreement; to settle with one another. —en neol., geom. concurrent, intersecting. —tir= /ı/ caus. of kesiş=.

kesit neol. crosscut, cross section; sectional area.

ke'siyüşşekl كأس الشكل A lrnd. calyciform, calyx-shaped.

keski كسكى chisel; shoe knife, shoemaker's paring knife; hatchet. — âleti cutter, edge-tool. — çeliği steel cutter. — demiri iron cutter. — ile al= /ı/ to chisel off. — ile kes= /ı/ to cut with a chisel, to chisel. — kalemi cold chisel; parting tool (lathe). — makinesi bookbinding cutting machine, paper knife.

keskin كسكين 1. sharp, keen; pungent; acute. 2. decided, severe; peremptory. 3. edge (of a cutting instrument). 4. slang sodomite. 5. Ott. hist. master rider. — git= to go along at a very rapid pace. — gözlü sharp-sighted, keen-sighted. — nişancı mil. marksman, dead shot. — sirke küpüne zarar Sour vinegar harms its own jar said of one whose bad temper does him harm. — soğancık iron ball with a point, formerly used by dervishes in self-inflicted torture. — söyle= to speak peremptorily. — şarap strong wine. — viraj sharp turning, hairpin bend. — yazı clear and legible writing. — zekâlı sagacious, ingenious, sharp-witted.

keskinlen=ⁱʳ, **keskinleş**=ⁱʳ كسكيناشمك كسكينلنمك to become sharp or pungent, to be sharpened. —dir=, —tir= /ı/ caus.

keskinlet=ⁱʳ كسكينلتمك /ı/ to make sharp, to sharpen.

keskinlikᵍⁱ كسكينلك 1. sharpness, keenness; clearness. 2. pungency. 3. shrewdness. 4. edgewise position. —ine koy= /ı/ to set edgewise.

keslân (. —) كسلان A lrnd. lazy, slothful.

kesme كسمه 1. verbal n. of kes= 1. 2. neol. geom. sector. 3. ling. hiatus. 4. decided, definite; fixed (price). 5. cut, faceted. 6. prov. a kind of sweet cut in squares. 7. open-work embroidery. 8. tinsmith's shears. 9. soft rock stratum. 10. archaic large arrowhead; large arrow. 11. archaic horse armor, bard. — al= slang to pinch one's cheek. — ev archaic, same as kesmelik³. — işareti apostrophe. — kalıp stencil, stencil paper. — kaya soft rock stratum. — makarna a kind of flat macaroni. — resim cut-out picture. — şeker lump sugar, cube sugar. — taş hewn stone, ashlar. — yazı Arabic calligraphy a kind of ornamental writing made by cutting out the letters and pasting them on colored paper.

kesmece كسمجه 1. on condition of being cut for examination (in buying a watermelon, etc.). 2. in a lump lot (something that is bought); for a lump sum.

kesmelikᵍⁱ كسملك 1. quarry for building stone. 2. stratum of soft rock. 3. archaic artificial cave in a hillside used as a dwelling place.

kesmez كسمز not sharp, blunt.

kesmikᵍⁱ, **kesmük**ᵍⁱⁱ كسمك كسميك 1. chaff. 2. clot or film of cream or curd in milk. 3. archaic wooden dog collar.

kesper كسپر a kind of crossbred sheep.

kesr كسر A cf. kesir 1.

Kesra (. —) كسرى A hist. Khosru, Chosroes (king of Persia).

kesre كسره A 1. Arabic script vowel sign (ِ), indicating a short ı or i. 2. lrnd. a single break or breakage. —i hafife vowel sign for i. —i sakîle vowel sign for ı.

kesret 1 كثرت A lrnd. 1. great quantity or number, abundance, excess. 2. multitude. 3. phil. plurality. —i ilâh mezhebi polytheism.

—**i kelâm** overmuch talk. —**i seher** frequency or excess of sleeplessness. —**i tekrar** tautology. — **üzere** in abundance, in great number; frequently.

kesret=^{der} 2 كَسْرَتْمَك *lrnd.* /ı/ 1. to harm, damage (a person's honor, etc.). 2. to mortify, subdue (one's passions); to defeat.

kesretiye (.. —.) كَسْرَتِيَه A *phil.* pluralism.

kesretle كَسْرَتْلَه *lrnd.* frequently; abundantly.

kesretli كَسْرَتْلُو abundant, excessive, great many, much.

kesrî (. —) كَسْرِي A *math.* fractional. — **aded** fractional number.

kestane (. —.) كَسْتَانَه Gk 1. chestnut, *bot.*, *Castanea dentata*. 2. chestnut colored, maroon. — **ağacı** chestnut tree. — **dorusu** chestnut bay. — **fişeği** firecracker. —. **kabuğundan çıkmış da kabuğunu beğenmemiş** The chestnut emerged from its shell and did not like the look of it. *Said for a person who disdains his origin, who is ashamed of his early background.* — **karası** strong north wind blowing over the Black Sea on September 26. — **kargası** jay, *zool.*, *Garrulus glandarius*. — **kebabı** roasted chestnuts. — **markası** token or tally, deposited by a sentry or watchman. — **palamudu** a small species of bonito. — **saçlı** brown haired. — **suyu** very weak coffee. — **şekeri**, — **şekerlemesi** maron glacé, candied chestnuts. — **turpu** turnip radish. —**ci** chestnut man, chestnut seller. —**cik** *anat.* prostate. —**lik** chestnut grove.

kestere كَسْتَرَه wood betony, *bot.*, *Betonica officinalis*.

kestir=^{ir} كَسْدِرْمَك كَسْدِيرْمَك 1. /ı, a/ *caus.* of **kes**= 1 ¹⁻³. 2. /ı/ to guess, estimate, discern, perceive, clearly understand. 3. *mil.* to locate, find the place (of). 4. to have a nap. —**ip at**= /ı/ to settle offhand, settle once and for all. —**il**= *pass.* of **kestir**=.

kestirme كَسْدِرْمَه *verbal n.* of **kestir**=. — **aleti** artillery direction-finding apparatus. — **cevap** decisive or short answer. —**den git**= 1. to take a shortcut. 2. to speak or act directly. — **hattı** *mil.* datum line. — **istasyonu** bearing station. — **merkezi** artillery direction-finding station. — **noktası** guide mark, adjusting mark; benchmark. — **yol** shortcut.

keş 1 كَش 1. *slang* simpleton, idiot. 2. *prov.* dry sour curd; skim milk cheese. — **et**= /ı/ *slang* to bring to confusion, to shame. —**ten gel**= to remain indifferent, not to care.

-**keş 2** كَش P *lrnd.* who pulls, draws, drinks, bears, endures, suffers, smokes, *as in*, **afyonkeş, barkeş, cefakeş, dilkeş, peşkeş, serkeş**.

keşakeş (. —.) كَشَاكَش P *lrnd.* confusion, turmoil, struggle; conflict; uncertainty.

keşan 1 كَشَان [**Kâşan 2**] painted tile, Dutch tile.

-**keşan 2** (. —) كَشَان P *lrnd., pl. of* -**keş 2**. *as in* **mihnetkeşan**.

keşan 3 (. —) كَشَان P *lrnd.* drawing, dragging. — **ber keşan**, — **keşan** dragging along; all struggling, pulling and fighting.

keşef كَشَف P *lrnd.* tortoise; tortoise shell.

keşende كَشَنْدَه P *lrnd.* who or that pulls, attracts, bears, endures.

keşer=^{ir} كَشَرْمَك *prov.* 1. to fade (color of cloth). 2. to die.

keşf كَشْف A *same as* **keşif**.

keşfet=^{der} كَشْفَتْمَك /ı/ 1. to discover, explore. 2. to make an estimate of the cost, value, etc. (of), to examine and estimate cost, value, etc. 3. *mil.* to reconnoiter. 4. to guess, divine, find out. 5. to reveal, to bring to light.

keşfî (. —) كَشْفِي A *lrnd.* pertaining to discovery, estimation or reconnoitering.

keşfiyat (.. —) كَشْفِيَات A *lrnd.* discoveries.

keşide (. —.) كَشِيدَه P 1. drawing (lots, in a lottery; bill, check). 2. *lrnd.* pulled, drawn, traced, endured; drunk. 3. *Arabic calligraphy* lengthening line between two letters. — **et**= /ı/ 1. to draw (a bill, check, lot). 2. *lrnd.* to draw (line), give (feast), send (telegram). — **tarihi** date of drawing.

keşideci كَشِيدَه جِي drawer (one who issues an order or bill of exchange).

keşidekamet (... —.) كَشِيدَه قَامَت P *lrnd.* tall of stature.

keşif^{şfi} كَشِف [**keşf**] 1. discovery, exploration. 2. estimate, estimation (of cost, value, condition of things). 3. *mil.* reconnaissance, reconnoitering; a spotting. 4. guess, divination, a finding out. 5. revelation, a bringing to light. 6. *myst.* revelation of mysteries to a saint. — **ağı** *mil.* scouting net. — **arabası** *mil.* scout car. —**i avret** *lrnd.* indecent exposure. — **bedeli** estimated cost or value. — **birliği** *mil.* reconnaissance troop, reconnoitering party. — **defteri**, — **evrakı** estimates, reports on estimated cost. — **gemisi** scouting vessel. — **hizmeti** *mil.* reconnaissance duty. — **kıtası** same as **keşif birliği**. — **kolu** *mil.* reconnaissance column, patrol column. — **kuvveti** reconnaissance force. — **muharebesi** combat of reconnaissance forces. — **müfrezesi** same as **keşif kolu**. — **raporu** expert report, report of a survey or evaluation. — **subayı** spotting officer. — **şebekesi** *mil.*, same as **keşif ağı**. —**i taarruz** *lrnd., mil.* offensive reconnaissance. — **tayyaresi**, — **uçağı** *mil.* reconnaissance plane. —**ini yapma** *com.* valuation.

keşifname (.. —.) كَشِفْنَامَه P estimate of quantities and costs.

keşikᵍⁱ كشيك 1. *prov.* turn (of duty, work, etc.). 2. *archaic* guard, patrol.
keşikçi كشيكجى *archaic* sentinel.
keşikhane (..—.) كشيكخانه *archaic* guardhouse, police station.
keşir كشور *prov.* carrot.
keşiş كشيش [P .—] Christian priest; monk; hermit. **K— Dağı** Mount Olympus near Bursa (now Uludağ).
keşişhane (..—.) كشيشخانه monastery, cloister.
keşişleme كشيشلمه 1. southeast wind (as blowing from Keşiş Dağı to Istanbul). 2. southeast point of the compass. 3. sirocco. **—nin gün doğusundan yana kertesi, — kerte doğu** southeast by east. **— kerte kıble, —nin kıbleden yana kertesi** southeast by south. **— rüzgârı** southeast wind.
keşişlikᵍⁱ كشيشلك 1. monachism, monkhood; priesthood. 2. monastery.
keşke كاشكه [kâşki] I wish, *e. g.*, **— bilseydik** I wish we had known.
keşkekᵍⁱ كشكك P wheat boiled with meat. **—lik** pearled wheat for making **keşkek**.
keşki كاشكى same as **keşke**.
keşkül كشكول P 1. sweetened milk or custard with almonds and pistachio. 2. boat-shaped beggar's cup. **—i fukarâ, —fukara** same as **keşkül**¹.
keşle— كشلمك *slang* 1. /a/ to take no notice, to pay no attention to. 2. to become stupid; to be woolgathering.
keşmekeş كشمكش P *lrnd.* great confusion, disorder. **— içinde** in great disorder and confusion.
Keşmir (.—) كشمير *geog.* Kashmir. **— şalı** Cashmere shawl with a plain ground and palm motifs in the corners.
keşsavakᵍⁱ كشساواك *Arm slang* foolish scapegrace, rake.
keşşaf (.—) كشاف A 1. *lrnd.* explorer, discoverer, investigator. 2. scout. **—lık** *mil.* a scouting, reconnaissance.
keşti (.—) كشتى P *lrnd.* boat, ship, vessel. **—i bâde** drinking cup in the shape of a ship. **—i gam** *poet.* vessel of sorrow, *i. e.* the world. **K—i Nûh** Noah's ark. **—i zer** 1. boat-shaped goblet of gold. 2. crescent of the moon, new moon. 3. the sun.
keştiban (.——) كشتيبان P *lrnd.* boatman, seaman, sailor; captain; pilot. **—î** (.——) P seamanship.
keştigâh (.——) كشتيگاه P *lrnd.* seaport, anchorage.
keştiger (.—.) كشتيگر P *lrnd.* shipbuilder, boat builder.
keştinişin (.—.—) كشتى نشين P *lrnd.* seamen; on boardship. **—ân** (.—.——) P *pl.*

keştisaz (.——) كشتى ساز P *lrnd.* ship-builder, boatbuilder. **—î** (.———) P shipbuilding.
keştisüvar (.—.—) كشتى سوار P *lrnd.* embarked in a ship or boat. **— ol=** to go on board ship, to embark.
keştişikeste (.—...) كشتى شكسته P *lrnd.* shipwrecked.
ket 1 كت obstacle. **— vur=** /a/ to handicap, impede, hinder.
ket 2 كت starch.
ketaib (.—.) كتائب A *lrnd., pl. of* **ketibe**.
ketal كتال starched and glazed cotton or linen stuff.
ketb كتب A *lrnd.* a writing, composing. **— et=, — ü tahrir et=** /ı/ to write, compose, inscribe.
kete كته *prov.* cake of rice flour.
ketebe كتبه A *lrnd., pl. of* **kâtib. —i aklâm** chancery clerks.
ketebehu كتبه A *lrnd.* He wrote it (first word in a colophon to a manuscript).
keten كتن [kettan] 1. flax, *bot.*, *Linum usitatissimum*. 2. flax (fiber), flaxen, linen. **— bezi** linen cloth. **— elyafı** flax fibers. **— fırçası** flax comb. **— helva, — helvası** cotton candy. **—i hindî** *lrnd.* Indian hemp. **— ipliği** linen yarn, linen thread. **— kâğıdı** linen paper. **— kuşu** linnet, *zool.*, *Carduelis cannabina*. **— lifi** flax fiber. **— tarağı** hatchel. **— teli** gold or silver gilt thread for embroidery. **— tohumu** flax seed. **— tohumu lâpası** flax seed poultice. **— tohumu yağı** linseed oil. **— üstüpüsü** tow.
ketenci كتنجى 1. flax weaver, linen weaver. 2. seller of linen cloth.
ketencikᵍⁱ كتنجك grass wrack, *bot.*, *Zostera marina*.
kentencilikᵍⁱ كتنجيلك 1. linen weaving, flax spinning. 2. linen trade.
ketencigiller *neol.* flax family, *bot.*, *Linaceae*.
ketf كتف A *lrnd.* shoulder blade.
kethüda (..—) كتخدا P *lrnd.*, same as **kâhya. —yi bevvabân** *Ott. hist.* chief of the doorkeepers guarding the **Bâb-ı Hümayun** and the central door of the palace. **— bey** *Ott. hist.* office of the minister for Home Affairs. **—yi kassaban** *Ott. hist.* chief butcher of the Palace. **— kâtibi** *Ott. hist.* secretary to the **Kethüda bey. —yi Sadrı âli** *Ott. hist.*, same as **Kethüda bey. — yeri** *Ott. hist.* 1. colonel of the thirty-second regiment of Janissaries. 2. colonel of the local cavalary bodies **Sipahi** and **Silâhtar**.
kethüdalıkᵍⁱ كتخدالق office and rank of a **kethüda. — ağırlığı** money collected from the village people by village **kethüdas**.
ketibe (.—.) كتيبه A *lrnd.* army, military force. **—i beyza** military force with glittering

arms. —**perver** (. — . . .) P protector of the soldiers.

ketifᵗᶠⁱ كتف A same as **ketf**.

ketimᵗᵐⁱ كتم var. of **ketm**.

ketm كتم A lrnd. a hiding, concealing, keeping a secret. —**i adem** hidden world before the creation. —**et=** /ı/ to conceal, hide; to keep (secret).

ketrepetre كتره پتره P lrnd. nonsense, nonsensical talk.

kettan (. —) كتّان A lrnd., same as **keten**.

ketūm (. —) كتوم A discreet, reticent; keeping a secret. — **davran=** to behave discreetly, to keep silent. —**iyet**, —**luk** discretion.

kev كو P lrnd. wise; sage.

kevakib (. —.) كواكب A lrnd., pl. of **kevkeb**. —**i cariye** planets. —**i fırk** stars α, β, η, δ Cephei. —**i mersude** observed and tabulated stars. —**i muz'afa** double, multiple or clustered stars. —**i mütehayyire** planets. —**i sabite** fixed stars. —**i sahabiye** nebulous stars. —**i seyyare** planets. —**i ulviye** the planets Mars, Jupiter and Saturn.

kevakibşinas (. —..—) كواكب شناس P lrnd. astronomer; astrologer.

kevden كودن P lrnd. weak in mind, dull, stupid.

keveke كوكه prov. crisp, brittle.

kevel كول P lrnd. 1. cloak of sheepskin 2. jaded, spiritless horse.

keven كون prov. gum tragacanth.

kevgir كوگير [kefgir] skimmer, perforated ladle. — **taşı** stone sewer grating.

kevikᵍⁱ كويك prov. 1. wooden hook; hooked rod or stick. 2. husk; straw. —**lik** strawhouse, strawshed. —**sin=** /a/ to condescend (to), stoop (to).

kevkeb كوكب A lrnd. star; anything round and shining. —**i Samus** P Samian earth.

kevkebe كوكبه A lrnd. 1. star. 2. great concourse of attendants, crowd.

kevkebî (..—) كوكبى A lrnd. astral, starry.

kevken كوكن prov. hooked stick, rod.

kevn كون A lrnd. 1. existence; state, condition. 2. world. — **ü fesad** being and dissolution (of organisms); the world. — **ü mekân** the world and space; the universe.

kevneyn (. —) كونين A lrnd. the two worlds, corporeal and spiritual.

kevnî (. —) كونى A lrnd. cosmic.

kevniyat (..—) كونيات A lrnd. cosmology.

kevr كور A lrnd. 1. a wrapping around the head in a spiral form (turban). 2. plenty, increase, abundance. 3. large herd of camels.

kevser كوثر A 1. w. cap., name of a river in Paradise. 2. lrnd. Islam; prophecy of Islam. 3. lrnd. abundance, multitude. — **gibi** very tasteful. **K— Suresi** name of the one hundred and eighth sura of the Quran. — **şarabı** paradisical beverage.

key 1 كى P lrnd. What time? When?

key 2 كى P lrnd. 1. great king, sovereign. 2. w. cap., name or surname of the old legendary Persian monarchs.

keyʸʸⁱ **3** كى A lrnd. a marking with a brand; cauterizing.

keyabad (. — —) كياباد P lrnd. 1. royal residence, palace. 2. mystic regions of God's presence, knowledge and might.

keyan (. —) كيان P lrnd., pl. of **key 2**.

keyanî (. — —) كيانى P lrnd. royal; pertaining to the Persian Achemenian dynasty.

Keyaniyan (. —.—) كيانيان P lrnd. kings of the Persian Achemenian dynasty.

keyareng (. —.) كيارنگ P lrnd. pure, fair, white, clear.

keyd كيد A lrnd. stratagem, trick, fraud.

keydullah كيدالله A lrnd. God's catching a sinner in his misdeeds.

keyf كيف A same as **keyif**.

keyfe كيف A lrnd. How? In what manner?

keyfemâ (..—) كيفما lrnd. in whatever manner, in whatever way. —**ttefak** A at will, at pleasure. —**yeşa** (..—.—) A 1. as he pleases, as he wills. 2. arbitrarily, just anyhow.

keyfer كيفر P lrnd. retribution, reward or punishment.

keyfet=ᵈᵉʳ كيفتمك to amuse oneself; to enjoy oneself.

keyfî (. —) كيفى A 1. arbitrary, despotic. 2. lrnd. qualitative, modal. — **muamele** arbitrary proceeding, arbitrary treatment. — **olarak** arbitrarily. — **tahlil** qualitative analysis.

keyfiyet كيفيت A 1. matter, state of affairs, circumstance. 2. phil. modality, quality, 3. lrnd. mode, condition; intoxicating quality (in a drug). 4. Arabic gram. gender. —**i arıza** lrnd. accidental, temporary condition. —**i erbaa** phil. the four prime conditions (heat, cold, moisture, dryness). —**i hâl** lrnd. condition or circumstances. —**i istidadiye** lrnd. proneness to change. —**i mahsuse** lrnd. condition perceptible to the senses. —**i rasiha** lrnd. permanent condition. — **zarfı** gram. qualitative adverb.

keyfiyeten (../..) كيفيةً A lrnd. qualitatively.

Keyhusrev كيخسرو P name of a legendary king of Persia; a great monarch.

keyifʸᶠⁱ كيف [keyf] 1. pleasure, delight, joy, enjoyment, merriment. 2. disposition, humor, spirits. 3. health; bodily and mental condition. 4. arbitrariness, arbitrary action. 5. slight intoxication, state of being slightly drunk; hilarious, tipsy. —**ince** same as **keyfine göre**.

keyiflen=

— **benim, köy Mehmet Ağanın** It's my concern; no one else need interfere. **—ini boz=** 1. /ın/ to spoil one's joy. 2. to feel unwell. **—i bozuk** in low spirits, depressed. **—im böyle istiyor** It pleases me so; I want it so. **— çat=** to enjoy oneself. **—ini çıkar=** /ın/ to enjoy, to savor, to have a good time (of). **—i düzel=** /ın/ 1. to become good humored. 2. to recover from sickness. **—i gel=** /ın/ to feel in good humor, to become pleased. **—in gıcır mı?** *slang* Are you well? **—ine göre** at his pleasure. **— hâlinde** tipsy, slightly drunk. **—ine hizmet et=** /ın/ to follow fancies (of), to please servilely. **— için** for pleasure, for fun. **—in iyi mi?** Are you well? **—i iyi ol=** /ın/ to feel well. **—i kaç=** /ın/ to be out of humor, to be depressed, annoyed or vexed. **—ini kaçır=** /ın/ same as **keyfini boz=** ¹. **—imin kâhyası mısın?** Don't interfere in my affairs; it's none of your business. **—iniz nasıl?** How are you? **— ol=** to be tipsy, to become slightly drunk. **—i olma=** 1. not to feel well. 2. not to feel like, not to feel up to. **— sor=** to inquire about one's health. **— sür=** to have a pleasant and comfortable life; to enjoy pleasure. **— ver=** /a/ to intoxicate, to make tipsy. **—i yerinde** 1. in good spirits, in good humor. 2. in good health. **—i yerine gel=** same as **keyfi düzel=**. **— yetiştir=** to make oneself merry with drink.

keyiflen=ⁱʳ 1. to become gay or merry; to enjoy oneself. 2. to get drunk. **—dir=** /ı/ *caus.*

keyifli 1. merry, joyous, gay, in good humor. 2. tipsy.

keyifsiz 1. in bad humor. 2. indisposed, unwell, out of sorts. **—len=** to become indisposed or unwell. **—lik** indisposition; ailment.

keykirde 1 *archaic* excitement, anxiety, fear.

keykirde=ʳ **2** *archaic* to be excited, anxious; to fear.

Keykubad (..—) P *name of the first king of the legendary Key dynasty of ancient Persia; a great king.*

keyl A *lrnd.* 1. bushel. 2. a measuring with a bushel. **— et=** /ı/ to measure.

keyldar (.—) P *lrnd.* public measurer of grain, etc.; keeper of the standard grain measures.

keylî (.—) A *lrnd.* measurable with a bushel.

keylûs (.—) A *physiol.* chyle; half-digested food.

keymus (.—) A *physiol.* chyme.

keynunet (.—.) A *lrnd.* existence, a being.

keys A *lrnd.* shrewdness, intelligence.

Keysanî (.——) A *Isl. rel.* member of the Keysaniye sect. **—ye** (.——.) *name of a Muslim sect.*

Keyvan (.—) P *lrnd.* the planet Saturn.

keyvanı, keyvene, keyveni Kurd *prov.* 1. female cook (esp. at weddings). 2. organizer of picnics. 3. female housekeeper.

keyyalⁱⁱ (.—) A *lrnd.* public measurer. **—iye** (.——.) fee paid to the public measurer.

keyyis A *lrnd.* shrewd, intelligent.

kez *prov.* time, e. g., **bu kez** this time, **her kez** always, **üç kez** three times.

keza (.—) A also, likewise, in like manner, ditto. **— ve keza** *lrnd.* and so forth.

kezalik (.—.) A *lrnd.* also, likewise, in the same way.

kezbi *prov.* 1. a kind of black bug destroying melons, cucumbers, etc. 2. blight on melons and cucumbers caused by this insect.

kezekᵍⁱ *prov.* turn (of duties), allotted turn, stint.

kezle=ʳ *prov.* /ı/ to wait for an opportunity (to do).

kezm A *lrnd.* 1. a suppressing or controlling one's anger. 2. a stopping up, closing an outlet.

kezvi *prov.*, *var.* of **kezbi**.

kezzab (.—) A *lrnd.* habitual liar.

kezzapᵇⁱ [*Arabic* **kezzab**] hydrochloric acid.

-kı *cf.* **-gı 1.**

kıbab (.—) A *lrnd., pl.* of **kubbe.**

kıbal *prov.* shape, manner, style, attire, cut.

kıbale, kıbalet (.—.) A *lrnd.* midwifery.

kıbel A *lrnd.* part, side; presence. **—i şer'-i şeriften** on the part of the canonical law.

kıble A 1. direction of Mecca (to which a Muslim turns in worship). 2. south; south wind. 3. place or person towards which or whom everyone turns. **—i âlem** *lrnd.*, title assumed by Oriental sovereigns. **—ye dön=** to turn toward Mecca. **— gösteren** same as **kıblenüma. —i hacet** *lrnd.* person from whom aid is expected, one who supplies another's needs. **— keşişleme** south southeast. **—nin keşişlemeden yana kertesi** southeast by east. **— lodos** south southwest. **—nin lodostan yana kertesi** southwest. **— rüzgârı, — yeli** south wind.

kıblegâh (..—) P direction of Mecca; any place one faces during prayer. **—i hâcet** *lrnd., same as* **kıble-i hacet.**

kıblenâme (..—.) P *var.* of **kıblenüma.**

kıblenüma (...—) قبلهنما P 1. compass with the card so constructed as to show the direction of Mecca. 2. mariner's compass.

kıblerû (..—) قبلهرو P lrnd. one whose face is turned in the direction of Mecca.

kıbleteyn (..—) قبلتين A lrnd. the two **kıbles**, places or directions for worship, *i. e.*, Mecca and Jerusalem.

Kıbrıs قبرس *geog.* Cyprus. — **dokuması** Cyprus calico (with black hand-painting, used for bed coverings, etc.). — **elması**, — **taşı** diamond-cut rock crystal (of Cyprus). —**î** (..—) *lrnd.*, —**lı** of or from Cyprus, Cypriote.

kıcı 1 قجی *prov.* 1. snowflake; hoarfrost. 2. hailstone.

kıcı 2 قجی *archaic* any bitter pungent herb, as mustard, cress, etc.

kıcık 1 قیجیك *prov., var. of* **gıcık 2.**

kıcık 2 قیجیك *prov.* irritation, rage. —**ına git=** /ın/ to irritate, provoke. — **ver=** to act as a mischiefmaker. —**la=** /ı/ 1. to irritate, enrage. 2. to cause doubt or suspicion.

kıç قیچ 1. buttocks, bottom, butt, behind, rump. 2. *naut.* stern, poop. 3. *prov.* leg, foot. —**a** *naut.* astern, abaft, aft. — **altı kamarası** stern cabin. — **at=** 1. to lash out with both feet (horse). 2. *vulg.* to desire eagerly or passionately. — **attır=** /a/ *slang* to get the better (of someone). — **ayak** hind foot. — **aynalık levhası** *naut.* sternplate. — **aynalık tahtası** *naut.* backboard. — **bacak** hind leg. — **bayrağı** stern flag. — **bodoslaması** *naut.* sternpost. — **dikmesi** *naut.* dog shore. —**a düş=** *naut.* to drop astern. — **feneri** stern lamp, poop lantern (of a ship). — **güverte** quarterdeck. — **halatı** stern fast. — **ıskarmozu** fashion piece (of a ship). —**ını kaldırma=** *colloq.* not to budge. —**tan kara** moored by the stern. — **kasarası** poop deck. —**ının kılı ağar=** *slang* to become old (said in contempt). —**ının kılları ile balık yakala=** *slang* to be very fortunate. —**ı kırık** *slang* of no importance. — **kısmı** afterbody (of a ship). — **koltuğu** stern hawser, poop hawser, checkrope. — **küpeştesi** taffrail. — **omuzluğu** stern quarter. — **palamarı** sternfast. — **postaları** stern frames. — **serp=** *archaic,* same as **kıç at=**. — **taraf** quarterdeck. —**ına tekmeyi at=** *joc.* to drive away, to kick out. — **topu** sternchaser; *aero.* rear gun, afterguhn. — **üstü otur=** *colloq.* to remain helpless. — **yelkeni** after sail. —**ını yırt=** *vulg.* to cry and shout excitedly.

kıçın kıçın قیچین قیچین backwards; astern. — **git=** to go more and more backward; to have sternway (ship).

kıdem قدم A 1. seniority, priority of service; precedence. 2. *lrnd.* antiquity; eternal existence in the past. —**e göre** by seniority, according to the length of service.

kıdemce (.'.) قدمجه same as **kıdeme göre**.

kıdemen (.'.) قدماً A *lrnd.* by seniority.

kıdemî (..—) قدمی A *lrnd.* pertaining to seniority, etc. —**yet** (..—.) A priority, precedence; eternity in the past.

kıdemli قدملی senior in service.

kıdemsiz قدمسز junior (in service). —**lik** junior status, shortness of service.

kıdık 1 قدیك *prov., var. of* **gıdık 1.**

kıdık 2 قدیك *prov.* small basket.

kıdıkla= قدیقلهمق same as **gıdıkla=**.

kıdve, kıdvet قدوه قدوت A *lrnd.* example, model, person or thing imitated; leader, chief.

kıdvetülebrar (....—) قدوة الابرار A *lrnd.* example of equity, type of good men or saints.

kıf قیف *archaic* cup, goblet.

kıfar (.—) قفار A *lrnd., pl. of* **kafr.**

kıfı قفی *prov.* good spirits, good humor; joke.

kıft قفت *archaic* near, associated; comrade. — **et=** /ı/ to encourage, stimulate.

kığ, kığı قیغ قیغی *prov.* dung of sheep, goat, rabbit, camel, etc. in pellets.

kığılcım قیغیلجم same as **kıvılcım**.

kığır= قیغیرمق *archaic* /ı/ to invite, call.

kığırdan= قیغیردانمق *archaic* to howl or whine continuously (dog).

kığırıcı قیغیرجی *archaic* public crier.

kığış= قیغیشمق *archaic* to rattle or clash together. —**tı** rustling, rattling sound.

kığla= قیغلامق *prov.* to dung in roundish pellets.

kıh ? *child language* dirty, bad.

kıhf, kıhıf قحف A *lrnd.* skull. —**î** (.—) A cranial. —**iyat** (.——) phrenology.

kık قیق *archaic* dry, dried up.

kıkır قیقیر thin, dry, hard, rattling. — **kıkır** giggling. — **kıkır gül=** to giggle, chuckle. — **poğaca** cake made with mutton drippings and pieces of crackling.

kıkırda= قیقیردامق 1. *slang* to die (said in contempt). 2. to rustle, rattle or crackle (from thinness and dryness).

kıkırdak قیقیرداق 1. cartilage, gristle; *sc.* chondrus. 2. greaves, crackling. — **bilgisi** chondrology. — **doku** *anat.* cartilaginous tissue, gristly tissue. — **halka** *anat.* cartilaginous ring. — **poğaçası** pastry prepared with cracklings. — **tutkalı** chondrin. — **zarı** *anat.* perichondrium.

kıkırdaklı قیقیرداقلی cartilaginous, gristly. — **balıklar** cartilaginous fishes, sharks and reys, *zool.,* Elasmobranchii.

kıkırdan= قیقیردانمق to rustle, rattle, crackle.

kıkırdat= قیقیرداتمق /ı/ *caus. of* **kıkırda=**.

kıkırtı قیقیردی giggling; snicker.

kıl 1 قبيل 1. hair, bristle (of swine, etc.); made of hair, bristle. 2. a hair's breadth. 3. *archaic* string (of a musical instrument). — **barak** 1. Shetland pony (bred in Turkey). 2. *prov.* long-haired dog. —**ına bile dokunulmaz** a hair of whose head must not be touched, sacrosanct. — **biti** crab louse, *zool.*, *Phthirius pubis*. — **burun** narrow neck of land. — **çadır** haircloth tent. — **çek=** *slang* to flatter, to sponge. — **çuval** haircloth sack. — **damar** *anat.* capillary vessel. —**ını dök=** to shed its hair. — **fırça** brush of bristles. — **gibi** thin as a hair. — **gömlek** hairshirt. — **kadar** the smallest quantity, the slightest degree. — **kaldı** /a/ It was within a hair's-breadth of... *e. g.*, — **kaldı· boğulacaktı** He nearly drowned. — **kalem** miniature-painter's brush made of one hair. —**dan kıla** *archaic* minutely, thoroughly. —**ını kıpırdatmadan** without turning a hair. — **kıran***. —**ı kırk yar=** to split hairs. —**ı kırk yaran** hairsplitter, too meticulous. —**ı kırk yarma** hairsplitting, subtlety. — **kumaş** haircloth. — **kuyruk***. —**ını oynatmadan** *same as* **kılını kıpırdatmadan**. — **şaşmadan** with scrupulous care. — **testere** fretsaw, scrollsaw.

kıl=ar 2 تخليو 1. /ı/ to render, make, as in, **mümkün kıl=**. 2. to perform, as in, **namaz kıl=**.

kılâa¹ (. —) قدم A *lrnd.*, pl. of **kal'a 3**. — **u bıka** castles and buildings, *e. g.*, the whole territory.

kılâa (. —.) قلاع A *lrnd.* sail.

kılâde (. —.) قلاده A *lrnd.* necklace.

kılağı قيلاغى قلاغى burr from whetting; wire-edge. —**sını al=** /ın/, —**la=** /ı/ to give a fine edge to a cutting instrument (by removing the **kılağı**). —**lı** very sharp, keen. —**sız** blunt, dull.

kılağuz قلاغوز قولاغوز قيلاغوز *same as* **kılavuz**.

kılaptan قلابدان gilt copper wire or thread, gold wire wound on silk, trimming of imitation gold thread. — **işi** imitation gold embroidery. — **işleme** worked with imitation gold thread. — **şerit** imitation gold lace braid. — **tel** gilt thread (for embroidery). —**cı** maker or seller of imitation gold thread or lace. —**lı** worked or trimmed with imitation gold thread.

kılav قيلاو a disease of sheep causing foaming of the mouth; staggers (in beasts).

kılavuz قلاوز قلاووز قيلاغوز 1. guide, leader. 2. *naut.* pilot. 3. go-between (in arranging a marriage). 4. *tech.* gimlet; screw-tap. 5. *mining* adit, gallery. — **aç=** /a/ to open a screw thread (into). — **burgu** slender, long gimlet point of an auger. — **çavuş** *Ott. hist.* 1. herald leading in the imperial procession. 2. bugleman in military exercises. — **dingil** leading axle. — **filâması** *naut.* pilot flag. — **halatı** *naut.* leading rope, guide rope. —**u karga olanın burnu boktan kurtulmaz** (*lit.* He who takes a crow for his guide will never have his nose far from dung.) If you take bad advice you will regret it. — **kol** *tech.* conductor rod. — **lokomotif** pilot engine. — **makara** *tech.* guide pulley. — **mihver** *same as* **kılavuz dingil**. — **resmi** *same as* **kılavuz ücreti**. — **sandalı** *naut.* pilot boat. — **suları** *naut.* pilot waters, pilot's fairway. — **tel** leading wire, guide wire. — **ücreti** pilotage, pilotage fee. — **yamağı** *Ott. hist.* guide who leads imperial processions.

kılavuzla=ʳ قيلاوزلامق /ı/ 1. to lead, guide, conduct, pilot. 2. to open a thread (screw).

kılavuzlu قيلاوزلى *tech.* threaded.

kılavuzluk^gu قيلاوزلوق pilotage, a piloting. — **et=** to act as a guide, pilot, go-between, etc.

kılavuzsuz قيلاوزسز 1. without a pilot. 2. *tech.* not threaded, without threads.

kılbaz (. —) قلباز *slang* flatterer, coaxer; cringer.

kılcal *neol.*, *phys.* capillary. — **boru** *phys.* capillary tube. — **damar** *anat.* capillary, capillary vessel. —**lık** capillarity; *phys.* capillarity, capillary action.

kılçık^gi قيلچق 1. fishbone, fishspine. 2. *bot.* awn (of wheat, barley). 3. string (of beans). — **at=** *wrestling* to shake oneself free and throw off the opponent. —**ını çıkar=** /ın/ 1. to bone (a fish). 2. to string (beans). —**lı** 1. bony (fish). 2. *bot.* awned. 3. stringy (beans). 4. beset with difficulties.

kılçıksız قيلچقسز 1. without bones or spines (fish). 2. awnless. — **arpa** awnless or beardless barley. — **buğday** spelt, *bot.*, *Triticum spelta*.

kıldır=ʳ قيلديرمق /ı/ *caus.* of **kıl= 2**. —**ıl=** *pass.*

kılefte, kılefteci قلفته جى قلفته Gk *slang* thief.

kılgı *neol.* practice, exercise, act. —**la=** /ı/ to practice. —**lı** practical.

kılıbık^gi قيليبيق henpecked husband. —**lık** condition of a henpecked husband, submission to one's wife.

kılıç^ci قيليچ قليچ قلج 1. sword; saber. 2. swordfish. 3. coulter of a plow. 4. *arch.* brace. 5. a card game played with fifty-two cards. 6. *Ott. hist.* yeoman's fief of the yearly value of three thousand aspers. —**ına** edgewise, on edge. — **ağzı** edge of a sword. — **alayı** *Ott. hist.* Sultan's procession, after accession, to gird on the sword of sovereignty. — **artığı** survivors of a lost battle. — **askısı** baldric. — **at=** to deal out sword-cuts; to slaughter indiscriminately. — **atla=** *Ott. hist.* to jump over a sword placed on the ground, as a kind of oath upon undertaking a dangerous enterprise. — **bacak** bandylegged, bowlegged; bandy legs. — **bağı** sword belt. — **balığı** swordfish, zool., *Xiphias gladius*. — **balığıgiller** the swordfishes, zool., *Xiphiidae*. — **çal=** /a/ to deal blows with a sword. — **çat=** mil. to stack swords. — **çatısı** mil. stack of swords. — **çek=** to draw or unsheathe the sword. — **darbesi** sword cut, saber cut. —**a dayan=** 1. to lean on a sword. 2. to throw oneself on to the point of a sword. — **demiri** sword blade. — **düellosu** duel with swords. — **dürt=** /a/ to stab with a sword. — **eri** good swordsman. —**tan geç=** to be put to the sword. —**tan geçir=** /ı/ to put to the sword. — **gagalı** avocet, zool., *Recurvirostra avocetta*. — **hakkı olarak** by right of conquest. — **hamayili** baldric. — **kabzası** hilt of a sword. — **kabza korkuluğu** basket hilt. — **kaftan gönder=** Ott. hist. to send a saber and robe of honor to a chieftain who is to be conciliated. — **kalkan oyunu** a Turkish folk dance performed with shield and sword. — **kaşı** guard of a sword. — **kayışı** sword or saber belt. — **kesesi** saber scabbard. — **kını** saber sheath, scabbard. —**ı kınına koy=** to put the sword into the scabbard, to sheathe a sword; to cease fighting. —**ını kır=** mil. to quit the service. — **kırlangıcı** swift, zool.!, *Apus apus*. — **kırlangıçları** swifts, zool., *Apodidae*. —**ına koy=** /ı/ to set on edge, edgewise (stones, timbers). — **kösteği** guard cord of a sword. — **kuşağı** sword belt worn around the waist. — **kuşan=** to gird on a sword. — **kuyruk** swordtail, zool., *Xiphophorus*. — **otu** prov. 1. yellow centaury. 2. common tutsan. — **oynat=** /da/ to dominate over, to predominate. — **oyunu** 1. sword dance. 2. sword game. — **pabucu** ferrule of a scabbard. — **püskülü** sword knot. — **savur=** to brandish the sword. — **siperliği** basket hilt. — **süngü** bayonet. — **tak=** 1. same as **kılıç kuşan=**. 2. /a/ to gird on a sword (to). — **talimi** sword drill. — **üşür=** /a/ archaic to charge with swords. — **vur=** to deal out blows with a sword. — **yarası** sword-cut. — **yürüt=** /a/ archaic to put to the sword.

kılıççı 1. sword seller. 2. clever swordsman.

kılıçhane sword factory.

kılıçla=ʳ /ı/ archaic, same as **kılıçtan geçir=**.

kılıçlama edgewise, set on edge; slung from the shoulder, crosswise. — **kaç=** 1. to warp edgeways (plank). 2. to swerve in running away. —**sına koy=** /ı/ to put edgewise.

kılıçlı armed with a sword, wearing a sword. — **bağlama** arch. wall tie.

kılıf [gılâf] 1. case, cover. 2. anat., zool. tunic; biol. sheath. —**lı** having a case, cover, tunic, sheath.

kılıkᵍⁱ 1. outward form, shape; appearance, aspect; phil. form. 2. dress, costume. 3. prov. portrait, picture. 4. archaic behavior, attitude. — **çek=**, — **çıkar=** prov. to draw or paint a likeness. — **değiştir=** to change form or costume. — **kıyafet** external appearance, dress, attire. — **kıyafet düşkünü** wearing worn or shabby clothes. — **kıyafet köpeklere ziyafet** in a most shabby condition, wretched, miserable.

kılıkçı prov. photographer.

kılıklandır=ⁱʳ neol. /ı/ to imagine.

kılıklı 1. well shaped, well dressed. 2. having such and such an appearance or dress, e. g., **dilenci kılıklı bir adam** a man looking like a beggar. 3. prov. beautiful, handsome. — **kıyafetli** well dressed.

kılıksız ill dressed, shabby looking, untidy. —**lık** untidiness, bad condition.

kılın=ⁱʳ 1. pass. of **kıl=** 2. 2. prov. /a/ to intend (to do). 3. /a/ prov. to cringe, flatter.

kılınçᶜⁱ 1 archaic 1. character, temper; behavior. 2. a cringing, flattering. — **et=**, — **eyle=** /a/ to cringe, flatter.

kılınçᶜⁱ 2 same as **kılıç**.

kılır prov. caltrop (plant). — **otu** same as **kılır**.

kılkıl A prov. small jug.

kılkıran baldness, alopecia.

kılkuyrukᵍᵘ 1. unstable and untrustworthy person; joc. wretched and very poor fellow. 2. pintail duck; zool., *Anas acuta*.

kılla [kulle] prov. money box.

kıllama prov. tasseled girdle.

kıllan=ⁱʳ to become hairy; to begin to show a beard.

kıllav prov. a cringing, flattering. — **et=** to cringe, flatter.

kıllet A lrnd. littleness, fewness, paucity. —**i fehm** stupidity. —**i matar** scarcity of rain. —**i mübalât** lack of consideration, insufficient attention.

kıllı 1. hairy, bristly; shaggy. 2. prov. the one who is it in children's games. — **bebek** one who behaves in a manner unsuitable to his age.

kıllıkᵍⁱ prov., same as **kıllı**². —**çı** trickster, cheater.

kılma verbal n. of **kıl=** ².

kılsız hairless, beardless, without bristles.

kılu archaic creation.

kılur=ᵘʳ archaic, caus. of **kıl=** 2.

kımıl قيميل [kaml] *prov.* an insect pest of cereals, *zool.*, *Aelia rostrata*.
kımılda=ᵉ قيميلدامق to move slightly, to stir, to be in slight motion or agitation.
kımıldan=ᵉʳ قيميلدانمق *same as* **kımılda=**. —**ma** slight motion, movement, agitation.
kımıldat=ᵉʳ قيميلدتمق /ı/ to cause to move, to agitate, shake.
kımıl kımıl قيميل قيميل wiggling, fidgety.
kımıltı قيميلدى motion, movement, agitation.
kımırt kımırt قيميرت قيميرت *prov.* little by little, slowly.
kımış=ᵉʳ قيميشمق *prov.* to fidget.
kımız قيميز koumis, kumiss (fermented mare's milk).
kımkım قيم قيم *prov.* slow, acting or moving without haste or rapidity.
kımlan=ᵉʳ قيملنمق *archaic* to prepare to fly (bird), to make a motion as if to rise.
kımra=ᵉʳ, **kımraş=**ᵉʳ قيمراشمق *prov.*, *same as* **kımılda=**, **kımıldan=**.
kın 1 قين 1. sheath, scabbard. 2. *bot.* ocrea. —**ından çıkar=** /ı/ to unsheathe. — **geçir=** /a/ to fit with a sheath or scabbard. —**ına koy=** /ı/ to sheath. — **tak=** /a/ *same as* **kın geçir=**.
kın 2 قين *archaic* torment, pain, torture.
kınⁿⁿⁱ **3** قن A *can. law* slave born in the family, whose father and mother are slaves.
kına 1 قنا قينا قد [hınna] 1. henna. 2. the henna plant, *bot.*, *Lawsonia inermis*. — **ağacı** henna, henna tree. — **basma**, — **basması** *prov.*, *same as* **kına gecesi**. —**ya çık=** *prov.* to go to the room of the guests at the **kına gecesi** (the bride). — **çiçeği** balsam, *bot.*, *Impatiens balsamina*. — **çiçeğigiller** *neol.*, *bot.*, *Balsaminaceae*. — **düğünü** *prov.*, *same as* **kına gecesi**. — **ezme**, — **ezmesi** *prov.* ceremony held in the family after the guests of the **kına gecesi** have left. — **gecesi** night next before the wedding day, a women's entertainment when the bride is taken to the public bath and has her fingers and toes freshly tinged with henna. — **gibi** very fine (powder). — **keklik** red legged partridge, *zool.*, *Alectoris rufa*. — **koy=**, — **sür=**, — **vur=**, — **yak=** /a/ to apply henna (to), to tinge with henna. —**lar yak=** /a/ to be in great joy, to be highly pleased or delighted (at). — **yakın=** to tinge oneself with henna.
kına=ʳ **2** قيناموق /ı/ 1. to blame, reproach. 2. *archaic* to punish.
kınaᵃⁿⁱ **3** (.—) قناع A *lrnd.* woman's kerchief or hood, yashmak, veil.
kınacık قيناجيق rust of plants, *bot.*, *Puccinia graminis*.
kınakᵍⁱ **1** قيناق قنايه *archaic* 1. claw, talon. 2. finger joint.

kınakᵍⁱ **2** قناع *prov.* shame.
kınakına قينه قينه قناقنا Sp Peruvian bark, Cinchona bark, *chem.* quinquina. — **ağacı** Cinchona tree. — **çiçeği**, — **sulfatosu** *chem.* quinine sulfate.
kınala=ʳ قيناله‌مق /ı/ to tinge or treat with henna.
kınalı قينالى 1. tinged with henna; mixed or prepared with henna. 2. golden red (hair). — **keklik** rock partridge, *zool.*, *Alectoris graeca*. — **yapıncak** golden red grapes.
kınamsı=ʳ قناميسمق /ı/ to find fault with everything.
kınamsıkᵍⁱ قناميسق hypercritical, sarcastic.
kınan=ᵉʳ قنانمق *pass. of* **kına=** 2.
kınat=ᵉʳ قناتمق /ı, a/ *caus. of* **kına=** 2.
kındır=ᵉʳ قنديرمق *archaic* /ı/ 1. to provoke, to irritate. 2. to egg on to some act, to encourage.
kındıra قنديره *prov.* small reed, rush.
kındıraçᶜⁱ قنديراج spokeshave.
kındırıkᵍⁱ قنديريق *prov.* 1. dwarf, squat. 2. ajar (door).
kınık=ᵉʳ **1** قنيقمق *archaic* to feel appetite; to desire ardently.
kınıkᵍⁱ **2** قنيق *prov.* 1. desire, wish. 2. greedy, gluttonous.
kınkanatlılar *neol.* beetles, *zool.*, *Coleoptera*.
kınla=ʳ قينلامق /ı/ to sheathe (sword).
kınnapᵇⁱ قنّاب [*Arabic* **kınnab**] string, twine.
kınnare (.—.) قنّاره A *lrnd.* slaughterhouse.
kıntıma قينتيمه *prov.* 1. food. 2. fresh spring grass.
kıntıraçᶜⁱ قينطراج *var. of* **kındıraç**.
kıp=ᵃʳ قيپمق /ı/ to wink, blink (eye).
Kıpçakᵍⁱ قپجاق Kipchak (a Turkish tribe occupying the region north of the Caspian in the Middle Ages).
kıpıkᵍⁱ قيپيق partly closed (eyes); winking; blinking. — **gözlü** winking, blinking, having partly closed eyes. —**lık** *path.* ptosis.
kıpıl=ᵉʳ قيپيلمق *pass. of* **kıp=**.
kıpır=ᵉʳ قيپيرمق to wink (the eyes).
kıpırda=ᵉʳ قيپيرداموق to move slightly and quickly, to stir.
kıpırdakᵍⁱ قيپيرداق quivering, restless.
kıpırdan=ᵉʳ قيپيردانمق to keep on moving or quivering of itself.
kıpırdat=ᵉʳ قيپيرداتمق *caus. of* **kıpırda=**.
kıpır kıpır قيپير قيپير wiggling, fidgeting. — **kayna=** to bubble; to boil. — **oyna=** to keep fidgeting.
kıpırtı قيپيردى slight and quick movement, a stirring.
kıpıt=ᵉʳ قيپيتمق *caus. of* **kıp=**.
kıpkırmızı قيپقرمزى quite red, very red bright red.

kıpkızıl قِپْقِزِل 1. scarlet, glaring red. 2. ardent communist.

kıpma قِپْمَه a winking, blinking (of the eye).

Kıpt قِپْط A Copt. **—ça** (.'.) 1. the Coptic language. 2. in Coptic; Coptic.

Kıptî (.—) قِپْطى 1. Copt, Coptic. 2. Gypsy. **—ce** (.—.) 1. Coptic language; in Coptic. 2. the Romany language; in Romany.

kır 1 قِر countryside, uncultivated land. **— balosu** open air ball. **— bekçisi** field watchman. **— çiçeği** field flower, wild flower. **—da gez=** to lead a nomad life. **— incir kuşu** tawny pipit, zool., Anthus campestris. **— kırlangıcı** barn swallow, zool., Hirundo rustica. **— koşusu** crosscountry race. **— kurdu** coyote, zool.; Canis latrans. **— romanı** pastoral novel. **— sansarı** polecat, zool., Mustela putorius. **— serdarı** obs. chief of rural police. **— sıçanı** field vole, zool., Microtus arvalis.

kır 2 قِر grey; greyness. **— at** grey horse. **— donlu** having a grey coat (horse). **— döküm demiri** grey pig iron. **— düş=** /a/ to turn grey. **— kişi** archaic grey haired man. **— madde** anat. grey matter, substantia grisea. **— saçlı** grey haired. **— sakal** greybeard, veteran. **— sakallı** grey bearded.

kır=ᵃʳ **3** قِرْمَق 1. /ı/ to break; split (wood); to rough-grind (corn), to crush, bruise (grain). 2. /ı/ to hurt, offend, injure (feelings, etc.), to break (heart). 3. /ı/ to break the back (of); to break up. 4. /ı/ to kill, destroy in large numbers; to decimate. 5. /ı/ to mitigate, abate, break (severity of cold, etc.). e. g., **lodos soğuğu kırdı** The southwest wind broke the cold spell; to reduce, lower (price); to buy at a discount (bill, etc.). 6. /ı/ auto. to throw the wheel over; naut. to put the helm down, as in **direksiyonu kır=, dümeni kır=**. 7. /ı/ to fold, crease; pleat, kilt. 8. /ı/ to make a large gain, to do great business. 9. colloq. to take to one's heels, to make off, to clear out. **—ıp dök=** /ı/ to destroy. **kır dümeni** colloq. Go away. Be off with you. **—ıp geçir=** /ı/ to tyrannize; to destroy. **—an kırana** wrestling with full force, as in **kıran kırana güreştiler, kıran kırana savaştılar** They fought with all their might. **—dığı kozlar kırkı aş=** to make many gross blunders.

kıraatᵗⁱ قِرَاءَت A 1. a reading; reading lesson. 2. special method of pronouncing each word of the Quran. **— et=** /ı/ 1. to read. 2. to recite artistically and solemnly (the Quran). **— ilmi** science of reciting the Quran. **— kitabı** reading book, reader.

kıraathane (...—.) قِرَاءَتْخَانَه P public reading room; coffee house where newspapers are kept.

kırab (.—) قِرَاب A lrnd. scabbard of a sword.

kıracakᵗⁱ قِرَاجَق nutcrackers.

kıraçᶜⁱ قِرَاچ unfit for cultivation (land), left fallow.

kırağı قِرَاغى قِرَاغى hoarfrost, rime. **— çal=** to become frostbitten, to be injured by frost. **— düş=** to have a frost. **—lı** covered with hoarfrost, rimy.

kırakᵗⁱ قِرَاق prov. edge, border, side; shore.

kıral قِرَال Sl king. **— gibi** majestically; kinglike. **— hânedanı** royal dynasty. **— ilân et=** /ı/ to proclaim king. **— katili** regicide (person). **— katli** regicide (act). **— naibi** regent. **— taraftarı** royalist. **—dan ziyade kıral taraftarı ol=** to be more royalist than the king. **—cı** royalist. **—cılık** royalism.

kıraliçe (...'.) قِرَالِيچَه Sl queen.

kıralî (.——) قِرَالى lrnd. royal, kingly.

kıraliyet (.——.), **kırallık**ᵗⁱ قِرَالِيَت kingdom, realm, royalty. **— sarayı** royal palace. **— tacı** royal crown, king's crown. **— unvanı** royal title.

kıran 1 قِرَان 1. who breaks, kills, cuts; breaking, destroying. 2. murrain. **— gir=** /a/ 1. to be struck by an epidemic. 2. to vanish as though stricken by a plague.

kıran 2 قِرَان prov. 1. same as **kırak**. 2. horizon. 3. treeless bare top of a mountain; hillside, slope.

kıran 3 (.—) قِرَان A lrnd. 1. conjunction of planets. 2. a joining oneself to another as a companion; company. 3. a performing under one vow and at the same time the rites of the greater and of the lesser pilgrimage at Mecca. **—ı nahseyn** conjunction of the two malignant planets Saturn and Mars. **—ı sa'deyn** conjunction of the two beneficent planets, Venus and Jupiter.

kıranta (.'..) قِرَانْتَه It man whose hair, mustache or beard is beginning to turn grey; grey-haired, grizzled. **— bıyık** grey mustache.

kırat قِرَاط A 1. carat. 2. quality, value, character. **—ı örfî** lrnd. traditional carat (weight of four or five equal barley grains). **—ı şer'î** lrnd. canonical carat. **—lık** of ... carats.

kırba قِرْبَه A 1. waterskin, leather water bag or water bottle; leather milk bag. 2. rickets or potbelly, rachitis. 3. wine-bibber. **— ol=** to be rickety or potbellied (child). **—cı** 1. maker or seller of water skins. 2. man who cures rickets by incantation. **—cık** anat. utricle, utriculus.

kırbaçᶜⁱ قِرْبَاچ whip, scourge; riding whip, horsewhip. **— darbesi** blow of a whip, lash. **— değneği** whip handle. **— ipi** whipcord, lash (of a whip). **— kayışı** thong of a whip.

kırbaçla=

— **kurdu** whip worm, a parasitic worm of the genus *Trichocephalus*. — **sapı** *same as* **kırbaç değneği**. —**ı şaklat=** to crack the whip. — **vur=** /a/ to strike with a whip. — **ye=** to be whipped, flogged, lashed, scourged.

kırbaçla=ᴵʳ قرباجلامق /ı/ to whip, flog, lash, scourge. —**n=** *pass.*

kırbaviyüşşekl قرباویاشکل A *lrnd., zool.,* Asciviacea.

kırcaş=ᴵʳ قرجاشمق *archaic* to crowd together.

kırcı قرجی *prov.* icy snow; small grained hail.

kırcılda=ᴵʳ قرجيلدامق *archaic, same as* **gıcırda=**.

kırcın قرجين murrain among cattle, epizooty.

kırç 1 قرج *prov.* icy snow.

kırç=ᵃʳ 2 قرجمق *prov.* to cut off at a single stroke or blow; to break off.

kırçal قرجال *prov.* grey-haired (man, animal).

kırçan 1 قرجان *prov.* hoarfrost, white frost, rime; windy rain.

kırçan 2 قرجان *prov., same as* **kırcın**. —**lan=** to be seized with murrain.

kırçıl قرجيل 1. mixed or sprinkled with grey. 2. *prov.* hoary, old person.

kırçıla (..'.) قرجيله [**gırcıla**] *naut.* houseline, marline.

kırçıllan=ᴵʳ قرجيللانمق to become sprinkled with grey; to become hoary.

kırçoz قرجوز *slang* whose hair is beginning to turn grey, grizzled.

kırçozlaş=ᴵʳ قرجوزلاشمق to begin to turn grey (hair).

kırd قرد A *lrnd.* monkey. —**e** A female monkey; she-ape.

kırdır=ᴵʳ قيردرمه /ı, a/ *caus. of* **kır=** 3 ¹⁻⁴, ⁷⁻⁸.

kırede قرده A *lrnd., pl. of* **kırd**.

kırf قرف A 1. *prov.* ear of wheat. 2. *prov.* bread crust. 3. *lrnd.* rind, peel. —**ı cerf et=** /ı/ *prov.* to destroy.

kırfacan قرفاجان *prov.* in distress.

kırgı 1 قرغی *prov.* waste stony land; treeless places on the slope of a hill.

kırgı 2 قرغی *prov.* 1. falcon. 2. sparrow hawk.

kırgıl قرغيل *archaic* grizzled, grey-haired.

kırgım قرغم *prov.* wedding present given to a bride.

kırgın قرغين 1. disappointed; hurt, offended, resentful, broken. 2. *prov.* murrain. 3. *archaic* massacre; plague. —**lık** 1. disappointment; offense, resentment. 2. physical weariness.

Kırgız قرغيز Kirghiz (Cossacks). — **bozkırı** the Kirghiz Steppe.

kırıkᵏ¹ قريق 1. broken, cracked, fractured; *phys.* refracted; indisposed. 2. break, crack; fracture; fragment, splinter. 3. coarsely ground cereals. 4. of mixed race. 5. *slang* boy; *prov.* lover. 6. *prov.* clearing cultivated as a field (in a forest). — **al=** to get a failing grade. — **bul=** *prov.* to find faulty. — **çizgi** broken line. — **çoğul** *neol., gram.* broken plural. — **dökük** 1. in pieces, smashed; down. 2. odds and ends of; metal, scrap, etc. 3. broken (English, etc.). — **döl**, — **dölü** *prov.* bastard. — **düzen** disorderly, untidy. — **ışın** *phys.* refracted ray. — **not**, — **numara** bad mark (in school). — **renkler** broken colors. — **sar=** to set and bind up a broken bone. — **tahtası** splint (to immobilize a fractured bone). — **ver=** to give a bad mark.

kırıkçı قيريقجی bonesetter. —**lık** bonesetting (as a profession).

kırıklıkᵏ¹ قيريقلق indisposition; a being out of sorts.

kırıl=ᴵʳ قيريلمق قيريلمق 1. *pass. of* **kır=** 3. 2. /a/ to be hurt, offended by someone. —**an cevizler bini geçti** (*lit.* The broken walnuts are more than a thousand.) Your faults are past endurance. —**abilir** breakable.

kırılır قيريلير fragile, brittle, breakable.

kırılma قرلمه 1. *verbal n. of* **kırıl=**. 2. breaking, break; *phys., optics* refraction; refracting. 3. coquetry. — **düzeyi** *optics* plane of refraction. — **haddi** breaking point. — **indeksi**, — **indisi** index of refraction. — **kıvılcımı** break-spark. — **mukavemeti haddi** breaking point. — **ölçer** refractometer. — **payı** *com.* breakage. — **yeri** point of fracture.

kırım 1 قيريم 1. slaughter, carnage. 2. fold, pleat. 3. *prov.* discount. — **kırım kırıt=** to make excessively coquettish gestures.

Kırım 2 قريم *geog.* Crimea. — **eyeri** Tatar saddle. —**lı** Crimean.

kırımsa قرمسه *prov.* hail.

kırın=ᴵʳ قيرنمق *same as* **kırıt=**.

kırınım *neol., phys.* diffraction.

kırıntı قيرندی 1. fragment; crumb. 2. *prov.* dried fruits eaten as tidbits. 3. *slang* small pieces of hashish. — **külte** *neol., geol.* detrital rock. —**lı** crumby, crumbled.

kırış=ᴵʳ 1 قريشمق 1. to become wrinkled. 2. to kill or destroy one another. 3. *prov.* to bet, wager. 4. *prov.* to be haughty, to assume airs; to romp. 5. *prov.* to butt.

kırış 2 قريش 1. *verbal n. of* **kır=** 3. 2. *archaic* battle. — **kopar=** *prov.* to make a clamor, noise, etc. — **tut=** *prov.* 1. to sulk, pout. 2. to be obstinate.

kırıştır=ᴵʳ قيريشديرمق 1. *caus. of* **kırış=** 1. 2. to flirt with a man (woman).

kırıt=ᵘʳ فِيرَتْمَق قَرَيَتْمَى to behave in a coquettish manner. —**ış** coquetry.
kırıtkan قِيرِيتقَان coquettish; flighty.
kırk 1 قِرْق forty. — **ambar** 1. person of encyclopedic knowledge. 2. general dealer. 3. *naut.* mixed cargo. 4. skatefish, *zool.*, *Raia batis.* — **anahtar sahibi**, — **anahtarlı** owner of many estates, very rich man. —**ayak***. — **bayır** third stomach of a ruminant, omasum. — **bir kere maşallah** a thousand times bravo! *said when a person is unusually good, industrious, nice, etc.* — **budak** large candelabra used in the ceremonies of the Bektashi order. —**ı çık** /ın/ to have completed forty days after childbirth (woman). — **evin kedisi** one who is always in and out of other people's houses; at home everywhere. — **geçit** very winding river. — **ikindi** afternoon rains (which continue about forty days in certain regions of Anatolia). — **kapının ipini çek**= to apply to many places. —**lara karış**= 1. to disappear, to make oneself scarce. 2. to be lost; to die. — **kilit** pewter grass, horsetail, *bot.*, *Equisetum.* — **merdiven** 1. very steep ascent. 2. a variety of Damascus steel in sword blades; sword with a many-notched back. —**ından sonra saz çal**= to take up something rather late in life. — **yılın başı**, — **yılda bir** very seldom, on very rare occasions. — **yıllık Yani olur mu Kâni?** People don't change easily.
kırk=ᵃʳ **2** قِرْقْمَق /ı/ to clip, shear.
kırkayakᵏ¹ قِرْقآيَاق 1. centipede. 2. millipede.
kırkı قِرْقِى scissors. —**cı** sheep shearer.
kırkıl=ᵘʳ قِرْقِلْمَق *pass. of* **kırk**= 2.
kırkım قِرْقِم 1. a clipping, shearing. 2. shearing season. 3. fleece; crop of wool. — **makinesi** shearing machine. —**cı** sheep shearer, clipper of goats, camels, etc.
kırkıncı قِرْقِنْجِى fortieth.
kırkıntı قِرْقِنْدِى قِرْقِنْتِى a clipping, clippings.
kırkla=ʳ قِرْقْلَامَق 1. /ı/ to make forty (a thing); to do something forty times. 2. to have passed forty days since birth (child). 3. to complete forty days after an event. 4. to reach the age of forty.
Kırklar قِرْقْلَر *Isl. myst.* the Forty, Forty Saints.
kırklı قِرْقْلِى 1. being born within forty days of someone else. 2. having forty parts.
kırklıkᵏ¹ **1** قِرْقْلِق 1. consisting of forty. 2. forty years old. 3. clothes for a newborn child, layette. 4. coin of forty paras.
kırklıkᵏ¹ **2** قِرْقْلِق shearing clippers.
kırkma قِرْقْمَه 1. *verbal n. of* **kırk**= 2. 2. haircut so as to cover the forehead. 3. *prov.* lock of hair, ringlet.
kırktır=ᵘʳ قِرْقْدِرْمَق /ı, a/ *caus. of* **kırk**= 2.

kırlağan قِيرْلَاغَان 1. plague. 2. evil man. — **sürüsü** 1. host of calamities. 2. troop of evil men.
kırlağıçᶜ¹, **kırlağuç**ᶜᵘ قِرْلَاغُوج archaic, same as **kırlangıç**.
kırlangıçᶜ¹ قِرْلَانْغِيج 1. swallow, *zool.*, *Hirundo*; martin, *zool.*, *Delichon*. 2. same as **kırlangıç balığı**. 3. *Ott. hist.* light, swift galley. 4. *prov.* quack eye doctor. — **balığı** gurnard, *zool.*, *Trigla hirundo.* — **dönümü** swallows' migration time, early October. — **fırtınası** storms occurring about the end of March. — **kuyruğu** carpentry dovetail, fantail. — **otu** celandine, *bot.*, *Chelidonium maius.*
kırlaş=ᵘʳ قِيرْلَاشْمَق to become grey.
kırlı 1 قِيرْلِى mixed with grey.
kırlı 2 قِرْلِى stranger, nomad.
kırlıkᵏ¹ قِيرْلِق open country.
kırma قِرْمَه 1. *verbal n. of* **kır**= 3. 2. coarsely ground corn, crushed or cracked grain, groats. 3. pleats (of a skirt, etc.); pleated, kilted. 4. a folding; fold; folded; broken; folding, collapsible (gun, etc.). 5. hybrid, half-breed, mongrel. 6. cramped variety of Arabic handwriting. — **değirmeni** mill for cracking grain. — **kebabı** cut-up, quickly cooked chicken. — **makinesi** jawbreaker, stone crusher. — **peyke** folding seat. — **tabanca** breach-loading pistol. — **taş** broken stones (for road making).
kırmacı قِرْمَجِى 1. bookbinding folder (person). 2. pleater. 3. miller of groats, owner of a cracking mill; seller of groats or cracked grain.
kırmahane قِرْمَهَانَه bookbinding folding loft.
kırmala=ʳ قِرْمَلَامَق /ı/ to pleat, kilt.
kırmalı قِرْمَلِى pleated, kilted; folded.
kırmız قِرْمِز A 1. kermes, cochineal (red dye). 2. kermes insect, *zool.*, *Coccus ilicis*; cochineal insect, *zool.*, *Coccus cacti.* — **böceği** same as **kırmız²**. — **macunu** kermes paste or elixir. — **madeni** mineral kermes, trisulphide of antimony. — **meşesi** kermes oak, *bot.*, *Quercus coccifera.*
kırmızı قِرْمِزِى A red. — **alklar** *bot.*, *Rhodopyceae.* — **ayaklı kerkenez** red footed falcon, *zool.*, *Falco vespertinus.* — **balık** goldfish, *zool.*, *Carassius auratus.* — **biber** cayenne pepper, red pepper, *bot.*, *Capsicum annuum.* — **boyunlu dalgıç** red necked grebe, *zool.*, *Podiceps griseigena.* — **çaylak** common kite or glede, *zool.*, *Milvus milvus* or *Milvus migrans.* — **dal bakkam** brazilwood logs. — **dipli mumla davet et**= /ı/ to invite especially. — **doğan** marsh harrier, *zool.*, *Circus aeruginosus.* — **dut** red mulberry, *bot.*, *Morus rubra.* — **fener** *slang* brothel. — **gagalı dağ kargası** chough, *zool.*, *Pyrrhocorax pyrrhocorax.* — **gömlek** thing that can never

be hidden. — **havuz balığı** same as **kırmızı balık**. — **havyar** red caviar. — **kantariyum** common centaury, bot., Centaurium umbellatum or Erythraea centaurium. — **kayıt com.** red ink entry. — **keklik** rock partridge, zool., Alectoris graeca. — **körlüğü** Daltonism, red-green blindness. — **oyalı alklar** bot., Rhodephyceae. — **patlıcan** prov. tomato. — **sandal** red sandalwood. — **sırtlı örümcek kuşu** red-rumped shrike, zool., Lanius collurio. — **sülügen** red lead, minium. — **şebboy** stock, gilliflower, bot., Matthiola incana. — **tilki** red fox, zool., Vulpes vulpes. — **yaban mersini** cowberry, bot., Vaccinium vitis idaea. — **yakut** red ruby. — **yüksük otu** purple foxglove, bot., Digitalis purpurea. —**ca** reddish, somewhat red.

kırmızılan=", **kırmızılaş=**" to grow red, to redden. —**dır=**, —**tır=** /ı/ caus.

kırmızılat=" /ı/ to make red, to redden.

kırmızılı partially red, which has red parts.

kırmızılıkᵍⁱ redness, ruddiness.

kırmızımsı, kırmızımtrak reddish, somewhat red.

kırnakᵍⁱ 1. archaic slave girl, slave woman. 2. prov. pretty, nice, beautiful woman. 3. prov. servant.

kırp=ᵃʳ 1. /ı/ to clip, shear; to trim. 2. /ı/ to cut down slightly (expense, etc.). 3. to wink (the eye).

kırpıkᵍⁱ clipped, shorn, cut down.

kırpıl=" pass. of **kırp=**.

kırpıntı clippings.

kırpma 1. verbal n. of **kırp=**. 2. clipped.

kırtas (.—) A lrnd. writing paper.

kırtasî (.——) A lrnd. 1. pertaining to writing paper or stationery. 2. bureaucratic. 3. anat. papyraceous, papery. — **işler** desk work. — **muamele** bureaucratic formalities.

kırtasiye (.—..) [based on **kırtas**] stationery, writing materials; office expenses.

kırtasiyeci (.—...) 1. stationer. seller of writing materials. 2. bureaucrat. —**lik** bureaucracy, red tape.

kırtıl 1 prov. 1. cereals, grain. 2. coarsely ground wheat meal. 3. corn bread.

kırtıl 2 prov. 1. lands, estates, real property; untilled or barren field. 2. land tax, pasture tax. —**cı** tax collector.

kırtipil slang shabby, wretched, miserable; insignificant.

kıs=ᵃʳ **1** 1. /ı/ to reduce, cut (expenses). 2. to lower (voice); to turn down (lamp, radio). 3. to fold back (ears); to put its tail between its legs (dog). 4. to squeeze, tighten, pinch.

kıs 2 A lrnd. compare and judge, as in — **alâ hâzâ** and so forth, and so on. — **aleyh-ilbevaki** You can imagine what follows.

kısa short; brief (time); brief; concise. — **dalga** radio short wave. — **dalgalı diatermi** med. short wave diathermy. — **devre elec.** short circuit. — **geç=** /ı/ to refer briefly (to a subject); to state briefly. — **görüşlü** narrow minded, short sighted. — **günün kârı** iron. It is better than nothing. — **hece** short syllable. — **hizmetli** mil. short service recruit — **kafalı** short headed, brachycephalic. — **kes=** /ı/ to cut short (a matter). — **kesilmiş** cut short, close cropped (hair). — **Mahmude, — Mahmut** wall germander, bot., Teucrium chamaedrys. — **ömürlü** short-lived, ephemeral. — **saplı** short handled; bot. short stalked, subsessile. — **sür=** to take a short time, not to last long. — **tut=** /ı/ to cut short (matter). — **vadeli borç** short term liability. — **vadeli istikraz** short loan. — **vadeli poliçe, — vadeli senet** short dated bill, short bill. — **vadeli sigorta poliçesi com.** short term policy. — **vadeli yatırım** current investment. — **yoldan reddet=** /ı/ to refuse flatly.

kısaca (..'.) in short, shortly, briefly. —**sı** in a word, briefly.

kısacıkᵍⁱ short and little, tiny, very short.

kısaçᶜⁱ a pair of pincers, pliers; claw (of a crab).

kısaçla=ʳ /ı/ to hold or pinch with pincers, etc.

kısal=" to become short, to shorten, to shrink in length.

kısalıkᵍⁱ shortness, brevity.

kısalt=" /ı/ to shorten, to abbreviate, to abridge. —**ıl=** pass.

kısaltma abbreviation. — **kondansörü** shorting condenser.

kısaret (.—.) A lrnd. a bleaching, a fulling. — **et=** /ı/ to bleach, to full.

kısas 1 [Arabic.—] retaliation, reprisal. — **et=** /ı/ to retaliate, to punish according to lex talionis; to put to death (a murderer). —**a kısas** an eye for an eye. — **suretiyle** by the law of retaliation.

kısas 2 A lrnd., pl. of **kıssa**. **K—ı Enbiya** History of the Prophets. **K— Suresi** the twenty-eighth sura of the Quran.

kısasen ('.—.) A lrnd. in retaliation.

kısaülhimar (.—..—) A lrnd. squirting cucumber, bot., Ecballium elaterium.

kısıkᵍⁱ 1. hoarse, choked (voice). 2. turned down (radio, lamp), narrowed (eyes). 3. prov. very narrow pass. — **sesli** hoarse voiced.

kısıklı قيصقلى 1. flowing in a mere trickle. 2. w. cap., name of a suburb at Üsküdar.
kısıklık[ᵍ¹] قيصقلق chokedness, hoarseness.
kısıl=[ⁱʳ] قيصيلى pass. of **kıs=** 1.
kısım[ˢᵐⁱ] 1 قسم [kısm] 1. part, piece; section, division. 2. kind, sort, e. g., **kadın kısmı** women folk. — **âmiri** head of a section. —**ı aşarî** lrnd., algebra mantissa. —**ı âzamı** /ın/ the bulk, the greater part (of). — **kısım** in parts or divisions, in several portions. — **kıymeti** astr. value of division. —**ı küllî** mil. the bulk, the main part. —**ı tam** lrnd., algebra characteristic.
kısım 2 قصمى handful.
kısıntı قيصنتى 1. restriction. 2. abstinence.
kısır قيصر barren, sterile; unproductive. — **döngü** neol., log. vicious circle.
kısırgan=[ⁱʳ] قيصرغانى /ı, dan/ to be chary of giving, to grudge (someone something).
kısırlaş=[ⁱʳ] قيصرلشمى to become barren, sterile, unproductive. —**tır=** /ı/ to render sterile (to remove sex organs). —**tırma** verbal n. of **kısırlaştır=**.
kısırlık[ᵍ¹] قيصرلك barrenness, sterility.
kıska قسقا prov. small onion, scallion.
kıskaç[ᶜ¹] قيصقاج 1. pincers, pliers, nippers; surg. forceps. 2. claw (of a crab). — **gözlük** pince-nez. — **hareketi** mil. pincer movement. —**varî** forceps-like.
kıskan=[ⁱʳ] قيصقانمى /ı/ to be jealous (of), to envy; /ı, dan/ to be jealous because of, e. g., **karısını o adamdan kıskanıyor** He is jealous of that man because of his wife.
kıskandır=[ⁱʳ] قيصقاندرمى /ı/ caus. of **kıskan=**; to arouse someone's jealousy.
kıskanıl=[ⁱʳ] قيصقانلمى /ı/ to be the object of envy or jealousy, to be envied.
kıskı قيصقى wedge, cleat.
kıs kıs قس قس imitates the sound of suppressed laughter. — **gül=** to laugh under one's breath; to snicker.
kıskıvrak (ˊ..) قيص قيوراق tightly bound or squeezed; tightly coiled up; neat and tidy. — **bağla=** /ı/ to bind tightly. — **yakala=** /ı/ to catch so that escape is impossible.
kısm قسم A same as **kısım** 1.
kısmen (ˊ.) قسماً A partly, partially.
kısmet قسمت A 1. chance, destiny, luck, godsend. 2. chance of marriage (for a woman). 3. lrnd. division, distribution. —! God knows. If fate will have it... —**i açık** 1. favored by fortune, fortunate, lucky. 2. sought after (girl in marriage). —**i açıl=** 1. to be in luck; /dan/ to have luck or success (in); to have the good luck (to). 2. to have many suitors, to be sought after (girl in marriage). —**i askeriye** Ott. hist. division of a dead soldier's inheritance among his heirs. —**i ayağına gel=** to have unex-pected luck or success. —**i çık=** /ın/ to be asked for in marriage. — **ise** God willing, if fate so decrees. —**i kıt** short on luck or success. —**inde ne varsa kaşığında o çıkar** You can't avoid your destiny. — **olma=** not to be possible; not to succeed.
kısmetli قسمتلى fortunate, lucky.
kısmetsiz قسمتسز unfortunate, unlucky.
kısmık[ᵍ¹], **kısmır** قيصمير prov. avaricious, greedy, stingy.
kısmî (.—) قسمى A partial. — **kabul** com. qualified acceptance. — **körlük** partial blindness. — **örtme** astr. partial eclipse. — **seçim** bye-election. — **taahhüt** com. partial bond. — **tediye** com. part payment. — **teftiş** com. limited audit.
kısrak[ᵍ¹] قيصراق mare.
kısrık[ᵍ¹] قيصريق naturally timid, shamefaced; awkward.
kıssa قصه A anecdote, story, tale; fable, legend. —**dan hisse** from tale to moral.
kıssagüzar (...—) قصه گذار P lrnd., same as **kıssahan**.
kıssahan (..—) قصه خوان P lrnd. teller of stories, narrator; moralist.
kıssakütah (...—) قصه كوتاه P lrnd. in short, to be brief; finally.
kıssaperdaz (...—) قصه پرداز P lrnd., same as **kıssahân**.
kıssis (.—) قسيس A lrnd. Christian priest.
kıst قسط A 1. lrnd. an executing justice, acting with justice; justice. 2. lrnd. share, lot, portion; proportionate part.
kıstak[ᵍ¹] neol. isthmus.
kıstas 1 قسطاس [kıstas 2] criterion.
kıstas 2 (.—) قسطاس A lrnd. large balance or pair of scales; especially the scales of God's justice.
kıstelyevm قسط اليوم A deduction from salary or wages as a penalty for unjustified absence.
kıstı قسطى prov. ornamental articles of gold or silver on a necklace.
kıstır=[ⁱʳ] قيصدرمى caus. of **kıs=** 1.
kıstırma قيصديرمه prov. 1. a kind of pastry with cheese, ground meat and vegetables. 2. narrow waistcoat for women; narrow baggy trousers.
kısu قيصو archaic suffering, pain; trouble.
kış 1 قيش winter, winter cold. — **armudu** winter pear. — **arpası** winter barley. **K— Baba** Jack Frost. — **bahçesi** winter garden. — **buğdayı** winter wheat. —**ı çıkar=** /da/ to spend the whole winter. — **ekimi** a sowing of winter grain. — **ekini** winter grain. — **elması** winter apple. —**ı et=** 1. to stay somewhere till winter comes. 2. to reach the winter. —**ı geçir=** to pass or spend the winter, to winter; zool. to hibernate. — **gör=** to experience winter or wintery weather.

— günü wintery day. **— kıyamet** severe winter. **—ta kıyamette** in the depths of winter. **— limanı** winter harborage. **— mesaisi** winter work. **— mevsimi** winter season, winter time. **— ordugâhı** *mil.* winter quarters. **— seferi** winter campaign. **— sömestresi** winter term. **— uykusu** *zool.* hibernation. **— uykusuna gir=** *zool.* to hibernate. **— üstü** towards winter. **— üzümü** grapes kept for the winter. **— ye=** to experience severe wintery weather. **— yeli** east wind (in southeast Anatolia).

kış 2 قِش Shoo! (noise made to scare away birds etc.). **— kış et=** to shoo, to call out «Shoo!»; /ı/ to shoo (away).

kışala=ʳ قِشالامە /ı/ to shoo away (birds, etc.).

kışçı قِشچى *slang* person who lets himself be imprisoned to pass the winter inside.

kışın (.'.) قِشين in the winter, during winter.

kışırˢʳⁱ قِشر [kışr] *Irnd.* bark, peel, crust, rind. **—ı arz** crust of the earth. **— bağla=** to form a crust, to crust. **—ı dimağ** cerebral cortex. **—ı muh** *anat.* pallium. **—ı sin** enamel (of a tooth).

kışkır=ʳ قِشقرمە to flare up, to be excited, to make an attack.

kışkırt=ʳ قِشقرتمە /ı/ to incite, excite; to provoke.

kışkırtı قِشقرتى incitement, provocation, challenge.

kışkırtıcı قِشقرتيجى provocative, inciting; provoker.

kışla 1 (.'.) قِشلا 1. barracks. 2. winter shelter for cattle. **— avlusu** barracks yard, barracks square. **— gemisi** *naut.* receiving ship. **— hakkı** *Ott. hist.* a kind of sheep tax. **— hapsi** detention in barracks. **— hastahanesi** military hospital. **— hizmeti** barracks service. **— karakolu** barracks guard. **— komutanı** barracks master. **—ya koy=** /ı/ to put into barracks, to barrack. **— muzipliklerı** barrack-room jokes.

kışla=ʳ 2 قِشلامە 1. to become wintery or cold. 2. to winter.

kışlakᵍⁱ قِشلاق winter quarters (for animals, nomads or an army).

kışlakıye قِشلاقيە *Ott. hist.* tax on winter quarters.

kışlıkᵍⁱ قِشلق 1. suitable for the winter; hibernal, wintery. 2. winter residence. **— ev, — ikametgâh** winter house, winter residence.

kışr قِشر A *Irnd., same as* **kışır**.

kışrî (.—) قِشرى .A *Irnd.* cortical, crustaceous. **— hayvanlar** crustacean animals. **—ye** (.—.) *zool., Crustacea.*

kıt 1 قِط scarce, little, few. **— ekmeği** *prov.* food sent by the neighbors to a house where somebody has died. **—a git=**

prov. to bring food to a bereaved family. **— kanaat** *colloq.* hardly enough, scantily. **— kanaat geçin=** to live modestly or thriftily, to live in poor circumstances. **—ı kıtına hesapla=** /ı/ to cut it fine, to allow no margin. **—ı kıtına idare et=** /ı/ just to be able to make both ends meet. **—ı kıtına yetiş=** to be barely sufficient.

kıt 2 قِت archaic 1. side; presence (of a person). 2. opinion, idea; *e. g.,* **benim kıtımda** in my opinion.

kıt'a 1 قطعه A 1. continent. 2. *mil.* detachment. 3. strophe; piece of poetry of two or more couplets, complete in itself as to idea. 4. stage (on bus or streetcar route). 5. piece (item in an inventory). 6. size, format. 7. *geom.* segment. **—i askeriye** *Irnd.* military unit. **—i daire** *geom.* segment of a circle. **—i harkafiye** *anat.* ilium. **— kıt'a** in sections; in separate pieces. **—i küre** *Irnd.* segment of a sphere.

kıtaᵃⁱ 2 (.—) قطاع A *geom.* sector. **—ı daire** sector of a circle.

kıtaat (..—) قطعات A *mil.* troops. **—ı fenniye** engineer corps. **—ı fenniye subayı** engineer officer.

kıtalⁱⁱ (.—) قتال A *Irnd.* massacre, carnage; slaughter.

kıt'atülferes قطعة الفرس A *Irnd., astr.* the constellation Equuleus.

kıtıkᵍⁱ قِتيق 1. tow; refuse, stuffing (of a mattress, etc.). 2. *neol., anat.* panniculus. **—lı harç** mortar mixed with tow.

kıtıpıyos قِتيپيوس *slang* ordinary, trifling, unimportant fellow.

kıtır قِتير 1. *colloq.* lie, invention. 2. crackling sound; crisp. 3. popcorn. **— at=** to tell lies, to invent. **— kıtır kes=** /ı/ to kill or massacre ruthlessly, to kill in cold blood. **— kıtır ye=** /ı/ to eat with a crackling noise. **— yuvarla=** same as **kıtır at=.**

kıtırcı قِتيرجى liar, inventor.

kıtırda=ʳ قِتيردامە to make a crunching or crackling sound.

kıtırtı قِتيردى crunch, crack (sound).

kıtlama قِتلامە a drinking tea holding a piece of sugar in the mouth.

kıtlaş=ʳ قِتلاشمە to become scarce.

kıtlıkᵍⁱ قِتلق scarcity, lack; dearth, famine. **—ında** in default (of), failing, in the absence (of), for want (of). **—tan çıkmış gibi ye=** to devour one's food ravenously. **—ına kıran mı girdi?** *colloq.* there are plenty (of), *e. g.,* **ekmek kıtlığına kıran mı girdi?** There is plenty of bread. **— yılı** year of dearth and famine.

kıtmir 1 (.—) قطمير A 1. *myth.,* name of

the dog of the Seven Sleepers of Ephesus. 2. *l. c.* dog.

kıtmîr 2 (. —) قطمیر A *lrnd.* shell of the date stone; white speck on a date stone. **— u nakîr** the smallest imaginable particle.

kıvam (. —) قوام A right moment (to do something); propitious point or state; right quantity or dose; proper degree of consistency or density; proper degree of ripeness. **—ında** at the right time, at the propitious point, in the right quantity or dose, in the proper consistency, well-baked, ripe, properly. **—ını bul=, —a gel=** to come to the right consistency, density or degree, to be at the best possible moment. **—ında konuş=** to speak properly. **—ında ye=** to eat with temperance or moderation.

kıvamlan=ᵗʳ قیوامـلنمق to acquire a proper degree of consistency or maturity, to come to the right point. **—dır=** /ı/ *caus.*

kıvamlı قیوامـلی having reached the proper degree of consistency or maturity.

kıvamsız قیوامـسز not at the proper degree of consistency or maturity.

kıvan=ᵗʳ قوانمق *prov.* 1. /a/ to be glad (of), to rejoice (over). 2. /la/ to boast, to be proud (of).

kıvanç *neol.* 1. pleasure, joy. 2. proper pride. **— duy=** /dan/ to be delighted or pleased (with), to feel proud (of).

kıvandır=ᵗʳ قواندیرمق *prov.* /ı, la/ to be delighted (with).

kıvılcım قیویلجیم spark. **—la ateşleme** spark ignition. **— bujisi** spark plug. **— çak=** to strike sparks (from). **— çakış uzunluğu** *phys.* spark length. **— saç=** to spark, to emit sparks. **— sayısı** sparking rate. **— siperi** spark arrester. **— söndürücü** spark extinguisher. **—lı** sparking. **—sız** sparkless.

kıvır=ᵗʳ قیویرمق /ı/ 1. to curl, coil, to twist. 2. to hem, fold. 3. *colloq.* to lie, to invent a story. 4. *colloq.* to succeed in doing. 5. *colloq.* to dance undulatingly, to dance while swaying, swinging or undulating one's hips. 6. *slang* to eat greedily. 7. *prov.* to steal.

kıvırcıkᵏˡ قیویرجیق 1. crisp, curly (hair). 2. a kind of small-tailed, curly-haired sheep or its mutton. **— koyunu** a kind of small-tailed and curly-haired sheep. **— lâhana** broccoli, curly kale. **— salata** crisp lettuce, lettuce with curly leaves.

kıvırdım قیویردم *prov.* trousseau, marriage outfit.

kıvır kıvır قیویر قیویر in curls. **— et=** 1. /ı/ to make full of folds or curls. 2. to fold or curl oneself, to writhe, undulate. **— oyna=** to undulate and sway in dancing. **— yürü=** to walk with swaying and undulating hips.

kıvırma قیویرمه 1. *verbal n.* of **kıvır=**. 2. *sewing* folded and whipped seam.

kıvırt=ᵗʳ قیویرتمق /ı, a/ *caus.* of **kıvır=** ¹⁻².

kıvır zıvır قیویر زیویر *colloq.* trifling, odds and ends, nothing substantial, insignificant.

kıvra=ʳ قیورامق *prov.* to walk rapidly.

kıvrakᵏˡ قیوراق 1. brisk, alert, swift, agile; tidy, dextrous; coquettish. 2. *prov.* woman's outdoor mantle; light head covering (for women). **— buğday** *prov.* spring wheat. **— oyun** brisk dance.

kıvraklıkᵏˡ قیوراقلق briskness, alertness, swiftness, agility; elegance.

kıvran=ᵗʳ قیورانمق 1. /dan/ to writhe (with pain, etc.), to suffer greatly (from), to have great trouble, to be in distress; to be agitated. 2. /ı/ *prov.* to go around or about, to take a turn around.

kıvrıkᵏˡ قیوریق 1. curled, twisted, coiled, plaited. 2. hemmed, folded; fold. 3. cuff, turnup (on trousers, sleeve, glove, etc.). **—lı** having curls, folds; cuffed. **—lık** curliness.

kıvrıl=ᵗʳ قیورلمق 1. *pass.* of **kıvır=** ¹⁻². 2. to curl up, coil up, twist about. 3. to be squeezed into a tight place.

kıvrılı قیورلی curled, coiled, twisted.

kıvrılma قیورلمه 1. *verbal n.* of **kıvrıl=**. 2. *geol.* fold, crumpling.

kıvrılt=ᵗʳ قیورلتمق /ı/ to make or let curl, coil or twist.

kıvrım قیوریم 1. curl, twist, fold; twine, winding. 2. *anat.* gyrus, convolution. 3. *geol.* fold; *geol.* undulation. **— bağırsak** *anat.* ileum. **— kıvrım** in curls, full of twists and turns. **— kıvrım kıvrıl=, — kıvrım ol=** to be doubled up with pain.

kıvrımlan=ᵗʳ قیورملنمق to form itself into a curl or curls.

kıvrımlı قیورملی curled, twisted, folded.

kıvrıntı قیورنتی a winding, turn, twist, coil.

kıy=ᵃʳ ¹ قیمق 1. /ı/ to chop up fine. 2. /a/ not to spare, to spend, to make a sacrifice (of); to bring oneself to do an injury (to). 3. /a/ to slaughter, massacre. **—ama=** 1. to spare the life of; to have pity on. 2. to grudge (expense). 3. to be unable to bring oneself (to do something); not to have the heart to do. **—a bak=, —a kıya bak=** to look sharply or furiously.

kıy 2 قی *archaic* side, border. **—ında** near, at the side (of).

kıyadet (. —.) قیادت A *lrnd.* a leading, guidance. **— et=** /a/ to lead.

kıyafet (. —.) قیافت A 1. dress, attire, costume; general appearance and dress (of a person). 2. physiognomy; aspect. **— balosu**

kıyafetli

fancy dress ball. **— değiştir=** to change dress or costume; to change form or appearance, to disguise oneself. **— düşkünü** poorly dressed, ill-dressed, shabby. **bir —e gir=** to take on some particular form or appearance. **— ilmi** physiognomy. **— tebdil et=** same as **kıyafet değiştir=**.

kıyafetli قیافتلی in some particular costume or shape.

kıyafetname (. — . — .) قیافتنامه P lrnd. 1. book on costume. 2. treatise on physiognomy. 3. written description of a person.

kıyafetsiz قیافتسز ill-dressed, untidy, shabby.

kıyak[1] قیاق 1. colloq. nice, pretty, smart, elegant. **—çı** slang reckless gambler.

kıyam (. —) قیام A 1. a rising, standing up; becoming erect. 2. revolt, rebellion, mutiny. 3. Isl. rel. standing position in prayer; prayer. 4. resurrection. 5. phil. existence. **— et=** 1. to get up, to stand up, to rise. 2. to revolt, rebel. 3. to rise from the dead. 4. /a/ to set (to, to do). **— filâması** naut. blue peter. **— halinde** in a standing posture.

kıyamet (. — .) قیامت A 1. resurrection of the dead; last judgment; doomsday. 2. great disaster; tumult, disturbance. **— alâmeti!** How dreadful! **— gibi** lots of. **— günü** day of the last judgment, doomsday. **— kadar** lots. **—e kadar** till kingdom come. **— koptu** There was a great tumult; a great row took place. **—i kopar=, —leri kopar=** to make a great fuss, to shout and scold terribly. **— mi kopar?** Why all the fuss? Is it really important? **K— Sûresi** name of the seventy-fifth sura of the Quran. **— teorisi** neol., biol. theory of catastrophe.

kıyas (. —) قیاس A 1. comparison, a comparing; conjecture; analogy. 2. log. syllogism, argument. 3. rule; opinion. **—la** /a/ by analogy (to, with); by comparison. **—ı bâtıl** lrnd. absurd comparison, worthless conclusion, misleading analogy. **— et=** /ı, la/ to compare; to conclude by analogy. **— et!** Draw your own conclusions. **—ı fâsid** lrnd., log. paralogism. **—tan hariç** beyond comparison, beyond imagination. **—ı iknaî** lrnd., log. syllogism or argument that satisfies reason, but does not absolutely prove. **—ı iktiranî** lrnd., log. categorical syllogism. **—ı istikranî** lrnd., log. absolute syllogism. **—ı istisnaî** lrnd., log. conditional or hypothetical syllogism. **— kabul etmez** incomparable. **—ı kâzib** lrnd. false comparison, analogy or conclusion. **—ı lûgavî** lrnd. lexicographical regular form. **—ı matvî** lrnd., log. enthymeme. **—ı mevsûlünnetâyiç** lrnd., log. prosyllogism. **—ı mukassem** lrnd., log. dilemma. **—ı müdellel** lrnd., log. epichirema. **—ı mülhak** lrnd., log. episyllo-

gism. **—ı mürekkeb** lrnd., log. polysyllogism. **—ı müselsel** lrnd., log. sorites. **—ı sahihül-erkân** lrnd., log. syllogism correct in its three members. **bu — üzre** by analogy with this, at this rate; in this way. **—ımca** in my opinion.

kıyasat (. — —) قیاسات A lrnd., pl. of **kıyas**. **—ı müteselsile** lrnd., log. polysyllogism.

kıyasça (. —′.) قیاسجه according to analogy or rule.

kıyasen (. —′.) قیاساً A by comparison, by analogy (with).

kıyasıya قیاسیه murderous, merciless; ruthlessly.

kıyasî (. — —) قیاسی A 1. lrnd. regular, in accordance with rule. 2. gram. regular. 3. log. analogical, analogous.

kıyasla=[1] قیاسلامق /ı/ to compare; to conclude by analogy.

kıydır=[1] قیدیرمق /ı, a/ caus. of **kıy= 1**.

kıyem قیم A lrnd., pl. of **kıymet**.

kıyı قیی 1. shore, coast; bank. 2. edge, side, border. 3. anat. limbus. **bir —da** aside, in some place or corner. **— balıkçılığı** coastal or inshore fishery. **—da bucakta** in out of the way places, in holes and corners. **—ya çekil=** to withdraw to a distance, to get out of the way. **—ya çık=** to go on shore, to land. **— düzlüğü** coastal plain. **— gemiciliği** coastal shipping. **—dan git=** 1. to go along a coast, to coast; to follow the river bank. 2. to go along the edge of a road. **—ya in=** to land, to disembark. **— iste=** to hug the coast. **—dan kıyıdan** along the shore; very cautiously. **— kordonu** geol. littoral cordon. **—da köşede** same as **kıyıda bucakta**. **— sıra** along the shore, coastwise. **— suları** shallow water near the shore, the shallows.

kıyıcı 1 قیییجی 1. shore fisherman. 2. gatherer of flotsam and jetsam. 3. frequenter of the shore. 4. coast guard.

kıyıcı 2 قیییجی 1. cutter, chopper, mincer (of tobacco, etc.). 2. pitiless or cruel person.

kıyık[1] قییق 1. ground, chopped up. 2. prov. sack needle, packing needle. 3. archaic cruel, pitiless, tyrannical.

kıyıl=[1] قییلمق 1. pass. of **kıy= 1**. 2. to have a feeling of debility, ache, e. g., **her tarafım kıyılıyor** I am aching all over.

kıyım قییم 1. a cutting or chopping up. 2. manner of mincing, cutting or chopping up. 3. single quantity of cut or chopped up (material). **— kıyım ol=** same as **kıyıl=**[2].

kıyımlı قییملی cut, chopped up, e. g., **ince kıyımlı tütün** finely cut tobacco.

kıyın=[1] قیینمق archaic to have a sensation of aching and debility (organ of body).

kıyıntı قیینتی 1. stomach pains; aching of the limbs, languor. 2. anything chopped up.

—**lı** 1. mixed or soiled with finely chopped particles. 2. aching (organ).

kıyış=ᵗʳ قيشمى 1. to come to a final agreement. 2. to act warmly or eagerly toward one another.

kıylükalˡⁱ (—.—) قيل و قال [kilükal] *lrnd.* gossip.

kıyma قيمه 1. *verbal n. of* **kıy**= 1. 2. chopped meat. 3. finely chopped. — **tahtası** chopping board. —**lı** prepared or filled with ground meat.

kıymet قيمت A 1. value, worth; esteem. 2. price, cost. —**i adediye** *lrnd., math.* numerical value. —**i ahlâkıye** *lrnd.* moral value. — **artışı** *com.* appreciation, increase in value. — **biç**= /a/ to estimate the value (of), to evaluate. —**ini bil**= /ın/ to value or appreciate properly, to realize the worth (of). —**ten düş**= to depreciate, to fall in value. —**i hakikiye** *lrnd.* true value. —**i harbiye** *lrnd.* combative value. — **hesapları** *com.* impersonal accounts. — **itibariyle** ad valorem, according to value. —**i itibariye** *lrnd.* nominal value, face value. —**i ittihadiye** *lrnd., chem.* valence. — **koy**= /a/ to value, appraise, tax. —**i mevzua** *lrnd.* price fixed by the seller. —**i mutlaka** *lrnd.* absolute value. —**i nakdiye** *lrnd.* money value, value of currency. — **nazariyesi** *phil.* axiology. —**i rayice** *lrnd.* current rate, market value. — **takdir et**= /a/ to estimate the value (of). — **tenezzülü** diminution or decrease in value. — **ver**= /a/ to attach importance (to), to set value (on), to esteem. —**i zatiye** *lrnd.* personal worth.

kıymetdan (..—) قيمتدان P *lrnd.* appreciative, a good judge of worth (of men or affairs).

kıymetlen=ᵗʳ قيمتلنمك to increase in value, to become valuable. —**dir**= /ı/ 1. to raise the value (of), to utilize, to make profitable use (of). 2. to estimate.

kıymetli قيمتلى valuable, precious. — **evrak** securities, stocks. — **mektup** insured letter, money letter. — **mürsele** *lrnd.* articles of value sent by post. — **paket** parcel with value declared.

kıymetnaşinas (..—.—) قيمت ناشناس P *lrnd.* who does not know the value (of), unappreciative; ungrateful.

kıymetsiz قيمتسز worthless, useless, of no use, valueless. — **senet**, — **vesika** invalid paper. —**lik** worthlessness, uselessness, valuelessness.

kıymetşinas (...—) قيمت شناس P *lrnd.* appreciative, who knows the value (of a thing or person); grateful.

kıymettar (..—). قيمتدار P valuable, precious.

kıymıkᵗⁱ قيميق splinter. —**lan**= to splinter, get splinters. —**lı** full of splinters.

kıynakᵗⁱ قيناق و قينق 1. *prov.* kernel of a nut, half or quarter of a nut kernel; segment (of an orange). 2. *archaic* claw, talon.

kıynaşıkᵗⁱ قيناشق *prov.* half open (eye).

kıynaştır=ᵗʳ قيناشديرمق *prov.* /ı/ to open just a little.

kıyye قيه A *lrnd.* okka (about 1300 grams).

kız 1 قز 1. girl, daughter. 2. virgin, maiden. 3. female servant; *obs.* female slave. 4. *cards* queen. 5. *obs.* nun. —**lar ağası** *Ott. hist.* chief black eunuch of the imperial harem. — **al**= to marry a girl. — **almak kız ver**=, — **alıp ver**= to intermarry. —**lar anası** *obs.* abbess of a convent. — **böceği** dragonfly, *zool.*, Libellula. — **değiştir**= *prov.* to marry each other's sisters. —**ını dövmeyen dizini döver** *proverb* Keep your daughter in order or you will regret it later. —**ın dünürlüğüne var**= *prov.* to go to ask a girl's hand in marriage. — **evlât** daughter. — **gibi** *colloq.* new, untouched; beautiful. — **kaçır**= to kidnap a girl, to elope with a girl. — **kalbi** bleeding heart, *bot.*, Dicentra. —**kardeş***. —**ı kısrağı** his womenfolk. — **kilimi** a kind of **kilim** woven by nomad girls. **K— Kulesi** Maiden's Tower or Tower of Leander at the juncture between the Bosphorus and the Sea of Marmara. — **kurusu** spinster, old maid. — **kuşu** lapwing, pewit, *zool.*, Vanellus vanellus. — **lisesi** girls' high school (lycée). — **memesi** *colloq.* grapefruit. — **oğlan**, — **oğlan kız** virgin; young and fresh. —**ım sana söylüyorum, gelinim sen anla** *colloq.* I am telling you, my daughter, but I mean you, my daughter-in-law! *said in reference to an allusive remark, an indirect attack.* — **tarafı** the bride's relatives. **K— Taşı** Maiden's Column, the ruined column of Marcian in Istanbul. — **ticareti** white slave traffic. — **ver**= /a/ to give a girl in marriage (to). — **yaşmağı** *obs.* loose open veil worn over the head by girls.

kız=ᵃʳ 2 قيزمق 1. to be angry, cross, ill-tempered; /a/ to be angry, vexed (with). 2. to get hot (iron, oil, etc.). 3. to be in heat, to get sexually excited (animal).

kız 3 قز *archaic* scarce, scanty; scarcity.

kızakᵗⁱ قيزاق و قزاق 1. sledge, sled, sleigh; runner of a sleigh. 2. *naut.* ways, sliding ways. 3. *tech.* slide, sliding carriage, slide or guide bars, chute. —**a çek**= /ı/ 1. to lay on the stocks (a ship). 2. to fire, dismiss (person). —**tan in**= to be launched (ship). —**tan indir**= /ı/ to launch from the ways (ship). —**tan indirilme** launching (of a ship). — **kay**= 1. to slide downhill on a sled. 2. to skate, to slide on ice. —**a koy**= /ı/ to lay down (a

kızalak

ship). — **yap**= to slide, to glide. —**lık** *carpentry* joist.
kızalak[1] قیزالاق wild red poppy, *bot., Papaver rhoeas.*
kızamık[1] قیزامق قیزامیس قزامورہ قیزامورہ measles, rubeola. — **çıkar**= to have the measles. —**çık** German measles. —**lı** suffering from the measles.
kızan 1 قیزان *prov.* child, lad, youth; little girl.
kızan 2 قیزان *prov.* rut, sexual excitement (of an animal). —**a gel**=, — **ol**= to rut, to be affected with rut. —**la**=, —**sa**= *same as* **kızana gel**=.
kızar=" قیزارمه 1. to turn red, to become rosy, to blush. 2. to be roasted, toasted, fried; to be soutéed. —**ıp bozar**= to grow red and pale by turns, to be much confused. —**mış ekmek** toast. —**ıp morar**= to blush deeply (in great embarrassment or rage). —**t**= /ı/ *caus. of* **kızar**=. —**tma** 1. *verbal n. of* **kızart**=. 2. roasted, roast meat.
kızdır=" قیزدرمه /ı/ 1. to make angry, to irritate, excite. 2. to heat, to make hot or warm. —**ıp soğut**= *tech.* to anneal. —**ıl**= *pass. of* **kızdır**=.
kızdırma قیزدرمه 1. *verbal n. of* **kızdır**=. 2. *prov.* fever. — **fırını** *tech.* annealing oven or furnace.
kızgın قیزغین قزغین 1. hot, red hot. 2. angry, enraged. 3. in heat; in rut (animal). — **ateşleme borusu** *tech.* hot air igniter. — **boru** *tech.* glow tube. — **boru ile ateşleme** *tech.* hot air ignition. — **dam** *prov.* Turkish bath. — **gülle** *obs.* red hot cannon ball. — **istim müvellidesi** *tech.* steam superheater. — **kızgın bak**= to look angrily. — **tel** *tech.* hot wire.
kızgınlaş=" قیزغینلشمه to grow angry.
kızgınlık[1] قیزغینلق anger, rage; rut.
kızıl قیزیل قزیل قزل 1. red; ruddy. 2. scarlet fever, scarlatina. 3. communist. 4. *prov.* gold. 5. *obs.* yarn or thread of goat or camel hair, etc. 6. *prov.* hot tempered. **K**—**lar** the Reds. **K**— **Adalar** Princes' Islands in the Sea of Marmara. — **ağaç** alder, *bot., Alnus.* — **akbaba** griffon vulture, *zool., Gyps fulvus.* — **akçe** gold coin. — **ardıç** common juniper, *bot., Juniperus communis.* — **aşı boyası** red ocher. **K**— **ay***. **K**— **baş***. — **başlı örümcek kuşu** redheaded butcher bird, woodchat shrike, *zool., Lanius senator.* — **behmen** root of the common meadow sage, *Salvia campestris,* or of the winter cherry, *Physalis flexuosa.* — **boya** *same as* **kızıl kök.** — **boz** white and red roan (horse). — **buğday** spelt, *bot., Triticum spelta.* — **cahil** utterly ignorant. —**a çal**= to verge on red. — **çam** cluster pine, *bot., Pinus bruttia.* — **çubuk** wild cornel, *bot., Cornus sanguinea.* — **deli** raving madman. **K**— **Deniz** Red Sea. — **derili** American Indian. — **dipli bal mumu ile davet et**= /ı/ to invite insistently. — **doru** sorrel, bay (horse). — **elâ** red spotted trout, *zool., Salmo fario.* **K**— **Elma** 1. *a legendary Turkish land in Central Asia.* 2. *archaic* the city of Rome. **K**— **Enternasyonal** International League of Anarchists. — **erik** red plum, red egg plum. — **erik fırtınası** storm occurring in the last week of July. — **gerdan,** — **gerdan kuşu** European robin, *zool., Erithacus rubecula.* — **gerdanlı incir kuşu** red-throated pipit, *zool., Anthus cervinus.* — **geyik** red deer, *zool., Cervus elaphus.* — **göz** roach (fish), *zool., Leuciseus rutilus.* **K**— **haç***. — **hastalığı,** — **humma** scarlet fever. — **ıssı** *prov.* dog days. — **kanat** roach (fish), *zool., Leuciseus rutilus.* — **kantaron** red gentian, *bot., Gentiana purpurea.* — **kantarongiller** *bot., Gentianaceae.* — **Karaman** a kind of fat tailed sheep of poorer quality than the common Karaman. — **karınca** red ant, *zool., Formica sanguinea.* — **kaz** redbreasted goose, *zool., Branta ruficollis.* — **keklik** red legged partridge, *zool., Alectoris rufa.* — **kırlangıç** red rumped swallow, *zool., Hirundo daurica.* — **koyun** a kind of Karaman sheep. — **kök** madder root (root of *Rubia tinctorum,* used as a red dye). — **kurt** 1. red mite (pest of birds). 2. scarlet plant louse, *zool., Trombidium hirsutissimum.* 3. harvest bug, *zool., Leptus autumnalis.* 4. *prov.* Damn you! — **kuruş** red cent. — **kuyruk** redstart, redtail, *zool., Phoenicurus phoenicurus.* — **mangır** *obs.* copper coin. — **oluk** *prov.* gullet, esophagus. **K**— **Ordu** Red Army. — **ötesi** infrared. — **öygen** *prov., same as* **kızıl oluk.** — **pul** 1. small spangle; sequin. 2. *obs.* a small copper coin. — **saçlı** red haired, carroty. — **sakal** red beard. — **söğüt** red willow, *bot., Salix rubra.* — **su yosunları** *bot.* 1. *Rodophyceae.* 2. *Florideae.* — **süci** *archaic* red wine. — **şahin** long legged buzzard, *zool., Buteo rufinus.* — **şap** light purple, lilac. — **ünük** *prov.* gullet. — **varatika** red scabious, *bot., Scabiosa stricta.* — **yaban mersini** hairgrass. — **yaprak** agrimony, *bot., Agrimonia eupatoria.* — **yara** *path.* carbuncle. — **yel** east or south wind. **K**— **Yıldız** *astr.* Mars. — **yonca** red clover, *bot., Trifolium pratense.* — **yumurta** 1. red egg. 2. Easter egg. — **yürük** *prov.* erysipelas.
Kızılay قزیلآی قیزیلآی Red Crescent (Turkish Red Cross).
Kızılbaş قیزیل باش قزیل باش قزل باش 1. a religious sect related to the Alevis. 2. a military class in the army of Shah Ismail. 3. *colloq.* person of loose morals.

kızılca قِزِلْجه reddish, ruddy. — **buğday** same as **kızıl buğday**. — **karga** chough, European crow, zool., *Pyrrhocorax pyrrhocorax*. — **kıyamet** terrible quarrel, noise or clamor. — **kıyamet kop=** for a fearful uproar to take place. — **turna** scarlet ibis, zool., *Eudocimus ruber*.

kızılcıkᵍⁱ قِزِلْجِق 1. cornelian cherry, bot., *Cornus mas*. 2. cornel, dogwood. — **ağacı** cornel tree. — **sopası** 1. dogwood stick. 2. bastinado, birching. — **sopası ye=** to be bastinadoed with a dogwood stick. —**giller** bot., *Cornaceae*.

Kızılhaç قِزِلْ خاچ Red Cross.

kızıllıkᵍⁱ قِزِلْلِق 1. redness, ruddiness. 2. obs. scarlet fever. 3. prov. rouge. — **otu** 1. centaury, bot., *Erythraea centaurium*. 2. comfrey, bot., *Symphytum officinale*. 3. alkanet, bot., *Anchusa officinalis*.

kızılsağı قِزِلْ ساغی قِزِلْ صاغی قِزِلْ صاغو archaic reddish.

kızıltı قِزِلْتی redness, red spot.

kızımtul قِزِمْتِل archaic rufous, somewhat ruddy.

kızın=ⁱʳ قِزِنْمَق prov. to warm, to become warm.

kızış=ⁱʳ قِزِشْمَق 1. to get angry or excited; to increase in fury or violence. 2. to become heated. —**tır=** /ı/ caus.

kızkardeş قِزْقارْدَش sister. — **kanı** dragon's blood (red resin exuding from the fruit of the palm *Daemonorops Draco*).

kızlıkᵍⁱ 1 قِزْلِق girlhood, maidenhood; virginity. — **adı** maiden name. — **zarı** hymen, virginal membrane, maidenhead.

kızlıkᵍⁱ 2 قِزْلِق archaic dearth, scarcity.

-kiⁿⁱ 1 کی (in a few cases, with vowel assimilation, -kı, -kü) added to temporal adverbs or adverbially used nouns belonging to (a certain time), e. g., **bu seneki** this year's, **bugünkü** today's, **yarınki** tomorrow's, **deminki** of a minute ago, **sabahki** the morning's, this morning's, **dünkü** yesterday's.

-kiⁿⁱ 2 کی added to directional adverbs forms adjective, as in **aşağıki**, **yukarıki**, **ileriki**, **karşıki**.

-kiⁿⁱ 3 کی added to nouns and pronouns in locative case forms locative adjective, e. g., **evdeki** that is in the house, **ondaki** which is his, **buradaki** which is here.

-kiⁿⁱ 4 کی added to nouns and pronouns in genitive case forms a possessive pronoun, e. g., **benimki** mine, **onlarınki** theirs, **herkesinki** everybody's, **babamınki** my father's, **ayınki** the moon's.

ki 5 کی P 1. who, which, that, e. g., **bir adam ki söz dinlemez** a man who does not listen to advice; **bilmem ki ne yapmalı?** I really don't know what one ought to do. 2. that, e. g., **herkes bilir ki dünya yuvarlaktır** Everybody knows that the earth is round. 3. after **öyle**, **o kadar**, (so) that, e. g., **bavul o kadar ağırdı ki kaldıramadım** The trunk was so heavy that I couldn't lift it. also with suppression of second clause, e. g., **o.kadar eğlendik ki!** We had such a good time. 4. And what do you know! e. g., **davete geldim ki kimseler yok** I came to the party, and what do you know, no one was there. 5. seeing that, since, e. g., **öğretmen gitmiş olmalı ki çocuklar oynuyorlar** The teacher must have left since the children are playing. 6. in order to, e. g., **herkes bir iş tutar ki para kazansın** Everybody takes a job in order to earn money. 7. following a negative statement, indicates effect, e. g., **vaktim yok ki seninle uğraşayım** I have no time to bother with you, also with suppression of second clause, e. g., **ona güvenemezsin ki** You can't rely on him. 8. at end of interrogative sentence, I wonder, e. g., **beğenecek mi ki?** Will he like it, I wonder?

=**ki** 6 کی cf. =**gı** 1.

kibar 1 کِبار [**kibar** 2] distinguished, select; belonging to the upper class; noble; rich. —**lar** people of rank or quality. — **adam** gentleman, distinguished man. —**lar âlemi** the polite world, world of fashion, high society, upper class world. — **hırsız** well dressed swindler. — **lokması** grand, magnificent (thing).

kibar 2 (.—) کِبار A lrnd., pl. of **kebîr**, nobles, grandees. —**ı rîşat** biol. quill feather.

kibarane (.—.—.) کِبارانه , **kibarca** (..′.) کِبارجه in a refined manner, politely, in a civil way.

kibariye (.—..) کِباریه A bot., *Capparidaceae*.

kibarlaş=ⁱʳ کِبارْلاشْمَق 1. to become more refined in one's manners. 2. to assume an air of superiority.

kibarlıkᵍⁱ کِبارْلِق refined manners, gentility, nobility; gentle birth. — **tasla=** to play the fine gentleman, to put on fine airs. — **tut=** 1. to become pretentious or disdainful. 2. to assume a gentlemanly manner.

kibaş (.—) کِباش A lrnd., pl. of **kebş**.

kiber کِبَر A lrnd. great old age, being full of years.

kibirᵇʳⁱ کِبْر [Arabic **kibr**] haughtiness, pride, conceit. —**ine dokun=** to affect one's pride, to be humiliated. —**ine yedireme=** /ı/ to esteem beneath one's dignity.

kibirlen=ⁱʳ کِبِرْلَنْمَك to become haughty, proud.

kibirli کِبِرْلی haughty, proud. —**lik** haughtiness.

kibirsiz کِبِرْسِز free from haughtiness.

kibrit کِبْریت .[Arabic .—] 1. match. 2. lrnd. sulfur. —**i ahmer** lrnd. philosopher's stone

kibritçi

— **çak=** to light or strike a match. — **çöpü** match stick. — **kutusu** match box. — **suyu** dilute sulfuric acid.
kibritçi کبریتجی 1. match-seller. 2. *colloq.* stingy person. —**lik et=** *colloq.* to show stinginess.
kibritî (..—) کبریتی A *lrnd.* 1. sulfurous. 2. bright yellow.
kibritiyet (..—.) کبریتیت A *lrnd.* sulfate.
kibritlik[ġi] کبریتلك match stand.
kibriya (..—) کبریا A *lrnd.* 1. divine greatness. 2. magnificence, power, grandeur. —**î** (..——) A almightiness.
kibriyapenah (..—.—) کبریا پناه P *lrnd.* the abode of consummate greatness, God.
kiçi کیچی *archaic* small. —**rek** smaller, smallish.
kifa (.—) کفا A *lrnd.* 1. sufficiency. 2. equal, like.
kifaf (.—) کفاف A *var. of* **kefaf**. —**lan=** /la/ to be contented (with frugal food).
kifah (.—) کفاح A *lrnd.* fight, battle.
kifar (.—) کفار A *lrnd., pl. of* **kâfir**.
kifaye (.—.) کفایه A *lrnd., same as* **kifayet**.
kifayet (.—.) کفایت A sufficiency; ability, capacity, efficiency. — **et=** 1. to suffice, to be sufficient. 2. /la/ to be contented, satisfied (with). — **edecek kadar** in a sufficient degree or amount, sufficiently. —**i mertebe** *lrnd.* in sufficient degree.
kifayetli کفایتلی having sufficient capacity or ability, adequate.
kifayetsiz کفایتسز inadequate; inept, inefficient. —**lik** inadequacy, inadequateness; ineptitude, lack of efficiency.
kifoskolyoz کیفوسقولیوز F *path.* kyphoskoliosis, curvature of the spine.
kihal[ii] 1 (.—) کهال A *lrnd., pl. of* **kehl**.
kihal[ii] 2 (.—) کهال A *lrnd.* kohl; eye-salve.
kihalet (.—.) کهالت A *lrnd.* art of the eye-salve maker or oculist.
kihter کهتر P *lrnd.* smaller, junior, younger; very small. —**î** (..—) P smallness, littleness. —**în** (..—) P the least, the smallest, youngest.
kik کیك E 1. *naut.* gig. 2. *slang* nose.
kikirik[ġi] کیکیریك *colloq.* John Bull.
kiklâ (.'—) کیکلا ballan, wrasse, *zool.*, *Labrus maculatus.*
kiklon کیکلون Gk cyclone.
kiklotron کیکلوترون Gk *phys.* cyclotron.
kil کیل [gil 3] fuller's earth, clay. — **ermeni***.
kila (.'.) کیلا It *naut.* keel.
kilâb کلاب A *lrnd., pl. of* **kelb**.
kilâr کیلار Gk *same as* **kiler**. —**dar** (.——) P *lrnd.* clerk of the imperial pantry.

kile کیله [Arabic **keyl**] bushel (36 1/2 kilos). — **ile** by bushels.
kilem کلم A *lrnd., pl. of* **kelime**.
kiler کیلر / کلار [kilâr] pantry, larder, storeroom. — **ağası** *obs.* head butler. — **harcı** *Ott. hist.* major or commissary in a Janissary regiment. — **kethüdası** *Ott. hist.* chief clerk of the palace pantry. — **odası** *Ott. hist.* office of the palace pantry.
kilerci کیلرجی butler. — **başı** *Ott. hist.* head butler in the palace.
kilermeni کل ارمنی [gil-i ermeni] red bole (a kind of soft, red clay).
kilid کلید P *lrnd., same as* **kilit**. —**i genc-i hakîm** *lrnd.* (*lit.* The sage's treasury key.) The formula **bismillahi'r-rahmani'r-rahîm**. —**i iman** *lrnd.* confession of the unity of God and the apostleship of Muhammad, confession of faith.
kilim کلیم [gilim] 1. woven matting, rug without a pile, kilim. 2. *anat.* tapetum. —**i kebeyi ser=** *colloq.* to settle in a place.
kilimci کلیمجی seller or maker of kilims. — **ile kör hacı** anybody.
kilindir کلندر Gk *archaic* nippled pitcher.
kilis[ısi] 1 کلس A *lrnd., var. of* **kils**.
kilis 2 کلیس tench, *zool.*, *Tinca tinca*. — **balığı** *same as* **kilis 2**.
kilise کلیسه Gk church. K— **Babaları** Church Fathers. — **buhuru** incense. — **hamursuzu** host, consecrated wafer. — **tarihi** ecclesiastical history.
kilit[di] کلیت / کلید [kilid] Gk 1. lock, latch, padlock. 2. *naut.* shackle of a chain cable. 3. linchpin. 4. white patch on a horse's muzzle and lip. — **aç=** to unlock a lock. — **ağızlığı** keyhole. — **altında** under lock and key. — **başı** *naut.* quarter irons. — **çarkı** locking wheel, hook. — **çengeli** locking notch. — **çubuğu** lock bar. — **deliği** keyhole. — **dili** bolt of a lock. — **dişlisi** lockwheel. — **gibi ağız** very discreet person. — **gibi ol=** to be loyally locked together, to be loyal in solidarity, to be close-knit. — **gövdesi** lockblock. — **harbisi** *naut.* shackle bolt. — **kapağı** keyhole cover, escutcheon. — **köprüsü** hasp of a lock. — **kutusu**, — **mahfazası** lockbox. — **mandalı** clasp of a lock. — **mili** *naut.*, *same as* **kilit harbisi**. — **noktası** *mil.* key position. — **perdesi** *same as* **kilit kapağı**. — **sandığı** *same as* **kilit kutusu**. — **sürgüsü** latch. — **taşı** *arch.* keystone (of an arch). — **topu** lock handle, knob of a lock or latch. — **vur=** /a/ to lock (a door), to attach a lock (to). —**e vur=** /ı/ to lock (prisoner, etc.), to lock (up or in). — **yayı** lock spring. — **yeri** *same as* **kilit noktası**. —**çi** locksmith. —**çik** *naut.* thole pin, double thole.

kilitle= كليتلمك /ı/ to latch, lock.
kilitleme كليتلمه a locking. **— aygıtı** locking device. **— dişlisi** lockgear. **— somunu** locknut.
kilitli كليتلى locked.
kilitsiz كليتسز without a lock.
kiliz كليز rush, reed, flag. **— balığı** tench, *zool., Tinca tinca.*
kilizma (..́..) كليزما *var. of* **kirizma.**
kilizman, kilizmen كليزمان reed plot.
kilk كلك P *lrnd.* reed pen.
killi كيللى clayey, muddy. **— külte** *geol.* clay rock. **— şist** *geol.* clay slate.
kilo (.́.) كيلو F kilo, kilogram (2.2046 pounds). **— al=** to put on weight. **— kaybet=, — ver=** to lose weight, to grow thin.
kilogram كيلوغرام F kilogram (2.2046 pounds).
kilometre (...́.) كيلومتره F kilometer (0.621 miles). **— dol=** /ın/ *slang* to become old. **— doldur=** *slang* to spend time. **— hesabı** measuring in kilometers. **— kare** square kilometer. **— saati, — sayacı** *auto.* kilometer recorder. **— taşı** kilometer stone.
kilosikl كيلوسيكل F *elec.* kilocycle.
kilovat كيلووات F kilowatt. **— saati** kilowatt-hour. **— saat sayacı** kilowatt-hour meter.
kils كلس A *geol.* limestone. **—î** (.—) A calcerous, chalky.
kilte كلته A *lrnd.* 1. bunch, faggot, handful, armful. 2. *anat.* glomerulus.
kilükal[lı] (—.—) قيل و قال A *same as* **kıylükal.**
kilüs كيلوس *same as* **keylûs.** **— damarı** *anat.* chyliferous vessel. **— taşıyıcı** *anat.* chyliferous.
kilya 1 (.́.) كيليا It *naut.* keel.
Kilya 2 (.́.) كيليا *geog.* Kilia (in Bessarabia).
kilye كليه A *lrnd.; same as* **külye.**
kim 1 كم 1. who? who, whoever. 2. *archaic* who, which, that (relative pronoun). 3. *archaic* that (conjunction). **—i** some (of them), *e. g.*, **kimi geldi kimi gitti** Some came; some went. **—imiz** some of us. **—in arabasına binerse onun türküsünü çağırır** Whoever gives him a ride, he sings that man's tune. **— bilir** Who knows? **— kime, dum duma** This is a chaotic situation in which nobody knows what's happening to the rest. **—e ne?** What does it matter to any one? **— o?** Who is it? **— oluyor?** Who does he think he is? **— olursa olsun** whoever it may be. **— vurduya git=** to be killed in a confused scuffle. **—i zaman** sometimes.
kim[mmi] **2** كم A *lrnd.* calyx, spathe.
kimesne كمسنه *archaic, same as* **kimse.**
kimlik[ği] *neol.* personal identity. **— belgesi, — cüzdanı** identity card.
kimono كيمونو F kimono.
kimse كمسه someone, somebody, anyone, anybody; *w. negative* nobody, no one. **— kendi memleketinde peygamber olmaz** Nobody is a prophet at home. **—si yok** He has no one; he has no friends.
kimsecik[ği] كيمسه جك not a single soul. **—ler yok** There's not a single soul (here).
kimsesiz كيمسه سز without relations or friends, without support or protection. **— çocuklar** homeless children. **—lik** a having nobody to look after one; destitution.
kimüs كيموس F *physiol.* chyme.
kimya (.—) كيميا A 1. chemistry; *obs.* alchemy. 2. *colloq.* rare and precious thing. **—yi ahmer** *lrnd.* philosopher's stone. **—yi can** *poet.* wine. **—yi cedid** *lrnd.* chemistry. **— doğrulumu** *neol., bot., zool.* chemotropism. **—yi ekber** *lrnd.* the highest alchemy (which would make gold and give perpetual youth). **—yi fizikî** *lrnd.* physical chemistry. **— formülü** chemical formula. **—yi gayriuzvî** *lrnd.* inorganic chemistry. **— göçümü** *neol., biol.* chemotaxis. **— harbi** chemical warfare. **—yi harurî** *lrnd.* thermochemistry. **— ile tedavi** chemotherapy. **— ilmi** chemistry. **— işareti** chemical notation. **— itibariyle** chemically. **— kinetiği** chemical kinetics. **—yi maâni** *poet.* study of truth. **— muadelesi** chemical equation. **— mühendisi** chemical engineer. **— mühendisliği** chemical engineering. **—yi saadet** *lrnd.* elixir of happiness. **— sanayii** chemical industry. **— teknolojisi** chemical technology. **—yi uzvî** P *lrnd.* organic chemistry.
kimyaca (.—́.) كيمياجه chemically. **— mücerret** chemically inert. **— saf** chemically pure.
kimyacı *neol.* chemist, teacher of chemistry. **—lık** science or profession of chemistry.
kimyaeser (.—..) كيميا اثر P *lrnd.* which acts like a charm.
kimyager (.—.) كيمياگر P chemist. **—lik** chemist's profession.
kimyasal *neol.* chemical. **— eşdeğer** *neol.* chemical equivalent. **— fonksion, — görev** *neol.* chemical function. **— ilgi** *neol.* chemical affinity. **— işlem** *neol.* chemical operation. **— reaksion** *neol.* chemical reaction.
kimyevî (..—́) كيميوى A chemical. **— analiz** chemical analysis. **— enerji** chemical energy. **— gübre** artificial fertilizer. **— hususiyet** chemical property. **— imtizaç** chemical combination. **— maddeler, — mevad** chemicals. **— muamele** chemical treatment. **— taamül** chemical reaction. **— unsurlar** chemical elements.
kimyon كيمون Gk cumin, *bot., Cuminum cyminum.* **—giller** *bot., Zygophyleaceae.* **—î** (.——) 1. sage green. 2. uncordial, cool (relation). **—lu** containing cumin, flavored with cumin.
kin (—) كين P grudge, malice, hatred, deepseated enmity. **—ini al=** to work off a

kinayat

grudge. — **bağla**= /a/ to hold a grudge (against). — **besle**=, — **güt**=, — **tut**= /a/ to bear a grudge. — **tutmaz** not vindictive, without rancor.

kinayat (. — —) كنايات A *lrnd.*, *pl.* of **kinaye**.

kinaye (. —.) كنايه A 1. allusion, hint, indirect remark, innuendo. 2. metaphor. — **at**= to hint (at), to allude or insinuate. — **ile**, — **suretiyle**, — **tarikiyle**, — **yoluyla söyle**= to use hints, allusions or innuendoes.

kinayeli كنايه لى allusive. — **kinayeli gülümse**= to grin knowingly, to smile meaningfully.

kinayetâmiz (. —. — —) كنايت آميز P *lrnd.* mixed with allusions or innuendoes (language).

kinci كينجى vindictive, nourishing a grudge.

kindar (. —) كيندار [*Persian* — —] vindictive.

kine (—.) كينه P *lrnd.*, same as **kin**. —**cu** (—. —) P malevolent, vindictive. —**dar** (—. —) P revengeful, malicious. —**gâh** (—. —) P field of battle, place of a quarrel. —**hah** (—. —) P malevolent, spiteful. —**keş** (—..) P vindictive. —**meşhun** (—.. —) P full of enmity or revenge. —**ver** (—..) P vengeful, rancorous.

kinematikᵍⁱ كينماتيك F kinematics; kinematical.

kinetik كنتيك F kinetics; kinetic. — **bilimi** kinetics. — **enerji** kinetic energy.

kinikᵍⁱ كينيك Gk *phil.* cynic.

kinin كينين F quinine. — **sülfatı** quinine sulphate.

kinizm كينيزم Gk *phil.* Cynicism.

kinli كينلى vindictive, nourishing a grudge.

kinver (—.) كينور P *lrnd.* vindictive, cherishing a grudge.

kip 1 *neol.*, *gram.*, *log.* mood.

kip 2 كيپ *prov.* tight, narrow; fit, suitable. — **gel**= /a/ to fit, to be suited (to). —**e kip** exactly the same.

kipi كيپى *prov.* fit, suitable.

kiple=ʳ كيپله مك /ı/ *prov.* to strengthen. —**ş**= to become strong or firm. —**ştir**= /ı/ 1. to make strong or firm. 2. to approach, to bring near.

kiplikᵍⁱ 1 *neol.*, *gram.*, *log.* modality.

kiplikᵍⁱ 2 كيپلك *prov.* elegance.

kir 1 كير dirt, filth. — **fitili** roll of dead skin rubbed from the body in a bath. — **götür**= not to show the dirt. — **kabar**= to come loose (dead skin). — **kaldır**= *same as* **kir götür**=. — **tut**= to show dirt (material).

kir 2 (—) كير P *lrnd.* penis.

kira (. —) كيرا A 1. rent, hire, hiring; tenancy (of land, a house). 2. rent, hire (money). — **arabası** hired vehicle, taxi, cab. — **bedeli** rent (money). — **beygiri** horse of a livery stable. — **et**= /ı/ to rent out. — **evi** a rentable house. — **ile** on hire, on lease. — **ile otur**= to live in rented quarters. — **ile tut**= /ı/ to rent, to hire, to take on hire. — **kontratosu**, — **mukavelesi** lease, rental contract. — **müddeti** term of hire, length of lease. —**da ol**= 1. rented, hired, let. 2. *same as* **kira ile otur**=. —**da otur**= *same as* **kira ile otur**=. — **parası** rent (money). — **sözleşmesi** *same as* **kira kontratosu**. — **tahdidi** rent control. —**ya ver**= /ı/ to let out on hire, to let, to rent. — **vergisi** rental tax.

kiracı (. —.) كيراجى tenant, renter, lodger. —**ya çıkmasını söyle**= to give notice to a tenant. —**nın kiracısı** subtenant. —**lık** tenantry.

kirala=ʳ كيرالامق /ı/ 1. to rent, hire, let, let out on hire or on lease. 2. to rent, hire, take on hire or on lease. 3. *naut.* to charter.

kiralama كيرالامه lease, letting. — **ve ödünç verme kanunu** lend-lease act.

kiralan=ⁱʳ كيرالانمق to be rented, hired, to have been let.

kiralıkᵍⁱ كيرالق for rent, for hire. — **kasa** safe-deposit box. — **mülk** leasehold estate. — **oda** room to let.

kiralıyan كيرالايان leasor; lessee; *naut.* charterer.

kiram (. —) كرام A *lrnd.*, *pl.* of **kerim**.

kiramun kâtibîn (. — — —. —) كرام كاتبين A *lrnd.* recording angels.

kiraren (. —ʹ.) كرارًا A *lrnd.* time and again. — **ve mimaren** many a time and oft.

kirasız كيراسز rentfree.

kiraz كراز Gk cherry. — **ağacı** cherry tree. — **ağızlık** cherry wood cigarette holder. — **ayı** May. — **biberi** *prov.* inedible decorative pepper. — **çubuk** *same as* **kiraz ağızlık**. — **dudak**, — **dudaklı** cherry-lipped. — **elması** very small kind of apple. — **eriği** sour cherry, *bot.*, *Prunus cerasus*. — **meltemi** June breeze. —**lık** cherry orchard.

kirbas (. —) كرباس A *lrnd.*, *same as* **kirpas**.

kirçᶜⁱ كرچ *prov.* dry fir needle or twig.

kirdar 1 (. —) كردار P *lrnd.* work, business; habitual action, habit.

-kirdar 2 (. —) كردار who habitually does (so and so), *as in* **bedkirdar** evil acting, wicked.

kirde كرده P thin, crustless cake of corn bread, kind of corn bread. —**li kebap** roast meat wrapped in **kirde**.

Kirdigâr (.. —) كردگار P *lrnd.* God the Omnipotent.

kireçᶜⁱ كرچ lime, chalk. — **dağı** calcareous mountain. — **fıçısı** lime tub, mortar trough. — **fırını** lime kiln. — **gibi** deathly pale; very white, like lime. — **harcı** lime mortar. — **kaymağı** calcium chloride. — **kesil**= to become deathly pale, to blanch.

— **kuyusu** lime pit. — **ocağı** limestone quarry. — **söndür=** to slake lime. — **suyu** lime water. — **sütü** milk of lime. — **taşı** limestone. — **tavası** large wooden trough in which lime is slaked. — **yak=** to burn lime. — **yeren** neol., zool. calcifugous. —**çi** lime burner; lime seller. —**çil** neol., zool. calcicole.

kireçhane (.. — .) lime storehouse.

kireçle=ʳ /ı/ 1. to put in lime, to add lime (to). 2. to whitewash, limewash.

kireçleş=ⁱʳ to calcify, become calcareous. —**me** calcification. —**tir=** /ı/ to calcify, change into lime, make calcareous.

kireçli calcareous, chalky; mixed with lime. — **su** chalky water. — **süngerler** zool., Calcispongiae. — **toprak** calcareous earth.

kireçsile=ʳ /ı/ neol., chem. to calcine, convert into calx by heat. —**me** neol., chem. calcination (converting into calx). —**me** neol., chem. calcination (being converted into calx). —**yen** neol., chem. calcinatory.

kiremidî (.. — —) brick-red.

kiremitᵈⁱ Gk red roof tile. — **ağızlığı** arch. antefix. — **fabrikası** tile factory. — **harmanı** tile works. — **imalâthanesi** same as **kiremit fabrikası**. — **kalıbı** tile mold. — **kapla=** /a/ to cover with roof tiles, to tile. — **ocağı** tile kiln. — **ört=** /a/ same as **kiremit kapla=**. — **rengi** brick colored, brick red. — **tozu** brick dust. — **yağı** obs. olive oil rendered siccative by throwing a red hot brick into it.

kiremitçi tile maker; tile seller, tile layer. —**lik** tile making, tile selling.

kiremithane tile factory.

kiremitli roofed with tiles, tiled.

kiren Gk cornel, cornelian cherry.

Kirene geog. Cyrene (ancient city in Libya). — **okulu** phil. Cyrenaic School. —**cilik** phil. Cyrenaicism.

kirez colloq., same as **kiraz**.

kiri=ʳ, **kirik=**ⁱʳ, **kirin=**ⁱʳ prov. to be obstinate.

kirinci prov. camel of three to seven years.

kiriş 1. joist, plank (set up edgewise); rafter. 2. catgut, bowstring; violin string. 3. geom. chord. 4. anat. tendon. — **germe** prov. straight way, straight line. —**i kır=** slang to take to one's heels, to run away. — **koy=** /a/ to fit with joists. — **tak=** /a/ to string. —**çi** 1. maker or seller of catgut. 2. obs. executioner (using a catgut bowstring to strangle a criminal).

kirişhane catgut factory.

kirişle=ʳ /ı/ 1. to joist, put in rafters. 2. to string (a bow). —**me** 1. building joisting, joist, girderage. 2. board set on edge; set on edge, edgewise.

kirişli joisted. — **köprü** girder bridge. — **tavan** trabeated ceiling.

kirişme P lrnd. coquettish glances, signs, actions. —**bâz** (... —) P, —**perdaz** (.... —) P, —**tıraz** (.... —) P coquetting, coquette.

kirizma, **kirizme** (..'.) a trenching of land (by spade). — **et=**, — **yap=** /ı/ to double-trench.

kirle=ʳ archaic /ı/ same as **kirlet=**.

kirlen=ʳ 1. to become dirty or soiled. 2. to become morally soiled, defamed or blemished; to lose her virginity (girl). 3. to become canonically unclean (by pollution, menses, etc.); to have her monthly period (woman).

kirlet=ⁱʳ /ı/ 1. to make dirty, to dirty, soil. 2. to soil, besmirch (one's name), to defile (virgin). 3. to make canonically unclean. —**il=** pass. —**tir=** /ı, a/ caus. of **kirlet=**.

kirli 1. dirty, soiled, filthy. 2. blemished, disreputable. 3. canonically unclean. —**ye at=** /ı/ to put aside for washing. — **çamaşır** ("dirty linen") a person's misdeeds. — **çamaşırlarını ortaya çıkar=**, — **çamaşırlarını meydana dök=** to show up someone's misdeeds. — **çıkın** person who does not show his wealth. — **hanım peyniri** a kind of cream cheese. — **kan** dark blood. — **kokoş** colloq. untidy child. — **kukla** colloq. untidy girl or woman. — **sepeti** laundry basket. — **su** slops.

kirlilikᵍⁱ 1. dirtiness, filthiness. 2. canonical impurity, uncleanness.

kirloz colloq. untidy and dirty person.

kirm P lrnd. worm. —**i bâdâme** silkworm. —**i çirâğ** glowworm. —**i çûp** wood boring insect. —**i ibrişim**, —**i kaz** silkworm. —**i palâs** clothes moth. —**i pile** silkworm. —**i şebçirâğ**, —**i şebefrûz**, —**i şebtâb** glowworm; firefly.

kirman 1 (. —) P lrnd. fortress.

Kirman 2 P a city in Iran.

kirmanî (.. — —) P obs. a kind of good sword.

kirmen prov. wooden spindle.

kirmhurde P lrnd. wormeaten.

kirmiz A same as **kırmız**.

kirpas [kirbâs] obs. linen cloth.

kirpi 1. hedgehog, zool., Erinaceus europaeus. 2. porcupine, zool., Erethizon dorsatum. 3. obs., mil. large hedgehog-like ball for defense. — **balığı** porcupine fish, zool., Diodon hystrix.

kirpikᵍⁱ **1** eyelash; zool.,

bot., cilium. — **çat=** *archaic* to close the eyes, to sleep.

kirpik[gi] **2** كرپيك *carbuncle* (stone).

kirpikli كرپيكلى *zool.* ciliferous; *bot.* ciliated. **—ler** *neol., zool.* Ciliata.

kirş كرش A *biol.* paunch, rumen.

kirti كرتى *prov.* true, right, correct.

kirtil كرتيل fishing basket.

kirtü كرتو *archaic, same as* **kirti.** **—n=** /a/ to believe (in), trust (in).

kis 1 (—) كيس A *lrnd.* 1. purse, money bag. 2. *anat.* pouch, sac.

kis 2 كيس [kils] *prov.* lime.

kisa (.—) كسا A *lrnd.* woolen cloth; rug, carpet. **K— Ehli** the family of the Prophet Muhammad.

kisb كسب A *lrnd.* gain, acquisition. **— ü kâr** business, trade; earning, gain.

kisbet 1 كسبت A *lrnd.* acquisition, acquiring.

kisbet 2 كسبت [kisvet] 1. *lrnd.* costume, garb. 2. *same as* **kispet.**

kisbî (.—) كسبى A 1. *phil., biol.* acquired. 2. *lrnd.* who earns. **— bilgi** acquired knowledge.

kise (—.) كيسه P *lrnd., same as* **kese. —i dem'iye** *anat.* lachrymal sac. **—i divanî** *Ott. hist.* purse containing 416-450 piasters. **—i havaiye** *anat.* aerial sac. **—i Mısrî** *Ott. hist.* purse containing 600 piasters. **—i Rumî** *Ott. hist.* purse containing 500 piasters. **—i safravî, —i safraviye** *anat.* gall bladder. **—i sephiye** *anat.* swim bladder. **—i şi'riye** *anat.* capillary follicle.

kisebür (—..) كيسه بر P *lrnd.* pickpocket, cutpurse.

kisedar (—.—) كيسه دار P *lrnd.* purse bearer or treasurer of a great office. ' **— efendi razı olmaz** I cannot afford it. **— şal** Cashmere shawl with borders two or three inches wide.

kiseduz (—.—) كيسه دوز P *lrnd., Ott. hist.* purse maker.

kisiye (—.—.) كيسيه A *lrnd.* marsupials, *zool.,* Marsupialia.

kispet كسبت [kisvet] 1. leather pants, tights of a Turkish wrestler. 2. costume, garb.

Kisra (.—) كسرى A *hist.* Chosroes.

Kisrevî (..—), **Kisrî** (.—) كسروى A pertaining to Chosroes.

kist كست Gk *path.* cyst. **— ameliyatı** cystectomy, cystotomy.

kisve, kisvet كسوه A *lrnd.* 1. garment, costume; special costume of a class. 2. cloth covering of the Kaaba at Macca. **— giy=** to dress oneself in the costume of an official class. **—ini kendi diker, —ini kendi iler** He is dependent on no one.

kiş 1 كيش check (at chess). **— et=** /1/ to put in check (the king).

kiş 2 (—) كيش P *lrnd.* 1. religious faith. 2. quiver (for arrows). 3. one's habits or practice.

-kiş 3 (.—) كيش P *lrnd.* having (such and such) habits or manners, *as in* **bedkiş, kâfirkiş.**

kişele=[r] كيشله *prov.* /1/ to shoo away.

kişi كيشى individual, person, human being; one. **— bilmediğinin düşmanıdır** Man hates what he does not understand. **— dokunulmazlığı** *neol.* personal inviolability, immunity from arrest or prosecution. **— ettiğini bulur** What a person gets is the result of what he has done. **— oğlu** of gentle birth, noble.

kişifçi كشفجى [keşifçi] *prov.* inquisitive, maliciously curious.

kişifle=[r] كشفله [keşf] *prov.* /1/ to peep, to observe secretly.

kişik[gi] كيشيك *prov.* 1. help. 2. *same as* **keşik 1.**

kişilen=[ir] كيشيلن *archaic* to assume airs, to boast.

kişilik[gi] كيشيليك 1. personality. 2. for (so many) persons, *e. g.,* **beş kişilik araba** five-passenger car. 3. humanity, benevolence. **— dışı** *phil.* impersonal. **— dokunulmazlığı** *same as* **kişi dokunulmazlığı.** **— giyesi, — kaftan** *archaic* gala dress. **—siz** *neol.* without individuality.

kişir كشير *same as* **keşir.**

kişirti كشرتى *archaic* neigh, whinny.

kişizade (..—.) كيشى زاده of gentle birth, noble; of a good family. **—lik** nobility.

kişkir=[ir] كشكير *prov.* /1/ to incite, excite, to provoke. **—i ver=** /a/, **—t=** /1/ *same as* **kişkir=.**

kişle=[r] كيشله *prov.* /1/ to shoo away.

Kişmir كشمير *geog.* Cashmere. **— şalı** Cashmere shawl. **—î** (..—) 1. of or from Cashmere. 2. dark skin.

kişmiş كشمش P kind of small seedless raisin (smaller than sultana).

kişne=[r] كيشنه مك to neigh, to whinny. **—me,** **—yiş** neigh, whinny.

kişniş كشنش [Persian **kişniç**] 1. coriander, *bot.,* Coriandrum sativum. 2. *prov., var. of* **kişmiş.** **— şekeri** coriander candy. **— üzümü** *same as* **kişmiş.**

kişt كشت P *lrnd.* 1. seed; sown seed. 2. sown field. **— et=** to sow.

kiştban (.—) كشتبان P *lrnd.* 1. sower, farmer. 2. field watcher.

kişte كشته P *lrnd.* sown.

kiştkâr (.—) كشتكار P *lrnd.* sower, farmer. **—î** (.——) P husbandry.

kiştzar (.—) كشتزار P *lrnd.* arable field, sown field.

kişver كشور P *lrnd.* country, region. **—dar** (..—) P lord of the land, sovereign. **—gir** (..—) P conqueror of countries. **—hüda**

(...—) P sovereign, king. —**küşa** (...—), —**sitan** (...—) P conqueror of countries.

kitab (.—) كتاب A lrnd., same as **kitap**. **K—ı hakîm** lrnd. the Quran. —**ı hükmî** lrnd. letter addressed by a judge to another judge. **K—ı Mukaddes** the Bible. **K—ı Mübin** lrnd. the Quran.

kitabe (.—.) كتابه A inscription; epitaph. — **levhası** panel for an inscription. —**i seng-i mezar** lrnd. epitaph. —**li** having an inscription or epitaph.

kitaben (.—'.) كتابًا A lrnd. in writing, in black and white.

kitabet (.—.) كتابت A lrnd. 1. literary composition, correct writing; literary style. 2. writing lesson; essay writing. 3. office and functions of a scribe or secretary. 4. can. law the agreement between slave and master, recorded in a court, under which a slave was to receive his freedom. — **dili** book language. —**i resmiye** official style.

kitabeviⁿⁱ (..'..) كتاب أوى bookstore, bookshop, bookseller's.

kitabî (.——) كتابى A 1. pertaining to books. 2. bookish; stilted, pedanfic. 3. believer in a book of sacred scripture. 4. Ott. hist. librarian (of the Sultan). 5. obs. a kind of striped muslin. — **konuş**= to speak in a bookish or stilted language.

kitabiyat (.———) كتابيات A bibliography.
kitabiye (.—..) كتابيه A bot. bast tissue, phloem.

Kitabullah (.—.—) كتاب الله A the Quran.

kitakse, kitaksi (.'..) كيناكسى Gk slang /a/ look at! e. g., **herife kitaksi** Look at the man. — **et**= /a/ to look (at).

kitapᵇⁱ كتاب [kitab] 1. book. 2. sacred scripture. 3. lrnd. writing; letter. — **ehli** believer in the books of revelation (as distinguished from pagans), cf. **ehl-i kitap**. —**a el bas**= to swear on a sacred book. —**a el basarım** I am quite certain about something. — **kurdu** 1. bookworm, zool. larva of various beetles, esp., Anobium hirtum. 2. one much given to reading, a bookworm. — **madeni** large library of books. — **meraklısı** an enthusiastic reader of books. — **sarayı** public library. —**a uydur**= to do something dishonest in an apparently honest way; to get around a law or agreement.

kitapçı كتابجى 1. bookseller. 2. Ott. hist. librarian to a personage of note. —**lık** the book trade.

kitaphane (..—.) كتابخانه 1. library. 2. bookshop.

kitaplıkᵍⁱ كتابلق 1. bookcase, book shelves. 2. neol. library.

kitapsız كتابسز 1. not possessing a book. 2. not believing in a sacred book, pagan.

kitara (.'.) كتارا It guitar.

kitle 1 كتله A same as **kütle 1**.

kitle=ʳ **2** كتلمك colloq., var. of **kilitle**=.

kitli كتلى colloq., var. of **kilitli**.

kitman (.—) كتمان A lrnd. concealing, keeping in; concealment. —**ı esrar** keeping of secrets.

kitre كتره A gum tragacanth.

kiyan (.—) كيان P lrnd. 1. star. 2. central point, center.

kiyaniyat (.—.—) كيانيات A lrnd. cosmogony.

kiyanus (.——) كيانوس Gk chem. cyanogen. — **hamızı** cyanic acid.

kiyaset (.—.) كياست A shrewdness; sagacity. —**li** intelligent. —**siz** dull, stupid.

kizb A, **kizib**ᶻᵇⁱ كذب lrnd. a speaking falsely, falsehood, lie. —**î** (.—) A false; lying. —**iyat** (..—) lies.

kizir كزير var. of **gizir 2**.

klâkson (.'.) قلاقسون F auto. horn.
klân قلان F sociol. clan.
klâpa (.'.) قلاپه G lapel.
klarinet قلارينت F mus. clarinet.
klâsikᵍⁱ قلاسيك F classic; classical.
klâsör قلاسور F file.
klaviye, klavye قلاويه F mus. keyboard.
klefte قلفته Gk slang, same as **kılefte**.
kliket قليكت F pinging (of an engine). —**leş**= to ping, to knock.
klinikᵍⁱ قلينيك F clinic.
kliring قليرينگ E com. clearing, set off.
klişe قليشه F prin. half-tone.
klor قلور F chlorine.
kloş قلوش F bell-shaped (skirt, garment, etc.). — **etek** circular skirt; full skirt (cut on the cross).

klüb, klüpᵇⁱ قلوب F same as **kulüp**.

ko=ʳ قومه same as **koy**= **2**.
koalisyon قواليسيون F coalition.
kobat قوبات [kavvad] prov. vulgar; rude; ugly.
kobay قوباى F guinea pig, cavy.

koca 1 قوجه 1. husband. 2. elderly. man, elder. — **başı** headman. —**ya var**= to marry (woman). —**ya ver**= to give in marriage (woman). — **yarpuzu** a kind of wild rosemary, bot:, Cachris libanotis. — **yemişi***.

koca 2 قوجه 1. old, aged; ancient. 2. large, great; famous. **K— Balkan** the main range of the Balkan Mountains. — **baş***. — **bebek** big baby. — **kalıp** bulky man; fellow. — **karı***.

koca=ʳ **3** قوجامق to grow old.
kocabaş قوجه باش 1. cattle. 2. large beet.
kocakarı قوجه قارى impolite old woman.

kocal=

— **ilâcı** folk remedy. — **lâkırdısı** old wives' tale, nonsense. — **soğuğu** cold spell about the middle of March.
kocal=ᵢᵣ, kocala=ᵣ قوجالمق to grow old.
kocalakᵍⁱ قوجه لاوه a very large species of kite, Arabian kite, zool., *Milvus Arabicus*.
kocalaş=ᵢᵣ قوجالاشمق to grow old, to age.
kocalı قوجه لى having a husband, married.
kocalıkᵍⁱ قوجه لق 1. old age. 2. state of being a husband.
kocalt=ᵢᵣ قوجالتمق /ı/ to cause to grow old.
kocaman قوجامان قوجمان large, huge, enormous.
kocasız قوجه سز unmarried (woman); widow.
kocat=ᵢᵣ قوجاتمق /ı/ to cause to become old.
kocayemiş, kocayemişi قوجايمش قوجايمشى arbutus, strawberry tree, bot., *Arbutus unedo*.
kocu=ʳ قوجو same as **kocun=**.
kocun=ᵘʳ قوجنمق same as **gocun=**. —**dur=** /ı/ caus.
kocuş=ᵘʳ 1 قوجشمق archaic to embrace one another.
kocuş 2 قوجش archaic embrace.
koç 1 قوچ 1. ram. 2. sturdy and brave young man. 3. archaic man. — **başı** 1. mil. battering ram. 2. brave. — **boynuzu** 1. ram's horn. 2. melilot, bot., *Melilotus officinalis*. 3. naut. cleat. — **burun** hooked nose. — **burunlu** Roman nosed, hook nosed. — **katımı** ramming season. — **katımı fırtınası** storm occurring about the 20th of November. — **otu** green-winged meadow orchis, bot., *Orchis morio*. — **yiğit** handsome and brave young man. — **yumurtası** ram's testicles, sweetbreads.
koç=ᵃʳ 2 قوچمو archaic to hug.
koçaç قوچاج Sl obs. coachman.
koçakᵍⁱ قوچاق prov. 1. brave (man). 2. generous.
koçaklama قوچاقلامه a name given to heroic songs in Turkish folk music.
koçan قوچان 1. corn cob. 2. stump; check stub. 3. heart (of a vegetable).
koçkar قوچقار prov. very large and powerful ram used for fighting.
koçlan=ᵢᵣ قوچلنمق 1. to become a ram. 2. to act violently or bravely.
koçu قوچو Hung archaic 1. a kind of large carriage (used for picnic parties). 2. closed cattle shed. 3. granary. — **arabası** ox cart. —**cu** coachman.
koçuş=ᵘʳ قوچشمق same as **kocuş=** 1.
kod قود F code.
kodaman قودامان 1. great, notable, influential; magnate. 2. large; clumsy. —**lar** humorous notables, important people.
kodes قودس Gk slang prison.
kodeş, kodoş قودش قودوش Arm colloq. pimp.
kodukᵍᵘ قودوك archaic new-born donkey.

kof قوف 1. hollow, dry or rotten inside. 2. ignorant and stupid; weak.
kofana قوفانا Gk large **lüfer** (bluefish).
koflan=ᵢᵣ قوفلنمق to become hollow inside (through decaying).
koflukᵍᵘ قوفلق hollowness; emptiness; ignorance.
kofti قوفتى Gk slang lie; trick.
koğ=ᵃʳ 1 قوغمق same as **kov=** 1.
koğ 2 قوغ prov., same as **kov** 2.
koğa قوغه same as **kova**.
koğala=ʳ قوغالامق same as **kovala=**.
koğalıkᵍⁱ قوغه لق bullrush, bot., *Scirpus lacustris*.
koğla=ʳ قوغلامق same as **kovla=**.
koğu قوغو same as **koğ** 2.
koğucu قوغوجى same as **kovucu**.
koğukᵍᵘ قوغوق same as **kovuk**.
koğul=ᵘʳ قوغلمق same as **kovul=**.
koğula=ʳ قوغولامق same as **kovula=**.
koğuş 1 قوغش same as **kovuş** 1.
koğuş=ᵘʳ 2 قوغشمق same as **kovuş=** 3.
kokᵏᵘ 1 قوك E coke. — **kömürü** coke.
kok=ᵃʳ 2 قوقمق 1. to smell, to have a smell. 2. to stink. 3. to go bad; to spoil. 4. to be at hand, to give signs of being about to happen.
kokakᵍⁱ قوقاق prov. dirty; stinking, smelly.
kokar قوقار 1. that smells. 2. fetid, stinking.
kokarca قوقارجه polecat, zool., *Mustela putorius*.
kokartᵈⁱ قوقارت F cockade.
koket قوكت F coquette, coquettish.
kokla=ʳ قوقلامق 1. /ı/ to smell; to nuzzle. 2. to get the wind of (some coming event). —**yanın burnu düşer** It is very unpleasant, stinking. —**n=**, —**nıl=** 1. to be smelled. 2. to be enjoyed (as a mere taste).
koklaş=ᵢᵣ قوقلاشمق 1. to smell one another. 2. to caress and kiss one another. —**tır=** caus.
koklat=ᵢᵣ قوقلاتمق 1. /ı, a/ caus. of **kokla=**. 2. to cause to smell. 3. to give just a whiff of; to give in very minute quantity.
kokmuş قوقمش 1. rotten, spoiled, putrid. 2. very lazy; dirty man.
kokona (..'.) قوقونه Gk elderly Greek woman.
kokoniça (...'.) قوقونيچه Gk young girl.
kokoreç قوقورج Gk dish of sheep's lungs.
kokoroz قوقوروز Rom 1. ear of corn; the corn plant. 2. any pointed misshaped thing. 3. slang ugly (person). —**lan=** to be defiant or threatening. —**lu** dressed in a very showy way.
kokot قوقوت F prostitute.
kokoz قوقوز 1. slang very poor; hard up. 2. obs. senile, doting; decrepit. —**la=** to become penniless or poor. —**luk** destitution.
kokteyl ('.) قوكتيل E cocktail party.
koku قوقو 1. smell, scent, odor; perfume. 2. indication or inkling of something as yet

unseen. 3. *slang* cocaine. — al= 1. to perceive a smell, to catch a whiff of. 2. to receive an inkling. —sunu al= /ın/ 1. to perceive the smell of. 2. to get an inkling or have a presentiment of something. —su çık= 1. to be divulged (secret). 2. to give signs of its approach.

kokulu قوقولو 1. having a smell. 2. sweet smelling, fragrant; perfumed. — **sarı yonca** fragrant yellow melilot, *bot.*, *Melilotus officinalis.*

kokusuz قوقوسز without smell; scentless.

kokuş=ur قوقوشمق to go bad, to be spoiled.

kokuşukᵍᵘ قوقوشق spoiled, with a bad smell.

kokut=ur قوقوتمق 1. /ı/ to give out a smell; to cause to smell (a place). 2. to smell (bad). 3. to sicken, disgust.

kol قول 1. arm; foreleg of an animal. 2. sleeve. 3. branch; subdivision. 4. side, direction. 5. neck (of a musical instrument). 6. team; troop. 7. patrol. 8. wing (of an army, of a building); column of troops. 9. handle; bar. 10. strand (of rope). **—larını aç=** /a/ to receive with open arms. — **ağası***. **—a al=** *archaic* to extend a protecting hand. — **at=** to put forth branches, ramify, extend, develop; to branch out. — **bur=**, — **bük=** 1. to twist one's arm violently. 2. to break one's power. **—u bükül=** 1. for one's arm to be twisted in a struggle. 2. to be weakened or destroyed (one's power). **—unu bük=** /ın/ to twist someone's arm. — **çavuşu** *Ott. hist.* herald or messenger of the corps of Janissaries. — **çek=** /a/ *archaic* to paraph, to sign. **bir — çengi** 1. a group of dancing girls. 2. animated, high-spirited; talking loudly and heartily. **—a çık=** to turn out to go on patrol. — **demiri** iron bar behind a door to keep it closed. — **düğmesi** cuff link. — **emeği** manual labor. — **gez=** to go about as a patrol, to go the rounds. — **gibi** as thick as a person's arm (flowing water etc.). **—una gir=** /ın/ to take someone by the arm. — **kalemi** radius (bone). — **kanat** one's limbs. — **kanat kalma=** to be thoroughly exhausted. **—u kanadı kırıl=** to be thoroughly broken and dismayed. — **kanat kop=** to be left with no power whatsoever. — **kanat ol=** /a/ to take someone under protection. — **kapağı** turned-back part of a sleeve, cuff. — **kayığı** patrol boat. — **kemiği** humerus. **—unu kes=** /ın/ to break someone's power and leave him destitute. — **kırılır yen içinde, baş yarılır börk içinde** *proverb* (lit. The arm breaks inside the sleeve; the head breaks inside the cap.) Private things should be kept private. — **kola** arm in arm. — **kola ver=** to give an arm to another. **—una kuvvet** Strength to his arm. Bravo. — **nizamı** *mil.* column. — **ordu***. — **oyunu** a kind of dance. **—larını sallıya sallıya gel=** to come empty handed. — **saati** wrist watch. **—u teni** his arms and his body, limbs and trunk. — **uzat=** to ramify, to extend. **—u uzun** one whose power or influence is extensive, powerful and influential. — **vur=** to patrol. **—u yetişir** powerful. — **yor=** to work hard. — **yürüt=** to splice a rope by following the strand.

kola (́.) قولا It starch, starch paste. — **vur=**, — **yap=** /a/ to starch (clothes). **—cı** one who does laundry work, washing, starching and ironing (shirts, etc.).

kolaçan قولاچان *colloq.* a walking about (especially with an eye to pilfering). — **çevir=** to go around; to roam about. **—a çık=** to wander about seeing what can be picked up. — **et=** /ı/ to sound out, spy out.

kolağasıⁿⁱ قول آغاسی *Ott. hist.* adjutant major, lieutenant commander.

kolakᵍᵘ قولاق قولدبه *prov.* 1. one who has lost a hand or arm. 2. left-handed.

kolala=ʳ (...́.) قولالمق /ı/ to starch. **—n=** *pass.* **—t=** /ı, a/ *caus.*

kolalı قولالی starched.

kolan 1 قولان 1. broad band or belt; girth. 2. binding around the bottom of a tent. 3. rope of a swing. — **aşır=** 1. to throw the end of bight of a girth over a saddle, a pile of bales, etc. 2. to act in some outrageous manner. **—ı boşla=** to let go the girth. **—ı çek=**, **—ı kas=** to tighten up the girth. — **salıncağı** swing suspended on leather thongs or ropes. — **vur=** to girth a horse; to swing a standing swing. — **yeri** the part of a horse where the girth is bound.

kolan 2 قولان *archaic, same as* **kulan.**

kolay قولای easy; easy way to do something; means. **—ına bak=** /ın/ to look for the easiest way of doing something. **—ını bul=** /ın/ to find an easy way. — **gele**, — **gelsin** May it be easy (said to someone at work).

kolayca (..́.) قولایجه easily; fairly easy.

kolayda قولایده handy.

kolayla=ʳ قولایلامق to facilitate; to have nearly finished (a job, money, food, etc.); to get well into a job. **—n=**, **—ş=** to become easy; to be nearly finished. **—ştır=**, **—t=** *caus. of* **kolayla=**.

kolaylıkᵍⁱ قولایلق 1. easiness; facility in working. 2. means; easy circumstances, comfort. — **göster=** /a/ to help, to make things easy. **—la** easily.

kolbağıⁿⁱ قول باغی *prov.* bracelet.

kolbaşı قول باشی head of a troup; foreman.

kolcu قولجی 1. watchman, custom house guard. 2. agent for servants. — **kadın** *formerly* female

kolçak police agent sent to investigate prostitutes. **—luk** occupation of a watchman.

kolçakᵏᵘ قولپی 1. *archaic* piece of plate armor for the protection of either the upper arm or the forearm; gauntlet. 2. *archaic* mitten. 3. *archaic* cuff protector, armlet. 4. *prov.* bracelet.

koldaş قولداش *archaic* associate; companion; mate. **—lık** companionship.

kolej قولژ F a school of lycée level teaching in English or other foreign language.

kolektör قوللكتور F *auto.* collector, collector, ring, ship ring, commutator (of a dynamo).

kolera (..'.) قولرا قولرە Gk cholera.

kolgan قولغان *prov.* blessed thistle, *bot.*, *Carduus benedictus;* Spanish thistle, *bot.*, *Carduus acarna*. **— dikeni, — otu** *same as* **kolgan.**

kollaᵣ قوللامق /ı/ 1. to search; to keep under observation. 2. to look after, to protect. **—n=**, **—nıl=** *pass.*

kollab قوللاب *var. of* **kullâb 2.**

kolleksiyon قوللكسیون F collection.

kollu قوللو 1. having arms; having sleeves. 2. having (so many) contingents (military force). 3. having (so many) strands (rope). 4. branched, forked.

kollukᵏᵘ 1 قوللوق 1. cuff. 2. anything worn on the arm.

kollukᵏᵘ 2 قوللوق *archaic* police.

kolomborna قولومبورنە *obs.* a variety of gun.

kolon قولن F 1. *typogr.* column. 2. *anat.* colon.

kolonborne قولونبورنە *same as* **kolomborna.**

kolonya (..'.) قولونیە It eau de Cologne.

kolordu قولاوردو army corps.

koloridiye (..'..) قولوریدیە Gk young Spanish mackerel.

kolpo (.'.) قولپو It *slang* the right moment (to do something), opportunity (in games).

koltukᵏᵘ قولتوق 1. armpit. 2. armchair. 3. hawker; dealer in old clothes. 4. out of the way spot; blind alley. 5. small wine shop. 6. ceremony during a wedding when the bridegroom gives his arm to the bride. 7. *slang* house where couples meet secretly. **— altı** armpit; space under the arm. **— altına al=** /ı/ to take under one's protection or under one's arm. **— bakkal** small grocer (branch of a larger establishment). **— değneği** crutch. **— değneği ile** with the help of others. **— dersi** *Ott. hist.* extracurricular lessons in a medresse. **— dirsek** *arch.* console (of a portal etc.) **—a gir=** to marry. **—una gir=** /ın/ to give one's arm to some one, to put one's arm through another's. **— halatı** *naut.* mooring rope, breastfast. **—u kabar=, —ları kabar=** to swell with pride. **— kapısı** servant's entrance (in a big house). **— meyhane, — meyhanesi** small wine shop in an out-of-the-way place. **—ta ol=** *colloq.* to be another's guest, to go to an entertainment at another's expense. **— sarrafı** petty money changer. **—una sığın=** /ın/ to be under the wing of someone. **— taşı** *arch.* voussoir, archstone. **— ver=** /a/ to flatter. **—a ver=** to confide (a bride). to the female friends who will assist her to her chamber in her husband's house. **— veziri** *Ott. hist.* the Bostancıbaşı who had the privilege of supporting the Sultan by his arm on state occasions. **— yastığı** bolster on which the elbow can rest. **— zaviyesi** *fort.* shoulder angle.

koltukçu قولتوقچی 1. old clothes man. 2. maker or seller of armchairs. 3. keeper of a small out-of-the-way tavern. 4. flatterer, hypocrite.

koltuklaᵣ قولتوقلامق /ı/ 1. to support by the arm. 2. to take something under the arm. 3. to flatter. **—n=** *pass.*

koltuklu قولتوقلی having arms (chair); armchair.

koltuklukᵏᵘ قولتوقلق gusset at the armpit of a garment; dress shield.

kolye (.'.) قولیە F necklace.

kolyos, kolyoz قولیوس قولیوز Gk chub mackerel, *zool., Scomber colias.*

kolza قولزا F rape, rapeseed, *bot., Brassica napus.*

kom قوم 1. *prov.* winter station for flocks. 2. *archaic* rough wayside inn or shelter.

koma 1 قوما 1. *verbal n. of* **ko=.** 2. put, set down. 3. brought forward (matter). **— koş** Run hard.

koma 2 قومە *mus.* one of nine equally divided parts between two consecutive whole tones, in the Turkish music system of 24 unequal intervals.

koma 3 قوما *same as* **kuma.**

koma 4 (.'.) قومە F *med.* coma. **—ya gir=** to go into a coma.

komalak, komalika (...'.) قومالاق قومالیقە It *same as* **gomalak.**

komana قومنە It *naut., same as* **gomena.**

komanda قوماندە It *same as* **kumanda.**

kombina قومبینە F combine, factories, mills.

kombinezon قومبینەزون F 1. slip (underclothing). 2. arrangement, way.

komedi, komedya (..'.) قومدی قومدیا F 1. comedy. 2. farce.

komfor قومفور F modern accommodations; ease, comfort.

komiser قومیسر F superintendent of police.

komisyon قومیسیون F 1. commission, committee. 2. percentage. **—cu** commission agent. **—culuk** commission (business).

komita (..'.) قومیتا F revolutionary

line of guards; cordon. 4. ribbon, broad ribbon of an order. 5. umbilical cord. — **altına al=** /ı/ to cordon off, to isolate (by a sanitary measure).

korgeneral *neol.* corps commander, lieutenant general.

koridor قورى‍دور F corridor; passage.

korindon قورى‍ندون F *min.* corundum.

kork=ᵃʳ قورقمق /dan/ to be afraid, to fear. **—tuğu başına gel=**, **—tuğuna uğra=** to encounter the very thing one was afraid of.

korkakᵍᵘ قورقاق 1. timid; cowardly. 2. coward. **— karga** *slang* easily frightened, jumpy, nervous. **—lık** timidity; cowardice.

korku قورقو 1. fear, fright, terror, dread. 2. alarm; anxiety, care. 3. danger, peril. 4. threat, menace. **— dağları bekler** Of course one is afraid. **— ver=** /a/ to frighten.

korkulu قورقولى dangerous, frightening; perilous; dreadful. **— rüya** nightmare. **— rüya görmektense uyanık durmak hayırlıdır** It is better to remain awake than to have a nightmare; better to take precautions than to suffer.

korkulukᵍᵘ قورقولوك 1. scarecrow. 2. banister, balustrade; parapet. 3. guard of a sword hilt. 4. mere figurehead.

korkunçᶜᵘ قورقونج terrible, terrifying. **—luk** fearsomeness.

korkusuz قورقوسز 1. fearless, intrepid. 2. safe; undisturbed; quiet. **—luk** fearlessness; safety.

korkut=ᵘʳ قورقوتمق /ı/ *caus.* of **kork=**. 1. to frighten, alarm; to cause to be anxious. 2. to threaten, menace, to drive away by threats. **—ul=** *pass.*

korlu قورلو having glowing embers (fire, ashes).

korlukᵍᵘ قورلوك 1. fire of red hot embers. 2. *prov.* brazier.

korna, korne (′.) قورنه It car horn.

korniş قورنش F cornice.

korniza (′..) قورنيزه It cornice.

korno (′.) قورنو It 1. horn; powder horn (of a gun). 2. oil can.

koro (′.) قورو It chorus.

koroydo (′..) قوروي‍دو Gk *slang* idiot, fool.

korporasyon قورپوراسيون F corporation.

korsan قورسان It pirate; corsair. **— yelkeni** lateen sail. **—lık** piracy.

korse قورسه F corset.

korta, korte (′.) قورته It dating. **— et=**, **— yap=** to flirt, to date.

koru 1 قورو small wood, grove.

koru=ʳ **2** قورومق 1. to protect, defend; to watch over. 2. to cover (expenses).

korucu قوروجى rural guard; forest watchman. 2. *Ott. hist.* Janissary, old both in service and years but still in active service.

korukᵍᵘ قوروك unripe grape, sour grape. **— lüferi** medium sized **lüfer** caught in August. **— suyu** verjuice.

korulukᵍᵘ قورولق 1. small wood, grove, coppice. 2. wooded district.

koruma قوروما verbal n. of **koru= 2**.

korun 1 *neol., anat.* cornea. **— tabakası** stratum corneum.

korun=ᵘʳ **2** قورونمق 1. to defend oneself; to take shelter. 2. /dan/ to avoid.

korunakᵍᵘ قوروناق *prov.* shelter, refuge.

korunga قورونغه sainfoin, *bot., Onobrychis sativa.*

korunma قورونمه defense; a seeking protection or shelter.

korunukᵍᵘ قورونوك *prov.* 1. sheltered place. 2. protégé.

korut=ᵘʳ قوروتمق /ı, a/ *caus.* of **koru= 2**.

koruyucu قورويجى 1. protecting, protective. 2. defender. **— tababet** preventive medicine.

korvet قورووت F *naut.* corvette. **— kaptanı** commander. **— süvarisi** senior commander.

korza (′.) قورزه It *naut.* fouling (of two cables or chains).

koskoca (′..) قوصقوجه enormous; very eminent. **—man** huge, very big.

koskos قوصقوص puffed up with conceit. **—lan=** *slang* to be puffed up with conceit; to swagger.

Kostantaniye, Kostantiniye قسطنطينيه A former name of İstanbul, Constantinople.

kostüm قوستوم F costume. **—lük** material (for making costumes).

koş=ᵃʳ **1** قوشمق 1. to run; to go in haste, to race about. 2. /ı, a/ to harness; to put harnessed beasts to a vehicle. 3. /ı, a/ to give as escort or companion. 4. to put to work. 5. /ı/ to lay down (condition). **—up yat=** to keep on racing about.

koş 2 قوش *prov.* a pair. **— koş=** to put to or drive a pair of beasts.

koşa قوشه 1. *archaic*, same as **koş 2**. 2. *neol., phil.* concomitant.

koşaltı قوشالدى a pair of animals yoked or harnessed together.

koşma قوشمه 1. *verbal n.* of **koş= 1**. 2. musical composition played and sung in free form. **—ca** tag (children's game).

koştur=ᵘʳ قوشدرمق 1. *caus.* of **koş= 1**. 2. to run about and tire oneself (in doing something). 3. to dispatch.

koşu 1 قوشو 1. race; racing. 2. *archaic* class, order. 3. *archaic* a kind of merry dance air or song. **bir —** quickly, with a dash. **— atı** race horse. **— devesi** racing camel. **— kopar=** to run off all together (as though in a race). **—da koş=** to run in a race. **— meydanı** an open place, a race course. **— yolu** race course, track.

koşu 2 فوشو obs., var. of koçu.
koşucu فوشجی runner.
koşukᵍᵘ فوشو archaic ballad; folk song.
koşul=ᵘʳ فوشلی pass. of koş= 1.
koşulu فوشیلو 1. harnessed; put to (carriage). 2. mil. horse-drawn.
koşum فوشم فوشوم 1. act of harnessing. 2. harness. 3. archaic a single run. bir —da 1. at one run. 2. at one harnessing. — hayvanı carriage horse, draft horse. — kayışı trace (of a harness). —lu harnessed, with harness on.
koşun 1 فوشون archaic 1. troops, military forces. 2. line, row (of people). — bağla= to stand in line.
koşun=ᵘʳ 2 فوشنم archaic 1. to run about idly. 2. to force one's company on another.
koşuntu فوشندی archaic 1. followers; rabble. 2. accomplices.
koşuş 1 فوشش verbal n. of koş= 1.
koşuş=ᵘʳ 2 فوششم to run together; to crowd in; to make a concerted rush. —tur= /ı/ caus.
koşut neol. parallel. —luk parallelism.
kota 1 فوطه prov. water buffalo.
kota 2 (´.) فوطه F fin. quoted (on the stock exchange); com. quota.
kotan فوطان قوطان Georgian prov. very large plow.
kotar=ᵘʳ فوتارم to dish up (food); to serve out, especially in pişirip kotar=, cf. pişir=.
kotas, kotaz فوطاس قوطاز [Persian kutas] archaic 1. plume of yak's hair (used as an ornament on a horse). 2. yak, zool., Bos grunniens. 3. woman's turban. 4. bird's crest.
kotra 1 (´.) فوطره E cutter (boat).
kotra 2 (´.) فوطره Sl prov. pen for small animals.
kov=ᵃʳ 1 فوودم فوغمم /ı/ 1. to drive away; to send away in disgrace. 2. to turn back; to repel. 3. to persecute; to denounce, to slander.
kov 2 فوع prov. tittle-tattle; scandal; gossip. — et=, — geç= to slander.
kova فوغا قووا bucket.
kovala=ʳ فوالامم قوغالامم قوغلی قووا لامم /ı/ 1. to pursue, run after, chase. 2. to endeavor to obtain.
kovalakᵍᵘ فوغالو prov. 1. who gives himself airs; braggart; boasting. 2. wild, unreasonable, flighty.
kovalamaca فوغالاماجه game of tag.
kovalan=ᵘʳ قوغالانم pass. of kovala=.
kovan 1 فوغان قووان 1. hive. 2. cartridge case; shell case. — çiçeği, — otu foxglove, bot., Digitalis; a kind of rosemary, bot., Cachrys libanotis. — resmi Ott. hist. tax on beehives.
kovan 2 فوغان that drives away or pursues.

kovcu فوجی قوغجی archaic informer, slanderer.
kovdur=ᵘʳ فودرمه قوغدرمم /ı, a/ caus. of kov= 1.
kovla=ʳ فولامه قغلامم prov. /ı/ to calumniate; to denounce; to backbite.
kovucu فوجی قوغجی 1. who chases, drives away. 2. archaic, same as kovcu.
kovukᵍᵘ فووق قوغوق hollow; cavity. —lu having a hollow.
kovul=ᵘʳ فوغولم pass. of kov= 1.
kovula=ʳ فوغولامم /ı/ prov. to calumniate; to denounce. —n= pass.
kovuş 1 فووش قوغوش large room; dormitory; ward. — ağacı baulk of timber; beam, joist. — tut= to hold akimbo (arms).
kovuş 2 فوغنش قوغش verbal n. of kov= 1.
kovuş=ᵘʳ 3 فوغشم prov. /la/ to pursue one another; to drive one another away. —tur= /ı, a/ caus.
kovuşturma neol. legal proceedings, prosecution.
koy 1 قوى 1. small bay or inlet. 2. nook.
koy=ᵃʳ 2 قومم 1. /ı/ to put, place, set. 2. /ı/ to let go; to leave. 3. /ı/ to allow, permit. 4. /ı/ to suppose. 5. /a/ slang to affect, afflict, sadden, impress, touch. —dunsa bul I can't find it anywhere. —up git= /ı/ to leave a thing or someone and go away.
koya قوه archaic pellet regurgitated by a bird of prey after digesting its food. —sını at= to regurgitate its pellet (bird of prey).
koyakᵍᵘ قوياق prov. valley.
koyar قويار archaic confluence of two streams.
koyu قوی 1. thick; dense (liquid, darkness). 2. deep, dark (color). 3. true, genuine. 4. fervent, extreme.
koyukᵍᵘ قويوق prov. sad, touching.
koyul=ᵘʳ 1 قويولم قيولم to become dense.
koyul=ᵘʳ 2 قويولم قيولم pass. of koy= 2. 1. to be put, placed. 2. /a/ to be busied with; to set to (work, etc.), to begin. 3. /a/ to fall on, to attack. 4. archaic to be poured, to fall into.
koyulan=ᵘʳ, koyulaş=ᵘʳ قويولانمم قويولاشمم to become dense, to become dark (color). —dır=, —tır= /ı/ caus.
koyulat=ᵘʳ قويولاتمم /ı/ 1. to make thick, to thicken (fluid). 2. to make deep (color), to deepen in color.
koyult=ᵘʳ قويولتم /ı/ 1. to render dense. 2. to thicken (soup etc.). 3. to darken (color).
koyulukᵍᵘ قويولق 1. thickness, density (of a fluid). 2. depth (of color). 3. extremity.
koyun 1 قويون قوين 1. sheep. 2. mild, spiritless person; simpleton. — bakışı sheepish, silly look. — bakışlı silly, simpleton

(in look). — **başlı**, — **beyinli** stupid. —**un bulunmadığı yerde keçiye Abdurrahman Çelebi derler** (lit. During a scarcity of sheep, they call a goat **Abdurrahman Çelebi**.) If the best is not at hand, the second-best will do. — **dede** colloq. fool. — **emini** Ott. hist. receiver-general of the sheep tax. — **eti** mutton. — **gibi** stupid, simpleton. — **gözü***, — **gözlü** 1. blue or green-eyed. 2. silly, simpleton (in looks). — **kaval dinler gibi** listening without understanding. — **kenesi** sheep tick, zool., Melophagus ovinus. — **kıran** common tutsan, bot., Hypericum androsaemum. — **otu** agrimony, bot., Agrimonia eupatorium; hemp agrimony, bot., Eupatorium cannabinum. — **saman yemez** proverb (lit. A sheep will not eat chopped straw.) What is being done is not good enough. — **sarmaşığı** orach, bot., Atriplex. — **yılı** the year of the sheep, the eighth year in the old Turkish cycle of years.

koyun^ynu 2 قویون قویـن 1. bosom; breast. 2. breast pocket. —**una al**= /ı/ to take to bed with one. —**una gir**= /ın/ to go to bed with someone. —**una koy**= /ı/ to put into one's bosom or breast pocket. — **koyuna** in each other's arms. — **saati** pocket watch.

koyungözü^nü قویون گوزی feverfew, bot., Chrysanthemum parthenium.

koyuntu قویـنتی prov. grief, sorrow.

koyuver=^ir, **koyver**=^ir قویـو ویر مك قویـویـر مك /ı/ 1. to let go; to allow. 2. just to put down.

koz قوز 1. walnut. 2. trump (at cards). — **helvası** nougat. — **kabuğuna gir**= to creep into any hole in order to hide oneself. — **kaybet**= to lose one's case (at law or in an argument). — **kır**= 1. to play a trump. 2. to commit an indiscretion, to make a faux pas. — **oyna**= to play trumps. —**unu pay et**=, —**unu paylaş**= /la/ to settle accounts; to share expenses; to come to an agreement.

koza قوزه 1. silk cocoon. 2. any small round thing. 3. a kind of bean.

kozak^ğı قوزاق 1. cone of a coniferous tree. 2. cone-shaped.

kozalak^ğı قوزالاق 1. cypress cone, cone. 2. small stunted thing. 3. obs. a small disc placed over soft wax seals for their protection. — **mahallesi** slang graveyard. —**lı** coniferous.

kozbekçileri قوزبكجیلری Ott. hist. servant whose job was to carry the Sultan's clothes.

köçek^ği 1 كوچك [kûçek] 1. boy dancer; man dancer. 2. camel foal. 3. archaic small thing; young (of any animal). — **fistanı** boy dancer's kilt. — **oğlanı** boy dancer.

köçek 2 كوچك P Or. mus. a **makam** starting with e' and ending like **saba**.

köçekçe كوچكچه tune or music used while a man is dancing.

köçekle=^r كوچكله مك to give birth to a foal.

köfte كوفته P meat balls. —**ci** maker and seller of meat balls.

köftehor كوفته خور P cunning rogue (said half affectionately). —**!** Lucky dog!

köfter كوفتر Gk kind of grape sweet (made by boiling down grape juice and drying it in thin cakes).

köftün^nü كوفتون Gk oil cake (food for cattle).

köhne كهنه P old; worn out; antiquated; second-hand. —**gi** (..—) P lrnd. agedness.

köhnelen=^ir, **köhneleş**=^ir كهنه لنمك كهنه لشمك to become old, worn and dilapidated.

köhnelik^ği كهنه لك the condition of being old and worn out.

kök 1 كوك 1. root; base. 2. root (of a tooth). 3. origin. — **at**= same as **kök sal**=. — **bacaklılar** neol., zool., Rhizopoda. — **boya**, — **boyası** madder (root). —**ünden buda**= /ı/ to root out. — **işareti** neol., alg. radical. —**ünü kazı**= /ın/ to extirpate, eradicate. —**ü kazıl**= to be extirpated, utterly destroyed. —**ünü kes**= /ın/ to wipe out, to extirpate (a thing). —**ünden kesip at**= /ı/ to reject or settle a matter once and for all. —**üne kibrit suyu!** Damn the whole mess! —**ünden kopar**= /ı/ to eradicate. —**ünü kurut**= /ın/ to exterminate. — **mantar** bot., Mycorhiza. — **sal**= to send out roots, to be deeply rooted. — **sök**= to do a very difficult job. —**ünden sök**= /ı/ to pull out by the roots, to root out. — **söktür**= to force someone (to do something). —**ten sürme** by descent. — **tut**= to take root.

kök 2 كوك P tuning peg of a stringed instrument. — **et**= /ı/ to tune (a stringed instrument).

kökçü كوكچی herbalist.

köke كوكه It archaic an obsolete kind of ship high in the freeboard.

köken كوكن 1. prov. stem of a melon or squash plant. 2. prov. nursery bed (for seedling plants). 3. prov. one's native place. 4. neol., gram. radical. —**inde büyü**= to grow up at home, not to see the world.

kökle=^r 1 كوكله مك to tune (musical instrument).

kökle=^r 2 كوكله مك /ı/ 1. to uproot; to clear roots from the ground. 2. to secure with stitches through the thickness (mattress). 3. drivers' slang to step on the accelerator. —**n**= pass. 1. to take root; to put forth roots. 2. to become firmly established. —**ş**= to take root. —**ştir**= /ı/ caus. of **kökleş**=.

köklü كوكلی having roots; rooted. — **kerevez** turnip-rooted celery.

köknar كوكنار Gk fir, bot., Abies.

kökün كوكن كوكین 1. same as **köken**. 2. from the root, radically.

köle كوله male slave, slave. —**niz** your very

humble servant. — **doyuran** a filling food. **—n olayım** *colloq.* Please. I beg you.
köleleştir=ᴵʳ كولشتيرمك to reduce to slavery.
kölelikᵍⁱ كوللك slavery.
kölemen كولمن 1. *hist.* Circassian slave brought up as a warrior; Mameluk (in Egypt). 2. *Ott. hist.* corps of military slaves.
kömür كومور 1. charcoal. 2. coal. 3. coal black. — **çarp=** /ı/ to overcome (charcoal fumes). — **gibi** 1. like coal. 2. as black as coal. — **gözlü** black eyed. — **ocağı** coal mine.
kömürcü كومرجى 1. coal dealer; stoker. 2. burner of charcoal. — **çırağına dön=** to get black all over.
kömürleş=ᴵʳ كومورلشمك to become carbonized. **—me** carbonization.
kömürlükᵍⁱ كومورلك 1. coal hole; coal cellar. 2. *naut.* bunker.
könçekᵍⁱ كنجك *prov.* drawers, trousers.
köpekᵍⁱ كوپك 1. dog. 2. vile person; cur. 3. *print.* letter remaining under a page or format. — **ayası** horehound, *bot., Marrubium vulgare.* — **balığı** shark, dogfish, *zool., Mustelus vulgaris.* — **bile yemez** very bad (food). — **dişi** canine tooth. — **gibi** doglike; cringing. — **gibi kıvrıl=** 1. to coil oneself up lazily while sleeping or resting. 2. to wriggle about like a fawning dog. **—ler güler buna** too funny for anything. — **kenesi** dog tick, *zool., Haematopinus piliferus.* — **memesi** tumor or bubo under the armpit. — **oğlu** *colloq.* son of a dog. **—i öldürene sürdürürler** *proverb* It is the man who kills the dog who gets driven out. It is the guilty one who suffers. — **pençesi** wild convolvulus, hooded bindweed, *bot., Calystegia sepium.* — **tasması** dog's leather collar. — **üzümü** black nightshade, *bot., Solanum nigrum.* — **yese kudurur** very insulting and harsh.
köpekle=ʳ كوپكلەمك 1. to cringe like a beaten dog. 2. to yield in humiliation.
köpekleş=ᴵʳ كوپكلشمك to become like a dog by panting, crouching, whining etc.
köpeklikᵍⁱ كوپكلك 1. quality of a dog. 2. lowdown behavior; baseness.
köpoğlu كوپوغلى [köpek oğlu] *colloq.* scoundrel, rat. — **köpek** dog, son of a dog; great scoundrel (term of violent abuse). **—luk** dirty trick; meanness.
köprü كوپرو كيپرو 1. bridge. 2. *dentistry* bridge. 3. hasp (of a lock). 4. *slang* a cheating (in gambling). — **altı çocukları** deserted children. **—den geçinceye kadar ayıya dayı derler** *proverb* They call the bear "uncle" until they have crossed the bridge. You have to play up to a person who can do you harm until you have gotten what you want. — **gözü** arch of a bridge. — **kur=** wrestling to bridge. — **mahmuzu** fender of a bridge. — **tombazı** bridge pontoon.
köprübaşı كوپروباشى 1. square giving access to a bridge. 2. *mil.* bridgehead.
köprücü كوپروجى 1. bridge-building specialist. 2. *mil.* pontoon soldier.
köprücükᵍⁱ كوپروجك *anat.* collar bone.
köprülü كوپرولى having a bridge; bridged over.
köpükᵍⁱ كوپوك كيپوك 1. froth; foam. 2. scum; seeds; lather.
köpüklen=ᴵʳ كوپوكلنمك 1. to foam. 2. to be covered with froth, foam etc. **—dir=** /ı/ *caus.*
köpüklü كوپوكلى frothy, foamy; foaming.
köpür=ᵘʳ كوپورمك كيپورمك 1. to froth; to foam; to foam (at the mouth). 2. to lather, make suds. 3. to effervesce. 4. to become furious, enraged. **—t=** /ı/ *caus.*
kör 1 كور [kûr 5] 1. blind; without foresight. 2. careless, blundering. 3. blunt (knife, point, etc.). 4. fine-meshed (net). 5. eyeless (needle). 6. dim. — **barsak*.** — **boğaz** 1. appetite (contemptuously). 2. gluttonous. — **döğüşü** confusion, muddle. **bir — döğüşüdür gidiyor** It is a complete muddle. — **duman** *prov.* heavy fog. — **düğüm** 1. knot that cannot be untied, snarl, tangle. 2. deadlock. — **ebe*.** — **gözlü** 1. blind. 2. ungrateful. — **hat** rail. siding (the dead end). **—ün istediği bir göz, Allah vermiş iki göz** *proverb* The blind man prayed for an eye; God has granted him two *said when some one receives much more than what he expected.* **—ün istediği iki göz, biri elâ biri boz** *proverb* The blind man wishes he had two eyes, one brown, the other gray *said when some one wishes to have something above his worth.* — **kadı** outspoken, downright. — **kadıya körsün de=** to call a spade a spade. — **kandil** dead drunk. — **kaya** submerged rock. **—ünü kır=** /ın/ to humble the pride (of). — **kör parmağım gözüne** as plain as a pikestaff. — **körüne, —ü körüne** blindly; carelessly; at random. — **kuyu** a dry well. — **kütük** dead drunk. — **nişancılık** shooting at random (without a target). — **nümayiş** stupid show, senseless parade. — **ocak** childless family. — **oğlu*.** — **olası, — olasıca** *colloq.* Damn! — **olası herif** the cursed fellow. — **ölür badem gözlü olur, kel ölür sırma saçlı olur** When the blind man dies, they say he had almond eyes; when a baldheaded one dies they say he had golden hair *exaggerated praise of the dead or the past.* **—ünü öldür=** to have control over one's temper. — **sıçan** mole, *zool., Talpa europaea.* — **talih** bad luck, evil destiny. — **tane** bunted grain; smut-ball. — **taşı, kelin başı** The blind man's stone, the bald headed man's head *said when an evasive*

answer is necessary. **—ün taşı rast geldi** The blind man's stone hit the mark *said when some unlikely person has achieved success.* **— tırnak** injured and deformed fingernail. **— topal** incompletely, somehow, so so. **—le yatan şaşı kalkar** (*lit.* If you sleep with a blind man you will wake up crosseyed.) If you associate with someone with troubles you will have troubles too. **— yılan** blind worm or snake (actually a legless lizard), *zool., Anguis fragilis.*

kör 2 كور [gûr 1] *archaic* grave, tomb.
kör 3 كور F *cards* hearts.
körbağırsakᵍⁱ كور باغرصاغى *anat.* caecum, appendix.
körbaht كور بخت P *lrnd.* of blind fortune, unlucky, unfortunate.
körbarsakᵍⁱ كور با رصاغى *var.* of **körbağırsak**.
kördil كور دل P *lrnd.* foolish, unfeeling; lazy.
körebe كور ابه blindman's buff; the blindfolded player.
körel=ⁱʳ كور لمك *prov.* to become blind, blunt or dim. **—me** *neol., biol.* atrophy.
köreşe كور شه frozen crust on snow.
körfez كور فز Gk gulf; bay; inlet.
körle=ʳ كور له مك /ı/ 1. to blind; to blunt. 2. to damp, discourage. 3. to bring to nought. **—me** an acting as though blind. **—meden, —mesine** blindly, at random. **—n=** *pass.* of **körle=**. **—ş=** to become blind. **—t=** /ı/ same as **körle=**.
körlükᵍᵘ كور لك 1. blindness, bluntness. 2. lack of foresight; blundering.
köroğlu كور اوغلو 1. *w. cap.* hero of a popular legend. 2. *colloq.* wife. **K—nun Ayvazı** an inseparable companion. **bir K— bir Ayvaz** just a wife and husband, without children.
körpe كورپه young, tender, fresh; very young and fresh. **— fidan** fresh and handsome youth. **—lik** freshness; tenderness; youth.
körşe كور شه same as **köreşe**.
körü=ʳ كور مك /ı/ *prov.* to blow with a bellows (fire, etc.).
körükᵍᵘ كور لك 1. a pair of bellows. 2. folding roof, cover (of a car etc.). **—çü** 1. bellows maker. 2. one who fans the flame, instigator, agitator.
körükle=ʳ كور كله مك /ı/ 1. to fan a flame with bellows. 2. to encourage, incite. **—n=** *pass.* **—t=** /ı, a/ *caus.* of **körükle=**.
körüklü كور كلى 1. having bellows. 2. having a folding hood (carriage). **— bavul** expanding suitcase.
kös 1 كوس [kus 2] big drum used in **Mehter** music. **— dinlemiş** too sophisticated to be impressed; callous, insensitive.
kös 2 كوس in **kös kös yürü=** to walk in a pensive or dejected manner.
köse كوسه P 1. with little or no beard. 2. sparsely timbered. **— sakal** very sparse beard.
köseğen كوسه گن sensitive plant (a kind of mimosa).
köseği كوسه گى 1. poker. 2. piece of wood burnt at the end.
kösele كوسه له · كوسا له [*Persian gosale*] stout leather (used for soles). **— gibi** very tough. **— kova** leather bucket. **— suratlı** shameless. **— taşı** 1. sandstone (used for polishing marble). 2. shoemaker's lapstone.
köselikᵍⁱ كوسه لك a being beardless or scant of beard.
kösem, kösemen كوسه من كوسه 1. ram or goat that leads the flock; bellwether. 2. ram trained to fight. 3. daredevil.
kösemlikᵍⁱ كوسه ملك leadership. **— et=** to act the leader.
köskötürüm كوس كوتوروم completely paralyzed.
kösnü 1 كوسنى *prov.* mole (animal).
kösnü=ʳ **2** كوسنه مك *prov.* to be in heat (female beast).
kösnükᵍᵘ كوسنوك *archaic* 1. lustful. 2. in heat (female beast).
köstebekᵍⁱ كوسته بك mole, *zool., Talpa europaea.* **— illeti** kind of scrofula (which a mole was supposed to cure).
köstekᵍⁱ كوسته ك 1. watch chain. 2. fetter, hobble. 3. brake. **—i kır=** *colloq.* to break one's fetters, to run away. **— vur=** /a/ to hobble (horse).
köstekle=ʳ كوسته كله مك /ı/ 1. to tether or fetter (horse, etc.). 2. to tie up, prevent (matter etc.). **—n=** *pass.*
köstekli كوسته كلى furnished or secured with a chain etc.; tethered, fettered.
Köstence كوسته نجه *geog.* Constanza.
köstere كوسته ره *var.* of **küstere**.
köşe كوشه [gûşe] 1. corner; angle. 2. nook; retreat. **— başı** street corner. **— başı yazıcısı** public scribe. **— bucak** every hole and corner. **—de bucakta** here and there; everywhere. **—sine çekil=, bir —ye çekil=** to withdraw into one's corner; to go into retirement; to withdraw from public life. **— doktoru** doctor who has no patients. **— kadısı** stay-at-home. **— kapmaca** puss in the corner. **— köşe** 1. every hole and corner. 2. angular, full of corners. **— müftüsü** (*lit.*, street-corner lawyer) pettifogging hatcher of quasilegal rascality. **— ol=** *archaic* to go into retirement. **—ye otur=** to get married (girl). **— sarrafı** petty moneychanger. **— taşı** cornerstone. **— ustası** *archaic* deputy warden of a trade guild in a large city. **— yer** out of the way place, retired spot. **—dar şal** Cashmere shawl with a plain ground and a design of palms in the corners.
köşebentᵈᵗ كوشه بند P angle-iron.

köşek^ġı كوشاك archaic camel colt (of less than a year). —le= same as köçekle=.
köşelek^ġı كوشەلەك archaic 1. very small camel colt. 2. anything very small of its kind.
köşeleme كوشەلەمە angular; having angles or corners; in an angular way, angularly, diagonally.
köşeli كوشەلى cornered, angled.
köşelik^ġı كوشەلىك 1. quality or functions of a corner or angle. 2. thing or piece of furniture special to a corner. 3. arch. cornerstone; cornerpiece.
köşk^kü كوشك P 1. villa; summerhouse; pavilion. 2. afterdeck cabin. 3. in the card game called fitil a score of twenty points. —lü fire lookout.
kötek^ġı 1 كوتەك a beating, cudgeling. — at=, — çek= /ı/ to give a beating. — ye= to get a beating.
kötek^ġı 2 كوتەك umbra (fish), zool., Umbrina cirrhosa.
kötrüm كوترم same as kötürüm.
kötü كوتو bad, wicked, evil. — günler hard times. — kadın prostitute; disreputable woman. — kişi ol= to become a bad person in the eyes of someone. — kötü düşün= to be worried and brooding. — söyle= 1. to talk evil (of). 2. to use harsh words. — yola sap= to become a prostitute.
kötüle=^r كوتولە /ı/ 1. to speak ill of, slander. 2. to become a wreck (from illness). —n= 1. to become bad. 2. to be the subject of evil talk.
kötüleş=^ır كوتولەش to become bad, to deteriorate. —tir= /ı/ caus.
kötülük^ġü كوتولوك 1. badness; wickedness. 2. bad act; wrong; harm. — et= /a/ to do harm or evil.
kötümse=^r neol. /ı/ to think ill of.
kötümser neol. pessimistic; derogatory. —lik pessimism.
kötürüm كوتورم paralyzed; crippled. — ol= to be paralyzed. —lük paralysis.
köy كوى [kûy] village; country (as opposed to town). — adamı villager. — ağası village headman. — ahalisi inhabitants of a village; the peasants. — başı 1. entrance to a village. 2. headman of a village. — muhtarı headman of a village. — odası village social room; guesthouse for travelers. — vur= to attack and sack a village.
köydaş, köydeş (.—) كوىداش a person from the same village.
köylü كوىلى 1. belonging to a village; villager, peasant. 2. fellow villager. 3. rough, bucolic. —lük a being born in a village.
köz كوز embers.
kral قرال Sl same as kıral.

krank قرانك E in krank mili crankshaft.
kravat قراوات F necktie.
kredi قرەدى F credit.
krem قرەم F face cream, hand cream.
krema قرەما It cream (of milk etc.).
kremayer قرەماىەر F mech. rack.
kremşantiye قرەمشانتىە F whipped cream.
krep قرەپ F 1. crepe. 2. French pancake. —döşin F crêpe de Chine.
kreş قرەش F public nursery for infants, crèche.
kriko (.'.) قرىكو It jack, lifting jack. —ya al= /ı/ to jack up.
kristal^ll قرىستال F 1. crystal. 2. slang cocaine.
kriz قرىز F crisis.
kroki قروكى F sketch, architect's drawing; plat.
krom قروم F chromium.
kromatik^ġı قروماتىك F chromatic; colored. — iplik chromatic fiber.
kron قرون F crown, koroner (coin).
kropi, krupi (.'.) قروپى It naut. knot. — bağı figure of eight knot.
kruvazör قروازور F cruiser.
=ku 1 قو cf. =gı 1.
kû 2 (—) كو P lrnd. where?
kû 3 (—) كو P lrnd. 1. street; road; thoroughfare. 2. district.
-kûb (—) كوب P lrnd. that knocks, pounds, stamps, as in paykûb.
kuba (——) قوبا A lrnd. ringworm, dry scab.
kubad قوباد prov. 1. same as kobat. 2. common (accent or way of speaking). —lık coarseness.
kubaş=^ır قوباش prov. to share in doing something; to be partners in any work.
kubaşık^ġı قوباشىق prov. job done together.
kubaşma قوباشما lending a hand to one another.
kubat قوبات same as kubad.
kubbe قبە A 1. dome, cupola. 2. poet. vault (of heaven), sky. — altı Ott. hist. the apartments in Topkapı Saray Palace where councils of state and public receptions used to be held. — çevir= archaic 1. to make a dome. 2. to devise a plan. —leri çınlat= make the welkin ring. — destar Ott. hist. a dome shaped turban. —i ezrak lrnd. the blue vault, i. e. the sky, firmament. — gibi 1. dome shaped, convex. 2. lumpy, ugly. K—i Hadra the Green Dome name of the Mausoleum of Mevlâna Jalaleddin-i Rumi in Konya. — kalıbı frame over which a dome is built. —i lâciverdî lrnd. sky. —i minâ lrnd. the azure vault, the sky. — veziri Ott. hist. vezir appointed as a member of a council of state. —i zerbeft lrnd., lit. a starlit night. —i zerin lrnd. the sun; the dawn.
kubbelen=^ır قبەلەن to become dome shaped,

convex, tumid. **—dir=** caus.
kubbeli قبه لى domed; dome shaped, convex.
kubbetülarz قبة الارض A lrnd. center of the surface of the habitable portion of the globe.
Kubbetülislâm (....—) قبة الاسلام A lrnd., geog., a name of the city of Balkh.
kûbe (—.) كوبه P lrnd. 1. beater, pounder, pestle. 2. a kind of drum or tomtom.
kubeb قبب A lrnd., pl. of **kubbe**.
kûbekû (—.—) كوبكو P lrnd. street by street; from place to place.
kubh قبح A lrnd. 1. a being ugly; ugliness. 2. unseemliness; defect. **—iyat** (..—) A pl. ugly acts.
kuble قبله A lrnd. kiss.
kubuh[bhu] قبح A var. of **kubh**.
kubûr 1 (.—) قبور A lrnd., pl. of **kabir 1**.
kubur 2 قبور 1. holster; quiver; long case. 2. horse pistol. 3. hole in a latrine. **— gibi** like a case, i. e. tight fitting. **— piştovu** horse pistol. **—luk** quiver.
kûc (—) كوج P lrnd. squinting (eye); squint eyed.
kucak[ğı] قوجاق 1. breast; embrace; lap. 2. armful. **—ta** in arms (infant). **— aç=** /a/ to receive with open arms. **—ına al=** to embrace; to take on one's lap. **— çocuğu, —ta çocuk** a child in arms, small baby. **—ına düş=** /ın/ to fall into the midst of (danger, trouble, etc.). **—ta gezdir=** /ı/ to carry about in arms (infant). **— kucağa** 1. in one another's arms. 2. very close together. **—ına otur=** /ın/ to sit on somebody's lap. **—ında yat=** /ın/ to lie in someone's arms.
kucakla=[r] قوجاقلامق /ı/ 1. to embrace, to take in one's arms. 2. to surround; to include. **—n=** pass. **—ş=** /la/ to embrace one another. **—t=** /ı, a/ caus. of **kucakla=**.
kûçe (—.) كوچه P lrnd. 1. narrow street, alley. 2. small region of a town. 3. hamlet. **—i bastan** (lit., the old alley) the world. **—i bazar** the byways and market places. **—i serbest** blind alley.
kûçek[ği] (—.) كوچك P same as **köçek 2**.
kuçu kuçu قوچو قوچو 1. call to a dog. 2. child's language dog, bow-wow.
kûd (—) كود P lrnd. 1. heap, mound (corn). 2. dunghill; manure.
kudama قضاما A prov. roasted chickpeas.
kuddam (.—) قدّام A lrnd. the front.
kuddas (.—) قدّاس A lrnd. 1. Christian Holy Communion, Mass. 2. consecrated wafer, the Host.
kuddise قدّس A lrnd. may he or it be blessed. **—sirruhu** may his grave be hallowed (said of a saintly person).
kuddus (.—) قدّوس A lrnd. most holy, all-holy (God). **—î** (.——) A pertaining to the all-holy God. **—iyet** (.——.) quality sanctity.
kûdek[ki] (—.) كودك P lrnd. boy, lad, infant. **—î** (—.—) P 1. childhood, infancy. 2. childish act, childishness.
kudema (..—) قدما A lrnd., pl. of **kadîm 1**, 1. the ancients. 2. eminent people; elders.
kudret قدرت A 1. power; might; strength; capacity. 2. the omnipotence of God. 3. wealth. 4. nature. **— hamamı** thermal spring. **— helvası** manna. **— sahibi** man of wealth. **— topu** thunder. **—im yetişmez** 1. I am not strong enough. 2. I can't afford it.
kudretintisab (....—) قدرت انتساب P lrnd. endued with power.
kudretli قدرتلى 1. powerful; capable. 2. rich, wealthy.
kudretsiz قدرتسز powerless; feeble; incapable. **—lik** feebleness.
kudretyab (..—) قدرت ياب P lrnd. who finds the power; powerful.
kuds قدس A lrnd. 1. holiness, sanctity, purity. 2. paradise; heaven. 3. w. cap. Jerusalem. 4. w. cap., a name of the Archangel Gabriel. **K—i Şerif** Jerusalem.
kudsî (.—) قدسى A lrnd. sacred, holy, divine.
kudsîyan (.——) قدسيان P lrnd. inhabitants of paradise, angels.
kudsiyat (.——) قدسيات A lrnd. 1. poems or verses containing expressions which none but saints could utter. 2. sacred things.
kudsiyet قدسيت A lrnd. holiness, sanctity, purity.
kudubet (.—.) قدوبت [gudûbet] colloq. 1. surly, grim (countenance). 2. ugly faced.
kudum 1 قدوم Or. mus. a small double drum used for rhythm in Mevlevi music; it is played with special small sticks.
kudum 2 (.—) قدوم A lrnd. a coming, arriving; arrival. **—î** (.——) A pertaining to an arrival.
kudumiye (.——.) قدوميه Ott. hist. 1. offering or present to one who arrives or by one who arrives. 2. poem of congratulation on an arrival.
kudumzen قدومزن P lrnd. a player of the **kudüm**.
kudur=[ur] قودورمق 1. to be infected with rabies; to go mad. 2. to become as rabid as a mad dog.
kudurgan قودورغان easily enraged.
kudurmuş قودورمش mad (dog); gone mad, furious; rabid.
kudurt=[ur] قودورتمق /ı/ caus. of **kudur=**.
kuduruk[ğu] قودوروق gone mad, furious.
kuduz قودوز، قودز، قوطوز، قوتوز

kudüm 1. hydrophobia, rabies. 2. suffering from hydrophobia; rabid, mad (dog). — **böceği** Spanish blister fly, zool., *Cantharis vesicatoria*. — **otu** the herb *Cynanchum monspeliacum*.

kudüm قدوم same as **kudum** 1.

Kudüs قدس [kuds] Jerusalem.

kûf (——) كوف P *lrnd.* 1. large owl. 2. weaver's sley carrying the reed.

kûfi (——.) كوفى A round wickerwork coracle (used on the Tigris).

Kûfe كوفه *geog.* the city of Kufa.

Kûfî (——) كوفى 1. The Cufic script of Arabic writing. 2. of or from the city of Kufa.

kufl[iü] قفل A *lrnd.* lock, bolt. **—i asman** P (*lit.*, the lock of heaven) misbelief, heresy. **—i Rumi** padlock. **—ger** P locksmith. **—küşa** P (..—) picklock.

kûft (——) كوفت P *lrnd.* 1. blow; a pounding; a bruising. 2. calamity; grief.

kûfte (——.) كوفته P *lrnd.* 1. beaten; pounded; bruised. 2. fatigued, beaten up. 3. struck by calamity; distressed. 4. meat ball.

kûftegi (—.—) كوفتگى P *lrnd.* 1. bruise. 2. jadedness.

kufûl[iü] 1 (.—) قفول A *lrnd.*, *pl.* of **kufl**.

kufûl[iü] 2 (.—) قفول A *lrnd.* a coming or going back, returning (from a journey); return. **— et=** to return.

kuğu كوغو mute swan, zool., *Cygnus olor*.

kuğur=[ur] كوغورمه *prov.* to coo.

kûh 1 (——) كوه P *lrnd.* 1. mountain, hill. 2. chain of mountains. **—i ateşfeşan** volcano. **K—i Kaf** 1. a mythical mountain, home of the legendary anka bird. 2. dreary, lonely, inaccessible place. **—i revende** huge horse.

kuh 2 (——) كوخ A *lrnd.* hut, hut woven of reeds.

kûhan (——) كوهان P *lrnd.* 1. hump. 2. saddle. **—i sevr** 1. hump on an ox's back. 2. the Pleiades.

kûhandaz (———) كوهانداز P *lrnd.* 1. humped. 2. saddled (horse).

kuhçe (——.) كوهچه P *lrnd.* little mountain; big hill.

kûhe (——.) كوهه P *lrnd.* 1. mound. 2. hump. 3. wave, billow. 4. saddle; pommel.

kûhefgen (——..) كوه افگن P *lrnd.* (*lit.*, demolisher of mountains) very destructive.

kûhî 1 (——) كوهى P *lrnd.* of or from the mountains, alpine; highlander.

kûhî 2 (——.) كوهى [based on **kûh** 2] in **— ev** narrow and gloomy house.

kûhistan (—.—) كوهستان P *lrnd.* 1. hilly, mountainous region; highlands. 2. *w. cap.*, *geog.* Persian Iraq (ancient Parthia).

kûhken (——.) كوهكن P 1. *lrnd.* underminer of mountains. 2. *w. cap.*, title of *Ferhad the lover of Shirin*.

kûhkûb (——) كوهكوب P *lrnd.* 1. that tramples the mountains; powerful horse or mule. 2. *w. cap.*, name of *Ferhad*.

kûhpare (——.) كوهپاره P *lrnd.* mountain, hill.

kûhpeyker (——..) كوهپيكر P *lrnd.* in the form of a mountain; large, gigantic.

kûhsar (——) كوهسار P *lrnd.* mountainous, hilly.

kûhvar (——) كوهوار P *lrnd.* gigantic.

kuka 1 (.'.) قوقه Gk ball (of wool etc.).

kuka 2 قوقا *Ott. hist.* a special kind of plumed headdress worn by field officers of the Janissaries.

kuka 3 قوقا Gk coconut (wood or root).

kukla قوقله Gk 1. doll; puppet. 2. very small man. **— gibi oynat=** /ı/ 1. to use one like a puppet. 2. to deceive one by pretending to be doing real work.

kûknar (——) كوكنار P *lrnd.* poppyhead; poppy seed; poppy sap.

kûknarhane (———.) كوكنارخانه P place where a concoction of poppy seed is sold as a beverage.

kûknarî (———) كوكنارى P *lrnd.* 1. pertaining to the poppy. 2. opium eater.

kuknus قوقنوس قوقنس same as **kaknus**.

kuku قوقو F cuckoo.

kukula (.'.) قوقوله Gk a Greek monk's cowl.

kukulete (...'.) قوقولته It hood; cowl. **—li** hooded; having a cowl.

kukulya (.'.) قوقوليه Gk silkworm cocoon. **— fırtınası** storm occurring about the middle of April.

kukulyacı قوقوليه جى 1. Gypsy fortuneteller. 2. dealer in cocoons. **— kıyafetli** dressed like a Gypsy (woman).

kukumav قوقوماو Gk small species of diurnal owl. **— gibi** alone; lonely; sitting apart by himself. **— gibi düşünüp dur=** to look worried and thoughtful.

kukuriko قوقوريكو *child's language* cock, rooster.

kukuvaya (...'.) قوقوايه Gk 1. owl. 2. kind of bonito.

kul قول 1. slave. 2. creature, human being, man (in relation to God). 3. *Ott. hist.* Janissary. **—unuz** your servant, I. **— hakkı** one's duty to one's neighbor. **— kâhyası**, **— kethüdası** *Ott. hist.*, title of the general of the Buluk Janissaries. **— köle ol=**, **— kurban ol=** /a/ to be greatly devoted to. **— oğlu** *Ott. hist.* Janissary who is the son of a Janissary. **— ol=** /a/ to be the slave of

somebody, to do everything asked of one. — **taifesi** Janissaries. — **yapısı** man-made, perishable.
kula 1 (´.) نُولْ قُولْ russet, dun (horse).
kulaⁿ¹ **2** (. —) قَدَع A *path*. aphtha. —**î** (. — —) A aphthous.
kûlâb (— —) كُولَاب P *lrnd.* 1. pond, lake. 2. large wave.
kulaçᶜ¹ قُولَاچْ fathom. — **aç=** to extend the two arms to the full. — **at=** 1. to take soundings. 2. to swim with an overarm stroke. — **kulaç** in full measure, freely.
kulaçla=ʳ قُولَاچْلَمَهْ /ı/ 1. to fathom; to measure with the extended arms. 2. to walk swiftly.
kulağakaçan قُولَاغَ قَاچَانْ earwig, *bot.*, *Forficula*.
kulakᵍ¹ قُولَاقْ 1. ear. 2. attention. 3. ear-shaped projection or handle. 4. flap. 5. peg (of a violin). 6. moldboard (plow). 7. guard (around a keyhole etc.). 8. slip of paper (attached to a letter). 9. branch pipe. 10. small meat ball (put in soup). — **aç=**, —**ğını aç=** to open one's ears; to listen to advice, to listen carefully. —**ı ağır** hard of hearing; deaf. — **altı bezi** *anat*. parotid gland. — **as=** /a/ to lend an ear, to pay attention. — **asma** Don't listen (to him). —**tan âşık ol=** /a/ to fall in love by report. — **belâsı** *colloq.* noise. — **beyazı** (*lit.*, the white of the ear) prominence of the mastoid process behind the ear. —**ı (bir şeydey) ol=** to lend one's ear to something. — **biti** earwig. — **bur=**, — **bük=** to pull one's ears. —**ını bük=** /ın/ to tip someone off about something. —**ına çalın=** to hear. —**ına çan çal=** /ın/ to talk to a person in a loud voice. —**ını çek=** /ın/ 1. to box one's ears. 2. to give a slight punishment. — **çınla=** to have a ringing in the ears. —**ı çınlasın** I hope his ears are ringing *said when making a kind reference to one who is absent*. — **davulu** *anat.* tympanum. —**a davul çalın=** to pay no attention to what is said. — **del=** 1. to pierce an earlobe (for earrings). 2. to make an earsplitting clatter. 3. to be understood (matter). —**ı delik** 1. alert, intelligent. 2. who is very quick in hearing news. — **demiri** moldboard of a plow. —**larını dik=** to prick up the ears. — **dol=** *archaic* to be persuaded. —**ları dol=** to get tired of hearing the same thing over and over again. —**ını doldur=** /ın/ to impress something on a person; to persuade or brief someone. —**ı dolgun** well informed. — **dolgunluğu** 1. hearsay. 2. knowledge acquired by listening to others. —**tan dolma** 1. hearsay. 2. acquired through hearing only (learning); hearsay. —**ını ensesinden göster=** (*lit.* to point to the ear with the opposite hand behind one's neck) to do something in a clumsy way. — **erimi** earshot. —**ına gir=** to understand; to be persuaded. —**ına girmedi** He paid no attention. — **kabart=** to prick up one's ears. —**ğa kaçan***. —**ına kar suyu kaç=** to be in trouble; to feel suspicious (about something). — **karıştıracağı**, — **karıştıracak** earpick. — **kepçesi** *anat.* earlap. — **kesil=** to be all ears, to listen attentively. — **kıkırdağı** cartilage of the ear. — **kıs=** to lay back the ears (beast). — **kiri** earwax. —**ı kirişte** He is all ears. —**ına koy=** to prime someone, to drop him a hint. —**tan kulağa** secretly passed on (news etc.). —**ına kurşun** May (the devil's) ear be plugged with lead *said when someone mentions good fortune, his own or another's.* —**ında küpe olsun** Let it (the advice you have just been given) be an earring for your ear. — **memesi** earlobe. — **menzili** earshot. — **misafiri** one who overhears. — **otu** houseleek, *bot.*, *Sempervivum tectorum*. — **ov=** *archaic*, same as **kulak bur=**. —**tan pamuk at=**, —**tan pamuğu çıkar=** to become attentive, to listen to advice. —**ları paslan=** (*lit.*, for the ears to become rusty) not to have heard good music for some time. —**ına pire kaç=** to become suspicious. **bir** —**ı sağır ol=** /a/ to shut one's ears to something, to wink at it. —**ına sok=** /ın/ to force someone's attention on something. —**ına söyle=** /ın/ to whisper in one's ear. —**larını tıka=** to shut one's ears. — **tozu** 1. the sensitive spot behind the ear. 2. eardrum. — **tut=** /a/ *archaic* to lend an ear, to listen. — **uğultusu** a ringing in the ears. — **ver=** /a/ to listen, to pay attention (to). — **vur=** *archaic* to listen. — **yağı** *anat.*, cerumen. — **yolu** *anat.* auditory meatus. — **yumuşağı** lobe of the ear. — **zarı** eardrum.
kulakçı قُولَاقْچِى ear specialist.
kulakçıkᵍ¹ قُولَاقْچِق *biol.* auricle.
kulakçın قُولَاقْچِين earflap.
kulaklı قُولَاقْلِى 1. having ears. 2. possessing earlike appendages. 3. having handles. 4. *slang* dagger. — **iğne** needle. — **keser** ship carpenter's broad-edged two-handled adze.
kulaklıkᵍ¹ قُولَاقْلِق 1. earflap. 2. headphone, earpiece. 3. hearing aid.
kulampara قُولَامْپَارَه [Persian **gulampare**] sodomite, pederast. —**lık** pederasty.
kulan قُولَانْ *archaic* young foal; wild ass.
kulapa قُولَاپَه common spurge laurel, *bot.*, *Daphne laureola*.
kulbe قُلْبَه P *lrnd.* plow. —**ran** (.. —) P that drives a plow; plowman.
kule قُلَه [**kulle**] tower; turret. — **sofileri**, — **sofuları** *Ott. hist.* servants to

kulel تَمَلَل A *lrnd., pl. of* **kulle.**
the eunuchs who guarded the harem gates in the Sultan's palace.
kulhuvallahi (...—.) قُلْ هُوَ اللّٰه A *lrnd.* Say, He is God. — **ahad Allahüssamad** Say: He is God, the One, the Eternal.
kulis قُولِيس F *theater* back stage; wings.
kulkas (.—) قُلْقَاس A the plant and root of *Colocasia esculenta.*
kulkulᵘ تَقَلْقُل A *lrnd.* 1. cheerful, ready to help. 2. noise (made by water etc.).
kullâb 1 (.—) كُلَّاب A *lrnd.* hook.
kullâb 2 كُلَّاب [**kullab 1**] 1. machine by which gold thread is wound on silk, etc. 2. pin in the heel of a gate on which it pivots.
kullan=ʳ قُوللَنمَق /ı/ 1. to use, to employ. 2. to treat (in any manner); to deal tactfully with, to humor. 3. to direct; to drive (car, etc.). 4. to take habitually (food, drink, tobacco etc.). 5. *archaic* to appoint (to an office, etc.). —**dır**= /ı, a/ *caus.* —**ıl**= *pass. of* **kullan**=.
kullanılmış قُوللَنِلمِش second hand, used, not new.
kullanış قُوللَنِش *verbal n. of* **kullan**=. —**lı** handy; serviceable. —**sız** not useful; not practical.
kullanma قُوللَنمَه *verbal n. of* **kullan**=.
kullapᵇⁱ قُولَّاب *var. of* **kullâb 2.**
kulle قُلَّه A *lrnd.* 1. top, summit, peak. 2. crown of the head. 3. metal boss. 4. tower. 5. large jar.
kullevi (..—) قُلَّوِي A *lrnd.* piled up in many coils (a kind of turban).
kullukᵍᵘ قُوللُّق 1. slavery, servitude. 2. worship; piety. 3. *Ott. hist.* military service in the Janissary corps. 4. *archaic* guardhouse; police station.
kullukçu قُوللُّقچِي 1. Janissary stationed at a guardhouse; subaltern in the Janissary corps. 2. *archaic* official; soldier.
kulmaş قُلمَاش *archaic* trickster; deceiver; mean.
kulp قُلب قُلْب قُولُب 1. handle (of a jug etc.). 2. pretext. —**a boz**= to become aware of a trick and take the necessary precautions. —**unu bul**= /ın/ to find a way of settling a matter. —**unu bulama**= to be confused, not to know what to do. **bir** —**una getir**= to seize an opportunity (to say something). —**unu kaybet**= to be at a loss to know what to do. —**u kulağı yok** I do not know how to handle it. — **tak**= /a/ to find a pretext; to fasten on someone (blame or ridicule).
kulplu قُلبلِي having a handle. — **tas** metal cup with a curved handle.
kulpsuz قُلبسِز without a handle.
kulûb (.—) قُلُوب A *lrnd., pl. of* **kalb 1.**

kuluçka (..′.) قُلُوچقَه Sl 1. broody hen. 2. *colloq.* utterly indolent, lazy. — **devri** incubation period (also of a disease). — **makinası** incubator. — **ol**= to be ready for brooding (hen). —**ya otur**= to sit on eggs (bird). —**ya yat**= to incubate.
kulum قُلُوم *obs.* one arm of an archery bow.
kulumber, kulumbur قُلُومبِر قُلُومبُور It 1. swivel gun, carronade. 2. *naut.* head of a mast above the top or crosstrees. — **makarası** *naut.* topblock.
kulun قُلُون قُلُن *prov.* newborn foal. — **at**= to abort (mare). — **dişleri** milk teeth of a camel, horse, etc.
kulunçᶜᵘ قُلُنج A 1. colic; cramp. 2. stiff neck. 3. lumbago. — **kır**= to cure lumbago by massage. — **otu** galangal, rhizome of *Alpinia galanga.* —**i rihî** *lrnd.* flatulent colic.
kulunla=ʳ قُلُنلَامَق *prov.* to foal.
kulübe قُلُبَه قُولُبَه قَلِيبَه Gk 1. hut; shed. 2. sentry box. 3. booth, covered stall.
kulüpᵇᵘ قُلُوب F club (organization).
Kulzüm قُلزُم A 1. *geog.* Kolzum (medieval port at the site of modern Suez). 2. *l. c.* sea.
kum 1 قُم 1. sand; gravel. 2. gravel (disease). — **balığı** sand eel, *zool., Ammodytes.* — **gibi** a great many. — **gibi kayna**= to swarm in countless numbers. — **havuzu** sandbox. — **inci** seed pearls. — **kalıbı** *metallurgy* sand mold. — **karınca** any very small variety of ants swarming in multitudes. — **otu** sedge, *bot., Carex.* —**a otur**= to run aground on a sandbank (ship). —**da oyna**= to remain emptyhanded. — **saati** hourglass. — **saati mide** hourglass waistline. — **taşı** sandstone.
kum 2 قُم *archaic* great wave; storm.
kuma قُمَه second wife (of two).
kumanda (..′.) قُمَانْدَه It 1. military command (order). 2. command (authority). — **et**= /a/ to command, to give a command.
kumandan قُمَانْدَان F military commander; major (in some armies). —**i** (..—.) *lrnd.* —**lık** commandership.
kumandar قُمَانْدَار *obs., same as* **kumandan.**
kumandarya (...′.) قُمَانْدَاريَا the Comaderia wine of Cyprus.
kumanya (..′.) قُمَانيَا It 1. ship's provisions; portable rations of a soldier. 2. small stern locker of a boat. — **üstü** deck covering of the stern locker in a boat.
kumar قُمَار [*Arabic* **kımar**] gambling. — **kâğıdı** playing cards. — **oku** 1. arrow used in gambling (by Arabs). 2. headless, featherless arrowshaft. — **oyna**= 1. to gamble. 2. to risk one's life in any dangerous enterprise. — **oyunu** 1. game of chance. 2. dangerous enterprise.

kumarbaz (..—) قومارباز P gambler. **—î** (..——) P lrnd. **—lık** gambling.
kumarcı قوماجى gambler. **—lık** gambling.
kumarhane (..—.) قومارخانه P gambling den.
kumarî (.——) قاموری A 1. w. cap. of or from the Comorin district of India. 2. aloes wood (from Comorin).
kumaş 1 قماش A 1. tissue; fabric, material; cloth; texture. 2. quality. **— topu** a roll of cloth.
kumaş= 2 قماشى prov., same as **kubaş=**.
kumbara (.'..) قومباره [from Persian humbara] 1. moneybox (for savings). 2. bombshell. **— çivisi** hobnail. **—cı** bombardier.
kumbarahane (...—.) قومباره خانه Ott. hist. barracks on the Golden Horn for the two corps; bombardiers and sappers and miners.
kumcu قومجى dealer in sand (for building, etc.).
kumız قومیز same as **kımız**.
kumkuma قومقم A large bodied, narrow necked vase or bottle; ink bottle, used in such expressions as **sır kumkuması** one full of secrets.
kumlu قوملو 1. sandy; gravelly; gritty. 2. speckled with small spots (cloth, etc.).
kumlukᵍᵘ قوملق sandy place; sands; sandy.
kumpanya (..'.) قومپانیا It commercial company; firm.
kumpas قومپاس F 1. calipers, compass. 2. print. composing stick. 3. consideration and calculation. 4. trick, plot. **—ı iyi kurdu** slang He laid his plans well. **— kur=** slang to calculate, plot, take counsel. **— salla=** slang to be distracted; not to pay attention.
kumpaslı قومپاسلى arranged; concerted; plotted; secretly or treacherously planned.
kumral قومرال 1. reddish yellow; light brown (hair). 2. light chestnut (horse). 3. olive (skin). **—lık** duskiness (of skin).
kumru قومرو [Arabic **kumrî**] turtledove, zool., Streptopelia turtur; ring dove, zool., Columba palumbus. **— göğsü** shimmering, changeable color (like a dove's breast).
kumsal قومسال 1. sandy. 2. sandy place; sand beach.
kûn (—) کون P lrnd. buttocks; anus.
kunda قونده kind of large poisonous spider.
kundakᵍⁱ 1 قونداق 1. swaddling clothes. 2. bundle of rags. 3. bun (of hair). 4. bundle of oily rags for incendiary purposes. **—tan beri** from the cradle. **— bezi** 1. cloth for swaddling clothes. 2. rags for an incendiary bundle. **— çocuğu**, **—taki çocuk** a baby in arms. **—ı çözülmemiş** quite young; quite new. **— koy=** /a/ 1. to set fire (to a house, etc.). 2. to be guilty of arson. **— sok=** /a/ 1. to set fire. 2. to sabotage. 3. to make mischief between two people.
kundakᵍⁱ 2 قونداق Gk 1. stock (of a gun). 2. gun carriage.
kundakçı قونداقجى 1. gunstock maker. 2. incendiary. 3. one who wrecks (a project, etc.). 4. mischiefmaker. **—lık** 1. arson. 2. wrecking.
kundakla= قونداقلامه /ı/ 1. to swaddle. 2. to set fire to. 3. to wreck, sabotage. 4. to do the hair up in a bun. **—n=** pass.
kundaklı قونداقلى 1. swaddled. 2. filled with combustibles.
kundura (.'..) قوندوره Gk shoe. **— bağı** shoelace. **— boyası** shoe polish.
kunduracı قوندوره جى shoemaker. **— sabunu** soapstone, steatite. **—lık** shoemaking.
kunduz قوندوز A beaver, zool., Castor faber. **— böceği** cantharides. **— hayası** castor sacs, castor, castoreum.
kûne (—.) کونه P lrnd. posteriors, buttocks.
kunfüz قنفذ A lrnd. hedgehog, zool., Erinaceus Europaeus.
kûnî (——) کونى P lrnd. sodomite.
kunla=, **kunna=** قونلامه قوننامه [**kulunla=**] prov. to bring forth young (animal).
kunneb قنب A lrnd. hemp, hemp fiber, yarn (cf. **kınnap**).
kunt قونت 1. strong, stout; thick. 2. solid. 3. rather thick-headed. **—luk** 1. strength, stoutness, solidity. 2. thick headedness.
kuntrat, kunturat قونتراط It same as **kontrat**.
kunut 1 (.—) قنوت A lrnd. 1. a serving and worshipping God humbly and obediently. 2. devotion; obedience. 3. special form of prayer used by Muslims in connection with the supererogatory service of night worship. **— et=** to worship God steadfastly, humbly and reverently. **— oku=** to recite the **Kunut** prayer.
kunut 2 (.—) قنوط A lrnd. a despairing; despair.
kupa 1 (.'.) قوپه It 1. cup, goblet; wineglass. 2. cupful. 3. cards hearts.
kupa 2 (.'.) قوپه F same as **kupe 2**.
kupal 1 قوپال archaic clumsy, big, coarse.
kûpâlᵘ **2** (——) کوپال P lrnd. 1. mace, ponderous club. 2. big-headed, thick-necked man.
kûpe 1 (—.) کوپه P lrnd. cupping glass.
kupe 2 قوپه F brougham, coupé.
kûpel (—.) کوپل P lrnd. flower, blossom.
kûpele (—..) کوپله P lrnd. 1. flower, blossom, bloom of a tree. 2. arch decorated

with flowers and branches. 3. hair of the head. 4. bubble. 5. crown of the head. 6. lock; padlock.
kupes (.'.) قوبیس Gk boce, bogue (a kind of sea bream), *zool.*, *Box vulgaris.*
kupkuru قوپ قورو bone-dry.
kupon قوپون F 1. coupon. 2. sufficient cloth to make a suit.
kupür قوپور F cutting (of newspaper etc.).
kur 1 قور *archaic* 1. row, file, series. 2. tier, course of masonry. 3. band. 4. steel or metal girdle.
kur 2 قور F 1. course (of studies etc.). 2. rate of exchange.
kur 3 قور F courtship; flirtation.
kur=ar **4** قورمق /ı/ 1. to set up, establish; to organize. 2. to plan; to meditate. 3. to set (trap). 4. to cock (gun); to wind (clock etc.). 5. to pitch (tent). 6. to prime (person). 7. to make (pickles). 8. to brood over something. —a **kura** by brooding over something. —a **kura çıldır=** to brood and go mad.
kûr 5 (—) کور P *lrnd.* blind.
kur'a 1 قرعه A 1. a drawing of lots; lot cast or drawn. 2. military conscription; year or class of conscripts. **— at=**, **— çek=** to draw lots. **—ya gir=** to reach military age. **— isabet etti** /a/ 1. The lot has fallen (to him). 2. He has been recruited by drawing lots. **— neferi** conscript.
kura 2 (.—) قری A *lrnd.*, *pl. of* **kariye.**
kûrab (——) کوراب P *lrnd.* 1. mirage. 2. one too thirsty to drink much.
kurabiye (.—..) قرابیه [gurabiye] 1. cake made with almonds or nuts. 2. *slang* beautiful child. **— gibi** very crisp. **— saat** small hunting watch.
kur'acı قرعجی officer charged with the drawing of lots for military service.
kurada 1 قورادە [kurada 2] 1. dried up and shriveled; worn out. 2. decrepit. **—sı çık=** to become very thin and worn out.
kurada 2 (.—.) قراضه A fragment, small particle (of gold or silver); filings.
kurakgi قوراق 1. dry, arid. 2. drought. **—lık** drought.
kural *neol.* rule. **—lı** regular. **—sız** irregular.
kuram *neol.* theory.
Kur'an 1 (.—) قرآن A the Quran. **—ı Kerim** the Holy Quran.
kuran 2 قوران F 1. breeze, draft. 2. electrical current. **—der** draft, breeze.
kûran 3 (——) کوران P *lrnd.*, *pl. of* **kûr 5.**
Kur'anhan (.——) قرآنخوان P *lrnd.* 1. one who recites or studies the Quran. 2. official dismissed to private life (as having no occupation but to read the Quran).

Kur'ani (.——) قرآنی A pertaining to the Quran, Quranic.
kuraza (.—.) قراضه A *lrnd.*, same as **kurada 2.**
kurbbü قرب A *lrnd.* 1. nearness, proximity. 2. neighborhood. 3. nearness of relationship; intimacy. **—i Hüda** spiritual nearness to God. **—i mesafe** shortness of a distance. **—ünde** neighboring, near.
kurbağa قوربغا قوربغا 1. frog. 2. stargazer, *zool.*, *Uranoscopus scaber.* **— adam** frogman. **— kaya balığı** kind of goby, *zool.*, *Mesogobius batrachocephalus.*
kurbağacıkgi قوربغەجق 1. little frog. 2. tumor on the tongue. 3. handle of a window frame; wire cutters.
kurbağalama قوربغەلامە frog-style; the breast stroke in swimming.
kurban 1 قربان A 1. sacrifice; victim. 2. ram. **K— ayı** *lunar calendar* the month of Zulhijja. **K— Bayramı** the Muslim Festival of Sacrifice. **— et=** /ı, a/ to sacrifice (to). **— git=** /a/ to fall a victim to. **— kes=** to kill as a sacrifice. **— ol=** /a/ to sacrifice oneself (for), to be a victim. **— olayım** Please! **— payı** part of a sacrificed sheep given to the poor. **— ver=** to lose as casualties.
kurban 2 (.—) قربان A *lrnd.* an approaching, approximation.
kurban 3 قربان قربان [from Arabic *guraban*] *archaic* the two flat-edged parts of the arms of an archery bow.
kurbanlıkgi قربانلق animal destined for sacrifice. **— koyun** 1. sheep for sacrifice. 2. mild uncomplaining man. **— koyun gibi** not knowing that you are near your destined unpleasant end.
kurbet 1 قربت A *lrnd.* 1. near relationship; intimacy. 2. nearness to God.
kurbet 2 قربت *prov. for* **gurbet.**
kurbiyet (.—.) قربیت A *lrnd.* nearness, proximity; intimacy.
kurca قورجە *obs.* irritation; itching. **— çıbanı** irritable ulcer.
kurcala=r قورجالامق /ı/ 1. to meddle with; to fiddle about with, tamper with. 2. to scratch, rub, irritate. **—ştır=** *archaic*, same as **kurcala=.**
kurcata (.'.) قورجەتە It *naut.*, same as **gurcata.**
kurd قورد same as **kurt 1. — ağzı** 1. dovetail (in cabinet making). 2. *naut.* fairlead. **— ayağı** clubmoss, *bot.*, *Lycopodium clavatum.*
kurdala=r قوردالامق *prov.*, same as **kurcala=.**
kurdela (.'.) قوردەلا It same as **kordelâ.**
kurdeşen قوردەشن 1. rash (nettle rash, harvest bug bites etc.). 2. harvest bug; *bots.*
kurdur=ur قوردورمق قوردورمق /ı, a/ *caus. of* **kur= 4.**

kûre (—.) كُورَه A *lrnd.* furnace of clay; smelting furnace.
kureba (..—) قُرَباء A *lrnd., pl. of* **karib.**
kurena (..—) قُرَناء A *lrnd., pl. of* **karin 1**, 1. companions, associates. 2. a chamberlain of the Sultan. 3. the verses of the Quran that are usually recited after the **Fatiha** in worship.
Kureşi (..—) قُرَشى A *same as* **Kureyşî.**
kurevi (..—) قُرَوى A *lrnd.* pertaining to a town or city, urban; villager.
kureybe قُرَيبَه A *obs., anat.* utricle.
kureybî (..—) قُرَيبى A *obs., anat.* utricular, utriculate.
Kureyş قُرَيش A the Quraysh (the Prophet's tribe). — **Suresi** *name of the 106th sura of the Quran.* —**î** (..—) A *of the tribe of Quraysh, Qurayshite.*
Kureyşülbitah (....—) قُرَيش البِطاح A the Quraysh sects who dwelt in the valleys around Mecca.
kurgan قُرغان 1. fortification; castle, fortress. 2. *archaeol.* tomb; mound; tumulus.
kurgaz قُرغاز *prov.* 1. very thin, mere skin and bone. 2. dry, arid (air).
kurgu قُرغو 1. fancy; fear; fantasy. 2. winding key, clock key, watch stem. —**lu** fanciful, haunted by fantasies.
kurha قُرحَه A *lrnd.* 1. *same as* **karha.** 2. small spot of white hair on the forehead of a horse, blaze.
kûri (——) كورى P *lrnd.* blindness.
kuriye (..'.) قورِيَه F courier.
kurkku قُرك [Persian **gurk**] *prov.* broody hen.
kurlağan, kurluğan قُرلاغان قُرلُغان قُرلوغن *archaic* whitlow.
kurma قُرمَه 1. *verbal n. of* **kur**= 4. 2. portable. 3. that winds up (toy etc.).
kurmay *neol., mil.* staff. — **subay** staff officer.
kûrmih (——) كورميخ P *lrnd.* wooden peg to which a horse is tethered.
kûrmuş (——) كورموش P *lrnd.* 1. mole, *zool., Talpa europaea.* 2. common shrew, *zool., Sorex araneus.*
kurna قُرنَه قُرناء A 1. basin of a bath or fountain. 2. *lrnd.* corner in a room; projecting corner. — **başı soygunu gibi** stark naked, very poor. — **hakkı** fee for the use of a basin in a public hot bath. — **kâtibi** *obs.* clerk in a public slaughter house.
kurnaz قُرناز sly, cunning; shrewd. —**lık** cunning, shrewdness.
kuron قُرون F 1. *dentistry* crown (of a tooth). 2. *same as* **kron.**
kurra (.—) قُرّاء A 1. *lrnd., pl. of* **kari 1**, readers (especially, of the Quran). 2. devout and holy man (given to sacred reading).

kurre قُرَّه A *lrnd.* a being cool and cheerful (eye).
kurretülayn قُرَّةُ العَين A *lrnd.* 1. blessed object. 2. anything that cools the eyes. 3. freedom from inflammation or redness of the eyes. 4. tranquility of mind, happiness.
kurs 1 قُرص A 1. small flat disk. 2. medical lozenge. 3. pastil of incense. —**i âfitab, —i hurşid** *lrnd.* disk of the sun. —**i nân** *lrnd.* cake or small loaf of bread. —**i sîmîn** P *lrnd.* the moon. —**i varak** P *bot.* leaf blade, limb.
kurs 2 قُرس F course (of lessons etc.). — **gör**= to attend courses. — **görmüş** one having attended courses.
kursakgı قُرصاغى قُرصَغى 1. craw of a bird; stomach. 2. dried bladder or its membrane. —**ı boş** whose maw is empty; hungry. — **düdük** child's bagpipe whistle. —**ından sakallı** bearded under the chin only.
kursaklı قُرصاقلى 1. greedy; full of guts. 2. goiterous person.
kurşakgı قُرشاقى *archaic, same as* **kuşak.**
kurşun قُرشون 1. lead. 2. bullet. 3. lead seal. — **at**= to fire a gun. — **boku** dross of lead. —**a diz**= /ı/ to execute by shooting. — **dök**= to perform the custom of melting lead and pouring it into cold water over the head of a sick person. — **erimi** musket shot, range of a musket. — **gibi** like lead, very heavy. — **ipi** plummet line. — **kâğıdı** lead foil. — **kalem, — kalemi** pencil, lead pencil. — **kalıbı** bullet mold. — **levha** sheet lead. — **merhemi** ointment of subacetate of lead. — **sirkesi** solution of subacetate of lead, Goulard's extract. — **tavası** ladle for melting lead. — **tuzu** subacetate of lead. — **yarası** bullet wound.
kurşuncu قُرشونجى 1. maker or caster of lead as a cure for the evil eye. 2. maker of or dealer in bullets. — **kadın** woman who performs the ceremony of lead melting.
kurşunî (..—) قُرشونى lead colored, gray.
kurşunla= قُرشونلَمَك /ı/ 1. to cover or seal with lead. 2. to shoot with a gun. —**n**= *pass.*
kurşunlu قُرشونلى mixed, covered or lined with lead.
kurtdu **1** قورت 1. wolf, *zool., Canis lupus.* 2. worm, maggot. — **bağrı, — baharı** common privet, *bot., Ligustrum vulgare.* — **boğan** wolfsbane aconite, monkshood, *bot., Aconitum Napellus.* — **dök**= to pass a worm. —**larını dök**= 1. to sow one's wild oats. 2. to achieve a long desired object. — **dumanlı havayı sever** *proverb* The wolf loves foggy weather. A rogue works in the dark. — **eşeni** *same as* **kurdeşen.** — **gibi** clever and grasping. — **gidişi** jog-trot. — **helvası** dittany of Crete, *bot., Origanum dictamnus.* —**la koyun bir**

kurt

yerde condition of perfect security. — **kapanı** 1. pit for trapping wolves. 2. a wrestling trick. —**unu kır**= to satisfy one's whims. — **kocayınca köpeklere maskara olur** *proverb* When the wolf becomes old he becomes a laughing-stock to the dogs *said when young people are disrespectful of their elders' opinions.* — **köpeği** wolf dog, wolfhound. — **kula** sorrel and gray (horse). — **kuş yuvasına döndü** Everybody has gone home. — **lengi** *same as* **kurt gidişi.** — **mantarı** puffball, *bot.*, *Lycoperdon pratense*. — **masalı** story told to explain away something. — **masalı oku**= to invent all sorts of pretexts in order to get out of doing something. — **pençesi** 1. bistort, snakeweed, *bot.*, *Polygonum bistorta*. 2. tormentil, *bot.*, *Potentilla tormentilla, Tormentilla officinalis*. — **sineği** blowfly, maggotfly, bluebottle. — **tırnağı** *same as* **kurt pençesi.** — **vur**= /a/ to become green and corky (timbers). — **yemez ağacı** catalpa, *bot.*, *Catalpa syringifolia*. — **yemiş** wormy, wormeaten. — **yeniği** 1. wormhole in wood. 2. tender spot; secret anxiety (due to some wrong done).

kurt 2 قُرط A *lrnd.* earring.

kurtar=ᵘʳ قُرْتارمَق /ı/ 1. to save, rescue. 2. to redeem (something pawned). 3. to recover (one's losses at a game). —**ıl**= *pass.*

kurtarma قُرتارمَه *verbal n. of* **kurtar**=. — **ve yardım** *law* salvage.

kurtlan=ᵘʳ قُرتْلَنمَق 1. to become maggoty or worm-eaten. 2. to become agitated or impatient; to fidget. —**dır**= /ı/ *caus.*

kurtlu قُرتْلُو 1. maggoty, wormy. 2. uneasy, suspicious; fidgety. — **bakla** fidgety. — **kaşar**, — **peynir** fidgety child.

kurtluca قُرتْلُوجَه 1. somewhat wormy, maggoty. 2. worm killer, *bot.*, *Aristolochia bracteata*.

kurtul=ᵘʳ قُرتُولمَق 1. to escape, to get free. 2. to be saved, redeemed. 3. to slip out. 4. to give birth (pregnant woman).

kurtuluş قُرتُولُش *verbal n. of* **kurtul**=, escape; salvation; release (from imprisonment or military occupation). — **yok** There is no way of escape.

kuru 1 قُورو 1. dry; dried. 2. withered, dead (plant). 3. emaciated, thin. 4. bare, mere. 5. dry land. — **ağrı** wasted, troubled; dull pain. — **baş**, — **başına** all alone. — **beyinli** ignorant and flighty. — **boynuz çek**= to apply a cupping horn without drawing blood, without scarification. — **çaylarda boğul**= to toil without reward. — **direk** *naut.* bare poles. — **direk git**= to scud under bare poles. — **duvar** 1. bare wall. 2. wall put up without mortar. — **ekmek** dry bread (bread and nothing else). — **erik** prune, prunes. —**dan git**= to go by land. — **gösteriş** mere show. — **gürültü** mere clamor; just rumor. — **hastalık** tuberculosis. — **havuz** drydock, floating dock. — **iftira** sheer calumny. — **incik** the thin shinbone, fibula. — **incir** dried fig. — **istimle temizleme** dry cleaning. — **kadid** mere skin and bones. — **kafa** skull. **bir** — **kafa kal**= to be left all alone (widow). — **kafes** mere skeleton, skin and bones. — **kahve** roasted coffee beans (ground or not ground). — **kahveci** seller of coffee. — **kalabalık** useless crowd. — **kalabalık et**= to hang around and do nothing. — **kalıp** mere carcass, body and nothing else. — **kaşkaval** simpleton. — **kaval** senseless chatterer. — **kaymak** buttery cream drained of all milk. — **kursak** dry membrane used like tissue paper between illuminated pages of a manuscript. — **kuruya** 1. uselessly, in vain. 2. without good reason, mere. — **lâf** 1. nonsense. 2. impossible promises. — **oda** unfurnished room. — **ot** hay; dried herb. — **örü** dry stone wall. — **poğaça** flaky pastry. — **sandalye** ordinary chair. — **sıkı***. — **şişe** cupping glass applied dry. — **tahta** bare boards. — **tahtada kal**= to lose one's furniture, to be destitute. — **tekne** hulk. — **toprakta** on the bare earth. — **ün** a mere name; an empty sound. — **üzüm** raisins. —**nun yanında yaş da yanar** (*lit.* By the side of the dry the green also burns.) The innocent suffer with the guilty. — **yaygara** mere clamor. — **yemiş** dried fruits. — **yerde** on the bare earth.

kuru=ʳ 2 قُورومَق 1. to dry, become dry. 2. to dry up, wither up. 3. to become thin. 4. to become paralyzed, withered (limb).

kurucu قُوروجى founder; organizer.

kurud (.—) قُرُود A *lrnd.*, *pl. of* **kırd**, monkeys.

kuruh (.—) قُرُوح A *lrnd.*, *pl. of* **karh**, **karha**, wounds.

kurul 1 *neol.* council; committee.

kurul=ᵘʳ 2 قُورولمَق 1. *pass. of* **kur**= 4. 2. to pose; to swagger. 3. to settle oneself comfortably.

kurula=ʳ قُورولامَق /ı/ to wipe dry; to dry. —**n**= *pass.*

kurulda=ʳ قُرولدامَق to rumble.

kurultay قُورولتاى council, assembly, congress.

kurulu قُورولى 1. established; set up. 2. strung (bow); wound up (clock, etc.). 3. ready to fire (gun).

kurulukᵍᵘ قُورولِق 1. dryness. 2. thinness, leanness. 3. drought.

kuruluş قُورولُش 1. *verbal n. of* **kurul**= 2. 2. foundation; structure. 3. *mil.* distribution of forces.

kurum 1 قورم soot. **— tut=** to be full of soot.

kurum 2 قُرُم قورم 1. pose; conceit. 2. manner or time in which a thing is arranged, set up, instituted, etc.; composition, system, arrangement. 3. *neol.* association; society. **—undan beri** since its foundation, building, institution, establishment. **—unu boz=** /ın/ to disarrange, to change the arrangement or system (of). **—u bozul=** to be humiliated. **—undan geçilmiyor** His conceit is intolerable. **— kurum kurul=** to be exceedingly puffed up. **— sat=** to give oneself airs.

kuruma قوروما *verbal n. of* **kuru= 2**.

kurumlan=ᵘʳ قورومْلَنْمَق to be puffed up, to give oneself airs.

kurumlu قوروملى 1. conceited, puffed up. 2. shaped, arranged, constituted. 3. sooty.

kurumsakᵏᵘ قورومْساق *prov.* pander for his own wife.

kurumsuz قورومْسُز 1. without conceit; modest. 2. lacking arrangement, badly arranged. 3. free from soot.

kurun 1 (.—) قرون A *lrnd., pl. of* **karn**, ages. **—i âhire** the period of history since the conquest of Istanbul (1453), Modern Era. **—i hâliye** contemporary times. **—i maziye** bygone times. **—i ûlâ** ancient times, Antiquity. **—i vusta** Middle Ages. **—i vustaî** medieval.

kurun=ᵘʳ 2 قورونمق to dry oneself.

kuruntu قورونتى 1. strange fancy; unfounded suspicion. 2. illusion; melancholy. **—lu** neurotic; melancholic; hypochondriac; afflicted with unfounded fears or suspicions.

kurusıkı قوروسیقى 1. blank shot. 2. empty threat. **— at=** 1. to fire a blank shot. 2. to utter empty threats.

kuruş غروش قروش [guruş] piaster. **—luk** piaster piece; piaster's worth. **—u kuruşuna** just barely enough, to the penny.

kurut=ᵘʳ 1 قورومتق /ın/ to cause to dry; to cause to shrivel.

kurut 2 قوروت *prov.* dried milk product.

kurut 3 (.—) قروط A *lrnd., pl. of* **kurt 2**.

kurutma قورتْمَه *verbal n. of* **kurut= 1**. **— kâğıdı** blotting paper.

kurutucu قوروتوجى drying, siccative; drier.

kurutul=ᵘʳ قوروتولمق *pass. of* **kurut= 1**.

kuruyası (....') قورویاسى *optative form of* **kuru= 1**. **—ca ağız** May that tongue be withered (a curse).

kurvet قوروت *same as* **korvet**.

kurye قوریه F *same as* **kuriye**.

kurza ('.) قورزه It *naut.* fouling of a ship's two cables.

kus=ᵃʳ 1 قوصمق /ı/ 1. to throw up, vomit. 2. to show an old stain (of cloth after being dyed or cleaned). **—acağım geliyor** 1. I feel like vomiting. 2. I am utterly disgusted.

kûs 2 (—) كوس *lrnd., same as* **kös 1**. **—i gaza** drum signal announcing a holy war. **— oyunu** kind of checker game formerly played on horseback. **—i rahil, —i rihlet** 1. drum sounded to break camp. 2. death knell.

kusar (.—), **kusara** (.——) قصارى A *lrnd.* the utmost of one's strength or ability.

kûse (—.) كوسه P *lrnd., same as* **köse**.

kûsec (—.) كوسج A *lrnd., same as* **köse**.

kuseybe قصيبه A *anat.* bronchiole.

kuseyra (..—) قصيرا A *lrnd.* 1. one's utmost strength or ability. 2. the shortest rib, a twelfth rib. **—yân** (..——) A the pair of shortest ribs.

kuskuğukᵏᵘ قوسقوغوق archaic ringdove, wood pigeon, *zool., Columba palumbus*.

kuskun قوسقون 1. crupper strap (of a horse harness); stern cable (of a ship). **—ü düşük** 1. drooping rumped, broken-down (horse). 2. down and out, too wretched to bother about his dress. **—una kuvvet kamçıya bereket de=** to run away with great speed. **— yeri** rump (of horse).

kuskunsuz قوسقونسز 1. without a crupper; free, unbridled. 2. neglected, broken-down.

kuskus قوسقوس A dough made into small pellets (used in pilaf); semolina.

kusmukᵏᵘ قوصميق vomit, vomited matter.

kussara (.——) قصارى A *lrnd., same as* **kusara**.

kustan (.—), **kustanî** (.——), **kustaniye** (.—..) قُطان قُطانيه A *lrnd.* rainbow.

kustur=ᵘʳ قوصدرمق *caus. of* **kus= 1**.

kusturucu قوصدروجى 1. that makes one vomit, emetic. 2. repulsive; nauseating. **— ilâç** an emetic.

kusukᵏᵘ قوصوق *same as* **kusmuk**.

kusul=ᵘʳ قوصلمق to be vomited; to get vomited.

kusuntu قوصنتى vomited matter.

kusur 1 قصور A 1. fault, defect; deficiency, imperfection. 2. failure to do one's duty. 3. *same as* **küsur**. **—a bakma=** to overlook an offense, to forgive. **— et=** to be at fault, to neglect; to fail. **— etme=** to spare no effort. **— kal=** 1. to remain over. 2. to remain wanting, deficient.

kusur 2 (.—) قصور A *lrnd., pl. of* **kasr 1**, castles; palaces.

kusurlu قصورلو 1. faulty, defective. 2. incomplete, deficient.

kusursuz قصورسز 1. without defect, perfect; complete. 2. faultless, innocent.

Red 44.

kusva قصوى فصوا A *lrnd.* 1. very far, very distant. 2. extreme; extreme limit; extremity.
kuş 1 قوش 1. bird. 2. hawk or falcon. 3. bald spot on the rump of an old horse. 4. *prov.* paper kite. **— u açılmış** the point of whose hip has become bare of hair (horse), *i. e.* old. **— bakışı** bird's-eye view. **— başı*. — a benzet=** /ı/ to spoil something by trying to improve it. **— beyinli** of limited intelligence; stupid, bird-brained. **— burnu*. — dili*. — a dön=** to look a mess, to be ruined, spoiled. **— ekmeği** marsh mallow, *bot.*, *Malva sylvestris.* **— gibi** very light, very agile and nimble. **— gibi uçup git=** to die quickly after a very short illness. **— gibi ye=** to eat very little. **— gömü*. — kadar canı var** very frail, easily hurt. **— kafesi** bird cage. **— kafesi gibi** small and beautiful (house). **— kanadı*. — kirazı** wild cherry, *bot.*, *Cerasus padus, Cerasus avium.* **— kondur=** /a/ to embellish greatly and try to make attractive. **— konmaz*. —u kuş ile tutarlar** Men catch birds with birds. **— kuşla=** *archaic* to hunt birds. **— kuyruğu** *prov., same as* **kuş palazı. — lokumu** kind of sweet cake shaped in small balls. **— misali** like a bird, with the quickness and ease of a bird's flight. **— palazı*. — sütü** *covert way of referring to alcoholic beverages.* **— tarağı** bird's crest. **— tüyü*. — uçmaz kervan geçmez** desolate, deserted. **— uçumu** as the crow flies. **— uçurma=** not to allow anyone or anything to go through. **— uçurmaz** very alert and capable. **— uykusu** sleep from which one awakes at the slightest sound. **— üvezi** bird's rowan, fruit of the beam tree, *bot.*, *Pyrus aria.* **— üzümü*. — yemi*.**
kûş 2 (—) كوش P *lrnd.* a striving, laboring; exertion. **— et=** to strive, to exert oneself.
-kûş 3 (—) كوش P *lrnd.* who strives, labors, exerts himself, *e. g.*, **atakûş.**
kûşa (——) كوشا P *lrnd.* who strives, labors, endeavors. **— ol=** to strive, endeavor.
kûşab (——) كوشاب P *lrnd.* grape juice, molasses.
kuşakᵍⁱ قوشاق 1. girdle; sash; belt; cummerbund. 2. diagonal timber tie between posts, cincture. 3. generation. 4. *print.* band. 5. *neol.* zone. **—ı berk** *archaic* one whose faith is strong. **—çı** maker or seller of girdles.
kuşakla=ʳ قوشاقدمق /ı/ to brace, tie (wall etc.).
kuşaklama قوشاقدمه diagonally.
kuşam قوشام *used in* **giyim kuşam.**
kuşan=ʳ 1 قوشانمق 1. to gird oneself; to put on a sash. 2. /ı/ to gird on (a sword). 3. to dress, *in* **giyin— kuşan=.**
kûşan 1 (——) كوشان P *lrnd.* striving, laboring. **— ol=** to strive, labor, endeavor.

kuşane (. —.) قوشانه *same as* **kuşhane.**
kuşantı قوشانتى *archaic, in* **giyinti kuşantı** clothes.
kuşat=ʳ قوشاتمق /ı/ 1. to wind (a thing) around someone's waist. 2. to gird on. 3. to surround, envelop; to besiege. **—ıl=** *pass.*
kuşbaşıⁿⁱ قوشباشى 1. in small pieces. 2. in big flakes (snow). **— et** small pieces of meat. **— kebap** pieces of meat roasted on skewers.
kuşbaz (.—) قوشباز bird fancier; bird catcher. **—lık** bird-raising.
kuşburnuⁿᵘ قوشبورنى قوشبرڧ 1. beak. 2. hip (of the dog-rose). 3. *prov.* dog-rose, *bot.*, *Cynorrhodon.*
kuşçu قوشچى falconer; bird fancier. **— başı** *Ott. hist.* Sultan's head falconer.
kuşdiliⁿⁱ قوشدىلى 1. thieves' slang. 2. childish language (with an **f** or other letter substituted for each initial consonant or prefixed to each initial vowel).
kûşe 1 (—.) كوشه P *lrnd.*, *same as* **gûşe.**
kûşe 2 كوشه P *lrnd.* labor, toil, effort.
kuşe 3 قوشه F *used in* **kuşe kâğıdı** heavily glazed paper.
kûşenişin (—..—) كوشه نشين P *lrnd.* solitary; hermit, anchorite.
kuşgömüⁿᵘ قوشگومى fillet of meat cut from each side of the backbone.
kuşhane (. —.) قوشخانه 1. aviary for hawks. 2. small saucepan.
kûşiş (—.) كوشش P *lrnd.* 1. an act of working; labor, effort. 2. strife, warfare. **— et=** to strive; to endeavor.
kuşkanadıⁿⁱ قوش قنادى 1. bird's wing. 2. *med.* diphtheria. 3. *med.* a kind of eye sore.
kuşkonmaz قوشقونماز 1. asparagus, *bot.*, *Asparagus officinalis.* 2. a decorative pot plant.
kuşku قوشقو suspicion.
kuşkulan=ʳ قوشقولانمق to feel nervous or suspicious. **—dır=** /ı/ *caus.*
kuşkulu قوشقولى suspicious.
kuşla=ʳ قوشلامق *school slang* to study very hard.
kuşlakᵍⁱ قوشلاق district abounding with birds.
kuşlu قوشلى on or with which there is a bird or birds. **— riyâl** *formerly* Austrian or American dollar; eagle dollar. **— saat** cuckoo clock.
kuşlukᵍᵘ قوشلق 1. place where birds are kept, aviary. 2. forenoon; lunch.
kuşluk yemeği قوشلق يمگى early lunch; brunch.
kuşmar قوشمار *archaic* a kind of bird trap.
kuşpalazı قوش پالازى *med.* diphtheria.
kuşsüdüⁿᵘ, **kuşsütü**ⁿᵘ قوش سودى قوش سوت (*lit.*, bird's milk) a non-existent or unobtainable thing; *euphemistic way of referring to alcoholic beverages.* **—nden başka her şey vardı** There was every conceivable thing to

eat. **— ile besle=** to look after someone with all possible care.

kuştüyü[nü] تحوش تويى 1. feather. 2. soft.

kuşur (.—) قشور A lrnd., pl. of **kışr**.

kuşüzümü[nü] قوشن اوزومى currants.

kuşyemi[ni] قوش يمى bird seed.

kut 1 (—) قوت A lrnd. food, nourishment; livelihood, sustenance. **—i lâyemût** bare subsistence. **—i lâyemût geçin=** to live in utter poverty. **—i Mesih** (lit., the Messiah's food.) 1. wine. 2. dates. **—i rûh** spiritual food. **—i uşşak** (lit., lovers' fare) kisses, smiles, sweet words.

kut 2 (—) قوت A lrnd. fortress, castle.

kut 3 قوت luck, good luck; prosperity, happiness.

kûtah (— —) كوتاه P lrnd. short. **—bâl** (— — —), **—bâlâ** (— — — —) P short of stature. **—bin** (— — —) P short-sighted, dim sighted. **—binî** (— — — —) P short-sightedness. **—dest** (— —.) P short-handed; slow; weak. **—endiş** (— —.—) P short sighted; imprudent; indiscreet. **—endişi** (— —.— —) P imprudence, indiscretion. **—î** (— —) P 1. shortness. 2. shortcoming, deficiency. **—nazar** (— —..) P 1. short-sighted; careless, improvident. 2. stingy, avaricious.

kutan قوتان var. of **kotan**.

kutb قطب A lrnd., same as **kutup**. **—i arz** pole of the earth. **—i bûruc** pole of the spheres. **—i cenûbî** South Pole. **—i felek** pole of the spheres. **K—i resâlet** the Prophet Muhammad. **—i sema** the north pole of the heavens. **—i şimalî** North Pole. **—i zamân** the chief saint of the age.

kutbeyn قطبين A lrnd. the two poles.

kutbî (.—) قطبى A polar. **—yet** (.—.) polarity.

kutbül'aktab (…—) قطب الاقطاب A lrnd. the chief of the greatest saints.

kutbül'arifin (..—.—) قطب العارفين A lrnd. the chief of wise men.

kûteh (—.) كوته P lrnd., var. of **kûtah**.

kutla=[r] قوتلامق /ı/ to celebrate, congratulate. **—n=** to be celebrated.

kutlu قوتلو lucky, fortunate; auspicious; happy.

kutlula=[r] قوتلولامق /ı/ to offer congratulations to someone (on a feast day, etc.).

kutn قطن A lrnd., same as **kutun**. **—î** (.—) A of cotton; of absorbent cotton.

kutnu قطنى [kutni] obs. kind of silk and cotton cloth.

kutr قطر A same as **kutur**. **—en** (.'.) A diametrically. **—î** (.—) A diametrical; diagonal.

kutsal neol. sacred.

kutsuz neol. unlucky; inauspicious. **—luk** bad luck.

kutta[ı] (.—) قطّاع A lrnd., pl. of **katı 2**. **—i tarîk** brigands; highwaymen.

kuttal[li] (.—) قتّال A lrnd., pl. of **katil 1**.

kutu 1 قوطو قوطى small box or case with a cover. **— gibi** small and cosy (room, house). **— inciri** boxed figs. **— kapağı** 1. lid of a small box. 2. reticent man. **— kapağı hotoz** a kind of headdress formerly worn by women.

kutu[uu] **2** (.—) قطوع A lrnd. 1. a passing over a road or through the water, a traversing. 2. bird's migrating. 3. a failing, drying up (water in a well).

kutu[uu] **3** (.—) قطوع A lrnd., pl. of **katı 2**, 1. cuts, sections. 2. camel saddlecloths. **—i mahrutiye** geom. conic sections.

kutuat (.— —) قطوعات A lrnd., pl. of **kutu 3**.

kutub (.—) قطوب A lrnd., pl. of **kutb**.

kutun[tnu] قطن [kutn] lrnd. 1. cotton. 2. cotton plant, bot., Gossypium.

kutup[tbu] قطب [kutb] 1. geog. pole (of the earth); elec. pole. 2. axle of a millstone. 3. chief, center of influence; most eminent person. 4. chief of God's saints upon earth. 5. polestar. 6. axis around which a business revolves. **— kuşağı** geog. polar zone, frigid zone. **— uzaklığı** polar distance. **— yıldızı** North Star, Polaris.

kutur[ru] قطر [kutr] 1. diameter. 2. lrnd. region, district.

kuud (.—) قعود A 1. the sitting posture (in the namaz). 2. a sitting. **— et=** to sit.

kuur (.—) قعور A lrnd., pl. of **ka'r 5**.

kuva (.—) قوى A lrnd., pl. of **kuvvet**. **—i külliye** mil. main force. **K—i Milliye** hist. the National Independence Army.

kuvafür قوافور F 1. hair styling; hair style. 2. colloq. hair dresser.

kuvars قوارص F geol. quartz.

kuvvani (.— —) قوّانى A phil. dynamic. **—yet** (.— —.) A dynamism.

kuvve قوّه A lrnd. 1. same as **kuvvet**. 2. mil. effective force. **—i âhize** lrnd. 1. power, faculty of taking or receiving. 2. magical power of bewitching. **—i asabiye** psych. innervation. **—i bahriye** lrnd. naval power, maritime power. **—i baide** lrnd. remote potency, bare possibility. **—i bâsıra** sense of sight; sight. **—i cazibe** power of attraction. **—den fiile çıkar=**, **—den fiile getir=** /ı/ to put into execution (a project); to produce or execute. **—i gıdaiye** lrnd. food value. **—i hâfıza** retentive power, memory. **—i hayaliye** imagination. **—i hayvaniye** lrnd. animal strength; vitality. **—i hazıma** ability to digest. **—i icraiye** executive power. **—de**

kal= to remain merely as a project, not to be put into execution. **—i karibeye getir=** /ı/ to bring into a state of preparedness, to mature to the point of action. **—i kazaiye** *lrnd.* jurisdictional power. **—i lâmise** *lrnd.* sense of touch. **—i maliye** *lrnd.* financial strength, wealth. **—i mâneviye** courage, morale. **—i masike** *lrnd.* power of retention. **—i mekniye** potential. **—i muharrike** *lrnd.* motive power. **—i müdrike** 1. perceptive faculty, sense. 2. the intellect. **—i müfekkire**, **—i mütefekkire** *lrnd.* ability to consider. **—i mütehayyile** *lrnd.* imagination. **—i nâbite**, **—i nâmiye** power of vegetative growth. **—de ol=** to be a possibility, to exist as a project. **—de olarak** potentially. **—i samia** sense of hearing. **—i şamme** sense of smell. **—i şehvaniye** appetite; lust. **—i te'yidiye** authority to confirm. **—i vâhime** *lrnd.* imagination (in reference to its inference of probabilities). **—i zaika** the sense of taste. **—i zakire** memory. **—i zatiye** *lrnd.* intrinsic faculty, personal quality. **—i zihniye** power of intellect.

kuvvet قوت A 1. strength; power; force; vigor. 2. faculty; quality. 3. potency; possibility. 4. luxuriance. **—le** strongly, greatly. **— al=** /dan/ to receive strength or courage. **—lerin ayrılığı** *pol.* separation of powers. **—lerin birleşmesi** *pol.* concentration of powers. **— bul=** to grow in strength, to be strengthened. **—ten düş=** to weaken, to lose strength, **—i hâfıza** *lrnd.* great power of memory. **—i hayal** *lrnd.* 1. imagination. 2. lively imagination. **— ilâcı** tonic (medicine). **—i kalb** 1. firmness of heart. 2. assurance, confidence. **—i tâli** *lrnd.* vigor, dominancy of one's star. **— taşı** stone to be lifted as a trial of strength.

kuvvetlen=ᶦʳ قوتلنمك to become strong; to be strengthened. **—dir=** /ı/ *caus.*

kuvvetli قوتلى 1. strong, powerful, mighty. 2. vigorous; healthy. 3. luxuriant, flourishing.

kuvvetpezir (...—) قوتپذير P *lrnd.* acquiring strength, strong.

kuvvetsiz قوتسز weak, feeble, without strength. **—lik** weakness, feebleness.

kûy (—) كوى P *lrnd.* 1. district, quarter. 2. main street, thoroughfare.

kuyd قيود only used to emphasize **kayıd**, as in **kayıd kuyd**.

kuyrukᵍᵘ قيروق قويروق 1. tail; appendix. 2. follower; retinue. 3. queue. 4. train (of a dress). 5. corner (of the eye). 6. breech of a gun. **— acısı** rancor, grudge; desire for vengeance for some wrong suffered. **—una baka baka** very dejectedly. **—una bas=** /ın/ to provoke. **—tan dolma** breech-loading (gun). **—u ele ver=** to be caught by the tail, to be in great straits. **— kakan** wheatear, *zool.*, *Oenanthe oenanthe*. **— kapağı** the bare tail place of some animals. **—u kapana kısıl=** *same as* **kuyruğu ele ver=**. **— kemiği** 1. bones of a beast's tail. 2. rump bone, the *os sacrum* and *os coccyx*. **— kıs=** 1. to catch and pinch a tail. 2. to threaten. 3. to be frightened; to crouch down (to hide oneself). **—unu kıs=** 1. to put the tail between the legs. 2. to be cowed. **— kısıl=**, **—u kısıl=** 1. to be caught and pinched or held fast. 2. to be hurt, vexed, annoyed. **—unu kıstır=** /ın/ to put into a very tight position, to have someone by the tail. **— ol=** 1. to form a line one behind another; to line up. 2. /a/ to follow blindly, to be partial (to). **— omurları** *neol., anat.* coccyges. **—unu omuzlayıp git=** to run away. **— salan** *same as* **kuyruk sallıyan**. **— salla=** 1. to wag the tail. 2. to fawn and flatter. **— sallıyan** pied wagtail, or white wagtail (bird), *zool., Motacilla alba*. **—u sıkış=** to be in trouble. **— sokumu** coccyx. **—unu tava sapına çevir=** to disgrace thoroughly; to thrash someone. **—una teneke bağla=** /ın/ to make a laughingstock of someone. **—u titret=** *slang* to die. **— üstü** 1. upper surface of the tail. 2. pip (disease of poultry). **— yağı** fat rendered down from the tail of the fat-tailed sheep.

kuyruklu قويروقلو قيروقلو 1. tailed, having a tail. 2. *prov.* scorpion. 3. *obs.* banker's license. **— biber** cubeba, *bot., Cubeba officinalis*. **— buyrultu** *Ott. hist.* decree bearing the signature of the minister of finance and certified by the grand vizier. **— fişek** rocket. **— imza** *Ott. hist.* signature of the minister of finance. **— kurbağa** tadpole. **— piyano** grand piano. **— saat** grandfather clock. **— sarraf** *obs.* banker who holds a government authorization. **— sürme** eyelid stain (antimony) somewhat overdone. **— yalan** an oversize lie. **— yıldız** 1. comet. 2. great luck.

kuytu قويتى قويتو 1. sheltered from the wind; snug; dark; hidden. 2. sheltered nook; remote spot.

kuytulan=ᶦʳ قويتولانمق *archaic* to become sheltered under the lee of a wall, etc.

kuyu قيو قويو قمحى 1. well; pit. 2. borehole. 3. mine shaft. **— bileziği** stone forming the mouth of a well. **— dolabı** 1. waterwheel over a well. 2. turning frame or windlass for lifting a bucket. **— fındığı** kind of hazelnut (which is buried to give it a special flavor). **— gibi** 1. like a well, very deep. 2. gloomy, dark (place). **—sunu kaz=** /ın/ to lay a trap for someone. **— kebabı** whole sheep or lamb roasted by burying it in a pit previously heated. **— suyu** well water; hard water. **— yalımı** side of a well shaft.

kuyucu کویجی well digger; well driller.
kuyud (. —) کیود A lrnd., pl. of **kayd**.
kuyudat (. — —) کیودات A lrnd. registrations.
kuyulu کویولو furnished with wells, shafts or pits.
kuyum کویوم gold or silver trinkets; jewelry.
kuyumcu کویومجی goldsmith; jeweler. — **tozu** borax.
kuyumcubaşı کویومجی باشی Ott. hist. chief jeweler in the Palace.
kûyyaft (— —) کوی یافت P lrnd. found in a street; foundling.
kûz 1 (—) کوز A lrnd. jug, mug; drinking cup.
kûz 2 (—) کوز P lrnd. 1. hump, hunchback; crooked back. 2. sky.
Kuzah قزح A pre-Islamic myth., name of a demon presiding over clouds and meteors.
kuzahiye قزحیه anat. iris (of the eye).
kuzat (. —) قضات A lrnd., pl. of **kazi**.
kûze (—.) کوزه P lrnd. 1. earthen mug. 2. flowerpot.
kûzepez (—..) کوزه پز P potter; brick maker.
kuzey 1. neol. north. 2. archaic sunless side of a mountain.
kuzgun قوزغون raven, zool., Corvus corax. — **ayağı** buckhorn plantain, bot., Plantago coronopus. **K—** Denizi, **K—** Gölü Caspian Sea. — **kılıcı** gladiolus, bot., Gladiolus byzantinus. — **otu** common brake fern, bot., Pteris aquilina. —**a yavrusu bülbül gelir** proverb A crow thinks its child is a nightingale. —**a yavrusu şahin görünür** proverb A crow thinks its child is an eagle.
kuzguncukᵍᵘ قوزغونجق 1. little raven. 2. small wicket with a window grill in the gate of a prison. 3. w. cap., name of a district on the Bosphorus.
kuzguni (..—) قوزغونی black as a raven.
kuzine (.'.) قوزینه Gk kitchen; kitchen stove.
kuzu قوزو 1. lamb. 2. mild person. 3. small fruit growing anomalously on a larger one. 4. wicket in a large door or gate. — **başı ye=** to have a feast on an early spring day. — **çevirmesi** lamb broiled on a spit. — **çıbanı** small boil appearing near a larger one. — **derisi** lambskin; especially Astrakhan lambskin. — **dişi** milk tooth. — **dolması** stuffed and roasted lamb. — **gibi**, — **gibi adam** a man as quiet and gentle as a lamb. — **göbeği**, — **göbeği mantarı** button mushroom. — **kestanesi** a small variety of chestnut (eaten raw). — **kulağı** sheep's sorrel, bot., Rumex acetosella. — **kulağı tuzu** potassium oxalate. — **mantarı** lycoperdon nuts, bot., Elaphomyces gramlatas, Elaphomyces muricatus. —**m** a familiar form of address. — **palamudu** small tunny. — **sarması** stuffed lamb chitterlings. —**cağız**, —**cuk** little lamb, pet lamb.
kuzula= قوزولامق to lamb. —**ş=** to become as mild as a lamb.
kuzulu قوزولی 1. big with young (sheep). 2. accompanied by a lamb. 3. with a small wicket (large door or gate). — **cedvel** thick marginal line with a fine line by its side. — **kapı** gate in which there is a small wicket.
-kü کو cf. **-gı 1**.
küb کوب F cube; cubic.
kübera (..—) کبرا A lrnd., pl. of **kebir**.
kübra (.—) کبری A lrnd., fem. of **ekber**, 1. greater, greatest. 2. major premise (of a syllogism).
küca (.—) کجا P lrnd. 1. where?, whither? 2. wheresoever.
küçekᵏⁱ کوچک same as **köçek 2**.
küçücükᵍᵘ ('..) کوچوجک very small; tiny; darling.
küçükᵍᵘ کوچک 1. small, little. 2. young; younger. 3. insignificant, paltry; inferior. 4. child; young animal. — **ağaçkakan** lesser spotted woodpecker, zool., Dendrocopus. — **aptes** urination. — **ay** pop. February. — **ayı** Little Dipper, astr., Ursa Minor. — **aylar** shorter lunar months. — **azı dişi** anat. premolar. — **baldıran** fool's-parsley, bot., Aethusa. — **baş hayvan** sheep, goats, etc. — **başlı** stupid. **K—** Bayram the Feast of Sacrifice. —**ten beri** from childhood. — **beyaz balıkçıl** little egret, zool., Egretta garzetta. — **beyin** anat., cerebellum. **K— Çuka Adası** geog. Cerigo, Cythera. — **çulluk** snipe, zool., Gallinago media. — **dağları ben yarattım de=** to be very conceited. **K— Değirmenlik** geog. Antimilo. — **dil** anat. uvula. — **dilini yut=** to be greatly surprised. — **direkler** upper masts of a ship. — **düş=** to look small; to feel ashamed. — **düşür=** /ı/ to cause someone to feel small. — **elçi** envoy of the lowest grade, minister resident. — **gezegen** neol., same as **küçük seyyare**. — **gör=** /ı/ to belittle, to regard as inferior. — **göz demiri** naut. bower anchor. — **Hindistan cevizi ağacı** nutmeg tree, bot., Myristica fragrans. — **ısırgan otu** small nettle, dwarf stinger, bot., Urtica urens. — **karakol** mil. picket. — **köyün büyük ağası** The great master of a small village, said of a self-important man. **K— Mevlûd** pop. the month of **Rebiülâhır**. — **parmak** little finger or toe. **K— Paskalya** Christmas. — **saka kuşu** goldfinch, zool., Carduelis carduelis. — **san'atlar** arts and crafts. — **seyyare** small planet, asteroid, planetoid. — **su dök=** to urinate. — **tonos demiri** naut. kedge anchor. — **tövbe ayı** pop.

the sixth month in the lunar year, **Cumadela-hır**. — **zabit** noncommissioned officer.

küçükle=ᵣ كوچوكله مك /ı/ to despise; to slight. **—ş=** to grow small, smaller. **—ştir=** /ı/ caus. of **küçükleş=**.

küçüklü كوچوكلى intermixed with small. **— büyüklü** some large, some small; young and old.

küçüklükᵍᵘ كوچوكلك 1. smallness, littleness. 2. childhood. 3. pettiness; indignity.

küçükse=ᵣ كوچوكسه مك /ı/ to despise; to belittle.

küçül=ᵘʳ كوچولمك 1. to become small; to be reduced. 2. to wane. 3. to feel insignificant. **—t=** /ı/ caus. **—tücü** humiliating.

küçümen كوچومن prov. rather small, tiny.

küçümse=ᵣ كوچومسه مك /ı/ to belittle.

küçürekᵍⁱ كوچوره ك rather small; tiny.

kudur (. —) كدر A lrnd., same as **küduret**.

kudurat (. — —) كدورات A lrnd., pl. of **küduret**.

küduret (. —.) كدورت A lrnd. 1. a being annoyed or grieved; grief, sadness. 2. a being turbid, muddy; turbidity; murkiness.

küf كوف mold, moldiness. **— bağla=** to become moldy. **— tadı** moldy taste. **— tut=** same as **küf bağla=**.

küfat (. —) كفات A lrnd., pl. of **kâfi**, they who are each sufficient; capable men.

küfe كوفه [from Arabic **kuffe**] 1. large deep basket (usually carried on the back). 2. slang buttock. **— ile getiril=** to be so drunk one has to be carried home in a basket.

küfeci كوفه جى 1. basket maker. 2. porter (who carries goods in a basket on his back).

küfeği, küfeki كوفكى 1. same as **kefeki**. 2. same as **kefeki taşı**.

küfelâ (. . —) كفلا A lrnd., pl. of **kefil**.

küfeli كوفه لى who carries goods in a basket on his back.

küfelikᵍⁱ كوفه لك 1. basketful. 2. man so drunk that he has to be carried home in a basket.

küffar (. —) كفار A lrnd., pl. of **kâfir**, unbelievers; blasphemers.

küflen=ⁱʳ كوفلنمك 1. to turn moldy. 2. to suffer from neglect. **—dir=** /ı/ caus.

küflenmiş كوفلنمش 1. moldy. 2. neglected. 3. out of date.

küflü كوفلى 1. moldy. 2. dead from neglect. 3. out of date. **— para** hoarded money.

küfr كفر A lrnd., same as **küfür**. **—i cahudî** a knowing inwardly but not confessing outwardly. **—i inadî** in spite of knowledge inwardly and confession outwardly (by tongue), not to accept the religion of Islam. **—i inkârî** a denying God's existence. **—i nifâkî** a confessing by tongue but denying inwardly (in one's heart).

küfran (. —) كفران A lrnd. callous denial or contempt of a favor; ingratitude. **—ı nimet** ingratitude.

küfret=ᵈᵉʳ كفر ايتمك 1. /a/ to curse; to swear. 2. to blaspheme.

küfrgû (. —) كفرگو P lrnd. blasphemer.

küfriyat (. — —) كفريات A lrnd. blasphemous acts or things.

küft كفت P lrnd. a pounding, hammering etc.

küftoros كوفتروس Gk calking iron.

küfuf (. —) كفوف A lrnd., pl. of **kef** 2.

küfürᶠʳᵘ كفر [**küfr**] 1. blaspheming, cursing; blasphemy; swearing. 2. unbelief; infidelity; misbelief. **—ü bas=** to curse and swear.

küfürbaz (. . —) كفرباز P swearing; foul mouthed. **—lık** swearing.

küfür küfür كوفور كوفور imitates the rustling of the wind.

küfüvᶠᵛᵘ, **küfv**ᵛᵘ كفو A lrnd. an equal in rank or social status. **—ü ol=** /ın/ to be the equal and peer of another.

kühʰᵘ كه P var. of **kûh** 1.

kühen كهن P lrnd. 1. old, aged; ancient, antique. 2. worn with age, dilapidated. **— gürg** (lit., the old wolf) the world. **— harabât** (lit., the old ruin) the world. **—pîr** a very old man.

küheylan (. . —) كهيلان A purebred Arab horse.

kühhan (. —) كهان A lrnd., pl. of **kâhin**.

kühlˡᵘ كحل A lrnd. kohl, collyrium, antimony reduced to a fine powder and used for the eyes. **—i cevahir** 1. collyrium mixed with ground pearls (used medicinally). 2. any rare or precious object or person. **—i Farsi**, **—i havlân** juice of boxthorn used as a collyrium. **—i Kirmani** sarcocolla (Persian gum or balsam used in dressing wounds). **—i Sudan** a certain black metallic granular crystal from which a collyrium is made.

kühuf (. —) كهوف A lrnd., pl. of **kehf**.

kühûlˡᵘ (. —) كهول A lrnd., pl. of **kehl**.

kühûlet (. —.) كهولت A lrnd. 1. a getting towards middle age and beginning to turn gray; middle age. 2. laziness, indolence.

kükre 1 كوكره aggressive from rage or sexual desire (beast).

kükre=ᵣ 2 كوكره مك 1. to become infuriated with rage or sexual desire. 2. to foam at the mouth. 3. to roar (lion). **—ş=** same as **kükre=** 2. **—t=** /ı/ caus. of **kükre=** 2.

kükürtᵈᵘ كوكرت sulfur. **— çiçeği** flowers of sulfur. **— kurşunu** min. galena, lead sulfide. **—lü** sulfurous.

kül 1 كول 1. ashes. 2. ash colored. 3. ruined. **— bastı***. **— et=** /ı/ 1. to reduce to ashes. 2. to ruin. **— gibi** like ashes (color). **— kedisi** one who feels the cold, who likes warmth. — **kesil**= to turn pale. — **kömür ol**= to be utterly ruined. — **ol**= 1. to be reduced to ashes. 2. to be utterly ruined. — **öksüzü** *archaic* orphan who has lost both parents. — **paparası** *same as* **kül yakısı**. — **pidesi** bread baked in ashes. — **poğaçası** raised bread baked under hot ashes. — **rengi** ash color; gray. —**ünü savur**= /ın/ (*lit*., to scatter the ashes of a person) to ruin someone. — **suyu** lye from wood ashes. — **üzre otur**= to be in great poverty. — **yakısı** cauterization by hot ashes. — **ye**= *slang* to make a mistake in one's accounts, to miscalculate. — **yut**= *slang* to be duped.

kül[llü] A *lrnd*. the whole, all. —**i atîk izz** Every ancient thing is valued. —**i matir** by every manner of flight; in all kinds of ways; altogether. —**i nefsi zaikatülmevt** Every soul tastes death (inscribed usually on tombs). —**i tavili ahmak** *proverb* All tall people are stupid. —**i vâhid** every one. —**i yevm** every day.

külâh P 1. conical hat or cap. 2. anything of the shape of a conical hat. 3. extinguisher; cover. 4. trick, deceit. 5. spire (of a minaret etc.). —**ıma anlat** You are telling me lies. —**ları değiş**=, —**ları değiştir**= /la/ *colloq*. to fall out, to quarrel. —**ıma dinlet** *colloq*. Don't tell me about it. — **et**= to play a trick. — **giydir**= /a/ to play a trick on someone. —**ını havaya at**= to throw one's hat in the air for joy. — **kap**= to get some advantage for oneself by cunning. —**ı Mevlevî** a Mevlevi dervish's conoidal felt hat. —**ı nemedin** *lrnd*. felt cap or hat. — **peşinde** one trying to secure some advantage for himself by cunning. — **salla**= /a/ to flatter, toady. —**ını ters giydir**= to be very cunning. —**ı zengele** *lrnd*. a kind of fool's cap worn by a criminal paraded through the streets. —**çı** 1. maker or seller of caps. 2. trickster.

külâhdar (. — —) P *lrnd*. crowned sovereign. —**î** (. — — —) P *lrnd*. sovereignty.

külâhlı 1. wearing a conical cap. 2. having a conical roof.

külâle (. — .) P *lrnd*., *same as* **gülâle**.
külbastı grilled cutlet, chop.
külbe P *lrnd*. 1. hut. 2. cell. —**i ahzan** house of woe.
külbek[ki] P *lrnd*. a little hut or cell.
külbütör F *auto*. rocker arm.
külçe [küliçe] 1. metal ingot. 2. heap, pile. 3. bunch (of keys). — **gibi otur**= to collapse from fatigue. **bir — inci** a mass, tassel or boss of pearls. — **külçe** 1. in ingots. 2. in masses, cakes, layers.
külçer a kind of darnel which grows among wheat; perhaps a kind of vetch.

küldür used in **paldır küldür**.
külef A *lrnd*., *pl*. *of* **külfet**.
küleh P *lrnd*., *var*. *of* **külâh**.
külek[ği] 1. wooden tub or wide shallow pail. 2. *obs*. palisaded top to a ship's mast.
külenc P *lrnd*. colic.
külfet A 1. trouble, inconvenience (necessary to accomplish something). 2. great expense. 3. ceremonious behavior. — **et**= to inconvenience oneself. —**i ihticacdan vareste** *lrnd*. free from the troublesome task of adducing proofs; self-evident.
külfetli 1. troublesome; laborious. 2. expensive. 3. ceremonious, forced, unnatural.
külfetsiz 1. easy; without inconvenience. 2. unceremonious; natural; spontaneous; informal. 3. not involving great expense. —**ce** unceremoniously; easily.
külhan P stokehole of a bath. — **beyi** a rough, rowdy. —**cı** stoker of a bath.
külhanî (. — —) P 1. urchin, young scamp; rascal. 2. *same as* **külhancı**.
küliçe (. — .) P *lrnd*. 1. disk of the sun or moon. 2. cake made with flour and butter. 3. flat disk of cast metal, wax, etc. —**i sîm** 1. disk of cast silver. 2. the moon.
küllâbi (. — —) *same as* **güllâbi**.
külle= /ı/ to cover with ashes; to sprinkle, treat with ashes. —**me** 1. *verbal n*. 2. mildew of vines. —**n**= *pass*. *of* **külle**=, 1. to be reduced to ashes. 2. to smolder; to cool down, to die down. —**t**= /ı, a/ *caus*. *of* **külle**=.
küllî (. —) A *lrnd*. 1. total, universal, general. 2. abundant, numerous, great. — **küsuf** total eclipse.
külliyat (. — —) A *lrnd*. 1. complete works of an author. 2. general, universal (things); universals.
külliye (. — .) A *lrnd*. 1. a collection of buildings of an institution, usually composed of schools, a mosque, lunatic asylum, hospital, kitchen, etc. 2. *same as* **külliyet**.
külliyen (. — .) A *lrnd*. 1. totally; entirely. 2. *w*. *neg*. not at all, absolutely not.
külliyet (. — .) A 1. totality; entirety. 2. abundance, great quantity. —**li** abundant; a good many.
küllü containing or mixed with ashes. — **su** lye water.
küllük[ğü] 1. ash hole, ash heap. 2. ash tray.
küllüm in **küllüm at**= *slang* to tell a lie.
külllüma (. . —) A *lrnd*. all that, all which, whatever.
külot F undershorts, briefs, men's underpants; riding trousers.

külsum (.—) كلثوم A *lrnd.* chubby, fat cheeked.
külte كلته A 1. bunch, handful. 2. *same as* **külçe**. 3. *neol., geol.* rock.
kültür كولتور F culture. **—lü** cultured.
külûh (.—) كلوخ P *lrnd.* 1. clod of earth. 2. unburnt brick; brickbat. 3. untutored man; dull, stupid; boor.
külûhendaz (.—.—) كلوخ انداز P *lrnd.* apertures in a fortified wall (through which stones and combustibles were thrown). **—an** (.—.——) P festival celebrated at the close of the month Shaban (in Iran).
külünkᵍᵘ كولونك گلنك P iron crowbar; pick; mace. **— kazma** mattock with two broad points or with one broad and one tapering point.
külüstür كولوستور *slang* 1. shabby; out of date. 2. poor in quality; worthless.
külüstürleş⁼ⁱʳ كولوسترلشمك to become worn out or out-of-date.
külye كليه A *lrnd.* kidney. **—tan** (..—), **—teyn** A the two kidneys. **—vi** (..—) A pertaining to kidneys, renal, nephritic.
küm 1 كوم Kurd *prov.* heap.
küm 2 كوم *prov.* small sheepfold.
kümᵐᵐᵘ **3** كم A *lrnd.* sleeve.
kümat (.—) كمات A *lrnd., pl. of* **kemi 2**.
kümbet كنبت [gümbed] 1. *lrnd.* vault, cupola, dome; arch, bend; cup. 2. *slang* the behind.
kümdet كمدت A *lrnd.* 1. a fading or changing of color. 2. great grief.
küme كومه 1. heap, mound, pile; mass. 2. hill. 3. straw or reed hut. 4. hide, blind (for shooting). **— küme** in heaps, piles, mounds.
kümelen⁼ⁱʳ كوملنمك to come together in heaps.
kümena (..—) كمنا A *lrnd., pl. of* **kemin 1**, men in ambush.
kümes كومس Gk 1. poultry house; coop. 2. hut. **— hayvanları** poultry.
kümeyt كميت A *lrnd.* 1. dark reddish roan horse. 2. deep red wine. **—i hâme** pen (for writing). **—i muhlif** brown bay horse.
kümun (.—) كمون A *lrnd.* a concealing oneself; lying in ambush.
kümültü كوملدى *archaic* small hut (for keepers or huntsmen).
kün 1 كن A *imperative of* **kân, yekûn** *lrnd.* be, be thou, exist thou. **— fekân** (..—) Be! and it was. **— feyekün***.
-kün 2 كن P *lrnd.* that makes or does (so or so), *as in* **elkenkün**.
künâ (.—) كنا P *lrnd.* who makes or does.
künad (.—) كناد P *lrnd.* May He make or do. God grant.
künam (.—) كنام P *lrnd.* den, lair of any wild beast; bird's nest; pasture; house, dwelling.
-künan (.—) كنان P *lrnd.* making or doing so and so, *as in* **nâlekünan**.
künasat (.——) كناسات A *lrnd., pl. of* **künase**.
künase (.—.) كناسه A *lrnd.* sweepings, rubbish.
künat (.—) كنات A *lrnd., pl. of* **kâni 3**.
künbed كنبد P *same as* **kümbet**.
künc كنج P *lrnd.* 1. corner, angle; nook. 2. hole, cellar, dungeon. 3. pleat, wrinkle, fold. 4. lump.
küncayiş (.—.) كنجايش P *lrnd.* capacity, holding, containing. **—pezir** (.—..—) P capable of being held or contained.
küncide (.—.) كنجيده P *lrnd.* oil cake.
küncü كنجى *prov.* sesame.
küncüd كنجد P *lrnd.* sesame, *bot., Sesamum orientale*.
küncüde, küncüdekᵏⁱ كنجده P *lrnd.* 1. a grain of sesame. 2. freckle, mole. 3. sarcocolla.
küncül كنجل P *lrnd.* 1. contracted, contorted, puckered. 2. contracted in the sinews (hand, foot, finger, or toe). 3. fallen on the embers and shrivelled (cake of bread). **—ek** P a wrinkle.
künd كند P *lrnd.* 1. brave, bold, valiant. 2. blunt, dull.
kündager (.—.) كنداگر P *lrnd.* 1. wise, learned. 2. brave, bold.
kündamuye (.——.) كندامويه P *lrnd.* hair on a new born child's head.
kündaver (.—.) كنداور P *lrnd.* 1. wise, learned. 2. brave.
künde كنده P 1. fetter, hobble. 2. trap; ambush. 3. *archaic* block set up to shoot at. 4. *lrnd.* log of wood or timber. 5. *lrnd.* potter's wheel. 6. *lrnd.* blockhead, man of dull understanding. **—ye al**⁼ *wrestling* to throw by a trick. **—den at**⁼ to trip someone up. **—i çeharbend** *lrnd.* (*lit.*, the fourfold fetter, *i. e.* on the soul) 1. the body. 2. the world. **—ye düşür**⁼ *same as* **kündeye al**⁼. **—i hizem** *lrnd.* a log of firewood.
kündgûş (.—) كندگوش P *lrnd.* hard of hearing, somewhat deaf.
kündî (.—) كندى P *lrnd.* 1. bravery, valor. 2. bluntness, dullness.
kündür كندر P *lrnd.* frankincense, olivanum, fragrant gum-resin of *Boswellia thurafera*. **—i Rumi** dry resin from Chian turpentine.
kündzeban (..—) كندزبان P *lrnd.* slow of speech; stammerer.
kündzihn كندذهن P *lrnd.* dull of intellect.
künende كننده P *lrnd.* maker, doer, factor.
kün feyekün (.'...) كن فيكون A *lrnd.* Be!

and it is; and it will be (referring to Divine creation out of chaos).

künge گُنگه *prov.* sweepings, rubbish; chip or splinter of wood.

küngüre كُنگُره P *lrnd.* battlement; turret; pinnacle. **—dar** (...—) P battlemented; turretted; pinnacled.

küngürle= گُنگُرلَنمَك *prov.* to feel drowsy or sleepy.

künh كُنه A essence, reality, truth (of a thing). **— ve hakikatine vakıf ol=** to be aware of the truth and reality of it. **—üne var=** /ın/ to get to the bottom of a matter, to learn thoroughly.

künkᵍᵘ كُنك P earthenware water pipe. **— döşe=** to lay down water or drainage pipes. **— otu** Bermuda grass, *bot.*, *Cynodon dactylon*.

künke كُنكه *var. of* **künge**.

künud (.—) كُنود A *lrnd.* a being ungrateful; ingratitude.

künun 1 (.—) كُنون A *lrnd.* a covering, curtaining, veiling.

künun 2 (.—) كُنون [*for* **eknûn**] P *lrnd.* now; God willing.

künuz (.—) كُنوز A *lrnd.*, *pl. of* **kenz**.

künye كُنيه A patronymic. **—si bozuk** of bad reputation; who has a bad record. **— defteri** register of names, especially army list. **—sini sil=** *colloq.* to exile, to banish.

küp 1 كُپ 1. large earthenware jar. 2. *slang* drunk. **—lere bin=** to get into a rage. **—ünü doldur=** to grow rich; to feather one's nest. **— gibi** enormously stout. **— yıka=** *colloq.* to be rakish, spendthrift; to have a drunken spree.

küpᵇᵘ **2** كُپ F *same as* **küb**.

küpe كُپه 1. earring. 2. natural or artificial abnormal lobe (to an ear, etc.), dewlap. 3. fuchsia, *bot.*, *Fuchsia hybrida*. **— askısı** pendant of an earring. **— çiçeği** *same as* **küpe** ³. **— kösteği** guard to an earring. **— tak=** to wear earrings.

küpeli كُپه‌لى 1. wearing earrings. 2. having a dewlap. **— keçi** Syrian goat, or a variety with appendages hanging from the throat.

küpeşte (..'.) كُپشته Gk *naut.* 1. handrail of banisters; rail of a balustrade or of the bulwarks of a ship. 2. gunwale of a boat.

küplü كُپلُو 1. *slang* wineshop. 2. *slang* drunkard.

kür كُر F health cure.

küraᵃᵘ (.—) كُراع A *lrnd.* 1. thin part of the shank of a sheep or ox. 2. sharp, rocky ridge of a mountain summit. **—i** (.——) A pertaining to the shins of sheep or oxen.

küran (.—) كُران P *lrnd.* dun horse.

kürat (.—) كُرات A *lrnd.*, *pl. of* **küre**.

kürbet كُربت A *lrnd.* care, anxiety; grief, distress.

Kürd كُرد 1. a Kurd; the Kurds. 2. Kurdish.

kürdan كُردان F toothpick.

kürde كُرده P *archaic* a Kurdish war knife.

Kürdî (.—) كُردى P 1. Kurdish. 2. Kurdish carpet. 3. *Or. mus.* one of the simple **makams**. **—li hicazkâr** *Or. mus.* a compound **makam** invented by Hacı Arif Bey about a century ago.

Kürdistan (..—) كُردستان P country of the Kurds.

küre 1 كُره A 1. globe; sphere. 2. ball. **—i âb** *lrnd.* the water which surrounds the globe; hydrosphere. **—i arz** the earth. **—i arz u mâ** *lrnd.* the earth. **—i ateş** *lrnd.* the region of elemental fire above the air. **—i ayn** *lrnd.* eyeball. **— dilimi** *neol.* spherical ungula. **—i esir** *lrnd.* the sky. **—i hacerî** *geol.* lithosphere. **—i hâk** *lrnd.* the earth. **—i haricetülmerkez** *lrnd.* (Ptolemaic system) an eccentric sphere. **—i hava** *lrnd.* atmosphere. **— kesmesi** *neol.* spherical sector. **— kuşağı** *neol.* spheric zone. **—i lâciverd** *lrnd.* the sky. **—i levniye** *astr.* chromosphere. **—i mücesseme** *lrnd.* globe (terrestrial or celestial). **—i nesimî** *lrnd.* atmosphere. **—i sema** *lrnd.* celestial globe. **—i sulbe** *lrnd.* lithosphere. **—i zemin** *lrnd.* the earth. **—i ziya, —i ziyaiye** *lrnd.* photosphere.

küre 2 كُره [**kûre**] *archaic* clay furnace; smelting furnace.

küre 3 كُره P *lrnd.*, *same as* **kürre**.

küre=ʳ **4** كُرَمَك to shovel up; to clear away (with a shovel).

kürecikᵍⁱ **1** كُرجك 1. small globe or ball. 2. small clay furnace.

kürecikᵍⁱ **2** كُرجك corpuscle.

kürekᵍⁱ كُرك 1. shovel. 2. oar; paddle. 3. baker's peel. 4. hard labor, penal servitude. **— at=** to stretch the oar well in rowing. **— cezası** *law* condemnation to the galleys; hard labor with exile. **— çek=** to row. **— gibi dil** impolite and insolent talker. **— kemiği** shoulder blade. **— kürek** by the shovel.

kürekçi كُركجى 1. oarsman, rower. 2. maker or seller of oars or shovels. **— bedeliyesi** *Ott. hist.* tax collected from the people to provide oars for the fleet.

küřele=ʳ كُره‌لَمَك *same as* **küre=** 4.

kürema (..—) كُرما A *lrnd.*, *pl. of* **kerim**.

küren=ⁱʳ كُرنمك *pass. of* **küre=** 4.

küreng كُرنك P *lrnd.*, *same as* **küran**.

kürevî (..—) كُروى A spherical; globular. **— heyet** spherical astronomy.

küreviyat (..——) كُرويات A *lrnd.* spherical trigonometry.

küreyvat (..—) كريوات A *biol.*, *pl. of* **küreyve**, globules; corpuscles. —ı **beyza** white corpuscles. —ı **hamra** red corpuscles.

küreyve كريوه A *biol.* corpuscle; globule.

kürkᵏᵘ كورك fur; fur coat. — **giydir=** /a/ 1. to make someone wear a fur coat. 2. to confer a robe of honor upon a person. — **kabı** the outer face of a fur garment. — **kapla=** /a, ı/ to line with fur. — **sırçası** a shining white hair in a fur, showing that the fur is not dyed. — **tahtası** a square of fur as usually prepared for sale by the pair. — **tulum**, — **tulumlu** a pair of squares of fur. — **zağrası** fur-covered lapel, reverse of a coat.

kürkçü كوركجى furrier. — **dükkânı** furrier's shop. — **başı** *Ott. hist.* servant in charge of the Sultan's fur coats.

kürklü كوركلو 1. of fur; fur trimmed; furbearing (animal). 2. wearing a fur coat.

kürmih كرميه P *lrnd.* nail having a large broad head; large-headed peg, pin or stake.

kürrase (.—.) كراسه A *lrnd.* 1. a lift of five sheets of paper, the unit of eastern bookbinding. 2. a small portion of the Quran, bound separately; a section of eight pages in a handwritten book.

kürre كره P *lrnd.* foal, colt. —**i âb** the white horses of the sea, *i. e.* foam flecked waves.

kürretâz (..—) كره تاز P *lrnd.* a breaker of colts; who knows how to ride a young horse.

kürsî (.—) كرسى A *lrnd.* 1. *same as* **kürsü**. 2. throne; seat of honor. 3. the upper heaven supporting the throne of God. 4. center of a government (person or place). 5. knowledge, power or dominion of God; knowledge; power, dominion. 6. evenness, regularity of curve in the under part of a line of handwriting. —**i hâk** footstool or basis of the universe, the earth. —**i hat** equality and elegance of handwriting. —**i hükûmet** seat of government. —**i memleket** capital of a country. —**i şeşkûşe** (*lit.*, the six-cornered basis) the world. —**i zer** the sun.

kürsidar (.——) كرسيدار P *lrnd.* seated on a throne, enthroned. —ı **meclis-i Tûr** the prophet Moses.

kürsinişin (.—.—) كرسى نشين P *lrnd.* seated on a throne, enthroned; ruler, governor; preacher.

kürsü كرسى A 1. chair, seat; professorship (in a university). 2. pulpit; dais, raised floor, platform. 3. base, pedestal; footstool; bezel in which a stone is set. 4. *same as* **kürsî**⁶. — **hocası**, — **şeyhi** a preacher in the mosque. — **taşı** pedestal stone.

kürsülü كرسيلى 1. standing on a base or pedestal. 2. having a chair in the university.

kürsüsüz كرسيسز 1. without a base or pedestal. 2. of which the under contour of the lines is irregular.

Kürtᵈᵘ كرد *same as* **Kürd**.

kürtaj كورتاژ F *med.* curetting, curettage; abortion.

Kürtçe كردجه the Kurdish language.

kürtün كورتون *prov.* large and clumsy packsaddle.

kürub (.—) كروب A *lrnd.*, *pl. of* **kerb**.

kürum (.—) كروم A *lrnd.*, *pl. of* **kerm**.

kürur (.—) كرور A *lrnd.* 1. times of repetition. 2. folds as doubled over and over. —**i edvar** repetition of the ages.

kürü=ʳ كوروملك *same as* **küre=** 4.

küs=ᵉʳ 1 كوسمك 1. to be offended; to sulk or pout. 2. to be retarded in growth; to be dwarfed or stunted.

küs 2 كوس offended; sulky.

küsahat (.—.) كساحت A *med.* 1. palsy of the hands or feet. 2. rickets.

-küsar (.—) كسار P *lrnd.*, *same as* -**güsar**.

küsbe كسبه P *same as* **küspe**.

küsegen كوسكن 1. *archaic* easily offended, moody; touchy, susceptible. 2. sensitive plant, *bot.*, *Mimosa sensitiva*.

küskü كوسكو 1. pointed crowbar; iron wedge. 2. firedog; kind of iron poker. 3. half-burned piece of wood.

küskün كوسكون 1. disgruntled; offended. 2. dwarf, stunted (plant, etc.). —**lük** vexation; a being sulky.

küs küs كوس كوس dejectedly, in a forlorn manner.

küskütükᵍᵘ (.'..) كوس كوتوك 1. stiff and paralyzed like a log or block. 2. helplessly drunk.

küsme كوسمه verbal n. of **küs=** 1.

küsnü=ʳ كوسنمك *same as* **kösnü=** 2.

küspe كسپه P residue of crushed seeds; oil cake.

küstah كستاخ [*Persian* .—] insolent, impertinent; shameless. —**âne** (.——.) P insolently; bold. —**î** (.——) P, —**lık** insolence, effrontery.

küstere كوستره *var. of* **küstüre**.

küstü كستو *prov.* short-sleeved jacket.

küstümotu كوستم اوتى mimosa, *bot.*, *Mimosa pudica*.

küstür=ᵘʳ كوستورمك /ı/ caus. of **küs=** 1.

küstüre كوستره 1. carpenter's long plane; jack-plane. 2. grindstone. 3. a kind of hard sandstone used for grindstones and millstones. —**ye tut=** to sharpen on a grindstone.

küsud (.—) كسود A *lrnd.*, *pl. of* **kesad**.

küsuf[fü] (. —) كُسوف A *lrnd.* solar eclipse. **—i cüz'i** partial eclipse. **—i küllî** total eclipse.
küsur (. —) كسور A *lrnd., pl. of* **kesir 1.** 1. fractions. 2. broken pieces, fragments. 3. remainder (of money, etc.). **bir — yıldır** It has been over a year since...
küsurat (. — —) كسورات A *lrnd.* groups of fractions, fractions. **—ı aşariye** the science of decimal fractions.
küsü كوسى كوسو *archaic* sulkiness, feeling of offense.
küsülü كوسولو sulky, offended; on bad terms.
küsün=[ür] كوسنمك *archaic* to sulk.
küsüş=[ür] كوسشمك to be mutually hurt, offended or sulky.
-küş كُش P *lrnd.* 1. that kills; that oppresses, *e. g.*, **merdümküş.** 2. that extinguishes, *e. g.*, **zebunküş.** 3. that cures, *e. g.*, **safraküş.**
-küşa (. —) كُشا P *lrnd.* 1. that opens, expands, unties, solves, *e. g.*, **dilküşa.** 2. that breaks, conquers, *e. g.*, **kişverküşa.**
küşad (. —) كشاد P *lrnd.* 1. an opening; inauguration. 2. an opening (at chess or backgammon). 3. a variety of backgammon. **— et**= /ı/ to inaugurate, to open (exhibition, hospital, etc.).
küşade (. —.) كشاده P *lrnd.* 1. opened; open, expanded. 2. cheerful (face). **—dest** (. —..) P open-handed; generous. **—dil** (. —..) P open-hearted; cheerful. **—ebrû** (. —..—) P with a cheerful face. **—gî** (. —.—) P openness; expansion. **—hâtır** (. —.—.) P pleased, cheerful. **—lik** openness. **—rû** (. —.—) P beaming, cheerful, happy-faced. **—zeban** (. —..—) P eloquent.
küşayende (. —..) كشاينده P *lrnd.* opener; expounder.
küşayiş (. —.) كشايش P *lrnd.* 1. cheerfulness, gaiety. 2. an opening, expanding. 3. a being serene; serenity, clearness. **—i hâtır** serenity, cheerfulness of mind.
küşende كشنده P *lrnd.* that kills, killer; fatal, mortal.
küşiş كشش P *lrnd.* an act of killing, slaughter.
küşne كشنه P *prov.* a kind of vetch (given as fodder to oxen).
küştar (. —) كشتار P *lrnd.* slain man, slaughtered; sacrifice.
küşte كشته P *lrnd.* 1. killed, murdered. 2. slain man; corpse of one slain.
küştegân (. . —) كشتگان P *lrnd.* 1. the slain. 2. corpses of the slain. **—ı zinde** (*lit.*, the living slain) martyrs.
küştegî (. . —) كشتگى P *lrnd.* death; murder.

küştengâh (. . —) كشتنگاه P *lrnd.* place of execution, slaughter or sacrifice.
küştenî (. . —) كشتنى P *lrnd.* fit or destined to be killed.
küştere كشتره *same as* **küstere.**
küşti (. —) كشتى P *lrnd.* wrestling; fighting. **—ca** (. — —) P place for wrestling, arena. **—gâh** (. — —) P place where wrestlers exercise their strength, gymnasium.
küştigir (. — —) كشتىگير P *lrnd.* wrestler. **—î** (. — — —) P, **—lik** quality, occupation or act of a wrestler; wrestling.
küşud (. —), **küşude** (. —.) كشود كشوده P *lrnd.* opened; open.
küşüfte كشفته P *lrnd.* 1. opened. 2. divided; cleft, split. 3. separated; scattered, dispersed. 4. faded; withered; annihilated.
küşümlen=[ir] كوشوملنمك *prov.* to feel ashamed, shy.
küşümlü كوشوملى *prov.* shy, bashful; considerate.
küt 1 كُت 1. blunt; not pointed. 2. paralyzed. **— bucak, — köşe** *geom.* obtuse angle.
küt 2 كُت imitates the noise of knocking on a door or of the heart beating, etc. **— diye vurdu** He gave it a sharp blow. **— küt at**= to beat repeatedly or violently (heart).
kütah (. —) كوتاه [kûtah] *colloq. for* **kûtah,** used only in **gençliğini (ömrünü) kütah et**= not to have enjoyed one's youth or life.
kütle 1 كتله A 1. heap; block; mass. 2. great quantity; aggregate. 3. group; social body.
kütle=[r] **2** كوتلەمك to thud, to knock.
kütleş=[ir] كوتلشمك to become blunt.
kütlet=[ir] كوتلتمك /ı/ to hit or knock with a great thud.
kütlü 1 كوتلو *prov.* with the seed in it (cotton).
kütlü 2 كوتلى *prov.* dignified, serious-minded.
küttab (. —) كتّاب A *lrnd., pl. of* **kâtib,** writers; clerks.
küttedek (. ..) كوتەدك with a bang.
kütüb كتب A *lrnd., pl. of* **kitab,** books. **—i münzele** the revealed Scriptures. **—i mütedavile** books in common use. **—i semaviye** the inspired writings, holy scriptures. **—i siyer** books on the biography of the Prophet Muhammad. **—i tefasir** exegetical works on the Quran.
kütübhane (. . — .) كتبخانه *same as* **kütüphane.**
kütük[gü] كوتوك 1. tree stump; baulk; log. 2. stock (of a vine). 3. ledger, register. 4. cartridge pouch. 5. *archaic* old and experienced (person). **— gibi** 1. dead drunk. 2. stiff as a log; swollen. **—e kaydet**= to inscribe, enroll in the register or archives. **— ol**= to become a log or like a log.
kütüklük[gü] كوتوكلك belt with cartridge pouches attached.

kütüphane (..—.) كتبخانه P 1. library; bookcase. 2. bookshop.

kütür كوتور crisp, fresh (fruit). — **kütür** 1. *noise made when eating crisp fruit*, etc. 2. a crunching sound.

kütürde= كوتورده مك to give out a crashing or crunching sound. —t= /ı/ *caus*.

kütürdü, kütürtü كوتوردى *sound of something cracking or of an apple or cucumber being eaten*.

küub 1 (.—) كعوب A *lrnd.*, pl. of **kâ'b 2**.

küub 2 (.—), **küubet** (.—.) كعوب كعوبت A *lrnd.* 1. the breasts' filling out at the age of puberty. 2. a having full, prominent breasts.

küulⁱⁱ (.—) كحول A *lrnd.* alcohol. —î (.——) A alcoholic.

küus (.—) كؤوس A *lrnd.*, pl. of **ke's 2**, cups.

küvet كوت F 1. basin for washing hands, sink. 2. *photogr.* developing tray.

küveys كويس A *anat.* saccule.

küy=ᵉʳ كويمك *prov.* to wait; to watch patiently (for).

küz كوز *archaic* 1. var. of **köz**. 2. piece of dry gristle. 3. anything bored and dried up.

küzaz (.—) كزاز A *lrnd.* 1. spasm, or violent shivering from cold. 2. tetanus.

küzbere كزبره P coriander, *bot.*, *Coriandrum sativum*.

küzeşt كذشت P var. of **güzeşt**.

küzzab (.—) كذاب A *lrnd.*, pl. of **kâzib 1**, liars.

küzzam كظم A *lrnd.*, pl. of **kâzım**, silent.

L

l, L the fifteenth letter of the Turkish alphabet. =la= 1, =le= ل forms a denominal verb, as in avla=, kireçle=.

-la 2, -le ل after vowels -yla, -yle [ile] 1. with.... 2. .... and. (*In meaning* 1., *if word to which it is suffixed is a pronoun, it has genitive suffix, e. g.*, **benimle** with me).

lâ 3 (—) لا A *lrnd.* 1. not. 2. no. — **de**= to say no. — **şey***.

lâ 4 لا F *mus.* la.

lâ 5 (—) لا P *lrnd.* fold, stratum. — **ber lâ**, — **lâ** in folds; pleated; in strata.

lâahlâki (—.——) لا اخلاقى A *phil.* amoral; nonmoral. —**ye mezhebi** amoralism.

lâakalⁱⁱ (—..) لا اقل A *lrnd.* at least.

lâalettâyin (—..——) A, **lâalettayin** (´..—.) لا على التعيين at random; any; any ...whatsoever.

lâalle لعل A *lrnd.* perhaps.

lâanasl (—..) لا عن اصل A *lrnd.* without any foundation, false.

Lâazer (.—.) لازر A *Bib.* Lazarus.

la'b لعب A same as **lu'b**.

lâbada (´..) لابادا Gk patience dock, *bot.*, *Rumex obtusifolius*, *Rumex patientia*.

lâbe (—.) لابه P *lrnd.* flattering words.

lâbeis (—..) لا بأس A *lrnd.* It does not matter.

lâberah (—.—) لا براه A *lrnd.* There is no going back.

lâbirent لابيرنت F labyrinth.

lâbis (—.) لابس A /ı/ *lrnd.* wearing, dressed (in).

laboratuvar لابوراتوار F laboratory.

lâbüd 1 (—.) لابد A *lrnd.* necessary; indispensible; unavoidable.

lâbüd 2 (—.) لابد *mus.* peg of a lute, tuning key.

lâcerem (—..) لا جرم A *lrnd.* necessarily; of course; by all means.

lâcevab (—.—) لا جواب A *lrnd.* 1. unable to answer; silenced. 2. unanswerable.

lâceverd (—..) لاجورد P *lrnd.* lapis lazuli; azure.

lâceverdhum (—...) لاجوردهم P *lrnd.* azure vault, sky.

lâceverdî (—..—) لاجوردى P of lapis lazuli; azure.

lâcivert (—..) لاجورد [lâceverd] dark blue; navy blue.

lâçin لاچين 1. peregrine (falcon). 2. *archaic* bold and determined; steep.

laçka (´.) لاچقا It 1. *naut.* Let go. Slacken off (rope). 2. play, slack (in machinery). — **et**= /ı/ to slacken, cast off (a rope). — **ol**= to get slack.

lâd (—) لاد P *lrnd.* 1. wall; footing of a wall. 2. base, foundation; reason, cause. 3. rows of bricks or turfs (in a wall).

lâde (—.) لاده P *lrnd.* stupid, idiot; ugly.

lâden (—.) لادن P labdanum; resin of cistus plants.
lâdes (—.) لادس [Persian **yadast**] a bet with the wishbone of a fowl. — **kemiği** wishbone. — **tutuş=** /la/ to pull a wishbone with one another.
lâdinga لادنغه obs. cartridge-belt.
lâdinî (———) لادينى A lrnd. lay; not connected with religion; secular.
lâedri (—..) لاادرى A lrnd. anonymous author. — **ye** phil. agnosticism; the agnostics.
lâemtefiha (—..——) لاامت فيها A lrnd. There is no doubt about it.
lâene (—..) لاانا A phil. non-ego.
lâf 1 لاف [**lâf 2**] 1. word; talk; chat. 2. empty words; boasting; idle talk; nonsense. — **açmazı** slang witty and subtle words. —**ı ağzında kal=** not to have time to answer; to be interrupted. —**ı ağzına tıka=** to interrupt somebody at once, to shut someone up. — **altında kalma=** to be quick to retort. — **anlamaz** 1. stupid. 2. obstinate; incorrigible. — **anlat=** /a/ to make one understand; to persuade. — **aramızda** between you and me. — **at=** 1. to chatter. 2. /a/ to make insinuating remarks (to women). —**ını bil=** to weigh one's words; to be considerate. —**a boğ=** /ı/ to drown in a flood of words (subject). — **çatlat=** to talk big, to boast. —**ı çiğne=** to beat around the bush. —**a dal=** to be lost in conversation. — **değil** It is no trifle; this is serious; this is not idle talk. — **ebesi** 1. a great talker; chatterbox. 2. quick at repartee. — **et=** 1. /ı/ to gossip about. 2. to talk, to chat. —**ını et=** /ın/ to talk (about something or someone). — **işit=** to be rebuked. — **kıtlığında asmalar budayım** You are talking nonsense. — **körük** loud boaster. — **lâfı açar** One topic leads to another. — **ola** Nonsense! —**ı mı olur?** not worth mentioning. — **ola beri gele** That has nothing to do with the question. — **olsun diye** just for something to say; for the sake of conversation. —**la peynir gemisi yürümez** proverb (lit. A ship loaded with cheese won't go with talk.) Talk does not accomplish what is necessary. — **söyledi balkabağı** You are talking nonsense. —**a tut=** /ı/ to engage someone in conversation (preventing him from working, etc.). — **ur=**, — **vur=** archaic to brag.
lâf 2 (—) لاف P lrnd., same as **lâf 1**. — **ü güzaf** empty words; boasting.
lâfazan لافازان [**lâfzen**] windbag; braggart. —**lık** blustering; chatter; small talk.
lâfızᶠᶻⁱ لفظ [**lafz**] 1. word. 2. law letter. — **ve mâna** law letter and spirit. —**ı murad** lrnd. 1. said but not meant. 2. person or thing of no account. —**ı vâhid** P 1. a single word.

2. the same word. —**ı zaid** P lrnd. redundant word.
lâfi (——) لافى P lrnd. boastful, braggart.
Lâfis (——) لافيس P lrnd., a demon who suggests wicked thoughts to people while they are at prayer; Satan, who tempts one to lie.
lâfz لفظ A same as **lâfız**.
lâfza لفظة A lrnd. a single word; utterance.
lâfzan (.'.) لفظا A lrnd. verbally; literally. — **ve mânen** in word and sense.
lâfzbelâfz لفظ بلفظ A lrnd. word by word; word for word.
lâfzen (—.) لفظاً P lrnd. braggart, boaster. —**î** (—.—) P boasting.
lâfzî (.—) لفظى A lrnd. verbal, literal. — **tefsir** law literal interpretation.
lag لغ P lrnd. fun, joke, jest.
lâgarv (—.) لاغرو A lrnd. no wonder.
lağ (—) لاغ P lrnd. fun, joke, jest.
lâğam لغم var. of **lağım**.
lağapᵇⁱ لقب prov., var. of **lâkap**.
lâğar (—.) لاغر P thin and weak; lean; weedy, skinny (animal); lanky. —**î** (—.—) P lrnd. emaciation; thinness.
lağım لغم 1. sewer; drain. 2. mil. explosive mine. 3. underground tunnel; adit. — **aç=** 1. to dig a drain. 2. mil. to tunnel for a mine; to mine. — **at=** 1. to fire a mine. 2. to burst from internal pressure (sewer). — **fitili** mil. fuse (mine). — **geri tep=** mil. to explode backwards by the gallery (mine). — **haznesi** mil. chamber of a mine. — **karşıla=** mil. to countermine. — **kaz=** 1. to excavate a sewer. 2. mil. to drive the gallery of a mine. — **kuyusu** sinkhole to a sewer; cesspool. — **patla=** to burst (a drain or sewer). — **yolu** gallery of a mine.
lağımcı لغمجى 1. sewerman. 2. mil. sapper. —**başı** Ott. hist. colonel of the corps of sappers and miners.
lağımla=ʳ لغمله /ı/ to mine, to undermine.
lağv لغو A 1. cancellation; annulment; suppression; abrogation. 2. lrnd. thoughtless and improper conversation. 3. lrnd. thing of no value; futile, vain.
lağvet=ᵈᵉʳ لغو ايتمك /ı/ to cancel; to abrogate; to abolish.
lağvî (.—) لغوى A lrnd. insignificant, worthless.
lâğviyat (.——) لاغويات A lrnd. vain words or acts; improprieties.
lâğz لغز P lrnd. slip; slipping of the foot; slide.
lağzân (.—) لغزان P lrnd. slipping; sliding; slippery.
lâğzide (.—.) لغزيده P lrnd. who has

lâğziş slipped. **—pâ, —pay** (. — . —) P whose foot has slipped.

lâğziş لغزش P lrnd. a slipping; slide; slip of the tongue or of the pen.

lâh (—) لاخ P lrnd., suffix indicating a place where something abounds, as in **divlâh, rudlâh, senglâh**.

lâha (—.) لاغه P lrnd. piece, patch.

lâhaddeleh لاحدله A lrnd. to which there is no limit, boundless.

lâhallaleh لاحله A lrnd. to which there is no solution, insoluble.

lâhana (.'..) لاهنا Gk cabbage. **— turşusu** pickled cabbage.

lâhasıl (.—.) لاحاصل A lrnd. 1. unproductive. 2. fruitless; useless, vain.

lâhavle (—.'.) لاحول A My God! (expression of anger). **— çek=** to say lâhavle. **— velâ kuvvete illâ billâh** lrnd. There is no power nor strength but in God (expression of impatience or annoyance).

lâhayrefih (...—) لاخيرفيه A lrnd. useless, worthless.

lâhd لحد A lrnd., same as **lâhit**.

Lâhey, Lâhi لاهى F geog. the Hague.

lâhidʰᵈⁱ لحد [lâhd] var. of lâhit.

lâhif (—.) لاحف A lrnd. complaining, sorrowing.

lâhifülkalb (—...) لاحف القلب A lrnd. deeply grieving.

lâhikᵏⁱ 1 لحق [lâhk] lrnd. alluvial soil.

lâhikᵏⁱ 2 (—.) لاحق A lrnd. 1. added; joined. 2. succeeding to a post; present holder of an office, incumbent. 3. who reaches to.

lâhika (—..) لاحقه A 1. gram. suffix. 2. lrnd. appendix, additional note.

lâhimʰᵐⁱ 1 لحم [lâhm] lrnd. meat; flesh; pulp of a fruit. **—i zaid** med. sarcoma.

lâhim 2 (—.) لاحم A lrnd. 1. flesh-eating, carnivorous. 2. who provides meat for others.

lâhinʰⁿⁱ 1 لحن [lâhn] lrnd. note; tone; melody.

lâhin 2 (—.) لاحن A lrnd. who makes mistakes in reading; who mispronounces.

lâhis (—.) لاحس A lrnd. greedy, craving, covetous.

lâhitʰᵈⁱ لحد [lâhd] archeol. sarcophagus; lrnd. walled tomb.

lâhiz (—.) لاحيز P lrnd. flood, torrent.

lâhkᵏⁱ لحم A lrnd., same as **lâhik** 1.

lâhlâha لاحلاح P lrnd. pastille composed of linaloa, labdanum, musk and camphor. **—i amberî** 1. pastille as above with ambergris added. 2. hours of darkness, the night.

lâhlâhiye (.———) لحلحيه lrnd., bot., Colchicaceae.

lâhm لحم A same as **lâhim** 1.

lâhmacun (.—.) لحم آجين [lahmül'acîn] a kind of meat pizza, flat bread baked with ground meat, pepper, and tomatoes.

lâhmî (.—) لحمى A 1. med. sarcomatous. 2. lrnd. fleshy. **—ye** bot., Crassulaceae.

lâhmül'acin (...—) لحم العجين A lrnd., same as **lâhmacun**.

lâhn لحن A lrnd. 1. same as **lâhin**. 2. a mispronouncing, a verbal mistake. 3. a speaking in a conventional language.

Lahor (.'.) لاهور geog. Lahore.

lahs لحس A lrnd. a licking; an eating.

lâht لحت P lrnd. ⸱ bit; piece; lump; part, portion; section. **—i ciger** one's own child; one's beloved.

lahtduz (.—) لحت دوز P lrnd. mender of old clothes.

Lâhur (—.) لاهور same as **Lâhor**. **— şalı** Lahore shawl.

Lâhuraki (—.—'.) لاهوركى Gk merino (imitating Lahore shawls).

lâhurî (—.—) لاهورى A material of which Lahore shawls are made.

lâhus (——) لاهوس A lrnd. very ill-omened, inauspicious; who brings ill luck.

lâhut (——) لاهوت A lrnd. divinity. **—i âlem** the divine universe.

lâhûtî (———) لاهوتى A lrnd. divine; spiritual. **—yan** (————) P angels. **—yet** (———.) A divine nature.

lâhza لحظ A 1. instant. 2. lrnd. a single glance. **—da** in an instant, very quickly.

lâicabiye (.———.) لا ايجابيه A phil. indeterminism.

laih (—.) لائح A same as **layih**.

laikᵏⁱ 1 (—.) لائق same as **lâyık** 1.

lâikᵍⁱ 2 (—.) لائيك F lay; secular. **—leştir=** to secularize. **—lik** secularism, laicism.

lâilâc (.—) لاعلاج A lrnd. irremediable; incurable.

lâilaheillallah (.—...—) لا اله الا الله A rel. formula There is no god but God.

lâim (—.) لائم A lrnd. who blames, reproaches. **—e** (—..) A reproach, censure.

lâin 1 (.—) لعين A lrnd. 1. accursed; execrable. 2. Satan, the accursed.

lâin 2 (—.) لاعن A lrnd. who curses.

lajverd (—.) لاجورد P var. of **lâciverd**.

lâkᵏⁱ (—) لاك P 1. gum lac. 2. lrnd. wooden trough, tray or bowl.

lâkanet (.—.), **lâkaniyet** (.———.) لقانت لقانيت A lrnd. a comprehending quickly; shrewdness of comprehension.

lâkapᵇⁱ لقب A 1. nickname; by-name. 2. surname. **— tak=** /a/ to give a nickname (to).

lâkayd (—.), **lâkayt**ʸᵈⁱ (—.) لا قيد A indifferent; careless; nonchalant. **— kal=** /a/

lâmaddiye

to be indifferent. **—âne** (—.—.) P indifferently.
lâkaydî (—.—) لا قيدى P *lrnd.* indifference; nonchalance. **—i tam** *phil.* ataraxy, tranquillity. **—ye mezhebi** *phil.* quietism.
lâke لاکه F 1. lacquer. 2. lacquered.
lâkelam (..—) لاکلام A *lrnd.* 1. indisputable, without question. 2. without a word.
lâkerda (..'.) لاکرده Gk salted tunny; sliced, pickled tunny. **— kur=** to pickle sliced tunny.
lâkırdı لاقردى 1. word. 2. talk; words. **—yı ağzında çiğne=** to try to evade. **— ağzından dökül=** 1. to talk unwillingly. 2. to be obviously lying. **—yı ağzından kap=** to interrupt. **—yı ağzına tıka=** to shut somebody up. **— altında kalma=** to be quick to retort. **—ya boğ=** /ı/ to drown in a flood of words (subject). **— çıkar=** to start gossip; to start a rumor. **—ya dal=** to be lost in conversation. **— et=** 1. to talk. 2. to gossip. **—sını et=** /ın/ to talk about something or someone. **—yı ezip büz=** to try not to tell something, to be evasive. **— karıştır** to draw a red herring across the trail. **— kavafı** great talker; chatterbox. **— sı mı olur?** not worth mentioning. **— taşı=** to spread gossip. **—ya tut=** /ı/ to engage someone in conversation (preventing him from working, etc.).
lakırdıcı لاقردىجى chatterbox; loquacious.
lâkim (.—) لاقم A *lrnd.* swallowed (thing).
lâkin (—.) لاکن A but; still; yet; however.
lâkît[ıı] (.—) لقيط A *lrnd.* a foundling.
lâklâk[kı, ğı] 1 (.—) لقلق A *lrnd.* stork.
lâklâk[ğı] 2 لقلاق 1. clucking noise made by storks. 2. senseless chatter. **— et=** to chatter.
lâklaka لقلقه A 1. clucking noise made by storks. 2. senseless chatter; talk.
lâklakıyat (...—) لقلقيات A prattle, idle talk.
lâkoz لاقوز Gk a kind of large gray mullet, *zool., Epinephelus aeneus.*
lâkpüşt (—.) لاکپوشت P *lrnd.* tortoise. **—i deryaî** sea turtle. **—i sahraî** land tortoise.
lâkt لقط A *lrnd.* a picking up a thing found by chance.
lakve لقوه A *lrnd.* facial paralysis.
lâl[ıı] 1 (—) لال P *lrnd.* mute; speechless. **— ü ebkem** speechless; dumbfounded.
lâ'l[ıı] 2 لعل A 1. ruby; garnet. 2. red ink. **—i âbdar** *poet.* 1. most brilliant ruby. 2. ruby lip. **—i felek** *poet.* sun. **—i hoşab** *same as* **la'li âbdar. —i kehruba** *poet.* sweet lip. **—i müzab** *poet.* red wine. **—i nâb** *poet.* clear, lustrous ruby. **—i nasufte** *poet.* 1. undrilled ruby. 2. original air or composition; elegant saying or discourse on a new topic. **—i revan** *poet.* red wine. **—i şekerbar** *poet.* sweet lips. **— yakut** 1. garnet. 2. carbuncle.
lâla ('.) لالا [Persian ——] 1. manservant assigned to the care of a child. 2. *Ott. hist.*, title of address by the Sultan to his grand vezir. **— paşa** *Ott. hist.* a vezir who was tutor to the reigning sultan when a child. **— paşa eğlendir=** to keep people amused or flattered. **— paşa oyununa çık=** to be disobedient and insolent (child). **—lık** office or duty of a **lâla.**
lalânga لالانغا [Persian **lâleng**] a kind of pancake.
lâle 1 (—.) لاله [lâle 2] 1. iron ring (formerly put round the neck of convicts). 2. forked stick for picking figs. **— zinciri** *naut.* pendant, rudder chains.
lâle 2 (—.) لاله P tulip. **L— Devri** *Ott. hist.* Tulip Age (early 18th century). **— soğanı** tulip bulb. **— tarlası** tulip bed.
lâleberg (—..) لاله برك P *lrnd.* 1. tulip petal. 2. rosy cheek.
lâlefâm (—.—) لاله فام P *lrnd.* tulip colored.
lâlegûn (—.—) لاله گون P *lrnd.* tulip colored.
lâlehad[ddi] (—..) لاله خد P *lrnd.* having rosy cheeks.
lâleli لاله لى having tulips, decorated with tulips.
lâlelik[ği] لاله لك 1. tulip bed. 2. vase for tulips.
lâlereng (—..) لاله رنك P *lrnd.* tulip-colored.
lâleruh (—..) لاله رخ P *lrnd.* rosy cheeked.
lâleveş (—..) لاله وش P *lrnd.* tuliplike.
lâlezâr (—.—) لاله زار P *lrnd.* tulip bed; tulip garden.
lâlgûn (.—) لعلگون P *lrnd.* red.
la'lî (.—), **la'lin** (.—), **la'line** (.—.) لعلى لعلين لعلينه P *lrnd.* 1. ruby, ruby colored; red. 2. set with rubies.
la'listan (..—) لعلستان P *lrnd.* country producing rubies; mine of rubies.
lâm 1 (—) لام *lrnd.*, Arabic script, name of the letter ل. (This is the twenty-third letter of the Arabic, the twenty-sixth letter of the Ottoman alphabet. In chronograms it has the numerical value of 30. In dates, it is the abbreviation for **Şevval**).
lâm 2 لام [lâm 1] Arabic script, name of the letter ل. **— cim istemez** no excuse; no objections. **—ı cimi yok** It must be done; there is no question about it.
lâm 3 لام F 1. metal plate. 2. microscope slide.
lâma 1 لاما F sheet of metal. **— demiri** sheet iron.
-lama 2, **-leme** ـلمه adverb of manner (esp., for position), as in **çaprazlama, dikleme, köşeleme, kurbağalama, uzunlama.**
lâmaddiye (—.—.) لامادّيه [Arabic ———.] *phil.* immaterialism.

lâmahale (—.—.) لا محال A *lrnd.* unavoidable.
lâmantıkî (—..—) لامنطقى A *phil.* illogical.
-lamasına, -lemesine لاماسنه *adverb of mode* (*esp. position*), *e. g.*, **uzunlamasına, diklemesine.**
lâmba 1 (´.) لامبه It 1. lamp. 2. radio tube. — **gömleği** incandescent mantle. — **karpuzu** globe of a lamp. — **şişesi** lamp glass.
lâmba 2 (´.) لامبه Gk *arch.* cornice; mortise; rabbet. —**lı** grooved or filleted.
lâme 1 لامه F spangled (material).
lâme 2 لامه F *same as* **lâma 1.**
lâme 3, lâmek^kı (—.) لام لا مك P *lrnd.* 1. piece of cloth worn over the turban. 2. wrap for the whole body.
lâmekân (..—) لامكان A *lrnd.* beyond all space, God.
lâmelif لام الف A *name of the compound Arabic letter* لا. — **çevir=** to take a short stroll.
lâmi^ii **1** (—.) لامع A *lrnd.* which shines or flashes; bright, flashing.
lâmi 2 (——) لامى A *lrnd.* pertaining to the Arabic letter ل.
lâmia (—..) لامعه A *lrnd.* shining.
lâmih (—.) لامح A *lrnd.* flashy, sparkling.
lâmis (—.) لامس A *lrnd.* feeling; touching.
lâmise (—..) لامسه A *lrnd.* the sense of touch.
lâmiünnûr (—..—) لامع النور A *lrnd.* which diffuses light; bright, brilliant.
lâmpasa (´..) لامپاسا untidy, long and loose garment; large and untidy; uncouth.
-lan=^ır **1, -len=**^ir لنمك 1. *pass. of* **—la= 1**, *as in* **taşlan=**. 2. *refl. of* **—la=**, *as in* **pudralan=**.
-lan 2, -len لن *after vowels* **—ylan, —ylen** (´.) [**ilen**] *prov., and vulg., var. of* **-la 2.**
lan 3 لان *same as* **ulan.**
la'n 4 لعن A *lrnd.* a cursing; imprecation.
lânazir (..—) لا نظير A *lrnd.* matchless; unique; incomparable. —**a-leh** (..—..) A unique, matchless.
lânda (´.) لاندا It *naut.* chain of a shroud (on a ship).
lândo, lândon (´.) لاندو لاندون F landau.
lâne (—.) لانه P *poet.* nest. —**gir** (—.—) P that builds a nest.
la'net A, **lânet** (—.) لعنت 1. malediction; damnation; imprecation. 2. peevish; cross. — **et=** to curse. — **oku=** /a/ to curse. — **olsun** Damn him (or it)!
lânetle=^r لعنتلمك /ı/ to curse.
lânetleme (—...) لعنتلمه 1. act of cursing. 2. accursed.
lânetli (—..) لعنتلى cursed; excommunicated.
la'netullah (´..—) لعنة الله A *lrnd.* the curse of God. —**i aleyh** May God's curse be upon him.
lângır lungur لانغر لونغر *colloq.* loud and vulgar (accent); uncouth talk; noisy and clumsy, loutish.
lângust لانغوست F spiny lobster; crayfish.
lânüsellim (´...) لانسلم A *lrnd.* We do not accept the point. No.
lâpa لاپا 1. watery boiled rice, thick rice soup, mush. 2. *med.* poultice. — **gibi** soft; mushy. — **lâpa** in large flakes (snow).
lâpacı لاپاجى 1. flabby; languid; milksop. 2. fond of sloppy dishes.
lapçın, lâpçin لاپچين slipper (laced at the side). — **ağızlı** windbag.
lâpina (..´.) لاپينه wrasse, *zool.*, *Labrus merula.*
lâp lâp لاپ لاپ flop! flop! — **ye=** to eat greedily, smacking the lips.
Lâpon (..´) لاپون It Laplander.
Lâponya (..´.) لاپونيا It *geog.* Lapland.
lappadak (´..) لاپادك suddenly.
—lar, —ler لر *pl. suffix, as in* **karlar, erler.**
—larca, —lerce لرجه many a..., *e. g.*, **yıllarca** for years, **kilolarca** by the kilo, many kilos.
lâreyb لاريب A *lrnd.* no doubt; doubtless; undoubted.
lâreybefih (´..—) لاريب فيه A *lrnd.* in which there is no doubt.
lâreybî (..—) لاريبى A *lrnd.* undoubted; indubitable; emanating from the Quran.
Lâristan (—.—) لارستان P *geog.* Luristan.
larmo (´.) لارمو It *naut.* in — **yakası** luff of a sail.
lasak^kı لصقى A *lrnd.* pleurisy with adhesions.
lâsani (.——) لا ثانى A *lrnd.* incomparable, without a second, matchless.
lâsık^kı (—.) لاصق A *lrnd.* adherent.
lâsiyemâ (—..—) لاسيما A *lrnd.* especially.
lâskine لاسكينه F a kind of card game.
lâsta (´.) لاستا It *naut.* cargo capacity; tonnage.
lâstarya لاستاريا large dark Scotch kale or colewort.
lâstik^ği لاستيك F 1. rubber. 2. tire. 3. galoshes. 4. *knitting* ribbing. — **pompası** tire pump. — **yaması** rubber patch for tires.
lâstikli لاستيكلى made of rubber; elastic; flexible; double entendre; elusive.
-laş=^ır, **-leş=**^ir لش [**-le= 1, =ş=**] 1. to become ... *as in* **zorlaş=, güçleş=**. 2. reciprocal action, *as in* **haberleş=, mektuplaş=**.
lâşe (—.) لاشه P *lrnd.* 1. corpse; carcass. 2. putrid thing; thing no longer fit for use and past repair.

lâşebiħeleh (ʹ...) لا شبيله A lrnd. to whom there is no similar, unequalled.

lâşek[kki] (ʹ.) لا شاك A lrnd. without doubt; certainly.

lâşekkefih (ʹ..—) لا شاك فيه A lrnd. in which there is no doubt.

lâşey (ʹ.) لا شى A lrnd. a thing of no account; mere trifle.

lâşka (ʹ.) لا شقه It same as **laçka**.

Lât (—) لات A hist., name of one of the chief gods of the pre-Islamic Arabs.

lâta 1 (ʹ.) لا ط It wooden board.

lâta 2 (ʹ.) لا طه It gown (formerly worn by **Ulema**); a priest's frock.

lâtail (.—.) لا طائل A lrnd. useless, unprofitable.

lâtarna لا تا رنه [**lâterna**] barrel organ.

lâtenahi (..—) لا تناهى A lrnd. endless; infinite.

lâterna (.ʹ.) لا تارنا It same as **lâtarna**.

lâteşbih (ʹ..) لا تشبيه A anything but ...; far from being. — **ve lâtemsil** anything but ...; far from being ....

latha لطخ A lrnd. stain, spot.

lâtif (.—) لطيف A fine; pleasant; charming; gracious; delicious.

lâtife (.—ʹ) لطيفه A 1. joke; jest. 2. lrnd. anecdote; witticism. —**den anla**= to appreciate a joke. — **bertaraf** joking apart; seriously (speaking). —**ye çevir**= /ı/ to change into a joke (a serious talk). — **et**= to joke. —**i gaybiye** lrnd. grace bestowed on one by God through the intercession of some invisible saint. — **lâtif gerek** Politeness should not be neglected even in a joke. — **olarak**, — **yollu**, — **yoluyla** as a joke. —**ci** same as —**gû**.

lâtifegû (.—.—) لطيفه گو P lrnd. fond of joking; witty person. —**yi** (.—.——) P witticism.

lâtifeperdaz (.—..—) لطيفه پرداز P lrnd. joker; witty person. —**ân** (.—..——) P pl. —**âne** (.—..——.) P jokingly. —**î** (.—..——) P joking.

lâtilokum (—...) لا فى الحقوم [rahatülhulkum] Turkish delight.

Lâtin 1 لاتين 1. Latin. 2. Eastern Catholic. — **çiçeği** garden nasturtium, bot., Trapaeolum. — **harfleri** Latin characters.

lâtin 2 لاتين It naut. lateen sail. — **yelken**, — **yelkeni** lateen sail.

Lâtince (..ʹ.) لاتينجه Latin language; in Latin.

lâtma لطمه A lrnd. slap; reproach.

lâtmahâr (..—) لطم خوار P lrnd. who has been slapped, scolded.

lâtmet=[der] لطم ايتمك lrnd. /ı/ 1. to slap. 2. to reproach.

lâtüad[ddi] لا نعد A lrnd. countless, innumerable.

lâübali (..—–) لا ابالى A free and easy; too familiar; offhand.

lâübalileş=[ir] لا ابالى لشمك to be too free and easy.

lâübalilik[ği] لا ابالى لك too free and easy behavior; excess of familiarity.

lâübaliyane (...——.) لا ابا ليانه P in a familiar way; carelessly; in a free and easy manner.

lâv لاو F lava.

lâva (ʹ.) لاوا It naut. Pull. Hoist away. — **et**= to pull a boat up, to pull on the oars.

lâvabo (..ʹ.) لاوابو F washbasin.

lâvaj لاواژ F washing; spilling; bathing; enema. — **yap**= to wash; to spill; to treat with an enema; to take a shower.

lâvallah لا والله A lrnd. No, by God!

lâvanta (.ʹ.) لاوانطه It 1. lavender water. 2. perfume. — **çiçeği** lavender (flower). — **sür**= to use perfume.

lâvaş لواش [Persian .—] prov. flat bread.

lâvaşa لواشه thin, flat ingot of silver.

lâvdanum (ʹ..) لاودنوم pharm. laudanum.

lâve 1 لاوه F washed (coal).

lâve 2 لعوه A lrnd. 1. greedy; miserly. 2. slatternly.

lâ ve naam لا و نعم A lrnd. no and yes (the right or faculty of giving a refusal or assent).

lâvha لوح A same as **levha**.

lâvman لوومان F med. enema.

lavta 1 (ʹ.) لاوطه 1. med. obstetric forceps. 2. obs. obstetrician, midwife.

lavta 2 (ʹ.) لوطه G mus. an instrument like the **ud** now out of use. —**cı** 1. lute player. 2. maker or seller of lutes.

lâvücud (..—) لا وجود A phil. nonexistence.

lây 1 (—) لاى P lrnd. 1. mud. 2. sediment.

-lây 2 (—) لاى P who speaks, as in herzelây.

lâya'kil (.ʹ.) لا يعقل A lrnd. unconscious; beside oneself; very drunk.

lâya'lem (.ʹ..) لا يعلم A lrnd. that does not know.

lâya'ni (ʹ..—) لا يعنى A lrnd. 1. that means nothing, has no signification. 2. useless; of no importance.

lâyecûz (.ʹ.—) لا يجوز A lrnd. illicit.

lâyemut (..—) لا يموت A lrnd. immortal; undying. —**iyet** (.—.—..) A immortality.

lâyenbagi (...—) لا ينبغى A lrnd. which should not be; improper.

lâyenfek[kki] (ʹ..) لا ينفك A lrnd. inseparable.

lâyenkati (ʹ...) لا ينقطع A lrnd. incessantly; without interruption.

Red. 45.

lâyenkesir (.'....) لا يَنْكَسِر A *lrnd.* unbreakable.
lâyetebeddel (.'....) لا يَتَبَدَّل A *lrnd.* unchangeable.
lâyetecezza (.'....) لا يَتَجَزَّا A *lrnd.* indivisible.
lâyetegayyer (.'....) لا يَتَغَيَّر A *lrnd.* immutable, inalterable.
lâyetehammel (.'....) لا يَتَحَمَّل A *lrnd.* unbearable.
lâyetenahi (...— —) لا يَتَناهى A *lrnd.* unending, infinite. —**yet** *phil.* infinity.
lâyezal[li] (..—) لا يَزال A *lrnd.* permanent; eternal, everlasting.
lâyezul[li] (..—) لا يَزول A *lrnd.* eternal, imperishable.
lâyık[fi] **1** (—.) لا ئِق A [**lâyık 2**] worthy; suitable; fitting, befitting, deserving; appropriate. —**ını bul=** to get one's deserts. — **değil** It is unworthy; it is a shame. — **gör=** /ı, a/ to deem worthy or suitable, to find fitting. — **ol=** /a/ to be worthy of; to merit.
lâyık[kı] **2** (—.) لا يِقُه A *same as* **lâyık 1**. —**iyle** properly; adequately. —**ı vechile** properly; thoroughly.
-lâyın لا يِن *var. of* **-leyin** *as in* **akşamlayın**.
lâyih (—.) لا يِح A *lrnd.* 1. obvious, evident, clear. 2. bright, splendid. — **ol=** 1. to be evident (as on a page). 2. /a/ to flash upon the mind.
lâyiha (—..) لا يِحه A 1. bill (proposed law); project. 2. memorandum expressing one's viewpoint on a subject.
lâyik[kı] لا ئِيك F *same as* **lâyık 2**.
lâyuad[ddi] (.'...) لا يُعَدّ A *lrnd.* innumerable, countless. — **ve lâyuhsa** countless, innumerable.
lâyugleb (.'...) لا يُغْلَب A *lrnd.* unconquerable; invincible.
lâyuhal[lli] (.'...) لا يُحَلّ A *lrnd.* unlawful.
lâyuhsa (.'.—) لا يُحْصى A *lrnd.* innumerable.
lâyuhti (.'.—) لا يُخْطى A *lrnd.* infallible.
lâyu'kal (.'...) لا يُعْقَل A *lrnd.* incomprehensible.
lâyu'lem (.'..) لا يُعْلَم A *phil.* unknowable.
lâyu'ref (.'..) لا يُعْرَف A *phil.* unknowable.
lâyusber (.'..) لا يُسْبَر A *lrnd.* unendurable, beyond patience.
lâyutak (..—) لا يُطاق A *lrnd.* beyond one's power; unendurable.
lâyüdrek (.'..) لا يُدْرَك A *lrnd.* 1. unattainable. 2. incomprehensible.
lâyüfhem (.'..) لا يُفْهَم A *phil.* inconceivable; which cannot be understood.
lâyüfna (..—) لا يَفْنى A *lrnd.* imperishable.
lâyüs'el (.'..) لا يُسْئَل A *lrnd.* irresponsible; omnipotent; God.

lâyüzal[li] (.'.—) لا يَزال *same as* **lâyezal**.
Lâz لاز Laz (of the southeast coast of the Black Sea).
lâza لازه *prov.* tray or small trough.
lâzale (.—.) لا زال A *lrnd.* May it never fail; may it last for ever.
Lâzca (.'.) لازجه in the Laz language; the Laz language.
lâzeval[li] (..—) لا زوال A *lrnd.* immortal; eternal. —**e leh** for whom there is no death, never failing, eternal.
lâzık[kı] (—.) لازِق A *lrnd.* adhering, adherent.
lâzım (—.) لازِم A 1. necessary; requisite. 2. *gram.* intransitive (verb). 3. *lrnd.* inseparable. —**ı gayri müfarik** necessary, indispensible, inseparable. — **gel=** to be necessary. — **melzûm, — ve melzûm** *lrnd.* 1. an inherent quality and the substance in which it is inherent. 2. an adherent and the one to whom he is attached. 3. a necessary consequence and its conditioning precedent. 4. a proposition and its corollary. — **ol=** to be necessary.
lâzımlı لازِملى *colloq.* necessary; unavoidable.
lâzımlık[fı] لازِملِق chamber pot.
lâzımüleda (—...—) لازِم الأدا A *lrnd.* that has to be fulfilled, obligatory.
lâzımülicra (—...—) لازِم الإجرا A *lrnd.* required (performance of an act). — **hüküm ve karar** *law, res adjudicata*.
lâzımülinkiyad (—....—) لازِم الإنقياد A *lrnd.* submission to which is incumbent.
lâzımüttekrim (—...—) لازِم التكريم A *lrnd.* the honoring of whom is a duty.
lâzib (—.) لازِب A *lrnd.* 1. adherent, adjacent; contiguous. 2. inherent. 3. permanent.
lâzime (—..) لازِمه A *lrnd.* 1. a necessary thing; natural consequence. 2. corollary. 3. obligation. 4. requisite (for a journey, etc.); ship's stores. —**ci** ship chandler.
Lâzistan (..—) لازستان *geog.* the Laz country.
Lâzkiye (—..) لاذقيه *geog.* Latakia.
=**le=** 1 لَك *cf.* =**la=** 1.
—**le** 2 لَ *cf.* —**la** 2.
leali (.—.) لآلى A *lrnd., pl. of* **lülü**.
leb لَب P *lrnd.* 1. lip. 2. edge; margin; border. —**i âftab** shadow. —**i cû** river bank. —**i cuybâr** shore. — **demeden leblebiyi anla=** to understand instantly. —**i derya** seashore. —**i hadra** the horizon. —**i sagar** rim of the wine cup.
lebabet (.—.) لبابت A *lrnd.* a being endowed with an intelligent mind; intelligence.
lebaçe (.—.) لباچه P *lrnd.* a full and long robe with sleeves; judge's robe.
lebad (.—), **lebade** (.—.) لباده P *lrnd., same as* **libade**.

lebaket (.—.) لياقت A *lrnd.* a being clever; cleverness, intelligence, skill.
lebaleb (.—.) لباب P *lrnd.* brimful.
lebbeleb, lebberleb لبرلب P *lrnd.* lip to lip.
lebbeste لب بست P *lrnd.* whose mouth is sealed; with closed lips.
lebbeyk, lebbeyke لبيك A *lrnd.* At your service! —**zen** P a yes-man.
leben لبن A *lrnd.* 1. milk. 2. curdled milk.
lebenî (..—) لبنى A *lrnd.* containing or producing milk; milklike; *chem.* lactic. — **kils** *chem.* milk of lime.
lebib (.—) لبيب A *lrnd.* intelligent.
lebik[k1] (.—) لبيك A *lrnd.* clever, intelligent.
lebin لبن A *lrnd.* sun-dried bricks. —**e** A a single sun-dried brick.
leblab (.—) لبلاب A *lrnd.* any twining, climbing plant, ivy. —**iye** *bot.*, *Hederacaea*.
leblebi لبلبي 1. roasted chickpeas. 2. *slang* pistol bullet. — **unu** flour of roasted chickpeas.
leblebici لبلبيجي maker or seller of roasted chickpeas.
lebriz (.—) لبريز P *lrnd.* overflowing, brimful.
lebs 1 لبس A *lrnd.* a proposing to anyone anything obscure or confused; confusion.
lebs 2 لبث A *lrnd.* a delaying, stopping, tarrying; delay.
lebteşne لب تشنه P *poet.* thirsty.
lebun (.—) لبون A *lrnd.* a milch beast.
lebve لبوه A *lrnd.* lioness.
lec, lecac (.—), **lecacet** (.—.) لجاج لجاجت A *lrnd.* dispute; quarrel; contention.
leccac (.—) لجاج A *lrnd.* quarrelsome; obstinately perverse.
leclâc (.—) لجلاج P *lrnd.* 1. doubting, wavering, undecided. 2. stuttering, stammering. 3. silver; quicksilver. 4. *w. cap.*, name of the legendary inventor of chess, the patron saint of gamblers.
leclec لجلج A *lrnd.* doubtful, unsteady, wavering.
leclece, leclecet لجلجه ، لجلجت A *lrnd.* a stammering from uncertainty, a being repetitious, tautological.
lecuc (.—) لجوج A *lrnd.* given to perverse contention, quarrelsome.
leçek[k1] لچك P square handkerchief folded and tied over the head.
lede لدى A *lrnd.* at a time (of so and so), on (such and such occurring) *e. g.*, **ledelvusul** on its arrival.
ledelhace (.'.—.) لدى الحاجه A *lrnd.* in case of necessity.
ledelicab (.'.——) لدى الايجاب A *lrnd.* when required.

ledelihtiyac (.'...—) لدى الاحتياج A *lrnd.* when needed.
ledelmuayene (...—..) لدى المعاينه A *lrnd.* on inspection; on examination.
ledettahkik (.'...—) لدى التحقيق A *lrnd.* on investigation.
ledg لدغ A *lrnd.* a venomous beast's biting or stinging; bite, sting.
lediğ (.—) لديغ A *lrnd.* 1. bitten by a serpent; stung by a scorpion. 2. who bites and stings with venomous words.
ledün لدن A *lrnd.* consciousness of God.
ledünî (..—) لدنى [*based on* **ledün**] derived from or existing in God. —**yat** (..——) A mysteries of the Divine nature; the real truth of a thing; trivial secrets.
leff[ff1] لف A *lrnd.* an enclosing, enclosure; a wrapping up. — **ü neşir** rhetorical figure which consists of naming a series of subjects, and subsequently naming their respective attributes.
leffen (.'.) لفاً A *lrnd.* enclosed.
leffet=[der] لفتمك /1/ to enclose (in a letter, etc.).
lefif لفيف A 1. *lrnd.* folded; involved; mixed. 2. *Arabic gram.* the root of which contains two of the letters و and ى (word).
lefk[k1] لفق A *lrnd.* a sewing and joining two things together.
Lefkoşe لفقوشه *geog.* Nicosia (Cyprus).
leftere لفتره P *lrnd.* vile, mean, low (fellow).
leğen لگن [*Persian* **leken**] 1. large bowl; basin. 2. *anat.* pelvis. — **ibrik** bowl and ewer. — **örtüsü** an unnecessary thing (when the essentials are missing).
leğençe لگنچه P small metal washbowl.
Leh 1 له 1. Polish, Pole. 2. *archaic* Poland.
leh 2 له A 1. for him or it. 2. in favor of him or it. 3. belonging to him; on the side of. —**inizde** in your favor. — **ve aleyh** for and against.
lehât (.—) لهات A *anat.* uvula.
lehaz (.—) لحاظ A *lrnd.* outer corner of the eye.
lehb لهب A *lrnd.* 1. flame, blaze. 2. *same as* **leheb.**
lehban (.—) لهبان A *lrnd.* burning with thirst.
lehce لهجه A *lrnd.*, *same as* **lehçe 1.**
lehçe 1 لهجه [lehce] 1. dialect. 2. speech, language. 3. *archaic* dictionary. 4. *archaic* face, visage, appearance.
Lehçe 2 (.'.) لهجه Polish, Polish language.
leheb لهب A *lrnd.* 1. flame, a flaming. 2. a thirsting; thirst. 3. dust flying in the air.
leheban (..—) لهبان A *lrnd.* a fire's flaming, a blazing.

lehef لهف A *lrnd.* a lamenting, lament.
lehf لهف A *lrnd.* Alas!
lehfan (. —) لهفان A *lrnd.* lamenting, complaining.
lehfet لهفت A *lrnd.* grief for a loss or disappointment.
lehib (. —) لهيب A *lrnd.* glow and heat of a fire; a flaming.
lehif (. —) لهيف A *lrnd.* lamenting, complaining.
lehim لهم [*Arabic* lıham] 1. solder. 2. solder joint.
lehimle=ʳ لهملمك /ı/ to solder. —t= /ı, a/ *caus.*
lehimli لهملى soldered.
Lehistan (.. —) لهستان P *geog.* Poland.
Lehli لهلى Polish, Pole.
lehüm (´.) لهم A *lrnd.* for them; to them.
lehv لهو A *lrnd.* amusement; play. —**iyat** (. — —) A amusements, entertainments.
leim (. —) لئيم A *lrnd.* abject; despicable; mean, base; miserly. —**an** (. — —) P mean, miserly, despicable men.
lejand لژاند F legend.
lejyon لژيون F legion.
lekᵏⁱ لك P *lrnd.* 1. a hundred thousand. 2. weak of mind, foolish, stupid. — **u pek a** gadding; rude, unskillful.
leke لكه P 1. stain; spot of dirt; mark, spot. 2. shame, dishonor. 3. speck (in the eye or on a fingernail). — **çıkar=** to remove a stain. — **et=** /ı/ to stain. — **getir=** /a/ to dishonor; to stain (the character of). — **ol=** to become stained or soiled. — **sabunu** soap for spots. — **sür=** /a/ to besmirch (someone's name). — **toprağı** fuller's earth. — **tut=** to stain easily. — **yap=** to stain; /ı/ to soil.
lekeci لكه جى dry cleaner, clothes cleaner.
leked لكد P *lrnd.* kick, blow, cuff.
lekedar (.. —) لكدار P *lrnd.* stained, polluted.
lekedhar (.. —) لكدخوار P *lrnd.* who is kicked.
lekedkûb (.. —) لكدكوب P *lrnd.* kicked, trampled under foot; smitten with calamity.
lekedzede لكدزده P *lrnd.* kicked, cuffed, trodden.
lekedzen لكدزن P *lrnd.* that kicks, striking; kicker.
lekele=ʳ لكه لمك /ı/ 1. to stain; to soil. 2. to cast aspersions on. —**n=** *pass.* —**t=** *caus. of* **lekele=**.
lekeli لكه لى spotted; stained; dishonored; of ill repute. — **humma** typhus fever; spotted fever.
leken لكن *prov.* a kind of snowshoe.
lekesiz لكه سز spotless; immaculate.

leklek, lekleke لكلك P *lrnd.* idle talk, chatter.
lektör لكتور F foreign language lecturer.
lemᵐⁱ 1 لمع A *lrnd.* a gleaming, shining, flashing; gleam, flash.
lem 2 لم A *lrnd.* not, *as in* **lemyezel**.
lem'a لمعه A *lrnd.* gleam, flash.
leman لمعان 1. *var. of* **lemean**. 2. *w. cap.* woman's name.
lem'ariz (.. —) لمعه ريز P *lrnd.* gleaming, shining.
-leme لمه *cf.* **-lama 2**.
lemeân (.. —) لمعان A 1. *lrnd.* gleaming, shining. 2. *phys.* luminescence.
lemeât (.. —) لمعات *lrnd., pl. of* **lem'a**.
lemehan (.. —) لمحان A *lrnd.* a glittering, shining; sparkle, flash.
lemehat (.. —) لمحات A *lrnd., pl. of* **lemha**.
—**lemesine** لمسنه *cf.* —**lamasına**.
lemf لمف F *same as* **lenf**.
lemh لمح A *lrnd.* 1. glancing, glance. 2. glittering, sparkling. —**i basar** at a glance.
lemha (. —) لمحه A *lrnd.* 1. glance. 2. flash, sparkle. —**i ula** the first glance.
lemhatülbasar لمحة البصر A *lrnd.* at a glance.
lems لمس A *lrnd.* touch, a touching or feeling. —**et=** /a/ to touch, to feel. —**î** tactile.
lemterema (...´ —) لم ترما *lrnd.* especially, above all.
lemyekün لم يكن A *lrnd.* it was not. **L— Suresi** *name of the ninety eighth sura of the Quran*.
lemyezel لم يزل A *lrnd.* eternal (God).
—**len= 1** لنك *cf.* —**lan= 1**.
—**len 2** لن *cf.* —**lan 2**.
lendüha (. — —) لندوها huge and clumsy.
lenf لنف *physiol.* lymph. — **damarları** lymph ducts.
lenfa (´.) لنفا F *physiol.* lymph. —**i dahilî** endolymph. — **damarları** lymph ducts. — **düğümü** lymph gland, lymph node. —**i haricî** perilymph.
lenfavî (.. —) لنفوى A 1. *physiol.* lymphatic. 2. *psych.* phlegmatic.
leng لنك P *same as* **lenk**. —**ân** (. —), —**âne** (. —.) P halting, limping; limpingly.
lenger لنكر P 1. large, deep copper dish. 2. *naut.* anchor. — **anası** body of an anchor. — **at=**, — **bırak=** to anchor.
lengerdar (.. —) لنكردار P *lrnd.* 1. at anchor, anchored. 2. heavy; grave; steady.
lengerendaz (... —) لنكر انداز P *lrnd.* anchored. — **ol=** 1. to anchor. 2. to stay long (in a place).
lengergâh (.. —) لنكركاه P *lrnd.* anchorage, harbor; port.
lengeri لنكرى big copper plate.

lengerkarar (...—) لنگر قرار P *lrnd.* permanently fixed, set to stay.
lengerli لنگرلی 1. at anchor. 2. firm, steady.
lengî (.—) لنگی P *lrnd.* lameness; a limp.
lenkᵍⁱ لنك P *lrnd.* lame. — **fahte** *Or. mus.* a fast rhythmic pattern of ten beats.
lentiye لنتیه It *naut.* spring on a ship's cable.
lento (.′.) لنتو F *arch.* lintel.
lep لپ *var. of* **leb**.
lepiska (..′.) لپسقا G 1. flaxen (hair), fair. 2. *w. cap.*, *obs.* Leipzig. — **saçlı** flaxen-haired.
lepra لپرا L *med.* leprosy.
—ler لر *cf.* **—lar**.
—lerce (.′.) لرجه *cf.* **—larca**.
lerci لرجی musk deer.
lermo (.′.) لرمو It *naut.* stay of a staysail.
lerzan (.—) لرزان P *lrnd.* trembling; shivering.
lerze لرزه P *lrnd.* tremble; a trembling, shivering.
lerzebahş (..—) لرزه بخش P *lrnd.* trembling; causing a shiver.
lerzenakᵏⁱ (..—) لرزه ناك P trembling.
lerzende لرزنده P *lrnd.* trembling.
lerziş لرزش P *lrnd.* a trembling.
lesˢʼⁱ لسع A *lrnd.* a stinging or biting serpent, scorpion; bite, sting.
—leş= 1 لش *cf.* **—laş=**.
leş 2 لش P carcass. — **kargası** hooded crow, *zool., Corvus cornix.* **—ini ser=** /ın/ to beat up (somebody).
leş 3 لش It *naut., only in* — **bağı** bowline hitch.
leşçi لشجی *slang* murderer.
leşger, leşker لشگر، لشكر P *lrnd.* army; troops. **—gâh** (..—) P camp. **—î** (..—) P pertaining to an army, military. **—keş** P who leads an army; captain, commander. **—şiken** P who breaks up armies.
let 1 لت P *lrnd.* 1. cudgel; club; mace. 2. blow. — **ur=** *archaic* /a/ to beat.
letᵗᵗⁱ 2 لتّ A *lrnd.* 1. a pounding, crushing, bruising. 2. a wetting and stirring up (flour, etc.).
letafet (.—.) لطافت A charm; grace, elegance.
letaif (.—.) لطائف A *lrnd., pl. of* **lâtife**.
letaifülhiyel (.—....) لطائف الحیل A *lrnd.* arts of finesse, tricks of diplomacy.
letalet (.—.) لتالت P *lrnd.* in pieces, fragments; fragile.
lete 1 لته *same as* **nete** 1.
lete 2 لته P *lrnd.* fragment, shred. — **lete** in pieces; broken in bits.
letenban (..—) لتنبان P *lrnd.* greedy fellow, glutton.

letre لتره P *lrnd.* 1. torn, ragged; broken. 2. coarse; fat. — **letre** in pieces, piecemeal.
lev 1 لو A *lrnd.* if.
levᵛⁱ 2 لوع A *lrnd.* a suffering and being impatient; love-pang.
leva 1 (.′.) لوا *same as* **lâva**.
lev'a 2 لوعه A *lrnd.* love-pang; grief.
levahikᵏⁱ (.—.) لواحق A *lrnd., pl. of* **lâhika**.
levaim (.—.) لوائم A *lrnd., pl. of* **laime**, reproaches.
levamiⁱⁱ (.—.) لوامع A *lrnd., pl. of* **lâmia**.
levanta (..′.) لوانطه It *same as* **lâvanta**.
Levanten لوانتن F Levantine.
levaşe (.—.) لواشه P *lrnd., same as* **yavaşa**.
levayih (.—.) لوایح A *lrnd., pl. of* **lâyiha**.
levazım (.—.) لوازم A 1. *mil.* supplies; provisions; quartermaster general's department. 2. necessities; materials. 3. sewing supplies. — **bürosu** supply office. — **çavuşu** supply sergeant. — **dairesi** quartermaster general's department; commissariat. — **müdürü** *mil.* quartermaster. — **sınıfı** supply corps. — **subayı** *mil.* commissary officer.
levazımat (.—.—) لوازمات *lrnd.* necessary things; provisions; equipment.
leve لوه F *cards* trick. — **yap=** to take a trick.
levend 1 لوند *naut.* portchain to a ship's portlid.
levend 2 لوند P *lrnd.* 1. free, independent; adventurer; irresponsible. 2. servant, laborer. 3. a handsome, strong youth. 4. *Ott. hist.* irregular military force.
levendane (..—.) لوندانه P *lrnd.* 1. free and easy, roistering. 2. stately and athletic.
levh لوح A *lrnd.* any flat surface for writing, tablet. **—i dû reng** the world of day and night, of weal and woe. **—i emles** *phil., tabula rasa.* **—i hamuşî** silence. **—i hâtır** memory. **L—i Mahfûz** *Isl. rel.* tablet of God's decrees preserved to the end of time.
levha لوحه A 1. picture; framed inscription. 2. signboard. 3. metal plate. 4. slab.
levhaşallah (...—) لوحش الله [la-evhaş-hu-llah] A *lrnd.* May God not leave him desolate. God forbid.
levinᵛⁿⁱ لوین *var. of* **levn**.
levisᵛˢⁱ لویس *var. of* **levs**.
levlâ (.—) لولا A *lrnd.* if...not; if there had not been.
levlâk (.—), **levlâke** (.—.) لولاك *Isl. rel.* but for thee (the spheres would not have been created) *symbolic name of the Prophet Muhammad.*
levm لوم A *lrnd.* blame, reproach.
levmet=ᵈᵉʳ 1 لوم ایتمك /ı/ to blame, to reproach.

levmet 2 لومة A *lrnd.* any act deserving reproof.
levn لون A *lrnd.* 1. color. 2. sort, kind.
levrekᵍⁱ لوررك Gk sea bass, *zool.*, *Labrax lupus*.
levs لوث A *lrnd.* dirt; filth. **—iyat** (. — —) dirty things, filthy affairs.
levvam (. —) لوّام A *lrnd.* blamer; faultfinder.
levz 1 لوز A *lrnd.* almond, *bot.*, *Amygdalus communis*.
levz 2 لوز A *lrnd.* 1. sheltered part of a valley. 2. refuge, asylum, retreat.
levze لوزه A 1. *anat.* tonsil. 2. *lrnd.* a single almond. **—tan** (. . —) A the two tonsils.
levzî (. —) لوزى *lrnd.* 1. almondlike. 2. tonsillar.
leyal (. —), **leyalî** (. — —) ليال ليالى A *lrnd.* nights.
—leyin (.'.) ليين temporal adverb, as in **geceleyin, sabahleyin**.
leyl ليل A *lrnd.* night. **L— Suresi** name of the ninety-second sura of the Quran.
leylâ 1 (. —) ليلا A *lrnd.* very dark (night).
leylâ 2 (. —) ليلا A *lrnd.* 1. the odor of black wine or the beginning of its intoxicating influence. 2. *w. cap.*, woman's name, especially, that of the celebrated sweetheart of Majnun.
leylâkᵍⁱ **1** ليلاك |**leylak 2**| lilac, *bot.*, *Syringa vulgaris*.
leylâkᵏⁱ **2** ليلاك A *lrnd.*, same as **leylâk 1**. **—î** lilac, lavender violet.
leyle ليله A *lrnd.* night. **L—i Beraet** a name of the fifteenth night of the month of Şaban. **—i garra** night which is the eve of Friday. **L—i Kadr** the Night of Power (the 27th of Ramazan). **—i leylâ** 1. very dark night. 2. thirtieth night of a lunar month. **L—i Mirac** same as **Mi'rac Gecesi**, the night of the Prophet Muhammad's journey to heaven. **—i şeyba** the last night of a lunar month. **—i vasl** the last night of a lunar month.
leylekᵍⁱ ليلك P stork, *zool.*, *Ciconia ciconia*. **—in attığı yavru** abandoned, discarded (person). **— gibi** very tall. **—in ömrü lâklâkla geçer** The stork spends all his life in chattering said about idle talk or vain expectation. **— yuvası gibi saç** untidy, unkempt (hair); a bird's-nest of hair.
leylen (.'.) ليلا A *lrnd.* at night, by night.
leyli 1 (. —) ليلى A 1. boarder (at a school). 2. *lrnd.* nocturnal. **— mektep** boarding school.
Leylî 2 (. —) ليلى same as **Leyla 2**².
leymûn (: —) ليمون A *lrnd.*, same as **limon**.
leys ليث A *lrnd.* 1. lion. 2. eloquent speaker. **—i ıffırin** 1. a jungle lion. 2. a man of fifty (who is then most fierce and cunning in attack).
leyse ليس A *lrnd.* 1. It is not. 2. There is not...
leysiye ليسيه A *phil.* nihilism.
leyte ليت A *lrnd.* If only; I wish that.
leytülaal, leyt ve laalle ليت لعل ليت و لعل A *lrnd.* needless delays; futile pretexts; indecision.
leyyin ليّن A *lrnd.* soft; mild.
leyyinül'asa (. . . . —) ليّن العصا • A *lrnd.* who punishes lightly; gentle.
leyyinülcanib (. . . —) ليّن الجانب A *lrnd.* of a mild, pliant disposition.
lezaiz (. — .) اللذائذ *lrnd.*, *pl.* of **lezize**, delights.
lezam (. —) لزام A *lrnd.* indispensibility, inseparability; persistence.
lezez اللذذ A *Ott. hist.* collective name for the lunar months Şevval, Zilkade, Zilhicce.
leziz (. —) لذيذ A delicious; relishing; tasty, savory.
lezukᵏᵘ (. —) لزوق A *obs.* adhesive tape.
lezyon لزيون F *med.* lesion.
lezzat (. —) لذات A *lrnd.*, *pl.* of **lezzet**. **—ı hissiye** sensual pleasures.
lezzet لذت A 1. taste; flavor. 2. pleasure, enjoyment. **— al=** to find pleasure (in something); /dan/ to enjoy. **— bul=** to find pleasure (in something). **— duy=** to enjoy. **—i kalmadı** There is no pleasure in it any more. **— ver=** /a/ to give pleasure; to give flavor (to a thing).
lezzetiye لذتيه A *phil.* hedonism.
lezzetlen=ⁱʳ لذتلن to become tasty.
lezzetli لذتلى tasty, delightful.
lezzetsiz لذتسز insipid; tasteless.
lezzetyab (. . —) لذت ياب P *lrnd.* finding pleasure.
-lı 1, —li, —lu, —lü لى لو 1. having, provided with. 2. coming from; belonging to (person). 3. *attached to adjectives, in duplication*, partly...partly, as in **büyüklü küçüklü, allı yeşilli**.
=lı 2, =li, =lu, =lü لى لو *after consonants* **=ılı, =ili, =ulu, =ülü** *passive adjective showing state resulting from a process*, e. g., **kapalı, döşeli, asılı, ekili, gömülü, kurulu**.
lıca ليجه *prov.*, *var.* of **ılıca 1**.
-lıkᵍⁱ**, -lik, -luk, -lük** لك لو لق 1. *attached to adjective: abstract noun*, as in **iyilik, güzellik**. 2. *attached to substantive:* abounding in (place), as in **taşlık, dağlık**. 3. container; intended for, as in **çaydanlık, tuzluk**. 4. *after a number:* of so many... **üç günlük**, as in **üç günlük seyahat** a three-day trip.
-li 1 لى لو *cf.* **-lı 1**.

-li 2 لی لو *cf.* **lı 2.**

li 3 لی A *lrnd.* 1. for. 2. in favor of; on account of. 3. to, belonging to, *as in* **liecl, lisebebin.**

liam (.—) لأم لآم A *lrnd., pl. of* **leim.**

lian (.—) لعان A *lrnd.* a calling down God's curse upon one another; especially, such a curse by husband and wife when the husband has accused the wife of adultery.

libâ (.—) لبأ A *lrnd.* beestings, colostrum.

libab (.—) لباب A *lrnd., pl. of* **lebib.**

libâde (.—.) لبادة [**lebade**] felt coat worn in rainy weather.

liban (.—) لبان A *lrnd.* 1. milk. 2. a sucking; lactation.

libas (.—) لباس A *lrnd.* garment. —ı **müstear** mortal body.

libre (.́.) لبره It pound (weight). —**lik** weighing so many pounds.

licam (.—) لجام A *lrnd.* bridle.

lice لیجه *same as* **lıca.**

lider لیدر E leader. —**lik** leadership.

lieb لأب A *lrnd.* on the father's side, paternal.

liebeveyn لأبوین A *lrnd.* having the same father and the same mother, full (brother or sister).

liecl لأجل A *lrnd.* for the purpose of; on the score of. —**i tahsil** for studying.

lif لیف [*Arabic* —] 1. fiber. 2. vegetable sponge, luffa. 3. palm fibers (used for scrubbing in a bath). — **halat** hemp rope. — **lif** fibrous.

lifafe (.—.) لفافة A *lrnd.* 1. bandage. 2. enveloping membrane.

lifî (— —) لیفی A *lrnd.* fibrous.

lifti لیفتی Gk mortise chisel.

lig لیغ E sports league.

ligadura (...́.) لیغادوره It *same as* **likatura.**

ligam (.—) لگام P *lrnd.* bridle; bit. —**riz** (.——) P slack rein, full speed.

ligarazihi (....́.) لغرضه A *lrnd.* for his own selfish ends.

liğen لگن P *same as* **leğen.**

liha (.—) لحی A *lrnd., pl. of* **lihye.**

lihaf (.—) لحاف A *lrnd.* blanket; sheet; quilt. —**i çeşm** the upper eyelid.

lihakᵏⁱ (.—) لحاب A *lrnd.* bow case.

liham 1 (.—) لحام A *lrnd., pl. of* **lahm.**

liham 2 (.—) لحام A *lrnd.* solder.

lihaz (.—) لحظ A *lrnd.* observing attentively; observation; scrutiny.

lihaza (.—.) لهذا A *lrnd.* for this reason; therefore.

lihyani (.——) لحیانی A *lrnd.* having a long or bushy beard.

lihye لحی A *lrnd.* beard. —**dâr** (..—) P bearded.

-likᵍⁱ **1** لك *cf.* **-lık.**

likˢⁱ **2** لیك *same as* **lig.**

lik 3 (—) لیك P *lrnd.* but, yet.

lika 1 (.́—) لیقة [*Arabic* —.] *obs.* raw silk.

lika 2 (.—) لقا P *lrnd.* face; aspect.

-lika 3 (.—) لقاء A *lrnd.* faced, *as in* **hublika, hurlika.**

lika 4 (.—) لقا A *lrnd.* an encountering, a meeting (a person).

likâf (.—) لكاف A *lrnd.* donkey saddle.

likatura (...́.) لیغاطوره It [**ligatura**] *naut.* spun yarn.

likaullah (.—.—) لقاءالله A *lrnd.* man's standing in God's presence on the day of judgment.

likidasyon لیكیداسیون F *com.* liquidation.

likin (—.) لیكن P *lrnd.* but, yet.

likorinoz (...́.) لیقورینوز Gk smoked mullet.

likör لیكور F liqueur.

lillâh (.—.) لله A *lrnd.* 1. for God; for God's sake. 2. to God; by God.

lilvaktᵗⁱ لوقت A *lrnd.* on the instant.

lima (.—) لما A *lrnd.* What for? Why?

limam (.—) لمام A *lrnd.* occasional times of repetition. —**en** (.—.) A at intervals, now and then.

liman لیمان Gk 1. harbor; seaport. 2. *obs.* calm. — **açıkları** the offing (of a port). — **amelesi** longshoreman, dock worker. — **dairesi** harbormaster's office. — **işçisi** longshoreman. — **nizamnamesi** harbor regulations. — **reisi** harbormaster. — **reisliği** harbormaster's office. — **rüsumu** harbor taxes.

limanla=ʳ لیمانلمه 1. to come into harbor. 2. to die down (wind or sea).

limanlıkᵏⁱ لیمانلق 1. place serving as a harbor. 2. calm (sea).

limaslahatin (..́...) لمصلحة A *lrnd.* on business.

limba (.́.) لیمبه It *obs.* a kind of barge.

lime (—.) لیمه narrowish long slice. — **lime** in strips; in tatters, in rags. — **lime kes=** to cut into long narrow slices.

limmî (.—) لمّی A *phil.*, *a priori.*

limon لیمون It lemon. — **ağacı** lemon tree. — **çiçeği** lemon blossom. — **gibi** pale. — **kabuğu** lemon peel. — **küfü** lemon mold; bluish green. — **sarısı** lemon yellow. — **suyu** lemon juice. — **tuzu** salts of lemon; potassium oxalate; citric acid; lemonade powder.

limonata (...́.) لیمناطه It lemonade. — **gibi** fresh, cool and pleasant (weather).

limonî (.——) لیمونی A 1. pale yellow. 2. capricious; touchy.

limonlu لیمونلی flavored with lemon.

limonlukᵍⁱ لیمونلق 1. greenhouse. 2. lemon squeezer.

limüellifihi (....'..) لمؤلفه A *lrnd.* by the author.

linç لينج E lynching. — **et=** /1/ to lynch.

linet (—.) لينت A gentle looseness of the bowels.

linkᵍⁱ لنك trotting pace of a horse, trot.

linkle=ʳ لنكله مك to trot.

liperi (.'..) ليپاری Gk a kind of mackerel.

lipsos (.'.) ليپسوس Gk a large red scaled fish, *zool.*, *Scarpaena scrofa.*

lir لير F *mus.* lyre.

lira (.'.) ليرا ليره It lira (Turkish monetary unit). —**nın üstü** change for one lira. —**lık** so many liras worth.

liret ليرەت It Italian lira.

lirikᵍⁱ ليريك F lyrical.

-lis (—) ليس P *lrnd.* licker, as in **kâselis.**

lisam (.—) لثام A *lrnd.* veil or net covering the mouth (to disguise the face).

lisan (.—) لسان A 1. language. 2. *lrnd.* tongue. —**i hâl** *lrnd.* the manner, looks or condition of a person or thing as appealing directly to the heart or mind without making use of words. —**âşina** (.——.—) P *lrnd.* linguist.

lisanen (.—'.) لسانا A *lrnd.* orally; verbally.

lisanî (.——) لسانی A *lrnd.* lingual; linguistic. —**yat** (.———) *lrnd.* linguistics. —**yun** (.———) *lrnd.* linguists; philologists.

lisans ليسانس F 1. *university* bachelor's or master's degree. 2. *com.* import or export license. — **yap=** to take a degree.

lisansiye ليسانسيه F Bachelor or Master of Arts.

Lisanullah (.—.—) لسان الله A *lrnd.* the Quran.

lisanüssevr (.—..) لسان الثور A *lrnd.* borage, *bot.*, *Borago officinalis.*

lisat (.—) لساة A *lrnd.*, *pl.* of **lise** 2.

lise 1 (.'.) ليسه F high school, lycée.

lise 2 لثه A *lrnd.* 1. gums (of the teeth). 2. uvula.

lisebebin (..'..) لسببٍ A *lrnd.* for some reason; not with reason.

liste (.'.) ليسته It list. —**ye geçir=** /1/ to enter on the list.

litre (.'.) ليتره It liter.

liv (—) ليو P *lrnd.* the sun.

liva (.—) لوا A 1. brigade; brigadier; rear admiral. 2. flag, banner, ensign. 3. *Ott. hist.* subdivision of a province.

livan (——) ليوان A *lrnd.*, same as **eyvan.**

livar (——) ليوار Gk fish pond (for keeping live fish for use).

livâta (.—.) لواطه A *lrnd.* sodomy, pederasty.

liyaz (.—) لواز A *lrnd.* a covering,

sheltering, protecting oneself; a taking shelter; refuge.

live (—.) ليوه P *lrnd.* flatterer; coaxer; deceiver.

livechillah (...—) لوجه الله A *lrnd.* for the sake of God, as a duty to God.

livre ليوره F livery.

liyakatᵗⁱ (.—.) لياقت A merit; capacity; suitability. — **göster=** to prove capable or deserving. — **sahibi** capable.

liyakatli لياقتلى capable, efficient.

liyakatsiz لياقتسز incapable, inefficient.

liyezon ليەزون F liaison.

liyme ليمه same as **lime.**

liynet لينت same as **linet.**

lizalike (.—.) لذلك A *lrnd.* for this reason.

lobut لوبوت لوبود [*Arabic* **nebbut**] cudgel; Indian club.

loca (.'.) لوجه It 1. box (at a theater), loge. 2. Masonic lodge.

loça (.'.) لوچه It *naut.* hawse pipe.

loda (.'.) لوده heap of straw covered with earth.

lodos لودوس Gk southwest wind; southwesterly gale. — **poyraz** capricious; now one way, then the other. — **poyraz mukataası** vagabondage, idleness.

lodosla=ʳ لودوسلامق to blow from the southwest (wind); to become mild (weather).

lodoslukᵍᵘ لودوسلق exposed to the southwest.

Lofça (.'.) لوفچه Sl Lowicz (in Poland); *l. c.* very large nail.

loğ لوغ *prov.* stone roller (used to roll the clay roof of a house). — **ağacı** wooden handle for a stone roller. — **taşı** stone roller.

loğla=ʳ لوغلامق /1/ to roll and compact with a roller (a clay roof).

loğap لوغاپ [**lûab**] *prov.* jelly.

loğusa (.'..) لوغوسه Gk woman after childbirth. — **otu** aristolochia. — **şekeri** a red sugar (used in preparing **loğusa şerbeti**). — **şerbeti** a drink offered people visiting the mother of a newborn baby.

loğusalıkᵍⁱ لوغوسه‌لق childbed; lying-in, confinement.

loka لوقه *obs.* untidy.

lokalᵗⁱ لوقال 1. clubroom; club. 2. local.

lokanta (..'.) لوقانته It restaurant. —**cı** restaurant keeper, restaurateur.

lokavt لوق‌آوت E *com.* lockout.

lokma لقمه A 1. morsel. 2. a small ball of fried sweet dough. 3. *anat.* condyle; rounded head of a bone. —**sı ağzında büyü=** not to have any appetite. **bir — bir hırka** enough to keep body and soul together. — **dök=** to make fritters. — **göz**, — **gözlü** popeyed. — **lokma** in small pieces.

Lokman لقمان A name of two legendary sages

one regarded as the father of medicine, the other as a famous storyteller. — **hekimin ye dediği** recommended by the doctor as good to eat *said of an attractive woman or delicious food*. — **ruhu** ether. — **Suresi** *name of the thirty-first sura of the Quran*.

Lokmanhikmet لقمان حكمت P *lrnd*. wise as Lokman.

Lokmanî (.——) لقمانى A *lrnd*. wise, sage.

lokomotif لوقوموتيف F railway engine, locomotive. — **garajı** engine shed.

lokra (´.) لوقره a kind of sparrow.

lokum لوقوم [**rahatülhulkum**] 1. Turkish delight. 2. *playing cards* diamonds.

lololo لولولو nonsense; empty words.

lombar لومبار It *naut*. port in a ship's side. — **ağzı** gangway. — **kapağı** port lid.

lomboz لومبوز It *naut*. porthole; deadlight; scuttle for air.

lonca (´.) لونجه It guild; corporation.

Londra (´.) لوندره It *geog*. London.

londrin لوندرين It *obs*. a kind of cloth.

longa لونغا instrumental dance music.

lop 1 لوپ round and soft. — **et** boned meat. — **inciri** a kind of large green fig. — **lop yut**= to bolt down (food). — **yumurta** hardboiled egg.

lop[bu] 2 لوپ F *anat*. lobe. —**çuk** lobule.

loppadak لوپدك falling suddenly (as a great lump).

lopur lopur لوپور لوپور greedily. — **yut**= to gobble down greedily.

lor لور P of goat milk curds. — **peyniri** soft goat milk cheese.

lorta (´.) لورطه Gk shoemaker's last, size of a last.

lostarya (.—´.) لوستاريا It small tavern.

lostra (´.) لوستره It shoe polish. —**cı** shoeshine boy.

lostromo (..´.) لوستروموl It *naut*. chief of the crew; boatswain.

losyon لوسيون F a kind of eau de cologne.

loş لوش dark; gloomy; dim.

loşluk[gu] لوشلق darkness, gloominess, dimness.

lotarya (..´.) لوتاريا It lottery.

Lozan (´.) لوزان F *geog*. Lausanne.

lök لوك 1. awkward; clumsy; sluggish. 2. *prov*. male camel. — **gibi otur**= to sit heavily and lazily.

lökün لوكون putty.

lövye لويه F gear lever, crowbar.

-lu 1 لو cf. **-lı** 1.

-lu 2 لو cf. **-lı** 2.

-lû 3 لو archaic for **-lı** 1. e. g., **devletlû**, **misillû**.

-lu 4, **-lü** لو *obs*. for **-lı** 2.

luab (.—) لعاب A 1. *anat*. saliva. 2. *lrnd*. mucilage. 3. *obs*. confectioner's jelly. —**ı**

ankebut P *lrnd*. 1. cobweb. 2. any fine gauzelike work. —**ı gâv**, —**ı gevezn** P *lrnd*. 1. brightness of sun or of lightning. 2. white paper. 3. dew; snow. —**ı mekes** P *lrnd*. 1. honey. 2. wine. —**ı şems** gossamer, fine threads floating in the air.

luabî (.——) لعابى A *lrnd*. salivary; saliva-like.

lu'b لعب A *lrnd*. game; toy.

lu'bet لعبت A *lrnd*. game; toy.

lu'betbaz (..—) لعبت باز P *lrnd*. 1. player; puppet player. 2. conjurer.

lu'betgâh (..—) لعبتگاه P *lrnd*. place where games are played.

lubiyat (.——) لعبيات [*based on Arabic*] *lrnd*. games, amusements.

lûgat[ti] 1 لغت A 1. dictionary. 2. word, term. 3. *lrnd*. language; dialect. — **kitabı** dictionary. — **parala**= to talk nonsense.

lûgat 2 (.—) لغات A *lrnd*., *pl*. of **lûgat** 1.

lûgatçe لغتچه P vocabulary, glossary.

lugavi (..—) لغوى A *lrnd*. pertaining to the words of a language. —**yat** (..——) lexicological questions. —**yun** (..——) lexicologists.

lugaz لغز A *lrnd*. riddle; enigma; puzzle.

luhud (.—) لحود A *lrnd*., *pl*. of **lahd**.

luhuk[ku] 1 (.—) لحوق *lrnd*. a joining, a reaching.

luhuk[ku] 2 لحوق [*Arabic* lu'uq] *obs*. electuary.

luhum (.—) لحوم A *lrnd*., *pl*. of **lahm**.

-luk[gu] لوك *cf*. **-lık**.

Luka (—´.) لوقا *Bib*. Luke.

lukata 1 لقاط A *lrnd*. a thing found and picked up.

lukata 2 (..—) لقطا A *lrnd*., *pl*. of **lakît**.

lukta لقط A *lrnd*. anything found by chance and the owner of which is unknown.

lûl[lü] (—) لول P *lrnd*. shameless, bold, impudent.

lule (—.) لوله P *lrnd*., *same as* **lüle**.

lûli (——) لولى P *lrnd*. 1. nice, delicate. 2. public singer. 3. courtesan.

lûmbar لومبار *same as* **lombar**.

lûmbuz لومبوز *same as* **lomboz**.

lûs[ssu] لص A *lrnd*. thief; robber.

lûstra لوسترا *same as* **lostra**.

lusuk[ku] (.—) لصوق A *lrnd*. a sticking, adhering; adhesion.

Lût (—) لوط A *Bib*. Lot, Abraham's nephew. — **Denizi** the Dead Sea. — **kavmi** the people of Sodom and Gomorrah.

lûtf لطف A *same as* **lûtuf**. — **et**= to do a favor.

lûtfen (´.) لطفاً A please; kindly — **ve keremen** graciously, generously.

lûtfî (.—) لطفى A pertaining to kindness or grace.

lûtfullah اطفنا الله A 1. the grace of God. 2. *w. cap.*, *man's name.*
lûti (— —) لوطى A *lrnd.* pederast.
lûtr لوطر F otter, otterskin.
lûtufᵗᶠᵘ الطف [lûtf] kindness, goodness, favor. **— gör=** to receive a favor.
lûtufdide (..—.) الطف ديده P *lrnd.* who has received a favor.
lûtufkâr (..—) الطفكار P kind, gracious. **—âne** (..— —.) P graciously. **—î** (..— —) P graciousness.
lûtufname (..—.) الطفنامه P gracious letter. **—niz** (..—..) *lrnd., polite form for your letter.*
lûub لعب same as **lû'b.**
-lü 1 لو لى *cf.* **-lı 1.**
-lü 2 لو لى *cf.* **-lı 2.**
-lü 3 لو لى *cf.* **-lu 4.**
lübᵇᵇᵘ لبّ A 1. *lrnd.* kernel; marrow; essence. 2. heart; mind; understanding.
lüban (.—) لبان A *lrnd.* 1. frankincense. 2. business, occupation.
lübbi (.—) لبّى A *lrnd.* pertaining to the kernel or marrow.
Lübnan (.—) لبنان A *geog.* Lebanon.
lübs لبس A *lrnd.* a putting on a garment.
lübûb (.—) لبوب A *lrnd., pl. of* **lüb.**
lücce لجّ A *lrnd.* 1. great crowd. 2. high sea; the deep.
lücmᶜᵐᵘ لجم. A *lrnd., pl. of* **licam.**
lüema (..—) لئام A *lrnd., pl. of* **leim,** the mean, miserly, despicable.
lüfer لوفر bluefish, *zool., Pomatomus saltatrix.*
lühüvᵛᵛᵘ لهو A *lrnd.* a being constantly diverted with a frivolous thing.
-lük 1 لك *cf.* **-lık.**
lükᵏᵘ **2** لك P 1. gum-lac. 2. *lrnd.* anklebone. **— boyası** a red dye obtained from gum-lac.
lüknet لكنت A *lrnd.* stammering, stuttering.
lüks لوكس F luxury. **— kâğıt** fancy paper. **— koltuk** extra good seats (in a theater etc.)

— lâmbası pressurized kerosene lamp with an incandescent mantle. **— mevki** de luxe class. **— nüsha** de luxe edition.
lükûnet (.—.) لكونت A *same as* **lüknet.**
lüle لوله [lûle] 1. spout. 2. pipe, tube. 3. bowl of a tobacco pipe. 4. curl; fold. 5. *obs.* a kind of water measure. **— lüle** curly (hair). **— taşı** meerschaum.
lüleci لوله جى maker or seller of pipe bowls. **— çamuru** pipe clay.
lü'lü لؤلؤ A *lrnd.* pearl. **—i meknûn** 1. a pearl concealed in its shell. 2. a virgin. **—i munazzad** 1. pearls neatly strung. 2. beautiful and regular teeth. **—i şahvar** a pearl worthy of a king; very precious pearl. **—bar** (..—), **—feşan** (...—), **—paş** (..—) P scattering gems.
lümaşel لوماشل F *geol.* lumachelle.
lüp لپ windfall. **— diye yut=** to gulp down. **—e kon=** to get something gratis or without effort.
lüpçü لپچى one who lives by his wits; parasite.
lüple= لوپله مك to gulp down.
lüseyn لسين A *anat.* uvula.
lüsus (.—) لصوص A *lrnd., pl. of* **lûs.**
lüsûsiyet (.—..) لصوصيت A *lrnd.* a robbing; robbery.
lüsün لسن A *lrnd., pl. of* **lisan.**
lüzub (.—) لزوب A *lrnd.* an adhering tenaciously; tenacity, toughness.
lüzûcet (.—.) لزوجت A *lrnd.* viscosity. **—li** viscous.
lüzûci (.— —) لزوجى A *lrnd.* viscous. **—yet** (.— —.) A viscosity.
lüzukᵏᵘ (.—) لزوك A *lrnd.* a sticking, adhering; adherence.
lüzumᵐᵘ (.—) لزوم A a being necessary, indispensible; necessity; need. **—unda** in case of necessity. **— gör=** /a/ to require, to deem necessary. **— görülürse** if needed, if necessary. **—lu** necessary. **—suz** unnecessary.

M

m, M 1 *the sixteenth letter of the alphabet.*
=m 2 *after consonants* =ım, =im, =um, =üm *(single) act of...*, *as in* **büküm, dolam, gelişim, içim, kırım, yudum.**
-m 3 *after consonants* -ım, -im, -um, -üm, *my, as in* **masam** *my table*, **kolum** *my arm*, **kollarım** *my arms.*
ma 1 مَ *A lrnd.* with, *as in* **maaile.**
ma 2 (—) ماء *A lrnd.* water. **—i cârî** running water, flowing water. **—i leziz** sweet water. **—i mukattar** distilled water. **—i râkid** stagnant water. **—i zerrin** gold wash.
mâ- 3 (—) ما *A lrnd.* what, that which, *as in* **mâdun, mâfevk.**
ma 4 ما *prov.* There! There it is. Take it.
=ma= 5, =me= 2 ما *not, e. g.,* **koşma** Do not run. **gelmedi** He did not come.
=ma 6, =me 3 ما ، مه 1. *the act of ..., e. g.,* **okuma salonu** reading room. 2. *adj. or substantive with participle meaning, often preceded by* -dan, *e. g.,* **dökme demir** cast iron, **kırma taş** broken rocks, **eskiden bozma elbise** a dress made from an old one.
maa مَعَ *A lrnd., same as* **ma 1.**
maab 1 (.—) مَعاب *A lrnd.* defect, fault, blemish.
-maab 2 (.—) مآب *A same as* **-meab.**
maabid (.—.) مَعابِد *A lrnd., pl. of* **ma'bed.**
maabir (.—.) مَعابِر *A lrnd., pl. of* **ma'ber.**
maacin (.——) مَعاجين *A lrnd., pl. of* **ma'cun.**
maad (.—) مَعاد *A* 1. *lrnd.* a place or condition to which one returns; an ultimate state; result, outcome. 2. *lrnd.* resurrection; a return; future state. 3. *myst.* goal; knowledge of God.
maada (——) ما عدا *A* 1. besides, except; in addition to. 2. rest, remainder (of a thing). **—sı** the rest of it.
maadib (.—.) مآدِب *A lrnd., pl. of* **me'debe.**
maadin (.—.) مَعادِن *A lrnd., pl. of* **maden.** **—i seb'a** the seven precious metals (gold, silver, copper, tin, iron, lead, platinum).
maadiyat (.—.—) مَعادِيّات *A lrnd.* eschatology.
maahaza (...—) مَعَ هٰذا *A lrnd.* nevertheless, in spite of this.
maahid (.—.) مَعاهِد *A lrnd., pl. of* **ma'hed.**
maaile (.'...) مَعَ عائِلَ *A* together with the whole family, as a family.
maaka ماءكَ *A lrnd.* a continued sobbing.
maalesef (.'...) مَعَ الأَسَف *A* unfortunately; with regret.
maalî (.——) مَعالي *A lrnd.* greatnesses, eminences, sublime matters.
maaliftihar (.'...—) مَعَ الاِفتخار *A lrnd.* with pride, with pleasure.
maalkasem (.'...) مَعَ القَسَم *A lrnd.* under oath.
maalkerahe (.'..—.) مَعَ الكَراهَة *A lrnd.* reluctantly, with repugnance.
maalmemnuniye (.'..—..) مَعَ المَمنونِيَّة *A lrnd.* with pleasure.
maamafih (.'..) مَعَ ما فيه *A* nevertheless, however; yet.
maan (.') مَعاً *A lrnd.* together, in company with.
maani (.—.) مَعاني *A lrnd., pl. of* **mânâ 1.**
maarif (.—.) مَعارِف *A* 1. education, public instruction. 2. *lrnd., pl. of* **ma'rifet.** **—i dünya** *lrnd.* man of worldwide celebrity. **— emini** *obs.* regional education officer. **— işleri** educational matters. **— müdürü** director of education in a province. **M—i Umumiye**

maarifçi

Nezareti *Ott. hist.* Ministry of Public Instruction. **M— Vekâleti** Ministry of Education.
maarifçi معارفچى official in the system of public education. **—lik** *abstr. n.*
maarifmend (.—..) معارفمند P *lrnd.* man of knowledge. **—an** (.—..—) P learned men.
maarifperdaz (.—..—) معارفپرداز P *lrnd.* versed in science; learned; great scholar.
maarifperver (.—...) معارفپرور P *lrnd.* promoter of knowledge.
maarik[ki] (.—.) معارك A *lrnd., pl. of* **ma'reke.**
maasi (.—.) معاصى A *lrnd., pl. of* **ma'siyet.**
maasim (.—.) معاثم A *same as* **measim.**
maasir (.—.) معاثر A *same as* **measir.**
maaş (.—) معاش A 1. salary; allowance (to widows etc.). 2. *lrnd.* a living, a subsisting; livelihood; subsistence. **—at** (.——) A *lrnd.* salaries, allowances.
maaşir (.—.) معاشر A *lrnd., pl. of* **ma'şer.**
maaşlı معاشلى receiving a salary, on salary, salaried.
maatteessüf (.'....) مع التأسف A unfortunately; I am sorry, I regret.
maayib (.—.) معايب A *lrnd.* faults; blemishes.
maayiş (.—.) معايش A *lrnd., pl. of* **maişet.**
maaz (.—) معاذ A *lrnd.* refuge.
maazalik (.—.) مع ذلك A *lrnd.* nevertheless; all the same.
maazallah (..'..) معاذ الله A God forbid!
maazir (.——) معاذر A *lrnd., pl. of* **mi'zar.**
maaziyadetin (.'—..) مع زيادة A *lrnd.* abundantly, amply.
maba'd (—.) A, **mabad** (——) ما بعد 1. sequence, continuation; remainder. 2. *lrnd.* beyond. **—i var** to be continued.
maba'düttabia (....—.) ما بعد الطبيعة A *lrnd.* metaphysics.
mabaki (.——) ما باقى A *lrnd.* that which remains, the remainder.
mabal ما بال *prov., var of* **vebal.**
ma'bed معبد A *lrnd., same as* **mabet.**
ma'ber معبر A 1. *lrnd.* place of passage, pass, ferry, ford. 2. *arch.* nave (of a church).
mabet[di] (—.) معبد [ma'bed] place of worship, temple.
mabeyin (—..) مابين [mabeyn] 1. relation between two people; between. 2. *Ott. hist.* room between the women's quarters and the men's quarters (in a large house). 3. *Ott. hist.* the private apartments of the Palace (where the Sultan usually received viziers, etc). **—de** between them. **—imizde** between us. **—leri bozuk** They are on bad terms. **—i hümayun** *Ott. hist.* the private apartments of the Palace where the Sultan received visitors on ordinary occasions, and in which the male officers of the household were on duty. **— müşiri** *Ott. hist.* marshal of the Sultan's household.
mabeyn مابين A *lrnd.* 1. *same as* **mabeyin.** 2. interval, intervening thing or space.
mabeynci (—..) مابينجى *Ott. hist.* court chamberlain.
mabeynihüma (....—) مابينهما A *lrnd.* the relation between them.
mabihiliftihar (.....—) ما به الافتخار A *lrnd.* cause of pride.
mabihülihticac (.....—) ما به الاحتجاج A *lrnd.* the basis of an argument.
mabihilihtiyac (.....—) ما به الاحتياج A *lrnd.* what is necessary.
mabihilkıvam (....—) ما به القوام A *phil., obs.* substratum.
mablak مابلق spatula; putty knife.
ma'bud (.—) معبود A *lrnd.* 1. *same as* **mabut.** 2. served, worshipped.
ma'bude (.—.) A, **mabude** (——.) معبوده goddess.
mabut[du] (——) معبود [ma'bud] God; idol.
=maca, =mece ماجه *forms certain nouns from verbs, e. g.,* **darılmaca, kesmece, boğmaca, bilmece.**
Macar ماجار 1. Hungarian. 2. *archaic* Hungary. 3. *l. c., slang* louse. **— üzümü** mistletoe berries. **—ca** (..'.) the Hungarian language. **—istan** (..'.—) Hungary.
macera (—.—) ماجرا A 1. event, occurrence. 2. adventure. 3. romance. **— ara= to seek adventure. — romanı** adventure novel. **—cı** adventurer. **—lı** adventurous, hazardous.
maceraperest (—.—..) ماجراپرست P *lrnd.* adventurer.
macid (—.) ماجد A *lrnd.* illustrious.
macin (—.) ماجن A *lrnd.* shameless; licentious; one careless and indifferent as to what he says or does.
ma'cun (.—) A, **macun** (——) معجون 1. paste; putty; cement. 2. a medicated preparation of sugar like soft taffy. 3. *slang* hashish. **— bıçağı** putty knife. **— küsteresi** fillister plane. **—la tıka=** to stop up, to bung up.
macuncu معجونجى maker or seller of medicated taffy. **— mablağı** spatula of a taffy seller.
macunla=[r] معجونلا to stop up with putty.
macunluk[ğu] معجونلق taffy container.
maç ماچ F *sport* game, match. **— yap=** to compete; to play at.
maça (.'.) ماچا *cards* spade. **— beyi** 1. jack of spades. 2. conceited and ostentatious person. **— beyi gibi kurul=** to sit in a disrespectful, insolent pose. **— kızı** *cards* queen of spades.
maço (.'.) ماچو It sledge hammer.

maçuna (..´.) ما جونه It *naut*. crane, masting machine; shears. **— dikmesi** gibbet. **— gemisi** shear hulk. **— ücreti** cranage.

madalle مضلّ A *lrnd*. a cause of error, a point where one is likely to go astray or to lose his way.

madalya (..´.) ماليه It medal.

madalyon ماليون It medallion.

madam 1 مادام F madam, married lady (used only of non-Muslim women).

madam 2 (.—) مادام A *lrnd*. 1. while it lasts. 2. while, since, as.

madama (..´.) مادامه F *archaic* European lady.

madamki مادامكه *same as* **mademki**.

madamülhayat (.—..—) مادام الحيات A *lrnd*. as long as one lives.

=madan, =meden (.´.) مادن مدن without..., before..., *e. g.*, **gelmeden** without coming, before coming. **— evvel, — önce** before..., *e. g.*, **gelmeden evvel** before coming, **oturmadan önce**.

madara (...´) مادارا *slang* 1. common, unpleasant; silly, trifling. 2. an embarrassing a teacher in class. **— ol=** to be proved to be a liar; to feel humiliated.

madde مادّه [*Arabic* —.] A 1. matter, substance. 2. material. 3. subject. 4. article; paragraph (of a regulation or law). 5. pus, matter. **—i asliye** *gram*. radical, theme. **— madde** 1. divided into separate articles. 2. article by article, item by item. **—i sincabiye** *anat*. grey matter.

maddeci مادّه جى materialist. **—lik** materialism.

maddeten (.´..) مادّةً A materially; substantially.

maddi (.—) مادّى A material; physical; materialistic; substantial. **— hata** *law* error of fact. **— mallar** *law* corporal goods.

maddiyat (..—) مادّيات [*Arabic* ———] *lrnd*. material things; materialism.

maddiye (.—.) مادّيه [*Arabic* ———.] *phil*. materialism.

maddiyet (.—.) مادّيت [*Arabic* ———.] *lrnd*. materiality.

maddiyun (.——) مادّيون [*Arabic* ———] *phil*. materialists. **— mezhebi** materialism.

made (—.) ماده P *lrnd*. female. **—gân** (—.—) P *pl*. females. **—gi** (—.—) P female nature, femininity.

ma'delet A, madelet (—..) معدلت *lrnd*. justice, equity. **—nişan** (.....—) P, **—ünvan** (....—) P just, righteous, equable.

madem (—´.) [**madam 2**], **mademki** (—.´.) مادام مادامكه since, as; while.

ma'den A, maden (—.) معدن 1. mine; ore; mineral; metal. 2. metallic. 3. mine of learning, virtue, etc. (person). 4. treasure. **— amelesi** miner; pitman. **— cevheri** mineral ore. **— damarı** lode; vein. **— direği** pit-prop. **— filizi** ore. **— katranı** crude naphtha. **— kömürü** coal. **— kuyusu** mine shaft. **— mühendisi** mining engineer. **— ocağı** mine; pit. **— suyu** mineral water. **— tuzu** rock salt. **— yağı** mineral oil. **— yatağı** ore strata. **— zifti** mineral pitch; bitumen.

madenci (—..) معدنجى 1. miner; mining expert. 2. metallurgist. 3. mine owner. **—lik** 1. mining. 2. metallurgy.

ma'denî (..—) A, **madenî** (—.—) معدنى mineral, metal; metallic. **—leşme** mineralization. **—lik** metallic quality.

madeniyat (—.——) معدنيات A 1. metallic things. 2. minerals. 3. mineralogy; mining.

madeniyet (—.—.) معدنيت A metallic quality.

madensi *neol*., *chem*. metalloid.

mader (—.) مادر P *lrnd*. mother. **— ender** (—...) P stepmother. **—âne** (—.—.) P motherly, in a maternal manner.

maderî (—.—) مادرى P *lrnd*. maternal; motherhood, motherliness. **—yet** (—.—.) motherhood; motherliness.

madernâmî (—.——) مادرنامى P *lrnd*. metronymic.

maderşahî (—.——) مادرشاهى P *lrnd*. matriarchal. **—lik** matriarchy, matriarchate.

maderzad (—.—) مادرزاد P *lrnd*. innate, congenital.

madg مضغ A *lrnd*. mastication. **— et=** to chew.

=madık *cf*. **=dık 2**.

=madın, =medin مادن مدن *archaic for* **=madan**, etc.

Mâdi (——) مادى A *archaic* Median; Mede.

mâdih (—.) مادح A *lrnd*. eulogist, praiser.

madik^gi مادك *slang* trick, ruse; deceit. **— at=, — et=, — oyna=** /a/ to cheat, to deceive. **—ci** cheat, trickster.

madiyan (—.—) ماديان P *lrnd*. mare.

madrabaz (—.—) مادراباز طرابات Gk 1. middleman. 2. cheat, impostor. **— kayığı** boat that goes to fishing stations, buys up cheap fish, and retails them. **—lık** 1. the business of a middleman. 2. cheating.

madrıb مضرب A *lrnd*. 1. place or time of striking. 2. place of pitching a tent.

madrub (.—) مضروب A *lrnd*. 1. struck, beaten. 2. forged; wrought; coined. 3. *math*. multiplied; multiplicand.

madrubunfih (.—.—) مضروب فيه A *math*. multiplier.

madrus (.—) مضروس A *lrnd*. 1. bitten. 2. cased with rough stones. 3. set with sharp projections.

ma'dud (.—) A, **madud** (——) معدود *lrnd.* 1. numbered, enumerated. 2. /dan/ regarded, considered; counted (as). **—at** (.——) A items counted, things sold by number.

ma'dum (.—) A, **madum** (——) معدوم *lrnd.* nonexistent. **—at** (———) A nonexistent things. **—iyet** (——..) A, **—luk** nonexistence.

mâdumülcism (.—..) معدوم الجسم A *lrnd.* nonexistent as a substance.

madun (——) مادون A *lrnd.* inferior, subordinate. **—unda** below him (in grade).

madunüşşuur (——..—) مادون الشعور A *psych.* subliminal, subconscious.

madut^du (——) معدود *var. of* **madud**.

mafa (.'.) مفا *var. of* **mapa**.

mafât (.—) مافات A *lrnd.* that which has gone out of reach or possession; a thing lost; opportunity missed.

mafe (—.) مافـ *var. of* **mahfe**.

mafer [**mihfer**] مافر lathe chisel.

mafevk^kı مافوق A *lrnd.* that which is above; superior. **—ında** above him, above it.

mafevkattabia (....—.) مافوق الطبيعة A *lrnd.* supernatural.

mafilbal^li (..—) مافي البال A *lrnd.* what is in one's heart or mind.

mafiş (—'.) مافيش [*Arabic* ——] *colloq.* 1. nothing left; finished. 2. a kind of very light fritter.

mafizzamir (...—) مافي الضمير A *lrnd.* that which is in the heart or mind; secret thought, hidden intention.

mafraş مفرش *colloq., var. of* **mefreş**.

mafsal مفصل A joint, articulation. **—ı gayri müteharrik**, **—ı mevsuk** *anat.* immovable articulation. **—ı müteharrik** *anat.* movable articulation, diarthrosis, synarthrosis. **—î** (..—) A *lrnd.* pertaining to joints, articular; articulate.

ma'fu (.—) معفو A *lrnd.* pardoned, absolved, forgiven; condoned.

ma'fun (.—) معفون A *lrnd.* fetid, putrid, stinking.

ma'fuv^vvu معفو *same as* **ma'fu**.

mafzul^lü (.—) مفضول A *lrnd.* surpassed, overcome, conquered.

magafir (.—.) مغافر A *lrnd., pl. of* **miğfer**.

magak^kı (.—.) مغاك P *lrnd.* 1. pit, abyss. 2. grave. **—ı gar** the grave. **—ı zulmet** 1. abyss of darkness. 2. the world. 3. human body. **—çe** (.—.) P a little pit.

magamız (.—.) مغامض A *lrnd.* very low ground.

maganim (.—.) مغانم A *lrnd., pl. of* **mağnem**.

magasil (.—.) مغاسل A *lrnd., pl. of* **mağsel**.

magazi (.—.) مغازى A *lrnd.* campaigns, especially campaigns against the enemies of Islam.

magazil (.—.) مغازل A *lrnd., pl. of* **miğzel**.

magazin مغازن E magazine, periodical.

magib (.—) مغيب A *lrnd.* a being absent or hidden; absence; concealment.

magrib 1 مغرب A *lrnd.* 1. west. 2. sunset.

Magrib 2 مغرب A *geog.* Morocco. **—i aksâ** Morocco. **—i edna** Tripoli of Barbary. **—i evsat** Tunis and Algiers. **— hattı** a style of Arabic writing peculiar to northwestern Africa. **— ocakları** *hist.* Tripoli, Tunis, and Algiers under Ottoman administration. **—i sayf** *astr.* midsummer point of sunset. **— tilkisi** fennec, *zool., Canis zerda.* **—an** (.—), **—eyn** A the two points of solstitial sunset.

Magribî (..—) مغربي A Moor; Moroccan.

Magosa (.'.) ماغوسا *geog.* Famagusta (in Cyprus).

magz مغز *var. of* **mağz**.

mağ ماغ a kind of pigeon with its head and the tips of its pinions all of one color.

mağara مغاره [*Arabic* .—.] 1. cave, cavern. 2. pit.

mağarib (.—.) مغارب A *lrnd., pl. of* **mağrib**.

Mağaribe (.—..) مغاربه A *lrnd., pl. of* **Magribî**.

mağaza مغازه 1. large store; shop. 2. *obs.* storehouse; storeroom, cellar. **—cı** shopkeeper.

mağbin مغبن A *anat.* groin; armpit.

mağbun (.—) مغبون A *lrnd.* 1. deceived; swindled; imposed upon, defrauded. 2. foolish, weak in mind.

mağbut (.—) مغبوط A *lrnd.* 1. envied or imitated by others; enviable. 2. happy, fortunate, prosperous.

mağdur (.—) مغدور A wronged, unjustly treated; sufferer, victim; *law* injured party. **—iyet** (.——.), **—luk** a being unjustly treated; a suffering loss.

mağfiret مغفرت A *lrnd.* forgiveness of sins, remission; grace. **—i zünûb** forgiveness of sins. **—âşiyan** (...—.—), **—nişan** (....—), **—penah** (....—) P who has attained mercy, deceased (monarch).

mağfur (.—) مغفور A *lrnd.* one whose sins are forgiven; pardoned, forgiven.

mağfurunleh (.—..) مغفورله A *lrnd.* deceased.

=mağın, **=meğin** مغين *obs., adverb* as..., since....

mağlata مغلط A *lrnd.* matter that leads one into error; argument devised to mislead one; fallacious argument, sophistry.

mağlataperdaz (....—) مغلط پرداز P *lrnd.* propounder of fallacies.

mağlubiyet (.—..) مغلوبيت A defeat.

mağlukᵏᵘ (.—) مغلوق A lrnd. shut, barred, locked, bolted.
mağlûlˡⁱⁱ (.—) مغلول A lrnd. 1. fettered, shackled, pilloried. 2. parched with thirst.
mağlupᵇᵘ (.—) مغلوب A conquered, overcome, defeated. — **ol**= to be beaten, conquered.
mağmum (.—) مغموم A lrnd. 1. sad, anxious. 2. gloomy, overclouded. —**iyet** (.—..), —**luk** sadness; gloom.
mağmur (.—) مغمور A lrnd. 1. mean, abject, obscure, without rank or dignity. 2. overwhelmed, overflowed. —**iyet** (..—.), —**luk** abjectness, obscurity.
mağmuz (.—) مغموز A lrnd. accused, suspected.
mağnem مغنم A lrnd. spoil, plunder, booty.
mağnezya (..'.) مغنزيا L magnesia.
mağnezyum مغنزيوم L magnesium.
Mağnisa ('—.) مغنيسا archaic, geog., name for **Manisa**.
mağnolya (..'.) مغنوليا F archaic, same as **manolya**.
mağrem مغرم A lrnd. debt that must be paid.
mağrib مغرب A var. of **magrib 1**.
mağrukᵏᵘ (.—) مغروق A lrnd. 1. sunk, foundered (ship). 2. drowned; submerged. —**in** (.——) A pl.
mağrur (.—) مغرور A 1. proud, conceited, haughty. 2. law deceived. — **ol**= to be proud, to be puffed up.
mağrurâne (.——.) مغرورانه A proudly, haughtily.
mağruren (.—'.) مغرورا A 1. proudly and confidently. 2. /a/ trusting and relying on.
mağruriyet (.—..) مغروريت A pride, conceit.
mağrurlan=ᵃʳ مغرورلانمق to become foolishly proud and conceited.
mağrurlukᵍᵘ (.—..) مغرورلق foolish pride and conceit.
mağrus (.—) مغروس A lrnd. planted.
mağsel مغسل A lrnd. place where corpses are canonically washed.
mağsub (.—') مغصوب A lrnd. taken away by violence, ravished.
mağsubünminh (.—..) مغصوب منه A law from whom a thing has been taken by violence, despoiled.
mağsulˡⁱⁱ (.,—) مغسول A lrnd. washed, cleaned.
mağşi (.—) مغشى A lrnd. bewildered; taken unawares. —**yün aleyh** fainted.
mağşuş (.—) مغشوش A lrnd. alloyed, adulterated, base (coin, etc.) —**iyet** (.——.) A state of being adulterated.
mağz مغز P lrnd. 1. brain; chief matter or essence of anything. 2. marrow. 3. pulp, pith, kernel. 4. intellect; sense. —**i Kur'an** heart of the Quran. —**i püşt** 1. spinal marrow. 2. sperm, semen.
mağzaba مغضبه A lrnd. cause of anger; anger, rage; a being angry.
mağzdar (.—) مغزدار P lrnd. marrowy; kernelly, kerneled; having sense or wit, pithy. —**î** (.——) P the condition of that which has brain, marrow, wit, etc.
mağzine (.—.) مغزينه P lrnd. brain.
mağzub (.—) مغضوب A lrnd., only in **mağzubün aleyh** against whom anger is felt; an object of Divine wrath.
mah (—) ماه P lrnd. 1. moon. 2. month. 3. beautiful girl or boy. —**ı âlemâra** the world-adorning moon. —**ı hal** the present month. —**ı kamerî** lunar month. —**ı Kaşgar** beautiful Turkish girl or boy. —**ı Ken'an**, —**ı Ken'anî** (lit. Moon of Canaan) Joseph, son of Jacob. —**ı Mukanna**, —**ı müzevver**, —**ı Nahşeb** a luminous appearance resembling the moon, produced from a well at the foot of mount Siyam by the juggler Mukanna every night during a period of four months. —**ı nev** new moon; first month. —**ı ruze**, —**ı sıyam** the month of Ramazan. —**ı si-ruze** 1. moon thirty days old, i. e. very small. 2. delicate, weak, and sickly mistress. —**ı Siyam** same as **mahı Mukanna**. **M**—**ı Yemanî** the luminous countenance of the Prophet Muhammad; the Prophet.
mahabbet محبت A same as **muhabbet**.
mahabib (.——) محابيب A lrnd., pl. of **mahbub**.
mahabis (.—.) محابس A lrnd., pl. of **mahbes**.
mahacir مهاجر colloq., var. of **muhacir**.
mahadim (.——) مخاديم A lrnd., pl. of **mahdum**.
mahafet (.—.) مخافت A lrnd. a fearing, fear, dread. —**ullah** (.—..—) A the fear of God.
mahafil (.—.) محافل A lrnd., pl. of **mahfil**.
mahakᵏᵏⁱ, (.—) محاق A lrnd. dark of the moon (that part of the month when the moon is invisible).
mahakim (.—.) محاكم A lrnd., pl. of **mahkeme**. —**i adliye**, —**i nizamiye** regular courts of law. —**i şer'iye** canonical law.
mahalˡⁱⁱ **1** محل A 1. place, locality. 2. place of stay, abode; post. 3. occasion; reason. —**inde** at his post; on the spot. —**i ikamet** abode, dwelling. — **kalma**= to be no longer necessary. —**ine masrûf** well spent. —**i vak'a** the scene of action. — **yoktur** It is out of place; there is no reason.
mahalˡⁱⁱ **2** (.—) محال A lrnd., pl. of **mahal 1**.
mahalakallah (....—) ما ضل الله A

mahale (.—.) محاله A *lrnd.* 1. device, stratagem. 2. remedy; skill, cunning. 3. power, ability.
mahalib (.—.) محالب A *lrnd.*, *pl. of* **mahleb**.
mahallât (..—) محلّات A *lrnd.*, *pl. of* **mahalle**.
mahalle محلّ A 1. street; quarter; district. 2. ward (in a city or town). — **bekçisi** night watchman of the district. — **beyi** tough of the district. — **çapkını** timid womanizer. — **çocuğu** street urchin, guttersnipe. — **dilberi** street corner beauty. — **karısı** common woman; quarrelsome and ordinary woman, fishwife. — **mektebi** local school. — **tavrı** vulgar manner.
mahallebi محلّبی [*Arabic* **mahallebiye**] sweet pudding made with milk and rice flour. — **çocuğu** mother's darling, milksop. —**ci** 1. maker and seller of milk dishes. 2. soft person, weakling.
mahalleli محلّلی 1. a man of a certain district. 2. inhabitants of a quarter.
mahallî (..—) محلّی A local. — **idare** local government.
mahalsiz محلسز 1. groundless, ill-founded; out of place. 2. insignificant.
mahamid (.—.) محامد A *lrnd.*, *pl. of* **mahmedet**.
mahamil (.—.) محامل A *lrnd.*, *pl. of* **mahmil 1**.
mahana ماهانه *colloq.*, *var. of* **bahane**.
mahane (——.) ماهانه P *lrnd.* monthly (wages).
maharet (.—.) مهارت A skill, proficiency. —**li** skillful, efficient. —**siz** clumsy, unskillful.
maharib (.—.) محارب A *lrnd.*, *pl. of* **mihrab**.
maharic (.—.) مخارج A *lrnd.*, *pl. of* **mahrec**.
maharim (.—.) محارم A *lrnd.*, *pl. of* **mahrem**.
mahasal[ii] (.´.) ماحصل A *lrnd.* 1. result, yield. 2. gist, tenor of a discourse. —**ı ömr** 1. one's child. 2. the result of one's lifelong efforts.
mahasin (.—.) محاسن A *lrnd.*, *pl. of* **hüsn**, 1. personal charms, beautiful features (especially the beard). 2. good works, virtues, merits. —**e el vur=** *archaic* to stroke one's beard.
mahaşerallah (....—) ماحشر الله A (*lit.*, whom God has assembled together) very crowded.
mahat محط A *lrnd.* 1. a place where loads are set down, or travelers alight in journeying; a station. 2. port, wharf.
mahatim (.——) مخاتیم A *lrnd.*, *pl. of* **mahtum**.
mahavif (.—.) مخاوف A *lrnd.*, *pl. of* **mahafet**.

mahazar ماحضر A *lrnd.* what is ready, what is available.
mahazır (.—.) محاضر A *lrnd.*, *pl. of* **mahzar**.
mahazi (.—.) مخازی A *lrnd.* ignominious deeds or habits.
mahazil (.——) مخازیل A *lrnd.*, *pl. of* **mahzul**.
mahazin (.—.) مخازن A *lrnd.*, *pl. of* **mahzen**.
mahazir (.——) محاذیر A *lrnd.*, *pl. of* **mahzur 1**.
mahbemah (—.—) ماه به ماه P *lrnd.* from month to month, monthly, month by month.
mahbes محبس A prison. —**i âmâl** prison of ambitions.
mahbez, mahbeze مخبزه A *lrnd.* bakery.
mahbub (.—) محبوب A *lrnd.* 1. beloved. 2. catamite. —**i cihan** P beloved of the whole world. —**i Huda** the Prophet Muhammad.
mahbube (.—.) محبوبه A belovéd woman.
mahbun (.—) محبون A 1. *lrnd.* hoarded, laid up (provisions). 2. *pros.* a foot changed so that its first syllable becomes short.
mahbus (.—) محبوس A imprisoned; prisoner.
mahbushane (..—.) محبوسخانه P prison, jail.
mahbusîn (.——) محبوسین A *lrnd.* prisoners.
mahbusiyet (..—.) محبوسیت A *lrnd.* captivity, imprisonment.
mahcer محجر A *lrnd.* 1. socket corner, or region around the eye. 2. eye, peeping out from under a veil.
mahcir محجر A *lrnd.* 1. an inclosed place. 2. depressed place.
mahcub (.—) محجوب A 1. *lrnd.* curtained; veiled; secluded. 2. *same as* **mahcup**. —**âne** (.——.) P shyly, bashfully. —**iyet** (.——.) shyness, bashfulness; modesty.
mahcup[bu] (.—) محجوب [**mahcub**] shy, bashful, ashamed. —**luk** bashfulness; modesty.
mahcur (.—) محجور A *law* under interdiction; not allowed to dispose of his property.
mahcuz (.—) محجوز A *law* seized (goods or property).
mahçe (—.) ماهچه P *lrnd.* small gilded crescent on the top of a flagpole, minaret, or dome.
mahçehre (—..) ماه چهره P *lrnd.* with a face fair as the moon.
mahdud 1 (.—) محدود A *same as* **mahdut**.
mahdud 2 (.—) محدود A *lrnd.* 1. furrowed, trenched. 2. scored, gashed.
mahdudiyet (.——.) محدودیت A limitedness.
mahdum محدوم A 1. son. 2. *lrnd.* served, waited on; lord, master. **M—ı Kâinat** the Prophet Muhammad (upon whom all beings and inanimate things wait in service). —**e** daughter. —**iyet** 1. sonship. 2. lordship.
mahdur (.—) محدور A *lrnd.* veiled, curtained.

mahdure (. —.) مخدوره A *lrnd.* kept veiled (woman), chaste, modest.
mahdutᵈᵘ محدود [**mahdud**] 1. limited; bounded. 2. restricted. 3. few, not much. 4. *phil.* definite.
mahe (—.) ماهه P *lrnd.* a crescent-shaped gouge or auger.
ma'hed معهد A *lrnd.* place of refuge; meeting place.
mahfaza محفظه A 1. case (for jewelery, etc). box; casket. 2. sheath; capsule; cover. —**lı** kept in a case; having a cover.
mahfe محفه A *lrnd.* frame across a camel's back with a seat on each side.
mahfel محفل *colloq.*, *var.* of **mahfil.**
mahfi (. —) مخفى A *lrnd.* hidden, concealed; secret; clandestine. —**ce** secretly.
mahfil (..') محفل A 1. place of resort. 2. circle (of society); club; assembly, council. 3. private pew or gallery in a mosque. 4. Masonic lodge. —**i âli** high court, *esp.* the highest court; God's presence. —**i kaza** *obs.* public court of justice. —**i şerif** *same as* **mahfil-i âli.**
mahfiyen (. —.) مخفيا A *lrnd.* secretly.
mahfuf (. —) محفوف A *lrnd.* 1. encompassed, surrounded. 2. besieged by want.
mahfukᵏᵘ (. —) محفوق A *lrnd.* 1. affected with palpitations of the heart. 2. bereft of reason; mad.
mahfur (. —) محفور A *lrnd.* dug, excavated.
mahfuz 1 (. —) محفوظ A *lrnd.* 1. kept, treasured; protected; looked after; safe; guarded. 2. committed to memory. — **hisse** *law* compulsory portion, legal portion. — **mahal** *mil.* shelter. — **mallar** *law* separate estate.
mahfuz 2 (. —) محفوض A *lrnd.* depressed, submissive, abased.
mahfuzat (. — —) محفوظات A 1. treasures. 2. things committed to memory. 3. musical works committed to memory.
mahfuzen (. —'.) محفوظا A under guard or protection; in custody.
mah gelme⁼ᶻ ماه گلمك *colloq.* to be insufficient.
mahıvʰᵛⁱ محو A *var.* of **mahv.**
mahi 1 (— —) ماهى P *lrnd.* fish.
mahi 2 (— —) ماحى A *lrnd.* obliterating, defacing; annihilating.
mahid (—.) ماهد A *lrnd.* who spreads out; God, as spreader of the heavens and earth.
mahifüruş (— — . —) ماهى فروش P *lrnd.* fishseller.
mahigir (— — —) ماهيگير P *lrnd.* fisherman.
mahipüşt (— — . .) ماهى پشت P *lrnd.* fishbacked, ridged; ridge.
mahir (—.) ماهر A expert, skillful, well versed. —**ane** (—.—.) P skillfully. —**lik** skill.

mahis (. —) محيص A *lrnd.* a turning away; a flying, escaping, retreating; refuge.
mahitab (—. —) ماهتاب [**mahtab**] *lrnd.* 1. moonlight. 2. *same as* **maytap, mehtap.**
mahiyan 1 (—. —) ماهيان P *lrnd.*, *pl.* of **mahi 1.**
mahiyan 2 (—. —) ماهيان P *lrnd.*, *pl.* of **mah.**
mahiyane 1 (—. —.) ماهيانه P *lrnd.* fish broth.
mahiyane 2 (—. —.) ماهيانه P *lrnd.* monthly pay or allowance.
mâhiye (—..) ماهيه [*based on Persian* **mah**] *lrnd.* 1. monthly allowance. 2. per month. 3. *same as* **mahya.**
mahiyet (—..) ماهيت A 1. the reality; true nature of a thing; character. 2. *phil.* entity; essence.
mahiz (. —) محيض A *lrnd.* menstruation.
mahk محق A 1. *lrnd.* effacement, obliteration. 2. *myst.* annihilation in God.
mahkeme محكمه A court of justice. —**i asliye** court of first instance. —**de dayısı ol**= to have an influential friend in a powerful position. —**lerin dereceleri** *law* instances. — **duvarı** *slang* shameless, brazenfaced. — **kadıya mülk olmaz** Place and power are not everlasting. **M—i Kübra** Day of Judgment. —**i şer'iye** canonical court.
mahkemelikᵍⁱ محكمه لك matter for the courts. — **ol**= to have a dispute which can only be settled in a court of law.
mahki (. —) محكى A *lrnd.* told, narrated, related.
mahkukᵏᵘ **1** (. —) محقوق A *lrnd.* worthy, fit, proper.
mahkûkᵏᵘ **2** (. —) محكوك A *lrnd.* 1. incised, engraved. 2. scratched out, erased; rubbed. —**ât** (. — —) A engravings, inscriptions.
mahkûm (. —) محكوم A 1. sentenced, condemned, judged; convict. 2. doomed. — **et**= /ı/ to sentence, to condemn. —**iyet** (. — —.) A condemnation; sentence.
mahkûmünaleyh (. — ...) محكوم عليه A *law* judicially condemned.
mahkûmünbih (. — ..) محكوم به A *law* matter upon which judgment has been passed.
mahlâs محلاص A *lrnd.* 1. pseudonym. 2. second name given at birth, *e. g.,* **Mehmed Tarık.**
mahleb محلب A 1. mahaleb (European cherry), *bot.,* Prunus mahaleb; the fruit of mahaleb, used for flavoring. 2. *lrnd.* honey.
mahlûᵘᵘ (. —) مخلوع A *lrnd.* dethroned, deposed.
mahlûc (. —) محلوج A *lrnd.* carded, ginned.
mahlûkᵏᵘ **1** (. —) مخلوق A 1. creature. 2. *lrnd.* created.

mahlûk

mahlûkᵏᵘ 2 (.—) محلوك A *lrnd.* shaved.
mahluka (.—.) مخلوقة A *lrnd.* a plagiarized poem.
mahlûkat (.——) مخلوقات A creatures; all creation.
mahlûlˡᵘ̈ 1 (.—) محلول A *lrnd.* 1. melted, dissolved; *chem.* solution. 2. vacant (office). 3. solved; untied; undone. 4. *law* escheated (property). 5. made lawful, legitimate.
mahlûlˡᵘ̈ 2 (.—) مخلول A *lrnd.* perforated; skewered.
mahlulât (.——) مخلولات A *law* escheated properties.
mahlûliyet (.——.) محلوليت A *law* escheat.
mahlut (.—) مخلوط A mixed; adulterated; mixture; *mech.* mixture of gas and air.
mahmedet محمدت A *lrnd.* 1. praiseworthy act or quality. 2. a praising, praise. —**sâz** (...—) P who praises.
mahmel محمل A *lrnd.* velvet.
mahmi (.—) محمى A *lrnd.* guarded, protected. — **devlet** *pol.* protected state, protectorate.
mahmidet محمدت same as **mahmedet**.
mahmil 1 محمل A *lrnd.* 1. camel litter for women. 2. the sacred litter which carried the Sultan's yearly offering for sacred uses to Mecca and Medina. — **kadısı** *Ott. hist.* judge appointed to accompany the pilgrims to Mecca.
mahmil 2 محمل [mahmil 1] *prov.* built-in cupboard.
mahmiye (.—.) محميه A *lrnd.* protected city, metropolis.
mahmud (.—) محمود A 1. *lrnd.* lauded, eulogized, praiseworthy. 2. *w. cap.*, man's name.
mahmude (.—.) محموده A scammony plant, *bot.*, *Convolvulus scammonia*.
mahmudi (.——), **mahmudiye** (.——.) محمودى، محموديه *Ott. hist.* a twenty-kurush gold coin issued by Sultan Mahmud II.
mahmulˡᵘ̈ (.—) محمول A 1. *lrnd.* borne, carried; loaded (on an animal). 2. *lrnd.* placed or based on a thing; attributed. 3. *gram.* attribute. 4. *log.* predicate. 5. *rhet.* heavy (style).
mahmule (.—.) محموله A *lrnd.* 1. same as **mahmul**. 2. load, lading of a beast. 3. red wheat.
mahmulen (.—.) محمولاً A *lrnd.* loaded, carrying a burden.
mahmum (.—) محموم A *lrnd.* 1. suffering from fever, feverish. 2. warmed, heated. —**âne** (.——.) P feverishly.
mahmur (.—) مخمور A 1. sleepy, languid (eye). 2. heavy after a drunken sleep; stupid from a recent debauch. — **bakış** soft, tender look. — **çiçeği** mountain saffron, *bot.*,

Colchicum Ritchii; African rue, *bot.*, *Peganum harmala*. — **çorbası** sour soup (used for a hangover).
mahmurâne (.——.) مخمورانه P soft, tender look.
mahmurlaş=ⁱʳ مخمورلاشمق to become languid.
mahmurlukᵍᵘ مخمورلق heaviness after a drunken sleep; pleasant sleepy feeling. —**unu boz**= to take something to settle the stomach after a debauch.
mahmuz مهميز، مهموز، مهمزان ماهموز [Arabic **mihmaz**] 1. spur. 2. cockspur. 3. ram, rostrum (of a warship). 4. *arch.* spur (of a bridge). — **vur**= /a/ to spur, to give the spur. —**la**= /ı/ to spur on (a beast). —**lu** armed, furnished with spurs, spurred.
mahnukᵏᵘ (.—) مخنوق A *lrnd.* strangled; choked. —**an** (.—.) A by strangling.
mahpare (——.) ماه پاره same as **mehpare**.
mahperver (—..) ماه پرور P *lrnd.* moonlit.
mahpeyker (—..) ماه پيكر P *lrnd.* beautiful, charming.
mahpus محبوس var. of **mahbus**.
mahra محرا [Arabic .—] *prov.* a wooden case for carrying grapes.
mahrama محرمه A var. of **makrama**.
mahrec مخرج A *lrnd.* 1. outlet. 2. origin, source; training place. 3. vocal organs; articulation. 4. *math.* denominator. 5. *Ott. hist.*, name of the lowest order of judges with the right of promotion in the Turkish hierarchy.
mahrekᵏⁱ محراك A orbit (of a planet etc.); trajectory.
mahrem محرم A 1. confidential; secret; intimate; confidant. 2. prohibited; within the forbidden degrees of relationship for marriage. —**i esrar** confidant.
mahremâne (..—.) محرمانه P confidential (remark, etc.), confidentially.
mahremiyet (..—.) محرميت A secrecy, the condition of a confidant. —**ine gir**= /ın/ to infringe on someone's privacy.
mahru (.—) ماه رو P *poet.* lovely, beautiful.
mahrub 1 (.—) مخروب A *lrnd.* destroyed, ruined, desolated.
mahrub 2 (.—) محروب A *lrnd.* robbed, plundered.
mahrukᵏᵘ (.—) محروق A *lrnd.* burnt, consumed by fire; combustible. —**at** (.——) A fuel; combustibles.
mahrum (.—) محروم A deprived, destitute, disappointed. — **kal**= /dan/ to remain deprived of; to be disappointed. —**âne** (.——.) P deprivedly, in a disappointed manner.
mahrumiyet (.——.) محروميت A deprivation,

privation, destitution. — **bölgesi** underdeveloped area.
mahrumluk[ğu] محرو ملغى *same as* **mahrumiyet**.
mahrur (. —) محرور A *lrnd*. heated, warmed; burning with fever, wrath or grief. **—âne** (. — —.) P heatedly, burning.
mahrus (. —) محروس A *lrnd*. guarded, protected.
mahruse (. —.) محروسة A city, capital.
mahrut (. —) مخروط A *geom*. cone.
mahrutî (. — —) مخروطى A conical, conic. **— çadır** bell tent. **— dişli** *mech*. cone pulley. **—yat** (. — — —) A *math*. the mathematics of conic sections. **—yet** (. — — .) A conical state.
mahruz (. —) محروض A *lrnd*. bad, base.
mahsub (. —) محسوب A 1. counted, taken into account, calculated. 2. *law* set off, deduction. **— et=** /1, a/ to reckon in an account; to account (for). **—ât** (. — —) A *pl.*
mahsuben (. —'.) محسوباً A on account, to the account (of).
mahsud 1 (. —) محسود A *lrnd*. envied.
mahsud 2 (. —) محصود A *lrnd*. reaped, cut, harvested.
mahsûf (. —) مخسوف A *lrnd*. eclipsed.
mahsul[lü] (. —) محصول A 1. product; produce, crop. 2. result.
mahsulât (. — —) محصولات A products, crops. **—ı arziye** *lrnd*. agricultural produce. **—ı sınaiye** *lrnd*. industrial products.
mahsuldar (. — —) محصولدار P productive, fruitful, fertile.
mahsulsüz محصولسز unproductive, infertile.
mahsun (. —) محصون A *lrnd*. surrounded by a wall, fortified.
mahsup[bu] (. —) محسوب A *var. of* **mahsub**.
mahsur 1 (. —) محصور A 1. shut up, confined, cut off; besieged, blockaded. 2. limited, hindered, disabled.
mahsur 2 (. —) محسور A *lrnd*. dim-sighted; wearied, fatigued (eye).
mahsus 1 (. —) مخصوص A 1. /a/ special, proper, peculiar (to). 2. /a/ reserved (for). 3. (.'..) not seriously meant; especially, on purpose.
mahsus 2 (. —) محسوس A *lrnd*. perceived, felt; perceptible.
mahsusan (. —.) مخصوصاً A 1. purposely. 2. expressly.
mahsusat (. — —) محسوسات A *lrnd., pl. of* **mahsus 2**.
mahsusiyet (. — —.) مخصوصيت A *biol*. specificity.
mahşer محشر 1. the last judgment. 2. great crowd, great confusion. **— midillisi** little mischief-maker. **—î** (. . —) A *lrnd*. crowded.

mahşud (. —) محشود A *lrnd*. around whom people collect.
mahşur (. —) محشور A *lrnd*. 1. raised from the dead. 2. collected, congregated, assembled.
mahtab (— —) ماهتاب P *lrnd., same as* **mehtab**.
mahtube (. —.) مخطوبة A *lrnd*. betrothed (girl).
mahtum (. —) مختوم A *lrnd*. 1. sealed. 2. stamped, weighed, measured.
mahtumülebsar (. —..—) مختوم الابصار A *lrnd*. whose eyes are blind as if sealed up.
mahtun (. —) مختون A *lrnd*. circumcised.
mahtut (. —), **mahtute** (. —.) مخطوط A *lrnd*. written, drawn as a line.
ma'hud (. —) A, **mahud** (— —). معهود 1. *usu. derogatory* known, so well known, notorious; to whom allusion has been made. 2. *lrnd*. undertaken by agreement, stipulated.
mahudane (— — —.) ماهودانه P *pharm*. croton ends, seeds of *Croton tiglium*.
mahude (— — .) معهوده A disreputable (woman).
mahuf (. —) مخوف A *lrnd*. feared, frightful, terrible.
mahun ماهون 1. American mahogany tree, *bot.*, *Swietenia Mahogoni*. 2. mahogany.
mahunya (.. '.) ماهونيا E mahonia, a variety of barberry.
mâhur (— .) ماهور P *Or. mus*. 1. one of the oldest **makams**. **— buselik** a compound **makam** consisting of parts of **mahur** and **buselik**. **—ek** *obs.* a makam.
mahut[du] (— —) معهود A *var. of* **mahud** [1].
mahv محو A a destroying, annihilating. **— ü harab** *lrnd*. utterly destroyed. **— ü isbat** *lrnd*. alteration (of a building, writing, etc.). **— ü isbat et=** /1/ *lrnd*. to alter. **— ol=** to perish.
mahvar (— —), **mahvare** (— —.) ماهوار ماهواره P *lrnd., same as* **mehvar**.
mahviyet محويت A modesty, humility; unobtrusiveness.
mahya (.. '.) ماهيه [Persian **mahiye**] lights strung between minarets during Ramazan to form words or pictures.
mahz محض A *lrnd*. pure, unmixed, mere. **—i keramet** a pure miracle. **—i nimet** a mere blessing.
mahza (. —), **mahzan** (.' .) محضاً A *lrnd*. merely, entirely, only.
mahzar محضر A *lrnd*. 1. place where one is present, presence. 2. judicial report or decree, protocol, minute. 3. round robin signed by all present.
mahzen مخزن A 1. underground storeroom; granary, cellar. 2. *prov.* cistern. **—i evrak** the archives. **— kapağı** trap door of a cellar, etc.

mahzub (. —) مَحْضُوب A *lrnd.* dyed, tinted, tinged, stained.

mahzuf (. —) مَحْذُوف A *lrnd.* 1. cut off, curtailed. 2. *gram.* elided. 3. *rhet.* understood without being expressed (word). 4. *pros.* from which a long syllable is dropped at the end (foot).

mahzulᵘ (. —) مَحْذُول A *lrnd.* abandoned, left without aid; forsaken; frustrated. **—en** (.—′.) A dejectedly.

mahzun 1 (. —) مَحْزُون A *lrnd.* stored, treasured.

mahzun 2 (. —) مَحْزُون A sad, grieved, saddened, sorry. **—ane** (.——.) P sadly, gloomily. **—iyet** (.——.), **—luk** sadness, gloom, grief.

mahzur 1 (. —) مَحْذُور A 1. feared; something to be guarded against; danger. 2. objection, inconvenience.

mahzur 2 (. —) مَحْظُور A *lrnd.* 1. forbidden; restricted, special. 2. enclosed.

mahzurat (.——) مَحْذُورَات A *lrnd.*, pl. of **mahzur 1**.

mahzurlu مَحْذُورْلِى inconvenient; dangerous; disapproved.

mahzuz (. —) مَحْظُوظ A *lrnd.* 1. pleased, delighted, glad, cheerful. 2. favored, fortunate. **—ât** (.——) A pl. **—iyet** (.——.) joy, pleasure.

mai 1 (. —.) مَائِى A *lrnd.*, same as **mavi**.

mai 2 (.——) مَائِى A *lrnd.* pertaining to water, aquatic.

maib (. —) مَعِيب A *lrnd.* fault, disgrace, blemish; vicious; immodest.

maide (. —..) مَائِدَة A *lrnd.* 1. laid table. 2. feast. **M—i Mesih** the table set for Jesus and his disciples. **—i seniye** the Sultan's table. **M— Suresi** name of the fifth sura in the Quran. **—i Süleyman** famous table set causing enmity among the conquerors of Andalusia.

maidesalar (—..—.) مَائِدَه‌سَالاَر P butler.

mail (. —.) مَائِل A 1. leaning, inclined; tending towards; inclined to. 2. oblique, slanting. **—i inhidam** *lrnd.* about to collapse (house).

maile (. —..) مَائِلَه A *lrnd.* slope; declivity.

mailiyet (. —...) مَائِلِيَّت A *lrnd.* 1. obliquity. 2. inclination.

main مَعِين A 1. *geom.* rhombus; lozenge. 2. *lrnd.* flowing over the surface of the ground (water); pure, clear (water). 3. *poet.* wine of paradise (flowing like a river).

maişet (. —.) مَعِيشَت A 1. *lrnd.* means of subsistence, livelihood; maintenance; living. 2. *Ott. hist.* food ration given to jurisprudents, religious teachers, etc. **—i zenk** *lrnd.* life of privation, *i. e.*, the torment of hell.

maişetgâh (...—) مَعِيشَتْگَاه P *lrnd.* place where one earns his living.

maiyet 1 مَعِيَّت A suite of an official; attendants; company, retinue. **—inde** in his company or suite; under him. **— memuru** official attached to the suite of an official of higher rank.

maiyet 2 (—..) مَعِيَّت [based on Arabic] *chem.* hydrate. **—i fahim** carbohydrate; saccharide.

maiyeten (...′.) مَعِيَّةً A *lrnd.* as a retinue.

majeste مَاژَسْت F majesty; His Majesty.

majör مَاژُور F *mus.* major (mode, scale, etc.).

majüskül مَاژُوسْكُول F capital letter.

=makᵏⁱ **1, =mek**ᵏⁱ مَك، ماك ending of the infinitive. (When any possesive suffix or a case suffix starting with a vowel is attached, the suffix; **=ma, =me** replaces **=mak, =mek**; in writing however, the dative is **=mağa, =meğe** and accusative **=mağı, =meği**).

makᵏⁱ **2** (—) مَاك A *lrnd.* inner corner of the eye, canthus.

maka (..′) مَاكَا F a card game, macao.

makabir (. —.) مَقَابِر A *lrnd.*, pl. of **makber, makbere**.

makablⁱⁱ (—.) مَاقَبْل A *lrnd.* that which goes before; antecedent. **—e şümul** *law* retroaction.

mak'ad 1 مَقْعَد A *lrnd.* 1. place of sitting, seat. 2. covering (of a sofa); cushion; 3. the behind, anus, rear.

ma'kad 2 مَعْقَد A *lrnd.* 1. place where a knot is tied; joint; node. 2. contract; bargain.

makadir (.——) مَقَادِير A *lrnd.*, pl. of **mikdar**. **—i müştereke** *math.* commensurable quantities.

makalⁱⁱ (. —.) مَقَال A *lrnd.* speech, saying; word.

makalat (.——) مَقَالاَت A *lrnd.*, pl. of **makale**.

makale (. —.) مَقَالَه A 1. article (in a newspaper etc.). 2. *lrnd.* speech, word.

makalid (.——) مَقَالِيد A *lrnd.* 1. keys, locks. 2. treasures.

makam 1 (. —) مَقَام A 1. place; abode. 2. one's place, rank, station; degree of esteem (in which one is held), state, dignity, post. position, office. 3. tomb of a saint. **—ında** 1. after the manner of, by the way of, in token of, *e. g.*, **takdir makamında** by way of appreciation. 2. in one's office, officially, *e. g.*, **onu makamında ziyaret ettim** I visited him in his office. **—ı ceberut** *myst.* the state of direct relation with the divine attributes. **M—ı İbrahim** *Isl. rel.* a stone associated with Abraham, near the Kaaba in the courtyard of the Great Mosque of Mecca. **M—ı Mahmud** *Isl. rel.* place assigned to the Prophet Muhammad (as interceding in the Last Judgment for all prophets and saints). **M—ı Musalla** *lrnd., same as* **Makamı İbrahim**. **— otomobili** an official car. **—ı sadakat** *lrnd.* faithful or loyal frame of mind.

makam 2 مقام P *Or. mus.* a concept of melodic creation which determines tonal relations, tessitura, starting tone, reciting tone and the finalis, as well as an overall indication of the melodic contour and patterns. Its closest counterpart in Western music is the medieval concept of mode. **— tuttur=** 1. to strike up a tune. 2. to annoy by constant repetition.

makamat (. — —) مقامات A *lrnd., pl. of* **makam 1, makame. M—ı Rıdvan** higher and still higher heavens; the eighth heaven.

makame (. — .) مقامه A 1. *literature* sermon, discourse, address. 2. *lrnd.* assembly; meeting.

makân (— —) ما كان A *lrnd.* as it was.

makarᵣᵣ¹ مقرّ A *lrnd.* seat, station, dwelling, residence, center. **—ı hükûmet** seat of government. **—ı saltanat** *Ott. hist.* the capital.

makara (. .'.) مقره ما قره متاره (*Arabic* **bekre**) 1. pulley, block; reel, spool, bobbin. 2. *anat.* trochlea. 3. *mech.* drum. **— dili** sheave of a block. **— gibi söyle=** to chatter incessantly. **—ları koyuver=** *colloq.* to burst into peals of laughter. **— pernosu** *naut.* pin (of a ship's block). **— rule** *naut.* fiddle block. **—ları salıver=** *same as* **makaraları koyuver=**. **— sapanı** *naut.* strop (of a ship's block). **— yuvası** slot of a pulley, mortise. **—ları zaptedeme=** *colloq.* to be unable to control one's laughter. **— zıvanası** axle (of a pulley). **—cı** 1. maker or seller of blocks or pulleys. 2. seller of reels of cotton. **—lı** having a pulley or block.

makarna (.'.) مقارنه It macaroni.

makarnacı مقارنجی 1. seller or maker of macaroni. 2. one who is fond of macaroni. 3. *joc.* an Italian.

makas مقاص [*Arabic* **mikas**] 1. scissors; shears. 2. *rail.* switch. 3. *auto.* road springs. 4. claw (of a lobster etc.). 5. *wrestling* scissors hold. 6. *colloq.* obstinate person. 7. *slang* Enough! Shut up! **— al=** /dan/ *slang* to pinch one's cheek with the first and second fingers. **— ateşi** *mil.* cross fire. **— bendi** *wrestling* cross-leg throw. **— dili** *rail.* switch rail. **— geç=** *same as* **makas al=**. **— gülle** chain shot. **— hakkı** the remnants after cutting out a suit. **—ı kapa** *slang* Shut up! **— kolu** *rail.* switch lever. **— payı** 1. seam allowance. 2. margin. **— vur=** to cut off (cloth, etc.). **— yap=** *slang* to cheat on the money belonging to the owner of a taxi (driver). **— yaprak-**

ları *auto.* leaves of the road springs. **— yeri** *rail.* crossover.

makasçı مقاصچی 1. maker or seller of scissors. 2. *rail.* switchman.

makasdar (. . —) مقاصدار P tailor's cutter.

makasıd (. — .) مقاصد A *lrnd., pl. of* **maksad**.

makasır (. — —) مقاصیر A *lrnd., pl. of* **maksure**.

makasla=ᵣ مقاصلا 1. to cut with scissors. 2. to pinch one's cheek with the first and second fingers. 3. *slang* to rob; plagiarize. 4. *wrestling* to down by a crossleg throw.

makaslama مقاصلامه crosswise.

makatᵈ¹ مقاط A *same as* **mak'ad**.

makatıⁿ (. — .) مقاطع A *lrnd., pl. of* **makta' 1**.

makatil (. — .) مقاتل A *lrnd., pl. of* **maktel**.

makber مقبر A *lrnd.* tomb, grave.

makbere مقبره A *lrnd.* 1. cemetery, burial place. 2. grave, tomb.

makbuh (. —) مقبوح A *lrnd.* reproved and detestable.

makbulⁱᵘ (. —) مقبول A accepted; acceptable; liked, esteemed. **—e geç=** to be received with pleasure, to be welcome, to come in handy. **— ol=** to be accepted, to be liked. **—iyet** (. — — .), **—lük** acceptability.

makbur (. —) مقبور A *lrnd.* buried.

makbuz (. —) مقبوض A 1. receipt (for payment). 2. *lrnd.* received, grasped. **—at** (. . —) A receipts.

makdem مقدم A *lrnd.* an arriving, arrival.

makderet مقدرت A *lrnd.* power, ability.

makdis مقدس A *lrnd.* holy place; Jerusalem. **—î** (. . —) A native of Jerusalem.

makduh (. —) مقدوح A *lrnd.* reviled, criticized.

makdur (. —) مقدور A *lrnd.* 1. divinely decreed and preordained. 2. one's best effort; all that it is possible for one to do. **—i beşer** humanly possible. **—at** (. — —) A *pl.*

Makedonya (. . .'.) ماكدونیا Gk *geog.* Macedonia. **—ca** language of Macedonia. **—lı** native of Macedonia.

ma'kes, makes (— .) معكس *lrnd.* place of reflection; reflector. **— ol=** /a/ to reflect.

maket ماكت F sketch; outline; model.

makferlân (. . .) مقفرلان E Inverness cape (woman's cloak with cape).

makhur (. —) مقهور A *lrnd.* overwhelmed by violence, overcome, defeated; crushed by irresistible might. **—i kahr-ı ilâhî** crushed by the irresistible Divine might. **—âne** (. — — .) P defeatedly. **—en** (. —.) A abjectly, overwhelmed.

maki 1 ماكی F *geog.* scrub, bush, brushwood-covered heath.

maki 2 ماكی *zool.* lemur.

makina, makine (..'.) ماکینه ماکینا It 1. machine, engine; sewing machine. 2. *colloq.* car, automobile; typewriter; safety razor. *rail.* locomotive. 3. *slang* pistol. **—yı boz=** *slang* to get diarrhea. **— çek=** /a/ to sew with a machine. **— dairesi** *naut.* engine room. **— gibi adam** a very regular and industrious person. **— ile yaz=** /ı/ to type (letter etc.). **— işi** machine made. **—yı kır=** *vulg., slang* to get venereal disease (man). **— mühendisi** mechanical engineer. **— subayı** *naut.* engineer officer. **— yağı** lubricating oil, machine oil.

makineleş=ⁱʳ ماکینلشمك to become like a machine. **—tir=** /ı/ to mechanize.

makineci ماکینه جی mechanic; engine driver.

makineli ماکینه لی fitted with a machine; engine-driven. **— tüfek** machine gun.

makinist ماکینست F engine driver; mechanic. **—lik** profession of engine driving.

mâkir (—.) ماکر A *lrnd.* deceiver, cheat; one who devises plots.

mâkis 1 (—.) ماکث A *lrnd.* abiding, durable; permanent.

makis 2 (.—) مقیس A *lrnd.* comparable, compared.

makiyaj ماکیاژ F a making up; makeup. **— yap=** to make up (face).

makiyan (—.—) ماکیان P *lrnd.* hen, fowl.

makkapᵇⁱ مثقب *colloq., var.* of **matkab**.

=makla beraber, =mekle beraber مقرله بر آبر ، مكله بر آبر though ....-ing, *e. g.,* **kalmakla beraber** though staying, **gelmekle beraber** though coming.

=maklıkᵍⁱ, **=meklik**ᵍⁱ مكلك followed by possessive suffix, formal infinitive, *e. g.,* **gelmekliğiniz lâzım** It is necessary that you come.

maklûᵘⁿ (.—) مقلوع A *lrnd.* plucked up; removed from its place.

maklûb (.—) مقلوب A *lrnd.* 1. turned over, overturned. 2. transposed, inverted; reversed. 3. palindrome, anagram. **—iyet** (.——.) A inversion.

maklûm (.—) مقلوم A *lrnd.* clipped, pared.

makrama مقرمه [Arabic **mikrama**] *lrnd.* handkerchief; kerchief; napkin; face towel.

makrebe مقربه A *lrnd.* relationship, connection.

makrosefali ماقروسفالی F *path.* macrocephalia.

makrosit ماقروسیت F *path.* macrocyte.

makroskopikᵍⁱ ماقروسقوپیک F *physiol.* macroscopic.

makruh (.—) مقروح A *lrnd.* wounded; ulcerated.

makrun (.—) مقرون A *lrnd.* joined; near; connected, related. **—iyet** (.——.) A nearness; relatedness.

makruz (.—) مقروض A *lrnd.* lent.

maksad A, **maksat**ᵈⁱ مقصد intention, purpose, aim, object.

=maksızın, =meksizin مقسزین مكسزین without ....-ing., *e. g.,* **okumaksızın** without reading, **gitmeksizin** without going.

maksim مقسم A *lrnd.* place of partition or division.

maksimum ماکسیموم L *neol., math.* maximum.

maksud (.—) مقصود A *lrnd.* intended, wished for; intention, purpose, object. **—i kün fekân** the object of God's «Be, and it was» (in the Quran), *i. e.* the Prophet Muhammad.

maksûm (.—) مقسوم A 1. *lrnd.* divided; distributed. 2. *math.* dividend. **—ünaleyh** (.—...) A *math.* divisor.

maksur (.—) مقصور A *lrnd.* shortened; contracted; limited.

maksure (.—.) مقصوره A *Ott. hist.* private enclosure in a mosque for the Sultan.

makşur (.—) مقشور A *lrnd.* peeled, barked.

maktaᵃⁱ **1** مقطع A 1. *lrnd.* place where a thing is cut off; cutting (in a wood). 2. *math.* section. 3. *pros.* stop, pause; end. 4. *lrnd.* a bone implement on which reed pens are nibbed. **—ı kelâm** *lrnd.* a pause in speaking; end of a discourse.

=makta 2, =mekte مقده مكده imperfect predicative, *e. g.,* **pencereden bakmaktayım** I am looking out of the window.

=maktansa, =mektense مقدنسه مكدنسه |**=mak-dan-ise**| rather than ....-ing. **gelmektense** rather than coming, **kalmaktansa** rather than staying.

maktel مقتل A *lrnd.* 1. place of execution. 2. place of a murder.

maktuᵘᵘ (.—) مقطوع A 1. fixed (price). 2. *lrnd.* cut off, cut through; separated, separate. 3. *lrnd.* interrupted; stopped. **—a** (.—.) A clipping (of a newspaper etc.). **—an** (.—'.) A at a fixed price. **—at** (.——) A *lrnd.* cuttings, clippings.

maktulⁱᵘ (.—) مقتول A *lrnd.* killed, slain. **—en** (.—'.) A murdered, killed. **—în** (.——) A the murdered.

maktur (.—) مقطور A *lrnd.* smeared with tar or pitch, tarred.

ma'kud (.—) معقود A *lrnd.* 1. tied; knotted. 2. concluded (treaty).

ma'kulⁱᵘ (.—) A, **makul**ⁱᵘ **1** (——) معقول 1. reasonable, wise; prudent; rational. 2. conceivable, comprehensible.

makul 2 (.—) مقول A *lrnd.* uttered, spoken; said; pronounced.

ma'kulat 1 (.——) معقولات A 1. *lrnd.* conceivable and comprehensible matters. 2. *phil.* noumenon.

makulât 2 (.——) مقولات A *lrnd., pl.* of **makule**.

makule (.—.) مَقُول A 1. kind, sort; *colloq.* contemptible thing. 2. *log.* category.

makulî (.——) مَقُولی A *log.* categorical.

ma'kuliyet (.—..) مَعقُولِيت A *lrnd.* reasonableness.

ma'kum (.—) مَعقُوم A *lrnd.* barren, sterile; unprolific.

ma'kûs (.—) مَعكُوس A *lrnd.* 1. inverted, inverse; reversed. 2. contrary, perverse, opposed. 3. reflected. 4. bad, unfortunate, unlucky.

ma'kûsen (.—.) مَعكُوسًا A *lrnd.* inversely, to the contrary. — **mütenasib** *math.* inversely proportional.

makzi (.—) مَقضی A *lrnd.* finished, settled; perfected, completed; decreed; paid (debt).

makziyünaleyh (.—...) مَقضیّ عَليه A *law* one against whom a judicial sentence has been pronounced.

mal 1 مال [mal 2] 1. property; possession; wealth, riches. 2. goods. 3. *colloq.* scamp, scoundrel. 4. *slang* pretty girl or woman; *slang* loose (woman). 5. *slang* money. 6. *slang* heroin; cigarette. 7. *prov.* an animal owned (goats, sheep, cows, etc.). — **ayrılığı** *law* separate ownership of property of married people. — **beyanı** declaration of property. — **birliği** *law* common ownership of property of married people. — **bul=** to find treasure. — **bulmuşa dön=** to be greatly delighted. — **bulmuş Magribi gibi** overjoyed. — **canın yongasıdır** *proverb* It is hard to part with anything one owns. — **canlısı** fond of money, avaricious, greedy. — **defteri** *Ott. hist.* public register of revenue. — **defterdarı** *Ott. hist.* controller of the public revenue. — **edin=** 1. to become owner of property. 2. /ı/ to appropriate; to be especially interested in. — **edinme=** to take no account of, not to worry about. —**a el koy=** *law* to sequester. — **et=***. —**ın gözü** *slang* rascal; evil person. — **kaçır=** 1. *com.* to conceal goods. 2. to run goods by a customs house, to smuggle goods. —**ı malına** (selling goods) at cost price. — **meydanda** You can see how it is. It is no secret. — **müdürü** head of the finance office (in a district). — **mülk** goods, property. — **ol=***. — **ortaklığı** *law* matrimonial joint ownership of property. — **sahibi** 1. proprietor; landowner; landlord. 2. rich man. — **sahibi mülk sahibi, nerede bunun ilk sahibi?** Everything in this world is transitory. — **sandığı** 1. financial office (for collection of taxes, etc.). 2. cashbox in a pay or receipt office. — **yap=** to get rich.

mal^II 2 (—) مال A *lrnd.*, same as **mal 1** ^1,2. —**i gaybî** property of an unknown owner, treasure trove. —**i Karûn** (*lit.* The wealth of Korah) great wealth. — **melâl** *colloq.* for

mal menal. — **menal** goods; property; goods and chattels. —**i menkul** chattel (goods); movables. —**i mirî** public money; public revenue. —**i natık** livestock, slaves and cattle. — **ol=***. —**i sâmit** mute property, *i. e.* gold, silver, etc. —**i uhrevî** blessings of the future life.

-mal 3 (—) مال P *lrnd.* that rubs, wipes, as in **destmal, rumal.**

mala مالا [*Persian* —.] trowel; mason's trowel. —**cı** plasterer; polisher.

malafa مالافا *mech.* arbor, mandrel.

malak^gı مالاک young buffalo calf.

malakârî (..——) مالاکاری P *arch.* trowel work.

malâkelâm (...—) مالاکلام A *lrnd.* indisputable.

malakit مالاقیت F *min.* malachite.

malakof مالاقوف crinoline, hoop skirt.

malala=^r مالالا /ı/ to work, smooth or polish with a trowel; to trowel. —**t=** /ı, a/ *caus.*

malama 1 مالاما Gk *prov.* stock of sheaves not yet threshed; in the heap, not yet winnowed.

malama 2 مالاما Gk *slang* gold lira.

malâmal^ll (———) مالامال P *lrnd.* brimful.

malamat مالامات [**melâmet**] *prov.* dirty, filthy; base; disgraced.

malanihaye (...—.) مالانهایه A *lrnd.* endless, infinite.

malârya (.'.) مالاریا It malaria.

malâyanî (...'.) مالایعنی A *lrnd.* useless; meaningless nonsense. —**at** (....—) A nonsense.

malâyu'lem (...'.) مالایعلم A *lrnd.* that which is not known. **M— mezhebi** *phil.* agnosticism.

malâyutak^kı (...—) مالایطاق A *lrnd.* unbearable; insupportable.

malbahş (—.) مالبخش P *lrnd.* wealth-giving.

maldar (——) مالدار P *lrnd.* rich, wealthy. —**î** (———) P, —**lık** wealthiness, wealth.

mal dö Pott مال دو پوت F *med.* Pott's disease.

ma'lef معلف A *lrnd.* crib, stall, manger.

malemyekun (.'..) مالمیکن A *lrnd.* that which does not exist; mere words.

malen (—'.) مالاً A *lrnd.* 1. financially. 2. in goods or property.

malet=^der مالت /ı/ 1. to take possession of, to appropriate. 2. to be greatly interested in.

malezim (.'.) مالازم A *lrnd.* that which is necessary.

malgama (.'.) مالغاما Gk amalgam.

=malı, =meli ملی having to ..., obliged to ......, forced to ..., must, *e. g.*, **bu işi yapmalı** He must do this job.

malıç^cı مالیچ ceramics slip.

malî 1 (——) مالی A pertaining to property; financial; fiscal. — **sene** fiscal year

malî 2 (——) مالی A lrnd. full.

mali 3 مالی in **— taşı** large stone used as an anchor.

malide (——.) مالیده P lrnd. rubbed, wiped; polished.

malihulya ما خولیا ما خلیا ما یخولیا [Persian ————] lrnd. 1. melancholy. 2. whim, fancy.

malik[ki] (—.) مالك A 1. possessor, owner; owning, possessing. 2. lrnd. king, lord. 3. lrnd., w. cap., name of an angel, especially the keeper of hell. 4. w. cap., name of the founder of one of the four great Muhammedan law schools; title of the Imam of Medina. **M—i mülk ve melekût** lrnd. God, the Lord of earthly and spiritual dominion. **— ol=** /a/ to have, to possess, to own. **— olma= (kendine)** to lose all self-control, to be beside oneself. **M—i yevmeddin** God, Lord of the Day of Judgment.

malikâne (—.—.) مالكانه P lrnd. state lands held in fief by a private owner; large estate.

malike (—..) مالكه A lrnd. 1. woman proprietor. 2. queen.

Maliki (—.—) مالكی A Isl. rel. Maliki, pertaining to the school of canonical law of Imam Malik; follower of the Maliki school, Malikite.

malikiyet (—...) مالكیت A 1. ownership. 2. lrnd. sovereignty.

malikülmülk (—...) مالك الملك A lrnd. God, Lord of the kingdoms of heaven, earth and hell.

maliş (—.) مالش P lrnd. a rubbing, polishing, furbishing; friction; a shampooing.

malişgâh (—.—), **malişgeh** (—..) مالشگاه مالشگه P lrnd. 1. place of rubbing (one's face). 2. place of adoration or prostration; temple.

malişger (—..) مالشگر P lrnd. 1. barber. 2. one who scrubs or shampoos the bathers in a warm bath.

maliyat (.——) مالیات A lrnd., pl. of **maliye**, 1. financial matters. 2. science of finance.

maliye (—..) مالیه A 1. finance; finance office. 2. financial. **— tahsil şubesi** tax office. **M— Vekâleti** Ministry of Finance. **M— Vekili** Minister of Finance. **—ci** financier; economist.

maliyet (—..) مالیت A 1. cost. 2. lrnd. costliness. **— fiati** cost price, prime cost.

maliyun (—.—) مالیون A lrnd. economists, financiers.

Malkoçoğlu مالقوچ اوغلی swindler, trickster.

mallan=[ir] ماللنمق to become wealthy.

malol=[ur] مال اولمق /a/ to cost.

malperest (—..) مالپرست P lrnd. who worships money, avaricious.

malt مالت F malt. **— hülâsası** malt extract.

Malta (.'.) مالطه مالطا مالط It geog. Malta. **— eriği** loquat, bot., Eriobotrya japonica. **— gibi** very dear expensive (place). **— haçı** arch. Maltese cross. **— muşmulası** same as **malta eriği**. **— palamudu** pilot fish, zool., Naucrates ductor. **— taşı** Malta stone, fine, white sandstone.

maltız مالطیز It 1. brazier. 2. w. cap., archaic Maltese. **— keçisi** a variety of domestic goat famous for giving birth to two kids at a time.

ma'lûl[ü] (.—) معلول A 1. diseased, ill; invalid. 2. defective; disabled. 3. phil. effect. **— gazî** disabled soldier. **—en** (.—.) A as an invalid. **—in** (.——) A lrnd. disabled soldiers. **—iyet** (.——.) infirmity, defectiveness; defect. **—iyet sigortası** insurance against disability. **—lük** infirmity.

ma'lûm (.—) معلوم A 1. known. 2. gram. active (voice). 3. math. given. 4. Yes! Just so! **—unuzdur ki** You already know that... **—u ilâm et=** to tell something that is known to all. **— ol=** 1. to be or become known. 2. /a/ to be sensed (in advance); to be revealed to.

ma'lûmat (.——) معلومات A information; knowledge, learning. **—ı cüz'iye** lrnd. 1. a knowledge of details. 2. slight information. **— kabilinden** for (your) information. **—ı külliye** lrnd. 1. knowledge of principles. 2. considerable knowledge or learning. **—ı ol=** 1. /dan/ to know about. 2. to have knowledge of. **— sahibi** man of learning, learned. **— sat=** to affect information or learning. **— ver=** to inform; to supply information or knowledge. **—ım yok** /dan/ I know nothing (about that). **—ı zaruriye** lrnd. necessary intuitive knowledge.

malûmatfüruş (.——.—) معلومات فروش P lrnd. one who poses as learned, pedant; pedantic. **—luk** pedantry.

malûmatlı (.——.) معلوماتی معلومات لی well-informed, learned or experienced.

malûmatsız (.—..) معلوماتسز uninformed, ignorant.

malûmattar (.———) معلومات دار P lrnd. informed; aware.

ma'lûmiyet (.——.) معلومیت A lrnd. state of being known.

ma'lûmülinniye (.—....) معلوم الانیه A log. proposition the categorical nature of which is known (as in Fire burns).

malzade (——.) مال زاده P lrnd. 1. child of a slave. 2. illegitimate child, bastard.

malzeme مالزمه [Arabic **malezime**] materials, necessaries; provisions, stock; stuff.

=mam, =mem مم مام (pl. **=mayız**, etc.) negative aorist first pers. sing., e. g., **bakmam, gelmem**.

mama 1 (.'.) ماما P 1. infants language

mamma, mother. 2. *slang* owner or matron of a brothel.

mama 2 (..′) ما ما 1. baby's food. 2. *infant's language* food.

mamafih (.′.′.) مع ما فيه *var. of* **maamafih**.

mamaliga (...′.) ماما ليغه Rom dish made of corn flour.

mamaza (.′..) ما مضى A *lrnd.* that which has passed away; the past.

=**mamazlık**ᵍ¹, =**memezlik**ᵍ¹ ما مازلوه noun formed by negative infinitive, e. g., **bakmamazlık**, **gelmemezlik**.

mamelekᵏⁱ (.′..) ما ملك A *lrnd.* all that one possessess; property, estate.

mamı ما مى *archaic* midwife. —**lık** midwifery.

mamiran (———) ماميران P *lrnd.* celandine, swallow-wort, *bot.*, *Chaledonium majus*.

mamisa (——.) ما ميثا A *lrnd.* red horn poppy, *bot.*, *Glaucium corniculatum*.

ma'mulˡᵘ (.—) معمول A 1. *lrnd.* manufactured. 2. *Arabic gram.* governed by another (word).

ma'mulât (.——) معمولات A manufactures; manufactured goods, products.

ma'mulün bih (.—..) معمولٌ به A *lrnd.* rule, agreement, etc. according to which action takes place; observed and practiced.

ma'mur (.—) معمور A *lrnd.* flourishing, prosperous; cultivated, inhabited.

ma'mure (.—.) معموره A *lrnd.* 1. prosperous and cultivated place. 2. inhabited place, city, town.

ma'muriyet (.——.), **mamurluk**ᵍᵘ معموريت معمورلو flourishing condition, prosperity.

Ma'muretül'aziz (.—.…—) معمورة العزيز *obs.*, *geog.* Elâzığ.

mamut ماموت F *zool.* mammoth.

=**man** *neol.*, forms nouns of agent when added to some verbs, as in **okutman**, **uzman**.

ma'na 1 (.—) A, **mâna** (——) معنى 1. meaning, significance, sense; interpretation. 2. expression (of a face etc.). 3. reason, motive; object. 4. *lrnd.* truth, reality, essence, spiritual realm; vision, dream. — **çıkar**= /dan/ 1. to get the meaning of a thing. 2. to put a false interpretation on. —**da gör**= /ı/ *archaic* to see in a dream or vision. —**lar ilmi** semantics. — **ver**= /a/ to interpret. — **vereme**= /a/ to be unable to make sense (of something); to be somewhat suspicious (of a thing).

mana 2 (.′.) مانا F *social anthropol.* mana.

manahnüfih (.′…) ما نحن فيه *lrnd.* about which we are discoursing, the subject under discussion.

mânalı (——.) معنالى 1. having a meaning or sense; significant. 2. suggestive, allusive, expressive.

mânasız (——.) معناسز 1. meaningless, senseless; insignificant. 2. expressionless, inexpressive. 3. nonsense, absurd.

manassa (.′.) منصّه A *lrnd.*, *var. of* **minassa**.

manastır (.′.′) ماناستر Gk 1. monastery. 2. *w. cap.*, *geog.* a town in Yugoslavia (modern Bitolj). — **kemeri**, — **tonozu** *arch.* square vault.

manav ماناو fruit seller, vegetable man. —**lık** profession of a fruit seller.

manca (.′.) مانجا It *colloq.* food; meal.

mancana (.′.′.) مانجانا It *naut.* scuttle, water cask.

mancınıkᵍ¹ منجنيق A 1. catapult, ballista. 2. spinning wheel for silk thread.

manda 1 ماندا 1. water buffalo. 2. very fat person. — **gözü** 1. very big, huge. 2. *slang* large size twenty-five kuruş coin (now out of use). — **göz mercan balığı** kind of red sea bream, *zool.*, *Pagellus centrodontus*.

manda 2 ماندا F *intern. law* mandate.

mandal مندال A 1. latch; bolt; catch; tumbler. 2. clothespin. 3. *Or. mus.* small metal pieces used to change the tension on the strings of a **kanun** to give sharps and flats. 4. *naut.* cleat; toggle.

mandaline (...′.) مندلينه *colloq.*, *same as* **mandarina**.

mandalla=ʳ ماندالاماق مندللامق 1. to shut with a latch or bolt. 2. /ı/ to hang laundry up with clothespins. 3. *naut.* to toggle. —**n**= *pass.*

mandallı ماندالّى مندلّلو 1. fastened by a latch, etc. 2. secured with clothespins. 3. *naut.* toggled.

mandapost ماندابوست F postal money order.

mandar ماندار Gk tie of a yard in a merchant ship.

Mandaren ماندارن F Mandarin.

mandarina (...′.) ماندارينه It tangerine, mandarin, *bot.*, *Citrus nobilis deliciosa*.

mandater ماندارتر F *pol.* mandatory.

mande 1 (—.) مانده P 1. *lrnd.* remaining, left; balance, residue. 2. *Ott. hist.* retired, pensioner. — **anbarı** *Ott. hist.* storehouse for old, unserviceable stores or surplus in a dockyard. —**ye kal**= to be left over as arrears. — **tezkeresi** *Ott. hist.* treasury certificate for arrears of pay.

-**mande 2** (—.) مانده P *lrnd.* 1. left, remaining, *as in* **hazinemande**, **pesmande**. 2. fatigued by, *as in* **amelmande**.

mandegî (—.—) ماندگى P *lrnd.* exhaustion, inability to work.

mandepsi (.′.′) ماندهپسى *slang* trick, deceit. —**ye bas**= to be cheated. —**ye düşür**= to cheat, to trick.

mandıra 1 (.′..) ماندرا Gk dairy farm; cowshed; sheep pen. — **koyunu** ewe kept for

mandıra

breeding. — **köpeği** 1. cattle dog. 2. brutal man. — **sütü** dairy milk, farm milk.
mandıra 2 ما نذرا a form of Turkish folk music.
mandolin ماندولين F *mus.* mandolin.
mandoz ماندوز Gk block, pulley.
manej مانژ F manège.
ma'nen (´.) A, **manen** (—.) معناً 1. morally (as opposed to materially); virtually; in truth. 2. *lrnd.* in sense; as regards the meaning. — **ve maddeten** morally and materially.
manend (—.) مانند P *lrnd.* resembling, similar.
manende (—..) مانندﻩ P *lrnd.* resembling, like.
maneska مانسقه It *naut.* tackle pulley with two double blocks.
manet مانت F *auto.* control lever (on the steering wheel).
ma'nevî (..—) A, **manevi** (—.—) معنوى 1. moral (as opposed to material); spiritual; virtual. 2. *lrnd.* significative; logical. — **borç** moral obligation. — **cebir** *law* compulsion, constraint. — **evlâd** adopted child. —**lik** *abstr. n.* of **manevi**.
mâneviyat (..— —) معنویّات 1. moral and spiritual matters. 2. morale. —**ı bozul=**, —**ı kırıl=** to be discouraged or dispirited.
mâneviyet (..—.) معنویّت A spirituality.
mâneviyun (..— —) معنویّون A *lrnd.* those occupied with spiritual things.
manevra (.´.) مانوره *var.* of **manevre**.
manevre (.´.) مانوره ۰ مناوره F 1. *mil., naut.* maneuver, maneuvers. 2. *mech.* an operating, a working; *rail.* a shunting. 3. *colloq.* trick; stratagem. — **çevir=** *colloq.* to play a trick, to maneuver. — **fişeği** *mil.* blank cartridge. — **kemeri** *mil.* shoulder belt, Sam Browne belt. — **yap=** 1. *rail.* to shunt. 2. *mil.* to maneuver. —**cı** *colloq.* trickster.
manga (´.) مانغه [**manka**] 1. *mil.* squad. 2. *mil.* mess. 3. small crowd. — **kolu** *mil.* squad column. — **kumandanı** *mil.* squad leader.
mangal مانقال مانغال [Arabic **menkal**] brazier. — **göbeği**, — **içi** the portable inner pan of a brazier. — **kömürü** charcoal. — **tablası**, — **tahtası** tray upon which a brazier stands.
manganez مانغانز F *chem.* manganese.
mangır مانغر مانغیر 1. *Ott. hist.* copper coin of a very small value. 2. *colloq.* money. 3. small disc of pressed charcoal dust (placed on the bowl of a **nargile**).
mangiz مانگیز Rom *slang* money. — **erit=** to spend money extravagantly.
mahiii 1 (— —) مانع A obstacle, impediment, hindrance; preventing, hindering. — **ol=**

/a/ to prevent, to hinder, to stop. — **tedbirler** *law* preventive measures.
mani 2 (—.) مانی [Arabic **manı**] a form of Turkish folk music. — **söyle=** to sing a folk song.
mani 3 مانی F *psych.* mania.
mani 4 مانی It *prov.* continually. — **mani** always, continually.
mania (—..) مانعه A obstacle, difficulty; barrier.
manialı (—...´) مانعه لی having obstacles. — **arazi** uneven country. — **yarış** obstacle race.
mânidar (.— —) معنیدار P significant; expressive; full of meaning.
manifatura (...´.) مانیفاتوره It textiles; drapery. —**cı** cloth-seller. —**cılık** cloth-seller's profession.
manifesto (...´.) مانیفستو It *com.* manifesto.
manikᵍⁱ مانیك *prov.* puppy; pussy.
manika (.´.) مانیقه F *naut.* windsail for ventilation.
manikür مانیکور F manicure.
maniple (.´.´) مانیپل F *teleg.* sending key.
manipülasyon مانیپولاسیون F manipulation.
manipülatör مانیپولاتور F *teleg.* 1. signalling key. 2. telegraph operator.
manita (.´.) مانیته *slang* swindle. — **yap=** to swindle. —**cı** swindler. —**cılık** swindling.
manivelâ (...´.) مانیول مانیوله It crank, lever.
mank مانك *prov.* stupid, imbecile.
manka مانقا مانقه *var.* of **manga**. —**daş** archaic comrade, companion.
mankafa (.´..) مانقفا منقفه 1. dull, stupid; awkward fool. 2. big, huge. 3. *vet.* suffering from chronic glanders (horse). — **balığı** a variety of wrasse. — **karpuz** huge watermelon. —**lık** 1. stupidity, blockheadedness. 2. *vet.* glanders.
mankala 1 مانقاله [Arabic **mankale**] board with hemispherical hollows in it, used for playing a game with pebbles.
mankala 2 منقاله *archaic* one whose opinion or advice is generally accepted, a man of authority.
manken مانکن F 1. mannequin. 2. scarecrow. —**lik** condition or profession of a mannequin.
mano (.´.) مانو It *gamblers' slang* money; share. — **al=** to take a share.
manolya (..´.) مانولیا F magnolia, *bot., Magnolia grandiflora.* —**giller** *bot., Magnoliaceae.*
manometre (...´.) مانومتره F *phys.* manometer.
mansapᵇⁱ منصب [**munsab**] *geog.* mouth of a river.
mansıb منصب A *lrnd.* 1. high office or rank, state office. 2. origin or source to which a thing

manyetize

is referred. **—i kaza** judge's office, appointment. **— ol=** to be appointed to an office of state.

mansıbdar (..—) منصبدار P holder of an office of state, official.

mansub (.—) منصوب A 1. *lrnd.* appointed to an office. 2. *lrnd.* set upright, erected. 3. *Arabic gram.* accusative (noun); subjunctive (verb). **— mirasçı** *law* testamentary heir.

mansube (.—.) منصوبه A *lrnd.* 1. *fem.* of **mansub**. 2. clever move at chess by which the adversary is caught in a trap; chess; a kind of backgammon. 3. trap, contrivance.

mansubebaz (.—.—)منصوبه باز P *lrnd.* 1. one who lays traps at chess. 2. cunning, wily.

mansur (.—) منصور A 1. *lrnd.* aided by God; victorious, triumphant. 2. *Or. mus.* melody in the key of «A»; a *ney* in «A».

mansure (.—.) منصوره A 1. *same as* **mansur**[1]. 2. *w. cap., Ott. hist.,* short for **Asakir-i Mansure-i Muhammediye**.

mansuriyet (.——.) منصوريت A victory, triumph.

mansus (.—) منصوص A *lrnd.* 1. supported by divine authority from the Quran or by a tradition from the Prophet; authoritative, indisputable. 2. manifested, declared. 3. attributed and traced to its author or source.

Manş مانش F *geog.* the English Channel. **— Denizi** the English Channel.

manşet مانشت F 1. cuff. 2. newspaper headline.

manşon مانشون F 1. muff. 2. *mech.* muff coupling; gas mantle.

mantar مانطار Gk 1. mushroom; fungus, toadstool. 2. cork; cork for a bottle; cork sole. 3. *slang* lie, invention. **— ağacı** cork tree, cork oak, *bot., Quercus suber.* **— at=** *slang* to tell lies. **—a bas=** to be duped. **— biçim** *anat.* fungiform. **— burgusu** corkscrew. **— doğuran** *bot.* phellogen, cork cambium. **— gibi** 1. mushrooming, growing fast. 2. like cork, corky; rotten. **— gibi yerden bit=** to mushroom, to appear suddenly; to grow very quickly and abundantly. **— kavı** German tinder, amadou. **— meşesi** cork tree, cork oak, *bot., Quercus suber.* **— özü** *biochem.* suberin. **— pabuç** shoe with cork soles or high cork heels. **— tabakası** cork layer, *periderm.* **— tabancası, — tüfeği** pop gun.

mantarcı مانطارجی 1. mushroom seller. 2. *slang* liar; swindler. **—lık** *slang* lying, swindling.

mantarla= مانطارلامق /1/ 1. to line or fit with cork. 2. *slang* to deceive.

mantarlaş=ir مانطارلاشمق to become suberized. **—ma** *bot.* suberization.

mantarlı مانطارلی 1. prepared with mushrooms (dish). 2. fitted with a cork, corked.

mantı 1 مانتی dish prepared with paste, ground meat and yogurt.

mantı 2 مانتی It *naut.* tie (to fasten a yard to a mast). **— makarası** tie lock.

mantık[ğı] منطق A 1. logic, reasoning faculty. 2. *lrnd.* reasonable and intelligible speech, speech. **— dışı** alogical. **— ilmi** logic. **— öncesi** prelogical. **—ı remzî** symbolic logic. **—ı surî** formal logic.

mantıkan (..'.) منطقاً A logically; reasonably.

mantıkçı منطقچی logician.

mantıki (..—) منطقی A logical; reasonable. **—yat** (..——) A *lrnd.* matters, problems, syllogisms, pertaining to logic. **—yun** (..——) A logicians.

mantıklı منطقلی , **mantıksal** *neol.* logical; reasonable.

mantıksız منطقسز illogical, unreasonable. **—lık** unreasonableness.

mantıkapan مانتی قپان It *naut.* runner and tackle, tie block, double whip.

Mantık-uttayr منطق الطير A *lrnd.,* name of a famous ethical work by Sheikh Feridüddin-i Attar.

manti مانتی It *same as* **mantı 2**.

mantilya (..'.) مانتيليه، مانتيليا It *naut.* lift of a yard on shipboard. **— doğrult=** to adjust lifts.

mantin مانتين F a heavy silk cloth.

mantinato, mantinota (...'.) مانتيناتو، مانتينوته It *slang* kept woman; mistress.

mantis مانتيس F *math.* mantissa.

manto (.'.) مانطو F woman's coat.

mantol[lü] مانتول F *chem.* menthol.

mantoluk[ğu] مانطولق material for a coat.

mantuk[ku] (.—) منطوق A *lrnd.* spoken, uttered; expressed in words; tenor of a discourse, sense. **—unca** according to the tenor of so and so.

mantuka (.—.) منطوقه A *lrnd.* uttered word or saying.

mantunita (...'.) مانتونيته *same as* **mantinato**.

manusa مانوسه *obs.* a kind of striped or designed cloth (worn by peasants).

manya (.'.) مانيا L mania.

manyak[ğı] مانياك F maniac.

manyaluka مانيالوقه a kind of ornamental carpet.

manyat مانيات It 1. fishing boat with three pairs of oars. 2. a kind of fishing net. 3. *w. cap., Ott. hist.* Mainote; Mainote mountaineer; pirate.

manyatizma (...'.) مانياتيزم F 1. mesmerism. 2. magnetism. **— yap=** /a/ to mesmerize. **—cı** mesmerist. **—cılık** mesmerization.

manyetize مانيه تيزه F 1. mesmerized. 2. magnetized. **— et=** /1/ 1. to mesmerize. 2. *phys.* to magnetize.

manyeto (..'.) مانیه تو F *elec.* magneto. **—lu ateşleme tertibatı** magneto-electric ignition.
manyezi مانیه زی F *chem.* magnesia.
manyeziyum مانیه زیوم F *chem.* magnesium.
manyok[tu] مانیوك F manioc, tapioca plant, cassava, *bot.*, *Manihot utilissima*.
manzar منظر A *lrnd.* 1. object of sight, view; lookout. 2. face; appearance, aspect. **—ı çeşm** pupil of the eye. **—ı inayet ol=** to be the object of kindness. **—ı nimhaye** the sky.
manzara منظره A view, sight, spectacle, panorama. **—lı** 1. having a nice view. 2. *archaic* lookout, balcony.
manzum (.—) منظوم A 1. written in rhyme and meter; in verse. 2. *lrnd.* arranged, threaded on a string or in a row.
manzumat (.——) منظومات A *lrnd.*, *pl. of* **manzume**.
manzume (.—.) منظومه A *lrnd.* 1. composition in rhyme or verse, verses, poem. 2. row, series. 3. system, complex. **—i şemsiye** solar system.
manzur (.—) منظور A *lrnd.* 1. seen, looked upon. 2. considered. 3. admired. **—ı âliniz oldu mu?** Have you seen it? *lrnd.*, addressing a superior.
manzurat (.——) منظورات A *lrnd.* seen or admired things.
mapa ماپا It *naut.* 1. eye bolt. 2. hooded lantern.
mapamondo (...'.) It, **mapamundi** (...'.) L ماپاموندو ماپاموندی *naut.* map of the world in two hemispheres.
mar 1 (—) مار P *lrnd.* 1. snake, serpent. 2. curl, ringlet. **—i sermadide** torpid snake.
mar[rn] 2 (—) مار A *lrnd.* that passes, that has passed.
marabut مرابط *var. of* **murabıt**.
maral مارال *same as* **meral**.
maran (——) ماران P *pl. of* **mar** 1.
marangoz مارانغوز مرانغز مارانغوس It carpenter; cabinetmaker. **— balığı** sawfish, *zool.*, *Pristis pectinatus*. **— baltası** adze. **— çaprazı** carpenter's triangular file. **— işi** cabinetmaker's work. **— kalemi** carpenter's chisel. **— keseri** large two-handled adze. **— kılavuzu** carpenter's auger. **— mengenesi** carpenter's clamp. **—luk** carpentry, cabinetmaking.
maraz 1 مرض A 1. disease; sickness, illness. 2. worry, pain; evil. **—ı sakıt** *obs.*, *med.* epilepsy.
ma'raz 2 معرض A *lrnd.* 1. place where anything appears or any event takes place; occurrence; occasion. 2. exhibition.
maraza ماراضا [muaraza] *colloq.* quarrel, row. **— çıkar=** to provoke a quarrel. **— et=** /la/ to quarrel.
marazî (..—) مرضی A *lrnd.* pertaining to illness, pathological; easily indisposed; morbid. **— teşrih** pathological anatomy. **—yat** (..——) A pathology. **—yun** (..——) A pathologists.
marda مارد ا 1. discarded goods; rubbish. 2. gratuity (beyond a price settled in a bargain).
ma'rec معرج A *lrnd.* place of ascent; ladder; ascent.
ma'reke معركه A *lrnd.* battlefield; battle.
mareşal[li] مار ه شال F *mil.* marshal. **—lik** rank or position of a marshal, marshalship.
margarin مارغارین F margarine.
margarit مارغاریت F daisy, *bot.*, *Bellis perennis*.
margarita (...'.) مارغاریتا It *naut.* sheepshank. **— bağı** sheepshank.
margezide (—.—.) مارگزیده P *lrnd.* snakebitten.
margir (——) مارگیر P *lrnd.* 1. snake catcher. 2. cunning cheat, sly rogue.
marhaba (.'..) مرحبا *prov. for* **merhaba**.
marhar (——) مارخوار P *lrnd.* 1. snake-eating. 2. elk; reindeer.
Marhasa مرخصه *same as* **Merhasa**.
marıl مارل *prov. for* **marul**.
mari banyosu[nu] ماری بانیوسی double boiler.
mârid (—.) مارد A *lrnd.* obstinate, perverse.
ma'rife معرفه A 1. *lrnd.* knowledge. 2. *Arabic gram.* definite noun.
ma'rifet A, **marifet** (—..). معرفت 1. skill, talent; skilled trade; clever thing. 2. contrivance; curiosity. 3. intervention, means, mediation. 4. *lrnd.* knowledge; spiritual knowledge; information. **—iyle** by means of, by way of, through. **— ehli** 1. talented, able. 2. person with spiritual knowledge. **— et=** to do an odd or an unwished thing. **— nazariyesi** *phil.* gnosiology; epistemology. **—i nefs** *myst.* self-knowledge. **— sat=** to pretend to have skill or to be clever.
marifetli معرفتلی skilled, talented; skillful; cleverly made.
Marifetname (—..—.) معرفتنامه P *name of the famous work by İsmail Hakkı Bey regarding the «Divân» culture*.
marifetperver معرفتپرور P *lrnd.* skilled, talented. **—âne** (.....—.) P skillfully. **—î** (.....—) P skillfulness.
marifetullah (....—) معرفت الله A *myst.* knowledge of God; mystical contemplation.
marik[ki] (—.) مارق A *lrnd.* apostate; schismatic. **—a** schismatics.
marinata (...'.) مارینا تا It a kind of sauce.
maristan (—.—) مارستان P *lrnd.* 1. place abounding in snakes. 2. *var. of* **bimaristan**.
mariz 1 (.—) مریض A *lrnd.* sick, ailing; diseased; morbid, depressed.

**mariz² ** (ـض.) مارِض A lrnd. diseased, sick.
mariz 3 مارِيز slang a beating, cudgeling. **— at=** /a/ to beat. **—ine kay=** /ın/ to fall upon (somebody) and give him a good hiding. **— uçlan=** /a/ to beat heavily.
marizâne (.ــــ.) مريضانه P lrnd. sickly, unhealthily.
marizle=ʳ مارِيزلمك /ı/ to beat. **—n=** to get a thrashing.
marj مارْج F margin.
markᵏ¹ مارْك G mark (monetary unit of Germany).
marka (´.) مارْقه It 1. mark; sign; brand. 2. stamp; trademark. 3. ticket. 4. initials on clothing. 5. football foul. **— kalıbı** stencil plate.
markacı مارْقه‌جى 1. football foul player. 2. slang cheat. **—oğlu** slang cheat; swindler.
markala=ʳ مارْقه‌لامق /ı/ to mark. **—n=** to be marked.
markalı مارْقه‌لى 1. marked; bearing the mark of. 2. stamped.
marke et= مارْكه ايتمك F football to foul.
marketöri مارْكتورى F inlaid work; marquetry.
marki مارْكى F marquess.
markiz مارْكيز F marchioness.
markizet مارْكيزت F marquisette, a kind of fine cotton cloth.
Marko (´.) مارْقو in **— Paşa** Ott. hist., Abdulhamit II's chief physician renowned for his patience in listening to his patients. **— Paşa'ya derdini anlat** Don't bother me with your troubles.
Marksizm مارْكسيزم F Marxism.
marmahî (ــــ) مارْماهى P lrnd. eel.
Marmara مرمره It geog. the Marmora, the Marmara.
marmara et=ᵈᵉʳ مرمره ايتمك naut. to pump out (the bilge water of a ship).
marmarine مارْمارينه Gk a kind of pastry prepared with spinach.
marmelâtᵈ¹ مارْمه‌لاد F marmalade.
marmot مارْموت F marmot, zool., Arctomys.
marmühre (ــ..) مأمهره P lrnd. snakestone (held to be an antidote for snakebites).
marn مارْن F geol. marl; diorite sand.
marnel مارْنل It naut. experienced seaman.
marodaj مارودای F law a looting, marauding.
maroken مارْكن F Morocco leather.
marpa (ــــ) مارْپا P lrnd. snake-footed; octopus.
marpuçᶜᵘ مارْپوچ [Persian **marpiç**] tube of a nargile; elastic tube. **—cu** maker or seller of flexible tubes.
marpuş (ــــ) مارْپوش P lrnd. slough of a snake.
marre (ــ.) مارّه A lrnd. passers-by (the street).

marrin (ــــ) مارّين A lrnd. people passing by. **— ve âbirin** those who come and go; passers-by.
mars 1 مارْس 1. backgammon game lost without taking a piece. 2. a being silenced and dumbfounded. **— ol=** 1. backgammon to be badly beaten. 2. to be dumbfounded.
Mars 2 مارْس F astr. Mars.
marsama مارْصمه same as **barsama**.
marsapet مارْساپت It naut. foot rope. (on which sailors stand while furling sail). **— ayağı** stirrup, yard foot rope. **— bağı, — cevizi** Turk's head knot, rose lashing.
marsıkᵏ¹ مارْصيق imperfectly burnt charcoal (giving off poisonous fumes). **— gibi** black and ugly (person).
marsıvan مارْصوان [Persian **merzeban**] 1. lrnd. warden of a frontier district. 2. ass, donkey. **— eşeği** donkey, ass; blockhead, idiot. **— otu** bot., Tanacetum balsamite.
Marsilya (´..) مارْسيليا It geog. Marseilles.
marş مارْش F 1. mil. Forward march! 2. mus. march. 3. mech. treadle. **—a bas=** auto. to press the starter. **— düğmesi** auto. starter button.
marşandiz مارْشانديز F rail. freight train.
Mart مارْت F the month of March. **— dokuzu** the 9th of March (according to the Gregorian calendar); day of the vernal equinox; name of a storm that usually occurs during the third week of March. **— havası** changeable weather. **— havası gibi** unreliable, inconstant (person). **— içeri pire dışarı** When March comes in the fleas go out, said when an undesirable person comes in and causes somebody to leave the place. **— kapıdan baktırır kazma kürek yaktırır** proverb March causes one to look out through the door and to burn the (handles of the) pickaxe and shovel. It can be very cold in March. **— kedisi** 1. kitten born in March. 2. slang a rascal.
martağan مارْطغان 1. Ott. hist. a special form of turban. 2. the martagon lily, Turk's-cap lily, bot., Lilium martagon.
martaval مارْطوال colloq. nonsense; lies. **— at=, — oku=** to talk nonsense; to tell lies. **—cı** liar, swaggerer. **—cılık** lying, swaggering.
martı مارْتى [old It. **martin**; Piri Reis calls them **Mart kuşları**] herring gull, zool., Larus argentatus. **— gübresi** gull manure, guano.
martıka (.´.) مارْتيقه It a two-masted sailing vessel used along the Black sea coast.
martila (..´ــ) مارْتيلا It small hammer (used by goldsmiths, etc.).
martin مارْتين F Martini rifle.
martoloz, martulos مارْتولوز مارْتولوس

ma'ruf Gk Ott. hist. Christian sailor from the Danube in the pay of Turks in their forts.

ma'ruf (.—) A, mâruf (——) معروف 1. lrnd. known, well-known, renowned. 2. Isl. rel. that which is approved by canonical law. 3. lrnd. munificence; gift, alms. —at (.——) A pl. —iyet (.———.) A notoriety, reputation.

marul مارول مرول Gk romaine lettuce; Cos lettuce, bot., Lactuca sativa. —cu seller of lettuce. —cuk Christmas rose, bot., Helleborus niger.

Marut (——) ماروت A Isl. rel., name of a fallen angel confined in a pit at Babylon with his companion Harut.

ma'ruz (.—) A, mâruz (——) معروض 1. /a/ exposed to. 2. presented, submitted, offered. 3. lrnd. request (to a superior), petition. — kal= /a/ to be subjected to.

mâruzat (———) معروضات A lrnd. matters submitted (to a superior); petitions, statements.

marya (.'.) مارية ماريا Gk 1. ewe; female sheep; female animal. 2. young fish, fry. — ağı a special kind of fishing net. — balık small refuse fish from a catch. — keçi she-goat.

maryol ماريول It rogue, cheat. —luk cheating.

mas⁵⁵¹ مص A lrnd. a sucking, absorbing; absorption. — et= /i/ to absorb.

masa (.'.) ماصا It 1. table. 2. office desk. 3. department in a government office. 4. bankrupt's effects. — örtüsü tablecloth.

masabih (.——) مصابيح A lrnd., pl. of misbah. —i nücum stars used by travellers to direct their way. M— Suresi name of the forty-first sura of the Quran.

mas'ad مصعد A lrnd. place of rising; ascent; step, ladder, staircase.

masadak^{kı} (.'.) ماصدق A lrnd. that which is true; that which confirms the truth; confirmatory; confirming.

masadır (.—.) مصادر A lrnd., pl. of masdar.

masaf^{ffı} 1 (.—) مصاف A lrnd., pl. of masaf 2.

masaf^{ffı} 2 مصف A lrnd. place where troops are drawn up in line; battlefield; battle.

masahif (.—.) مصاحف A lrnd., pl. of mushaf.

masaib 1 (.—.) مصائب A var. of mesaib.

masaib 2 (.—.) مصاعب A lrnd. difficulties, troubles.

masaid (.—.) مصاعد A lrnd., pl. of mas'ad.

masaj ماساژ F massage. — yap= to massage. —cı masseur.

masal ماصال ماسال [Arabic mesel] 1. story, tale; fairy tale. 2. lie, invention. — oku= /a/ 1. to read or tell a tale. 2. to lie, to try to deceive. — söyle= /a/ to tell a tale. —cı story teller.

masalih (.—.) مصالح A lrnd., pl. of maslahat.

masallama neol., path., psych. an inventing stories or tales. — tutkunluğu mythomania.

masam (.—) مصام A lrnd. place where a horse stands.

masani^{ii} (.—.) مصانع A lrnd., pl. of masna, masnaa.

ma'sar معصر A lrnd. place where olives, grapes, etc. are pressed, oil press.

mâsara (—..) معصرة A prov. wine press, oil press.

masari^{ii} 1 (.—.) مصارع A lrnd., pl. of masra 2.

masari^{ii} 2 (.——) مصاريع A lrnd., pl. of mısra.

masarif 1 (.—.) مصارف A pl. of masraf.

masarif 2 (.——) مصاريف A lrnd., pl. of masruf.

masarifat (.—.—) مصارفات A pl. of masarif 1.

masarika (...'.) ماساريقة A anat., zool. mesentery.

masat^{dı} مصاد [Arabic mishad] steel (for sharpening knives). —a vur= /ı/ to sharpen on a steel (knife).

masatıb (.—.) مصاطب A lrnd., pl. of mastaba.

masbah مصبح A lrnd. daybreak; morning.

masbuu (.—) مصبوع A lrnd. proud, arrogant.

masbuğ (.—) مصبغ A lrnd. dyed, tinged, imbued with.

masdar مصدر A lrnd. 1. source, origin. 2. same as mastar¹. —ı mimî Arabic gram. infinitive beginning with the letter م. —î (..—) A 1. pertaining to a place of origin. 2. pertaining to an infinitive, infinitival.

masdariye مصدرية A Ott. hist., name of a duty levied on exports, also on newly pressed grape juice. —ci excise officer, customs house officer.

masdariyet مصدريت A lrnd. quality of an infinitive or of a verbal noun.

masduka (.—.) مصدوقة A lrnd. truth, true saying; truism.

masdum (.—) مصدوم A lrnd. smitten; bruised, knocked.

masdur (.—) مصدور A lrnd. 1. having pain in the chest. 2. grieved, vexed, annoyed.

masebak^{kı} ماسبين A lrnd. what has preceded, the past; precedent.

maselef ماسلف same as masebak.

ma'seret A, mâseret (—..) معسرت lrnd. difficulty.

masfuf (.—) مصفوف A lrnd. arranged in line.

mashara مسخرة A lrnd., same as maskara.

mashub (.—) مصحوب A, lrnd. 1. accompanied. 2. carried with one (thing).

mashuben (.—'.) مصحوبا A lrnd. in the company of, accompanied by.

mâsıyet (—..) معصيت A lrnd. 1. a rebelling, disobeying; disobedience, rebellion. 2. sin.

masif 1 ما سيف F massive, solid.
masif 2 (.—) مصيف A lrnd. summer residence.
masikᵏⁱ (—.) ماسك A lrnd. that holds, holding, retentive.
masir (.—) مصير A lrnd. dwelling, home, residence.
masiva (—.—) ما سوا A lrnd. 1. the rest, all else. 2. all else besides God, i. e. the world, the flesh, the vanities of life. —**dan geç=**, —**yı terket=** to renounce all things save love for God.
ma'siyet معصيت A var. of **mâsıyet**.
maskal, maskala مصقل A var. of **mıskal, mıskala**.
maskalla=ʳ مصقالادم to polish, to burnish (steel etc.).
maskara مسخره [mashara] 1. buffoon, laughing-stock. 2. ridiculous; dishonored. 3. droll child, little dear. 4. masquerade, masquerader (in a carnival). —**ya al=**, —**ya çevir=** /ı/ to make a fool of, to ridicule; to disgrace. —**sını çıkar=** /ın/ 1. to ridicule. 2. to spoil. — **et=** /ı/ to make a laughing-stock of. — **gibi** ridiculous, clownish. — **ol=** to be ridiculed.
maskaralan=ⁱʳ مسخره لنى 1. to make oneself a laughingstock; to be ridiculous. 2. to play the buffoon.
maskaralaş=ⁱʳ مسخره لشمك to grow ridiculous.
maskaralıkᵏⁱ مسخره لك 1. buffoonery. 2. making oneself ridiculous. 3. shame, dishonor. — **et=** to act the fool; to be funny.
maskarata (…′.), **maskaret** (…′) مسقاره ت It toe cap (of a shoe).
maskat مسقط A lrnd. place where a thing falls. —**i re's** one's birthplace.
maske (.′.) ماسكه F mask. —**yi at=**, —**yi indir=** to throw off the mask. —**sini indir=** /ın/ to unmask somebody, to expose (a person).
maskele=ʳ ماسكه لمك 1. to mask, to hide. 2. to camouflage, to blacken (the lights). —**me** verbal n.
maskeli ماسكه لى masked. — **balo** masked ball, fancy ball. — **örümcek kuşu** masked shrike, zool., Lanius nubicus. — **ötleğen kuşu** barred warbler, zool., Sylvia nisoria.
maskulᵘ̈ (.—) مصقول A lrnd. polished, burnished.
masl مصل A 1. lrnd. whey strained off from sour curds. 2. anat. serum. —**ı dem** anat. blood serum.
maslahat مصلحت A 1. business; affair. 2. lrnd. the proper course; the right thing to do. — **için** for a good cause.
maslahatgüzar (….—) مصلحتگذار P lrnd. 1. chargé d'affaires. 2. agent acting for another. —**lık** the position of a chargé d'affaires.

maslahatlı مصلحتلى one who has some business affair in a public office.
maslahatperdaz (….—) مصلحتپرداز P lrnd. performing a business.
maslakᵏⁱ مصلك 1. stone trough (for watering animals). 2. running faucet. 3. water tower.
maslıkᵏⁱ مصلى archaic hashish; dope.
maslî (.—) مصلى A anat. serous.
maslub (.—) مصلوب A lrnd. 1. hanged. 2. Bib. crucified. —**en** (.—′.) A by hanging.
masmana ماصمانا [Arabic masbana] prov. soap factory.
masmavi (.′—.) ماسماوى very blue, deep blue.
masnaᵃⁱ, **masnaa** مصنع A lrnd. cistern, tank.
masnuᵘᵘ (.—) مصنوع A lrnd. 1. manufactured; artificially made. 2. artificial, false.
masnuat (.——) مصنوعات A manufactured goods. —**i İlâhiye** creations of the Divine Power.
mason ماسون F Freemason, Mason. —**luk** Freemasonry.
masör ماسور F masseur.
masra 1 ماصره var. of **masura**.
masraᵃⁱ **2** (.—) مصرع A lrnd. arena; field of battle.
masraf مصرف A 1. expense; outlay. 2. ingredients. 3. trimming. —**ı çek=** to bear the expenses. —**tan çık=** to get into great expense; to undergo expense. —**ını çıkar=** to pay for itself. — **et=** to spend money, to incur expense. —**a gir=** to have expense. — **gör=** to be in charge of expenditure; to incur expense. —**tan kaç=** to avoid expense. — **kapısı aç=** to cause expense. —**lar** expenses. —**lı** expensive, costly. —**sız** without expense; cheap.
masruᵘᵘ (.—) مصروع A lrnd. in an epileptic fit; epileptic.
masruf (.—) مصروف A lrnd. 1. spent (money), expense. 2. bestowed; used. 3. turned back or aside; diverted.
masset=ᵈᵉʳ مصّ ايتمك to absorb.
mast (—) ماست P lrnd. yogurt .
mastaba مصطبه A 1. stone bench used as a seat. 2. Egyptian arch. mastaba.
mastaki (.′.) مصطكى Gk same as **mastika**.
mastar مصدر [masdar] 1. gram. infinitive. 2. gauge. —**a vur=**, —**la=** /ı/ to gauge.
mastara مسطره [based on Arabic] surveying alidade.
mastela (.′.) ماستله It small tub.
mastgeran (—.—) ماستگران P lrnd. maker of yogurt. —**ı Hassa** Ott. hist. the yogurt-maker in the Sultan's palace kitchen.
mastı ماستى turnspit (dog).
mastıbacakᵏⁱ ماستىباجاق same as **bastıbacak**.

mastika

mastika (..´.) ماستيقا ما ستقا Gk 1. raki flavored with mastic. 2. gum mastic.

mastor, mastur ماستور Gk *slang* drunk, drowsy. **—laş=** to be drunk.

masturi (..´.) ماستوری Gk *naut.* the broadest part of a ship.

ma'sum (.—) A, **masum** (——) معصوم 1. innocent; guiltless. 2. little child. **—âne** (———.) P innocently. **—iyet** (———.) A, **—luk** innocence.

masun (.—) مصون A *lrnd.* preserved, guarded, safe; inviolable.

masuniyet (.———.) مصونیت A security; inviolability; immunity. **—i şahsiye** *law* inviolability. **—i teşriiye** *law* parliamentary privilege.

ma'sur (.—) معصور A *lrnd.* squeezed, pressed.

masura (..´.) ماسوره ماصره ماسره مصره P 1. bobbin. 2. weaver's shuttle. 3. spout. 4. *obs.* a measure of water (1/4 of a **lüle**).

maş (—) ماش P green gram, mung bean, *bot.*, *Phaseolus aureus*, *Phaseolus mungo*.

maşa ماشا [*Arabic* mihassa] tongs; pincers. **— gibi** dark and thin (person). **— gibi kullan=** /ı/ to use someone as a tool for one's selfish purposes. **— kadar** *colloq.* small (newborn baby). **— varken elini yak=** (*lit.*, to burn one's hand when tongs are available) to do something in an unnecessarily difficult way.

maşaallah (———..) ماشاء الله A *lrnd.*, same as **maşallah**.

maşacı ماشاجی gipsy who makes and sells tongs.

maşala=ʳ ماشالاس /ı/ to wave the hair with a curling iron.

maşalı ماشالی ماشاللو ماشلی having tongs or pincers. **— gözlük** pince-nez. **— saat** watch or clock with lever-escapement.

maşalıkᵏⁱ ماشالوی a being the tool of somebody. **— et=** /a/ to be the cat's-paw (of).

maşallah (——..) ماشاالله [maşaallah] 1. (*lit.* What (wonders) God has willed!) Wonderful, how marvellous (used to express admiration or wonder; also to avert the evil eye). 2. blue bead, charm (worn by children to avert the evil eye). **—ı var** /ın/ He is unusual to-day *said when a person is unusually good, nice, industrious, etc.*

maşatlıkᵏⁱ ماشاطلو |*from Arabic* meşhed] non-Muslim (especially Jewish) cemetery.

ma'şer معشر A *lrnd.* company, community. **—î** (..—) A collective.

maşi (——) ماشی A *lrnd.* walking, on foot, pedestrian.

maşita (—..) ماشط A *lrnd.* woman hair dresser especially called to do a bride's hair.

maşive (—...) ماشی A *lrnd.* 1. same as maşı. 2. beast used for riding or carrying loads or for slaughtering. 3. woman having many children.

maşiyen (—..) ماشیا A *lrnd.* on foot, walking.

maslah مشلح A loose open-fronted cloak without sleeves.

maşraba A, **maşrapa** مشربه metal drinking pot, mug.

maşrıkᵏⁱ مشرق A *lrnd.* the place where the sun rises, east, Orient. **M—i Azam** Grand Lodge (of Freemasons). **—î** (..—) A eastern, oriental.

maşt مشت A *lrnd.*, *var.* of **muşt** 2.

ma'şukᵏᵘ (.—) A, **mâşuk**ᵏᵘ (——) معشوق 1. beloved. 2. *myst.* God as the sole object of love.

ma'şuka (.—.) معشوقة A beloved woman.

ma'şukıyet (.———.) معشوقیت A *lrnd.* state of being loved.

mat 1 (—) مات P *chess* checkmate. **— et=** 1. /ı/ to checkmate. 2. to defeat; to silence. **— kal=** to remain silenced, confused, speechless. **— ol=** to be checkmated; to be heavily defeated.

mat 2 مات F mat, dull (color).

matâᵃⁱ **1** (.—) متاع A *var.* of **meta'**.

mata 2 (.´.) ماطا It *naut.*, name of a block in a corner of a boat's sail, by which it is set or furled.

mataahhar (...´.) ماتأخر A *lrnd.* that which has come after, subsequent.

matabiⁱⁱ (.—.) مطابع A *lrnd.*, *pl.* of **matbaa**.

matabih (.—.) مطابخ A *lrnd.*, *pl.* of **matbah**.

mataf (.—) مطاف A *lrnd.* a going round, circuiting; place around which people walk in procession in religious ceremonies.

matafora (...´.) ماتافوره *var.* of **metafora**.

matafyon ماتافیون It *naut.* lacehole (of an awning). **— bağı** eyelet knot, roband hitch. **— yakası** eyelet leach.

matah متاع [matâ] contemptuous goods, thing. **bir — mı sandın?** Did you think it was something precious?

matahir (.—.) مطاهر A *lrnd.*, *pl.* of **mathere**.

mataht (..´) ماتحت A *lrnd.* that which is beneath.

matahtessera (....—) ماتحت الثری A *lrnd.* what is under the earth.

mataım (.—.) مطاعم A *lrnd.*, *pl.* of **mat'am**.

mataın (.—.) مطاعن A *lrnd.*, *pl.* of **mat'an**.

matakaddem (...´.) ماتقدم A *lrnd.* that which has preceded; the past. **—den beri** from of old, heretofore. **— ve mataahhar** precedent and subsequent (acts, etc.).

mataliⁱⁱ (.—.) مطالع A *lrnd.*, *pl.* of **matla**.

matalib (.—.) مطالب A *lrnd.*, *pl.* of **matlab**.

mat'am مطعم A *lrnd.* place of eating, restaurant.

matamih (.—.) مَطَامِع A lrnd., pl. of **matmah**.
matamir (.——) مَطَامِير A lrnd., pl. of **matmure**.
mat'an مَطْعَن A lrnd. 1. place for thrusting in a spear. 2. point of attack, vulnerable place.
matar مَطَر A lrnd. rain, shower.
matara (..'.) مَطَرَه [mathere] 1. metal or leather water bottle (for traveler's use); flask, canteen. 2. chemist's matrass.
matarıkᵏⁱ (.—.) مَطَارِك A lrnd., pl. of **mıtrak**, **mıtraka**.
matarid (.—.) مَطَارِد A lrnd., pl. of **mıtred**.
matarih (.—.) مَطَارِح A lrnd., pl. of **matrah**.
matavi (.——) مَطَاوِى A lrnd., pl. of **matvi**.
mataya (.——) مَطَايَا A lrnd., pl. of **matiye**.
matbaa مَطْبَعَه A printing press, press; printing office. **M—i Âmire** Ott. hist. State Press. **—cı** printer. **—cılık** printing.
matbah مَطْبَخ A lrnd. kitchen. **—ı âmire** Ott. hist. kitchen of the Sultan's Palace. **—ı has** Ott. hist. the Sultan's private kitchen. **—ı şerif** 1. kitchen in a Mevlevi convent. 2. *Mevlevi Order* the first place in which a Mevlevi novice begins his training.
matbuuᵘᵘ (.—) مَطْبُوع A 1. printed. 2. lrnd. natural, innate. 3. lrnd. agreeable; charming. **—a** A printed matter.
matbuat (.——) مَطْبُوعَات A the Press, newspapers, periodicals, etc. **— cürümleri** offenses against the Press law. **— hukuku** laws governing the Press. **— hürriyeti** freedom of the Press. **— kanunu** Press law.
matbuh (.—) مَطْبُوخ A lrnd. 1. cooked. 2. *chem.* calcined. 3. decoction.
mate (—.) مَاتَ A lrnd. He died (word used in obituary texts).
matem (—.) مَاتَم A mourning; sorrow, grief. **M— Âyini** *Isl. rel.* ceremony held on the tenth of Muharrem. **— havası**, **— marşı** funeral march. **— tut=** to mourn, to go into mourning; to grieve, to lament.
matematikᵍⁱ مَاتَمَاتِيك F mathematics; mathematical. **—ci** mathematician, mathematics teacher.
matemdar (—.—) مَاتَمْدَار P lrnd. mournful; grieved, full of sorrow.
matemgede (—...) مَاتَمْگَدَه P lrnd. house of mourning.
matemî (—.—) مَاتَمِى A lrnd. mournful, sorrowful.
matemkünan (—..—) مَاتَمْكُنَان P lrnd. mournfully; grieving.
matemli (—..) مَاتَمْلِى mournful, in mourning.
matemzede (—...) مَاتَمْزَدَه P lrnd. mourning, in mourning.
materyalᵘ مَاتَرْيَال F material.
materyalist مَاتَرْيَالِست F *phil.* materialist; materialistic.

materyalizm مَاتَرْيَالِيزم F *phil.* materialism.
mathere مَطْهَرَه A lrnd., same as **matara**.
mathun (.—) مَطْحُون A lrnd. ground (in a mill), pulverized.
ma'tıf مَعْطِف A lrnd. 1. bend, elbow. 2. fold, crease.
matine مَاتِينَه F matinee.
matir (.—) مَطِير A lrnd. raining, rainy.
matiye مَطِيَّه A lrnd. beast of burden.
matiz 1 مَاتِيز Gk *slang* very drunk. **—lik** drunkenness.
matiz 2 مَاتِيز Gk *naut.* long splice.
matkab, matkapᵇⁱ مَطْقَاب [miskab] drill gimlet, auger. **— yayı** bow with which a drill is worked.
matlaᵃⁱ (.—) مَطْلَع A 1. lrnd. place or time of the rising of a heavenly body. 2. lrnd. appearing, arising (as the sun or stars). 3. *pros.* the first verse of a poem. 4. *myst.* manifestation of God to a saint as he recites the Quran. **—ı felek-i mail** *astr.* oblique ascension of a heavenly body. **—ı itidal** *astr.* point where the sun rises at the equinox. **—ı üstüvaî** *astr.* the right ascension of any heavenly body.
matlab مَطْلَب A lrnd. 1. demand, wish. 2. question, proposition.
matlubat (.——) مَطْلُوبَات A lrnd., pl. of **matlûp**.
matlûlᵘ (.—) مَطْلُول A lrnd. wet (with dew); damp, moist.
matlûpᵇᵘ (.—) مَطْلُوب A 1. lrnd. desired, wished for, demanded. 2. *fin.* debt, due; credit. **—a kaydet=** to pass to one's credit. **— ol=** /ı/ to be desired; to be asked for. **— sabit oldu** It is now proved.
matmaᵃⁱ (.—) مَطْمَع A lrnd. a desired thing; lure.
matmah مَطْمَح A lrnd. an object looked at. **—ı nazar** regarding, with a view to.
matmazel مَاتْمَازِل F Miss, Mademoiselle.
matmuᵘᵘ (.—) مَطْمُوع A lrnd. greedily desired, coveted; longed for.
matmur (.—) مَطْمُور A lrnd. 1. concealed in the earth. 2. stored in a subterranean pit.
matmure (.—.) مَطْمُورَه A lrnd. 1. subterranean chamber for storing grain. 2. dungeon; grave.
matmus (.—) مَطْمُوس A lrnd. 1. blind, bereft of sight. 2. obliterated, effaced.
matmusülayn (.—..) مَطْمُوسُ العَين A lrnd. 1. whose eye is completely obliterated. 2. Antichrist (as being one-eyed).
matrabaz مَطْرَبَاز Gk same as **madrabaz**.
matrah مَطْرَح A 1. *fin.* category of taxed goods or of taxpayers; standard by which a tax is assessed. 2. lrnd. place into which a thing is thrown.
matrakᵍⁱ مَطْرَق مَطْرَاق مَاتْرَاق

Red 47.

matraka [Arabic mıtrak] 1. stout stick, cudgel; mace. 2. *slang* joke, a mocking. 3. *school slang* easy and pleasant lesson. **—a al=** /ı/ *slang* to make fun of. **— geç=** *slang* to joke, tease.

matraka مطرقة A 1. *lrnd.* quarryman's hammer. 2. *anat.* malleus.

matrakuka مطرقوقه [based on **matrak**] *slang* penis.

matraporlar ماطراپورلر *zool.* Madreporaria (corals).

matriks ماتريكس *anat.* matrix, womb.

matris ماتريس F *print.* plate; matrix.

matrud (.—) مطرود A *lrnd.* driven away, banished, expelled.

matruh (.—) مطروح A 1. *math.* remainder. 2. *fin.* imposed tax. 3. *lrnd.* thrown, flung, cast.

matruhunanh (.—..) مطروعنه A *math.* minuend.

matruhunminh (.—..) مطروع منه A *math.* subtrahend.

matrukku (.—) متروك A *lrnd.* 1. weak of intellect, flabby, relaxed. 2. wet with rain after being dried (fodder).

matruş (.—) مطروش [based on Persian **teraş**] shaven, shaved.

Matta متى A *Bib.* Matthew.

mattalli (.—) مطال A *lrnd.* one who habitually puts off payment (of a debt).

ma'tuf (.—) A, **mâtuf** (——) معطوف 1. *lrnd.* /a/ directed; imputed; aiming at. 2. *lrnd.* bent, inclined. 3. *gram.* joined to a preceding word or clause by a conjunction. **— ol=** /a/ to be directed to, to be aimed at.

mâtufunaleyh (——...) معطوف عليه A *gram.* a word to which another is joined by a conjunction.

ma'tuh (.—) A, **matuh** (——) معتوه *lrnd.* weak in mind, dotard. **—âne** (———.) P in a dotardly manner. **—luk** dotage.

ma'tukku (.—) معتوق A *lrnd.* freed, emancipated; freedman.

mat'umat (.——) مطعومات A *lrnd.* edibles, victuals.

mat'un (.—) مطعون A *lrnd.* 1. reviled, scorned, reprehended. 2. stabbed with a spear. 3. struck with the plague. **—en** (.—'.) A infected with pestilence.

matvi (.—) مطوى A *lrnd.* folded, doubled; rolled up. **—yen** (.—.) A folded; enclosed.

matya ماتيه F 1. purulent ulcer, virulent sore. 2. pus, matter. **— et=** /ı/ 1. to turn a pimple into a virulent sore. 2. to exasperate by a trifling disagreement. **— olmuş** become virulent (sore or abcess).

maun 1 ماغون F *same as* **mahun**.

maun 2 (.—) ماعون A *lrnd.* 1. assistance; incumbent alms. 2. anything whereby one is benefited. 3. any kind of household utensils as kettles, pots, etc. **M— Sûresi** *the 107th sura of the Quran.*

maunet (.—.) معونت A *lrnd.* 1. help, assistance. 2. maintenance, provisions, food and necessaries.

maülverd (—..) ماءالورد A *lrnd.* rose water.

maürremad (—..—) ماءالرماد A *lrnd.* lye.

mav ماو mew (of a cat), miaow.

mavakaaı (...') ماوقع A *lrnd.* occurrence, event.

maval ماوال *[Arabic* **mevval**] *colloq.* lie; story. **— oku=** to tell stories, to lie.

mavera (..—) ماوراء A *lrnd.* that which is beyond. **—sında** /ın/ in the space or degree beyond it. **—yi benefşevî** *obs., phys.* ultraviolet. **M—yi Kafkas** Transcaucasia. **M—yi Ürdün** Transjordan. **—î** (—.——) A which lies beyond; transcendental.

Maveraünnehr (..—..) ماوراءالنهر A *geog.* Transoxiana.

mavi (—.) ماوى A blue. **— asâ** *Ott. hist.* staff carried by naval dignitaries at ceremonies. **— baştankara** blue titmouse or blue tit, *zool., Farus caeruleus.* **— boncuk hikâyesi** story of the blue bead *said of someone who tries to keep the same good relations with various persons.* **M— Deniz** *obs.* the China Sea. **— doğan** hen harrier, *zool., Circus cyaneus.* **— güğüm** endive, *bot., Cichorium endivia.* **— güvercin** stock dove, *zool., Columba oenas.* **— kâğıt al=** /dan/ *chauffeur's slang* to be fired. **— kâğıt ver=** /a/ *chauffeur's slang* to fire, to dismiss. **— kordele** *naut.* blue ribbon (first prize), cordon bleu. **— kuzgun** European roller, *zool., Coracias garrulus.* **— kuzgunlar** rollers, *zool., Coraciidae.* **— takım** *Ott. hist.* a military unit of the **Asakir-i Mansûre** in blue uniform.

mavileş=ir ماويلشمك to turn blue. **—tir=** /ı/ to render blue, to blue.

mavilikği ماويلك blue color, blueness.

mavimsi, mavimtrakgı ماويمسى ماويمتراق bluish.

maviş (—.) ماويش blue-eyed, fair-haired, fair-skinned.

mavla=r ماولامق to mew.

mavna ماونا *var. of* **mavuna 1.**

mavro ماورو Gk *slang* negro. **— oskisi** Egyptian pound (money).

mavuç ماووچ It *naut.* caulker's iron hook for scraping out oakum, rave hook.

mavuna 1 ماونة *[Arabic* **maune**] barge, lighter. **— ücreti** lighterage.

mavuna 2 ماونة *naut.* trestle tree, cheek, hoop piece (of a mast). **— yatağı** hound, knee, cheek (of a mast).

mavunacı ماونجى lighterman, bargeman. **—lık** profession of a bargeman.

maya 1 مايه [**maye**] 1. ferment, leaven;

yeast; virus. 2. essence, root, origin. 3. *lrnd.* capital (in trade), stock; wealth, money. 4. abilities, talent (of a person); knowledge. 5. brood stock; brood beast. 6. *archaic* she camel. 7. *slang* saucy. — **bozan** *chem.* antiferment. **—sı bozuk** of base origin; of bad character. **— otu** common hop, *bot., Humulus lupulus.*

maya 2 مايه [**maye 2**] a kind of folk song. =**maya gör**=, =**meye gör**= ماية گورمك، مه يه گورمك not to happen once, *e. g.*, **bir kırgınlık olmaya görsün, artık bir daha düzelmez** Once a break occurs it is impossible to mend.

mayala=ʳ ماياله /ı/ 1. to ferment, to leaven. 2. to increase; to accumulate. **—n=** *pass.* **—ndır=, —lat=** /ı, a/ *caus.*

mayalı مايه لو ماياه لى 1. leavened, fermented. 2. possessed of substance, strength, wealth, value.

mayalıkᵏı ماياه لو 1. anything serving as a ferment. 2. animal kept for breeding.

mayasıl مايا سيل ماياسيل A 1. hemorrhoids, piles. 2. chilblains. **— otu** 1. lesser celandine, *bot., Ranunculus Ficaria.* 2. *name given to various medicinal herbs.*

mayasız ماياسز 1. unfermented, unleavened. 2. lacking substance, strength, capital, talent, nobility or value.

maydanoz مغداونوس ماي دانوز [*Arabic* **bakdunis, makdunis**] parsley, *bot., Carum petroselinum.* **—lu köfte** dish of ground meat containing parsley.

maye 1 (—.) مايه P *lrnd., same as* **maya 1.** **—i itibar** essential point that gains esteem. **M—i Sıdk** *a name of Abu Bakr.* **—i şeb** darkness of night. **—i zindegânî** means of life, livelihood.

maye 2 (—.) مايه *Or. mus.*, collective names for three **makams** which end in b', a', and g' respectively.

mayedar (—.—) مايه دار P *lrnd.* 1. substantial, strong. 2. rich, man of substance or property. 3. leavened; impregnated. **—î** (—.——) P, **—lık** essence; strength; wealth.

mayehoş (—.—) مايه خوش P *lrnd.* sweet or agreeable to the taste.

mayelikᵏı (..—) مايه ليك A *lrnd.* that which befits.

mayenkasem (...′.) ماينقسم A *lrnd.* divisible. **—iyet** (....—.) A *math.* divisibility.

mayerdom مايردوم L *hist.* major-domo.

mayestro (..′.) مايسترو It chef d'orchestre, conductor of an orchestra.

mayetehallel (....′.) ماي تحلل A *lrnd., chem.* soluble. **—iyet** (.....—.) A solubility.

mayhoş ماي خوش [**mayehoş**] 1. pleasantly acid,

tart. 2. *colloq.* slightly strained (friendly relations). **—luk** pleasant acidity, tartness.

mayın مايين E 1. *mil.* floating mine, mine. 2. *slang* stupid, blockhead. **— dök=** to lay mines. **— gemisi** mine layer. **— tara=** to sweep mines. **— tarayıcı gemi** mine sweeper. **— tarlası** mine field.

mayınla=ʳ ماييننله /ı/ *mil.* to mine. **—n=** *pass.*

Mayıs 1 مايس L May (month). **— böceği** May bug, cockchafer, *zool., Melolontha vulgaris.* **— çiçeği** Mayflower, *bot., Ipigaea repens;* lily of the valley, *bot., Convallaria majalis.*

mayıs 2 مايس fresh stable manure; dried cattle dung (used as fuel).

=**mayız,** =**meyiz** ماييز ميز *pl. of* =**mam,** *etc., negative aorist,- 1st person pl.* We do not...

mayiii (—.) مايع A liquid, fluid. **—i dimağii şevkî** *obs., anat.* cerebrospinal fluid. **—at** (—.—) A *lrnd., pl.* **—iyet** (—.—.) A liquidity, fluidity.

mayistra (..′.) مايسترا ماي سطره It *naut.* 1. mainsail, sail; mizzen. 2. northwest wind. **— sereni** mainyard. **— yelkeni** mainsail.

maymun مايمون ميمون A 1. monkey, ape. 2. *colloq.* ugly and queer person; droll (person). **— balığı** monk fish, angelfish, *zool., Squatina vulgaris.* **— ekmeği ağacı** monkey bread, baobab, *bot., Adansonia digitata.* **— gibi** monkey-like; ridiculous; apish. **— gözünü açtı** *colloq.* He has learned his lesson; you can't deceive him again. **— iştahlı** inconstant, fickle. **— kadar** small and funny. **— suratlı** ugly and sour-faced.

maymuncu مايمونجى Gipsy exhibitor of monkeys; dealer in monkeys.

maymuncukᵏu مايمونجك 1. little monkey. 2. picklock. 3. long iron hooks for holding window shutters open.

maymunlukᵏu مايمونلك 1. quality or nature of a monkey. 2. drollery; apishness.

maymunsular *neol., zool., Lemuridae.*

mayn ماين E *same as* **mayın.**

mayna (′.) ماينه It 1. *naut.* Down with. Down it. 2. *colloq.* an ending; end. **— et=** /ı/ 1. *naut.* to haul down; to lower. 2. to cease work. **— ol=** 1. to be hauled down. 2. to come to a stop; to calm down.

mayo (′.) مايو F bathing suit. **—lu** wearing a bathing suit.

mayolika (..′.) مايوليقا It *pottery* Majolica.

mayonez ماي ونز F mayonnaise. **—li** dressed with mayonnaise.

mayordom مايردوم It *hist.* major-domo.

maytapbı مايتاب 1. *colloq., var. of* **mehtab.** 2. small fireworks, Bengal light. **—a al=** /ı/

ma'yûb

slang to make fun of. **— et=** /ı/ *slang* to make fun of.

ma'yûb (. —) مَعِيوب A *lrnd.* shameful; vicious; defective; found fault with. **—at** (. — —) A *pl.* **—en** (. —.) A defectively, shamefully.

mayuhdes (. .'.) ما يحدث A *lrnd.* whatever occurs.

mayu'kes (. .'.) ما يعكس A *lrnd.* convertible.

mayu'ref (. .'.) ما يعرف A *lrnd.* whatever is known. **—iyet** (. . . . .) *obs., phil.* cognoscibility.

mayüfhemiyet (. . . .'.) ما يفهميت A *obs., phil.* conceivability.

=maz, =mez ما نـ مز *neg. aorist participle* 1. He does not. 2. that never does . . . . *e. g.*, **o buraya gelmez** He does not come here.

maza (. .') مَضَى A *lrnd.* It is over and done with. **— ma maza** Let byegones be byegones.

mazabit (. —.) مَضَابِط A *lrnd., pl.* of **mazbata**.

mazaci (. —.) مَضَاجِع A *lrnd., pl. of* **mazca**.

mazahir (. —.) مَظَاهِر A *lrnd., pl .of* **mazhar** 1.

mazaik (. —.) مَضَائِك A *lrnd., pl. of* **mazik**.

mazak (. — .) مَا نَ و rock gurnard (fish), *zool.*, Trigla lineata.

mazalle مَظَلّ A *lrnd.* 1. shadowy place. 2. parasol; tent, pavilion.

mazamîn (. ——) مَضَامِين A *lrnd., pl. of* **mazmun**.

mazamir (. ——) مَضَامِير A *lrnd., pl. of* **mızmar**.

mazanne مَظِنّ A *lrnd.* a suspect person or place; suspicion, conjecture. **—i hayr** 1. person from whom only goodness is expected. 2. supposed saint. **—i kiram** saintly persons. **—i su law** suspected person.

mazar (. —) مَضَار A *lrnd., pl. of* **mazarrat** 1.

mazarib (. —.) مَضَارِب A *lrnd., pl. of* **mızrab**.

mazarrat 1 مَضَرّت A *lrnd.* harm, injury; detriment. **—ı dokun=** to harm; to be detrimental.

mazarrât 2 (. . —) مَضَرَّت A *lrnd., pl. of* **mazarrat** 1.

mazarratlı مَضَرَّتى harmful, injurious; detrimental.

mazbata مَضْبَط A official report; protocol; minutes (of a meeting).

mazbut (. —) مَضْبُوط A 1. well protected (house etc.); solid. 2. decent; level headed; correct. 3. neat, compact, correct (style, etc.). 4. *lrnd.* recorded, written down. 5. *lrnd.* fixed in the mind; decided. 6. *lrnd.* taken possession of, conquered. 7. *lrnd.* administered by the State (pious foundations). **—iyet** (. — . .) solidity; correctness.

mazca مَضْجَع A *lrnd.* 1. place of repose; bed. 2. grave, tomb.

=mazdan evvel, =mezden evvel ما نـ دنـ اول مزدنـ اول *same as* **=madan evvel**. *e. g.*, **oturmazdan evvel** before sitting down, **yemezden evvel** before eating.

=mazdın ön, =mezdin ön ما نـ دنـ اوڭ مزدنـ اوڭ *archaic, same as* **=madan evvel**.

ma'zeret A, **mazeret** (—. .) مَعْذِرَت excuse; apology. **— beyan et=** to offer an excuse, to apologize. **—i şer'iye** *lrnd.* valid legal reason.

mazeryun (—. —) ما نـ ريون P *lrnd.* spurge olive, mezeron, *bot.*, Daphne mezereum; spurge laurel, *bot.*, Daphne laureola.

mazg مَضْغ A *lrnd., var. of* **madg**.

mazgal 1 ما نـ غال مَزْغَل Gk 1. embrasure (in a parapet), loophole. 2. *mil.* slit in a machine gun shield. **— deliği** *fort.* loophole. **— siperi** *fort.* merlon. **— şevi** crenel, embrasure.

mazgal 2, **mazgala** ما نـ غال مَزْغَل *var. of* **mıskal** 2, **mıskala**.

mazgallı ما نـ غالى embrasured. **— barbata** *fort.* crenellation, castellation.

mazgalsız ما نـ غالسـز embrasureless, in barbette.

mazhar 1 مَظْهَر A *lrnd.* 1. the object of (favors, honor, etc.); manifestation. 2. honored, distinguished.

mazhar 2 مَظْهَر A *mus.* a kind of tambourine used in religious music.

mazhariyet مَظْهَرِيَّت A *lrnd.* distinction; attainment; acquisition; success.

mazharzen مَظْهَر زن P a player of the **mazhar**.

mazı ما نـ و [*Persian* mazu] 1. arbor vitae, *bot.*, Thuya orientalis. 2. gall nut; oak apple. **— böceği** gallfly, *zool.*, Cynips. **— meşesi** dyer's oak, gall oak, *bot.*, Quircus lusitanica. **— tuzu** tannic acid; gallic acid.

mâzığ (—.) ما ضغ A *lrnd.* that chews, masticates.

mazığa (—. .) ما ضغ A *lrnd.* organ of mastication; maxilla.

=mazız, =meziz (.'.) ما نـ ز obs. for **=mayız**, etc.

mazi (——) ما ضى A 1. past, bygone; the past. 2. *gram.* past tense, preterite. **—i nakli** Turkish *gram.* reported past, *e. g.*, **gitmiş**. **—i şuhudi** Turkish *gram.* witnessed past, *e. g.*, **gitti**.

mazia (. —.) مَضِيعَ A *lrnd.* 1. perdition. 2. place of danger or destruction.

mazife (. —.) مَضِيفَ A *lrnd.* grief, sadness, care.

mazik (. —) مَضِيق A *lrnd.* 1. narrow place, pass, strait, narrows. 2. difficulty; difficult affair.

mazim (. —) مَظيم A lrnd. injured, oppressed, wronged.
maziperest (— ...) ماضى پرست P lrnd. who worships the past.
mazir (. —) مَظير A lrnd. acid, sour (milk).
maziz (. —) مَظيض A lrnd. a being grieved, a being sad.
mazleme مَظلم A lrnd. oppression, tyranny, cruelty, injustice.
=**mazlık**, =**mezlik** مازلك neg. infinitive, var. of =**mamazlık**, etc., e. g., **anlaşmazlık**.
mazlûm (. —) مَظلوم A 1. wronged, oppressed. 2. quiet, modest; inoffensive. —**âne** (. — —.) P 1. like an injured man. 2. quietly, mildly. —**in** (. — —) A lrnd., pl. those who have been wronged, oppressed. —**iyet** (. — —.), —**luk** tractability; mildness.
mazmaza مَضمَضة A lrnd. 1. a rinsing the mouth with water. 2. mouth lotion, gargle.
mazmum (. —) مَضموم A 1. lrnd. added; joined. 2. gram. marked with **zamma** (letter).
mazmun (. —) مَضمون A 1. lrnd. signification, meaning, tenor, sense; contents (of a letter). 2. lrnd. witticism, pun. 3. obs., law thing for which some person is guarantee.
mazmundar (. — —) مَضموندار P lrnd. witty saying.
mazmunperdâz (. — . —) مَضمون پرداز P lrnd. one who says witty things.
mazmunteraz (. — . —) مَضمون تراز P lrnd. inventor of anagrams.
maznukᵘ (. —) مَظنوك A lrnd. troubled with a cold in the head.
maznun مَظنون A 1. law suspected, accused, defendant. 2. lrnd. thought, surmised.
mazohizm مازوحيزم F psychiatry masochism.
mazot مازوت F 1. Diesel oil, fuel oil. 2. slang drink. 3. slang cigarettes. — **al**= slang to have a meal. — **enjektörü** fuel injector (of a Diesel engine). — **pompası** fuel pump (of a Diesel engine). —**u yerinde ol**= /ın/ chauffeur's slang to be drunk.
mazrıb مَضرب A lrnd. place of striking.
mazrub (. —) مَضروب A 1. lrnd. struck, beaten. 2. lrnd. coined; wrought; forged. 3. math. multiplied; multiplicand.
mazrubeyn (. — .) مَضروبين A math. the multiplier and multiplicand.
mazrubunfih (. — . .) مَضروب فيه A math. multiplier.
mazruf (. —) مَظروف A lrnd. 1. things contained, contents. 2. enclosed in an envelope. —**ı zarfı aştı** The contents outshone the container.
mazrufat (. — —) مَظروفات A lrnd. enclosures.

mazrufen (. — ′ .) مَظروفاً A lrnd. under cover; enclosed (letter, etc.).
mazrur (. —) مَضرور A lrnd. 1. harmed, injured. 2. who has suffered loss.
ma'zub (. —) A, **mâzub** (— —) مَعضوب lrnd. 1. weak, infirm. 2. crippled, paralyzed.
ma'zubüllisan (. — . . —) مَعضوب اللسان A lrnd. who has an impediment in his tongue.
maz'uf (. —) مَضعوف A lrnd. weakened, enfeebled.
mazulᵘ (— —) مَعزول A lrnd. dismissed (from a post); out of office.
mâzulen (— — ′ .) مَعزولاً A lrnd. in retirement; discharged.
mâzulîn (— — —) مَعزولين A lrnd. dismissed officials.
mazuliyet (— — . .) مَعزوليت A condition of being dismissed. — **maaşı** salary paid to an official dismissed from his post.
ma'zur (. —) A, **mâzur** (— —) مَعذور excusable; excused; having a valid excuse. — **gör**=, — **tut**= /ı/ to excuse, to hold one excusable. —**iyet** (. — —.) A excusableness; excuse.
mazut مازوت var. of **mazot**.
me 1 lamb's bleat, baa.
=**me 2** cf. =**ma 5**.
=**me 3** cf. =**ma 6**.
me 4 name of the letter **m**.
mea (. —) مَعا A var. of **mia**.
-**meab** (. —) مآب A home of, abode of, as in **celâletmeab**, **şevketmeab**.
meabî (. — —) مآبى A med. endemic; local (disease).
meabir (. — .) مَعابر A same as **maabir**.
meacin (. — —) مَعاجين A same as **maacin**.
mead (. —) مَعاد A same as **maad**.
meadib (. — .) مآدب A lrnd., pl. of **me'debe**.
meadin (. — .) مَعادن A same as **maadin**.
meahiz (. — .) مآخذ A lrnd., pl. of **me'haz**.
meakil (. — .) مآكل A lrnd., pl. of **me'kel**, **me'kele**. — **ve meşarib** food and drink.
mealᵘ (. —) مآل A lrnd. meaning, purport (of a sentence), content.
mealen (. — ′ .) مآلاً A lrnd. with regard to the meaning; giving the substance of (an article, etc.).
mealperver (. — . .) مآل پرور P lrnd. full of meaning.
mealsiz مآلسيز senseless, meaningless.
meani (. — —) مَعانى A same as **maani**.
measim (. — .) مآثم A lrnd. sins, iniquities.
measir (. — .) مآثر A lrnd. 1. illustrious acts; memorials, signs; apostolic and historical or legendary traditions. 2. glories, excellencies.
mebad (. —), **mebada** (. — —) مَبادا P lrnd. By no means! God forbid! lest.
mebadi (. — —) مَبادى A lrnd., pl. of **mebde**,

mebahis

—**i âliye** spirits that move the spheres. —**i nihayat** worship, alms, fasting and pilgrimage (the four pillars of Islam). —**i ulâ** first principles. —**i ulûm** first principles of the sciences.

mebahis (. —.) مباحث A lrnd., pl. of **mebhas**.

mebalii (. —) مبال A lrnd. urethra.

mebaliğ (. —.) مبالغ A lrnd., pl. of **meblağ**.

mebani (. — —) مبانى A lrnd. 1. pl. of **mebna**. 2. base, foundation.

mebdeei مبدأ A 1. beginning; origin; source; cause. 2. place or time of beginning. 3. first principle, axiom. 4. *myst.* starting point (from which a saint proceeds to a knowledge of God). —**i arz** lrnd. 1. the equator. 2. the ecliptic. —**i metali** *obs., astr.* the first celestial meridian, the equinoctial colure. —**i meyl** *obs., astr.* equinoctial line. —**i semt** *astr.* azimuth; base line. —**i tezad** *phil.* principle of contrariety. —**i tûl** *astr.* 1. the base meridian of longitude. 2. the first point of Aries. —**iyet** (. . —.) lrnd. beginning; origin.

meberrat (. . —) مبرّات A lrnd. good works.

mebğuz (. —) مبغوض A lrnd. hated, detested; odious.

mebhas (. —) مبحث A lrnd. 1. treatise, chapter; subject. 2. science. —**i ensice** *obs.* histology. —**i esvat** *obs.* phonetics. —**i gayat** *obs.* teleology.

mebhur (. —) مبهور A lrnd. panting, out of breath, breathless.

mebhus (. —) مبحوث A lrnd. above-mentioned. —**ün anh** (. — . .) A thing in question; about whom discussion is made, aforementioned.

mebhut (. —) مبهوت A lrnd. bewildered, dumbfounded. —**iyet** (. — —.) bewilderment.

mebiii (. —) مبيع A lrnd. sold; offered for sale. —**de ayıp dâvası** *obs., law* action of warranty regarding defects of property sold.

mebit (. —) مبيت A lrnd. 1. place where one passes the night, sleeping place. 2. a passing the night.

mebiz (. —) مبيض A *anat., zool.* ovary. —**i âlâ** *bot.* superior ovary. —**i esfel** *bot.* inferior ovary.

meblâğ (. —) مبلغ A amount; sum of money.

meblûuu (. —) مبلوع A lrnd. swallowed, swallowed up.

meblûlü (. —) مبلول A lrnd. wetted, moistened; watered.

mebna (. —) مبنى A lrnd. 1. foundation. 2. building, structure.

mebni (. —) مبنى A 1. lrnd. /a/ owing to, in view of. 2. lrnd. built, constructed; erected.

3. lrnd. based, grounded. 4. *Arabic gram.* indeclinable word.

mebniünaleyh (. — . . .) مبنى عليه A lrnd. 1. built on (foundation etc.). 2. acted on (consideration).

mebrud (. —) مبرود A lrnd. cooled; chilled.

mebrur (. —) مبرور A lrnd. laudable, praiseworthy, worthy.

mebruz (. —) مبروز A lrnd. openly shown, displayed; opened (letter).

mebsus (. —) مبثوث A lrnd. scattered, dispersed; spread out; divulged, noised abroad.

mebsut (. —) مبسوط A 1. lrnd. spread, extended; expanded, dilated, stretched out. 2. lrnd. detailed, told in detail. 3. *math.* direct.

mebsuten (. —.) مبسوطاً A *math.* directly. —**mütenasip** *math.* directly proportionate.

mebşure (. —.) مبشوره A lrnd. gracefully proportioned; with beautiful skin (woman).

mebtun (. —) مبطون A lrnd. diseased in the belly.

mebtute (. —.) مبتوته A *can. law* finally repudiated; divorced (wife).

me'bun (. —) مأبون A lrnd. infamous; catamite.

meb'us (. —) A, **mebus** (. —) مبعوث 1. deputy, member of the Grand National Assembly. 2. lrnd. sent (as a messenger); sent (with a divine mission); messenger. 3. lrnd. raised from the dead.

meb'usan (. . —) مبعوثان P members of the Assembly (Legislature). **M— Meclisi** 1. Legislature. 2. capitol building.

mebuslukğu مبعوثلق membership in the Assembly.

mebzul (. —) مبذول A lavish, abundant, ample, overly common. —**iyet** (. — —.), —**luk** lavishness, abundance.

mecaatü (. —.) مجاعت A lrnd. a becoming hungry; hunger, famine.

mecadil (. —.) مجادل A lrnd., pl. of **micdel**.

mecalü (. —) مجال A 1. power, ability; strength. 2. lrnd. possibility; opportunity. —**i kalma=** /ın/ to have no more power left.

mecalî (. — —) مجالى A lrnd., pl. of **mecla**.

mecalis (. —.) مجالس A lrnd., pl. of **meclis**.

mecalsiz مجالسز powerless, weak, exhausted. —**lik** feebleness; exhaustion.

mecamiii (. —.) مجامع A lrnd., pl. of **mecma**.

mecamir (. —.) مجامر A lrnd., pl. of **micmer**.

mecanikkı (. —.), **mecanik**kı (. — —) مجانيك A lrnd., pl. of **mencenik**.

mecanin (. — —) مجانين A lrnd., pl. of **mecnun**.

mecari (. — —) مجارى A lrnd., pl. of **mecra**.

mecaz (. —) مجاز A 1. metaphor, figure of speech. 2. lrnd. path, way, passage. —**i meşhur** lrnd. commonly used figure of speech.

mecazen (.—'.) مَجازاً A figuratively, metaphorically.

mecazî (.——) مَجازى A 1. figurative, metaphorical. 2. spiritual, mystical.

mecbub (.—) مَجبوب A *lrnd.* whose genitals are cut off.

mecbulü (.—) مَجبول A *lrnd.* formed by nature, innate; natural; naturally endowed.

mecbur (.—) مَجبور A 1. /a/ compelled, constrained, forced. 2. *lrnd.* reestablished after having been in distressed circumstances. 3. /a/ devoted, dedicated. — ol= to be compelled, forced (to do).

mecburen (.—'.) مَجبوراً A by force, compulsorily.

mecburî (.——) مَجبورى A compulsory, obligatory, forced. — hizmet compulsory service. — iniş *aero.* forced landing. — istikamet one way. — sigorta obligatory insurance.

mecburiyet (.——.) مَجبوريت A compulsion, obligation; necessity.

meccan (.—) مَجّان A *lrnd.* gratuitous, free.

meccanen (.—'.) مَجّاناً A freely, gratis.

meccanî (.——) مَجّانى A *lrnd.* free, gratis.

mecd مَجد A *lrnd.* glory, honor; grandeur, greatness, splendor. M— Suresi *a name of the opening sura of the Quran.*

mecdud (.—) مَجدود A *lrnd.* fortunate, lucky, happy.

mecdulü (.—) مَجدول A *lrnd.* 1. slim but strong; wiry (person). 2. firmly twisted (rope).

mecdur (.—) مَجدور A *lrnd.* pockmarked; suffering from smallpox (person).

=**mece** مَج مَج *cf.* =maca.

mecel مَجل A *anat.* ampulla.

mecellât (..—) مَجلّات A *lrnd., pl. of* mecelle.

mecelle مَجلّه A 1. *lrnd.* volume, book. 2. *law* civil code.

mecelleş=lr مَجلّشمك مَجلّشمك [becelleş=] *colloq.* /la/ to wrangle.

mecenne مَجنّه A *lrnd.* 1. place haunted by demons. 2. madness.

mecerre مَجرّه . A *lrnd.* the Milky Way.

Mecesti (..—) مَجسطى A Almagest, Ptolemy's great astronomical treatise.

mechel مَجهل A *lrnd.* 1. trackless desert. 2. dubious affair.

mechud (.—) مَجهود A *lrnd.* 1. endeavor, care. 2. oppressed with labor, fatigued.

mechulü (.—) مَجهول A 1. *same as* meçhul. 2. *gram.* passive (verb, voice).

mechulât (.——) مَجهولات A 1. unknown. 2. unknown matters.

mechuliyet (.——.) مَجهوليت A a being unknown; uncertainty; obscurity.

meci (.—) مَجى A *lrnd.* a coming, an arrival.

mecid (.—) مَجيد A *lrnd.* most illustrious, glorious; Most Glorious (God).

Mecidî (.——) مَجيدى A *lrnd.* pertaining to the Sultan Abdulmejid.

Mecidiye (.——.) مَجيديه A *Ott. hist.* silver coin of 20 piasters; 20 piasters. — altını Ottoman gold lira. — nişanı *Ott. hist.* The Mecidiye Order.

mecitdi مَجيد *colloq., same as* mecidiye.

meclâ (.—) مَجلى مَجلا A *lrnd.* polishing place; mirror.

meclis مَجلس A 1. assembly, council; meeting. 2. place of assembly; *lrnd.* place where one sits. 3. social gathering. 4. *lrnd.* session, sitting (of a council, court, etc.). 5. scene (of a play). M—i Âyan *lrnd.* the Senate. M—i Has 1. *Ott. hist.* cabinet meeting. 2. *lrnd.* private meeting. —i hoş /ın/ of pleasant manner in society. —i idare board of managers. — kur= 1. to sit in council. 2. to come together. M—i Mahsus *Ott. hist., same as* Meclisi Has. M—i Meb'usan *Ott. hist.* Parliament. — odası council chamber; board room. — soruşturması *same as* meclis tahkikatı. M—i Şer' *Ott. hist.* Court of Canon Law of Islam. — tahkikatı parliamentary inquiry. M—i Vâlâyı Ahkâm-ı Adliye *Ott. hist.* law court established in 1837 to deal with cases of high officials. —i vükelâ *lrnd.* the cabinet.

meclisârâ (..——) مَجلس آرا P *lrnd.* illuminating the meeting; who is good company.

meclisefruz (...——) مَجلس افروز P 1. *lrnd.* who adorns the society he is in. 2. *obs., name of a makam in Oriental music.*

meclisnüvis (...—) مَجلس نويس P *lrnd.* secretary of a meeting.

meclûb (.—) مَجلوب A *lrnd.* 1. drawn, attracted. 2. brought, sent for. 3. won over (to a cause). —în (.——) A *pl.* —iyet (.——.)· A a being drawn or attracted; attraction.

mecmaaı مَجمع A 1. *lrnd.* place of assembly; assembly, meeting. 2. *lrnd.* place of junction. 3. *anat., confluens.* —i bahreyn *same as* mecmaülbahreyn. —i nehreyn *lrnd.* meeting of the two rivers (Tigris and Euphrates).

mecmaa مَجمعه A *lrnd.* 1. *same as* mecmua. 2. *same as* mecma.

mecmaülbahreyn (....—) مَجمع البحرين A 1. *lrnd.* confluence of the two seas. 2. *myst.* point where the divine and created existence meet and through which God and man communicate.

mecmer, mecmere مَجمر مَجمره A *lrnd.* 1. censer, incense burner, chafing dish. 2. perfumed candle.

mecmuuu (.—) مَجموع A 1. the whole, all;

total, sum total, aggregate. 2. *lrnd.* assembled, collected; gathered together.
mecmua (. —.) مجموعة A 1. periodical, magazine, review. 2. *lrnd.* collection. 3. manuscript with mixed contents. 4. *lrnd.* system (*e. g.,* solar system, etc.). **—i fünun** *lrnd.* 1. encyclopedia. 2. very learned person.
mecmuan (. —ˊ.) مجموعا A *lrnd.* totally, wholly; in all.
mecmuiyet (. — ..) مجموعیت A *lrnd.* wholeness, totality.
mecnub (. —) مجنوب A *lrnd.* 1. affected with pleurisy. 2. affected by the south wind.
mecnun (. —) مجنون A 1. mad, insane. 2. madly in love. 3. *w. cap.*, *name of the famous lover and hero of the eastern romance, «Leila and Majnun».* **—i âkil ve meczub-i kâmil** *lrnd.* A sane lunatic, one perfect in ecstasy, *i. e.* a true dervish. **—âne** (. — —.) P madly. **—iyet** (. — —.) A *lrnd.*, **—luk** madness, insanity.
mecra (. —) مجری A 1. canal, conduit, watercourse. 2. course, direction of events. 3. *anat.* meatus. **— bacası** *arch.* manhole.
mecruh (. —) مجروح A *lrnd.* 1. wounded. 2. rejected, refused. **—in** (. — —) A *pl.* the wounded.
mecrur (. —) مجرور A 1. *lrnd.* pulled, drawn, dragged. 2. *Arabic gram.* put in the genitive case (noun).
Me'cuc (. —) مأجوج A a mythical tribe of dwarfs.
mec'ulᵘ (. —) مجعول A *lrnd.* made; created; prepared.
me'cur (. —) مأجور A *lrnd.* 1. hired, rented. 2. recompensed, paid, remunerated; rewarded.
Mecus (. —) مجوس A the Magians, fire worshippers.
Mecusî (. — —) مجوسی A a Magian, fire worshipper; pertaining to the Magi. **—lik**, **—yet** (. — —.) A Magianism, Zoroastrianism.
meczub (. —) مجذوب A 1. *colloq.* crazy, insane. 2. *myst.* attracted by divine grace and entirely given to piety and contemplation; obsessed by divine love. 3. *lrnd.* attracted, drawn. **—in** (. — —) A *pl.*
meczubiyet (. — —.) مجذوبیت A 1. *colloq.* madness. 2. *myst.* state of spiritual ecstasy. 3. *lrnd.* attractedness; attraction.
meczum 1 (. —) مجذوم A *lrnd.* afflicted with leprosy, leprous.
meczum 2 (. —) مجزوم A *lrnd.* 1. cut, amputated. 2. decided on, settled. 3. *Arabic gram.* made quiescent (final consonant).
meczupᵇᵘ (. —) مجذوب A *var. of* **meczub 1**. **—luk** madness.
meczur (. —) مجذور A *math.* a perfect square.

meç مچ Sl rapier, small sword, foil. **— talimi** fencing exercise. **— ustası** fencing master.
meçhulᵘ (. —) مجهول [mechul] 1. unknown. 2. *math.* unknown quantity. **—lü** *math.* with unknown quantities. **—ümdür** I don't know it.
medᵈᵈⁱ مدّ A 1. high tide; flow of the tide. 2. *lrnd.* a stretching, extending; spreading; extension; prolongation. 3. *lrnd.* extent of the sight. 4. *Arabic gram.* the sign over آ ; a pronouncing the letter ا by extending its usual phonetic value. 5. *lrnd.* a helping, assisting. **—i basar** 1. *lrnd.* range of vision, eyesight. 2. *med.* presbyopia, far-sightedness. **— ü cezr** tides. **— ü cezr si'ası** *geog.* tidal amplitude. **—i cüz'i** *geog.* neap tide. **—i kâmil** *geog.* spring tide. **—i küllî** *geog.* high tide. **—i nazar** *lrnd.* as far as the eye can see. **—i yed** *lrnd.* an extending a helping hand.
meda-ᵃⁱ (. —) مدی A *lrnd.* the utmost stretch or limit, *as in* **medalavam, medaleyyam.** (*cf.* **medel'avam, medeleyyam**).
medafiⁱⁱ (. — .) مدافع A *lrnd., pl. of* **midfa'**.
medahil (. — .) مداخل A *lrnd., pl. of* **medhal**.
medain (. — .) مدائن A 1. *lrnd., pl. of* **medine**. 2. *w. cap., collective name of seven cities flourishing in the reign of* **Nuşirevan** *according to the legendary history of Iran.* **M—i Kisra** the cities of Cyrus.
medamiⁱⁱ (. — .) مدامع A *lrnd., pl. of* **medma**.
medar (. —) مدار A 1. point on which a question turns; center of movement. 2. means, help. 3. *astr.* orbit; *astr.* tropic. **—ı cedî** *astr.* the tropic of Capricorn. **—ı iftihar** object of pride. **—ı kelâm** *lrnd.* subject of conversation. **—ı maişet** means of subsistence. **— ol**= /a/ to be a means (of), to help. **—ı seretan** *astr.* the tropic of Cancer. **—ı yevmî** *astr.* circle of daily revolution of any point in the heavens.
medareyn (. — —) مدارین A *astr.* the two tropics (Capricorn and Cancer).
medarî (. — —) مداری A *geog., astr.* tropical.
medaric (. — .) مدارج A *lrnd., pl. of* **medrec, medrece.**
medarikᵏⁱ (. — .) مدارک A *lrnd.* the four sources of the canon law of Islam; the Quran, the customs of the Prophet Muhammad, the consensus of the elders, and analogy.
medaris (. — .) مدارس A *lrnd., pl. of* **medrese.**
medayih (. — .) مدایح A *lrnd., pl. of* **mediha**.
medbuğ (. —) مدبوغ A *lrnd.* tanned (hide).
meddah (. —) مداح A 1. public story teller and mimic. 2. *lrnd.* one who praises, eulogist. **—lık** quality and occupation of a public story teller; toadying.

medde مَدَّ A the Arabic sign (ـٓ) indicating the long **a**.
meddücezirʳⁱ مَدّ و جَزْر A *lrnd*. tide, ebb and flow.
me'debe مَأدُبَ A *lrnd*. feast, banquet.
meded مَدَد A 1. help, aid. 2. Help! 3. *obs., law* helper; reinforcement. — **bekle=**, — **um=** to hope for help, to expect help.
meded-Allah (...—) مَدَدَ الله A O God! Help me, God!
mededhâh (..—) مَدَدْخواه P *lrnd*. one who asks for aid. —**âne** (..——.) P in a manner of asking for aid. —**î** (..——) P asking for aid.
mededkâr (..—) مَدَدْكار P helper, protector. —**âne** bringing help. —**î** (..——) P *lrnd*. help, aid, assistance, succor.
mededres مَدَدْرَس P *lrnd*. who comes to one's help, helper. —**ân** (...—) P helper. —**î** (...—) P helping.
medela'vam (...—), **medeleyyam** (...—) مَدَى الأيَّام A *lrnd*. to the end of time.
medelbasar مَدَى البَصَر A *lrnd*. as far as the eye can see.
medeng مَدَنك P *lrnd*. wooden latchkey.
medeni (..—) مَدَنِي A 1. civilized; cultured; civil; civic. 2. *lrnd*. city dweller; native of Medina; native of Istanbul. — **cesaret** moral courage. — **haklar** civil rights. — **haklardan iskat** loss of civic rights. — **haklardan istifade ehliyeti**, — **hakları kullanma ehliyeti** *law* legal capacity. — **hal** the state of being married or unmarried. — **hukuk** civil law. — **ölüm law** civil death. **M— Süver** suras of the Quran promulgated at Medina.
medeniyet مَدَنِيَّت A civilization. —**siz** uncivilized.
meder مَدَر A *lrnd*. 1. clods; sundried bricks. 2. cities; towns.
medetᵈⁱ مَدَد *var. of* **meded**.
medfen مَدْفَن A *lrnd*. burial place; tomb; grave.
medfuᵘᵘ (.—) مَدْفوع A *lrnd*. 1. expelled, repelled. 2. paid out, defrayed, disbursed. —**at** (.——) A payments, disbursements.
medfun (.—) مَدْفون A buried.
medh مَدْح A a praising, eulogizing; praise, eulogy. — **et=** *same as* **methet=**.
medhalˡⁱ (..—) مَدْخَل A *lrnd*. 1. entrance; inlet; door. 2. beginning; introductory principles. 3. *Or. mus.* a piece with no set rhythmic pattern used instead of **peşrev**. 4. influence, connection. —**i olma=** /da/ to have nothing to do with; to have no connection with.
medhaldar (..—) مَدْخَلْدار P involved in; participating.
medhiyat (..—) مَدْحِيَّات A *lrnd., pl. of* **medhiye**.

medhiye مَدْحِيَّة A eulogy. —**ler oku=** /a/ to recite eulogies in praise of someone.
medhulˡⁱ (.—) مَدْخول A *lrnd*. 1. blamed; suspected; accused. 2. entered into; penetrated. —**i biha** consummated in marriage (woman).
mehdûle (.—.) مَدْخولَة A *lrnd*. woman consummated in marriage.
medhur (.—) مَدْحور A *lrnd*. driven away, banished.
medhuş (.—) مَدْهوش A *lrnd*. bewildered, confounded. —**âne** (.——.) P astoundedly. —**iyet** (.——.) A bewilderment.
medid (.—) مَدِيد A 1. *lrnd*. long, extensive, extended. 2. *pros.* meter characterized by the trochaic beginning of each foot (—.——/ —.—/—.——).
medihᵈʰⁱ 1 مَدِح *var. of* **medh**.
medih 2 (.—) مَدِيح A *lrnd*. praiseworthy act; laudable.
mediha (.—.) مَدِيحَة A 1. *lrnd*. eulogy, panegyric. 2. *w. cap., woman's name*.
medihagû (.———) مَدِيح‌گو P *lrnd*. applauder, praiser.
medihasenc (.——.) مَدِيح‌سنج P *lrnd*. eulogizer. =**medik** مَدِك *cf.* =**madık** 2. =**medin** 1 مَدِن *cf.* =**madın**.
medin 2 (.—) مَدِين A *lrnd*. indebted, in debt; debtor.
Medine 1 (.—.) مَدِينَة A *geog.* Medina. — **çiçeği** everlasting flower, *bot., Gnaphalium*. — **fıkarası** in rags and tatters. —**i Münevvere** Medina.
medine 2 (.—.) مَدِينَة A *lrnd*. town, city.
Medinetünnebi (.—...—) مَدِينَة النبي A Medina.
Medinetürresulullah (.—...—..) مَدِينَة الرَّسول الله A Medina.
Medinetüsselâm (.—...—) مَدِينَة السَّلام A Baghdad.
medkukᵏᵘ (.—) مَدْقوق A *lrnd*. pounded, ground, pulverized.
medlûlˡⁱ (.—) مَدْلول A *lrnd*. 1. inferred, deduced, understood. 2. sense, meaning. —**ünce**, —**ü üzere** according to its sense.
medmaᵃⁱ (.—) مَدْمَع A *lrnd*. 1. lachrymal gland; eye. 2. tears.
medrec, medrece مَدْرَج A *lrnd*. road, path.
medrese مَدْرَسَة A *Ott. hist.* Muslim theological school, medresse; high school; college of a university. —**ye düş=** *iron.* to be the subject of futile discussion (matter). —**i meşaiye** school of Aristotelian philosophy, peripatetic school.
medreseli مَدْرَسَه‌لِى educated at a medresse.
medresenişin (....—) مَدْرَسَه‌نشين P *lrnd*. boarding at a medresse.
medrus (.—) مَدْروس A *lrnd*. 1. worn out; obliterated, defaced. 2. studied.
med'uvᵛᵛᵘ مَدْعو A *lrnd*. invited, called,

medüz

summoned. —en (..´.) A invited, as a guest; by invitation. —în (...—) A pl.

medüz مدوز F 1. w. cap., Gk. myth. Medusa. 2. jellyfish, zool., Callinema ornata.

medyum مديوم F spiritualism medium.

medyun (.—) مديون A lrnd. indebted, in debt. —i şükran ol= /a/ to be indebted, to owe thanks (to).

mefahir (.—.) مفاخر A lrnd., pl. of **mefharet**.

mefarikᵏⁱ (.—.) مفارق A lrnd., pl. of **mefrak**.

mefariş (.—.) مفارش A lrnd., pl. of **mefreş**.

mefasıl (.—.) مفاصل A lrnd., pl. of **mafsal**.

mefasid (.—.) مفاسد A lrnd., pl. of **mefsedet**.

mefatih (.——) مفاتيح A lrnd., pl. of **miftah**.

mefatihülgayb (.——..) مفاتيح الغيب A lrnd. keys to occult matters, i. e. direct divine inspiration and magic arts.

mefatir (.——) مفاطير A lrnd., pl. of **muftir**.

mefaze (.—.) مفازه A lrnd. desert, wilderness.

meferʳʳⁱ مفرّ A lrnd. refuge, asylum.

mefhar مفخر A lrnd. thing in which one glories, object of glory; glory. **M—i Kâinat** (lit. Glory of the Universe.) the Prophet Muhammad.

mefharet مفخرت A lrnd. subject of glory; cause of pride; pride.

mefhum (.—) مفهوم A 1. conception, idea; phil. notion, concept. 2. sense, meaning. 3. lrnd. understood. —iye (.——.) A phil. conceptualism.

mefkaret مفقرت A lrnd. poverty, need.

mefkud (.—) مفقود A lrnd. 1. nonexistent, missing. 2. lost, disappeared. —iyet (.——.) A nonexistence, lack; absence.

mefkûkᵏᵘ (.—) مفكوك A lrnd. separated; freed, liberated.

mefkur (.—) مفقور A lrnd. hurt, hit or diseased in the vertebrae; broken-backed.

mefkûre (.—.) مفكوره [based on Arabic] ideal. —ci idealist. —cilik idealism. —vî (.—.—) idealistic.

meflûc (.—) مفلوج A 1. paralyzed. 2. completely helpless. —en (.—´.) A in a paralyzed state.

meflûlˡᵘ̈ (.—) مفلول A lrnd. notched, chipped, broken (sword).

mefrağ (.—) مفرغ A lrnd. 1. place of issue; spout. 2. a flowing out.

mefrakᵏⁱ مفرق A lrnd. place where the hair naturally parts; crown of the head.

mefreş مفرش A lrnd. large leather bag (for keeping mattresses and quilts in).

• **mefret** مفرط A archaic big, gigantic.

mefruğ (.—) مفروغ A lrnd. vacated; assigned; ceded.

mefruğunbih (.——.) مفروغ به A law vacator or assignor (of a thing).

mefruğunleh (.——.) مفروغ له A law vacatee or assignee (of a thing).

mefrukᵏᵘ 1 (.—) مفروق A lrnd. separated, divided, disjoined.

mefrukᵏᵘ̈ 2 (.—) مفروك A lrnd. rubbed or crushed between the fingers.

mefruş (.—) مفروش A 1. furnished; carpeted. 2. spread on the ground.

mefruşat (.——) مفروشات A furniture; carpets, mats etc.

mefruz 1 مفروض A lrnd. 1. supposed, hypothetical. 2. ordained of God (act), obligatory.

mefruz 2 (.—) مفروز A law separated; divided into plots (land).

mefruzat (.——) مفروضات A lrnd. 1. ordinances of God. 2. suppositions; points fixed by hypothesis.

mefruzüledâ (.—..—) مفروض الادا A lrnd. duties that one is obliged to carry out.

mefsaka مفسقه A lrnd. place of evildoing.

mefsedet مفسدت A lrnd. mischief, plot, intrigue; seditious act, villainy.

mefsedetpişe (...—.) P lrnd. evildoer, villain.

mefsud (.—) مفصود A lrnd. one whose vein has been opened; bled; lanced.

mefsuh (.—) مفسوخ A lrnd. annulled; abrogated, abolished, void. —iyet (.——.) A nullity, abolishment, voidance.

meftah مفتح A lrnd. treasure; store.

meftuh (.—) مفتوح A 1. lrnd. opened; captured, conquered (country). 2. Arabic gram. letter marked with a **fetha**.

meftukᵏᵘ (.—) مفتوق A lrnd. ruptured.

meftulˡᵘ̈ (.—) مفتول A lrnd. twisted, spun.

meftum (.—) مفطوم A lrnd. weaned.

meftun (.—) مفتون A 1. distracted with love, madly in love; admiring; fascinated; charmed. 2. lrnd. tested by fire; tested.

meftûnâne (.——.) مفتونانه P in a fascinated manner; admiringly.

meftuniyet (.——.) مفتونيت A lrnd. a being madly in love, intense admiration, fascination.

meftur 1 (.—) مفتور A lrnd. created; innate, natural, by nature.

meftur 2 (.—) مفطور A lrnd. 1. languid, listless, wearied. 2. lukewarm. —âne (.——.) P wearily, languidly. —iyet (.——.) A languidness, weariness.

meftut (.—) مفتوت A lrnd. crumbled, broken small.

mef'ulˡᵘ̈ (.—) مفعول A 1. gram. object, complement; passive. 2. lrnd. made, done. 3. lrnd. subjected to some action, passive. —i gayri sarih gram. indefinite object. —i sarih gram. definite object.

mef'ulün anh (. — ..) مفعول عنه A gram. ablative.
mef'ulün bih (. — ..) مفعول به A gram. accusative.
mef'ulün fih (. — ..) مفعول فيه A gram. locative.
mef'ulün ileyh (. — ...) مفعول اليه A gram. dative.
mef'ulün leh (. — ..) مفعول له A gram. complement expressing the motive of the action, dative of purpose.
mef'ulün maah (. — ...) مفعول مع A gram. instrumental case.
megafon مغافون F megaphone.
megaloblâst مغالوبلاست F med. megaloblast.
megaloman مغالومانى P psychiatry megalomaniac.
megalomani مغالومانى F psychiatry megalomania.
megalosefal[li] مغالوسفال F med. megacephalic.
megalosit مغالوسيت F med. megalocyte, macrocyte.
meges مگس P lrnd. fly. —**i engübîn** bee. —**gîr** (.. —) P spider. —**nâk** (.. —) P infested with flies. —**ran** (.. —) P fan; fly flap. —**vâr** (.. —) P like a fly.
meğer مگر (Persian meger) but, however; unless, and yet; only; perhaps. — **ki** provided that; unless; only. —**se** and all the while.
=**meğin** مگين cf. =**mağın**.
meğre=[r] مگرك archaic, same as **mele**=, to bleat.
meh مه var. of **mah** 1.
mehabet (. —.) مهابت A lrnd. 1. awe, dread, fear. 2. reverence, greatness, majesty. —**li**, -**lû** (. — . —) majestic, awe-inspiring.
mehabil (. —.) مهابل A lrnd., pl. of **mehbil**.
mehafil (. —.) محافل A lrnd., var. of **mahafil**.
mehalik[ki] (. —.) مهالك A lrnd., pl. of **mehleke**, **mehlike**.
meham[mmi] (. —) مهام A lrnd., pl. of **mühim**.
mehanet (. —.) مهانت A lrnd. a being contemptible, despicable; baseness, contemptible state; poverty.
mehar (. —) مهار P lrnd. leading rein of a camel; reins, bridle.
meharet (. —.) مهارت A var. of **maharet**.
mehasin (. —.) محاسن A var. of **mahasin**.
mehat محط A var. of **mahat**.
mehatürrıhâl[li] (. . . . —) محط الرحال A lrnd. traveler's halting place.
me'haz مأخذ A 1. source of origin (book, etc.). 2. authority (used in writing a book), reference. — **havzası** physical geog. reception basin.
mehbil مهبل A anat. vagina. —**i** (.. —) A vaginal.
mehbit مهبط A lrnd. place of descent or fall.
mehcur (. —) مهجور A lrnd. 1. left, forsaken, deserted, abandoned. 2. disappointed and frustrated. —**iyet** (. — —.), —**luk** a being abandoned or forgotten; disappointment.
mehcüv[vvü] مهجو A lrnd. satirized, lampooned.
mehçe مهچه P lrnd., same as **mahçe**.
mehd مهد A lrnd. 1. cradle. 2. womb; mother. —**i mina** the sky. —**i Musa** Moses' cradle of bulrushes. —**i ülyayı saltanat** Ott. hist. the Sultan's mother. —**i zuhur** cradle (of a movement, religion, etc.).
mehdi (. —) مهدى A 1. lrnd. guided, rightly guided. 2. w. cap., Isl. rel. the twelfth Imam of the Shias expected to return to purify Islam. 3. w. cap., Isl. rel. the Muslim Messiah (who will appear in due time to deliver the faithful), Mahdi.
mehdum (. —) مهدوم A lrnd. destroyed, pulled down, demolished.
mehek[kki] مهك A lrnd., same as **mehenk**.
mehel مهل or محل [Arabic mahal] only in **meheldir** It serves him right.
mehengir مهنگير [pehengîr] carpenter's marking gauge; mech. surface gauge.
mehenk[gi] مهنك [Arabic mihak] 1. touchstone, Lydian stone. 2. test, standard. — **taşı** touchstone, Lydian stone. —**e vur**= /ı/ to test.
mehenkçi مهنكچى 1. goldsmith who tests metals. 2. person who has a special gift in weighing-up a matter or people's character.
mehere مهره A lrnd., pl. of **mahir**.
mehib (. —) مهيب A lrnd. 1. awful, dreadful. 2. venerable, revered; grave.
mehil 1 مهل [mehl] time, term, permitted delay, days of grace.
mehil 2 (. —) مهيل A lrnd. formidable, dreadful (place).
mehin (. —) مهين A lrnd. insignificant; abject, contemptible; weak in judgment.
mehire (. —.) مهيره A lrnd. 1. very expert or clever. 2. free and with a dowry (woman).
mehl مهل A lrnd., same as **mehil 1**.
mehle مهله prov. the best end of a neck of mutton.
mehleke مهلكه lrnd., var. of **mehlike**.
mehlika (.. —) مهلقا P lrnd. fair as the moon, beautiful (person).
mehlike مهلكه A lrnd. 1. dangerous place, precipice; danger, peril. 2. a dying; death.
mehmaemken (. —..) مهما امكن A lrnd. as far as possible.
Mehmetçik[ği] محمدچك name epitomizing the Turkish common soldier.
mehmum (. —) مهموم A lrnd. grieved, depressed, sad.
mehmus (. —) مهموس A lrnd. 1. whispered. 2. hidden, concealed. —**en** (. —'.) A secretly.
mehmuz (. —) مهموز A Arabic gram. marked

with **hemze**, hamzated; ending in **hemze** (poem or verse).

mehpare (. —.) مهپاره P lrnd. very beautiful (person). **—gân** (. —. —) P pl.

mehperest مهپرست P lrnd. worshipper of the moon; lover. **—ân** (...—) P lovers.

mehr مهر A lrnd. marriage settlement or dowry. **—i muaccel** can. law. part of a wife's dowry paid by the husband upon marriage. **—i müeccel** can. law. part of dowry paid by the husband in case of divorce or widowhood.

mehrû (. —) مهرو P lrnd. having a face like a moon, beautiful. **—yan** (. — —) P pl.

mehşid (. —) مهشید P lrnd. moonlight, moon.

mehtâb (. —) P, **mehtâp**[b¹] (. —) مهتاب 1. moonlight, full moon. 2. same as **maytap**. **—iye** (. —..) terrace or roofless pavilion, where the moonlight can be enjoyed.

mehter مهتر [Persian **mihter**] 1. Ott. hist. band of musicians which played at palaces; musician. 2. Ott. hist. groom, tent pitcher, door man in a public office. 3. Ott. hist. superior servant, chamberlain. 4. Ott. hist. official who announced the award of promotions or decorations. 5. lrnd. greater, superior. **— başı** 1. Ott. hist. chief of the band of musicians. 2. Ott. hist. chief of the tent-pitchers. **—i raht** lrnd. attendant on the baggage, tents, etc. **— takımı** band (of musicians).

mehterân (..—) مهتران P lrnd., pl. of **mehter**. **—ı alem** Ott. hist. 1. military band that saluted their lord's banner with music. 2. Imperial standard bearers. **—ı hayme** Ott. hist. 1. body of irregular horsemen who accompanied the pilgrim caravans to Mecca. 2. the tent-pitchers.

mehterhane (..—.) مهترخانه P Ott. hist. 1. military band in the suite of a vizier or prince; «Janissary band» consisting of wind and percussion instruments. 2. special place of the military band.

mehtûk[ü] (. —) مهتوك A lrnd. torn, rent; violated.

mehûl[ü] (. —) مهول A lrnd. frightful, dreadful, horrible.

me'huz (. —) مأخوذ A lrnd. 1. taken, obtained. 2. quoted (from), referred (to). 3. borrowed.

me'huzat (. — —) مأخوذات A pl., fin. receipts. **— ve medfuat** fin. receipts and payments.

me'huze (. — —) مأخوذه A log. lemma.

mehvar (. —) مهور P lrnd. moonlike; monthly. **—e** (. —.) P monthly stipend.

mehveş مهوش P lrnd. 1. like the moon; beautiful as the moon. 2. sweetheart.

mehyum (. —) مهیوم A lrnd. bewildered, distracted.

mehzum (. —) مهزوم A lrnd. crushed, smashed; defeated, routed. **— kıl=** /ı/ to rout, defeat.

mejeng مژنك P lrnd. disagreebleness; ugliness. **=mek** ماك cf. **=mak** 1.

mekabir (. —.) مقابر A lrnd., var. of **makabir**.

mekadir (. — —) مقادیر A lrnd., var. of **makadir**.

mekâmin (. —.) مکامن A lrnd., pl. of **mekmen**.

mekân (. —) مکان A 1. place, site; residence, abode. 2. phil. space. 3. lrnd. position, rank. **—dan münezzeh** to whom no place or limit can be assigned (God). **—i refi'** lrnd. exalted position or place. **— tut=** to establish oneself; to get settled. **— zarfı** gram. adverb of place.

mekânen (. —'.) مکاناً A lrnd. with regard to space; concerning a place.

mekânet (. —.) مکانت A lrnd. 1. rank, position; authority. 2. gravity; dignity.

mekânî (. — —) مکانی A 1. lrnd. pertaining to place. 2. phil. spatial; spatially.

mekanik[ği] مکانیك F 1. mechanics. 2. mechanical. **— fren** auto. mechanical brake. **—cilik** neol., phil. mechanism. **—sel** neol. mechanical.

mekanizm مکانیزم F phil. mechanism.

mekanizma (...'.) مکانیزما It mechanism.

mekâre (. —.), **mekâri** (. — —) مکاره same as **mekkâre**, **mekkâri**.

mekârih (. —.) مکاره A lrnd. 1. pl. of **mekruh**. 2. trouble, suffering, tribulation.

mekârim (. —.) مکارم A lrnd., pl. of **mekremet**. **—kâr** (. —. —) P very kind person.

mekâsib (. —.) مکاسب A lrnd., pl. of **mekseb**.

mekâtib 1 (. —.) مکاتب A lrnd., pl. of **mekteb**.

mekâtib 2 (. — —) مکاتیب A lrnd., pl. of **mektub**.

mekbul[ü] (. —) مکبول A lrnd. fettered; prisoner, captive.

meke مکه [Mekke] prov. corn.

me'kel (. .') مأکل A lrnd. 1. an eating, a devouring; that which can be eaten; livelihood, subsistence. 2. profitable affair.

me'kele (. .'.) مأکله A lrnd. 1. food storeroom, pantry. 2. food; edible.

meker مکر only in **teker meker** head over heels.

mekere مکره A lrnd., pl. of **mâkir**.

mekfuf (. —) مکفوف A lrnd. 1. closed, drawn together. 2. restrained, kept back. 3. blind.

mekfûl[ü] (. —) مکفول A lrnd. mortgaged, pledged, bailed; guaranteed.

mekhûl[ü] (. —) مکحول A lrnd. with eyes blackened with kohl.

mekide (.—.) مَكِيدَه A lrnd. a using a stratagem; deceit, fraud, stratagem.

mekik^gi مَكِيك [Persian **mekûk**] weaver's shuttle. **— doku=** /arasında/ to shuttle back and forth between. **— kalemi, — masurası** bobbin of a shuttle.

mekil (.—) مَكِيل A lrnd. a measuring (grain).

mekin (.—) مَكِين A lrnd. 1. firmly fixed, well established. 2. grave, authoritative, dignified.

mekinet (.—.) مَكِينَت A lrnd., same as **mekânet**.

mekis (.—) مَكِيث A lrnd. grave, sedate, dignified.

mekkâr (.—) مَكَّار A lrnd. habitually deceitful; cheat.

mekkâre مَكَّارَه [mükâri] lrnd. 1. animal let out on hire, packhorse. 2. goods carried by hired pack animals. 3. packhorses of an army.

mekkâreci مَكَّارَه جِى 1. person who hires out pack animals and looks after them. 2. soldier in charge of military pack animals.

mekkârî (..—) مَكَّارِى A same as **mekkâre**.
mekkâs (.—) مَكَّاس A lrnd. tax-collector.
Mekke مَكَّة A geog. Mecca. **— belesan ağacı** bdellium tree, balsamodendron, kua, bot., Commiphora africanum. **— pelesengi** balm of Gilead, balsam of Mecca, bot., Commiphora opobalsamum. **— samanı** camel's hay, geranium grass, bot., Andropogon Schoenanthus.

mekkî (.—) مَكِّى A lrnd. belonging to Mecca, Meccan.

=mekle beraber مَكْلَه بَرابَر cf. **=makla beraber**.
=meklik^gi مَكْلِك cf. **=maklık**.
meklûb (.—) مَكْلُوب A lrnd. affected with canine rabies, suffering from hydrophobia.
meklûm (.—) مَكْلُوم A lrnd. wounded, hurt.
mekmen مَكْمَن A lrnd. ambush, hiding place.
mekmûn (.—) مَكْمُون A lrnd. hidden, concealed.
meknî (.—) مَكْنِى A lrnd. hidden, concealed, latent.
meknûn (.—) مَكْنُون A lrnd. laid up, hidden, concealed; secret.
meknûs (.—) مَكْنُوس A lrnd. swept (house).
meknûz (.—) مَكْنُوز A lrnd. 1. hidden, laid up in a treasury; stored away; buried (treasure). 2. intrinsic, inherent (meaning).
mekr مَكْر A lrnd. a plotting, deceiving; deceit, trick, artifice. **—i mahmud** justifiable stratagem (used for a good purpose). **—i mezmum** blameworthy trick for a bad purpose.
mekrehet مَكْرَهَت A lrnd. a hating; loathing; abhorrence, disgust.
mekremet مَكْرَمَت A lrnd. kindness, beneficence; generosity; honor, glory.
mekremetli, mekremetlû (...—) مَكْرَمَتْلُو

A Ott. hist. endowed with noble qualities official title for addressing a letter to a professor of canon law.

mekrub (.—) مَكْرُوب A lrnd. 1. distressed, afflicted, oppressed with grief. 2. strong.

mekruh (.—) مَكْرُوه A 1. abominable, disgusting. 2. can. law not forbidden by God but looked upon with horror and disgust by Muslim teachers (act). 3. disliked, disagreeable (thing).

mekruhat (.——) مَكْرُوهَات A lrnd. things canonically held in detestation.

mekruhiyet (.—..) مَكْرُوهِيَت A disgust, abomination.

mekrümet مَكْرُمَت A lrnd., same as **mekremet**.

meks 1 مَكْث A lrnd. a staying, pausing, delaying; stay, halt, delay. **— et=***.

meks 2 مَكْس A lrnd. 1. a defrauding someone by taking his wares at a price below their market value. 2. a collecting taxes or tribute; tribute, tax; fee exacted by a collector as a bribe for his not giving trouble.

mekseb مَكْسَب A lrnd. earning, gain, livelihood; place of gain.

meksefe مَكْسَفَه A obs., elec. condenser.
mekset=^der مَكْسَت to halt, to pause.
meksir مَكْسِر A lrnd. 1. place of fracture. 2. place of creasing or folding; crease.
=meksizin مَكْسِزِين cf. **=maksızın**.
meksub (.—) مَكْسُوب A lrnd. earned, gained, acquired, merited.
meksuf (.—) مَكْسُوف A lrnd. eclipsed (sun or moon).
meksur (.—) مَكْسُور A lrnd. 1. broken, fractured. 2. gram. consonant marked with the vowel **kesre**.
mekşuf (.—) مَكْشُوف A lrnd. uncovered; exposed, unveiled; manifested, discovered, revealed; explored.
=mekte مَكْتَه cf. **=makta 2.**
mekteb مَكْتَب A same as **mektep**. **M—i Aklâm** Ott. hist. a special secondary school for training civil servants. **M—i Âlî** Ott. hist. school for higher education. **M—i Fünûn-i Harbiye, M—i Harbiye** Ott. hist. War Academy. **M—i Maarif-i Adliye** Ott. hist. a school founded in 1839 for the training of government officials. **M—i Mülkiye** Ott. hist. school for civil servants (former name for Siyasal Bilgiler Fakültesi). **M—i Ulûm-i Harbiye** same as **M—i Harbiye**. **—i inas** Ott. hist. girls' school. **M—i Sultanî** Ott. hist., a name of the Galatasaray Lycee. **M—i Tıbbiye** Ott. hist. medical school.
=mektense (..'.) مَكْتَنْسَه cf. **=maktansa**.
mektep^bl مَكْتَب [mekteb] 1. school. 2. slang brothel. **—i as=** school slang to play truant. **—e başlat=** slang to sell. **— çocuğu** 1. school

mektepli child. 2. raw, inexperienced. **— gemisi** training ship. **— görmemiş** 1. illiterate. 2. ill-mannered, rude. **— görmüş** educated. **— kaçağı** truant. **— medrese görmüş** educated.

mektepli مكتبلى 1. school child, pupil. 2. who has a school diploma. 3. officer who has graduated from a military school. **—lik** abstr. n.

mektub (. —) مكتوب A 1. same as **mektup**. 2. lrnd. written. **—i sami** Ott. hist. vezirial letter to a functionary.

mektubat (. — —) مكتوبات A pl. 1. written documents; texts. 2. letters.

mektûbî (. — —) مكتوبى A Ott. hist. chief secretary of a ministry or province.

mektûf (. —) مكتوف A lrnd. whose hands are pinioned behind his back; clamped together.

mektûm (. —) مكتوم A lrnd. 1. kept secret; hidden, concealed. 2. phil. esoteric. **— tut=** /ı/ to keep secret.

mektûmât (. — —) مكتومات A lrnd. matters kept secret; official peccadillos and delinquencies.

mektûme (. —.) مكتومه A 1. same as **mektûm**. 2. w. cap., name of the well **Zemzem** at Mecca.

mektupᵇᵘ مكتوب A [mektub] letter. **— üstü** address on a letter.

mektupçu مكتوبجى chief secretary of a ministry or province. **— kalemi** Ott. hist. office of the grand vizier's private secretary. **—luk** office and functions of a **mektupçu**.

mektuplaş=ᵗʳ مكتوبلشمق to be in correspondence (with). **—ma** verbal n.

me'kûlˡü (. —) مأكول A lrnd. 1. eaten. 2. edible.

me'kûlat (. — —) مأكولات A comestibles. **— ve meşrubat** food and drink.

mekyulˡü (. —) مكيول A lrnd. measured with a grain measure.

mekzebe, mekzube (. —.) مكذبه ، مكذوبه A lrnd. lie.

mekzum (. —) مكظوم A lrnd. 1. vexed, sad, sorrowful. 2. suppressed, restrained, checked (emotion).

melâᵃⁱ 1 (. —) ملأ A lrnd. 1. a being full; a filling. 2. a body of men, assembly; crowd. 3. people, the public. 4. disposition, habit. 5. nobility, high rank; nobles. **—i âlâ** the sublime assembly, court of heaven.

melâ 2 ملا A lrnd. desert.

mel'ab ملعب A lrnd. a place of amusement or recreation; playground.

mel'abe ملعبه A lrnd. game; toy. **—i sübyan** child's toy.

melâbis (. —.) ملابس A lrnd., pl. of **melbes**.

melah ملخ P lrnd. grasshopper, locust. **—ı âbî** shrimp. **—ı piyade** small locust whose wings are not yet grown.

melâhatᵗⁱ (. —.) ملاحت A lrnd. beauty; sweetness; goodness, elegance. **—li** 1. beautiful, sweet. 2. pleasant (voice etc.).

melâhi (. —.) ملاهى A lrnd., pl. of **melha**.

melâhif (. —.) ملاحف A lrnd., pl. of **milhafe**.

melâhim (. —.) ملاحم A lrnd., pl. of **melhame**.

melâib (. —.) ملاعب A lrnd., pl. of **mel'ab**.

melâikᵏⁱ 1 ملائى A lrnd., pl. of **mil'aka**.

melâikᵏⁱ 2 (. —.) ملائك A lrnd., pl. of **melek**. **— otu** angelica, archangelica, bot., Archangelica officinalis.

melâike (. —..) ملائكه A 1. angel. 2. lrnd., pl. of **melek**.

melâin 1 (. — —) ملاعين A lrnd., pl. of **mel'un**.

melâin 2 (. —.) ملاعن A lrnd., pl. of **mel'anet**.

melâlˡⁱ (. —) ملال A lrnd. 1. depression; melancholy. 2. weariness, fatigue. **— gel=** /a/ to become depressed or weary.

melâlaver (. — —.) ملال آور P lrnd. tiring, wearying, wearisome.

melâlet (. —.) ملالت A lrnd., same as **melâl**. **— çek=** to suffer from depression.

melâmet (. —.) ملامت A lrnd. reproach, blame, censure, criticism.

melâmetger (. —..) ملامتگر P lrnd. censurer, blamer; criticizer.

Melâmetî (. —. —) ملامتى A same as **Melâmî**.

Melâmetiye (. —. —.) ملامتيه A same as **Melâmiye**.

melâmetzede (. — . ..) ملامت زده P lrnd. blamed, censured, reproved. **—gân** (. —...—) P pl.

Melâmî (. — —) ملامى A 1. sect of Sunni dervishes who subject themselves to public reproach by disregarding the outward rites of religion. 2. member of the **Melâmî** sect.

melâmih (. —.) ملامح A lrnd., pl. of **lemha**.

Melâmilikᵍⁱ (. — —.) ملاميلك state or condition of the **Melâmî** sect.

Melâmiye (. — —.) ملاميه A the **Melâmî** sect.

Melâmiyun (. — — —) ملاميون A lrnd. those who belong to the **Melâmî** sect.

mel'anet ملعنت A lrnd. abominable deed; diabolism; curse, damnation. **—kârane** (...——.) P abominably; malignantly, diabolically.

mel'anetpişe (...—.) ملعنت پيشه P lrnd. malignant, diabolical.

melankoli ملنقولى F melancholia.

melankolikᵍⁱ ملنقوليك F melancholic.

melanurya ملنوريا It melanure (fish), zool., Oblada melanura.

melâs سلاس F molasses.

melâset (.—.) ملاست A *lrnd.* a being smooth, smooth and sleek, smoothness, sleekness.

melâz (.—) ملاذ A *lrnd.* place of refuge, shelter, asylum; stronghold.

melbes ملبس A *lrnd.* garment.

melbus (.—) ملبوس A *lrnd.* 1. clothed, draped, clad. 2. put on, worn.

melbusât (.——) ملبوسات A *lrnd.* things worn; garments, clothes.

melce[ei] ملجا A refuge, asylum. — **hakkı** *law* right of asylum, right of sanctuary.

melduğ (.—) ملدوغ A *lrnd.* stung by a scorpion; bitten by a snake.

mele[=r] ملك مه ملك مر ملك to bleat.

melek[gi] ملك A angel. — **gibi** angel-like, angelic; sweet-natured. **M— Girmez** *Ott. hist.*, name given to the Janissary barracks that used to be at Bahçekapı in Istanbul. — **otu** angelica, longwort, *bot.*, *Angelica*; archangel, angelica, *bot.*, *Archangelica officinalis.*

melekât (..—) ملكات A *lrnd.*, *pl. of* **meleke.** **—ı akliye** mental faculties.

melekçehre ملك چهره P *lrnd.* angel-faced, beautiful.

meleke ملكه A 1. natural capability. 2. *phil.* faculty. 3. mastery, readiness, skill; experience.

melekhaslet ملك خصلت P *lrnd.* having an angel's nature, good.

melekî (..—) ملكى A *lrnd.* pertaining to angels, angelic.

melekper ملك پر P *lrnd.* angel-winged.

melekrû (..—) ملك رو P *lrnd.* angel-faced.

meleksıfat ملك صفت P *lrnd.* of angelic qualities.

meleksima (..——) ملك سيما P *lrnd.* angel-faced.

melekût (..—) ملكوت A *lrnd.* 1. supreme dominion, power, authority. 2. God's spiritual kingdom; Heaven.

melekutî (..——) ملكوتى P *lrnd.* pertaining to the Kingdom of Heaven. **—yan** (..———) P those belonging to the Kingdom of Heaven.

melekülmevt ملك الموت A *lrnd.* the angel of death, Azrail.

melel ملل A *lrnd.*, *same as* **melâl.**

meleme 1 مرمه *verbal n. of* **mele=.**

meleme 2 مرمه *prov.* 1. incapable, awkward. 2. slow, gentle.

meles 1 ملس swaybacked horse.

meles 2 ملس A *archaic* a kind of fine silk cloth.

meleş ملش ewe that bleats continually.

melevan (..—) ملوان A *lrnd.* the two alternating times, day and night.

melez ملز [*Arabic meles*] 1. half-breed, cross-bred, mulatto, hybrid. 2. tawny. 3. mixed; mixture. **—le=** to cross (in breeding).

melfuf (.—) ملفوف A *lrnd.* wrapped up; enclosed (in a letter); enclosure. **—at** (.——) A enclosures.

melfûfen (.∴.) ملفوفاً A *lrnd.* enclosed, as an enclosure.

melfûz (.—) ملفوظ A *lrnd.* uttered, pronounced, spoken, expressed.

melfûzat (.——) ملفوظات A *lrnd.* words, sayings, speeches, utterances.

melha ملهى A *lrnd.* toy; amusement.

melhame ملحمه A *lrnd.* bloody battle, slaughter.

melhem ملحم [**merhem**] 1. ointment, salve. 2. healing, cure. — **ol=** /a/ to be a cure for an ailment. — **sür=** /a/ to apply a salve.

melhub (.—) ملهوب A *lrnd.* inflamed; kindled.

melhûd (.—) ملحود A *lrnd.* laid in a sarcophagus, entombed.

melhûf (.—) ملهوف A *lrnd.* distressed; sighing, sad; afflicted.

melhufülkalb (.—..) ملهوف القلب A *lrnd.* pained at heart, distressed and sad.

melhuz (.—ʹ) ملحوظ A *lrnd.* 1. expected, anticipated, probable. 2. contemplated, thought of; observed.

melhuzat (.——) ملحوظات A *lrnd.* things anticipated, pondered, intended; anticipations, thoughts.

melî 1 (.—) ملى A *obs.*, *law* rich, wealthy. **=meli 2** ملو *cf.* **=malı.**

melih (.—) مليح A *lrnd.* pretty, beautiful, gentle, sweet.

melihülkelâm (.—..—) مليح الكلام A *lrnd.* charming in conversation.

melik[ki] **1** ملك A 1. king, sovereign. 2. God, the sovereign Lord. **M—i Müteal** the Most High God. **M—i Nimruz** 1. Adam. 2. the Prophet Muhammad. 3. Rustem (the Persian hero).

melik[ki] **2** (.—) مليك A *lrnd.* king, sovereign, lord.

melikâne (.——.) ملكانه P kingly, royal; majestic.

melike (.—.) ملكه A queen.

melikî (.——) ملكى A pertaining to a sovereign, royal.

melikiyet (.——.) ملكيت A kingliness.

melisa (.∴.) مليسا It lemon balm, bee-balm, *bot.*, *Melissa officinalis*; molucca balm, shell flower, *bot.*, *Muluccella laevis.*

melkut (.—) ملقوط A *lrnd.* 1. picked up. 2. foundling.

mellâh (.—) ملّاح A *lrnd.* boatman, seaman, sailor. **—ân** (.——) P, **—în** (.——) A *pl.* **—lık** seamanship.

melmûs (.—) ملموس A *lrnd.* felt, touched (by the hand).

melmûsât (. ——) ملموسات A *lrnd*. 1. tangible things. 2. touches.
melodi ملودى F melody.
melodram ملودرام F melodrama.
melon ملون F bowler hat. **— şapka** derby hat, bowler hat.
melsa (.—) ملسا A *lrnd*. 1. smooth, bare. 2. delicate wine gliding smoothly down the throat.
melsûk[ku] (.—) ملصوص A 1. *lrnd*. adhering, joined; attached. 2. *ling*. agglutinated.
meltem ملتم off-shore breeze that blows daily for a period in summer.
mel'ub (. —) ملعوب A *lrnd*. slobbering (mouth, etc.).
me'luf (.—) مألوف A *lrnd*. accustomed; usual, habitual, ordinary. **—iyet** (. ——.) habit.
melûl[lü] (. —) ملول A low spirited; sad, vexed, melancholy. **— melûl bak=** to look mournful, to wear a sad expression. **—âne** (. ——.) P low-spiritedly; in a sad manner.
melûm 1 (. —) ملوم A *lrnd*. blamed, reproached; badly spoken of.
me'lum 2 (. —) مألوم A *lrnd*. subjected to pain; grieved, pained; sad.
mel'un (. —) ملعون A cursed, damned, accursed, execrated; cursed man.
melzum (. —) ملزوم A *lrnd*. inseparable, connected. **—iyet** (. ——.) inseparableness.
=mem مم cf. **=mam**.
memalik[ki] **1** (. —.) ممالك A *lrnd*., *pl*. of **memleket**. **M—i Mahruse, M—i Mahrusei Şahane** the Imperial Ottoman dominions (as divinely protected). **M—i Müctemiai Amerika Cumhuriyeti, M—i Müttehidei Amerika** the United States of America. **M—i Osmaniye, M—i Şâhane** the Ottoman Empire.
memalik[ki] **2** (. ——) ممالك A *lrnd*., *pl*. of **memlûk**.
memat (. —) ممات A death. **—î** (. ——) A pertaining to death.
memba[ai] منبع [menba'] 1. spring, fountain. 2. source, origin.
memdûd (. —) ممدود A 1. *lrnd*. extended, stretched, prolonged. 2. *gram*. long vowel. 3. *chem*. diluted.
memdûh (. —) ممدوح A *lrnd*. praised, eulogized; praiseworthy. **—at** (. ——) A *pl*. praiseworthy acts or qualities. **—iyet** (. ——.) praiseworthiness.
meme مم 1. teat, nipple; breast; udder, dug. 2. any nipple-shaped prominence; knob, tumor. 3. lobe (of the ear). 4. burner (of a lamp). 5. *naut*. crown of the anchor. 6. *mech*. nozzle. 7. *artillery* anvil. **—de** suckling (baby). **— başı** nipple of a teat. **— bezi** *anat*. mammary gland. **— düğmesi** tip of the nipple. **— em=** to suckle (infant). **— gülü** tip and orifice of the nipple. **— ve kapsül** *artillery* anvil and cap. **—den kes=** /ı/ to wean. **— pusu** gummy excretion found in the nipple of newly-lambed ewes. **— süngeri** *anat*. sebaceous gland of the nipple of a nursing woman. **— ucu** tip of the nipple. **— üzümü** kind of finger-shaped grapes. **— ver=** /a/ to suckle (a baby). **—den yar=** /ı/ *prov*. to wean.
memecik[ği] ممجك *anat*. papilla.
memeli ممه لى 1. having teats; mammiferous (animal). 2. *mach*. equipped with nozzles, burners, etc. **— hayvanlar** mammals.
memelik[ği] ممه لك cover to protect a sore teat or to prevent sucking.
mememsi 1. *neol*., *anat*. papillary. 2. like a teat.
me'men (.'.) مأمن A *lrnd*. place of security; refuge, stronghold. **M—i Rıza** · the Kaaba.
memer[rri] ممر A *lrnd*. place of passage, passage; path. **—i nâs** 1. public thoroughfare. 2. transit of man, *i. e*. death.
memeş ممش saliva dripping from the mouth of an ox.
=memezlik[ği] ممه زلك cf. **=mamazlık**.
memhûr (. —) ممهور A *lrnd*. sealed, signed with a seal.
memhûre (. —.) ممهوره A *lrnd*. dowered (wife).
memhûs (. —) ممهوس A *lrnd*. 1. furbished, polished. 2. strongly and compactly built (person).
memhuv[vvü] ممحو A *lrnd*. obliterated, done away with.
memkûr (. —) ممكور A *lrnd*. 1. colored with red ocher. 2. smeared with the blood of his prey (lion).
memlâha ممحه A *lrnd*. salt works, salt pit.
memleket ممالكت A dominion; country; town; a person's home district; native land.
Memleketeyn ممالكتين A *Ott. hist*. the two countries, *i. e*. Wallachia and Moldavia.
memleketli ممالكتلى 1. inhabitant of a town. 2. fellow countryman.
memlû (. —) ممالو A *lrnd*. full; filled.
memlûh (. —) ممالوح A *lrnd*. salted, pickled.
memlûhât (. ——) ممالوحات A *lrnd*. salted meats; pickles.
memlûk[kü] (. —) ممالوك A *lrnd*. 1. possessed, owned as absolute property. 2. purchased slave; *w. cap*., *hist*. **Mameluke**. **—âne** (. ——.) P pertaining to a slave; as a slave; most obediently. **—iyet** (. ——.) slavery.
memlûl[lü] (. —) ممالول A *lrnd*. 1. baked under hot ashes (bread). 2. tired of, weary of, disgusted with.
memnu[uu] (. —) ممنوع A forbidden, prohibited; prevented. **— hakların iadesi** *law*

rehabilitation. — mıntıka prohibited zone. — silâhlar prohibited arms.

memnuat (.— —) ممنوعات A *lrnd.* prohibited things.

memnuiyet ممنوعیت A prohibition. — müddeti *law* time of widowhood.

memnun (.—) ممنون A 1. pleased, happy, glad; delighted; satisfied. 2. *lrnd.* under an obligation; obliged. 3. *lrnd.* diminished; stinted, grudged.

memnunen (.—'.) ممنوناً A gladly, with pleasure.

memnuniyet (.— —.) ممنونیت A pleasure, gladness, delight, gratitude. —le with pleasure, gladly.

memnunluk^gu ممنونلق pleasure, gladness, contentment.

memsûh 1 (.—) ممسوح A *lrnd.* 1. wiped with the hand, especially in an ablution. 2. anointed. 3. visited by God with good or evil.

memsûh 2 (.—) ممسوخ A *lrnd.* changed, metamorphosed into the shape of a beast.

memsûn (.—) ممثون A *lrnd.* having bladder pain; diseased in the bladder.

memsûs 1 (.—) ممسوس A *lrnd.* 1. touched, felt, tangible. 2. diabolically possessed.

memsûs 2 (.—) ممصوص A *lrnd.* 1. sucked, absorbed. 2. emaciated by disease; bony.

memşa (.—) ممشی A *lrnd.* privy.

memtul^lü (.—) ممطول A *lrnd.* hammered into shape (sword blade etc.).

memtur (.—) ممطور A *lrnd.* rained upon, wetted with rain.

memul^lü (.—) مأمول A hoped, expected, desired; thing hoped for; hope.

me'mun (.—) مأمون A *lrnd.* 1. made safe, secured. 2. confided in, trusted; firm, constant. 3. *w. cap.*, name of the seventh Abbaside Caliph.

memur (.—) مأمور A 1. official; employee; agent; officer. 2. /a/ charged with; ordered to, appointed, commissioned. — et= /i/ to appoint, to commission; to authorize. — sicili civil servant's register. — ve müstahdem official and employee. —un şahsî kusuru *law* civil liability for misfeasance for a public officer.

me'muren (.—'.) مأموراً A *lrnd.* officially; commissioned, authorized.

me'murin (.— —) مأمورین A officials. — kanunu *law* civil service regulations.

memuriyet (.— —.) مأموریت A official duty; appointment; office, charge; post.

memurluk^gu مأمورلق quality and duties of an official; official post.

memzuc (.—) ممزوج A *lrnd.* incorporated, blended, mixed.

men^n'i 1 منع A a preventing, hindering, prohibiting; prohibition, hindrance; inhibition.

men 2 من A *lrnd.* whosoever.

men^nni 3 منّ A *lrnd.* manna.

men 4 من [*Arabic* menn] *lrnd.*, a Persian unit of weight, about forty to eighty pounds.

men^nni 6 منّ A *lrnd.* 1. a giving as of grace and favor; gift; a doing a kindness. 2. a casting a former gift or kindness in the face of its recipient; taunt, reproach.

men'a منعا A *lrnd.* news of the death of a person.

menaat^ti (.—.) مناعت A *lrnd.* a being inaccessible; inaccessibility; impregnability.

menab (.—) مناب A *lrnd.* a being the deputy or substitute of another; place where anyone acts as a substitute.

menabi^i (.—.) منابع A *lrnd.*, *pl. of* menba.

menabir (.—.) منابر A *lrnd.*, *pl. of* minber.

menabit (.—.) منابت A *lrnd.*, *pl. of* menbet, menbit.

menacik^kı (.— —) مناجیق A *lrnd.*, *pl. of* mancınık.

menadil (.— —) منادیل A *lrnd.*, *pl. of* mendil.

Menaf (.—) مناف A *rel. hist.*, name of a pagan Arabian god.

menafi (.—.) منافع A *lrnd.*, *pl. of* menfaat.

menafiz (.—.) منافذ A *lrnd.*, *pl. of* menfez.

menaha (.—.) مناحه A *lrnd.* place of lamentation (for the dead); house of mourning.

menahi (.— —) مناهی A *lrnd.*, *pl. of* menhi.

menahic 1 (.—.) مناهج A *lrnd.*, *pl. of* menhec.

menahic 2 (.— —) مناهج A *lrnd.*, *pl. of* minhac.

menahil 1 (.—.) مناهل A *lrnd.*, *pl. of* menhel.

menahil 2 (.—.) مناهل A *lrnd.*, *pl. of* münhal 2, münhül.

menahir (.—.) مناهر A *lrnd.*, *pl. of* menhar 2.

menahis (.—.) مناحس A *lrnd.*, *pl. of* nahs.

menaî (.— —) مناعی A *lrnd.*, *pl. of* men'a.

menaif (.—.) منائف A *lrnd.* mountain peaks.

menair (.—.) منائر A *lrnd.*, *pl. of* menare.

menajer منائجر F *sports* manager.

menakıb (.—.) مناقب A *lrnd.*, *pl. of* menkabe.

menakır (.—.) مناقر A *lrnd.*, *pl. of* minkar 2.

menakib (.—.) مناكب A *lrnd.*, *pl. of* menkib.

menakir 1 (.—.) مناكر A *lrnd.*, *pl. of* münker.

menakîr 2 (.— —) مناقیر A *lrnd.*, *pl. of* minkar.

menal^lü (.—) منال A *lrnd.* possession; wealth, property; goods, chattels.

menam (.—) منام A *lrnd.* 1. sleep; dream. 2. bed, bedroom. —e (.—.) A bed, bedroom. —î (.— —) A pertaining to dreams, oneiric.

menar (.—) منار A *lrnd.* 1. lighthouse. 2. road sign. 3. minaret.

Red 48.

menare (.—.) مَنارَه A *lrnd.* 1. candlestick; lighthouse. 2. *same as* **minare**.
menas (.—) مَناص A *lrnd.* refuge, asylum.
menasıb (.—.) مَناصِب A *lrnd., pl. of* **mansıb**. **—ı sitte** *Ott. hist.* the functions of the heads of the financial departments of the six State offices: **Nişancı, Defterdar, Reisülküttab, Defter Emini, Şıkkı Sâni,** and **Şıkkı Sâlis**.
menasik[kı] (.—.) مَناسِك A *lrnd., pl. of* **mensek, mensik**.
menasim (.—.) مَناسِم A *lrnd., pl. of* **mensim**.
menaşir 1 (.——) مَناشِير A *lrnd., pl. of* **menşur**.
menaşir 2 (.—.) مَناشِر A *lrnd., pl. of* **minşar**.
menat 1 (.—) مَناط A *lrnd.* point of suspension.
Menat 2 (.—) مَنات A *rel. hist.,* name of one of the three chief gods of the pagan citizens of Mecca.
menatık[kı] (.—.) مَناطِق A *lrnd., pl. of* **mıntıka**.
menaya (.——) مَنايا A *lrnd., pl. of* **meniye**.
menazım (.—.) مَناظِم A *lrnd., pl.* rows, orders.
menazır (.—.) مَناظِر A *lrnd.* 1. *pl. of* **manzara**. 2. perspective. **—î** (.—.—) A in perspective; perspectively.
menazırüttasvir (.—...—) مَناظِرُالتَّصْوِير A *lrnd.* stereography. **—î** (.—...——) A stereographic.
menazil (.—.) مَنازِل A *lrnd., pl. of* **menzil**. **—i kamer** the twenty-eight lunar mansions.
menba[ıı] مَنْبَع A *same as* **memba**.
menbet, menbit مَنْبِت A *lrnd.* place where plants grow.
menbûş (.—) مَنْبُوش A *lrnd.* uncovered, opened, rifled (grave).
menbûz (.—) مَنْبُوذ A *lrnd.* 1. foundling, bastard, abandoned by the wayside. 2. fit only to cast away (beast).
menca (.—) مَنْجا A *lrnd.* 1. elevated spot to which one can escape for safety from a flood. 2. a fleeing (for safety); safety.
mencat (.—) مَنْجات A *lrnd.* source of safety; means of escape.
mencelâb (..—) مَنْجَلاب A *lrnd.* polluted water (into which a dog or carrion has been thrown).
mencem مَنْجَم [*Arabic* mincem] *lrnd.* handle of a balance.
mencenik[kı] مَنْجَنِيك A *var. of* **mancınık**.
mencud (.—) مَنْجُود A *lrnd.* 1. afflicted, distressed. 2. perishing. 3. dead.
mencuk[ku] (.—) مَنْجُوك A *lrnd.* 1. crescent shaped ornament on a flagstaff. 2. umbrella, sunshade. 3. flag, banner.
-mend مَنْد P *lrnd.* possessing, endued with, *as in* **derdmend, hiredmend**.

mendebur مَنْدَبُور [*Persian* **mendbur**] 1. good for nothing; lazy. 2. miserable; wretch; disgusting.
mendel 1 مَنْدَل P *lrnd.* magic circle.
mendel 2 مَنْدَل P *lrnd.* lignaloes (wood for incense), *Aquilaria agallocha*.
mendeme مَنْدَمَه A *lrnd.* source of regret; cause of repentance; act of repentance.
menderes مَنْدَرِس Gk 1. winding path or course of a river, meander. 2. *w. cap.* the Meander River.
mendil مَنْدِيل A 1. handkerchief. 2. napkin, towel. **— atma** *Ott. hist.* a throwing the handkerchief (by the Sultan as an indication of his choice of a pretty girl at the Palace). **— salla=** /a/ to wave one's handkerchief.
mendirek[ği] مَنْدِرَك Gk artificial harbor; breakwater.
mendub (.—) مَنْدُوب A *lrnd.* 1. laudable, good and pious (act). 2. lamented, mourned for (after death).
menduf (.—) مَنْدُوف A *lrnd.* carded or teased (cotton).
menekşe مَنَكْشَه [*Persian* **benefşe**] 1. violet, *bot., Viola odorata*. **— gülü** Bengal rose, China rose, *bot., Rosa chinensis*. **— kökü** orris root, *bot., Iris florentina;* root of the sweet flag, *bot., Acorus calamus*. **—giller** *neol., bot.,* Violacae.
menend مَنَنْد [**manend**] resembling, similar.
menengiç[ci] مَنَنْكِيج *same as* **meneviş**.
menenjit مَنَنْجِيت F *path.* meningitis.
men'et=[der] مَنْعَتْمَك /ı/ to prevent, to forbid; to hinder.
menevî (..—) مَنَوِى A *anat.* seminal, spermal.
meneviş مَنَوِيش 1. fruit of the terebinth tree, *bot., Pistacia terebinthus*. 2. wavy appearance of watered silk. 3. bluing of steel, mottled or moiré appearance (metal).
menevişlen=[ir] مَنَوِيشْلَنْمَك to acquire a wavy appearance or a blue finish on the surface (silk, metal).
menevişli مَنَوِيشْلِى watered (silk); blued, browned, moiréd (metal).
menevşe مَنَوْشَه *prov. for* **menekşe**.
menfa (.—) مَنْفا A *lrnd.* place of exile.
menfaat[ti] مَنْفَعَت A use; advantage; profit; benefit; interest. **—ine** /ın/ for the benefit of. **— değeri** insurable value. **— değerinden yüksek sigorta** overinsurance. **— düşkünü** *same as* **menfaatperest**.
menfaatbahş (...—) مَنْفَعَتْبَخْش P *lrnd.* advantageous, beneficial; useful.
menfaatdar (...—) مَنْفَعَتْدار P who has an advantage or benefit.
menfaatli مَنْفَعَتْلِى useful; beneficial.
menfaatperest مَنْفَعَتْپَرَسْت P *lrnd.* self-seeking,

always looking for gain; utilitarian. —î, —lik selfishness, self-interest.

menfes مَنْفَس A *lrnd*. breathing hole, vent.

menfez مَنْفَذ A *lrnd*. passage, hole; outlet, vent.

menfi (. —) مَنْفِى A 1. negative; contrary, perverse. 2. antagonistic; adverse. 3. *lrnd*. banished, exiled. — **aded** negative number. —**lik** negation; contrariness. —**yen** (. —ʹ .) A *lrnd*. as an exile.

menfûh (. —) مَنْفُوخ A *lrnd*. 1. blown, blown into. 2. inflated, swollen; fat.

menfûr (. —) مَنْفُور A *lrnd*. abhorred, loathed, shunned. —**iyet** (. — —.), —**luk** loathsomeness.

menfûş (. —) مَنْفُوش A *lrnd*. teased, plucked (cotton or wool).

mengeçᶜⁱ *prov*. large shuttle (for wool).
mengel *prov*. bangle.
Mengele, Mengelûs (. . —) P *archaic, geog*. Bengal.
mengene (ʹ . .) Gk press, vise, screw-jack, clamp.
menguş P *lrnd*. earring.

menhar 1 A *lrnd*. place where animals are slaughtered for sacrifice.

menhar 2 A *lrnd*. nostril.

menhec A *lrnd*. wide road, highway. —**i sedâd** the way of righteousness.

menhel A *lrnd*. 1. watering place, place of drinking. 2. halting place.

menhi (. —) مَنْهِى A *lrnd*. forbidden, prohibited. —**yat** (. — —) A *pl*. forbidden things.

menhûb (. —) A *lrnd*. plundered, snatched away by force. —**ât** (. — —) A *pl*. booty, spoil.

menhûs (. —) A inauspicious, ill-omened; unlucky; cursed.

menhûş (. —) A *lrnd*. bitten (by a snake).

menhût (. —) A *lrnd*. cut out, hewn (wood or stone).

meni 1 مَنِى A *anat*. semen, sperm.
meniⁱⁱ **2** A *var*. of **men 1**.
meni 3 (. —) P *lrnd*. egoism, selfishness.
meniⁱⁱ **4** (. —) A *lrnd*. unapproachable, unassailable; inaccessible, impregnable.

menin (. —) A *lrnd*. dust.

-**meniş** P *lrnd*. natured, charactered, as in **büzürgmeniş, harmeniş**.

meniye (. —.) A *lrnd*. death.

menkabe, menkıbe A 1. legend; narrative. 2. exploit, heroic deed.

menkıbevî (. . . —) A legendary.

menkib A *lrnd*. shoulder, shoulder joint.

menkuᵘᵘ (. —) A *lrnd*. infused, soaked, macerated; infusion. —**at** (. — —) A *pl*.

menkûb 1 (. —) A *lrnd*. fallen from prominence, out of favor; miserable, disgraced.

menkub 2 (. —) A *lrnd*. hollowed, dug; undermined.

menkûbiyet (. — —.) A disgrace, a being out of favor.

menkûha (. —.) A *lrnd*. wife.

menkulⁱⁱ (. —) A 1. transported, conveyed; movable. 2. told, narrated; traditional. — **dâvası** *law* action concerning goods and chattels. — **kıymetler** stocks and bonds. — **mallar** movable goods. — **mülkiyeti** *law* movable property, personal property. — **rehni** *law* pledge.

menkulât (. — —) A *lrnd*. 1. movables. 2. legends, traditions.

menkûr 1 (. —) A *lrnd*. denied; ignored.

menkur 2 (. —) A *lrnd*. pierced, bored; incised.

menkûs (. —) A *lrnd*. 1. inverted; read backwards. 2. head downwards; topsy-turvy. 3. suffering from a relapse.

menkuş (. —) A *lrnd*. 1. drawn as a picture. 2. ornamented, colored, painted. 3. impressed on the memory.

menkut (. —) A *lrnd*. 1. spotted; dotted (letter). 2. date verse in which only the dotted letters are reckoned.

menkuz (. —) A *lrnd*. taken to pieces; demolished; annulled.

mennaᵃ¹ (. —) A *lrnd*. one who strongly prohibits; hinderer; refuser.

mennah (. —) A *lrnd*. giver, bestower; God as the All-Gracious.

mennan (. —) A *lrnd*. very kind and munificent; God as the All-Bounteous.

mennane (. —.) A *lrnd*. married for her wealth and taunting her husband with his obligation to her (woman).

menolun=ᵘʳ to be prevented or forbidden.

menopoz F *physiol*. menopause.

mensec A *lrnd*. weaver's workshop.

mensekᵏⁱ A *lrnd*. 1. a being religious; piety, devotion. 2. place of sacrifice, especially in the valley of Mina near Mecca. 3. religious rites and ceremonies of sacrifice, especially of the pilgrimage of Islam. 4. religious worship; place of worship.

mensi (. —) A *lrnd*. forgotten, neglected.

mensim A *lrnd*. 1. foot of a camel 2. mark, sign, trace. 3. way, road, path. 4. mode, manner, aspect.

mensiyat (. . —) A *lrnd*., *pl*. of **mensi**.

mensub (.—) منسوب A /a/ related to, connected with, belonging to.

mensubat (.——) منسوبات A lrnd. 1. things related or attributed to a person, thing, or place. 2. one's relatives.

mensubin (.——) منسوبين A lrnd. those connected with a person or place.

mensubiyet (.———.) منسوبيت A relationship; connection; membership (of a society, etc.).

mensûc (.—) منسوج A 1. lrnd. woven; textile. 2. lrnd. interwoven.

mensucat (.——) منسوجات A textiles.

mensûh (.—) منسوخ A lrnd. canceled, annulled, abolished. —**iyet** (.——.) A obliteration, annulment.

mensûkᵏᵘ (.—) منسوك A lrnd. ranged in a line, row or series; arranged.

mensupᵇᵘ (.—) منسوب var. of **mensub**.

mensûr (.—) منثور A lrnd. 1. in prose, not metrical. 2. scattered, strewed.

menşeᵉⁱ منشأ A 1. place of origin; source; beginning; root. 2, qualification, degree (education). — **işaretleri** com. indication of origin. — **şehadetnamesi** com. certificate of origin.

menşele منشل A lrnd. ring joint of the little finger.

menşeli منشألى originating from, exported from.

menşur (.—) منشور A lrnd. 1. diffused, scattered, published. 2. geom. prism. 3. royal patent of rank, office, etc. —**i kaim** rectangular prism. —**i mail** geom. oblique prism. —**î** (.——) A prismatic.

menşurnüvis (.—..) منشورنويس P lrnd. writer of letters-patent. —**an-ı bağ** nightingales; larks.

menta (.'.) منتا Gk peppermint.

menteşe منتشا hinge.

menteşeli منتشألى 1. hinged. 2. w. cap., name of a Turkish Prince who, following the fall of the Seljuk dynasty, founded a sovereign principality in southwest Asia Minor.

menun (.—) منون A lrnd. 1. time; the world. 2. death; fate.

me'nus (.—) مأنوس A lrnd. 1. to which one is accustomed, familiarized. 2. in common use; current; usual, habitual. —**iyet** (.——.) A familiarity, habit.

menut (.—) منوط A lrnd. /a/ depending on; bound to.

menvi (.—) منوى A lrnd. intended; intention, purpose.

menzele منزل A lrnd. 1. station, rank, dignity, post of honor. 2. stopping place.

menzil منزل A 1. halting place; station; goal, place of destination. 2. lrnd. stage, day's journey. 3. lrnd. inn, caravanserai; house, mansion; hotel. 4. artillery range (of a gun). 5. mil. transport branch of an army; lines of communication. 6. astrol. mansion of the moon. — **arabası** obs. stagecoach, diligence. — **beygiri** obs. post horse. — **boz**═ archery to break a record. —**i ceberut** myst. the state of direct relation with the divine attributes. — **dik**═ archery to erect a stone at the place where the record-breaking arrow falls. —**i maksuda ulaş**═ to attain one's object. — **oku** arrow shot to a great distance. — **sür**═ archaic to travel with all speed. — **taşı** archery stone erected at the place where the arrow of the best competitor falls and on which the name of the winner and the date of the occasion was inscribed. — **topu** long range gun. —**ine var**═ to reach one's destination.

menzilci منزلجى post rider, courier.

menzile, menzilet منزلت A lrnd. high station, rank. —**li, —lû** (...—) high in rank, honorable.

menzilgâh (..—), **menzilgeh** منزلگاه P lrnd. halting place.

menzilhane (..—.) منزلخانه P lrnd. posting house for horses. —**ci** man in charge of a post station for horses.

menzilli منزللى 1. having a range of; long ranged. 2. having stages.

menzilşinas (...—) منزلشناس P lrnd. 1. one who knows stations and camping grounds. 2. one who knows his own station; holy man.

menzuᵘᵘ (.—) منزوع A lrnd. plucked out, torn up.

menzûf (.—) منزوف A lrnd. 1. weakened by loss of blood. 2. parched with thirst; one whose tongue is dry from thirst.

menzûlˡᵘ (.—) منزول A lrnd. paralyzed; suffering from apoplexy.

menzûr (.—) منذور A lrnd. vowed, promised, dedicated.

merʳ¹ مرء A lrnd. man.

mer'a (.—) مرعى A pasture, pasturage.

meraciⁱⁱ (.—.) مراجع A lrnd., pl. of **merci**.

meradet (.—.) مرادت A lrnd. a being or becoming perversely obstinate; obstinate and rebellious perversity.

merafıkᵏⁱ (.—.) مرافق A lrnd., pl. of **mirfak**.

merah (.—) مراح A lrnd. place of repose; home.

merahan (.——) مراحاً A lrnd. joyousness, gladness; exuberant joy, turbulent mirth.

merahil (.—.) مراحل A lrnd., pl. of **merhale**.

merahim 1 (.—.) مراحم A lrnd., pl. of **merhamet**.

merahim 2 (.—.) مراهم A lrnd., pl. of **merhem**.

merai (.—.) مراعى A lrnd., pl. of **mer'a**.

merakᵏⁱ (.—) مراك A 1. curiosity. 2. whim,

passion, great interest, fancy; caprice. 3. anxiety; depression; *med.* hypochondria, melancholy. —**ta bırak**= /ı/ to cause anxiety (to someone). —**tan çatla**= to become extremely curious. —**ına dokun**= 1. /ın/ to make one uneasy, to alarm one (matter). 2. to become uneasy and troubled. — **edin**= /ı/ to take up a whim. — **et**= 1. /ı/ to be anxious about a person. 2. /ı/ to be curious (about). 3. /a/ to be greatly interested (in something), to have a passion (for a thing). — **etme** Don't worry. — **getir**= to have melancholia, to become a hypochondriac. —**ı kalk**= /ın/ to become curious or interested (about). —**ını mucib ol**= /ın/ to excite someone's curiosity. —**ı ol**= /a/ to have a passion for; to make a hobby of something. — **sar**= /a/ to have a great passion for, to devote oneself to a hobby.

Merakeş (. —.) مراكش *geog.* Morocco.
merakıd (. —.) مراقد A *lrnd.*, pl. of **merkad**.
merakî (. ——) مراقى 1. whimsical. 2. afflicted with unfounded fears; hypochondriac.
merakib (. —.) مراكب A *lrnd.*, pl. of **merkeb**. —**i bahriye** sea transportation. —**i berriye** overland transportation.
merakiz (. —.) مراكز A *lrnd.*, pl. of **merkez**.
meraklan="مراقلنمق to be anxious. —**dır**= /ı/ *caus.*
meraklı مراقلى 1. whimsical; anxious; sensitive. 2. curious, inquisitive. 3. /a/ interested in, fond of. 4. meticulous, particular, extremely careful. —**lık** curiosity; anxiety.
meraksız مراقسز 1. careless; untroubled, insensitive. 2. uninterested, indifferent. —**lık** indifference, lack of interest.
meralli (. —) مرال doe, roe.
mer'alık (. —.) مرعالق well pastured; pasturage.
meram (. —) مرام A intention, purpose, aim; desire. — **anlat**= /a/ to explain what is meant. —**ını anlat**= to explain oneself. — **et**= /a/ to intend, wish, design to do.
meramet (. —.) مرامت [**meremmet**] a repairing; temporary repairs. — **et**= /ı/ to repair temporarily, to patch up. —**çi** mender, tinker, cobbler.
merametle=r مرامتلك /ı/ to mend in a rough manner. —**n**= *pass.* —**t**= /ı, a/ *caus.* of **merametle**=.
meramsızlıkti مرامسزلوك *psych.* abulia, loss of will power.
meranet (. —.) مرانت A 1. *lrnd.* softness; smoothness. 2. *phys.* ductility.
merare (. —.) مراره A *anat.* gall bladder.
meraret (. —.) مرارت A *lrnd.* a being bitter, bitterness. —**li** bitter, painful.
merasıd (. —.) مراصد A *lrnd.*, pl. of **mırsad**.
merasi 1 (. ——) مراسى A *lrnd.*, pl. of **mersa**.

merasi 2 (. ——) مراثى A *lrnd.*, pl. of **mersiye**.
merasim 1 (. —.) مراسم A 1. ceremonies; established usages; celebrations. 2. ceremony, commemoration. 3. protocol. —**i aza** *lrnd.* the ceremonial duties of mourning or condolence. — **duruşu** *mil.* review order. — **geçişi** *mil.* ceremonial parade review. — **kıt'ası** military detachment taking part in ceremonies. —**i pursîş-i hâtır** *lrnd.* inquiries after one's health.
merasim 2 (. ——) مراسيم A *lrnd.*, pl. of **mersûm**.
merasimperest (. —...) مراسيمپرست P *lrnd.* devoted to established usages; formalist.
meraşid (. —.) مراشد A *lrnd.*, pl. of **merşed**.
mer'at (. —) مرآت A *lrnd.* aspect, appearance; beautiful look.
meratili (. —.) مراتع A *lrnd.*, pl. of **merta**.
meratib (. —.) مراتب A *lrnd.*, pl. of **mertebe**. — **silsilesi** stages of appeal; the usual channels.
mer'atilayn (. —..) مرآتالعينين A *lrnd.* outward appearance.
meravih 1 (. —.) مراوح A *lrnd.*, pl. of **mirvaha**.
meravih 2 (. ——) مراويح A *lrnd.*, pl. of **mervaha**.
Meravize (. —..) مراوزه A *lrnd.*, pl. of **Mervezi**.
meraya (. ——) مرايا A *lrnd.*, pl. of **mir'at**.
merazibe (. —..) مرازبه A *lrnd.*, pl. of **merzüban**.
merbai مربع A *lrnd.* dwelling place for the spring or autumn season. —**nişin** (... —) P inhabitant of a spring resort.
merbat مربط A *lrnd.* place where cattle are tied; stable, stall.
merbub (. —) مربوب A *lrnd.* one who has a lord or master; slave.
merbut (. —) مربوط A 1. bound, tied; attached, appended, connected. 2. dependent. 3. captive balloon. — **kıt'alar** *mil.* undivisioned units. — **ol**= /a/ 1. to be attached, appended, to be tied, connected. 2. to depend, to be dependent on.
merbutat (. ——) مربوطات A *lrnd.* attached documents; attachments.
merbuten (. —'.) مربوطا A *lrnd.* attached as an appendage.
merbutiyet (. —..) مربوطيت A 1. devotion; attachment. 2. connection. 3. dependence.
merc 1 مرج A *lrnd.* meadow, grass plot.
merc 2 مرج A *lrnd.* disturbance, mixture, confusion.
mercan مرجان [*Arabic* .—] coral, *zool.*, *Corallium rubrum;* made of coral. — **ada**, — **adası** atoll, coral island. — **balığı** red sea bream, *zool.*, *Pagellus erythrinus*, *Pagrus*

mercanköşk

†*pagrus*. — **biberi** cherry pepper, *bot.*, *Capsicum cerasiforme*. — **çiçeği** coral creeper, **coral pea**, *bot.*, *Kennedya*. — **kayaları** coral reef, atoll. — **kırı** roan (horse). — **odunu** red sandalwood tree, *bot.*, *Adenanthera pavonina*. — **otu** pearlweed, pearlwort, *bot.*, *Sagina procumbens*. — **terlikleri** red leather slippers. — **yılanı** coral snake, *zool.*, *Micrurus corallinus*.

mercanköşkᵏᵘ مرجان گوشك [**mercengûş**] sweet marjoram, *bot.*, *Majorana hortensis*.

mercanlar *neol.*, *zool.*, *Corallidae*.

mercekᵍⁱ *neol.* lens.

mercengûş (..—) مرجن گوش [**merzenguş**] same as **mercanköşk**.

merciⁱⁱ مرجع A 1. place to which recourse is made; source to which a thing is referred; recourse, reference. 2. competent authority; department or office concerned. —**i hâs ü âm** person to whom all classes have recourse. —**i kül** place to which all recourse is made.

mercimekᵍⁱ مرجمك P lentil, *bot.*, *Lens esculenta*. —**ği fırına ver**= to have a secret love affair; to come to terms (with). — **kemiği** *anat.* lenticular bone, — **taşı** *geol.* pisolite.

mercûᵘᵘ (.—) مرجو A *lrnd.* 1. requested; asked for. 2. hoped; expected.

mercuh (.—) مرجوح A *lrnd.* 1. preferred. 2. outweighed, excelled, surpassed. —**iyet** (.——.) A superiority.

mercum (.—) مرجوم A *lrnd.* stoned to death.

mercülbahreyn (...—) مرج البحرين A *lrnd.* place where two seas unite; place where Mevlana Jalaleddin Rumî and Shams-i Tabrizî first encountered each other.

merd مرد *same as* **mert** 1. —**i garib** stranger, foreigner. —**i Hüda** man of God; saint. —**i merdan** a man among men, one excelling amongst others. —**i neberd** warrior, soldier.

merdan (.—) مردان P *lrnd.*, *pl. of* **merd**. —**ı merd** a man worth many men. —**ı ulvî** 1. the seven planets. 2. seven spiritual beings held to be guides and rulers of the faithful.

merdane 1 (.—.) مردانه P *lrnd.* manly, in a brave manner.

merdane 2 (.—.) مردانه [**verdane**] 1. printer's inking cylinder. 2. rolling pin; roller.

merdanegî (.—.—) مردانگى P *lrnd.* manliness.

merdbeçe مرد بچه P *lrnd.* brave son of a brave father.

merdefgen مردافگن P *lrnd.* (*lit.*, that overthrows men) heroic, powerful; warrior.

merdevjen مردوژن P *lrnd.* brave; hero.

merdî (.—) مردى P *lrnd.* manliness; virility, valor; bravery.

merdiven مردوبن مردبون مردون [Persian

nerdban] ladder; steps; stairs, staircase. — **babası** newel of a staircase. — **basamağı** step of a staircase. — **böğürü** *arch.* string board. — **daya**= /a/ to be nearing (a certain age), *e. g.*, **kırkına merdiven daya**= to be nearing one's forties. — **korkuluğu** balustrade of a staircase. — **sahanlığı** landing on a staircase, stair-head.

merdud (.—) A, **merdut**ᵈᵘ (.—) مردود *lrnd.* rejected, repulsed; rebutted. —**iyet** (.—..) A rejectedness.

merdüm مردم P *lrnd.* man, human being, person. —**i çeşm** pupil of the eye. —**ân** (..—) P *pl.*

merdümâzar (..——) مردم آزار P *lrnd.* mantormenting, oppressor.

merdümekᵏⁱ مردمك P *lrnd.* 1. little man. 2. pupil of the eye. 3. lentil.

merdümevbâr (...—) مردم اوبار P *lrnd.* man-consuming; vampire.

merdümgiriz (...—) مردم گریز P *lrnd.* misanthrope; misanthropic; unsociable.

merdümhar (..—) مردم خوار P *lrnd.* cannibal, man-eating; tyrant.

merdümhiz (..—) مردم خیز P *lrnd.* where men abound, populous (country).

merdümhor مردم خور P *lrnd.* devouring men; fierce warrior.

merdümî (..—) مردمى P *lrnd.* 1. human nature, humanity. 2. bravery, generosity.

merdümkeş مردم كش P *lrnd.* leader.

merdümküş مردم كش P *lrnd.* murderer; murderous.

merdümnüvaz (...—) مردم نواز P *lrnd.* courteous, kind. —**î** (...——) P, —**lık** courtesy, kindness.

merdümperest مردم پرست P *lrnd.* hero worshipper.

merdümpira (..——) مردم پیرا P *lrnd.* teacher; guide, leader.

merdümzad (..—), **merdümzâde** (..—.) مردم زاده مردم زاد P *lrnd.* man, human, human being.

me'rebe مأربه A *lrnd.* a business, matter of business.

merede مرده A *lrnd.*, *pl. of* **mârid**.

merekᵍⁱ مرك *prov.* barn.

meremet مرمت *var. of* **meremmet**.

meremmet مرمت A *lrnd.*, *same as* **meramet**.

meret مرت [Arabic **marid**] damned person; cursed thing.

merfuᵘᵘ (.—) مرفوع A *lrnd.* 1. raised, elevated; exalted, removed to a higher place or station. 2. removed, abolished. 3. *Arabic gram.* marked with the vowel point **zamma**.

merg 1 مرگ P *lrnd.* meadow, pasturage.

merg 2 مرگ P *lrnd.* death.

mergâmerg (. — .), **mergamergî** (. — . —) مَرگامَرگ مَرگامَرگی P lrnd. plague, pestilence.

mergûb (. —) A, **mergup**^bu (. —) مَرغوب lrnd. desirable, desired; longed for, sought after. **—iyet** (. — —.) A desirability.

mergzar (. —) مَرغزار P lrnd. meadow, park, wood. **—ı ukba** Paradise.

merhaba (.'..) مَرحبا A 1. Hello. Good day. Greetings. How do you do? Welcome! 2. lrnd. Be at ease. Be in comfort. **—yı kes=** /la/ to terminate one's friendly relations (with someone). **—sı ol=** /la/ to have a slight aquaintance (with somebody). **— siperi** loophole in the wall just facing the inner facade of a fortress gate (for the defense of the stronghold when the enemy succeeds in forcing the gate).

merhabalaş=^ır مَرحبالاشمق /la/ to greet one another.

merhale مَرحَله A 1. stage; phase. 2. a day's journey. **— merhale** by stages.

merhamet مَرحمَت A mercy, compassion; pity; tenderness of heart; kindness. **—e gel=** to become merciful. **— maraz getirir** proverb He who is kind may suffer for it.

merhametdisar (....—) مَرحمَت دثار P lrnd. full of mercy, compassionate.

merhameten (...'.) مَرحمةً A for mercy's sake; kindly.

merhametgüster مَرحمَتگستر P lrnd. merciful, kind. **—î** (.....—) P mercifulness, tenderness.

merhametli مَرحمَتلی merciful; tender-hearted, kind.

merhametpenah (....—) مَرحمَتپناه P lrnd. merciful.

merhametperver مَرحمَتپرور P lrnd. mercifulness, pitying. **—âne** (.....—.) P mercifully. **—î** (.....—) P mercifulness.

merhametsiz مَرحمَتسز merciless, pitiless. **—lik** mercilessness, cruelty.

merhametşiar (....—) مَرحمَت شعار P lrnd. merciful, kind. **—î** (....——) P mercifulness.

Merhasa مَرحَصا Syriac hist. Armenian bishop.

merhem مَرهَم A same as **melhem**.

merhemsaz (..—) مَرهَمساز P lrnd. cure, healing.

merhûb (. —) مَرهوب A lrnd. feared, dreaded, dreadful; lion.

merhûm (. —) مَرحوم A one whom God has taken into his mercy; deceased, the late.

merhume (. — .) مَرحومه A deceased (woman).

merhûn (. —) مَرهون A law 1. pledge, pawned. 2. contingent.

merhûz (. —) مَرحوض A lrnd. 1. washed (cloth). 2. thrown into a sweat by an attack of fever.

mer'i 1 (. —) مَرعی A law 1. observed, in force, valid. 2. respected.

mer'i 2 (. —) مَرئی A lrnd. visible, seen.

meri 3 (. —) مَری A gullet, anat. esophagus.

Meriç^cı مَریچ geog. the Maritza River.

merîd (. —) مَرید A lrnd. obstinately rebellious, stubborn, perverse.

meridyen مَریدین F geog. meridian. **— dairesi** meridian circle. **— düzlem** neol. meridian plane.

Merih مَریخ A astr. the planet Mars. **—li** Martian.

merinos مَرینوس Sp. merino (sheep).

mer'iyat (..—) مَرئیات A lrnd. visible objects.

mer'îyülicra (.—..—) مَرعی الاجرا A lrnd. observed, in force.

Meriye مَریه geog. Almaria in Spain.

mer'iyet (.—.) مَرعیّت A a being valid or in validity. **—e gir=** to come into force.

merkad مَرقَد A lrnd. 1. resting place, bed. 2. grave, tomb; mausoleum, sepulcher.

merkeb A, **merkep**^bı مَرکَب 1. donkey, ass. 2. lrnd. mount (horse, etc.); ship. **—çi** donkeyman.

merkez مَرکَز A 1. center; administrative center, capital; central office. 2. police station; mil. main force. 3. manner, condition, e. g., **vaziyet bu merkezde** This is how the matter stands. 4. lrnd. where a spear etc. is driven into the ground to stand. **— kumandanı** garrison commander. **—i kürrî** lrnd. geocentric. **—i sıklet** 1. phys. center of gravity; focal point. 2. mil. center of combat, principal attack. **—ci** adherent of centralization. **—cil** neol. centripetal.

merkezî (..—) مَرکَزی A central; principal, main.

merkezileş=^ır مَرکَزیلَشمك to centralize. **—tir=** /ı/ caus.

merkeziyet (..—.) مَرکَزیّت A a being central; centralization.

merkezkaç neol., phys. centrifugal. **— kuvvet** centrifugal force.

merkezlen=^ır مَرکَزلَنمك 1. to center. 2. to be centralized. **—dir=** /ı/ caus.

merkûb (. —) مَرکوب A lrnd. 1. ridden, mounted. 2. shoe, boot, overshoe.

merkum (. —) مَرقوم A lrnd. 1. the said (person), the above-mentioned (used contemptuously). 2. marked, written; recorded. **—ân** (. — —) P pl. **—e** (. — .) A fem. of **merkum**. **—ûn** (. — —) A pl. of **merkum**.

merkûz (. —) مَرکوز A lrnd. 1. erected, set up. 2. implanted; fixed, fastened. **—iyet** (. — —.) A erectness; implantation.

Merkür مَرکور F astr. Mercury (planet).

merlânos مَرلانوس It whiting (fish), zool., Merlangus merlangus:

merlengeç

merlengeç[ci] مرلنگیج mastic tree, *bot., Pistacia lentiscus.*
merlos مرلوس It hake (fish), *zool., Merluccius vulgaris.*
mermahûr (. — —) مرما هور A enchanter's nightshade, *bot., Circaae lutetiana.*
mermer مرمر A marble. **— gibi** 1. like marble; hard, unfeeling. 2. quite white. **— kaymağı** prepared chalk. **— kireci** lime from burned marble. **— ocağı** marble quarry. **— sıva** finest hard-finish stucco. **— taklidi** marbling, scagliola. **— tülbendi** book muslin. **—ci** 1. marble cutter. 2. seller of marble. **—lik** marble paving.
mermerşahî مرمرشاهى book muslin.
mermi مرمى A projectile, shell. **— yolu** *mil.* trajectory. **—iyat** (. . —) A *lrnd., pl.*
mermuz (. —) مرموز A *lrnd.* 1. expressed by signs, indicated symbolically. 2. suggested obscurely, hinted at. **—ât** (. — —) A things indicated, indicated symbolically.
merrat (. —) مرّات A *lrnd., pl.* of **merre** many times, repeatedly. **—la** (. —.) repeatedly, again and again.
merre مرّة A *lrnd.* one time, once. **—i vâhide** one time, only once.
merretân (. . —) مرّتان A *lrnd.* two times, twice.
merreten (. . .) مرّةً A *lrnd.* at one time, once. **— bâde merreten, — bâde uhra** time after time, repeatedly.
mersa (. —) مرسى مرسا A *lrnd.* anchorage, harbor, port.
merserize مرسریزه F *text.* mercerized.
mersin 1 مرسين [A .—] 1. myrtle, *bot., Myrtus communis.* 2. sturgeon, *zool., Acipenser sturio.* **— marinası** the largest kind of sturgeon, *zool., Acipenser huso.*
Mersin 2 مرسين *geog.,* name of a coastal town in Turkey.
mersiye مرثیه A elegy; dirge.
mersiyehan (. . . —) مرثیه خوان P *lrnd.* reciter of elegies, dirge singer. **—î** (. . . — —) P, **—lık** dirge singing.
mersûd (. —) مرصود A *lrnd.* observed, watched (star, etc.); lain in wait for.
mersûm (. —) مرسوم A *lrnd.* 1. drawn, designed; traced. 2. mentioned; abovementioned, aforesaid (was used in referring to Christians in the Ottoman Empire). 3. accustomed, usual. 4. *Ott. hist.* stipend authorized by warrant; tax authorized by edict.
mersumat (. — —) مرسومات A *Ott. hist.* 1. things authorized or commanded. 2. taxes.
mersûmhar (. — —) مرسوم خوار P *Ott. hist.* stipendiary, person on salary.
mersus (. —) مرصوص A *lrnd.* strong, solid, cemented.

merşed مرشد A *lrnd.* the right way; a firm resolution.
mert[di] **1** مرد [**merd**] 1. man. 2. brave, manly man, manly. 3. fine in character; dependable; decent.
mert 2 مرت P *lrnd.* alive; energetic; active.
mertçe مردجه in a manly manner, straightforwardly.
merta[aı] (. —) مرتع A *lrnd.* pasture, pasturage.
mertebanî (. . — —) مرتبانى A *lrnd.* a kind of bluish green pottery originally made at Martaban; bluish green. **— tabak** plate, etc. of Japan ware, Celadon ware.
mertebe مرتبه A 1. degree; rank, grade; position. 2. *math.* order. 3. *lrnd.* step, stair. **—i âliye** a high degree. **—i bâlâ** superior degree. **—ler silsilesi** hierarchy, hierarchical order.
mertebet مرتبة A *lrnd.* rank, degree.
mertek[gi] مرتك squared balk of timber, beam, post.
mertlik[gi] مردلك bravery; manliness.
mertûb (. —) مرطوب A *lrnd.* moist, juicy.
mer'ûb (. —) مرعوب A *lrnd.* frightened. **—en** (. —'.) A in fear.
merv مرو P marjoram, *bot., Origanum.*
mervaha مروحه A *lrnd.* windy place, desert.
mervarid (. — —) مرواريد P *lrnd.* pearl.
Mervezî (. . —) مروزى A *lrnd.* from the city of Merv.
mervî (. —) مروى A *lrnd.* related, narrated, told; tradition.
Meryem مريم A Mary, Miriam. **— Ana** the virgin Mary. **— Ana fırtınası** name of a storm occurring about the middle of October. **— eli** rose of jericho, *bot., Anastatica hierochuntica.* **—iye** (. . —.) common sage, garden sage, *bot., Salvia officinalis.*
merz مرز P *lrnd.* 1. limit, border; frontier district. 2. land, cultivated field.
merza (. —) مرضى A *lrnd., pl.* of **mariz 1.**
merzaga مرزغه A *lrnd.* marshy place, bog.
merzagi (. . —) مرزغى A *lrnd.* marshy.
merzat (. —) مرضات A *lrnd.* a being pleased, satisfied; satisfaction, pleasure.
merzban (. —) مرزبان P *lrnd.* warden of a frontier.
merzbum (. —) مرزبوم P *lrnd.* region, country.
merzencûş (. . —) مرزنجوش A same as **mercanköşk.**
merzengûş (. . —) مرزنگوش P *lrnd.,* same as **mercanköşk.**
merzûk[ku] (. —) مرزوق A *lrnd.* fed, rationed; possessed of all necessaries and comforts; fortunate, lucky. **—at** (. — —) A rations. **—iye** (. . — —.) food ration.

merzulᵘ (.—) مرذول A lrnd. treated with contempt; disgraced.
merzüban (..—) مرذبان A lrnd., same as **merzban**.
merzübum (..—) مرزبوم P lrnd. country, place of residence.
mesˢˢⁱ 1 مس A lrnd. 1. a touching; contact, touch. **—i cünun** a touch of insanity. **— et=***. **—i hacet** case of necessity, case.
mes 2 مس colloq., for **mest** 1.
mesa (.—) مسا A lrnd. evening.
mesaat (.—.) مساءت A lrnd. a doing evil to another, an ill-treating, offending.
mesab (.—) مثاب A lrnd. a place of assembly; a place to which one returns, a dwelling.
mesabe (.—.) مثابه A lrnd. point, degree; quality, nature. **—sinde** of the nature of; in the position of, e. g., **müdür mesabesinde** in the position of a director.
mesacid (.—.) مساجد A lrnd., pl. of **mescid**.
mes'adet مسعدت A lrnd. happiness; fortune.
mesafᶠⁱ مصف A lrnd. place where ranks are drawn up; battlefield.
mesafât (.— —) مسافات A lrnd., pl. of **mesafe**.
mesafe (.—.) مسافه A distance; space, interval. **— modülü** astr. distance modulus. **— ölçme âleti** range finder.
mesağ (.—) مساغ A can. law lawfulness; permissibility. **—i şer'i** canonical permissibility.
mesaha (.—.) مساحه A a measuring, measurement of land; a surveying; measure (of road, field, etc.). **— et=** /ı/ to measure (land, etc.). **— fenni**, **— ilmi** science of surveying, mensuration. **— memuru** surveyor. **—i sathiye** math. superficies; superficial area. **— şeridi** tape measure (of a surveyor). **— zinciri** measuring chain.
mesahatᵗⁱ (.—.) مساحت A lrnd., same as **mesaha**.
mesahif (.—.) مصاحف A lrnd., pl. of **mushaf**.
mesai (.— —) مساعى A efforts, work; activities. **— saatleri** working hours.
mesaib (.—.) مصائب A lrnd., pl. of **musibet**.
mesail (.—.) مسائل A lrnd., pl. of **mesele**. **—i şetta** various problems, different matters.
mesaj مساژ F message, notice.
mesakᵏⁱ (.—) مساق A lrnd. 1. place of driving. 2. an urging onward; impulse, momentum.
mesakıt (.—.) مساقط A lrnd., pl. of **maskat**.
mesakin 1 (.—.) ساكن A lrnd., pl. of **mesken**.
mesakin 2 (.— —) مساكين A lrnd., pl. of **miskin** 1.
mesalib (.—.) مثالب A lrnd., pl. of **meslebe**.
mesalih (.—.) مصالح A lrnd., var. of **masalih**.
mesalikᵏⁱ (.—.) مسالك A lrnd., pl. of **meslek**.

mesalis (.—.) مثالث A lrnd., pl. of **mesles**.
mesamᵐᵐⁱ (.—) مسام A lrnd., pl. of **mesemme**.
mesamat (.— —) مسامات A lrnd., pl. of **mesame**.
mesame (.—.) مسامه [Arabic **mesam**] lrnd. pore, hole. **—li** porous.
mesamiⁱⁱ (.—.) مسامع A lrnd., pl. of **misma**.
mesamîr (.— —) مسامير A lrnd., pl. of **mismar**. **—î** (.— — —) A pertaining to nails.
mesane (.—.) مثانه A anat. urinary bladder.
mesani (.— —) مثانى A lrnd. 1. pl. of **mesna**, **mesnat**. 2. verses recited repeatedly, especially the **Fatiha**. 3. the Quran; a section of the Quran.
mesanid (.—.) مساند A lrnd., pl. of **mesned**.
mesarʳⁿ (.—) مسار A lrnd., pl. of **meserret**.
mesatır (.—.) مساطر A lrnd., pl. of **mistar**.
mesavi 1 (.— —) مساوى A lrnd. evil acts or states.
mesavi 2 (.— —) مساوى A lrnd., pl. of **mesva**.
mesba'a مسبعه A lrnd. region abounding with lions and other ferocious beasts.
mesbukᵏᵘ 1 (.—) مسبوق A lrnd. 1. preceded, having a precedent. 2. surpassed, outrun. **— hizmetine binaen** for services rendered by him.
mesbukᵏᵘ 2 مسبوك A lrnd. cast in a mould.
mescen مسجن A lrnd. prison, jail.
mescid A, **mescit**ᵈⁱ مسجد 1. small mosque. 2. lrnd. place of worship, temple. **M—i Aksa** the mosque just south of the Dome of the Rock, in Jerusalem. **M—i Haram**, **M—i Şerif** The mosque which surrounds the Kaaba of Mecca. **M—i Zırar** a mosque set up near Medina to distract the community of Islam and demolished by command of the Prophet Muhammad.
mescud (.—) مسجود A lrnd. worshipped, adored. **M—i Melek Adam** (before whom the angels were commanded to prostrate themselves).
mescum (.—) مسجوم A lrnd. flowing, shed (tears).
mescun (.—) مسجون A lrnd. imprisoned; prisoner.
mesdud (.—) مسدود A lrnd. shut, closed; obstructed; barred; plugged up.
me'sede مأسده A lrnd. place abounding with lions; a lion's haunt.
mesel مثل A 1. proverb; parable, saying. 2. instance, example. **— kur=** archaic to quote a parable. **— ol=** to become a parable. **— ur=** archaic, same as **mesel kur=**.
meselâ (..—) مثلا A for example, for instance.

mes'ele A, **mesele** سَائِل مَسْئَلة 1. problem, question, matter; point under consideration; affair. 2. thesis, proposition. 3. *lrnd.* an asking alms. — **çıkar=** 1. to raise a question. 2. to make a fuss (about something). **—i müste'hire** *obs., law* prejudicial question; interrogatory action. **—i nâs** *lrnd., law* money or things collected as alms.

mesem[mmi] مَسَمّ A, *lrnd.* eye of a needle; small hole, pore.

meserret مَسَرَّت A a being joyful; joy, rejoicing. **—âver** (...—.) P *lrnd.* joyful. **— bahş** P *lrnd.* joy-inspiring. **—efza** (....—) P *lrnd.* joy-increasing. **—engiz** (....—) P *lrnd.* mirth-exciting. **—üslûb** (....—) P *lrnd.* joyful.

mesfû[uu] (.—) مَسْفُوع A *lrnd.* smitten with the evil eye.

mesfûh (.—) مَسْفُوح A *lrnd.* poured out; shed.

mesfûk[kü] (.—) مَسْفُوك A *lrnd.* shed, spilled (blood).

mesfûr (.—) مَسْفُور A *lrnd.* written; above-mentioned (not used about respected persons).

mesgabe مَسْغَبَة A *lrnd.* hunger.

mesh 1 مَسْح A *lrnd.* a wiping a thing with the palm of the hand; an anointing; a stroking, rubbing. **—i cebin et=** to place the forehead on the ground as a sign of reverence. **— ver=** *same as* **mesver=**.

mesh 2 مَسْخ A *lrnd.* 1. a changing a man into a beast; metamorphosis; a deforming. 2. a plagiarizing; plagiarism.

meshet=[der] مَسْح ایتمك 1. to wipe with the palm of the hand especially in ablution. 2. to anoint.

meshuf (.—) مَسْهُوف A *lrnd.* 1. afflicted with unquenchable thirst. 2. greatly desirous.

meshuk[ku] (.—) مَسْحُوك A *lrnd.* 1. pounded, pulverized. 2. bruised.

meshur (.—) مَسْحُور A *lrnd.* enchanted, bewitched, charmed.

meshut (.—) مَسْحُوط A *lrnd.* disapproved, hated; unsightly, hateful.

Mesih 1 (.—) مَسِيح A 1. the Messiah, the Anointed, Jesus Christ. 2. *l. c.* wiped with the hand; anointed. **M—i Deccal** Antichrist.

mesih 2 (.—) مَسِيخ A *lrnd.* metamorphosed, changed into a beast; deformed, hideous; monster.

Mesiha (.—.) مَسِيحا A *lrnd.* the Messiah; Christ. **—dem** (.—..) P, **—nefes** (.—...) P *lrnd.* having healing breath like Jesus.

Mesihî (.——) مَسِيحى A *lrnd.* pertaining to Christ, Christian. **—yet** (.——.) A Christianity. **—yun** (.————) A Christians.

mesil 1 (.—) مَسِيل A *lrnd.* river bed, stream of water.

mesil 2 (.—) مَثِيل A *lrnd.* like, similar.

mesir (.—) مَسِير A *lrnd.* 1. an act of going; motion. 2. orbit; period. 3. rate, pace. **—i has proper** motion of a body. **—i mutedil** equable motion. **—i şems** the ecliptic. **—i vasat** mean motion.

mesire (.—.) مَسِيرَة A 1. promenade, excursion spot. 2. *lrnd.* space traveled in a given time; a journeying. **—gâh** (.—.—) P excursion spot.

meskat 1 مَسْقَط A *lrnd., same as* **maskat**.

meskat 2 (.—) مَسْقاط A *lrnd.* place of drinking; drinking fountain; bucket.

mesken مَسْكَن A dwelling, house; home. **— masuniyeti** *law* inviolability of one's house, security of domicile. **— zammı** allowance for lodging.

meskenet مَسْكَنَت A *lrnd.* 1. poverty. 2. lack of spirit, sluggishness.

meskub[bu] **1** (.—) مَسْقُوب A *lrnd.* bored, pierced.

meskûb[bu] **2** (.—) مَسْكُوب A *lrnd.* 1. poured out, shed. 2. molded.

meskûk[kü] (.—) مَسْكُوك A *lrnd.* coined (money). **—at** (.——) A 1. coins. 2. numismatics.

meskûn[nu] (.—) مَسْكُون A inhabited, habitable. **— yer** settlement.

meskût (.—) مَسْكُوت A *lrnd.* silenced; passed over in silence. **— geç=** /ı/ to keep silence (about a matter).

meslah مَسْلَح A *lrnd.* place where animals are slaughtered, slaughterhouse, shambles.

meslebe مَسْلَبَة A *lrnd.* defect, cause of reproach.

meslek[ği, ki] مَسْلَك A 1. profession, career. 2. *lrnd.* moral character; principle. 3. *lrnd.* mode of acting or thinking, system, way, path. **— hastalıkları** *med.* occupational diseases. **— sahibi** 1. one who has a profession. 2. man of sound principles. **—ten yetişme** professional.

meslekî (..—) مَسْلَكى A of a profession, professional.

meslekli مَسْلَكلى 1. having a profession. 2. *lrnd.* man of principle, principled.

meslekesiz مَسْلَكسز 1. having no profession. 2. *lrnd.* unprincipled. **—lik** 1. a being without profession. 2. unprincipledness.

meslektaş مَسْلَكداش colleague.

mesles مَثَلَّث A *lrnd.* triple twisted or third string of a lute.

meslûb (.—) مَسْلُوب A *lrnd.* 1. seized as spoil, snatched away. 2. stripped, spoiled; robbed (of one's senses).

meslûbülakl (.—..) مَسْلُوب العَقل A *lrnd.* bereft of reason, insane, mad.

meslûh (.—) مَسْلُوخ A *lrnd.* skinned, flayed (sheep).

meslûl[lü] (.—) مَسْلُول A *lrnd.* 1. unsheathed. 2. tuberculosis patient.

meslût (. —) مسلوط A *lrnd.* 1. subjugated to the power of another. 2. thin line of hair about the jaw.

mesmu[uu] (. —) مسمع A *lrnd.* 1. heard; listened to; audible. 2. valid.

mesmuat (. — —) مسموعات A *lrnd.* 1. things heard. 2. rumors, hearsay.

mesmum (. —) مسموم A *lrnd.* 1. poisoned; poisonous. 2. killed by poison. **—en** (. —′.) A by poison, poisoned.

mesmur (. —) مسمور A *lrnd.* 1. nailed, riveted. 2. lean and spare but having the bones and muscles firmly knit together. 3. unhappy, uncomfortable.

mesna, mesnat (. —) مثنى مثنات A *lrnd.* 1. bend, crease. 2. double-twisted or second string of a lute.

mesned مسند A 1. thing leaned upon, support, basis. 2. office of dignity; rank. 3. *phil.* attribute. 4. *mech.* fulcrum. **—i âsudegân** *poet.* the grave. **—i cem** *lrnd.* wind. **M—i Meşihat** *Ott. hist.* rank and position of the Şeyhülislâm.

mesnedârâ (. . — —) مسندآرا P *lrnd.* adorning a high office, a great man.

mesnedgâh (. . —) مسندگاه P *lrnd.* 1. place leaned against or rested upon, support. 2. official residence of a functionary.

mesnednişin (. . . —) مسند نشين P *lrnd.* occupying a high office.

mesnevi (. . —) مثنوى A *pros.* 1. poetry composed in rhymed couplets each couplet being of a different rhyme but the whole of one meter. 2. *w. cap.*, title of several works of this kind, especially the mystical poem of Mevlana Jalaladdin Rumi. **M—i Şerif** the **Mesnevi** of Mevlana Jalaladdin Rumi composed in the thirteenth century.

Mesnevihân (. . — —) مثنوى خوان P *lrnd.* one who recites the **Mesnevi**.

mesneviyat (. . — —) مثنويات A *lrnd.* works written in the form of a **mesnevi**.

mesnun (. —) مسنون A *lrnd.* 1. customary, prescribed by tradition; according to the traditions of the Prophet. 2. circumcised.

mesrah مسرح A *lrnd.* wide pasture, pasturage.

mesrûd (. —) مسرود A *lrnd.* mentioned, set forth, indicated. **—at** (. — —) A *pl.* matters mentioned.

mesruk[ku] (. —) مسروق A *lrnd.* stolen.

mesrur (. —) مسرور A *lrnd.* glad, joyful, happy. **—iyet** (. — —.) A gladness, joy.

messah (. —) مساح A *lrnd.* land measurer, surveyor.

messet=[der] مسيتمك 1. /a/ to touch, to be in contact. 2. to occur, arise (need).

mest 1 مست [mesh 1] light thin-soled boot (worn indoors or inside overshoes). **— pabuç** a set of inner boots and overshoes.

mest 2 مست P 1. drunk, intoxicated. 2. enchanted. **—i elest** *lrnd.* eternally drunk. **—i gurur** *lrnd.* intoxicated with pride. **—i hâb** *lrnd.* sleeping heavily. **—i harab** *lrnd.* dead drunk, intoxicated. **—i müdam** *lrnd.* perpetually drunk; habitual drunkard.

mestan 1 (. —) مستان P *lrnd.* drunkards.

mestan 2 (. —) مستان [*Persian* **mestane**] 1. *lrnd.* who acts as though drunk. 2. *prov.*, common name for a cat.

mestane (. —.) مستانه P *lrnd.* 1. drunken; intoxicated; like a drunkard; intoxicatedly. 2. habitually drunk. **—lik** drunkenness.

mestî (. —) مستى P *lrnd.* 1. intoxication, drunkenness. 2. *myst.* bewilderment arising from contemplation.

mestur 1 (. —) مستور A *lrnd.* 1. concealed, hid, secret. 2. covered, veiled. 3. good, honest, abstaining from what is unlawful.

mestur 2 (. —) مسطور A *lrnd.* 1. written; lined, delineated. 2. abovementioned, aforesaid.

mesture (. —.) مستوره A *lrnd.* 1. modest and virtuous, veiled to all strange men. 2. *lrnd.* covered, hidden, secret, *e. g.*, **tahsisatı mesture**. 3. *obs., law* secret document sent by the judge in order to ascertain the character of a proffered witness.

mesubat (. — —) مثوبات A *lrnd.*, *pl.* of **mesube**.

mesube (. —.) مثوبه A *lrnd.* reward; heavenly reward; recompense.

mes'ud (. —) مسعود A *same as* **mesut**. **—âne** (. — —.) P *lrnd.* happily, in a happy way. **—iyet** (. — —.) *lrnd.* happiness.

me'suf (. —) مأسوف A *lrnd.* vexed, grieved.

mes'ul[lü] (. —) مسئول A 1. /dan/ responsible; answerable. 2. *lrnd.* asked, questioned; demanded, asked for. **— müdür** editor in chief (of a newspaper etc.). **— olmamak şartiyle** *com.* without recourse.

mes'ulat (. — —) مسئولات A *lrnd.* matters asked about, things asked for; petitions, prayers.

mes'uliyet (. — . .) مسئوليت A responsibility; liability. **— kabul etme**= to decline responsibility. **—ten kaç**= to shun responsibility. **— müşteriye ait** *com.* without guarantee. **— satıcıya ait** *com.* guaranteed. **— sigortası** liability insurance.

mes'uliyetli (. — . . .) مسئوليتلى 1. responsible. 2. involving responsibilities.

me'sum (. —) مأثوم A *lrnd.* held guilty of sin, suspected (person).

me'sur 1 (. —) مأثور A *lrnd.* handed down by tradition, traditional; legendary.

me'sur 2 (. —) مأسور A *lrnd.* bound, imprisoned; captive.

mesut[du] (. —) مسعود [**mes'ud**] prosperous

and happy; fortunate, happy; blessed. **—luk** happiness.

mesva (. —) مثوى A *lrnd.* dwelling, residence, home.

mesver=ir مسح دير ملك [mesh ver=] *colloq.* /a/ to wipe the head and feet with wet hands in ablution.

meşacir (. —.) مشاجر A *lrnd., pl. of.* **meşcer, meşcere.**

meşagil (. —.) مشاغل A *lrnd., pl. of* **meşgale.**
meşahid (. —.) مشاهد A *lrnd., pl. of* **meşhed.**
meşahir (. — —) مشاهير A *lrnd., pl. of* **meşhur.**
meşail (. —.) مشاعل A *lrnd., pl. of* **meş'al, meş'ale.**
meşaim (. — —) مشائم A *lrnd., pl. of* **meş'um.**
meşair (. —.) مشاعر A *lrnd., pl. of* **meş'ar.**
meşairülhac (. — ...) مشاعرالحج A *lrnd.* the stations at which the ceremonies of the great pilgrimage of Islam are performed.

meşakkkı (. —) مشاق A *lrnd., pl. of* **meşakkat.**
meşakil (. —.) مشاكل A *lrnd., pl. of* **müşkil.**
meşakkatti مشقّت A hardship, trouble, suffering. **— çek=** to suffer hardship, to go through great suffering. **—li** difficult, troublesome, exhausting, wearisome.

meş'alli مشعل A *lrnd., same as* **meş'ale.**
meş'aldar (.. —) مشعلدار P *lrnd.* torchbearer.
meş'ale مشعل A torch, lantern. **—i dil** heart's torch. **—i gîtifürûz** *lrnd.* the world-illuminating sun; the Prophet Muhammad. **—i haverî, —i rûz, —i subh** *lrnd.* the sun.

meşammmı (. —) مشام A *lrnd.* sense of smell; smell, nose.

meş'ar مشعر A *lrnd.* 1. a station where a prescribed religious rite is performed during the great pilgrimage at Mecca. 2. any one of the five senses.

meşarili (. —.) مشارع A *lrnd., pl. of* **meşra.**
meşarib (. —.) مشارب A *lrnd., pl. of* **meşreb.**
meşarikkı (. —.) مشارق A *lrnd., pl. of* **maşrık, meşrık.**
meşarit (. — —) مشارط A *lrnd., pl. of* **mişrât.**
meşayih (. —.) مشايخ A *lrnd., pl. of* **şeyh.**
meşayim (. —.) مشايم A *lrnd., pl. of* **meşime.**
meşbu (. —) مشبوط A *chem.* saturated; satiated.

meşbukkü (. —) مشبوك A *lrnd.* interlaced like lattice work.

meşcer مشجر A *lrnd.* place planted with trees; grove, wood.

meşcere مشجرة A *lrnd.* ground planted with or abounding in trees.

meşcuuu (. —) مشجوع A *lrnd.* surpassed in bravery.

meşcûc (. —) مشجوج A *lrnd.* wounded in the scalp; battered on the head.

meşdûddü (. —) مشدود A 1. *lrnd.* tied, bound, fastened. 2. firmly twisted (Bursa silk).

meşdûh (. —) مشدوه A *lrnd.* astonished, amazed, perplexed.

meşe مشه 1. oak, *bot.*, *Quercus*. 2. oak wood or timber. 3. oaken. **— odunu** 1. oak wood (as firewood). 2. *colloq.* blockhead. **—cik** wall germander, *bot.*, *Teucrium chamaedrys*. **—lik** oak forest.

meş'emet مشأمت A *lrnd.* inauspiciousness, unfortunate event.

meşfuuu (. —) مشفوع A *lrnd., law* real property claimed or purchased by the next neighbor by right of pre-emption.

meşgale مشغلة A occupation, business; preoccupation.

meşgûf (. —) مشغوف A *lrnd.* inflamed with love; frantic, mad.

meşgûllü (. —) مشغول A busy, occupied, preoccupied. **—iyet** (. — —.) A occupation, preoccupation.

meşhed مشهد A *lrnd.* 1. place of martyrdom; battlefield. 2. a place where **şehids** have been buried. 3. *w. cap., name of a city in Khorasan, Mashhad*. **M—i Hüseyin** the mausoleum of Hüseyin at Kerbala.

meşher مشهر A *lrnd.* exhibition, exposition.
meşhûddü (. —) مشهود A *lrnd.* witnessed, seen. **— suç** *law* witnessed crime. **—at** (. — —) A *pl.*

meşhûm (. —) مشهوم A *lrnd.* 1. ingenious, persevering and successful; brave, quick, witty. 2. terror-stricken, frightened.

meşhûn (. —) مشحون A *lrnd.* filled; loaded.
meşhur (. —) مشهور A famous; notorious; generally known. **—i âlem** *lrnd.* known to the whole world.

meşhurat (. — —) مشهورات A *lrnd.* things commonly current and taken for granted; common sayings.

meşi مشى A *lrnd., same as* **meşy.**
meşib (. —) مشيب A *lrnd.* gray hair, hoariness; old age.

meşid (. —) مشيد A *lrnd.* plastered or whitewashed with lime.

meşiet (. —.) مشيئت A *lrnd.* a willing, will; the will of God.

meşihat (. —.) مشيخت A 1. *Ott. hist.* office of the **Şeyhülislâm**. 2. *lrnd.* sheikhdom.

meşihatpenah (. — .. —) مشيخت بناه P *Ott. hist.* **Şeyhülislâm.**

meşime (. —.) مشيمة A *anat.* caul, chorion, afterbirth, placenta. **—i dünya** *lrnd.* the sky. **—i şeb** *lrnd.* heart of the night. **—î** (. —. —) A *anat.* chorionic.

meşin مشين [mişîn 3] leather in general; roan; sheepskin leather. **— gibi** thick and brown (human skin). **— suratlı** thick skinned.

meşkkı 1 مشق A *lrnd.* 1. model of writing, calligraphical model (for pupils). 2. an exercising or practicing; lesson (in certain arts); singing lesson. — al= /dan/ to receive a model or lesson (from a teacher). — hocası writing master, teacher of calligraphy. — ol= /a/ to serve as a model. — ver= /a/ to give a lesson.

meşk[ki] 2 مشك P lrnd. waterskin.

meşket=[der], meşkeyle=[r] مشد يتمله مشدايلك A lrnd. 1. to practice. 2. /ı/ to take as a model.

meşkhane (.—.) مشقخانه P lrnd. school of music.

meşkûk[kü] 1 (.—) مشكوك A 1. lrnd. doubtful, doubted. 2. phil. ambiguity.

meşkuk[ku] 2 (.—) مشقوق A lrnd. cleft, split, cracked, slit.

meşkûkât (.——) مشكوكات A lrnd. 1. pl. doubtful matters. 2. phil. amphibology.

meşkûkiyet مشكوكيت A lrnd. doubtfulness.

meşkûl[lü] (.—) مشكول A lrnd. hobbled, fettered (horse).

meşkûr (.—) مشكور A lrnd. 1. worthy of thanks or praise, laudable. 2. acknowledged with thanks and gratitude. —e (.—.) A fem.

meşlah مشلح A lrnd., same as maşlah.

meşmul[lü] (.—) مشمول A lrnd. 1. included, contained, enveloped, surrounded. 2. agreeable. —at (.——) A contents.

meşmum (.—) مشموم A lrnd. fragrant, perfumed; odors; musk. —at (.——) A perfumes, scents.

meşnuk[ku] (.—) مشنوق A lrnd. hanged.

meşra[aı] مشرع A lrnd. 1. path, road; thoroughfare. 2. drain, canal; spout.

meşreb A, meşrep[bi] مشرب 1. natural disposition, temperament; character. 2. lrnd. drinking place; drink, water; a drinking.

meşrık[kı] مشرق A lrnd., same as maşrık. —eyn (..—) A east and west.

meşru[uu] (.—) مشروع A lawful, legal; legitimate. — müdafaa law necessary defense, self-defense.

meşruat (.——) مشروعات A lrnd. acts ordained or permitted by God's law.

meşrub (.—) مشروب A lrnd. 1. drink. 2. drunk, drinkable.

meşrubat (.——) مشروبات A drinks.

meşruh (.—) مشروح A lrnd. commented on, explained, illustrated.

meşruhat (.——) مشروحات A lrnd. written comments, explanations.

meşruiyet (.—..) مشروعيت A lrnd. lawfulness, legality; legitimacy.

meşrum (.—) مشروم A lrnd. cloven, slit.

meşrut (.—) مشروط A lrnd. bound by conditions, stipulated.

meşruta (.—.) مشروطة A law mortmain, inalienable trust or estate.

meşruten (.—'.) مشروطا A conditional, depending upon. — tahliye law release on probation (prisoner).

meşruti (.——) مشروطى A lrnd. constitutional. — hükûmet constitutional government. — kırallık constitutional kingdom.

meşrutiyet (.——.) مشروطيت A constitution, constitutional government. M— Devri Ott. hist. Constitutional Period (1875-1876, 1908-1918).

meşşaiye (.——.) مشائية A phil. peripateticism.

meşşaiyun (.———) مشائيون A phil. peripatetics. — felsefesi peripateticism.

meşşata (.—.) مشاطة A lrnd. hairdresser, hairdresser for a bride.

meşta (.—) مشتا A lrnd. winter quarters, winter resort.

meştum (.—) مشتوم A lrnd. reviled, cursed.

meş'um (.—) مشؤم A inauspicious, ill-omened, sinister.

meş'uf (.—) مشعوف A lrnd. lovesick.

meş'un (.—) مشعون A lrnd. disheveled (hair).

meş'ur (.—) مشعور A 1. lrnd. perceived, understood. 2. phil. conscious.

meşveret مشورت A lrnd. 1. consultation, mutual deliberation. 2. council.

meşy مشى A lrnd. a walking, walk.

met[ddi] مد A same as med.

meta[aı] (.—) متاع A 1. goods, merchandise. 2. stuff, object. —i ma'rûf obs., law generous provision (by a husband for his divorced wife).

metab (.—) متاب A lrnd. a repenting, being converted from sin; repentance.

metabolizm, metabolizma (.…'.) متابوليزم متابوليزما F biol. metabolism.

metafizik[ği] متافيزيك F metaphysics.

metafora (.…'.) متافورا It naut. davit. — ventosu davit guy.

metaib (.—.) متاعب A lrnd. fatiguing things; difficulties, toils; afflictions.

metakarp متاقارپ F anat. metacarpus.

metal[li] متال F metal; print. type metal. — yatak auto. metal bearing.

metalib (.—.) مطالب A lrnd., same as matalib.

metalik متاليك F 1. of metal, metallic. 2. obs., same as metelik.

metamorfoz متامورفوز F metamorphosis.

metanet (.—.) متانت A 1. solidity, firmness, tenacity. 2. resistance, fortitude; courage. — göster= to show firmness, to be unyielding.

metanetli متانتلى firm, able to resist, strong; tenacious.

metanetsiz متانتسز weak, lacking in firmness, yielding. —lik weakness.

metapsişik[ği] متاپسيشيك F metapsychical.

metastaz متاستاز F med. metastasis.

metatars مـتاتارس F *anat., zool.* metatarsus.
metazori مـتا ذوری Gk *slang* by force and threats, by violence.
metbu[uu] (. —) متبوع A *lrnd.* 1. followed, obeyed. 2. sovereign, chief, leader. **—i müfahham** august sovereign. **—i şer'î** one whom the canon law requires to be obeyed. **—iyet** (. — —.) A sovereignty.
metelik[ği] متاليك مته لك [**metalik**] F *obs.* coin of 10 paras. **— etmez** not worth a cent. **—e kurşun at=** to be penniless. **— verme= /a/** not to care anything about.
meteor متئور F meteor. **— taşı** meteorite.
meteorit متئوريت F meteorite.
meteoroloji متئورولوژی F meteorology.
meteorolojik[ği] متئورولوژیك F meteorological.
meteris متريس *var. of* **metris**.
methal مدخل A *var. of* **medhal**.
methet=[der] مدح ایتمك /ı/ to praise.
metin[tni] 1 متن [**metn**] text.
metin 2 (. —) متين A firm, strong, solid; trustworthy.
metis متيس F *biol.* half-breed, of mixed blood, metis.
metizmenos متيزمنوس Gk *slang* intoxicated with hashish.
metn متن A *lrnd., same as* **metin** 1.
metod F, **metot**[du] متود method, system.
metre 1 (´.) متره F meter. **— kare** F square meter. **— küp** F cubic meter.
-metre 2 (´.) متره F -meter, as in **ampermetre**.
metres متره س F mistress, kept woman.
metrik[ği] متريك F metric. **— sistem** metric system.
metris متريس [Persian **maters**] *mil.* trench, entrenchment.
metro 1 متره *It same as* **metre** 1.
metro 2 متره F subway.
Metrofça متره فچ Sl *Ott. hist., geog.* Mitrovtza.
metronom متره نوم F *mus.* metronome.
metropol[lü] متروپول F metropolis. **—lük** state of being a metropolis.
metropolit متروپوليت F 1. Greek bishop. 2. metropolitan. **—lik** bishopric, diocese.
metruk[ku] (. —) متروك A 1. left, abandoned, deserted; neglected. 2. obsolete. 3. *law* left at death (property).
metrukât (. — —) متروكات A *law* effects of the deceased person.
metrukiyet (. — — .) متروكيت A abandonment; destitution; a being left unused.
Metta متى A *Bib., same as* **Matta**.
met'ub (. —) متعب A *lrnd.* tired, fatigued, jaded.
meunet (. — .) مؤنت A *lrnd.* 1. daily food; provisions. 2. trouble, hardship.

me'va (. —) مأوى A *lrnd.* home; shelter.
mevacib (. — .) مواجب A *lrnd.* salary; appropriations. **—hâr** (. — . —) P salaried; stipendiary.
mevad[ddi] (. —) مواد A *lrnd., pl. of* **madde**. **—ı gaita** *biol.* excrement. **—ı infilâkıye** explosives.
mevahib (. — .) مواهب A *lrnd., pl. of* **mevhibe**.
mevaid 1 (. — .) موائد A *lrnd., pl. of* **maide**.
mevaid 2 (. — .) مواعد A *lrnd., pl. of* **mev'id**.
mevaid 3 (. — —) مواعيد A *lrnd., pl. of* **mev'ud, miad**.
mevaiz (. — .) مواعظ A *lrnd., pl. of* **mev'iza**.
mevakıf (. — .) مواقف A *lrnd., pl. of* **mevkıf**.
mevakıt (. — .) مواقت A *lrnd., pl. of* **mevkit**.
mevaki[ii] (. — .) مواقع A *lrnd., pl. of* **mevki**.
mevakib (. — .) مواكب A *lrnd., pl. of* **mevkib**.
mevakit (. — —) مواقيت A *lrnd., pl. of* **mikat**.
mevali (. — —) موالى A *lrnd., pl. of* **mevlâ**. **—i kiram** *Ott. hist.* the chief judges of the Empire.
mevalid 1 (. — .) مواليد A *lrnd., pl. of* **mevlid**.
mevalid 2 (. — —) مواليد A *lrnd., pl. of* **mevlûd, milâd**. **—i selâse** the three kingdoms of nature, *i. e.* animal, vegetable and mineral.
mevani[ii] (. — .) موانع A *lrnd., pl. of* **mani** 1, **mania**.
mevarid (. — .) موارد A *lrnd., pl. of* **mevrid**.
mevaris (. — —) مواريث A *lrnd., pl. of* **miras**.
mevasık[kı] (. — .) مواثق A *lrnd., pl. of* **mevsık**.
mevasıl (. — .) مواصل A *lrnd., pl. of* **mevsil**.
mevasik[ki] (. — —) مواثيق A *lrnd., pl. of* **misak**.
mevasim (. — .) مواسم A *lrnd., pl. of* **mevsim**.
mevaşi (. — —) مواشى A *lrnd., pl. of* **maşiye**, cattle, livestock.
mevat (. —) موات A *lrnd.* 1. inanimate thing; stock, block. 2. piece of waste land.
mevatın (. — .) مواطن A *lrnd., pl. of* **mevtın**.
mevazi[ii] (. — .) مواضع A *lrnd., pl. of* **mevzi**.
mevazin (. — .) موازين A *lrnd., pl. of* **mizan**.
mevbık[kı] (. — .) موبى A *lrnd.* 1. dangerous, fatal place; prison. 2. *w. cap.* the valley of Gehenna where children were sacrificed to Moloch.
mevc موج A *lrnd.* wave, ripple, billow, surge.
mevcamevc (. — .) موجاموج P *lrnd.* full of waves, in great waves.
mevcdar (. —) موج دار P *lrnd.* wavy, undulatory.
mevce موجه A *phys.* wave; *lrnd.* a single wave, ripple. **—i derya** wave of the sea. **— uzunluğu** *phys.* wave length. **—dar** (. . —) P *lrnd., same as* **mevcdar**.
mevcelen=[ir] موجلنمك to rise in waves, to become wavy. **—dir=** /ı/ *caus.*
mevceli موجلى wavy; waved.

mevchiz (. —) موج خیز P *lrnd.* rising in waves, rough (sea).
mevcûb (. —) موجوب A *lrnd.* made necessary; burdened with an obligation.
mevcud (. —) موجود A 1. existing, existent. 2. present; the number present (at an assembly); stock, supply; *mil.* effective force. **— ol=** 1. to exist, to be. 2. to be present.
mevcudat (. — —) موجودات A *lrnd.* 1. all existing things, creation, the universe. 2. *com.* assets. **— ve muvazene defteri** *com.* inventory record.
mevcuden (. —´.) موجوداً A *law* by way of summoning (through the police).
mevcudiyet (. — —.) موجودیت A 1. existence; being. 2. presence. **bir — göster=** to show personality; to make oneself felt. **— hükmü** *log.* existential judgment.
mevcutᵈᵘ موجود *var. of* **mevcud**.
mevczar (. —) موجزار P *lrnd.* place full of billows.
mevczen موج زن P *lrnd.* billowy; boisterous.
mevduᵘᵘ (. —) موضوع A *lrnd.* placed in the charge of a person; entrusted.
mevduat (. — —) موضوعات A 1. *lrnd.* entrusted things. 2. *com.* deposits. **— hesabı** *com.* deposit account. **— yerine kaim olan evrak** *com.* deposit currency.
mevdud (. —) مودود A *lrnd.* beloved, held dear.
mevecat (.. —) موجات A *lrnd.*, *pl. of* **mevce**.
meveddet مودت A *lrnd.* affection, love; friendship. **—li** loving, affectionate.
mevfur (. —) موفور A *lrnd.* 1. plentiful, abundant, numerous, much. 2. complete, perfect; entire.
mevhibe موهبه A *lrnd.* 1. gift, present. 2. talent, natural capacity. **—i ilâhiye** talent bestowed by God.
mevhil موحل A *lrnd.* deep miry place, swamp.
mevhin موهن A *lrnd.* part or half of the night.
mevhûb (. —) موهوب A *lrnd.* given, granted, presented, conferred; gift. **—at** (. — —) A granted things, gifts, donations.
mevhum (. —) موهوم A *lrnd.* imagined, fancied; imaginary; fictitious. **— adet** *math.* imaginary number. **— hat** *sc.* dotted line, imaginary line. **—at** (. — —) A illusions. **—e** (. —.) A 1. imaginary. 2. fiction.
mevhun (. —) موهون A *lrnd.* enervated, weakened, despised.
mev'id موعد A *lrnd.* 1. place or time agreed on; appointment. 2. promise, agreement. **—i mülâkat** appointment, rendezvous.
meviş موش *var. of* **meneviş**.
mev'iza موعظه A *lrnd.* exhortation, admonition; sermon.

mevkıd موقد A *lrnd.* fireplace, hearth.
mevkıf موقف A *lrnd.* halting place, station, post, stop; railway station.
mevkiⁱⁱ موقع A 1. place, site, locality. 2. situation, position; case, circumstance. 3. special place, class (of passengers), first class (in train etc.). **—i fiile koy=** to put into practice, to do. **—i iktidar** government (in power). **— kumandanı** *mil.* commandant. **— tâyini bezi** *mil.* ground strip signal.
mevkib موكب A *lrnd.* 1. procession, mounted retinue (of a ruler). 2. army, large detachment. **—i hac** procession of the pilgrims (on the way to Mecca).
mevkiban (.. —) موكبان P *pl. of* **mevkib**. **—ı seher** angels.
mevkibdar (.. —) موكبدار P *lrnd.* head of a procession.
mevkibrev موكب رو P one who goes in a procession.
mevkiî (.. —) موقعى A *lrnd.* pertaining to a special place, local.
mevkili (. —.) موقعلى A having a first-class compartment or seat.
mevkin, mevkine موكن A *lrnd.* bird's nest.
mevkit موقت A *lrnd.* stated time or season.
mevkuf (. —) موقوف A 1. stopped, arrested; detained, prisoner. 2. /a/ dependent upon, subject to. 3. given in trust for some pious use; held in abeyance (payment).
mevkûfat (. — —) موقوفات A *lrnd.* 1. properties held in mortmain by a perpetual trust (for pious uses). 2. stores in government storehouses. 3. payments held in abeyance. **M— Kalemi** *Ott. hist.* The Public Stores Office or the Suspended Payments Office in the Ministry of Finance. **—çı, —î** (. — — —) *Ott. hist.* controller of the Office of Suspended Payments.
mevkufen (. —´.) موقوفاً A *law* under arrest; in custody.
mevkufîn (. — —) موقوفین A *lrnd.* persons under arrest; prisoners.
mevkufiyet (. — ..) موقوفیت A 1. detention, arrest. 2. a being held in mortmain. 3. dependence.
mevkûlⁱⁱ (. —) موكول A *lrnd.* entrusted to a representative, committed (to the care of).
mevkut (. —) موقوت A *lrnd.* fixed for a certain period. **—e** (. —.) A periodical (paper, brochure etc.).
mevlâ (. —) مولى A 1. *w. cap.* God. 2. *lrnd.* master, lord, patron. 3. *lrnd.* freedman, manumitted slave.
mevlâna (. — —) مولانا A 1. *lrnd.* our lord title of respect applied to great religious personages and judges. 2. *w. cap.*, title of the great mystic Jalaladdin Rumî.

Mevlevî

Mevlevî (..—) مولوى A Mevlevi, member of the order of dervishes founded by Mevlana Jalaladdin Rumi, called also the «whirling dervishes.» — **âyini** vocal composition of four parts, accompanying the ceremony performed by the Mevlevi dervishes. — **külâhı** a Mevlevi dervish's high conical felt cap. —**i mânevî** a title of Jalaladdin Rumi. — **musikisi** music having special characteristics, played and sung in the **Mevlevihanes.**

Mevlevihane (..— —.) مولوىخانه P lodge of Mevlevi dervishes.

Mevlevilik[ti] مولوىلك state of being a Mevlevi.

mevleviyet (..—.) مولويت A lrnd. 1. rank, functions or jurisdiction of a molla or judge of the canon law. 2. w. cap. state of being a **Mevlevi.**

mevlid مولد A lrnd. 1. place or time of birth. 2. nativity, birth. 3. birthday. 4. same as **mevlûd** [1, 2]. **M— Alayı** Ott. hist. procession of the Sultan to the mosque on the anniversary of the Prophet Muhammad's birthday. **M—i Şerif** anniversary of the Prophet's birthday (twelfth of **Rebiülevvel**).

mevlûd[dü] (.—) مولود A 1. w. cap. poem written by Süleyman Çelebi depicting the birth of the Prophet Muhammad, sung only by special singers; the chanting of the Nativity Poem. 2. a religious meeting held in memory of a deceased person, in which the Mevlûd is chanted. 3. birthday; the Prophet Muhammad's birthday. 4. lrnd. born; child, son. 5. lrnd. one of the natural kingdoms (animal, vegetable, mineral). **M— Kandili** evening of the Feast of the Birth of the Prophet. **M— oku=** to chant the Nativity Poem of the Prophet.

mevlûdât (.— —) مولودات A lrnd. those born during a certain period such as one year.

mevlûdhan (.— —) مولودخوان P chanter of the **Mevlûd.**

mevrid مورد A lrnd. place of arrival, destination.

mevrud (.—) مورود A lrnd. 1. arrived at, reached. 2. touched upon, mentioned.

mevrudat (.— —) مورودات A lrnd. things that have arrived (letters, etc.), mail.

mevrude (.—.) مورودة same as **mevrudat.**

mevrus (.—) موروث A lrnd. inherited, hereditary. —**iyet** (.— —.) A heredity.

mevsık[kı] موثق A lrnd. a trusting, confiding in; treaty, compact.

mevsil موصل A lrnd. place of joining, joint, junction.

mevsim موسم A 1. season; proper time (for anything), period. 2. spring and fall. — **hastalıkları** seasonal diseases. —**î** (.— —) A astr. seasonal.

mevsimlik[ti] موسملك suitable for spring or autumn; seasonal.

mevsimsiz موسمسز untimely, unseasonable; out of place.

mevsûf (.—) موصوف A 1. lrnd. indued with a quality, qualified, distinguished; characterized, endowed. 2. gram. substantive qualified by an adjective. —**iyet** (.— —.) A qualification.

mevsûk[ku] (.—) موثوق A lrnd. reliable, trusted; authentic, documented. —**an** (.—'.) A reliably; authentically. —**iyet** (.— —.) A authenticity; reliability.

mevsul[lü] (.—) موصول A 1. lrnd. joined; united. 2. lrnd. arrived, attained. 3. Arabic gram. relative pronoun.

mevsulunnetayic (.— ..—.) موصول النتائج A phil. polysyllogism.

mevsum (.—) موسوم A lrnd. 1. marked, signed, branded. 2. named, called.

mevt موت A 1. lrnd. a dying, death. 2. myst. a dying to self. —**i ahmer** 1. violent death. 2. myst. violent struggle with self. —**i ahdar** myst. a withdrawing from worldly possessions and being contented with a very scanty living. —**i ebyaz** natural death. —**i esved** 1. black death, i. e. death by strangulation or drowning. 2. patient endurance of all tribulations. —**i fevat**, —**i fücaat**, —**i müfacat** sudden death. —**i müchiz** speedy death.

mevta (.—) موتا A 1. corpse. 2. lrnd., pl. of **meyit**, the dead. —**i** (.— —) A lrnd. deathlike, deadly.

mevtalûd (.— —) موتآلود P lrnd. stained with death.

mevtan (.—) موتان A lrnd. 1. faint, fainted. 2. crazy, insane.

mevtı (.—) موطى A lrnd. place trodden or stood upon. —**i kadem ol=** to be trodden upon.

mevtın موطن A lrnd. homeland, home; residence.

mevtî (.—) موطى A lrnd. pertaining to death, deathlike, deathly.

mevtu[uu] (.—) موطوء A lrnd. 1. trampled under foot; beaten, trampled on. 2. sexually known.

mev'ud (.—) موعود A lrnd. 1. promised, appointed, agreed upon. 2. predestined.

mevvac (.—) موّاج A lrnd. billowy, rough (sea).

mevzek[ti] موزك [Persian **mevîzek**] 1. stavesacre, bot., Delphinium staphisagria. 2. seeds of stavesacre.

mevzi[ü] موضع A place, locality, situation; position. — **al=** mil. to take up a position. — **harbi** mil. stationary war.

mevziî (.— —) موضعى A local; regional; positional. — **coğrafya** regional geography. — **irticaflar** geog. local perturbations.

mevziileş=ⁱʳ موضعیلشمك to become localized. **—tir=** /ı/ caus.

mevzuᵘᵘ (.—) موضوع A 1. subject; subject treated of; proposition. 2. *lrnd.* placed, laid; situated. 3. *lrnd.* instituted; laid down as true and indubitable. 4. *lrnd.* conventional, customary. **—i bahs** in question, under discussion. **— hukuk** positive law. **— ve mahmul** *log.* subject and attribute of a proposition.

mevzua (.—.) موضوعه A *log.* postulate, axiom.

mevzuat (..—) موضوعات A 1. pl. of **mevzu.** 2. regulations, conventions, legislations; laws of the country.

mevzun (.—) موزون A 1. well balanced, well proportioned; symmetrical. 2. weighed, of full weight. 3. that scans correctly (verse). **—ât** (.——) A pl. **—iyet** (.—..) A balance; good balance.

mevzuubahis موضوع بحث *same as* **mevzu-i bahs.**

mey 1 می P *poet.* wine; intoxicating drink. **—i gülfam, —i gülgûn** red wine. **—i nâb** neat wine.

meyʸⁱ 2 میع A *lrnd.* 1. a flowing, running. 2. a melting, becoming fluid.

mey'a میعه A *lrnd.* 1. storax. 2. early part, prime of any state; bloom of youth. 3. a flowing of anything poured out. **—i saile** liquid storax, sweet gum tree, *bot., Liquidambar styraciflua.* **—i yabise** the inner bark of *Liquidambar orientale* (after the liquid storax of commerce is distilled from it).

meyadin (.——) میادین A *lrnd.*, pl. of **meydan.**

meyama (.'..) میامه Gk *naut.* earing of a sail.

meyamin 1 (.—.) میامن A *lrnd.*, pl. of **meymenet.**

meyamin 2 (.——) میامین A *lrnd.*, pl. of **meymun.**

meyan 1 میان [piyan] licorice. **— balı** licorice extract. **— kökü** root of licorice plant, *bot., Glycyrrhiza glabra.*

meyan 2 (.—) میان P *lrnd.*, same as **miyan. —larında** in the midst of them, among them, between them.

meyane (.—.) میانه P 1. sauce made with butter and flour. 2. correct degree of cooking (helva etc.), *as in* **meyanesi geldi.**

meyasir (.—.) میاسر A *lrnd.*, pl. of **meysere.**

meyaşam (.——) میاشام P *lrnd.* addicted to wine, wine drinker.

meyazib (.——) میازیب A *lrnd.*, pl. of **mizab.**

meybuhtec میبختج [*Persian* **meypuhte**] *lrnd.* boiled wine.

meydan 1 میدان A 1. open space; public square, the open. 2. arena, ring, ground; field, area. 3. one's surroundings, the world around. 4. *myst.* universe. 5. *dervish orders* open space for religious ceremony in a dervish convent. 6. opportunity, occasion; possibility. **—da** 1. in the open, houseless; unprovided for. 2. lying about, exposed. 3. clear, evident, obvious. **—i ağber** *lrnd.* the world, earth. **— al=** to make progress by taking advantage of an opportunity; to get on in the world. **— ara=** 1. to seek space. 2. to look for opportunity. **—a at=** /ı/ to put forward, to suggest, to bring up. **—a atıl=** to go headlong (into a thing), to throw oneself into action. **— baklası** *colloq.* woman who does not veil herself in the presence of men. **— başı** *Ott. hist.* disciplinary officer of the recruits of the Janissary corps. **— bırak=** *same as* **meydan ver=. —da bırak=** /ı/ 1. to leave somebody in the cold, to neglect intentionally. 2. to leave in the open. **—ı boş bul=** to make use of an opportunity in the absence of rivals. **— bul=** to find an opportunity; to get on. **—a çık=** 1. to come out into the open; to appear. 2. to be revealed, to be found out (secret etc.); to be brought to light. 3. to come forth, to show oneself. 4. to grow up (child). **—a çıkar=** /ı/ 1. to bring to light; to expose to view. 2. to make public, to publish; to reveal. 3. to bring up to maturity (child). **— dayağı** a public flogging. **— dayağı çek=** /a/ to give someone a beating. **— düğünü** wedding feast open to everybody (in a village). **—a düş=** to set forth zealously to do something. **—a gel=** 1. to be accomplished, to come into existence. 2. to come to maturity. **—a getir=** /ı/ 1. to accomplish, to achieve; to create. 2. to bring forward (into view). **—a gir=** *archaic* to go to war, to fight. **—i harb** *lrnd.* battlefield. **— hizmeti** *mil.* service outside the barracks. **—da kal=** to be left destitute, to be homeless. **— kethüdası** *same as* **meydan başı. — korkusu** psychopath. agoraphobia. **— muharebesi** pitched battle. **— oku=** /a/ to challenge. **— sazı** the largest variety of the **bağlama** used in folk music. **—ı siyaset** 1. *archaic* place of execution. 2. the field of politics. **—ı siyaset ustası** *Ott. hist.* executioner, hangman. **— süpürgesi** 1. long-handled rough broom. 2. streetwalker, loose woman. **— şuarası** *lrnd.* minstrels. **— topu** *mil.* field gun. **— ver=** /a/ to give opportunity; to tolerate. **—a vur=** /ı/ to show openly, to make public.

meydan 2 (.—) میدان P *lrnd.* wine glass.

meydancı میدانجی 1. dervish who supervises the whirling dervishes during a ritual ceremony of the Mevlevis. 2. dervish in charge of the housework of a dervish convent. 3. runner on call in a bank.

meydangâh (.——) میدانگاه P *lrna.* public square.

meydanî (.——) میدانی A *obs.* a kind of

Red 49.

meydanlık

expensive cloth of cotton mixed with silk, having dark red or purple stripes, made especially in Damascus and India.

meydanlık[^ṣ1] (. — .) سيدانلي open space, square. =meye gör=[^ür] ميه كورمك cf. =maya gör=.

meyelân (..—) ميلان A lrnd. an inclining towards; tendency; inclination; affection.

meyfüruş (..—) ميفروش P poet. wine seller, tavern keeper.

meygûn (.—) ميكون P poet. wine colored, red.

meygüsar (..—) ميكسار P lrnd. 1. wine drinker. 2. cupbearer.

meyhane (.—.) ميخانه P wine shop, tavern. **— fıçısı** constant tippler. **—ci** tavern keeper, barkeep. **—cilik** profession of a tavern keeper.

meyhar, meyhor (.—) ميخوار P lrnd. wine drinker, wine bibber.

meyhoş ميخوش P lrnd., same as **mayhoş**.

meyil[^yli] ميل [meyl] 1. a leaning, inclining; inclination, tendency. 2. deviation, deflection; declination (of a heavenly body). 3. slope. 4. affection, love; propensity. **— zaviyesi** angle of inclination. **—li** inclined; leaning; oblique; sloping.

=meyiz ميز cf. =mayız.

meykede ميكده P poet. wine shop, tavern.

meykeş ميكش P lrnd. wine drinker.

meyl ميل A lrnd., same as **meyil**. **—i a'zam** astr. greatest declination of a heavenly body. **—i a'zam hattı** geom. line of the greatest inclination. **—i küllî** astr. total declination or obliquity of the ecliptic. **—i mutlak** astr. common declination of a star.

meylen (.'.) ميلًا A by inclination; by affection.

meylet=[^der] ميل اتمك 1. to incline, to be inclined. 2. to swerve, to deviate, to turn upwards or downwards. 3. /a/ to have a liking or propensity (for). **—tir=** /ı/ caus.

meyliyat (.——) ميليات A lrnd. inclinations, tendencies.

meymene ميمنه A lrnd. right wing of an army.

meymenet ميمنت A a being lucky, fortunate; auspiciousness, fortune. **—li** auspicious, lucky; prosperous.

meymenetsiz ميمنتسز 1. inauspicious, unlucky. 2. disagreeable (person). **—lik** abstr. n.

meymun (.—) ميمون A 1. lrnd., same as **maymun**. 2. fortunate, happy; auspicious, prosperous.

meyn مين A lrnd. a speaking falsely; a lie.

meyperest ميپرست P addicted to drink; given to drinking wine. **—ân** (...—) P drunkards. **—î** (...—) P addiction to drinking; drunkenness.

meysere ميسره A lrnd. 1. left wing of an army. 2. riches, wealth.

meysir ميسر A lrnd. dice game, any gambler's game.

meysur (.—) ميسور A lrnd. made easy, facilitated (by God). **—at** (.——) A matters facilitated by God.

meyt ميت A lrnd., same as **meyyit**.

meyte ميته A lrnd. carrion, beast that has died and is unfit for food. **—har** (..—) P eater of carrion.

me'yus (.—) مأيوس A desperate, hopeless, despairing. **—âne** (.——.) P desperately, in despair. **—iyet** (.——.) A despair, desperateness; hopelessness.

meyva, meyve ميوه [Persian miva] fruit. **—i dil** (lit. fruit of the heart.) 1. one's own beloved child. 2. poem or witty saying (of one's own composition). **—bar** (..—) P same as **meyvedar**. **—ci** fruit seller. **—cilik** fruit trade, fruit culture. **—dar** (..—) P lrnd. fruit-yielding, fruitful. **—dışı** neol., bot. exocarp. **—füruş** (...—) P lrnd. fruit seller. **—hâ** (..—) P pl., lrnd. fruit. **—hane** (..—.) P hothouse. **—hoşk** P lrnd. dried fruit; fruit market. **—içi** neol., bot. endocarp. **—li** having fruit; fruitful. **—lik** 1. fruit garden. 2. receptacle for fruit. 3. having fruit. **—ortası** neol., bot. mesocarp. **—siz** fruitless; without fruit. **—sizlik** lack of fruit; fruitlessness. **—yaprak** neol., bot. carpel.

meyyal[^li] (.—) ميّال A lrnd. /a/ inclined towards, very fond of.

meyyit ميّت A lrnd. 1. dead man, corpse. 2. dying, moribund. **—âne** (..—.) P 1. deathlike. 2. dismal.

meyzer ميزر a kind of cloth woven in the Mardin district.

meyzin ميزن colloq., var. of **müezzin**.

=mez مز cf. =maz.

meza (.'.) مزه It naut., same as **meze** 2.

mezabıt (.—.) مضابط A lrnd., pl. of **mazbata**.

mezabih (.—.) مذابح A lrnd., pl. of **mezbah**.

mezabil (.—.) مزابل A lrnd., pl. of **mezbele**.

mezabir (.—.) مزابر A lrnd., pl. of **mizber**.

mezad (.—) مزاد A same as **mezat**.

mezahib (.—.) مذاهب A lrnd., pl. of **mezheb**. **M—i Erbaa** the four orthodox schools of Islam, Hanefi, Şafii, Mâliki and Hanbeli.

mezahim (.—.) مزاحم A lrnd. difficulties, troubles; obstacles.

mezahir 1 (.—.) مظاهر A lrnd., pl. of **mazhar** 1.

mezahir 2 (.—.) مزاهر A lrnd., pl. of **mizher**.

mezaik[^kı] (.—.) مضائق A lrnd., pl. of **mazik**.

mezak[^kı] 1 (.—) مذاق A lrnd. 1. a tasting; taste. 2. palate. 3. joking, humor, fun.

mezak[^ṣ1] 2 (.—) مزاح [mizah] prov. joking, fun. **—a al=** /ı/ to make fun of.

mezalik^kı (.—.) مَزالِو A lrnd., pl. of **mezlaka**.

mezalim (.—.) مَظالِم A oppressions, atrocities, cruelties, injustices.

mezam^mmı (.—) مَنام A lrnd., pl. of **mezamet**.

mezamet (.—.) مَنامَت A lrnd. mutual disparagement.

mezamir (.——) مَنامير A lrnd., pl. of **mezmur, mizmar**.

mezar (.—) مَزار A 1. tomb, grave. 2. lrnd. a visiting; place of visiting. — **bozan** violator of graves. — **eş=** to rob a grave. — **kaçkını** sickly person. — **kitabesi** epitaph. —**ı zâr** the weeping grave. —**cı** gravedigger. —**cılık** profession of a gravedigger.

mezari^iı 1 (.—.) مَزارِع A lrnd., pl. of **mezraa**.

mezari^iı 2 (.——) مَزاريج A lrnd., pl. of **mezru 1**.

mezarik^kı (.——) مَزاريك A lrnd., pl. of **mızrak**.

mezaristan (.—.—) مَزارِستان P lrnd. graveyard, cemetery.

mezarlık^ğı (.—.) مَزارلو graveyard, cemetery.

mezarna (.ˊ.) مَزارنه It naut. coamings.

mezat^dı مَزاد [mezad] auction; auction place; auction sale. —**a çıkar=**, —**a koy=** /ı/ to put up for sale by auction. — **malı** goods bought at an auction; cheaply bought, bargain. —**çı** auctioneer.

mezaya (.——) مَزايا A lrnd., pl. of **meziyet**. —**şinas** (.——.—) P one who appreciates good qualities.

mezbah مَذبَح A lrnd. 1. slaughterhouse. 2. altar.

mezbaha مَذبَحَه A slaughterhouse.

mezbele مَزبَلَه A refuse heap, dunghill.

mezbelekeşan (.…—) مَزبَلَه كَشان P Ott. hist. scavengers of the Sultan's palace.

mezbelelik^ği مَزبَلَه لِك place like a dunghill, very dirty place.

mezbub (.—) مَذبوب A lrnd. 1. infested with flies; persecuted by flies. 2. crazy, mad; furious.

mezbuh (.—) مَذبوح A lrnd. slaughtered, slain; sacrificed. —**âne** (.——.) P desperate, desperately, homicidal, suicidal.

mezbur (.—) مَذبور A lrnd. 1. aforesaid, abovementioned. 2. written, recorded.

mezbure (.—.) مَذبوره same as **mezbur**.

mezc مَزج A a mixing, blending; mixture. — **et=** /ı/ to mix, blend, combine.

=**mezden evvel** مَزدَن اَوَّل cf. =**mazdan evvel**.
=**mezdin ön** مَزدِن اُون cf. =**mazdın ön**.

meze 1 مَزه P 1. savory tidbits that accompany drinking; appetizer, relish, snack; hors d'oeuvres. 2. lrnd. pleasant taste, flavor. 3. pleasantry, joke. —**ye al=** /ı/ fig. to make fun of.

meze 2 (.ˊ.) مَزه [meza] naut. razee. — **et=** /ı/ tc razee. — **borda** broadside. — **kapak** double-banked frigate. — **korvet** gun vessel. — **marinaye** hook on a short handle, in boats. — **volta** half turn, marline hitch.

mezeci مَزه جی seller of snacks.

mezegî (..—) مَزه گی P lrnd. agreeable flavor, sweetness.

mezelik^ği مَزه لِك tidbits to accompany a drink, appetizer.

mezellet مَذَلَّت A lrnd. abjectness, baseness; contempt; humiliation.

mezemmet مَذَمَّت A lrnd. a blaming, reproaching; blame, reproach; scorn, contempt; shame, disgrace, abuse.

mezen 1 مَزَن A lrnd. custom, habit, manner; state.

me'zen 2, me'zene مَأذَنه A lrnd. gallery where the **ezan** is proclaimed.

mezestra, mezestre (.ˊ.) مَزِستره It naut. halfmast. — **et=** /ı/ to hoist the flag at halfmast.

mezgeldek^ği, **mezgerdek**^ği مَزگَلدَك مَزگَردَك prov. little bustard.

mezgid مَزگید same as **mezit**.

mezheb A, **mezhep**^bi مَذهَب 1. religious opinion; religious sect; religion, creed; doctrine. 2. way or path followed, course; manner, mode of conduct. 3. phil. school of thought, system. —**i geniş** too tolerant in matters of morals. — **hürriyeti** freedom of confession of faith. —**ine sığmaz** It is out of the limits of his principles; completely beyond his understanding.

mezhur (.—) مَذخور A lrnd. laid up in store, stored.

mezid (.—) مَزید A lrnd. an increasing; increase, abundance; increased, augmented, abundant.

mezillet مَزَلَّت A lrnd. 1. a slipping, sliding, falling; slip of the foot. 2. a blundering in speech.

mezit مَزیت whiting (fish), zool., Gadus euxinus.

meziyat (.——) مَزیات A lrnd., pl. of **meziyet**.

meziyet مَزیت A 1. excellence, virtue, merit, good quality. 2. ability, talent, value. —**li** excellent, virtuous, capable. —**siz** having no virtue or quality.

=**meziz** مَزیز cf. =**maziz**.

mezk^kı مَزك A lrnd. a tearing.

mezkûm (.—) مَزكوم A lrnd. troubled with a cold in the head.

mezkûr (.—) مَذكور A mentioned, aforementioned; the said. —**at** (.——) A things mentioned.

mezlaka مَزلَقَه A lrnd. 1. slippery place.

2. state or affair that causes one to fall into error.
=**mezlik**ᵗⁱ مَزلِك cf. =**mazlık**.
mezmum (.—) مَذموم A lrnd. blamed, blameworthy; despised, scorned.
mezmur (.—) مَزمور A lrnd. 1. w. cap., Bib. Psalm. 2. sung with a flute accompaniment.
mezraa مَزرعَ A lrnd. arable field.
mezruᵘᵘ 1 (.—) مَزروع A lrnd. sown, cultivated.
mezruᵘᵘ 2 (.—) مَزروع A lrnd. measured by the cubit.
mezruat 1 (.— —) مَزروعات A lrnd. 1. seeded fields. 2. crops.
mezruat 2 (.— —) مَزروعات A lrnd. things measured by the cubit.
mezrukᵏᵘ (.—) مَزروك A lrnd. injected. —at (.— —) A injectable medicines.
me'zun (.—) مَأذون A 1. permitted, allowed; authorized. 2. graduated from, graduate. 3. on leave on holiday; excused (from performing some duty). —**en** (.—´.) A on leave. —**in** (.— —) A lrnd. graduates.
mezuniyet' (.— — .) مَأذونيّت A 1. permission, authorization. 2. leave, furlough. 3. graduation.
mezura (.´.) مَزورا It 1. tapeline, tape measure. 2. measuring cup, measuring beaker.
mezzah (.—) مَزّاح A lrnd. jester, joker.
mezzo مَزّو It naut. buntline.
mezzo-soprano (.´...´.) مَزّوسوپرانو It mezzo-soprano.
mı, mi, mu, mü مى adverb of interrogation, e. g., aldı mı? Did he take it?
mıcır مِجير 1. grit used for road surfacing. 2. coal dust. 3. slang worthless person.
mıcırıkᵏⁱ مِجيريك prov. 1. crushed, squashed (tomatoes, grapes etc.). 2. careless and untidy.
mıdrab مِضراب A same as **mızrab**.
mığlâkᵏⁱ 1 مِغلى A same as **mığlâk** 2.
mığlâkᵏⁱ 2 (.—) مِغلاك A lrnd. lock, bolt, bar, latch.
mığrı مِغرى Gk conger eel, zool., Conger conger.
mığsel مِغسل A lrnd. tub or other vessel used for washing.
mığvel مِغول A lrnd. long small sword; dagger.
mıh مِيخ [Persian **meh, mîh**] nail; peg. — **çak**= to drive in a nail. — **değmiş** hurt in the foot by a nail (horse). — **kes**= to cut, make nails. — **sök**= to pull out a nail.
mıhla=ʳ مِيخلمَق /ı/ 1. to nail. 2. to set (precious stone etc.). 3. to nail somebody down. 4. slang to stab.
mıhladız مِيخلديز colloq., var. of **mıknatıs**.
mıhlama 1 مِيخلمَه 1. a studding (box etc.), an ornamenting with nails. 2. slang a manner of dice throwing.

mıhlama 2 مِيخلمَه Syriac prov. dish made of pastırma, onions and eggs.
mıhlan=ⁱʳ مِيخلنمَق 1. to be nailed (to be fixed). 2. to be set (precious stones etc.).
mıhlât (.—) مِخلات A lrnd. fodder sack, nosebag.
mıhlayıcı مِيخلايجى 1. one who nails. 2. setter of precious stones.
mıhleb مِخلب A lrnd. claw, nail, talon of a rapacious bird.
mıhlı مِيخلى 1. furnished with nails, rivets, pegs etc.; nailed. 2. set (gem etc.)
mıhrez مِحرز A lrnd. shoemaker's awl.
mıhsıçtı مِيخ صيچدى slang, vulg. very stingy, miserly.
mıhyat مِخيط A lrnd. needle.
mıhzefe مِحذفه A lrnd. stick slit at the end for throwing a stone; sling.
=**mık**ᵏⁱ, =**mik**ᵏⁱ, =**muk**ᵏᵘ, =**mük**ᵏᵘ مِيك substantive-forming suffix added to the root of an infinitive, e. g., çiğnemik, kusmuk.
mıkbaza مِقبضه A lrnd. hilt, handle.
mıkdaha مِقدحه A lrnd. steel for kindling fire; fire-steel.
mıkdam (.—) مِقدام A lrnd. brave, enterprising; dauntless.
mıklâ (.—) مِقلى A lrnd. frying pan.
mıklâd (.—) مِقلاد A lrnd. 1. key, lock. 2. storeroom, repository.
mıklat (.—) مِقلات A lrnd., same as **mıkla**.
mıkleb مِقلب A lrnd. 1. tuck of the binding of a book. 2. iron hoe.
mıknaⁿⁱ, **mıknaa** مِقنع مِقنعه A lrnd. woman's muffler.
mıknatıs مِقناطيس Gk magnet; lodestone. —**î** (...—) A magnetic. —**iyet** (...— .) A lrnd. magnetism.
mıknatısla=ʳ مِقناطيسلمَق /ı/ to magnetize. —**n**= to be magnetized.
mıknatıslı مِقناطيسلى magnetic.
mıkraⁿⁱ (.—) مِقرع A lrnd. mallet for breaking stones, large pickax.
mıkraa مِقرعه A lrnd. 1. instrument for beating. 2. cudgel for beating a drum.
mıkrıs مِقريس prov. very stingy.
mıktaⁿⁱ مِقطع A 1. lrnd. cutting instrument. 2. obs. small flat piece usually made of ivory used to support a reed pen when splitting the nib.
mıkvel مِقول A lrnd. the tongue as the organ of speech.
mıncıkla=ʳ مِنجقلمَق /ı/ to squeeze and squash; to pinch repeatedly. —**t**= /ı, a/ caus.
mıncık mıncık مِنجق مِنجق 1. squashed. 2. miry, muddy, sticky. — **et**= /ı/ to spoil (by squeezing or breaking into pieces).
mıntaka, mıntıka مِنطقه A 1. zone, region, district; mil. sector. 2. lrnd. ecliptic. 3. lrnd.

girdle, sash. —**i bâride** *lrnd.* frigid zone. **—i hârre** *lrnd.* torrid zone. **—i mûtedile** *lrnd.* temperate zone.

mıntakatülbürûc (.....—) منطقة البروج A *astr.* the zodiac.

mırılda=ʳ, mırıldan=ʳ مرالدامه مرالدانمه to mutter to oneself, to grumble; to murmur.

mırıl mırıl مرل مرل muttering, grumbling.

mırıltı مرلتى a grumbling; a muttering; a murmuring.

mırın kırın مرن قرن a grumbling. **— et=** to grumble.

mırla=ʳ مرلامه to purr (cat).

mır mır مرمر 1. grumbling; grumbler. 2. *slang* rowdy, rough. **— balığı** worm eel, *zool.*, Echelus myrus.

mırmırık[ᵗⁱ] مرمريه *colloq.* fermented; heady.

mırnav مرناو miaow.

mıs'ad (.—) مصعاد A *lrnd.* rope by which one climbs trees, ladder.

mısbah (.—) مصباح A *lrnd.* light, lantern, lamp, torch.

mısdak[ᵏⁱ] (.—) مصداق A *lrnd.* criterion; authority, proof. **—ınca** according to the sense of. **—iyat** (.———) A criteriology.

mısfat (.—) مصفات A *lrnd.* strainer.

Mısır[ˢʳⁱ] 1 مصر [*Arabic* **Mısr**] 1. Egypt; Cairo. 2. *lrnd., l. c.* city, town; limit, boundary. **—ı Atîk** *hist.* ruined city of Fustat. **— baklası** Egyptian lupin, *bot.*, Lupinus thermus. **— buğdayı** *obs.* corn. **— dikeni** Egyptian thorn, *bot.*, Acacia Arabica. **— gülü** jonquil, *bot.*, Narcissus jonquilla. **— tavuğu** turkey. **— turnası** ibis, *zool.*, Ibis. **— zeri mahbubu, — zincirli altını** *Ott. hist.*, names of a gold coin minted in Egypt.

mısır 2 مصر [**Mısır** 1] corn, *bot.*, Zea mays. **— ekmeği** corn bread. **— fitili** *obs.*, artillery cord made of corn silk to prime a gun for firing.

Mısırlı مصرلى an Egyptian.

mıska مسقه *var. of* **muska**.

mıskal[ⁱⁱ] 1 (.—) مصقال A *mus.* panpipe. **— kamışı gibi** close together.

mıskal[ⁱⁱ] 2 مصقل A 1. burnisher. 2. polished speaker. **—a vur=** /ı/ to burnish (steel etc.).

mıskale مصقله A burnisher.

mıskalî (.——) مصقلى A *lrnd.* panpipe player.

mısmıl مسمل archaic clean, pure.

mısra[ᵃⁱ] (.—) مصراع A 1. *pros.* line of poetry. 2. *lrnd.* one half of a double door. **—i âzade** *pros.* a single line. **—i berceste** *pros.* the best and most powerful line in a poem.

Mısran (.—) مصران A *lrnd.* two cities, especially Basra and Kufa.

Mısrî (.—) مصرى A *lrnd.* 1. Egyptian. 2. of or from Egypt.

=mıssa, =misse مصه *obs. for* **=mışsa** etc.

mıstar مسطر A *lrnd.* 1. geometrical rule by which straight lines are drawn, ruler. 2. parallel threads stretched on a piece of cardboard (used for ruling lines by those who copy manuscripts); lined paper placed under a sheet of paper to aid writing in straight lines.

mısvat (.—) مصوات A *lrnd.* clamorous, very noisy (person).

=mış 1, =miş, =muş, =müş مش 1. *suffix forming dubitative mood, 3rd person sing.,* e. g., **açmış**. 2. *suffix forming past participle,* e. g., **geçmiş hâdise** past event.

=mış 2 etc. after vowels **=ymış** etc. مش [**imiş**] (He is) said to be, e. g., **alıkmış** He is said to be an imbecile.

=mışçasına, =mişçesine etc. after vowels **=ymışçasına** etc. مشجسنه [**imişçesine**] as if, e. g., **büyümüşçesine** as if grown up.

=mışık 1 etc. مشك *prov.*, 1st pers., pl. of past narrative, e. g., **kalmışık**.

=mışık 2, etc. after vowels. **=ymışık** etc. [**imişik**] *prov.*, 1st pers. pl., added to adjectives We are said to be, e. g., **yemişik** We are said to have eaten.

mışılda=ʳ مشيلدامه to breathe heavily in sound sleep.

mışıl mışıl مشيل مشيل sound of heavy breathing in sleep. **— uyu=** to sleep soundly.

=mışın 1 etc. (pl. **=mışınız,** etc.) *colloq., prov.* variant of the past narrative 2nd pers. sing. ending **=mışsın**, e. g., **kalmışın**.

-mışın 2 etc. after vowels. **-ymışın** etc. (pl. **-mışınız** etc.) مشك [**imişin**] *colloq., prov.*, variant of second pers. sing. ending **-mışsın** You are said to be, e. g., **ahmakmışın** You are said to be a fool.

=mışken, =mişken etc. مشكن [=**mış** + **iken**] usually preceded by the adverb **hazır**, having, readily, e. g., **hazır kalkmışken gidelim** Now that we have stood up, let us go.

=mışsa, =mişse etc. مشسه 1. if (... is) said to have, e. g., **kalmışsa** if he has stayed. 2. if ... has/is [past participle].

=mıştı, =mişti etc. مشتى 3rd. pers. past perfect (he) had, e. g., **kalmıştı** He had stayed.

mıtal[ⁱⁱ] (.—) مطال A *lrnd.* a putting off (the payment of a debt).

mıt'am (.—) مطعام A *lrnd.* given to feeding others, hospitable.

mı'tar (.—) معطار A *lrnd.* one who habitually uses perfume, highly perfumed (person).

mıtfaha مطفه A *lrnd.* skimmer, ladle.

mı'tir (.—) معطير A *lrnd., same as* **mı'tar**.

mıtlak[ᵏⁱ] (.—) مطلاك A *lrnd.* one who often divorces his wives.

mıtrab (.—), **mıtrabe** (.—.) مطراب A *lrnd.* very lively, very joyful and merry.

mıtrak[kı], **mıtraka** مطرقه مطرقة A *lrnd.* beating implement; hammer, mace; cudgel.
mıtred مطرد A *lrnd.* spear; dart.
mıtrıb مطرب A *lrnd.*, same as **mutrib**.
mıtva[aı] (. —) مطواع A *lrnd.* extremely submissive and obedient.
mıymıntı يمينتى slow, lazy and exasperatingly passive.
=**mız** etc. م after consonants =**ımız** etc. [pl. of -**m 3**] our.
mızfar (. —) مظفّا A *lrnd.* very successful.
mızık[ğı] مزيك 1. foolish complaint, peevishness. 2. a not obeying the rules of a game (when losing).
mızıka (.'.) مزيقه It military band.
mızıkalı مزيقه لى *Ott. hist.* one of the band players in the Sultan's palace.
mızıkçı مزيقجى 1. unreliable, unpredictable (person). 2. one who does not obey the rules of a game when he is losing. 3. peevish.
mızıklan=[ır] مزيقلنمق to find excuses for spoiling a game.
mızmar (. —) مضما A *lrnd.* exercise ground for training horses.
mızmız مزمز 1. hesitant, unable to make up his mind. 2. unpleasantly particular. 3. slow and lazy.
mızmızlan=[ır] مزمزلنمق to become querulous and unduly particular.
mızmızlık[ğı] مزمزلق hesitancy.
mızrab (. —) مضراب A *mus.* plectrum.
mızrak[ğı] مزراق [*Arabic* . —] spear, lance; javelin. — **çuvala sığmaz** The spear will not go into the sack (expression used to deride an obvious falsehood).
mızraklı مزراقلى armed with a spear or lance; lancer. — **ilmihal** *obs.* standard elementary schoolbook.
mi مى *adverb of interrogation,* cf. **mı**.
mia معا A *anat.* intestine. —**i a'ver** blind gut, caecum. —**i dikakî** ileum. —**i galiz** large intestine. —**i isna aşer** duodenum. —**i müstakim** rectum. —**i rakik** small intestine. —**i saimî** jejunum.
miaî (. — —) معائى A *anat.* intestinal.
miad (— —) ميعاد A 1. fixed period (for the renewal of clothes, etc. issued to soldiers or pupils). 2. *lrnd.* fixed place or time; rendezvous. 3. *lrnd.* day of the Last Judgment. —**ını doldur**= to have completed its appointed time, to become old. —**ı gel**= to reach the time (of replacement, renewal).
miat (. —ı) ميعات A *lrnd.*, pl. of **mie**.
mi'ber معبر A *lrnd.* 1. ferry boat. 2. bridge.
miblâ[aı] مبلغ A *lrnd.* gluttonous, voracious; glutton.
mibred مبرد A *lrnd.* file; rasp.
mibree مبرع A *lrnd.* penknife.

mibtan (. —) مبطان A *lrnd.* big bellied; paunchy; slave to his belly.
mibvele مبوله A *lrnd.* urinal, chamber pot.
mibza[aı] (. —), **mibzağ** مبزغ مبزع A *lrnd.* lancet.
mibzer مبزر A *lrnd.* drill for sawing.
micana ميجانه It *naut.*, same as **mizana**.
micdaf (. —) مجداف A *lrnd.* oar, paddle.
micdel مجدل A *lrnd.* strong fortress, castle, citadel.
micen[nni], **micenne** مجنّه A *lrnd.* 1. shield. 2. protection.
mi'cer معجر A *lrnd.* woman's scarf worn over the head.
michar (. —) مجهار A *lrnd.* who habitually speaks loudly; who habitually speaks out bluntly.
micmer, **micmere** مجمره A *lrnd.*, same as **mecmer**.
micred مجرد A *lrnd.* dentist's instrument for scraping teeth.
miczaf (. —) مجذاف A *lrnd.*, same as **micdaf**.
miçaço (. .'.) ميچاجو It *naut.* screw jack.
miço (.'.) ميچو It 1. cabin boy. 2. boy waiter in a tavern.
midad (. —) مداد A *lrnd.* ink.
midak[kkı] مدق A *lrnd.* implement for knocking or pounding, pestle of a mortar.
mi'de A, **mide** (—.) معده 1. stomach. 2. good taste. — **ağzı** *anat.* cardia. — **ayakları taşır** (*lit.* The stomach carries the feet.) Strength depends on one's nourishment. — **baygınlığı** sinking sensation in the stomach. — **bezi** gastric gland. — **borusu** esophagus. — **boz**= 1. to cause suspicion or unrest. 2. to cause indigestion. — **bozukluğu** indigestion. —**si bulan**= /ın/ 1. to be nauseated. 2. to feel suspicious, to be upset. — **bulantısı** nausea. —**sine dokun**= /ın/ to cause indigestion — **dolgunluğu** fullness and oppression of stomach, indigestion. — **düşüklüğü** *path.* ptosis of the stomach. — **ekşimesi** acidity of the stomach. — **fesadı** indigestion. — **fesadına uğra**= to have a bad stomach from overeating. — **iltihabı** gastritis. —**si kabul etme**=, —**si kaldırma**= /ın/ 1. to be unable to digest. 2. not to tolerate unseemly behavior. — **kapısı** pylorus. — **kaynaması** feverish and disordered condition of the stomach. —**ye otur**= to lie heavy on the stomach. — **şişkinliği** distension of the stomach. — **tevessüü** dilatation of stomach. — **usaresi** *physiol.* gastric juice. — **zaafı** indigestion, dyspepsia.
mideci معده جى who thinks only of his belly; self-seeker.
midesiz معده سز 1. eating anything. 2. having bad taste.
mi'devî (.'. —) A, **midevî** (—. —) معدوى

1. pertaining to the stomach; gastric, stomachic. 2. good for the stomach.
midfaᵃˡ مدفع A lrnd. cannon, gun.
midhat مدحت A lrnd. á praising; praise; laudable action.
midhatger مدحتگر P lrnd. praiser. —î (...—) P, —lik condition of one who praises.
Midilli مدللو Gk 1. geog. Mytilene; hist. Lesbos. 2. l. c. small shaggy pony.
midrar (.—) مدرار A lrnd. that gives copious rain (cloud).
midye میدیه Gk mussel, zool., Mytilus edulis. — **dolması** mussels stuffed with rice.
mie ماه A lrnd. hundred.
mie'tan (..—), **mie'teyn** مئة مئتين A lrnd. two hundred.
mifad (.—) مقاد A lrnd. 1. spit, skewer. 2. poker for fire.
mifsad مفصد A lrnd. lancet, fleam.
miftah (.—) مفتاح A lrnd. 1. key. 2. code. 3. exercise book with answers for beginners.
mifzalˡˡ (.—) مفضال A lrnd. preeminent in beneficence; one who excels greatly.
migren میگرن F path. migraine.
miğ (—) میغ P lrnd. cloud; fog, mist.
miğfer مغفر A helmet. —î (..—) A lrnd. helmet-shaped.
miğnakᵏˡ (.—) میغناك P lrnd. hazy, foggy; cloudy, overcast.
miğtas مغطی A lrnd. small cup for bathing the eye.
miğzel مغزل A lrnd. spinning spindle.
miğzeliyüşşekl مغزلی الشكل A anat., fusiformis.
mih 1 (—) میخ P lrnd., same as **mıh**.
mih 2 مه P lrnd. great.
Mihabad (.——) مه آباد P hist., name of the most ancient prophet known to the old Zoroastrian Persians.
mihad (.—) مهاد A lrnd. bed, mattress, carpet (used to sit on).
mihan (.—) مهان P lrnd., pl. of **mih 2**.
mihanikᵏˡ (——.) مینیك A mechanics.
mihanikî (——.—) مینیكی A mechanical. —**ye** (——.—.) phil. mechanism. —**yet** (——.—.) mechanicalness; automatism.
mihaşˢˢˡ محش A lrnd. scythe.
mihber مخبر A phys., chem. test tube, flask.
mihcem, mihceme محجم محجمه A lrnd. cupping glass.
mihekᵏˡ محك A lrnd., same as **mehenk**.
mihen محن A lrnd., pl. of **mihnet**.
mihenkˢˡ محنك [mihek] same as **mehenk**.
mihfer, mihfere محفره A lrnd. digging implement, spade; pick.
mihî 1 (——) میخی P lrnd. 1. furnished with nails. 2. cuneiform. 3. dervish's stitched and patched cassock.

mihî 2 (.—) مهی P lrnd. greatness; superiority.
mihin (.—), **mihine** (.—.) مهین P lrnd. greatest, most superior.
mihkan, mihkana محقن A lrnd. enema, syringe.
mihlâc (.—) محلاج A lrnd. 1. carding-bow. 2. rolling-pin.
mihlakᵏˡ محلق P lrnd. razor.
mihman (.—) مهمان P lrnd. guest.
mihmandar (.——) مهماندار P lrnd. 1. host; hospitable person. 2. officer appointed to receive and entertain a foreign ruler or a distinguished personality; one who has charge of receiving and entertaining guests. —î (.———) P, —lık 1. hospitality, a waiting upon guests. 2. the office of a person who is in charge of entertaining distinguished guests.
mihmandost (.——) مهماندوست P lrnd. hospitable.
mihmanhane (.——.) مهمانخانه P lrnd. 1. inn, caravanserai; any place where travellers are lodged and entertained. 2. the world.
mihmanî (.——) مهمانی P lrnd. 1. hospitality. 2. entertainment, banquet, feast. —**i has** banquet to which only select friends are invited. —**i hitan** circumcision feast. —**i iyd** banquet on a religious festival.
mihmanlıkˢˡ (.—.) مهمانلق 1. quality of a guest. 2. entertainment, feast.
mihmannevaz, mihmannüvaz (.—.—) مهمانواز P lrnd. hospitable. —î (.—.——) P, —lık hospitality, hospitableness.
mihmanperver (.—..) مهمانپرور P lrnd. hospitable. —**âne** (.—..—.) P hospitably. —î (.—..—) P, —lik hospitableness; hospitality.
mihmansera, mihmanseray (.—.—) مهمانسرا P lrnd., same as **mihmanhane**.
mihnet محنت A trouble, affliction; torment, misery. — **çek=** to suffer, to be afflicted. —**abad** (..—) P poet. 1. abode of trouble. 2. the world. —**dide** (..—.) P lrnd. afflicted, suffering. —**gede, —kede** P poet. abode of trouble.
mihnetkeş محنتكش P lrnd. afflicted, suffering. —**an** (...—) P bearers of hardship, sufferers. —î (...—) P, —lik misery, suffering.
mihnetzede محنتزده P afflicted, distressed.
mihr مهر P lrnd. 1. sun. 2. love, friendship, affection. —**i muaccel** can. law the part of the wife's dower paid to her by her husband on consummation of the marriage. —**i müeccel** can. law the part of the dower agreed to be paid to a wife if divorced or widowed. **M—i Şeriat** the Prophet Muhammad.
mihrab محراب A same as **mihrap**. —**ı Cemşid**

mihrace lrnd. the sun. —**î** (.—.—) A 1. pertaining to a mosque niche. 2. shaped like a mihrab.
mihrace (.—.) مهاجه [based on Persian **mihrağ**] maharajah.
mihraf (.—) محراف A lrnd. surgeon's probe.
mihrak[k1] 1 محرق A phys. focus.
mihrak[ki] 2 (.—) محراك A lrnd. poker for stirring a fire.
mihrap[b1] (.—) محراب [mihrab] niche of a mosque indicating the direction of Mecca.
mihras (.—) مهراس A lrnd. very large mortar (for pounding grain).
mihrecan (..—) مهرجان A [from P **mihrgân**] time of the autumnal equinox.
mihrgân (.—) مهرگان P 1. day of the autumnal equinox (in Old Persia). 2. autumn. 3. *mus.*, name of a tune.
mihrî (.—) مهري P lrnd. 1. pertaining to the sun, solar. 2. pertaining to affection; affectionate.
mihriban (..—) مهربان P lrnd. affectionate, friendly, loving; friend. —**î** (..—.—) P, —**lık** friendship; affection; kindness.
mihrimah (..—) مهرماه P Persian calendar, name of the seventh month of the solar year.
mihsab (.—) محساب A lrnd. abacus.
mihter مهتر P lrnd. greater, superior. —**ân** (..—) P pl. —**î** (..—) P greatness, superiority. —**în** (..—) P greatest, supreme.
mihver محور A pivot; axle; axis.
=**mik**[ği] ملك cf. =**mık**.
mika (..') ميقا F mica.
mik'ab مكعب A same as **mikâp**. —**î** (..—) A cubic.
Mikado (..'.) ميقادو Jap Mikado.
Mikâil (.—.) ميكائل A Michael.
mikâp[b1] مكعب [mik'ab] cube; cubic; cubic measure.
mikaşist ميقاشيست F geol. mica schist.
mikat (—.—) ميقات A lrnd. 1. fixed time; place appointed for a certain time or action. 2. place on the road to Mecca where pilgrims assume the garb worn during the rites of the pilgrimage.
mikdar (.—) مقدار A 1. same as **miktar**. 2. lrnd. degree, rank, value. —**ı kâfi** enough, sufficient. —**ı mutavassıt** math. parameter.
Miken ميكن Gk geog. Mycenae.
Mikenai ميكناى Gk Mycenaean.
mikhâl[li] (.—), **mikhal**[li] مكحال A lrnd. stylus with which kohl is applied to the eye.
mikleb مقلب A lrnd., same as **mıkleb**.
miknese مكنسة A lrnd. broom.
miknet مكنت A lrnd. power, might. —**li**, —**lû** (..—) archaic powerful, mighty.
mikram (.—) مكرام A lrnd. munificent, kind.
mikraz (.—) مقراض A lrnd. scissors; snuffers.

mikrobiyoloji ميقروبيولوژى F microbiology.
mikrofilm ميقروفلم F microphotograph, microfilm.
mikrofon ميقروفون F microphone.
mikrokok[ğu] ميقروقوق F bacteriology micrococcus.
mikrolit ميقرولیت F min. microlite.
mikrometod ميقرومتد F med. micromethod.
mikrometre (..'.) ميقرومتر F micrometer.
mikron ميقرون F micron.
mikrop[bu] ميقروب F 1. microbe. 2. colloq. evil person. 3. slang policeman. 4. slang clever gambler.
mikrosefal[li] ميقروسفال F microcephalus; microcephalic.
mikroskop[bu] ميقروسقوب F microscope.
miksar (.—) مكثار A lrnd. very talkative; great talker.
miksefe مكثفة same as **mükessife**.
miktar (.—) مقدار [mikdar] 1. quantity, amount, measure. 2. portion, part; proportion. 3. dose.
mikyal[li] (.—) مكيال A lrnd. any measure for measuring grain.
mikyas (.—) مقياس A 1. scale (for measuring lengths); measuring instrument. 2. proportion; standard size; measure. 3. lrnd. the Nilometer at Cairo. —**ı amel** psychophysiol. ergograph. —**ı hassasiyet**, —**ı his** psychophysiol. esthesiometer. —**ı mâ** hydrometer. —**ı matar** meteor. rain gauge.
mikyasülharare (.—..—.) مقياس الحراره A obs., phys. thermometer.
mil 1 ميل A 1. stylus (with which kohl is applied to the eye); metal stylus. 2. axle; axletree; pivot; crowbar; axis. 3. probe, surgical sound. — **kalemi** stylus. — **yatağı**, — **yuvası** mech. step bearing.
mil 2 ميل F mile. —**i bahrî** lrnd. nautical mile. —**i berrî** lrnd. statute mile. — **taşı** milestone.
mil 3 ميل prov. silt; clay.
milâd (—.—) ميلاد A 1. w. cap. birth of Christ; Christmas Day. 2. lrnd. nativity, birthday. **M—dan evvel** before Christ, B. C. **M—ı İsa** 1. Christmas. 2. Christian era. **M—dan sonra** after Christ, A. D.
Milâdî (—.—.—) ميلادى A lrnd. 1. pertaining to the Birth of Christ. 2. pertaining to the Christian era; A. D.
milâhat[ti] (.—.) ملاحت A lrnd. seamanship, navigation.
mi'lâk[k1] (.—) معلاك A lrnd. stirrup strap.
mil'aka ملعقة A lrnd. spoon.
mil'akatraş ملعقةتراش P lrnd. maker of wooden spoons. —**lık** profession of a spoon maker.
mildiyu ميلديو F bot. mildew.
milel ملل A lrnd., pl. of **millet**. —**i erbaa**

the four communities of the Ottoman Empire, i. e. Muslims, Jews, Armenians and Greeks.

milh ملح A lrnd. salt; chemical salt.

milhafe ملحفة A lrnd. blanket; wrapper.

milhî (. —) ملحى A lrnd. saline, pertaining to salt. **—yet** (. —.) A saltiness; brackishness.

miligram ميليغرام F milligram.

mililitre (...'.) ميليليتره F milliliter.

milim ميليم F thousandth.

milimetre (...'.) ميليمتره F millimeter.

milimikron ميليميقرون F millimicron.

milis ميليس F militia. **— kuvvetleri** territorial forces.

militarizm ميليتاريزم F militarism.

milk[ki] ملك A lrnd., same as **mülk**.

milkat ملقط A lrnd. instrument for picking things up; forceps.

milkî (. —), **milkiye** (. —.) ملكى ملكيه A lrnd. pertaining to the state; pertaining to the civil administration of the state.

millet ملت A 1. nation; people; nationality. hist. religious community; group defined by religion and language. 2. colloq. crowd, folk. **—i beyza** lrnd. the whole of Islam. **M—ler Cemiyeti** League of Nations. **—i İslam** lrnd. 1. Islam. 2. the Muslims. **M— Meclisi** the National Assembly. **—i Mesihiye** lrnd. the Christians, Christendom. **M— Partisi** the National Party. **— vekili** deputy, member of the Turkish National Assembly. **— vekili dokunulmazlığı** Parliamentary immunity.

milletlerarası[nı] ملتلرآراسى A international. **M— Adalet Divanı** International Court of Justice, World Court. **M— İş Hukuku** International Labor Law. **M— Posta İttihadı** Universal Postal Union. **— teamül** international custom. **M— Tediyât Bankası** Bank of International Settlements. **— ticaret hukuku** international mercantile law.

millî (. —) ملى A national. **M— Eğitim Bakanlığı** the Ministry of Public Education. **— kıyafet** national costume. **— marş** national anthem. **M— Müdafaa Vekâleti** Ministry of Defense. **— takım** national team.

millileştir=[ir] ملليلشتيرمك /1/ to nationalize.

milliyegâh ملى يكاه Or. mus., name given to the **sultaniyegâh makamı** for a certain period.

milliyet ملت A 1. nationality; nationalism. 2. religious community. **—çi** nationalist. **—çilik** nationalism.

milliyetperver ملتپرور P nationalist. **—î** (.....—) P, **—lik** nationalism.

milyar ميليار F a thousand million.

milyarder ميلياردر F billionaire.

milyon ميليون F million.

milyoner ميليونر F millionaire.

milzab (. —) مزآب A lrnd. extremely stingy, very avaricious.

mim 1 م [**mim 2**] 1. name of the letter م. 2. sign, mark. **— koy=** /a/ to make a mark against something; to tick off.

mim 2 م A lrnd., Arabic script, name of the letter م (the letter is the twenty-fourth letter of the Arabic and twenty-seventh of the Ottoman alphabets. Its numerical value is 40. It is used as an abbreviation for the month **Muharrem** and for **temme**).

mi'mar (. —) A, **mimar** (— —) معمار architect. **— arşını** architect's cubit measuring about 78 centimeters. **— kademi** foot measuring half of an **arşın**. **M—ı kârhane-i kudret** lrnd. God. **—başı** Ott. hist. chief architect.

mi'marî (. — —) A, **mimarî** (— — —) معمارى A architecture; architectural. **—ye** (. — —.) fee paid to an architect.

mimarlık[ğı] معمارلوك architecture; architectural.

mimber منبر var. of **minber**.

mimî (— —) ميمى A lrnd. pertaining to **mim** (م).

mimik ميميك F mimic.

mimle=[r] ميملمك /ı/ 1. to mark with م. (item, etc.). 2. to mark down (as suspect, etc.). **—n=** pass.

mimli ميملى 1. notorious; marked (person), politically suspect. 2. marked with م.

mimraz (. —) ممراض A lrnd. delicate in health.

min من A lrnd. from; of; by means of; among.

mina 1 (— —) مينا P lrnd. 1. glass, glass bottle. 2. enamel. 3. sky, azure vault; blue.

mina 2 (—.) مينا ميناى A lrnd. port, harbor; anchorage.

minafam (— — —) ميناى فام P lrnd. azure, light blue; crystalline.

minakâr (— — —) ميناكار P lrnd. enameler. **—î** (— — — —) P 1. enameler's profession. 2. enameler's work.

minakop ميناقوب umbra (fish), zool., Umbrina cirrhosa.

min'am (. —) منعام A lrnd. exceedingly munificent.

minarat (. — —) منارات A lrnd. minarets.

minare (. —.) منارە [**menare**] minaret. **M—i Beyza** lrnd. the White Minaret at Damascus where it is believed that Jesus Christ will descend to rule on earth, before the Day of Judgment. **— boyu** height of about 20 or 30 meters. **—yi çalan kılıfını hazırlar** He who steals a minaret will have a proper cover prepared beforehand said of one who ventures to do something illegal. **— gibi** very tall; very high. **— gölgesi davul tozu** colloq. nonsense. **—lere kaftan giydir=** to illuminate the conical upper part of the minarets on special religious occasions. **— kırması** very tall person. **— külâhı** conical top of a minaret.

minareci مناره جى 1. person who repairs the conical top part of a minaret. 2. *slang* burglar who uses a ladder.

minassa منصّة A *lrnd.* 1. highly decorated raised seat on which the bride is exhibited to public view. 2. marriage chamber. 3. any place of exhibition.

minba'd من بعد A *lrnd.* hereafter, henceforth.

minbaz منبض A *lrnd.* carder's mallet.

minber منبر A pulpit (in a mosque). —**i nüh paye** P *lrnd.* the ninth heaven, the throne of God.

mincel منجل A *lrnd.* sickle, reaping hook.

mincihetin (..´..) من جهة A *lrnd.* in one respect, from one point of view.

mincümle من جمله A *lrnd.* 1. from among; out of. 2. for instance.

mindef مندف A *lrnd.* large bent bow used for teasing cotton; carder's mallet.

mindel مندل A *lrnd.* ambitious, greedy, covetous.

minder مندر A 1. cushion (to sit on); mattress. 2. wrestling ring. — **altı et=** /ı/ to shelve (a matter); to hide, to hush up. — **altına git=** to be shelved and forgotten. —**e çık=** *Ott. hist.* to become a minor government official. — **çürüt=** 1. to be fond of sitting, to sit idly. 2. to stay too long (on a visit). — **çürüten** persistent bore. —**e geç=** *Ott. hist.* to move up to a higher seat; to pass from an inferior grade to a higher one. — **ser=**, —**i ser=** to sit and settle comfortably; to make oneself at home. — **tuhafı** *Ott. hist.* public storyteller and mimic, monologist.

mine مينا [mina 1] 1. enamel. 2. dial (of a clock). — **çiçeği** 1. pigeon's-grass, vervain, *bot., Verbena officinalis.* 2. common garden verbena, *bot., Verbena hybrida.* —**ci** enameler. —**cilik** enameler's profession.

minel'an (..—) من الآن A *lrnd.* henceforth.

minelarş ilel ferş من العرش الى الفرش A *lrnd.* from the highest heaven to the outspread surface of the earth.

minelbab ilel mihrab (..—...—) من الباب الى المحراب A *lrnd.* (lit., from the door to the apse) the whole house; from end to end; entirely.

minele= مينه لمك /ı/ to enamel. —**n=** *pass.* —**t=** /ı, a/ *caus.* of **minele=**.

minelevvel من الأول A *lrnd.* from the beginning, from the first.

minelezel من الأزل A *lrnd.* from the beginning of eternity.

minelgaraib (...—.) من الغرائب A *lrnd.* How odd!

mineli مينه لى enameled.

minelkadim (...—) من القديم A *lrnd.* since ancient times, from days of old.

minen منن A *lrnd., pl.* of **minnet**.

mineral[ü] مينرال F mineral. — **yağlar** mineral oils. —**leştir=** *geol.* /ı/ to mineralize.

mineraloji مينرالوژى F mineralogy.

minessera ilâssüreyya (...—.—..—) من الثرى الى الثريا A *lrnd.* from the earth to the Pleiades.

min evvelihi ilâ âhirihi (......—.— —...) من اوله الى آخره A *lrnd.* from end to end, in fullest details.

minfah (.—) منفاخ A *lrnd.* a pair of bellows.

min gayri haddin (....´.) من غير حدٍّ A *lrnd.* if I might presume; although it is not for me to say.

min gayri resmin (....´.) من غير رسمٍ A *lrnd.* unofficially.

minh منه A *lrnd.* from him, from it, *as in* **mef'ulü minh.**

minha منها A *lrnd.* 1. from her, from it; from them. 2. *math.* subtrahend.

minhac (.—) منهاج A *lrnd.* 1. highway, wide road. 2. method, way.

minhar (.—) منخار A *lrnd.* nostril.

minhays من حيث A *lrnd.* in respect of, in connection with. —**el mecmû** in all, altogether.

minicik[ği] (.´.) مينيجك tiny, very small.

minik[ği] مينك dear little thing, small and sweet.

minimini مينى مينى tiny, very small.

minimum مينيموم L minimum.

minkale منقله A *math.* protractor.

minkar (.—) منقار A *lrnd.* 1. bird's beak. 2. stone cutter's chisel. —**î** (.——) A 1. beak shaped. 2. having an aquiline nose.

minkaş (.—) منقاش A *lrnd.* tweezers, pincers.

minküllilvücuh (....—) من كل الوجوه A *lrnd.* on all sides, all around; in every way.

minnacık[ği] مين نه جك *colloq.* very tiny.

minnet منت A 1. obligation (for a kindness received), indebtedness. 2. ungrudged kindness, favor. 3. taunt (for a former kindness). 4. *lrnd.* praise, thanks. — **altında kal=** to remain under obligation. — **çek=** to be indebted (for some kindness). — **efendimizin** You will do me a great kindness. — **et=** /a/ 1. to ask a favor; to bow (to). 2. to cast a favor in someone's teeth. — **size kaldı** To grant this favor is in your hands.

minnetdide (..—.) منت ديده P *lrnd.* one who has received a kindness.

minnetkâr (..—) منتكار P *lrnd.* beneficient, benefactor. —**âne** (..——.) P *lrnd.* beneficient (act), beneficiently.

minnetkeş منتكش P *lrnd.* one who is under obligation. —**ân** (...—) P *pl.*

minnetşinas (...—) منت شناس P *lrnd.* one who appreciates a favor; grateful. —**ân** (...——) P *pl.* —**âne** (...——.) P gratefully. —**î** (...——) P, —**lık** gratefulness, gratitude.

minnettar (..—) منتدار P grateful, indebted.

—âne (.. — —.) P gratefully. **—î** (.. — —) P, **—lık** gratitude.
minör مینور F *mus.* minor.
minre's من رأس A *lrnd.* from the beginning, again.
minser منسر A *lrnd.* 1. beak of a bird of prey. 2. troop of horseman; vanguard.
minşar (. —) منشار A *lrnd.* saw. **—î** (. — —) A saw-like, serrated.
minşefe منشفة A *lrnd.* towel.
minşel منشل A *lrnd.* fleshhook or fork with which meat is taken out of a pot.
mintan منتان [**nimten**] 1. a kind of heavy outer shirt. 2. shirt. **—lık** cloth for a shirt.
mintarafillâh (.. .. —) من طرف الله A *lrnd.* 1. by divine dispensation. 2. fortunately; as a godsend.
minu (— —) مینو P *lrnd.* 1. paradise; heaven, sky. 2. emerald.
minuta (. .'.) مینوطه It *naut.* log glass, hour glass, sand glass.
minüskül مینوسکول F 1. small letter, miniscule. 2. *university slang* small, unimportant.
minval[1] (. —), منوال A *lrnd.* method, manner, way.
minyatür مینیاتور F *art* miniature. **—cü** miniaturist.
minyon مینیون F dainty, tiny and delicate.
minzar (. —) منظار A *lrnd.* looking glass, mirror.
mîr (—) میر P *lrnd.* chief, lord, leader; commander, captain. **—im!** Sir! My dear friend! **—i alem** leader of troops. **—i âşıkan** cockscomb, *bot., Celosia cristata*. **—i kelâm** good speaker, eloquent orator. **—i kıbtiyan** *Ott. hist.* officer representing the Gypsy community (in affairs connected with the Government). **—i liva** *Ott. hist., same as* **mirliva**. **—i mîran** *Ott. hist.* pasha who governs a province.
mira میرا It surveyor's rod, levelling rod.
mi'rac (. —) A, **mirac** (— —) معراج *lrnd.* 1. *w. cap.* the Prophet Muhammad's ascent to heaven. 2. place of ascent; ladder, especially ladder by which souls and angels ascend to heaven. **M— Gecesi** the night of the Prophet Muhammad's miraculous journey to heaven (the 26th of Recep).
Mi'raciye (. — ٮ.) معراجیه A a poem recounting the miraculous journey of the Prophet Muhammad to heaven.
Mi'racname (. — —.) معراجنامه P *same as* **Mi'raciye**.
mirahor, mirahur (. — —) میراخور P *Ott. hist.* Master of the Horse.
miralay میرالای A *mil.* colonel. **—lık** rank and functions of a colonel.
miran (— —) میران P *lrnd., pl. of* **mîr**.

mirar (. —) مرار A *lrnd., pl. of* **merre**.
miraren (. —'.) مراراً A *lrnd.* repeatedly; frequently. **— ve kirâren** again and again, repeatedly.
miras (— —) میراث A inheritance; heritage; estate. **—a ehliyet** *law* capacity of succeeding. **—ın iktisabı** *law* devolution of inheritance. **—tan iskat** *law* disheritance. **—a kon=**. **— ye=** to inherit, to come into an inheritance.
mirasçı میراثجی heir; heiress; successor.
mirashar (— — —), **mirashor** (— — .) میراثخور P *lrnd.* heir, heiress.
mirasyedi میراثیدی 1. one who has inherited a great fortune. 2. spendthrift. **—lik** extravagance, squandering.
mir'at (. —) مرآت A *lrnd.* mirror, looking glass.
mircel مرجل A *lrnd.* copper cauldron, large kettle.
mirdas (. —) مرداس A *lrnd.* stone thrown down a well to ascertain its depth and whether there is water in it.
mirfak[1] مرفق A *lrnd.* elbow.
mirfaka مرفقة A *lrnd.* cushion on which to rest the elbow.
mirfed مرفد A *lrnd.* large bowl; drinking cup.
mîrî (— —) میری A *lrnd.* 1. belonging to the state; public. 2. the state treasury. 3. government tax or duty. **—sini al=** *archaic* /ın/ to collect government tax (on something). **— anbarı** *Ott. hist.* government storehouse. **— için** for the government account. **— malı** public money or property.
mîrilû (— — —) میریلو *Ott. hist.* men recruited as soldiers with pay to serve in long wars and when the regular army is insufficient.
mirkak[1] (. —) مرقاق A *lrnd.* rolling pin.
mirkam مرقم A *lrnd.* 1. pen, stylus for writing with. 2. gnomon, sun dial.
mirkat (. —) مرقاة A *lrnd.* ladder; staircase.
mirliva (. . —) میرلوا *obs.* commander of a brigade, major general. **—lık** the rank of a major general.
mirsâd (. —), **mirsad** مرصاد مرصد A *lrnd.* 1. place of observation; ambush; outlook; observatory. 2. broad open way. **—i ibret** place serving as an example and warning.
mirsat (. —) مرساة A *lrnd.* anchor.
mirvaha مروحة A *lrnd.* fan; ventilator.
mirvahacunban (.. .. —) مروح جنبان P one who moves the fan. **—î** (.. . — —) P moving the fan.
mirza (— —) میرزا P prince; son of a great lord; gentleman.
mirzab (. —) مرزاب A *lrnd.* water pipe; spout from a roof.
mis 1 مس [**misk**] *colloq., same as* **misk**. **— gibi** 1. sweetly scented; fragrant; delicious.

2. in a perfect manner. — **sabunu** perfumed soap.
mis 2 مِسّ P *lrnd.* copper.
misaferet (. — ..) مُسافَرَت A *lrnd.* 1. a being a guest. 2. *Ott. hist.* internment of the ambassadors and citizens of hostile countries in war time.
misafir (. — .) مُسافِر A 1. guest; visitor; company. 2. traveler; stranger. 3. speck in the eye. — **ağırla=** to entertain a guest. — **çarşafı** 1. fine sheet. 2. hypocritical spy. — **et=** /ı/ to have as a guest. — **gibi otur=** 1. to live in a house ready to leave at a moment's notice. 2. to sit in a constrained posture. — **konağı** guesthouse for travelers in a village. — **odası** living room; guest room. — **ol=** /a/ to be a guest; to stay as a guest. — **tohumu** *slang* bastard. — **umduğunu yemez, bulduğunu yer** *proverb* A guest eats what he finds, not what he expects.
misafireten (. — ...) مُسافِرَةً A as a guest.
misafirhane (. — . — .) مُسافِرخانَه P public guesthouse for travellers.
misafirlik[ği] مُسافِرلِك a being a guest; visit. — **et=** to be a guest; to visit. —**e git=** to go on a visit, to pay a visit.
misafirperver (. — ...) مُسافِرپَرْوَر P hospitable. —**lik** hospitality.
misak[kı] (— —) مِيساق A *law, pol.* compact; solemn promise; pact, treaty. **M—ı Millî** the National Pact of 1920.
misal[li] (. —) مِثال A 1. example, model; precedent. 2. match, like. 3. *phil.* idea. 4. *lrnd.* dream. 5. *lrnd.* command, edict. — **getir=** to give an example. —**i meymun** *Ott. hist.* Sultan's monogram. —**siz** matchless; unprecedented.
mi'sam مِعْصَم A *lrnd.* wrist.
mi'sar 1 (. —), **mi'sar** مِعْصَر A *lrnd.* instrument for crushing or squeezing, press.
mis'ar 2 (. —) **misar** مِسْعَر A *lrnd.* poker for stirring a fire.
misas (. —) مِساس A *lrnd.* a touching, feeling, handling.
misbah مِسْبَح A *biol.* fin; bladder; float.
misbar (. —) مِسْبار A *lrnd.* surgical probe or sound or tent.
misen[nni] مِسَنّ A *lrnd.* hone, grindstone.
misfat (. —) مِصْفاة A *lrnd.* filter used in purifying water.
misfen مِسْفَن A *lrnd.* 1. adze, hatchet. 2. file.
mishal مِسْحَل A *lrnd.* 1. tool for smooothing, file, plane. 2. versed in reciting the Quran. 3. eloquent orator.
misil[sli] مِثْل [**misl**] similar, equal; equal amount; as much again. —**i görülmemiş** The like of which has never been seen; unique.
—**iyle mukabele** *law* retortion; *intern. law* retaliation by a State upon subjects of another. —**i müşterek** *math.* common multiple. —**i müşterek-i asgar** *arith.* lowest common multiple. —**i müşterek-i âzam** *arith.* highest common factor. —**i yok** matchless. —**leme** *same as* **misliyle mukabele**. —**li**, —**lu** like, similar. —**siz** matchless.
misina مِيسِينا It *fishery* gut (between line and hook).
misistra (.'.) مِسْتَرَه *obs.* short steel-pointed goad or dart.
misk[kı] مِسْك A musk. — **çiçeği** field scabious, field knautia, *bot., Knautia arvensis.* — **faresi** European muskrat. — **gibi kokuyor** fragrant. — **göbeği** musk bag, musk pod. — **ile anber** as desired, perfect. — **keçisi** musk deer, *zool., Moschus moschiferus.* — **kedisi** civet cat, *zool., Viverra civetta*; zibeth, *zool., Viverra zibetha.* — **otu** musk plant, *bot., Mimulus moschatus.* — **rengi** dark grey, pepper-and-salt color. — **samuru** mink, *zool., Mustela lutreola.* — **torbası** musk bag.
miskab مِسْقَب A *lrnd., same as* **matkap**.
miskal[li] **1** (. —) مِثْقال A weight of 1 ½ drams (for precious stones).
miskal[li] **2** مِسْكَل [*Arabic* **miskel**] *lrnd.* Panpipe. — **kamışı** 1. Panpipe reed. 2. anything packed close like a Panpipe.
miskam (. —) مِسْقام A *lrnd.* sickly, unhealthy, infirm.
miskat (. —) مِسْقات A *lrnd.* drinking cup, drinking vessel.
miskçi مِسْكچى dealer in musk, perfumer.
misket 1 مِسْكَت F 1. muscatel grape. 2. scented fruit. — **şarabı** muscatel wine. — **üzümü** muscatel grape.
misket 2 مِسْكَت F *artillery* 1. musket (gun): 2. grape-shot.
miskî (. —) مِسْكى A *lrnd.* 1. musky, pertaining to musk. 2. of the color of musk, dark pepper-and-salt color. 3. sugar plum.
miskin 1 مِسْكين [A .—] 1. idle, lazy, abject; poor spirited. 2. poor, wretched. 3. leprous; leper. —**ler dergâhı**, —**ler tekkesi** leper hospital.
miskin 2 (. —) مِسْكين P *lrnd.* 1. musky. 2. black.
miskinhane (.. — .) مِسْكينخانَه P *lrnd.* 1. leper hospital. 2. den of idlers.
miskinleş=[ir] مِسْكينلَشْمَك to become idle; to become poor or wretched.
miskinlik[ği] مِسْكينلِك 1. abjectness, indolence. 2. poverty; wretchedness. 3. leprosy.
miskiye (. — .) مِسْكِيَّة A *zool., Viveridae.*
misl مِثْل A *lrnd., same as* **misil**.
misliler *neol., zool., Viveridae.*
misma[aı] مِسْمَع A *med.* 1. ear. 2. stethoscope.

mismar (.—) مِسْمَار A *lrnd.* nail, peg, pin.
—î (.——) A nail shaped; cuneiform.
=**misse** مِسّ *cf.* =**mıssa**.
mistaçu, mistaçyo (..'.) مِسْتَاجُور سْتَاجْيُو It *naut.* spritsail yard.
mistar مِسْطَر A *lrnd.*, same as **mıstar**.
mister مِيسْتَر F *rel. of antiquity* mystery.
mistikᵍⁱ مِيسْتِيك F mystical.
mistika, mistiko (..'.) مِسْتِيقَا مِسْتِيقُو It *naut.* a kind of sailing boat similar to a schooner.
mistisizm مِيسْتِيسِيزْم F mysticism.
misvakᵏⁱ (.—) مِسْوَاك A stick of wood beaten into fibers at one end and used as a toothbrush.
— **ağacı** toothbrush tree, *bot.*, Salvadora persica.
misyon مِيسْيُون F mission.
misyoner مِيسْيُونَر F missionary. —**lik** function and quality of a missionary.
=**miş 1** مِشّ *cf.* =**mış 1**.
=**miş 2** (.'.) مِشْ *cf.* =**mış 2**.
miş 3 (—) مِيش P *lrnd.* sheep.
mi'şar 1 (.—) مِعْشَار A *lrnd.* one tenth, a tenth part.
miş'ar 2 مِشْعَر A *lrnd.*, same as **meş'ar**.
=**mişçesine** مِشْچَسِنَه *cf.* =**mışçasına**.
mişezar (—.—) مِيشَزَار P *lrnd.* an oak grove.
=**mişik 1** (.'.) مِشِك *cf.* =**mışık 1**.
-**mişik 2** (.'.) مِشِك *cf.* -**mışık 2**.
=**mişin 1,** =**mişiniz** (.'..) مِشِك *cf.* =**mışın 1**.
-**mişin 2,** -**mişiniz** (.'..) مِشِك *cf.* -**mışın 2**.
mişin 3 (——) مِيشِين P *lrnd.*, same as **meşin**.
mişkât (.—) مِشْكَاة A *lrnd.* recess in the wall, lamp niche.
=**mişken** (.'.) مِشْكَن *cf.* =**mışken**.
=**miş'li** *neol., gram.* dubitative, indeterminate.
mişmiş مِشْمِش A *lrnd.* apricot.
mişrakᵏⁱ (.—) مِشْرَاك A *lrnd.* place exposed to the sun.
mişrat (.—), **mişrat** مِشْرَاط A *lrnd.* surgeon's lancet; scarificator.
=**mişse** (.'.) مِشَّ *cf.* =**mışsa**.
=**mişti** (.'.) مِشْتِى *cf.* =**mıştı**.
mişvar (.—) مِشْوَار A *lrnd.* pace, manner of going, course (events); behavior.
mişvare (.—.) مِشْوَارَه A *lrnd.* honeycomb.
mişvargâh (.——), **mişvergeh** مِشْوَارْگَاه P *lrnd.* place of display; arena.
mişvel مِشْوَل A *lrnd.* small sickle.
—**î** (..—) A falciform.
mit مِيت F myth.
mithare مِطْهَرَه A *lrnd.*, same as **mathere**.
mitil مِيتِل *prov.* case of a quilt; pillow case.
miting مِيتِنْگ F public meeting, demonstration. — **yap**= to hold a public demonstration.

mitoloji مِيتُولُوژِى F mythology.
mitolojikᵍⁱ مِيتُولُوژِيك F mythological.
mitra (.'.) مِيتْرَا Gk 1. chimney cowl, chimney pot. 2. miter (of bishop).
mitralˡˡ مِيتْرَال F *anat.* mitral, mitral valve.
— **darlığı** *path.* mitral stenosis.
mitralyöz مِيتْرَالْيُوز F machine gun.
mi'vel مِعْوَل A *lrnd.* stonemason's pointed pick for cutting stone.
miyah (.—) مِيَاه A *lrnd., pl. of* **ma 2**.
—**ı harre** hot springs, hot wells.
miyan (.—) مِيَان P *lrnd.* 1. medium; middle, center. 2. waist, loins. 3. interval. 4. *Or. mus.*, name of the third line of a **beste** or song.
miyanbâlâ (.———) مِيَان بَالَا P *lrnd.* of middle stature.
miyanbend (.——) مِيَان بَنْد P *lrnd.* belt, girdle.
miyanbeste (.—..) مِيَان بَسْتَه P *lrnd.* ready, girded.
miyancı مِيَانْجِى a go-between, mediator. —**lık** mediatorship.
miyandar (.——) مِيَانْدَار P *same as* **miyancı**.
miyane (.—.) مِيَانَه P *lrnd.* 1. middle; middling; moderate. 2. interval. 3. middle pearl in a necklace. 4. *same as* **meyane**².
miyanegî (.—.—) مِيَانَگِى P *lrnd.* 1. middle, half. 2. mediation.
miyangîr (.——) مِيَانْگِير P *lrnd.* mediator, intercessor; reconciler.
miyanhâli (.———) مِيَان خَالِى P *lrnd.* 1. hollow within. 2. separated by an interval.
miyanhane (.——.) مِيَانْخَانَه 1. *mus.* middle tone. 2. *lrnd.* middle part of the arms and of an archery bow.
miyankadᵈᵈⁱ (.—.) مِيَان قَد P *lrnd.* of a middle stature.
miyanser (.—.) مِيَانْسَر P *lrnd.* 1. crown of the head. 2. small, gem-studded crown.
miyansera, miyanseray (.—.—) مِيَان سَرَا مِيَان سَرَاى P *lrnd.* middle; square, court of a house.
mi'yar (.—) A, **miyar** (——) مِعْيَار 1. standard; measure. 2. *chem.* reagent.
miyasma (..'.) مِيَاسْمَا Gk miasma.
miyav مِيَاو a meowing (cat); meow.
miyavla= مِيَاوْلَه to meow. —**t**= /ı/ to cause to meow.
miyokard مِيُوكَارْد F *anat.* myocardium.
miyokardit مِيُوكَارْدِيت F *path.* myocarditis.
miyopᵇᵘ مِيُوپ F shortsighted. —**i** shortsightedness, myopia.
miyozit مِيُوزِيت F *med.* myositis.
=**miz 1** مِز *cf.* =**mız**.
miz 2 (—) مِيز P *lrnd.* 1. guest. 2. stool on which a tray of food is placed; table.
mi'zab (.—), **mîzâb** (——) مِيزَاب مِثْعَب A *lrnd.* eavestrough; gargoyle, spout by which rain

mizabe

runs from a roof. **M—i Rahmet** the spout from the roof of the Kaaba of Mecca.
mizabe (.—.) ميزابه A *anat.* sulcus.
mizac (.—) مزاج A same as **mizaç**. **—i beden** *lrnd.* bodily constitution, state of health. **—i şahsî** *psych.* idiosyncrasy.
mizacdan (.——) مزاجدان P *lrnd.* tactful, knowing dispositions and ways of humoring them.
mizacgir (.——) مزاج گير P *lrnd.* who humors the whims of others. **—âne** (.———.) P tactfully, considerately. **—î** (.———) P knowing how to deal with people's dispositions.
mizaç[cı] (.—) مزاج [mizac] 1. temperament; disposition. 2. humor, whim, mood. 3. *lrnd.* state of health. **—ına hizmet et=** to humor, to tolerate the whims of others. **—a mugayir** contrary to one's liking.
mizaçsız مزاجسز unwell. **—lık** ill health.
mizah (.—) مزاح A a joking, joke; humor. **— mecmuası** humor magazine. **—çı** 1. humorist. 2. joker. **—î** (.——) A humorous.
müzahnüvis (.—.—) مزاح نويس P *lrnd.* humorist.
mizan 1 (——) ميزان A 1. *lrnd.* balance; pair of scales; measure; weight. 2. *arith.* proof, check. 3. *bookkeeping* trial balance. 4. *lrnd.* mind, judgment, logic. 5. *lrnd.* justice, equity. 6. *astr.* constellation and sign *Libra*.
mizan- 2 (.—) ميزان A meter, as in **mizanülharare, mizanülhava**.
mizana (..'.) ميزانه It *naut.* mizzen.
mizandri ميزاندرى F *psychiatry* misandry, hatred of men by women.
mizanpaj ميزانپاژ F *print.* paging, page-setting, making up (in pages).
mizansen ميزانسن F *theat.* set.
mizantrop ميزانتروپ F misanthrope, manhater.
mizanülharare (.—..—.) ميزان الحراره A *lrnd.* thermometer.
mizanülhava (.— ...) ميزان الهوا A *lrnd.* barometer.
mi'zar (.—) A, **mizar** (——) معنار *lrnd.* 1. covering, veil. 2. excuse.
mizban (——) ميزبان P *lrnd.* master of the house, host. **—ân** P *pl.* **—î** (————) P hospitality.
mizber مزبر A *lrnd.* reed pen.
mizebbe مذبّه A *lrnd.* implement for driving away flies, fly swatter, fly flap.
mi'zene مأذنه A *lrnd.* special place inside a mosque, where the muezzin recites the call to prayer.
mizer ميزر F misere, a card game.
mizher مزهر A *lrnd.* a kind of lute played with a bow.
mizitra (.'.) ميزيتره Gk fresh cheese, cheese curds.

mizkâr (.—) منت كار A *lrnd.* that always begets male offspring.
mizmar (.—) مزمار A 1. *anat.* glottis. 2. *lrnd.* a kind of flute, pipe. **—zen** (.—.) P flute player.
mizofobi ميزوفوبى F *psychiatry* mysophobia, morbid dread of dirt.
mizojini ميزوژينى F *psychiatry* misogyny, hatred of women.
mizopedi ميزوپدى P *psychiatry* misopedia, dislike of children.
mizvac (.—) مزواج A *lrnd.* who marries often (woman).
mobilya (.'.) موبيليه It furniture. **—lı** furnished.
moda 1 ('.) مودا It fashion. **—sı geç=** /ın/ 1. to be out of fashion. 2. to be forgotten. **—ya uy=** to keep up with fashions, to be fashionable.
moda 2 مودا It *naut.* close reef.
model مودل F 1. model, pattern; example. 2. mannequin; artist's model. 3. fashion magazine. **—ci** pattern maker.
modern مودرن F modern. **—izm** modernism.
modistra (..'.) موديستر It dressmaker.
modulasyon مودولاسيون F *mus.* modulation.
Moğol موغول مغل P Mongol. **—ca** (.'.) Mongolian language. **—istan** P Mongolia.
mola ('.) مولا It 1. act of slacking off or letting go; rest, pause. 2. *naut.* Let go. Ease off. **— et=** 1. /ı/ to slacken, to ease off. 2. to rest oneself. **— iskota** *naut.* Let go the main sheet. **— taşı** stone by the road on which porters can rest their loads. **— ver=** to rest oneself; to halt; to cease work for a while.
molada مولاده *obs.* aged female slave.
molekül مولكول F *chem.* molecule. **— derişmesi** molecular concentration.
molla (.'.) ملا |*from Arabic* mevla| 1. theological student, mullah. 2. *Ott. hist.* chief judge; doctor of Muslim law. **M—yı Rum** *lrnd.*, a title of *Mevlana Jalaladdin Rumî.* **—lık** *abstr. n.* **—yâne** as becomes a mullah.
moloz مولوز Gk 1. rough stone; rubble. 2. useless; good for nothing. **— döşek** stone bedding. **— duvar** wall of rough stones. **—lu pilâv** *slang* pilav with plenty of meat in it. **— taşı** rubble stone. **—laş=** *slang* to become ugly and old. **—luk** soil full of rough stones.
moment مومانت F *mech.* momentum.
monarşi (...) مونارشى F monarchy.
monat[dı] مونات F *phil.* monad.
monden (.'.) موندن F fancy, elegant, modern.
monla منلا *var. of* **molla**.
monografi مونوغرافى F monography.
monogram مونوغرام F monogram.

monoklü موُنوُقل F monocle.
monolog موُنوُلوُغ F monologue.
monopleji موُنوُپلیژى P monoplegia.
monopol (...ˈ.) موُنوُپوُل F monopoly.
monotip موُنوُتیپ F print. monotype.
monoton موُنوُطوُن F monotonous.
monsenyör موُنسِنیوُر F monsignor.
monşer موُنشِر F colloq. my dear.
montaj موُنتاژ F mech. mounting, fitting, setting.
mor موُر 1. violet, purple. 2. a kind of brown, as in **mor koyun, mor inek**. — **et**= /ı/ slang to cause to be ashamed, to humiliate. — **ol**= slang 1. to have a good hiding. 2. to feel ashamed. — **salkım** wisteria. — **tavuk** purple gallinule (bird). — **yakut** 1. hyacinth. 2. amethyst.
morar=ır موُرارمق 1. to become purple. 2. to become bruised. —**t**= /ı/ to make purple.
moratoryum (...ˈ.) موُراتوُریوُم L moratorium.
more موُره Albanian Hey there!
morela (.ˈ.) موُرِله It naut. fid, wooden marline spike.
moren (..ˈ) موُرِن F geol. moraine.
morfem (..ˈ) موُرفِم F ling. morpheme.
morfin (..ˈ) موُرفین F morphine. — **at**= slang to speak biting words. — **koy**= school slang to fool the teacher.
morfinizm موُرفینیزم F morphinism, morphine habit.
morfinoman موُرفینوُمان F morphinomaniac, morphine addict.
morfinomani موُرفینوُمانى F morphinomania.
morfoloji موُرفوُلوُژى F ling. morphology.
morg موُرغ F morgue, mortuary.
morina (..ˈ.) موُرینه It white sturgeon, zool., Huso huso.
morlan=ır, **morlaş**=ır موُرلانمق موُرلاشمق to become purple.
morlukğu موُرلوُق purpleness.
mornel موُرنِل It naut. marline, houseline.
Mors 1 موُرس F Morse (telegraph). — **alfabesi** Morse alphabet, Morse code.
mors 2 موُرس F walrus, zool., Odobenus rosmarus.
mort موُرت F slang dead; death. — **ol**= to die.
morti (.ˈ.) موُرتى It slang dead. —**yi çek**= to die.
mortla=r موُرتلامق slang 1. to die. 2. to lose (in gambling). —**t**= 1. /ı/ to kill. 2. to clear out an opponent (in gambling).
morto, mortu (.ˈ.) موُرتوُ It slang, same as **morti**. —**yu çek**= slang to die. —**cu** 1. the imam officiating at a funeral. 2. the driver of a hearse.
morukğu موُروُق Arm slang 1. old man; dotard. 2. father. —**la**=, —**laş**= to age, to grow old.

morumsu, morumtrakğı موُروُمتراق purplish.
Moskof موُسقوُف 1. hist. Moscovite, Russian; colloq. the Russians. 2. ruthless. — **bezi** Russian duck. — **camı** min. Muscovy glass, muscovite. — **toprağı** geol. holystone, tripoli. —**ça** (.ˈ.) colloq. Russian, Russian language. —**luk** abstr. n.
Moskova (.ˈ..) موُسقوُوه geog. Moscow.
mosmor (.ˈ.) موُصموُر very purple, all purple.
mostariye (.ˈ..) موُسطاریه [Arabic **mustâr**] lrnd. new, strong wine.
mostra (.ˈ.) موُستره It 1. sample, pattern. 2. hunting decoy bird. —**sını boz**= /ın/ colloq. to act in such manner as to disgrace and humiliate another. — **ol**= slang to make an exhibition of oneself.
mostralıkğı موُسترهلق 1. a thing that is meant only for sample but not for sale. 2. slang person who shows off but does nothing in action.
motif موُتیف F art, mus. pattern, motif.
motor موُطوُر F 1. motor; auto. engine. 2. motorboat. 3. slang one who is made a fool of. — **kaputu** auto. hood. —**u bozul**= slang to have diarrhea. —**bot** motorboat. —**cu** motorman, driver.
motorize موُطوُریزه F motorized.
motosiklet موُطوُسقلِت F motorcycle. —**li** motorcyclist.
motör موُطوُر F same as **motor**. —**lü** 1. having a motor; motorized. 2. motor train. —**tren** F motor train.
motris موُتریس F electric locomotive.
mozaikki موُزاییک F mosaic.
mozakğı, **mozalak**ğı موُزالاق prov. young pig.
möble موُبله F furnished.
Mösyö (.ˈ.) موُسیوُ F 1. Monsieur, M. 2. foreign gentleman.
-msı, -msi, etc., after consonants **-ımsı,** etc., مسى adjectival suffix. 1. attached to adjective somewhat, as in **acımsı, kırmızımsı**. 2. attached to substantive resembling, somewhat like, e. g., **kışlamsı** resembling barracks.
-msi, -msu, -msü مسى cf. **-msı**.
-mtırakğı متراق var. of **-mtrak**.
-mtrakğı, after consonants **-ımtrak, -imtrak,** etc., متراق adjectival suffix somewhat..., slightly, —ish, as in **acımtrak, mavimtrak**.
mu 1 مى cf. **mı**.
mu 2 (—) موُ P lrnd. hair; the hair; fiber.
muabber مُعبّر A lrnd. interpreted (dream).
muabbir مُعبّر A lrnd. interpreter of dreams; soothsayer. —**in** (...ˈ—) A pl.

muaccel مُعَجَّل A *can. law* promptly paid, paid down, paid in ready money. —**ât** (..—) A *pl.* of **muaccele**.

muaccele مُعَجَّلة A *can. law* sum of money paid down at the conclusion of bargains, especially those parts of the price paid at once on the purchase of real property.

muaccelen (..′..) مُعَجَّلاً A *com.* 1. hurriedly. 2. promptly paid down.

muacceliyet مُعَجَّليَّت A *com.* maturity, due date. — **kesbet=** to fall due, to mature for payment.

muaccib مُعَجِّب A *lrnd.* surprising, astonishing.

muaccil مُعَجِّل A *lrnd.* who causes to make haste; that admits no delay. —**en** (..′..) A in haste.

muacciz مُعَجِّز A *lrnd.* annoying; that bothers; importunate. —**lik** annoyance, importunity.

muadat (.——) مُعاداة A *lrnd.* an acting with enmity; enmity, hostility.

muaddel مُعَدَّل A *lrnd.* modified, corrected.

muaddid مُعَدِّد A *lrnd.* counter, indicator (electricity, gas, water).

muaddil مُعَدِّل A *lrnd.* modifying, adjusting, straightening; modifier.

muaddile مُعَدِّلة A *astr.* equatorial.

muaddilünnehar (.....—) مُعَدِّل النهار A *astr.* equinoctial line.

muadelât (.—.—) مُعادلات A *lrnd., pl.* of **muadele**.

muadele (.—..) مُعادلة A 1. *math.* equation. 2. *lrnd.* a being mutually equal, equality.

muadelet (.—..) مُعادلت A *lrnd.* a being equivalent, equivalence.

muadil (.—.) مُعادل A equivalent; alike; similar.

muaf (.—) مُعاف A 1. exempted; free (from). 2. *med.* immune. 3. *lrnd.* pardoned, forgiven. — **tut=** /ı, dan/ to exempt (from).

muafat (.——) مُعافات A *lrnd.* 1. an excusing, exempting, exemption. 2. a restoring to health, preserving in health (God); health, safety, security.

muafiyet (.—..) مُعافيت A 1. exemption. 2. *lrnd.* immunity. 3. *lrnd.* a being excused.

muaflıkᵏⁱ (.—..) مُعافلق same as **muafiyet**.

muahat (.——) مُعاخات A *lrnd.* 1. an entering into a brotherhood; fraternity; brotherly love. 2. intimate friendship.

muahazat (.—.—) مُواخَذات A *lrnd., pl.* of **muaheze**.

muahedat (.—.—) مُعاهَدات A *lrnd., pl.* of **muahede**.

muahede (.—..) مُعاهَدة A 1. treaty, pact. 2. *lrnd.* a mutually entering into an alliance or covenant; a swearing mutually. — **akdi** conclusion of a treaty.

muahedename (.—..—.) مُعاهَدةنامه P treaty, agreement.

muahezat (...—) مُواخَذات A *lrnd.* criticisms; blaming, reproving.

muaheze مُواخَذة A *lrnd.* a calling to account, a chiding, reproving, blaming; reprimand, censure, criticism. — **et=** /ı/ to criticize; to blame.

muahezekâr (.—..—) مُواخَذةكار P *lrnd.* reproving; critical.

muahhar مُؤَخَّر A 1. deferred, subsequent; consequent. 2. posterior. —**an**, —**en** (..′..) A subsequently; latterly; later.

muahid (.—.) مُعاهِد A 1. *law* contracting; signatory (of a treaty etc.). 2. *Ott. hist.* non-Muslim who has taken an oath of fealty and agreed to pay tribute to the Sultan; tributary, subject. —**eyn** (.—.—) A the two mutual signatories (of a treaty). —**în** (.—.—) P *pl.* the contracting parties.

muahiz (.—.) مُؤاخِذ A *lrnd.* one who reproaches; criticizer.

muakabe (.—..) مُعاقَبة A *lrnd.* an inflicting a consequence on another; a punishing, retaliating; punishment.

muakade (.—..) مُعاقَدة A *lrnd.* a mutually making a contract, agreement, treaty etc.; league, alliance.

muakale (.—..) مُعاقَلة A *lrnd.* a contending as to intellect or wisdom; a disputing (with another) for superiority of genius.

muakid (.—.) مُعاقِد A *lrnd.* who mutually make a contract or agreement.

muakkab مُعَقَّب A *lrnd.* followed, pursued; succeeded.

muakkad مُعَقَّد A *lrnd.* 1. knotted; involved, intricate. 2. obscure, difficult speech.

muakkib مُعَقِّب A *lrnd.* 1. follower, pursuer. 2. one who follows up legal procedure in government offices. —**în** (...—) A *pl.*

mualecat (.—.—) مُعالَجات A *lrnd., pl.* of **mualece**.

mualece (.—..) مُعالَجة A *lrnd.* a treating one medically; medical treatment.

muallâ (..—) مُعَلَّى A 1. *lrnd.* exalted, sublime. 2. *phil.*. transcendent.

muallâkᵏⁱ مُعَلَّق A 1. hung, hanging; suspended. 2. left in suspense; uncertain. —**ta kal=** 1. to remain in suspense, uncertain. 2. to remain suspended.

muallâkat (...—) مُعَلَّقات A 1. *lrnd.* suspended things. 2. *pre-Islamic Arab hist.* hung up for public attention in the temple of Mecca. **M—ı Seb'a** the celebrated seven Arabic poems hung up in the Kaaba at Mecca.

muallâkıyet. (...—.) مُعَلَّقيَّت A *lrnd.* suspense.

muallel مُعَلَّل A *lrnd.* having a cause.

muallem معلّم A *lrnd.* taught, trained, instructed.

muallil معلّل A *lrnd.* one who offers a reason; who makes an excuse.

muallim معلّم A *obs.* school teacher, teacher; master. **M—i Evvel** *lrnd.* 1. Aristotle. 2. Satan. 3. *l. c.* headmaster. **—i sâni** Farabi.

muallimât (...—) معلّمات A *lrnd., pl. of* **muallime.**

muallime معلّمة A *obs.* schoolmistress, woman teacher.

muallimhane (...—.) معلّمخانه P *Ott. hist.* school for teachers.

muallimîn (...—) معلّمين A *lrnd., pl. of* **muallim.**

muallimlik[ki] معلّملك *obs.* profession of a teacher; teaching job.

muamelât (—.—) معاملات A *lrnd., pl. of* **muamele. —ı ticariye** commercial transactions.

muamele (—..) معامله A 1. a dealing with another, a treating another (well, ill etc.); treatment; a behaving, conducting oneself (towards another); conduct. 2. formality, procedure; transaction. 3. business; interest on money. 4. *slang* sexual intercourse. **— görmüş** approved and marked for action (of an application or decision). **— vergisi** tax on transactions, tax on turnover.

muameleci معامله‌جى 1. broker, moneylender. 2. real estate agent. **—lik** money lending.

muamma (..—) معمّا A 1. mystery; obscure, enigmatic. 2. riddle, puzzle. 3. *lrnd.* riddle whose solution depends on changing the letters in a key word.

muammagû (..——) معمّاگو P *lrnd.* composer of enigmas.

muammem معمّم A *lrnd.* turbaned, crowned.

muammer معمّر A *lrnd.* blessed with long life, long lived.

muammerîn (...—) معمّرين A *Arab. hist.* persons famous for having reached great age, the long-lived ones.

muanaka (—..) معانقه A *lrnd.* an embracing one another; embrace.

muanber معنبر A *lrnd.* perfumed with ambergris.

muanede (—..) معانده A *lrnd.* a perversely opposing; a being stubborn; obstinacy.

muanid (—.) معاند A *lrnd.* obstinate, stubborn, unyielding.

muanik[ki] (—.) معانق A *lrnd.* one who embraces (another).

muannid معنّد A *lrnd.* obstinate, perverse, unyielding. **—âne** (...—.) P stubbornly, obstinately. **—lik** obstinacy.

muanven معنون A *lrnd.* marked with a title or inscription (book, letter), having a title, entitled.

muar (.—) معار A *lrnd.* lent.

muaraza (.—..) معارضه A *lrnd.* 1. controversy. 2. quarrel; noisy dispute.

muarefe (.—..) معارفه A *lrnd.* a being mutually acquainted; acquaintance.

muarekât (.—.—) معاركات A *lrnd., pl. of* **muareke.**

muareke (.—..) معاركه A *lrnd.* a fighting, battle, fight; squabble.

muarız (.—.) معارض A /a/ against, opposing, hostile; opponent, antagonist. **—în** (.—.—) A *lrnd.* opponents.

muarra (..—) معرّا A *lrnd.* 1. bared, uncovered, naked, nude. 2. void, exempt from.

muarreb معرّب A *lrnd.* Arabicized.

muarref معرّف A 1. *Arabic gram.* made definite (noun), having the definite article. 2. *lrnd.* explained, described, made known; *phil.* definite.

muarrif معرّف A 1. *Arabic gram.* that makes definite (noun). 2. *hist.* person who mentioned in thanksgiving the names of benevolent people just before the Friday noon prayer in a mosque; master of ceremonies. 3. *lrnd.* that explains, makes known, who makes known. **—ân** (...—) P *pl.*

muarrik[ki] معرّق A *lrnd.* producing perspiration.

muasaret معاصرت A *lrnd.* a being contemporary (with), contemporaneousness.

muasır (.—.) معاصر A contemporary. **—în** (.—.—) A *pl.*

muasker معسكر A *lrnd.* military camp, place of encampment.

muassel معسّل A *lrnd.* sweetened with honey, honeyed.

muaşaka (.—..) معاشقه A *lrnd.* a making love, flirtation.

muaşeret (.—..) معاشرت A a having social relations with another, social intercourse. **— âdabı** rules of social behavior, good manners, etiquette.

muaşık[ki] (.—.) معاشق A *lrnd.* one who loves; lover.

muaşir (.—.) معاشر A *lrnd.* who associates with another. **—an** (.—.—) P *pl.*

muaşşer معشّر A 1. *lrnd.* made ten; divided into ten; made up of ten elements or parts. 2. *geom.* decagon. 3. *pros.* in stanzas of ten couplets each. 4. *lrnd.* tithed.

muaşşir معشّر A *Ott. hist.* tithe collector.

muatat (.——) معاطات A *lrnd.* 1. a giving, submitting. 2. a handing things to one another.

muateb (.—.) معاتب A *lrnd.* reproved, reprehended.

muatebe (.—..) معاتبه A *lrnd.* a reproving, blaming; reproof, reprimand.

muatib (.—.) معاتب A *lrnd.* reprover, blamer.

Red 50.

muattal مُعَطَّل A 1. abandoned, deserted; neglected. 2. vacant, disused; idle (factory). 3. unoccupied, jobless.

muattar مُعَطَّر A lrnd. perfumed, fragrant, scented.

muattarsaz (...—) مُعَطَّرْسَاز P perfuming; perfumer.

muattıs مُعَطِّس A lrnd. sternutative (medicine), sternutatory.

muavaza (.—..) مُعَاوَضَه A 1. a returning like for like, a compensating; compensation. 2. exchange, barter. —lı involving unfair dealings behind the scene.

muavazeten (.—·..) مُعَاوَضَةً A by way of compensation; in exchange.

muavedet (.—..) مُعَاوَدَت A lrnd. a returning to a former habit or action; a recurrence.

muavenet (.—..) مُعَاوَنَت A a helping, aiding; help, assistance, support. —i ma'neviye moral aid.

muavin (.—.) مُعَاوِن A 1. one who helps, helper; assistant. 2. assistant director; assistant principal; assistant official. 3. football halfback. —e (.—..) A woman helper.

muavvak[kı] مُعَوَّق A lrnd. detained, delayed; hindered.

muavvec مُعَوَّج A lrnd. bent, curved. — yazı Arabic calligraphy a kind of curved writing.

muavvik[kı] مُعَوِّق A lrnd. that detains, hinders; detainer.

muavvizetan (....—), **muavvizeteyn** (....—) مُعَوِّذَتَان، مُعَوِّذَتَيْن A lrnd., name of the last two suras of the Quran.

muayede (.—..) مُعَايَده A lrnd. a visiting one another on festive occasions; an exchanging the compliments of the feast day. —i humayun Ott. hist. an imperial state levee held at bayram.

muayene (.—..) مُعَايَنَه A an inspecting, scrutinizing, examining; inspection, examination. — et= /ı/ to inspect, scrutinize; to examine; to test. — memuru customshouse inspector. — ücreti examination fee. —ci same as muayene memuru.

muayenehane (.—·..—.) مُعَايَنَه خَانَه P consulting room of a doctor.

muayyeb مُعَيَّب A lrnd. blamed, found fault with (thing); immoral, vicious.

muayyebat (...—) مُعَيَّبَات A lrnd. faults; obscenities; shameful things.

muayyen مُعَيَّن A 1. definite; determined, known. 2. lrnd. appointed.

muayyenat (...—) مُعَيَّنَات A obs., adm. supplementary rations given by the government to government officials or soldiers.

muayyeniyet مُعَيَّنِيَّت A lrnd. a being determined, definiteness. —çilik obs., phil. determinism.

muayyin مُعَيِّن A lrnd. determining, determiner.

muazadet (.—..) مُعَاضَدَت A lrnd. a helping one another; assistance, support, mutual aid.

muazere مُعَاذَره A lrnd. a begging to be excused, an apologizing.

muazzam مُعَظَّم A 1. great, enormous. 2. esteemed great, respected; important.

muazzamat (...—) مُعَظَّمَات A lrnd. great and important affairs.

muazzeb A, **muazzep**[bi] مُعَذَّب tormented, pained; worried.

muazzez مُعَزَّز A lrnd. exalted, glorified: esteemed, honored; cherished. — tut= /ı/ to hold dear; to honor. —en (.·..) A with great honors; with respect.

muazzib مُعَذِّب A lrnd. that torments or pains, tormenting, worrying.

muazzir مُعَذِّر A lrnd. who offers an excuse or apology.

mubah (.—) مُبَاح A can. law neither commanded nor forbidden by religious law; allowed, tolerated, permissible. —at (.——) A harmless or lawful things. —lık canonical toleration.

mubalağa مُبَالَغَه A same as **mübalâğa**.

mubarek[gi] (.—.) مُبَارَك A same as **mübarek**.

mubassır مُبَصِّر A obs., school adm. superintendent; usher at a school.

mubayaa (.—..) مُبَايَعَه A a purchasing; commercial transactions; purchase; wholesale buying. — ağnamı Ott. hist. sheep bought at a certain price. — et= /ı/ to buy wholesale. — zahiresi Ott. hist. provisions purchased by the government at a special price.

mubayaacı (.—...) مُبَايَعَجِي A 1. stockbroker; purchasing agent. 2. Ott. hist. agent for the wholesale purchase of grain, and especially of obsolete coins for the mint.

mubayaat (.—.—) مُبَايَعَات A purchases, commercial transactions.

mubed (—.) مُبَد same as **mubid**.

mubemu (—.—) مُوبَمُو P lrnd. hair by hair; minutely.

mubid (—.) مُوبِد P lrnd. Zoroastrian priest, learned doctor of the Magi. —ân (—.—) P the chief priest of the fireworshippers.

muceb (—.) مُوجِب A lrnd. made necessary, required, requirement. —ince obs., same as **mucibince**.

mu'cem مُعْجَم A lrnd. 1. dotted, distinguished by dots (Arabic letters). 2. arranged alphabetically (letters, as opposed to the **ebced** arrangement).

mucer (—.) مُوجَر A lrnd. hired, let out for hire.

mucez (—.) موجز A *lrnd.* short, laconic; epitome, summary.
muciⁱⁱ (—.) موجع A *lrnd.* which gives pain; painful.
mucib 1 (—.) موجب A a rendering necessary, causing; cause, motive, reason; requirement; necessary consequence. **—ince** as required in accordance with, *e. g.*, **program mucibince** in accordance with the program. **bir — çek=** *law* to pass a petition, etc. as approved. **—den çık=** *law* to be approved (decree, etc.). **—i ibret** example, means of warning to others. **— ol=** /ı/ to cause; to entail. **— sebepler** leading motives, main reasons. **—i şer'i** legal reason requiring some act.
mu'cib 2 موجب A *lrnd.* that causes admiration; wonderful, beautiful.
mucibat (—.—) موجبات A *lrnd.*, *pl.* of **mucib 1, mucibe**.
mucibe 1 (—..) موجبه A *lrnd.* 1. same as **mucib 1**. 2. act of vital spiritual importance as being a sufficient reason in itself for reward or punishment in the future life.
mu'cibe 2 موجبه A *lrnd.*, same as **mu'cib 2**.
mucid (—.) موجد A same as **mucit**.
mucipᵇⁱ (—.) موجب A same as **mucib 1**.
mucir (—.) موجر A *law* who lets or hires out.
mucitᵈⁱ (—.) موجد A who invents, inventing; inventor.
muciz 1 (—.) موجز A *lrnd.* laconic, concise.
mu'ciz A, **mûciz 2** (—.) معجز *lrnd.* that makes one incapable and powerless; overpowering; perplexing.
mu'cizâsar (—.——) معجزآثار P *lrnd.* wonderful.
mu'cizat (..—) A, **mûcizat** (—.—) معجزات *lrnd.*, *pl.* of **mucize**.
mu'cize A, **mûcize** (—..) معجزه miracle.
mu'cizedâ (...—) معجزادا P *lrnd.* having superior behavior.
mu'cizegû (...—) معجزه‌گو P *lrnd.* saying miraculous things.
mucizevî (—..—) معجزوی A miraculous.
mu'ciznüma (...—) P, **mûciznüma** (—..—) معجزنما *lrnd.* displaying wonders; wonderful.
mucur موجور Arm *prov.* 1. scoriae, dross, scales. 2. rubbish, refuse. 3. *w. cap.* a town in Anatolia.
muço (.'.) موچو It *naut.*, same as **miço**.
mudaᵃˡ (—.) مودع A *lrnd.* lodged; consigned; deposited.
mudallaᵃˡ مضلع A *lrnd.*, *geom.* polygon.
mudârebat (.—.—) مضاربات A *lrnd.*, *pl.* of **mudarebe**.
mudarebe (.—..) مضاربه A *lrnd.* 1. a fighting, contending with another, striking; combat, conflict. 2. a kind of commercial cooperation in which one of the partners supplies the capital while the other does the actual work, sleeping partner.
mudarib (.—.) مضارب A *lrnd.* 1. combatant; fighter. 2. one of the two partners in a commercial cooperation in which one puts up the capital while the other does the actual work.
mudcer مضجر A *lrnd.* grieved; offended.
mudcir مضجر A *lrnd.* that vexes or annoys.
mudhalˡⁱ مدخل A *lrnd.* made to enter; inserted, imported.
mudhikᵏⁱ مضحك A *lrnd.* that causes laughter, droll, ridiculous, comic.
mudhikât (..—) مضحكات [*based on Arabic*] *lrnd.* drolleries.
mudhike مضحكه [*based on Arabic*] *lrnd.* drollery, comedy.
mudiⁱⁱ (—.) مودع A 1. *com.* depositor. 2. *lrnd.* one who entrusts (something to another).
mu'dil A, **mudil 1** (—.) معضل *phil.* complex.
mudilˡⁱⁱ 2 مضل A *lrnd.* who leads astray.
mu'dilât (..—) A, **mudilât** (—.—) معضلات *lrnd.* complexities.
mu'dile A, **mudile** (—..) معضل *psych.* complex.
mufa موفى A *lrnd.* paid, performed in full.
mufad (.—) مفاد A *lrnd.* purport, contents; expression, meaning. **—ınca** in accordance with.
mufagame (.—..) مفاغم A 1. *anat.* anastomosis. 2. *lrnd.* a kissing.
mufarakat (..—..) مفارقت A *lrnd.* 1. a departing, leaving, departure. 2. separation; absence.
mufarikᵏⁱ (.—.) مفارق A *lrnd.* separate; separable.
mufassal مفصل A detailed, fully described. **— defter** *Ott. hist.* the detailed domesday book of a province containing all information about the population, land tenure, crops, taxes, etc.
mufassalan ('...) مفصلاً A *lrnd.* in detail, at length.
mufi (——) موفی A *lrnd.* who pays in full; who performs faithfully; fulfiller.
mufla ('.) موفله F *chem.* muffle, muffle furnace.
muflon موفلون F a kind of thick lining attached to overcoats with buttons.
muftir مفطر A *lrnd.* who ends his fast at its canonical conclusion.
mugaddi (..—) مغذّی A *physiol.* nutritious, nourishing.
mugaderet (..—..) مغادرت A *lrnd.* a leaving.
mugalâta (.—..) مغالطه A *lrnd.* a striving

mugalatat to mislead in argument; a using sophistry in arguing; sophistry; fallacy.

mugalatat (. — . —) مغالطات A *lrnd.*, *pl. of* **mugalâta**.

mugalebe (. — . .) مغالبه A *lrnd.* a striving to surpass or overcome; an overpowering.

mugammedülcenah (. . . . . —) مغمدالجناح A *obs., zool., Coleoptera.*

muganni (. . —) مغنی A singer, male singer.

muganniye (. . — .) مغنيه A professional woman singer in the Arabic style.

mugayeret (. . — . .) مغايرت A *lrnd.* a being mutually opposed, contrary; opposition; difference; disagreement.

mugayir (. — .) مغاير A /a/ opposed, contrary, adverse to. —**i edeb** contrary to good manners; uncivil.

mugaylân (. . —) مغيلان P [Arabic **ümmü gaylân**] *lrnd.* Egyptian thorn, *bot.*, *Acacia arabica.* —**gâh** (. . — —) P, —**istan** (. . — . —) P, —**zar** (. . — —) P place of thorny acacias, the world.

mugayyeb مغيّب A *lrnd.* 1. hidden, invisible. 2. supernatural.

mugayyebat (. . . —) مغيّبات A *lrnd.*, *pl.* 1. concealed things. 2. mysteries, secrets.

mugayyer مغيّر A *lrnd.* changed, altered.

mugayyir مغيّر A *lrnd.* that changes, alters.

mugber مغبر *var. of* **mugber**.

mugîs (. —) مغيث A *lrnd.* who gives aid, helper.

mug (—) مغ P 1. Magian, fireworshipper. 2. tavern keeper. —**an** (. —) P *pl.*

mugbeçe مغبچه P *poet.* 1. Magian boy. 2. boy waiter at a tavern. 3. attractive youth. —**gân** (. . . —) P *pl.*

mugber مغبر A 1. offended, hurt, vexed. 2. *lrnd.* soiled with dust, dusty.

mugfel مغفل A *lrnd.* deceived, cheated; seduced.

mugfil مغفل A *lrnd.* deceitful; deceptive; deceiver; seducer.

mugkede مغکده P *poet.* 1. Magian fire temple. 2. tavern.

muglâk[kı] مغلق A 1. obscure; complicated, confused. 2. *lrnd.* locked, latched. —**at** (. . —) A *pl.* obscure things.

mugli (. —) مغلی A *lrnd.* 1. that makes a thing expensive; who asks an extravagant price. 2. that sets a pot boiling.

muglim مغلم A *lrnd.* libidinous; pederast.

mugmed مغمد A *lrnd.* sheathed (sword).

mugni 1 (. —) مغنی A *lrnd.* 1. that suffices to make one independent; God. 2. who causes one to become rich, enriching.

mugni 2 مغنی A *obs.* a musical instrument with 39 strings.

mugpeçe مغپچه A *var. of* **mugbeçe**.

mugrak[kı] مغرق A *lrnd.* drowned; overwhelmed.

mugtab (. —) مغتاب A *lrnd.* backbiter, slanderer.

mugtariyet (. — . .) مغتاريت A *obs., phil.* heteronomy.

mugtasab مغتصب A *lrnd.* taken away by violence; ravished.

mugtasıb مغتصب A *lrnd.* who takes away by violence, ravishes, or constrains to act, usurper.

mugtebit مغتبط A *lrnd.* envied, enviable; happy.

mugtedi (. . —) مغتدی A *lrnd.* nourished, fed (with).

mugtenim مغتنم A *lrnd.* 1. who takes spoil by a raid or by war. 2. who profits from an opportunity.

mugterib مغترب A *lrnd.* 1. who goes to a foreign place; who lives among strangers. 2. setting (sun).

mugtesel مغتسل A *lrnd.* 1. washing place; bathroom. 2. washing water.

mugtesil مغتسل A *lrnd.* one who washes his whole body.

mugtezi (. . —) مغتذی A *lrnd.*, same as **mugtedi**.

mugzib مغضب A *lrnd.* one who provokes to anger; irritant.

muh[hhu] **1** مخ A *lrnd.* 1. marrow. 2. brain, cerebrum. 3. substance, essence.

muh[hhu] **2** مخ A *lrnd.* egg yolk.

muhabbet محبت [**mahabbet**] 1. love, affection. 2. friendship; friendly chat. — **çiçeği** reseda, garden mignonette, *bot.*, *Reseda odorata.* — **et**= /la/ to have a friendly chat. — **kuşu** lovebird, *zool.*, *Melopsittacus undulatus.* — **otu** mandrake, *bot.*, *Mandragora officinarum.* — **tellâlı** procurer, pimp. — **tılsımı** love charm.

muhabbetâmiz (. . . — .) محبت آميز P *lrnd.* friendly.

muhabbetârâ (. . . — —) محبت آرا P *lrnd.* love-adorning.

muhabbethane (. . . — .) محبت خانه P a kind of complicated embroidery.

muhabbetkâr (. . . —) محبت کار P *lrnd.* loving, affectionate.

muhabbetleş=[ir] محبت لشمك 1. to have a loving friendship for each other. 2. to enjoy a friendly chat together.

muhabbetli محبتلی affectionate, loving; friendly.

muhabbetname (. . . — .) محبت نامه P 1. love letter. 2. friendly letter.

muhabbetzede محبت زده P *lrnd.* smitten with love, love-stricken.

muhaberat (. — . —) مخابرات A *lrnd.*, *pl. of* **muhabere**, correspondence, communication.

muhabere (. — . .) مخابره A 1. correspondence

(by letter); mutual communication. 2. *mil.* signals. **— et=** to correspond, to communicate. **— gemisi** dispatch boat. **— güvercini** carrier pigeon, homing pigeon. **— köpeği** messenger dog. **— memuru** telegraphing clerk of a post office, operator. **— şebekesi** intelligence net.
muhabereci مخابره جى *mil.* soldier or officer of the signals corps.
muhabir (.—.) مخابر A correspondent.
muhacat 1 (.——) محاجات A *lrnd.* a propounding riddles to each other.
muhacat 2 (.——) مهاجات A *lrnd.* a satirizing in verse, lampooning each other.
muhaccel محجّل A *lrnd.* placed in the wedding chamber.
muhacemat (.—.—) مهاجمات A *lrnd., pl.* of **muhaceme.**
muhaceme (.—..) مهاجمه A *lrnd.* sudden onslaught; concerted attack.
muhaceret (.—..) مهاجرت A a moving from one country to another (emigration, immigration). **— vizesi** immigration visa.
muhacim (.—.) مهاجم A 1. *lrnd.* assailant; attacking; raider. 2. *soccer* forward. **— hattı** *soccer* forward line, rush line. **—în** (.—.—) A *lrnd., pl.*
muhacir (.—.) مهاجر A emigrant; fugitive; refugee; Turk who has immigrated from a Balkan country. **— arabası** a kind of four-wheeled wagon. **— kuşlar** passenger birds, migratory birds.
muhacirîn (.—.—) مهاجرين A 1. Meccans who followed the Prophet Muhammad in settling in Medina. 2. *lrnd.* emigrants; refugees.
muhadaa (.—..) مخادعه A *lrnd.* a mutually deceiving; deception.
muhaddeb محدّب A 1. convex. 2. *lrnd.* humpbacked.
muhadded محدّد A *lrnd.* 1. limited, terminated. 2. defined.
muhadder محدّر A *lrnd.* 1. veiled; concealed. 2. benumbed.
muhadderat (...—) محدّرات A *lrnd., pl.* of **muhaddere.**
muhaddere محدّره A *lrnd.* veiled, modest (woman), virtuous lady.
muhaddid محدّد A *lrnd.* limiting, circumscribing; defining.
muhaddir محدّر A 1. *med.* narcotic. 2. *lrnd.* which benumbs, benumbing.
muhaddirat (...—) محدّرات A *lrnd.* narcotics, anodynes.
muhaddis محدّث A *Isl. rel.* traditionist well versed in Muslim tradition. **—în** (...—) A *pl.*
muhaddiş محدّش A *lrnd.* 1. that scratches. 2. disturbing, irritating.

muhadene, muhadenet (.—..) مخادنت مخادنه A *lrnd.* mutual friendship.
muhadese (.—..) محادثه A *lrnd.* a mutual conversing, conversation; narration.
muhadi مهادى A *lrnd.* deluder, deceiver.
muhafaza (.—..) محافظه A 1. a guarding, protecting, defending; protection; care. 2. conservation, preservation; a keeping; maintenance. **— altına al=** /ı/ 1. to guard, keep, protect. 2. to cover (roof etc.); to shelter. **— et=** /ı/ 1. to guard, protect, keep, maintain. 2. to conserve, preserve. 3. to cover.
muhafazakâr (.—..—) محافظه كار P conservative. **—âne** (.—..—.) P conservatively. **—lık** conservatism.
muhafazalı محافظه لى well protected; sheltered; secure; unexposed.
muhafazasız محافظه سز unprotected, unsheltered; exposed.
muhafete (.—..) مخافته A *lrnd.* a speaking in a very low voice; a reading low or mutteringly.
muhaffef مخفّف A 1. *Arabic gram.* not doubled in pronunciation (consonant). 2. *lrnd.* lightened, alleviated.
muhaffif مخفّف A 1. *law* extenuating. 2. *Arabic gram.* who pronounces a consonant without doubling. 3. *lrnd.* that lightens or alleviates; lightening.
muhafız (.—.) محافظ A 1. who guards, protects, defends; guard, defender; warden; keeper (of a museum). 2. commander of a fort. **— alayı** presidential guard. **— kıt'ası** bodyguard. **—în** (.—.—) A *lrnd., pl.* **—lık** guardianship.
muhak[kı] (.—) محاك A *lrnd., same as* **mahak.**
muhakât (.——) محاكات A *lrnd.* a relating, telling stories to one another.
muhakemat (.—.—) محاكمات A *lrnd., pl.* of **muhakeme.**
muhakeme (.—..) محاكمه A 1. an applying to the court. 2. a hearing of a case in court; trial. 3. judgment, discernment. 4. *phil.* reasoning. **— et=** /ı/ 1. to hear (a case), to decide (a case). 2. to judge, to reason. **—nin iadesi** reopening of a case; revision of a judgment. **—nin men'i kararı** *law* nonsuit.
muhakkak[kı] محقّق A certain, sure; well known; without doubt, certainly.
muhakkar محقّر A *lrnd.* contemptible; despicable, insignificant.
muhakkarat (...—) محقّرات A venial sins; mortal sins deemed small by the sinner.
muhakkem محكّم A 1. *Isl. rel.* one to whom the option is given of recantation from Islam or death. 2. *lrnd.* appointed judge or arbiter.
muhakkık[kı] محقّق A 1. *myst.* mystic who has attained to the degree of perfection called

hakikat. 2. *Arabic calligraphy, name of a decorative style of writing.* 3. *lrnd.* who investigates, scrutinizes closely; verifier, confirmer.

muhakkıkane (...—.) مُحَقِّقانه P *lrnd.* scrutinizing (method etc.), scrutinizingly.

muhakkıkîn (...—) مُحَقِّقين A *lrnd.* philosophers; authorities.

muhakkir مُحَقِّر A *lrnd.* insulting; insulter. —**âne** (...—.) P insultingly.

muhal[ı] (.—) مُحال A impossible, inconceivable; *phil.* absurd.

muhalâa (.—..) مُخالَعه A *lrnd.* a divorcing one's wife at her desire.

muhalâsat (.—..) مُخالَصت A *lrnd.* a mutually feeling and acting sincerely; sincerity; sincere friendship.

muhalât (.——) مُحالات A *lrnd.*, *pl. of* **muhal**, impossibilities, absurdities.

muhalâta (.—..) مُخالَطه A *lrnd.* conversing, mixing together in society; an associating with another; intercourse.

muhalâtât (.—.—) مُخالَطات A *lrnd.* intercourse, associations.

muhalefe (.—..) مُحالَفه A *lrnd.* a taking oath mutually.

muhalefet 1 (.—..) مُخالَفت A a being contrary, an opposing; opposition, contrariness; *pol.* the opposition. — **et=** /a/ to oppose. — **lideri** *pol.* leader of the chief opposition party. — **sözcüsü** *pol.* spokesman for the opposition. —**e geç=** *pol.* to join the opposition. —**i hava** bad weather (hindering transportation).

muhalefet 2 (.—..) مُحالَفت A *lrnd.*, same as **muhalefe.**

muhalif 1 (.—.) مُخالِف A 1. opposing, opposed, contrary, contradictory. 2. adversary, antagonist, opponent. —**i akl** *lrnd.* irrational. —**i ırak** *Or. mus.* a makam.

muhalif 2 (.—.) مُحالِف A *lrnd.* confederate, sworn ally.

muhallâ 1 (..—) مُحَلّى A *lrnd.* empty, emptied.

muhallâ 2 (..—) مُحَلّى A *lrnd.* ornamented, jewelled, adornment.

muhallak[ı] مُحَلَّق A 1. *lrnd.* shaven. 2. *lrnd.* furnished with rings. 3. *w. cap., name of a place in Mina where pilgrims usually have their heads shaved.*

muhallas مُخَلَّص A *lrnd.* saved, delivered, redeemed.

muhallebi مُحَلَّبى A same as **mahallebi.**

muhalled مُخَلَّد A *lrnd.* eternal, durable, immortal. —**at** (...—) A immortal works; classics.

muhallef مُخَلَّف A *lrnd.* left behind (by a deceased person).

muhallefat (...—) مُخَلَّفات A *lrnd.* effects bequeathed or left; inheritance.

muhallefe مُخَلَّفه A *lrnd.* widow.

muhalli مُخَلِّى A *lrnd.* emptying, vacator.

muhallid مُخَلِّد A *lrnd.* eternalizing, immortalizing.

muhallil مُحَلِّل A 1. *chem.* solvent. 2. *lrnd.* who makes or pronounces another to be in lawful possession. 3. *lrnd.* one who marries a woman divorced triply by her husband and then divorces her, thus making it lawful for her first husband to marry her again.

muhallilat (...—) مُحَلِّلات A *lrnd.* solvents.

muhallis مُخَلِّص A *lrnd.* that saves, redeems; savior, deliverer.

muhallit[u] مُخَلِّط A *lrnd.* who mixes, confuses, jumbles; mixer, confounder, disturber.

muhamat (.——) مُحاماة A *lrnd.* a repelling aggression, protecting; a guarding, defending; protection, defense.

muhami (.——) مُحامى A *lrnd.* defender, advocate, lawyer.

Muhammed مُحَمَّد A 1. Muhammad, the Prophet and founder of the Islamic religion. 2. *lrnd., l. c.* much praised, praiseworthy.

Muhammedî (...—) مُحَمَّدى A pertaining to Muhammad; Muhammadan, Muslim.

muhammen مُخَمَّن A *com.* estimated.

muhammer 1 مُخَمَّر A *lrnd.* leavened, fermented.

muhammer 2 مُحَمَّر A *lrnd.* called a donkey.

muhammes 1 مُخَمَّس A 1. *pros.* stanza consisting of five lines. 2. *Or. mus.* a rhythmic pattern of 32 beats. 3. *lrnd.* pentagon, pentangular.

muhammes 2 مُحَمَّص A *lrnd.* parched, roasted (coffee beans, etc.).

muhammin مُخَمِّن A estimator. —**lik** the profession of an estimator.

muhanat (.——) مُخَنَّثات [**muhannes**] vile, wretched; mean, cowardly.

muhanna (..—) مُحَنَّى A *lrnd.* tinged with henna.

muhannat مُحَنَّط A *lrnd.* embalmed. —**an** (..'..) A in an embalmed state.

muhannes مُخَنَّث A *lrnd.* 1. effeminate. 2. catamite. 3. vile, mean.

muhannit مُحَنِّط A *lrnd.* embalmer.

muharebat (.—.—) مُحارَبات *lrnd., pl. of* **muharebe.**

muharebe (.—..) مُحارَبه A war; battle. — **ağırlığı** *mil.* first line baggage. — **bölgesi** *mil.* zone of action. — **grupu** *mil.* fighting cadre. — **idare yeri** observation post of the commanding officer. — **ileri karakolu** *mil.* outpost. — **kademesi** *mil.* echelon of attack. — **keşfi** *mil.* battle reconnaissance. — **meydanı** battlefield. — **tertibatı** battle array.

muharese (.—..) محارسه A *lrnd.* a keeping, preserving.
muhareşe (.—..) محارشه A *lrnd.* an inciting to attack; incitement.
muharib A, **muharip**^bi (.—.) محارب 1. belligerent, combatant; warrior. 2. *lrnd.* mutually at war. **—lik** state of being a warrior, fighting qualities; belligerency.
muharref محرّف A *lrnd.* altered in form (word); anagram; perverted as to language; falsified. **—at** (...—) A 1. anagrams. 2. falsified things.
Muharrem محرّم A 1. *Arabic lunar calendar*, name of the first month. 2. *l. c., lrnd.* forbidden, unlawful; made sacred.
muharremat (...—) محرّمات A *lrnd.* 1. things forbidden by canonical law; sacred things. 2. *w. cap.* months of Muharram.
muharremiye محرّميه A *lrnd.* 1. gift given at the New Year, which begins with Muharram. 2. congratulatory New Year's poem.
Muharremülharam (..,...—) محرّم الحرام A *lrnd.* the month of Muharram.
muharrer محرّر A *lrnd.* written.
muharrerat (...—) محرّرات A *lrnd.* written papers, writings; correspondence.
muharrib محرّب A *lrnd.* that ruins, spoils, injures.
muharrif محرّف A *lrnd.* who alters or falsifies a writing; anagrammatist.
muharrik^ki محرّك A 1. mover, moving; *anat.* motor. 2. *lrnd.* inciter; provoker. 3. *lrnd.* stimulant; drive. **—i fesad** *lrnd.* stirrer up of troubles, promoter of mischief. **—i kulûb** *lrnd.* God, the Mover of Hearts. **— sinirler** *anat.* motor nerves.
muharrikiyet محرّكيت A *lrnd.* motivity.
muharrir محرّر A writer, author; editor. **—i memâlik** *Ott. hist.* secretary of land or tax registry.
muharriran (...—) محرّران P *lrnd.* writers, authors. **—ı felek** *lrnd.* the sun, the moon and the five planets.
muharririn (...—) محرّرين A *lrnd.,* pl. of **muharrir.**
muharrirlik^ği محرّرلك authorship; state of being a writer.
muharris محرّص A *lrnd.* that excites to greediness.
muharriş محرّش A *lrnd.* that irritates or scratches; irritating, itching.
muhasama (.—..) محاصمه A *lrnd.* hostility, contention, opposition; dispute.
muhasamat (.—.—) محاصمات A *lrnd.* hostilities.
muhasara (.—..) محاصره A a surrounding, besieging, blockading; siege, blockade.

muhasebat (.—.—) محاسبات A *lrnd.* accounts. **M— Divanı** Court of Audit.
muhasebe محاسبه A 1. an examining, balancing accounts. 2. accountancy, bookkeeping. 3. the accounts office (of a business etc.). 4. *lrnd.* a reckoning with, calling to account. **— kalemi** accounting or auditor's office for the finance of a government department. **— memuru** bookkeeper in a government office. **—sini yap=** /ın/ to call to account; to draw up a balance sheet (of acts etc.).
muhasebeci محاسبه جی accountant; chief accountant; auditor. **—lik** accountancy.
muhasım (.—.) محاصم A *lrnd.* 1. adversary (at law), opponent; antagonist. 2. hostile.
muhasımîn (.—.—) محاصمين A *lrnd.* the opponents (in war, etc.).
muhasır (.—.) محاصر A *lrnd.* that shuts in, besieges, invests; besieger. **—în** (.—.—) A *pl.*
muhasib A, **muhasip**^bi (.—.) محاسب 1. accountant; bookkeeper; auditor of accounts. 2. *lrnd.* who reckons, reckoner. **—lik** accountancy.
muhassal محصّل A *lrnd.* gotten, produced, extracted; result; product. **—ı kelâm** sum and substance of a speech.
muhassala محصّله A 1. *phys.* resultant. 2. *lrnd.* product; result.
muhassalan (..'..) محصّلاً A *lrnd.* in brief, summarily.
muhassan (..'.) محصّن A *lrnd.* fortified; impregnable by nature.
muhassas محصّص A *lrnd.* appropriated, assigned (to). **—at** (...—) A appropriations; salaries.
muhassen محسّن A *lrnd.* beautiful; approved of.
muhassenât (...—) محسّنات A *lrnd.* 1. beautiful things; good works, virtues. 2. advantages.
muhasser محسّر A *lrnd.* troubled; despised; tired; pining.
muhassıl محصّل A 1. *lrnd.* who gets, produces, extracts. 2. *Ott. hist.* tax collector. **—lık** functions of a tax collector.
muhassıs محصّص A *lrnd.* one who appropriates.
muhassin محسّن A *lrnd.* 1. beautifier. 2. who approves of, who admires.
muhassir محسّر A *lrnd.* one who causes loss (to another); injurious, detrimental.
muhaşşa (..—) محشّى A *lrnd.* annotated.
muhaşşi 1 (..—) محشّی A *lrnd.* annotator.
muhaşşi 2 (..—) محشّی A *lrnd.* that makes one fear, awe inspiring.
muhat 1 (.—) محاط A *lrnd.* 1. surrounded, encircled. 2. comprehended.
muhat 2 (.—) مخاط A *biol.* mucus.

muhatab (.—.) مخاطب A 1. one spoken to by another; *gram.* second person. 2. *com.* drawee. 3. *Ott. hist.* doctor of canon law who attended the lectures, called "Huzur Dersleri" taking place during Ramazan in the presence of the Sultan.

muhataba (.—..) مخاطبة A a talking to one another; conversation.

muhatabat (.—.—) مخاطبات A *lrnd.*, *pl.* of muhataba.

muhatap[b1] (.—.) مخاطب [muhatab] *same as* muhatab.

muhatara (.—..) مخاطرة A *com.* danger; risk. —lı dangerous, perilous; risky. —sız safe.

muhatarat (.—.—) مخاطرات A *lrnd.*, *pl.* of muhatara.

muhatıb (.—.) مخاطب A *lrnd.* who addresses another.

muhatî (.—.) مخاطي A *anat.* mucous.

muhattat مخطط A *lrnd.* 1. striped; ruled with lines. 2. *anat.* striated. 3. *lrnd.* drawn.

muhattıt مخطط A *lrnd.* who draws lines.

muhaverat (.—.—) محاورات A *lrnd.*, *pl.* of muhavere.

muhavere (.—..) محاورة A a talking, disputing with another; conversation, talk; dialogue.

muhavvat محوط A *lrnd.* surrounded by a wall; enclosed.

muhavvel محول A *lrnd.* 1. changed, transformed, altered. 2. turned over to, referred. —ât (...—) A alterations.

muhavven محون A *lrnd.* accused, suspected of perfidy.

muhavvil محول A *lrnd.* that changes, transmutes, alters.

muhavvile محولة A *elec.* transformer.

muhayyeb مخيب A *lrnd.* disappointed, frustrated.

muhayyel مخيل A imagined; imaginary.

muhayyelât (...—) مخيلات A *lrnd.* fancies; imaginations.

muhayyem مخيم A *lrnd.* 1. tent shaped. 2. erected, pitched (tent); tented; camp. 3. living in a tent (man). —gâh (...—) P *lrnd.* army camp.

muhayyer 1 مخير A 1. *lrnd.* who has a choice or option. 2. *law* left to free choice, optional. 3. *com.* on approval (goods to be purchased). 4. *Or. mus.* the note a". 5. *Or. mus.* one of the oldest mâkams. 6. *art* a kind of moired paper. — al= /ı/ to buy something on approval, to take on trial. — **buselik** *Or. mus.* a compound **makam**, composed about four centuries ago. — **kürdî** *Or. mus.* a compound **makam** composed about a century and a half ago. — **perdesi** *Or. mus.*, *same as*

muhayyer[4]. — **sünbüle** *Or. mus.* a makam composed by Sultan Selim III one and a half centuries ago.

muhayyer 2 مخير A *lrnd.* bewildered, perplexed.

muhayyib مخيب A *lrnd.* that disappoints, disappointing; frustrating.

muhayyil مخيل A *lrnd.* that causes day-dreaming.

muhayyile مخيلة A imagination, fancy.

muhayyir 1 مخير A *lrnd.* bewildering, astonishing. —i ukûl most astonishing.

muhayyir 2 مخير A *lrnd.* who gives freedom of option.

muhazara (.—..) محاضرة A 1. a conversing or disputing face to face; debate. 2. *lrnd.* a reciting literary sayings or anecdotes. 3. *lrnd.* a being mutually present.

muhazarat (.—.—) محاضرات A *lrnd.*, *pl.* of muhazara.

muhazat (.——) محاذات A *lrnd.* 1. mutually lining up; opposition, conjunction. 2. a facing.

muhazeret (.—..) محاذرت A *lrnd.* a being cautious of each other; caution.

muhazi (.——) محاذي A *lrnd.* 1. a being in line with another. 2. equal, similar to; parallel.

muhazzab مهذب A *lrnd.* tinged, dyed.

muhazzar مخضر A *lrnd.* 1. made green, verdant. 2. made flourishing; blessed.

muhazzir محذر A *lrnd.* who warns menacingly, threatener.

muhbir مخبر A who gives information, informant; informer; newspaper correspondent, reporter.

muhcil مخجل A *lrnd.* who makes ashamed.

muhdes محدث A *lrnd.* 1. recently made; not ancient. 2. innovation. 3. modern (author).

muhdesât (..—) محدثات A *lrnd.* modern things.

muhdis محدث A *lrnd.* who creates; innovator.

muheyh مخيخ A *anat.* cerebellum.

muhib[bb1] محب A 1. who loves, affectionate friend. 2. *myst.* sympathizer (of dervish orders).

muhibban (..—) محبان P *lrnd.* friends, loved ones.

muhibbane (..—.) محبانه P *lrnd.* friendly, affectionately.

muhibbe محبة A *lrnd.* woman friend.

muhif (.—) مخيف A *lrnd.* that frightens, terrifies, threatens; terrible, formidable, dreadful.

muhik[kk1] محق A *lrnd.* 1. who executes justice. 2. who does any act conscientiously. 3. who speaks the truth. 4. true, right, justifiable. — **sebepler** *law* cogent grounds. —ane (..—.) P correct, just (act); rightly.

muhil[lll] **1** مخل A *lrnd.* that injures or

violates; who troubles or spoils; disturber. —i âsayiş disturber of the peace.

muhil 2 (. —) محيل A com. assignor, transferer.

muhisssi محس A lrnd. that feels, is aware of, perceives.

muhiş (—.) موحش A lrnd. solitary and desolate, dreadful (place), terrible, horrible.

muhit (. —) محيط A 1. surrounding; the circle in which one moves; environment, milieu. 2. lrnd. which surrounds, comprehends, takes in or holds; comprehending. 3. geom. circumference. 4. lrnd. ocean. —i daire geom. circumference of a circle, periphery. —i (.. —) A lrnd. peripheral.

muhitülmaarif (. — .. — .) محيط المعارف A lrnd. encyclopedia.

muhkem محكم A firm, strong; sound; tight.

muhkemât (.. —) محكمات A lrnd. the incontrovertible verses of the Quran.

muhlis مخلص A lrnd. sincere; sincere friend. —âne (.. —.) P sincerely, in a friendly manner.

muhmid محمد A lrnd. that allays, extinguishes.

muhnikkı مخنى A lrnd. throttling; asphyxiating.

muhraka محرقة A 1. lrnd. fireplace in the stokehole of a public bath. 2. Bib. burnt offering, burnt sacrifice.

muhrez محرز A lrnd. gained, earned; obtained.

muhrib مخرب A lrnd. that destroys.

muhrikkı محرق A lrnd. 1. burning, destroying. 2. very touching, moving (voice etc.).

muhripbi محرب |muhrib| navy destroyer.

muhriz محرز A lrnd. who earns, gains, gets, obtains.

muhsan محصن A 1. lrnd. guarded, preserved. 2. law married, and therefore naturally kept chaste (man).

muhsin محسن A lrnd. beneficient, benefactor. —e (...') A fem.

muhtac A, muhtaçcı (. —) محتاج /a/ in want, needy, indigent. —ı beyan lrnd. needing explanation. —ı himmet lrnd. needing help. —in (. — —) A the needy. —iyet (. — ..) lrnd., —lık need, indigence; poverty.

muhtakir محتكر A lrnd. who despises.

muhtallı 1 (. —) محتال A lrnd. artful, crafty.

muhtallı 2 محتال A lrnd. conceited, arrogant, proud; self-important.

muhtar 1 (. —) مختار A 1. lrnd. chosen, elected. 2. free to chose; independent; autonomous.

muhtar 2 (..') مختار |muhtar 1| head man, elder (of a quarter or village).

muhtariyet (. — —.) مختاريت A freedom of action, autonomy.

muhtarlıktı مختارلى 1. the duties and state of an elder (man). 2. village administered by an elder.

muhtasssı مختص A lrnd. 1. special; appropriate, proper (to a thing). 2. sincerely attached (to a person).

muhtasar مختصر A 1. shortened, abridged, summarized; abbreviated; short, brief. 2. frugal, unpretentious. — müfid brief but to the point, pithy.

muhtasaran (..'..) مختصرا A in brief, concisely.

muhtasid محتصد A lrnd. reaper.

muhtasım مختصم A lrnd. disputant, wrangler; adversary.

muhtassan (..'.) مختصا A lrnd. especially, particularly.

muhtassîn (.. —) محتصين A lrnd., pl. of muhtas, those connected with, followers (of a person or order).

muhtatıb 1 مختطب A lrnd. 1. who asks a woman in marriage. 2. who delivers an address or sermon.

muhtatıb 2 محتطب A lrnd. who cuts or collects firewood.

muhtatıf مختطف A lrnd. 1. snatcher, seizer, carrier off. 2. dazzling, blinding (light).

muhtazar, muhtazır محتضر A lrnd. dying, in the agony of death. —ane (... —.) P agonizing.

muhtaziii محتضع A lrnd. humble, modest, submissive.

muhtebes محتبس A lrnd. imprisoned, confined; suppressed.

muhtebir مختبر A lrnd. who ascertains, tries, proves; expert. —ane (... —.) P expertly.

muhtebis محتبس A lrnd. that confines; who restrains himself; restrainer, detainer.

muhtebit مختبط A lrnd. night beggar.

muhtecib محتجب A lrnd. veiled, hidden; secluded.

muhtecibat (... —) محجبات A lrnd. veiled women.

muhted محتد A lrnd. keen, vehement, fierce (in anger or in battle); furious.

muhtediii محتدع A lrnd. deceived, cheated.

muhtefi (.. —) مختفى A lrnd. hidden, concealed, clandestine..

muhtekir محتكر A who hoards grain or goods to make a profit, profiteer. —ane (...— .) P lrnd. in the manner of a profiteer. —in (... —) A lrnd., pl.

muhtellii مختل A lrnd. spoiled; injured; disturbed.

muhtelefünfih مختلف فيه A lrnd. controversial..

muhteliii مختلع A lrnd. who puts away his wife for a consideration given to him by her.

muhtelic مختلج A lrnd. quivering, shaking agitated, disturbed.

muhtelif مختلف A various; different.
muhtelikᵏⁱ مختلوا A lrnd. deviser, forger (of a lie).
muhtelis مختلس A lrnd. embezzler, pilferer.
muhtelit مختلط A mixed, composite; joint; complex. — **aded** math. complex number. — **hakem mahkemesi** joint tribunal of arbitration. — **hayat sigortası** mixed insurance. — **tedrisat** coeducation.
muhtellüşşuur (....—) مختل الشعور A lrnd. mentally afflicted, insane.
muhtemel محتمل A 1. possible. 2. probable, likely.
muhtemelât (...—) محتملات A lrnd. possibilities, probabilities.
muhtemelen (..'..) محتملا A 1. possibly. 2. probably.
muhtemi (..—) محتمی A lrnd. who diets; who restrains himself, abstinent.
muhtemil محتمل A lrnd., same as **muhtemel**.
muhtemir مختمر A lrnd. 1. leavened; fermenting; fermented. 2. whose head and face are wrapped in a muffler (woman).
muhtenikᵏⁱ مختنق A lrnd. choked, throttled.
muhteraᵃⁱ (..—) مخترع A lrnd. invented. —**at** (..——) A inventions.
muhterem محترم A honored, respected, esteemed, venerable.
muhteriⁱⁱ مخترع A lrnd. 1. who invents, inventor. 2. contriver; calumniator. —**ane** (...—.) P inventively.
muhterib محترب A lrnd. engaged in war; fighting a battle. —**in** (...—) A pl.
muhterif محترف A lrnd. who works and earns his subsistance; artisan, artificer.
muhterikᵏⁱ محترق A lrnd. burning, burned.
muhteris محترص A inordinately desirous, covetous.
muhteriz محترز A lrnd. who takes precautions; cautious; reserved; timid, hesitating. —**ane** (...—.) P cautiously.
muhtesib محتسب A 1. Ott. hist. superintendent of police who has charge of examining weights, measures, provisions, etc. 2. lrnd. reckoner, calculator.
muhteşem محتشم A majestic, magnificent; great, powerful.
muhteva (..—) محتوا A contents.
muhtevi محتوى A lrnd. containing, including.
muhteviyat (...—) محتويات A lrnd. contents.
muhtezen محتزن A lrnd. 1. stored up, preserved. 2. hidden.
muhtezin محتزن A lrnd. 1. who stores up, hoarder of wealth. 2. who conceals.
muhtezir محتذر A lrnd. cautious, circumspect.
muhtır محطر A lrnd. who reminds.
muhtıra مطره A memorandum; note. — **defteri** diary, notebook.

muhtî مخطی A lrnd. who errs; who commits a fault; culprit; sinner. —**yane** (..—.) P sinner-like; mistakenly.
muhyi (.—) محیی A lrnd. 1. giving life; reanimating. 2. who quickens, resuscitates the lifeless (God).
muhzır محضر A 1. Ott. hist. officer of a court of justice who summoned persons and produced them in court. 2. lrnd. who presents or causes to be present.
muhzıra محضره A 1. Ott. hist., title of the colonel of the 28th Buluk Regiment of Janissaries, captain of the guard of the grand vizier. 2. lrnd. summoning officer.
muhzin محزن A lrnd. saddening.
muid (.—) معید A lrnd. tutor; supervisor (in a school).
muin (.—) معین A law 1. who helps, assists; helper, auxiliary. 2. God, the Helper.
muinli معینی Ott. hist. recruit having somebody to support his family in his absence on military service.
muinsiz معینسز Ott. hist. recruit excused from military service, not having anyone else to support his family.
muir (.—) معیر A lrnd. lender.
muizᶻᶻⁱ معز A lrnd. 1. who honors or exalts. 2. God, the Exalter.
muje (—.) موژه P lrnd. sorrow, grief, affliction.
mujikᵍⁱ موژیک Russ muzhik, Russian peasant. =**muk**ᵍᵘ 1 موق cf. =**mık**.
mukᵏᵘ 2 (—) موق A lrnd. inner corner of the eye.
mukᵏᵘ 3 (—) موك P lrnd. sting of an insect.
mukaar مقعر A concave.
mukabbeb مقبب A lrnd. 1. covered with a dome; vaulted. 2. shaped like a dome.
mukabbel مقبل A lrnd. kissed.
mukabbız مقبض A anat. constrictor. —**i ev'iye** vasoconstrictor.
mukabbil مقبل A lrnd. who kisses.
mukabele مقابله A 1. a facing another; a confronting. 2. a reciprocating; returning like for like; reward; retaliation. 3. a being in opposition, resistance; retort, reply. 4. a collating, comparing; comparison. 5. a recitation of the Quran. 6. myst. orders ceremony of whirling or **zikr**. —**de bulun=** 1. to return (an action). 2. to retort, reply. — **et=** 1. to reciprocate, to retaliate; to retort; to return hostile action; to return fire; to resist. 2. /ı/ to confront; to collate, to compare. — **oku=** to recite the Quran by heart. —**i saffeyn** lrnd. an encountering of opposing lines of battle. —**bilmisl** A lrnd. reprisal.

mukabeleci مقابرجى 1. official who collates documents. 2. reciter of the Quran.
mukabeleten (. —ʹ. . .) مقابلة A in return, reciprocally.
mukabil (. —ˑ) مقابل A 1. facing another, opposite; the opposite. 2. equivalent; corresponding. 3. /a/ in return, in exchange, in compensation for; thing given in return. —**inde** /ın/ opposite; in return; against. — **dâva** law counterclaim; cross action. — **hücum** mil. counterattack. — **taraf** opposite side; opponent.
muk'ad مقعد A lrnd. who is forced to sit; paralyzed in the lower limbs; crippled.
mukaddem مقدّم A lrnd. 1. in front, put forward. 2. previous, former. 3. prior, preferable, first, antecedent. 4. /dan/ ago, before. — **cidar** anat. claustrum.
mukaddema (.ʹ. . —) مقدّما A previously; in the past; before.
mukaddemat (. . . —) مقدّمات A 1. lrnd., pl. of **mukaddeme**. 2. log. premises; elements. —**ı ilm** lrnd. propaedeutic. —**ı vâhiye** lrnd. nonsensical premises.
mukaddeme مقدّمة A 1. introduction; preface. 2. forerunner of an event, preliminary. 3. rudiment, first principle, element; premise.
mukadder مقدّر A 1. decreed by providence, predestined, foreordained; fate. 2. inevitable. 3. lrnd. estimated, appraised.
mukadderat (. . . —) مقدّرات A 1. divinely appointed events, preordained things; destiny, fate. 2. lrnd. weighed or measured things.
mukaddes مقدّس A sacred, holy; sanctified. **M— İttifak** hist. Holy Alliance.
mukaddesat (. . . —) مقدّسات A lrnd. sacred things.
mukaddim مقدّم A lrnd. that causes to precede; who places before and gives preference to.
mukaddimat مقدّمات A lrnd., pl. of **mukaddime**.
mukaddime مقدّمة A lrnd., var. of **mukaddeme**.
mukaddir مقدّر A lrnd. 1. who estimates, estimator. 2. God, the predestinater.
mukaddirülâcal (. . . . — —) مقدّر الاجال A lrnd. the preordainer of the time of man's death, God.
mukaffa (. . —) مقفّى A lrnd. rhymed.
mukaffel مقفّل A lrnd. locked.
mukallakᵏı مقلّق |from Turkish **kılık**| lrnd. in the guise of (so and so).
mukalled مقلّد A lrnd. imitated, mimicked.
mukallib مقلّب A lrnd. transforming, changing.
mukallibülkulûb (. . . . . —) مقلّب القلوب A lrnd. the Converter of hearts (God).
mukallid A, **mukallit**ᵈⁱ مقلّد imitator, mimicking; mimic. —**ane** (. . . —.) P mimickingly. —**lik** mimicry.

mukamere (. —. .) مقامرة A lrnd. a gambling together, gambling.
mukamir (. —.) مقامر A lrnd. who gambles, fellow gambler, gambler.
mukanfez مقنفذ A lrnd. spiny, bristly.
mukanfezülcild مقنفذ الجلد A. zool., Echinodermata.
mukannaʿ (. . —) مقنّع A lrnd. helmeted.
mukannen مقنّن A law fixed by civil law; fixed, regular.
mukannin مقنّن A lrnd. who institutes laws or regulations, institutor.
mukantar مقنطر A lrnd. 1. furnished with arches, arched. 2. heaped up, complete.
mukantara مقنطرة A 1. lrnd. sundial. 2. astr. small circle of the celestial sphere parallel to the horizon, almucantar.
mukantarat (. . . —) مقنطرات A lrnd., pl. of **mukantara**.
mukaraa (. —. .) مقارعة A lrnd. 1. a striking one another in battle. 2. a casting lots.
mukarebet (. —. .) مقاربت A lrnd. a being or becoming mutually near; approaching; approximation.
mukarenet (. —. .) مقارنت A 1. pol. rapprochement. 2. astr. conjunction. 3. lrnd. a becoming associated with another; a drawing near; association. 4. lrnd. sexual intercourse.
mukarib (. —.) مقارب A lrnd. that approaches; near, neighboring.
mukarin (. —.) مقارن A lrnd. associated, joined, connected.
mukarnes (. —.) مقارنس A lrnd. 1. lofty circular building or parlor decorated with pictures, to which one ascends by a winding or spiral staircase. 2. that rises by stages to the middle (ceiling). 3. a kind of turban. 4. varicolored; decorated.
mukarreb مقرّب A lrnd. 1. placed or drawn near; allowed to approach, admitted. 2. one near the throne, courtier. 3. cherub. —**ân** (. . . —) P, —**în** (. . . —) A pl.
mukarrer مقرّر A lrnd. 1. decided; certain, sure. 2. established; fixed. —**at** (. . . —) A pl. decisions.
mukarrib مقرّب A 1. lrnd. who brings nearer; who lets one approach. 2. Ott. hist. teacher who interpreted Quranic texts in the presence of the Sultan during Ramazan. 3. anat. adductor.
mukarrin مقرّن A lrnd. who puts near together.
mukarrir مقرّر A 1. lrnd. who narrates, narrator. 2. Ott. hist. assistant teacher, lecturer. 3. lrnd. who fixes, establishes; confirmer.
mukasat (. —. —) مقاسات A lrnd. an enduring, suffering.

mukaseme (. — ..) مقاسم A *lrnd.* a mutually sharing, dividing; apportioning.

mukassar مقصّر A *art* foreshortened.

mukassat مقسّط A *lrnd.* paid in installments. **—an** (..′..) A in installments.

mukassem مقسّم A *lrnd.* divided, distributed, portioned out.

mukassır مقصّر A *lrnd.* who makes anything deficient, who fails in duty; culpable.

mukassi (..—) مقسّي A *lrnd.* oppressive; stuffy.

mukassim مقسّم A *lrnd.* who divides or distributes.

mukaşkış مقشقش A *lrnd.* that stimulates and heals.

mukaşkışetan (....—) مقشقشتان A *lrnd.* the two suras of the Quran entitled **Yâ eyyuhelkâfiruna** and **El-ihlâs**, the 109th and 112th suras.

mukaşşer مقشّر A *lrnd.* barked, skinned, peeled.

mukaşşir مقشّر A *lrnd.* that peels, skins; peeler.

mukataa (. — ..) مقاطع A 1. *Ott. hist.* a farming out of public revenue; rent paid to the **Evkaf** for cultivated land turned into building land or gardens; sale of a business for a lump sum. 2. *lrnd.* a cutting off relations with each other. **—cı** tax farmer. **—lı** subject to the **mukataa** rent.

mukatele (. — ..) مقاتل A *lrnd.* slaughter; battle.

mukatil (. —.) مقاتل A *lrnd.* who fights; combatant. **—ûn** (. — . —) A fighters.

mukatta⁽¹⁾ مقطّع A *lrnd.* 1. cut or broken into many pieces; broken off. 2. interrupted; fragmentary (poetry); divided to show its scansion (poetry).

mukattaât (...—) مقطّعات A 1. *literature* short poems. 2. *lrnd.* things broken into fragments. 3. *lrnd.* abbreviations.

mukattar مقطّر A *chem.* 1. distilled. 2. made to fall in drops. **—ât** (...—) A *pl.*

mukavelât (. — . —) مقاولات A *lrnd., pl.* of **mukavele. — muharriri** notary public.

mukavele (. — . .) مقاوله A contract; a mutually conversing and coming to an agreement; agreement. **— akdet=** to make a contract. **—i zımniye** *law* quasi contract.

mukaveleli مقاوله لي 1. that has been settled by agreement. 2. bound by contract, acting under an agreement.

mukavelename (....—.) مقاوله نامه P deed, indenture; written agreement, pact.

mukavelevî (.—..—) مقاولوي A *law* bilateral, contractual.

mukavemet مقاومت A 1. a resisting; resistance; endurance. 2. opposition. **— koşusu** long distance race.

mukavil (. — .) مقاول A *lrnd.* who comes to an agreement with another.

mukavim (. — .) مقاوم A 1. that resists, resisting; resistant. 2. strong, enduring; unyielding.

mukavva (.′.) مقوّى A 1. cardboard; pasteboard. 2. *lrnd.* strengthened; fortified.

mukavves مقوّس A *lrnd.* arched, bow shaped; curved.

mukavvi (..—) مقوّي A *lrnd.* that strengthens, strengthening, invigorating; tonic. **—yat** (..——) A *pl.*

mukavvim مقوّم A 1. *lrnd.* who makes upright, straight or correct. 2. *biochem.* substratum.

mukayaza (. — ..) مقايضه A *lrnd.* an exchanging, substituting; exchange, substitution.

mukayesat (. — . —) مقايسات A *lrnd., pl.* of **mukayese.**

mukayese (. — ..) مقايس A a comparing, comparison. **— et=** /ı/ to compare. **—li** comparative.

mukayyed, mukayyet[dı] مقيّد A 1. bound; limited; restricted. 2. registered. 3. diligent, attentive. **— ol=** 1. /la/ to be bound, to be restricted. 2. to be registered. 3. /a/ to attend diligently (to something), to take care (of).

mukayyi[i] (..—) مقيّي A *med.* which causes vomiting, emetic. **—ât** (..——) A *pl.*

mukayyid مقيّد A *lrnd.* 1. who registers; registrar. 2. who binds, restricts. **—in** (...—) A *pl.* **—lik** registrarship.

mukbil مقبل A *lrnd.* 1. fortunate, prosperous. 2. that advances, approaching. **—ân** (..—) P, **—in** (..—) A *pl.* the fortunate.

mukdim مقدم A *lrnd.* diligent, laborious, persevering. **—âne** (..—.) P diligently, perseveringly.

mukın (—.) موقن A *lrnd.* who knows for certain; firmly believing.

mukır[rrı] مقرّ A *lrnd.* who confesses a fault; confessor. **—âne** (..—.) P confessedly.

mukim (. —) مقيم A who stays, dwells; dweller, resident; stationary.

mukle مقله A *lrnd.* eyeball; the black, also the white, of the eye; pupil of the eye.

mukmir مقمر A *lrnd.* moonlit (night).

mukni[iı] مقنع A *lrnd.* satisfying; convincing.

mukri[iı] مقرئ A *lrnd.* who causes or teaches one to read or recite (the Quran).

mukriz مقرض A *lrnd.* money-lender.

muksit مقسط A *lrnd.* who acts or distributes with justice and equity; God, the Just and Equitable.

mukşair[rrı] مقشعرّ A *lrnd.* 1. upright, standing on end (hair), bristling. 2. whose hair stands on end from terror.

muktahim مُقْتَحِم A *lrnd.* who throws himself upon a thing with no thought of danger.

muktasir مُقْتَصِر A *lrnd.* 1. who restricts or contents himself. 2. who is brief.

muktataf مُقْتَطَف A *lrnd.* gathered, culled, eclectic. —**ât** (..—) A eclectics; anthology.

muktatıf مُقْتَطِف A *lrnd.* who culls.

muktáza (..—) مُقْتَضَى A *lrnd.* 1. required, needed, requirement, need; exigency. 2. marginal note on an official document. —**sınca** according to the requirements of, in accordance with.

muktazayat (..——) مُقْتَضَيَات A *lrnd.* requisites; requirements.

muktazi (..—) مُقْتَضِى A *lrnd.* necessary; inevitable. —**yat** (..——) A *pl.* necessary or inevitable consequences.

muktebes مُقْتَبَس A *lrnd.* quoted (passage etc.) acquired from another. —**at** (...—) A *lrnd.* quotations.

muktebis مُقْتَبِس A *lrnd.* one who quotes from another. —**in** (...—) A those who quote from others.

mukteda (..—) مُقْتَدَى A *lrnd.* imitated, followed, taken as a model; guide; example. —**bih** (..—.) A followed; guide; example.

muktedi (..—) مُقْتَدِى A *lrnd.* who follows or imitates a model; follower, imitator.

muktedir مُقْتَدِر A 1. able, capable. 2. powerful; mighty.

muktefa (..—) مُقْتَفَى A *lrnd.* followed; chosen.

muktefi (..—) مُقْتَفِى A *lrnd.* who follows, follower.

mukterib مُقْتَرِب A *lrnd.* approaching, brought near; near.

mukterin مُقْتَرِن A *lrnd.* in close conjunction.

mukteriz مُقْتَرِض A *lrnd.* who borrows money, borrower.

muktesid مُقْتَصِد A economical; careful (in spending money).

mukteza (..—) مُقْتَضَى *var. of* **muktaza.**

muktezi (..—) مُقْتَضِى *var. of* **muktazi.**

mulaj مُولاژ F 1. *archaic* casting, molding. 2. *med.* moulage.

mu'lem مُعْلَم A *lrnd.* marked with a special distinguishing mark or badge.

mu'len مُعْلَن A *lrnd.* made known, publicly proclaimed.

mu'lim مُعْلِم A *lrnd.* who marks with a special mark or badge.

mu'lin مُعْلِن A *lrnd.* who proclaims; revealer.

mum 1 مُوم [mum 2] 1. candle; *elec.* candlepower; watt. 2. wax. — **ağacı** 1. wax palm, *bot.*, *Ceroxylon andicola.* 2. wax myrtle, *bot.*, *Myrica cerifera.* —**la ara**= /ı/

1. to seek eagerly, to search very diligently. 2. to search for something very difficult to find. 3. to miss bitterly. — **burnu** snuff, burned end of the wick of a candle. — **cilâsı** 1. *art* encaustic (painting). 2. wax polish. —**a çevir**= /ı/ to cause to become submissive and obedient. — **çiçeği** waxflower, *bot.*, *Cerinthe minor;* honeywort, *bot.*, *Cerinthe retorta.* — **damlalığı** socket, sconce (of a candlestick). — **dibi mum ortası** game played with a candle placed on a table. — **dibine ışık vermez** *proverb* (*lit.* A candle does not illuminate its own base.) One who helps others sometimes is unable to help himself; some persons of authority neglect to use this authority in the interest of their relatives. — **dikmelik** candle frame (in a church). — **direk** bolt upright; very straight. —**a dön**= to become like wax in someone's hands. — **gibi** 1. straight as a candle. 2. very neat and trim. — **heykelciliği** ceroplastics, wax modelling. — **kirpisi** *same as* **mum dikmelik.** — **kuvveti** *phys.* candlepower. — **külâhı** candle extinguisher. — **makası** snuffers. — **ol**= to become submissive and obedient. — **söndü** the candle was extinguished, *alluding to a Bektashi ceremony in which the lights were put out and which was popularly imagined to be immoral;* immoral, improper. — **yapıştır**= /a/ to make a mark against (something); to make a note of; to keep in mind.

mum 2 (—) مُوم P *lrnd.* wax.

mumaileyh (——..) مُومَى اِلَيْه A *lrnd.* aforementioned (man).

mumaileyha (——..—) مُومَى اِلَيْهَا A *lrnd.* aforementioned (woman).

mumaileyhim (——...), **mumaileyhima** (——..—) A مُومَى اِلَيْهِم *lrnd.*, *pl. of* **mumaileyh, mumaileyha.**

mumbar (.—) مُومْبَار [Persian **mubar**] *lrnd.*, *same as* **bumbar.**

mumcu مُومْجِى 1. maker or seller of candles. 2. *obs.* matchlockman. 3. *Ott. hist.* one of the twelve officers of the Janissary corps in the early days of its organization.

mumdil مُومْدِل P *lrnd.* tender hearted.

mumhala مُومْحَالَا *only in the expression* — **gibi** 1. awake. 2. restless, always on the move.

mumhane (.—.) مُومْخَانَه *Ott. hist.* candle factory.

mumi (——) مُومِى P *lrnd.* waxen, waxed, waxy.

mumise (—..) مُومِسَه A *lrnd.* unchaste, adulterous (woman).

mumiyan (—.—) مُومِيَان P *lrnd.* small waisted, slim.

mumla= مُومْلَا 1. /ı/ to wax. 2. to put a mark or seal on (a thing). —**t**= /ı, a/ *caus.*

mumlu موملو مومی 1. containing wax, prepared with wax. 2. furnished with candles. — **kâğıt** wax paper.

mumlukᵍᵘ مومّو candlepower; wattage.

mumya مومیا [Persian **mumiya**] 1. mummy. 2. shriveled, sallow man. — **ol=** 1. to become a mummy. 2. to be sallow and shriveled like a mummy. —**laş=** to become a mummy.

munafıkᵏⁱ (. — .) منافق A same as **münafık**.

mundar موندار colloq., var. of **murdar**.

munfasıl منفصل A lrnd. 1. separated, disjoined. 2. removed from office; retired. —**an** (..´..) A in a separated manner, disjointedly. —**în** (...—) A pl.

munfasım منفصم A lrnd. broken without separation, crushed.

munhafız منخفض A lrnd. 1. depressed, low, subjected. 2. soft, hushed.

munhasır منحصر A same as **münhasır**.

munis (—.) مونس A 1. sociable, companionable, good-natured, friendly; familiar. 2. tame.

munkabız منقبض A lrnd. 1. contracted, retracted. 2. constipated; shriveled. 3. disturbed (from anger, fear, or shame); tongue-tied.

munkalib منقلب A lrnd., same as **münkalib**.

munkaşir منقشر A lrnd. skinned, peeled.

munkatı منقطع A lrnd. 1. cut off; separated. 2. interrupted, broken off; come to an end.

munsabᵇᵇⁱ منصب A lrnd. 1. poured, flowing, forming a mouth (river). 2. same as **mansap**. — **ol=** /a/ to flow (into).

munsabığ منصبغ A lrnd. 1. tinged, dyed. 2. baptized.

munsarif منصرف A 1. Arabic gram. declinable (noun). 2. lrnd. turning away; averted; departing.

munsarih منصرح A lrnd. evident, manifest.

munsarim منصرم A lrnd. cut or broken through; separated; cut off from others.

munsif منصف A lrnd. just, equitable, fair. —**âne** (..—.) P 1. just, equitable, reasonable (act). 2. in an equitable manner, fairly. —**lik** equity, reasonableness.

muntabıⁱ منطبع A lrnd. 1. stamped; printed. 2. having a certain natural disposition or character. 3. docile, yielding, obedient.

muntabıh منطبخ A lrnd. cooked, done; baked, roasted.

muntabıkᵏⁱ منطبق A lrnd. fitting, equal, even; coincident.

muntafi منطفی A lrnd. extinguished; extinct.

muntalıkᵏⁱ منطلق A lrnd. loosed, released, gone, loosened, relaxed.

muntasıb منتصب A lrnd. erect, standing upright, set up.

muntasıh منتصح A lrnd. who accepts good advice, who takes warning. —**âne** (...—.) P submissively; ready to take advice.

muntavi منطوی A lrnd. 1. folded up, wrapped 2. contained, expressed in a document.

muntazam منتظم A 1. regular, well arranged; tidy, orderly. 2. in a line, drawn up. —**an** (..´..) A regularly, in an orderly manner.

muntazar منتظر A lrnd. awaited, expected. — **haklar** law expectancy, contingent interest, remainder.

muntazır منتظر A lrnd. who waits expectantly, watching for; ready and waiting. —**an** (..´..) A awaiting.

munzamᵐᵐⁱ منضم A added, additional; supplementary; extra; appended. — **hat** telephone extension line. — **nesç** anat. conjunctive tissue. — **tahsisat** supplementary estimates.

mur (—) مر P lrnd. 1. ant. 2. symbol of poverty and weakness. 3. rust.

murabaha (.—..) مرابحة A usury. —**cı** usurer. —**cılık** usury.

murabba 1 مربع 1. math. square; squared; square of a number. 2. pros. poem of four verses or four lines, quatrain. 3. lrnd. made four; divided into four; fourfold. 4. Or. mus. a **makam** used in old times; a musical instrument used in old times; the old name of the **beste** composition form.

murabba 2 (..—) مربّا A preserved fruit; confectionary.

murabıt (.—.) مرابط A lrnd. one who devotes himself to a life of religious seclusion; Muslim hermit, marabout.

Murabıtîn (.—.—) مرابطین A hist. Almoravides.

murad (.—) مراد A wish, desire; intention; aim. — **da o!** That's all he wants! —**ına er=** to attain one's desire. — **et=** /ı/ archaic to purpose, to resolve, to wish determinedly. — **şudur ki** This is what is meant.

muradbahş (.—.) مرادبخش P lrnd. giver of one's desires; God.

murafaa (.—..) مرافعة A law a mutually referring a dispute to a court of justice, a pleading before a court; a hearing in court, trial.

murahhas مرخّص A delegated, deputed; delegate, envoy; plenipotentiary. — **heyet** delegation with full power. —**iyet**, —**lık** delegation.

murakaba, murakabe (.—..) مراقبة A 1. control, supervision, inspection, censure; banking audit. 2. myst. a going into ecstasy; ecstasy; contemplation; meditation. 3. lrnd. a watching and waiting; vigilance.

murakıb, murakıpᵇⁱ (.—.) مراقب A 1. supervisor, auditor. 2. myst. one who goes into ecstasy; a contemplative person. 3. lrnd. who watches and waits.

murakka⁸¹ مُرَقَّع A 1. patched cloak (of a dervish). 2. Arabic calligraphy collage, decorative page composed of pieces of writing which are patched together. 3. patched.

murakkaat (...—) مُرَقَّعات A Arabic calligraphy collection or album of calligraphical collages.

murakkam مُرَقَّم A lrnd. numbered.

murakkapuş (..——) مُرَقَّع پوش P lrnd. clothed in patched garments (dervish).

murane (——.) مُورانه P lrnd. like an ant; very small; humbly, modestly.

murassa⁸¹ مُرَصَّع A 1. set with jewels, jeweled. 2. rhet. having words which are homophonous in each member (clause).

murassas مُرَصَّص A lrnd. 1. covered with lead or tin. 2. made compact, compactly joined together.

muratᵈ¹ (.—) مُراد same as **murad**.

murc مُرج Arm prov. mason's point, chasing-chisel.

murçalᵘ (——) مُورچال P lrnd. entrenchment for besieging a fortified place.

murçe (—.) مُورچه P lrnd. 1. small ant. 2. insignificant man, contemptible fellow. 3. honeycomb in a piece of metal.

murd مُورد P myrtle, bot., Myrtus communis.

murdar (.—) مُردار P 1. dirty, filthy; unclean. 2. indecent, corrupt, foul. — **ağacı** common purple loosestrife, bot., Lythrum salicaria. — **ilik** anat. spinal marrow.

murdarhane (.——.) مُردارخانه P a point in backgammon whence there is no opening for a move.

murdarhâr (.——) مُردارخوار P lrnd. carrion crow, vulture.

murdarla⁼ᵣ مُردارلامق 1. to soil, to make filthy. 2. to discharge faeces. —n= pass.

murdarlıkᶠ¹ مُردارلق 1. filthiness, dirtiness; filth, dirt. 2. indecency.

mu'reb مُعرَب A Arabic gram. declined, declinable (noun).

mu'rız مُعرِض A lrnd. that turns away.

murina (..'.) مُورينا Gk moray, zool., Muraena helena.

muris (—.) مُورِث A 1. law testator. 2. lrnd. that causes, brings about.

muriza (..'.) مُوريزه Gk naut. reef earing.

murtabıt مُرتَبِط A lrnd. connected, related, attached to, dependent upon. — **suçlar** law connected offenses.

murtad مُرتَدّ [mürted] colloq. apostate from Islam. —**lık** apostasy.

murtaza (...') مُرتَضى A lrnd., same as **mürtaza**.

Musa 1 (——) مُوسى A 1. Moses. 2. l. ¹c. razor. — **ağacı** fire thorn, bot., Pyracantha coccinea.

musâ 2 (—.) مُوصى A law appointed executor; appointed legatee.

musaad مُصعَد A lrnd. 1. high, lofty. 2. distilled. 3. concentrated or rectified by boiling (beverage).

musaare مُصاعَره A lrnd. a turning the head away in disgust or contempt.

musab (.—) مُصاب A lrnd. stricken by illness or calamity; afflicted, struck, hit; victim.

musabbag مُصبَّغ A lrnd. dyed.

musabere (.—..) مُصابَره A lrnd. an exercising patience (towards one another); forbearance, endurance.

mûsa-bih (——.) مُوصى به A law legacy, bequest.

musabin (.——) مُصابين A lrnd., pl. the afflicted; victims.

musabiyet (.——.) مُصابيَّت A lrnd. a being afflicted by calamity or illness.

musadakatⁱⁱ (.——.) مُصادَقت A lrnd. sincere mutual friendship.

musadda⁸¹ مُصَدَّع A lrnd. 1. troubled with a headache. 2. worried, disturbed.

musaddakᵏ¹ مُصَدَّق A lrnd. confirmed, proved, true; certified, verified.

musadder مُصَدَّر A lrnd. 1. having a chief seat; placed in the seat of honor. 2. having an initial word (sentence).

musaddıⁱⁱ مُصَدِّع A lrnd. 1. that gives a headache. 2. disturber, troubler.

musaddıkᵏ¹ مُصَدِّق A lrnd. that confirms or ratifies; who accepts as true.

musadefe, musadefet (.—..) مُصادفه مُصادفت A lrnd. a meeting, encountering, finding, lighting on; a chance meeting.

musademat (.—.—) مُصادَمات A lrnd., pl. of **musademe**.

musademe (.—..) مُصادَمه A 1. collision; clash. 2. mil. skirmish, encounter. — **iğnesi** firearms striker.

musadere (.—..) مُصادَره A same as **müsadere**.

musadıf (.—.) مُصادِف A lrnd., same as **müsadif**.

Musaf مُصاف colloq., var. of **Mushaf**.

musafaa مُصافاه A lrnd. 1. a striking one another; a fight. 2. an embracing one another; an embrace.

musafaha (.—..) مُصافَحه A lrnd. a handshaking. — **et**= /la/ to shake hands; to greet one another.

musafat (.——) مُصافات A lrnd. a behaving sincerely, an acting with pure affection towards (somebody), true friendship, sincerity.

musaffa (..—) مُصَفّى A lrnd. purified, clarified, fine, clear; pure, refined.

musaffef مُصَفَّف A lrnd. arranged in a line or lines.

musaffi (..—) مصفّى A *lrnd.* that makes pure, fine or dear; purifier, clearer; refining.

musaffir مصفّر A *lrnd.* 1. that dyes yellow. 2. who whistles.

musafih (.—.) مصافح A *lrnd.* who takes another's hand in his own; who shakes hands.

musaggar مصغّر A 1. *gram.* diminutive (noun). 2. *lrnd.* made small.

musahabat (.—.—) مصاحبات A *lrnd.*, *pl. of* **musahabe.** —ı ahlâkıye *obs.* civics.

musahabe, musahabet[ti] (.—..) مصاحبت A a having a friendly conversation; company.

musaheret (.—..) مصاهرت A *lrnd.* a being related by marriage.

musahhaf مصحّف A *lrnd.* corrupted or changed (written word); misspelled, inaccurate.

musahhah مصحّح A *lrnd.* corrected.

musahhih مصحّح A 1. *print.* proofreader. 2. *lrnd.* who corrects; corrector. —in (...—) A *lrnd.*, *pl.* —lik proofreading.

musahib (.—.) مصاحب A 1. *hist.* gentleman-in-waiting (on the Sultan). 2. *lrnd.* who keeps company with another, companion, associate, friend. —ân (.—.—) A *pl.*

musahibe (.—..) مصاحبه A *lrnd.* lady-in-waiting.

musahiblik[gi] مصاحبلك the function of a gentleman-in-waiting.

musakka مصقّع A stewed vegetable especially eggplant with ground meat.

musal[li] (—.) موصل A *lrnd.* joined, brought into contact, united.

musalâha (.—..) مصالحه A *lrnd.* a making peace with another; reconciliation, pacification.

musalâhat (.—.—) مصالحات *lrnd.*, *pl. of* musalaha.

mûsa-leh (—..) موصى له A *law* legatee, devisee.

musalih (.—.) مصالح A *lrnd.* 1. mutually at peace. 2. maker of peace.

musalla (..—) مصلّى A *Isl. rel.* 1. public place for prayer. 2. open place near a mosque for performing a funeral service. — taşı stone on which the coffin is placed during the funeral service.

musallat مسلّط A that pertinaciously attacks, worries; worrying, annoying. — et= /ı, a/ to set one to attack or worry another. — fikir *psych.* obsession. — ol= /a/ to worry, pester, fall upon; to infest a place (robbers, etc.).

musalleb مصلّب A *lrnd.* hardened, dried; made compact.

musallî (..—) مصلّى A *lrnd.* engaged in worship; who says his prayers regularly; devout.

musallit مسلّط A *lrnd.* who causes someone to pester another continuously.

musammem مصمّم A *lrnd.* decided upon, determined; intended.

musammet مصمّت A *lrnd.* 1. made silent or speechless; silenced (complaining). 2. solid (not hollow). 3. complete (a thousand).

musandıra (..'..) مصندره 1. large closet in a wall for storing mattresses, etc. 2. fixed slab at the end of a sofa frame; sideboard.

musanna[aı] مصنّع A 1. *phil.* fictitious. 2. *lrnd.* made with skill, artistically fashioned.

musannef مصنّف A *lrnd.* 1. arranged in classes or kinds; classified. 2. composed or compiled (book).

musannefat (...—) مصنّفات A *lrnd.* literary works.

musannif مصنّف A *lrnd.* classifier; compiler of a book; author. —i fakir the author (when speaking of himself). —an (...—) P, —in (...—) A *pl.* authors, writers.

musap[bı] (.—.) مصاب A *var. of* **musab.**

musaraa (.—..) مصارعه A *lrnd.* 1. a wrestling together; wrestling. 2. contest, struggle.

musaraha (.—..) مصارحه A *lrnd.* a saying something openly to another; explicitness. —ten (.—'...) A said openly or explicitly.

musari[iı] (.—.) مصارع A *lrnd.* who wrestles, wrestler.

musarra[aı] مصرّع A *pros.* in couplets and lines (poem).

musarrah مصرّح A *lrnd.* openly, explicitly (set forth). —an (..'..) A clearly and explicitly.

musattah مسطّح A *lrnd.* made flat, leveled.

musavver مصوّر A 1. imagined; formed; figured. 2. illustrated, depicted.

musavvir مصوّر A *lrnd.* 1. who depicts, shapes; forms; God (the Former of all). 2. artist, designer, portrait painter. 3. the imaginative faculty.

musavvit مصوّت A *lrnd.* that makes a sound, noise, or cry; sonorous.

musayaha (.—..) مصايحه A *lrnd.* a crying aloud to one another; a shouting.

musayefe (.—..) مصايفه A *lrnd.* a bargaining or hiring for the summer.

musaykal مصيقل A *lrnd.* polished, burnished.

Musevi (—.—) موسوى A 1. Jew; Jewish. 2. Mosaic, belonging to Moses. 3. *Isl. rel.* follower of Musa, son of Jafer-i Sadık.

Mushaf مصحف A 1. the Quran. 2. *l. c.* book, volume, written page. — kesesi cloth case in which a Quran is kept.

musır[rrı] مصرّ A persistent; persevering. —âne (..—.) P in a persistent manner, pertinacious, insistent (acts).

musi (——) موصى A 1. *law* who appoints

an executor or legatee. 2. *lrnd.* who commands or recommends.

musib (.—) مصيب A *lrnd.* that hits the mark; right, appropriate.

musibet (.—.) مصيبت A 1. calamity, evil. 2. ill-omened, foul. 3. tiresome person. —! you pest! **bir — bin nasihattan yeğdir** *proverb* A single misfortune is more effective than a thousand warnings. **—li** calamitous.

musikar (—.—) موسيقار P *lrnd.* 1. pipe made of unequal reeds; Pandean pipe. 2. an old **makam**; a wind instrument used in old times. 3. a bird whose bill is perforated with holes through which it emits a musical sound, the mythical singing swan. **—ı hatayi** a kind of ancient musical wind instrument. **—î** (—.——) P a player of **musikar**.

musiki (—.—) موسيقى A music. **— makamatı** the twelve original airs of Oriental music with their modern variations.

musikişinas (—.—.—) موسيقيشناس P musician; lover of music.

musil (—.) موصل A *lrnd.* 1. leading to, joining. 2. carrier, bearer.

musile (—..) موصلة A *lrnd.*, *fem. of* **musil**.

Musile-i Sahn, Musile-i Süleymaniye موصلۀ صحن موصلۀ سليمانيه A *Ott. hist.* highest degree of a teacher in the medresses of Fatih and Süleymaniye.

mu'sir 1 معسر A *lrnd.* poor, needy.

musir 2 (—.) موسر A *lrnd.* rich, wealthy.

muska موسقة [nusha] 1. written charm, amulet. 2. triangular thing shaped like an amulet. 3. *archery* amulet-shaped piece of leather pasted to the hilt of a bow. **— böreği** a kind of pastry stuffed with cheese or ground meat having an amulet shape. **— fişeği** three-cornered squib.

muskavarî (..——) موسقه وارى P dangling; after the fashion of an amulet.

muslih مصلح A *lrnd.* who puts to rights; corrector, restorer; reconciler.

muslihane (..—.) مصلحانه P peacefully, reconciliatory.

muslihîn, muslihûn (..—) مصلحين A *lrnd.* reconcilers; restorers.

muslin موسلين F muslin.

muslukᵗᵘ موصلق [maslak] 1. tap, spigot. 2. *colloq.* toilet. **— taşı** stone basin under a tap, sink. **—çu** 1. one who sells or repairs taps. 2. *slang* swindler, thief.

musmul مصمل *archaic, var. of* **mısmıl**.

muson موسون F monsoon.

mustabir مصطبر A *lrnd.* patient.

mustafa مصطفى A *lrnd.* 1. chosen; elect. 2. *w. cap.*, title of the Prophet Muhammad (as the elect of God). **M—vî** (...—) A pertaining to Muhammad, Muhammadan.

mustahfız مستحفظ A *Ott. hist.* commander of a fort.

mustalah مصطلح A *lrnd.* 1. idiomatic; technical (term). 2. full of idioms or technical expressions (discourse).

mustalahât (...—) مصطلحات A *lrnd.* conventional or technical terms; idioms.

mustaripᵇⁱ مضطرب *same as* **muztarib**.

mustatil مستطيل A *geom.* rectangle. **—î** (...—) A rectangular.

musütürde (—...) موسترده P *lrnd.* 1. one whose head is shaved. 2. an order of dervishes who shave their heads and beards.

muş 1 موش F steam launch.

=**muş 2** مش *cf.* =**mış 1**.

=**muş 3** مش *cf.* =**mış 2**.

muş 4 (—) موش P *lrnd.* mouse, rat. **—i deştî** field mouse; mole; hamster. **—i düpa** jerboa. **—i hurma** polecat; fennec. **—i kûr** mole, blind mouse. **—i perende** 1. bat. 2. squirrel. **—i sahraî** *same as* **muş-i deştî**. **—i sultaniye** common dormouse.

muşabakᵏⁱ مشاباك [*from Arabic* müşebbek] openwork embroidery.

muşamba (..'.) موشامبا [muşemma] 1. oiled silk; wax cloth, oilcloth; tarpaulin. 2. linoleum. 3. raincoat, waterproof. **— döşe=** to lay linoleum. **— fener** folding lantern made of oilcloth. **— gibi** very dirty (clothes, etc).

=**muşçasına** مشجاسنه *cf.* =**mışçasına**.

muşekᵏⁱ (—.) موشك P *lrnd.* little mouse; muskrat. **—i perran** flying squirrel, pteromys.

muşemmaᵃⁱ مشمع A *lrnd.*, *same as* **muşamba**.

muşer موشر [*Arabic* müeşşer] *prov.* a kind of curved saw.

muşgir (——) موشگير P *lrnd.* that catches mice; rat catcher.

muşhar (——) موشخوار P *lrnd.* owl.

muşikâf (—.—) موشكاف P *lrnd.* 1. who splits hairs, hair splitting. 2. strict critic, subtle reasoner. **—âne** (—.—.) P meticulously, minutely, with greatest care. **—î** (—.——) P minute criticism.

=**muşken** ('.) مشكن *cf.* =**mışken**.

muşmula موشمولا Gk 1. medlar, *bot.*, *Mespilus germanica*. 2. *slang* old, shrivelled. **— gibi** all creases and wrinkles. **— suratlı** having a wrinkled face.

=**muşşa** ('.) مشّ *cf.* =**mışsa**.

muşt 1 مشت P *lrnd.* 1. fist. 2. blow with the clenched fist. 3. handful. **—i hâk** 1. a handful of earth. 2. the earth, the world and its vanities. 3. man.

muşt 2 مشط A 1. *anat.* shoulder blade. 2. *lrnd.* comb.

muşta موشته مشته [muşt 1] 1. fist. 2. blow

muştala= with the fist. 3. short handle, hilt (of a sword etc.). 4. metal instrument used by shoemakers, for pounding and smoothing seams.

muştala=ʳ موشته لامق 1. /ı/ to give a blow with the fist. 2. to pound, to thump.

muştefşar (..—)مشتافشا P lrnd. 1. fabulous kind of soft gold capable of being molded by hand. 2. small golden scent box held in the hand by great people.

=muştu 1 (´.) مشد ف cf. =mıştı.

muştu 2 موشنو مشنو [müjde] prov. piece of good news, glad tidings. —**cu** bringer of good tidings.

muştula=ʳ مشتو لامق /ı, a/ to give good news (to a person).

muştulukᵍᵘ موشتونوق present given to a bringer of good news.

muştülkadem مشط القدم A anat. metatarsus.

muştülyed مشط اليد A anat. metacarpus.

muştvare (.—.) مشتواره P lrnd. handful.

muştzen مشت زن P lrnd. professional boxer. —**lik** boxing.

=muşuk 1 (´.) مشك cf. =mışık 1.

=muşuk 2 مشك cf. =mışık 2.

=muşun 1, =muşunuz (´...) مشنك cf. =mışın 1.

=muşun 2, =muşunuz (´...) مشنك cf. =mışın 2.

mut 1 موت luck, fortune; happiness.

mut 2 مط [Arabic müdd] archaic a grain measure.

mu'taᵃⁱ **1** (.—) A, **mûta** (——) معطى 1. data. 2. lrnd. given, presented.

mutaᵃⁱ **2** (.—) مطاع A lrnd. obeyed.

muta 3 (——) مطاء A lrnd. 1. caused to be trampled under foot. 2. led to commit folly.

mutaassıb A, **mutaassıp**ᵇⁱ متعصّب 1. fanatical; bigoted; fanatic. 2. zealous, ardent. —**âne** (....—.) P fanatically. —**în** (....—) A lrnd. fanatics.

mutaazzım متعظّم A lrnd. proud, haughty, arrogant.

mutabakat مطابقت A 1. a being mutually conformable; conformity; agreement; congruity. 2. math. congruity, congruence.

mutabıkᵏⁱ (.—.) مطابق A 1. conformable, agreeing. 2. math. identical. — **kal=** /da/ to agree (upon).

mu'tad (.—) A, **mûtad** (——) معتاد customary; habitual, usual habit, custom.

mutaf 1 (.—) مطاف A lrnd., same as **mataf**.

mutaf 2 مِناف [Persian **mutab**] spinner of goat hair; maker of articles woven of goat hair. —**çı** colloq., same as **mutaf**. —**çılık** the trade of making articles of goat hair.

nutagazzıb متغضّب A lrnd. who becomes angry, irritable.

mutahhar مطهّر A lrnd. canonically clean, purified; sacred. —**iyet** cleanness, purity.

mu'takᵏⁱ معتق A can. law freed, emancipated; freedman.

mu'takadat (...—) A, **mûtakedat** (—..—) معتقدات lrnd., pl. points of belief or of faith.

mutalâa (.—..) مطالعه A same as **mütalâa**.

mutalebat (.—.—) مطالبات A lrnd. things demanded, demands, claims.

mutalebe (.—..) مطالبه A lrnd. 1. claim, title; demand. 2. a seeking, demanding; requisition.

mutaliⁱⁱ (.—.) مطالع A lrnd. who reads and studies. —**in** (.—.—) A pl.

mutallâ (..—) مطلّى A lrnd. gilt; ornamented with gold.

mutallaka مطلّقة A law divorced wife.

mutallakârî (..———) مطلّاكاری P lrnd. gilding; gilded work.

mutallikᵏⁱ مطلّق A lrnd. one who divorces his wife.

mutalsem مطلسم A lrnd. protected by a talisman.

mutantan متطنطن A lrnd. accompanied by pomp and circumstance; pompous; ostentatious, gorgeous.

mutaraha (.—..) مطارحه A lrnd. a talking together, a bandying words; a contending in improvisation.

mutarede (.—..) مطارده A lrnd. an attacking one another furiously; mutual attack.

mu'tariza A, **mutariza** (—...) معترضه parenthesis, bracket.

mutarra (..—) مطرّى A lrnd. 1. juicy, fresh. 2. fragrant, perfumed, scented with aromatics. 3. polished, glazed.

mutarrez مطرّز A lrnd. bordered, fringed; embroidered.

mutasabbi (...—) متصبّى A lrnd. who acts as a child. —**yâne** (...—.) P acting in a childish manner.

mutasabbir متصبّر A lrnd. who constrains himself to patience.

mutasaddıkᵏⁱ متصدّق A lrnd. who gives alms. —**în** (....—) A pl.

mutasaddır متصدّر A lrnd. who acts as a chief; who occupies the chief seat. —**âne** (....—.) P acting as chief. —**în** (....—) A pl.

mutasaddî 1 (...—) متصدّى A lrnd. who sets about a task, who dares to do some act; venturesome; audacious.

mutasaddiⁱⁱ **2** متصدّع A lrnd. split, cracked.

mutasaffî (...—) متصفّى A lrnd. clarified, free from sediment; purified.

mutasallib متصلّب A lrnd. 1. determined, obdurate. 2. hardened, solidified. —**âne** (....—.) P obdurate (manner).

mutasallif تَصَلُّف A *lrnd.* pedant. —**âne** (....—.) P pedantically.

mutasanniⁱⁱ تَصَنُّع A *lrnd.* pretending to be skilled; who affects, feigning. —**âne** (....—.) P affectedly, putting on airs. —**în** (....—) A *pl.*

mutasarrıf مُتَصَرِّف A 1. *lrnd.* who uses and disposes of a thing at will. 2. *lrnd.* possessor, occupant; master. 3. *Ott. hist.* governor of a Sancak.

mutasarrıfe تَصَرُّف A *psych.* faculty of the mind by which ideas are set in order for use.

mutasarrıflıkᵏ¹ تَصَرُّفْلِك post and jurisdiction of a **mutasarrıf**.

mutasarrım تَصَرُّم A *lrnd.* 1. cut through. 2. dexterous, clever. —**în** (....—) A *pl.*

mutasavver تَصَوُّر A 1. imagined; contemplated. 2. projected, intended.

mutasavvıf تَصَوُّف A who becomes a Sufi; Sufi, mystic. —ı **mübtıl** mystic who asserts extravagant nonsense.

mutasavvıfa تَصَوُّفَه A the Sufis.

mutasavvıfâne (....—.) تَصَوُّفَانَه P in a mystical way, mystically.

mutasavvıfîn (....—) تَصَوُّفِين A *pl. of* **mutasavvıf**.

mutasavvıt تَصَوُّت A *lrnd.* sounding, resonant.

mutasavvır تَصَوُّر A *lrnd.* 1. depicting. 2. who forms an idea upon (something).

mutasayyıf تَصَيُّف A *lrnd.* who remains in a place during summer.

mu'tasım مُعْتَصِم A *lrnd.* 1. who holds fast, clings to. 2. abstaining, refraining (from disobedience by the grace of God).

mutasyonizm مُتَاسْيُونِيزم F *phil.* mutationism.

mûtat (——) مُعْتَاد *var. of* **mûtad**.

mutatabbıⁱⁱ تَطَبُّع A *lrnd.* who has acquired some nature, disposition or habit.

mutatabbib تَطَبُّب A *lrnd.* quack doctor.

mutatahhir تَطَهُّر A *lrnd.* 1. purified, cleansed, washed. 2. sanctified.

mutataım تَطَعُّم A *lrnd.* who tastes, tries.

mutatarrıkᵏ¹ تَطَرُّق A *lrnd.* that seeks access, that finds the way.

mutatarrib تَطَرُّب A *lrnd.* alive with joy. —**âne** (....—.) P in a joyful manner. —**în** (....—) A *pl. of* **mutatarrib**.

mutatarrıf تَطَرُّف A *lrnd.* that goes or keeps apart, aside.

mutatavvıkᵏ¹ تَطَوُّق A *lrnd.* 1. who puts on his neck a ring collar or necklet; collared. 2. who assumes responsibility.

mutatavvıⁱⁱ تَطَوُّع A *lrnd.* 1. obedient. 2. volunteer (in a holy war). 3. who performs a religious act of supererogation.

mutatayyib تَطَيُّب A *lrnd.* 1. who perfumes himself. 2. pleasant, agreeable, fragrant.

mutatayyir تَطَيُّر A *lrnd.* 1. who draws a bad omen from birds. 2. who views as a bad omen —**âne** (....—.) P ominously. —**în** (....—) A *pl.*

mutavaat (.—..) مُطَاوَعَت A 1. *gram.* reflexive form of a verb. 2. *lrnd.* a submitting, yielding, complying, conforming; submission; obedience; compliance.

mutavassıf مُتَوَصِّف A 1. endued with a quality, qualified. 2. described; celebrated.

mutavassıl مُتَوَصِّل A *lrnd.* 1. that tries to reach or gain admittance. 2. desirous of becoming united; arrived.

mutavassıt مُتَوَسِّط A 1. that intervenes, interposes; who mediates; intercessor, mediator. 2. intermediary, medium; middle term; mean. — **kaplar** *phys.* communicating tubes. — **nisbet** mean proportional. —**în** (....—) A *pl.*

mutavele, mutavelet (.—..) مُطَاوَلَه A *lrnd.* a delaying payment; procrastination.

mutaviⁱⁱ (.—.) مُطَاوِع A 1. *gram.* intransitive formed from a transitive. 2. *lrnd.* obedient, compliant, submissive.

mutavvakᵏ¹ مُطَوَّق A *lrnd.* 1. furnished with a ring, collar; ringed, collared. 2. collar; shaped.

mutavvel مُطَوَّل A *lrnd.* 1. made long, prolonged, extended. 2. prolix.

mu'tayat (.——) مُعْطَيَات A *math., phil., pl. of* **mu'ta 1**, data.

mutayebat (.—.—) مُطَايَبَات A *lrnd., pl. of* **mutayebe**.

mutayebe (.—..) مُطَايَبَه A *lrnd.* a jesting, joking together; joke, pleasantry.

mutayyeb مُطَيَّب A *lrnd.* 1. made good, pleasant; clean. 2. spiced, perfumed, aromatized.

Mutayyebe مُطَيَّبَه A *a name of the city of Medina*.

mutazaccır تَضَجُّر A *lrnd.* distressed, oppressed; annoyed, grieved.

mutazallim تَظَلُّم A *lrnd.* who complains of injustice. —**âne** (....—.) P complainingly. —**în** (....—) A *pl.*

mutazammın تَضَمُّن A 1. which comprises, contains; comprising, containing. 2. *law* who stands bail, guarantor, surety; responsible.

mutazannın تَظَنُّن A *lrnd.* who thinks, surmises or suspects.

mutazarrıf تَظَرُّف A *lrnd.* affectedly witty or graceful; affecter of elegance. —**âne** (....—.) P putting on an air, of an affectedly graceful way. —**în** (....—) A *pl.*

mutazarrır تَضَرُّر A who suffers injury, injured, harmed, suffering loss.

mutazarri تَضَرُّع A *lrnd.* who humbles himself obsequiously; who humbles himself in prayer; humbled; suppliant. —**âne** (....—.) P humbly. —**în** (....—) A *pl.*

mutazavvıⁱⁱ تَضَوُّع A *lrnd.* fragrant when stirred (musk).
mutazayyıkᵏⁱ تَضَيُّق A *lrnd.* narrow, close, confined; straitened.
mutbikᵏⁱ مُطْبِق A *lrnd.* continuous, incessant (fever).
mutçulukᵍᵘ *neol., phil.* eudaemonism.
mu'teber A, **muteber** (—..) مُعْتَبَر 1. held in consideration; of good repute; esteemed, respected. 2. valid, legal (document etc.), solvent.
mu'teberan (...—) مُعْتَبَران P *lrnd.* the notables, the men of repute (of a people or town).
mutedᵈᵈⁱ مُعَدّ A *lrnd.* 1. numbered, counted, computed. 2. accounted of importance. 3. ready, prepared.
mu'tedil A, **mutedil** (—..) مُعْتَدِل 1. moderate, temperate; mild, soft. 2. equable, uniform. 3. *chem.* neutral. —**âne** (...—.) P moderately; mildly.
mu'tekad مُعْتَقَد A *lrnd.* believed, credited, held (as an article of creed).
mu'tekadât (...—) مُعْتَقَدات A *lrnd.* things believed or deemed credible; articles of faith.
mu'tekid A, **mutekid** (—..) مُعْتَقِد 1. who firmly believes; follower (of a creed or sect); believer; religious. 2. firmly persuaded, confident.
mu'tekif مُعْتَكِف A *lrnd.* who retires for a period of fasting and prayer.
mu'telˡˡⁱ مُعْتَلّ A 1. *Arabic gram.* having for radicals the letters و or ى (word). 2. *lrnd.* affected with a disease, diseased, infirm; defective.
mu'temed A, **mûtemed** (—..) مُعْتَمَد 1. relied on, confided in; reliable, trustworthy. 2. man entrusted with the finances of a department, fiduciary.
mu'temir مُعْتَمِر A *lrnd.* who visits, visitor; visitor to Mecca in the minor pilgrimage.
mu'tena (..—) A, **mûtena** (—.—) مُعْتَنى 1. carefully attended to, important; painstaking. 2. select, refined; elaborate.
mu'teref مُعْتَرَف A *lrnd.* confessed; acknowledged, admitted.
mu'terif A, **muterif** (—..) مُعْتَرِف *lrnd.* who confesses; confessor; confessing, acknowledging, admitting.
mu'teriz A, **muteriz** (—..) مُعْتَرِض *lrnd.* who objects, opposes, rejects; opposing, objecting; opposer, objector.
mu'terize A, **muterize** (—...) مُعْتَرِضة A *lrnd.*, same as **mutariza**.
mu'tesif A, **mûtesif** (—..) مُعْتَسِف *lrnd.* 1. who takes a wrong direction. 2. oppressive; harsh; exacting, extortionate.
mu'tezil A, **mûtezil** (—..) مُعْتَزِل *lrnd.* who secedes and separates himself; seceding; dissenter, separatist, schismatic.
Mu'tezile A, **mutezile** (—...) مُعْتَزِلة Mutazila, *name of a Muslim sect.*
mu'tezim مُعْتَزِم A *lrnd.* 1. who goes straight on his course; who patiently endures. 2. constant, steady, firm.
mu'tezir مُعْتَذِر A *lrnd.* who offers an excuse; who complains. —**âne** (...—.) P in an apologetic manner.
mutfakᵏⁱ مُطْفَأة [*Arabic* matbah] kitchen. —**takımı** set of kitchen utensils.
mutfî (.—) مُطْفِئ A *lrnd.* that puts out fire; who extinguishes; fire extinguisher.
mutiⁱⁱ 1 (.—) مُطِيع A obedient, submissive.
mu'ti (.—) A, **muti**ⁱⁱ 2 (——) مُعْطي *lrnd.* who gives; giver; bestower; God (giver of all things).
mutikᵏⁱ (—.) مُعْتِق A *lrnd.* who frees a slave.
mut'im مُطْعِم A *lrnd.* who feeds, gives to eat, gives the means of subsistence.
mutlakᵏⁱ مُطْلَق A 1. absolute, unconditional, autocratic. 2. absolutely, certainly. 3. *lrnd.* freed; unrestrained. — **haklar** absolute rights.
mutlaka (.'.—) مُطْلَقا A absolutely, without fail.
mutlakıyet (..—.) مُطْلَقِيَّت A 1. monarchy; autocracy. 2. absolutism.
mutlu مُوطْلُو lucky, fortunate. —**luk** happiness, good fortune, luck.
mutmain مُطْمَئِنّ A tranquil; peaceful; satisfied, assured.
mutrib مُطْرِب A poet. 1. musician, minstrel, singer. 2. *myst. orders* special place for musicians and singers in a Mevlevi lodge. —**i felek** *poet.* the planet Venus.
muttaliⁱⁱ مُطَّلِع A *lrnd.* informed, aware. — **ol**= /a/ to become aware of.
muttarid مُطَّرِد A *lrnd.* flowing freely and in a straight and onward course; in succession; regular, uniform. —**en** (...'.) A regularly; in regular succession.
muttasıf مُتَّصِف A endowed with some quality; qualified.
muttasıl مُتَّصِل A 1. adjoining, joined. 2. continuous, uninterrupted; continually. —**an** (..'..) A 1. in conjunction. 2. continuously.
muvacehat (.—.—) مُواجَهات A *lrnd.*, pl. of **muvecehe**.
muvacehe (.—.) مُواجَهة A *lrnd.* a being face to face, confrontation. —**sinde** /ın/ in the presence of; in the face of; before.
muvaceheten (.—...) مُواجَهةً A *lrnd.* face to face, in each other's presence.
muvadaa (.—..) مُوادَعة A *lrnd.* 1. a forsaking enmity and becoming reconciled; reconciliation. 2. a taking leave; farewell.

muvafakatᵗⁱ (.—..) مُوافَقَت A an agreeing, consenting; agreement, consent. — **et**= /a/ to agree, to consent.

muvaffakᵏⁱ مُوَفَّق A successful. — **ol**= /da/ to be successful.

muvaffakıyat (...——) مُوَفَّقِيات A lrnd., pl. of **muvaffakıyet**.

muvaffakıyet مُوَفَّقِيَت [A ...—.] success; victory. —**li** successful. —**sizlik** failure.

muvaffıkᵏⁱ مُوَفِّق A lrnd. who guides to success, God.

muvafıkᵏⁱ (.—.) مُوافِق A agreeable, suitable; favorable. — **rey** affirmative vote.

muvahhad مُوَحَّد A lrnd. 1. declared to be one and unique. 2. distinguished by a single dot (letter of the alphabet).

muvahhid مُوَحِّد A rel. monotheist; Muslim. —**ane** (...—.) P in a monotheistic way.

muvahhidîn (...—) مُوَحِّدين A 1. pl. of **muvahhid**. 2. Almohades.

muvahhiş مُوَحِّش A lrnd. terrible, dreadful; desert, uninhabited (country).

muvakkaᵃⁱ مُوَقَّع A lrnd. made valid by being sealed or signed (document); decree, statute.

muvakkar مُوَقَّر A lrnd. honored, revered, respected; venerable.

muvakkat مُوَقَّت A fixed, stated (time or event); temporary; provisory. — **teminat** temporary guarantee.

muvakkaten (..'..) مُوَقَّتًا A lrnd. temporarily. — **icra** law provisional execution.

muvakkıf مُوَقِّف A lrnd. that stops or detains, detainer, hinderer.

muvakkiᵏⁱⁱ مُوَقِّع A lrnd. who affixes a signature to documents.

muvakkir مُوَقِّر A lrnd. honorer, respecter.

muvakkit مُوَقِّت A lrnd. 1. timekeeper at a mosque. 2. chronometer.

muvakkithane (...—.) مُوَقِّتخانه P clock room of the **muvakkit**.

muvaneset (.—..) مُوانَسَت A lrnd. 1. a cultivating an intimacy; friendly association; familiarity. 2. tameness, a being domesticated.

muvanis (.—.) مُوانِس A lrnd. familiar, accustomed to; companion.

muvaredat (.—.—) مُوارَدات A lrnd. 1. arrivals (of things or persons). 2. inspirations, thoughts.

muvarede, muvaredet (.—..) مُوارَده مُوارَدَت A lrnd. 1. a coming to a place together, arrival. 2. a reciting of the same verse extemporarily by two poets entirely unknown to one another.

muvasala (.—..) مُواصَلا A communication. — **hatları** lines of communication.

muvasalat (.—..) مُواصَلَت A an arriving, arrival.

muvasebe (.—..) مُواثَبَه A lrnd. a leaping, rushing upon one another.

muvassal مُوَصَّل A lrnd. joined to another thing.

muvassi (..—) مُوَصِّي A lrnd. who commands or recommends.

muvazaa (.—..) مُواضَعَه A 1. law simulation, fictitious transaction. 2. lrnd. a pretending to agree with one another for some ulterior motive. —**lı** simulated, false; feigned.

muvazaatan (.—...) مُواضَعَةً A lrnd. in pretence, false, feignedly.

muvazat (.—..) مُوازات A lrnd. a being parallel; a being coincident; coincidence. — **nazariyesi** psych. parallelism.

muvazebet (.—..) مُواظَبَت A lrnd. assiduity, perseverance, continuance.

muvazene (.—..) مُوازَنَه A a balancing one another; equilibrium; balance.

muvazeneli مُوازَنَه‌لى 1. balanced; level headed. 2. in equilibrium.

muvazenesiz مُوازَنَه‌سز unbalanced; undependable.

muvazenet (.—..) مُوازَنَت A balance.

muvazıb (.—.) مُواظِب A lrnd. assiduous, persevering.

muvazi (.—.) مُوازى A 1. parallel; in line with another. 2. coincident.

muvazin (.—.) مُوازِن A lrnd. 1. equal in weight. 2. well balanced.

muvazzaf مُوَظَّف A 1. mil. regular (army); on the active list (officer). 2. lrnd. having a duty; charged with. 3. lrnd. salaried, paid. — **hizmeti** mil. active service. — **subay** mil. active officer.

muvazzah مُوَضَّح A lrnd. made clear; manifest. —**an** (.'..)= A clearly, evidently.

muvazzih مُوَضِّح A lrnd. who makes clear; explainer.

mu'vec مُعْوَج A lrnd. bent, crooked, curved.

muy (—) مُوى P lrnd., same as **mu 2**.

muye (—.) مُويَه P lrnd. weeping, lamentation, wailing. —**ger** (—..) P, —**zen** (—..) P weeper, wailer.

muyi (——), **muyin** (——) مُويى P lrnd. made of hair; made of fur.

muyine (——.) مُويينَه P lrnd. 1. fur. 2. fur coat.

muylu مُويلو [Arabic **muhl**] trunnion of a cannon; hub of a car. — **yatağı** trunnion plate.

muymul مُويمُل same as **boymul**.

muytab (——) مُويتاب P lrnd. hair rope maker.

muz 1 مُوز [A —] banana, bot., Musa paradisiaca; plantain, bot., Musa sapientum. — **gibi ol**= slang to be ashamed; to feel shy.

-muz 2 مُز cf. **-mız**.

muzaaf 1 (.—.) مُضاعَف A lrnd. doubled,

muzaaf twofold; multiplied. — **usulü** *bookkeeping* double entry.

muzaaf 2 مضنّف A *lrnd.* 1. weakened, considered weak. 2. doubled; double, multiplied.

muzaafe (.—..) مضاعف A *lrnd.* a doubling, a making double; a multiplying.

muzad^{ddı} (.—) مضاد A *lrnd.* a mutually opposing; contrary. —**i istitbab** *med.* contraindication. —**i taaffün** antiseptic, disinfectant.

muzaf (.—) مضاف A 1. *gram.* a noun or verbal noun that is governed or modified by another noun or a pronoun, *e. g.,* the second word in **Ahmet'in yaptıkları, tahta parçası,** and the first word in **Bab-ı Saadet.** 2. *lrnd.* added to, annexed; related; appended to, dependent on.

muzafat (.——) مضافات A *lrnd.* things annexed; appendages, additions.

muzaffer مظفّر A victorious, triumphant; made successful. —**âne** (...—.) P victoriously. —**en** (.'...) A victoriously, triumphantly.

muzafferiyet (...—.) مظفّریت A victory, triumph; success.

muzafünileyh مضاف الیه A *gram.* a noun or pronoun that governs or modifies an adjacent noun, showing ownership, location, component material, or other attribute of the governed noun, *e. g.,* the first word in the following: **Kayseri valisi, adamın söyledikleri, demir kapı.**

muzahat (.——) مضاهات A *lrnd.* resemblance.

muzaheret (.—..) مظاهرت A help, support; backing.

muzahi (.——) مضاهی A *lrnd.* resembling, like.

muzahir (.—.) مظاهر A *lrnd.* one who supports; supporter, helper.

muzallel مظلّل A *lrnd.* shaded over.

mu'zam معظم A *lrnd.* the main part, the mass, bulk of a thing; major part. —**at** (..—) A *pl.*

muzammer مضمّر A *lrnd.* 1. fully resolved upon but kept secret (matter). 2. concealed, suppressed (hate); conceived in the mind.

muzammir مضمّر A *lrnd.* 1. who secretly resolves on some act or cherishes some feeling. 2. *pros.* meter which has most commonly the form: ——./—.—./.——./—.—/ .

muzariⁱⁱ مضارع A 1. *Turkish gram.* a tense used in narration, to describe habitual action, or to state a generalization (aorist, *e. g.*, **gider**). 2. *lrnd.* like, resembling.

muzarib (.—.) مضارب A *lrnd., same as* **mudarib.**

muzayaka (.—..) مضایقه A *lrnd., same as* **müzayaka.**

muzcir مضجر A *lrnd.* wearisome, troublesome, irksome; annoyer.

muze (—.) موزه P *lrnd.* boot, high boot. —**duz** (—.—) P boot maker.

muzga مضغه A *lrnd.* a little bit; enough for a mouthful; piece of meat.

muzika (..'.) موزیقه It *same as* **mızıka.**

muzır^{rrı} مضرّ A harmful; detrimental; vexatious; mischievous; destructive. —**lık** harmfulness, mischievousness.

muzi (.—) مضی A *lrnd.* which illumines; luminous, illuminating.

mu'zib A, **muzib** (—.) معذب A teasing, tormenting, plaguing; mischievous. —**lik** teasing, mischievous behavior.

muzik^{kı} (.—) مضیق A 1. *anat.* isthmus 2. *lrnd.* that makes narrow, that oppresses.

muzlim مظلم A *lrnd.* 1. dark, darkened; gloomy, sinister. 2. dull, obscure.

muzmahil^{lli} مضمحل A *lrnd.* dispersed, come t naught, annihilated.

muztaciⁱⁱ مضطجع A *lrnd.* that lies dow·· especially on the side. —**an** (...'.) A in a reclining fashion.

muztar مضطر A *lrnd.* forced, compelled.

muztarib مضطرب A worried, disturbed; agitated; suffering. —**âne** (...—.) A *lrnd.* worriedly.

muztarim مضطرم A *lrnd.* 1. kindled, blazing. 2. excited.

müayese (.—..) موایسه A *lrnd.* a driving to desperation.

mübaade, mübaadet (.—.—) مباعده مباعدت A *lrnd.* a being distant; a removing far; distance.

mübaale (.—..) مباعله A *lrnd.* a toying and dallying with one another; amorous dalliance.

mübadat (.——) مبادات A *lrnd.* an openly treating someone with enmity; undisguised treatment, especially with enmity.

mübadelât (.—.—) مبادلات A *lrnd., pl. of* **mübadele.**

mübadele مبادله A 1. a mutually exchanging, bartering; exchange; substitution. 2. exchange of populations. — **et=** /ı/ to exchange.

mübadere, mübaderet مبادره مبادرت A *lrnd.* a making haste; a setting about doing something.

mübadil (.—.) مبادل A 1. *lrnd.* exchanging; subject to exchange (of population, etc.). 2. *int. law* Turkish immigrant from Greece after the 1921-2 war, settled on land of an exchanged Greek.

mübadir (.—.) مبادر A *lrnd.* who sets about doing a thing; who makes haste.

mübagama مباغمه A *lrnd.* a speaking softly, gently, and lovingly to one another.

mübagat (.——) مباغات A *lrnd.* harlotry, adultery, fornication.

mübagate (.—..) مباغته A *lrnd.* surprise

attack; a coming on someone by surprise; sudden arrival; sudden occurrence.

mübagaza (. — ..) مباغضه A *lrnd.* a hating one another, mutual rancor.

mübahasat (. — . —) مباحثات A *lrnd., pl. of* **mübahase.**

mübahase (. — ..) مباحثه A *lrnd.* discussion, dispute. — et= to discuss.

mübahat (. — —) مباهات A *lrnd.* a contending for glory; a vaunting; a boasting with a just pride.

mübahele, mübahelet (. — ..) مباهله مباهلت A *lrnd.* a cursing, wishing evil to another; a cursing one another.

mübahhal[ii] مبخّل A *lrnd.* very avaricious.
mübahhar مبخّر A *lrnd.* fumigated; perfumed.
mübahi (. — —) مباهى A *lrnd.* who glories, boasts with just pride.

mübahis (. — .) مباحث A *lrnd.* who discusses or argues; disputant.

mübaid مبعد A 1. *lrnd.* who drives a thing away to a distance. 2. *anat.* adductor.

mübalağa (. — ..) مبالغه A 1. an exaggerating, exaggeration. 2. *lrnd.* a using one's utmost strength; utmost exertion. — et= to exaggerate. — ile overly. — ile ismi fail *Arabic gram.* the active participle of the intensive verb form. —cı exaggerator. —lı exaggerated.

mübalât (. — —) مبالات A *lrnd.* a heeding, caring, minding, regarding; heed, attention, consideration. —kâr (. — — —) P heedful.

mübalâtsız (. — —.) مبالاتسز indifferent, careless, heedless.

mübarat (. — —) مبارات A *lrnd.* a separation or dissolution of marriage by mutual consent.

mübarek[gi] (. — .) مبارك A 1. blessed, holy, sacred; bountiful, auspicious. 2. good; beautiful. 3. *colloq.* worthless, strange (person). —! Bless it! — ağzını aç= to start speaking evil. — olsun 1. Good luck with it. 2. Congratulations.

mübarekbad (. — . —) مبارك باد P *lrnd.* congratulations.

mübarekî (. — . —) مباركى P *lrnd.* 1. blessedness, auspiciousness. 2. felicitations; good luck.

mübareklik[gi] مباركلك blessedness; holiness, bountifulness.

mübareze (. — ..) مبارزه A *lrnd.* single combat of champions; contest; duel.

mübariz (. — .) مبارز A *lrnd.* champion, warrior, combatant; duellist.

mübasara (. — ..) مباصره A *lrnd.* a striving to see first. —i hilâl a striving between two persons as to who will see the new moon first.

mübaşele, mübaselet (. — ..) مباسله مباسلت A *lrnd.* a valorously charging an enemy.

mübasete (. — ..) مباسطه A *lrnd.* a forgetting to be shy and becoming free and easy in manner and conversation.

mübaşeret (. — ..) مباشرت A *lrnd.* 1. a setting about doing something; a beginning. 2. a having sexual intercourse.

mübaşir (. — .) مباشر A 1. usher (in a court); process server. 2. official who conveys the order of a department; agent.

mübaşiriye (. — . — .) مباشريه same as **mübaşirlik.** — akçesi *Ott. hist.* tax imposed to pay the salaries of the ushers.

mübaşirlik[gi] مباشرلك the duty of an usher or agent.

mübatana (. — ..) مباطنه A *lrnd.* a striving in conversation to ascertain the inner thoughts or intentions of one another.

mübataşa (. — ..) مباطشه A *lrnd.* a mutually attacking in fight; fierce struggle, contest.

mübattan مبطّن A *lrnd.* 1. whose belly has fallen in (from hunger); having a small, lank belly. 2. having a large belly, paunchy.

mübayaa (. — ..) مبايعه *var. of* **mubayaa.**
mübayenet (. — ..) مباينت A 1. conflict (of statements, etc.); divergence. 2. *lrnd.* a being separated; separation, severance.

mübayin (. — .) مباين A *lrnd.* 1. conflicting; different; opposed; repugnant. 2. separated, severed; separate.

mübda[aı] مبدع A *lrnd.* originated; created; invented; innovated.

mübdaât (. . —) مبدعات A *lrnd.* inventions; creations; innovations.

mübdi[ii] 1 مبدع A *lrnd.* who originates, creates, invents, innovates; innovator (especially heretic).

mübdi[ii] 2 مبدى A *lrnd.* who originates, begins, creates; originator, beginner; creator, doer of a marvelous thing; God. **M—i Muid** 1. God, who creates, causes to die and finally raises again. 2. *l. c.* experienced warrior.

mübeccel مبجّل A *lrnd.* honored, reverenced, highly esteemed.

mübeddel مبدّل A *lrnd.* changed, altered.
mübeddil مبدّل A *chem.* converter.
mübeddile مبدّله A *elec.* transformer.
mübehhec مبهّج A *lrnd.* rendered charming.
mübehhic مبهّج A *lrnd.* joy-inspiring, recreative.

mübekki (. . —) مبكّى A *lrnd.* that causes to weep.

mübelliğ مبلّغ A *lrnd.* 1. who informs; informer. 2. special person in a large mosque who repeats certain formulas after the Imam.

müberhen مبرهن A *lrnd.* proven; authentic.
müberka[aı] مبرقع A 1. *lrnd.* veiled, masked. 2. *obs., Or. mus.* a makam which ends in a' (or, according to others, in b')

müberra

müberra (..—) مُبَرَّا A *lrnd.* exempt, free; absolved; guiltless of, exonerated.
müberred مُبَرَّد A *lrnd.* chilled, cooled.
müberrid مُبَرِّد A *lrnd.* that chills, cools, refreshing, cooling; refrigerator.
mübeşşer مُبَشَّر A *lrnd.* to whom joyful tidings have been announced; joyful because of good news.
mübeşşir مُبَشِّر A *lrnd.* 1. that bears good news, herald; announcing glad tidings. 2. evangelist.
mübeşşirât (...—) مُبَشِّرَات A *lrnd.* heralds of coming rain *i. e.* winds.
mübeşşirîn (...—) مُبَشِّرِين A *lrnd., pl. of* **mübeşşir.**
mübevveb مُبَوَّب A *lrnd.* 1. arranged in chapters. 2. furnished with doors.
mübevvil مُبَوِّل A *med.* diuretic.
mübeyyaz مُبَيَّض A *lrnd.* 1. whitened; whitewashed; bleached. 2. brightened, clear (countenance). 3. written in a clean copy.
mübeyyen مُبَيَّن A *lrnd.* set forth in words, described, explained, declared.
mübeyyin مُبَيِّن A *lrnd.* that declares, sets forth; explanatory, declarer; stating.
mübeyyiz مُبَيِّض A 1. *Ott. hist.* clerk who makes a fair copy from a draft. 2. *lrnd.* whitener, whitewasher; bleacher. **—in** (...—) A *pl.* **—lik** copying (letters etc.); work of a copyist.
mübezzir مُبَذِّر A *lrnd.* extravagant, squandering; squanderer.
mübhem مبهم A *var. of* **müphem.**
mübhic مبهج A *lrnd.* that pleases, charming; joy inspiring, recreative.
mübi[ii] (.—) مبيع A *lrnd.* who sells, seller.
mübin (.—) مبين A *lrnd.* 1. manifest, evident, clear, 2. distinguisher; explainer.
mübni (.—) مبنى A *lrnd.* who causes to build; founder; author. **—i fesad** instigator of troubles.
mübrem مبرم A 1. inevitable; urgent. 2. *lrnd.* inexorable (decree etc.).
mübrez مبرز A *lrnd.* manifested, shown openly; patent.
mübrid مبرد A *lrnd.* that cools; refreshing. **—en** (..'.) A in the cool of the day or night.
mübrim مبرم A *lrnd.* 1. wearisome; importunate. 2. dull or insipid in conversation.
mübriz مبرز A *lrnd.* who manifests, displays; displayer.
mübsar مبصر A *lrnd.* seen, perceived. **—i bilvasıta** indirectly seen by means of light and color (thing). **—i bizzat** essentially visible, as light or color. **—ât** (..—) A *pl.* visible objects.
mübşer مبشر A *lrnd.* exhilarated with good news; brightened; gladdened.

mübta[a1] (.—) مبتاع A *lrnd.* bought, purchased.
mübteda 1 (..—) مبتدأ A 1. *gram.* subject of a clause. 2. *lrnd.* time or place of beginning, commencement; begun (thing). **— ve haber** *gram.* subject and predicate.
mübteda[a1] **2** مبتدع A *lrnd.* originated; introduced; innovation.
mübtedi 1 (..—) مبتدى A beginner, novice.
mübtedi[ii] **2** مبتدع A *lrnd.* who originates, introduces; innovator, inventor.
mübtediyan (..——) مبتديان P *lrnd., pl. of* **mübtedi 1.**
mübtediyane (..——.) مبتديانه P *lrnd.* in an inexperienced way.
mübtega (..—) مبتغى A *lrnd.* sought, sought after; desirable.
mübtehic مبتهج A *lrnd.* cheerful, rejoicing; exultant.
mübtehil مبتهل A *lrnd.* humble and earnest in prayer; supplicator, suppliant.
mübtel مبتل A *lrnd.* moistened, wetted, damped.
mübtelâ 1 (..—) مبتلا *var. of* **müptelâ.**
mübtelâ[a1] **2** مبتلع A *lrnd.* swallowed, swallowed up.
mübteli[ii] مبتلع A *lrnd.* that swallows.
mübtena (..—) مبتنا *var. of* **mübteni.**
mübteni (..—) مبتنى A *lrnd., same as* **müpteni.**
mübtesim مبتسم A *lrnd.* smiling; smiler.
mübtezel مبتذل A *var. of* **müptezel.**
mübtıl مبطل A *lrnd.* 1. who abolishes, cancels, frustrates, defeats; that renders vain; defacer, destroyer. 2. who talks nonsense or asserts falsehoods.
mübti (.—) مبطى A *lrnd.* slow, dilatory.
müca'ad مجعد A *lrnd.* curly (hair).
mücab (.—) مجاب A *lrnd.* answered, accepted (prayer).
mücadelât (.—.—) مجادلات A *lrnd., pl. of* **mücadele.**
mücadele (.—..) مجادله A 1. struggle, strife; combat, contention. 2. dispute. **— et= /la/** to fight. **—ci** one who likes to struggle; contestant.
mücadil (.—.) مجادل A *lrnd.* who disputes, contends.
mücahedat (.—.—) مجاهدات A *lrnd., pl. of* **mücahede.**
mücahede (.—..) مجاهده A *lrnd.* 1. a combating; a fighting (for Islam). 2. an endeavoring, a doing one's best; endeavor, strife, effort.
mücahid (.—.) مجاهد A combatant, fighter, champion (of Islam). **—âne** (.—.—.) P like a champion; heroic. **—în** (.—.—) A *pl. of* **mücahid.**

mücahiz (. —.) مجاهز A *lrnd.* who equips. **M—i ervah** 1. (*lit.* He who equips spirits.) God. 2. the Prophet Muhammad. **—i kân** (*lit.* That which equips mines.) the sun.

mücalese, mücaleset (. —..) مجالست A *lrnd.* a sitting with another.

mücalis (. —.) مجالس A *lrnd.* who sits with another; seated with another.

mücamaa, mücamaat (. —..) مجامعت A *lrnd.* copulation.

mücamele (. —..) مجامله A 1. *lrnd.* an acting with kindness and consideration; kindness, courtesy. 2. *int. law* comity of nations.

mücanebet (. —..) مجانبت A *lrnd.* a becoming apart, aloof; an avoiding, abstaining; abstention.

mücaneset (. —..) مجانست A *lrnd.* a being of the same kind as others, homogeneity; uniformity.

mücanib (. —.) مجانب 1. *math.* asymptote. 2. *lrnd.* that keeps away or aloof.

mücanis (. —.) مجانس A *lrnd.* of the same kind as another; homogeneous, similar.

mücaraha (. —..) مجارحه A *lrnd.* a wounding one another, fighting.

mücaseret (. —..) مجاسرت A *lrnd.* a daring; venture; bold attempt. **— et=** to venture.

mücasir (. —.) مجاسر A *lrnd.* venturer, audacious.

mücavebe (. —..) مجاوبه A *lrnd.* an answering one another.

mücavede, mücavedet (. —..) مجاوده مجاودت A *lrnd.* a competing in liberality; munificence, liberality.

mücaveret (. —..) مجاورت A *lrnd.* 1. a being a neighbor, a being near; a keeping near another for safety. 2. a taking residence in the vicinity of a sacred place, esp. at Medina or Mecca.

mücavib (. —.) مجاوب A *lrnd.* who answers; answerer.

mücavir (. —.) مجاور A *lrnd.* 1. who dwells near to another; neighbor. 2. contiguous, adjacent. 3. resident in the vicinity of a sacred place, esp. in Medina or Mecca.

mücaviran (. —. —) مجاوران P *lrnd., pl. of* **mücavir. —ı felek** the seven planets.

mücaz (. —) مجاز A *lrnd.* 1. permitted; lawful. 2. licensed, licentiate. 3. *Ott. hist.* a graduate of a medresse.

mücazat (. ——) مجازات A *lrnd.* 1. a punishing; punishment; retribution. 2. a compensating, requital of good or evil, compensation.

mücazebe (. —..) مجاذبه A *lrnd.* a contending in pulling or attracting; mutual attraction.

mücazefe (. —..) مجازفه A *lrnd.* a selling or buying by estimate of bulk.

mücber مجبر A *lrnd.* compelled, forced, constrained.

mücbir مجبر A that compels; compelling; inevitable. **— sebep** force majeure, superior power.

mücbire مجبره A *lrnd.* compelling; inevitable. **—i mutavassıta** a Muslim sect.

mücebbir مجبّر A *lrnd.* setter of broken bones, bone setter.

mücedded مجدّد A renewed; new.

müceddeden (..'..) مجدّدا A *lrnd.* 1. newly, recently. 2. again, anew, afresh.

mücedder مجدّر A *lrnd.* suffering from smallpox; pitted with smallpox.

müceddid مجدّد A *lrnd.* who renews, renovates, innovator. **—âne** (... —.) P like a renovator. **—în** (... —) A *pl. of* **müceddid.**

müceffi مجّف |*from Arabic* **mücevvef**| *lrnd.* 1. hollow; hollow part; cavity. 2. bore of a gun.

müceffef مجفّف A *lrnd.* dried.

müceffif مجفّف A *lrnd.* that dries, desiccates. **—at** (... —) A *pl.*

mücehhez مجهّز A 1. /la/ equipped, furnished with. 2. rigged out (ship); armed (with).

mücehheze مجهّزه A *lrnd.* young girl who has a trousseau.

mücehhiz مجهّز A *lrnd.* 1. who equips. 2. shipowner.

mücelcel مجلجل A *lrnd.* adorned with small bells.

mücellâ (.. —) مجلّى A *lrnd.* 1. polished, burnished; shining. 2. made manifest.

mücelled مجلّد A *lrnd.* bound (book); volume.

mücelledât (... —) مجلّدات A *lrnd.* bound books, volumes.

mücelli (.. —) مجلّى A *lrnd.* that polishes, polisher.

mücellid A, **mücellit**di مجلّد bookbinder. **—hane** (... —.) P bookbinder's shop. **—lik** bookbinding.

mücelliyat (... ——) مجلّيات A *med.* detergent.

mücennah مجنّح A 1. *lrnd.* winged. 2. *pros.* having an initial and final anagram (couplet).

mücerreb مجرّب A *lrnd.* tried, proven by experience. **—an** (... —) P those proven by experience. **—at** (... —) A tried or proven things.

mücerred A, **mücerret**di مجرّد 1. abstract; incorporeal. 2. isolated; single; unmarried. 3. naked; simple; pure. 4. *gram.* nominative. 5. *colloq.* merely, simply; positively. **— alacak** *law* abstract claim. **— kullar** the bachelors. **— resmi** *Ott. hist.* tax received from bachelors.

mücerredat (... —) مجرّدات A *lrnd.* incorporeal beings; beings of the spirit world; abstract things; abstraction.

mücerrediyet مجرّديت 1. bareness. 2. incorporeity. 3. celibacy.

mücerrib مجرّب A *lrnd.* who tries by

mücerrid experiment; experimenter, trier, prover. —**ân** (...—) P, —**in** (...—) A pl.

mücerrid A, **mücerrit**^ddi مجرّد elec. isolating; insulating; insulator.

mücessed مجسّد A lrnd. to which a body has been given; who has a body.

mücessem مجسّم A 1. personified. 2. geom. of three dimensions. 3. lrnd. solid, possessed of a solid body; corporeal. — **zekâ** personified intelligence.

mücessemat (...—) مجسّمات A 1. geom. triangular solids. 2. lrnd. solid bodies. —**ı Eflâtuniye** geom. the five regular solids of Plato: tetrahedron, hexahedron, octahedron, dodecahedron and icosahedron. —**ı müteşabihe** geom. similar solids.

mücesseme مجسّمة A 1. phil. anthropomorphism. 2. lrnd. statue.

mücevher مجوهر A 1. set with pearls or diamonds; bejewelled; jewel. 2. pros. date verse in Arabic script of which only the dotted letters are calculated according to the **ebced** system.

mücevherat (...—) مجوهرات A jewellery.

mücevvef مجوّف A lrnd. hollowed out, hollow.

mücevver مجوّر A lrnd. considered to be tyrannical.

mücevvez مجوّز A lrnd. 1. canonically lawful. 2. tolerated.

mücevveze مجوّزة A lrnd. a turban of many plaited folds, formerly worn as part of the uniform of Turkish functionaries.

mücevvid مجوّد A lrnd. who reads the Quran in accordance with rule.

müchiz مجهز A lrnd. that kills off quickly; quick, sudden (death).

mücib (.—) مجيب A lrnd. who answers; who accepts (prayer); God, who answers prayers.

mücid^ddi مجدّ A lrnd. who works earnestly; diligent. —**ane** (..—.) P diligently.

müciz (.—) مجيز A lrnd. who permits; who licenses; permitter, approver.

müclâ (.—) مجلى A lrnd. driven from home, exiled.

mücmel مجمل A lrnd. 1. concise, succinct summary. 2. abstract. —**en** (.'..) A concisely.

mücrim مجرم A culpable, guilty; culprit, criminal, sinner. —**in** (..—) A pl. —**iyet** (..—.) guilt, culpability.

mücteba (..—) مجتبى A lrnd. specially selected, chosen; the Prophet Muhammad as chosen by God.

müctehid مجتهد A 1. can. law expounder of Islamic laws. 2. lrnd. who strives hard to acquire correct and sound views.

müctemi^ii مجتمع A lrnd. collected together; well put together, compact. —**an** (.'..) A all together; collectively.

müctena (..—) مجتنى A lrnd. 1. gathered (products). 2. gained.

müctenib مجتنب A lrnd. who abstains; abstaining, avoiding, aloof.

müctenih مجتنح A lrnd. 1. that leans, inclined. 2. who spreads his elbows in the prostration of worship.

mücteri^ii مجترئ A lrnd. bold; endued with fresh courage.

müctes^ssi مجتث A pros. meter with iambic variations, e. g., (.—.—/..——/.—.—/——).

müctevir مجتور A lrnd. who is a neighbor; neighboring.

mücver مجوّر cookery croquette.

müd^ddü مدّ A lrnd. a measure for grain, double handful.

müdaabe, müdaabet (.—..) مداعبة A lrnd. a playing together, a jesting with another; fun.

müdaase (.—..) مداعسة A lrnd. a fighting with spears.

müdabere, müdaberet (.—..) مدابرة A lrnd. a turning one's back on another; a shunning, avoiding.

müdafaa (.—.) مدافعة A a repelling, defense, resistance. — **et=** /ı/ to defend. — **hakkı** law right of defense. — **hattı** mil. line of defense. — **vergisi** tax for the benefit of national defense. —**name** (.—..—.) P law written defense. —**sız** undefended, defenseless.

müdafaat (.—.—) مدافعات A lrnd., pl. of **müdafaa**.

müdafi^ii مدافع A 1. who repels, defends, defender. 2. law counsel for the defense. 3. soccer back.

müdahalât (.—.—) مداخلات A lrnd., pl. of **müdahale**.

müdahale (.—..) مداخلة A interference; intervention. — **et=** /a/ to interfere.

müdahene (.—..) مداهنة A flattery, sycophancy. —**ci** flatterer, sycophant. —**li** flattering. —**siz** free from flattery.

müdahere (.—..) مداهرة A lrnd. a hiring a person or thing for a long term.

müdahhan مدخّن A lrnd. smoked, smoky; fumigated.

müdahhar مدّخر A lrnd. 1. stored; hoarded. 2. treasured.

müdahhir مدّخر A lrnd. who stores, hoards.

müdahil (.—.) مداخل A lrnd. who meddles; meddler, intervener. — **avukat** law attorney of an intervening party.

müdahin (.—.) مداهن A lrnd. who flatters; flatterer, sycophant.

müdam (.—) مدام A *poet.* 1. continual, perpetual; continually, all the time. 2. wine, old wine.

müdame (.—.) مدامه A *poet.* wine.

müdanat (.——) مداناة A *lrnd.* 1. a bringing near. 2. a being near; approximation.

müdani (.—) مداني A *lrnd.* 1. that draws near, approaches. 2. near, like, similar (used especially in the negative as **bimedanî**).

müdara (.—) مداراة P [müdarat] a dissembling; dissimulation; feigned friendship. **— et=** to dissemble.

müdarat (.——) مداراة A *lrnd.*, same as **müdara.**

müdarese (...) مدارسة A *lrnd.* a studying mutually, giving or taking a lesson.

müdari (.——) مدارى A *lrnd.* who dissembles; dissembler.

müdavat (.——) مداواة A *lrnd.* a treating medically; medical treatment.

müdavele (.—..) مداوله A *lrnd.* 1. a causing to circulate. 2. an exchanging. **—i efkâr** exchange of views. **— et=** /ı/ to circulate, to exchange.

müdavemet (.—..) مداومت A 1. a being assiduous; persevering; assiduity; perseverance. 2. unremitting attention (to work); a frequenting (school etc.). **— et=** to be constant in doing a duty, to be assiduous.

müdavere, müdaveret (.—..) مداوره مداورت A *lrnd.* 1. a circling about one another; a going around. 2. a trying to persuade or manage; an administering.

müdavi (.——) مداوى A *lrnd.* who treats or cures. **— tabip** doctor in attendance.

müdavim (.—.) مداوم A 1. who frequents; frequenter, regular visitor. 2. *lrnd.* assiduous, persevering. **—in** (.—.—) A *pl.*

müdayene (.—..) مداينه A *lrnd.* a buying or selling on credit; a getting into debt. **— et=** to buy or sell on credit.

müdbir مدبر A *lrnd.* whose affairs are in a bad state; who has come down in the world; unfortunate. **—lik** decline, ruin.

müddahar مدخر A *lrnd.* stored, hoarded; treasured up.

müddahir مدخر A *lrnd.* who stores (for future use); hoarder.

müddea (..—) مدعا A *law* 1. claimed; asserted. 2. claim; accusation, plea. 3. subject of a claim (before a court); thesis.

müddeaaleyh (..—..) مدعى عليه A *law* defendant.

müddeat (..—) مدعات A *lrnd.*, *pl.* of **müddea.**

müddei (..—) مدعى A 1. *law* accuser; prosecutor, plaintiff. 2. *lrnd.* who makes an assertion, who contests; who makes a claim, claimant. **—i umumi** *law* public prosecutor. **—i umumilik** *law* public prosecutor's office, directorate of public prosecutions.

müddeiyan (..——) مدعيان A *lrnd.* the two parties in a controversy or suit.

müddeiyat مدعيات A *lrnd.* assertions; contests.

müddesir مدثر A *lrnd.* who covers, is covered with a wrap. **M— Suresi** name of the seventy-fourth sura of the Quran.

müddet مدت A a space of time, period, interval. **—i ömr** lifetime. **—i örfiye** *Ott. hist.* time limitation according to the rules of each province.

müdebber مدبر A *lrnd.* 1. ably conducted, properly managed (matter). 2. *can. law* a slave to whom freedom has been promised upon the death of his owner.

müdebbir مدبر A *lrnd.* 1. prudent and efficient manager. 2. *can. law* who promises freedom, upon his own death, to a slave.

müdebbiran (...—) مدبران A *lrnd.*, *pl.* of **müdebbir. —ı felek** *lrnd.* the seven planets.

müdebbirâne (...—.) مدبرانه P *lrnd.* efficiently, prudently; wisely.

müdebbirat (...—) مدبرات A *lrnd.* angels. **—ı emr** angels charged with the execution of God's decrees.

müdebbire مدبره A *lrnd.* angel.

müdebdeb مدبدب A *lrnd.* pompous, gorgeous; magnificent.

müdehhen مدهن A *lrnd.* oiled; anointed.

müdehhin مدهن A *lrnd.* greasy; anointed.

müdekkik[ki] مدقق A *lrnd.* who investigates minutely; research scholar. **—ane** (...—.) P minutely, meticulously. **—in** (...—) A *pl.*

müdellel مدلل A *lrnd.* proved, supported by evidence; well grounded.

müdemmag مدمغ A *lrnd.* stupid, idiotic.

müdemmer مدمر A *lrnd.* utterly destroyed, annihilated.

müdemmir مدمر A *lrnd.* who destroys; annihilator, destroyer.

müdennes مدنس A *lrnd.* defiled, polluted, contaminated, dirty.

müdennis مدنس A *lrnd.* defiler, polluter, profaner.

müderhem مدرهم A *lrnd.* moneyed, rich.

müderris مدرس A 1. *obs.* university professor. 2. *Ott. hist.*, a grade in the hierarchy of the Ulema. **—in** (...—) A *pl.* **—lik** professorship.

müdesser مدثر A *lrnd.* covered with a cloak or wrap.

müdessi (..—) مدسى A *lrnd.* 1. who corrupts or tempts; seducer. 2. who conveys secret intelligence.

müdessir مدثر A *lrnd.* who covers.

müdevven مدون A *lrnd.* 1. collected into a

müdevvenât müdevvenât مُدَوَّنَات A *lrnd.* collected writings, complete works.

müdevver مُدَوَّر A 1. round, circular, spherical. 2. *lrnd.* transferred (from), handed down. 3. *bookkeeping* transferred (to a new balance sheet). **—iyet** circularity, roundness.

müdevvin مُدَوِّن A *lrnd.* collector of poems into a book, compiler of an anthology.

müdevvir مُدَوِّر A *lrnd.* who causes to turn in a circle, who revolves, who makes (a thing) round.

müdgam مُدْغَم A 1. *Arabic gram.* combined with another, as though inserted in it (consonant), coalescent. 2. *lrnd.* inserted, introduced.

müdhiş مُدْهِش A *lrnd.* 1. terrible, fearful, horrible; awful. 2. enormous; terrific; extraordinary; excessive.

müdir[rri] **1** مُدِرّ A *lrnd.*, same as **müdrir**.

müdir 2 (.—) مُدِير A *lrnd.*, same as **müdür**. **—ân** (.——) P administrators, managers. **—e** (.—.) A directress, directrix. **—iyet** (.——.) directorate, administration, management.

müdmic مُدْمِج A *lrnd.* who rolls, wraps up, folds up.

müdmin مُدْمِن A *lrnd.* confirmed in (debauchery, etc.).

müdn مُدُن A *lrnd.*, *pl. of* **medine**.

müdrec مُدْرَج A *lrnd.* interpolated, inserted in.

müdrik[ki] مُدْرِك A 1. /ı/ that perceives, comprehends; perceiving, comprehending. 2. *lrnd.* who overtakes, reaches, attains to.

müdrikât (..—) مُدْرَكَات A *pl.*, *psych.* powers of the senses.

müdrike مُدْرِكَة A *psych.* intellect, mind.

müdrir مُدِرّ A *med.* diuretic.

müdür مُدِير [müdir 2] 1. director, manager, administrator. 2. official governing a subdistrict.

müdürlük[gü] مُدِيرلِك office and functions of a manager, directorate; head office.

müebbed مُؤَبَّد A perpetual, eternal (in the future). **— hapis** life sentence. **—en** (..'.) A eternally, in perpetuity.

müeccel مُؤَجَّل A 1. *can. law* (a sum) agreed to be paid to a wife if she is divorced or widowed. 2. *lrnd.* fixed for some future time; extended; put off. **—iyet** (...—.) postponement (of debate).

müeccil مُؤَجِّل A *lrnd.* who appoints a time for a future event.

müedda (..—) مُؤَدَّى A *lrnd.* 1. paid. 2. meaning, significance, tenor. 3. contents (of a document). **—sınca** as they say (a proverb etc.).

müeddeb مُؤَدَّب A *lrnd.* 1. well behaved, modest; courteous. 2. well instructed, learned.

müeddeben (..'..) مُؤَدَّبًا A *lrnd.* courteously.

müeddi (..—) مُؤَدِّي A *lrnd.* 1. who pays. 2. causing; performing.

müeddib مُؤَدِّب A *lrnd.* that instructs in behavior; who educates well; instructor.

müekked مُؤَكَّد A *lrnd.* made firm, strengthened; reiterated, confirmed; corroborated. **—en** (.'..) A repeatedly; emphatically.

müekkel مُؤَكَّل A *lrnd.* appointed, representative, charged (with).

müekkid مُؤَكِّد A *lrnd.* that makes firm, strengthens, reiterates, warns repeatedly.

müekkil مُؤَكِّل A *lrnd.* client (of a lawyer).

müellef مُؤَلَّف A *lrnd.* put together, composed, compiled; written.

müellefât (...—) مُؤَلَّفَات A *lrnd.* written works, literary compositions.

müellif مُؤَلِّف A author, writer, compiler, composer. **— hakkı** author's rights. **—âne** (...—.) P *lrnd.* like an author. **—în** (...—) A *pl. of* **müellif**.

müellim مُؤَلِّم A *lrnd.* painful, grievous; very sad, distressing.

müemmen مُؤَمَّن A *lrnd.* assured; secure, safe; sure; safeguarded.

müennes مُؤَنَّث A 1. *gram.* feminine (gender). 2. *lrnd.* female.

müerrah مُؤَرَّخ A *lrnd.* dated (document). **—an** ('...) A bearing the date of, dated.

müesses مُؤَسَّس A *lrnd.* 1. founded, established; placed on a base. 2. well indoctrinated.

müessesat (...—) مُؤَسَّسَات A *lrnd.* institutions; organizations. **—ı hayriye** pious foundations, benevolent institutions.

müessese مُؤَسَّسَة A institution, establishment, foundation.

müessif مُؤَسِّف A 1. regrettable; deplorable. 2. sad.

müessir مُؤَثِّر A 1. that produces an effect; effective; influential. 2. touching, moving; affecting. 3. *psych.* agent. **— fiil** *law* assault and battery. **—iyet** effectiveness.

müessis مُؤَسِّس A who founds, who lays a foundation, who establishes; founder. **—an** (..'.—) P, **—în** (...—) A *pl.*

müevvel مُؤَوَّل A *lrnd.* that gives rise to suspicion; explained in an unnatural sense on some slight ground (word); explained away.

müevvil مُؤَوِّل A *lrnd.* who explains away; who explains.

müeyyed مُؤَيَّد A *lrnd.* 1. strengthened, corroborated, confirmed. 2. fortified; assisted, supported.

müeyyid مُؤَيِّد A *lrnd.* 1. that strengthens, corroborates; strengthening. 2. who aids, supports; God.

müeyyide مُؤَيِّدَه A lrnd. corroborative statement, confirming action; law sanction.

müezza (—.—) مُؤَذَّى A lrnd. tormented, tortured; afflicted; grieved.

müezzi (—.—) مُؤَذِّى A lrnd. that torments, tortures, afflicts, annoys.

müezzin مُؤَذِّن A one who calls Muslims to prayer, muezzin. —in (...—) A lrnd., pl. —lik occupation of a muezzin.

müfacat (.——) مُفَاجَاَت A lrnd. a happening suddenly.

müfad (.—) مُفَاد A lrnd. expression, meaning.

müfadat (.——) مُفَادَات A lrnd. a paying ransom, ransoming. —ı üsera an exchanging of war prisoners.

müfagama (.—..) مُفَاغَمْ A 1. biol. anastomosis. 2. lrnd. a kissing.

müfahare, müfaharet (.—..) مُفَاخَرَه مُفَاخَرَت A lrnd. a boasting, contending for glory; honest pride.

müfahham مُفَخَّم A 1. Arabic gram. pronounced with a very broad sound (letter of the alphabet). 2. lrnd. illustrious, august; glorious.

müfahhar مُفَخَّر A lrnd. glorified, glorious, exalted.

müfahir (.—.) مُفَاخِر A lrnd. who boasts justly.

müf'am مُفْعَم A lrnd. full, high (river).

müfarakat⁽ⁱⁱ⁾ (.—..) مُفَارَقَت A lrnd., same as mufarakat.

müfavaza (.—..) مُفَاوَضَه A lrnd. 1. a being a copartner; unlimited partnership. 2. equality.

müfavazaten (.—...) مُفَاوَضَةً A lrnd. in unlimited partnership.

müfavız (.—.) مُفَاوِض A lrnd. a copartner.

müfaz (.—) مُفَاض A lrnd. made abundant, ample, full, wide.

müfazünfih (.—..) مُفَاضٌ فِيه A lrnd. fully gone into (matter).

müfazzal⁽ⁱⁱ⁾ مُفَضَّل A lrnd. 1. considered to be excellent; excelling greatly. 2. pronounced superior, preferred.

müfazzalünaleyh مُفَضَّلٌ عَلَيه A lrnd. to whom another is preferred.

müfekkir مُفَكِّر A lrnd. that ponders, deliberates; who thinks deeply.

müfekkire مُفَكِّرَه A psych. capacity to think.

müferrak⁽ᵏⁱ⁾ مُفَرَّق A lrnd. 1. parted, separated. 2. dispersed, scattered.

müferric مُفَرِّج A lrnd. that removes sorrow; exhilarating; God, who dispels grief.

müferrid مُفَرِّد A lrnd. who retires to lead a solitary religious life.

müferrih مُفَرِّح A 1. med. exhilarating medicine, exhilarant. 2. lrnd. that makes cheerful, exhilarating.

müferrik⁽ᵏⁱ⁾ مُفَرِّق A lrnd. that separates, scatters, disperses.

müfesser مُفَسَّر A lrnd. explained, commented on; annotated.

müfessir مُفَسِّر A lrnd. who expounds; commentator on the Quran. —in (...—) A pl.

müfettih مُفَتِّح A lrnd. 1. med. medicine that removes obstructions. 2. lrnd. who opens.

müfettin مُفَتِّن A lrnd. 1. that tries one much; that seduces. 2. that bewitches.

müfettiş مُفَتِّش A who examines, investigates; inspector. —i emval-i hassa Ott. hist. official who inspected the Sultan's property. —lik inspectorship.

müfevvaz مُفَوَّض A lrnd. committed or entrusted to the care of. —a A who contracted marriage with a renunciation of legal dowry (wife).

müfezzi⁽ⁱⁱ⁾ مُفَزِّع A lrnd. that frightens; that threatens; menacing.

müfhim مُفْهِم A lrnd. that completely silences, that reduces one to silence.

müfid (.—) مُفِيد A 1. useful, advantageous. 2. lrnd. that conveys a meaning.

müfik⁽ᵏⁱ⁾ (.—) مُفِيق A lrnd. 1. recovering from an illness, etc. 2. admirable, excellent (poet).

müfiz (.—) مُفِيض A lrnd. who bestows, gives abundantly.

müfkir مُفْقِر A lrnd. that impoverishes; God, who makes poor whom he will.

müflih مُفْلِح A lrnd. successful, prosperous, happy; righteous. —âne (..—.) P prosperously. —in (..—), —un (..—) A pl.

müflik⁽ᵏⁱ⁾ مُفْلِي A lrnd. wonderful (poet).

müflis مُفْلِس A bankrupt, insolvent; penniless. —an (..—) P, —in (..—) A lrnd., pl. —lik bankruptcy, insolvency.

müfni (.—) مُفْنِى A lrnd. that annihilates, destroys; destructive.

müfrağ مُفْرَغ A lrnd. cast in a mold.

müfred مُفْرَد A 1. gram. singular. 2. pros. a single couplet. 3. lrnd. single, separate; isolated. 4. lrnd. simple, not compound.

müfredat (..—) مُفْرَدَات A 1. details; particulars. 2. enumeration, detailed inventory. — cetveli inventory. — programı detailed program giving items (of a school curriculum).

müfrez مُفْرَز A lrnd. separated; detached.

müfreze مُفْرَزَه A mil. detachment (of troops).

müfrid مُفْرِد A obs., phys. isolator.

müfriğ مُفْرِغ A 1. anat. excretory. 2. lrnd. ejecting.

müfrit مُفْرِط A lrnd. 1. who exceeds bounds, excessive, beyond bounds. 2. exaggerated; extremist.

müfsid مُفْسِد A disturber of the peace;

müfsih

mischief-maker; intriguer; corrupter; seditious (person). **—lik** mischief-making; intrigue.

müfsih مفصح A *lrnd.* clear, eloquent.

müft مفت P *lrnd.* without payment, gratis. **—e git=** to go for nothing.

müftaal[i] مفتعل A *lrnd.* 1. invented, originally composed. 2. unusual, unprecedented. 3. false, spurious.

müftakir مفتقر A *lrnd.* in need; poor.

müftasid مفتصد A *lrnd.* who opens a vein, who bleeds; bled.

müftazih مفتضح A *lrnd.* exposed and disgraced for evil deeds; infamous.

müftehir مفتخر A /la/ who glories in; proud (of).

müfteri (..—) مفترى A slanderer, false accuser.

müfterik[ki] مفترق A *lrnd.* that separates from others; that goes to pieces; dispersed, scattered.

müfteris مفترس A *lrnd.* that takes prey (wild beast); rapacious.

müfteriyat (..——) مفتریات A *lrnd.* calumnies, accusations.

müfthar (.—) مفتخار P *lrnd.* who eats for nothing or gratuitously, sponger, parasite.

müfti (.—) مفتى A official expounder of Muhammedan law, mufti. **—i kanun** *same as* **nişancı. —lik** office and rank of a mufti.

Müftilenam (...—) مفتى الانام A *Ott. hist.* (*lit.*, legal counsel of mankind) Sheikh-ul-Islam of the Ottoman Empire.

müftü مفتى *same as* **müfti.**

mühab (.—) مهاب A *lrnd.* dreaded (things), awful, revered (man).

mühaba (.—.) محابا A *lrnd.* a treating with respect and consideration; respect, regard.

mühaceze (.—..) مهاجزه A *lrnd.* a whispering, speaking secretly.

mühakât (.——) مهاكات A *lrnd.* a treating someone as a fool; contempt.

mühamese (.—..) مهامسه A *lrnd.* a secretly whispering together.

mühan (.—) مهان P *lrnd.* looked upon with contempt, despised, slighted.

müharat (.——) مهارات A *lrnd.* a poking fun at another, a making fun of.

mühce مهجه A *lrnd.* life, soul, spirit; blood; heart's blood.

mühda (.—) مهدى A *lrnd.* given as a gift, offered, presented.

mühder مهدر A *lrnd.* shed with impunity (blood), unavenged blood.

mühdi (.—) مهدى A *lrnd.* who gives, makes a present.

mühdir مهدر A *lrnd.* who allows shed blood to go unavenged.

mühelhel مهلهل A *lrnd.* 1. fine, delicate, exquisite. 2. delicately composed (verse).

mühellil مهلل A *lrnd.* who pronounces the formula **lâilâheillallah.**

mühendis مهندس A 1. engineer. 2. *lrnd.* geometrician. **—i felek** *lrnd.* 1. astronomer; astrologer. 2. the planet Saturn. **M— Mektebi** Engineering School.

mühendishane (...—.) مهندسخانه P *hist,* school of engineering. **M—i bahri-i Hümayun** *Ott. hist.* The Imperial Naval Engineering School. **M—i berr-i Hümayun** *Ott. hist* school for artillery officers. **M—i Sultanî** *Ott. hist.* school of sciences.

mühendisin (...—) مهندسين A *lrnd., pl. of* **mühendis.**

mühendislik[ği] مهندسلك profession of an engineer, engineering.

mühenned مهند A *lrnd.* of Indian steel (sword).

mühevvil مهول A *lrnd.* that terrifies; terrifying, horrible.

müheykel مهيكل A *lrnd.* huge, giant; clumsily built.

müheymen مهيمن A *lrnd.* 1. in whom men confide, who inspires trust; protector. 2. *one of the names of God.*

müheyya (..—) مهيا A *lrnd.* disposed in order, prepared, ready.

müheyyi (..—) مهيئ A 1. *med.* predisposing. 2. *lrnd.* that puts in shape, forms or prepares.

müheyyic مهيج A that stirs up, excites; stimulant, exciting, stirring.

mühezzeb مهذب A *lrnd.* improved, emended, corrected; polite.

mühezzib مهذب A *lrnd.* that improves one morally.

mühib (.—) مهيب A *lrnd., same as* **mehib.**

mühim[mmi] مهم A important, urgent; considerable; indispensable.

mühimmat (..—) مهمات A *pl.* 1. requisites; munitions of war; ammunition. 2. urgent, important matters; indispensable things. **—ı cumhur** urgent affairs of the nation. **—ı kırtasiye** all kinds of stationery requisites.

mühimme مهمه A *Ott. hist.* important or urgent affair. **— defteri** *Ott. hist.* book of records of the Imperial Assembly of State. **— odası** bureau for the management of pressing affairs of importance in a Government Ministry.

mühimmenüvis (....—) مهم نويس P *lrnd.* secretary charged with drafting documents of importance.

mühimse=[r] مهمسمك /ı/ to consider important.

mühimter مهمتر P *lrnd.* more important, more urgent. **—in** (...—) P most important or urgent.

mühin (. —) مُهين A *lrnd*. 1. despiser, contemner. 2. vile, base, despicable.
mühlet مُهلَت A fixed term of respite; delay; grace. — **iste=** to ask for delay.
mühlik[ki] مُهلِك A *lrnd*. that destroys, kills; destructive, fatal, deadly; dangerous.
mühliye مُضلِيه same as **mülhiye**.
mühmel مُهمَل A 1. *lrnd*. neglected, unattended; abandoned. 2. *lrnd*. meaningless, insignificant. 3. *gram*. undotted (letter).
mühmelât (. . —) مُهمَلات A *lrnd*. words devoid of definite meaning, expletives.
mühmil مُهمِل A *lrnd*. who neglects, neglectful; careless, indifferent, unconcerned.
mühr 1 مُهر *lrnd.*, same as **mühür**. **—i cem**, **—i fâm**, **—i hum** seal of silence; silence. **—i hümayun** *Ott. hist*. imperial seal confided to the Grand Vizier as his symbol of office. **—i Meryem** Solomon's seal, *bot., Polygonatum officinale*. **—i nübüvvet** seal of the prophecy impressed on the shoulder of the Prophet Muhammad. **—i Süleyman** 1. same as **Mühri Meryem**. 2. the geometrical figure known as Solomon's seal. **—i yezdan** (*lit.*, the seal of God) virginity.
mühr 2 مُهر A *lrnd*. colt.
mührbend مُهربَند P *lrnd*. sealed.
mühre مُهره P 1. *lrnd*. stone found in the head of a serpent. 2. iron or bone polishing instrument; hammer. 3. *lrnd*. stone or glass bead; a kind of small shell resembling a pearl. 4. *calligraphy* shell used for giving smoothness and glossiness to paper. 5. *lrnd*. callosity on the skin; crust of a sore. 6. *arch.* concha. 7. *lrnd*. chessman, counter (in backgammon or checkers). **—i divar** rough stone used in building a wall. **—i hâk** 1. the world. 2. the human body. **— ü hokka** 1. ball and cup. 2. earth and heaven. **—i kâğıt** paper polisher. **—i nerd** backgammon man or piece. **—i püşt** vertebra of the spine, backbone. **—i sim**, **—i simâbi** moon and stars. **—i şeşder** piece used at backgammon. **— tahtası** smooth, hard board on which paper is polished. **— taşı** rounded stone for grinding, polishing, etc. **—i tesbih** bead of a rosary. **—i zer** the world-illuminating sun.
mührebaz (. . —) مُهرهباز P *lrnd*. polished, burnished. **—î** (. . — —) P deceit, stratagem.
mühredâr (. . —) مُهرهدار P *lrnd*. polished, glazed, burnished by rubbing.
mührele=[r] مُهرهلَك /ı/ to polish or burnish with a round burnisher. **—n=** *pass*. **—t=** *caus*.
mühreli مُهرهلی polished, burnished.
mühresenk[ki] مُهرهسَنك P *lrnd*. onyx (for making beads).
mührezen مُهرهزَن P *lrnd*. paper-polisher.

mühtecel مُحتَجَل A *lrnd*. newly conceived or advised.
mühtecene مُحتَجَنه A *lrnd*. deflowered before maturity.
mühteci مُحتَجی A *lrnd*. who satirizes and is satirized (poet); a lampoonist.
mühtedi (. . —) مُحتَدی A *lrnd*. 1. who embraces the true faith, converted to Islam. 2. who obtains and follows a right direction.
mühtez[zzi] مُحتَزّ A *lrnd*. trembling, vibrating, moving, agitated.
mühud (. —) مُهود A *lrnd., pl. of* **mehd**.
mühur (. —) مُهور A *lrnd., pl. of* **mehr**.
mühür[hrü] مُهر [**mühr 1**] 1. seal; signet ring; impression of a seal. 2. whorl of hair on the crown of the head. 3. black stain on a cat's palate. **—ünü bas=** /a/ 1. to seal; to stamp. 2. to be certain (of a thing), to swear that it is right. **— kaz=** to engrave a seal. **— kazıcı** seal engraver. **— mumu** sealing wax. **—ünü yala=** to go back on one's promise or agreement. **—cü** engraver of seals.
mühürdar (. . —) مُهردار P *Ott. hist*. 1. keeper of the seals. 2. private secretary of a minister or high official. **—lık** office or rank of a **mühürdar**.
mühürle=[r] مُهرلَك /ı/ to seal; to stamp with a seal. **—n=** *pass*. **—t=** *caus. of* **mühürle=**.
mühürlü مُهرلو sealed, under seal; stamped.
müj مُژ P same as **müje**.
müjd مُژد P same as **müjde**.
müjde مُژده P 1. good news, joyful tidings. 2. present given to a bearer of good news. **—ler olsun** Good news! **—aver** (. . — .) P *lrnd*. bringing good tidings. **—beha** (. . . —) P *lrnd*. gift to the bringer of glad tidings.
müjdeci مُژدهجی messenger carrying joyful news. **—başı** *Ott. hist*. official communicating to the Sultan the good news on the occasion of the departure to and arrival from Mecca of the **sürre alayı**.
müjdeğan (. . —) مُژدهگان P *lrnd*. a piece of good news. **—e** (. . — .), **—î** (. . — —) P *lrnd*. present given to the bringer of good news.
müjdeha (. . —) مُژدها P *lrnd*. Good news!
müjdele=[r] مُژدهلَك /ı, a/ to announce good news.
müjdelik[gi] مُژدهلِك present given to a messenger who brings good tidings.
müjderes, müjderesan (. . . —) مُژدهرسان P *lrnd*. messenger, bringer of good news.
müje مُژه P *poet*. eyelash.
müjek[ki] مُژَك P *lrnd*. a little eyelash.
müjgân (. —) مُژگان [*Persian* **müjegân**] *poet., pl. of* **müje**.
=mük[gü] مَك *cf*. **=mık**.

mükâⁿⁱ (.—) کَا۰ A *lrnd.* a whistling; whistle.

mükâab کَعَبْ A *lrnd.* cube shaped; cube.

mükâbere (.—..) کَابَرَه A *lrnd.* a vying for greatness and superiority, a putting on airs of greatness; assumption, pride; conceit.

mükâfaha (.—..) کَافَه A *lrnd.* 1. a confronting, facing, coming face to face with another. 2. a fighting, an encountering in open fight; a refuting in argument. — **et=** 1. to confront. 2. to fight.

mükâfahaten (.—́...) کَافَةً A *lrnd.* face to face, openly.

mükâfat (.——) کَافَاتْ A a compensating, recompensing; reward, compensation, retribution. — **ver=** to give a reward.

mükâfaten (.——́.) کَافَاةً A as a reward.

mükâfi (.—.) کَافِ A 1. *lrnd.* alike; equal; equivalent. 2. *geom.* parabolic (curve).

mükâfil (.—.) کَافِل A *lrnd.* who is a joint security of any agreement or undertaking.

mükâhhal کَحَّل A *lrnd.* 1. tinged with kohl. 2. covered with green (land). —**i bittab'** whose eyes are by nature tinged black in the edges of the lids.

mükâlebe (.—..) کَالَبَه A *lrnd.* an acting like a dog by snarling, attacking with words etc.; a being malignant, hurting one another. — **et=** to attack, to hurt one another.

mükâlemat (.—.—) کَالَمَاتْ A *lrnd.*, pl. of **mükâleme**.

mükâleme (.—..) کَالَمَه A 1. a talking together, conversation. 2. dialogue; conference; diplomatic negotiation. — **memuru** commissioner to a conference; officer with the flag of truce.

mükâlemename (.—..—.) کَالَمَنَامَه P *lrnd.* conversation handbook.

mükâri (.——) کَارِی A *lrnd.* who hires out mules, horses, etc.; muleteer. —**i müflis** *obs.*, *law* muleteer who cheats his customers, there being neither money nor mules for use.

mükâşefe (.—..) کَاشَفَه A 1. *adm.* investigation. 2. *myst.* God's manifesting Himself openly to a saint; spiritual communion with God; ecstasy. 3. *lrnd.* a manifesting sentiments to one another. — **ilmi** the knowledge of God given by Himself to a saint. — **mezhebi** mysticism.

mükâşeha (.—..) کَاشَه A *lrnd.* a cherishing a secret grudge against another.

mükâteb (.—.) کَاتَبْ A *can. law* promised freedom on payment of a stipulated price (slave).

mükâtebat (.—.—) کَاتَبَاتْ A *lrnd.*, pl. of **mükâtebe**.

mükâtebe (.—..) کَاتَبَه A 1. a corresponding with one another in writing; correspondence. 2. *can. law* a giving a slave a covenant to set him free on payment of a price. — **et=** /la/ to correspond.

mükâteme (.—..) کَاتَمَه A *lrnd.* a concealing (one's secret); concealment, silence. — **et=** to conceal one's thoughts.

mükâtib (.—.) کَاتِبْ A *lrnd.* 1. who corresponds by letter with another; correspondent. 2. *can. law* who agrees with his slave to set him free on payment of a stipulated price.

mükâvaha (.—..) کَاوَهَ A *lrnd.* a railing at one another; an abusing each other face to face. — **et=** to rail at one another.

mükâyede (.—..) کَایَدَه A *lrnd.* a making use of a device to outwit another; circumvention. — **et=** to circumvent.

mükâyele (.—..) کَایَلَه A *lrnd.* a measuring one another up; a giving measure for measure. — **et=** to measure up one another.

mükâyese (.—..) کَایَسَه A *lrnd.* a contending in sagacity or ingenuity; a using cunning in buying or selling. — **et=** to claim superiority in sagacity or ingenuity.

mükâzebe (.—..) کَاذَبَه A *lrnd.* a telling lies to one another; a lying; falsehood. — **et=** to lie to one another.

mükebbir کَبِّر A *lrnd.* 1. that enlarges, magnifies or honors. 2. who pronounces the formula **Allahü ekber**. —**e** same as **mi'zene**.

mükedder کَدَّر A 1. grieved, sad, vexed. 2. *lrnd.* made turbid, disturbed. 3. *lrnd.* reproached, rebuked. —**âne** (...—.) P *lrnd.* sorrowfully, sadly; distressedly.

mükeddir کَدِّر A *lrnd.* 1. which grieves, distresses. 2. that makes turbid, disturber. 3. who rebukes. —**at** (...—) A annoyances, vexations; distressful events.

mükeffen کَفَّن A *lrnd.* shrouded, wrapped in a winding sheet.

mükehhalⁱⁱ کَحَّل same as **mükâhhal**.

mükelleb کَلَّب A *lrnd.* 1. trained to hunt (dog). 2. fettered.

mükellef کَلَّف A /la/ 1. charged with, bound, obliged, liable. 2. richly adorned, elaborate, pompous. 3. taxable, taxpayer; conscripted. —**in** (...—) A *lrnd.* taxpayers; conscripts.

mükellefiyet کَلَّفِیَّتْ 1. obligation, liability. 2. charge; imposition of duties, obligatory service.

mükellel کَلَّل A *lrnd.* crowned; ornamented with jewels.

mükemmel کَمَّل A completed, complete in all points; perfect, excellent. —**en** (...́.) A perfectly. —**iyet** perfection.

mükemmil کَمِّل A *lrnd.* who completes, perfects, supplements.

mükenna کَنَّی A *lrnd.* surnamed.

mükerrem مُكَرَّم A *lrnd.* honored, revered; respected. **—en** (...َ.) A with great honor.
mükerrer مُكَرَّر A 1. repeated; reiterated; duplicate. 2. *lrnd.* double refined; double distilled. **— iskonto** *com.* compounded discounts. **— sigorta** *com.* reinsurance. **—at** (...—) A *lrnd.* repeated things.
mükerreren (..َ..) مُكَرَّرًا A *lrnd.* repeatedly; again and again.
mükerrir مُكَرِّر A 1. *law* one who repeats an offense, recidivist. 2. *lrnd.* who repeats, reiterates.
mükesser 1 مُكَثَّر A *lrnd.* 1. made much or many. 2. plural.
mükesser 2 مُكَسَّر A *lrnd.* broken, fractured; fractional.
mükessif مُكَثِّف A *lrnd.* condensing. **—e** *elec.* condenser.
mükessir مُكَسِّر A *lrnd.* who breaks (a thing) into pieces.
mükevkeb مُكَوْكَب A *lrnd.* star-studded.
mükevven مُكَوَّن A *lrnd.* called into being, created; produced.
mükevvenât (...—) مُكَوَّنات A *lrnd.* creatures; the creation, universe.
mükevvin مُكَوِّن A *lrnd.* who creates, produces; creator.
mükeyyif مُكَيِّف A *lrnd.* which intoxicates, makes merry; stimulant.
mükeyyifat (...—) مُكَيِّفات A *lrnd.* intoxicants, narcotics; stimulants.
mükezzeb مُكَذَّب A *lrnd.* declared to be false.
mükezzib مُكَذِّب A *lrnd.* who declares a saying to be false or a man to be a liar.
mükhale, mükhüle مُكحَلة A *lrnd.* kohl case.
mükibbᵇᵇⁱ مُكِبّ A *lrnd.* who applies himself to a thing; assiduous, persistent; diligent.
mükra مُكْرى A *lrnd.* hired, hired out.
mükreh مُكْرَه A *lrnd.* forced to do a thing; compelled. **—en** (.َ..) A by force.
mükrem مُكْرَم A *lrnd.* honored; noble; kind, munificent.
mükri مُكْرى A *lrnd.* who hires out, gives for hire.
mükrih مُكْرِه A *lrnd.* who forces one to do some act, compeller.
mükrim مُكْرِم A *lrnd.* who honors; hospitable, kind; courteous. **—âne** (..—.) P kindly, hospitably.
müksir مُكْثِر A *lrnd.* that increases a thing or multiplies it; rich, wealthy.
müktahil مُكْتَحِل A *lrnd.* who applies kohl.
müktefi مُكْتَفى A *lrnd.* satisfied and content.
mükten مُكْتَن A *lrnd.* covered up, concealed, hidden.
mükteri مُكْتَرى A *lrnd.* who hires out; hirer, renter.
mükterib مُكْتَرِب A *lrnd.* grieved, sad; afflicted.

mükteseb مُكْتَسَب A *lrnd.* acquired, earned. **— hak** vested interest.
müktesebât (...—) مُكْتَسَبات A *lrnd.* acquirements; acquisitions; attainments.
müktesepᵇⁱ مُكْتَسَب *same as* **mükteseb**.
müktesib مُكْتَسِب A *lrnd.* who earns, acquires, acquirer.
mül مُل P *poet.* wine.
mülâabe (.—..) مُلاعبة A *lrnd.* a playing or amusing oneself; a playing or joking with another. **— et=** to play or joke with one another.
mülâbese (.—..) مُلابسة A *lrnd.* 1. a being intimate with; intimacy. 2. a meddling with. 3. connection, relation. **—siyle** in connection with, in consideration of.
mülâhadet مُلاحدة A *lrnd.* an acting hypocritically; a feeling hatred or dislike; hate, dislike. **— ehli** enemies; intriguers. **— et=** to act hypocritically; to hate, dislike.
mülâhaza (.—..) مُلاحظة A *lrnd.* 1. consideration; observation; reflection. 2. a looking attentively and critically at a thing. **— et=** to observe, consider. **—siyle** in consideration of. **—sında ol=** to be of the opinion that. **—sız** without consideration; thoughtless, inconsiderate.
mülâhazat (.—.—) مُلاحظات A *lrnd., pl. of* **mülâhaza**. **— hanesi** column for remarks. **— hanesini açık bırak=** to be slow in judging a person.
mülâhham مُلَحَّم A *lrnd.* fleshy, corpulent. **—lık** fleshiness.
mülâhhas مُلَخَّص A *lrnd.* briefly summed up, epitomized (discourse etc.); summary.
mülâib (.—.) مُلاعب A *lrnd.* who plays and amuses himself.
mülâkat (.——) مُلاقات A a meeting one another; a meeting; interview, audience. **— yap=** /la/ to have an interview with.
mülâki (.—.) مُلاقى A *lrnd.* who meets with another; who interviews. **— ol=** /a/ to meet with.
mülâkkab مُلَقَّب A *lrnd.* called, designated; surnamed; nicknamed.
mülâmese (.—..) مُلامسة A *lrnd.* a touching; a handling. **— et=** to touch one another.
mülâsaka, mülâsakatᵗⁱ (.—..) مُلاصقت A *lrnd.* an adhering, being joined to, touching; contact, junction.
mülâsıkᵏⁱ (.—.) مُلاصق A *lrnd.* contiguous, in actual contact, touching. **—lık** contiguity.
mülâtafa (.—..) مُلاطفة A *lrnd.* a pleasantly joking with one another; affability, courtesy. **— et=** to joke with one another.
mülâtafat (.—.—) مُلاطفات A *lrnd., pl. of* **mülâtafa**.
mülâtame (.—..) مُلاطمة A *lrnd.* a mutually striking, slapping or boxing; a fight with hands,

Red 52.

mülâtıf fists or sticks. — **et=** to fight with one another.

mülâtıf (. — .) ملاطف A lrnd. who pleasantly jokes with another; courteous, polite, affable.

mülâttıf ملطّف A 1. med. attenuant, diluent (drug). 2. lrnd. who shows kindness; kind, courteous.

mülâttıfat (. . . —) ملطّفات A med. attenuating medicines.

mülâyemet (. — . .) ملايمت A lrnd. 1. looseness of the bowels. 2. a being mild, gentle, kind; mildness, gentleness. 3. a suiting, fitting, agreeing with.

mülâyim (. — .) ملايم A 1. suitable, mild, gentle, affable; soft, submissive. 2. free in the bowels. **—lik** mildness.

mülâzemet (. — . .) ملازمت A 1. Ott. hist. a serving as an unpaid beginner in an official post, novitiate. 2. lrnd. a holding to a thing so as never to quit it; constant attendance; persistence. **— et=** to serve as a novice for a post.

mülâzim (. — .) ملازم A 1. obs. mil. lieutenant. 2. Ott. hist. novice; assistant functionary. 3. lrnd. adherent, inseparable; constant, persistent. **—i evvel** obs. first lieutenant. **—i sani** obs. second lieutenant.

mülâzime (. — . .) ملازمه A Or. mus. ritornello in an instrumental composition (e. g., **peşrev**), refrain.

mülâzimlik[ği] ملازملك 1. obs. mil. lieutenancy. 2. Ott. hist. novitiate.

mülci ملجى A lrnd. compelling, forcing.

mülebbes ملبّس A lrnd. 1. clothed, dressed. 2. made intricate (matter); falsified, intentionally corrupted.

müleffef ملفّف A lrnd. wrapped, folded up.

mülekâ (. . —) ملكا A lrnd., pl. of **melik 2**.

mülemma ملمّع A lrnd. 1. bright, gilded; parti-colored. 2. poet. composed half in one language and half in another (poem). 3. soiled, smeared. **—ger, —kâr** (. . . —), **—sâz** (. . . —) P 1. gilder, plater. 2. hypocrite, double dealer.

mülevven ملوّن A lrnd. colored, tinged; variegated.

mülevves ملوّث A soiled, dirty, filthy; nasty. **—lik** filthiness.

mülevvin ملوّن A lrnd. that colors; coloring, tingeing.

müleyyen ملیّن A lrnd. 1. softened, soothed. 2. moved (bowels).

müleyyin ملیّن A 1. laxative. 2. lrnd. that softens or soothes; softening.

mülfam (. —) ملفام P poet. wine colored, red.

mülga (. —) ملغى A abolished; suppressed.

mülhak[kı] ملحق A added to, appended, joined to; annexed, attached; dependent (on). **— bütçe** subsidiary budget.

mülhakat (. . —) ملحقات A lrnd. 1. things added. 2. places subordinate (to a center of government).

mülhem ملهم A /dan/ 1. inspired; revealed by inspiration. 2. suggested.

mülhid ملحد A 1. who swerves from a true and proper direction. 2. atheist; irreligious; heretic. **—lik** atheism.

mülhim ملهم A lrnd. who reveals truth to man by inspiration (God); inspirer.

mülhiye ملوخيا Gk 1. Jew's-mallow, bot., Corchorus olitorius. 2. dish prepared with the leaves of Jew's-mallow.

mü'lim 1 مؤلم A lrnd. which causes pain, painful.

mülim[mmi] **2** ملمّ A lrnd. 1. who approaches puberty. 2. hard, firm, strong.

mülimme ملمّة A lrnd. calamity, accident.

mülk[kü] ملك A 1. possession; property; real estate. 2. sovereignty, dominion; state. 3. rel. the whole creation as the domain of God; God's supreme sovereignty and dominion. **— al=** to buy landed property. **—i beka** lrnd. a future state, realm of eternity. **—i hakikî ve mecâzî** lrnd. God's kingdom of the real and the spiritual. **— sahibi** landowner. **—i yemin** can. law property acquired or held by conquest or purchase.

mülkdâr (. —) ملكدار P lrnd. 1. landowner; rich in possessions. 2. sovereign, king; God. **—î** (. — —) P lrnd. 1. pertaining to a sovereign. 2. government; sovereignty.

mülki (. —) ملكى A belonging to the state; civil; civilian. **— idare** civil administration. **— teşkilât** administrative organization.

mülkiye ملكيه A civil service; school for civil servants.

mülkiyet ملكيت A lrnd. 1. quality of being a freehold; proprietorship. 2. possession. **— dâvası** law claim in rem. **—i edebiye** law rights over intellectual (non-material) property. **— hakkı** law property right. **—i muhafaza mukavelesi** law reservation of ownership.

mülklen=[ir] ملكلن to become an owner of property.

müllâk[kı] (. —) ملّاك A lrnd., pl. of **malik**.

mülsak[kı] ملصق A lrnd. adhering; adjoining.

mültahi (. . —) ملتحى A lrnd. bearded.

mültahik[kı] ملتحق A lrnd. that joins; joining.

mültakım ملتقم A lrnd. that swallows at a mouthful.

mültakıt ملتقط A lrnd. 1. who picks up. 2. who comes by chance upon a thing.

mültakim ملتقم A lrnd. that meets (another).

mültasık[kı] ملتصق A lrnd. adjoining, contiguous.

mültebis مُلتَبِس A lrnd. intricate, difficult (matter); obscure, entangled (thing).
mülteca (..—) مُلتَجا A lrnd. place of refuge; refuge, asylum.
mülteci (..—) مُلتَجِی A who takes refuge, refugee. —yan (..——) P lrnd., pl. —yane (..——.) P lrnd. like a refugee.
mültefet مُلتَفِت A lrnd. esteemed, considered with great respect.
mültefit مُلتَفِت A 1. attentive, courteous, kind. 2. who takes notice of. —ane (...—.) P lrnd. kindly, friendly.
mültehib مُلتَهِب A 1. med. inflamed, infected. 2. lrnd. flaming, kindled, burning.
mültehif مُلتَهِف A lrnd. flaming, blazing, on fire.
mülteim مُلتَئِم A lrnd. closed, healed (wound).
mülteka (..—) مُلتَقا A lrnd. 1. place or time of meeting; junction. 2. confluence of two rivers; meeting of seas.
mültekayülebhur مُلتَقَی البحور A geog. junction of the seas.
mültemes مُلتَمَس A lrnd. asked for as a favor; protected, backed; protegé.
mültemi' مُلتَمِع A lrnd. 1. which flashes, gleams; brilliant, shining. 2. that suddenly seizes and carries off.
mültemis مُلتَمِس A lrnd. who asks as a favor. —ane (...—.) P beseechingly. —în (...—) A pl. of mültemis.
mültesikᵏⁱ مُلتَصِق A lrnd., same as **mültasık**.
mültevi مُلتَوی A lrnd. twisted, distorted.
mültezem مُلتَزَم A lrnd. considered important and supported by all means; favored.
mültezim مُلتَزِم A 1. Ott. hist. contractor or farmer of any branch of the public revenue; contractor. 2. lrnd. who cleaves to; adherent, follower. —âne (...—.) P favoringly. —în (...—) A pl. of mültezim. —lik quality or functions of a revenue farmer.
mülûkᵏᵘ (.—) مُلوک A lrnd., pl. of melik 1. —âne (.——.) P royal, regal, sovereign; kingdom.
mülûkî (.——) مُلوکی A lrnd. pertaining to kings, royal, regal. — sakız helvası a kind of sweet.
mülzem مُلزَم A lrnd. beaten in an argument, reduced to silence.
mülzim مُلزِم A lrnd. who convinces and reduces to silence.
mülzime مُلزِمه A lrnd. paperweight.
mümacede (.—..) مُماجَده A lrnd. a contending for glory, a glorying in. — et= to contend for glory.
mümahhas مُمَحَّص A lrnd. 1. tried, proved. 2. strong, hardy.
mümalaha (.—..) مُمالَحه A lrnd. an eating salt together (as a pledge of friendship); an eating together. — et= to eat together.
mümanaat (.—..) مُمانَعت A an opposing, hindering, preventing; opposition, prevention. — et= to oppose, prevent.
mümaresat (.—.—) مُمارَسات A lrnd., pl. of mümarese.
mümarese, mümareset (.—..) مُمارَست A an applying oneself; skill acquired by practice; dexterity; training, exercise.
mümasˢˢⁱ (.—) مُماسّ A 1. geom. tangent. 2. lrnd. that touches, is in contact; touching. — hattı geom. tangential line, tangent.
mümaselet (.—..) مُماثَلت A 1. phil. analogy, similitude. 2. math. homothety. 3. lrnd. a being similar or equal; similarity, equality.
mümasil (.—.) مُماثِل A 1. /a/ alike, similar; equal. 2. geom. homothetic, similar. 3. phil. analogous.
mümaşat (.—.—) مُماشات A lrnd. 1. a walking together. 2. an acting considerately and making concessions; a complying. 3. a feigned approval, flattery. — et= to make concessions to, to approve in order to flatter.
mümatele (.—..) مُماطَله A lrnd. a putting off, deferring a claimant; deferring a payment, a being dilatory in carrying out a promise. — et= to put off, defer.
mümbit مُنبِت var. of münbit.
mümecced مُمَجَّد A lrnd. made glorious, glorified.
mümehhed مُمَهَّد A lrnd. 1. laid out, leveled, smoothed. 2. well arranged.
mümehhid مُمَهِّد A lrnd. 1. who lays and spreads out in order. 2. who arranges well and solidly.
mümellekᵏⁱ مُمَلَّک A law put into one's possession (property).
mümellikᵏⁱ مُمَلِّک A lrnd. who puts into possession of (property).
mü'men مُؤمَن A lrnd. believed, trusted, relied on.
mümessekᵏⁱ مُمَسَّک A lrnd. mixed with musk, musky.
mümessel مُمَثَّل A lrnd. 1. produced as a sample or example. 2. pictured, represented.
mümessil مُمَثِّل A 1. representative; delegate; agent. 2. lrnd. who produces a thing as a sample or example. 3. lrnd. editor. 4. lrnd. actor. 5. lrnd. assimilator. —lik state of being a representative; delegation; agency.
mümeyyez مُمَيَّز A lrnd. distinguished by some mark or quality.
mümeyyiz مُمَيِّز A 1. examining clerk, chief clerk. 2. examining official (at a school). 3. lrnd. that distinguishes a person by some mark or quality, distinguishing; discriminating;

characteristic, distinctive. —lik functions of a **mümeyyiz**.

mümezzakᵏⁱ مُمَزَّق A lrnd. torn to shreds, mangled.

mümhil مُمْهِل A lrnd. who grants a delay for payment of a debt; granting a delay.

mümidᵈᵈⁱ مُمِدّ A lrnd. 1. who helps, assists, comes to the rescue. 2. who prolongs a term; extender, prolonger.

mümilⁱˡⁱ 1 مُمِلّ A lrnd. that makes one tired, bores, disgusts; wearisome, annoying.

mümil 2 (.—) مُمِيل A lrnd. that causes to lean, incline or swerve.

mümiletülkulüb (.—...—) مُمِيلَةُ القُلُوب A lrnd. who draws all hearts to her.

mü'min A, mümin (—.) مُؤْمِن who believes or trusts, believer; believer in Islam.

mü'minat (..—) مُؤْمِنَات A lrnd. believing women.

mü'mine مُؤْمِنَة A 1. lrnd. a believing woman. 2. w. cap., woman's name.

mü'minîn (..—) مُؤْمِنِين A lrnd. believers, the faithful.

mümit (.—) مُمِيت A lrnd. that kills or causes to die; one of the names of God.

mümkin مُمْكِن same as **mümkün**.

mümkinât (..—) مُمْكِنَات A lrnd. possibilities, potentialities.

mümkün مُمْكِن [mümkin] 1. possible, potential, feasible. 2. log. contingent. — **mertebe** as far as possible. —**ü yok** colloq. It is impossible.

mümriz مُمْرِض A lrnd. that makes one ill, causing disease.

mümsikᵏⁱ مُمْسِك A lrnd. 1. who holds firmly, tenacious. 2. who restrains himself; reticent. 3. stingy, miser. —**lik** 1. tenacity; reticence. 2. stinginess, meanness.

mümtahan مُمْتَحَن A lrnd. examined; experienced, tried.

mümtahin مُمْتَحِن A lrnd. who tries, proves, examines; examiner, expert.

mümtaz (.—) مُمْتَاز A 1. distinguished, select, privileged; eminent, excellent. 2. autonomous. —**iyet**, —**lık** being distinguished or privileged; autonomy.

mümtedᵈᵈⁱ مُمْتَدّ A lrnd. extended, prolonged, stretched.

mümteli مُمْتَلِئ A lrnd. full, filled.

mümteniⁱⁱ مُمْتَنِع A 1. log. absurd. 2. lrnd. who refuses and stands aloof; impossible, unattainable.

mümteniat (...—) مُمْتَنِعَات A lrnd. unattainable things, impossibilities.

mümtesil مُمْتَثِل A lrnd. who conforms to, follows, obeys.

mümtezic مُمْتَزِج A lrnd. 1. who accommodates himself to the disposition of another; accommodating; fitting in with; compatible. 2. mingled, mixed, compounded.

mümtir مُمْطِر A lrnd. 1. who makes rain fall (God). 2. rainy.

mümza مُمْضَى A lrnd. signed; finished, settled.

mümzi مُمْضِي A law who signs and executes (document); signing; signatory.

münaam مُنْعَم A lrnd. surrounded with comfort and luxury; benefited.

münacat (.——) مُنَاجَات A 1. silent and fervent prayer, inward supplication to God. 2. piece used as a prayer in religious music.

münada (.——) مُنَادَى A 1. gram. vocative case. 2. lrnd. called out, shouted, proclaimed; cry, proclamation. 3. lrnd. person or thing addressed.

münadât (.——) مُنَادَات A lrnd. shout, invocation, proclamation.

münademe, münademet (.—..) مُنَادَمَت A lrnd. a being a confidential companion.

münadi (.——) مُنَادِي A who calls or shouts out; herald; public crier.

mün'adil مُنْعَدِل A lrnd. straying, deviating.

mün'adim 1 مُنْعَدِم A lrnd. come to naught, annihilated, destroyed.

münadim 2 (.—.) مُنَادِم A congenial companion. —**în** (.—.—) A pl.

münafaka, münafakat (.—..) مُنَافَقَت A lrnd. an acting hypocritically in religion; religious hypocrisy. — **et=** to act hypocritically.

münafat (.——) مُنَافَات A lrnd. 1. a driving each other off; a repelling. 2. mutual irreconcilability; incompatibility.

münaferat (.—.—) مُنَافَرَات A lrnd., pl. of **münaferet**.

münaferet (.—..) مُنَافَرَت A lrnd. 1. a mutual aversion, dislike of one another. 2. a contending with one another as to superiority of claims to honor. — **et=** to dislike one another.

münafese, münafeset (.—..) مُنَافَسَت A lrnd. a disputing, contending or vying as to the possession of some highly prized quality; personal quarrels, envy, malice. — **et=** to envy, dispute, quarrel.

münafıkᵏⁱ (.—.) مُنَافِق A 1. hypocrite (especially in religion). 2. tell-tale, backbiter; double dealer. —**ane** (.—.—.) P lrnd. hypocritical (act); hypocritically. —**în** (.—.—) A lrnd., pl. of **münafık**. —**lık** hypocrisy, double dealing.

münafi (.——) مُنَافِي A lrnd. that excludes; incompatible, irreconcilable; opposed to.

münaggas مُنَغَّص A lrnd. rendered miserable, made wretched, irksome and melancholy (life).

münakalât (.—.—) مُنَاقَلَات A pl. of

münakale. — vekâleti ministry of communication.

münakale (.—..) مناقله A transport, communication, transfer.

münakasa (.—..) مناقصه A a selling by Dutch auction, successively lowering the price.

münakasat (.—.—) مناقصات A lrnd., pl. of münakasa.

münakaşa (.—..) مناقشه A a disputing, wrangling, dispute, lively discussion, argument. — et= /ı/ to discuss, dispute.

münakaşat (.—.—) مناقشات A lrnd., pl. of münakaşa.

münakaza (.—..) مناقضه A lrnd. a proposition's being contradictory to another; a denying an assertion and stating something incompatible with it; contradiction, opposition.

münakeha (.—..) مناكحه A lrnd. a contracting a marriage; a marrying.

münakehat (.—.—) مناكحات A lrnd., pl. of münakeha.

münakız (.—.) مناقض A lrnd. contradictory, contrary, opposite.

mün'akid منعقد A 1. law agreed upon, ratified, concluded (treaty etc.). 3. lrnd. knotted, tied; bound.

mün'akis منعكس A lrnd. 1. reflected, reversed (as a figure in a mirror). 2. inverted. 3. reflex.

münakkah منقح A lrnd. 1. corrected, polished (literary composition); carefully revised. 2. trimmed, cleaned. —iyet a carefully revising; a trimming.

münakkas منقص A lrnd. lessened.

münakkaş منقش A ornamented with a design; embroidered.

münakkat منقط A lrnd. dotted; spotted.

münakkıs منقص A lrnd. that lessens the quantity of a thing; lessening, reducing.

münakkid منقد A same as münekkid.

münakkile منقله A lrnd. head wound penetrating to the bone.

münasafa, münasafet (.—..) مناصفة A law a dividing into two equal parts; a halving with another. — üzre by way of sharing in halves.

münasafeten (.—'...) مناصفة A lrnd. in halves.

münasat (.—.—) مناسات A lrnd. a forgetting. — et= to forget.

münasebat (.—.—) مناسبات A lrnd., pl. of münasebet, relations (between nations or people).

münasebet (.—..) مناسبت A 1. a being fit, suitable, proper, analogous, proportionate, reasonable; fitness; proportion; reason. 2. a being related, relation, connection; motive, object. 3. favorable occasion, opportunity. —iyle in connection with, on the occasion of. — al= to be proper, opportune. — düş= to occur (fitting occasion).

münasebetdar (.—..—) مناسبتدار P lrnd. related.

münasebetli مناسبتلی 1. having a relation. 2. reasonable. — münasebetsiz 1. reasonable and unreasonable. 2. in season and out of season.

münasebetsiz مناسبتسز 1. unreasonable, absurd. 2. unseemly, unsuitable. —lik unreasonableness; absurdity; silly act.

münasib A, münasip^bi (.—.) مناسب 1. fit, suitable, proper, opportune. 2. reasonable. — gör= /ı/ to think proper; to approve (of).

mün'atıf منعطف A lrnd. swerving, bent, inflected.

münavaha (.—..) مناوحه A lrnd. a lamenting to another (woman). — et= to lament.

münavebe (.—..) مناوبه A an occurring or acting alternately; alternation; a taking turns. — ile by turns.

münavebeten (.—...) مناوبةً A lrnd. alternately.

münavele (.—..) مناوله A lrnd. a stretching out the hand, offering or giving.

münazaa (.—..) منازعه A a disputing angrily; angry dispute, quarrel; litigation. — et= to quarrel, dispute. —lı in dispute; controversial.

münazaat (.—.—) منازعات A lrnd., pl. of münazaa.

münazara (.—..) مناظره A a debating, disputing; debate, argument, discussion.

münazarat (.—.—) مناظرات A lrnd. disputations, argumentation.

münazaünfih (.—...) منازع فيه A lrnd. about which there is a dispute, controversial.

münazır (.—.) مناظر A lrnd. 1. who debates with another, debator; dialectician. 2. parallel, equal. —în (.—.—) A those who debate.

münazi^i (.—.) منازع A lrnd. disputant, opponent, litigant, claimant.

mün'azil منعزل A lrnd. 1. dismissed from office. 2. retired from the world.

münazzaf منظف A lrnd. made scrupulously clean; purified, purged.

münazzam منظم A lrnd. arranged, regulated.

münazzım منظم A lrnd. who arranges, regulates.

münbagi (..—) منبغی A lrnd. proper, suitable.

münbais منبعث A lrnd. 1. caused, resulting. 2. sent, sent out.

münbasit منبسط A lrnd. 1. spread out, dilated, extended; expansive. 2. rejoicing, exultant, glad.

münbit مُنْبِت A fertile (land). **—lik** fertility, richness of soil.

münceli (..—) مُنْجَلِى A *lrnd.* 1. manifest, visible, apparent; bright. 2. put aside, removed (veil).

müncemid مُنْجَمِد A *lrnd.* frozen; coagulated; solidified.

müncer[rri] مُنْجَرّ 1. /a/ resulting in, leading to. 2. *lrnd.* drawn, attracted. **— ol=** /a/ 1. to be attracted or drawn. 2. to result in.

müncezib مُنْجَذِب A *lrnd.* drawn, attracted.

münci مُنْجِى A *lrnd.* that saves from danger; rescuer, deliverer.

münciz مُنْجِز A *lrnd.* who complies with a request; who performs a promise.

mündefi[ii] مُنْدَفِع A *lrnd.* pushed away, repelled, repulsed; removed. **—at** (...—) A pus discharge, etc. (from a wound).

mündehiş مُنْدَهِش A *lrnd.* terrified.

mündemic مُنْدَمِج A 1. *lrnd.* entering in, contained in. 2. *phil.* immanent.

münderic مُنْدَرِج A *lrnd.* inserted; published, written.

mündericat (...—) مُنْدَرِجَات A contents (of a letter or book).

münderis مُنْدَرِس A *lrnd.* in utter ruin, obliterated.

münebbih مُنَبِّه A 1. *med.* stimulus; stimulant, excitant (coffee etc.). 2. *lrnd.* who awakens, rouses; rousing, awakening, warning. **—li saat** alarm clock.

münecci مُنَجِّى A *lrnd.* rescuer, deliverer.

müneccim مُنَجِّم A 1. astronomer. 2. astrologer. **M— Başı** *Ott. hist.* chief astrologer of the Sultan. **—lik** state or occupation of an astrologer.

münehhi مُنَهِّى A *lrnd.* that forbids, forbidding.

münehhiyat (...—) مُنَهِّيَات A *lrnd.* forbidden things.

münekker مُنَكَّر A 1. *Arabic gram.* indeterminate, indefinite. 2. *lrnd.* disguised, incognito.

münekkes مُنَكَّس A *lrnd.* overturned, inverted.

münekkid مُنَقِّد A criticizing; criticizer; critic. **—lik** criticism; occupation of a critic.

münevver مُنَوَّر A *lrnd.* 1. enlightened; educated, intellectual. 2. *lrnd.* lighted up, illuminated.

münevvim مُنَوِّم A *med.-* that puts to sleep; soporific; narcotic.

münevvir مُنَوِّر A *lrnd.* illuminating, enlightening; illuminator.

münezzeh مُنَزَّه A /dan/ freed, exempt from (any unworthy thing); pure; blameless.

münezzel مُنَزَّل A *lrnd.* sent down.

münezzil مُنَزِّل A *lrnd.* who sends down; *rel.* revealer.

münfail مُنْفَعِل A 1. annoyed, offended. 2. *chem., phil.* passive. **—iyet** passivity, passiveness.

münfatır مُنْفَطِر A *lrnd.* cracked, burst; torn.

münfecir مُنْفَجِر A *lrnd.* 1. that bursts forth and flows; flowing. 2. that breaks (dawn), dawning.

münfehim مُنْفَهِم A *lrnd.* understood, comprehended.

münfek[kki] مُنْفَكّ A 1. *path.* dislocated (joint). 2. *lrnd.* separated, severed.

münfelik[ki] مُنْفَلِق A *lrnd.* split, cleft.

münferic مُنْفَرِج A 1. *geom.* separated by an interval, wide apart. 2. *lrnd.* tranquil, contented, happy. **— zaviye** *geom.* obtuse angle.

münferid مُنْفَرِد A separate, alone, isolated. **—en** (..'..) A separately, singly, alone.

münferik[ki] مُنْفَرِق A *lrnd.* sundered, severed, dispersed.

münfeseh 1 مُنْفَسِخ A *lrnd.* disintegrated, broken up.

münfeseh 2 مُنْفَسِح A *lrnd.* expanding, opening (place).

münfesih مُنْفَسِخ A *lrnd.* 1. dissolved, broken off (contract etc.). 2. abolished, annulled.

münfetih مُنْفَتِح A *lrnd.* opened, open.

münfık[ki] مُنْفِق A *lrnd.* who spends money freely (on his family); who disposes of his goods easily.

münhadi[ii] مُنْخَدِع A *lrnd.* deceived, cheated.

münhadib مُنْحَدِب A *lrnd.* humped; convex.

münhadir مُنْحَدِر A *lrnd.* that descends; sloping.

münhafız مُنْخَفِض A *lrnd.* depressed, low.

münhal[iii] **1** مُنْحَلّ A 1. vacant, vacated (job, seat, office). 2. *chem.* decomposed; dissolved. 3. *lrnd.* loosened, opened, untied. 4. *lrnd.* solved (problem).

münhal[ii] **2** مُنْخَل A *lrnd.* fine sieve.

münhali[ii] مُنْخَلِع A *lrnd.* dethroned; abdicated.

münhani مُنْحَنِى A *geom.* bent, curved; curve; arc. **—lik** curvedness; convexity; concavity.

münhanik[ki] مُنْخَنِق A *lrnd.* choked, strangled.

münharif مُنْحَرِف A 1. *geom.* trapezium; quadrilateral. 2. *lrnd.* turned to one side, deviating, swerving; leaning; crooked. 3. *lrnd.* indisposed; changed.

münharifülhatır (....—.) مُنْحَرِفُ الخَاطِر A *lrnd.* disturbed in mind; hurt, vexed, offended.

münharifülmizac (.....—) مُنْحَرِفُ المِزَاج A *lrnd.* indisposed.

münhasır مُنْحَصِر A restricted, limited. **—an** (..'..) A exclusively.

münhasif مُنْخَسِف A 1. *astr.* eclipsed (moon). 2. *lrnd.* blinded (eye). 3. *lrnd.* extinguished, put into the shade (by something better).

münhat[tti] مُنْحَطّ A *lrnd.* 1. descending, falling off. 2. depressed; low lying (place) lowered; diminished; degraded.

münhazım مُنهَضِم A lrnd. digested.
münhebit مُنهَبِط A lrnd. that comes down, descends, falls.
münhedim مُنهَدِم A lrnd. fallen down; demolished; in ruins.
münhemik^ki مُنهَمِك A lrnd. /a/ assiduously occupied; absorbed in, indulging in.
münhezim مُنهَزِم A routed, put to flight, utterly defeated. —en (..'..) A. in rout, in disorderly flight; dispersed.
münhi مُنهِى A lrnd. that announces, communicates intelligence; reporter. —yan (..—) P bringers of news.
münhül^lü مُنحَلّ var. of münhal 2.
münib (.—) مُنِيب A 1. lrnd. who renounces sin and turns to God; repentant, penitent. 2. *order of dervishes* dervish who has passed his novitiate. 3. lrnd. plentiful and repeated (rain); abundant rainfall.
münif (.—) مُنِيف A lrnd. high, exalted, illustrious.
mün'im مُنعِم A lrnd. who confirms a gift or favor; beneficient, benevolent, gracious, generous; benefactor. —i biçûn u çirâ the Benefactor without how or why; God. —âne (..—.) P beneficiently, generously.
münir (.—) مُنِير A lrnd. that gives light; luminous, bright; illuminating.
münkad (.—) مُنقاد A lrnd. submissive, docile; obedient.
münkah مُنقَح A lrnd. polished, corrected (literary composition).
münkali^i مُنقَلِع A lrnd. torn up; uprooted; extracted.
münkalib مُنقَلِب A /a/ changed, transformed, converted.
münkariz مُنقَرِض A extinct (family, race); exterminated; perished; destroyed. — ol= to die out.
münkasım مُنقَسِم A lrnd. divided into parts.
münkazi (..—) مُنقَضِى A lrnd. ended, finished, expired (period).
münker مُنكَر A 1. *can. law* unlawful, not allowed. 2. *w. cap.*, name of one of the two angels that question the dead. 3. lrnd. denied, disbelieved, ignored; unacknowledged.
münkerât (..—) مُنكَرات A lrnd. things not allowed by canonical law. —ı mevt horrors of death.
münkesif مُنكَسِف A *astr.* eclipsed (sun).
münkesir مُنكَسِر A lrnd. 1. broken. 2. annoyed, vexed; broken-hearted. — hat *geom.* broken line.
münkesirülhal (....—). مُنكَسِرُالحال A lrnd. broken-down, unfortunate.
münkeşif مُنكَشِف A lrnd. 1. revealed, brought to light, disclosed; discovered. 2. uncovered; displayed.

münkir مُنكِر A who denies or disbelieves unbeliever; atheist. —in (..—) A atheist.
münsakib مُنثَقِب A lrnd. perforated, pierced, bored.
münsecil مُنسَجِل A lrnd. registered, written (by a judge).
münsecim مُنسَجِم A lrnd. flowing smoothly.
münsecir مُنسَجِر A lrnd. loose, flowing (hair).
münsed^ddi مُنسَدّ A lrnd. closed, blocked up, obstructed.
münselib مُنسَلِب A lrnd. 1. taken away, removed. 2. stripped, despoiled; snatched away.
münselih مُنسَلِخ A lrnd. 1. stripped off; skinned. 2. finished, in its last day (lunar month).
münselik^ki مُنسَلِك A lrnd. who takes and follows a road, series or progression.
münşaat (..—) مُنشَآت var. of münşeat.
münşaib مُنشَعِب A lrnd. branched out in subdivisions; subdivided.
münşail مُنشَعِل A lrnd. flaming, blazing, on fire.
münşak^kkı مُنشَقّ A lrnd. split, rent, torn.
münşeat (..—) مُنشَآت A 1. writings, literary compositions. 2. letters; sets of examples of letters.
münşel^lü مُنشَلّ A lrnd. which rushes down in torrents.
münşerih مُنشَرِح A lrnd. cheerful; rejoicing.
münşet^tti مُنشَتّ A lrnd. subdivided, branched, separated, scattered.
münşi مُنشِى A 1. composer in prose; writer, author. 2. secretary, clerk. —i felek *poet.* the planet Mercury.
münşid مُنشِد A lrnd. reciter of poems.
müntahab مُنتَخَب A chosen, selected; choice; elected.
müntahabât (...—) مُنتَخَبات A lrnd. extracts, selections of writings, anthology.
müntahib مُنتَخِب A lrnd., same as müntehib 1.
müntahil مُنتَحِل A lrnd. who falsely assumes to himself the merit of another's writings; plagiarist.
müntahir مُنتَحِر A lrnd., same as müntehir.
müntakid مُنتَقِد A lrnd. who criticizes, critic.
müntakil مُنتَقِل A lrnd. 1. that moves from one place to another, migrating. 2. transferred; passed away. 3. passed on, inherited. 4. of quick perception, intelligent.
müntakim مُنتَقِم A lrnd. 1. who takes vengeance; avenger. 2. God, the Great Avenger.
müntakiş مُنتَقِش A lrnd. who gets a thing engraved or ornamented with figures.
müntakiz مُنتَقِض A lrnd. that goes to pieces; disintegrated; demolished.
müntebih مُنتَبِه A lrnd. awake, vigilant watchful, attentive.

müntefiⁱⁱ **1** منتفع A *lrnd.* who profits, who gains an advantage; gainer.
müntefi 2 (—.—) منتفى A *lrnd.* driven away, repulsed, rejected; exiled, banished.
müntefih منتفخ A *lrnd.* swollen; inflated.
müntefil منتفل A *lrnd.* who does more than is required; who performs a supererogatory act of divine worship.
münteha منتهى A limit, extreme limit, extremity; end, utmost, extent.
müntehab منتخب A same as **müntahab**.
müntehi منتهى A *lrnd.* that reaches a limit or comes to an end, ending; final, last.
müntehib 1 منتخب A *pol.* who selects, chooses; elector. —**i evvel** *pol.* primary elector. —**i sani** *pol.* electoral delegate.
müntehib 2 منتهب A *lrnd.* who takes as spoil; plunderer.
müntehil منتحل A *lrnd.*, same as **müntahil.**
müntehir منتحر A who commits suicide; suicide (person).
müntehiz منتهز A *lrnd.* who seizes an opportunity.
müntekis منتكس A *lrnd.* upside down, inverted; headlong.
müntemi منتمى A *lrnd.* related to, of the same family.
münten منتن A *path.* infected; contaminated.
müntesib منتسب A *lrnd.* /a/ connected with; related to, belonging to (one of superior rank).
müntesic منتسج A *lrnd.* woven, interwoven, interlaced.
müntesikᵏⁱ منتسق A 1. *phil.* coordinate. 2. *lrnd.* arranged in a regular order.
müntesir منتثر A *lrnd.* scattered, dispersed.
münteşir منتشر A 1. published, propagated. 2. diffused; disseminated; scattered. 3. expanded, spread out. — **muhayyile** *psych.* diffused imagination.
münteziⁱⁱ منتزع A *lrnd.* 1. that plucks, pulls up or away. 2. separated, detached.
müntic منتج A *lrnd.* that produces a result; causing; resulting in.
müntif منتف A *lrnd.* that plucks (hair), that depilates.
müntin منتن A *lrnd.* 1. stinking, fetid. 2. *path.* contagious.
münzalim منظلم A *lrnd.* who submits quietly to oppression; oppressed, wronged.
münzecir منزجر A *lrnd.* prohibited, forbidden.
münzel منزل A *lrnd.* made to descend; sent down, revealed to man from God.
münzevi (..—) منزوى A retired to a solitary place; recluse, hermit. —**yâne** (..——.) P in the manner of a recluse.
münzic منضج A *lrnd.* that makes ripe, that matures.

münzil منزل A *lrnd.* who causes to descend; who sends down.
münzir منذر A *lrnd.* who warns, cautions; who threatens; who dissuades.
müphem مبهم A vague; indefinite; dubious.
müphemât (..—) مبهمات A *lrnd.* vague and indefinite things.
müphemiyet (..—.) مبهميت A *lrnd.* vagueness; lack of precision.
müpteda مبتدأ *var. of* **mübteda 1.**
müptedi مبتدى *var. of* **mübtedi 1.**
müptelâ (..—) مبتلا A 1. subject to, addicted to; having a passion for; in love with. 2. suffering from.
müpteni مبتنى [**mübteni**] 1. built, raised, erected. 2. /a/ established, based (on).
müptezel مبتذل A 1. lavish, profuse, plentiful, common. 2. commonplace and vulgar; too cheap.
mürʳʳᵘ **1** مر A *lrnd.* myrrh. — **ağacı** myrrh tree, *bot., Commiphora myrrha.*
mürʳʳᵘ **2** مر A *lrnd.* bitter.
müraat (.——) مراعات A *lrnd.* 1. a showing respect for a rule; observing a rule; conformity. 2. regard, respect, consideration.
mürabaa (.—..) مرابع A *lrnd.* a hiring or contracting for the spring season.
mürabaha (.—..) مرابحه *var. of* **murabaha.**
mürabata (.—..) مرابط A *lrnd.* 1. a hovering with a corps of cavalry about an enemy's frontier. 2. a being vigilant, assiduous and persevering, especially in religious exercises.
mürabıt (.—.) مرابط A *lrnd., var. of* **murabıt.**
müracaatᵗⁱ **1** (.—.) مراجعت A 1. a making a reference, referring, applying to a person or thing; reference, recourse, application. 2. *lrnd.* a returning, return. — **et**= /a/ to have recourse to, refer to, apply.
müracaat 2 (.—.—) مراجعات A *lrnd., pl. of* **müracaat 1,** applications, references.
müracaha (.—..) مراجح A *lrnd.* a vying as to preferability or as to forbearance.
müradefe, müradefet (.—..) مرادفت A *lrnd.* 1. a riding behind another on the same beast. 2. a being synonymous with another (word). — **et**= to travel on the same beast with someone.
müradif (.—.) مرادف A *lrnd.* 1. synonymous. 2. riding behind another on the same beast; companion.
mürafakat (.—..) مرافقت A 1. an accompanying another on a journey; companionship. 2. *phil.* coincidence. — **et**= /a/ to accompany someone on a journey.
mürafıkᵏⁱ (.—.) مرافق A *lrnd.* who accompanies another; fellow traveler.

mürafiⁱⁱ مرافع A *law* a litigant in a suit carried to a court of justice.
mürahaka, mürahakatⁱⁱ (.—..) مراحقة مراحقت A *lrnd.* an approaching the age of puberty.
mürahene, mürahanet (.—..) مراهنة مراهنت A *lrnd.* a betting; a depositing bets (especially at a horse race). — **et=** to bet.
mürahham مرحّم A *lrnd.* 1. paved, cased or ornamented with marble. 2. curtailed, abbreviated (word).
mürahhil مرحّل A *lrnd.* who orders to depart on a journey; who sends away.
mürahikᵏⁱ (.—.) مراهق A *lrnd.* on the verge of puberty.
mürai 1 (.——) مرائى A hypocritical; hypocrite.
mürai 2 (.——) مراعى A *lrnd.* who conforms to a rule, etc., observer.
mürailikᵍⁱ (.——.) مرائيلك hypocrisy.
müraiyane (.———.) مرائيانه P *lrnd.* hypocritically.
mürakabe (.—..) مراقبة A *var. of* **murakaba**.
mürakıb (.—.) مراقب A *var. of* **murakıb**.
müramat (.——) مراماة A *lrnd.* a competing with someone by throwing the javelin or shooting arrows. — **et=** to compete.
mürasada (.—..) مراصدة A 1.*lrnd.* a watching; watchful observation. 2. a lying in wait and spying. — **et=** to watch, to spy.
müraselât (.—.—) مراسلات A *lrnd., pl. of* **mürasele**.
mürasele (.—..) مراسلة A 1. *Ott. hist.* a judge's letter of appointment. 2. *lrnd.* a mutually sending letters or messages; correspondence. — **et=** to correspond.
müravaga (.—..) مراوغة A *lrnd.* 1. a wrestling together. 2. a striving to persuade or deceive.
müravaza (.—..) مراوضة A *lrnd.* an endeavoring to conciliate; a putting the best face on a matter to another so as to persuade him.
müravede (.—..) مراودة A *lrnd.* 1. a paying court to another assiduously with an object. 2. an asking, desiring, wooing; wish, desire; amicable relation.
mürayat (.——) مرايات A *lrnd.* an acting ostentatiously or hypocritically; hypocrisy, dissimulation. — **et=** to act hypocritically, ostentatiously.
mürazaa (.—..) مراضعة A *lrnd.* a suckling (child). — **et=** to suckle.
mürciⁱⁱ مرجى A *chem.* reducing agent, reducer.
mürd 1 مرد P *lrnd.* dead (said of animals).
mürd 2 مرد A *lrnd., pl. of* **emred**.
mürdab (.—) مرداب P *lrnd.* backwater of a stream; creek, lagoon.
mürdad (.—) مرداد P *lrnd.* 1. name of the fifth Persian month (July). 2. name of an angel of the Zoroastrians. 3. name of the seventh and eighth days of the months.
mürdasenc, mürdaseng (.—.) مرداسنگ P *lrnd., same as* **mürdeseng**.
mürde مرده P *lrnd.* dead (person); corpse. — **bacı** *Ott. hist.* tax levied on sheep in transit to Istanbul for slaughter.
mürdedil مرده‌دل P *lrnd.* lifeless; cold-hearted, callous.
mürdegân (..—) مردگان P *lrnd.* the dead.
mürderig (..—) مرده‌ریگ P *lrnd.* effects of a dead person, anything hereditary.
mürdeseng مرده‌سنگ P *lrnd.* litharge, lead monoxide.
mürdeşu, mürdeşuy (..—) مرده‌شو مرده‌شوی P *lrnd.* washer of the dead.
mürdüm مردم damson plum, *bot., Prunus insititia.* — **eriği** damson.
mürebba (..—) مربّى A *lrnd.* 1. nourished and brought up. 2. *same as* **murabba 2**.
mürebbi (..—) مربّى A who brings up and educates (child); educator; trainer.
mürebbiye (..—.) مربّية A governess.
müreccah مرجّح A *lrnd.* preferred; preferable. **—iyet** preference.
müreccep مرجّب A *lrnd.* treated with honor; honored; venerable.
müreccih مرجّح A *lrnd.* who prefers; who honors and respects.
müreda (..—) مرداء A *lrnd., pl. of* **merid**.
müreddef مردّف A *lrnd.* said or repeated (after something else).
müreffeh مرفّه A comfortable, luxurious; prosperous, well to do.
müreffehen (.'..) مرفّها A *lrnd.* comfortably off; in easy circumstances.
müreffih مرفّه A *lrnd.* that makes one's life easy, comfortable, luxurious.
mürehheb مرهّب A *lrnd.* frightened.
mürehhib مرهّب A *lrnd.* that frightens, terrific, appalling.
mürekkeb مركّب A *same as* **mürekkep**. — **aded** complex number. — **balığı** cuttlefish, *zool., Sepia officinalis.* **—i kurumadan** immediately afterwards, very quick. — **yalamış** experienced; well educated.
mürekkebât (...—) مركّبات A *lrnd.* compounds, compound medicines.
mürekkebe مركّبة A *bot.* composite.
mürekkepᵇⁱ مركّب [**mürekkeb**] /dan/ 1. composed (of); combined; *chem.* compound; *geom.* compound. 2. ink. 3. *log.* complex. **—çi** maker or seller of ink.
mürekkeple=ʳ مركّبله /i/ to ink; to cover with ink. **—n=** *pass.* **—t=** *caus. of* **mürekkeple=**.

mürekkepli مركبلي inky; filled with ink. **— kalem** fountain pen.
mürekkeplik[ɡi] مركبلك 1. inkstand. 2. inking roller, inker.
mürekkib A, **mürekkip**[bi] مركب 1. component. 2. who composes or makes up; composing.
müressem مرسم A lrnd. traced, designed; embellished with lines.
müressim مرسم A lrnd. who draws; painter.
müreşşah مرشح A lrnd. nurtured, reared; trained.
müretteb مرتب A 1. planned; prepared; invented. 2. mil. destined for; allotted. 3. lrnd. set in order, regularly arranged.
mürettebat (...—) مرتبات A 1. complement, crew (of a ship, plane etc.). 2. appropriation, allocations. 3. mil. troops allotted to or destined for some place or duty.
mürettib مرتب A same as **mürettip**. **— hatası** misprint.
mürettibhane (...—.) مرتبخانه P print. composing room, case room.
mürettibin (...—) مرتبين A lrnd. compositors, typesetters.
mürettil مرتل A lrnd. who recites the Quran in the slowest of the three acknowledged modes.
mürettip مرتب [mürettib] 1. print. compositor, typesetter. 2. lrnd. that sets in order, arranges. **—lik** profession of a typesetter.
mürevvah مروح A lrnd. 1. perfumed, highly scented. 2. rested, made comfortable.
mürevvak[ki] مروق A lrnd. strained, filtered; clear.
mürevvec مروج A lrnd. current, saleable; usual.
mürevvic مروج A lrnd. 1. that gives currency (to a thing). 2. propagating (ideas etc.). 3. who pushes or facilitates things; supporter. **—i efkâr** publication promoting a viewpoint (a newspaper etc.).
mürevvih مروح A lrnd. 1. who perfumes. 2. who causes one to rest.
mürg مرغ P lrnd. bird. **—i âb, —i âbi** same as **mürgab**. **—i âfitab-âlem** fire. **—i âmin** angel flying in the air and continually calling out «Amen» (any prayer coinciding with this call being granted). **—i aşk** the bird of love; love. **—i âzer-efruz** the fire-kindling bird, phoenix. **—i bağ, —i bam** nightingale. **—i bigâhhan** cock that crows out of season. **—i bismillâhi** the words **Bismillâhi** written in the shape of a bird. **—i bivakt** same as **—i bigâhhan. —i çemen** nightingale. **—i dânâ** parrot. **—i dil** poet. the heart, mind, soul. **—i felek, —i gerdûn** angel, cherub. **—i guşt-ruba** kite. **—i hak-gû** name of a bird which is said to suspend itself by the claws and to cry «hak hak» the whole night till the blood drops from its mouth. **—i hânegi** domestic fowl. **—i hoşhân** nightingale. **—i ilâhi** the human soul, the spirit. **—i İsa** bat. **—i leb** word, speech. **—i Mecnun** the bird said to have built its nest on Mecnun's head. **—i nâme, —i nâmeaver, —i nâmeber** carrier pigeon. **—i ruz** the sun. **—i seher, —i seherhan** 1. nightingale. 2. cock. 3. ringdove. 4. early rising worshipper. **M—i Sidre** the Angel Gabriel. **—i subh** nightingale. **—i Süleyman** hoopoe. **—i şeb ü rûz** moon and sun. **—i şebahenk** nightingale. **—i şebâvîz** same as **mürgi hakgû. —i şebhân, —i şebhîz** nightingale. **—i tarab** 1. nightingale. 2. musician, singer. **—i yâkut-per** fire. **—i zer** 1. sun. 2. golden flagon. **—i zerrîn, —i zerrîn-bâl, —i zerrîn-per** 1. sun. 2. name of a bird. **—i zîrek, —i zîrek-sar** starling.
mürgab (.—) مرغاب P lrnd. waterfowl; duck.
mürgan (.—) مرغان P lrnd., pl. of **mürg. —i Sidre** angels.
mürgâne (.—.) مرغانه P lrnd. bird's egg.
mürgbaz (.—) مرغباز P lrnd. cockfighter, cock feeder.
mürgdil مرغدل P lrnd. chicken-hearted, timid.
mürgek[ki] مرغك P lrnd. little bird; chicken. **—i dânâ** the wise bird, parrot.
mürid (.—) مريد A 1. myst. orders novice in an order of dervishes; disciple. 2. lrnd. desirous. **—ân** (.——) P lrnd. pl. **—âne** (.——.) P lrnd. pertaining to a novice in an order; as becomes a disciple. **—i** (.——) P, A, **—iyet** (.—..), **—lik** quality or state of a novice; discipleship.
mürnel مرنل It naut., same as **mornel**.
mürsel مرسل A lrnd. sent with a message or mission; envoy, messenger; apostle.
mürselât (..—) مرسلات A lrnd., pl. of **mürsele,** 1. things sent by mail etc. 2. messengers, apostles. 3. angels. **M— Sûresi** name of the seventy-seventh sura of the Quran.
mürsele مرسله A lrnd. 1. sent. 2. angel. 3. message; letter.
mürselin (..—) مرسلين A lrnd., pl. of **mürsel,** prophets; apostles.
mürselünileyh مرسل اليه A postal service addressee; consignee.
mürsil مرسل A 1. postal service who sends; sender, consigner. 2. anat. afferent.
mürsile مرسله A phys. transmitter; transmitting station.
mürşid مرشد A 1. who guides to the right road. 2. spiritual guide spiritual teacher. 3. head of a religious order **—i âgâh** same as **—i kâmil. —i a'zam** the Prophet Muhammad. **—i kâmil** myst. supreme teacher, perfect guide. **—âne** (..—.) P in the manner of a

guide. **—in** (..—) A *lrnd.*, *pl. of* **mürşid**.
—lik the quality of a spiritual teacher.
mürtagib مرتغب A *lrnd.* desirous; supplicator; beseecher.
mürtahil مرتحل A *lrnd.* 1. who starts on a journey, goes away. 2. who dies; dead.
mürtahis مرتخص A *lrnd.* who buys cheap; who accounts a thing cheap.
mürtahiz مرتحض A *lrnd.* disgraced, shamed.
mürtai (..—) مرتعى A *lrnd.* grazing, at pasture, feeding.
mürtaib مرتعب A *lrnd.* who fears; frightened.
mürtaid, mürtaiş مرتعش مرتعد A *lrnd.* quivering, tremulous; shivering.
mürtaki (..—) مرتقى A *lrnd.* that ascends; ascended; progressing.
mürtakib مرتقب A *lrnd.* who waits and watches; watcher, keeper, awaiting; expectant.
mürtaza (..—′) مرتضى A *lrnd.* 1. with whom one is pleased; agreeable; chosen, approved. 2. *w. cap.*, a title of the Caliph Ali. **—vî** (...—) A pertaining to **Mürtaza**.
mürtazi[ii] 1 مرتضع A *lrnd.* who sucks; sucking.
mürtazi 2 (..—) مرتضى A *lrnd.* 1. pleased, satisfied, content. 2. belonging to **Mürtaza**.
mürtebit مرتبط A *lrnd.*, *same as* **murtabıt**.
mürteca (..—) مرتجى A *lrnd.* hoped or prayed for.
mürtecel مرتجل A *lrnd.* extemporized, impromptu; done offhand.
mürteci[ii] 1 مرتجعى A *pol.* reactionary.
mürteci 2 مرتجى A *lrnd.* who hopes, prays for.
mürtecil مرتجل A *lrnd.* who extemporizes, composes, impromptu; extempore speaker. **—âne** (...—.) P extemporaneously. **—en** (../..) A extempore; extemporarily.
mürted[ddi] مرتد A who apostatizes from Islam; apostate; renegade.
mürtedi[ii] مرتدع A *lrnd.* who abstains from a forbidden thing.
mürtedif مرتدف A *lrnd.* that follows; follower.
mürtefi[ii] مرتفع A *lrnd.* 1. that rises high; high; elevated, exalted. 2. removed.
mürtefid مرتفد A *lrnd.* who receives a gift; gainer, receiver of profit.
mürtehin مرتهن A *lrnd.* who pledges, leaves as a pawn, security or hostage.
mürtekib A, **mürtekip**[bi] مرتكب 1. corrupt, dishonest; taking bribes. 2. *lrnd.* who commits a sin. **—in** (..—) A *lrnd.*, *pl.*
mürtekiz مرتكز A *lrnd.* standing upright; erect.
mürtes[ssi] 1 مرتشى A *lrnd.* spread abroad (news etc.).
mürtes[ssi] 2 مرتث A *lrnd.* carried from the field (a wounded man).

mürtesem مرتسم A 1. *geom.* projection. 2. *lrnd.* delineated. **—i şakulî** *geom.* vertical projection. **—i ufkî** *geom.* horizontal projection.
mürtesim مرتسم A *lrnd.* drawn; pictured.
mürteşi (..—) مرتشى A *lrnd.* who accepts bribes, corrupt.
mürteşih مرتشح A *lrnd.* filtered, infiltrated.
mürtezık[kı] مرتزق A *lrnd.* who asks or expects means of subsistence; dependent, stipendiary.
mürtezika مرتزقة A *Ott. hist.* servants of a department of government as salaried dependents.
müruc (.—) مروج A *lrnd.*, *pl. of* **merc** 1.
mürur (.—) مرور A a passing along in space or time; passage, lapse of time. **— et=** to pass (in space or time). **—i eyyam** the course of time. **— hakkı** *law* right of passage. **— tezkeresi** permit to pass; pass. **— u ubur** a passing along; traffic. **—i zaman** *law* prescription; limitation (time after which an action cannot be taken).
mürüriye (.——.) مروريه A 1. permit to pass; pass. 2. fee paid for passage; toll.
mürüvvet مروت A 1. munificence; generosity; blessing. 2. feast on some family occasion when the house is open to all comers (for a birth, marriage, circumcision). **—e endaze olmaz** There is no limit to generosity; give all you can. **— et=** to be generous; to act generously. **—ini gör=** /ın/ to live to see (children grow up and marry). **—li, —mend** P generous, considerate of others.
mürüvvetsiz مروتسز ungenerous; inconsiderate. **—lik** lack of generosity, inconsiderateness.
mürvarid (.——) مرواريد P *lrnd.*, *same as* **mervarid**.
mürver مرور elder tree, *bot., Sambucus nigra*.
mürvet مروت *colloq.*, *var. of* **mürüvvet**.
mürzi[ii] مرضع A *lrnd.* suckling an infant (woman).
müsaadat (.—.—) مساعدات A *lrnd.*, *pl. of* **müsaade**, favors, facilities.
müsaade (.—..) مساعده A 1. permission; permit. 2. *lrnd.* a favoring, favor; a permitting. **— et=** /a/ to give permission.
müsaadekâr (.—..—) مساعده كار P tolerant.
müsaafe (.—..) مساعفه A *lrnd.* tolerance; permission.
müsab (.—) مساب A *lrnd.* rewarded.
müsabaka (.—..) مسابقه A competition; rivalry. **—ya gir=** to compete. **— imtihanı** competitive examination.
müsabakat[ti] (.—..) مسابقات A *lrnd.*, *same as* **müsabaka**.
müsaberet (.—..) مسابرت A *lrnd*

müsademe

a determinedly undertaking; a persevering in. — **et=** to begin and persevere.
müsademe (.—..) مصادر A same as **musademe**.
müsaderat (.—.—) مصادرات A *lrnd.*, pl. of **müsadere**.
müsadere (.—..) مصادره A *lrnd.* a confiscating; confiscation, seizure, capture. — **et=** /ı/ to confiscate.
müsadif (.—.) مصادف A *lrnd.* 1. who finds, falls on; encountering. 2. coinciding; happening.
müsafaa (.—..) مصافع A *lrnd.* 1. an embracing one another; embrace. 2. a fencing with one another; fight. — **et=** 1. to embrace one another. 2. to fight.
müsafaha (.—..) مصافق A *lrnd.*, same as **musafaha**.
müsafat (.——) مسافات A *lrnd.* 1. an acting foolishly, folly. 2. a treating medically.
müsaferet (.—..) مسافرت A *lrnd.* 1. a being a guest. 2. a traveling; journey.
müsafir (.—.) مسافر A same as **misafir**.
müsağ (.—) مساغ A *lrnd.* lawful; allowed.
müsahane (.—..) مساهنه A *lrnd.* 1. a meeting face to face. 2. a mixing in friendly intercourse; etiquette.
müsahele (.—..) مساهل A *lrnd.* 1. a treating gently, a being easy with another. 2. a neglecting, acting in a loose, negligent manner; carelessness, indifference. — **et=** to connive at another's faults, to overlook.
müsahelekâr (.—..—) مساهلكار P *lrnd.* tolerant.
müsaheme (.—..) مساهم A *lrnd.* 1. a contending in shooting arrows. 2. a mutually casting lots by arrows. — **et=** to contend in shooting arrows.
müsahere (.—..) مساهره A *lrnd.* a being mutually sleepless; a watching (with another). — **et=** to watch together.
müsaheret (.—..) مصاهرت A same as **musaheret**.
müsahhan مسخّن A *lrnd.* heated; hot.
müsahhar 1 مسخّر A *lrnd.* enchanted, bewitched, fascinated; beguiled.
müsahhar 2 مسخّر A *lrnd.* taken, subdued, conquered.
müsahhin مسخّن A *lrnd.* that warms, heats, heating.
müsahhir مسخّر A *lrnd.* that compels, subdues, conquers.
müsahim (.—.) مساهم A *lrnd.* 1. sharer, partner. 2. shareholder.
müsaid, müsaitᵈⁱ (.—.) مساعد A 1. favorable, convenient. 2. permitting, consenting.
müsakat (.—..) مساقات A *lrnd.* 1. a mutually giving to drink; a drawing water at the same time. 2. a contracting to water and tend trees or vines for a share of the produce.
müsakata (.—..) مساقط A *lrnd.* a letting fall in succession; a causing to fall.
müsakkab مثقّب A *lrnd.* pierced, bored; worm-eaten.
müsakkaf مسقّف A *lrnd.* roofed.
müsakkafat (...—) مسقّفات A *lrnd.*, pl. 1. roofed buildings, house property. 2. waqf income derived from house property. — **vergisi** tax on house property.
müsakkalˡⁱ مثقّل A *lrnd.* made heavy; overloaded.
müsakkib مثقّب A *lrnd.* that pierces or bores; instrument for boring.
müsakkil مثقّل A *lrnd.* that makes heavy; oppressive, distressing, painful (load, sleep etc.).
müsalefe, müsalefet (.—..) مسالفت A *lrnd.* 1. a travelling (with another). 2. a preceding; precedence. 3. a striving to be before another. — **et=** to travel with one another.
müsalemet (.—..) مسالمت A *lrnd.* a being mutually at peace; peace, reconciliation; tranquility.
müsalemetkâr (.—..—) مسالمتكار P *lrnd.* peace-loving, peaceful.
müsalemetüslûb (.—...—) مسالمت اسلوب P *lrnd.* friendly.
müsalim (.—.) مسالم A *lrnd.* 1. mutually at peace; reconciled. 2. cultivator of peace and amity.
müsamaha (.—..) مسامح A 1. tolerance; forbearance. 2. negligence; indulgence. — **et=** to be willfully blind to an impropriety.
müsamahakâr (.—..—) مسامحكار P tolerant; noncensorious; indulgent. —**âne** (.—..——.) P indulgently, tolerantly.
müsamahalı مسامحلی indulgent to an impropriety.
müsamerat (.—.—) مسامرات A *lrnd.*, pl. of **müsamere**.
müsamere (.—..) مسامره A 1. evening entertainment, entertainment. 2. *myst.* God's conversing with the human soul in secret.
müsamih (.—.) مسامح A *lrnd.* tolerating; lenient, indulgent.
müsanaha (.—..) مسانح A *lrnd.* a being evident; manifestation, occurrence.
müsanede, müsanedet (.—..) مساندت A *lrnd.* an assisting, aiding; mutual help, support. — **et=** to support, aid.
müsanehe (.—..) مسانه A *lrnd.* a contracting or hiring by the year; a giving annually. — **et=** to hire annually.
müsaraa, müsaraatˡⁱ (.—..) مسارعت A *lrnd.* a making haste; haste, hurry. — **et=** to hurry.
müsaraka, müsarakatˡⁱ (.—..) مسارقت A *lrnd.* a doing an act by stealth; theft.
müsatere (.—..) مساتره A *lrnd.* a veiling,

concealing; a being concealed, veiled. — **et=** to conceal.

müsavat (. — —) مساوات A a being mutually equal; equality. **—çı** *phil.* equalitarian. **—çılık** *phil.* equalitarianism.

müsaveme (. —..) مساومه A *lrnd.* a bidding against, raising the price; bargaining, bidding.

müsavere (. —..) مساوره A *lrnd.* a springing upon, attacking; attack, assault. **— et=** to attack.

müsavi (. — —) مساوى A 1. equal, equivalent. 2. the sign "=". **—lik** equality.

müsavim (. —.) مساوم A *lrnd.* who bargains, chaffers; bargainer, haggler.

müsayefe (. —..) مسايفه A *lrnd.* a fighting with swords, duelling.

müsbet مثبت A 1. proved, established, demonstrated. 2. positive; *elec.* positive; the positive sign. **— aded** *math.* positive number. **— cevap** an answer in the affirmative. **— felsefe** positivism. **— hukuk** positive law. **— ilimler** sciences. **— kafalı** realistic.

müsbiğ مسبغ A *lrnd.* 1. who confers abundant benefits (God). 2. who makes a thing full or ample.

müsbit مثبت A *lrnd.* that proves; prover, establisher. **— evrak** documents of proof.

müsebba' مسبع A 1. *poet.* in stanzas of seven couplets each (poem). 2. *Or. mus.* time. 3. *geom.* heptagon. 4. *lrnd.* made seven, composed of seven parts or elements.

müsebbeb مسبب A *lrnd.* caused, brought about.

müsebbib مسبب A 1. who furnishes with necessaries; author, instigator. 2. *lrnd.* cause, motive. 3. *lrnd.* that produces, causes; producing, causing. **—i hakiki** the true Cause, God.

müsebbibülesbab (.....—) مسبب الاسباب A *lrnd.* God, the great Producer of all secondary causes.

müsebbih مسبح A *lrnd.* who recites litanies; praiser of God; teller of beads.

müsebbiha مسبحه A *lrnd.* forefinger of the right hand (raised in solemnly calling on God).

müsebbihan (...—) مسبحان P *lrnd., pl.* of **müsebbih.** **—ı felek** the angels.

müsebbihane (...—.) مسبحانه P *lrnd.* in praise.

müsebbihîn, müsebbihûn (...—) مسبحين A *pl. of* **müsebbih.**

müsebbit مثبت A *lrnd.* who fixes, establishes; establisher, prover.

müsecca' مسجع A *pros.* rhymed (prose).

müseccel مسجل A 1. officially registered; matriculated. 2. notorious (thief, etc.); marked (person). 3. enrolled in a canonical law court.

müseccil مسجل A *lrnd.* 1. registrar. 2. recorder of matters in the archives of a canonical law court.

müsedded مسدد A *lrnd.* rightly directed.

müseddes مسدس A 1. *poet.* having six feet to each couplet or six couplets to each stanza. 2. *geom.* hexagon. 3. *lrnd.* made six; divided into six; composed of six elements or parts. **—i âlem** the universe, as having six sides or directions (front and back, right and left, up and down).

müsekkin مسكن A *med.* that quiets, calms; calming, sedative, anodyne.

müsellâh مسلح A armed. **—an** (..'..) A with arms in their hands; armed.

müsellem مسلم A 1. admitted by all; granted; incontestable. 2. *Ott. hist.* engaged in military service in lieu of tax payment.

müsellemât (...—) مسلمات A *lrnd.* incontestable matters, truisms.

müsellemîn (...—) مسلمين A *Ott. hist.* recruits free from tax payment.

müsellimlik[gi] مسلملك *Ott. hist.* freedom from tax payment (recruits).

müselles مثلث A 1. *geom.* triangle; triangular. 2. *lrnd.* syrup or wine reduced to a third by boiling. 3. *lrnd.* made three, composed of three parts; triple. **—i kürevi** spherical triangle. **—i müstevi** plane triangle.

müsellesât (...—) مثلثات A *lrnd.* trigonometry.

müsellim مسلم A 1. *Ott. hist.* administrative official under the **vali.** 2. *lrnd.* who delivers (anything to a person). **— kaldıran** *obs.* a long pipe with a large amber mouthpiece.

müsellis مثلث A 1. *Christ. rel.* who accepts the doctrine of the Trinity. 2. *Isl. rel.* Muslim who rejects Ali as a rightful caliph but acknowledges Abubakr, Omar and Othman. 3. *lrnd.* that triples. 4. *lrnd.* that divides into three.

müselsel مسلسل A *lrnd.* 1. in links as a chain; linked; connected. 2. consecutive; successive. 3. handed down in its original words (apostolic tradition). **—en** (...'.) A in consecutive order, successively.

müsemma (..—) مسمى A *lrnd.* 1. named, bearing a name; called. 2. appointed time. **— binnakiz** bearing a name that is opposed to his real nature.

müsemmat مسمط A *poet.* in strophes all of the same meter and with a refrain ending each strophe.

müsemmen مثمن A 1. *poet.* poem in stanzas of eight couplets; couplet of eight feet. 2. *mus.* a rhythmic pattern of eight beats. 3. *geom.* octagon; octangular. 4. *lrnd.* made up of eight parts or elements.

müsemmim مُسَمِّم *A lrnd.* who poisons; poisoning; poisonous.

müsenna (..—) مُثَنَّى *A lrnd.* 1. *gram.* made dual, dualized (word). 2. double-dotted (letter). 3. the third string on an **ud**. 4. doubled, twofold. 5. made up of two parts or elements.

müsennat 1 (..—) مُثَنَّات *A lrnd., pl. of* **müsenna. —ı fevkaniye** the letter ت. **—ı tahtaniye** the letter ى.

müsennat 2 (..—) مُثَنَّات *A lrnd.* dam, dike.

müsennem مُسَنَّم *A lrnd.* 1. shaped like a house roof; raised in a heap or mound; protuberant. 2. depicted in relief.

müsennen مُسَنَّن *A* 1. *lrnd.* serrated, toothed. 2. *anat.* serratus.

müserrec مُسَرَّج *A lrnd.* saddled.

müsevvid مُسَوِّد *A* who writes a rough draft, secretary. **—lik** profession of a secretary who drafts letters.

müseyyeb مُسَيَّب *A lrnd.* reckless; negligent; untidy; devil-may-care (fellow). **—ane** (...—.) P recklessly; carelessly. **—lik** negligence through self-indulgence; untidiness; recklessness.

müseyyef مُسَيَّف *A lrnd.* girt with a sword.

müshil مُسْهِل *A* purgative, laxative.

müs'id مُسْعِد *A lrnd.* that makes one happy and prosperous; liberal; helping.

müsil (.—) مُسِيل *A lrnd.* that causes to flow.

müsim^mmi مُسِمّ *A lrnd.* poisonous.

müsin^nni مُسِنّ *A lrnd.* aged, very old.

müsir (.—) مُثِير *A lrnd.* that excites, incites.

Müsire Suresi سُورَةُ المُثِير *A name of the ninth sura of the Quran.*

müskir مُسْكِر *A lrnd.* intoxicating; intoxicating drink.

müskirat (..—) مُسْكِرَات *A* intoxicants, alcoholic drinks.

müskit مُسْكِت *A* that silences, silencing.

Müslim مُسْلِم *A* Moslem, Muslim, Mohammedan.

Müsliman (..—) مُسْلِمَان *P lrnd., pl. of* **Müslim.**

Müslime مُسْلِمَة *A lrnd.* Muslim woman.

Müslimin, Müslimûn (..—) مُسْلِمِين مُسْلِمُون *A lrnd., pl. of* **Müslim.**

Müslüman مُسْلُمَان [**Müsliman**] 1. a Muslim, Mohammedan. 2. pious. **— Kardeşler** the Moslem Brotherhood. **—ca** (...'.) 1. in a Muslim way. 2. honestly, honorably. **—lık** quality and belief of a Muslim; Islam.

müsmin مُسْمِن *A lrnd.* 1. fat and fleshy. 2. fattening (food, medicine etc.).

müsmir مُثْمِر *A* fruit-bearing, fruitful, productive; successful.

müsned مُسْنَد *A* 1. *gram.* predicate, attribute.

2. *Isl. rel.* uninterruptedly traced to one of the companions of the Prophet Muhammad (apostolic tradition). 3. *lrnd.* Himyaritic character (of script). 4. *lrnd.* made to lean against, to rest or stand on; supported. **—iyet** (..—.) *phil.* imputability.

müsnedünileyh مُسْنَدٌ إِلَيْهِ *A gram.* subject (of a proposition).

müspet مُثْبَت *var. of* **müsbet.**

müsri^ıı مُسْرِع *A lrnd.* that hastens; quickening.

müsrif مُسْرِف *A* extravagant; prodigal; spendthrift. **—ane** (..—.) P extravagantly, lavishly. **—lik** extravagance.

müsta'bid مُسْتَعْبِد *A lrnd.* who enslaves.

müsta'bir مُسْتَعْبِر *A lrnd.* who asks for an interpretation of dreams. **—in** (...—) *A pl.*

müstabki (..—) مُسْتَبْقِى *A lrnd.* who causes to last or remain; who continues, preserves or reserves.

müstabtın مُسْتَبْطِن *A lrnd.* 1. that enters the innermost recesses of a thing; deep-seated. 2. who tries to understand the inner condition or truth of a matter.

müstabzı^ıı مُسْتَبْضِع *A lrnd.* one who gives capital to another for trading on condition that he has part of the profit.

müsta'cel مُسْتَعْجَل *A* required to be done quickly; urgent, pressing (matter). **—en** (.—'..) *A* in haste; urgently.

müstaceliyet مُسْتَعْجَلِيَّة *A* urgency. **— kararı** *law* declaration or vote of urgency.

müsta'cib مُسْتَعْجِب *A lrnd.* who wonders; amazed. **—en** (..'..) *A* wonderingly.

müsta'cil مُسْتَعْجِل *A* who hastens; who asks one to make haste.

müsta'fi (..—) مُسْتَعْفِى *A* 1. one who resigns (an office); resigned. 2. who asks to be pardoned, excused, relieved.

müstagal^ııı مُسْتَغَلّ *A lrnd.* 1. from which a revenue comes (real property). 2. mortgaged.

müstagallât (...—) مُسْتَغَلَّات *A lrnd.* landed property in mortmain from which an income accrues to the trust.

müstagas (..—) مُسْتَغَاث *A lrnd.* called to for aid; invoked.

müstagis (..—) مُسْتَغِيث *A lrnd.* who calls out for help.

müstağfir مُسْتَغْفِر *A lrnd.* who asks for pardon; penitent, repentant.

müstağni (..—) مُسْتَغْنِى *A* /dan/ 1. that has no need; independent, satisfied. 2. disdainful, conceited. **—yane** (..——.) P independently.

müstağrak^kı مُسْتَغْرَق *A lrnd.* 1. completely sunk, overwhelmed; submerged. 2. completely lost (in thought, study, etc.); immersed.

müstağreb مُسْتَغْرَب *A lrnd.* deemed strange, unusual; surprising.

müstağrib مُسْتَغْرِب *A lrnd.* who deems strange

or unusual; who wonders at; amazed. **—ane** (...—.) *P* amazedly. **—in** (...—) *A pl. of* **müstağrib.**

müstağrik[kı] مستغرق *A lrnd.* immersed, plunged; engrossed; absorbed. **—i hûn** immersed in blood. **—i ziya** full of light.

müstahak[kkı] مستحق *A* 1. merited, due. 2. who merits; who has a right or is entitled to a thing; worthy, deserving; entitled to. 3. due reward; punishment; deserts. **—tır** It serves him right. **—ını bul=** to get one's deserts. **— ol=** /a/ to be entitled to; to deserve.

müstaham[mmı] مستحم *A lrnd.* place in which to wash, bath.

müstahber مستخبر *A lrnd.* 1. heard, learned. 2. information received.

müstahberat (...—) مستخبرات *A lrnd.* news or information received.

müstahbir مستخبر *A lrnd.* who inquires, investigates, learns by inquiry.

müstahcer مستحجر *A lrnd.* petrified, turned to stone.

müstahdem مستخدم *A* employed, employee; servant. **—in** (...—) *A pl.* employees, staff; personnel.

müstahdim مستخدم *A lrnd.* who asks another to serve him; who employs a servant, employer.

müstahfaz مستحفظ *A lrnd.* to whom the defense of a place is entrusted.

müstahfız مستحفظ *A* 1. *Ott. hist., mil.* reservist. 2. *lrnd.* who appoints one to defend a place. **—in** (...—) *A pl.* **—lık** service in the reserve.

'müstahfi (..—) مستخفي *A lrnd.* 1. who hides; hidden; clandestine. 2. invisible, imperceptible.

müstahif[ffı] مستخف *A lrnd.* who considers as light; who despises as of no weight; despiser.

müstahib[bbı] مستحب *A lrnd.* 1. who holds an act to be canonically laudable or worthy of love. 2. who holds dear; loving, affectionate.

müstahik[kkı] مستحق *A lrnd., same as* **müstahak.**

müstahil 1 (..—) مستحيل *A lrnd.* who deems absurd; absurd, impossible.

müstahil 2 مستحل *A lrnd.* who deems or pronounces a thing to be canonically lawful.

müstahilât (..——) مستحيلات *A lrnd., pl. of* **müstahil 1,** absurdities, impossibilities.

müstahim[mmı] مستحم *A lrnd.* who bathes himself with hot water, who goes to a hot bath.

müstahkar مستحقر *A lrnd.* looked upon with contempt, contemptible, despised; insignificant.

müstahkem مستحكم *A* 1. fortified; strong to resist. 2. strengthened, consolidated; solid; firm. **— mevki** *mil.* fortified place.

müstahkır مستحقر *A lrnd.* who regards as contemptible; despiser.

müstahlâs مستخلص *A lrnd.* 1. liberated, released, set free. 2. extracted as pure.

müstahleb مستحلب *A lrnd.* drawn by sucking, milking and the like; emulsion.

müstahlef 1 مستخلف *A lrnd.* appointed successor or substitute.

müstahlef 2 مستحلف *A lrnd.* asked to take an oath.

müstahlib 1 مستحلب *A lrnd.* that draws forth a thing by milking, sucking or the like; milker.

müstahlib 2 مستحلب *A lrnd.* that tears with the nails or claws.

müstahlif 1 مستخلف *A lrnd.* who appoints a successor or substitute.

müstahlif 2 مستحلف *A lrnd.* who asks a person to take an oath.

müstahlis مستخلص *A lrnd.* 1. who rescues; deliverer. 2. who extracts as a pure essence.

müstahmil مستحمل *A lrnd.* who carries a burden.

müstahrec مستخرج *A lrnd.* extracted; deducted, inferred.

müstahric مستخرج *A lrnd.* that extracts; who deduces, infers.

müstahsal[lı] مستحصل *A* produced; product. **—ât** (...—) *A pl.*

müstahsen مستحسن *A* 1. *lrnd.* admired, approved; preferred. 2. *mus.* a kind of **ney** that plays the **la/ dügâh** as **fa/ acem.**

müstahsil مستحصل *A* 1. who produces; producer. 2. productive. **— kuvvet** productive capacity.

müstahzar مستحضر *A* 1. ready made drug, preparation. 2. *lrnd.* ready made, prepared. 3. *lrnd.* asked to be present; ordered to be brought.

müstahzarat (...—) مستحضرات *A lrnd.* prepared drugs, medical preparations.

müstahzır مستحضر *A lrnd.* 1. who asks a person to be present, brought. 2. preparer (of ready drugs).

müstaid[ddı] مستعد *A lrnd.* 1. /a/ inclined, disposed to (illness). 2. clever, capable, able. 3. ready, prepared for action.

müstaiddan (...—) مستعدان *P lrnd.* the capable (people).

müstaiddane مستعدانه *P lrnd.* ably, capably.

müstaiddîn مستعدين *A lrnd., pl. of* **müstaid.**

müstain (..—) مستعين *A lrnd.* who asks aid.

müstainen (..—'.) مستعيناً *A lrnd.* depending on one's help.

müstair (..—) مستعير *A lrnd.* 1. who asks a thing as a loan; borrower. 2. who speaks metaphorically.

müstakar[rrı] مستقر *A* 1. permanent dwelling place, settled abode. 2. settled, stationary; confirmed.

müstakbah مستقبح *A lrnd.* disapproved; detestable; abominable.

müstakbel مستقبل *A* 1. future; the future. 2. *gram.* future tense. **—ât** (...—) *A pl.*

müstakbeliyat (...——) مستقبليات A *lrnd.* future events or states.
müstakbih مستقبح A *lrnd.* who regards as ugly or odious.
müstakbil مستقبل A *lrnd.* who advances to meet or greet; who meets. —**in** (...—) A *pl.*
müstakdim مستقدم A *lrnd.* 1. that precedes, leads or outstrips. 2. venturesome, bold.
müstakırʳⁿ مستقر A *lrnd.* 1. settled, stationary, fixed. 2. stable, firm. —**an** (...'.) A firmly, steadily.
müstakısˢˢⁱ مستقص A *lrnd.* who asks one to retaliate; anxious for retaliation.
müstakilˡˡⁱ مستقل A 1. independent; free; apart. 2. *lrnd.* absolutely; solely; expressly. 3. *lrnd.* on purpose.
müstakillen (...'.) مستقلا A 1. independently. 2. absolutely; solely; expressly.
müstakim (..—) مستقيم A 1. straight, direct. 2. upright, honest. — **hat** *geom.* straight line.
müstakimâne (..——.) مستقيمانه P honestly; correctly.
müstakimülcenah (.....—) مستقيم الجناح A *zool.* orthoptera.
müstakraz مستقرض A *econ.* borrowed. —**at** (...—) A borrowed money.
müstakrib مستقرب A *lrnd.* 1. who wishes to approach. 2. who deems near.
müstakriz مستقرض A *lrnd.* who borrows money. —**in** (...—) A *pl.*
müstaksi (..—) مستقصى A *lrnd.* who investigates completely.
müstaktab مستقطب A *phys.* polarized.
müstaktıb مستقطب A *phys.* polarizer.
müstaktır مستقطر A *lrnd.* that distills; that causes to drip.
müstaktil مستقتل A *lrnd.* fearless of death, heroic; seeking to be killed.
müsta'li (..—) مستعلى A *lrnd.* 1. high, exalted, elevated. 2. ascending; overtopping; superior, dominating.
müsta'lim مستعلم A *lrnd.* who asks for information; anxious to know, curious.
müstalki (..—) مستلقى A *lrnd.* lying supine, sleeping on his back.
müsta'mel مستعمل A 1. used, made use of; second hand, old. 2. *lrnd.* employed (especially as collector of taxes). —**ci** *obs.* dealer in second hand wares.
müsta'mer مستعمر A *lrnd.* made to flourish; colonized.
müstamerat (...—) مستعمرات A *lrnd., pl.* of **müstamere**.
müstamere مستعمره A colony. —**ci** colonist.
müsta'mil مستعمل A *lrnd.* who uses, makes use of; user, employer. —**in** (...—) A *pl.*
müsta'mir مستعمر A *lrnd.* who causes to reside or live; colonizer; colonist.

müstankıs مستنقص A *lrnd.* anxious to lower the price of an article (purchaser).
müstansır مستنصر A *lrnd.* who asks for help.
müstantıkᵏⁱ مستنطق A 1. *law* examining magistrate. 2. *lrnd.* who questions. —**lık** state or office of an examining magistrate.
müsta'raz مستعرض A *anat., geol.* transverse.
müsta'reb مستعرب A *lrnd.* who becomes a naturalized Arab; Arabicized.
müsta'rıkᵏⁱ مستعرق A *lrnd.* who perspires, who goes to bed in order to sweat.
müsta'rib مستعرب A *lrnd.*, same as **müsta'reb**.
müstas'ab مستصعب A *lrnd.* accounted difficult; difficult (business).
müstasbah مستصبح A *lrnd.* illuminated.
müstasfi مستصفى A *lrnd.* 1. who deems a thing clear, pure or choice. 2. who chooses, selects or takes the best part or the whole.
müstasgar مستصغر A *lrnd.* deemed small, insignificant.
müstasgır مستصغر A *lrnd.* who deems small, despises; despiser. —**âne** (...—.) P despisingly.
müstashab مستصحب A *lrnd.* 1. held in possession or carried on the person. 2. taken into another's company.
müstashır مستسخر A *lrnd.* who laughs and mocks; mocker, scorner.
müstashib مستصحب A *lrnd.* who takes someone into his company. —**en** (...'.) A accompanying.
müstas'ıb مستصعب A *lrnd.* who regards as difficult.
müsta'sım مستعصم A *lrnd.* who grasps firmly.
müstasveb مستصوب A *lrnd.* approved of.
müstasvib مستصوب A *lrnd.* who regards as reasonable, who approves.
müstatiⁱⁱ (..—) مستطيع A *lrnd.* 1. who consents. 2. able.
müstatil مستطيل A *same as* **mustatil**.
müstatref مستطرف A *lrnd.* 1. deemed new or curious. 2. newly acquired.
müstatrib مستطرب A *lrnd.* 1. that invites to gaiety. 2. who seeks after amusement. —**âne** (...—.) P in a manner of seeking amusement.
müstavzıh مستوضح A *lrnd.* 1. who asks for an explanation. 2. who tries to make manifest.
müstazhir مستظهر A *lrnd.* 1. who leans, relies upon. 2. who implores help; who finds strength or support. —**en** (...'.) A relying upon.
müstazılˡˡⁱ مستظل A *lrnd.* 1. that seeks shade, that is in the shade; shady. 2. who seeks protection or help.
müsta'zım مستعظم A *lrnd.* 1. who regards as great, grand or momentous. 2. who magnifies himself, conceited.
müstaz'if مستضعف A *lrnd.* who accounts one weak or of no account.

müstean (..—) مستعان A lrnd. whose aid is implored; God.

müstear (..—) مستعار A 1. lit. metaphorical, figurative. 2. Or. mus. a compound **makam** composed about three centuries ago. 3. lrnd. temporary. 4. lrnd. asked or obtained as a loan; borrowed.

müsteb'ad مستبعد A regarded as remote or improbable; far-fetched.

müsteban (..—) مستبان A lrnd. made clear; evident, manifest.

müstebdel مستبدل A lrnd. exchanged for.

müstebdi[i] مستبدع A lrnd. who regards as new, original or as an innovation.

müstebdil مستبدل A lrnd. who gives in exchange; who takes as a substitute.

müstebend مستبند P lrnd. sad, sorrowful.

müstebhir مستبحر A lrnd. 1. vast as a sea, widespread. 2. abounding in wealth, learning or eloquence; erudite.

müstebid[ddi] مستبد A same as **müstebit**. —**âne** (...—.) P lrnd. despotic (action, etc.), tyrannically, despotically.

müstebin (..—) مستبين A lrnd. 1. that makes evident, manifests or declares. 2. who investigates in order to make evident; evident.

müstebit[ddi] مستبد [müstebid] 1. despotic, tyrannical; tyrant, despot. 2. who acts alone, absolute in action; independent. —**lik** despotism.

müstebşir مستبشر A lrnd. 1. who rejoices at good news. 2. communicator of good news; who asks a present on announcing a happy event.

müstecab (..—) مستجاب A lrnd. 1. answered, worthy of answer. 2. accepted (request); acceptable, agreeable.

müstecabüddavat[ii] (..—.——) مستجابالدعوات A lrnd. 1. whose prayers are accepted by God. 2. where prayers are accepted (time or place).

müste'cer مستأجر A lrnd. hired, rented.

müstechil مستجهل A lrnd. 1. who considers as ignorant, thinks lightly of, despises. 2. that makes one speak or act frivolously or ignorantly. —**âne** (...—.) P despisingly.

müstecid[ddi] مستجد A lrnd. 1. who renews or renovates. 2. who innovates; innovator.

müste'cir 1 مستأجر A who rents; tenant; hirer.

müstecir 2 (..—) مستجير A lrnd. who implores protection, who takes refuge; suppliant. —**âne** (..——.) P as becomes a suppliant.

müste'ciren (..'..) مستأجرا A lrnd. as a tenant; on lease.

müsteclib مستجلب A lrnd. that draws, attracts, brings or brings about.

müstecmi[ii] مستجمع A lrnd. 1. that collects or asks others to come together. 2. that come together or assemble. 3. collected, quiet (mind).

müsted'a (..—) مستدعى A lrnd. asked for; desired; sought; petitioned; request; petition.

müstedam (..—) مستدام A lrnd. perpetual; continual.

müsted'ayat (..——) مستدعيات A lrnd., pl. of **müsted'a**.

müstedbir مستدبر A lrnd. 1. who turns his back upon, who puts or leaves behind. 2. who looks back at; who sees or understands afterward or too late.

müstedel[lll] مستدل A lrnd. deduced, inferred; convinced by argument.

müsted'i (..—) مستدعى A lrnd. who requests, asks, demands; petitioner; claimant.

müstedim (..—) مستديم A lrnd. that lasts or continues; enduring; continual, perpetual, everlasting.

müstedin (..—) مستدين A lrnd. who asks a loan or borrows.

müstedir (..—) مستدير A lrnd. 1. round, circular, spherical. 2. that circles or circuits.

müstedrik[ki] مستدرك A lrnd. who seeks to understand; perceiver.

müstefad (..—) مستفاد A lrnd. 1. gained, got as profit; received, acquired. 2. inferred, understood.

müstefhem مستفهم A lrnd. wishing to be understood; asked about.

müstefhim مستفهم A lrnd. who seeks to understand, who asks about a thing.

müstefid A, **müstefit**[di] (..—) مستفيد who profits. — **ol=** /dan/ to profit by; to learn from; to enjoy (rights, etc.). —**âne** (..——.) P lrnd. profitingly.

müstefiz (..—) مستفيض A lrnd. who is favored, benefited. — **ol=** to profit, to learn. —**âne** (..——.) P benefitingly.

müstefreşe مستفرشه A lrnd. taken as a concubine (female slave); concubine.

müstefrig مستفرغ A 1. lrnd. who vomits. 2. med. emetic.

müstefsir مستفسر A lrnd. who asks for an explanation or comment; questioning, inquisitive. —**în** (...—) A pl.

müstefti (..—) مستفتى A lrnd. who consults a mufti; who asks a legal opinion.

müsteftih مستفتح A lrnd. 1. that manages to open or conquer. 2. who begins.

müstehab[bbi] مستحب A lrnd. 1. considered to be canonically laudable; approved, desirable. 2. recommended but not enjoined by religious law.

müsteham (..—) مستهام A lrnd. distracted, perplexed, astonished.

müstehan (..—) مستهان A lrnd. despised, despicable; abject, base.

müstehas (..—) مستحاث A geol. fossilized. —**at** (..——) A 1. fossils. 2. paleontology.

Red 53.

müstehase (..—.) ستحاث A *lrnd.* fossil.
müstehcen مستهجن A 1. obscene. 2. *lrnd.* loathed, loathsome.
müstehcin ستهجن A *lrnd.* who loathes, abhors.
müstehdi (..—) مستهدى A *lrnd.* who asks for guidance, who seeks direction.
müstehdif مستهدف A *lrnd.* upright, erect.
müstehlek^ki مستهلك A *lrnd.* consumed, wasted.
müstehlik^ki مستهلك A *lrnd.* consuming, consumer.
müstehzi (..—) مستهزى A who jeers, mocks; jeering, mocking, sarcastic, ironical. —yane (..——.) P sarcastically, ironically.
müstekbir ستكبر A *lrnd.* proud, haughty. —âne (...—.) P proudly, haughtily. —în (...—) A *pl.*
müstekin^nni ستكن A *lrnd.* that seeks to hide himself; hidden.
müstekinne ستكنة A *lrnd.* 1. hidden, hiding. 2. hidden hate, rancor, hatred.
müstekmel ستكمل A *lrnd.* completed, perfect.
müstekmil ستكمل A *lrnd.* seeker after perfection; who completes, perfects.
müstekra (..—) ستكرى A *lrnd.* hired, rented.
müstekreh ستكره A disgusting; loathsome, abominable.
müstekri (..—) ستكرى A *lrnd.* who hires or rents, renter.
müstekrih ستكره A *lrnd.* who loathes, abominates, is disgusted.
müsteksir ستكثر A *lrnd.* who deems many or much; who considers something to be too much.
müstekşif ستكشف A *lrnd.* who seeks to discover, desirous of uncovering.
müstelez^zzi ستلذ A *lrnd.* savory, relishable, pleasant. —ât (...—) A delicacies.
müsteliz^zzi ستلذ A *lrnd.* who relishes.
müstelzim ستلزم A *lrnd.* 1. who deems necessary. 2. which necessitates; requiring, exacting.
müste'men ستأمن A *lrnd.* to whom application is made for safety, quarter or amnesty.
müstemend ستمند P *lrnd.* sad, humble; unhappy, afflicted; poor. —âne (...—.) P wretchedly, humbly.
müstemhil ستمهل A *lrnd.* who asks for delay, respite.
müstemi^ii ستمع A *lrnd.* 1. who hears; who listens; listener, hearer. 2. who learns by oral instruction. —în (...—) A *pl.*
müstemid^ddi ستمد A *lrnd.* who asks for help; petitioner for aid against an enemy. —âne (...—.) P in a manner of asking for help.
müste'min ستأمن A 1. *lrnd.* who applies for safety, quarter or amnesty. 2. *Ott. hist.* alien in the Ottoman dominions.
müstemir^rri ستمر A *lrnd.* continual, perpetual, long; lasting, constant; firm, solid. —ren (...'.) A perpetually.
müstemlek^ki ستملك A *lrnd.* taken into possession.
müstemlekât (...—) ستملكات A *pl.* of müstemleke.
müstemleke ستملكة A colony.
müstemli (..—) ستملى A *lrnd.* who asks one to write.
müstemti^ii ستمتع A *lrnd.* 1. one who has the benefit of a thing; who enjoys an advantage. 2. who being at Mecca for the great pilgrimage is able also to perform the lesser.
müstenbat ستنبط A *lrnd.* 1. reached, got at, brought to light. 2. inferred.
müstenbi (..—) ستنبى A *lrnd.* who asks for information.
müstened ستند A *lrnd.* 1. leaned upon, relied on. 2. authority relied on.
müstenfir ستنفر A *lrnd.* that runs away in fright; who shuns, avoids.
müstenid ستند A *lrnd.* that leans upon, rests upon; relying upon, based on. —en (.'..) A /a/ relying (on), based (on).
müste'nif ستأنف A 1. *law* who appeals, appellant (in a law suit). 2. *lrnd.* that begins; that begins again.
müste'nifünaleyh ستأنف عليه A *law* defendant; appellee.
müstenim (..—) ستنيم A *lrnd.* who feigns sleep; who sleeps.
müstenir (..—) ستنير A *lrnd.* who seeks for light, illuminated.
müste'nis ستأنس A *lrnd.* accustomed, habituated; familiar; tamed (wild beast).
müstenkcr ستنكر A *lrnd.* denied; ignored.
müstenkif ستنكف A who refuses or holds back from; abstainer. — kal= to hold back from; to abstain.
müstenkir ستنكر A *lrnd.* who ignores, denies.
müstensih ستنسخ A 1. who makes a copy; transcriber. 2. copying press; hectograph.
müstenşık^kı ستنشق A *lrnd.* who snuffs up into his nostrils.
müstenşid ستنشد A *lrnd.* who asks one to compose or recite a poem.
müstentic ستنتج A *lrnd.* that brings about a result.
müsterah (..—) ستراح A *lrnd.* 1. place of comfort or rest. 2. lavatory, privy.
müsterak^kı ستراق A *lrnd.* stolen; embezzled.
müsterca 1 (..—) سترجا A *lrnd.* hoped or asked for.
müsterca^aı 2 سترجع A *lrnd.* demanded back.
müsterci 1 (..—) سترجى A *lrnd.* who hopes or asks for.
müsterci^ii 2 سترجع A *lrnd.* w. o asks for a gift or loan to be returned to him.

müsteredddi مسترّد A *lrnd.* demanded back; revoked; recalled.

müsterfih مسترفه A *lrnd.* who takes his ease; who seeks comfort.

müsterha (..—) مسترخا مسترخى A *lrnd.* relaxed; loose.

müsterham مسترحم A *lrnd.* implored, begged.

müsterhis مسترخص A *lrnd.* who considers a price cheap.

müsterhi (..—) مسترخى A *lrnd.* 1. hanging loosely. 2. relaxed, flabby; easy.

müsterhim مسترحم A *lrnd.* who asks God's mercy; who humbly asks a favor.

müsterhin مسترهن A *lrnd.* who asks a pledge or hostage; pawn-broker.

müsterih مستريح A resting, at ease; at rest. **—âne** (..——.) P calmly.

müsterşi (..—) مسترشى A *lrnd.* who demands a bribe. **—yane** (..——.) P in the manner of a bribeseeker.

müsterşid مسترشد A *lrnd.* who seeks the right way, who finds the right road. **—âne** (...—.) P in the manner of a seeker of the right way. **—în** (...—) A *pl.*

müsterzel مسترذل A *lrnd.* treated as mean and vile; rejected, disapproved.

müsterzil مسترذل A *lrnd.* who renders vile; who considers or finds contemptible.

müstes'ad مستسعد A *lrnd.* deemed auspicious or lucky; rendered happy, favored, gratified.

müste'salˡˡ مستأصل A *lrnd.* uprooted, eradicated; totally destroyed.

müsteshil مستسهل A *lrnd.* who considers as smooth or easy. **—âne** (...—.) P deeming smooth and easy.

müstes'id مستسعد A *lrnd.* 1. who considers auspicious or lucky. 2. who asks for help. 3. desirous of happiness.

müste'sil مستأصل A *lrnd.* that uproots, that totally destroys, extirpator.

müstesinⁿⁿⁱ مستسن A *lrnd.* 1. travelled (road). 2. who keeps to a right course. 3. who becomes old; aged.

müsteskalˡˡ مستثقل A *lrnd.* regarded as disagreeable; received coldly.

müsteski (..—) مستسقى A *lrnd.* 1. dropsical. 2. who asks for a drink; who prays for rain.

müsteskil مستثقل A *lrnd.* 1. who considers a thing heavy, disagreeable, or unbearable. 2. who treats coldly. **—âne** (...—.) P in a cold manner; rudely.

müsteslim مستسلم A *lrnd.* resigned, submissive; humble.

müstesna مستثنى مستثنا A 1. excluded, excepted; except; exception. 2. extraordinarily, exceptional. **— evkaf** *Ott. hist.* independent estates in mortmain not subject to State control. **— eyaletler** *Ott. hist.* provinces exempted from the general rules of taxation and control.

müstesni (..—) مستثنى A *lrnd.* who makes an exception from a general rule.

müsteşar (..—) مستشار A permanent undersecretary of a ministry; councillor. **—î** (..——) P *lrnd.*, **—lık** *abstr. n.*

müsteşfi 1 (..—) مستشفى A *lrnd.* who seeks a cure.

müsteşfiˡˡ **2** مستشفع A *lrnd.* who asks another to intercede.

müsteşhed مستشهد A *lrnd.* 1. asked to be a witness or to give evidence. 2. cited in proof (document). **—at** (...—) A *pl.* things proved.

müsteşhid مستشهد A *lrnd.* 1. who asks one to witness or give evidence. 2. who cites proof.

müsteşrif مستشرف A *lrnd.* 1. who looks attentively; who takes a view of. 2. /a/ on the verge of; inclined to.

müsteşrikᵏⁱ مستشرق A orientalist. **—în** (...—) A *lrnd.*, *pl.*

müstetab (..—) مستطاب A *lrnd.* approved; pleasant, agreeable.

müstetemᵐᵐⁱ مستتم A *lrnd.* full, completed, perfect.

müstetıbᵇᵇⁱ مستطب A *lrnd.* who asks for a prescription or remedy from a physician.

müstetimᵐᵐⁱ مستتم A *lrnd.* 1. who makes full, completes. 2. who asks for a thing to be completed or perfected.

müstetir مستتر A *lrnd.* veiled, concealed; hidden.

müstevcib مستوجب A *lrnd.* 1. which necessitates, causes. 2. meriting, proper, worthy of.

müstevdaᵃˡ مستودع A *com.* 1. committed for safe keeping; deposited. 2. depositary, depositee, bailee. **—at** (...—) A *pl.* deposits.

müstevdiˡˡ مستودع A *com.* who entrusts for safekeeping; depositor, depositary.

müstevfa (..—) مستوفا A *lrnd.* received in full or made full, ample.

müstevfi (..—) مستوفى A *lrnd.* 1. who receives or pays in full. 2. sufficient, ample to cover outlay.

müstevhiş مستوحش A *lrnd.* 1. who finds a place lonely, wild; who feels lonely; alienated. 2. frightened, afraid.

müstevi (..—) مستوى A 1. level, uniform. 2. *geom.* plane. 3. *Arabic gram.* of common gender. **—yen** (..—´.) A *lrnd.* uniformly, equally.

müstev'ib مستوعب A *lrnd.* 1. containing or covering the whole. 2. who extirpates.

müstevkiˡˡ مستوقع A *lrnd.* who expects; expectant; sustained by hope.

müstevli مستولى A 1. that overcomes or

invades; invading; invader. 2. spreading over; predominant, prevalent, epidemic.

müsteykın ستيقن A *lrnd.* who feels sure of a matter.

müsteykız ستيقظ A *lrnd.* awake, watchful, vigilant.

müstezad (..—) مستزاد 1. *pros.* having a supplement to each couplet or line (poem). 2. *lrnd.* increased, supplemented.

müstezak^{kı} (..—) مستذاب A *lrnd.* 1. tasted; tried and liked. 2. known from experience.

müstezil^{lli} مستذل A *lrnd.* 1. who renders submissive or abject. 2. who despises.

müste'zin مستأذن A *lrnd.* who asks permission.

müstezkir مستذكر A *lrnd.* who remembers, recollects.

müsûl^{lü} (.—) مثول A *lrnd.* 1. a standing respectfully (before a superior). 2. a resembling; resemblance.

müsveddat (..—) مسودات A *lrnd.*, pl. of **müsvedde**.

müsvedde مسوده A 1. rough copy, draft. 2. manuscript for a printer. 3. *slang* imbecile, simpleton. **—lik** paper for rough drafts.

=müş 1 مش *cf.* =mış 1.
=müş 2 مش *cf.* =mış 2.

müşa^{aı} (.—) مشاع A 1. *law* owned in common, undivided. 2. *lrnd.* spread, made known to everyone (rumor etc.).

müşaabe (.—..) مشاعبه A *lrnd.* 1. a staying aloof. 2. a departing, dying. **—et=** to depart.

müşaare (.—..) مشاعره A *lrnd.* a contending or excelling in poetry; poetic contest. **—et=** to contend in poetry.

müşabehet (.—..) مشابهت A 1. resemblance; analogy. 2. *chem.* homology.

müşabih (.—.) مشابه A /a/ like, similar, resembling.

müşacere (.—..) مشاجره A *lrnd.* a contending together, disputing; controversy. **—et=** to struggle, dispute.

müşafehat (.—.—) مشافهات A *lrnd.*, pl. of **müşafehe**.

müşafehe (.—..) مشافهه A *lrnd.* a conversing together. **—et=** to converse together.

müşafih (.—.) مشافه A *lrnd.* who converses with another face to face.

müşagabe (.—..) مشاغبه A 1. *lrnd.* a brawling; a squabbling, raising tumults; brawl. 2. *phil.* eristic.

müşahed (.—.) مشاهد A *lrnd.* seen; observed.

müşahedat (.—.—) مشاهدات A *lrnd.*, pl. of **müşahede**. **—ı gaybiye** sights of spiritual mysteries.

müşahede (.—..) مشاهده A 1. a seeing, beholding, witnessing; sight, vision, contemplation; an observing; observation; an experiencing a thing. 2. *myst.* the highest degree of perfection in contemplating the divine essence; revelation. **—altında** subject to medical observation. **—et=** /ı/ to see, witness, observe.

müşahere (.—..) مشاهره A *lrnd.* a hiring or contracting by the month, a paying monthly; monthly wages.

müşahereten (.—.'..) مشاهرة A *lrnd.* by the month, monthly.

müşahhas مشخص A 1. personified, identified; individually perceived. 2. *phil.* concrete. 3. *lrnd.* recognized, acknowledged; specified.

müşahhasât (...—) مشخصات A *lrnd.* the sciences.

müşahhıs مشخص A *lrnd.* 1. observer; distinguisher. 2. skilled in diagnosis; diagnostician.

müşahid A, **müşahit**^{di} (.—.) مشاهد A *lrnd.* 1. who sees, beholds; spectator. 2. observer.

müşakele, müşakelet (.—..) مشاكله A *lrnd.* 1. a being of the same form, similarity; resemblance. 2. a variety of metaphor where a word is used consecutively once in a natural and once in a figurative sense.

müşakil (.—.) مشاكل A *lrnd.* of the same form, similar; resembling.

müşar (.—) مشار A *lrnd.* indicated, signified.

müşarata (.—..) مشارطه A *lrnd.* a making conditions, a stipulating with each other. **—et=** to stipulate.

müşarebe (.—..) مشاربه A *lrnd.* a drinking together. **—et=** to drink together.

müşarefe مشارفه A *lrnd.* 1. a being or becoming near; proximity. 2. a contending together for nobility or distinction.

müşareket (.—..) مشاركت A 1. *gram.* reciprocal form of the verb. 2. *lrnd.* a being partner or participant with another; partnership; participation. **—i ihsasat** *psych.* synesthesia. **—et=** to be a partner with one another, participate.

müşareze, müşarezet (.—..) مشارضت A *lrnd.* 1. a picking a quarrel. 2. a showing bad temper. **—et=** to quarrel.

müşarik^{ki} مشارك A *lrnd.* who participates; participant; associate, partner.

müşarileyh (.—..) مشاراليه A *lrnd.*, same as **müşarünileyh**.

müşariz (.—.) مشارض A *lrnd.* who quarrels; who shows bad temper, ill-disposed.

müşarünbilbenan (.—...—) مشارباليبنان A *lrnd.* (lit., pointed out with the finger) noted, celebrated.

müşarünbilenamil (.—...—.) مشاراالأنامل A *lrnd.*, same as **müşarünbilbenan**.

müşarünileyh (.—...) مشاراليه A *lrnd.* the aforesaid, aforementioned (used for high officials and celebrities).

müşa'şa⁰¹ مُشَعْشَع A lrnd. brilliant, shining; gorgeous, splendid.
müşatara, müşataret (.—..) مُشاطرة • مُشاطَرَت A lrnd. a going halves with another; halving. **— et=** to halve something with someone.
müşateme (.—..) مُشاتَمَة A lrnd. a reviling or abusing one another.
müşatır (.—.) مُشاطِر A lrnd. who shares by halves.
müşavere, müşaveret مُشاوَرَة • مُشاوَرَت A mutual consultation, deliberation; council, conference.
müşavir (.—.) مُشاوِر A who counsels, is counselled; councilor; consultant; adviser. **—lik** the rank and office of a councilor.
müşayaa (.—..) مُشايَعَة A lrnd. 1. a following and overtaking. 2. a conforming to, agreeing with. 3. an accompanying a departing traveller to see him off. **— et=** /a/ to escort, accompany a departing guest.
müşbi⁰¹ مُشْبِع A chem. saturating; saturant.
=müşçesine مُشْجَسِنَه cf. **=mışçasına**.
müşebba⁰¹ مُشْبَع A 1. lrnd. satisfied, full. 2. chem. saturated.
müşebbeh مُشَبَّه A 1. lrnd. compared, likened; like, resembling. 2. rhet. the unnamed object intended to be understood in a figurative comparison.
müşebbehe مُشَبِّهَة A lrnd. anthropomorphism.
müşebbehünbih مُشَبَّهٌ بِه A rhet. the thing named in a figurative comparison to represent something not named.
müşebbehünfih مُشَبَّهٌ فِيه A rhet. that to which a thing is likened in a simile.
müşebbekᵏⁱ مُشَبَّك A lrnd. 1. reticulated, like a net or lattice-work. 2. same as **muşabak**.
müşeccer مُشَجَّر A lrnd. 1. written characters formed in the shape of a tree. 2. figured with trees and leaves (garment). 3. poem written in the shape of a tree.
müşedded مُشَدَّد A 1. Arabic gram. doubled (consonant), geminated. 2. lrnd. made strong; made tight, firm; increased in violence.
müşeddid مُشَدِّد A lrnd. increasing the violence; reinforcing, aggravating.
müşeddide مُشَدِّدَة A phys. amplifier.
müşehhi مُشَهِّي A lrnd. 1. that gives appetite. 2. lust-exciting.
müşekkekᵏⁱ مُشَكَّك A lrnd. thrown into doubt.
müşekkel مُشَكَّل A lrnd. 1. well shaped; of imposing form; beautiful, handsome. 2. huge.
müşemmes مُشَمَّس A lrnd. exposed to the sun, sunned.
müşemmis مُشَمِّس A lrnd. 1. who exposes a thing to the sun. 2. who worships the sun.
müşennef مُشَنَّف A lrnd. adorned with earrings.
müşerref مُشَرَّف A honored, exalted. **— ol=** to be honored, to feel honored and proud. **— oldum** I am glad to meet you.
müşerrih مُشَرِّح A 1. who expounds, explains, annotates; commentator. 2. anatomist, dissector.
müşevvekᵏⁱ مُشَوَّك A lrnd. thorny.
müşevveş مُشَوَّش A lrnd. confused, dubious (matter); perplexed. **—iyet** (...—.) A confusion.
müşevvikᵏⁱ مُشَوِّق A that incites; inciting; encouraging; instigator, provoker.
müşeyyed مُشَيَّد A lrnd. 1. strongly built with lime mortar, strongly cemented. 2. high (edifice).
müşeyyid مُشَيِّد A lrnd. who builds and strengthens.
müşezzeb مُشَذَّب A lrnd. 1. lopped, pruned. 2. tall and comely, well proportioned.
müşfikᵏⁱ مُشْفِق A tenderly or compassionately kind; tender, compassionate.
müşfikane (..—.) مُشْفِقانَه P tenderly, kindly.
müşhid مُشْهِد A lrnd. who calls a witness; who brings evidence.
müş'ir 1 مُشْعِر A 1. mech. index, pointer. 2. lrnd. pointing out, marking, informing.
müşir 2 (.—) مُشير A 1. mil. obs., same as **müşür**. 2. lrnd. who makes a sign or signal; that points out, indicates; indicative.
müşirân (.——) مُشيران P mil. field marshals.
müşirâne (.——.) مُشيرانَه P lrnd. special to a **müşir**.
müş'ire مُشْعِرَة A mech. dial, scale (of a pressure gauge etc.).
müşiriyet (.——.) مُشيريَّت A mil. rank and position of a field marshal.
müşkᵏᵘ مُشك P musk.
müşkâlûd (.——) مُشك آلود P lrnd. musky; full of musk.
müşkbar (.—) مُشك بار P lrnd. diffusing musk.
müşkbid (.—) مُشك بيد P lrnd. flower of the willow, Egyptian willow.
müşkbû (.—) مُشك بو P lrnd. 1. musk-scented; musky. 2. fragrant.
müşkdem مُشك دم P lrnd. black songbird.
müşkefşan (..—) مُشك افشان P lrnd. 1. diffusing musk. 2. fragrant.
=müşken (.'.) مُشكن cf. **=mışken**.
müşkfam (.—) مُشك فام P lrnd. musk-colored, black.
müşkfüruş (..—) مُشك فروش P lrnd. 1. seller of musk; perfumer. 2. polite, amiable person; agreeable speaker.
müşkî (.—) مُشكى P lrnd. 1. musky. 2. dark-colored.
müşkil مُشكل A same as **müşkül**.
müşkilât (..—) مُشكلات A 1. difficulties. 2. doubts.
müşkile مُشكله A lrnd. 1. difficulty. 2. doubt.

müşkilküşa (...—) مشکل کشا P *lrnd.* solver of difficulties. **—î** (...— —) P, **—lık** (...—.) *lrnd.* the solving, overcoming or removing of difficulties.

müşkilpesend مشکل پسند P same as **müşkülpesent**. **—ân** (....—) P *pl.* **—âne** (....—.) P fastidiously; in a manner of making difficulties.

müşkilter مشکلتر P *lrnd.* very difficult. **—în** (...—) P most difficult.

müşkin (.—) مشکین P *lrnd.* 1. musky. 2. dark; black. **—i vefadar** wild rose, sweet briar. **—cu** (.— —), **—çah** (.— —), **—hal** (.— —) P mole on the face of a beauty.

müşkinhitam (.—.—) مشکین ختام P *lrnd.* of a musky flavor (wine).

müşkinkülâh (.—.—) مشکین کلاه P *lrnd.* dark hair of a beauty.

müşkinmühre (.—..) مشکین مهره P *lrnd.* the earth.

müşkinsinan (.—.—) مشکین سنان P *lrnd.* (*lit.*, black spear head) eyelash of a beauty.

müşksar (.—) مشک سار P *lrnd.* perfumed with musk, musky.

müşkû (.—) مشکو P *lrnd.* 1. palace; the female apartments in a palace. 2. *w. cap.*, *name of the palace built for Shirin by Khusrau Parviz*.

müşkül مشکل A 1. difficult, hard; difficulty. 2. doubtful, obscure.

müşkülât (..—) مشکلات A difficulties; intricacies; doubts. **— çıkar=** to raise difficulties.

müşküle (..'.) مشکله a kind of grapes (ripening in late autumn). **— üzümü** same as **müşküle**.

müşkülleş=ir مشکلاشمک to become difficult. **—tir=** /ı/ *caus.*

müşkülpesentdi مشکل پسند [müşkilpesend] one who is fond of difficulties, hard to please; fastidious; exacting.

müşmeiz مشمئز A *lrnd.* disgusted.

müşrefiye مشرفیه A *arch.* moucharaby; projecting oriel window or enclosed balcony.

müşrif مشرف A *lrnd.* 1. high, overlooking; overhanging. 2. on the point of, near; on the verge of. **—i harab** on the point of falling down (building).

müşrikki 1 مشرک A 1. who attributes a partner or partners to God; syntheist. 2. who believes in a plurality of Gods; polytheist; pagan.

müşrikki 2 مشرق A *lrnd.* 1. shining brightly. 2. rising (sun etc.).

müşrikîn (..—) مشرکین A syntheists; polytheists.

müşriklikği مشرکلک syntheism; polytheism.

müşrikûn (..—) مشرکون A same as **müşrikîn**. **=müşse** مشسع *cf.* **=mışsa**.

müşt مشت P *lrnd.*, same as **muşt** 1.

müştagil مشتغل A *lrnd* /la/ occupied, busy.

müştail مشتعل A *lrnd.* 1. burning with a flame; blazing, flaming. 2. inflammable.

müştakkı 1 (.—) مشتاق A /a/ filled with desire, longing, pining.

müştakkkı 2 مشتق A which derives, which branches off; derived; *gram.*, *math.* derivative.

müştakane (.— —.) مشتاقانه P *lrnd.* desirous of seeing, longing; longingly.

müştakkat (..—) مشتقات A *lrnd.*, *pl. of* **müştak 2**.

müştebih مشتبه A *lrnd.* 1. doubtful, ambiguous; intricate. 2. whose canonical lawfulness is uncertain.

müştebihât (...—) مشتبهات A *lrnd.* doubtful things especially those whose canonical lawfulness is doubtful.

müştebikki مشتبک A *lrnd.* interlaced, interlacing; intricate.

müştedddi مشتد A *lrnd.* waxed strong, violent, severe.

müşteha (..—) مشتها A *lrnd.* longed for with appetite, desired; desirable. **—yât** (..— —) A things longed for.

müştehi (..—) مشتهی A 1. that has an appetite or desire; who desires, longs for. 2. appetizing; tonic. **—yât** (..— —) A desires, wishes, appetites.

müştehir مشتهر A *lrnd.* publicly known, famous; named, called.

müştekâ (..—) مشتکی A *lrnd.* one complained of.

müşteki مشتکی A who complains; complainant. **—yâne** (...—.) P complainingly.

müştemel مشتمل A *lrnd.* contained, comprised.

müştemelât (...—) مشتملات A 1. contents; things of which a thing consists. 2. outhouses, annexes.

müştemil مشتمل A *lrnd.* which contains, containing; comprising. **—ât** (...—) A same as **müştemelât**.

müştera (..—) مشتری A bought, purchased.

müşterekki مشترک A 1. common, shared by several. 2. cooperative. 3. *math.* commensurable. **— bahis** *horse race* parimutuel. **— borçlu** *law* co-debtor. **— duvar** *law* wall common to' two houses, party-wall. **— hâkimiyet** *law* condominium; joint ownership. **— harekât** *mil.* combined operation. **— hukuk** common law. **— mülkiyet** *law* co-ownership. **— sigorta** *com.* joint insurance.

müştereken (..'..) مشترکاً A in common; jointly.

müşteri 1 مشتری A 1. customer, purchaser; buyer; client. 2. *lrnd.* desirous (for), interested (in), open (to). **— avla=** to try to attract customers by artifice.

Müşteri 2 مشتری A *astr.* Jupiter.

müşterik^{ki} مُشْتَرَك A lrnd. who owns a thing in common with others; sharer. —en (..´..) A by sharing. —în (...—) A pl. of müşterik.
=müştü (.´.) مُشدى cf. =mıştı.
=müşük 1 (.´.) شُلك cf. =mışık 1.
-müşük 2 (.´.) شُلك cf. -mışık 2.
-müşün 1, -müşünüz 1 (.´..) شُلك مُشَك cf. -mışın 1.
-müşün 2, -müşünüz 2 (.´..) شُلك مُشَك cf. -mışın 2.
müşür شُيِر [müşir 2] field marshal.
müt'a مُطْعَة A lrnd. 1. kind of temporary marriage practiced among Shi'i Muslims. 2. can. law present given to a divorced wife in addition to the stipulated dower. 3. advantage, benefit.
[Note: mütaa- (..—) see mütea-]
mütabaat^{tı} مُتَابَعَت A lrnd. 1. a following, imitating. 2. a conforming oneself to, submitting, obeying; conformity, obedience. — et= /a/ to imitate, obey.
mütabi^{iı} (..—.) مُتَابِع A lrnd. that follows; follower; following, succeeding. —în (.—.—) A pl.
mütacere, mütaceret (.—..) مُتَاجَرَت A lrnd. a trading; trade, commerce. — et= to engage in commerce, trade.
mütahattır مُتَخَطِّر A lrnd. 1. that occurs to the mind. 2. who remembers.
mütalâa (..—..) مُطَالَعَة A 1. a reading, studying; study. 2. observation, remark; opinion. — et= /ı/ to read, study.
mütalâat (..—.—) مُطَالَعَات A lrnd., pl. of mütalâa.
mütareke (.—..) مُتَارَكَه A 1. truce, armistice. 2. lrnd. a mutually abandoning, giving up.
mütarik^{kı} (.—.) مُتَارِك A lrnd. 1. who leaves, abandons by mutual action. 2. who abandons warfare by a truce with another; trucemaker.
mütasaıb مُتَصَعِّب A lrnd. which becomes difficult.
mütasyon مُتَاسْيُون F biol. mutation.
müteabbed مُتَعَبَّد A lrnd. place of worship.
müteabbid مُتَعَبِّد A lrnd. devout, constant in divine worship; worshipper. —âne (....—.) P devoutly. —în (....—) A pl. of müteabbid.
müteabbis مُتَعَبِّس A lrnd. frowning, morose, austere. —âne (....—.) P frowningly. —în (.....—) A pl.
müteaccib مُتَعَجِّب A lrnd. astonished, amazed. —âne (....—.) P in astonishment, amazedly.
müteaccil مُتَعَجِّل A lrnd. who makes haste, hasty. —âne (....—.) P hastily. —în (....—) A pl. of müteaccil.
müteaccin مُتَعَجِّن A lrnd. that becomes like dough.
müteaddi مُتَعَدِّي A 1. gram. transitive, active. 2. lrnd. aggressive.

müteaddid مُتَعَدِّد A numerous, many; several.
müteadi (..—.) مُتَعَادِي A lrnd. mutually hostile and aggressive.
müteadil (..—.) مُتَعَادِل A lrnd. 1. mutually equal; parallel to each other. 2. mutually just.
müteaffif مُتَعَفِّف A lrnd. who abstains from sin; chaste, incorruptible.
müteaffin مُتَعَفِّن A rotten and fetid; putrid; stinking.
müteahhid مُتَعَهِّد A 1. same as müteahhit. 2. lrnd. who has undertaken to do something; engaging in, undertaking. —âne (....—.) P lrnd. like a contractor. —în (....—) A lrnd., pl. of müteahhid.
müteahhir مُتَأَخِّر A lrnd. 1. subsequent; latest, last. 2. modern, man of the modern times.
müteahhirîn, müteahhirûn (....—) مُتَأَخِّرِين مُتَأَخِّرُون A lrnd. the moderns, modern men.
müteahhit^{di} مُتَعَهِّد [müteahhid] contractor, surveyor.
müteahid (..—.) مُتَعَاهِد A lrnd. mutually bound by contract or treaty; confederate; contractor.
müteakıb (..—.) مُتَعَاقِب A 1. following on each other's heels, successive; subsequent upon. 2. /ı/ following immediately after.
müteakıben (..—´..) مُتَعَاقِبًا A lrnd. subsequently; successively.
müteakkid مُتَعَقِّد A lrnd. 1. fastened together, tied, knotted. 2. congealed; concreted.
müteakkıl مُتَعَقِّل A lrnd. who conceives in the mind, comprehends; intelligent, wise. —âne (....—.) P intelligently, wisely.
müteakkis مُتَعَكِّس A lrnd. reflected, inverted.
müteâl^{li} (..—) مُتَعَال A ❋1. phil. transcendent. 2. lrnd. supreme, high (God).
müteali (..—.) مُتَعَالِي A lrnd. 1. high, lofty, exalted. 2. transcendental.
müatealim (..—.) مُتَعَالِم A lrnd. 1. known to each other. 2. known of all.
müatealli مُتَعَلِّي A lrnd. 1. high, exalted. 2. mounting, ascending.
müteallik^{kı} مُتَعَلِّق A /a/ dependent upon, connected with; related, concerning; gram. dependent (of a verb).
müteallikat (....—) مُتَعَلِّقَات A 1. lrnd. children; family, relatives. 2. gram. dependencies. 3. accessories.
müteallil مُتَعَلِّل A lrnd. 1. who amuses himself to pass the time; who delays action. 2. who makes a pretext.
müteallim مُتَعَلِّم A lrnd. who studies; taught, instructed; learner, student, scholar; learned. —âne (....—.) P in a scholarly manner. —în (....—) A students.
müteami (..—.) مُتَعَامِي A lrnd. who feigns

müteamil

blindness, who pretends not to see. —**yâne** (..—.—.) P feigning blindness.

müteamil (..—.) مُتَعَامِل A 1. customary, usual. 2. *lrnd.* having relations with each other; transacting business with one another.

müteammid مُتَعَمِّد A *lrnd.* 1. who acts intentionally, deliberately. 2. who resolves; resolved. —**âne** (....—.) P intentionally, deliberately. —**în** (....—) A *pl.* of **müteammid**.

müteammikᵏⁱ مُتَعَمِّق A *lrnd.* that probes into the depths; entering deeply into a matter.

müteammim مُتَعَمِّم A general, in common use; current.

müteanni مُتَأَنِّي A *lrnd.* who takes trouble; worried; tired, fatigued. —**yane** (....—.) P worriedly.

müteannid مُتَعَنِّد A *lrnd.* obstinate, stubborn. —**âne** (....—.) P stubbornly. —**în** (....—) A *pl.* of **müteannid**.

müteannit مُتَعَنِّت A *lrnd.* who finds fault; who seeks the humiliation of another.

mütearız (..—.) مُتَعَارِض A *lrnd.* opposed to each other, contrary; conflicting, contradictory.

mütearif (..—.) مُتَعَارِف A *lrnd.* 1. acquainted with one another. 2. well-known.

mütearife (..—..) مُتَعَارِفَه A *lrnd.* axiom.

mütearrız مُتَعَرِّض A that opposes or attacks; attacking; aggressive; aggressor.

mütearrib مُتَعَرِّب A *lrnd.* 1. who becomes an Arab. 2. who adopts the life of a nomad Arab.

mütearrif مُتَعَرِّف A *lrnd.* 1. who seeks to know. 2. known.

mütearris مُتَعَرِّس A *lrnd.* fond of his wife.

müteasir (..—.) مُتَعَاسِر A *lrnd.* difficult, hard.

müteassıb مُتَعَصِّب A same as **mutaassıb**.

müteassım مُتَعَصِّم A *lrnd.* 1. who holds tight. 2. protected, kept safe.

müteassif مُتَأَسِّف A *lrnd.* 1. that goes astray. 2. who acts inconsiderately or with violence.

müteassir مُتَعَسِّر A *lrnd.* hard, difficult; arduous.

müteaşir (..—.) مُتَعَاشِر A *lrnd.* consorting with each other; intimate, familiar.

müteaşşikᵏⁱ مُتَعَشِّق A *lrnd.* 1. in love. 2. who feigns to be in love.

müteatıf (..—.) مُتَعَاطِف A *lrnd.* mutually kind, affectionate.

müteati (..—.) مُتَعَاطِي A *lrnd.* who exchange things with each other.

müteattıf مُتَعَطِّف A *lrnd.* favorably inclined. —**âne** (....—.) P favorably.

müteattıl مُتَعَطِّل A *lrnd.* idle, unemployed.

müteattır مُتَعَطِّر A *lrnd.* perfumed; highly scented.

müteavin (..—.) مُتَعَاوِن A *lrnd.* helping each other.

müteavvız مُتَعَوِّض A *lrnd.* who takes in lieu of.

müteavvic مُتَعَوِّج A *lrnd.* bent, crooked, curved.

müteavvid مُتَعَوِّد A *lrnd.* accustomed, habituated.

müteavvikᵏⁱ مُتَعَوِّق A *lrnd.* hindered, impeded.

müteavviz مُتَعَوِّذ A *lrnd.* who seeks shelter, who takes refuge.

müteayyib مُتَعَيِّب A *lrnd.* 1. faulty. 2. who considers faulty, reproacher, accuser.

müteayyin مُتَعَيِّن A *lrnd.* 1. manifest, visible; determined, fixed. 2. distinguished, conspicuous.

müteayyiş مُتَعَيِّش A *lrnd.* who manages to sustain himself; supported by his own industry.

müteazid (..—.) مُتَعَاضِد A *lrnd.* supporting, helping each other.

müteazım (..—.) مُتَعَاظِم A *lrnd.* 1. proud, haughty; pompous. 2. important, serious.

müteazzım مُتَعَظِّم A *lrnd.*, same as **mutaazzım**.

müteazzıv مُتَعَضِّي A *lrnd.*, same as **müteazzi**.

müteazzi مُتَعَضِّي A *lrnd.* having organs, organic; organized.

müteazzib مُتَعَزِّب A *lrnd.* bachelor, unmarried. —**âne** (....—.) P in the manner of a bachelor. —**în** (....—) A *pl.*

müteazzil مُتَعَزِّل A *lrnd.* retired; removed from office.

müteazzir مُتَعَذِّر A *lrnd.* 1. who offers an excuse; deserving pardon. 2. difficult, impossible (as excusing failure).

müteazziz مُتَعَزِّز A *lrnd.* 1. highly esteemed, excellent; powerful. 2. haughty, self-exalting.

mütebadil (..—.) مُتَبَادِل A *lrnd.* 1. taking each other's place. 2. interchangeable; alternate. — **zaviye** *geom.* alternate angle.

mütebadir (..—.) مُتَبَادِر A *lrnd.* 1. which immediately comes to mind. 2. who exerts himself striving to be first.

mütebaggız مُتَبَغِّض A *lrnd.* 1. who manifests hatred, hating. 2. hateful.

mütebagız (..—.) مُتَبَاغِض A *lrnd.* full of mutual hatred, rancorous.

mütebahhir 1 مُتَبَخِّر A *lrnd.* 1. vaporized. 2. a perfumer of his person; perfumed.

mütebahhir 2 مُتَبَحِّر A *lrnd.* 1. vast as the sea; vastly rich. 2. very learned, widely read, erudite. —**âne** (....—.) P 1. profoundly. 2. deeply learned. —**în** (....—) A *pl.*

mütebahi (..—.) مُتَبَاهِي A *lrnd.* vying in glory. —**yane** (..—.—.) suited to a proud person.

mütebahtir مُتَبَخْتِر A *lrnd.* swaggering.

mütebaid (..—.) مُتَبَاعِد A 1. *lrnd.* who goes far away; remote, distant; estranged. 2. *geom.* divergent.

mütebaki 1 (..—.) مُتَبَاقِي A 1. remaining, outstanding; remainder. 2. balance; surplus.

mütebaki 2 (..—.) مُتَبَاكِي A *lrnd.* who

forces himself to shed tears; feigning to weep. —yâne (..—.—.) P forcedly weeping.

mütebariz (..—.) مُتَبارِز A *lrnd.* prominent, outstanding.

mütebasbıs مُتَبَصْبِص A *lrnd.* 1. fawning, cringing. 2. toadying, flattering; flatterer. —âne (....—.) P flatteringly; fawningly. —in (....—) A *pl.*

mütebassır مُتَبَصِّر A *lrnd.* 1. who looks, examines attentively. 2. considerate, prudent. —âne (....—.) P prudently.

mütebayi' (..—.) مُتَبايِع A *lrnd.* mutual buying and selling, trading. —ân (..—'.—) A buyer and seller.

mütebayin (..—.) مُتَبايِن A 1. *math.* incommensurable. 2. *lrnd.* distinct, different; contrasting.

mütebeddi' مُتَبَدِّع A *lrnd.* innovating; innovator.

mütebeddil مُتَبَدِّل A *lrnd.* changed, self-altered.

mütebekkim مُتَبَكِّم A *lrnd.* 1. dumb, silent; faltering. 2. that sticks in one's throat (word).

mütebellid مُتَبَلِّد A *lrnd.* bewildered, stupid; lazy.

mütebellih مُتَبَلِّه A *lrnd.* stupid, idiotic; ignorant.

mütebellil مُتَبَلِّل A *lrnd.* 1. wet, moistened. 2. juicy.

mütebellir مُتَبَلِّر A 1. *chem.* crystallized. 2. *lrnd.* very evident; as clear as crystal.

mütebenna (...—) مُتَبَنّى A *lrnd.* claimed or adopted as a son.

mütebenni (...—) مُتَبَنّي A *lrnd.* who claims or adopts as a son.

müteberrek[ki] مُتَبَرَّك A *lrnd.* blessed, holy, sacred.

müteberri' 1 مُتَبَرِّع A *lrnd.* who relinquishes property from a pious motive; who does voluntarily that which is not obligatory.

müteberri 2 مُتَبَرِّى A *lrnd.* free, clear; innocent.

müteberrid مُتَبَرِّد A *lrnd.* who cools himself; that is cooled.

müteberrik[ki] مُتَبَرِّك A *lrnd.* 1. blessed through some holy person or thing. 2. who deems sacred. —en (....'.) A sacredly.

müteberrir مُتَبَرِّر A *lrnd.* pious, devout; dutiful.

müteberriz مُتَبَرِّز A *lrnd.* that becomes manifest, evident.

mütebessil مُتَبَسِّل A *lrnd.* 1. stern or determined looking. 2. who makes a show of courage.

mütebessim مُتَبَسِّم A smiling. —âne (...—.) P smilingly.

mütebeşbiş مُتَبَشْبِش A *lrnd.* who shows joy.

mütebettil مُتَبَتِّل A *lrnd.* retired from the world in celibacy and devotion; recluse.

mütebevvil مُتَبَوِّل A *lrnd.* that urinates.

mütebeyyin مُتَبَيِّن A *lrnd.* 1. manifest, evident, conspicuous; clear. 2. proved.

mütecadil (..—.) مُتَجادِل A *lrnd.* mutually contentious.

mütecahil (..—.) مُتَجاهِل A *lrnd.* who pretends ignorance. —âne (..—.—.) P with feigned ignorance.

mütecaid (..—.) مُتَجَعِّد A *lrnd.* 1. curly (hair). 2. wrinkled, shriveled.

mütecanib (..—.) مُتَجانِب A *lrnd.* 1. removed to one side. 2. who holds aloof, abstains; estranged.

mütecanis (..—.) مُتَجانِس A of the same kind, alike; homogenous.

mütecasir (..—.) مُتَجاسِر A *lrnd.* daring, presuming; audacious; presumptuous. —âne (..—.—.) P audaciously. —in (..—.—) A *pl. of* **mütecasir**.

mütecavib (..—.) مُتَجاوِب A *lrnd.* mutually answering, answering one another.

mütecavir (..—.) مُتَجاوِر A *lrnd.* neighboring, adjacent, nigh, near by.

mütecaviz (..—.) مُتَجاوِز A 1. /ı/ that exceeds, exceeding. 2. invader, aggressor. 3. that passes bounds; transgressing; exorbitant; presumptuous. —âne (..—.—.) P *lrnd.* 1. aggressively. 2. presumptuously. —in (..—.—) A *lrnd., pl. of* **mütecaviz**.

mütecazib (..—.) مُتَجاذِب A *lrnd.* mutually attracting, pulling or contending.

mütecebbir مُتَجَبِّر A *lrnd.* overbearing, insolent, haughty. —âne (....—.) P haughtily; insolently.

müteceddid مُتَجَدِّد A *lrnd.* 1. renewed, renovated. 2. new, recent. 3. innovator; modernist following the latest fashion. —âne (....—.) P 1. in a renewed fashion. 2. modernistic. —in (....—) A *pl. of* **müteceddid**.

müteceffif مُتَجَفِّف A *lrnd.* drying, dried.

mütecehhiz مُتَجَهِّز A *lrnd.* equipped, fitted out.

mütecelli (...—) مُتَجَلّي A *lrnd.* 1. visible, manifest; becoming manifest. 2. illuminated; splendid.

mütecellid مُتَجَلِّد A *lrnd.* courageous, daring, challenging. —âne (....—.) P daringly. —in (....—) A *pl. of* **mütecellid**.

mütecemmi' مُتَجَمِّع A *lrnd.* collected together, assembled; congregated. —in (....—) A *pl.*

mütecemmil مُتَجَمِّل A *lrnd.* 1. embellished; beautiful. 2. good, pleasant, kind.

mütecenni مُتَجَنّي A *lrnd.* 1. who gathers fruit or produce. 2. who imputes an offense falsely.

mütecennib مُتَجَنِّب A *lrnd.* that keeps aloof; who avoids or abstains.

mütecennin مُتَجَنِّن A *lrnd.* mad, insane. —**âne** (....—.) P madly, insanely.

mütecerred مُتَجَرَّد A *lrnd.* 1. stripped, bared; naked. 2. unmarried, bachelor. 3. isolated; withdrawn from the world.

mütecerrid مُتَجَرِّد A *lrnd.* 1. stripped, unclothed, naked. 2. who divests himself of all else and devotes himself to something. 3. unmarried, single. 4. who separates himself; incorporeal, immaterial.

mütecessid مُتَجَسِّد A *lrnd.* which assumes a body, embodied; incarnate, corporeal.

mütecessim مُتَجَسِّم A 1. which becomes like a solid body. 2. corporeal; personified.

mütecessis مُتَجَسِّس A inquisitive, prying, curious. —**âne** (....—.) P inquisitively, curiously. —**în** (....—), A *lrnd., pl. of* **mütecessis**.

mütecevvif مُتَجَوِّف A *lrnd.* hollow, cavernous.

mütecevviz مُتَجَوِّز A *lrnd.* 1. who does anything casually, lenient. 2. perfunctory, careless (in prayer). 3. who uses metaphor. —**âne** (....—.) P perfunctorily. —**în** (....—) A *pl. of* **mütecevviz**.

mütecezzi (...—) مُتَجَزِّى A *lrnd.* which becomes divided into parts; divisible into parts; divided; disintegrated.

mütedafiii (..—.) مُتَدَافِع A *lrnd.* employed in pushing and thrusting each other; repulsing (in battle). —**an** (..—'..) A in a repulsing manner. —**âne** (....—.) P repulsingly.

mütedahil (..—.) مُتَدَاخِل A 1. *lrnd.* confusedly intermixed, entering each other; overlapping. 2. *lrnd.* in arrears (of payments etc.). 3. *math.* commensurable. 4. *phil.* interpenetrable.

mütedair (..—.) مُتَدَائِر A *lrnd.* concerning, relative.

mütedarikki (..—.) مُتَدَارِك A *lrnd.* 1. that catches up with and overtakes. 2. who prepares, supplies. 3. *pros.* meter consisting of four dactyl-like feet (—.—/—.—/—.—/—.—).

mütedavel (..—.) مُتَدَاوَل A *lrnd.* in common use, current.

mütedavi (..—.) مُتَدَاوِي A *lrnd.* who takes a medicine, who uses a remedy; who doctors himself.

mütedavil (..—.) مُتَدَاوِل A current, in common use. — **kıymet** current asset. — **sermaye** floating capital, working capital.

mütedebbir مُتَدَبِّر A *lrnd.* who deliberates prudently. —**âne** (....—.) P prudently.

mütedeffin مُتَدَفِّن A *lrnd.* buried; hidden, concealed.

mütedelli مُتَدَلِّي A *lrnd.* 1. hanging, dangling. 2. lowered. 3. approaching. 4. submissive, humble. 5. *same as* **mütedellil**.

mütedellil مُتَدَلِّل A *lrnd.* who acts in a coquettish way; lively, merry. —**âne** (....—.) P coquettishly.

mütedenni مُتَدَنِّي A *lrnd.* 1. who stoops to baseness. 2. retrograde; decadent; degenerate. —**yâne** (....—.) P retrogradely.

mütedennis مُتَدَنِّس A *lrnd.* soiled, defiled, polluted.

mütederriii مُتَدَرِّع A *lrnd.* clad in mail or chain-armor.

mütederris مُتَدَرِّس A *lrnd.* studying, taking lessons from a teacher.

mütedessir مُتَدَثِّر A *lrnd.* wrapped in a cloak, muffled up in a plaid.

mütedeyyin مُتَدَيِّن A *lrnd.* religious, pious.

müteeddi مُتَأَدِّي A *lrnd.* payer.

müteeddib مُتَأَدِّب A *lrnd.* 1. well-bred; well-behaved; polite. 2. well-instructed, learned. —**âne** (....—.) P politely. —**în** (....—) A *pl. of* **müteeddib**.

müteehhil مُتَأَهِّل A married.

müteekkid مُتَأَكِّد A *lrnd.* which becomes confirmed by repetition or addition; confirmed; strengthened.

müteellif مُتَأَلِّف A *lrnd.* that is familiar with, accustomed to; associated, familiar, intimate.

müteellim مُتَأَلِّم A *lrnd.* afflicted, pained; suffering; grieved, sad. —**âne** (...—.) P sadly.

müteemmil مُتَأَمِّل A *lrnd.* who contemplates, reflects; reflecting; contemplative, meditative. —**âne** (....—.) P contemplatively, reflectingly.

müteemmir مُتَأَمِّر A *lrnd.* who becomes a prince; who obtains or exercises sovereign power.

müteenni مُتَأَنِّي A *lrnd.* slow and cautious in action, who takes time to reflect; circumspect. —**yâne** (....—.) P cautiously.

müteessif مُتَأَسِّف A grieved, sorry; regretful. —**âne** (....—.) P sorrowful, regretful (word, act etc.); regretfully. —**en** (...'..) A regretfully.

müteessir مُتَأَثِّر A 1. hurt, touched, grieved, afflicted; sad. 2. /dan/ influenced. —**âne** (....—.) P *lrnd.* grievedly. —**en** (...'..) A *lrnd.* grieving.

müteeyyid مُتَأَيِّد A *lrnd.* that becomes strengthened, confirmed, corroborated.

müteezzi مُتَأَذِّي A *lrnd.* 1. hurt, annoyed, vexed. 2. oppressed; grieved.

mütefahhir مُتَفَخِّر A *lrnd.* who prides himself; proud, haughty. —**âne** (....—.) P proudly.

mütefahhıs مُتَفَحِّص A *lrnd.* who searches or inquires after; investigator, examiner. —**âne** (....—.) P investigating, examining.

mütefahir (..—.) مُتَفَاخِر A who boasts; boasting.

mütefakkih مُتَفَقِّه A *lrnd.* learned in

jurisprudence; skilled in the divine law of Islam. **—âne** (.... —.) P learnedly. **—în** (.., —) A pl.
mütefakkid مُتَفَقِّد A lrnd. 1. who seeks a lost object. 2. who investigates.
mütefattın مُتَفَطِّن A lrnd. shrewd, discerning, considerate.
mütefattır مُتَفَطِّر A lrnd. cracked, fissured; split, cleft, divided.
mütefavit (.. — .) مُتَفَاوِت A lrnd. dissimilar, various; unequal.
mütefavvız مُتَفَوِّض A lrnd. receiver of property from the government.
mütefazıl (.. — .) مُتَفَاضِل A lrnd. 1. who vies for pre-eminence; ambitious for superiority. 2. superior.
mütefazzıl مُتَفَضِّل A lrnd. 1. who affects to be superior; who assumes a superiority over his fellows. 2. superior, excellent, eminent. **—âne** (.... —.) P acting in a superior way. **—în** (.... —) A pl. of **mütefazzıl**.
mütefecciˀ مُتَفَجِّع A lrnd. complaining, groaning.
mütefeccir مُتَفَجِّر A lrnd. breaking (dawn).
mütefehhim مُتَفَهِّم A lrnd. 1. who understands little by little. 2. who affects to understand.
mütefekkir مُتَفَكِّر A who thinks, reflects; thoughtful, pensive; thinker. **—âne** (.... —.) P lrnd. thinkingly, thoughtfully. **—în** (.... —) A lrnd., pl. of **mütefekkir**.
mütefellıkki مُتَفَلِّق A lrnd. 1. split, cracked, burst. 2. breaking (dawn).
mütefennin مُتَفَنِّن A learned in art or science; scientist. **—âne** (.... —.) P scientifically.
müteferriˁ مُتَفَرِّع A lrnd. 1. that has branches, branched out, ramifying. 2. derived, derivative; accessory; subordinate.
müteferriât (.... —) مُتَفَرِّعَات A lrnd. 1. branches, offshoots, ramifications. 2. subdivisions, derivatives.
müteferric مُتَفَرِّج A lrnd. who diverts himself, who goes out in the open air for recreation. **—în** (.... —) A pl.
müteferrid مُتَفَرِّد A lrnd. that is separate; isolated; sole, unique. **—âne** (.... —.) P solely, uniquely. **—în** (.... —) A pl. of **müteferrid**.
müteferriğ مُتَفَرِّغ A 1. law who receives into his possession a house or land. 2. lrnd. at leisure; vacant, empty.
müteferrih مُتَفَرِّح A lrnd. who rejoices; cheerful.
müteferrikki مُتَفَرِّق A lrnd. 1. separated, dispersed; scattered. 2. various, miscellaneous.
müteferrika مُتَفَرِّقَة A 1. money for miscellaneous expenses; petty cash. 2. sundries. 3. Ott. hist. the department of a police-station dealing with petty offenses, licenses, etc.

müteferrikat (.... —) مُتَفَرِّقَات A lrnd. disunited fragments; details. **M— baskısı** Müteferrika print, printed by İbrahim Müteferrika (d. 1754), the first Turkish printer.
müteferrikabaşı مُتَفَرِّقَه باشی Ott. hist. chief of the Müteferrika office.
müteferris مُتَفَرِّس A lrnd. who is perceptive; who observes.
müteferriş مُتَفَرِّش A lrnd. 1. spread out. 2. that stretches himself; which spreads its wings.
müteferriz مُتَفَرِّز A lrnd. separated as a portion; apportioned; portioned out.
mütefessih 1 مُتَفَسِّخ A lrnd. disintegrated; rotten; degenerate.
mütefessih 2 مُتَفَسِّح A lrnd. spacious, roomy.
mütefettit مُتَفَتِّت A lrnd. broken in pieces, crumbled, crumbling.
mütefevvih مُتَفَوِّه A lrnd. who speaks; who utters used usually for those who use bad language.
mütefevvikki مُتَفَوِّق A lrnd. superior. **—ane** (.... —.) P in a superior manner. **—în** (.... —) A pl. of **mütefevvik**.
müˀtefikki مُؤْتَفِك A lrnd. overturned, inverted.
müˀtefikât (.... —) مُؤْتَفِكَات A lrnd. 1. certain boisterous winds which favor vegetation. 2. w. cap. the "Cities of the Plain" destroyed in the time of Lot.
mütegabi (.. — .) مُتَغَابِي A lrnd. who feigns stupidity. **—yâne** (.. — . — .) P with feigned stupidity.
mütegabin (.. — .) مُتَغَابِن A lrnd. mutually defrauding.
mütegaddi مُتَغَدِّي A lrnd. 1. that takes nourishment. 2. who breakfasts or lunches.
mütegaffil مُتَغَفِّل A lrnd. careless, heedless.
mütegafil (.. — .) مُتَغَافِل A lrnd. who feigns negligence; who pretends to be unmindful. **—âne** (.. — . — .) P in the manner of feigned carelessness. **—în** (.. — . —) A pl. of **mütegafil**.
mütegalib (.. — .) مُتَغَالِب A lrnd. who competes.
mütegallib مُتَغَلِّب A lrnd. who assumes the mastery wrongfully or tyrannically; tyrannical; tyrant; usurper. **—âne** (.... —.) P in a cruel and violent manner; tyrannically.
mütegallibe مُتَغَلِّبَة A lrnd. usurpers; oppressors.
mütegamiz (.. — .) مُتَغَامِز A lrnd. winking at one another. **—în** (.. — . —) A pl.
müteganni مُتَغَنِّي A lrnd. who sings; singer. **—yâne** (.... —.) P singingly.
mütegannic مُتَغَنِّج A lrnd. who uses coquettish airs; coquettish.
mütegarrib مُتَغَرِّب A lrnd. in a strange

mütegarrid place; who travels in foreign lands; stranger. —în (....—) A pl.

mütegarrid مُتَغَرِّد A lrnd. warbling, humming, songster.

mütegarrir مُتَغَرِّر A lrnd. 1. who rushes into danger. 2. proud, haughty.

mütegassil مُغْتَسِل A lrnd. who washes his body.

mütegaşşi مُتَغَشِّى A lrnd. 1. that covers itself; covering, enveloping. 2. who goes into ecstasy.

mütegavvil مُتَغَوِّل A lrnd. 1. that assumes divers appearances. 2. capricious, fickle.

mütegayir (..—.) مُتَغَايِر A lrnd. different, diverse.

mütegayyib مُتَغَيِّب A lrnd. that is bodily absent; absent; hidden, invisible.

mütegayyim مُتَغَيِّم A lrnd. cloudy (sky).

mütegayyir مُتَغَيِّر A 1. changed, altered, changeable. 2. spoiled, putrid. —âne (....—.) P changeably.

mütegazzil مُتَغَزِّل A lrnd. who recites an ode; writer of erotic poetry. —în (....—) A pl.

mütehabb[bbi] (..—) مُتَحَابّ A lrnd. mutually loving, mutually friendly.

mütehabbir مُتَخَبِّر A lrnd. who asks diligently for information; who is well informed.

mütehabbis مُتَحَبِّس A lrnd. shutting oneself up; shut up, imprisoned, restricted. —âne (....—.) P self-restrainedly.

mütehaccir مُتَحَجِّر A lrnd. 1. that becomes stone, petrified. 2. hard as stone.

mütehaci (..—.) مُتَهَاجِى A lrnd. mutually satirizing or lampooning (poets). —yâne (..—.—.) P satirizingly.

mütehacim (..—.) مُتَهَاجِم A lrnd. who rush and crowd on each other, who attack each other; assailant. —âne (..—.—.) P attackingly. —în (..—.—) A assailants.

mütehaddi[ii] 1 مُتَحَدِّع A lrnd. knowingly deceived.

mütehaddi 2 مُتَحَدِّى A lrnd. who contends; challenging.

mütehaddib مُتَحَدِّب A lrnd. humpbacked.

mütehaddid مُتَحَدِّد A lrnd. 1. sharp, keen. 2. angry, irritable.

mütehaddir 1 مُتَحَدِّر A lrnd. that descends slowly.

mütehaddir 2 مُتَخَدِّر A lrnd. covered, veiled.

mütehaddis مُتَحَدِّث A lrnd. 1. which comes to pass; occurring. 2. arising (from); due (to).

mütehadi[ii] (..—.) مُتَحَادِع A lrnd. 1. feigning to be duped. 2. mutual in deceiving.

mütehaffız مُتَحَفِّظ A lrnd. who takes care of himself; cautious, vigilant. —în (....—) A pl.

mütehaffif مُتَخَفِّف A lrnd. 1. light of weight. 2. frivolous of manner. 3. who puts on boots; booted.

mütehafit (..—.) مُتَهَافِت A lrnd. 1. rushing consecutively on or against a person (a crowd). 2. that hits itself against something repeatedly. —âne (..—.—.) P falling repeatedly against.

mütehakkid مُتَحَقِّد A lrnd. filled with hate.

mütehakkik[kı] مُتَحَقِّق A lrnd. truly existing, real; found to be true.

mütehakkim مُتَحَكِّم A 1. who assumes wrongfully the role of judge or arbitor. 2. despotic; domineering; arrogant. —âne (....—.) P domineeringly. —în (....—) A pl. of **mütehakkim**.

mütehalif 1 (..—.) مُتَخَالِف A lrnd. mutually opposed; diverse.

mütehalif 2 (..—.) مُتَحَالِف A lrnd. bound together by oath, covenant or treaty.

mütehalik[kı] (..—.) مُتَهَالِك A lrnd. who rushes blindly and foolishly into a dangerous course; precipitate; enthusiastic. —âne (..—.—.) P enthusiastically; with much eagerness. —en (..—'..) P with great enthusiasm.

mütehallik[kı] مُتَخَلِّق A lrnd. who acquires some special moral quality or habit; endowed with; possessing.

mütehallıt مُتَخَالِط A lrnd. mixed; confused.

mütehalli 1 مُتَحَلِّى A lrnd. embellished; adorned.

mütehalli 2 مُتَخَلِّى A lrnd. 1. that becomes empty or free from some particular thing. 2. unoccupied, free, disengaged.

mütehallid مُتَخَلِّد A lrnd. that becomes everlasting.

mütehallif مُتَخَلِّف A lrnd. that differs; varying, fluctuating; diverging.

mütehallil 1 مُتَحَلِّل A lrnd. 1. melting; melted, dissolved. 2. resolved, reduced.

mütehallil 2 مُتَخَلِّل A lrnd. 1. harmed; spoiled. 2. that intervenes (time).

mütehallim مُتَحَلِّم A lrnd. who affects to be patient, meek or wise.

mütehallis مُتَخَلِّص A lrnd. 1. free, freed, clear, safe. 2. who adopts a pseudonym (poet).

mütehamık[kı] (..—.) مُتَحَامِق A lrnd. who feigns madness.

mütehami (..—.) مُتَحَامِى A lrnd. who guards himself, shuns, avoids. —yâne (..—.—.) P guardedly.

mütehammık[kı] مُتَحَمِّق A lrnd. who becomes stupid; who acts or talks stupidly.

mütehammız مُتَحَمِّض A lrnd. which turns sour; acidified.

mütehammi مُتَحَمِّى A lrnd. 1. who takes care of himself. 2. who observes a diet.

mütehammil مُتَحَمِّل A 1. enduring, patient. 2. lrnd. that carries a burden; who takes on himself a burden; who undertakes a responsibility. —âne (....—.) P *lrnd.* 1. patiently. 2. with endurance. —în (....—) A *pl.*

mütehammir متخمّر A 1. *chem.* fermenting; leavened. 2. *lrnd.* drunk with wine.

mütehanni متحنّى A *lrnd.* bent, crooked, curved.

mütehannin متحنّن A *lrnd.* who yearns for another; yearning, pining.

müteharib (..—.) متحارب A *lrnd.* mutually at war.

müteharim (..—.) متهارم A *lrnd.* who feigns extreme old age or decrepitude. —âne (..—.—.) P with feigned decrepitude. —în (..—.—) A *pl. of* müteharim.

müteharis (..—.) متحارش A *lrnd.* clawing and scratching each other.

müteharrık[kı] متهرّئ A *lrnd.* torn, ragged; pierced.

müteharri متحرّى A *lrnd.* who searches; inquisitive, prying.

müteharrik[kı] متحرّك A 1. moving, movable; portable; mobile. 2. *Arabic gram.* accented with short vowels (consonant).

müteharrim متحرّم A *lrnd.* 1. inviolable to others and restricted in action by any one of certain religious states or acts; forbidden, unlawful. 2. self-denying, abstaining. —âne (....—.) P self-denyingly. —în (....—) A *pl. of* müteharrim.

müteharris متحرّس A *lrnd.* who guards himself.

müteharris متحرّش A 1. *physiol.* irritated. 2. *lrnd.* who obtains by force or by importunity.

mütehasım (..—.) متخاصم A *lrnd.* mutually disputing or litigating; adversary, opponent (in a law suit).

mütehasımeyn (..—..) متخاصمين A *lrnd.* the two litigants in a suit, plaintiff and defendant, adversaries (at law).

mütehasid (..—.) متحاسد A *lrnd.* envious of each other.

mütehassıl متحصّل A *lrnd.* produced, resulting.

mütehassın متحصّن A *lrnd.* 1. who retires to a stronghold and fortifies himself there. 2. garrisoned (troops).

mütehassına متحصّنة A *lrnd.* woman whose virtue is unassailable.

mütehassıs متخصّص A specialist; expert.
— **doktor** medical specialist.

mütehassir 1 متحسّر A who grieves, regrets the absence of a person or thing desired; longing, repining, disappointed. —âne (....—.) P longingly. —în (....—) A *lrnd., pl. of* **mütehassir 1**.

mütehassir 2 متخثّر A *lrnd.* thick, curdled; coagulated.

mütehassis متحسّس A 1. moved with emotion; touched. 2. *lrnd.* who listens or inquires anxiously; who looks for information. —âne (....—.) P *lrnd.* in a moving manner.

mütehaşi (..—.) متحاشى A *lrnd.* withdrawing, avoiding; shrinking, refraining.

mütehaşşi[i] متخشّع A *lrnd.* submissive, modest, subdued, humble.

mütehaşşid متحشّد A *lrnd.* 1. collected as a military force, mobilized. 2. concentrated.
— **kuvvetler** *mil.* assembled forces. —în (....—) A *pl. of* **mütehaşşid**.

mütehaşşin متخشّن A *lrnd.* coarse, harsh, hard.

mütehatıb (..—.) متخاطب A *lrnd.* addressing one another.

mütehattır متخطّر A *lrnd.* who remembers.

mütehatti متخطّى A *lrnd.* 1. who oversteps a limit, who transgresses. 2. mistaken, erring.

mütehattim 1 متحتّم A *lrnd.* absolutely necessary, inevitable, incumbent.

mütehattim 2 متختّم A *lrnd.* who wears a seal ring on his finger.

mütehavin (..—.) متهاون A *lrnd.* who despises, neglects or holds as if of little account; negligent.

mütehavir (..—.) متحاور A *lrnd.* conversing with one another.

mütehavvif متخوّف A *lrnd.* terrified, frightened.
—âne (....—.) P in terror.

mütehavvil متحوّل A 1. that turns or changes; changing; changed. 2. changeable, variable.
—**i mutavassıt** *math.* parameter.

mütehayyil متخيّل A *lrnd.* who imagines, fancies, imagining, fanciful. —âne (....—.) P imaginary; fancifully.

mütehayyile متخيّلة A *lrnd.* the imagination.

mütehayyir متحيّر A *lrnd.* amazed, bewildered, dazzled. —âne (....—.) P amazedly. —în (....—) A *pl.*

mütehayyiz متحيّز A *lrnd.* occupying a special place; distinguished. —ân (....—) P, —în (....—) A *pl.*

mütehazzı[ı] متخضّع A *lrnd.* humble, modest.
—âne (....—.) P humbly.

mütehazzır متحضّر A *lrnd.* present; in attendance.

mütehazzib متحزّب A *lrnd.* collected in groups, parties or a confederation.

mütehazzin متحزّن A *lrnd.* sad, sorrowful.
—âne (....—.) P sorrowfully.

mütehazzir متحذّر A *lrnd.* careful, vigilant, circumspect.

mütehecci متهجّى A *lrnd.* who spells out the letters of a word.

müteheccid متهجّد A *lrnd.* 1. who stays awake at night. 2. who rises in the night and performs a supererogatory service of worship.

müteheddi (...—) متهدّى A *lrnd.* who goes right; guided aright (by God).

müteheddim مُتَهَدِّم A *lrnd.* falling in ruin, pulled down, ruined.
mütehekkim مُتَهَكِّم A *lrnd.* who mocks, mocker. —**âne** (....—.) P mockingly.
mütehellil مُتَهَلِّل A *lrnd.* bright and smiling.
mütehennic مُتَهَنِّج A *lrnd.* quickened (foetus).
mütehettik[kı] مُتَهَتِّك A *lrnd.* 1. torn, rent. 2. dishonored; shameless.
mütehevvid مُتَهَوِّد A *lrnd.* turned Jew.
mütehevvir مُتَهَوِّر A *lrnd.* 1. thoughtlessly rash; impulsive, impetuous. 2. furious. —**âne** (....—.) P rash, impetuous (act); furiously.
müteheyyi مُتَهَيِّئ A *lrnd.* ready, prepared for.
müteheyyib مُتَهَيِّب A *lrnd.* 1. that inspires awe. 2. struck with awe.
müteheyyic مُتَهَيِّج A *lrnd.* excited, stirred up. —**âne** (....—.) P excitedly. —**en** (....—.) A with excitement.
müteheyyim مُتَهَيِّم A *lrnd.* bewildered, perplexed. —**âne** (....—.) P in bewilderment. —**în** (....—) A *pl.* of **müteheyyim**.
mütehezzic مُتَهَزِّج A *lrnd.* who hums or sings a ballad tune. —**âne** (....—.) P with a hum. —**în** (....—) A *pl.* of **mütehezzic**.
mütehezziz مُتَهَزِّز A *lrnd.* which moves or vibrates.
mütekabbız مُتَقَبِّض A *lrnd.* contracted, shrunk.
mütekabbil مُتَقَبِّل A *lrnd.* who accepts.
mütekabil (..—.) مُتَقَابِل A 1. opposite each other; reciprocal; mutual, correspondent. 2. *math.* contrary. — **dâva** *law* counterclaim, cross-action. — **sigorta** reciprocal insurance.
mütekabilen (..—'..) مُتَقَابِلًا A *lrnd.* reciprocally, mutually.
mütekabiliyet (..—...) مُتَقَابِلِيَّت A *law* reciprocity. — **esası** rule of reciprocity.
mütekâbir (..—.) مُتَكَابِر A *lrnd.* proud, haughty.
mütekaddim مُتَقَدِّم A 1. that precedes, preceding; enterprising. 2. former, ancient. 3. who presents himself; presented, submitted. —**în** (....—) A the ancients, men of old.
mütekaddis مُتَقَدِّس A *lrnd.* holy, sanctified.
mütekadim (..—.) مُتَقَادِم A *lrnd.* ancient; prior to.
mütekâfi (..—.) مُتَكَافِئ A *lrnd.* equal, of the same degree. —**yen** (..—'..) A in a manner of equality, on the footing.
mütekâhil (..—.) مُتَكَاهِل A *lrnd.* negligent, careless, lazy.
mütekaid (..—.) مُتَقَاعِد A *same as* **mütekait**. —**en** (..—'..) on retirement. —**în** (..—.—) A *pl.* of **mütekaid**.
mütekais (..—.) مُتَقَاعِس A *lrnd.* whose back goes in and breast sticks out; pigeon-breasted.
mütekait[dı] (..—.) مُتَقَاعِد [**mütekaid**] retired on a pension; pensioner.

mütekâlib (..—.) مُتَكَالِب A *lrnd.* snarling mutually like dogs; jumping at each other like dogs. —**âne** (..—.—.) P in the manner of dogs. —**în** (..—.—) A those who act like dogs.
mütekallib مُتَقَلِّب A *lrnd.* 1. that rolls over and over; changeful (events). 2. reversed, inverted, converted; versatile.
mütekallid مُتَقَلِّد A *lrnd.* 1. who wears a necklace, collar or sword. 2. who assumes command, sovereignty. —**în** (....—) A *pl.*
mütekallil مُتَقَلِّل A *lrnd.* reduced, little, few.
mütekallis مُتَقَلِّص A *physiol.* shrunken; contracted.
mütekâmil (..—.) مُتَكَامِل A 1. perfect, perfected; complete; mature. 2. developed by evolution.
mütekamir (..—.) مُتَقَامِر A *lrnd.* gambling together.
mütekammis مُتَقَمِّص A *lrnd.* who wears a shirt.
mütekarib (..—.) مُتَقَارِب 1. *math., phys.* convergent. 2. *lrnd.* that draws near; mutually approaching; near. 3. *pros.* epical meter with trisyllabic feet (. — — /. — — /. — — /. —).
mütekarin (..—.) مُتَقَارِن A *lrnd.* united together, adjacent.
mütekarrib مُتَقَرِّب A *lrnd.* 1. that approaches, approaching; near. 2. who draws near to God. —**în** (....—) A *pl.*
mütekarrih مُتَقَرِّح A *lrnd.* ulcerated, eaten up with sores.
mütekarrir مُتَقَرِّر A *lrnd.* 1. established, confirmed. 2. fixed, determined, decided.
mütekasır (..—.) مُتَقَاصِر A *lrnd.* lacking in doing duty; unequal to the performance of a thing. —**în** (..—.—) A *pl.*
mütekasif (..—.) مُتَكَاثِف A *lrnd.* 1. thick, condensed. 2. concentrated.
mütekasil (..—.) مُتَكَاسِل A *lrnd.* lazy; negligent; indolent. —**âne** (..—.—.) P lazily. —**în** (..—.—) A *pl.* of **mütekasil**.
mütekasim (..—.) مُتَقَاسِم A *lrnd.* 1. mutually dividing. 2. making an oath with each other.
mütekâsir (..—.) مُتَكَاثِر A *lrnd.* increased, multiplied; abundant.
mütekassi مُتَقَصِّي A *lrnd.* who investigates thoroughly.
mütekatır (..—.) مُتَقَاطِر A *lrnd.* dripping.
mütekati[ii] (..—.) مُتَقَاطِع A 1. *geom.* intersecting. 2. *lrnd.* parted from each other.
mütekatil (..—.) مُتَقَاتِل A *lrnd.* mutually killing or fighting.
mütekattı مُتَقَطِّع A 1. *math.* discontinued. 2. *med.* intermittent. 3. *lrnd.* cut into pieces.
mütekattır مُتَقَطِّر A *lrnd.* dripping.
mütekavvi مُتَقَوِّي A *lrnd.* that acquires strength, strong.

mütekavvil مُتَقَوِّل A *lrnd.* who asserts falsely; teller of lies about another. **—âne** (....—.) P in a lying manner. **—în** (....—) A *pl. of* **mütekavvil**.

mütekavvim مُتَقَوِّم A *lrnd.* corrected, straightened; straight.

mütekavvis مُتَقَوِّس A *lrnd.* arched, bent, curved.

mütekâyid (..—.) مُتَكَايِد A *lrnd.* mutually deceitful. **—âne** (..—.—.) P deceitfully. **—în** (..—.—) A *pl. of* **mütekâyid**.

mütekayyid مُتَقَيِّد A *lrnd.* 1. who pays attention, takes special care; attentive. 2. who imposes restraint on himself. **—âne** (....—.) P attentively. **—în** (....—) A *pl. of* **mütekayyid**.

mütekayyih مُتَقَيِّح A *lrnd.* purulent, suppurating (sore).

mütekazı (..—.) مُتَقَاضِى A *lrnd.* 1. who continually duns; dun. 2. importunate.

mütekebbir مُتَكَبِّر A proud, haughty, arrogant. **—âne** (....—.) P peculiar to a proud person; arrogantly. **—în** (....—) A *pl. of* **mütekebbir**. **—lik** pride, haughtiness.

mütekeddir مُتَكَدِّر A *lrnd.* 1. sad, sorrowful, grieved. 2. turbid; misty; dusty. **—âne** (....—.) P sadly. **—în** (....—) A those who are sad.

mütekeffil مُتَكَفِّل A *law* who stands surety for, guaranteeing; responsible for. **—âne** (....—.) P in surety for. **—în** (....—) A *pl. of* **mütekeffil**.

mütekehhil مُتَكَحِّل A *lrnd.* whose eyes are blackened with kohl. **—în** (....—) A *pl.*

mütekehhin مُتَكَهِّن A *lrnd.* who is or pretends to be a soothsayer; predictor. **—âne** (....—.) P in the manner of a soothsayer. **—în** (....—) A *pl. of* **mütekehhin**.

mütekellif مُتَكَلِّف A *lrnd.* who takes great pains, who attempts more than is required; troubler. **—âne** (....—.) P painstakingly. **—în** (....—) A *pl. of* **mütekellif**.

mütekellil مُتَكَلِّل A *lrnd.* crowned; turbaned.

mütekellim مُتَكَلِّم A 1. *gram.* first person. 2. *lrnd.* that speaks; speaker; orator. 3. *lrnd.* scholar of theology as deduced from the Quran alone.

mütekellimîn (....—) مُتَكَلِّمِين A *Isl. rel.* scholars of theology.

mütekemmil مُتَكَمِّل A *lrnd.* complete; perfect. **—âne** (....—.) P in a complete manner. **—în** (....—) A *pl. of* **mütekemmil**.

mütekemmin مُتَكَمِّن A *lrnd.* who hides in ambush, ambushed.

mütekerrih مُتَكَرِّه A *lrnd.* 1. who loathes; who shows aversion. 2. who does a thing unwillingly. **—âne** (....—.) P loathingly.

mütekerrir مُتَكَرِّر A which occurs repeatedly; recurring.

mütekessir 1 مُتَكَثِّر A *lrnd.* multiplied; enriched.

mütekessir 2 مُتَكَسِّر A *lrnd.* broken in pieces.

mütekeşşif مُتَكَشِّف A *lrnd.* uncovered, displayed, manifested.

mütekevvin مُتَكَوِّن A *lrnd.* that comes into existence; which happens.

mütekeyyif مُتَكَيِّف A *lrnd.* 1. described, defined in form and quality. 2. intoxicated.

mütekeyyis مُتَكَيِّس A *lrnd.* who pretends to be shrewd. **—âne** (....—.) P with feigned shrewdness. **—în** (....—) A *pl. of* **mütekeyyis**.

mütelâffız مُتَلَفِّظ A *lrnd.* who pronounces, articulates.

mütelâfi (..—.) مُتَلَافِى A *lrnd.* who corrects an error or omission, compensator.

mütelâhhiz مُتَلَحِّظ A *lrnd.* 1. whose mouth waters with desire. 2. stingy, miserly.

mütelâhık[kı] (..—.) مُتَلَاحِق A *lrnd.* successive, following in a continued series; reaching, touching.

mütelâhız (..—.) مُتَلَاحِظ A *lrnd.* eyeing each other; looking askance at one another. **—în** (..—.—) A *pl.*

mütelâhi (..—.) مُتَلَاهِى A *lrnd.* 1. amusing themselves together. 2. engaged in play; who frivolously amuses himself. **—yâne** (..—.—.) P engaging in self-amusement.

mütelâhime (..—..) مُتَلَاحِم A *lrnd.* that cuts through the scalp (wound); flesh wound on the head.

mütelâib (..—.) مُتَلَاعِب A *lrnd.* playing together.

mütelâin (..—.) مُتَلَاعِن A *lrnd.* cursing or invoking maledictions on each other.

mütelâki (..—.) مُتَلَاقِى A *lrnd.* that come together, join one another; meeting.

mütelâkkıb مُتَلَقِّب A *lrnd.* called by a surname; surnamed, titled. **—în** (....—) A *pl.*

mütelâkkım مُتَلَقِّم A *lrnd.* that swallows in leisurely fashion.

mütelâkki مُتَلَقِّى A *lrnd.* 1. who meets, encounters. 2. who conceives. 3. who hears and communicates by turns.

mütelâkkiyan (....—) مُتَلَاقِيَان A *Isl. rel.* the two recording angels.

mütelâsık[kı] (..—.) مُتَلَاصِق A *lrnd.* mutually touching or adhering, adjacent, adherent.

mütelâ'sim مُتَلَعْثِم A *lrnd.* 1. who is hesitant in answering. 2. answering foolishly or stammeringly. **—âne** (....—.) P answering in a reluctant manner. **—în** (....—) A *pl. of* **mütelâ'sim**.

mütelâşi (..—.) متلاشی A *lrnd.* flurried. —**yâne** (..—.—.) P flurriedly.
mütelâtıf (..—.) متلاطف A *lrnd.* mutually courteous.
mütelâtım (..—.) متلاطم A *lrnd.* dashing together (waves).
mütelâttıf متلاطف A *lrnd.* who acts pleasantly, kind. —**âne** (....—.) P kindly.
mütelâttıh متلطخ A *lrnd.* daubed, smeared.
mütelâzzi متلاظی A *lrnd.* flaming, blazing.
mütelebbis متلبس A *lrnd.* who wears a dress, dressed, clad. —**în** (...—) A *pl.*
müteleclic متلجلج A *lrnd.* who mumbles in speaking, mumbled.
mütelehhi متلهی A *lrnd.* who amuses himself; player.
mütelehhib متلهب A *lrnd.* flaming, blazing.
mütelehhif متلهف A *lrnd.* who sighs, laments. —**âne** (....—.) P piningly. —**în** (....—) A *pl. of* **mütelehhif**.
müteleib متلاعب A *lrnd.* who plays, amuses himself.
mütele'li متلألی A *lrnd.* glittering, sparkling.
mütelemmiⁱⁱ متلمع A *lrnd.* 1. that sparkles; glittering. 2. who snatches, seizes.
mütelemmis متلمس A *lrnd.* 1. who often touches and feels. 2. who seeks repeatedly.
mütelessim متلثم A *lrnd.* 1. who veils his mouth. 2. who kisses.
mütelevvin متلون A 1. variegated; changeable. 2. fickle, variable, capricious. —**âne** (....—.) P *lrnd.* in a changeable manner.
mütelevvis متلوث A *lrnd.* soiled, filthy.
müteleyyin متلین A *lrnd.* softening; softened.
müteleyyis متلیث A *lrnd.* 1. who affects boldness. 2. courageous, bold. —**âne** (....—.) P courageously, boldly.
mütelezzic متلزج A *lrnd.* sticky, viscous.
mütelezziz متلذذ A who enjoys the sense of taste; relishing; pleased. —**âne** (....—.) P relishingly.
mü'telif 'A, **mütelif** (—..) مؤتلف *lrnd.* 1. associated, familiar. 2. congruous, suitable, appropriate; in accord. **M— Devletler** *hist.* the Entente Powers.
mütemacid (..—.) متماجد A *lrnd.* contending together for glory.
mütemadi (..—.) متمادی A 1. which continues, continuing; continuous. 2. continually, ever and anon. —**yen** (..—'..) A continually; continuously. —**yet** (..—..) *math.* continuity.
mütemahhıt متمخط A *lrnd.* who clears his nose.
mütemalikᵏⁱ (..—.) متمالك A *lrnd.* who has power and ability; able.
mütemarız (..—.) متمارض A *lrnd.* who feigns illness, malingering; malingerer. —**âne**

(..—.—.) P malingeringly. —**în** (..—.—) A *lrnd., pl. of* **mütemarız**.
mütemasil (..—.) متماثل A 1. *math.* homologue. 2. *lrnd.* alike, equal.
mütemattır متمطر A *lrnd.* 1. that falls in drops (rain); rainy (weather). 2. who is out in the rain.
mütemavit (..—.) متماوت A *lrnd.* 1. who feigns to be dead. 2. hypocrite in religion.
mütemayil (..—.) متمایل A *lrnd.* leaning; inclined. —**âne** (..—.—.) P *lrnd.* inclining.
mütemayin (..—.) متماین A *lrnd.* false, lying; liar.
mütemayinalûd (..—.——) متماین آلود P *lrnd.* false in friendship or love.
mütemayiz (..—.) متمایز 1. *Ott. hist., name of a civil rank corresponding to army colonel.* 2. *log.* distinct. 3. *lrnd.* distinguished (for); extraordinary.
mütemeccid متمجد A *lrnd.* who becomes glorious, illustrious; glorified.
mütemeccis متمجس A *lrnd.* who becomes a Magian, fire worshipper.
mütemeddih متمدح A *lrnd.* who strives for praise; who praises himself; boastful. —**âne** (....—.) P boastfully. —**în** (....—) A *pl. of* **mütemeddih**.
mütemeddin متمدن A *lrnd.* 1. civilized. 2. settled in a town.
mütemehdi متمهدی A *lrnd.* who claims to be a Mahdi. —**yâne** (....—.) P in the manner of one who pretends to be a Mahdi.
mütemehhid متمهد A *lrnd.* spread (carpet, etc.).
mütemehhir متمهر A *lrnd.* who is shrewd and experienced; skillful, intelligent. —**în** (....—) A *pl.*
mütemekkin متمكن A *lrnd.* who settles in a place; settled; established.
mütemellikᵏⁱ 1 متملك A *lrnd.* who is in possession of a thing.
mütemellikᵏⁱ 2 متملق A *lrnd.* fawning, cringing. —**âne** (....—.) P fawningly.
mütemellil متملل A *lrnd.* who enters or is of a nationality or religion.
mütemelmil متململ A *lrnd.* suffering, disturbed, restless; agitated.
mü'temen مؤتمن A *lrnd.* trusted, sure.
mütemenna متمنی A *lrnd.* 1. desired, wished for. 2. asked, begged for.
mütemenni متمنی A *lrnd.* 1. who desires, wishes for. 2. who asks, begs. —**yâne** (....—.) P desiringly.
mü'temer مؤتمر A *lrnd.* congress; council; conference.
mütemerkiz متمركز A *lrnd.* concentrated; assembled.

mütemerrid مُتَمَرِّد A perversely, obstinate, rebellious; recalcitrant. —âne (....—.) P obstinately. —în (....—) A pl. of **mütemerrid**.

mütemerrin مُتَمَرِّن A lrnd. accustomed, habituated to, versed in.

mütemeshir مُتَمَشِّر A lrnd. who jokes, jests, who makes fun of. —âne (....—.) P jokingly.

mütemeskin مُتَمَسْكِن A lrnd. 1. who feigns poverty. 2. poor.

mütemessih مُتَمَسِّح A lrnd. 1. who takes water into his hand to apply to the body in ablution. 2. who rubs himself.

mütemessik[ki] مُتَمَسِّك A lrnd. who holds fast.

mütemessil مُتَمَثِّل A lrnd. 1. that has the form of a thing. 2. who applies a proverb.

mütemeşşi مُتَمَشِّي A lrnd. that walks or creeps about; proceeding; going on.

mütemeşşik[ki] مُتَمَشِّك A lrnd. who studies.

mütemetti[ü] مُتَمَتِّع A lrnd. 1. who profits; possessed of. 2. enjoying, delighting in. 3. who takes advantage of his presence at Mecca on a pilgrimage of reverence to perform in the same year the full pilgrimage.

mütemevvic مُتَمَوِّج A 1. wavy, billowy; rough (sea). 2. fluctuating.

mütemevvil مُتَمَوِّل A lrnd. wealthy, rich. —âne (....—.) P wealthily. —în (....—) A pl. of **mütemevvil**.

mütemeyyi[ü] مُتَمَيِّع A lrnd. viscously or fluidly plastic.

mütemeyyiz مُتَمَيِّز A lrnd. separate, distinct, distinguished. —ân (....—) P, —în (....—) A pl.

mütemezzik[ki] مُتَمَزِّق A lrnd. torn, mangled.

mütemmem مُتَمَّم A lrnd. finished, perfected, complete.

mütemmim مُتَمِّم A that finishes, perfects, consummates; completing, perfecting; additional; complementary; math. supplementary; supplemental; gram. complement. — **ceza** law complementary punishment, additional punishment. — **cüzü** essential, component part.

mütenaci (..—.) مُتَنَاجِي A lrnd. who whisper secrets to each other. —**yâne** (..—.—.) P whisperingly.

mütenadi (..—.) مُتَنَادِي A lrnd. calling out to each other.

mütenadim (..—.) مُتَنَادِم A lrnd. mutually sociable and chatty; engaged in familiar talk.

mütenadir (..—.) مُتَنَادِر A lrnd. that becomes scarce.

mütenafi (..—.) مُتَنَافِي A lrnd. negative.

mütenafir (..—.) مُتَنَافِر A lrnd. hating each other, opposed to one another.

mütenafis (..—.) مُتَنَافِس A lrnd. striving mutually for some exquisite thing.

mütenahhi مُتَنَحِّي A lrnd. that is aside, that becomes distant.

mütenahi (..—.) مُتَنَاهِي A that reaches a limit or end; ending; finite.

mütenahiz (..—.) مُتَنَاهِز A lrnd. who mutually hurry to be first.

mütenahnih مُتَنَحْنِح A lrnd. 1. whose throat rattles with phlegm as he breathes. 2. who repeatedly clears his throat of phlegm. —âne (....—.) P with a rattling throat. —în (....—) A pl. of **mütenahnih**.

mütena'im مُتَنَعِّم A lrnd. who lives in comfort; loaded with favors, fortunate. — **ol**= /dan/ to enjoy.

mütenakıs (..—.) مُتَنَاقِص A lrnd. gradually diminishing, dwindling.

mütenakız (..—.) مُتَنَاقِض A 1. mutually contradictory (two propositions). 2. inconsistent.

mütenakih (..—.) مُتَنَاكِح A lrnd. intermarrying, allied by intermarriage.

mütenakir (..—.) مُتَنَاكِر A lrnd. who feigns ignorance.

mütenakkil مُتَنَقِّل A lrnd. which passes from place to place; movable.

mütenasik[ki] (..—.) مُتَنَاسِك A lrnd. arranged in a continuous line or series; proportional.

mütenasır (..—.) مُتَنَاصِر A lrnd. who aid and support one another.

mütenasi (..—.) مُتَنَاسِي A lrnd. who pretends to forget.

mütenasib مُتَنَاسِب A 1. proportional; symmetrical. 2. well proportioned; well built.

mütenasih (..—.) مُتَنَاسِخ A lrnd. that passes by metempsychosis into another body (soul).

mütenasil (..—.) مُتَنَاسِل A lrnd. begotten in succession.

mütenasir (..—.) مُتَنَاثِر A lrnd. mutually scattered, dispersed.

mütenassıb مُتَنَصِّب A lrnd. 1. that stands erect. 2. persistent.

mütenassıh مُتَنَصِّح A lrnd. 1. who takes good advice. 2. who affects to give good advice. —**âne** (....—.) P taking good advice.

mütenassır مُتَنَصِّر A 1. who becomes a convert to Christianity. 2. lrnd. who prepares to help another.

mütenaşid (..—.) مُتَنَاشِد A lrnd. who recite poetry to each other.

mütenatıh (..—.) مُتَنَاطِح A lrnd. mutually butting.

mütenavib (..—.) مُتَنَاوِب A same as **mütenavip**.

mütenaviben (..—'..) مُتَنَاوِباً A lrnd. alternately; alternatively.

mütenavil (..—.) مُتَنَاوِل A lrnd. 1. who receives. 2. who takes food, etc. —în (..—.—) A pl.

Red 54.

mütenavim (..--.) مُتَناوِم A *lrnd.* who feigns sleep. —**âne** (..—.—.) P with feigned sleep. —**în** (..—.—) A *pl. of* **mütenavim**.

mütenavipᵇⁱ (..—.) مُتَناوِب |**mütenavib**| alternating; alternate. — **cereyan** *elec.* alternating current.

mütenazır (..—.) مُتَناظِر A 1. corresponding; symmetrical. 2. *lrnd.* related to each other; parallel, similar, contrary. 3. *lrnd.* facing one another; opposite each other.

mütenaziⁱⁱ (..—.) مُتَنازِع A *lrnd.* engaged in a dispute with one another.

mütenazzım مُتَنَظِّم A *lrnd.* in a line, series or order; arranged.

mütenazzıf مُتَنَظِّف A *lrnd.* 1. scrupulously clean. 2. overnice in affecting cleanliness.

mütenazzır مُتَنَظِّر A *lrnd.* 1. that looks attentively; beholder. 2. who acts with circumspection. 3. who expects. —**âne** (....—.) P looking attentively.

mütenebbi مُتَنَبِّى A *lrnd.* 1. who falsely claims to be a prophet; pseudo-prophet. 2. *w. cap., surname of an Arabian poet*.

mütenebbih مُتَنَبِّه A 1. awake; watchful, vigilant; on his guard. 2. cautious and circumspect.

mütenebbit مُتَنَبِّت A *lrnd.* that grows from the ground (plant).

müteneddim مُتَنَدِّم A *lrnd.* regretfully sorry, penitent. —**âne** (....—.) P penitently. —**în** (....—) A *pl. of* **müteneddim**.

müteneffil مُتَنَفِّل A *lrnd.* who performs an act of supererogatory worship.

müteneffir مُتَنَفِّر A who feels aversion (for); hating, abhoring. —**âne** (....—.) P loathingly.

müteneffis مُتَنَفِّس A *lrnd.* 1. that breathes and lives; possessed of breath. 2. who rests to catch his breath.

müteneffiz مُتَنَفِّذ A *lrnd.* having authority. —**ân** P *pl.*

mütenekkir مُتَنَكِّر A *lrnd.* unknown, unrecognizable; disguised; incognito. —**âne** (....—.) P disguisedly.

mütenekkiren (...'..) مُتَنَكِّرًا A *lrnd.* incognito.

mütenemmil مُتَنَمِّل A *lrnd.* swarming and creeping like ants.

mütenemmir مُتَنَمِّر A *lrnd.* 1. savage or agile as a leopard. 2. scolding loudly, roaring. 3. surly, sulky, growling. —**âne** (....—.) P in the manner of a leopard.

mütenessıkᵏⁱ مُتَنَسِّق A *lrnd.* ranged in a regular row or series; monotonous.

mütenessim مُتَنَسِّم A *lrnd.* 1. who inhales; breathing. 2. fragrant, sweet-scented. —**âne** (....—.) P sweet-scentedly.

mütenessir مُتَنَثِّر A *lrnd.* scattered, dispersed.

müteneşşıt مُتَنَشِّط A *lrnd.* lively.

müteneşşib مُتَنَشِّب A *lrnd.* that penetrates and holds (pointed thing).

müteneşşif مُتَنَشِّف A *lrnd.* that imbibes moisture; spongy.

müteneşşir مُتَنَشِّر A *lrnd.* spread out, opened out; scattered.

mütenevviⁱⁱ مُتَنَوِّع A of various kinds, diverse.

mütenevvih مُتَنَوِّح A *lrnd.* 1. oscillating 2. crying; singing mournfully. —**âne** (....—.) P crying in a mournful way.

mütenevvir مُتَنَوِّر A luminous, illumined.

mütenezzih مُتَنَزِّه A *lrnd.* 1. who goes out for a walk for amusement. 2. pure, free (from vice or stain). —**âne** (....—.) P in the manner of one who takes a walk. —**în** (....—) A *pl. of* **mütenezzih**.

mütenezzil مُتَنَزِّل A *lrnd.* 1. which comes down; diminishing. 2. who condescends, stoops. —**âne** (....—.) P condescendingly. —**en** (..'..) A condescending. —**în** (....—) A *pl. of* **mütenezzil**.

müterabbiⁱⁱ مُتَرَبِّع A *lrnd.* who sits four-square.

müteradif (..—.) مُتَرادِف A 1. synonymous. 2. *lrnd.* consecutive. 3. *phil.* equivocal.

müterafiⁱⁱ (..—.) مُتَرافِع A *lrnd.* mutually appealing to a judge.

müterafıkᵏⁱ (..—.) مُتَرافِق A 1. mutually associated. 2. concurrent (with). 3. concomitant.

müterahhil مُتَرَحِّل A *lrnd.* who saddles and departs; traveller.

müterahhim مُتَرَحِّم A who feels compassion; compassionate, merciful, tender. —**âne** (....—.) P compassionately.

müterahi (..—.) مُتَراخي A *lrnd.* slow; tardy; sluggish.

müterakib (..—.) مُتَراكِب A *lrnd.* piled one upon another (tiles, etc.).

müterakim (..—.) مُتَراكِم A accumulated; accumulating.

müterakkab مُتَرَقَّب A *lrnd.* watched for, expected.

müterakkıb مُتَرَقِّب A *lrnd.* 1. who hopes or expects; expectant. 2. who watches, guards.

müterakkıs مُتَرَقِّص A *lrnd.* dancing; oscillating.

müterakki مُتَرَقِّي A who advances; which grows or increases; progressive. — **vergi** progressive taxation. —**yâne** (....—.) P progressively.

müterasil (..—.) مُتَراسِل A *lrnd.* 1. mutually corresponding. 2. alternating.

müterassad مُتَرَصَّد A *lrnd.* watched, observed, waited for.

müterassıd مُتَرَصِّد A 1. who watches, observes; watcher. 2. who lies in wait. —**âne** (....—.) P watchingly. —**în** (....—) A *pl. of* **müterassıd**.

müterazı (..—.) مُتَراضي A *lrnd.* pleased and contented with each other.

müterazzi مُتَرَضّي A *lrnd.* who seeks to please.

mütercem مُتَرجَم A *lrnd.* translated; interpreted.

mütercim مُتَرجِم A who translates, interprets; translator; interpreter. —**âne** (...—.) P *lrnd.* in the manner of a translator. —**în** (...—) A *pl.* of **mütercim**.

müterecci مُتَرجّي A *lrnd.* 1. who hopes, expects. 2. who requests.

mütereddi مُتَرَدّي A *lrnd.* depraved; degenerate.

mütereddid مُتَرَدّد A 1. who doubts, hesitates; hesitating, undecided, irresolute. 2. *lrnd.* who frequents a place; that goes and comes. 3. *med.* remittant. — **irade** *psych.* velleity. —**âne** (...—.) P undecidedly. —**în** (...—) A *pl.* of **mütereddid**.

mütereffıkⁿ مُتَرَفِّق A *lrnd.* gentle, courteous, kind. —**ane** (...—.) P gently. —**în** (...—) A *pl.* of **mütereffık**.

müterefiiᵘ مُتَرَفِّع A *lrnd.* high; exalted in rank.

müterefiih مُتَرَفِّه A *lrnd.* living in ease. —**âne** (...—.) P comfortably. —**în** (...—) A *pl.* of **müterefiih**.

müterehhib مُتَرَهِّب A *lrnd.* who devotes himself to the service of God; hermit; recluse. —**âne** (...—.) P in a devout way. —**în** (...—) A *pl.* of **müterehhib**.

müterekkib مُتَرَكِّب A /dan/ consisting of parts, composed (of).

müterekkin مُتَرَكِّن A *lrnd.* 1. strongly propped; well supported; strong, firm. 2. grave, sedate, steady.

müteremrim مُتَرَمرِم A *lrnd.* 1. silent, mute. 2. who moves the lips without speaking. —**âne** (...—.) P mutely. —**în** (...—) A *pl.* of **müteremrim**.

müterennim مُتَرَنِّم A *lrnd.* that sings, warbles; singing; singer.

müteressib مُتَرَسِّب A *lrnd.* depositing (sediment); precipitated.

müteressim مُتَرَسِّم A *lrnd.* which takes shape and becomes pictured in the mind.

müteressif مُتَرَشِّف A *lrnd.* who sips or sucks in.

müteressih مُتَرَشِّح A *lrnd.* oozing out.

müterettib مُتَرَتِّب A *lrnd.* 1. arranged in order; classified. 2. existent, resultant; established. 3. /a/ charged (with), entrusted (to, as a duty).

müterevvih مُتَرَوِّح A *lrnd.* 1. who fans himself. 2. who smells something.

mütesabıkⁿ (..—.) مُتَسابِق A *lrnd.* striving to precede one another.

mütesabi (..—.) مُتَصابي A *lrnd.* acting like a young man; amorously inclined; fallen in love. —**yâne** (..—.—.) P in a youthful manner.

mütesaddi مُتَصَدّي A *lrnd.* who sets out to do, who attempts, presumes, is intent upon.

mütesadım (..—.) مُتَصادِم A *lrnd.* colliding with each other.

mütesadif (..—.) مُتَصادِف A that meets by chance; which happens by chance; coincident.

mütesafıh (..—.) مُتَصافِح A *lrnd.* shaking hands with each other.

mütesağır (..—.) مُتَصاغِر A *lrnd.* who affects to be of small account; little in one's own esteem.

mütesahhin مُتَسَخِّن A *lrnd.* growing warm or hot.

mütesahib (..—.) مُتَصاحِب A *lrnd.* who protects, who backs up a protégé. —**în** (..—.—.) A *pl.*

mütesahil (..—.) مُتَساهِل A *lrnd.* 1. mutually indulgent; easy going towards each other. 2. careless, negligent. —**âne** (..—.—.) P carelessly. —**în** (..—.—) A *pl.* of **mütesahil**.

mütesaid مُتَصَعِّد A *lrnd.* that ascends; high.

mütesaib (..—.) مُتَثائِب A *lrnd.* who yawns, gapes.

mütesaid (..—.) مُتَصاعِد A *lrnd.* that mounts, ascends.

mütesail (..—.) مُتَسائِل A *lrnd.* who begs. —**âne** (..—.—.) P in the manner of a beggar. —**în** (..—.—) A *pl.* of **mütesail**.

mütesakıt (..—.) مُتَساقِط A *lrnd.* falling; falling gradually or successively.

mütesakil (..—.) مُتَساقِل A *lrnd.* 1. mutually hanging back; heavy, slow, sluggish. 2. reluctant, slow in going to battle.

mütesakkıb مُتَثَقِّب A *lrnd.* 1. pierced, perforated; worm-eaten. 2. who bores.

mütesakkıf مُتَسَقِّف A *lrnd.* 1. who becomes a bishop. 2. roofed, ceilinged.

mütesalib (..—.) مُتَصالِب A *lrnd.* x-shaped, intersecting.

mütesalif (..—.) مُتَسالِف A *lrnd.* related as brothers-in-law.

mütesalih 1 (..—.) مُتَصالِح A *lrnd.* who feigns deafness.

mütesalih 2 (..—.) مُتَصالِح A *lrnd.* mutually at peace or making peace. —**în** (..—.—) A *pl.*

mütesalim (..—.) مُتَسالِم A *lrnd.* at peace with one another.

mütesallıtᵘ مُتَسَلِّط A *lrnd.* that exercises power or jurisdiction over another; aggressive; dominant. —**âne** (...—.—.) P aggressively; despotically. —**în** (...—.—) A *pl.* of **mütesallıt**.

mütesamih (..—.) مُتَسامِح A *lrnd.* mutually tolerant.

mütesanid (..—.) مُتَسانِد A *lrnd.* mutually

mütesavi supporting or aiding; solidary; joint (responsibility).
mütesavi (..—.) مُتَسَاوِ A *lrnd.* equal to one another, parallel. **—yen** (..—ً.) A equally.
mütesayif (..—.) مُتَسَايِف A *lrnd.* fighting or fencing each other (with swords).
mütesebbib مُتَسَبِّب A *lrnd.* causer.
müteseccid مُتَسَجِّد A *lrnd.* who prostrates himself in worship. **—âne** (....—ً.) P prostratedly. **—în** (....—) A *pl. of* müteseccid.
müteseil مُتَسَئِل A *lrnd.* who asks alms, beggar.
mütesekkin مُتَسَكِّن A *lrnd.* calm, tranquil.
müteselli مُتَسَلِّي A who takes comfort, consoles himself; comforted; solaced. **— ol=** to find consolation. **—yâne** (....—.) P in a solaced manner.
mütesellib مُتَسَلِّب A *lrnd.* in mourning (widow).
mütesellih مُتَسَلِّح A *lrnd.* armed.
mütesellim مُتَسَلِّم A 1. *Ott. hist.* deputy lieutenant-governor and local collector of taxes and tithes. 2. *lrnd.* who takes or receives a thing from another custodian.
müteselsil مُتَسَلْسِل A 1. in continuous succession; in continuous links like a chain; uninterrupted (sequence); *law* joint. **— alacaklılar** *law* joint creditors. **— borçlular** *law* joint debtors.
müteselsilen (..ً..) مُتَسَلْسِلاً A *lrnd.* continuously; successively, in succession.
mütesemmi مُتَسَمِّي A *lrnd.* 1. named. 2. who calls himself (so and so).
mütesemmim مُتَسَمِّم A *lrnd.* poisoned.
mütesemmin مُتَسَمِّن A *lrnd.* that has grown fat; fattened.
mütesennih مُتَسَنِّه A *lrnd.* 1. become old, altered, spoilt by time. 2. moldy, moldering.
müteserri[i] 1 مُتَسَرِّع A *lrnd.* who makes haste; active, quick, hasty.
müteserri 2 مُتَسَرِّي A *lrnd.* who takes a concubine.
mütesettir مُتَسَتِّر A *lrnd.* covered; veiled; screened.
mütesevvi مُتَسَوِّي A *lrnd.* even, level, equal.
mütesevvib مُتَسَوِّب A *lrnd.* who does an act that merits reward; who performs a supererogatory service of worship.
müteseyyib 1 مُتَسَيِّب A *lrnd.* widow, widowed.
müteseyyib 2 مُتَسَيِّب A *lrnd.* careless, prodigal in expense. **—âne** (....—.) P prodigally. **—în** (....—) A *pl. of* müteseyyib 2.
müteseyyid مُتَسَيِّد A *lrnd.* who pretends to belong to the Prophet's lineage.
mütesabih (..—.) مُتَشَابِه A resembling one another; similar, alike.

müteşabihat (..—.—) مُتَشَابِهَات A *lrnd.* the ambiguous or parabolic verses of the Quran.
müteşacir (..—.) مُتَشَاجِر A *lrnd.* 1. squabbling together, hostile, contentious. 2. mutually interlaced. **—âne** (..—.—.) P contentiously. **—în** (..—.—) *pl. of* müteşacir.
müteşahhıs مُتَشَخِّص A *lrnd.* standing up as a visible object; distinguished.
müteşaib مُتَشَعِّب A *lrnd.* branched, ramified; forked.
müteşaim (..—.) مُتَشَائِم A *lrnd.* who draws an evil omen from an event.
müteşair 1 (..—.) مُتَشَاعِر A who affects to be a poet, poetaster.
müteşair 2 مُتَشَعِّر A *lrnd.* hairy.
müteşaki (..—.) مُتَشَاكِي A *lrnd.* complaining of or to each other.
müteşakil (..—.) مُتَشَاكِل A *lrnd.* 1. resembling each other. 2. suitable, agreeable to one another.
müteşatim (..—.) مُتَشَاتِم A *lrnd.* reviling each other.
müteşavir (..—.) مُتَشَاوِر A *lrnd.* mutually consulting and deliberating.
müteşebbih مُتَشَبِّه A *lrnd.* resembling, similar. **—âne** (....—.) P resemblingly. **—în** (....—) A *pl. of* müteşebbih.
müteşebbik[i] مُتَشَبِّك A *lrnd.* 1. mutually interlaced. 2. intricate, complicated, intertwined.
müteşebbis مُتَشَبِّث A 1. who seriously sets to work, begins to do it; enterprising. 2. who has initiative. **—în** (....—) A *lrnd.* the enterprising people.
müteşecci[i] مُتَشَجِّع A *lrnd.* who pretends to have courage. **—âne** (....—.) P with affected courage. **—în** (....—) A *pl. of* müteşecci.
müteşeddid مُتَشَدِّد A *lrnd.* becoming hard, firm, severe.
müteşeddik[i] مُتَشَدِّق A *lrnd.* 1. who mouths his words in speaking; talkative. 2. who tries to be eloquent. **—âne** (....—.) P talkatively. **—în** (....—) A *pl. of* müteşeddik.
müteşeffi 1 مُتَشَفِّي A *lrnd.* 1. who appeases his own wrath by vengeance. 2. who becomes cured.
müteşeffi[i] 2 مُتَشَفِّع A *lrnd.* 1. who acts as an intercessor. 2. who begs one to intercede.
müteşehhi مُتَشَهِّي A *lrnd.* who has a longing; desirous, eager.
müteşehhib مُتَشَهِّب A *phys.* incandescent.
müteşehhid مُتَشَهِّد A *lrnd.* 1. who seeks to become a martyr. 2. who recites the profession of Islamic faith or the ascription of praise ending with that profession.
müteşe'im مُتَشَئِم A *lrnd.* who prophecies evil.

müteşekki مُشْتَكي A /dan/ who complains; complainer, lamenter.
müteşekkikᵏⁱ مُشَكِّك A lrnd. who doubts, doubting; scrupulous.
müteşekkil مُشَكَّل A 1. /dan/ consisting, composed (of). 2. lrnd. formed, shaped.
müteşekkir مُشَكِّر A who gives thanks, thankful, grateful. —ane (....—.) P lrnd. gratefully.
müteşelşil مُتَشَلْشِل A lrnd. pouring out, flooding (like a waterfall).
müteşemmil مُشَمِّل A lrnd. wrapped up; cloaked.
müteşemmim مُشَمِّم A lrnd. who sniffs gently; who perceives by smell.
müteşemmir مُشَمِّر A lrnd. girt up; ready for work.
müteşemmis مُشَمِّس A lrnd. sunned, exposed to the sun.
müteşennic مُشَنِّج A lrnd. 1. shrivelled, wrinkled. 2. gangrenous.
müteşennif مُشَنِّف A lrnd. who wears earrings.
müteşerriⁱⁱ مُشَرِّع A lrnd. 1. who conforms to the canon law. 2. skilled in canonical law. —ane (....—.) P in an orthodox manner.
müteşerrif مُشَرِّف A lrnd. who receives an honor; honored.
müteşetti مُشَتِّي A lrnd. who has taken winter quarters; who winters.
müteşettit مُشَتِّت A lrnd. 1. dispersed, scattered. 2. disordered.
müteşevvikᵏⁱ مُشَوِّق A lrnd. eager; wishful, desirous. —ane (....—.) P desirously. —în (....—) A pl. of **müteşevvik**.
müteşevviş مُشَوِّش A lrnd. confused, complicated; doubtful.
müteşeytın مُشَيْطِن A lrnd. like Satan in evil or in wiles; devilish, satanical.
müteşeyyiⁱⁱ مُشَيِّع A lrnd. who assumes the qualities of a Shi'i. —în (....—) A pl.
müteşeyyid مُشَيِّد A lrnd. firmly built.
müteşeyyih مُشَيِّخ A lrnd. 1. middle aged or old. 2. who pretends to be aged. 3. who affects to be a Sheikh; elder.
mütabıkᵏⁱ (..—.) مُطابِق A lrnd. mutually agreeing or corresponding; suited, agreeable to.
mütabiⁱⁱ (..—.) مُتابِع A lrnd. consecutive, gradual; proportioned; uniform. —an (..—'..) A consecutively.
mütali (..—.) مُتالي A lrnd. successive, consecutive.
mütetavil (..—.) مُتَطاوِل A lrnd. 1. long or high. 2. who assumes an air of superiority.
mütetebbiⁱⁱ مُتَتَبِّع A lrnd. 1. who follows up, pursues. 2. who investigates with perseverance; researcher, searcher.

mütetevvic مُتَتَوِّج A lrnd. who wears a crown; crowned.
mütevacih (..—.) مُتَواجِه A lrnd. face to face, opposite.
mütevafıkᵏⁱ (..—.) مُتَوافِق A 1. math. commensurable. 2. lrnd. in accord with one another; agreed; congruous. — zaviyeler geom. corresponding angles.
mütevafir (..—.) مُتَوافِر A lrnd. abundant, copious, numerous.
mütevaggil مُتَوَغِّل A lrnd. 1. who goes to a great distance. 2. who occupies himself greatly; who goes deeply into a matter. —în (....—) A pl.
mütevahhid مُتَوَحِّد A lrnd. sole, unique; isolated; without companion.
mütevahhiş مُتَوَحِّش A lrnd. 1. timid; frightened, scared. 2. desolate, deserted, solitary.
mütevaid (..—.) مُتَواعِد A lrnd. who mutually promise; bound to each other by promise. —în (..—.—) A pl.
mütevakil (..—.) مُتَواكِل A lrnd. acting mutually as deputies or representatives.
mütevakka (...—) مُتَوَقَّى A lrnd. feared and shunned.
mütevakkıd مُتَوَقِّد A lrnd. in combustion, on fire.
mütevakkıf مُتَوَقِّف A lrnd. 1. at a stop; standing still. 2. /a/ dependent (on), contingent.
mütevakkır مُتَوَقِّر A lrnd. respected, dignified. —ane (....—.) P in a dignified manner. —în (....—) A pl. of **mütevakkır**.
mütevakki 1 مُتَوَقِّي A lrnd. who takes pains or precautions to guard against or avoid.
mütevakkiⁱⁱ **2** مُتَوَقِّع A lrnd. who hopes, expects, who desires. —ane (....—.) P hopefully.
mütevali (..—.) مُتَوالي A lrnd. 1. that follow one another. 2. consecutive, successive, continuous.
mütevalid (..—.) مُتَوالِد A lrnd. successively generated and born.
mütevaliyen (..—'..) مُتَوالِياً A lrnd. successively, continuously, consecutively.
mütevari (..—.) مُتَواري A lrnd. that goes behind something, hidden from view; concealed, retired. — ol= to be lost to sight.
mütevarid (..—.) مُتَوارِد A lrnd. that come successively (news etc.); arriving.
mütevaris (..—.) مُتَوارِث A lrnd. inherited; hereditary.
mütevasıkᵏⁱ مُتَواثِق A lrnd. bound mutually by compact.
mütevasıl (..—.) مُتَواصِل A joined together; connected with one another.
mütevasi (..—.) مُتَواصي A lrnd. mutually

mütevasib (..—.) مُتَواصِب A *lrnd.* mutually springing on or attacking.

mütevatir (..—.) مُتَواتِر A *lrnd.* spread from mouth to mouth; generally admitted, well known truth.

mütevatirat (..—.—) مُتَواتِرات A *lrnd.* generally known truth.

mütevatiren (..—'..) مُتَواتِرًا A *lrnd.* by general report; by general admission.

mütevattın مُتَوَطِّن A *lrnd.* who settles in a place, resident.

mütevazı (..—.) مُتَواضِع A humble, modest. —**âne** (..—.—.) P modestly, humbly. —**in** (..—.—.) A *lrnd., pl.* of **mütevazı**.

mütevazi (..—.) مُتَوازِي A *lrnd.* parallel.

mütevazin (..—.) مُتَوازِن A equal in weight; balancing one another; balanced.

mütevaziyen (..—'..) مُتَوازِيًا A *lrnd.* in parallel.

mütevazzı مُتَوَضِّي A *lrnd.* who performs an ablution.

mütevazzıh مُتَوَضِّح A *lrnd.* clear, open, conspicuous, evident.

müteveccii مُتَوَجِّع A *lrnd.* 1. in pain, suffering; pained. 2. sorry for another; grieved for. —**âne** (...—.) P 1. grievedly. 2. like one in pain.

müteveccid مُتَوَجِّد A *lrnd.* enraptured with religious ecstasy.

müteveccih مُتَوَجِّه A /a/ 1. that turns his face (towards a person or thing); facing. 2. aimed at. 3. favorably disposed towards; favorably inclined toward. 4. which falls to the share of.

müteveccihâne (....—.) مُتَوَجِّهانه P *lrnd.* as one who is inclined towards.

müteveccihen (...'..) مُتَوَجِّهًا A *lrnd.* in the direction of; bound for.

müteveccihîn (....—) مُتَوَجِّهين A *lrnd., pl.* of **müteveccih**.

müteveddid مُتَوَدِّد A *lrnd.* who displays love, who has friendly inclinations. —**âne** (....—.) P in a friendly manner.

müteveffa مُتَوَفَّى A deceased, dead; the late.

müteveffık^{kı} مُتَوَفِّق A *lrnd.* successful.

mütevehhim مُتَوَهِّم A *lrnd.* who has imaginary fears; suspecting, fearing. —**âne** (....—.) P suspiciously. —**in** (.....—) A *pl.* of **mütevehhim**.

mütevekkil مُتَوَكِّل A who puts all his trust in God; resigned. —**âne** (....—.) P trustingly; resignedly.

mütevekkilen (...'..) مُتَوَكِّلًا A *lrnd.* confiding, relying. — **alallah** trusting in God.

mütevelli مُتَوَلِّي A administrator, especia the trustee of a pious foundation.

mütevellid مُتَوَلِّد A 1. born; come 2. caused, resulting. —**ât** (....—) A *lrı*../dan/ female children.

mütevellih مُتَوَلِّه A *lrnd.* lost in wonder or perplexity; amazed, stupified. —**âne** (....—.) P lost in wonder.

müteverrık^{kı} مُتَوَرِّق A *lrnd.* that has leaves.

müteverrıt مُتَوَرِّط A *lrnd.* fallen into an abyss; involved in great trouble.

müteverriⁱⁱ مُتَوَرِّع A *lrnd.* piously scrupulous; continent, abstinent. —**âne** (....—.) P abstinently.

müteverrim مُتَوَرِّم A *path.* 1. tubercular. 2. swollen.

mütevessık^{kı} مُتَوَثِّق A *lrnd.* 1. firm, immovable. 2. relying upon; authenticated. —**ane** (....—.) P firmly.

mütevessiⁱⁱ مُتَوَسِّع A *lrnd.* wide, spacious; extensive; comprehensive.

mütevessid مُتَوَسِّد A *lrnd.* lying or leaning on a cushion. —**en** (...'..) A lying.

mütevessih مُتَوَسِّخ A *lrnd.* soiled, dirty.

mütevessil مُتَوَسِّل A *lrnd.* 1. who has recourse to God or man in full trust. 2. studious of obtaining nearness of access. —**en** (...'..) A confidingly, relying.

müteveşşih مُتَوَشِّح A *lrnd.* 1. who puts on a sword suspended from the shoulder. 2. decked out, adorned.

mütevettir مُتَوَتِّر A *lrnd.* stretched tight.

müteveyyil مُتَوَيِّل A *lrnd.* wailing; a wailer.

mütevezziⁱⁱ مُتَوَزِّع A *lrnd.* dividing, dealing.

mütevvec مُتَوَّج A *lrnd.* crowned.

mütevvic مُتَوِّج A *lrnd.* that crowns.

müteyakkın مُتَيَقِّن A *lrnd.* sure, convinced; certified.

müteyakkız مُتَيَقِّظ A awake, vigilant; watchful, circumspect. —**âne** (....—.) P *lrnd.* vigilantly.

müteyemmen مُتَيَمَّن A *lrnd.* fortunate, auspicious, of good omen.

müteyemmim مُتَيَمِّم A *lrnd.* who uses sand when water is not to be had for performing ablutions. —**âne** (....—.) P in the manner of one who performs an ablution in form.

müteyemmimen (...'..) مُتَيَمِّمًا A *lrnd.* in the manner of performing ablution in form.

müteyemmin مُتَيَمِّن A *lrnd.* who regards himself as fortunate. —**en** (...'..) A auspiciously.

müteyessir مُتَيَسِّر A *lrnd.* 1. attained, accomplished; successful. 2. easy.

mütezad^{ddı} مُتَضاد A *lrnd.* mutually opposed, contrary.

mütezahif (..—.) مُتَزاحِف A *lrnd.* mustering like troops. —**âne** (..—.—.) P in the manner of mustering troops. —în (..—.—) A *pl. of* **mütezahıf**.

mütezahıkᵏⁱ (..—.) متضاحك A *lrnd.* who laughs at or with another, laughing together.

mütezahim (..—.) متزاحم A *lrnd.* crowding and disturbing each other; crowded, squeezed together, thronging (people). —în (..—.—) A *pl.*

mütezahir (..—.) متظاهر A *lrnd.* visible, manifest.

mütezaif (..—.) متضاعف A *lrnd.* increased to twice as much; doubled.

mütezakir (..—.) متذاكر A *lrnd.* 1. mutually remembering. 2. mutually conferring, consulting.

mütezakkım متزقّم A *lrnd.* who swallows food in leisurely fashion. —âne (....—.) P eating at leisure. —în (....—) A *pl. of* **mütezakkım**.

mütezallıl متظلّل A *lrnd.* 1. that goes into shade. 2. who seeks or finds protection.

mütezarib (..—.) متضارب A *lrnd.* beating one another.

mütezavic (..—.) متزاوج A *lrnd.* 1. marrying each other. 2. resembling each other in form or sound (words).

mütezavil (..—.) متزاول A *lrnd.* mutually vying, contending.

mütezavir (..—.) متزاور A *lrnd.* 1. mutually visiting. 2. turning aside, deviating. —în (..—.—) A *pl.*

mütezayıkᵏⁱ (..—.) متضايق A *lrnd.* narrow, straitened (in mind or place).

mütezayid (..—.) متزايد A which increases, increasing; multiplied. — **vergi** *fin.* progressive taxation.

mütezebbid متزبّد A *lrnd.* 1. foaming, frothing. 2. having cream on the surface (milk). 3. very angry.

mütezebzib متزبذب A *lrnd.* 1. tossed about; wavering. 2. capricious. 3. agitated, confused, restless.

mütezehhid متزهّد A *lrnd.* ascetic; pious, devout. —âne (....—.) P piously. —în (....—) A *pl. of* **mütezehhid**.

mütezehhir متزهّر A *lrnd.* blossoming, flowering.

mütezekki متزكّي A *lrnd.* 1. that becomes purified. 2. who gives alms. 3. very pious.

mütezekkir متذكّر A *lrnd.* 1. who remembers, who recalls to mind. 2. talking things over in consultation.

mütezellikᵏⁱ متزلّق A *lrnd.* slippery; slidden, fallen down.

mütezellil متذلّل A *lrnd.* 1. humble, submissive; meek. 2. humiliated, debased; contemptible, servile. —âne (....—.) P 1. humbly. 2. contemptibly.

mütezelzil متزلزل A *lrnd.* shaken, convulsed; trembling.

mütezemmil متزمّل A *lrnd.* who wraps himself in a cloak.

mütezenbir متزنبر A *lrnd.* who assumes a haughty manner; who is oppressive in behavior.

mütezendikᵏⁱ متزندق A *lrnd.* 1. who becomes a Magian; who is a worshipper of fire. 2. atheist, impious.

mütezevvıkᵏⁱ متذوّق A *lrnd.* 1. who tastes. 2. who enjoys a pleasure.

mütezevvic متزوّج A *lrnd.* who takes a spouse; married. —în (....—) A *pl.*

mütezevvid متزوّد A *lrnd.* who makes provision for a journey. —în (....—) A *pl.*

mütezeyyin متزيّن A *lrnd.* adorned, ornamented.

müthiş مدهش *var. of* **müdhiş**.

müt'ib متعب A *lrnd.* tiring, fatiguing.

mütimᵐᵐⁱ متمّم A *lrnd.* that completes, perfects.

mütlif متلف A *lrnd.* destroying.

müttahiz متّخذ A *lrnd.* who takes to himself; who adopts, who seizes.

müttaki متّقي A *lrnd.* 1. God-fearing, pious, devout. 2. who takes care of himself, who avoids danger, or impropriety.

müttakin متّيقن A *lrnd.* sure of, certain.

müttefakᵏⁱ متّفق A *lrnd.* agreed.

müttefikᵏⁱ متّفق A 1. that conforms, agrees; agreeing. 2. in league with, allied; ally, confederate. 3. unanimous.

müttefikan (.'..) متّفقاً A 1. unanimously. 2. in agreement.

müttefikürrey متّفق الرأي A *lrnd.* unanimously in agreement.

müttehaz متّخذ A 1. accepted, adopted. 2. current, in use.

müttehem متّهم A accused, suspected (of).

müttehid متّحد A united; agreeing; unanimous; in accord. —en (.'..) A *lrnd.* unanimously; unitedly. —iyet unity.

müttehim متّهم A 1. who accuses or suspects; accusing. 2. accused, suspected; guilty.

müttekâ متّكا A *lrnd.* anything leaned upon; cushion, bolster; arm rest.

müttesiᵘ متّسع A *lrnd.* 1. large, broad, spacious. 2. dilated.

mütun (.—) متون A *lrnd., pl. of* **metin 1**, texts; original texts.

müvaade (.—..) مواعده A *lrnd.* an appointing a place or time of meeting; a promising.

müvaaze (.—..) مواعظ A *lrnd.* a preaching; exhortation.

müvacehe (.—..) مواجهه A *same as* **muvacehe**.

müvalât (.——) موالات A *lrnd.* mutual confidence and reliance; friendship, love.

müvecceh موجّه A lrnd. 1. /a/ directed towards; sent to. 2. suitable, reasonable, right.

müveffer موفّر A lrnd. made numerous; plentiful.

müvekkil موكّل A same as **müekkil**.

müvellâ مولّى A lrnd., law set in charge over a thing, charged.

müvelled مولّد A lrnd. 1. begotten, born. 2. adopted from another language (word); invented. 3. can. law foreign as to parentage but home-born and adopted as a slave. —**ât** (...—) A pl.

müvellid مولّد A 1. that generates, begets; begetting; generator; math. generant. 2. lrnd. who or that causes to be born. —**i kuvvet** psych. dynamogenic. —**i levn** art chromatogenous.

müvellide مولّدة A lrnd. midwife.

müvellidül-humuza مولّد الحموضة A chem. oxygen.

müvellidül-ma مولّد الماء A chem. hydrogen.

müverrah مورّخ A lrnd. dated. —**ân** (...) A at a dated time.

müverrih مورّخ A who dates; chronicler; historian. —**în** (...—) A pl.

müvessah موسّخ A lrnd. soiled, befouled.

müvessiⁱⁱ موسّع A lrnd. that enlarges, widens.

müvessih موسّخ A lrnd. who soils, befouls.

müvesvis موسوس A naturally suspicious, troubled by scruples; apprehensive. —**lik** suspiciousness.

müveşşah موشّح A 1. pros. with two or more pairs of rhymes in each verse (poem). 2. lrnd. in which the first word determines the last (clause). 3. lrnd. attired or adorned with a baldric.

müveşşahat (...—) موشّحات A lrnd. a sort of ode.

müvezziⁱⁱ موزّع A 1. postman; paper boy. 2. lrnd. who distributes, distributing. —**lik** occupation of a postman.

müyaveme (.—..) مياومة A lrnd. a contracting, hiring or working by the day. —**et=** to hire by the day.

müyavim (.—.) مياوم A lrnd. that hires or contracts by the day.

müyemmen ميمّن A lrnd. 1. made prosperous. 2. congratulated.

müyesser ميسّر A /a/ facilitated by God; favorable (any happy matter).

müyessir ميسّر A lrnd. who facilitates matters and so gives success.

- **müz 1** مز cf. - **mız**.
- **müz 2** F myth. the muse.

müzab (.—) مذاب A lrnd. melted, fused; liquified, liquid.

müza'fer مزعفر A lrnd. 1. colored or flavored with saffron. 2. a kind of pilav.

müzah (.—) مزاح A same as **mizah**.

müzahaf (.—.) مزاحف A pros. 1. altered from its original form (prosodial foot). 2. in which an altered foot occurs (couplet).

müzahame (.—..) مزاحمة A lrnd. 1. a hindering, disturbing, pressing upon; hindrance, obstruction. 2. crowd, mob, throng.

müzaheret (.—..) مظاهرت A same as **muzaheret**.

müzahgû (.——) مزاح‌گو P lrnd. joker. —**yâne** (.———.) P jokingly.

müzahim (.—.) مزاحم A lrnd. that throngs, mobs, opposes by thronging. —**ol=** to throng, to give trouble.

müzahref مزخرف A lrnd. 1. adorned, ornamented; varnished. 2. falsified; deceitful.

müzahrefat (...—) مزخرفات A lrnd. 1. exaggerations and interpolations, lies. 2. excrement; filth.

müzakerat (.—.—) مذاكرات A lrnd. negotiations. —**ruznamesi** agenda.

müzakere (.—..) مذاكرة A 1. discussion, consultation, conference, negotiation. 2. lrnd. the rehearsing of their lesson by pupils amongst themselves; a reciting of the previous lessons in class. 3. psych. deliberation. —**et=** /ı/ to talk over, to discuss (a subject).

müzakereci (.—...) مذاكره‌جى 1. master who hears students reciting their lessons, tutor. 2. Ott. hist. official who goes over and corrects documents in a government office.

müzakir (.—.) مذاكر A lrnd. 1. who converses and consults with another. 2. usher to a school; tutor to a student.

müzaraa 1 (.—..) مزارعة A lrnd. a letting or taking land for a share of the harvest; share cropping.

müzaraa 2 (.—..) مذارعة A lrnd. a selling or buying by the **arşın** (cubit: distance shoulder to fingertip).

müzarebe (.—..) مضاربة A lrnd., same as **mudarebe**. —**et=** to fight.

müzavece (.—..) مزاوجة A lrnd. a marrying. —**et=** to marry.

müzavele (.—..) مزاولة A lrnd. 1. a laboring, endeavoring; labor, endeavor. 2. a causing something to be near to another thing.

müzayaka (.—..) مضايقة A 1. hardship, straits; difficulty. 2. scarcity, want, necessity; distress.

müzayede (.—..) مزايدة A sale by auction; auction. —**ile sat=** to sell by auction.

müzayele (.—..) مزايلة A lrnd. a departing from, abandoning, quitting. —**et=** to abandon, quit.

müzcat (.—) مزجاة A lrnd. a small matter, trifle.

müzd مزد P lrnd. remuneration, premium, reward; pay. —**i dendan** (lit., tooth hire)

money distributed to the poor at the time of feasting.
müzdad (.—) مزداد A *lrnd.* increased, augmented.
müzdahim مزدحم A *lrnd.* crowded, thronging.
Müzdelife مزدلفة A *lrnd.*, name of a place near Mecca between mount Arafat and the valley of Mina.
müzdevic, müzdevice مزدوج مزدوجه A 1. *lrnd.* coupled, united, wedded. 2. *bot.*, *math.* conjugate.
müzdver مزدور P *lrnd.* hired servant, hireling. **—i dev** (*lit.*, hireling of the devil) 1. idle mischief-maker. 2. man in government service. **—î** (..—) P, **—lik** 1. the quality of a hired servant. 2. bodily labor; service.
müze موزه F museum.
müzebzeb مذبذب A *lrnd.* in utter confusion; hesitating, irresolute.
müzebzib مذبذب A *lrnd.* vacillating, hesitating; capricious, inconstant.
müzecilikᵍⁱ موزه جیلك museology.
müzeffet مزفت A *lrnd.* pitched, pitchy, tarred.
müzehheb مذهب A worked, ornamented or plated with gold; gilt, gilded.
müzehhib مذهب A gilder; gold-embroiderer.
müzekkâ مزكى A *lrnd.* purified; cleared, justified.
müzekker مذكر A 1. *gram.* masculine. 2. *lrnd.* male; masculine. **—i semai** (*lit.*, male by hearsay) henpecked husband.
müzekkere 1 مذكره A memorandum; note, warrant.
müzekkere 2 مذكره A *lrnd.* 1. masculine. 2. masculine in manners (woman).
müzekki مزكى A *lrnd.* 1. who pays the canonical poor-rate on property. 2. who ascertains the character of a proffered witness.
müzekkir مذكر A *lrnd.* 1. that reminds; adviser, admonisher. 2. praiser (especially of God).
müzekkire مذكره A *lrnd.*, same as **müzekkere 1**.
müzelikᵍⁱ موزه لك 1. worthy of a museum; precious. 2. queer, strange and antiquated.
müzellel مذلل A *lrnd.* made low, abject; humiliated.
müzellil مذلل A *lrnd.* that abases, humbles, humiliates.

müzelzel مزلزل A *lrnd.* shaken; shaking.
müzemmel مزمل A *lrnd.* wrapped in a cloak or wrap. **M— Suresi** a name of the seventy-third sura of the Quran.
müzemmil مزمل A *lrnd.* who wraps up and hides in his garments.
müzerkeş مزركش A *lrnd.* embroidered with gold wire.
müzevva مزوى A *lrnd.* having a corner; angular.
müzevveb مذوب A *lrnd.* melted; liquefied.
müzevvec مزوج A *lrnd.* married; paired, coupled.
müzevver مزور A *lrnd.* corrupted, sham; falsified.
müzevvir مزور A who falsifies; trickster; sneak; mischief-maker. **—âne** (...—.) P sneakingly. **—în** (...—) A *lrnd.*, *pl. of* **müzevvir**. **—lik** trickery; tale-telling.
müzeyyel مذيل A *lrnd.* 1. appendaged; having an appendix or addendum. 2. having an answer appended below (document). 3. tailed; skirted, long-skirted. **—ât** (...—) A appendages; addenda.
müzeyyelen (..'..) مذيلاً A *lrnd.* as an appendix or addendum.
müzeyyen مزين A *lrnd.* embellished, decorated; adorned.
müzeyyif مزيف A *lrnd.* who mocks, who deems contemptible; derisive. **—âne** (...—.) P derisively.
müzeyyin مزين A *lrnd.* that embellishes, decorates.
müzhere مزهره A *lrnd.* place abounding with flowers, flower garden.
müziⁱⁱ مذيع A *lrnd.* who divulges a secret.
müz'ic مزعج A troublesome, annoying; vexatious.
müzikᵍⁱ موزيك F western style music. **—li** musical.
müzilⁱⁱⁱ 1 مذل A *lrnd.* that abases; who renders abject; God, the abaser of the haughty.
müzil 2 (.—) مزيل A *lrnd.* that removes, abolishes.
müzmin مزمن A *lrnd.* of long duration, chronic (disease).
müzminleş=ⁱʳ مزمنلشمك to become chronic.
müznib مذنب A *lrnd.* sinner, culprit; criminal, faulty. **—âne** (..—.) P sinfully. **—în** (..—) A *pl. of* **müznib**.

N

N, n 1 *The seventeenth letter of the alphabet.*
═n═ 2   ن   *after consonants* ═ın═,
═in═ *etc.* 1. *reflexive, as in* **yıkan**═,
giyin═, **sarın**═, **tutun**═, **bölün**═. 2. *(only after vowel and* -l*) passive, as in* **okun**═,
sallan═.
═**n 3**   ك   *archaic for* ═yın *etc., plural imperative, e. g.,* **din** *say,* **kon** *put,* **beklen** *wait.*
-**n 4**   ك   *after consonants* -ın 3, -in 2, -un 6, -ün 6, *pl.* -nız, *etc., possessive of second person singular* (familiar) *your, e. g.,* **odan** *your room,* **evin** *your house.*
na 1   نه   *There. There it is. Take it.* — **kafa** *What a fool I (he, etc.) was! What was I thinking about?* — **sana** *So much for you! There! Take that!*
nâ- 2 (—)   نا   P *negative prefix* non-, un-, dis-, mis-, *as in* **nâbina, nâehl.**
-**nâ 3** (—)   نا   P *lrnd. place, as in* **tengna.**
naam 1   نعم   A *lrnd.* yes.
naam 2   نعم   A *lrnd.* domesticated animals (*esp.* camels or sheep).
naam 3 (.—)   نعام   A *lrnd.* ostrich. —**ât** (.——) *pl.*
naamet (.—.)   نعامت   A *lrnd.* stupidity like that of the ostrich; utter ignorance.
nâaşina (——.—)   ناآشنا   P *lrnd.* not acquainted, stranger, unknown.
naat[ti]   نعت   *var. of* **na't.**
nab 1 (—)   ناب   P *lrnd.* 1. pure, clear, limpid. 2. unmixed, unadulterated, unalloyed.
nâb 2 (—)   ناب   A *lrnd.* 1. tusk, canine tooth. 2. ivory.
nabaliğ (——.)   نابالغ   P *lrnd.* underage, unripe, immature.
Nabati (..—)   نبطی   A *hist.* Nabatean.
nabayeste (——..)   نابایسته   P *lrnd.* improper, unlawful.

nabazan (..—)   نبضان   A *lrnd.* 1. a pulsating; pulsation. 2. a twanging a bowstring; twang.
nabeca (—.—)   ناجا   P *lrnd.* inopportune, out of place.
nabedid (—.—)   نابدید   P *lrnd.* out of sight, invisible; disappeared. — **ol**═ to disappear.
nabehencar (—..—)   نابهنجار   P *lrnd.* misplaced; wrong, improper.
nabehengâm (—..—)   نابهنگام   P *lrnd.* unseasonable, untimely.
nabehired (—...)   نابخرد   P *lrnd.* unwise.
nabehre (—..)   نابهره   P *lrnd.* 1. great, choice, excellent. 2. bad, spurious, abject. 3. worthless.
nabekaide (—.—..)   ناقاعده   P *lrnd.* against the rule.
nabekâr (—.—)   ناکار   P *lrnd.* useless, good for nothing.
nabeled (—..)   نابلد   P *lrnd.* unfamiliar with a place; unacquainted with the ways and manners of a country; ignorant of, not at home in a situation.
nabemahal[III] (—...)   نابمحل   P *lrnd.* untimely, out of place.
nabemevsim (—...)   نابمموسم   P *lrnd.* premature, out of season.
naberca (—.—)   نابرجا   P *lrnd.* displaced, out of place.
nabesud (—.—)   نابسود   P *lrnd.* 1. useless, disadvantageous. 2. unused, quite new.
nabız[bzı] **1**   نبض |nabz| 1. pulse. 2. pulsation. —**ı at**═ to pulsate. — **atışı**, — **atması** pulsation. —**ına bak**═ /ın/ to feel one's pulse. —**ına gir**═ to win someone's favor. —**a göre şerbet ver**═ to feel the atmosphere; to feel one's way with a person. —**ını tut**═, —**ını yokla**═ /ın/ 1. to feel the pulse (of). 2. to sound out somebody's intentions.

nâbız 2 (—.) نابض A lrnd. 1. beating (artery), throbbing (pulse). 2. thrower, darter.
nâbi 1 (—.) نابی A lrnd. high, elevated.
nâbi' 2 (—.) نابع A lrnd. welling up; flowing.
nabice (—..) نابجه A lrnd. calamity, evil, misfortune.
nabiga (—..) نابغه A lrnd. 1. man of magnificence or of exalted rank; genius. 2. a suddenly famous poet.
nabih (—.) نابه A lrnd. 1. important, grave (affair). 2. great, celebrated (man).
nabina (———) نابینا P lrnd. blind, weak-sighted; unseeing. —i (————) P blindness.
nabit (—.) نابت A lrnd. growing, which grows. — ol= to grow (plant).
nâbud (——) نابود P lrnd. nonexistent. — et= /ı/ to destroy, annihilate. — ol= to disappear. —i (———) P nonexistence.
nabz نبض A same as nabız 1. —a A one beat. —âşina (.—.—) P same as nabzgîr.
nabzgîr (.—) نبض‌گیر P lrnd. who feels the pulse of another and suits his action to its requirements; timeserver.
nabzî (.—) نبضی A lrnd. pulsatory.
nâcâiz (——.) ناجائز A lrnd. illicit; unlawful; not allowed.
nacak[1] ناجاق large axe with a hammer at the back.
nacar ناجار prov., var. of neccar.
na'ce نعجه A lrnd. ewe.
nâci (—.) ناجی A lrnd. 1. who is saved; especially, who avoids eternal damnation. 2. w. cap. Noah (as having escaped the flood). 3. one who escapes; swift.
nacins (—.) ناجنس P lrnd. of inferior quality.
nacis (—.) ناجس A lrnd. incurable (disease).
naciz (—.) ناجذ A lrnd. wisdom tooth.
nacud (——) ناجود A lrnd. 1. any vessel for holding wine; large goblet. 2. wine. 3. blood.
naçar (——) ناچار P 1. who has no remedy; forced by necessity; helpless, in distress. 2. reluctantly; of necessity.
naçesban, naçespan (—.—) ناچسبان P lrnd. unseemly, improper.
naçide (——.) ناچیده P lrnd. ungathered.
nâçiz (——) ناچیز P lrnd. 1. of no account; insignificant. 2. modest; humble.
nâçizâne (———.) ناچیزانه P lrnd. humbly, in a humble manner.
nâçizî (———) ناچیزی P lrnd. insignificance, nothingness.
nâdan (——) نادان P 1. tactless, unmannerly; indelicate. 2. ignorant, uneducated. —i (———) P lrnd. tactlessness; unmannerliness.

nâdaniste (———..) نادانسته P lrnd. ignorantly; unwittingly.
nadas نطاس نداس نداط ناداس 1. preliminary plowing of land for cleaning before preparing the seed bed; fallowing. 2. arable field fallowed and cleaned. — et= /ı/ to fallow and clean an arable field, to prepare land for sowing the following year.
nademsaz (—.—) نادمساز P lrnd. at variance, out of harmony, discordant.
naderberaber (—..—.) نادربرابر P lrnd. impertinent, irrelevant; incongruous, unconnected.
nadi 1 (—.) نادی A lrnd. public crier; who convokes.
nadi 2 (—.) نادی A lrnd. 1. council; assembly. 2. place of assembly.
nadic (.—) نضیج A lrnd., same as nazic.
nadide (——.) نادیده P 1. rare; precious. 2. never seen before.
nadidenî (——.—) نادیدنی P lrnd. not fit to be seen; invisible.
nadim (—.) نادم A regretful; sorry; penitent. — ol= to regret; to be sorry.
nadimâne (—.—.) نادمانه P lrnd. regretfully.
nadimiyet (—.—.) نادمیت A lrnd. regret; penitence.
nadir (—.) نادر A rare, unusual; rarely, seldom.
nadirât (—.—) نادرات A rare and unusual things. —tan very rare.
nadire (—..) نادره A lrnd. 1. rarity. 2. anecdote, witticism.
nadiredan (—..—.) نادره‌دان P lrnd. knowing rare, mysterious things; intelligent, learned.
nadiregû (—..—) نادره‌گو P lrnd. one who says witty or wise things.
nadiren (—'..) نادراً A rarely, seldom.
nadireperdaz (—...—) نادره‌پرداز P lrnd. witty, intelligent.
nadiresenc (—...) نادره‌سنج P lrnd. witty; who tells witty stories.
nadireza (—..—) نادره‌زا P who produces witticisms.
nadirî (—.—) نادری P lrnd. rareness, rarity.
nadürüst (—..) نادرست P lrnd. incorrect; unjust. —i (—..—) P incorrectness; unsoundness; a wrong.
naehl (—.) ناأهل P lrnd. incapable; inexpert; unqualified; unfit.
naendiş (—.—) ناندیش P lrnd. requiring no thought; clear, evident.
nâf (—) ناف P lrnd. navel; middle of a thing. —i arz (lit. center of the earth) Mecca. —i hefte Tuesday.
nafaka نفقه A 1. livelihood, means of subsistence. 2. law maintenance allowance, alimony. — bağla= /a/ to assign a subsistence

nafe

allowance to. **—sını temin et=** to earn one's living.

nafe (—.) نافه P *lrnd.* 1. perfume obtained from the musk deer. 2. fur from the belly of an animal. 3. the hair of one's beloved.

nâfercam (—.—) نافرجام P *lrnd.* 1. coming to a bad end. 2. trifling; useless (thing).

nâferiz (—.—) نافريز P *lrnd.* which spreads perfume.

nafi[ii] **1** (—.) نافع A useful, profitable; beneficial.

nafi 2 (—.) نافى A *lrnd.* 1. that denies; negative. 2. that drives away.

nafia (—..) نافعه A public works; Ministry of Public Works. **N— Vekâleti** Ministry of Public Works.

nafice (—..) نافجه P *lrnd.* a bag of musk; musk-pod.

nâfih (—.) نافخ A *lrnd.* that blows with the breath.

nafile (—..) نافله A 1. useless, in vain; purposeless, wasted. 2. a voluntary or supererogatory act of worship. **—!** It's no use! Don't persist. **— yere** uselessly; in vain.

nafir (—.) نافر A *lrnd.* timid, shy.

nafiz (—.) نافذ A 1. influential. 2. *lrnd.* penetrating.

nafize (—..) نافذه A *lrnd.* orifice of the body.

naftalin نافتالين F naphthalene.

nagâh (——) ناگاه P *lrnd.* 1. suddenly; unexpected.

nagam نغم A *lrnd.* singing; vocal music.

nagamat (..—) نغمات A *lrnd.,* pl. of **nağme.**

nagamkâr (..—) نغمكار P *lrnd.* melodious.

nagamperver نغمپرور P *lrnd.* who likes music.

nagamsaz (..—) نغمساز P *lrnd.* who sings.

nagant ناغانت mil. an old-fashioned kind of pistol.

nâgeh (—.) ناگه P *lrnd., var.* of **nagâh.**

nâgehan (—.—) ناگهان P *lrnd.* suddenly. **—î** (—.——) P sudden.

nâgehzuhur (—..—) ناگهظهور P *lrnd.* unexpected.

nagüvar (—.—), **nagüvare** (—.—.) ناگوار P *lrnd.* unpleasant to eat; indigestible.

nagüzir (—.—) ناگزير P *lrnd.* unavoidable; inevitable.

nağış ناغش *prov., same as* **nakış.**

nağız (—.) ناغض A *lrnd.* 1. tremulous, undulating. 2. cartilage (of the shoulder blade).

nağme نغمه A 1. tune; song. 2. musical note. 3. *colloq.* roundabout way of saying something. **—yi değiştir=** to change one's tune; to tone down. **— yap=** *colloq.* to say something pretending not to care about the matter at hand. **—ger, —hîz** (..—), **—keş,** **—perdaz** (...—), **—saz** (..—), **—seray** (...—) *same as* **nağmezen.**

nağmezen نغمهزن P *lrnd.* singer, musician; warbler.

nağz نغز P *lrnd.* good, beautiful; first-rate, excellent.

nah 1 ناه *colloq., same as* **na 1.**

nah 2 نخ P *lrnd.* 1. rope. 2. raw thread of yarn of any sort. 3. carpet (beautiful on both sides and having a long pile).

naha[ai] (.—) نخاع A *lrnd.; same as* **nuha.**

nahafet (.—.) نحافت A *same as* **nehafet.**

nahah (——) ناخواه P *lrnd.* unwillingly, involuntarily.

nahak[kkı] (—.) ناحقه P unjust, iniquitous. **— yere** unjustly, unfairly; unnecessarily. **—lık** injustice.

nahalef (—..) ناخلف P *lrnd.* a bad follower; degenerate; vicious.

nahan (——) ناخوان P *lrnd.* 1. who does not read. 2. illegible.

nahast 1 (——) ناخواست P *lrnd.* unsolicited, undesired.

nahast 2 (——) ناخاست P *lrnd.* unable to rise.

nahaste (——.) ناخاسته P *lrnd.* 1. not risen; unfermented. 2. not come to pass.

nahb 1 نخب A *lrnd.* 1. a drawing out, extracting, extraction. 2. a selecting, choosing. 3. copious draught (drunk to the health of a friend).

nahb 2 نحب A *lrnd.* a weeping most violently; violent weeping. **—e** A fit of violent weeping.

nahcir (.—), **nahçir** (.—) نخچير P *lrnd.* 1. hunting, chase; game, prey. 2. hunting groud.

nahçirgâh (.——) نخچيرگاه P *lrnd.* hunting ground.

nahçirgir (.——) نخچيرگير P *lrnd.* hunter.

nahemta (—.—) ناهمتا P *lrnd.* unparalleled, incomparable.

nahemvar (—.—) ناهموار P *lrnd.* unequal, uneven, irregular; unbecoming, improper.

nahencar (—.—) ناهنجار P *lrnd.* rough, uneven; improper.

nahham (.—) نحام A *lrnd.* 1. one who breathes hard; one who often clears his throat. 2. miserly; miser.

nahhas 1 (.—) نخاس A *lrnd.* slave trader, cattle dealer.

nahhas 2 (.—) نحاس A *lrnd.* smelter, worker or seller of copper; coppersmith.

nahır ناخر *prov.* cattle; fold. **—cı** herdsman, drover.

nâhi 1 (—.) ناهى A *lrnd.* that forbids; prohibiting.

nahi 2 (—.) ناهی A *lrnd.* writer on syntax, syntactician.

nahib 1 (—.) ناهب A *lrnd.* who plunders, pillages.

nahib 2 (.—) نحيب A *lrnd.* a weeping and wailing bitterly.

nahib 3 (.—) نهيب A *lrnd.* timid, fearful, cowardly.

nahid 1 (—.) ناهد A *lrnd.* swelling, prominent (breast).

nahid 2 (——) ناهيد P *lrnd.* 1. the planet Venus. 2. young girl.

nahif (.—) نحيف A *lrnd.* thin, weak, fragile.

nahikᵏⁱ (—.) ناهق A *lrnd.* neighing; braying.

nahilʰⁱⁱ **1** نخل A *lrnd.*, same as **nahl 1, 2**.

nahil 2 (.—) نخيل A *lrnd.* palm tree; palm grove.

nahil 3 (.—) نحيل A *lrnd.* lean, slender.

nâhil 4 (—.) ناخل A *lrnd.* who selects, who sifts.

nahil 5 (—.) ناهل A *lrnd.* thirsty.

nahir 1 (.—) نحير A *lrnd.* stab in the pit of the throat (slaughtered camel).

nahir 2 (.—) نخير A *lrnd.* a snoring, snorting; snorting sound.

nahir 3 (.—) نخير P *lrnd.* ambush, lurking place.

nahire 1 (.—.) نحيره A *lrnd.* the first or last day of the lunar month; the last night of the month.

nahire 2 (.—..) ناحيره A *lrnd.*, same as **nahire 1**.

nahis 1 (—.) ناحس A *lrnd.* lean, disastrous (year); unpropitious.

nahis 2 (.—) نحيس A *lrnd.* unfortunate, barren (year); unlucky (date).

nahit (.—), **nahite** (.—.) نحيت A *lrnd.* 1. sob, moan. 2. nature; origin; disposition.

nahivʰᵛⁱ نحو [nahv] *gram.* syntax.

nahiye (—..) ناحيه A 1. administrative subdivision of a *kaza;* township. 2. district; region. 3. *anat.* region. — **müdürü** governor of a township.

nahiyevi (—..—) ناحيوى A 1. *lrnd.* regional. 2. *med.* local.

nahiz (.—) نحيز P *lrnd.* 1. ambush. 2. defective; coarse.

nahizgâh (.——) نحيزگاه P *lrnd.* ambush, lurking place.

nahlⁱⁱ **1** نخل A *lrnd.* palm tree.

nahlⁱⁱ **2** نخل P *lrnd.* 1. tree or bush of any kind. 2. date palm. 3. festoon, thyrsus. —**i matem**, —**i Muharrem** coffin. —**i tabut** funeral wreath, garland for a coffin. —**i Tur** the Burning Bush of Mount Sinai that appeared to Moses.

nahlⁱⁱ **3** نخل A *lrnd.* 1. a sifting, bolting (flour etc.). 2. a picking, choosing; choice, selection.

nahlⁱⁱ **4** نحل A *lrnd.* 1. honeybee. 2. gift. **N— Suresi** *name of the sixteenth sura of the Quran.*

nahlâra (.——) نخل‌آرا P *lrnd.* adorned with palm trees.

nahlbend نخلبند P *lrnd.* 1. maker of artificial flowers; engraver or molder of waxwork ornaments in the form of trees; ceroplast, wax modeller. 2. gardener.

nahlbün نخلبن P *lrnd.* palm tree.

nahle 1 نخله A *lrnd.* a single palm tree.

nahle 2 نحله A *lrnd.* one honeybee.

nahlistan (..—) نخلستان P *lrnd.* palm grove; country of date palms.

nahliye 1 نخليه A *lrnd.*, *bot.*, Palmaceae.

nahliye 2 نحليه A *lrnd.*, *zool.*, Aphides.

nahlzar (.—) نخلزار P *lrnd.* palm grove.

nahme نخم A *lrnd.* expectorated phlegm, mucus.

nahmet نخمت A *lrnd.* beauty, elegance.

nahnaha نحنحه A *lrnd.* a hemming, clearing the throat.

nahoş (—.) ناخوش P 1. disagreeable, unpleasant. 2. unwell, ailing.

nahoşgüvar (—..—) ناخوشگوار P *lrnd.* 1. difficult to digest. 2. unwholesome (meat).

nahoşî (—.—) ناخوشى P *lrnd.* 1. unpleasantness. 2. indisposition.

nahoşlukᵗᵘ ناخوشلق same as **nahoşî**.

nahoşnud (—.—) ناخوشنود P *lrnd.* discontented, dissatisfied. —**î** (—.——) P discontentedness, displeasure.

nahr نحر A *lrnd.* 1. a stabbing, a slaughtering. 2. throat; the upper part of the breast. 3. a having the right hand placed upon the left over the breast while standing erect at prayer. 4. the beginning of the day, month, or new moon.

nahre نخره A *lrnd.*, *med.* necrosis.

nahs نحس A *lrnd.* 1. evil fortune, inauspiciousness. 2. dark and mysterious affair. 3. either of the two inauspicious planets, Mars and Saturn. —**i asgar** Mars. —**i ekber** Saturn.

nahsan (.—), **nahseyn** نحسان A *lrnd.* the two inauspicious planets Mars and Saturn.

nahtⁱⁱ نحت A *lrnd.* a chopping, planing, shaving (wood). — **san'atı** sculpture.

nahuda 1 (—.—) ناخدا P *lrnd.* godless, atheist.

nahuda 2 (—.—) ناخدا P *lrnd.* ship's captain.

nahudaters (—.—.) ناخداترس P *lrnd.* not God-fearing.

nahufte (—..) ناخفته P *lrnd.* 1. not lying down; not sleeping. 2. unstaunched (blood).

nahun (—.) ناخن P *lrnd.* 1. fingernail;

nahunaftab

claw; hoof. 2. nib of a pen. —ı **âftab***. — **be dendan** (lit., with fingernail between the teeth) amazed or regretful. —ı **hâme** nib.

nahunaftab (—.——) ناف آفتاب P lrnd. fire.

nàhunbür, nâhunbüra ناخن بر ، ناخن برا P lrnd. small knife or scissors for paring the nails.

nahune (—..) ناخنه P lrnd. 1. any nail-like thing; plectrum of a lute etc. 2. onyx in the eye.

nahvᵛⁱ نحو A lrnd. 1. same as **nahiv**. 2. direction, side. 3. margin, quarter, region.

nahvet نخوت A lrnd. haughtiness, conceit, self-importance.

nahvetfürüş (...—) نخوت فروش P lrnd. conceited, proud.

nahvetpişe (..—.) نخوت پیشه P lrnd. conceited, haughty.

nahvi (.—) نحوی A lrnd. 1. syntactical, grammatical. 2. grammarian.

nahviyin (.——), **nahviyûn** (.——) نحویین ، نحویون A lrnd. grammarians, teachers of syntax.

nahz نخز A lrnd. 1. a puncturing, pricking or stabbing with a pointed instrument. 2. hurting by words.

nai 1 (—.) ناعی A lrnd. one who officially proclaims the death of a person.

naiⁱⁱ **2** (—.) نائع A lrnd. 1. ready to faint from hunger. 2. thirsty.

naib نائب A 1. regent. 2. substitute. 3. Ott. hist. substitute judge. —**i fail** gram. subject of a passive verb.

naibe (—..) نائبه A lrnd. 1. fem. of **naib**. 2. intermittent fever, ague. 3. calamity, disaster.

naibülharem (—....) نائب الحرم A Ott. hist. judge-substitute of Medina.

nailⁱⁱ (—.) نائل A lrnd. who obtains, who attains. — **ol**= /a/ to obtain, to acquire, to attain. —**iyet** (—.—.) A attainment, acquisition.

nâim 1 (—.) نائم A lrnd. who sleeps; sleepy.

naim 2 نعم A lrnd. soft; easy; gentle.

naim 3 (.—) نعیم A lrnd. 1. pleasure, luxury, ease. 2. God's bounty to His creatures. 3. name of the fourth of the eight paradises mentioned in the Quran. —**i ayn** sparkle of the eye with happiness; delight. —**i dünya** conveniences and luxuries of life. —**i ilâhî** favors or graces of God.

naim 4 (—.) ناعم A lrnd. 1. soft. 2. young and tender. —**at** (—.—) A pl.

nâime (—..) ناعمه A lrnd. 1. delicate (woman). 2. zool., Mollusca.

naipᵇⁱ (—.) نائب [**naib**] regent. —**lik** 1. regency. 2. substitution. 3. judgeship.

nair (—.) نائر A lrnd. on fire; shining, bright.

naire (—..) نائره A lrnd. fire; flame; inflammation. —**i adavet** enmity. —**i harb ü kıtal**, —**i kifah** flames of war and battle.

-nâk 1 (—) ناک P lrnd. having plenty of, laden with, as in **derdnâk, gamnâk**.

nakᵏⁱ **2** نقع A lrnd. 1. firm, clayey soil on which water collects. 2. dust; cloud of dust.

nâka (—.) ناقة A lrnd. a she-camel.

nakabet (.—.) نقابت A lrnd., same as **nikabet**.

nâkabil (——.) ناقابل P 1. impossible. 2. incapable. —**i icra** impossible to carry out, impracticable.

nâkabul (—.—) ناقبول P lrnd. not consenting, unpleasant; unacceptable.

nâkâfi (———) ناکافی P lrnd. insufficient.

nakahatᵗⁱ نقاهت A same as **nekahet**.

nakaisˢⁱ (..—.) نقائص A lrnd., pl. of **nakisa**.

nakale نقله A lrnd., pl. of **nâkil 1**.

nâkâm (——) ناکام P lrnd. dissatisfied; disappointed. —**î** (————) P dissatisfaction; disappointment.

nakarat (..—) نقرات A 1. mus. the part repeated in songs, usually the second line refrain. 2. tiresome repetition, nagging.

nakare 1 (.—.) نقاره P 1. mus. a small kettledrum used in **mehter** music. 2. Ott. hist. military band that played in a public place or in front of the residence of a governor. — **faslı** mus. kettledrum solo (an interlude in a musical performance). —**hane** (.—.—.) same as **nakkarhane**. —**zen** (.—..) P lrnd. kettledrum player.

nakâre 2 (——.) ناکاره P lrnd. 1. useless, worthless. 2. idle, lazy. —**gi** (——.—) P idleness; uselessness.

nakari (.——) نقاری P lrnd. 1. kettledrummer. 2. maker or seller of kettle-drums.

nakâste (——.) ناکاسته P lrnd. undiminished, unaltered (regard).

nakavet (.—.) ناکاوت same as **nekavet**.

nakavt نقاوت E sports knockout.

nakayiⁱⁱ (..—.) نقایع A lrnd., pl. of **nakia**. —**i mevt** mortals.

nakb نقب A lrnd. 1. a digging a hole or tunnel through a wall, into a rock etc. 2. large hole or tunnel dug in wall, rock etc. —**zen** P digger; miner.

nakdᵈⁱ نقد A same as **nakid**. —**i can** lrnd. one's life given in support of a cause. —**i can et**= to sacrifice one's own life for a cause. — **ü cins** lrnd. cash and merchandise, coin and kind. —**a nakd** lrnd. in ready money successively paid down; prompt payment.

nakden (.'.) نقداً A lrnd. in cash, for ready money.

nakdî (. —) نقدِه A *lrnd.* cash; in ready money. **— kıymet** cash value. **— teminat** *law* pecuniary warrant, guarantee.

nakdine (. — .) نقدينه P *lrnd.* 1. ready money; cash. 2. valuable goods.

nâkerde (— . .) ناكرده P *lrnd.* not done, undone.

nâkes (— .) ناكس P *lrnd.* mean; despicable (person). **—î** (— . —) P, **—lik** meanness, despicableness.

nâkeşide (— . — .) ناكشيده P *lrnd.* 1. not drawn. 2. not drunk, unconsumed.

nakıd (— .) ناقد A *lrnd.* 1. examiner, essayer of coins. 2. clever.

nakıl نقل [nahl 1] palm branch. **— çiçeği** phlox.

nâkıliyet (— . . .) ناقليت A *same as* **nakiliyet**.

nakır (— .) ناقر A *lrnd.* 1. that hits the mark (arrow). 2. that excavates or perforates.

nakıs 1 (— .) ناقص A 1. minus; below zero (centigrade). 2. *lrnd.* deficient; defective. **— borçlar** *law* imperfect obligations.

nakıs 2 نقص *var. of* **naks**.

nakısulakl (— . . .) ناقص العقل A *lrnd.* deficient in intellect, unintelligent.

nakış[ks1] نقش A 1. embroidery. 2. design; drawing; decoration. 3. *Or. mus.* a variant of **murabba**, **ağırsemaî** and **yürüksemaî** in which every repeat is followed by a melodic passage. **— işle=** to embroider. **— işleri** embroidery, stitching. **—lı** embroidered; ornamented.

nakız[kz1] **1** نقض *var. of* **nakz**.

nâkız 2 (— .) ناقض A *lrnd.* 1. abrogating, violating. 2. contradicting.

naki 1 نقيّ A *lrnd.* clean, pure; exquisite.

naki[ii] **2** (. —) نقيع A *lrnd.* 1. potable, drinkable; that quenches thirst. 2. bountiful, copious (water).

nakia (. — .) نقيعه A *lrnd.* 1. feast given to a returned traveler. 2. wedding supper. 3. beast slaughtered for the entertainment of a guest.

nakib 1 (— .) ناقب A *lrnd.* that perforates, pierces.

nakib 2 (. —) نقيب A *lrnd.* chief, leader; warden of a guild or community.

nakiban (. — —) نقيبان P *lrnd.* chiefs, leaders. **—i bar** angels, archangels.

nakibe (. — .) نقيبه A *lrnd.* 1. soul, spirit; mind. 2. nature, disposition.

nakibüleşraf (. — . . —) نقيب الاشراف A 1. *lrnd.* chief of the descendants of the Prophet. 2. *Ott. hist.* representative at Istanbul of the Sherif of Mecca.

nakid[kd1] نقد [nakd] ready money, cash.

nâkil 1 (— .) ناقل A 1. *elec.* conductor. 2. *lrnd.* narrator. 3. translator; adapter. 4. *lrnd.* transporting, transferring.

nakil[kli] **2** نقل [nakl] 1. transport, transfer. 2. removal. 3. translation; adaptation. 4. narration. **—i hane** a move; change of address. **— kafilesi** *mil.* convoy. **—i mekân** 1. change of place. 2. change of residence. **— ve tâyin** transfer and appointment. **— vasıtaları** means of transport.

nakil 3 (— .) ناكل A *lrnd.* 1. who refrains or withdraws. 2. timid; weak.

nakile 1 (— . .) ناقله A *lrnd.* narrator, translator (woman).

nakile 2 (. — .) نقيله A *lrnd.* 1. patch on a boot, etc. 2. foreign (woman).

nakiliyet (— . — .) A, **nakiliyet** (— . . .) نقليت *elec.* conductivity.

nakir (. —) نقير A *lrnd.* 1. hollowed (wood) or stone; small groove in a date stone. 2. poor, mean, despised. 3. nature, origin, kind. **— ü kıtmir** the hole and skin of a date stone; a mere trifle; minutely.

nakis 1 (. —) نقيص A *lrnd.* defective; deficient; faulty.

nakis 2 (— .) ناكس A *lrnd.* who hangs down his head; humbled, depressed.

nakisa (. — .), **nakise** (. — .) نقيصه A *lrnd.* 1. defect. 2. shame, disgrace. **— getir=** /a/ to bring dishonor upon.

nakit[di] ناقد [nakd] ready money, cash.

nakiz (. —) نقيض A *lrnd.* contradictory, opposite. **—i müddea** *phil.* antithesis.

nakiza (. — .), **nakize** (. — .) نقيضه A *lrnd.* contradiction; contrary proposition, refutation.

nakkab (. —) نقّاب A *lrnd.* 1. who pierces. 2. examiner, scrutinizer.

nakkad (. —) نقّاد A *lrnd.* 1. examiner of coins. 2. prompt, ready. 3. critic.

nakkal[li] (. —) نقّال A *lrnd.* 1. narrator, story teller. 2. transcriber. 3. carrier.

nakkare (. — .) نقّاره *var. of* **nakare 1**.

nakkarhane (. — — .) نقّارخانه P *Ott. hist.* 1. military band. 2. place in a palace where the drums are beaten at stated intervals.

nakkaş (. —) نقّاش A 1. decorator; artist. 2. *lrnd.* sculptor; carver; engraver. **—ı âlem**, **—ı ezel** *lrnd.* God. **—î** (. — —) P, **—lık** drawing; painting; engraving.

nakl[li] نقل A *same as* **nakil 2**.

naklen (′ .) نقلاً A *lrnd.* 1. by transfer. 2. by tradition.

naklî (. —) نقلى A *lrnd.* 1. pertaining to transport. 2. traditional. 3. narrative.

nakliyat (. — —) A, **nakliyat** (. . —) نقليات 1. transport; means of transport, shipping. 2. *lrnd.* things handed down by tradition. **— birliği** *mil.* transport unit. **— gurubu** *mil.* convoy. **— resmi** transport tax. **— sigortası** insurance against risks of carriage; transport insurance. **—cı** shipping agent.

nakliye (. —.) A, **nakliye** (. . .′) نقليه 1. means of transport. 2. transport expenses. **— gemisi** transport ship. **— kıt'ası** *mil.* transport troops. **— komisyoncusu** forwarding agent. **— senedi** letter of carriage; way bill. **— sınıfı** *mil.* army service corps; military transport. **— takımı** *mil.* ferry. **—ci** shipping agent.

naklüddem نقل الدم A *med.* blood transfusion.

nakmet نقمت A *lrnd.* vengeance, an act of revenge or retaliation.

nakr نقر A *lrnd.* 1. a carving, inscribing; incising; sculpture. 2. a striking, beating; blow. 3. a blaming, chiding; reproach. 4. a blowing a horn, a trumpeting. 5. a bird's pecking with its beak; peck.

nakris نقرس A *med.*, same as **nıkris**.

naks نقص A *lrnd.* deficiency; imperfection. **—ı din** imperfection in a person's religion.

nakş نقش A *lrnd.*, same as **nakış**. **—ı bi gubar** cries of the oppressed. **—ı divar** (lit., a fresco on a wall) person without spirit or energy. **—ı kül** the universal design, *i. e.* all creation. **—ı nik** happy time. **—ı parmur** honeycomb. **—ı zerkâr** writing done in gold letters, chrysography.

nakşâbâd (. — —) نقش آباد P *lrnd.* wine and its enjoyments; strong drink.

nakşbaz (. —) نقشباز P *lrnd.* who plays cautiously and skillfully; intriguer.

nakşbeharam (. . . —) نقش بحرام P *lrnd.* (lit., embellishment to no purpose) a handsome foe.

nakşbend نقشبند P *lrnd.* 1. who adorns. 2. painter; embroiderer. 3. *w. cap.*, title of a great Muslim mystic. **—i havadis** the Designer of all existences, *i. e.* God.

nakşbendî (. . —) نقشبندى P *lrnd.* 1. art of painting or embroidering. 2. *w. cap.* the nakshbendi order of dervishes; a dervish of this order.

nakşberâb (. . —) نقش برآب P *lrnd.* (lit. writing on water) building on sand; words thrown away.

nakşet=ᵈᵉʳ نقش اتمك /ı/ 1. to decorate, to design. 2. to imprint.

nakşperdaz (. . —) نقش پرداز P *lrnd.* painter.

nakur (— —) ناقور A *lrnd.* trumpet.

nakus (— —) ناقوس A *lrnd.* church-bell; bell.

nakusî (— — —) ناقوسى A *Or. mus.*, name of a makam.

naküşade (—. —.) ناكشاده P *lrnd.* undisclosed; closed.

nakz نقض A annulment; a quashing; abrogation. **—ı ahdet**= *lrnd.* to break a treaty; to violate an engagement.

nakzen (′.) نقضاً A *lrnd.* by annulment; in violation.

nakzet=ᵈᵉʳ نقض اتمك /ı/ 1. to annul; to quash. 2. to violate; to contradict.

nal 1 نعل [na'l 2] 1. horseshoe. 2. iron point of a plow. 3. *archaic* a figure tattooed on the skin. **—ları at**= *slang* to die. **— çak**= to nail shoes on a horse; to shoe. **—ları dik**= *slang* to die. **— döğ**= *archaic* to prick a tattoo figure on the skin, to tattoo. **— kes**= 1. to make horseshoes. 2. *archaic* to tattoo. **—ını sökmek için ölmüş eşek arar** to try to make a profit out of nothing, with no effort. **— tokmağı** shoeing mallet (wooden hammer).

na'l 2 نال A *lrnd.* 1. same as **nal 1**. 2. *lrnd.* shoe, sandal, slipper. 3. *lrnd.* metal ferrule on a sheath.

nâlⁱⁱ **3** (—) نال P *lrnd.* 1. slender yellow reed; tube, pipe. 2. reed pen. 3. threads or pith inside of a reed pen. 4. sugar cane. 5. lamenting, complaining.

nâlân (— —) نالان P *lrnd.* moaning, lamenting. **— ol**= to moan, to lament.

nâlâyıkᵏⁱ (— —.) نالايق P *lrnd.* unworthy, unsuitable.

nalbaha (. . —) نعل بها P *hist.* horseshoe money; a forced contribution collected from villagers.

nalband, nalbantᵈⁱ نعلبند ـ نعلبنت P blacksmith, farrier. **—î** (. . —) P *lrnd.*, **—lık** horseshoeing.

nalbeki نعلبكى very small plate or saucer.

nalbur نعلبر P 1. hardware dealer. 2. smith who makes horseshoes.

nalça نعلچه P iron tip on a boot.

nalçala= نعلچه لمق /ı/ to tip a boot with iron.

nalçalı نعلچه لى tipped with iron (boot or shoe). **— gem** bridle bit with a horseshoe-shaped projection in the center.

nale (—.) ناله P *lrnd.* moan, groan.

nalekâr (—. —) ناله كار P *lrnd.* moaner, groaner.

nalekünân (—. . —) ناله كنان P *lrnd.* uttering complaints, groaning.

nalende (—. .) نالنده P *lrnd.* moaning, groaning; complaining.

nalet (—.) نعلت *colloq.*, same as **lânet**.

nalın نعلين [Arabic na'leyn] pattens, clogs.

nalıncı نعلينجى clog maker. **— keseri** 1. clog maker's adze. 2. egoist; selfish. **— keseri gibi kendine yont**= to think only of one's own advantage.

naliş (—.) ناليش P *lrnd.* moan, groan; lamentation. **—ker** (—. .) P moaning, groaning.

nalla= نعللمق ـ نعل لمق 1. /ı/ to shoe (a

horse). 2. *slang* to settle someone's account, to kill.

nallama نَـلَّـمـه *verbal n. of* **nalla=**. **— çekici** shoeing hammer. **— kerpeteni** blacksmith's tongs.

nallan=ır نَـلَّـنـمـق *pass. of* **nalla=**.

nam 1 (—) نَـام P 1. name, title. 2. fame, renown; reputation. 3. named. **—ıma** 1. in my name, on my behalf, for me. 2. addressed to me. **—ına** 1. in the name of, on behalf of. 2. addressed to. **—ında** named, called. **—ı altında** 1. under the name of. 2. disguised as. **— ü hesabına, — ve hesabına** on behalf of, for. **—ı ile** 1. with the name or title of. 2. disguised as. **— kazan=** to become famous, to be renowned. **—a muharrer** *com.* to the order. **—ı müstear** pseudonym, penname. **— ve neng** *lrnd.* reputation and honor. **— ve nişanı kalmadı** It has left no trace; it has totally disappeared. **— ver=** 1. to acquire a reputation. 2. to get a bad name.

na'm 2 نَـعـم A *lrnd.* a being happy; happiness. **—i ayn** sparkle in the eyes from happiness.

na'ma (.—) نَـعـمـاء A *lrnd.* boon, blessing; gift.

nama'dud (———) نَـامَـعـدود P *lrnd.* unlimited, boundless; innumerable.

namağlûb (———) نَـامَـغـلـوب P invincible; undefeated.

namahdud (—.—) نَـامَـحـدود P *lrnd.* boundless, unlimited.

namahrem (—..) نَـامَـحـرم P 1. canonically a stranger. 2. not intimate; not having access to the harem. 3. uninitiated. **—iyet, —lik** state or condition of being canonically a stranger.

namahsur (—.—) نَـامَـحـصـور P *lrnd.* immense, infinite, unbounded.

namakbullü (—.—) نَـامَـقـبـول P *lrnd.* unacceptable.

nama'kullü (—.—) نَـامَـعـقـول P *lrnd.* unreasonable; unwise.

nama'lûm (—.—) P, **namalûm** (———) نَـامَـعـلـوم *lrnd.* unknown.

nama'ruf (—.—) نَـامَـعـروف P *lrnd.* unknown, unfamiliar.

namatbuuu (—.—) نَـامَـطـبـوع P 1. not printed. 2. *lrnd.* not to one's taste, unpleasant; unacceptable.

namaver (——.) نَـامَـآور P *lrnd.* famous, renowned; illustrious.

namaz 1 نَـمـاز [namaz 2] ritual worship; prayer, namaz. **— ayları** the months of special divine services for women, *i. e.* **Receb, Şaban** and **Ramazan**. **— bezi** 1. scarf (worn by a woman during worship). 2. cloth or carpet spread out on which to perform the namaz. **— bozan** 1. a kind of fern. 2. anything that prevents or invalidates the namaz. **—ı bozul=** /ın/ to be invalidated (prayer). **— kıl=** to perform the namaz. **— kıldır=** to conduct the namaz. **—ı kılındı** /ın/ 1. His burial service has been read. 2. *colloq.* He is dead. **— seccadesi** carpet spread out on which to perform the namaz. **— vakti** time of the namaz.

namaz 2 (.—) نَـمـاز P *lrnd., same as* **namaz 1**. **—ı pişin** noon service. **—ı şâm** evening prayer.

namazgâh (.——) P, **namazgeh** (.—.) نَـمـازگـاه place for public worship in the open air, place of prayer.

namazgüzar (.—.—) نَـمـازگـزار P *lrnd.* one who performs the namaz.

namazlağı نَـمـازلـغـى *prov.* carpet used in the performance of the namaz.

namberdar (—.—) نَـامـبـردار P *lrnd.* who exalts his name, becomes famous.

namcu, namcuy (——) نَـامـجـو P *lrnd.* who seeks fame, aspiring.

namdar (——) نَـامـدار P *lrnd.* famous, celebrated. **—î** (———) P, **—lık** renown, fame.

name 1 (—.) نَـامـه P letter, dispatch, message; love letter. **—i â'mal** *lrnd.* register of one's deeds kept by the recording angels. **—i çehariüm** *lrnd.* the fourth book, the Quran as succeeding the Pentateuch, Psalms and Gospel. **—i hümayun** *Ott. hist.* autograph letter from the Sultan. **— oku=** 1. to read out a dispatch. 2. to recite commonplaces.

-name 2 (—.) نَـامـه P written document, *as in* **kanunnâme, mukavelename, nizamname**.

nameber (—..) نَـامـبـر P *lrnd.* bearer of a letter; carrier pigeon.

namecat (—.—) نَـامـجـات A *lrnd., pl. of* **name**, letters, dispatches.

namefhum (—.—) نَـامـفـهـوم P *lrnd.* 1. meaningless. 2. unintelligible.

name'mullü (—.—) P, **namemul**lü (———) نَـامَـأمـول *lrnd.* unexpected; unhoped for.

namerbut (—.—) نَـامـربـوط P *lrnd.* disconnected; loose.

namerd (—.) نَـامـرد P *same as* **namert**. **—âne** (—.—.) P *lrnd.* cowardly; unmanly; contemptible. **—î** (—.—) P *lrnd.* cowardice; violence; cruelty.

nameres (—..) نَـامـرس P *lrnd.* who delivers a letter, mailman; messenger.

namergub (—.—) نَـامـرغـوب P *lrnd.* disliked, disagreeable.

namer'i 1 (—.—) نَـامـرعـى P *lrnd.* 1. not in force, obsolete. 2. not observed.

namer'i 2 (—.—) نَـامـرئـى P *lrnd.* invisible.

namertdi (—.) نَـامـرد [namerd] unmanly, cowardly, despicable; vile! **—e muhtaç ol=** to be obliged to ask help from one whom one

Red 55.

despises. **—e muhtaç olma**= to depend on no one for one's living, to be under obligation to no one. **—çe** (..'.) cowardly; unmanly, contemptible (action). **—lik** cowardice; cruelty.

namerzi (—.—) نامرضى P *lrnd.* unsatisfactory, disapproved.

namesbukᵏᵘ (—.—) نامسبوك P *lrnd.* unique, unparalleled.

namesmuᵘᵘ (—.—) نامسموع P *lrnd.* unheard, unheard of.

namestur (—.—) نامستور P *lrnd.* uncovered.

names'ud (—.—) نامسعود P *lrnd.* 1. unblessed; wretched. 2. inauspicious, unfortunate.

nameşruᵘᵘ (—.—) نامشروع P illegal; illegitimate.

namevzun (—.—) نامورون P 1. *lrnd.* ill-proportioned. 2. not metrical; badly composed (verse or prose).

namıkʰ (—.) نامق A 1. *lrnd.* who writes, writer. 2. *w. cap.*, *man's name*.

nami 1 (—.) نامى A *lrnd.* germinating, growing, flourishing.

nami 2 (——) نامى P *lrnd.* illustrious, celebrated; celebrity.

namihrban (—.—)نامهربان P *lrnd.* unfriendly; unaffectionate.

nâmiye (—..) ناميه A *lrnd.* growth. **—bar** (—..—) P life-giving.

namizac (—.—) نامزاج P *lrnd.* indisposed; ill.

namkör نامكور *colloq.*, *var of* **nankör**.

namlı 1 نامى *famous, renowned*.

namlı 2 نامى It barrel (of a gun), blade (of a sword). **— ağız kapağı** muzzle cover. **— ağzı seviyesi** firing angle. **— ceketi** barrel casing. **— matkabı** D-bit for a horse. **—cık** sub-caliber rifle.

namlu ناملو *var. of* **namlı 2**.

namurad (—.—) نامراد P *lrnd.* whose wishes are not gratified; disappointed. **—î** (—.——) P disappointment, dissatisfaction.

namus (——) ناموس A 1. honor; honesty; good name. 2. *archaic law*. 3. *lrnd.* angels. **— belâsı** for the sake of one's honor; unwillingly. **—una dokun**= /ın/ to affect someone's honor, to hurt someone's pride. **—i ekber** *lrnd.* the archangel Gabriel. **—uyla yaşa**= to live honestly, to lead a decent honorable life.

namuskâr (———) ناموسكار P honest, upright; honorable. **—âne** (————.) *lrnd.* honorably.

namuslu ناموسلى honorable, honest; modest; chaste.

namussuz ناموسسز dishonest, shameless; scoundrel. **—luk** shamelessness; dishonesty.

namutasavver (—....) نامتصور P *lrnd.* unthinkable, unimaginable.

namuvafıkᵏ¹ (—.—.) ناموافق P *lrnd.* 1. unsuitable. 2. disagreeing, differing.

namübarekᵏⁱ (—.—.) نامبارك P unfortunate, inauspicious.

namülâyim (—.—.) نامليم P *lrnd.* difficult, hard; uncompromising.

namünasib (—.—.) نامناسب P *lrnd.* unfitting, unsuitable; improper.

namüsaid (—.—.) نامساعد P unfavorable.

namüstehakᵏᵏ¹ (—...) نامستحق P *lrnd.* unworthy; undeserving.

namüstaid (—...) نامستعد .P *lrnd.* inept, incapable; stupid.

namütenahi (—..—.) نامتناهى P infinite, boundless, endless; infinitely. **— hesap** infinitesimal calculus. **— kesir** interminate fraction. **—lik, —yet** infinitude, endlessness.

namver (—.) نامور P *lrnd.* renowned, famous; celebrated. **—î** (—.—) P fame, celebrity.

namz نامض *var. of* **nabz**.

namzed (—.) نامزد P *lrnd.*, *same as* **namzet**.

namzetᵈⁱ نامزد [namzed] 1. candidate; designated; applicant (for a post). 2. betrothed. 3. *mil.* cadet. **— göster**= /ı/ to nominate as a candidate.

namzetlikᵗⁱ نامزدلك candidacy. **—ini koy**= to be a candidate.

nan 1 (—) نان P *lrnd.* bread; livelihood; food. **—ı aziz** one's daily bread; bread (as being a sacred and precious thing). **—ı haram** living earned by unlawful means. **—ı helâl** lawful bread, bread earned by honest labor. **— ü nemek** bread and salt; obligation for a kindness received. **— ü nemek haini** ungrateful, treacherous. **— ü nemek hakkı** claim to gratitude due from a recipient to a benefactor or from a guest to his host. **—ı tenk** bread in thin cakes.

-nan 2, نن **-nen,** *after vowels* **-ynan, -ynen** *prov.*, *var. of* **-la**= 2, **-le**=.

nanaᵃⁱ (.—) نعناع A *lrnd.*, *same as* **nâne.**

nanay نانا Romany *slang* There isn't...

nâne (—.) نانه [nana] 1. peppermint, *bot.*, *Mentha piperita*. 2. garden mint, *bot.*, *Mentha viridis*. **— likörü** creme de menthe. **— molla** *joc.* a timid and useless weakling. **— ruhu** oil of peppermint. **— suyu** peppermint water. **— şekeri** peppermint drop. **— ye**= *colloq.* to commit a blunder, to say something silly, to commit an indiscretion, *e. g.*, **yediği naneye bak!** What a silly thing to do! **—li** containing peppermint.

nancu, nancuy (———) نانجوى P *lrnd.* beggar.

nanhah (——) نانخواه P *lrnd.* beggar (for bread).

nanhor (— —) نان خور P *lrnd.* servant, domestic, dependent.

nanik[tı] نا نياك Arm *slang* long nose. **— yap=** to thumb one's nose.

nanizm نا نيزم F *path.* nanism, dwarfishness.

nankör نا نكور [Persian — —] 1. ungrateful, unthankful. 2. treacherous. **—î** (—.—) P *lrnd.*, **—lük** ingratitude. **—lük et=** to show ingratitude.

nanpare (— —.) نا نپاره P piece of bread; livelihood. **—ye muhtaç ol=** to be destitute.

nanpez (—.) نا نپز P *lrnd.* baker.

nansuk[tu] نا نسوك F nainsook, fine cotton fabric, fine muslin.

nanu (— —) نا نو P *lrnd.* nurse's lullaby.

napak[kı] (— —) نا پاك P *lrnd.* unclean, foul, filthy. **—î** (— — —) P, **—lik** uncleanness, foulness.

napaydar (— — —) نا پايدار P *lrnd.* transitory; unstable.

naperva (—.—) نا پروا P *lrnd.* 1. fearless, heedless. 2. inconsiderate, thoughtless.

napesend (—..), **napesendide** (—..—.) نا پسند ، نا پسنديده P *lrnd.* not approved, disapproved.

napeyda (—.—) نا پيدا P *lrnd.* not found, nonexistent.

Napoli (..'.) نا پولي It *geog.* Naples.

Napoliten نا پوليتان It Neapolitan.

napuhte (—..) نا پخته P *lrnd.* 1. not cooked; raw. 2. immature, unripe. 3. inexperienced.

nar 1 نار [Persian —] pomegranate, *bot.*, Punica granatum. **— bülbülü** European robin, *zool.*, Erithacus rubecula. **— çiçeği rengi** coral red; bright scarlet. **— gibi** well roasted, well toasted. **— kabuğu** pomegranate shell. **— taneleri** pomegranate seeds.

nar 2 (—) نار A 1. fire. 2. hell fire. 3. *lrnd.* pain, injury, torment. **—ı beyza** *lrnd.* white heat, incandescence. **—ı Farisiye** *lrnd.* erysipelas. **—a yak=** /ı/ to injure. **—ına yan=** /ın/ to suffer through the fault of (another person); to be the victim of. **—ı zırar** *lrnd.* a certain fiery appearance said to have been seen in the Yemen and used there as an era in chronology.

na'ra A, **nara** (—.) نعره loud cry, shout. **— at=** to shout out, to yell at the top of one's voice.

nârast (— —) نا راست P *lrnd.* 1. not right; untrue, false. 2. crooked; incorrect; not upright. **—î** (— — —) P dishonesty, unrighteousness.

narcıl نا رجيل A *lrnd.* coconut.

nardenk[kı] نا ردنك P *lrnd.* syrup made with pomegranate or damson juice.

nardin (— —) نا ردين P mat-grass, *bot.*, Nardus stricta.

narefşan (—.—) نا رافشان P *lrnd.* pouring out hot tears.

narefte (—..) نا رفته P *lrnd.* not gone; not frequented.

narenc (—.) نا رنج P *lrnd.* orange, *bot.*, Citrus aurantium. **—î** (—.—) P orange colored.

narenciye نا رنجيه Citrus fruits; *bot.*, Citrus.

nares (—.) نا رس P *lrnd.* unripe.

naresa (—.—) نا رسا P *lrnd.* 1. unworthy, unfit. 2. illbred.

naresaî (—.—) نا رسائي P *lrnd.* 1. unworthiness; unfitness. 2. unmannerliness, ill breeding.

nareside (—.—.) نا رسيده P *lrnd.* 1. that has not arrived. 2. unripe, immature.

nareva (—.—) نا روا P *lrnd.* undeserved, unjust; unworthy.

nârezen (—..) نا رزن P *lrnd.* shouting at the top of the voice.

nargile نا رگيله P water-pipe, hookah, narghile, hubble-bubble. **— başı** earthen cup of a water-pipe. **— iç=** to smoke a water-pipe. **— kamışı** suction tube of a water-pipe.

nargiller *neol., bot.,* Punicaceae.

narh نرخ P officially fixed price. **— koy=** /a/ to set a fixed price (on commodities). **— tâyin et=** to set a market price.

nari (— —) نا ري A *lrnd.* 1. pertaining to fire. 2. full of fire, fiery. 3. hellish; destined to perdition.

narin (—.) نا رين [Persian — —] slender, slim, delicate, tender. **— kale** *hist.* inner fort, citadel. **—lik** 1. slimness, slenderness of frame. 2. elegance of manner.

nariyet (— — —.) نا ريت A *lrnd.* 1. the quality or nature of fire. 2. quality of being predestined to hell fire.

nark[kı] نا رك var. of **narh**.

narpistan (—.—) نا رپستان P *lrnd.* having breasts round as pomegranates.

narven (—.) نا روين P *lrnd.* 1. wych-elm. 2. pomegranate tree.

nâs 1 (—) نا س A *lrnd.* people, men, mankind, the public. **N— Sûresi** name of the last sura of the Quran.

nass[ssı] **2** نص A *lrnd.* a verse of the Quran decisive of any point in canon law; dogma; incontrovertible proof. **—ı kat'î** dogma.

na's 3 نعس A *lrnd.* 1. a being drowsy; drowsiness. 2. weakness.

nâsaf (— —) نا صاف P *lrnd.* unclean, dirty; impure.

nasafet 1 (.—.) نصافت A *lrnd.* a taking half of the property of a person.

nasafet 2 نصفت A *lrnd.*, same as **nısfet**.

nasaih (.—.) نصائح A *lrnd.*, *pl.* of **nasihat**

na'san (.—) نعسان A *lrnd.* drowsy, sleepy

Nasâra (.——) نَصَارَى ، نَصَارا A lrnd., pl. of **Nasrani**, Christians.
nâsavab (—.—) نَا صَوَاب P lrnd. not right, incorrect; wicked.
nasayih نَصَايِح A var. of **nasaih**.
nâsaz (——) نَا سَاز P lrnd. 1. discordant; improper. 2. not in order, untoward.
nâsazî (———) نَا سَازِى P lrnd. discordance, bad behavior.
nâsazkâr (———) نَا سَازكَار P lrnd. rendering dissonant or absurd; dissenting. **—î** (————) P discordance, dissension.
nasb نَصب A 1. same as **nasp**. 2. Arabic gram. a governing word putting a noun in the accusative or a verb in the subjunctive. 3. lrnd. a setting up, erection.
nasbet=[der] نَصب ايتمك /ı/ 1. to nominate, to appoint to an office. 2. Arabic gram. to put a word in the accusative or a verb in the subjunctive. 3. lrnd. to erect.
na'se نَعسه A lrnd. a nap, a dozing, short sleep.
nâsencide (—.—.) نَا سَنجيده P lrnd. 1. unmeasured. 2. unconsidered.
nâsere (—..) نَا سَره P lrnd. of light weight or base alloy (money).
nâseza (—.—) نَا سَزا P lrnd. unbecoming, unseemly.
nasfet نَصفت A lrnd., same as **nısfet**.
nasıb (—.) نَا صب A 1. Arabic gram. that governs a word in the accusative or a verb in the subjunctive. 2. lrnd. who appoints one to an office. 3. lrnd. that sets up or erects a thing.
Nasıbiye (.—..) نَاصِبيه A Isl. hist., name of a subdivision of the Kharijiya sect.
nâsıf 1 (—.) نَاصف A lrnd. manservant.
nâsıf 2 (—.) نَاصف A math. bisector.
nâsıh (—.) نَاصح A lrnd. advisor, counsellor.
nâsık[kı] (—.) نَا سِك A lrnd. who arranges and regulates.
nasıl نَصل ناصل How? What sort? **—sa** in any case, somehow or other. **—sınız?** How are you? How do you do? **— ki** just as...so; as a matter of fact. **— nasıl?** What did you say? Say it again.
nâsır 1 (—.) نَاصر A lrnd. one who helps, helper; auxiliary or ally.
nasır 2 نَاصر [nasur] a corn, wart, callus. **— bağla=** to get corns, to become calloused.
nasırlan=[ır] نَاصِرلَنمَق 1. to get corns. 2. to become calloused or callous.
nasırlaş=[ır] نَاصِرلَشمَك to become calloused, thick skinned.
nasırlı نَاصِرلى warty, with corns; callous; calloused.
Nasıra (—..) نَاصِره A Bib. Nazareth.
nasıye (—..) نَاصِيه A lrnd., same as **nasiye**.
nâsi 1 (——) نَاسى A lrnd. who forgets.

nâsi[iı] **2** (—.) نَاصع A lrnd. 1. pure, unmixed. 2. clear, limpid.
nasib (.—) نَصيب A lrnd., same as **nasip**.
nasibe (.—.) نَصيبه A lrnd. 1. a lot, portion. 2. anything erected for a signal.
nasic (—.) نَاسج A lrnd. who weaves; weaver.
nasicülhiyel (—....) نَاسج الحيل A lrnd. weaver of plots, intriguer.
nasif (.—) نَصيف A lrnd. half; half measure for grain.
nasigâlide (—.—.) نَا گاليده P lrnd. 1. who has never thought of (so and so). 2. unthought of. 3. inconsiderate, heedless.
nasih 1 (.—) نَصيح A lrnd. advisor, counsellor.
nasih 2 (—.) نَاسخ A lrnd. 1. effacing, canceling; abrogating. 2. who copies. 3. transformer (of men by transmigration of their souls). **— âyet** a verse or passage of the Quran that abrogates an earlier passage.
nasihat[iı] (.—.) نَصيحت A advice, counsel, admonition. **— dinle=** to listen to advice. **— et=** /a/ to advise. **— tut=** to follow advice. **— ver=** /a/ to give advice, to advise. **— yollu** as advice, in the nature of counsel.
nasihatâmiz (.—.——) نَصيحت آميز P lrnd. mixed with good advice, advisory.
nasihatpezir (.—..—) نَصيحت پذير P lrnd. who accepts advice.
nasik[kı] (—.) نَاسك A lrnd. pious, devout.
nasip[bı] (.—) نَصيب [nasib] lot, share, portion; one's lot in life. **— al=** myst. to be initiated into a dervish order. **—ini al=** /dan/ to enjoy. **— ol=** /a/ to fall to one's lot (good thing). **— olursa** if destiny should will it, all being well.
nasipas (—.—) نَا سپاس P lrnd. ungrateful. **—î** (—.——) P ingratitude.
nasipli (—.) نَصيبلى receiving a share; happy, fortunate.
nasipsiz (—.—.) نَصيبسز who has no share; luckless.
nasir 1 (—.) نَاثر A lrnd. prose writer.
nasir 2 (.—) نَصير A lrnd. helper, auxiliary; aid.
nasiye (—..) نَاصيه A lrnd. forehead. **—i hâl** first appearance of a situation. **—de mestur olan** written on the forehead (by the finger of destiny).
nasl نَصل A lrnd. spearhead; arrowhead.
nasp[bı] نَصب [nasb] appointment, nomination.
nasr نَصر A lrnd. help, assistance; salvation. **—ı müezzer** efficacious assistance. **N— Sûresi** name of the hundred and tenth sura of the Quran.
Nasrani (.——) نَصرانى A lrnd. Nazarene; Christian. **—ye** a Christian woman. **—yet** A Christianity; Christian doctrine.

nasri (.—) نصرى A *lrnd.* pertaining to victory and God's assistance.

Nasriye نصريّه A *lrnd.*, name of a sect who affirmed that God was incarnate in the Caliph Ali.

nassi (.—) نصّى A *phil.* dogmatic. **—ye** A dogmatism.

Nasturi نسطورى A same as **Nesturi**. **—ye** A Nestorianism.

nasuh (.—) نصوح A *lrnd.* 1. who gives advice. 2. sincere, pure. 3. sincere oath or declaration of repentance. **— nusuh tövbesi** *colloq.* never again.

nasur (——) ناسور A *lrnd.* 1. fistula. 2. same as **nasır 2**.

nasut (——) ناسوت A *lrnd.* humanity; human nature. **— âlemi** this world as the mortal world. **—î** (———) A human.

nâsüfte (—..) ناسوفته P *lrnd.* undrilled, unbored.

nâsütude (—.—.) ناسوده P *lrnd.* not well spoken of; worthless, base.

na'ş نعش A corpse; bier or coffin with a corpse.

nâşad (——) ناشاد P *lrnd.* unhappy, not cheerful.

nâşayan (———) ناشايان P *lrnd.* undeserving.

nâşayeste (———..) ناشايسته P *lrnd.* unseemly; unworthy.

nâşekib (—.—), **nâşekiba** (—.——) ناشكيب ناشكيبا P *lrnd.* impatient, unsteady, helpless.

nâşekibai (—.———) ناشكيبائى P *lrnd.* impatience.

nâşenide (—.—.) ناشنيده P *lrnd.*, same as **naşinide**.

naşıt (—.) ناشط A *lrnd.* cheerful, active, lively.

naşi (——) ناشى A 1. /dan/ hence, arising out of this; because of. 2. springing from; originating. **— ol=** 1. to originate. 2. to happen.

naşid (—.) ناشد A *lrnd.* who recites or writes poetry.

nâşigüfte (—...) ناشگفته P *lrnd.* unblown, unopened (blossom).

nâşinas (—.—) ناشناس P *lrnd.* who does not know, ignorant. **—î** (—.——) P ignorance.

nâşinide (—.—.) ناشنيده [naşenide] *lrnd.* unheard, unheard of; original. **—lik** originality.

naşir (—.) ناشر A 1. publisher. 2. *lrnd.* that spreads out, that scatters; that diffuses. **—i efkâr** organ (newspaper, periodical etc.)

naşire (—'..) ناشره A *anat.* 1. extensor muscle. 2. *lrnd.* that spreads abroad blessings or afflictions (angel, wind, cloud etc.)

naşirlikᵗⁱ ناشرلك publishing business.

naşita (—.—) ناشته P *lrnd.* having an empty stomach, hungry, fasting.

naşiz (—.) ناشز A 1. *lrnd.* palpitating with emotion (heart). 2. *lrnd.* swollen and throbbing (artery). 3. *law* obstinately disobedient (wife).

naşüste (—..) ناشسته P *lrnd.* unwashed, unclean.

na'tⁱⁱ 1 نعت A 1. poem praising the Prophet Muhammad; eulogy. 2. *lrnd.* epithet, description; praise. 3. *lrnd.* qualificative adjective.

nat'ⁱⁱ 2 نطع A *lrnd.* 1. leather used as a seat, carpet, table etc. 2. sheet of leather on which a criminal was seated when about to be decapitated.

nâtab (——) ناتاب P *lrnd.* weak, infirm.

nâtamam (—.—) ناتمام P incomplete, imperfect. **—î** (—.——) P, **—iyet** (—.——.) A *lrnd.* incompleteness.

nâteraş (—.—) ناتراش P *lrnd.*, same as **natıraş**.

nâters (—.) ناترس P *lrnd.* fearless.

na'tgû (.—) نعتگو P *lrnd.* who recites eulogies to the Prophet.

nath نطح A *lrnd.* an animal's butting or goring with his horn.

na'than (.—) نعتخوان P *lrnd.* one who chants a poem in praise of the Prophet Muhammad.

natıh (—.) ناطح A *lrnd.* that butts, gores or tosses.

natıkᵏᵘ (—.) ناطق A *lrnd.* 1. who speaks; that expresses. 2. rational (animal). 3. indicating, expressing. **— hayvan** the reasoning and articulating animal, man.

natıka (—..) ناطقه A faculty of speech, eloquence. **—lı** eloquent. **—perdaz** (—...—) P, **—pira** (—..——) P *lrnd.* eloquent.

natıkıyet (—...) ناطقيت A *lrnd.* eloquence.

natır ناطر [natur] attendant in a woman's bath.

nâtıraş (—.—), **nâtıraşide** (—.——.) ناتراش ناتراشيده P *lrnd.* 1. unshaved. 2. unsmoothed. 3. impolite, uncultivated.

natokafa (.'...) ناتوكفا Gk *slang* thick-headed, idiot. **— natomermeri** thick-headed idiot.

natrun (.—) ناترون A *min.* natron, native sodium carbonate.

natukᵏᵘ (.—) نطوق A *lrnd.* 1. eloquent. 2. talkative.

natur (——) ناطور A *lrnd.* 1. watchman of a garden or vineyard. 2. same as **natır**.

natüvan (—.—), **natüvana** (—.——) ناتوان ناتوانه P *lrnd.* not strong, weak.

naure (——.) ناعوره A *lrnd.* water wheel, machine for raising water for irrigation.

nauzübillâh (.—..—) نعوذبالله A same as **neuzübillâh**.

nâümid (—.—) نااميد P *lrnd.* hopeless, in despair. **—î** (—.—.——) P despair.
nâüstüvar (—..—) نااستوار P *lrnd.* unsteady.
nav (—) ناو P *lrnd.* rain pipe; channel, ditch; trough.
nauçağan ناوچاغان double-flowered datura.
navçe (—.) ناوچه P *lrnd.* 1. small mold for ingots. 2. small boat.
navdan (——) ناودان P *lrnd.* channel; milldam; spout.
nave (—.) ناوه P *lrnd.* channel; trough.
navek^{ki} (—.) ناوك P *lrnd.* 1. small arrow. 2. small pipe or tube. **—i kalbî** imprecation or sigh from the bottom of one's heart. **—i seherî** (*lit.*, an early morning arrow) imprecation or complaint uttered by a sleepless victim against his oppressor.
navekendaz (—..—) ناوك انداز P *lrnd.* archer.
naver (—.) ناور P *lrnd.* possible.
naverd (—.) ناورد P *lrnd.* fight, battle.
naverdgâh (—.—) ناوردگاه P *lrnd.* battlefield.
naverdhah (—.—) ناوردخواه P *lrnd.* eager for combat; combatant.
navlun ناولون [*Arabic* .—] freight paid for goods on a ship.
nay 1 (—) نای P *lrnd.* 1. *same as* **ney 1.** 2. reed, *bot., Phragmites communis.* 3. nostril; the nostrils. **—i bini** *lrnd.* air passage of the nose, the nostrils. **—i gülâ** *lrnd.* passage of the throat, windpipe. **— ü nuş** music and wine. **—i Türkî** *lrnd.* trumpet, clarion.
na'y 2 نعی A *lrnd.* announcement of death.
-nay 3 نای *lrnd., same as* **-na 3.**
nayab (——) ناياب P *lrnd.* 1. undiscoverable, unattainable. 2. rare, scarce.
nayban (——) نايبان P *lrnd.* flute player.
nayçe (—.) نايچه P *lrnd.* 1. small flute. 2. small reed used by weavers.
nayeksan (—.—) نايكسان P *lrnd.* unequal, dissimilar.
nayenban (—.—) ناي انبان P *lrnd.* bagpipe.
nayî (——) نايى P *lrnd.* 1. flute player, flutist. 2. maker or seller of flutes.
nayiha (—..) نائحه A *lrnd.* hired female mourner.
Nayman نايمان *hist.,* name of an ancient Turkish tribe.
naymeşk^{ki} (—.) ناىمشك P *lrnd.* bagpipe.
nayzen (—.) نايزن P *lrnd., same as* **neyzen.**
naz ناز [P —] 1. mincing air, coquetry; whims; smirking. 2. *Or. mus.* a **makam** which forms a pair with **niyaz. —ını çek=** /ın/ to put up with someone's whims. **— et=** to feign reluctance. **—ı geç=** for one's whims to be tolerated; to be a socially acceptable person. **— u nimet içinde büyü=** to grow up amid fondling and favors. **— u niyaz ile** with reluctance. **— sat=** *same as* **naz et=. — uykusu** sleep taken because of luxury and indolence. **— yap=** *same as* **naz et=.**
nâzad (——) نازاد P *lrnd.* barren; not born.
nazair (.—.) نظائر A *lrnd.*, *pl. of* **nazire.**
nazan (——) نازان P *lrnd.* who shows shyness (real or affected).
nazar نظر A 1. a looking, glancing at a thing; look, glance; sight. 2. the malignant look of an evil eye; the evil eye. 3. a considering; consideration. 4. a regarding with favor or esteem; regard. 5. *lrnd.* the favor of a prominent person. 6. *lrnd.* a facing a place, being opposite to it. **—ımda** in my opinion, as I see it. **—ında** as he sees it, in his opinion. **—a al=** /ı/ to take into account. **— at=**, **— atfet=** /a/ to glance (at). **— boncuğu** bead worn to avert the evil eye. **— boncuğu gibi** single; conspicuous. **—ı değ=** /ın, a/ to cause illness or misfortune by the evil eye. **— değmesin** May the evil eye not reach it. *i. e.* God preserve it (ejaculation politely used when praising a thing). **—ı dikkatini celbet=** /ın/ to attract the attention (of). **—dan düş=** to fall from favor into disgrace. **— ehli** person of insight or prudent consideration. **— et=** *archaic* /a/ 1. to look at a thing. 2. to reflect on a matter. 3. to have respect or consideration for a person or thing. **—ı ibret** *lrnd.* an accepting a bad example as something to be shunned. **—ı itibara al=** /ı/ to take into consideration. **—da ol=** to be in favor. **— sal=** /a/ to glance towards a person or thing. **—ı şefkat** *lrnd.* commiseration. **— takımı** ornaments worn by children as a protection against the evil eye.
nazara نظاره a kind of card game.
nazaran (.'.) نظاراً A /a/ according to, after; in respect of, with regard to; in proportion to; seeing that.
nazarbaz (..—) نظرباز P *lrnd.* who casts glances; coquettish. **—î** (..——) P coquettishness.
nazarbend نظربند P *lrnd.* 1. bandage over the eyes. 2. fascination (of a conjuror). 3. prisoner under a keeper's eye. **—î** (...—) P imprisonment under the eye of a keeper, confinement.
nazare نظاره [*nazar*] *only in* **nazareye al=** /ı/ to make fun of.
nazarendaz (...—) نظرانداز P *lrnd.* who glances, looks.
nazaret (.—.) نظارت A *same as* **nezaret.**
nazargâh (..—) نظرگاه P *lrnd.* 1. place of sight; space open to vision; one's range of vision. 2. one who has the power of the evil eye.

nazari (..—) نظری A 1. theoretical; speculative. 2. *lrnd.* visual.
nazariyat (..— —) نظریات A matters deduced or inferred by reasoning; theories. **—çı** theorist.
nazariye (..—.) نظریه A theory. **—i a'dad** *lrnd.* arithmology.
nazarlık[ğı] نظرلوه charm against the evil eye, amulet.
nazarpira (..— —) نظرپیرا P *lrnd.* that pleases the eye.
nazc نضج A *lrnd.* 1. a ripening, a coming to maturity; ripeness, maturity. 2. a becoming thoroughly cooked.
nazende (—..) نازنده P *lrnd.* disdainful; coquetting; graceful.
nazenin (—.—) نازنین P 1. delicately beautiful, graceful; amiable, nice. 2. petted, spoiled. 3. whippersnapper (sarcastically). 4. *obs., Or. mus.* a **makam**.
nazıc (—.) ناضج A *lrnd.* 1. ripe, mature. 2. well cooked.
nâzım 1 (—.) ناظم A 1. who arranges, who puts in order; *mech.* regulator. 2. *lrnd.* who composes poetry; versifier. **N—ı kâinat** *phil.* Demiurge.
nazım[zmı] **2** نظم [**nazm**] versification, verse, poetry.
nazır (—.) ناظر A 1. who watches; spectator. 2. minister (of state). 3. superintendent. 4. /a/ overlooking, facing.
nazıre (—..) ناظره A *lrnd.* the eye, the sight.
nazırlık[ğı] ناظرلوه ministry.
nazi[ii] (—.) نازع A *lrnd.* 1. that pulls or drags; that pulls out. 2. a homesick wanderer, foreigner, stranger.
naziat (—.—) نازعات A *lrnd.* angels of death who drag out the souls of the wicked. **N— Suresi** *name of the seventy-ninth sura of the Quran.*
nâziba (— — —) نازیبا P *lrnd.* not ornamental, unseemly, ugly, ungraceful. **—î** (— — — —) P ugliness.
nazîc (.—) نضیج A *lrnd.* 1. ripe. 2. thoroughly cooked. 3. mature.
nazif (.—) نظیف A *lrnd.* clean, cleanly; neat.
nazifüsseravil (.—..— —) نظیف السروایل A *lrnd.* chaste.
nazik[ği] (—.) نازك P 1. delicate; easily damaged; elegant. 2. polished (in manner), polite, refined, courteous. 3. agreeable, pleasing.
nazikâne (—.—.) نازکانه P typical of a refined and kindly person; delicate; delicately.
nazikeda (—:.—) نازک ادا P *lrnd.* delicate in tone or manner.
nazikendam (—..—) نازك اندام P *lrnd.* delicately soft and graceful.
nazikhayalân (—..— —) نازك خیالان P *lrnd.* those whose minds are occupied with divine works, theistic philosophers.
naziklik[ği] نازكلك A delicacy; refinement; polished manner; courtesy.
nazikmizac (—..—) نازك مزاج P *lrnd.* delicate in habit of thought or act.
nazil (—.) نازل A *lrnd.* 1. that descends; descending. 2. that alights; alighting. 3. which happens. **— ol=** to descend, alight.
nazile (—..) نازله A *lrnd.* calamity, disaster, misfortune (as descending from heaven).
nazir 1 (.—) نظیر A *lrnd.* 1. anything opposite or parallel. 2. match, like. 3. point opposite to another in a circle; *astr.* the nadir. **—i evc** *astr.* the nadir of the apogee, the perigee or inferior apsis. **—i şems** *astr.* point of the ecliptic opposite the sun's place.
nazir 2 (.—) نضیر A *lrnd.* 1. gold or silver. 2. vivid, splendid, bright.
nazire (.—.) نظیره A 1. a poem written to resemble another poem in form and subject; imitative piece of poetry. 2. *lrnd.* a similar thing. **— söyle=** to compose a piece of poetry or utter a witticism as parallel to what another has composed.
naziş (—.) نازش P *lrnd.* act of proud contempt or disdain; boasting; blandishment.
nazlaç[cı] نازلاچ same as **nazlı aş**.
nazlan=[ır] نازلانمق 1. to behave coquettishly; to be coy. 2. to show contempt or disdain. 3. to feign reluctance; to behave in an affected manner.
nazlı نازلى 1. coquettish; coy. 2. wayward; petted, spoiled. 3. reluctant. 4. ticklish (job, etc.). **— aş** pudding or blanc-mange of coarsely pounded rice. **— büyü=** to grow up capriciously and wayward.
nazm نظم A 1. *same as* **nazım 2**. 2. *lrnd.* a ranging things in a line or series. 3. *lrnd.* line, row, series of things in order.
nazmen (.'.) نظماً A in verse.
nazmi (.—) نظمی A *lrnd.* pertaining to verse or versification.
nazperver, nazperverd (—..)نازپرور، نازپرورد P *lrnd.* delicately brought up; spoiled child.
nazra, nazre نظره A *lrnd.* 1. one look, glance. 2. regard, compassion, pity. 3. sternness, awfulness. 4. ugliness; untidiness; deformity. 5. a blight of the evil eye. 6. fault, defect. **—i ulâ** first glance; at first sight.
nazret نضرت A *lrnd.* 1. brightness, splendor, beauty. 2. freshness of countenance. 3. affluence, fortune; pleasure.
nazzam (.—) نظّام A *lrnd.* 1. arranger; stringer (of pearls etc.). 2. versifier.
nazzare (.—.) نظّاره A *lrnd.* a body of spectators or observers.
-ncı, -nci, [-ncu, -ncü *do not occur*]. *after*

consonants -ıncı, -inci², -uncu², -üncü *after number form ordinal numbers, e. g.* **onuncu** the tenth.

=ndı, =ndi, *etc., after consonants* **=ındı, =indi,** *etc., prov., or archaic, var. of* **=ntı,** *e. g.* **çalkandı.**

ne 1 نه P 1. What? *with substantive* what. 2. whatever. 3. How? *with adjectives* how. 4. Which? **—den*. — dense*. —ler** all sorts of things; what things! **—si** his what? What relation of his? **—sine** 1. What do you bet? 2. Why should he have... *e. g.,* **otomobil onun nesine?** Who is he to have a private car? **— acep?** *prov.* Why? I wonder why. **— acı!** How bitter! **— âlâ memleket!** How wonderful! *said sarcastically of a profitable but unjust act.* **— âlem!** *archaic* What is the use? Is there any reason for it? **— âlemdesiniz?** How are you? **— alıp veremiyor?** What is the matter with him? What does he want? **— ara?** *archaic for* **nere?** Where? **— arar?** What is such a thing doing here? It does not exist, *e. g.,* **onda para ne arar?** Don't look for money where he is concerned. **— arıyor?** What is he looking for? What does he want? **— buyrulur?** 1. What do you think? 2. You see how it is. **— buyurdunuz?** What did you say? **— canı var ki...?** He hasn't got much strength or energy. **— cehennemdesin?** *colloq.* Where are you? *said angrily.* **— çare!** What can one do? **— çiçek olduğunu bilirim** /ın/ I know what sort of a person he is. **— dedim de sözünü dinlemedim?** Why didn't I listen to you? **— demeğe?** Why? **— demek?** 1. what does it mean? 2. How unreasonable! **— demek olsun?** 1. Of course not. 2. How unreasonable! **— denir?** What can one say? Words fail me. **— denlû?** *archaic* How? What sort? **— dersin** Words fail me. **—dir ki** *same as* **ne var ki, ne diye?** for what purpose? Why? **— doğrarsan aşına, o çıkar kaşığına** What you put in the soup is what you get when you eat it. **— fayda!** What is the use? **— gezer!** *same as* **ne arar. — gibi?** What sort? **—ler gördüm!** What didn't I see! I saw all sorts of things. **— günlere kaldık!** What an evil time we are in! **— güzel!** How nice! **— hacet!** What need is there! **— haddine!** How dare he! **— hâl ise** whatever the circumstances may be, in any case. **— hâli varsa görsün** Well, let him go his own way! **— haltetmeye ......** What a mistake .....! **— hikmetse** Heaven knows why! Strangely enough. **— için?** *same as* **niçin. — idiği belirsiz** No one knows anything about him *said of a doubtful chracter.* **— ise!** fortunately! Well, never mind; anyway. **— iyi!** How nice! **— kadar?** How much? so much. **— kumaştır!** O what a scoundrel he is! **—me lâzım!** 1. What is that to me? It is none of my business. 2. but still; all the same. **— mutlu!** How lucky! How fortunate! **— mümkün!** Impossible! **— münasebet** How? Of course not! **—yin nesi** Who on earth is (that person)? **— o?** What is that? What happened? **— olacak** What of it? What do you expect? **— de olsa** still, all the same; after all. **— olur!** oh, please! kindly. **— olursun!** Please! Will you? **— olduğumu bilemedim** I lost control of myself. **— oldum delisi** parvenu. **— olur ne olmaz** just in case. **— olursa olsun** come what may, never mind what happens. **— satıyorsun?** What are you talking about? **—den sonra** long after, belatedly. **— sularda** What's the position? How does it stand? **— şüphe** most certainly, no doubt at all. **— tan** *archaic* no wonder. **— vakit?** When? **— var?** What is it? What is going on? What is the matter? **— var ki** 1. but. 2. in fact. **— var ne çok?** *colloq.,* *same as* **ne var ne yok? — var ne yok?** What is the news? How are things getting on? **— vazifen!** What business is it of yours? How does it concern you? **— yaparsın?** What can you do? **— yaparsın ki** It can't be helped but... **— yapıp yapıp** in some way or other, by every possible means. **— yüzle?** How dare he! How can he bring himself (to do that)? **— zahmet** Why trouble about it? **— zaman?** When? At what time? **— zarar!** What's the harm? What does it matter? So what?

ne 2 نه P not; neither; nor. **— deveyi gördüm ne deveciyi** (*lit.* I saw neither camel nor camel driver.) I know nothing about it. **— kokar ne bulaşır** harmless, passive (person). **— o ne bu** neither that nor this, neither one. **— od var ne ocak** poverty-stricken. **— sakala minnet ne bıyığa** Avoid being under an obligation to any one; if you want your work done do it yourself. **— Şamın şekeri ne Arabın yüzü** I would rather not have it! (in spite of its being very attractive or advantageous). **— şap ne şeker** neither one thing nor the other. **— şiş yansın ne kebap** (*lit.,* so that neither the skewer nor the mutton be burnt) so that neither party suffers damage.

nebᵇ'¹ نبع A *lrnd.* a welling of water.

nebahatᵗⁱ (.—.) نباهت A *lrnd.* a being noble, great and famous; nobility, celebrity.

nebail (.—.) نبائل A *lrnd., pl. of* **nebile.**

nebalet (.—.) نبالت A *lrnd.* a being of noble family, shrewd and intelligent.

nebat (.—) نبات A 1. plant. 2. *lrnd.* vegetation.

nebatat (.——.) نباتات A plants. **— bahçesi** botanical garden. **— ilmi** botany. **—ı maiye** *lrnd.* aquatic plants.

nebatî (. — —) نَبَاتِى A vegetable; botanical. **— kuvvet** the power of growth in an organism. **— yağ** vegetable oil. **—yun** (. — — —) A lrnd. botanists.

nebayed (. —.) نَبَايَـ P lrnd. It is not required or proper.

nebbal[li] (. —) نَبَّال A lrnd. maker or seller of arrows.

nebbar (. —) نَبَّـار A lrnd. 1. loud-voiced; clamorous. 2. eloquent.

nebbaş (. —) نَبَّاش A law grave robber.

nebe نَبَا A lrnd. communication; information, news. **N— Suresi** name of the seventy-eighth sura of the Quran.

nebean (. . —) نَبَعَان A lrnd. gushing; welling up. **— et=** /dan/ to gush, well up.

nebehre نَبَهْرَه P lrnd. 1. not fit for currency, short of weight or of bad alloy. 2. bad and unsaleable. 3. vile, despicable.

neberd نَبَرْد P lrnd. fight, battle. **—azma** (. . — —) P veteran, warrior. **—e** P warlike, brave. **—gâh** (. . —) P battlefield.

nebevi (. . —) نَبَوِى A pertaining to a prophet; prophetic.

nebık[bkı] نَبِك [nebk] lrnd. fruit of the lotus tree. **— ağacı** lotus tree, bot., Zizyphus lotus.

nebi (. —) نَبِى A prophet, heavenly messenger.

nebih (. —) نَبِيه A lrnd. celebrated, famous, noble.

nebil (. —) نَبِيل A lrnd. noble and talented.

nebile (. —.) نَبِيلَه A lrnd. virtuous and beautiful (woman).

nebir (. —), **nebire** (. —.) نَبِيرَه P lrnd. grandchild.

nebise (. —.) نَبِيسَه P lrnd. a son's child, grandchild.

nebiyun (. — —) نَبِيُّون A lrnd., pl. of **nebi**.

Nebiyülmelhame نَبِى الْمَلْحَمَه A the Prophet of Peace a title of the Prophet Muhammad.

nebk نَبْك A lrnd., same as **nebık**.

nebl نَبْل A lrnd. arrow, Arabian arrow. **—e** A a single arrow.

nebr نَبْر A lrnd. 1. an elevating, exalting, raising up. 2. a raising the voice, shouting, yelling.

nebre نَبْرَه A lrnd. 1. eminence. 2. a rise of the voice from the bass range to a higher range. 3. shriek of terror. 4. tumor.

nebş نَبْش A lrnd. 1. an unearthing buried treasure, a robbing a grave. 2. an extracting information. 3. a laying open, manifesting.

nebt نَبْت A lrnd. 1. vegetation, verdure, pasture. 2. a growing, sprouting (as herbage).

nebve نَبْوَه A lrnd. eminence, high ground.

nebze نَبْذَه A particle, bit. **bir —** a little bit.

necabet (. —.) نَجَابَت A a being noble-born and noble-minded, nobility. **—li** noble.

necadet (. —.) نَجَادَت A lrnd. a being successfully bold and enterprising; successful boldness.

necah (. —) نَجَاح A lrnd. success; victory. **— bul=** to meet with success, to be successful.

necahat[ti] نَجَاحَت A lrnd. 1. patience. 2. munificence.

necaib (. —.) نَجَائِب A lrnd., pl. of **necib**, **necibe**, 1. noble. 2. the most excellent chapters or verses of the Quran.

necaset (. —.) نَجَاسَت A 1. excrement. 2. impurity, canonical uncleanness. **—li** soiled with uncleanness.

Necaşi (. — —) نَجَاشِى A Negus, Emperor of Abyssinia.

necat (. —) نَجَات A salvation; safety; escape. **— bul=** to find a way of escape, so as to avoid a danger or evil.

neccad (. —) نَجَّاد A lrnd. maker of cushions and mattresses; upholsterer.

neccam (. —) نَجَّام A lrnd. astronomer, astrologer.

neccar (. —) نَجَّار A lrnd. carpenter. **—î** (. — —) P carpenter's craft, carpentry.

necd نَجْد A lrnd. 1. high place, eminence, highland. 2. w. cap., the Nejd (interior part of the Arabian peninsula).

necdet نَجْدَت A lrnd. a being bold; boldness.

nece 1 نَجِه In what language?

nece 2 نَجِه colloq., same as **nice**.

Necef نَجَف A 1. geog. Najaf (in Irak). 2. l. c. rock crystal. 3. l. c., lrnd. high piece of land in a valley; dam for keeping out water.

necefe نَجَفَه A lrnd. a hanging lamp or ball hung in a mosque, mausoleum, etc.

necend نَجَنْد P lrnd. unhappy, wretched, miserable.

neces نَجَس A lrnd. a being canonically unclean; canonical uncleanness; canonically unclean.

neci نَجِه of what trade? **—dir?** What is his trade?, What does he do?

necib (. —) نَجِيب A lrnd., same as **necip**.

necibüttarafeyn (. — . . . .) نَجِيب الطَّرَفَين A lrnd. noble on both sides (father and mother).

necid (. —) نَجِيد A lrnd. 1. successfully venturesome; brave, strong. 2. sad, sorrowful, vexed.

necil (. —.) نَجِيل A lrnd. noble, honorable.

necip[bi] (. —) نَجِيب [necib] 1. noble, of high lineage. 2. chem. noble.

necis (. —.) نَجِيس A lrnd. 1. nasty, incurable (disease). 2. dirty, filthy.

necl نَجْل A lrnd. a man's child; issue, son.

necm نَجْم A lrnd. 1. star. 2. asterism. 3. the Pleiades. **—i sâkıb** bright star; Saturn. **N— Sûresi** name of the fifty-third sura of the Quran.

necmî (.—) نجمى A 1. pertaining to the stars. 2. *w. cap.*, man's name.
necs نجس A *lrnd.* dirty, filthy, nasty.
necva (.—) نجوى A *lrnd.* 1. a whispering; whisper. 2. a thing whispered; a secret. 3. a whisperer, teller of secrets.
neda (.—) ندا ندى A *lrnd.* 1. moisture, damp, wet. 2. gift; bounty.
nedamet (.—.) ندامت A a regretting, being sorry for; regret, remorse. — çek=, — et=, — getir= to regret.
nedametkâr (.—.—) ندامتكار P *lrnd.* regretful.
nedavet (.—.) نداوت A *lrnd.* a being moist, damp; moisture.
nedb ندب A *lrnd.* 1. a lamenting or weeping and reciting the virtues of a dead person. 2. an inciting; inviting; incitement; invitation.
nedbe ندبه A *path.* scar, cicatrice.
neddaf (.—) نداف A *lrnd.* carder of cotton. —î (.——) P, —lık business of a cotton carder.
nedeb ندب A *lrnd.* a being scarred; scar.
nedem ندم A *lrnd.* a repenting; repentance, regret.
neden ندن A 1. Why? What for?, For what reason? 2. *neol.* cause. —se (..'.) for some reason or other; somehow or other.
nedf ندف A *lrnd.* a carding cotton. — et= /i/ to card.
nedib (.—) نديب A *lrnd.* scarred.
nedid (.—), **nedide** (.—.) نديد نديده A *lrnd.* like, equal, match, fellow.
nedif (.—) نديف A *lrnd.* carded (cotton etc.).
nedim (.—) نديم A 1. boon companion, intimate friend. 2. courtier; court buffoon.
nedime (:—.) نديمه A lady of the court.
nedman (.—) ندمان A *lrnd.* 1. sorry, regretful. 2. companion, convivial associate.
nedret ندرت A rarity.
nedve ندوه A *lrnd.* council, assembly; an assembling, convoking.
nef[1] نفع A *lrnd.* an advantaging, benefiting; advantage; profit. —ine to one's own advantage. —i hazine the maxim that the first consideration in official matters must be the Public Purse.
nefa[a1] (.—) نفاع A *lrnd.* use, profit, advantage.
nefad (.—) نفاد A *lrnd.* a coming to an end; ending; end; finish; exhaustion; extinction.
nefahan (..—) نفحان A *lrnd.* 1. the wind's blowing; breeze. 2. an odor's diffusing itself; exhalation. 3. a giving a gift of money, donation. —ı nesim a gentle wind, zephyr.
nefahat (..—) نفحات A *lrnd.*, *pl.* of **nefha** 1.
nefais (.—.) نفائس A *lrnd.*, *pl.* of **nefise**.
nefak[k1] (.—) نفاق A *same as* **nifak**.

nef'an (.'.) نفعاً A *lrnd.* for the benefit of (so and so).
nef'anlilbeşer (.'....) نفعاً للبشر A *lrnd.* for the benefit of man.
nefaset (.—.) نفاست A exquisiteness, beauty, excellence.
nefaz (.—) نفاذ A *lrnd.* 1. a penetrating and going clear through (a thing); penetration. 2. a being obeyed (an order). — et= to penetrate and go through, to traverse.
nefed نفد A *same as* **nefad**.
nefel نفل A *lrnd.* spoils taken from the enemy.
nefer نفر A 1. a single individual; person. 2. private soldier. —ât (..—) A *pl.* soldiers. —î (..—) A pertaining to an individual or to a private soldier.
neferiye نفريه very small bunch of grapes; aborted bunch.
nefes نفس A 1. breath; a breathing. 2. moment, duration of a breath. 3. breath with healing power (blown upon the sick). 4. *Bektashi order* hymn. 5. *slang* hashish. — al= 1. to breathe, to take a breath; to inhale. 2. to breathe freely again. 3. to leak (airtight vessel). — aldırma= to give no rest, not to give any respite. — borusu *anat.* trachea. — çek= 1. to take a whiff (of tobacco etc.). 2. *slang* to smoke hashish. —ini çek= to draw a long breath like a sigh. — darlığı asthma. — et= /a/ to cure by breathing on someone and casting a spell. — genişle= to feel more at ease, to be rid of a difficulty. — kesil= not to be able to breathe. — nefese out of breath, panting. — nefes iç= /i/ 1. to sip. 2. to smoke a pipe by puffs. —i tutul= to be unable to breathe; to have an attack of asthma. — tüket= to talk oneself hoarse. bir — tütün one puff of a pipe; a puff of tobacco smoke. —i vâpesin *lrnd.* the last breath. — ver= 1. to breathe out. 2. /a/ to give someone time for breathing.
nefesle=[r] نفسلمك /i/ to breathe upon one in order to cure him. —n= to breathe; to take a short rest; to have a breather; to breathe again (with relief). —ş= to smoke hashish.
nefeslik[81] نفسلك 1. the time passed in taking a breath. 2. ventilator; vent-hole. bir — canı kalmış He looks wretched; he is worn out.
nefh 1 نفخ A *lrnd.* 1. a blowing, puffing (with the mouth). 2. an inspiring, breathing into. —i ruh 1. the breathing of the angel Gabriel upon the Virgin Mary (by which she conceived). 2. God's breathing the breath of life into Adam. —i Sûr a blowing a trumpet; especially, the blowing of the last trumpet for the Resurrection.
nefh 2 نفح A *lrnd.*, *same as* **nefahan**.

nefha 1 نَفْخَة A lrnd. 1. a single blast of breath. 2. a swelling of the abdomen, tympanitis. —**i uhra** the second blast of the trumpet, when the dead shall rise. —**i ûlâ** the first blast of the trumpet by the archangel, when all alive will die.

nefha 2 نَفْحَة A lrnd. 1. a single puff of wind; a breath. 2. a single whiff of an odor; odor. 3. a single act of giving; gift.

nefi'ʻii 1 نَفْع A var. of nef.

nef'i 2 نَفْعِي A phil. utilitarian.

nefihᶠʰⁱ نَفْخ var. of nefh 1.

nefir 1 (. —) نَفِير P 1. anat. tube. 2. a kind of musical instrument used until two centuries ago. 3. lrnd. clamor, hubbub, noise.

nefir 2 (. —) نَفِير A lrnd. 1. a body of men, crowd, small party of less than ten men. 2. an assembling for a common purpose. —**i âm** hist. 1. a general levy of all able-bodied men for public defense. 2. a general rising; expedition.

nefisᶠˢⁱ **1** نَفْس [nefs 1] 1. self, one's own personality. 2. the essence of anything, its very substance or reality. 3. seminal fluid. 4. soul; spirit; life. 5. the carnal man, the flesh, the spirit of concupiscence. —**ine** in himself. —**ini beğen=** to think a lot of oneself, to be conceited. —**i çekeme=** /ı/ not to be able to endure; to detest, abhor (a thing). —**ine düşkün** self-indulgent. —**i emmare** lrnd. inordinate appetite, concupiscence. —**i hayvani** animal spirit (common to man and beast). —**in ibramiyle** lrnd. with the continued incitement of the flesh. —**i İstanbul** the city of Istanbul proper (not its suburbs). —**ini kır=** to mortify one's lusts or pride. —**ini körlet=** to take the edge off one's appetite or desire; to have a snack to satisfy one's hunger for the moment. —**i kül** lrnd. 1. the universal soul. 2. the throne of God; the tablets of divine decrees. —**i levvame** lrnd. the carnal mind when resisted but still unsubmissive; the voice of conscience. —**ine mağlûp ol=** to be overcome by one's desires. —**i mutmaine** lrnd. the carnal mind when conquered and obedient to all pious impulses; the pious and tranquil mind of a saintly person. — **mücadelesi** inner struggle. —**i mütefekkir** phil. ego. —**i mütekellim** gram. the first person. —**i nâtıka** lrnd. human reason. —**i nefis** lrnd. the precious soul, dear life. —**i nefsine** each one for himself. —**i tayıka** lrnd. the flesh, the passions. —**ine uy=** to conform to the carnal mind, i. e. to sin. —**ine yedir=** /ı/ to swallow one's pride, to swallow or endure (an affront). —**ine yedireme=** /ı/ to be unable to bring oneself (to do something). —**ini yen=** to master oneself. —**ini zaptet=** to control one's passions.

nefîs 2 (. —) نَفِيس A excellent, exquisite; rare; fine.

nefîse (. —.) نَفِيسَة A lrnd. an exquisite or beautiful object.

nefiyᶠʸⁱ نَفْي [nefy] lrnd. 1. banishment, exile. 2. negation. — **edatı** gram. the negative particle. — **ve icab,** — **ve isbat** lrnd. negation and affirmation or assertion.

nefl نَفْل A lrnd. a voluntary act of religion, a work of supererogation.

nefr نَفْر A lrnd. 1. a being frightened and running away. 2. a dispersing of the pilgrims from the valley of Mina after the ceremonies are completed.

nefret نَفْرَت A 1. disgust, loathing. 2. lrnd. a running away in terror; flight, aversion. — **et=** /dan/ to detest, to hate; to feel an aversion (for).

nefrin (. —) نَفْرِين P lrnd. 1. curse, imprecation. 2. horror; terror.

nefrit نَفْرِيت F path. nephritis.

nefs 1 نَفْس A same as nefis 1.

nefs 2 نَفْث A lrnd. 1. a blowing (as a necromancer when making incantations or playing tricks). 2. a puffing slightly; a slight puff of breath.

nefsa (. —) نَفْسَاء A lrnd. woman after childbirth.

nefsani (. — —) نَفْسَانِي A 1. sensual, carnal. 2. lrnd. spiteful, malignant.

nefsaniyet (. — —.) نَفْسَانِيَّت A 1. sensuality. 2. lrnd. spite, selfishness. —**çi** one who bears malice, a spiteful man. —**li** spiteful, rancorous.

nefsen (́.) نَفْسًا A lrnd. by oneself, of one's own accord; willingly.

nefsî (. —) نَفْسِي A lrnd. pertaining to the soul or to self; sensual.

nefsperest نَفْسپَرَست P lrnd. selfish.

nefsüddem نَفْثُ الدَّم A path. a spitting of blood.

nefsülemr نَفْسُ الأَمْر A lrnd. essence and reality of a matter. —**de** in essence, in reality.

nefsüşşeytan (. . . —) نَفْثُ الشَّيْطَان A lrnd. (lit. Satan's breath) poetry.

neft نَفْط P 1. naphtha. 2. hist. Greek fire. — **yağı** naphtha.

neftendaz (. . —) نَفْت اَنْدَاز P lrnd. that throws naphtha; soldier especially trained in the use of Greek fire.

neftî (. —) نَفْتِي P of a dark brownish green color.

nefûr (. —) نَفُور A lrnd. frightened, scared, timid (beast).

nefy نَفْي A same as nefiy. — **et=** 1. to banish, exile. 2. to deny.

nefz نَفْض A lrnd. 1. a shaking; a shaking off. 2. a reading or reciting the whole Quran

negatif

3. a looking carefully around one; an examining a thing closely.

negatif نگاتیف F negative.

negüfte نگفته P lrnd. unsaid; not spoken; unexpressed.

nehad (.—) نهاد P lrnd. manner, custom.

nehafet (.—.) نحافت A lrnd. a being thin, lean; leanness, thinness.

nehale (.—.) نهاله var. of **nihâle**.

nehar (.—) نهار A lrnd. day; daytime. **—en** (.—'.) A by day.

neharî (.——) نهاری A lrnd. 1. day student. 2. lrnd. pertaining to the day, diurnal.

neharir (.——) نهارير A lrnd., pl. of **nihrir**.

nehat (.—) نهت A lrnd. side, tract, quarter.

nehb نهب A lrnd. a seizing as spoil; a taking spoil; spoil, booth. **— et=, — ü garet et=** /ı/ to pillage, to plunder.

nehc نهج A lrnd. 1. a highway; the right way. 2. method, system.

nehec نهج P lrnd., same as **nehc**.

neheng نهنگ P lrnd. 1. crocodile, alligator. 2. shark; water-dragon or similar monster. 3. sword. 4. writing pen. 5. all-devouring fortune; the world. **—i felek** the zodiacal signs of Cancer and Pisces. **—i iltikam** sword that swallows victims like a crocodile. **—i sebz, —i siyah** sword. **—i zir-i haftan** a glittering sword.

nehengân (..—) نهنگان P lrnd., pl. of **neheng**. **—ı niyam** swords in their sheaths.

nehhab (.—) نهاب A lrnd. spoiler, plunderer.

nehhac (.—) نهاج A lrnd. guide.

nehib (.—) نهيب P lrnd. 1. fear, terror. 2. grief, anxiety.

nehikᵏⁱ (.—) نهيق [nehk 1] lrnd. a braying.

nehim (.—) نهيم A lrnd. 1. insatiable, voracious. 2. vociferation.

nehirʰʳⁱ **1** نهر [nehr] river, stream. **N—i Âsi** the Orontes River. **—i cerrar** lrnd. mighty river.

nehîr 2 (.—) نهير A lrnd. affluent; copious, much, many.

nehiyʰʸⁱ نهى [nehy] 1. a prohibiting; prohibition. 2. gram. negative imperative. **—i gaib** third person of the negative imperative. **—i hazır** negative imperative in the second person.

nehkᵏⁱ **1** نهق A lrnd. a braying.

nehkᵏⁱ **2** نهك A lrnd. 1. a wearing someone out. 2. a doing anything too much. 3. a punishing or tormenting. 4. a weakening, emaciating.

nehlân (.—) نهلان A lrnd. 1. that drinks a lot; thirsty. 2. satiated with drink.

nehle نهله A lrnd. a single first drink.

nehm نهم A lrnd. 1. a breathing stertorously; panting. 2. a vociferating; a roaring.

nehme, nehmet نهمه نهمت A lrnd. 1. a being very keen (desire). 2. a vociferation, roar, growl.

nehr نهر A lrnd., same as **nehir 1**. **—en** (.'.) A by river. **—eyn** A two rivers. **—î** (.—) A pertaining to a river.

nehy نهى A same as **nehiy**. **— et=** /ı/ to prohibit. **— edici hüküm** law prohibition, restraint.

nehz نهض A lrnd. 1. a rising, getting up. 2. a setting out on a journey; departure.

nehzat نهضت A lrnd. a single rise or departure.

nejad (.—) نژاد lrnd., var. of **nijad**.

nekahet (.—.) نقاهت A 1. convalescence. 2. lrnd. a being intelligent, intelligence.

nekais (.—.) نقائص A same as **nakais**.

nekaiz (.—.) نقائض A lrnd., pl. of **nakiza**.

nekâlˡˡ (.—), **nekâle** (.—.) نكال نكاله A lrnd. exemplary punishment, chastisement.

nekâre (.—.) نكاره P lrnd. good for nothing, worthless, useless.

nekâret (.—.) نكارت A lrnd. 1. a being very intelligent, shrewd, cunning; intelligence, shrewdness, cunning. 2. a matter's being very serious, grave; seriousness, gravity of an event.

nekave (.—.) نقاوه A lrnd., same as **nukave**.

nekavet (.—.) نقاوت A lrnd. a being clean, good, and choice; purity, cleanness; excellence.

nekbet نكبت A lrnd., same as **nikbet**.

neked نكد A lrnd. 1. want, poverty; distress. 2. inauspicious, sinister; distressing.

nekef 1 نكف A lrnd. 1. a refusing, turning away; refusal. 2. a declining, turning away from. 3. a brushing away one's tears with one's hand.

nekef 2 نكف A lrnd., pl. of **nekefe**.

nekefe نكفه A anat. 1. lymphatic gland of the side of the neck. 2. either of the two processes of the **ramus** of the lower jawbone.

nekefetan (...—) نكفتان A anat. the two horns or processes of the **ramus** of the lower jawbone.

nekere نكره A lrnd. denial, negation.

nekes نكس [nâkes] mean, stingy. **—lik** stinginess.

nekf نكف A lrnd. 1. same as **nekef 1**. 2. a finding again a lost trace, and continuing to follow it up. 3. a coming to an end, an ending, finishing.

nekhet نكهت A lrnd. 1. a single breathing towards another. 2. a single whiff of an odor. 3. fragrance, perfume. 4. smell of the breath.

Nekîr 1 (.—) نكير A 1. one of the two angels who question men in their graves (the other is **Münker**). 2. l. c. wonderful, extreme of its kind.

nekir 2 نكر A lrnd. very intelligent, acute, cunning.

nekkâd (.—) نكاد A lrnd. woeful, calamitous.

nekr نکر A *lrnd.* understanding, sagacity; acuteness, cunning.

nekre نکره A 1. funny, entertaining, quaintly odd or witty; witty saying. 2. *gram.* indefinite (noun).

nekregû (..—) نکره‌گو P *lrnd.* who makes odd and witty remarks.

neks 1 نکث A *lrnd.* 1. a taking or pulling a thing to pieces, separating it into its component parts, dissection; disintegration. 2. a breaking, violating a pact.

neks 2 نکس A *lrnd.* 1. an inverting, turning upside down, inversion. 2. a bending one's head down. 3. a causing a relapse of a disease. 4. a reading or reciting backwards (especially a chapter of the Quran).

neks 3 نکص A *lrnd.* a turning or starting back, abstaining or desisting; retreat.

nekûh (.—) نکوه P *lrnd.* who blames, censures, criticises. **—ende** (.—..) P blamer, accuser, censurer. **—ide** (.——.) P 1. who has blamed. 2. blamed, despised, rejected; blameworthy.

nekuhiş (.—.) نکوهش P *lrnd.* reproach, blame, scorn; words of blame. **— et=** /a/ to cast blame, censure, criticism on a person.

nekünad (..—) نکناد P *lrnd.* May He avert, forefend!

neli نه‌لی having what in it? containing what?

nelikᵏⁱ نه‌لک the character or nature (of a thing).

nem 1 نم P 1. moisture, dampness; moist, damp; dew. 2. suspicion. **— al=**, **— kap=** to absorb moisture, become damp.

nemᵐᵐⁱ **2** نم A *lrnd.* 1. a carrying a tale secretly to make mischief; an acting the talebearer; talebearer, mischief-maker. 2. a diffusing a smell; diffusion.

nema (.—) نما A *lrnd.* 1. a growing; growth. 2. an increasing, augmenting; increase, augmentation. 3. interest on money; profit. **— al=** to take or charge interest. **— bul=** to grow, to increase.

nemadar (.——) نمادار P *lrnd.* growing, flourishing.

nemaikᵏⁱ (.—.) نمائک A *lrnd.*, pl. of **nemika**.

nemaim (.—.) نمائم A *lrnd.*, pl. of **nemime**.

nemâkᵏⁱ (..—) نماک P *lrnd.* beauty, splendor, grace.

nemalan=ⁱʳ نمالانمق to increase (money). **—dır=** /ı/ *caus.* to make profitable.

nemarikᵏⁱ (.—.) نمارک A *lrnd.*, pl. of **nümruka**.

nemat نمط A *lrnd.* 1. way, manner, method. 2. covering, blanket, coverlet. 3. kind, sort, variety. 4. sect or party in a community. **—ı vahid üzere** in one manner, uniformly.

Nemçe (ʹ.) نمچه Sl Austria; Austrian.

— arpası pearled barley used for a kind of pudding, pearl barley. **— Devleti** *hist.* the Austrian Empire. **—ce** German language. **—li** German, Austrian.

nemdar (.—) نمدار P *lrnd.* damp, moist, humid.

nemdide (.—.) نمدیده P *lrnd.* 1. mildewed; damp. 2. bathed in tears, weeping.

nemed نمد P *lrnd.* felt cloth. **—in** (..—) P felt, of felt, made of felt. **—pare** (..—.) P a piece of felt cloth. **—puş** (..—) P clad in felt; poor. **—saz** (..—) P maker of felt cloth.

nemedzin (..—) نمدزین P *lrnd.* 1. folded felt used as a saddle or pillion. 2. felt cloth placed under or over a saddle.

nemekᵏⁱ نمک P *lrnd.* 1. salt. 2. flavor.

nemekâb (..—) نمک‌آب P *lrnd.* salt water, brine.

nemekbeharam (....—) نمک‌بحرام P *lrnd.* untrue to salt eaten together, *e. g.*, ungrateful, faithless.

nemekbend نمک‌بند P *lrnd.* who rubs salt on a wound as a torture.

nemekberciğer نمک‌برجگر P *lrnd.* (lit. who has salt sprinkled on his liver) whose feelings are hurt.

nemekçeş نمک‌چش P *lrnd.* 1. a taste of food taken to try its saltiness. 2. a very small quantity of salt put into a newborn infant's mouth. **—î** (...—) P the ceremony of placing salt in an infant's mouth.

nemekdan (..—) نمکدان P *lrnd.* 1. saltcellar. 2. mouth of a beauty.

nemekharam (...—) نمک‌حرام P *lrnd.*, same as **nemekbeharam**.

nemekhelâl (...—) نمک‌حلال P *lrnd.* faithful, loyal, true.

nemekîn (..—) نمکین P *lrnd.* 1. salted, flavored with salt. 2. wet with tears (eyes). 3. full of delight (lips). 4. full of eloquence and wit, beautiful.

nemekine (..—.) نمکینه P *lrnd.* special dish of salted food.

nemekperver نمک‌پرور P *lrnd.* 1. salted, prepared with salt. 2. one who eats another's salt, *e. g.*, servant.

nemekşinas (...—) نمک‌شناس P *lrnd.* (lit., who knows and acknowledges the salt that he eats) grateful, loyal; worthy, faithful in service.

nemekzar (..—) نمکزار P *lrnd.* salt marsh; saltworks.

nemekzede نمکزده P *lrnd.* 1. who has salted something. 2. salted.

nemel 1 نمل A *lrnd.* 1. a climbing (as into a tree). 2. a being asleep and helpless (the hand).

nemel 2 نمل A *lrnd.*, same as **neml 1**.

nemelâzımlıkğı *neol.* the attitude of one who says **"neme lâzım"** "What's that to me?" indifference, unconcern.

nemeli (..—) نملى A *lrnd.* pertaining to the ant; antlike. **—ye** (..—.) A *zool.*, *Formicidae*.

nemer نمر A *lrnd.* 1. leopard. 2. a being spotted like a leopard. 3. a being angry and snarling; fierce as a leopard; fierceness; ferocity; rage.

nemeş نمش A *lrnd.* 1. spottedness, spots; freckles. 2. variegation of a tissue in spots or stripes.

nemhurde نم خورده P *lrnd.* mildewed, moldy, discolored from dampness.

nemika (.—.) نميقه A *lrnd.* written letter, note, epistle.

nemime (.—.) نميمه A *lrnd.* 1. a secret-whispering; sound of a whisper. 2. talebearing, mischief-making, slander. 3. sound of a pen when writing.

nemimekâr (.—.—) نميمه كار P *lrnd.* slanderer, talebearer.

nemir (.—) نمير A *lrnd.* 1. abundant and potable (water); sweet and clear (water). 2. unsullied, untarnished.

neml 1 نمل A *lrnd.* ant. **N— Suresi** *name of the twenty-seventh sura of the Quran*.

neml 2 نمل A *lrnd.* 1. a climbing as into a tree. 2. a carrying tales mischievously.

nemle نمله A *lrnd.* 1. an ant. 2. a kind of herpetic eruption, herpes. 3. talebearing, mischief-making. 4. lying, falsehood. **—i caversiye** miliary fever.

nemlen=ir نملنمك to become damp. **—dir=** /ı/ *caus.*

nemli نملى moist, damp. **—lik** moistness, dampness.

nemmâlli نمّال A *lrnd.* whisperer of secrets, backbiter.

nemmam (.—) نمّام A *lrnd.* 1. secret-whisperer, backbiter, spy. 2. wild thyme. **—î** (.——) P talebearing, backbiting, calumniation.

nemmamelmelikki نمّام الملك A *lrnd.* wild thyme.

nemmas (.—) نمّاس A *lrnd.* whisperer, backbiter, talebearer.

nemnâkki نمناك P *lrnd.* damp, humid, moist. **—î** (.——) P moistness, humidity.

Nemrud (.—) نمرود A Nimrod (an impious king who is said to have cast Abraham into the flames).

nemrutdu نمرود [Nemrud] cruel; very obstinate; very contrary; unmanageable. **—luk** cruelty, tyranny, obstinacy. **—luğu tut=** /ın/ to have a fit of obstinacy.

nems نمس A *lrnd.* 1. a keeping a secret, concealing; concealment. 2. a making a person one's confident.

Nemse نمسه *var. of* **Nemçe**. **— böreği** a kind of meat patty.

nemş نمش P *lrnd.* 1. a whispering; whisper. 2. a talebearing; a lying; falsehood, fraud, deceit.

nemûkkü (.—) نموك P *lrnd.* mark, target for missiles.

nemum (.—) نموم A *lrnd.* mischievous, secret talebearer; calumniator, spy.

nemuzec (.—.) نموذج A *lrnd.* exemplar, model.

-nen نن *cf.* **-nan 2**.

nene ننه *same as* **nine**.

neng ننگ P *lrnd.* 1. shame, dishonor, ignominy. 2. shameful thing or act. 3. decency; self-respect. 4. fight; dispute. **— ü namus** honor and self-respect.

nengname (.—.) ننگنامه P *lrnd.* 1. a written account of a combat. 2. prose or verse written with irony or as satire.

nengsar (.—) ننگسار P *lrnd.* a transformation by metempsychosis into an inferior condition; transmigration.

nenni ننى *same as* **ninni**.

ner نر P *lrnd.* 1. male, masculine; a male. 2. large, strong, chief of its kind. **— ü mâde** male and female.

nercis نرجس A *lrnd.* narcissus.

nerd نرد P *lrnd.* backgammon. **—baz** (.—) P backgammon player.

nerde نرده *var. of* **nerede**.

nerden (.'.) نرده ن *var. of* **nereden**.

nerdüban (..—) نردبان P *lrnd.*, *same as* **merdiven**.

nere 1 نره 1. what place? what part? 2. *prov.* where? **—m?** what part of me? **—n?** what part of you?

nere 2 نره P *lrnd.*, *same as* **nerre**.

nerede نرده where? wherever. **— ise** before long, presently. **— kaldı ki** how much less...; let alone that...

nereden نرده ن from where? whence. **— nereye?** What a coincidence! Who would have thought of it?

nereli نره لى where from? of what place? **—siniz?** Where are you from? Where were you born?

nereye نره يه to what place? whither. **— giderse gitsin** Let him go where he will; wherever he goes.

nergâv (.—) نرگاو P *lrnd.* bull.

nergeda (..—) نرگدا P *lrnd.* impudent, shameless; sturdy beggar; audacious fellow.

nergis 1 نرگس [nergis 2] 1. narcissus. 2. marigold, *bot.*, *Calendula officinalis*.

nergis 2 نرگس P *lrnd.* 1. *same as* **nergis 1**

2. the eye of a beauty. —**dan** (..—) P bed of narcissus plants. —**e** (.—.) P 1. figure of a narcissus carved in ivory or bone and placed on the roof of a house. 2. the Pleiades. —**î** (..—) P pertaining to, resembling or perfumed with narcissus or marigold.

nerh P *lrnd.*, same as **narh**.

neri (.—) P *lrnd.* 1. masculinity, virility. 2. the male organ.

Nerim (.—), **Neriman** (.——) P name of a famous hero of Persian legend, great-grandfather of Rustam.

nerine (.—.) P *lrnd.* 1. male, masculine. 2. virility.

nerm P *lrnd.* 1. soft, pliant. 2. mild, gentle. 3. lax, flabby; weak. 4. *mus.* · low (note). — **acem** *mus.* the note f'. — **hisar** *obs.*, *mus.* the note f♯ or b♭'. — **hüseynî** *obs.*, *mus.* the note e'. — **nerm** slowly, gently.

nermâhen (.—.) P *lrnd.*, (*lit.* soft iron) 1. lazy, indolent, idle. 2. weak, infirm, impotent.

nermâvaz (.——) P *lrnd.* soft voiced.

nermbür P *lrnd.* 1. carpenter's and blacksmith's clamp. 2. flatterer, wheedler.

nermdil P *lrnd.* 1. compassionate, tender-hearted. 2. timid.

nermgû (.—) P *lrnd.* soft-spoken.

nermhû (.—) P *lrnd.* soft-natured, gentle.

nermî (.—) P *lrnd.* 1. softness, pliancy. 2. mildness; gentleness. 3. laxity, weakness.

nermîn (.—) P *lrnd.* soft; gentle; mild.

nermiyet (.—.) P *lrnd.* softness, mildness.

nermsar (.—) P *lrnd.* kind, meek, forbearing.

nerre P *lrnd.* 1. male; male organ. 2. wards of a key. 3. main trunk of a tree. 4. wave, billow. 5. beggar. —**dev** (..—) P great, frightful demon. —**gâv** (..—) P bull.

nesa 1 A *lrnd.* nerve or tendon extending from the hip to the heel; femoral artery.

nesa 2 (.—) P *lrnd.* shady place.

nesaic (.—.) A *lrnd.*, *pl.* of **nesice**.

nesaikki (.—.) A *lrnd.*, *pl.* of **nesike**.

nesaim (.—) A *lrnd.*, *pl.* of **nesim**.

nesakkı A *lrnd.* 1. order, method; arrangement, management. 2. row, string of pearls or beads. 3. an orderly line or series of any kind. 4. style, mode of writing, manner. 5. the constellation Orion.

Nesatıre (.—..) A *lrnd.*, *pl.* Nestorians.

nesayih (.—.) A *lrnd.*, *pl.* of **nasihat**.

nesc A *lrnd.*, same as **nesic 1**. —**i ankebut** cobweb. —**i beşere-i muhati** *anat.* epithelium. —**i lifî** fibrous tissue. — **et**= /ı/ to weave, knit, interlace.

neseb A 1. family, genealogy. 2. inherited nobility. 3. affinity; relationship. — **dâvaları** *law* petitions concerning legitimacy. —**i muttasıl** *lrnd.* uninterrupted lineage. —**i sahih olmıyan çocuk** child of uncertain parentage, illegitimate child.

neseben (.'..) A *lrnd.* by descent; by family.

nesebî (..—) A *lrnd.* relating to one's family; genealogical.

nesebname (..—.) P *lrnd.* written genealogy.

nesem, nesemat (..—) A *lrnd.*, *pl.* of **neseme**.

neseme A *lrnd.* 1. a single breathing out, exhalation of the breath. 2. life, spirit, soul. 3. a breathing creature, especially a man, human being. 4. slave (male or female).

nesf A *lrnd.* 1. a pulling down; demolition. 2. a crumbling to dust, pulverizing. 3. a biting.

nesh A *lrnd.* 1. an abolishing; abolition; abrogation. 2. an effacing; effacement. 3. same as **nesih**. 4. a transcribing a book. 5. a transforming; especially, a transmigration of the soul from one human body to another. — **et**= /ı/ 1. to abolish, to cancel, abrogate. 2. to transcribe. —**î** (.—) A 1. pertaining to copying. 2. a kind of Arabic writing. —**ül-âyet bil-âyet** abrogation of one verse of the Quran by another.

nesi 1 (.—) A *lrnd.* 1. very forgetful. 2. one who is of no account.

nesi 2 (.—) A *lrnd.* thing forgotten or not worth remembering.

nesib (.—) A *lrnd.* 1. a celebrating in verse (mistress). 2. well-descended; fit, worthy.

nesibî (.——) A *lrnd.* 1. pertaining to the custom of mentioning a mistress in the exordium of a poem. 2. one who habitually mentions a mistress in a poem; amatory, fond of women.

nesicsci **1** [nesc] A 1. a weaving; tissue. 2. a knitting; web, net. 3. an uttering a lie.

nesic 2 (.—) A *lrnd.* woven; web, tissue. —**i vahid** 1. matchless tissue. 2. great scholar.

nesice (.—.) A *lrnd.* 1. anything woven, web. 2. tissue.

nesihshi [nesh] *a style of Arabic script*. naskhi.

nesikki (.—) A *lrnd.* gold; silver

nesike (.—.) نسیکه A *lrnd.* 1. sacrificial victim. 2. large nugget of gold or silver.

nesil[ⁱⁱ] نسل [nesl] 1. generation; descendants; family. 2. child, issue. **—i münkarız oldu** His family is extinct.

nesim (.—) نسیم A 1. *poet.* gentle breeze, zephyr. 2. *obs.*, *Or. mus.* a **makam** related to sabâ. **—î** (.——) A atmospheric.

nesir[ˢʳⁱ] نثر [nesr 2] prose. **—ci** prose writer.

nesk[ᵏⁱ] 1 نسك A *lrnd.* a drawing up and arranging a discourse; arrangement.

nesk[ᵏⁱ] 2 نسك A *lrnd.* 1. religious piety. 2. anything a man is bound to do as an ordinance of God.

nesket نسكت A *lrnd.* a being religious; piety, devotion.

nesl نسل A *lrnd.*, *same as* **nesil.** **—î** (.—) A pertaining to issue and posterity.

nesm نسم A *lrnd.* gently blowing (wind).

nesnas (.—) نسناس A *lrnd.* anthropoid ape; gorilla.

nesne نسنه 1. thing; anything. 2. *gram.* object.

nesnel *neol.* objective. **—leştirme** *neol.*, *phil.* objectivation.

nesr 1 نسر A *lrnd.* 1. vulture. 2. *a name of the ancient Arabian idol Nisroch.* **—i tair** the constellation Aquila. **—i vaki** the constellation Lyra.

nesr 2 نثر A 1. *same as* **nesir.** 2. *lrnd.* a scattering broadcast; a dispersing. **—en** ('.) A in prose.

nesrin (.—) نسرین P *poet.*, name of several varieties of the rose.

nessab (.—) نساب A *lrnd.* genealogist.

nessac (.—) نساج A *lrnd.* 1. knitter; weaver. 2. liar.

nesta'lik[ᵏⁱ] (..—) نستعلیق A *Arabic calligraphy*, a Persian style of writing, taliq.

nesta'likgûy (..——) نستعلیقگو P *lrnd.* an emphatic and correct speaker.

nester, nesteren, nesterin (..—), **nesterun** (..—) نستر نسترن نسترین نسترون P *lrnd.* dog rose, *bot.*, Rosa canina.

nestuh (.—) نستوه P *lrnd.* brave, warlike; determined.

Nesturi (.——) نسطوری A Nestorian. **—ye** (.——.), **—yun** (.——) A the Nestorians; Nestorianism.

nesyan (.—) نسیان A *lrnd.* very forgetful.

nesyen نسیا A *lrnd.* forgotten. **— mensiyen** as a thing forgotten, out of mind.

neşa نشا A *lrnd.* starch (from wheat).

neşaet (.—) نشاءت A *lrnd.*, *same as* **neş'et.**

neşaf (.—) نشاف P *lrnd.* imbecility, stupidity.

neşaid (.—.) نشائد A *lrnd.*, *pl. of* **neşide.**

neşak[ᵏⁱ] نشاق A *lrnd.* a smelling a thing, inhaling it.

neşastec (.—.) نشاستج A *lrnd.* starch.

neşat (.—) نشاط A *lrnd.* a being eager, brisk, lively, ready; cheerfulness, gaiety; alacrity; briskness. **—lı, —mend** (.—.) P in good spirits; gay, cheerful.

neşd نشد A *lrnd.*, *same as* **nişdet.**

neş'e نشئه A 1. gaiety, merriment; joy. 2. slight intoxication; merry humor. **—si yerinde** He is in good humor.

neşefe نشفه A *lrnd.* porous pumice stone.

neş'elen[ⁱʳ] نشءلنمك to grow merry; to become slighty drunk. **—dir=** /ı/ *caus.*

neş'eli نشءلی merry; in good humor.

neş'esiz نشءسز in bad humor; out of sorts, sad.

neş'et نشءت A 1. a coming into existence; origin. 2. *lrnd.* a growing up and becoming strong; adolescence. **— et=** /dan/ 1. to originate, to come into existence. 2. *lrnd.* to grow up. 3. *lrnd.* to graduate from school. **—i uhra** *lrnd.* departure of the soul from the body. **—i ulâ** *lrnd.* the entrance of the soul into the body.

neşf نشف A *lrnd.* 1. an imbibing fluid (porous substance). 2. a penetrating, soaking into a porous substance (fluid). 3. a dying off wholesale.

neşid (.—) نشید A *lrnd.*, *same as* **neşide.**

neşide (.—.) نشیده A *lrnd.* 1. verses which people recite alternately; verse, poetry. 2. loud cry, shout. **N—ler Neşidesi** *Bib.* the Song of Songs. **—han** (.—.—) P reciter of poems.

neşinide (.——.) نشینیده P *lrnd.* 1. who has not heard. 2. never before heard, unheard of.

neşir[ˢʳⁱ] نشر [neşr] 1. a spreading broadcast, a scattering; a being scattered. 2. a publishing, diffusing; publication, promulgation.

neşr نشر A *lrnd.* 1. *same as* **neşir.** 2. God's raising the dead; the dead's being raised; resurrection. 3. *lrnd.* a sprouting, coming into life (herbage). **—en** ('.) A by way of publication.

neşret=[ᵈᵉʳ] نشر ایتمك /ı/ 1. to spread abroad. 2. to publish; to diffuse. 3. *lrnd.* to raise, to resurrect (the dead).

neşriyat (.——) نشریات A publications.

neşşaf (.—) نشاف A *lrnd.* that sucks up, imbibes; bibulous. **— kâğıt** blotting paper.

neşter نشتر P lancet.

neşur (.—) نشور A *lrnd.* that diffuses greatly.

neşv نشو A *lrnd.* a growing (plant), growth. **— ü nema bul=** to grow, flourish and increase in size; to develop.

neşvan (.—) نشوان A *lrnd.* 1. intoxicated, drunk. 2. all agog with news.

neşve نشوه A *lrnd.* 1. intoxication. 2. exhilaration. 3. odor, smell. **—bahş** P exhilarating;

intoxicating. —dar (..—), —mend P exhilarating.

netac (.—) نَتاج A lrnd. a beast's bringing forth young.

netaic (.—.) نَتائج A lrnd., pl. of netice. —i vahîme evil consequences.

netameli (.—..) نَتامِل ill-omened; sinister; best avoided (person or thing).

netayic (.—.) نَتايج A lrnd., same as netaic.

nete 1 (.'.) نَت It naut. a putting a place in order; properly stowed; shipshape. — et= /ı/ to clear away and put in order, to tidy up; to disentangle.

nete 2 نَت same as nite.

netf نتف A lrnd. a plucking out hair, feathers etc.

netice (.—.) نَتيجه A 1. consequence, result; effect. 2. a logical consequence; conclusion. 3. lrnd. young of a beast at one birth, litter. —i istidlâl phil conclusion. —i kelâm lrnd. 1. in short, in conclusion. 2. conclusion arrived at by a discourse. —i lâzıme corollary. bir —yi münüc ol= 1. to give a result, produce an effect. 2. to infer, to draw a conclusion. 3. to point to a conclusion (premises).

neticebahş (.—..) نَتيجه‌بخش P lrnd. that produces a result.

neticelen=ir نَتيجه‌لنمك to come to a conclusion.

neticepezir (.—..—) نَتيجه‌پذير P lrnd. producing a result.

neticesiz نَتيجه‌سز useless, futile, inconclusive.

netn نتن A lrnd. stench, bad smell.

neuzübillâh (.—..—) نعوذ بالله A lrnd. (lit. We take refuge in God.) God help us! God defend us! God forbid!

nev'vi 1 نَوع A same as nevi 1.

nev 2 نو P lrnd. 1. new; fresh. 2. young.

neva (.—) نوا P 1. lrnd. tune, melody. 2. Or. mus. a very old simple makam. 3. lrnd. means; food, provisions; wealth; power. 4. a person's child or grandchild. — kürdî a compound makam composed a century and half ago by Sultan Selim III. — perdesi the note "d" above high "c." — puselik a compound makam composed a century and a half ago by Sultan Selim III. — teli treble string of an instrument.

nevâbâd (.——) نوآباد P lrnd. newly equipped, built up or inhabited.

nevabit (.—.) نوابت A lrnd. 1. growing organisms. 2. inexperienced youths.

nevaceste (.—..) نواجسته P lrnd. newly planted vineyard or orchard.

nevacib (.—.) نواجب A lrnd. the esoteric senses of verses of the Quran.

nevaciz (.—.) نواجذ A lrnd., pl. of naciz.

neyad (.—) نواد P lrnd. 1. hole in the ground for concealing treasure. 2. injury, loss.

nevade (.—.) نواده P lrnd. grandson, a son's son.

nevadir (.—.) نوادر A lrnd., pl. of nadire.

nevafil (.—.) نوافل A lrnd., pl. of nafile.

nevager (.—.) نواگر P lrnd. singer; musician.

nevahi 1 (.——) نواهی A lrnd., pl. of nehy, prohibitory precepts; prohibitions.

nevahi 2 (.——) نواحی A lrnd., pl. of nahiye.

nevahtti (.—) نواخت P lrnd. 1. a caressing; caress. 2. a touching, performing on a musical instrument.

nevahte (.—.) نواخته P lrnd. 1. who has caressed or played. 2. caressed, petted; touched, played, struck.

nevai (.——) نوائی P lrnd. 1. pertaining to song. 2. pertaining to wealth.

nevaib (.——) نوائب A lrnd., pl. of naibe.

nevair (.—.) نوائر A lrnd., pl. of naire.

nevakıs (.—.) نواقص A lrnd., pl. of nakisa, defects.

nevakis (.——) نواقیس A lrnd., pl. of nakus.

nevâlti (.—) نوال A lrnd. 1. gift, present. 2. share, lot, portion.

nevale (.—.) نواله A 1. food, meal; one's daily bread, portion. 2. lrnd. a single thing given as a gift. — düz= to provide food. —çin ol= to eat a snack.

nevalelen=ir نوالنمك /dan/ to take a taste (of).

nev'ama (.'.—) نوعما A lrnd. in a certain manner; a kind of; so to speak.

nevami (.—.) نوامی A lrnd., pl. of namiye.

nevamis (.——) نوامیس A lrnd., pl. of namus.

nevamuz (.——) نوآموز P lrnd. learner, novice; inexperienced.

nev'an نوعاً A as to its species or kind; in a way, in a manner.

nev'arus (..—) نوعروس P poet. newly married woman. —an-ı bahar, —an-ı çemen opening flowers.

nevasaz (.——) نواساز P lrnd. singer, musical performer.

nevase (.—.) نواسه P lrnd. grandchild, daughter's child.

nevasıb (.—.) نواصب A lrnd., pl. of nasıb 1.

nevasi (.—.) نواصی A lrnd., pl. of nasiye.

nevat (.—) نوات A lrnd. a single date stone.

nevay (.—) نوای P lrnd., same as neva.

nevayende (.—..) نوآینده P lrnd. newly come; novel.

nevayin (.——) نوآیین P lrnd. 1. new fashion; novelties, wonders; of a new kind. 2. one who introduces a new fashion.

nevaz (.—) نواز P 1. who caresses, pets; who treats one kindly, e. g., bendenevaz, garibnevaz. 2. who plays, sounds a musical instrument, e. g., berbatnevaz.

nevazan (.——) نوازان P lrnd., same as nevaz.

Red 56.

nevazende (.—..) نوازنده P *lrnd.*, same as **nevaz.**

nevazır (.—.) نوازظ A *lrnd.*, *pl.* of **nazire.**

-nevazi (.——) نوازى P *lrnd.*, *abstr. n.* of **nevaz.**

nevazil (.—.) نوازل A 1. head cold. 2. *lrnd.*, *pl.* of **nazile.** — ol= to have a cold. —li having a cold in the head.

nevaziş (.—.) نوازش P *lrnd.* act of caressing, petting, treating kindly; caresses, kindness, courtesy. — et= /a/ to bestow caresses, treat kindly. —ci, —ger P one who caresses; a habitually kind man.

nevazişkâr (.—.—) نوازشكار P *lrnd.* caressing, soothing. —ane (.—.——.) P caressingly.

nevazişli نوازشلى who caresses or treats kindly, kindly disposed.

nevazişname (.—.—.) نوازشنامه P *lrnd.* letter conveying kind sentiments (to an inferior or junior).

nevb نوب A *lrnd.* 1. an occurring in turn; occurrence. 2. a recurring; recurrence. 3. a calamity's befalling.

nevbahar (..—) نوبهار P 1. spring season. 2. a **makam.** —i (..——) P 1. pertaining to the spring season, vernal. 2. *mus.* the twenty-seventh among the thirty tunes.

nevbare, nevbave (.—.) نوباره • نوباوه P *lrnd.* first fruits, early fruit.

nevbenev نوبنو P *lrnd.* ever new.

nevber نوبر P *lrnd.* 1. first fruits; first born. 2. newborn child. 3. girl whose breasts begin to show.

nevbet نوبت A *same as* **nöbet.**

nevcivan (..—) نوجوان P *lrnd.* youth, young man. —i (..——) P, —lık quality or acts of youth; prime of life, youth.

nevdaran (.——), **nevdarane** (.——.), **nevdarani** (.———) نوداران • نودارانه • نودارانى P *lrnd.* a small present given upon a new acquisition or joyful news.

nevdere نودره P *lrnd.* beloved son, a darling.

nevdevlet نودولت P *lrnd.* newly prosperous, newly rich; parvenu, upstart.

neve نوه P *lrnd.* grandson, especially, son's son.

neved نود P *lrnd.* ninety.

nevede نوده P *lrnd.* grandchild.

nevend نوند P *lrnd.* 1. horse, swift or ambling horse; vehicle; ship; boat. 2. postmessenger. 3. intelligent person; intelligence.

nevende نونده P *lrnd.* quick or ambling (horse); ambling horse.

nevendül[lü] (..—) نونده‌ول P *lrnd.* great-grandchild; great grandson of the male line.

neverd 1 نورد P *lrnd.* 1. a turning, revolving; revolution. 2. a circling, circuiting; gyration. 3. an encircling. 4. a rolling or folding a thing on itself; roll; fold. 5. a weaver's beam. 6. tournament; combat. 7. hem around a piece of cloth. 8. journey, travel. 9. a like, fellow, match.

-neverd 2 نورد P *lrnd.* that goes around, as in **cihanneverd, rehneverd.**

neverde نورده P *lrnd.* 1. wrap, shirt, chemise. 2. roll, document inscribed on a roll. 3. twisted, folded, coiled; creased.

neverdide (..—.) نورديده P *lrnd.* 1. that has rolled or folded up; folded, rolled, twisted. 2. that has gone or travelled. 3. gone around or over.

neveser نوأثر P *Or. mus.* a compound **makam** composed a century and half ago by the famous musician İsmail Dede.

nevfel نوفل A *lrnd.* 1. sea, lake, great river. 2. generous man. 3. gift, bounty. 4. handsome youth. 5. wild beast's cub.

nevh نوح A *lrnd.* 1. a lamenting, moaning; a mourning a deceased relative. 2. a dove's cooing long and vociferously.

nevha نوحه A *lrnd.* a wail or lament; lamentation, moan, keening. — et= to wail and lament vociferously. — kopar= to set up a loud wailing.

nevhagâh (..—) نوحه‌گاه P *lrnd.* place of mourning.

nevhager نوحه‌گر P *lrnd.* a woman wailing aloud for the dead; hired mourner. —i (...—) P lamentation.

nevhaste (.—.) نوخاسته P *lrnd.* 1. newly risen; youth, young man. 2. newly sprouted; newly appeared, new.

nevhat 1 (.—) نوحط A *lrnd.*, *pl.* of **nevha.**

nevhat[tı] **2** نوحات P *lrnd.* youth with down on his upper lip. —i (..—) P first appearance of a beard.

nevheves نوهوس P *lrnd.* 1. who shows fresh enthusiasm for a thing; who starts off on a thing enthusiastically. 2. who has a new desire every day; frivolous; capricious.

nevhiz (.—) نوخيز P *lrnd.* new-risen, fresh, tender.

nevi[vi] **1** نوع [nev 1] 1. sort, kind, variety. 2. *literature* genre. 3. *biol.* species. —i beşer the human race, mankind. — nevi of various kinds. —i şahsına münhasır of its own kind, *sui generis.*

nev'i 2 (.—) نوعى A *lrnd.* specific, pertaining to species or variety.

nevi 3 (.—) نوى P *lrnd.* newness; novelty.

nevicad (.——) نوايجاد P *lrnd.* 1. newly invented. 2. newly introduced.

nevid (.—) نويد P *lrnd.* 1. good tidings, good news. 2. promise of a good thing.

nevim نوم A *lrnd.*, *var.* of **nevm.**

nev'ima (..—) نوعما A *var.* of **nev'ama.**

nevin نوین P *lrnd.* 1. prince. 2. the most excellent of anything.
-nevis (.—) نویس P *lrnd.*, same as **-nüvis**.
nevişt نوشت P *lrnd.* an act of writing; writing. **—i Huda** that which God has written; divine predestination, fate, destiny.
nevişte نوشته P *lrnd.* 1. that has written; written. 2. a writing, dispatch, letter.
neviştecat (...—) نوشتیات A *lrnd.* writings.
nev'iyet نوعیت A *lrnd.* specificity.
nevk[ki] نوک P *lrnd.* 1. tip, point, end. 2. tip of the beak or bill of a bird. 3. tips of eyelashes. **—i kalem** point or nib of a pen. **—i zeban** tip of the tongue.
nevkâr (.—) نوکار P *lrnd.* new to work or business.
nevkise (.—.) نوکیسه P *lrnd.* newly-rich; parvenu.
nevküşâde (..—.) نوکشاده P *lrnd.* newly opened.
nevl نول A *lrnd.* freight.
nevm نوم A *lrnd.* a sleeping, slumbering; sleep, slumber. **—i sınai** *psych.* hypnosis. **—î** (.—) A pertaining to sleep.
nevmid (.—) نومید P without hope, despairing, desperate. **— ol=** to be in despair. **—âne** (.——.) P desperate, desperately. **—î** (.——) P *lrnd.* despair, hopelessness.
nevnihal[li] (..—) نونهال P *lrnd.* 1. a young seedling tree; sapling. 2. slim, graceful body.
nevniyaz (..—) نونیاز P *lrnd.* 1. anything newly produced. 2. beginner, tyro, novice.
nevpeyda (..—) نوپیدا P *lrnd.* new, newly produced.
nevr 1 نور only in **nevri dön=** for one's mood to change; to become moody or angry.
nevr 2 نور A *lrnd.* 1. a being bright, brilliant; brightness. 2. white blossoms; bloom. **—e** A a single flower or white blossom.
nevralji نورالژی F *med.* neuralgia.
nevregân (..—) نورگان *bookbinding* curved knife for cutting leather.
nevres نورس P *lrnd.* newly attained; freshly ripe or mature, adolescent.
nevreside (..—.) نورسیده P *lrnd.* 1. new, fresh, germinating. 2. newly arrived. **—gân** (..—.—) P *pl.*
nevresm نورسم P *lrnd.* new, newly produced; novelty.
nevreste نورسته P *lrnd.* newly sprouted; young shoot, sapling.
nevroz نوروز F *psychiatry* neurosis.
Nevruz (.—) نوروز P 1. the Persian New Year's Day (March 22). 2. one of the most ancient compound **makams** of Turkish music. **—i âmme**, day of the vernal equinox. **—i büzürg** same as **Nevruz-i hassa**. **—i hâra** *obs.* a makam. **—i harzemşah** New Year's Day of the king of Kharezm, the 19th day of the sun in Aries, 9th of February. **—i hassa** (*lit.*, great or special New Year's Day) the 6th day after the vernal equinox (held as a royal levee). **—i mizan** day of the autumnal equinox. **— otu** 1. *name of certain herbs and roots reputed to be antidotes for poisonous bites and stings.* 2. toad-flax, *bot.*, *Linaria vulgaris*. **—i sultanî** same as **Nevruz-i âmme**.
Nevruziye (.——.) نوروزیه 1. a kind of sweet offered as a present on the Persian New Year's Day. 2. poem offered as a New Year present.
nevsal (.—), **nevsale** (.—.) نوسال P *lrnd.* youthful.
nevşah (.—), **nevşeh** نوشاه P *lrnd.* 1. young king. 2. bridegroom.
nevşüküfte نوشکفته P *lrnd.* new-blown (rose); beginning to blossom out.
nevt نوط A *lrnd.* 1. a hanging, appending a thing; appendage. 2. a small parcel added to a beast's load; small basket of provisions, etc. hung on a beast's saddle.
nevtî (.—) نوتی A *lrnd.* seamen, sailor.
nevvab (.—) نواب A *lrnd.* one who naturally takes another's place in his absence or at his death; successor.
nevvah (.—) نواح A *lrnd.* professional wailer over the dead. **—a** (.—.) A *fem.*
nevyafte (.—.) نویافته P *Ott. hist.* population increase between two censuses.
nevvere (.´..) نوّر A *lrnd.* may (God) glorify.
nevzad (.—) نوزاد P *lrnd.* newly born (child).
nevzade (.—.) نوزاده P *lrnd.* 1. that has newly given birth. 2. newly born. **—gân** (.—.—) P *pl.* **—gân-ı çemen** sprouts, shoots, buds, blossoms.
nevzemin (..—) نوزمین P *lrnd.* in a new style or mode.
nevzuhur (..—) نوظهور P *lrnd.* newly appeared, new.
ney 1 نی |nay| a reed flute played especially in Mevlevi music. **— başparesi** mouthpiece of a reed flute. **— üfle=** to play the **ney**.
ney 2 نی A *lrnd.* 1. raw, rare, underdone (meat). 2. a being distant, long or extensive; distance.
Neyded نیده a legendary name of Medina.
neyi (.—) نیی P *lrnd.* ney player.
neyin (.—) نیین P *lrnd.* made of reeds.
neyistan (..—) نیستان P *lrnd.* reed marsh, reed bed, bamboo jungle.
neyl نیل A *lrnd.* a having obtained, a possessing any good thing; possession, enjoyment.

neyle= نیه باد short for **ne eyle=**.
neypare (.—.) نی پاره P *lrnd.* a piece of reed.
neysan (.—) نیسان P *lrnd.* reedlike; tall, slim and straight.
neyşeker نیشکر P *lrnd.* sugar cane. **—i had** down on a youth's cheek.
neyyir (.—) نیّر A *lrnd.* very bright and luminous; bright star; the sun; the moon.
neyyire (.—.) نیّره A *lrnd.* a striking retribution of providence.
neyyireyn (.—.) نیّرین A *lrnd.* both luminaries, the sun and the moon.
neyzar (.—) نیزار P *lrnd.* reed bed, reed marsh.
neyzen نیزن P a **ney** player. — **bakışı** a looking askance.
nez[zı] نزع A *lrnd.* 1. same as **nezi**. 2. a pulling or tearing away; removal.
nezafet (.—.) نظافت A *lrnd.* a being clean; cleanliness.
nezahet (.—.) نزاهت A purity, cleanness; decency, decorum. **—li** free from unpleasant accompaniments; pleasant, delightful and healthy.
nezaket (.—.) نزاکت P 1. delicacy; refinement; good breading, politeness. 2. a matter requiring delicacy. — **sahibi** person of refined manners. — **sat=** to show off an exaggerated politeness. **—li** refined, delicate; polite.
nezalet (.—.) نذالت A *lrnd.* a being mean-spirited, meanness, baseness.
nezaret (.—.) نظارت A 1. extensive view and outlook, prospect, view. 2. inspection; supervision, superintendence. 3. administration; direction; Ministry. — **altında** under surveillance. — **et=** /a/ to superintend, direct, inspect.
nezd نزد P *lrnd.* 1. immediate vicinity of a person or thing, the presence of a person. 2. opinion or judgment of a person. **—inizde** 1. near you. 2. in your opinion.
nezdik[ki] (.—) نزدیک P *lrnd.* 1. near, nigh; approximating in quality. 2. closely related.
nez'et=[der] نزع اتمك *lrnd.* /ı/ to tear away; to remove.
nezf نزف A *lrnd.* 1. same as **nezif** 1. 2. a weakness or faintness from a hemorrhage. 3. an exhausting the water of a well; a well's drying up. **—i dimagî** cerebral hemorrhage. **—i fail** active hemorrhage. **—î** A hemorrhagic
nezh نزه A *lrnd.* purity of life and character; pure, chaste.
nezi[zı] نزع [nez] death agony.
nezif[zfı] 1 نزف [nezf] path. hemorrhage.
ınezif 2 (.—) نزیف A *lrnd.* 1. faint from loss of blood. 2. parched with thirst; feverish. 3. intoxicated.
nezih (.—) نزیه A 1. pure in life and character. 2. quiet, healthy and pleasant (place).
nezil 1 (.—) نزیل A *lrnd.* guest, foreigner; visitor.
nezil 2 (.—) نذیل A *lrnd.* poor-spirited, mean, abject.
nezir[zrı] 1 نذر [nezr] a vowing or devoting; vow; thing vowed.
nezir 2 (.—) نذیر A *lrnd.* 1. one who warns or admonishes with threats; warning or admonition accompanied by a threat. 2. prophet who calls men to virtue with warnings of God's wrath.
nezire (.—.) نذیره A *lrnd.* thing done, given or sacrificed in fulfillment of a vow; especially, a child dedicated to God; Nazarite.
nezkeb نزکب *archaic* woman's kerchief.
nezl نذل A *lrnd.* poor-spirited, mean, vile.
nezle نزله A head cold. — **ol=** to catch cold. — **otu** feather geranium, Jerusalem oak, *bot.*, *Chenopodium botrys*.
nezr نذر A same as **nezir** 1.
nezret=[der] نذر ایتمك /ı, a/ 1. to vow. 2. to promise to give (as a vow).
nıkat (.—) نقاط A *lrnd.*, pl. of **nokta**.
nıkmet نقمت A *lrnd.*, same as **nakmet**.
nıkris نقرس A *med.* gout, podagra. **—e uğra=** to have the gout. **—li** gouty.
-nın نك cf. **-ın** 4.
nısab (.—) نصاب A 1. *can. law* the minimum income above which the Muslim tax of **zekât** becomes payable. 2. the number necessary for a quorum. 3. *lrnd.* the proper condition of a thing. **—ını bul=** to acquire the proper degree or condition.
nısf نصف A *lrnd.*, same as **nısıf**. **—en** (..) A half; in half.
nısfet نصفت A *lrnd.* justice, equity.
nısfılleyl نصف الليل A *lrnd.* midnight.
nısfınnehar (...—) نصف النهار A *lrnd.* 1. the meridian. 2. midday.
nısfî (.—) نصفی A *lrnd.* pertaining to a half.
nısfiye (.—.) نصفیه A 1. a **ney** half as long (as another, specified **ney**). 2. *lrnd.* a half-sequin piece. 3. *lrnd.* pertaining to a half. — **limon** a partly ripe lemon.
nısfiyet (.—.) نصفیت A *lrnd.* quality of half, of being half. — **üzre** by way of halving, by halves.
nısıf[sfı] نصف [nısf] half. — **daire** semicircle. — **kutur** radius. — **küre** hemisphere.
nışadır (.—.) نشادر [Persian **nuşadır**] salamoniac; ammonia. — **kaymağı** ammonium carbonate. — **ruhu** ammonia water. **—î** (.—.—) *lrnd.* pertaining to ammonia.

nışasta نشاستَ [Persian .—.] starch (from wheat etc. used for food). — **aharı** starch sizing.

-nız, -niz, -nuz, -nüz after consonants **-ınız**, etc. [pl. of **-n**] ڭز possessive second person plural your.

niac (.—) نِعاع A lrnd., pl. of **na'ce**.

niâlli (.—) نِعال A lrnd., pl. of **nal** 1. —**î** (.——) A pertaining to sandals.

niam نِعَم A lrnd., pl. of **ni'met**.

niamat (..—) نِعَمات A lrnd., pl. of **ni'met**.

nibah (.—) نِباح A lrnd. 1. a barking or howling. 2. a bleating. 3. a hissing (snake); hiss.

niballi 1 (.—) نِبال A lrnd., pl. of **nebl**.

ńiballi 2 (.—) نِبال A lrnd., pl. of **nebil**.

nibeşte نِبشتَ P lrnd. 1. that has written. 2. written; book.

nicad 1 (.—) نِجاد A lrnd. cord passed over one shoulder to suspend a sword; baldric.

nicad 2 (.—) نِجاد A lrnd., pl. of **necd**.

nicar (.—) نِجار A lrnd. stock, source, origin of a thing.

nicaret (.—.) نِجارَت A lrnd. quality or art of a carpenter, carpentry.

nice (.'.) نیجَ 1. how many! many a...; 2. how? in what manner or degree? 3. however many, howsoever. — **bir?** for how long? — **kimseler** many a person; how many persons! — **nice** very many. — **olur?** How will it be? What will happen? — **senelere** Many happy returns of the day (a formal greeting on feast days). —**lik** neol. quantity.

niçin نیچین why? for what? —**ci** protester who continually asks: why?

nidddi نِدّ A lrnd. equal, fellow, match, peer.

nida (.—) نِدا A 1. a shouting, proclaiming, shout, cry; proclamation. 2. gram. interjection. — **et**═ to shout, to proclaim; to cry out.

nidilân (—.—) نِدِلان A lrnd. nightmare.

nifakkı (.—) نِفاق A 1. discord, enmity, strife. 2. insincerity in friendship with secret enmity; hypocrisy, duplicity. 3. lrnd. a pretending to embrace Islam. — **ehli** person who acts with hypocrisy or duplicity in friendship or in religion.

nifalli (.—) نِفال A lrnd., pl. of **nefel**.

nifar (.—) نِفار A lrnd. 1. a being terrified, frightened and running away (animal). 2. a mobbing in haste and agitation (people).

nifas (.—) نِفاس A lrnd. 1. period of forty days after childbirth. 2. lochial discharges. —**î** (.——) 1. lochial. 2. puerperal.

nigâh (.—) نِگاه P lrnd. glance, look.

nigâhban (.——) نِگاهبان P lrnd. watchman, guard. —**î** (.———) P, —**lık** office or function of a guard; custody.

nigâhdar (.——) نِگاهدار P lrnd. guardian, keeper, custodian.

nigâhdaşti (.———) نِگاهداشتی P lrnd. 1. watch; custody. 2. a thing in charge.

-nigâr 1 (.—) نِگار P lrnd. who paints, depicts, represents, as in **vakayinigâr**.

nigâr 2 (.—) نِگار P lrnd. 1. picture, portrait; idol. 2. figure, image, statue. 3. beautiful woman, sweetheart; beauty. 4. superficial ornamentation of any kind. 5. a compound **makam** of Turkish music at least six centuries old. —**ı âlem** the prettiest creature in the world; beloved by all. —**ı hâtır** (lit. an embellishment of one's mind) matter kept in mind.

nigâre (.—.) نِگارَه P lrnd. figure, pattern, design.

nigârende (.—..) نِگارَندَه P lrnd. who depicts; painter.

nigârhane (.——.) نِگارخانَه P lrnd. 1. temple of an idol. 2. picture gallery, studio.

nigarin (.——) نِگارین P lrnd. adorned, embellished; beautiful; beauty.

nigârinekki نِگارینَک P Or. mus., name of a **makam**.

nigâristan (.—.—) نِگارستان P lrnd. 1. picture gallery. 2. collection of anecdotes, etc.

nigâriş (.—.) نِگارش P lrnd. an act of depicting; painting, drawing. —**pezir** (.—..—) P depicted.

nigâşte (.—.) نِگاشتَ P lrnd. 1. who has depicted. 2. depicted, painted; written.

nigeh نِگَه P lrnd., var. of **nigâh**. —**ban** (..—) P same as **nigâhban**.

nigehdâr (..—) نِگَهدار P lrnd., same as **nigâhdar**.

nigehendaz (...—) نِگَهانداز P lrnd. who casts a look at a thing. — **ol**═ /a/ to look at a thing.

nigende نِگَندَه P lrnd. 1. a particular kind of ornamental sewing; seam; quilting seam. 2. anything buried and hidden; buried treasure.

nigeran (..—) نِگَران P lrnd. 1. who looks, beholds. 2. who expects. 3. who reflects, meditates. — **ol**═ to look, to expect; to reflect.

nigerende نِگَرَندَه P lrnd. onlooker, spectator.

nigin (.—) نِگین P lrnd. 1. ring, seal, signet. 2. precious stone set in a finger ring. —**i saltanat** royal signet. —**say** (.——) P engraver of seals.

nigû (.—) نِگو P same as **nigûn**.

nigûn (.—) نِگون P lrnd. head downwards, inverted, upside down. —**baht** (.—.) P unfortunate. —**sar** (.——) P head downwards; inverted. —**taşt** (.——) P sky, spheres.

-nih ∻ P lrnd. that puts, places, *as in* kademnih.
nihab (.—) نهاب A lrnd., pl. of nehb, spoils.
nihad 1 (.—) نهاد P lrnd. character, disposition.
-nihad 2 (.—) نهاد P lrnd. put, placed, set, *as in* pişnihad.
nihade (.—.) نهاده P lrnd. 1. that has put. 2. put, placed, laid.
nihaf (.—) نهاف A lrnd., pl. of nahif.
nihai (.——) نهائى A final, ultimate.
nihal[ii] (.—) نهال P lrnd. sapling, shoot, twig.
nihale 1 (.—.) نهال [nihalî] table mat.
nihale 2 (.—.) نهال P lrnd. 1. same as nihal. 2. a lurking-place for hunters; hunting place. 3. carpet. —gâh (.—.—) P same as nihalgâh.
nihalgâh (.——) نهالگاه P lrnd. place of young trees, forest; hunting forest.
nihalî (.——) نهالى P lrnd. 1. same as nihale 1. 2. carpet. —çe small carpet.
nihalistan (.—.—) نهالستان P lrnd. place planted with young trees.
nihan (.—) نهان P lrnd. 1. concealed; hidden, secret. 2. laid by, treasured up. 3. inner thoughts; the inner man.
nihandan (.——) نهاندان P lrnd. any receptacle in which a thing may be hidden; storehouse, cellar.
nihandar (.——) نهاندار P lrnd. one who keeps anything secret, concealer.
nihanhane (.——.) نهانخانه P lrnd. private or secret room.
nihanî (.——) نهانى P lrnd. pertaining to what is hidden; secret, private.
nihas (.—) نحاس A lrnd. nature, origin; disposition.
nihavend (.—.) نهاوند P Or. mus. one of the oldest makams. —i kebir a compound makam about four centuries old.
nihaye (.—.) نهايه A lrnd., same as nihayet.
nihayet (.—.) نهايت A 1. end; extremity, extreme. 2. at last; at most. — bul= to come to an end; to finish. — derecede extremely. — ver= /a/ to bring to an end, to put an end to. —siz endless; infinite; countless; endlessly.
nihayetülemr (.—...) نهايةالامر A lrnd. at the end, at length.
nihayetünnihaye (.—...—.) نهايةالنهايه A lrnd. after all, when all is said and done.
nihrir (.—) نحرير A lrnd. sagacious, wise, experienced.
nihüft (.—) نهفت P lrnd. 1. a hiding, concealing; concealment. 2. hiding place. 3. private chamber. 4. hidden, secret.

nihüfte نهفته P lrnd. covered, concealed; hidden, secret.
nijad (.—) نژاد P lrnd. family, origin; parentage; race.
nijend نژند P lrnd. 1. miserable, wretched; vexed, angry. 2. poor, mean.
nik[ki] (—) نيك P lrnd. 1. good, excellent. 2. lucky, auspicious. — ü bed good and evil.
nika (.—) نقا A lrnd., pl. of naki 1.
nikab 1 (.—) نقاب A lrnd. 1. veil with two holes for the eyes; veil. 2. mask. —ı hazra the sky. —ı nil night.
nikab 2 (.—) نقاب A lrnd. very learned and well informed.
nikabet (.—.) نقابت A lrnd. quality, office, function of a dean or registrar.
nikâh (.—) نكاح A 1. engagement; marriage. 2. marriage portion (paid by the bridegroom to the bride). — düş= for a marriage to be possible (*i. e.* for the parties not to be within the prohibited degrees of relationship). — et= /ı/ to become engaged to; to marry. —ı kaç= for the marriage to be annulled. — kıy= to perform the ceremony of marriage.
nikâhî (.——) نكاحى A lrnd. pertaining to marriage, to the marriage contract or to a wife's dowry.
nikâhla=[r] نكاحلامق /ı, la/ to betroth or marry (a couple). —n= to become engaged or married.
nikâhlı نكاحلى engaged; married.
nikâhsız نكاحسز unmarried; out of wedlock. — yaşa= /la/ to live together without being married.
nikahter (—..) نيك اختر P lrnd. lucky.
nikân (——) نيكان P lrnd., pl. of nik, the good, the righteous.
nikât (.—) نكات A lrnd., pl. of nükte.
nikâyet (.—.) نكايت A lrnd. a routing, defeating, destroying an enemy; rout, defeat, destruction.
nikbet نكبت [nekbet] lrnd. great calamity, misfortune; disgrace. —hane (..—.) P house of troubles; poverty-stricken household. —î (..—) P fallen, disgraced, ruined. —zede P struck down by misfortune.
nikbin نيكبين [*Persian* ——] optimistic; optimist. —lik optimism.
nikel نيكل F nickel.
nikelâj نيكلاژ F nickel plating.
nikendiş (—.—) نيك انديش P lrnd. friend, well-wisher.
nikfal[ii] (——) نيك فال P lrnd. of good augury, auspicious.
nikfor (—.) نيكفر Gk obs. a variety of blue fig.

nikhah (— —) نیك خواه P *lrnd.* well-wishing, friendly.
nikhu, nikhuy (— —) نیك خو P *lrnd.* of good disposition or habits; good-natured, well-bred. —**yi**, —**î** (.— —) P good-temperedness; goodness of habits.
niki (— —) نیکی P *lrnd.* goodness.
nikkâr (— —) نیك كار P *lrnd.* philanthropist; beneficient.
niknam (— —) نیك نام P *lrnd.* 1. good name, good reputation. 2. who has a good name or reputation. —**î** (— — —) P, —**lık** good repute, good name.
nikrev (—.—) نیكرو P *lrnd.* quick or pleasant-going (horse).
nikriz نكریز P *Or. mus.* one of the oldest makams.
niksiret (— —.) نیك سیرت P *lrnd.* virtuous, good, moral.
nikter (—.) نیكتر P *lrnd.* better. —**în** (—.—) P best.
nikû (— —) نیكو P *lrnd.* good; beautiful, elegant. —**siyer** (— —..) P well-disposed; of good manners or habits. —**yi** (— — —) P goodness; elegance.
nil 1 نیل [Persian —] 1. indigo. 2. *lrnd.* indigo plant, *bot.*, *Indigofera tinctoria*.
Nil 2 (—) نیل A *geog.* the Nile. —**i mübarek** the Nile. —**i Sudan**, —**i Zenc** the Niger.
Nilâb (— —) نیلاب P *geog.* 1. the Nile. 2. the Indus.
nilfam (— —) نیلفام P *lrnd.* 1. indigo-colored. 2. black; dark.
nilgûn (— —) نیلگون P *lrnd.* indigo-colored, deep blue; black, dark. —**bahr** (— — —.) P the azure sky. —**hayam** (— — — .—), —**perdeha** (— —..—), —**vita** (— —.—) P the heaven, spheres.
nilî (— —) نیلی P *lrnd.* 1. of the color of indigo, deep blue; blueness. 2. mixed or colored with indigo.
nilüfer نیلوفر [Persian .—.] water lily, *bot.*, *Nymphea*.
nim 1 (—) نیم P *lrnd.* half.
nim- 2 (—) نیم P *mus.* half (a prefix before names of rhythmic patterns).
nimâl نمال A *lrnd.*, pl. of **neml** 1.
nimbismil (—..) نیم بسمل P *lrnd.* half-slaughtered (sheep etc. *i. e.* the throat of which has been insufficiently cut).
nimcan (—.—) نیم جان P *lrnd.* half dead (with fright).
nimcezire (—.—.) نیم جزیره P *lrnd.* peninsula.
nimcivan (—.—) نیم جوان P *lrnd.* middle-aged.
nimçe (—.) نیمچه P *lrnd.* 1. short-skirted garment. 2. short sword; short-barreled gun.

nimdevr (—.) نیم دور P *Or. mus.* a fast rhythmic pattern of 18 beats.
nime 1 (—.) نیمه P *lrnd.* half.
ni'me 2 نعم A *lrnd.* How good! How excellent!
ni'melbedel نعم البدل A *lrnd.* What a good replacement!
ni'mennasir (...—) نعم النصیر A *lrnd.* How good is the Helper! God the great Helper.
ni'met نعمت A 1. blessing, benefaction; favor. 2. good fortune; happiness; comfort. 3. food (especially bread). —**i ayağı ile tep=** to spurn a piece of luck.
ni'methar (..—) نعمت خوار P *lrnd.* who subsists on benefactions.
ni'metşinas (...—) نعمت شناس P *lrnd.* grateful.
nimhab (— —) نیم خواب P *lrnd.* half-asleep, dozing; half-sleep.
nimkâr (— —) نیم كار P *lrnd.* 1. lukewarm, inefficient. 2. half-made.
nimlâhza (—..) نیم لحظه P *lrnd.* 1. a split second. 2. a rapid glance.
nimperde (—..) نیم پرده P *mus.* semitone.
nimpertev (—..) نیم پرتو P *lrnd.* dull, dim (light).
nimpuht (—.), **nimpuhte** (—..) نیم پخت، نیم پخته P *lrnd.* 1. half-cooked. 2. half-ripe.
nimr نمر A *lrnd.* leopard.
nimreng (—.) نیم رنگ P *lrnd.* of a faint or undecided color.
nimres (—.) نیم رس P *lrnd.* half-finished, half-ripe; half-mature.
nimresmi (—.—) نیم رسمی P *lrnd.* semi-official.
nimruz (— —) نیم روز P *lrnd.* 1. midday, noon. 2. the south, the direction of the sun at midday. 3. *mus.* the 29th among the 30 tunes.
nimsal[l] (— —) نیم سال P *lrnd.* middle-aged.
nimşeb (—.) نیم شب P *lrnd.* midnight.
nimşeffaf (—.—) نیم شفاف P *lrnd.* translucent.
nimtaht (—.) نیم تخت P *lrnd.* couch (with one arm or end to it).
nimten (—.), **nimtene** (—..) نیم تن، نیم تنه P *lrnd.* 1. bust. 2. short-bodied coat, a kind of jacket with elbow-length sleeves. 3. *name of an imaginary race of creatures shaped like men cloven from head to foot, one half being male and the other female*.
nimtereng (—..) نیم ترنگ P *lrnd.* low voice, murmur, mutter.
nimtih (—.) نیم تیه P *lrnd.* 1. half a load. 2. divided in two.
-nin نك cf. **-ın** 4.
nine نینه grandmother.
Nineva نینوا *hist.* Nineveh.
ninni نینی lullaby. — **söyle=** to sing a lullaby.

nir (—) نِر A *lrnd.* 1. yoke. 2. fringe, border.
niran (— —) نِيرَان A *lrnd.*, *pl. of* **nar 2, nir, nur.**
nirenc (—.) نِيرَنْج A [**nireng**] *lrnd.* 1. magic, enchantment; charm, incantation; talisman; witchcraft. 2. trick. **—ât** (—.—) A incantations, fascination.
nireng (—.) نِيرَنْك P *lrnd.*, *same as* **nirenc.**
nirengi (..—) نِيرَنْكِى P surveyor's triangulation. — **noktası** trigonometrical point; landmark, reference mark, guide mark.
nirengsaz (—.—) نِيرَنْكْسَاز P *lrnd.* 1. sorcerer, magician. 2. trickster. **—î** (—.——) P deceit, subtlety.
niru (——) نِيرُو P *lrnd.* strength, power, might.
nirumend (——.) نِيرُومَنْد P *lrnd.* strong, powerful. **—î** (——.—) P power, strength.
nisa (.—) نِسَاء A *lrnd.* women, womankind. N—**i Kasri Sûresi** name of the sixty-fifth sura of the Quran. N— **Suresi** name of the fourth sura of the Quran.
Nisabur (—.——) نِيسَابُور P *var. of* **Nişabur.**
nisacet (.—.) نَسَاجَت A *lrnd.* art of weaving.
nisai (.——) نِسَائِى A 1. pertaining to women. 2. gynecological.
nisaiye (.—..) نِسَائِيَّه A diseases peculiar to women; gynecology. **—ci** gynecologist.
Nisan (——) نِيسَان A April. — **balığı** April fool.
nisar 1 (.—) نِثَار A *lrnd.* 1. a scattering things broadcast; dissemination. 2. things so scattered broadcast; money which is thrown among the people at marriages or on other festive occasions.
-nisar 2 نِثَار P *lrnd.* scattering, strewing, *as in* **zernisar.**
nisbet نِسْبَت A 1. relationship; relation. 2. ratio, proportion; proportional number. 3. comparison. 4. spite, spiteful or defiant act. **—le** /a/ in comparison (with). **—i ceybiye** trigonometry logarithmic sine. — **et=** 1. /a/ to act spitefully. 2. /ı/ to compare. 3. /ı, a/ to attribute. — **kabul etme=** to bear no ratio or comparison. **—i sübutiye** *lrnd.* relation of positive inherency as a quality. — **ver=** /a/ to say something out of spite. **—i zılliye** trigonometry tangential ratio; logarithmic tangent.
nisbetçi نِسْبَتْجِى spiteful, defiant.
nisbeten (.'..) نِسْبَةً A 1. relatively; in comparison; in proportion. 2. in order to spite, spitefully.
nisbî (.—) نِسْبِى A 1. proportionate; proportional. 2. relative. — **temsil** *pol.* proportional representation. **—ye** (.—.) relativism. **—yet** (.—.) relativity.

nisevi (..—) نِسْوِى A *lrnd.* pertaining to women.
nispet نِسْپَت *var. of* **nisbet.**
nisti (——) نِيسْتِى P *lrnd.* nonexistence.
nisvan (.—) نِسْوَان A *lrnd.* women.
nisvi (.—) نِسْوِى A *lrnd.*, *same as* **nisevi.**
nisyan (.—) نِسْيَان A *lrnd.* a forgetting; forgetfulness; oblivion.
niş 1 (—) نِيش P *lrnd.* 1. sting of a wasp etc. 2. sharp point. 3. fang of a snake, tusk of a boar.
niş 2 نِيش F recess in a wall; niche.
Nişabur (———) نِيشَابُور P 1. *same as* **Nişapur.** 2. a compound **makam** about five centuries old.
nişaburek[ki] (———.) نِيشَابُورَك P *Or. mus.* a compound **makam** about three centuries old.
nişadır نِشَادُر *var. of* **nışadır.**
nişahte (.—.) نِشَاخْتَه P *lrnd.* 1. who has set up, planted, erected. 2. set up; planted; erected.
nişan 1 نِشَان [**nişan 2**] 1. sign, mark; indication. 2. target. 3. order, decoration. 4. engagement, betrothal; token given on betrothal. 5. a distinguishing sign or mark; scar. 6. *Ott. hist.* royal monogram usually set over letters-patent, public buildings etc. — **al=** /a/ to take aim at (something). — **at=** to shoot, to fire. **—a at=** to shoot at a target. **—dan dön=** to break off an engagement. **—a geçir=** to shoot into a mark (arrow). — **halkası** engagement ring. — **kabağı** *obs.* gourd set up as a mark or target. — **koy=** to make a mark. — **oku** arrow made to fly true and hit a mark. — **tablası** round target. — **tak=** /a/ 1. confer a medal of honor. 2. to betroth. — **ver=** 1. /dan/ to give signs (of so and so); to bear a resemblance to. 2. /a/ to give a token of engagement. 3. /a/ to confer a decoration on a person. **—a vur=** to hit the target. — **yap=** to arrange an engagement. — **yüzüğü** engagement ring.
nişan 2 (.—) نِشَان P *same as* **nişan. —ı hâkani** *Ott. hist.* imperial monogram. **—ı iftihar** *Ott. hist.*, an Ottoman order of special merit. **—ı imtiyaz** name of the highest Ottoman order. **—ı şefkat** *Ott. hist.*, decoration conferred by the Sultan upon ladies of distinction.
-nişan 3 (.—.) نِشَان P *lrnd.* 1. which is a sign or mark of (so and so); which is marked or set up in (so and so), *as in* **belâgatnişan, mâdeletnişan.** 2. fixing, planting, impressing, *as in* **hâtırnişan.**
nişancı نِشَانْجِى 1. marksman, a good shooter. 2. *Ott. hist.*, title of an officer whose duty it was to inscribe the Sultan's imperial monogram over all imperial letters-patent. **—lık** marksmanship.

nişande (.—.) نِشانده P *lrnd.* 1. that has set up, erected or planted a thing. 2. set up, erected, planted.

nişane (.—.) نِشانه P 1. sign, mark, trace. 2. target at which missiles are aimed.

nişangâh (.——) نِشانگاه P 1. back sight (of a gun). 2. *lrnd.* butt, target. **— dürbünü** telescopic sight. **— sürmesi** slide of a back sight. **— yatağı** bed of a back sight.

nişangîr (.——) نِشانگير P *lrnd.* 1. one who takes notes. 2. that receives a mark or impression. 3. cabinetmaker's tool for making lines or distances.

nişanî (.——) نِشانى P *lrnd.*, same as **nişancı**.

nişanla=ᵣ نِشانلمق 1. /ı/ to mark. 2. /a/ to take aim at. 3. /ı, la/ to engage (one's son or daughter) to another. **—n=** to become engaged to.

nişanlama نِشانلامه engagement.

nişanlı نِشانلى 1. engaged to be married. 2. fiancé; fiancée. 3. marked with a sign or mark, etc.

Nişapur (.——) نِشاپور P *geog.*, name of a celebrated city in the north of Khurasan.

nişasta نِشاسته [Persian .—.] same as **nışasta**.

nişat (.—) نِشاط A same as **neşat**.

nişdan (.—), **nişdet** نِشدت A *lrnd.* 1. a seeking a thing by proclamation. 2. a proclaiming a thing found in order to discover its owner. 3. a putting one on his oath; proposing to put someone on his oath.

nişest نِشست P *lrnd.* a sitting down; a being seated.

nişeste نِشسته P *lrnd.* 1. who has sat; seated. 2. aground, stranded (ship). 3. sagged, subsided (wall, etc.).

nişesteni (...—) نِشستنى P *lrnd.* 1. (thing) on which to sit. 2. (place) in which to reside.

nişestgâh (..—), **nişestgeh** نِشستگاه P *lrnd.* 1. seat, place to sit. 2. part of the body on which one sits, buttocks.

nişib (.—) نِشيب P *lrnd.* 1. low ground, bottom. 2. slope, declivity; descent. **— ü firaz** 1. descent and ascent. 2. ups and downs. **—gâh** (.——) P descent; low place.

nişimen (.—.) نِشيمن P *lrnd.* 1. seat; place of sitting; assembly. 2. place where one resides. 3. bird's nest. **—div** (.—.—) P home of the demon, *i. e.* the world. **—gâh** (.—.—) P assembling place.

-nişîn (.—) نِشين P *lrnd.* who sits, sitting, seated; that lives, as in **postnişîn**, **tahtnişîn**.

nişter نِشتر P *lrnd.*, same as **neşter**.

nişve نِشوه A *lrnd.* 1. a smelling; perceiving an odor. 2. a hearing information.

nitac (.—) نِتاج A *lrnd.*, same as **netac**.

nitaf (.—) نِطاف A *lrnd.*, pl. of **nutfe**, clear waters.

nitah (.—) نِطاح A *lrnd.* a butting (ram).

nitakᵏⁱ (.—) نِطاقه A *lrnd.* 1. a kind of apron or petticoat; the ordinary working garment of an Arab woman. 2. girdle, waist belt.

nite نِته archaic how. **— ki** same as **nitekim**.

nitekim (..'.) نِتكيم even as; just as; thus; as a matter of fact.

nitele=ᵣ *neol.* /ı/ to qualify. **—me** verbal n.

nitelikᵍⁱ *neol.* quality.

niv (—) نِيو P *lrnd.* brave, bold.

nivâr (——) نِوار P *lrnd.* the space between the earth and the sky, atmosphere.

nivâre (———.) نِواره P *lrnd.* rolling pin.

nive (—.) نِوه P *lrnd.* weeping, tears; wailing, moans.

nivend (—.) نِوند P *lrnd.* intellect, mind, understanding.

niver (—.) نِور P *lrnd.* production, produce; creatures. **—i nivâr** productions of the sky, meteors of all kinds.

nivmerd (—.) نِومرد P *lrnd.* hero.

niyâ (.—) نِيا P *lrnd.* grandfather, ancestor.

niyabet (ı—.) نِيابت A 1. regency, regentship. 2. *Ott. hist.* office of a deputy judge. 3. *lrnd.* an acting as a deputy or substitute. **— et=** /a/ to act as deputy or substitute. **—i saltanat** regency.

niyabeten (.—'..) نِيابةً A *lrnd.* as a substitute.

niyagân (.——) نِياگان P *lrnd.*, pl. of **niyâ**.

niyah (.—), **niyahat**ᵘ (.—.) نِياح، نِياحت A *lrnd.* a vociferously wailing for the dead; lamentation, moan.

niyam 1 (.—) نِيام P *lrnd.* sheath, scabbard.

niyam 2 (.—) نِيام A *lrnd.*, pl. of **nâim 1**.

niyam 3 (.—) نِيام A *lrnd.* a sleeping; sleep, slumber. **—en** (.—'.) A in sleep, sleeping.

niyâr (.—) نِيار A *lrnd.*, pl. of **nâr 2**.

niyat 1 (.—) نِيات A *lrnd.*, pl. of **niyet**.

niyât 2 (.—) نِياط A *lrnd.*, pl. of **nevt**, things suspended.

niyât 3 (.—) نِياط A *lrnd.* 1. a suspensory loop, string or thong. 2. the heart-string by which the heart is suspended; the heart. 3. the descending aorta. 4. a prolongation of a sandy desert between other lands.

niyâyiş (.—.) نِيايش P *lrnd.* act of praising God or of blessing and praying for a person; benediction.

niyaz (.—) نِياز P 1. entreaty, supplication; prayer. 2. *myst. orders* salutation (of a dervish to his superior). 3. need; wish. 4. *Or. mus.* a **makam** which forms a pair with **nâz**. **— et=** to ask as a favor, to entreat for.

niyazî (.——) نِيازى P *lrnd.* 1. pertaining

niyaziyan

to entreaty. 2. supplicant. 3. *w. cap., man's name.*
niyaziyan (.———) نیازیان P *lrnd.* supplicants; the needy.
niyazkâr (.——) نیازکار P *same as* **niyazmend**.
niyazmend (.—.) نیازمند P *lrnd.* supplicant. —î (.—.—) P, —lik quality or act of a supplicant; supplication, entreaty.
niye نیه Why? What for?
niyendele=ʳ گنده لك [**nigende**] *archaic* to stitch or quilt a thing thoroughly.
niyet نیت A 1. a firmly resolving; resolve, intention; purpose. 2. formal resolve to perform some religious act. —**i boz=** to change one's mind. —**i bozuk** having an evil intention. — **çek=** to have one's fortune told (by drawing slips of paper bearing various prophecies). — **et=** /a/ to resolve; to intend. — **hayır âkıbet hayır** The intention is good, may the issue be good. — **kuyusu** wishing well. — **tut=** when consulting a fortuneteller to think of the matter about which one is inquiring.
niyetli نیتلی 1. who has an intention. 2. who has resolved to fast.
-niyuş 1 (.——) نیوش P *lrnd.* who hears, who listens, as in **hakikatniyuş.**
niyuş 2 (.—) نیوش P *lrnd.* hearing, listening; attention.
niyuşa (.——) نیوشا P *lrnd.* who hears, listens.
niyuşe نیوشه P *lrnd.* a listening attentively; eavesdropping.
niyuşende نیوشنده P *lrnd.* hearer, listener.
niyuşide (.——.) نیوشیده P *lrnd.* who has listened or heard; heard, hearsay.
-niz 1 ڭز *cf.* **-nız.**
-niz 2 نیز P *lrnd.* also; too; even.
nizaᵃⁱ (.—) نزاع A 1. a contending, quarreling; quarrel, dispute; litigation. 2. *lrnd.* an exile's being homesick; homesickness. — **et=** /la/ to contend, dispute. —**i lâfzî** *lrnd.* a mere verbal contention. —**cı** contentious; quarrelsome. —**lı** disputed.
nizam (.—) نظام A 1. order, regularity. 2. law, regulation; system, method. 3. line, row or string of things arranged in order. 4. *Ott. hist.* regular troops; regular soldier. N—**ı Cedid** *Ott. hist.,* the new system inaugurated by Sultan Selim III; especially, the new regular troops then organized. —**a getir=**, —**a koy=** /ı/ to put in order.
nizamât (.——) نظامات A *lrnd., pl. of* **nizam.** —**ı cedide** *lrnd.* the new ordinances of the Ottoman Empire by which feudalism was legally abolished.
nizamen (.—ʹ.) نظاماً A *lrnd.* according to law; legally.

nizamî (.—̣—) نظامی A *lrnd.* pertaining to order or law; legal; regular; regularized.
Nizamiye (.——.) نظامیه A Regular Army. — **Hazinesi** *Ott. hist.* military treasury. — **kapısı** the main entrance to a barracks.
nizamla=ʳ نظاملمق /ı/ to put in order. —**n=** *pass.*
nizamlı نظاملی 1. in order, straight; regular. 2. legal.
nizamname (.——.) نظامنامه P regulation.
nizamsız نظامسز 1. in disorder; irregular. 2. illegal. —**lık** 1. disorder; irregularity. 2. illegality.
nizar 1 (.—) نزار P *lrnd.* 1. thin, lean; meager, emaciated. 2. slender, slim.
nizar 2 (.—) نظار A *lrnd.* sagacity, perspicacity, insight.
nizaret (.—.) نظارت A *lrnd.* threat, menace.
nizarî (.——) نزاری P *lrnd.* leanness; slenderness.
niza'sız (.—.) نزاعسز free from contention or dispute. — **kaza** *law* voluntary jurisdiction.
nize (—.) نیزه P *lrnd.* 1. spear, lance, javelin. 2. a length of dried reed, each section of which can be made into a pen. —**i âteşin** *poet.* a beam of sunlight. —**i barkeş** a spear bearing an enemy's head. —**i bidberg** spear with a head shaped like a willow leaf.
nizebaz (—.—) نیزه باز P *lrnd.* spearsman.
nizebekef (—...) نیزه بکف P *lrnd.* 1. whose spear is in his hand. 2. the sun illuminating the world (with its rays compared to lances).
nizedar (—.—) نیزه دار P *lrnd.* armed with a spear, spearman.
nizezen (—..) نیزه زن P *lrnd.* spearman.
nobran نوبران arrogant; discourteous, churlish, ill-bred. —**lık** ill-breeding; arrogance.
noda نوده [**loda**] *prov.* straw heap covered with earth.
nodul نودول *prov.* nail at the end of an ox-goad. —**la=** /ı/ 1. to push with such a nail. 2. to goad, to incite.
Noel نوئل F Christmas. — **Baba** Father Christmas, Santa Claus.
nohudi (.——) نخودی P chickpea color.
nohutᵈᵘ نخود [*Persian* —] chickpea, *bot., Cicer arietinum.* — **oda bakla sofa** small-roomed house. — **yakısı** a cut kept open by means of a chickpea. —**lu** mixed with chickpeas.
noksan نقصان A 1. deficient; defective, missing. 2. deficiency, defect, shortcoming. — **gör=** to suffer a falling off. —**lık** deficiency, defect.
nokta نقطه A 1. point, dot; period, full stop. 2. spot, speck. 3. center punch. 4. *mil.* isolated sentry; military or police post, pill box. 5. dot (in Morse). 6. particular place in space, point,

direction. —i ihtirak *lrnd.* focus (of a mirror lens or a conic section.). —i inkılâb *astr.* a solstitial point of the ecliptic. —i itidal *astr.* equinoctial point of the ecliptic. —i itidal-i harîfi *astr.* autumnal equinoctial point. —i itidal-i rebii *astr.* vernal equinoctial point. —i kül *lrnd.* center of all. —i nazar point of view. —i necmiye *anat.* asterion. — nokta 1. dotted, spotted. 2. each dot distinctly apart; point by point. —sı noktasına exactly, in every way. — ol= *slang* 1. to run away. 2. to drop into a drunken slumber. —i ruşentar pergâr *lrnd.* (*lit.* The point of the most glorious compasses.) 1. the north celestial pole. 2. center of the earth. 3. the Prophet Muhammad. —i tekatu *geom.* point of intersection. —i temas *geom.* point of contact (of two circles).

noktabaşı نقطه باشى *Ott. hist.*, a seventeenth-century tax.

noktadar (..—) نقطه دار P *lrnd.* dotted, that has dots.

noktala=ᵣ نقطه لامق /ı/ to dot, punctuate; to mark with a center punch.

noktalı نقطه لى dotted; punctuated; speckled. — virgül semicolon.

noktasız نقطه سز undotted.

nonoş نونوش little pet.

normalⁱⁱ نورمال F 1. normal. 2. *geom.* normal. —leş= to become normal.

Norveç (´.) نوروج *geog.* Norway. —çe Norse. —li a Norwegian.

not نوط F 1. note; memorandum. 2. mark, grade (in school). — et= /ı/ to note down. — tut= to take notes. — ver= /a/ 1. to give marks (to). 2. to pass judgment (on).

nota (´.) نوطه It 1. musical note; written music. 2. diplomatic note. 3. bill; memorandum.

noter نوتر F notary public.

nöbet 1 نوبت [nevbet] 1. turn (of duty etc.); watch (of a sentry etc.). 2. onset (of fever); fit. 3. set performance of a military band. — ateşi a rolling barrage of infantry fire, a fire by file. — bekle= 1. to stand guard. 2. to await one's turn. — çal= to play before a sovereign or governor (band). — gel= to have a fit (of fever etc.).

nöbet 2 نوبت [nebat] *only in* — şekeri a kind of crystallized candy.

nöbetçi نوبتجى 1. on guard; on duty. 2. sentry; watchman. — eczahane pharmacy whose turn it is to be on night call. — zabit officer of the watch, orderly officer.

nöbethane (..—.) نوبتخانه P *lrnd.* 1. guard-house, station of a guard. 2. military band that performed at stated times daily at court. 3. place where the band assembles.

nöbetî (..—) نوبتى A *lrnd.* 1. man on a turn of duty. 2. member of a military band which played at court.

nöbetleş=ⁱʳ نوبتلشمك /la/ to take turns; to take turn and turn about. —e in turn, by turns. —me a taking turns; *agr.* rotation of crops. =ntı, =nti, *etc., after consonants* =ıntı, *etc.* نتى deverbal noun designating a movement or agglomeration produced by an action, as in, akıntı, birikinti, sarsıntı, sızıntı, süprüntü.

nuas (.—) نعاس A *lrnd.* drowsiness; stupor; doze.

nufus (.—) نفوس A *var. of* **nüfus**.

Nuh (—) نوح A Noah. — der peygamber demez He is very obstinate. —un gemisi Noah's Ark. — Nebiden kalma antidiluvian; very old. — Sûresi name of the seventy-first sura of the Quran. — teknesi wishbone.

nuhaʳᵃ¹ (.—) نخاع A *anat.* spinal marrow. —i şevkî spinal cord.

nuhale (.—.) نخاله A *lrnd.* 1. bran. 2. the finest choice of anything.

nuhas (.—) نحاس A *same as* **nühas**.

nuhat 1 (.—) نخاط A *lrnd.* sob; inward weeping.

nuhat 2 (.—) نحات A *lrnd., pl. of* **nahi 2**, writers on syntax, grammarians.

nuhbe نخبه A *lrnd.* chosen, selected (person or thing).

nuhûlⁱⁱⁱ (.—) نحول A *lrnd.* a being emaciated, lean; leanness, emaciation.

nuhur (.—) نحور A *lrnd., pl. of* **nahr**.

nuhuset (.—.) نحوست A *lrnd.* a being unlucky, inauspicious; evil omen. —li unlucky, inauspicious.

nuhust نخست P *lrnd.* first, the first.

nuhustin (..—) نخستين P *lrnd.* the first, the very first.

nuhustzad (..—) نخستزاد P *lrnd.* first-born, eldest son.

nukaba (..—) نقباء A *lrnd., pl. of* **nakib 2**, elders of communities, especially the Prophet Muhammad's twelve chief disciples in Medina.

nukalâ (..—) نقلاء A *lrnd., pl. of* **nakil 1**, 1. narrator. 2. transcribers. 3. movers, removers.

nukat نقط A *lrnd., pl. of* **nokta**.

nukave (.—) نقاوه A *lrnd.* 1. the pure, excellent, the cream of anything. 2. purity, cleanness. 3. the refuse and siftings of wheat.

nukbe نقبه A *lrnd.* 1. hole. 2. face; color or complexion. 3. petticoat.

nûkdar (——) نوكدار P *lrnd.* 1. beaked. 2. pointed.

nuker (.—.) نوكر P *lrnd.* servant, manservant. —î (.—.—) P, —lik service, attendance.

nukra 1 نقره A *prov.* 1. a swelling and

nukra

puncture in the skin made by the warble fly. 2. hole or defect in a hide of leather.

nukra 2 نُقْرَه A *lrnd.* 1. natural round depression where water can collect. 2. hollow at the back of the neck. 3. eye, socket. 4. lump of smelted gold or silver. **—i ham** pure silver.

nukud (.—) نُقُود A *lrnd., pl. of* **nakd.**

nukulᵘ̈ (.—) نُقُول A *lrnd., pl. of* **nakl,** narratives, traditions, histories.

nukuş (.—) نُقُوش A *lrnd., pl. of* **nakş.**

nûlᵘ̈ (—) نُول P *lrnd.* 1. beak of a bird. 2. spout of a vessel.

nu'man (.—) نُعْمان A *lrnd.* 1. blood. 2. red anemone, red peony.

numara نُومَرو ، نُمْره ، نُومَرو It 1. number; mark. 2. trick; performance. 3. item, event (in an entertainment). 4. size or number (shoe etc.). **—sını ver=** /a/ to form a bad opinion of. **— yap=** *slang* to play a part; to act up.

numaracı نُمْرَهجى *slang* tall talker, charlatan.

numarala=ʳ نُمْرَهلاش /ı/ to mark with numbers; to number.

numaralı نُمْرَهلى numbered, marked with a number.

numune (.—.) نُمُونه P *same as* **nümune.**

-nun 1 نك *cf.* **-ın 4.**

nun 2 [nun 3] name of the letter ن (twenty-eighth letter of the Ottoman and Persian alphabets, twenty-fifth of the Arabic. In chronograms it has the numerical value of 50. In dates of documents it represents the month of Ramazan).

nun 3 (—) نُون A *lrnd.* 1. *same as* **nun 2.** 2. fish; fishes. 3. edge of a sword; sword. 4. inkstand. 5. dimple in the chin. 6. eyebrow.

nune (—.) نُونه A *lrnd.* 1. one fish. 2. dimple.

nur (—) نُور A 1. light; brilliance. 2. halo, the spiritual light of saintliness. 3. glory. **N—i Âlem** *lrnd.* the light of the world, *i. e.* the Prophet Muhammad. **N—i Azra** *lrnd.* the glory, halo of the Virgin Mary. **—i çeşm** *lrnd.* one's darling child. **— damlası** a lovely child. **—i dide** *lrnd., same as* **nur-i çeşm. — içinde yatsın** May he sleep in radiance, *said when mentioning a beloved dead one.* **—i ilâhi** the divine glory. **—i iman** the glory of the faith that surrounds a believer. **— in=** for divine light to come down (from heaven). **N—i Mübin, N—i Nuhustin, N—i Pesin** *lrnd.* the Prophet Muhammad. **—i sade** *lrnd.* unmixed effulgence, God's effulgence. **—i tecelli** *myst.* illumination. **— topu** a lovely child. **— yüzlü** benevolent looking (old person).

nuran (——) نُوران A *lrnd.* (lit., the two lights) the two daughters of the Prophet Muhammad.

nurani (———) نُورانى A 1. shining with light, luminous. 2. formed from the glory of God; of blessed aspect. 3. glorious; blessed; majestic.

nuraniyet (———.) نُورانيّت A 1. a having a saintly aspect. 2. luminosity; gloriousness; light, splendor.

nurbahş (—.) نُوربَخْش P *lrnd.* 1. light-giving, glorious. 2. given by the glory of God.

nurefşan (—.—) نُورافْشان P *lrnd.* light-diffusing.

nureyn (—.) نُورَيْن A *lrnd., same as* **nuran.**

nuri (——) نُورى A *lrnd.* splendid, bright, clear.

nurlan=ⁿ نُورلانْمَق to become bright, luminous, surrounded with a halo of glory.

nurlu (—.) نُورلو 1. luminous, bright. 2. illumined with a halo.

nursuz (—.) نُورسُز 1. having no light; dim. 2. malicious. **— pirsiz** malicious looking, ugly and unlovely.

nurün-alâ nur (—...—) نُورعلى نُور A *lrnd.* much better, even more excellent.

nusara (..—) نُصَرا A *lrnd., pl. of* **nasîr 2.**

Nusayrî (..—) نُصَيْرى A *lrnd.* an adherent of the Nusairiye sect.

Nusayriye (..—.) نُصَيْريّه A *lrnd.,* name of a community and religious sect found in the northern parts of Syria.

nusb نُصْب A *lrnd.* 1. obelisks or stones set up; idols set up to be worshipped. 2. evil, calamity; sickness, disease.

nush نُصْح A *lrnd.* a giving advice; admonition, advice.

nusha, nuska نُسْخه [nüsha] *colloq.* amulet, charm.

nusret نُصْرَت A *lrnd.* 1. victory. 2. help, succor; especially, God's help (in battle).

nusretcu (..—) نُصْرَتْجُو P *lrnd.* who seeks victory by divine aid.

nusreteser نُصْرَت اَثَر P *lrnd.* victorious.

nusretintisab (....—) نُصْرَت انْتِساب P *lrnd.* related to divine aid; victorious.

nusrettev'em نُصْرَت تَوأَم P *lrnd.* victorious.

nussah (.—) نُصّاح A *lrnd., pl. of* **nasıh.**

nussar (.—) نُصّار A *lrnd., pl. of* **nâsır 1.**

nusuᵘ̈ (.—) نُصُوع A *lrnd.* 1. a being pure; purity. 2. a being clear, manifest, evident. 3. a being satisfied with drink.

nusub نُصُب A *lrnd., same as* **nusb.**

nusulᵘ̈ (.—) نُصُول A *lrnd., pl. of* **nasl.**

nusus (.—) نُصُوص A *lrnd., pl. of* **nas 2.**

-nuş 1 (—) نُوش P *lrnd.* who drinks, *e. g.* **bâdenûş.**

nûş 2 (—) نُوش P *lrnd.* 1. a drinking; carouse. 2. a drink of any kind; anything drunk, especially, a sweet, agreeable and wholesome drink. 3. medicine; remedy; antidote, balm; the elixir of life. 4. life; health. 5. sweet;

pleasing, agreeable; salutary, healing. — et≡ 1. to drink, to carouse. 2. to take (medicine).

nuşa (— —) نوشا P *lrnd.* drinker.

nûşâbe (— — .) نوشابه P *lrnd.* 1. any pleasant or remedial drink. 2. water of life.

nûşanûş (— — —) نوشانوش P *lrnd.* 1. a repeated or consecutive drinking; a carousing. 2. Drink! 3. with full cups; with emptied glasses.

nûşbâd (— —) نوشباد P *lrnd.* 1. May it be salutary, pleasant. 2. *name of a tune in Oriental music.*

nûşdârû (— — — —) نوشدارو P *lrnd.* efficacious remedy; elixir, balm; antidote; wine.

nûşe (— .) نوش P *lrnd.* Here's health to you! Your health!

nûşende (— . .) نوشنده P *lrnd.* drinker; carouser. —**gân** (— . . —) P *pl.*

nûşhand (— .) نوشخند P *lrnd.* a sweet smile or laugh.

nûşide (— — .) نوشیده P *lrnd.* 1. that has drunk. 2. drunk down, drunk off. —**gi** (— — . —) P a drinking; draught.

nûşîn (— —) نوشین P *lrnd.* 1. sweet, pleasant to drink. 2. salutary to drink or to take as a medicine. 3. pleasant, sweet, enjoyable.

nûşînbâde (— — — .) نوشین باده P 1. *lrnd.* pleasant and life-giving wine. 2. *mus., the 26th of the 30 tunes.*

nûşîne (— — .) نوشینه P *lrnd.* 1. pleasant, life-giving wine. 2. *name of a tune in Oriental music.*

nûşînrevan (— — . —) نوشین روان P *lrnd.* 1. sweet life, sweet soul. 2. *w. cap.,* king Nushirevan.

Nuşirevan (— — . —) نوشیروان P *name of a Sassanid king.*

nûşlebina (— . — —) نوشلبینا P *Or. mus.,* a tune.

nutaf نطف A *lrnd., pl. of* **nutfe.**

nutfe نطفه A *lrnd.* 1. seminal fluid. 2. remnant of water in a vessel; a little water remaining in a bottle. 3. sea; lake; great river.

nutfetan (. . —) نطفتان A *lrnd.* the two seas, *i. e.* the Persian Gulf and the Red Sea.

nutkᵏᵘ نطق A *same as* **nutuk.** —**î** (. —) A pertaining to speech.

nutuᵘᵘ (. —) نطوع A *lrnd., pl. of* **nat 2.**

nutukᵗᵏᵘ نطق [**nutk**] 1. faculty of speech; speech. 2. speech, oration, discourse. — **at≡,** — **çek≡** *deprecatory* to give a long drawn out speech. —**a gel≡** to begin to speak. — **irad et≡** to make a speech; to deliver a discourse. —**u tutul≡** to be tongue-tied, to be confused and silent.

nuumet (. — .) نعومت A *lrnd.* a being soft to the touch; softness, smoothness.

nuut (. —) نعوت A *lrnd., pl. of* **na't 1.**

nuuz (. —) نعوظ A *lrnd.* 1. a becoming erected; erection. 2. morbid priapism.

nûye (— .) نویه P *lrnd.* tender shoot, twig, sucker.

-nuz *cf.* **-nız.**

nuzar (. —) نضار A *lrnd.* 1. gold; silver; virgin gold. 2. wood, timber.

nuzaz (. —) نضاض A *lrnd.* pure, unmixed; the best (sort of people).

nûzdeh (— .) نوزده P *lrnd.* nineteen. —**üm** (— . .) P nineteenth.

nuzub (. —) نضوب A *lrnd.* 1. flowing, running, seeping (water in the earth). 2. a becoming sunken (eye). 3. a departing, fading away (prosperity). 4. a dying; death.

nuzzar (. —) نظار A *lrnd., pl. of* **nazır.**

nübea (. . —) نبآء A *lrnd., pl. of* **nebi'.**

nübelâ (. . —) نبلاء A *lrnd., pl. of* **nebil.**

nübüvvet نبوّت A *lrnd.* prophethood, prophetic mission; gift of prophecy.

nüceba (. . —) نجباء A *lrnd., pl. of* **necib.**

nücum (. —) نجوم A *lrnd., pl. of* **necm.** —**i ahz** mansions of the moon (28 in number). —**i devri kamer** *astr.* sidereal month.

nücumî (. — —) نجومی A *lrnd.* 1. pertaining to the stars, sidereal; astrological; astronomical. 2. astronomer; astrologer.

nüdbe ندبه A *lrnd.* eulogizing; lamentation; elegy.

nüdema (. . —) ندما A *lrnd., pl. of* **nedim.**

nüfur (. —) نفور A *lrnd.* 1. a being frightened and running away (animal). 2. an abhorring, shunning. 3. a departing from the valley of Mina after the performance of the ceremonies at Mecca.

nüfus (. —) نفوس A *pl. of* **nefs 1,** 1. people; souls. 2. inhabitants, population. 3. person; inhabitant. — **cüzdanı,** — **kâğıdı** identity card. — **kütüğü** state register of persons. — **memurluğu** Registry of Births, etc. — **sayımı,** — **tahriri** census. — **tezkeresi** identity papers.

nüfusça (. — ' .) نفوسجه as regards persons, *e. g.,* — **zayiat yokmuş** There was no loss of life.

nüfuslu نفوسلی inhabited (region).

nüfuz (. —) نفوذ A 1. personal influence, weight or power. 2. a penetrating, traversing. 3. a seeing the inmost parts of a thing; insight; mental penetration; permeation. — **et≡** /a/ to penetrate; to go into; to influence. —**i nazar** insight. — **sahibi** influential person. — **ticareti yap≡** to make selfish profit out of one's own high position. —**iyet** (. — — .) P *phys.* permeability. —**lu** influential, powerful. —**suz** without influence.

nüh نه P *lrnd.* nine. — **felek** the nine

nüha heavens. — **pâye** 1. the nine heavens. 2. pulpit (of a preacher in a mosque).

nüha 1 (.—) نُهَا A lrnd., same as **nuha**.

nüha 2 نُهَى A lrnd. 1. intellect. 2. pl. of **nühye**, understandings.

nühak[kı] (.—) نُهَاق A lrnd. a braying; a bray of a donkey.

nühas (.—) نُحَاس A lrnd. 1. copper; copper coin. 2. flameless smoke. **—î** (.——) A pertaining to copper; like copper; copper, coppery.

nühur (.—) نُحُور A lrnd., pl. of **nehr**.

nühuz (.—) نُهُوض A lrnd. a raising oneself, rising up (against any one or to do him honor).

nühüft نهفت P lrnd. 1. concealed, covered. 2. *Or. mus.* one of the most ancient compound **makams**.

nühüfte نهفته P lrnd. covered, concealed, hidden.

nühüm نهم P lrnd. ninth. — **çarh** the ninth or highest sphere; the heaven of heavens.

nühye نُهْيَة A lrnd. intellect, intelligence, reason. — **ehli** reasonable person.

nühyek[ki] (.—) نهيك P lrnd. one part in nine; one ninth.

nühze, nühzet نُهْزَة A lrnd. opportunity, occasion.

nükâs (.—) نُكَاس A lrnd. return of a malady, relapse.

nüket نُكَت A lrnd., pl. of **nükte**.

nükle, nüklet نُكْلَة A lrnd. punishment, chastisement.

nüks نُكْس A med. relapse.

nükset[der] نُكْس يتملك to return and cause a relapse (disease).

nükte نُكْتَة A 1. subtle point; nicety (of language); witty remark; epigram. 2. lrnd. speck, spot. — **saç=** to make witty remarks.

nükteâmiz (..——) نكته آميز P lrnd. full of subtleties (discourse).

nüktearay (..——) نكته آراى P lrnd. adorned with subtle sayings.

nüktebin (.—) نكته بين P lrnd. who perceives delicate points, hair-splitter.

nükteci نكته جى witty; a wit (person).

nüktedân (..—) نكته دان P lrnd. witty; who appreciates niceties of language or argument.

nüktegû (..—) نكته گو P lrnd. subtle, keen, witty in discourse.

nükteli نكته لى witty, subtle (of speech).

nükteperdaz (...—), **nükteperver** نكته پرداز، نكته پرور P lrnd. subtle, keenly appreciative of niceties; delighting in fine niceties.

nüktepeyvend نكته پيوند P lrnd. subtle, ingenious.

nüktepira (..——) نكته پيرا P lrnd. who writes subtleties.

nüktesenc نكته سنج P lrnd. weigher of words, orator.

nükteşinas (...—) نكته شناس P lrnd. sagacious, understanding subtleties or mysterious meanings.

nükteza (..—) نكته زا P lrnd. producing witty remarks.

nükûb (.—) نكوب A lrnd. 1. a swerving, declining; declination. 2. a blowing in an oblique direction (wind). 3. a becoming the warden of a guild or fraternity.

nükûl[lü] (.—) نكول A lrnd. an abstaining or withdrawing through fear or fickleness; withdrawal. — **et=** /dan/ to withdraw, retract, recant.

nüküs[ksü] نكس var. of **nüks**.

-nüma نما P lrnd. 1. that shows, e. g., **cihannüma**. 2. that appears or seems, e. g., **hoşnüma**.

nümayan (.——) نمايان P lrnd. apparent, manifest, evident. **—lık** manifestness, clearness.

nümayende (.—..) نماينده P lrnd. one who shows; one who appears.

nümayiş (.—.) نمايش P 1. demonstration, political demonstration. 2. appearance, simulation; show, pomp. **—i âb** lrnd. semblance of water in a sandy place, mirage.

nümayişçi نمايشچى demonstrator.

nümayişgâh (.—.—) نمايشگاه P lrnd. place of a demonstration.

nümayişkâr (.—.—) نمايشكار P lrnd. who demonstrates, who makes a show; who simulates. **—âne** (.—.——.) P lrnd. 1. demonstrative (act); done to make a show. 2. affected (manner).

nümruke نمرقه A lrnd. small cushion placed between the rider and his saddle.

-nümud (.—) نمود P lrnd. show, appearance, aspect, e. g., **saadetnümud**.

nümudar (.——) نمودار P lrnd. 1. model, pattern; copy (of a thing). 2. appearing, exhibiting.

nümude (.—.) نموده P lrnd. 1. who has shown, manifested. 2. shown, exhibited; model, copy.

-nümun (.—) نمون P lrnd. that shows, exhibits, manifests, e. g., **rahnümun**.

nümune (.—.) نمونه P sample; pattern; instance, example; model. — **çiftliği** model farm. **—i imtisal** lrnd. an example to be followed.

nümunehane (...—.) نمونه خانه P obs. model-room, museum.

nümunelik[ği] نمونه لك 1. pattern, sample. 2. slang ridiculous, absurd.

nümur (.—) نمور A lrnd., pl. of **nimr**.

nümuzec (.—.) نموزج [from Persian **nümude**] lrnd. exemplar, model.

nümür نمر A lrnd., pl. of **nimr**.

nümüvᵛᵛᵘ نمو A *lrnd.* an increasing by growth, a growing; growth; a flourishing. — **bul**= to grow and flourish.

-nün نك *cf.* **-ın 4.**

nüsafe (.—.) نسافة A *lrnd.* 1. chaff blown away by the wind. 2. froth.

nüsah نسخ A *lrnd., pl. of* **nüsha.**

nüsalⁱⁱ (,—) نسال A *lrnd.* moulting fur or down.

nüsale (.—.) نسالة A *lrnd.* 1. a single tuft of fur, a single feather or tuft of down. 2. surgical lint.

nüsgˢᵘ نسغ A *lrnd.* sap.

nüsha نسخة A 1. copy, reproduction in writing, a single written or printed paper or book; edition. 2. issue, number (of a newspaper etc.). 3. *same as* **nusha.** 4. *lrnd.* cooking recipe; doctor's prescription.

nüskᵏᵘ نسك A *lrnd.* 1. sacrificial victim. 2. divine worship, adoration, piety.

nüssâkᵏⁱ (.—) نساك A *lrnd., pl. of* **nasik.**

nüsur (.—) نسور A *lrnd., pl. of* **nesr 1.**

nüşare (.—.) نشارة A *lrnd.* sawdust.

nüşhar (.—) نشخوار P *lrnd.* a chewing the cud; cud.

nüşre نشرة A *lrnd.* amulet, charm to drive away madness or disease.

nüşşab (.—) نشاب A *lrnd.* Arabian arrows. **—e** (.—.) A a single Arabian arrow.

nüşur (.—) نشور A *lrnd.* 1. God's raising the dead to life, resurrection. 2. a being freshened by rain (vegetation).

nütuᵘᵘ نتوء A *med.* swelling (wound or sore); apophysis.

nüvah (.—) نواح A *lrnd.* a wailing and lamenting the dead; wail.

-nüvaz (.—) نواز *var. of* **-nevaz.**

nüvaziş (.—.) نوازش *var. of* **nevaziş.**

nüve نوه [*based on* **nevat**] 1. *biol.* nucleus. 2. focus, center.

nüveyt نويت A 1. *bot.* nucleolus. 2. *anat.* ossicle.

Nüvi (.—) نوى P *lrnd.* the Quran.

nüvid (.—) نويد P *same as* **nevid.**

-nüvis (.—) نويس P *lrnd.* who writes; author, writer, composer, *as in* **hoşnüvis, vak'anüvis.**

nüvisende (.—..) نويسنده P *lrnd.* writer, one who writes.

nüvvab (.—) نواب A 1. nabob (a title used in India). 2. *lrnd., pl. of* **naib.**

nüyub (.—) نيوب A *lrnd., pl. of* **nab 2.**

-nüz نز *cf.* **-nız.**

nüzale, nüzalet (.—.) نزالة نزالت A *lrnd.* emitted semen, emission.

nüzeha (..—) نزها A *lrnd., pl. of* **nezih.**

nüzelâ (..—) نزلاء A *lrnd., pl. of* **nezil 2.**

nüzera (..—) نزراء A *lrnd., pl. of* **nezir 2.**

nüzhet نزهت A *lrnd.* 1. pleasure, delight. 2. pleasantness (of a place). 3. recreation. **—efza** (...—), **—feza** (...—) P increasing delight.

nüzhetgâh (..—) نزهتگاه P *lrnd.* quiet, beautiful, restful place.

nüzhetpezir نزهت‌پذیر P *lrnd.* that gives pleasant distraction; that has charming quiet.

nüzlᵘ̈ نزل A *lrnd.* 1. an overnight stop, camping place. 2. provisions, especially, provisions for a march or journey. — **emini** *Ott. hist.* commissary-general of an army.

nüzûlᵘ̈ 1 (.—) نزول A 1. apoplexy, stroke. 2. *lrnd.* a descending; an alighting; descent. — **et**= *lrnd.* to descend, alight. — **isabet et**= to have an apoplectic stroke.

nüzûlᵘ̈ 2 نزول A *lrnd., pl. of* **nezl.**

nüzûlet (.—.) نزولت A *lrnd.* a being mean-spirited; meanness, vileness.

nüzullü (.—.) نزوللی apoplectic.

nüzur 1 (.—) نزور A *lrnd.* a vowing or devoting a thing to God.

nüzur 2 (.—) نزور A *lrnd., pl. of* **nezr.**

nüzülᶻⁱᵘ̈ نزل *var. of* **nüzl.**

O

o, O 1 *The eighteenth letter of the Turkish alphabet.*

o! 2 (—) اوْ oh!, ah!, O!

oⁿᵘ **3** او *all oblique cases are based on* **on-**, *pl.* **onlar**, *archaic* **olar** 1. that; those, *e. g.*, **— adam** that man. 2. he, she, it. **— anda** at that moment. **— bir** *same as* **öbür**. **— bu** whether this or that. **— çocuklar** those children. **— duvar senin bu duvar benim** (*lit.* That wall is yours and this wall is mine.) swinging on both sides, very drunk. **— gibi** such as. **— gün bugün** since that day. **— hilâlde** *lrnd.* at that time, then. **— kadar** 1. so much; so. 2. That's all. **— saat** at that instant. **—na sebep** *colloq.* because of it, therefore. **— takdirde** in that case. **— taraflı olma=** to pay no attention, to take no notice of something. **— tarakta bezi yok** He is not interested in that thing. **— vakit bu vakit** since that time.

oba اوبه ٬ اوبا ٬ 1. large nomad tent (in several sections). 2. nomad (family). 3. *sociol.* encampment.

obje اوبژه F object; matter; thing.

objektif اوبژكتيف F objective. **— hukuk** law. **— hüsn-i niyet** good faith, bonafides.

obligasyon اوبليغاسيون F *fin.* obligation; debenture; bond.

obrukᵍᵘ اوبروك *prov.* 1. steep; precipitious; broken (ground). 2. pit. **—luk** 1. brokenness of ground. 2. patchy piece of ground fallen away in places.

obrul=ᵘʳ اوبرلمق *prov.* 1. to break partly and fall away so as to leave a jagged breach. 2. to be dislocated or shaken.

observatuvar اوبسروالوار F observatory.

obur اوبور greedy; gluttonous. **—laş=** to become gluttonous. **—luk** gluttony.

obüs اوبوس F *mil.* shell; howitzer.

Ocakᵍ¹ **1** اوجاق January. **— ayı** January.

ocakᵍ¹ **2** اوجاق ٬ اوجیم 1. furnace, hearth, kiln, fireplace; oven, range. 2. chimney. 3. stone-quarry, mine. 4. family line; dynasty; home. 5. political body, guild; fraternity. 6. *Ott. hist.* Janissary corps. 7. bed (in a kitchen garden). 8. cook's galley on board a ship. **— ağası** *Ott. hist.* chief of the Janissary corps. **—ı bat=** to be exhausted; to go to pieces. **— bucak** every corner of the house. **— çekirgesi** house-cricket. **—ı daim yanan** (*lit.*, whose hearth is always alight) a family or dynasty that will never be extinct. **— dayısı** *Ott. hist.* dey (the commander of the Janissaries in the North African provinces). **—ına düş=** /ın/ to seek the protection (of); to be at the mercy (of). **— gömleği** iron sheet placed in a furnace as protection against a back draft. **— halkı** *Ott. hist.* the Janissaries. **— ihtiyarları** *Ott. hist.* famous veterans of the Janissary corps. **—ına incir dik=** /ın/ to ruin (a family). **— kaşı** stone stand for saucepans, etc. in front of the hearth. **— kurumu** chimney soot. **— kuşu** *same as* **ocak çekirgesi**. **— külâhı** hood over a hearth. **— sehpası** andiron. **— siperi** fire screen. **—ı söndü** (*lit.* His hearth has become extinguished.) His family line has died out. **—ını söndür=** /ın/ to ruin the family (of); to extinguish the dynasty (of). **— süngüsü** poker. **— takımı** fire tongs. **— taşı** hearthstone. **— yap=** to found a family or dynasty. **— yaşmağı** mantlepiece.

Ocakᵏ¹ **3** (. —) اوجاق ٬ اوجیم [**ocak 2**] *Ott. hist.* Janissary corps. **—ı Bektaşiyan** Janissary corps.

ocakbaşı اوجاق باشی *Ott. hist.* cook in the Sultan's kitchen.

ocakçı اوجاقجی 1. chimneysweep. 2. stoker. —**lık** profession of a chimneysweep.

ocaklı اوجاقلی 1. having a fireplace, furnace etc. 2. belonging to a political body; member of a guild.

ocaklık[ğı] اوجاقلق 1. fireplace; hearthstone; chimney. 2. *Ott. hist.* family estate given by the Sultan. 3. a timber serving as a base for a superstructure. — **demiri** *naut.* sheet anchor.

od اود *archaic* 1. fire. 2. poison. — **ocak temin et=** to acquire a home. — **taşı** a kind of coarse sandstone. —**a ver=**, —**a vur=** /ı/ to set on fire. —**lara yan=** to burn inwardly, to be deeply grieved. — **yok ocak yok** without fire or hearth; poverty-stricken.

oda اودا اوده اوطه 1. room, chamber. 2. office; department. 3. *Ott. hist.* Janissary barracks. — **hapsi** *law* confinement to one's room. — **müziği** chamber music. — **takımı** set of furniture for a room.

odabaşı اوطه باشی 1. janitor in a large establishment. 2. man in charge of the rooms of an inn.

odacı اوطه جی 1. person employed to clean and watch the rooms of an office or a public establishment; office boy. 2. servant at an inn. —**lık** work of an office boy.

odak[ğı] *neol., phys.* focus.

odalar اوطلر 1. *Ott. hist.* Janissary barracks. 2. *w. cap.* the Chambers of Commerce and Industry.

odalık[ğı] اوطه لق concubine, odalisk.

odaşık[ğı] اوطه شق *prov.* roommate.

oditoryum (...̄.) اوديتوريوم E auditorium.

odun اودون اودن 1. firewood; log; cudgel. 2. stupid, coarse fellow. — **ağa blokhkafa**. — **at=** /a/ to cudgel. — **gibi adam** stupid, coarse person. — **kes=** to cut firewood. — **yar=** to chop wood. — **yarıcı** woodchopper.

oduncu اودونجی 1. seller of firewood. 2. woodcutter. —**luk** cutting or selling wood.

odunlaşma اودونلشمه *bot.* lignification.

odunluk[ğu] اودونلق 1. woodshed. 2. forest where firewood is cut; tree suitable for firewood.

of! اوف ugh! *expression of grief, pain, disgust, or annoyance.*

ofis اوفيس F 1. office, department. 2. private office.

ofla=[r] اوفله مه اوفلی to ejaculate "ugh!". —**yıp pofla=** to say "ugh" from weariness or heat.

oflaz اوفلاز *prov.* beautiful, fine; perfect.

ofort اوفرت F *art* etching.

ofsayd اوفسايد E *football* offside.

ofset اوفست E *soccer* offside.

oftalmoskop[bu] اوفتالموسكوپ F *med.* ophthalmoscope.

oğ=[ur] اوغمه اوغی /ı/ 1. to rub and press with the hand; to massage. 2. to polish. 3. to rub and crumble in the palm of the hand.

oğala=[r] اوغالامه اوغالی /ı/ 1. to rub and press with the hand. 2. to break up small, to crumble by hand. —**n=** *pass.* —**t=** /ı, a/ *caus. of* **oğala=**.

oğdur=[ur] اوغديرمه /ı, a/ *caus. of* **oğ=**.

oğlak[ğı] اوغلاق kid. — **takım yıldızı** *astr.* the constellation Capricorn.

oğlan اوغلان 1. boy; youth. 2. servant. 3. catamite. 4. *cards* jack. — **yatağı** the womb. —**cı** pederast. —**cık** little boy.

oğlu اوغلی *cf.* **oğul** 1.

oğma اوغمه *verbal n. of* **oğ=**.

oğmaç[cı], **oğmak**[kı] اوغماچ اوغماق *prov.* freshly made **tarhana**, a kind of thick soup.

oğra=[r] اوغرامه *same as* **uğra=**.

oğraş=[ır] اوغراشمی *colloq. for* **uğraş=** 2.

oğru اوغری اوغرو *same as* **uğru** 2.

oğrun اوغرون *prov.* secretly; sneakingly.

oğul[lu] 1 اوغل اوغول 1. son. 2. swarm of bees. —**um** my son. — **arısı** young bee in a swarm. — **balı** virgin honey, the first honey from a fresh swarm. — **edin=** /ı/ to adopt as a son. — **oğlu** son of one's son, grandson. —**dan oğula** from father to son. —**u ol=** to have a son. — **otu** lemon balm, *bot.*, *Melissa officinalis*.

oğul=[ur] 2 اوغلمه *pass. of* **oğ=**.

oğulcuk[ğu] اوغلجق 1. little son. 2. *biol.* embryo.

oğulduruk[ğu] اوغلدرق *prov.* womb.

oğulluk[ğu] اوغللق 1. sonship; duty of a son. 2. adopted son. 3. *prov.* stepson.

oğun=[ur] اوغنمی *prov.* to faint, to lose consciousness.

oğur اوغر *prov., same as* **uğur** 1.

oğuştur=[ur] اوغشديرمه 1. to rub the hands against each other. 2. to rub the body with the two hands. —**ma** *verbal n.* —**ul=** *pass. of* **oğuştur=**.

Oğuz 1 اوغز 1. *name of a legendary Turkish king.* 2. *name given to the Turkish tribes inhabiting southwestern Asia.* — **Han** a famous early Turkish king in Asia.

oğuz 2 اوغز *archaic* 1. pure of heart and mind; good; good fellow. 2. robust lad. 3. peasant. 4. simple, inexperienced; stupid. —**ca** very simple.

oğuzlan=[ır] اوغزلنمه 1. to act with simplicity or stupidity. 2. to be or pretend to be naive.

oğuzluk[ğu] اوغزلق 1. simplicity, stupidity. 2. inexperience.

Oğuzname (..—.) اوغزنامه P 1. tale of King Oğuz and his wonderful exploits. 2. wonderful tale; fabulous legend.

oh! اوخ good, delightful! — **çek=** to rejoice

oha!

over another's misfortunes. **— de=** 1. to breathe a sigh of satisfaction. 2. to rest. **— olsun** It serves him right.

oha! (.'—) اوها *vulg.* Hey you! Stop! Whoa!

ohşa=ʳ اوخشامق ، اوخشمق archaic, same as **okşa=**.

oje اوژه F fingernail polish.

okᵏᵘ اوق 1. arrow. 2. beam, pole (of a carriage). 3. any long straight piece of wood at right angles to another part. 4. porcupine's quill. **— at=** to shoot arrows. **— atımı** bowshot-distance, furlong. **— gezi** notch of an arrow. **— gibi** like an arrow; very swift. **— kertesi** same as **ok gezi**. **— menzili** distance of a bowshot. **— meydanı** archery ground. **— meydanında buhurdan yak=** to try to heat a field with an incense burner; to hope for great results from inadequate measures. **— sep=** to send a shower of arrows. **—a tut=** to shower arrows over one. **— yaydan çıktı, — yayından fırladı** (lit. The arrow has left the bow.) What is done is done; there is no going back. **— ye=** to receive an arrow wound. **— yeleği** the feather of an arrow. **— yılanı** a kind of water snake, zool., *Zamenis gamonensis*. **— yıldız** Barnard's star.

okaliptüs (...'.) اوقالیپتوس F eucalyptus, bot., *Eucalyptus glauca*.

okar اوقار bittern, zool., *Botaurus stellaris*.

okçu اوقجی 1. maker or seller of arrows. 2. archer, bowman. **— tekkesi** hall where archery is taught and practiced.

okka اوقه ، اوقیه oke, a weight of 400 dirhems or 2.8 lb. **—nın altına git=** to be the victim; to bear the brunt. **— çek=** to weigh heavy. **— dört yüz dirhem** Facts are facts. **— her yerde dört yüz dirhem** Men are the same everywhere; things are much the same wherever you go.

okkalı اوقه لی 1. weighing so many okes. 2. weighty, heavy; important; grave. **— kahve** large cup of Turkish coffee. **— küfür** heavy and vulgar oath.

okkalıkᵏⁱ اوقه لق 1. an oke of something. 2. container of one oke capacity.

okla=ʳ اوقدمق ، اوقلمق 1. /ı/ to shoot with an arrow. 2. /ı/ to furnish with arrows. 3. to dart like an arrow.

oklağı, oklağu اوقدغو prov. for **oklava**.

oklava اوقدوا cookery rolling-pin. **— yutmuş gibi** very stiff (person).

oklu اوقلی 1. furnished with arrows. 2. having quills. **— Besmele** Arabic calligraphy decorative arrangement of the Besmele. **— kirpi** porcupine.

oklukᵍᵘ اوقلی quiver.

okra=ʳ اوقرامق archaic to whinny as a horse does at sight of food; to neigh. **—t=** /ı/ caus.

oksijen اوقسیژن F oxygen; hydrogen peroxide.

oksitᵈⁱ اوقسید F chem. oxide.

oksitle=ʳ اوقسیدله مك /ı/ to oxidize. **—n=** to be oxidized. **—nme** oxidation. **—yen** oxidizing agent.

okso (.'.) اوقسو Gk slang Go away!

oksula=ʳ اوقسولامق slang /ı/ to get rid of, to drive away.

okşa=ʳ اوقشامق ، اوخشمق ، اوخشامق 1. to caress with the hand, to stroke, pat, fondle. 2. /ı/ to flatter. 3. /ı/ colloq. to beat. 4. /a/ to resemble, remind one of. **—ma** verbal n. **—n=** pass. of **okşa=**.

okşaş اوقشاش ، اوخشاش archaic like, resembling; resemblance.

okşat=ᵘʳ اوقشاتمق ، اوخشاتمق /ı, a/ caus. of **okşa=**.

okşayış اوقشایش 1. caress; petting. 2. prov. resemblance.

oktant اوقطانت F mariner's quadrant, octant.

oktav اوقتاو F mus. octave.

oktruva اوقتروا F octroi, city toll.

oku=ʳ 1 اوقومق 1. to read; to decipher. 2. /ı/ to study, to learn. 3. /ı/ to chant, to sing, to recite (literary composition); to read or recite (prayer). 4. archaic /ı/ to proclaim, to announce publicly; to invite; to call. 5. /a/ slang to curse, to swear (at). 6. slang /a/ to spoil thoroughly.

oku 2 اوقو prov. formal invitation to a wedding.

okul neol. school. **—daş** schoolmate. **—lu** who has been to school; pupil.

okuma اوقومه verbal n. of **oku=**. **— yazma** literacy. **— yitimi** psychopath. word blindness, alexia.

okumamış (..'..) اوقومامش ignorant, illiterate. **—lık** illiteracy.

okumuş اوقومش well-read, learned; educated.

okun=ᵘʳ اوقونمق pass. of **oku=** 1.

okunaklı اوقوناقلی legible, readable.

okunur اوقونور readable; worthy of being read.

okur اوقور reader; literate.

okut=ᵘʳ اوقوتمق /ı/ 1. caus. of **oku=** 1. 2. colloq. to sell. **—ma** verbal n.

okutman neol. lecturer (at a university).

okuttur=ᵘʳ اوقوتدرمق 1. /ı/ same as **okut=**. 2. /ı, a/ caus. of **okut=**. **—ul=** pass. of **okut=**.

okuyucu اوقویجی 1. reader. 2. singer. 3. one who recites incantations; exorcist. 4. person who goes around and invites people to a wedding.

okuyuş اوقویش verbal n. of **oku=** 1.

oküler اوقولر F ocular, eyepiece.

okyanus اوقیانوس Gk ocean.
Okyanusya (..'.) اوقیانوسیا *geog.* Oceania.
ol 1 اول *wherever a case or plural suffix is added, the word is* **an-**, *archaic* 1. that; those. 2. he, she, it. **— babda** in that respect, in this connection. **— bir** the other. **— dem** 1. that moment, at that instant. 2. immediately afterwards. **— vechile** in that way, by those means.
ol=ur **2** اولمق 1. to be; to exist; to happen, occur. 2. to become; to have, to catch (sickness); to be completed; to be cooked, prepared; to ripen; to mature; *colloq.* to get drunk. 3. to be suitable; to fit. 4. /dan/ to lose, to be bereft (of). **—abilir** possible; perhaps. **—abilirlik** *neol.* possibility. **—acak** 1. So fate has willed! 2. *contemptuous* who calls himself..., *e. g.,* **o baban olacak adam** that confounded father of yours. **—amazlık** *neol.* impossibility **—arak** being, as, *e. g.,* **memur olarak** as an official, **kat'i olarak söylüyorum** I tell you definitely. **ilk defa olarak** this being the first time. **sarhoş olarak** being in a drunken condition. **—ası*.** **—du!** That's all right; it is all done; ready! (in children's games). **—dukça** rather; fairly, quite. **—ma** *verbal n. of* **ol=** 2. **—madık** 1. without precedent. 2. impossible, unacceptable, *e. g.,* **—madık iş** an unusual event, **—madık iş değil** It may well happen; it is not unusual. **—madık olmaz** Anything may happen; nothing is impossible. **—madık söz** unseemly, unreasonable words. **—mamış** unripe; not yet matured. **—maz** impossible; wrong, unsuitable. **—maz!** No! It's impossible! You mustn't do it! **—mazlı** *neol., log.* absurd. **—mazlılık** *neol., log.* absurdity. **—mıyacak** 1. unseemly, unsuitable, unlikely. 2. impossible. **—muş** completed; ripe; mature. **—sun** 1. let it be. 2. if only, at least. 3. So be it! All right. I don't mind. **—ur** All right. Good. **—an biten, —up biten** event; happening; what is going on. **—du bitti** 1. It's completed; it's all over and done with. 2. *neol., fait accompli.* **—muş bitmiş iş** *fait accompli.* **—du da bitti maşallah!** Well, it worked! *said of something rushed through as a hasty expedient.* **—mıyacak duaya âmin de=** to occupy oneself with useless matters. **—a gel=** to be, become, happen fortuitously, occasionally or frequently. **—sa gerek** probable. **—acak gibi değil** It's impossible; it can't be done. **—acak iş değil** It's absurd. That's impossible. **—ur iş değil** It's incredible. **—a ki, —a kim** *archaic* It may be; perchance; possible. **—mıya ki** ... Beware lest... **—acağı nedir?** What is its lowest price? *said while bargaining in buying something.* **—du olacak** The inevitable has happened; now that the thing has gone so far, one may as well... **—du olanlar** The worst has happened. **—dum olası** right from the beginning, all along. **—maz olaydı!** I wish it had not happened. **—an oldu** What's done is done; it's too late now; no use crying over spilled milk. **—maz olmaz** There is nothing which can't happen; anything may happen. **—ur olmaz** any, whatever; anybody; whoever. **—sa olsa** at the very most; in the last resort. **—sun olsun** at the very most. **—acak olur** What will be, will be. **—ur olur** You never know. It may happen after all. **—ur mu olur** Of course it may happen; one never knows.
olağan اولغان 1. that commonly happens, usual; frequent; everyday. 2. possible, probable. **— iş** usual, commonplace. **— üstü** *neol.* extraordinary.
olama اولمه a removing the suckers of a vine.
olâmesa اولامسا Gk *slang* thoughtlessly, rashly.
olanakğı *neol., phil.* possibility. **—lı** possible. **—sız** impossible. **—sızlık** impossibility.
olanca (..'.) اولنجه utmost; to the full.
olar اولر *archaic, same as* **onlar**.
olası اولاسی which may be, happen or suit; possible, probable; reasonable. **—cılık** *neol., phil.* probabalism. **—lık** *neol., phil.* probability.
olay *neol.* event; *phil.* phenomenon. **—cılık** *phil.* phenomenalism.
olaydı, olaydım اولایدی اولایدم *short for* **olsa idi** *used in expressions as* **gelmez olaydı** I wish to heaven he hadn't come, **görmez olaydım** I wish I had not seen him.
oldur=ur اولدرمق /ı/ 1. to bring into being; to cause to be or become. 2. to bring to perfection; to cause to mature; to bring to a state of fitness. 3. to cause to ripen.
oldurgan *neol., gram.* causative.
olgu *neol., phil.* fact, event. **—culuk** positivism.
olgun اولغون 1. ripe, mature. 2. experienced, accomplished.
olgunlaş=ır اولغونلاشمق to become ripe, mature or experienced.
olgunlukğu اولغونلك ripeness, maturity; accomplishment. **— imtihanı** matriculation examination, university entrance exam.
oligarşi اولیغارشی F oligarchy.
Olimpiyad اولیمپیاد F Olympiad.
olta 1 (.'.) اولطه اولتا Gk fishing line. **— iğnesi** fishhook. **— yemi** bait.
olta 2 (.'.) اولطه اولتا It *same as* **volta**.
olukğu اولوق 1. an open trough like a gutter for water etc. to flow in; gutter pipe. 2. channel dug out for flowing water, groove. 3. carpenter's gouge. 4. *anat.* sulcus. **— gibi ak=** to flow in abundance. **— oluk** in streams. **—çuk** *anat.* sulculus.

oluklu اولقلو اولقلو channeled, hollowed out as a trough or gutter; grooved. **— kalem** gouge. **— mil** channeled probe. **— sac** corrugated iron.

olum neol. an act of existing. **—la=** gram., log. /ı/ to affirm. **—lama** log. affirmation. **—lu** gram., log. positive, affirmative. **—sal** log. contingent. **—sallık** log. contingency. **—suz** gram., log. negative.

oluş 1 اولش 1. verbal n. of **ol=** 2. 2. phil. genesis. 3. geol. formation. **—unda** in itself, in reality.

oluş=ur **2** neol. to come into existence, to be. **—tur=** /ı/ caus. **—um** geol. formation.

olut neol., fait accompli.

om 1 اوم F elec. ohm.

om 2, oma اوم اوما prov. rounded prominence (like the head of a bone); protuberance.

omaca اوماجه prov., same as **omca**.

omaçcı اوماچ prov., same as **oğmaç**.

ombra ('.) اومبره It umber (paint).

omca, omça اومجه اومچه prov. 1. stock of a vine; tree stump, log. 2. rump bone, ischium.

omlet اوملت F omelet.

omur neol., anat. vertebra. **— deliği** vertebral foramen.

omurga اومورغه اوکورغه الرغ 1. anat. backbone; spine. 2. naut. keel. **— kanalı** anat. rachidian canal. **—lılar** zool., Vertebrata.

omurilikği neol., anat. spinal marrow. **— kanalı** medullary canal. **— kovuğu** medullary cavity. **— soğanı** spinal bulb.

omuz اوموز امز امز shoulder. **—una al=** /ı/ 1. to shoulder. 2. to undertake. **—dan at=** /ı/ 1. to get rid of. 2. to get out of a task. **— başı** point of the shoulder. **— çaprazı** shoulder strap. **— çek=** 1. to shrug the shoulders. 2. to pretend not to know. **— çevir=** /a/ to turn a cold shoulder to. **—la dayan=** /a/ to help; to support. **— kaldır=** to shrug the shoulders, to pretend not to know. **— kayışı** soldier's shoulder belt. **— küreği** shoulder blade. **— omuza** 1. shoulder to shoulder. 2. very crowded. **— öpüş=** 1. to kiss one anothers' shoulders on meeting (as a sign of affection). 2. to be equal to; to be neck and neck with. **— sırığı** yoke, shoulder piece (for carrying buckets, etc.). **— silk=** to shrug the shoulders as a sign of indifference; to pretend not to know. **— şalı** shawl. **—da taşı=** /ı/ 1. to carry on the shoulder. 2. to honor, to hold in high esteem. **— ver=** /a/ to help; to support. **—a vur=** 1. /ı/ to shoulder, to carry on the shoulder. 2. to strike the shoulder.

omuzdaş اومزداش companion. **—lık** companionship.

omuzla=r اومزلامق /ı/ 1. to shoulder; to assist. 2. to hit with the shoulder. 3. slang to carry off, to shoulder and make off with. **—n=** pass. **—t=** /ı, a/ caus. of **omuzla=**.

omuzlukğu اومزلوق 1. epaulet; shoulder strap. 2. naut. quarter; bow.

on 1 اون ten. **— bir** eleven. **— defa** ten times. **— iki*. — kaidesi** 1. math. numeration. 2. sociol. statistics. **— minare boyu** very high, very deep. **— numara** highest classroom grade. **— para etmez** worth nothing. **— paralık et=** to disgrace badly; to cheapen. **— parmak** the two hands. **— parmağı kara, — parmağında on kara** "His ten fingers have ten black stains" said of one who is ready to calumniate people. **— parmağında on marifet** very skillful. **— parmağım yakasında** I won't let him get out of this; I shall never forgive him. **— sekiz bin âlem** myst. the whole universe.

on=ar **2** اوکمق اونمق 1. to heal up. 2. to improve, mend (person).

ona=r اوناسمق prov. /ı/ to approve; to prefer, choose, like. **—n=** pass.

onanizm اونانيزم F psychiatry onanism; masturbation.

onar 1 اونر ten each; ten at a time. **— onar** by tens; ten by ten.

onar=ır **2** اوکارمق /ı/ 1. to cure, to heal. 2. to mend, repair, put in order.

onarım neol. repair, restoration.

onart=ır اوکارتمق /ı, a/ caus. of **onar=** 2.

onaş=ır neol., phil. to consent. **—ma** consent.

onat اونات prov. 1. regular, in good order. 2. useful. 3. good-natured; good.

onay neol. convenient, suitable. **—la=** /ı/ to approve, to ratify. **—lı** approved, certified.

onbaşı اونباشى mil. corporal. **—lık** corporalship.

onca ('.) اونجه according to him (her); in his or her opinion; as far as he or she is concerned.

onda اونده math. tenth. **— bir** one tenth; one in ten.

ondalıkğı اوندهلق 1. a tenth part; ten percent. 2. tithe. **— kesir** decimal fraction. **— sayı** decimal number. **—çı** one who works on a ten percent commission.

ondur=ur اوکدرمق /ı/ caus. of **on=** 2.

ondülâsyon اوندولاسيون F permanent wave, permanent (hair).

ondüle اوندوله F curled, curly.

ongun اونغون 1. prov. flourishing, prosperous. 2. prov. blessed, happy. 3. anthropology totem. **—culuk** totemism.

oniki اون ايكى twelve. **O— Ada** geog. the Dodecanese. **— parmak, — parmak barsağı**

anat. duodenum. — **telli** a twelve-stringed guitar.
onlar اونلر *pl. of* **o** 3.
onlu اونلو 1. having ten parts. 2. ten (of a suit at cards).
onlukᵘ اونلق 1. of ten parts. 2. ten kuruş piece, ten para piece; ten lira bill. 3. worth ten kuruş.
onmadıkᵗⁱ اونمدك ،اوكمادن 1. not cured; not healed; incurable. 2. unfortunate; incorrigible. — **babanın onmadık oğlu** Like father like son. — **baş** a sore head. — **hacı** 1. sore-headed pilgrim. 2. unfortunate. —**lık** 1. incurableness. 2. helplessness.
onmaz اونمكز 1. that will not heal of itself; incurable. 2. that will not come right; incorrigible. —**lık** incurability.
ons اونس ounce.
onsuz اونسز without him, her, it.
onul=ᵘʳ اونولمق to heal up. —**maz** incurable. —**t**= /ı/ *caus. of.* **onul**=.
onun انك his, her, hers, its; of him, her, it. —**la beraber** 1. together with him, her, it. 2. for all that; at the same time. — **için** 1. for him. 2. therefore, so, for this reason, because of it.
onuncu اونجى tenth.
onur اوكور It dignity, self-respect, honor. —**una dokun**= to hurt someone's pride.
onurga اوكورغه archaic, same as **omurga**.
onurla=ʳ اوكورلمق /ı/ to do honor (to). —**n**= 1. *pass.* 2. /la/ to have the honor (of). —**ndır**= /ı/ to honor.
onurlu اوكورلو proud; having self-respect; dignified.
opalⁱⁱ اوپال F opal.
oparlör اوپارلور F loudspeaker.
opera (..'.) اوپرا F opera; opera house. — **komik** comic opera.
operasyon اوپراسيون F *med.* operation.
operatör اوپراتور F 1. surgeon. 2. *mech.* operator.
operet اوپرت F operetta.
optikᵗⁱ اوپتيك F *phys.* optics; optical.
or اور archaic dike; earthwork protected by a ditch. — **beyi** dike commandant. — **kaz**= to ditch.
ora 1 اورا that place. —**da** there, at that place. —**dan** from there, thence. —**larda** in those parts; at those places. —**ları** those places, those parts. —**sı** that place; that affair. —**ya** there; to that place. —**sı benim burası senin diye dolaş**= to go around aimlessly from place to place. —**ya kadar** up to that place. —**larda olma**= not to pay any attention; to pretend not to hear or know. —**sı öyle** That is so.

ora=ʳ 2 اورامق *archaic* /ı/ to reap with a sickle.
ora=ʳ 3 اورامق *archaic* /ı/ to dig a ditch.
oracıkta اوراجقده just there.
orain اورائين *slang* heroin.
orakᵗⁱ اوراق sickle, reaping hook. — **böceği**, — **çekirgesi** field cricket; grasshopper. —**a git**= to go reaping. — **kuşu** the great green grasshopper. —**çı** reaper.
orakla=ʳ اوراقلامق /ı/ to reap. —**n**= *pass.*
oralı اورالى of that place; born there. — **olma**= to feign indifference; to pay no attention.
oramiralⁱⁱ *neol.* vice-admiral.
oran اوران ،اورن *archaic* 1. measure; scale. 2. proportion; symmetry; estimate. 3. moderation. 4. ratio, rate.
oranla=ʳ اورانلامق *archaic* /ı/ to measure, plan, contrive or estimate. —**ma** *verbal n.* —**n**= *pass. of* **oranla**=. —**t**= /ı, a/ *caus. of* **oranla**=.
oranlı اورانلى *archaic* 1. measured; according to measure. 2. proportioned, symmetrical; suitable. 3. moderate.
oransız اورانسز *archaic* 1. unmeasured. 2. badly proportioned, asymmetrical; clumsy. 3. immoderate, excessive.
orantı *neol., math.* ratio. —**lı** proportional. —**lı orta** mean proportional.
orası اوراسى *cf.* **ora** 1.
orat=ʳ اوراتمق /ı, a/ *caus. of* **ora**= 2.
oratoryo (..'..) اوراتوريو It *mus.* oratorio.
ordinaryüs (..'..) اوردينارويس L senior professor holding a chair in a university.
ordinat اوردينات F *math.* ordinate.
ordino (.'..) اوردينو It 1. delivery order; license; order. 2. certificate of ownership.
ordövr اوردوور F hors d'œuvre; appetizer.
ordu 1 اوردو 1. army; army corps. 2. camp. 3. crowd; multitude; host. — **bozan** 1. spoil-sport. 2. firebrand. 3. *colloq.* varicose veins. 4. *w. cap., name of a city in northern Anatolia.* — **çıkar**= to send or to lead out an army. — **emri** order of the day, general order. — **evi** officers' club. **O—yi Hümayun** *Ott. hist.* Imperial Army; Imperial Camp. — **kadısı** *Ott. hist.* judge-advocate of an army on active duty in the field. — **kaldır**= to break up a camp. — **kur**= 1. to form a camp. 2. to encamp. — **merkezi** army headquarters. — **sokakları** the alleys between rows of tents in a camp.
Ordu 2 اوردو Urdu. — **lisanı** the Urdu language.
orducu اوردوجى *Ott. hist.* craftsman accompanying the army.
ordugâh (..—) اوردوگاه P military camp; encampment.
org اورگ F *mus.* organ.

organ اورغان F *anat.* organ.
organikᵍⁱ اورغانیك F organic. **— külte** organic rock.
organizma (...ˊ.) اورغانیزما F *biol.* organism.
orgeneral *neol.* full general; army commander.
Orhon اورخون *geog.* Orkhon (river in Central Asia).
orijinalⁱⁱ اوریژینال F 1. original. 2. unusual.
orkestra (..ˊ.) اورکسترا It *mus.* orchestra. **— şefi** conductor.
orkide (..ˊ.) اورکیده F orchid.
orkinos اورکینوس Gk a very large kind of tunny fish, *zool., Orcynus vulgaris.*
orkit اورکیت F *path.* orchitis.
orman اورمان forest; thicket; wood. **— horozu** blackcock. **— hukuku** forest laws. **— kanunu** *colloq., obs.* a public flogging of an offender by the police. **— kebabı** roasted or stewed mutton chops. **— kibarı** *colloq.* bear. **— kolcusu** forest-keeper; forester. **— mühendisi** forest engineer. **— sıçanı** wood-mouse, *zool., Mus sylvaticus.* **— taşla=** to try to find out one's thoughts in a roundabout way. **— tırmaşık kuşu** tree creeper, *zool., Certhia.*
ormancı اورمانجی forester, forest guard.
ormancılıkᵍⁱ اورمانجیلیغ 1. forestry. 2. the science of forestry. **O— Fakültesi** school of forestry.
ormanlıkᵍⁱ اورمانلیق thickly wooded, covered with trees; woodland.
ornat=ⁱʳ *neol., chem.* /ı, a/ to substitute.
orojeni اوروژنی F *geol.* orogeny, orogenesis.
orojenik اوروژنیك F *geol.* orogenic.
orospu اوروسپو اوروسبی [*Persian* **rûspî**] prostitute, whore, harlot. **— bohçası gibi** very untidy. **—luk** 1. prostitution. 2. dirty trick.
orostopoğlu, orostopollu اوروستوپوغلی اوروستوپوللی *slang* son of a bitch; scoundrel. **—luk** dirty trick.
orsa (ˊ.) اورصا اورسا It *naut.* the weather side. **— alabanda** Hard a-lee. Down the helm. **— alabanda yap=** to be hove to. **— boca et=** 1. to tack and veer; to cruise about. 2. to luff and fall off. 3. to pace up and down as on the quarter deck. **— boca git=** *colloq.* to struggle along; to sway about, to lurch; to be in confusion. **— dur=** to remain with head to wind, lying to (ship). **— et=** to luff, to go nearer the wind. **— git=** to hug the wind, to be close-hauled. **— pupa çemberi** hoop on the boom to which the boomguy is fastened. **— pupa palangası** boom-guy tackle. **—sına seyret=** to fetch, to sail by the wind.
orsala=ʳ اورسالامق to hug the wind. **—t=** to make a ship luff up in the wind.
ort 1 اورت *archaic* fire.
ort=ᵃʳ 2 اورتمق *archaic* to burn, singe, scorch or parch.

orta اورته اورطه 1. middle; midst; center; central. 2. mean (in quantity, degree or condition), medium; middling. 3. space around one; the public; the present scene of events. 4. *Ott. hist.* battalion of the Janissaries. **—da** 1. in the middle. 2. obvious; in sight. **—sından** /ın/ through. **—ya al=** /ı/ to set in the middle; to surround. **— aksak** *Or. mus.* a rythmic pattern. **O— Asya** Central Asia. **—ya at=** /ı/ to make a suggestion. **— baklası** *colloq.* bold woman. **—ya bir balgam at=** *vulg.* to drop a malicious hint at a time when an affair is going on nicely. **— baştarda** *obs., naut.* small war galley. **—da bırak=** /ı/ to leave in the lurch. **— boy** middle size, medium length. **— boylu** of medium height (person). **—sını bul=** /ın/ 1. to find a middle course. 2. to reconcile. 3. to divide into two equal parts. **— camii** *Ott. hist.* mosque of the Janissary corps. **— çağ*. —ya çık=** 1. to come into being. 2. to come to light. **—ya çıkar=** 1. /ı/ to bring to light; to discover. 2. to expose. **— damar*. — dere** *arch.* valley-channel (of roof). **— derece, — derecede** medium, middling; fairly good. **— deri** *biol.* mesoderm. **— direk** *naut.* mainmast. **O— Doğu** Middle East. **—ya dök=** /ı/ to disclose, to make public. **— elçi** minister plenipotentiary. **—da fol yok yumurta yokken** *colloq.* with no obvious reason. **— halli** neither poor nor rich; moderate. **— hizmetçisi** housemaid. **— işi** housework. **—da kal=** 1. to be left destitute. 2. to be in a difficult situation. **—dan kaldır=** /ı/ to do away with; to remove. **—dan kalk=** 1. to disappear; to be removed. 2. to be destroyed. **— karar** moderate (quantity, state or degree). **—dan kaybol=** to disappear. **—ya koy=** /ı/ to bring up (a matter); to expose, present for consideration. **— kulak** *anat.* middle ear, tympanum. **— kulak iltihabı** *path.* mesotitis. **— kuşak** *neol., geog.* temperate zone. **— malı** 1. common to all; common possession. 2. prostitute. **— mektep** junior high school. **— muavin** *soccer* center halfback. **— muhacim** *soccer* center forward. **— okul*. — oyunu** theatrical representation with a central stage. **— öğretim** *neol.* secondary education. **— parmak** middle finger. **— sahan** *arch.* central nave. **O— Şark** the Middle East. **— taş devri** *prehistory* mesolithic age. **— terim** *neol., log.* middle term. **—ya vur=** /ı/ to expose; to disclose; to make public. **— yaşlı** middle-aged. **O— Zaman, O— Zamanlar** the Middle Ages.
ortaçᶜⁱ *neol., gram.* participle.
Ortaçağ اورته چاغ the Middle Ages.
ortadamar *neol., biol.* median vein.
ortakᵍⁱ اورتاق 1. partner; associate;

accomplice. 2. common, in common, shared. 3. fellow-wife (in a polygamous household). — **çarpan** *neol., math.* ratio of a geometrical progression. — **fark** *neol., math.* ratio of an arithmetical progression. — **kat** *neol., math.* common multiple. — **ol=** 1. /a/ to participate (in something), to share. 2. /la/ to become a partner (with). — **ölçülmez sayılar** *neol., math.* incommensurable numbers. — **ölçülür sayılar** *neol., math.* commensurable numbers. — **tam bölen** *neol., math.* common divisor. — **yaşama** *neol., bot.* symbiosis. — **yaşar** *neol., bot.* symbiont. —**çı** share cropper.

ortaklaş=ᵘʳ اورتاقلشمق ' to enter into partnership with another. —**a** 1. as a partner; in common. 2. sharing equally. 3. collectively. —**ma** *verbal n.*

ortaklıkᵏ¹ اورتاقلق ' 1. partnership. 2. firm, company. 3. condition of a wife in a polygamous household.

ortala=ʳ اورتالامق ' /ı/ 1. to divide in the middle. 2. to split the difference (in an affair). 3. to set in the midst (thing). 4. to reach the middle. 5. *soccer* to center.

ortalama اورتالاما ' 1. *verbal n. of* **ortala=**. 2. average, medium; mean.

ortalıkᵏ¹ اورتالق ' 1. one's immediate surroundings; the world around. 2. the face of nature. 3. people, the public. — **açıldı**, — **ağardı** Dawn has broken. — **ı birbirine kat=** to cause alarm and confusion; to turn the place upside down. — **bozulmuş** Conditions have degenerated; morals have deteriorated. — **karardı** 1. Evening has closed in, it is nightfall. 2. It is very cloudy. — **karıştı** Trouble has broken out. —**ta kimse yok** There is no one about. — **süpür=** to sweep up. —**ı topla=** to tidy up, to put a place in order. —**ı toz pembe gör=** to see the world through rose-colored glasses. —**ı tut=** to fill the air (smell, smoke).

ortanca 1 (...́) اورتانجه ' middle; middle child (of three).

ortanca 2 (.́.) اورتانجه ' It hydrangea, Chinese guilder-rose, *bot., Hydrangea hortensia.*

ortaokul *neol.* junior high school.

ortaşım *neol., psych.* association.

Ortodoks اورتودوقس ' F Greek Orthodox. —**luk** Orthodoxy, the Greek Orthodox Community.

ortografi اورتغرافی ' F orthography, correct spelling.

ortopedi اورتوپدی ' F orthopedics.

ortoz اورتوز ' F *min.* orthoclase, common feldspar.

ortutᵈᵘ اورتوت ' *prov.* dried vine stem.

oruçᶜᵘ اوروج ' [ruze] 1. fasting, fast. 2. abstinence. — **aç=** to break a canonical fast at its close. — **boz=** 1. *same as* **oruç aç=**. 2. to violate a fast in an uncanonical manner. — **tut=** to fast. — **ye=** not to observe the fast. —**lu** fasting (person). —**suz** not fasting.

orun اورن ' *archaic* 1. place, site. 2. office, employment, post. —**suz** homeless; jobless.

orya (.́.) اوریا ' It *cards* diamonds.

oski اوسکی ' Arm *slang* gold lira.

Osman عثمان ' Othman, the third Caliph. — **Zunûreyn** Othman of the two glories, i. e. husband of the two daughters of the Prophet Muhammad.

Osmanî (. — —) عثمانی A *Irnd.* 1. Ottoman. 2. *an old Ottoman coin.* — **nişanı** Ottoman order or decoration, medal.

Osmaniyan (. — — —) عثمانیان P the Ottomans.

Osmanlı عثمانلی ' 1. Ottoman. 2. brave and noble. 3. a kind of a game in backgammon. — **kademi** *obs.* Ottoman foot measuring half of an **arşın**, nearly 15 inches. — **küşadı** a variety of backgammon. — **lirası** the Ottoman gold lira.

Osmanlıca عثمانلیجه ' the Ottoman Turkish language.

Osmanlılıkᵏ¹ عثمانلیلق ' 1. quality of being an Ottoman. 2. the Ottomans. 3. valor and nobility.

osur=ᵘʳ اوصورمق ' to break wind, to fart.

osurgan اوصورغان ' who habitually breaks wind. — **böceği** stag beetle, *zool., Lucanus cervus.*

osurukᵍᵘ اوصوروق ' fart. —**u cinli** *slang* very irritable person. —**unu düğümle=** /ın/ *slang* to threaten, to frighten.

oş 1 اوش ' *archaic* 1. here. 2. that.

oş 2, oşt اوشت ' Go away! (cry used to drive away a dog).

ot 1 اوت ' 1. grass, herb; small plant; weed; fodder. 2. medicine; depilatory. 3. poison; venom. 4. *slang* dope; hashish. — **çekirgesi** common grasshopper. — **tutun=** to remove hair by means of a depilatory. — **ye=** *chauffeurs' slang* to use dope. — **yeri** any part of the body from which superfluous hair is removed by a depilatory. — **yiyen** *zool.* herbivorous. — **yoldur=** /a/ *colloq.* to give trouble (to), to oppress.

ot 2 اوت ' *same as* **od.**

otacı اوتاجی ' 1. *archaic* physician, doctor. 2. *prov.* one who treats eye diseases with powdered herbs. —**lık** profession of a physician or an eye doctor.

otağ, otakᵏ¹ (. —) اوتاغ، اوتاق ' P large and luxurious tent, state tent, pavilion. —**ı hümayun** *Ott. hist.* imperial tent. —**çı** 1. tent maker. 2. servant in charge of a tent.

otağgeran (. — . —) اوتاغگران ' P *lrnd.* makers of luxurious tents.

otala=ʳ اوتالامه اوتمى *prov.* /ı/ 1. to poison. 2. to treat medically.

otar=ıʳ اوتاریه اوتومه *archaic* /ı/ to pasture (an animal). —**ıl=** *pass.*

otarşi اوتارشى F 1. autarchy. 2. economic self-sufficiency.

otçul *neol.*, *zool.* herbivorous.

otel اوتل F hotel. —**ci** hotel-keeper.

otla=ʳ 1 اوتلامه اوتمى 1. to graze, to be out to pasture. 2. to lead a bovine existence, to vegetate. 3. *slang* to sponge.

otla=ʳ 2 اوتلامه اوتمى *archaic* to burn; to scorch.

otlakᵍᵘ اوتلاق 1. pasture, pasturage, grassland. 2. well stocked with grass, grassy. — **lüferi** medium sized bluefish (caught in August).

otlakçı اوتلقجى *slang* sponger. —**lık** *slang* occupation of a sponger.

otlakıye اوتلقيه pasture tax; pasture rent.

otlan=ıʳ 1 اوتلانمه اوتنمى 1. to be at pasture; to graze. 2. to be pastured on by animals (pasture). 3. to be overgrown with grass.

otlan=ıʳ 2 اوتلانمى *archaic, pass. of* **otla=** 2.

otlat=ıʳ اوتلاتمه اوتاتمى /ı/ to pasture (cattle); to feed. —**ıl=** *pass.* —**tır=** /ı, a/ *caus. of* **otlat=**.

otlu اوتلو اوتلى grassy, full of herbs.

otlubağa اوتلوبغى اوتى باغه toad.

otlukᵍᵘ اوتلق اوتنوه 1. place for grass, herbs, or hay; hayrick, haystack; hayloft. 2. grassy. 3. pasture. 4. priming powder (for a gun).

oto اوتو F auto, car, automobile.

otobüs اوتوبوس F bus.

otokar اوتوقار F motor coach.

otoklav اوتوقلاد F autoclave.

otokrasi اوتوقراسى F autocracy.

otokrat اوتوقرات F autocrat.

otolit اوتوليت F *zool.* otolith.

otoman اوتومان F ottoman, divan.

otomat اوتومات F automaton.

otomatikᵍᵘ اوتوماتيك F automatic. — **gibi** *chauffers' slang* very talkative and fidgety.

otomatizm اوتوماتيزم F *psych.* automatism.

otomobil اوتومبيل F car, automobile. — **idare et=**, — **kullan=** to drive a car. — **lâstiği** tire.

otonomi اوتونومى F autonomy.

otopsi اوتوپسى F autopsy, post mortem examination.

otoray اوتوراى F rail-car.

otorite اوتوريته F authority; influence.

otoriter اوتوريتر F bossy, authoritarian.

otosist اوتوسيست F *anat.* otocyst.

otoskopᵇᵘ اوتوسقوپ F autoscope.

otsu, otsul *neol.*, *bot.* herbaceous.

otur=ᵘʳ اوتورمه اوتورمى 1. to sit; to sit down, to sit up. 2. to sit still doing nothing; to rest. 3. to dwell, to live, to reside; to stay. 4. to fit well; to settle, to sink (building); to settle (liquid). 5. to be stranded, to run aground (ship). 6. *colloq.* to cost, *as in* **pahalıya otur=**.

oturakᵍᵘ اوتوراق اوتراق 1. seat; *naut.* thwart. 2. chamber-pot. 3. the posterior; place on which a thing stands (bottom, foot, stand). 4. *archaic* halting place; residence; halting, resting; seated, sedentary. 5. *archaic* retired on a pension, pensioner. 6. *prov.* bedridden, paralytic. 7. *prov.* drinking party with dancing women. — **âlemi** orgy with drink and women dancers. — **tahtası** thwart-seat (in a boat).

oturakçı اوتوراقجى *archaic* dealer in ready-made goods.

oturaklı اوتوراقلى 1. well settled; solidly based. 2. imposing-looking (person); sound and dignified (person). 3. well chosen, suitable (words).

oturma اوتورمه *verbal n. of* **otur=**. — **odası** living room.

oturt=ᵘʳ اوتورتمه اوترتمى /ı/ *caus. of* **otur=**, 1. to seat, place, let have a seat. 2. to set, mount (jewel). 3. to allow to rest; to let dwell. 4. to run aground (ship). 5. to cause to incubate (bird). 6. to place right, to make fit.

oturtma اوتورتمه 1. *verbal n. of* **oturt=**. 2. *a dish of ground meat with vegetables*. 3. set, mounted (gem).

otuz اوتوز thirty. — **bir** *a kind of card game*. — **bir çek=** *slang* to masturbate.

otuzar اوتوزر thirty each, thirty at a time.

otuzlukᵍᵘ اوتوزلق of thirty, thirty years old.

otuzuncu اوتوزنجى thirtieth.

ov=ᵃʳ اوومه اومى *same as* **oğ=**.

ova اووه اووا ovا 1. plain, grassy plain; lowland. 2. meadow.

ovacıkᵍᵘ اووجق 1. small field, meadow, paddock. 2. *w. cap.*, name of several small towns in Turkey.

ovalˡⁱ اووال F oval.

ovala=ʳ اووالمه اووه لامه اوغالامه *same as* **oğala=**.

ovalıkᵍᵘ اووالق اووه لك level and extensive, grassy land; plain.

ovdur=ᵘʳ اوودرمه اوغدرمى *same as* **oğdur=**.

ovma اوومه *verbal n. of* **ov=**.

ovogon F *neol.*, *bot.* oogonium. — **dağarcığı** ovisac, sporangium. —**lu mantarlar** oomycetes.

ovolit F *neol.*, *geol.* oolite. —**li** oolitic. —**li kalker** oolitic limestone.

ovul=ᵘʳ اوولمى *same as* **oğul=**.

ovuştur=ᵘʳ اووشترمى *same as* **oğuştur=**.

oy 1 *neol.* 1. opinion, view. 2. vote. — **sandığı** ballot box. — **ver=** to vote.

oy=ᵃʳ 2 اويمق 1. to carve, to engrave, to incise; to scoop out; to excavate. 2. to cut out in decorative designs (paper, etc.).

oya اويا ، اويه ، pinking; embroidery on the edge of a garment. — **gibi** very fine and pretty. —**cı** worker or seller of pinking or embroidery.

oyala=ʳ 1 اويالمق ، اويالامق /ı/ 1. to detain, to put one off so as to waste time. 2. to distract somebody's attention; to amuse a child to keep him quiet.

oyala=ʳ 2 اويالمق ، اويالامق /ı/ to pink, to embroider.

oyalan=ⁱʳ اويالانمق 1. pass. of oyala=. 2. to loiter, to waste time; to tarry. 3. /la/ to distract oneself.

oyalı اويالى pinked, ornamented on the edge.

oyan اويان prov. bridle with its bit, reins and accessories. — **vur=** /a/, —**la=** /ı/ to put the bridle on a horse, to bridle.

oydur=ᵘʳ, **oydurt=**ᵘʳ اويدرمق ، اويدرتمق /ı, a/ caus. of **oy=** 2. —**ul=** pass.

oygala=ʳ اويغلمق same as **oyulgala=**.

oylaşıkᵏⁱ neol., phil. deliberative.

oylaşım neol., phil. deliberation.

oylukᵍᵘ اويلق same as **uyluk**.

oylum اويلم ، اويلوم 1. hollowed out; holed, carved. 2. excavation, pit. 3. pockmark. — **oylum** 1. curling (smoke). 2. in bunches.

oyma اويمه 1. verbal n. of **oy=** 2. 2. carving; sculpture, engraving; decoration by hollowing out. 3. excavated, hollowed out; carved, engraved, cut in, incised. — **işi** work produced by carving. — **kalemi** stone cutter's chisel.

oymacı اويماجى maker or seller of carvings; engraver.

oymakᵏⁱ اويماق 1. subdivision of a great tribe; tribe; phratry. 2. troop of boy scouts. 3. prov. thimble. — **beyi** scoutmaster, leader of boy scouts.

oymalı اويمالى carved, engraved. — **yaprak** bot. lobate leaf.

oyna=ʳ اويناماق ، اوينامق 1. to play; /ı/ to play (a game); to gamble. 2. to dance, to skip and jump about. 3. to move; to vibrate; to palpitate; mech. to be loose, to have too much play; to slip (ground in a landslide). 4. /ı/ to perform (a play); to play (a card). 5. /la/ to risk, to stake in a venture. 6. to amuse oneself; to jest. —**ya oynaya** joyfully, with much pleasure.

oynakᵏⁱ اويناق ، اوينك 1. playing, moving; mobile; playful, frisky; unstable, unreliable; fickle, flirtatious (woman); mech. loose, having much play, shifting; handy (airplane). 2. anat. joint. 3. mus. a rhythmic pattern of nine beats. — **kemiği** colloq. kneecap. — **yeri** articulation, joint. —**lık** lightness of character, frivolity.

oynama اوينامه verbal n. of **oyna=**.

oynan=ⁱʳ, **oynanıl=**ⁱʳ اويناتنمى ، اويناتلمى pass. of **oyna=**.

oynaş 1 اويناش 1. playfellow. 2. sweetheart, lover; paramour.

oynaş=ⁱʳ 2 اويناشمق to play with one another; to joke together. —**ma** 1. verbal n. 2. sweetheart; paramour.

oynat=ⁱʳ اويناتمق 1. /ı/ caus. of **oyna=**. 2. to go out of one's head. —**ıl=** pass. —**ma** verbal n. of **oynat=**.

oynayış اويناييش verbal n. of **oyna=**.

oysaki (..'..) اويسه كه whereas, yet; however.

oyucu اويوجى who carves, excavates, engraves, incises, etc.

oyukᵍᵘ 1 اويوك 1. hollow, grooved; hollowed out. 2. hollow part of a thing, cavity; pit.

oyukᵍᵘ 2 اويوك archaic scarecrow.

oyuklan=ⁱʳ اويوقلانمق to become hollow.

oyul=ᵘʳ اويولمق pass. of **oy=** 2.

oyulga 1 اويولغه a basting, sewing loosely together, tacking.

oyulga=ʳ 2, **oyulgala=**ʳ اويولغمق ، اويولغلامق /ı/ to baste together (cloth etc.), to tack.

oyulgan=ⁱʳ اويولغانمق pass. of **oyulga=**. —**a oyulgana gel=** to slide up in a toadying and hypocritical manner.

oyum اويوم 1. a digging or scooping out; a hollowing. 2. pit, hollow; hole. 3. taproot (of a plant). — **oyum oy=** /ı/ to dig in many holes. —**la=** to form a taproot (plant).

oyun اويون 1. game; play; dance; joke. 2. spectacle, play; performance. 3. trick, deception. — **al=** to win a game. — **boz=** to spoil the game. —**a çık=** to appear on the stage for a performance. — **çıkar=** 1. to play well. 2. to play a trick; to bring about some trouble. — **et=** /a/ to play a trick, to deceive. —**a gel=** to be deceived. — **havası** one of the characteristic musical works especially composed for dancing: Zeybek, Horon, Bar, Ağırlama, Karşılama, Halay, Çiftetelli, Kasap, Hora, Sirto, Longa, Köçekçe, Tavşanca, etc. — **kâğıdı** playing cards. — **oyna=** 1. to play. 2. to play a trick, to deceive. — **oyuncak** an easy matter, trifle. — **ver=** to lose a game. — **yandı** The game is lost. — **yap=** same as **oyun et=**.

oyunbaz (..—) اويونباز 1. playful. 2. deceitful; swindler.

oyunbozan اويون بوزان 1. killjoy, spoilsport; quarrelsome. 2. who keeps making fresh difficulties; who goes back on his word at the last moment. —**lık** abstr. n. —**lık et=** to be a killjoy.

oyuncak

oyuncak[gi] اويونجاغه ' اويوبجى ' اوينجى ' اويونجاق '
1. toy, plaything. 2. trifle, easy job. 3. laughingstock. —**çı** maker or seller of toys.

oyuncu اويونجى ' 1. player; gambler. 2. actor; dancer. 3. comedian; trickster.

oyuntu اويونتى ' اويونتو ' اويندى ' 1. excavation, hollow. 2. the material scooped out.

ozan اوزان ' اوزانق ' 1. wandering minstrel. 2. *neol.* poet. 3. *archaic* talkative, bragging; boastful. —**la**= *archaic* to babble, chatter.

ozon اوزون ' F *chem.* ozone.

Ö

ö 1, Ö *the nineteenth letter of the Turkish alphabet.*

ö 2 (—) اوٴ ' ugh! (used to indicate disgust).

öbek[gi] اوبك ' heap; mound; group. — **öbek** in groups; scattered around in heaps.

öbür اوبر ' *var. of* **o bir**, *the other.* —**kü**, —**sü** *colloq.*, —**ü** the other one; that one. — **dünya** the other world, the next world. — **gün** the day after tomorrow.

öc اوج ' 1. revenge. 2. *archaic* bet; wager. — **al**= /dan/ to avenge oneself on. — **çıkar**= /dan/ *colloq.* to take revenge on. — **ko**=, — **tut**= *archaic* to lay a wager, to bet.

öcü اوجى ' *child's language* ogre, bogyman.

öcür=[ür], **öcüş**=[ür] *archaic* /la/ 1. to bet with somebody. 2. to pull the wishbones of a fowl with another.

öç[cü] اوج ' *var. of* **öc.**

öd 1 اوٴد ' 1. gall, bile; gall bladder. 2. courage; guts. — **kavuğu**, — **kesesi** gall bladder. —**ü kop**=, —**ü patla**= to be badly frightened.

öd 2 عود ' [ud 2] 1. *Irnd.* aloe wood. 2. wood, piece of wood or timber. — **ağacı** agallocum, Indian aloe tree, *bot.*, *Aloexylon Agallocum.*

öde=[r] اوده مك ' اوده مك ' 1. /ı/ to pay back (a debt). 2. /ı/ to indemnify. 3. *com.* to amortize.

ödek[gi] 1 اودك ' *prov.*, *same as* **ödlek.**

ödek[gi] 2 اودك ' *archaic* indemnity; compensation.

ödem اودم ' F *path.* edema.

ödeme اوده مه ' *verbal n. of* **öde**=. — **emri** order of payment. — **kabiliyeti** *com.* solvency. —**lerin tatili** suspension of payments. —**li** cash on delivery (C.O.D.).

öden=[ir] اودنمك ' *pass. of* **öde**=.

ödenek[gi] *neol.* appropriation, allowance.

ödenti *neol.* fee (to a society, etc.).

ödeş=[ir] اوده شمك ' /la/ to settle accounts (with one another); to pay (one another).

ödet=[ir] اودتمك ' /ı, a/ *caus. of* **öde**=.

ödev *neol.* 1. duty; obligation. 2. homework (of a pupil), exercise. — **bilgisi** deontology, ethics. —**li** charged with (an official duty).

ödeyiş اوده يش ' *verbal n. of* **öde**=.

ödlek[gi] اودلك ' timid, cowardly; pusillanimous.

ödül *neol.* reward, prize.

ödün *neol.* compensation.

ödünç اودنج ' اودنج ' loan, borrowed. — **al**= /ı/ to borrow. — **ver**= to lend; to lend money.

ödünle=[r] *neol.* /ı/ to compensate. —**me** compensation.

ödünlü *neol.* commutative (justice).

öf اوف ' Ugh! (expressing disgust)

öfke اوفكه ' anger, rage, wrath. — **baldan tatlıdır** It is very difficult not to get angry. —**yle kalkan ziyanla oturur** A person who loses his temper suffers in the end. — **topuklarına çık**= to fly into a rage. —**ci** irascible, irritable (person).

öfkelen=[ir] اوفكه لنمك ' to grow angry. —**dir**= /ı/ to anger, to irritate, to infuriate.

öfkeli اوفكه لى ' irritated; angry; irritable; hot-headed, impetuous.

öfkesiz اوفكه سز ' calm; not easily irritated.

öfle=[r] اوفله مك ' to ejaculate ughs.

öğ 1 اوك ' *archaic* mind, intelligence. —**ünü der**= to collect one's mind, to be sensible.

öğ=[er] 2 اوكمك ' *same as* **öv**=.

öğdül اوكدل ' *archaic, same as* **ödül.**

öğe *neol., phil.* element.

öğendire اوكندره ' *var. of* **üvendire.**

öğle اويله ' اوكله ' 1. noon, midday. 2. the noon worship of a Muslim. 3. the noon call to prayer. —**n** *colloq. for* **öğle.** —**nde**, —**ne** *colloq.* at noon. —**ye**, —**yin** (.'..) at midday, at noon. —**den evvel** in the forenoon, a.m.

—den sonra in the afternoon, p. m. **— üstü** around noon. **— yemeği** noon meal, lunch.

öğren=[ir] اوگرنمك /ı/ 1. to learn; to hear; to be informed. 2. to become accustomed (to), to get familiar (with). **—ci** neol. pupil, student. **—il=** pass. **—iliş**, **—ilme** verbal n. of **öğrenil=. —im** neol. education, instruction. **—iş**, **—me** verbal n. of **öğren=**.

öğret=[ir] اوگرتمك 1. /ı, a/ to teach; to suggest. 2. /ı/ to instruct; to advise. 3. /a/ to teach a lesson.

öğreti neol., phil. doctrine.

öğretici اوگرتيجی 1. teacher, instructor. 2. instructive; inspiring.

öğretil=[ir] اوگرتلمك pass. of **öğret=**.

öğretim neol. instruction.

öğretmen neol. teacher, instructor. **— okulu** teacher's training school. **—lik** teaching; teacher's profession.

öğü اوكو archaic great owl, zool., Bubo maximus.

öğün 1 اوكون same as **övün 1**.

öğün=[ür] 2 اوكونمك same as **övün= 2**.

öğür 1 اوكور archaic 1. habit, second nature; habituated; used, accustomed to. 2. broken in, quiet, trained (animal). 3. of the same age; equal. **— ol=** to get used to, to be very familiar with.

öğür=[ür] 2 اوكورمك 1. to make a noise when vomiting, to retch. 2. to low, bellow.

öğürde=[r] اوكوردمك archaic 1. to sob, to cry sobbingly. 2. to retch.

öğürdüş=[ür] اوكورد شمك archaic 1. /la/ to race, to compete (animal). 2. /a/ to be accustomed to, to get the habit of.

öğürlük[gü] اوكورلك archaic familiarity, friendship.

öğürt=[ür] اوكورتمك /ı/ caus. of **öğür= 2**.

öğürtle=[r] اوكورتلمك اوبورتلمك archaic to pick, to choose; to pick and cleanse, to rid of refuse.

öğürtü اوكورتو a retching.

öğüş 1 اوكوش same as **övüş**.

öğüş 2 اوكش، اوكوش archaic much, many.

öğüt[dü] 1 اوكت، اوكوت advice, counsel, admonition.

öğüt=[ür] 2 اوكوتمك same as **övüt=**.

öğütle=[r] اوكوتلمك 1. to advise, to admonish. 2. /ı, a/ to recommend. **—n=** pass.

öhö اوهو expression of contempt or derision.

ökçe اوكچه 1. heel of a shoe or boot; heel. 2. arch. spur on a door (that supports it and turns in a socket in the threshold). **—sine bas=** /ın/ slang to follow closely, to pursue and control. **—leri çek=** slang 1. to get ready (to start). 2. to run off, to walk away. **— kemiği** heel bone, calcaneus. **—li** heeled (shoe).

ökçesiz اوكچه سز 1. heelless, flat (shoe). 2. slang coward.

Öklid اوقليد F geom. Euclid. **— geometrisi** Euclidean geometry. **—den başka** non-Euclidean. **— mesafesi**, **— uzayı** Euclidean space.

ökse=[r] 1 اوكسمك prov. /ı/ to long for, to desire; to miss.

ökse 2 اوكسه، اكسه Gk 1. birdlime. 2. man hunter (woman). **—ye bas=** to fall into a trap. **— çubuğu** birdlimed stick. **— inciri** mistletoe fig, bot., Ficus diversifolia. **— otu** mistletoe, bot., Viscum album. **— otugiller** neol., bot., Loranthaceae.

öksele=[r] اوكسه لمك /ı/ to smear with birdlime. **—n=** 1. to become smeared with birdlime. 2. to become birdlime.

ökseli اوكسه لی smeared with birdlime, containing birdlime.

öksü=[r] 1 اوكسمك /ı/ same as **ökse= 1**.

öksü 2 اوكسو halfburned piece of wood, firebrand.

öksüle=[r] اوكسولمك 1. to kindle fire with a firebrand. 2. to provoke, to stir up.

öksür=[ür] اوكسورمك to cough; to have a cough. **—me** verbal n. **—t=** /ı/ caus. of **öksür=**. **—tücü** causing a cough, irritating to the throat.

öksürük[gü] اوكسوروك، اوكروك cough, a coughing. **— otu** coltsfoot, bot., Tussilago farfara. **—lü** 1. having a cough (person). 2. accompanied by a cough (disease).

öksüz اوكسوز 1. orphan; motherless. 2. without relations or friends. **— babası** charitable man. **— balığı** red gurnard, zool., Trigla lyra. **— kendi göbeğini kendi keser** proverb (lit. An orphan cuts his own navel-string.) A person who has no friends has to help himself in everything. **— parmak** ring finger. **— sevindiren** a common cheap thing. **— vardiya** naut. dogwatch. **—lük** orphan status; orphanage.

öküz اوكوز، اوكز، اكز 1. ox. 2. dull, heavy, stupid (person). 3. gambler's slang loaded dice. **—ün altında buzağı ara=** (lit., to search for a calf under an ox) to hunt for something in the most unlikely place. **— arabası** ox-cart. **— arabası gibi** very slow. **—ü bacaya çıkar=** to undertake an impossible job. **—ü bıçağın yanına götür=** to make things unnecessarily difficult. **—e boynuzu yük olmaz** It is not a burden for one to serve his friends or relatives. **— boynuduruğa bakar gibi** in horror and disgust. **—e boyunduruğu kuyruğundan vurur** He is very incapable and awkward. **— damı** ox-stall, cow-shed. **— dili** bugloss, common alkanet, bot., Anchusa officinalis.

ökuzlük

— **gibi** blockhead, very stupid. — **gözü mountain alkanet**, arnica, *bot.*, *Arnica montana*. — **kafalı** blockhead. — **öldü ortaklık ayrıldı** *proverb* (*lit.* Now that the ox is dead, the partners have parted.) There is no more reason to keep up the relationship *said when the particular cause for friendship has disappeared*. — **soğuğu** the six cold days in the latter part of April after the sun has entered Taurus.

ökuzlükᵘ اوكوزلك ' 1. stupid and unreasonable affair. 2. dull, heavy stupidity.

öl=ᵘʳ 1 اولمك ' 1. to die. 2. to fade, wither, lose freshness. 3. to suffer terrible grief or anxiety; to be exhausted. — **düm Allah!** *colloq.* Impossible! — **düm Allah de=** *colloq.* to be in dismay, to be greatly distressed. — **me eşeğim ölme**, — **me eşeğim ölme çayır çimen bitecek** *colloq.* (*lit.* Don't die my donkey; the grass will grow some day.) Hold on, better days will come. Oh, what a long time to wait! — **ür müsün öldürür müsün?** *colloq.* Should one kill or die? *said when one is very angry with something but is unable to do anything about it*. — **üp ölüp diril=** to go through great distress or illness.

öl 2 اول ' *prov.* wet and muddy (place).

ölç=ᵉʳ اولچمك ' /ı/ 1. to measure. 2. to consider, to weigh. — **üp biç=** 1. to measure and cut out. 2. to decide a matter after consideration; to consider all around.

ölçekᵏⁱ اولچك ' 1. measure of capacity (for grain). 2. measure, scales. — **çizgisi** scale on a map.

ölçer=ⁱʳ اولچر ' *archaic* /ı/ 1. to stir up a fire. 2. to provoke.

ölçme اولچمه ' *verbal n.* of **ölç=**.

ölçtür=ᵘʳ اولچديرمك اولچدرمك ' /ı, a/ *caus.* of **ölç=**.

ölçü اولچو ' 1. measure; measurement; dimensions; quantity; proportion. 2. moderation. 3. *mus.* measure. — **al=** 1. to take the measure or capacity of. 2. to take warning. — **sünü al=** /ın/ to take the measurements (of), to measure (something). — **yü bildir=** *archaic* to teach a person his place. — **yü kaçır=** to pass the limit; to overdo. — **şeridi** measuring tape. — **ver=** to be measured (for a suit of clothes).

ölçül=ᵘʳ اولچلمك ' *pass.* of **ölç=**.

ölçüle=ʳ *neol.* /ı/ to adjust, to arrange; to calibrate. — **me** calibration, gauging.

ölçülü اولچولو ' 1. measured; well balanced, well proportioned. 2. temperate, moderate. — **balon** *phys.* gauge glass.

ölçüm اولچوم ' 1. measure; a measuring. 2. dimension. 3. appraisal, estimate; consideration. 4. behavior, air, manner. — **ü boz=** to change the established course of affairs. — **ünü boz=** to alter one's behavior for the worse. — **et=** to give oneself airs; to be vain.

ölçümle=ʳ اولچوملمك ' /ı/ to measure or consider a thing carefully and repeatedly. — **n=** *pass.*

ölçüsüz اولچوسز ' 1. unmeasured; unmeasurable, measureless. 2. immoderate; excessive.

ölçüş=ᵘʳ اولچشمك ' /la/ to measure oneself with or against another. — **tür=** /ı/ *caus.*

ölçüt *neol.* criterion.

öldür=ᵘʳ اولديرمك اولدرمك ' /ı/ 1. *caus.* of **öl= 1**, to kill. 2. to sauté (onions) — **esiye** to death, with the intention of killing; ruthlessly. — **me** *verbal n.* — **t=** /ı, a/ *caus.* of **öldür=**. — **tül=** *pass.* of **öldürt=**. — **ücü** 1. killer, killing. 2. mortal, fatal, deadly. — **ül=** *pass.* of **öldür=**. — **üş** *verbal n.* of **öldür=**.

öleş 1 اولش ' [leş] *prov.* dead body, corpse.

öleş= 2 اولشمك ' *prov.*, same as **üleş= 2**.

ölet اولت ' *prov.* epidemic.

ölgün اولكون ' 1. almost dead; faded, withered; exhausted, enervated. 2. calm (sea).

ölker اولكر ' *prov.* 1. nap, pile (of cloth). 2. down (on fruit). — **siz** napless, pileless. — **siz şeftali** nectarine.

ölme اولمه ' *verbal n.* of **öl= 1**.

ölmez اولمز ' 1. that never dies, who will not die; immortal, undying, eternal. 2. hard-wearing, resistant. — **dikeni** butcher's broom, *bot.*, *Ruscus aculeatus*. — **oğlu** *colloq.* hard wearing, resistant, enduring. — **otu** immortelle, everlasting flower, *bot.*, *Xeranthemum inapertum*. — **leştir=** /ı/ to immortalize. — **lik** immortality.

ölmüş اولمش ' 1. dead; faded, withered. 2. lacking energy or vitality.

ölü اولو اولی ' 1. dead, deceased; corpse, dead body. 2. lifeless, feeble, faded, withered. 3. *gambler's slang* loaded dice; marked playing card. — **aşkı** necrophilia, love of the dead. — **benzi** corpse-like skin, sallow skin. — **deniz** *naut.* swell. — **sü dirisine bin=** to be in confusion, to hurry in great alarm. — **fiatına** very cheap. — **gibi** corpselike; motionless. — **gömme** burial, interment. — **gözü gibi** very dull, lusterless. — **yü güldürür** too funny. — **sü kandilli**, — **sü kınalı** *slang* the cursed fellow, the wretch. — **korkusu** necrophobia. — **nokta** *mach.* dead point. — **zaviye** *mil.* dead angle.

ölücü اولوجی ' mortal.

ölüm اولوم اولم ' death. — **Allahın emri Death is God's decree** *said when making a vital and risky decision*. — **e bağlı tasarruflar** *law* dispositions because of a death. — **cezası** *law* capital punishment. — **dirim** life and death. — **dirim dünyası** this world. — **döşeği**

death bed. **—ü göze al=** to risk one's life. **— hak miras helâl** *prov.* (*lit.* Death is God's will; inheritance is legitimate.) There is nothing wrong in coming into an inheritance. **— kalım** life and death. **—ün ötesi kolay** (*lit.* What is on the other side of death is easy.) This is a hard world to live in. **— sigortası** life insurance. **—üne susa=** to scorn life; to court death.

ölümcül اولومجیل اولومجل ۱ 1. causing death, mortal, fatal. 2. in the state of death, dying.

ölümlü اولوملی ۱ mortal, transitory. **— dünya** this mortal world.

ölümlükᵍᵘ اولوملك ۱ a sum of money saved by one to be spent on his own funeral.

ölümsü *neol.* deathlike, mortal.

ölümsüz اولومسز ۱ immortal. **—lük** immortality.

ömr عمر A *cf.* **ömür**.

ömrevbar (..—) عمر اوبار P *lrnd.* life-consuming.

ömürᵐʳᵘ عمر [ömr] 1. life; existence; age. 2. enjoyment of life, happiness. 3. odd, amusing, pleasant. **—ünde** *with neg.* in all his life, never. **— adam** very pleasant man, funny person. **—i aziz** *lrnd.* precious life. **—üne bereket** May your life be blessed. **—i billâh** *colloq.* It has always been and will be so. **—ünüz çok olsun** (*lit.* May your life be long.) God reward you! Thank you. **— çürüt=** to waste one's life; to waste one's time unnecessarily. **—ü oldukça** as long as one lives, for the rest of one's life. **—ler olsun!** May you live long *said by an elder person to a younger one when he kisses the older person's hand in respect.* **— törpüsü** long and exhausting affair; trying and difficult person. **—üm vefa ederse** should my life be spared, if I live long enough. **—lü** long lived; enduring. **—süz** short lived.

ön اون اوڭ ۱ 1. front; space in front (of a thing); foremost; fore, front; *neol.* preliminary. 2. breast, chest. 3. the future. 4. /dan/ *archaic* previous, before, previously. **—de** in the front; before; ahead. **—den** from the front; in front. **—e** to the front. **—ünde** /ın/ in front of; before, in the presence (of). **— aks** *auto.* front axle. **— al=** *mil.* to precede, to go or come before. **— ünü al=** /ın/ to prevent, to avoid. **—ü ardı** the beginning and the end. **—üne ardına bakma=** to be careless, not to mind what is happening around one. **—ünü ardını bil=** to be tactful and considerate. **—ünde ardında dolaş=** /ın/ to follow persistently. **—ünü ardını düşün=** to think well before acting, to be prudent and considerate. **—üne arkasına bakmadan** rashly, thoughtlessly, without considering the consequences. **— ayak** 1. forefoot. 2. prompter; instigator; leader in mischief. 3. the first to do something, pioneer. **—üne bak=** to hang one's head. **—üne bak** Look out. Be careful. **— bilgi** *neol., phil.* beginnings, preliminaries, first principles. **— cam** *auto.* windshield. **—den çekişli** *auto.* front-wheel drive. **—e düş=** to go in front, to show the way. **—üne geç=** /ın/ to avoid; to take measures against. **—üne gelen** whomever he comes across, everybody. **—üne kat=** /ı/ to drive and follow after. **—ünü kes=** /ın/ to bar the way (of), to waylay. **—ünde perende atama=** /ın/ not to be able to play tricks on. **—ü sıra** /ın/ in front of, ahead of. **—ünde sonunda** in the end, sooner or later. [*For other compounds see* **önce — önyüzbaşı**].

önce (.'.) اوكجی ۱ 1. first, at first. 2. before, previously; /dan/ prior to, before. **—den** 1. from the beginning; first of all. 2. beforehand. **—ki** the preceding, former. **—leri** at first, formerly.

öncel *neol.* predecessor; former. **— düzen** *phil.* preestablished harmony.

öncelikᵍⁱ *neol.* 1. preceding act, precedent. 2. earnest money.

öncü اوكجی ۱ vanguard; advance guard.

öncül *neol., phil.* premise.

önder اوندر ۱ leader, chief. **—lik** leadership.

öndin اكدین ۱ *archaic* formerly, previously; at first.

öndüçᶜᵘ اوكدوج ۱ *archaic* forerunner.

öneği اوكگی ۱ *archaic* obstinate, perverse; intractable. **—leş=** to become obstinate. **—lik** obstinacy, perversity.

önekᵏⁱ *neol., gram.* prefix.

önem *neol.* importance. **—li** important. **—se=** /ı/ to consider important. **—siz** unimportant.

öner=ⁱʳ *neol.* /ı/ to propose, to suggest.

önerge *neol.* proposal, motion.

önerme *neol.* proposition.

önerti *neol.* antecedent.

öngörü *neol.* farseeing, prudence. **—lü** farsighted, prudent.

önkol اوك قول *anat.* forearm. **— kemiği** radius.

önle=ʳ اوكله ۱ /ı/ to prevent, to check; to resist, to face. **—n=** *pass.* **—yici** preventive.

önlükᵍᵘ اوكلك ۱ apron.

önoda اوك اوطه ۱ 1. antechamber. 2. *neol., anat.* anterior cavity.

önoluş *neol., biol.* preformation.

önrapor *neol.* preliminary report.

önsel *neol., phil., a priori.*

önsezi *neol., psych.* presentiment.

önsöz اوك سوز ۱ foreword, preface.

önürdü اوكوردو اكورو ۱ *archaic* before; first; previously. **—cü** vanguard, pioneer.

önürt=ᵘʳ اوكرت ۱ *archaic* /ı/ 1. to advance,

önyüzbaşı

to push forward. 2. to make one superior or eminent.
önyüzbaşı *neol., mil.* lieutenant commander.
öp=ᵉʳ اوپمك to kiss. **— babanın elini!** Now what next! What's to be done now? **— de başına koy** You should be grateful even for small mercies. **— eşiği çık dışarı** (*lit.* Kiss the threshold and get out.) You remain empty handed. You lose everything. **—erken ısırır** He is not to be trusted; his smiling face is deceptive. **—erle=** *slang* to kiss each other. **—me** *verbal n. of* **öp=**. **—tür=** /ı, a/ *caus. of* **öp=**.
öpü اوپو kiss. **—cük** kiss.
öpül=ᵘʳ اوپلمك *pass. of* **öp=**.
öpüş 1 اوپوش 1. *verbal n. of* **öp=**. 2. kiss.
öpüş=ᵘʳ 2 اوپوشمك /la/ 1. to kiss one another. 2. to kiss and be reconciled. **—tür=** /ı/ *caus*.
ör=ᵉʳ **1** اورمك 1. to plait; to knit; to darn. 2. to interlace; to interweave. 3. to build (wall); to lay bricks or stones in building.
ör 2 اور *archaic* fence; artificial barrier, hurdle.
örcin اورجين *archaic* rope ladder.
ördekᵍⁱ اوردك 1. duck. 2. urinal (for using in bed). 3. *slang* blockhead, stupid. 4. *chauffeurs' slang* customer picked up on the way (on a long journey). **— avla=** *chauffeurs' slang* to pick up customers on the way. **— balığı** striped wrasse, *zool.*, *Habrus mixtus*. **— başı** greenish blue, duck-head green. **— edalı** bandylegged. **— gagası** light orange color.
ördür=ᵘʳ اوردرمك /ı, a/ *caus. of* **ör= 1**.
örekᵍⁱ اورك *archaic* network of a tissue, wall, etc.; *building* netting (of a wall). **— çamuru** coarse plaster, mortar for building. **— ipi** plumb line.
öreke اوركه 1. distaff. 2. midwife's stool. **— taşı** flat surfaced rock in the sea.
örele=ʳ اورله مك *archaic* /ı/ to plait, intertwine or knit together temporarily. **—n=** *pass*. **—t=** /ı, a/ *caus. of* **örele=**.
ören اورن ruin; ruined remains (of a wall or building). **— gülü** white bryony. **— yavşanı** common wormwood, *Artemisia absinthium*.
örf عرف A 1. common usage, extra-judicial civil usage. 2. oppressive government; tyranny. 3. sovereign right. 4. *Ott. hist.* turban (worn by Sultans and judges). 5. *lrnd.* benefit, favor; generosity, kindness. 6. *lrnd.* comb of a cock; neck feathers of a cock. 7. *lrnd.* colloquial or technical language. **— ve âdet** usage and custom. **— ü âdet hukuku** *law* consuetudinary law, common law. **—i âm** *lrnd.* 1. common

usage, general custom. 2. popular dialect. **—i belde** *lrnd.* 1. the usage of a town or country. 2. local dialect. **—i hâs** *lrnd.* the technical language of a special class. **—i nâs** *lrnd.*, same as **örfi âm**. **—i şer'î** *lrnd.* technical language of the canon law.
örfen (.'.) عرفاً A 1. according to common usage. 2. conventionally, colloquially; technically. 3. by sovereign right. 4. extrajudicial, arbitrary.
örfî (.—) عرفى A 1. *law* conventional, customary; *lrnd.* colloquial, technical (language). 2. *law* extrajudicial, sovereign, arbitrary (right, etc.). **— idare** state of siege, martial law.
örgen *neol., biol., phil.* organ. **—leş=** to become a living organism. **—lik** organism.
örgü اورگو 1. plaited, knitted thing; plait; a plaiting or knitting. 2. tress of hair; rush mat. 3. *neol., anat.* plexus. 4. technique of building (of a wall etc.).
örgüçᶜᵘ اورگوج *same as* **hörgüç**.
örkᵏᵘ اورك *prov.* tether. **—le=** /ı/ to tether.
örme اورمه 1. *verbal n. of* **ör= 1**. 2. plaited, knitted; interwoven; darned; built (wall). **— işleri** passementerie, trimmings.
örnekᵍⁱ اورنك Arm 1. specimen, sample, pattern, model. 2. example. **— al=** to take as example. **—ini çıkar=** /ın/ to make a copy of.
örneklikᵍⁱ اورنكلك 1. model, sample. 2. serving as a model or sample.
örs اورس anvil. **— kemiği** *anat.* incus.
örsele=ʳ اورسه لمك /ı/ 1. to handle roughly, to misuse. 2. to spoil, to rumple, to wear out. 3. to exhaust, to weaken. **—n=** *pass*. **—t=** /ı, a/ *caus*.
ört=ᵉʳ اورتمك /ı/ 1. to cover; to wrap; to veil. 2. to conceal, to hide. 3. to shut (door, window etc.). 4. to roof (house).
örtbas اورتباص *only in* **— et=** /ı/ to use every endeavor to hide or suppress; to hush up (some unpleasant fact or defect).
örtenekᵍⁱ *neol., biol.* mantle.
örttür=ᵘʳ اورتدرمك /ı, a/ *caus. of* **ört=**.
örtü اورتو 1. cover; wrap; blanket. 2. roof. **—cü** covering, concealing; who covers.
örtül=ᵘʳ اورتلمك *pass. of* **ört=**. **—me** *verbal n.*
örtülü اورتولو 1. covered; wrapped up; concealed. 2. shut, closed (door, etc.). 3. roofed. 4. obscure (speech). **— ödenek** *neol.* secret funds.
örtün=ᵘʳ اورتنمك 1. to cover oneself, to veil oneself. 2. /ı/ to cover oneself with.
örü 1 اورى *prov.* 1. texture, web; plaited or woven thing; mode of plaiting;

a darning. 2. enclosed space; barrier, division. 3. wall, building. **— balçığı** clay mortar. **— taşı** rough building stone.

örü 2 اورو ' اورى archaic upright, standing. **— dur=** to stand upright.

örü 3 اورى prov. pasture.

örücü اورومى ' اورىجى mender; darner.

örül=ᵘʳ اورولمك ' اورلمك pass. of **ör= 1**. **—me** verbal n.

örülü اورولى ' اورلو ' اورملو ' اورلو 1. plaited, woven, interlaced; darned. 2. built (wall). 3. enclosed (by a wall or stakes).

örümcekᵍⁱ اورومجك ' ارمجك spider; cobweb. **—ler** spiders, zool., Arachnida. **— ağı** spider's web, cobweb. **— al=** to sweep away cobwebs. **— kafalı** colloq. old-fashioned, incapable of accepting new ideas. **— kuşu** shrike, zool., Lanius.

örümceklen=ⁱʳ اورمجكلنمك 1. to become covered with cobwebs. 2. path. to feel as if covered with cobweb while feverish (mouth, eyes). **—dir=** /ı/ caus.

örümcekli اورمجكلى covered with cobwebs.

örümceksi neol., biol. arachnoid, cobweblike.

östaki borusu neol., anat. Eustachian tube.

öşr عشر A cf. **öşür**.

öşürᵒˢʳᵘ عشر [öşr] 1. tithe. 2. lrnd. a tenth part. **—cü** tithe collector.

öt=ᵉʳ 1 اوتمك 1. to sing (bird); to crow (cock). 2. to resound, to echo; to ring. 3. to talk foolishly, to chatter. 4. slang to vomit.

öt=ᵉʳ 2 اوتمك archaic /dan/ to pass, to pass on.

öte اوته 1. the further side; what is on the further side. 2. further, beyond. 3. the rest; other; the other side. **—de** over there, further on. **—den** from the other side; from beyond. **—si** what follows; the rest. **—ye** further on; to the other side. **— beri***. **—den beri** heretofore; from of old. **—de beride** here and there. **—den beriden** from here and there. **—si berisi** 1. this side and that, here and there. 2. some parts. **—ye beriye** here and there; back and forth; on all sides. **—den beriden bahset=** to talk of various things. **—sini beri et=** /ın/ to look at a matter from all sides; to do all that is possible. **—si can sağlığı** That's all that one can do. **— gün** prov. a few days ago. **—sine var=** /ın/ to surpass, to exceed that which is usual.

öteberi اوته برى 1. this side and that; here and there. 2. this and that; various things. **— al=** to buy various things; to do shopping.

öteğen اوتگن ' اوتوگن archaic 1. that sings habitually (bird). 2. that makes continuous noise.

öteki اوتكى ' اوتكى the other; the other one. **— beriki** 1. this one and that, the one and the other. 2. the people, anybody. **— gün** the other day.

ötelem neol., phys. transition.

ötleğen اوتلگن ' اوتوگى ' اوتنگس 1. white throat warbler, zool., Sylvia communis. 2. archaic singing.

ötleği اوتنگى ' اوتلى bearded vulture, lammergeier, zool., Gypaetus barbatus.

ötlekᵍⁱ اوتلك same as **ödlek**.

ötme اوتمه verbal n. of **öt= 1**.

ötre اوترى ' اوتورى ' اوترى Arabic script, the vowel sign for o, ö, u, ü.

ötrü اوترو archaic, same as **ötürü**.

öttür=ᵘʳ اوتدرمك ' اوتدرمك /ı/ caus. of **öt= 1**.

ötücü اوتىجى 1. that sings habitually (bird). 2. that sounds or resounds habitually.

ötün=ᵘʳ اوتونمك archaic to pardon, to forgive.

ötürü اوترو ' اوتورى ' اوتورو /dan/ by reason of, because of; respecting, concerning.

ötüş=ᵘʳ 1 اوتوشمك 1. to sing or crow with one another. 2. to sound or ring together.

ötüş 2 اوتوش verbal n. of **öt= 1**.

öv=ᵉʳ اوكمك ' اومك /ı/ to praise, to commend.

öveçᶜⁱ اوكج prov. two-year-old ram.

övül=ᵘʳ اوكلمك pass. of **öv=**.

övün 1 اوكون meal.

övün=ᵘʳ 2 اوكونمك to praise oneself, to boast, brag.

övünçᶜᵘ اوكونج boasting.

övüngen اوكونگن boaster, boastful, vainglorious.

övünme اوكونمه verbal n. of **övün= 2**.

övür 1 اوكور archaic, same as **öğür 1**.

övür=ᵘʳ 2 اوكورمك same as **öğür= 2**.

övüş اوكوش a praising, praise.

övüt=ᵘʳ اوكوتمك 1. to grind. 2. to eat heartily. **—me** verbal n. **—ücü** 1. that grinds. 2. molar (tooth). **—ül=** pass. of **övüt=**.

öyke اويكه archaic, same as **öfke**.

öyken اويكن prov. the lungs, the lights.

öykün=ᵘʳ اويكونمك ' اويكنمك prov. to look up to for guidance, to follow; to imitate.

öyle اويله ' اويله so, in that manner; such, like that. **— mi?** Is that so? **—si** such, the like, that sort. **—sine** in such manner; exceedingly. **—yse** same as **öyle ise**. **— gel=** /a/ to suppose, to think; to seem. **— ise** in that case; if so, then. **— olsun** all right; so be it; as you wish. **— şey yok** Oh no! Of course not! **— ya!** Of course! Oh, yes! **—ce** in that manner; somewhat, so. **—likle** thus, in that manner.

öyükᵍᵘ اويوك prov., var. of **höyük**.

öyün=ᵘʳ اويونمك ' اويكنمك var. of **övün= 2**.

öz 1 اوز 1. genuine, real, essential; pure. 2. own; self. 3. pith, marrow, cream; essence of a thing. **— ad** first name. **— anne** one's own mother. **— bakır** pure copper. **—ü göyün=** archaic /a/ to feel compassion (for). **— gözüyle** with his own eyes. **— ışınları** bot. medullary rays. **— özü** archaic he himself. **—ü özüne** archaic spontaneously, voluntarily. **—üm** I, myself. **— saygısı** neol. self-respect. **— söyle=** to speak wisely and to the point. **—ü sözü bir** sincere, genuine. **—ü sözü doğru** honest and correct, trustworthy. **— Türkçe** pure Turkish.

öz 2 اوز archaic brook, rivulet.

Özbekᵍⁱ اوزبك Uzbek, the Uzbeks. **—ce** (..'.) the Uzbek language, in Uzbek.

özbeöz (.'..) اوزباوز real, true, genuine.

özdekᵍⁱ اوزدك 1. archaic trunk, stem, stock (of a tree or plant). 2. neol., phil. matter. **—çilik** neol., phil. materialism.

özdekle=ʳ اوزدكمك archaic to glean. **—yip bözdekle=** archaic to be cringing and humble.

özden اوزدن 1. sweetbread, pancreas. 2. archaic earring, pendant.

özdenlikᵍⁱ neol., phil. aseity.

özdeş neol., phil. identical. **—le=** /ı/ to perceive as identical. **—lik** identity.

özdevim neol., phil. automatism.

özdışı neol., phil. extrinsic.

özdirençᶜⁱ neol., phys. resistivity.

öze neol., phil. /a/ proper, special (to).

özel neol. 1. private, personal. 2. special. **— ad** gram. proper noun. **— okul** private school.

özelikᵍⁱ neol. specialty, property.

özellikᵍⁱ neol. special feature, peculiarity, characteristic. **—le** particularly, specially.

özen=ⁱʳ 1 اوزه نمك 1. to take pains, to try hard. 2. /a/ to take pains about; to desire ardently. 3. /a, dan/ to try to imitate (others), to have a passing fancy (to do something). **—ip bezen=** to take great pains, to go to great trouble. **—e bezene** with particular care, painstakingly.

özen 2 اوزن pains, a painstaking; care. **— bezen** 1. trinkets, ornaments. 2. ceremony.

özendir=ⁱʳ اوزنديرمك /ı/ caus. of **özen= 1.**

özengi اوزنكى same as **üzengi**.

özenli neol. painstakingly; careful.

özensiz neol. 1. carelessly; careless. 2. superficial; not elaborate.

özenti اوزنتى 1. affectation. 2. pseudo-, counterfeit, mock. 3. showing off. **— muharrir** pseudo-writer.

özerkli neol. autonomous. **—lik** autonomy.

özet neol. summary. **—le=** /ı/ to summarize.

özge اوزكه 1. other, another, different. 2. peculiar; uncommon; rare. 3. stranger. **—ci** neol., phil. altruist. **—cilik** altruism.

özgül neol., specific. **— ağırlık** specific weight. **—lük** specificity.

özgür neol. free. **—lük** freedom.

özindükleme neol., phys. self-induction.

özle=ʳ اوزله مك /ı/ to wish for, to long for; to yearn for.

özlem neol. 1. a yearning, longing. 2. phil. aspiration, ardent desire.

özlen=ⁱʳ 1 اوزلنمك pass. of **özle=**.

özlen=ⁱʳ 2, **özleş=**ⁱʳ اوزلشمك 1. to become pasty. 2. to acquire pith, substance, pulp. **—dir=**, **—tir=** /ı/ caus.

özlet=ⁱʳ اوزلتمك /ı, a/ caus. of **özle=**.

özleyiş اوزله يش verbal n. of **özle=**.

özlü اوزلى 1. having substance, sappy, pithy, pulpy. 2. of a sticky or pasty consistency. 3. substantial, pithy; laconic. **— toprak** 1. potter's clay. 2. fertile soil. **—lük** abstr. n.

özlükᵍᵘ اوزلك 1. substance of a thing, marrow, pith, essence. 2. self; identity. 3. egotism. selfishness.

özne neol., phil., gram. subject.

öznel neol., phil. subjective. **—cilik** phil. subjectivism.

özr عذر A lrnd., same as **özür**. **—i mâfât** excuse for past faults.

özrhah (.—) عذرخواه P lrnd. who apologizes, apologizer. **—âne** (.——.) P apologetic; as an excuse. **—î** (.——) P, **—lık** apologizing.

özrpezir (..—) عذرپذير P lrnd. 1. who accepts excuses. 2. excusable.

özsu neol., bot. juice, sap.

özümle=ʳ, **özümse=**ʳ neol., biol. /ı/ to assimilate. **—me** assimilation. **—me dokusu** assimilation tissue. **—n=** pass.

özüneroslukᵍᵘ neol., phil. autoeroticism.

özünlü neol., phil. intrinsic.

özürᶻʳᵘ عذر 1. defect, impediment. 2. excuse, hindrance. 3. apology; pardon. **— bul=** 1. /a/ to find fault with. 2. to invent an excuse. **— dile=** /dan/ to beg to be excused, to ask pardon. **—ü kabahatinden büyük** His excuse is worse than his fault said when one's excuses make matters worse.

özürlü عذرلى 1. defective, faulty. 2. who has an excuse.

özürsüz عذرسز 1. free from defect. 2. inexcusable. **— pürüzsüz** free from all defect.

özveren neol. unselfish, self-denying.

özveri neol. renunciation, self-denial. **—li** unselfish, self-denying.

P

p, P the twentieth letter of the Turkish alphabet.

pa (—) پا P *lrnd.* 1. foot; leg. 2. foundation, base; footing. 3. power; constancy; firmness, durability.

pabend (—.) پابند P *lrnd.* fetter, hindrance; fettered. **—ân** (—.—) P prisoners in fetters.

paberca, pabercay (—.—) پابرجا پابرجای P *lrnd.* 1. firm, constant, persevering. 2. enduring, everlasting, eternal.

paberehne (—...) پابرهنه P *lrnd.* barefoot; barefooted.

paberencen (—...) پابرنجن P *lrnd.* anklet, ankle ornament.

paberikâb (—..—) پابركاب P *lrnd.* whose foot is in the stirrup, ready to depart.

pabest (—.), **pabeste** (—..) پابست P *lrnd.* foot-bound, fettered, captive.

pabuç[cu] پابوش [Persian *pâpuş*] 1. shoe; slipper. 2. tag of an electric wire. 3. *naut.* shoe of an anchor. 4. *arch.* base, basement. **—umu alırsın** You can't get anything out of me. **—tan aşağı** most vile and contemptible. **—u başına giydir=** /ın/ *colloq.* to make someone do the wrong thing. **— bırakma=** /a/ *colloq.* not to be discouraged (by something or somebody). **—u büyük** *colloq.* Big Shoes, *i. e.* hodja who cures people by prayer. **—u büyüğe okut kendini** *colloq.* You had better get yourself exorcized by Big Shoes, *i. e.* Something must be wrong with your mind. **—larını çevir=** /ın/ to cause somebody to understand that he is not wanted, to dismiss someone in a polite manner. **—ları dama atıl=** /ın/ to lose favor, to fall into discredit. **—umda değil** *colloq.* I don't care. **—larını eline ver=** /ın/ to fire (a person). **— eskit=** to follow up something energetically. **— ızmaridi** a large variety of seabream. **— kadar dili var** He has a tongue as long as a shoe *said of one who answers back in a rude manner.* **— pahalı** I can't compete with him. It's time to give up and quit. **— parala=** *same as* **pabuç eskit=**. **— tarağı** instep of a shoe. **— tart=** to strut slowly along. **— tartan** dungbeetle; woodlouse. **—u ters giydir=** /a/ to cause to leave in a hurry, to chase away; to put into confusion. **—una tuz ek=** /ın/ *colloq.* to put salt into a visitor's shoes (to hasten his departure). **— üzengi** stirrup fitted with a shoe, Oriental stirrup.

pabuççu پابوجچی 1. maker or seller of shoes; cobbler; shoemaker. 2. attendant who looks after people's shoes in mosques. **— kölesi** shoemaker's iron last. **— somakisi** shoemaker's lapstone. **—luk** shoemaking.

pabuçlu پابوجلی having shoes.

pabuçluk[tu] پابوجلیی place where shoes or slippers are kept in an entrance of a house.

pabuçsuz پابوجسیز without slippers. **— kaç=** to run away, to be routed.

pabus (——) پابوس P *lrnd.* 1. kissing of the foot; kissing a superior's foot ceremonially. 2. one who kisses another's foot in token of reverence. 3. one who assumes a humble position. **—î** (————) P foot-kissing, reverence, adoration.

pacame (——.) پاجامه P *lrnd.* pair of drawers, trousers.

paça پاچه [*paçe*] 1. sheep's feet, trotters; dish made from trotters. 2. lower part of the leg; lower part of the trouser leg. **—sını çekecek hali yok** He is hopelessly awkward and incapable. **— dondurması** trotter jelly.

paçacı

—**sı düşük** untidy, slovenly, awkward, clumsy. —**günü** the day after a wedding, when a dish of trotters is eaten. —**sını kurtar=** to escape, to get through safely. —**larını sıva=** 1. to roll up one's trousers. 2. to prepare to set about some important business; to get down to a job. —**suyu** hot jelly from trotters. —**sından tutup at=** /ı/ to turn someone out roughly.

paçacı یا جه جی 1. dealer in sheep's trotters. 2. small restaurant where trotters are eaten.

paçal یا چال proportion of various grains legally permitted in bread.

paçarız یا چارز مجارز Gk crosswise; intricate. — **aç=** to disentangle. — **düş=** to fall foul of a thing and get tangled in it.

paçavra (.ˊ.) یا چاوره مجاوره 1. rag. 2. miserable rag (newspaper). 3. worthless. 4. *slang* pertinacious and shameless person, importunate. —**ya çevir=** /ı/ 1. to insult and ridicule completely. 2. to make a mess of something, to spoil. —**sını çıkar=** /ın/ to crush, to smash, to spoil something so as to make it utterly useless. — **et=** /ı/ same as **paçavraya çevir=**. — **gibi** ragged; in rags. — **hastalığı** *colloq.* influenza.

paçavracı یا چاوره جی old clothes man.

paçe (—.) یا چه P *lrnd., same as* **paça**.

paçefürüş (—..—) یا چه فروش P *lrnd., same as* **paçacı**.

paçoz, paçuz یا چوز 1. *slang* harlot; prostitute. 2. gray mullet, *zool., Mugil cephalus*.

padam (——) یا دام P *lrnd.* trap made of horse hair for catching birds; bird tied by a foot to decoy others.

padaş (——) یا داش P *lrnd.* 1. reward, retribution (good or bad). 2. companion.

padavra (.ˊ.) یا داوره بداوره [**pedavra**] shingle; thin board (used under tiles). —**sı çıkmış, — gibi** so thin that his ribs stick out.

pader (—.) یا در P *lrnd.* a trembling of the limbs.

padergil (—..) یا درگل P *lrnd.* 1. stuck in the mire. 2. embarrassed, entangled, bewildered.

paderpa (—.—) یا در پا P *lrnd.* foot to foot, side by side.

paderrikâb (—..—) یا درّکاب P *lrnd.* mounted on horseback; prepared for a journey.

padılbot یا دل بوت E paddle boat.

padişah (—.—) یا دشاه P sovereign, ruler, king; the Sultan of the Ottoman Empire. —**ın atı bana baktı** (*lit.* The Sultan's horse looked at me.) foolish pride, vainglory. — **otu** broadleaved hog-fennel, *bot., Peucedanum ostruthium*.

padişahâne (—.—.) یا دشاهانه P royal, imperial; royally.

padişahî (—.——) یا دشاهی P *lrnd., same as* **padişahlık**.

padişahlık[ki] یا دشاهلق 1. sovereignty. 2. empire, kingdom, realm. 3. the period of a sovereign's rule. 4. state and glory of a sovereign; royal, imperial.

padişahzade (—..—.) یا دشاهزاده P prince, son of a king or Sultan.

padişeh (—..) یا دشه P *lrnd., same as* **padişah**.

padzehr (—.) یا دزهر P *lrnd., same as* **panzehir**.

pafta (.ˊ.) یا فته [*Persian* **bafte**] 1. section of a large map. 2. metal decoration on a horse's harness. 3. screw plate. 4. large colored spot. — **kolu** die stock. — **lokması** screw die. — **pafta** covered with spots; stained with spots.

pağurya (.ˊ.) یا غوریه Gk 1. small crab. 2. *slang* one who walks sidewise with one shoulder lowered.

pah یا ه chamfer, bevel. —**ını al=** /ın/ to bevel, to chamfer.

paha یا ها [**baha 1**] price, value. —**da ağır** high priced; costly. — **biç=** /a/ to set a value (on), to estimate. — **biçilmez** priceless, invaluable. —**ya çık=** to rise in price, to become expensive. —**dan düş=**, —**dan in=** to fall in price. — **kat'et=**, — **kes=** /a/ to settle the price (of). —**sı yok** priceless, invaluable.

pahacı یا هاجی who sells at a high price.

pahalan=[ır], **pahalaş=**[ır] یا هالان یا هالاش to become more expensive.

pahalı یا هالی expensive, costly. —**ya otur=** /a/ to be very expensive.

pahalılaş=[ır] یا هالیلاش to become expensive.

pahalılık[ki] یا هالیلق 1. expensiveness, costliness. 2. dearth, scarcity of provisions.

pahıl یا خیل [**bahil 1**] *prov.* uncharitable; stingy.

pahla=[r] یا هلا /ı/ to chamfer, to bevel.

pak[ki] (—) یا ک P clean, pure; holy.

pâkân (——) یا کان P *lrnd.* the Saints of God. —**ı hıtta-i evvel** the angels who bear the throne of God, the cherubim and seraphim.

pakbaz (——) یا کباز P *lrnd.* 1. who plays without cheating. 2. who loses all his money at gambling. 3. pious; saint. 4. honorable lover. —**i çarh** moon, moonlight. —**ân** (———) P *pl.* —**âne** (———.) P loyally, honorably.

pakbazî (———) یا کبازی P *lrnd.* 1. purity of mind. 2. pure and loyal love.

pakdamen (———.) یا کدامن P *lrnd.* chaste, pure; incorrupt, just. —**î** (——.—) P, —**lik** purity.

paket یا کت It 1. package, parcel. 2. small box (of cigarettes etc.). 3. *slang* buttocks. — **postanesi** parcel post. — **taşı** rectangular paving stone.

paketle= باكتله مك /ı/ to package, to make into a parcel.

pakî (——) پاكى P lrnd. 1. purity, chastity; cleanliness. 2. razor.

pakize (——.) پاكيزه P lrnd. 1. pure, chaste; innocent. 2. good, excellent, choice.

pakizegi (——.—) پاكيزه كى P lrnd. purity, goodness, excellence; beauty.

pakizehuy (——.—) پاكيزه خوى P lrnd. of excellent disposition.

pakizeruy (——.—) پاكيزه روى P lrnd. beautiful of face.

pakla= باكله مك /ı/ 1. to clean, to cleanse. 2. to clear (of an accusation); to acquit. 3. to use up, to take away. 4. to kill. —n= pass. —t= /ı, a/ caus.

paklık[tı] باكلك cleanness, cleanliness; purity.

pakmeşreb (—..) باك مشرب P lrnd. pure of disposition; noble.

pakûb (——) پاكوب P lrnd. 1. who kicks, stamps or prances. 2. dancer; jumper, tumbler.

pakzad (——) پاكزاد P lrnd. of noble birth, of honorable descent.

pala 1 (..') پالا scimitar. — **bıyık** 1. one whose mustache is long, full and curved. 2. slang unfledged, immature. — **çal=** 1. to brandish a scimitar. 2. to swagger about, to strive. — **çek=** 1. to draw a scimitar. 2. to attack with a scimitar. — **salla=** same as **pala çal=**. — **sürt=** to have lived through many experiences.

pala 2 (..') پالا It 1. long steering-oar, paddle. 2. long flat plank thinned at the two edges.

pala 3 (..') پالا 1. long quilted saddle-cloth. 2. prov. rug; rag.

palâğz (—.) پالاغز P lrnd. 1. slip of the foot, false step. 2. offense, error, sin.

palağzide (—.—.) پالاغزيده P lrnd. 1. whose foot has slipped. 2. who has fallen into error.

palaheng (——.) پالاهنك P lrnd. 1. halter, bridle, rein, rope. 2. moral bond. 3. the Milky Way.

palalık[tı] پالالق edge of a rafter. —**ına koy=** to set up on edge (timber).

palamar پالامار It naut. hawser, mooring rope. —**ı çöz=** slang to take off, to slip the cable. — **gözü** hawse-hole. —**ı kopar=** same as **palamarı çöz=**.

palamut[du] **1** پالاموت Gk bonito; short-finned tunny, zool., Pelamys sarda.

palamut[du] **2** پالاموت Gk valonia oak, bot., Quercus aegilops; acorn of the valonia oak.

palan پالان [Persian ——] broad soft saddle without a frame.

palandız پالاندز stone in which the faucet of a public fountain is fixed.

palânduz (———) پالاندوز P lrnd. maker of pack-saddles.

palanga (.'.) پالانغه It same as **palanka 1**.

palânî (———) پالانى P lrnd. maker of pack-saddles.

palanka 1 (.'.) پالانقه It tackle for hoisting, pulley-block. — **donat=** to rig a tackle; to reeve a tackle with its rope.

palanka 2 (.'.) پالانقه .پالانغه Hung 1. closed fortification of earth works; fort. 2. redoubt (of a fortress).

palas 1 پلاس [pelâs] 1. coarse textile. 2. rag.

palas 2 پلاس F 1. sumptuous hotel or big building. 2. school slang comfortable, very easy (thing). 3. slang pleasant (person); comfortable (place). — **geç=** to pass the time comfortably.

palaserte (...'.), **palasertiye** (...'..) پالاسرته پالاسرتيه It naut. chain wale on a ship's side.

palaska (.'.) پالاسقه Hung 1. cartridge belt, bandolier. 2. ammunition box on board a ship.

palas pandıras پلاس پاندراس hastily, abruptly, suddenly.

palastrupa, palasturpa (...'.) پالاستروپا پالاسطرپا It naut. wad for a cannon.

palâvan (———), **palâven** (———.) پالاوان پالاون P lrnd. colander, strainer, skimmer.

palavra 1 (.'.) پالاوره Sp slang idle talk, boast; swagger; lie. — **at=**, — **savur=**, — **sık=** to lie; to boast, to brag.

palavra 2 (.'.) پالاوره It naut. main deck (of a man-of-war); upper tween-deck.

palavracı پالاوره جى braggart; boasting.

palây (——) پالاى P lrnd. 1. straining. 2. augmenting. 3. led horse. —**iş** (——.) P filtration, percolation.

palaz پلاز 1. young of a duck, goose or pigeon. 2. fat.

palazla=[r], **palazlan=**[r] پالازلامق پالازلانمق 1. to grow fat. 2. to grow up (child). 3. to become wealthy. 4. slang to become defiant; to stand up for oneself; to answer back.

paldım پالدم [pardüm] crupper, crupper strap. —**ı aş=** to go beyond the limit, to attempt something above one's head. — **kemiği** anat. coccyx.

paldır küldür پالدر كلدر with a great clatter.

paldum پالدم [pardüm] same as **paldım**.

paleng (—.) P, **palenk**[tı] (—.) پالنك lrnd. a kind of rustic leather shoe.

palet 1 پالت It naut. mat used on board ship to prevent chafing, paunch, mat.

palet 2 بالت F 1. palette. 2. *auto.* blade; articulated track of a caterpillar vehicle. —li tracked (vehicle).

palide (— —.) باليد P *lrnd.* 1. strained, purified. 2. searched, investigated.

palikarya (..ˊ.) باليقاريه Gk Greek youth; Greek rowdy.

palto (ˊ.) بالتو F overcoat.

palûde (— —.) بالوده P *lrnd.* 1. strained, filtered, cleared, skimmed. 2. *same as* **palûze**.

palûze بالوزه [palûde] blancmange, starch pudding.

palyaço (.ˊ.) باليازو It clown, buffoon, harlequin.

palyoş بالیوش short sword, dagger, hunting knife.

pamal[li] (— —) بامال P *lrnd., same as* **paymal**.

pambuk[gu] بامبوق *var. of* **panbuk**.

pami (ˊ.) بامى Gk *slang* Let's go. Come on. Be quick.

pamuk[gu] باموق [panbuk] cotton. — **ağacı** cotton tree, *bot., Gossypium arboreum.* — **at**= to card cotton. — **unu at**= /ın/ to scold. — **balı** white honey (from cotton fields), cotton honey. — **balığı** blue shark, *zool., Carcharias glaucus.* — **barutu** guncotton. — **bezi** cotton cloth. — **elması** cotton boll. — **fidanı** cotton plant, *bot., Gossypium herbacium.* — **gibi** soft as cotton. — **gibi at**= /ı/ to throw into utter confusion. — **ipliği** cotton thread, cotton yarn. — **ipliğiyle bağla**= /ı/ to make an unsatisfactory or temporary arrangement. — **otu** cotton weed, *bot., Diotis candidissima*; cotton grass, *bot., Eriophorum polystachion.* — **tarağı** cotton gin. — **taşı** travertine.

pamukaki (..—.) باموقاكى Gk cotton yarn used for embroidery, twist.

pamukçu باموقچى seller of raw cotton.

pamukçuk[gu] باموقچق *path.* thrush, aphtha.

pamukla=[r] باموقله /ı/ to decorate, wad or quilt with cotton. —**n**= 1. *pass.* 2. to be covered with a thin coat of mold or mildew. —**t**= /ı, a/ *caus. of* **pamukla**=.

pamuklu باموقلى 1. of cotton; cotton cloth. 2. wadded or quilted.

pamüzd[dü] (—.) بامزد P *lrnd.* wage earned by foot-labor; reward to messengers.

pan بان F breakdown (of a car). — **yap**= to have a breakdown (car).

panat بانت It *naut.* studding sail, bonetta sail.

panayır بانایر Gk fair, market. — **oyuncusu** tumbler, showman.

panbuk[gu] بنبوق *prov., same as* **pamuk**.

pancar بانجار Arm beet, *bot., Beta vulgaris.* — **gibi ol**=, — **kesil**= to turn red as a beet. — **şekeri** beet sugar.

pancur بانجور F slatted shutters.

pandantif بانداتیف F 1. pendant (necklace). 2. *arch.* pendentive.

pandemi باندمى F *path.* pandemia.

pandili باندیلى Gk tambourine used in the old Turkish theatrical show.

pandispanya (...ˊ.) باندسپانیه It sponge cake, plain cake. — **gazetesi** *slang* made-up stories, lies.

pandomima (..ˊ.) باندومیما Gk pantomime. — **koptu** An amusing quarrel broke out; it was quite a row. — **oyna**= to pantomime.

pandufla (.ˊ.) باندوفله *var. of* **pantufla**.

pane بانه F fried in bread crumbs; breaded (fried meat etc.).

paneta (.ˊ.) پانتا It *naut., same as* **panat**.

pangadoz, pangodoz بانقادوز *slang* slovenly, drunkard (old man).

panihade (—.—.) بانهاد P *lrnd.* who has set foot on, who has arrived.

panik[gi] بانیك F panic. —**e kapıl**= to panic. — **kır**= *slang* to slip away, to run off. — **yarat**= to cause a panic.

pankardit بانکاردیت F *path.* pancarditis.

pankreas بانقراس F pancreas.

pano بانو F 1. painter's panel. 2. ornamental panel on a door or wall. 3. *mil.* ground strip-signal.

panorama (...ˊ.) بانورامه F panorama.

pansad (—.) بانصد P *lrnd.* five hundred.

pansıman بانسمان F dressing for a wound. — **yap**= /ı/ to dress (a wound).

pansiyon بانسیون F boarding house.

pansiyoner بانسیونر F boarder.

pantalon بانتالون F *same as* **pantolon**.

panteizm بانتئیزم F *phil.* pantheism.

pantol بانتول *colloq.* trousers, pants.

pantolon بانتولون [pantalon] trousers, pants.

pantufla (.ˊ.) بانتوفله F 1. slippers, felt slippers. 2. *slang* stealing, swindling. —**cı** 1. maker or seller of slippers. 2. *slang* thief, swindler.

panya (ˊ.) بانیه stern-painter of a boat. —**yı çöz**= 1. to let go the stern-painter. 2. to slip away quietly.

panzdeh (—.) بانزده P *lrnd.* fifteen. —**üm** (—..) P fifteenth.

panzehir[hri] بانزهر [Persian **panzahr**] bezoar-stone, antidote. — **otu** tame poison; swallow-wort, *bot., Cynanchum vicetoxicum.* — **taşı** 1. bezoar-stone. 2. opal.

Papa (ˊ.) بابا It the Pope.

papafingo (...ˊ.) بابافینغو It *same as* **babafingo**.

papağan بابغان A parrot; parakeet. — **gibi ezberle**= to learn by heart without understanding the meaning, like a parrot. — **yemi** seeds of bastard saffron, safflower-seeds, seeds of *Carthamus tinctorius*. **—lık** *psych.* psittacism.

papak[ε¹] بابق high cylindrical lambskin cap (Persian or Turkman).

papalık[ε¹] بابالو the Holy See, Papacy.

papara 1 (.′.) بابارا ، بابره 1. dish made from pieces of dry bread and broth. 2. anything insipid and unpalatable. **— ye=** *colloq.* to get a bad scolding.

papara 2 (.′.) بابره flute played during the performance of old Turkish theatrical shows.

papas 1 باباس Gk same as **papaz**.
papas 2 باباس *colloq.*, same as **paspas**.
papatya (.′.) باباتیه ، باباتیا ، باباتیه daisy, camomile, *bot.*, *Anthemis nobilis*. **— falı** fortune telling with daisy petals.

papaz باباز ، بابس |**papas 1**] 1. priest; monk. 2. *cards* king. **— balığı** blue damsel fish, *zool.*, *Chromis chromis*. **—a dön=** to be in need of a haircut. **— her gün pilâv yemez** *proverb* (lit. A priest doesn't eat pilav every day.) Good things don't happen every day. **— kaçtı** a card game. **— karası** 1. a strong, deep red country wine. 2. a particular shade of black cloth worn by Greek priests. **—a kızıp perhiz boz=** (lit., to get angry with the priest and break one's fast) to cut off one's nose to spite one's face. **— otu** hellebore, *bot.*, *Helleborus albus*. **— otu tozu** veratrine. **— ravendi** garden rhubarb, *bot.*, *Rheum rhaponthicum* monk's rhubarb, *bot.*, *Rumex alpinus*. **— uçtu** same as **papaz kaçtı**. **— uçur=** *colloq.* to have a drinking party. **— yahnisi** mutton stewed with wine or vinegar.

papazi (.——) بابزی F fine shirt material.
papazlık[ε¹] بابازلق ، بابسلق duties and office of a priest; priesthood.

papel بابل Sp *slang* 1. Turkish lira note. 2. marked card. **—ci** cardsharp.
papirüs (.′.) بابیروس F papyrus. **—giller** *bot.*, *Cyperaceae*.
papiyon بابیون F bow tie. **— somunu** *mach.* winged nut. **— vidası** *mach.* thumb screw.
papuç[cu] بابوج [**papuş**] same as **pabuç**.
papura بابوره heavy plow drawn by two yoke of oxen.
papuş (——) بابوش P *lrnd.* shoe, slipper, sandal.
papyebüvar بابی بووار F blotting paper.
papyekuşe بابی قوشه F surface-coated paper, art paper.
papyemaşe بابی ماشه F papier maché, pulped paper.

para باره [**pare 1**] 1. money, currency; coin. 2. para (one fortieth of a kurush). **— arslanın ağzında** (lit. Money is inside the mouth of a lion.) Earning money is a hard struggle. **— bas=** to coin money, to mint. **—yı bayıl=** *colloq.* to pay. **— boz=** to change money. **— canlı, — canlısı** money-lover. **— cezası** *law* fine, penalty. **— cicoz** *slang* The money is all gone. **— cüzdanı** purse, pocketbook; wallet. **— çek=** /dan/ 1. to draw money (from a bank). 2. to squeeze money out of somebody. **—ya çevir=** *com.* to realize assets. **—dan çık=** to have to spend money. **— çıkar=** 1. to issue money. 2. to make money. **—sını çıkar=** to pay its own cost. **— darbet=** to mint. **—yı denize at=** to waste money. **— dök=** /ı/ to spend a lot of money. **— et=** to be worth (something). **— etme=** 1. to be worth nothing. 2. to have no effect; to be in vain. **beş — etmez** He is not worth a cent. **— farkı** rate of exchange. **— göz, — gözlü** money-lover. **— hesabı** *banking* cash account. **— hukuku** monetary law. **— ile değil** very cheap. **— kazan=** to earn money. **— kes=** 1. to coin money. 2. *colloq.* to earn a lot of money. **— kır=** *colloq.* to earn a lot of money. **— kopar=** /dan/ to exact money from somebody. **— oyunu** 1. betting, gambling. 2. risking money on any speculative transaction. **— parayı çeker** Money breeds money. **—sıyla rezil ol=** to pay a lot of money for some work and end up with the job badly done. **— sızdır=** /dan/ to squeeze money out of somebody. **—sını sokağa at=** to throw money away. **—yı sökül=** *slang* to have to pay. **—yı tedavülden kaldırma** demonetization. **— tut=** 1. to have money. 2. to save money. **—yı veren düdüğü çalar** Pay the piper and call the tune. **— yap=** to earn money; to save money. **— yatır=** /a/ *com.* to invest. **— ye=** 1. to spend money freely. 2. to accept a bribe. **— yedir=** to bribe.

parabol[lü] بارابول F *geom.* parabola.
parabolik[ɛ¹] بارابولیك F parabolic.
paraçol باراچول It 1. *naut.* knee, bracket (of timber or iron). 2. *naut.* console, corbel. 3. light one-horse carriage without springs.
paradi بارادی F gallery (in theater).
paraf باراف F paraph, flourish at the end of a signature.
parafazi بارافازی F *psych.* paraphasia.
parafe بارافه F initialed, approved. **— et=** /ı/ to initial.
parafin بارافین F paraffin wax.
parafudr بارافودر F *elec.* static shield.
paragat باراغات *var. of* **paraketa 1**.
paragraf باراغراف F 1. paragraph. 2. paragraph sign.
paraka (.′.) باراكه *var. of* **paraketa 1**.
paraketa 1 (..′.) باراكته Gk *fishing* long fishing line with a number of

paraketa

hooks. — **oltası** float with several fish-hooks suspended from it.

paraketa 2, parakete (...'.) بالاگته براگته
بالا قط It *naut.* log for gauging speed of a ship. — **at=** to heave the log. — **dolabı** log reel. — **hesabı** dead reckoning. — **savlusu** log-line. — **tahtası** log-boat, log-ship.

parala=ᴿ بالالمق بالالدى بالالدس /ı/ to break, tear or cut in pieces.

paralan=" 1 بالالنمق بالالنى بالالدنو *pass. of* **parala=**, 1. to be broken, torn or cut to pieces. 2. to go to pieces. 3. to strain every nerve. 4. to exert oneself greatly.

paralan=" 2 بالالنى to become rich.
paralat=" بالالدى /ı, a/ *caus. of* **parala=**.
paralel بالالل F parallel. — **kenar** *neol., geom.* parallelogram. —**lik** parallelism. — **yüz** *neol., geom.* parallelepiped.

paralı بالالى بالالى 1. rich, having money. 2. requiring payment, not free. — **pullu** rich, wealthy.

paralıkᴷⁱ بالالق of so many paras. **bir — et=** /ı/ to ruin somebody's reputation; to disgrace.

paralojizm بالالوژزم F *log.* paralogism.
parametre (...'.) بالامتره F *math.* parameter.
paramparça (...'.) بالام بارچه all in pieces; ragged, tattered.
parankima (...'.) بالنكيما L *biol.* parenchyma.
paranoya (...'.) بالانويا F *path.* paranoia.
parantez بالانتز F parenthesis, bracket.
parapet بالابت It *naut.* 1. parapet. 2. bulwarks of a ship.

parasız بالاسز 1. without money; penniless. 2. free, without paying. — **pulsuz** penniless. — **tellâl** person who spreads gossip. —**lık** poverty; pennilessness.

Paraşam بالاشام *obs., var. of* **Berrüşşam**.
paraşüt بالاشوت F parachute. —**çü** 1. parachutist. 2. *slang* person who tries to get into places without payment.

paratifo (...'.) بالاتيفو It F *med.* paratyphoid (fever).

paratoner بالاتونر F. lightning conductor, lightning rod.

paravan, paravana (...'.) بالاوان F folding screen.

parazit بالازيت F 1. *biol.* parasite. 2. *radio* atmospherics, static; cross-talk.

parça بارچه P 1. small piece; piece, fragment; bit. 2. length of cloth. 3. *mus.* piece. 4. *slang* pretty woman. 5. *slang* dope. —**sı** used contemptuously of a person of a certain category, as in **bakkal parçası** a very ordinary grocer, **hizmetçi parçası** a miserable servant. — **başına** per piece; piece-work. — **bohçası** rag bag. — **emniyetli** *mil.* splinter-proof. — **mal** piece goods, parcels, sundry goods. — **parça** 1. in pieces; in bits. 2. by separate pieces; in installments. 3. tattered, in rags. — **parça et=** /ı/ to break into pieces, to tear into pieces. — **parça sat=** /ı/ 1. to sell piecemeal. 2. to sell retail. — **purça** *same as* **parçak purçak**. — **tesirli bomba** *mil.* fragmentation bomb.

parçacı بارچه جى 1. seller of piece goods. 2. seller of spare parts, dealer in accessories.

parçak purçakᴷⁱ بارچاق بورچاق *colloq.* in rags, in fragments, much broken or torn.

parçala=ᴿ بارچه لمق بارچه لدس /ı/ to break into pieces, to cut into parts. —**n=** 1. *pass.* 2. to exert oneself greatly to please another. —**ndır=**, —**t=** /ı, a/ *caus. of* **parçala=**.

parçalı بارچه لى - بارچه لو 1. pieced; in parts. 2. mended, patched. 3. sarcastic; biting; piquant. — **bohça** patchwork cover for a bundle of clothes. — **bohça gibi** composed of ill-assorted pieces. — **conta** *auto.* detachable rim, interchangeable rim. — **kalıp** piece mold. — **komedi** episodic play, revue strung together on a simple theme. — **tarz** newsreel style.

pardesü بارده سو F light overcoat.
pardı باردى half-burned piece of wood.
pardon باردون F Pardon me. Excuse me.
pardüm (—.) باردوم P *lrnd., same as* **paldım**.
pare 1 (—.) باره P *lrnd.* 1. piece, portion, fragment; part. 2. money, coin. — **pare** all in pieces.

-pare 2 (—.) باره P *lrnd.* piece, fragment, *as in* **mehpare, yekpare**.

parela, parele (..'.) بارله It *naut.* parallel block, block of the very largest kind.

parenc (—.) بارنج P *lrnd.* fee paid to a messenger for his trouble, tip.

parılda=ᴿ بارلدامق بارلدى to gleam, to glitter; to twinkle. —**ma** *verbal n.* —**t=** /ı/ *caus.*

parıl parıl بارل بارل gleamingly; glittering brightly; flashing. — **parla=** to shine very brightly. — **yan=** to burn in flames.

parıltı بارلتى glitter, gleam, flash.
parima بارما It *naut.* boat's painter.
parin (——.), **parine** (——.) بارين P *lrnd.* last year, of the last year.

parite بارته F *com.* parity.
parkᴷⁱ بارك F 1. public garden, park. 2. parking place (for automobiles). 3. play pen. 4. *mil.* park, depot.

parke باركه F parquet, parqueted floor; small cobblestones.

parla=ᴿ بارلامق بارلدس 1. to shine. 2. to burn and blaze up. 3. to rise in life, to become distinguished; to acquire influence. 4. to break out suddenly in anger, to flare up. 5. *colloq.* to look smart. 6. to cause to fly at a quarry (falcon).

parlakᴷⁱ بارلاق 1. bright, brilliant, shining. 2. beautiful, pretty, handsome.

3. successful, influential. 4. *slang* good looking (lad). —**lık** 1. brilliance. 2. beauty. 3. influence; ability.
parlâmento (...´.) پارلامنتو It parliament.
parlat=ᵗ پارلاتمق 1. /ı/ *caus. of* **parla**=. 2. /ı/ to polish, to burnish. 3. *slang* to drink. —**ma** *verbal n.*
parlâtoryo (...´.) پارلاتوریو It reception or visitor's room in a special institution, parlor.
parlayış پارلایش *verbal n. of* **parla**=.
parmakᵍⁱ پارمس پارمق پرماق 1. finger; toe. 2. spoke (of a wheel). 3. bar, rail, rod; single bar of a railing. 4. a measure of length (1.25 inch); a tenth of an **arşın**. 5. touch or taste of something. —**ı ağzında kal**= 1. to be greatly astonished. 2. to be lost in admiration. — **at**= to make trouble, to interfere. — **bas**= 1. /a/ to draw attention (to a point). 2. to dip one's thumb into ink and press it on a document as a signature; to fingerprint. —**ımı basarım** /a/ I'll take my oath on it. —**ını bile oynatma**= not to move a finger. —**ına dola**= /ı/ to keep bothering about something, to fret. —**la gösteril**= to be a person of distinction, to be famous. — **hesabı** 1. counting on the fingers. 2. *pros.* syllabic meter. — **ısır**= to bite one's finger in astonishment. —**ı içinde** He has a hand in it, he has a finger in it. — **izi** fingerprint. — **kadar** very small, tiny. — **kaldı** almost, nearly. — **kaldır**= to raise the hand *asking for permission to speak, at a meeting.* — **kalemleri** the long bones of the fingers and toes. — **kapı** 1. gate of rails or bars. 2. hinged window-grating. 3. bier. — **karıştır**= /a/ to meddle. — **kemikleri** *anat.* phalanges. —**ını koy**= /a/ to take a hand in a matter. —**ında oynat**= /ı/ to twist somebody around one's little finger. —**ına sar**= /ı/ *same as* **parmağına dola**=. —**la sayıl**= to be counted on one's fingers; to be very rare. —**ını sok**= /a/ to meddle with something. — **tatlısı** pastry made in the shape of fingers. —**ının ucunda çevir**= /ı/ to do something easily and skillfully. — **usulü** *pros.* system of syllabic meter. —**ı uzun bal yemez, kısmeti olan yer** *proverb* A benefit sometimes falls not to the one who worked for it, but to another who happens to be lucky. — **üzümü** a long kind of grape. —**larını ye**= to like a dish very much.
parmakçı پارمقجی 1. lathe-operator making railings, banisters, or wheel-spokes. 2. firebrand; inciter.
parmakla=ʳ پارمقلامق پارمقدس /ı/ 1. to finger; to meddle with. 2. to stir up, to incite. —**n**= *pass.* —**t**= /ı, a/ *caus. of* **parmakla**=.
parmaklıkᵍⁱ پارمقلق railing, balustrade; banisters; grating; grill.
parmıcan پارمیجان It Parmesan cheese.

parola (..´.) پارولا It watchword; password; parole.
parpa پارپا young turbot.
par par پار پار *only in* — **parla**= to shine brightly. — **yan**= to burn in flames.
pars 1 پارس P leopard, *zool., Felis pardus.* — **gibi bacaklarından ayır**= /ı/ to tear to pieces.
Pars 2 (—) پارس P *geog.* Persia proper; the Province of Shiraz.
parsa 1 (.´.) پارسا P money gathered up from the crowd. —**yı başkası topladı** Someone else got the benefit. — **topla**= to make a collection of money from a crowd, to pass the hat.
parsa 2 (——) پارسا P *lrnd.* pious, holy; chaste; conscientious.
parsal 1 پارسال old, worn (clothes); in tatters.
parsalˡⁱ **2** (——) پارسال P *lrnd.* last year.
parsayî (———) پارسایی P *lrnd.* piety, holiness, conscientiousness; blamelessness.
parsel پارسل F plot (of land).
parselle=ʳ پارسللمك /ı/ to subdivide.
parseng (—.) پارسنك P makeweight.
Parsi (——) پارسی P *lrnd.* 1. Persian. 2. the ancient language of Persia proper.
parşömen پارشومن F parchment, vellum. — **kâğıdı** parchment paper.
partal پارتال *same as* **parsal 1**.
parter پارتر F parterre (in a theater).
parti پارتی F 1. political party; party (social). 2. game. 3. consignment (of goods). 4. bargain, something acquired very cheaply. —**yi kaybet**= to lose the game. —**yi vur**= to do a good stroke of business.
partici پارتیجی partisan. —**lik** partisanship.
partili پارتیلی member of a political party.
partisyon پارتیسیون F *mus.* score.
partizan پارتیزان F partisan. —**lık** partisanship.
parya (.´.) پاریا F pariah, outcast.
pas 1 پاس 1. rust; tarnish. 2. dirt. — **aç**= 1. to clean off rust. 2. *colloq.* to have a drink. — **bağla**= to rust, to get rusty. — **lâlesi** yellow crocus; brown iris, *bot., Iris lurida.* — **tut**= to rust.
pas 2 پاس E 1. *soccer* pass; *bridge* pass. 2. *card* stake. — **geç**= *slang* to give up. — **ver**= /a/ *slang* to give an encouraging glance (woman), to make a pass at (man to woman).
pas 3 (—) پاس P *lrnd.* 1. watch of the day or night, three hours. 2. care; vigilance. 3. attention, regard. 4. solicitude, anxiety; fear, terror. 5. part, portion.
pasa پاسا carpentry covering, beading, batten.
pasaj پاساژ F 1. arcade with shops. 2. passage (of a writing).
pasakᵍⁱ پاساك dirty and untidy clothes; dirt, filth.

pasaklı پاساقلى dirty, filthy; slovenly, untidy in dress.
pasaparola (....'.) پاصاپارولا پاساپارولا It 1. *mil.* verbal command passed along the ranks. 2. *naut.* a passing a watchword, password. 3. *slang* in agreement; coming to an understanding. — **et**= to pass the word along.
pasaport پاساپورط پاساپورت It passport. —**unu al**= *colloq.* to be fired. —**unu ver**= *colloq.* /a/ to fire.
pasavan پاساوان F safe-conduct pass.
pasban (——) پاسبان P *lrnd.* watchman, guard, sentinel. —**ı felek** the planet Saturn.
pasbanî (———) پاسبانى P *lrnd.* watching, the duty and action of a sentry.
pasdar (——) پاسدار P *lrnd.* 1. watchman, guard, sentinel. 2. trustworthy and loyal man.
pasdarî (———) پاسدارى P *lrnd.* 1. watchmanship, guardianship. 2. loyalty to duty.
pasebük[kü] (—..) پاسبك P *lrnd.* agile, swift.
pasif پاسيف F 1. passive. 2. *com.* liabilities, debts. — **korunma** civil defense. — **mukavemet** passive resistance.
pasitade (—.—.) پاستاده P *lrnd.* standing on foot, ready, in order.
paskal پاسقال F 1. comic of the old Turkish theater. 2. buffoon, clown. —**lık** comicalness, funny actions.
paskalya (..'.) پاسقاليه بصقاليه بصقلى پاسقاليه Gk Easter. — **çiçeği** daisy, marguerite, *bot.*, *Bellis perennis*; a kind of lilac. — **çöreği** special bread-like cake for Easter. — **yumurtası** eggs dyed in gay colors for the Easter season. — **yumurtası gibi** over made-up (woman). —**lık** made for Easter.
paslan=[ır] پاسلنمق 1. to become tarnished or rusty. 2. to be coated (tongue). —**dır**= /ı/ *caus.* —**ış**, —**ma** *verbal n.* of **paslan**=.
paslaş=[ır] پاسلشمق 1. *soccer* to pass the ball to each other. 2. *slang* to exchange amorous glances, to make passes at each other.
paslı پاسلو پاسلى 1. rusty, dirty. 2. pale, faded.
pasmantarı[nı] ('...) پاسمنطارى *bot.* uredo. —**giller** *neol.*, *Uredinales*.
paso (.'.) پاسو It 1. pass (on a railway etc.); free pass; reduced-rate pass. 2. *colloq.*, used in **benden paso!** I have had enough of it; it is none of my concern. I'm through.
paspas پاسپاس [papas 2] doormat.
pasta 1 ('.) پاستا It sweet cake; pastry; tart.
pasta 2 ('.) پاستا Gk pleat, fold.
pastacı پاستاجى pastry seller.
pastahane (..—.) پاستهخانه pastry shop.
pastal پاسطال بصطال بيصطال bundle of tobacco leaves.
pastav پاستاو بصتاو Hung 1. a whole piece of broadcloth or other woolen cloth. 2. large castanet used by the leading actor in the old Turkish theater. —**la pazarlık** wholesale bargain.
pastırma پسترمه پاسطرمه پاصدرمه پاستيرمه pressed meat cured with garlic and other spices. — **çemeni** cummin used in preparing **pastırma**. —**sını çıkar**= /ın/ to give somebody a beating. — **yazı** spell of warm sunny weather late in November. —**cı** maker or seller of **pastırma**.
pastika (..'.) پاستقا It *naut.* snatch block, fair-leader.
pastil پاستيل F *pharm.* pastille, lozenge.
pastinay پاستيناى F common parsnip, *bot.*, *Pastinaca sativa*.
pastörize پاستوريزه F pasteurized.
pastra ('.) پاسترا Gk a card game.
pasuh (—.) پاسخ P *lrnd.* answer.
pasüvar (—.—) پاسوار P *lrnd.* agile walker, good walker.
pasvan (——) پاسوان P *lrnd.*, same as **pasban**.
-**paş** (—) پاش P *lrnd.* diffusing, scattering, as in **ziyapaş**.
paşa پاشا 1. *Ott. hist.* pasha the highest title of civil and military officials. 2. *mil.* general; navy admiral. **P**— **Eli** *Ott. hist.* European Turkey. — **bardağı** greatly valued thing. — **kapısı** *Ott. hist.* 1. Sublime Porte. 2. government office (in the provinces). — **ol**= *colloq.* to get very drunk.
paşalı پاشالى *Ott. hist.* 1. officer in the service of a Pasha. 2. who has a Pasha (to back him).
paşalık[ğı] پاشاليق 1. the quality, rank and function of a Pasha. 2. territory ruled by a Pasha.
paşazade (..—.) پاشازاده son of a pasha.
paşib (——) پاشيب P *lrnd.* 1. very steep descent, steep decline. 2. ladder.
paşide (——.) پاشيده P *lrnd.* sprinkled, scattered; diffused.
paşina (———), **paşine** (——.) پاشينه پاشينا P *lrnd.* heel. —**i der** projecting pivot below a door on which it turns.
paşmak[ğı] پاشماق بشماق same as **başmak**.
pat 1 پات flat, snub (nose).
pat 2 پات بات 1. thud. 2. with a thud, suddenly. — **küt** noise of repeated blows (sharp and dull in turn). — **pat** thuds; footfalls.
pat 3 پات 1. starwort, *bot.*, *Aster*. 2. diamond pin shaped like an aster.
pat 4 پات F *chess* stalemate.
pata 1 ('.) پاتا It *cards* drawn game; deadlock. — **çak**= *slang* to wave the hand in greeting.

pata 2 (′.) باطه باتَه باتا It *naut.* bridle of a bowline to a sail.

patadak^(tı), **patadan** باتادك باتادن *suddenly.*

patagos باتاغوس Gk *slang* five-kurush coin.

patak^(tı) باتاق *colloq.* beating.

patakla=^r باتاقلامق /ı/ to give a beating to somebody; to beat. **—n=** *pass.*

patalya (.′.) باتاليه It 1. *naut.* very small boat, dinghy, punt. 2. decoy-bird.

patata (..′.) باتاتا It *colloq.*, *var.* of **patates**.

patates (...′) باتاتس Gk potato, *bot.*, Solanum tuberosum.

patavatsız باتاوات سز who talks at random and thoughtlessly; tactless. **—lık** thoughtlessness, tactlessness.

paten باتن F skate.

patent باتنت F *same as* **patenta**.

patenta (.′.) باتنتا It 1. patent, patent right, license. 2. letters of naturalization. 3. *naut.* bill of health. **—sı altına al=** /ı/ to domineer (over).

patentalı باتنتالى 1. having naturalization papers. 2. possessing a license, licensed.

patır باتر tapping sound. **— kütür** with the noise of footsteps, noisily, hastily. **— patır** sound as of tapping or the fall of feet.

patırda=^r باتردامق to make a continuous knocking noise. **—t=** /ı/ 1. *caus.* 2. *slang* to have a smattering of a foreign language.

patırdı باتردى 1. noise; row. 2. tumult, disturbance. **— çıkar=** to make a row, to cause a commotion. **— et=** 1. to make a great deal of noise. 2. to cause a disturbance. **— gürültü, — kütürtü** great noise, trampling, stamping. **—ya pabuç bırakma=** not to be scared off by noisy dispute. **—ya ver=** /ı/ to put into confusion, to cause a disturbance. **—lı** very noisy; rowdy.

patik^(ği) باتيك child's shoe.

patika (.′.) باتيقه Sl footpath, track.

patinaj باتيناژ F 1. ice skating. 2. *auto.* skidding; slipping. **— yap=** 1. to skate. 2. to slip; to skid. **— zinciri** *auto.* anti-skid chain.

patis باتيس F a fine kind of cambric.

patiska (.′.) باتيسقه F cambric.

patla=^r باتلامق 1. to burst, to explode; to burst open. 2. to occur suddenly, to arrive suddenly. 3. to crack, to crackle. 4. to break out, to blurt out. 5. to burst out (with impatience, anger etc.). 6. /a/ *colloq.* to cost. **—ma** (′..) Keep calm. Wait a moment.

patlak^(ği) باتلاق 1. burst; torn open; cracked. 2. place where a thing has burst. **— gözlü** popeyed. **— ver=** 1. to burst; to burst out (rebellion). 2. to be discovered or divulged.

patlama (...′) باتلامه explosion.

patlangaç^(cı), **patlangıç**^(cı) باتلانغيچ anything that explodes with a noise, firecracker; popgun.

patlat=^r باتلاتمق 1. /ı, a/ *caus.* of **patla=**. 2. /ı/ to infuriate. 3. /a/ *colloq.* to hit, to sap.

patlayıcı باتلاييجى explosive.

patlayış باتلاييش *verbal n.* of **patla=**.

patlıcan باتليجان باطليجان [badincan] eggplant, *bot.*, Solanum melongena. **— inciri** purple fig. **—giller** *neol.*, *bot.*, Solanaceae.

patolog^(ğu) باتولوغ F pathologist.

patoloji باتولوژى F pathology.

patolojik باتولوژيك F pathological.

patos باتوس F *prov.* tractor.

Patrik^(ki) باطريك بطريق Gk Patriarch.

Patrikhane (..—.) بطريقخانه P Patriarchate.

Patriklik^(ği) بطريقلك office and functions of a Patriarch; Patriarchate.

patrisa (..′.) باتريسا It *naut.* topgallant backstay.

patron باطرون F 1. employer, head or owner of a firm or business. 2. pattern, model.

patrona (..′.) باطرونا باتروونه It *Ott. hist.* vice-admiral of the fleet. **— gemisi, —i hümayun** vice-admiral's flagship.

pattadak, pattadan (..′.) باتادك باتادن *var.* of **patadak**.

pavend (—.) باوند P *lrnd.*, *same as* **pabend**.

paviyon باويون F 1. detached building. 2. night club.

pavkır=^r باوقيرمق *prov.* to howl (wolf, etc.).

pavurya (.′.) باورى *var.* of **pağurya**.

pay 1 باى 1. share; lot, portion. 2. part, proportional part. 3. *mech.* margin, tolerance. 4. *neol.*, *math.* numerator. 5. reproach; blame. **— al=** /dan/ to get a share. **—ını al=** 1. to get one's share. 2. to get a bitter lesson. 3. to be scolded. **— bırak=** to leave a margin (for seams or trimming). **— biç=** /dan/ 1. to take as an example; to compare. 2. to deduce, to judge (from). **— et=** /ı/ to share out, to divide. **— ver=** /a/ 1. to reprove or scold. 2. to answer back.

pay 2 (—) باى P *lrnd.*, *var.* of **pa**.

payab (——) باياب P *lrnd.* 1. power of endurance, resistance or action; matter within the limits of one's power. 2. stability, durability, duration. 3. shallow. 4. end, limit.

payam بايام *prov.* almond.

payan (——) بايان P 1. *lrnd.* end, extremity; limit, boundary; edge, margin. 2. *lrnd.* result. 3. *myst.* an experience of union with God.

payanda (.′.) بايَنده [payende] 1. prop, support. 2. *arch.* pillar, stanchion. **—ları çöz=**

payandala= *slang* to run away, to go off, to break bounds. **— kemer** *arch.* flying buttress. **— ver=, — vur=** /a/ to prop up, to shore.

payandala= با ینداز • لا سد /ı/ to prop up.

payansız (— —.) با یا نسـ *Irnd.* endless, unending, unlimited.

payapay با یا پای *colloq.* completely.

paybaf (— —) با یا ف P *Irnd.* weaver.

paybend (—.) با یبند P *var.* of **pabend**.

paybest (—.), **paybeste** (—..) با یبست یا بسه P *same as* **pabest, pabeste**.

payda *neol., math.* denominator. **—ları eşitle=** to reduce to a common denominator. **—dan kurtar=** to eliminate the denominator.

paydam (— —) با یدام P *Irnd., same as* **padam**.

paydar (— —) با یدار P *Irnd., same as* **payidar**.

paydaş *neol.* participator, partner. **—lı** having sharers. **—lık** participating, sharing. **—lık kanunu** law of participation.

paydos با یدوس Gk 1. cessation from work; break, rest. 2. *cry given to workmen to knock off work.* 3. Enough! Quit it! **— borusu çal=** to quit work. **— et=** to quit work, to stop working.

paye 1 (—.) با یه P 1. degree of rank; honorary grade. 2. dignity, esteem. 3. *arch.* pillar, prop, support. 4. *Irnd.* step, rung of a ladder. 5. *Irnd.* footing, foundation basis. **—i fetva** *Ott. hist.* the rank of Şeyhülislam. **—i mücerrede** *Ott. hist.* honorary rank held without official duties. **— paye** *Irnd.* step by step, by degrees. **— ver=** /a/ 1. to show deference to. 2. to esteem unduly.

-paye 2 (—.) با یه P *Irnd.* attaining the rank of, *as in* **asmanpaye**.

payedar (—.—) با یدار P *Irnd.* having rank. **—i** (—.——) P, **—lık** a having a rank.

payeli (—..) با یه لی با یلی 1. having a rank. 2. *arch.* supported by pillars.

payendaz (—.—) با ینداز P *Irnd.* 1. carpets spread on the pavement for the public entry of a king. 2. gift laid at the feet. 3. doormat.

payende (—..) با ینده P *Irnd.* 1. standing; on foot. 2. lasting, enduring; eternal. 3. *same as* **payanda**.

payendegân (—..—) با ینده گان P *Irnd.* eternal things.

payendegi (—..—) با ینده گی P *Irnd.* permanence, durability, everlastingness.

paygâh (— —) با یگاه P *Irnd.* 1. rank, position; dignity. 2. place for depositing shoes at the entrance of a house. 3. the landing at the bottom of a staircase.

payidar (—.—) با یدار |paydar| *Irnd.* permanent, constant; stable, firm; enduring. **— ol=** to be everlasting or permanent. **—i** (—.——) P, **—lık** (—.—.) 1. permanence. 2. stability, firmness.

payimal (—.—) با یمال |paymal| *Irnd.* 1. trampled upon, trodden under foot; oppressed, destroyed; despised. 2. defeated; ill-treated; ruined. 3. abject, wretched, miserable. **—i** (—.——) P devastation, ruin.

payitaht (—..) با یتخت |paytaht| capital city, seat of government.

payiz (— —), (—.) با ییز P *Irnd.* 1. autumn. 2. old age.

paykâr (— —) با یکار P *Irnd.* 1. minor tax-collector. 2. servant; garbage collector.

paykûb (— —) با یکوب P *Irnd., same as* **pakûb**.

payla= با یلا با یله مک /ı/ 1. to give one his due; to scold. 2. to assign a share to.

paylâgz (—.) با یلاغز P *Irnd., same as* **palâgz**.

paylaş= با یلاش با یلشمك /ı/ to divide and share out, to share. **—ıl=** to be shared out. **—ma** *verbal n.* of **paylaş=. —tır=** /ı, a/ *caus.*

paylat= با یلات با یلتمك /ı, a/ *caus.* of **payla=**.

paymaçan (— — —) با یماجان P *Irnd.* 1. place for leaving the slippers. 2. penance practiced by the Sufis in which the offender is made to stand on one foot, his left hand touching his right ear, and his right hand touching his left ear.

paymal (— — —) با یمال P *Irnd., same as* **payimal**.

paymüzd (—.) با یمزد P *Irnd., same as* **pamüzd**.

paytaht (—.) با یتخت P *Irnd., same as* **payitaht**.

paytak 1 با یتاق • با یطاق • با یطاق knock-kneed; bandy-legged.

paytak 2 با یتق |beydak| 1. *chess* pawn. 2. *Irnd.* foot soldier. **— yolu** *obs.* path, byway.

payton با یطون *prov., var.* of **fayton**.

puyvend (—.) با یوند P *Irnd., same as* **pavend**.

payzen (—.) با یزن P *Irnd.* 1. prisoner in chains. 2. culprit; vagabond. 3. barefoot. **— kıyafetli** in the garb of a prisoner or ne'er-do-well. **— payzen gez=** to go barefoot.

payzib (— —) با یزیب P *Irnd.* bangle, anklet.

pazar با زار |bazar| 1. market, market place; bazaar. 2. *w. cap.* Sunday. 3. bargaining, bargain; trade. **P—a** on Sunday. **— başı** *archaic* warden of a market. **— boz=** 1. to close an open-air market. 2. to break a bargain. 3. to spoil another's plans. **—a çıkar=** /ı/ to put on sale. **— et=** to bargain. **P— günü** Sunday; on Sunday. **— kayığı** *Ott. hist.* large heavy rowboat carrying passengers and freight to the villages on the Bosphorus. **— kayığı gibi**

pazarcı بازارجى seller in an outdoor market.
pazarla=ʳ بازارلامق com. to market. —**ma** marketing.
pazarlaş=ʳ بازارلشمق /la/ to bargain; to agree on a price.
pazarlıkᵍⁱ بازارلق 1. a bargaining, bargain; deal. 2. agreement, understanding. —**lı alış veriş** sale by bargaining, by negotiating.
Pazartesi (..'..) بازارئرتەسى Monday. —**ne**, —**ye** on Monday.
pazede (—..) بازده P lrnd. 1. who has set his foot. 2. trampled, trodden under foot. —**i adem** who has gone to annihilation, annihilated.
pazen (—.) بازن [**bazen 1**] cotton flannel.
Pazend (—.) بازند P lrnd., name of one of the Zoroastrian books; commentary on the Zend.
pazenkᵍⁱ بازنك P lrnd. pimp, pander.
pazı 1 بازو [Persian **paju**] chard, bot., Beta vulgaris cicla.
pazı 2 بازو بازو [**bâzû**] 1. arm; brachium. 2. strength, muscle. — **kemiği** anat. humerus.
pazı 3 بازو Gk prov. 1. a kind of thin bread. 2. a lump of dough big enough for one loaf of bread.
pazıbend بازبند [**bâzûbend**] armlet; amulet worn round the arm.
pazval بازوال shoe-maker's knee-strap.
pazvant بازوانت بازوانت [**pasban**] watchman, night watchman.
pazvend (—.) بازوند [**bazubend**] lrnd. armlet.
peçe پچه It veil. —**le=** /ı/ to veil; to camouflage. —**leme** camouflage. —**li** veiled.
peçeta (..'.) پچته Sp peseta (coin).
peçete (..'.) پچته It napkin, table napkin.
peçiçᶜⁱ پچیج Hind a game like parcheesi in which sea shells are used instead of dice.
peçuta پچوته large bonito, zool., Pelamys sarda.
peçvakᵏⁱ (.—) پچواك P lrnd. interpreter, translator.
pedagogᵍᵘ پداغوغ F pedagogue.
pedagoji پداغوژى F pedagogy.
pedal پدال F pedal.
pedavra (..'.) پداورا Gk same as **padavra**.
peder پدر P father. —**âne** (..—.) P fatherly, paternal.
pederender پدراندر P lrnd. step-father.
pederî (..—) پدرى P lrnd. 1. fatherly, paternal. 2. fatherhood, paternity.
pederlikᵍⁱ پدرلك 1. fatherhood. 2. foster father.
pedershahî (..——) پدرشاهى P sociol. patriarchal. —**lik** (..——.) patriarchal system, patriarchate.
pedikür پدیکور F pedicure.
pedrud (.—) پدرود P lrnd., same as **bedrud**.
peftere پفتره P var. of **befter**.
pegâh (.—) پگاه P lrnd. early morning, in the early morning.
peh په Bravo! — **peh!** Well done! — **peh de=** colloq. to praise.
pehengir پهنگیر P lrnd., same as **mehengir**.
pehle پهله [**pehlû**] the side stone of a tomb.
Pehlevî (..—) پهلوى P Pahlavi.
pehlivan پهلوان [Persian **pehlevân**] 1. wrestler. 2. champion, mighty man, valor; hero. — **salatası** oil and vinegar eaten with bread. —**ı sipihr** lrnd. the celestial warrior, the planet Mars. — **tekkesi** Ott. hist. wrestler's lodge. — **yakısı** cantharides; blister-plaster. — **yakısı aç=** to cause immense suffering.
pehlivanâne (..——.) پهلوانانه P lrnd. special to a champion; heroic; heroically.
pehlivanî (..——) پهلوانى P lrnd. 1. heroic. 2. same as **pehlivanlık**.
pehlivanlıkᵍⁱ پهلوانلق quality or act of a wrestler; heroism.
pehlû (.—) پهلو P lrnd. 1. side. 2. wing of an army. — **be pehlû** P side by side.
pehlûbüzürg (.—..) پهلوبزرك P lrnd. surrounded by numerous supporters; great, noble.
pehlûdar (.——) پهلودار P lrnd. 1. helper; generous, beneficent. 2. sarcastically equivocal (word), insolent in speech.
pehn پهن P lrnd. 1. wide, broad, large; spacious. 2. flat.
pehna (.—) پهنا P lrnd. 1. width, breadth, spaciousness. 2. flatness.
pehnaver (.—.) پهناور P lrnd. wide, broad; ample. —**î** (.—.—) P wideness, breadth.
pehpehle=ʳ پهپهلمك /ı/ to flatter; to applaud.
pehriz پهریز var. of **perhiz 1**.
pejmürde پژمرده P 1. shabby, worn out, ragged. 2. faded, withered; decayed; broken down.
pejmürdegi (...—) پژمردگى P lrnd. 1. shabbiness; wretched appearance. 2. sorrow, anxiety, affliction.
pejmürderuy (...—) پژمرده روى P lrnd. woe-begone; pale-faced.
pekᵏⁱ **1** پك 1. very, much, extremely; often. 2. violently, impetuously. 3. loudly. — **âlâ** 1. very good. 2. all right, very well. — **çok** very much, a great many; greatly. — **iyi** very good, excellent, very well; all right; highest grade (in classroom grading.) — **oku=** to read out loud. — **pek** at most.
pekᵏⁱ **2** پك 1. hard, firm; unyielding; strong. 2. violent, severe. 3. tight, firmly fixed. 4. loud,

fast. — **başlı** obstinate, hard-headed. — **canlı** hardy; stoical. — **gözlü** bold, courageous. — **söyle=** to speak harshly. — **yürekli** hard hearted. — **yüzlü** brazen faced; thick skinned, callous.

pekçe پكجه 1. rather hard, rather violent, somewhat hard. 2. somewhat loudly or violently. — **koş=** to run fairly fast. — **söyle=** 1. to speak somewhat loudly. 2. to talk pretty harshly.

pekdoku neol., bot. collenchyma.

Peke sarnıcı neol., biol. reservoir of Pecquet, cisterna chyli.

peki پكی [short for **pek iyi**] all right, very well.

pekin neol., phil. certain; authentic. —**lik** certitude.

pekiş=ⁱʳ پكشمك to become hard, tight or firm. —**me** verbal n. —**tir=** /ı/ caus.

pekiştirme پكشديرمه 1. stiffening, hardening. 2. neol., gram. intensive.

pekit=ⁱʳ پكتمك /ı/ 1. to make hard or firm, to strengthen. 2. reinforce, to fortify.

pekitme پكتمه arch. strengthening, stiffening. — **ayağı** buttress, prop. — **demiri** armature. — **duvarı** reinforcement wall. — **kirişi** ceiling beam.

pekleş=ⁱʳ پكلشمك to get firm, to harden, tighten. —**tir=** caus.

peklikᵍⁱ پكلك 1. hardness, firmness. 2. violence, severity. 3. stinginess. 4. constipation. — **çek=** to suffer from constipation.

pekmez پكمز 1. grape juice boiled to a sugary solid or a heavy syrup. 2. slang blood. — **akıt=** slang to spill blood. —**in olsun, sineği Bağdat'tan gelir** proverb Parasites soon gather round one who has money. — **toprağı** marl. —**ci** seller of grape-molasses. —**li** sweetened with grape-molasses.

peksimet پكسمت Gk hard biscuit.

pelâs (.—) پلاس P lrnd., same as **palas 1**.

pelâspâre (.—.) پلاسپاره P lrnd. rags, tattered clothes.

pelâspûş (.—.) پلاسپوش P lrnd. 1. clothed in rags. 2. clad in dervish garb.

pele پله P lrnd. 1. scale of a balance. 2. step, stair, rung of a ladder.

pelekᵏⁱ پلك P lrnd. eyelid.

peleng پلنگ P lrnd. 1. leopard, panther. 2. warrior, hero.

pelengâheng (..—.) پلنگاهنگ P lrnd. leopard-like; eager to attack.

pelengâne (..—.) پلنگانه P lrnd. like a leopard; heroic.

pelengî (..—) پلنگی P lrnd. quality or disposition of a leopard.

pelengîn (..—) پلنگین P lrnd. leopardlike.

pelengîne (..—.) پلنگینه P lrnd. coat or rug of leopard skin.

pelengir پلنگیر [pehengir] carpenter's wooden gauge.

pelenkᵍⁱ پلنك same as **peleng**.

pelesenkᵍⁱ پلسنك [belesan] balm, balsam. — **ağacı** 1. xylobalsamum, wood of the balsam tree. 2. wood of Cuaiacum officinale. — **yağı** balm of Gilead, balm of Mecca.

pelid (.—) پلید P lrnd. dirty, filthy, nasty; foul. —**î** (.——) P dirtiness, filthiness; dirt, filth.

pelin پلین wormwood, bot., Artemisia absinthium. — **ruhu** 1. tincture of wormwood. 2. absinthe. — **şarabı** obs. vermouth. — **tuzu** potassium carbonate.

pelit پلیت [bellût 1] 1. acorn. 2. valonia. — **ağacı** valonia oak, bot., Quercus aegilops.

pelte پلته [palide] flavored gelatine dessert; jelly-like; flabby.

peltekᵍⁱ پلتك stutterer, lisper, one who speaks indistinctly; lispingly.

pelteklen=ⁱʳ, **peltekleş=**ⁱʳ پلتكلنمك پلتكلشمك to lisp; to begin to stammer.

pelteklikᵍⁱ پلتكلك stammering, lisping, lisp.

peltelen=ⁱʳ پلتهلنمك 1. to gel. 2. to become flabby. —**dir=** /ı/ caus.

pelteleş=ⁱʳ پلتهلشمك same as **peltelen=**. —**tir=** caus.

pelür پلور F onion-skin. — **kâğıdı** onion-skin paper.

pelüş پلوش F text. plush, shag.

pembe پنبه [penbe] pink, rose color; rosy. — **gör=** /ı/ to see things through rose-colored glasses, to be optimistic.

pembeleş=ⁱʳ پنبهلشمك to turn pink.

pembelikᵍⁱ پنبهلك rose color, rosiness.

pembezar (..—) پنبهزار [penbezar] a fine shirting material.

penagâh (.——) پناگاه P lrnd. place of refuge, shelter or protection.

penah 1 (.—) پناه P lrnd. 1. a taking refuge, a seeking refuge or protection. 2. place of refuge, shelter or protection; asylum, stronghold; protection, refuge. 3. protector, one to whom one flees for refuge.

-**penah 2** (.—) پناه P lrnd. who affords protection, who is a refuge, as in **risaletpenah**.

-**penahî** (.——) پناهی P lrnd., forms abstr. nouns, as in **adaletpenahî**, **vezaretpenahî**.

penbe پنبه P lrnd. 1. cotton. 2. anything soft. — **ipliği** cotton thread. —**bez** P cotton carder. —**dar** (..—) P padded or quilted with cotton. —**çul** (..—) P a fine shirting material. —**dehan** (...—) P who speaks little, taciturn. —**dergûş** (...—) P who refuses to heed advice or warning; deaf; negligent, heedless. —**duz** (..—) P cotton carder.

—riz (..—) P cotton-spinning (machine); cotton-spinner. **—zar** (..—) P cotton field. **—zen** P dresser of cotton.

penc پنج P 1. lrnd. five. 2. dice five. 3. art cinquefoil, ornamental foliation with five cusps or points. **— biçare** lrnd. (lit. the five helpless ones.) the planets Mercury, Venus, Mars, Jupiter, and Saturn. **— cihar dice** a five and a four. **— ü dü*. — ü se*. — ü yek*.**

pencah (.—) پنجاه P lrnd. fifty. **—üm** (.—.) P fiftieth.

pencberg پنج برگ P art cinquefoil.

pence پنجه P lrnd. 1. same as **pençe**. 2. any group of five things or five people. 3. handle, hilt. **—i âfitab** the spreading rays of the sun. **—i âl-i abâ** drawing made in the form of the palm of a hand, in which the names of the Prophet Muhammad, Ali, Hasan, Hüseyin and Fatma are written. **—i biçare** same as **penç biçare. —i çınar** leaf of the plane tree. **— der pence** with fingers locked in fingers (in a trial of strength). **—i duzdide** five intercalary days added to the Persian year. **—i elmas, —i fulâd** a steel hand with a strong spring with which athletes try their strength. **—i hurşid** same as **pence-i âfitab.**

pencegir (..—) پنجه گیر P lrnd. who locks fingers with another in a trial of strength. **— ol=** to make a trial of strength with another.

pencere (.'..) پنجره P window. **— boşluğu** window bay. **— eteği** wall from window to floor. **— kanadı** leaf of a window. **— peykesi** window seat. **— yanağı** recess for a window.

pencgâh (.—) پنجگاه P Or. mus. one of the most ancient compound **makams.**

pencgâne (.—.) پنجگانه P lrnd. composed of five elements or members; consisting of five parts.

pencidü پنج و دو |penc ü dü| dice a five and a two.

pencikᵏⁱ پنجك Ott. hist. title deed delivered from the customs house to the owner of a slave on payment of the duty.

pencikli پنجكلی sold by title deed. **— köle** slave sold in this way.

pencpa (.—), **pencpaye** (.—.) پنجپا پنجپایه P lrnd. 1. crab. 2. the sign Cancer.

pencşembih پنجشنبه P lrnd., same as **Perşembe.**

pencüm, pencümin (..—) پنجم پنجمین P lrnd. fifth.

pencüse پنج و سه P dice a five and a three.

pencüyek پنج و یك P dice a five and a one.

pençe پنجه [pence] 1. paw, claw, the whole hand. 2. strength, violence. 3. talon; sole (for shoe-repair). 4. Ott. hist. official signature of high officials. 5. prov. handful. **— at=** /a/ 1. to lay hands on, to seize. 2. to claw. **— pençe in patches. — pençe yanaklar** fresh-pink cheeks (as though they had just been slapped). **— vur=** /a/ to re-sole (shoe).

pençele=ʳ پنجه لمك /ı/ 1. to claw, to paw. 2. to seize, to grasp. **—n=** pass.

pençeleş=ⁱʳ پنجه لشمك /la/ 1. to lock fingers with another and have a trial of strength. 2. to come to grips with; to engage in fierce contest; to struggle.

pençeli پنجه لی 1. having claws. 2. formidable, fierce. 3. repaired, resoled (shoe). 4. Ott. hist. marked with the official signature. **— ferman** Ott. hist. decree bearing the official signature of the Sultan.

pend پند P lrnd. advice, counsel; admonition, exhortation.

pendifrankᵏⁱ پندی فرانی Gk slang blow, slap. **— at=** /a/ to slap.

pendir پندیر [penir] prov., same as **peynir.**

pendname (.—.) پندنامه P lrnd. book of counsel and advice.

peneplen پنه پلن E geol. peneplain.

peni پنی E penny; pence.

penir (.—) پنیر P lrnd., same as **peynir.**

peniz et= پنیز ایتمك /ı/ slang to expose, to disclose (secret).

pens پنس F 1. pliers. 2. tailor. pleat.

pense پنسه F combination pliers.

pentafil پنتافیل Gk creeping cinquefoil, five-finger grass, bot., Potentilla reptans.

pepe پپه stutterer, stammerer.

pepele=ʳ پپه لمك to stammer, to stutter.

pepeme, pepeyi پپمه پپیی a stammering, stuttering; stammerer, stutterer. **—lik** a stammering; the quality of a stutterer.

perʳʳⁱ 1 پر P lrnd. 1. wing, feather. 2. the arm and hand. 3. ray of light. 4. leaf. **— u bâl*.**

-per 2 پر P lrnd. flying, that flies, as in **tizper.**

perakende (.—..) پراكنده P 1. com. retail. 2. lrnd. dispersed, scattered, disconnected. 3. lrnd. confused, disturbed. **—ci** retailer. **—dil** (.—...) P, **—hatır** (.—.—.) P lrnd. whose mind is distressed, disquieted.

peran (.—) پران P lrnd., same as **perran.**

peraver (.—.) پراور P lrnd. flying; swift.

perçem پرچم P 1. tuft of hair; long lock on the top of the head. 2. forelock of a horse. 3. fringe or tassel tied round the neck of a spear.

perçin پرچین [Persian .—] rivet; a clenching of a nail; a riveting of a bolt; a putting a nut on the protruding end of a bolt.

perçinle=ʳ پرچین لمك /ı/ 1. to rivet, to clench. 2. to fasten. **—n=, —ş=** pass.

perçinli پرچینلی riveted; fastened.

perdah پرداه پرداخ [perdaht] 1. polish,

perdahçı

glaze; gloss. 2. finishing shave. — **vur**= /a/ to finish, polish, burnish.

perdahçı بردهچی 1. polisher, burnisher. 2. *slang* boring talker; braggart; swindler.

perdahla=ʳ بردهلامق /ı/ 1. to finish, polish, burnish. 2. *slang* to swindle; to bore by talking. 3. *slang* to swear at, to abuse. —**n**= *pass*. —**t**= /ı, a/ *caus. of* **perdahla**=.

perdahlı بردهلی polished, shining.

perdahsız بردهسز unpolished; dull; matt.

perdaht (.—) بردافت P *lrnd*. 1. a completion, finishing. 2. an embellishing, a touching up; polishing, glazing; polish, glaze, gloss.

perdahte (.—.) بردافته P *lrnd*. 1. finished, polished, completed. 2. put in order; adorned.

perdar (.—) بردار P *lrnd*. 1. feathered, feathery; fledged. 2. winged.

-perdaz (.—) برداز P *lrnd*. 1. that works, does, effects, finishes, *as in* **maslahatperdaz**. 2. that occupies with, arranges, *as in* **kasideperdaz**.

perdazış (.—.) بردازش P *lrnd*. an act of making, arranging, polishing, finishing.

perde برده P 1. curtain; screen; movie screen; tapestry hung as a curtain. 2. partition shutting off the women's quarters. 3. veil; feminine honor; modesty, chastity. 4. *theater* act of a play. 5. *anat.* membrane. 6. *path.* cataract of the eye. 7. *mus.* note; the pitch of a note. 8. *mus.* fret of a stringed instrument. 9. *poet.* the sky. —**i ankebut** 1. *lrnd*. spider web, cobweb. 2. *anat.* arachnoid membrane of the brain and spinal marrow. — **arası** *theater* intermission. — **arkasında** secretly. — **ayaklılar** *zool.*, Palmipedes. —**i bini** *obs.*, *anat.* septum of the nose. —**i bülbül**, —**i çağane** *names of notes in Turkish music.* — **çek**= /a/ to veil; to conceal. —**i çeşm** *lrnd*. 1. the eyelid. 2. veil before the eyes. —**i der** *lrnd*. curtain hung before a door. —**i dil** *lrnd*. 1. *anat.* pericardium. 2. blood of the heart. —**i dirsâl** *lrnd*. (*lit.*, veil of olden years.) 1. sky. 2. *name of a note in Oriental music.* —**i Ehrimenî** *lrnd*. (*lit.*, the veil of Ahriman) lusts of the flesh; wicked spirits. —**i fânus** *lrnd*. the oiled or waxed cloth covering a lantern. —**i heftreng** *lrnd*. 1. the world; ever changing fortune. 2. the vicissitudes of life. 3. the seven heavens. —**i hicaz** *name of a note in Turkish music*. —**i iffet** *lrnd*. modesty, chastity in a woman. —**i İsagiray** *lrnd*. the fourth heaven. —**i İzidî** *lrnd*. veil interposed by God, divine mystery. —**i kumarî** *name of a note in Turkish music*. —**i mükeddir** *lrnd*. dusty veil; lusts of the flesh; wicked spirits. —**i nâmus** *lrnd*. honor, reputation. —**i nilgûn** *lrnd*. the sky. —**si sıyrık** shameless. —**i uşşak** *name of a note in Turkish music*. —**i yakut**

lrnd. 1. the seventh heaven. 2. *name of a note in Turkish music*. —**si yırtık** immodest; adulterous (woman). —**i zanbûr** *lrnd*. 1. a kind of embroidered curtain. 2. *name of a note in Turkish music*. —**i zanbûrî** *lrnd*. the sky. —**i zücacî** *lrnd*. (*lit.*, crystalline veil) 1. the sky. 2. dark cloud. 3. dark night.

perdebaz (..—) بردهباز P *lrnd*. 1. musician; singer. 2. player of a shadow show.

perdeberdar (...—) بردهبردار P *lrnd*. who lifts the curtain.

perdeberendaz (....—) بردهبراندار P *lrnd*. who throws up the veil and exhibits herself; who divulges.

perdebirun (..——) بردهبرون P *lrnd*. bold, unabashed, impudent. —**âne** (..———.) P boldly, impudently.

perdeci بردهچی 1. maker or seller of curtains. 2. *Ott. hist.* doorkeeper.

perdedar (..—) بردهدار P *lrnd*. 1. door-keeper, curtain holder. 2. curtained; veiled, screened. 3. confident. —**i felek** the moon. —**i harem** eunuch of the Sultan's women's apartments.

perdedarî (..——) بردهداری P *lrnd*. 1. office of a chamberlain. 2. keeping secrets.

perdeder بردهدر P *lrnd*. 1. impudent, immodest man; ravisher of women; slanderer or defamer of women. 2. betrayer of secrets. —**î** (...—) P immodesty; a slandering; defamation.

perdederide (...—.) بردهدریده P *lrnd*. immodest, shameless.

perdegi (..—) بردهگی P *lrnd*. 1. concealed by a curtain, veil or cover; modest, chaste woman. 2. keeper of the curtain of a house or room, chamberlain. —**i heftreng** the world; time; fortune. —**i rez** wine.

perdegiyan (..——) بردهگیان P *lrnd*. modest women. —**ı saltanat** women of the imperial family.

perdekâr (..—) بردهکار P *lrnd*. curtained (place).

perdekeş بردهکش P *lrnd*. one who draws or withdraws a curtain.

perdele=ʳ بردهلهمك بردهله /ı/ 1. to cover with a curtain or veil, to conceal. 2. *mil.* to screen or shelter. —**n**= *pass*. —**t**= /ı, a/ *caus. of* **perdele**=.

perdeli بردهلی 1. curtained, veiled; screened. 2. webbed; membranous. 3. having a cataract. 4. modest, chaste.

perdelikᵍⁱ بردهلك cloth for a curtain.

perdenişin (...—) بردهنشین P *lrnd*. 1. who lives behind a curtain or veil; who lives in seclusion. 2. modest woman; who remains constantly at home veiled from the eyes of men. 3. who is admitted to the intimacy of a grandee; angel, as being admitted to the Divine presence.

perdenişinan (...— —) پَرده نشينان P lrnd., pl. of **perdenişin**. **—ı bar** 1. those admitted to the intimacy of God. 2. men who have penetrated all religious truth. 3. the angels of heaven.

perdepuş (..—) پَرده پوش P lrnd. who has closed a curtain or veil; who keeps a secret.

perdesera پَرده سرا P lrnd. curtain, pavilion.

perdesira (...—) پَرده سرا P lrnd. musician, singer.

perdesiz پَرده سیز 1. without veil or curtain; unscreened. 2. shameless, immodest. **—lik** 1. lack of curtains. 2. immodesty, unchastity.

perdeşinas (...—) پَرده شناس P lrnd. 1. musician, singer. 2. man of intelligence, especially one versed in theology, law, or mystical philosophy.

pereme پَرَمه Gk heavy two-oared boat. **—ci** boatman.

peren پَرن P lrnd. the Pleiades.

perend پَرند P lrnd. 1. plain silk material. 2. shining surface of a polished sword; sword.

perendaver (..—.) پَرنداور P lrnd. 1. grained, damascened (sword). 2. shining sword, blade.

perende 1 (...'.) پَرنده P somersault. **— at=** to turn a somersault. **—den at=** to cheat, dupe, deceive. **— atama=** not to be able to challenge (another person)

perende 2 پَرنده P lrnd. 1. flying, volatile. 2. bird, flying creature. **— ve çerende** birds and cattle.

perendebaz (...—) پَرنده باز P lrnd. tumbler, acrobat.

perenduş, perendvar (..—) پَرندوش پَرندوار P lrnd. the night before last.

perese پَرسه 1. mason's plumbline; level. 2. direction, bearing. 3. state, condition. **—ye al=** 1. to measure from a horizontal line. 2. to weigh (a matter). **—sine düş=** to happen just at the right time, to be in the very nick of time. **bir —ye geldi ki** It came to such a point that... **—sine getir=** to choose the right moment for something.

-perest پَرست P lrnd. who serves, worships; worshiping, as in **ateşperest, putperest**.

perestar (..—) پَرستار P lrnd. 1. servant, slave. 2. worshiper.

perestaran (..— —) پَرستاران P lrnd. 1. servants. 2. worshipers. **—ı hayal** 1. worshipers of vain imaginations; poets and writers of fiction. 2. worldly minded people.

perestarâne (..— —.) پَرستارانه P lrnd. worshipingly.

perestarî (..— —) پَرستاری P lrnd. servitude; worship.

pereste پَرسته P lrnd. worshiped, adored

perestende پَرستنده P lrnd. 1. worshiper, adorer. 2. servant.

perestide (..—.) پَرستیده P lrnd. 1. worshiped. 2. served.

perestiş پَرستش P a worshiping; adoration. **— et=** /a/ to worship, to adore.

perestişkâr (...—) پَرستشکار P lrnd. adoring, worshiping; adorer. **—ân** (...— —) P adorers; worshipers **—âne** (..— —.) P adoringly. **—î** (...— —) P, **—lık** servitude; adoration.

pergâlⁱⁱ (.—) پَرگال P lrnd., same as **pergel**.

pergâle (.—.) پَرگاله P lrnd. piece, fragment. **— pergâle** in pieces.

pergâr (.—) پَرگار P lrnd., same as **pergel**. **—î** (.— —) P drawn with compasses.

pergârvar (.— —) پَرگاروار P lrnd. 1. like a pair of compasses. 2. bewildered; beating round and round a subject.

pergel پَرگل [pergâr] pair of compasses. **—leri aç=** to take long steps.

pergelle=ʳ پَرگلله /ı/ 1. to measure with a pair of compasses. 2. to think out in all detail. **—n=** pass. **—t=** /ı, a/ caus.

perger پَرگر P 1. same as **pergâr**. 2. collar or ring for the neck, especially a jeweled collar of gold.

pergune (.—.) پَرگونه P lrnd. ugly, hideous.

perhaş (.—) پَرخاش P lrnd. 1. fight, combat. 2. quarrel, altercation. **—cû** (.— —) P hot for fighting, pugnacious. **—çı** pugnacious person.

perhiz 1 پَرهیز [perhiz 2] 1. diet, regimen of an invalid. 2. an abstaining from anything forbidden; abstinence, continence. 3. a fearing and avoiding what is forbidden; caution, circumspection. 4. myst. abstinence from seeking all things but God. 5. Christian or Jewish fast. **— et=** 1. to diet. 2. to abstain. **— tut=** to fast, to keep a fast.

perhiz 2 (.—) پَرهیز P lrnd., same as **perhiz 1**. **—âne** (.— —.) P food given to the sick; diet. **—î** (.— —) P fit for diet; digestible.

perhizkâr (.— —) پَرهیزکار P 1. fasting, on a diet. 2. continent, sober; chaste. **—âne** (.— — —.) P special to an abstinent or a cautious man. **—î** (.— — —) P, **—lık** abstinence, sobriety, chastity.

perhizli پَرهیزلی 1. on a diet. 2. fasting.

peri 1 پَری P 1. fairy, good djinn. 2. beautiful person. **— bacası** geol. earth pillar. **— gibi** very beautiful, fairylike. **— hastalığı** epilepsy; hysteria. **—si hoşlanma=** to dislike. **— illeti** epilepsy. **—si pis** He likes dirt; he is never clean.

peri 2 (.—) پَری P lrnd. 1. feathered; winged, pinioned. 2. pertaining to feathers or wings.

pericik

pericikᵍⁱ پریجك 1. little fairy. 2. bolt of a door. 3. epilepsy, hysteria.
peridar (.——) پری‌دار P *lrnd.* 1. one possessed of a demon; insane. 2. wizard who has a familiar spirit; a necromancer. 3. place haunted by fairies or demons. —**i** (.———) P 1. insanity, diabolical possession. 2. witchcraft. 3. epilepsy.
peride (.—.) پریده P *lrnd.* 1. flown away. 2. faded (color).
periefsa (.—.—) پری‌افسا P *lrnd.* witch who controls spirits, exorcist.
perigirifte (.—...) پری‌گرفته P *lrnd.* possessed by a spirit; soothsayer.
perihan (.——) پری‌خوان P *lrnd.* exorcist, magician.
perili پریلی 1. haunted; possessed by a demon or spirit. 2. inauspicious, sinister.
peripeyker (.—..), **periru** (.——) پری‌پیکر ، پری‌رو P *poet.* fairy-faced, beautiful.
periruh (.—.), **periruhsar** (.—.—) پری‌روح ، پری‌روحسار P *poet.* angel-cheeked, fairy-faced, very beautiful.
periruz (.——) پری‌روز P *lrnd.* the day before yesterday.
perişan 1 (..—) پریشان [**perişan 2**] 1. scattered, disordered, disheveled, in confusion. 2. perplexed, perturbed, bewildered. 3. wretched, ruined; routed. —**et=** /ɪ/ to scatter; to ruin; to rout.
perişan 2 (.——) پریشان P *lrnd.*, same as **perişan 1**. —**cilve** (.———..) P beautiful in mad disorder; scattering brightness. —**hâl** (.——.) P in a ruined state, very wretched.
perişanî (.———) پریشانی P *lrnd.* 1. state of disorder, ruin, or wretchedness; confusion, distress, perplexity. 2. *Ott. hist.* headgear worn by certain minor officials. —**i hâtır** wretchedness or distraction of mind.
perişanlıkᵍⁱ (..—.) پریشانلق wretchedness, confusion.
perişeb (.—.) پریشب P *lrnd.* the night before last.
periton پریتون F *anat.* peritoneum. —**kovuğu** peritonial cavity.
peritonit پریتونیت F *path.* peritonitis.
perivar (.——) پریوار P *lrnd.* fairylike.
periveş (.—.) پریوش P *lrnd.* fairylike, fairy-faced.
perizad (.——) پریزاد P *lrnd.* fairy-born, very beautiful.
perkende پرکنده It *naut.* small brig, brigantine.
perki پرکی Gk perch, *zool., Perca fluviatilis.*
perkiş=ⁱʳ پرکش same as **pekiş=**.
perkit=ⁱʳ پرکت same as **pekit=**.
perküşa (..—) پرکشا P *lrnd.* flying.
permeçe (../.) پرمچه Gk *naut.* small hawser, towrope.
permi پرمی F permit, warrant.
perniyan (..—) پرنیان P *lrnd.* richest brocaded or painted Chinese silk. —**huy** (..——) P (*lit.*, of a silky disposition) kind, tenderhearted, affable.
perno (./.) پرنو It *naut.* pin on which the sheave of a block turns.
pero (./.) پرو It single pear-shaped gem. —**küpe** pendant earring.
peron پرون F *rail.* platform.
perpi پرپی *archaic* 1. a kind of charcoal or stone used as an antidote to snake bites. 2. monkshood, wolfsbane, *bot., Aconitum napelus.*
perran (.—) پرّان P *lrnd.* which flies; in flight.
perre پرّه P *lrnd.* 1. wing; side, border. 2. bolt of a door, bolt of a lock. 3. spindle; paddle or cog of a wheel.
perrende پرّنده P *lrnd.* flying, volatile; flier.
Pers 1 پرس P Persian.
pers 2 پرس *archaic* confused; upset; sullen. —**ol=** to get upset, to be confused.
pers 3 پرس only in **ters pers**, fallen and bruised.
persenkᵏⁱ پرسنك [**parseng**] refrain; word continually repeated *as* «you see», «you know».
personel پرسونل F personnel, staff.
Perşembe پرشنبه [**pençşembih**] Thursday. —**nin gelişi Çarşambadan belli olur** It is sure by Wednesday how Thursday will come. From such bad beginnings a bad ending is inevitable.
pertab, pertav (.—) پرتاب ، پرتو P *lrnd.* 1. leap, jump; run taken before a jump. 2. a throwing; cast; bowshot. —**al=** to take a run before a jump. —**et=** 1. to jump. 2. to shoot (arrow, etc.).
pertavsız پرتاوسز [**pertevsuz**] magnifying glass, burning glass.
pertev پرتو P *lrnd.* ray, light. —**efşan** (...—) P, —**endaz** (...—), —**paş** (..—) P, —**riz** (..—) P which scatters, casts, shoots out rays; brilliant; luminous. —**siz** dull, lusterless.
pertevsuz (..—) پرتوسوز [*based on Persian*] *lrnd.*, same as **pertavsız**.
perubalˡⁱ (..—) پربال P *lrnd.* 1. pinions and wings. 2. riches and power.
peruka (./.) پروکا It wig. —**cı** maker or seller of wigs. —**lı** wigged·
perukâr پروکار It hairdresser; barber.
perupay (..—) پرپای P *lrnd.* riches; power; influence.
perva (.—) پروا P 1. fear, anxiety; restraint. 2. heed, attention; concern.
pervane (.—.) پروانه P 1. moth (that hovers

round a candle). 2. flywheel; propeller; paddle wheel; sails of a windmill. 3. lrnd. guide, escort. 4. lrnd. sovereign mandate; diploma; letters-patent. — **balığı** sunfish, zool., Mola mola. — **ol**= /a/ to show great attention and devotion (to someone).

pervar (.—), **pervare** (.—.) پَروار ، پَروارَه P lrnd. a feeding, fattening (of cattle); fattened.

pervari (.——) پَرواری P lrnd. fattened, stall-fed.

pervasız (.—.) پَرواسز free from concern or apprehension, fearless; without restraint. —**lık** fearlessness.

pervaz 1 پَرواز [Persian .—] border, cornice, molding, fringe.

pervaz 2 (.—) پَرواز P 1. lrnd. flight, a flying; soaring. 2. myst. the soaring of the spirit away from worldly trivialities.

-pervaz 3 (.—) پَرواز P lrnd. that flies, as in **bülendpervaz**.

-perver پَرور P lrnd. that nourishes, caring for, as in **canperver**.

perverde پَرورده P lrnd. 1. nourished, fed. 2. brought up, educated; bred, reared.

perverdegâr (...—) پَروردگار P lrnd. 1. protector, nourisher; God. 2. king.

perverende پَرورنده P lrnd. cherishing; cherisher, protector.

perveriş پَرورش P lrnd. 1. a feeding, nourishing, maintaining, caring for. 2. an educating, training; education; learning.

perverişâmuz (...—) پَرورش آموز P lrnd. learned man; spiritual teacher; philosopher; God, the great teacher of all wisdom.

perverişyab (...—) پَرورشیاب P lrnd. nourished; educated.

perverişyâfte (...—.) پَرورشیافته P lrnd. cared for; nourished; educated.

pervin (.—) پَروین P lrnd. the Pleiades.

perviz (.—) پَرویز P lrnd. victorious, successful; fortunate; powerful.

pervizen (.—.) پَرویزن P lrnd. sieve, sifter.

pes 1 پس [pest] 1. low, soft (voice). 2. low (of a note), designates the lower octave of an instrumental or vocal range. — **perdeden konuş**= to talk with a deep voice. — **ses** gruff; bass (voice or note).

pes 2 پس [bes 3] 1. That beats all! It's the limit! 2. wrestling I accept my defeat! — **de**= to submit, to give in. — **dedirt**= /a/ to make somebody give up. — **et**= to accept one's defeat.

pes 3 پس P lrnd. 1. hinder part, back of a thing. 2. pursuit after a thing.

pes 4 پس P archaic then, therefore, consequently; moreover; however.

pesadest (.—.) پَسادست P lrnd. bargain or sale on credit; credit.

pesekᵍⁱ پَسَك tartar (of the teeth).

-pesend 1 پَسَند P lrnd. approving, admiring, loving, as in **dilpesend, hoşpesend**.

pesend 2 پَسَند P lrnd. 1. a liking, approving; approved, approbation. 2. art a kind of gilding used especially to decorate the beginning of a chapter in hand written books. — **et**= /ı/ to approve, to like.

pesendide (..—.) پَسَندیده P lrnd. 1. liked, approved, admired; pleasing, agreeable. 2. Or. mus. a **makam** starting with c″, wandering up and down several times, finally ending on g′. —**gi** (..—.—) P approbation; approvedness.

pesin (.—) پَسین P lrnd. hindmost, last, latest.

pesmande (.—.) پَسمانده P lrnd. 1. remaining behind; left; survivor. 2. remainder of a thing, leftover. —**hor** (.—..) P eater of leftovers.

pesnihad (..—), **pesnihade** (..—.) پَسنهاد ، پَسنهاده P lrnd. treasure, store; heritage.

pespaye (.—.) پَسپایه P mean, common, vulgar.

peşşam (.—) پَسشام P lrnd. meal taken shortly before daybreak during Ramazan.

pest پست P 1. same as **pes 1**. 2. lrnd. low; humble; poor. 3. lrnd. vile, mean, base, perverted. —**ân** (.—) P pl. the poor; the vile or degraded.

peste پَسته P lrnd. pistachio nut.

pestenkerani (...——) پَستنکرانی nonsensical, idiotic, common, vulgar.

pester پَستَر P lrnd. further behind, latter.

pesterin (..—) پَستَرین P lrnd. hindmost; latest, last.

pestfıtret پستفطرت P base natured; small-minded.

pesti (.—) پَستی P lrnd. lowness; baseness.

pestil پَستیل fruit pulp dried in thin layers on cloth. —**i çık**= to be beaten or crushed. —**ini çıkar**= /ın/ 1. to beat someone to a jelly. 2. to tire extremely. 3. to crush. — **gibi ol**= to be too tired to move, to be exhausted.

pesüpiş (..—) پَسوپیش P lrnd. back and front.

pesüs پَسوس [Persian **pıhsoz**] open earthenware oil-lamp.

peszinde پَسزنده [based on Persian] phil. survivor. —**lik** survival, surviving.

peş 1 پش [peş 2] space behind, back. —**ini bırakma**= /ın/ to keep at (something), to pursue continually. —**inde dolaş**= /ın/ to pursue (a matter); to go around with someone. —**ine düş**= /ın/ to follow, to run after. —**inden koş**= /ın/ to run after. —**i sıra** 1. behind him, following him; with him. 2. afterwards. —**ine tak**= /ı/ to bring along with one. **—ine takıl=** /ın/ to attach oneself to someone.

peş 2 بش [piş 1] edging of a garment.

peşekâr بشکار [pişekâr] name of one of the two staple characters in the old Turkish theater (Orta oyunu).

peşenkᵍⁱ بشنك |Persian **peşaheng**] leading beast in a string or caravan.

peşiman (. — —) پشیمان P lrnd., same as **pişman**. **—î** (.— — —) P regretfulness; regret.

peşin پشین [pişin] 1. paid in advance; ready (money), prepayment. 2. in advance, former, first, in the first place. **— al=** to buy for cash. **— cevap** answer given before the question is asked. **— hüküm** presupposition. **— para** cash, ready money, spot cash. **— söyle=** to tell in advance, to prognosticate. **— yargı** neol., phil. prejudice.

peşinat (. — —) پشیناة sum paid down, advance payment.

peşinci پشینجی one who deals for cash, cash-customer.

peşinen (. — ' .) پشیناً in advance, beforehand.

peşiz (. —), **peşize** (. — .) پشیز پشیزه P lrnd. very small coin; mite.

peşkeş پشكش [pişkeş] P gift or offering brought to a superior. **— çek=** /ı, a/ to make a present of a thing that does not belong to one.

peşkir پشكیر P table napkin, napkin; towel. **— ağası** Ott. hist. chief servant in charge of the table napkins.

peşkirci پشكیرجی 1. maker or seller of napkins. 2. Ott. hist. servant who has charge of and who places the table napkins.

peşkün پشكون arch. glass dome of a public bath. **— atla=** colloq. to show great courage.

peşm پشم P lrnd. wool; down; camel or donkey hair. **—i devat** cotton, wool or any spongy substance placed in an inkholder.

peşme پشمه same as **beşme**.

peşmelba پشملبا F ice cream with peaches and syrup, peche Melba.

peşmin (. —) پشمین P lrnd. woolly; woolen.

peşmine (. — .) پشمینه P lrnd. woolen; woolen cloth or garment; dervish garment made of a coarse kind of woolen cloth.

peşminepuş (. — . —) پشمینه پوش P lrnd. 1. clad in russet. 2. dervish; peasant.

peşrev پشرو [pişrev] 1. Or. mus. the best-known form of music, usually of four parts, used with long rhythmic patterns and played at the beginning of a classical musical performance. 2. lrnd. forerunner, harbinger. 3. wrestling preliminary movements of wrestlers. 4. artillery grapeshot. 5. archery a kind of arrow having a bone-edged tip.

peşşe پشه P lrnd. gnat; mosquito. **—dar** (. . —) P gnat-tree; elm, bot., Ulmus campestris.

peştahta پشتخته [piştahta] P. 1. small desk; counter (in a shop). 2. money-changer's board. **— saati** clock made to stand on a table.

peştemal پشتمال [destmal] large bath towel, waist cloth. **— kuşan=** to finish one's apprenticeship and become a master workman.

peştemaliye (. . — . .) پشتمالیه Ott. hist. fee paid by an apprentice to his master on leaving his apprenticeship to work independently.

peştemallıkᵍⁱ پشتمالّق money paid for the goodwill of a business, goodwill. **— ver=** to buy the goodwill.

Peşte (. ' .) پشته geog. Budapest; Pest.

petekᵍⁱ پتك 1. honeycomb. 2. any circular disk. 3. prov. large pottery jar. 4. arch. part of a minaret between the upper gallery and the eave of the conical roof. **— göz** zool. compound eye (of insects). **— gözü** cell in a honeycomb.

petgir (. —) پتگیر P lrnd. hair sieve, sieve.

petrolⁱⁱ پترول F petroleum. **— kuyusu** oil well. **— şirketi** oil company.

petyare (. — .) پتیاره P lrnd. 1. evil, misfortune, calamity. 2. difficulty; trouble; severity. 3. dishonor. 4. trick, fraud, stratagem. 5. quarrel, strife.

pey 1 پی 1. earnest-money, money on account; deposit. 2. bid (at an auction). **— akçesi** earnest money, deposit. **— sür=** to run up the bidding. **—i tutulmaz** that cannot be taken as serious, that cannot be relied on. **— ver=** to pay a deposit. **— vur=** to make a bid.

pey 2 پی [pay 2] lrnd. 1. foot. 2. footstep, track; trace. 3. sinew, tendon.

peyam (. —) پیام P lrnd. 1. news; message; tidings. 2. divine revelation. **—aver** (. — — .) P messenger, envoy.

peyamber (. — .) پیامبر P lrnd. messenger; prophet.

peyapey (. — .) پیاپی P lrnd. 1. step by step; by degrees. 2. incessantly, continuously.

peyda (. —) پیدا P 1. existent. 2. manifest, visible. 3. born; produced; discovered. **— et=** /ı/ to procure, to beget, to create; to acquire. **— ol=** to come into being; to be manifested; to appear.

peydahla=ʳ پیداحلا /ı/ colloq., same as **peyda et=**. **—n=** pass.

peyderpey پی در پی P step by step, by degrees, little by little; in succession.

peyem پیم P lrnd., var. of **peyam**.

peygale (. — .) پیغاله P lrnd. wine, cup of wine; wine-cup.

peygam (. —) پیغام P lrnd. 1. message, news,

tidings. 2. divine commandments, divine revelation.

peygamber 1 پیغمبر، پیغامبر [**peygamber 2**] prophet; the Prophet Muhammad. **— ağacı** lignum vitae, *bot., Guaiacum officinale, Guaiacum sanctum.* **— arpası** common cultivated oat, *bot., Avena sativa.* **— çiçeği** cornflower, *bot., Centaurea cyanus;* lily of the valley, *bot., Convallaria majalis.* **— devesi** the praying mantis, *zool., Mantis religiosa.* **— dikeni** blessed thistle, *bot., Cuicus benedictus.* **— kabuğu** cascarilla bark, eleuthera bark. **— kuşu** white wagtail, *zool., Motocilla alba.* **— öküzü** 1. *slang* blockhead, fool. 2. *prov., same as* **peygamber devesi.** **— reçinesi, — zamkı** guaiacum resin.

peygamber 2 (. — .) پیغمبر، پیغامبر P *lrnd*. 1. *same as* **peygamber 1.** 2. messenger. **—ân** (. — . —) P prophets. **—âne** (. — . — .) P special to a prophet or apostle, prophetically. **—î** (. — . —) P special to a prophet or messenger; prophetical office.

peygamberlik[ti] پیغمبرلك prophethood; prophecy.

peygamgüzar (. — . —) پیغامگذار P *lrnd*. messenger. **—î** (. — . — —) P delivery of a message; office of a messenger.

peygule (. — .) پیغوله P *lrnd*. 1. corner, angle. 2. narrow street, bypath; blind alley.

peygulenişin (. — . . —) پیغولهنشین P *lrnd*. living in retirement.

peygulezar (. — . —) پیغولهزار P *lrnd*. place full of nooks and blind corners.

peyk[ki] پیك P 1. satellite; follower. 2. *archaic* running footman, messenger. **—i ecel** *lrnd*. angel of death. **—i felek** *lrnd*. the moon.

peykân (. —) پیكان P *lrnd*. 1. spearhead; arrowhead. 2. arrow; spear.

peykâr (. —) پیكار P *lrnd*. battle, strife. **—perest** (. — . .) P warlike; warrior.

peyke پیكه [**paygâh**] wooden bench. **— kurusu** *slang* person who sleeps the night on the benches of a coffee house.

peyker 1 پیكر P *lrnd*. 1. form, figure. 2. face, countenance; portrait.

-peyker 2 پیكر P *lrnd*. visaged, featured, *as in* **mahpeyker, peripeyker.**

peykerperest پیكرپرست P *lrnd*. worshipper of an idol, idolator.

peyle[r] پیلمك، بیلهمك /ı/ 1. to pay a deposit on something (to seal a bargain). 2. to make sure of getting something. 3. to book, to engage. **—n=** *pass*. **—ş=** to conclude a bargain by the payment of a deposit.

-peyma (. —) پیما P *lrnd*. who measures, *e. g.,* **badpeyma, badepeyma, badiyepeyma.**

peyman (. —) پیمان P *lrnd*. 1. oath; promise, pledge. 2. agreement, compact, treaty.

peymane (. — .) پیمانه P 1. *lrnd*. cup, goblet, bowl. 2. *myst*. the heart of a perfected devotee filled with divine love. 3. measure for dry or liquid goods. **—si dol=** to come to an end (allotted life span).

peymanekeş (. — . .) پیمانهكش P *lrnd*. who empties a goblet, wine-bibber.

peymanepeyma (. — . . —) پیمانهپیما P *lrnd*. drinker of wine.

peymaneşiken (. — . . .) پیمانهشكن P *lrnd*. breaker of wine cups.

peymanşiken (. — . .) پیمانشكن P *lrnd*. oath-breaker. **—î** (. — . . —) P breach of faith.

peymude (. — .) پیموده P *lrnd*. measured; who has measured.

peynir پنیر، پینیر [**penir**] cheese. **— ağacı** a kind of cotton plant, *bot., Bombax eriodendron.* **— dişi** the last remaining tooth of an old man. **— dişli** toothless. **— ekmekle ye=** /ı/ to do something easily as a matter of course. **— kurdu** cheese mite, *zool.; Tyroglyphus domesticus.* **— mayası** rennet. **— şekeri** a softish white candy flavored with bergamot. **— tatlısı** a kind of sweet. **— tekerleği** flat round cake of cheese.

peynirci پنیرجی maker or seller of cheese. **—lik** cheesemaking.

peynirlen=[ir], **peynirleş=**[ir] پنیرلنمك، پنیرلشمك to become cheesy; to coagulate (milk).

peynirli پنیرلی mixed with cheese, containing cheese.

peyrev پیرو، پیرو P *lrnd*. 1. who follows in another's footsteps; follower; imitator. 2. minor player in an orchestra. **—î** (. . —) P, **—lik** *abstr. n.*

peysefid (. . —) پیسفید P *lrnd*. unfortunate, who succeeds in nothing; inauspicious.

peysiper پیسپر P *lrnd*. 1. trampled upon, kicked about. 2. who walks, traveling; traveler.

peyvend 1 پیوند P *lrnd*. 1. bound, fastened; connection, union, junction; bond, fastening. 2. place of junction; joint.

-peyvend 2 پیوند P *lrnd*. reaching, touching; belonging to, *as in* **asmanpeyvend, nüktepeyvend.**

peyvest 1 پیوست P *lrnd*. 1. conjunction, coherence; meeting, reunion. 2. an arriving; an attaining; attainment. 3. spiritual union with the Supreme Being.

-peyvest 2 پیوست P *lrnd*. united, uniting (with), *as in* **ebedpeyvest.**

peyveste پیوسته P *lrnd*. 1. joined, united; arrived. 2. that has attained. 3. continuously, continually, always, unceasingly. 4. concrete, material, corporeal.

peyvestegân (. . . —) پیوستگان P *lrnd*. animals; vegetables; minerals.

peyvestegi (. . . —) پیوستگی P *lrnd*. 1. relation,

peyzaj union, junction. 2. continuity, conjunction. 3. spiritual union with God.

peyzaj پیزاژ F landscape, landscape picture.

pezevenkᵉⁱ بزونك ، پوزه ونك ، پوزوونك [Persian **pazhawand**] vulgar pimp, procurer; scoundrel. **—lik et=** to procure, to pimp.

-pezir (.—) پذیر P lrnd. that accepts or admits; admitting, accepting, as in **halelpezir, suretpezir**.

pezira (.——) پذیرا P lrnd. accepting, hearing, obeying. **—i** (.———) P acceptance; obedience; reception.

pezire (.—.) پذیره P lrnd. 1. acceptance, submission; obedience. 2. reception, a meeting, encounter.

peziriş (.—.) پذیرش P lrnd. acceptance, receipt; obedience.

peziruftar (.—.—) پذیرفتار P lrnd. one who accepts, submits or obeys. **—i** (.—.——) P acceptance, submission, obedience.

pezirüfte (.—..) پذیرفته P lrnd. accepted, admitted; approved. **—gi** (.—..—) P acceptedness.

pıhtı پیختی P coagulated (liquid); clotted blood.

pıhtılan=ⁱʳ پیختیلانمق to become coagulated; to clot. **—ma** verbal n.

pıhtılaş=ⁱʳ پیختیلاشمق same as **pıhtılan=**. **—tır=** /ı/ caus.

pılıpırtı پیلی پیرتی old rubbish; belongings. **—yı topla=** to pack up one's belongings.

pınar پیکار ، پکار ، بکار spring, fountain; source. **— başı** fountainhead.

pır پیر a whirring, a whizzing. **— diye uçtu** It flew away. **— pır edip lamba söndü** The lamp spluttered and went out. **— pır et=** to whiz, to whirr.

pıranga, pıranka (.'.) پرانغا ، پرانقا ، پرانکا var. of **pranga**.

[For other words beginning with **pır-** see **pr**.]

pırasa (.'.) پراسا [**prasa**] leek, bot., Allium porrum. **— bıyıklı** having a very long heavy mustache. **— olsa yemem** colloq. I couldn't eat anything more.

pırılda=ʳ پیریلدامق to glitter, to gleam, to glisten.

pırıldakᵉⁱ پیریلداق mil. signal lamp.

pırılpırıl پیریل پیریل same as **parılparıl**.

pırıltı پیریلتی same as **parıltı**.

pırla=ʳ پیرلامق 1. to flutter (young bird). 2. to run away suddenly.

pırlagıçᵉⁱ, **pırlaguç**ᶜᵘ پیرلاغیچ ، پیرلاغوچ archaic 1. child's toy made to spin with a loop of string. 2. scarecrow.

pırlakᵉⁱ پیرلاق lure, decoy.

pırlan=ⁱʳ پیرلانمق to flutter and try to fly (young bird).

pırlangıçᵉⁱ پیرلانغیچ archaic, same as **pırlagıç**.

pırlanta (.'.) پیرلانته ، پیرلانتی It brilliant (diamond); set with brilliants.

pırna ('.) پیرنا Gk slang raki.

pırnal, pırnar پیرنال ، پیرنار holly oak, holm oak, bot., Quercus ilex. **—lık** region planted with holly bushes and the like.

pırpı پیرپی var. of **perpi**.

pırpırı پیرپیری ، پیرپیرو Gk 1. slang shabbily dressed; dissolute rake; wretch. 2. Ott. hist. cloak of red felt worn by constables. **— kıyafeti** shabby costume.

pırpıt پیرپیت Gk prov. 1. coarse homemade cloth. 2. old, worn out, shabby. 3. kind of wrestlers' trousers.

pırt=ᵃʳ پیرتمق prov. 1. to slip out. 2. to be disjointed (limb).

pırtı 1 پیرتی prov. 1. belongings, clothes. 2. worn out clothes or things.

pırtı 2 پیرتی Arm slang Shut up! Be quiet!

pırtıkᵉⁱ پیرتیك torn, ragged; in rags.

pırtla=ʳ پیرتلامق to bulge out.

pırtlakᵉⁱ پیرتلاق bulging; that easily slips off (shell, skin etc.)

pısırıkᵉⁱ پیسیریق shy, diffident, weak, incapable. **—lık** weakness; shyness, timidity.

pıskır=ⁱʳ پیسقیرمق prov. to sneeze; to blow one's nose.

pıt پیت only in **pıt yok** there is not a sound.

pıtırda=ʳ پیتیردامق to make a tapping sound, to crackle. **—t=** /ı/ caus.

pıtırdı پیتیردی light tapping or crackling sound.

pıtır pıtır پیتیر پیتیر lightly, softly (imitates the sound of rapid footsteps).

pıtpıt پیتپیت imitating a soft repeated noise, e. g., **— yürüyerek geldi** He came with light footsteps.

pıtrakᵉⁱ پیتراق ، پوتراق ، پوتراق ، بوتراق 1. plant bearing innumerable burrs. 2. knurl or gnarl in a tree. 3. name of various densegrowing shrubs. 4. burr (of a burdock). 5. prov. puckered, wrinkled, crumpled in folds. **— gibi** covered with fruit. **—lı** knurly, knotted.

piçᶜⁱ **1** پیچ 1. illegitimate child, bastard. 2. impudent or disagreeable child. 3. offshoot, sucker. 4. cuticle (nail). 5. small, incomplete or deficient replica of anything. **— et=** /ı/ to spoil by frequent interruption; to spoil. **— kurusu** naughty, tiresome child. **— ol=** to be spoiled or disturbed.

piçᶜⁱ **2** (—) پیچ P lrnd. 1. twist, curl, plait, twisted; complicated, intricate. 2. moral distortion such as, suffering, envy, hatred, perplexity. 3. crookedness, bend, fold, wrinkle. **— ender piç** very intricate, curled, or involved. **— piç** full of twists or turns. **— u puç**

1. clumsy and crooked. 2. unsightly and good for nothing.

piçan (— —) مپيچان P. lrnd. complicated, twisted. — ol= 1. to twist, wind, curl oneself. 2. to be in agony of suffering.

piçapiç (— — —) پيچاپيچ P lrnd. 1. full of twists and turns. 2. involved, intricate.

piçdar (— —) پيچدار P lrnd. crooked, curled, twisted, wrinkled.

piçe (—.) پيچه P lrnd. 1. curl, ringlet. 2. fillet.

piçide (— —.) پيچيده P lrnd. 1. twisted, curled, coiled; bent, crooked. 2. wrinkled, puckered; distorted; averted. —gi (— —.—) P, —lik a twisting, twist; distortion.

piçin پيچين archaic monkey, little monkey. — yılı the ninth year in the old Turkish cycle of twelve.

piçiş (—.), پيچش P lrnd. a turning, twisting, bending; curve, contortion.

piçleş=ir پيچاشرلك to become spoiled.

piçota پيچوتا the largest kind of **palamut** (bonito).

piçpa (— —) پيچپا P lrnd. crab.

piçtab (— —), **piçutab** (—.—) پيچتاب P lrnd. 1. a twisting and curling; a writhing. 2. pain, inward distress.

pide (′.) پيده Gk a slightly leavened flat bread. — gibi very flat. —ci baker or seller of flat bread.

pih (—) په P lrnd. fat, grease, tallow.

pijama (..′.) پيژاما F pajamas.

pijuhende (.—..) پژوهنده P lrnd. examining, searching; diligent seeker.

pikkı **1** پيك It naut. gaff topsail.

pikkı **2** پيك E cast iron.

pikkı **3, pika** (′.) پيكا F cards spade.

pikapbı, pı پيكاپ E 1. phonograph (with record changer). 2. pickup, small truck.

pike 1 پيكه F piqué (cotton fabric); quilting.

pike 2 پيكه F aero. diving. — et= to dive (aircraft). — hücumu dive bombing. — uçağı dive bomber. — uçuşu diving flight.

piket پيكت F cards piquet.

piknikgı پيكنيك E picnic.

piko (′.) پيكو F purl of lace, picot.

pil 1 پيل F electric battery, dry cell.

pil 2 (—) پيل P lrnd. elephant. —i âbkeş (lit., water-carrying elephant) rain cloud. —i havai (lit., elephant of the air) rain cloud.

pilaj پيلاژ var. of **plâj**.

pilâki (..′.) پيلاكى Gk 1. stew of fish or beans with oil and onions, eaten cold. 2. slang simpleton, idiot.

pilân پيلان var. of **plân**.

pilâv پيلاو P pilaf, boiled rice prepared with butter, meat fat, etc. —dan dönenin kaşığı kırılsın (lit. Whoever turns away from the pilaf, may his spoon be broken.) Let us stick to our plan. I shall certainly do it. Nothing will scare me out of it.

pilbalâ (— — —) پيلبالا P lrnd. big, huge, elephantine, gigantic.

pilban (— —) پيلبان P lrnd. elephant driver or keeper.

pile (—.) پيله P lrnd. silkworm's cocoon; silkworm.

pilever (—..) پيله ور P lrnd. petty dealer, huckster, peddler.

pili پيلى F var. of **pli**.

piliçci پيلچ Sl 1. young chicken. 2. slang pretty girl. — çıkar= to hatch eggs.

pilmürg (—.) پيلمرغ P lrnd. turkey.

pilot پيلوت F pilot. — ol= slang to get drunk.

pilpaye (— —.) پيلپايه P arch. pillar, prop; pier.

pilsem (—.) پيلسم P lrnd. massive and strong.

pilten (—.) پيلتن P lrnd. 1. huge, gigantic. 2. huge war horse. 3. w. cap. Rustam, the Persian Hercules.

pilvar (— —) پيلوار P lrnd. 1. like an elephant, great, heavy. 2. elephant's load, very much.

pilzehre (—..) پيلزهره P lrnd. powerful or bold as an elephant.

pilzur (— —) پيلزور P lrnd. strong as an elephant.

pimpis (′.) پيمپيس very dirty, filthy.

pin 1 پين E mech. pin.

pin 2 پين prov. poultry house, coop.

pindar (.—) پندار P lrnd. 1. idea; thought; fancy, imagination; judgment. 2. pride, conceit.

pine (—.) پينه P lrnd. patch. —duz (—.—) P patcher, mender.

pinekgi پينك [Persian **pînegî**] doze, slumber, nap.

pinekle=r پينكله mek 1. to doze, to have a broken sleep. 2. to sit idly as if asleep; to waste time. —me verbal n.

pinel پينل It 1. naut. weathervane on board ship, dogvane. 2. pennon on a spear or lance.

pines (′.) پينس Gk pinna, a kind of mussel, zool., Pinna nobilis.

pingân (.—) پنگان P lrnd. 1. cup, bowl; small cup. 2. cupping instrument.

pinhan (.—) پنهان P lrnd. hidden, concealed, secret; clandestine, mysterious. —î (.— —) P, —lık concealment; secrecy; mystery.

pinpirlikgi پينپيرلك joc. old and decrepit (person).

pinpon پينپون slang dotard; decrepit.

pinti پينتى miserly, stingy; sordid, shabby. —le=, —len=, —leş= to become dirty and shabby from miserliness. **—lik** miserliness, meanness; shabbiness.

pinyalⁱⁱ دىنيال It *obs.* rapier.

pipet پيپت F *chem.* pipette, dropping tube, dropper.

pipo (..) پيپو It tobacco pipe.

pir 1 (—) پير P 1. patron saint; spiritual teacher; sage; founder of an order of dervishes; chief of a convent of dervishes. 2. *lrnd.* old man; old. **— aşkına** just for love, without asking anything in return. **—i berna** *lrnd.* 1. youthful old man. 2. the world; the spheres. **— ü berna** *lrnd.* old men and youths; old age and youth; old and young. **— ü civan** *lrnd.* old and young. **—i çihl sâle** *lrnd.* 1. man forty years old; maturity of intellect. 2. Adam. **—i dihkan** *lrnd.* 1. old villager, old rustic. 2. old wine. **—i dumuy** *lrnd.* 1. elderly man whose hair is sprinkled with gray. 2. the world of day and night, of good and bad fortune. **—i duta** *lrnd.* 1. an old man bent with age. 2. sky; spheres. **—i fâni** *poet.* saintly old man. **—i felek** *lrnd.* the planet Saturn. **—i fertut** *lrnd.* decrepit old man. **—i harabat** *poet.* 1. old man who keeps a disreputable wine shop. 2. *myst.* spiritual guide and preceptor; devotee, perfect in spiritual excellencies and dead to all worldly vanities. **P—i Kenân** *lrnd.* (*lit.*, the old man of Canaan) Jacob. **—i mugan** *poet.* 1. elder of the Magi. 2. superior of a dervish lodge. 3. keeper of a wineshop. **— ol!** Bravo! Well done! **—i sâlhurde** *lrnd.* 1. old man. 2. old wine. **—i sani** *myst.* second chief of a dervish order. **—i serendib** *lrnd.* (*lit.* The old man of Ceylon.) Adam *said to have come down in Ceylon when banished from Paradise.* **—i tarikat** *lrnd.* chief of a dervish order; spiritual guide. **— yoluna git**= to perish in vain. **—i zâl** *lrnd.* grayheaded old man.

pir 2 پر complete, full *never used independently*, e. g., **kış bir geldi amma pir geldi** Winter was late in coming but it came in full.

-pira (——) پيرا P *lrnd.* 1. who adorns, polishes or finishes off; who cleanses, shaves, clips, *as in* **belagatpira, nazarpira.** 2. who composes or writes, *as in* **nüktepira.**

piraçol پراچول It *naut.*, same as **paraçol.**

pirahen (——.) پيرهن P *lrnd.* shirt, chemise.

piramen (——.) پيرامن P *lrnd.*, same as **piramun.**

piramitᵈⁱ پيراميد F pyramid. **— kavak** *neol.* Lombardy poplar, *bot.*, *Populus pyramidalis.*

piramun (———) پيرامون P *lrnd.* circumference, border, margin; environs.

pirân (——) پيران P *lrnd.*, *pl. of* **pir 1.**

pirâne (——.) پيرانه P *lrnd.* special to an old man; senile.

piraste (——.) پيراسته P *lrnd.* adorned, decked out; clipped, trimmed; cleansed, made. **—gi** (——.—) P, **—lik** adornment.

piraye (——.) پيرايه P *lrnd.* embellishment, ornament, decoration. **—bahş** (——..) P that adds embellishment, that adorns.

pirayende (——..) پيرآينده P *lrnd.* who adorns, embellishes, or trims.

pirayiş (——.) پيرايش P *lrnd.* 1. an adorning, cleansing; a composing or arranging. 2. ornament, decoration.

pire 1 پيره 1. flea, *zool.*, *Pulex irritans.* 2. aphid or any similar insect on plants. **—yi deve yap**= to exaggerate grossly. **— gibi** very agile, very quick. **— için yorgan yak**= (*lit.*, to burn a blanket to get rid of a flea) to cause great damage to oneself in order to avenge a trifle. **—yi nalla**= (*lit.*, to shoe a flea) to attempt the useless and impossible. **— otu** 1. fleabane, fleawort, *bot.*, *Plantago psyllium.* 2. insecticide for fleas.

Pire 2 (..) پيره *geog.* Piraeus.

pire 3 (—.) پيره P *lrnd.* assistant to the chief of a dervish convent who acts for him on occasions.

pireboli, pirebolu پيره بولى Gk bee-bread, propolis.

pirelen=ⁱʳ پيرەلن 1. to become infested with fleas. 2. to hunt for fleas on oneself. 3. to be worried by suspicion or fear; to feel uneasy; to be in a bad temper. **—dir**= /ı/ *caus.*

pireli پيرەلى 1. full of fleas. 2. suspicious, uneasy.

pirehen (—..) پيرهن P *lrnd.*, same as **pirahen.**

pirezen (—..) پيرزن P *lrnd.*, same as **pirzen.**

pirî (——) پيرى P *lrnd.* 1. old age, age. 2. special to an old man, senile. 3. quality or office of an elder or patron saint.

pirina (..'.) پيرينا Gk cake of crushed olives from which the oil has been extracted, oil cake.

pirinçᶜⁱ **1** پرنج [birinc] rice; rice plant, *bot.*, *Oryza sativa.* **— kağıdı** 1. rice paper. 2. tissue paper. **— örgüsü** *knitting* moss stitch. **—i su kaldırmaz** He is very touchy. **—in taşını ayıkla**=, **—i taşından ayır**= (*lit.*, to separate the rice from the stones) to deal with a difficult problem, to do an exasperating job. **—in taşını ayıkla!** (*lit.* Pick out the stones from the rice!) What a tiresome job! This is a mess!

pirinçᶜⁱ **2** پرنج [birinc] brass.

piristu (..—), **piristuk**ᵏᵘ (..—), **pristük**ᵏᵘ پيرستو P *lrnd.* swallow, martin.

pirlikᵍⁱ (—.) پيرلك 1. quality, office or act

of an elder or patron saint. 2. *lrnd.* old age, age.

pirmerd (—.) پیرمرد P *lrnd.* old man.

pirohu پیروهو Sl dish of ground meat, flour, and yogurt boiled together.

Pironculuk (.'...), **Pironiye** (..—.) پیرونجیلیك پیرونیه *phil.* Pyrrhonism, radical scepticism.

pirpiri پیرپیری *same as* pırpırı.

pirpirim پیرپریم *prov.* purslane, *bot.*, Portulaca oleracea.

pirsâl (——) پیرسال P *lrnd.* old man, aged.

piruhi پیروهی *var. of* pirohu.

piruz (——) پیروز P *lrnd.* victorious; prosperous, successful; fortunate; auspicious.

piruze (——.) پیروزه P *lrnd.* turquoise. —**çadır** (——.—.), —**çarh** (——..) P *poet.* the sky.

piruzi (———) پیروزی P *lrnd.* victory, success, fortune, luck; auspiciousness.

pirüpâk[ki] (—.—) پیروپاك P *lrnd.* spotlessly clean, immaculate.

piryan (.—) پریان P *lrnd.* roast. —**kebabı** lamb roasted whole on a spit.

piryol 1 پریول It cask wide at the bottom and narrow at the top; cylindrical iron vessel.

piryol 2 پریول «turnip» watch (old-time pocket watch).

pirzen (—.) پیرزن P *lrnd.* old woman.

pirzola (.'..) پیرزوله It chop, cutlet.

pis 1 پیس [Persian —] 1. dirty, filthy, foul; obscene. 2. mean, vile; stingy, miserly. — **ağız**, — **ağızlı** foul-mouthed. — **boğaz**. — **herif** dirty fellow; wretch, dirty dog. — **lâf**, — **lâkırdı** dirty words, filthy talk. —**i pisine** in vain, uselessly. — **pis düşün**= to brood; to look worried and distraught. — **pis gül**= to laugh in a scoffing manner, to grin unpleasantly.

pis 2 (—) پیس P *path.* leprosy.

pisboğaz پیسبوغاز greedy; so greedy that he eats anything at any time. —**lık** greediness.

pisendam (—.—) پیس‌اندام P *lrnd.* leprous.

pisender پیسندر P *lrnd.* stepson.

piser پیسر P *lrnd., same as* püser.

pisi پیسی *child's language* pussy-cat, cat. — **pisi** puss, pussy.

pisibalığı پیسی‌بالغی plaice, *zool.*, Pleuronectes platessa.

.**pisik**[gi] پیسیك *prov.* cat.

pisin پیسین F 1. fish pond; swimming pool. 2. *rel.* piscina.

piskopos پیسكوپوس Gk bishop. —**luk** bishopric; rank of a bishop; bishop's house.

pisle= پیسله 1. /ı/ to soil, to dirty. 2. /ı/ to spoil, to make a mess of. 3. to relieve oneself; to dirty something (an animal or baby). —**n**=, —**ş**= to become dirty and soiled; to get into a mess —**t**= /ı/ to make dirty; to soil.

pislik[ği] پیسلیك 1. dirt, mess. 2. dirtiness, filthiness. 3. obscenity. — **götür**= /ı/ to be very dirty (place). — **parmağından ak**= to be very filthy.

pist 1 پیست Scat! *word used to drive away a cat.*

pist 2 پیست F 1. *sports* running track. 2. *aero.* runway.

pistan (.—) پستان P *lrnd.* breast; teat, nipple.

piste پسته P *lrnd.* pistachio nut. —**i şekerfişan** *poet.* lips of a beauty.

piston پیستون F 1. piston. 2. *slang* backing; influence. — **kır**= *chauffeurs' slang* to make use of a car without the permission of the owner. — **kolu** *auto.* connecting rod.

pistonlu پیستونلی 1. having a piston. 2. *slang* having a backer.

piş 1 (—) پیش P *lrnd.* 1. before, in front; front part. 2. future; further, beyond.

piş=[er] **2** پیشمك 1. to be cooked or baked. 2. to ripen, to mature. 3. to be perfected; to become experienced. 4. to be overcome by the heat. 5. to be chafed or inflamed by heat or perspiration. —**memiş** uncooked; unbaked; immature; inexperienced, unripe. —**miş armut gibi eline düş**= to fall into one's hands like a ripe pear. —**miş aşa su kat**= to spoil a completed affair. —**miş kelle gibi** always grinning.

pişadest (——.) پیشادست P *lrnd.* 1. a ready-money bargain. 2. for ready money, not on credit.

pişaheng (——.) پیشاهنگ P *lrnd.* leader; vanguard.

pişamed (——.) پیشامد P *lrnd.* 1. a coming forward, advance. 2. a getting on in rank, wealth or power. 3. occurrence, event.

pişan (——) پیشان P *lrnd.* the utmost extremity in front, the farthest of all.

pişani (———) پیشانی P *lrnd.* 1. forehead, brow, front. 2. effrontery, impudence, insolence; pride; obstinacy. —**bend** (———.) P fillet for the hair. —**dar** (————) P brazen faced.

pişapiş (———) پیشاپیش P *lrnd.* onwards and still onwards.

pişbaz (——) پیشباز P *lrnd.* one with open arms to receive a friend or favor; a meeting.

pişbin (——) پیشبین P *lrnd* foreseeing; wise, prudent, sagacious.

Pişdadiyan (——.—) پیشدادیان P the Pishdadians, first dynasty of the kings of Persia.

pişdar پیشدار [*based on Persian*] vanguard.

-**pişe 1** (—.) پیشه [Persian -peşa] *lrnd.* who exercises the art or habit named, *as in* cefapişe.

pişe 2 (—.) پیشه [Persian **peşva**] lrnd. 1. craft, trade, profession. 2. habit, custom. 3. a kind of small flute. **—i ateş** sin, diabolical deeds. **—gâh** (—.—), **—geh** (—..) P workshop.

pişeğen پیشه‌گن that cooks easily (beans, etc.).

pişekâr (—.—) پیشه‌کار P lrnd. 1. clever man; artisan. 2. conjurer. 3. same as **peşekâr**.

pişendiş (—.—) پیشندیش P lrnd. who anticipates; who thinks beforehand. **—î** (—.—.—) P forethought.

pişever (—..) پیشه‌ور P lrnd. artisan; craftsman. **—î** (—..—) P craftsmanship.

pişgâh (——), **pişgeh** (—.) پیشگاه ، پیشگه P lrnd. space in front, front.

pişhane (——.) پیشخانه P lrnd. 1. porch, portico, vestibule, entrance hall. 2. tents of state sent in advance when traveling.

pişi (——) پیشی P lrnd. a being forward, in advance; precedence, superiority.

pişik پیشیک diaper rash; inflamed sore in the groin or armpit resulting from heat or perspiration.

pişim پیشیم act of being cooked or baked; amount cooked at one time.

pişin (——) پیشین P lrnd., same as **peşin**.

pişine (——.) پیشینه [Persian **peşîne**] lrnd. 1. former, first, prior. 2. old, ancient.

pişini (———) پیشینی P lrnd. 1. priority, precedence. 2. oldness; related to ancient times. **—yan** (————) P pl. the ancients.

pişir=ir پیشیرمک /ı/ 1. to cook, to bake. 2. to ripen, to cause to mature. 3. to plan (a course of action); to hatch (a plot). 4. to cause a sore (perspiration). 5. to learn well (lesson etc.). **—ip kotar=** 1. to cook and serve up (food). 2. to settle (a question). 3. to finish off (a job).

pişirim پیشیریم act of cooking; amount that one will cook at one time. **—lik** amount for cooking at one time.

pişirme پیشیرمه verbal n. of **pişir=**.

pişirt=ir پیشیرتمک /ı, a/ caus. of **pişir=**.

pişkadem (—..) پیشقدم [Persian **peşkadem**] lrnd. 1. leader. 2. deputy leader in a dervish lodge.

pişkâr (——) پیشکار P lrnd. 1. assistant, helper; servant. 2. disciple; steward, bailiff.

pişkeş (—.) پیشکش P lrnd., same as **peşkeş**.

pişkeşçi پیشکشچی officer who registered all presents offered. **—i şehriyarî** Ott. hist. registrar of presents in the Sultan's palace.

pişkeşneviz (—..—) پیشکش‌نویز P same as **pişkeşçi**.

pişkin پیشکین 1. well cooked, well baked. 2. ripe, mature; experienced. 3. hard baked, well hardened. **— kalem** ripe-cut, well-seasoned reed pen.

pişkinlikği پیشکینلک 1. a being well cooked or ripened. 2. maturity; experience, knowledge of the world. 3. behavior of a thick-skinned person.

pişman (.—) پیشمان [**peşiman**] regretful, sorry; penitent, repentent. **— ol=** /a/ to repent.

pişmaniye (.—..) پیشمانیه candy made of sugar and oil with soapwort whipped into fibers.

pişmanlıkği پیشمانلق regret, penitence. **— çek=** to be sorry, repent. **— navlunu** deadfreight.

pişmüzd (—.) پیشمزد P lrnd. pay given in advance.

pişnamaz (—..) پیشنماز P lrnd., Isl. rel. prayer-leader. **—î** (—.—) P duty of a prayer leader.

pişnihad (—.—) پیشنهاد P lrnd. 1. custom, manner; pattern, aim; intention, design. 2. a proposing, submitting; proposition. **—ı hatır et=** /ı/ to propose to one's mind.

pişres (—.) پیشرس P lrnd. early mature, ripening early; first fruits.

pişrev پیشرو P lrnd., same as **peşrev**.

piştahta (—..) پیشتخته P lrnd., same as **peştahta**.

pişter (—.) پیشتر P lrnd. prior, more forward; further on. **—in** (—.—) P most advanced, first, foremost.

pişti پیشتی 1. a kind of ball game. 2. a kind of card game.

piştov پیشتو F pistol. **—u dokuz patlar** He is very irritable or hot-tempered. **— tası** metal cup on the butt end of a pistol.

pişva (——) پیشوا P lrnd. 1. leader, commander. 2. teacher, exemplar, pattern, model. **—yî** (————) P leadership.

piyade 1 (.—.) پیاده P 1. pedestrian. 2. foot soldier; infantry. 3. chess pawn. 4. man of small capacity or knowledge. **— kaldırımı** foot pavement, sidewalk (of a street).

piyade 2 پیاده It light rowboat.

piyale (.—.) پیاله P 1. lrnd. cup, cup of wine. 2. lrnd. eye of a beauty. 3. myst. one's soul's beloved, God; divine presence intoxicating the beholder. **—i cevr** cup filled to the brim.

piyan 1 پیان It naut. seizing (of a rope).

piyan 2 پیان Gk prov., same as **meyan 1**.

piyanço (..) پیانچو slang louse.

piyango (..) پیانقو It lottery, raffle. **— çek=** 1. to draw a lottery, to draw lots. 2. school slang to have an oral examination. **— vur=** /a/ to win in a lottery.

piyanist پیانیست F pianist.

piyano (..´.) پیانو It 1. piano. 2. *mus.* piano, softly, quietly. — **çal=** to play the piano.

piyasa (..´.) پیاسا It 1. a going out for a pleasant stroll. 2. rate of exchange; current price; the market. 3. open space, public place. —**ya çık=** 1. to go out for a walk. 2. to come on the market (goods). —**ya düş=** 1. to be plentiful. 2. to go on the streets (woman). — **et=** to walk about. — **rayici** market price, market value.

piyastos پیاستوس Gk *slang* a taking hold of, catching. — **et=** /ı/ to catch, to seize. — **ol=** to be caught, (culprit).

piyata (..´.) پیاتا It plate, dinner plate.

piyaz پیاز P 1. chopped onions. 2. dish principally flavored with onion (beans etc.). 3. *slang* flattery. — **doğra=** *slang* to lie. —**ları bas=** *slang* to applaud, to flatter. —**ı ver=** *slang* to flatter.

piyazcı پیازجی 1. seller of **piyaz**. 2. *slang* flatterer.

piyazla=ʳ پیازلامق /ı/ 1. to marinate. 2. *slang* to sing the praises of, to flatter.

piyes پیس F *theat.* play.

piyiz پییز *slang* raki. — **kay=** to go uninvited to a table where drinking is going on. —**len=** to drink raki.

pizişkᵏⁱ پزشك P *lrnd.* physician.

plâçka پلاچقا Alb spoil, booty. —**cı** raider, freebooter.

plâfon پلافون F *cards* a kind of bridge game.

plaj پلاژ F beach, bathing beach.

plâkᵍⁱ پلاك F 1. phonograph record. 2. plate, plaque.

plâka پلاكه It 1. number plate (car etc.); plate, plaque. 2. *print.* plate. 3. *archaic* great flat rock in the middle of the sea. — **ayarı** plane of polished steel used by mechanics to test plane surfaces. — **lâmbası** *auto.* license plate lamp.

plân پلان F plan, scheme; design. — **atışı** *artillery* mapfire. — **kur=** to scheme.

plânçete (..´.) پلانچته It surveyor's plane-table.

plânketa (..´.) پلانكته It bar-shot, chain-shot.

plânlama پلانلاما *econ.* a planning.

planlı پلانلی planned; designed. — **ekonomi** planned economy. — **tarım** planned agriculture.

plânör پلانور F *aero.* glider. —**cülük** gliding (as a sport).

planya (.´.) پلانیا It carpenter's long-plane (used to make straight edges) — **et=** to plane off.

plâsiye (.´..) پلاسیه F commercial traveler, agent.

plâsman پلاسمان F *fin.* investment.

plâstikᵍⁱ پلاستیك F plastic.

plâterina (..´.) پلاترینا Gk sand-smelt, atherine, *zool.*, *Atherina presbyter*.

plâtin پلاتین F *chem.* platinum.

plâzma (´.) پلازما L *biol.* plasma. — **bozulumu** *neol.* plasmolysis.

plebisit پلبیسیت F *pol.* plebiscite.

plevra (´.) پلورا Gk *anat.* pleura. —**î** (..—) pleural.

pli پلی F *sewing* pleat.

plise پلیسه F *sewing* pleated, pleating.

plonjon پلونژون F 1. *soccer* a throwing oneself at full length on the ground to catch the ball. 2. a diving.

plûtokrasi پلوتوكراسی F plutocracy.

poca (´.) پوجا It *naut.* leeward direction of a ship's sailing. — **alabanda** 1. Veer ship. 2. Down with the helm. Hard to leeward. — **et=** to bear away to leeward, to veer.

pocala=ʳ پوجالامق *naut.* to veer, to bear away.

podra (´.) پودرا var. of **pudra**.

pof پوف *pop.*, imitates a popping noise.

pofla=ʳ پوفلامق 1. to burst with a pop. 2. to puff violently, to snort.

pofur pofur پوفور پوفور puffing regularly.

pofurda=ʳ پوفوردامق to puff regularly, to snort.

pofyos پوفیوس *slang* 1. empty, hollow. 2. worthless, rubbish.

poğaça (.´.) پوغاچا It cake of very fat pastry baked usually without any stuffing, flaky pastry. —**cı** maker or seller of **poğaça**.

poğama پوغاما crane for lifting heavy weights, derrick.

poh پوه *prov.*, var. of **bok**.

pohpoh پوهپوه 1. flattery, applause. 2. Bravo! —**u bol** a flatterer.

pohpohla=ʳ پوهپوهلامق /ı/ to applaud, to flatter. —**n=** pass.

poker پوكر E poker (game). —**ci** poker player.

pokruva پوكروا *naut.* main trysail-yard.

polat پولاد var. of **pulat**.

poliça, poliçe (..´.) پولیچه It 1. bill of exchange, draft; insurance policy. 2. receipt for money.

poligon پولیگون F 1. *geom.* polygon. 2. *artillery* range; ground for firing practice.

poliklinikᵍⁱ پولیكلینیك F clinic for out-patients.

polim پولیم Gk *slang* lie, falsehood. — **at=** to tell lies. — **yap=** to show off.

polis پولیس F the police; policeman.

politika (..´.) پولیتیقه Gk 1. politics; policy. 2. cunning or flattery in conversation.

politikacı پولیتیقه‌جی 1. politician. 2. one who

Polonez

knows when to use flattery or cunning in his talk. **—lık** 1. party politics. 2. flattery.

Polonez پولونز F Polish.

Polonya (.'.) پولونیا It geog. Poland. **—lı** Pole, Polish.

Pomak[gu] پوماق Pomak, Bulgarian Muslim.

pomata (.'.) پوماط It pomade.

pompa (.'.) پومپه It pump. **—la=** /ı/ to pump.

pompon پومپون F powder puff; pompon, tassel.

pompuruk[gu] پومپوروق slang old, aged.

ponje پونژه F a kind of thin silk cloth, pongee.

ponza (.'.) پونزه It pounce; pumice; rottenstone.

popo پوپو child's language buttock.

porfir پورفیر F min. porphyry.

porselen پورسلان F 1. porcelain. 2. porcelain insulator.

porsiyon پورسیون F a dish of food, helping, portion.

porsu=[r] پورصومه same as **pörsü=**.

porsuk[gu] 1 پورسوک same as **pörsük**.

porsuk[gu] 2 پورسوق badger, zool., Meles. **— ağacı** common yew, yew tree, bot., Taxus baccata. **—giller** bot., Taxaceae.

porta پورطه It Ott. hist. gate where duty is collected. **— akçesi** due paid at a gate.

portakal پورتقال orange; common orange tree, bot., Citrus aurantium. **—i** (..——) of orange color.

portatif پورتاتیف F portable, movable.

porte پورته F mus. staff.

Portekiz پورتکیز geog. Portugal; Portuguese. **—ce** Portuguese language. **—li** a Portuguese.

portföy پورتفوی F 1. purse, pocket book, wallet. 2. bill case, portfolio.

portmanto پورتمانطو F coat hanger; coat stand.

portolon پورطولون It naut. chart, plan.

portre پورتره F portrait.

portuc, portuç[cu] پورتوچ It naut. peak, storeroom, locker, caboose.

posa (.'.) پوصا 1. sediment, dregs. 2. tartar (of wine, or of the teeth). **—sını çıkar=** /ın/ 1. to extract the sediment of. 2. to squeeze almost to death.

posalan=[ır] پوصالانمق to deposit a sediment; to settle (as dregs).

posalı پوصالی full of sediment or tartar.

posbıyık[gı] پوسبییق large bushy mustache; having a bushy mustache.

post پوست [Persian —] 1. skin, hide, undressed skin. 2. tanned skin with the fur on, especially when used as a rug. 3. post, office, position. 4. the official post of the Sheikh in a mystical order. **—unu çıkar=** /ın/ to beat to death. **— elden git=** to lose one's job, position, life. **—a geç=** 1. to take possession

of an official position. 2. myst. to become sheikh of a dervish lodge. **— kalpak** sheepskin cap. **— kap=** to get an office (possibly by fraud or cunning). **— kavgası** quarrel over official positions. **— kubbesi** seat of the sheikh in a dervish lodge. **—u kurtar=** to save one's skin. **— nakibi** dervish whose duty is to spread the sheepskins. **—a otur=** to become sheikh. **—una otur=** 1. to take possession of one's official post. 2. to assume airs. **—una saman doldur=** /ın/ to kill. **—u ser=** to settle oneself down in a place or a post (with the intention of staying). **—u yoluk** slang wretch, miserable fellow.

posta (.'.) پوسته It 1. mail; post, postal service. 2. mail train, mail steamer; train, boat, service. 3. mil. orderly, watch, sentry. 4. shift, gang, relay. 5. naut. pair of timbers prepared and set up in ship-building; frame, timbers. **— arabası** mail coach. **— et=** /ı/ to pick someone up (policeman); to take to the police station. **— havalesi** postal order. **P— İttihadı** Universal Postal Union. **—yı kes=** to cease frequenting a place; to cut relationships. **— kur=** slang to plot against somebody. **— polisi** policeman on a beat. **— pulu** postage stamp. **— yap=** to go and return according to schedule (boat, etc.).

postacı پوستهجی mailman; post office clerk.

postahane پوستهخانه post office.

postal پوستال 1. heavy army shoe; heelless slipper or shoe of soft leather. 2. colloq. loose woman, prostitute.

postala=[r] پوستهلهمق /ı/ to mail, to post. **—n=** pass.

postane (.—.) پوستانه [postahane] post office.

posteki پوستکی var. of **pösteki**.

postin (.—) پوستین P lrnd. 1. fur cloak, coat, or jacket. 2. made of leather, skin or fur. **—duz** (.——) P furrier.

postlimini پوستلیمینی F law postliminium.

postnişin (..—) پوستنشین [Persian —.—] lrnd. established in an office of dignity; head of a religious order.

postrestant پوسترستانت F general delivery, poste restante.

poşu پوشو P same as **puşu**.

pot 1 پوت Arm 1. crease, fold, pleat. 2. baggy, too full (dress). 3. blunder; slip (of the tongue). 4. slang poker (game). **— gel=** 1. to go wrong, to turn out badly. 2. to be baggy, to be too full (dress). **— kır=** to make a blunder, to commit a faux pas. **— yap=** slang to play poker. **— yeri** defect.

pot 2 پوت 1. small boat used for crossing rivers, raft, punt. 2. wooden floor of a cattle shed.

pota (ˊ.ˋ) بوطه بوتا بوته P 1. crucible. 2. clay pot set up as a target.

potansiyel پوتانسیل F potential.

potaş 1 پوتاس slang shabby (man).

potas 2, potasyum (.ˊ.) پوتاس پوتاسیوم F chem. potassium.

potin بوطین بوتین [botin] F boot.

potlan= بوتلانمق to get creased or rumpled.

potlu بوتلی creased, rumpled; in folds.

potluk[gu] بوتلق bagginess in a garment.

potpuri پوت پوری F mus. musical production, potpourri.

potrak[gi] بوتراق very puckered, rumpled.

potrel بوترل [putrel] arch. I-beam, T-beam.

potuk[gu] **1** بوتوق بوطوق بوتوك puckered; full (dress); in pleats; fold, pleat.

potuk[gu] **2** بوتوق بوطوق prov. young camel; young buffalo.

potuklan= بوتوقلنمق بوتوقلنمق to become wrinkled or pleated.

potur بوتر بوطر بوتور 1. full gathered knee-breeches worn with tight leggings. 2. pleat, fold; corrugation. 3. puckered, pleated, gathered. —**lu** wearing the breeches known as **potur**; peasant.

poyra (ˊ.ˋ) پویره hub of a wheel; axle-end (of a car). — **deliği** hole in the center of the hub of a wheel. — **zıvanası** metal lining of a hub, hub-lining.

poyralık[gi] پویره لق 1. log of hard wood out of which hubs are made. 2. pine timber (for a rafter).

poyraz پویراز Gk northeast wind; northeast point of the compass. — **kuşu** oyster catcher, zool., Haematopus ostralegus.

poyrazla= پویرازلامق to change to the northeast (wind).

poz پوز F 1. pose. 2. phot. exposure. — **ver=** 1. to expose. 2. to pose (for a photograph).

pöç, pöçük[gu] پوچك Arm prov. tail; coccyx.

pöf پوف Ugh!

pörçük pörçük[gu] پورچك پورچك in bits and pieces.

pörsü= پورسمك to shrivel up, to become wrinkled or withered.

pörsük[gu] پورسك shrivelled up, withered.

pörtle= پورتله مك prov. to protrude (eyes).

pörtlek[gi] پورتلك protruding (eye).

pösteki پوستكی P sheepskin; sheepskin rug used to sit on. —**sini çıkar=** colloq. /ın/ to beat to death. — **ol=** to become limp. — **say=** (lit., to count the hairs on a sheepskin) to be engaged on a useless and tedious task. — **saydır=** /a/ to give someone tiresome but useless work to do; to weary; to give trouble (to).

—**sini ser=** /ın/ to flay someone, to give someone a severe thrashing. —**yi ser=** /a/ to stay long. —**yi sudan çıkar=** to get settled; to better one's work or position.

prafa (ˊ.ˋ) پرافه a kind of card game for three.

pragmacı (ˊ...) neol., phil. pragmatist. —**lık** pragmatism.

pragmatizm پراگماتیزم F phil. pragmatism.

pranga, pranka (ˊ.ˋ) پرانغه پرانغا پرانكا It fetters attached to the legs of criminals; penal servitude. — **kaçağı** jailbird; burglar. —**ya vur=** /ı/ to put in fetters or to hard labor.

prangabend پرانغه بند P lrnd. condemned to imprisonment with hard labor. —**lik** abstr. n.

prasa (ˊ.ˋ) پراسه Gk same as **pırasa**.

prasya (ˊ.ˋ) پراسیا It naut. brace of a ship's yard.

pratik[gi] پراتیك F 1. practical; handy. 2. practice; skill.

pratika (.ˊ.) پراتیقه It naut. clean bill of health, pratique. — **al=** to take out a clean bill of health.

prazvana (.ˊ.) پرازوانه [berazban] shank of a blade; metal socket; ferrule.

prens پرنس F prince.

prenses پرنسس F princess.

prensip[bi] پرنسیپ F principle.

prenslik[gi] پرنسلك princedom; principality.

pres پرس F press, pressing machine.

prevantoryum (...ˊ.) پره وانتوریوم F sanitarium for tuberculosis suspects.

prez پرز F slang a pinch of heroin.

prim پریم F 1. premium. 2. prize.

priz پریز F 1. elec. socket. 2. mech. drive. — **direkt** auto. direct drive.

problem پروبلم F problem.

profesör پروفسور F professor. —**lük** professorship.

profesyonel پروفسیونل F professional.

profil پروفیل F profile. —**li** sectional (iron).

program پروغرام F program. —**lı** systematical, methodical.

proje پروژه F project.

projektör پروژكتور F projector.

propaganda (...ˊ.) پروپاغنده F propaganda. —**cı** propagandist.

prospektüs (.ˊ.) پروسپكتوس F prospectus, handbill.

prostela (.ˊ.) پروستله Gk apron.

protektora پروتكتورا F pol. protectorate.

Protestan پروتستان F Protestant. —**lık** Protestantism.

protesto (.ˊ.) پروتستو It 1. protest. 2. objection. — **çek=** to make a formal protest. — **et=** /ı/ to protest.

protokol[lü] پروتوقول F protocol.

prova 1 (ˊ.ˋ) پروا It 1. trial. 2. print.

prova proof. 3. *theat.* rehearsal. 4. *tailor.* fitting. **—larını yap=** /ın/ *naut.* to carry out trials (of a vessel).

prova 2 (.'.) بروه بروا It *naut.* bow, head. **—da** ahead. **— çanaklığı** foretop. **— direği** foremast. **—sından es=** /ın/ *slang* to vex, provoke a person; to irritate (someone). **—dan rüzgâr** head wind.

provadifortuna (.'....'.) بروه واد يفترِ تونا It *com.* protest of average.

pruva (.'.) بروه بروا same as **prova 2**.

psikanalist پسيكنَالست F psychoanalyst.
psikanaliz پسيكنَاليز F psychoanalysis.
psikiyatri پسيقياتيرى F psychiatry.
psikolog[ğu] پسيقولوغ F psychologist.
psikoloji پسيقولوژى F psychology.
psikolojik[ği] پسيقولوژيك F psychological.
psikopat پسيقوپات F psychopath.
psikoterapi پسيقوتراپى F psychotherapy, psychotherapeutics.
psikoz پسيقوز F *med.* psychosis.

pu 1 (—) پو P *lrnd.* a running, going; a running about.
-pu 2 (—) پو P *lrnd.* that runs, that goes, e. g., **cihanpu.**
puç[cu] (—) پوچ P *lrnd.* 1. good for nothing, rotten; empty. 2. clumsy, uneven, unsightly. **— burunlu** snub-nosed.
puçmağz (—.) پوچ مغز P *lrnd.* blockhead, dunce.
pud (—) پود P *lrnd.* weft, woof.
puding پودينغ E 1. *cookery* pudding. 2. *geol.* conglomerate.
Pudkal پودقال *hist.* inhabitants of Podolia (in Poland). **— kazakları** Cossacks of Podolia.
pudra (.'.) پودرا F powder, face powder.
puduk[ğu] پودوك same as **potuk 2**.
puf پوف F big circular cushion to sit on. **— böreği** puff pastry stuffed with meat or cheese.
pufla 1 (.'.) پوفلا down, eiderdown. **— gibi** very soft.
pufla=[r] **2** پوفلامسى to blow, to puff.
puğur پوغور same as **buğur 1**.
puhte پخته P *lrnd.* 1. thoroughly cooked. 2. ripe, mature; experienced.
puhtegân (..—) پختگان P *lrnd.* men of mature experience. **—ı hakikat** men matured, skilled in the knowledge of sacred truth; wise men; saints.
puhtegî (..—) پختگى P *lrnd.* ripeness; maturity; mature experience.
puhtehâr (..—) پخته خوار P *lrnd.* 1. one who eats whatever is ready cooked; lazy. 2. son-in-law who lives with his wife's parents; beggar.
puhu پوهو eagle owl, *zool.*, *Bubo bubo*.
pul پول 1. stamp (postage, etc.). 2. thin round disc; piece (in checkers and backgammon); cymbal (in the hoop of a tambourine). 3. spangle, sequin. 4. scale (of a fish). 5. washer (for a screw); nut (of a bolt). 6. small coin, mite; *colloq.* money. **bir — etme=** to be worthless. **— iğnesi** very fine sewing needle; spangle-needle. **— kaya** *geol.* schist. **— pul** in scales; in spots. **— pul ayrılma** *geol.* exfoliation. **bir —a sat=** /ı/ *archaic* to disregard entirely; to act disloyally (against). **— şişe** a kind of bottle made of very thin greenish glass.

pulâd (— —) پولاد P *lrnd.* steel.
pulat[dı] پولاد 1. steel. 2. strength. **— gibi** very hard and strong.
pulatarına پولاتارينا thin-lipped gray mullet, *zool.*, *Mugil auratus*.
pulcu پولجى 1. seller of stamps. 2. collector of postage stamps, philatelist.
pulkanatlılar *neol.*, *zool.*, *Lepidoptera*.
pulla=[r] پوللامسى /ı/ 1. to put stamps (on a letter). 2. to decorate with spangles. **—n=** 1. *pass.* 2. *art* to be exfoliated (oil painting).
pullu پوللى 1. bearing stamps. 2. scaly. 3. spangled; spotted. **— yılancık** *path.* simple squamous erysipelas. **— zırh** scale-armor.
pulluk[ğu] پوللوق *Sl* heavy plow.
pulpare (.—.) پولپاره P *arch.* line of small decorative disks on a ceiling or wall.
pulsuz پولسز 1. without stamps. 2. without scales. 3. without money, impecunious. **—luk** impecuniousness.
puluç[cu] پولوچ پولوج archaic sexually impotent.
punar پونار same as **pınar**.
punç[cu] پونچ E punch (beverage).
punt[du] پونت It 1. *naut.* position of a ship (on the open sea). 2. appropriate time. **—unu bul=** /ın/, **—una getir=** /ı/ to find a suitable opportunity for doing something. **— tayini** finding a ship's position by astronomical calculations.
punta (.'.) پونتا lathe-center.
puntal, puntel پونتال It *naut.* stanchion.
punto (.'.) پونتو It *print.* size of type, point.
punya (.'.) پونيا It *naut.* clew garnet.
pupa (.'.) پوپا It *naut.* the after direction of a ship or boat; stern wind. **— et=** to run into another vessel's stern. **—dan gel=** to come right astern, to follow after a vessel's stern. **— git=** to go with the wind right aft. **— hava**, **— rüzgâr** stern wind. **— yelken git=** 1. to sail before the wind. 2. to be in a lucky way.
pupla (.'.) پوپلا same as **pufla 1**.
pur 1 (—) پور P *lrnd.* son. **P—i Arabî** a surname of the famous mystic Muhiddin Ibn-

el Arabi. **P—i Âzer** Abraham. **P—i Meryem** Jesus.

pur 2 (—) پُر [**bur 1**] *prov.* stony, rocky, unfit for cultivation.

puro (´.) پورو *cigar.*

pus 1 بوس ،بُوس 1. mist, haze, slight fog. 2. bloom (on fruit); moss (on trees and plants). 3. gum, resin; blight, mildew. 4. condensation (on a cold glass). 5. web (made by insects on leaves). 6. crust (formed on the nipples of ewes).

pus 2 بوص F inch.

pus 3 (—) بوس [**bûs 2**] 1. a kissing. 2. *lrnd.* cajolery, deceptive soft words.

pus=ᵃʳ **4** بوسمق *colloq.* 1. to crouch down; to lie in ambush. 2. to become downcast, grieved, or offended; to become very quiet. 3. to become misty.

pusar=ⁱʳ بوسارمق *prov.* to become misty.

pusarıkᵍⁱ بوسارق ،بوسرك ،بوساره *prov.* 1. hazy, misty, rainy; haze, mist, slight fog. 2. mirage.

pusat بوصاط ،بوساط ،بوسات ،بوصات *archaic* 1. arms, armor; equipment, instruments of war. 2. apparatus, tools, gear.

pusatçı بوساتجى 1. *obs. theat.* clown with a slapstick or sword. 2. *Ott. hist.* man who danced and clowned in advance of a column of warriors on the march.

pusatlan=ⁱʳ بوساتلنمق to be armed; to put on armor. —**dır=** *caus.*

pusatlı بوساتلى ،بوصاتلى *archaic* equipped; armed; clad in armor.

puse (—.) بوسه [**buse**] kiss.

puselikᵍⁱ (—..) بوسه لك *var. of* **buselik 1**.

puside (——.) بوسيده P *lrnd.* 1. rotten, decayed. 2. faded, withered; discolored (from a bruise). —**gi** (——.—) P, —**lik** rottenness, fadedness, discoloration.

pusla (´.) بوصله *same as* **pusula 1, 2**.

puslan=ⁱʳ بوسلانمق ،بوصلانمق to become misty, cloudy, moldy. —**dır=** /ı/ *caus.*

puslu بوصلى ،بوسلو 1. hazy, misty. 2. having bloom or condensation on it.

pusu بوسو ،بوسى ،بوصو ambush. —**ya düşür=** /ı/ to cause to fall into an ambush, to trap. — **kur=** to lay an ambush. —**ya yat=** to lie in wait.

pusula 1 (´..) بوصوله note, short letter; memorandum; list.

pusula 2 (´..) بوصوله ،بوصله ،بوسله ،بوصل ،بوصول It *naut.* compass. — **dolabı** binnacle. —**yı şaşır=** to lose one's bearings; to be bewildered.

pusulan=ⁱʳ بوصولانمق to lie in wait.

pusval بوصوال measure (used by makers of slippers called **yemeni**).

-puş (—) بوش P *lrnd.* 1. who wears, who puts on, *as in* **siyahpuş, sebzpuş**. 2. who covers over and forgives, *as in* **hatapuş**.

puşa (——) بوشا P *lrnd.* covering, concealing.

puşe (—.) بوشه P *lrnd.* curtain, veil.

puşegân (—.—) بوشه گان P *myst.* state or place where the devotee loses conciousness of externals just before the divine essence is manifested to him.

puşende (—..) بوشنده P *lrnd.* 1. that covers; who wears. 2. who covers over, forgives and forgets. —**gi** (—..—) P garment, covering.

puşide (——.) بوشيده P *lrnd.* 1. covered; closed; hidden. 2. forgiven, pardoned. 3. covering; quilt. 4. a kind of scarf worn round the head. —**çeşm** (——..) P 1. who has closed his eyes; whose eyes are bound. 2. blind; hoodwinked, deceived. —**gi** (——.—) P ambiguity, dubiousness.

puşidenî (——.—) بوشيدنى P *lrnd.* suitable to be covered, veiled or worn; clothing, dress.

puşiş (—.) بوشش P *lrnd.* 1. a covering, forgiving, or wearing; cover, garment, dress. 2. coverlet, sheet, blanket.

puşt 1 بوشت P catamite.

puşt 2 بشت P *lrnd.* 1. back; outside, surface of a thing. 2. support, backer; protection, assistance; strength. —**i pa** instep, convex or upper part of the foot.

puşte بشته P *lrnd.* 1. hill; hillock; mound. 2. heap, stack, pile.

puştiban, puştivan (..—) بشتيبان ،بشتوان P *lrnd.* 1. prop, bar, support. 2. supporter, protector.

puştlukᵍᵘ بوشتلق 1. quality and act of a sodomite. 2. untrustworthiness, changeableness, fickleness.

puştvare (.—.) بشتواره P *lrnd.* burden, load; as much as a man can carry on his back.

puşu بوشى 1. *Ott. hist.* light turban (worn by soldiers). 2. kerchief worn round the head.

put 1 بوت [**büt**] 1. idol, god. 2. the cross. — **gibi** like a statue, very quiet and rigid. — **gibi dur=** to stand like a graven image. — **kesil=** to become as motionless as a statue.

put 2 بوت twisted silk thread.

puta بوته *archaic* 1. target. 2. a kind of arrow.

pute (—.) بوته P *lrnd., same as* **pota**.

puthane (.—.) بوتخانه [**büthane**] P place of pagan worship.

putkıran بوت قيران *eccl.* iconoclast.

putla=ʳ بوتلامس to foal (camel).
putlaştır=ⁱʳ بوتلاشدیرمك /ı/ to idolize.
putperest بوتپرست [bütperest] idolator, pagan. —lik idolatry, paganism.
putrel بوترل F same as potrel.
puvan پوان F₊ sports point; score.
puvantaj پوانتاژ F 1. time keeping (at a factory). 2. scoring, marking (of a game).
puy (—) بوی P lrnd., same as pu 1.
puya, puyan (— —) پویا پویان P lrnd. 1. running, trotting; runner. 2. plunged in.
puyapuy (— — —) پویاپوی P lrnd. continued running; in haste, galloping.
puye (—.) پویه P lrnd. a running, rushing; canter.
puyende (—..) پوینده P lrnd. running; runner.
puyepuy (—.—) پویه پوی P lrnd., same as puyapuy.
puyiş (—.) پویش P lrnd. a running or going about; a trotting up and down.
puz (—) پوز P lrnd. muzzle, the environs of the mouth. —bend (—.) P muzzle, muzzle-strap.
puzine (— —.) پوزینه P lrnd. ape, monkey.
puziş (—.) پوزش P lrnd. excuse, apology. —pezir (—..—) P 1. admitting excuse, excusable. 2. accepting excuses.
püf پوف gentle puff, breath. — de= /a/ to puff out, extinguish. — et= to blow out; to blow on; to puff. — noktasını bul= to find the delicate vital spot (of a thing).
püfkerde پفكرده P lrnd. blown out, extinguished with a puff.
püfkür=ᵘʳ بوفكورمك prov. to puff with a sound; to blow out.
püfle=ʳ بوفلمك /ı/ to blow upon, to blow out, to puff.
püfteri بوفتری [peftere] falconer's lure, decoy whistle, decoy-bird.
püfür püfür بوفور بوفور noise of a gentle breeze. — es= to blow gently.
pül پل P lrnd. 1. bridge. 2. arch. P—i Sırat Isl. rel. the Bridge of Sirat, leading to Paradise.
pünez پونز F thumbtack.
pür 1 پر P lrnd. full, filled.
pür- 2 پر P lrnd. full of, as in pürhiddet, pürneş'e.
pürapür (—.) پراپر P lrnd. filled to the brim, brimfull.
pürazamet (..—.) پرعظمت P full of haughtiness, grandiosely.
pürbad (—.) پرباد P lrnd. 1. full of wind, inflated. 2. puffed up with vanity.
pürçek⁽ⁱⁱ⁾ پرچك prov. curled, curly; curl. —len= to become curly; to curl. —li with curly hair.

pürçin (.—) پرچین P lrnd. full of wrinkles.
pürçük⁽ᵍⁱⁱ⁾ پرچك prov., same as pürçek.
pürdil پردل P lrnd. 1. courageous; magnanimous; generous. 2. wise, intelligent. —ân (..—) P pl.
püre 1 پوره F cookery purée.
püre 2 پره prov., same as pire 1.
pürefşan (..—) پرافشان P name of a mode in Oriental music.
püren پورن prov. pine needle.
pürgayz پرغیظ P lrnd. wrathful, raging.
pürgulûl (..—) پرغلول P lrnd. deceitful, treacherous.
pürgurur (..—) پرغرور P lrnd. overconfident, very proud.
pürhiddet پرحدت P angry, raging.
pürhun (.—) پرخون P lrnd. full of blood.
pürkeyf پركیف P joyful.
pürkine (.—.) پركینه P lrnd. malicious, spiteful.
pürmaye (.—.) پرمایه P lrnd. valuable, costly.
pürmelal⁽ⁱⁱ⁾ (..—) پرملال P lrnd. sorrowful.
pürneşe پرنشه P joyful, very cheerful.
-pürs پرس P lrnd. who inquires, as in hatırpürs.
pürsa (.—) پرسا P lrnd. inquiring; who inquires.
pürsale (.—.) پرساله P lrnd. aged, old.
pürsan (.—) پرسان P lrnd. who inquires. — ol= to inquire.
pürsende پرسنده P lrnd. inquirer, interrogator.
-pürsi (.—) پرسی P lrnd., verbal n. of -pürs, as in hatırpürsi.
pürsiş پرسش P lrnd. question, interrogation.
pürsuz (.—) پرسوز P lrnd. blazing; burning.
pürtük⁽ᵍⁱⁱ⁾ پرتوك rough, uneven, knobby; knob, small protuberance. — pürtük full of knobs, knobby. —len= to become knobby. —lü knobby, rough.
pürüz پوروز [pürz] 1. shagginess; roughness; unevenness. 2. irregularity. 3. roughness on the surface of a casting. 4. nap, pile of cloth; fluff. 5. hitch, difficulty. — ayıkla=, — temizle= to settle a matter; to clear away difficulties.
pürüzlen=ⁱʳ پوروزلنمك 1. to become rough or shaggy. 2. to be beset with difficulties. —dir= /ı/ caus.
pürüzlü پوروزلو 1. rough, shaggy. 2. covered with ink stains or splashes of paint. 3. uneven, irregular. 4. beset with difficulties.
pürüzsüz پوروزسز 1. even, smooth. 2. without defects.
pürz پرز P lrnd. nap, pile of cloth; down.
püs پوس prov. resin, gum (of a tree).
püser پسر P lrnd. son, boy, lad. —i hande adopted son.

püskül پوسکول ، یوسکل ، پسکل ، پسکول 1. tassel; tuft. 2. difficulties.
püsküllen=ⁱʳ پوسکوللنمك 1. to become like a tassel; to acquire a tassel or appendage like a tassel. 2. to entail troublesome consequences, to grow worse.
püsküllendir=ⁱʳ پوسکوللندیرمك /ı/ 1. to tease out into a tassel; to attach a tassel. 2. to cause to become difficult or complicated. 3. to cause to branch out in annoying directions; to exaggerate greatly.
püsküllü پوسکوللی 1. tasseled. 2. difficult, complicated. — belâ 1. serious calamity. 2. a great nuisance.
püskür=ⁱʳ پوسکورمك ، پسکرمك ، پوسکرمك 1. to blow out water from the mouth; to spray (liquid). 2. to foam at the mouth, to splutter. 3. to scatter, drive away. 4. to erupt (volcano). 5. prov. to laugh immoderately.
püskürgeç ᶜⁱ پوسکورگج atomizer.

püskürme پوسکورمه 1. verbal n. of püskür=. 2. anything splashed about; scattered about (of water etc.). 3. a kind of baggy trousers. — ben beauty spots scattered about over the face. — boya spray paint. — fişek floral shell (in fireworks). — memesi mech. injection nozzle. — pompa fuel pump. — yaldız spray gilding. —lik pulverizer.
püskürt=ⁱʳ پوسکورتمك /ı/ caus. of püskür=.
püskürtü neol., geol. lava.
püskürük ᵍᵘ neol., geol. eruptive, volcanic. — külte eruptive rock.
püsür پوسور Gk colloq. 1. filth, rubbish. 2. unpleasant additions and accessories (children, relatives). —lü beset with difficulties or unnecessary things.
püşt پشت P lrnd., same as puşt 2.
pütür pütür پوتور پوتور roughened, chapped (hands).

R

r, R 1 the twenty-first letter of the Turkish alphabet.
=r 2 with positive verb stems only after a consonant, if the stem has more than one syllable, =ır, =ir, =ur, =ür; if the stem has one syllable, =ar, =er. By rare exception, some monosyllabic stems ending in l, n, or r take =ır=, =ir= etc. that generally does, that may do, e. g., yanar that burns, inflamable, yazar who writes, writer, giderim I always go, I may go.
-ra, -re ه - obs., postposition of direction, e. g., başıra onto his head.
raad (. —) رعاد A lrnd. 1. that thunder much, thundering (clouds). 2. garrulous, talkative. 3. threatening, menacing. 4. electric catfish, zool., Malapterurus electricus.
rab ᵇᵇⁱ 1 رب A 1. w. cap. the Lord, God. 2. lrnd. master, lord; ruler. 3. lrnd. possessor, owner, proprietor. R—im my God.
ra'b 2 رعب A lrnd. 1. a fearing, a being frightened; fear, terror. 2. threat, menace.
rabbani (. — —) ربانی A lrnd. 1. divine, godly. 2. devout. —yet (. — —.) A divinity, deity. —yun (. — — —) A devout men.
rabbe (—.) ربّه A lrnd. stepmother, foster mother.

Rabbena (..—) ربّنا A lrnd. our Lord; O God!
Rabbi ربّی A lrnd. my God, as in ya Rabbi!
Rabbülerbab (...—) ربّ الارباب A lrnd. Lord of Lords, God the Almighty.
rabih (—.) رابح A lrnd. 1. who gains (in commerce). 2. profitable, lucrative. —a (—..) A profitable business.
rabıt ᵇᵗⁱ 1 ربط [rabt] 1. a binding, connecting; connection, bond. 2. grammatical construction. — edatı gram. conjunction.
rabıt 2 (—.) رابط A lrnd. 1. that ties or binds, binding, connecting. 2. courageous, firm of purpose. 3. ascetic, hermit.
rabıta (—..) رابطه A 1. tie, bond; connection. 2. orderly arrangement, congruity; propriety. 3. log. copula.
rabıtalı رابطه لی 1. in good order; regular. 2. well-conducted, decent, excellent.
rabıtasız رابطه سز 1. disordered, irregular. 2. incoherent, unconnected, rambling, disorderly. 3. bad, worthless, improper. —lık 1. disorder, irregularity. 2. bad behavior, impropriety.
rabi ⁱⁱ (—.) رابع A lrnd. fourth.
rabian (—'..) رابعا A lrnd. fourthly.

rabit (.—) رابط A *lrnd.* 1. tied, bound, fastened. 2. hermit, devotee.

rabt ربط A *lrnd.*, *cf.* **rabıt** 1. —**ı kalb et**= /a/ to set one's heart on.

rabtet=^{der} ربط ايتمك /ı, a/ to bind, connect, fasten.

rabtiye ربطیه same as **raptiye**.

Raca (.'.) راجا Hind Hindu Rajah.

raciⁱⁱ 1 (—.) راجع A *lrnd.* 1. returning. 2. concerning, relating to. — **ol**= /a/ to concern, to fall on one (responsibility, etc.)

raci 2 (—.) راجى A *lrnd.* 1. who hopes or expects. 2. who asks as a favor.

racif (—.) راجف A *lrnd.* 1. that shakes. 2. shaking fever.

racih (—.) راجح A *lrnd.* preponderant; preferable.

racil (—.) راجل A *lrnd.* 1. on foot, pedestrian. 2. ignorant.

racilen (—'..) راجلا A *lrnd.* on foot, walking.

racis (—.) راجس A *lrnd.* that thunders, roars, brays.

racon راجون It *slang* custom, rule. — **kes**= 1. to judge and condemn. 2. to show off.

ra'd 1 رعد A *lrnd.* 1. thunder. 2. threat. **R— Sûresi** the thirteenth sura of the Quran.

rad 2 (—) راد P *lrnd.* 1. wise; sage. 2. generous, liberal, munificent; brave, valiant. 3. narrator, historian, poet.

rad^{ddi} 3 راد A *lrnd.* 1. that repels or rejects. 2. who gives back.

radansa (.'.) رادانسا It *naut.* iron thimble or cringle for a rope. —**lı halat** lizard.

radar رادار E radar. —**cı** school *slang* sneak, tale-bearer.

radde رادّه [Arabic —.] point, degree. —**lerinde**, —**sinde** approximately; about (such and such an hour).

ra'de رعده A *lrnd.* shiver, shake, tremor.

ra'dendaz (..—) رعدانداز P *lrnd.* thundering.

radi 1 (——) رادى P *lrnd.* 1. wisdom; intelligence. 2. liberality, generosity; boldness.

radi 2 (—.) رادى A *lrnd.* 1. that pelts, batters, strikes. 2. who falls, tumbles into. 3. who perishes, lost.

radif (—.) رادف A *lrnd.* that follows, succeeds another; that comes after.

radife (—..) رادفه A *lrnd.* the second blast of the trumpet at the Resurrection.

radikalⁱⁱ راديقال F radical. —**izm** *phil.* radicalism.

radike 1 (.'.) راديكه It chicory, *bot.*, *Cichorium intibus.*

radike 2 (.'.) راديكه It dandelion, *bot.*, *Taraxacum officinale.*

radiyallahü anh (...—..) رضى الله عنه A *rel. formula* May God be well pleased with him *used after naming any companion of the Prophet Muhammad.*

radmenis (—..), **radmerd** (—.) رادمنش، رادمرد P *lrnd.* noble and generous; munificient.

radyatör رادياتور F 1. radiator. 2. *auto.* cooling radiator. — **buhar borusu** *auto.* radiator tube. — **pancuru** *auto.* radiator shell.

radyo (.'.) راديو F radio.

raf 1 راف P shelf. —**a koy**= /ı/ 1. to put on the shelf. 2. to shelve and forget.

ra'f 2 رعف A *lrnd.* a bleeding of the nose.

rafadan رفدان 1. soft-boiled egg. 2. *slang* raw and inexperienced.

rafız (—.) رافض A *lrnd.* who leaves, forsakes, deserts.

rafıza (—..) رافضه A *Isl. rel.* a sect of the Shiites who renounced their allegiance to Zaid, the grandson of Husain.

rafızî (—.—) رافضى A 1. pertaining to the **rafıza** sect. 2. schismatic, heretic; Shi'i. —**lik**, —**yet** A heresy.

rafiⁱⁱ (—.) رافع A *lrnd.* 1. who raises, lifts. 2. who exalts; God, the Exalter of His people. 3. who erects.

rafia (—..) رافعه A 1. *lrnd.* raising. 2. *anat.* levator (muscle).

rafih (—.) رافه A *lrnd.* 1. easy, comfortable, luxurious. 2. who leads an easy, luxurious life.

rafz رفض A *lrnd.* 1. a leaving, forsaking, abandoning; abandonment, desertion. 2. schism, heresy.

ragad رغد A *lrnd.* 1. ample, plentiful, abundant; comfortable, luxurious. 2. in comfortable circumstances.

ragaib (.—.) رغائب A *lrnd.*, *pl.* of **ragibe**. **R— Gecesi**, **R— Kandili** night preceding the first Friday in the month of Rejeb, regarded as the anniversary of the conception of the Prophet Muhammad.

Ragaibiye (.—...) رغائبيه A *lrnd.* poem written on the occasion of the Night of **Ragaib**.

ragıb (—.) راغب A *lrnd.* desirous, eager; willing, wishing.

ragibe (.—.) رغيبه A *lrnd.* thing desired; gift, reward.

ragif (.—) رغيف A *lrnd.* thin cake of bread baked without hard crust; loaf of bread.

rağ (—) راغ P *lrnd.* lower part of a mountain; fields, meadows on a mountain slope.

rağbet رغبت A 1. inclination, desire. 2. demand. —**ten düş**= to be out of favor; to be no longer in demand. — **et**= /a/ to wish (for); to esteem, to like. — **gör**= to be in demand.

rağbetli رغبتلى 1. desirous; having an inclination for something. 2. in demand, sought after, liked.

rağbetlû (..—) غَبْطَلُو Ott. hist. esteemed, estimable (title given to non-Muslims who had no official title).

rağbetsiz رَغْبَتْسِز 1. who feels no desire (for something). 2. unesteemed, not sought after. **—lik** 1. a being without inclination. 2. lack of esteem, a not being in demand.

rağm رَغْم A 1. spite. 2. lrnd. a rubbing in the dust (the nose of a person). **—ına** /ın/ out of spite for.

rağmen (.'.) رَغْماً A /a/ in spite of.

rah 1 (—) راه P lrnd. 1. road, way, path. 2. course, rule; system; custom. 3. name of a mode in Oriental music; time. **—ı adem** death. **—ı beka** 1. the road to eternity, death. 2. name of a note in music. **—ı birah** 1. road that is not a thoroughfare; mountain pass. 2. improper, irregular way. **—ı fenâ** death. **—ı güldâr** the world; time, life, fortune. **—ı güriz** way of escape, line of retreat. **—ı Hak** the way of God. **—ı hüsrevanî** name of a note in music. **—ı kehkeşan** the milky way. **—ı kur** unfrequented road, difficult track. **—ı kûfte** frequented road, well-beaten track. **—ı nârefteye git=** to strike out in new paths. **— rah** marked with stripes; striped, variegated. **—ı rast** the right way. **—ı ruh** mus., the seventh among the thirty tunes. **—ı şah** public thoroughfare, highway. **—ı tecrid** myst. path of contemplative abstraction.

rah 2 (—) راح A lrnd. wine. **—ı beka** name of a note in music.

raha 1 (.—) رَهَا A lrnd. ease, freedom from care, comfort.

raha 2 (—.) راح A lrnd. palm of the hand.

rahamahullah رَحَمَهُ اللّٰه A lrnd. May God's mercy be upon him said of a deceased person.

rahamet (.—.) رَحَمَت A lrnd. a being soft, gentle and melodious (speech or voice).

rahamut (..—) رَحَمُوت A lrnd. great pity, compassion and kindness.

rahamuz (———) راه آمُوز P lrnd. 1. guide. 2. teacher.

rahaset (.—.) رَهَاسَت A lrnd. 1. a being soft, tender, pliant. 2. a being cheap; cheapness.

rahat راحَت [Arabic —.] 1. ease, rest; comfort, tranquillity; quiet. 2. at ease, comfortable; tranquil; easy; comfortably, quietly. 3. mil. At ease! **—ına bak=** to mind one's own comfort. **—ınıza bakın** Please don't worry; it really doesn't matter. **— bat=** /a/ to be stupid enough to throw away a comfortable position. **— döşeği** one's death bed. **— dur** 1. Don't fidget. 2. mil. At ease! **— et=** 1. to be at ease. 2. to make oneself comfortable, to rest. **—ı lokum** colloq. for **rahatülhulkum**. **— rahat** easily; amply.

— verme= /a/ to annoy, to harass. **— yüzü görme=** to have no peace.

rahatefza, rahatfeza (—..—) راحَت افزا P lrnd. 1. increasing comfort, quieting, soothing. 2. Or. mus., one of the compound makams.

rahatla= راحَتلَنمَك 1. to become comfortable, to feel relieved; to get calmed. 2. to have no more anxiety. **—n=, —ş=** to rest, to take one's ease; to calm oneself.

rahatlık^{ğı} راحَتلِق ease; comfort; quiet, tranquillity.

rahatnişin (—..—) راحَت نِشين P lrnd. who sits in ease and comfort; living in tranquillity.

rahatsız راحَتسِز 1. uncomfortable; disagreeable. 2. uneasy, anxious; unquiet. 3. indisposed, unwell, ill. **— et=** /ı/ 1. to bother, to inconvenience. 2. to annoy, to disturb. **— olmayın** Don't let me disturb you.

rahatsızlık^{ğı} راحَتسِزلِق discomfort, uneasiness, illness. **— ver=** /a/ same as **rahatsız et=**.

rahatülervah (—...—) راحَت الارواح A Or. mus., one of the oldest compound makams.

rahatülhulkum (—...—) راحَت الحُلقوم A lrnd., same as **lâtilokum**.

rahaver, rahaverd (——.) راه آوَر ، راه آوَرد P lrnd. present brought by a traveler.

rahavet (.—.) رَخاوَت A 1. softness, limpness. 2. slackness, lethargy. **— çök=** to feel lazy.

rahban (——) رَهبان P lrnd. guard, road, patrol.

rahber (—.) رَهبَر P lrnd., same as **rehber**.

rahdan (——) راهدان P lrnd. road guide.

rahdar (——) راهدار P lrnd. 1. guard, road patrol. 2. toll collector; customhouse officer. 3. highwayman, bandit.

rahgüzar (—.—), **rahgüzer** (—..) راهگُذَر ، راهگُذار P lrnd. place by which the road passes.

rahi 1 (——) راهى P lrnd. 1. pertaining to a road or to travelling. 2. about to travel; traveling.

rahi 2 (.—) رَخى A lrnd. 1. comfortable, ample (means of subsistance). 2. easy, free from sorrow or anxiety.

rahi 3 (——) راحى A anat. pertaining to the palm of the hand, palmar.

rahib 1 (—.) راهِب A same as **rahip**.

rahib 2 (.—) رَحيب A lrnd. wide, spacious, extensive.

rahiban (—.—) راهِبان P lrnd., pl. of **rahib 1**.

rahibe (—..) راهِبه A 1. nun. 2. priestess.

rahik^{kı} (.—) رَحيق A lrnd. 1. pure, unmixed, genuine. 2. wine, choice wine.

rahil 1 (.—) رَحيل A lrnd. 1. a moving, departure; migration; journey. 2. saddled

rahil

(camel); strong in journeying (camel). **— göçü** departure to the next world.

rahil 2 (—.) راحل A *lrnd.* who journeys, departs or migrates; traveler.

Rahil 3 (— —) راحيل A *Bib.* Rachel.

rahile (— ..) راحلة A *lrnd.* 1. camel that is ridden, saddle-camel. 2. beast of burden. 3. caravan, company traveling together.

rahim[hmi] **1** رحم [rahm 1] *anat.* uterus, womb. **—i mader** *lrnd.* mother's womb.

rahim 2 (—.) راحم A *lrnd.* who feels compassion, who shows pity; compassionate, merciful.

rahim 3 (.—) رحيم A *lrnd.* 1. pitiful, merciful, compassionate; kind. 2. all-merciful God.

rahim 4 (.—) رخيم A *lrnd.* 1. soft, gentle, quiet. 2. gentle-voiced, softspoken (girl).

rahimane (.— —.) رحيمانه P *lrnd.* with compassion, mercifully.

rahimin (—.—) راحمين A *lrnd.*, *pl. of* **rahim 2**.

rahin (—.) راهن A *lrnd.* who pledges, who gives security, pledger.

rahip[bi] (—.) راهب [rahib 1] 1. monk. 2. priest. **—lik** 1. monkhood. 2. priesthood.

rahis (.—) رخيص A *lrnd.* 1. cheap, of little value. 2. soft (garment). 3. sudden, quick (death).

rahiye (— ..) راحية [rah 1, -iye 3] traveling expenses.

rahl[li] رحل A *lrnd.* 1. small camel saddle, saddle. 2. traveler's kit. 3. reading desk. 4. resting place, abode, dwelling.

rahle رحله A low reading desk.

rahm[mi] **1** رحم A *lrnd.*, *same as* **rahim 1**.

rahm 2 رحم A *lrnd.* a pitying; compassion.

Rahman (.—) رحمان A All-Compassionate. **— Suresi** the fifty-fifth sura of the Quran.

Rahmanî (.— —.) رحمانى A *lrnd.* pertaining to the All-Compassionate God; bestowed by God; divine. **—yun** (.— — —) A *myst.* a certain class of saints.

rahmet 1 رحمت A 1. God's mercy, compassion, forgiveness and grace. 2. rain (as a mercy). **— deryası** ocean of divine grace. **— düş=** to rain. **— oku=** /a/ 1. to pray for God's mercy and grace on the dead; to pray for the soul of. 2. to regret something lost. **— okut=** /a/ 1. to cause one to regret. 2. to make one long for a lost thing; to be a greater evil or nuisance (than). **— olsun canına** May God bless his soul. **—i Rahmana kavuş=** to pass away, to go to one's eternal rest. **— yağ=** to rain.

rahmet=[der] رحم ايتمك /a/ *lrnd.* to have mercy on, to show compassion.

rahmetli, rahmetlik[ği] رحمتلك the deceased, the late. **— ol=** to die.

rahmetullah (. . . —) رحمة الله A *lrnd.* God's compassion and mercy. **—i aleyhi** May God bless his soul *said for a deceased person*.

rahmi 1 (. —) رحمى A *lrnd.* merciful, compassionate.

rahmi 2 (. —) رحمى A *anat.* uterine.

rahname (— — .) راهنامه P *lrnd.* road-book, map, chart.

rahne رخنه P *lrnd.* 1. rent, breach, fissure. 2. gash, wound. 3. breach of friendship, violation of a pact.

rahnedar (. . —) رخنه دار P *lrnd.* 1. notched, cracked. 2. damaged; broken up. **— ol=** to be broken up or cracked.

rahnelen=[ir] رخنه لنمك to become rent, cracked, fissured; to be damaged. **—dir=** /ı/ *caus.*

rahneverd (— . .) راهنورد P *lrnd.* 1. traveled; messenger. 2. quick, fleet.

rahnişin (—.—) راهنشين P *lrnd.* 1. traveler, wanderer. 2. peddler. 3. toll-gatherer. 4. robber.

rahnüma, rahnümun (. . —) راهنما راهنمون P *lrnd.* showing the way; guide.

rahrev (—.) راهرو P *lrnd.* traveler.

rahrevan (—.—) راهروان P *lrnd.* travelers. **—ı ezel** God's predestined, saints. **—ı gerdûn** the seven planets. **—ı seher** 1. travelers at dawn. 2. vigil keepers till dawn; devotees. **—ı tarikat** the dervishes.

rahrevi (—.—) راهروى P *lrnd.* travel, journey.

rahş رخش P *lrnd.* 1. gleam, flash, glitter. 2. *w. cap., name of Rustam's charger.* 3. swift horse. 4. rainbow. **—i bahar** vernal breezes or clouds. **—i sabâ-reftâr** a very swift horse.

rahşa, rahşan (. —) رخشان P *lrnd.* gleaming, glittering, shining.

rahşe رخشه P *lrnd.* flash, flame, blaze.

rahşende رخشنده P *lrnd.* gleaming, glittering, shining.

rahşiş رخشش P *lrnd.* gleaming, flashing, glittering, shining.

rahşiye (. —.) رخشيه P *lrnd.* poem written in praise of a horse.

raht رخت P *lrnd.* 1. luggage; household effects; furniture. 2. harness; trappings of a horse. 3. hinge of a window or door. 4. *arch.* rise (of a stair); riser. **— ve baht** one's all. **— çek=** to carry one's effects. **—ı hâb** bed clothes, night dress. **—ı hesti** the material of one's existence, one's being; reason, understanding. **—ını vur=** /ın/ to harness a horse.

rahtban (. —) رختبان P *same as* **rahtvan**.

rahtla=[r] رختلمك /ı/ to harness a horse.

rahtlı رختلى fitted up, equipped.

rahtvan (. —) رختوان P *lrnd.* gold-embroidered surcingle used on a state occasion. **— ağası** *Ott. hist.* a kind of chief equerry to a grandee.

rahum (. —.) صَهُومٌ ‎ A *lrnd.* pitying, merciful; kind.

ràhv رَهْوٌ ‎ A *lrnd.* 1. soft; loose; relaxed. 2. limp, flaccid.

rahvan رَهْوَانْ ‎ [**rahvar**] amble; ambling horse; ambling pace. — **git=**, — **yürü=** to amble.

rahvar (——), **rahver** (—.) راهوار ـ راهور ‎ P *lrnd.* quick, easy, ambling-paced (horse); good roadster.

rahzen (—.) رَهْزَنْ ‎ P *lrnd.* 1. highway robber. 2. musician; singer. —**î** (—.—) P highway robbery.

rai 1 (——) رَاعٍ ‎ A *lrnd.* 1. shepherd, herdsman. 2. ruler, king, guardian, protector.

rai 2 (——) رَائِي ‎ A *lrnd.* one who sees, seer.

rai 3 (——) رَائِي ‎ A *lrnd.* pertaining to or containing the letter ر.

raib 1 (—.) رَاعِبْ ‎ A *lrnd.* 1. who fears; frightened. 2. magician.

raib 2 (.—) رَعِيبْ ‎ A *lrnd.* afraid, terrified.

raic (—.) رَائِجْ ‎ A *lrnd.*, *same as* **rayic**.

raid (—.) رَاعِدْ ‎ A *lrnd.* 1. thundering. 2. menacing, vituperative.

raide (—..) رَاعِدَه ‎ A *lrnd.* surpassingly beautiful (woman).

raif (—.) رَائِفْ ‎ A *lrnd.* clement, benign.

raiha (—..) رَائِحَه ‎ A *lrnd.*, *same as* **rayiha**.

raikᵏⁱ (—.) رَائِقْ ‎ A *lrnd.* 1. pleasantly astonishing; beautiful, handsome. 2. pure, genuine, clear.

raiş (—.) رَائِشْ ‎ A *lrnd.* who offers a bribe; broker employed to conciliate the favor of an official by presents.

raiyet رَعِيَّتْ ‎ A 1. *Isl. hist.* people under a ruler, subject community. 2. *lrnd.* flock at pasture.

raiyetperver رَعِيَّتْ پَرْوَرْ ‎ P *lrnd.* who cherishes his subjects, nourisher of his people. —**âne** (.....—.) P beneficent and just. —**î** (.....—) P, —**lik** beneficence and justice to subjects.

rakᵏᵏⁱ **1** رَقّ ‎ A *lrnd.* 1. parchment, vellum. 2. sheet or leaf of parchment; document written on parchment.

-rakᵍⁱ **2, -rek**ᵍⁱ رَك ‎ *diminutive of some adjectives (final -k is dropped), as in* **ufarak, küçürek**.

-rakᵍⁱ **3, -rek**ᵍⁱ رَك ‎ *archaic, comparative form of adjective, as in* **kiçirek** *smaller,* **yeğrek** *better.*

rakabat (..—) رَقَبَاتْ ‎ A *lrnd.*, *pl. of* **rakabe**.

rakabe رَقَبَه ‎ A *lrnd.* 1. neck. 2. slave (purchased with money); prisoner.

rakabet (.—.) رَقَبَتْ ‎ A *same as* **rekabet**.

rakabi (..—) رَقَبِي ‎ A *anat.* cervical.

rakadan (..—) رَقَدَانْ ‎ A *lrnd.* a leaping or frisking for joy, exultation.

rakaikᵏⁱ (.—.) رَقَائِقْ ‎ A 1. *lrnd.* subtleties, abstruse points. 2. *myst.* transcendental points of doctrine.

rakam رَقَمْ ‎ A 1. figure, numeral; number. 2. *lrnd.* arithmetic. 3. *lrnd.* writing; written character; cipher. —**i evvel** *myst.* the halo of divine glory whence proceeded the spirit of the Prophet Muhammad.

rakamî (..—) رَقَمِي ‎ A *lrnd.* pertaining to figures, numerical; arithmetical.

rakamkeş رَقَمْكَشْ ‎ P *lrnd.* who writes down figures.

rakamla=ʳ رَقَمْلَه ‎ /ı/ to mark with numbers.

rakamlı رَقَمْلِي ‎ having numbers or figures.

rakampezir (...—) رَقَمْ پَذِيرْ ‎ P *lrnd.* that can be expressed in numerals.

rakamzede رَقَمْ زَدَه ‎ P *lrnd.* written, put on paper.

rakamzen رَقَمْ زَنْ ‎ P *lrnd.* that writes.

rakaş رَقَشْ ‎ A *lrnd.* spottedness, mottledness.

rakdᵈⁱ رَقْدْ ‎ A *lrnd.* 1. sleep; a sleeping. 2. dullness, lethargy, stagnancy.

rakde رَقْدَه ‎ A *lrnd.* a sleep, a nap, a dozing.

raket رَاكِتْ ‎ F racket.

rakı رَاقِي ‎ [**arak 2**] raki, arrack. — **âlemi** a drinking party. — **çek=** to produce raki.

rakıcı رَاقِيجِي ‎ 1. maker or seller of raki. 2. raki addict. —**lık** manufacturing of raki; profession of a raki maker.

rakım (—.) رَاقِمْ ‎ A 1. altitude above the sea level. 2. who writes or marks. —**ı huruf** *same as* **rakımülhuruf**.

rakımülhuruf (—...—) رَاقِمُ الْحُرُوفْ ‎ A *lrnd.* the writer of this, *i. e.* I, the writer.

rakiⁱⁱ (—.) رَاكِعْ ‎ A *lrnd.* 1. who bows his head in worship, who bows down (in prayer). 2. who displays humility and lowliness.

rakian (—'..) رَاكِعَانْ ‎ A *lrnd.* bowing down in humility or respect.

rakib 1 (.—) رَقِيبْ ‎ A 1. rival. 2. *lrnd.* watchman, scout; guardian; God, the Universal Guardian.

rakib 2 (—.) رَاكِبْ ‎ A *lrnd.* one who mounts, embarks or travels on an animal, a vehicle, or a vessel, riding; mounted; rider.

rakiban (.——) رَقِيبَانْ ‎ P *lrnd.*, *pl. of* **rakib 1**.

rakiben (—'..) رَاكِبَاً ‎ A *lrnd.* /a/ riding on, riding in, mounted; on board.

rakid (—.) رَاكِدْ ‎ A *lrnd.* still, motionless, silent.

rakikᵏⁱ (.—) رَقِيقْ ‎ A 1. *lrnd.* slender; fine; tender, soft-hearted. 2. *lrnd.* thin; weak. 3. servile; enslaved; slave.

rakim (.—) رَقِيمْ ‎ A *lrnd.* a writing, inscription; book.

rakime (.—.) رقیمه A *lrnd.* writing, inscription, document; letter.

rakiz (—.) راكز A *lrnd.* 1. who sets up, drives in, plants in the ground. 2. firm, immovable.

rakka (.—) رقّاء A *lrnd.* enchanter, wizard.

rakkas (.—) رقّاص A 1. pendulum. 2. *lrnd.* professional male dancer.

rakkase (.—.) رقّاصه A dancing girl.

rakor راقور F joint, coupling, connection, junction, union (of pipes).

raks رقص A 1. a dancing; dance; any of various dances performed to music. 2. *phys.* regular oscillation, vibration, pulsation. — **aksağı** a rhythmic pattern of nine beats. — **et=**. —**a gel=**, —**a gir=** to begin dancing. —**ı keçûl** *lrnd.* 'the lasvicious dance of the East. —**ı rubah** *lrnd.* willful negligence.

raksan (.—) رقصان P *Or. mus.* a rhythmic pattern of fifteen beats.

rakset=[der] رقصەتمك 1. to dance. 2. *phys.* to oscillate, to vibrate, to beat rhythmically.

rakskünan (..—) رقص كنان P *lrnd.* dancing, vibrating, pulsating.

rakşa (.—) رقشاء A *lrnd.* speckled, spotted, mottled.

rakta (.—) رقطاء A *lrnd.* 1. speckled, spotted (animal). 2. in which the letters are alternately dotted and undotted (composition).

ralânti رالانتی F *auto.* a throttling down; throttled down. — **hava ayar vidası** air-adjusting screw for slow running. — **memesi** pilot jet.

ram (—) رام P *lrnd.* 1. tame, gentle, quiet. 2. submissive, obedient. — **et=** /ı/ to subjugate, to cause to yield. — **ol=** /a/ to submit, to yield oneself to another.

ramak[kı] رمق A 1. the least possible quantity or degree of anything. 2. the remaining spark of life in a dying man. 3. *lrnd.* the minimum of food sufficient to keep life going. — **kaldı** It almost happened; all but.

Ramazan رمضان A *Arabic calendar* Ramazan, the ninth month of the year during which Muslims fast between dawn and sunset. — **Bayramı** the three-day feast at the end of Ramazan. — **keyfi** bad temper caused by fasting. — **tiryakisi** quick-tempered person.

Ramazaniye رمضانیه 1. eulogy written on the occasion of Ramazan. 2. provisions, groceries bought for use during Ramazan.

rami 1 (—.) رامی A *lrnd.* 1. who throws or shoots; archer. 2. *astr.* the constellation Sagittarius.

rami 2 رامی F China-grass, ramie, *bot.*, *Boehmeria nivea*.

ramiş (—.) رامش P *lrnd.* 1. rest, repose, tranquillity. 2. joy, pleasure. 3. music. —**i can** name of a tune in Oriental music.

ramişgâh (—.—) رامشگاه P *lrnd.* place of repose, chamber, couch.

ramişger (—..) رامشگر P *lrnd.* musician; singer. —**î** (—..—) P *abstr. n.*

ramişhar (—.—) رامشخوار P *lrnd.*, name of a tune in Oriental music.

ramişî (—.—) رامشی P *lrnd.* 1. pertaining to music. 2. musician; singer.

ramiz (—.) رامز A *lrnd.* 1. who makes a sign or signal. 2. who uses an allusion or abbreviation.

rampa 1 (.'.) رامپا It ramp; loading platform.

rampa 2 (.'.) رامپا It *naut.* 1. act of boarding an enemy's ship in battle, casting grappling hooks for the purpose of boarding. 2. a ship's going alongside another or a wharf. — **et=** 1. /a/ to board an enemy's ship. 2. *slang* to accost (a woman). 3. *slang* to join a party uninvited.

rampacı رامپاجی *Ott. hist.* warrior boarding the enemy's ship.

ran 1 (—) ران P *lrnd.* the thigh.

-ran 2 (—) ران P *lrnd.* that drives, urges, impels, as in **hükümran, kâmran.**

ra'na (.—) A, **râna** (——) رعنا *lrnd.* 1. beautiful, pretty, tender, delicate. 2. admirable, graceful; exquisite, perfect. 3. stupid, silly. — **bil=** /ı/ to know perfectly.

ra'nai (.——) رعنائی P *lrnd.* 1. beauty; exquisiteness. 2. stupidity.

ra'naifüruş (.——.—) رعنافروش P *lrnd.* a beautiful but silly coquette.

randa (.'.) راندە It *naut.* spanker.

rande (—.) راندە P *lrnd.* who has driven; driven out or away; rejected, outcast. —**gân** (—.—) P exiles.

randevu راندەوو F appointment, rendezvous. — **evi** house where couples meet secretly. —**cu** keeper of a house where couples meet secretly.

randıman راندمان F yield, produce; profit; output. —**lı** profitable; productive.

ranza (.'.) رانزە It bunk; berth.

rapor راپور F 1. report; statement. 2. medical certificate, doctor's report.

raportör راپورتور F reporter.

rap rap راپ راپ imitates the sound of marching.

rapt ربط *var.* of **rabt.**

raptiye ربطیه [rabtiye] paper clip; thumbtack.

rasad رصد A a watching, observing; astronomical or meteorological observation.

rasadgâh (..—) رصدگاه P *lrnd.* place from whence spying or observing is done, observatory.

rasadhane (..—.) رصدخانه P observatory; meteorological station.

rasadî (..—) رصدى A lrnd. pertaining to astronomical or meteorological observation.

rasadnişin (...—) رصدنشين P lrnd. observer; astronomer.

rasaf رصف A lrnd. stones or bricks built together into a dam, wall or pavement.

rasafe رصفه A lrnd. pavement stone.

rasafet (.—.) رصافت A same as **rasanet**.

rasanet (.—.) رصانت A lrnd. 1. a being firm, solid and strong; firmness, solidity. 2. a being grave, calm, wise; gravity, sedateness, wisdom. —**li** firm, solid, strong; grave.

rasas (.—) رصاص A lrnd. lead (metal). —**ı ebyaz** tin; pewter. —**ı esved** lead. —**î** (.——) A 1. gray. 2. tinsmith.

rasayiî (.—.) رصائع A lrnd., pl. of **rasia**.

rasgel=ⁱʳ راست گل var. of **rastgel**=.

rasıd (—.) راصد A observer, watch. —**ân** (—.—) P lrnd., pl.

rasıkâri (..——) رسیکاری carpentry marquetry.

rasi (—.) راسى A lrnd. 1. firmly fixed, immovable. 2. anchored.

rasia (.—.) رصیعه A lrnd. 1. ornamental metal stud. 2. plaited loop, tassel.

rasib (—.) راسب A lrnd. 1. which sinks, subsides as a deposit. 2. firmly fixed, firm, immovable. 3. grave, sedate, moderate.

rasif (.—) رصیف A lrnd. 1. well and strongly made, firmly built. 2. sound, valid.

rasih (—.) راسخ A lrnd. 1. firm, stable, fixed, established. 2. well-grounded in science, learned, well-versed. —**i dem** staunch, not short-winded; constant. —**în**, —**un** (—.—) A learned men.

rasim (—.) راسم A lrnd. who designs, delineates, sketches, writes.

rasime (—..) راسمه A lrnd. ceremony; pageant; custom.

rasin (.—) رصین A lrnd. 1. firm, strong, stable. 2. grave, calm, cool.

rasla=ʳ راستلمس var. of **rastla**=.

raspa (.'.) راسپه It 1. rasp; grater; naut. scraper. 2. slang gluttony. — **et**= /ı/ to scrape; to rasp. — **taşı** pumice stone, holystone. —**cı** 1. scraper (man). 2. slang greedy.

raspala=ʳ راسپالامق 1. /ı/ to scrape, to rasp. 2. /a/ slang to accost, to edge up (to a person).

rassad (.—) رصّاد A lrnd. 1. astronomical observer; astronomer. 2. one who habitually waits and watches; robber, bandit. —**an** (.——) P pl.

rast (—) راست P 1. straight; right, correct, proper. 2. in order; successful. 3. Or. mus., one of the oldest makams. 4. lrnd. straightforward, honest, righteous. 5. lrnd. true; complete, perfect. 6. lrnd. firm, sound; sure, certain. 7. lrnd. right, right side. —**ı cedid** Or. mus., a **makam** similar to rast. — **git**= to go well, to succeed. — **perdesi** mus. the note g.

rastan (——) راستان P lrnd. 1. straightbacked men. 2. those who are sound and healthy. 3. the upright, the honest, virtuous, righteous.

rastbalâ (———) راست بالا P lrnd. 1. straight of stature. 2. cypress.

rastbaz (——) راست باز P lrnd. who plays well or fairly; faithful, trustworthy.

rastbin (——) راست بين P lrnd. impartial, seeing right, of sound judgment.

raste (—.) راسته P lrnd. row of shops, street with shops on each side; market-place.

rastgel=ⁱʳ راست گلمك 1. /a/ to encounter; to meet by chance, to come across; to hit the mark. 2. to succeed, to turn out right.

rastgele راست گله 1. by chance; chance. 2. haphazard, at random.

rastgetir=ⁱʳ راست گتيرمك /ı/ 1. to succeed in meeting; to hit the mark. 2. to cause to succeed.

rastgû (——) راست گو P lrnd. truth teller, honest. —**yan** (———) P pl.

rasthane (——.) راست خانه P lrnd. most conscientious, straightforward, unbiased.

rastıkᵍⁱ راستق [rasuht] 1. cosmetic used for blackening the eyebrows, kohl. 2. smut ball (disease of wheat). — **çek**= /a/ to blacken (the eyebrows). — **mürekkep** ink that will not wash off the paper; indelible ink. — **taşı** antimony, kohl.

rastî (——) راستى P lrnd. straightness, honesty, loyalty.

rastiver (——.) راستيور P lrnd. true, honest, just, right.

rastkâr (——) راستكار P lrnd. one who acts justly, does right or performs well; just, pious.

rastla=ʳ راستلمق /a/ to meet by chance, to coincide (with). —**ş**= to meet one another.

rastsaz (——) راست ساز P lrnd. attuned, in tune, in unison.

rasuht (—.) راسخت P lrnd., same as **rastık**.

rasyonel راسيونل F rational, well planned, well organized.

raşa 1 راشا F com. repurchase, buying back.

raşa 2 (.'.) راشا G obs. rash, shalloon, serge.

ra'şan (.—) رعشان A lrnd. trembling.

ra'şe رعشه A lrnd. tremble, shiver; tremor, shudder. —**dar** (..—) P, —**li**, —**nak** (..—) P trembling, tremulous; shivering.

raşi (—.) راشى A lrnd. who bribes, briber. — **ve mürteşi** the briber and the bribed.

raşid (—.) راشد A lrnd. 1. well-directed; well guided, who follows a right course. 2. of age. —**în** (—.—) A pl.

raşitikᵍⁱ راشینیاك F rickety, rachitic.
raşitizm راشینزم F rickets, rachitism.
ratanet (.—.) رطانت A lrnd. a speaking unintelligibly.
ratb رطب A lrnd. 1. moist, damp. 2. fresh, green; tender, soft. —ü yâbis 1. fresh and dry 2. relevant and irrelevant; suitable or unsuitable.
ratbüllisan (...—) رطب اللسان A lrnd. eloquent, melodious.
ratib (—.) رطب A lrnd. 1. moist, damp, humid. 2. tender, soft, pliant, supple.
ratıkᵏⁱ (—.) راتق A lrnd. who repairs, mends, darns; who draws together two sides.
ratib 1 (.—) رطيب A lrnd. 1. moist, damp, wet. 2. fresh, green; tender, soft.
ratib 2 (—.) راتب A lrnd. 1. fixed, firm, settled. 2. daily allowance of food, ration.
ratibe (—..) راتبه A lrnd. 1. fixed allowance, pay, salary; rations. 2. fixed duty or function, especially religious duty which is incumbent as being a practice of the Prophet Muhammad.
ratibehar (—..—) راتبه خوار P lrnd. dependent; pensioner.
ratinec (——.) راتینج A lrnd. 1. common turpentine. 2. rosin, pitch.
ratl رطل A lrnd. 1. rotl (weight of about one lb). 2. cup of wine, goblet. —ı girân large cupful of wine, bumper.
ratlkeş رطل كش P lrnd. one who drinks cups of wine.
rauf (.—) رؤوف A lrnd. clement, benign; All-Clement God.
ravakᵏⁱ رواق P pure clarified strained settled honey.
ravend (—.) راوند P rhubarb, bot., Rheum officinale.
ravi (—.) راوى A lrnd. narrator. —yân (—.—) A pl.
ravnt راوند E sports a round.
ravza روضه A lrnd. 1. garden, meadow; oasis in a desert. 2. tomb of a saint; w.- cap. the tomb of the Prophet. 3. Paradise. 4. a kind of five-stringed musical instrument. —i bağ-ı refi' the Garden of Paradise where the Prophet Muhammad will dwell. —i Muharrem a Muharrem meeting for mourning the death of Hasan and Husain. R—i Mutahhara, —i Nebi the Prophet's tomb. —i rıdvan Garden of Paradise, Paradise.
ravzahan (..—) روضه خوان P lrnd. one who recites elegies for Hasan and Husain.
ravzat (.—) روضات A lrnd., pl. of **ravza**.
ray 1 راى F rail (railway, etc.).
ra'y 2 رعى A lrnd. 1. a pasturing, feeding (cattle); a tending flocks. 2. a browsing the herbage (cattle). 3. submission.
ray 3 (—) راى P lrnd., same as **rey**.
raya (——) رعايا var. of **reaya**.

rayat (——) رعايات A lrnd., pl. of **rayet**.
rayegân (—.—) رايگان [raygân] lrnd. 1. gratis, gratuitous. 2. spent in vain. 3. abundant; current.
rayet 1 (—.) رايت A lrnd. flag.
ra'yet⁼ᵈᵉʳ 2 رعيتمك /ı/ lrnd. to pasture.
raygân (——) رايگان P lrnd., same as **rayegân**. —har (———) P sponging parasite.
rayic (—.) رايج A 1. current (coin or price), market price; current value. 2. in demand; salable. 3. in common use, general. — akça money in circulation, currency. — usûlü com. ad valorem.
rayiha (—..) رايحه A fragrance, aroma, scent. —dar (—..—) P lrnd, —lı scented, fragrant.
rayma (.'.) رايما E mech. reamer. —la= /ı/ to ream.
raz (—) راز P lrnd. secret; mystery; concealed thing. —ı derûn secret of the heart. —ı nihân concealed secret. —ı zemin (lit., mystery of the earth) vegetation.
razakı رازاقى A [razıkî] a variety of white grape (from which the best raisins are made).
razban (——) رازبان P lrnd. confidant.
razdan (——) رازدان P lrnd. 1. who knows secrets or mysteries. 2. confidant.
razdar (——) رازدار P lrnd. confidant; trusty, faithful.
razı (—.) راضى A 1. satisfied, contented, willing, approving, pleased. 2. resigned, submissive.
razıkᵏⁱ (—.) رازق A lrnd. who feeds, who provides daily bread.
razıkî (—.—) رازقى A same as **razakı**.
Razi 1 (——) رازى P lrnd. inhabitant of the city of Ray in Iran.
raziⁱⁱ 2 (.—) رضيع A lrnd. 1. foster brother. 2. suckling, infant.
raziyane (—.—.) رازيانه P same as **rezene**.
razlaş⁼ᵣ (—..) رازلاشمق to talk over secrets with one another.
raziyallahü anh (...—..) رضى الله عنه A same as **radiyallâhü anh**.
=**rdı**, =**rdi**, etc., after consonants =**ardı**, =**erdi**, or =**ırdı**, =**irdi**, etc. (see rule under =**r2**) (=**r**= + =**idi**) دى [he] used to ..., [he] would ...
re 1 ر 1. the letter r. 2. name of the letter ر (the tenth letter of the Arabic alphabet, and the twelfth letter of the Ottoman alphabet. In chronograms, it has the numerical value of 200).
re 2 ر mus. re.
-**re 3** ر cf. -**ra 1**.
reaksiyon رە آقسيون F reaction.
realist رەآلست F realistic.

realite رآليته F reality.
realizm رآليزم F realism.
reasürans رآسورانس F reinsurance.
reaya (. — —) رعايا A 1. *Ott. hist.* the tax-paying subjects of the Ottoman Empire; non-Muslim subjects of the Ottoman Empire; the Christian subjects. 2. *lrnd.*, *pl. of* **raiyet**. — **ve beraya** the tribute-paying and the free.
rebb'i ربع A *lrnd.* spring or autumn resort, dwelling, home, camp.
rebab (. —) رباب A an ancient Oriental three-stringed violin, still popular, with a body made of a coconut shell.
rebabe (. — .) ربابه A *lrnd.*, *same as* **rebab**.
rebabî (. — —) ربابى A 1. rebab-player or maker. 2. pertaining to a rebab.
rebabzen (. — .) ربابزن P *lrnd.* player of the rebab.
rebiii (. —) ربيع A *lrnd.* spring, spring season.
rebib (. —) ربيب A *lrnd.* 1. stepson. 2. raised in one's house. —**e** (. — .) A stepdaughter.
rebiî (. — —) ربيعى A *lrnd.* pertaining to spring, vernal.
Rebiülahir (. — . — .) ربيع الآخر A Arabic calendar the fourth month.
Rebiülevvel (. — . . .) ربيع الأول A Arabic calendar the third month.
rebubî (. — —) ربوبى A *lrnd.* divine; theological (learning).
rebun (. —) ربون A *lrnd.* earnest money.
recc'i 1 رجع A *lrnd.* a bringing back, returning.
reccci 2 رجّ A *lrnd.* a shaking violently, a being shaken violently; violent agitation, commotion.
reca (. —) رجاء A *lrnd.* 1. *same as* **rica 1**. 2. a hopefully expecting, desiring; hope, expectation, desire.
recâmend (. — .) رجامند P *lrnd.* 1. expectant. 2. solicitous, requesting. —**î** (. — . —) P expectancy, solicitousness.
Receb رجب A Arabic calendar the seventh month. —**ân** (. . —) A *lrnd.* the months **Receb** and **Şaban**.
recefan (. . —) رجفان A *lrnd.* 1. a shaking violently (earth). 2. a thundering with reverberation. 3. tremor, emotion.
recez رجز A *pros.* meter characterized by the spondaic beginning of each tetrasyllabic foot (most commonly : — — . — / — — . — / — — . — / — — . —).
recf رجف A *lrnd.* a violently shaking, a being violently shaken; commotion, agitation.
recfe رجفه A *lrnd.* a single shake, tremor, commotion.

recil (. —) رجيل A *lrnd.* 1. vigorous, stout in walking. 2. that goes on foot.
recim (. —) رجيم A *lrnd.* 1. pelted and driven away. 2. stoned to death. 3. cursed, execrated; reviled.
recm رجم A 1. *can. law* a stoning to death. 2. *lrnd.* a pelting; a reviling; a missile used in pelting.
recmet=der رجم ايتمك /ı/ 1. *can. law* to stone to death. 2. *lrnd.* to pelt.
recül رجل A *lrnd.* 1. full-grown man; male. 2. efficient, able man; capable. —**i devlet** statesman.
recüliyet (. — . .) رجوليت A *lrnd.* manhood, virility, manliness.
reçel رچل |Persian riçal| jam, fruit preserve.
reçete (. . .) رچته It prescription, recipe.
reçina (. . .) رچينه It resin, colophony; pitch. —**lı** resinous.
reçine (. . .) رچينه *var. of* **reçina**.
redddi 1 رد A 1. a repelling or rejecting; repulse, rejection, expulsion; a refusing, refusal. 2. a refuting; refutation. 3. a repudiating; repudiation. 4. a disclaiming, disowning. 5. *lrnd.* a restoring, restoration; return. 6. *lrnd.* a returning a salutation. 7. *can. law* a distributing the residue of the estate of a deceased person among those entitled to share when there is no other direct heir. —**i cevab et**= to answer. —**i hâkim** *law* rejection of the judge. —**i kelâm et**= to speak in reply.
redd'i 2 ردع A *lrnd.* a turning or driving from; a deterring, restraining, prohibiting.
redaet (. — .) رداءت A *lrnd.* worthlessness; viciousness; badness.
reddet=der 1 رد ايتمك 1. to reject; to repel; to refuse, to repudiate, to refute. 2. *lrnd.* to return (answer).
reddet 2 ردت A *lrnd.* defect, fault, deformity.
reddiye ردية A *lrnd.* article written to refute some thought or doctrine, refutation.
redi (. —) ردى A *lrnd.* bad, corrupt, depraved, wicked.
redif (. —) رديف A 1. *Ott. hist.* reserve, reservist. 2. *lrnd.* one who rides behind another on the same beast. 3. *pros.* word repeated at the end of every couplet of a poem. — **askeri** troops of the militia or reserve.
redingot ردنكوت F frock coat.
redm ردم A *lrnd.* 1. a shutting, closing up (gap). 2. a bolting (door). 3. embankment, rampart, dike; wall or barrier (particularly that between Gog and Magog).
ree رع A *var. of* **rie**.
reeskont رعسكونت F *com.* rediscount.
refr'i 1 رفع A *same as* **refi 1**.
reffffi 2 رفت A *lrnd.*, *same as* **raf 1**.

refah (.—) رَفاه A easy circumstances; comfort, luxury, affluence.

refahet (.—.), **refahiyet** (.—..) رَفاهَت ، رَفاهِيَت A lrnd., same as **refah**.

refakatᵘ (.—.) رَفاقَت A 1. companionship, an accompanying. 2. mus. accompaniment. **—inde** /ın/ accompanied by, in the company of. **—iyle** /ın/ mus. accompanied by. **— et=** /a/ to accompany (someone).

referandum (...'.) فَراندوم F referendum.

refet=ᵈᵉʳ 1 رَفع ايتمك /ı/ lrnd. 1. to raise, to lift, to heighten. 2. to take away, to remove, to annul. 3. to promote. 4. to raise a number (to a certain mathematical power).

re'fet 2 رَأفَت A lrnd. a being clement and benign; benignity.

re'fetlû (..—) رَأفَتلو benign used as a title in addressing the commander-in-chief of the army by letter.

re'fetmeab (...—) رَأفَتمآب P lrnd. clement; very kind man. **—î** (...——) P benign, kind.

refhan (.—) رَفهان A lrnd. in comfortable or luxurious circumstances of life; one who lives comfortably.

refiʳⁱ 1 رَفع |ref 1| lrnd. 1. a raising, lifting, elevating. 2. a taking away or removing; removal; an annulling. 3. a promoting; advancement, promotion. **—i asâ** (lit., a taking up the staff) a departing, going away. **— kararı law** annulment.

refiⁱⁱ 2 (.—) رَفيع A lrnd. 1. high, elevated; eminent, illustrious, exalted. 2. lofty, tall. **—i caygâh** of exalted station.

refih (.—) رَفيه A lrnd. easy, comfortable, luxurious (life).

refikᵏⁱ (.—) رَفيق A 1. companion, associate; friend. 2. lrnd. husband.

refika (.—.) رَفيقه A 1. wife. 2. lrnd. female companion.

refiz (.—) رَفيض A lrnd. 1. left, forsaken; relinquished. 2. thrown away, rejected.

refleks رَفلَكس F physiol. reflex.

refref رَفرَف A 1. Isl. rel., name of the last of the four vehicles on which the Prophet Muhammad was borne on the occasion of his night journey. 2. lrnd. coverlet, quilt, blanket, rug. 3. lrnd. a fluttering (of wings); rapid motion of the waves. 4. green cloth of which carpets, etc. are made; pillow, cushion; floor-cloth.

refs رَفث A lrnd. a talking or acting obscenely; lasciviousness, obscenity.

refş رَفش A lrnd. 1. a beating, pounding, bruising, crushing. 2. shovel, spade.

reft رَفت P lrnd. 1. a going; departure. 2. outgo, expenditure.

reftar (.—) رَفتار P lrnd. 1. a mode of walking, gait. 2. graceful, affected or pompous air in walking. 3. mode of procedure; conduct.

refte رَفته P lrnd. that has gone, departed; past. **— refte** little by little, by degrees, gradually.

refteni (..—) رَفتَنى P lrnd. 1. about to depart, pass away; doomed to perish. 2. what is to come to pass.

reftiye رَفتيه Ott. hist. export duty.

refu (.—) رَفو P lrnd. 1. a mending, patching, darning. 2. a poet's introducing a phrase or a couplet from another work and so making a literary patchwork.

refuger (.—.) رَفوگَر P lrnd. mender of torn clothes; fine-drawer, darner.

refukâr (.——) رَفوكار P lrnd. worker of artistic patchwork. **—î** (.———) P 1. artistic patchwork. 2. darning, fine-drawing.

reg رَگ P lrnd. 1. blood vessel, vein or artery. 2. sinew, tendon, muscle. **—i can** 1. artery. 2. vital spot, most important point.

regaib (.—.) رَغائب A lrnd., same as **ragaib**.

regzen رَگزَن P lrnd. phlebotomist, bloodletter.

reh ره P lrnd., var. of **rah 1**.

reha (.—) رَها P lrnd. escape, salvation. **— bul=** /dan/ to escape.

rehabin (.——), **rehabine** (.—..) رَهابين ، رَهابِنه A lrnd. priests; monks.

rehai (.——) رَهائى P lrnd. freedom, release, escape, relief. **—bahş** (.——.) P giver of liberty, savior.

rehain (.—.) رَهائن A lrnd., pl. of **rehine**. **—i mevt** doomed to die.

rehakâr (.——) رَهاكار P lrnd. who liberates; liberator.

rehavet (.—.) رَخاوَت A var. of **rahavet**.

rehavi (.——) رَهاوى P lrnd. 1. Or. mus. one of the oldest compound **makams**. 2. musical clock, watch or box.

rehayab (.——) رَهاياب P lrnd. 1. who escapes; who finds an escape. 2. who recovers from an illness. **— ol=** /dan/ to recover (from).

rehayiş (.—.) رَهايش P lrnd. freedom, escape, liberation.

rehb رَهب A lrnd. a dreading, fearing; fear, terror.

rehbaniyet (.—..) رَهبانِيَت A lrnd. condition or acts of an ascetic; asceticism, monkhood.

rehber رَهبَر P 1. guide, guidebook, directory. 2. leader, chief. **—lik** a guiding; leadership.

rehbet رَهبَت A lrnd. a fearing; fear, terror. **—en** ('..) A in fear.

rehgüzar (..—), **rehgüzer** رَهگُذار ، رَهگُذَر P lrnd. place through which a road passes; frequented place.

rehide (.—.) رَهيده P lrnd. escaped from some calamity; dismissed, set free.

rehin 1 رهن ـ [rehn] pawn, pledge, security; hostage. **—e koy=** /ı/ to pawn, to pledge; to give as security.

rehin 2 (. —) رهين ـ A *lrnd*. 1. pawned, pledged; deposited as security, given as hostage. 2. about to; near. **—i iz'an** understood.

rehine (. —.) رهينة ـ A 1. hostage. 2. *lrnd*. object given as a pledge.

rehn رهن ـ A *lrnd*., *same as* **rehin 1**.

rehneverd رهنورد ـ P *lrnd*., *var. of* **rahneverd**.

rehnüma (.. —) رهنما ـ P *lrnd*., *var. of* **rahnüma**.

rehrev رهرو ـ P *lrnd*., *var. of* **rahrev**.

reht رهط ـ A *lrnd*. 1. a man's family, house, clan, tribe; one's relatives. 2. a small party of men.

rehyab (. —) رهياب ـ P *lrnd*. who discovers a way or a new mode of doing anything; who finds an opportunity.

rehzen رهزن ـ P *lrnd*., *var. of* **rahzen**.

reis[re'si] **1** رئيس ـ A *same as* **re's 1**.

reis 2 (. —) رئيس ـ A 1. head, chief, president; principle. 2. captain of a small merchant vessel, skipper; able bodied seaman. **R—i Cumhur** President of the Republic. **— efendi** *Ott. Hist., same as* **reisülküttab**.

reislik[ği] رئيسلك ـ presidency, leadership, chairmanship. **— hükûmeti** presidential government.

reisülküttab (. —..—) رئيس الكتاب ـ A *Ott. hist.* Minister of Foreign Affairs.

Reji رژی ـ F *obs.* Regie (administration of the Tobacco Monopoly).

rejim رژيم ـ F 1. regime, system of government. 2. *med.* diet. **— yap=** to diet.

rejisör رژيسور ـ F 1. *theat.* director. 2. movie director.

-rek[ği] **1** رك ـ *cf.* **-rak 2**.

-rek 2 رك ـ *cf.* **-rak 3**.

rekabet (. —.) رقابت ـ A 1. rivalry. 2. competition. **— memnuiyeti** *law* covenant in restraint of trade.

rekâket (. —.) ركاكت ـ A 1. *psych.* defect in speech; a stammering; stammer. 2. *lrnd*. incoherence; defect in style. 3. *lrnd*. a being thin, weak, slender; weakness, thinness, flimsiness.

rekânet (. —.), **rekâniyet** (. —..) ركانت ، ركانيت ـ A *lrnd*. soundness, sedateness, dignity.

rek'at[tı] A, **rekât**[tı] ركعت ـ 1. *Isl. rel.* a complete act of worship with the prescribed postures, a unit of the namaz. 2. a kneeling in worship.

rekb ركب ـ A *lrnd*., *pl. of* **râkib 2**.

rekeat (.. —) ركعات ـ A *lrnd*., *pl. of* **rek'at**.

rekeke ركك ـ A *lrnd*., *pl. of* **rekik**.

rekik[kı] (. —) ركيك ـ A *lrnd*. 1. incorrect, dubious, not reliable. 2. thin, slender, weak. 3. shallow, flimsy, poor.

rekin (. —) ركين ـ A *lrnd*. 1. immovable, firmly rooted; firm, reliable. 2. grave, steady, quiet, tranquil (man).

reklâm رقلام ـ F advertisement. **—cılık** advertising.

rekolta, rekolte (..'.) رقولته ـ F harvest, crop.

rekor رقور ـ F *sports* record. **— kır=** to break the record. **—cu** record-breaker.

rekortmen رقورتمن ـ *sports* record-holder.

rektör رقتور ـ F president (of a university).

rekz 1 ركز ـ A *lrnd*. a setting up, erecting, planting; erection.

rekz 2 ركض ـ A *lrnd*. 1. a stamping with the foot; a kicking. 2. a running, a running away. 3. a making a horse go faster by spurring him with the heels.

rekza ركضة ـ A *lrnd*. a single stamp or kick. **—i cebril** *a name of the well* **Zamzam** *at Mecca*.

rekzet=[der] ركزايتمك ـ /ı/ to set up, erect; to plant.

reli (.'.) رلی ـ *naut.* futtock shroud, futtock rigging.

rem رم ـ P *lrnd*. terror, flight; a being scared.

remad (. —) رماد ـ A *lrnd*. ashes. **—î** (.——) A ashy; of, from or like ashes; ashcolored.

reman (. —) رمان ـ P *lrnd*. timid, fugitive.

reme رمه ـ P *lrnd*. 1. flock, herd. 2. multitude, mob, company; troop, army.

remed رمد ـ A *lrnd*. inflammation of the eye, ophthalmia.

remel رمل ـ A 1. *pros.* meter characterized by the trochaic beginning of each tetrasyllabic foot (most commonly: —.——/—.——/—.— —/—.—). 2. *mus.* a medium-fast rhythmic pattern of 28 beats.

remende رمنده ـ P *lrnd*. running away in fear or disgust; wild, terrified, timid.

remide (. —.) رميده ـ P *lrnd*. fugitive; scared; disturbed, afflicted.

remil[mli] رمل ـ [reml] geomancy. **— at=**, **— dök=** to tell the future by geomancy.

remim (. —) رميم ـ A *lrnd*. rotten, moldering, putrefying (bones, etc.).

remiz[mzi] رمز ـ [remz] symbol; abbreviation used in writing; enigmatical expression. **—lendir=** /ı/ to symbolize. **—li** symbolical.

remkerde رمكرده ـ P *lrnd*. put to flight, fugitive.

reml رمل ـ A *lrnd*. 1. *same as* **remil**. 2. sand. **—î** (. —) A 1. geomantic. 2. pertaining to sand, sandy.

remmal[li] رمّال ـ A geomancer. **—lik** quality, art, remuneration of a geomancer.

remy رمى A *lrnd.* a throwing, projection, shot, discharge.
remyet=[der] رميتمك /ı/ to throw, shoot, fire (missile).
remz رمز A *lrnd.* 1. same as **remiz**. 2. sign; nod; wink.
remzâşina (.—.—) رمز آشنا P *lrnd.* knowing signs and symbols.
remzet=[der] رمز ايتمك /ı/ 1. to make a sign; to allude, hint. 2. to symbolize, typify.
remzi (.—), **remziye** رمزى ، رمزيه A *lrnd.* allegorical, symbolic, in code, in cipher.
Ren 1 رن F *geog.* the Rhine.
ren 2 رن F reindeer. — **geyiği** reindeer, *zool.*, *Rangifer tarandus*.
renanet (.—.) رنانت A *lrnd.* a ringing, resounding, echoing.
renc رنج P *lrnd.* 1. pain, stress; suffering. 2. trouble, fatigue, toil. 3. harm, injury, ill, offense. 4. sickness, disease, wound. 5. annoyance, vexation; grief, anxiety; affliction.
rencber رنجبر P *lrnd.*, same as **rençper**.
rence رنجه P *lrnd.* 1. pain, trouble, injury; vexation, sorrow. 2. afflicted, vexed, sad.
rencide (.—.) رنجيده P pained, tormented; injured, hurt; annoyed, vexed. — **et=** /ı/ to hurt (someone's feelings), to annoy.
rencidegi (.—.—) رنجيدگى P *lrnd.* affliction, sadness.
renciş رنجش A *lrnd.* a feeling pain, suffering, or annoyance; offense, indignation. —**i hâtır** a feeling hurt or annoyed.
rencur (.—) رنجور P *lrnd.* 1. pained, distressed, suffering. 2. infirm, sick, afflicted. **—î** (.——) P 1. anguish. 2. sickness.
rençper رنجبر [**rencber**] 1. day laborer, laborer; workman. 2. farm hand; farmer. — **başı** laborer's foreman. —**lik** occupation of a laborer or farmhand.
-rend رنده P *lrnd.* which scrapes, grates, as in **cigerrend**.
rende رنده P 1. carpenter's plane. 2. grater. 3. shave.
rendele=[r] رنده لمك /ı/ 1. to plane. 2. to grate. 3. to shave. —**n=** *pass.*
rendide (.—.) رنديده P *lrnd.* planed, scraped; polished.
reng رنگ P 1. *lrnd.*, same as **renk**. 2. *archaic* trick, device. — **ü bû** 1. color and fragrance. 2. prosperity and a flourishing condition. 3. youth, beauty, and freshness. — **et=** /a/ *archaic* to play a trick (on a person).
rengâmiz (.——) رنگ آميز P *lrnd.* 1. painted, dyed, stained. 2. fickle, inconstant, deceitful.
rengârenk[gi] (.—.) رنگارنگ P of various colors, multicolored, variegated.
rengâver (.—.) رنگاور P *lrnd.* 1. colored. 2. deceitful, fraudulent.

rengin (.—) رنگين P *lrnd.* 1. colored, tinctured, painted in many colors. 2. charming, beautiful, elegant. 3. allegorical, figurative. — **semaî** *Or. mus.* 1. rhythmic pattern similar to **yürük semai** but slower. 2. secular vocal composition which uses this rhythmic pattern.
renin (.—) رنين A *lrnd.* 1. an emitting a twanging, humming, buzzing or whizzing sound. 2. a crying out aloud; a ringing, resounding, echoing.
renk[gi] رنك [**reng**] 1. color, hue. 2. sort, kind, variety. —**i at=** to grow pale. —**i belli değil** of uncertain character. —**i çalık** 1. faded, discolored. 2. pale. — **gideren** *neol.*, *chem.* decolorant, bleach. —**i kaç=** to turn pale. — **körlüğü** *med.* color-blindness, achromatopsy. — **küre** *neol.*, *astr.* chromosphere. — **renk** of various colors, variegated. —**ten renge gir=** 1. to keep changing color; to be greatly embarrassed. 2. to be inconstant, to use every kind of subterfuge. — **renk ol=** to change color, to grow red in the face (from emotion). —**i uç=** /ın/ same as **rengi at=**. — **verme=** to appear unmoved, to conceal one's feelings. —**i yok** 1. colorless. 2. unreliable.
renkle=[r] رنكله مك /ı/ to color, to give a color to. —**n=** 1. *pass.* 2. to get color. —**ndir=** /ı/ to give color, to lend color (to).
renkli رنكلى having color; colored; colorful. — **filim** color film. — **fotoğraf** color photograph. — **işitme** *psych.* color hearing, synesthesia. —**lik** coloredness; multicoloredness.
renkölçer *neol.*, *chem.* colorimeter.
renkseçmezlik[gi] *neol.*, *psych.* dyschromatopsia, poor color discrimination.
renksiz رنكسز 1. colorless, white; pale. 2. nondescript, lacking personality, dull. —**lik** colorlessness.
renkteş *neol.*, *bot.* homochromous. —**lik** homochromatism.
rennan (.—) رنان A *lrnd.* resonant, sonorous.
repertuvar رپرتوار F *theat.* repertory.
re's 1 رأس A *lrnd.* 1. head; uppermost, foremost or most important part of a thing. 2. summit, promontory. 3. headman, chief. 4. head (of cattle); individual. 5. source, origin, fountain, beginning. 6. the very point or degree of some quality, age, etc. —**i kâr***. —**i sene** the beginning of the year.
-res 2 رس P *lrnd.* that brings, as in **destres**, **feryadres**, **müjderes**.
res[ssi] **3** رص A *lrnd.* a well constructed with stones.
resa (.—) رسا P *lrnd.* attaining, reaching; arriving.
resail (.—.) رسائل A *lrnd.*, pl. of **risale**.

resale رساله A *same as* **risale**.
resalet رسالت A *same as* **risalet**.
-resan (. —) رسان P *lrnd*. that brings, as in **şerefresan**.
resanet (. — .) رسانت A *lrnd*., *var. of* **rasanet**.
resas (. —) رصاص A *lrnd*., *var. of* **rasas**.
resaset (. — .) رصاصت A *lrnd*. a being old, worn and tattered; raggedness; unsightliness.
resçek=ᵉʳ رسچك *same as* **restçek=**.
re'sen 1 (ʼ.) رأساً A *lrnd*. on one's own account, on one's own initiative. **— yemin** *law* oath by order of court.
resen 2 رسن A *lrnd*. cord, rope; halter. **—baz** (..—) P rope-dancer, tumbler. **—bend** P bound with ropes.
resentab (..—) رسن تاب P *lrnd*. 1. rope-maker. 2. plotter, one who prepares rope for the necks of people. **—î** (..———) P *abstr. n.*
reseptör رسپتور F *phys*. receiver.
resid 1 (. —) رسيد P *lrnd*. mark made against an item in an account to show that the entry has been cancelled. **— et=** /ı/ to cancel an item in account as received.
-resid 2 (. —) رسيد P *lrnd*. arrived, attained, as in **nevresid**.
-reside 1 (. — .) رسيده P *lrnd*. struck by, befallen, as in **ecelreside**.
reside 2 (. — .) رسيده P *lrnd*. 1. arrived; that has reached to and touched. 2. mature, ripe; adult. **—i hitam** finished. **—gi** (. — . —) P maturity, perfection; ripeness.
resif رصيف F *geol*. reef.
re'sikâr (ʼ. —) رأسكار P *lrnd*. supreme authority (of a business, etc.); highest post.
resil (. —) رسيل A *lrnd*. messenger; envoy.
resimˢᵐⁱ رسم [**resm**] 1. picture, photograph; drawing; design; illustration. 2. the art of drawing or painting. 3. due, toll, perquisite. 4. state ceremony, ceremony; *lrnd*. practice, custom, manner; etiquette, formality. 5. *lrnd*. mark, trace, vestige. 6. *lrnd*. ordinance, law, rule. 7. *myst*. mere outward religious observance. **— al=** 1. to photograph. 2. to collect taxes. **—ini al=** /ın/ 1. to draw, to make a picture, to take the photograph (of). 2. to collect a duty (on something). **— çek=**, **— çıkar=** to take a photograph. **—ini çıkar=** /ın/ to take a picture (of). **—ini çıkart=** to have one's photo taken. **—i geçit** military review, parade. **—i küşad** inauguration. **—i müsennem** *lrnd*. a drawing in profile, a section. **—i selâm**, **—i tâzim** *mil*. salute. **— yap=** to draw, to paint. **— yazı** pictography.
resimci رسمجى 1. photographer; artist; picture dealer. 2. draftsman.
resimle=ʳ رسمله /ı/ to illustrate (book).
resimli رسملى illustrated.
resis (. —) رثيث A *lrnd*. 1. old, worn, ragged. 2. wounded, covered with wounds and dying.
resm رسم A *same as* **resim**.
resmen (ʼ.) رسماً A 1. officially; ceremoniously. 2. as a mere matter of form.
resmet=ᵈᵉʳ رسم ايتمك /ı/ 1. to draw; to picture. 2. to describe (a circle, etc.).
resmi (. —) رسمى A 1. official; ceremonious; formal. 2. done as a matter of form. **— elbise** uniform; dress suit. **— evrak** legal documents. **— makam** official position, government agency.
resmiyat (..—) رسميات A *lrnd*. 1. matters of ceremony and state. 2. customary acts or words, or those of mere form and ceremony. 3. official matters, acts, words, or writings.
resmiyet رسميت A official character of something, formality; primness.
ressam رسام [*Arabic* .—] artist, painter; designer. **—lık** art or profession of painting.
rest رست F *cards* a staking all one's chips in poker.
restahiz (. — —) رستاخيز P *lrnd*. 1. general scramble to escape. 2. general resurrection.
restçek=ᵉʳ رست چكمك to stake all, to act boldly; to dare to do something.
reste 1 رسته P *lrnd*. 1. straight line. 2. row, rank, series; row of houses or shops; market, fair. 3. custom, manner, fashion.
reste 2 رسته P *lrnd*. 1. escaped, saved, delivered, free. 2. free from the cares and vanities of the world.
restegân (..—) رستگان P [*pl. of* **reste 2**.] *lrnd*. free, escaped.
restgâr (. —) رستگار P *lrnd*. safe, free, escaped. **—î** (. ——) P safety, escape, freedom.
resthiz (. —) رستخيز P *poet. for* **restahiz**.
resto (ʼ.) رستو It 1. cry used by waiters to cancel an order. 2. *slang* Enough! Stop! Shut up!
resûlˡᵘ̈ (. —) رسول A 1. *rel*. prophet; apostle. 2. *lrnd*. messenger, envoy.
resuli (. ——) رسولى P *lrnd*. function, act or condition of a messenger, envoy or apostle.
Resulullâh (. — . —) رسول الله A *lrnd*. the Apostle and Prophet of God, Muhammad.
Resulussakaleyn (. — . . . .) رسول الثقلين A *lrnd*. Muhammad, as God's Apostle to the inhabitants of the earth (human beings and jinns).
re'sülmalˡⁱ (..—) رأس المال A *fin*. capital.
resye رشيه A *lrnd*. stiffness of the joints, arthritis, rheumatism, gout.
reşˢˢⁱ رش A *lrnd*. 1. a sprinkling. 2. a slight sprinkle of rain.
reşad (. —) رشاد A *lrnd*. 1. a pursuing a

reşadet

straight course, orthodoxy; a following a right road. 2. *w. cap.*, *man's name*.

reşadet (. —.) رشادت A *lrnd.* a doing what is right; good conduct.

reşadetlû (. — . —) رشادتلى *Ott. hist.*, *a form of address in writing to the head of a dervish lodge*.

reşakatⁱⁱ (. —.) رشاقت A *lrnd.* a being slender of waist, graceful and light of motion; gracefulness.

reşaş (. —), **reşaşe** (. —.) رشاش رشاشه A *lrnd.* a few rain drops, a light shower.

Reşatᵈⁱ رشاد [reşad] 1. *man's name*. 2. short for **Reşat altını**. — **altını** Ottoman gold lira (coined during the reign of Sultan Rashad).

reşehat (..—) رشحات A *lrnd.*, *pl. of* **reşha**. —ı **sehab-ı mekremet** (*lit.*, drops from the clouds of generosity) gifts, benefactions.

reşf رشف A *lrnd.* a sucking in, a sipping.

reşh رشح A *lrnd.* a sweating, oozing; exudation.

reşha رشحه A *lrnd.* a dropping, dripping, distilling; a drop of sweat or dew.

reşhapaş (..—) رشحاپاش P *lrnd.* that scatters drops of fluid.

reşhayab (..—) رشحایاب P *lrnd.* sweating, dripping.

reşid (. —) رشيد A 1. who has become an adult. 2. *lrnd.* who follows the right road; orthodox; righteous; well conducted; capable and careful. 3. *lrnd.* who ordains all things rightly (God).

reşidiye (. —..) رشيديه A confection of honey and sesame oil in white flexible threads.

reşih (. —) رشيح A *lrnd.* sweat, perspiration.

reşikᵏⁱ (. —) رشيق A *lrnd.* of an elegant stature or form, slender, graceful and light in motion.

reşkᵏⁱ رشك P *lrnd.* 1. envy, jealousy. 2. object of envy or jealousy. —**âver** (. — .) P jealous, envious. —**engiz** (..—) P that excites envy. —**în** (. —) P jealous, envious.

reşme رشمه *prov.* chain or leather noseband (for a horse). — **gem** chain bit. —**li** having a headstall.

retᵈᵈⁱ رد *var. of* **red 1**.

retaim (. —.) رتائم A *lrnd.*, *pl. of* **retime**.

retel رتل A *lrnd.* 1. evenness and luster of the teeth. 2. neat and regular arrangement.

retil رتل A *lrnd.* 1. even and lustrous (teeth); who has even and lustrous teeth. 2. regularly arranged.

retime (. —.) رتيمه A *lrnd.* a thread wound round the finger as a reminder.

retkᵏⁱ رتق A *lrnd.* 1. a joining together, a closing up a gap. 2. a mending, repairing; filling a breach; a remedying. — **ü fetk-ı umur** administration of affairs.

retme رتم A *lrnd.*, *same as* **retime**.

retret رترت F *com.* redraft, cross-bill; renewed bill.

retuş رتوش F a retouching.

-rev 1 رو P *lrnd.* that goes along, as in **rahrev, tizrev.**

revᵛⁱ **2** روع A *lrnd.* fear, fright, terror.

reva (. —) روا P lawful, permissible, proper, suitable, worthy. — **gör**= /1, a/ to deem lawful or proper.

revabıt (. —.) روابط A *lrnd.*, *pl. of* **rabıta**.

revac (. —) A, **revaç**ᶜⁱ رواج a being in demand; a being current. —**landır**= /1/ to cause something to be in demand. —**lı** current, in demand. —**sız** not in demand, not current, unsaleable.

revafız (. —.) روافض A *Isl. rel.* the Shiites; heretics.

revah (. —) رواح A *lrnd.* 1. ease. 2. afternoon, evening.

revaid (. —.) رواعد A *lrnd.*, *pl. of* **raide**.

revakᵏⁱ (. —) رواق A porch, portico; pavillion. —ı **bîsütûn** *poet.* the heavens, the sky. —ı **leyl** *poet.* darkness.

revaki (. — —) رواقى A *lrnd.* stoic philosopher. —**ye** (. — ..) A stoicism. —**yun** (. — — —) A Stoics.

revan 1 (. —) روان P *lrnd.* 1. that goes, that moves along; flowing, going easily. 2. current; fluent.

revan 2 (. —) روان P *lrnd.* soul, spirit, life. —**bahş** (. —.) P, —**bahşa** (. — . —) P that gives life.

revane (. —.) روانه P *lrnd.* 1. that goes, passes along; flowing. 2. current, in practice, in common use. — **ol**= 1. to go along. 2. to flow.

revanegi (. —. —) روانگى P *lrnd.* 1. a running, flowing; mobility. 2. currency.

revani (. —.) روانى [revganî] a kind of sweet made with semolina.

revanş روانش F *sports* revenge. — **maçı** return match.

revarev (. —.) رو ارو P *lrnd.* 1. a continued going, advancing, proceeding. 2. by degrees, consecutively.

revatib (. —.) رواتب A *lrnd.*, *pl. of* **ratibe**.

revayih (. —.) روايح A *lrnd.*, *pl. of* **rayiha**.

revazin (. —.) روازن A *lrnd.*, *pl. of* **revzen, revzene**.

revende رونده P *lrnd.* 1. that goes, departs. 2. that goes along, progresses; traveler.

revendegân (...—) روندگان P *lrnd.*, *pl. of* **revende**. —**i âlem** 1. they who depart this life. 2. travelers. 3. the seven planets.

revendegi (...—) روندگى P *lrnd.* rapidity of motion.

reverans روﺭانس F a bowing in salute; bow, courtesy.
revgan روغن P lrnd. 1. oil, butter; fat, grease. 2. varnish; ointment. —ı sade clarified butter used in cooking. —ı zeyt olive oil.
revganî (..—) روغاني P lrnd., same as revani.
revh روح A lrnd. 1. gentle breath of air; pleasant refreshing wind. 2. ease, rest, repose, tranquility; comfort; happiness.
revhanî (.——) روحاني A lrnd. pleasant, agreeable, airy.
revhaniyet (.—..) روحانيت A lrnd. pleasantness, agreeableness. —li cheerful.
revi (.—) روي A pros. main rhyme letter. —i mukayyed a main rhyme letter not followed by a vowel. —i mutlak main rhyme letter followed by a vowel.
revir روير G 1. infirmary (at a school or factory). 2. mil. small military hospital; naut. sickbay.
reviş رويش P lrnd. 1. a going, going along, gait. 2. trend; conduct; way, mode, manner. 3. movement, motion.
reviyet رويت A lrnd. 1. careful consideration; reflection; vigilance. 2. ability. —siz inconsiderate, unreflecting.
revizyon رويزيون F revision. —dan geçir= mech. /ı/ to overhaul.
revkʰⁱ روك A lrnd. 1. veil, curtain. 2. portico. 3. a being clear, bright (wine). 4. horn. 5. prime of youth; first or best part of anything.
revnakʰⁱ رونق A lrnd. 1. brightness, splendor; brilliance, sparkle; beauty. 2. prime of youth, height of prosperity or power. —dar (..—) P bright, beautiful, splendid. —efza (...—) P giving splendor; sparkling. —lı brilliant, splendid; in full prime; beautiful.
revnaknüma (...—) رونقنما P Or. mus. a compound makam composed about a century ago.
revnaksız رونقسز lusterless, dull.
revolver رولور F pistol, revolver.
revü روو F theat. revue.
revzen, revzene روزن ، روزنه P lrnd. window, aperture; loophole.
revzeni (..—) روزني P lrnd. a kind of hand-woven colored silk cloth.
rey راي [Arabic ray 3] 1. opinion, judgment. 2. pol. vote. 3. lrnd. a seeing, perception. —i âm pol. public opinion. —i âma müracaat pol. plebiscite, referendum. — beyan et= to express an opinion. — ehli a man of sound judgment. —e koy= /ı/ to put to the vote. — pusulası ballot. — sandığı ballot box. — topla= to take a vote. — ver= to vote.
reyahin (.——) رياحين A lrnd., pl. of reyhan.

rey'an (.—) ريعان A lrnd. the first or best part of anything. —ı şebab prime of youth.
reyb ريب A lrnd. doubt, suspicion; doubtful event.
reybî (.—) ريبي A phil. sceptical, sceptic. —ye A scepticism. —yun (.——) A sceptics.
reyean (..—) ريعان A lrnd. 1. a growing, increasing, augmenting. 2. a yielding an increase; yield. 3. a remaining over, being in excess.
reyel'ayn رأي العين A lrnd., same as reyül'ayn.
reyhan (.—) ريحان A 1. sweet basil, bot., Ocimum basilicum. 2. lrnd. the support of life, sustenance.
reyhanî (.——) ريحاني A 1. Arabic calligraphy kind of monumental writing similar to cufic. 2. lrnd. pertaining to sweet basil.
reyn رين A lrnd. dirt, filth (physical and moral); rust.
reyül'ayn رأي العين [reyel'ayn] lrnd. with one's own eyes. — gör= /ı/ to see for oneself.
reyya (.—) ريّا A lrnd. 1. quenching her thirst (woman). 2. agreeable smell, scent.
reyyan (.—) ريّان A lrnd. 1. satisfied with drink, free from thirst, refreshed. 2. flourishing; vigorous. 3. full of sap, juicy.
rez رز P lrnd. grapevine, vine.
rezaᵃⁱ (.—), **rezaat** (.—.) رضاع ، رضاعت A lrnd. a sucking milk from the breast.
rezail (.—.) رذائل A lrnd., pl. of rezile.
rezalet (.—.) رذالت A 1. scandal; scandalous behavior; disgrace. 2. a being vile, corrupt; vileness, baseness. — çek= to suffer disgrace. — çıkar= to cause a scandal.
rezanet (.—.) رزانت A lrnd. a being grave and sensible; modest; sobriety, sensibleness; dignity.
rezaya (.——) رزايا A lrnd., pl. of rezie.
reze رزه P 1. hinge of two loops; hinge made with a pintle. 2. a kind of lock that works by the pressure of the thumb to open the door, thumb lock. — dişisi brace of a hinge. — erkeği pintle of a hinge. — yuvası socket in which the pin of a hinge turns.
rezele=ʳ رزهلمك /ı/ 1. to furnish with hinges. 2. to bolt.
rezeli رزهلي furnished with hinges; bolted.
rezene رزنه [raziyâne] common fennel, bot., Foeniculum vulgare.
rezie (.—.) رزية A lrnd. calamity, affliction, disaster.
rezil (.—) رذيل A 1. vile, base; disreputable; disgraced. 2. scoundrel. — et= /ı/ to disgrace, to hold up to scorn. — ol= to be disgraced; to be put to shame.
rezilâne (.——.) رذيلانه P 1. meanly,

rezile shamefully, disgracefully. 2. scandalous, infamous.

rezile, rezilet (. —.) رذيلت ـ رذيله A *lrnd.* any mean, disreputable or disgraceful act or habit; vileness, worthlessness.

rezillik[ti] رذيللك 1. disreputableness, infamy. 2. scandal.

rezin (. —) رزين A *lrnd.* 1. firm, sound, solid. 2. modest, grave, patient.

rezm رزم P *lrnd.* fight, battle, war. **—azma** (. — —) P experienced in war, warlike. **—dide** (. —.) P experienced in warfare; veteran. **—gâh** (. —), **—geh** P battlefield. **—hah** (. —) P eager for battle, brave.

rezzak[ı] (. —) رزاق A *lrnd.* God, the Provider of the needs of men and beasts.

rezze رزه A same as **reze**.

rı var. of **re** 1 [2].

rıbat (. —) رباط A *lrnd.* 1. bond, band, tie. 2. inn; military station on a frontier. 3. lodge for dervishes. 4. nerve, tendon.

rıbh ربح A *lrnd.* gain, profit in trade; interest. **—î** (. —) A 1. pertaining to profit, of the nature of interest. 2. usurer.

rıbka ربقه A *lrnd.* neck rope for a lamb; collar, yoke. **—i İslâm** the bonds of Islam. **—i itaat** subjection and obedience.

rıdvan (. —) رضوان A *lrnd.* 1. a being pleased, satisfied, gratified; a being resigned; satisfaction, contentment. 2. paradise. 3. *w. cap., Isl. rel.,* name of the door-keeper of Paradise.

rıdvanî (. — —) رضوانى A *lrnd.* pertaining to Paradise, heavenly; angel, sainted human spirit.

rıfk[ı] رفق A *lrnd.* gentleness, softness, suavity of manner.

rıfz رفض A *lrnd.* the doctrine of the **Revafız** sect.

rıh (—) ريح [rig] sand sprinkled on a freshly written page to dry the ink.

rıhdan (— —) ريحدان [rigdan] sand-sprinkler.

rıhtım ريحتم P quay, wharf; dike.

rık[kı] رق A *lrnd.* 1. slavery, bondage. 2. slave, bondsman.

rık'a 1 رقعه [ruk'a] *Arabic script* a cursive style of writing (used in Turkey) (the style used in this dictionary).

rıka[aı] 2 (. —) رقاع A *lrnd., pl. of* **ruk'a**.

rıkab (. —) رقاب A *lrnd., pl. of* **rakabe**.

rıkai (. — —) رقاعى A *lrnd.* 1. special to billets or petitions. 2. professional scribe. 3. cursive handwriting.

rıkkiyet رقيت A *lrnd.* servile condition, slavery, servitude.

rıtl رطل A *lrnd., var. of* **ratl**.

rıza 1 رضا A 1. consent, acquiescence. 2. resignation. 3. satisfaction, approval. 4. *w. cap., man's name.* **— göster=** /a/ to consent, to resign oneself (to). **—yı hak** God's approval (of man's action or conduct). **—sı ol=** to give one's consent, to approve.

rıza[aı] 2 (. —), **rızaat**[ti] (. —.) رضاعت ـ رضاع A *lrnd., same as* **reza**.

rızacû (. — —) رضاجو P *lrnd.* who seeks approbation, who strives to please.

rızadade (. — — .) رضاداده P *lrnd.* 1. who has given his acquiescence, who has consented. 2. approved.

rızaen (. —'.) رضاءً A *lrnd.* with free consent or approval.

rızaenlillâh (. —' . . —) رضاء لله A *lrnd.* for God's sake.

rızaî (. — —) رضائى A *lrnd.* 1. pertaining to consent, approbation or resignation. 2. *w. cap.* pertaining to a person named Riza.

rızamend (. — .) رضامند P *lrnd.* consenting, permitting; resigned. **—î** (. — . —) P, **—lik** acquiescence, approval, resignation.

rızk[kı] رزق A 1. one's daily food, sustenance (provided by God). 2. the necessities of life. **—ını çıkar=** to earn one's daily bread. **—ı hasen** *lrnd.* the good things of life enjoyed without toil. **—ı maksûm** *lrnd.* portion appointed by God. **—ı mazmûn** *lrnd.* food and necessities granted by God.

riayet (. —.) رعايت A 1. a respecting; observance; respect, esteem; respectful treatment; consideration, regard, kind attention. 2. a conforming to, an obeying; conformity, obedience. 3. *lrnd.* a guarding and protecting.

riayeten (. —' . .) رعاية A /a/ out of respect for; in consideration of.

riayetkâr (. — . —) رعايتكار P respectful; considerate. **—âne** (. — . — .) P *lrnd.* considerately, respectfully. **—î** (. — . — —) P *lrnd.,* **—lık** politeness, respect, consideration.

riayetlû (. — . —) رعايتلو *lrnd.* honored, honorable, respected (one of the polite titles formerly used by Muslims in letters to non-Muslims).

riayetsiz رعايتسز disrespectful; irreverent. **—lik** disrespect, irreverence.

riba (. —) ربا A *lrnd.* usury.

ribahar (. — —) رباخوار P *lrnd.* usurer.

ribat (. —) رباط A *lrnd., same as* **rıbat**.

ribatat[ti] 1 (. — .) رباطت A *lrnd.* a being firm and resolute; firmness, resolution.

ribatat 2 (. — —) رباطات A *lrnd., pl. of* **ribat**.

ribet (. —.) ريبت A *lrnd.* doubt, misgiving, suspicion; suspicious thing.

rica 1 (. —) رجا [reca] request. **— et=** /ı, dan/ to request (something from someone). **— minnet** after much beseeching.

ric'a 2 رجعه A *lrnd.* 1. a returning to earth after death. 2. a receiving again a divorced wife.

ricacı (. —.) جاجى ‎- who makes a request.
ricakâr (.——) جاكار ‎- P *lrnd.* making or containing a request; intercessor.
ricalⁱⁱ (. —) رجال ‎- A *lrnd.* men; men of importance, high officials; dignitaries. **—i gayb myst.** saints who know far-away events and become present wherever they wish. **—i kibar** the great civil functionaries.
ricaname (.——.) رجانامه ‎- P *lrnd.* letter of request.
ric'atⁱⁱ رجعت ‎- A 1. retreat. 2. *astr.* retrograde motion in a planet; period of retrogradation. 3. *lrnd.* return. 4. *lrnd.*, same as **ric'a 2²**. **—i kahkari** *lrnd.* shameful retreat.
ric'i (. —) رجعى ‎- A *lrnd.* aiming at retreat; retractive.
ricl رجل ‎- A *lrnd.* foot.
rics رجس ‎- A *lrnd.* 1. filth, dirt, abomination; filthiness, uncleanness. 2. the devil; diabolical suggestions, wiles. 3. sin of believing in or worshipping gods other than God. 4. unlawful thing, sin, offense.
ricz رجز ‎- A *lrnd.*, same as **rics**.
rida (. —) رداء ‎- A *lrnd.* woolen cloak, scarf for the shoulders.
riddet ردت ‎- A *lrnd.* apostasy (from the Islamic religion).
ridf ردف ‎- A 1. *pros.* long vowel preceding the final consonant of the rhyme. 2. *lrnd.* back end of a thing, rump.
rie رئه ‎- A *anat.* lung. **—vi** (. . —) A pulmonary.
rifade (. —.) رفاده ‎- A *lrnd.* surgical pad, compress.
rifah (. —) رفاه ‎- A *lrnd.*, same as **refah**.
Rifai (.——) رفاعى ‎- [**Rufai**] member of the Rufaiyah dervish order. **—lik** *abstr. n.* **—ye** the Rufaiyah dervish order.
rif'atⁱⁱ رفعت ‎- A *lrnd.* a being or becoming high, sublime; eminence; sublimity; high rank.
rif'atlû رفعتلو ‎- *lrnd.* eminent (formerly the official form of address to major or civil functionary of comparable rank).
rifd رفد ‎- A *lrnd.* 1. gift, present, favor. 2. help, assistance.
rig (—) ريگ ‎- P *lrnd.* sand; a kind of gold-colored dust used formerly for sprinkling on freshly-written ink. **—i revan** moving sand.
rigdan (——) ريگدان ‎- P *lrnd.* sandbox. **—lık** *colloq.* sandbox.
rigistan (—. —) ريگستان ‎- P *lrnd.* sandy region.
rignâk (——) ريگناك ‎- P *lrnd.* sandy.
rigzâr (——) ريگزار ‎- P *lrnd.* sandy region.
rih (—) ريح ‎- A *lrnd.* 1. wind. 2. rheumatic or neuralgic discomfort. **—i tayyar** rheumatic pains, rheumatism.
rihalⁱⁱ (. —) رحال ‎- A *lrnd.*, *pl. of* **rahl**.

rihale (. —.) رحاله ‎- A *lrnd.* horse saddle; light racing saddle.
rihan (. —) رهان ‎- A *lrnd.* a betting, a staking; bet, wager, stake.
rihlet رحلت ‎- A *lrnd.* 1. a departing, migrating, traveling; change of abode, migration. 2. a passing away, death.
rihte (—.) ريخته ‎- P *lrnd.* poured, spilled, shed.
rihtegân (—. —) ريختگان ‎- P *lrnd.* melters of brass or copper; *Ott. hist.* casters of cannon.
rikᵏⁱ (—) ريق ‎- A *lrnd.* 1. saliva, spittle. 2. first and best of a thing.
rik'a رقعه ‎- [**ruk'a**] same as **rık'a 1**.
rikâb 1 (. —) ركاب ‎- A *lrnd.* 1. stirrup. 2. retinue of a prince. 3. the Royal Presence. **— ağaları** *Ott. hist.* the Sultan's equerries of state. **— arzuhali** *Ott. hist.* petition presented to the Sultan when he was on horseback. **—i Hümayun** *Ott. hist.* the Sultan's presence when on horseback on a state occasion.
rikab 2 (. —) رقاب ‎- A *lrnd.* 1. a waiting for, watching. 2. a watching for the departure of a rival.
rikab 3 (. —) رقاب ‎- A *lrnd.*, *pl. of* **rakabe**.
rikâbdar ركابدار ‎- P *lrnd.* stirrup-holder, equerry.
rikâbi (. ——) ركابى ‎- A same as **rikâbdar**.
rik'at ركعت ‎- *var. of* **rek'at**.
rikâz (. —) ركاز ‎- A *lrnd.* treasures buried in the earth.
rikkatⁱⁱ رقت ‎- A 1. compassion, mercy; tenderness. 2. *lrnd.* slenderness, delicacy, slimness. **—i kalb** *lrnd.* tender-heartedness, compassion. **—âmiz** (. . ——) P, **—engiz** (. . . —) P *lrnd.* piteous; deplorable. **—li** tender-hearted, compassionate.
rikze رقزه ‎- A *lrnd.* a single buried treasure.
rim 1 (—) ريم ‎- P *lrnd.* 1. pus, matter; filth, impurity. 2. dross of metal.
Rim 2 ريم ‎- Sl *obs.* Rome. **— Papa 1.** the Pope. **2.** *colloq.* very old man, grayhead.
rimah (. —) رماح ‎- A *lrnd.*, *pl. of* **rümh**.
rimalⁱⁱ (. —) رمال ‎- A *lrnd.*, *pl. of* **reml**.
rimayet (. —.) رمايت ‎- A *lrnd.* a shooting a missile; a throwing stones, darts etc.; a shooting.
rimel ريمل ‎- cosmetic for the eyelashes, mascara.
rimnakᵏⁱ (——) ريمناك ‎- P *lrnd.* 1. dirty, filthy; corrupt, purulent. 2. mixed with dross.
rina (. .) رينا ‎- sting ray, *zool., Dasyatis pastinaca*.
rind رند ‎- P 1. *poet.* jolly, unconventional, humorous man. 2. *lrnd.* vagabond. **—an** (. —) P *lrnd.*, *pl.* **—âne** (. —.) P *poet.* in an Epicurean spirit. **—î** (. —) P *lrnd.*, **—lik** Epicureanism.
rindmeşreb رندمشرب ‎- P *lrnd.* having a jolly and unconventional temperament, Epicurean.

ringa (ˊ.) رِنگَه‎ Gk herring, zoo.., *Clupea harengus.*

rintᵈⁱ ـدِ‎ var. of **rind**.

risale (.—.) رِسَالَه‎ A 1. treatise; pamphlet, brochure. 2. *lrnd.* message, epistle, letter. 3. *lrnd.* periodical. **—i mahsusa** monograph.

risalet (.—.) رِسَالَت‎ A *lrnd.* 1. mission of a prophet; apostleship. 2. office and functions of a messenger.

Risaletpenah (.—..—) رِسَالَتْپَنَاه‎ P *lrnd.* in whom the office of apostle resides; the Prophet Muhammad. **—î** (.—..——) P apostolic, apostolical.

risman (——) رِسْمَان‎ P *lrnd.* rope, cord; thread. **—baz** (———) P rope-dancer.

riş 1 (—) رِش‎ A *lrnd.* 1. plumage, feathers. 2. beard. **—i sefid** 1. an old man. 2. elder, chief man of a town.

riş 2 (—) رِش‎ P *lrnd.* wound, sore.

-riş 3 (—) رِش‎ P *lrnd.* wounded, sore; wounding, as in **dilriş.**

rişa 1 رِشَا‎ A *lrnd.*, pl. of **rişvet.**

rişa 2 (.—) رِشَا‎ A *lrnd.* rope; well-rope.

rişdar (——) رِشْدَار‎ P *lrnd.* 1. bearded. 2. wounded, sore.

rişe 1 (—.) رِشَه‎ A *lrnd.* a single feather.

rişe 2 (—.) رِشَه‎ P *lrnd.* 1. tendril; fiber; fibrous roots. 2. rough or ragged fringe. **—i nâhun** hang-nail.

rişedar (—.—) رِشَه‌دَار‎ P *lrnd.* fringed, fibrous.

rişgâv (——) رِشْگَاو‎ P *lrnd.* stupid fellow, simpleton, ass.

rişhand (—.) رِشْخَنْد‎ P *lrnd.* a laughing up one's sleeve; jeer, jest, taunt; jester; laughing-stock.

rişi (——) رِشِی‎ A *lrnd.* 1. plumose, plumous. 2. pinnate, pinnated.

rişte رِشْتَه‎ P *lrnd.* 1. yarn, thread; twine. 2. clue; link; tie, connection. 3. Guinea-worm, jigger. 4. vermicelli.

riştekeş رِشْتَه‌کَش‎ P *lrnd.* drawing thread; reducing to order.

rişvet رِشْوَت‎ A same as **rüşvet 1.**

ritimᵗᵐⁱ رِتِم‎ F rhythm.

ritmikᵍⁱ رِتْمِیک‎ F rhythmic.

riv (—) رِو‎ [Persian **rêv**] *lrnd.* trick, device, stratagem; cunning, fraud, treachery.

rivayet (.—.) رِوَایَت‎ A 1. narrative, tale; rumor. 2. tradition. 3. a variant reading of a word of the Quran handed down by a pupil of one of the masters of reading.

rivayetkerde (.—...) رِوَایَت‌کَرْدَه‎ P *lrnd.* narrated, told.

riya (.—) رِیَا‎ A hypocrisy, dissimulation.

riyah (.—) رِیَاه‎ A *lrnd.*, pl. of **rih.**

riyakâr (.——) رِیَاکَار‎ P hypocrite; hypocritical. **—âne** (.———.) P *lrnd.* hypocritical (conduct); in a hypocritical manner. **—î** (.———) P *lrnd.*, **—lık** hypocrisy.

riyalˡⁱ رِیَال‎ Sp silver dollar, real.

riyale رِیَالَه‎ It *Ott. hist.* 1. rear-admiral. 2. rear-admiral's ship. **— bey** rear-admiral of the fleet.

riyaset (.—.) رِیَاسَت‎ A presidency, chairmanship. **R—i Cumhur** Presidency of the Republic. **— divanı** presidential board.

riyasetpenah (.—..—) رِیَاسَت‌پَنَاه‎ P *lrnd.* His Excellency the President. **—î** (.—..——) P *lrnd.* presidential.

riyasız (.—.) رِیَاسِز‎ free from hypocrisy, sincere; genuine.

riyaz (.—) رِیَاض‎ A *lrnd.*, pl. of **ravza.**

riyazat (.——) رِیَاضَات‎ A *lrnd.*, pl. of **riyazet.**

riyazet (.—.) رِیَاضَت‎ A 1. ascetic discipline, mortification of the flesh; asceticism, mortification. 2. *lrnd.* prison punishment (with only dry bread for food and no smoking or reading). **—i bediniye** *obs.* gymnastics. **— çek=** to undergo ascetic austerities. **— et=** 1. to train and discipline oneself. 2. to practice ascetic austerities.

riyazetkeş (.—..) رِیَاضَتْ‌کَش‎ P *lrnd.* ascetic.

riyazi (.——) رِیَاضِی‎ A 1. mathematical. 2. *lrnd.* pertaining to training and discipline.

riyaziyat (.—.—) رِیَاضِیَات‎ A *lrnd.* 1. mathematical questions; mathematics. 2. a practicing ascetic austerities.

riyaziye (.—..) رِیَاضِیَه‎ A mathematics.

riyaziyun (.———) رِیَاضِیُّون‎ A *lrnd.* mathematicians.

-riz (—) رِیز‎ P *lrnd.* that sheds, pours out, scatters, as in **eşkriz, hunriz.**

rizan (——) رِیزَان‎ P *lrnd.* shedding; scattering, pouring.

rize (—.) رِیزَه‎ P *lrnd.* small fragment, grain, crumb, bit. **— rize** in fragments, in particles, grains, or shreds.

rizeçin (—.—) رِیزَه‌چِین‎ P *lrnd.* a picker up of crumbs, one who lives on scraps.

rizekâr (—.—) رِیزَه‌کَار‎ P *lrnd.* one who does very fine work.

riziko (..ˊ.) رِیزِکو‎ It *com.* risk.

riziş (—.) رِیزِش‎ P *lrnd.* a shedding, pouring forth, falling off.

=rken, after consonants **=arken, =erken,** or **=ırken, =irken, =urken, =ürken** (see rule under **=r** 2)ـکَن‎ [**=r + iken**] while... -ing, e. g., **beklerken** while waiting.

=rmış, =rmiş, =rmuş, =rmüş, after consonants **=armış, =ermiş,** or **=ırmış, =irmiş, =urmuş, =ürmüş** (see rule under **=r** 1)ـمِش‎ [**=r + =miş**] 1. (he) is said to... 2. (he) is said to have been used to (do something).

=rmışçasına, =rmişçesine, etc., after consonants =armışçasına, =ermişçesine, or =ırmışçasına, =irmişçesine, etc. (see rule under =r 1) ـرْمُشْجَـ [=r + =mışçasına] as if (doing something).

=rmış gibi, =rmiş gibi, etc., after consonants =armış gibi, =ermiş gibi, or =ırmış gibi, =urmuş gibi, etc. (see rule under =r 1) ـرْمِشْ گبى [=r + =mış gibi] as if (doing something).

=rmiş ـرْمِشْ cf. =rmış.

=rmişçesine ـرْمِشْچَسِنَه cf. =rmışçasına.

rob ـرُبْ F dress.

roba (ˊ.) ـرُبَه It 1. ornamental piece on the breast of a gown, etc. 2. robe.

robdöşambr ـرُبْدُوشَامْبِر F dressing gown.

roda (ˊ.) ـرُودَه It naut. coil of rope, coiled rope.

rodaj ـرُودَاژْ F mech. a running in. —**da** running in. — **yap**= to grind in (valve).

Rodos ـرُودُوسْ geog. Rhodes. —**lu** a Rhodian.

roka ـرُوقَه Gk rocket, bot., Eruca sativa. — **salatası** rocket used for salad.

roket ـرُوكَتْ F rocket. — **at**= to launch a rocket.

rolü ـرُولْ F role, part.

rolo (ˊ.) ـرُولُو It naut. ship's article.

rom ـرُمْ F rum (drink).

Roma (ˊ.) ـرُومَا It geog. Rome. —**lı** a Roman.

roman 1 ـرُومَانْ F novel, story.

Roman 2 ـرُومَانْ F Romanesque.

romancı ـرُومَانْجى novelist.

Romanya (ˊ.ˊ.) ـرُومَانْيَا geog. Rumania. —**lı** Rumanian.

romatizma (..ˊ.) ـرُومَاتِيزْمَه F rheumatism. —**lı** rheumatic (person).

Romen ـرُومَنْ F a Roman.

rondelâ (.ˊ.) ـرُونْدَلَا It mech. washer.

ropbu ـرُبْ F var. of **rob**. —**luk** material for a dress.

rosto (ˊ.) ـرُوسْتُو It roast meat.

rot ـرُوتْ E auto. rod.

rota (ˊ.) ـرُوطَه It course of a ship.

roza (ˊ.) ـرُوزَه It rose-diamond.

rozbif ـرُوزْبِيفْ F roast beef.

rozet ـرُوزَتْ F rosette.

rölâns ـرُولَانْسْ F cards a raising the bid.

römorkku ـرُومُورْكْ F trailer (vehicle).

römorkaj ـرُومُورْكَاژْ F towage, haulage; towing.

römorkör ـرُومُورْكُورْ F 1. tugboat. 2. tractor (motor). — **yedeğinde** towed by a tug.

Rönesans ـرُونَسَانْسْ F Renaissance.

rönons ـرُونُونْسْ F cards renounce.

röntgen ـرُونْتْگَنْ G 1. X-ray. 2. slang a watching secretly. — **çek**= to take an X-ray picture. — **işlet**= slang to watch secretly.

röntgenci ـرُونْتْگَنْجى 1. X-ray specialist. 2. person who watches others secretly, Peeping Tom.

röportaj ـرُوپُورْتَاژْ F 1. a reporting. 2. set of articles on a topical subject.

rötar ـرُوتَارْ F delay. —**lı** delayed (train, etc.).

=**rsa**, =**rse**, afer consonants =**arsa**, =**erse**, or =**ırsa**, =**irse** etc. (see rule under =r 1) ـرْسَه if... (does something).

ru 1 (—) ـرُو P lrnd. 1. face, visage, countenance. 2. appearance, aspect. 3. surface. 4. myst. the light of God's countenance. —**yi ırak** Or. mus. a compound makam six or seven centuries old, seldom used. —**yi türş** sour face.

-**ru 2** (—) ـرُو P lrnd. which grows, growing, as in **hodru**.

ruaf (.—) ـرُعَافْ A lrnd. a bleeding at the nose; blood that flows from the nose. —**î** (.——) A pertaining to hemorrhage from the nose.

ruam (.—) ـرُعَامْ A vet. glanders.

rubbu **1** ـرُبْ A obs. 1. quarter; quarter of a kurush. 2. an eighth of a cubit. 3. rhumb.

rub 2 (—) ـرُبْ P lrnd. a sweeping; broom.

ru'b 3 ـرُعْبْ A lrnd., same as **ra'b 2**.

ruba 1 ـرُبَا It clothes; clothing.

ruba 2 (ˊ.) ـرُبَا It naut. a bringing by the lee; boxhauling.

rubab (.—) ـرُبَابْ A lrnd., same as **rebab**.

rubah (——) ـرُوبَاه P lrnd. fox. —**âne** (.———) P special to the fox, foxlike, crafty. —**î** (———) P 1. quality or act of a fox. 2. vulpine, cunning.

rubai (.——) ـرُبَاعِى A 1. poet. verse of four half-lines, quatrain. 2. Arabic gram. word of four radicals. 3. lrnd. of four elements (thing).

rubaiyat (.—.—) ـرُبَاعِيَاتْ A poet. collection of quatrains.

rubar ـرُوبَارْ P prov. comparison, collation. — **et**= to compare.

rubeh (—.) ـرُوبَه P lrnd., same as **rubah**.

ruberah (—.—) ـرُوبَرَاه P lrnd. prepared, ready for a journey.

ruberu (—.—) ـرُوبَرُو P lrnd. face to face; opposite.

rub'iye ـرُبْعِيَّه A obs. gold quarter-lira piece.

rububu var. of **rub 1**.

rubya (ˊ.) ـرُبْيَه rupee.

rud (—) ـرُودْ P lrnd. 1. river, stream. 2. lute, viol. 3. string of a musical instrument.

rudad (——) ـرُودَادْ P lrnd. occurence, event.

rudade (——.) ـرُودَادَه P lrnd. which has happened.

rudaverd (——.) ـرُودَآوَرْدْ P lrnd. brought by a river.

rudbar (——) ـرُودْبَارْ P lrnd. 1. large river.

rude

2. country intersected with rivers; land on a river.
rude (—.) ‎رود‎ P lrnd. 'gut, bowel, intestine. —**gân** (—.—) pl.
rudlâh (——) ‎رودلاع‎ P lrnd. place abounding in rivers.
Rufai (.——) ‎رفاعى‎ A same as **Rifai**.
rufat (.—) ‎رفات‎ A lrnd. moldering, crushing.
rugan ‎روغن‎ [revgan] 1. patent leather. 2. same as **revgan**. —**la**= /ı/ to varnish, polish. —**lı** 1. varnished, polished. 2. patent leather.
rugerdan (—.—) ‎روگردان‎ P lrnd. disobedient; one who renounces. —**î** (—.——) P desertion.
ruh 1 (—) ‎روح‎ A 1. soul, spirit, breath of life. 2. essence, tincture, volatile fluid. 3. energy, activity. 4. ghost. —**i aklî** lrnd. man's conceptive spirit. — **argınlığı** neol. psychasthenia. —**i a'zam** lrnd. the supreme spirit, spirit of the Prophet Muhammad. —**u bile duymaz** He won't even notice. — **bilim***. — **çağırma** necromancy. — **düşümü** neol. psycholepsy. —**i emin** lrnd. the faithful spirit, the angel Gabriel. — **göçü** neol. metempsychosis. — **hâleti** psychological condition; morale, mood. —**i hassas** lrnd. the perceptive faculty. — **hastalığı** psychopathy, mental disease. —**i hayalî** lrnd. the reflective faculty. —**i hayvanî** lrnd. animal spirit (common to man and brute). — **hekimliği** psychiatry. —**i ilâhî** lrnd. spirit of God. —**i ilka** lrnd. 1. the angel Gabriel. 2. the Quran. —**i insanî** lrnd. 1. the spirit of the Prophet Muhammad. 2. man's rational soul. —**i kudsî** lrnd. the spirit in saints by which they comprehend divine truth. —**i küllî** lrnd. God's universal spirit. —**i mükerrem** lrnd. the angel Gabriel. —**i nebatî** lrnd. the principle of life in plants, vegetable spirit. —**i nefsanî** lrnd. man's intelligent soul. — **ölçümü** neol. psychometry. — **ötesi***. —**i revan** lrnd. a living soul. — **sayrılığı** neol. psychopathy. —**i tabiî** lrnd. animal life. — **tedavisi** psychotherapy. —**unu teslim et**= to give up the ghost, to die. —**i tutya** chem. zinc oxide. —**i zikrî** lrnd. the memory.
ruh 2 ‎روح‎ P 1. lrnd. cheek; face, countenance. 2. myst. manifestation of God's grace; God's unity; divine command.
ruh 3 ‎رخ‎ P 1. chess. rook, castle. 2. lrnd. roc (name of a mythical bird).
ruham (.—) ‎رخام‎ A lrnd. marble, alabaster.
ruhan (—´.) ‎روحا‎ A in spirit, mentally.
ruhanî (———) ‎روحانى‎ A 1. spiritual; immaterial; holy, saintly. 2. clerical. 3. angel; ghost.

ruhaniyat (——.—) ‎روحانيات‎ A lrnd. spiritual matters.
ruhaniyet (——..) ‎روحانيت‎ A lrnd. 1. spirituality; saintliness. 2. spiritual influence.
ruhaniyun (——.—) ‎روحانيون‎ A lrnd. angels; ghosts.
ruhbahşa (—.—) ‎روحبخش‎ P lrnd. life-giving.
ruhban (.—) ‎رهبان‎ A lrnd., pl. of **rahib** 1. —**iyet** A monastic life.
ruhbilim neol. psychology.
ruhefza (—.—) ‎روحافزا‎ P 1. obs., Or. mus. a makam starting like **nazenin** and ending on **aşiran**. 2. lrnd. enlivening; cheering.
ruhî (——) ‎روحى‎ A 1. psychic. 2. psychological, mental.
ruhiyat (—.—) ‎روحيات‎ A phil. spiritualism.
ruhiyet (—..) ‎روحيت‎ A 1. spiritual state; temperament. 2. psychism.
ruhiyun (—.—) ‎روحيون‎ A phil. spiritualists.
ruhlan= ‎روحلن‎ to become animated, to revive. —**dır**= /ı/ caus.
ruhlu ‎روحلو‎ 1. having a soul or spirit, animated. 2. lively; vivid, full of feeling. 3. spirituous (liquor). 4. spirit-level.
ruhm ‎رحم‎ A lrnd. pity, mercy, compassion; forgiveness.
ruhperver (—..) ‎روحپرور‎ P lrnd. nourishing the mind or soul.
ruhs ‎رخص‎ A lrnd. cheapness, lowness of price.
ruhsal neol. psychic.
ruhsar (.—), **ruhsare** (.—.) ‎رخسار‎ P lrnd. cheek; face, countenance.
ruhsat ‎رخصت‎ A 1. permission; permit; license. 2. lrnd. leave, dismissal. 3. lrnd. dispensation by God in respect to the lightening of a religious duty.
ruhsatcu (..—) ‎رخصتجو‎ P lrnd. who asks for permission.
ruhsatiye ‎رخصتيه‎ license.
ruhsatlı ‎رخصتلى‎ 1. authorized; on leave. 2. licensed.
ruhsatname (..—.) ‎رخصتنامه‎ P permit; credentials.
ruhsatsız ‎رخصتسز‎ 1. without permission; unauthorized. 2. unlawful, secret.
ruhsude (—.) ‎روحسوده‎ P lrnd. a doing homage to a superior (by touching the ground with one's face).
ruhsuz ‎روحسز‎ 1. lifeless, inanimate. 2. spiritless, inactive; dull. —**luk** lifelessness, spiritlessness.
Ruhulkudüs (—...) ‎روح القدس‎ A 1. Isl. rel. the Angel Gabriel. 2. Christ. rel. the Holy Ghost.
Ruhullah (..—) ‎روح الله‎ A lrnd. Jesus Christ.
ruj ‎روژ‎ F lipstick.
ruk'a ‎رقعه‎ A lrnd. 1. slip of paper for a short note. 2. written memorial, petition. 3. same as

rık'a 1. 4. patch; piece of material used as a patch.
rukaba (..—) رُقَباء A *lrnd.*, *pl. of* **rakib 1.**
rukad (.—) رُقاد A *lrnd.* a sleeping, sleep.
rukud (.—) رُقود A *lrnd.* a sleeping; sleep.
rukum (.—) رُقوم A *lrnd.*, *pl. of* **rakam.**
—**i ulûm** man's senses and perceptive powers as indicative of God's omniscience.
rukye رُقْيه A *lrnd.* charm, incantation, spell.
—**han** (..—) P enchanter; sorcerer.
rulet رولت F roulette.
rulman رولمان F mech. bearing.
rulo (´.) رولو F 1. roll (of paper). 2. roller.
Rum 1 رُم [**Rum 2**] Greek of Turkish citizenship.
Rum 2 (—) رُم A *hist.* 1. the Byzantines; the Byzantine Empire. 2. Asia Minor. 3. the Ottoman Empire.
rumal[ii] (——) رومال P *lrnd.* who rubs his face upon anything (as an act of reverence).
— **ol=** to prostrate oneself in reverence.
rumalî (———) رومالى P *lrnd.* a rubbing the face.
rumalide (———.) رومالیده P *lrnd.* who has rubbed his face, who has done reverence to.
rumat (.—) رُمات A *lrnd.*, *pl. of* **rami 1.**
Rumanya (.´.) رومانیه *geog.* Rumania. —**lı** Rumanian.
Rumca (´.) رومجه Modern Greek.
rume (—.) روم P *lrnd.* hair about the pubes or body.
Rumeli روم ایلی European Turkey, Rumelia.
— **Hisarı** *name of the fortress built by Mehmed the Conqueror in 1452 on the European side of the Bosphorus.*
Rumen رومن F Rumanian. —**ce** the Rumanian language.
Rumi (——) رومى A *lrnd.* 1. pertaining to the ancient Romans or to the Byzantine Greeks. 2. pertaining to the Ottomans, to Turkey, or to Anatolia. — **sene** *calendar* a modification of the Muslim era which uses solar years, numbering them 584 years less than the Western calendar (i. e. 1984 A.D. = 1400 Rumi).
Rumiyan (—.—) رومیان P *lrnd.* the Romans; the Byzantines.
Rumiyane (—./—.) رومیانه P *lrnd.* pertaining to the Romans or to the Byzantine Greeks.
Rumiye (—..) رومیه A *lrnd.* Rome.
Rumlaş=[ır] رُملاشمق to become a Greek of Turkish citizenship. —**tır=** /ı/ *caus.*
Rumluk[tu] رُملك 1. district inhabited by Turkish subjects of Greek race. 2. Hellenism (within Turkey).
rumuz (.—) رُموز A [*pl. of* **remz**] 1. symbol; abbreviation; initial; cipher. 2. *lrnd.*: signs, nods, *etc.* —**i kimyeviye** *lrnd.* the chemical symbols. —**ât** (.——) A formula; abbreviations.

runüma (—.—) رُونما P *lrnd.* 1. who shows his face; which appears. 2. which occurs, happens. 3. present made to a bride by the bridegroom on first seeing her face.
runümaî, runümayi (—.——) رُونمائى رُونمایى P 1. a showing of the face; appearance; occurrence. 2. *same as* **runüma.**
runümun (—.—) رُونمون P *lrnd., same as* **runüma.**
rupuş (——) رُوپوش P *lrnd.* veil covering the whole face; covered, concealed, disappearing out of sight.
rupye (.´.) روپیه rupee.
Rus روس F Russian. —**ça** the Russian language; in Russian.
rusefid (—.—) رُوسفید P *lrnd.* honored, illustrious, excellent; select; honest, righteous.
rusg رُسغ A *lrnd.* wrist; ankle.
rusgülkadem رُسغ القدم A *anat.* metatarsus.
rusgülyed رُسغ الید A *anat.* metacarpus.
rusiyah (—.—) رُوسیاه P *lrnd.* 1. black-faced. 2. shamed, disgraced; unfortunate, mean, abject.
Ruslaş=[ır] رُسلاشمق to become Russian. —**tır=** /ı/ to Russify. —**tırma** Russification.
rusta (——) رُوستا P *lrnd.* 1. village; market place. 2. rustic, peasant.
rustahiz (..—), (———) روستاخیز P *lrnd.* Day of Resurrection.
rustaî (———) روستائى P *lrnd.* 1. rustic, pastoral. 2. villager, peasant. 3. boorishness, clownishness.
Rusya (´.) روسیا *geog.* Russia. —**lı** native of Russia.
ruşen (—.) روشن P *lrnd.* 1. bright, shining; sparkling; lighted up, illuminated. 2. clearly visible, manifest, conspicuous.
ruşena (—.—) روشنا P *lrnd., same as* **ruşen.** —**î** (—.——) P brightness, luminousness; light.
ruşenbasar (—...) روشن بصر P *lrnd.* clear-sighted, keen-sighted.
ruşenbeyan (—..—) روشن بیان P *lrnd.* clear and eloquent in expression.
ruşendil (—..) روشن دل P *lrnd.* 1. of enlightened mind; sage; saint. 2. in good faith.
ruşeni (—.—) روشنى P *lrnd.* brightness, luminousness; light.
Ruşeniye (—...) روشنیه A name of an order of dervishes affiliated with the Khalwati order.
ruşenrevan, ruşenzamir (—..—) روشن روان روشن ضمیر P *lrnd.* of enlightened mind.
ruşinas (—.—) روشناس P *lrnd.* 1. who recognizes a face. 2. known by sight; casual acquaintance. —**î** (—.——) P acquaintance.

rutubet (. —.) رطوبت A dampness, humidity; moisture.
rutubetlen=ⁱʳ رطوبتلنمك to become damp, wet, or moist. **—dir**= /ı/ *caus*.
rutubetli رطوبتلى moist, damp, humid, wet.
ruud (. —) رعود A *lrnd.*, *pl. of* **ra'd 1**.
ruunet (. —.) رعونت A *lrnd.* 1. a being stupid, foolish, silly; stupidity, foolishness. 2. pride, arrogance; ignorance.
ruunetli (. —..) رعونتلى 1. stupidly ignorant, foolishly proud and haughty. 2. coquettish, silly.
ruva رووا F *cards* king.
ruy 1 (—) روى P *lrnd., same as* **ru 1**.
ruy 2 (—) روى P *lrnd.* brass; bronze.
ruya (— —) رؤيا [**rüya**] A *same as* **rüya**.
ru'yan (. —) رعيان A *lrnd., pl. of* **rai 1**.
ruyaru (— — —) رويارو P *lrnd.* 1. face to face. 2. opposite.
ruyende (—..) رويند ه P *lrnd.* which grows, growing.
ruyin (— —) روئين P *lrnd.* of bronze or brass; brazen.
ruz (—) روز P *lrnd.* day; daytime. **R—i Ceza, R—i Dad** Day of Judgment. **—i elest** time of the creation of Adam; day of the original covenant between God and man. **R—i Hesab** Day of Judgment. **— ü şeb** day and night; by day and by night.
ruze (—.) روزه P *lrnd.* 1. fast, fasting. 2. day.
ruzedar (—. —) روزه دار P *lrnd.* fasting, who is keeping his fast.
ruzefza (—. —) روزافزا P *lrnd.* which increases the days.
ruzefzun (—. —) روزافزون P *lrnd.* increasing daily.
ruzehar (—. —) روزه خوار P *lrnd.* who unlawfully breaks a fast.
ruzeküşa (—..—) روزه كشا P *lrnd.* 1. who lawfully breaks his fast. 2. a slight repast taken by a Muslim to break his fast.
ruzgâr (— —) روزگار P *lrnd.* 1. time; space of time; period, age. 2. world; fortune. 3. one's life or circumstances; good fortune, prosperity. **— geçir**= to pass one's life.
ruzgârdide (— — —.) روزگارديده P *lrnd.* who has experienced various turns of fortune; who has seen the world and its vicissitudes.
ruzgüzar (—. —) روزگزار P *lrnd.* 1. means of living; livelihood. 2. occupation.
ruzî (— —) روزى P *lrnd.* 1. one's daily bread, one's means of living. 2. portion, lot, portion.
ruzidih (— —.) روزىده P *lrnd.* giver of daily bread, God.
ruzihâh (— — — —) روزى خواه P *lrnd.* one who asks for his daily bread.

ruzihâr (— — —) روزى خوار P breadeater, a dependent.
ruzine (— —.) روزينه P *lrnd.* daily; daily allowance, pay or ration.
ruzinedar (— —. —) روزينه دار P *lrnd.* one who receives a daily allowance, pensioner.
ruziresan (—..—) روزى رسان P *lrnd.* one who provides, God.
ruziyane (—. —.) روزيانه P *lrnd.* daily allowance, pay, or ration.
ruzmerre (—..) روزمرّه P *lrnd.* 1. daily or constant occurrence; everyday, common. 2. daily occupation.
ruznamçe (— — —.) روزنامچه P *Ott. hist.* rough day-book of current financial transactions in a government office. **—ci** clerk in charge of financial transactions.
ruzname (— — —.) روزنامه P *lrnd.* 1. order of the day, agenda. 2. calendar; journal, diary. 3. daily cash-book. 4. daily paper.
-rüba (. —) ربا P *lrnd.* that steals or carries off; stealing, attracting, *as in* **dilrüba**.
rübai (. — —) رباعى A *lrnd., same as* **rubai**.
rübubiyet (. —..) ربوبيت A *lrnd.* 1. ownership; lordship. 2. Godhead, deity, divinity.
rübude (. —.) ربوده P *lrnd.* seized, plundered, robbed; attracted, carried off.
rübudeakl (. —..) ربوده عقل P *lrnd.* robbed of one's senses, bewildered.
rübudedil (. —..) ربوده دل P *lrnd.* whose heart is stolen, in love.
rüchan (. —) رجحان A *lrnd.* 1. preference, preponderance. 2. advantage. **— hakkı** preferential right, privilege, priority.
rüchaniyet (. —..) رجحانيت A 1. a being preferable, having priority; superiority. 2. *gram.* comparative.
rücuᵘᵘ (. —) رجوع A *lrnd.* 1. a returning, reverting; return; a going back on one's word. 2. recision. 3. a turning to, recourse. **— hakkı** right of recovery, right of recourse. **—a kefil** *law* counter-guaranty.
rüculet (. —.), **rüculiyet** (. —..) رجولت، رجوليت A *lrnd., same as* **recüliyet**.
rücum (. —) رجوم A *lrnd.* 1. missiles. 2. shooting stars.
rüesa (..—) رؤسا A *lrnd., pl. of* **reis 2**.
Rüfai (. — —) رفاعى A *same as* **Rifai**.
rüfeka (..—) رفقا A *lrnd., pl. of* **refik**.
rüft رفت P *lrnd.* a sweeping. **— ü rub et**= /ı/ to sweep.
Rüha (. —) رها A *former name of* Urfa.
rühn, rühun (. —) رهون A *lrnd., pl. of* **rehn**.
rükban (. —) ركبان A *lrnd., pl. of* **râkib 2**.
rükbe ركبه A *lrnd.* knee.
rükeb, rükebat (..—) ركب، ركبات A *lrnd., pl. of* **rükbe**.

rükn رکن A lrnd. 1. pillar, column. 2. prop, support. 3. fundamental principle; influential person.

rükûᵘᵘ (.—) رکوع A Isl. rel. a bowing down in prayer so that the palms of the hands touch the knees; bowing the head in humility and reverence.

rükûb (.—) رکوب A lrnd. a mounting and riding on a beast or vehicle.

rükûd (.—), **rükûdet** (.—.) رکود ، رکودت A lrnd. 1. a becoming stagnant; stagnation. 2. a being still, calm; stillness, quiet.

rükûn (.—) رکون A lrnd. 1. a leaning, inclining; inclination. 2. a leaning on; trust; reliance.

rükûnet (.—.) رکونت A lrnd. 1. a being sound, steady, sedate; soundness, sedateness. 2. a being firmly rooted; firmness, immovability.

rükünᵏⁿᵘ رکن var. of **rükn**.

rüküş رکوش a comically dressed, helpless little woman. — **hanım** same as **rüküş**.

rümh رمح A lrnd. spear, lance. —**î** (.—) A like a spear, sharp.

rümman (.—) رمان A lrnd. pomegranate. —**e** (.—.) A a single pomegranate. —**î** (.——) A pomegranate-colored, ruby-colored, ruby. —**iye** (.—..) A bot., Punicaceae.

rümuz (.—) رموز A lrnd., same as **rumuz**.

rüptör روپتور F elec. interruptor, circuit-breaker.

rüselâ (..—) رسلا A lrnd., same as **rüsül**.

rüstakᵏᴵ (.—) رستاق A lrnd. cultivated rural district with villages; village. —**î** (.——) P villager; pertaining to a village.

rüste رسته P lrnd. grown. —**i hâk** produce of the earth; men, beasts and vegetation; animated nature.

rüsub (.—) رسوب A lrnd. a sinking to the bottom (in fluid), dregs, sediment. —**î** (.——) A 1. sedimentary. 2. precipitate.

rüsuh (.—) رسوخ A lrnd. 1. a being firm, stable, fixed, tight. 2. a being well-versed in a science. —**î** (.——) A constant, stable. —**iyet** A firmness, stability.

rüsum (.—) رسوم A lrnd., pl. of **resm**. —**i âdâb** the conventional usages of good manners. —**i âdiye** established forms or usages. —**i ayniye** customs paid in kind. —**i din** rites and external ceremonies of religion.

rüsumat (.——) رسومات A lrnd., pl. of **rüsum**, 1. dues, taxes, charges, tolls. 2. as sing. Custom, Customs Administration. —**ı örfiye** tolls and charges arbitrarily imposed. —**ı zecriye** prohibitory duties, duties on prohibited articles.

rüsül رسل A lrnd., pl. of **resûl**.

rüsva, rüsvay (.—) رسوا ، رسوای P publicly disgraced, infamous; object of scorn. —**yı âlem** the object of universal scorn. —**î**, —**yi** (.——) P lrnd., —**lık** disgrace, ignominy; disgraceful act.

rüşd رشد A 1. majority; a coming of age. 2. lrnd. a taking or following a right road, orthodoxy; rectitude, right judgment.

rüşdî (.—) رشدی A pertaining to right judgment and action.

rüşdiye رشدیه A Ott. hist. high school.

rüşeym رشیم A biol. embryo, germ. —**at** (..—) pl. —**atın tekevvünü** embryogeny. —**î** (..—) A embryonic. —**iyat** embryology.

rüşvet 1 رشوت A bribe; bribery. — **al**= to accept, receive a bribe. —**i kelâm** complimentary words before criticizing. — **ye**= to accept bribes.

rüşvet 2 رشوت ، رشوه ت It naut. ship's spare rigging stores, place where spares are kept.

rüşvetçi رشوتچی taker of bribes; dishonest official.

rütbe رتبه A degree; grade; rank. — **al**= to rise in rank. —**li** having high rank.

rütbet رتبت A lrnd., same as **rütbe**.

rütbetlû (..—) رتبتلو of high rank (title given to high ecclesiastics).

rüteb رتب A lrnd., pl. of **rütbe**.

rütebi (..—) رتبی A lrnd. pertaining to rank. — **sayılar** ordinal numbers.

rüteylâ (..—) رتیلا A lrnd. venomous insect whose bite is fatal; tarantula.

rüus (.—) رؤوس A lrnd., pl. of **res**, 1. heads. 2. Ott. hist. grade of the Ulema. 3. diploma in theology.

rüvat (.—) رواة A lrnd., pl. of **ravi**.

rüveyda رویدا A lrnd. Gently! Softly!

rü'ya (.—) A, **rüya** (——) رؤیا A dream, vision. — **gör**= to have a dream. — **tabiri** interpretation of dreams.

rüyet رؤیت A lrnd. 1. a seeing, perceiving; visibility; perception; vision. 2. examination; supervision. —**i dâva** law the hearing of a suit. — **et**= /a/ 1. to examine (a disputed question). 2. to supervise.

rüzelâ (..—) رذلا A lrnd., pl. of **rezil**.

rüzgâr (.—) روزگار P wind, breeze. — **altı** naut. lee side. — **avla**= 1. to go at full gallop. 2. to get nothing. — **ekip fırtına biç**= to sow the wind and reap a storm; to be punished with a greater evil than what one has done to another. — **gelecek deliklerı tıka**= to take all the necessary precautions. — **gülü** compass rose. — **ile git**= 1. to sail with the wind. 2. to trim one's sails to suit the occasion. — **payı** wind allowance in shooting. — **üstü** naut. windward side. — **yakası** naut. leech of a sail. —**ı yakaya al**= naut. to shiver the sails by luffing. —**lı** windy, breezy.

S

S the twenty-second letter of the Turkish alphabet.
═sa 1, ═se ﺳـ [ise] if (he) ..., e. g., **kalsa** if he stays, **gitse** if he goes.
-sa 2, -se, after vowels **-ysa, -yse** (.'.) ﺳـ [ise] if (he) ..., e. g., **çoksa** if it is too much; **evdeyse** if he is at home.
-sa═ 3, -se═ ﺳــﻤﺴــ ﺳــﻤــ to deem ..., as in **mühimse═**.
-sa 4 (—) ﺳـ P lrnd. that rubs, rubbing, as in **cebinsa**.
-sa 5 (—) ﺳـ P lrnd. like, as in **ambersa**.
saᵃⁱ 6 (—) ﺻﺎع A lrnd. a dry measure of about a gallon.
saa ﺳـ A lrnd., same as **sia**.
saabib (.——) ﺛﻌﺎﺑﻴﺐ A lrnd. threads of saliva flowing from the mouth.
saadet (.—.) ﺳﻌﺎدت A happiness; prosperity, felicity. **—le** Good-by! Good luck! said to a departing person. **— ahlâkı** phil. eudaemonism. **— asrı** the period of the lifetime of the Prophet Muhammad. **—i ebediye** lrnd. eternal happiness. **—i tamme, —i uzma** lrnd. beatitude.
saadetencam (.—..—) ﺳﻌﺎدت اﻧﺠﺎم P lrnd. propitious.
saadethane (.—.—.) ﺳﻌﺎدت ﺧﺎﻧﻪ P abode of bliss, place of felicity term of politeness used in speaking to another of his house.
saadetihtiva (.—...—) ﺳﻌﺎدت اﺣﺘﻮا P lrnd. surrounded by blessedness, blessed.
saadetintiva (.—...—) ﺳﻌﺎدت اﻧﻄﻮا P lrnd. prosperous; felicitous.
saadetinzimam (.—...—) ﺳﻌﺎدت اﻧﻀﻤﺎم A lrnd. prosperous; salutary.
saadetli, saadetlû (.—.—) ﺳﻌﺎدﺗﻠﻰ ﺳﻌﺎدﺗﻠﻮ 1. prosperous, happy, fortunate. 2. official title formerly given to generals, etc.

saadetmenat (.—..—) ﺳﻌﺎدت ﻣﻨﺎط P lrnd. auspicious.
saadetmend (.—..) ﺳﻌﺎدت ﻣﻨﺪ P lrnd. 1. prosperous, happy, fortunate. 2. spiritually elect. **—î** (.—..—) P happiness, prosperity.
saadetnümud (.—..—) ﺳﻌﺎدت ﻧﻤﻮد P lrnd. happy; august; felicitous.
saadetünvan (.—..—) ﺳﻌﺎدت ﻋﻨﻮان P lrnd. blessed in Paradise.
saalib (.—.) ﺛﻌﺎﻟﺐ A lrnd., pl. of **sa'leb**.
saatᵗⁱ 1 ﺳﺎﻋﺖ A 1. hour; time; time of day. 2. an interval of time; moment; a while. 3. watch, clock. 4. meter (electric, gas, etc.). **— ayarı** 1. regulation of a watch or clock; correct time. 2. regulator of a watch. **— başı** 1. end of an hour. 2. general pause in conversation. **— be saat** from hour to hour. **— beşte** at five o'clock. **— bu saat** Make the best of the present time. **— çemberi, — dairesi** astr. hour circle. **bir — evvel** as soon as possible. **— gibi** like a clock, very regular, accurate; smoothly (running). **— kaç?** What time is it? **— kaçta?** at what time? when? **— kösteği** watch chain. **— kulesi** clock tower. **—i kur═** to wind a watch. **— makinesi** clockworks. **—i muhtar** lrnd. the propitious moment. **—ler olsun** colloq. for **sıhhatler olsun**. **— onbirde** at the eleventh hour; very late; very late in life. **—i saatine** at the right time, punctually. **— tahtası** dial of a clock. **— tası** bell of a striking clock. **— tut═** to time (race, etc.). **— vur═** to strike the hour. **— zarfı** watch case.
saat 2 (——) ﺳﺎﻋﺎت A lrnd., pl. of **saat 1**.
saatçi (—..) ﺳﺎﻋﺘﺠﻰ 1. watchmaker; watch repairer. 2. watch seller. **—lik** trade of a maker, seller or repairer of watches.

saatçiyan (...—) ساعتچیان Ott. hist. watch makers in the Sultan's palace.

saatlikᵍⁱ ساعتلك 1. lasting so many hours. 2. shelf on which a clock stands.

sa'b 1 صعب A lrnd. 1. hard, difficult, arduous. 2. obstinate, refractory, troublesome.

sabᵇᵇⁱ **2** صبّ A lrnd. a pouring, pouring out.

saba 1 (.—) صبا A 1. poet. light breeze blowing from the east. 2. Or. mus. one of the oldest and most characteristic **makams**. — **berâber** sweet and pleasant like the morning breeze. — **perdesi** mus. the note d' flat. — **puselik** Or. mus. a compound **makam** composed 150 years ago. — **zemzeme** Or. mus. a compound **makam**.

saba 2 (.—) صبا A same as **seba 2**.

sababet (.—.) صبابت A lrnd. a being deeply in love; deep love.

sabah 1 صباح [sabah 2] 1. morning; in the morning; forenoon. 2. dawn, daybreak. 3. tomorrow, tomorrow morning. —**ları** in the morning, mornings. —**tan** 1. already early in the morning; from early morning. 2. from tomorrow. — **akşam** all the time. —**ı bul**= to stay awake all night; to work through the night. —**a çıkma**= not to live till morning, to die during the night. —**a doğru** toward morning. —**ı et**= same as **sabahı bul**=. —**a karşı** towards morning. — **ola hayır ola** Let's wait for the morning (hoping for something good to happen). — **oldu** It is morning. — **sabah** early in the morning. — **vakti** daybreak, morning. — **yıldızı** the morning star, Venus.

sabah 2 (.—) صباح A lrnd., same as **sabah 1**. —**ı mahşer** morning of the Day of Judgment. —**ı şerifiniz hayrolsun**, —**ı şerifler hayırlar olsun** Good morning.

sabahat (.—.) صباحت A 1. lrnd. beauty. 2. w. cap., woman's name.

sabahçı صباحجى 1. early riser. 2. working or remaining till daybreak. 3. pupil who goes to school only in the mornings. — **kahvesi** coffeehouse that stays open all night, or opens very early in the morning.

sabahgâh (..—) صباحگاه P lrnd. morning.

sabahkiⁿⁱ صباحكى this morning's.

sabahla=ʳ صباحلامق 1. to sit up all night, to pass the whole night. 2. to become morning. —**t**= /ı/ caus.

sabahleyin (..´..) صباحلين in the morning, early.

sabahlı akşamlı صباحلى آقشاملى mornings and evenings, always.

sabahlıkᵍⁱ صباحلك 1. dressing gown, house coat. 2. special to the morning.

saban صابان plow. — **ağacı** wooden pole or beam of a plow. — **bıçağı** plow blade. — **burnu** sharp end of the sole of a plow. — **demiri** plowshare. — **izi** furrow. — **kayışı** thong that fastens the yoke to the pole of the plow. — **kemiği** anat. vomer bone. — **keskisi**, — **kılıcı** plow blade. — **kulağı** mold board. — **oku** pole of a plow. — **ökçesi** heel of the foot of the plow. — **sapı** plow handle. — **sür**= to plow, to drive the plow. — **tabanı** slade, sole. — **zıvanası** pin of the pole to which the yoke of the animals is fastened.

sabankıran صبانقیران restharrow, bot., Ononis repens.

sabareftar (.—.—) صبارفتار P poet. graceful of gait.

sabavet (.—.) صباوت A lrnd. infancy, childhood.

sabaya (.—.—) صبایا lrnd., pl. of **sabiye**.

sabbağ (.—) صبّاغ A lrnd. 1. dyer. 2. liar, one who gives a false coloring to a statement.

sabbar (.—) صبّار A lrnd. very patient; having great fortitude.

sabg صبغ A lrnd. 1. dyeing; dye. 2. a dipping. 3. a baptizing, immersing.

sabıkᵏⁱ (—.) سابق A 1. former, previous, preceding. 2. foregoing. — **ve esbak** the most recent and his predecessor (minister, etc.). — **ve lâhik** 1. a predecessor and the incumbent (of an office, etc.). 2. a senior and a junior traditionist of one generation.

sabıka 1 (—..) سابقه A 1. former misdeed; previous conviction. 2. antecedent; bad antecedent. —**i meşi'et-i ilâhiye** lrnd. a previous act of the will of God. —**i mükerrere sahibi** person who has been convicted repeatedly.

sabıka 2 (—.—), **sabıkan** (—..) سابقا سابقاً A lrnd. formerly, previously.

sabıkalı سابقه‌لى previously convicted, confirmed criminal, recidivist.

sabıkasalâr (—..——) سابقه‌سالار P lrnd. captain of an advanced guard or company; leader; the Prophet Muhammad.

sabıkıyet (—...) سابقیت A lrnd. 1. precedence. 2. precedent to all time, eternity in the past.

sabıkîn, sabıkun (—.—) سابقین سابقون A lrnd., pl. of **sabık**, religious leaders; important persons (of a nation etc.). —**i evvelûn** the first Muslims.

sabırᵇʳⁱ صبر [sabr] 1. patience; forbearance. 2. endurance, fortitude. 3. aloes. — **taşı** 1. folk tales stone to which troubles are told in private. 2. very patient person. —**ın sonu selâmet** Patience is rewarded. —**ı tükendi** His patience was exhausted.

sabırlı صبرلى 1. patient, forbearing. 2. firm, enduring.

sabırsız صبرسز 1. impatient. 2. lacking in fortitude, weak. —**lan**= to grow impatient. —**lık** impatience.

sabi 1 (.—) صبى A *lrnd.* male child, boy. **—i muabbir** *archaic law* a talking child who knows what he is talking about.
sabiii **2** (—.) سابع A *lrnd.* seventh.
Sabi 3 (——) صابى A *hist.* Sabean; pagan, idolator.
sabia (—.—), **sabian** (—..) سابعا ، سابعاً A *lrnd.* seventhly.
sabih 1 (—.) سابح A *lrnd.* that swims, swimming; floating. **— havuz** floating drydock.
sabih 2 (.—) صبيح A *lrnd.* beautiful, comely.
sabiha (.—.) صبيحة A 1. *lrnd.* beautiful woman. 2. *w. cap., woman's name.*
sâbihat (—.—) سابحات A *lrnd.* 1. ships, boats. 2. the stars. 3. spirits of men of faith.
sabir (—.) صابر A *lrnd.* patient; long-suffering; forbearing. **—in** (—.—) A *pl.*
sabit (—.) ثابت A 1. fixed, stationary; firm, steadfast. 2. permanent, constant, unchanging; enduring, lasting. 3. settled, established; sound, valid, real. 4. proved, demonstrated; sure. **— balon** captive balloon. **— fikir** fixed idea. **— kalem** indelible pencil. **— seviye kabı** *mech.* float chamber (of a carburetor).
sabite (—..) ثابتة A 1. *astr.* fixed star. 2. *math.* constant.
sabitkadem (—...) ثابت قدم P *lrnd.* 1. firm and steadfast, resolved. 2. who keeps his word; persistent.
sabiye (.—.) صبية A *lrnd.* girl, female child.
sabotaj سابوتاژ F sabotage.
sabr صبر A *lrnd., same as* **sabır.** **—i cemil** enduring a calamity bravely. **—i Eyyüb** great patience like that of Job.
sabren صبراً A *lrnd.* in or by patience, with fortitude. **— katlet=** /ı/ to put to death in any way other than in a fight; to kill by any slow process or in cold blood. **— yemin et=** to take an oath under duress.
sabret=der صبر ايتمك 1. to be patient. 2. /a/ to endure. **—en derviş muradına ermiş** *proverb* Patience is rewarded.
sabrî (.—) صبرى A *lrnd.* pertaining to patience.
sabuh (.—) صبوح A *poet.* a morning draught, drink taken in the morning.
sabuklama *neol.* delirium.
sabun صابون [*Arabic* ——] soap. **— otu** soapwort, *bot., Saponaria officinalis.* **— taşı** soapstone, steatite.
sabuncu صابونجى soap maker; soap seller. **—luk** soap manufacturing.
sabunhane (..—.) صابونخانه soap factory.
sabunî (———) صابونى A *lrnd.* 1. pertaining to soap. 2. maker or seller of soap. 3. soaplike. 4. emerald clouded like mottled soap.
sabuniye صابونيه A *lrnd.* a starch confection.
sabunla=r صابونلامق /ı/ to soap, to wash with soap. **—n=** 1. *pass.* 2. *gambler's slang* to be completely cleaned out. **—ş=** to become like soap. **—şma** saponification. **—t=** /ı/ *caus. of* **sabunla=**.
sabunlu صابونلى soapy.
sabunlukgu صابونلق 1. soap dish. 2. washcloth.
sabur 1 صبر *var. of* **sabır.**
sabur 2 (.—) صبور A *lrnd.* 1. patient; endured with fortitude. 2. forebearing; long-suffering, the All-patient God. **—âne** (.——.) P patiently.
sabura (.'.) صابوره Gk *naut.* ballast.
sac 1 ساج ، صاج 1. sheet iron; made of sheet iron. 2. thin iron plate for cooking or baking.
sac 2 (—) صاج A 1. teak tree, East Indian oak, *bot., Tectona grandis.* 2. teak timber.
sacayağım, **sacayak**gu صاج آياغى ، صاج آياق 1. trivet. 2. trio. **— yürü=** *mil.* to march with one company in front and two in the rear separated by an interval.
saciii (—.) ساجع A *lrnd.* who speaks in rhymed and balanced prose.
sacid (—.) ساجد A *lrnd.* who prostrates himself in worship.
saç 1 صاچ hair of the head, hair. **— ağart=** to live long and become gray-haired. **—ına ak düş=** to begin to go gray (hair). **— bağı** hair band, bow. **—ı başı ağarmış** grown old. **—ını başını yol=** to tear out one's hair (in despair) **— biçimi** hairdo, hair style. **—ı bitmemiş** (*lit.*, whose hair has not grown) infant. **—ı bitmedik yetim** orphaned while still a baby. **— boyası** hair dye. **— bölüğü** *prov.* braid. **—ın çingenesi** hair on the neck too short to be combed or braided. **—larımı değirmende ağartmadım** (*lit.* I did not get my hair white at the mill.) I have not lived all these years for nothing. **—ı el elinde** 1. one subject to another's orders; not free to act on one's own. 2. married woman. **—ları iki türlü ol=** to have one's hair partly gray. **— kıran*. — ör=** to braid the hair. **— saça baş başa gel=** to come to blows. **—ı sakalı ağarmış** old and gray. **—ına sakalına bakmadan** disregarding his age. **— sakal birbirine karışmış** with hair and beard intermingled, untrimmed, unkempt. **— sakala karışmış** unshaved, shabby and neglected. **—a sakala kır serpil=** to be sprinkled with gray (hair and beard). **— salıver=** to let one's hair grow long. **—ını süpürge et=** to exert oneself greatly, to work very unselfishly, to be unsparing in one's efforts. **— teli** a single hair.
saçcı **2** صاچ same as **sac 1.**
saç=ar 3 صاچمق 1. to scatter, to sprinkle. 2. to sow broadcast. **—ıp savur=** to spend money recklessly, to throw money away.
saçakgu صاچاق ، صاچق 1. eaves of a house.

2. fringe. —ı ateş sardı Fire has enveloped the eaves of the house. Matters have taken a dangerous turn. — bulut neol. cirrus (cloud).

saçaklan= ᵗʳ صاچاقلانمق 1. to get eaves or fringes. 2. to become fringed.

saçaklı صاچاقلی 1. eaved, fringed. 2. untidily dressed.

saçaklıkᵏⁿ صاچاقلق arch. architrave; entablature.

saçı صاچی prov. coins, candy, millet, rice, etc., strewn over a bride or cast to the public to be scrambled for; shower of presents brought to the bride. — kıl= to scatter coins, etc., at a wedding.

saçıkᵏⁿ صاچق disordered, scattered.

saçıl=ᵗʳ صاچیلمق pass. of saç= 3.

saçın=ᵗʳ صاچنمق archaic to rub oneself with perfume; to sprinkle oneself with perfume.

saçıntı صاچنتی things thrown and scattered about.

saçıştır=ᵗʳ صاچیشدیرمق /ı/ to sprinkle, scatter, sow.

saçkıran صاچ قیران med. loss of hair, alopecia.

saçlı صاچلی haired, hairy. — sakallı of mature age. — yıldız archaic comet.

saçma صاچمه 1. verbal n. of saç= 3. 2. anything scattered or sprinkled. 3. b-b's, buckshot, small shot (for hunting). 4. cast net. 5. nonsense; nonsensical; absurdity. — ağ cast net. — sapan nonsense, incongruous talk. —cı nonsense talker.

saçmala=ʳ صاچمه لامق to talk or act in an unreasonable manner.

saçula (..'.) ساچوله It wooden mold for casting metal, wooden form.

sad 1 صاد name of the letter ص (This letter is the seventeenth letter of the Ottoman and the fourteenth letter of the Arabic alphabets. In chronograms it has the numerical value of 90 and is the abbreviation for the month Sefer).

sad 2 صد P lrnd. one hundred. — çendan a hundredfold. — hezar a hundred thousand.

sa'dᵈⁱ **3** سعد A lrnd. prosperity, happiness. auspiciousness; lucky, auspicious. —i asgar the planet Venus. —i ekber the planet Jupiter.

sadᵈᵈⁱ **4** (—) سادّ A 1. lrnd. that obstructs, closes or bars. 2. med. cataract.

sada (.—) صدی A 1. sound, voice; cry. 2. echo.

Sa'dabad (.——) سعدآباد P a name given, in the Tulip Period, to the picnic park at the Sweet Waters of Europe (Kâğıthane).

sadakᵍⁱ **1** صداق quiver.

sadakᵏⁿ **2** صدق A lrnd. 1. He has spoken the truth used especially at the end of a recital of the Quran in the expression sadak-allâhü'l-azîm. 2. used as mâsadak.

sadaka صدقه alms, charity. —i fıtr lrnd. alms which Muslims are required to give at the end of the fast of Ramazan.

sadakallah (.'..—) صدق الله A lrnd. God is the Speaker of truth.

sadakat 1 (..—) صدقات A lrnd., pl. of sadaka.

sadakatᵗⁱ **2** (.—.) صداقت A 1. faithfulness, faithful friendship; fidelity, devotion, loyalty. 2. hypocritical friendship, flattering those in power. — göster= /a/ to show loyalty.

sadakatalem (.—...) صداقت عالم P lrnd., same as sadakatkâr.

sadakatkâr (.—.—) صداقت كار P lrnd. sincere, faithful, devoted. —âne (.—.——.) P lrnd. faithfully, devotedly. —î (.—.——) P lrnd. 1. faithfulness, fidelity, devotion. 2. faithful, devoted.

sadakatli صداقتلی faithful, devoted.

sadakatsemir (.—..—) صداقت سمیر P lrnd. faithful.

sadakatsiz صداقتسز disloyal, unfaithful.

sadakatşiar (.—..—) صداقت شعار P lrnd. faithful.

sadakor سادکور It raw silk (cloth).

sadalı (.—.) صدالی ling. sonorous, voiced.

sadanüvis (.—.—) صدانویس P lrnd. phonograph.

sadaret (.—.) صدارت A Ott. hist. 1. office rank and functions of the Grand Vizier. 2. office and functions of the Kazaskers of Rumeli and Anadolu. — kaimmakamı, — kaymakamı Ott. hist. official representing the Grand Vizier in Istanbul while he was on a campaign. — kethüdası Ott. hist. chief assistant to the Grand Vizier. —i uzma the Grand Vizierate.

sadaretpenah (.—..—) صدارت پناه P lrnd. the Grand Vizier. —î (.—..——) P Grand Vizierial.

sadasız صداسز ling. unvoiced.

sadat (——) سادات A lrnd., pl. of seyyid, princes, lords, especially the descendants of the Prophet Muhammad.

sadberkᵏⁱ صد برك P lrnd. hundred-petal (rose). — gülü cabbage rose.

sade (—.) ساده P 1. mere, simple; simply, merely, just, only. 2. unmixed, pure; plain, unadorned. 3. simple-minded, artless; ingenuous. 4. single (flower). 5. unsweetened (coffee); unstuffed (pastry). — güzel natural beauty. — suya plain, mere; unimportant. — suya çorba soup made without fat, clear soup. — yağ clarified butter; cooking fat.

sadece (—'..) ساده جه 1. simply, merely. 2. somewhat plain.

saded صدد A lrnd. point or object in view; objective, intention, scope. —inde bulun= /ın/ to have the intention of. —e gel= to come to the point under discussion. —den hariç extraneous to the question, off the point.

sadedil (—..) ساده دل P lrnd. simple-minded, ingenuous; guileless, naive. —**âne** (—..—.) P simple-mindedly, artlessly, naively. —**î** (—..—) P, —**lik** simpleness of heart, ingenuousness, naiveté.
sadef صدف A same as **sedef 2**.
sadefçe صدفچه P lrnd. a small piece of mother-of-pearl, a small shell.
sadefe صدفه A 1. lrnd. single shell of a mollusk; mother-of-pearl shell. 2. anat. external ear, concha.
sadefî (..—) صدفى A shell-like.
sadefkâr (..—) صدفكار P craftsman who does inlaid work with mother-of-pearl. —**î** (..——) P 1. inlaid or worked with mother-of-pearl. 2. art of inlaying ornaments with mother-of-pearl.
sadegi (—.—) سادگى P lrnd. 1. simplicity, guilelessness; purity. 2. simpleness, plainness.
sadekâr (—.—) ساده كار P lrnd. 1. goldsmith who does especially plain unornamented work. 2. plain-working, plain-dealing; plain; unornamented. —**î** (—.——) P unornamented goldsmithery.
sadeleş=ir ساده لش to become plain or simple; to be simplified. —**tir**= /ı/ to render simple, simplify. —**tirme** simplification; simplifying.
sadelevh (—..) ساده لوح P lrnd. 1. ingenuous; simpleton. 2. pure in heart.
sadelikği (—..) سادهلك plainness, simpleness; unadornedness; simplicity.
sademat (..—) صدمات A lrnd., pl. of **sadme**.
sademe صدمه A same as **sadme**.
saderu (—.—) ساده رو P lrnd. smooth-faced, beardless, shaved. —**yan** (—.——) pl.
sadetdi ساده د A same as **saded**.
sa'deyn سعدين A lrnd. the two lucky planets, Jupiter and Venus.
sadıkği (—.) صادق A true, sincere; faithful; honest, devoted.
sadıkane (—.—.) صادقانه P sincerely; faithfully.
sadırdri 1 صدر A var. of **sadr**.
sadır 2 (—.) صادر A lrnd. that comes forth, issues, emanates; emanating. — **ol**= 1. to emanate (decree, etc.). 2. to take place, to happen. — **ve vârid** he who goes and he who comes. —**a defteri** register book for outgoing letters and documents.
sadikkı (..—) صديق A lrnd. true, sincere; faithful friend.
sadin (—.) سادن A lrnd. hereditary doorkeeper or servitor of the Kaaba at Mecca.
sadis (—.) سادس A lrnd. sixth.
sadisen (—'..) سادسا A lrnd. sixthly, for the sixth time.
sadist ساديست F sadist.

Sa'diye (.—.) سعديه A name of an order of dervishes.
sadizm ساديزم F sadism.
sadme صدمه A lrnd. 1. collision; sudden blow or misfortune. 2. explosion.
sadpare (.—.) صدپاره P lrnd. a hundred pieces, in a hundred pieces.
sadr صدر A lrnd. 1. breast, chest; heart. 2. front, prominence. 3. post of honor; most important person; chief minister. —**ı a'zam** same as **sadrazam**. —**a geç**= to take the chief seat in an assembly; to become Grand Vizier. **S**—**ı Rum** Ott. hist. the Kazasker of Rumelia. **S**—**ı Sudur** Ott. hist. Prime Minister, Grand Vizier. —**a şifa verecek bir şey** something satisfactory.
sadrazam (.—.—) صدر اعظم |sadrı a'zam| Ott. hist. the Grand Vizier.
Sadreyn صدرين A Ott. hist. the two Kazaskers of Rumeli and Anadolu.
sadrî (.—) صدرى A lrnd. pertaining to the chest, pectoral.
sadrnişin (..—) صدرنشين P lrnd. sitting in the highest place of honor.
sa'dullah سعد الله A 1. lrnd. blessed by God. 2. w. cap., man's name.
sa'düddin (..—) سعدالدين A 1. lrnd. uplifting religion. 2. w. cap., man's name.
saf 1 (—) صاف A 1. pure, unadulterated. 2. clear, limpid. 3. sincere, unfeigned. 4. simple, ingenuous, naive. — **kan** purebred, thoroughbred (horse).
saffı 2 صف A row, line; rank. — **bağla**= to stand in line. —**ı cemaat** lrnd. line of worshippers in a mosque. — **düz**= to draw up a line of battle. —**ı harb** line of battle. —**ı harb gemisi** warship, battleship. —**tan haric** hors de combat, out of the fight. —**ı niâl** lrnd. place by the door where shoes are left on entering. —**ı nialde otur**= to sit out of humility in the place where shoes are left. — **saf** in rows, in ranks.
safa (.—) صفا A 1. enjoyment, pleasure, delight. 2. freedom from anxiety; peace, ease. 3. lrnd. a being clear, clearness, limpidness. 4. Or. mus. a **makam** starting one octave higher than **saba**, but ending on a' like **saba**. — **bulduk** Thank you, said in reply to the greeting **safa geldiniz**. — **et**= to amuse and enjoy oneself. — **geldiniz** Welcome! — **geldine git**= to visit somebody on his return from a journey. —**yı hâtır** peace and quiet of mind; ease and comfort. —**yı hâtır ile** with tranquillity, with pleasure and joy. —**ya mest kapla**= (lit., to put shoes on pleasure) to prolong the duration of pleasure. —**lar olsun** May it be enjoyable. — **pezevengi** slang

a pleasure addict. — **sür=** to lead a life of pleasure; to enjoy oneself.

safaâyin (.———) صفا آيين P lrnd. sincere; friendly.

safabahş (.—.) صفابخش P lrnd. pleasant, delightful.

safacu (.——) صفاجو P lrnd. pleasure-seeking. —**yan** (.———) P pl.

safahat (..—) صفحات A lrnd., pl. of **safha**.

safaih (.—.) صفائح A lrnd., pl. of **safiha**.

safalan='' (.—..) صفا لنمك to feel pleasure. —**dır=** /ı/ caus.

safalı (.—.) صفالى that gives pleasure or enjoyment, pleasant.

safârâ (.——) صف آرا P lrnd. one who draws up in array. —**yî** (.———) P marshalling of troops; parade.

safayab (.——) صفاياب P lrnd. full of pleasure.

safbeste صف بسته P lrnd. ranged in rank or file, ranked.

safder صف در P lrnd. who breaks ranks; hero, brave. —**ân** (..—) P pl. —**âne** (..—.) P pertaining to a hero, heroic. —**î** (..—) P, —**lik** heroism.

safderun 1 (..—) صافدرون |safderun 2| 1. sincere, candid. 2. simple; simpleton.

safderun 2 (—.—) صافدرون P lrnd., same as **safderun 1**. —**âne** (—.——.) P with sincerity or simpleness of heart. —**î** (—.——) P sincerity; simpleness.

safdil 1 صافدل |safdil 2| simple-hearted, ingenuous; naive, credulous.

safdil 2 (—.) صافدل P lrnd., same as **safdil 1**. —**âne** (—.—.) P simple-heartedly. —**î** (—.—) P simple-heartedness.

Safer صفر A the second month of the Arabic lunar year. —**ân** (..—) A lrnd. the two months, Muharrem and Sefer.

Safevi (..—) صفوى A hist. Safavid.

saffat (——) صافات A lrnd. (the angels) arranged in ranks about God's throne. **S— Suresi** a name of the thirty-seventh sura of the Quran.

saffet صفت [safvet] purity; sincerity; ingenuousness; simpleness of heart.

saffeyn صفين A lrnd. two opposing lines drawn up for battle.

safh صفح A lrnd. 1. a turning away, averting the face. 2. an overlooking, excusing; pardon.

safha صفحه A 1. phase. 2. lrnd. surface, face. 3. lrnd. leaf, page; plate.

safi 1 (—.) صافى [Arabic ——] 1. clear, limpid. 2. pure; sincere. 3. mere; net (quantity). — **su** just plain water and nothing else.

safi 2 (.—) صفى A lrnd. 1. pure, clear, limpid. 2. true, sincere. 3. choicest; choice object (picked by a leader from the spoils).

safih (.—) صفيح A lrnd. 1. broad-surfaced things; slabs, tablets, swords, etc. 2. the sky.

safiha (.—.) صفيحه A lrnd. 1. thin leaf or sheet; metal plate, plaque. 2. surface. 3. page.

safil (—.) سافل A lrnd. 1. low; lower part. 2. mean, humble, poor.

safin (—.) صافن A 1. anat. the large vein on each side of the foot, saphena vein. 2. lrnd. standing still with one foot resting on the tip of the toe (animal).

safinat (—.—) صافنات A lrnd. fleet, thoroughbred horses.

safir 1 صفير [Arabic .—| sapphire.

safir 2 (.—) صفير A lrnd. a whistling, hissing; whistling noise, hiss.

safir 3 (—.) سافر A lrnd. 1. who goes traveling; traveler. 2. scribe.

safire (—..) سافره A lrnd. body of travelers.

safirî (.——) صفيرى A 1. ling. sibilant. 2. lrnd. resembling a whistle; whistling.

Safiyullâh (.—.—) صفى الله A lrnd. Adam.

safiyet (—..) صافيت A simplicity; purity.

safizm صفيزم F psychiatry sapphism.

saflık صافى 1. simplicity, ingenuousness; naiveté. 2. purity, clearness.

safra 1 صفراء It naut. ballast. — **at=** to get rid of useless persons or things.

safra 2 صفرا [safra 3] bile, gall. — **bastır=** to have a snack. —**sı bulan=**, —**sı kabar=** to be nauseated. — **kesesi** anat. gall bladder.

safra 3 (.—) صفرا A lrnd. yellow.

safraküş (.—.) صفرا كش P lrnd. early breakfast.

safralı صفرالى bilious; feeling sick or giddy.

safralık صفرالك breakfast.

safran صفران F 1. saffron, bot., Crocus sativus. 2. coloring matter of saffron.

safravi (..—) صفراوى A lrnd. bilious; biliary.

safsaf صفصاف A willow, bot., Salix. —**iye** Salicaceae.

safsata سفسطه A lrnd. false reasoning, sophistry; quibbling, nonsense. —**ya düş=** to use silly arguments. —**cı** sophist; nonsense-talker. —**la=** to use sophistry, to argue falsely. —**lı** full of sophistry or nonsense.

safşiken صفشكن P lrnd. who breaks through the enemy's ranks; valiant.

Safura (.—.) صفوره صافورا صفوريا A Bib. Zipporah, wife of Moses.

safvet صفوت A lrnd., same as **saffet**.

safzen صفزن P lrnd., same as **safşiken**. —**î** (..—) P, —**lik** heroism in attacking and routing the enemy.

sagair (..—) صغائر A lrnd., pl. of **sagire**. — **ve kebair** the small sins and the great.

sagar 1 (—.) ساغر P 1. lrnd. drinking-cup, goblet, bowl, chalice. 2. myst. any means by which one attains perception of divine truth; saint's heart; spiritual ecstacy. **—ı gerdân** the cup that goes around from hand to hand. **—ı sahbâ** wine cup.

sagar 2 نَغَر A *lrnd.* pass, road, gap in a frontier; especially in the frontier of Muslim territory and subject to invasion by non-Muslim nations.

sagir (. —) صَغِير A *lrnd.* small, little, young. **— ü kebir** the young and the old.

sagire (. — .) صَغِيرَه A *lrnd.* small sin, venial sin.

sagu (´. .) ساگو Malay common sago palm, *bot., Sagus rumphii.*

sağ 1 صاغ 1. alive; sound in body, healthy, well. 2. safe; trustworthy, whole; strong. **— akçe** good money, genuine coin. **— ayakkabı değil** He is not reliable. **— duyu*. — esen** *archaic* alive and in good health. **— kal=** 1. to remain alive. 2. to remain in good health. **— kalanlar** the survivors (after a disaster or battle). **— kazığa bağla=** /ı/ to make safe or sure; to secure, to ensure. **— kurtul=** to escape with one's life; to come out safe and sound. **— ol!** (*lit.* May you be well and strong.) Thank you. **— ol=** to be alive; to be in good health. **— olsun** Bless him *said to soften a reproachful criticism.* **— para** *same as* sağ akçe. **— sâlim, — selâmet** safe and sound. **— yağ*.**

sağ 2 صاغ right, right-hand; the right-hand side. **—a** to the right. **—da** on the right hand, on the right side. **—dan** from the right (side). **— açık** *soccer* right wing, right winger. **—a bak!** *mil.* Eyes right! **— bek** *soccer* right back. **—dan gel** *slang* Let it be of the best *said by coffeehouse waiters.* **—dan geri!** Right about face! **— gözünü sol gözünden kıskan=** to be extremely jealous. **— kol** 1. right arm. 2. right wing or troops. 3. right-hand man. **— kol ağası** *Ott. hist.* senior adjutant commanding the right wing of a battalion. **— kulağını sol eliyle göster=** to do a thing the hard way. **— muavin** *soccer* right half-back. **— müdafi** *soccer* right fullback. **—a sola** right and left; on both sides; in all directions. **—da solda** on both sides; everywhere. **—dan soldan** from all directions. **—ına soluna bak=** to look about one. **—ına soluna bakma=** to act without consideration. **—a sola bakmadan** carelessly, without consideration for others. **—ı solu belli olmaz** You never know what he is going to do next. **—ını solunu bilme=, —ını solunu şaşır=** to be confused or bewildered. **—ı solu yok** unpredictable, eccentric; tactless; devil-may-care. **— yap** *chauffeurs' slang* Pull over to the right.

sağ=ᵃʳ **3** صاغمَق 1. /ı/ to milk. 2. /ı/ to fleece; to despoil. 3. /ı/ to extract honey from the hive. 4. to pour out rain (cloud). 5. /ı/ to unwind.

sağal=ⁱʳ صاغالمَق *prov.* to be cured, to get well. **—t=** /ı/ *caus.*

sağanakᵍ¹ صاغاناق 1. heavy rainstorm, downpour, shower; squall. 2. sudden loss or damage.

sağcı صاغجى *pol.* rightist, right-wing sympathizer.

sağdıçᶜⁱ صاغدِچ 1. bridegroom's best man. 2. intimate friend of the bride or bridegroom; intimate friend. **— emeği** useless efforts.

sağdır=ⁱʳ صاغدِرمَق /ı, a/ *caus. of* **sağ=** 3.

sağduyu *neol.* common sense.

sağı صاغى *archaic* bird droppings.

sağıl=ⁱʳ صاغِلمَق 1. *pass. of* **sağ=** 3. 2. to glide along the ground, to uncoil itself (snake).

sağım صاغِم 1. a milking. 2. quantity of milk taken at one time, quantity of honey taken at one time. 3. *prov.* milk-giving animal. **—lı** kept for milking; in milk (animal). **—lık** dairy animal.

sağır صاغِر 1. deaf; deaf person. 2. giving no sound, dull; indistinct (sound or voice). 3. opaque (glass); closed up, sham (door). 4. having a low conductivity of heat (kettle, etc.). 5. echoless (room, etc.), soundproof **— et=** /ı/ to deafen. **— işitmez uydurur** *proverb* The deaf person does not hear what is said but he makes it up, *said when a person says something he has overheard wrongly.* **— kef, — nun** the Turkish letter ڭ representing the sound of **ng**. **— sultan bile duydu** Everybody knows about it. **— yılan** viper, adder, *zool., Vipera berus.*

sağırlaş=ⁱʳ صاغِرلَشمَق to grow deaf. **—tır=** /ı/ to deafen.

sağırlıkᵍ¹ صاغِرلِق 1. deafness. 2. indistinctness, dullness or nasal quality of a sound. **—a vur=** to pretend not to hear.

sağış 1 صاغِش 1. *verbal n. of* **sağ=** 3.

sağış 2 صاغِش *archaic* mode of counting, account, number. **— günü** Day of Judgment.

sağışla=ʳ صاغِشلامَق /ı/ *archaic* to count, calculate, figure.

sağışsız صاغِشسِز *archaic* innumerable.

sağla=ʳ **1** *neol.* /ı/ 1. to make safe, secure, certain. 2. to obtain, to get.

sağla=ʳ **2** صاغلامَق to keep to the right.

sağlam صاغلام 1. sound, whole; safe, in good health. 2. healthy; healthful; wholesome. 3. sure; honest, trustworthy, reliable. 4. firm, strong; decided. **— ayakkabı değil** He is unreliable. **—a bağla=** /ı/ to make safe or sure. **—a git=** *slang* to beat someone mercilessly. **— kaba kotar=** /ı/ to make profitable. — **kazığa bağla**= *same as* **sağlama bağla**=. — **rüzgâr** a steady wind.

sağlama صا غلامه 1. *arch.* strut. 2. *neol., math.* proof, check. —**lık** *arch.* reinforcement.

sağlamla=ʳ صا غلاملامه /ı/ 1. to secure, to make safe, to ensure. 2. to strengthen, to fortify. —**n**= *pass.* —**ş**= to become sound, safe, strong. —**ştır**=, —**t**= /ı/ *caus.*

sağlamlıkᵍ¹ صا غلاملك soundness, wholeness; safety; health; sureness, trustworthiness; firmness, solidity.

sağlan=ʳ *pass. of* **sağla**= 1.

sağlat=ʳ /ı, a/ *caus. of* **sağla**= 1.

sağlıcakla (..˙.) صا غيجقله *prov.* in good health, happily. — **gidiniz** Have a good trip.

sağlıkᵍ¹ 1. صا غلغ 1. health, good health. 2. a being alive; life; lifetime. —! All's well! — **olsun** Never mind; it's all right; forget it. **S— ve Sosyal Yardım Bakanlığı** Ministry of Health and Social Aid.

sağlıkᵍ¹ 2 صا غلغ inquiry or answer as to the location of a place. — **al**= /ı/ to ask directions, ask the way; to have something recommended. — **ver**= /ı, a/ to show the way; to recommend.

sağlı sollu صا غلى صوللى on both sides, right and left.

sağma صا غمه *verbal n. of* **sağ**= 3.

sağmal صا غمال 1. milch, kept for milking (cow, etc.); milk-giving (animal). 2. *slang* fit to be fleeced (person). — **inek** *slang* person who is continually cheated. — **keçi** milch-goat. — **koyun** ewe milked for dairy purposes.

sağnakᵍ¹ صا غناقده صنغناق *same as* **sağanak**.

sağrakᵍ¹ صا غره صغره صاغراق صوراق *archaic* 1. drinking bowl; pot with a spout. 2. a measure for liquids. — **sür**= to serve drinks.

sağrı صا غرى 1. rump. 2. leather made from the rump of a horse. 3. mountain ridge. — **kemiği** *anat.* sacrum.

sağrıpuş (—.—) صا غريپوش P *lrnd.* horse cloth to cover the rump.

sağsız صا غسز *prov.* poor in health, unhealthy.

sağu (—.) صا غو *archaic* eulogy, elegy, lamentation. — **sağ**= to chant or recite the virtues of a dead person in a dirge.

sağucu (—..) صا غوجى professional mourner.

sağyağ صا غياغ cooking butter.

sahʰʰ¹ صح A *Ott. adm.* official flourish on a document (to show that it had been examined or registered). — **çek**= /a/ to write the word **sah** on a document.

saha 1 (—.) ساحه A 1. court, open space, courtyard, quadrangle. 2. field, area, region; ground (soccer, etc.).

saha 2 (.—) سخى A *lrnd.* generosity, beneficence.

saha 3 (.—) سخاء A *anat.* membrane of the brain, meninx.

sahabe (.—.) صحبه A *Isl. hist.*, *pl. of* **sahib**, companions of the Prophet Muhammad.

sahabet (.—.) صحابت A *lrnd.* support, protection, patronage.

sahabetkâr (.—.—) صحابتكار P *lrnd.* protecting, supporting (person).

sahabî (.——) صحابى A *lrnd.* who was one of the companions of the Prophet Muhammad.

sahaf (.—) صحاف [**sahhaf**] dealer in secondhand books.

sahafet (.—.) سخافت A *lrnd.* a being thin and slender; thinness; a being weak of mind, weak in intellect.

sahaif (.—.) صحائف A *lrnd.*, *pl. of* **sahife**.

sahakâr (.——) سخاكار P *lrnd.* liberal, generous.

sahan صحن [**sahn** 1] A copper food dish; dish of food.

sahanlıkᵍ¹ صحنلق 1. landing on a staircase. 2. platform of a street car; footplate of a locomotive. 3. marble-topped stand to put dishes on. 4. amount of food in a **sahan**.

sahapsız صحابسز *prov. for* **sahipsiz**.

sahara (.—.) صحارى A *lrnd.*, *pl. of* **sahra**.

sahare (.—.) صحاره *lrnd.* waterproof chest.

sahari (.——, .—.) صحارى A *lrnd.*, *same as* **sahara**.

sahat 1 ساعت *prov. for* **saat**.

sahat 2 (——) ساحات *lrnd.*, *pl. of* **saha** 1.

sahaver (.—.) سخاور P *lrnd.* liberal, munificent. —**âne** (.—.—.) P generously. —**î** (.—.—) P generosity, munificence.

sahavet (.—.) سخاوت A munificence, generosity. —**kâr** (.—.—) P *lrnd.*, —**li** generous, beneficent.

sahb صحب A *lrnd.*, *pl. of* **sahib**.

sahba (.—) صهبا A *poet.* wine, red wine.

sahhaf (.—) صحاف A *lrnd.*, *same as* **sahaf**.

sahhar (.—) سحار A *lrnd.* wizard, sorcerer, magician; charming, bewitching. —**e** (.—.) A sorceress, witch. —**î** (.——) A magic, sorcery, witchcraft.

sahın صحن *var. of* **sahn** 1.

sahit (—.) ساخط A *lrnd.* angry, furious.

sahi 1 (—.) صحى [**sahih**] really, truly. —**den** indeed, truly.

sahi 2 (.—.) سخى A *lrnd.* generous, liberal, open-handed.

sahi 3 (—.) ساهى A *lrnd.* who makes a mistake.

sahib (—.) صاحب A 1. possessing, endued with (quality). 2. owner, possessor. 3. protector, master, patron. 4. *lrnd.* companion, consort, disciple. **S—i Asâ** *lrnd.* Moses. —**i ayâr** *Ott. hist.* assayer. —**i arz** *Ott. hist.*

sahibdil

owner of a fief. **S—i Beyan** *lrnd.* The Prophet Muhammad. **—i cemal** *lrnd.* beautiful, handsome. **— çık=** /a/ to claim ownership (of something); to stand as protector or patron (to someone). **—i devlet** 1. *lrnd.* prosperous man. 2. *Ott. hist., title given to the Grand Vizier.* **—i emel** *lrnd.* ambitious person. **—i firaş** *lrnd.* bedridden. **—i hane** *lrnd.* master of the house. **S—i Hût** *lrnd.* (*lit., lord of the fish*) Jonah. **S—i Kadib** *lrnd.* (*lit., master of the sword*) the Prophet Muhammad. **—i menzil** *lrnd.* champion archer. **—i namus** *lrnd.* 1. lawgiver. 2. the Prophet Muhammad. 3. man of honor. **—i nazar** *lrnd.* 1. clear-sighted. 2. seer; pious. **—i rey** *lrnd.* 1. whose opinion and counsel is adopted. 2. Vizier. **—i rüşd** *lrnd.* 1. man of good judgment. 2. man of the true religion. **S—i Sıffin** *lrnd.* (*lit., Lord of the battle of Siffin*) the Caliph Ali. **—i sikke** *lrnd.* sovereign who has the right to coin money. **—i sikke ve hutbe** *lrnd.* sovereign who coins money in his own name and is publicly prayed for in mosques. **S—i Yasin** *lrnd.* he to whom the call was addressed, the Prophet Muhammad. **S—i Yed-i Beyza** 1. *lrnd.* (*lit., Lord of the white hand*) Moses. 2. any distinguished man who effects wonders. **—i zaman** *lrnd.* (*lit., master of the time*) man of authority and prosperity.

sahibdil (—..) صاحب دل P *lrnd.* 1. courageous. 2. pious man, saintly person.

sahibe (—..) صاحبه A *lrnd.* lady companion or possessor.

sahibhuruc (—..—) صاحب خروج P *lrnd.* great conqueror, especially one who acquires sovereignty though of obscure origin.

sahibkemal[li] (—..—) صاحب كمال P *lrnd.* perfect, excellent (person).

sahibkıran (—..—) صاحب قران P *lrnd.* (*lit., lord of a fortunate conjunction*) *title given to prosperous or victorious monarchs.* **—î** (—..——) P pertaining to a sovereign; heroic; royal, imperial.

sahibzuhur (—..—) صاحب ظهور P *lrnd.* man who rises from obscurity and makes himself conspicuous or powerful.

sahici (—..) صاحيجى real, genuine, true.

sahif (.—) خفيف A *lrnd.* 1. thin, flimsy; slim, slender. 2. weak, shallow, silly.

sahife (.—.) صحيفه A *lrnd.* a page, leaf, sheet. **—i mütelemmis** *lrnd.* sealed letter given to a person to carry, which contains a warrant for him to be put to death. **—i zemin** *lrnd.* surface of the earth. **—i zer** *lrnd.* the sun.

sahih (.—) صحيح A *lrnd.* 1. true, correct, accurate. 2. sound, valid, good, perfect.

sahihan (.—'.) صحيحا A *lrnd.* truly, rightly, really.

sahik[kı]**1** (.—) سحيق A *lrnd.* far, distant, very remote.

sahik[kı]**2** سحيق A *lrnd.* pounded, bruised; rubbed.

sahil 1 (—.) ساحل A shore, coast, bank. **—i selâmet** *lrnd.* safety from danger.

sahil 2 (.—) صهيل A *lrnd.* a neighing; neigh.

sahileş=[ir] صاحيلشمك to turn out to be right; to be confirmed; to be fulfilled. **—tir=** /ı/ *caus.*

sahilhane (—.—.) ساحلخانه P *lrnd.* house on the seashore or bank of a river.

sahilsaray (—..—) ساحلسراى P *lrnd.* palace on the seashore or bank of a river.

sahin 1 (.—) سخين A *lrnd.* 1. thick, stout; tough, hard. 2. coarse, gross.

sahin 2 (.—) سخينه A *lrnd.* warm, hot; inflamed.

sahip[bi] (—.) صاحب A *same as* **sahib.** **—lik** ownership, protection.

sahipsiz صاحبسز 1. having no owner, ownerless. 2. without a protector; abandoned. **—lik** ownerlessness; unprotectedness, destitution.

sahir 1 (—.) ساهر A *lrnd.* that remains awake, vigilant, sleepless, watchful.

sahir 2 (—.) ساحر A *lrnd.* who works magic, enchanter, necromancer, sorcerer.

sahire (—..) ساحره A *lrnd.* enchantress, sorceress, witch.

sahk[kı] سحق A *lrnd.* a pounding; rubbing violently; bruising, pulverizing.

sahla=[r] صحله مك /ı/ to mark with the paraph صح. **—n=** *pass.* **—t=** /ı/ *caus. of* **sahla=.**

sahleb سحلب *var. of* **salep.**

sahn 1 صحن A *lrnd.* 1. *same as* **sahan.** 2. area, square; yard, courtyard, esplanade. 3. *anat.* outer cavity of the ear. **—i azîm** the earth's surface. **—i çemen** lawn. **—i dûreng** the world. **—i gülistan** middle of a flower garden. **S— Medarisi, S— Medreseleri** *Ott. hist.* the medresses in the court of the Fatih Mosque in Istanbul. **S—i Seman** *Ott. hist.* Court of the Eight Medresses attached to the great mosque of Mehmet Fatih in Istanbul. **—i sîm** 1. a sheet of white paper. 2. the moon's disc.

sahn 2 سخنه A *lrnd.* heat.

sahne صحنه A scene; stage. **—ye koy=** /ı/ *theater* to stage, to produce. **—ye koyan** *theater* producer.

sahr صحر A *lrnd., pl. of* **sahre.**

sahra (.—) صحرا A 1. open country, open plain; wilderness, desert. 2. *mil.* field. **—i adem** the desert of nonexistence, death. **S—i Kebir** the Sahara. **— topu** *mil.* field gun.

sahragerd (.—.) صحراگرد P *lrnd.* desert traveler.

sahraî (.——) صحرائى A *lrnd.* pertaining to wild open country; wild, desert, uninhabited.

sahraneverd (.—..) صحرا نورد P *lrnd.* who travels in the wide open spaces. **—î** (.—..—) P a traversing, wandering in a desert.

sahranişin (.—.—) صحرا نشین P *lrnd.* living in the wilds, nomadic. **—î** (.—.——) P *lrnd.* nomadic life.

sahravî (.——) صحراوی A *lrnd.*, same as sahraî.

sahre صخر A *lrnd.* rock.

sahrıc, sahrınç صهرج ، صهرنج A *lrnd.*, same as sarnıç.

saht سخت P *lrnd.* 1. hard, strong, firm, solid; vehement, severe, intense, violent. 2. austere, harsh, stern; rough, difficult, arduous. 3. stubborn, obstinate. 4. miserly, stingy. 5. very, extremely.

sahtâviz (.——) سخت آویز P *lrnd.* that takes firm hold.

sahtbünyad (..—) سخت بنیاد P *lrnd.* strongly built; firmly constituted.

sahtcan (.—) سخت جان P *lrnd.* 1. tenacious of life. 2. hard-hearted.

sahtçeşm سخت چشم P *lrnd.* bold, impudent.

sahtdil سخت دل P *lrnd.* 1. hard-hearted; cruel. 2. brave.

sahte سخته [P —.] 1. false, spurious, counterfeit, sham. 2. made, arranged, artificial. **— hareket** *mil.* demonstration. **—ci** same as sahtekâr.

sahtegi (..—) سختگی P *lrnd.* falseness, hypocrisy.

sahtekâr (..—) سخته کار P who counterfeits or forges; liar. **—lık** forgery, counterfeiting, falsification.

sahtelik[ʰ] ساختهلك falsity, spuriousness; hypocrisy.

sahtevekar (..—) سخت وقار P *lrnd.* who assumes an air of dignity. **—lık** *lrnd.* pretended dignity.

sahtgir (.—) سختگیر P *lrnd.* who seizes firmly or violently; who attacks, punishes or reprimands severely.

sahtguş (.—) سخت گوش P *lrnd.* hard of hearing, deaf.

sahtî (.—) سختی P *lrnd.* hardness, harshness; severity. **—keş** (.—.) P who endures hardships, etc. bravely.

sahtiyan (..—) سختیان P Morocco leather.

sahtiyancı سختیانجی dresser or seller of Morocco leather. **—lık** dressing or selling Morocco leather.

sahtiyanî (..——) سختیانی P *lrnd.* 1. pertaining to or made of Morocco leather. 2. maker or seller of Morocco leather.

sahtlık[ʰ] سختلك *lrnd.* 1. hardness; firmness; sternness; severity. 2. difficulty. 3. distress, poverty.

sahtligâm (..—) سخت لگام P *lrnd.* hard mouthed; hard headed.

sahtmağz سخت مغز P *lrnd.* tough brained; obstinate, headstrong.

sahtpa, sahtpay (.—) سخت پا P *lrnd.* firm of foot; steady; constant.

sahtpençe سخت پنجه P *lrnd.* close fisted, avaricious.

sahtru (.—) سخت رو P *lrnd.* of an austere, severe countenance.

sahur 1 سحور [A .—] meal taken before dawn during the Ramazan fast. **—a kalk=** to rise from one's sleep to take this meal.

sahur 2 (——) سحور A *lrnd.* 1. sleeplessness, wakefulness. 2. sheath into which the moon is supposed to enter when eclipsed.

sahv صحو A *lrnd.* 1. a recovering from drunkenness, a becoming sober after intoxication; *myst.* return to reality after mystical experience. 2. a departing, being dispersed (clouds), cloudlessness, clearness.

sai (——) ساعی A *lrnd.* 1. one who exerts himself in walking or running; foot-messenger; courier, messenger. 2. one who endeavors, attempts or strives after; studious, diligent; earnest, eager. 3. *obs.* collector of tithes and other revenues.

saib 1 (—.) صائب A *lrnd.* that hits the mark; right, straight, sound, valid.

saib 2 (—.) سائب A *lrnd.* wind blowing up fresh before or at the beginning of rain.

saibe (..) سائبة A *lrnd.* camel, especially a female camel, set at complete liberty.

said 1 (.—) سعید A *lrnd.* auspicious, prosperous, fortunate, lucky, happy.

said 2 (—.) صاعد A *lrnd.* that mounts, ascends; ascending.

said 3 (—.) ساعد A *lrnd.* forearm. **—i billûr** beautiful white arm.

said 4 (.—) صعید A *lrnd.* 1. high land; high region, upland. 2. Upper Egypt. 3. the earth; surface of the earth. **S—i Mısır** Upper Egypt.

saiğ 1 (—.) سائغ A *lrnd.* 1. easy and pleasant to swallow. 2. permissible, lawful. **— ve laiğ** pleasant to swallow and light to digest.

saiğ 2 (—.) صائغ A *lrnd.* goldsmith, silversmith.

saik[ʰ] (—.) سائق A that urges, impels to do some act; driving, impelling; factor, motive, reason.

saika 1 (—..) سائقة A cause, motive, incentive.

saika 2 (—..) صاعقة A *lrnd.* thunderbolt, lightning.

sail[ʰ] **1** (—.) سائل A *lrnd.* 1. who begs, beggar. 2. who asks, enquires, interrogates; questioner. 3. who requests, supplicates. 4. that flows, flowing; fluid, liquid.

sail[ʰ] **2** (—.) صائل A *lrnd.* that makes attacks, actively aggressive, presumptuous, arrogant.

sailiyet (—...) ساﺋﻠﻴﺖ A *lrnd.* liquidity.
saillikᵏⁱ (—..) ساﺋﻠﻠﻚ *lrnd.* 1. beggary. 2. fluidity, liquidity.
saim (—.) صاﺋﻢ A *lrnd.* who keeps a fast.
saime (—. .) صاﺋﻤﻪ A *lrnd.* animal or animals pasturing at liberty.
sair 1 (—.) ساﺋﺮ A 1. that remains, the rest of, other. 2. *lrnd.* that goes, moves, travels. 3. *lrnd.* that becomes known, current.
sair 2 (.—) سعير A *lrnd.* 1. flaming fire, flame. 2. partition of hell.
sairfilmenam (—...—) ساﺋﺮﻓﻰاﻟﻤﻨﺎم A somnambulist.
sait (—.) صاﺋﺖ A 1. *gram.* vowel. 2. *lrnd.* that cries, sounds, resounds.
sak 1 (—) ساق A *lrnd.* 1. shank, shin. 2. stem of a tree, stalk, trunk. 3. leg of a triangle.
sakᵏᵏ¹ **2** صكّ A *lrnd.* 1. legal document. 2. book of legal formulas.
sakᵏ¹ **3** صاح *prov.* awake, vigilant.
=**sak 4**, =**sek** ساق [*pl. of* =**sam 3**, etc.] if we..., *e. g.*, **kalsak** If we stay.
-**sak 5**, -**sek** *after vowels* -**ysak**, -**ysek** (.'.) ساق [*pl. of* -**sam 4**, etc.] if we are... *e. g.*, **uyanıksak** If we are awake. **gençsek** If we are young.
saka 1 ساﻗﺎ [sakka] 1. water carrier. 2. *Ott. hist.* corporal of the Janissaries. — **beygiri** 1. water carrier's horse. 2. sponging parasite. — **beygiri gibi dolaş**= to run about on errands. — **kuşu** goldfinch, *zool.*, Carduelis carduelis. — **meşki** waterskin.
sa'ka 2 صعقة A *lrnd.* 1. thunderbolt; crashing noise of a thunderbolt. 2. blast of the trump at the resurrection. 3. a fainting, falling into a swoon.
saka 3 (—.) ساﻗﻪ A *lrnd.* rear of an army, rear guard.
sakaf سقف A *same as* **sakf**.
sakağı صاﻗﺎﻏﻰ glanders; farcy.
sakakᵍ¹ صغاﻗﻪ صغو double chin; dewlap.
sakal صاﻗﺎل 1. beard, whiskers. 2. *naut.* dolphin striker under the end of a bowsprit. 3. *print.* form having irregular and untidy folds. 4. *fine arts* a kind of brush used in gilding. — **akı** old age. — **başı çevir**= to leave (in shaving) the side face unshaven as a token that the beard will be allowed to grow. — **başı dağıt**= to threaten. — **bırak**= to let the beard grow. —**ı bit**= /ın/ 1. to begin to grow (beard). 2. *same as* **işin sakalı bit**=. — **cücüğü** man's weak point, where he is most sensitive. — **dağıt**= /a/ to scatter around unwanted advice. —**ı değirmende ağart**= to grow old having learned nothing; to be green and ignorant. —**ımı değirmende ağartmadım** (*lit.* I have not made my beard white in a mill,

i. e. with flour.) I have grown gray with experience. — **döken** a kind of itch causing the beard to fall out. — **duasına çık**= to pray for a beard to grow, *said when one hopes for the impossible.* —**ı ele ver**= 1. to allow oneself to be led by the nose. 2. to allow all one's secrets to be guessed. —**ına gül**= /ın/ 1. to deceive. 2. to ridicule, to make a fool of. —**ı kana boyanmış** (*lit.*, whose beard has become dyed with blood) decapitated, slaughtered. — **koyver**= *same as* **sakal bırak**=. — **oynatmaz** eaten without moving the mouth, ripe and delicious (fruit). — **salıver**= *same as* **sakal bırak**=. —**ı saydır**= to lose one's prestige, to be no longer respected. —**ını sıvazla**= to smooth one's beard. —**ına soğan doğra**= to make game (of), to consider a fool. S—**ı Şerif** some hairs of the Prophet Muhammad's beard. —**ımı uzatsam değecek** very close. —**ım yok ki sözüm geçsin** People listen to the advice of old people.
sakalân (..—) ثقلان A *lrnd.*, *same as* **sakaleyn**.
sakalet (.—.) ثقالت A *lrnd.* 1. a being or becoming burdensome, oppressive, oppressiveness, unpleasantness, ugliness, eyesore. 2. a being or becoming heavy, weightiness; preponderancy.
sakaleyn ثقلين A *lrnd.* the two races of beings that inhabit the earth, men and djinn.
Sakalibe (.—..) صقالبه A *lrnd.* the Slavs.
sakallan=ⁱʳ صقاللنمق to grow a beard.
sakallı صقاللى bearded. — **bebek** childish old man.
sakam (.—) A, **sakam** سقم *lrnd.* ailment, disease.
sakamet (.—.) سقامت A *lrnd.* 1. ailment, disease, infirmity. 2. defect, fault; vice. 3. ill, harm, danger, something to fear. —**li** 1. harmful, dangerous. 2. defective.
sakomonya (...'.) سقمونيا Gk scammony (purgative).
sakandırıkᵍ¹ صقندرق chin strap.
sakangur, sakankur سقنقور A 1. skink, *zool.*, Scincus officinalis. 2. coarse book-muslin.
sakar 1 صقار سقر white patch on a horse's forehead, blaze.
sakar 2 صقر 1. who always breaks things, awkward person. 2. sinister, ill-omened, unlucky.
sakar 3 سقر A *lrnd.* hell.
sakarca صقارجه white-fronted goose.
sakarin سقارين F saccharine.
sakarlı صقارلى 1. having a white blaze (horse). 2. ill-omened, unlucky (person).
sakarlıkᵍ¹ صقارلق clumsiness, awkwardness.
sakaroz ساقاروز F *chem.* saccharose.
sakat سقط A 1. unsound, defective. 2. invalid,

disabled, crippled, maimed. 3. broken, cracked, damaged.

sakatat (..—) سقطات A 1. offal. 2. *lrnd*. defects, mistakes, blunders. —çı seller of offal.

sakati (..—) سقطى A *lrnd*. dealer in damaged or inferior articles, in things of small value.

sakatla=ʳ سقطلە /ı/ to injure, damage, mutilate. —n= *pass*.

sakatlıkᵏⁱ سقطلق infirmity, defect, mistake, blemish.

sakayan (..—) سقایان P *Ott. hist.*, water carriers in the Sultan's palace.

sakb ثقب A 1. *lrnd*. a perforating; boring, piercing; perforation, small hole; puncture. 2. *anat*. canal, sinus.

sakf سقف A *lrnd*. 1. roof. 2. ceiling. 3. sky. —î (.—) A pertaining to a roof or ceiling.

sâkıb (—.) ثاقب A *lrnd*. 1. that pierces, penetrates, perforates; piercing, penetrating. 2. that shines brightly, penetrating the gloom. 3. sure, certain, decisive.

sakıfᵏᶠⁱ سقف A *var.* of **sakf**.

sakın 1 صاقین 'Beware. Take care. Don't.

sakın=ʳ **2** صاقنمق 1. to take care of oneself by flinching, standing out of the way, etc. 2. to be cautious in word and deed. 3. to protect oneself or one's property for fear of the consequences.

sakınca *neol*. objection, drawback.

sakıngan صاقنغان timid, prudent, cautious, retiring.

sakınıcı صاقنیجى cautious person who avoids risks.

sakınma صاقنمه *verbal n.* of **sakın**= 2. —sı **olma**= to be heedless.

sakırda=ʳ صاقردامق to shiver with chattering teeth.

sakırdı صاقردى a shivering with cold or fear.

sakırga صاقرغه tick, dog tick.

sakır sakır صاقر صاقر shivering, trembling. — **titre**= to shiver with chattering teeth.

sakıt (—.) ساقط A *lrnd*. 1. that falls, falling, dropping down. 2. fallen in esteem; become of no account. 3. aborted.

sakıye (—..) ساقیه A *lrnd*. 1. female cupbearer. 2. small irrigation channel; water wheel, any contrivance for raising water.

sakız صاقز 1. chewing gum, mastic; masticatory. 2. resin, gum. 3. *w. cap.* Chios (Island). S— **Adası** Chios. — **ağacı** mastic tree, *bot.*, Pistacia lentiscus. S— **alı** scarlet dye of Chios; scarlet cloth of Chios. S— **bademi** Chios almonds, roundish soft-shelled almonds. — **çiğne**= 1. to chew gum. 2. /a/ to tell lies to humor a person. — **dikeni** gum-thorn, *bot.*, Acorna gummifera. — **gibi** 1. very white and clean. 2. sticky. — **kabağı** vegetable marrow. — **leblebisi** a kind of salted roast pea. — **merhemi** pitch plaster. S— **rakısı** mastic raki of Chios.

sakızlan=ʳ صاقزلانمق 1. to become sticky like mastic. 2. to become resinous. —**dır**= /ı/ *caus*.

sakızlı صاقزلى 1. mixed with resin or gum-mastic. 2. *w. cap.* a Sciot.

saki (——) ساقى A 1. *poet*. cupbearer. 2. *lrnd*. distributor of water. 3. *myst*. spiritual teacher to a novice; God, as the universal teacher. —**i ecel** *poet*. death. —**i şeb** *poet*. the moon.

sakib (—.) ساكب A *lrnd*. 1. who pours out. 2. pouring forth, flowing (blood, tears or water).

sakil (.—) ثقیل A 1. heavy, ponderous. 2. burdensome, oppressive, wearisome; disagreeable, tedious. 3. indigestible; unwholesome. 4. harsh (word or sound). 5. ugly, unbecoming, sluggish, indolent. 6. *Or. mus.* a medium-fast rhythmic pattern of forty-eight beats.

sakilikᵍⁱ (———.) ساقیلك the occupation of a cupbearer.

sakillikᵍⁱ (.—.) ثقیللك ugliness, offensiveness; heaviness.

sakim (.—) سقیم A *lrnd*. 1. defective, faulty, harmful, wrong. 2. diseased, sick, ailing.

sakin (—.) ساكن A 1. quiet, motionless, stationary. 2. calm; calmed, appeased, allayed. 3. who dwells, who lives; dweller; inhabitant. 4. *gram*. quiescent (letter).

sakiname (———.) ساقینامه P *lrnd*. ode addressed to a cupbearer.

sakinan (—.—) ساكنان P *lrnd*. inhabitants. —**i gerdûn** angels; stars. —**i hâk** inhabitants of the world.

sakinleş=ʳ (—...) ساكنلشمك to become quiet, to calm down. —**tir**= /ı/ *caus*.

sakit (—.) ساكت A *lrnd*. 1. silent, mute; taciturn. 2. dead.

sakiya (—.—) ساقیا P *poet*. O cupbearer!

sakiyan (—.—) ساقیان P *poet., pl.* of **saki**.

sakka (.—) سقاء A *lrnd., same as* **saka 1**.

sakkâkᵏⁱ (.—) سكاك A *lrnd*. clerk who drafts legal documents issued from a court.

saklⁱⁱ صقل A *lrnd*. 1. a polishing, furbishing. 2. a grooming a horse well.

sakla=ʳ صاقلەمق /ı/ 1. to hide, conceal. 2. to keep secret. 3. to keep, store, save for future use. 4. to preserve, shield from danger.

Saklâb (.—) سقلب P *hist*. the Slavs.

saklambaçᶜⁱ صاقلامباچ hide-and-seek (game).

saklan=ʳ صاقلانمق 1. *pass.* of **sakla**=. 2. to hide. —**ış**, —**ma** *verbal n.* —**tı** nook, corner, hiding place.

saklat=ʳ صاقلاتمق /ı, a/ *caus.* of **sakla**=.

saklayıcı صاقلایجى 1. protecting, preserving. 2. concealing, secretive.

saklı صاقلى 1. hidden, concealed, secret.

sako 2. put aside, preserved. 3. *mil.* absentee (conscript or reservist).

sako صاقو. It sack coat, loose jacket.

sakoleta (...′.) صاقولته سقولته صاقولنه It *artillery* case shot, canister.

saksağan صقصغان صقـغان magpie, *zool.*, *Pica pica*.

saksı صاقسى flowerpot; vase. — **çiçeği** plant grown in pots or hothouses. — **dibi** a kind of fez. — **güzeli** kidneywort, navelwort, *bot.*, *Cotyledon umbilicus*. —**lık** shelf for flowerpots.

Saksonya, Saksunya (.′.) ساقسونيا 1. Saxony. 2. *l. c.* Dresden china, Dresden ware.

sakulete (...′.) ساقولته *var. of* **sakoleta**.

saky سقى A 1. a giving to drink. 2. a watering, an irrigating; irrigation. 3. a tempering (steel etc.).

sal 1 صال 1. raft. 2. stretcher. 3. inner, middle, flattish part of each arm of an archery bow. 4. *prov.* coffin.

sâlⁱⁱ 2 (—) سال P *lrnd.* year. —**i hâl** the current year.

salⁱⁱ 3 صال F hall.

sal=ᵃʳ 4 صالمق 1. /ı/ to set free, to let go; to let hang down, to drop. 2. /ı, a/ *prov.* to send, to dispatch. 3. /ı, a/ to throw, fling; to spread out; to send forth (shoots, smoke); to cast (shadow); to lay (foundation); to throw into a cooking-pot. 4. /ı, a/ to insert. 5. /a/ to postpone, put off. 6. /ı/ to impose (tax). 7. /a/ to be aggressive; to hurl oneself in attack.

salâ 1 (.—) صلا A 1. *Isl. rel.* a chant from the minarets on occasions of the Friday **namaz**, a call to a funeral service, and similar sacred occasions. 2. *lrnd.* any cry or proclamation in a loud voice, challenge. 3. *obs.* fight with stones between two groups of boys. —**!** *obs.* Listen. Look here. — **et=** to proclaim publicly. — **veriliyor** A special call is being given from the minaret.

sala 2 (.′.) سالم It hall.

salâbet (.—.) صلابت A *lrnd.* strength, hardiness, firmness, toughness. —**i ahlâk** firmness of character. —**i diniye** strength of religion. —**li** firm, rigid, stiff; tough, strong; hardy, sturdy.

salaburun صالابرون صلبرون It *naut.* leech line.

salaca صلجه *archaic* 1. slab on which corpses are placed for washing. 2. bier on which a corpse is borne.

salacakᵍ¹ صلجاى same as **salaca** ¹.

salâh (.—.) صلاح A 1. improvement. 2. *lrnd.* a being good; goodness, soundness. 3. *lrnd.* a doing what is right, righteousness. — **bul=** to improve. —**a doğru git=** to get better, improve. —**i hâl** *lrnd.* 1. improvement in character. 2. the best thing to do under the circumstances. — **kesbet=** to improve (conditions).

salâhan (.—.—) صلاحوان P *lrnd.* 1. caller to worship, muezzin. 2. public crier, herald. 3. proclaimer of a challenge.

salâhiyet (.—..) صلاحيت A authority, power, right to do something; competence, fitness. — **dairesi** the limits of one's authority; the sphere of one's competence. —**i tamme** *lrnd.* full powers. —**i yok** He has no authority or right (to do this).

salâhiyetdar (.—..—) صلاحيتدار P same as **salâhiyettar**.

salâhiyetli صلاحيتلى 1. authorized, competent. 2. the department or authority concerned.

salâhiyetname (.—..—.) صلاحيتنامه P *lrnd.* credentials; written authority.

salâhiyetsiz صلاحيتسز having no authority.

salâhiyettar (.—..—) صلاحيتدار [salahiyetdar] authoritative, competent.

salahur صلاخور *an ancient title like the old English "esquire"; knight free from taxes but charged with the keeping of a fortress*.

salakᵍ¹ 1 صالاق silly, doltish.

salakᵍ¹ 2 صالاق *archaic* pole furnished with chains carrying iron balls at the end, a weapon.

salakᵍ¹ 3 صالاق *archaic* pasturage, place where travelers camp.

salam 1 صلام It salami.

sal'am 2 صلعم A *lrnd.* contraction in writing of the ejaculatory phrase **sallâllahu aleyhi ve sellem**.

salamandra (...′.) سالامندره F portable stove.

salamon 1 صالمون It salmon, *zool.*, *Salmo salar*.

Salamon 2 صالمون Heb Solomon (when used to mean Jews in general).

salamura (...′.) صالامورا It brine for pickling; anything pickled in brine.

salapurya (...′.) صالاپوريه It a kind of small lighter (boat). — **gibi** very large (shoe).

sâlar (—) سالار P *lrnd.* chief, leader; commander.

salariye (.—.—.) سالاريه Ott. *hist.* a kind of agricultural tax.

salaş صالاش Hung booth; market stall; temporary shed.

salaşpur صلاشپور loosely woven cotton fabric (used for linings etc.).

salât (.—) صلاة A 1. *Isl. rel.* ritual prayer. 2. *lrnd.* prayer, supplication; invocation. —**ı aşâ** the evening prayer. —**ı fecr** morning prayer. —**ı hamse** the five prayers of the day. —**ı havf** short prayer performed just before a battle. —**ı îd** prayer performed on feast days. —**ı istiska** prayer for rain. —**ı**

sefer short prayer performed just before a journey.

salata (.'.) صلطه صلدت It 1. salad; lettuce. 2. *print.* sheets of paper disorderly or carelessly put in the machine. 3. *school slang* senile teacher. —cı lettuce seller.

salatalıkᵍ¹ صلدته لو 1. anything used as salad. 2. cucumber.

salâtüselâm (.—..—) صلدت وسلام A *lrnd.* prayer in moments of danger. — **getir**= to pronounce the formula calling God's benediction on the Prophet (during prayer or in times of peril).

salâvat (..—) صلوات A *lrnd.*, *pl. of* **salât**, prayers. — **getir**= *same as* **salâtüselâm getir**=.

salâzma (———) سال آزما P *lrnd.* who has experienced the good and evil of many years, old and experienced.

salb صلب A *lrnd.* 1. an executing by hanging; hanging; impaling. 2. a crucifying, crucifixion.

salben (.'.) صلبًا A *lrnd.* by hanging.

salbet=ᵈᵉʳ صلب ايتمك /ı/ to hang; to crucify.

salbur سلبر *archaic* sandals made of rope and straw.

salcı صالجى conductor or builder of rafts.

salça (.'.) صالچه It 1. tomato paste; tomato sauce. 2. gravy. —lı having sauce. —lık sauce dish; gravy boat.

saldır=ⁱʳ صالديرمك 1. to make an attack. 2. /a/ to rush upon; to hurl oneself (upon). 3. /ı, a/ to rush someone to a place. —**gan** aggressive; aggressor. —ıcı aggressive. —ı *neol.*, —ım aggression, attack. —ış *verbal n. of* **saldır**=.

saldırma صالديرمه 1. *verbal n. of* **saldır**=. 2. large knife.

saldırmazlıkᵍ¹ صالديرمازلق nonaggression.

saldırt=ⁱʳ صالديرتمك /ı, a/ *caus. of* **saldır**=.

saldide (———.) ساليده P *lrnd.* full of years, old man.

sâle (—.) ساله P *lrnd.* of (so many) years of age.

sa'leb ثعلب A *lrnd.* 1. fox. 2. *same as* **salep**.

salepᵇˡ (—.) سالب [sa'leb] salep (root of *Orchis mascula*); a hot drink made from the powdered root of salep.

salepçi سالپجى maker or seller of hot salep drink. — **güğümü** 1. salep-maker's kettle. 2. *slang* plotter of mischief.

salepgiller *neol.*, *bot.*, *Orchidaceae*.

salgı صالغى *biol.* secretion.

salgın صالغين 1. contagious, infectious; epidemic. 2. invasion; aggression. 3. aggressive; savage, apt to make attacks (animal). 4. general tax levied on a community; annual tribute.

salhane (.—.) سالخانه صالخانه [selhhane] slaughterhouse.

salhorde (—..) سالخورده P *lrnd.* old, aged.

salı صالى Tuesday.

salıkᵍ¹ 1 صاليق *same as* **sağlık** 2.

salıkᵍ¹ 2 صالوق *archaic* halberd, iron mace.

salıkla=ⁱʳ صالقلامق /ı/ *prov.* to describe, to show the way.

salın=ⁱʳ 1 صالينمق 1. to swing, wave; to sway. 2. to loiter along swaying from side to side. 3. to oscillate. —**ıp bulan**= *archaic* to lunge swaggeringly along. —**ı bulanı yürü**= to walk with a rolling gait, to waddle. —**a salına yürü**=, —**ı salını yürü**= to walk along lungingly, swaggeringly.

salın=ⁱʳ 2 صالينمق *pass. of* **sal**= 4.

salıncakᵍ¹ صالنجاق swing; hammock. —**ta kolan vur**= to swing as high as possible on a rope swing. — **sandalye** rocking chair. —**lı** rocking; having rockers; having a swing.

salındır=ⁱʳ صالنديرمق /ı/ *caus. of* **salın**= 1.

salıngaçᶜˡ *neol.* pendulum.

salınım *neol.* 1. *phys.* oscillation. 2. *astr.* libration.

salınış, salınma صالينش صالينمه *verbal n. of* **salın**= 1.

salıntı صالينتى 1. swell (at sea). 2. a swaying about. —**lı** 1. swollen, running with a swell (sea). 2. swaying, tottering.

salıver=ⁱʳ صاليورمك 1. to let go, to set free; to release. 2. to allow to grow (beard, etc.). —**dir**= /ı, a/ *caus.* —**il**= *pass.* —**me** *verbal n. of* **salıver**=.

salib 1 (.—) صليب A *same as* **salip**. S—i **Ahmer** *obs.* Red Cross.

salib 2 (—.) سالب A *lrnd.* 1. who or which takes away; seizer, spoiler, plunderer. 2. negative, privative.

salibe (—..) سالبه A *log.* negative proposition.

salibî (.——) صليبى A *lrnd.* 1. pertaining to a cross; cruciform. 2. Christian. —**ye fasilesi** *bot.*, *Brassicaceae*. —**yun** (.———) A Christians.

salif (—.) سالف A *lrnd.* that goes before, preceding.

salife (—..) سالفه A *lrnd.* preceding command; preceding event.

salifüzzikr (—...) سالف الذكر A *lrnd.* above-mentioned.

salih (—.) صالح A *lrnd.* 1. good, serviceable; valid. 2. upright, righteous, pious. 3. suitable, proper. — **ve talih** the righteous and the sinful.

saliha (—..) صالحه A *lrnd.* 1. pious woman. 2. good work, pious act. 3. *w. cap.*, *woman's name*.

salihat (—.—) صالحات A *lrnd.* 1. good works. 2. righteous women.

salik^(kı) (—.) سالك A 1. *lrnd.* who follows (a profession); who follows a road. 2. *myst.* follower of the road of virtue and piety; a class of dervishes above the novitiate; devotee. —**i hâlik** mistaken aspirant who never can attain to holiness. —**i meczub** aspirant after perfection who has received a divine call; fit guide for others. —**i mücerred** aspirant after perfection who lacks the divine call and can never become a real guide to others. —**i râh-ı Hüda** mystic, ascetic. —**i vâsıl** aspirant who has reached saintly perfection.

salikân (—.—) سالكان P *lrnd.* 1. travelers. 2. aspirants and devotees who strive after holiness. —**ı arş** 1. angels. 2. saints, holy men.

salikîn (—.—) سالكين A *lrnd., pl. of* **salik**.

salim (—.) سالم A 1. safe, sound, free from suffering, defects, etc. 2. *lrnd.* healthy. 3. *Arabic gram.* that none of the radicals ا و س (root); regular (noun plural form).

salimen (—'..) سالما A *lrnd.* in safety, safely and soundly.

salimîn (—.—) سالمين A *lrnd., pl. of* **salim**.

salip^(bi) (.—) صليب [salib 1] cross, crucifix.

salis (—.) ثالث A *lrnd.* third.

salise (—..) ثالثة A *lrnd.* 1. the sixtieth part of a second (of time or angle). 2. *Ott. hist.* the third grade of a rank or order.

salisen (—'..) ثالثاً A *lrnd.* thirdly; in the third place.

saliyan (—.—), **saliyane** (—.—.) ساليان ساليانه P *lrnd.* 1. annual, yearly. 2. a yearly stipend or allowance.

salkı 1 صالقى *archaic* 1. hanging pendulously. 2. relaxed, flaccid. 3. defective, deformed, paralyzed. — **otur**= to loll languidly.

salkı=^r **2** صالقى *archaic* to hang pendulously. —**lan**= to become relaxed, flaccid and pendulous. —**lık** laxity, flaccidity.

salkım صالقم صالقيم صلقم 1. hanging bunch of grapes, flowers etc.; cluster. 2. any tree that bears flowers in hanging bunches (acacia, wisteria, etc.). 3. hanging, pendant. 4. shrapnel, canister shot. — **ateş** *fireworks* rocket ending in a shower of stars. — **küpe** earring with a pendant. — **saçak** hanging about untidily or in rags. — **salkım** hanging in bunches. — **söğüt** weeping willow, *bot.*, *Salix babylonica;* Egyptian willow, *bot.*, *Salix aegyptica.* — **topu** cannon for firing scattering missiles.

salkımlan=^r صالقملن to form into bunches.

salkulak^(ğı) صالقولاق *prov.* one who does not pay attention to what is said; careless in listening.

sallâ 1 صلى A *lrnd.* May (God) command.

salla=^r **2** صاللسه /ı/ 1. to swing or rock to and fro; to shake; to wag. 2. to put off, to leave in suspense. 3. *slang* to hit, deliver (a blow). 4. to mind, to care, to pay attention.

sallabaş صالله باش afflicted with an involuntary shaking of the head.

sallâllahu aleyhi ve sellem (..—. ... ...) صلى الله عليه وسلم A *rel. formula* May God commend and salute him! *used after mentioning the name of the Prophet Muhammad, usually abbreviated in writing as* **S.A.S.**

sallama=^r صاللمسى /ı/ *slang* to pay no attention, not to care.

sallan=^r صاللن 1. *pass. of* **salla**= 2. 2. to be about to fall. 3. to loiter, lounge about, waste time. —**ı bullanı** with a swinging, swaggering gait. —**dır**= /ı/ 1. *caus. of* **sallan**=. 2. to hang, to execute by hanging. —**ış**, —**ma** 1. *verbal n. of* **sallan**=. 2. rolling, swaggering gait.

sallantı صاللنتى 1. a rocking, rolling. 2. suspense, a leaving in suspense. —**da bırak**= /ı/ to leave in suspense.

sallapata, sallapati (..—'.) صاللپاتى *colloq.* 1. without reflection; suddenly. 2. careless, tactless.

sallasırt صاللسرت *colloq.* rough hoisting of a load on to one's shoulder. — **et**= /ı/ to hoist on to the shoulders, to shoulder.

sallayış صاللیش *verbal n. of* **salla**= 2.

sallı صاللى 1. large and wide, open mouthed; straggling, ill-planned (building). 2. furnished with rafts.

salma صالمه 1. *verbal n. of* **sal**= 4. 2. a kind of stew containing rice. 3. *Ott. hist.* sent out on a round or expedition (troops or policemen). 4. local rate levied on villages. 5. long hanging sleeve. 6. special room for bird breeding. 7. *prov.* beam. 8. let out to pasture (animal), sent out freely, untethered. 9. running continuously (water). — **deve gibi gezin**= to saunter about so as to disturb passers-by. — **ipi** lasso, lariat. — **karakollukçu** the police of Istanbul in the time of the Janissaries. — **salıver**= to let go freely, to pasture (animal). — **su** water allowed to run freely. — **tomruğu** *Ott. hist.* police cell.

salmalık^(ğı) صالمه لق 1. mussels for stewing. 2. *prov.* pasture.

salman صالمان *prov.* set free, loose, untied (animal).

salmastra (..'.) صالماسطره صالماسترا It 1. cord wound around something to protect it against chafing. 2. gasket. 3. packing, stuffing. — **kutusu** stuffing box.

salname (——.) سالنامه P *lrnd.* yearbook, annual; almanac.

salon صالون F room for receiving guests, hall.

saloz صالوز Gk *slang* fool; stupid; imbecile.

salozlaş=ᵻʳ صالوزلشمق to become stupid, to become foolishly petrified.
salpa 1 (´.) صالپه It *naut.* Anchor's aweigh.
salpa 2 صالپه slovenly, untidily dressed; loose, slack. —**lık** untidiness, slovenliness.
salsalⁱⁱ (.—) صلصال A *lrnd.* clay mixed with sand; hardened clay which yields a sound. —**î** (.— —) A claylike.
salt صالط mere, simple, merely, solely.
salta 1 (´.) صالته It a standing on the hind legs (dog, etc.) — **dur**=, — **et**= to stand on the hind legs.
salta 2 (´.) صالته a kind of short jacket.
salta 3 (´.) صالته It *naut.* a slackening off (a tight rope).
salta 4 صالته صالط A *lrnd.* sovereignty, dominion.
saltadora, saltadura (...´.) صالته دوره It *naut.* Jacob's-ladder with wooden rungs.
saltamarka (..´.) صالته مارقه سالتامارقه It *same as* **salta 2.**
saltanat سلطنت A 1. sovereignty, dominion, sultanate. 2. authority, rule. 3. pomp, magnificence, state. — **arabası** *Ott. hist.* royal coach. — **kaim makamı** *Ott. hist.* prince representing the Sultan in Istanbul while the Sultan was on a campaign. — **kayığı** *Ott. hist.* the imperial rowboat. **S—ı Seniye** *lrnd.* the Ottoman Government. — **sür**= 1. to rule as Sultan. 2. to live in great splendor. —**lı** regal, magnificent; pompous, showy. —**sız** without display or parade.
saltiye (´..) سالتیه It *naut., same as* **salta 3.**
salûs 1 (— —) ثالوث A *lrnd.* trinity; the Trinity.
salûs 2 (— —) سالوس P *lrnd.* hypocritical, flatterer. —**i** (— — —) P hypocrisy, deceit.
salvele صلوله A *lrnd., short for* **salâtüselâm** (prayer for the Prophet).
salvo (´.) سالوو It artillery salvo.
salya 1 (´.) صالیا سالیه [**salyar**] saliva. —**sı ak**= 1. to water with desire (mouth). 2. to slobber.
salya 2 (´.) صالیا سالیه It *naut.* Haul out. — **et**= /ı/ to shift from one side to the other.
salyalı صالیه لی 1. who slobbers. 2. stupid, idiotic.
salyan (— —), **salyane** (— —.) سالیانه سالیان صالیانه صالیان [**saliyan, saliyane**] *Ott. hist.* yearly tax, esp. an oppressive tax.
salyangoz صالیانغوز Gk 1. snail, *zool.*, *Helix.* 2. climbing snail flower, *bot., Phaseolus caracalla.* 3. *anat.* cochlea. — **kanalı** *anat.* cochlear duct. — **merdiven** corkscrew stairs, winding stairs; spiral staircase.
salyar صالیار سالیار صالیه Gk archaic, *same as* **salya 1.**

samᵐᵐⁱ **1** (—) سامّ A *lrnd.* 1. poisonous, venomous. 2. poisonous wind; simoom; blight. — **vur**= to scorch, to blight (poisonous wind). — **yeli***.
Sam 2 سام A *Bib.* Shem (son of Noah).
=**sam 3**, =**sem** [*pl.* =**sak**, etc.] if I ..., *e. g.*, **kalksam** If I get up, **gitsem** If I go.
-**sam 4**, -**sem** سم سم سم *after vowels* -**ysam**, -**ysem** [*pl.* -**sak**, etc.] if I am ..., *e. g.*, **evdeysem** If I am at home. **ahmaksam** If I am an idiot.
samame (.—.) صمامه A *med.* embolism.
saman 1 صامان صمان straw, cut straw. — **alevi gibi** like a straw flame flaring suddenly but extinguishing quickly; quick, passing flame or passion. — **altından su yürüt**= to intrigue covertly; to do something in an underhanded way. — **anızı** stubble left standing in a field. — **çöpü** chaff. — **gibi** insipid, tasteless. — **kâğıdı** tracing paper. — **kapan***. — **nezlesi** hay fever. — **rakısı** smoky spirits, whisky. — **rengi** straw color. — **suyu** straw-colored gilding. — **tozu** chaff. — **uğrusu***. — **yemez** *colloq.* hard to deceive; clever. — **yolu***.
saman 2 (— —) سامان P *lrnd.* 1. wealth, wellbeing. 2. comfort, rest. 3. power, ability. 4. order, arrangement, disposition.
samanî 1 (.— —) صمانى straw color; straw-colored.
Samanî 2 (— — —) سامانى A *hist.* Samanid. —**yan** (— — — —) P *lrnd., pl.*
samankapan صامان قپان amber.
samanlı صمانلى صامانلى 1. containing chaff, not well winnowed. 2. mixed with chaff or cut straw.
samanlıkᵍ¹ صامانلق place for storing straw; straw rick.
samansûz (— — —) سامانسوز P *lrnd.* destroyer of wealth; disturber of the peace.
samanuğrusuⁿᵘ, **samanyolu**ⁿᵘ صامان اوغریسى صامان یولى the Milky Way.
samed صمد A *lrnd.* perpetual, eternal, sublime; lord, protector; God, the eternal, the most high.
samedanî (..— —) صمدانى A *lrnd.* divine. —**yet** (..—..) A deity, divinity.
samem صمم A *lrnd.* 1. a being or becoming deaf; deafness. 2. a turning a deaf ear to what is said. —**i lâfzî** *psych.* word deafness, auditory aphasia. — **ruhî** *psych.* auditory agnosia.
samg صمغ A *lrnd., same as* **zamk**. —**î** (.—) A gummy.
sami 1 (— —) سامى A *lrnd.* 1. high, lofty, elevated. 2. illustrious.
samiⁱⁱ **2** (—.) سامع A *lrnd.* that hears; listener; *school* auditor. — **sıfatiyle** *school* as an auditor, auditing.

Sami 3 (——) سامى A Semite; Semitic.
samia (—..) سامعه A *physiol.* the sense of hearing; ear.
samih (—.) سميح A *lrnd.* generous, bountiful, liberal.
sâmiha (—..) سامحه A 1. *lrnd.* generous woman. 2. *w. cap.*, woman's name.
samiin (—.—) سميعين A *lrnd.*, *pl.* of **sami 2**, the listeners, the audience.
samim (.—) سميم A *lrnd.* the inmost essential part of a thing; the choicest part of a thing; essence. —**âne** (.——.) P from the heart, sincerely.
samimî (.——) سميمى P cordial, sincere. —**yet** (.—..) A cordiality, sincerity.
samin (—.) ثامن A *lrnd.* eighth. —**en** (—'..) A eighthly.
samir (—.) ثامر A *lrnd.* in fruit; fruitful.
Samirî (—.—) سامرى A *Bib.* Samaritan. —**ye** (—...) Samaria.
samit (—.) صامت A 1. *gram.* consonant. 2. *lrnd.* silent; mute. 3. *lrnd.* in gold and silver (wealth as opposed to an estate in slaves and cattle). — **ü lerzân** silent and trembling. — **ve natık** immovable and movable (goods).
samlah (.—) صملاح A *anat.* earwax, cerumen.
samma (.—) صمّاء A *lrnd.*, *fem.* of **asam 2**, 1. deaf. 2. inexorable, headstrong. 3. hard, solid (rock). 4. hard part of the duodenum.
samme (—.) سامّه A *lrnd.* poisonous animal.
samsa صامسا [**sembuse**] a kind of pastry sweetened with syrup.
samsam (.—), **samsame** (.—.) صمصام A *lrnd.* sword that does not bend, sharp sword, saber.
samsun صامسون *archaic* mastiff.
samsuncu صامسونجى *Ott. hist.* keeper of the mastiffs (used against the enemy). —**lar** keepers of the Sultan's mastiffs.
samt صمت A *lrnd.* a being silent, silence.
samur سامور [**semmur**] sable, *zool.*, *Martes zibellina*; sable fur. — **kaşlı** having eyebrows as thick as sable fur. — **kürk** sable-skin coat. — **kürkü sırtına al=** to take the blame, to bear the responsibility.
samuriye سمّوريه *zool.*, Mustelinae.
samut (.—) صموت A *lrnd.* silent, noiseless; speechless.
samyeli[nl] صامیلى very hot unwholesome wind, simoom. — **vurmuş Mayıs çirozu** *slang* very thin, skinny person.
san 1 صان 1. esteem, reputation; surname. 2. *archaic* estimate (as to number or quantity). 3. *archaic* review of troops. 4. *archaic* subdivision; piece. — **san doğra=** /ı/ to cut to pieces. — **ver=** to be passed in review.
san 2 صانئه [**sam 1**] *archaic* a yellow blight that attacks wheat, disease of grain crops (causing yellowness).
san 3 صان *archaic* aspiration.
san 4 صان *archaic*, same as **sanki**.
san 5 (—) سان P *lrnd.* way, fashion, mode, appearance.
-san 6 (—) سان P *lrnd.* equal, like, resembling, *e. g.*, **yeksan**.
san=[ır] **7** صانمى /ı/ 1. to deem, suppose, think. 2. to imagine. 3. *archaic* to desire, to wish.
=san 8, **=sen** [*pl.* **=sanız**, etc.] if you..., *e. g.*, **istesen** if you want.
-san 9, **-sen**, *after vowels* **-ysan**, **-ysen** (.'.) [*pl.* **-sanız**] if you are ..., *e. g.*, **bekârsan** If you are single.
sana 1 سانا [*dat. of* **sen 1**] to you.
sana=[r] **2** صانامق *archaic* /ı/ 1. to estimate by guess or judgment; to estimate the quantity or value of. 2. to esteem and respect. 3. to scrutinize, minutely investigate; to dissect. 4. to sneer at, to pull to pieces figuratively
sanaat (.—.) صناعت A *lrnd.*, same as **sınaat 1**.
sanacı صاناجى [*based on* **sana=** 2] estimator.
sanacık[ğı] (.—.) سناجك *lrnd.*, *pl.* of **sancak**.
sanadid (.——) صناديد A *lrnd.*, *pl.* of **sındid**.
sanadik[kı] (.——) صناديق A *lrnd.*, *pl.* of **sanduk**.
sanai (.——) صناعى A *lrnd.*, same as **sınai**.
sanal *neol.* conjectural. — **sayı** imaginary number.
san'at[tı, ti] صنعت A 1. art; craft; trade, calling. 2. skill, ability. 3. industry. 4. skillful act; trick. —**la** artistically. — **altın bileziktir** (*lit.* A craft is a golden bracelet.) A worker with a skill can always find work. —**çı** artisan, craftsman.
san'atger صنعتگر P *lrnd.* craftsman, artisan.
san'atkâr (..—) صنعتكار P artisan; artist; actor. —**âne** (..——.) P artistically.
san'atkârî (..——) صنعتكارى P *lrnd.* 1. profession of an artisan or artist. 2. skill, artistic ability.
san'atlı صنعتلى made with skill and ingenuity, ingenious.
sanatoryum (...'.) سناتوريوم F sanitarium.
sanavber صنوبر A 1. stone pine, *bot.*, *Pinus pinea*; pine, fir, larch. 2. *lrnd.* cone of a coniferous tree.
sanavberhiram (....—) صنوبرخرام P *lrnd.* graceful as the tall pine; swaying like a fir tree in walking.
sanavberî (...—) صنوبرى A shaped like a pine cone. —**ye** *bot.*, Coniferae.
sanavberkamet (...—.) صنوبرقامت P *lrnd.* of a lofty stature.
sanayi[ii] (.—.) صنايع A industries. —**i nefise** *lrnd.* fine arts.
sanc=[ır] صانجمق *archaic* 1. to set up in

the earth (lance, etc.) 2. to stick a sharp-pointed thing into.
sancakᵏⁱ صانجاو سنجق سانجاق 1. flag, banner; standard. 2. *naut.* starboard side of a ship. 3. *Ott. hist.* subdivision of a province. 4. *archaic* pole stuck into the ground by one end. — **aç**= to unfurl a flag. — **beyi** *Ott. hist.* governor of a sancak. — **boğ**= *mil.* to give a signal asking for help. — **kaldır**= to raise a rebellion. **S—ı Şerif** *lrnd.* the flag of the Prophet only unfurled for a holy war.
sancakdar (..—) ساتجقدار P *lrnd.* standard bearer.
sancı 1 صانجى صانجو 1. stomach ache, colic; stitch. 2. travail, labor pain.
sancı=ʳ 2 صانجيمق صانجمق 1. to ache (stomach etc.). 2. *archaic, same as* **sanc**=.
sancıl=ʳ صانجيلمق *archaic, pass. of* **sanc**=.
sancılan=ʳ صانجيلانمق صانجيلانمق 1. to have stomach ache or similar internal pain. 2. to have labor-pains. —**dır**= /ı/ *caus.*
sancılı صانجيلى having a stomach ache.
sancış=ʳ صانجيشمق *archaic* to thrust into one another (lance, etc.); to fight with bayonets.
sancıt=ʳ صانجيتمق صانجتمق /ı/ *caus. of* **sancı**= 2.
sanç=ʳ صنجمق *var. of* **sanc**=.
sand صند A Egyptian acacia, *bot., Acacia arabica.*
sandal 1 صندال A 1. sandal (shoe). 2. white sandalwood, *bot., Santalum album.*
sandal 2 صندال Gk rowboat.
sandal 3 صندال a kind of silk or satin cloth, brocade, sendal. **S— Bedesteni** the municipal auction rooms at Istanbul.
sandalcı صندالجى boatman.
sandalî (..—) صاندالى A *lrnd.* 1. throne. 2. made of sandalwood.
sandalos ساندلوس *var. of* **senderus.**
sandalya, sandalye (..′.) صانداليه صندليه [sandalî] 1. chair. 2. office, post. — **kavgası** struggle for a post or position. — **sazı** cane for making chairs.
sandıkᵏⁱ صنديق صاندوق سنديق [sanduk] 1. chest, coffer, box. 2. cash box; cash department (of a government or business). 3. cofferdam. 4. old-fashioned fire pump. 5. box for measuring sand, etc. — **at**= to construct a cofferdam. — **balığı** boxfish, *zool., Ostracion.* — **defteri** cash-book. — **emini** cashier, treasurer. — **eşyası** clothes, etc. forming part of a bride's dowry. — **odası** storeroom. —**a para at**= to hoard money. — **sepet** box and basket, bag and baggage. —**ı sepeti kaldır**= to go away carrying bag and baggage. —**çe** *var. of* **sandukçe.** —**çı** maker or seller of chests, boxes, etc.
sandıkkâr (..—) صنديककار P cashier.

sandıkla=ʳ صنديقلامق /ı/ to box, to crate.
sandıklama صنديقلاما encasing, nesting (of boxes).
sandıklı صنديقلى 1. furnished with a chest, box or case. 2. thin board used for veneer. 3. *Ott. hist.* a kind of gold coin of the time of Mahmud II. — **saat** clock in a tall case, grandfather clock.
sandukᵏᵘ (.—) صندوق A *lrnd.* box, case.
sanduka (.—′.) صندوقة A *lrnd.* sarcophagus.
sandukçe (.—.) صندوقچه P *lrnd.* small box.
sandukdar (.——) صندوقدار P *lrnd.* cashier.
sandukkâr (.——) صندوقكار P *lrnd.* cashier.
sandviç صاندويچ E sandwich.
sanekallah (—..—) صانك الله A *lrnd.* May God protect you.
sanem صنم A *lrnd.* 1. idol, image or picture that is worshipped. 2. idol of one's heart, beloved object.
sanemperest صنم پرست P *lrnd.* idolatrous; idolator.
sanevber صنوبر A *lrnd., same as* **sanavber.**
sangı صانغى *archaic* confused, stupified, dizzy. —**la**= to feel stupid and confused. —**lık** confusion of mind, stupification; stupidity.
sanı صانو صانى 1. imagination, supposition, surmise, idea. 2. suspicion. — **san**= to have a surmise, suspicion or idea.
sanıcı صانيجى who thinks or meditates, who imagines or surmises.
sanıkᵏⁱ *neol.* suspected, accused.
=**sanız 1,** =**seniz** سـكـز سـاكـز ـكـز [*pl. of* =**san 7,** etc.] if you..., *e. g.,* **bilseniz** If you only knew, **kalsanız** If you stay.
-**sanız 2,** -**seniz 2,** *after vowels* -**ysanız,** -**yseniz** (′...) سـه سـكـز سـه ساكز ـسـه كـز [*pl. of* -**san 8,** etc.] if you are..., *e. g.,* **yorgunsanız** If you are tired, **evdeyseniz** If you are at home.
sani 1 (—.) ثانى A *lrnd.* second.
sani 2 (—.) ثانى A *lrnd.* that turns one away.
saniⁱⁱ 3 (—.) صانع A *lrnd.* worker, maker, creator; the Creator. **S—i âlem** the Maker of the Universe.
saniⁱⁱ 4 (.—) صنيع A *lrnd.* 1. made, manufactured. 2. done; act, deed.
sani'a (.—.) صنيعه A *lrnd.* 1. deed, act, action. 2. invention, ruse.
sanih (—.) سانح A *lrnd.* 1. that crosses one's path, that presents itself. 2. that occurs to the mind; that happens.
saniha (—..) سانحه A *lrnd.* 1. sudden thought; inspiration. 2. event, occurrence, incident.
sanihat (—.—) سانحات A *lrnd., pl. of* **saniha.**
saniya (—′..) ثانيا A *lrnd., var. of* **saniyen.**
saniye (—..) ثانيه A 1. second, moment; second hand. 2. *Ott. hist.* second grade of officials. —**si saniyesine** to the very second,

saniyen right on time. —li with a second hand (watch). —li tapa *artillery* time-fuse.
saniyen (—´..) ساني A *lrnd.* 1. secondly, in the second place. 2. for the second time.
sankᵍⁱ, sankı 1 صانق صانغ ساني صانغ *archaic* bird dung.
sankı 2 صنقى *archaic, same as* sangı.
sankılat=ⁱʳ صانقلت *archaic* /ı/ to chain up (a falcon) in preparation for taking it out to hunt.
sanki صانكى as if, as though, supposing that.
sankim صانكم *archaic, same as* sanki.
sanlı صانلو esteemed, well known, reputed.
sanrı *neol., psych.* hallucination. —la= to hallucinate.
sansar صانسار 1. stone marten, *zool., Martes foina;* polecat. 2. marten fur. — gibi stealthy, sly.
sansör سانسور *F* censor.
sansun صومصون *same as* samsun.
sansür سانسور *F* censorship.
sant^{dı} سانت *var. of* sand.
santabarba (..´..) صانتابربا *It naut.* 1. gun room of a man-of-war. 2. afterhold, after magazine.
santigram سانتغرام *F* centigram.
santim سانتم *F* 1. centimeter. 2. centime.
santimetre, santimetro (..´.) سانتمتره *F* centimeter. — kare square centimeter. — küp cubic centimeter.
santral سانترال *F* 1. telephone exchange. 2. powerhouse. 3. central. 4. *slang* brain, intelligence.
santrfor سانترفور *F soccer* center-forward.
santur صانطور *A* musical instrument similar to the kanun, placed on a stand and played with wooden mallets. The strings are made of steel and the sound is similar to that of a piano. —î (.——) dulcimer player.
santurlu سانطورلو pompous, splendid, showy.
sanu صانو *archaic, same as* sanı.
sanzatu سانزاتو *F* cards no trumps.
sap 1 صاپ 1. handle. 2. stalk, stem. 3. a single thread. 4. stack. — çek= to remove stacks of wheat to the threshing ground. — demeden samanı anla= to be very quick on the uptake. — derken saman de= to talk random nonsense. —ına kadar utterly, to the core. —ı silik *colloq.* tramp, vagabond.
sap=ᵃʳ 2 صاپس 1. to swerve, to deviate, to diverge, to turn off into a different direction. 2. to go astray; to fall into error.
sapa صاپ off the road; out of the way, secluded; devious. — düş= to be off the main road; to be remote or inaccessible. — yer secluded spot. — yol bye-road, side-street.

sapak^{gı} *neol.* abnormal. —lık abnormality.
sapan صاپان 1. sling for throwing stones. 2. sling for hoisting heavy articles; catapult. 3. *naut.* strop (of a block on board ship). 4. straddle between the legs. —ı açık wide in the straddle of his hind legs (horse). — balığı thresher shark, *zool., Alopias vulpinus.* — taşı sling pebble. — taşı peşinden yetişemez A pebble from a sling could not catch him *said of one running away very fast*.
sapanorya (..´.) ساپانوريه *Gk slang* ugly, shapeless (person).
saparna (..´.) صاپارنه *Sp* sarsaparilla, root of *Smilax officinalis*.
saparta (..´.) صاپارطه *It* 1. *colloq.* severe scolding. 2. naval artillery double broadside. —yı ye= to get a good scolding.
sapasağlam (..´..) صاپاصاغلم well and sound, very strong.
sapçık^{gı} *neol., bot.* tigella.
sapık^{gı} صاپيق 1. gone astray, perverted; eccentric; crazy. 2. harmless lunatic.
sapınç^{cı} *neol.* deviation.
sapır sapır, sapır sopur صاپير صاپير صاپير صوپور imitates the noise of continuously falling things. — dökül= to fall continuously with a rattling noise.
sapıt=ⁱʳ صاپيتمق 1. to go off one's head; to talk nonsense. 2. to cause to go astray; to go astray.
sapkı *neol., phil.* perversity, perverseness.
sapkın 1 صاپقين 1. *phil.* perverse; astray, off the right road. 2. *geol.* deviated, erratic.
sapkın 2 صاپقين harpoon, fish spear.
sapla=ʳ صاپلامق /ı, a/ 1. to thrust into (a sharp pointed thing); to pierce. 2. to spit, skewer.
saplama صاپلامه 1. *verbal n. of* sapla=. 2. *mech.* stud. 3. *Ott. hist.* person who is not a devşirme but who finds his way into the Janissary corps.
saplan=ⁱʳ صاپلانمق /a/ *pass. of* sapla=.
saplantı *neol., phil.* fixed idea.
saplat=ⁱʳ صاپلاتمق /ı, a/ *caus. of* sapla=.
saplı صاپلى 1. having a handle; stalked. 2. sticking into a thing. 3. bowl or pot with a handle; scoop, ladle. — kal= to stick to some old habit, etc. — meşe pedunculate oak.
sapma صاپمه 1. *verbal n. of* sap= 2. 2. *phys.* deviation.
sapsağlam (.´..) صاپصاغلم very strong; very healthy.
sapsarı (.´.) صاپصارى very yellow, bright yellow; very pale.
sapsız صاپسيز without a handle; stemless, stalkless. — balta 1. one without backing or influence. 2. idle, good-for-nothing. — meşe British oak, *bot., Quercus robur.*
sapta=ʳ *neol.* to fix.
saptır=ⁱʳ صاپديرمق /ı, a/ *caus. of* sap= 2.
sar=ᵃʳ 1 صارمق 1. /ı/ to wind, wrap around; to

bandage. 2. /ı/ to clasp to one's bosom; to embrace; to cling (to). 3. /ı/ to surround (as with a military force). 4. /ı/ to wind (wool, etc.) 5. /ı/ to comprehend, take in. 6. /ı/ to captivate, interest. 7. /a/ to climb (vine, etc.). 8. /ı/ to busy oneself about anything. —ıp sarıştır=, —ıp sarmala= /ı/ to wrap carefully.

sar^rn 2 سار A that exhilarates and makes happy.

sar'a 1 صرع صرعا صرعى A epilepsy; epileptic fit. —sı tuttu He is in a fit of epilepsy.

sara 2 (— —) سارا P lrnd. 1. pure, excellent. 2. w. cap. Sarah, Abraham's wife.

saraç^ci سراج [Arabic serrac] saddler, leather worker.

saraçhane (..—.) سراجخانه harness shop.

saraçlık^ğı سراجلق trade of a saddler, saddlery.

sarahat (..—.) صراحت A clearness; explicitness.

sarahaten (.—'..) صراحةً A lrnd. openly, explicitly, clearly.

sarak^ği, saraka صاراق صاراقه Gk 1. slang ridicule, mockery. 2. post, pillory. —ya al=, — et= /ı/ to ridicule, to mock, deride. —a sar= /ı/ 1. to hold up to ridicule, to mock. 2. to bind to a stake.

sarakacı صاراقجى mocker.

sar'alı صرعلى epileptic.

sarar=^ır صارارمق to turn yellow; to grow pale. —t= /ı/ caus. —tma 1. verbal n. 2. pale-skinned.

saray 1 سراى [saray 2] 1. palace; mansion. 2. government house, government office. — ağası Ott. hist. gentleman attendant at the Palace. — altı a famous quality of tobacco grown at Manisa. — kapı dövmesi dish prepared chiefly with chicken and okra. — lokması a sweet made of flour, eggs and sugar. — nazırı same as saray ağası. — patı China aster.

saray 2 (.—) سراى P lrnd., same as saray 1. S—i Asafî Ott. hist., name of the Grand Vizier's department. S—i Atik Ott. hist. the first palace built by Sultan Fatih in Istanbul. —i beka the next world. S—i Cedid Ott. hist. the Topkapı Palace. —i fena this world. —i hümayûn the Imperial Palace. —i sipenc the world.

Saray 3 (— —) سراى A lrnd. Sara, the wife of Abraham.

Saraybosna سراى بوسنه geog. Sarajevo.

Sarayburnu سراى بورنى geog. Saray Point (in Istanbul).

saraydar (.— —) سرايدار P lrnd. 1. keeper of the palace 2. steward, major domo.

Sarayiçi سراىيچى the place in Edirne where the old palace used to be.

saraylı سرايلى 1. attached to a palace; brought up in a palace; palace servant or slave. 2. having palaces.

sarban (— —) ساربان P lrnd. 1. camel-driver. 2. baggage man in a caravan.

sardalya, sardalye, sardela (..'.) ساردلا ساردليه ساردليه It sardine, pilchard, zool., Arengus pilchardus.

sardır=^ır صاردیرمق صاردرمق /ı, a/ caus. of sar= 1.

sardoğan صاردوغان a kind of hawk.

sardun ساردون Gk a kind of rope (made of the fibers of the lime tree).

sardünya (..'.) ساردونيه ساردونيا It 1. geranium, bot., Pelargonium. 2. w. cap. Sardinia (island). —giller neol., bot., Geraniacea. S—lı Sardinian.

Sare (— .) ساره A Sarah, Abraham's wife.

sarf صرف A 1. a spending, expending; expenditure; consumption. 2. lrnd. a changing, altering; a turning aside or away; a diverting, averting. 3. lrnd. use, utilization; exertion. 4. grammar. —ı gayret et= to make great efforts, to exert oneself. — ve istihlâk et= to spend and use up. —ı makderet et= to exert oneself. — ü nahiv grammar; grammar and syntax.

sarfet=^der صرفایتمك /ı/ 1. to spend, to expend. 2. to change (money).

sarfınazar صرف نظر A putting aside; apart from; regardless of, notwithstanding. — et= /dan/ 1. to overlook, to disregard. 2. to relinquish.

sarfî (.—) صرفى A lrnd. 1. grammatical. 2. grammarian; etymologist. 3. pertaining to expenditure.

sarfiyat (..—) صرفيات A expenses, expenditure; consumption.

sarfiyun (..—) صرفيون A lrnd. grammarians.

sargı صارغى bandage.

sarhoş سرخوش P 1. drunk, intoxicated; drunkard. 2. happy, delighted. — anahtarı key to a watch. —luk drunkenness.

sarı صارى 1. yellow. 2. blond. 3. pale, haggard. 4. yolk. 5. brass. — ağaç smoke tree, bot., Cotinus. — ağız maigre (fish), zool., Sciena aquila. — altın pure gold; a Turkish gold lira piece. — arı wasp. — asma golden oriole, zool., Oriolus oriolus. — aşı boyası geol. yellow ocher. — bakır brass. — balık a kind of scaled fish of the carp family. — benek anat. macula. — benizli sallow skinned. — boya 1. yellow paint, yellow dye. 2. yellow berries of Rhamnus infactorius. — çalı barberry, bot., Berberis vulgaris. — çam yellow fir, Scotch pine, bot., Pinus sylvestris. — çıyan 1. yellow centipede, zool., Cermatia nobilis. 2. unpleasant-looking blond person. — çiğdem yellow crocus, bot., Crocus sativus. — çizme giy= (lit., to wear yellow boots) to be well off in the world, to be of importance or rank. — **çizmeli Mehmet Ağa** an unknown person; just anybody; a nobody. — **diken** spotted golden thistle, common yellow thistle, *bot., Scolymus maculatus*. — **diş** a kind of sword made in Khorasan. — **doğan** *same as* **sardoğan**. — **göz** a kind of seabream, *zool., Cantharus lineatus*. — **güğüm** dandelion, *bot., Taraxacum officinale*. — **halile** the fruit of *Terminalia citrina*. — **humma** yellow fever. — **kanat** medium sized **lüfer** (fish). — **kantaryun** large flowered St. John's wort, *bot., Hypericum colycinum*. — **kavak** plane tree. — **kebe** great owl, *zool., Bubo maximus*; brown owl, *zool., Otus vulgaris*. — **kız** slang gold coin. — **melhem** *colloq.* sulfur ointment. — **ot** small pine plank or board (used in building). — **papa** a fine yellow variety of peach. — **papatya** golden marguerite, ox-eye camomile, *bot., Anthemis tinctoria*. — **pat** corn marigold, corn chrysanthemum, *bot., Chrysanthemum segetum*. — **sabır** the finest quality of aloes. — **salkım** laburnum, *bot., Cytisus laburnum*. — **samur** 1. otter. 2. otter fur. — **sandal** siskin, *zool., Carduelis spinus*. — **sırma** gold thread, gold lace. — **sinir** yellow fibrous tissue, esp. the tendon of the neck. — **sütleğen** sun spurge, wartwort, *bot., Euphorbia helioscopia* — **şebboy** wallflower, bleeding heart, *bot., Cheiranthus cheiri*. — **teneke** brass in thin sheets. — **yağ** clarified butter. — **yağız** sorrel (horse). — **yakut** topaz. — **yasemin** yellow jasmine, *bot., Gelseminum sempervirens*. — **yonca** honey lotus, king's clover, *bot., Melilotus officinalis*. — **zambak** yellow asphodel, *bot., Asphodeline lutea*. — **zincifre** *min.* yellow cinnabar.

sarıca صاریجه 1. yellowish. 2. *Ott. hist.*, name of a class of Turkish irregular militia. 3. wasp.

sarıcı صاریجی one who habitually winds, binds, wraps, etc.

sarıcıkᵏ¹ صاریجیق yellow hammer, oriole, *zool., Oriolus*.

sarığıburma صاریغی بورمه a kind of sweet pastry.

sarıkᵏ¹ صاریق turban. — **boyna geç**= (lit., for a turban to come down about one's neck) to be worsted in a squabble. — **ı burma***. — **sar**= to wear a turban. — **teli** *Ott. hist.* band of gold tissue worn in the turban by high functionaries of the law and by pashas of high grade. — **ucu** the pendulous end of a turban.

sarıkçı صاریقجی 1. servant who took care of his master's turbans. 2. one skilled in winding turbans.

sarıklı صاریقلی 1. turbaned, wearing a turban. 2. hodja.

sarıl=ⁱʳ صارلمق *pass. of* **sar**= 1.

sarılgan *neol.* 1. winding. 2. *bot.* climbing.

sarılı 1 صاریلی wound, fastened, surrounded.

sarılı 2 صاریلی 1. mixed with yellow color. 2. wearing yellow.

sarılıkᵏ¹ صاریلیق 1. yellowness. 2. jaundice.

sarılış=ⁱʳ صاریلشمق /la/ to embrace each other.

sarım 1 صاریم 1. *verbal n. of* **sar**= 1. 2. bandage. 3. *elec.* a turn of winding (coil, etc.).

sarım 2 (—.) صارم A *lrnd.* 1. sharp, trenchant. 2. determined, who acts with courage and decision.

sarımsakᵏ¹ صاریمساق *same as* **sarmısak**.

sarımsı, sarımtırakᵏ¹ صاریمسی صاریمتراق yellowish.

sarın=ⁱʳ صارنمق /a/ 1. to wrap oneself in. 2. to gird oneself. —**ma** *verbal n.*

sarışın صاریشین blond.

sari 1 (—.) ساری A contagious, epidemic.

sari 2 (——) ساری *archaic* to, towards, in the direction of, *i. e.* **cennet sari pervaz et**= to wing one's flight towards heaven. **şehir sari git**= to go in the direction of the city.

sari 3 (——) ساری P common dress of Hindu women of all classes, sari.

sar'i 4 (.—) صرعی A *lrnd.* epileptic.

sarif (—.) صارف A *lrnd.* 1. who spends, expends. 2. that averts, diverts, repels.

sarih (.—) صریح A 1. clear, explicit, evident, manifest. 2. *lrnd.* pure, unmixed.

sarihan (.—'.) صریحاً A *lrnd.* explicitly, in clear terms.

sarikᵏ¹ (—.) سارق A *lrnd.* who steals or robs; thief, robber.

sarir (.—) صریر A *lrnd.* 1. a creaking, a scratching of a pen; creak. 2. a grating of a door. 3. a making a prolonged and loud noise; noise. —**i hâme** the scratching of a pen.

sark=ᵃʳ صارقمق 1. to hang loosely, to hang down. 2. /dan/ to lean out (of a window, etc.) 3. /a/ to come down on, to attack suddenly. 4. *archaic* to bow down. 5. *archaic* to have a surplus. —**aç** *neol.* pendulum.

sarkan صارقان 1. hanging. 2. *archaic* surplus, balance.

sarkı صارقی woman's short jacket with gold embroidery.

sarkıkᵏ¹ صارقیق pendulous; hanging loosely; flabby; drooping.

sarkıl=ⁱʳ صارقلمق to hang down; to be suspended.

sarkın=ⁱʳ صارقنمق 1. to hang down; to lean over. 2. /a/ to attack, to molest, to worry.

sarkıntı صارقنتی 1. molestation. 2. robbery, spoliation; violence.

sarkıntılıkᵏ¹ صارقنتیلق 1. act of molestation or robbery. 2. importunate or insulting behavior to a woman. — et═, — yap═ to molest, to beset (a lady).

sarkıt 1 *neol., geol.* stalactite.

sarkıt═" **2** صَارْقْتَى /a/ 1. *caus. of* **sark**═. 2. *slang* to hit, to deal a heavy blow. —ıl═ *pass.*

sarkıtma صَارْقْتِمَه 1. *verbal n. of* **sarkıt**═ 2. 2. pendant, ornamental dangling end of a belt.

sarkma صَارْقْمَه *verbal n. of* **sark**═.

sarma صَارْمَه 1. *verbal n. of* **sar**═ 1. 2. dish made of rice and meat wrapped up in grape leaves. 3. wound, wrapped and enveloped with. 4. *wrestling* a tripping with the leg. 5. *embroidery* raised satin stitch. 6. tow, oakum. — **dal** *arch.* ornamental foliage, foliated scroll. —**ya getir**═ /ı/ to get (one's adversary) into the clasp of the leg.

sarmal *neol.* 1. *phys.* spiral. 2. *bot.* helicoidal cyme. — **damarlar** spiral ducts, spiral vessels.

sarman صَارْمَان 1. huge, enormous. 2. yellow cat.

sarmaş═" **1** صَارْمَاشْمَق /la/ to embrace one another; to be intertwined.

sarmaş 2 صَارْمَاش interlaced, intertwined. — **dolaş** 1. in a close embrace; close embrace. 2. inextricably intertwined. — **dolaş ol**═ to embrace one another; to be very close friends.

sarmaşıkᵍ¹ صَارْمَاشِيق 1. common ivy, hedera, *bot.*, *Hedera helix*. 2. intertwined, interwoven. —**giller** *neol., bot., Araliaceae.*

sarmaştır═" صَارْمَاشْدِيرْمَق /ı/ *caus. of* **sarmaş**═ 1.

sarmısakᵍ¹ صَارْمِيْسَاق garlic, *bot.*, *Allium sativum*. —**ı balla yemesini icad et**═ to think of something original but useless. — **dişi** a clove of garlic. — **otu** water germander, *bot.*, *Tencrium scordium*; garlic mustard, *bot.*, *Alliaria officinalis*. —**lı** flavored with garlic.

sarnıçᶜ¹ صَارْنِيج [sahrınç] cistern; tank. — **gemisi** tanker. —**lı** furnished with a cistern or tank.

sarp صَرْپ 1. very steep, difficult to ascend. 2. hard, difficult. 3. inaccessible, intractable, unyielding. —**a sar**═ to become difficult or very complicated and serious.

sarpa (′.) صَارْپَه Gk sea bream, *zool.*, *Pagellus centrodontus*.

sarplaş═" صَارْپْلاشْمَق to become steep; to become difficult or impracticable. —**ma** 1. *verbal n.* 2. *geog.* escarpment. —**tır**═ /ı/ *caus.*

sarpon, sarpun صَارْپُون prov. 1. pit for storing grain, silo. 2. baker's dough-tub.

,sarraf (.—) صَرَّاف A 1. money-changer; banker. 2. clever critic. —**ı sühan** *lrnd.* person who uses and appreciates beautiful language. —**ân** (.—) P *lrnd., pl. of* **sarraf**. —**iye** (.—..) rate of exchange; money-changer's commission. —**lık** profession of a money changer; money-changer's fee.

sars═ᵃʳ صَارْسْمَق /ı/ 1. to shake; to joggle, to give a shock (to). 2. to agitate; to upset.

sarsakᵍ¹ صَارْسَاق 1. walking with a wavering gait; shaky, shaking from feebleness. 2. palsied. 3. untidy, clumsy; idiot. — **pursak** 1. trembling, shaky. 2. awkwardly. — **sursak** shakingly; idiotic. —**lık** 1. clumsiness, shakiness. 2. palsy.

sarsar صَرْصَر A *lrnd.* extremely cold wind; intense cold.

sarsıkᵍ¹ صَارْسِيق walking with a quivering gait; shaky. —**lık** shakiness.

sarsıl═" صَارْسِيلْمَق *pass. of* **sars**═. —**ış**, —**ma** *verbal n.*

sarsıntı صَارْسِينْتِي 1. a being shaken, shock; jolt. 2. concussion. 3. earthquake; disaster.

sarsma صَارْسْمَه 1. a shake; a shaking; joggle. 2. shaken, shaky.

sart 1 صَارْت Gk rope made of reeds.

Sart 2 (—) صَارْت P man of Persian origin in Tatary.

Sart 3 صَارْت F *geog.* Sardis (in Lydia).

sartiya (′..) صَارْتِيَا It *naut.* topgallant shroud.

saruc (——) صَارُوج A *lrnd.* 1. plaster, cement. 2. quicklime.

sarvan (——) صَارْوَان P *lrnd., same as* **sarban**.

Sasan (——) سَاسَان P name of the remote ancestor of the Sassanid dynasty of Persian kings. —**i asgar** the father of Ardshir Babek. —**i ekber** the older Sassan, the remote ancestor.

Sasani (———) سَاسَانِي P *hist.* Sassanid. —**yan** (————) P *lrnd.* Sassanids.

sası صَاسِي the smell of decaying vegetable matter or of mold; smelling moldy. — **sası kok**═ to smell of decay and mildew.

sat═ᵃʳ صَاتْمَق /ı/ 1. to sell. 2. to make a false show (of); to pretend to be. 3. *slang* to get rid of (somebody). 4. *colloq.* to palm off, to foist. —**ıp sav**═ /ı/ to sell all one has. —**a sava geçin**═ to be reduced to such straits that one has to sell one's belongings to live.

satakᵍ¹ صَاتَاق *archaic* market.

satan صَاتَان *prov.* 1. leg (in man); hind leg (of an animal). 2. straddle of the hind legs.

sataş═" صَاتَاشْمَق /a/ 1. to become aggressive; to seek a quarrel. 2. to annoy, interfere with; to tease. 3. *archaic* to meet by chance; to come upon. 4. *archaic* to meet with, to encounter (something unpleasant).

sataşkan *neol.* aggressive; aggressor, meddler with other people.

saten صَاتَن F satin.

sa'ter سَعْتَر A summer-savory, *bot.*, *Satureia hortensis*.

sath سَطْح A *lrnd., same as* **satıh**. —**ı arz** surface of the earth. —**ı cevherî**, —**ı hakikî**

sathan

geometrical superficies. —ı **mail** *phys.* inclined plane, slope. —ı **müstedir** curvilinear surface.
sathan (.'.) سطحاً A *lrnd.* superficially.
sathî (.—) سطحى A 1. pertaining to the surface. 2. superficial. —**ce** superficially.
sathiyat (..—) سطحيات A *lrnd.* superficial things.
sathiyen (.—'.) سطحياً A 1. superficially. 2. on the surface.
satı 1 صاتى a selling, sale. —**ya çıkar=** /ı/ to present for sale. — **pazarı** offer with a view to sell, a cheap bargain.
satı'' 2 (—.) ساطع A *lrnd.* raised up; bright, clear; evident.
satıcı صاتيجى salesman, seller; peddler, dealer; —**lık** quality or trade of a seller, dealer, or street-peddler, salesmanship.
satıhᵗʰı سطح [sath] surface; exterior surface, superficies; plane.
satıl=ır صاتيلمق *pass.* of **sat=**.
satılıkᵍı صاتيليق for sale; on sale.
satılmış صاتيلمش 1. sold. 2. hireling; corrupt. 3. consecrated, vowed.
satım صاتيم sale. —**lık** percentage received by a dealer, commission on a sale.
satın صاتين *only in* — **al=** /ı/ to buy, to purchase. — **alıcı** purchaser.
satır 1 سطر A a line of writing. — **başı** paragraph indentation.
satır 2 ساطير [satur] 1. large knife for cutting meat, cleaver. 2. tobacco cutter. 3. executioner's sword. 4. *gambler's slang* trick. — **at=** /a/ to exterminate.
satış صاتيش a selling, manner of selling; sale. —**a çıkar=** /ı/ to offer for sale.
satir (—.) ساتر A *lrnd.* that covers, hides, conceals.
satlıcan صاتليجان [zatülcenb] *colloq.* pleurisy.
satrançcı شطرنج A 1. chess. 2. check pattern. 3. checkered. —**baz** (..—) P *lrnd.* chess player. —**lı** with a check pattern; checkered.
sattır=ır صاتديرمق /ı, a/ *caus.* of **sat=**.
satur (——) ساطور A *lrnd., same as* **satır 2**.
satvet سطوت A *lrnd.* 1. spring, leap, rush, attack. 2. a conquering, might in battle, force, power.
satvetmedar (...—) سطوت‌مدار A *lrnd.* powerful, mighty.
sav 1 صاو *archaic* 1. word; saying. 2. news. 3. thesis, assertion.
sav=ar 2 صاومق 1. to send away, to turn away; to dismiss, to get rid (of). 2. to avoid, to escape (from). 3. to get over (an illness). 4. to pass away, to come to an end.
sava 1 ساوه *prov.* 1. glad tidings, good news. 2. verbal message or invitation.

sava 2 صلّ *prov.* small anvil.
savab (.—) صواب A *lrnd.* 1. right, right action. 2. correct judgment. 3. *same as* **sevab**.
savabdide (.——.) صواب‌ديده P *lrnd.* approved, deemed correct.
savabendiş (.—.—) صواب‌انديش P *lrnd.* who has correct judgment.
savabnüma (.—.—) صواب‌نما P *lrnd.* showing the right way; seeming right.
savacı صاوه‌جى *archaic* bringer of good tidings, harbinger; messenger.
savaikkı (.—.) صواعق A *lrnd., pl.* of **saika 2**.
savakᵍı 1 صاواق 1. cistern from which water is distributed. 2. weir to a mill-pond, sluice.
savakᵍı 2 صاواق *prov.* 1. stupid, foolish, simpleton. 2. wild, very impulsive or violent.
savamiıı (.—.) صوامع A *lrnd., pl.* of **savmaa**.
savarif (.—.) صوارف A *lrnd.* vicissitudes of fortune. —**i dehr** changes of fortune.
savarım (.—.) صوارم A *lrnd., pl.* of **sarım 2**.
savaş 1 صاواش 1. struggle, fight; battle, war. 2. effort, endeavor. — **grupu** *mil.* section, cell.
savaş=ır 2 صاواشمق 1. to struggle, to fight, to dispute. 2. /la/ to work and struggle hard (at a thing).
savaşçı صواشچى combatant, fighter, warrior.
savaşıcı صواشيجى who struggles, fights; who endeavors, works.
savaşkan صواشقان fighter, combatant.
savat 1 صوات engraving in black on silver; niello, Tula work.
savat 2 صوات *archaic* 1. watering place for cattle. 2. place for fattening cattle.
savatir (.——) سواطير A *lrnd., pl.* of **satur**.
savatla=r 1 صاواتلامق /ı/ to ornament with Tula work.
savatla=r 2 صاواتلامق *archaic* /ı/ to fatten cattle at pasture.
savatlı صواتلى *archaic* fattened, ready for slaughter.
savb صوب A *lrnd.* 1. direction, quarter. 2. course, the right way.
savcı *neol.* attorney general, public prosecutor. —**lık** attorney generalship, public prosecutor's office.
savdır=ır صاودرمق /ı, a/ *caus.* of **sav=** 2.
sa've صعوه A *lrnd.* fire-crested wren.
savıl=ır صاويلمق *pass.* of **sav=** 2.
savlıı صول A *lrnd.* a springing on one, an attacking, assaulting; attack.
savla صولا It *naut.* signal halyard.
savlecan (..—) صولجان A *lrnd.* long bat curved at one end with which horsemen strike the ball in the game of horse-shinny.

savlet صولت A *lrnd.* impetuous assault, attack, onslaught.

savm صوم A *lrnd.* a fasting; fast. —**ı Davud** observing fast every other day.

savma صاومه *verbal n. of* **sav=** 2.

savmaa صومعه A *lrnd.* hermit's cell; monastery.

savmaanişin (.... —) صومعه نشين P *lrnd.* hermit, recluse.

savmış صاومش *archaic* 1. gone, gone by; come to an end. 2. lost; past use; spoiled.

savn صون A *lrnd.* a keeping, preserving, protecting; preservation, protection.

savruk[gu] صاوروق awkward, clumsy; untidy; too hasty. —**luk** untidiness, awkwardness.

savrul=[ur] صاورلمق *pass. of* **savur=**.

savsa صاوصه صاوسه 1. slow. 2. a sly prowling for immoral purposes. — **ver=** *slang* to creep into a woman's bed stealthily. —**cı** a prowling rake.

savsak[gı] صاوساق negligent, dilatory. — **savsak** prowling about.

savsakla=[r] صاوساقلامق /ı/ to put off doing something; to put someone off with excuses or pretexts.

savt 1 صوت A *lrnd.* 1. sound; voice; noise, cry. 2. a form used in religious music by certain orders. —**i bülend** loud voice. —**i hazin** a touching voice. —**i taklidî** onomatopoeia.

savt 2 صوط A *lrnd.* 1. whip, lash; riding whip. 2. a blow with a whip; a flogging, lashing.

savtî (.—) صوتى A *lrnd.* pertaining to sound; phonetic.

savuk[gu] صاووق صاوق *archaic, same as* **soğuk**.

savul=[ur] صاوولمق to stand aside, to get out of the way.

savun=[ur] صاونمق to defend oneself. —**ma** defense.

savur=[ur] صاورمق /ı/ 1. to toss about violently, to throw into the air; to blow about. 2. to winnow. 3. to brandish (sword). 4. to blow violently. 5. to bluster, to brag. 6. to spend extravagantly. —**ma** *phys., geog.* deflation. —**t=** /ı, a/ *caus. of* **savur=**.

savuş=[ur] صاوشمق 1. to slip away, to go away stealthily. 2. to pass, to cease (illness). —**maz** incurable, chronic.

savuştur=[ur] صاوشديرمق /ı/ 1. to ward off. 2. to escape, avoid (some disagreeable thing or person). —**ul=** *pass.*

=**savuz**, =**sevüz** صاووز *archaic for* =**sak 4**, *etc.*

savvag (.—) صوّاغ A *lrnd.* goldsmith, silversmith. **S— Çarşısı** *name of the goldsmith market in the Covered Market of Istanbul.*

sa'y 1 سعى A 1. *can. law* a slave's working to obtain the means of purchasing his freedom. 2. *lrnd.* an exerting oneself; endeavor, effort, exertion; an exerting oneself in walking or running, as a foot messenger, or as a pilgrim between Safa and Merva. —**i beliğ** working with great effort.

-say 2 (—) ساى P *lrnd., var. of* **-sa 4**, **-sa 5**.

say 3 صاى *prov.* 1. flat stone. 2. rock, virgin soil.

say=[ar] 4 صايمق /ı/ 1. to count, to enumerate. 2. to take into account; to regard, to count as. 3. to esteem, to respect, to value. 4. to deem, to suppose, to imagine to be. —**ıp dök=** /ı/ to recount at length.

saya 1 صايه ساي upper part of a shoe.

saya 2 صايه ساي *Ott. hist.* collector of the sheep tax. — **çuhası** a kind of coarse woolen twilled cloth used as carpet, etc. — **fesi** tall fez with top inclined to one side. — **ocağı** company and attendants of a sheep tax collector.

saya 3 صايه ساي *archaic* embroidered waistcoat.

sayacı صايجى person who cuts and sews the upper part of shoes.

sayaç[cı] *neol., elec.* meter.

sayban سايبان P *same as* **sayvan**.

sayd صيد A *lrnd.* 1. a hunting, hunt, chase; a fishing. 2. prey, game; anything acquired by stratagem or violence. —**i mâhi** fishing. — **ü şikâr** the chase.

Sayda صيدا A *geog.* Sidon.

saydam *neol.* transparent. — **tabaka** *anat.* cornea.

saydelâni (..——) صيدلانى A *lrnd.* 1. pharmacological. 2. chemist.

saydele صيدله A *lrnd.* pharmacology.

saydgâh (.—) صيدگاه P *lrnd.* hunting ground.

saydger صيدگر P *lrnd.* hunter, fisher.

=**saydı**, =**seydi** (.'.) سيدى if he had ... e. g., **baksaydı** If he had looked.

saydır=[ır] صايديرمق /ı, a/ *caus. of* **say= 4**.

saydi (.—) صيدى A *lrnd.* pertaining to hunting or fishing.

saye (—.) سايه P *lrnd.* 1. shadow; shade. 2. protection, assistance, favor. —**sinde** thanks to; under the auspices of. —**i bîcan** lifeless shadow. —**i Hüda** (*lit.,* the shadow of God) the Caliph. —**i medîd** lengthy shadow. — **sal** /a/ 1. to give shade. 2. to protect.

sayeban (—.—) سايبان ساي بان P *lrnd.* 1. baldachin. 2. protector; refuge.

sayedar (—.—) سايه دار P *lrnd.* 1. shady, umbrageous; shady place. 2. affording protection; protector.

sayeefgen (—...), **sayeendaz** (—..—) سايه افگن ساي انداز P *lrnd.* 1. casting a shade, shady. 2. affording protection.

sayefiken (—...) سايه فكن P lrnd. spreading a shade, shading.

sayegâh (—.—) سايه گاه P lrnd. shady place; tent.

sayegüster (—...) سايه گستر P lrnd. 1. shade-diffusing, shady. 2. benevolent, friendly.

sayende (—..) سايهنده P lrnd. that touches, rubs, chafes.

sayenişin (—..—) سايه نشين P lrnd. 1. who has sat in the shade. 2. who has seen few troubles, protected.

sayeperest (—...) سايه پرست P lrnd. that likes the shade, protection or secrecy.

sayeperver (—...) سايه پرور P lrnd. nourished in the shade or under protection.

sayepuş (—.—) سايه پوش P lrnd. 1. parasol. 2. arbor.

sayerev (—..) سايه رو P lrnd. 1. that goes about in the dark; who goes about by night clandestinely as a lover, devotee or thief.

sa'yet=ᵈᵉʳ سعيئت to endeavor, to exert oneself.

sayezâr (—.—) سايه زار P lrnd. shadowy place.

sayf صيف A lrnd. summer.

sayfa صحيفه same as **sahife**.

sayfî (.—) صيفى A lrnd. pertaining to summer. — **inkılâp** astron. summer solstice.

sayfiye صيفيه A summer house; country house; villa. — **ye git**= to go into the country.

saygı صايغى 1. respect, esteem. 2. thoughtfulness, consideration. 3. archaic computation, calculation of chances.

saygılı صايغيلى respectful, considerate; good-mannered.

saygısız صايغيسز having no regard or respect; inconsiderate, disrespectful. —**lık** inconsiderateness, lack of respect.

sayha صيحه A lrnd. cry, shriek, clamor. —**i ümid** a cry of hope.

sayı صايى 1. number; enumeration. 2. reckoning. 3. number, issue (of a newspaper) —**ya gelmez** innumerable. —**m suyum yok** children's games Count me out; I'm taking no part.

sayıcı صايجى 1. one who counts. 2. official teller of sheep for taxation. 3. auto. mileage recorder, odometer.

sayıkla=ʳ صايقلامق 1. to talk in one's sleep or in a delirium; to rave. 2. to talk nonsense. 3. /ı/ to dream (of something longed for). —**ma** verbal n.

sayıl=ʳ صايلمق pass. of **say**= 4.

sayılama neol., math. 1. numeration, numbering. 2. statistics.

sayılı صايلى 1. counted, numbered; limited in number. 2. marked, special. — **gün** a red-letter day.

sayım صايم a counting; census. — **vergisi** tax on the number of animals.

sayın 1 neol. esteemed, excellent.

sayın=ʳ **2** صاينمق archaic to consider carefully; to act cautiously.

sayısal neol., math. numeric, numeral. — **değer** numerical value.

sayısız صايسز innumerable; unnumbered.

sayış 1 صايش verbal n. of **say**= 4.

sayış=ʳ **2** صايشمق to settle accounts with one another.

sayıştay neol., new name of the Divan-ı Muhasebat, the Exchequer and Audit Department.

sayıştır=ʳ صايشدرمق caus. of **sayış**= 2.

sayi سايى colloq., var. of **sai**.

sayis (—.) سايس A lrnd., var. of **seyis**.

saykalⁱⁱ صيقل A lrnd. 1. polisher, burnisher. 2. polish, burnish. — **ver**= /a/ to polish, furbish, burnish (metal, etc.). —**cı** 1. polisher, burnisher. 2. flatterer.

saykalla=ʳ صيقللامق /ı/ 1. to polish, burnish. 2. to flatter grossly. —**n**= pass.

saylav neol. deputy, member of parliament.

sayma صايمه verbal n. of **say**= 4.

saymaca صايمه جى 1. in counting, numerically. 2. nominal; considered as.

saymamazlıkᵏⁱ صايمامازلق same as **saymazlık**.

sayman neol. accountant. —**lık** accountant's office; accountancy.

saymazlıkᵏⁱ صايمازلق disrespect, irreverence.

sayref, sayrefi (..—) صيرف صيرفى A lrnd. 1. money-changer; banker. 2. shrewd; cunning fellow; cheat.

sayrı, sayru صايرو صايرى سايرو سايرى archaic ill, sick, ailing. —**lık**, —**luk** sickness, disease.

sayruret (.—.) صيرورت A lrnd. 1. a being, becoming. 2. a changing from one state into another.

sayvan سايوان صايوان [Persian **sayban**] 1. flounce, fringe, frill. 2. awning, roof, tent. 3. anat. the external ear, auricle. 4. bot. umbel. —**iye** bot., Umbelliferae.

sayyad (.—) صياد A lrnd. hunter. —**ı bîinsaf** merciless hunter. —**ı ecel** Death, Angel of Death. —**î** (.——) A hunting.

sayyag (.—) صياغ A lrnd. goldsmith, silversmith.

sayyağı صايغى صاينى same as **sağyag**.

sayyib صيّب A lrnd. that pours rain (cloud).

saz 1 ساز P 1. musical instrument; any string instrument played by plucking. 2. a group of music players. — **çal**= to play a musical instrument. —**a git**= to go to a place of amusement where Oriental music is played. — **semaisi** Or. mus. an instrumental form in four movements, usually played following a **fasıl**. — **söz** music and conversation; party. — **şairi** minstrel who improvises songs and music. — **takımı** Oriental orchestra.

saz 2 سز rush, rushes, bot., *Juncus;* reed, bot., *Phragmites;* flag, bot., *Iris pseudacorus.* — **benizli** pale. — **kalem** reed pen, calamus.

saz 3 (—) سز P *lrnd.* 1. means, appliances; arms, apparatus. 2. goods, effects, substance. 3. learning, talent, ability. 4. order, regularity. 5. good works standing to one's credit in heaven. —**ı râh** traveler's luggage. — **ve selb** arms, etc. taken as spoil.

-saz 4 (—) سز P *lrnd.* 1. that makes, does, arranges, prepares or adjusts, *as in* **çaresaz.** 2. made, arranged, prepared, *as in* **nâsaz.** 3. tuned, in tune, *as in* **rastsaz.**

sazak[k1] سزك *prov.* 1. very cold north wind. 2. marshy place, bog.

sazan سزان carp, *zool., Cyprinus carpio.*

sazcı سزجی 1. maker or seller of musical instruments. 2. lute player.

sazende (—..) سازنده P 1. player of a musical instrument; musician. 2. *lrnd.* that makes, does, performs; one who arranges or composes. —**gi** (—..—) P, *lrnd.,* —**lik** musical performance.

sazgâr (— —) سازگار P *lrnd.* 1. accordant, consonant, harmonizing. 2. yielding, favorable, suitable. —**î** (— — —) P accord, harmony; consent, adjustment.

saziş (—.) سازش P *lrnd.* a making, performing, disposing; performance, arrangement, contrivance.

sazkâr (— —) سازکار P *lrnd.* 1. in accordance, consonant, harmonizing. 2. *Or. mus.* a compound **makam** more than six centuries old.

sazlık سزلق place covered with rushes, reed-bed; marshy place.

se 1 name of the letter **s.**

se 2 ث name of the letter ث (the fifth letter of the Ottoman and fourth letter of the Arabic alphabets. In chronograms it has the numerical value of 500).

se 3 ﺳﻪ P *dice games* three.
=se 4 ﺳﻪ *cf.* **=sa 1.**
-se 5 ﺳﻪ *cf.* **-sa 2.**
-se= 6 ﺳﻪ *cf.* **-sa= 3.**

seb[bbl] **1** سب A *lrnd.* a vituperating, reviling, cursing; blaspheming, blasphemy, swearing.

seb[b'1] **2** سبع A *lrnd.* seven.

seb'a 1 سبع A *lrnd.* seven. —**i iklim** the seven climates.

Seba 2 سبا A Saba (ancient town in South Arabia). — **Kraliçesi** Queen of Sheba.

seba 3 صبا *same as* **saba 1.**

sebâdü (.—.) سه باد و P *backgammon* two and three (in dice).

sebahr سبحر *Or. mus.* an old compound **makam** about six centuries old, out of use at the present time.

sebaik[k1] (.—.) سبائك A *lrnd., pl. of* **sebike.**

sebak[k1] **1** سبق A *lrnd.* He or it preceded, used especially in **masebak.**

sebak 2 سبق A *lrnd.* 1. lesson, task. 2. wager, stake or competition prize. —**âmuz** (..— —) P teacher. —**han** (..—) P pupil, student. —**taş** (..—) P fellow student, classmate.

sebat (.—) ثبات A 1. stability, firmness, perseverance, constancy. 2. a being settled, established, a becoming fixed, stationary, firm, fast. — **et=**, — **göster=** to be persevering; to exhibit firmness of mind.

sebatkâr (.— — —) ثباتكار P enduring; persistent, persevering. —**âne** (.— — — .) P *lrnd.* perseveringly, persistently.

sebatlı ثباتلی stable, persevering, enduring.

sebatsız ثباتسز unstable, fickle; lacking perseverance. —**lık** instability.

sebaya (.— —) سبايا A *lrnd., pl. of* **sebi 1,** prisoners of war, captives.

sebayidü (.—..) سه باى دو P *lrnd.* three and two (in dice).

sebbabe(.— .) سبّابه A *lrnd.* forefinger; index finger; the second toe.

sebbabegeza (.—..—) سبّابه گزا P *lrnd.* who bites his forefinger as a gesture of astonishment; astonished.

sebbah (.—) سبّاح A *lrnd.* who swims habitually, swimmer.

sebbak[k1] (.—) سبّاك A *lrnd.* melter, founder of metals.

sebbet=[der] سبّت *lrnd.* to curse, to vituperate.

sebeb سبب A *lrnd., same as* **sebep.** —**i bâdi** *phil.* primary cause. —**i hafif** one movent consonant followed by one quiescent. —**i sakil** two movent consonants in succession as part of a foot. —**i tam** *phil.* efficient cause.

sebebî (..—) سببی A *lrnd.* causal, of the nature of a means; intermediary, causative.

sebebiyet سببیت A *phil.* causality. — **ver=** /a/ to cause.

sebel سبل A *lrnd.* 1. nebula of the eye. 2. disease or web in the eye. 3. trailing appendages of a rain cloud; rain.

sebep[bi] سبب [**sebeb**] 1. cause, reason. 2. source, means; occasion. —**iyle** by reason of, owing to, due to. — **ol=** /a/ to cause; to be the means (of).

sebeplen=[ir] سببلنمك to earn one's living; /dan/ to get a small profit out of something. —**dir=** /ı/ *caus.*

sebepli سببلی having a reason or excuse.

sebepsiz سببسز without any reason, causeless. — **iktisap** *law* unjustifiable enrichment.

sebh سبح A *lrnd.* 1. a swimming. 2. a going or gliding along.

sebhale سبحله A *lrnd., short for the formula* **sübhanallah.**

sebi 1 سبی A *lrnd.* 1. a making one

sebi a prisoner of war and leading him into captivity. 2. a captivating. — **et**= 1. to seize and carry into captivity. 2. to captivate.

sebi 2 (.—) سبى A *lrnd.* captive.

seb'î 3 سبعى A *lrnd.* pertaining to the number seven.

sebike (.—.) سبيكة A *lrnd.* 1. ingot, bar of cast metal. 2. golden scepter of a ruler.

sebil (.—) سبيل A 1. free distribution of water; public fountain. 2. *lrnd.* road, path, way. — **et**= /ı/ to spend lavishly, squander. —**ini tahliye et**= /ın/ to set free (prisoner). —**ci** man who distributes water gratis (but generally begs).

sebilhane (.——.) سبيلخانه P building where water is distributed free. — **bardağı gibi** all in a row (slightly derogatory).

seb'in (.—) سبعين A *lrnd.* seventy.

sebkᵏı **1** سبق A *lrnd.* 1. a going before; precedence. 2. an anticipating another, anticipation. 3. a predeceasing another.

sebkᵏⁱ **2** سبك A *lrnd.* 1. a casting or running metal into a mold. 2. an arranging words and phrases with propriety; a molding of phrases. —**i kelâm** arrangement, context and tenor of a discourse or passage.

sebkat سبقت A *lrnd.* a preceding in time; antecedence, precedence.

sebkürabt سبك ربط P *lrnd.* coordination of phrases; coherence; grammatical construction.

seblâ (.—) سبده A *lrnd.* having long eyelashes.

seblet سبلت A *lrnd.* mustache, whiskers.

sebt 1 سبت A *lrnd.* Saturday, Sabbath.

sebt 2 ثبت A *lrnd.* a registering, an inscribing. —**i sicl et**= /ı/ to register, to inscribe in the court rolls.

Sebte سبتة A *geog.* the town of Ceuta. — **Boğazı** Straits of Gibraltar.

sebtet=ᵈᵉʳ ثبت ايتمك /ı/ to put down, to set down, to write down.

sebu 1 (.—) سبو P *lrnd.* jug, pitcher, mug.

sebuᵘᵘ **2** سبع A *lrnd.* predatory beast or bird, beast of prey.

sebuh (.—) سبوح A *lrnd.* who swims, swimmer.

sebui (..—) سبعى A *lrnd.* pertaining to a beast of prey. —**yet** quality of a beast of prey.

seb'un (.—) سبعون A *lrnd.* seventy.

sebükᵏü سبك P *lrnd.* 1. light; flighty, inconsiderate. 2. fast, fleet. 3. dexterous.

sebükbar (..—) سبكبار P *lrnd.* 1. lightly-laden. 2. free from care.

sebükdil سبكدل P *lrnd.* light-hearted, cheerful.

sebükhimmet سبك همت P *lrnd.* light-minded, unambitious.

sebükhired سبك خرد P *lrnd.* flighty in judgment, injudicious.

sebükhiz (..—) سبك خيز P *lrnd.* vigilant, quick, brisk, active.

sebükmağz سبكمغز P *lrnd.* 1. stupid, silly. 2. fickle, inconstant, irresolute.

sebükmaye (..—.) سبكمايه P *lrnd.* 1. of a frivolous disposition. 2. of small value, cheap. 3. ignorant.

sebükmeşreb سبكمشرب P *lrnd.* lightminded, frivolous.

sebükmizac (...—) سبكمزاج P *lrnd.* weak; fickle, inconstant, irresolute.

sebükpay (..—) سبكپاى P *lrnd.* light of foot.

sebükpervaz (...—) سبكپرواز P *lrnd.* swift-winged.

sebükrev سبكرو P *lrnd.* 1. who travels quickly. 2. frivolous, indiscrete.

sebükruh (..—) سبكروح P *lrnd.* merry, jovial.

sebükseng سبكسنك P *lrnd.* 1. light. 2. lightly esteemed. 3. flighty.

sebüktoz سبكتاز P *lrnd.* running swiftly.

sebz سبز P *lrnd.* 1. green; dark blue. 2. fresh, tender.

sebzbaht سبزبخت P *lrnd.* fortunate, lucky.

sebze سبزه P vegetable; green plant. — **çorbası** vegetable soup. —**ci** vegetable seller.

sebzevat سبزوات *pl. of* **sebze**. —**çı** vegetable seller. —**lı** having vegetables.

sebzezar (..—) سبزه زار P *lrnd.* 1. kitchen garden. 2. green field.

sebzi (.—) سبزى P *lrnd.* 1. greenness, verdure. 2. luxuriance of plants. 3. prosperity, pleasantness.

sebzpa (.—) سبزپا P *lrnd.* unlucky, unauspicious.

sebzpuş (.—) سبزپوش P *lrnd.* 1. clothed in green. 2. angel; the prophet Elijah or any one of the seventy saints always existent on earth. 3. dressed in dark blue or in mourning. 4. ascetic recluse.

secᶜ'ˡ **1** سجع A *lrnd.* 1. *same as* **seci**. 2. a pigeon's cooing; coo.

secᶜᶜⁱ **2** سج A *lrnd.* 1. a pouring out, a shedding. 2. a flowing out, gushing out violently.

secavend (.—.) سجاوند P *lrnd.* marks of subdivision in manuscripts of the Quran.

secavendî (.—.—) سجاوندى P *lrnd.* embellishment of manuscripts with gold or red ink.

secaya (.—.) سجايا A *lrnd., pl. of* **seciye**.

seccac (.—) سجاج A *lrnd.* 1. that pours, that rains down. 2. that is shed and streams copiously.

seccade (.—.) سجاده A 1. prayer rug. 2. small carpet. —**ci** 1. maker or seller of prayer rugs. 2. servant whose duty it is to look after the prayer rug of a great man.

seccadenişin (.—..—) سجاده نشين P *lrnd.* religious

leader or chief in a congregation or dervish order.

seccan (.—) سجّان A *lrnd.* jailer.

secde سجده A act of prostrating oneself in worship. **— et=** to prostrate oneself in worship. **— gülü** ornamental rose made in the margin of the Quran to indicate the act of prostration. **—ye var=** *same as* **secde et=**.

secdegâh (..—), **secdegeh** سجده گاه ، سجده گه P *lrnd.* place of adoration, mosque.

secencel سجنجل A *lrnd.* mirror.

seciᶜⁱ سجع [sec 1] *stylistic* rhymed prose; rhyming word in a piece of rhymed prose.

secin (.—) سجين A *lrnd.* imprisoned, incarcerated.

seciye سجيّه A moral quality; character; natural disposition. **—li** of high moral character, excellent. **—siz** untrustworthy; vicious.

secl سجل A *lrnd.* a bucket filled with water.

secn سجن A *lrnd.* an imprisoning, incarceration. **—et=** /ı/ to imprison.

seç=ᵉʳ سچمك /ı/ 1. to choose, select, to elect. 2. to perceive, to distinguish, to see, to discern.

seçi *neol., phil.* choice.

seçici سچيجى who chooses or distinguishes; selector; selective.

seçikᵍⁱ *neol.* distinct, clear.

seçil=ⁱʳ سچيلمك *pass. of* **seç=**.

seçim سچيم 1. *pol.* election, polls. 2. choice, preference.

seçiş سچيش *verbal n. of* **seç=**.

seçkin سچكين choice, distinguished; outstanding.

seçme سچمه 1. *verbal n. of* **seç=**. 2. selected, choice. **—ce** *com.* allowing the purchaser to pick and choose. **—cilik** *neol., phil.* eclecticism.

seçmen *neol.* voter.

seçtir=ⁱʳ سچيرمك /ı, a/ *caus. of* **seç=**.

sedᵈᵈⁱ سدّ A 1. barrier, obstacle; dam, bank; fence, rampart. 2. a closing, obstructing, barring, barricading; obstruction. **—i âhenin** iron door. **—i bâb** closing a door. **— çek=** /a/ to build a barrier. **S—i Çin** Great Wall of China. **—i hail** a barring; obstacle. **S—i İskender** *hist.* Alexander's Rampart. **—i nutk** *lrnd.* silence. **—i ramak** *lrnd.* a bare subsistence; the last remains of life; a keeping one alive. **S—i Ye'cuc ve Me'cuc** the Wall of Gog and Magog.

seda 1 (.—) صدا A *same as* **sada**.

seda 2 ثدى A *lrnd.* breast, teat.

sedab (.—) سداب A rue, *bot., Ruta graveolens*. **—î** (.——) A *lrnd.* pertaining to rue.

sedacet (.—.) سذاجت A *lrnd.* simplicity of mind or manners; good nature, geniality.

sedad (.—) سداد A *lrnd.* 1. a right and proper word, action or line of conduct, rectitude. 2. a straight direction.

sedaya (..—) ثدايا A 1. *zool.*, Mammalia. 2. *lrnd., pl. of* **seda 2**.

seddad (.—) سدّاد A *anat.* obturator.

seddet=ᵈᵉʳ سدايتلمك /ı/ to bar, obstruct, barricade.

sedebiye سدبيه A *bot., Rutaceae*.

sedef 1 سدف [sedab] rue, *bot., Ruta graveolens*. **— otu***.

sedef 2 صدف A mother-of-pearl; shell producing mother-of-pearl; made of mother-of-pearl. **— hastalığı** *path.* psoriasis. **—çi** worker in mother-of-pearl, one who produces furniture inlaid with mother-of-pearl.

sedefi (..—) صدفى A *lrnd.* orange-red.

sedefkâr (..—) صدفكار P *lrnd., same as* **sedefçi**. **—î** (..——) P *lrnd.* furniture inlaid with mother-of-pearl.

sedeflenme صدفلنمه iridescence.

sedefotuⁿᵘ سدف اوتى rue, *bot., Ruta graveolens*. **—giller** *neol., bot., Rutaceae*.

sedene سدنه A *lrnd., pl. of* **sadin**.

sedi ثدى A *lrnd., same as* **seda 2**.

sedid (.—) سديد A *lrnd.* 1. right, well-directed. 2. in a right and proper state, who takes the right course of action. 3. efficient in obstructing, obstacle.

sedir 1 سدير [sadr] platform at the head of a room with a divan on it; divan, sofa.

sedir 2 سدير F cedar, *bot., Cedrus*.

sedrebeki سدره بكى *colloq.* nonsense.

Sedum (.—) سدوم A *Bib.* Sodom.

sedye (.'.) سدیه It stretcher. **—ci** stretcher-bearer. **—lik** a stretcher case.

seele سئله A *lrnd., pl. of* **sail 1**.

sefa صفا A *same as* **safa**.

sefahet (.—.) سفاهت A foolish squandering; dissipation. **— et=** to be wastefully extravagant.

sefain (.—) سفائن A *lrnd., pl. of* **sefine**. **—i harbiye** warships.

sefalet (.—.) سفالت A poverty; misery. **— çek=** to suffer privation. **—e düş=** to be reduced to poverty.

sefaret (.—.) سفارت A ambassadorship; embassy; legation.

sefarethane (.—.—.) سفارتخانه P embassy building, legation.

sefaretname (.—.—.) سفارتنامه P *Ott. hist.* report written by an Ottoman ambassador regarding his official work, his experiences, and his observations while in foreign lands.

sefaric (.—.) سفارج A *lrnd., pl. of* **sefercel**.

sefat سفط A *lrnd.* sack or basket of plaited palm leaves, rushes, etc.

sefatic (.—.) سفاتج A *lrnd., pl. of* **seftece**.

sefeh سفه A *lrnd.* levity of conduct, folly.

sefele سَفَلة A *lrnd., pl. of* **sâfil.** **—i nas** the rabble.

sefer 1 سَفَر A 1. journey, voyage, travel. 2. campaign, cruise. 3. state of war. 4. time, occurrence. 5. *myst.* stage of progress of the heart to or from God. 6. *can. law* three days' journey. **— aç=** to start hostilities. **—e eş=** *archaic* to go to war. **— et=** to go on a journey, campaign, or cruise. **—e git=** to go to war, to go on a campaign.

Sefer 2 صَفَر A *colloq. for* **Safer.**

seferber سَفَربَر P 1. mobilized for war. 2. *lrnd.* ready for a journey. **—î** (...—) P *lrnd.* pertaining to a campaign or to a trip. **—lik** mobilization; state of war.

sefercel سَفَرجَل A *lrnd.* quince, *bot.*, *Cydonia vulgaris.*

sefere سَفَرة A *lrnd., pl. of* **sâfir 3.**

sefergüzin (...—) سَفَرگُزين P *lrnd.* traveling; traveler.

seferi (..—) سَفَرى A 1. *Isl. rel.* traveling and therefore exempt from fasting during Ramazan (person). 2. *lrnd.* pertaining to travel or campaigning; in campaign; prepared for war.

seferle=ʳ سَفَرلَمَك *archaic* to go on a campaign; to make war.

seferli سَفَرلى who is on a campaign or journey; mobilized.

seferlikᵍⁱ سَفَرلك 1. sufficient for one time. 2. special to traveling or campaigning.

sefertasıⁿⁱ سَفَرطاسى traveling food box (with several metal dishes fastened together).

seffakᵏⁱ (.—) سَفّاك A *lrnd.* 1. a great shedder of blood and tears. 2. eloquent, powerful speaker.

sefid (.—) سَفيد P *lrnd.* 1. white. 2. unsoiled, unsullied. 3. bright, beaming, free from shame or grief (face). **— ü siyah** white and black.

sefidac (.—.—) سَفيداج P *lrnd.* white lead, ceruse.

sefidî (.——) سَفيدى P *lrnd.* 1. whiteness. 2. clearness; brightness.

sefidkâr (.——) سَفيدكار P *lrnd.* whose actions are laudable.

sefidname (.——.) سَفيدنامه P *lrnd.* the record of one whose acts are resplendent and righteous.

sefidriş (.——)سَفيدريش P *lrnd.* 1. graybearded. 2. elder of a village.

sefih (.—) سَفيه A spendthrift, prodigal; dissolute. **—âne** (.——.) P *lrnd.* in a spendthrift manner. **—î** (.——) P *lrnd.*, **—lik** prodigality, dissoluteness.

sefil (.—) سَفيل A 1. poor, miserable; destitute. 2. mean, base, low. **—ân** (.——) P the miserable. **—lik** misery, poverty.

sefine (.—.) سَفينه A *lrnd.* 1. ship, vessel, boat. 2. memorandum, notebook, book. **S—i Nuh** Noah's Ark.

sefir (.—) سَفير A ambassador; envoy. **—e** (.—.) A ambassadress. **—lik** ambassadorship.

sefk سَفك A *lrnd.* a pouring out, shedding (blood etc.). **—i dima** bloodshed.

seftece سَفتجه A *lrnd.* bill of exchange, draft, check.

sefuf (.—) سَفوف A *lrnd.* medicinal powder.

seg سَگ P *lrnd.* 1. dog; hound. 2. a brute of a man, vile wretch. **—i divâne** mad dog.

segâbi (.——) سَگابى P *lrnd.* beaver, castor.

segâh (.—) سَگاه P *Or. mus.* an ancient and characteristic **makam.** **— perdesi** b' flat.

segân (.—) سَگان P *lrnd., pl. of* **seg.**

segâne (.—.) سَگانه P *lrnd.* doglike, canine.

segban (.—) سَگبان P *Ott. hist.* keeper of the Sultan's hounds (incorporated later with the Janissaries).

segcan (.—) سَگجان P *lrnd.* 1. dog-souled, malignant, cruel. 2. patient, longsuffering.

segdil سَگدل P *lrnd.* 1. dog-hearted, fierce; selfish. 2. longsuffering.

segman سَگمان F *auto.* piston-ring, packing-ring, shoe.

segsar (.—) سَگسار P *lrnd.* doglike; voracious; grasping.

segsiret (.—.) سَگسيرت P *lrnd.* doggish, churlish, snappish.

seğir=ⁱʳ سَگرمك to twitch nervously; to tremble.

seğirdim سَگردم 1. recoil (of a gun). 2. distance run in a race. 3. *archaic* attack; raid. 4. banquette in a fortification. **— yap=** to recoil.

seğirdiş=ⁱʳ سَگرديشمك /la/ 1. to run with one another. 2. to struggle.

seğirme سَگرمه nervous twitch; vibration, tremor.

seğirmename (...—.) سَگرمه نامه *archaic* book of mad stories, of impossibilities.

seğirt=ⁱʳ 1 سَگرتمك to run, to hasten.

seğirt=ⁱʳ 2 سَگرتمك /ı/ *caus. of* **seğir=.**

seğirtme سَگرتمه 1. *verbal n. of* **seğirt=** 1. 2. fishing line without bait.

seğmen سَگمن [**segban**] 1. servant in charge of dogs. 2. *prov.* young man, armed and in national costume who takes part in a wedding procession.

seğrekᵍⁱ سَگرك *same as* **seyrek.**

seha (.—) سَها A *lrnd., same as* **saha 2.**

sehab (.—) سَحاب A *lrnd.* cloud; clouds. **—ı muzi** nebula. **—ı rahmet** rain cloud.

sehâbûd (.——) سَحابآلود P *lrnd.* cloudy.

sehabe (.—.) سَحابه A *lrnd.* 1. a single cloud. 2. *astr.* nebula.

sehabî (.——) سَحابى A *lrnd.* 1. of the nature of clouds; cloudy. 2. nebulous.

sehaib (.—.) سَحائب A *lrnd., pl. of* **sehab** **—i meftûre** motionless and heavy clouds.

sehanet 1 (. —.) سَخانَتْ A *lrnd.* a being warm or hot; warmth, heat.
sehanet 2 (. —.) سَخانَتْ A *lrnd.* a being or becoming thick, coarse, hard; thickness.
seher 1 سَحَر A time just before dawn; early morning.
seher 2 سَهَر A *lrnd.* 1. a being sleepless at night, insomnia. 2. a remaining awake voluntarily.
seheran (.'..) سَحَرًا A *lrnd.* early morn; in the early morning.
sehere سَحَرَة A *lrnd.*, *pl. of* **sahir 2**.
sehergâh (..—) سَحَرگاه P *lrnd.* morning, dawn.
seherhiz (..—) سَحَرخيز P *lrnd.* early riser.
seherî (..—) سَحَرى A *lrnd.* pertaining to early morn.
sehhar (. —) سَحّار A *lrnd.*, *same as* **sahhar**.
sehi (. —) سَهى P *lrnd.* straight as an arrow; erect (as a cypress). —**bâlâ** (. ———) P, —**kad** (. —.) P, —**kamet** (. ——.) P tall and graceful.
sehil[hli] سَهل [sehl] *obs.* 1. easy; simple. 2. smooth and soft.
sehim[hmi] سَهم [sehm 1] *com.* lot; share, portion; treasury bond.
sehiv[hvi] سَهو [sehv] *lrnd.* mistake; inadvertence.
sehl سَهل A *lrnd.*, *same as* **sehil**. —**i mümteni**, —**i müşkil** *stylistic* piece of simple, clear writing done with great skill. —**en** (.'.) A easily.
sehm 1 سَهم A *lrnd.* 1. *same as* **sehim**. 2. arrow. 3. pole, mast, staff. 4. the sinking of any part of a building because of pressure.
sehm 2 سَهم P *lrnd.* fear, terror, dread. —**gin** (. —), —**nâk** (. —) P frightful, terrible.
sehpa (. —) سَهپا P 1. tripod; three legged stool or table. 2. easel. 3. gallows. —**ya çek**= /ı/ to hang.
sehreng سَهرنگ P *lrnd.* three colored silk material.
sehtar (. —) سَهتار P *lrnd.*, *name of a stringed musical instrument resembling the* **rebab**.
sehv سَهو A *lrnd.*, *same as* **sehiv**. —**i kalem** a slip of the pen. —**i sarih** a clear mistake.
sehven (.'.) سَهوًا A *lrnd.* by mistake, inadvertently.
sehviyat (..—) سَهويات A *lrnd.* mistakes.
sek=[er] **1** سَك 1. to hop; to run in a series of jumps. 2. to ricochet; to miss.
sek[ki] **2** سَك F dry (wine), champagne.
=**sek 3** سَك سَك *cf.* =**sak 4**.
-**sek 4** سَك سَك *cf.* -**sak 5**.
sekalet (. —.) سَقالَت A *lrnd.*, *same as* **sakalet**.
sekb سَكب A *lrnd.* a pouring out, shedding.
sekenat (..—) سَكَنات A *lrnd.*, *pl. of* **sekne**.

sekene سَكَنَة A *lrnd.*, *pl. of* **sakin**, inhabitants.
sekeran (..—) سَكَران A *lrnd.* a being drunk, intoxication.
sekerat (..—) سَكَرات A *lrnd.*, *pl. of* **sekre**, fits of intoxication.
sekeratülmevt (..—..) سَكَراتُالمَوت A *lrnd.* death agony.
seki 1 سَكى سَكى 1. stone seat; raised bank of earth (in a tent serving as a couch). '2. *geog.* terrace. 3. pedestal.
seki 2 سَكى white sock on a horse.
sekil سَكيل *prov.*, *same as* **seki 2**.
sekine, sekinet (. —.) سَكينَة سَكينَت A *lrnd.* 1. tranquillity, serenity; composure, calm. 2. anything that gives tranquillity of mind; comfort. 3. *Bib.* the presence of God dwelling in a mysterious manner in the Ark of the Covenant.
sekir[kri] سَكر [sekr] *lrnd.* drunkenness, intoxication.
sekit=[ir] سَكت *archaic* /ı/ 1. to calm; to cause to cease. 2. to scold; to reproach.
sekiz سَكيز eight. — **yüzlü** *neol.*, *geom.* octahedron. —**er** eight each; eight at a time. —**gen** *neol.*, *geom.* octagon. —**inci** eighth.
sekizle=[r] سَكيزله /ı/ to make (things) eight. —**n**= to become eight.
sekizli سَكيزلى 1. having eight. 2. the eight (of a suit of cards).
sekizlik[gi] سَكيزلك worth or containing eight.
sekme سَكمه *verbal n. of* **sek**= **1**.
sekne سَكنه A *lrnd.* 1. rest, pause; quiescence, cessation of motion. 2. stop on a letter of a word (in pronouncing).
sekr سَكر A *lrnd.*, *same as* **sekir**.
sekran (. —) سَكران A *lrnd.* drunk, intoxicated. —**iyet** A drunkenness.
sekre سَكره A *lrnd.* 1. drunkenness; insensibility. 2. agony of death, pang of sorrow, depth of woe.
sekreter سَكرتر F secretary.
seksek سَك سَك hop-scotch.
seksen سَكسن eighty. —**er** eighty each; eighty at a time. —**inci** eightieth. —**lik** 1. worth or containing eighty. 2. octogenarian.
sekson سَكسون *Ott. hist.* hound from Saxony. —**cu** group of the Janissary corps in charge of the **seksons**.
sekt سَكت A *lrnd.* interval of silence between two musical notes; a short hiatus between phrases in reading and recitation (without taking a breath).
sekte سَكته A 1. stoppage, interruption of any action or business. 2. pause; interval. 3. apoplexy. 4. stagnation. 5. *lrnd.*, *same as* **sekt**. —**i dimağiye** *path.* paralysis of the brain. —**i kalb** *path.* heart failure. — **ver**=

sektedar

/a/ to give a respite, to relax. — **vur**= /a/ to interrupt, to cause to stop.

sektedar (..—) سکته دار P lrnd. 1. disturbed, interrupted. 2. defective. 3. prejudiced.

sektelen=ⁱʳ سکته لن to be hindered or interrupted.

sektir=ⁱʳ سکته دیر /ı/ caus. of **sek**= 1. —**me** verbal n.

sekvestro (..´.) سکوستروا It law sequestration. — **et**= /ı/ to sequester, to impound, to destrain.

sel 1 سیل A torrent; flood, inundation. — **gider kum kalır** proverb (lit. The torrent passes on but the sand remains in its place.) Depend not on transitory things but on essential things. —**i suyu kalmamış** completely dry (food or fruit). — **yatağı** torrent bed, ravine.

selⁱⁱⁱ **2** سل A lrnd. a drawing forth from a sheath. —**i seyf et**= to draw the sword.

Selacıka (.—..) سلاجقه A lrnd. the Seljuk dynasty; the Seljuks.

selâm (.—) سلام A 1. salutation, greeting, salute. 2. lrnd. peace, concord; safety, security. 3. lrnd. source, means or assurance of immunity, especially, God as the giver of immunity. 4. lrnd. soundness, freedom from imperfection. 5. each one of the four sections of the vocal music used during a Mevlevi service. — **ağası** Ott. hist. Master of Ceremonies who accompanied the Grand Vizier. — **al**= to acknowledge a salute or another's bow. —**i âm** Ott. hist. public reception at court. — **çavuşu** Ott. hist. attendant whose duty was to salute the people for the Sultan on certain occasions such as the celebrations of bayram and anniversaries of accession to the throne. He also offered prayer at the close of the ceremonies. — **dur!** Present arms! —**a dur**= to rise respectfully to receive the salute of a superior. — **et**=, — **gönder**= /a/ to send one's compliments. —**i hâs** Ott. hist. audience at court by special permission. — **otu** herb lovage, lovage, bot., Levisticum officinale. —**ı sabahı kes**= /la/ to cease relations with; to ignore somebody completely. — **söyle**= to send one's compliments. — **ver**= /a/ to salute, to greet. — **verip borçlu çık**= to be in debt because of a mere greeting, said of a person who takes the opportunity for asking a favor the moment one greets him.

selâmaleyküm (.—..´.) سلام علیکم colloq. for **selâmünaleyküm**.

selâmet (.—.) سلامت A 1. safety, security; freedom from danger or illness. 2. soundness, liberation. 3. successful result. 4. lrnd. freedom from defect or error (sentence). —**le!** Good-by and good luck. — **bul**=, —**e çık**= to gain safety, to turn out well.

selâmetbaş (.—.—)سلامت باشی P lrnd. Peace be (with you). May you prosper.

selâmetle=ʳ سلامتله /ı/ to see somebody off; to wish somebody Godspeed.

selâmla=ʳ (.—..) سلاملمق /ı/ to salute, to greet.

selâmlaş=ⁱʳ سلاملشمق /la/ to greet or salute each other.

selâmlıkᵍⁱ (.—.) سلاملق 1. the part of a large Muslim house reserved for males. 2. Ott. hist. public procession of the Sultan to a mosque at noon on Fridays.

selâmünaleyküm (.—...´.) سلام علیکم A lrnd. Peace be with you (the formal greeting of Muslims). — **demeden** without so much as by your leave; brusquely and tactlessly.

selâmünkavlen (.—...) سلام قولن A lrnd., euphemism for paralysis, stroke.

Selânikᵍⁱ (.—´.) سلانیك geog. Salonika, Thessalonike. — **dönmesi** a person whose ancestors were converted from Judaism to Islam at the time of Sabbatai Sebi (Zevi) in 1666. —**li** 1. of Salonika. 2. Salonika Jew.

selâse (.—.) ثلاثه A lrnd. three. —**i gassale** 1. three cups of wine taken on an empty stomach for purging out corrupt humors. 2. the first three cups of wine drunk at a drinking party (after which shyness is gone).

selâset (.—.) سلاست A lrnd. fluency of speech; smoothness of style. —**le** fluently. —**li** fluent.

selâsil (.—.) سلاسل A lrnd., pl. of **silsile**. —**i müjgîn** hair of the beloved.

selâsin, selâsun (.——) ثلاثین A. lrnd. thirty.

selâtin (.——) سلاطین A lrnd., pl. of **sultan**. — **camii** mosque built by a sultan. — **meyhane** Ott. hist., name of a certain class of great wine shops.

selb سلب A lrnd. 1. a taking by force, a seizing and carrying off. 2. a depriving; negation. 3. myst. a power's depriving one of self-will; a devotee's being or becoming a mere passive instrument in the hands of an exterior power.

selbet=ᵈᵉʳ سلب ایتمك /ı/ 1. to carry off, to take by force; to deprive forcibly. 2. to deny, negate.

selbî (.—) سلبی A lrnd. negative, privative.

selc سلج A lrnd. snow. —**î** (.—) A pertaining to snow, snowy.

Selcukᵏᵘ, **Selçuk**ᵍᵘ سلجوق hist. Seljuk. —**î** (.——) A Seljuk. —**iyan** (.———) P the Seljuks. —**lu** Seljuk.

sele سله [selle] flattish wicker basket. — **zeytini** a kind of olives especially prepared with comparatively little salt.

seleb سلب A lrnd. 1. spoil lawfully acquired from an enemy (arms, clothes, etc.). 2. clothes, garments.

selef سلف A 1. predecessor; ancestor. 2. man of old. 3. lrnd. advance of money; loan without interest. — **ve halef** predecessor and successor; ancestor and descendant.

selefî (..—) سلفى A *lrnd.* 1. pertaining to a predecessor. 2. pertaining to an advance of money.

Selefke سلفكه *same as* **Silifke**.

selem سلم A *lrnd.* money paid in advance for a commodity.

seleserpe *var. of* **sereserpe**.

selgi *archaic* loose.

selh A *lrnd.* 1. a flaying. 2. the thirtieth day of a lunar month. 3. a plagiarist's changing each word in a poem while preserving the original sense.

selhhane (.—.) P *lrnd.*, *same as* **salhane**.

selib (.—) A *lrnd.* 1. carried off as spoil, seized. 2. bereft of one's senses.

selika (.—.) A *lrnd.* 1. good taste. 2. natural ability to speak or write. **—dar** (.—.—) P, **—mend** (.—..) P, **—şiar** (.—..—) P possessed of genius or good taste; of good disposition.

selim (.—) A 1. *lrnd.* free from defect or danger; safe, sound. 2. *path.* benignant (tumor).

selimî (.——) A *Ott. hist.* a peculiar kind of smooth turban worn by officers of the Sultan's Palace. **—ye** a kind of silk material.

selinti *prov.* 1. small torrent caused by rain; bed made by a torrent. 2. mud left by a torrent.

selis (.—) A fluent; easy-flowing (style).

selit (.—) A *lrnd.* aggressive, vituperative.

selle A *lrnd.*, *same as* **sele**.

sellebaf (..—) P *lrnd.* basket maker or seller.

sellemehüsselâm (.'....—) A *colloq.* without ceremony; without being announced; unexpectedly; rudely.

selman (.—) A *w. cap.*, man's name. **— et=** *slang* to beg, to ask for alms.

selmek[ki] *Or. mus.* an ancient compound makam.

selsal[li] (.—) A *lrnd.* pure, limpid stream; cool, pleasant to drink, delicious.

selsebil (..—) A *lrnd.* 1. a spring in Paradise. 2. ornamental fountain. 3. cool, pleasant to drink (water). 4. mellow wine.

selva 1 A *lrnd.* 1. quail, *zool., Coturnix coturnix*. 2. honey.

selva (.'.) Sp *lrnd.* the forest trees of a region or country considered collectively, silva.

selvet A *lrnd.* 1. consolation, comfort.

2. ease, affluence, happiness. 3. philter that makes one forget sorrow.

selvi *same as* **servi**.

selvise (..'.) *naut.*, *var. of* **servise**.

sem[mmi] 1 A *lrnd.* poison. **—i Babilî** (*lit.* Babylonian poison) wine. **—i helahil** instantaneously fatal poison. **—i katil** killing poison.

sem[m'i] 2 A *lrnd.* 1. a hearing, listening, an obeying. 2. ear. **—i mülevven** *psych.* colored hearing.

=**sem** 3 *cf.* =**sam** 3.

-**sem** 4 *cf.* -**sam** 4.

sema 1 (.—) A sky, heaven. **—yi lâciverd** the blue sky.

sema 2 (.—) A 1. a whirling dance performed during a Mevlevi service. 2. *lrnd.* hearing; mention. **— et=** to whirl in an ecstatic state. **—i râh** whirling done while traveling.

semacet (.—.) A *lrnd.* a being ugly; ugliness. **—i ibtidâ** ugliness at the beginning of a speech.

Semaderek[gi] Gk *same as* **Semendirek**.

semafor Gk *naut.* semaphore.

semahane (.——.) P *lrnd.* dervish meeting-house for religious music and whirling.

semahat (.—..) A *lrnd.* generosity, munificence.

semahatlû (.—.—) *archaic* bountiful, munificent.

semahatpişe (.—.—.) P *lrnd.* bountiful, munificent.

semaî 1 (.——) A *lrnd.*, *same as* **semavi**.

semaî 2 (.——) A 1. *Or. mus.* a rhythmic pattern with three beats; a form special to vocal music; a form used by minstrels in folk music. 2. *lrnd.* based upon what has been heard; founded on custom, traditional. **— kahvesi** coffee house where **semaî** singers gather together.

semaim (.—.) A *lrnd.*, *pl. of* **semum**.

sem'an 1 (.'.) A *lrnd.* 1. by hearing, hearingly. 2. willingly. **— ve taaten** most willingly; you have only to command.

Sem'an 2 (.—) A *Bib.* Simon; Simeon.

seman 3 (.—) A *lrnd.* eight.

semanet (.—.) A *lrnd.* a being fat, fatness.

semanin (.—.) A *lrnd.* eighty.

semaniye A *lrnd.* eight.

semanun (.——) A *lrnd.* eighty.

semar (.—) A *lrnd.* fruit.

semasire (.—..) A *lrnd.*, *pl. of* **simsar**.

semavat (.——) A *lrnd.*, *pl. of* **sema 1**.

semaver Rus samovar.

semavi (.——) A *lrnd.* pertaining

to the sky or heaven; celestial; heavenly. **— arz** celestial latitude. **— mihanik** celestial mechanics.
semazen (.—.) ﺳﻤﺎزن P *lrnd.* a Mevlevi who performs the **sema'**, whirler.
sembolᵘ̈ ﺳﻤﺒﻮل F symbol.
sembuse (.—.) ﺳﻤﺒﻮﺳﻪ P *lrnd.* a triangular pastry.
semc ﺳﻤﺞ A *lrnd.* ugly, hideous of feature.
semdar (.—) ﺳﻤﺪار P *lrnd.* poisonous; venomous.
seme ﺳﻤﻪ *prov.* 1. stupid, foolish. 2. confused, perplexed.
semekᵏⁱ ﺳﻤﻚ A *lrnd.* fish. **—e** A a single fish.
semen 1 ﺳﻤﻦ A *path.* fatness, obesity. **— gel=** to get fat.
semen 2 ﺳﻤﻦ A *can. law* price, value.
semen 3 ﺳﻤﻦ P *lrnd.* jasmine. **—ber** P jasmine-breasted. **—bu** (..—) P fragrant as jasmine.
semend ﺳﻤﻨﺪ P *lrnd.* roan, strawberry or sorrel horse; horse.
semender ﺳﻤﻨﺪر P *lrnd.* 1. the mythical salamander. 2. common salamander, *zool., Salamandra maculosa.*
Semendirekᵍⁱ ﺳﻤﻨﺪرك *geog.* Samothrace.
semenistan (...—) ﺳﻤﻨﺴﺘﺎن P *lrnd.* jasmine garden, jasmine patch.
semer 1 ﺳﻤﺮ Gk 1. packsaddle; pad (used by porters for carrying heavy weights). 2. *slang* buttocks. **—ini daya=** 1. to put up an animal in its stable. 2. to put a man out of office. **—i döv=** to hesitate before taking up a burden or responsibility. **— vur=** to put a packsaddle on a beast. **—ini yere vur=** to resign an office or duty.
semer 2 ﺳﻤﺮ A *lrnd.* 1. fruit. 2. property, wealth.
semer 3 ﺳﻤﺮ A *lrnd.* 1. evening conversations; tale told by night. 2. night assembly; evening party.
semerat (..—) ﺳﻤﺮات A *lrnd., pl. of* **semere**.
semerci ﺳﻤﺮﺟﻰ maker of packsaddles. **—lik** packsaddle making.
semere ﺳﻤﺮه A 1. fruit; profit; result. 2. crop; produce, product. **—dar** (...—) P *lrnd.*, **—li** 1. fruitful. 2. profitable.
semerle=ʳ ﺳﻤﺮﻟﻪ /ı/ to saddle with a packsaddle.
semerli ﺳﻤﺮﻟﻰ 1. having a packsaddle (animal). 2. wearing a pad (porter). 3. having a hump, hooked (nose). 4. coarse, vulgar.
semiᵐⁱ **1** ﺳﻤﻰ *var. of* **sem 2**.
sem'i 2 (.—) ﺳﻤﻌﻰ A *lrnd.* pertaining to hearing; acoustic.
semiⁱⁱ **3** (.—) ﺳﻤﻴﻊ A *lrnd.* 1. that hears, listens; quick of hearing. 2. God, the All-Hearing.

semih (.—) ﺳﻤﻴﺢ A *lrnd.* liberal, generous, munificent.
semin 1 (.—) ﺳﻤﻴﻦ A *lrnd.* 1. fat, fleshy. 2. rich (food).
semin 2 (.—) ﺳﻤﻴﻦ A *lrnd.* high-priced, valuable, expensive.
semir=ⁱʳ **1** ﺳﻤﺮﻣﻚ ﺳﻤﻮرﻣﻚ ﺳﻤﺮﻣﻚ to grow fat.
semir 2 (.—) ﺳﻤﻴﺮ A *lrnd.* 1. evening entertainment, night gossip. 2. intimate companion, fond of nocturnal conversations. 3. *used also in compounds, e. g.,* **sadakatsemir**.
semirgin ﺳﻤﺮﮔﻦ fat and lazy.
semirt=ⁱʳ ﺳﻤﺮﺗﻤﻚ /ı/ *caus. of* **semir= 1**, to fatten.
semiz ﺳﻤﺰ fat, fleshy, overweight. **— boya** *art* fatty paint. **—ce** rather fat.
semizle=ʳ ﺳﻤﺰﻟﻪ to grow fat. **—t=** *caus.*
semizlikᵍⁱ ﺳﻤﺰﻟﻚ fatness, fleshiness.
semizotu ﺳﻤﺰاوﺗﻰ purslane, *bot., Portulaca oleracea.* **—giller** *neol., bot., Portulacaceae.*
semmakᵏⁱ (.—) ﺳﻤﺎك A *lrnd.* fisherman.
semmî (.—) ﺳﻤّﻰ A *lrnd.* pertaining to poison; poisonous; poisoned. **—yat** (..—) A poisons; poisonous substances. **—yet** A poisonousness.
semmur (.—) ﺳﻤّﻮر A *lrnd., same as* **samur**. **—iye** *zool., Mustalidae.*
semn ﺳﻤﻦ A *lrnd.* clarified butter.
sempati ﺳﻤﭙﺎﺗﻰ F sympathy.
sempatikᵍⁱ ﺳﻤﭙﺎﺗﻴﻚ F likable, attractive.
semra (.—) ﺳﻤﺮاء A *lrnd.* dark, brown, swarthy (woman).
semt ﺳﻤﺖ A 1. region, neighborhood; quarter in which one lives. 2. direction. 3. *astr.* azimuth. **—i kadem** *astr.* nadir. **— semt** in certain places; in every quarter.
semtî (.—) ﺳﻤﺘﻰ A *lrnd.* pertaining to a quarter, direction or azimuth.
semtürre's ﺳﻤﺖ اﻟﺮأس A *astr.* zenith.
semuh (.—) ﺳﻤﻮح A *lrnd.* very bountiful, munificent.
semum (.—) ﺳﻤﻮم A *lrnd.* hot, poisonous wind of the desert, simoom.
sen 1 ﺳﻦ you (sing.) (Among educated people **sen** is used within the family, but not by a child to his parents, and to servants. Cf. **siz**.) **—de** with you; you have it. **— ağa ben ağa koyunları kim sağa** «You are a gentleman, I am a gentleman, so who is to milk the sheep?», *said to one who does not want to do his job.* **— de** you too. **— kim oluyorsun?** Who are you? What is it to you? **— misin*.** **— necisin?** *same as* **sen kim oluyorsun? — sağ ben selâmet** That's the end of it. **— sen, ben ben** *said to indicate selfish argument between two persons.* **— sen ol** forever; never. **— sen ol bir daha bunu yapma** Now don't forget, you mustn't do this again.

=sen 2 ڛان ر ڛاڮ cf. =san 8.
-sen 3 ڛان ر ڛاڮ cf. -san 9.
sena 1 (.—) ثَنا A praise, eulogy. — et= /ı/ to praise, to commend.
sena 2 سَنا A lrnd. 1. light, splendor, brightness; flashing (lightning). 2. senna, bot., Cassia. —i kâzib bladder senna, bot., Colutea.
senabik (.—.) سَنابك A lrnd., pl. of sünbük.
senabil (.—.) سَنابل A lrnd., pl. of sünbüle.
senacil (.—.) سَناجل A lrnd., pl. of secencel.
senâgû (.——) ثَناگُو P lrnd. praiser, eulogist. —yâne (.———.) P praisingly. —yi (.———) P a praising.
senahan (.——) ثَناخوان P lrnd. 1. who praises, praiser, eulogist. 2. your humble servant, I.
senakâr (.——) ثَناکار P lrnd., same as senahan. —âne (.———.) P praisingly. —î (.———) P sincere; my, your humble servant's (in a letter).
senam (.—) سَنام A lrnd. 1. camel's hump. 2. summit, pinnacle; sand hill. 3. central part (of anything).
senamekki (...—) سَنامَكی A same as sinameki.
senaryo (..'.) سَناریو It scenario.
senato (..'.) سَناتو It senate.
senaver (.—.) ثَناور P lrnd. 1. praiser, eulogist. 2. your humble servant. —âne (.—.—.) P praisingly. —î (.—.—) P a praising.
senaya (.—.) ثَنایا A lrnd., pl. of seniye.
-senc سَنج P lrnd. that weighs; who ponders and speaks or acts, as in sühansenc.
sence (.'.) سَنجه according to you, in your opinion.
sencer سَنجر P lrnd. fortress; barricade.
sencide (.—.) سَنجیده P lrnd. 1. who has weighed, pondered, thought over, uttered or done. 2. weighed, pondered, tried, proved. 3. well-ordered, arranged.
sencileyin (.'...) سَنجِلَین archaic like you.
sendan (.—) سَندان A lrnd., same as sindan.
sendele=ᵗ سَندَلَمك to totter; to stagger. —t= /ı/ caus.
sendere سَندَره thin board, shingle.
senderus (..—) سَندَروس A copal; gum juniper, sandarac.
sendika (..'.) سَندیقا F trade union. —cı trade unionist. —cılık trade unionism.
sene سَنه A year. —i Arabiye lrnd., same as sene-i kameriye. — be sene from year to year, year by year. —i Hicriye lrnd. year of the Hegira. —i kameriye lrnd. lunar year of the Muslim calendar. —i kebise leap year. —i Milâdiye lrnd. year of the Christian era. —i Rumiye, —i şemşiye lrnd. solar year of the Turkish calendar. (See under Rumi.)

sened سَنَد A 1. same as senet. 2. lrnd. argument in support of an assertion. 3. lrnd. prop, stay or support leaned upon; person on whom one relies. — ittihaz et= /ı/ to hold as a proof.
senedat (..—) سَنَدات A lrnd. title-deeds.
senedî (..—) سَنَدی A lrnd. pertaining to a voucher or document.
senek^{gi} سَنَك prov. wooden pitcher; jug.
senelik^{gi} سَنَلِك 1. for a year; of a year. 2. a year old. 3. yearly. 4. yearly rent.
senet^{di} سَنَد [sened] promissory note; title deed; instrument; voucher; receipt.
senetleş=ⁱʳ سَنَدلَشمك to exchange documents of proof.
senetli سَنَدلی based on written proof; accompanied by written proof.
senetsiz سَنَدسِز without any receipt. — sepetsiz without giving or demanding any written proof.
senevat سَنَوات A lrnd., pl. of sene.
senevî 1 (..—) سَنَوی A annual, yearly; annually.
senevî 2 (..—) ثَنَوی A lrnd. who believes or affirms the doctrine of two creators, one of good, the other of evil; dualist. —ye A religion of the Magi or dualists. —yet A dualism.
senfoni سَنفونی F mus. symphony.
senfonik^{gi} سَنفونیك F mus. symphonic. — orkestra symphony orchestra.
seng سَنگ P lrnd. 1. stone; rock. 2. weight; heaviness. 3. gravity, authority, dignity. 4. value, worth; esteem. —i asiyab millstone. —i felâhan sling pebble. —i hârâ a very hard stone. —i ibret Ott. hist., name of an obelisk in front of Topkapı Palace where the heads of executed persons were exposed to the public view as a warning. —i imtihan 1. touchstone. 2. test, trial. —i melâmet reproach cast at one. —i musa 1. touchstone. 2. hone for sharpening razors. —i musalla same as musalla taşı. —i râh impediment, obstacle. — ü sebu (lit., stone and pitcher) the breaker and the broken; servitude. —i siyah 1. black stone or rock. 2. touchstone. 3. black stone in the Kaaba at Mecca. —i yede magic stone producing rain, stone of rain.
sengdil سَنگدل P lrnd. hard-hearted, cruel, merciless.
sengendaz (..—) سَنگَنداز P lrnd. 1. that throws stones. 2. fault-finder. 3. machine for throwing rocks in war, catapult. 4. holiday celebrated before Ramazan (when wine jars are broken).
sengî (.—) سَنگی P lrnd. stony, of stone; heavy.
sengin (.—) سَنگین P lrnd. 1. stone, of stone; stony; hard as stone. 2. heavy; important.

— **semaî** *Or. mus.* a kind of **yürüksemaî** with slower movements in six beats.

sengistan (..—) سنگستان P *lrnd.* stony or rocky country.

senglâh (.—) سنگلاخ P *lrnd.* rocky, stony place.

sengpuşt سنگپشت P *lrnd.* tortoise, turtle.

sengriz (.—) سنگريز P *lrnd.* flinging stones; stoned.

sengrize (.—.) سنگريزه P *lrnd.* small stones; pebbles; gravel.

sengru (.—) سنگرو P *lrnd.* brazen-faced; impudent.

sengsar (.—) سنگسار P *lrnd.* a stoning to death.

sengsebu (..—) سنگسبو P *myst.* orders penance undergone by an offender who stands in the presence of the chapter with a pitcher-full of stones suspended round his neck.

sengtraş (.—) سنگتراش P *lrnd.* stonecutter, mason. —**î** (.——) P stone-cutting, masonry.

seni 1 سنى you (*Sing.*, *objective*). Sometimes used as a term of abuse usually in conjunction with **gidi**. — **gidi** You little rascal!

seni 2 (.—) سنى A *lrnd.* high, exalted, grand.

seni 3 (.—) سنى A *lrnd.* at the age for shedding the incisor milk teeth (domestic quadruped).

senin سنين your. —**ki** yours. —**le** with you.

seniye سنيه A *lrnd.* one of the four front teeth.

=**seniz 1** سنيز *cf.* =**sanız 1**.
-**seniz 2** سنيز *cf.* -**sanız 2**.

senk[gi] سنك *var.* of **seng**.

senkron سنكرون F *auto.* in step.

senkronik[gi] سنكرونيك F *mech.* synchronous.

senktraş سنكتراش *var.* of **sengtraş**.

senli benli سنلى بنلى familiar; unpretentious, free-and-easy. — **konuş**= to talk intimately, to have a confidential talk.

senlik[gi] سنلك 1. yourself. 2. suitable for you, fitting you exactly.

sen misin سن ميسن Is it you? *When used with a present participle it forms an idiom indicating an unexpected and unpleasant development:* It serves you right for doing so and so, *e. g.*, **evinde bir tek çocuk gürültüsünden şikayet ediyordu, sen misin şikâyet eden, bitişik komşuya altı çocuklu bir aile geldi** He was complaining of the noise made by a single child in the house, then one day a family of half a dozen children came to live in the next flat.

sentetik[gi] سنتتيك F *chem.* synthetic.

sentez سنتز F synthesis.

sep=[er] سپمك *prov.* 1. to sip noisily; to gobble. 2. to sprinkle (rain or fluid); to drizzle, to scatter.

sepa (.—) سپا P *lrnd.*, *var.* of **sehpa**.

seped سپد P *lrnd.*, same as **sepet**.

sepek[gi] سپك pivot of a millstone.

sepele=[r] سپلمك same as **serpele**=.

sepet سپت [**seped**] 1. basket; anything made of wickerwork; wickerwork. 2. basket full. 3. *motor.* sidecar. — **havası çal**= *slang* to make a person feel that he is not wanted; to dismiss. — **işi** basket work, wickerwork. — **kafalı** *colloq.* blockhead. — **kulpu kemer** *arch.* basket-handle arch. — **örgü** wickerwork. —**te pamuğu olma**= /ın/ *colloq.* to have an empty brain. — **sandık** basketwork trunk covered with leather.

sepetçi سپتچى maker or seller of baskets. — **söğüdü** osier willow, basket willow, *bot.*, *Salix viminalis*.

sepetle=[r] سپتلمك /ı/ *colloq.* to get rid of a tiresome person; to fire, to dismiss.

sepetleme سپتلمه 1. *verbal n.* of **sepetle**=. 2. woven like a basket, of wickerwork. 3. slanting (cut). — **vur**= to strike and cut slantingly.

sepetli سپتلى having a basket. — **fistan** crinoline, hoop-skirt.

sepetlik[gi] سپتلك 1. substance suitable for making baskets. 2. place where baskets are kept. 3. *anat.* front part of the abdomen.

sepi سپى 1. dressing for hides, tanning. 2. a dying of furs. — **çubuğu** small stick for beating furs. — **ver**= /a/ to dress a fur. —**de yatır**= /ı/ to leave (a hide) to soak in lime or tan liquor. —**ci** tanner.

sepid (.—) سپيد P *lrnd.*, same as **sefid**.

sepidedem (.—..) سپيدهدم P *lrnd.* dawn, early morning.

sepile=[r] سپيلهمك /ı/ to tan; to prepare furs.

sepken سپكن anything sprinkled, shower of rain; slight fall of snow.

Septe سپته *var.* of **Sebte**.

sepya (.'.) سپيا F sepia (color).

ser 1 سر P *lrnd.* 1. head. 2. headman, chief; commander. 3. top, summit, apex. 4. end, point, extremity. —**i bâlin** bedside of a sıck person. —**i bâm** the air space just over a roof. — **ü berg** taste for a thing with means to obtain it; desire, lust. — **ü bün** 1. beginning and end; totally. 2. foundation of a matter. — **ü çeşm** With pleasure! —**de delikanlılık var** What else do you expect of a youth? —**i divar** top of a wall; the sky over a wall. —**i har** 1. scarecrow. 2. fool. —**i hayl** captain of a host. —**i kûy** *same as* **serkûy**. —**i menzil** goal. —**i mu** *same as* **sermu**. —**i pa** toe. — **ü pa** 1. head and foot; all. 2. wish and means to accomplish. — **ü saman** means and power. — **ver**= to devote one's life (to a

serbeste

cause). — **verip sır verme**= rather to die than tell a secret. **—i zeban** tip of the tongue.

ser 2 F greenhouse; hothouse.

ser 3 A lrnd. blood revenge, revenge for homicide.

ser=ᵉʳ **4** /ı/ 1. to spread out on the ground; to spread over. 2. to hang up, to spread out on a line. 3. to beat down to the ground. 4. to neglect (one's job).

=**ser 5** archaic, joined to the root of a verb, forms the participle of a duty or necessity, e. g., **yazıser** who has to write, **yürüyüser** that has to walk.

-**sera 1** (. —) P lrnd., var. of **-seray 2**.

sera 2 A lrnd. earth, ground, land.

serab (. —) P lrnd. 1. same as **serap**. 2. nothingness, emptiness.

serabalâ (. — — —) P lrnd. ascending, rising, uphill.

serabil (. — —) A lrnd., pl. of **sirbal**.

serabistan (. — . —) P lrnd. 1. region of mirages. 2. land of delusion; the world of vanity.

seraçe (. —.) P lrnd. 1. small house; inner apartment. 2. palace, mansion.

seradib (. — —) A lrnd., pl. of **serdab**.

serağaz (. — —) P lrnd. a beginning, prelude.

seraheng (. — .) P lrnd. 1. vanguard; patrol. 2. leader of an orchestra.

serahur (. — —) P Ott. hist. Master of the Horse (title of the men of the second regiment of the Ottoman household cavalry).

serair (. — .) A lrnd., pl. of **serire**.

serairhane (. — . — .) P lrnd. house of secrets. **—i tabiat** place where secrets of nature are stored.

serairülasar (. —. . — —) A lrnd. mysteries, occult meanings of the names of God.

serairürrebubiye (. — . . . — . .) A lrnd. mysteries of the Godhead.

serakᵏı F geol. serac, ice pinnacle.

seraka A lrnd., pl. of **sarik**.

serâmac (. — —) P lrnd. yoke.

seramed (. — .) P lrnd. leader, chief. **—ân** (. — . —) P pl.

seran (. —) P lrnd., pl. of **ser 1**, chiefs, generals.

Serandib (. — —) P cf. **Serendib**.

serapᵇı (. —) [serab] mirage.

serapa (. — —) P lrnd. from head to foot, totally, wholly.

seraperde (. — . .) P lrnd. 1. curtain, especially at the door of a royal palace or pavilion. 2. a royal pavilion. **—i kühlî** 1. sky. 2. night. 3. black cloud.

serar (. —) A lrnd. 1. the next to the last night of a lunar month. 2. the best of a race. 3. myst. a saint's spiritual union with God.

seraser (. — .) P lrnd. 1. from beginning to end; from end to end; whole, entirely. 2. a kind of brocade.

serasime (. — . .), **serasime** (. — — .) P lrnd. astonished, confounded; stupified, confused.

serasker P Ott. hist. 1. commander-in-chief. 2. Minister of War. **S— Kapısı** Office of the Minister of War, War Ministry. **—i** (. . . —) P, **—lik** office and duties of the Minister of War.

ser'aşer P lrnd. head of a section of ten verses of the Quran.

seratan (. . —) A 1. astr. the sign Cancer. 2 path. cancer; disease in the feet of horses. 3. lrnd. crab. **— medarı** geog. Tropic of Cancer.

seravil (. — —) A lrnd. a pair of drawers, breeches, or trousers.

seray 1 (. —) P var. of **saray 1**.

-**seray 2** (. —) P lrnd. who sings, as in **nağmeseray**.

seraya (. — .) A lrnd., pl. of **seriye**, small detached military forces.

seraydar (. — —) P lrnd. house steward; person left in charge of a house; servant of all work.

serayende (. — . .) P lrnd. that sings; singer, chanter.

serazad (. — —) P lrnd. free, independent.

serb 1 A anat. omentum.

serb 2 A lrnd. 1. herd, flock. 2. a man's household. 3. road, way, mode, manner.

serbaz (. —) P lrnd. 1. who stakes his life in a cause; brave; foolhardy. 2. Persian soldier. 3. bare-headed, uncovered.

serbeceyb P lrnd. whose head hangs on his breast from shame or modesty.

serbeha (. . —) P lrnd. price of blood, ransom.

serbemühr P lrnd. 1. the mouth of which is sealed, sealed (bag, etc.) 2. veiled, concealed.

serbend P lrnd. 1. bandage for the head; fillet; turban. 2. stopper, cork.

serberhatᵗı P lrnd. obedient, compliant.

serbes var. of **serbest**.

serbeser P lrnd. 1. equal; square, balanced. 2. from end to end. 3. head to head.

serbest P 1. free, independent. 2. unreserved, frank; bold. 3. easy, unconstrained. **— meslek** independent business. **— mıntıka** free zone. **— tevdiat** fin. free deposits. **—ce** (. . ' .) freely; with ease.

serbeste P lrnd. 1. attached to some

serbesti

service. 2. whose head is fastened to a place; whose head is bandaged. 3. covered, concealed; veiled.

serbesti (..—) سربستى P lrnd. freedom; liberty. **— mezhebi** liberalism.

serbestiyet سربستيت [based on **serbest**] freedom.

serbestle=ʳ سربستلمك to get free, to feel relieved.

serbestlikᵍⁱ سربستلك freedom; independence; frankness.

serbesücûd (...—) سرسجود P lrnd. whose head is constantly bowed in worship.

serbevvabin (..——) سربوّابين P Ott. hist. chamberlains of the Sultan's court.

serbezanu (..——) سربزانو P lrnd. whose head is bent towards his knees in thought or sorrow.

serbezemin (...—) سربزمين P lrnd. whose head touches the ground in profound reverence.

serbülend سربلند P lrnd. lofty, high-headed; excellent, eminent, glorious. **—î** (...—) P eminence, exaltation.

serbüride (..—.) سربريده P lrnd. beheaded, decapitated.

serc سرج A lrnd. riding saddle.

serçe سرچه house sparrow, zool., *Passer domesticus*. **— parmak** little finger or toe. **— yuvası** Ott. hist. a kind of turban worn by some theological students. **—giller** neol., zool., *Passeridae*.

serçeşme سرچشمه P 1. lrnd. fountain head. 2. Ott. hist. officer commissioned to raise irregular troops.

serçin (.—) سرچين P 1. lrnd. the best of anything picked or selected. 2. Ott. hist. tax gathered at so much per head. **— derçin** all manner of taxes gathered in.

serd 1 سرد A lrnd. a setting forth consecutively; proper arrangement of a discourse; exposition (of a subject); consecutive. **— et=***. **— ve ferd** consecutive and single.

serd 2 سرد P lrnd. 1. cold, cool, chilly. 2. disagreeable, unpleasant, unsympathetic. 3. hard; harsh, ugly.

serdab (.—), **serdabe** (.—.) سرداب P lrnd. 1. cellar, underground reservoir. 2. underground room (used in hot weather).

serdar (.—) سردار P lrnd. military chief, general; commander. **—ı ekrem** commander-in-chief. **—ı gâlib** the victorious commander. **—ı ülemâ** hist. 1. the best learnéd man of the time. 2. teacher of the Sultan. **—ân** (.——) P the commanders. **—î** (.——) P, **—lık** rank and functions of a **serdar**.

serdefter سردفتر P lrnd. 1. Chancellor of the Exchequer. 2. head name on a list or roll.

serdengeçti سردنگچتى 1. Ott. hist. troops selected for a desperate enterprise, forlorn hope, suicide squad. 2. person who renounces his life for a cause.

serdet=ᵈᵉʳ سردتمك /1/ to set forth; to expound.

serdî (.—) سردى P lrnd. coldness; chilliness. **—i heva** coldness of weather. **—i tabiat** sternness of character.

serdir=ⁱʳ سردرمك /1, a/ caus. of **ser=** 4.

serdrey سردراى P lrnd. whose opinion is disagreeable; cynical.

serdrû (.—) سردرو P lrnd. morose; disagreeable; insipid.

serdümen سردومن naut. quartermaster.

sere 1 سره span between the thumb and first finger.

sere 2 سره archaic blockhead; stupid; fool.

serebat (..—) سربات A lrnd. the fingers.

seref سرف A lrnd. 1. prodigality; waste. 2. inordinate use, abuse.

serefgen سرافگن P lrnd. who throws away his head, who loses or stakes his head by his devotion; self-sacrificing; dauntless.

serefkende سرافكنده P lrnd. who hangs his head in sorrow or shame; confused; abashed.

serefraz (..—) سرافراز P lrnd. who holds his head high, tall; stately, eminent, superior. **—î** (..——) P stateliness, superiority, tallness.

Serehs سرخس geog. Sarakhs, city in Khurasan.

seren سرن naut. yard; boom, spar. **— biçmesi** plank (sawn from the middle of a pine log for flooring). **— yelken** square sail.

serencam (..—) سرانجام P lrnd. 1. end, conclusion, result. 2. event, occurrence.

serend سرند a kind of yew tree, bot., *Taxus*.

serendaz (..—) سرانداز P lrnd. 1. that throws heads about. 2. who devotes his life to a cause; fearless, dauntless. **—ân** (..——) P fearless, dauntless men of courage. **—î** (..——) P fearlessness, bravery.

Serendib (..—) سرنديب A lrnd. the island of Ceylon.

serengüşt سرانگشت P lrnd. fingertip.

sereserpe سرسرپه free and unrestrained; nonchalant; with disordered clothing.

seretan (..—) سرطان A same as **seratan**.

sereyan (..—) سريان A lrnd. 1. spreading over; infecting. 2. penetrating every part of a thing.

serferaz, serfiraz (..—) سرفراز P lrnd., same as **serfraz**.

serfüru (..—) سرفرو P lrnd. with a humble head, submissive. **— et=** to humble oneself; to yield; to submit.

sergen سرگن prov. shelf made close to the ceiling.

sergerdan (..—) سرگردان P lrnd. 1. whose head turns round, giddy. 2. perplexed, bewildered.

sergerde سرگرده P *lrnd.* chief; leader of a band (of bandits or irregulars).
sergerm سرگرم P *lrnd.* whose brain is heated, excited; intoxicated. **—î** (..—) P excitement.
sergeşte سرگشته P *lrnd.* bewildered, perplexed; stupified. **—gân** (...—) P the bewildered, perplexed. **—gi** (...—) P astonishment, bewilderment, perplexity.
sergi سرگی 1. exhibition, show; shop-front; temporary display of goods. 2. *prov.* anything spread; mat, carpet. 3. *Ott. hist.* order for payment of money from a public office. **— halifesi** *Ott. hist.* clerk of a pay office. **— kalemi** *Ott. hist.* the pay office at the treasury. **— ol=** *colloq.* to get exhausted and fall in a heap.
sergici سرگیجی keeper of a stall for the sale of goods.
sergile=ʳ سرگیله /ı/ to exhibit.
sergin 1 سرگین 1. laid or spread out. 2. ill, laid up. **— ver=** to lie sick in bed.
sergin 2 (.—) سرگین P *lrnd.* dung, manure.
sergirân (..—) سرگران P *lrnd.* 1. whose head is heavy with drink, intoxicated. 2. whose head aches.
sergüzeşt سرگذشت P adventure.
sergüzin (..—) سرگزین P *lrnd.* the best, choicest.
serhadᵈᵈⁱ سرحد P frontier. **—dar** (..—) P *lrnd.* soldier in garrison on a frontier. **—ât** (..—) P *lrnd.* frontiers.
serhadli سرحدلی 1. same as **serhaddar**. 2. having a frontier. 3. *Ott. hist.* a kind of travelling clothes worn by high government officials. **— mesti** rather tight-fitting boot fastened with hooks and eyes.
serhadlikᵍⁱ سرحدلك 1. place that serves as a frontier. 2. *Ott. hist.* a kind of light half-boot with a flap that buttons or hooks at the side.
serhademe (.'...) سرخدمه P head servant in an office.
serhalife (..—.) سرخلیفه P *Ott. hist.* head clerk in a government office.
serhalka ('..) سرحلقه P *lrnd.* 1. first ring of a chain. 2. chief of a party.
serhan (.—) سرخوان P *lrnd.* head singer, head chanter.
serhas سرخس P *lrnd.* fern. **—ı müzekker** common male fern, *bot., Dryopteris filix-mas.*
serhatᵗⁱⁱ سرخط P *lrnd.* 1. head line or copy set before a pupil. 2. original document.
serhaylˡⁱ سرخیل P *lrnd.* 1. commander of a regiment, troop, or body of men. 2. head, chief. **—i şeyatin** Satan.
serheng سرهنگ P *lrnd.* 1. halberdier, yeoman of the guard; policeman, watchman. 2. leader, champion. **—ân** (..—) P halberdiers; champions.

serhoş (.—) سرخوش P *lrnd.*, same as **sarhoş**. **—âne** (.——.) P in a drunken manner. **—î** (.——) P 1. drunkenness; intoxication. 2. exhilaration, delight.
serîⁱⁱ 1 (.—) سریع A 1. quick; swift, rapid, speedy. 2. *pros.* meter characterized by a trochaic-iambic foot (—..—/—..—/—.—).
seri 2 سری F series. **— halinde imal** mass production.
serian (.—'.) سریعاً A *lrnd.* quickly, speedily.
serikâr (..—) سرکار P *lrnd.* 1. supervisor; head of a business. 2. direction of public affairs. **—da bulunanlar** the leaders; the authorities.
seril=ⁱʳ سریل *pass.* of **ser=** 4.
serili سریلی stretched out or spread on the ground.
serin سرین cool; cool weather or air; chilly. **— kanla** coolly.
serinle=ʳ سرینله to cool, to become cool or chilly. **—n=** 1. to become cool. 2. to cool, to feel cool.
serinleş=ⁱʳ سرینلش to become gradually cool or cold. **—tir=** *caus.*
serinlet=ⁱʳ سرینلت /ı/ *caus.* of **serinle=**.
serinlikᵍⁱ سرینلك coolness; chilliness.
serir (.—) سریر A *lrnd.* 1. couch; throne. 2. bed. **—i basarî** *anat.* thalamus. **—i felek** constellation of the Big Dipper. **— ü efser** throne and crown.
serirârâ (.———) سریرآرا P *lrnd.* adorning the throne, ruling.
serire (.—.) سریره A *lrnd.* 1. secret, mystery. 2. heart, mind, the inner man.
serirî (.——) سریری A 1. *med.* clinical. 2. *lrnd.* pertaining to a couch or throne.
seririyat (...—) سریریات A *med.* clinical instruction. **—ı dahiliye** clinic for internal diseases. **—ı hâriciye** clinic for external diseases.
serirnişin (.—.—) سریرنشین P *lrnd.* enthroned, sitting on a throne.
seriülinfialˡⁱ (.—...—) سریع الانفعال A *lrnd.* quick to take offense, touchy.
seriülintikalˡⁱ (.—...—) سریع الانتقال A *lrnd.* quick-witted.
seriüzzevalˡⁱ (.—..—) سریع الزوال A *lrnd.* ephemeral, transient.
seriye سریّه A *lrnd.* small expeditionary corps; detached military expedition.
serkafile (.—..) سرقافله P *lrnd.* chief, leader of a caravan or troop.
serkâr (.—) سرکار P *lrnd.* steward; administrator, manager, supervisor.
serkaside (..—.) سرقصیده P *lrnd.* choice poem, masterpiece.
serkatar (..—) سرقطار P *lrnd.* leader of a file; first in a herd of camels or mules.
serkâtib (.—.), **serkâtibî** (.—.—) سرکاتبی P

serkerde سرکرده P *lrnd.* 1. secretary, confidential clerk. 2. chief clerk.
serkerde سرکرده P *lrnd.*, same as **sergerde**.
serkeş سرکش P unruly, rebellious, disobedient. **—âne** (..—.) P *lrnd.* rebelliously. **—î** (..—) P *lrnd.*, **—lik** disobedience, rebelliousness.
serkûb (.—) سرکوب P *lrnd.* 1. that knocks heads, head-striking. 2. knock on the head. 3. club, mace. 4. rebuke, reprimand.
serkûbe (.—.) سرکوبه P *lrnd.* 1. heavy mace. 2. sharp reproof.
serkûçek[ki] (.—.) سرکوچک P *lrnd.* man of no importance; vile, low, worthless.
serkûfte (.—.) سرکوفته P *lrnd.* 1. whose head has been pounded, broken-headed. 2. rebuked, reprimanded.
serkûn سرکون P *lrnd.* leader, chief (of a troop).
serkurena (...—) سرکرنا P *lrnd.* the Sultan's chief intimate.
serkûy (.—) سرکوی P *lrnd.* entrance to a street or quarter.
serlevha سرلوحه P title, heading.
serma (.—) سرما P *lrnd.* winter; cold; frost.
sermâdide (.——.) سرمادیده P *lrnd.* torpid from the cold.
sermaye (.—.) سرمایه P 1. capital, stock (of a business). 2. first cost. 3. fortune, estate, property. 4. acquired knowledge, ability. 5. *slang* prostitute. **—yi kediye yüklet=** to reduce one's property to what a cat can carry, to be bankrupt. **— koy=** /a/ to invest capital. **—i mübahat** *lrnd.* a cause of just pride. **— teşkili** capitalization, capital formation. **—ci** one who furnishes capital to traders.
sermayedar (.—.—) سرمایه دار P capitalist. **—ân** (.—.——) P capitalists.
sermayeli سرمایه لی 1. possessing capital. 2. able.
sermayesiz سرمایه سیز 1. without capital. 2. without attainments. **—lik** 1. lack of capital. 2. lack of knowledge.
serme سرمه 1. *verbal n. of* **ser=** 4. 2. spread out, laid out.
sermed سرمد A *lrnd.* the eternal presence of God; eternity. **—î** (..—) A eternal, everlasting. **—iyet** A eternity.
sermenzil سرمنزل P *lrnd.* station, final halting place.
sermest سرمست P *lrnd.* drunk, intoxicated (with joy, etc.). **—î** (..—) P intoxication.
sermu (.—) سرمو P *lrnd.* 1. end of a hair. 2. the very least space, quantity or degree; one iota.
sermuharrir سرمحرر P *obs.* editor-in-chief.
sermuri (.——) سرموری P *lrnd.* very small, minute.
sermuze (.—.) سرموزه P *lrnd.* overshoe, galosh.
sermürettib سرمرتب P *printing* chief compositor.

sername (.—.) سرنامه P *lrnd.* heading, superscription (of a writing).
sernayi (.——) سرنایی P *Mevlevi order* chief of the flute players.
sernigûn (..—) سرنگون P *lrnd.* 1. head downwards; inverted. 2. abject; depressed.
sernüvişt سرنوشت P *lrnd.* written on the forehead; destiny, predestination, fate.
serp=[er] سرپ /1, a/ 1. to sprinkle. 2. to scatter (with the hand). 3. to fall in a sprinkle or light shower. 4. *archaic* to push aside. 5. *archaic* to pat, stroke.
serpantin سرپانتین F 1. paper streamer. 2. *geol.* serpentine.
serpaş (.—) سرپاش P *lrnd.* small skullcap of steel or iron worn by warriors, capeline.
serpele=[r] سرپله to sprinkle in small drops (rain).
serpenah (..—) سرپناه P *lrnd.* helmet; mail fringe to a helmet protecting the neck.
serpençe سرپنجه P *lrnd.* 1. tip of the hand or of an animal's claws. 2. power, might; tyranny; powerful. 3. blow with the hand or talons. **—gî** (...—) P strength of fist, violence.
serpenek[gi] سرپنک *colloq. for* **serpenah**.
serpil=[ir] سرپل 1. *pass. of* **serp=**. 2. to stretch oneself out to rest. 3. to grow apace (child).
serpin=[ir] سرپن 1. to sprinkle over oneself. 2. to sprinkle slightly.
serpinti سرپنتی 1. drizzle; slight rain, sleet or snow. 2. spray from a falling liquid. 3. traces left behind; repercussion. **—sine uğra=** /ın/ 1. to feel the effects of some remote cause. 2. to be harmed as a consequence of something.
serpiştir=[ir] سرپشتر 1. to sprinkle in small quantities. 2. to scatter or distribute small amounts of money. 3. to begin to drop (rain).
serpiyadegân (..—.—) سرپیادگان P *Ott. hist.* the officers of the Janissaries.
serpme سرپمه 1. *verbal n. of* **serp=**. 2. sprinkled about; sprinkled with. 3. *fishing* cast-net. 4. *arch.* rough-cast, spatter dash. 5. *art* spotted, speckled (ornaments). **— altın** speckled gilding. **— boya** sprinkle painting; spray painting.
serptir=[ir] سرپتر /1, a/ *caus. of* **serp=**.
serpuş (.—) سرپوش P *lrnd.* headgear.
serpuşe (.—.), **serpuşide** (.——.) سرپوشه P *lrnd.* 1. headgear. 2. cover (of anything).
serra (.—) سرا A *lrnd.* 1. happiness, prosperity. 2. joy, gladness. **— ve zarra** 1. prosperity and adversity. 2. joy and sorrow.
serrişte سررشته P *lrnd.* clue, pretext, occasion. **— ver=** to afford a means, pretext or occasion.

sersam (. —) سرسام P lrnd. brain fever; delirium.

sersar (. —) سرسار A lrnd. who vociferates noisily or talks nonsensically; garrulous.

sersebük^kü سربسباك P lrnd. light-headed, vain.

sersebz سرسبز P 1. lrnd. flourishing, prosperous, happy. 2. myst. saintly. —î (.. —) P 1. luxuriance; prosperity. 2. saintliness.

sersefil (.´..) سرسفيل very miserable, thoroughly wretched.

sersem سرسم [sersam] 1. stunned, bewildered, stupified; unconscious. 2. foolish, scatterbrained, silly. — **sepelek**, — **sepet** stupid.

sersemle=^r, **sersemleş=**^ir سرسملمك 1. to be stunned or stupified; to lose one's head. 2. to become silly, absent-minded, or forgetful.

sersemlik^ği سرسملك 1. stupefaction, confusion. 2. stupidity; wool-gathering.

serseri (.. —) سرسرى P 1. vagabond, tramp, vagrant. 2. loose (mine, etc.). — **ce** (.. —´.) in the manner of a vagabond. — **lik** vagrancy, vagabondage. — **yâne** (.. — —.) P like a vagabond.

sersühan سرسخن P lrnd. the colored heading of a paragraph in old manuscripts.

serşar (. —) سرشار P lrnd. 1. brimful. 2. abundant. —î (. — —) P abundance, copiousness.

sert سرت 1. hard, rough. 2. sharp, severe, harsh, stern, austere. 3. strong, violent (wind). 4. potent; pungent. 5. fiery, mettlesome (horse). — **alçı taşı** geol. anhydride. — **buğday** hard wheat. — **çelik** tempered steel. — **doku** neol., bot. sclerenchyma. — **sessiz** neol., gram. mute. — **söyle=** to speak sharply. — **tabaka** anat. sclerotic tissue.

sertab (. —) سرتاب P lrnd. 1. that refuses or avoids. 2. overlapping part of the cover of a book in old style binding.

sertabbah (.. —) سرطبّاخ P Ott. hist. chief cook.

sertabib (.. —) سرطبيب P lrnd. head physician of a hospital.

sertac (. —) سرتاج P lrnd. 1. crown; ornament for a woman's head. 2. chief, honored person.

sertapa (. — —) سرتاپا P lrnd. from head to foot; wholly, entirely.

sertaser (. —.) سرتاسر P lrnd. from end to end; wholly, entirely.

serteraş (.. —) سرتراش P lrnd. 1. barber. 2. whose head is shaved.

serteser سرتسر P lrnd., same as **sertaser**.

sertir (. —) سرتير P lrnd. 1. chief arrow. 2. chief, leader; great, wise, learned.

sertiz (. —) سرتيز P lrnd. 1. sharp pointed (sword, thorn, etc.). 2. eyelashes of the fair.

sertlen=^ir, **sertleş=**^ir سرتلنمك سرتلشمك to become hard, severe, violent. — **dir=**, — **tir=** caus. — **diril=**, — **tiril=** pass. of **sertlendir=**, **sertleştir=**.

sertlik^ği سرتلك 1. hardness, harshness, severity. 2. violence; potency.

serv سرو P poet. 1. same as **servi**. 2. graceful youth or woman, a beauty.

servakt^ti سروقت P lrnd. one's private moments; convenient, leisure time; one's private room.

servazad (. — —) سروآزاد P lrnd. straight-grown cypress.

servendam (.. —) سرواندام P lrnd. tall and graceful as the cypress.

server سرور P lrnd. chief, prince, head. — **i enbiya**, — **i kâinat** the Prophet Muhammad. — **ân** (.. —) P pl. of **server**. —î (.. —) P, — **lik** quality of a chief; superiority.

servet ثروت A riches, wealth. — **li** wealthy.

servi سروى [serv] cypress, bot., Cupressus sempervirens. — **altı** slang the grave. — **boylu** of a slender and graceful stature. — **kavağı** lombardy poplar, bot., Populus fastigiata. — **yağı** oil of juniper. — **giller** neol., bot., Cupressiceae. — **lik** place abounding in cypresses.

servinaz (.. —) سرویناز P lrnd. 1. young and graceful cypress. 2. beautiful woman, sweetheart.

servis سرویس F 1. service. 2. department (in a bank, etc.). — **kapısı** side door (of an apartment, etc.).

servise (..´.) سرویسه It naut. service. — **takımı** service ropes, the running rigging of a ship.

servistan (.. —) سرویستان P lrnd. cypress grove.

serzede سرزده P lrnd. 1. that has been knocked on the head, who has been scolded. 2. that has happened.

serzeniş سرزنش P 1. reproach, reproof, reprimand. 2. lrnd. a knocking on the head. —i **ruzgâr** lrnd. fortune's frowns; blow dealt by fortune.

serzenişkâr (... —) سرزنشکار P lrnd. reproachful.

ses سس 1. sound; noise; voice; cry. 2. note, tone. — **le** vocal, aloud. — **bilgisi** neol., gram. phonology. — **çıkar=** 1. to speak. 2. to blab. — **çıkarma=** to say nothing, to condone. — **ini çıkarma=** to say nothing, to give no opinion. — **çıkma=** 1. to be quiet. 2. not to be heard (news). — **i çıkma=** not to say anything. — **i çıkmaz** taciturn. — **et=** 1. to make a noise. 2. to shout; to call. — **ini kes=**, — **i kesil=** to cease speaking, to be reduced to silence. — **ini kıs=** to lower one's voice. — **kirişleri** anat. vocal cords. — **sada çıkma=** to get no news whatsoever. — **sada yok** not a sound to be heard. — **şeritleri** anat.

vocal cords. — **takdim ve tehiri** *gram.* metathesis. — **türemesi** *neol., gram.* epenthesis. — **uyumu** *neol., gram.* vowel harmony in Turkish words. — **ver=** to give out a sound; to say something. — **verme=** not to answer (when called). — **yitimi** *neol., path.* aphonia.

sesle=ʳ سله‌مك سسله‌مك *prov.* /ı/ to hearken, to give ear.

seslen=ⁱʳ سسلنمك سسله‌نمك 1. /a/ to call out (to somebody). 2. to reply to one calling. 3. to speak, to say something. —**dir=** /ı/ *caus.*

seslenim *neol., physiol.* phonation.

sesli سسلی 1. having such and such a voice. 2. noisy; voiced; sounding. 3. talking (film). 4. voiced; vowel. — **benzeri** *neol., gram.* semivowel. — **oku=** to read aloud. — **taş** *geog.* phonolite, clinkstone. — **uyumu** *neol., gram.* vocalic harmony.

sessiz سسیز 1. voiceless. 2. quiet, silent, meek. 3. *music* having a poor tune. 4. *gram.* consonant. —**lik** quietness, silence, meekness.

set ست same as **sed**.

seten ساتن *var. of* **saten**.

setirᵗʳⁱ 1 ستر *var. of* **setr**.

setir 2 (.—) ستیر A *lrnd.* 1. covering, protecting; covered, concealed. 2. chaste, modest.

setire (.—.) ستیره A *lrnd.* 1. chaste, modest, veiled (woman). 2. cover.

setr ستر A *lrnd.* a covering, concealing, veiling, hiding; cover, protection. —**i avret** a covering of one's private parts.

setre ستره old-fashioned form of frock-coat.

setret=ᵈᵉʳ ستره‌تمك /ı/ to cover, to veil; to hide, to conceal.

setri (..') ستری *same as* **setre**.

settar (.—) ستّار A *lrnd.* 1. who habitually covers or veils. 2. the Veiler (of sin), God.

settarül'uyub (.—..—) ستّارالعیوب A *lrnd.* 1. God, who veils the shortcomings of men. 2. *l. c.* worn-out clothes still adequate to cover one's nakedness.

sev=ᵉʳ سومك سوه‌مك 1. to love; to like. 2. to pet, fondle, caress —**sinler!** How nice! *said sarcastically.*

seva (.—) سوا A *lrnd.* 1. equal, like; equality. 2. another; all else.

sevab (.—) ثواب A 1. God's reward for a pious act or good conduct on earth. 2. merit acquired by a good action; good deed. 3. meritorious in God's sight; that entitles to future reward. — **et=** 1. to do a good act. 2. to live virtuously. —**a gir=**, — **işle=**, — **kazan=**, —**a nail ol=** to acquire merit in God's sight.

sevabıkᵏı (.—.) ثوابق A *lrnd., pl. of* **sabıka** 1. —**ı ahval** memoranda as to the past life of an individual.

sevabit (.—.) ثوابت A *lrnd., pl. of* **sabite**.

sevad (.—) سواد A *lrnd.* 1. blackness, black clothes; black. 2. darkness. 3. writing, black ink. 4. figure of a person in the distance. 5. populous region, cultivated district; suburbs. —**i a'zam** 1. large city; Mecca. 2. the majority of Muslims, those faithful to the Caliph. 3. *myst.* the microcosm of poverty and need out of which the universe is developed. —**i hat** 1. writing ink. 2. writing; rough-draft. 3. blackness of down on the cheek.

sevadhan (.——) سوادخوان P *lrnd.* who can read a writing, reader of a book.

sevadülayn (.—..) سوادالعین A *lrnd.* iris and pupil of the eye.

sevadülbatn (.—..) سوادالبطن A *lrnd.* liver.

sevadülkalb (.—..) سوادالقلب A *lrnd.* the black core supposed to exist in the heart.

sevadülmuslimin (.—...—) سوادالمسلمین A *lrnd.* the general mass of Muslims.

sevadülvech (.—..) سوادالوجه A *lrnd.* shame, disgrace.

sevahil (.—.) سواحل A *lrnd., pl. of* **sahil** 1.

sevahir (.—.) سواهر A *lrnd., pl. of* **sahire**.

sevai (.——) سوائی A a kind of silk dress material.

sevakıb (.—.) ثواقب A *lrnd.* shiny stars.

sevaki (.—.) سواقی A *lrnd., pl. of* **sakiye**, irrigation ditches.

sevalib (.—.) سوالب A *lrnd., pl. of* **salibe**.

sevalif (.—.) سوالف A *lrnd., pl. of* **salife**.

sevalis (.—.) ثوالث A *lrnd., pl. of* **salise**.

sevamᵐᵐı (.—) سمام A *lrnd., pl. of* **samm**.

sevani (.—.) ثوانی A *lrnd., pl. of* **saniye**.

sevanih (.—.) سوانح A *lrnd., pl. of* **saniha**.

sevapᵇı ثواب *same as* **sevab**.

sevaplan=ⁱʳ ثواب قازانمق to acquire merit. —**dır=** /ı/ *caus. of* **sevaplan=**.

sevaplı ثوابلی meritorious.

sevatir (.——) سواطیر A *lrnd., pl. of* **satur**.

sevayi (.——) سوائی *same as* **sevai**.

sevb سوب A *lrnd.* 1. garment, robe. 2. piece of cloth. 3. burial-shroud.

sevda (.—) سودا A 1. love, passion; intense longing; strong wish or desire. 2. melancholy; spleen; black bile. 3. intense longing for power, ambition. 4. greed for gain. 5. *lrnd.* scheme, project; trade, commerce, business. 6. *lrnd.* blackness. — **çek=** to be deeply in love. —**yi hâm** *lrnd.* crude aspiration, scheme or project. **bir —dan vazgeç=** to give up an idea.

sevdager (.—.) سوداگر P *lrnd.* 1. merchant, trader. 2. melancholic. —**î** (.—.—) P, —**lik** *lrnd.* trade, commerce.

sevdaî (.——) سودائی P *lrnd.* 1. pertaining to trade. 2. melancholic.

sevdakede (.—..) سوداکده P *lrnd.* 1. shop. 2. the world.

sevdalan=ⁱʳ سودالنمك to fall in love.
sevdalı سودالى 1. madly in love. 2. melancholic, monomaniacal.
sevdaperest (.—..) سوداپرست P lrnd. 1. slave to his own desires; ambitious. 2. sensual.
sevdavî (.——) سوداوى P lrnd. 1. melancholic, atrabilious; amorous. 2. pertaining to the black bile.
sevdazede (.—..) سودازده P lrnd. 1. in deep love. 2. melancholic.
sevdir=ⁱʳ سودرمك سوديرمك /ı, a/ caus. of sev=.
seveban (..—) نواب A lrnd. 1. a recovering health; recovery. 2. a returning; return.
sevgend سوگند P lrnd. oath, a swearing.
sevgi سوگى 1. love, affection. 2. compassion.
sevgili سوگيلى 1. beloved; dear, darling. 2. lovable.
sevi 1 سوى archaic love, affection.
sevi 2 (.—) سوّى A lrnd. 1. equal; uniform. 2. even, level. 3. straight, erect.
sevici سويجى 1. one who loves or likes. 2. lesbian. 3. archaic lover. —**lik** lesbianism, Sapphism.
sevil=ⁱʳ سويلمك pass. of sev=.
sevim سويم 1. love, affection. 2. affability, charm. —**li** lovable, affable; genial, charming. —**siz** unattractive, unlikable.
sevin=ⁱʳ سونمك 1. to be glad, to be pleased. 2. /a/ to be happy, to rejoice (at).
sevinçᶜⁱ سوينج joy, pleasure, delight. —**inden yere basma**= to jump for joy. —**li** joyful.
sevindir=ⁱʳ سوينديرمك /ı/ caus. of sevin=, to please.
seviniş, sevinme سوينش verbal n. of sevin=.
sevirᵛʳⁱ سور [sevr] 1. astr. the constellation Taurus. 2. lrnd. bull.
seviş 1 سوييش mode of loving; manner of caressing.
seviş=ⁱʳ **2** سويشمك 1. to love or caress one another; to make love. 2. to like one another, to be good friends.
seviye سويّه A 1. level, rank, degree. 2. equality; (social) standing. —**li** of good standing.
sevkᵏⁱ سوق A 1. a driving, urging, inciting. 2. a sending, shipping. 3. dispatch (of troops, etc.). —**ı tabii*. — ü idare** 1. management, control. 2. mil. leadership and administration of an army.
sevket=ᵈᵉʳ سوقتمك /ı/ 1. to drive, impel. 2. to urge, incite. 3. to send.
sevkıtabii (.'..——) سوق طبيعى A instinct, impulse.
sevkıyat (..—) سوقيات A dispatch of troops, consignment of goods.

sevkülceyş سوق الجيش A mil. strategy. —**î** (...—) A strategic.
sevm سوم A lrnd. 1. an asking, offering or setting a price. 2. a price asked, a set price.
sevme سومه verbal n. of sev=.
sevr ثور A lrnd., same as sevir.
sevre ثوره A lrnd. cow.
sevret سورت A lrnd. 1. assault, attack. 2. tyranny, power, despotism. 3. virulence (of poison); strength (of wine). 4. ardor, impetuosity. 5. fierceness (of a battle), severity (of cold).
sevsen سوسن A lrnd. any iridaceous plant such as the iris, ixia, and gladiolus.
sevsene سوسنه A lrnd. iris.
sevsengûş (..—) سوسنگوش P lrnd. having ears shaped like lilies (horse).
sevsenî (..—) سوسنى A lrnd. pertaining to the iris. —**ye** bot., Iridaceae.
sevsenzeban (...—) سوسن زبان P lrnd. unable to speak, silent, mute.
sevü, sevükᵍᵘ سوى archaic, same as sevi 1.
=**sevüz** سوز cf. =savuz.
seyadet (.—.) سيادت A lrnd. 1. nobility, chieftainship; dominion, rule. 2. a being a descendant of the Prophet Muhammad.
seyadetintisab (.—...—) سيادت انتساب P lrnd. related to the princely line of the Prophet Muhammad.
seyadetlû (.—.—) سيادتلو descended from the Prophet Muhammad.
seyahat (.—.) سياحت A 1. journey, trip, voyage; expedition. 2. myst. religious vagabondage. — **çeki** traveler's check. — **et**= to travel.
seyahatname (.—.—.) سياحتنامه P book of travels.
=**seydi** سيدى cf. =saydı.
seydudet (.—.) سيدودت A lrnd. 1. a being or becoming a master, lord, prince; rank, noble lineage. 2. a being a descendant of the Prophet Muhammad.
seyekᵏⁱ (.'.) سه يك P dice games three and one.
seyelân (..—) سيلان A 1. a flowing, streaming. 2. an incursion spreading over a country, flood. 3. phys. flux. — **et**= to stream, pour, flow, flux. —**ı dem** path. hemorrhage. —**ı meni** path. spermatorrhoea.
seyeran (..—) سيران A lrnd., same as seyran.
seyf سيف A lrnd. sword. —**i sârım** sharp sword.
seyfî (.—) سيفى A 1. pertaining to the sword. 2. pertaining to the military or naval service. 3. w. cap., man's name.

seyfüddin سیف الدین A *lrnd.* the sword of religion, religion's soldier.
seyfullah سیف الله A *lrnd.* 1. the sword or soldier of God. 2. *w. cap.*, man's name.
seyikᵍⁱ سیك *prov.* surgical splint.
seyikle= سیكله مك /ı/ to tie up with splints, to splint.
seyirʸʳⁱ 1 سیر [seyr] 1. a moving in a course, going along, progress, motion. 2. spectacle, show; something to be seen. 3. a looking on, seeing any spectacle or action. 4. a going about for air and recreation; excursion; travel, voyage. 5. *myst.* spiritual progress. 6. *Or. mus.* the succession of tones creating the characteristics of the **makams**. **— e çık=** to go for a walk or ride, to make an excursion. **— jurnalı** *naut.* log book. **— kılavuz kitabı** *naut.* sailing directions. **—i müstevi** *naut.* plane sailing. **—i mütevazi** *naut.* parallel sailing. **— tecrübesi** *naut.* trial trip. **— var** There is something to be seen; there is a spectacular sight. **— yeri** place of amusement.
seyir=ⁱʳ 2 سیرمك سیر لمك, *same as* **seğir=**.
seyirci سیرجی spectator; one who merely looks on. **— kal=** to be a mere spectator.
seyirme سیرمه tremulous vibration in a nerve or muscle; nervous twitch.
seyis سایس ساییس A 1. groom, horse keeper. 2. who manages property.
seyishane (..—.) سایس خانه P 1. baggage of a prince or grandee (when traveling). 2. sumpter-horse, pack-horse. **— beygiri** baggage horse.
seyl سیل A *lrnd.*, *same as* **sel 1**.
seylâb (.—), **seylâbe** (.—.) سیلاب سیلابه P *lrnd.* flood, torrent. **—i eşk** floods of tears.
Seylân سیلان *geog.* Ceylon. **— taşı** garnet, carbuncle. **—î** 1. Ceylonese, Singhalese. 2. Ceylon garnet, Ceylon carbuncle.
seylâverd (.—.) سیلاورد P *lrnd.* brought by a torrent.
seylgâh (.—) سیلگاه P *lrnd.* 1. place where a torrent flows, torrent bed. 2. the world.
seylhiz (.—) سیلخیز P *lrnd.* streaming (eye); torrent.
seylrâm (.—) سیلرام P *lrnd.* pouring forth a torrent.
seyman سیمن *same as* **segban**.
seyr سیر A *lrnd.* 1. *same as* **seyir 1**. 2. a behaving. **— ü menakıb** the deeds, qualities and history of a great man. **— ü sülûk***.
seyran (.—) سیران P 1. a walking or riding for pleasure; pleasure trip, excursion. 2. a looking on, seeing, contemplating. 3. *myst.* dream. **—a çık=**, **— et=** to go for a trip, to make an excursion.
seyrangâh (.——) سیرانگاه P *lrnd.* place of recreation, a place of public promenade, pleasure spot.
seyrekᵍⁱ سیرك wide apart, open; few and far between; at infrequent intervals; rare; rarely; loosely woven, sparse. **—ce** (...') somewhat infrequent; quite rare.
seyrekleş=ⁱʳ سیركلشمك to become infrequent; to be at wide intervals. **—tir=** /ı/ *caus.*
seyreklikᵍⁱ سیركلك 1. distance of intervals; rarity of occurence, infrequency. 2. looseness of texture.
seyrel=ⁱʳ سیرلمك سیركلمك *same as* **seyrekleş=**. **—t=** /ı/ *caus.*
seyret=ᵈᵉʳ سیرتمك 1. /ı/ to look, see (spectacle). 2. to move, to go along. 3. *lrnd.* to behave, conduct oneself. **— sen!** Now you'll see (what's going to happen).
seyrgâh (.—) سیرگاه P *lrnd.*, *same as* **seyrangâh**.
seyrifilmenam (....—) سیر فی المنام A *lrnd.* somnambulism.
seyrisefain (...—.) سیر سفاین A art and science of navigation; navigation.
seyrüsefer سیر و سفر A traffic (of vehicles, etc.). **— memuru** traffic policeman.
seyrüsülûkᵏᵘ̈ (...—) سیر و سلوك A *lrnd.* special training of a religious order.
seyyaf (.—) سیاف A *lrnd.* 1. maker or seller of swords. 2. swordsman. 3. executioner.
seyyah (.—) سیاح A traveler; tourist. **— ver=** *myst.* orders to decree a period of traveling for a member of the order. **—in** (.——) *lrnd.*, *pl.*
seyyalⁱⁱ (.—) سیال A *lrnd.* fluid, liquid.
seyyale (.—.) سیاله A *lrnd.* fluid. **—i berkıye** electric current.
seyyan (.—) سیان A *lrnd.* two equal things. **— tut=** to make no distinction between two things or persons.
seyyanen (.—'.) سیانا A *lrnd.* in equal parts, share and share alike.
seyyar سیار A habitually moving; itinerant; mobile; portable. **— satıcı** street peddler, itinerant peddler. **— tekke** *slang* car used as a hideout for taking drugs. **— ticaret memuru** travelling salesman.
seyyarat (.——) سیارات A *lrnd.*, *pl.* of **seyyare**.
seyyare (.—.) سیاره A *astr.* planet.
seyyi سیئی A *lrnd.* bad, evil.
seyyiat (..—) سیئات A *lrnd.*, *pl.* of **seyyie**.
seyyib, seyyibe ثیب A *lrnd.* 1. no longer a virgin; married woman. 2. widow.
seyyid سید A *lrnd.* master, lord, chief; Seyyid (descendant of the Prophet). **S—i Kâinat** the Prophet Muhammad.
seyyidan (..—) سیدان A *lrnd.* the two

princes: the Prophet Muhammad's two grandsons.
seyyide سيّدة A *lrnd.* lady; princess; queen; a female descendant of the Prophet Muhammad. **S—i nisa-ül-âlemin** Fatima, daughter of the Prophet.
Seyyidetülarab سيّدة العرب A *Isl. hist.* Fatima, the Prophet's eldest daughter.
Seyyidetülmuhadderat (.......—) سيّدة المخدّرات A *lrnd.* (*lit.*, Queen of the veiled ones.) Muslim princess of a sovereign house.
seyyidî (..—) سيّدى A *lrnd.* pertaining to a master or lord; pertaining to a descendant of the Prophet Muhammad.
seyyidlik[gi] سيّدلك the quality of a lord or master, *esp.*, a descendant of the Prophet Muhammad.
Seyyidülafak[kı] (...——) سيّد الآفاق A *Isl. rel.* the Prophet Muhammad.
seyidülasfiya (.....—) سيّد الاصفياء A *lrnd.* an eminently pious learned man.
Seyyidülebrar (....—) سيّد الابرار A *Isl. rel.* the Prophet Muhammad.
Seyyidülenam (....—) سيّد الانام A *Isl. rel.* the Prophet Muhammad.
Seyyidülenbiya (.....—) سيّد الانبياء A *Isl. rel.* the Prophet Muhammad.
Seyyidülkevneyn سيّد الكونين A *Isl. rel.* the Prophet Muhammad.
Seyyidülmürselin (.....—) سيّد المرسلين A *Isl. rel.* the Prophet Muhammad.
Seyyidüssadat (...——) سيّد السادات A *Isl. rel.* the Prophet Muhammad; lord of lords; any descendant of the Prophet, eminently distinguished for virtue and learning.
Seyyidüssakaleyn سيّد الثقلين A *Isl. rel.* the Prophet Muhammad.
seyyie سيّئة A *lrnd.* evil thing, evil; evil act; sin, evil consequence. **—sini çek**= /ın/ to suffer the consequence of an evil act.
sez=[er] سزمك /ı/ to perceive, feel; to discern.
seza (.—) سزا P 1. fit, suitable, becoming; convenient. 2. merited punishment or reward; merited. **—dır** Serves him right. **—sını ver**= /ın/ to inflict a merited punishment (on).
sezaryen سزاريان F *surg.* Caesarean (operation).
sezavar (.——) سزاوار P *lrnd.* /a/ worthy of, deserving. **—î** (.———) P, **—lık** worthiness, deservingness.
sezdir=[ir] سزدرمك /ı, a/ *caus.* of **sez**=.
sezgi *neol.* 1. perception, discernment. 2. *phil.* intuition. **—cilik** *phil.* intuitionism. **—li** intuitive.
sezi *neol.* feeling; intuition.
sezil=[ir] سزلمك *pass.* of **sez**=.
sezin=[ir], **sezinle**=[r], **sezinse**=[r] سزينمك سزينلمك سزينسمك /ı/ to be aware (of), to be conscious (of); to have an inkling (of).

sezinti *neol.* perception; inkling.
seziş, sezme سزيش سزمه *verbal n.* of **sez**=.
sezü سزو cork oak, cork tree, *bot.*, *Quercus suber.*
-sı 1 سى *cf.* **-ı 3.**
-sı 2, -si, *etc.* سى somewhat like, resembling, as in **kadınsı.**
sı=[r] **3** سمق سمك archaic /ı/ 1. to break; to demolish, smash, knock to pieces. 2. to defeat, scatter, annihilate (an enemy). 3. to reject.
sıbağ (.—) صباغ A *lrnd.* dye, pigment.
sıbg صبغ A *lrnd.* dye.
sıbgat صبغت A *lrnd.* 1. a mode of dyeing; dye. 2. the law of God as communicated to the Prophet Muhammad. 3. Christian baptism by immersion.
sıbgatullâh (...—), **sıbgat-ül-İslâm** (....—) صبغة الله صبغة الاسلام A *Isl. rel.* the true faith received in the heart.
sıbt سبط A *lrnd.* 1. family, progeny; tribe. 2. a son's son, a daughter's son.
sıbteyn سبطين A *lrnd.* the two sons of Ali, Hasan and Huseyn.
sıbyan (.—) صبيان A *pl.* of **sabi 1.** **— mektebi** *Ott. hist.* primary school.
sıcacık[gi] (.'..) صجاجق warm; pleasantly hot.
sıcak[gı] صجاق 1. hot; heat. 2. public bath. 3. warm, hearty. **—lar bastı** The weather has become suddenly warm; it is very hot. **—a git**= to go to a public bath. **— kanlı** 1. amiable; lovable. 2. warm-hearted. **(bu) —a kar mı dayanır** Such expenditure couldn't go on like that. **— renkler** *art* bright colors. **— sıcak** fresh and hot (food). **—ı sıcağına** while the iron is hot; at once. **— terazisi** *obs.* thermometer. **— tut**= /ı/ to keep warm. **— yüzlü** amiable; attractive. **—lık** 1. heat; warmth. 2. *archeol.* sudatorium. **—ölçer** *neol.* thermometer.
sıç=[ar] صيچمق *vulgar* 1. to defecate, excrete. 2. to befoul or spoil something.
sıçan صيچان rat; mouse. **— çıktığı deliği bilir** *proverb* A child estranged from his parents will some day be reconciled. **— derisi** various furs of small animals; moleskin. **— dişi** a fine edging to linen, hemmed seam. **—a dön**= to get very wet. **— düşse başı yarılır** completely empty. **— giremediği deliğe bir de kabak bağlarmış** *cf.* **fare.** **— kırı** mouse-colored (horse); dark gray. **— kulağı** chickweed, *bot.*, *Cerastium arvense;* water mouse-ear, *bot.*, *Myosotis stricta.* **— kuyruğu** 1. mousetail, black grass, *bot.*, *Alopecurus agrestis;* mousetail, blood strange, *bot.*, *Mysosurus minimus.* 2. rat-tailed file; round tapering file. **— oluğu** *arch.* gutter overhang. **— otu** arsenic (as rat poison). **— tüyü** mouse

color. — **yılı** *hist.* the Rat year (the first year in the Turkish cycle of twelve years). **— yolu** 1. covered way outside a fortification; military zigzag. 2. underground passage, gallery for a landmine. **—cıl** kite, *zool., Milvus regalis.*

sıçıl=ᴵʳ صيجلامس *vulgar* 1. *pass.* of **sıç=**. 2. to be covered with one's own dirt. 3. to be filthy. 4. to be damaged (things).

sıçırgan, sıçırtgan صيجرغان، صيجرتغان *vulgar* unable to control one's bowels or bladder, incontinent.

sıçra=ʳ صيجرامه 1 to leap, spring, jump. 2. to start; to spurt out, to hop. 3. to splash. 4. to attack and spring upon, to bounce upon.

sıçrama صيجرامه *verbal n.* of **sıçra=**. **— tahtası** springboard.

sıçrantı صيجرنتى particles that fly, splash, spurt from a thing.

sıçraş=ᴵʳ صيجراشمق to leap, spring, jump with, upon, or over one another.

sıçrat=ᴵʳ صيجراتمق *caus.* of **sıçra=**. **—ma** *verbal n.* **—ma menteşesi** a kind of hinge.

sıçrayış صيجرايش *verbal n.* of **sıçra=**.

sıçtır=ᴵʳ صيجديرمك /ı/ *vulgar, caus.* of **sıç=**.

sıdakᵏᴵ (. —) صداق A *lrnd.* marriage settlement (portion which the husband engages to give to his future wife).

sıddikᵏᴵ (. —) صدّيق A *lrnd.* eminently truthful, true, sincere, *title given to Abu Bakr.*

sıddika (. — .) صدّيقة A *lrnd.* truthful lady, *title given to Mary, the Mother of Jesus, and to Aisha, wife of the Prophet Muhammad.*

sıddikî (. — —) صدّيقى A *lrnd.* 1. pertaining to a most truthful man or saint. 2. pertaining to Abu Bakr. **—yet** (. — . .) A the quality of utmost veracity.

sıddikûn (. — —) صدّيقون A *lrnd.* saints who bear witness to God's truth.

sıdıkᵈᵏᴵ صدى *var.* of **sıdk**.

sıdkᵏᴵ صدق A 1. truth, veracity; sincerity. 2. *lrnd.* reality; correctness. **—ı derun** *lrnd.* inward honesty, truthfulness of heart. **— ile çalış=** to give one's all, to put one's heart into one's work. **—ı sıyrıl=** /dan/ to lose faith in a person.

sıfakᵏᴵ (. —) صفاق A 1. *lrnd.* any thin membrane beneath the skin. 2. *anat.* fascia.

sıfat 1 صفت A 1. quality, attribute. 2. appearance, aspect. 3. *gram.* adjective. 4. character, capacity. **— ve mevsuf** *gram.* an adjective and the noun it modifies.

sıfat 2 (. —) صفات A *lrnd., pl.* of **sıfat 1**. **—ı âliye** *phil.* the transcendentals. **—ı cemaliye** *lrnd.* God's attributes such as mercy and compassion. **—ı ilâhiye** *lrnd.* divine attributes. **—ı selbiye** *lrnd.* the negative attributes of God (as uncreated, unbegotten, and undying).

—ı sübutiye *lrnd.* attributes special to God only, such as might, power, glory, etc.

Sıffîn (. —) صفّين A *Isl. hist.* place near the right bank of the Euphrates famous for the great battle between Ali and Muawiya.

sıfır صفر [sıfr] zero, naught; nothing. **— numara** *slang* excellent. **— numara traş** the closest possible haircut. **—a sıfır elde var bir** add zero to zero and carry one (*i. e.,* the barest minimum). **—ı tüket=** *colloq.* to exhaust one's means; to be destitute.

sıfr صفر A *lrnd.* 1. *same as* **sıfır**. 2. empty.

sıfrülyed صفراليد A *lrnd.* 1. empty-handed, poor. 2. utterly disappointed.

sıgar 1 (. —) صغار A *lrnd., pl.* of **sagir**. **— ü kibâr** young and old.

sıgar 2 صغر A *lrnd.* 1. a being small; smallness. 2. a being young. 3. a being insignificant; insignificance. **—i cirm** smallness of body. **—i cürm** smallness of guilt.

sığ 1 صيغ 1. shallow. 2. shoal, sandbank. **—a düş=** to be driven onto a shallow (ship). **—a otur=** to run aground (ship).

sığ=ᵃʳ 2 صيغمق /a/ to fit into; to be contained by.

sığa 1 *neol., phys.* capacity.

sığa=ʳ 2 صيغامق 1. to tuck up, roll up (skirts, shirt sleeves etc.) 2. to rub with the hand; to smooth, to massage.

sığa 3 صغا *archaic, same as* **sığ 1**.

sığaca صيغاجا saw for cutting thick timber.

sığan=ᴵʳ صيغانمق *same as* **sıvan= 2**.

sığdır=ᴵʳ صيغديرمك /ı, a/ to make a thing go into (a receptacle); to cram in, squeeze in, force into. **—ama=** (içine veya aklına) /ı/ not to be able to comprehend or digest.

sığın 1 صيغين moose, elk. **— çatalı** antlers of a stag. **— topuğu** horn cup.

sığın=ᴵʳ 2 صيغينمق /a/ 1. to take shelter (in); to take refuge (with). 2. to squeeze oneself and crouch (into a narrow place).

sığınakᵍᴵ *neol.* shelter (alpine, air raid, etc.).

sığınca, sığıncakᵍᴵ صيغنجى، صيغنجاك *archaic* refuge, shelter.

sığındır=ᴵʳ صيغنديرمك /ı/ *caus.* of **sığın= 2**.

sığıntı صيغنتى *derogatory* 1. one who takes refuge or to whom shelter has been given. 2. parasite.

sığır صيغير 1. ox; bull, cow, buffalo. 2. cattle. **— baldıranı** water-hemlock, cowbane, *bot., Cicuta virosa.* **— dili***. **— eti** beef. **— gözü***. **— kuyruğu***. **— mantarı***. **— şeridi** tapeworm, *zool., Taenia saginata.* **— topuğu** a kind of drinking cup.

sığırcıkᵍᴵ صيغرجيك starling, *zool., Sturnus vulgaris.*

sığırdiliⁿᴵ صيغرديلى 1. oxtongue, bugloss, *bot., Anchusa.* 2. ox tongue, salted and smoked.

3. book opened lengthwise. — **yutmadım** I haven't eaten an ox's tongue (and acquired his patience). I am sick of telling you! **—giller** *neol., bot., Anchusa.*

sığırgözüⁿᵘ ﺻﻴﻐﺮﮔﻮزى corn marigold, *bot., Chrysanthemum segetum,* ox-eye daisy, *bot., Chrysanthemum leucanthemum.*

sığırkuyruğu ﺻﻴﻐﺮﻗﻮﻳﺮوﻏﻰ great mullein, *bot., Verbascum thapsus;* mullein, cow's lungwort, *bot., Verbascum.*

sığırmantarıⁿⁱ ﺻﻴﻐﺮ ﻣﺎﻧﻄﺎرى lycoperdon nuts, *bot., Elaphomyces granulatus, Elaphomyces muricatus.*

sığırlıkᵍⁱ ﺻﻴﻐﺮﻟﻖ 1. nature of an ox. 2. bovine stupidity; boorishness.

sığırtmaçᶜⁱ ﺻﻴﻐﺮﺗﻤﺎج ﺳﻐﺮﺗﻤﺎج herdsman, drover.

sığış 1 ﺻﻴﻐﺶ ﺻﻐﻴﺶ *verbal n.* of **sığ= 2.**

sığış=ⁱʳ **2** ﺻﻴﻐﺸﻤﻖ /a/ to squeeze or fit into a confined space with difficulty. **—ma** *verbal n.* **—tır=** /ı, a/ *caus. of* **sığış=.** **—tırıl=** *pass.*

sığlıkᵍⁱ ﺻﻴﻐﻠﻖ 1. shallowness. 2. shallow, sandbank.

sıhhatᵗⁱ ﺻﺤّﺖ A 1. health. 2. truth; truthfulness, correctness. **—te bulun=** to be in good health. **S— ve İçtimaî Muavenet Vekâleti** *obs.* Ministry of Public Health and Welfare. **—ler olsun** Good health to you! *said to one having had a bath, haircut or a shave.* **—ini tahkik et=** /ın/ to ascertain the truth (of).

sıhhatli ﺻﺤّﺘﻰ in good health, healthy.

sıhhî (. —) ﺻﺤّﻰ A pertaining to health; hygienic.

sıhhiye ﺻﺤّﻴﻪ [*based on* **sıhhî**] 1. sanitary matters. 2. public health. **S— Vekâleti** *obs.* Ministry of Health.

sıhhiyun (. — —) ﺻﺤّﻴﻮن A *lrnd.* specialists in sanitary matters.

sıhr ﺻﻬﺮ A *lrnd.* 1. affinity by marriage; in-law relationship. 2. relation by marriage, especially, son-in-law, father-in-law. **—î** (. —) A pertaining to relationship by marriage, to relations-in-law.

sıhriyet ﺻﻬﺮﻳّﺖ A *lrnd.* relationship by marriage.

sık 1 ﺻﻴﻖ 1. close together; dense, thick. 2. frequently occurring; frequent, often; numerous. 3. closely woven; tight. **— doku=** to investigate minutely, to be very particular. **— sık** frequently; often.

sık=ᵃʳ **2** ﺻﻴﻘﻤﻖ /ı/ 1. to squeeze, to press; to wring out, to juice. 2. to tighten; to put pressure on. 3. to cause annoyance, embarrassment, or discomfort. 4. to dun (for payment). 5. to put financial pressure on someone. 6. to discharge (firearm).

sıkboğaz ﺻﻴﻖ ﺑﻮﻏﺎز urgently. **— et=** /ı/ to take by the throat; to force someone to do something.

sıkça (. .́) ﺻﻴﻘﺠﻪ somewhat close, dense, or frequent; often.

sıkı ﺻﻴﻘﻰ 1. tight; firmly driven or wedged in. 2. severe, strict; severe menace or reprimand. 3. hurried, brisk (pace). 4. high, heavy (gale). 5. tight-fisted, stingy. 6. pressing necessity, fatigue, or trouble; straits. 7. wad used in small-arms. 8. *school slang* nice, pleasant. **— bas!** Hold tight! Don't give way. **— bas=** to use one's authority (against others in doing something). **— çalış=** to work hard. **—ya dayan=** to stand hard work, to brave trouble. **— dur=** to hold fast; to sit tight. **— düzen** discipline; orderliness. **— es=** to blow a gale. **—ya gel=** to meet with great difficulty, to be hard put to it. **—yı görünce** when pressed, compelled, or threatened. **— isen** *vulgar* If you dare! **—ya koy=** /ı/ to press somebody hard; to try to force someone to do something. **— tut=** 1. to hold tight. 2. to rule or control firmly. **—yı ye=** to receive a severe threat or reprimand. **— yönetim** *neol.* martial law. **— yürü=** to walk briskly.

sıkıcı ﺻﻴﻘﻴﺠﻰ tiresome, boring.

sıkıfıkı ﺻﻴﻘﻰ ﻓﻴﻘﻰ close together, intimate.

sıkıl=ⁱʳ ﺻﻴﻘﻠﻤﻖ 1. *pass.* of **sık= 2.** 2. to be bored, annoyed, uneasy, ashamed.

sıkıla=ʳ ﺻﻴﻘﻴﻼﻣﻖ /ı/ *same as* **sık= 2.**

sıkılcım ﺻﻴﻘﻠﺠﻢ *archaic* crowdedness; narrowness; tightness.

sıkılgan ﺻﻴﻘﻠﻐﺎن bashful, shy; easily embarrassed; awkward. **— olmıyan** unconstrained. **—lık** shyness, bashfulness.

sıkılıkᵍⁱ ﺻﻴﻘﻴﻠﻖ 1. tightness, firmness, closeness. 2. briskness, violence. 3. tight-fistedness, stinginess.

Sıkılıye (. . .́ .) ﺻﻘﻠﻴّﻪ A *lrnd., geog.* Sicily.

sıkım ﺻﻴﻘﻢ 1. *verbal n.* of **sık= 2.** 2. *prov.* one handful squeezed by the hand. **—lık** *in* **bir sıkımlık canı var** You could knock him down with a feather *said of a very weak person.*

sıkın=ⁱʳ ﺻﻴﻘﻴﻨﻤﻖ *prov.* to restrain, constrain oneself.

sıkıntı ﺻﻴﻘﻨﺘﻰ ﺻﻴﻘﻨﺘﻰ 1. discomfort; distress; embarrassment; weariness; worry. 2. financial straits. 3. boredom, annoyance, suffering. 4. *archaic* anything squeezed out, as juice, oil etc. **— bas=** to be distressed, to be bored, fed up. **— çek=** to suffer annoyance or inconvenience. **—ya düş=** to be hard up. **—ya geleme=** to have no stamina to withstand hardship. **—da ol=** to be in straits. **— ver=** to annoy.

sıkıntılı ﺻﻴﻘﻨﺘﻴﻠﻰ 1. one who has trouble or suffers from boredom. 2. that gives trouble, embarrass-

sıkış ment or annoyance; depressive. — **Raziye** person who gets tired of everything very quickly.

sıkış 1 صيقش *verbal n. of* **sık=** 2.

sıkış=ᵗʳ **2** صيقشير 1. to be closely pressed together; to be crowded together. 2. to be in trouble. 3. to become urgent. 4. to be squeezed, tightened.

sıkışıkᵍ¹ صيقشق 1. closely pressed together, close; crowded. 2. congested. 3. tight. **—lık** closeness, compactness.

sıkıştır=ᵗʳ صيقشتيريم صيقشديرم 1. /ı/ *caus. of* **sıkış=** 2. 2. /ı/ to force by importunity. 3. /ı/ to cross-question closely; to torture judicially, to oppress. 4. /a, ı/ to slip (money etc.) quietly into another's hand as a gift or alms. 5. /ı/ to hasten, quicken, press. **—ıl=** *pass.* **—ma** 1. *verbal n.* 2. *mech.* compression.

sıkıt 1 *neol., chem.* condensed, compressed.

sıkıtᵏᵗⁱ **2** سقط [sıkt] *physiol.* miscarriage.

sıkkın صيقين 1. annoyed, disgusted; distressed. 2. in difficulty, in need.

sıkla=ʳ صيقدرم 1. to sob. 2. *archaic* to whistle.

Sıklâb (. —) صقلب A *lrnd.* a Slav.

sıklan=ᵗʳ صيقدنم *same as* **sıklaş=**. **—dır=** /ı/ *caus.*

sıklaş=ᵗʳ صيقدشم 1. to become frequent (in time or space). 2. to be closely woven. 3. to be close together. **—tır=** /ı/ *caus.*

sıklat=ᵗʳ صيقدتم *caus. of* **sıklan=**

sıklet ثقلت A 1. heaviness, weight. 2. oppressiveness, pressure. 3. uneasiness, languor, oppression of the body. 4. tedium; depression. **— çek=** to be bored. **—i izafiye** *phys.* specific gravity. **— merkezi** *phys.* center of gravity. **—i mutlaka** *phys.* absolute gravity. **— ver=** to annoy, bore. **—i zatiye** *lrnd.* specific gravity.

sıkletâver (. . — .) ثقلت آور P *lrnd.* tedious.

sıklıkᵍ¹ **1** صيقليق 1. frequency (of repetition). 2. densely populated. 3. density of texture or arrangement.

sıklıkᵍ¹ **2** صيقلى صيقايى صيقلير سقى *archaic* a whistling. **— çal=**, **— ver=** to whistle.

sıkma صيقمه 1. *verbal n. of* **sık=** 2. 2. squeezed; pressed; pressed out. 3. a kind of tightly fitting trousers. 4. *prov.* a kind of brassiere.

sıkt ثط A *lrnd., same as* **sıkıt** 2.

sıktır=ᵗʳ صيقديرم صيقديريرم *caus. of* **sık=** 2. **—ıl=** *pass.*

sıla صله A 1. a being united with one's friends or family; reunion. 2. visit to one's native place. 3. *lrnd.* a doing something to recall oneself to the mind of friends or relations after long absence. 4. *Arabic gram.* relative pronoun. **—sını çek=** /ın/ to feel homesick (for). **—ya git=** to visit one's native country, to go home. **— hastalığı** homesickness, nostalgia. **—i rahm** *lrnd.* 1. a visit to one's relations. 2. message, letter or present sent to relatives from a distance.

sılacı صلەجى who sets off to visit his home; on leave (soldier).

sılât (. —) صلات A *lrnd., pl. of* **sıla**, acts or things that serve to unite people.

sımah (. —) صماخ A *lrnd.* channel of the ear, ear-hole; ear.

sımam (. —), **sımame** (. — .) صمام صمامه A 1. *path.* embolism. 2. *lrnd.* stopper, plug, cork.

sımız=ᵗʳ صيميزم *archaic* to break one's oath.

sımızdı صمزدى disloyalty; disloyal person.

sımsıkı (. ˙. .) صيم صيقى very tight; squeezed; narrow.

-sın 1, -sin, *etc.* سڭ |*pl.* -sınız, *etc.*| 2nd. *pers. sing., familiar form* you are, *e. g.* **kimsin?** Who are you?

=sın 2, =sin, *etc.* سين *imperative 3rd pers. sing.,* may he, *e. g.,* **kalsın** May he stay. Let him stay.

sın=ᵃʳ **3** صينى *archaic* 1. to break, to become broken. 2. to be routed; to be scattered. 3. to be penniless, bankrupt.

sına=ʳ صينامه صناميه /ı/ 1. to try, to test. 2. to sniff in order to recognize.

sınaatᵗⁱ **1** (. — .) صناعت A *lrnd.* 1. craft; art; industry. 2. trick of the trade; method of procedure.

sınaat 2 (. — —) صناعات A *lrnd., pl. of* **sınaat 1**. **—i hams** *logic* the five methods of argument. **—i seb'** the liberal arts.

sınaî (. — —) صناعى A 1. pertaining to craftsmanship; industrial. 2. artificial. **— haklar** *law* patent rights. **— müessese** industrial enterprise.

sınamsa=ʳ صناماسه *archaic* to be over-nice, hypercritical.

sınamsıkᵍ¹ صناميسيق *archaic* over-nice, hypercritical, hard to please.

sınan=ᵗʳ, **sınanıl=**ᵗʳ صينانم صناناليم *pass. of* **sına=**. **—mış** 1. tried and liked. 2. recognized and befriended.

sınar - صينار *archaic* 1. experienced, accustomed to, easily adapting himself to circumstances. 2. that sniffs at another of his own kind, recognizes and befriends it (animal). **—a andır=** to put one in mind of a similar animal. **—ına çek=** to run true to form (often in a bad sense).

sınat=ᵗʳ صيناتم /ı, a/ *caus. of* **sına=**.

sınav *neol.* examination. **—la=** /ı/ to examine, test.

sıncan سنجان *same as* **sincan**.

sındı صيندى *archaic* large shears.

sındık^{ği} صنديق *archaic* which has been broken or defeated; scene of a defeat.
-sındır 1 (.´.), **-sindir**, *etc.* ـسـْـندر You are surely ..., *e. g.*, **yorgunsundur** You must be tired.
sındır=^{ır} **2** صنديرمه *archaic* /ı/ 1. to defeat utterly, to wipe out, to rout. 2. to break.
sındırgı, sındırık^{ği} صنديرغى صنديريجه *archaic* place of defeat; defeat, rout.
sındid (.—) صنديد A *lrnd.* chief, lord, king.
sıngın, singun سنغين مينغون *archaic* 1. broken; defeated, routed. 2. break, smash; defeat, rout.
-sını سنى *cf.* **-ı 3**.
sınıf صنف [*Arabic* **sınf**] 1. class; category. 2. sort, kind. 3. classroom. **—ta çak=** school slang to fail to repeat the class. **—ta kal=** to fail (in one's class). **—la=** *neol.* to classify. **—lama** *phil.*, *biol.* classification.
sınık^{ği} صنيق *same as* **sıngın**.
sınır سنير صنير صنور Gk frontier, border; boundary, limit. **— açı** *geom.* limit angle. **— dışından** from abroad. **— koy=** 1. to limit. 2. to fix a boundary.
sınırdaş صنورداش having a common frontier; bordering.
sınırla=^r صنورلمه to border, to limit. **—ma** *neol.* 1. *phil.* determination. 2. *math.* definition. **—yıcı** *neol.*, *phil.* limitative.
sınırlı صنورلى 1. having a boundary. 2. limited. 3. *neol.*, *math.* definite.
sınırnâme (..—.) صنورنامه *Ott. hist.* title deed issued by the Kadi by imperial decree to solve the lawsuits caused by pasture problems.
sınırsız صنورسز 1. having no boundary. 2. *phil.*, *math.* unlimited, indefinite.
-sınız, -siniz, *etc.* ـسـْـنز [*pl. of* **-sın 1**, *etc.*] 2nd person pl. (*also polite form of sing.*) You are ..., *e. g.*, **neredesiniz?** Where are you?
-sınızdır, -sinizdir, *etc.* (.´..) ـسـْـنزدر you are surely ..., *e.g.*, **açsınızdır** You must be hungry.
sınv صنو A *lrnd.* 1. a stem of two branches growing from one root. 2. brother; son.
sıpa 1 صپا year-old donkey foal; year-old fawn.
sıpa 2 (.—) صپا P *same as* **sehpa**.
sıpırt=, sıpıt= صپـْـرتمه صپـْـتمه slang to get rid of; to turn out, to drive away.
sır^{rrı} **1** سرّ A 1. secret; mystery. 2. secrecy. **— aç=** to reveal a secret, to confide a secret. **—a kadem bas=** to disappear. **— kâtibi** *Ott. hist.* private secretary. **— küpü** one who keeps secrets. **— ol=, — olup git=** to disappear. **— sakla=** to keep a secret. **— tut=** 1. /ı/ to keep (a thing) secret. 2. to keep a confided secret. **—ı vahdet** *myst.* a devotee's withdrawing for meditation; retreat. **— ver=** to betray a secret.

sır 2 سر صر صير [*Arabic* **sirr**] 1. glaze (of pottery). 2. silvering of a mirror. **— sür=, — ver=** /a/ to glaze (pottery).
sıra 1 صيره صره 1. row, file, rank. 2. order, sequence. 3. series. 4. regularity. 5. turn. 6. opportune moment; right time. 7. bench; desk. 8. line of writing. 9. in a row, line or layer; range. 10. along; by. **—da** in a row. **o —da** just at the moment that..., as ..., *e. g.*, **o —da kapı açıldı** Just at that moment the door was opened. **—sında** 1. in his or its turn. 2. when necessary. **—ya bak=** to pay attention to time or turn. **— bekle=** to wait one's turn, to line up. **— dağları*. — duvarı** a wall supporting a terrace. **—sı düştü** The right moment for it has come. **— düşür=** to find a favorable opportunity. **— evler** row houses. **—sı gelmişken** by the way. That reminds me. **—sına getir=** to find a suitable opportunity. **—sına göre** according to circumstances. **— gözet=** 1. to wait for a suitable moment. 2. to respect somebody's turn or seniority. **— ile** in rows; in turn; in order. **—sı ile** respectively. **— karpuzu** melons, large and small, just as they come (not picking and choosing). **—sına koy=** /ı/ 1. to put into its proper place. 2. to set to rights. **— malı** ordinary goods (not specially made). **— sıra** in rows, courses or layers.
-sıra 2 صره صيره *forms an adverb of place or time, e. g.*, **ardısıra, önüsıra**.
sıraca صراجه *path.* scrofula. **— otu** figwort, great pilewort, *bot.*, *Scrophularia*. **—lı** scrofulous.
sıradağ, sıradağlar صيره داغ صيره داغلر mountain chain, mountain range.
sırala=^r صيره لمه 1. /ı/ to arrange in a row; to set up in order. 2. /ı/ to enumerate a series. 3. to begin to walk by holding on to one thing after another (child). **—n=** 1. *pass.* 2. to stand in line. **—t=** /ı/ *caus. of* **sırala=**.
sıralı صيره لى 1. in a row; in due order. 2. at the right moment. **— sırasız** in and out of season; at odd times.
sırasız صيره سز 1. out of order, irregular. 2. poorly timed. 3. improper.
Sırat (.—) صراط A 1. *Isl. rel.* the bridge Sirat from this world to Paradise, more slender than a hair and sharper than a sword. 2. *l. c.*, *lrnd.* road, path. **—ı geç=** to get through danger, to arrive safely. **— köprüsü** 1. *same as* **Sırat 2**. 2. steep and treacherous road. **S—ı müstakim** *lrnd.* straight road, *i. e.*, the Islamic religion.
sıravari (..—.) صراوارى in a line or row.
Sırbistan (..—), **Sırbiye** صربستان صربيه *geog.* Serbia.
sırça صرچه 1. glass. 2. rock-crystal.

3. spun glass; glass bead. 4. paste (false diamond). 5. long glossy hairs (in some furs). **— boya** *art* scumble, glaze. **— gömlek** *ceramics* slip, engobe. **— işleri** small glassware; glass trinkets. **— parmak** *archaic, same as* **serçe parmak. — saray** greenhouse.

sırçan صرچان *prov.* 1. spindle. 2. ball (of wool or cotton thread).

sırdaş سرداش fellow-holder of a secret; confidant, intimate. **—lık** intimate friendship, intimacy.

sırf صرف A pure, mere, sheer, only.

sırık^ɢⁱ صيرينك صرينه سيرينه صير ك pole; stick (for climbing plants). **— la atlama** *sports* pole vault, pole jump. **— domatesi** a kind of tomatoes needing supporting sticks for the vines. **— gibi** *colloq.* tall and ugly (person). **— gibi boy büyüt=** to grow in size but not in sense. **— gibi dur=** to stand aside and do nothing. **— hamalı** porter carrying loads on poles.

sırıkla=ʳ صريقلمه /ı/ 1. to lift with a pole. 2. *slang* to carry off, to steal.

sırım صريم صرم leather thong; strap. **— arabası** wagon of which the body is suspended on leather straps. **— gibi** wiry (person). **— örgüsü** braided thong.

sırıt=ⁱʳ صيرتمق صرتمن صريتش 1. to grin, to show the teeth. 2. to come out, to appear, to become manifest (defect); to be a fiasco. 3. to be frozen. **—a kal=** to remain grinning like a dead person.

sırıtkan صرتغان given to grinning.

sırla=ʳ **1** صرلامه سرلامن /ı/ 1. to glaze (pottery). 2. to silver (mirrors).

sırla=ʳ **2** صرلامه سرلمن *myst. orders* /ı/ 1. to close, shut (door, etc.). 2. to bury (the dead).

sırlı 1 صرلو glazed; silvered (mirror).

sırlı 2 سرلى having a secret; mysterious.

sırma صرمه سيرمه 1. lace or embroidery of silver or silver gilt thread. 2. golden (hair). 3. stripes (indicating the rank of an officer). **— gümüşü** 1. pure silver for drawing into wire. 2. silver with a small admixture of gold. **— işi** gold or silver embroidery. **— işlemeli** worked with gold or silver thread. **— saçlı** auburn, golden haired. **— şerit** broad gold or silver lace.

sırmakeş صرمكش P *lrnd.* maker of gold or silver thread; embroiderer in gold or silver.

sırmakeşhane (...—.) صرمكشخانه P factory where gold or silver thread is made.

sırmalı صرملى embroidered with gold or silver thread.

sırnaş=ⁱʳ صرناشمك /a/ to annoy, to worry (a person).

sırnaşık^ɢⁱ صرناشق tiresome, worrying; pertinacious, importunate. **—lık** importunity.

Sırpᵇⁱ صرب the Serbian people; Serb; Serbian. **—ça** (.ˊ.) Serbian (language). **—lı** Serbian (person).

sırran, sırren (.ˊ.) سرّاً A *lrnd.* secretly, in secret. **— ve alenen, — ve cehren** privately and publicly.

sırret=ᵈᵉʳ سرّايتمك /ı/ *myst. orders* to close (door).

sırrî (.—) سرّى A *lrnd.* 1. pertaining to a secret, mysterious. 2. mystical. **—yûn** (.——) A mystics.

sırrol=ᵘʳ سرّاولمك to disappear.

sırsıklam (.ˊ..) صرصقلام very wet; soaked to the skin. **— âşık** *colloq.* madly in love.

sırt صرت صيرت 1. upper part of a person's back, back. 2. ridge of an animal's back; ridge (of a mountain). 3. back of a knife, sword, etc. 4. fur from the middle strip along the back of a beast's skin. **—ına al=** /ı/ 1. to shoulder. 2. to undertake. **—ından at=** /ı/ to get rid of, to free oneself from. **—ından çıkar=** /ın/ to get something at another's expense. **—ını daya=** /a/ to lean upon (something); to depend upon (somebody). **—ından geçin=** /ın/ to live at somebody's expense. **— ipi** *neol., biol.* dorsal cord. **—ı kara** 1. a kind of bluefish. 2. *slang* double six in dice. **— kaşağısı** long handled instrument to scratch the back, back-scratcher. **—ı kaşınıyor** He is itching for a beating. **—ı kavi** 1. strong in the back. 2. well supported by friends. 3. warmly clad. **— köyleri** villages perched high up on a mountain range. **— omurları** *neol., biol.* dorsal vertebra. **—ı pek** warmly clad. **—ı sıra** succeeding one another. **— sırta ver=** 1. to stand back to back. 2. to support and help one another. **— üstü yat=** to lie flat on one's back. **—ına vur=** /ı/ to toss (a load) up on to one's back, to shoulder. **—ı yere gel=** to be completely defeated. **—ını yere getir=** /ın/ to overcome, to get the better of. **—ı yufka** scantily clad. **— yüzgeci** *neol., biol.* dorsal fin.

sırtar 1 صرتار a kind of lizard (with thick skin on the back). **— balığı** fresh-water bream.

sırtar=ⁱʳ **2** صرتارمن to grin.

sırtar=ⁱʳ **3** صرتارمن 1. to arch its back (cat). 2. to set oneself up in opposition (to or against). 3. to pile up (clouds).

sırtla=ʳ صرتلامن صيرتلدكن /ı/ 1. to take on one's back, to shoulder. 2. to back, to support.

sırtlan 1 صرتلان hyena.

sırtlan=ⁱʳ **2** صرتلانمن 1. *pass. of* **sırtla=**. 2. to become broad or high in the back.

sıska صيسقه [istiska] 1. dropsy; dropsical. 2. rickety (child). 3. thin and weak, puny. **—lık** dropsy; rickets.

sıtma صيتمه ستمه malaria; fever. **— ağacı** eucalyptus, blue gum tree, *bot., Eucalyptus* *globulus*. — **görmemiş ses** a rich, deep voice. **—ya tutul=**, **—lan=** to get malaria, to come down with a fever. **—lı** malarial.

sıva 1 صِوَا صِوَه plaster. — **harcı** plaster prepared for use as stucco.

sıva=ʳ **2** صِوَامَاق صِوَامَق /ı/ 1. to plaster; to stucco; to daub, bedaub. 2. *colloq.* to accuse, vituperate, ridicule; to soil.

sıva=ʳ **3** صِوَهمَق صِوَمَق same as **sığa 2**.

sıvacı صِوَاجی plasterer. — **kuşu** nuthatch, *zool.*, *Sitta europea*.

sıvakᵍⁱ صِوَاق *prov.*, same as **sıva 1**.

sıvala=ʳ صِوَالَامَق /ı/ same as **sıva= 2**. **—n=** *pass*.

sıvalı 1 صِوَالی plastered, stuccoed.

sıvalı 2 صِوَالی with sleeves rolled up.

sıvama صِوَامَه 1. *verbal n.* of **sıva= 2**, **sıva= 3**. 2. laid on like plaster. 3. covered with; washed over with. — **çamuru**, — **hamuru** *ceramics* lute. — **kel** bald all over.

sıvan=ʳ **1** صِوَانْمَق *pass.* of **sıva= 2**.

sıvan=ʳ **2** صِوَانْمَق *pass.* of **sıva= 3**.

sıvaş=ʳ صِوَاشْمَق 1. to become sticky; adhesive. 2. to adhere, to stick to. 3. to be dirtied with some sticky substance.

sıvaşıkᵍⁱ صِوَاشِد same as **sıvışık**.

sıvaştır=ʳ صِوَاشْدِرْمَق /ı/ *caus.* of **sıvaş=**.

sıvat=ʳ صِوَاتْمَق /ı, a/ *caus.* of **sıva= 2**, **sıva= 3**. **—ıl=** *pass*.

sıvazla=ʳ صِوَازْلَامَق /ı/ to stroke, to caress, to pet.

sıvı *neol.*, *phys.* liquid, fluid.

sıvıkᵍⁱ صِوِد 1. semifluid. 2. sticky. 3. bedaubed. 4. *slang* tiresome, importunate. **—lık** semifluidity, stickiness.

sıvırya (..'.) صِوِریا *Gk* 1. continually. 2. one after the other. 3. in full swing. 4. *slang* brimful, completely full.

sıvış 1 صِوِش same as **sıvık**.

sıvış=ʳ **2** صِوِشْمَق same as **siviş= 2**.

sıvışıkᵍⁱ صِوِشِد 1. sticky, adhesive. 2. annoying, troublesome. **—lık** stickiness.

sıyagatᵗⁱ (.—.) صِیَاغَت *A lrnd.* the art or occupation of a goldsmith or silversmith.

sıyağ صِیَاغ *A lrnd.*, *pl.* of **sıyga**.

sıyah (.—) صِیَاح *A lrnd.* 1. a calling aloud, a shouting to one another. 2. loud cry, shout or exclamation. **—ı matem** wails of mourning.

sıyam (.—) صِیَام *A lrnd.* an abstaining from food, fasting; fast.

sıyanet (.—.) صِیَانَت *A lrnd.* a preserving, protecting; preservation, protection. — **et=** /ı/ to preserve, to protect.

sıyga صِیْغَه *A* 1. *gram.* form taken by a word when conjugated; mood, tense. 2. *lrnd.* form taken by metal when cast in a mold. 3. *lrnd.* form, shape; state, condition. **—ya çek=** /ı/ to cross-examine.

sıyır=ʳ صِیِرمَق سِیِرمَق /ı/ 1. to tear, peel off; to strip off. 2. to skim off (cream.) 3. to touch in passing, to graze. 4. to draw (sword.) 5. to polish off, finish up. **—ma** 1. *verbal n.* 2. torn off, stripped off. 3. stripped of its outer skin or peel. **—t=** /ı, a/ *caus.* of **sıyır=**.

sıyrıkᵍⁱ صِیِرِد 1. peeled, skinned; abraded; abrasion. 2. brazen faced. **—lık** 1. abrasion. 2. brazen-facedness.

sıyrıl=ʳ صِیِرِلْمَق 1. *pass.* of **sıyır=**. 2. /dan/ to slip off, sneak away; to squeak through, to get out of a difficulty.

sıyrın=ʳ صِیِرِنْمَق *archaic* 1. to peel, flake off of its own accord. 2. to slip away like an eel.

sıyrıncakᵍⁱ صِیِرِنْجَق *archaic* slippery.

sıyrıntı صِیِرِنْتی 1. scrapings (from a kitchen utensil), peelings. 2. scratch.

-sız 1, -siz, *etc.* without, -less, as in **onsuz** without him, **şüphesiz** doubtless.

-sız 2, -siz ('.) ـْ *archaic for* **-sınız**, *etc.*

sız=ᵃʳ **3** صِزْمَق 1. to ooze; to trickle; to leak. 2. to leak out (secret, etc.). 3. /a/ *mil.* to infiltrate. 4. to drop into a drunken slumber. **—dır=** 1. /ı/ *caus.* 2. *colloq.* /ı, dan/ to squeeze (money) out (of). **—dırıl=** *pass*.

sızı صِزی 1. ache, pain. 2. grief.

sızıltı صِزِلْتی 1. lamentation, complaint. 2. discontent. — **çıkar=** 1. to complain, murmur. 2. to give rise to murmurings of discontent. **—ya meydan verme=** not to give cause to complain.

-sızın, -sizin ـسِزِن *adverbial suffix to infinitives* 1. without (doing so and so). 2. before (doing so and so).

sızıntı صِزِنْتی 1. oozings, tricklings, leakage. 2. an oozing out (of secrets, information, etc.).

sızır=ʳ صِزِرْمَق same as **sızdır=**.

sızla=ʳ صِزْلَامَق 1. to ache, smart. 2. to suffer sharp pain. **—n=** 1. to moan with pain; to groan. 2. to lament, to complain. **—t=** /ı/ *caus*.

-sızlıkᵍⁱ, **-sizlik**ᵍⁱ, *etc.* ـسِزْلِك *abstr. n.* of word ending in **-sız**, *etc.* lack of, as in **kararsızlık**, indecision.

-si 1 ـسی *cf.* **-ı 3**.

-si 2 ـسی *cf.* **-sı 2**.

si 3 سی *mus.* ti.

si 4 سی *P lrnd.* thirty. — **vü dü** thirty-two (*i. e.*, the teeth).

sia سَعَه *A* 1. *phys.* capacity, power. 2. width, breadth; capaciousness. **—i hal** comfortable living, plentifulness.

siayet (. —.) سعایت A 1. *lrnd.* an accusing or informing against; calumny, accusation. 2. *obs., law* a paying a part of his wages (slave who is working himself free); work performed in this way.

sib (—) سیب P *lrnd.* apple. — **ü sücud** (*lit.,* an apple and a prostration) a small gift offered in hopes of some favor. **—i zakan, —i zenah, —i zenahdân** chin of a beauty.

sibaᵃⁱ (. —) سباع A *lrnd., pl. of* **sebu 2**.

sibahatᵗⁱ (. —.) سباحت A *lrnd.* a swimming; swimming.

sibakᵏⁱ (. —) سباق A *lrnd.* 1. preceding context (of a discourse or writing). 2. race, contest. — **ü siyak** the whole context of a word.

siberg سه برگ P *lrnd.* three-leaved; clover.

sicalˡⁱ (. —) سجال A *lrnd., pl. of* **secl**.

sicilˡˡⁱ سجل A 1. register; judicial record. 2. *mil.* qualification. **—i ahval** register of service of an employee. **— et=** *same as* **—e kaydet=**. **—i kadı** *same as* **kadı sicili**. **—e kaydet=** /ı/ to enter into the register of a court of record.

sicillât (. . —) سجلات A *lrnd., pl. of* **sicil**. **—a geçir=** /ı/ to enter into the court rolls.

sicilli سجلی 1. registered. 2. previously convicted.

Sicilya (. .´.) سجیلیا *geog.* Sicily.

sicim سجیم string, cord. — **gibi yağmur** pelting rain.

sicn سجن A *lrnd.* prison, dungeon.

sidad (. —) سداد A *lrnd.* 1. stopgap. 2. stopper, cork, plug. 3. fault, defect.

sidikᵍⁱ سیدك، سیدیك، سیدیاك urine. — **borusu** *anat.* ureter. — **borucukları** *biol.* urinary ducts. — **damlaması** *path.* incontinence of urine. — **kavuğu** *anat.* bladder. — **şekeri** *path.* diabetes. — **torbası** *anat.* urinary bladder. — **tutulması** *path.* retention of urine. — **yarışı** futile rivalry; dispute about trifles. — **yarışına çık=** to compete over useless things. — **yolu** *anat.* urethra. — **yolları** *anat.* urinary canal. — **zoru** *path.* difficulty in passing water.

sidikli سیدكلی 1. stained by urine. 2. suffering from incontinence of urine.

sidrat (. —) سدرات A *lrnd., pl. of* **sidre**.

sidr سدر A *lrnd.* 1. lotus tree, *bot.,* Rhamnus nabeca. 2. ground lotus leaf used as soap.

sidre سدره A *lrnd.* 1. one lotus tree or one variety of lotus tree. — **beyi** a drunken bragger. **—kad** P, **—kamet** (. . —.) P tall and stately of stature.

sidrenişinân (. . . — —) سدره نشینان P *lrnd.* the angels.

sidretülmünteha سدرة المنتهی A *lrnd.* the lotus tree in the seventh heaven.

sidretünnebi (. . . . —) سدرة النبی A the lotus tree of the Prophet that miraculously separated in the middle in order that Muhammad should pass in safety as he dozed on his camel during a certain night journey.

siesbe (— . .) سی اسبه P *lrnd.* three-horsed (messenger); swift, expeditious.

sif E *com.* C.I.F.

sifad (. —) سفاد A *lrnd.* an animal's copulating with its mate.

Sifahan (. . —) اصفهان P *lrnd., geog.* Isfahan.

sifalˡⁱ (. —), **sifale** (. —.) سفال، سفاله P *lrnd.* earthenware; sherd.

sifalger (. —.) سفالگر P *lrnd.* potter.

sifalin (. — —) سفالین P *lrnd.* made of clay, earthenware.

sifaline (. — —.) سفالینه P *lrnd.* 1. glassware, earthenware. 2. artificial pearl.

sifalpare (. — —.) سفالپاره P *lrnd.* potsherd.

sifilis سیفلیس F *med.* syphilis.

sifle سفله A *lrnd.* mean, base, vile.

sifon سیفون F 1. siphon. 2. toilet flush tank. 3. S-trap.

sifos سیفوس *slang* 1. futile, useless. 2. finished, no more.

sifr سفر A *lrnd.* 1. book, writing. 2. any one of the five books of the Pentateuch.

sifri سیفری *archaic for* **sivri**.

sift سفت P *lrnd.* shoulder.

siftah سفتاح [*istiftah*] *colloq.* 1. first sale of the day; first sale of a new commodity. 2. for the first time. **— et=** 1. to make the first sale of the day. 2. /a/ to eat something for the first time in the season. **— senden bereket Allahtan** I hope you will bring me good luck *said to the first customer, but also used figuratively.*

siftahla=ʳ سفتاحله 1. to make the first sale of the day. 2. to begin.

siftin=ⁱʳ سفتنلك 1. to wriggle about and scratch oneself. 2. to approach a person in a cringing, fawning manner.

siga (— .) صیغه *same as* **sıyga**.

-sigâlˡⁱ (. —) سگال P *lrnd.* who thinks, reflects, *as in* **bedsigâl**.

sigâliş (. —.) سگالش P *lrnd.* thought, reflection.

sigara (.´. .) سیگاره Sp cigarette. **— böreği** small fried pastry roll stuffed with meat or cheese. **— iskemlesi** small table or stand. **— tablası** ash tray.

sigaralıkᵍⁱ سیگارالق cigarette case.

sigorta (.´. .) سیگورته، سیگورطه It 1. insurance. 2. security. 3. insurance company.

4. *elec.* fuse. **— acentası** insurance agent. **— bedeli** insurance money. **— değeri** insurable value. **— et=** /ı/ to insure. **— menfaati** insurable interest. **— mukavelenamesi, — poliçesi** insurance policy. **—ya yatır=** /ı/ to cover by insurance. **—cı** insurance agent. **—lı** insured.

sigorya سیغوریا It *slang* for sure, surely.
siğil سیگل شیبل سیئیل گیوران گل 1. wart, a small callosity. 2. congenital callosity on the inner surface on the shank of a horse. 3. white stocking on a horse's leg. 4. quoin for elevating the breech of a cannon. **— çek=** to draw back a quoin in aligning a cannon. **— iskemlesi** quoin bed of a cannon. **— otu** dandelion or spurge with which warts are cured. **— sür=** to advance a quoin in pointing a cannon.
siğillen=[ir] سیگللنمك to become affected with warts.
siğilli سیگللی 1. warty; having a callosity. 2. white stockinged (horse). 3. furnished with a quoin.
sih (—) سیخ A *lrnd.* roasting-spit, skewer.
siham (.—) سهام A *lrnd.*, pl. of **sehm** 1.
sihan سخن A *lrnd.* 1. thickness. 2. density.
sihir[hri] سحر [sihr] 1. magic; sorcery, witchcraft. 2. charm, spell, incantation; fascination.
sihirbaz سحرباز [sihrbaz] who practices magic; magician, sorcerer, witch. **—lık** magic; sorcery, witchcraft.
sihirkâr (..—) سحرکار [sihrkâr] enchanting, fascinating.
sihirle=[r] سحرلمك /ı/ to enchant, bewitch. **—n=** pass.
sihirli سحرلو 1. enchanting, bewitching. 2. enchanted, bewitched.
sihper (—.) سهپر P *lrnd.* callow, unfledged.
sihr سحر A *lrnd.*, same as **sihir**, 1. fascinating, enchanting. 2. magician. **—i helâl** 1. natural magic. 2. magic employed in self defense. 3. charm of eloquence; eloquent words; poetry. **—i kelâm** magic of oratory; enrapturing eloquence.
sihrâmiz (.——), **sihrâferin** (.—.—) سحرآمیز سحرآفرین P *lrnd.* magical; fascinating.
sihrbaz (.—) سحرباز P *lrnd.*, same as **sihirbaz.** **—âne** (.——.) P magical; magically. **—î** (.——) P magic, sorcery, witchcraft.
sihrbenan (..—) سحربنان P *lrnd.* wonderful artist or writer.
sihrbeyan (..—) سحربیان P *lrnd.* stirring (words) of magic expression.
sihren (.'.) سحراً A *lrnd.* by magic, by witchcraft.
sihrî (.—) سحری A *lrnd.* magical, pertaining to magic.

sihrkâr (.—) سحرکار P *lrnd.*, same as **sihirkâr.**
sik[ki] 1 سیك سیك penis.
sik=[er] 2 سیكمك /ı/ 1. to have sexual intercourse (with). 2. *vulgar* to injure seriously or to ruin; to deceive.
sika ثقة A *lrnd.* person worthy of trust; reliable person.
sikal[li] (.—) ثقال A *lrnd.*, pl. of **sakil.**
sikat (.—) ثقات A *lrnd.*, pl. of **sika.**
sikaye (.—.) سقایه A *lrnd.* 1. place where water is distributed. 2. drinking vessel, cup. 3. drink prepared by steeping raisins in water, served out gratis to pilgrims at Mecca.
sikayet (.—.) سقایت A *lrnd.* the office and functions of the hereditary distributor of water and of raisin water at Mecca.
sikayetülhac[cci] (.—...) سقایة الحج A *lrnd.* water furnished to the pilgrims.
sikek[ki] سكك A *lrnd.*, pl. of **sikke** 1.
sikencübin سكنجبین A *lrnd.*, same as **sikengübin.**
Sikender سكندر P Alexander the Great.
sikengübin (...—) سكنگبین P *lrnd.* oxymel, vinegar with honey.
sikil=[ir] سیكلمك pass. of **sik=** 2.
sikiş 1 سیكش sexual intercourse.
sikiş=[ir] 2 سیكشمك /la/ to have sexual intercourse together, to copulate. **—tir=** /ı/ caus.
sikke 1 سكه A 1. coin; die. 2. design on a coin or medal. 3. *lrnd.* level road. **— bas=, — darbet=** to coin money, to mint. **—i hasene** money. **— ve hutbe** the right of minting coins and of mention in the **hutbe,** two prerogatives of the Sultan.
sikke 2 سكه A headdress special to any dervish order; religious garment. **—i şerif** headdress worn by a Mevlevi dervish.
sikkedar (..—) سكه دار P *lrnd.* keeper of the dies in a mint.
sikkehane (..—.) سكه خانه P *lrnd.* mint.
sikkeken سكه کن P *lrnd.* die-sinker for a mint. **—lik** department for die-sinkers in a mint.
sikkele=[r] سكه لمك /ı/ to coin, to affix the die to (metal).
sikkeli سكه لو 1. stamped with a die. 2. wearing a dervish cap.
sikkepuş (..—) سكه پوش P *lrnd.* Mevlevi dervish who wears the special headdress.
sikkesuret (..—.) سكه صورت P *lrnd.* having a face like a coin *said of a person who uses exaggerated makeup.*
sikkeşinas (...—) سكه شناس P *lrnd.* coin specialist, numismatist.
sikketülhadid (....—) سكة الحدید A *lrnd.* railroad.
sikkezen سكه زن P *lrnd.* coiner in a mint.
sikkin (.—) سكین A *lrnd.* knife.
sikl 1 سیقل F *phys.* cycle.

sıkl

sıklⁱⁱ 2 نَقْل A *lrnd.* 1. weight. 2. load, burden. **—i izafi** specific gravity. **—i mutlak** absolute gravity.

siklon سِيكْلُون F cyclone.

siktir=ⁱʳ سِكْتِيرمَكْ /ı, a/ *caus.* of **sik= 2. —!** *vulgar* Off with you! Go to hell! **— et=** to drive away. **—ici** *vulgar* base, low, vulgar.

sikûşe (.—.) سِه كُوشَه P *lrnd.* triangle.

sikvestro (..'.) سِقْوِسْتْرُو It *law,* same as **sekvestro.**

sil=ᵉʳ 1 سِلْمَكْ /ı/ 1. to wipe. 2. to wash and scrub; to rub off or out; to rub down. 3. to polish. 4. to erase. 5. to remove the excess of anything (skim foam off beer, level off a heap of grain, etc.). 6. to plane. **—ip süpür=** /ı/ to sweep away and carry off entirely; to make a clean sweep of.

silⁱⁱⁱ 2 سِلّ A *lrnd., path.* tuberculosis.

sil'a سِلْعَه A *lrnd.* goods, merchandise.

silâh 1 سِلاح [silâh 2] A weapon, arm. **— altı** under arms. **— arma** trophy, weapons grouped ornamentally. **— at=** to fire. **— başı** call to arms, alarm. **— başına** To arms. **— çat=** to pile arms. **— çek=** to threaten with arms. **—a davran=** to take up and prepare to use a weapon. **— kuvveti** armed force. **— omuza** Shoulder arms. **— patla=** to break out (war). **—a sarıl=** to resort to arms.

silâh 2 (.—) سِلاح A *lrnd.,* same as **silâh 1.**

silâhcame (.——.) سِلاحْجامَه P *lrnd.* armor; coat of mail.

silâhçı سِلاحْجِى armorer.

silâhdar (.——) سِلاحْدار P 1. *Ott. hist.* the regular Ottoman guards of the Janissary period. 2. *lrnd.* custodian of the arms (of a great personage); sword-bearer. **S— Ağa** *Ott. hist.* the sword-bearer of the Sultan. **—ân** (.———) P *lrnd.,* pl. of **silâhdar.**

silâhendaz (.—.—) سِلاحْاَنْداز P *lrnd.* 1. common soldier; fusilier. 2. marine. **—lık** service or quality of the marines.

silâhhane (.——.) سِلاح خانَه P armory; arsenal.

silâhla=ʳ سِلاحْلَمَق /ı/ to arm. **—n=** to take up arms; to arm oneself. **—ndır=** /ı/ to arm.

silâhlanma سِلاحْلَنْمَه a being armed; armament. **— yarışı** *pol.* arms race.

silâhlı سِلاحْلِى armed. **— bitaraflık** *pol.* armed neutrality.

silâhlıkᵍⁱ سِلاحْلِق belt for carrying weapons.

silâhsız سِلاحْسِز unarmed. **—a ayır=** /ı/ *mil.* to allot to non-combatant duties.

silâhsızlan=ʳ سِلاحْسِزْلَنْمَق to be disarmed. **—dır=** /ı/ to disarm. **—ma** *pol.* disarmament.

silâhşor 1 سِلاحْشُور [silâhşor 2] warrior; knight; musketeer.

silâhşor 2 (.——) سِلاحْشُور P 1. *lrnd.* armed guard of a palace. 2. *Ott. hist.,* title of the first regiment of the Ottoman household cavalry.

sildir=ⁱʳ سِلْدِيرْمَكْ /ı, a/ *caus.* of **sil= 1.**

-sile (—.) سِيلَه *cf.* **-ile 2.**

silecekᵍⁱ سِلَه جَكْ large bath towel.

silgi سِلْكِى 1. duster for cleaning a blackboard. 2. sponge for wiping a slate. 3. eraser.

sili (——) سِلِى P *lrnd.* 1. slap on the face; box on the ear; buffet. 2. misfortune. **—i Hüdai** a misfortune viewed as divine retribution.

silici سِلِيجِى 1. professional cleaner or polisher. 2. one who planes boards for construction work. 3. *auto.* windshield wiper.

Silifke (..'.) سِلِفْكَه *geog.* Silifke, the ancient Seleucia.

silikᵍⁱ سِلِيكْ 1. rubbed out; worn. 2. indistinct; insignificant. 3. second rate. 4. flat, planed off. **— gözlü** whose eyes are flat from atrophy, etc. **—lik** 1. indistinctness; insignificance. 2. flatness.

silin=ⁱʳ سِلِنْمَكْ *pass.* of **sil= 1.**

silindir سِلِنْدِر F 1. cylinder. 2. roller (for road-making). **— ateşi** *mil.* curtain fire, barrage fire. **— kapağı** *auto.* cylinder head. **— şapka** top hat.

silindiraj سِلِنْدِراژ F rolling.

silinti سِلِنْتِى wipings, anything wiped off.

silis سِلِيس F *chem.* silica.

silsre, silistre (..'.) سِلِسْتْرَه Gk *naut.* boatswain's pipe, sifflet.

silkᵏⁱ 1 سِلْك A *lrnd.* 1. career, profession. 2. line, series, order. 3. thread or cord for stringing beads, etc. **—i askeri** military career. **—i leâli** a string of pearls.

silk=ᵉʳ 2 سِلْكْمَكْ /ı/ 1. to shake, to shake off. 2. to pounce, make a copy of a drawing, etc. by perforating holes in it and shaking a colored powder through the holes.

silkele=ʳ سِلْكَلَمَكْ /ı/ to shake off (dust, etc.). **—n=** *pass.*

silki سِلْكِى shaky, that moves with sudden unequal motion or with convulsive starts.

silkil=ⁱʳ سِلْكِلْمَكْ *pass.* of **silk= 2.**

silkilen=ⁱʳ سِلْكِلَنْمَكْ to become convulsively shaky, tremulous. **—dir=** /ı/ *caus.*

silkin=ⁱʳ سِلْكِنْمَكْ 1. to shake oneself. 2. to shake off the effects of something; to shake oneself free. 3. to move with convulsive starts.

silkinti سِلْكِنْتِى 1. shake; a shaking or trembling. 2. anything shaken off.

silkiş=ⁱʳ سِلْكِشْمَكْ to shake itself (bird), to flutter.

silkme سِلْكْمَه 1. *verbal n.* of **silk= 2.** 2. dish of finely chopped eggplant or squash and meat. 3. *art* design produced by shaking fine charcoal through pinholes.

silktir=ᶦʳ ‏سلكتر‎ /ı, a/ *caus.* of **silk=** 2.

sille ‏سله‎ ‏سيله‎ [sili] box on the ear, slap. **— at=** /a/ to box an ear or slap a face. **— tokat birbirine girdiler** They engaged in fist-fighting. **— ye=** to get a box on the ear or slap on the face.

sillî (. —) ‏سلّى‎ A *path.* pertaining to tuberculosis, tubercular.

silme ‏سلمه‎ ‏سلمه‎ 1. *verbal n.* of **sil=** 2. 2. wiped; washed, scrubbed. 3. planed or molded with a special plane, shaven. 4. leveled to the rim (measure of grain.) 5. *arch.* moulding, moulure. **— tahtası** board for leveling off a measure of grain.

silsile ‏سلسله‎ A 1. chain; line, series. 2. dynasty; pedigree; genealogy. 3. chain of promotions through seniority. 4. *geog.* mountain range. **—i meratib** *lrnd.* hierarchy. **— yürü=** to take place by right of seniority through successive grades (promotion).

silsiledar (. . . —) ‏سلسله دار‎ P *lrnd.* 1. chained. 2. guardian in charge of the bell chain at a ruler's gate.

silsilemu (. . . —) ‏سلسله مو‎ P *lrnd.* with hair in ringlets (like chains), curly haired.

silsilename (. . . — .) ‏سلسله نامه‎ P *lrnd.* genealogical tree, written pedigree.

silsilezülf ‏سلسله زلف‎ P *lrnd.* curly haired.

sim, sim 1 (—) ‏سيم‎ P 1. silver; silver money. 2. money, coin. 3. silvering on mirrors. 4. imitation silver, electroplate. 5. wire. **— şerit** imitation silver braid.

sim 2 ‏سم‎ *prov.* sign, symbol.

sima 1 (— —) ‏سيما‎ P 1. face, features. 2. figure, personage.

sima 2 (— —) ‏سيما‎ A *lrnd.* 1. mark, token, badge. 2. a mark on the forehead (from prostration in worship).

simaᵃᶦ **3** (. —) ‏سماع‎ A *lrnd.*, same as **sema 2**.

simâb (— —) ‏سيماب‎ P *lrnd.* quicksilver, mercury.

simâbdil (— — .) ‏سيماب دل‎ P *lrnd.* chicken-hearted, timid.

simâbî (— — —) ‏سيمابى‎ P *lrnd.* 1. of quicksilver, like quicksilver. 2. white; bright, glittering.

simar (. —) ‏سمار‎ A *lrnd.*, *pl.* of **semer 2**, **semere**.

simat 1 (. —) ‏سماط‎ A *lrnd.* 1. order, series, line, row. 2. same as **somat**.

simat 2 (. —) ‏سمات‎ A *lrnd.*, *pl.* of **sime**, 1. marks, traces, brands marked by burning. 2. moral qualities.

simaver (— — .) ‏سيماور‎ P *lrnd.* rich.

simber (— .) ‏سيمبر‎ P *lrnd.* having a bosom like silver, fair-breasted.

sime ‏سمه‎ A *lrnd.* sign, mark.

simendam (— . —) ‏سيم اندام‎ P *lrnd.* with silvery limbs, fair.

simendûd (— . —) ‏سيم اندود‎ P *lrnd.* washed or plated with silver.

simge *neol.* symbol. **—cilik** symbolism.

simger (— .) ‏سيمگر‎ P *lrnd.* silversmith. **—i** (— . —) P art and occupation of a silversmith.

simgûn (— —) ‏سيمگون‎ P *lrnd.* silver colored; white.

simhakᵏᶦ (. —) ‏سمحاق‎ A *anat.* periosteum, pericranial membrane. **—i** (. — —) pericranial.

simin (— —) ‏سيمين‎ P *lrnd.* 1. made of silver. 2. silver-like, white. 3. bright. **—ber** (— — .) P with a silver bosom, fair-breasted. **—ten** (— — .) P fair-bodied.

simitᵈᶦ ‏سميد‎ ‏سميت‎ [*Arabic semiz*] 1. roll of bread in the shape of a ring. 2. life buoy. 3. *naut.* grummet (of ropes). 4. anything in the shape of a ring. 5. *school slang* zero. **—çi** maker or seller of simits.

simkâr (— —) ‏سيمكار‎ P *lrnd.* a worker in silver filigree inlay upon other metals.

simkarî (— — —) ‏سيمكارى‎ P *lrnd.* 1. the art or profession of a silver-inlayer. 2. silver filigree inlaid on other metals.

simkeş (— .) ‏سيمكش‎ P *lrnd.* 1. gold or silver wire-drawer. 2. that attracts silver. 3. persistent beggar.

simkeşhane (— . — .) ‏سيمكشخانه‎ P shop that makes silver wire.

simkûb (— —) ‏سيمكوب‎ P *lrnd.* beater of silver leaf, silver-beater.

simreng (— .) ‏سيمرنگ‎ P *lrnd.* white, shiny.

simsar (. —) ‏سمسار‎ A 1. broker. 2. middleman; commission agent. **—iye** brokerage, broker's commission. **—lık** 1. profession of a broker. 2. brokerage.

simsiyah (.' . .) ‏سمسياه‎ jet black.

simt ‏سمط‎ A *lrnd.* 1. string with beads on it; long necklace. 2. strap hanging from the saddle used to tie loads down. 3. anything hanging down pendulously. 4. stanza ended with a kind of chorus.

simtî (. —) ‏سمطى‎ A *lrnd.* arranged in stanzas with a kind of chorus to each (poem).

simürg (— .) ‏سيمرغ‎ P *lrnd.*, name of a mythical bird inhabiting the mountain of Elburz. **—i ateşînper** the sun.

simya (— —) ‏سيميا‎ A *lrnd.* alchemy. **—ger** (— — .) P alchemist.

sin 1 ‏س‎ name of the letter ‏س‎ (fifteenth letter of the Ottoman and fourteenth letter of the Arabic alphabets. In chronograms it has the numerical value of 60).

sinⁿⁿᶦ **2** ‏سنّ‎ A *lrnd.* 1. age, span of life;

sin

one's time of life. —**i bülûğ** age of puberty. —**i inhitat** age when vigor begins to decrease. —**i kühûlet** age when gray hairs begin to show. —**i sagar** time of infancy. —**i vukuf** age when growth ceases.

sin[nni] 3 سِنّ A lrnd. tooth. —**i katı'** anat. incisive tooth. —**i lâhime** anat. carnassial tooth. —**i nâbi** anat. canine tooth.

sin 4 سين سِن 1. tomb, grave. 2. pit.

sin=[er] 5 سِنمَك سنكمك 1. to crouch down (to hide oneself); to be hidden. 2. to be humiliated, to be cowed. 3. to subside and be absorbed; to be swallowed, digested. 4. to /a/ sink (into), to penetrate. —**e sine** 1. so as to sink in. 2. crouchingly, stealthily. —**e sine yağmur yağ=** to come down as a soaking rain.

Sin 6 سين صين A lrnd. China.

-sin 7 سِن سن cf. **-sın** 1.

=sin 8 سَك cf. **=sın** 2.

sinagrit[di] سِناغرِيت Gk same as **sinarit**.

sinameki سِنامَكى A senna, bot., Cassia acutifolia. — **gibi** slow and unattractive.

sinan (.—) سِنان A lrnd. 1. steel spearhead. 2. weapon of defense. —**î** (.——) A 1. pertaining to a spearhead. 2. maker of steel spearheads.

sinara, sinare (..'.) سِناره٬ سِنارو Gk fishhook.

sinarit سِنارِيت Gk dentex (fish), zool., Dentex vulgaris.

sincab (.—) سِنجاب P lrnd., same as **sincap**.

sincabî (.——) سِنجابى P 1. dark gray. 2. lrnd. of gray squirrel fur.

sincan سِنجان matrimony vine, bot., Lycium halimifolium.

sincap[bı] سِنجاب [sincab] 1. European squirrel, zool., Sciurus vulgaris. 2. squirrel fur.

sincefre, sincerf سِنجفره A lrnd., same as **zincifre**.

Sind سِند geog. 1. Sind. 2. the river Indus.

sindan (.—) سِندان P lrnd. 1. blacksmith's anvil. 2. plate of a door-knocker.

sinderus سِندرس same as **senderus**.

Sindî (.—) سِندى A 1. Sindian, of Sind. 2. the Sind language.

sindik[kı] سِندِيك F 1. receiver in bankruptcy. 2. guild-warden.

sindika سِندِيقه F same as **sendika**.

sindir=[ır] 1 سِندِرمَك سِكدِرمَك /ı/ caus. of **sin=** 4. —**e sindire** permeating; very thoroughly.

-sindir 2 سِندِر cf. **-sındır** 1.

sindirici سِندِرِيجى 1. digestive. 2. subduing, subsiding.

sindiril=[ır] سِندِرِلمَك pass. of **sindir=** 1.

sindirim neol. digestion. — **sistemi** physiol. digestive system.

sine (—.) سِينه P poet. bosom, breast. —**ye çek=** /ı/ to put up with, to resign oneself to. —**ye elif çek=** to rend one's heart (with passion). — **tamburu** a kind of lute that is rested upon the shoulder or breast in playing.

sinebend (—..) سِينه بند P lrnd. 1. bodice, stomacher. 2. child's bib. 3. breast-band of an animal.

sineçak[kı] (—.—) سِينه چاك P lrnd. whose breast is rent open; grieved, sorrowing.

sinek[ği] سِنَك 1. fly, zool., Musca. 2. cards clubs. — **avla=** to putter about, to idle. — **kâğıdı** flypaper. —**ten yağ çıkar=** (lit., to extract oil out of a fly) to profit from small things. — **kapan** Venus's-fly-trap, fly-catcher, bot., Dionaea muscipula. — **yutan** spotted flycatcher, zool., Muscicapa striata. —**çil** zool., Muscicapa.

sinekkaydı سِنَك قايدى (lit. a shave on which the fly slipped.) a very smooth shave. — **tıraş** same as **sinekkaydı**.

sinekli سِنَكلى containing flies, full of flies, flyblown.

sineklik[ği] سِنَكلِك 1. fly-whisk; fly swatter. 2. place abounding with flies.

sinekeman (—..—) سِينه كمان P mus. a cello with extra strings.

sinema ('..) سِينه ما F motion picture, cinema, picture show.

sinepuş (—.—) سِينه پوش P lrnd. breastplate.

sinesuz (—.—) سِينه سوز P lrnd. tormented, distressed; tormenting, distressing.

sinezen (—..) سِينه زَن P lrnd. one who beats his breast (in mourning). —**ân** (—..—) P beating the breast.

sinezenlik[ği] سِينه زَنلِك a beating the breast (the self-imposed torture of the Shiite Muharrem ceremony).

sinh سِنخ A 1. anat. root of a tooth, alveolus. 2. lrnd. root, source, basis, origin.

sini 1 سِينى A round metal tray.

sini 2 (——) سِينى A lrnd. 1. Chinese. 2. China ware, porcelain.

sini 3 (——) سِينى P lrnd. 1. Chinese; of or from China. 2. round metal tray used as a table for meals. 3. Dutch tile, painted tile.

sini 4 (——) سِينى A 1. lrnd. pertaining to the letter س 2. anat. sigmoid.

-sini 5 سِنى cf. **-ı** 3.

sinici 1 سِينيجى 1. maker of metal trays. 2. Ott. hist. servant who had charge of metal trays.

sinici 2 سِنيجى 1. that habitually shrinks into some cavity. 2. that is easily digested.

sinik[ği] سِنِك crouching, cowed.

sinin (.—) سِنِين A lrnd., pl. of **sene**. —**i sâlife** past years.

sinir 1 سِنِر 1. nerve, sinew; fiber. 2. bot. rib, vein, bundle of fiber. 3. string. 4. nervous habit. 5. colloq. sensitiveness. — **adam** colloq. an enervating

person. — **ağrısı** *path.* neuralgia. **—leri altüst ol=** /ın/ to be upset. **— argınlığı** *neol.* neurasthenia. **—leri ayakta ol=** /ın/ for one's nerves to be on edge. **— boğumları** *anat.* neural ganglions. **—leri boşan=** to have a nervous fit. **— çekilmesi** contraction of a sinew or tendon. **— çiftleri** *neol., anat.* neural pairs. **—ine dokun=** /ın/ to irritate; to get on one's nerves. **— hastalığı** neuralgia. **— kavrulması** cramp, spasm. **— kesil=** to become all nerves. **—i tut=** to have a fit of nerves. **— tutulması** cramp.
sinir=ᵢʳ 2 سِنگِرمَك سَپِيَرمَك سِپَرمَك *archaic* 1. to digest (food). 2. /ı/ to conceal.
sinirbilim *neol.* neurology.
sinirce *neol.* neurosis.
sinirdoku *neol., histology* neural tissue.
sinirkanatlılar *neol., zool.* neuroptera.
sinirle=ʳ سِپَرلَمَك *archaic* to free from sinews, to hamstring.
sinirlen=ᵢʳ سِپَرلَنْمَك 1. to become irritated; to have one's nerves set on edge. 2. to be hamstrung. **—dir=** /ı/ *caus.*
sinirli سِپَرلي 1. on edge, irritable; nervous. 2. sinewy, wiry. **— ot, — yaprak** ribwort plantain, *bot., Plantago lanceolata.* **—lik** 1. a state of nerves, irritability. 2. wiriness.
-siniz سِكز *cf.* **-sınız.**
-sinizdir سِكزدر *cf.* **-sınızdır.**
sinle 1 سِنله *archaic* 1. graveyard, cemetery. 2. tomb.
sinle=ʳ 2 سِنْلَمَك سِگْلَمَك سِنْگلَمَك *archaic* to make a low whining or moaning noise (animal). **—n=** to make a low moaning noise to oneself. **—t=** /ı/ *caus.*
sinmez سِنْمَز 1. indigestible. 2. hard to swallow. 3. that will not be absorbed.
sinnen (.́.) سِنًّا *A lrnd.* in point of age.
sinnevr سِنَّوْر *A lrnd.* cat. **—i cebelî** mountain cat.
sinnî (.—) سِنِّي *A lrnd.* 1. pertaining to age. 2. dental.
sinsi سِنْسِي stealthy; slinking, sneaking; insidious. **—lik** stealthiness; underhand dealing.
sintina, sintine (.́.) سِنْتِنَه stage *naut.* bilgeways and pump well of a ship; bilge. **— suyu** bilge water.
sinyalᵘ سِنيَال *F* signal.
sipa (.—) سِپَا *P lrnd.*, same as **sehpa.**
sipah (.—) سِپَاه *P lrnd.* military force, troops, army. **—ân** (.—) *P pl.*
sipahdar (.—) سِپَهْدَار *P lrnd.* captain or general.
sipahi (.—) سِپَاهِي *P* 1. *Ott. hist.* cavalry soldier (holder of fief in knight service), spahi. 2. *lrnd.* belonging to the army. **S— Ocağı** name of a fashionable riding school in Istanbul.

— oğlanı *Ott. hist.* special cavalry corps in the army. **—lik** quality of being a **sipahi.**
sipahiyan (.———) سِپَاهِيَان *P pl. of* **sipahi.**
sipahiyane (.———.) سِپَاهِيَانَه *P* soldierly, military.
sipahsalâr (.———) سِپَهْسَالَار *P lrnd.* commander-in-chief. **—î** (.————) *P* relating to the commander.
-sipar 1 (.—) سِپَار *P lrnd.* who commits or consigns to, *as in* **cansipar.**
sipar 2 سِپَار *slang* cigarette.
sipare (———.) سِپَاره *P lrnd.* any one of the thirty sections into which the Quran is divided for daily recitation.
sipari سِپَاري *slang* money (paid for a party, etc.).
sipariş (.—.) سِپَارِش *P* 1. *com.* order. 2. commission. 3. allotment of pay (made by a soldier to a relative). **—ât** (.—.—) *pl.*
sipas (.—) سِپَاس *P lrnd.* 1. kindness, grace, favor. 2. praise, thanksgiving. 3. obligation, gratitude.
sipasdar (.——) سِپَاسْدَار *P lrnd.* thankful, grateful (person).
sipasgüzar (.—.—) سِپَاسْگُزَار *P lrnd.* who feels and expresses gratitude, grateful. **—î** (.—.——) *P* gratitude, thanksgiving.
sipasî (.——) سِپَاسِي *P lrnd.* grateful, thankful.
sipeh سِپَه *P lrnd.*, same as **sipah. —i belâ** the army of calamities.
sipehbed, sipehbüd سِپَهْبُد *P lrnd.* chief, lord, general; ruler.
sipehsalâr (..——) سِپَهْسَالَار *P lrnd.*, same as **sipahsalar.**
sipenc سِپَنْج *P lrnd.* 1. three or five, very few; three and five (at dice). 2. fifteen. 3. period of a few days' or years' duration; temporary, transitory state. 4. temporary abode; the world.
sipenchane (..—.) سِپَنْجْخَانَه *P lrnd.* the world.
sipencî (..—) سِپَنْجِي *P lrnd.* temporary, transitory.
sipend سِپَنْد *P lrnd.* wild rue, *bot., Peganum harmala;* wild rue seed.
sipendan (..—) سِپَنْدَان *P lrnd.* 1. same as **sipend.** 2. mustard; cress or broad-leafed pepperwort.
siper سِپَر *P* 1. shield; shelter; protection; guard; screen. 2. trench; rampart. 3. peak of a cap. 4. top-slide (lathe). **— al=** to take shelter behind something, to parry a blow. **—e al=** /ı/ to take under one's protection. **—i berkî** *lrnd.* lightning rod. **— ol=** /a/ to shield with one's own body. **—i saika** lightning conductor. **—i şems** peak (of a cap). **— tahtası** *auto.* dashboard.
siperdar (..—) سِپَرْدَار *P lrnd.* shield-bearer.

siperde سپرده P *lrnd.* 1. who has consigned, committed, entrusted. 2. consigned, committed, entrusted.
siperendaz (...—) سپرانداز P *lrnd.* who throws away his shield, who surrenders.
sipergam سپرغم P *lrnd.* sweet basil, *bot.*, *Ocimum basilicum.*
siperlen=ᵢʳ سپرلنمك to take shelter.
sipihr سپهر P *lrnd.* 1. sky, heavens. 2. fortune; the world; time. 3. *Or. mus.* a compound **makam** more than six centuries old. —**i berin** the ninth or highest heaven. —**i bukalemun** 1. the varying sky. 2. fickle fortune.
sipihrasitan (..—.—) سپهرآستان P *lrnd.* whose threshold is exalted as the spheres.
sipihrşinas (...—) سپهرشناس P *lrnd.* astrologer.
sipürde سپرده P *mus.* a **ney** tuned in a special way.
sipsi سپسی 1. *prov.* whistle; boatswain's pipe. 2. *prov.* reed (of a clarinet). 3. *slang* cigarette.
sipsivri سپسوری very sharp (point). — **çıkagel=** to appear unexpectedly (when undesired). — **kal=** to be suddenly deserted by everyone; to be destitute.
si'r 1 سعر A *lrnd.* established market price.
sir 2 (—) سیر P *lrnd.* 1. full, satiated with food or drink. 2. full of sap, well-watered. 3. nauseated.
sir 3 (—) سیر P *lrnd.* garlic. — **der levzine,** — **ü levzine** any unpleasant supplement to a pleasant introduction; a having one's joys alloyed with sorrows. — **ü piyâz** garlic and onion.
sirab (——) سیراب P *lrnd.* 1. who has drunk his fill and is satiated. 2. full of sap and moisture, juicy; fresh.
sirac (.—) سراج A *lrnd.* 1. lamp, light, candle. 2. the sun. —**ı ehli cennet** title of the Caliph Umar. —**ı râh-ı hidâyet** the light of the right path, the Prophet Muhammad.
siracüddin (.—.—) سراج الدين A *lrnd.* 1. the light of religion. 2. *w. cap., man's name.*
Siracülmü'minin (.—...—) سراج المؤمنين A *lrnd.* the Quran.
siracünnihar (.—..—) سراج النهار A *lrnd.* the sun.
siran (——) سيران A *lrnd., pl.* of **sevr.**
sirayet (.—.) سرايت A a spreading, propagation; contagion, infection.
sirbalᵘ (.—) سربال A *lrnd.* shirt.
sirçeşm (.—.) سرچشم P *lrnd.* satisfied, satiated; contented.
sireng (—.) سرنك P *lrnd.* 1. many colored, iridescent. 2. griffin; anything impossible or which the mind cannot grasp. 3. impenetrable mystery; the unsearchable God.
siret (—.) سيرت A *lrnd.* 1. moral quality; conduct; character. 2. biography. —**i hasene** good character. —**i suretine uymaz** whose appearance belies his character.
sirhan (.—) سرحان A *lrnd.* wolf.
siri (——) سيری P *lrnd.* satiety; fullness, abundance.
sirişkᵏⁱ سرشك P *lrnd.* 1. a tear. 2. a drop of fluid. —**bar** (..—) P shedding tears.
sirişt سرشت P *lrnd.* 1. nature, temperament, constitution. 2. mixture, mixed mass. 3. form, figure; disposition. —**i hûb** sweet nature, lovely character.
sirişte سرشته P *lrnd.* 1. mixed and kneaded. 2. formed, fashioned. 3. endued, endowed with. 4. implanted (quality).
sirkᵏⁱ **1** سيرك F circus.
sirk=ᵉʳ **2** سيركك *archaic for* **silk= 2.**
sirkatᵗⁱ سرقت A *law* a stealing, theft.
sirke سركه P 1. vinegar. 2. sour, morose look. 3. nit (in the head). —**i dih sâle** 1. ten year old wine. 2. enmity, grudge.
sirke ebru (...—) سركه ابرو P *lrnd.* crabbed fellow.
sirkefüruş (...—) سركه فروش P *lrnd.* 1. seller of vinegar. 2. sour faced, morose. —**i** (...——) P vinegar selling.
sirkelen=ᵢʳ سركه لنمك 1. to become vinegar. 2. to become infested with nits.
sirkeli سركه لی 1. mixed or flavored with vinegar. 2. infested with nits.
sirkencübin, sirkengübin (...—) سركنجبين P *lrnd.* oxymel, honey and vinegar.
sirkin=ᵢʳ سركنتی *archaic for* **silkin=.** —**ti** *same as* **silkinti.**
sirküler سيركولر F general letter of authorization.
sirnaz (——) سرناز P *lrnd.* full of coquettish blandishments.
siroko (.'.) سيروكو It very hot wind, sirocco.
sirto (.') سيرتو Gk music composed in Turkish **makams** for dances in the Greek style.
sirud (.—) سرود P *lrnd.* three-stringed guitar.
sirvâlᵘ (.—) سروال A *lrnd.* trousers, pants.
sis سيس 1. fog, mist. 2. *prov.* freckle; freckles. 3. *archaic* small brown or reddish spots on the coat of a horse.
sisad سصد P *lrnd.* three hundred.
sisam (——) سيسام A 1. *same as* **susam 1.** 2. *w. cap.* Island of Samos.
siskin=ᵢʳ سسكنمك *archaic* to start up in terror from sleep. —**dir=** /ı/ *caus.*
sislen=ᵢʳ سسلنمك 1. to become damp and foggy. 2. to be misted over (glass). 3. *prov.* to become freckled. —**dir=** /ı/ *caus.*
sisli سسلی 1. foggy, misty; hazy. 2. *prov.* freckled. 3. *archaic* spotted (horse). — **kır** flea-bitten gray horse.

sistem سیستم F system. **—li** systematical. **—leştir=** /ı/ to systematize.

sistire (`.`..) سیستره Gk 1. instrument for scraping the dough off a bread board, baker's peel. 2. carpenter's scraper.

sişembih (—..) شنبه سشنبیه P lrnd. Tuesday.

sit 1 (—) صیت A lrnd. fame, reputation. **— u şöhret** fame and reputation.

sit 2 (—) صیت A lrnd. 1. loud, vehement (voice, sound). 2. loud-voiced, clamorous. **—i safa** joyous noise.

sitᵗᵘ 3 ست A lrnd. lady.

sitᵗᵘ 4 ست A lrnd. six.

sita 1 (.—) ستا P lrnd. 1. praise, eulogy.

-sita 2 (.—) ستا P lrnd. who praises, who panegyrizes, *as in* **hodsita.**

sita 3 (.—) ستا P lrnd. 1. threefold, triple. 2. composed of three elements; a thing of three elements; three-stringed lute.

sitabr ستبر P lrnd., same as **sitebr.**

sitad (.—) ستاد P lrnd. 1. a taking. 2. a buying.

sitade (.—.) ستاده P lrnd. 1. that has taken; taken, carried away. 2. that has risen or stood erect; standing; erect.

sitam (.—) ستام P lrnd. ornamented part of a saddle.

-sitan 1 (.—) ستان P lrnd. that takes or receives, *as in* **dilsitan.**

sitan 2 (.—) ستان P lrnd. country or region where something abounds.

sitane (.—.) ستانه P lrnd. threshold.

sitare (.—.) ستاره P lrnd. 1. star. 2. fortune, felicity. 3. three-stringed lute. 4. three-die backgammon. 5. open tent or pavilion. **—i dümdar** comet. **—i rahşân** bright star.

sitaredan (.—.—) ستاره‌دان P lrnd. astrologer.

sitaregân (.—.—) ستارگان P lrnd. the stars.

sitareli ستاره‌لی 1. starry. 2. lucky, fortunate. 3. in good condition; well-shaped, regular.

sitaresiz ستاره‌سز 1. unfortunate, unlucky. 2. ill-conditioned, miserable, poor. 3. misshapen, irregular.

sitaresuhte (.—.—.) ستاره‌سوخته P lrnd. ill-fated.

sitareşinâs (.—..—) ستاره‌شناس P lrnd. astronomer.

sitayende (.—..) ستاینده P lrnd. who praises.

sitayiş (.—.) ستایش P a praising; praise, eulogy, commendation. **— et=** /ı/ to praise, to eulogize.

sitayişgâh (.—.—) ستایشگاه P pros. portion of a poem devoted to eulogy.

sitayişger (.—..) ستایشگر P lrnd. who praises, eulogist.

sitayişkâr (.—.—) ستایشکار P praising, praiseful.

sitayişname (.—.—.) ستایش‌نامه P pros. eulogy.

sitebr ستبر P lrnd. thick, coarse, hard, stiff. **—î** (..—) P thickness, stoutness.

sited ستد P lrnd., same as **sitad.**

sitem ستم P 1. reproach, rebuke. 2. lrnd. wrong, injury; ill-treatment, cruelty. **— et=** /a/ to reproach.

sitemâlûd (..——) ستم‌آلود P lrnd. full of reproach.

sitemâmiz (..——) ستم‌آمیز P lrnd. unjust, cruel (words).

sitemdide (..—.) ستم‌دیده P lrnd. unjustly treated, ill-treated; oppressed. **—gân** (..—.—) P the oppressed.

sitemger ستمگر P lrnd. cruel, tyrant.

sitemî (..—) ستمی P lrnd. tyrannical, unjust, cruel.

sitemkâr (..—) ستمکار P reproachful. **—ân** (..——) P the unjust, the cruel (persons).

sitemkeş ستمکش P lrnd. unjustly treated, oppressed.

sitemreside (...—.) ستم‌رسیده P lrnd. reproached.

sitil 1 ستل [*Arabic* satl] prov. 1. small copper pail, large metal bucket (for watering horses). 2. large drinking cup with a handle, dipper. 3. silver brazier (for incense or coffee). 4. barber's hanging water reservoir with tap. 5. pot for boiling pitch.

sitil 2 ستیل F style; stylish.

sitiz (.—) ستیز P lrnd., same as **sitize.**

sitize (.—.) ستیزه P lrnd. quarreling, strife; fight; contention. **—cu** (.—.—) P, **—hu** (.—.—) P, **—kâr** (.—.—) P quarrelsome. **—ru** (.—.—) P ugly; cross, morose.

sitr ستر A lrnd. cover, covering; curtain, veil, screen.

sitte ستّه A lrnd. six. **—i sevir** *calendar* six days in April when the sun is in Taurus, known as a time of bad weather.

sitti ستّی A lrnd. My lady. Madam.

sittin (.—) ستّین A 1. a great many, *only in* **— sene** for a very long time. 2. lrnd. sixty; sixtieth.

sittûn (.—) ستّون A lrnd. sixty, sixtieth.

siva (.—) سوا A lrnd., same as **seva.**

sivar (.—) سوار A lrnd. bracelet. **—ı zerrin** golden bracelet.

sivil 1 سیویل F 1. civilian; in mufti. 2. plain-clothes policeman. 3. *slang* naked.

sivil 2, sivilce سیویل سیویلجه pimple, pustule.

siviş 1 سیویش سیویشمك a slipping away or disappearing. **— yılı** *solar calendar* the year in thirty-three of the lunar calendar not counted siviş= in numbering subsequent years, to keep harmony with the solar year.

siviş=ᶦʳ 2 سورشمك سورشمك to slip away, disappear, decamp.

sivişik⁼ⁱ سورشيك same as sıvışık.

sivişken سورشكن slippery, that slips away.

siviştir=ⁱʳ سورشدرمك /ı/ caus. of siviş= 2.

sivri سوری 1. sharp pointed; tapering. 2. tall and slim. — akıllı odd and self-opinionated, eccentric. — başlı 1. sharply tapering at one end. 2. obstinate, perverse. — boylu very tall (person). — bucak geom. acute angle. — burun 1. with a pointed nose. 2. palamut (fish). — kafalı obstinate. — köşe same as sivri bucak. — kulaklık 1. pointed, sharp-eared. 2. a kind of large sheath-knife. — kuyruk zool., oxyuris. — sıçan shrew. — sinek*.

sivril=ⁱʳ سوریلمك 1. to become pointed, to become prominent. 2. to make rapid progress in one's career.

sivrilce سوریجه same as sivilce.

sivrileş=ⁱʳ سوریلشمك to become pointed. —tir= /ı/ caus.

sivrilik⁼ⁱ سوریلك sharp-pointedness, taperingness.

sivrilt=ⁱʳ سوریلتمك /ı/ caus. of sivril=.

sivrisinek⁼ⁱ سوری سنك mosquito.

siy=ᵉʳ سیمك 1. to urinate against a wall (dog). 2. to be sexually excited (male animal).

siya (.́.) سیا It naut. a reversing oars and rowing backwards. —! Back oars! — et= to backwater.

siyab (.—) ثیاب A lrnd., pl. of sevb.

siyabullah (.—..) ثیابالله A lrnd. the curtains of the Kaaba at Mecca.

siyadet (.—.) سیادت A lrnd., same as seyadet.

siyah 1 سیاه [siyah 2] 1. black; black color. 2. dark; dark-colored. 3. Negro. 4. slang opium. — kalem pen and ink (drawing). — tilki black Siberian fox.

siyah 2 (.—) سیاه P lrnd. 1. same as siyah 1. 2. unlucky, inauspicious. 3. the fourth line on the cup of Jemshid. 4. the fourteenth book in the Zendavesta of Zoroaster.

siyahân (.——) سیاهان P lrnd. 1. Negroes. 2. dark skinned people. 3. thieves, robbers. 4. black locks of a beauty (as a robber of hearts).

siyahbaht (.—.) سیاه بخت P lrnd. unlucky.

siyahçerde (.—..) سیاه چرده P lrnd. 1. very dark skinned. 2. the beloved.

siyahçeşm (.—.) سیاه چشم P lrnd. 1. black-eyed. 2. the black-eyed hawk.

siyahdest (.—.) سیاه دست P lrnd. 1. avaricious, stingy. 2. unfortunate.

siyahdil (.—.) سیاه دل P lrnd. black-hearted, malevolent.

siyahfam (.——) سیاه فام P lrnd. black-colored.

siyahhane (.——.) سیاه خانه P lrnd. 1. haunted or ill-fated house. 2. prison.

siyahımsı, siyahımtırak⁼ⁱ سیاهمسی سیاهمترك somewhat black, blackish.

siyahi (.——) سیاهی P 1. Negro. 2. lrnd. blackness; darkness.

siyahkâm (.——) سیاه کام P lrnd. disappointed, unhappy.

siyahkâr (.——) سیاه کار P lrnd. evil-doing; sinner.

siyahkâse (.——.) سیاه کاسه P lrnd. avaricious, miser.

siyahkilim (.—.—) سیاه کلیم P lrnd. poor, wretched.

siyahlan=ⁱʳ, siyahlaş=ⁱʳ سیاهلنمك سیاهلشمك to become black, to turn black.

siyahlat=ⁱʳ سیاهلتمك /ı/ to blacken.

siyahlık⁼ⁱ سیاهلك 1. blackness. 2. a figure in the dark.

siyahlika (.—.—) سیاه لقا P lrnd. 1. black-faced. 2. disgraced.

siyahmağz (.—.) سیاه مغز P lrnd. 1. black-kerneled. 2. black-marrowed. 3. mad, insane.

siyahmest (.—.) سیاه مست P lrnd. dead drunk.

siyahname (.——.) سیاه نامه P lrnd. evildoer, worthless wretch.

siyahpuş (.——) سیاه پوش P lrnd. 1. clothed in black; mourner. 2. groom. 3. Christian priest or monk.

siyahru (.——) سیاه رو P lrnd. 1. black-faced. 2. disgraced. —yi (.———) P disgrace.

siyahruz (.——) سیاه روز P lrnd. unlucky (person).

siyahzeban (.—.—) سیاه زبان P lrnd. 1. foul-mouthed. 2. who brings bad tidings.

siyak⁼ⁱ (.—) سیاق A lrnd. 1. the after-context of a word, arrangement of ideas. 2. methods of expression; logical sequence. 3. style, manner. —ı baid log. round-about method of syllogism when the middle term is the subject of the minor premise and predicate of the major premise. — ü sibak the whole context of a word.

siyakat⁼ⁱ (.—.) سیاقت A 1. Ott. hist. style of writing used in treasury accounts and documents; the finance cipher. 2. lrnd. con-catenation, series. — kırması cramped, broken hand-writing similar to siyakat. — vavı a perverse, ugly man.

siyan (.—) سیان A lrnd., same as seyyan.

siyanen (.—́.) سیانا A lrnd. equally.

siyasa neol. politics, diplomacy.

siyasal neol. political. S— Bilgiler Fakültesi College of Political Science.

siyaset (.—.) سياست A 1. politics; policy; diplomacy. 2. *lrnd.* managing, governing, ruling; government. 3. *lrnd.* an administering property; administration. 4. *lrnd.* capital punishment. **—i bedeniye** *lrnd.* bodily service of a ruler to his people. **— et=** 1. to use policy or diplomacy. 2. *lrnd.* to administer; to govern, to rule, to run. 3. *lrnd.* to punish; to put to death, to execute. **— çeşmesi** *Ott. hist.* place of execution in Topkapı Palace. **— meydanı** place of execution. **—i mülk** *lrnd.* administration of the state, of the body politic. **—i nefsiye** *lrnd.* religious administration of a community.

siyaseten (.—'..) سياةً A politically, diplomatically.

siyasetgâh (.—.—) سياستگاه P *lrnd.* place of execution.

siyasi (.——) سياسى A 1. political, diplomatic. 2. *lrnd.* pertaining to administration or government. **— müsteşar** parliamentary secretary.

siyasiyat (.—.—) سياسيات A *lrnd.* diplomacy; politics.

siyasiyûn سياسيون A *lrnd.* politicians, diplomats.

siyatik^gi سياتيك F *path.* sciatica.

siyeç^ci سياج |*Arabic* **siyac**] *prov.* fence, enclosure, hedge or wall; hedge or wall with thorns set on it.

siyeh سيه P *lrnd.*, same as **siyah 2**.

siyer سير A *lrnd.* 1. rules of Muslim conduct. 2. the canon laws of Islam. 3. biography. **S—i Kebir** the larger book of the Prophet Muhammad's biography.

-siyle سيله *cf.* **-ile 2**.

siyret سيرت A *lrnd.*, same as **siret**.

siz 1 سز |*pl. of* **sen 1**| you, *also used politely for singular*. **— bilirsiniz** as you like; you know best. **—den iyi olmasın** *said when praising an absent person.* **—lere ömür!** May your life (be long), *said to indicate the death of a third person*. **— sağ olunuz!** May you have good health! *used on mentioning the death of a friend*.

-siz 2 سز *cf.* **-sız 1**.
-siz 3 سز *cf.* **-sız 2**.

sizcileyin سزجلين *archaic* like you.

sizdeh (—.) سزده P *lrnd.* thirteen. **—üm** (—..) P thirteenth.

sizin 1 سزڭ your; yours.
-sizin 2 سزن *cf.* **-sızın**.
sizinki^ni سزڭكى yours.
-sizlik^gi سزلك *cf.* **-sızlık**.

skolâstik^gi سكولاستيك F scholastic.

smokin سموكن E dinner jacket, tuxedo.

soba صوبا Sl 1. stove. 2. hothouse. 3. *slang* meeting place of rowdies. **— borusu** stovepipe. **— boyası** black lead. **— üzümü** hothouse grapes. **—cı** maker, repairer, or installer of stoves.

sobra (.'.) صوبره It *naut.* a counterbracing the yards. **— et=** /ı/ to back (the main top sail); to lie to (ship).

soda (.'.) صودا It soda.

sodyum صوديوم F sodium.

sof صوف [**suf**] cloth made with the hair of goats, camels etc.; camlet; mohair; alpaca.

sofa صوفا |*Arabic* **suffa**| 1. hall, anteroom. 2. stone bench. 3. sofa. 4. raised flower bed. 5. *Ott. hist.* military ward. **— kur=** *Ott. hist.* to meet in order to discuss the misbehavior of a member of the fire brigade (discipline committee). **— taşı** large flagstone at the foot of a staircase.

sofalı صوفالى 1. furnished with a porch, bench, etc. 2. *Ott. hist.* who remains in attendance in an anteroom (servant). **— çeşme** public fountain with a wide-eaved roof. **—lar** *Ott. hist.* a certain class of young men joining the Janissary organization.

sofi (.—) صوفى A *lrnd.* mystic, Sufi; devotee. **—yân** (..—) P *pl.* **—yâne** (..—.) P pertaining to a devotee or dervish; piously. **—ye** A, **—ye mezhebi** *phil.* mysticism. **—yûn** (..—) A mystics.

sofra صفره A 1. dining table; wooden or metal tray serving as a table. 2. meal; mealtime. 3. portable mat of leather, etc., serving as a table for meals. 4. anus. **— başında** at the table. **— başına geç=** to sit down to a meal. **— bezi** tablecloth. **— kaldır=** to clear away (after a meal). **— kur=** to set the table. **—sı meydanda** generous. **— örtüsü** tablecloth. **— takımı** table service. **—cı** butler.

softa صوفته [**suhte**] 1. *Ott. hist.* Muslim theological student. 2. bigot, fanatic. 3. behind the times, old-fashioned. **—lık** *abstr. n.*

sofu صوفو [**sofi**] 1. religious, devout. 2. fanatic. **— soğan yemez yerse kabuğunu komaz** *proverb* A fanatic will not eat onions, but if he does, he will not leave so much as its peel, *said of one who is strict toward others but self-indulgent*.

sofuluk^gu صوفولك religious devotion; punctiliousness in the observance of religious duties; fanaticism.

sofyan صوفيان *Or. mus.* a rythmic pattern of four beats.

soğan صوغان 1. onion, *bot., Allium cepa.* 2. bulb. **— cücüğü** heart of an onion. **— zarı** onion skin. **—cı** seller of onions. **—cık** pickling-onion, scallion. **—lı** prepared with onions.

soğanlık^gi صوغانلق 1. onion bed or garden. 2. place for storing onions.

Red 65.

soğla صوغله *prov.* soil where water is found by digging.

soğu=ʳ صوغومق صوغيمق 1. to become cold, to cool. 2. /dan/ to lose love, desire or enthusiasm; to be chilly in one's relations; to cease to care (for).

soğukᵍᵘ صغون صوغون صؤیه 1. cold; cold weather. 2. frigid, unfriendly; unemotional in disposition. 3. out of place, in bad taste. **— adam** unlovable person. **— al=** to catch a cold. **— algınlığı** *path.* a cold, chill. **— bastı** Cold weather has set in. **— bez*. — damga** embossed stamp. **— davran=** /a/ to behave coldly. **— dur=** to look on coldly. **— düş=** to be out of place, in bad taste (deed or word). **— hava deposu** deep freeze depot. **— iplik** *bookbinding* relief line made on leather-bound books. **— kaç=** *same as* **soğuk düş=. — kanlı*. — neva** unlovable. **— soğuk** unpleasantly; stupidly. **— söz** unfriendly word. **— yakmış** frost-bitten (vegetation.).

soğukbez صوغوزبز cotton cloth, jaconet.

soğukkanlı صوغوق قانلی 1. cool-headed, calm. 2. cold, unsympathetic.

soğukla=ʳ صوغوقلمق to catch cold. **—ma** cold, chill. **—t=** /ı/ *caus.*

soğuklukᵍᵘ صغوقلی 1. cold, coldness. 2. chilliness of manner. 3. cooling room in a public bath; tepidarium. 4. a cold sweet.

soğul=ᵘʳ صوغلمق صوغولمق سغلی *archaic* 1. to sink down into the earth and disappear (water, worm, etc.). 2. to become dry, to dry up.

soğulcan صوغلجان صوغوجان *same as* **solucan.**

soğulma *neol., geog.* low water.

soğum صوغم *archaic* satiety, repletion, satisfaction. **—suz** insatiable. **—suzluk** insatiability.

soğur=ᵘʳ *neol.* to absorb. **—ma** absorption.

soğuş=ᵘʳ صوغشمق *archaic* 1. to sink into the earth (water, etc.) 2. to sink, to subside from the surface. 3. to become dry (fluid).

soğut=ᵘʳ صوغتمق /ı/ *caus. of* **soğu=,** to cool.

soğutkan *neol.* refrigerant.

sohbet صحبت A friendly intercourse; conversation, chat, talk. **— et=** to have a chat. **—i yârân** a gathering of friends for conversation.

sok=ᵃʳ صوقمق 1. /ı, a/ to thrust into, to insert; to introduce; to drive into. 2. to involve, entail. 3. /ı, a/ to let in. 4. /ı/ to sting or bite (insect or snake). 5. to injure, to calumniate. 6. *slang* to punish.

sokakᵍⁱ سوقاق صوقاغن ـ قاغی ـ و قاغی [zukak] 1. road, street, alley. 2. outside, out of doors. **—a at=** /ı/ to turn out into the street. **—a atsan on lira eder** It's worth at least ten liras. **— aynası** window mirror. **— başı** entrance to a street. **—a çık=** to go out. **— çocuğu** street urchin. **— dili** The ordinary language of the people. **—a düş=** to take to the streets (woman). **— halkı** the rabble. **— havadisi** unimportant rumors. **— kadını** street-walker. **— kapısı** street-door of a house. **— kızı** 1. girl who is fond of being out. 2. street-walker. **— süpürgesi** 1. coarse broom made of twigs. 2. loose woman. **—a uğra=** to rush out into the street. **—ta yemek ye=** to eat out (at a restaurant, etc.).

sokma صوقمه 1. *verbal n. of* **sok=.** 2. introduced from outside; imported.

sokman صوقمان سقمان صقمان *archaic* a kind of high boot.

sokra صوقره سـقره صوغره *Gk naut.* butt seam between two plank ends in a ship's side. **— başı** butt end of a plank.

sokran=ⁱʳ صقرانمق صوقرانمق *prov.* to murmur and mutter in anger, to grumble.

soktur=ᵘʳ صوقدرمق /ı, a/ *caus. of* **sok=.**

soku صوقو *prov.* 1. stone mortar for pounding. 2. mallet, pestle. 2. stick or rod used for pushing something in, ramrod.

sokul=ᵘʳ صوقولمق صوقلی 1. *pass. of* **sok=.** 2. to push, worm, insinuate oneself into a place; to cultivate friendly relations with.

sokulgan صوقولغان who pushes in, insinuates himself everywhere; quick to make friends, sociable. **—lık** sociability.

sokum صوقوم صوقم 1. act of inserting; single quantity pushed in at one time. 2. place where a thing is inserted. 3. a kind of cheese sandwich made with thin bread. 4. *prov.* mouthful, morsel.

sokur صوقور *archaic* 1. mole. 2. blind; one-eyed.

sokuş=ᵘʳ صوقشمق /a/ to push oneself gently or secretly into a place or amongst others, to sneak in, to infiltrate. **—tur=** /ı/ *caus.*

sol 1 صول left; left side. **—a** to the left. **—da** on the left. **— açık** *soccer* left wing. **— eli bekle=** to wait for the left hand *said jokingly to a person who is late for dinner.* **—dan geri!** *mil.* Left about face! **—dan geri dön=** to turn left about, to retire. **— iç** *soccer* left inner. **— kol** 1. left hand. 2. left wing. **— muavin** *soccer* left halfback. **— müdafi** *soccer* left full-back, left back. **—da sıfır** unimportant; nonexistent; a mere nothing. **— tarafından kalk=** to get out of bed on the wrong side. **— yap** *chauffeur's slang* Steer to the left.

solˡᵘ **2** صول F *mus.* sol. **— anahtarı** treble clef.

sol=ᵃʳ **3** صولمق 1. to fade; to wilt. 2. to become pale.

solakᵍⁱ صولاغن 1. left-handed. 2. *Ott. hist.* guardsman in attendance on the Sultan in processions.

solakan (..—) صولاقان *same as* **solak**[2].
solcu صولجى *pol.* leftist.
soldur=ᵘʳ صولدرمق صولديرمك /ı/ *caus. of* **sol**= 3.
solfato (..'.) صولفاتو It quinine sulfate.
solfej صولفژ F *mus.* solfeggio.
solgun صولغون pale; faded; wilted.
solist صوليست F *mus.* soloist.
solla=ᵃʳ صڭللامق to cross over to the left side of the road (driver).
solma صولمه *verbal n. of* **sol**= 3.
solmaz صولماز صولمز 1. unfading. 2. fast (color).
solu=ᵃʳ صولومق to breathe heavily, to pant.
solucan صولجان صوغولجان صوغولان 1. common earthworm, *zool.*, *Lumbricus terrestris*. 2. ascarid, round worm. 3. shrewd cheater; sneaky person. — **gibi** 1. pale and thin. 2. unpleasant (person).
soluğan صولوغان 1. short of breath; asthmatic. 2. shortness of breath; asthma. 3. roaring (horse). 4. *geog.* swell (of the sea).
solukᵍᵘ 1 صولوق صوليق faded; withered; pale.
solukᵍᵘ 2 صولوق صولق 1. breath; a breathing; a panting. 2. *prov.* a short time, while. **bir —ta** in a flash. — **al**= to breathe; to take a breath, to recover oneself. — **aldırma**= /a/ not to allow one time to take a breath, not to give a break. — **alma** *physiol.* inspiration. — **borusu** *anat.* trachea. —**u Bağdatta al**= to flee the country, to escape. —**u daral**= 1. hardly to be able to breathe. 2. to escape narrowly. — **deliği** *biol.* stigma. — **soluğa** panting, out of breath. —**u soluğuna** without taking breath, all at once, instantly. — **verme** *physiol.* exhalation.
soluklan=ᵃʳ صولوقلانمق to take a long and easy breath; to have a rest. —**dır**= /ı/ *caus.*
solunum *neol.* respiration. — **sistemi** respiratory system.
solut=ᵘʳ صولوتمق /ı/ *caus. of* **solu**=. —**maz sancı** 1. hard work. 2. wearying, tedious, troublesome (action or thing).
som 1 صوم 1. solid, not hollow. 2. massive. — **duvar** solid wall.
som 2 صوم ivory from a fish tooth, rhinoceros horn, etc.
som 3 صوم F salmon, *zool.*, *Salmo salar*. — **balığı** *same as* **som** 3.
soma 1 صومه *archaic* useless, fruitless. —**ya çalış**= to work for nothing. —**sına gel**= to come to no purpose. — **yere çalış**= to work without useful result.
soma 2 (.'.) صومو raki without aniseed.
somakᵏı سماق صماق [*Arabic* **summak**] sumac, *bot.*, *Rhus coriaria*.
somaki (.—.) سماقى صماقى [*Arabic*

summaki] porphyry. — **sıva** stucco imitating porphyry scagliola.
somat صماط [**simat** 1] long mat or table on which food is set in a line; any table with food on it (used especially in dervish lodges).
somun صومون Gk (?) 1. loaf (of bread). 2. large soft thing (such as a camel's foot). 3. nut (to a bolt). — **ayak** clubfoot. — **gibi şiş**= to swell out like a loaf, to puff out, to be puffed out.
somuncu صومونجى *colloq.* sponger.
somur=ᵘʳ صومورمق *same as* **somurt**=.
somurdan=ᵃʳ صومورداتمق *archaic* to sulk, pout, grumble.
somurt=ᵘʳ صومورتمق to pout, to sulk, to frown.
somurtkan صومورتقان sulky. —**lık** sulkiness.
somut *neol.*, *gram.*, *phil.* concrete.
somye (.'.) صوميه F spring mattress.
son 1 صوڭ 1. end; last; ultimate; latter, final. 2. result, issue. 3. afterbirth. —**unda** finally, in the end. — **bahar***. —**dan bir evvelki** penultimate, next to the last. — **defa** last time; for the last time. — **derece** the utmost, most; extremely. —**unu düşün**= /ı/ to think of the consequences (of an act). —**unu getir**= /ın/ to succeed, to bring to a successful conclusion. —**unu getireme**= /ın/ to fail to achieve. — **günlük** ease and comfort in one's old age. —**a kalan dona kalır** The one who is last freezes. Hurry or you will lose out. — **kozunu oyna**= to use one's last resources. — **körlük** blindness as to results. — **nefes** one's last breath. — **pişmanlık akçe etmez** It is too late for repentance. — **posta** *colloq.* the last time.
son=ᵃʳ 2 صوڭمق *archaic* to become low (fire); to become dull (light).
sonbahar صوڭ بهار autumn, fall.
sonda (.'.) سوندا It 1. surgeon's probe. 2. bore; catheter.
sondaj سونداژ F test bore, exploratory well.
sondalama سوندالامه *same as* **sondaj**.
sondur=ᵘʳ صوندرمك /ı/ to stretch.
sonekᵏı (.'.) *neol.*, *gram.* suffix.
sonlu *neol.*, *math.* finite.
sonra (.'.) صوڭره • صكره • صوڭره 1. in the future, hereafter; then, afterwards; /dan/ later (than), after. 2. a later time; consequence, sequel, latter part of a series. —**dan** not at the time; later. —**ları** later. —**ya at**=, —**ya bırak**= /ı/ to postpone, to put off. —**sını düşün**=, —**yı düşün**= to think of the consequences. —**dan görme** newly-rich; upstart. —**dan olma** 1. comparatively recent. 2. upstart. —**sı sağlık** 1. That's all. 2. Never mind. Forget it.
sonraki صوڭره كى 1. who comes later. 2. that

sonrasız

happens later. —**ler** successors; those who come later; posterity.

sonrasız *neol.* eternal, endless. —**lık** eternity.

sonsuz صونسز 1. endless, eternal, infinite. 2. useless, without results. — **vida** *auto.* wormscrew. —**luk** 1. infinity endlessness. 2. vastness, boundlessness.

sontakı *neol., gram.* postposition.

sonucu[nu] صوڭوجى صوڭ اوجى *archaic,* same as **sonuç**.

sonuç[cu] *neol.* 1. result, consequence. 2. end, outcome; conclusion.

sonuçla=[r] *neol.* 1. /ı/ to bring to an end, to conclude. 2. to result in. —**n=** *pass.* —**ndır** *caus.*

sonuk[ğu] صوڭوق صوڭوك *archaic* 1. low (fire), extinct. 2. dull, lusterless, dim. —**luk** 1. lowness, extinction (of a fire). 2. dullness, lusterlessness.

sonuncu (.'.) صوڭنجى last, final; latter.

sop صوپ 1. *only in* **soy sop**. 2. *neol., sociol.* clan.

sopa صوپا صوپه صوپ 1. thick stick, club, cudgel. 2. blow (with a club), a beating. 3. stripe in cloth. — **at=**, — **çek=** /a/ to give a beating (to). — **düşkünü** deserving a beating. — **ye=** to get a beating, to be clubbed.

sopalı صوپالى 1. armed with a stick. 2. having broad stripes (cloth). — **taka** a certain cloth with stripes of gold thread.

sor=[ar] 1 صورمق /ı, a *or* dan/ to ask, to inquire (about). —**ma** (.'.) 1. Don't ask me! 2. Terrible! 3. Wonderful! —**a sora** by dint of repeated questions.

sor=[ur] 2 صورمق /ı/ to suck up (a fluid with a noise), to slurp, sip.

sora (.'.) صوره *colloq., var. of* **sonra**.

sorak[ğı] صوراق *archaic* question, enquiry.

sorav *neol.* responsibility.

sordur=[ur] صوردرمق صورديرمق /ı, a/ *caus. of* **sor=** 1.

sorgu صورغى 1. question, inquiry. 2. interrogation. —**ya çek=** /ı/ to cross-examine. — **hâkimi** coroner, examining magistrate.

sorguç[cu] صورغوچ سرغوچ 1. crest, aigrette (worn on the head). 2. plume (of a helmet). —**lu** plumed, tufted, crested.

sorgula=[r] صورغولمق صورغيلمق /ı/ to cross-examine.

sorgun, sorkun صورغون صورقون ben-tree, moringa, *bot., Moringa aptera.*

sorti صورتى F *elec.* outlet.

soru 1 صورى صورو question, interrogation. — **günü** Day of Judgment. — **işareti** question mark. — **sıfatları** interrogative adjectives.

soru=[r] 2 صورمق to suck noisily, to slurp.

soruk[ğu] صوروق *archaic, same as* **soru**.

sorul=[ur] صورولمق pass. of **sor=** 1.

sorum *neol.* responsibility. —**lu** /dan/ responsible (for). —**suz** irresponsible. —**suzluk** irresponsibility.

soruş=[ur] 1 صوروشمق verbal n. of **sor=** 1, question.

soruş=[ur] 2 صوروشمق to ask one another, to inquire. —**tur=** 1. to make investigations. 2. /ı/ to inquire (about), to investigate. —**turma** verbal n. investigation.

sorut=[ur] صورتمق *prov.* to pout, to look cross or disdainful.

sorutkan صورتقان صورتيقان *prov.* sulky, peevish; disdainful. —**lık** disdain, peevishness.

sosis سوسيس F sausage.

sosyal[li] سوسيال F social.

sosyalist سوسياليست F socialist.

sosyalizm سوسياليزم F socialism.

sosyete سوسيته F 1. the upper classes. 2. society.

sosyetik[ği] سوسيتيك F *ironical* belonging to high society.

sosyoloji سوسيولوجى F sociology.

sovuk[ğu] صوووق *same as* **soğuk**.

sovut=[ur] صووتمق /ı/ *same as* **soğut=**.

Sovyet سويت Soviet.

soy 1 صوى 1. family; race, lineage; ancestors; descendants. 2. of pure blood, noble. 3. good. 4. sort, kind; species. — **adı***. — **ağacı** family tree. — **at** thoroughbred horse. —**a çek=** to take after one's family. — **maden** bullion, precious metal. — **sop***. — **soya çeker** Heredity is strong.

soy=[ar] 2 صويمق /ı/ 1. to strip; to undress. 2. to rob; to sack. 3. to peel; to flay. —**up soğana çevir=** /ı/ to rob completely.

soya 1 صويا F soybean, *bot., Glycine Soja.*

soya 2 صويه *prov.* middle toe and claw of a bird of prey.

soya 3 صويه *prov.* 1. inclined, sloping, gently rising (ground). 2. superficial.

soya 4 صويه *prov.* clasp knife.

soyadı[nı] صوى آدى family name, surname.

soyca صويجه as a family; as regards family.

soycak[ğı] صويجغين *colloq.* the whole family (including relatives).

soydaş صويداش 1. of the same kind or race. 2. *biol.* consanguineous.

soydur=[ur] صويدرمق صويديرمق /ı, a/ *caus. of* **soy=** 2.

soyga صويغه decoy used in fowling.

soygun صويغون 1. pillage, spoliation. 2. undressed, stripped. 3. robbed. — **ver=** to be plundered, pillaged.

soyguncu صويغونجى plunderer, pillager. —**luk** plundering, fleecing.

soygunluk[ğu] صويغونلق 1. a being half undressed; nakedness. 2. robbery.

soyka صويقه *prov.* 1. garment. 2. garment taken off the body of a dead person; dead

soyla=ʳ صويله‌مك archaic /ı/ 1. to investigate, to inquire after. 2. to exalt, to honor.

soylu صويلى of a good family, noble. **—luk** nobility.

soyma صويمه verbal n. of **soy=** 2.

soymantı صويمانتى prov. 1. any vegetable product usually peeled to be eaten. 2. the peel or skin of vegetables such as cucumber. 3. cudgel made of a young stripped sapling.

soymukᵍᵘ صويموق prov. edible inner bark of the pine tree.

soysal neol. civil; civilized.

soy sop صوى سوپ family and relations. **soyu sopu belli** that comes from a good family..

soysuz صويسز 1. of bad race. 2. degenerate good-for-nothing, worthless.

soysuzlaş=ʳ صويسزلاشمق to degenerate.

soysuzlukᵍᵘ صويسزلق 1. degeneracy. 2. worthlessness; perversity.

soytarı صويطارى |Arabic sa'teri| clown, buffoon. **—lık** buffoonery.

soyucu صويجى brigand, thief.

soyul=ᵘʳ صويولمق 1. pass. of **soy=** 2. 2. to peel off.

soyuluş صويولش 1. verbal n. of **soyul=**. 2. neol., biol. philogeny.

soyun=ᵘʳ صويونمق 1. to undress (oneself); to take off good clothes (in order to work). 2. to join a mystical order. **—up döken=** to change into comfortable clothes. **—dur=** /ı/ caus.

soyuntu صويونتى 1. anything stripped off, peel, bark, etc. 2. spoils of war.

soyut neol., phil., gram. abstract. **—la=** to abstract, to isolate. **—lama** abstraction.

söbe سوبه prov. oval.

söbekᵍⁱ سوبك prov. 1. urinal attached to a baby's cradle. 2. oval. 3. metal axis around which the millstone turns.

söbü سوبى same as **söbe**.

söğ=ᵉʳ سوكمك same as **söv=**.

söğe سوكه same as **söve**.

söğülme سوكولمه prov. roast; roast meat.

söğüş سوكوش boiled meat; cold meat; vegetable served with no dressing.

söğüşle=ʳ سوكوشله‌مك /ı/ slang to swindle.

söğütᵈᵘ سوكوت willow, bot., Salix: **— yaprağı** 1. willow leaf. 2. a very thin kind of dagger. **—giller** neol., bot., Salicaceae. **—lü** covered with willows. **—lük** willow grove.

sök=ᵉʳ سوكمك 1. /ı/ to tear down; to pull up. 2. /ı/ to rip open; to undo; to unravel; to dismantle. 3. /ı/ to break through (obstacle); to surmount (difficulty). 4. /ı/ to break up (land). 5. /ı/ to decipher. 6. to succeed. 7. to take effect (purgative). 8. to appear, come out; to break (down). 9. to flow (mucus).

sökel سوكل prov. diseased, infirm. **—lik** illness.

söktür=ᵘʳ سوكديرمك /ı, a/ caus. of **sök=**.

sökükᵍᵘ سوكوك 1. unraveled; unstitched; ripped, burst open. 2. dropped stitch in knitting; tear. **— ör=** to repair a tear.

sökül=ᵘʳ سوكولمك 1. pass. of **sök=**. 2. slang to be forced to give or pay. **—üp atıl=** to be utterly eradicated.

sökün سوكون an appearing suddenly. **— et=** 1. to appear suddenly. 2. to burst in suddenly in a crowd. 3. to crop up; to come one after the other.

söküntü سوكونتى 1. rip in a seam; place where knitting has unraveled. 2. sudden rush of a crowd. 3. undone or broken-up things.

söküotuⁿᵘ سوكواوتى bird's foot trefoil, bot., Ornithopus.

sölgü سولكى same as **sölpük**.

sölpü=ʳ سولپمك to hang flabbily; to be flabby or sluggish.

sölpükᵍᵘ سولپوك flabby; lax.

sömestr سومستر F semester.

sömür=ᵘʳ سومورمك 1. /ı/ to gobble down; to devour. 2. to graze (cow). 3. to exploit, to seize for private gain (natural resources, public property).

sömürge neol. colony. **—ci** colonist.

sömürt=ᵘʳ سومورتمك /ı/ caus. of **sömür=**.

sön=ᵉʳ سونمك 1. to be extinguished, to go out (fire). 2. to be deflated. 3. to become slack, to flap (sail). **—dür=** /ı/ caus. **—dürül=** pass.

sönükᵍᵘ سونوك 1. extinguished; extinct. 2. dim; tarnished; lusterless. 3. obscure, undistinguished. 4. washed out. 5. deflated. 6. slack (sail). **—lük** abstr. n.

sönüm neol. 1. phys. damping (of a pendulum). 2. com. periodic debt reduction.

söv=ᵉʳ سومك /a/ to curse, to swear. **—üp say=** /a/ to swear (at). **—dür=** /ı, a/ caus.

söve سوه ، سوه 1. door or window frame. 2. posts on a wagon for holding up the load. **— taşı** door frame.

sövel=ⁱʳ سوه‌لمك prov. 1. to stand up. 2. to grow long or tall. **—t=** /ı/ caus.

söven سون prov. stick used for making fences.

söviş 1 سوكوش ، سوكش verbal n. of **söv=**.

söviş=ᵘʳ **2** سوكشمك /la/ to curse and swear at each other. **—üp sayış=** to swear violently at one another. **—tür=** /ı, la/ caus. of **söviş=**.

söyke, söykekᵍⁱ سويكك archaic support.

söyken=ⁱʳ سويكنمك archaic to lean against.

söyle=ᵣ سويلەمەك سويلەمك 1. to speak, to say, to tell. 2. to declare, utter, explain. 3. to betray, disclose, divulge. 4. to sing. **—me** *verbal n.*
söylen=ⁱʳ سويلەنمك 1. *pass. of* **söyle=**. 2. to grumble, mutter. **—il=** *pass.* **—iş** *verbal. n.* **—ti** *neol.* rumor.
söyleş=ⁱʳ سويلەشمك سويلشمك /la/ 1. to talk over, discuss (something). 2. to converse or consult with one another. **—tir=** /ı/ *caus.* **—tiril=** *pass.*
söylet=ⁱʳ سويلەتمك سويلتمك /a, ı/ *caus. of* **söyle=**. **—il=** *pass.* **—tir=** *caus. of* **söylet=**.
söylev *neol.* speech.
söyleyiş سويلەيش 1. *verbal n. of* **söyle=**. 2. *neol.* pronunciation. **—ine göre** 1. according to what he said. 2. from his manner of speaking.
söyün=ᵘʳ سوينمك سوينمك *prov., same as* **sön=**. **—dür=** /ı/ *caus.*
söz سوز 1. word; speech, talk. 2. promise, agreement. 3. rumor, gossip. 4. influence. 5. remark, observation. **—de*.** **— aç=** /dan/ to start a conversation (about). **— ağızdan dökülüyor** You can tell by the way he is speaking that he is lying. **—ü ağıza tık=**, **—ü ağzına tıka=** to interrupt somebody abruptly, to shut someone up. **— al=** to obtain a promise. **— altında kalma=** not to remain silent when insulted or attacked. **— anla=** to show understanding; to be reasonable. **— anlamaz** unreasonable, obstinate. **— anlar** reasonable. **— anlat=** /a/ to persuade. **— aramızda** between you and me. **— arasında** in the course of the conversation; by the way. **— at=** 1. to make an insulting or cutting remark (to somebody). 2. to make improper remarks (to a stranger, usually a girl). **—e atıl=** to butt in unnecessarily into a conversation. **— ayağa düştü** Important affairs have got into the hands of the rabble. **—ü bağla=** to bring a speech to a conclusion. **—ünü bal ile kes=** /ın/ to apologize and interrupt a conversation. **— başı** chapter heading, paragraph. **—ünü bil=** to be tactful and considerate in talking. **—ünü bilmez** tactless. **— bir Allah bir** I am a man of my word. **— bir et=** to unite with others (against someone or something). **— birliği** unanimity, agreement. **—e boğ=** /ı/ to drown a subject in a torrent of words. **—ü bol** one who is generous with words and fine promises. **— bölükleri** *neol., gram.* parts of speech. **— çat=** *archaic* to put words together, to speak. **—ü çevir=** to change the subject. **—ünden çık=** /ın/ to disregard the advice of (someone). **—ü çiğne=** to mumble. **—ünü değiştir=** to change one's tone. **— dinle=** to listen and follow advice. **— dizimi** *gram.* word order; syntax. **—ünden dön=** to go back on one's word. **—ünde dur=** to keep one's word. **— düşmez** /a/ It is not his place to speak. **— düşür=** to bring the conversation (to a subject). **— ebesi** 1. quick at repartee. 2. chatterbox. **— ehli** 1. eloquent person. 2. reasonable man. **— eri** 1. spokesman; good talker. 2. influential, whose word goes. **—ünün eri** man of his word. **—ünü esirgeme=** not to hold back one's words, to speak out one's opinion plainly. **— esle=** *archaic* to take advice, to be obedient. **— et=** 1. to talk, gossip (unfavorably about somebody). 2. to raise an objection. **—ü geçen** aforesaid; abovementioned. **—ü geçer** His words have weight; he is influential; what he says goes. **— geçir=** /a/ to make one's influence felt; to make somebody listen to one. **— gel=** /a/ to be subject to criticism. **—e gel=** to be gossiped about. **— gelişi** for example; supposing that; for the sake of argument. **—ün gelişi** in the course of a conversation. **— götürmez** It is beyond question; there is no room for discussion. **— işit=** to be scolded. **— kaldır=** not to take offense at a joke or a contradiction. **— kaldırmaz** who cannot take a joke against himself; who cannot stand being contradicted. **—e kapıl=** to be taken in by persuading words. **— kavafı** chatterbox, talker. **— kes=** 1. to decide, to agree. 2. to conclude a marriage agreement. **—ünü kes=** /ın/ to interrupt a person, to cut somebody short. **— kesimi** agreement to marry, engagement. **— kesiş=** /la/ to agree together on a matter of business. **—ün kısası** in short, the short of it is. **— ol=** to be the subject of gossip. **— olur** People will talk about it; there will be gossip. **— olsun diye** without meaning what one says; just to say something. **—üm ona** so-called, alleged, *e. g.,* **sözüm ona doktor** the alleged physician, **sözüm ona gidecekti** He was supposed to go (but he did not). **— onun** 1. What he says is right. 2. It is his turn to speak. **— öğret=** /a/ to put words into one's mouth, to prompt (another). **— sağırlığı** *psych.* auditory aphasia, word deafness. **— sahibi** 1. who has a say (in a matter). 2. master of words, eloquent. **— sat=** to boast, to brag. **— sav** chit chat. **—ün sırası gelmişken** by the way, now that we have mentioned it. **—üm söz** You have my word, I promise solemnly. **— sözü açar** One topic leads to another. **— söğesi** a trivial word, an expletive. **— tekerle=** 1. to blurt out; to let slip out inadvertently. 2. to coin a parable or proverb. **—ünü tut=** 1. to keep one's word. 2. /ın/ to take the advice of, to obey. **— ver=** /a/ to promise, to give one's word. **—üm yabana** *colloq.* Pardon the expression. **—ümü yabana atma** Don't disregard what I say. **— yitimi** *neol.* aphasia.

— **yok** There is nothing to say to that; quite true! —**üm yok** Well and good; I have no objections.
sözcü 1. spokesman. 2. *prov.* talker.
sözde 1. in word only. 2. so-called; as though, as if. 3. supposing that supposedly. 4. pseudo.
sözleş=ir /la/ 1. to agree together (on something); to make an appointment. 2. to dispute.
sözleşme 1. *verbal n. of* **sözleş**=. 2. agreement, contract. 3. appointment.
sözlü 1. agreed together; having promised. 2. engaged to be married. 3. in words, verbal, oral.
sözlükğü *neol.* dictionary, vocabulary.
spekülâsyon F speculation.
spiker (´.) E announcer (radio).
spor 1 F sports, games.
spor 2 F *biol.* spore. — **kesesi** sporangium.
sporcu athlete, game player; sportsman.
sporlular *neol., zool., Sporozoa.*
sportmen E athlete.
stad, stadyum F stadium.
staj F 1. apprenticeship; training. 2. course of instruction; probation. — **gör**=, — **yap**= to be under training.
stajyer F apprentice, probationer.
statü F rules of an organization.
statüko F status quo.
steno F 1. stenography. 2. stenographer.
stenografi F shorthand (writing), stenography.
step F steppe.
stepne E *auto.* spare tire.
stilo F fountain pen.
stokku F stock, inventory.
stor window shade.
strangola (.´.) It *naut.* a frapping (action and result). — **et**= to frap (a rope).
strateji F *mil.* strategy.
stratejikği F *mil.* strategical.
su 1 1. water, fluid. 2. sap, juice. 3. stream, brook; mass of water. 4. broth; gravy. 5. temper (of steel). 6. luster (of a jewel). 7. disposition (of a person). 8. *embroidery* running pattern. —**dan** of no significance, empty (talk), insubstantial (pretext). —**lar***. — **al**= to leak, make water (ship). — **altı** underwater. — **arkı** irrigation channel. — **askıları** *neol., bot., Characeae.* — **aygırı** hippopotamus. —**da balık sat**= to sell the fish in the water; to promise what cannot be fulfilled. — **bas**= /ı/ to flood a place (water). — **baskını** flood. — **başı***. —**yun başı** 1. source, spring, fountain. 2. water-side, shore. 3. center; most important part (of a business).

—**yu başından kes**= 1. to cut off at its source. 2. to nip in the bud. — **bendi** water reservoir, dike, dam. — **biberi** water pepper, *bot.*, *Polygonum hydropiper*. —**da boğul**= to be drowned. —**ya boğul**= to be overwhelmed with an excess of water. — **bölümü çizgisi** *geog.* watershed. — **böreği** a pastry made by boiling the sheets of dough before baking. — **cenderesi** hydraulic press. — **çek**= 1. to draw water from a well or cistern. 2. to absorb. 3. to carry water. —**yunu çek**= to be exhausted, to be used up. —**yu çekilmiş değirmene dön**= to become completely useless. —**yu mu çıktı?** /ın/ What's wrong with it? — **çiçeği** chicken pox, *path.* varicella. — **çulhası** water spider. — **çulluğu** common sandpiper, *zool., Tringa hypoleuca*; snipe. — **damarı** subterranean vein of water. — **dolabı** wheel for raising water. — **dök**= 1. to urinate. 2. to spill water. — **dökmelik** urinal. — **dökün**= to bathe with a basin and dipper. —**ya düş**= 1. to fail, to come to naught. 2. to fall into water. — **et**= to leak, make water (ship). — **geçmez**, — **geçirmez** waterproof. — **gemesi** water rat, *zool., Arvicola amphibius*, —**yu getiren de bir testiyi kıran da** For some people it's all the same whether you exert yourself or you are useless (indicating lack of appreciation). — **gibi** 1. like water. 2. easily, smoothly. 3. fluently. — **gibi aziz ol** Be as worthy as water *said in thanks to one who offers water.* — **gibi bil**= to know perfectly. — **gibi git**= to be spent like water (money). — **gibi oku**= /ı/ to read fluently. —**yuna git**=, —**yunca git**= /ın/ not to go counter to a person; to treat with tact; to flatter when necessary. —**yu görmeden paçaları sıva**= to tuck up one's trousers before seeing a stream; to count one's chickens before they are hatched. —**ya göster**= /ı/ to give something a quick rinse-through. — **götürür** It bears examination; disputable. — **götürmez** indisputable. —**ya götürür susuz getirir** (*lit.* He takes one to the stream and brings him back without having had a drink.) very cunning and crafty. — **güllesi** globular bottle for water. — **hattı** *naut.* water line. — **havuzu** *chem.* vat. — **hazinesi** water tank. — **hızarı** sawmill worked by water. — **hızası** 1. water level. 2. water-level (instrument). — **ıtrıfili** marsh trefoil, buckbean, *bot., Menyanthes trifoliata.* — **içmek gibi** very easy. — **içinde** easily; certainly. — **içinde kal**= 1. to get very wet. 2. to sweat heavily. — **in**= /a/ to have a cataract (eye). — **inmesi** accumulation of humour in some part of the body. — **kabağı** white gourd, vegetable marrow, *bot., Cucurbita pepo*. — **kaçır**= 1. to leak. 2. *slang* to annoy, to disturb. — **kaldır**= 1. to take up or absorb water (rice, etc., when cooking). 2. not to take offense at a joke or a contradiction. — **kaldırmaz** 1. who cannot stand being contradicted; who cannot take a joke about himself. 2. indisputable; beyond question. — **kamışı** reedmace, cattail, small bulrush, *bot., Typha latifolia*. — **kamışıgiller** *neol., Typhaceae*. — **kap**= to imbibe water and fester (wound). — **katılmamış** unadulterated, pure. — **keleri** newt. — **kemeri** aqueduct. — **kendiri** Virginian hemp, water hemp, *bot., Acnida cannabiona*. — **keneviri** bur marigold, water hemp, *bot., Bidens tripartita*. — **kerdemesi** watercress, *bot., Nasturtium officinale*. — **kerevizi** water parsnip, *bot., Sium latifolium*. — **kesimi** *naut.* draft of water of a vessel, water line. —**yu kesiyor** It is very blunt (knife). — **kireci** *geol.* hydraulic lime. — **koyver**= 1. to extract water (cooking vegetables). 2. *slang* to become impudent, to overdo it. — **kulesi** 1. water tower. 2. *rail.* tank. — **malikesi** *lrnd.* 1. mermaid. 2. the common seal. — **maydanozu** marshwort, *bot., Sium repens*. — **medüzleri** *zool.* hydromedusa. — **mercimeği** duckweed, water lentil, *bot., Lemna minor*. — **mercimeğigiller** *neol., bot., Lemnaceae*. — **mermeri** 1. alabaster. 2. stone deposited from water. — **oku** adder's tongue, arrowhead, *bot., Sagitteria sagittifolia*. — **oyuğu** undermining, underwashing; erosion (of banks). — **örümceği** water spider, *zool., Argyoneta aquatica*. — **patlangıcı** underwater firecracker. — **perisi** nymph. —**yuna pirinç salınmaz** He is not reliable. — **raziyanesi** samphire, sea fennel, *bot., Crithmum maritimum;* water hemlock, *bot., Cicuta virosa*. — **rezenesi** meadowsweet, *bot., Filipendula rubra*. — **saati** 1. *archaeol.* clepsydra, water clock. 2. water meter. —**ya sabuna dokunma**= to avoid meddling; to refrain from attacking. — **samuru** smaller otter. — **sayacı** *neol.* water meter. —**yu seli kalmamış** all dried up (food). —**yu sert** 1. hard-tempered (steel). 2. harsh (person). — **sıçanı** water vole, water rat, *zool., Arvicola amphibius*. — **sığırı** water buffalo, *zool., Bubalus bubalis*. — **sineği** mayfly, ephemerid. — **yunun suyu** a distant relationship; only a remote connection. — **sümbülü** water hyacinth, *bot., Eichhornia crassipes*. — **tabakası** underground water level. — **tavuğu** European coot, *zool., Fulica atra*. — **tedavisi** *med.* hydrotherapeutics. — **terazisi** *phys.* hydrostatic balance. — **teresi** watercress, *bot., Nasturtium officinale*. —̇ **testisi su yolunda kırılır** *proverb* The pitcher is broken on trips to the fountain. One must endure the results of one's behavior. —**yuna**

tirit simple, uninteresting, scanty. —**yu tokmakla kesiyor** *same as* **suyu kesiyor**. — **topla**= to have an accumulation of fluid (wound). —**dan ucuz** extremely cheap. — **uyur düşman uyumaz** *proverb* One must be always alert and careful. — **üstü** above-water. — **ver**= /a/ 1. to water. 2. to give water to. 3. to temper (steel). — **yaldız** gilding wash. — **yap**= *same as* **su et**=. — **yarpuzu** water mint, *bot., Mentha aquatica* — **yelvesi** water rail, *zool., Rallus aquaticus*. **bir** — **yıka**= to wash once (clothes, etc.). — **yılanı** water snake. — **yolcu***. — **yolu** 1. water conduit; aqueduct. 2. *biol.* urinary passage. 3. watermark (in paper). — **yoncası** buckbean, marsh trefoil, *bot., Menyanthes trifoliata*. — **yoncası** buckbean, marsh trefoil, *bot., Menyanthes trifoliata*. — **yosunu** seaweed, *bot., Alga marina*. —**yu yumuşak** 1. good-natured. 2. soft-tempered (steel). — **yürümüş** /a/ It has begun to rise (sap of trees); they have begun to bud (trees).

su 2 (—) سُوء A *lrnd.* evil, badness.
su 3 (—) سُو P *lrnd.* side, quarter, direction.
-su[nu] **4** ـسُو *cf.* **-ı 3**.
-su 5 ـسُو *cf.* **-sı 2**.

sual[li] **1** (. —) سُؤَال A 1. question; inquiry. 2. problem. 3. *lrnd.* request, petition. 4. *lrnd.* a begging alms, begging. — **aç**= /a/ to interrogate. — **cevab** question and answer; dialogue. — **et**= /a/ to ask. — **sor**= /a/ 1. to put a question. 2. to ask a question. — **takriri** interpellation.
sual 2 (. —) سَعَال A *lrnd., var. of* **süal**.
sualât (. — —) سُؤَالَات A *lrnd., pl. of* **sual 1**.
sualli سُؤَالِى containing a question. — **cevaplı** in the form of question and answer.
suavi (. — —) سَاعُوف A *lrnd.* who patiently undergoes vigils or fatigues; active and industrious.
su'ban (. —) ثُعْبَان A *lrnd.* large snake; mythical serpent of enormous size, dragon.
subaşı[nı] **1** صُوبَاشِى 1. source, spring, fountain. 2. waterside.
subaşı 2 صُوبَاشِى *Ott. hist.* 1. police superintendent. 2. farm manager.
subay *neol.* officer.
subesu (—. —) سُوبَسُو P *lrnd.* from side to side; on all sides; side by side.
subh صُبْح A *lrnd.* dawn, daybreak. —**i âherîn** the real dawn. —**i düruğ**, —**i evvel**, —**i evvelîn**, —**i kâzib** false dawn. — **ü mesa** morning and evening. —**i mustatil** false dawn. —**i mustatir** *same as* **subh-i sadık**. —**i mülemma nikab** false dawn. —**i sadık**, —**i sani** the real dawn, the real break of day. — **ü şâm** morning and evening. —**i yeküm** false dawn.

subha سبحه A *lrnd.* 1. rosary. 2. litany, consisting of the repetition, thirty-three times, of each of the three formulas. 3. act of divine worship.
subhan (.´.) صبحى A *lrnd.* at dawn.
subhdem, subhgâh (.—) صبحدم صبحگاه P *lrnd.* daybreak; at daybreak; early in the morning.
subhî (.—) صبحى A *lrnd.* pertaining to daybreak.
subilim *neol.*, hydrology.
subkütan سبكوتان F *med.* subcutaneous.
subra (´.) سبرا F dress shield.
sucu صوجى water seller.
sucukᵍᵘ صوجوق 1. savory sausage. 2. confection made of grape juice boiled and dried on strings of nuts. 3. soft, lax, flabby. **—unu çıkar=** /ın/ 1. to beat, pummel. 2. to tire out, to exhaust. **— gibi ıslan=, — kesil=, — ol=** to be wet through, to be drenched, soaked.
sucul *neol., bot., zool.* hydrophyte, hydrophilous.
suç صوچ 1. fault; offense; guilt. 2. crime; sin. **— at=** /a/ to attribute an offense to. **—unu bağışla=** to forgive an offense. **— et=** to commit an offense, to sin. **—undan geç=** /ın/ to overlook somebody's offense. **— işle=** to commit an offense or crime. **— ortağı** *law* accomplice, accessory. **— tasnii** *law* simulation of infringements. **— üstü*. — yüklet=** /a/ to lay the blame on.
suçla=ʳ صوچلامق /ı, la/ to accuse, to lay the blame (on). **—n=** /la/ to be accused. **—ndır=** /ı/ 1. to accuse. 2. to find guilty. **—ndırıl=** *pass.*
suçlu صوچلى guilty; culprit; sinner. **— bulun=** 1. to be guilty. 2. to be found guilty. **— çıkar=** /ı/ to find guilty. **— dur=** to stand like a culprit in a shamefaced way. **—ları geri verme, —ların iadesi** *law* extradition. **—luk** guilt; guiltiness.
suçsuz صوچسز not guilty, innocent. **—luk** innocence.
suçüstü صوچ اوستى *law* red-handed. **— yakalanmış** caught in the act.
sud (—) سود P *lrnd.* 1. profit, gain. 2. advantage, benefit, utility.
sudaᵃ¹ (.—) صداع A *lrnd.* 1. headache. 2. annoyance, trouble.
sudakᵍⁱ صداق pike perch, walleye, *zool.*, *Lucioperca.*
Sudan سودان [A ——] 1. *geog.* the Sudan. 2. *lrnd.* negroes. **—î** (———) A *lrnd.* pertaining to the Sudan, Sudanese; of or from the Sudan. **—lı** Sudanese.
sudaver (——.) سوداور P *lrnd.* profitable; advantageous.

sude (—.) سوده P *lrnd.* 1. rubbed, worn, chafed. 2. dust, powder, scrapings.
sudg (.—) صدغ A *anat.* temple. **—î** (.—) A templar.
sudhar (——) سودخار P *lrnd.* usurer.
sudi (——) سودى P *lrnd.* pertaining to advantage.
sudmend (—.) سودمند P *lrnd.* profitable, advantageous; useful. **—î** (—.—) P profit, gain, advantage.
sudur 1 (.—) صدور A *lrnd.* an issuing, emanating; emanation. **— et=** to issue, to be issued; to take place.
sudur 2 (.—) صدور A *lrnd., pl. of* **sadr**. **—i kirâm** *Ott. hist.* Kaziaskers. **—i nâs** chiefs, ministers.
suf (—) صوف A *lrnd.* wool.
sufar (——) سوفار P *lrnd.* 1. small, narrow hole; eye of a needle. 2. notch at the end of an arrow.
sufeyha صفيحه A *anat.* lamella.
sufi (——) صوفى A *same as* **sofi**.
sufistai (—.—.) سوفسطائى A *lrnd.* 1. sophistic. 2. sophist. **—ye** (—.—..) A the sophist school of philosophers. **—yun** (—.—.—) sophists.
suflör سوفلور F *theat.* prompter.
sufret صفرت A *lrnd.* 1. yellowness; yellow color. 2. paleness.
sufuf (.—) صفوف A *lrnd., pl. of* **saf 2**.
suga (.´.) سوغا It *naut.* Belay. **— et=** to belay, to tighten (rope, screw).
sugur (.—) ثغور A *lrnd., pl. of* **sagar 2**, passes, narrows, straits; frontiers.
suğr صغر A *lrnd.* a being insignificant; insignificance.
suğra! صغرى A 1. *logic* minor premise, minor. 2. *lrnd.* less; least, smallest. 3. *lrnd.* younger, youngest.
suhan (——) سوهان P *lrnd.* file; rasp; grater. **—i ruh** worry, nuisance, pest.
suhen سخن P *lrnd.* 1. word, expression; remark, saying; discourse, talk. 2. *myst.* revelation or divine command. **—i âbberdâr** equivocal speech. **—i bikr** original saying; clever original turn of phrase. **—i dehlizî** baseless rumor; gossip, petty scandal. **—i gaibî** communication from the unseen world; a foretelling, predicting. **—i gılâfî** ambiguous language. **—i zinde** elegant speech, brilliant talk.
suhenârâ (..——) سخن آرا P *lrnd.* eloquent.
suhençin (..—) سخن چين P *lrnd.* informer, tale-bearer, calumniator.
suhendân (..—) سخن دان P *lrnd.* eloquent; who knows the value of words; poet.
suhengû (..—) سخن گو P *lrnd.* eloquent.

suhenperdaz, suhenpira (...—) سخن پرداز سخن پیرا P lrnd. eloquent.

suhenran (..—) سخن ران P lrnd. orator, rhetorician.

suhensenc سخن سنج P lrnd. weigher of words; prudent; poet.

suhensera (...—) سخن سرا P lrnd. orator; excellent writer.

suhenver سخنور P lrnd. eloquent.

suhenza (..—) سخن زا P lrnd. that brings forth words.

suhre سخره A 1. lrnd. ridiculous fellow, laughingstock. 2. prov. person or animal reduced to subjection and obedience; one who is compelled to work for nothing.

suhriye سخریّه A lrnd. mockery, scoffing; ridicule.

suhte (—.) سوخته P lrnd. 1. burnt, scorched, singed. 2. hurt, injured, vexed, grieved. 3. lost, squandered. 4. *same as* **softa**.

suhtecan (—.—) سوخته جان P lrnd. pained, suffering.

suhtedil (—..) سوخته دل P lrnd. whose heart is inflamed, grieved.

suhtegi (—.—) سوخته گی P lrnd. burning, burnt.

suhtekevkeb (—...) سوخته کوکب P lrnd. unfortunate, unlucky.

suhtepâ (—.—) سوخته پا P lrnd. whose feet are blistered from running.

suhtevat (—.—) سوخته وات P lrnd. the softas.

suhuf صحف A lrnd. 1. written books, pages or tablets. 2. sheets or tablets not yet written on. 3. the books of the minor prophets.

suhunet (.—.) سخونت A lrnd. hardness and thickness.

suhur (.—) صخور A lrnd., *pl. of* **sahr**.

suhuv, suhuvvet سخو سخوّت A lrnd. a being munificent; munificence.

sui- (—.) سوء A evil, mis-. **—ahlâk** (—..—) P lrnd. immorality; vice. **—amel** (—...) P lrnd. bad act, offense. **—hâl** (—.—) P misconduct. **—hareket** (—....) P lrnd. evil deed, misconduct. **—hazm** (—..) P lrnd. indigestion. **—idare** (—..—.) P misgovernment; maladministration. **—istimal** (—..——) P abuse; misuse; misappropriation. **—istimal et=** /ı/ to misuse, abuse, misappropriate. **—karin** (—..—) P lrnd. bad associate, bad companion. **—kasd** (—..) P lrnd., **—kast** malice aforethought; criminal attempt, plot. **—kastçı** one who makes attempt upon life, conspirator. **—misal** (—..—) P lrnd. bad example. **—mizac** (—..—) P lrnd. bad health. **—muamele** (—..—..) P lrnd. bad treatment. **—niyet** (—...) P evil intention. **—tali** (—.:—.) P lrnd. misadventure, ill fortune. **—tefehhüm** (—....) P misunderstanding. **—tefsir** (—..—) P lrnd. misinterpretation. **—telâkki** (—....) P lrnd. misconception. **—zan** (—..) P lrnd. suspicion, distrust.

sukᵏᵘ (—) سوق A lrnd. 1. market place, market. 2. public square.

sukalâ (..—) ثقلا A lrnd., *pl. of* **sakil**, heavy (men in any sense). **—i nâs** burdens to others, bores.

sukat 1 (.—) سقات A lrnd. they who give something to drink, cupbearers.

sukat 2 (.—), **sukata** (.—.) سقاط A lrnd. 1. crumbs and scraps that fall off. 2. anything of little value. **—çin** (.—.—) P gatherer of crumbs. **—hâr** (.—.—) P one who eats crumbs and left-overs.

sukbe ثقبه A lrnd. small hole, puncture, perforation; *anat.* foramen.

suki (——) سوقی A lrnd. pertaining to the market; dealer, tradesman.

sukub (.—) ثقوب A lrnd., *pl. of* **sakb**.

sukuf (.—) سقوف A lrnd., *pl. of* **sakf**. **—i büyût** house roofs. **—i münakkaşa** ornamental roofs.

sükûkᵏᵘ (.—) صکوک A lrnd., *pl. of* **sak 2**.

sukut (.—) سقوط A 1. a falling, fall. 2. a lapsing from a path, lapse, deviation. 3. abortion. 4. a becoming of no avail; downfall. **—ı ahlâk** lrnd. moral corruption. **— et=** 1. to fall; to drop. 2. to lapse. **—ı hayal** disappointment. **— sebepleri** *law* causes for discharge, termination, forfeiture.

sula=ʳ سولامق /ı/ 1. to water; to irrigate. 2. to thin, dilute with water, water down. 3. to temper (steel). 4. *slang* to pay cash, to pay in advance.

sulakᵉ¹ سولاق 1. watery, wet. 2. marshy. 3. water trough; water bowl.

sulama سولاما *verbal n. of* **sula=**.

sulan=ʳ سولانمق 1. *pass. of* **sula=**. 2. /a/ *slang* to flirt, bother. 3. *slang* to become silly or too familiar. **—dır=** /ı/ *caus.* **—ma** *verbal n. of* **sulan=**.

sular سولار 1. waters. 2. grades. 3. times. 4. condition, state. 5. phase of nature. **—ında** around, about (such and such a time), *e. g.,* saat yedi sularında about seven o'clock. **— karardı** Darkness has fallen; evening has closed in. **— kırıldı** It has got warm.

sulat=ʳ سولاتمق /ı, a/ *caus. of* **sula=**.

sulbᵇᵘ **1** صلب A lrnd. 1. the loins; spinal column. 2. offspring of one's loins, descendants.

sulbᵇᵘ **2** صلب A lrnd. 1. hard, firm; rigid, stiff. 2. tough, strong, solid. 3. hardy, sturdy.

sulban (.—) صلبان A lrnd., *pl. of* **salib 1**.

sulbi (.—) صلبی A lrnd. 1. pertaining to the loins. 2. sprung from one's loins, legitimate (son).

sulbiye صلبیه A *law* daughter of a deceased man.
sulbiyet صلبیت A *lrnd.* hardness, solidity, toughness.
suleha (..—) صلحاء A *lrnd., pl.* of **salih**.
sulfato (.—'.) صولفاتو It *same as* **solfato**.
sulh صلح A 1. peace; reconciliation; accord. 2. compromise, friendly arrangement. — **et**=*. — **hâkimi** justice of the peace; police-court magistrate. — **mahkemesi** minor court for petty offenses. — **ol**=*. — **ve salâh** *lrnd.* peace and amity. —**a sübhana yat**= to become docile or amenable.
sulhamiz (.—ˉ—) صلح آمیز P *lrnd.* conciliatory.
sulhan ('.) صلحاً A peaceably, pacifically.
sulhcu (.—) صلحجی P *lrnd.* peace-loving, pacifist. —**yane** (.——.) P pacifically.
sulhet=ᵈᵉʳ صلح اتمك to make peace; to be reconciled.
sulhî (.—) صلحی A *lrnd.* pertaining to peace, peaceable.
sulhiye صلحیه A *lrnd.* poem written in praise of peace.
sulhlaş=ⁱʳ صلحلشمك /la/ 1. to make peace together. 2. to effect a compromise. —**tır**= /ı, la/ *caus.*
sulhname (.—.) صلحنامه P *obs.* treaty of peace.
sulhol=ᵘʳ صلح اولمك /la/ to come to an amicable agreement; to settle a difference.
sulhperver صلح پرور P peace-loving, pacific.
sulpᵇᵘ صلب A *var.* of **sulb 2**.
sulta سلطه A *lrnd.* sovereignty; power; authority.
sultan 1 سلطان [**sultan 2**] 1. ruler, sovereign; sultan. 2. princess of the imperial house, Sultana; lord, master, chief. 3. *title of respect or affection.* — **börkü** cock's-comb, *bot.*, Celosia cristata.
sultan 2 (.—) سلطان A *lrnd., same as* **sultan 1**. —**ı cihan** the constraint of the world over a devout man. —**ı çerh** the sun. **S**—**ı Dervişan** the Prophet Muhammad. —**ı encüm** the sun. **S**—**ı Rum** the Sultan of the Ottoman Empire.
sultanî (.——) سلطانی A 1. pertaining to a sultan, imperial. 2. of fine quality (fruit, etc.). 3. *Ott. hist.* secondary school. 4. a seedless grape, sultana. 5. *Ott. hist.*, name of a gold coin (minted in Egypt and Cyrenaica). — **bamya** a fine variety of garden okra. — **cedid** *Or. mus.* a compound **makam**. — **hüzzam** *Or. mus.* a **makam** related to **hüzzam**, which is now not in use. — **ırak** *Or. mus.* a compound **makam** about three centuries old. — **tembel** extremely lazy. — **yegâh** *Or. mus.* a **makam** composed by the famous musician Ismail Dede Efendi about 150 years ago.
sultanlıkᵍⁱ سلطانلق 1. sovereignty; office of a sultan. 2. sultanate, country ruled by a sultan. 3. great happiness.
Sultanönü سلطان اوكی *Ott. hist., name of the* Eskişehir-Söğüt *region*.
Sultanülberreyn (.—...) سلطان البرین A *Ott. hist.* Sultan of the two continents (European and Asiatic Turkey).
sulu صولو 1. watery, wet; sappy; juicy. 2. fluid. 3. *slang* silly, importunate; too familiar. — **boya** water color (paint), aquarelle. — **gaz** petroleum. — **sepken** sleet. — **zırtlak** *prov.* lemon.
suluca (...') صولوجه 1. somewhat watery. 2. *slang* rather too familiar. 3. *prov.* a scalp disease.
sulukᵍᵘ **1** صولوق *prov.* 1. water crop of a bird. 2. vessel for holding water. 3. cheek, cross-piece of a horse's bit. 4. skin disease affecting a baby's head. — **zinciri** curb chain.
su'lûkᵏᵘ **2** (.—) صعالیك A *lrnd.* 1. pauper; vagrant. 2. thief, robber.
sululukᵍᵘ صولولق 1. wateriness; sappiness; juiciness. 2. *slang* a being importunate, silly, too familiar.
sumᵐᵐᵘ **1** صمّ A *lrnd.* 1. deaf. 2. surd.
sum 2 ثوم A *lrnd.* garlic.
sumakᵍⁱ صوماق *same as* **somak**.
sumat صوماط *same as* **somat**.
sumen سومن F blotter.
sumulˡᵘ (.—) صمول A *lrnd.* a being or becoming dry and hard.
sumut (.—) صموت A *lrnd.* a being silent, silence.
sunⁿᵘ **1** صنع A *lrnd.* 1. a making, manufacturing; manufacture. 2. a creating, forming; creation. 3. a doing an act; act, deed. —**i bedi** fine art. —**i beşer** man's handiwork. — **u taksir***.
sun= **2** صونمق /ı, a/ 1. to put forward, offer. 2. to present, hand, give.
-sun 3 سڭ *cf.* **-ın 7**.
-sun 4 سڭ *cf.* **-sın 1**.
=sun 5 سین *cf.* **=sın 3**.
suna صونه 1. pheasant. 2. tall and handsome (person).
sunakᵍⁱ صوناق 1. *archaic* mug, dipper. 2. *neol., archae.* altar.
sundur=ⁱʳ **1** صوندرمق /ı, a/ *caus.* of **sun**= **2**.
-sundur 2 ('.) سندر *cf.* **-sındır 1**.
sundurma صوندرمه penthouse, open shed; lean-to-roof.
sungur صنغر falcon.
sun'i (.—) صنعی A artificial; false; affected. —**lik** artificialness.
suntraş صونتراش [Persian **sumteraş**] *prov.* blacksmith's paring-iron.

suntur صونطور [Arabic **santur**] 1. dulcimer. 2. noise of hilarious festivity. **—lu** 1. severe (scolding). 2. resounding (oath). 3. splendid, magnificent; joyous (festivity).
sunuⁿ'ᵘ صنع var. of **sun** 1.
-sunu سنى cf. **—ı** 3.
sunuf (.—) صنوف A lrnd., pl. of **sınıf**.
sunul=ᵘʳ صونولى pass. of **sun**= 2.
sun'ullâh (..—) صنع الله A 1. lrnd. the work of God. 2. w. cap., man's name.
sun'utaksir (...—) صنع و تقصير A lrnd. wrongdoing; harmful negligence.
-sunuz (ˊ.) سڭز cf. **-sınız**.
-sunuzdur (ˊ..) سڭزدر cf. **-sınızdır**.
supapᵇⁱ سوباپ F valve. **— iteceği** auto. valve tappet.
supara سوباره [**sipare**] reading-book for children.
supya (ˊ.) سوبيه Gk cuttlefish, squid. **— kemiği** cuttle bone.
sur 1 (—) سور A city-wall, ramparts. **— dahilinde** within the city's walls.
sur 2 صور A 1. Isl. rel. the trumpet of the Day of Judgment. 2. lrnd. trumpet.
sur 3 (—) سور P lrnd. wedding feast; wedding or circumcision. **—i hümayun** Ott. hist. royal wedding; princely circumcision feast.
Sur 4 (—) صور geog. Tyre.
sura صورا E a kind of soft twilled silk, surah.
surah (——) سوراخ P lrnd. hole.
surat صورت [**suret**] 1. face, countenance. 2. sour face; angry look. **— as**= to frown, to make a sour face. **—ı asık** sour-faced, sulky. **—ına bak süngüye davran** Look at his face and get your bayonet ready said when mentioning a very ugly or disagreeable-looking person. **— davul derisi** brazen-faced, shameless. **—ı değiş**= to change one's manner and become hardened toward a person. **—ından düşen bin parça olur** very bad-tempered, angry-looking. **— düşkünü** very ugly. **— et**= to look sulky.
suratlı صورتلى sulky, sullen; frowning.
suratsız صورتسز ugly; sulky. **—lık** ugliness; sulkiness.
surdin سوردين F mus. sordino.
sure (—.) سوره Isl. rel. sura of the Quran. **S—i Âdiyet** a name of the 100th sura. **S—i Arusülkur'an** a name of the 55th sura. **S—i Fatiha** the first sura. **S—i İhlâs** a name of the 112th sura.
suret (—.) صورت A 1. form, shape, figure. 2. aspect, manner; method. 3. countenance; picture. 4. copy (of a document). 5. case, supposition. 6. math. numerator. **—inde** in the shape of; as. **bir —le** in some way or other; to such a degree that. **— al**= 1. to make a copy (of a document). 2. to take form.
— bağla= 1. to make some kind of arrangement. 2. to get into shape. **—i bima'na** lrnd. form without sense; doll, puppet. **— bul**= archaic to be put into effect. **— çıkar**= to make a copy (of a document). **— değiştir**= to change the expression of one's face; to put on an angry or dissatisfied look. **bir —e gir**= 1. to assume a form. 2. to be arranged in some special manner. **—ine gir**= /ın/ to assume the form of. **—i haktan görün**= to appear sincere. **—i kat'iyede** lrnd. absolutely. **—i hal** the state of affairs; how conditions are. **—i mahsusada** lrnd. in a special way; particularly. **—i mutlakada** lrnd. absolutely. **—i siretine uymaz** unreliable. **—i tesviye** the way to solve a matter. **— uğrusu** archaic hypocrite. **— yaz**= archaic to paint (pictures).
sûreta (—..) صورتا A lrnd. 1. outwardly, in appearance. 2. simulated; as a matter of form.
suretbend (—..) صورتبند P lrnd. artist, painter.
suretger (—..) صورتگر P lrnd. artist, painter.
suretnüma (—..—) صورتنما P lrnd. apparent.
suretperest (—...) صورتپرست P lrnd. 1. worshipper of idols. 2. who pays great attention to outward forms.
suretpezir (—..—) صورتپذير P lrnd. 1. that assumes a form or shape. 2. coming into being. **— ol**= to be brought about, to be put into effect.
suretyab (—.—) صورتياب P lrnd., same as **suretpezir**.
surh صرح same as **sürh**.
suri (——) صورى A 1. logic formal; pertaining to visible form, apparent. 2. lrnd. feigned, simulated.
Suriye (—..) سوريه [Arabic ——.] geog. Syria. **— damanı** Syrian coney, zool.; Procaria syriaca. **—li** Syrian, of Syria.
surna (——) سورنا P lrnd., same as **zurna**.
surnazen (——.) سورنازن P lrnd. player of a **zurna** (wind intrument).
surname (——.) سورنامه P poetry work written on the occasion of a wedding or circumcision feast.
surre صرّه A lrnd., same as **sürre** 2.
sursur صرصر A lrnd. mole-cricket.
sus 1 صوص 1. Be quiet. 2. silent, quiet.
sus 2 (—) سوس A lrnd. 1. licorice plant; bot., Glycirrhiza glabra. 2. maggot, weevil.
sus=ᵃʳ 3 صوصمق to be silent, to hold one's tongue, to stop talking, to be quiet.
susa=ʳ صوصامق 1. to be thirsty, to thirst. 2. /a/ to thirst (for), to long (for).
susakᵍⁱ 1 صوصه صيران صصه سوسه prov.

1. wooden bowl or scoop with a handle. 2. wooden ladle. 3. milk pail.
susakᵍⁱ 2 صوصاى صوصو *prov.* 1. thirsty. 2. imbecile, stupid. — **ağızlı** person who talks nonsense; inconsiderate. —**lık** 1. thirstiness, thirst. 2. stupidity.
susalıkᵍⁱ صوصالق صوصلي *archaic* 1. *med.* tympanites. 2. thirst.
susam 1 صوسام سوسام [**sisam**] sesame, *bot.*, *Sesamum indicum*. **S— Adası** the island of Samos.
susam 2 سوسام صوسام [*Persian* **susen**] any iridaceous plant or flower as the iris, ixia etc.
susamlı صوساملى 1. containing sesame. 2. *w. cap* of or from Samos, Samian.
susama صوساما *verbal n.* of **susa**=.
susan=ⁱʳ صوسانمق to feel thirsty.
susat=ⁱʳ صوساتمق صوساتني /ı/ *caus.* of **susa**=. —**ıl**= to be made thirsty.
susmalıkᵍⁱ *neol.* hush-money.
susmar (— —) سوسمار P *lrnd.* Lybian lizard, spinefooted stellion, *zool.*, *Uroprastix spinipes*.
suspus صوصپوس reduced to silence; silent and cowering.
susta 1 سوسته *only in* **susta dur**= 1. to stand on its hind legs (dog, etc.) 2. to be very obsequious.
susta 2 (ˊ.) سوسته safety catch.
sustalı سوستهلى 1. having a safety catch. 2. switchblade. — **çakı** switchblade.
sustur=ᵘʳ صوصدرمق صوصديرمك /ı/ to silence, to cause to stop talking, to shut up, cut off. —**ucu** *mech.* silencer. —**ul**= *pass.* of **sustur**=.
susu صوصو like water, tasting like water.
susuz صوصز 1. waterless, dry, arid. 2. thirsty. 3. untempered (steel). — **bırak**= /ı/ to leave to suffer or die from thirst. —**luk** 1. waterlessness, aridity. 2. thirst.
sutaş سوتاش F *tailor.* braid, trimming. —**lı** braided.
sutuᵘᵘ (.—) سطع A *lrnd.* 1. a rising, diffusing in the air; diffusion (dawn or lightning). 2. an exhalation. 3. a being or becoming obvious (odor).
sutur (.—) سطور A *lrnd., pl.* of **satır** 1.
sutyen سوتين F brassiere.
suubet (..—.) صعوبت A *lrnd.* a being difficult, difficulty. —**i telâffuz** *path.* inability to articulate words, anarthria. —**li** difficult.
suud (.—) صعود A *lrnd.* an ascending; ascension, ascent. — **et**= to ascend, to climb.
suvakᵍⁱ صواقه 1. *var.* of **savak**. 2. fountain.
suvar=ⁱʳ صوارمق صوارمك /ı/ 1. to water (animal). 2. to temper (steel). —**ıl**= *pass.*
suvarım صوارم 1. manner of watering. 2. amount of water given at one irrigation.
suvat صواد *prov., same as* **savat** 2.
suver صور A *lrnd., pl.* of **suret**.

suy (—) سوى P *lrnd., same as* **su** 2.
suyolcu (.ˊ..) صو يولجى man responsible for maintenance of water conduits.
suz 1 (—) سوز P *lrnd.* 1. a burning, conflagration; inflammation. 2. anguish, torment, torture. —**i ciger** suffering. — **ü güdaz** 1. a burning and melting. 2. a sorrowing and weeping, pining.
-**suz** 2 سز *cf.* -**sız** 1.
-**suz** 3 (—) سوز P *lrnd.* that burns, consumes, destroys, *as in* **dilsuz**.
suzan (— —) سوزان P *lrnd.* 1. burning, inflaming. 2. ardent, fervent.
suzen (—.) سوزن P *lrnd.* 1. needle; pin. 2. pricker —**i İsa** The pin of Jesus, *a pin reputedly found in the robe of Jesus as he ascended to heaven so that he could rise no higher than the sphere of the sun*. —**bâl** (—.—) P *same as* **suzenper**.
suzenper سوزن پر P *lrnd.* unfledged, with feathers yet like stubs or pins.
suzendan (..—) سوزندان P *lrnd.* pin or needle case.
suzende (—..) سوزنده P *lrnd.* burning, kindling. —**gi** (—..—) P conflagration; the act of burning.
suzeni (—.—) سوزنى P *lrnd.* 1. a kind of fine embroidery. 2. pertaining to pins or needles. 3. maker or seller of needles.
suzidil (—..) سوز دل P 1. *Or. mus.* a **şed makam** two centuries old. 2. *lrnd.* heart-ache.
suzidilarâ (—..— —) سوز دل آرا P *Or. mus.* a **makam** composed by Sultan Selim III 150 years ago.
suzinakᵏⁱ (—.—) سوزناك P *Or. mus.* a simple **makam** about two centuries old.
suziş (—.) سوزش P *lrnd.* 1. a burning. 2. a suffering; passion. —**li** 1. burning, inflaming. 2. touching, sad, moving.
-**suzluk**ᵍᵘ سوزلك *cf.* -**sızlık**.
suznâkᵏⁱ (— —) سوزناك P *lrnd.* 1. burning, flaming. 2. pained; grieved, suffering. 3. *same as* **suzinak**.
sü 1 سو *archaic* soldier.
-**sü**ⁿᵘ 2 سو *cf.* -**ı** 3.
-**sü** 3 سى *cf.* -**sı** 2.
süada (..—) ساده A *lrnd., pl.* of **said** 1.
süalᵘ (.—) سؤال A *lrnd.* cough.
sübᵇᵘ سبع A *lrnd.* a seventh.
sübai (—.—) سباعى A *lrnd.* 1. of seven letters (word). 2. of seven parts.
sübat (.—) سبات A *lrnd.* 1. rest, repose; sleep, drowsiness. 2. lethargy, coma. —**î** (.— —) A pertaining to sleep, drowsiness or coma; lethargic.
sübekᵍⁱ سبك صوباك *prov., same as* **söbek**.
sübha صبى A *lrnd., same as* **subha**.

sübhan (.—) سبحان A *lrnd.* a reciting of the glories of God, His names and attributes; especially a reciting of the formula **sübhanallah**.

Sübhanallah (.—.—) سبحان الله A *lrnd.* 1. Praise be to God! 2. Oh my God!

sübhanehu (.—..) سبحانه A *lrnd.* 1. Glory be to Him. 2. the Most Holy, *used as a name of God*.

sübhanî (.——) سبحانى A *lrnd.* pertaining to God, divine. **—yet** (.—..) A divinity.

sübjektif سوبژەكتيف F *phil.* subjective.

süblime سوبليمه F *chem.* corrosive sublimate; sublimate, mercuric chloride.

sübur (.—) سبور A *lrnd.* 1. a destroying; annihilation. 2. a perishing, ruin, perdition. 3. a suffering loss; privation, destitution.

sübut (.—) ثبوت A *lrnd.* 1. a being proved, certain, sure; certainty. 2. a being valid, true; truth, validity, reality. 3. a being existent; reality. 4. a being permanent, invariable; permanence. 5. a being settled and established; firmness, steadfastness. 6. evidence, proof, testimony. **— bul=** to become proved, established, demonstrated. **— delili** certain proof.

sübutet (.—.) ثبوتت A *lrnd.* 1. steadiness, firmness; courage. 2. a being reliable; sureness, reliability.

sübuti (.——) ثبوتى A *lrnd.* positive and inherent; incontestable.

sübül سبل A *lrnd., pl. of* **sebil**.

sübye 1 سبيه 1. sweet drink prepared from pounded almonds, melon seeds, etc. 2. emulsion.

sübye 2 (.′.) سبيه *var. of* **supya**.

sübye 3 (.′.) سبيه It *naut.* unrigged mast; single whip. **— armalı** fore-and-aft rigged.

sücud (.—) سجود A *Isl. rel.* 1. a prostrating oneself in worship. 2. a bowing down. **— et=**, **—a var=** to prostrate oneself in worship.

sücun (.—) سجون A *lrnd., pl. of* **sicn**.

sücü سجى *archaic* wine.

südasi (.——) سداسى A *lrnd.* 1. composed of six elements. 2. word of six letters.

südde سده A 1. *lrnd.* threshold; gateway. 2. *biol.* obstruction, stoppage in a passage of the body. **— boncuğu** bead of carbonate of lime, powdered and taken as a remedy in obstruction of the spleen. **—i saadet, —i seniye** *Ott. hist.* the Sultan's court.

süded سدد A *lrnd., pl. of* **südde**.

südre=ʳ سدرماك *archaic* to get drunk.

südreme سدرمه 1. a getting drunk. 2. a talking like a drunkard.

südsi (.—) سدسى A *lrnd.* pertaining to a sixth.

südud (.—) سدود A *lrnd.* a being in a right state, direction or way.

südüs سدس A *lrnd.* a sixth.

süfeha (..—) سفها A *lrnd., pl. of* **sefih**.

süfelâ (..—) سفلا A *lrnd., pl. of* **sefil**.

süfera (..—) سفرا A *lrnd., pl. of* **sefir**.

süfl سفل A *lrnd.* sediment, dregs.

süflâ (.—) سفلى A *lrnd.* lower, lowest.

süflâni (.——) سفلانى A *lrnd.* low, lower, inferior.

süfli (.—) سفلى A *lrnd.* 1. low, inferior; common, low-down. 2. menial; shabby. **—lik** *abstr. n.* **—yat** (..—) A low and common things. **—yet** 1. baseness, lowness, meanness. 2. shabbiness. **—yeyn** A the planets Venus and Mercury. **—yin** (..—) A the rabble.

süft سفت P *lrnd.* hole, perforation.

süfte سفته P *lrnd.* 1. bored, perforated. 2. newly coined (expression).

süftegûş (..—) سفته گوش P *lrnd.* 1. whose ear is pierced; slave. 2. obedient, submissive.

süftger سفتگر P *lrnd.* borer of pearls.

süfün سفن A *lrnd., pl. of* **sefine**.

sügvar (.—) سگوار P *lrnd.* mournful, afflicted, sorrowful. **—î** (.——) P mournfulness, sorrow.

süğlün سگلون *same as* **sülün**.

süğü سگو *archaic* 1. bayonet. 2. spear.

Suha (.—) سها A *lrnd.* a small star in Ursa Major.

sühan سخن P *lrnd., same as* **suhen**.

sühar (.—) سهار A *lrnd.* sleeplessness.

süheyl سهيل A *lrnd.* the star Canopus.

süheylâ (..—) سهيلا A *lrnd.* 1. good-natured woman. 2. *w. cap., woman's name*.

sühulet (.—.) سهولت A 1. a being easy, gentle; facility, ease, gentleness. 2. easy circumstances. **— göster=** to offer facilities. **—bahş** (.—..) P *lrnd.* offering ease or facilities. **—li** easy.

sühunet (.—.) سخونت A *lrnd.* 1. a being warm of heart; heat. 2. fever; temperature.

sükkân (.—) سكان A *lrnd., pl. of* **sâkin**.

sükker سكر A *lrnd.* 1. sugar. 2. anything sweet as sugar. **—i mükerrer** sugar candy. **—i uşer** a kind of red manna gathered from the leaves of the Calotropis shrub. **—î** (..—) A pertaining to sugar.

sükkerîn (..—) سكرين P *lrnd.* made of sugar, mixed with sugar, sugared.

süklüm püklüm سكلوم بكلوم in a crestfallen manner; hanging the head.

sükna سكنى A *lrnd.* habitation, quarters.

süksün سكسون *prov.* back of the neck, nape.

sükûn (.—) سكون A rest, calm, quiet, repose, tranquillity. **— bul=** to be calmed, appeased, rested.

sükûnet (.—.) سكونت A quiet, calm, rest.

sükûnetgâh (.—.—) سكونتگاه P *lrnd.* resting place.

sükûnetli سکونتلی quiet, peaceful, calm.
sükût (. —) سکوت A silence; reticence. **— et=** to be silent. **— hakkı** hush-money.
sükûtî (. — —) سکوتی A taciturn; reticent.
sülâf (. —), **sülafe** (. —.) سلاف سلافه A lrnd. 1. wine. 2. fruit juice; pure juice. 3. the clear, fine part of anything.
sülale (. — .) سلاله A family, line; descendants.
sülâma (. — .) سلامی A lrnd. bone of the finger or toe, phalange.
sülâsi (. — —) ثلاثی A 1. lrnd. related to a group of three, composed of three elements. 2. *Arabic gram.* composed of three radical consonants, triliteral Arabic root.
Süleyman (. . —) سلیمان A Suleyman; Solomon. **— Peygamber** King Solomon. **—î** (. . — —) A lrnd. 1. pertaining to King Solomon. 2. agate, onyx.
süline (. ʹ .) سولینه Gk razor-fish, solen.
süllâ سلی ثمد A lrnd. departed greatness; ruined power.
süllâf (. —) سلاف A lrnd., pl. of **salif**.
sülle ثله A lrnd. crowd of people.
süllem سلم A lrnd. ladder, flight of steps, staircase.
sülme ثلمه A lrnd. crack, notch, dent.
sülpü=ᵘʳ سولپومك archaic to hang loosely, flabbily.
sülpükᵍᵘ̈ سولپوك archaic 1. lax, relaxed, flabby 2. devoid of energy. **— kulaklı** drooping-eared, hang-eared.
süls ثلث A lrnd. 1. a third, the third part. 2. *same as* **sülüs**. **—ân** (. —) A two-thirds. **—î** (. —) A *calligraphy* pertaining to large letters.
sülûc (. —) سلوج A lrnd., pl. of **selc**.
sülûkᵏᵘ̈ (. —) سلوك A lrnd. 1. an entering upon, a following a road; a following a career. 2. a belonging to a religious order. 3. contemplative life. **— et=** /a/ to enter, follow the career (of). **— ehli** dervish, hermit.
süliğen سولیغن سولوكان سولوكن red lead. **—li** containing red lead; mixed or colored with red lead.
sülükᵏᵘ̈ سولوك 1. leech, *zool., Hirudo medicinalis*. 2. tendril (of a vine). **— gibi** sticking like a leech. **— tutun=** to apply leeches to oneself. **—cü** 1. leech-fisher; leech-merchant. 2. one who applies leeches. **—giller** *zool., Hirudinea*. **—lü** abounding with leeches.
sülümen سولومن It corrosive sublimate, mercuric chloride.
sülün سولون سولكون pheasant, *zool., Phasianus colchicus*. **S— Bey** a brisk, lively little man. **— gibi** tall and graceful.
sülüsˡˢᵘ̈ ثلث [**süls**] *calligraphy* a style of Arabic script with large letters.

süm 1 سم P lrnd. hoof of a quadruped.
süm=ᵉʳ **2** سومك archaic 1. to butt with the nose in sucking (young animal). 2. to push about roughly or disrespectfully.
süm'a سمعه A lrnd. 1. a word or act heard of or to be heard of. 2. fame, report, rumor.
sümbükᵏᵘ̈ سمبوك archaic hoof.
sümbül سنبل [**sünbül**] 1. hyacinth, *bot., Hyacinthus orientalis*. 2 *poet.* curly locks and ringlets of a beauty. **—i hataî** angelica, *bot., Archangelica officinalis*. **—i ıkliti**, **—i rumî** Celtic valerian, Celtic spikenard, *bot., Valeriana celtica*. **—i teber** garden tuberose, *bot., Polyanthes tuberosa*. **—i ter** *poet.* youthful beard.
sümbülî (. . —) سنبلی P 1. pertaining to a hyacinth; of the dark color of the wild hyacinth. 2. cloudy, overcast (sky).
sümdükᵍᵘ̈ سومدك *prov.* 1. avaricious; greedy. 2. impudent.
sümeyra (. . —) سمیرا A lrnd. petite brunette.
sümkür=ᵘʳ سومكورمك to blow one's nose. **—t=** /ı/ *caus.*
sümme ثم A lrnd. 1. then, afterward. 2. again, also; and again.
sümmettedarik (. ʹ . . — .) ثم الاستدارك A lrnd. then, the preparation *said of something entered on without preparation, on the spur of the moment.*
sümn ثمن A lrnd. an eighth.
sümpare (. — .) سمپاره P lrnd. emery.
sümre, sümret سمره سمرت A lrnd. darkness, brownness, swarthiness.
sümsükᵍᵘ̈ uncouth; imbecile; spiritless. **—lük** imbecility; spiritlessness.
sümter سمتر *prov.* a kind of wheat.
sümum (. —) سموم A lrnd., pl. of **sem 1**.
sümükᵍᵘ̈ سومك سوموك mucus (of the nose).
sümüklü سوموكلی 1. covered with mucus; slimy. 2. snivelling. **— böcek** 1. snail, *zool., Helix*. 2. slug, *zool., Limax*.
sümüksü *neol., biol.* pituitary.
sümünᵐⁿᵘ̈ سمون *var. of* **sümn**.
sümür=ᵘʳ سومورمك *same as* **sömür=**.
sümüvᵛᵛᵘ̈ سمو A lrnd. a being high, exalted; elevation; eminence.
sün=ᵉʳ **1** سونمك to stretch, to become stretched out, extended.
-sün 2 سون *cf.* **-sın 1**.
-sün 3 سون *cf.* **-ın 7**.
=sün 4 سنك *cf.* **=sın 2**.
sünayi (. . — —) ثنائی A lrnd. 1. biliteral (word). 2. composed of two elements or parts. **—ye** *phil.* dualism.
sünbükᵏᵘ̈ سنبك A lrnd. 1. toe, front tip of a hoof. 2. tip of anything.
sünbül سنبل P *same as* **sümbül**.

sünbülât (..—) سنبلات A *lrnd., pl. of* **sünbüle**.
sünbüle سنبل A *lrnd.* 1. an ear of grain. 2. a single spike of flowers. 3. *astr.* the constellation Virgo. 4. *Or. mus.* an old compound makam. **—i nihavend** *Or. mus.* a makam composed of the makams **sünbüle** and **nihavend**. **— perdesi** *mus.* the note a'' flat.
sündür=ür 1 سوندورمك /ı/ *caus. of* **sün**= 1. **=sündür 2** (ˊ.) سكّدر *cf.* **=sındır 1**.
sündüs سندس A *lrnd.* fine silk brocade. **—î** (..—) A of brocade; like brocade; pertaining to brocade.
süne سونه 1. drake. 2. an insect pest of cereals, *zool., Eurygastrum*.
sünen سنن A *lrnd., pl. of* **sünnet**.
sünepe سونه په slovenly (person); sluggish. **—lik** slovenliness.
sünger سونگر Gk 1. sponge. 2. anything soft or porous as a sponge. **S— Adası** the island of Symi (north of Rhodes). **— doku** *neol., biol.* spongeous tissue. **— geçir**= to pass the sponge over, to cancel. **— gibi** like a sponge, porous; humid and compressible. **— kâğıdı** blotting paper. **—le sil**= /ı/ to wipe off the slate. **— taşı** pumice stone. **—iye** sponge cake. **—li** furnished with sponge; mixed with or made up of sponge.
süngü سونگو 1. bayonet. 2. spine (of the back). **—sü ağır** 1. slow-moving. 2. unlovable, disagreeable. **— davran** *mil.* Fix bayonets. **—sü düşük** /ın/ subdued, depressed, crestfallen. **— süngüye** 1. with fixed bayonets. 2. at close quarters (fight). **— tak** *mil.* Fix bayonets. Charge with bayonets.
süngüle=r سنگولمك /ı/ to bayonet. **—n**= *pass.*
süngülü سنگولو with fixed bayonets. **— ampul** bayonet-base light bulb.
sünh سنح A *lrnd.* 1. an appearing, presenting itself; an occurring (to the mind). 2. prosperity, blessing, good luck.
sünne سنه A *lrnd., same as* **sünnet**.
sünnet سنت A *Isl. rel.* 1. Sunnah (practices and rules not laid down in the Quran but derived from the Prophet's own habits and words). 2. ritual circumcision. **— düğünü** circumcision feast. **— ehli** Sunni Muslims. **— et**= /ı/ 1. to circumcise. 2. to amend. **—i müekkede** a supererogatory act of worship, etc., seldom omitted by Prophet Muhammad (omission of which would be an impropriety). **— ol**= to be circumcised. **—i ratibe** a usual supererogatory act of worship practiced by the Prophet Muhammad (omission of which is irreverent). **—i zâide** a supererogatory act of worship more often omitted than practiced by the Prophet Muhammad (omission of which is not blameworthy). **—çi** circumciser.

sünnetle=r سنتلمك /ı/ *slang* to eat up entirely, to finish off.
sünnetli سنتلی circumcised.
Sünni (.—) سنّی A *Isl. rel.* Sunni. **—lik** the Sunni branch of Islam.
sünuh 1 (.—) سنوح A *lrnd.* an occurring to the mind; occurrence; manifestation. **— ve sudur et**= to occur, to appear; to emanate.
sünuh 2 (.—) سنوح A *lrnd.* 1. a being firm, solid in knowledge; stability, constancy. 2. a being well grounded in science.
sünuhat (.——) سنوحات A *lrnd., pl.* occurrences, manifestations.
-sünü سنی *cf.* **-ı 3**.
sünükğü سوكك archaic bone.
-sünüz (ˊ.) سكز *cf.* **-sınız**.
-sünüzdür (ˊ..) سكزدر *cf.* **-sınızdır**.
süphan (.—) سبحان A *lrnd., same as* **sübhan**.
süprül=ür سوپرلمك *same as* **süpürül**=.
süprüntü سپرنتی 1. sweepings, rubbish. 2. rabble. **—cü** 1. street-sweeper; garbage collector. 2. person dealing in sweepings or rubbish. **—lük** rubbish-heap.
süpür=ür سوپورمك /ı/ 1. to sweep; to brush (clothes). 2. to sweep away, to clear the table.
süpürge سوپورگه 1. broom. 2. brush. 3. heath, heather. **— ağacı** tree-heath, brierroot, *bot., Erica arborea*. **— darısı** broom corn, *bot., Andropogon sorghum*. **— hesabı** *colloq.* a thrashing, beating. **— otu** black heath, bell heather, *bot., Erica cinerea*. heather, common ling, *bot., Calluna vulgaris*. **— sapı ye**= to get the stick. **—ci** 1. maker or seller of brooms. 2. street sweeper. **—lik** *arch.* plinth.
süpürt=ür سوپورتمك /ı, a/ *caus. of* **süpür**=.
süpürücü سوپوروجی sweeper.
süpürül=ür سوپورولمك *pass. of* **süpür**=.
sür=er سورمك 1. /ı/ to drive away; to banish. 2. /ı/ to drive in front; to advance, push forward. 3. /ı/ to drive (vehicle). 4. /ı/ to push forth (root, stem, branch). 5. /ı/ to rub on, smear. 6. /ı/ to plow. 7. /ı/ to spend (time, life). 8. /ı/ to sell, to market; to circulate. 9. to push on; to go on; to continue, to extend. 10. to pass (time). 11. to germinate (seeds); to shoot out, protrude. 12. to purge (bowels). **—üp at**= /ı/ to drive away, expel. **— gitsin** Let it be. Don't worry.
süradikkı (.—.) سرادك A *lrnd.* 1. awning, tent, pavilion. 2. curtain before the door of a house or tent. **—at** (.—.—) A *pl.*
sürahi (.—.) صراحی A decanter, water bottle.
sür'attı سرعت A a being quick; speed, velocity, haste. **—le** quickly. **—i intikal** *lrnd.* quick-wittedness, perspicacity. **— katarı** express

train. — **topçuları** *Ott. hist.* an artillery corps formed in 1774. —**li** quick; hurried.
sürc *lrnd.* a stumbling, stumble; slip, mistake. —**i lisan** slip of the tongue.
sürç=ᵉʳ to stumble; to slip; to make a mistake. —**tür**= /ı/ *caus.*
sürdür=ᵘʳ 1. /ı, a/ *caus.* of **sür**=¹⁻⁸. 2. /ı/ to let continue, to make last. —**t**= *caus.* —**ül**= *pass.*
süre *neol.* period; extension.
süregen *neol.* 1. continued, lasting. 2. *path.* chronic.
sürekᵍⁱ 1. drove (of cattle). 2. duration. 3. fast driver. — **avı** drive (shooting). — **tatar** fast-going messenger.
sürekli lasting, prolonged, continuous. —**lik** 1. continuality. 2. *neol., math.* continuity.
süreksiz transitory, transient. —**lik** transitoriness.
Süreyya A 1. *lrnd.* the Pleiades. 2. *lrnd., l. c.* aloe, American aloe, *bot., Agave Americana.* 3. *l. c., Or. mus.* a fast rythmic pattern of five beats.
sürfe 1 A *lrnd.* caterpillar; maggot; teredo.
sürfe 2 P *lrnd.* cough.
sürgü 1. bolt (of a door). 2. sliding bar. 3. bedpan. 4. roller. 5. plasterer's trowel. 6. harrow; till. 7. *prov.* diarrhea. — **taşı** 1. stone roller used for leveling fields. 2. levigating stone. 3. whetstone; grindstone.
sürgüle=ʳ /ı/ 1. to bolt, to fasten with a bolt. 2. to roll (road). 3. to harrow (field). 4. to smooth (plaster). 5. to grind, hone, whet. —**n**= *pass.*
sürgülü 1. bolted. 2. sliding. — **cetvel**, — **hesap cetveli** slide-rule. — **pergel** beam-compass.
sürgün 1. a driving or chasing; banishment, exile. 2. an exile; exiled. 3. place of exile. 4. shoot, sucker (of a plant). 5. *prov.* diarrhea. — **ağı** trawl-net, seine. — **avı** drive. — **et**= /ı/ to exile. — **evi vurgun evi** The house of the exile is the home of the afflicted. —**e git**= to go into banishment.
sürgünlükᵍᵘ 1. banishment, exile; place of exile. 2. *prov.* diarrhea; purgative.
sürh P *lrnd.* 1. red, ruddy yellow, golden. 2. vermilion; red lead. — **ile yaz**= to write with red ink.
sürhâb (. —) P *lrnd.* 1. red fluid. 2. bitter tears. 3. rouge for the face. —**î** (. — —) P red duck; ruddy goose.
sürhbad (. —) P *lrnd.* erysipelas.
sürhçeşm P *lrnd.* 1. red-eyed. 2. cruel, bloodthirsty. 3. executioner.

sürhî (. —) P *lrnd.* 1. redness. 2. ruddle.
sürhlükᵍᵘ redness.
sürhser P *lrnd.* 1. red-headed. 2. Kizilbash.
Sürhşeban (..—) P *lrnd.* Moses.
sürhzenburan (..— —) P *lrnd.* 1. wasps. 2. burning embers. 3. henna-tinged fingertips.
sürm A *anat.* rectum.
sürme 1 P kohl, collyrium. —**i dünbaledar** *lrnd.* small streak of collyrium at the outer corner of the eye. —**i hâkbin** *lrnd.* legendary collyrium that enabled the eyes to see into the depths of the earth. —**i hifa** *lrnd.* collyrium that conferred invisibility. — **mili** stibium style. —**i Süleyman** *lrnd.* Solomon's stibium by which he saw all secret things; collyrium which makes one see the hidden treasures of the earth. — **taşı** antimony.
sürme 2 1. *verbal n.* of **sür**=. 2. something that is drawn, pulled. 3. bolt, sliding bar. 4. drawer, till. 5. sliding, drawing in and out. 6. smut (of wheat). 7. move (chess, etc.). — **cam** sliding sash with its glass. — **çekmece** drawer that slides in and out. — **hapı** laxative pill. — **kapı** sliding door.
sürmedan (..—) P *lrnd.* small box in which kohl is kept.
sürmele=ʳ /ı/ 1. to bolt (a door). 2. to put on kohl.
sürmeli 1. having a bolt; bolted. 2. sliding. 3. tinged with kohl.
sürmelikᵍⁱ *same as* **sürmedan**.
sürpriz F surprise.
sürrakᵏⁱ (. —) A *lrnd., pl.* of **sarik**.
sürrat (. —) A *lrnd., pl.* of **sürre 1**.
sürre 1 A *lrnd.* navel.
sürre 2 A 1. *lrnd.* purse, bag of money. 2. *Ott. hist.* gifts sent to Mecca by the Sultan annually. — **alayı** procession which accompanied the **sürre**. — **devesi** an oddly-dressed person. — **devesi gibi dolaş**= to loaf about with an air of being busy. — **emini** the official entrusted with the delivery of the **sürre**.
sürrevi (..—), **sürri** (.—) A *lrnd.* pertaining to the navel.
sürsat (. —) *Ott. hist.* 1. forced contributions. 2. permission to sell or export grain.
sürstarya (..'.) F *law* demurrage.
sürşarj F surcharge (postage stamp).
sürt=ᵉʳ 1. /ı/ to rub one thing against another; to rub with the hand. 2. /ı/ to wear down by friction. 3. to wander about aimlessly. — **Allah kerim** Just wander about to see what happens, *said of vagabonds, who wander about aimlessly.*

sürtme سورتمه 1. *verbal n.* of **sürt=**. 2. *neol., phys.* rubbing. 3. *slang* a method of dice-throwing. — **boya** *art* scumble.

sürttür=ür سورتديرمك /ı, a/ *caus.* of **sürt=**.

sürtükᵏü سورتوك 1. always walking the streets (woman). 2. street-walker. —**lük** *abstr. n.*

sürtül=ür سورتولمك *pass.* of **sürt=**.

sürtün=ür سورتنمك 1. /a/ to rub oneself (against). 2. to drag oneself along; to creep. 3. to toady; to demean oneself. 4. to seek a quarrel, to behave in a provocative manner. —**me**, —**üş** *verbal n.*

sürtüş=ür سورتشمك /la/ to rub against each other. —**tür=** /ı, a/ *caus.*

süruc (.—) سروج A *lrnd., pl.* of **serc**.

sürud (.—) سرود A *lrnd.* 1. song, chant. 2. vocal and instrumental music. 3. saying, discourse. —**i hezâr** song of the nightingale. —**gû** (.——) P, —**sera** (.—.—) P 1. singer. 2. poet; speaker.

sürur (.—) سرور A *lrnd.* joy, pleasure, gladness. —**î** (.——) A pertaining to gladness; joyful.

süruş (.—) سروش P *lrnd.* 1. angel; the archangel Gabriel. 2. divine message.

sürü 1 سورو 1. herd, flock. 2. crowd, a multitude of people; gang. **bir —** a lot of. —**den ayrılma=** 1. to join the crowd, to do as others do. 2. to cease to be a baby and go in company with others (child). —**den ayrılanı kurt kapar** (*lit.* The wolf will devour a lamb out of the flock.) One who separates himself from social life is bound to face many hardships. —**süne bereket** *slang* heaps of. —**ye katıl=** same as **sürüden ayrılma=**. — **sepet** in great numbers, all together; all the lot. — **sürü** in droves, in flocks.

sürü=ʳ **2** سورومك 1. to drag along the ground. 2. to procrastinate.

sürücü سوروجى 1. drover; driver (of a vehicle). 2. man in charge of post horses, especially those carrying the mail. 3. *Ott. hist.* head of the group of the boys selected for the Janissary corps.

sürükle=ʳ سوروكلمك 1. to drag along the ground, to drag. 2. to drag someone to a place against his will. 3. /ı/ to carry with one (audience, readers). 4. to involve, to lead to, to entail.

sürüklen=ir سوروكلنمك /a/ 1. to drag oneself; to be dragged. 2. to drag on, to be protracted. —**dir=** /ı/ *caus.*

sürükleyici سوروكلييجى fascinating, attractive.

sürül=ür سورلمك *pass.* of **sür=**. —**me** *verbal n.*

sürüm سوروم 1. act of driving, rubbing, etc. 2. rapid sale, great demand (for some article).
— **sürüm sürün=** to suffer great misery; to lead a life of wretchedness or beggary. —**lü** finding a ready sale, in great demand. —**süz** hard to sell; not in demand.

sürün=ür سورينمك 1. /ı/ to rub on, to rub in. 2. /a/ to rub oneself against. 3. to drag oneself along the ground, to grovel; to live in misery, to live a wretched life.

sürünceme سورينجمه delay; negligence; a matter's dragging on. —**de kal=** to drag on, to be long drawn out.

süründür=ür سوروندورمك /ı/ *caus.* of **sürün=**.

sürüngen *neol., zool.* reptile.

sürür 1 سرور mercuric sulfide; vermilion varnish.

sürür 2 سرور A *lrnd., pl.* of **serir**.

sürüş=ür سورشمك /la/ to rub against or rub together. —**tür=** /ı/ 1. to rub together. 2. to rub in slowly and gently, to massage. —**türül=** *pass.*

sürüt=ür سورتمك /ı/ *caus.* of **sürü=**.

sürütme سوروتمه سورتمه /ı, a/ 1. *verbal n.* of **sürüt=**. 2. drag-net, trawl, a kind of fish hook.

Süryani (.——) سريانى A *lrnd.* 1. Christian who uses Syriac as a liturgical language. 2. Syriac language. —**ce** Syriac.

süs 1 سوس 1. ornament, decoration. 2. elegance of dress; toilet. 3. luxury. —**e düşkün** very fond of finery. — **saltanat** great luxury. —**ü ver=** (kendine) to play the part of...

süs=ᵉʳ **2** سوسمك to butt, to toss, to gore (with the horns).

süsen سوسن P iris. — **kökü** orris root.

süsle=ʳ سوسلمك /ı/ to adorn, to embellish, to decorate. —**yip püsle=** /ı/ adorn with great care.

süsleme سوسلمه *verbal n.* of **süsle=**. —**lik** decorative.

süslen=ir سوسلنمك to adorn oneself, to deck oneself out. —**dir=** same as **süsle=**.

süslü سوسلو 1. ornamented, decorated. 2. carefully dressed. 3. luxurious. — **püslü** elaborately dressed.

süst سست P *lrnd.* 1. feeble, infirm; languid. 2. slack, relaxed; idle, negligent; slow. 3. soft, tender. 4. vain, worthless (words). —**azm** P weak of purpose. —**baht** P unfortunate, unlucky. —**endam** (..—) P debilitated.

süstî (.—) سستى P *lrnd.* looseness, laxness; feebleness, impotence; worthlessness.

süstpay (.—) سستپاى P *lrnd.* slow of pace.

süstpeyman (..—) سستپيمان P *lrnd.* untrue to engagements, faithless.

süstrey سستراى P *lrnd.* weak minded.

süstür=ür سوسديرمك /ı, a/ *caus.* of **süs=**.

süsüş=ür سوسشمك to butt each other. —**tür=** *caus.*

süt سوت سود 1. milk, milk-like juice. 2. *chauffeurs' slang* gasoline, petrol. **— ağzı** beestings (colostrum). **—ten ağzı yanan yoğurdu üfliyerek yer** He who burns his mouth with hot milk blows his yogurt. **— ana, — anne** wet-nurse; foster mother. **— baba** foster father. **— başı** cream. **— beyaz** milk white, snow white. **—ü bozuk** base, characterless, villain. **— çal=** to get infected or sick from milk (baby). **— camı** a kind of Venetian milk glass. **— çıbanı** pustules in nursing infants. **— damarı** *anat.* 1. milk vein. 2. milk-duct, lacteal. **— dişi** milk tooth. **— dökmüş kedi gibi** in a crestfallen manner. **— gibi** white and clean. **—üne havale et=** /ı/ to leave (matters) to a person's sense of honor. **— hırası** *prov.* pining from bad milk (infant). **— hülâsası** condensed milk. **— kardeş, — kardeşi** foster brother or sister. **— kebabı** meat in pieces parboiled in milk, then skewered and roasted. **—ten kes=** to wean. **— kesildi** The milk has turned sour. **— kesimi** weaning. **— kesmiği** clot or film of cream or curd in milk. **— kırı** milk-white (horse). **— kızı** foster daughter. **— kökü** the root of *Polygala senega*, senega-root, snake-root. **— kuzusu** 1. suckling lamb. 2. baby. **— liman, — limanlık** dead calm. **— mavisi** light sky-blue. **— nine** wet-nurse, foster mother. **— oğlu** foster son. **— otu** milkwort, *bot.*, *Polygala vulgaris*. **— sağ=** to milk. **— suyu** whey. **— şekeri** *chem.* milk-sugar, lactose. **— tozu** milk powder, dried milk. **— ver=** /a/ to suckle, to nurse. **— vurgunu** suffering from bad milk (child); rickety. **— yüzü** 1. cream. 2. film on the surface of boiled milk.
sütçü سوتجى milkman, dairyman. **—lük** dairying trade.
süthane (. —.) سوتخانه dairy.
sütlaçᶜⁱ سوتلاج rice-milk, rice-pudding.
sütleğen سوتلكن سوتلوكن euphorbium, gum-plant, *bot.*, *Euphorbia resinifera*.
sütlü سوتلى 1. milky, in milk. 2. prepared with milk. **— aş** *prov.* rice-milk. **— mısır** fresh corn.
sütlüce سوتلوجه 1. somewhat milky. 2. petty spurge, *bot.*, *Euphorbia peplus*. 3. *w. cap.*, name of a quarter in Istanbul.
sütlükᵍᵘ سوتلك 1. dairy. 2. milk-jug, milk-pot.
sütne سوتنه short for **süt nine**.
sütre ستر A *mil.* cover.
sütsüz سوتسز 1. without milk; dry; having no milk. 2. base, mean.
sütude (. —.) ستوده P *lrnd.* 1. praised, glorified. 2. praiseworthy, laudable. **—gi** (. —.—) P praise, glorification. **—sıfat** (. —...) P, **—şiyem** (. —...) P of laudable qualities.
sütuh 1 (. —) سطح A *lrnd.*, *pl. of* **sath**. **—ı müteşabihe** similar surfaces. **—ı mütevaziye** parallel surfaces.
sütuh 2 (. —) ستوه P *lrnd.* 1. tired, exhausted; distressed, suffering. 2. stupefied, astonished.
sütun (. —) ستون P 1. pillar, column; prop, support. 2. column (in a newspaper). 3. beam (of light). **— başlığı** *arch.* capital. **— oturmalığı, — sekisi** *arch.* stylobate.
sütur 1 (. —) ستر A *lrnd.*, *pl. of* **sitr**.
sütur 2 (. —) ستور P *lrnd.* animal; quadruped, beast of burden; horse, mule. **—ban** (. — —) P groom. **—dan** (. — —) P stable.
sütürde ستورده P *lrnd.* shaved, erased, cut off.
sütüre ستوره P *lrnd.* razor.
sütürg ستورك P *lrnd.* 1. huge, gigantic, colossal. 2. strong, powerful. 3. violent, vehement, fierce; quarrelsome.
süvar (. —) سوار P *lrnd.* mounted on an animal, riding in a vehicle; rider, horseman. **— ol=** /a/ to mount, to ride. **—ân** (. — —) P *pl. of* **süvar**.
süvari (. — —) P, **süvari** سواری 1. cavalryman; cavalry; mounted. 2. captain (of a ship). **— alayı** cavalry regiment. **— askeri** cavalryman. **— polisi** mounted police.
süvarilikᵍⁱ (. —..) سواریلك career and duties of a cavalryman or a captain.
süve سوه سوا same as **söve**.
süver سور A *lrnd.*, *pl. of* **sure**. **S—i Medenî** suras of the Quran promulgated at Medina.
süveter (..'.) سوتر E sweater.
süveyda (..—) سویدا A *lrnd.* 1. petite and black (woman). 2. the reputed black core of the heart. 3. black dot.
süveykᵏⁱ سویك A *bot.* tigella.
Süveyş سویش *geog.* Suez. **— Kanalı** Suez Canal.
süyuf (. —) سیوف A *lrnd.*, *pl. of* **seyf**.
süyulᵘ (. —) سیول A *lrnd.*, *pl. of* **seyl**.
süyüm سویوم *prov.* 1. the first strand of yarn spun out of a fresh distaff. 2. one strand of yarn.
süz=ᵉʳ 1 سوزمك /ı/ 1. to strain, to filter. 2. to half-close the eyes from drowsiness, intoxication or rapture; to look attentively at something through half-closed eyes; to examine closely.
-süz 2 سز *cf.* **-sız 1**.
süzdür=ᵘʳ سوزدرمك /ı, a/ *caus. of* **süz= 1**.
süzekᵍⁱ سوزك *prov.*, same as **süzgeç**.
süzgeçᶜⁱ سوزكج 1. strainer, filter. 2. rose, spray-head (of a watering can). 3. close examination.
süzgü سوزكو fine filter. **— taşı** porous stone used as a filter.

süzgün سوزگون 1. languid, half-closed (eye). 2. grown thin. — bakış languid glance.
-süzlük^gü سزلك cf. -sızlık.
süzme سوزمه 1. verbal n. of süz= 1. 2. strained, filtered. 3. run (honey). 4. slang rascal. — yoğurt yogurt partially dried by hanging in a cloth bag.
süzük^gü سزوك drawn, strained (face, etc.).
süzül=^ür سزلل pass. of süz= 1.
süzüntü سوزنتى dregs.

Ş

ş, Ş 1 the twenty-third letter of the alphabet.
-ş 2, ش after consonants -ış, -iş, -uş, -üş, dimunitive, especially for names, e. g., Aliş, İbiş, Memiş.
=ş= 3, after consonants =iş=, =ış=, =uş=, =üş=, reciprocal and collective action, as in bekleş=, dövüş=, kaçış=.
şab^bb1 1 (—) شاب A lrnd. young, youthful; youth.
şa'b 2 شعب A lrnd. 1. people; tribe (of the Arabs). 2. division of a thing; a thing divided up. 3. fissure, cleft, suture in the skull.
şâb 3 (—) شاب P lrnd. alum. —i firengî European alum. —i rumî white pepper.
Şa'ban 1 (.—) A, Şaban (——) شعبان 1. the eighth month of the Muslim year. 2. man's name. 3. slang stupid, imbecile.
şaban 2 شابان archaic petrified, astounded.
şabaş (——) شاباش P lrnd. Well done! —î (———) P praise, applause.
şabbe (—.) شابة A lrnd. young (woman).
şabbıemred (—...) شابامرد A lrnd. beardless youth.
şa'beze شعبذه A lrnd. a practicing jugglery; jugglery, trickery.
şabla شابلا archaic, same as şaplak.
şablon شابلون Gk mech. pattern.
şabrak^gı شابراق horse cloth, saddle blanket.
sad (—) شاد P lrnd. merry, joyful; happy. — ol= to rejoice, to be merry.
şadab (——) شاداب P lrnd. 1. full of sap, luxuriant, flourishing. 2. fresh, pleasant. 3. merry, joyous. —î (———) P 1. luxuriousness; freshness. 2. joyousness.
şadan (——) شادان P lrnd. rejoicing, happy, glad.
şadbehr (—.) شادبهر P lrnd. whose lot and portion is happy; happy situation.
şaddil (—.) شاددل P lrnd. cheerful.
şadhâb (——) شادضواب P lrnd. refreshing sleep.

şadırda=^r شاردامس to make a splashing, gurgling noise, to gush. —t= /ı/ caus.
şadırdı شاردى a gushing; a spouting.
şadırvan شاردوان [Persian —.—] fountain of water (with a jet in the middle); reservoir with faucets at the sides for ablutions, usually attached to a mosque. — külâhı the conical roof of a fountain.
şadi (——) شادى P lrnd. joy, happiness, gladness.
şadkâm (——) شادكام P lrnd. happy, contented, rejoicing, gratified. —î (———) P happiness, gratification, content.
şadlık^gı (—.) شادلك joy, happiness.
şadman (——) شادمان P lrnd., same as şaduman.
şadmane (——.) شادمانه P lrnd. joyful, joyfully.
şadmanî (———) شادمانى P lrnd. joy, happiness.
şadmerg (—.) شادمرگ P lrnd. sudden death from joy; dying easily or from joy.
şadnâk^kı (——) شادناك P lrnd. cheerful, joyous.
şaduman (—.—) شادمان [şadman] P lrnd. cheerful, joyful; pleased. —lık joy, happiness.
şaf (—) شاف [Arabic şiyâf] med. suppository.
şafak^gı شفق A 1. morning twilight, dawn. 2. lrnd. evening twilight, dusk. — at= 1. to dawn; to become dusky. 2. /da/ to realize the truth of something and be scared. — sökmesi break of dawn.
şafakalûd (..——) شفق آلود P lrnd. like the dawn, rosy.
şafakgûn (..—) شفقگون P lrnd. twilight-colored, red.
şafi 1 (—.) شافى A lrnd. 1. health-giving (thing), healing, therapeutic. 2. satisfactory; categorical (answer).
şafi^iı 2 (—.) شافع A lrnd. who intercedes;

interceding; intercessor. —**i ruz-i cezâ** the Prophet Muhammad.

şafii (—.—) شافعى A 1. *Isl. rel.* Shafii, pertaining to the school of canonical law of Imam-ı Shafii; follower of the Shafii school, Shafiite. — **köpeği** dirty-faced person. **—ye**, **—lik** the Shafii school of canonical law.

şafiye (—..) شافيه A *lrnd.*, same as **şafi** 1. **Ş— Suresi** one of the names of the first sura of the Quran.

şaft شافت E *mech.* shaft.

şaful شافول small wooden tub for carrying honey.

şagaf 1 (.—) شغاف A 1. *anat.* pericardium. 2. *med.* angina pectoris.

şagaf 2 شغف A *lrnd.* 1. deep love, longing, yearning. 2. pericardium, midriff.

şagalⁱⁱ (.—) شغال P *lrnd.* jackal.

şagil (—.) شاغل A *lrnd.* that occupies one; busy, occupied, attentive.

şagird (—.) شاگرد P same as **şakird**.

şah 1 (—) شاه P 1. Shah. 2. king, monarch. 3. *chess* king. 4. *Or. mus.* a compound **makam** six centuries old. 5. *mus.* the longest kind of **ney**. **—ımı ben bu kadar severim** I can't risk any more; this is all I am willing to do. **— beyt** *poetry* the best couplet of an ode. **—ı encüm** *lrnd.* the sun. **— iken şahbaz oldu** He has become finer and finer used only ironically. **Ş—ı Kerbelâ** Husain, son of the Caliph Ali. **Ş—ı Kevneyn** *lrnd.* Lord of the two Worlds, the Prophet Muhammad. **Ş—ı Levlâk** *lrnd.* the Prophet Muhammad. **Ş—ı Merdan** *lrnd.* the Caliph Ali. **Ş—ı Risalet** *lrnd.* the Prophet Muhammad. **Ş—ı Velâyet**, **Ş—ı Zülfikar** *lrnd.* the Caliph Ali.

şah 2 (—) شاخ P *lrnd.* 1. branch, bough, twig. 2. fork, prong, arm (of anything). 3. horn (of a beast). 4. drinking-horn; powder-horn, horn for blowing. 5. a lock of hair: **—a kalk=** to rear, to stand up on its hind legs (horse). **—ı âhû** 1. buck's horn. 2. false promise. **—ı gül** 1. rose branch. 2. branched horn of a buck.

şah- 3 (—) شاه P great or good of its kind, as in **şahdamar, şaheser**.

şaha (—.) شاخه P *lrnd.* 1. two-pronged fork. 2. two-armed yoke.

şahadet (.—.) شهادت A *lrnd.*, same as **şehadet**.

şahamet (.—.) شهامت A *lrnd.*, same as **şehamet**.

şahan (——) شاهان P *lrnd.*, *pl. of* **şah** 1.

şahane (——.) شاهانه P royal, imperial; regal, magnificent.

şahapᵇⁱ شهاب [şihab] meteor; shooting star.

şahbâlⁱⁱ (——) شهبال P *lrnd.*, same as **şehbal**.

şahbâlâ (———) شاه بالا P *lrnd.* bridegroom's best man at his wedding.

şahbaz (——) شاهباز [Persian ——] 1. royal falcon. 2. champion, hero. 3. fine, handsome. 4. rough daredevil, bully.

şahbender (—..) شاهبندر P *lrnd.*, same as **şehbender**.

şahbuy (——) شاهبوى P *lrnd.* ambergris.

şahdamar, şahdamarıⁿⁱ شاه دامار شاه داماری 1. *anat.* aorta. 2. a great artery (of trade, etc.).

şahdane (——.) شاهدانه P *lrnd.* 1. large and lustrous pearl; largest bead in a rosary. 2. hempseed.

şahdar (——) شاخدار P *lrnd.* 1. branched, forked. 2. horned.

şahdaru (———) شاهدارو P *lrnd.* wine.

şaheser (—..) شاه اثر P masterpiece.

şahgâm (——), **şahgâne** (——.) شاهگام شاهگانه P *lrnd.* fit for a king, great and noble (of its kind).

şahimʰᵐⁱ شحم [şahm] *lrnd.* 1. fat; grease. 2. pulp of fruit. 3. pith of a plant.

şahısʰˢⁱ **1** شخص [şahs] 1. person, individual. 2. personal features. **— zamiri** *gram.* personal pronoun.

şahıs 2 (—.) شاخص A *lrnd.* surveyor's rod.

şahıs 3 (—.) شاخص A *lrnd.* 1. fixed staringly, wide open (eye). 2. whose eyes are fixed and looking up. 3. projecting, standing out or upright; projection, process.

şahi (——) شاهى P *lrnd.* 1. royal, imperial. 2. kingship. 3. cotton longcloth. 4. shahi (Persian coin). 5. an ancient form of brass muzzle-loading cannon. 6. a kind of candy (made of starch and egg).

şahid 1 (—.) شاهد A 1. witness. 2. supporting citation, example (from a well-known work); *gram.* example. 3. control (in an experiment). 4. *Isl. rel.* recording angel. 5. the Prophet Muhammad as the witness of the one God. **—i âdil** *lrnd.* a legally competent witness. **—i ayn** *lrnd.* eye-witness. **—i hâl** *lrnd.* witness of the event. **— ol=** /a/ to witness. **— tepe** *geol.* outlier. **— tut=** /ı/ to call on one to witness; to accept as witness. **—i zûr** *lrnd.* false witness.

şahid 2 (—.) شاهد P *lrnd.* 1. beautiful woman; handsome man. 2. pretty boy, catamite. **—i bâzâr** streetwalker. **—i devran** famous beauty. **—i ziba** very beautiful.

şahidbaz (—.—) شاهدباز P *lrnd.* sodomite; whore monger. **—î** (—.——) P sodomy; prostitution.

şahide (—..) شاهده A *lrnd.* tombstone.

şahidlikᵍⁱ (—..) شاهدلك 1. a giving evidence, testimony. 2. a being witness to something. **— et=** /a/ to give testimony.

şahik̄¹ (—.) شاهق A lrnd. high, lofty (mountain or edifice).
şahika (—..) شاهقه A lrnd. summit, peak.
şahin (—.) شاهين P 1. peregrine falcon, zool., Falco peregrinus. 2. tongue of a balance. — bakışlı with fierce and piercing eyes. —ci Ott. hist. falconer in charge of the peregrine falcons.
şahinşah (—.—) شاهنشاه P same as şehinşah.
şahit^dı (—.) شاهد same as şahid 1.
şahlan=ᵣ 1 شاهلنمق 1. to buck, rear (horse). 2. to become angry and threatening; to get out of hand.
şahlan=ᵣ 2 (—..) شاهلانمق lrnd. to become branched; to get horns.
şahlı شاهلى 1. branched, branchy. 2. horned, antlered.
şahlık^ǧı شاهلق 1. quality of a shah; sovereignty. 2. kingdom.
şahm شحم A lrnd., same as şahım.
şahmerdan (—.—) شاهمرذان P 1. battering-ram; pile-driver; beetle (heavy hammer). 2. w. cap., same as Şah-ı Merdan.
şahmî (.—) شحمى A 1. lrnd. fatty, adipose. 2. chem. aliphatic.
şahmühre (—..) شاه مهره P lrnd. precious stone said to be found in a serpent's mouth or a dragon's head.
şahname (——.) شاهنامه P 1. w. cap., the Book of Kings (historical poem written by Firdausi). 2. lrnd. poetical history; epic.
şahnameci شاهنامه جى Ott. hist. official court poet who glorified dynastic history.
şahnay (——) شاهناى P lrnd. large trumpet.
şahne شحنه A obs. 1. police magistrate, director of the police of a town. 2. tax gatherer, tithe gatherer. —i bazar the police inspector of a market place. Ş—i çeharum the fourth great lawgiver, the Prophet Muhammad. Ş—i çeharum hisar (lit., the Lord of the fourth heaven.) 1. the sun. 2. Jesus Christ. Ş—i Çeharum kitab the Lord of the fourth sacred book, the Prophet Muhammad. Ş—i deryay-ı ışk the Prophet Muhammad. —i divan Ott. hist. the police superintendent under the Council of State. Ş—i gavga-i kıyamet the Prophet Muhammad. Ş—i iklim-i adl u dad the Caliph Umar. Ş—i kişver-i sıdk the Caliph Abu Bakr. Ş—i mülk-i Haya the Caliph Othman. Ş—i Necef the Caliph Ali. —i pencüm hisar the planet Mars. —i şeb watchman. —i şeb ü seher the Prophet Muhammad.
şahnış, şahnişin (..—) شاهنشين P bay window on an enclosed balcony.
şahper (—.) شاهپر P lrnd. pinion of a bird's wing.
şahrah (——) شاهراه P lrnd. main road, highway.
şahreg (—.) شاهرگ P lrnd. principal vein; artery.
şahrem شخرم 1. a bursting, cracking; crack, fissure. 2. segment between two fissures, flake. — şahrem çatla= 1. to be covered with cracks (skin). 2. to flake.
şahrud (——) شاهرود P lrnd. 1. great river. 2. bass string of a lute. 3. bass viol.
şahs شخص A lrnd., same as şahıs 1.
şahsan (.'.) شخصا A lrnd. personally, in person.
şahsar (——) شاخسار P lrnd. branchy tree; full of branches; branchy place, forest, thicket, grove.
şahsî (.—) شخصى A personal, private (matter). — hâl law status, civil status.
şahsiyat (..—) شخصيات [Arabic .——] 1. personal matters. 2. lrnd. personalities. —a dökül= to descend to personalities (discussion).
şahsiyet (.—.) شخصيت A 1. personality; character. 2. important person. — hakları personal interests.
şahsüvar (—.—) شاهسوار P lrnd. a good horseman.
şahtane (.—.) شاهدانه P same as şahdane.
şahtar (——) شاهتار P lrnd. chief string of a musical instrument.
şahtere شاهتره P common fumitory, bot., Fumaria officinalis. —giller neol., Fumariaceae.
şahtur شختور A large raft-like boat used as a ferry on large rivers.
şahûr (——) شاهور P lrnd. kiln, furnace.
şahvar (——) شاهوار P lrnd. 1. fit for a king, royal. 2. fine pearl fit for a king.
şahveş (—.) شاهوش P lrnd. royal in appearance, kingly.
şahzade (——.) شاهزاده P lrnd., same as şehzade.
şaibe (—.) شائبه A lrnd. 1. stain; defect. 2. trace, indication (of doubt etc.). 3. foulness, pollution. 3. sunspot.
şaibedar (—..—) شائبه دار P lrnd. stained; tarnished.
şaik̄¹ (—.) شائق A lrnd. desirous, yearning.
şair 1 (—.) شاعر A 1. poet. 2. minstrel; public singer. —i a'zam poet laureate.
şair 2 (.—) شعير A lrnd. barley.
şairan (—.—) شاعران P lrnd., pl. of şair 1.
şairane (—.—.) شاعرانه P poetical; in a poetical manner.
şaire 1 (—..) شاعره A lrnd. poetess.
şaire 2 (.—.) شعيره A lrnd. a grain of barley.
şairlik^ǧı شاعرلك 1. the quality of a poet or minstrel. 2. poetical writing. — sat= to pretend to be a poet, to poeticize.

şak¹ 1 شاق loud clacking noise (as of wood against wood, the crack of a whip, a box on the ear). — **şak vur**= to strike repeatedly and noisily.

şakᵏ¹ 2 شقّ A lrnd. a splitting, fissuring, slitting; crack, fissure. — **et**=*. —**ı şefe et**= to open the lips, to speak.

şakᵏ¹ 3 (—) شاقّ A lrnd. difficult, arduous, toilsome.

şaka 1 شاقه ~ شقا ~ شاقَ joke, fun; jest. —**ya boğ**= /ı/ to try to pass off (a matter with a joke). — **derken kaka olur** colloq. A joke may easily become a serious matter. —**ya gelme**= 1. not to be able to take a joke. 2. not to be a joking matter. 3. not to be joked with, to be very severe. —**ya getir**= /ı/ 1. to tell a serious matter jokingly. 2. to calm down a dispute by giving the conversation a joking flavor. — **gibi gel**= to be incredible (matter). — **götürmez** 1. not a joking matter, serious. 2. He can't take a joke. — **iken kaka olur** colloq., same as **şaka derken kaka olur**. — **kaldır**= to be able to take a joke. — **maka**, — **maka derken** By taking things calmly one can accomplish a lot without trouble, e. g., **şaka maka sekiz saat çalışmışız** We have worked eight hours without even noticing it. — **söyle**= to joke. —**ya vur**= /ı/ to pretend to take something as a joke. — **yap**= to make fun, to joke. —**sı yok** not to be trifled with; in earnest.

şaka 2 شقاء A lrnd. 1. a being miserable, wretched; wretchedness, misery. 2. insolence; villainy.

şakacı شاقه جى joker, jester.

şakacıktan شاقه جقدن 1. as a joke. 2. doing something serious under the pretense of a joke. 3. without noticing (difficulty, etc.).

şakaikᵏ¹ شقائق A lrnd., var. of **şakayık**.

şakakᵍ¹ (.—) شقاق temporal portion of the skull, temple.

şakalaş=ⁱʳ شاقه لشمك /la/ to joke with one another.

şakaşuka شاقه شوقه colloq. joke, pleasantry.

şakavet (.—.) شقاوت A lrnd., same as **şekavet**.

şakayıkᵏ¹, ᵍ¹ (.—.) شقايق A peony, bot., Paeonia officinalis; anemone. — **ı nu'man** poppy anemone, crown anemone, bot., Anemone coronaria.

şakı=ʳ شاقيمق ~ شاقيماق 1. to sing loudly (nightingale, canary). 2. archaic to flash, gleam, glitter.

şakırda=ʳ شاقرداماق 1. to rattle and clatter together, to jingle. 2. to sing vociferously (nightingale). —**t**= caus.

şakır şakır شاقر شاقر rattling or rushing noise like a heavy rainfall. — **yıka**= to wash with a splashing noise, to wash thoroughly.

şakır şukur شاقر شوقر a hollow rattling, banging noise.

şakırtı شاقرتى repeated or continuous clatter or rattle.

şakıt شاقط ~ شاقت moray eel, zool., Muraena helena; lamprey, zool., Petromyzon marinus.

şaki 1 (.—) شقى A lrnd. 1. brigand, robber; rebel, outlaw. 2. miserable, wretched. 3. sinner, evil-doer.

şaki 2 (——) شاكى A lrnd. 1. complaining; complainant. 2. bristling with arms, heavily armed.

şakikᵏ¹ (.—) شقيق A lrnd. 1. a half of anything cleft in two. 2. uterine brother.

şakika (.—.) شقيقه A lrnd. 1. uterine sister. 2. pain affecting one half of the head or face, migraine. 3. rain or lightning (as cleaving the clouds). 4. fissure, crack, crevice.

şakikıye (.—..) شقيقيه A bot., Ranunculaceae.

şakile (—..) شاكله A lrnd. 1. mode, manner. 2. resemblance, likeness.

şakilikᵍ¹ شقيلك lrnd. 1. robbery, rebelliousness. 2. act of one sinning against God or rebelling against the law.

şakir (—.) شاكر A lrnd. 1. thankful, grateful. 2. God, the requiter of good deeds.

şakird (—.) شاكرد [şagird] A 1. lrnd. pupil; apprentice; disciple. 2. Ott. hist. female slave (while being brought up under an experienced hand in the Harem).

şakirdan (—.—) شاكردان P lrnd., pl. of **şakird**.

şakirdâne (—.—.) شاكردانه P lrnd. befitting a pupil or apprentice (conduct).

şakirdlikᵍ¹ شاكردلك 1. quality of a pupil or apprentice; apprenticeship; discipleship. 2. wages paid to an apprentice.

şâkiriyet (—...) شاكريت A lrnd. thankfulness, gratitude.

şakket=ᵈᵉʳ شقّ ايتمك lrnd. to cleave; to split.

şakla=ʳ شاقلاماق to make a loud, cracking noise.

şaklaban شاقلابان 1. mimic, jester, buffoon. 2. amusing person. 3. charlatan. —**lık** mimicry, buffoonery.

şaklat=ʳ شاقلاتمق /ı/ 1. to crack (whip). 2. to cause a loud cracking noise.

şakra=ʳ شاقراماق same as **şakı**=.

şakrakᵍ¹ شاقراق noisy, mirthful; vivacious; chatty. — **kuşu** bullfinch, zool., Pyrrhula pyrrhula. —**lık** noisy mirth.

şakşakᵍ¹ شاق شاق ~ شق شق 1. a large kind of castanet; slap-stick. 2. applause; toadying. —**çı** toady; yes-man. —**çılık** base adulation.

şakulˡᵘ (—.) شاقول A plumb-line; plummet. —**î** (———), (—.—) A perpen-

şakulla=

dicular. **—iyet** (—.—.) verticality, perpendicularity.
şakulla=ʳ **şakulle=**ʳ شاقوللمق /ı/ 1. to set up with a plumb-line. 2. to plan, to measure.
şal شال P 1. shawl, especially a Cashmere shawl. 2. homespun woolen cloth.
şalâki (——.) شالاکی Gk 1. alpaca. 2. French merino.
şalbend (—.) شالبند P lrnd. a kind of shawl worn as a turban.
şalgam شلغم P turnip, bot., Brassica rapa.
şali شالی 1. camlet; alpaca. 2. bunting.
şallakᵍ¹ شلّاك 1. naked; shameless. 2. charm, trinket, especially watch-charm. **— mallak** 1. stark naked. 2. a mob of roughs.
şaltakᵍ¹ شالطاق prov. quarrelsome; noisy, clamorous. **—cı** quarrelsome person.
şalter شالتر G elec. switch.
şalupa (..′.) شالوپه It sloop, long boat.
şalvar شالوار |şelvar| baggy trousers, shalwar. **—bend** P trouser string. **—lı** wearing baggy trousers.
Şam 1 شام |Şam 2| A 1. Damascus. 2. Ott. hist. Syria. **— alacası** striped silk and cotton material for dresses. **— babası** 1. a kind of pastry. 2. colloq. father who has no authority over his family. **— çöveni** jointed glasswort, bot., Salicornia herbasia. **— fıstığı***. **— hırkası** a kind of comfortable jacket worn by men at home. **— işi** Damascus work (material, etc.). **— kitabesi** Damascus muslin (for dresses). **— kumaşı** cloth of Damascus. **— tabanı** an inferior kind of Damascus steel.
Şam 2 (—) شام A lrnd., same as **Şam 1**.
—ı cennetmeşam (lit., Damascus, redolent of Paradise) Damascus. **—ı Şerif** Damascus.
şam 3 (—) شام P lrnd. evening. **—ı muğber** dreary evening. **— ü seher** evening and morning.
şamᵐᵐ¹ **4** (—) شام A lrnd. that smells.
şam'a شمعا A lrnd. wax-taper, candle.
şam'alı شمعلی made of wax. **— kibrit** wax match.
şamama شمامه |şemame| 1. muskmelon. 2. undersized, weak (child or man).
şamandıra (..′..) شامندره 1. buoy, float. 2. float (for a wick); burner (of a kerosene lamp). 3. ball (of a ball-cock). **— kabı** auto. float chamber.
şamar شامار a slap on the face; a box on the ear, slap. **— at=** /a/ to give a slap on the face or box on the ear. **— oğlanı** 1. Ott. hist. youth who bore the blame for other peoples' faults; scapegoat. 2. schoolboy. **— ye=** to get a box on the ear or a slap on the face.
şamarla=ʳ شامارلا /ı/ to slap.

şâmât (——) شامات A lrnd., pl. of **şame 1**.
şamata شاماته great noise, uproar, hubbub. **— et=** to make a great noise. **— teli** tinsel in strips. **—cı** noisy, uproarious, quarrelsome (person). **—lı** noisy.
şamdan شمعدان |şem'dan| candlestick. **— ağası** Ott. hist. valet of the candlesticks in a grandee's house. **— hokkası** the cup or removable hollowed part of a candlestick for holding the candle. **— külâhı** candle extinguisher. **— pulu** socket, sconce (of a candlestick).
şamdancı شمعدانجی 1. maker and seller of candlestick. 2. person in charge of candlesticks in a department or house. **— başı** Ott. hist. chief candle-maker in the palace.
şame 1 (—.) شامه A lrnd. black mole on the skin.
şame 2 (—.) شامه P lrnd. woman's veil. **—keş** (—..) P who has a veil on her head. **—küşa** (—..—) P who has opened her veil.
şamfıstığıᵐ¹ شامفستیغی pistachio nut.
şamgâh (——) شامگاه P lrnd. evening, eventide.
Şamî (——) شامی A lrnd. 1. pertaining to Damascus or Syria. 2. man from Damascus or Syria.
şamih (—.) شامخ A lrnd. 1. high, lifted up. 2. lofty, proud.
şamil (—.) شامل A /ı or a/ lrnd. that contains, comprises, comprehends, including, comprehensive.
Şamkârî (———) شامکاری P lrnd. of Damascus workmanship.
Şamlı شاملی from Damascus (person).
şamme (—.) شامّه A lrnd. sense of smell.
şampanya (..′.) شامپانیه F champagne.
şampanze شامپانزه F chimpanzee.
şampiyon شامپیون F champion.
şampuvan شامپوان F shampoo.
şan 1 (—) شان A 1. fame, renown. 2. dignity, honor, glory, reputation. 3. state, quality, aspect. 4. display, pomp, importance. **—ına düş=** to befit one's station or dignity. **—ı insaf** that befits justice. **— kazan=** to become famous. **—ından ol=** to befit one's dignity. 2. to be peculiar to, to be characteristic of. **— ver=** 1. to become famous. 2. slang to encourage, to spoil. **—ına yakış=** to befit one's station and dignity.
şan 2 شأن [şe'n 2] lrnd. 1. matter, business, affair. 2. event, occurrence.
şan 3 شان F a singing.
şane (—.) شانه P lrnd. 1. comb. 2. honeycomb. 3. shoulderblade; the body of the hand or foot. **—dân** (—.—) P comb-case. **—saz** (—.—) P combmaker. **—zede** (—...) P

who has combed; combed, combed out; curried. **—zen** (—..) P comber; hairdresser.

şangırda= شا نغرُدامق to rattle; to crash, to make the noise of breaking glass. **—t=** /ı/ caus.

şangır şıngır, şangır şungur شانغر شينغر شا نغر شونغور imitates the noise of breaking glass.

şangırtı شا نغرتى the noise of breaking glass.

şanjan شانجان F shot (silk, etc.).

şanjiman شانجمان F auto. gear, shift.

şankr شانقر F med. canker, chancre.

şanlı شانلى 1. famous, renowned. 2. great, glorious, dignified. 3. fine looking; showy, magnificent. **— şöhretli** magnificent and imposing.

şano (´.) شانو It stage (theatre). **—ya çık=** to appear on the stage.

şans شانس F luck. **—lı** lucky. **—sız** hapless, unlucky.

şantaj شانتاژ F blackmail, extortion. **—cı** blackmailer, extortionist.

şantiye شانتيه F 1. yard; shipyard. 2. building constructor's supply shed.

şantöz شانتوز F female singer.

şanziman شانزيمان var. of şanjman.

şap 1 شاب [şeb 2] 1. alum. 2. coral reef. **Ş— Denizi** the Red Sea. **— gibi** very salty. **— gibi don=, — gibi kal=** 1. to be astounded. 2. to be greatly embarrassed and disconcerted. **— illeti** foot-and-mouth disease of cattle. **— kayışı** a very tough strap. **— kesil=** to become bitter. **— ocağı** alum mine. **—a otur=** (lit., to be grounded on a coral reef) to be in a hopeless dilemma, to be greatly disconcerted. **—a sok=** (lit., to plunge into alum water) to adopt some heroic remedy.

şap 2 شاپ smack; a smacking noise.

şapçı شاپجى slang pederast.

şaphane (.—.) شاپخانه P alum factory.

şapırda= شاپرداسق to make a smacking noise; to make a loud splashing noise. **—t=** /ı/ caus.

şapır şapır, şapır şupur شاپر شاپر شاپر شپور imitates the smacking of lips. **— öp=** to kiss with a loud smacking noise.

şapırtı شاپرتى smacking noise of the lips.

şapka (´.) شاپقه Polish 1. hat. 2. truck (of a ship's mast). 3. cowl (of a chimney). 4. circumflex. **—yı ters giy=, —yı yere vur=** to show anger. **—cı** maker or seller of hats; hatter. **—lı** 1. wearing a hat. 2. having a circumflex.

şapla= شاپلامق to make a smacking noise (with the lips or hand).

şaplak شاپلاق smack on the face.

şaplat= شاپلاتمق /ı/ caus. of şapla=.

şappadak (´...) شاپپاداق all at once, suddenly.

şaprak شابراق saddle covering.

şapşak شاپشاق prov. wooden pot or mug. **— at=, — salla=** to toady, to flatter.

şapşal شاپشال untidy, slovenly. **—lık** untidiness.

şap şap شاپ شاپ imitates the sound of repeated kissing.

şar 1 (—) شار P lrnd. town, city. **Ş— Dağı** Mount Scardus in Macedonia.

şa'r 2 شعر A lrnd. hair.

-şar 3 شر cf. -ar 3.

şarab (.—) شراب A 1. lrnd., same as şarap. 2. lrnd. beverage. 3. fruit syrup. **—ı nâb** clear and pure wine. **—ı nûhî** a thousand-year-old wine. **—ı tahur** any canonically pure drink.

şarabdâr (.——) شرابدار P lrnd. butler.

şarabhâr (.——) شرابخوار P lrnd. wine-bibber.

şarabhorde (.—..) شرابخورده P lrnd. drunk with wine.

şarabî 1 (.——) شرابى wine-colored.

şarabi 2 (.——) شرابى A lrnd. wine merchant.

şarampol شرامپول Hung mil. stockade; palisade. **— çek=, — çevir=** to construct a stockade.

şarap شراب [şarab] wine. **—ın hurmeti** unlawfulness of wine. **— tortusu** crude tartar.

şarapçı شراپجى wine merchant. **—lık** wine trade.

şaraphane (.——.) شراپخانه 1. wine factory. 2. storehouse for wine. 3. large wine-cask, vat.

şarapnel شراپنل E mil. shrapnel.

şarbon شاربون F 1. med. anthrax. 2. smut (of wheat).

şârık (—.) شارق A lrnd. 1. rising and shining (sun, etc.). 2. eastern side.

şârıka (—..) شارقه A lrnd. 1. which rises and shines. 2. flash, ray or beam of light.

şarılda= شارلداسق to flow with a splashing noise. **—t=** /ı/ caus.

şarıl şarıl شارل شارل imitating the sound of running water. **— ak=** to flow with a splashing noise.

şarıltı شارلتى a gurgling, splashing noise. **—lı** having a splashing noise; flowing.

şa'ri 1 (.—.) شعرى A lrnd. pertaining to hair; capillary.

Şari'i A, **şâri'i 2** (—.) شارع lrnd. 1. law-giver, legislator; Prophet Muhammad. 2. that enters; that leads or points to. 3. who begins, commences. 4. highway, thoroughfare; street.

şârib 1 (—.) شارب A lrnd. mustache.

şârib 2 (—.) شارب A lrnd. that drinks.

şaribülleben (—....) شارب اللبن A lrnd. who drinks milk.

şaribülleyl vennehar (—.....—) شارب الليل والنهار A who drinks day and night, hopeless drunkard.

şarid (—.) شارد A lrnd. 1. wild, shy or

şarih

refractory (animal). 2. unusual but popular (rhyme, poem, etc.).
şarih (—.) شارح A lrnd. commentator, annotator; that annotates or comments.
şa'riye شعريه A lrnd., same as şehriye 1.
şa'riyet شعريت A lrnd. capillarity.
şarj شارژ F artillery charge.
şarjör شارژور F mil. drum for feeding ammunition to automatic arms.
şark[kı] 1 شرق A 1. the east. 2. eastern, oriental. Ş—ı Karib lrnd. the Near East.
şark[kı] 2 شارك a loud clapping or slamming noise.
şarkada شرفاده prov. 1. inconsiderately impulsive in his speech and action. 2. quarrelsome; mischievous.
şarkadak[ğı] (.'..) شارفاده imitates the noise of a thing falling. — bayıl= to fall down in a swoon.
şarkan (.'.) شرقا A lrnd. in an eastern direction.
şarkı شرقى song (the most common secular vocal form). — devr-i revanı Or. mus. a rhythmic pattern of thirteen beats. — oku=, — söyle= to sing. —cı 1. singer. 2. song writer.
şarkî (.—) شرقى A Eastern, Oriental.
Şarkiyat (..—) شرقيات |Arabic .——| Orientalism; the study of Oriental languages and literature. —çı Orientalist.
Şarkiyun (.——) شرقيون A lrnd. Orientalists.
şarklı شرقلى an Oriental. —laş= to become an Oriental. —lık state of being an Oriental, Oriental mentality.
şarla=[r] شارلامق same as şarılda=. —t= /ı/ caus.
şarlatan شارلاتان F charlatan; quack. —lık charlatanism, quackery.
şarmöz شارموز F a kind of silk cloth.
şarpa شارپا F colloq. scarf.
şar şar شارشار same as şarıl şarıl.
şart شرط A 1. condition, stipulation; article of agreement. 2. gram. conditional clause. 3. can. law a pronouncing on oneself a conditional divorce from a wife; divorce that will be executed on certain conditions. —ı âzam lrnd. indispensable condition. — et= to invoke a divorce (under certain conditions). — koş=, — koy= to lay down a condition, to make a stipulation. — ol= to become inevitable. — olsun May I be divorced from my wife (if this be not true). — şurt tanıma= not to be bound by conditions and stipulations.
şartî (.—) شرطى A 1. gram. conditional. 2. phil. hypothetical. —yet conditionality.
şartla=[r] شرطلامق to wash clothes or vessels in accordance with the requirements of canon law. —n= pass.

şartlaş=[ır] شرطلاشمق to agree to conditions. —ma 1. verbal n. 2. contract.
şartlı شرطلى 1. having a condition attached. 2. who takes the oath called şart. 3. conditional.
şartname (.—.) شرطنامه P list of conditions; specification; contract.
şartröz شارترز F chartreuse (liquor).
şartsız شرطسز unconditional, free from all conditions.
şasi شاسى F chassis.
şast شست P lrnd. 1. sixty. 2. hook; handle used in drawing a crossbow —a al= to take as a mark in shooting.
şastüm شستم P lrnd. sixtieth, in the sixtieth place.
şaş=[ar] شاشمق 1. to be surprised or bewildered. 2. /dan/ to miss one's way, to go astray; to deviate. 3. to miss its object (missile, blow, etc.). —a kal= to be bewildered. —acak şey surprising thing, strange thing.
şa'şaa A, şaşaa (—..) شعشعه glitter, splendor, sparkle.
şa'şaadar (...—) شعشعه‌دار P lrnd. brilliant, sparkling; gorgeous.
şa'şaalan=[ır] شعشعه‌لنمك to glitter, sparkle; to be magnificent or pompous. —dır= /ı/ caus.
şa'şaalı شعشعه‌لى glittering; gorgeous, magnificent.
şa'şaapaş (...—) شعشعه‌پاش P lrnd. glittering, brilliant.
şaşala=[r] شاشالامق to be bewildered or confused.
şaşı شاشى squinting, squint-eyed; crosseyed.
şaşıla=[r] شاشيلامق prov., same as şaşılaş=.
şaşılacak[ğı] شاشيلاجق surprising; wonderful.
şaşılaş=[ır] شاشيلاشمق to squint, to become crosseyed.
şaşılık[ğı] شاشيلق squint, crossed eyes.
şaşır=[ır] شاشيرمق 1. to be confused (about something). 2. /ı/ to lose (the way, etc.). 3. to become bewildered or embarrassed; to lose one's head. —ma verbal n.
şaşırt=[ır] شاشيرتمق 1. caus. of şaşır=. 2. to transplant (seedlings).
şaşırtma شاشيرتما 1. verbal n. of şaşırt=. 2. zigzag. 3. tongue-twister. 4. a transplanting. —ca tongue-twister, puzzle.
şaşkaloz شاشقالوز slang, contemptuous crosseyed.
şaşkın شاشقين 1. bewildered, confused. 2. stupid, silly. —a dön= to be stupefied.
şaşkınlaş=[ır] شاشقينلاشمق to become bewildered.
şaşkınlık[ğı] شاشقينلق bewilderment; stupidity.
şat[tı] 1 شط A lrnd. 1. large river. 2. the Tigris.
şat 2 شات flat-bottomed boat; lighter.
şataf شطف arch. bevel.
şatafat شطفات luxury; ostentatious living. —lı showy, pretentious.
şataret (.—.) شطارت A same as şetaret.

şathiyat (..—) شطحيات [Arabic .——| lrnd. satirical and flippant writings.
şatıh شطح A lrnd. 1. ravings of an ecstatic. 2. satire.
şâtır (—.) شاطر A lrnd. 1. gay, vivacious; agile. 2. Ott. hist. running attendant (formerly employed by high officials when on horseback). 3. myst. who has broken with the world.
şâtim (—.) شاتم A lrnd. foul-mouthed, vituperative.
şato (.'.) شاتو F castle, chateau.
şatr شطر A lrnd. 1. half; a halving, bisection. 2. part, portion; side. 3. hemistich.
şatranç شطرنج A same as satranç.
şattaraban شطربان same as şedaraban.
Şattülarab شط العرب A geog. the united Tigris and Euphrates from their junction to the sea.
şavk^kı شوك [şafak] colloq. light, sunlight.
şavt شوط A lrnd. 1. a run, one heat or course in running. 2. one of the seven runs around the Kaaba. —ı bâtıl beam of sunlight through a hole in the wall (which appears to turn around).
şavul شاول colloq., var. of şakul.
şayak^gı شاياق a kind of homespun woolen cloth, serge.
şayan (——) شايان P fitting, suitable; worthy, deserving. —ı dikkat notable, remarkable. —ı hayret astonishing. —ı takdir praiseworthy.
şayed (—.) شايد P 1. same as şayet. 2. lrnd. lest.
şayegân (—.—) شايگان P lrnd. 1. fit, proper. 2. wide, extensive, plentiful, bounteous. —î (—.——) P 1. fitness. 2. wideness, plentifulness.
şayeste (—..) شايسته P lrnd. worthy, deserving. —gî (—..—) P suitableness, worthiness.
şayet (—'.) شايت |sayed| if, perchance.
şayi^ii (—.) شايع A 1. lrnd. divulged, spread abroad, commonly known. 2. law shared in common. — mal co-ownership. — ol= to become commonly talked of.
şayia (—..) شايعه A news spread about, rumor.
şayian (—'..) شايعاً A law by parcenary, jointly.
şayiat (—.—) شايعات A lrnd. rumors.
şayka (.'.) شايقه Hung a kind of boat used in the Black Sea.
şaz^zzı (—) شاذ A lrnd. 1. contrary to general rule, irregular. 2. exceptional, rarely used; exception.
Şazeliye (—...) شاذلیه Isl. rel., name of a mystical order.
şe the twenty-third letter of the Turkish alphabet.
şeair (.—.) شعائر A lrnd., pl. of şiar, signs, symbols, sacred observances (especially such as are of divine appointment).
şeamet شآمت A lrnd. a being inauspicious, evil omen. —li inauspicious, ill-omened.
şeb 1 شب P lrnd. night. Ş—i Arus the nuptial night, name of the night on which Mevlana Jalaleddin passed away. —i aşk a night of love. —i deycûr an extremely dark, moonless night. —i hicrân a desolate night, a night of separation. — ta-be-seher all night, until morning. —i târik a dark night. — ü rûz night and day. —i yelda longest winter night. — zindedâr vigilant during night; who spends the night in wakeful prayer. — zindedâr-ı sohbet who spends the whole night in friendly conversation and discussion.
şeb^bbi 2 شب A lrnd. alum.
şebab (.—), şebabet (.—.) شباب شبابت A lrnd. youth; youthfulness.
şebabi (.——) شبابى A lrnd. pertaining to youthfulness.
şebabik^kı (.——) شبابيك A lrnd., pl. of şibak 1, şübbak, şübbake.
şebah شبح A lrnd. form and figure, apparition.
şebaheng (.—.) شب آهنگ P lrnd. 1. that which works by night. 2. the nightingale. 3. the morning star.
şebahet (.—.) شباهت A lrnd. a resembling, resemblance.
şeb'an 1 (.—) شبعان A lrnd. satisfied (with food); satiated, full.
şeban 2 (.—.) شبان P lrnd., pl. of şeb 1.
şebane (.—.) شبانه P lrnd. 1. nocturnal. 2. left overnight, stale. —rûz (.—.—) P same as şebanrûz.
şebangâh (.——) شبانگاه P lrnd. evening; night.
şebanrûz (.——) شبانروز P lrnd. night and day, the civil day, twenty-four hours.
şebâviz (.——) شباويز P lrnd., a certain night-hooting bird said to hang by one foot, probably an owl.
şebboy شب بوى P wallflower, stock, bot., Matthiole.
şebçirag (..—) شب چراغ P lrnd. 1. a very brilliant mythical gem. 2. carbuncle. 3. glow-worm, firefly.
şebdiz (.—) شبديز P lrnd. 1. horse of a dark rusty color; noble, generous steed. 2. w. cap., name of a famous horse belonging to King Khusrau-Parviz of Persia.
şebe شبه P lrnd. 1. jet, black amber, black coral. 2. night, duration of a night.
şebefruz (..—) شب فروز P lrnd. illuminating the night.
şebek^gi 1 شبك 1. a long-tailed monkey, zool., Cercopithecus. 2. ugly and impudent.

şebek 2 شباك a kind of boat with a long narrow stern used in the Mediterranean.
şebeke شبكه A 1. net. 2. lattice work; grating; reticulation. 3. network (of railways etc.). 4. band (of robbers, etc.); ring (of dealers, etc.). 5. *anat.* the arachnoid membrane of the brain. 6. a university student's transport pass. **—i ankebutiye** *lrnd.*, same as **şebeke** [5]. **—i meşimiye** *lrnd.* the arachnoid membrane of the encephalon.
şebekî (..—) شبكى A *lrnd.* reticular, reticulated.
şebengiz (..—) شبانگيز P *lrnd.* 1. bat. 2. henbane root.
şebeş شبش *prov.* snaffle-bit for a baggage horse.
şebgerd شبگرد P *lrnd.* 1. that goes about by night; watchman, night-patrol. 2. thief, robber. 3. the moon.
şebgir (.—) شبگير P *lrnd.* 1. person who remains awake and active by night. 2. traveler that sets out before dawn. 3. nightingale; any night-singing bird. 4. early dawn; the morning. **—î** (.——) ·P sleeplessness, insomnia.
şebgûn (.—) شبگون P *lrnd.* the color of night, black; dark night.
şebhane (.—.) شبخانه P *lrnd.* 1. place to pass the night. 2. free hostel for the poor.
şebhengâm (..—) شبهنگام P *lrnd.* 1. evening, nightfall. 2. night, nighttime; at night.
şebhiz (.—) شبخيز P *lrnd.* 1. who rises at night (to pray or to work). 2. who watches in the night.
şebhun (.—) شبخون P *lrnd.* night assault. **— sal=** to make a night attack.
şebî (.—) شبى P *lrnd.* belonging to the night, nocturnal.
şebih (.—) شبيه A *lrnd.* 1. like, similar, resembling. 2. portrait. **— yaz=** *obs.* to make a portrait.
şebike (.—.) شبكه P *lrnd.*, same as **şebeke**.
şebistan (..—) شبستان P *lrnd.* 1. women's apartments in a house. 2. apartment, room, closet where night-devotions are performed in solitude. 3. bedroom.
şebkülâh (..—) شبكلاه P *lrnd.* nightcap.
şebnem شبنم P *poet.* dew.
şebpere شبپره P *lrnd.* bat.
şebreng شبرنگ P *lrnd.* 1. black, dark; obscure. 2. black (horse).
şebrev شبرو P *lrnd.* 1. that goes about by night; who travels in the night. 2. night patrol. 3. night-devotee; holy man. 4. robber, thief.
şebtab (.—) شبتاب P *lrnd.* 1. which shines by night, the moon. 2. firefly, glow-worm. 3. very lustrous (pearl, etc.).
şebtaz (.—) شبتاز P *lrnd.* 1. who makes a rushing attack by night. 2. nocturnal surprise.

şebzindedar (...—) شب‌زنده‌دار P *lrnd.* vigilant at night.
şec[cci] شجّ A *lrnd.* a breaking, wounding a head.
şecaat[ti] (.—.) شجاعت A *lrnd.* a being or becoming brave; courage, bravery, valor. **— arzederken merd-i kıptî sirkatini söyler** The gipsy boasting of his courage tells of his theft, said when someone in boasting of one's qualities confesses his defects. **—li** brave, valiant.
şecce شجّه A *lrnd.* wound in the head.
şecen شجن A *lrnd.* 1. branchlet, rootlet of a tree; branch. 2. branch road in a valley. 3. grief, anxiety; want. 4. love.
şecer شجر A *lrnd.* tree.
şecerat (..—) شجرات A *lrnd.*, *pl.* of **şecere**.
şecere شجره A 1. genealogical tree, pedigree. 2. *lrnd.* a single tree or shrub. **—li** having a pedigree; of good family.
şeceristan (...—) شجرستان P *lrnd.* place set with trees, grove.
şeci[ii] (.—) شجيع A *lrnd.* brave, bold, courageous.
şecic (.—) شجيج A *lrnd.* whose scalp is fractured; wounded in the head.
şed 1 شد A [**sed 2**] *Ott. hist.* special kind of belt worn by masters of trades. **— bağla=** to bestow a belt on a novice.
şed[ddi] **2** شد A *lrnd.* 1. a making hard, firm, or tight; a strengthening. 2. a running with all one's might, rushing; a run, a rush. 3. a doubling a consonant, gemination. 4. *same as* **şedde**. 5. *Or. mus.* a transposal of a scale to a new pitch without altering the intervals of the scale. **—i araban** *same as* **şedaraban**. **—i rahl** a saddling (of animals), departure.
şedaid (.—.) شدائد A *lrnd.*, *pl.* adversities; severities, severe trials.
şedaraban شدعرابان [**şedd-i araban**] *Or. mus.* a **şed makam** more than five centuries old.
Şeddad (.—) شدّاد A *lrnd.* 1. *name of an impious king who built the gardens of Iram*. 2. *l. c.* tyrant, oppressor. **—âne** (.——.) P pertaining to **Şeddad**, like **Şeddad**.
şedde شدّه A *Arabic script* gemination mark (ّ). **—li** 1. bearing the gemination mark, doubled (consonant). 2. perfect, utter (donkey, fool, etc.).
şedid (.—) شديد A *lrnd.*, *same as* **şedit**.
şediden (.—'.) شديدًا A *lrnd.* violently, strongly.
şedidüşşekime (.—..—.) شديد الشكيمه A *lrnd.* hard-mouthed; determined, unyielding.
şedit[di] شديد [**şedid**] 1. hard, strong, firm. 2. violent, severe, vehement. 3. bad, disastrous.
şef شف F chief, leader. **— garson** head waiter.
şef'a شفعه A *lrnd.*, *same as* **şüf'a**.

şefaat^{ti} (.—.) شفاعت A an interceding; intercession. — et= to intercede. —çi intercessor.

şefakat^{ti} شفقت same as şefkat. —nisâr (....—) P scattering tenderness.

şefe شف A lrnd. lip.

şefetan (..—), şefeteyn شفتان شفتين A lrnd. two lips.

şefetülerneb شفة الأرنب A lrnd. harelip.

şefevat (..—) شفوات A lrnd. lips.

şefevî (..—) شفوى A lrnd. labial.

şeffaf شفاف [A .—] transparent, translucent. —lık transparency.

şefiⁱⁱ (.—) شفيع A 1. lrnd. intercessor. 2. law part owner or next-door neighbor to a landed property offered for sale (who possesses the right of preemption). —i câr P next door neighbor who claims preemption. —i müznibîn, —i rûz-i ceza the Prophet Muhammad as being the intercessor for sinners on the Day of Judgment.

Şefiül-ümem (.—...) شفيع الأمم A Isl. rel. the Intercessor for mankind, the Prophet Muhammad.

Şefiülvera (.—...) شفيع الورى same as Şefiül-ümem.

şefif (.—) شفيف A lrnd. thin, transparent (tissue or veil).

şefik^{kı} (.—) شفيق A lrnd. 1. compassionate, kind, benevolent. 2. w. cap., man's name.

şefkat^{ti} شفقت A 1. compassion, tender kindness; affection. 2. pity, concern, solicitude. —li compassionate; affectionate.

şefkatsiz شفقتسز hard-hearted, pitiless. —lik lack of affection and pity.

şeflik^{ği} شفلك duties of a chief; chief office.

şeftali (.—.) شفتالى [Persian şeftâlû] 1. peach. 2. kiss. — ağacı peach tree, bot., Prunus persica. — al= to kiss on the cheek. — sokağı lonely street. — ver= to give a kiss.

şeftren شفترن F guard (of a train).

şegab شغب A lrnd. factious contention.

şegaf 1 (.—) شغاف A anat. pericardium.

şegaf 2 شغف A lrnd. 1. pericardium. 2. deep love.

şegafî (.—-) شغافى [şegaf 1] anat. pertaining to the pericardium.

şegal^{li} (.—) شگال P lrnd. jackal.

şeh ش P same as şah 1.

şehâ (.—) شها P lrnd. O king!

şehab (.—) شهاب A same as şihab.

şehadet (.—.) شهادت A 1. a witnessing, seeing; testimony, evidence. 2. a thing witnessed. 3. a testifying to Islam. 4. death of a Muslim in battle; martyrdom. 5. lrnd. a being present and perceptible; perception, perceptibility. — âlemi the visible world. — et= /a/ to bear witness (to). — getir= to pronounce the formula "There is no god but God, Muhammad is the apostle of God". — mertebesi Isl. rel. the honor of martyrdom. —e nail ol= to attain martyrdom; to die on the field of battle. — parmağı index finger. —i zûr lrnd. false witness, perjury.

şehadetname (.—.—.) شهادتنامه P testimonial; certificate, diploma.

şehamet (.—.) شهامت A lrnd. a being ingenious; a being bold, brave, courageous; dauntless courage, valor. —li bold and efficient.

şehametlû (.—.—) شهامتلو lrnd. valorous and successful, title formerly given by the Turks to the Shah of Persia.

şehba (.—) شهبا A lrnd. ash-colored (verging to white).

şehbal^{li} (.—) شهبال P lrnd. the longest feather in a bird's wing.

şehbaz (.—) شهباز P same as şahbaz.

şehbender شهبندر P Ott. hist. consul (in a foreign country).

şehbenderhane (...—.) شهبندرخانه P consulate.

şehbenderlik^{ği} شهبندرلك rank and duties of a consul.

şehd شهد A lrnd. honey.

şehdab (.—), şehdabe (.—.) شهداب شهدابه P lrnd. honey-water; mead.

şehdâmiz (.—.) شهدآميز P lrnd. mixed with honey.

şehdane (.—.) شهدانه P lrnd., same as şahdane.

şehdiye شهديه a large kind of boat used for carrying timber.

şehevat (..—) شهوات A lrnd., pl. of şehvet. —ı nefsaniye carnal appetites.

şehevî (..—) شهوى A lrnd. sensual; lustful.

şehi^{iyi} 1 (.—) شهى A lrnd. desirable, appetizing, delicious.

şehi 2 (.—) شهى P lrnd., same as şahi.

şehid (.—) شهيد A lrnd. 1. same as şehit. 2. lrnd. God the all-witnessing. 3. witness. —i Kerbelâ the martyr of Kerbelâ, Huseyin, the Prophet's grandson.

şehiden (.—.) شهيدا A lrnd. 1. as a martyr. 2. as a witness.

şehik^{kı} (.—) شهيق A lrnd. 1. an inhalation of breath. 2. a sobbing; sob; hiccough.

şehim (.—) شهيم A lrnd. active, intelligent and efficient; ingenious, sagacious.

şehinşah (..—), şehinşeh شهنشاه P King of kings, a title of the Shah of Iran. —ı felek poet. the sun.

şehir^{hri} 1 شهر [şehr 2] city, town. — dışı suburb. — meclisi town council.

şehir^{hri} 2 شهر A var. of şehr 1.

şehir 3 (.—) شهير A lrnd. celebrated, famous, well-known.

şehirci شهرجى town planner. **—lik** town planning.
şehirli شهرلى townsman; citizen.
Şehislâm (..—) شيخ الاسلام A var. of **Şeyhülislâm**.
şehitᵈⁱ شهيد |**şehid**| one who dies in battle for Islam, martyr. **—lik** 1. death in battle, martyrdom. 2. cemetery or monument for those who die in battle.
şehka شهقة A lrnd. a loud cry or scream. **—yi bükâ** a sob.
şehkâr (.—) شهكار P lrnd. great and magnificent work; masterpiece.
şehlâ (.—) شهلا A 1. having a slight cast in the eye. 2. of a bluish or light gray color (eye); whose eyes are bluish or light gray.
şehlevend شهلوند P lrnd. tall and handsome man.
şehm شهم A lrnd. 1. intelligent, sagacious; efficient. 2. bold, brave, audacious.
şehname (.—.) شهنامه P lrnd., same as **şahname**.
şehnaz (.—) شهناز P Or. mus. one of the most ancient compound **makams**. **— puselik** a compound **makam** six centuries old.
şehnişin (..—) شهنشين P same as **şahnişin**.
şehper شهپر P lrnd., same as **şahper**.
şehr 1 شهر A lrnd. month. **—i haram** a sacred month of the pre-Islamic Arabs during which war was held unlawful. **—i savm** the month of Ramazan.
şehr 2 شهر P lrnd., same as **şehir 1**.
şehrah (.—) شهراه P lrnd., same as **şahrah**.
şehrara (.——) شهرآرا P lrnd. that adorns the city.
şehraşub (.——) شهرآشوب P lrnd. that disturbs the city.
şehrayin (.——) شهرآيين P lrnd. illumination of a town (for a festival).
şehrbend شهربند P lrnd. 1. city walls. 2. prison; captive.
şehreg شهرگ P lrnd. aorta.
şehreh شهره P lrnd., same as **şahrah**.
şehremanetiⁿⁱ (..—..) شهرامانتى Ott. hist. prefecture of a large town.
şehreminiⁿⁱ (.'.—.) شهرامينى Ott. hist. prefect of a large town.
şehrî 1 (.—) شهرى A lrnd. monthly, every month.
şehrî 2 (.—) شهرى P lrnd. 1. urban; urbane. 2. polite, well-mannered.
şehristan (..—) شهرستان P lrnd. 1. large city. 2. country full of cities.
şehriyar (..—) شهريار P lrnd. sovereign; the Sultan. **—âne** (..——.) P pertaining to the Sultan, imperial. **—î** (..——) P imperial, royal; regal dignity. **—lık** sovereignty.
şehriye 1 شعريه |**şa'riye**| vermicelli.

şehriye 2 شهريه A lrnd. monthly salary.
şehrnaz (.—) شهرناز P Or. mus. a compound **makam** about two centuries old.
şehrüssabr شهرالصبر A lrnd. the month of patience, Ramazan.
şehsüvar (..—) شهسوار P lrnd., same as **şahsüvar**.
şehtane (.—.) شهتانه P same as **şahdane**.
şehvan (.—) شهوان A lrnd. longing with a keen appetite; desirous; greedy, hungry.
şehvani (.——) شهوانى A sensual; lustful.
şehvar (.—) شهوار P lrnd., same as **şahvar**.
şehvat (.—) شهوات A lrnd., pl. of **şehvet**. **—ı nefsaniye** lusts of the flesh.
şehvet شهوت A 1. lust, sexual desire. sensuality. 2. lrnd. desire, appetite. **—engiz** (...—) P lrnd. lust-exciting; lascivious. **—li** sensual, voluptuous.
şehvetperest شهوتپرست P lrnd. slave to lust. **—î** (.…—), **—lik** sensuality, debauchery.
şehzade (.—.) شهزاده P prince; a Sultan's son. **—gân** (.—.—) P lrnd., pl.
şekᵏᵏⁱ شك A lrnd. a doubting, feeling uncertain; doubt, suspicion; uncertainty. **— ve şübhe** doubt and misgiving.
şeka شقا A lrnd. wretchednes; misery; sin. perdition.
şekaim (.—.) شكائم A lrnd., pl. of **şekime**.
şekâset (.—.) شكاست A lrnd. a being perverse and refractory; perversity.
şekât (.—) شكات A lrnd. 1. a complaining; complaint. 2. malady; blemish.
şekavet (.—.) شقاوت A lrnd. 1. villainy, brigandage. 2. a being wretched and miserable; misery, wretchedness.
şekayıkᵏⁱ, ᵍⁱ (.—.) شقايق A same as **şakayık**.
şeker شكر P 1. sugar. 2. candy. 3. a sweet, darling; sweet. **—im!** colloq. Honey! Darling! **— ağacı** sugar tree, bot., Myoporum platycarpum. **Ş— Bayramı** the feast after Ramazan. **— çiğne=** to make false promises. **— gibi** very sweet; charming; good-natured. **— hastası** diabetic. **— hastalığı, — illeti** diabetes. **— kamışı** sugar cane, bot., Saccharum officinarum. **— kellesi** sugar loaf. **— kestir=** to clarify sugar. **— tortusu** molasses.
şekerâb (..—) شكرآب P. lrnd. 1. a slight misunderstanding or coolness between friends. 2. politeness shown between two enemies.
şekerâviz (..——) شكرآويز P lrnd. 1. anything pleasant or delightful. 2. loose end of the turban (especially of the Mevlevi dervishes).
şekerbar (..—) شكربار P lrnd. raining sweetness, mellifluous.
şekerci شكرجى 1. confectioner. 2. candy-seller; sugar merchant. **— boyası** poke weed, bot., Phytolacco. **— boyasıgiller** neol., bot., Phytolaccaceae. **— çöğeni** stems of soapwort used by

confectioners. **—lik** 1. candy store. 2. sugar industry.
şekerdan (..—) شکردان P lrnd. sugar bowl.
şekere شکره P lrnd. rapacious bird trained to hunt, small species of hawk.
şekergüftar (...—) شکرگفتا‍ر P lrnd. sweet-spoken.
şekerha (..—) شکرخا P lrnd. who eats sugar; who speaks sweetly.
şekerhab (..—) شکرخواب P lrnd. sweet sleep; morning doze.
şekerhand, şekerhande شکرخند شکرخنده P lrnd. 1. a smiling sweetly. 2. charming, amiable, sweet.
şekerî (..—) شکری P lrnd. pertaining to sugar.
şekerin (..—) شکرین P lrnd. sweet; sugared. **—e** confection.
şekeristan (...—) شکرستان P lrnd. sugarcane plantation.
şekerkand[di] شکرقند P lrnd. candy.
şekerle=[r] شکرلمك /ı/ to sugar, to sweeten, to preserve in sugar.
şekerleb شکرلب P lrnd. sweet-lipped, sweetheart.
şekerleme شکرلمه 1. candy; candied fruit. 2. a doze, nap. 3. verbal n. of **şekerle=**.
şekerlen=[ir] شکرلنمك pass. of **şekerle=**.
şekerleş=[ir] شکرلشمك to turn to sugar; to become very sweet.
şekerli شکرلی 1. sweetened with sugar, containing sugar; sugared. 2. having diabetes.
şekerlik[ği] شکرلك sugar bowl.
şekerpare (..—.) شکرپاره P 1. lrnd. lump of sugar. 2. a kind of apricot. 3. kind of pastry.
şekerrenk[gi] شکررنك P 1. light brown. 2. cool, uncordial (relations).
şekerriz (..—) شکرریز P lrnd. 1. who scatters sugar, mellifluous. 2. sweet or elegant (language).
şekerrize (..—.) شکرریزه P lrnd. pieces of candy.
şekerrizî (..——) شکرریزی P lrnd. 1. the scattering of pieces of candy at weddings. 2. pleasant conversation.
şekersi شکرسی 1. sugar-like. 2. neol., geol. saccharoid. **— mermer** geol. saccharoid marble.
şekersizlik[ği] شکرسزلك lack of sugar.
şekerşiken شکرشکن P lrnd. sweet-spoken.
şekevat (..—) شکوات A lrnd., pl. of **şekva**.
şeki (.—) شکی A lrnd. given to complaining, querulous. **—mizac** (.—.—) P querulous.
şekib (.—) شکیب P lrnd. 1. patience; fortitude. 2. long-suffering, patient.
şekiba (.——) شکیبا P lrnd. patient, enduring, long-suffering. **—î** (.———) P patience, fortitude, long-suffering.

şekibende (.—..) شکیبنده P lrnd. patient, long-suffering.
şekil[kli] شکل |şekl| 1. form, shape; figure. 2. plan, diagram. 3. kind, sort, manner. 4. features; physiognomy; appearance. **bir —e gir=** 1. to take a shape or form. 2. to come out somehow or other. **— itibariyle** as a matter of form. **bir —e koy=** /ı/ to manage a matter somehow or other. **—i musattah** geom. plane figure. **—i mücessem** geom. solid figure. **—i münkalib** geomancy any one of the four figures in which the "houses" of fire and earth are both "singles". **—e riayeten** for form's sake. **— unsuru** gram. morpheme. **— bilim** neol. morphology. **—ci** phil. formalist. **—cilik** phil. formalism. **— değişimcilik** neol., phil. transformism. **— değişimi** neol., phil. transformation. **—deş** neol., biol. homomorphous. **—deşlik** neol., biol. homomorphism.
şekilperest شکل‌پرست P lrnd. formalist.
şekilsiz شکلسز 1. shapeless, amorphous, uncouth, untidy. 2. without diagrams or figures.
şekime (.—.) شکیمه A lrnd. 1. bridle bit. 2. determination; perseverance.
şekker شکر P lrnd., var. of **şeker**.
şekkiyun (..—) شککیون A phil. sceptics. **— mezhebi** scepticism.
şekl شکل A same as **şekil**. **— ü şemail** appearance.
şeklen (.'.) شکلاً A in appearance, in form.
şeklî (.—) شکلی A 1. relating to form, formal. 2. having diagrams. **—yat** (.——) morphology. **—ye** (.—.) phil. formalism.
şekûr (.—) شکور A lrnd. 1. thankful, grateful. 2. God, who rewards the righteous.
şekva (.—) شکوی A lrnd. 1. complaint. 2. disease, malady. **—cı** complainant.
şekve شکوه A lrnd., same as **şekva**.
şel[lli] شلّ A lrnd. a being or becoming paralyzed or maimed (arm).
şelâle (.—.) شلاله A waterfall.
şelel شلل A 1. lrnd. a being withered, paralyzed, or maimed and motionless. 2. anat. macula.
şelf شلف E geog. shelf.
şellâle (.—.) شلّاله A same as **şelâle**.
şelvar (.—) شلوار P same as **şalvar**.
şem[mmi] 1 شمّ A lrnd. 1. a smelling, perceiving, examining or enjoying by the sense of smell. 2. the sense of smell.
şem[m'i] 2 شمع A lrnd. 1. wax candle, taper. 2. candle. **—i âlemtâb** the sun. **—i asel** beeswax. **—i efruhte** lighted candle. **—i felek** the sun. **—i ilâhi** the Quran. **—i kâfur** candle made of white wax or spermaceti. **—i külbe-i ahzân** the candle of the house of sorrow, i. e. Joseph. **—i küşte** extinguished candle. **—i meclisârâ** the candle adorning a gathering, a

şem'a beautiful woman who gives pleasure to a social gathering. **—i sabah, —i seher** the sun. **—i şebefruz** the night-illuminating candle.. **—i şebistân** night candle.

şem'a 1 شمع A *lrnd., same as* **şam'a.**

şema 2 شما F diagram, plan; outline.

şemail (. —.) شمائل A *lrnd.* 1. features. 2. habits, dispositions.

şemailname (. —. —.) شمائل نامه P *lrnd.* description of a person's features.

şemaim (. —.) شمائم A *lrnd., pl. of* **şemime.**

şemame (. —.) شمامه A *lrnd.* 1. thing valued for its fragrance; pomander; scent. 2. panpipe. **—i amber** pastille perfumed with ambergris. **—i kâfûr** *poet.* 1. the sun; moon; star. 2. daylight, break of day.

şematet (. —.) شماتت A *lrnd.* a rejoicing at another's misfortune.

şem'dan (. —) شمعدان P *lrnd., same as* **şamdan.**

şemen شمن P *lrnd.* 1. idolator, idol. 2. priest of the shamanists, Shaman. **—i** (. . —) P of the Shaman religion.

şem'i (. —) شمعى A *lrnd.* 1. pertaining to wax; like wax. 2. maker or seller of wax-tapers.

şemim (. —) شميم A *lrnd.* 1. smelling, scenting; odor, perfume, scent. 2. a smelling, perceiving or enjoying by smell.

şemime (. —.) شميمه A *lrnd.* odor, smell.

şem'istan (. . —) شمعستان P *lrnd.* place ablaze with lighted candles.

şeml شمل A *lrnd.* an including, comprehending, covering.

şemle شمله A *lrnd.* cloak, wrapper, shawl.

şemmame (. —.) شمامه A *lrnd., same as* **şamama.**

şemmas (. —) شماس A Christian church deacon. **—lık** deaconship.

şemme شمه A *lrnd.* 1. a single sniff, a single whiff (of an odor). 2. a very small quantity of something. 3. hint (of reproach, etc.).

şemmî (. —) شمى A *physiol.* pertaining to smell, olfactory.

şempanze شپانزه F *same as* **şampanze.**

şems شمس A *astr.* the sun; *lrnd.* sunshine. **Ş—i Münir** 1. the bright sun. 2. *Or. mus.* a compound **makam** several centuries old and now out of use. **Ş— Suresi** a name of the ninety-first sura of the Quran.

şemsâbâd (. — —) شمس آباد P *lrnd.* sunny.

şemse شمسه A art decorative figure of the sun, rosette.

şemsî (. —) شمسى A *astr.* pertaining to the sun, solar.

şemsisiper شمس سپر P *lrnd.* 1. peak of a cap. 2. cloth protecting the head.

şemsiye شمسيه A 1. umbrella, parasol. 2. *zool.,* Heliozoa. **— ağacı** umbrella tree, *bot.,* Sophora japonica. **—ci** maker or seller of umbrellas. **—li** carrying an umbrella. **—lik** 1. used for making umbrellas (cloth, etc.). 2. umbrella stand.

şemspâre (. —.) شمس پاره P *lrnd.* 1. a piece of the sun. 2. very bright.

Şemsüddin (. . —) شمس الدين A 1. *lrnd.* the sun of religion. 2. *man's name.*

şemşir (. —) شمشير P *lrnd., same as* **şimşir** 2. **—i Hindî** a kind of sword made in India. **—i tâbdar** bright sword.

Şem'un (. —) شمعون A *Bib.* Simon.

şen 1 شن 1. joyous, cheerful. 2. cultivated, inhabited, civilized. **— ve şuh** joyous and gay.

şe'n 2 شأن A *lrnd.* matter, business, affair.

şenaatⁱⁱ (. —.) شناعت A a being abominable, detestable; shameless, abominable act; foulness, wickedness.

şenair (. —.) شنائر A *lrnd., pl. of* **şenar.**

şenar (. —) شنار A *lrnd.* disgrace, infamy; shameful transaction.

şenayiⁱⁱ (. — —) شنائع A *lrnd., pl. of* **şenia.**

şenbih شنبه P *lrnd.* 1. a day of the week. 2. Saturday.

şendere شندره 1. stave of a cask. 2. thin board. 3. goatfish, *zool.,* Mullus surmulletus.

şendikᵍⁱ شندك *prov.* crowd of people; visitors.

şenel=ⁱʳ شنل *colloq., same as* **şenlen=**. **—t=** /ı/ *caus.*

şeng شنگ P *lrnd.* 1. lively, merry, cheerful. 2. thief, robber.

şengaret شنگرت A *lrnd.* bad temper; bad disposition.

şengerf شنگرف P *lrnd.* native cinnabar; vermilion.

şengül شنگل *archaic* cheerful, lively; playful.

şeniⁱⁱ 1 شنيع A bad, infamous, abominable; vile, immoral.

şe'ni 2 (. —) شأنى A *phil.* real.

şenia (. —.) شنيعه A *lrnd.* abominable, immoral or shameless act.

şenide (. —.) شنيده P *lrnd, same as* **şinide.**

şe'niyet (. —.) شأنيت A *phil.* reality.

şenlen=ⁱʳ شنلن 1. to become cheerful, gay, joyful. 2. to become inhabited and prosperous. **—dir=** /ı/ *caus.*

şenlet=ⁱʳ شنلت /ı/ *caus. of* **şenlen=**.

şenlikᵍⁱ شنلك 1. cheerfulness, gaiety, merriment. 2. public rejoicings, illumination. 3. prosperity, increase in amenities. 4. *prov.* population. **— görmemiş** *prov.* ill-bred; uncouth. **—li** full of gaiety; prosperous. **—siz** void of gaiety, solitary, waste.

şennâr (. —) شنار *var. of* **şenar.**

şerʳʳⁱ 1 شر A 1. evil, wickedness. 2. harm, injury; suffering, misfortune. 3. bad, wicked. **—ine lânet!** A curse upon his wickedness! God forbid! **—ine ninni** A lullaby to his mischief.

God save us from his wickedness. — **ü fesad** evil and wickedness.

şer[r1] **2** ش A *lrnd.* 1. the law of God. 2. road, highway. **—i şerif** the canonical law of Islam.

-şer 3 ش *cf.* **-ar 4.**

şerafet (.—.) شرافت A *lrnd.* a being noble, illustrious; nobility; a being of the descendants of the Prophet Muhammad (more particularly through his grandson Hasan).

şerair (.—.) شرائر A *lrnd., pl. of* **şerire.**

şerait شرائط *pl. of* **şart, şerita.**

şer'an (´.) شرعاً A *lrnd.* in accordance with canon law, canonically. **— ve kanunen** by canon law and by civil law.

şerar (.—) شرار A *lrnd.* sparks of fire.

şerare (.—.) شراره A *lrnd.* a spark of fire.

şerarefigen (.—...) شراره فگن P *lrnd.* scattering sparks.

şeraret (.—.) شرارت A *lrnd.* a being bad, wicked; a sinning, wickedness.

şeraset (.—.) شراست A *lrnd.* a being of an evil, mischievous disposition, maliciousness, evil nature.

şerat شرط A *lrnd.* 1. sign or signal, token. 2. insignificant (property).

şeratan (..—) شرطان A *lrnd.* the two stars α and β Arieties.

şerayi[ii] (.—.) شرايع A *lrnd., pl. of* **şeriat.**

şerayin (.——) شرايين A *lrnd., pl. of* **şiryan.**

şerazet (.—.) شرازت A *lrnd.* 1. a being or becoming very dry and hard. 2. harshness, severity, malignity.

şerazim (.—.) شرازم A *pl. of* **şirzime.**

şerbet شربت A 1. sweet fruit drink. 2. solution or suspension of a solid in a liquid. 3. medicinal drink, especially a laxative. **— al=** to take a laxative. **— otu** *same as* **şerbetçi otu.**

şerbetçi شربتجی maker or seller of sweet fruit drinks. **— otu** common hop, *bot., Humulus lupulus.* **—lik** profession of making or selling fruit drinks.

şerbetdar (..—) شربت دار P *lrnd.* servant who had charge of preparing fruit drinks.

şerbethane (..—.) شربت خانه P *lrnd., euphemism for* wineshop.

şerbetlen=[ir] شربتلنمك to be rendered magically immune to a disease.

şerbetli شربتلی 1. having a fruit drink. 2. dissolved. 3. rendered magically immune to snake bites and the like. 4. notorious, incorrigible.

şerbetlik[gi] شربتلک suitable for use in making a fruit drink.

şerc شرج A *anat.* anus.

şeref شرف A 1. honor, excellence, glory. 2. legitimate pride, exaltation. 3. superiority, distinction. **— bul=** 1. to be honored. 2. to increase in value. **—i hamidî** *obs. mus.* the makam, **Şerefnüma.** **—ül-mekân bilmekîn** The honor of a house depends on the dweller.

şerefbahş, şerefbahşa (...—) شرف بخش P *lrnd.* that honors; who honors (by his presence).

şerefe شرفه [**şürfe**] 1. gallery of a minaret (from which the call to prayer is made). 2. *lrnd.* pinnacle, battlement, ornament to a wall.

şerefefza (...—) شرف افزا P *lrnd.* who honors, that honors.

şerefiye (..—.) شرفیه 1. tax on the increase in land value due to building, betterment tax. 2. honorarium, royalty.

şereflen=[ir] شرفلنمك 1. to acquire honor, to be honored. 2. to increase in value. **—dir=** /ı/ *caus.*

şerefli شرفلی 1. highly esteemed, honored. 2. favored or distinguished (district).

şerefnüma (...—´) P *Or. mus.* a **makam** composed at the end of the 19th century.

şerefresan (...—) شرف رسان P *lrnd.* bringer of honor.

şerefriz (..—) شرف ریز P *lrnd.* scattering honors.

şerefsadır (..—.) شرف صادر P *lrnd.* which has had a praiseworthy outcome.

şerefsanih (..—.) شرف سانح P *lrnd., same as* **şerefsadır.**

şerefsiz شرفسز 1. not held in any special esteem. 2. dishonest, unworthy.

şerefsudur, şerefsünuh (...—) شرف صدور P *lrnd., same as* **şerefsadır.**

şerefyab (..—) شرفیاب P *lrnd.* honored, dignified.

şerefyafte (..—.) شرفیافته P *lrnd.* who has found honor, honored.

şereh شره A *lrnd.* a being or becoming exceedingly greedy; greed; ravenousness. **—âlûd** (..——) P, **—ân** (..—) A exceedingly greedy, ravenous.

şeremet شرمت 1. brazen-faced, loquacious scoundrel. 2. spirited, mettlesome. 3. obstinate, intractable.

şerer شرر A *lrnd.* 1. sparks. 2. malicious acts, discords. **—feşan** (...—), **—nâk** (..—) P scattering sparks.

şergil شرگیل [**şergir**] *archaic, same as* **şergir.**

şergir (.—) شرگیر P *lrnd.* 1. rebellious; malignant, malicious. 2. attacking, mistreating, oppressing.

şerh شرح A 1. an explaining, expounding; explanation. 2. commentary. 3. *lrnd.* a cutting, dissecting.

şerha شرحا A *lrnd.* 1. cut, split. 2. wound.

şeri

3. slice. — **şerha doğra**= /ı/ to cut into pieces.
şeri 1 شرى var. of şer' 2.
şer'î 2 (. —) شرعى A Isl. rel. pertaining to the religious law, canonical, canonically legal.
şeriatᵗⁱ (. — .) شريعت A Isl. rel. canonical law; law, law code. **— evi** colloq. the vulva. **— evine gir**= colloq. to have sexual intercourse. **—in kestiği parmak acımaz** The finger that the law cuts off does not hurt. Just punishment is not resented.
şeriatçı شريعتجى 1. Ott. hist. official in the office of the **Şeyhülislâm**. 2. an upholder of the religious law.
şerif (. —) شريف A 1. sacred. 2. noble. 3. lrnd. descendant of Muhammad. 4. Sherif. 5. Ott. hist., title of the governor of Mecca.
şeriha (. — .) شريحه A lrnd. thin slice (of meat).
şerikᵏⁱ (. —) شريك A partner, shareholder; companion. **—i cürm** accomplice. **—e** fem. of şerik. **—lik** partnership; companionship.
şerir (. —) شرير A lrnd. 1. bad, wicked. 2. rebellious, scoundrel. **—e** (. — .) A evil deed, wickedness. **—lik** wickedness, evil, evil-doing.
şeritᵈⁱ شريط A 1. tape, ribbon. 2. band, belt. 3. film (movie). 4. tapeworm. **— arşın** tape measure. **— halkası** zool. proglottis.
şerita (. — .) شريطه A lrnd. condition, stipulation, article of agreement.
şeritgiller neol., zool., Taenia.
şeritle=ʳ شريطلامك /ı/ to bind or decorate with tape or ribbon. **—n**= pass.
şeritli شريطلى bound or decked with tape or ribbon, beribboned.
şer'iyat (. — —) شرعيات A lrnd. canonical obligations. **—çı** same as şeriatçı.
şer'iyet شرعيت |Arabic . — .| lrnd. canonical legality.
şerli شرلى 1. tainted with evil, wicked. 2. quarrelsome.
şerm شرم P lrnd. shame, bashfulness, modesty. **—alûd** (. — —) P bashful, ashamed, shamefaced. **—ende** P who blushes with shame or diffidence, confused, disconcerted. **—endegi** (. . . —) P modesty; shame. **—gin** (. —) P bashful, ashamed. **—ide** (. — .) P, **—în** (. —) P, **—nâk** (. —) P ashamed.
şermsar (. —) شرمسار P lrnd. abashed, ashamed. **—î** (. — —) P bashfulness.
şerrah (. —) شراح A lrnd. commentator.
şerren (.'.) شرا A lrnd. in respect of evil, by evil, wickedly.
şerrî (. —) شرى A lrnd. pertaining to evil.
şerrülhalef شرالخلف A lrnd. a successor in evil.
şersuf (. —) شرسوف A anat. rib cartilage; gristle, soft bone. **—î** (. — .) A epigastric.

şerze شرزه P lrnd. fierce, enraged, that growls and bares its teeth.
şest شست P lrnd., same as şast.
şeş 1 شش P lrnd. six. **— beş** six and five in backgammon. **—i beş gör**= 1. to squint. 2. to be thoroughly confused. **—i beş göster**= /a/ to hit someone so hard that he sees stars.
şeş=ᵉʳ **2** ششله prov. to untie, unravel.
şeşder شش در P lrnd. 1. backgammon board. 2. the world. **—i fena, —i teng** the world.
şeşgâh (. —) ششگاه P Or. mus. a compound **makam** several centuries old, no longer extant.
şeşhane (. — .) ششخانه P 1. rifle, barrel of a gun. 2. lrnd. anything with six chambers or compartments. **—ci** rifleman, sharp-shooter.
şeşhaneli ششخانه لى 1. armed with a rifle. 2. rifled in the bore. **— tüfek** rifle.
şeşper ششپر P lrnd. mace or battle-axe with six edges, halberd. **— ok** six-feathered large bolt or shaft for a crossbow or catapult.
şeşsad ششصد P lrnd. six hundred.
şeşsale (. — .) ششساله P lrnd. 1. six years old. 2. of six years' duration.
şeşta, şeştar (. —) ششتا P lrnd. a six-stringed lute.
şeştari (. — —) ششتارى P lrnd. a striped cloth.
şeşüdü شش و دو P six and two in backgammon.
şeşüm ششم P lrnd. sixth.
şeşüse شش و سه P six and three in backgammon.
şeşüyek شش و يك P six and one in backgammon.
şetaraban شطعربان same as şedaraban.
şetaret (. — .) شطارت [sataret] lrnd. merriment, gaiety, cheerfulness. **—li** merry, gay.
şetimᵗᵐⁱ شتم var. of şetm.
şetm شتم A lrnd. a reviling; abuse, invective. **— ü la'n et**= /a/ to curse, vituperate.
şetmet=ᵈᵉʳ شتم ايتمك lrnd. /a/ to revile, to abuse.
şetta (. —) شتى A lrnd. 1. divided, distinct. 2. various, different; scattered.
şettam (. —) شتام A lrnd. who reviles habitually.
şev شيب [şib 2] 1. slope, declivity, sloping. 2. slant; bevel. **—ine** 1. sloping. 2. not at right angles.
şevahid (. — .) شواهد A lrnd., pl. of şahid 1.
şevahikᵏⁱ (. — .) شواهق A lrnd., pl. of şahika.
şevahin (. — —) شواهين A lrnd., pl. of şahin.
şevaib (. — .) شوائب A lrnd., pl. of şaibe.
şevakil (. — .) شواكل A lrnd., pl. of şakile.
şevarıkᵏⁱ (. — .) شوارق A lrnd., pl. of şarika.
şevari'ⁱⁱ (. — .) شوارع A lrnd., pl. of şâri 2.
şevarib (. — .) شوارب A lrnd., pl. of şarib 1.
şevende شونده P lrnd. 1. existing, that exists; that is, was, or will be. 2. that goes.
şevher شوهر P lrnd. husband. **—dar** (. . —) P married woman. **—dide** (. . — .) P who has had a husband.
şevkᵏⁱ **1** شوق A 1. eagerness, ardor. 2. mirth.

3. lrnd. desire, ardent yearning. —i cedid Or. mus. a makam. —e gel= 1. to become eager. 2. to grow merry.

şevk¹ 2 شوق same as şavk.

şevk¹ 3 شوك A lrnd. thorn, prickle; thistle.

şevkaver (. —.) شوق آور P lrnd. 1. giving eagerness, bringing joy. 2. Or. mus. a compound makam which has not been greatly used.

şevke شوكه A lrnd. 1. a single thorn, prickle; a thorny plant. 2. thing shaped like a thorn; sting; point (of an instrument or weapon).

şevkefza (..—) شوق افزا P lrnd. 1. increasing joy and eagerness. 2. Or. mus. a makam supposedly composed by Sultan Selim III.

şevkengiz (..—) شوق انگیز P lrnd. pleasure-giving.

şevkeran (..—) شوکران P lrnd. poison hemlock, bot., Conium maculatum.

şevket شوكت A 1. imperial majesty and pomp. 2. might, power. — ve iclâl ile, — ve ikbal ile with pomp and honors, with majesty and prosperity. —li mighty, majestic.

şevketlû (..—) شوكتلو majestic, title especially given to the Sultan.

şevketmakrûn (...—) شوكت مقرون P lrnd. imperial, royal, glorious.

şevketmasir (...—) شوكت مصير P lrnd. imperial, royal, glorious.

şevketmeab (...—) شوكت مآب P lrnd. 1. of imperial majesty, majestic. 2. Your Majesty. —i (...——) P lrnd. imperial.

şevketpenah (...—) شوكت پناه P lrnd. 1. majestic. 2. Your Majesty. —i (...——) P lrnd. imperial.

şevketsimat (...—) شوكت سمات P lrnd. marked with imperial majesty.

şevketvaye (..—.) شوكت وایه P lrnd. majestic.

şevkıdil شوق دل P Or. mus. a compound makam about two centuries old.

şevki 1 (.—) شوقی A lrnd. 1. ardent, yearning. 2. cheerful; full of eagerness.

şevki 2 (.—) شوكی A 1. anat. spinal. 2. lrnd. pertaining to a thorn; resembling a thorn.

şevklen=ⁱʳ شوقلنمك to grow eager, to become enthusiastic. —dir= /ı/ caus.

şevkli شوقلی 1. eager, desirous. 2. merry, lively, gay.

şevklika (..—) شوقلیقا A Or. mus. a rythmic pattern.

şey'i (.—) شیئی A phil. objective.

şevksiz شوقسز cold, dull, calm. —lik 1. coldness, calmness. 2. dullness.

şevkütarab شوق و طرب P Or. mus. a makam composed by Sultan Selim III.

şevlen=ⁱʳ شولنمك to become sloping, to slope, to incline. —dir= /ı/ caus.

şevli شولی sloping; beveled. — gönye square beveled at the edge.

Şevval¹¹ (.—) شوّال A Isl. calender, name of the tenth month.

şey شی A 1. thing. 2. often used when one cannot find the right word or name. What do you call it? What's his name? bir — a thing, something. bir —ler something or other. bir — değil 1. It is nothing; it doesn't matter. 2. You're welcome (in reply to thanks). bir —dir oldu I am sorry it happened but it can't be helped now.

şeyatin (.——) شیاطین A lrnd.,˙ pl. of şeytan 1.

şeyb شیب A lrnd. whiteness, grayness of the hair.

şeyba (.—) شیبا A lrnd. white-haired (woman).

şeybiye (.—.) شیبیه A bot. lichens.

şeyd شید P lrnd. hypocrisy, flattery; deceit.

şeyda (.—) شیدا P lrnd. mad, insane; in love, madly in love. —lık, —yi (.——) P insanity.

şeyh شیخ A 1. head of a religious order; head preacher or teacher, sheikh. 2. head of a family or tribe. 3. lrnd. old man, elder. Ş—i Ekber lrnd., title of Muhiddin-i Arabi. —i fani lrnd. a mortal old man. —in kerameti kendinden menkul It is the Sheikh himself who tells of his own miracles, said of a person who brags about his own achievements. Ş—i Necdî lrnd. (lit. the old man of Nejd) Satan (who appeared as an old man to counsel the murder of the Prophet Muhammad).

Şeyhan (.—) شیخان A lrnd. the two sheikhs, Imam Abu Hanifa and Imam Abu Yusuf.

Şeyheyn شیخین A lrnd. the two Caliphs Abubakr and Umar.

şeyhuhet (.—.), şeyhuhiyet (.—..) شیخوخت شیخوخیت A lrnd. a growing old; old age.

Şeyhülharem شیخ الحرم A Ott. hist. the governor of the town and province of Medina.

Şeyhülislâm (...—) شیخ الاسلام A Ott. hist. Sheikhulislam (dignitary responsible for all matters connected with the canon law, religious schools, etc., and coming next to the Grand Vizier in precedence).

Şeyhülmürselin (....—) شیخ المرسلین A lrnd. (lit., the most senior of the prophets) Noah.

şeyhzade (.—.) شیخ زاده P son of a sheikh.

şeyle شیله prov., same as şöyle.

şeyn شین A lrnd. disgrace; vice; defect.

şeypur (.—) شیپور P lrnd. 1. clarinet. 2. brass trumpet with a large mouth used in battle.

şeytan 1 شیطان [şeytan 2] 1. Satan; devil. 2. crafty person. 3. clever (child). Ş— Akıntısı the Devil's Current, name of a strong current *along the Bosphorus from Rumelihisar to Kandilli and Akıntı Burnu*. **— aldat=** 1. to be deceived by the devil. 2. to be subject to nocturnal emissions. **— arabası** 1. thistle-down floating in the air. 2. hand-driven trolley used by railwaymen. 3. *colloq*. bicycle. **—ın ard ayağı** crafty fellow; mischief-maker. **—ın ayağını kır=** to decide to do something after a long interval. **—ları ayaklandı** 1. His evil propensities have been aroused. 2. He has become very mischieveous again. **— azapta gerek** It is right for the devil to be in constant torment. He had it coming to him. It serves him right. **—ın bacağını kır=** *same as* **şeytanın ayağını kırmak**. **— bacaklı** *colloq*. short-legged. **—ları başına toplan=**, **—ları başına üşüş=** to become furious. **— bezi** velveteen. **— boku** asafetida. **—a çarık giydirir** He could cheat the devil himself; he is very cunning. **— çarmığı** *naut*. Jacob's-ladder. **— çarpmış keçi yavrusu gibi titre=** *colloq*. to be in great fear. **— çarşısı** 1. conjurer's shop. 2. a row of toy-shops. 3. a conclave of demons in a bad man's heart. **— çekici** 1. malignant person. 2. a clever urchin. **— diyor ki** I am very tempted (to do something irresponsible or desperate). **— dürt=** /ı/ to do something bad all of a sudden. **—ı eşeğe ters bindirir** He is more cunning than the devil. **— feneri** 1. Chinese lantern plant, *bot.*, *Physalis alkekengi*. 2. Japanese lantern, Chinese lantern. **— gibi** very clever. **—ın işi yok** by pure bad luck. **—ın kıç bacağı** *same as* **şeytanın ard ayağı**. **— kösteği** a double-fetter for a horse. **— kulağına kurşun** May the devil's ear be filled with lead, *said after mentioning one's good fortune*. **— kuşu** horseshoe bat, *zool.*, *Rhinolophus ferrumequinum*. **—a külâhı ters giydirir** He is very clever and sly. **— minaresi** hermit crab with shell. **— oyunda gerek** The devil is always ready to play a trick. Beware of possible trouble. **— örümceği** 1. gossamer. 2. delicate muslin gauze cloth. **—a pabucunu ters giydirir** *same as* **şeytana külâhı ters giydirir**. **—a parmak ısırt=** to outdo the devil, to do something diabolical. **— saçı** water hemp, hemp weed, *bot.*, *Eupatorium cannabinum*. **— şalgamı** snake-bryony, *bot.*, *Bryonia dioica*. **—ı şişeye sokar** *same as* **şeytanı eşeğe ters bindirir**. **— taşla=** to throw stones at the devil according to custom during the pilgrimage at Mecca. **—ları tepesine çık=** /ın/ to lose one's temper. **— tersi** asafetida. **— tırnağı** 1. hang-nail (on a finger). 2. the perfume onycha of the ancients. **— tüyü** devil's hair; talisman supposed to give personal attraction, the attractiveness of a person that makes him lovable. **—a uy=** to let oneself be led astray; to yield to temptation. **—ın yattığı yeri bil=** to know the most unimaginable things.

şeytan 2 (. —) شیطان A *Irnd.*, *same as* **şeytan 1**. **—ı leytan** very crafty fellow.

şeytanca (. ́.) شیطانجه 1. devilish; very crafty. 2. cunningly.

şeytanet شیطنت A *Irnd.* act of deviltry, devilish malice; craftiness.

şeytanetkâr (...—) شیطنتکار P devilish. **—ane** (...— —.) P in a devilish manner, craftily.

şeytanî (. — —) شیطانی A *Irnd.* diabolical, infernal. **—yet** (. — . .) A deviltry, craftiness.

şeytanlıkᵍ¹ شیطانلق deviltry, craftiness; slyness; malicious cunning.

şezere . ́. . شذره A *Irnd.* in dispersion.

şezlong شزلونغ F chaise longue.

şezre . ́. . شذره A *Irnd.* 1. gold dust. 2. small gilt bead; small pearl; small bead.

şıkᵏᵏ¹ 1 شق A 1. one of two alternatives. 2. *Irnd.* half of anything cut in two. **—ı evvel** *Ott. hist.* the finance accounts of the first division of the Ottoman Empire, relating to Turkey in Europe. **—ı evvel defterdarı** *Ott. hist.* Minister of Finance. **—ı sâlis** *Ott. hist.* the third division of the Ottoman Empire including Hungary, Mesopotamia, Syria, Egypt and Arabia. **—ı sani** *Ott. hist.* the second financial division of the Ottoman Empire comprising all Asia Minor.

şıkᵏ¹ 2 شیك F chic; smart, elegant.

şıkakᵏ¹ (. —) شقاق A *Irnd.* a contending, quarreling, opposing; contention, strife, partiality.

şıkıkᵍ¹ شیقیق *prov*. poppy.

şıkırda=ʳ شیقیردامق to rattle, to click repeatedly, to jingle. **—t=** /ı/ *caus*.

şıkırdım شیقیردم 1. *slang* boy. 2. *prov*. abundant, plentiful.

şıkır şıkır شیقیر شیقیر 1. *imitates a jingling or clinking noise*. 2. dazzling, shiny, bright.

şıkırtı شیقیردی a jingling noise, clinking.

şıkkırık شیقیریق *prov*. latch.

şıklıkᵍ¹ شیقلق elegance, smartness.

şıl شیل *prov*. affected with purulent ophthalmia.

şıla=ʳ شیلامق *prov*. to shine, to twinkle.

şılakᵍ¹ شیلاق *prov*. bright, shining.

şıldır şıldır شیلدیر شیلدیر *in* **— bak=** to stare with wide-open eyes (baby).

şıllıkᵍ¹ شیللیق gaudily dressed (woman); loose woman.

şımar=ʳ شیمارمق to be spoiled by indulgence; to lose one's self-control.

şımarıkᵍ¹ شیماریق spoiled (child); impertinent. **—lık** conceit, rudeness.

şımart=ʳ شیمارتمق /ı/ *caus*. of **şımar=**. **—ıl=** *pass*.

şıngır شِنْغِر *noise imitating the breaking of glass crash.* — şıngır *same as* şıngır.
şıngırda=ʳ شِنْغِرْدامِ *same as* şangırda=. —t= /ı/ *caus.*
şıngırtı شِنْغِرْدى *same as* şangırtı.
şıp شِب 1. *noise of a drop falling.* 2. *easily, quickly, at once.* — diye *immediately, all of a sudden.* —ın işi*. — sevdi*.
şıpıdık⁾ı شِپِدِك *open-heeled slipper.*
şıpılda=ʳ شِپِلدامِ *to make a lapping noise, to lap (water).*
şıpınişi شِپِنشى *colloq. very quickly and easily.*
şıpır şıpır شِپِر شِپِر *dripping, with a dripping sound.*
şıpırtı شِپِرْدى *splash.* —lı *splashing.* —lı hava *rainy weather.*
şıpıtık⁾ı شِپِتِك *same as* şıpıdık.
şıpka (ˊ.) شِپْقَه *naut. rope or wire net (used on a ship); torpedo-net.*
şıplan شِپْلان *slang quickly, immediately.*
şıppadak (ˊ..) شِپادك *colloq. at once, quickly.*
şıpsevdi شِپْ سَوْدى *colloq. quick to fall in love; susceptible.*
şıpşak⁾ı شِپْ شاپ *colloq. at once, quickly.*
şıpşakla=ʳ شِپْ شاقْلَمِ /ı/ *slang to hear very quickly (news, gossip); to remember.*
şıpşıp شِپْشِپ *slipper without any back.*
şıra شِرَه [Persian şire] 1. *grape juice.* 2. *slang liquid opium.* —lı 1. *juicy.* 2. *prov. sweetened (drink).*
şırak⁾ı شِراپ *imitates a sudden sharp noise crash.* — diye yere düştü *It fell down with a thud.*
şırakkadak⁾ı شِراقْدامِ *colloq. all of a sudden.*
şırfıntı شِرْفِنْتى *common woman.*
şırılda=ʳ شِرِلْدامِ *to flow in a stream with a babbling sound; to make a gurgling sound (running water).* —t= /ı/ *caus.*
şırıl şırıl شِرِل شِرِل *imitates the noise of gently running water.* — ak= *to flow in a stream or with a babbling sound.*
şırıltı شِرِلْتى *noise of running water, splashing, gurgling.*
şırınga شِرَنْغَ شِرِنْغَ شِرَنْغَ شِرِنْغَه *It* 1. *enema.* 2. *hypodermic syringe, injection.*
şırla=ʳ شِرْلَمِ *to rain or flow in torrents.*
şırlağan 1 شِرْلَغان [Persian şırevgen] *sesame oil.*
şırlağan 2 شِرْلَغان *prov.* 1. *hissing noise (on the fire).* 2. *current of water; a flowing, running (of water); plashing.* —lı *watery, running (eye).*
şırlop شِرْلوپ 1. *eggs served with yogurt.* 2. *slang lie; nonsense.*
şırp شِرْپ *click of a pair of scissors; whir of a sword.* — diye kes= /ı/ *to cut off with a whir or click.*

şırpadak⁾ı شِرْپادك *suddenly.*
şırvan, şırvanı شِرْوانى 1. *loft over a shop, stable, etc.* 2. *raised part at one end of a shop.*
şıvgın شِوْغِن *prov.* 1. *shoot, twig.* 2. *fir or pine (used for making masts).* 3. *sleet.*
Şia (—.) شيعَه A 1. *the Shiite sect of Muslims.* 2. *lrnd., l. c. party, clique of companions or adherents.*
şiab (.—) شِعاب A *lrnd., pl. of* şi'b 5.
şian (.—) شِأن A *lrnd., pl. of* şe'n 2.
şiar 1 شِعار A 1. *countersign, watchword; token by which friends know one another in battle, as a war cry, flag, badge or sign.* 2. *habit, characteristic, trait.* 3. *Isl. rel. any one or the whole of the ceremonies of the pilgrimage at Mecca.* 4. *lrnd. badge, sign, token.*
-şiar 2 (.—) شِعار P *lrnd. marked by, distinguished for, as in* belagatşiar, sadakatşiar.
şib 1 شِب 1. *a coarse, open kind of canvas.* 2. *a kind of coarse gauze.*
şib 2 (—) شِب P *lrnd.* 1. *descent, slope.* 2. *a falling in fortune.* — ü feraz *descent and ascent; ups and downs.*
şib 3 (—) شِب A *lrnd., same as* şeyb.
şibᵇⁱ 4 شِبع A *lrnd.* 1. *a being satisfied with food, satiety, fullness.* 2. *enough food to satisfy hunger for once.*
şi'b 5 شِعب A *lrnd.* 1. *road; pass between two mountains.* 2. *small watercourse.*
şibakᵏⁱ 1 (.—) شِباك A *lrnd.* 1. *lattice.* 2. *net.*
şibakᵏⁱ 2 (.—) شِباك A *lrnd., pl. of* şebeke.
şibh 1 شِبه A *lrnd. a like, similar thing.*
şibh 2 شِبه A *resembling, quasi.* —i akid *law quasi contract.* —i cezire *peninsula.* —i cümle *gram. an exclamation that expresses the sense of a clause.* —i cürüm *law quasi delict.* —i intifa *law quasi usufruct.* —i mâden *chem. metalloid.* —i main *geom. rhomboid.* —i münharif *geom. trapezoid.* —i zıl *astr. penumbra.*
şibihʰⁱ شِبه [şibh] *same as* şibh 1, 2.
şibl شِبل A *lrnd. whep, cub.*
şibr شِبر A 1. *lrnd. span (of space).* 2. *astr. arc of about a degree.*
şid (—) شيد P *lrnd.* 1. *light; the sun.* 2. *glory, splendor, halo.*
şidad (.—) شِداد A *lrnd., pl. of* şedid, *hard, strong; severe, violent, vehement.*
şiddet شِدَّت A 1. *hardness, violence; terror, severity.* 2. *strength; intensity.* 3. *lrnd. great hardship, affliction, suffering.* — göster= *to act severely.* —i hal *lrnd.* 1. *hardness of the times, pressure of circumstances.* 2. *poverty, want, distress.* — sebepleri *law aggravating*

şiddetlen=

circumstances. **—i sefalet** *lrnd.* extreme poverty.

şiddetlen=ⁱʳ شدتلنمك 1. to become severe and violent. 2. to become intensified, to be aggravated. **—dir=** /ı/ *caus.*

şiddetli شدتی شدتمو severe, violent, vehement; strong.

şidurgu شيدورغو a musical instrument with four strings.

şif شيف *prov.* cotton boll.

şifa (.—) شفاء A 1. a restoring to health; restoration. 2. a recovering health; recovery. 3. a healing, cure, remedy for a disease. **— bul=** to recover health. **—yı bul=, —yı kap=** *ironical* to fall ill; to turn out badly. **— niyetine** May it do you good (said to a person taking medicine). **— olsun** May it bring you health (said to one having a drink or taking medicine). **— ver=** /a/ to restore to health, to heal.

şifabahş (.—.) شفابخش P *lrnd.* healthful, salutary.

şifah (.—) شفاه A *lrnd., pl. of* **şefe, şife**.

şifahane (.—.) شفاخانه P *lrnd.* 1. hospital. 2. lunatic asylum.

şifahen (.—.) شفاهاً A orally, verbally.

şifahi (.——) شفاهی A oral, verbal.

şifalı (.—.) شفالی healing; wholesome.

şifapezir (.—.—) شفاپذير P *lrnd.* curable.

şifaresan (.—.—), **şifasaz** (.——) شفارسان شفاساز P *lrnd.* healthful, salutary.

şifayab (.——) شفایاب P *lrnd.* restored to health.

şife شفه A *lrnd., same as* **şefe**.

şifle=ʳ شفله *prov.* /ı/ to separate cotton from the boll.

şifre (.'.) شيفره F cipher; code. **— aç=, — çöz=** to decode, decipher. **—li** in cipher; with abbreviations.

şifte (—.) شيفته P *lrnd.* 1. insane, crazy. 2. madly enamored. 3. strongly inclined.

şiftegi (—.—) شيفتگی P *lrnd.* 1. loss of one's senses. 2. greed.

şiğil, şiğir شكيل شبير [Persian **zihgir**] *archaic* 1. ring without a stone. 2. hobble.

şihab (.—) شهاب A *lrnd.* 1. flame, flashing fire. 2. *same as* **şahap**. 3. energetic, efficient man. **—ı sakıb** 1. bright flame. 2. active, daring man.

Şii (.—) شیعی A Shiite. **—lik, —yet** Shiism.

şiirˢⁱʳʳⁱ شعر [şi'r 3] A poetry, poem, verse.

şikâf (.—) شكاف P *lrnd.* 1. that splits, slits, cleaves. 2. split, cleft, fissure. 3. ornamentation made by a mixture of paint and gilt (used especially for hand-written books).

şikâfe (.—.) شكافه P *lrnd.* plectrum.

şikâfende (.—..) شكافنده P *lrnd.* that splits, rends or cracks.

şikâfezen (.—..) شكافزن P *lrnd.* musician.

şikâfiş (.—.) شكافش P *lrnd.* a splitting, cleaving, rending.

şikâfte (.—.) شكافته P *lrnd.* that has split; split, cleft.

şikakᵏⁱ (.—) شقاقه A *lrnd., same as* **şıkak**.

şikâr 1 (.—) شكار P 1. prey; victim; plunder, booty, spoil. 2. *obs.* anything rare and much sought after. 3. *lrnd.* chase, hunt. **— bir şey mi?** Is it such a rarity? **— pazar** *obs.* a cheap bargain.

-şikâr 2 (.—) شكار P *lrnd.* seizing, hunting, *as in* **dilşikâr**.

şikârgâh (.——) شكارگاه P *lrnd.* hunting country, hunting ground.

şikârî (.——) شكاری P *lrnd.* 1. hunter. 2. used in hunting. 3. bird or beast of prey.

şikâyat (.——) شكايات A *lrnd., pl. of* **şikâyet**.

şikâyet (.—.) شكايت A a complaining; complaint. **— hakkı** *law* right of petition. **—çi** complainant.

şikâyetname (.—.—.) شكايتنامه P written complaint.

şike شيكه F *sports* prearranged defeat of the opponent team in return for money; a putting on a rigged game.

şikem شكم P *lrnd.* 1. abdomen, belly. 2. womb.

şikembe شكمبه P *lrnd., same as* **işkembe**.

şikembende شكمبنده P *lrnd.* slave to his belly, glutton.

şikemdar (..—) شكمدار P *lrnd.* big-bellied, paunchy.

şikemhar (..—) شكمخوار P *lrnd.* glutton.

şikemperest, şikemperver شكمپرست شكمپرور P *lrnd.* pamperer of his belly, epicure, glutton.

şikemran (..—) شكمران P *lrnd.* laxative.

şikemrev شكمرو P *lrnd.* diarrhea.

-şiken 1 شكن P *lrnd.* that breaks, fractures, defeats, destroys, *as in* **hatırşiken, haysiyetşiken**.

şiken 2 شكن P *lrnd.* fold, wrinkle, curl.

şikenc شكنج P *lrnd.* 1. ply, fold, wrinkle. 2. trick, fraud, deceit. 3. tune, musical melody. 4. torture, torment.

şikence شكنجه P *lrnd., same as* **işkence**.

şikest شكست P *lrnd.* 1. break, fracture. 2. defeat, rout; destruction. 3. broken, impaired.

şikeste شكسته P 1. *Arabic calligraphy* shikasta (a style of writing used in Iran). 2. *lrnd.* broken; defeated; injured, destroyed. 3. fracture.

şikestebal (...—) شكسته بال P *lrnd.* broken-hearted, distressed in mind.

şikestebazu (...——) شكسته بازو P *lrnd.* 1. whose arm is broken. 2. whose power is broken.

şikestebend شكسته بند P *lrnd.* 1. binder of

fractures, surgeon. 2. mender of any injury or damage. 3. bandage.

şikestebeste شکسته بسته P *lrnd.* 1. broken and bandaged. 2. shattered and repaired. 3. fast and loose; worthless.

şikestedil شکسته دل P *lrnd.* broken-hearted, grieved.

şikestegi (...—) شکستگی P 1. fracture, rupture. 2. chagrin, affliction, grief.

şikestehal (...—) شکسته حال P *lrnd.* distressed, indigent.

şikestehatır (...—.) شکسته خاطر P *lrnd.* offended, annoyed.

şikestezeban (....—) شکسته زبان P *lrnd.* 1. who speaks in broken accents; stammerer. 2. with a broken nib (pen).

şil 1 شل P *lrnd.* javelin, halbert.

şil 2 شیل *prov.*, same as **şıl**.

şilep[bl] شلپ G tramp steamer; cargo boat.

Şili شیلی F *geog.* Chile.

şilin شیلین E shilling.

şilte شلته thin mattress.

Şilyak[kı] (.—) شلیاک A *astr.* Lyra.

şimal[li] **1** (.—) شمال A 1. north. 2. *lrnd.* left side or direction. 3. *lrnd.* left hand, left arm. —**i şarki** northeast. — **yıldızı** North Star.

şimal 2 شمال *prov.* vigorous shoot or branch.

şimalen (.—'.) شمالا A to the north, in a northern direction.

şimali (.——) شمالی A northern, north.

şimden gerü شمدن گری *archaic* from now on, henceforth.

şimdi شمدی شیمدی now, at present; the present time. —**den** 1. henceforth, from now on. 2. at this very moment; already. —**ki** the present; the actual (state, time, etc.). —**ye değin**, —**ye dek**, —**ye kadar** until now. —**den tezi yok** the sooner the better, with all speed. —**cik** just now; this very moment. —**lik** for the present, at present.

şime (—.) شیمه A *lrnd.* natural quality or habit.

şimendifer شمندفر F railway; train.

şimşad (.—) شمشاد P *lrnd.* 1. boxwood, *bot.*, *Buxus sempervivens*. 2. graceful figure; gracefully grown young person.

şimşek[gi] شیمشک lightning; a flash of lightning. — **ağacı** spiny broom, aspalathus, *bot.*, *Calycotome spinosa*. — **çaktı** There was a flash of lightning. — **gibi** like lightning, very quick. — **taşı** meteorite.

şimşekli شمشکلی flashing. — **fener** flashing light (lighthouse).

şimşir 1 شمشیر P boxwood, *bot.*, *Buxus sempervivens*.

şimşir 2 (.—) شمشیر P *lrnd.* sword, saber. —**baz** (.——) P 1. sword-player. 2. swordsman. —**zen** (.—.) P swordsman, warrior. —**zenan** (.—.—.) P warriors. —**zenlik** swordsmanship.

şin 1 شین A name of the letter ش (sixteenth letter of the Ottoman and fifteenth letter of the Arabic alphabets. In chronograms it has the numerical value of 300).

şin 2 (—) شین A same as **şeyn**.

şina (.—), **şinab** (.—) شنا شناب P *lrnd.* a swimming.

şinager (.—.) شناگر P *lrnd.* swimmer.

şinah (.—) شناه P *lrnd.* a swimming.

şinaht (.—) شناخت P *lrnd.* knowledge.

şinahte (.—.) شناخته P *lrnd.* 1. known, understood. 2. an acquaintance. —**gân** (.—.—) P acquaintances.

şinanay شاناناى *colloq.* 1. indicates joy and merriment. 2. glaring, gaudy. 3. refrain, tra-la-la.

şinar (.—) شنار P *lrnd.* 1. a swimming. 2. unlucky, bad, inauspicious.

-şinas (.—) شناس P *lrnd.* who knows, recognizes, e. g., **hakşinas**, **kadirşinas**.

şinav (.—) شناو P *lrnd.*, same as **şina**, **şinab**.

şinaver (.—.) شناور P *lrnd.* 1. swimmer. 2. floating. —**i** (.—.—) P a swimming.

şindi, şindik (.'.) شندى شندك *prov.*, same as **şimdi**.

şinel شنل F Spanish cloak, mantle.

şinev شنو P *lrnd.* who hears.

şinevende شنونده P *lrnd.* that hears, hearer; listener.

şinide (.—.) شنیده P *lrnd.* heard, who has heard.

şinik[gi] شنیك Gk measure of cereals equalling a quarter bushel.

şinşile شنشیل F chinchilla, the skin and fur of *Chinchilla laniger*.

şip[bi] شب same as **şib 1**.

şir 1 (—) شیر P *lrnd.* 1. lion. 2. brave man, hero. —**i asuman**, —**i çerh** the constellation Leo. —**i felek**, —**i gerdun** 1. the constellation Leo. 2. the sun. **Ş— ü Hurşid** the Persian order of the Lion and the Sun. **Ş—i Huda** the Caliph Ali. —**i jiyan** 1. furious lion. 2. brave man. —**i made** lioness. —**i ner** 1. male lion. 2. very brave man. —**i sipihr** 1. the constellation Leo. 2. the sun.

şir 2 (—) شیر P *lrnd.* milk. —**i mader** mother's milk. —**i mürg** bird's milk, non-existent thing. — **ü şeker** in perfectly good accord.

şi'r 3 شعر A *lrnd.*, same as **şiir**. —**i şair** excellent poetry.

şira 1 شیرا same as **şıra**.

şira 2 (.—) شراء A *lrnd.* 1. a buying; purchase. 2. a selling; sale.

şira[a1] **3** (.—) شِراع A *lrnd.* 1. sail (of a ship). 2. string (of a musical instrument).

şi'ra 4 (.—) شِعرى A *lrnd.* the Dog-Star, Sirius. **—i Şamiye** Procyon, in Canis Minor. **—i Yemaniye** Sirius.

şira'küşa (..'.—) شراع كشا P *lrnd.* that spreads sail.

şiran (——) شيران P *lrnd.*, *pl. of* **şir 1**.

şirane (——.) شيرانه P *lrnd.* lion-like, bold, brave.

şirar (.—), **şirare** (.—.) شِرار ـ شِراره A *lrnd.*, *same as* **şerar, şerare**.

şiraz (——) شيراز 1. *geog.* Shiraz. 2. *obs., mus.* a **makam**.

şiraze (——.) شيرازه P 1. headband of a bound volume. 2. bond of union; thing that holds other things together. 3. order, regularity. 4. leg of a wrestler's trousers. **—si bozul=** to deteriorate beyond recovery (matter). **—den çık=** to lose one's mental balance. **—sinden çık=** *same as* **şirazesi bozul=**.

şirazebend (——..) شيرازه بند P *lrnd.* fastened with a headband; stitched together.

şirazegir (——.—) شيرازه گير P *lrnd.* submitting to a headband or to a bond of unity.

şirazekeş (——..) شيرازه كش P *lrnd.* who puts headbands to books; bookbinder.

şirban (——) شيربان P *lrnd.* lion keeper; keeper in a zoo.

şirbeçe (—..) شيربچه P *lrnd.* lion's whelp.

şirdan (——) شيردان P *lrnd.* 1. vessel for holding milk. 2. *same as* **şirden**.

şirdar (——) شيردار P *lrnd.* 1. having milk; giving milk. 2. sappy.

şirden شيردن [**şirdan**] second stomach of ruminants. **— dolması** dish like Scotch haggis.

şirdil (—.) شيردل P *lrnd.* lion-hearted, brave.

şi'ren ('.) شعرا A *lrnd.* in verse.

şirevjen (——..) شيراوژن P *lrnd.* conqueror of lions, brave, bold, strong.

şirgir (——) شيرگير P *lrnd.* 1. who captures lions; brave. 2. mad with drink; tipsy.

şirhar (——), **şirhare** (——.) شيرخوار ـ شيرخواره P *lrnd.* nursing baby.

şirhişt (—.) شيرخشت P *lrnd.* manna (collected in the east of Persia).

şirhuşk[ü] (—.) شيرخشك P *lrnd.* a kind of manna.

şiri 1 (——) شيرى P *lrnd.* 1. lion-like. 2. ferocity, bravery.

şiri 2 (——) شيرى P *lrnd.* 1. the quality of milk. 2. milky.

şi'ri 3' (.—) شعرى A *lrnd.* pertaining to poetry; poetic, poetical.

şirin 1 شيرين [**şirin 2**] 1. sweet; delicious. 2. charming, affable.

şirin 2 (——) شيرين P *lrnd.* 1. milky, sweet. 2. pleasant, gentle, affable. 3. *w. cap.*, name of a celebrated lady beloved of King Ferhad.

şirinavaz (————) شيرين آواز P *lrnd.* sweet-voiced.

şirincemal (——.—) شيرين جمال P as beautiful as **Şirin**.

şirineda (——.—) شيرين ادا P *lrnd.* 1. of sweet or graceful manners. 2. sweet-sounding.

şiringüftar (——.—.) شيرين گفتار P *lrnd.* sweet-spoken, eloquent.

şirini (————) شيرينى P *lrnd.* 1. sweetness; loveliness, agreeableness. 2. candy, sweets.

şirintab[b1] (——.) شيرين طبع P *lrnd.* of sweet disposition, sweet-tempered.

şirinzeban (——.—) شيرين زبان P *lrnd.* with an enchanting tongue, eloquent, affable.

şiristan (—.—) شيرستان P *lrnd.* 1. district infested by lions. 2. country of brave men.

şirit[d1] شريط A *same as* **şerit**.

şirk[ki] شرك A *rel.* a giving companions or partners to God, polytheism. **— koş=** /a/ to attribute a partner to God, to be a polytheist.

şirket شركت A 1. *com.* company. 2. *law* partnership, joint ownership **—i âdiye** *law* ordinary partnership. **—i akd** *law* partnership by agreement. **—i akdi inan** *law* partnership in a specified thing only. **—i inan** *law* special joint-ownership, special limited partnership. **—i mudarebe** *law* a sleeping or silent partnership in business. **—i mufavaza** *law* unlimited partnership. **—i muhatara** *law* partnership in ventures of chance. **—i mülk** *law* joint ownership.

şirlan شيرلان *same as* **şırlağan 1**.

şirmerd (—.) شيرمرد P *lrnd.* 1. a courageous man. 2. a saint who accounts trials as nothing. **—an** (—.—) P heroes, holy men.

şirmürg (—.) شيرمرغ P *lrnd.* the bat.

şirpençe (—..) شيرپنجه P 1. large carbuncle, anthrax. 2. *anat.* lion's paw.

şirret شرّت A 1. evil disposition, malice. 2. evilly disposed, malicious; malicious person. 3. shrew, virago; quarrelsome. **—lik** evil disposition, malice.

şirrir (.—) شرّير A *lrnd.* most wicked, very mischievous.

şirseg (—.) شيرسگ P *lrnd.* dog used in hunting lions, hare-hunting dog.

şirsüvar (—.—) شيرسوار P *lrnd.* the sun.

şiryan (.—) شريان A *anat.* artery; aorta. **—ı nazil** the descending aorta. **—ı said** the ascending aorta. **—ı subati** the carotid artery. **—ı sezen** trachea. **—ı veridi** venous or pulmonary artery. **—i arterial**.

şirzime شرذمه A *lrnd.* 1. a piece of a thing; part, slice. 2. small, insignificant or dispersed body of men.

şist شيست F *geol.* schist. **—lik** schistosity.

şiş 1 شِيش 1. spit; skewer. 2. knitting needle. 3. rapier, fencing foil. 4. axle. **—e geçir=** /ı/ to skewer. **— iğne*. — kebabı*.**

şiş 2 شيش 1. a swelling, tumor. 2. swollen, swelled. 3. *slang* disagreeable (person).

şiş=ᵉʳ **3** شيشمك 1. to swell; to become inflated, blown out. 2. to grow fat; to be distended or congested. 3. *colloq.* to be puffed up with pride. 4. to be unable to continue for want of breath (runner); to get tired. 5. *slang* to feel embarrassed, disconcerted.

şişane (.—.) شيشانه *same as* **şeşhane²**.

şişe 1 شيشه [şişe 2] 1. bottle; flask. 2. lamp chimney. 3. cupping-glass. 4. molded or planed lath. **— çek=** /a/ to apply a cupping-glass. **— üfle=** to blow glass.

şişe 2 (—.) شيشه P *lrnd., same as* **şişe 1** ¹⁻³.

şişebâz (—.—) شيشه باز P *lrnd.* player at cups and bowls.

şişeci شيشه جى 1. maker or seller of bottles. 2. glass blower.

şişehane (..—.) شيشه خانه P *lrnd.* glassworks.

şişekᵏⁱ شيشك *prov.* lamb in its second year.

şişiğne شيش ايكنه knitting needle; netting needle.

şişin=ⁱʳ شيشنمك to become irritated.

şişir=ⁱʳ شيشيرمك /ı/ 1. *caus. of* **şiş= 3.** 2. *colloq.* to exaggerate. 3. *colloq.* to do something hastily and carelessly. 4. *school slang* to cram for an examination. 5. *colloq.* to incite a person by exaggerated and provocative words. 6. *slang* to stab. **—il=** *pass.*

şişirme شيشيرمه 1. *verbal n. of* **şişir=.** 2. blown (glass).

şişirt=ⁱʳ شيشيرتمك /ı, a/ *caus. of* **şişir=. —il=** *pass.*

şişkebabıⁿⁱ شيش كبابى meat roasted on a spit or skewers.

şişkin شيشكين 1. swollen, puffed up. 2. fat, paunchy. **—lik** distension, fullness; puffiness, swelling.

şişko (ʹ.) شيشقو very fat person.

şişle=ʳ شيشله مك /ı/ 1. to spit, to skewer. 2. *slang* to stab. **—n=** *pass.*

şişli شيشلى having a spit or skewer. **— baston** sword cane, sword stick.

şişman شيشمان fat, obese.

şişmanla=ʳ شيشمانله مك to grow fat. **—t=** /ı/ *caus.*

şişmanlıkᵏⁱ شيشمانلق fatness, obesity.

şita (.—) شتا A *lrnd.* winter.

şitab (.—) شتاب P *lrnd.* speed, haste; quickness. **— et=** /a/ to hurry, to hasten.

şitaban (.——) شتابان P *lrnd.* that goes quickly, hurried; in haste. **— ol=** to hurry, to rush.

şitai (.——) شتائى A *lrnd.* belonging to winter, wintry. **—ye** (.——.) poem about winter.

şitari (.——) شتارى *same as* **şeştari**.

şitevi (..—) شتاوى A *lrnd., same as* **şitai. — inkılâb** *astron.* winter solstice.

şitil شتيل *prov.* seedling plant (for planting out). **—le=** /ı/ to plant out (seedlings).

şiv شيو [*Persian* şib] *same as* **şev**.

şivaz شواظ A *lrnd.* flame without smoke, blaze.

şive (—.) شيوه P 1. accent, way of pronouncing. 2. *lrnd.* form, way, manner, style. 3. *lrnd.* gracefulness, coquetry. **—i lisan** *lrnd.* idiomatic expressions of a language. **—baz** (—.—) P, **—ger** (—..) P *same as* **şivekâr**.

şivekâr (—.—) شيوه كار P *lrnd.* who acts in a graceful, attractive or coquettish manner; elegant, stylish.

şiveli شيوه لى 1. graceful and attractive. 2. stylish, beautiful, charming. 3. idiomatic.

şiven (—.) شيون P *lrnd.* lamentation. **—gâh** (—.—) P place of lamentation.

şivenüma (—..—) شيون نما P *Or. mus.* a compound **makam** about three centuries old.

şivesiz (—..) شيوه سز 1. with a bad accent or pronunciation, unidiomatic. 2. without grace or style.

şivgar شيوغار *var. of* **cıvgar**.

şiyem شيم A *lrnd., pl. of* **şime**.

şizofreni شيزوفرنى F *psychiatry* schizophrenia.

şoban شوبان P *lrnd.* shepherd, herdsman.

şofben شوفبن F hot-water boiler.

şoför شوفور F chauffeur, driver. **—lük okulu** driving school.

şokᵏᵘ شوك F shock.

şol شول (all oblique cases are based on **şun**- *pl.* **şular**) *archaic for* **şu 1**.

şom شوم inauspicious, unlucky; sinister, gloomy. **— ağızlı** who always predicts misfortune.

şopar شوپار *slang* child.

şor 1 شور P *lrnd.* saltish, brackish.

şor 2 شور [*Arabic* şavr] *prov.* word, speech; conversation.

şorakᵏⁱ شوراق *archaic, same as* **çorak**.

şorba شوربا P *archaic, same as* **çorba**.

şorla=ʳ شورلامق *archaic* 1. to make a gurgling sound (water). 2. to flow with a splashing and gurgling noise.

şorolop شورولوپ 1. *imitates the sound of a thing gulped down*, swallowing all of a sudden. 2. *slang* lie.

şorulda=ʳ شورولدامق *same as* **şarılda=**.

şorultu شورولدى *same as* **şarıltı**.

şorulu شورلى *slang* boy; girl.

şorva شوروا *archaic, same as* **çorba**.

şose شوسه F macadamized road, highway.

şoson شوسون F galoshes.

şoven شوون F chauvinistic.

şöhre شهره A *lrnd.* 1. *same as* **şöhret**. 2. famous. **—i âfak** world-famous person or thing.

şöhret شهرت A 1. fame, reputation, renown. 2. name by which a man is known. **— al=** to become famous. **— bul=** to acquire fame, to become generally known. **— hastası** one who passionately seeks notoriety. **— kazan=** to acquire fame. **—i kâzibe** *lrnd.* undeserved reputation. **— ver=** to bring honor and fame (to).

şöhretgir (..—) شهرتگیر P *lrnd.* famous, celebrated.

şöhretgüzin (...—) شهرتگزین P *lrnd.* eager for fame, seeking fame.

şöhretli شهرتلی 1. famous, renowned. 2. remarkable. 3. having a name and reputation (good or bad).

şöhretsiz شهرتسز unknown to fame, obscure. **—lik** lack of fame, obscurity.

şöhretşiar (...—) شهرتشعار P *lrnd.* famous.

şöhretyab (..—) شهرتیاب P *lrnd.* that acquires fame or celebrity.

şölen شولن [*Persian* şilan] feast, especially, feast given in honor of somebody.

şömine شومینه F fireplace, European style of open fire.

şövale شواله F easel.

şövalye شوالیه F knight. **— yüzük** ring with a crest on it. **—lik** chivalry.

şöyle شویله 1. in that manner, so; just. 2. of that sort, such. **— bir** casually, for a moment. **— bir baktı** 1. He just glanced at it. 2. He looked with contempt. **— böyle** 1. so so. 2. not too well. 3. roughly speaking. **— böyle de=** to make excuses. **— dursun** let alone *e. g.*, **koşmak şöyle dursun, yürümek bile imkânsızdı** It was impossible to walk let alone run. **— ki** 1. in such a manner that. 2. as follows; that is to say. **—ce** in this manner. **—likle** in this way.

şu^{nu} 1 شو All oblique cases are based on **şun-,** *pl.* **şunlar** 1. this, that. 2. this thing; this person. **—na bak** Look at him (a belittling expression). **— bu** this and that, any one (of the people). **—ndan bundan bahset=** to talk about this and that. **—dur budur diyecek yok** (*lit.* There will be no one to say it is this or that.) There is nothing to be said against it. **— kadar** so much, so many. **— kadar ki**, **— var ki** only, but (used to introduce a remark).

-şu 2 (—) شو P *lrnd.* that washes, *e. g.* **hâkşu** washer of earth or sweepings.

şua^{aı} (.—) شعاع A 1. *phys.* ray of light. 2. *math.* vector.

şuab شعب A *lrnd., pl. of* şu'be.

şuai (.——) شعاعی A 1. *phys.* of the nature of rays of light, radial. 2. *geom.* vectorial.

şuabat (..—) شعبات A *lrnd., pl. of* şu'be.

şuara (..—) شعراء A *lrnd., pl. of* şair 1.

—i muhdesun modern poets. **— tezkeresi** biographies of poets. **Ş—i Yemani** the Dog Star, Sirius.

şubara شوبارا Sl a kind of round wadded cap.

Şubat شباط *Syriac* February.

şu'be (..) A, **şûbe** (—.) شعبه 1. branch, section, department, branch office. 2. division, ramification.

şubede (—..) شعبده P *lrnd.* jugglery, trick of deception. **—baz** (—..—) P 1. juggler, conjurer. 2. trickster, cheat.

şubelen=^{ir} شعبه لنمك to branch out, to ramify.

şuf'a شفعه A *lrnd.* 1. house or land of which one is part owner or which adjoins one's own property. 2. a right or claim of pre-emption in respect of such a house or land. **— hakkı** *law* right of pre-emption.

şufaa (..—) شفعاء A *lrnd., pl. of* şefi.

şugl^{lü} شغل A *lrnd.* occupation, business, work.

şuh (—) شوخ P *lrnd.* 1. lively, full of fun. 2. coquettish, unreserved, pert. **— u şeng** lively and coquettish. **—çeşm** (—.) P saucy-eyed, impudent.

şuhî (——) شوخی P *lrnd.* 1. pertness, coquettishness. 2. fun, joke, mirth.

şuhluk^{ğu} شوخلق 1. liveliness, playfulness. 2. coquettishness, freedom of manner.

şuhtabiat (—...) شوخ طبیعت P *lrnd.* of bold or saucy manners; naturally gay.

şuhum (.—) شحوم A *lrnd., pl. of* şahm.

şuhur (.—) شهور A *lrnd., same as* şühur.

şuhus (.—) شخوص A *lrnd., pl. of* şahs.

şukka شقه A *lrnd.* 1. a strip torn off; a breadth of cloth; a piece of cloth. 2. a slip of note paper; note, letter.

şukkalık^{ğı} شقه لق 1. slip of paper suitable for a note or letter. 2. piece of muslin in which a letter may be folded.

şukuk^{ku} (.—) شقوق A *lrnd., pl. of* şak 2.

şular شولر *archaic, pl. of* şol.

şu'le شعله A *lrnd.* 1. flame, blaze, flash. 2. light, splendor, luster. 3. lock or patch of white hair in a horse's coat. **—i cevvale** circle of fire produced by swinging around a burning brand.

şulebar (..—) شعله بار P *lrnd.* raining flames of fire, blazing.

şuledar (..—) شعله دار P *lrnd.* 1. flaming. 2. brilliant.

şulegir (..—) شعله گیر P *lrnd.* flaming.

şulehiz (..—) شعله خیز P *lrnd.* flaming, resplendent, brilliant.

şulelen=^{ir} شعله لنمك to flame, to blaze. **—dir=** /ı/ *caus.*

şuleli شعله لی flaming.

şulever شعله ور P *lrnd.* flaming, blazing.

şulide (——.) شولیده P *lrnd.* perturbed, perplexed, distracted.

şûm (—) شوم A *lrnd.* inauspiciousness; evil omen.

şunca (ʹ.) شونجه 1. so much, so many. 2. to such a degree.

şuncağız شونجغز this little one.

şuncalayın شونجالاين *archaic* 1. *same as* **şunca**. 2. like that.

şundakʰ شوندق ته *archaic* at once, immediately.

şunlar شونلر *pl. of* **şu** 1.

şur 1 (—) شور P *lrnd.*, *same as* **şor 1**.

şur 2 (—) شور P *lrnd.* 1. noise, tumult, uproar, riot. 2. sedition.

şura 1 (ʹ.) شوره this place; that place. **—da*. —dan*. —larda** in these parts. **—sı*.**

şura 2 (— —) شورى A council. **Ş—yı Devlet** the Council of State.

şurab (— —), **şurabe** (— —.) شوراب P *lrnd.* 1. salty, bitter or brackish water. 2. tears.

şuracıkʰ (ʹ..) شوره جك just this little spot. **—ta** right here; close by.

şurada (ʹ..) شوره ده here; there. **— burada** here and there.

şuradan (ʹ..) شوره دن from here, hence. **— buradan** from here and there, of this and that.

şuralı شوره لو 1. inhabitant of this place. 2. belonging to this place.

şurasıⁿⁱ (ʹ..) شوره سى this place; this fact. **— muhakkak** This much is certain. **—nı unutmayalım** Let's not forget this point.

şurba شوربه P *lrnd.* soup.

şurbaht (—.) شوربخت P *lrnd.* unfortunate; sordid. **—lık** ill-fortune, misfortune.

şurçeşm (—.) شورچشم P *lrnd.* evil-eyed, whose look brings misfortune.

şurda, şurdan شورده short for **şurada, şuradan.**

şure (—.) شوره P *lrnd.* 1. soil yielding salt; saltmarsh, nitrous earth; barren soil. 2. niter, saltpeter.

şureger (—..) شوره گر P *lrnd.* saltpeter manufacturer.

şurengiz (—.—) شورانگيز P *lrnd.* tumult-exciting, stirring quarrels.

şurezar (—.—) شوره زار P *lrnd.* brackish ground; barren soil.

şurî (— —) شورى P *Or. mus.* 1. an old compound **makam**. 2. a scale no longer extant.

şuride (— —.) شوريده P *lrnd.* 1. confused, disordered; disturbed. 2. mad with love, desperately in love.

şuridebaht (— —..) شوريده بخت P *lrnd.* unfortunate, ill-starred.

şuridegi (— —.—) شوريده گى P *lrnd.* 1. confusion, disorder. 2. madness; love.

şuridehal (— —.—) شوريده حال P *lrnd.* mad, distracted.

şuridehatır (— —.—.) شوريده خاطر P *lrnd.* troubled in mind; dejected, sad.

şuridelikⁱ شوريده لك 1. confusion, disorder. 2. madness.

şuristan (—.—) شورستان P *lrnd.* marsh, salt-marsh.

şuriş (—.) شورش P *lrnd.* confusion; tumult, sedition.

şursuf (.—) شرسوف A *same as* **şersuf**.

şurta شرطه A *lrnd.* 1. body of guards or policemen on patrol duty. 2. fair, favorable (wind).

şurupᵇᵘ شروب A 1. syrup. 2. sweet medicine.

şuşe (—.) شوشه P *lrnd.* 1. ingot of gold or silver. 2. heap of sand. 3. slab, gravestone, tablet. 4. lath, especially, a planed and molded lath.

şuub (.—) شعوب A *lrnd.*, *pl. of* **şa'b 2**.

şuubi (.— —) شعوبى A *lrnd.* 1. pertaining to the nations outside Islam, heathen, foreign. 2. pertaining to the sect called **Şuubiye**. **Ş—ye** name of a sect that exalts the non-Arab.

şuun (.—) شعون A *same as* **şüun**.

şuur 1 (.—) شعور A 1. a comprehending, understanding; comprehension; intelligence. 2. conscience; mind; consciousness. **—u bozuk** out of his senses. **—u git=** to be out of one's senses.

şuur 2 (.—) شعور A *lrnd.*, *pl. of* **şa'r 2**.

şuuraltı شعور آلتى *psych.* subconscious.

şuuri (.— —) شعورى A *lrnd.* 1. pertaining to the mind or consciousness. 2. conscious, consciously.

şuurlu شعور لى 1. intelligent; conscious (will etc.). 2. being conscious of; with comprehension, sensible, judicious.

şuursuz شعورسز 1. unconscious. 2. unreasonable; heedless, callous. **—luk** 1. heedlessness, unreasonableness. 2. unconsciousness.

şuvalla=ʳ شولامق *archaic* to sew together roughly, to tack.

-şuy 1 (—) شوى P *lrnd.*, *same as* **-şu 2**.

şuy 2 (—) شوى P *lrnd.* husband. **—dide** (— — —.) P who has had a husband; married woman.

şüban (.—) شبان P *lrnd.* shepherd, pastor. **Ş—ı vadii eymen** shepherd of the happy valley, Moses. **—firib** (.—.—) P lapwing; shrike.

şübbak (.—), **şübbake** (.—.) شبّاك A *lrnd.* 1. lattice. 2. net.

şübban (.—) شبّان A *lrnd.*, *pl. of* **şab 1**.

şübeh, şübehat (.. —) شبه A *lrnd.*, *pl. of* **şübhe**.

şübhe شبهه A *lrnd.*, *same as* **şüphe**.

şübubiyet (.— ..) شبوبيت A *lrnd.* youth, youthfulness.

şüca⁰¹ (.—) شجاع A *lrnd.* 1. bold, brave, valiant. 2. serpent; a certain very bold species of serpent. 3. the constellation Hydra.
şüc'an (.—), şücea (..—) شجعان A *lrnd.*, *pl.* of şeci.
şücun (.—) شجون A *lrnd.*, *pl.* of şecen.
şüd شد P *lrnd.* 1. departure. 2. He or it was or has been; he is dead; he or it is gone.
şüde شده P *lrnd.* 1. who has gone; which has been. 2. departed, dead. —gân (..—) P *pl.*
şüf'a شفعه A *lrnd.*, same as şuf'a.
şüfea (..—) شفعا A *lrnd.*, *pl.* of şefi.
şüheda (..—) شهدا A *lrnd.*, *pl.* of şehid.
şühud 1 (.—) شهود A *lrnd.*, *pl.* of şahid 1.
şühud 2 (.—) شهود A *lrnd.* 1. a being present and witnessing a thing, an eye-witness. 2. a being visible and existent; existence, visibility. — âlemi the material universe. — ehli 1. eye-witnesses, those who were present at anything. 2. saints who miraculously see all things.
şühur (.—) شهور A *lrnd.*, *pl.* of şehr 1. —i malûmat, —i selâse, —i sülse the months Şevval, Zilka'de and Zilhicce.
şükât (.—) شكات A *lrnd.*, *pl.* of şaki 2.
şükr⁰ü شكر A 1. a thanking, giving thanks; gratitude; thanksgiving. 2. *lrnd.* God's showing acceptance by rewarding a righteous man for his deeds. —ünü bil= to feel grateful (for a blessing). — et=*.
şükran (.—) شكران A thanksgiving, thanks, gratitude.
şükrane (.—.) شكرانه P *lrnd.* a thank offering; a sign of gratitude.
şükraniyet (.——.) شكرانيت A *lrnd.* gratitude, gratefulness.
şükret=ᵈᵉʳ شكر ايتمك /a/ to thank, to praise (God); to be thankful for.
şükrgüzar (..—) شكرگزار P *lrnd.* expressing gratitude; grateful, thankful. —i (..——) P thanksgiving; gratefulness.
şükûfe (.—.) شكوفه P *lrnd.* blossom of a fruit-bearing tree; flower.
şükûfedan (.—.—) شكوفه‌دان P *lrnd.* jug-shaped vase-holder.
şükûfezar (.—.—) شكوفه‌زار P *lrnd.* a garden in bloom; filled with flowers.
şükûfte (.—.) شكوفته P *lrnd.* open, expanded (flower).
şükûh (.—) شكوه P *lrnd.* majesty, magnificence, pomp.
şükûhî (.——) شكوهى P *lrnd.* pertaining to majesty or glory.
şükûhmend (.—.) شكوهمند P *lrnd.* majestic, awe-inspiring.
şükûk⁰ü (.—) شكوك A *lrnd.*, *pl.* of şek.
şükur (.—) شكور A *lrnd.*, *pl.* of şükr.

şükür⁰ʳü شكر A same as şükr.
şümar (.—) شمار P *lrnd.* 1. number, count; enumeration. 2. reckoning, calculation. 3. a giving or receiving an account. 4. a trial before a judge, especially the great trial at the Day of Judgment.
şümarende (.—..) شمارنده P *lrnd.* teller, numberer.
şümargâh (.——) شمارگاه P *lrnd.* place of the Last Judgment.
şümargir (.——) شمارگير P *lrnd.* enumerator, accountant, auditor.
şümu⁰⁰ (.—) شموع A *lrnd.*, *pl.* of şem 2.
şümul⁰ü (.—) شمول A an including; comprehending, covering; comprehensiveness, inclusiveness. —ü ol= /a/ to include, cover, embrace.
şümullendir=ⁱʳ شمول‌لندرمك /ı/ to extend, amplify, generalize.
şümullü شمول‌لى comprehensive.
şümus (.—) شموس A *lrnd.*, *pl.* of şems.
-şümür شمر P *lrnd.* who counts, reckons or enumerates.
şümürde شمرده P *lrnd.* 1. counted, reckoned, numbered. 2. who has counted, reckoned or enumerated.
şünud (.—) شنود P *lrnd.* 1. a listening, hearing. 2. what is heard, hearsay.
şünude (.—.) شنوده P *lrnd.* 1. that has heard. 2. heard.
şüphe شبهه [şübhe] 1. doubt; suspicion. 2. uncertainty. — bırak= to leave a doubt behind, to instill a suspicion. —ye düş= to begin to suspect, to have a suspicion. — et= /dan/ to suspect. — kurdu the sting of suspicion. — yok doubtless.
şüpheci شبهه‌جى suspicious person, sceptic. —lik scepticism.
şüphelen=ⁱʳ شبهه‌لنمك /dan/ to have a suspicion, to suspect. —dir= *caus.*
şüpheli شبهه‌لى 1. doubtful, uncertain. 2. causing suspicion, suspicious.
şüphesiz شبهه‌سز 1. doubtless, sure, certainly. 2. giving no grounds for suspicion. —lik doubtlessness, certainty.
şürb شرب A *lrnd.* a drinking. —i müdam a drinking incessantly, drunkenness. —i Yahud drinking wine clandestinely.
şürefa (..—) شرفا A *lrnd.*, *pl.* of şerif.
şürefat (..—) شرفات A *lrnd.*, *pl.* of şürfe.
şürekâ (..—) شركا A *lrnd.*, *pl.* of şerik.
şürfe شرفه A *lrnd.*, same as şerefe.
şürrah (..—) شراح A *lrnd.*, *pl.* of şarih.
şüru⁰⁰ (.—) شروع A *lrnd.* an entering upon (any act); commencement, beginning. — et= /a/ to commence, to make a beginning.
şürud (.—) شرود A *lrnd.* a fleeing, running away.

şuruh (. —) شروح A lrnd., pl. of şerh.
şurur (. —) شرور A lrnd., pl. of şer 1.
şurut (. —) شروط A lrnd., pl. of şart.
şüst شست P lrnd. an act of washing. — ü şu a washing and cleansing. — ü şu et= to cleanse by washing.
şüste شسته P lrnd. 1. who has washed. 2. washed, cleansed.
şüş شش P lrnd. the lungs. —i (. —) P pertaining to the lungs, pulmonary.
şüşpistan (.. —) ششپستان P lrnd. pendulous breasted (woman); old woman.
şüt شوت F soccer shoot. — çek= to shoot; to propel.
şütum (. —) شتوم A lrnd., pl. of şetm.
şütür شتر P lrnd. camel. —i dü kühan Bactrian camel. —i hamza camel renowned for its speed; swift, fast running.
şütürban (.. —) شتربان P lrnd. camel driver, camel attendant.
şütürbar (.. —) شتربار P lrnd. camel-load.
şütürdil شتردل P lrnd. 1. fainthearted, timid, cowardly. 2. camel-hearted, spiteful, vindictive.
şütürek^{ki} شترك P lrnd. 1. small camel. 2. man who makes a camel of himself (to amuse children). 3. wave, billow.
şütürgâv (.. —), şütürgâvpeleng (.. — ..) شترگاو شترگاوپلنگ P lrnd. giraffe.
şütürgâz (.. —) شترگاز P lrnd. root of the Asafetida plant (used in pickles); camel thorn.
şütürgiyah (... —) شترگیاه P lrnd. camel thorn.
şütürgürbe شترگربه P lrnd. camel-cat; i. e. any two things which are very disproportionate and incongruous and have no relation to each other.
şütürhar (.. —) شترخار P lrnd. camel thorn.
şütürhû (.. —) شترخو P lrnd. camel-tempered, vindictive as a camel.
şütürî (.. —) شتری P lrnd. acts or disposition of a camel.
şütürkürre شترکره P lrnd. 1. camel colt. 2. wave, billow.
şütürmur (.. —) شترمور P lrnd. mythical ant of large size.
şütürmürg شترمرغ P lrnd. ostrich.
şütürsüvar (... —) شترسوار P lrnd. 1. mounted on a camel. 2. mounted for a long journey.
şütürsüvari (... — —) شترسواری P lrnd. freed from observing fast-days (a dispensation allowed to travelers.)
şütürzühre شترزهره P lrnd. faint-hearted, timid.
şuun (. —) شوون A lrnd., pl. of şe'n 2.
şüyu^{uu} 1 (. —) شیوع A a being or becoming publicly talked of; publicity. — bul= to be noised abroad, to become common gossip.
şüyu^{uu} 2 (. —) شیوع A law undivided shares (in a property). —un izalesi division of an undivided property.
şüyuh (. —) شیوخ A lrnd., pl. of şeyh.
şüyuhet (. — .), şüyuhiyet (. — ..) شیوخت شیوخیت A lrnd., same as şeyhuhet, şeyhuhiyet.
şüzur (. —) شذور A lrnd., pl. of şezre.
şüzuz (. —) شذوذ A lrnd. a being an exceptional and isolated thing; irregularity, peculiarity.

T

t, T 1 *the twenty-fourth letter of the Turkish alphabet.*

-t= 2 *after vowels and liquids. In a few words after* -k-, *or* -p-, *it becomes* -ıt=, -it=, -ut=, -üt=; *causative, e. g.,* akıt=, getirt=, korkut=, ürküt=.

ta 1 (ˊ.) *cf.* **da 1.**

-ta 2 *cf.* **-da 2.**

ta 3 (—) P 1. *even until, even unto; until; even as far as.* 2. *there, lo.* 3. *lrnd. lest (before negative verbs).* — **kendisi** *his very self.* — **ki,** — **kim** *so that, in order that.* — **oraya kadar** *even to there, as far as there.*

taᵃˡ **4** *name of the letter* ت *(fourth letter of the Ottoman and Persian and third letter of the Arabic alphabets. In chronograms it has the numerical value of 400).*

ta 5 *name of the letter* ط *(nineteenth letter of the Ottoman and Persian and sixteenth letter of the Arabic alphabets. In chronograms it has the numerical value of 9).*

ta 6 P *lrnd.* 1. *fold, pleat, as in* **düta, yekta.** 2. *a leaf, sheet as of paper; an individual person or thing.* 3. *string of a musical instrument.* 4. *match, equal, peer.*

ta 7 A *lrnd. by (in oaths only), as in* **tallâhi.**

taab A *lrnd. a being or becoming tired; fatigue, exhaustion, weariness.*

taabbüdᵈᵘ A *lrnd. a worshiping; worship, adoration; devotion.* — **et=** /a/ *to worship, to adore.*

taabbüs A *lrnd. a putting on a sour, morose look, a frowning.* —**ât** (...—) A *frowns.*

taaccüb A *a marveling, a being astonished; wonder, astonishment.* — **et=** /a/ *to marvel, to be astonished (at).*

taaccül A *lrnd. a making haste; a causing to make haste, an urging, accelerating.*

taaddi A 1. *lrnd. a transgressing; a being unjust; oppression; transgression.* 2. *lrnd. a passing from one place or thing to another.* 3. *gram. a being active, transitive.* —**yât** (...—) A *pl.*

taaddüd A *lrnd. a multiplying; plurality.* — **et=** *to multiply, to become frequent.* —**i ezvac** *polyandry.* —**i ilâh** *polytheism.* —**i zevcat** *polygamy, bigamy, polygyny.*

taadi (.—.) A *lrnd. a carrying on mutual hostilities; an acting as enemies to one another, discord, enmity.*

taadül (.—.) A *lrnd. a being or becoming equal to one another; a becoming just to each other, equilibrium.* —**ât** (.—.—) A *equilibria.*

taaffüf A *lrnd. an abstaining from what is improper; a being chaste, pure; chastity, purity.*

taaffün A *a being rotten, a being fetid; putrefaction; stink.* — **et=** *to rot, to become fetid (from decay).*

taaffünât (...—) A *lrnd. rotten things; putrefactions.*

taahhüd A, taahhütᵈᵘ *an undertaking, an engaging to do something; engagement, obligation, contract.* — **et=** /ı/ *to undertake, to engage to do.* — **senedi** *contract.* —**ât** (...—) A *pl.*

taahhütlü *lrnd.* 1. *registered (letter, etc.).* 2. *slang good revolver.* — **git=** *slang to be arrested and go with the police.*

taahhütname (...—.) تعهدنامه P written undertaking, contract.

taahüd (.—.) تعاهد A *lrnd.* 1. an undertaking engagements with one another, a making a treaty together. 2. mutual engagement, contract, treaty. —ât (.—.—) A *pl.*

taakkud^dü تعقّد A *lrnd.* 1. a being tied (knot), a knitting together strongly. 2. a being agreed to (contract). 3. a coagulating or forming into lumps.

taakkul^lü تعقّل A *lrnd.* 1. a conceiving in the mind, a comprehending; comprehension; a conceiving by ready wit. 2. a becoming intelligent.

taakküs تعكّس A *lrnd.* a being or becoming inverted or reflected; inversion, reflection.

taakub (.—.) تعاقب A *lrnd.* 1. a following one another in succession; succession. 2. a pursuing one another; pursuit.

taakud (.—.) تعاقد A *lrnd.* a mutual bargaining or agreeing.

taaküs (.—.) تعاكس A *lrnd.* a being reechoed noise, rumor).

taalâ (.—.) تعالى A *lrnd.* May (His name) be exalted, *as in* **Allahütaalâ, Hak Taalâ.**

taali (.—.) تعالى A *lrnd.* a being or becoming high, elevated, sublime; elevation, height, sublimity.

taalik^ki (.——) تعاليم A *lrnd., pl. of* **ta'lika 1.**

ta'alli (..—) تعلّى A *lrnd.* a being or becoming high or elevated; highness, eminence. —yât (..——) A *pl.*

taallûk^ku تعلّك A *lrnd.* 1. a clinging and hanging to a thing; a fastening oneself to a thing. 2. a being or becoming related to or connected with; connection, relation. 3. a being or becoming attached by love; attachment. 4. a being or becoming suspended; suspension. 5. a being attached to the world and its vanities; worldly-mindedness. — et= /a/ to have connection with, to concern.

taallûkat (...—) تعلّقات A *lrnd.* relations; family connections.

taallül^lü تعلّل A *lrnd.* a seeking a pretext or excuse for avoiding something; excuse; evasion. —ât (...—) A *pl.*

taallüm تعلّم A *lrnd.* a studying and learning.

taallün تعلّن A *lrnd.* a becoming manifest; a becoming public.

taam (.—) طعام A *lrnd.* 1. food; meal. 2. a making a meal. — et= to have a meal, to eat.

taami (.—.) تعامى A *lrnd.* an affecting to be blind, a pretending not to see.

taamiye (.—..) طعاميه 1. *Ott. hist.* revenue devoted by religious institutions to the feeding of the poor. 2. *lrnd.* money allowed for food; expenses for provisions.

taammuk^ku تعمّق A *lrnd.* 1. a going deep; deepness, depth, profoundness. 2. a penetrating deeply into a matter; a speaking profoundly and mysteriously; penetration. —at (...—) A *pl.*

taammüd تعمّد A *law* an acting intentionally; premeditation. —ât (...—) A *lrnd., pl.*

taammüden (.´..) تعمّداً A *lrnd.* intentionally; with premeditation.

taammüdî (...—) تعمّدى A *lrnd.* intentional, premeditated.

taammüm تعمّم A a becoming general; generalization. — et= to become general, to spread.

taamül (.—.) تعامل A 1. custom, practice. 2. *chem.* reaction. —ât (.—.—) A *lrnd., pl.*

taan (.—) طعّان A *lrnd.* 1. habitually given to stabbing or prodding. 2. habitually censorious, evil-tongued.

taanni تعنّى A *lrnd.* 1. a striving, a making strenuous endeavors. 2. a giving trouble to a person; a taking trouble. 3. a suffering trouble or worry.

taannüd تعنّد A *lrnd.* a being or becoming obstinate; obstinacy. —at (...—) A *pl.*

taannüt^dü تعنّت A *lrnd.* 1. a trying to find out one's fault or sin; a finding fault with. 2. a troubling, badgering.

taanuk^ku (.—.) تعانق A *lrnd.* an embracing each other.

taaric (.——) تعاريج A *lrnd.* curves, curvatures, bends, turns; wavy lines, serpentines.

taarri تعرّى A *lrnd.* 1. a being or becoming naked. 2. a losing or getting rid of (something).

taarrub تعرّب A *lrnd.* 1. a becoming an Arab. 2. a being Arabicized (word).

taarruf تعرّف A *lrnd.* 1. a being or becoming known. 2. an inquiring with a view to learn; a seeking knowledge. 3. an acting according to customs (not according to the canon law of Islam).

taarruk^ku تعرّق A *lrnd.* a perspiring.

taarruz تعرّض A 1. an opposing, attacking; attack, aggression; assault. 2. molestation. 3. a meddling, interfering wrongfully; interference, meddling. 4. *lrnd.* a presenting itself before one, crossing one's path, offering itself (a thing). 5. *lrnd.* an exposing oneself to some occurrence. — et= /a/ 1. to attack, assault. 2. to violate (a woman). —ât (...—) A *lrnd., pl.*

taarruzî (...—) تعرّضى A *lrnd.* aggressive; offensive (attacking).

taarruzkâr (...—) تعرّضكار P *lrnd.* who meddles and interferes wrongfully or injuriously; aggressive. —âne (...——.) P *lrnd.* aggressively.

taaruz (.—.) تعارض A *lrnd.* 1. an opposing

taarüf (.—.) تعارف A *lrnd.* a recognising or being acquainted with one another; mutual acquaintance. — et= /la/ to recognize, know.

taassi تعصّي A *lrnd.* 1. a being rebellious and refractory; rebellion. 2. a being difficult, arduous.

taassub تعصّب A 1. a being a zealot, a becoming a bigot in religion; bigotry, fanaticism. 2. a being zealous, earnest, ardent; zeal, earnestness, ardor.

taassubkâr (...—) تعصّبكار P *lrnd.* fanatical. —ane (...——.) P *lrnd.* fanatically. —î (...——) P fanaticism.

taassup[bu] same as **taassub**.

taassür تعسّر A *lrnd.* a being or becoming difficult, arduous.

taasür (.—.) تعاسر A *lrnd.* 1. a being or becoming difficult in relations with each other. 2. a being or becoming difficult.

taasşi تعشّي A *lrnd.* an eating supper.

taasşuk[ku] تعشّق A *lrnd.* a falling in love. — et= /a/ to fall in love with.

taaşür (.—.) تعاشر A *lrnd.* a living together, associating together.

taat[ü] 1 (—.) طاعت A *lrnd.* act of obedience to God; act of piety.

ta'at 2 (——) طاعات A *lrnd.*, pl. of **taat** 1.

taatdar (—.—) طاعتدار P *lrnd.* pious. —î (—.——) P pious diligence in obeying God, piety.

taatgâh (—.—) طاعتگاه P *lrnd.* place where service is rendered to God; temple; mosque.

taatgüzin (—..—) طاعتگزين P *lrnd.* who seeks to serve God.

taattuf تعطّف A *lrnd.* 1. a being favorably or kindly inclined (toward an inferior). 2. an acting mercifully, a pitying. — et= /a/ 1. to incline favorably. 2. to be kind to. —at (...—) A *pl.*

taattul[lü] تعطّل A *lrnd.* 1. a being or becoming idle or unemployed. 2. a being void, empty or inactive.

taattur تعطّر A *lrnd.* a perfuming oneself.

taattus تعطّس A *lrnd.* a sneezing.

taattuş تعطّش A *lrnd.* 1. a being or becoming thirsty. 2. a pretending to be very thirsty or very desirous.

taattüh تعتّه A *lrnd.* 1. a becoming an imbecile. 2. a feigning imbecility.

ta'atuf (.—.) تعاطف A *lrnd.* a being kind and affectionate to each other.

taaviz (.——) تعاويذ A *lrnd.*, pl. of **ta'viz** 2.

taavün (.—.) تعاون A a helping one another; mutual assistance.

taavvuk[ku] تعوّق A *lrnd.* a being hindered or prevented; a being late.

taavvuz تعوّض A *lrnd.* a taking or receiving in exchange. —ı tams *biol.* menstruation.

taavvüc تعوّج A *lrnd.* a being or becoming bent or crooked. —ât (...—) A *pl.*

taavvüd تعوّد A *lrnd.* 1. an accustoming oneself to a habit. 2. a going to visit a sick person.

taavvüz تعوّذ A *lrnd.* a seeking for shelter, a taking refuge (in God).

taayyün تعيّن A 1. a being manifest, plain, visible. 2. a being determined; determination. 3. *lrnd.* a being or becoming existent as a real being (apart from idea or conception). 4. *lrnd.* a being or becoming individually distinguished, conspicuous. — et= 1. to become clear or manifest. 2. to be defined or determined. —i evvel *lrnd.* existent thing, God. —i sani *lrnd.* the second really existent thing, God's quality of oneness.

taayyünat (...—) تعيّنات A *lrnd.* separate individual existences.

taayyüş تعيّش A *lrnd.* an obtaining a living; means of subsistence. — et= to manage to live, to find the means of subsistence.

taayyuşgâh (...—) تعيّشگاه P *lrnd.* place where one lives.

taazi (.—.) تعازى A *lrnd.*, pl. of **ta'ziye**.

taazud (.—.) تعاضد A *lrnd.* an assisting one another.

taazum (.—.) تعاظم A *lrnd.* 1. a being or becoming great, important, serious; importance, seriousness. 2. a being or becoming proud; pride.

taazi تعزّى A *lrnd.*, same as **taazzuv**.

taazzum تعظّم A *lrnd.* 1. a pretending to be great. 2. a being proud; arrogance.

taazzuv تعزّو [based on Arabic] *lrnd.* a forming organs, a becoming a living organism; development.

taazzüb تعزّب A *lrnd.* a being or remaining long unmarried.

taazzül تعزّل A *lrnd.* a going apart, a separating oneself (from).

taazzür تعذّر A *lrnd.* 1. an offering an excuse or an apology; excuse, apology. 2. a being impossible or impracticable (so that an excuse exists for its non-occurrence); impossibility, impracticability; excusableness.

taazzüz تعزّز A *lrnd.* 1. a being or becoming high and highly esteemed; a being or becoming strong or powerful. 2. a being or becoming scarce, rare or beyond price. 3. a being or becoming difficult, insurmountable.

tab 1 (—) تاب P *lrnd.* 1. power, strength, ability. 2. heat, warmth, ardor. 3. light, radiance; glitter, flash; polish, burnish. 4. twist, curl, coil; wrinkle, plait. 5. bodily or mental pain, anguish; confusion, trouble. 6. anger, wrath, rage. 7. temper of a sword; keenness of a sword. — getir= /a/ to show the ability to do, bear, or resist. —ı gisû side curl. —ı hurşid 1. warmth of the sun. 2. freshness; radiance of youth. 3. plait, curl. — ü tâkat, — ü tüvan power and ability.

-tab 2 تاب P lrnd. 1. illuminating, shining, glowing, as in ateştab, cihantab. 2. twisting, spinning, as in muytab.

tab^(b'ı) 3 طبع A lrnd. 1. natural quality, natural temperament, disposition. 2. one's health or bodily condition. —ı şerif the noble health (of your honor, etc.). —ı yârân the disposition of friends.

tab^(b'ı) 4 طبع A same as tabı. — et=*.

tab'a طبعه A lrnd. a single printing. —i ulâ first edition.

tabaat^(ti) (.—.) طباعت A lrnd. printing; printer's art.

tababet (.—.) طبابت A the science of medicine, therapeutics.

tabahat^(ti) (.—.) طباخت A lrnd., var. of tıbahat.

tabak^(ğı) 1 طبق A 1. plate, dish. 2. lrnd. sheet; layer. — gibi flat. — yala= to idle, to sit around doing nothing.

tabak^(ğı) 2 دباغ [debbağ] tanner.

tabak^(ğı) 3 طباق prov. foot and mouth disease of animals.

tabaka 1 طبقه A 1. layer, stratum; level. 2. sheet (of paper). 3. rank, class of men. 4. prov. story (of a building). —i karniye anat. cornea. —i meşimiye anat. choroid coat. —i nâriye Ptolemaic cosmography the igneous stratum of the atmosphere, the region next below the sphere of the moon. —i türbiye Ptolemaic cosmography fifth stratum out of seven, counting downwards from the lunar sphere. (It consists of sands and earths). —i zemheririye Ptolemaic cosmography stratum of the atmosphere which is the place of origin of clouds, thunder, and lightning.

tabaka 2 طبق تاباقه It tobacco box, cigarette box.

tabakat (..—) طبقات A lrnd., pl. of tabaka 1.

tabakat-ül-arz (..—..) طبقات الارض A lrnd. geology.

tabakat-ül-fukaha (..—...—) طبقات الفقهاء A lrnd. biographies of teachers of Islamic canon law according to their ranks.

tabakatüşşuara (...'...—) طبقات الشعراء A lrnd. biographies of poets; classes of poets.

tabakça, tabakçe طبيقچه P lrnd. small plate, saucer.

tabakhane طباخانه tanning yard, tannery.

tabakla=^r طباقده /ı/ to tan (skin or hide). —n= pass. —t= /ı/ caus.

tabaklık^(ğı) 1 طباقلق trade of a tanner.

tabaklık^(ğı) 2 طباقلق plate-rack (in a kitchen).

tabakülarz طبقات الارض A lrnd. the earth.

taban 1 طابان تابان 1. sole (of a foot or shoe); heel. 2. firmness, boldness, pluck. 3. girder, wall-plate. 4. floor; base; plateau. 5. fine steel. 6. bed of a river. 7. a long, narrow strip of velvet (attached to two rods of sandalwood, formerly wound round the feet of babies). — ağacı longitudinal beam, girder. — at= to lay a wall-plate or girder in a building. — boya undercoat (paint). — çal= to run or walk quickly. — çek= to walk uninterruptedly for a long time. — çeliği arch. ground sill, sole-timber. — çukuru arch under the sole of the foot. — demiri Damascus steel. — döşeği arch. foundation-raft, sleeper. — fiatı fin. the lowest price in governmental purchases, especially on tobacco. — hatılı same as taban ağacı. — inciri small sweet fig ripening late on the tree. —ı kaldır=, —ları kaldır= to take to one's heels. — kılıç sword of Damascus steel. — kirişi same as taban ağacı. —a kuvvet by dint of hard walking; fleeing fast. — oku same as taban ağacı. — pabucu same as taban döşeği. — patlat= to walk until one's feet become blistered and sore. — savağı hose reel. — tabana, — tabana zıt diametrically opposite, utterly opposed, absolutely contrary. — tahtası floor plank. — tarla fertile plateau. — tep= to walk a long way; to tire oneself by walking. — terazisi builder's level. —ları yağla= 1. to prepare to go to a distant place on foot. 2. to run away. —ı yanık one who keeps going from place to place, wanderer. — yolu path.

taban 2 طبان agriculture roller.

tab'an 3 (.'.) طبعًا A lrnd. 1. by nature, naturally. 2. by printing; in print.

taban 4 (——) تابان P 1. lrnd. bright, luminous, radiant. 2. lrnd. shining, polished; sparkling.

tabanca (..'.) طبانجه 1. pistol, revolver; pistol shot. 2. spray gun, sprayer. 3. archaic slap on the face or head; blow, box. 4. slang wine bottle. — at= /a/ 1. to fire a pistol (at). 2. archaic to give a slap on the face. — boyası spray paint. — çek= /a/ to draw a pistol. — oyunu a game resembling marbles. — ye= 1. to receive a pistol shot. 2. archaic to receive a slap, cuff, etc.

tab'aniye (.—.) طبعانيه A phil. naturism.

tabankeş طبانكش lrnd. walking on foot; a great walker.

tabanla=^r 1 طبانله /ı/ to tread, press or kick.

tabanla=' 2 طبا نلامىه /ı/ to roll or harrow smooth.
tabanlı طبانى طبانو 1. soled. 2. brave, firm.
tabansız طبانسز 1. soleless. 2. weak, cowardly. —**lık** cowardice.
tabasbus تبصبص A *lrnd.* a cringing or fawning. — **et=** to fawn and flatter. —**i kelbâne**, —**i kelbî** a fawning like a dog. —**ât** (...—) A *pl.*
tabaşir (.——) طباشىر A *lrnd.* 1. same as **tebeşir**. 2. substance of a siliceous nature in bamboo (used in medicine).
tabaver (——.) تابا'ور P *lrnd.* able, possessing power.
tabayiⁱⁱ (.—.) طبا ئج A *lrnd.*, pl. of **tabiat**.
tabbah (.—) طبّاخ A *lrnd.* cook. —**în** (.——) A *pl.*
tabbalⁱⁱ (.—) طبّال A *lrnd.* drummer.
tabdade (——.) تابىاده P *lrnd.* 1. inflaming; inflamed. 2. lighted; heated.
tabdan (——) تابىان P *lrnd.* 1. a kind of skylight or upper window. 2. fireplace; stove. 3. forge; furnace.
tabdar (——) تابىار P *lrnd.* 1. luminous; gleaming, bright. 2. hot, burning; ardent, fervent. 3. twisted, curling; curly. 4. vexed, annoyed, uneasy.
tabdih (—.) تابىه P *lrnd.* 1. light-giving, illuminating. 2. heat-giving, heating. 3. power-giving, empowering. 4. twisting, spinning. 5. temper or edge-giving.
tabe 1 (—.) تابه P *lrnd.* 1. frying pan. 2. flat iron plate used in baking. 3. large, flat, thick tile, brick. 4. pane or plate (of glass). 5. any dish of fried food. —**i tabdan** pane of glass or a cloth or paper screen that covers a window. —**i zer** the golden frying pan, *i. e.* the sun.
tabe- 2 (—.) تابه P *lrnd.* until, *as in* **tabekıyamet, tabesabah.**
tabekey (—..) تاکى P *lrnd.* until when.
tabekıyamet (—..—.) تابقىامت P *lrnd.* until the Day of Judgment, forever.
tabelâ (..'.) تابلا It 1. sign (of a shop or firm). 2. list of food (in schools, hospitals, etc.). 3. soldier's ration book. 4. card of treatment (hung on a patient's bed in hospitals). 5. table (list). —**cı** sign-painter.
tabende (—..) تابنده P *lrnd.* 1. which shines, glows, sparkles. 2. which twists, bends, curls (a thing). 3. who averts his face. —**gi** (—..—) P luster, luminousness. —**izâr** (—...—) P having shining cheeks.
tabesabah (—..—) تابصباح P *lrnd.* until morning.
tabeserahü (—..—.), **tabesirruhü** (—....)

طابا ثراه A *rel.,formula* (*lit.* May his grave be pleasant.) May he rest in peace.
tabet=ᵈᵉʳ طبع ابتك /ı/ to print. —**tir=** /ı, a/ *caus.*
tabh طبخ A *lrnd.* a cooking; cookery.
tabhane 1 (——.) طبخانه P *lrnd.* 1. room artificially heated as a warm winter-room; hothouse, warming room. 2. hospital; madhouse.
tab'hane 2 (.—.) طبعخانه P *lrnd.* printing house.
tabhî (.—) طبخى A *lrnd.* pertaining to cooking.
tabhiye طبخىه fee paid to a baker for cooking a tray of food.
tabıᵇ'¹ طبع [**tab** 4] a printing, stamping, impressing; impression, edition (of a book).
tabih (—.) طابخ A *lrnd.* 1. that cooks; cook. 2. burning hot; burning fever. 3. who torments the people of hell (angel).
tabıha (—..) طابخه A *lrnd.* midday in the hot season.
tabılᵇ'ⁱ طبل *var. of* **tabl**.
tabiⁱⁱ 1 (—.) تابع A 1. that follows; following. 2. a follower of the practice of another; follower (of a leader). 3. dependent; subject (of a state or sovereign); servant. 4. imitating; conforming; submissive. 5. *Isl. rel.* follower in point of time, especially, one who lived after Muhammad was dead but had conversed with at least one of his companions. 6. *geog.* tributary (of a river). 7. *Arabic gram.* word in apposition. — **ve metbu'** 1. follower and the one followed. 2. subject and his sovereign. 3. consequent and antecedent. — **ol** /a/ 1. to follow, to be a follower, dependent, or imatator (of). 2. to depend (on). — **vadiler** *geog.* secondary valleys.
tabiⁱⁱ 2 (—.) تابع A printer; publisher, editor.
tab'î 3 (.—) طبعى A *lrnd.* natural, by nature.
tabiatⁱⁱ طبىعت [*Arabic* .—.] 1. nature. 2. natural quality, character, disposition. 3. natural refined taste, refinement. 4. habit. 5. regularity (of the bowels). —**iyle** naturally, of itself. —**i beşeriye** *lrnd.* human nature. — **bilgisi** biology. — **edin=** /ı/ to make a habit of. — **kanunu** law of nature. — **sahibi** a man of taste.
tabiatli طبىعتلى 1. having such and such a nature. 2. possessing good taste.
tabiatsiz طبىعتسز devoid of good taste; unrefined. —**lık** lack of taste and refinement.
tabiatüstü طبىعتۈستى supernatural.
tabib (.—) طبىب A *lrnd., same as* **tabip**. —**i adlî** doctor of forensic medicine, medical examiner of suspicious death cases. —**i ruhani-i hasse** *Ott. hist.* psychologist of the Palace (He

cured the sick by breathing on them and casting a spell). —**ân** (. — —) P *pl.* of **tabib.** —**î** (. — —) P quality, art and duty of a physician.
tabii 1 (. — —) طبیعى A 1. natural, normal. 2. naturally, of course. 3. *lrnd.* natural philosopher, naturalist. — **borçlar** *law* natural obligations. — **hukuk** *law* natural law. — **senatör** *neol.* appointed life-time senator.
tabii 2 (—.—) تابعى A *same as* **tabi 1⁵**.
tabiilikᵏⁱ طبیعیلك naturalness, normality.
tabiin (—.—) تابعین A *lrnd., pl.* of **tabi 1⁵**.
tabiiyat (.—.—) طبیعیات A *lrnd.* questions and facts of nature, matters of natural science.
tabiiye (..—.) طبیعیه A 1. natural history, natural science. 2. *phil.* naturalism. —**ci** teacher or specialist in natural science.
tabiiyet 1 (.——.) طبیعیت A *lrnd.* naturalness, normality.
tabiiyet 2 (—.—.) تابعیت A 1. nationality, allegiance. 2. *lrnd.* a conforming, dependence. —**sizlik** statelessness.
tabiiyun (.———) طبیعیون A *phil.* 1. naturalists. 2. specialists of natural science. — **mezhebi** naturalism.
tabipᵇⁱ (.—) طبیب [**tabib**] physician, doctor. —**lik** profession and practice of a physician.
ta'bir (.—) A, **tabir** (——) تعبیر 1. expression, term; phrase. 2. interpretation of a dream or vision. — **caizse** if I may say so. —**i diğerle** in other words. — **et**= /ı/ 1. to express in words. 2. to name, to designate. 3. to interpret (dream). —**ât** (.——) A *lrnd., pl.* of **ta'bir.** —**ci** interpreter of dreams.
tabirname (———.) تعبیرنامه P book on the interpretation of dreams.
tabistan (—.—) تابستان P *lrnd.* summer.
tabiş (—.) تابش P *lrnd.* 1. a shining; splendor, brilliance; light. 2. a glowing heat; inflammation. 3. a being able; power, strength. 4. a twisting; twist, curl. 5. a suffering from bodily or mental pain; grief, sorrow.
tabiun (—.—) تابعون A *lrnd., pl.* of **tabi 1⁵**.
tab'iye 1 (.—.) طبعیه A *lrnd.* printing expenses.
ta'biye 2 A, **tabiye** (—..) طابیه تعبیه 1. *mil.* tactics. 2. *lrnd.* a preparing, arranging for use. —**ci** tactician. —**vi** (—..—) A tactical.
tabkur طبقور *same as* **tapkur.**
tablˡⁱ طبل A 1. *anat.* tympanum. 2. *lrnd., same as* **davul.**
tabla (.'.) طبله طبلا A circular tray (commonly of wood); ashtray; flat disk; level surface; tray (put under a stove); pan of a balance; *arch.* cap (of a column).
tablakâr (..—) طبله كار P 1. itinerant vendor of goods who carries them on a circular tray on his head. 2. servant charged with carrying trays of food. —**ân** (..——) P *lrnd., pl.*

tablalı طبله لى 1. flat and circularly expanded at the top. 2. having a circular tray.
tablbaz (.—) طبلباز P *lrnd.* 1. drummer. 2. small hawking drum. —**ân** (.——) P *pl.*
tabldot تابل دوت F table d'hote.
tablekᵏⁱ طبلك P *lrnd.* small drum.
tablekâr (..—) طبله كار *same as* **tablakâr.**
tablhane (.—.) طبلخانه P 1. *Ott. hist.* military band of the Sultan's palace, (cf. **mehterhane**). 2. *lrnd.* band of music, concert of drums.
tabli (.—) طبلى A *lrnd.* pertaining to a drum; drumlike.
tabliye (.—.) طبلیه A *lrnd.* 1. drumlike. 2. flat tray-like circular receptacle or stand. 3. tribute; a payment of tribute.
tablo (.'.) تابلو F 1. picture. 2. tableau. 3. *auto.* instrument panel, instrument board.
tablzen طبلزن P *lrnd.* drummer.
tabnâkᵏⁱ (——) تابناك P *lrnd.* 1. shining, bright, brilliant. 2. passionate, fiery; hot, angry.
tabsıra تبصره A *lrnd.* 1. a making clearly seen and understood; demonstration; warning. 2. beacon, signpost.
tabsir (.—) تبصیر A *lrnd.* 1. an explaining and defining. 2. a causing to see with the eyes or mind. 3. a putting one on his guard, a making cautious and wary.
tabu (.'.) تابو F taboo.
tabulga تابولغا *same as* **tavulga.**
tabur طابور 1. battalion. 2. *archaic* camp surrounded with carts chained together for defense.
taburcu طابورجى 1. discharged from a hospital, especially, soldier passed fit for service after an illness. 2. *slang* released from jail. 3. *slang* dead person.
tabure (.'.) تابوره F footstool.
taburmacar, taburmacor طابورماجار طابورماجور F drum-major.
tabut تابوت [*Arabic* ——] 1. coffin, bier. 2. large egg-box. 3. *Bib.* the cradle of bulrushes of Moses; Ark of the Covenant.
tabutla= تابوتلا /ı/ to put into a coffin. —**n**= *pass.* —**ndır**=, —**t**= /ı, a/ *caus.* of **tabutla**=.
tabutlukᵗⁱ تابوتلق 1. place in a mosque courtyard where coffins are set. 2. *colloq.* place of torture (in a police station).
Tabutülahd (——..), **Tabutüssekine** (——..—.) تابوت العهد تابوت السكینه A *Bib.* the Ark of the Covenant.
tabya (.'.), **tabye** (.'.) طابیه [**tabiye 2**] bastion, redoubt; fort. — **sepeti** gabion. — **siperi** gabionade. — **topu** heavy gun for siege purposes.
tabzad (.—) طبعزاد P *lrnd.* innate, congenital.
tac (—) تاج P *lrnd., same as* **taç**. —**ı firuze** 1. the sky. 2. the crown of Keykhusrev. —**ı gerdun** (*lit.,* crown of the revolving sphere)

the sun. —ı **gül** corolla of a flower. —ı **ser** crown of the head; greatly honored person or thing. — **ü serir** the crown and the throne. —ı **Şem'** flame of a candle.

tacan=ᶦʳ ناجا نس archaic to assume the crown, to be crowned. —**dır**= /ı/ archaic to crown.

tacaver (— —.) ناج آور P lrnd. who possesses a crown; crowned; sovereign. —**âne** (— —. —.) P special to a king, royal, imperial. —**î** (— —. —) P sovereignty, royalty.

tacdar (— —) ناجدار P lrnd. wearing a crown; king, sovereign. —**ân** (— — —) P kings, rulers, sovereigns. —**ân-ı zaman** rulers of the time. —**âne** (— — —.) P royal, imperial. —**î** (— — —) P royalty, sovereignty; royal dignity.

tacdih (—.) ناج دهنده P lrnd. bestower of a crown, suzerain, prince.

tacduz (— —) ناجدوز P lrnd. maker of quilted dervish caps.

tace (—.) ناجه P lrnd. 1. cock's comb; bird's crest. 2. woman's headgear.

tacekᵏⁱ (—.) ناجك P lrnd. little crown.

tacgâh (— —) ناجگاه P lrnd. 1. capital city. 2. royal palace.

tachah (— —) ناج خواه P lrnd. who claims the crown, rightful sovereign.

tacib (. —) نجيب A lrnd. a filling with astonishment; a causing wonder, surprise.

Tacikᵍⁱ (—.) ناجيك P Tajik. —**istan** (— . . —) Tajikistan.

ta'cil (. —) A, **tâcil** (— —) تعجيل 1. a making haste, a causing, urging to hurry. 2. *phys.* acceleration. 3. *lrnd.* a paying down in ready money. — **et**= /ı/ 1. to hasten; to accelerate. 2. *lrnd.* to pay down (cash). —**ât** (. — —) A lrnd., pl. of **ta'cil**.

ta'cim (. —) تعجيم A lrnd. a marking a letter with its proper diacritical points.

ta'cin (. —) تعجين A lrnd. a kneading.

tacir (— .) تاجر A merchant, dealer.

ta'ciz (. —) A, **tâciz** (— —) تعجيز a bothering, worrying, troubling; a harassing. — **ateşi** *mil.* harassing fire. — **et**= /ı/ to annoy, to harass, to disturb. —**ât** (. — —) A lrnd., pl. of **taciz**.

tacizlikᵍⁱ تعجيزلك a worrying, importunity. — **getir**= to complain; to feel fed up. — **ver**= /a/ to harass.

tacpuş (— —) تاجپوش P lrnd. wearing a crown or turban; having a crest (bird).

tacver (—.) تاجور P lrnd. wearing a crown, crowned; sovereign, monarch. —**âne** (—. —.), —**î** (—. —.) P special to a crowned prince. —**lik** sovereignty.

taçᶜⁱ تاج [tac] 1. crown; dervish's headgear. 2. *bot.* corolla; *zool.* crest of a bird. — **giy**= to be crowned. — **yaprağı** *bot.* petal. — **yapraklı** gamopetalous.

taçend (—.) تاچند P lrnd. until when? how long?

taçla=ʳ تاجلمك /ı/ to crown. —**n**= *pass.* —**ndır**= /ı/ to crown.

taçlı تاجلو 1. crowned; crested. 2. marked with the figure of a crown.

taçsız تاجسز 1. without a crown. 2. *bot.* apetalous.

tadaccur تضجر A lrnd., same as **tazaccur**.

ta'dad (. —) A, **tâdad** (— —) تعداد lrnd. a counting, numbering, enumeration. — **et**= /ı/ 1. to count, to number. 2. to enumerate, to recount. —**ı nakıs** imperfect enumeration. — **ve terkîm** counting and writing the numbers; enumeration.

tadahhükᵏᵘ تضحك A lrnd., same as **tazahhuk**.

tadal=ᶦʳ طعم آلمك to taste, to relish.

tadan=ᶦʳ طعم آلنمك same as **dadan**=.

tadarrub تضرب A lrnd., same as **tazarrub**.

tadhiye تضحيه A lrnd. 1. a slaughtering a victim in sacrifice (shortly after sunrise). 2. a slaughtering in sacrifice during the four days of the **Kurban Bayramı**.

tadıcı طاد يجى one who tastes, taster.

tadım طاد م 1. the faculty of taste. 2. a tasting, taste. —**lık** just enough to taste.

ta'did (. —) تعديد A lrnd. 1. a counting, numbering; an enumerating. 2. a preparing as a store, a laying up ready for use.

ta'dil (. —) A, **tâdil** (— —) تعديل 1. adjustment, rectification, alteration, modification; amendment. 2. *lrnd.* a balancing; a putting in a right position. — **et**= /ı/ to adjust, modify, correct; to amend. — **mâbeyn-es-satreyn** *literature* interpolation.

tâdilât (. — —) تعديلات A modifications, amendments.

tâdilen (. —'.) تعديلا A lrnd. by way of modification or amendment.

ta'dim (. —) تعدم A lrnd. an annihilating; annihilation.

ta'diye تعديه A 1. *gram.* a making a verb transitive. 2. *lrnd.* a making or letting pass from one to another.

tadlil (. —) تضليل A lrnd. 1. a misleading; a leading into error, wickedness or perdition. 2. an accusing of error; a pronouncing to be astray.

tafahhus تفحص A lrnd. an investigating, an inquiring closely into; investigation. —**ât** (. . . —) A *pl.*

tafazzulˡᵘ تفضل A lrnd. 1. a being or becoming superior; superiority. 2. an assuming a superiority. 3. a doing a kindness; goodness, favor, kindness.

tafdil (. —) تفضيل 1. *gram.* comparison.

2. *Irnd.* a deeming as superior, a treating one as superior; preference.
tafl[li] طفل A *Irnd.* young and tender (child).
taflan طفلان Gk cherry laurel, *bot.*, *Prunus laurocerasus*.
tafra طفره A 1. pride, conceit. 2. *Irnd.* spring, leap, bound. 3. *Irnd.* a step in promotion. — **sat**= to give oneself airs. —**cı** *same as* **tafrafuruş**.
tafrafuruş (...—) طفره فروش P *Irnd.* 1. conceited. 2. bragging; boastful. —**luk** (...—.) conceit.
tafralı طفره لى conceited, proud, vain.
tafsil (.—) تفصيل A 1. an entering into details; detailed explanation; detail, particular. 2. *Irnd.* a dividing into portions or sections. — **et**= /ı/ to explain in detail. —**i mürekkeb** *log.* the fallacy known as division and disjunctive judgment.
tafsilât (.——) تفصيلات A full explanation. —**ı mâlâyânî** unnecessary explanation. —**ı meşruhâ** detailed information. — **ver**= to give detailed explanation. —**lı** detailed.
tafsilan (.—.) تفصيلا A *Irnd.* in detail.
tafta تافته [**tafte**] taffeta.
tafte (—.) تافته P *Irnd.* 1. turned, twisted, folded, bent. 2. burnt, heated; shining, illumined. 3. vexed, grieved, afflicted.
tafteciger (—.—.) تافته جگر P *Irnd.* (*lit.*, whose liver is inflamed) that suffers anguish; in love.
taftegi (—.—) تافتگى P vexation, fatigue; distortion.
tafzih (.—) تفضيح A *Irnd.* a reproaching; an exposing another's vices or faults, a putting to shame. —**ât** (.——) A *pl.*
tafzil (.—) تفضيل *var. of* **tafdil**.
tafziz (.—) تفضيض A *Irnd.* an ornamenting with silver; a silvering.
tagabün (.—.) تغابن A *Irnd.* a defrauding one another, a cheating one another; mutual deceit. **T— Suresi** name of the sixty-fourth sura of the Quran.
tagaddi تغدّى A *Irnd.* a being fed; nutrition. — **et**= to be fed, to be nourished.
tagaffül تغفّل A *Irnd.* a being careless, thoughtless; heedlessness, thoughtlessness.
tagallut تغلّط A *Irnd.* a falling into error, a mistaking. —**ât** (.——) A *pl.*
tagallüb تغلّب A *Irnd.* a gaining or assuming mastery over another; a prevailing upon; domination; mastery. — **et**= 1. to usurp power. 2. /a/ to make oneself master (of), to subjugate. —**ât** (.——) A *pl.*
tagallüf تغلّف A *Irnd.* a being or becoming covered by a case, sheath, and the like. —**i em'â** *med.* entanglement of the intestines.
tagammüd تغمّد A *Irnd.* a covering, wrapping, enveloping.
taganni تغنّى A 1. a singing, chanting. 2. *Irnd.* a being or becoming independent of aid; a being contented. —**yât** (...—) *pl.*
tagannüc تغنّج A *Irnd.* a using coquettish gestures, looks and blandishments; coquetry.
tagarrüb تغرّب A *Irnd.* 1. a being or arriving in a strange place as a stranger; estrangement. 2. a being in or going to the west.
tagarrüd تغرّد A *Irnd.* a making a prolonged sound as a bird's singing, a humming of an insect, etc.
tagarrür تغرّر A *Irnd.* an exposing oneself to danger rashly or from self-confidence; presumption, temerity.
tagassül تغسّل A *Irnd.* a washing the whole body, a bathing oneself.
tagaşşi تغشّى A *Irnd.* 1. a covering, enveloping. 2. a covering or wrapping oneself.
tagavvul تغوّل A *Irnd.* 1. a putting on the capricious aspects of a ghoul. 2. an assuming diverse appearances. 3. a being capricious.
tagavvur تغوّر A *Irnd.* a going deeply into a subject, getting to the bottom of it.
tagavvus تغوّص A *Irnd.* 1. a plunging, diving. 2. a going minutely into a subject.
tagayyuz تغيّظ A *Irnd.* 1. a being or becoming sultry. 2. a becoming furiously angry; fury, wrath, vehemence. 3. a roaring (fire). 4. a boiling and emitting a loud sound (pot).
tagayyüb تغيّب A *Irnd.* 1. a becoming absent; a becoming invisible, concealed. 2. a setting (sun, etc.). — **et**= to disappear.
tagayyüm تغيّم A *Irnd.* a being or becoming cloudy (sky); cloudiness. —**ât** (...—) A *pl.*
tagayyür تغيّر A *Irnd.* 1. a changing, a becoming another substance; change, variation. 2. a becoming spoiled or putrid; deterioration. 3. a changing color, becoming pale or red; pallor; blushing. 4. mutation. — **et**= to change, alter; to vary.
tagazzi تغذّى A *Irnd.*, *same as* **tagaddi**.
tagazzub تغضّب A *Irnd.* a being or becoming angry.
tagazzül تغزّل A *Irnd.* a composing an ode on love and pleasure. —**ât** (...—) A *pl.*
tagi (—.) طاغى A *Irnd.* rebellious; sinful; unjust; unrighteous. — **ve bagi** 1. rebellious and obstinate. 2. wicked.
tagut (——) طاغوت A *Irnd.* 1. devil, demon. 2. idol. 3. *w. cap.* an ancient idol at Mecca. 4. sorcerer; soothsayer.
tağa طاغا [*Arabic* **taka**] *prov.* window.
tağan طغان *prov.* frying pan.
tağar طغار *prov., same as* **dağar** 1, 2. — **dibi** bottom, depth; end.
tağarcık[gı] طغارجق *same as* **dağarcık**.
tağbir (.—) تغبير A *Irnd.* 1. a soiling with dust; a raising the dust. 2. a saddening or vexing.

tağdiye تغذيه A 1. a feeding, nourishing. 2. *mech.* feed, input. — et= /ı/ to feed, nourish.

tağfil (.—) تغفيل A *lrnd.* 1. a causing to be careless, thoughtless. 2. a taking unawares, being taken by surprise.

tağlağı, tağlağu طغلغى *prov., same as* **dağlağı.**

tağlib (.—) تغليب A *lrnd.* 1. a rendering superior or predominant; a pronouncing victorious; prevalence. 2. a making a word dominate in use over another as when "man" includes women.

tağlif (.—) تغليف A *lrnd.* 1. a making a case or sheath to a thing. 2. a putting a thing into its case or sheath. —**i süyûf** peace-making.

tağlik[kı] (.—) تغليق A *lrnd.* a shutting, fastening a door or gate. —**i ebvâb** 1. a closing the doors. 2. *literature* talking enigmatically. —**ât** (.——) A *pl.*

tağlit[ıı] (.—) تغليط A *lrnd.* 1. a causing to fall into error. 2. a judging or pronouncing one in error; an accusing one of an error. —**ât** (.——) A *pl.*

tağliz (.—) تغليظ A *lrnd.* 1. a making a thing thick, coarse, heavy, or clumsy. 2. a making an oath strong in its terms.

tağmid (.—) تغميد A *lrnd.* 1. a covering up and concealing. 2. a putting into its sheath (sword).

tağmis (.—) تغميس A *lrnd.* a plunging (into a liquid).

tağmiz (.—) تغميض A *lrnd.* 1. a half-shutting the eyes; a conniving at, an indulging. 2. a making the speech obscure, unintelligible.

tağniye تغنيه A *lrnd.* 1. a causing to become rich, independent of aid. 2. a singing or chanting.

tağrib (.—) تغريب A *lrnd.* 1. a causing to become a stranger; a banishing. 2. a sending or directing to the west.

tağrid (.—) تغريد A *lrnd., same as* **tagarrüd.**

tağrik[kı] (.—) تغريق A *lrnd.* 1. a drowning someone. 2. an overwhelming a person.

tağrim (.—) تغريم A *lrnd.* a causing to undertake a debt; a fining.

tağrir (.—) تغرير A *lrnd.* 1. a cheating a customer. 2. an exposing oneself to danger. 3. a temptation to presumption; overconfidence. —**ât** (.——) A *pl.*

tağris (.—) تغريس A *lrnd.* a planting trees.

tağsil (.—) تغسيل A *lrnd.* 1. a washing oneself with extra care; a taking a bath. 2. a causing to wash.

tağşiş (.—) تغشيش A *lrnd.* 1. an adulterating; adulteration. 2. a falsifying, garbling a story. 3. a nourishing envy, malice.

tağşiye تغشيه A *lrnd.* 1. a covering up; a putting a thing over something else as a cover. 2. a dazzling the eye (light).

tağtiye تغطيه A *lrnd.* a covering, or causing to cover the surface or body of a thing.

tağviye تغويه A *lrnd.* a leading astray, a misleading, a seducing.

tağyib (.—) تغييب A *lrnd.* 1. a causing to become absent. 2. a making disappear. 3. a backbiting.

tağyir (.—) تغيير A *lrnd.* 1. a changing a thing for something else; substitution. 2. an altering, varying, modifying; change, alteration. 3. a spoiling; deterioration. —**ât** (.——) A *pl.*

tağyiz (.—) تغييظ A *lrnd.* a causing to be furiously angry.

tağziye 1 تغذيه A *lrnd., same as* **tağdiye.**

tağziye 2 تغزيه A *lrnd.* a sending on a military expedition; an equipping one for a military expedition.

taha (——) طه A *lrnd., name of the twentieth sura of the Quran.*

tahabbür تحبر A *lrnd.* 1. an asking, an inquiring for information. 2. a being acquainted, conversant with; a knowing well.

tahabbüs تحبس A *lrnd.* 1. a shutting oneself up, a being shut up. 2. a restricting oneself.

tahaccüb تحجب A *lrnd.* a being veiled, a becoming curtained.

tahaccür تحجر 1. *geol.* petrifaction. 2. *lrnd.* a becoming stone or as hard as stone. —**ât** (...—) A *lrnd., pl.*

tahaddi تحدى A *lrnd.* a striving for superiority; competition.

tahaddu[uu] تحدع A *lrnd.* an ostentatiously deceiving.

tahaddüb تحدب A *lrnd.* 1. a being or becoming humpbacked. 2. a being or becoming convex. —**ât** (...—) A *pl.*

tahaddür 1 تحدر A *lrnd.* a descending gradually or slowly; gradual descent or flow.

tahaddür 2 تخدر A *lrnd.* a keeping or being kept veiled, a keeping modestly out of view (woman).

tahaddüs تحدث 1. *phil.* intuition. 2. *lrnd.* a coming into existence; a not being eternal as to the past; a coming to pass, an occurring; occurrence. 3. *lrnd.* a talking, conversing, conversation. —**ât** (...—) A *lrnd., pl.* —**î** (...—) intuitive. —**iye** (...—.) intuitionism.

tahaffuz تحفظ A *lrnd.* 1. a guarding oneself; preservation; conservation. 2. a committing to memory.

tahaffuzhane (...—.) تحفظخانه P quarantine station.

tahaffuzî (...—) تحفظى A *lrnd.* pertaining to

measures of precaution, precautionary; preventive.

tahaffuzkâr (...—) محتفظكار P cautious, guarding himself. **—âne** (...——.) P precautionally.

tahaffüf تحفّف A *lrnd.* 1. a being light, a becoming thin; lightness, levity. 2. a being or becoming booted.

tahakkud^dü تحقّد A *lrnd.* a being or becoming filled with hate; spite, malice, malevolence.

tahakkuk^ku تحقّق A 1. a proving to be true; a being realized; verification; realization, a carrying out (a decision). 2. *lrnd.* a really and truly existing; real existence, persistence, consistency. **—i aslî** *lrnd.* self-existence. **— et=** 1. to prove true; to be realized. 2. to come into existence; to come into effect. **— memuru** official charged with the final assessment of a tax. **— tarihi** date when tax becomes due.

tahakküm تحكّم A 1. arbitrary power; oppression. 2. *lrnd.* a being or becoming judge or arbiter; arbitration. **— et=** /a/ to dominate, oppress, tyrannize. **—ât** (...—) A *pl.*

tahal طحل A a having a diseased or enlarged spleen.

tahalli 1 تحلّي A *lrnd.* 1. a wearing ornaments; adornment. 2. a being adorned by excellent qualities.

tahalli 2 تخلّي A *lrnd.* 1. a being or becoming free from occupation. 2. an abandoning, leaving empty or alone; a being alone. 3. an occupying oneself exclusively with, a devoting oneself.

tahallûk^ku تخلّق A *lrnd.* 1. a being or becoming characterized with some special quality. 2. an assuming the appearance of any special moral quality.

tahallûs تخلّص A *lrnd.* 1. a being free, a becoming safe; safety; salvation. 2. adoption of a pseudonym.

tahallût تخلّط A *lrnd.* a being or becoming confusedly mixed; confusion.

tahallüb تحلّب A *lrnd.* 1. a gradually secreting and flowing from its organ (humor). 2. a flowing with its special secretion (organ). 3. a sweating, perspiring.

tahallüd تخلّد A *lrnd.* a becoming everlasting, an enduring forever.

tahallüf تخلّف A *lrnd.* 1. a differing, a not being consistent; a fluctuating; difference, divergence; variation; fluctuation. 2. a remaining behind; a being left behind; backwardness.

tahallül 1 تحلّل A *lrnd.* 1. a being melted, dissolved or decomposed; solution, decomposition. 2. a being resolved or reduced; resolution, reduction.

tahallül 2 تخلّل A *lrnd.* 1. a penetrating, a passing into or through; penetration. 2. time's intervening. 3. a disturbing; disturbance, discord.

tahammi تحمّي A *lrnd.* 1. a taking care of oneself. 2. an observing a diet or taking medical precautions; diet; care.

tahammuz تحمّض A 1. *chem.* oxidation. 2. *lrnd.* a becoming sour.

tahammül^lü تحمّل A 1. a supporting or carrying a burden. 2. an enduring suffering; endurance, long-suffering, patience, forbearance. 3. *lrnd.* an undertaking, accepting. **— et=** /a/ to endure, support, put up with. **—ât** (...—) A *lrnd., pl.* of **tahammül**.

tahammülfersa (....—) تحمّل‌فرسا P *lrnd.* intolerable.

tahammülgüdaz (....—) تحمّل‌گداز P *lrnd.* unendurable, intolerable.

tahammülsûz (...—) تحمّل‌سوز P *lrnd.* intolerable.

tahammülsüz تحمّل‌سز impatient, intolerant. **—lük** impatience, intolerance.

tahammür تحمّر A 1. a fermenting; fermentation. 2. *lrnd.* a becoming drunk with wine. 3. *lrnd.* a veiling the head leaving only the eyes visible (woman). **— et=** 1. to ferment. 2. *lrnd.* to muffle oneself. **—ât** (...—) A *lrnd., pl.* of **tahammür**.

tahan طحن *var. of* **tahin 1**.

tahanni تحنّي A *lrnd.* a being bent, a becoming crooked.

tahannut تحنّط A *lrnd.* a perfuming oneself with a mixture of camphor. (*cf.* **hanut 2**).

tahannüf تحنّف A *lrnd.* a being or becoming a follower of the true God and of the Hanefi school.

tahannün تحنّن A *lrnd.* a being affectionate towards one's young with tender noises (mother).

taharet (.—.) طهارت A 1. cleanliness, purity. 2. canonical purification (of the body). **— bezi** a very small towel (used for canonical ablutions). **— kâğıdı** toilet paper. **— podrası** depilatory powder.

taharethane (.—.—.) طهارت‌خانه P 1. washroom. 2. toilet.

taharetlen=^ir طهارت‌لنمك to cleanse and purify oneself.

taharir (.——) تحارير A *lrnd., pl.* of **tahrir**.

taharri (..—) تحرّي A 1. a searching for, seeking for; search. 2. a searching, an investigation, an inquiring into; investigation; research. 3. *myst.* a seeking the course most pleasing to God when such a course cannot be authoritatively known; a doing one's best. **— et=** /ı/ 1. to investigate, to seek. 2. to search for. **— memuru** plainclothes policeman, detective. **—yat** (...—) A *lrnd., pl.* of **taharri**.

taharruk^ku **1** تحرّك A *lrnd.* 1. a being or becoming torn, ragged; raggedness; tatters 2. a blustering of the wind.

taharrukᵏᵘ 2 تَحَرُّك A *lrnd.* 1. combustion. 2. a being in a state of fever, feverishness; anguish.

taharrüc تَحَرُّج A *lrnd.* 1. a passing an examination with honor (pupil). 2. a being clearly rendered or explained (opinion).

taharrüf تَحَرُّف A 1. *astr.* aberration. 2. *lrnd.* an inclining to one side; deviation, inclination. 3. *lrnd.* a becoming changed and corrupted (word).

taharrükᵏᵘ تَحَرُّك A 1. *lrnd.* a moving, stirring, shaking, vibrating; motion, vibration; oscillation. 2. *gram.* a being immediately followed in pronunciation by a vowel (consonant). —**iyet** motivity.

taharrüm تَحَرُّم A *lrnd.* 1. a being or becoming sacred or inviolable to others and restricted in action (man). 2. a performing an act which makes one inviolable and sacred. 3. an abstaining from any unworthy act. **T— Suresi** *a name of the sixty-sixth sura of the Quran.* —**ât** (...—) A *pl.* of **taharrüm**.

taharrüs تَحَرُّس A *lrnd.,* same as **taharrüz**.

taharrüş تَحَرُّش A *lrnd.* irritation, an itching. —**ât** (...—) A *pl.*

taharrüz تَحَرُّز A *lrnd.* a taking precautions; caution; precaution.

tahassulˡᵘ̈ تَحَصُّل A 1. *biol., psych.* reproduction. 2. *lrnd.* a resulting; an occurrence. 3. *lrnd.* a being existent, a becoming present; existence, presence. — **et=** to be produced, to result.

tahassun تَحَصُّن A *lrnd.* a withdrawing into a stronghold, a fortifying, entrenching oneself. — **et=** to retire to a fortress, to shut oneself up in a stronghold.

tahassus تَحَصُّص A *lrnd.* 1. a being or becoming endowed with a special quality. 2. a being or becoming particular.

tahassün تَحَسُّن A *lrnd.* a being or becoming beautiful, agreeable or admired.

tahassür 1 تَحَسُّر A a grieving, regretting the absence of a loved person or thing; a yearning, longing.

tahassür 2 تَحَسُّر A *lrnd.* a becoming thick, viscid; coagulation.

tahassürât (...—) تَحَسُّرات A *lrnd.* longings, yearnings.

tahassüs تَحَسُّس A 1. a being moved or impressed; feeling, sensation. 2. *lrnd.* a listening and inquiring earnestly. —**ât** (...—) A emotions, feelings.

tahasum (.—.) تَخاصُم A *lrnd.* a disputing with each other; mutual dispute, enmity.

tahaşşi تَحَشِّي A *lrnd.* a standing in awe of; fear, awe, dread.

tahaşşuᵘᵘ تَحَشُّع A *lrnd.* 1. a casting one's eyes humbly to the ground. 2. a being ostentatiously humble in demeanor; a humbling oneself; submissiveness, humility.

tahaşşüd تَحَشُّد A *lrnd.* a collecting together; concentration. —**ât** (...—) *pl.*

tahaşşül تَحَشُّل A *lrnd.* a being abject, a becoming despised.

tahaşşün تَحَشُّن A *lrnd.* a being coarse, a becoming harsh to the senses; roughness, hardness, asperity.

tahaşşür تَحَشُّر A *lrnd.* a being raised from the dead, resurrection.

tahatti (..—) تَخَطِّي A *lrnd.* an overstepping a limit, a transgressing, transgression.

tahattur تَخَطُّر A *lrnd.* an occurring to the mind; recollection. — **et=** /ı/ to call to mind, to remember. —**ı mübhem** *phil.* reminiscence.

tahattüm 1 تَحَتُّم A *lrnd.* a being or becoming necessary, incumbent, unavoidable; necessity.

tahattüm 2 تَخَتُّم A *lrnd.* 1. a putting a signet ring on one's finger. 2. an observing secrecy. 3. a withdrawing into oneself, seeing and saying nothing.

tahavif (.——) تَخاويف A *lrnd.,* pl. of **tahvif**, threatenings, menaces; things with which one is threatened.

tahavvüf تَخَوُّف A *lrnd.* a fearing; fear.

tahavvül تَحَوُّل A 1. a turning, a changing; change, transformation. 2. *lrnd.* a moving from place to place; motion, transition. —**i âni** *biol.* mutation.

tahavvülât (...—) تَحَوُّلات A *lrnd.* changes, transformations. —**ı külliye** great changes.

tahayül (.—.) تَخايل A *lrnd.* 1. an appearing, a seeming to be; appearance. 2. a being conceited, a becoming haughty, arrogant; conceit, pride, arrogance.

tahayyül تَخَيُّل A 1. a forming an idea of a thing, an imagining; imagination; idea, notion. 2. a fancying, a creating in the imagination; fancy. — **et=** /ı/ 1. to picture to oneself. 2. to fancy (an unreal thing).

tahayyülât (...—) تَخَيُّلات A *lrnd.* fancies; imaginations.

tahayyülî (...—) تَخَيُّلي A *lrnd.* pertaining to imagination or fancy, imaginary.

tahayyülkerde تَخَيُّلكرده P *lrnd.* imagined; fancied.

tahayyür تَحَيُّر A *lrnd.* 1. a being dazzled. 2. a being amazed, bewildered, perplexed; bewilderment, amazement; perplexity, confusion. —**ât** (...—) A *pl.*

tahayyüz تَحَيُّز A *lrnd.* 1. an acquiring special distinction or importance (of rank or position). 2. a being or becoming existent, comprehended or included in a place or class; existence.

tahazzuᵘᵘ تَحَضُّع A *lrnd.* a being or becoming humble; humility.

tahazzüb تحزّب A *lrnd.* a collecting into groups, parties, or troops.

tahazzün تحزّن A *lrnd.* a being or becoming sad; sorrowfulness, grief.

tahazzür تحزّر A *lrnd.* a being on one's guard, a becoming vigilant; care, vigilance, circumspection.

tahbir (.—) تحبير A *lrnd.* a telling, an informing.

tahbiz (.—) تحبيذ A *lrnd.* acclamation, a saying bravo!

tahcil 1 (.—) تحجيل A *lrnd.* a making one ashamed, a putting to shame; a humiliating.

tahcil 2 (.—) تحجيل A *lrnd.* a putting a bride into her bridal room.

tahdiⁱⁱ (.—) تحديع A *lrnd.* a deceiving, outwitting, tricking; deceit, guile.

tahdib (.—) تحديب A *lrnd.* 1. a making one's back humped. 2. a making protuberant, prominent, convex.

tahdid (.—) تحديد A 1. a limiting, a keeping circumscribed; limitation, circumscription. 2. a defining by a logical definition; definition. 3. a setting the limits or boundaries of a thing or place; delimitation. 4. *lrnd.* a sharpening, a whetting, a pointing. — **et=** /ı/ to limit. —**i sin** *law* age limit.

tahdidât (.——) تحديدات A *lrnd.* limitations; restrictions.

tahdidî (.——) تحديدى A *lrnd.* limitative, restrictive. — **hükümler** *law* restrictive provisions.

tahdikᵏⁱ (.—) تحديق A *lrnd.* a looking intently, a staring.

tahdir (.—) تحدير A *lrnd.* a making a woman veil herself and keep to the women's apartments.

tahdis (.—) تحديث A *lrnd.* 1. a talking, conversing with. 2. a relating a tale, especially, a tradition. — **et=** /ı/ to tell, relate, especially, to hand down a tradition received from one's own teacher.

tahdiş (.—) تحديش A *lrnd.* 1. a lacerating violently with the nails. 2. a perturbing the mind violently. —**i ezhan et=** to perturb public opinion. —**i hâtır et=** to cause great trouble of mind (to a person). —**ât** (.——) A disturbances.

tahekᵏⁱ تاهك *mus.* an exclamation used in counting time.

tahfif (.—) تخفيف A 1. a rendering light in weight, a lightening; an alleviating, a relieving; relief. 2. *gram.* a pronouncing a consonant without reduplication. — **et=** /ı/ to lighten; to relieve, to mitigate. — **kemeri** *arch.* discharging arch. —**î** (.——) A *law* mitigatory.

tahhan (.—) طحّان A *lrnd.* miller.

tahıl تخيل A *prov.* produce, especially grain cereals. — **biti** weevil.

tahille تحلة A *lrnd.* 1. a lawfully voiding an oath or vow. 2. any act by which an oath or vow is voided (such as a mental reservation or saying "God willing").

tahin 1 طاحين A sesame oil. — **helvası** sweet made of sesame oil and sugar.

tahin 2 (.—) طحين A *lrnd.* flour, meal.

tahine (—..) طاحنة A *lrnd.* grinder, molar tooth.

tahini (.——) طاحينى A of a yellowish gray color.

tahir 1 (—.) طاهر A 1. *lrnd.* clean, pure. 2. *w. cap., man's name.* 3. *Or. mus.* an ancient **makam**. — **buselik** *Or. mus.* a compound **makam** composed about two centuries ago. —**i sagir** *obs.* a **makam**.

tahir 2 (.—) طهير A *lrnd.* clean, pure.

tahiyat (..—) تحيات A *lrnd., pl.* of **tahiye**, salutations, greetings.

tahiye, tahiyet تحية A *lrnd.* 1. a saluting with good wishes, a greeeting; salutation. 2. an ascribing eternity and dominion to God.

tahkikᵏⁱ (.—) تحقيق A 1. an ascertaining, investigating, verifying. 2. *law* a proving by incontrovertible proof. 3. *myst.* the manifestation of God in His divine attributes. 4. *lrnd.* a holding to be real and true; an affirming; a making to be really existent, a giving real existence. — **et=** /ı/ to ascertain, verify, investigate. — **bil=** *archaic* 1. to know for certain. 2. to account certain. — **ehli** *lrnd.* 1. a person who minutely ascertains the verities. 2. a man of exact science; philosopher.

tahkikan (.—´.) تحقيقاً A *lrnd.* 1. really, truly. 2. for certain, for sure.

tahkikat (.——) تحقيقات A 1. investigation; research. 2. inquiry, trial, examination. — **hâkimi** examining judge.

tahkiki (.——) تحقيقى A *lrnd.* of the nature of or resulting from inquiry; sure, certain, confirmatory.

tahkikyafte (.——.) تحقيق يافته P *lrnd.* inquired into and found to be true.

tahkim (.—) تحكيم A *lrnd.* 1. a strengthening, a fortifying. 2. an appointing a judge or arbitrator; arbitration. 3. a holding in, a restraining; restraint, control. — **et=** /ı/ to fortify.

tahkimat (.——) تحكيمات A fortifications.

tahkimname (.——.) تحكيم نامه P *law* arbitration, agreement.

tahkir (.—) تحقير A a treating with contempt, an insulting; insult, scorn. — **et=**

ahkirâmiz

/ı/ to insult, to treat with disdain, to despise. —**ât** (. — —) A *lrnd.* insults.
tahkirâmiz (. — — —) تحقیرآمیز P *lrnd.* contemptuous, insulting.
tahkiye تحکیه A *lrnd.* narration, story-telling.
tahliⁱⁱ (. —) تخلیع A *lrnd.* 1. a freeing from shackles or tethers. 2. a walking with a shuffle as though the hips were out of joint.
tahlid (. —) تخلید A *lrnd.* a causing to live forever, a making eternal.
tahlif 1 (. —) تحلیف A *lrnd.* 1. a causing to take an oath. 2. an adjuring; adjuration. — **et**= /ı/ 1. to administer an oath. 2. to adjure.
tahlif 2 (. —) تخلیف A *lrnd.* 1. a leaving behind. 2. a making a person one's successor or representative.
tahlikᵏⁱ (. —) تحلیس A *lrnd.* a shaving very closely.
tahlil 1 (. —) تحلیل A 1. a solving, decomposing, or analyzing; analysis. 2. *lrnd.* a melting, dissolving. 3. *can. law* a making lawful; a legally voiding a vow or oath. — **et**= /ı/ to analyze.
tahlil 2 (. —) تخلیل A *lrnd.* 1. a pinning, skewering. 2. a making into vinegar; a pickling in vinegar.
tahlilî (. — —) تحلیلی A *sc.* analytical.
tahlim (. —) تحلیم A *lrnd.* 1. a rendering patient, meek, forbearing. 2. an esteeming one to be longsuffering; a deeming meek.
tahlis (. —) تخلیص A *lrnd.* 1. a liberating or rescuing; a keeping or making safe or free from embarrassment or danger; salvation, preservation. 2. a refining, a making pure; purification. —**i giriban** an escape.
tahlisiye تخلیصیه A lifeboat service; salvage. — **sandalı** lifeboat. — **simidi** life buoy.
tahlitᵘ (. —) تخلیط A *lrnd.* 1. a mixing, blending together; adulteration. 2. a bewildering, embarrassing, a confounding. — **et**= /ı/ 1. to blend, to mix; to adulterate, amalgamate. 2. to confuse, to perplex.
tahlitât (. — —) تخلیطات A *lrnd.* blendings, mixtures, amalgams.
tahliye 1 تخلیه A 1. an emptying, vacating; a discharging (of cargo). 2. a setting free (prisoner). 3. *lrnd.* a rendering free from embarrassment. — **et**= /ı/ 1. to discharge (cargo); to empty; to unload. 2. to set free. —**i sebil et**= (*lit.*, to disencumber the path of a person) to set at liberty.
tahliye 2 تحلیه A *lrnd.* an ornamenting, an adorning.
tahmet تحمت A *lrnd.* great rushing mass or crowd. —**i iblis** an assault of the devil.
tahmid (. —) تحمید A *lrnd.* a praising much; a praising God often by repeating the ejaculation **elhamdülillâh**. —**ât** (. — —) A praises.
tahmikᵏⁱ (. —) تحمیق A *lrnd.* a making stupid; a deeming or calling one a fool.
tahmil (. —) تحمیل A *lrnd.* 1. a loading, an imposing (one thing upon another); imposition. 2. an entrusting a matter or a duty. 3. an imputing, attributing an offense; imputation. — **et**= /ı/ 1. to load (ship). 2. to impose (a burden). 3. to trust or confer (a charge). 4. to impute (an offense).
tahmilât (. — —) تحمیلات A *lrnd.* burdens; imputations.
tahmin (. —) تخمین A an estimating; estimate, conjecture, guess. — **et**= /ı/ to estimate, calculate, conjecture. —**ât** (. — —) A *lrnd.* estimates.
tahminen (. —' .) تخمیناً A approximately.
tahminî (. — —) تخمینی A approximate, conjectural.
tahmir 1 (. —) تخمیر A *lrnd.* 1. a leavening; a causing fermentation (by adding curd; yeast, etc.) 2. a kneading to a proper consistency. 3. a veiling or concealing.
tahmir 2 (. —) تحمیر A *lrnd.* a calling one a donkey.
tahmis 1 (. —) تخمیس 1. *poetry* poem composed by adding three lines rhyming with the first line of each couplet of a **gazel**. 2. *lrnd.* a causing to be five, to be composed of five parts; a dividing into fifths.
tahmis 2 (. —) تحمیص A 1. *obs.* establishment for roasting and grinding coffee (for sale). 2. *lrnd.* a parching, roasting.
tahmis 3 (. —) تحمیس A *lrnd.* an angering, a provoking; irritation.
tahmisçi تحمیصجی a roaster and grinder of coffee.
tahmiz (. —) تحمیض A *lrnd.* a making sour; oxidization.
tahn طحن A *lrnd.* a grinding.
tahnet=ᵈᵉʳ طحنی ایتمك /ı/ to grind (in a mill).
tahnikᵏⁱ (. —) تحنیك A *lrnd.* a strangling, a choking; a drowning.
tahnit (. —) تحنیط A *lrnd.* 1. an embalming (of the dead). 2. a stuffing (of animals or birds).
tahra طحره *prov.* pruning hook, reaping-sickle.
Tahran (.' .) طهران *geog.* Teheran.
tahrib (. —) تخریب A *lrnd.*, same as **tahrip**.
tahribat (. — —) تخریبات A destruction.
tahribkâr (. — —) تخریبكار P *lrnd.* destructive, deadly.
tahric (. —) تخریج A *lrnd.* 1. a drawing or putting out, an extracting, expelling; extraction, expulsion, protrusion. 2. a sending forth a pupil perfect in his studies (by his teacher). 3. an explaining or rendering the meaning of a

saying. **—i menat** an educing a theological reason for a divine decree.

tahrif 1 (.—) تَحْرِيْن A 1. a changing, diverting, perverting. 2. a corrupting or distorting the orthography of a word; distortion. 3. a corruption of a tradition by an alteration of a letter or a vowel. 4. a corrupting a word of the Quran in recitation. 5. a falsifying of a document (by erasure or addition); fraudulent alteration. **— et=** /ı/ to falsify, distort, misrepresent, alter fraudulently.

tahrif 2 (.—) تَحْرِيْف A *lrnd.* 1. a deeming or pronouncing one a dotard. 2. a making or letting talk nonsense. 3. a being or becoming a dotard and talking nonsense.

tahrifat (.——) تَحْرِيفَات A *lrnd.* falsification of documents.

tahrik[kı] **1** (.—) تَحْرِيك A 1. a moving, a causing to move or vibrate. 2. an inciting, impelling, instigating; incitement, provocation. 3. an exciting; excitation. 4. *Arabic gram.* a marking a consonant with a vowel-point; a making a consonant movent. **— et=** /ı/ to incite, provoke, instigate.

tahrik[kı] **2** (.—) تَحْرِيق A *lrnd.* 1. a burning much or frequently. 2. a consuming by fire. 3. a causing to be very thirsty.

tahrik[kı] **3** (.—) تَحْرِيق A *lrnd.* 1. a tearing, a rending; laceration. 2. a lying outrageously.

tahrikâmiz (.———) تَحْرِيك آميز P *lrnd.* provocative, subversive.

tahrikât (.——) تَحْرِيكات A *lrnd.* provocations, instigations.

tahril تَحْرِيل [tahrir] a symmetrical marking or ornamentation.

tahrilli تَحْرِيلى ornamented with lines of color or embossed work. **— göz** an eye that naturally looks as if the eyelids were artificially darkened.

tahrim (.—) تَحْرِيم A *lrnd.* 1. a causing to be unlawful or sacred, a prohibiting, a making inviolable; prohibition; consecration. 2. a deeming to be prohibited, unlawful or sacred. **— et=** /ı/ 1. to prohibit, to declare unlawful. 2. to hold to be unlawful or sacred. **T— Suresi** *name of the sixty-sixth sura of the Quran.*

tahrimât (.——) تَحْرِيمات A *lrnd.,* pl. of **tahrim.**

tahrime (.—.) تَحْرِيمَه A *lrnd.* a saying **Allahüekber** at the beginning of the prayer.

tahrimî (.——) تَحْرِيمى A *lrnd.* 1. pertaining to divine prohibition or sacred ritual. 2. prohibitive; prohibited by Canon law.

tahrip[bı] (.—) تَحْرِيب [tahrib] a ruining, destroying, devastating; devastation, destruction. **— et=** /ı/ to destroy, ruin, devastate. **— maddesi** an explosive. **— mermisi, — tanesi** high explosive shell.

tahrir (.—) تَحْرير A 1. a writing, a setting forth in words; essay, composition. 2. a registering; registration. 3. *Ott. hist.* land survey for taxation purposes; land registers. 4. *lrnd.* a freeing from impurity, defect, or obscurity. 5. *lrnd.* an emancipating a slave, a giving freedom; manumission. 6. *lrnd.* an illuminating the pages of books; ornamental lines. **— çek=** *art* to draw ornamental lines around the gilding between the written lines. **— defteri** *Ott. hist.* written survey of a province. **— emini** *Ott. hist.* land surveyor. **—i emlâk** land registry. **— et=** /ı/ 1. to set down in writing, to write. 2. to draw up (a document). 3. to register. 4. *lrnd.* to free. **— heyeti** editorial board. **— müdürü** sub-editor. **—i nüfus** census.

tahrirât (.——) تَحْريرات A 1. documents; dispatches. 2. official letter; circular note. **— kalemi** secretariat. **— kâtibi** head secretary to a district director. **— müdürü** secretary general.

tahriren (.—´.) تَحْريرًا A *lrnd.* 1. in writing. 2. written.

tahrirî (.——) تَحْريرى A written. **— beyyine** *law* documentary evidence.

tahrirkeş (.—.) تَحْريركش P *lrnd.* 1. scribe, writer. 2. illuminator of manuscripts.

tahrirli تَحْريرلى same as **tahrilli.**

tahris[sı] (.—) تَحْريص A *lrnd.* 1. making greedy, grasping, or desirous. 2. an inciting to strive after something. **— et=** /ı/ 1. to make covetous. 2. to urge to strive for, to arouse ambition.

tahriş (.—) تَحْريش A 1. a scratching violently with the nails. 2. a being irritated (skin, etc.); irritation. **—ât** (.——) A *lrnd.* irritation.

tahriz (.—) تَحْريض A *lrnd.* an inciting, an instigating. **—ât** (.——) A *pl.*

tahsil (.—) تَحصيل A 1. an obtaining; acquiring; acquisition, acquirement; acquirement of learning or science; study, education. 2. a collecting (money); collection of taxes. 3. *lrnd.* a producing; production. 4. *lrnd.* an extracting, an educing. 5. *log.* a reducing a proposition to the categoric form. 6. *lrnd.* a working out the required letter (in enigmas). **—i emval kanunu** *law* concerning the collection of taxes or legal penalties. **— et=** /ı/ 1. to learn by study, to study. 2. to collect (dues etc.). 3. to produce; to obtain, acquire, gain. 4. to extract or educe. **— gör=** to study, to have education. **—i huruf-i muamma** *lrnd.* operation of finding the answer to an enigma.

tahsilât (.——) تَحصيلات A 1. money collected. 2. dues, taxes.

tahsildar (..—) تَحصيلدار |Persian .——| collector of moneys; tax collector; agent. **—ân**

tahsilî (. — —) P *lrnd., pl.* **—iye** collector's charges; expenses of collection. **—lık** tax collecting.

tahsilî (. — —) تحصیلی A *lrnd.* pertaining to tax collecting.

tahsiliye (. — ..) تحصیلیه A money collector's charges.

tahsin 1 (. —) تحسین A *lrnd.* 1. a deeming to be beautiful or good; approbation; admiration. 2. *obs.* certificate given as a prize in schools. 3. Well done! Bravo! 4. a making beautiful; an embellishing; embellishment, adornment. **— et=** /ı/ 1. to approve, to admire. 2. to embellish or adorn.

tahsin 2 (. —) تحصین A *lrnd.* a making difficult of access, a fortifying, surrounding with a wall. **— et=** /ı/ to fortify.

tahsinhan (. — —) تحسین خوان P *lrnd.* one who praises. **—î** (. — — —) P a praising.

tahsinkerde (. — ..)تحسین کرده P *lrnd.* praised, admired.

tahsinname (. — — .) تحسین نامه P *lrnd.* letter of appreciation.

tahsir 1 (. —) تحسیر A *lrnd.* a throwing into a fit of grief, a causing to mourn, fret or feel regret for a loss.

tahsir 2 (. —) تحسیر A *lrnd.* 1. a causing to suffer loss of goods, fortune or character; a ruining. 2. a deeming or calling one ruined or reprobate.

tahsis (. —) تخصیص A 1. an assigning to a special duty or purpose; assignment; appropriation. 2. a specially endowing; consecration. **— et=** /ı, a/ to assign, to appropriate.

tahsisat (. — —) تخصیصات A special appropriation (of revenue); money earmarked for a special purpose, allowance. **—ı mestûre** discretionary fund (in the government budget).

tahsisen (. — .) تخصیصاً A *lrnd.* especially, particularly.

tahşid (. —) تحشید A *lrnd.* a collecting into a body, an assembling; concentration.

tahşidat (. — —) تحشیدات A *mil.* concentration of troops.

tahşiye 1 تحشیه A *lrnd.* an annotating a writing or a book; annotation; marginal note.

tahşiye 2 تخشیه A *lrnd.* a frightening, a causing to fear.

taht 1 تخت A 1. throne, sovereign's throne. 2. *lrnd.* seat, bench, sofa, litter. **—ı âc** (*lit.*, throne of ivory.) *poet.* 1. day. 2. white things. **—ı âbnusî** ebony throne; *poet.* night. **—a çık=** to ascend the throne, to become king. **—ı firûze** *lrnd.* turquoise throne; the sky. **—a geç=** to succeed to the throne and sovereignty. **— gemisi** *Ott. hist.* the Sultan's special ship. **—ı hümayun** *Ott. hist.* the imperial throne. **—tan indir=** /ı/ to dethrone. **— kadıları** *Ott. hist.* judges of the canonical courts in Istanbul. **T—ı Muhammed** *Bektashi order* the Throne of Muhammad, the special steps on which the candles are placed for the **Ayini Cem** ceremony. **—ı nerd** *lrnd.* backgammon board. **— odası** *Ott. hist.* the Sultan's audience hall. **—a oturt=** /ı/ to enthrone. **—ı revan***. **T—ı Süleymanî** *lrnd.* the flying Throne of Solomon. **T—ı Takdisî** *lrnd.* 1. the ancient Persian throne with places for all the orders of the state on its different steps. 2. *name of a note in Oriental music.*

taht 2 تحت A *lrnd.* under surface (of a thing), space under (a thing); under, beneath. **—ı emniyete al=** /ı/ to secure; to make secure. **—ı emrimde** under my command, under my orders. **—ında müstetir** hidden underneath. **—ı mütezad kazıye** *log.* subcontrary proposition. **—ı nikâhında** (*lit.*, under his wedlock) married to him.

taht 3 (—) تا خت P *lrnd.* 1. a horse's cantering or galloping; a run, a gallop. 2. a marauding; plunder, spoil; assault, invasion. **— ü târâc** a marauding, a pillaging; assault, plunder. **— ü tâz** 1. run, race. 2. cavalry charge, assault.

tahta تخته P 1. board, plank. 2. wood; wooden. 3. anything made of boards with flat surface; blackboard. 4. slab, tablet or plate of metal or stone. 5. bed (in a garden). 6. a sheet of fur sewed and prepared for use in lining a garment. **bir —da** in cash; all at once (payment). **—dan** of wood, wooden. **— bacak** wooden leg. **— başı** something written at the upper end of a board (as the name at the head of a list); a chief man. **— bezi** scrub rag; coarse cloth (for cleaning the floor). **— biç=** to saw out planks. **— biti** bedbug, *zool.*, *Cimex lectularius.* **—ya, çamaşıra git=** to go out to work as a charwoman. **—sı eksik** *colloq.* half-witted. **—yı evvel** *lrnd.* 1. a board on which a child learns his letters. 2. *Isl. theol.* the tablet on which are inscribed God's decrees and revelations to man from all eternity. **— güvercini** *same as* **tahtalı güvercin**. **— havale** picket fence, palisade. **— işleri** cabinet-maker's work, woodwork. **—ya kaldır=** /ı/ to call the pupil to the blackboard. **— kaplı** boarded, planked. **— kehlesi** *same as* **tahta biti**. **— kılıç** wooden sword. **— kiremit** roof made of tile-shaped boards. **— kumu** sand used for scrubbing floors. **— kurdu** woodworm. **— kurusu** *same as* **tahta biti**. **— külâh** 1. wooden candle snuffer. 2. conical roof to a spire. **— pabucu, — papuç** clogs. **— perde** fence or partition of boards. **— sakal** 1. flat, even and longish beard. 2. whose beard is flat and broad.

tahtaboş تخت بوش *var. of* **tahtapuş**.
Tahtacı تختجى 1. *Takhtajy, member of an Alevi group in Anatolia*. 2. *l. c.* sawyer or cutter of boards.
tahtakoz تخت قوز *Gk slang* police.
tahtalı تختلو ,تختلى 1. planked; boarded. 2. laid out in beds (garden). 3. turtle dove, *zool., Streptopelia turtur;* ring dove, wood pigeon, *zool., Columba palumbus*. — **güvercin** *same as* **tahtalı**³. — **han**, — **köy** *slang* cemetery. — **köyü boyla=** *slang* to die. — **köye yolla=** *slang* to kill.
tahtani (.——) تحتانى *A lrnd.* 1. pertaining to the lower or under part of anything; lower. 2. ground floor (of a house).
tahtapuş تخت پوش *P* raised platform on a roof (with posts for clothes lines).
tahtarevalli تخت روللى [tahtı revan] *same as* **tahterevalli**.
tahtasenk^gi تخته سنك *P art* palette.
tahtdar (.—) تخت دار *P lrnd.* sovereign. —**i** (.——) *P* sovereignty.
tahtelarz تحت الارض *A lrnd.* subterranean.
tahtelbahir^hri تحت البحر *A* 1. a submarine. 2. *lrnd.* submarine.
tahtelcild تحت الجلد *A med.* subcutaneous.
tahtelhıfz تحت الحفظ *A lrnd.* under escort.
tahterevalli تخت روالى [tahtı revan] seesaw, teeter-totter.
tahtessıfır تحت الصفر *A lrnd.* below zero.
tahteşşuur (...—) تحت الشعور *A psych.* subconscious.
tahtgâh (.—) تختگاه *P lrnd.* 1. royal throne room. 2. capital. —**ı saltanat** residence of the sovereign, capital.
tahtıravan تخت روان *same as* **tahtırevan**.
tahtıravancı تخت روانجى *Ott. hist.* sedan-bearer. — **başı** *Ott. hist.* chief of the sedan-bearers at the Imperial Court.
tahtırevan (...—) تخت روان *P* litter; palanquin.
tahtie تخطئه *A lrnd., same as* **tahtiye**.
tahtim (.—) تختيم *A lrnd.* a sealing with a seal or signet.
tahtit^tı (.—) تخطيط *A lrnd.* 1. a marking with lines, a striping; a being marked or woven in stripes. 2. a writing, an inscribing; a being written or inscribed. —**i arazi** topography.
tahtiye تخطيه *A lrnd.* 1. a causing to fail or make a mistake. 2. a considering or pronouncing to have failed or mistaken; a blaming for a fault. 3. a making one overstep a limit. — **et=** /ı/ 1. to accuse of error; to pronounce in error. 2. to cause to fail or mistake. 3. to cause to transgress.
tahtnişin (..—) تخت نشين *P lrnd.* sitting on the throne; reigning prince; sovereign.
tahun (——), tahune (——.) طاحون ,طاحونه *A lrnd.* mill, grist-mill.

tahur (.—) طاهر *A lrnd.* 1. purifying, cleansing; that by which anything is purified or cleaned. 2. clean, pure.
tahvif (.—) تخويف *A lrnd.* 1. a frightening, menacing. 2. threat; intimidation. —**ât** (.——) *A pl. of* **tahvif**. —**en** (.—´.) *A* by frightening, threateningly.
tahvil (.—) تحويل *A* 1. a transforming, converting; transfer; conversion. 2. draft, security, commercial bill. 3. a changing, altering, transmuting. 4. *Ott. hist.* appointment of a high official or fief-holder. 5. *astrol.* a passing from one sign of the zodiac to another (sun, etc.). 6. *math.* a reducing a fraction. —**i düyun** *law* conversion of a public loan. — **kalemi** *Ott. hist.* the Exchequer Bill Office at the Ministry of Finance. — **kesedarı** *Ott. hist.* official in charge of high appointments.
tahvilât (.——) تحويلات *A* 1. *com.* debentures, bonds, securities. 2. *astrol.* passages of heavenly bodies from sign to sign.
tahvin (.—) تخوين *A lrnd.* a considering to be treacherous; accusing of treachery.
tahvit^tı (.—) تحويط *A lrnd.* 1. a surrounding with an enclosure. 2. a guarding, a protecting; protection, care.
tahyib (.—) تخييب *A lrnd.* a frustrating, disappointing; frustration, disappointment.
tahyil (.—) تخييل *A lrnd.* 1. a picturing to oneself, an imagining; a fancying; imagination, fancy. 2. a perceiving; perception. 3. a suspecting; suspicion. —**ât** (.——) *A pl.* —**î** (.——) *A* imaginary, imaginative.
tahyir 1 (.—) تحيير *A lrnd.* 1. a dazzling. 2. an amazing, bewildering, puzzling, confusing.
tahyir 2 (.—) تخيير *A lrnd.* 1. a preferring, a choosing; preference, choice. 2. a giving another the choice. —**ât** (.——) *A pl.* —**î** (.——) *A* optional.
tahzib 1 (.—) تحزيب *A lrnd.* 1. a collecting people into groups; a separating into groups. 2. a dividing the Quran into sixty portions.
tahzib 2 (.—) تخضيب *A lrnd.* a dyeing, a coloring intensely. —**i lihye et=** to dye one's beard.
tahzil (.—) تخذيل *A lrnd.* 1. a causing to act like a coward. 2. a defeating, routing, crushing. 3. a rendering abject and contemptible.
tahzin 1 (.—) تحزين *A lrnd.* 1. a making sad, a causing grief. 2. a reading or chanting the Quran in a plaintive tone.
tahzin 2 (.—) تخزين *A lrnd.* a placing, collecting in a treasury or storehouse.
tahzir 1 (.—) تحذير *A lrnd.* 1. a causing to be on the alert and circumspect; a cautioning, warning. 2. a threatening or menacing in order to produce circumspection; a causing to fear.

tahzir 2 (. —) تَحْضِير A *lrnd.* 1. a making green. 2. a bruising the skin and so discoloring it.

taınᵃⁿⁱ طَعَنِ *var. of* **ta'n 7.**

Taî (— —) طَائِي A belonging to the tribe of **Tay.**

taib (— .) تَائِب A *lrnd.* who repents, who forsakes sin and vows not to repeat it; penitent.

taif (— .) طَائِف A *lrnd.* 1. that goes round, revolves. 2. patrol, watchman. 3. apparition, specter.

taife (— . .) طَائِفَة A 1. class, sect or body of men; tribe. 2. crew of a ship; gang. 3. *lrnd.* that goes round, revolves. **—i bağiye** perverse and rebelling group. **—i nisa** *lrnd.* the women. **—i zükûr** *lrnd.* the men.

tail (— .) طَائِل A *lrnd.* profit, utility.

tair (— .) طَائِر A *lrnd.* 1. flying. 2. volatile. 3. bird, any winged thing. **—i feza-i ins** the human soul. **—i hayal** imagination. **T—i Kudüs** the angel Gabriel. **—i pürneş'e** a merry bird. **—i sidre** the angel Gabriel.

takᵏⁱ **1** طَاق thump, knock. **— tak vur=** to knock repeatedly, to strike with noise.

tâkᵏⁱ **2** (—) طَاق A 1. arch, vault. 2. *lrnd.* fold, stratum. **—i baziçereng** *lrnd.* the spheres, fortune. **—i ebru** *lrnd.* an arched eyebrow. **—i ezrak, —i hazra** *lrnd.* vault of the sky. **—i mukarnas** *lrnd.* the throne of Solomon; the sky, heaven. **—i târem** *lrnd.* vault of the sky. **— ü turum, — ü türümb** *lrnd.* magnificence; pomp; ostentation. **—i zafer** triumphal arch.

tak=ᵃʳ **3** تَغْمِير 1. /ı, a/ to affix, attach, append. 2. /ı, a/ to give as a present (to a bride). 3. /ı/ to put on; to wear. 4. /ı, a/ to give (a name). 5. /a/ *slang* to incur a debt; to cheat. 6. /ı/ *slang* to consider, to take notice of (person). 7. /dan/ *school slang* to fail (an examination). **—ıp takıştır=** to adorn oneself elaboratery.

tâkᵏⁱ **4** (—) تَاك P *lrnd.* vine; grape vine.

taka 1 طَاقَة small sailing boat.

taka 2 طَاقَة [*Arabic* —.] *prov.* 1. small upper window near the ceiling. 2. small doorless cupboard in a wall.

taka 3 طَاق a bolt of a certain kind of cloth.

takabbuz تَقَبُّض A *lrnd.* 1. a being or becoming contracted or shriveled; contraction. 2. a drawing oneself up because of dislike of a thing. **—ât** (. . . —) A *pl.*

takabbül تَقَبُّل A *lrnd.* a receiving willingly; an admitting, accepting. **— et=** /ı/ 1. to receive willingly. 2. to undertake (a task, etc.).

takaddese تَقَدَّسَ A *lrnd.* May He be sanctified. **— ve taalâ** May He be sanctified and exalted.

takaddüm تَقَدُّم A *lrnd.* a preceding; precedence; priority. **— et=** /a/ to precede, to anticipate. **—ât** (. . . —) A antecedents.

takaddür تَقَدُّر A *lrnd.* 1. a being, becoming possible and feasible. 2. a being foreordained by God.

takaddüs تَقَدُّس A *lrnd.* a being pure and holy; holiness, sanctity, purity.

takadim (. —.) تَقَادِم A *lrnd., pl. of* **takdime.**

takadir (. — —) تَقَادِير A *lrnd., pl. of* **takdir.**

takadüm (. —.) تَقَادُم A 1. *law* a being debarred a hearing as past date (claim). 2. *lrnd.* a being ancient or without beginning, a being eternal.

takahkur تَقَهْقُر A *lrnd.* a retreating hastily.

takalib (. — —) تَقَالِيب A *lrnd., pl. of* **taklib,** revolutions, vicissitudes; changes.

takallûs تَقَلُّص A a shrinking, contracting; contraction (of muscles, etc.).

takallüb تَقَلُّب A *lrnd.* 1. change, revolution; transformation. 2. a changing of events. 3. a rolling, tossing oneself. **—ât** (. . . —) A changes, revolutions.

takallüd تَقَلُّد A *lrnd.* 1. a putting on or wearing a necklace or collar. 2. a putting on or wearing a sword (slung on a baldric from the right shoulder). 3. a taking command and authority upon oneself. **—i kazâ** *law* acceptance of judgeship. **—i süyuf** a wearing of sword. **—ât** (. . . —) A *pl.*

takamaka طَقَمَاقَا E gum tacamahac, tacamahac resin.

takamür (. —.) تَقَامُر A *lrnd.* a gambling with one another.

takanakᵃⁱ طَاقَانَاق *prov.* attachment; relation.

takannun تَقَنُّن A *lrnd.* a becoming a law; a being finally fixed.

takarir (. — —) تَقَارِير A *lrnd., pl. of* **takrir.**

takariz (. — —) تَقَارِيظ A *lrnd., pl. of* **takriz 1.**

takarruh تَقَرُّح A *lrnd.* a being or becoming wounded or ulcerated; ulceration.

takarrüb تَقَرُّب A *lrnd.* 1. a being or becoming near; approach; proximity. 2. a worshipper's drawing near to God. **— et=** /a/ to approach. **— kesbet=** 1. to acquire or be favored with personal proximity. 2. to enjoy communion with God. **—ât** (. . . —) A *pl.*

takarrür تَقَرُّر 1. a being or becoming established; a being decided. 2. a being or becoming confirmed, proved. 3. *lrnd.* a being stationary. **— et=** to be decided or confirmed.

takas تَقَاص [*Arabic* . —] A 1. a setting off claims against each other; a clearing of indebtedness. 2. exchange of goods; compensation. **— et=** to balance off (mutual claims, debts, etc.). **— odası** clearing house. **— tukas ol=** to be all square (claims, accounts, etc.). **— usulü** *com.* clearing system.

takasir (. — —) تَقَاصِير A *lrnd., pl. of* **taksir.**

takasit (. — —) تَقَاسِيط A *lrnd., pl. of* **taksit.**

takassi نقصّی A *lrnd.* an investigating thoroughly.

takasur (. —.) تقاصر A *lrnd.* a shortcoming in duty.

takaşşuu تقشّع A *lrnd.* a spitting, an extracting phlegm.

takaşşür تقشّر A *lrnd.* a forming a skin, shell or bark.

takatᵗⁱ (—.) طاقت A 1. strength; power; *phys.* capacity. 2. potency; energy. — **getir**= /a/ to endure. —**i kalma**= to have no more strength left. —**i kesil**=, —**i tüken**= to get exhausted.

takatfersa (—..—) طاقت فرسا P *lrnd.* unbearable, beyond endurance.

takatgüdaz (—..—) طاقت گداز P *lrnd.* that wears out strength.

takatsiz طاقت سز powerless, weak; exhausted. —**lik** exhaustion; weakness.

takatşiken (—...) طاقت شکن P *lrnd.* weakening, exhausting.

takattur تقطّر A *lrnd.* 1. a falling drop by drop, dripping. 2. distillation.

takatuᵘᵘ (. —.) تقاطع A *lrnd.* 1. an intersecting; intersection. 2. a cutting off friendly relations with one another.

takatuka (...'.) طاقا طوق طاقترقه طا قطرقه [**taktuka**] 1. noise, tumult. 2. a large ashtray. 3. a kind of roller used in printing.

takatur (.—.) تقاطر A *lrnd.* a dropping, a dripping.

takavim (.——) تقاويم A *lrnd.*, *pl.* of **takvim**.

takavvi تقوّی A *lrnd.* a growing strong, acquiring strength.

takavvül تقوّل A *lrnd.* a fabricating an assertion, asserting falsely; a telling a lie about another. —**ât** (...—) A *pl.*

takavvüm تقوّم A *lrnd.* an acquiring the requisite degree of consistency; a becoming straightened.

takavvüs تقوّس A *lrnd.* 1. a being or becoming arched like a bow; curvature. 2. a taking up or bearing one's bow.

takavvüt تقوّت A *lrnd.* a providing food for oneself; alimentation.

takayyüd تقيّد A *lrnd.* a paying attention to; attention, care.

takayyüdat (...—) تقيّدات A *lrnd.* precautions, precautionary measures.

takayyüh تقيّح A *lrnd.* a suppurating; suppuration.

takaza 1 نقاضا [**takaza 2**] a taunting; taunt. — **et**= to taunt, to reproach mockingly.

takaza 2 (.—.) تقاضی A *lrnd.* 1. a dunning, exacting. 2. a continually and insistently urging one to do something.

takazzüh تقزّح A *phys.* iridescence.

takbib (.—) تقبيب A *lrnd.* a constructing a dome or cupola.

takbih (.—) تقبيح A a disapproving, a blaming; disapproval; blame. — **et**= /ı/ to blame, to censure; to disapprove.

takbihat (.——) تقبيحات A *lrnd.* disapproval; expressions of disapproval.

takbil (.—) تقبيل A *lrnd.* a kissing.

tâkçe (—.) طاقچه P *lrnd.* little arch, vault, or window.

takdim (.—) تقديم A 1. a presenting, an introducing; presentation. 2. an offering; offer. 3. *lrnd.* a giving precedence. — **et**= /ı, a/ 1. to introduce (one person to another). 2. to present, offer. 3. *lrnd.* to give precedence or preference (to). — **ü tehir** change of place of words or sentences in a writing. —**ât** A *lrnd.* presents, offerings.

takdime تقدمه A 1. *lrnd.* a present laid before a superior. 2. *Bib.* offering.

takdimen (.—'.) تقديماً A *lrnd.* by giving precedence or priority. — **müzakere** *law* discussion by priority.

takdir (.—) تقدير A 1. an appreciating a value; appreciation. 2. an estimating; estimate; a fixing beforehand a quantity; prearrangement. 3. supposition, hypothesis; a supposed case. 4. God's preordaining; providential foreordination; predestination, fate. —**e bağlı muamele** *law* discretionary act. — **böyle imiş** It was so decreed. — **et**= /ı/ 1. to appreciate; to know the value of; to understand. 2. to estimate. 3. to foreordain; to prearrange. — **hakkı** 1. judicial discretion. 2. valuer's commission. —**i ilâhi** divine dispensation; destiny. —**i kıymet** evaluation. — **salâhiyeti** *law* discretionary power. — **tedbiri bozar** God's decree overrides man's plans. — **topla**= to seek recognition.

takdirâmiz (.———) تقديرآميز P *lrnd.* appreciative.

takdirât (.——) تقديرات A *lrnd.*, *pl.* of **takdir**.

takdiren (.—'.) تقديراً A *lrnd.* 1. in consideration of; appreciating the fact that. 2. virtually. 3. by supposition.

takdirî (.——) تقديری A *lrnd.* 1. taken for granted, virtually existing; virtual. 2. supposed; estimated. 3. that happens by foreordination.

takdirkâr (.——) تقديرکار P 1. admirer. 2. appreciative.

takdirname (.——.) تقديرنامه P letter of appreciation.

takdis (.—) تقديس A 1. a making holy; sanctification. 2. a dedicating to the service of God; consecration. 3. a holding God to be All-Holy; veneration. — **et**= /ı/ 1. to sanctify, revere. 2. to celebrate the memory (of). 3. to dedicate to divine service. 4. to hold or pro-

ta key   **1088**

nounce God to be All-Holy. —ât (. — —) A *lrnd*. consecrations, dedications.

ta key (—.) تا کی P *lrnd.* whither? to what length? how long?

takfil (. —) تفقيل A *lrnd.* a locking a door.

takfiye تفقيه A *lrnd.* 1. a rhyming a verse in any particular manner. 2. a causing to follow, a setting on the track of.

takhir (. —) تقهیر A *lrnd.* an overwhelming with a superior force. —ât (. — —) A *pl.*

takı 1. *neol., gram.* particle, enclitic. 2. *prov.* wedding present put around one's neck (necklace, etc.).

takıl 1 تاقل *prov., var.* of **tahıl**.

takıl=ır **2** طاقىلمق طاقیلو 1. *pass.* of **tak= 3**. 2. /a/ to attach oneself to a person. 3. /a/ to annoy with ridicule or impudent attentions; to deride, to banter. —ıp kal= to be stuck.

takıldakgı طاقلداق mill clapper; mill hopper.

takılgan طاقلغان teaser, teasing.

takılı طاقلى affixed, attached.

takılış, takılma طاقلش طاقلمه *verbal n.* of **takıl 2**.

takım طاقم طاقیم تاقیم 1. a set, lot, or number (of things). 2. suit (of clothes); suit (of cards). 3. tea or dinner service. 4. squad of men; boat's crew; gang, *sports* team; *mil.* squad. 5. class (of people). 6. set of instruments. 7. cigarette holder. 8. *biol.* order. 9. *neol., gram.* compound. bir — some; certain; a set of. — aç= *slang* to run while walking. — adalar *geog.* archipelago. — takım in sets, in lots, in classes. — taklavat *colloq.* 1. in all detail; bag and baggage. 2. all together, the whole lot of them. — yatır= *slang* to defeat. — yıldız constellation.

takın=ır طاقنمق /ı/ 1. to assume, put on (airs). 2. to wear (ornaments).

takınakgı *neol., psych.* obsession. —lı obsessed.

takınıl=ır طاقنلمق *pass.* of **takın=**.

takıntı طاقنتى 1. connection (with a person). 2. affair with a woman. 3. small debt. 4. *school slang* temporary failure to pass an examination.

takırda=ır طاقردامق تاقردامك to make a tapping or knocking noise. —t= /ı/ *caus.*

takırdı طاقردى a repeated tapping or knocking noise.

takır takır طاقر طاقر 1. *imitates the noise of horses' hooves, etc.* 2. hard and dry. — vur= to knock repeatedly with a repercussion from each blow.

takır tukur طاقر طوقور 1. an alternation of tapping and knocking sounds. 2. with noise. 3. rough and dry.

takıştır=ır طاقشترمق /ı/ 1. to wear (ornament). 2. to fasten on neatly.

-takini **1** ده کى *cf.* **-daki**.

taki 2 (. —) تقى A *lrnd.* God-fearing, pious, who avoids sin.

ta'kib (. —) تعقيب A *lrnd.* same as **takip**. —ât (. — —) A persecution. —en (. — .) A following.

ta'kid (. —) تعقيد A *lrnd.* 1. a tying or knotting firmly. 2. a making speech obscure and puzzling; obscurity of language; amphibology. 3. a concluding a bargain or treaty. 4. a boiling (a thing till it becomes thick). —i lâfzî *literature* a making speech obscure. —i mânevi *literature* a making the meaning of a thing unintelligible. —ât (. — —) A *pl.*

ta'kil (. —) تعقيل A *lrnd.* 1. a making or letting be understood. 2. a causing to be intelligent or discreet.

ta'kim (. —) تعقيم A *lrnd.* 1. a sterilizing; sterilization. 2. a commanding silence, a silencing. 3. a rendering unfit for conception.

takipbi (— —) تعقيب |ta'kib| 1. a going after, a following. 2. a pursuing; pursuit. 3. a persecuting; persecution. 4. a following up an act with another act. 5. *law* execution. — et= /ı/ to follow; to pursue; to follow up.

takipçi تعقيبجى one whose profession is to follow up legal proceedings for other people.

ta'kir (. —) تعقير A *lrnd.* 1. a wounding much or severely. 2. a hocking; a hamstringing.

takiye تاقيه A *lrnd.,* same as **takke**.

takke طاقیه تقیه تاقيه |takiye| 1. skullcap (of linen for wearing under a turban). 2. nightcap. — at=, —sini havaya at= to throw one's hat into the air for joy. — kap= 1. to snatch the cap (from another's head). 2. to get money (out of a person by some trick). — külâh a thin felt cap worn under another.

takkeduz (.. —) طاقيه دوز P *lrnd.* 1. maker of linen skullcaps. 2. cheat, deceiver.

takkeci طاقيه جى seller of skullcaps.

takla, taklakgı طاقلە طاقلاق تاقلدە تقلە طقلدە تقدره somersault. — at= to turn a somersault. — attır= /a/ to twist someone around one's little finger. — kıl= to turn a somersault.

taklabaz (.. —) طاقلاباز P *lrnd.* tumbler, acrobat.

taklavat طاقلاوات *in* **takım taklavat**, *cf.* **takım**.

takliii (. —) تقليع A *lrnd.* a pulling up by the roots.

taklib (. —) تقليب A *lrnd.* 1. a turning over, an inverting; inversion. 2. a turning inside out, a reversing; reversal. 3. a changing the position, arrangement, or direction of a thing. 4. change, revolution, vicissitude. —i hükûmet *coup d'etat.*

taklibat (. — —) تقليبات A *lrnd.* changes, revolutions.

taklid (. —) تقليد A *lrnd.* 1. *same as* **taklit**.

2. a placing anything around the neck (as necklace, collar or a shoulder belt to a sword); a putting on a sword. 3. a conferring office. 4. blind or implicit obedience and imitation in matters of faith and ritual. —i harekât *psych.* echopraxia. —i kelâm *psych.* echolalia. —i kaza *Ott. hist.* appointment of a judge. —i seyf *Ott. hist.* the girding on by the Sultan of the sword of Othman (the equivalent of a coronation ceremony). —ât (. — —) A *lrnd.*, pl.

takliden (.—′.) تَقْليداً A *lrnd.* 1. by way of imitation or counterfeit. 2. by way of blind, implicit obedience.

taklidî (.——) تَقْليدى A *lrnd.* 1. imitative; counterfeit. 2. that arises out of blind or implicit obedience.

taklidsaz (.——).ـ P *lrnd.* who imitates.

taklil (.—) تَقْليل A *lrnd.* a diminishing; diminution, reduction. —ât (.——) A *pl.*

taklim (.—) تَقْليم A *lrnd.* 1. a cutting off the tip, a clipping. 2. a paring the nails.

taklis (.—) تَقْليس A *lrnd.* 1. an assuming an attitude of deference. 2. a meeting a prince, etc., upon his arrival with acclamation, music and the like.

taklit[di] تَقْليد [taklid] 1. an imitating; imitation. 2. imitated, counterfeit, sham. 3. a mimicking. — et= /ı/ 1. to follow blindly; to imitate. 2. to feign, to sham. 3. to gird on another (sword). 4. to confer (an office). —ini yap= /ın/ to mimic. —çi mimic.

takma طاقْما 1. *verbal n.* of **tak=** 3. 2. stuck on; attached. 3. false (beard, tooth, etc.). 4. prefabricated (house). — **ad** nickname. — **âletleri** make-up appliances. — **diş** false teeth. — **saç** false piece; wig.

takmis[si] (.—) تَقْميص A *lrnd.* to clothe another with a shirt.

taknin (.—) تَقْنين A *lrnd.* to lay down a law.

takoz طاقوز Gk 1. a short stake of wood, cleat or stopper; wooden wedge. 2. prop (used to shore up a ship on the ways). —a al= /ı/ *auto.* to store in a garage (car).

takri[iı] (.—) تَقْريع A *lrnd.* 1. a reprimanding severely; a reproving, chiding. 2. an agitating. —ât (.——) A *pl.*

takrib (.—) تَقْريب A *lrnd.* 1. a bringing near, a giving access, causing to approach; approximation, proximity. 2. means or pretext of access; motive. — et= /ı/ to bring near; to approximate. bir — ile by some means.

takriba (.—.) تَقْريباً A *lrnd.*, same as **takriben**.

takriben (.—.) تَقْريباً A approximately; about.

takribî (.——) تَقْريبى A *lrnd.* approximate.

takrin (.—) تَقْرين A *lrnd.* a causing to become a companion.

takrir (.—) تَقْرير A 1. statement; deposition; official note, report, memorandum. 2. delivery (manner of speaking), lecture. 3. *law* motion (in an assembly). 4. *lrnd.* a confirming, proving. 5. *lrnd.* a making stationary. 6. *law* official notification of transference of real property. —i âli *Ott. hist.* official statement given to the Sultan by the Grand Vizier. —i kelâm et= *lrnd.* to give utterance to words, to speak. —i sual *lrnd.* interpellation. —i sükûn *lrnd.* establishment of public order.

takrirlik[ği] تَقْريرلك paper of the proper size for official documents, foolscap paper. — **kâğıt** foolscap paper.

takriz 1 (.—) تَقْريض A *lrnd.* 1. a pronouncing or writing a eulogy on a literary work; eulogy (of a book). 2. favorable review; appreciatory preface by an important literary man for another's book.

takriz 2 (.—) تَقْريظ A *lrnd.*, same as **takriz 1**.

takrizan (.—′.) تَقْريضاً A *lrnd.* by way of eulogy.

takrizat (.——) تَقْريضات A *lrnd.*, *pl.* of **takriz 1, 2**.

taksa (.′.) تاقْسا F postage due. — **pulu** postage-due stamp. —**lı mektup** postage-due letter.

taksi (.′.) تاقْسى F taxi.

taksim (.—) تَقْسيم A 1. a dividing into parts; division; partition, distribution, *math.* division. 2. reservoir from which water is distributed. 3. *Or. mus.* an instrumental improvisation (corresponding to a vocal **gazel**). —i a'mâl *sociol.* division of labor. — **dâvası** *law* action for partition. — et= /ı/ 1. to divide. 2. to share out; to distribute. — geç= *Or. mus.* to play an improvisation. —i gurema *law*, *lrnd.* proportional division among creditors of a debtor's assets. —i miyah *geog.* divide, watershed. —i müsenna *lrnd.* dichotomy.

taksimat (.——) تَقْسيمات A 1. divisions, sections. 2. scale (of a measuring instrument).

taksir (.—) تَقْصير A *lrnd.* 1. a failure in duty, a being remiss; remissness. 2. fault; sin, trespass. 3. a shortening, abbreviating; a making too short. — et= 1. /ı/ to abbreviate. 2. to be remiss. 3. to commit a fault.

taksirat[tı] (.——) تَقْصيرات A *lrnd.* 1. *pl.* of **taksir**. 2. fault, sin; *colloq.* fate, destiny. —**ı haricinde** through no fault of his. —**lı iflâs** *law* culpable bankruptcy.

taksirli تَقْصيرلى 1. faulty. 2. guilty. — **suçlar** *law* imprudent offenses.

taksirsiz تَقْصيرسز faultless; innocent.

taksit تَقْسيط [*Arabic* .—] installment. —**le** by installments.

takşir (.—) تقشير A *lrnd.* a peeling, skinning.
taktakᵍⁱ طا قطا نه *prov.* wooden instrument for beating washing, laundry beetle.
taktaka طقطقه A *lrnd.* a clattering sound of hard bodies striking.
taktır⁼ⁱʳ طا قتيريه /1, a/ *caus. of* **tak**⁼. 3.
taktiʲⁱⁱ (.—) تقطيع A 1. *pros.* a scanning. 2. *lrnd.* a cutting up. — **et**⁼ 1. to scan (a verse). 2. *lrnd.* to cut up piecemeal. —**ât** (.——) A *pl.*
taktikᵍⁱ تاكتيك F tactics.
taktil (.—) تمتيل A *lrnd.* a killing.
taktir (.—) تقطير A 1. *chem.* a distilling; distillation. 2. *lrnd.* a pouring drop by drop; a dribbling. — **et**⁼ /1/ to distill. —**i yâbis** dry distillation. —**ât** (.——) A *pl.*
tak tuk طا ق طوق imitates the sound of knocking.
taktuka طا قتوقه تا قتوقه طقطوقه A *same as* **takatuka**.
takunya (..ˊ.), **takunye** (..ˊ.) طا قونيه Gk clog; sabot.
takuş tukuş طوقش طوقش with a clatter.
takva (.—) تقوى A *lrnd.* fear of God; piety. — **ehli** pious.
takvil (.—) تقويل A *lrnd.* a falsely attributing a saying to a person. —**ât** (.——) A falsely ascribed utterances.
takvim (.—) تقويم A 1. almanac, calendar. 2. *lrnd.* a straightening; a fixing, an adjusting; a putting in proper order, a making symmetrical, a giving a thing its proper consistency. **T—i Vekayi** *Ott. hist.*, name of the first Ottoman official gazette. — **yılı** calendar year.
takvimçe (.—.) تقويمچه P *lrnd.* small agenda.
takvis (.—) تقويس A *lrnd.* 1. a giving a thing the form of a bow, an arching, bending. 2. a being or becoming arched; curvature.
takvit (.—) تقويت A *lrnd.* a nourishing; alimentation.
takviye تقويه A 1. a strengthening, imparting strength. 2. reinforcement. — **et**⁼ /1/ to strengthen; to reinforce.
takviyet تقويت A *lrnd., same as* **takviye**. — **bul**⁼ to gain strength and support.
takyid (.—) تقييد A *lrnd.* 1. a binding. 2. a putting a condition; restriction. 3. a bewitching, a holding by a spell. — **et**⁼ /1/ 1. to bind, to limit with conditions; to restrict. 2. to bewitch.
takyidât (.——) تقييدات A *lrnd.* restrictions; restriction.
talʳⁱ 1 طلع A *lrnd.* 1. pollen. 2. flower-bud of the date palm.
talˡʰⁱ 2 طل A *lrnd.* drizzle.
tala⁼ʳ طالامه طلامه طالاموه *prov.* /1/ to plunder, to pillage, to loot.

talâb 1 (——) طالاب P *lrnd.* pond, large puddle.
talab⁼ⁱʳ 2, **talabı**⁼ʳ طالانمه طالابمه *archaic* 1. to palpitate, throb. 2. to be agitated; to be in a commotion. 3. to be desirous, to strive.
talabıkᵍⁱ طالابيق *archaic* palpitation; agitation.
talâkᵏⁱ 1 (.—) طلاق A repudiation, divorce (of a wife by her husband). —**ı bain** *can. law* an irrevocable divorce. —**ı selâse** *can. law* final and irrevocable divorce. **T— Suresi** name of the sixty-fifth sura of the Quran.
talakᵏⁱ 2 طلاق *archaic* band of slaves newly reduced to captivity.
talakᵍⁱ 3 طلاق *archaic, same as* **dalak** 1.
talâkatᵗⁱ (.—.) طلاقت A *lrnd.* 1. glibness of tongue; eloquence. 2. a being cheerful and open (countenance).
talâkatli طلاقتلى 1. eloquent. 2. bright, cheerful; open, genial.
talan 1 (——) طالان P *lrnd., same as* **talan** 2.
talan 2 طالان [**talan** 1] pillage, plunder; raid. — **et**⁼ /1/ to plunder; to sack, loot.
talan⁼ⁱʳ 3 طالانمه *pass. of* **tala**⁼.
talapı⁼ʳ, **talapsı**⁼ʳ طالابسيمه *archaic* to be in heat (female animal).
talas طالاس Gk *same as* **talaz**.
talasım (.—.) طلاسم A *lrnd., pl. of* **tılsım**.
talaş 1 طالاش 1. wood shavings; sawdust. 2. filings; raspings. — **kebabı** a kind of meat patty.
talâş 2 طالاش *colloq., same as* **telâş**.
tal'atᵗⁱ طلعت A *lrnd.* aspect, face, countenance; pleasant countenance.
tal'atefrûz, tal'atfürûz طلعت فروز P *lrnd.* scattering light, illuminating.
talâttuf تلطف A *lrnd.* an acting pleasantly, kindly; a favoring, showing kindness; favor, kindness.
talâttufât (...—) تلطفات A *lrnd.* favors, kindnesses.
talâttufan (..ˊ..) تلطفا A *lrnd.* by favor, kindly.
talâttufkâr (...—) تلطفكار P *lrnd.* of genial manners, affable; kind.
talâvet (.—.) طلاوت A *lrnd.* 1. beauty, grace, loveliness. 2. delay; expectancy.
talayiⁱⁱ طلايع A *lrnd., pl. of* **talia**.
talaz طالاز [**tales**] *archaic* 1. foaming wave, billow, surge. 2. whirlwind; cyclone. 3. a being ruffled up (silk, etc.).
talazlan⁼ⁱʳ طالازلانمه 1. to be rough (sea). 2. to be ruffled up, to swell out (silk, etc.). 3. to surge into a mass (driven sheep). —**dır**⁼ /1/ *caus.*
talazlı طالازلى rough (sea).
talazlıkᵍⁱ طالازليق *naut.* washboard.
tâle (—ˊ.) طال A *lrnd.* May it be long

(used in formulas of blessing), *e. g.,* **tâle beka.**
taleb طَلَب A *lrnd., same as* **talep.**
talebdar (..—) طَلَبْدار P *lrnd.* 1. suitor. 2. creditor.
talebe طَلَبَه 1. student; pupil; students. 2. *lrnd., pl. of* **talib.** **—i ilm** *lrnd.* students of Islamic learning.
tâle beka (—'..—) طالِعْ بَقاء A *lrnd.* Long may he live!
taleben (..'.) طَلَبًا A *lrnd.* by asking, seeking.
talebkâr (..—) طَلَبْكار P *lrnd.* 1. desirous; who asks for. 2. applicant. 3. suitor.
talebname (..—.) طَلَبْنامه P *lrnd.* written request.
talep[bl] طَلَب [taleb] 1. an asking; request. 2. a desiring, wishing, longing for; desire; *econ.* demand. 3. a seeking, a striving for, a looking for. **— et=** /ı/ 1. to request, ask for, seek for; to demand. 2. to desire, to long for.
taler (..') طالِرْ G *obs.* Austrian dollar, thaler.
tales same as **talaz.**
talh طَلْح A *lrnd.* gum Arabic acacia, *bot.,* Acacia vera.
tali[ii] **1** (—.) طالِع A 1. *same as* **talih 1.** 2. *lrnd.* that rises, rising (heavenly body); that appears, that comes inside; that happens; occurs.
tali 2 (—.) تالى A 1. secondary; subordinate; *math.* consequent term in proportion; *log.* consequent in a conditional proposition; *Ott. hist.* reserve battalion in the regular army. 2. *lrnd.* that follows; that succeeds; following. 3. *lrnd.* one who recites the Quran. **— had** *log.* consequent.
tali 3 طَلْى A *lrnd.* 1. a rubbing, smearing with an unguent. 2. a silvering or gilding.
talia (.—.) طَلِيعه A *lrnd.* scout; party of scouts, outpost, vanguard.
talib (—.) طالِب A *lrnd.* 1. *same as* **talip 2.** 2. student. **—i dünya** worldly-minded person. **—i ilm** student, scholar.
taliban (—.—) طالِبان P *lrnd., pl. of* **talib.**
talibe (—..) طالِبه A *lrnd.* girl student.
talid (—.) تالِد A *lrnd.* born in one's possession or inherited from one's parents (property, cattle, slaves).
talih 1 (—.) طالِع [tali 1] 1. good fortune, luck. 2. one's star. **—e bağlı** depending on luck. **—i yok** He has no luck.
talih 2 (—.) طالِح A *lrnd.* bad, wicked.
talihli (—..) طالِعْلى lucky, fortunate.
talihsiz (—..) طالِعْسِز who has no luck, luckless, unlucky. **—lik** lucklessness.
ta'lik[kı] **1** (.—) A, **talik**[kı] (——) تَعْلِيق 1. a postponing; postponement. 2. *lrnd.* a suspending; suspension. 3. a making a thing depend on something else. 4. *Arabic calligraphy* a Persian style of writing: ta'liq. 5. *poetry* a making the-sense of a first line depend on what follows. **— et=** 1. /ı/ to suspend; to put off, to postpone. 2. /ı, a/ to attach to, to cause to depend on. 3. /ı, a/ *lrnd.* to refer.
talik[kı] **2** (.—) طَلِيق A *lrnd.* 1. open (of countenance); eloquent. 2. freed; manumitted, emancipated.
tâlik[kı] **3** (—.) طالِق A *lrnd.* divorced, repudiated (woman).
ta'lika 1 (.—.) تَعْلِيقه A *lrnd.* 1. an appendix or marginal note to a writing. 2. coin or pendant suspended as an ornament.
talika 2 (..'.) طالِقه تالِيقه Sl 1. four-wheeled cart with its body suspended on straps. 2. light covered vehicle open at the sides.
talika 3 (—..) طالِقه طَبِيعْ A *lrnd., same as* **tâlik 3.**
ta'likat (.——) تَعْلِيقات A *lrnd.* marginal notes to a writing; annotation.
ta'lil (.—) تَعْلِيل A *lrnd.* 1. an assigning a cause or reason for anything; deduction. 2. a diverting, amusing; an engaging one's attention. **— et=** /ı/ 1. to amuse and divert. 2. to assign a reason for. **— yap=** to deduce.
ta'lim (.—) A, **tâlim** (—.) تَعْلِيم 1. a teaching; instruction. 2. exercise, practice; drill. **— et=** /ı/ 1. to teach; to drill. 2. to practice. **— fişeği** blank cartridge. **— meydanı** exercise ground, drill ground. **— ve taallüm** *lrnd.* a teaching and learning. **— ve terbiye** instruction, training. **T— ve Terbiye Hey'eti** Council of Educational Policy (attached to the Ministry of Education).
talimar طالِيمار [talyamar] *naut.* cutwater. **—lı** furnished with a cutwater.
ta'limat (.——) A, **tâlimat** (—.—) تَعْلِيمات 1. instructions; directions. 2. exercises. **—ı hafiye** *lrnd.* confidential instructions. **—ı resmiye** *lrnd.* official instructions. **— ver=** /a/ to give instructions.
tâlimatnâme (——.—.) تَعْلِيماتْنامه P 1. book of instructions; drill book. 2. regulations.
tâlimci (—..) drill master.
talimgâh (—.—) تَعْلِيمْگاه P *lrnd.* military drill-ground.
ta'limhane (.——.) P, **talimhane** (—.—.) تَعْلِيمْخانه *mil.* parade ground; drill-hall.
talimî (.——) تَعْلِيمى A *lrnd.* pertaining to instruction; educational; didactic.
talimli (—..) تَعْلِيمْلى instructed; practiced; drilled. **— maymun** one who acts only within the limits of what is taught him (like a well-trained monkey).
ta'limname (.——.) P, **talimname** (—.—.) تَعْلِيمْنامه *lrnd.* manual of instruction; drill-book.
talip[bl] (—.) طالِب [talib] 1. desirous, wishful;

seeking; striving for. 2. suitor; customer.
— ol= /a/ to seek (after), to aspire (to), to
strive (for). —li *colloq.* 1. desirous, 2. suitor.
talisiz (—..) طالسز *same as* **talihsiz.**
taliyat (—.—) تاليات A *lrnd.* 1. that recite
the praises of God (angels). 2. *art* accessories.
taliye 1 تاليه A *lrnd.* that follows, that reads
or recites.
ta'liye 2 (.—.) تعليه A *lrnd.* an exalting,
elevating. —i nâme a putting a headline to a
letter.
talk[k1] **1** طالو F 1. talc. 2. mica.
talk[k1] **2** طلق A *lrnd.* pains of childbirth,
birth pangs.
talk[k1] **3** طلق A *lrnd.* 1. free, loose,
unrestrained. 2. still, serene (day).
talküllisan (...—) طلق اللسان A *lrnd.* glib-
tongued, eloquent, speaking with fluency.
talkülyed طلق اليد A *lrnd.* munificent.
talkülyedeyn طلق اليدين A *lrnd.* very munificent,
open-handed.
talkım *neol., bot.* cyme.
talkın تلقين *colloq. for* **telkin.**
tallahi (.—.) تالله A by God (usually in
conjunction with **vallahi**).
taltif (.—) تلطيف A *lrnd.* 1. a gratifying;
kindness; favor. 2. appreciation; recompense.
— et= 1. /ı/ to gratify, to treat with kindness,
to show favor (to). 2. /ı/ to make kind remarks
about. 3. /ı, la/ to confer (a rank). —ât
(.— —) A *pl. of* **taltif.**
taltifen (.—'.) تلطيفا A *lrnd.* in gratification; appreciatively.
taltih[h1] (.—) تلطيخ A *lrnd.* a daubing and
soiling; a dirtying.
talu تالو *archaic* shoulder blade.
Talût (——) طالوت A *Quranic* Saul.
talvar طالوار *prov.* light structure consisting
of posts and a roof of branches, trellis.
talveg تالوگ F *geog.* thalweg.
talya (.'.) طالية It completed; full
count. — de= to call out "Tale", *i. e.* to have
completed a count, to have finished one's work.
talyamar طاليامار طاليا مار It *naut.*,
same as **talimar.**
talyon, talyun طاليون 1. yellow mallow, Indian
mallow, *bot., Abutilon.* 2. plaster of vegetable
juices.
talziye تلظيه A *lrnd.* a blazing, causing to
blaze.
tam 1 تام [*Arabic* tâmm] 1. complete,
entire; exact; completely, exactly. 2. perfect.
— adamına düşmüşsünüz You have found the
very man (for the job or for whom you are
looking, etc.) — aded *math.* whole number.
— bölen *neol., math.* divisor. — çark
1. *watchmakers' term* instrument for cutting
teeth in a wheel. 2. self-acting lathe or engine
for very accurate work. — gel= to fit well
(dress, shoes, etc.). — gideceği sırada just as
he was going. — gölge *astr.* umbra. — kan
full blood, full breed (horse). — kaza davaları
law administrative actions. — örtme *astr.*
total eclipse. — saat astronomical clock,
regulator; chronometer. — sayı *math.* whole
number. — siyah *print.* full black line. —ı
tamına exactly; precisely. — tertip fully,
thoroughly. — tezgâh 1. self-acting lathe.
2. watchmaker's dividing-machine. — üstüne
bas= *colloq.* to hit the mark. — vaktinde
at just the right moment. — yol full speed.
tam 2 طم A a turning and polishing on
a wheel (of copper etc.). — çarhı lathe for
turning and polishing metals.
tam 3 طم *prov., var. of* **dam 1,**
1. roof. 2. house.
ta'm 4 طعم A *lrnd.* 1. taste, flavor; agreeable
flavor. 2. an eating, tasting. 3. matter or virus
introduced into the animal system as in inoculation; graft. —ı bakarî, —ı cederî vaccine.
tama[a1] طمع A 1. a coveting; covetousness,
greed. 2. stinginess, avarice. 3. anything
coveted. 4. *Ott. hist.* pay of a soldier. — et=
/a/ to covet; to desire. —i ham *lrnd.* 1. un-
checked and unconcealed covetousness. 2. desire
for an impossible thing. — ucundan belâya
uğradı He suffered for his cupidity.
tamaan (..'.) طمعا A *lrnd.* /a/ by way of
covetousness; out of greed.
tamah طمع *var. of* **tama.**
tamahkâr (..—) طمعكار [tama'kâr] stingy,
avaricious, greedy. —lık stinginess, greed.
tama'kâr (..—) طمعكار P *lrnd., same as*
tamahkâr.
tamam (.—) تمام A 1. complete; finished;
ready; completely, exactly. 2. just right; true,
correct. 3. a being or becoming complete; completion. 4. a finishing, ending; end. 5. the
whole of a thing; complement. 6. dead; killed.
—! 1. That's right! 2. *used to express unpleasant
surprise.* There you are! What a mess! —iyle
wholly, entirely; in its entirety. — bul=
archaic to be completed; to be finished,
terminated. —ı ceyb *trigonometry* the cosine
of an arc. —ına dinle= /ı/ to listen to (a
story) as though it were true. — et= /ı/
1. to complete, finish, terminate. 2. to kill.
— gel= /a/ to be just right. —ı katı
trigonometry the cosecant of an arc. —ı kavs
trigonometry the complement of an arc. —ı
mümas *trigonometry* the cotangent of an arc.
—ı nisbeti zıllıye *trigonometry* a logarithmic
cotangent. — ol= 1. to be completed, finished,
ended. 2. to be killed. —ı semt *astr.* the
complement of the amplitude, *i. e.* azimuth;
the complement of the azimuth, *i. e.* the

amplitude. **—ı tamamına** exactly; precisely.
— yerine gel= 1. to reach the point of perfection. 2. to get exactly into place. **—ı zıl** *trigonometry* cotangent.
tamamca (...') تَمَامِى fairly complete. **—sına dinle=** /ı/ *same as* **tamamı tamamına dinle=**.
tamamen (.—'.) تَمَامًا A completely, entirely.
tamamî (.——) تَمَامِى A *lrnd.* 1. complementary, integral. 2. completeness, integrity. **—î icra** *lrnd.* complete execution. **—yet** (.—..) A *lrnd.* completeness; wholeness, integrity.
tamla=ᵃʳ تَمَامْلامَق /ı/ 1. to complete, finish. 2. to make good (a defect).
tamamlama تَمَامْلامَه . 1. *verbal n.* 2. *phil.* integration.
tamamlan=ᵃʳ تَمَامْلانمَق *pass. of* **tamamla=**. **—dır=** /ı, a/ *caus. of* **tamamlan=**.
tamamlayıcı تَمَامْلَيْجِى complementary; supplementary.
tamamlıkᵍⁱ تَمَامْلِق integrity, completeness.
taman تَامَان *prov.* you know; well; didn't I?, *e. g.*, **taman dün geldim** Didn't I come yesterday? **taman söyliyecektin** You know you're going to tell me.
tamat (——) طَامَات [**tammat**] high-sounding and boastful or deceptive words; bluster; nonsense.
tambur طَنْبُور [**tanbur**] an ancient form of lute, still in use.
tambura (.—.), **tambure** (.—.) طَنْبُورَه A any string instrument played by plucking. **— gibi** like a lute, *said of a very tight-fitting garment.* **—i Türkî** a kind of small lute. **—cı** player of the **tambura**.
tamburi (.——) طَنْبُورِى A a **tambur** player.
tamburzen (.—.) طَنْبُورزن P *lrnd.* a **tambur** player.
tamıᵃʳ (—.) طَامِع A *lrnd.* coveting, covetous.
ta'mid (.—) تَعْمِيد A *lrnd.* 1. a baptizing. 2. a propping up or supporting; a damming (a current).
ta'mikᵏⁱ (.—) تَعْمِيق A *lrnd.* 1. a making one's researches penetrate a matter; research; profound investigation. 2. a making deep, a deepening. **— et=** /ı/ 1. to go deeply into (something). 2. to deepen. **—at** (.——) A *pl.*
ta'mil (.—) تَعْمِيل A *lrnd.* 1. an appointing as governor or revenue agent. 2. a paying one his wages.
ta'mim (.—) A, **tâmim** تَعْمِيم 1. *adm.* circular (letter). 2. *lrnd.* a making general; generalization. **— et=** /ı/ 1. to announce through a circular. 2. to make general; to generalize. **— olun=** to be circulated. **—ât** A *lrnd.*, *pl.*
tâmimen (.—'.) تَعْمِيمًا A *lrnd.* by circular.

ta'mir (.—) A, **tâmir** (—.) تَعْمِير a repairing; repair; restoration. **—ât** (.——) A repairs.
tâmirhane (—.—.) تَعْمِيرخَانه P repair shop.
ta'miye, ta'miyet (.—) تَعْمِيَة A *lrnd.* 1. a blinding in both eyes, a making blind. 2. a making ineffective. 3. a making a phrase obscure or enigmatical. 4. enigma, riddle, puzzle.
ta'miyetâmiz (...——) تَعْمِيَت آمِيز P *lrnd.* enigmatic.
tamlama *neol.*, *gram.* status constructus; the genitive relationship.
tammaᵃⁱ (.—) طَمَّاع A *lrnd.* exceedingly covetous.
tammat (——) طَمَّات A *lrnd.* overwhelming calamities.
tamme (—.) طَمَّة A *lrnd.* an overwhelming calamity.
tammetülkübra (—....) طَامَّة الكُبْرَى A *lrnd.* the Day of Judgment, resurrection.
tampon تَامْپُون F 1. buffer. 2. *med.* wad, plug. 3. *auto.* bumper. 4. blotter. **— devlet** buffer state.
tams 1 طَمْث A *lrnd.* 1. a being menstruous; a bleeding; blood. 2. a deflowering (a woman).
tams 2 طَمْس A *lrnd.* 1. an effacing; obliterating, obliteration. 2. a converting into dust, destroying. 3. a becoming obliterated or corrupt.
tamtakır (.'..) تَامْ طَاقِر absolutely empty. **— kırmızı bakır**, **— kuru bakır** *colloq.* absolutely empty.
tamtam طَامْ طَامْ F tom-tom.
tamu طَامُو *archaic* hell, the bottomless pit.
tamukᵍᵘ طَامُون تَامُون تَمُون تَمُو *archaic* 1. *same as* **tamu**. 2. cave; pit; dungeon.
tan 1 طَانْ تَانْ طَالْى A dawn. **— ağar=**, **— at=** to dawn. **— yeri***.
tan 2 طَانْ تَانْ *archaic* amazement, astonishment; amazed, perplexed, confused (*cf.* **dan 6**). **— kal=** to be petrified with amazement.
tan 3 تَانْ *archaic* 1. trace, mark, sign, indication. 2. doubt, suspicion. **— değil** It is not a matter of doubt.
-tan 4 تَن *cf.* **-dan 1**.
tan=ᵃʳ 5 تَانْمَق *archaic* to be amazed (*cf.* **dan- 8**.)
tan=ᵃʳ 6 تَانْمَق *archaic* to deny.
ta'n 7 طَعْن A *lrnd.* 1. an offending, criticizing, censuring; wounding words, reproach; calumny. 2. a thrusting, stabbing with a spear and the like. **— et=***.
tanabir (.——) طَنَابِير A *lrnd.*, *pl.* of **tanbur**.
tanakᵍⁱ تَنَك *archaic* strange, queer.
ta'nâmiz (.——) طَعْن آمِيز P *lrnd.* implying blame (words).
tanassur تَنَصُّر A *lrnd.* conversion to Christianity. **— et=** to become a Christian.

tanaz طنز *archaic* joke, merriment.
-tan beri دن بری د ن بری د نبه د د ن به د *cf.*
-dan beri.
tanbur (. —) طنبور A *same as* **tambur**.
Tanca (.'.) طنجه *geog.* Tangiers in Morocco.
tandır طا ند ر طا ند ور تاند ور تنـد ور تا ند ور
[**tennur**] 1. oven made in a hole in the earth. 2. heating arrangement (consisting of a brazier put under a table with a covering over the table and the legs of those sitting around it). — **başında otur=** to sit around a **tandır**. — **ekmeği** bread baked in an earth oven. — **kebabı** dish of meat roasted in an oven. — **kebesi** large felt carpet thrown over a **tandır** in winter. — **kur=** to arrange a **tandır**.
tandırnâme (..—.) تاند ر نامه P an old wives' tale.
tane 1 (—.) دانه [**dane**] 1. grain, seed; pip, berry. 2. a single individual thing of any kind; piece. 3. bullet, cannon-ball. — **bağla=**, **—ye gel=** to form fruit or seed (plant). — **tane** in separate grains; one by one. — **tane söyle=** to speak each word distinctly.
ta'ne 2 طعنه A *lrnd.* 1. one spear thrust, stab. 2. a stroke of censure; taunt, sarcasm.
tanecik[1] دا ند جك 1. granule, little grain. 2. unique, only. **—li** granulous, granular.
tanele=[r] (—...) دا نه لمك /ı/ to separate into grains; to granulate. **—n=** 1. *pass.* 2. to produce grains or berries. **—ndir=**, **—t=** /ı/ *caus. of* **tanelen=**.
taneli (—..) دا ن ه لو دا ن ه لی 1. having grains or berries. 2. in separate grains.
tanen تا نـن F *chem.* tannin.
ta'net=[der] (—..) طعن ایتمك *lrnd.* to reproach, abuse.
ta'nezen طعنـزن P *lrnd.* 1. reviler, taunter, scoffer. 2. one who thrusts with a spear.
tangırtı طا نغردی a repeated clanging.
tangır tungur طا نغر طونغور loud clanging noise; noisily.
tango (.'.) تانغو Sp 1. tango. 2. *slang* loudly dressed woman.
tanı=[r] طا نیمق /ı/ 1. to know, to be acquainted with. 2. to recognize; to acknowledge; to listen to.
tanıdık[1] طا نیدیـق acquaintance. **— çık=** /la/ to have met before (each other).
tanık[1] طا نوق طا نیق witness. **— tepe** *neol., geol.* outlier. **—lık** 1. evidence. 2. a witnessing.
tanıl=[r] طا نیلمق *same as* **tanın=**.
tanım *neol.* definition.
tanıma طا نیمه *verbal n. of* **tanı=**, acknowledgment, recognition.
tanımla=[r] /ı/ *neol.* to define. **—ma** *same as* **tanım**.
tanımlı *neol., phil.* definite.

tanımsız *neol., phil.* indefinite.
tanın=[r] طا نینمق 1. *pass. of* **tanı=**. 2. to become known, to gain fame.
tanınmış طا نینمش well known; famous.
tanır=[r] طا کرمق *archaic* to be amazed, surprized, astounded.
tanış=[r] 1 طا نیشمق /la/ to get acquainted with one another; to be acquaintances.
tanış 2 طا نیش *colloq.* an acquaintance.
tanışık[1] طا نیشیق acquainted (with one another), an acquaintance. **—lık** mutual acquaintance.
tanıştır=[r] طا نیشدیرمق /ı, la/ *caus. of* **tanış= 1**, to introduce to one another, to cause to become acquainted.
tanıt=[r] 1 طا نیتمق /ı/ *caus. of* **tanı=**.
tanıt 2 *neol.* proof; evidence.
tanıtıl=[r] طا نیتلمق /a/ *pass. of* **tanıt=**.
tanıtla=[r] /ı/ *neol.* to prove. **—n=** *pass.*
ta'nif (.—) تعنیف A *lrnd.* a reproaching harshly, blaming severely; harshness; reproach. **—ât** (.—.—) A *pl.*
tanin (.—) طنین A *lrnd.* a booming, buzzing, humming or resounding noise.
taninendaz (.—.—) طنین انداز P *lrnd.* resounding, booming.
taninî (.——) طنینی P *mus.* interval of nine komas between two full notes.
ta'niye تعنیه A *lrnd.* a restraining; restraint.
tank[kı] تانک E 1. tank. 2. reservoir, depot (for liquids). **—çı** tank crew. **—savar** *mil.* anti-tank.
tanla=[r] 1 طا ککلامق *archaic,* to be amazed, surprised, astounded.
tanla=[r] 2 طا ککلامق *prov.* to dawn.
tanla 3 طاکلا [**tan ile**] *archaic* at dawn, in the early morning. **—cak**, **—cık** *same as* **tanla 3**. **—yın** at dawn.
tannan (.—) طنان A *lrnd.* sonorous, resounding; ringing.
tannaz (.—) طناز A *lrnd.* habitual jeerer; facetious, sportive. **—âne** (.——.) P facetiously; fun-making.
Tanrı تاکری تکری تنکری طاکری God. *l. c.* god. **T— Buyruğu** God's commandment, the Quran. **T— Dağları** *geog.* the Tien Shan Range. **— deveciği** wood louse. **—nın günü** every single day, every blessed day. **— hakkı için** by God. **— kayrası** *neol., phil.* providence. **— kulu** a servant of God, a righteous, pious man. **— kuşu** *archaic* peacock. **— misafiri** a stranger sent by God; unexpected guest. **—bilim** *neol.* theology. **—bilimsel** *neol.* theological. **—cı** *neol., phil.* theist. **—cılık** *neol., phil.* theism. **—ça** (.'.) goddess. **—kayral** *neol., phil.* providential.
tanrılaş=[r] تاکریلشمك to become a god, to be deified **—tır=** /ı/ to deify, to recognize as a god.

tanrılık تاڭرولیك 1. deity, godhead, divinity. 2. peculiar to God, holy, divine. 3. pious, God-fearing.
tanrısız *neol.* atheist. **—lık** atheism.
tansı, tansık *neol.* miracle.
tansıla= *neol.* to admire.
tansib (. —) تنصیب A *lrnd.* a setting up, erecting.
tansif (. —) تنصیف A *lrnd.* a halving, a dividing by two; bisection. **— tülbent** a kind of muslin used for a head covering.
tansir (. —) تنصیر A *lrnd.* a causing to become a Christian.
tansis (. —) تنصیص A *lrnd.* 1. a scrutinizing minutely (vouchers and details). 2. a supporting a thesis by scriptural quotation. **—ât** (. — —) A. *pl.*
tansiyon تانسیون F *physiol.* blood pressure.
-tan sonra دن صوڭره *cf.* **-dan sonra**.
tansuk طاڭسوق |*Persian* **tensuh**| *archaic* rare and exquisite, curious, rare (thing).
tantana طنطنه A pomp, display; magnificence. **—lı** pompous, showy; magnificent.
tantun طانطون *slang,* in **tantuna git=** to be lost, ruined, dismissed.
tanyeri طاڭ یری 1. daybreak on the eastern horizon; dawn. 2. east.
tanz طنز A *lrnd.* a sneering and jeering; sneer, jeer, sarcasm.
tanzic (. —) تنضیج A *lrnd.* 1. a ripening fruit (the sun). 2. a properly cooking food. 3. a preparing a secretion (an organ).
tanzif (. —) تنظیف A *lrnd.* a making clean, a cleaning, a purifying.
tanzifat (. — —) تنظیفات A town scavenger service.
tanzim (. —) تنظیم A 1. a putting in order; an organizing. 2. an arranging, regulating. **— et=** /ı/ 1. to put in order; to organize. 2. to reorganize; to arrange. 3. to edit. **— satışı** sale of foodstuffs by a municipality in order to regulate prices.
Tanzimat (. — —) تنظیمات 1. *Ott. hist.* the political reforms of Abdülmejid in 1839 and the period following. 2. *l. c., lrnd.* organic institutions; reforms, reorganization. **—i Hayriye** *Ott. hist.* "Beneficial Reforms" name of the law of 1839 introducing constitutional reforms. **—cı** *Ott. hist.* reformer.
tanzir 1 (. —) تنظیر A *lrnd.* 1. an imitating a poem. 2. a comparing one poem with another, holding or pronouncing it a parallel production. 3. a resembling, likening.
tanzir 2 (. —) تنضیر A *lrnd.* 1. a causing a plant to become luxuriant. 2. a making prosperous.
tap 1 طاب *archaic* enough, sufficient.

tap= 2 طاپمق 1. /a/ to worship to bow down. 2. /a/ to adore, to admire greatly. 3. *archaic* /ı/ to find, to meet with.
tapa طاپا تاپا طپه طبا It 1. stopper, cork; plug. 2. fuse (to a bomb). 3. mop (for oiling guns). **— burgusu** corkscrew.
tapala= تاپالامق /ı/ 1. to cork, to plug. 2. to fit with a fuse. **—n=** *pass.* of **tapala=**.
tapalı طاپالی furnished with a cork, plug, or fuse.
tapan طاپان *prov., same as* **taban 2**.
tapı طاپی *archaic* God.
tapıcı طاپیجی 1. worshipper. 2. *archaic* who habitually finds or meets with something.
tapıl= طاپیلمق *archaic* to be found.
tapın= طاپینمق 1. to bow down in worship. 2. /a/ to worship, adore.
tapınak طاپیناق place of worship, temple.
tapırda= طاپیرداموق طیپرداموق تاپرداموق to clatter, to make a clattering noise. **—t=** /ı/ *caus.*
tapış 1 طاپش a manner of worshipping.
tapış= 2 طاپشمق *archaic* to meet with, to meet or find each other. **—tır=** /ı/ *caus.*
tapkur طاپقور طیقور تاپقور *archaic* 1. a row, line; row of horses or cattle tethered in line; row of carts chained together wheel to wheel as a defense in time of danger. 2. camp surrounded with carts chained together for defense. 3. girth or surcingle. **— kokanı** 1. girth or surcingle. 2. tethering line.
tapon طاپون *slang* discarded; common, second-rate, worthless.
tapşır=, tapşur= تاپشیرمق تاپشورمق /ı, a/ *archaic* 1. to deliver, to give up to another. 2. to recommend, commit to the care of another. **—t=** /ı, a/ *caus.*
taptaze (. ' . .) تاپ تازه very fresh.
taptır= طاپدیرمق *caus.* of **tap= 2**.
tapu 1 طاپو تاپو title deed. **— defteri** *Ott. hist.* written survey of a province. **— resmi** *Ott. hist.* feudal dues collected from those who worked on the land. **— senedi** deed of real estate, extract from a land register. **— sicili** land register, official title register.
tapu 2 طاپو *archaic* 1. presence, rank, vicinity (of a person). 2. exalted person. 3. act of homage. **— et=, — kıl=** /a/ 1. to pay homage to; to submit to. 2. to worship. **— sağrağı** very large drinking bowl.
tapula= طاپولامق /ı/ to register with a title-deed (real estate). **—n=** *pass.*
tapunâme (. . — .) طاپونامه *Ott. hist.* title deed.
tapyoka (. ' .) تاپیوقا F tapioca.
târ 1 (—) تار P *lrnd.* 1. thread; yarn; string. 2. fiber; hair. 3. shred; tatter. 4. warp of cloth. 5. crown of the head; top, point (of anything). **—ı ankebût** spider web, cobweb.

—ı bam bass string of a musical instrument. —ı berkî telegraph. — ü pud warp and woof. — târ in shreds, in fiber.

târ 2 (—) P lrnd. 1. dark. 2. thick, turbid. — târ very dark or turbid. — ü tûr entirely dark.

tar 3 a plucked string instrument with a leather top, used in Azerbaijani folk music.

tara=ᵃʳ /ı/ 1. to comb. 2. to hackle. 3. to rake; to harrow. 4. to dredge. 5. to search minutely. 6. art to tint, paint with grey.

tarab A lrnd. joy, mirth; merrymaking.

tarabefza (...—) P lrnd. mirth-exciting; increasing enjoyment.

tarabengiz (...—) P 1. lrnd. joy-increasing; giving gladness. 2. Or. mus. an old makam.

tarabgâh (..—) P lrnd. place of enjoyment.

tarabnâk (..—) P lrnd. merry, mirthful.

Tarabulus var. of Trablus.

târâc (——) P 1. lrnd. pillage; marauding; plunder; scramble. 2. myst. removal of a devotee's free will in respect to all conditions and actions.

taracgâh (———) P lrnd. place where pillage takes place.

taracger (——.) P lrnd. pillager; marauder, robber; scrambler. —ân (——.—) P pillagers.

tarackerde (——..) P lrnd. pillaged.

taraça (..'.) It terrace.

taraf A 1. side, edge, border. 2. direction; district, region. 3. site, place. 4. part, portion. 5. end, extremity. 6. party (to a cause or dispute). 7. powerful protector or patron. 8. the behalf of a person, presence. —ıma towards me, to me. —ımca by me. —ımdan on my behalf; by me. —ına towards; to. —ından on the part of; by; from the direction of. —ınıza to you. —ınızdan on your behalf; by you. —lar law parties (in a transaction or proceeding). —ı âlinizce lrnd. in your high opinion. — çık= /a/ to become a protector (someone). —a çık= /dan/ to take the part (of), to side (with). — iltizam et= to adopt and support a side or cause. —a ol= /dan/ same as tarafa çık=. —ı sâmileri lrnd. their exalted presence, your Excellency. — taraf in various directions; in various places; on this side and that. — tut= to take sides; to support a cause or party. —ını tut= /ın/ same as taraf çık=. — yuları halter with two lead-ropes.

tarafâne (..—.) P lrnd. pertaining to a side; with partiality.

tarafdar (..—) P lrnd., same as taraftar. —âne (..——.) P partial, biased; partially. —î (..——) P partiality; partisanship.

tarafet (.—.) A lrnd. 1. a being newly produced or introduced. 2. a being a parvenu. —li new, recent.

tarafeyn A law the two parties, the two sides.

tarafgir (..—) P lrnd. partisan; partial, biased. —âne (..——.) P in a partial manner. —î (..——) P, —lik partisanship, partiality.

tarafiyet A lrnd. partisanship.

taraflı 1. having sides; having supporters. 2. supporter.

tarafsız neutral, impartial. —lık neutrality, impartiality.

taraftar (..—) P [tarafdar] 1. partisan. 2. supporter, follower. — ol= /a/ to be in favor of. —lık partiality.

taraif (.—.) A lrnd., pl. of tarife 2.

taraikᵏ¹ (..—.) A lrnd., pl. of tarika, tarikat.

tarakᵍ¹ 1. comb. 2. rake; harrow. 3. hackle; weaver's reed. 4. crest (of a bird). 5. drag. 6. gills (of a fish). 7. instep (of the foot). 8. scallop, zool., Pecten; cockle, zool., Cardium edule. 9. stone-mason's tooth-edged mattock. 10. serrated pattern (on cloth). — çekiç stone-mason's bush-hammer. — damarlı yaprak art pinnate leaf. — dişi tooth of a comb. — dubası dredger. — fırça veining-brush, graining-brush. — işi serrated (embroidery, etc.). — otu*. — servi Irish yew, bot., Taxus baccata. — vur= /a/ 1. to comb (one's hair). 2. to tooth (stone).

taraka (.—.) A lrnd. crash, loud knocking.

tarakçı maker or seller of combs.

tarakla=ʳ /ı/ 1. to comb, to hackle; to rake; to harrow. 2. to dredge. 3. to paint with zigzag lines. —ma verbal n. —n= pass. of tarakla=. —t= /ı, a/ caus. of tarakla=.

taraklı 1. having a comb. 2. crested (bird). 3. ornamented with toothed designs. 4. broadfooted. —lar neol., zool., Ctenophora.

taraklıkᵍ¹ 1. place or receptacle for combs. 2. material used for a comb.

tarakotuⁿᵘ teasel, bot., Dipsacus fullonum. —giller neol., bot., Dipsacaceae.

taralelli same as terelelli.

taralı combed.

tarama 1. verbal n. of tara=. 2. topography hatching, hachure. 3. research. 4. soft roe; red caviar. — muayene a searching investigation. — **resim** shaded drawing, hachure. — **vur=** to hachure.

taran=ᴵʳ 1 طالَنَم طَلانيم تارانيم تَمالَنيم 1. *pass. of* **tara=**. 2. to comb oneself, to comb one's hair.

taran 2 (— —) تاراں P *lrnd.* dark.

taranıkᵏ¹ طالاني combed; carded; raked.

tarantı طالانتى 1. refuse combed, raked or harrowed out. 2. the selected parts of anything.

tarassud ترصّد A 1. a watching, an observing; observation. 2. a dogging, lying in wait for. — **et=** /ı/ to watch, observe. —**ât** (...—) A *lrnd.*, *pl. of* **tarassud**.

taraş 1 تاراش *archaic* loot, booty.

taraş 2 طرش A *lrnd.* a being slightly deaf; deafness.

tarat=ᴵʳ 1 طالاتم /ı, a/ *caus. of* **tara=**.

tarat 2 (— —) تارات P *lrnd.* spoil, plunder; plundering expedition.

tarat 3 (— —) تارات A *lrnd.* 1. times, seasons. 2. times of repetition. 3. murderers; avengers of blood. —**i seb'** the seven stages in the development of a human being (1. clay; 2. seed; 3. blood; 4. flesh; 5. bones; 6. fleshly form; 7. birth).

tarator طاراتور sauce made with vinegar and walnuts.

taravet (.—.) طراوت A 1. a being fresh, juicy; freshness, juiciness. 2. bloom of youth. —**li** 1. fresh, juicy. 2. ruddy.

taraz طراز combings; fibers combed out. — **taraz**, — **turaz** dishevelled.

tarazla=ʳ طرازلامق /ı/ to clean the fiber of the cloth taken out of the loom. —**n=** 1. to become rough by combing or friction; to be frayed. 2. to be dishevelled.

tarbuş (.—) طربوش P *lrnd.* fez; skullcap.

tarçın تارچين طارچين P cinnamon. — **ağacı** common cinnamon tree, *bot.*, *Cinnamomum zeylanicum*. —**î** (..—) cinnamon color, light reddish brown.

tard طرد A 1. a sending or driving away, repelling or expelling; expulsion; repulsion. 2. degradation and expulsion of an officer.

tardet=ᵈᵉʳ طرد ایتمك /ı/ to expel, degrade.

tardî (.—) طردى A *lrnd.* repulsive, expulsive. —**ye** *lrnd.* a digression or episode in a poem.

tare 1 (— —) تاره P *lrnd.* dark, gloomy.

tare 2 (— —) تاره P *lrnd.* 1. a fiber; filament; a hair; a thread. 2. a lute-string.

tare 3 (— —.) تاره A *lrnd.* 1. time, season. 2. a time of repetition.

tarekᵏ¹ (— —.) تارك P *lrnd.* 1. crown of the head. 2. summit or point of anything.

tarem 1 (—.) تارم P *lrnd.* 1. nomad's tent of felt or goat's hair. 2. any high-roofed or domed structure. 3. high trellis for climbing plants. 4. the sky.

tarem 2 (—.) طارم P *lrnd.* 1. roof, dome, cupola. 2. the sky. —**i ahzar** the sky. —**i çarum** the fourth heaven, the sphere of the sun; the firmament. —**i firûzefâm**, —**i nilgûn** the blue sky. —**i pâk** heaven.

taret تاريت E *mil.* turret.

tareten (—'..) تارةً A *lrnd.* 1. at one time, once. 2. now; then. — **ba'de tareten**, — **ba'de uhra** time after time, repeatedly. — **ve tareten** from time to time.

tareyan (..—) طريان A *lrnd.* 1. a coming, arriving suddenly. 2. a happening.

tarf طرف A *lrnd.* 1. the eye; the eyelid. 2. a looking at, beholding. 3. a closing the eyelid.

tarfe طرفه A *lrnd.* one wink or twinkle with the eye.

tarfetül'ayn طرفة العين A *lrnd.* in the twinkling of an eye.

tarh 1 طرح A flower bed; garden border.

tarh 2 طرح A 1. a subtracting; subtraction. 2. an imposing a tax, imposition. 3. *lrnd.* a laying down, a placing, an establishing. 4. *lrnd.* a regulating, planning, laying out; plan; method, system. 5. *lrnd.* a throwing down or away. —**i esas** laying a foundation.

tarhana طرخانه ترخانه تارخانه [Persian .—.] preparation of dried curds and flour; soup made of this preparation. — **çorbası** soup made of **tarhana**.

tarhefgen طرح افگن P *lrnd.* who lays a foundation; who plans, who establishes a method.

tarhendaz (..—) طرح انداز P *lrnd.*, *same as* **tarhefgen**.

tarhun طرخون A tarragon, *bot.*, *Artemisia dracunculus*.

tarıkᵏ¹ (—.) طارق A *lrnd.* 1. morning star. 2. that comes or happens by night. 3. diviner by means of pebbles, seer. **T— Sûresi** the eighty-sixth sura of the Quran.

tarım *neol.* agriculture.

târi 1 (— —) تارى P *lrnd.* 1. dark, gloomy; sad. 2. darkness, gloom.

târi 2 (—.) طارى A *lrnd.* which comes, happens. — **ol=** to come, happen, befall.

tari 3 (.—) طرى A *lrnd.* fresh; sappy, juicy.

ta'rib (.—) تعريب A *lrnd.* 1. a rendering into Arabic; an arabicizing. 2. a speaking or declaring audibly; clearly and intelligibly. — **et=** /ı/ 1. to arabicize (a word). 2. to declare explicitly. —**ât** (.——) A *pl.*

tarid 1 (.—) طريد A *lrnd.* 1. driven away, banished, expelled; repelled. 2. seized and driven away.

tarid 2 (—.) طارد A *lrnd.* that drives away, repels, or expels.

taridan (.——), **tarideyn** (.—.) طَرِيدان ، طَرِيدَيْن A *lrnd.* two things that alternate with one another (as day and night).

ta'rif 1 (.—) A, **târif** (——) تَعْرِيف 1. description. 2. definition. 3. recipe. 4. *archaic* praise, commendation. **— et**= /ı/ to describe; to define. **—e uy**= to match the description.

tarif 2 (.—) طَرِيف A *lrnd.* new, fresh; rare, pretty.

ta'rifat (.——) تَعْرِيفات A *lrnd., pl. of* **ta'rif 1**.

ta'rife 1 تَعْرِيفَه A 1. price list. 2. timetable. 3. instruction sheet.

tarife 2 (.—.) طَرِيفَه A *lrnd.* new, fresh; rare.

tarifle=ʳ *neol.* to describe; to define. **—n**= *pass.* **—nmemiş** *math.* indefinite. **—nmiş** *math.* definite.

tarih 1 (—.) تاريخ |*Arabic* ——| 1. date. 2. history; annals. 3. epoch, era. 4. chronogram. **—inde** at the date of, dated. **—i Arab**, **—i Arabî** *lrnd., same as* **tarihi Hicrî**. **— at**= to put the date, to date. **—i Buhtunnasar** *lrnd.* "era of Nebuchadnezzar," beginning 742 B.C. **—i Celâli** *lrnd.* the era of Jalaladdin Malik Shah, the Seljuk Sultan of Khorasan, beginning 1079 A.D. **— düşür**= to compose a choronogram. **—i Fürs** *lrnd.* era of the Persians starting in 632 A.D. **—i Hicrî** the Muslim era, lunar year starting 622 A.D. **—i İlhanî** *lrnd., same as* **—i Celâli**. **—i İskender**, **—i İskenderî** *lrnd.* era of Alexander the Great, commencing 312 B.C. **—e karış**= to be a thing of the past, to be out of date. **—i Meliki** *lrnd., same as* **tarihi Celâli**. **—i Milâdî** the Christian era, A.D. **—i Rumî** era commencing 584 A.D., fiscal year in Muslim lands. **—i Safar** *lrnd.* the Julian era. **—i sıfr** *lrnd.* era of the Caesars, long used in Spain. **— söyle**= *same as* **tarih düşür**=. **—i tabiî** *lrnd.* natural history. **—i Türk** *lrnd.* the Turkish era, divided into ages of 10,000 years each, and into periods of 60, 12, and 10 years each, the total predestined duration of the earth being 300,000 ages. The period of twelve years is the one commonly used: in it each year receives the name of an animal. **—i umumî** general history. **— yaz**= to write a history.

tarih 2 (.—) طَرْح A *lrnd.* thrown down; knocked down; lying unconscious or dead.

tarihçe (—..) تاريخچه P short history.

tarihçi (—..) تاريخچى historian. **— kalemi** *Ott. hist.* an office of the financial administration.

tarihen (—.'.) تاريخًا A *lrnd.* historically.

tarihî (—.—) تاريخى A 1. historical. 2. *lrnd.* chronologist, chronicler.

tarihli (—..) تاريخلى dated.

tarihnüvis (—..—) تاريخ نويس P *lrnd.* historian.

tarihsel (—..) *neol.* historical.

tarihsiz (—..) تاريخسز undated.

tarihşinas (—..—) تاريخ شناس P *lrnd.* historian.

tarikᵏⁱ **1** (.—) طَرِيق A *lrnd.* 1. road, path, way. 2. street; alley. 3. method, manner; means. 4. hierarchy, line of service and promotion. 5. order of dervishes. **bir —le** in some way, by some means. **—i âm** public road, highway, thoroughfare. **— bedeli** *obs.* road tax. **—i ehli seyf** the military and naval services. **—i eklâm** the hierarchy of officials, the civil service. **—i hak** the right course. **—i has** private street not open to the public. **—i ilmî** the career, also the hierarchy, of the legal functionaries and professors of the canon law of Islam. **— maaşı** *Ott. hist.* revenues assigned to members of the ulema class. **—i müstakim** the right path. **—i ulema** the hierarchy of the learned in the canon law of Islam.

tarikᵏⁱ **2** (.—) تَارِك A *lrnd.* who forsakes, relinquishes or neglects; who departs, goes away. **—i dünya** who forsakes the world, hermit, nun. **—i edeb** neglectful of good manners.

tarikᵏⁱ **3** (——) تاريك P *lrnd.* dark; gloomy.

ta'rikᵏⁱ **4** (.—) تَعْرِيس A *lrnd.* a causing to perspire.

ta'rikᵏⁱ **5** (.—) تَعْرِيك A *lrnd.* 1. a rubbing, manipulating with the palm of the hand. 2. a boxing or twisting the ear of a culprit.

tarika (.—.) طَرِيقَه A *lrnd., same as* **tarikat**.

tarikat (.—.) طَرِيقَت A *lrnd.* 1. religious order, order of dervishes. 2. sect; hierarchy. 3. mysticism. 4. way, path, road. **— ehli** members of any order of dervishes; the mystics.

tarikatçı طَرِيقَتچى member of a religious order, dervish.

tarikbaht (——.) تاريك بخت P *lrnd.* unlucky, unfortunate (person).

tarikcan (———) تاريك جان P *lrnd.* wicked; unenlightened; wretched.

tarikçeşm (——.) تاريك چشم P *lrnd.* weak-sighted, short-sighted.

tarikdil (———.) تاريك دل P *lrnd.* 1. ignorant. 2. depraved.

tarikî (———) تاريكى P *lrnd.* darkness; gloom; obscurity.

tarikrûz (———.) تاريك روز P *lrnd.* whose days are blighted; unhappy, wretched.

ta'ris (.—) تَعْرِيس A *lrnd.* an alighting after a night's journey for a rest until dawn.

ta'riye تَعْرِيه A *lrnd.* a stripping, a causing to be naked.

ta'riz (.—) A, **târiz** (———) تَعْرِيض 1. a speaking allusively; a hinting; hint, allusion. 2. a blaming or censuring indirectly: allusive censure, innuendo. 3. *lrnd.* a making broad, a widening. —**de bulun**= /a/ to censure indirectly. — **et**= /a/ to censure by innuendo.

ta'rizan (.—´.) تَعْرِيضًا A lrnd. by hint, by allusion.

ta'rizât (.— —) تَعْرِيضَات A lrnd., pl. of **ta'riz**.

tarla طَارْلَا ، تَارْلَا ، تَارْلَهْ ، تَارْلِهْ arable field; garden bed. — **aç**= to clear the ground of bushes, etc., and reduce it to a field. — **et**= 1. to convert land into arable ground. 2. to spread out with a smooth surface. — **kuşu** skylark, zool., Alauda arvensis. — **sıçanı** harvest mouse, zool., Micromys minutus; short-tailed vole, zool., Microtus agrestis. — **tabanı** harrow; beam or roller used as a harrow.

tarlakoz طَارْلَاقُوزْ 1. fishing boat with two pairs of oars. 2. a kind of fishing net.

tarmar (— —) تَارْ ـ مَارْ P lrnd., same as **tarumar**.

tarpan طَارْپَانْ ، تَارْپَانْ tarpan, wild horse of Central Asia.

tarpoş طَارْپُوشْ [Persian **serpoş**] skull cap, fez.

tarrah (.—) طَرَّاحْ A lrnd. 1. one who habitually puts or lays down. 2. architect; founder.

tarraka (.—.) طَرَّاقَه A lrnd., same as **taraka**.

tarrar (.—) طَرَّارْ A lrnd. 1. one who snatches or seizes by force suddenly; plunderer, pillager; pickpocket, purse-snatcher. 2. stealer of hearts, beauty.

tarsii (.—) تَرْصِيع A 1. lrnd. an ornamenting with jewels. 2. rhet. a composing rhymed prose in which every word of one clause is balanced by a similar word in the other; homophony. — **ma' tecnis** rhet. homophony and homonymy. —**ât** (.— —) A pl. of **tarsi**.

tarsif (.—) تَرْصِيف A lrnd. 1. a joining the parts of a thing compactly together. 2. a constructing a sentence lucidly and grammatically.

tarsin (.—) تَرْصِين A lrnd. 1. a making sure and free from doubt. 2. a consolidating or making firm. —**i cidar** a consolidating a wall. —**ât** (.— —) A pl.

tarsis (.—) تَرْصِيص A lrnd. 1. a joining closely, a soldering, gluing. 2. a converting into lead.

tart=ᵗʳ طَارْ ـ تَمْ ، تَارْ ـ تَمَقْ /ı/ 1. to weigh. 2. to ponder in the mind; to estimate deliberately and maturely. 3. to weigh up (person). 4. archaic to poise or brandish (weapon). 5. archaic to toss off, to drink off.

tartakla=ᵗʳ طَارْ ـ تَقْلَامَقْ /ı/ 1. to tease, worry, badger, harass, torment. 2. to manhandle, assault. 3. to pull to pieces; to tease out (fibers). 4. prov. to lift something up to test its weight.

tartı طَارْقِ ، طَارْتِي ، طَارْلِي 1. a weighing. 2. weight, balance; scale; measure. —**ya gelmez** 1. imponderable. 2. immeasurable. —**ya vurul**= to be pondered.

tartıcı طَارْ ـ تِيجِي 1. weigher. 2. reflector, ponderer.

tartıl=ᵗʳ 1 طَارْ ـ تِمَقْ ، طَارْ ـ تِيلْمَقْ 1. pass. of **tart**=. 2. to totter, to vacillate. 3. to speak hesitatingly. 4. to intrude. 5. to be unwilling to go. 6. to throw oneself on another.

tartıl 2 neol., chem. gravimetric.

tartılı طَارْ ـ تِيلِي 1. weighed, balanced. 2. ponderable; well-pondered.

tartılma طَارْ ـ تِيلْمَه verbal n. of **tartıl**= 1.

tartın 1 طَارْ ـ طِينْ archaic continued roll or swagger in walking.

tartın=ᵗʳ 2 طَارْ ـ تَنْمَقْ archaic, same as **tartıl**= 1.

tartısız طَارْ ـ تِيسِزْ 1. unweighed, unbalanced. 2. not well thought out; imponderable. 3. without rule or measure, irregular.

tartış 1 طَارْ ـ تِيشْ verbal n. of **tart**=.

tartış=ᵗʳ 2 طَارْ ـ تِيشْمَقْ /la/ 1. to weigh one thing with another. 2. to struggle. 3. neol. to dispute, to argue. —**ma** verbal n.

tartib (.—) تَرْطِيب A lrnd. 1. a moistening, a wetting. 2. a freshening, refreshing.

tartkı طَارْ ـ تْقِي archaic 1. buckle of a girth-strap. 2. a gradual pulling in of the reins of a horse.

tartma طَارْ ـ تْمَه verbal n. of **tart**=.

tarttır=ᵗʳ طَارْ ـ تْدِيرْمَقْ /ı, a/ caus. of **tart**=. —**ıl**= pass.

tartura (..´.) طَرْطُورَه lathe wheel; wheel of a spinning wheel.

tarumar (—.—) تَارْ ـ وْمَارْ P lrnd. scattered; in disorder, in confusion. — **et**= /ı/ to rout.

tarz طَرْزْ A 1. mode, manner, style; method. 2. form, shape, appearance. 3. sort, variety. 4. demeanor. —**ı cedid** Or. mus. a **makam** starting with d″ and ending on f′. —**ı hal** method of solution (of a difficulty). —**ı hareket** behavior. —**ı itilâf** compromise. —**ı nevin** Or. mus. a compound **makam** composed a century ago.

tarziye تَرْضِيَه A 1. apology; satisfaction; a satisfying. 2. lrnd. a blessing one with the formula: "Radiyallahü anh". — **ver**= /a/ to give satisfaction (to an offended person), to make an apology.

tas 1 طَاسْ ، تَاسْ [tas 2] 1. cup or bowl (with a rounded bottom). 2. helmet. — **başlı** bald-headed. — **gibi** colloq. 1. bald, naked. 2. plain. — **giydir**= hist. to put a hot bowl on the head of a victim. — **mı kayboldu?** Has a bowl got lost? (asked in derision when women are making a great outcry). — **kebabı***. —**ı oku**= colloq. a kind of magic performed by reciting certain formulas over a bowl full of water. — **suratlı** round and plain-faced. —**ı tarağı topla**= to pack up and go. — **tasa başbaşa** colloq. a violent quarrel, a coming to blows.

tas 2 (—) طَاسْ P lrnd. bowl. —**i eflâk**, —**i gerdûn**, —**i nilgûn**, —**i sernigûn** the sky.

ta's 3 نَسّ A *lrnd.* 1. a perishing, a falling. 2. perdition, calamity, ruin, destruction.

tasa طاسه طه ناسه طاس [tase] 1. anxiety, care; grief, affliction. 2. *lrnd.* a choking sensation from grief or anxiety. **— çek=, —sını çek=** /ın/ to suffer anxiety or grief; to worry. **—mın on beşi** *colloq.* I don't care! **—sı sana mı düştü?** It's no concern of yours, why worry? **— ver=** /a/ to cause anxiety.

tasabbi تَصَبِّي A *lrnd.* an acting in a childish manner, a being childish.

tasabbun تَصَبُّن A *chem.* saponification.

tasabbur تَصَبُّر A *lrnd.* a constraining oneself, patience, endurance.

tasaddi تَصَدِّي A *lrnd.* a setting oneself to do something; a daring to do something.

tasaddu^uu تَصَدُّع A *lrnd.* 1. a becoming dispersed, scattered, dissipated. 2. a being split, cracked, fissured.

tasaddud تَصَدُّد A *lrnd.* a turning the eyes, intention, or effort toward.

tasadduk^ku تَصَدُّق A *lrnd.* a giving of alms. **—ât** (...—) A alms.

tasaddur تَصَدُّر A *lrnd.* a being promoted to, occupying, or claiming the chief seat (in an assembly or court).

tasaffi تَصَفِّي A *lrnd.* a being or becoming clarified, free from cloudiness, clear.

tasalan=^ır طاصلانى ناصلانس to become sad from anxiety or regret; to worry. **—dır=** /ı/ *caus.*

tasalı ناصلى ناسلى anxious and sorrowing; wistful; worried.

tasallûb تَصَلُّب A *lrnd.* 1. a becoming hardened; solidification. 2. a being hard, firm, inflexible. **—i şerayin** *path.* arteriosclerosis. **—ât** (...—) A *pl.* of **tasallûb**.

tasallûf تَصَلُّف A *lrnd.* an assuming excellency, a being vain and overweening; a boasting. **—ât** (...—) A *pl.*

tasallûfkâr (...—) تَصَلُّفكار P *lrnd.* presumptuous.

tasallût تَسَلُّط A 1. molestation. 2. *lrnd.* a usurpation of power; aggression. **—ât** (...—) A *lrnd.*, *pl.*

tasallüp^bü تَصَلُّب *var.* of **tasallûb**.

tasanif (.——) تَصانيف A *lrnd.*, *pl.* of **tasnif**.

tasannu^uu تَصَنُّع A *lrnd.* 1. an affecting to be skillful; feint, pretense. 2. gaudy decoration; artifice. **—ât** (...—) A *pl.*

tasar تاصار archaic project; draft; plan.

tasarı *neol.* 1. bill, draft law. 2. project, plan.

tasarım *neol., phil.* representation. **—la=** /ı/ to represent. **—lı** representative.

tasarif (.——) تَصاريف A *lrnd.* changes, vicissitudes.

tasarla=^r تاصارلامس 1. to plan, to project; to arrange (in one's mind). 2. to compose, to draft in outline, to sketch out. 3. to roughcast (clay model). **—yarak öldür=** /ı/ law to kill with premeditation. **—ma** *verbal n.* of **tasarla=**. **—n=, —nıl=** *pass.* of **tasarla=**. **—yış** *verbal n.* of **tasarla=**.

tasarlı *neol., phil.* virtual.

tasarruf تَصَرُّف A 1. disposal, power of disposal; possession. 2. economy, frugality, parsimony. 3. a saving (money), savings. 4. *lrnd.* a knowing a woman carnally. **—umda** at my disposal. **— bonosu** an income and profits tax in exchange for which bonds were given to be paid at certain future dates (issued after 1960). **— ehliyeti** *law* power of disposition. **— et=** 1. to save, economize. 2. /a/ to have the use and disposal (of); to possess. **— muameleleri** *law* acts of disposal. **— nisabı** *law* disposable portion of an estate. **— sandığı** savings bank.

tasarrufan (..·..) تَصَرُّفًا A *lrnd.* for economical purposes.

tasarrufat (...—) تَصَرُّفات A *lrnd.* 1. savings. 2. acts of disposal.

tasarrufkâr (...—) تَصَرُّفكار P *lrnd.* economical, thrifty.

tasarsız تاصارسز extemporary, improvised.

tasasız تاساسز 1. free from care; light-hearted. 2. thoughtless, indifferent.

tasaub 1 تَصَعُّب A *lrnd.* a being or becoming difficult; difficulty.

tasaub 2 (.—.) تَصاعب A *lrnd.* a being obstinate.

tasaud (.—.) تَصاعد A *lrnd.* an ascending, going up; ascension.

tasavir (.——) تَصاوير A *lrnd., pl.* of **tasvir**.

tasavvuf تَصَوُّف A 1. Islamic mysticism, Sufism. 2. *lrnd.* a being or becoming a Sufi. **— ehli** one who is versed in and who practices Sufism; Sufi. **— ilmi** Sufism. **—ât** (...—) A *pl.* **—î** (...—) A mystical, Sufi.

tasavvur تَصَوُّر A 1. a picturing to oneself, a forming an idea; idea; conception. 2. an imagining; imagination. 3. *phil.* representation. 4. *lrnd.* a taking shape and form. 5. *log.* term representing an idea.

tasavvurât (...—) تَصَوُّرات A *lrnd.* conceptions; ideas.

tasavvurî (...—) تَصَوُّرى A *lrnd.* 1. imaginary; theoretical. 2. *phil.* representative, cognitive.

tasavvut تَصَوُّت A *gram.* intonation.

tasayyud تَصَيُّد A *lrnd.* 1. a capturing game or fish; hunting. 2. a going out in pursuit of game or fish.

tasayyuf تَصَيُّف A *lrnd.* a remaining during summer, passing the summer in a place.

tasdi^u (.—.) تَصْدِيع A *lrnd.* 1. a giving one a headache. 2. a troubling one by a request or importunity. 3. a paying a visit (used by the visitor as an expression of politeness). **— et=** /ı/ 1. to disturb, pester. 2. to pay a visit to somebody. **—ât** (.——) A *pl.*

tasdik[k1] (. —) تَصْديق A 1. a confirming; confirmation. 2. an affirming, asserting; affirmation, assertion. 3. a ratifying; ratification; a certifying; certification. — et= /ı/ to confirm, affirm, ratify, certify.

tasdikan (. —′.) تَصْديقًا A *lrnd.* in confirmation.

tasdikat (. — —) تَصْديقات A *lrnd.*, *pl.* of **tasdik**.

tasdikî (. — —) تَصْديقى A *lrnd.* affirmative, confirmatory.

tasdikli تَصْديقلى certified, ratified.

tasdikname (. — —.) تَصْديقنامه P 1. letter of confirmation; certificate. 2. *education* certificate given to a student who leaves a school without graduating.

tasdiksaz (. — —) تَصْديقساز P *lrnd.* confirmatory.

tasdir (. —) تَصْدير A *lrnd.* 1. a promoting one to the chief place or presidency of a court or assembly. 2. a prefacing a written composition; a beginning a letter with a preamble or exordium. 3. a causing an order, etc. to go forth. —ât (. — —) A *pl.*

tasdiye تَصْديه A *lrnd.* a clapping the hands in beating time or as a call.

tase (—.) تاسه P *lrnd.*, same as **tasa**.

tasfif (. —) تَصْفيف A *lrnd.* a ranging in a row or lines; a drawing up troops in line of battle. —ât (. — —) A *pl.*

tasfih (. —) تَصْفيح A *lrnd.* 1. a clapping the hands. 2. a flattening, a spreading out by pressure. —ât (. — —) A *pl.*

tasfik[k1] (. —) تَصْفيق A *lrnd.* 1. a striking a thing so as to cause a sound. 2. a clapping the hands. —ât (. — —) A *pl.*

tasfir (. —) تَصْفير A *lrnd.* 1. a dyeing or tinging yellow. 2. a whistling; whistle. 3. a reducing to zero; an exhausting, a finishing. —ât (. — —) A *pl.*

tasfiye تَصْفيه A 1. a cleaning or clarifying (a liquid). 2. a purifying (from alloy or admixture); purification. 3. liquidation; clearance; elimination; a winding up. 4. a making the heart or mind free from evil thoughts or intentions. — **bankası** clearing house. — **et=** /ı/ 1. to clean, clarify, refine. 2. to clear up (a matter). 3. to liquidate, to eliminate. —**i kalb et=** to purify the heart. — **memuru** liquidator.

tasfiyehane (. . . —.) تَصْفيه‌خانه P refinery.

tasgir (. —) تَصْغير A 1. *lrnd.* a making smaller. 2. *gram.* a putting into the diminutive form. —ât (. — —) A *pl.*

tashif (. —) تَصْحيف A *lrnd.* 1. a corrupting a word by incorrectly reading, writing or copying its diacritical points; orthographical mistake. 2. an artful corruption of a word by which eulogy becomes satire. 3. a corrupting a tradition by an alteration of diacritical points. —ât (. — —) A *pl.*

tashih (. —) تَصْحيح A 1. a correcting; correction; rectification; adjustment. 2. *print.* a reading proofs. 3. *lrnd.* a restoring health; a being restored to health. — **et=** /ı/ 1. to correct, rectify. 2. to read proof sheets. —**i mizac et=** to recover one's health. —ât (. — — —) A *lrnd.*, *pl.*

tashin (. —) تَصْحين A *lrnd.* a staging (a play).

tasım تاصم 1. *archaic* supposition. 2. *archaic* system, rule; custom. 3. *neol.*, *log.* syllogism.

tasımla=[r] تاصملمك *archaic* /ı/ 1. to plan, project. 2. to imagine; to estimate.

tasi[ii] (—.) تاسع A *lrnd.* the ninth (in order or succession). —**an** (—′..) A ninthly.

tas'ib (. —) تَصْعيب A *lrnd.* a rendering difficult. —ât (. — —) A *pl.*

tas'id (. —) تَصْعيد A *lrnd.* 1. a causing to rise. 2. a distilling or volatilizing; distillation; sublimation; volatilization; evaporation.

ta'sil (. —) تَعْسيل A *lrnd.* a mixing with honey; a causing to be as sweet as honey. —**i kelâm et=** to sweeten one's speech.

Tasin (— —) طسٓ A *lrnd.* the letters ط and س standing at the head of the twenty-seventh sura of the Quran. —**mim** the letters س, ط, and م standing at the head of the twenty-sixth sura of the Quran.

ta'sir 1 (. —) تَعْصير A *lrnd.* a pressing (fruit for the juice).

ta'sir 2 (. —) تَعْسير A *lrnd.* a making difficult. —ât (. — —) A *pl.*

ta'sirhane (. — —.) تَعْصيرخانه P *lrnd.* oil press, oil-pressing mill.

taskebabı[nı] طاس‌كبابى meat cut in small pieces and stewed with vegetables in a baking dish covered with a bowl.

taskil (. —) تَصْقيل A *lrnd.* a polishing, burnishing. —**i seyf et=** to polish one's sword. —ât (. — —) A *pl.*

tasla=[r] طاسلامك /ı/ to pretend to something one does not possess; to make a show of.

taslak[k1] طاسلاق 1. anything in the rough, not yet perfected; rough draft; sketch; model. 2. rough, not finished. 3. naked, hairless. — **kalemi** sculptor's boaster, roughing-chisel. —**çı** pattern maker.

taslakla=[r] طاسلاقلامك /ı/ to rough-hew (a sculpture); to outline (picture, plan).

taslib (. —) تَصْليب A *lrnd.* 1. a crucifying or hanging. 2. a making the sign of the Cross; a painting or forming in the shape of a crucifix. 3. a rendering hard and firm; solidification. —ât (. — —) A *pl.*

taslit[ii] (. —) تَسْليط A *lrnd.* a causing someone to pester another. — **et=** /ı, a/ to cause to fall upon, to pester, to vex.

tasliye, tasliyet تَصْليه A *lrnd.* 1. an

tasliyehan invoking blessing on the Prophet Muhammad with the formula **Sallallâhu aleyhi ve sellem**. 2. a benediction with this formula.

tasliyehan (...—) تصليه خوان P *lrnd.* reciter of the formula of benediction.

tasma طاسما ٖطاسمو تسمه تصمه ٖتاصمه طسم [**tasme**] 1. collar (of a dog etc.). 2. strap (of clogs). 3. *arch.* ring (of a column). 4. *slang* fool, idiot.

tasmala=ʳ طاسمالمق /ı/ to put a strap or collar (on). —n= *pass.* —t= /ı, a/ *caus.* of **tasmala**=.

tasme (—.) تسمه P *lrnd., same as* **tasma**.

tasmim (.—) تصميم A *lrnd.* a resolving firmly to do some act; firm intention or resolution; determination. — et= to firmly resolve upon. —ât (.——) A resolutions, firm intentions.

tasmimkerde (.—..) تصميمكرده P *lrnd.* fully resolved on and determined.

tasmimle=ʳ تصميملمك to resolve and determine to do.

tasmit 1 (.—) تسميط A *prosody* a composing a poem in stanzas of from four to ten distichs each, the last of which in each stanza is a kind of chorus and must rhyme with the first distich of the poem, of which these last distichs may be repetitions.

tasmit 2 (.—) تصميت A *lrnd.* a silencing; a remaining silent; silence.

tasniⁱⁱ (.—) تصنيع A 1. *lrnd.* an inventing; invention, fabrication. 2. *phil.* fiction. 3. a forming with art or with skill; a making. — et= /ı/ to fabricate (lies etc.).

tasniât (.——) تصنيعات A *lrnd.* inventions, falsehoods.

tasnif (.—) تصنيف A 1. a separating into classes, kinds or varieties; classification. 2. *lrnd.* a composing or compiling; composition; compilation; musical composition. —i ârâ *lrnd.* counting of ballots. — et= /ı/ to classify; to compose, to compile. — **nazariyesi** taxonomy.

tasnifât (.——) تصنيفات A *lrnd.* literary compositions, works, writings.

tasnim (.—) تصنيم A *lrnd.* a forming an image or idol.

tasrif (.—) تصريف A 1. *gram.* a declining a noun; declension; conjugation; inflection. 2. *gram.* a deriving a word according to a rule; derivation. 3. *lrnd.* a using as one wills, an applying a thing according to one's judgment or fancy; use, application. —ât (.——) A *lrnd., pl.*

tasrifî (.——) تصريفى A *ling.* inflectional. — **diller** inflectional languages.

tasrih (.—) تصريح A an expressing directly and clearly; clear interpretation or expression. — et= /ı/ to make clear, to specify.

tasrihât (.——) تصريحات A *lrnd.* explanation; explanations, specifications.

tasrihen (.—ʼ.) تصريحاً A *lrnd.* by way of clarification; explicitly.

tasrihkerde (.—..) تصريحكرده P *lrnd.* explicitly mentioned.

tastamam تاس تمام ٖطاس نام complete; perfect.

tastih (.—) تطيح A *lrnd.* 1. a making smooth or level. 2. a projecting a solid surface on a plane.

tastir (.—) تسطير A *lrnd.* a writing, an inscribing.

tasvib (.—) تصويب A *lrnd., same as* **tasvip**. —ât (.——) A *lrnd., pl.*

tasviben (.—ʼ.) تصويباً A *lrnd.* in approval, approvingly.

tasvibkâr (.——) تصويبكار P *lrnd.* approving.

tasvibkerde (.—..) تصويبكرده P *lrnd.* approved.

tasvipᵇⁱ (.—) تصويب [**tasvib**] approval. — et= to approve (of).

tasvir (.—) تصوير A 1. picture; design. 2. a describing; description. 3. a forming, a shaping, a giving shape and form. 4. likeness, effigy. 5. handsome. — et= /ı/ 1. to picture, to represent by an effigy; to depict, to draw. 2. to describe. — **gibi** pretty as a picture. —i **miyah** *lrnd.* hydrography. —i **mücessem** *lrnd.* statue, physical image. —i **nim ruh** *lrnd.* profile portrait. —ât (.——) A *lrnd.* pictures; descriptions. —ci portrait painter. —î (.——) P descriptive.

tasvit (.—) تصويت A *lrnd.* 1. a causing to make a sound; a giving forth a sound; a calling out with a loud voice. 2. a rendering notorious.

taş 1 طاش تاش طش 1. stone; rock; made of stone. 2. hard as stone. 3. precious stone. 4. *chess and other games* piece, man. 5. allusion, innuendo. 6. *med.* calculus; tartar (on the teeth). 7. crust, deposit (in a boiler), lime (in a kettle). 8. *slang* money. — **arabası** *slang* idiot, fool, stupid. — at= /a/ 1. to throw a stone (at). 2. to direct an unpleasant allusion or innuendo (at somebody). — **atıp kolu yorulma**= to obtain something easily. **bir — atımı** a stone's throw away, quite near. — **bademi** wild almond. — **bağa** *prov.* tortoise. — **bağla**= to form a crust. — **balığı** rockfish. — **basma** lithograph; lithography. —**a bastır**= /ı/ to stone to death. —**a başvur**= to look for a remedy. — **bebek** doll. — **bebek gibi** very pretty but charmless (woman). — **bilim***. — **bina** stone building. — **çatlasa** whatever happens. —**a çek**= /ı/ to whet (knife). — **çıkar**= 1. to break stone (in a quarry). 2. /a/ *same as* **taş çıkart**=. — **çıkart**= /a/ to be greatly superior (to somebody); to surpass. — **devri** stone age. — **dik**= 1. to erect a stone. 2. *archery* to break a record. 3. *chess* to arrange the men in order. — **dolgu** filling-in (wall). — **döğen** *archaic* strong, sturdy. — **döşek** drain made of loose stones. — **döşeme** flagging, flag pavement; stone pavement. —**la dövün**= to regret something bitterly. — **düşür**= to pass a gallstone. —**tan ekmeğini çıkarır** He is very clever and industrious; he is able to make a living out of anything. — **evi** *jewelry* socket holding a precious stone. — **evi tırnağı** claw of a jewel setting (on a ring, etc.). —**ı gediğine koy**= to make a clever retort, to give as good as one gets. — **gibi** 1. very hard; solid. 2. heartless, cruel. — **hamuru** *arch.* stucco. — **iliği** vein in the structure of a stone. — **illeti** stone in the bladder, kidney, etc., calculus. — **kabası** dirt, earth clinging to quarried stone. — **kalem** slate pencil. — **kesil**= to be petrified; to be astounded or horrified. — **kesimi** art of stonecutting. — **kömürü** coal. — **kurdu** stone-boring worm. — **mantarı** *bot.* lichen growing on rocks. — **nanesi** dittany, stone-mint, *bot. Cunila origanoides.* — **ocağı** stone quarry. —**ı ölçeyim** *colloq.* (*lit.* Let me measure the stone.) God protect us, *said when pointing at a certain part of the body to describe an illness or wound.* — **pamuğu** asbestos. — **sektirme** ducks and drakes (game). —**ı sıksa suyunu çıkarır** He is incredibly strong; he is efficient and successful in every field. — **söve** door frame. — **tahta** slate. —**a tapma** litholatry. — **tekne** stone trough (generally for holding water). — **toprak** rough stone, rubble. — **tut**= *slang* to have money. —**a tut**= 1. to throw stones at (in ridicule). 2. to stone to death. 3. to hold to a grindstone (implement); to grind, to sharpen, to whet. — **yağı** *obs.* kerosene. — **yağar kıyamet koparken** When it rains stones and hell breaks loose, *used to describe a great disaster.* — **yalımı,** — **yelemi** *obs.* Portland cement. — **yerinde ağırdır** (*lit.* The stone is heavy in its proper place.) The value of a person is appreciated where he is known. —**ı yerine koy**= *same as* **taşı gediğine koy**=. — **yoncası** seven-headed crown-vetch; *bot., Coronilla glauca;* bird's-foot, *bot., Lotus corniculatus.* — **yont**= to cut, dress stone. — **yosunu** lichen. — **yuvarla**= /a/ to make bitter allusions (to), to inveigh (against somebody). — **yürekli** hard-hearted, cruel.

taş 2 طاش *archaic* 1. the outside, exterior. 2. outer, external.

taş=ᵃʳ 3 طشمر 1. to overflow, to run over; to boil over. 2. to exceed the bounds of moderation or decency; to go too far. 3. to lose one's patience. 4. to get above oneself; to be insolent. 5. to overlap. 6. to be in a ferment.

-**taş** 4 داش *cf.* -**daş**.

taşakᶠ¹ طاشاب testicle. — **bağı** 1. the spermatic cord. 2. gubernaculum of the testicle. 3. suspensory for the scrotum. — **torbası** scrotum. —**lı** 1. having testicles. 2. bold, virile, brave. —**sız** 1. without testicles. 2. wanting in courage, coward.

taşal=ⁱʳ طاشالمر *archaic* 1. to become stone, to petrify. 2. to become paralyzed with amazement or horror.

taşbilim *neol., geol.* lithology.

taşçı طاشجی stonemason; quarryman. — **kalemi** stonemason's chisel. — **mili** stonemason's crowbar or drill. — **tokmağı** bushhammer. —**lık** stonecutting; stonemasonry.

taşı=ⁱʳ طاشیمر /ı/ 1. to carry transport (from one place to another). 2. to bear, support, sustain. 3. to pass on (another's words); to spread (gossip).

taşıl *neol.* fossil.

taşım طاشیم a coming to the boil. **bir** — **kaynatmalı** One has to bring it to the boil once.

taşıma طاشیمه 1. *verbal n. of* **taşı**=. 2. carried. — **su ile değirmen dönmez** (*lit.* A mill will not turn with carried water.) An enterprise cannot succeed with inadequate means.

taşın=ⁱʳ طاشینمر طاشینی 1. *pass. of* **taşı**=. 2. to move one's belongings to another place; to move. 3. to go too often (to a place).

taşır=ⁱʳ طاشیرمر طاشرمد /ı/ 1. *caus. of* **taş**= 3. 2. to injure its hoof by excessive work (horse).

taşıt 1 *neol.* means of transportation, vehicle.

taşıt=ⁱʳ 2 طاشیتمر /ı, a/ *caus. of* **taşı**=.

taşıyıcı طاشیجی 1. that habitually bears or carries. 2. who spreads gossip.

ta'şir (. —) تعشیر A *lrnd.* 1. a causing to be ten; a dividing into tenths. 2. a tithing produce, taking the canonical tithe. 3. a doing an act ten times, or for the tenth time. 4. a dividing or making a copy of the Quran by sections each of ten verses (each section making a lesson for recitation) 5. a making a poem in stanzas of ten couplets, or of ten verses. —**ât** (. ——) A *pl.* —**î** (. ——) A pertaining to tithing.

ta'şiye تعشیه A *lrnd.* 1. a giving one his evening meal. 2. a pasturing cattle in the cool of the evening.

taşkaldıran طاشقالدیران the turnstone, *zool., Arenaria interpres.*

taşkın طاشقین 1. overflowing; overlapping. 2. excessive; exuberant. 3. insolent beyond bounds. — **ayak** *arch.* pier (of a wall, arch, etc.). — **coşkun** 1. seething or effervescing and overflowing. 2. very exuberant. — **saçak** eaves (of roof).

taşkınlıkᶠ¹ طاشقینلق 1. overflowingness. 2. excess; impetuosity. 3. insolence.

taşla=[r] **1** طاشلامسن /ı/ 1. to stone, to kill with stones. 2. to pave with stones.

taşla=[r] **2** طاشىرمق archaic /ı/ to throw out.

taşlama طاشلامه 1. verbal n. of **taşla= 1.** 2. folk poetry satiric poem.

taşlan=[ır] طاشلنمق pass. of **taşla= 1.**

taşlaş=[ır] طاشلاشمق to become petrified.

taşlat=[ır] طاشلاتمق /ı, a/ caus. of **taşla= 1.**

taşlı طاشلى 1. stony, rocky. 2. set with stones.

taşlık[ğı] طاشلق 1. stony, rocky place. 2. paved courtyard; stone threshold. 3. gizzard.

taşma طاشمه verbal n. of **taş= 3.**

taşra (..) طاشره 1. the outside. 2. the provinces. 3. archaic out; outwards. **—lı** living in the provinces; provincial. **—lık** 1. conditions of provincial life. 2. the provinces.

taşt طشت P lrnd. basin, bowl. **—ı sîmîn** poet. the moon. **—ı zerîn** 1. golden bowl, goblet. 2. poet. the sun.

taştdar (. —) طشتدار P lrnd. valet who has charge of the wash basin and ewer offered after meals.

taştger طشتگر P lrnd. maker of basins and bowls.

tat[dı] **1** طاد طات 1. taste, flavor; relish. 2. charm; sweetness. **— al=** /dan/ to taste; to enjoy the taste of. **—ını al=** /ın/ to acquire a taste (for); to enjoy. **—ına bak=** /ın/ to taste. **—ında bırak=** /ı/ not to overdo something. **—ını çıkar=** /ın/ to get the utmost enjoyment out of something. **—ı damağında kaldı** The flavor of it still lingers on one's palate; one still hankers after it. **—ına doyum olmaz** It is very tasty; one cannot have enough of it. **—ı git=**, **—ı kaç=** to lose its taste; to become unpleasant. **—ını kaçır=** /ın/ to spoil the enjoyment (of a party, etc.); to overdo something. **—ını tat=** /ın/ to have a taste (of). **—ını tuzunu boz=** /ın/ same as **tadını kaçır=**. **—ı tuzu kalmadı** It has lost all its charm; it no longer gives any pleasure. **— tuzu yok** tasteless, insipid. **—ına var=** /ın/ to get the full flavor (of), to enjoy. **—ından yenmez** too sweet.

Tat 2 (—) طات 1. Ott. hist., scornful name given by the Turks to subject Persians and Kurds. 2. l. c., archaic poor, wretch. 3. l. c., archaic stranger.

tat=[dar] **3** طاتمق /ı/ 1. to taste, to try the taste of. 2. to experience; to undergo.

tatabbu[uu] طبّع A lrnd. 1. an acquiring some particular nature and disposition. 2. an affecting the habits or disposition of another.

tatabbub طبّب A lrnd. 1. a studying medicine; a practicing medicine, especially as a beginner. 2. a pretending to be a physician.

tatabuk[ku] (. —.) طبّک A same as **tetabuk.**

tatafful[lü] طفّل A lrnd. a going uninvited to a feast for the sake of the food.

tatahhur طهّر A lrnd. 1. a becoming purified, cleansed; purity, cleanliness. 2. a performing an ablution; purification. 3. a keeping oneself pure from sin; moral purity. **—ât** (... —) A pl.

Tatar 1 تاتار Tatar; the Tatars. **— böreği** a kind of pastry (filled with ground meat and yogurt). **— Bucağı** Ott. hist. Bessarabia. **— Kazağı** the Cossack of the Dnieper.

tatar 2 تاتار |Tatar 1| courier, especially a government courier. **— ağası** Ott. hist. 1. head courier. 2. restless person who does not stay long in one place. **— çıkar=** to send out couriers. **— dolaması** Ott. hist. cloak worn by couriers. **— kalpağı** Ott. hist. headdress peculiar to government couriers. **— kaltağı** light, strong saddle-tree of a peculiar shape. **— kethüdası** Ott. hist. the superintendent of government couriers. **— oku** 1. crossbow. 2. shaft shot from a crossbow. **— yolu** highway, post road.

Tatarca (. . .) تاتارجه the Tatar language; in Tatar.

tatarcık[ğı] تاتارجق sandfly, midge, zool., Phlebotomus. **— humması** sandfly-fever.

tatari تاتارى half-cooked, underdone (food).

Tatari 1 (— — —) تاتارى P lrnd. Tatar, pertaining to the Tatars.

tatari 2 (..—) تاتارى carrier (pigeon).

Tataristan (...—) تاتارستان P Tatary, the land of the Tatars.

Tatarlık[ğı] تاتارلق 1. quality and mode of life of the Tatars. 2. territory inhabited by Tatars.

tatarrub طرّب A lrnd. a being or becoming lively and sprightly with joy.

tatarruf طرّف A lrnd. a withdrawing to one side and not mixing with others.

tatarruk[ku] طرّق A lrnd. 1. a seeking or finding a way of access to. 2. a thwarting, injuring. 3. a consecutively striking, a hammering.

Tatarsı تاتارسى resembling a Tatar, Mongoloid.

tataum 1 (. —.) طاعم A lrnd. 1. a feeding and entertaining one another on successive days. 2. a billing and cooing with one another; a being very friendly together.

tataum 2 طعّم A lrnd. a tasting, a trying the taste of.

tatavvu[uu] طوّع A lrnd. 1. an acting obediently and submissively. 2. a performing any religious act as a work of supererogation; any act performed in addition to the strict letter of religious requirement.

tatavvuan (. . ..) طوعًا A lrnd. supererogatively.

tatavvuât (...—) تطوّعات A *lrnd.* spontaneous actions, works of supererogation.

tatavvuk^ku تطوّك A *lrnd.* 1. a putting or having another put a necklace, collar or chain on one's own neck. 2. a taking upon oneself, an undertaking; a submitting to.

tatayyub تطيّب A *lrnd.* 1. a becoming pleasant, agreeable, delicious or fragrant. 2. a perfuming oneself.

tatayyur تطيّر A *lrnd.* an auguring evil, a considering as a bad omen. **—ât** (...—) A *pl.*

tatbik^kı (.—) تطبيق A 1. an applying or adapting; adaptation; application. 2. a making one thing correspond to another; a comparing one thing with another; comparison; collation. 3. *lrnd.* a covering or fitting anything like a lid or cover. 4. *lrnd.* stratification of minerals. **— edil=** to be brought into application, to come into force (law). **— et=** 1. /ı/ to apply (rule, expedient); to adapt. 2. /la/ to compare (one thing with another). 3. /ı, a/ to fit (lid, etc.). **— imzası** specimen signature. **— mühürü** official seal (of a person recognized by the authorities). **— sahasına koy=** /ı/ to put into practice.

tatbikan (.—'.) تطبيقاً A *lrnd.* /a/ 1. conformable (to). 2. according to.

tatbikat (.——) تطبيقات A 1. applications (of a law). 2. a putting into practice; practice. 3. *mil.* maneuvers. **—ta** in practice.

tatbikçi تطبيقجى *Ott. hist.* officer in a court or department who registers official seals for the purpose of comparing and identifying impressions that may be doubtful.

tatbikî (.——) تطبيقى A 1. comparative. 2. practical. **— ilimler** applied sciences. **— sanatlar** applied arts.

tatbil (.—) تطبيل A *lrnd.* a beating a drum, a drumming.

tatfif (.—) تطفيف A *lrnd.* a giving short weight or measure. **T— Suresi** name of the eighty-third sura of the Quran.

tatfiye تطفية A *lrnd.* an extinguishing a fire or light.

tathin (.—) تطحين A *lrnd.* a grinding. **—ât** (.——) A *pl.*

tathir (.—) تطهير A *lrnd.* 1. a cleaning, purifying; purification. 2. a disinfecting, disinfection. **— et=** /ı/ to clean, purify; to disinfect.

tathirât (.——) تطهيرات A *lrnd.* purification; disinfection.

tatık^kı, **tatım** طاتيم طاتين طاتو a taste; small bit eaten to try the taste.

ta'tif (.—) تطيف A *lrnd.* 1. a bending or inclining a thing. 2. a making a person incline kindly to an inferior.

ta'til (.—) A, **tatil** (—.) تعطيل 1. a suspension of work; holiday, vacation; rest. 2. stoppage (of any activity). 3. closed for a holiday (office, etc.). 4. *lrnd.* a denying the existence of God, atheism. **— et=** /ı/ 1. to suspend, to cause to cease. 2. to close (school, etc.) **—i eşgal** *lrnd.* stoppage of work, strike. **— günü** holiday, day off. **— ol=** to be closed (for a holiday). **— yap=** to take a holiday.

tatilname (———.) تعطيلنامه P *lrnd.* order of suspension (of a newspaper).

tat'im (.—) تطعيم A *lrnd.* 1. a giving food, a feeding. 2. a grafting or budding. 3. an inoculating, inoculation; vaccination.

ta'tir (.—) تعطير A *lrnd.* a perfuming.

ta'tis (.—) تعطيس A *lrnd.* a causing to sneeze.

ta'tiş (.—) تعطيش A *lrnd.* a causing to become thirsty.

tatla=^r طاتلامو /ı/ to sweeten, flavor (food). **—n=** to become sweet or tasty.

tatlı طاتلى طاتلو طاتو 1. sweet; pleasant, agreeable. 2. dessert; sweet. 3. flavored; savory, tasty. 4. fresh, drinkable (water). 5. kind (words). **— acı** bittersweet. **—ya bağla=** /ı/ to settle (a matter) amicably. **— bakış** 1. a sweet glance. 2. slight cast in the eye. **— belâ** a sweet curse (used as a term of endearment for a child). **— boyan** the licorice plant and root. **— can** one's precious soul. **— dil** soft words; a pleasant way of speaking. **— dil güler yüz** soft words and a pleasant manner. **— dil yılanı deliğinden çıkarır** *proverb* (lit. Soft words can bring a snake out of its hole.) Sweet words and pleasant manners can work wonders. **— dilli** soft-spoken. **— limon** sweet lemon, sweet lime, *bot.*, *Citrus pergamia*, or *Citrus limonum*. **— patates** sweet potato, *bot.*, *Ipomoea batatas*. **— sert** pleasantly harsh (words, manner). **— söz** soft words, pleasant speech. **— su** fresh water, drinkable water. **— su Frengi** Levantine. **— su kaptanı** inexperienced sailor. **— sülümen** calomel. **— tatlı** in a very sweet and agreeable manner; softly, pleasantly. **— yerinde nihayet ver=** /a/ to bring something to a conclusion in time (so as to avoid complications).

tatlıcı طاتليجى 1. maker or seller of sweets. 2. fond of sweet things, sweet-toothed.

tatlılan=^ır طاتليلانمق to become sweet or pleasant. **—dır=** /ı/ to render sweet, pleasant.

tatlılaş=^ır طاتليلاشمق to become sweet or pleasant. **—tır=** /ı/ to render sweet, pleasant.

tatlılı طاتليلى sweetened.

tatlılık^ğı طاتليلق 1. sweetness; pleasantness; agreeableness. 2. kindness; soft words.

tatlımsı طاتليمسى somewhat sweet.

tatlik^kı (.—) تطليق A *lrnd.* 1. a divorcing,

tatlıye

repudiating a wife. 2. a loosing (a beast and letting it go).

tatlıye تطليه A *lrnd.* an anointing; a coating over with paint, gilding.

tatma طعم 1. *verbal n. of* **tat= 3.** 2. the sense of taste, gustation.

tatmin (. —) تطمين A reassurance; satisfaction. — **et=** /ı/ 1. to satisfy. 2. to calm, reassure. — **ol=** to be satisfied.

tatminat (. — —) تطمينات A *lrnd.* satisfactions.

tatminkâr (. — —) تطمينكار P *lrnd.* satisfactory.

tatrib (. —) تطريب A *lrnd.* 1. a making lively, sprightly with joy and pleasure. 2. a trilling, quavering the voice in singing or chanting.

tatriz (. —) تطريز A *lrnd.* an embroidering a cloth or garment; embroidery.

tatsız طعم سز 1. tasteless, insipid; ill-flavored. 2. disagreeable. — **tuzsuz** insipid; stupid and dull.

tatsızlan= طعم سزلانمق 1. to become insipid. 2. to behave in a disagreeable manner. —**dır=** /ı/ *caus.*

tatsızlık طعم سزلك 1. insipidity, dullness. 2. disagreeable behavior.

tattır= طعم دير مك /ı, a/ to let taste.

tatula, tatura طاطوره P 1. thorn-apple, datura, *bot., Datura stramonium.* 2. bad-tasting thing.

tatvik (. —) تصويق A *lrnd.* 1. a putting a ring or necklace around the neck; a putting anything around the neck. 2. a giving power and ability to a person, an empowering, enabling.

tatvil (. —) تطويل A *lrnd.* 1. a lengthening, prolonging, stretching out. 2. prolixity. — **et=** /ı/ to prolong. —**i kelâm** a being talkative or contentious, speaking too much. —**ât** (. — —) *pl.*

tatyib (. —) تطييب A *lrnd.* 1. a making good, pleasant, agreeable, delicious or fragrant. 2. a perfuming. 3. a rendering tranquil and happy. —**i hatır et=** to calm, console, satisfy a person.

tatyiben (. —'.) تطييبا A *lrnd.* consolingly.

taun (— —) طاعون A *lrnd.* pest; plague; epidemic. —**i Amvas** *Isl. hist.* the first pestilence which attacked the Muslim conquerors of Syria. —**î** (— — — —) A pertaining to a plague; epidemic.

taus (—.) طاؤس A *lrnd., same as* **tavus.** —**i ateşber** *poet.* the sun. —**i felek,** —**i huld,** —**i kudsi** *poet.* angel. —**i maşrık** *poet.* the rising sun. —**i sidre** the angel Gabriel.

tav 1 طاو [*Persian* —] 1. the exact state of heat, dampness etc. (required for the manipulation of a material); proper heat (for tempering or hammering a metal). 2. opportune moment. 3. well-nourished condition, fatness. 4. water sprinkled (on paper, tobacco, etc., before pressing). 5. *slang* trick. —**ır** 1. well-tempered (iron). 2. at the right moment. —**ını bul=** to acquire the right condition (for working, etc.) —**ına düş=** to happen just at the right time. —**a düşür=** /ı/ *slang* to cheat, to deceive. — **fırını** tempering furnace. —**ı geçti** The best moment (for working) has passed. — **getir=** /a/ to find the necessary strength to do something. —**a getir=** /ı/ to bring to the correct heat. —**ına getir=** /ı/ to bring to the right condition. —**ı kaçır=** to miss the right moment; to let slip a suitable opportunity. —**ı savdı** *same as* **tavı geçti.** — **ver=** /a/ to bring to the requisite degree of dampness. —**ını ver=** /ın/ *same as* **tava getir=**.

tav 2 طاو *var. of* **dav 1.**

tav [v¹] **3** طوع A *lrnd.* a willingly submitting; willing submission; obedience.

tava طاوه [tabe 1] 1. frying pan. 2. fried food. 3. ladle (for melting metal). 4. trough for slaking lime. 5. ditch for letting sea water into a salt pan.

tavaf (. —) طواف A 1. *Isl. rel.* the ceremony of going around the Kaaba during the pilgrimage at Mecca. 2. a walking or running round a sacred thing or place; circumambulation.

tavafan (.. —) طوفان A *lrnd.* a going around a person, thing or place; a circumambulating; circumambulation, especially a circuit about the Kaaba at Mecca.

Tavagi, Tavagit (. — .) طواغى طواغيت A *lrnd., pl. of* **Tagut.**

tavahin 1 (. — .) طواحن A *lrnd., pl. of* **tahine.**

tavahin 2 (. — —) طواحين A *lrnd., pl. of* **tahun, tahune.**

tavaif (. — .) طوائف A *lrnd., pl. of* **taife.** —**i mülûk** *hist.* the nationalities into which a great empire breaks up.

tavain (. — —) طواعين A *lrnd., pl. of* **taun.**

tavali [ii] (. — .) طوالع A *lrnd., pl. of* **tali 1.**

tavamir (. — —) طوامير A *lrnd., pl. of* **tamar.**

tavan 1 طاوان 1. ceiling (of a room). 2. highest point reached (by an aircraft or a projectile). — **arası** attic. — **başa geç=,** — **başa yıkıl=** (*lit.,* for the ceiling to fall down on one's head) to be crushed or ruined; to be overcome by fear or shame. — **fiatı** *fin.* highest price in governmental purchases. — **göbeği** the central boss or ornament of a ceiling. — **kirişi** *arch.* ceiling joist. — **süpürgesi** long-handled broom for ceilings.

tav'an 2 (.'.) طوعا A *lrnd.* voluntarily; spontaneously. — **ve kerhen** willingly or under compulsion, willy-nilly.

tavan 3 (— —) طاوان P *lrnd.* 1. crime, trespass, sin. 2. impost, fine, tax.

tavanla= طاوانلمق /ı/ to apply a ceiling. —n= pass. —t= /ı, a/ caus. of tavanla=.
Tavasim, Tavasin (.——) طواسيم صواسين A the 26th, 27th and 28th suras of the Quran.
tavassul توصل A lrnd. a managing to reach, a gaining admittance to a person by means of endeavor; a seeking connection with.
tavassut توسط A 1. an intervening, interposing; intervention. 2. a mediating; mediation, interposition. — et= to intervene, to act as mediator.
tavaşi (.—.) طواشى A lrnd. eunuch.
tavattun توطن A lrnd. a settling in a place; a making a home (in a country). — et= to settle for permanent residence.
tavavis (.——) طواويس A lrnd., pl. of taus, tavus.
tavazzuh توضح A a becoming clear or manifest. — et= to become clear.
tavcı طاوجى slang 1. accomplice in a swindle (who runs up the price at an auction or pretends to put a high value on a worthless thing). 2. swindler, cheat. —lık the quality or profession of such a swindler.
tavd طود A lrnd. 1. mountain, hill. 2. camel's hump.
tavf طوف A lrnd., same as tavafan. — et= /ı/ to circumambulate.
tavhane (.—.) طاوخانه P lrnd. 1. same as tabhane 1. 2. shelter for the poor. — gibi in utter confusion.
tavır طور [tavr] A 1. mode, manner, kind. 2. attitude; arrogant manner. 3. lrnd. time (of repetition), turn. 4. mus. deviating realization of a melodic line. — sat= /a/ to give oneself airs.
tavırlı طورلى 1. having (such and such) a manner. 2. arrogant.
tav'î (.—) طوعى A lrnd. spontaneous.
ta'vic (.—) تعويج A lrnd. 1. a bending (a thing), a twisting. 2. an inlaying or ornamenting with ivory.
ta'vid (.—) تعويد A lrnd. an accustoming, a habituating.
ta'vik (.—) تعويق A lrnd. a delaying, hindering, preventing, impeding. — et= /ı/ 1. to hinder, prevent. 2. to delay. 3. to defer. —ât (.——) A pl. of ta'vik. —li bomba delayed-action bomb.
tavil (.—) طويل A lrnd. 1. long; tall. 2. lengthy. 3. pros. meter characterized by the iambic beginning of alternating 3 and 4 syllabic feet (.——/.——/.——/.——). T— Suresi one of the names of the fortieth sura of the Quran.
tavile (.—.) طويله A lrnd. 1. line or lines of horses picketed at pasture to a long rope. 2. tether for an animal. 3. same as tavla 2.

taviyet طويت A lrnd. 1. purpose, intention; mind, heart. 2. thought, the thoughts; secret intention. 3. man's character or disposition.
ta'viz 1 (.—) A, tâviz (——) تعويض lrnd. 1. concession; compromise. 2. a substituting; substitution. 3. a compensating one for something taken; compensation; replacement.
ta'viz 2 (.—) تعويذ A lrnd. 1. amulet, charm; incantation against evil. 2. a praying for protection; a commending one in prayer to God. 3. a fortifying or preserving from evil by amulet or incantation.
ta'vizat 1 (.——) تعويضات A lrnd., pl. of ta'viz 1. —ta bulun= to make concessions.
ta'vizat 2 (.——) تعويذات A lrnd., pl. of ta'viz 2, amulets, charms; incantations.
ta'vizen (.—'.) تعويضاً A lrnd. by way of replacement; as a substitute; in compensation.
tavk طوق A lrnd. 1. necklace, chain, collar. 2. power, ability, means. 3. bird's ruff. —i amberin poet. dark circle of young beard on the cheek. —i beşer man's ability. —i zerrîn gold necklace.
tavla 1 (.'.) طاوله It backgammon. bir — atalım Let's play a game of trick track. — pulu backgammon piece. — tahtası backgammon board.
tavla 2 (.'.) طاوله [tavile] stable for horses. — ipi long rope by which horses are picketed.
tavla= 3 طاوله مك /ı/ 1. to bring (a thing) to its best condition. 2. to sprinkle water on (paper, etc. before pressing). 3. to deceive, swindle. 4. archaic to grow fat and sleek.
tavlacı (.'..), **tavlakâr** (..—) طاوله جى طاوله كار 1. stable boy. 2. habitual backgammon player.
tavlan= طاوله نمك pass. of tavla= 3. —dır= /ı, a/ caus. of tavla= 3.
tavlat= طاوله تمك /ı, a/ caus. of tavla= 3.
tavlı طاولى 1. at its best condition. 2. damped (paper, tobacco). 3. red-hot (iron). 4. in prime condition (animal).
tavlun طاولون It naut. the orlop deck of a ship of war of the old style, lower deck.
tavr طور A lrnd., same as tavır. — ü hareket behavior. — ü hareket ruhiyatı behaviorism.
tavren (.'.) طوراً A lrnd. 1. by manner, in mode. 2. at one time of repetition.
tavsa= طاوساماق 1. to fall away from its prime; to cool down. 2. to decline, decay. —t= /ı/ caus.
tavsız طاوسز 1. not heated sufficiently; not tempered. 2. not in prime condition.
tavsif (.—) توصيف A lrnd. 1. a describing; description. 2. a praising, praise, eulogy.

tavsil

— **et=** /ı/ 1. to enumerate the qualities of something; to describe. 2. to praise, to eulogize. —**ât** (. — —) A *pl.*

tavsil (. —) تَوْصِيل A *lrnd.* a causing to reach and join another, a bringing or putting together.

tavsit (. —) تَوْسِيط A *lrnd.* a causing to be the means of, a causing to be a go-between.

tavsiye تَوْصِيه A a recommending; recommendation; advice, suggestion. — **et=** to recommend.

tavsiyeli تَوْصِيه لى 1. recommended. 2. backed, supported (by an influential person).

tavsiyename (. . . — .) تَوْصِيه نامه P letter of recommendation.

tavşan 1 طاوشان، طوشان، تاوشان hare, *zool.*, *Lepus europaeus*; rabbit. — **ağzı** pink (color). — **anahtarı** picklock. —**ı araba ile avla=** to hunt hares in a carriage; to do something calmly and easily. — **ayağı** hare's-foot clover, *bot.*, *Trifolium arvense*. — **bayırı aştı** The hare has gone over the hill; it's gone forever. — **bıyığı** sowbread, *bot.*, *Cyclamen*. — **boku** *vulgar* useless, good-for-nothing man. — **boku gibi ne kokar ne bulaşır** (*lit.*, like a hare's droppings, neither smelly nor messy) harmless but useless. — **dağa küsmüş de dağın haberi olmamış** The hare was cross with the mountain but the mountain was not even aware of it, *said when an insignificant person takes to heart the action of an important person*. — **dudağı** harelip. —**a kaç tazıya tut de=** to be tolerant toward a person and provoke another against him. — **kanı** bright carmine. — **kulağı** sowbread, *bot.*, *Cyclamen*. — **otu** corn panic-grass, Deccan grass, *bot.*, *Panicum colonum*. — **paçası** sowbread, *bot.*, *Cyclamen*. — **paçası yonca** hare's-foot clover, field clover, *bot.*, *Trifolium arvense*. —**ın suyunun suyu** a very distant connection. — **uykusu** 1. sleep with the eyes half closed; pretended sleep. 3. inattention. — **yatağı** hare's "form." — **yavrusu** leveret. — **yılı** fourth year of the Turkish cycle of twelve years. — **yürekli** timid.

tavşan 2 طاوشان، طوشان، تاوشان cabinet maker.

tavşan 3 طاوشان a boy dancer who performs a certain dance. — **oğlanı** *Ott. hist.*, name given to a certain class of dancers in the palace. — **raksı** *Ott. hist.*, a kind of dance imitating the movements of a hare.

tavşanca طاوشانجه a certain dance and its music.

tavşancıl طاوشانجیل eagle, vulture. — **otu** eagle's claw. — **taşı** 1. the stone *aetites*. 2. nicker-seed or nut fruit of *Caesalpinia bonduc*.

tavşanla= طاوشانلامق to become as thin as a hare.

tavşanlık^ti طاوشانلق fine joinery, carving.

tavtin (. —) تَوْطِين A *lrnd.* a settling, establishing a person in a permanent home.

tavtiye تَوْطِيه A *lrnd.* 1. a preparing the way for a subject by prefatory remarks; a preparing.

2. a treading down, a trampling. 3. a leveling by trampling, rolling, raking, etc.

tavuk^gu طاووق، تاووق، طاوق، تاوق hen. — **ayağı** skeleton key, picklock. — **ayağı yemiş** who prates unnecessarily; garrulous, indiscreet. — **balığı** local name for the whiting. — **biti** crab-louse. — **gelen yerden yumurta esirgenmez** Don't stint on eggs for the hatchery. Give a little if you hope to get something for it. — **götü** wart. — **götü tövbe tutmaz** *vulgar* A weak person won't reform for long. — **gözü** 1. chicken's eye. 2. chilblains. — **kanadı** 1. chicken wing. 2. fan (for fanning a fire). — **karası** night-blindness. — **kümesi** chicken-coop. — **otu** fowl meadow grass, *bot.*, *Poa palustris*. — **pençesi** air plant, floppers, *bot.*, *Bryophyllum pinnatum*. — **suyu** chicken broth. — **yılı** the tenth year of the Turkish cycle of twelve.

tavukçu طاووقجى raiser or seller of chickens. —**luk** dealing in poultry.

tavulga تاوولغه a species of buckthorn; purple willow; arbutus.

tavus طاووس، طاوس [taus] peacock, *zool.*, *Pavo cristatus*. — **kuşu** peacock. — **kuyruğu** 1. peacock's tail. 2. *slang* violent vomiting.

tavuslan=^ir طاووسلنمق to strut like a peacock.

tavuş 1 طاووش *prov.* a walking or pattering sound.

tavuş=^ur **2** طاووشمق *prov.* to creep along slowly and stealthily.

tavvaf (. —) طَوَّاف A *lrnd.* 1. one who habitually walks, runs or circles about anything. 2. one who joins in the sacred procession at Mecca or in other places.

tavvafiye (. — . .) طَوَّافِيه *Ott. hist.* fee paid night-watchmen of government offices.

tavvele طَوَّلَ A *lrnd.* May God prolong (his life).

tavzif (. —) تَوْظِيف A *lrnd.* 1. an entrusting with a duty. 2. an assigning a pay or allowances, an appointing as a salaried official.

tavzih (. —) تَوْضِيح A *lrnd.* 1. a making plain; a declaring explicitly; clear explanation. 2. an explicit declaration; explanatory correction. — **et=** to make clear, explain. —**ât** (. — —) A *pl.*

tavzihen (. — ´ .) تَوْضِيحاً A *lrnd.* by way of explanation.

tay 1 طاى، تاى colt, foal.

tay 2 طاى، تاى P 1. half a beast's load; bale. 2. counterpoise. — **dur=** to stand up (baby not able to walk yet).

tay 3 طاى، تاى *prov.* match, equal.

tay^yyi **4** طَىّ A *lrnd.* 1. a folding or rolling up. 2. a canceling or erasing of words. 3. a traversing of a space (of time or place); a leaving distance behind. —yi mekân a traversing of a space or place, a going from one place to another in a miraculous way regardless of distance.

taya طايه [dâye] child's nurse. — çocuğu spoiled child.

tayaran (..—) طيران A *lrnd.* 1. a flying, flight. 2. a being volatile.

Taybe طيبه A the pleasant city, Medina.

tayf طيف A 1. *lrnd.* specter, ghost. 2. *phys.* spectrum. 3. *lrnd.* stroke of paralysis or insanity (inflicted by a demon).

tayfa طايفه [taife] 1. band, troop. 2. crew; gang; sailor.

tayfbin (.—) طيف بين P *lrnd.* spectroscope.

tayfun طايفون Chin typhoon.

tayıkᵏⁱ (—.) تايق A *lrnd.* that desires, that yearns after.

tayın 1 تعيين [ta'yin] ration; small loaf issued to soldiers.

tayın=ⁱʳ **2** طاينس *archaic* to slip; to stumble.

tayiⁱⁱ (—.) طايع A *lrnd.* 1. obedient, submissive. 2. willing, acting cheerfully.

tayian (—.'.) طايعا A *lrnd.* willingly, obediently.

ta'yib (.—) تعييب A *lrnd.* a finding fault; a reproaching. — **et=** /ı/ to blame. —**ât** (.——) A *pl.*

ta'yid (.—) تعييد A *lrnd.* an observing a festival.

ta'yin (.—) A, **tayin** (——) تعيين 1. an appointing, designating; appointment, designation; determination. 2. same as **tayın 1**. 3. a pointing out, indicating a part to the eyes. —**i cihet** *phil.* orientation. — **et=** /ı/ 1. to appoint. 2. to decide, fix, settle, determine. 3. to point out; to assume (a point etc.). —**i ta'yinât** *lrnd.* rations and allowances.

ta'yinât (.——) تعيينات A *lrnd.* rations. — **bedeli** commutation of rations.

ta'yinci تعييني 1. contractor for supplies. 2. man who receives the rations of his squad.

ta'yinî (.——) تعييني A *lrnd.* determinative.

ta'yinkerde (.—..) تعيين كرده P *lrnd.* appointed, designated.

ta'yir (.—) تعيير A *lrnd.* a reproaching, reviling, disgracing. —**ât** (.——) A *pl.*

ta'yiş (.—) تعييش A *lrnd.* a causing to live; a giving the means of subsistence.

taylakᵏⁱ طايلاق *archaic* 1. young camel in his second year. 2. a young scapegrace.

taylasan (..—) طيلسان A *lrnd.* 1. cloth or shawl wound about the head as a turban or as a wrap. 2. the end of a turban hanging down.

tayr طير A *lrnd.* birds; winged things; bird. —**i hür** the hawk, falcon.

tayriyun (..—) طيريون A *lrnd.* ornithologists.

tayrunnutkᵏᵘ طير النطق A *lrnd.* speech, a word.

tayrüddevle طير الدوله A *lrnd.* the bird of Paradise.

tayrülleyl طير الليل A *lrnd.* owl.

Taysefun (..—) طيسفون A *hist.* the city of Ctesiphon (in Iran).

tayş, tayşan (.—) طيش طيشان A *lrnd.* a being light, frivolous; frivolity.

tayyar (.—) طيّار A *lrnd.* 1. extremely volatile. 2. given to flying; flying. 3. very swift (horse). 4. of a volatile, mercurial temperament (man). 5. high, towering (wave). 6. mercury.

tayyarat (.——) طيّارات A 1. *lrnd.* chance gains, gifts. 2. *Ott. hist., fin. adm.* unbudgeted revenues, a windfall.

tayyare (.—.) طيّاره A airplane, aircraft. — **gemisi** aircraft-carrier. — **meydanı** airport. —**ci** pilot. —**cilik** aviation, flying.

tayyebe ('..) طيّبه A *lrnd.* May (God) make (his grave) easy, pleasant. May he rest in peace.

tayyet=ᵈᵉʳ طيّ اتمك /ı/ to write off, to strike out, to delete.

tayyib طيّب A *lrnd.* 1. good, pleasant, pure. 2. in good health, well.

tayyibat (..—) طيّبات A *lrnd.*, *pl.* of **tayyibe**.

tayyibe طيّبه A *lrnd.* good word, benediction, praise. **T— Suresi** one of the names of the first sura of the Quran.

tayyör تايّور F tailor-made costume.

taz 1 (—) تاز P *lrnd.* a run, gallop, charge.

-taz 2 (—) تاز P *lrnd.* that runs, gallops, chases or pillages, as in **sebüktaz**.

tazaccuᵘᵘ تضجّع A *lrnd.* a being slothful, negligent, or backward in acting.

tazaccur تضجّر A *lrnd.* a being vexed, grieved or disgusted; vexation, grief, disgust.

tazahhükᵏᵘ تضحّك A *lrnd.* a laughing with affectation.

tazahükᵏᵘ (.—.) تضاحك A *lrnd.* 1. a laughing at or with each other. 2. a pretending to laugh.

tazallülⁱᵘ تظلّل A *lrnd.* 1. a going into or keeping under shade, a shading oneself. 2. a seeking or finding protection.

tazallüm تظلّم A *lrnd.* a complaining of wrong or oppression. — **et=** 1. to complain of an injustice. 2. to excite compassion; to play the martyr. —**i hal** a complaining about one's condition. —**ât** (...—) A *pl. of* **tazallüm**.

tazalüm (.—.) تظالم A *lrnd.* an acting unjustly towards one another; an injuring one another.

tazammun تضمّن A *lrnd.* 1. a comprising, containing; comprehension. 2. implication.

tazane (——.) تازانه P *lrnd.*, same as **taziyane**.

tazannuⁿ تظنّن A *lrnd.* a surmising; conjecture; guess.

tazarruᵘᵘ تَضَرُّع A *lrnd.* 1. a humbling oneself in prayer. 2. a humbling oneself obsequiously; supplication. — **et=** 1. humbly to beg. 2. to address a humble prayer. —**ât** (...—) A *pl.*

tazarrub تَضَرُّب A *lrnd.* a smiting oneself violently; agitation, commotion.

tazarruf تَظَرُّف A *lrnd.* an affecting wit or gracefulness; affectation. —**ât** (...—) A *pl.*

tazarruname (...—.) تَضَرُّع نامه P *lrnd.* letter of supplication.

tazarrur تَضَرُّر A *lrnd.* a suffering injury or loss.

tazarub (.—.) تَضَارُب A *lrnd.* a striking, beating or wounding one another.

tazavvuᵘᵘ تَضَوُّع A *lrnd.* a diffusing odors.

tazayüf (.—.) تَضَايُف A *lrnd.* 1. a being or becoming narrow; narrowness. 2. a being related; mutual relationship. 3. a collectively drawing near and hemming in; a mutually approaching.

tazayyukᵏᵘ تَضَيُّق A 1. *path.* stenosis. 2. *lrnd.* a being narrow.

taze (—.) تازه P 1. fresh; new; recent. 2. young, tender. 3. young girl. 4. raw; inexperienced. — **bahar** 1. early spring; early verdure. 2. early youth. — **biber** green pepper. — **can bul=** to revive, to find new life. — **ekmek** fresh bread. — **fasulye** green beans. — **fidan** 1. young plant. 2. handsome boy or girl. — **taze** quite fresh. — **yaprak** fresh grape leaves. — **yemiş** fresh fruit.

tazegân (—.—) تازه گان P *lrnd., pl. of* **taze**.

tazegi (—.—) تازه گی P *lrnd.* 1. freshness, newness, recentness. 2. youthfulness.

tazekâr (—.—) تازه کار P *lrnd.* one who touches up and freshens old things. —**i** (—.——) P a renewing.

tazele=ʳ تازه لمك /ı/ 1. to renew, to freshen up. 2. to replenish. —**n=** *pass.* —**ndir=** /ı/ *caus.* —**ş=** 1. to become fresh or new. 2. to become young. —**ştir=** /ı/ *caus.* —**t=** /ı, a/ *caus. of* **tazele=**.

tazelikᵍⁱ تازه لك 1. freshness, tenderness; youth. 2. newness, recentness.

tazende (—..) تازنده P *lrnd.* runner, galloper, charger.

tazene (—..) تازنه P *lrnd., same as* **taziyane**.

tazhir (.—) تظهیر A *lrnd.* 1. a contemning, disregarding. 2. a giving support. —**ât** (.——) *pl.*

tazı تازی طازی [tazi] greyhound; sleuth. — **gibi** very thin (person).

tazıla=ʳ تازیلمك to become thin. —**t=** /ı/ *caus.*

tazi (——) تازی P *lrnd.* 1. Arabic; Arabian. 2. Arabian horse. 3. *same as* **tazı**.

ta'zib (.—) تعذیب A *lrnd.* a torturing, an inflicting torment. —**ât** (.——) A *pl.*

taz'if (.—) تضعیف A *lrnd.* 1. a doubling; a multiplying; reduplication, multiplication. 2. a causing to become weak. — **et=** /ı/ 1. to double, multiply. 2. to weaken. —**ât** (.——) A *pl. of* **taz'if**.

ta'zil 1 (.—) تعذیل A *lrnd.* a blaming, rebuking severely.

ta'zil 2 (.—) تعزیل A *lrnd.* a removing, separating; removal, separation.

ta'zim (.—) تعظیم A 1. an honoring, reverencing and respecting. 2. *lrnd.* a treating as great, powerful or sacred. — **et=** /ı/ to do honor to, respect, revere.

ta'zimât (.——) تعظیمات A *lrnd.* honors; homage.

ta'zimen (.—'.) تعظیماً A *lrnd.* out of respect; as an honor; in reverence.

tazinijad (——.—) تازی نژاد P *lrnd.* of Arabian race.

ta'zir 1 (.—) تعزیر A *lrnd.* 1. a reproving, censuring; reproof. 2. a chastising, beating; a flogging; punishment. — **et=** /ı/ to reprove, reprimand.

ta'zir 2 (.—) تعذیر A *lrnd.* a seeking an excuse; a putting forth a vain excuse. — **et=** /ı/ to seek an excuse, to be remiss. —**ât** (.——) A *pl. of* **ta'zir 2**.

tazisüvar (——.—) تازی سوار P *lrnd.* mounted on an Arabian horse.

taziş (—.) تازش P *lrnd.* an act of running or galloping.

taziyan (—.—) تازیان P *lrnd., pl. of* **tazi**.

taziyane (—.—.) تازیانه P *lrnd.* 1. whip, lash. 2. stimulus, spur. 3. *mus.* plectrum made of cherry wood used for playing instruments of the **bağlama** group. 4. means.

ta'ziye, ta'ziyet تعزیت تعزیه A an offering consolation for a loss by death; condolence.

taziyetname (...—.) تعزیت نامه P letter of condolence.

ta'ziz (.—) تعزیز A *lrnd.* 1. an honoring the memory (of a person); a holding in esteem. 2. a causing to become expensive or rare. — **et=** /ı/ to honor the memory (of). —**ât** (.——) A *pl. of* **taziz**.

tazlil (.—) تظلیل A *lrnd.* 1. a shading, a casting a shade over. 2. a protecting.

tazmin (.—) تضمین A 1. a holding or making free of loss, an indemnifying; indemnification. 2. indemnity, a sum paid as damages. 3. *lrnd.* a quoting matter from another work (in a poem); quotation. 4. *lrnd.* an adding a letter to a rhyme already complete (so as to necessitate the same addition in all the rhymes of the piece). 5. *lrnd.* a making or accepting a person as surety or bail. — **et=** /ı/ 1. to indemnify. 2. to accept as surety. 3. to quote from another's works. —**i mezduc** *lrnd.* a placing homophonous words in any other position than that of the rhyme word. **—i zarar et=** *lrnd.* to indemnify and make good damage or loss.

tazminat (. — —) تضمينات A damages; indemnity, compensation; reparations. **— dâvası** law action for damages. **—ı harbiye** *lrnd.* war indemnity.

tazrir (. —) تضرير A *lrnd.* a subjecting to much injury or loss.

tazyiⁱⁱ (. —) تضييع A *lrnd.* 1. a causing to be lost or wasted and destroyed; a wasting or destroying. 2. an idling away one's time. **—i evkat** a waste of time. **—ât** (. — —) A *pl. of* **tazyi.**

tazyif (. —) تضييف A *lrnd.* a receiving and entertaining hospitably.

tazyikᵏ¹ (. —) تضييق A 1. pressure. 2. oppression; a cross-questioning, threatening, torturing in order to extract information. 3. a making very narrow. 4. *lrnd.* a reducing a besieged place to straits. **— et=** /ı/ 1. to press, put pressure on. 2. to oppress. 3. *lrnd.* to tighten; to make narrow. 4. *lrnd.* to reduce to extremity. **—i nesimi** *lrnd.* atmospheric pressure. **—ât** (. — —) A *lrnd., pl. of* **tazyik.**

te 1 *name of the letter* **t** *of the Turkish alphabet.*
te 2 ت *same as* **ta 4.**
-te 3 ده *cf.* **-da 2.**
teadül (. — .) تعادل A *lrnd., same as* **taadül.**
te'alâ (. — .) تعالى A *lrnd., same as* **ta'alâ.**
teali (. — .) تعالى A *lrnd., same as* **taali.**
teamül (. — .) تعامل A *lrnd., same as* **taamül.**
tearüf (. — .) تعارف A *lrnd.* a recognizing or being acquainted with one another.
teati (. — .) تعاطى A a giving to one another; exchange.
teavün (. — .) تعاون A *lrnd., same as* **taavün.**
teb تب P *lrnd.* 1. heat. 2. fever; fever and ague. 3. feverish anxiety or desire. **— ü tâb** 1. fever and restlessness. 2. anxiety or desire and restlessness of mind. 3. ardor.
tebaᵃ¹ تبع A *lrnd.* 1. a following; an imitating, conforming to or obeying. 2. follower; imitator. **—i tabiin** the disciples of those who learned from the companions of the Prophet Muhammad.
tebaa تبع A subjects; subject (of a state).
tebaan (. '. .) تبعا A *lrnd.* /a/ in conformity with.
tebab (. —) تباب A *lrnd.* a suffering loss; a being lost; loss, perdition.
tebadül (. — .) تبادل A *lrnd.* 1. a mutual exchanging of commodities; exchange. 2. a mutual substituting; permutation of letters, alternation of terms.
tebadür (. — .) تبادر A *lrnd.* 1. a being at once understood (meaning); sudden inspiration.

2. a competing to be quickest. **— et=** /a/ to occur to the mind; to strike one (idea).

tebagguz تبغّض A *lrnd.* 1. a manifesting hatred; hatred. 2. a becoming hateful; hatefulness.

tebaguz (. — .) تباغض A *lrnd.* a mutual hating; mutual hatred, mutual ill-will. **— et=** to hate one another.

tebah (. —) تباه P *lrnd.* 1. lost, gone; wasted. 2. spoiled, rotten, putrid. 3. devastated, ruined. 4. bad, useless; corrupt, wicked.

tebahhur 1 تبخّر A 1. evaporation. 2. *lrnd.* a perfuming, fumigating oneself by incense or smoke.

tebahhur 2 تبحّر A *lrnd.* 1. a penetrating the depths of science; a going deeply into a subject; erudition. 2. a being vastly rich or very learned.

tebahhurat (. . . —) تبحّرات A *lrnd., pl. of* **tebahhur 1.**

tebahi 1 (. — .) تباهى A *lrnd.* a vying in beauty, goodness or glory; a contending for pre-eminence.

tebahi 2 (. — —) تباهى P *lrnd.* corruption, destruction, ruin.

tebahkâr (. — —) تباهكار P *lrnd.* evildoer, sinner, vicious person. **—an** (. — — —) P *pl.* **—âne** (. — — — .) P corruptly; wickedly, viciously. **—i** (. — — — —) P, **—lık** the conduct or quality of a vicious man; sin, vice.

tebahtür تبختر A *lrnd.* a walking with a proud gait, strutting, swaggering pompous gait; swagger.

tebaiyet تبعيّت A *lrnd.* 1. a being the subject of a sovereign or state; allegiance; submission. 2. a following, an imitating, obeying. 3. a conforming. **— et=** /a/ 1. to submit (to), to become subject (to). 2. to conform.

tebaiyeten (. . —' . .) تبعيّة A *lrnd.* 1. as a follower, imitator, or conformer. 2. as a consequence; conforming to.

tebaki 1 (. — .) تباقى A *lrnd.* a remaining with one another.

tebaki 2 (. — .) تباكى A *lrnd.* 1. a constraining oneself to weep; forced tears. 2. a pretending to weep; feigned tears.

tebalüh (. — .) تباله A *lrnd.* a pretending to be stupid; feigned stupidity.

tebance (. — .) تبنجى *var. of* **tepançe.**

tebar 1 (. —) تبار A *lrnd.* perdition, destruction, ruin.

tebar 2 (. —) تبار P *lrnd.* family, dynasty; lineage.

tebarekâllah (. — . . —) تبارك الله A *lrnd.* God be exalted and blessed (exclamation of wonder).

tebareke (. — . .) تبارك A *lrnd.* (God) be blessed! (exclamation of piety or of mere wonder). **T— Sûresi** *name of the sixty-seventh sura of the Quran.*

tebarüz (. —.) تَبارُز A 1. a becoming manifest or prominent. 2. *lrnd.* a going forth to fight against each other as champions (in front of two hostile forces). **— ettir=** /i/ to show clearly, to emphasize, to demonstrate.

tebasbus تَبَصُّص A *lrnd.*, *same as* **tabasbus.**

tebassur تَبَصُّر A *lrnd.* a studying with special attention; diligent scrutiny. **— et=** /i/ to give attention, to scrutinize closely.

tebaşir 1 (. — —) تَباشِير P *lrnd.*, *same as* **tebeşir.**

tebaşir 2 (. — —) تَباشِير A *lrnd.* 1. good news, glad tidings. 2. indications, earnests, or beginnings of good tidings to come. **—i sabah, —i subh** the first glimmerings of dawn, the break of day.

tebaüd (. —.) تَباعُد A *lrnd.* 1. a being or becoming distant; remoteness. 2. a going to a distance, a withdrawing, a keeping at a distance; withdrawal. 3. an estranging oneself. 4. divergence.

tebayün (. —.) تَبايُن A 1. *lrnd.* a being mutually distinct and different; a being inconsistent or incommensurate with one another; contrast. 2. *phil.* antinomy. **—ât** (. —. —) A *pl.*

tebbet تَبَّت A *lrnd.* May she or it perish! **T— Sûresi** *one of the names of the one-hundred-eleventh sura of the Quran.*

tebcil (. —) تَبجيل A *lrnd.* 1. a treating with great honor, courtesy, respect or consideration; veneration, honoring. 2. honor and respect shown. **— et=** /i/ to treat with great respect and honor; to glorify.

tebcilât (. — —) تَبجيلات A *lrnd.* ceremonious acts of courtesy.

tebcilen (. —'.) تَبجيلًا A *lrnd.* in glorification (of).

tebdiⁱⁱ (. —) تَبديع A *lrnd.* a deeming or pronouncing to be an innovator (in religious matters).

tebdil (. —) تَبديل A 1. a changing, modifying; alteration, modification. 2. a converting into some other thing; change, conversion. 3. a giving in exchange; an exchanging; exchange. 4. in disguise, incognito; government spy; *obs.* detective. 5. *lrnd.* God's substituting one ordinance for another; abrogation and substitution. **—e çık=** to go out among the people for information and in disguise. **— gez=** to go about in disguise. **—i hava** change of air, change of scene. **— kayığı** *Ott. hist.* ordinary rowboat used by the Sultan or high officials to avoid observation. **—i kıyafet** disguise. **—i mekân** a changing one's residence. **— olun=** to be changed. **—i suret et=** *lrnd.* to change shape or appearance; to be transfigured. **— suretli** in disguise, incognito.

tebdilât (. — —) تَبديلات A *lrnd.*, *pl. of* **tebdil.**

tebdilen (. —'.) تَبديلًا A *lrnd.* 1. in exchange; as a change. 2. in disguise, incognito.

tebeddüⁱⁱ تَبَدُّع A *lrnd.* a being or becoming an innovator; innovation.

tebeddül تَبَدُّل A 1. a being changed. 2. change, alteration, vicissitude. **— et=** to undergo a change, to alter. **—ât** (. . . —) A changes, vicissitudes.

tebeh تَبَه P *lrnd.*, *same as* **tebah.**

tebehhül تَبَهُّل A *lrnd.* 1. a being earnest in endeavor; earnestness; strenuousness. 2. a cursing and reviling one another, a wishing evil upon each other.

tebehhüm تَبَهُّم A *lrnd.* a being doubtful, obscure and unintelligible (speech).

tebehhür تَبَهُّر A *med.* shortness of breath.

tebel تَبَل wrinkle; fold; corrugation.

tebelbül تَبَلبُل A *lrnd.* 1. languages being intermixed; confusion of tongues; Babel. 2. a being troubled with grief or anxiety; grief, anxiety. **—i elsine** confusion of tongues. **—ât** (. . . —) A *pl. of* **tebelbül.**

tebelleş تَبَلَّش obstacle that impedes or trips one up. **— ol=** /a/ 1. to pester, to worry. 2. to intrude, to be an obstacle.

tebellüdⁱⁱ تَبَلُّد A *lrnd.* a being or becoming bewildered and stupid.

tebellüğ تَبَلُّغ A *lrnd.* a receiving an official communication. **— et=** /i/ to receive a communication; to be informed. **—ât** (. . . —) A *pl. of* **tebellüğ.**

tebellüh تَبَلُّه A *lrnd.* a being or becoming idiotic; stupidity.

tebellül تَبَلُّل A *lrnd.* 1. a being or becoming moist or wet. 2. a becoming juicy, fresh, plump.

tebellür تَبَلُّر A 1. a being crystallized; crystallization. 2. a becoming clear. **— et=** 1. to crystallize. 2. to become crystal clear. **—ât** (. . . —) A *pl.*

tebeng تَبَنگ P *lrnd.* 1. large wooden tray or bowl. 2. mold for casting. 3. drum.

tebengi, tebengü تَبَنگى [*Persian* **tebenge**] thick pad of a pack-saddle. **— ağacı** lath or stretcher of wood worked into a pad to keep it stretched.

tebenni (. . —) تَبَنّى A *lrnd.* 1. a claiming or proclaiming as one's own offspring. 2. an adopting as a child; adoption (of a child). **— et=** /i/ to adopt as a child.

teber تَبَر P *lrnd.* 1. ax; hatchet. 2. halberd. 3. battle-ax.

teberdar (. . —) تَبَردار P *Ott. hist.* 1. a man furnished or armed with an ax, hatchet, or battle ax 2. halberdier. **—ân** (. . — —) P *pl.* **—ân-ı hassa** *Ott. hist.* special corps of halberdiers which marched by the side of the Sultan's horse in ceremonial processions.

teberkuᵘᵘ نَبَرْكُو A *lrnd.* a veiling one's face. —**i nisvân** the veiling of women.

teberra (..—) تَبَرَّى A *lrnd.* a withdrawing to a distance; a standing aloof.

teberrî تَبَرِّي A *lrnd.* a being justified; a being clear of blame or responsibility.

teberruᵘᵘ **1** تَبَرُّع A a giving property from pious motives; charitable gift, donation. — **et=** /ı/ to give as a free gift.

teberru 2 تَبَرُّؤ A *lrnd.* 1. a being or becoming clear, free, innocent; innocence; irresponsibility. 2. a making oneself clear, free, innocent of; a washing one's hands of.

teberruan (..'..) تَبَرُّعاً A *lrnd.* as a gift, as a charitable donation.

teberruat (...—) تَبَرُّعات A *lrnd.* donations.

teberrüd تَبَرُّد A *lrnd.* 1. a becoming cool or lukewarm (in a cause). 2. a cooling oneself with cold water, etc.

teberrükᵏᵘ تَبَرُّك A *lrnd.* 1. a receiving, anticipating, or deeming oneself possessed of a blessing (through some holy person or thing). 2. relic or sacred object through which blessings are anticipated. — **et=** to regard as a blessing; to consider as a good omen.

teberrükât (...—) تَبَرُّكات A *lrnd.* relics, sacred objects through which blessings are expected.

teberrüken (..'..) تَبَرُّكاً A *lrnd.* 1. counting something as a blessing or as a good omen. 2. bringing the blessing (of a holy man). 3. as a compliment.

teberrür تَبَرُّر A *lrnd.* a doing one's whole duty without omission; a being godly, devout.

teberrüz تَبَرُّز A *lrnd.* an appearing, coming forth.

teberzed تَبَرْزَد P *lrnd.* 1. white sugar-candy (cut with a hatchet). 2. rock salt.

teberzen تَبَرْزَن P *lrnd.* one who cuts or strikes with an ax, battle-ax, or halberd.

teberzin (..—) تَبَرْزين P *lrnd.* battle-ax carried at the saddle-bow.

tebessül تَبَسُّل A *lrnd.* 1. a wearing an austere or determined countenance; seriousness, austerity. 2. a making a show of courage (true or false).

tebessüm تَبَسُّم A 1. a smiling; smile. 2. *lrnd.* a glimmering with lightning (cloud); a commencing to open (flower). —**i hulya** smile caused by something imagined. —**i istifsar** a questioning smile. —**i zirleb** *lrnd.* (*lit.* a smile under the lip) sardonic smile, smile of derision. —**ât** (...—) A *lrnd.* smiles.

tebessümkünân (....—) تَبَسُّم‌كُنان P *lrnd.* with a smile, smilingly.

tebessür تَبَسُّر A *lrnd.* a breaking out in pustules on the skin.

tebeşbüş تَبَشْبُش A *lrnd.* a showing pleasure and joy upon seeing a friend.

tebeşir تَباشير [**tebaşir**] 1. chalk. 2. chalk mark or score. — **devri** *geol.* cretaceous period. —**e peynir bakışlı** 1. (*lit.* who looks at chalk as if it were cheese) ignorant; greedy, hungry. 2. cross-eyed. — **sistemi** *geol.* cretaceous system. — **tahtası** blackboard. —**li** mixed with or marked with chalk, chalky.

tebettül تَبَتُّل A *lrnd.* a renouncing the world, devoting oneself to a life of celibacy and devotion; devotional celibacy and retirement from the world.

tebevvül تَبَوُّل A *lrnd.* a urinating. — **et=** to urinate.

tebeyyün تَبَيُّن A *lrnd.* a being or becoming clear, manifest, visible, or conspicuous; clearness, distinctness; manifestation, conspicuousness. — **et=** to become clear; to be evident; to be proved or demonstrated.

tebhalⁱⁱ (.—), **tebhale** (.—.) تَبْخال P *lrnd.* 1. pustule breaking out upon the lip after fever. 2. bubble on wine.

tebhaledar (.—.—) تَبْخالدار P *lrnd.* 1. that has a pustule on the lip. 2. that has bubbles (wine).

tebhalenûş (.—.—) تَبْخالنوش P *lrnd.* drinker of bubbling wine.

tebhic (.—) تَبْهيج A *lrnd.* an adorning, beautifying.

tebhil (.—) تَبْخيل A *lrnd.* a deeming or pronouncing avaricious and miserly.

tebhir (.—) تَبْخير A *lrnd.* 1. a fumigating, a perfuming with incense, etc.; fumigation. 2. a vaporizing; vaporization. 3. a disinfecting; disinfection. — **et=** /ı/ to fumigate, vaporize, disinfect. —**ât** (.—.—) A *pl.*

tebhirhane (.—.—.) تَبْخيرخانه P fumigating station.

tebiⁱⁱ (.—) تَبيع A *lrnd.* 1. helper, assistant, auxiliary (in war). 2. servant; follower. 3. debtor who is or may be dunned; dun.

teb'id 1 (.—) تَبْعيد A *lrnd.* a sending to a distance, a banishing; banishment. — **et=** /ı/ to remove, to drive away, to banish.

te'bid 2 (.—) تَأْبيد A *lrnd.* a making one eternal.

teb'iden (.—'.) تَبْعيداً A *lrnd.* by removing to a distance; by banishment.

tebir (.—), **tebire** (.—.) تَبير P *lrnd.* drum, kettledrum. —**zen** (.—.) P drummer.

teb'iz (.—) تَبْعيض A *lrnd.* a dividing, a subdividing; division, partition.

tebkit (.—) تَبْكيت A *lrnd.* 1. a striking with

a stick; an assailing with rough or unseemly words. 2. a silencing in argument.

tebkiye A *lrnd.* 1. a weeping, wailing, lamenting. 2. a causing to weep; a hiring or causing to bewail a deceased person with tears and recitation of praises.

teblerze P *lrnd.* paroxysm of a fever; ague, intermittent fever.

tebligât (.——) A communications by word or letter; reports; notice, notification. **—ı resmiye** official communiquè.

tebliğ (.—) A 1. a delivering, transmitting, communicating; communication; transmission. 2. paper (read to a congress), essay. 3. *lrnd.* a causing to reach or attain. **— et=** /ı/ 1. to deliver, transmit, communicate (a message, etc.). 2. to cause to reach.

teblil (.—) A *lrnd.* a moistening, a wetting.

tebliye A *lrnd.* a causing to wear out, a being worn out.

tebn A *var. of* **tibn**.

tebniye A *lrnd.* a building, a constructing.

tebrid (.—) A *lrnd.* 1. a cooling; refrigeration. 2. a lessening the love or zeal of a person. **— et=** /ı/ to cool.

tebrik[ki] (.—) A a congratulating, a wishing joy; congratulation; felicitation. **— et=** /ı/ to congratulate, to felicitate.

tebrikât (.——) A *lrnd.* congratulations.

tebrikname (.——.) P letter of congratulation.

tebrir (.—) A *lrnd.* an acknowledging (a person) to have fulfilled his duty; an acquitting of fault or defect.

tebriye A *lrnd.* 1. a deeming one free of fault or responsibility, acquittal, absolution, exoneration. 2. a clearing oneself; a being set free. 3. *lrnd.* a curing, a releasing from suffering. **— et=** /ı/ 1. to absolve, acquit, exonerate. 2. *lrnd.* to cure. **—i zimmet et=** *lrnd.* to prove one's innocence.

Tebriz (.—) P 1. *geog.* Tabriz. 2. *l. c., Or. mus.* an old **makam**.

tebs *archaic, same as* **teps**.

tebsi *var. of* **tepsi 1**.

tebside (.—.) P *lrnd.* 1. hot, feverish. 2. swollen, pustuled or cracked from feverishness (lip). **—leb** (.—..) P whose lip is cracked from fever.

tebsil (.—) A *lrnd.* 1. a stripping off the skins of an onion. 2. a stripping of clothes or of property.

tebsim (.—) A *lrnd.* a causing to smile.

tebsir (.—) A *lrnd., same as* **tabsir**.

tebşir (.—) A a communicating good news; glad tidings. **— et=** to communicate good news; to cheer with glad tidings. **—ât** (.——) A *lrnd.* glad tidings.

tebtil (.—) A *var. of* **tebettül**.

tebvi (.—) A *lrnd.* a giving a lodging; esp., a furnishing a home to one's married female slave.

tebvib (.—) A *lrnd.* 1. a dividing into chapters. 2. an arranging in sorts and categories. 3. an arranging the parts of a treatise.

tebyaze (.—.) P *lrnd.* chill of fever and ague.

tebyin (.—) A *lrnd.* 1. a making clear, plain, manifest. 2. an explaining; explanation, exposition. 3. phrase that fully explains itself. 4. a separating, a distinguishing one thing from another. **— et=** /ı/ to set forth clearly.

tebyiz (.—) A 1. a making a fair copy; a fair copy. 2. *lrnd.* a causing to become white, bright, clean; a whitening, polishing or cleaning; a brightening a person's countenance, a making it beam with pride and joy. **— et=** /ı/ 1. to make a fair copy. 2. *lrnd.* to whiten.

tebzede P *lrnd.* attacked by fever. **—gân** (...—) P those attacked by fever.

tebzil (.—) A *lrnd.* a cracking, or splitting a thing.

tebzir (.—) A *lrnd.* 1. a being extravagant, prodigal, wasteful in expenditure; extravagance, wastefulness. 2. a disseminating. 3. a sowing, a seeding. **—ât** (.——) A *pl.*

tecadül (.—.) A *lrnd.* a contending together; controversy; litigation.

tecahüd (.—.) A *lrnd.* an earnestly striving, a doing one's utmost; effort, exertion.

tecahül (.—.) A *lrnd.* a pretending not to know; feigned ignorance. **—i ârif** assumed ignorance; figure of speech that is ironical, satirical or merely used as an embellishment. **—i ârifane** a making use of an assumed ignorance for the purpose of satire or irony. **— et=** to pretend ignorance. **—ât** (.—.—) A *pl. of* **tecahül**.

tecahülkâr (.—.—) P *lrnd.* pretending ignorance (person). **—âne** (.—.——.) P in the manner of pretending ignorance. **—î** (.—.——) P pretense of ignorance.

tecahür (.—.) A *lrnd.* 1. an appearing openly; manifestation. 2. a speaking or acting openly; openness.

tecalid (.——) A *lrnd.* members of the body; the whole body.

tecalüd (.—.) A *lrnd.* a fencing or fighting together with swords

tecalüs (.—.) A *lrnd.* a sitting down together.

tecanüb (.—.) A *lrnd.* 1. a being or

becoming separate and removed. 2. an avoiding, a keeping aloof from; abstention; alienation, estrangement.

tecanüs (. —.) تجانس A *lrnd.* homogeneity, homogeneousness; likeness, similarity resemblance.

tecarib (. — —) تجاریب A *lrnd.*, pl. of **tecribe, tecrübe.** **—i nazariye** theoretical experiments.

tecasür (. —.) تجاسر A *lrnd.* a daring, presuming; presumption. **— et=** /a/ to dare, presume, venture.

tecaud تجعد A *lrnd.* 1. a being or becoming curled, wrinkled, shrivelled. 2. a becoming curly and crisp (hair).

tecavezallâhu anhü (. —..— ...) تجاوز الله عنه A *lrnd.* May God forgive him.

tecavid (. — —) تجاوید A *lrnd.* gentle, beneficient shower.

tecavif (. — —) تجاویف A *lrnd.*, pl. of **tecvif.**

tecavüb (. —.) تجاوب A *lrnd.* 1. an answering one another; controversy or dispute. 2. a corresponding to one another.

tecavül (. —.) تجاول A *lrnd.* a going round and round each other. **—ât** (. — . —) A *pl.*

tecavür (. —.) تجاور A *lrnd.* a being neighbors to one another; mutual proximity.

tecavüz (. —.) تجاوز A 1. a going beyond bounds, transgressing; transgression; excess. 2. a going beyond the bounds of forbearance; insolence, presumption. 3. aggression, attack, offensive; invasion. 4. a passing beyond, an exceeding. 5. *lrnd.* an overlooking, pardoning (an offense); pardon. forgiveness. **— et=** 1. /a/ to go beyond the bounds, to transgress; to attack. 2. /ı/ to pass, to exceed. **—ât** (. — . —) A *lrnd.*, pl. of **tecavüz.**

tecavüzî (. — . —) تجاوزی A aggressive, offensive. **— harb** offensive war. **— ve tedafüi ittifak** offensive and defensive alliance. **— harekât** *mil.* offensive operations.

tecavüzkâr (. — . —) تجاوزکار P aggressive **—âne** (. — . — —.) P aggressive (action); aggressively. **—î** (. — . — —) P *lrnd.* aggressiveness.

tecazüb (. —.) تجاذب A 1. *lrnd.* a mutually pulling at a thing and contending for it; contest. 2. *lrnd.* a pulling one another about. 3. *phil.*, *phys.* sympathy.

tecbin (. —) تجبین A *lrnd.* a deeming or pronouncing someone a coward.

tecbir (. —) تجبیر A *lrnd.* 1. a restoring, setting (a broken bone). 2. a restoring to a state of competency or wealth.

Teccâl[ll] (. —) دجال A 1. antichrist; impostor. 2. fearing neither God nor man. (*cf.* **Deccal.**) **— çıktı** The end of the world has come.

tecdi[ii] (. —) تجدیع A *surg.* a mutilating; mutilation.

tecdid (. —) تجدید A *lrnd.*, same as **tecdit.** **—i iman** reaffirmation of one's faith. **—i vuzu** a renewing ablutions. **—ât** (. — —) A *pl. of* **tecdid.** **—en** (. —´.) A *lrnd.* a renewing.

tecdil (. —) تجدیل A *lrnd.* a throwing or knocking one to the earth.

tecdir (. —) تجدیر A *lrnd.* 1. a causing to be attacked by smallpox, a being attacked by smallpox. 2. sprouting with herbage in small patches (earth).

tecdit[di] (. —) تجدید [**tecdid**] a renewing; renewal. **— et=** /ı/ to renew; to renovate.

tecebbür تجبر A *lrnd.* 1. a being or becoming proud, overbearing or insolent; pride, arrogance, insolence. 2. a being reduced or set (broken or dislocated bone). 3. a recovering from sickness; recovery. 4. a having one's broken fortunes repaired. **—ât** (. . . —) *pl. of* **tecebbür.**

teceddüd تجدد A *lrnd.*, same as **teceddüt.** **—ât** (. . . —) A renovations, reformations.

teceddüt[dü] تجدد [**teceddüd**] a being renewed, renovated, regenerated; reform; renovation. **— et=** to be renewed.

teceffüf تجفف A *lrnd.* a being dried (garment).

tecehhüz تجهز A *lrnd.* a being prepared or equipped; equipment; preparation. **—i arûs** equipping a bride.

tecellâ (. . —) تجلى A *lrnd.*, same as **tecelli.**

tecelli (. . —) تجلى A 1. a being or becoming visible; manifest; manifestation. 2. *lrnd.* destiny; luck. 3. *lrnd.* Christ's being transfigured; the Transfiguration. 4. *myst.* manifestation of God to man. **— ba müşahede** *myst.* a manifestation of God's grace together with a perception thereof by a devotee. **— bi-müşahede** *myst.* a manifestation of God's power without the sinner's perception of its source. **—m bu** Just my luck! **— et=** 1. to be manifested, to be shown. 2. to appear; to happen. **—i sıfat** a manifestation of an attribute of God. **—i Zât** a manifestation of God's person.

tecelligâh (. . — —) تجلى گاه P *lrnd.* place of manifestation.

tecellihiz (. . — —) تجلى خیز P *lrnd.* 1. in which some favorable or agreeable manifestation takes place. 2. rising in splendor.

tecellisenc (. . —.) تجلى سنج P *lrnd.* that manifests his or its own self.

tecellisiz تجلى سز ill-fated, unfortunate.

tecelliyat (. . . —) تجلیات A *lrnd.* 1. manifestation of God's person or power. 2. the manifestations of Nature. 3. strokes of fate.

tecellizar (..——) تجلی زار P *lrnd.* place of manifestation.

tecellüd تجلّد A *lrnd.* 1. a being or becoming ostentatiously sturdy, brave or enduring; daring, open bravery. 2. display of unflinching firmness; moral courage.

tecemmüᵘᵘ تجمّع A *lrnd.* a coming together, an assembling. —ât (...—) A *pl.*

tecemmüd تجمّد A *lrnd.* a becoming frozen; congelation. —ât (...—) A *pl.*

tecemmül تجمّل A *lrnd.* 1. a being or becoming beautiful; beauty, adornment. 2. a dressing, adorning one's person.

tecemmülât (...—) تجمّلات A *lrnd.* 1. conveniences; articles of luxury. 2. odds and ends; a lot of junk. —ı **beytiye** furniture of a house.

tecen تجن wild he-goat, chamois buck.

tecenni (..—) تجنّی A *lrnd.* 1. a gathering fruit, a cutting. 2. a falsely imputing a fault; false accusation.

tecennüb تجنّب A *lrnd.* 1. a keeping away from, abstaining from; abstention, avoidance. 2. a being polluted.

tecennün تجنّن A a becoming insane; madness, insanity. — **et=** to become insane.

tecerruᵘᵘ تجرّع A *lrnd.* 1. a swallowing at a gulp. 2. a swallowing down grief or wrath; a bearing anger by self-restraint. — **et=** /ı/ to swallow. —ı **gussa** a being oppressed with sorrow or anxiety.

tecerrüd تجرّد A *lrnd.* 1. a separating oneself from others; isolation, solitude. 2. a giving up worldly interests for religion; exclusive devotion. 3. a being without a wife; celibacy. 4. a being or becoming nude; nudity. 5. a becoming incorporeal, immaterial; immateriality; a being abstract; abstractness. — **et=** /dan/ 1. to divest oneself (of); to withdraw (from). 2. to remain single; to be isolated. —**i evrak** the falling of leaves (in autumn).

tecerrüdgüzin (....—) تجرّدگزین P *lrnd.* who lives in solitude and religious contemplation.

tecessüd تجسّد A *lrnd.* an assuming a material body, a becoming incarnate; incarnation.

tecessüm تجسّم A 1. a becoming a solid body; an appearing like a solid body. 2. personification. 3. *lrnd.* a becoming vivid. — **et=** 1. to assume or appear like a solid body. 2. to be personified. — **ettir=** /ı/ to personify. —**i hayâl** a seeing a ghostly appearance. —**at** (...—) A *lrnd., pl. of* **tecessüm.**

tecessüs تجسّس A 1. an enquiring in a diligent or in a prying manner; search, scrutiny. 2. inquisitiveness, curiosity. —**ât** (...—) A *lrnd., pl.*

tecessüskâr (...—) تجسّسکار P inquisitive.

tecessi, tecessu تجشّی، تجشّو A *lrnd.* an eructating, belching.

tecevvüf تجوّف A *lrnd.* 1. a getting into the interior or cavity of a thing. 2. a being or becoming hollow.

tecevvüz تجوّز A *lrnd.* 1. a passing by, a permitting; indulgence; pardon. 2. a using language metaphorically; metaphor. 3. a being remiss in the performance of worship. —**ât** (...—) A *pl.*

tecevvüzen (..'..) تجوّزاً A *lrnd.* metaphorically.

tecezzi, tecezzü تجزّی، تجزّو A *lrnd.* a being divided into pieces. — **et=** to disintegrate, come apart.

tecfif (.—) تجفیف A *lrnd.* a drying.

tecfiye تجفیه A *lrnd.* an acting harshly, tyrannically, capriciously; a causing one to be treated harshly.

techil (.—) تجهیل A *lrnd.* 1. a showing up somebody's ignorance. 2. a deeming or proving one ignorant. 3. a causing one to remain in ignorance. — **et=** /ı/ 1. to show up someone's ignorance. 2. to cause to remain ignorant. —**ât** (.——) A *pl. of* **techil.**

techiz (.—) تجهیز A 1. a fitting out, an equipping. 2. a washing, swathing and arranging a corpse on the bier. — **et=** /ı/ 1. to equip, fit out. 2. to lay out a corpse.

techizat (.——) تجهیزات A 1. *pl. of* **techiz.** 2. equipment, the rigging out of a ship. —**ı askeriye** military equipment

techizî (.——) تجهیزی A *lrnd.* pertaining to equipment.

te'cic تأجیج A *lrnd.* 1. a stimulating a fire to burn fiercely. 2. a stimulating anger and hate.

tec'id (.—) تجعید A *lrnd.* a causing to curl; wrinkle, shrivel; a becoming corrugated.

te'cil (.—) A, **tecil** (——) تأجیل 1. a granting a respite or delay; a delaying, postponing. 2. a fixing or assigning a future term. —**ât** (.——) A *pl.*

tecim *neol.* commerce.

teckere تجکره [deskere] *prov.* handbarrow, litter, stretcher, bier.

teclid (.—) تجلید A *lrnd.* 1. a binding of a book. 2. a flaying. — **et=** /ı/ to bind (a book).

teclil (.—) تجلیل A *lrnd.* 1. a covering with a horsecloth. 2. a covering, an enveloping.

tecliye تجلیه A *lrnd.* 1. a polishing, scouring, making bright. 2. a showing, displaying, disclosing, a making clear and plain; manifestation; revelation. —**i seyf** a polishing a sword.

tecmiᵘ (.—) تجمیع A *lrnd.* 1. a collecting with care and diligence. 2. an assembling with others for Friday noon prayers.

tecmid (. —) تجميد A *lrnd.* 1. a causing to freeze; congealing. 2. a becoming congealed.

tecmil (. —) تجميل A *lrnd.* 1. a beautifying, an adorning; embellishment, adornment. 2. a being good, kind; goodness, kindness. **—ât** (. ——) A embellishments.

tecmir (. —) تجمير A *lrnd.* 1. a bringing together or coming together; a collecting, an assembling. 2. an incensing, fumigating with a censer. 3. a pilgrim's performing a ceremony of throwing stones at certain spots near Mecca.

teenid (. —) تجنيد A *lrnd.* a collecting a troop, a levying an army.

tecnin (. —) تجنين A *lrnd.* a making crazy or possessed.

tecnis (. —) تجنيس A *lrnd.* 1. a punning; play upon words. 2. a making homogeneous; resemblance, analogy. **—i gayri tam** homonymy where the letters and vowels of the two words differ. **—i mefrûk** a compound homonymy in which the two terms are not written alike. **—i mürekkebi tam** a perfect compound homonymy. **—i müstahil** a false homonymy where a trick enters into its production.

tecriⁱⁱ (. —) تجريع A *lrnd.* a causing to drink or swallow by gulps.

tecrib (. —) تجريب A *lrnd.*, same as **tecrübe**.

tecribe تجربه A *lrnd.*, same as **tecrübe**.

tecribeten (. ...) تجربةً A *lrnd.* experimentally.

tecribi (. . —) تجربي A *lrnd.* experimental.

tecrid (. —) تجريد A *lrnd.* 1. *same as* **tecrit**. 2. an abstracting; abstraction. 3. a denuding, a stripping of clothes; an uncovering, a baring. 4. a devotee's divesting himself of all worldly concerns, devoting himself to religious contemplation. 5. contemplative abstraction; a separating the performance of the pilgrimage from all other objects and desires; a performing the pilgrimage at Mecca without performing the supererogatory visit at the same time. **— et=** /ı/ to strip, bare, insulate, isolate; to free from. **—ât** (. ——) A *pl. of* **tecrid**.

tecriden (. —'.) تجريداً A *lrnd.* separately.

tecrih (. —) تجريح A *lrnd.* 1. a wounding; a wounding severely. 2. a judge's rejecting a witness by reason of bad character or other ineligibility.

tecrim (. —) تجريم A *lrnd.* 1. a finding guilty; an inculpating. 2. a fining an offender. **— et=** /ı/ 1. to find guilty. 2. to fine. **—ât** (. ——) A *pl. of* **tecrim**.

tecris (. —) تجريس A *lrnd.* a rendering one infamous by public exposure; exposure.

tecritᵈⁱ (. —) تجريد A [tecrid] insulation, separation, isolation. **— et=** /ı/ *var. of* **tecrid et=**.

tecrithane (. ——.) تجريدخانه P prison cell for solitary confinement.

tecrübe تجربه A 1. a trying, proving, making trial of; trial, test. 2. an experimenting; an experiencing; experiment, experience. **— et=** /ı/ 1. to try, test, prove. 2. to assay a metal. 3. to experiment; to experience. **—sini et=** /ın/ to try something out, experiment. **—yi göke çekmediler ya!** They have not withdrawn experiment up into the sky; there is no reason why one shouldn't try it. **— tahtası** something that can be experimented on with impunity. **— yemeği** *med.* test meal.

tecrübekâr (... —) تجربه‌كار P *lrnd.* experienced. **—âne** (... ——.) P in an experienced manner. **—î** (... ——) P, **—lık** experience.

tecrübeli تجربه‌لى experienced; proven by trial.

tecrübesiz تجربه‌سز inexperienced; untested. **—lik** inexperience.

tecrübî (. . —) تجربي A experimental.

tecsim (. —) تجسيم A *lrnd.* 1. a making material or corporeal. 2. a giving or attributing a solid body or form. **—ât** (. ——) A plastic ornamentation on a wall (reliefs etc.) **—î san'atlar** plastic arts.

tecsir (. —) تجسير A *lrnd.* a causing to be bold; an encouraging.

tecviⁱⁱ (. —) تجويع A *lrnd.* 1. a making hungry; a giving an appetite. 2. a starving one, keeping him without food; starvation.

tecvid (. —) تجويد A *lrnd.* 1. a reading, reciting, or chanting the Quran with proper pronunciation. 2. the art of reading, reciting or chanting the Quran with proper rhythm. 3. a making good, a doing well. **—i hurûf** *ling.* articulation of letters.

tecvif (. —) تجويف A 1. *lrnd.* a hollowing, an excavating; excavation; cavity, cavern. 2. *anat.* canal, passage, duct. **—ât** (. ——) A hollows, caverns. **—î** (. ——) A pertaining to a cavity or to a canal.

tecvir (. —) تجوير A *lrnd.* 1. a deeming unjust or tyrannical. 2. an upsetting, a throwing into confusion.

tecviz (. —) تجويز A *lrnd.* a deeming to be lawful, proper or expedient; a permitting; permission. **— et=** /ı/ to declare lawful, to permit. **—ât** (. ——) A *pl. of* **tecviz**.

tecyif (. —) تجييف A *lrnd.* 1. a becoming putrid. 2. a being terrified; fright, alarm.

tecziⁱⁱ (. —) تجزيع A *lrnd.* 1. a comforting, consoling; comfort, consolation, relief. 2. a causing to moan and repine.

teczim (. —) تجزيم A *lrnd.* a cutting.

teczir (. —) تجزير A 1. *lrnd.* a cutting off the root of a plant, a cutting up by the root. 2. *math.* an extracting a square root; extraction of a square root.

tecziye 1 تجزيه A 1. punishment. 2. *lrnd.*

tecziye a recompensing according to desert, reward. — **et=** /ı/ to punish.

tecziye 2 تجزیه A 1. *lrnd.* a dividing, portioning out. 2. *pros.* a suppressing one foot at the end of each hemistich. — **et=** /ı/ to divide into parts. **—i nisbet** *math.* the composition of a compound ratio into its component simple parts.

tedabir (.— —) تدابیر A *lrnd., pl. of* **tedbir**.

tedafuᵘᵘ, **tedafü**ᵘᵘ (.— .) تدافع A *lrnd.* 1. a mutually repelling one another; mutual repulsion. 2. a repelling by united or consecutive action.

tedafüî (.— . —) تدافعی A defensive.

tedahhun تدخن A *lrnd.* 1. a becoming flavored by smoke; smokiness. 2. a fumigating; fumigation.

tedahül (.— .) تداخل A *lrnd.* 1. a being or becoming confused and intermixed; interaction. *phys.* interference. 2. an interpenetrating so as to occupy the same space and form. 3. a being partially identical or alike. 4. arrears. 5. *said of two numbers of which one is exactly contained in the other a certain number of times.* **—de** in arrears. **—e bin=**, **—de kal=** to be or become in arrears (payments). **—ât** (. — . —) A *pl.*

tedai (.— .) تداعی A 1. *psych.* association of ideas. 2. *lrnd.* a summoning or inviting one another. 3. *lrnd.* a claiming as one's own in opposition to the claim of another. **—ye**, **—yun mezhebi** associationism.

tedarikᵏⁱ (. — .) تدارك A a preparing, procuring, or getting together any needful thing; preparation; provision. — **et=** /ı/ to procure, obtain, prepare, provide. — **gör=** to make necessary preparations.

tedarikât (.— . —) تداركات A *lrnd.* preparations (of necessary articles).

tedarikli تداركلی prepared; fitted out. — **bulun=** to be prepared with all requirements.

tedariksiz تداركسیز unprepared.

tedarük (. — .) تدارك A *lrnd.* 1. a coming up with, an overtaking. 2. a being continuous, continual, consecutive. 3. *same as* **tedarik**.

tedavi (. — .) تداوی A medical treatment; cure.

tedavir (. — —) تداویر A *lrnd., pl. of* **tedvir**, 1. recitations from the Quran delivered in a moderately quick style. 2. *astr.* epicycles.

tedavül (. — .) تداول A 1. a circulating; successive or alternate possession or use; succession or alternation. 2. a passing successively or alternately from hand to hand; a being in common use; circulation; currency. — **bankası** bank of issue. — **et=** to circulate, to be current. **—den kaldırma** demonetization.

tedbir (. —) تدبیر A 1. measure, plan, course, expedient; precaution. 2. a treating; treatment; cure. 3. a considering the requirements of a matter; circumspection; foresight. 4. a planning, arranging, regulating, managing any matter. 5. *lrnd.* a transmitting a tradition on the authority of another. 6. *lrnd.* a disciplining the soul. — **al=** to take the necessary measures. — **ehli** 1. a wise counselor. 2. a wise and successful administrator. — **ittihaz et=** *same as* — **al=**. **—i menzil** *sociol.* domestic economy. **—i mülk** *lrnd.* statesmanship. **—e takdir uymuyor** Human plans are subject to fate.

tedbirât (. — —) تدبیرات A *lrnd.* measures; plans; regulations.

tedbirli تدبیرلی provident, thoughtful; cautious.

tedbirsiz تدبیرسیز improvident; thoughtless. **—lik** thoughtlessness; incautiousness.

tedbirşinas (. — . —) تدبیرشناس P *lrnd.* shrewd in expedients; wise, prudent.

tedebbür تدبر A *lrnd.* a considering, deliberating; steps necessary to be taken; deliberation, meditation. — **et=** to ponder (over what is to be done). **—ât** (. . . —) A deliberations.

tedeffün تدفن A *lrnd.* a being or becoming buried.

tedehhi تدهی A *lrnd.* an acting with or as if with shrewdness and cunning.

tedehhün تدهن A *lrnd.* 1. an anointing oneself with oil. 2. a being anointed.

tedehhüş تدهش A *lrnd.* a being terrified.

tedemmüᵘᵘ تدمع A *lrnd.* a being in tears.

tedemmüğ تدمغ A *psych., physiol.* cerebration.

tedemmür تدمر A *lrnd.* a perishing; perdition.

tedenni تدنی A *lrnd.* 1. decline; decadence 2. a falling back; retrogression.

tedennüs تدنس A *lrnd.* a being soiled, a becoming defiled; defilement, pollution.

tederruᵘᵘ تدرع A *lrnd.* 1. a putting on or wearing a coat of mail. 2. a putting on or wearing a slip.

tederrübᵇᵘ تدرب A *lrnd.* 1. a becoming habituated; a being accustomed; custom, habit, habitude. 2. a being or becoming able, dexterous, bold; ability, dexterity, boldness.

tederrüc تدرج A *lrnd.* 1. an advancing, approaching gradually. 2. a becoming gradually accustomed to a thing; use, custom, habit.

tederrüs تدرس A *lrnd.* 1. a studying by lessons. 2. a studying, or taking lessons from a teacher; study. **—ât** (. . . —) A studies.

tedessür تدثر A *lrnd.* a wrapping and muffling oneself up.

tedeyyün تدین A *lrnd.* 1. a falling into debt. 2. a being or becoming of a certain religion. 3. a being or becoming pious.

tedfin (. —) تدفین A *lrnd.* a burying, an

interring; burial. —î (. — —) A related to interments.

tedhil (. —) تَدْهِيل A *lrnd*. a causing to enter, an inserting; introduction; insertion.

tedhin 1 (. —) تَدْهِين A *lrnd*. 1. a smoking, a scenting, medicating or drying by smoke. 2. a subjecting to smoke in order to destroy or drive away. 3. a giving out smoke.

tedhin 2 (. —) تَدْهِين A *lrnd*. an oiling or anointing.

tedhiş (. —) تَدْهِيش A 1. a terrifying; terror. 2. *lrnd*. an utterly perplexing and bewildering; bewilderment. — et= /ı/ to terrify. —ât (. — —) A terrorization. —ci terrorist, terrorizer.

te'dib (. —) A, **tedib** (— —) تَأْدِيب *lrnd*. 1. a chastening; a punishing for a fault; punishment. 2. a teaching polite manners; moral education. — et= /ı/ 1. to correct, punish; to chastise. 2. to instruct. —ât (. — —) A *pl*.

te'diben (. —'.) تَأْدِيبًا A *lrnd*. 1. as punishment. 2. as instruction.

tedirgin تَدِرْگِين not at ease, unsettled, stirred up, irritated, discomposed, troubled. — et= /ı/ to irritate, disturb, discompose, trouble, irk, provoke.

te'diyat (. — —) A, **tediyat** (. —.) تَأْدِيَات *lrnd.*, *pl.* of **te'diye**.

te'diye A, **tediye** (—..) تَأْدِيَة 1. a paying; payment. 2. *lrnd*. a fulfilling, an acquitting oneself of a duty; performance; fulfillment. 3. *lrnd*. a delivering over a trust to its owner. — et= /ı/ to pay. —li cash on delivery.

tedkik[ki] (. —) تَدْقِيق A 1. a minutely examining, investigating; close examination; scrutiny; investigation. 2. *lrnd*. a pounding, bruising or grinding finely; a making slender or fine. 3. *phil*. a corroborating a proof by evidences or indications. 4. *myst*. a saint's seeing by intuition and having no need of proof. — et= /ı/ to investigate carefully, to examine closely, to go into a matter. —i hutut ilmi *lrnd*. graphology.

tedkikat (. — —) تَدْقِيقَات A *lrnd* investigation, minute investigations; researches.

tedlik[ki] (. —) تَدْلِيك A *lrnd*. a rubbing, manipulating with the palm of the hand.

tedlis 1 (. —) تَدْلِيس A *lrnd*. 1. a deceiving or misleading. 2. a concealing. 3. a concealing the authority for a tradition in order to lead people to suppose it more trustworthy.

tedlis 2 (. —) تَدْلِيس A *lrnd*. 1. a smoothing, polishing. 2. a rubbing so as to make pliant.

tedliye تَدْلِيَة A *lrnd*. 1. a lowering from above by a rope. 2. a suspending. 3. a making fall into trouble or destruction through presumption.

tedmir (. —) تَدْمِير A *lrnd*. 1. a devastating and destroying. 2. God's destroying one; destruction. —ât (. — —) A *pl*.

tednis (. —) تَدْنِيس A *lrnd*. a soiling, polluting; defilement, pollution. —ât (. — —) A *pl*.

tedri[ii] (. —) تَدْرِيء A *lrnd*. a putting on armor.

tedrib (. —) تَدْرِيب A *lrnd*. an accustoming; a teaching, practicing, exercising; discipline; exercise, practice. —î (. — —) A *phil*. empirical, empiric.

tedric (. —) تَدْرِيج A *lrnd*. 1. an advancing by degrees. 2. a causing to move by slow steps.

tedricen (. —'.) تَدْرِيجًا A by degrees, gradually, little by little.

tedricî (. — —) تَدْرِيجِي A gradual.

tedris (. —) تَدْرِيس A instruction, a teaching. — et= to teach by lesson. —i idadi *lrnd*. preliminary instruction, propaedeutics. — ve **tederrüs** teaching and learning.

tedrisat (. — —) تَدْرِيسَات A instruction.

tedrisî (. — —) تَدْرِيسِي A *lrnd*. pertaining to teaching, instructional, didactic.

tedsim (. —) تَدْسِيم A *lrnd*. 1. a blackening the dimple in a child's chin (as a charm against the evil eye). 2. a making greasy. 3. the rain's lightly spattering the earth.

tedsiye تَدْسِيَة A *lrnd*. a perverting, seducing, corrupting; perversion, seduction, corruption.

tedvin (. —) تَدْوِين A *lrnd*. 1. a collecting the works of an author. 2. a registering, codifying; codification, consolidation. — et= /ı/ 1. to write or collect in a register or volume. 2. to codify. —ât (. — —) A codification.

tedvir (. —) تَدْوِير A *lrnd*. 1. a causing to revolve. 2. a directing (a business). 3. a reflecting repeatedly upon an idea, a revolving in the mind. 4. a transforming into a circle. 5. epicycle. — et= /ı/ 1. to cause to revolve. 2. to administer (a business). 3. to make round.

tedviye تَدْوِيَة A *lrnd*. a treating with medicine, medication.

tedyin (. —) تَدْيِين A *lrnd*. 1. a causing to go into debt. 2. a causing to follow a religion.

teebbi تَأَبِّي A *lrnd*. 1. an adopting a person as one's father; a finding a father in another. 2. a showing repugnance, a shrinking from (someone) in dislike.

teebbüd تَأَبُّد A *lrnd*. 1. a being or becoming wild, shy or unsociable. 2. a becoming solitary or wild (place); loneliness.

teebbüh تَأَبُّه A *lrnd*. a thinking highly of oneself.

teebbün تَأَبُّن A *lrnd*. a tracking, a tracing.

teeccüc تَأَجُّج A *lrnd*. 1. a fire's blazing furiously. 2. a day's being intensely hot.

teeccül تَأَجُّل A *lrnd*. a begging for a delay.

teeccüm تَاعَجُّم A *lrnd*. 1. a being in a fury. 2. a burning fiercely (fire).

teeddi (..—) تَأَدِّي A *lrnd*. 1. an acquitting oneself as by payment of a debt or performance of a duty; a paying. 2. a reaching, attaining an object.

teeddüb تَأَدُّب A *lrnd*. 1. a showing good manners. 2. a restraining oneself out of politeness (from some action); decorum. **— et=** to refrain from some action out of politeness.

teeddüben (.'..) تَأَدُّبًا A *lrnd*. out of politeness.

teeddüm تَأَدُّم A *lrnd*. an eating a condiment with bread.

teeffüf تَأَفُّف A *lrnd*. a crying out "Ough" in disgust or vexation.

teehhül تَأَهُّل A a marrying. **— et=** to marry. **—ât** (...—) A *lrnd*. marriages.

teehhür تَأَخُّر A *lrnd*. 1. a being postponed, delayed; postponement, delay. 2. a getting behind; a lagging. 3. a being late (in point of time); a being more recent. 4. a drawing backwards, a receding, retreating; retrogression. **— et=** 1. to be postponed, to be late. 2. to retire, to draw back. **—ât** (...—) A postponements, delay.

teekküd تَأَكُّد A *lrnd*. a being or becoming confirmed, strengthened, corroborated; confirmation.

teekkül تَأَكُّل A *lrnd*. 1. a being worn away by attrition. 2. a being fretted and annoyed; annoyance.

teellüf تَأَلُّف A *lrnd*. a being or becoming familiar, sociable; familiarity, sociability, friendliness. **—ât** (...—) A *pl*.

teellüh تَأَلُّه A *lrnd*. a worshipping, giving adoration; devotion; piety.

teellüm تَأَلُّم A *lrnd*. a being grieved or distressed; a suffering bodily or mental anguish; distress, grief, torment, sorrow. **— et=** to be distressed or pained. **—ât** (...—) A *pl*.

teemmi تَأَمِّي A *lrnd*. a taking to oneself a female slave.

teemmül تَأَمُّل A a pausing to reflect; reflection; deliberation; caution; *law* premeditation. **— et=** to reflect, deliberate.

teemmülât (...—) تَأَمُّلَات A *lrnd*. reflections, deliberations. **—ı amika** deep reflections.

teemmülsüz تَأَمُّلسُز 1. inconsiderate, rash, impulsive. 2. impulsively. **—lük** rashness, impulsiveness.

teemmüm تَأَمُّم A *lrnd*. 1. an adopting as mother. 2. a taking as one's object of attainment.

teemmür تَأَمُّر A *lrnd*. 1. a being or becoming ruler, prince or king; an exercising authority. 2. a consulting together; consultation.

teenni تَأَنِّي A *lrnd*. deliberateness, unhurried behavior, composure.

teennüs 1 تَأَنُّس A *lrnd*. 1. a becoming familiar, friendly; sociability, friendliness. 2. a becoming domesticated and tame.

teennüs 2 تَأَنُّث A *lrnd*. 1. a becoming or being effeminate or yielding. 2. a being or becoming feminine.

teerrüb تَأَرُّب A *lrnd*. 1. an attempting to exercise sagacity. 2. a pretending to penetration and sagacity.

teessi (..—) تَأَسِّي A *lrnd*. a receiving patience and comfort, a bearing oneself with fortitude; patience.

teessüf تَأَسُّف A a feeling grief, sorrow, sadness, regret; sorrowfulness; regret. **— et=** /a/ to be sorry (for). **—ât** (...—) A regrets.

teessüm تَأَسُّم A *lrnd*. 1. an avoiding sin. 2. a forsaking or repenting of sin.

teessür 1 تَأَثُّر A 1. grief. 2 a being affected; emotion. **— et=** *lrnd*. to be affected; to grieve. **—e kapıl=** to be seized by grief.

teessür 2 تَأَثُّر A *lrnd*. a delaying with frivolous excuses.

teessürat (...—) تَأَثُّرات A *lrnd.*, *pl*. of **teessür 1**.

teessüri (...—) تَأَثُّري A *psych*. affective. **—yet** affectivity.

teessüs تَأَسُّس A a being founded or established. **— et=** to be established.

teevvi تَأَوِّي A *lrnd*. 1. a seeking a place of rest or abode. 2. a collecting or trooping together.

teevvüd تَأَوُّد A *lrnd*. 1. a matter's weighing on one. 2. a bending under a burden.

teevvüh تَأَوُّه A *lrnd*. a crying out in sorrow. **—ât** (...—) A sighs.

teevvül تَأَوُّل A *lrnd*. an explaining a word or phrase by some slight but real analogy.

teeyyüd تَأَيُّد A 1. a being confirmed. 2. *lrnd*. a finding aid and support; aid, support. **— et=** to be confirmed.

teezzi (..—) تَأَذِّي A *lrnd*. 1. a being hurt; a being annoyed; pain, suffering. 2. a being ill-treated or wronged; oppression.

teezzür تَأَزُّر A *lrnd*. a wrapping oneself up; a being covered up.

tef 1 دَف [def 1] tambourine with cymbals. **— çal=** to play the tambourine. **— çalsan oynıyacak** It's all topsy-turvy. What a mess! **— gezdir=** to pass a tambourine around (to collect money). **—e koy=, —e koyup çal=** /ı/ to speak ill of publicly, to hold up to public ridicule. **— pulu** the bells or cymbals in the hoop of a tambourine.

tef 2 تَف P *lrnd*. 1. heat. 2. vapor. 3. light, flash, sparkle.

tefahhum تَفَحُّم A *chem*. a becoming carbonized; carbonization.

tefahhur تَفَخُّر A 1. a boasting; arrogance.

2. *lrnd.* a speaking or acting with pride. **—ât** (...—) A boasts.

tefahhus نَفَحُّص A *lrnd.*, same as **tafahhus**.

tefahhuş تَفَحُّش A *lrnd.* a being obscene in speech.

tefahüm (.—.) تَفاهُم A *lrnd.* a pretending or trying to understand.

tefahür (.—.) تَفاخُر 1. a boasting; arrogance. 2. *lrnd.* a mutually boasting, a vying in boasting. **— et=** /la/ to boast (about).

tefahürat (.—.—) تَفاخُرات A 1. *lrnd.* boasts. 2. *pros.* the metrical foot (.——).

tefa'il (.——) تَفاعيل A *lrnd.*, *pl. of* **tef'ile**.

tefakkud^(dü) تَفَقُّد A *lrnd.* 1. a seeking or inquiring for. 2. an investigating, a scrutinizing. **—ât** (...—) A inquiries, investigations.

tefakkuh 1 تَفَقُّه A *lrnd.* 1. a being learned in Muslim jurisprudence. 2. an understanding, a comprehending.

tefakkuh 2 تَفَتُّح A *lrnd.* a flower's opening.

tefakud^(dü) (.—.) تَفاقُد A *lrnd.* 1. a seeking for or inquiring after each other. 2. a losing one another.

tefakum (.—.) تَفاقُم A *lrnd.* a becoming formidable (matter).

tefakur (.—.) تَفاقُر A *lrnd.* a pretending to be poor; a being humble and submissive in manner.

tefarik^(kı) (.——) تَفاريق A *lrnd.* 1. fragments, sections, parts; separate things. 2. rarities fit to be offered as presents. 3. the dried tops of the herb patchouli, *bot.*, *Pogostema* (used as a perfume); the plant patchouli.

tefaruk^(ku) (.—.) تَفارُك A *lrnd.* a separating from one another.

tefarut (.—.) تَفارُط A *lrnd.* 1. a competing to get before one another. 2. a being overdue. **—i hümum** the crowding of anxieties on a person.

tefasil (.——) تَفاصيل A *lrnd.*, *pl. of* **tafsil**, detailed explanations; details.

tefasir (.——) تَفاسير A *lrnd.*, *pl. of* **tefsir**, comments, commentaries on the Quran.

tefassum تَفَصُّم A *lrnd.* a fissuring, cracking.

tefattun تَفَطُّن A *lrnd.* an understanding by sagacity.

tefattur تَفَطُّر A *lrnd.* a being cracked, fissured.

tefaül^(lü) (.—.) تَفاؤُل A *lrnd.* a drawing an augury from a thing; augury, omen.

tefavüt تَفاوُت A *lrnd.* 1. a being unequal to one another, a being dissimilar. 2. difference, disparity. **— et=** to differ (one from the other). **—i hasene** *Ott. hist.* factor based on the difference in length of the lunar and solar years and used in financial computations at the time of transition from a lunar calendar to a solar calendar.

tefayüd (.—.) تَفايُد A *lrnd.* an imparting instruction, information or profit to one another.

tefazul^(lü) (.—.) تَفاضُل A 1. *math.* remainder, difference after subtraction; difference. 2. *lrnd.* a competing with one another for preeminence. 3. *lrnd.* a being or becoming superior; superiority; excess. **—i matlaayn** *astr.* the ascensional difference.

tefazulî (.—.—) تَفاضُلي A *math.* differential. **— hesab** *math.* differential calculus.

tefazzul تَفَضُّل A *lrnd.* 1. a being superior; superiority. 2. kindness, goodness.

tefci^(iü) (.—) تَفجيع A *lrnd.* 1. a causing to cry out from suffering, a distressing. 2. a giving pain, an afflicting.

tefcir (.—) تَفجير A *lrnd.* 1. a causing to burst forth and flow. 2. a deeming or pronouncing to be a reprobate.

tefdiye تَفدِيَة A *lrnd.* a saying "May I be the ransom" (from an impending evil).

tefe تَفه [*Arabic* **daffa**] 1. frame which holds the reed of a hand loom. 2. *obs.* package, roll; book of gold leaf; hank of spun silk; machine for winding silk. 3. *obs.* flap of a saddle. **— başı** lady's garment embroidered with gold.

tefeccü^(üü) تَفَجُّع A *lrnd.* a lamenting, groaning; lamentation. **—ât** (...—) A lamentations.

tefeccür تَفَجُّر A *lrnd.* 1. a bursting forth and flowing. 2. a being profusely munificent. 3. the dawn's breaking. **—ât** (...—) A *pl.*

tefeci تَفَجي usurer.

tefecilik^(ği) تَفَجيلِك usury.

tefehhüm تَفَهُّم A *lrnd.* an understanding, comprehending gradually. **— et=** /ı/ to understand gradually, to perceive. **—ât** (...—) A *pl.*

tefekkür تَفَكُّر A a thinking, reflecting, pondering; reflection, meditation, thought. **— et=** to think, meditate. **— hürriyeti** freedom of thought. **— tarihi** intellectual history.

tefekkürat (...—) تَفَكُّرات A *lrnd.* reflections.

tefeli تَفَلي of close texture (cloth, etc.).

tefelluk^(ku) تَفَلُّق A *lrnd.* 1. a splitting, fissuring, bursting. 2. the dawn's breaking.

tefelsüf تَفَلسُف A *lrnd.* a philosophizing.

tefennün تَفَنُّن A *lrnd.* 1. a becoming versed in arts and sciences. 2. a using various styles or arguments in discourse.

teferru^(uu) تَفَرُّع A *lrnd.* a ramifying, a separating into branches or lesser subdivisions; ramification; a being subdivided. **— et=** 1. to ramify, branch out. 2. to be subdivided. 3. /a/ to belong to (as a branch).

teferruat (...—) تَفَرُّعات A details, accessories.

teferruğ تَفَرُّغ A *lrnd.* 1. a being at leisure, free and unoccupied. 2. a receiving possession of a house or land by sale, gift, etc.

teferruh تفرّح A *lrnd.* a being at ease; leisure, refreshment.

teferrukᵏᵘ تفرّك A *lrnd.* 1. a separating and splitting up into several or many portions or sections; a becoming separated or dispersed. 2. discrimination; differentiation. **—i ittisâl** *med.* the splitting of skin because of illness.

teferrüc تفرّج A *lrnd.* 1. a strolling for pleasure; pleasure trip; excursion. 2. a diverting oneself; diversion. **—ât** (...—) A *pl.*

teferrücgâh (...—) تفرّجگاه P *lrnd.* pleasure resort; promenade; excursion spot.

teferrüd تفرّد A *lrnd.* a standing out from others, a distinguishing oneself.

teferrüs تفرّس A *lrnd.* a perceiving by mental acumen; perspicacity. **— et=** to perceive by intuition, to discern by sagacity. **—ât** (...—) A sagacious findings.

teferrüş تفرّش A *lrnd.* 1. a being spread out (carpet, bed, etc.). 2. a stretching oneself out; a bird's spreading its wings for flight.

teferrüz تفرّز A *lrnd.* a becoming set off and separated as a portion.

tefer'un تفرعن A *lrnd.* a being or becoming like Pharaoh in pride and obstinacy.

tefessüh 1 تفسّخ A *lrnd.* a going to pieces by decay or otherwise; decomposition; putrifaction. **— et=** to decay.

tefessüh 2 تفسّح A *lrnd.* a being spacious; spaciousness.

tefettüt تفتّت A *lrnd.* a being broken or crumbled.

tefe'ül تفاؤل A a taking a good omen (from something). **— et=** to consult an oracle.

tefe'ülât (...—) تفاؤلات A *lrnd.* divination.

tefevvukᵏᵘ تفوّق A *lrnd.* a being superior; superiority

tefevvuz تفوّض A *lrnd.* a taking possession of a thing handed over.

tefevvüh تفوّه A *lrnd.* 1. a saying a word. 2. a saying unpleasant words; a gossiping.

tefevvühat (...—) تفوّهات A *lrnd.* insults. **—ta bulun=** to use insulting or blasphemous words.

tefeyyüz تفيّض A *lrnd.* a progressing; prosperity, progress. **— et=** to make progress, to prosper; to profit (morally). **—ât** (...—) A *pl.*

tefiz (.—) تفويض A *var. of* **tefviz**.

tefhim 1 (.—) تفهيم A *lrnd.* 1. a causing to understand. 2. a communicating something to somebody. **— et=** /ı, a/ to cause to understand, to communicate (something to someone).

tefhim 2 (.—) تفحيم A *lrnd.* 1. a blackening with charcoal. 2. a carbonizing; carbonization.

tefhim 3 (.—) تفخيم A *lrnd.* 1. an honoring, a treating with a great show of consideration. 2. a pronouncing with a full resonant voice (letter).

te'fif (.—) تأنيف A *lrnd., same as* **teeffüf**.

te'fikᵏⁱ (.—) تأفيك A *lrnd.* a telling a lie; mendacity. **—ât** (.——) A lies.

tef'ile تفعيلة A *pros.* the metrical foot (...).

tefkih (.—) تفقيه A *lrnd.* a teaching one Muslim jurisprudence.

tefkir (.—) تفكير A 1. *psych.* ideation. 2. *lrnd.* a pondering. 3. *lrnd.* a causing to think, ponder, meditate.

teflis (.—) تفليس A *lrnd.* a pronouncing one insolvent.

tefne تفنه *var. of* **defne**.

tefriⁱⁱ (.—) تفريع A *lrnd.* a making a branch diverge from a main stem or main subject; a dividing into branches or sections.

tefric (.—) تفريج A *lrnd.* 1. a banishing grief, dispelling care. 2. a parting, a separating by an interval.

tefrice تفرجه A *lrnd.* interstice, a cleft (between two things).

tefrid (.—) تفريد A *lrnd.* 1. a retiring, leading a solitary life (on account of devotion); asceticism of a Sufi. 2. an excelling in science, a being unique in scholarship. 3. a causing to be alone or apart.

tefriğ (.—) تفريغ A *lrnd.* 1. a causing to become empty. 2. a pouring out, a causing to gush out. 3. a causing to become free of fear or unpleasant forebodings. 4. a causing to be at leisure. **— ve teferruğ** *law* cession and seizing of real property. **—ât** (.——) A *pl.*

tefrih 1 (.—) تفريح A *lrnd.* a making glad, gladdening. **— et=** /ı/ to gladden, to cause to rejoice.

tefrih 2 (.—) تفريخ A 1. *physiol.* incubation. 2. *lrnd.* a beginning to send up shoots (grain). **— müddeti** *physiol.* incubation period.

tefrikᵏⁱ (.—) تفريق A 1. a separating things from one another; a distinguishing one from another by sight or definition; distinction. 2. a separating into portions; separation. 3. *lrnd.* a subtracting. 4. *lrnd.* a separate thing. 5. *lrnd.* analysis. **— et=** /ı/ to separate, to distinguish (one thing from another).

tefrika تفرقه A 1. an installment of a story in a newspaper. 2. *lrnd.* discord; disunion, misunderstanding. 3. *lrnd.* a scattering, disintegrating, separating and splitting up into sections or parties.

tefriş (.—) تفريش A *lrnd.* 1. a spreading (a carpet, etc.). 2. a carpeting or furnishing (a room). 3. a covering a floor with a carpet, etc. **— et=** /ı/ to spread (a carpet); to furnish; to cover (a floor).

tefrişât (.——) تفريشات A *lrnd.* furnishings.

tefritᵘ (.—) تفريط A *lrnd.* a doing less than one's duty; remissness; deficiency.

tefriz 1 (. —) تَفْرِيض A *lrnd.* a making a canonical duty obligatory.
tefriz 2 (. —) تَفْرِيز A *lrnd.* a separating a thing from a multitude or whole.
tefs تَفْس P *lrnd.* warmth, heat.
tefsan (. —) تَفْسَان P *lrnd.* warm, hot.
tefsid (. —) تَفْسِيد A *lrnd.* a spoiling, corrupting, injuring, disorganizing.
tefside (. — .) تَفْسِيدَه P *lrnd.* burned, warmed; very hot.
tefsideleb (. — ..) تَفْسِيدَه لَب P *lrnd.* chapped lipped; very thirsty.
tefsih 1 (. —) تَفْسِيح A *lrnd.* a causing to be ample, spacious.
tefsih 2 (. —) تَفْسِيخ A *lrnd.* a disintegrating; a causing to fall to pieces by decay.
tefsik[kı] (. —) تَفْسِيك A *lrnd.* a calling or making one profligate, depraving, perverting.
tefsir (. —) تَفْسِير A 1. an explaining, expounding; interpretation. 2. commentary on the Quran. 3. *rhet.* explanatory phrase. **—i celi** *poet.* clause where the obscure word is repeated with its explanation. **—i hafî** *poet.* clause when the obscure word is not repeated with the explanation. **— hükümleri** *law* interpretative provisions. **—ât** (. — —) A *lrnd., pl. of* **tefsir**. **—ci** commentator on the Quran.
tefsire تَفْسِيرَه A *med.* 1. a physician's inspecting urine for a diagnosis. 2. urine, urine-bottle to be offered to a physician for examination.
tefsirî (. — —) تَفْسِيرِي A *lrnd.* interpretative. **— hükümler** *law* variable rules, non-compulsive or non-imperative provisions.
teft تَفْت P *lrnd.* 1. warmth, heat. 2. haste, speed. 3. warmth of temper, hastiness in words or action.
tefte تَفْتَه P *lrnd.* 1. hot; heated. 2. disturbed; weighed down. **—dil** P heartsick.
tefter تَفْتَر *var. of* **defter**.
teftih (. —) تَفْتِيح A *lrnd.* 1. an opening things a lot. 2. an expelling wind from the stomach, a belching.
teftik[kı] **1** (. —) تَفْتِيك A *lrnd.* a teasing out into fibers with the fingers; a carding of cotton.
teftik[kı] **2** (. —) تَفْتِيك A *lrnd.* 1. a splitting, bursting, tearing a thing. 2. a spoiling, marring.
teftil (. —) تَفْتِيل A *lrnd.* a twisting as in spinning.
teftin 1 (. —) تَفْتِين A *lrnd.* 1. a trying, testing in order to seduce into a wrong course; an exciting sedition. 2. a seducing, an infatuating; a bewitching.
teftin 2 (. —) تَفْتِين A *lrnd.* 1. a causing to become shrewd and sagacious. 2. a making one to understand or to consider (a thing).
teftir 1 (. —) تَفْتِير A *lrnd.* 1. an allaying, an assuaging. 2. a wearing out, a tiring, a making weak and languid.
teftir 2 (. —) تَفْطِير A *lrnd.* a causing one to break the fast; a making breakfast.
teftiş (. —) تَفْتِيش A an investigating, examining, investigation; inquiry; inspection. **— et=** /ı/ to inspect. **— mahkemesi** court of inquiry. **— ve murakabe** inspection, supervision **—ât** (. — —) A *lrnd., pl.* **—î** (. — —) A inspectorial.
teftit (. —) تَفْتِيت A *lrnd.* a breaking and crumbling small.
tefviz (. —) تَفْوِيض A *lrnd.* a handing over or committing to the charge of somebody. **— et=** /ı, a/ to hand over, to commit to the charge of somebody. **T— Suresi** a name of the first sura of the Quran.
tefzi[ii] (. —) تَفْزِيع A *lrnd.* a striking with terror, a frightening.
tegaddi تَغَدِّى A *same as* **tagaddi**.
tegafül (. — .) تَغَافُل A *lrnd.* 1. a pretending to be unmindful; feigned ignorance or inattention. 2. a being unmindful and careless. **— et=**, **— göster=** to pretend to be unaware or unmindful, to pretend ignorance.
tegafülât (. — . —) تَغَافُلَات A *lrnd.* inattentive behavior.
tegalüb (. — .) تَغَالُب A *lrnd.* a competing for superiority.
tegamüz (. — .) تَغَامُز A *lrnd.* a making signs to one another by winking, nodding, etc. **—ât** (. — . —) A *pl.*
teganni تَغَنِّى *var. of* **taganni**.
tegayüb (. — .) تَغَايُب A *lrnd.* a being absent.
tegayür (. — .) تَغَايُر A *lrnd.* a being different from each other; difference, diversity. **—ât** (. — . —) A *pl.*
tegayyür تَغَيُّر A *lrnd., same as* **tagayyür**.
tegerg تَگَرْگ P *lrnd.* hail, sleet.
teğelti تَگَلْتِى saddle-pad; numdah.
teğet *neol., geom.* tangent.
teğmen *neol.* lieutenant.
teh تَه P *lrnd.* 1. bottom, deep or inner part. 2. fold, layer, ply. **—i derya** bottom of the sea.
tehaci (. — .) تَهَاجِى A *lrnd.* a satirizing one another.
tehacüm (. — .) تَهَاجُم A *lrnd.* 1. a rushing or crowding together. 2. a rushing at, an attacking one another; a concerted rush or attack. **— et=** /a/ to make a concerted rush. **—at** (. — . —) A *pl.*
tehadu[uu] (. — .) تَهَادُع A *lrnd.* a pretending to be deceived.
tehafüt (. — .) تَهَافُت A *lrnd.* a crowding together around something.
tehalüf 1 (. — .) تَخَالُف A *lrnd.* a differing from one another; difference, dissimilarity. **— et=** to differ from one another; to vary.

tehalüf 2 (. —.) تحالف A *lrnd.* a taking oath together in making a compact.

tehalük^(kü) (. —.) تهالك A *lrnd.* 1. a throwing oneself eagerly on to something. 2. keenness, zeal; ardor, desire. —**le arzu et**= /ı/ to desire ardently. —**ât** (. —. —) A *pl.*

tehami (. —.) تحامى A *lrnd.* a shunning, an avoiding; a guarding oneself.

tehamuk^(kü) (. —.) تحامق A *lrnd.* a feigning stupidity.

tehani (. —.) تهانى A *lrnd., pl. of* **tehniye**, felicitations, congratulations.

teharüc (. —.) تخارج A *law* a dividing property by the mutual consent of the coheirs (one taking the house, another the land, etc.).

teharüş (. —.) تخارش A *lrnd.* a fighting and tearing one another with tooth and claw.

tehasin (. — —) تحاسين A *lrnd., pl. of* **tahsin 1**, 1. embellishments. 2. ornamental writings.

tehassür تحسر A *same as* **tahassür 1**.

tehasüd (. —.) تحاسد A *lrnd.* a being envious of each other; mutual envy.

tehaşi 1 تحاشى A *lrnd.* a drawing aside, withdrawing, an avoiding; careful avoidance.

tehaşi 2 (. —.) تحاشى A *lrnd.* a shrinking and drawing back through fear; fear, dread.

tehaşu^(uu) (. —.) تخاشع A *lrnd.* a feigning submissiveness and humility; feigned or exaggerated humility.

tehaşüd (. —.) تحاشد A *lrnd.* a collecting as a troop, an assembling, a trooping together.

tehattür تختر A *lrnd.* a being languid, torpid, feverish or confused in intellect; languor, heaviness, torpor; feverishness, confusion of mind.

tehatub (. —.) تخاطب A *lrnd.* an addressing one another, a speaking to each other, dialogue.

tehatuf (. —.) تخاطف A *lrnd.* a trying together to seize and carry off.

tehatüm (. —.) تحاتم A *lrnd.* a contending with one another without reason; unfounded contest, contention.

tehatür (. —.) تحاتر A *lrnd.* a disputing about trifles; a convicting each other of uttering falsehood.

tehavil 1 (. — —) تحاويل A *lrnd., pl* of **tahvil**, 1. changes, vicissitudes. 2. *astr.* ingresses, entries of the sun, etc. into the signs of the zodiac. 3. commercial bills of exchange, drafts.

tehavil 2 (. — —) تحاويل A *lrnd., pl. of* **tehvil**.

tehavün (. —.) تهاون A *lrnd.* a regarding as of little account, a despising; contempt.

tehaya (. — —) تحايا A *lrnd., pl. of* **tahiye**.

tehcir (. —.) تهجير A *lrnd.* a causing to migrate; deportation. — **et**= /ı/ to deport.

tehciye تهجية A *lrnd.* 1. a spelling out the letters of a word. 2. a satirizing.

tehdid (. —) تهديد A *lrnd., same as* **tehdit**. — **et**= /ı/ to threaten.

tehdidâmiz (. — — —) تهديدآميز P *lrnd.* threatening; threateningly.

tehdidât (. — —) تهديدات A *lrnd.* threats.

tehdiden (. — ʹ.) تهديداً A *lrnd.* threateningly.

tehdidkâr (. — —) تهديدكار P menacing, threatening.

tehdim (. —) تهديم A *lrnd.* a demolishing greatly.

tehdit^(di) (. —) تهديد |**tehdid**| 1. threat, menace. 2. a threatening.

tehdiye تهدية A *lrnd.* a sending or giving as a present.

tehecci تهجى A *lrnd.* a spelling out the separate letters of a word.

teheccüd تهجد A *lrnd.* 1. a becoming awake after sleep. 2. prayer performed during the night.

teheddi تحدى A *lrnd.* a taking a right direction; a going right.

teheddüm تهدم A *lrnd.* 1. a falling down in ruins. 2. a becoming involved with another in high words through anger.

tehekküm تحكم A *lrnd.* 1. a mocking; mockery. 2. a being very angry. —**ât** (. . . —) A *pl.* —**en** (.ʹ. .) A sarcastically.

tehennüc تهنج A *lrnd.* a beginning to quicken (foetus).

tehettük^(kü) تهتك A *lrnd.* 1. a being or becoming torn. 2. one's honor's being attacked; disgrace, dishonor.

tehevvüd تهود A *lrnd.* a becoming a Jew.

tehevvük^(kü) تهوك A *lrnd.* a becoming perplexed, bewildered.

tehevvül تهول A *lrnd.* a being frightened, terrified.

tehevvüm تهوم A *lrnd.* a nodding the head in drowsiness.

tehevvür تهور A 1. a going into a sudden anger; sudden outburst of anger, fury. 2. rashness, impetuosity. — **et**= to burst into anger. —**ât** (. . . —) A *lrnd., pl. of* **tehevvür**.

teheyyü^(uu) تهيء A *lrnd.* 1. a preparing for; a being prepared. 2. a taking form, assuming its proper appearance; a becoming materially existent.

teheyyüb تهيب A *lrnd.* 1. an inspiring awe. 2. a feeling awe and dread.

teheyyüc تهيج A *lrnd.* a being raised (as anger or dust); emotion, excitement. — **et**= to become excited; to be overcome by emotion. —**ât** (. . . —) A *pl. of* **teheyyüc**. —**î** (. . . —) A *psych.* emotional. —**iyet** *psych.* emotivity.

teheyyüm تهيم A *lrnd.* 1. a walking grace-

fully; elegant walk. 2. a being bewildered, amazed; bewilderment.
tehezzüᵘᵘ تَهَزُّؤ A *lrnd.* a mocking at, an exposing to ridicule.
tehezzüb تَهَذُّب A *lrnd.* a becoming pruned and deprived of superfluities and defects; a being refined.
tehezzüc تَهَزُّج A *lrnd.* a humming or singing a tune; a warbling, shaking, trilling.
tehezzül تَهَزُّل A *lrnd.* a talking nonsense jokingly; a being jocose, facetious.
tehezzüz تَهَزُّز A *lrnd.* a moving and shaking about. —**ât** (...—) A vacillations; vibrations.
tehi (.—) تَهِى P *lrnd.* 1. empty. 2. void of weight, influence or effect.
tehiçeşm (.—.) تَهِى چَشم P *lrnd.* 1. whose eyeball has disappeared; blind. 2. wanting in discernment. 3. greedy, covetous.
tehidest (.—.) تَهِى دَست P *lrnd.* 1. poor. 2. avaricious. —**ân** (.—.—) P the poor. —**î** (.—.—) P poverty.
tehim (.—) تَهِيم A *lrnd.* accused; suspect.
tehimagz (.—.) تَهِى مَغز P *lrnd.* empty-brained. —**î** (.—.—) P empty-brainedness.
tehimeyan (.—.—) تَهِى ميان P *lrnd.* hollow. —**î** (.—.—) P hollowness.
te'hir (.—) A, **tehir** (——) تَأْخِير 1. a postponing, deferring, delaying; delay, postponement. 2. *law* adjournment, arrest (of judgment). — **et=** /ı/ to defer, postpone. —**ât** (.——) A *pl.* of **tehir**.
tehire (.—.) تَهِيره P *lrnd.* one's fate, lot, destiny, fortune.
tehiyat (..—) تَهِيَّآت A *lrnd.* preparations.
tehiye تَهِيَّه A *lrnd.* a preparing for; a being prepared. — **et=** /ı/ to prepare.
tehlikᵏⁱ (.—) تَهلِيك A *lrnd.* a killing, destroying greatly.
tehlike تَهلُكَه [**tehlüke**] *lrnd.* 1. danger. 2. risk. —**ye atıl=** to court danger. —**ye koy=**, —**ye sok=** /ı/ to endanger. —**li** dangerous, perilous. —**siz** without danger, safe; inoffensive.
tehlil (.—) تَهلِيل A *lrnd.* a pronouncing the profession of God's unity by **lâilâheillallah**. —**ât** (.——) A *pl.*
tehlilhan (.——) تَهلِيل خوان P *lrnd.* a chanter of the **tehlil**.
tehlüke تَهلُكَه A *lrnd., same as* **tehlike**.
tehniye, tehniyet تَهنِيَت A *lrnd.* 1. a felicitating, congratulating. 2. felicitation, congratulation.
tehniyetname (...—.) تَهنِيَت نامه P *lrnd.* letter of congratulation.
tehrib (.—) تَهرِيب A *lrnd.* a putting to flight.
tehrim (.—) تَهرِيم A *lrnd.* 1. a making old and feeble. 2. a showing respect and honor, a treating one as a senior. 3. a chopping up, a mincing.
tehşim (.—) تَهشِيم A *lrnd.* a showing great respect and honor.
tehtikᵏⁱ (.—) تَهتِيك A *lrnd.* a tearing, rending.
tehvid (.—) تَهوِيد A *lrnd.* a converting to Judaism.
tehvil (.—) تَهوِيل A *lrnd.* 1. a frightening, terrifying. 2. frightful object, dreadful thing. —**ât** (.——) A *pl.*
tehvim (.—) تَهوِيم A *lrnd., same as* **tehevvüm**.
tehvin (.—) تَهوِين A *lrnd.* 1. a lightening, a making easy and light; alleviation, facilitation. 2. a judging to be of little consequence, a making light of. 3. a despising, contempt. — **et=** /ı/ 1. to facilitate, alleviate. 2. to cheapen. —**ât** (.——) A *pl.*
tehviş (:—) تَهوِيش A *lrnd.* a throwing into confusion.
tehyib (.—) تَهيِيب A *lrnd.* 1. a causing to become formidable, dreadful. 2. a representing as formidable or dreadful. —**ât** (.——) A *pl.*
tehyic (.—) تَهيِيج A *lrnd.* an exciting, provoking, stimulating; excitement. — **et=** /ı/ to excite. —**ât** (.——) A *pl.*
tehzib (.—) تَهذِيب A *lrnd.* 1. a correcting, improving, beautifying. 2. a mending one's own manners and morals, self-improvement. —**i ahlâk** moral education. — **et=** /ı/ to correct, set right. —**ât** (.——) A *pl.*
tehzic (.—) تَهزِيج A *lrnd., same as* **tehezzüc**. —**at** (.——) A *pl.*
tehzil (.—) تَهزِيل A *lrnd.* 1. a ridiculing, mocking; ridicule, mock; satirization. 2. a causing to become thin and emaciated. —**ât** (.——) A *pl.*
tehziz (.—) تَهزِيز A *lrnd.* 1. a shaking, moving a thing about. 2. a causing to vibrate; vibration. —**ât** (.——) A *pl.*
tekᵏⁱ **1** تَك 1. a single thing. 2. odd number. 3. fellow, mate, equal. 4. single; unique. 5. alone, solitary. 6. only; merely; only once. 7. *mus.* clear drum beat, drum beat with clear tone; a word used in beating time. 8. odd (not even or not paired). 9. as long as, provided that. — **adam şirketi** one-man company. — **aded** odd number. — **aharlı** *art* single-sized (paper). — **ali** *art, name for a kind of paper.* — **anlamlı** *neol., phil.* univocal. **bir — at=** *colloq.* to have a drink. — **başına** 1. on one's own. 2. apart, alone. — **başına kal=** to remain all alone. — **bencilik** *neol., phil.* solipsism. — **bir** 1. only one. 2. *with negative predicate* not even one. — **mi çift mi?** odd or even? — **dizgin** that pulls to one side

and requires to be constantly checked by one rein (horse). — **düşüncelik** *neol., psych.* monoideism. — **elden** under one management or command; from one center. — **kürekle mehtaba çık=** 1. to start doing something without due preparation. 2. to attempt a joke tactlessly. — **meclisli hükûmet sistemi** *pol.* one-chamber system. — **sofyan** *Or. mus.* a rhythmic pattern. — **tanrıcılık** *neol., phil.* monotheism. — **taraflı akidler** one-sided contracts, unilateral transactions. — **tek** 1. one by one. 2. odd ones, not a pair. **—e tek kavga** single combat. — **tük***. — **vuruş** *mus.* a rhythmic pattern with eleven beats.

tek 2 تك quiet, motionless and noiseless; void of mischief or turbulence. — **dur=**, — **otur=** 1. to keep still; to be quiet. 2. to sit by oneself.

tek 3 تك *archaic, same as* **dek 2**.

tek 4 تك *archaic* in vain, useless; meaningless. — **değil** not in vain, significant.

tek[ki] **5** تك P *lrnd.* a running. — **ü pu** a running about. — **ü tâz** a galloping about.

tekâ (. —) تكا *mus.* a word used in counting time.

tekabbel Allah (. . . . —) تقبل الله A May it be acceptable in God's sight *said to one who has just performed a prayer or a pious act*.

tekabbül[ü] تقبل A *lrnd., same as* **takabbül**.

tekabül (. —.) تقابل A 1. *lrnd.* a coming face to face; a meeting. 2. *lrnd.* a compensating; compensation. 3. *phil.* opposition. — **et=** /a/ 1. to correspond, to be proportional (to). 2. to meet (a need etc.). **—i saffeyn** *lrnd.* the meeting of lines of battle. **—ât** (. —. —) A *pl. of* **tekabül**.

tekâbür (. —.) تكابر A *lrnd.* a being or becoming proud, an imagining oneself great, important; pride.

tekaffi تقفي A *lrnd.* 1. a following; imitating, taking as one's model. 2. a showing great respect for one.

tekâfu[üü] (. —.) تكافو A *lrnd.* 1. an equaling one another, a being congruous; equality. 2. a complete balancing of opposites in two consecutive clauses, antithesis.

tekâhül (. —.) تكاهل A *lrnd.* a being careless, negligent; carelessness, negligence.

tekâkire (. —..) تكاكر A *lrnd., pl. of* **tekûr**, emperors, princes, lords etc. of the Byzantine Empire.

tekâlif (. — —) تكاليف A *lrnd., pl. of* **teklif**, 1. proposals; terms. 2. duties, taxes. **—i örfiye** extraordinary tax, levy; taxes based on Common Law. **—i şakka** unjustified extraordinary taxes.

tekâlüb (. —.) تكالب A *lrnd.* an attacking one another like dogs.

tekâlüm (. —.) تكالم A *lrnd.* a speaking to one another; conversation.

tekâmül (. —.) تكامل A a being perfected; evolution. — **et=** to be in the process of being perfected; to mature, develop. — **kanunu** the law of evolution. **—ât** (. —. —) A *pl.* **—iye** *phil.* evolutionism.

tekâpu (. — —) تكاپو P *lrnd.* 1. sycophancy, base flattery. 2. a running about. — **et=** /a/ to toady (to).

tekarrür تقرر A *same as* **takarrür**.

tekarun (. —.) تقارن A *lrnd.* a being near to each other; a coming near to one another.

tekarüb (. —.) تقارب A *lrnd.* 1. an approaching one another. 2. a drawing near its close (time).

tekârüm (. —.) تكارم A *lrnd.* an acting in a consciously noble or generous manner.

tekâsüf (. —.) تكاثف A *phys.* a being dense; condensation; density. — **et=** to condense; to become dense.

tekâsül (. —.) تكاسل A *lrnd.* a being lazy and negligent; negligence, laziness. **—ât** (. —. —) A *pl.*

tekasüm (. —.) تقاسم A *lrnd.* 1. a taking an oath with one another. 2. a dividing with each other.

tekâsür 1 (. —.) تكاثر A *lrnd.* 1. a collecting in abundance, an abounding; a becoming numerous. 2. a disputing for superiority (in number, affluence or offspring). **T— Suresi** name of the one hundred and second sura of the Quran.

tekâsür 2 (. —.) تكاسر A *phys.* diffraction.

tekâşüf (. —.) تكاشف A *lrnd.* 1. an opening out the inmost thoughts to one another; mutual confidence. 2. a saint's power of second sight.

tekatu[uu] (. —.) تقاطع A *lrnd., same as* **takatu**.

tekâtüb (. —.) تكاتب A *lrnd.* a corresponding together by letters; mutual correspondence.

tekatül (. —.) تقاتل A *lrnd.* a killing one another.

tekâtüm (. —.) تكاتم A *lrnd.* 1. a practicing concealment towards one another. 2. a habitually concealing oneself or one's thoughts.

tekaüd (. —.) تقاعد A *lrnd., same as* **tekaüt**. **—en** (. —'. .) A by retirement.

tekaüdiye (. —. —.) تقاعدية 1. pension. 2. deduction from a salary for a pension.

tekaüt[dü] تقاعد [**tekaüd**] 1. retirement, pension. 2. retired, pensioned. — **et=** /ı/ to pension off. — **maaşı** retirement pay, pension. — **sandığı** retirement fund, superannuation fund. **—lük** a being pensioned; retirement on a pension.

tekâver (. —.) تكاور P *lrnd.* 1. swift runner; swift running. 2. courser. **—i eblak** *poet.*

1. the world of good and bad fortune. 2. day and night.

tekavül (. —.) تقاول A *lrnd.* 1. a talking together. 2. a mutually promising, a making an engagement together.

tekavüm (. —.) تقاوم A *lrnd.* standing up to oppose each other, a confronting each other.

tekâya (. —.) تكايا A *lrnd.*, *pl. of* **tekye**, dervish convents.

tekâyüd (. —.) تكايد A *lrnd.* a planning tricks against each other, a tricking one another. —ât (. —.—) A *pl.*

tekaza (. —.) تقاضى تقاضا A *lrnd.*, *same as* **takaza** 2.

tekâzüb (. —.) تكاذب A *lrnd.* an accusing one another of falsehood.

tekbib (. —) تكبيب A *lrnd.* a cutting meat into bits for roasting; a making **kebab**.

tekbir (. —) تكبير A 1. the affirmation **Allahu ekber**: God is most great. 2. a religious composition by Itrî, familiar in all Muslim countries. 3. *lrnd.* a making, calling, or esteeming great. — **al=**, — **getir=** to pronounce the formula "Allahu ekber." —ât (. —.—) A *pl. of* **tekbir**.

tekbiratüttahrim (. —.. —) تكبيرات التحريم A *Isl. rel.* call of the formula "Allahu ekber" at the commencement of a service of worship.

tekbiratüttesrik[ki] (. —.. —) تكبيرات التشريك A *Isl. rel.* the formula of conclusion of every service of worship beginning with "Allahu ekber".

tekbirhan (. —.—) تكبيرخان P *lrnd.* one who repeats the formula "Allahu ekber".

tekbirle=[r] تكبيرلمك *Isl. rel.* to pronounce the formula "Allahu ekber".

tekdelikliler *neol., zool.* monotremates.

tekdir (. —) تكدير A 1. scolding, a reprimanding; reprimand, scolding; punishment. 2. *lrnd.* a causing to become turbid or misty. 3. *lrnd.* a causing the heart to be clouded with grief; a grieving, an afflicting. — **et=** /ı/ 1. to scold, reprimand. 2. *lrnd.* to make turbid or clouded. 3. *lrnd.* to grieve, to afflict. —**i hâtır** *lrnd.* a saddening, troubling the heart of a person.

tekdirât (. —.—) تكديرات A *lrnd.* scoldings; punishments. —**ı sedide** hard scoldings.

tekdirî (. —.—) تكديرى A *lrnd.* of the nature of punishment.

tekdüşüncelik[ği] *neol., psych.* monoideism.

teke 1 تكه 1. he-goat. 2. shrimp, *zool.*, Crago vulgaris; prawn, *zool.*, Pandalus annulicorinus. 3. *w. cap.*, name of a Turkman tribe in Central Asia. — **burunlu** hook-nosed, aquiline-nosed. **T—** **eli** *hist.*, name of the coastal area between Alanya and Antalya, the ancient Pamphylia. — **sakalı** goat's beard, *bot.*, Tragopagon protensis. —**den süt çıkar=** *colloq.* to be very skillful in getting what one wants.

teke 2 تكه *var. of* **tekâ**.

tekebbüd تكبد A *biol.* a hardening. —**i rie** *med.* hepatization. —**i süflâ** *astr.* lower culmination. —**i ülya** *astr.* upper culmination.

tekebbür تكبر A *lrnd.* a being proud; pride, haughtiness. — **et=** to be haughty, to give oneself airs.

tekeddür تكدر A *lrnd.* 1. a being clouded with grief (heart); grief, sadness. 2. a becoming turbid, misty, or dusty; turbidity, mistiness; slight opacity. —**i hâtır** heart's sorrow.

tekeffüf تكفف A *lrnd.* a holding out the open palm for alms.

tekeffül تكفل A *law.* a becoming bail or surety. — **et=** /a or ı/ to stand surety (for), to guarantee.

tekehhül تكحل A *lrnd.* 1. a treating one's own eyes with kohl. 2. the earth's being or becoming dark with vegetation.

tekehhün تكهن A *lrnd.* 1. a being a soothsayer. 2. soothsaying. —ât (... —) A soothsayings.

tekel *neol.* monopoly. **T— İdaresi** Management of the State Monopolies. —**cilik** monopolism.

tekele 1 تكله *archaic* robe of honor worn by the **ulema**; *prov.* waistcoat.

tekele=[r] 2 تكله لمك 1. to be sexually excited (he-goat). 2. to become full grown (male kid). —**n=** 1. to assume the airs of a he-goat. 2. to assume airs of importance. —**ndir=** /ı/ *caus.*

tekelik[ği] تكه لك 1. manners or acts of a he-goat. 2. arrogance. — **sat=** to play the he-goat.

tekellüf تكلف A a taking great pains; a giving oneself unnecessary trouble; empty show; false display; ceremoniousness, formality.

tekellüfat (... —) تكلفات A *lrnd.* special or extraordinary acts and observances of ceremony.

tekellüflü تكلفلو on which great care has been expended; ornate, sumptuous; elaborate; bombastic.

tekellüfsüz تكلفسز plain; not overdone.

tekellüm تكلم A *lrnd.* a speaking, a talking. — **et=** to talk, to speak.

tekellüs تكلس A *lrnd.* a being calcified; calcification.

tekemmül تكمل A *lrnd.* a being perfected; perfection; evolution. — **et=** to be perfected. —ât (... —) A perfections; evolutions.

tekemmüm تكمم A *lrnd.* 1. a tucking the hands in the sleeves. 2. a being covered or enveloped in a wrap.

tekemmün تكمن A *lrnd.* a concealing oneself in an ambush, a lying in wait.

tekenni تكنى A *lrnd.* a being named with a patronymic or a name derived from a quality.

teker 1 1. wheel. 2. circular, round. **— arası** width of track. **— meker** head over heels (in falling). **— tabanı** rim of a cartwheel.
teker 2 one at a time. **— teker** one by one.
tekerle=ʳ 1. to roll. 2. to let slip out inadvertently; to blurt out.
tekerlekᵍⁱ 1. wheel (of a vehicle). 2. round disk. **— izi** rut or track of a wheel. **— kırıldıktan sonra yol gösteren çok olur** It is easy to give advice after the event. **— mili** axle of a wheel or trunk. **— pabucu** brake shoe. **— parmağı** spoke of a wheel. **bir — peyniri** one cake of cheese.
tekerleme 1. jingle. 2. playful formula used in folk narrative. 3. roller (wave).
tekerlen=ⁱʳ 1. *pass. of* **tekerle=**. 2. to roll round; to turn head over heels; to fall over. 3. *slang* to die. 4. *slang* to be fired. **—dir=** /ı/ *caus.*
tekerrüh A *lrnd.* 1. a disliking, a loathing; a showing an aversion to. 2. a doing an act unwillingly, under compulsion, with a bad grace.
tekerrüm A *lrnd.* an acting in a kind, generous manner, a showing nobleness of soul.
tekerrümen (..´..) A *lrnd.* out of noble and generous kindness.
tekerrür A 1. an occurring again or several times, repetition; recurrence. 2. *law* relapse, repetition of an offense. **— et=** to be repeated, to repeat itself. **—i zaid** *log.* truism. **—ât** (...—) A *lrnd., pl. of* **tekerrür**.
tekessüb A *lrnd.* an earning one's living with difficulty.
tekessüf A *lrnd.* a being dense; condensation; density.
tekessül A *lrnd.* a being lazy; indolence.
tekessür 1 A *lrnd.* 1. a becoming much or many; a multiplying; abundance; multitude. 2. a making a great display with the property of others.
tekessür 2 A *lrnd.* a being broken. **—i mizac** ill-health.
tekeşşüf A *lrnd.* a being uncovered, displayed, manifested; a manifesting oneself; display, manifestation.
tekevvün A 1. *lrnd.* a coming into existence; a being created; an originating; origination. 2. *phil.* genesis. **—i cibâl** *geol.* orogeny. **— et=** to come into existence, to originate, arise. **—i evvel** *phil.* preformation. **—i hayatî** biogenesis. **—i nev'î** phylogeny. **—ât** (.:.—) A *pl. of* **tekevvün**. **—î** (...—) A genetic.
tekeyyüf A *lrnd.* a becoming merry; a taking something that causes merriness.

tekeyyüs A *lrnd.* a pretending to be sagacious and shrewd.
tekfil (.—) A *lrnd.* 1. a causing to become surety, bail or guarantee. 2. a making oneself liable for the maintenance of a person.
tekfin (.—) A *lrnd.* a wrapping in a winding-sheet (corpse). **— et=** /ı/ to wrap in a winding-sheet. **—ât**ı (.——) A *pl. of* **tekfin**. **—î** (.——) A pertaining to the swathing of a corpse.
tekfir (.—) A *lrnd.* 1. an accusing of heresy or blasphemy (a Muslim). 2. a holding or pronouncing to be blasphemy. 3. God's blotting out a man's sins. 4. a performing expiation for violating a rash vow. 5. a covering up, a concealing. **— et=** /ı/ to pronounce to be a misbeliever or a blasphemer; to call a doctrine blasphemy. **—ât** (.——) A *pl of* **tekfir**.
tekfur [**tekûr**] *hist.* Christian princelet, local Christian ruler in Asia Minor. **T— Sarayı** the ruins of the palace of the Hebdomon on the land wall of Istanbul.
tekgözlükᵍᵘ monocle.
tekhil (.—) A *lrnd.* a treating an eye with kohl; an applying kohl to the eyes.
-tekiⁿⁱ *cf.* **-deki**.
te'kid (.—) A, **tekid** (——) 1. reiterating, corroborating, strengthening; confirmation; reiteration, corroboration. 2. a repeating (a message or order). 3. *gram.* word or phrase corroborative of another word or phrase in the same sentence or paragraph; intensive word or phrase. **— et=** /ı/ to confirm, to repeat.
te'kidât (.——) A *lrnd.* corroborations.
te'kiden (.—´.) A *lrnd.* in confirmation, as a repeat.
te'kidnâme (.——.) P letter of confirmation.
tekil 1 *neol., gram.* singular.
te'kil 2 (.—) A *lrnd.* 1. a giving to eat; an inviting one to eat. 2. an asserting or holding that a person did eat.
tekin 1 1. auspicious *not used with affirmative verbs; with neg.* ill-omened, haunted. 2. *prov.* deserted, empty (place). 3. unique. **— değil** 1. ill-omened, haunted, uncanny. 2. of unsound mind; with whom it is best to have nothing to do. **— dur=** *prov.* to keep quiet, to hold back.
tekin 2 *ancient Turkish hist.* prince.
tekinsiz *prov.* ill-omened, uncanny.
tekir 1. marked with irregularly rounded spots; tabby (cat). 2. ounce, snow leopard, *zool., Leopardus uncia*. **— balığı** striped goatfish, *zool., Mullus surmuletus*.

— **kedi** tabby cat. **T— Sarayı** *var. of* **Tekfur Sarayı**.
tekke [**tekye**] 1. dervish lodge. 2. *slang* den of scoundrels where hashish is taken. 3. *slang* place where idlers find refuge and food. **—yi bekliyen çorbayı içer** He who serves patiently will be rewarded eventually. **—ye kurban geldi** A God-sent opportunity has occurred. **—li** who lives in a lodge; lodge.
tekle=ʳ **1** 1. /ı/ to thin out, plant out (thick seedling plants). 2. to work singly (piston of a motor). 3. *slang* to stammer.
tekle 2 *archaic, same as* **tekele 1**.
teklif (. —) A 1. a proposing or offering for acceptance; proposal; offer. 2. motion (before an assembly). 3. etiquette, formal behavior, ceremony. 4. *lrnd.* custom; tax, obligation. **— et=** /ı, a/ 1. to propose; to offer formally or ceremoniously. 2. to submit. 3. to move (a motion). 4. to bid, tender. **—i hâm** an impossible nad out-of-place proposal. **—î mâlâyutâk** unbearable and impossible proposal. **— sahibi** 1. mover (of a motion or bill). 2. bidder, one who submits a tender. **— ve tekellüf** rules of etiquette and decorum. **— yok** There's no need for ceremony.
teklifât (. — —) A *lrnd.* 1. proposals, offers. 2. formalities.
teklifî (. — —) A *log.* obligatory.
teklifli 1. with whom one must stand on ceremony. 2. with decorum, observing the rules of etiquette.
teklifsiz 1. without ceremony. 2. free-and-easy, familiar, unconstrained. **—ce** unceremoniously. **—lik** unceremoniousness, absence of compliments.
teklikᵍⁱ *phil.* oneness, uniqueness.
teklil (. —) A *lrnd.* a crowning; coronation.
teklis (. —) A *lrnd.* 1. a plastering with plaster of Paris. 2. calcination.
tekme kick. **— at=** /a/ to give a kick. **— ye=** 1. to get a kick, to receive a blow. 2. to fall into disgrace.
tekmele=ʳ /ı/ to kick. **—n=** *pass.*
tekmil (. —) A 1. all; the whole of. 2. *lrnd.* a completing or perfecting; complete, perfect; *phil.* integration. 3. *lrnd.* a termination, a concluding; terminated, finished, ended. **—i enfas et=** to die. **— et=** /ı/ to complete, finish. **— ol=** to be completed.
tekmile A *lrnd.* 1. a completing, perfecting; completion. 2. finishing touch, complement.
tekmille=ʳ /ı/ 1. to complete, to finish. 2. *slang* to do away with, to kill.
tekmin (. —) A *lrnd.* a putting in ambush.

tekne 1. trough. 2. hull (of a ship); craft, sailing vessel. 3. body of certain stringed instruments originally made of or shaped like a half-gourd. 4. *print.* galley. **—de hamur** work ready to be accomplished. **— kazıntısı** (*lit.* the last scraping of dough from the trough) the youngest child of a numerous family. **— sarık** a kind of turban the top of which resembled a trough. **— taşı** stone trough for water. **— tavan** *arch.* 1. concave ceiling. 2. roof over a gate in a garden wall.
teknif (. —) A *lrnd.* a surrounding as with a border.
teknikᵍⁱ F 1. technique. 2. technical. **—çi** technician.
tekniker Gk technician, mechanic.
teknin (. —) A *lrnd.* a hiding, a covering up.
teknisyen F technician.
tekniye A *lrnd.* a surnaming a person or thing with a patronymic or a name derived from a quality.
tekrar (. —) A 1. repeating; repetition. 2. a happening again, a recurring; recurrence. 3. repeatedly; again. 4. *log.* tautology. **— et=** /ı/ to repeat. **— ol=** to happen again, to recur. **— alettekrar** A, **— betekrar** P, **— tekrar** over and over again.
tekraren (. —ʹ.) A *lrnd.* repeatedly, again and again.
tekrarla=ʳ /ı/ to repeat. **—n=** *pass.* **—t=** /ı, a/ *caus. of* **tekrarla=**.
tekrarlı *neol.* repeated.
tekrih (. —) A *lrnd.* a causing to be accounted an abomination; a making loathsome. **—ât** (. — —) A *pl.*
tekrim (. —) A *lrnd.* 1. a treating with respect, an honoring. 2. deference, mark of respect. **— et=** /ı/ to treat with great deference. **—ât** (. — —) A reverences, honors.
tekrimen (. —ʹ.) A *lrnd.* in honor of; with respect for.
tekrir (. —) A *lrnd.* 1. a repeating; repetition. 2. repetition of a word or clause for the sake of emphasis. **—i istidlâl** *log.* instance. **—i merdud** *log.* tautology. **—ât** (. — —) A repetitions.
Tekrur (. —) A *lrnd., a name given to the Sudan.*
teksib (. —) A *lrnd.* a causing to be earned or acquired.
teksif (. —) A a making dense. **— et=** /ı/ 1. to condense, compress. 2. to render opaque.
teksir 1 (. —) A 1. a causing to become much or many; a multiplying; augmentation, multiplication. 2. duplication (of copies);

teksir a multigraphing. — **et=** /ı/ 1. to multiply; to increase. 2. to duplicate. — **makinası** multigraph, mimeograph. **—i sevad** *lrnd.* a useless multiplication of words in a composition.

teksir 2 (. —) تكسير A 1. *lrnd.* a breaking much or violently; comminution. 2. *math.* a dividing so as to produce a fraction.

teksiye تكسية A *lrnd.* a robing, investiture.

tekşif (. —) تكشيف A *lrnd.* 1. an uncovering, a displaying, a manifesting; manifestation. 2. a causing to be uncovered, displayed or manifested.

tektaz (. —) تكتاز P *lrnd.* 1. a running about; searching, seeking. 2. haste, speed.

tektib (. —) تكتيب A *lrnd.* 1. a causing to be written; a teaching or causing to write; a writing. 2. a collecting and organizing as a troop or army.

tektim (. —) تكتيم A *lrnd.* a concealing; concealment.

tektük تك ترك 1. here and there; now and again. 2. one or two; occasional. **—ten geçin=** to live by chance with things picked up.

tekûr تكور *same as* **tekfûr**.

tekvin (. —) تكوين A 1. *lrnd.* a causing to come into existence; a creating, an originating; creation; production. 2. *w. cap., Bib.* Genesis. **— et=** /ı/ to produce, to originate. **—i evvel** *phil.* antecedent. **—i ferdi** *biol.* ontogenesis. **—ât** (. — —) A creations.

tekvinî (. — —) تكويني A 1. *lrnd.* pertaining to creation; creative. 2. *phil.* genetic; epigenetic.

tekvir (. —) تكوير A *lrnd.* 1. a wrapping the turban round the head in a spiral form. 2. a rolling or winding a thing into a ball or round mass, or around something. **T— Sûresi** *name of the eighty-first sura of the Quran.*

tekye تكيه A *lrnd.* 1. *same as* **tekke**. 2. a leaning on a thing with the back or elbow. 3. place of repose; anything upon which one leans, prop. **— et=** /a/ 1. to lean on or against. 2. to trust to for support; to confide in. **— vur=** /a/ *archaic* 1. to lean on or against. 2. to trust.

tekyedar (. . —) تكيه دار P *lrnd.* 1. dervish who lives in a lodge. 2. housekeeper or porter of a dervish lodge.

tekyegâh (. . —) تكيه گاه P *lrnd.* 1. place or person that can be leaned upon or trusted for support. 2. resting place; refuge, protection.

tekyelen=ⁱʳ تكيه لنك *archaic, same as* **tekye vur=**.

tekyenişin (. . . —) تكيه نشين P *lrnd.* dwelling in a lodge (dervish).

tekyezen تكيه زن P *lrnd.* that supports, supporting.

tekyil (. —) تكييل A *lrnd.* to measure by kiles.

tekzib (. —) A, **tekzip**ᵇⁱ تكذيب 1. a declaring to be a lie; a denying. 2. a contradicting; contradiction. **— et=** /ı/ 1. to proclaim false; to give the lie to; to deny. 2. to contradict. **—ât** (. — —) A *pl. of* **tekzib**.

tel 1 تل 1. wire; fiber. 2. a single thread or hair. 3. string (of a musical instrument). 4. silver or gold thread used to decorate a bride's hair. 5. made of wire; resembling wire. 6. telegram. **—e al=** /ı/ to record, on wire. **— çek=** 1. to draw wire; to enclose with wire. 2. to telegraph, to send a wire. **— çivi** brad. **— dokuma** fine screening made of woven wire. **—ine dokun=** /ın/ to touch somebody on his tender spot. **— dolap** flyproof food cupboard with wire screening, meat safe. **— gibi** slender as a fiber. **— halat** cable. **— kadayıf** a sweet pastry made from dough extruded in filaments; the partially dried dough from which the pastry is made. **— kafes** 1. iron cage; wire cage. 2. wirework. **— kakma** damascening. **— kır=** 1. to break a thread or wire. 2. to blunder. 3. *slang* to run away, to decamp. **— mania** *mil.* barbed wire entanglement. **—de oyna=** to show talent, to do a clever thing. **— örgü** wire netting, wire fence. **— şehriye** vermicelli. **—ler tak=, —ler takın=** 1. to dress oneself out for a holiday. 2. to rejoice greatly over something. **— tel** in fibers, single threads. **— vur=** to telegraph, to send a telegram. **— yazısı** telegram.

telˡˡⁱ **2** تل A *lrnd.* 1. hill, hillock. 2. artificial mound of earth. 3. sandhill.

telâ تلا It *tailor.* horsehair stiffening (of coat collars, etc.).

telâffuz تلفظ A 1. a pronouncing; pronunciation. 2. an uttering, utterance. **— et=** /ı/ 1. to pronounce. 2. to utter. **— kabiliyetsizliği** *med.* anarthria. **—ât** (. . . —) A *pl. of* **telâffuz**.

telâfi (. — .) تلافى A a making up for something lost, a repairing an error, compensation. **— et=** /ı/ to make up for, compensate. **—si imkânsız** irreparable. **—i mâfât** *lrnd.* a making good the past, a repairing an error or loss.

telâfif (. — —) تلافيف A *lrnd.* luxuriant entangled grass.

telâhhum تلحم A *lrnd.* 1. a becoming covered with flesh. 2. a becoming fat.

telâhhuz تلحظ A *lrnd.* 1. a watering of the mouth (from desire or anything acid). 2. a becoming stingy and miserly; stinginess, miserliness.

telâhi (. — .) تلاهى A *lrnd.* a playing, beguiling the time.

telâhukᵏᵘ (. — .) تلاحق A *lrnd.* a meeting and joining one another; conjunction, junction.

— **et=** to join one another, to follow or succeed one another.

telâhuz (. — .) تلاحظ A *lrnd.* a looking at one another.

telâki (. — .) تلاق A *lrnd.* a coming together, a meeting one another; meeting. — **et=** /la/ 1. to meet one another, to meet. 2. to encounter one another. — **noktası** point of junction.

telâkigâh (. — — —) تلاقى گاه P *lrnd.* place of meeting one another.

telâkki تلقّى A 1. mode of receiving or regarding; interpretation, view. 2. *lrnd.* a communicating and listening in turns. 3. *lrnd.* a receiving and accepting; reception. 4. *lrnd.* a meeting, an encountering face to face. — **et=** /ı/ 1. to consider; to regard (as good or bad, etc.). 2. *lrnd.* to receive (a piece of news). —**yât** (. . . —) A *pl. of* **telâkki**.

telâkkub تلقّب A *lrnd.* a taking or being called by a surname.

telâkkum تلقّم A *lrnd* 1. an eating or swallowing one's food in leisurely fashion. 2. water's rumbling in the body.

telâ'lüᵘᵘ تلألؤ A *lrnd.* a sparkling, shining.

telâmiz (. — —), **telâmize** (. — . .) تلامذه تلامیذ A *lrnd., pl. of* **tilmiz**.

telâsukᵏᵘ (. — .) تلاصق A *lrnd.* a sticking fast to one another; adherence. — **et=** /a/ to stick together, to adhere to one another.

tela'süm تلعثم A *lrnd.* hesitation; stuttering, stutter.

telâş (. —) تلاش 1. flurry, confusion. 2. alarm; hurry. 3. embarrassment, anxiety. —**a düş=** to be confused, alarmed, flurried. —**a gel=** to be hurried.

telâşçı تلاشجى 1. nervous, restless (person). 2. alarmist.

telâşi 1 (. — —) تلاشى A *lrnd.* a being aboilshed, abolition.

telâşi 2 (. — .) تلاشى *lrnd., var. of* **telâş**.

telâşlan= تلاشلن to become flurried or anxious. —**dır=** /ı/ *caus.*

telâşlı تلاشلى confused, flurried; agitated, upset.

telâşsız تلاشسز calm, composed; quietly.

telâtin (. — —) تلاتين Russ Russian leather.

telâttuf تلطّف A *lrnd., same as* **talâttuf**.

telâttuh تلطّخ A *lrnd.* a becoming smeared, a being daubed.

telâtuf (. — .) تلاطف A *lrnd.* an acting courteously and kindly to each other. —**ât** (. — . —) A *pl.*

telâtum (. — .) تلاطم A *lrnd.* the dashing together of waves; agitation, commotion.

telâtumgâh (. — . —), **telâtûmgeh** (. — . . —) تلاطمگاه تلاطمگه P *lrnd.* place where the waves hit against each other.

telâub 1 (. — .) تلاعب A *lrnd.* a playing together.

telâub 2 تلعّب A *lrnd.* a playing, an amusing oneself.

telâun (. — .) تلاعن A *lrnd.* a cursing one another.

telâzüm (. — .) تلازم A 1. *lrnd.* a being inserted within one another, a hanging together. 2. *phil.* inherence.

telâzzi (. . —) تلظّى A *lrnd.* a burning, flaming; blaze, flare.

telbis (. —) تلبيس A *lrnd.* 1. a causing a matter to assume the appearance of something different, a misrepresenting; misrepresentation. 2. a covering, concealing (the truth, the faults of goods on sale, etc.); a cheating, deceiving, lying. 3. a causing a garment to be worn.

telbisât (. — —) تلبيسات A *lrnd.* misrepresentations; false pretences; adulterations.

telbisle= تلبيسله /ı/ to misrepresent, to deceive.

telbisli تلبيسلى 1. who misrepresents and deceives. 2. in which deception is concealed.

telbiye تلبيه A *lrnd.* a pilgrim ejaculating the formula **lebbeyke** (at Mecca). — **et=** to ejaculate the formula **lebbeyke**.

telcie تلجيه A *law* simulation; fictitious transaction.

telcim (. —) تلجيم A *lrnd.* a bridling a horse.

tele تله P *lrnd.* 1. trap for beasts. 2. fold, enclosure for beasts.

telebbüs تلبّس A *lrnd.* 1. a putting on of clothes; a clothing oneself. 2. a being dubious, assuming an appearance that leads to doubt (matter). —**ât** (. . . —) A *pl.*

telecüc تلجلج A *lrnd.* a stammering.

telef تلف A a going to waste, destruction or death; ruin; perdition; death. — **et=** /ı/ to destroy, ruin, kill. — **ol=** 1. to be destroyed or ruined; to be killed. 2. to die.

telefat (. . —) تلفات A 1. *mil.* casualties. 2. losses of life (in an accident, etc.). — **ver=** to suffer losses (in battle). — **verdir=** /a/ to inflict losses.

teleferikᵏⁱ تله‌فريك F telpher, cable lift.

teleffüf تلفّف A *lrnd.* a being wrapped or enveloped in.

teleffüt تلفّت A *lrnd.* a turning towards, a taking notice of or paying attention to.

telefiyat (. . . —) تلفيات A *lrnd.* losses; deaths.

telefon تلفون F telephone. — **et=** /a/ to telephone.

telefonlaş= تلفونلش /la/ to talk over the telephone (with somebody).

telegraf تلغراف F *same as* **telgraf**.

telehhi تلهّى A *lrnd.* 1. an amusing oneself; amusement; play, diversion. 2. a becoming diverted from.

telehhüb تلهّب A *lrnd.* a blazing, flaming (fire).
telehhüf تلهّف A *lrnd.* a sighing, a moaning, lamenting bitterly. —**ât** (...—) A *pl.*
telekᵍⁱ تلك *prov.* feathers on the wings and tail of a bird. — **damarlı yaprak** *bot.* pinnate leaf.
teleke تلكه *zool.* remex.
tele'lü تلألؤ A *lrnd.* a flashing, gleaming, glittering (lightning or sword).
teleme تلمه 1. a kind of unsalted cheese. 2. a kind of milk curdled with yeast. — **peyniri** fresh unsalted cheese. — **peyniri gibi** soft, flabby.
telemmuᵘᵘ تلمّع A *lrnd.* a flashing, glittering (lightning, sword). —**ât** (...—) A *pl.*
telemmüs تلمّس A *lrnd.* a touching with the hand.
telemmüz تلمّذ A *lrnd.* a becoming a pupil; a learning like a student.
telepati تلپاتى F telepathy.
teles تلس [Arabic **tallis**] threadbare.
telesiʳ تلسيمك 1. to become threadbare. 2. to become thin-faced, bony; to pine away (infant).
teleskopᵇᵘ تلسقوپ F astronomical telescope.
telessüm تلثّم A *lrnd.* 1. a veiling the mouth (woman). 2. a carrying to the lips, a kissing.
televvün تلوّن A *lrnd.* 1. a changing color, appearance or disposition. 2. caprice, fickleness. 3. a having or acquiring a color or tinge. — **et=** to change color; to be changeable or inconstant.
televvünat (...—) تلوّنات A *lrnd.* caprices, ficklenesses.
televvüs تلوّث A *lrnd.* 1. a being soiled with filth. 2. stain; uncleanness. —**ât** (...—) A stains.
teleyyün تليّن A *lrnd.* 1. a becoming soft; softness. 2. a being mitigated; mitigation. —**i dimaği** *med.* softening of the brain, a becoming senile. —**ât** (...—) A *pl.*
telezzüc تلزّج A *lrnd.* 1. a becoming sticky, mucilaginous. 2. a being partly matted together (hair).
telezzüz تلذّذ A *lrnd.* 1. a deriving pleasure; a tasting something pleasant. 2. pleasure of the senses; intellectual enjoyment, pleasure, enjoyment. — **et=** to enjoy the taste of, to take pleasure in. — **felsefesi** hedonism.
telezzüzât (...—) تلذّذات A *lrnd.* pleasures, enjoyments.
telfif (.—) تفنيف A 1. *lrnd.* a folding or winding a thing on itself. 2. *lrnd.* a wrapping or enveloping a thing; a covering up. 3. *anat.* gyrus.
telfikᵏⁱ (.—) تلفيق A *lrnd.* 1. a collecting, putting together; a compiling. 2. a joining, adding a breadth to a cloth; a sewing together. — **et=** /ı/ to put together; to compile. —**at** (.——) A *pl.* of **telfik**.
telgraf تلغراف [telegraf] 1. telegraph; telegram. 2. *slang* a sitting beside a gambler and signaling secretly to the opponent. — **çek=** to send a telegram.
telgrafçı تلغرافجى telegrapher. —**lık** 1. occupation of a telegrapher. 2. telegraphy.
telgrafhane (..—.) تلغرافخانه telegraph office.
telgrafî (..—) تلغرافى P *lrnd.* telegraphic.
telgrafla= تلغراف لمق /ı/ to telegraph.
telgrafname (..—.) تلغرافنامه telegram.
telh تلخ P *lrnd.* bitter; acrimonious, malicious.
telhâb (.—), **telhâbe** (.—.) تلخاب P *lrnd.* bitter water; salt water
telhbar (.—) تلخبار P *lrnd.* 1. wild, unwholesome fruit. 2. that has bitter consequences.
telhgâm تلخكام *var.* of **telhkâm**.
telhgû (.—) تلخگو same as **telhgüftar**.
telhgüftar (..—) تلخگفتار P *lrnd.* who says biting or bitter things, speaking bitterly; harsh, sarcastic, sharp.
telhî (.—) تلخى P *lrnd.* bitterness.
telhib (.—) تلهيب A *lrnd.* 1. a making a fire blaze, flare. 2. a setting aflame with anger, etc.
telhiçeşide (.—.—.) تلخ چشيده P *lrnd.* who has experienced grief or disappointment.
telhid (.—) تلحيد A *lrnd.* a placing a corpse with its head in the niche in a grave.
telhif (.—) تلهيف A *lrnd.* a lamenting, regretting (anything neglected, missed or lost). —**ât** (.——) A *pl.*
telhin (.—) تلحين A *lrnd.* 1. a quavering voice while reading. 2. a chanting, singing. 3. a holding or pronouncing in error. —**ât** (.——) A *pl.*
telhis (.—) تلخيص A 1. *lrnd.* a making a summary or abstract. 2. *lrnd.* abstract, summary. 3. *Ott. hist.* condensed report drawn up at the Porte for submission to the Sultan. — **et=** /ı/ to summarize, to make an abstract of. —**ât** (.——) A *pl.* of **telhis**. —**çi** same as **telhisî**.
telhisen (.—'.) تلخيصاً A *lrnd.* in a summary form.
telhisî (.——) تلخيصى A *Ott. hist.* official charged with making summaries of reports for the Sultan.
telhiye تلهيه A *lrnd.* 1. a causing to play and amuse oneself. 2. a diverting or distracting one from a matter; anything by which time is beguiled.
telhkâm (.—) تلخكام P *lrnd.* having a bitter taste in the mouth; disappointed, balked. —**î** (.——) P, —**lık** bitterness of taste, disappointment.
telhlikᵍⁱ تلخلك *lrnd.* bitterness.

telhmizac (. —) تخمزاج P *lrnd.* whose disposition is disagreeable, splenetic, peevish.
telhnâkki (. —) تخناك P *lrnd.* 1. more or less bitter. 2. very bitter; bitterly.
telhru (. —) تخرو P *lrnd.* sour-faced, morose, sullen.
telhütürş تخ و ترش P *lrnd.* 1. bitter and sour. 2. troubles and miseries of the world.
telhzeban (.. —) تخزبان P *lrnd.* who says bitter things; speaking with bitterness or crossly.
telid (. —) تليد A *lrnd.* 1. born in foreign parts and educated at home. 2. home-born, hereditary (slave or cattle).
te'lif (. —) A, **telif** (— —) تأليف 1. a composing or an arranging a book; composition, compilation. 2. book. 3. a bringing together as friends, uniting in peace and concord; a reconciling. **—i beyn et=** *lrnd.* to reconcile two contending parties. **— et=** 1. /ı/ to write; to compile. 2. /ı, la/ to reconcile, to square (conflicting facts). **— hakkı** copyright. **—i havatır** *lrnd.* a winning confidence. **— ilmi** *lrnd.* the science of music. **—i kulûb** a pleasing, treating nicely. **—i lif ü sâbûn** (*lit.*, combining palm-fiber used in washing and soap) doing an impossibility. **—i nisbet** *lrnd.* composition of a ratio in mathematics.
telifât (. — —) تأليفات A *lrnd.* books, works.
telifiye (. — ..) تأليفيه A *phil.* sycretism.
telifkâr (. — —) تأليفكار P *lrnd.* reconciliatory. **—ane** (. — — —.) P in a reconciliatory way.
telifkerde تأليفكرده P *lrnd.* 1. composed, written. 2. work composed.
te'lih (. —) تأليه A *lrnd.* 1. a rendering devout in worship. 2. a deifying. **— et=** /ı/ to deify.
tel'in (. —) تلعين A a cursing violently, an anathematizing; curse, anathema. **— et=** /ı/ to curse. **—ât** (. — —) A *lrnd., pl. of* tel'in.
telkâri (. — —) تلكاری P woven of gold or silver thread; stuff woven thus, filigree.
telkib (. —) تلقيب A *lrnd.* a giving a surname or nickname. **— et=** /ı/ to surname. **—ât** (. — —) A *pl. of* **telkib**.
telkih (. —) تلقيح A *lrnd.* 1. /ı/ a grafting. 2. an inoculating; inoculation; vaccination. 3. fecundation. **— et=** to graft, inoculate, vaccinate. **—ât** (. — —) A *pl. of* **telkih**.
telkim (. —) تلقيم A *lrnd.* a causing to be eaten at a mouthful; a giving in morsels.
telkin (. —) تلقين A 1. a suggesting; suggestion, inspiration; inculcation. 2 a communicating orally. 3. an inculcating to a novice the articles of the Muslim faith. 4. final rites at a funeral. **— binefsihi** *psych.* autosuggestion, self-suggestion. **— et=** /ı, a/ 1. to suggest, inspire, inculcate. 2. to communicate orally. **— kabiliyeti** *phil.* suggestibility.
telkinat (. — —) تلقينات A *pl. of* **telkin**. **—a kapıl=** to be influenced by suggestions
telkinle=r /ı/ *neol., same as* **telkin et=**.
telkinli تلقينلی made by suggestion. **— tedavi** faith-healing.
telkiye تلقيه A *lrnd.* 1. a casting a thing upon or into a person (really or figuratively). 2. an infusing, inspiring.
tellâkki تلاك [**dellâk**] 1. bath attendant. 2. masseur, shampooer. **—lık** 1. the profession and state of a bath attendant. 2. fee or charge paid to a bath attendant.
tellâl تلال [**dellâl**] 1. town-crier. 2. broker. 3. middleman; pimp, bawd. **—iye** fee paid to a **tellâl**. **—lık** profession and state of a **tellâl**.
telle=r تللمك 1. to adorn with gold wire or thread. 2. to deck out; to embellish (a story). 3. to praise extravagantly. 4. to send a telegram. **—yip pulla=** /ı/ 1. to deck out with gold thread; to cover with decorations. 2. to embroider (a narrative with exaggerations).
telleme تلله *verbal n. of* **telle=**.
tellen=ir تللنمك *pass. of* **telle=**. **—dir=** /ı/ 1. *caus. of* **tellen=**. 2. *colloq.* to smoke a cigarette.
tellet=ir تللتمك /ı/ to cause to be furnished or arranged with wire, thread or fibers.
telli تللی 1. wired. 2. decorated with gold or silver wire or thread. **— bebek** extravagantly dressed; dandy. **— bez** a kind of fine cloth having gold or silver thread. **— cam** wired glass, safety glass. **— kâğıt** gilt paper. **— kavuk** *Ott. hist.* turban worn by the grand viziers. **— mürdeseng** flaky litharge. **— pullu** decked out; showy. **— sazlar** stringed musical instruments. **— turna** demoiselle crane, *zool.*, *Anthropoides virgo*.
telmiii (. —) تلميع A *lrnd.* 1. a causing to shine and glitter. 2. a coloring; a varying, diversifying. 3. a reciting a poem mixing two or three languages together. **—ât** (. — —) A *pl.*
telmih (. —) تلميح A *lrnd.* an alluding to a subject; allusion; hint. **—ât** (. — —) A *pl.*
telmihen (. —.) تلميحاً A *lrnd.* alluding.
telmihî (. — —) تلميحی A *lrnd.* allusive. **— istiare** allusive metaphor.
telmiz (. —) تلميذ A *lrnd., same as* **tilmiz**.
telsim (. —) تلثيم A *lrnd.* a kissing. **—ât** (. — —) A *pl.*
telsiz تلسز 1. without wire, radio. **— telefon** wireless telephone. **— telgraf** wireless telegraph. **—ci** wireless operator.
teltikgi 1 تنتيك 1. *prov.* deficiency,

teltik defect. 2. deficient, incomplete. 3. small balance of an account. — **doldur=** to make good a deficiency; to make an odd number even. — **gel=** to turn out deficient. —**i temizle=** to pay off a small balance of account.

teltik[ii] 2 تلتك *archaic, same as* **tetik 1**.

teltikli تلتكلی with a small balance owing (account), with a fractional amount, not a round sum (of money).

teltiksiz تلتكسز 1. round (sum); without fractions. 2. complete; whole. 3. fully paid.

telve تلوه 1. coffee grounds. 2. bore; tiresome, persistent man. 3. sot; man who stupifies himself with opium. — **falı** fortune-telling by the appearance of coffee grounds.

telvi[ii] (.—) تلویح A *lrnd.* a causing to be deeply affected (by love). —**ât** (.——) A *pl.*

telvih (.—) تلویح A *lrnd.* 1. an alluding to; distant allusion; scientific or technical allusion. 2. a making glitter and gleam (sword). 3. a making a signal by waving. —**ât** (.——) A allusions.

telvim (.—) تلویم A *lrnd.* a reproaching; an upbraiding. —**ât** (.——) A *pl.*

telvin (.—) تلوین A 1. *lrnd.* a coloring, a tingeing. 2. *lrnd.* a bringing a matter to a certain complexion. 3. *myst.* a devotee's being filled with ecstasy by a glimpse of the divine favor; rapture, ecstasy. — **et=** /ı/ to color. —**ât** (.——) A painting (of buildings).

telvis (.—) تلویث A *lrnd.* 1. a making filthy; a soiling. 2. an act that soils, act of soiling. — **et=** /ı/ to defile, to soil. —**ât** (.——) A *pl. of* **telvis**.

telviye تلویه A *lrnd.* a twisting, turning, bending much or often.

telyin (.—) تلیین A *lrnd.* 1. a softening, a making soft. 2. a mitigating; mitigation. 3. a loosening the bowels.

telziz (.—) تلزیذ A *lrnd.* a causing to become enjoyable or delicious.

temacüd (.—.) تماجد A *lrnd.* a contending with one another as to nobility or honor; a rehearsing the glory of oneself.

temadi (.—.) تمادی A *lrnd.* a continuing uninterruptedly; long continuation. — **et=** to continue.

tema'dün تمعدن A *lrnd.* a becoming metal, a being metallized.

temahhuk[ku] تمحق A *lrnd.* a being annihilated, a being destroyed.

temalük[ku] (.—.) تمالك A *lrnd.* 1. a maintaining self-possession. 2. a possessing the power and ability to do or say a thing; power, ability.

temam (.—) تمام A *same as* **tamam**.

temari (.—.) تماری A *lrnd.* a doubting and hesitating; doubt and hesitation.

temaruz (.—.) تمارض A *lrnd.* a feigning sickness; feigned sickness. — **et=** to pretend to be sick, to malinger. —**ât** (.—.—) A *pl. of* **temaruz**.

temas (.—) تماس A a touching one another; contact. — **et=** 1. /a/ to touch. 2. /a/ to touch on (a subject). 3. /la/ to make contact with, to get in touch with. —**a geç=** /la/ to get into touch with. —**a gel=** /la/ to come in touch, to meet. — **noktası** *geom.* point of contact.

temasih (.——) تماسیح A *lrnd., pl. of* **timsah**.

temasil (.——) تماثیل A *lrnd., pl. of* **timsal**.

temasüh (.—.) تماسخ A *lrnd.* metempsychosis, a transforming; metamorphosis.

temasük[ku] (.—.) تماسك A *lrnd.* 1. a holding fast to a thing. 2. a repressing, containing oneself.

temasül (.—.) تماثل A *lrnd.* 1. a being equal, like each other. 2. a being convalescent, convalescence. — **et=** to become like or equal to one another. —**ât** (.—.—) A *pl. of* **temasül**.

temaşa (.——) تماشا A 1. a walking about to see things. 2. public promenade. 3. spectacle, show, scene; the theater. —**ya çık=** to go out for a walk, to stroll about and watch things. — **et=** /ı/ to observe; to enjoy (the scene).

temaşacı تماشاجی spectator; lounger in a place of public promenading.

temaşagâh (.———) تماشاگاه P *lrnd.* 1. public promenade. 2. theater.

temaşager (.——.) تماشاگر P *lrnd., same as* **temaşacı**.

temaşahane (.———.) تماشاخانه P *lrnd.* 1. place where spectacles are seen; theater, etc. 2. the world. —**i garaib** place where strange things are exhibited.

temaşaî (.———) تماشائی P *lrnd.* spectacular.

temaşakâr (.———) تماشاکار P *lrnd.* spectator. —**î** (.————) P spectatorship.

temaşakede (.———..) تماشاکده P *lrnd.* place of amusement, theater.

temaşalık[ği] تماشالق public promenade; theater.

temattur تمطر A *lrnd.* 1. rain's falling in drops; weather's turning to rain. 2. a being caught by the rain, a going out into the rain.

temavüt (.—.) تماوت A *lrnd.* 1. a pretending to be dead or dying. 2. a pretending to have cast off worldliness.

temayül (.—.) تمایل A 1. an inclining, a leaning; inclination; bias. 2. tendency; liking. — **et=** /a/ to have an inclination (towards), a tendency (to). —**ât** (.—.—) A *pl. of* **temayül**.

temayüz (.—.) تمایز A a being distinguished or privileged. — **et=** to excel.

tembel تنبل [tenbel] lazy; lazy man. —e iş buyur sana akıl öğretsin If you ask a lazy man to do something he will give you better advice; i. e. he will try to get out of it.

tembelhane (..—.) تنبلخانه P 1. leper-house. 2. office where work is neglected. 3. house where lazy people are allowed to live on charity.

tembellen=ir, **tembelleş**=ir تنبللنمك تنبللشمك to grow lazy.

tembellikği تنبللك laziness.

tembih تنبيه var. of **tenbih**.

tembullü (.—) تنبول P betel-leaf.

temcid (.—) تمجيد A 1. rel. a chant sung from the minarets at night about an hour after the last service of worship during the months of Rejeb, Shaban, and Ramazan; it consists of an ascription of praise and an expression of amazement that any loving servant of God can sleep while God is awake and keeping watch. 2. lrnd. a glorifying God. — namazı voluntary worship between midnight and dawn. — yemeği supplementary meal eaten late in the evening during Ramazan. —ât (.——) A pl. of **temcid**.

temcis (.—) تمجيس A lrnd. 1. a converting one to Zoroastrianism. 2. a holding or pronouncing to be a Magian.

temcitdi تمجيد var. of **temcid**. — pilâvı thing that grows wearisome from repetition.

temdid (.—) تمديد A lrnd., same as **temdit**.

temdih (.—) تمديح A lrnd. a praising one much or often. —ât (.——) A pl.

temdin (.—) تمدين A lrnd. a civilizing, refining or polishing. — et= /ı/ to civilize.

temditdi (.—) تمديد [temdid] a stretching, lengthening; prolongation; extension. — et= to extend, to prolong.

temeccüs تمجس A lrnd. a becoming a Zoroastrian, Magian.

temeddüd تمدد A lrnd. a being stretched; a stretching when drawn; extension, lengthening.

temeddüh تمدح A lrnd. a boasting, a glorifying oneself without cause. —ât (...—) A pl.

temeddün تمدن A lrnd. 1. a becoming civilized, polished. 2. a leaving the nomadic life and settling in a town. — et= to become civilized.

temehdi تمهدى A lrnd. a claiming to be a Mahdi.

temehhüd تمهد A lrnd. 1. a becoming established on a secure foundation. 2. a having or acquiring power and ability. 3. a spreading out (carpet).

temehhül تمهل A lrnd. a taking time to consider; a proceeding slowly.

temehhür تمهر A lrnd. a being penetrating, ingenious; a becoming skillful.

temekkün تمكن A lrnd. 1. a taking up one's abode in a place; a being firmly fixed and well established. 2. a becoming possible. — et= to settle down in a place.

temekküs تمكث A lrnd. a stopping, staying, waiting.

temel تمل Gk 1. foundation; base. 2. basic, fundamental. —inden 1. fundamentally; at bottom. 2. altogether, thoroughly. — at= to lay a foundation. — bırak= colloq. to stay too long on a visit. — cümlecik gram. main clause. — çivisi largest size nail. — çivisi çak=, — çivisi kak= to have every intention of staying in a place or in the world. — direği main post in a building. — kak= to settle down permanently. — kemiği biol. sphenoid. — sal= to lay a foundation. — taşı foundation stone; basis. — tut= to become firm in its place; to settle down permanently.

temellen=ir تمللنمك to acquire a permanent foundation; to be firmly settled or based. —dir= /ı/ caus.

temelleş=ir تمللشمك 1. to become firmly established. 2. to settle down permanently. —tir= /ı/ caus.

temelli تمللى 1. having a foundation; true, authenticated. 2. well-founded; fundamental. 3. permanent. — geldi He came for good. — otur= to settle and live permanently in a place. — taş rock that is fixed.

temellûkku تملك A lrnd. a fawning servilely; sycophancy. — et= to fawn and flatter. —at (...—) A pl.

temellükkü تملك A lrnd. a taking possession. — et= to take possession of. —ât (...—) A pl.

temellül تملل A lrnd. 1. an adopting a religion or nationality. 2. a being depressed; depression, sadness; agitation.

temelmül تململ A lrnd. a tossing and turning about on one's bed.

temelsiz تملسز without foundation; unfounded, baseless.

temenna (..—) A, **temennah** تمنا Oriental salute (bringing the fingers of the right hand to the lips and then to the forehead). — çak= colloq. for **temenna** et=. — et= to salute.

temenni تمنى A 1. a desiring in one's heart and mind; desire, wish. 2. an asking for, a requesting. — et= 1. to desire, to wish. 2. to request, to ask. — sıygası gram. optative mood.

temenniyat تمنيات A lrnd. wishes; desiderata.

temennüüü تمنع A lrnd. 1. a being inaccessible, unapproachable, impregnable; strength, temerküz impregnability. 2. a being hindered, prohibited, excluded.

temerküz تَمَرْكُز A 1. a concentrating; concentration. 2. coalition. — **kabinesi** coalition cabinet. — **kampı** concentration camp.

temermür تَمَرْمُر A lrnd. a shaking, quivering, trembling.

temerrüd تَمَرُّد A same as **temerrüt**. —ât (...—) A pl.

temerrün تَمَرُّن A lrnd. 1. a being used to or versed in; use, habit. 2. an affecting shrewdness or dexterity; affectation.

temerrüt^dü تَمَرُّد [temerrüd] 1. lrnd. a being perversely obstinate; obstinacy, perverseness. 2. law default (in payment). — **et=** to be obstinate. — **faizi** com. interest for default, moratory interest.

temeshür تَمَشْهُر A lrnd. a playing the fool; ridicule; buffoonery. —ât (...—) A pl.

temeskün تَمَسْكُن A lrnd. a being poor; an assuming an appearance of poverty.

temessüh تَمَسُّح A lrnd. 1. Isl. rel. a carrying water or moisture with one hand to any part of the body. 2. a rubbing oneself. 3. an enjoying.

temessük^kü تَمَسُّك A lrnd. 1. a taking firm hold of a thing. 2. bill acknowledging a debt or claim; title deed. —ât (...—) A pl. title deeds.

temessül تَمَسُّل A lrnd. 1. an assuming a form; similitude, semblance. 2. a being assimilated; assimilation. 3. acculturation, assimilation. 4. an applying a proverb, speaking in a parable. — **et=** 1. to take on a form. 2. to be assimilated, to be absorbed into a foreign community. —ât (...—) A pl.

temeşşi تَمَشِّي A lrnd. 1. a walking about, creeping about. 2. an invading, a pervading. 3. a making progress, advancing; a performing, carrying out.

temeşşuk^ku تَمَشُّك A lrnd. 1. a taking as model or pattern. 2. a practicing (in writing, chanting, etc.).

temettü^üü تَمَتُّع A 1. lrnd. a profiting, deriving gain; profit, benefit, advantage. 2. com. dividend. 3. lrnd. an adding the performance of the greater pilgrimage to a mere visit of reverence to the sacred places at Mecca. — **et=** to profit, to use with advantage. — **vergisi** tax on profits. —ât (...—) A pl. of **temettü**.

temevvüc تَمَوُّج A lrnd. 1. a rising and falling of waves. 2. fluctuation, undulation. — **et=** 1. to fluctuate, undulate. 2. to wave (flags). —**e gel=** to rise in waves. —ât (...—) A undulations.

temevvül تَمَوُّل A lrnd. a becoming wealthy.

temevvüt تَمَوُّت A lrnd. death and postmortem change of one part of an animal body, while the rest continues to live, mortification.

temeyyü^üü تَمَيُّع A phys. a becoming liquid; liquefaction.

temeyyüh تَمَيُّه A lrnd. a becoming watery.

temeyyüz تَمَيُّز A a being distinguished; distinction. — **et=** to become distinguished or distinct. —ât (...—) A lrnd. distinctions.

temezzuk^ku تَمَزُّق A lrnd. a being torn; laceration.

temhid (.—) تَمْهِيد A lrnd. 1. a spreading on the ground. 2. an arranging, disposing, adjusting. 3. a pleading an excuse, pretext, a putting forward a pretension. —ât (.——) A pl.

temhik^kı (.—) تَمْحِيق A lrnd. an annihilating, destroying; annihilation.

temhil (.—) تَمْهِيل A lrnd. an appointing a future term, a granting a delay or respite. —ât (.——) A pl.

temhir (.—) تَمْهِير A lrnd. 1. a sealing by way of signature. 2. a sealing up. — **et=** /ı/ 1. to put a seal to, to sign with a seal. 2. to seal.

temhis (.—) تَمْحِيص A lrnd. a proving, trying, making an experiment; a testing, a putting to the test. —ât (.——) A pl.

temime (.—.) تَمِيمَة A lrnd. charm, amulet, talisman; large bead hung on a child as a protection against the evil eye.

te'min (.—) A, **temin** (——) تَأْمِين 1. a rendering safe or sure; assurance; confidence. 2. a securing. — **et=** /ı/ 1. to assure, ensure. 2. to render secure. 3. to inspire confidence. 4. to secure, procure.

te'minat (.——) A, **teminat** (————) تَأْمِينَات 1. security; deposit. 2. guarantee, assurance. — **akçesi** guarantee fund. — **mektubu** bond assuring performance of a contract. —**ı nakdiye** lrnd. pecuniary warrant. —**lı** secured. —**sız** unsecured, insecure.

te'minen (.—'.) تَأْمِينًا A lrnd. by giving assurance, guaranteeing.

te'mir تَأْمِير A lrnd. a making a commander.

temiz تَمِيز [Persian .—] 1. clean, pure; cleanly. 2. good; desirable; neat. 3. honest, honorable. 4. clear, net. 5. slang poker (game). — **bir dayak** a sound thrashing. —**e çek=** /ı/ to make a fair copy (of a writing) — **çevir=** slang to play poker. —**e çık=** to be cleared, to prove innocent. —**e çıkar=** /ı/ to clear one (of a charge). — **giyin=** to dress respectably. —**e havale et=** /ı/ slang 1. to clean up. 2. to kill. — **kan** oxygenated blood as it issues from the lungs. — **konuş=** to talk in a correct and polished manner. — **para** net sum of money (after deductions). — **patenta** a clean bill of health. — **raporu** certificate of good health. — **taş** diamond or precious stone without blemish. — **ye=** to eat good food in good places.

temizce (. .' .) تَمِيزَجِه fairly clean; cleanly, nicely.

temizle=ʳ تَمِيزلَمك /1/ 1. to clean; to clean up. 2. to clear away; to despoil, rob. 3. *slang* to kill, wipe out. 4. *slang* to cheat a person out of all his money in gambling; to clean someone out. **—me** *verbal n.* **—me işleri** public cleaning services. **—n=** *pass. of* **temizle=**. **—t=** /1, a/ *caus. of* **temizle=**.

temizleyici تَمِيزلَيجِى 1. cleansing. 2. cleaner.

temizlikᵍⁱ تَمِيزلَمكِ تَمِيزلَكِ 1. cleanliness; pureness; purity. 2. goodness, honesty. 3. act of cleaning; purge. **— işleri** scavenging service.

temkin (. —) تَمكِين A 1. a having control over oneself; self-possession; dignity, composure. 2. *lrnd.* a fixing, settling, establishing one permanently. 3. *lrnd.* a making possible. 4. *psych.* localization. **— erbabı** *lrnd.* person of self-possession, gravity and dignity.

temkinli تَمكِينلِى grave, dignified; self-possessed.

temkinsiz تَمكِينسِز lacking in dignity, frivolous.

temlie تَملِيَه A *lrnd.* 1. a filling. 2. *archery* a drawing the string of a bow to the utmost.

temlih (. —) تَملِيح A *lrnd.* 1. a salting too much; a salting. 2. a making an elegant remark.

temlikᵏⁱ (. —) تَملِيك A *lrnd.* 1. a giving into the possession of a person. 2. landed estate held in freehold by patent from the crown; assignment. **— edilemiyen haklar** *law* unassignable rights. **— edilmeme şartı** *law* restraint on alienation. **— et=** /1/ to give formal possession (of a property). **— ve temellük** a giving and taking possession.

temlikî (. — —) تَملِيكِى A *lrnd.* held by patent. **— muameleler** *law* conveyances. **—yet** quality of being held in freehold by patent.

temlikname (. — — .) تَملِيكنَامَه P *hist.* brief of ownership.

temlis (. —) تَملِيس A *lrnd.* a making smooth.

temliye تَملِيَه *same as* **temlie**.

temme, temmet تَمَّت تَمَّ A *lrnd.* the end.

Temmuz 1 تَمُّوز |Temmuz 2| July.

Temmuz 2 (. —) تَمُّوز A *lrnd., same as* **Temmuz 1**. **—iye** (. — ..) poem written in praise of summer.

temniⁱⁱ (. —) تَمنِيع A *lrnd.* 1. refusing or prohibiting. 2. a protecting, defending.

temniye تَمنِيَه A *lrnd.* a causing to be wished for or asked for.

tempo (.' .) تَمپُو It 1. *mus.* time; tempo. 2. manner, way. **— tut=** to keep time.

temr تَمر A *lrnd.* ripe date. **—i Hindi** (lit., the Indian date) tamarind, *bot.*, *Tamarindus indica*. **—e** a single dried date.

temren تَمرَن head of an arrow or spear.

temreyi تَمرَگِى *same as* **temriye**.

temrin (. —) تَمرِين A *lrnd.* 1. exercise (given to a pupil); practice. 2. an accustoming, teaching to do or to bear. **—at** (. — —) A exercises.

temrir (. —) تَمرِير A *lrnd.* a rendering bitter.

temriye تَمرِيَه skin disease; lichen.

temsil (. —) تَمثِيل A 1. a representing; representation (agency) 2. performance (of a play). 3. a comparing, likening; comparison; parable; symbol. 4. saying, maxim. 5. assimilation. 6. *lrnd.* a multiplying copies (of a book etc.); copy (of a book); edition. 7. *lrnd.* a causing to become similar, a making resemble; analogy. 8. *prov.* so to speak, supposing that, for example. **T— Bürosu** press bureau of a ministry. **— et=** /1/ 1. to represent. 2. to present (play). 3. to assimilate. 4. to compare. **— kudreti** *law* authority.

temsilât (. — —) تَمثِيلَات A *lrnd., pl. of* **temsil**.

temsilci تَمثِيلجِى representative.

temsilen (. —' .) تَمثِيلًا A *lrnd.* /1/ representing.

temsilî (. — —) تَمثِيلِى A *lrnd.* pertaining to a representation, etc., representative.

temsiye تَمسِيَه A *lrnd.* an asking after one's health in the evening, a wishing one a good evening.

temşit (. —) تَمشِيط A *lrnd.* 1. a combing the hair well. 2. a lady's maid's decking out a lady.

temşiye, temşiyet تَمشِيَت تَمشِيَه A *lrnd.* 1. a causing to walk; a walking. 2. a causing to make progress, advance; advancement. 3. an advancing; progress. **— et=** to push forward. **—i garaz et=** to further one's own selfish object. **— muameleleri, — tasarrufları** *law* acts of management. **— ver=** /a/ to give an impulse to a thing.

temteme تَمتَمَه A *lrnd.* a stuttering, a stammering.

temtiⁱⁱ (. —) تَمتِيع A *lrnd.* a causing to be profitably used or temporarily possessed by a person; a giving the use and enjoyment of a thing.

temtin (. —) تَمتِين A *lrnd.* a strengthening, a corroborating, a providing with something that adds to strength (as lining a cloth, fastening a tent with cords and pins, etc.).

temvih (. —) تَموِيه A *lrnd.* 1. a watering copiously or too much. 2. a tempering steel; a gilding or silvering metals by the liquid process. 3. a misrepresenting, a falsely making a thing appear desirable. **—ât** (. — —) A misrepresentations.

temvil (. —) تَموِيل A *lrnd.* a causing to become rich, a making wealthy.

temvit (. —) تَموِيت A *lrnd.* a causing to die, a killing.

temyiii (. —) تمييع A *phys.* a causing to be liquified.

temyil (. —) تمييل A *lrnd.* a causing to incline.

temyiz (. —) تمييز A 1. a separating, discerning and distinguishing; discernment; soundness of judgment. 2. *psych.* discrimination. 3. *law* appeal; reversal. **— erbabı** those who have reached years of discretion. **— et=** /ı/ 1. to distinguish. 2. *law* to appeal. **— kudreti** power of judgment, power of discernment. **— mahkemesi** court of appeal.

temyizen (. — '.) تمييزاً A *law* on appeal.

temzic (. —) تمزيج A *lrnd.* a mixing much, a thoroughly blending one thing with another.

temzikkı (. —) تمزيق A *lrnd.* a tearing much or violently; a tearing to pieces. **—at** (. — —) A *pl.*

temziye, temziyet تحميدت A *lrnd.* a praising, eulogizing; praise, commendation, eulogy.

ten 1 تن P the body; flesh. **— fanilası** undershirt. **— rengi** flesh color.

ten 2 تن *prov.* dew, dampness.

Ten 3 تن *archaic* the River Don.

-ten 4 دن *cf.* **-dan** 1.

Tenab (. —) تناب P *lrnd., geog.* the Danube.

tenaci (. —.) تناجى A *lrnd.* a whispering together, a telling secrets to one another.

tenadddı (. —) تناد A *lrnd.* a being dispersed, a fleeing in disorder from one another; dispersal, flight.

tenadi (. —.) تنادى A *lrnd.* 1. a calling out to one another. 2. an assembling together.

tenadüm (. —.) تنادم A *lrnd.* a being sociable and intimately friendly with each other; friendly intercourse and society.

tenadür (. —.) تنادر A *lrnd.* a becoming scarce.

tenafi (. —.) تنافى A *lrnd.* a being mutually exclusive; a seeking to ruin one another.

tenafüd (. —.) تنافد A *lrnd.* a pleading against each other before a judge.

tenafür (. —.) تنافر A *lrnd.* 1. a flying from one another in a panic; mutual repugnance, aversion. 2. incongruity in the letters of a word or in contiguous words. 3. a going to a judge to state their cases; a disputing before a judge.

tenafüs (. —.) تنافس A *lrnd.* a competing against another to gain something exquisite.

tenafüz (. —.) تنافذ A *lrnd.* a going to a judge to dispute their cases.

tenaggum تنغم A *lrnd.* a singing, chanting or humming a tune. **—at** (. . . —) A *pl.*

tenaggus تنغص A *lrnd.* one's life's being or becoming wretched.

tenahhi تنحى A *lrnd.* a withdrawing, a retiring.

tenahhul تنحل A *lrnd.* 1. a falsely arrogating to oneself (the verses or sayings of another). 2. a professing to belong to some religious society.

tenahhus تنحس A *lrnd.* 1. a diligently seeking to ascertain the full truth of a rumor. 2. a being hungry. 3. a fasting; an abstaining from meat.

tenahi (. —.) تناهى A *lrnd.* 1. a reaching a limit or object; arrival; termination; finish, completion. 2. an obeying a prohibition; abstention through obedience.

tenahnuh تنحنح A *lrnd.* 1. a clearing the throat; a hemming and hawing. 2. the breath's rasping in the air passages when clogged with phlegm.

tenai (. —.) تناءى A *lrnd.* a becoming distant; distance.

tenakkullü 1 تنقل A *lrnd.* a passing from place to place.

tenakkullü 2 تنقل A *lrnd.* any kind of fruit or cake eaten after taking liquor. **—ât** (. . . —) A *pl.*

tenakkus تنقص A *lrnd.* 1. a decrying, speaking ill of. 2. a becoming diminished; a diminishing, diminution.

tenakus (. —.) تناقص A *lrnd.* a diminishing, decreasing; decrease, diminution. **—ât** (. —. —) A *pl.*

tenakuş (. —.) تناقش A *lrnd.* a debating.

tenakuz (. —.) تناقض A a being contradictory (two propositions); contradiction. **—a düş=** to contradict oneself. **—ât** (. —. —) A *pl.*

tenaküh (. —.) تناكح A *lrnd.* the right to intermarry.

tenakür (. —.) تناكر A 1. *lrnd.* a pretending not to know; feigned ignorance. 2. *phil.* antipathy.

tenaküs (. —.) تناكث A *lrnd.* a mutually breaking a pact.

tenanin (. — —) تنانين A *lrnd., pl.* of **tinnin**.

tenanir (. — —) تنانير A *lrnd., pl.* of **tennur**.

tenasa (. — —), **tenasan** (. — —) تن آسا تن آسان P *lrnd.* whose body is at rest, at ease; self-indulgent.

tenasanî, tenasayî (. — — —) تن آسانى تن آسايى P *lrnd.* bodily ease, repose, quiet; indulgence.

tenasi (. —.) تناسى A *lrnd.* a pretending to have forgotten; feigned forgetfulness.

tenassub تنصب A *lrnd.* 1. a standing bolt upright. 2. a rising in a column (dust). 3. a being persistently assiduous or obstinate.

tenassuh تنصح A *lrnd.* 1. a pretending to give good advice. 2. a taking good advice.

tenassur تنصر A *lrnd., same as* **tanassur**.

tenassus تنصص A *lrnd.* an obtaining scriptural texts and authorities.

tenasuh (. —.) تناصح A *lrnd.* a giving advice to each other.

tenasur (. —.) تناصر A *lrnd.* an aiding and supporting one another; mutual aid and support.

tenasüb (. —.) تناسب A 1. a having a mutual relation and proportion; mutual proportion; symmetry (of proportion). 2. equality of ratio. 3. *math.* ratio. —i âdad *math.* equality of ratio between numbers. —i âza *math.* symmetry of the limbs. —î (. —.—) A *lrnd.* proportional.

tenasüh (. —.) تناسخ A *phil.* a soul's passing at death into another body of the same species, metempsychosis.

tenasühî (. —.—) تناسخى A *phil.* 1. metempsychic. 2. believer in metempsychosis.

tenasühiye (. —...) تناسخيه A *phil.* the doctrine of metempsychosis.

tenasühiyun (. —..—) تناسخيون A *phil.* the school believing in the transmigration of souls.

tenasül (. —.) تناسل A an issuing from one another, successive generation; reproduction. — âleti organ of generation.

tenasülî (. —.—) تناسلى A genital; sexual.

tenasüp[bü] (. —.) تناسب *var. of* **tenasüb**.

tenasür (. —.) تناثر A *lrnd.* 1. a being scattered and dispersed. 2. a people's falling and dying on all sides during an epidemic.

tenaşşut تنشط A *lrnd.* a being brisk, lively, active, alert; a cheerfully doing anything.

tenaşüd (. —.) تناشد A *lrnd.* a reciting verses to one another.

tenatuh (. —.) تناطح A *lrnd.* rams' butting each other.

tena'um تنعم A *lrnd.* 1. a living in comfort and luxury. 2. an enjoying in abundance the conveniences and comforts of life; enjoyment, ease, prosperity. —ât (...—) A *pl.*

tenaver (. —.) تناور P *lrnd.* 1 corpulent, bulky. 2. lazy; who favors his body. —ân (. —.—) P *pl.* —î (. —.—) P, —lik corpulency, laziness.

tenavüb (. —.) تناوب A *lrnd.* a taking turns; alternation.

tenavül (. —.) تناول A *lrnd.* 1. a taking as food, drink or medicine. 2. a taking in one's hand, a receiving. — et= to take food or drink.

tenavüm (. —.) تناوم A *lrnd.* a pretending to be asleep.

tenazu[uu] (. —.) تنازع A *lrnd.* a contending, quarreling or litigating with each other.

tenazur (. —.) تناظر A 1. *geom.* symmetry. 2. *astr.* a being in opposition to each other (planets). 3. *lrnd.* a being symmetrical. 4. a looking at each other, eyeing one another. —i matlaî *astr.* two planets' being equidistant from an equinoctial point on opposite sides of it. —i zamanî *astr.* two planets' being equidistant from a solstitial point on opposite sides of it. —î (. —.—) A symmetrical.

tenazül (. —.) تنازل A *lrnd.* 1. a dismounting or calling on each other to dismount. 2. a rushing down into a plain against each other (two bodies of men).

tenazzuf تنظف A *lrnd.* 1. a being clean or neat. 2. a being ostentatiously clean; a striving after neatness, purity.

tenazzum تنظم A *lrnd.* a being arranged in a line, string, series or in poetical meter.

tenazzur تنظر A *lrnd.* 1. a looking attentively and long. 2. an acting with circumspection. 3. a looking for with expectation.

tenbakû (. —.—) تنباكو P *lrnd.*, same as **tömbeki**.

tenbel تنبل P *lrnd.*, same as **tembel**.

tenbelid, tenbelit[di] (.. —) تنبليد P *lrnd.* 1. bundle placed on the top of an animal's load. 2. bag or bundle thrown on an animal's back and ridden like a saddle.

-ten beri دنبرى *cf.* **-dan beri**.

tenbih (. —) تنبيه A 1. an ordering, a commanding; order, command. 2. a warning. 3. a waking one from sleep or carelessness; stimulation. 4. *lrnd.* proclamation, order publicly proclaimed. — et= 1. /ı, a/ to warn, to enjoin. 2. /ı/ to excite (nerves); to stimulate. — kabiliyeti *psych.* excitability. — tedavisi nonspecific therapy. —ât (. —.—) A *lrnd.* warnings, orders.

tenbit (. —) تنبيت A *lrnd.* a causing a plant to germinate and grow.

tenbul (. —) تنبول P *lrnd.*, same as **tembul**.

tenbur (. —) تنبور P *lrnd.*, same as **tambur**.

tencere ('...) تنجره saucepan. — havaici herbs used in cookery for seasoning. —si kaynarken, maymunu oynarken when a person has comfortable living and is happy all around. — kebabı meat cooked in a covered stewpan. —de pişirip kapağında ye= to cook in a saucepan and eat from its lid; to live very economically. — tava hepsi bir hava *proverb* Everyone goes his own way; nobody cares. — tencereye dibin kara demiş *proverb* One kettle said to the other, "Your bottom is black." The speaker is even worse. — yuvarlandı, kapağını buldu (*lit.* The saucepan rolled away and found its lid.) He has found an associate like himself.

tencim (. —) تنجيم A *lrnd.* 1. a prognosticating or calculating any event by the aspect of the stars; astrology. 2. a paying by instalments.

tencis (. —) تنجيس A *lrnd.* 1. a rendering unclean, impure or unlawful to be used. 2. unclean thing worn as a charm (*e. g.* a dead man's bone).

tenciye تنجيه A *lrnd.* a delivering, saving.

tenciz (. —) تنجيز A *lrnd.* 1. a finishing, a completing. 2. a putting a functionary out of office at the completion of his term of service.

tendih تنديه P *lrnd.* who gives body and strength to an occupation, who exerts himself, diligent. —î (.. —) P persevering exertion.

tendiye تنديه A *lrnd.* 1. a slightly moistening. 2. an alternately watering and feeding cattle.

tendürüst تن درست P *lrnd.* healthy, vigorous, robust. —î (... —) P, —lük soundness of health and body.

tene تنه P *lrnd.* 1. body. 2. trunk or stem of a tree or plant. 3. spider web. 4. individual.

tenebbüü 1 تنبع A *lrnd.* a welling up from a spring (water).

tenebbüü 2 تنبى A *lrnd.* a claiming falsely to be a prophet or apostle.

tenebbüh تنبه A *lrnd.* 1. an awakening; a being awake. 2. a being vigilant and watchful; vigilance. 3. a watching over one's own thoughts or deeds; a taking care in consequence of advice or experience. 4. *physiol.* a becoming stimulated, stimulation. — et= to become wiser from some experience. —ât (...—) A *pl.*

tenebbüt تنبت A *lrnd.* vegetable growth; vegetation, germination. — et= to grow (plants). —ât (...—) A *pl.*

teneccüm تنجم A *lrnd.* 1 an observing the stars. 2. a lying awake all night; insomnia.

teneccüs تنجس A *lrnd.* a being unclean, impure or soiled; uncleanness, impurity.

teneddüm تندم A *lrnd.* a being sorry and penitent; repentance.

tenef تنف [*Arabic* **tanab**] *obs.* tent-rope.

teneffuu تنفع A *lrnd.* a benefiting, profiting; benefit, profit. — et= to benefit, profit.

teneffül تنفل A *lrnd.* 1. a doing more than the law requires; a saying prayers of supererogation. 2. a forager's taking more spoil than his companions.

teneffür تنفر A *lrnd.* a feeling an inclination to shun a person or thing; aversion, disgust, horror. — et= /dan/ to feel an aversion for, to be disgusted with.

teneffüs تنفس A 1. a breathing; respiration. 2. a pausing for breath; rest; recess. — et= to breathe; to pause for breath. —i sınaî *med.* artificial respiration; tracheotomy. —ât (...—) A *pl.*

teneffüshane (...—.) تنفسخانه P recreation room; place for resting.

tenekâr (..—) تنكار P *lrnd., same as* **tenkâr**.

teneke تنكه 1. tinplate; made of tinplate. 2. a can (especially a kerosene can); amount held by a kerosene can. — çal= (arkasından) to boo someone publicly. —sini eline ver= /ın/ *colloq.* to fire someone.

— **mahallesi** shanty town. —**ci** tinsmith. —**li** covered with tinplate.

tenekkür تنكر A *lrnd.* 1. a becoming unknown or unrecognizable. 2. a becoming incognito, a disguising oneself. 3. a falling into poverty or misery.

tenekküs تنكس A *lrnd.* a being turned upside down.

tenemmül تنمل A *lrnd.* a moving to and fro like ants.

tenemmür تنمر A *lrnd.* 1. an acting like a leopard in savageness, surliness or agility. 2. a threatening with a long growl. 3. a being angry, ill-humored. —ât (...—) A *pl.*

tenend تنند P *lrnd.* 1. spider. 2. idle person.

tenendeh تننده P *lrnd.* 1. weaver. 2. spider. 3. weaver's shuttle.

tenendû (..—) تنندو P *lrnd.* spider.

tenessukᵏᵘ تنسك A *lrnd.* a being ranged in a regular series or order.

tenessüb تنسب A *lrnd.* a claiming to belong to a certain family.

tenessükᵏᵘ تنسك A *lrnd.* a being devout, pious; piety, devotion.

tenessüm تنسم A *lrnd.* 1 a breathing; an inhaling; inspiration. 2. a smelling anything fragrant; a sniffing up a breeze. 3. a being fragrant; fragrance. —ât (...—) A *pl.*

tenessür تنسر A *lrnd.* a being disintegrated, scattered.

teneste تنست P *lrnd.* spider web.

teneşir تنشير [**tenşûy**] 1. rite of washing a corpse. 2. bench on which the corpse is washed. —**e gel=** *colloq.* to die. — **horozu** near death; doomed to death. — **kargası** very thin (person). — **paklar** /ı/ Only death will put an end to his wickedness. —**e sür=** to last till death (bad habit). — **tahtası** bench on which corpses are washed for burial.

teneşirlikᵏᶦ تنشيرلك 1. place for washing corpses (in the courtyard of a mosque). 2. *slang* about to die, at death's door. 3. one whose bad character will never change (except at death).

teneşşi (. —) تنشى A *lrnd.* 1. a smelling, a perceiving an odor especially if fragrant. 2. a becoming slightly intoxicated.

teneşşut تنشط A *lrnd.* a becoming lively, active, brisk.

teneşşüüü تنشى A *lrnd.* a rising up, getting up (to do some act).

teneşşüb تنشب A *lrnd.* a sticking into so as to adhere.

teneşşüd تنشد A *lrnd.* a quietly hunting up private information.

teneşşüf تنشف A *lrnd.* 1. a liquid's soaking into a substance. 2. a substance's imbibing moisture.

teneşşür تَنَشُّر A *lrnd.* 1. a spreading and opening out. 2. rumors' spreading.

teneşşüz تَنَشُّز A *lrnd.* a standing up to fight with another.

tenevvuh تَنَوُّه A *lrnd.* 1. a lamenting, mourning. 2. an oscillating. —ât (. . .—) A *pl.*

tenevvüüᵘᵘ تَنَوُّع A *lrnd.* a being of various sorts; variety. — et= to vary.

tenevvüât (. . .—) تَنَوُّعات A *lrnd.* varieties; diversities.

tenevvüm تَنَوُّم A *lrnd.* a going to sleep; a dreaming.

tenevvür تَنَوُّر A *lrnd.* 1. a being luminous or illuminated; enlightenment. 2. a becoming clear. — et= 1. to be enlightened. 2. to be made clear.

tenezzehe تَنَزَّه A *lrnd.* May (God) be held free from imperfection!

tenezzühʰᵘ تَنَزُّه A 1. a going out for a walk or ride for amusement; pleasure walk, excursion. 2. *colloq.* car, automobile; taxi. 3. *lrnd.* a becoming free from defect.

tenezzül تَنَزُّل A 1. a condescending; condescension. 2. *lrnd.* a coming down; a growing less in number, quantity or degree; decline. — buyur= to condescend. — et= /a/ to deign to, to deign to accept.

tenezzülen (. .'. .) تَنَزُّلاً A condescendingly; graciously; without being too proud.

tenezzür تَنَزُّر A *lrnd.* 1. a heeding a warning. 2. a making a vow to sacrifice something.

tenfih (. —) تَنْفِيح A *lrnd* 1. a blowing much with the mouth. 2. a blowing a thing up with the breath. 3. a causing a part of the body to swell. —ât (. ——) A *pl.*

tenfir (. —) تَنْفِير A *lrnd.* 1. a raising a feeling of aversion or disgust. 2. a causing to flee, a driving away. — et= /dan/ to cause aversion (for or from). —i kulûb a turning the hearts of the people from a ruler. —ât (. ——) A *pl.*

tenfis (. —) تَنْفِيس A *lrnd.* 1. a causing to breathe. 2. a consoling, comforting, refreshing. —ât (. ——) A *pl.*

tenfiş (. —) تَنْفِيش A *lrnd.* 1. a teasing (cotton or wool). 2. a bristling up (angry dog or cock). —ât (. ——) A *pl.*

tenfiz (. —) تَنْفِيذ A 1. *law* putting an order into execution. 2. *lrnd.* a causing to penetrate; a causing to force a way into or through a thing. — et= /ı/ 1. *law* to put into execution. 2. *lrnd.* to cause to penetrate. — kararları *law* award of an order for execution.

tenfizât (. ——) تَنْفِيذات A *lrnd.* orders put to execution.

teng تَنْگ P *lrnd.* 1. narrow, small; thin. 2. tight, fast. 3. miserable, poor, anxious. 4. near, close, neighboring 5. rare, scarce, unique. 6. difficult. 7. strap; girth; rope for binding a burden on an animal. 8. bale; half a horse-load. 9. gorge, narrow valley. 10. mouth of a beauty. 11. lever for working a screw, press or mill. 12. panel or canvas on which a picture is painted. — et= /ı/ to make narrow, thin, tight, miserable. — nân thin, round cake of bread.

tengâb (. —) تَنْگ آب P *lrnd.* shallow.

tengâteng (. —.) تَنْگاتَنْگ P *lrnd.* 1. continually narrow, thin, tight, miserable, near or rare. 2. in close contact, crowded.

tengây (. —) تَنْگای P *lrnd.* 1. gorge, defile. 2. strait, difficulty.

tengbar (. —) تَنْگبار P *lrnd.* 1. difficult of access; inaccessible. 2. into whose presence no flesh can penetrate (God). 3. rare, scarce; curious.

tengçeşm تَنْگچَشْم P *lrnd.* 1. narrow-eyed. 2. insatiable; stingy. —î (. . —) P stinginess.

tengdehan (. . —) تَنْگدَهان P *lrnd.* small-mouthed.

tengdest تَنْگدَسْت P *lrnd.* 1. close-fisted; avaricious. 2. poor. —î (. . —) P 1. poverty. 2. parsimony.

tengdil تَنْگدِل P *lrnd.* whose heart is straitened, sorrowful; heartsick. —î (. . —) P heartache, grief.

tenghâl (. —) تَنْگحال P *lrnd.* in narrow circumstances; poor. —î (. ——) P poverty; distress.

tenghavsala تَنْگحوصله P *lrnd.* narrow-minded.

tenghu, tenghuy (. —) تَنْگخوی P *lrnd.* narrow of disposition; easily-angered, bad-tempered.

tengî (. —) تَنْگی P *lrnd.* 1. narrowness, smallness. 2. thinness. 3. tightness. 4. poorness of circumstances, poverty. 5. nearness. 6. rarity. 7. hardness, difficulty.

teng'iş (. —) تَنْگعَيش P *lrnd.* 1. poor. 2. melancholy.

tengmaaş (. . —) تَنْگمعاش P *lrnd.* in narrow circumstances.

tengmeşreb تَنْگمَشْرَب P *lrnd* easily vexed.

tengnay (. —) تَنْگنای P *lrnd.* 1. narrowness. 2. narrow place; gorge, defile. 3. the world. 4. the human body. 5. the grave.

tengpeygule (. . —.) تَنْگپَيغوله P *lrnd.* 1. narrow hole, corner. 2. the world.

tengsâl (. —) تَنْگسال P *lrnd.* time of drought or scarcity. —î (. ——) P dearth, scarceness.

tengsar (. —) تَنْگسار P *lrnd.* weak of intellect, stupid.

tengyâb (. —) تَنْگياب P *lrnd.* hard to find, rare.

tengzarf تَنْگظَرف P *lrnd.* of small capacity.

tengzehre تَنْگزَهره P *lrnd.* 1. crestfallen, despondent. 2. timid.

tenha (.—) تنها P 1. scarcely populated, relatively deserted, uncrowded. 2. alone; lonely.
tenhaca (.—.') تنهاجه 1. somewhat solitary (place). 2. quite free from interruption of strangers; not so crowded.
tenhalaş="ᴵʳ تنهالاشمن 1. to be alone. 2. to become deserted or empty (place).
tenhalıkᵍ¹ تنهالوه 1. solitude. 2. deserted or lonely place. 3. deserted, lonely. 4. religious retirement.
tenhanişin (.—.—) تنهانشين P lrnd. who lives in solitude. —î (.—.——) P, —lik living in seclusion.
tenharev (.—.) تنهارو P lrnd. solitary wanderer.
tenhaver (.—.) تنهاور P lrnd. who goes alone. —î (.—.—) P, —lik lrnd. a going or traveling alone.
tenhayi (.——) تنهائى P lrnd., same as **tenhalık**.
tenhiye تنهيه A lrnd. 1. a prohibiting, forbidding; prohibition. 2. a causing to reach its object or destination.
tenide (.—.) تنيده P lrnd. 1. woven. 2. spider web.
te'nikᵏ¹ (.—) تأنيق A lrnd. a making wonderfully beautiful.
ten'il (.—) تنعيل A lrnd. 1. a causing to put on or wear shoes. 2. a shoeing (horse).
ten'im (.—) تنعيم A lrnd. 1. a causing one's life to be one of comfort and luxury. 2. a bestowing plenty. 3. an answering "yes".
tenis 1 تنيس E tennis.
te'nis 2 (.—) تأنيث A 1. gram. a putting into the feminine (adjective, etc.). 2. lrnd. a making effeminate, yielding, gentle.
te'nis 3 (.—) تأنيس A lrnd. a making familiar, sociable or friendly; a taming. — et= /ı/ 1. to familiarize, accustom. 2. to tame (a beast).
tenisçi تنيسجى tennis player.
te'niye تأنيه A lrnd. 1. a postponing, delaying; postponement. 2. a being tardy.
tenize (.—.) تنيزه P lrnd. edge, margin, side, border, skirt. —i kûh skirt of a mountain.
tenkâr (.—) تنكار P lrnd. crude borax, tincal.
tenkıye تنقيه A 1. med. enema; an administering an enema. 2. lrnd. a cleaning.
tenkid (.—) تنقيد A lrnd., same as **tenkit 1**. —ât (.——) A criticisms. —atta bulun= to criticize.
tenkih 1 (.—) تنكيح A lrnd. 1. a causing to be engaged or married. 2. a performing the service of betrothal or marriage (on someone). — et= /ı/ to perform the service of betrothal or marriage.
tenkih 2 (.—) تنقيح A 1. adm. a cutting down of expenses or salaries. 2. lrnd. a pruning (of a composition). — et= 1. to emend, prune (a composition) of defects. 2. to cut down (the number of employees). 3. to reduce (expenses or wages). —i menat law a pointing out the cause or motive of a law
tenkihat (.——) تنقيحات A lrnd. reduction in expenses; economies. —ı askeriye reduction of troops by rejection of unfit or unneccessary corps and individuals.
tenkil (.—) تنكيل 1. a repressing (a revolt). 2. a punishing, a making an example of. 3 lrnd. a prohibiting, diverting, turning (anyone aside). — et= /ı/ 1. to repress (a rebellion). 2. to punish so as to make an example of. 3. to divert, to turn aside. —ât (.——) A measures of suppression.
tenkir (.—) تنكير A 1. lrnd. a causing to become unrecognizable. 2. gram. a making a noun indefinite. —ât (.——) A pl.
tenkis 1 (.—) تنقيص A lrnd. a diminishing, decreasing a thing; diminution; reduction. — et= /ı/ to diminish, to curtail.
tenkis 2 (.—) تنكيس A lrnd. an inverting; inversion.
tenkiş (.—) تنقيش A lrnd. 1. a decorating with various colors or designs. 2. a being decorated. 3. an imprinting. —ât (.——) A pl.
tenkitᵈⁱ **1** (.—) تنقيد |tenkid| criticizing; criticism.
tenkitᵗⁱ **2** (.—) تنقيط A lrnd. vocalization of Arabic words by putting in the vowel points, a punctuating; punctuation.
tenkitçi تنقيدجى critic.
tenkiz (.—) تنقيذ A lrnd. a delivering one from peril or suffering; salvation, deliverance.
tenmikᵏ¹ (.—) تنميق A lrnd. a writing, a copying out; a writing a fine ornamental hand.
tenmiye تنميه 1. econ. investment (of money). 2. lrnd. a causing to grow. 3. lrnd. a feeding, sustaining. 4. lrnd. an adding fuel to a fire. — et= /ı/ 1. to make grow; to nourish; to develop. 2. to invest (capital). 3. to cultivate (friendly relations).
tennub (.—) تنوب A lrnd. Norway spruce, white fir, bot., Picea abies. —iye bot., Abietinae.
tennur (.—) تنور A 1. same as **tandır**. 2. lrnd. oven; fireplace. 3. lrnd. pit used as an oven. 3. lrnd. sterilizing oven; autoclave.
tennure (.—.) تنوره A wide skirt worn by the Mevlevi dervishes.
tennurepuş (.—.—) تنورپوش P lrnd. wearing a dervish's skirt; a Mevlevi dervish.
tennurhane (.——.) تنورخانه P lrnd. 1. bakehouse. 2. kitchen.

tennurtâb (.——) تنورتاب P *lrnd*. 1. one who feeds an oven. 2. fuel.
tenperest تن پرست P *lrnd*. 1. slave to one's own body; self-indulgent, sensual. 2. lazy, indolent. **—î** (...—) P, **—lik** self-indulgence.
tenperver تن پرور P *lrnd*. one who takes great care of his body; fond of comfort; soft. **—âne** (...—.) P in the manner of one who loves comfort. **—î** (...—) P, **—lik** fondness of comfort and ease; softness (of living).
tensib (.—) تنسيب A a judging to be fit and proper; approval, approbation. **—ine bırak=** /ı, ın/ to leave something to someone's discretion. **— et=** /ı/ to approve.
tensik[kı] (.—) تنسيق A 1. *lrnd*. a putting into proper order, an arranging, organizing; arrangement, organization. 2. *lrnd*. a ranging in a line or series. 3. *rhet*. an enumerating of attributes in a sequence. **— et=** /ı/ to reorganize, reform.
tensikat (.——) تنسيقات A 1. reforms, reorganization. 2. a combing out of inefficient officials. **—ı askeriye** *Ott. hist*. military ordinances and regulations.
tensim (.—) تنسيم A *lrnd*. 1. a causing to breathe or breathe freely. 2. an allowing breathing time to one. 3. a giving freedom to a slave.
tensir (.—) تنشير A *lrnd*. 1. a scattering, dispersing; a disintegrating. 2. a putting into prose.
tensiye تنسيه A *lrnd*. a causing to be forgotten; a causing to forget.
-ten sonra دن صكره *cf.* **-dan sonra.**
tensuh 1 (.—) تنسخ *lrnd*. a kind of perfumed paste made in pieces of ornamental shapes often used as personal ornaments; pastil.
tensuh 2 تنسخ P *lrnd*. rare and lovely, beautiful and choice.
tenşib (.—) تنشيب A *lrnd*. 1. a sticking a thing into a thing so that it holds fast; a fixing. 2. a setting oneself to work at a matter.
tenşif (.—) تنشيف A *lrnd*. 1. a making a liquid be imbibed by a porous substance; a wiping, sucking up water (with a cloth). 2. a drying up.
tenşim (.—) تنشيم A *lrnd*. 1. a making a beginning; a beginning to spoil (meat). 2. a raising the fame (of).
tenşir (.—) تنشير A *lrnd*. 1. a spreading wide open. 2. a spreading a rumor abroad. 3. a counteracting a charm or witchcraft.
tenşit[u] (.—) تنشيط A *lrnd*. a making lively, an enlivening. **— et=** /ı/ to make lively, to enliven. **—ât** (.——) A *pl*.
tenşûy (.—) تنشوى P *lrnd*. 1. washer of corpses. 2. *same as* **teneşir.**
tente 1 (.'.) تنته It awning.

tente 2 تنته P *lrnd*. spider web.
tenteli (.'..) تنته لى provided with an awning.
tentene ('..) تنتنه [dantel] lace. **—li** ornamented with lace.
tentif (.—) تنتيف A *lrnd*. a plucking up much hair.
tentür تنتور F *chem*. tincture.
tentürdiyot تنتور ديود F tincture of iodine.
tenumend (.—.) تنومند P *lrnd*. robust, corpulent; strong, powerful.
tenure (.—.) تنوره P *lrnd*. 1. breastplate or corselet of scale-armor. 2. ring of men; a forming a ring; a going around in a ring. 3. trough to conduct water to a mill wheel. 4. sheepskin bound round the waist by mendicant dervishes. 5. *same as* **tennure.**
tenük[kü] تنك P *lrnd*. thin, slender, slight, weak, delicate.
tenvi[iı] (.—) تنويع A *lrnd*. a causing a class to divide into varieties. **—ât** (.——) A *pl*.
tenvim (.—) تنويم A *lrnd*. a causing to sleep, a lulling to sleep. **—i sınai** hypnotism.
tenvin (.—) تنوين A *Arabic gram*. 1. nunnation (i. e., an indefinite noun-ending **an, in,** or **un**) (ً , ٍ , ٌ). 2. a vowel sign of nunnation. **— et=** /ı/ to nunnate a word or final letter in Arabic grammar. **—ât** (.——) A *pl*.
tenvir (.—) تنوير A 1. an illumining; illumination. 2. a becoming bright with light, luminous. 3. an enlightening **— et=** /ı/ 1. to illuminate. 2. to enlighten; to make clear. **— fişeği** *mil*. flare. **— mermisi** *mil*. star shell. **— tabancası** Very pistol.
tenvirât (.——) تنويرات A lighting (of a street).
tenvirî (.——) تنويرى A *lrnd*. pertaining to illuminations.
tenya ('..) تنيا F tapeworm, taenia.
tenzede تنزده P *lrnd*. who has submitted, submissive; taciturn, modest.
tenzih (.—) تنزيه A *lrnd*. 1. a considering free from defect. 2. a declaring and believing God to be free from defect. **— et=** /ı/ to absolve. **—ât** (.——) A *pl*.
tenzihî (.——) تنزيهى A *lrnd*. absolutory.
tenzilât (.——) تنزيلات A reduction of prices, etc.). **—lı** reduced in price. **—lı satış** bargain sale.
tenzir (.—) تنزير A *lrnd*. a frightening by warning.
tenzu تنزو *var. of* **tensuh 1. —yi** (..—) *name of a certain hue of deep green, almost black*.
tep=[er] 1 تپمك 1. to kick; to spurn. 2. to recoil; to recur (illness). 3. to dance (a folk dance). 4. /ı/ not to appreciate; to throw away (a good chance, job, etc.). **—e tepe kullan=** /ı/ to

tep wear continually and give it rough usage (garment, etc.).

tep 2 تَپ P lrnd. 1. a struggling convulsively; restlessness. 2. mental agitation.

tepâk[ki] (.—) تپاك P lrnd., same as **tep 2**.

tenzil (.—) تنزل A 1. a lowering, diminishing. 2. a subtracting; subtraction. 3. reduction (of prices). 4. a causing to alight at a place. 5. lrnd. God's sending down a revelation from heaven; divine revelation. 6. the Quran. **— et=** /1/ 1. to lower, diminish, reduce. 2. to subtract. 3. to cause to alight. 4. to send down as a revelation.

tepan (.—) تپان P lrnd. 1. kicking and struggling convulsively in a fit or in the agony of death. 2. mentally agitated.

tepançe (.—.) تپانچه P lrnd. slap on the face, box on the ears; blow.

tepas (.—) تپاس P lrnd. ascetic practice of mortifying the flesh by fasting and watching; asceticism.

tepe تپه 1. hill, mound, peak. 2. mountain peak, summit. 3. apex, summit of anything. 4. crown of the head; crest of a bird. **—den** 1. from above. 2. condescendingly. **— altını** gold coins arranged ornamentally around a woman's headgear **— aşağı git=** 1. to fall headlong. 2. to go downhill (business). **—si at=** to be infuriated. **—den bak=** /a/ to look down (on), to despise. **— başı** obs. a kind of embroidery in silk and gold thread; a garment so embroidered. **—sine bin=** /ın/ to pester; to bully. **—sinde bit=** /ın/ to pester, to worry. **— camı** bull's eye in a ceiling. **—sine çık=** /ın/ to presume on somebody's kindness; to become insolent. **— çiçeği** arch. flower-shaped ornament. **— damgası** soft spot on the skull of a newborn baby, fontanella. **—sinde değirmen çevir=** /ın/ to pester and disturb greatly in any way (especially those living on the next floor down). **— delen** castle on a towering crag. **— deliği** same as **tepe mazgalı**. **—sine dikil=** /ın/ to worry, to insist. **— göz*. —sinde havan döv=** /ın/ same as **tepesinde değirmen çevir=. —den inme** 1. sudden, unexpected. 2. from above, coming from a higher authortiy. **—sinden kaynar su dökül=** to be greatly disturbed and vexed. **— kemiği** the skull or its vertex. **— köşkü** arch. belvedere. **— mazgalı** arch. machicolation. **— penceresi** skylight. **— saçı** hair left in a tuft on the crown of the head in shaving. **— süsü** arch. crowning, coping (of a wall etc.). **— takla, — taklak** on one's head, upside down, head foremost. **—den tırnağa, —den tırnağa kadar** from head to foot. **— topu, — toparlağı** arch. ornamental globe of a building. **— üstü, —si üstü** head first, headlong.

tepecik[gi] تپه جك 1. small hill, mound. 2. bot. stigma.

tepegöz تپه گوز 1. whose forehead is so narrow that his eyes seem near his hair. 2. star-gazer (fish), zool., Uranoscopus scaber. 3. cyclops (legendary monster).

tepele=[r] تپه له مك /1/ 1. to knock on the head; to kill. 2. to thrash unmercifully.

tepeleme تپه له مه 1. verbal n. of **tepele=**. 2. brimful. 3. mound, heap; heaped.

tepelen=[ir] تپه له نمك pass. of **tepele=**.

tepelet=[ir] تپه له تمك /1, a/ caus. of **tepele=**.

tepeli تپه لى 1. crested (bird). 2 hilly. **— tarla kuşu** same as **tepeli toygar**. **— tavuk** Polish fowl. **— toygar** crested lark, zool., Galerida cristata.

tepelik[gi] تپه لك 1. button or similar ornament on bridal headgear. 2. anything that serves as a summit or crest. 3. full of hills, hilly (district). 4. ornamental knob (formerly worn on headgear).

tepengi, tepengû تپنگى تپنگو vars. of **tebengi, tebengû**.

tephir (.—) تپخير A var. of **tebhir**.

tepik[gi] تپيك prov. kick. **— tep=** to kick. **—le=** to give a kick, to kick

tepil=[ir] تپيلمك pass. of **tep=** 1.

tepin=[ir] تپينمك 1. to throw one's legs and arms about; to kick and stamp. 2. to dance (with joy or in anger). **—dir=** /1/ caus. **—me** verbal n. of **tepin=**.

tepir تپير 1. prov. a kind of hair sieve. 2. archaic a kind of tray used as a table for food.

tepirle=[r] تپيرله مك /1/ to sift or bolt. **—n=** pass. **—t=** /1, a/ caus. of **tepirle=**.

tepiş=[ir] 1 تپيشمك 1. to kick at one another, to kick one another. 2. to quarrel violently. 3. to dance (a dance together).

tepiş 2 تپيش verbal n. of **tep=** 1.

tepiş 3 تپيش P lrnd. 1. act of convulsively struggling; throes. 2. state of mental agitation. **—i kalb** palpitation of the heart.

tepişme تپيشمه verbal n. of **tepiş=** 1.

tepiştir=[ir] تپيشديرمك /1/ caus. of **tepiş=** 1.

tepke neol., phil. reflex.

tepki 1 neol. reaction.

tepki=[r] 2 neol. to react. **—me** reaction.

tepkili neol. reactive. **— uçak** jet plane.

tepkin neol. reactive.

tepme تپمه 1. verbal n. of **tep=** 1. 2. kick. 3. relapse (illness). 4. made or compressed by stamping with the feet. **— at=** to kick. **— keçe** felt made by trampling the wool under foot.

tepre=ʳ, tepren=ⁱʳ تپره‌مك تپره‌نمك 1. to move, to stir. 2. to struggle, to bestir oneself. 3. to rise, to get up from sitting or lying.
tepreş=ⁱʳ تپرشمك 1 same as **tepre=**, **tepren=**. 2. to recur (illness etc.). **—tir=** /ı/ caus.
tepret=ⁱʳ تپرتمك /ı/ caus. of **tepre=**.
teps تپس archaic 1. mitigation, cessation, extinction. 2. quieted, subsided. **— et=*.** **— ol=** 1. to be mitigated, allayed. 2. to be quieted, to subside.
tepser=ⁱʳ تپسرمك prov. 1. to be parched (lips). 2. to dry (wet clothes, etc.). 3. to stop, restrain, quiet or allay.
tepset=ⁱʳ تپستمك archaic /ı/ 1. to mitigate, to allay, to quiet. 2. to restrain, stop, prevent.
tepsi 1 تپسی small tray; tray. **— böreği** a large kind of pie cooked in a tray. **— kur=** to prepare a table for a convivial entertainment.
tepsi=ʳ 2 تپسمك prov. to subside; to become quieted or cooled.
tepsici تپسیجی 1. maker or seller of small trays. 2. Ott. hist. servant in charge of the trays. **— başı** Ott. hist. chief of the attendants who managed the trays, especially in the Sultan's palace.
tepsin=ⁱʳ تپسنمك prov., same as **tepsi=** 2.
tepsir=ⁱʳ تپسیرمك same as **tepser=**.
tepsit=ⁱʳ تپستمك prov. to stop, restrain, quiet or allay.
teptir=ⁱʳ تپتیرمك /ı/ caus. of **tep=** 1.
ter 1 تر 1. sweat, perspiration. 2. exudation. 3. vapor condensed in the form of dew. 4. wages or fees for certain kinds of labor. **— alıştır=** to wait till one's sweat has dried. **— bas=** 1. to sweat. 2. to sweat with terror or anxiety. 3. work hard. 4. to be greatly ashamed or embarrassed. **—e bat=** to perspire heavily. **— bıyık*. — boşan=** to perspire suddenly. **— dök=** same as **ter bas=**. **— döşeği** childbed. **— geç=** to pass lightly or carelessly over a matter. **— gözü** a drop of sweat. **— kebesi** very warm felt blanket for a horse. **— oğlanı** 1. archaic boy hired to do one's heaviest work. 2. Ott. hist. assistant to the collector of the head tax on Christian subjects. **—ini soğut=** to sit in a place to cool off. **—e yat=** to make oneself sweat by hot drinks and many blankets.
ter 2 تر P lrnd. 1. moist, damp; wet. 2. fresh, green; juicy. 3. graceful, easy, fluent. 4. easily affected. 5. quarrelsome, brawling, unfair. **— ü taze*.**
-ter 3 تر P lrnd., comparative termination of adjectives, as in **balâter, hoşter**.

terabbuᵘᵘ ترَبُّع A lrnd. a sitting crosslegged.
terabbus ترَبُّص A lrnd. 1. a waiting, hoping, expecting; hope, expectation. 2. an obstructing a person who tries to build a house on land he does not own or to live in such a house.
teracim 1 (. — .) تراجم A lrnd., pl. of **terceme. —i hal** biographies.
teracim 2 (. — —), **teracime** (. — . .) تراجیم A lrnd., pl. of **terceman**, interpreters.
teracuᵘᵘ (. — .) تراجع A lrnd. 1. a returning to one another after separation. 2. a returning to a former condition. 3. a retreating or retrograding; retreat, retrogression. 4. a speaking to one another, an answering each other.
teradüf (. — .) ترادف A lrnd. 1. a following one another, a being consecutive; succession. 2. a being synonymous. 3. a using in an enigma a synonym of the answer. 4. a using synonymous words so as to explain the meaning clearly.
terafuᵘᵘ (. — .) ترافع A law a mutually appealing to a judge; a trial by mutual appeal.
terafukᵏᵘ (. — .) ترافق A 1. lrnd. a being companions. 2. poet. a being so arranged as to lose neither sense, measure nor rhyme by transposition of the hemistichs.
terafüd (. — .) ترافد A lrnd. a helping one another; mutual help.
teragde ترغده P lrnd. stiff; paralyzed.
teraggum ترغّم A lrnd. a becoming vexed, a being annoyed.
teragub (. — .) تراغب A lrnd. a mutually and emulously having a desire for a thing.
terah ترح A 1. lrnd. a being or becoming unhappy; grief, anguish, care. 2. lrnd. a dying, a perishing; death, destruction. 3. astrol. the house of affliction of a planet.
terahhi ترحّی A lrnd. a coiling up (as a serpent).
terahhulᵘ ترحّل A lrnd. 1. a saddling one's animal and departing; departure. 2. an emigrating, traveling. **—ât** (. . . —) A pl.
terahhum ترحّم A lrnd. 1. a feeling compassion; compassion, mercy, pity. 2. a praying for God's mercy on a dead person by the formula **rahamahullah. — et=** /a/ to take pity (on).
terahhumen (. .´. .) ترحّماً A lrnd. mercifully; pityingly.
terahhus ترخّص A lrnd. 1. a taking things easily; a showing moderation toward others. 2. an obtaining leave. 3. a being let off easily, not being pushed to extremities. 4. a being low-priced (provisions).
terahi (. — .) تراخی A lrnd. 1. a being slow or tardy; sluggishness, backwardness, supineness. 2. a being protracted; protractedness. 3. a procrastinating as to performing the pilgrimage to Mecca.

terahül (. —.) تراحل A *lrnd.* a traveling together.

terahüm (. —.) تراحم A *lrnd.* a taking pity on each other; mutual compassion.

terahün^nü (. —.) تراهن A *lrnd.* 1. a mutually giving pledges or hostages. 2. a mutually laying wagers.

teraib (. —.) ترائب A *lrnd.* 1. the upper breast on which a necklace rests. 2. the bones of the upper breast: the pectoral ends of the first four pairs of ribs and the head of the sternum.

teraik^ki (. —.) تراىك A 1. refuse; leavings; things left unused. 2. matters left by God open to the free choice or rejection of mortals. 3. helmets.

terak^ki (. —) ترائك P *lrnd.* 1. crack, rent, fissure. 2. a cracking, bursting. 3. noise made in splitting or bursting. 4. a peal of thunder.

teraki 1 (. —.) تراقى A *lrnd.* an exalting oneself, a raising oneself.

teraki 2 (. —.) تراقى A *lrnd.* collar bones, clavicles.

terakib (. — —) تراكيب A *lrnd.* 1. compositions, compounds. 2. complex things. 3. systems.

terakide (. — —.) تراكيده P *lrnd.* cracked, cleft, split, burst.

Terakime (. — ..) تراكمه A *lrnd.*, *pl.* of **Türkmen.**

terakki ترقى A 1. an advancing, progressing; advancement, progress, advance. 2. an increasing; increase, augmentation, growth. 3. an ascending, ascent. 4. *Ott. hist.* advancement, increase of salary. — **et**= to make progress, to advance; to increase.

terakkicû (. . . —) ترقى جو P *lrnd.* desiring progress. —**yâne** (. . . — —.) P befitting one who desires progress. —**yi** (. . . — —) P a desiring progress.

terakkidar (. . . —) ترقى دار P *lrnd.* capable of progress.

terakkiperver ترقى پرور P *lrnd.* progressive. —**ân** (. . . . . —) P *pl.* —**âne** (. . . . . —.) P progressively.

terakkişiken ترقى شكن P *lrnd.* destroying progress. —**âne** (. . . . . —.) P in the manner of destroying progress.

terakkiyat (. . . —) ترقيات A *lrnd.* advances, improvement.

terakkub ترقب A *lrnd.* 1. a looking, a hoping, an expecting; hope, expectation. 2. a watching, a guarding. —**ât** (. . . —) A *pl.*

terakkus ترقص A *lrnd.* an oscillating; oscillation.

terakus (. —.) تراقص A *lrnd.* a dancing together.

teraküb (. —.) تراكب A *lrnd.* a uniting; union.

teraküm (. —.) تراكم A *lrnd.* a large collection, accumulation. — **et**= to collect, to accumulate. —**ât** (. —. —) A accumulations.

terane (. —.) ترانه P 1. tune, melody; refrain. 2. yarn, concocted story. 3. subterfuge; joke. 4. *lrnd.* piece of poetry complete in four hemistichs, of which at least the first, second and fourth must rhyme. 5. *lrnd.* handsome youth. 6. *myst.* love towards God and its ecstatic rites.

teranekâr (. —. —) ترانه كار P *lrnd* one who sings melodies, singer.

teraneli ترانه لى having a melody and tune.

teraneperdaz (. —. . —) ترانه پرداز P *lrnd.* a composer or singer of a **terane.** —**ân** (. —. . — —) P *pl.* —**î** (. —. . — —) P, —**lık** *lrnd.* song composition.

teraneriz (. —. —) ترانه ريز P *lrnd.* who pours forth melodies.

teranesaz (. —. —) ترانه ساز P *lrnd.* singing, singer.

teranesenc (. —. . —) ترانه سنج P *lrnd.* who composes or sings.

teranezar (. —. —) ترانه زار P *lrnd.* place full of melodies.

teranezen (. —. .) ترانه زن P *lrnd.* 1. one who sings, singer. 2. one who speaks.

terasül (. —.) تراسل A *lrnd.* 1. a sending messages to one another; correspondence. 2. an alternating with one another; alternation.

teraş (. —) تراش P *lrnd.* 1. *same as* **tıraş.** 2. who pares or shaves; who shapes by paring or shaving; who carves or hews. 3. pared, shaved, hewn, carved into shape; newly shaved. 4. shavings; chips. 5. brought into shape; educated, refined. — **ü heraş** (*lit.*, shavings and scratchings) rubbish.

teraşe (. —.) تراشه P *lrnd.* 1. that which is or ought to be trimmed away. 2. shaving, chip, splinter.

teraşide (. — —.) تراشيده P *lrnd.* 1. who has shaved, pared or hewn. 2. shaved, pared or hewn clean or into shape.

teraşiş (. —.) تراشش P *lrnd* 1. act of shaving, paring, carving or shaping. 2. graven image; piece of sculpture.

teraud ترعد A *lrnd.* a shaking, a quivering like jelly.

teravi (. — —) تراوى *var.* of **teravih.**

teravih (. — —) تراويح A *Isl. rel.* the supererogatory night service of the month of Ramazan performed immediately after the prescribed night service of worship (consisting of twenty genuflexions with an interval for rest and breathing after each two or four acts).

terazi 1 (. —.) ترازى [**terazu**] 1. balance, pair of scales. 2. equality; balance, equivalence. 3. acrobat's balancing pole. 4. *w. cap.*, *astr.* the constellation Libra. — **dili** the pointer of a balance. — **eli** handle of a balance. — **gözü** pan of a balance. — **kolu** arm of a balance. — **tablası** flat pan of a balance. —**ye vur=** /ı/ 1. to weigh. 2. to ponder.

terazi 2 (. — .) ترازى A *lrnd*. mutual satisfaction. —**i tarafeyn** with mutual consent.

terazili ترازىلى 1. having a balance or scales. 2. well-balanced.

terazisiz ترازىسز 1. without a balance or scales. 2. out of balance; uneven; irregular.

terazu (. — —) ترازو P *lrnd*. 1. same as **terazi 1**. 2. equity, justice. 3. mind, intellect. 4. balance of words in two consecutive phrases; symmetry of phrases. 5. any weighing, measuring or adjusting apparatus. 6. the Quran or the true religion as a moral balance. —**i cerh** the constellation Libra. —**i encüm** astrolabe. —**i felek** the constellation Libra. —**i kelâm** balance or symmetry of words in consecutive phrases. —**i kıyamet** the weighing of human actions on the day of judgment. —**i nazm** the theory of meters, prosody. —**i pulâdsencân** *poet*. 1. spear. 2. lance. —**i zer** the sun.

terazudan (. — — —) ترازودان P *lrnd*. case for a balance.

terazudar (. — — —) ترازودار P *lrnd*. 1. one who holds a balance. 2. official weighmaster. 3. well balanced.

terb ترب P *lrnd*. trick, deceit.

terbend تربند P *lrnd*. wet bandage on a wound.

terbıyık[1] تربیق youth whose mustache has just started.

terbi[ii] (. —) تربیع A 1. *lrnd*. a making square or four-sided. 2. *lrnd*. a doing any act four times or for the fourth time. 3. *lrnd*. a making a smaller number four. 4. *math*. a squaring a number. 5. *astr*. a planet's being in quartile aspect, quadrature. 6. *poetry* poem composed by adding two rhyming lines to the first line of each couplet of a gazel. 7. *lrnd*. an asserting four legitimate Caliphs as the immediate successors of the Prophet Muhammad. 8. *onom*. a composing a scheme in a square. —**i daire** *geom*. squaring of the circle. — **et=** /ı/ 1. to make four. 2. to square. —**i evvel** 1. *astrol*. the first quadrature of a planet. 2. same as **terbii eymen**. —**i eymen** *astrol*. right quadrature of a planet. —**i eyser** *astrol*. sinister quadrature of a planet. —**i sani** *astrol*., same as **terbii eyser**. —**i tabii** *astrol*. natural quartile aspect of Mercury or of Jupiter.

terbian (. —′.) تربیعا A *lrnd*. by squaring.

terbiat (. — —) تربیعات A *pl*. of **terbi**.

terbib (. —) تربیب A *lrnd*. 1. a raising, bringing up a child; nurture. 2. a preserving in or with fruit juice.

terbii (. — —) تربیعى A *lrnd*. related to squaring; squared, square.

terbiye تربیه A 1. a bringing up; a raising, nursing, training, educating; maintenance; training or education. 2. culture, good manners, good breeding. 3. a correcting, chastising; a teaching manners; correction, punishment, admonition. 4. a regulating or improving by the use of chemical or other agents; treatment. 5. a seasoning for food; sauce. 6. rein (of a cart horse). — **al=** to receive an education; to acquire good manners. —**sini boz=** to be rude. — **et=** /ı/ 1. to bring up, educate, train. 2. to correct, punish; to teach manners. 3. to flavor (with a sauce). — **ilmi** pedagogy. —**sini ver=** /ın/ to teach somebody his manners; to reprimand.

terbiyeci تربیه‌جى educator; pedagogue; trainer.

terbiyeli تربیه‌لى 1. well brought up; educated. 2. well behaved, good-mannered, polite. 3. flavored (with a sauce). — **maymun gibi** like a trained monkey, very well behaved.

terbiyesiz تربیه‌سز 1. badly brought up; ill-mannered; impolite, rude. 2. without a sauce or seasoning; insipid. —**lik** bad manners; rudeness; lack of education.

terbiyet تربیت A *lrnd*., same as **terbiye**.

terbiyetkerde تربیت‌كرده P *lrnd*. brought up, educated, trained.

terbiyetpezir (. . . . —) تربیت‌پذیر P *lrnd*. brought up; teachable, docile.

terbiyevi (. . . —) تربیوى [based on Arabic] *lrnd*. educational, pedagogic.

terceman (. . —) ترجمان A *lrnd*, same as **tercüman**.

terceme ترجمه A *lrnd*., same as **tercüme**.

terci[ii] (. —) ترجیع A *lrnd* 1. a causing to return or revert repeatedly; a making go and return repeatedly. 2. a frequently reciprocating, repeating or reproducing; repetition, reproduction; renewal; especially, a repeating a second time and in a louder tone each separate section of the public call to worship. 3. a making a trill or quaver in a song or cry; a bow's twanging; a reverberating; an echoing. 4. a saying in a time of trouble the formula **innalillâhi ve innaileyhi raciûn** (We belong to God and to Him we shall return). 5. an arranging in two or more members of a paragraph words of the same measure in the same order and ending in the same class of consonants so as to form a species of parallelism in sound. —**i bend***. — **et=** 1. to return, send or bring back. 2. to repeat.

terciât (. — —) ترجیعات A *lrnd*., *pl*. of **terci**.

tercib (. —) ترجیب A *lrnd*. 1. a respecting, venerating, honoring; respect, reverence, veneration. 2. a sacrificing to an idol in the month of Rejeb as was practiced by the pagan Arabs. —**at** (. — —) A *pl*. of **tercib**.

tercibend (. — .) ترجیع بند P *poetry* long poem with a recurrent couplet at the end of each stanza.

tercih (. —) ترجیح A an esteeming or declaring to be preferable; preference; priority. **— et=** /ı, a/ to prefer. **— bilâ müreccah** a giving priority without special reason.

tercihan (. — ′ .) ترجیحًا A *lrnd.* preferably, in preference.

tercihât (. — —) ترجیحات A *lrnd., pl. of* **tercih**.

terciibend (. — ..) ترجیع بند *var. of* **tercibend**.

tercim (. —) ترجیم A *lrnd.* 1. a stoning to death. 2. a placing a tombstone or a pile of stones over a grave.

terciye ترجیه A *lrnd.* a hoping, longing for, expecting; hope, expectation.

tercüman ترجمان A 1. interpreter; translator; dragoman. 2. *lrnd.* expounder. **— kalpağı** *obs.* tall bearskin hat (formerly worn by the dragomans of the European embassies).

tercümanlık[gi] ترجمانلق office or profession of an interpreter. **— et=** to act as interpreter.

tercüme ترجمه A 1. an interpreting or translating; translation; interpretation. 2. *lrnd.* an explaining or expounding; exposition, exegesis. 3. *poetry* an expressing a matter in both Arabic and Turkish words. **— et=** /ı, a/ to translate (into). **—i hâl** biography. **— odası** *Ott. hist.* office of translations at the Porte.

terdamen (. — .) تردامن P *lrnd.* 1. polluted, vicious, sinful. 2. whoremonger. **—î** (. — . —) P, **—lik** debauchery, immorality.

terdest تردست P *lrnd.* dextrous, adroit. **—ân** (.. —) P *pl.* **—î** (.. —) P dexterity, adroitness.

terdid (. —) تردید A *lrnd.* 1. the art of giving a surprising end to a story. 2. a causing to go and come repeatedly. 3. a frequently rejecting, repelling. 4. a throwing into doubt, vacillation or hesitancy. 5. a turning over and over again, a revolving in one's mind. 6. a repeating, renewing, reproducing; repetition, reproduction, reiteration. 7. a reverberating, a rumbling; a trilling the voice. 8. alternative. 9. an investigating the ultimate ground of a law; a clearing up an ambiguity. **— et=** 1. /ı/ to repeat. 2. to trill. 3. to reject. **—ât** (. — —) A *pl.*

terdif (. —) تردیف A *lrnd.* 1. a sending as escort or guide. 2. a causing to accompany. **—ât** (. — —) A *pl.*

terdifen (. — ′ .) تردیفًا A *lrnd.* as escort; as company; together with.

terdiye تردیه A *lrnd.* 1 a causing to fall. 2. a casting into destruction. 3. a wrapping one in a shawl or wrapper.

tere تره P garden cress, *bot.*, *Lepidium sativum*. **— otu***.

tereb ترب A *lrnd.* 1. a being soiled with dust; dustiness. 2. a being frustrated or crushed to earth by poverty; disappointment.

terebbi تربّی A *lrnd.* 1. a nursing, raising or educating; nurture, education. 2. a being raised or educated.

terebbüs تربّص A *lrnd.* a waiting, hoping, expecting; hope, expectation.

terebbü[üü] تربّع A *lrnd.* a sitting cross-legged.

terebbüb تربّب A *lrnd.* a claiming a right to, pretending to lord over.

terecci ترجّی A *lrnd.* 1. a hoping, expecting; hope, desire, expectation. 2. a requesting, supplicating; request, petition, supplication.

tereccuh ترجّح A *lrnd.* a leaning to one side (balance), preponderance. 2. an inclining towards, a preferring; a being deemed preferable.

tereci ترجى seller of cress. **—ye tere sat=** (*lit.*, to sell cress to the cress seller) to explain the obvious to an expert. **—ye tere satma** Don't try to take me in.

tereddi تردّى A *lrnd.* 1. a degenerating; degeneration; deterioration. 2. a falling; a perishing. 3. a wrapping oneself. **— et=** to deteriorate. **—yât** (. .. —) A *pl.*

tereddüd A, **tereddüt**[dü] تردّد A 1. a being doubtful, a hesitating in a matter; doubt, hesitation; indecision. 2. *lrnd.* a stammering and hesitating in speech. 3. *lrnd.* a going and coming repeatedly; a frequenting; frequentation. 4. *lrnd.* a reverberating; reverberation. 5. *med.* remittence. **— et=** 1. to hesitate; to be in suspense. 2. to frequent a place. **—ât** (. .. —) A *pl.*

teref ترف A *lrnd.* a having ease and plenty; luxury, enjoyment.

tereffu[uu] ترفّع A *lrnd.* 1. a becoming high; elevation. 2. a becoming exalted in rank or conceit. **— et=** 1. to be elevated. 2. to rise (prices, etc.). **—ât** (. .. —) A *pl.*

tereffuk[ku] ترفّق A *lrnd.* a being gentle, gracious, courteous; gentleness, tenderness; graciousness, courtesy, kindness.

tereffüh ترفّه A *lrnd.* a leading a life of plenty, ease and luxury; plenty, ease, luxury.

terehhüb ترهّب A *lrnd.* 1. a devoting oneself to God; a serving God with awe. 2. an embracing a monastic life. 3. a dreading, fearing.

terek[gi] 1 ترك 1. *prov.* shelf; small drawer in a cupboard. 2. *archaic* protruding border of a hat or headgear; *myst. orders* raised stripes on the headgear of a dervish.

terek[ki] 2 ترك P *lrnd.* 1. moat, ditch. 2. young girl, maid. 3. little or pet thing; fresh, juicy, moist.

terekât (..—) تَرَكات A *pl. of* **tereke 1**, *law* effects, property left by a person at death; estates.

tereke 1 تَرَكَ A *law* 1. estate of a deceased person; heritage. 2. sale of a dead man's effects.

tereke 2 تَرَكَ *prov.* grain, produce.

Terekeme تَرَاكَمَ [Terakime] Turkish tribesmen in Eastern Anatolia and Transcaucasia.

terekkuᵘᵘ تَرَكُّع A *lrnd* a bowing down in divine worship.

terekküb تَرَكُّب A *lrnd., same as* **terekküp**. —ât (...—) A compositions, compounds.

terekkün تَرَكُّن A *lrnd.* 1. a being strong; strength, firmness; a being firmly established. 2. a being impregnable (place); impregnability. 3. a being sedate, calm, and sober; gravity, sedateness.

terekküpᵇᵘ تَرَكُّب [terekküb] a being put together, composed or compounded; composition, combination. — et= to be composed or compounded.

terelelli (..′.) تَرَلَلْلِي feather-brained; frivolous.

terementi (..′.) تَرَمَنْتِي تَرَهْ مَنْتِي Gk turpentine; terebinth.

teremmi تَرَمِّي A *lrnd.* a throwing or shooting at a mark.

teremmüd تَرَمُّد A *lrnd.* a becoming reduced to ashes.

teremmül تَرَمُّل A *lrnd.* a being or becoming a widow.

teremmüm تَرَمُّم A *lrnd.* a mending or becoming restored gradually, becoming patched up.

teremmüz تَرَمُّز A *lrnd.* a making a sign with the hand.

teren تَرَن P *lrnd.* 1. dog-rose. 2. field; desert.

terenc تَرَنْج P *lrnd.* a tightening, squeezing, contracting; constriction.

terenci (..—) تَرَنْجِي P *lrnd.* a pinch of a person's flesh with the finger tips.

terencide (..—.) تَرَنْجِيدَه P *lrnd.* squeezed; tightened; contracted.

terencübin (...—) تَرَنْجُبِين P *lrnd.* manna.

tereng تَرَنْگ P *lrnd.* 1. twang of a bowstring. 2. any sharply resonant sound as that of a heavy blow, the jingle of money, etc.

terengâtereng (..—..) تَرَنْگاتَرَنْگ P *lrnd.* a continually repeated succession of twangs or other resonant sounds.

terengubin (...—) تَرَنْگُبِين P *lrnd.* manna.

terennüh تَرَنُّح A *lrnd.* a waving in the wind; an oscillating. —ât (...—) A *pl.* oscillation.

terennüm تَرَنُّم A 1. a singing, warbling, humming pleasantly; hum, warble, coo. 2. *lrnd.* a making a trilling or quavering sound; trill, quaver, twang. 3. *mus.* vocal refrain. — et= to sing, hum, warble.

terennümat (...—) تَرَنُّمَات A *lrnd., pl. of* **terennüm**.

terennümsaz (...—) تَرَنُّمْسَاز P *lrnd.* singing; singer. —î (...— —) P, —lık *lrnd.* singing.

terennümsenc تَرَنُّمْسَنْج P *lrnd.* singing. —î (....—) P singing.

tereotuⁿᵘ تَرَهْ اوتُو dill, *bot., Anethum graveolens.*

teres تَرَس 1. cuckold; pander, pimp. 2. scoundrel.

teressüb تَرَسُّب A *sc.* a sediment's settling; sediment, precipitation. — et= to be precipitated; to be deposited as sediment. —ât (...—) A sediment.

teressül تَرَسُّل A *lrnd.* 1. an acting as envoy or messenger. 2. an acting with deliberation, calmness and gentleness. 3. a speaking or reading in a deliberate manner.

teressüm تَرَسُّم A *lrnd.* 1. a taking shape, a picturing itself in one's mind. 2. an attentively examining or considering a trace, mark etc.; a studying; consideration, study. — et= 1. to be pictured. 2. to become evident. —ât (...—) A *pl.*

tereşşüf تَرَشُّف A *lrnd.* a sipping, a sucking.

tereşşüh تَرَشُّح A *lrnd.* 1. an oozing or trickling. 2. a body's dripping with moisture. — et= 1. to ooze or trickle. 2. to transpire, to ooze out (secrets, news, etc.). —ât (...—) A things that ooze out.

tereşşüş تَرَشُّش A *lrnd.* a being sprinkled.

teretizekᵏⁱ تَرَهْ تِيزَك P *lrnd.* garden cress.

terettüb تَرَتُّب A *lrnd.* 1. a being incumbent. 2. a being arranged in order or in classes; arrangement, classification. 3. a being composed and constituted; composition, constitution. 4. a becoming existent or established; a resulting; rise; existence. — et= 1. /a/ to be incumbent (upon) 2. to result, to happen as a consequence.

tereüf تَرَؤُّف A *lrnd.* a forcing oneself to be mild and merciful.

terevvüᵘᵘ تَرَوُّع A *lrnd.* a becoming frightened; fear, terror.

terevvüc تَرَوُّج A *lrnd.* a finding currency, a being or becoming current.

terevvüh تَرَوُّح A *lrnd.* 1. a fanning oneself. 2. a contracting a smell from any neighboring substance.

tereyağ تَرَه يَاغ *same as* **tereyağı**.

tereyağı تَرَه يَاغي 1. fresh butter. 2. *slang* soft, fresh, stupid (person). — gibi very soft (apple, pear, etc.). —ından kıl çeker gibi skillfully and easily.

terezzün تَرَزُّن A *lrnd.* a showing or affecting calmness or gravity.

terfend, terfende تَرْفَنْد تَرْفَنْدَه P *lrnd.* trick, wile, fraud.

terfiⁱⁱ (.—) تَرْفِيع A 1. an advancing the rank

or grade of a person; promotion; advancement. 2. a raising, exalting; elevation. 3. *lrnd.* a submitting a matter to one in authority. — **et=** 1. to be promoted. 2. to advance. — **ettir=** /ı/ to advance in rank. —**i rütbe** *lrnd.* promotion in rank. — **ve terakki** promotion, advancement.

terfian (. —ʹ.) ترفيعاً A *lrnd.* by way of promotion; on promotion.

terfiât (. — —) ترفيعات A *lrnd., pl. of* **terfi.**

terfid (. —) ترفيد A *lrnd.* an electing as lord over oneself.

terfih (. —) ترفيه A *lrnd* a causing to live in prosperity. — **et=** /ı/ to bring prosperity (to); to better the condition (of).

terfik[kı] (. —) ترفيق A *lrnd.* a causing to accompany another as attendant, guide or companion. — **et=** /ı/ to send as escort or companion. —**ân** (. —ʹ.) A as companion; by way of escort.

terfil (. —) ترفيل A 1. *lrnd.* an honoring. 2. *lrnd.* a letting down so as to touch the ground (skirt. etc.). 3. *prosody* a lengthening the final syllable of a prosodic foot.

terfürus (. . —) ترفرش P *lrnd.* 1. who fancies himself handsome without being so, conceited. 2. hypocrite; cheat, rogue.

tergib (. —) ترغيب A *lrnd.* a causing to desire; a stimulating, encouraging. —**ât** (. — —) A *pl.*

tergim (. —) ترغيم A *lrnd.* 1. a humbling, a humiliating one as if by rubbing his nose in the dirt. 2. a doing something to vex a person or in spite of him. —**i enf** a humiliating, vexing (a person).

tergimen (. —ʹ.) ترغيماً A *lrnd.* by way of humiliating, annoying or cursing.

terhab (. —) ترحاب A *lrnd.* a welcoming, saying **merhaba** to a person

terhande ترخنده P *lrnd.* joke; trick.

terhib 1 (. —) ترهيب A *lrnd.* a frightening, terrifying; a threatening.

terhib 2 (. —) ترحيب A *lrnd.* 1. a welcoming, saying **merhaba**. 2. a making spacious.

terhibat 1 (. — —) ترهيبات A *lrnd., pl. of* **terhib 1,** threats.

terhibat 2 (. — —) ترحيبات A *lrnd., pl. of* **terhib 2.**

terhiben (. —ʹ.) ترهيباً |**terhib 1**| *lrnd.* by frightening, threateningly.

terhibî (. — —) ترهيبى A *lrnd.* 1. terrorizing. 2. deterrent (punishment).

terhil (. —) ترحيل A *lrnd.* a causing or ordering to depart, a sending away.

terhim 1 (. —) ترحيم A *lrnd.* a praying for God's mercy to a dead person by the formula **rahamehullah.**

terhim 2 (. —) ترخيم A *lrnd.* 1. a curtailing, a truncating; curtailment, truncation. 2. a cutting off (the final syllable of a vocative); abbreviation, contraction. — **et=** /ı/ 1. to curtail, to truncate. 2. to abbreviate.

terhin (. —) ترهين A a pawning; a pledging. — **et=** /ı/ to pawn, to pledge. —**ât** (. — —) A *lrnd.* pawnings.

terhis (. —) ترخيص A 1. discharge (of a soldier after serving his time), demobilization. 2. *lrnd.* an authorizing; a permitting; authorization, permission; license, full power. — **et=** /ı/ 1. to discharge (soldier), to demobilize. 2. to authorize. — **tezkeresi** discharge papers of a soldier. —**ât** (. — —) A *pl.*

terhûn 1 (. —) ترهون P *same as* **tarhun.**

terhûn 2 (. —) ترهون P *lrnd.* ruffian, cutthroat, murderer.

teri (. —) ترى P *lrnd.* 1. wetness; wet; dampness; moisture. 2. greenness, luxuriance. 3. freshness; youth. 4. fluency of composition or expression.

te'rib 1 (. —) تأريب A *lrnd.* 1. a making strong and firm. 2. a sharpening, a whetting. 3. a making intelligent, keen and firm.

ter'ib 2 (. —) ترعيب A *lrnd.* a frightening, terrifying. — **et=** /ı/ to frighten.

terib 3 ترب A *lrnd.* 1. dusty. 2. frustrated, crushed to earth; disappointed.

teribe (. —.) تربة A *lrnd.* the upper breast on which the necklace rests.

ter'id (. —) ترعيد A *lrnd.* a trilling; quavering the voice in chanting (forbidden in chanting the Quran).

ter'if (. —) ترعيف A *lrnd.* a causing blood to flow from the nose.

te'rik[kı] (. —) تأريك A *lrnd.* a making sleepless and restless.

terike (. —.) تركه A *lrnd* 1. an old maid. 2. anything left, abandoned, neglected (as a woman by lovers or a pasture not grazed by cattle). 3. iron helmet.

terim 1 F *neol.* term; technical term

terim 2 (. —) تريم A *lrnd.* 1. obedient, submissive to God's will. 2. polluted, stained with dust or sins.

-terin (. —) ترين P *lrnd., superlative* most, -est, *as in* **balâterin.**

ter'is (. —) ترعيس A *lrnd.* a causing to be head and chief.

ter'iş (. —) ترعيش A *lrnd.* a causing to shiver or tremble.

terit (. —) تريت P *lrnd., same as* **tirit.**

terk[kı] **1** ترك A 1. a quitting, forsaking, abandoning, deserting, leaving, relinquishing; abandonment; desertion. 2. a refraining from, renouncing; renunciation. 3. a leaving undone, an omitting, neglecting; omission; neglect. 4. a leaving and perpetuating. 5. an abandoning self for the sake of love to God; self-renunciation. 6. a leaving property at death. —i dünya *lrnd.* a renouncing the world. —i edeb *lrnd.* a breach of good manners. — et=*. —i hayat *lrnd.* a dying. —i saltanat *lrnd.* abdication. —i ser *lrnd.* a sacrificing one's life in a cause.

terkki 2 ترك P *lrnd.* 1. iron helmet, casque. 2. seam; breadth of cloth between seams.

terkend, terkende تركنده P *lrnd.* a trick, trickery.

terkeş تركش *var. of* **tirkeş**.

terket=der ترك ايتمك /ı/ 1. to leave, to abandon. 2. to give up. 3. to renounce.

terki 1 تركى 1. surface of the back of a Turkish saddle. 2. anything strapped to the back of a saddle. **—ye al=** /ı/ to take as pillion rider. **—ye as=** /ı/ to suspend behind one's saddle. **— bağı** strap for fastening things to the back of a saddle. **— yeri** place behind a saddle on a horse's back where things may be carried in straps.

terkiii 2 (.—) ترقيع A *lrnd.* 1. a patching. 2. a mending or putting to rights.

terkib (.—) تركيب A *lrnd.* 1. *same as* **terkip**. 2. a mounting, a furnishing with arms and a mount. 3. the employing a compound word to shadow out a simple one as **merdümkeş** for **mürşid**. —i atfî *gram.* conjunction. —i bend *var. of* **terkibbend**. —i isnadî *gram.* indicative phrase or sentence. —i izafî *gram.* compound of two nouns one governing the other, status constructus. —i ta'dadî *lrnd.* compound numeral. —i tavsifi *gram.* compound of a substantive and its adjective.

terkibât (.— —) تركيبات A *lrnd.* compositions, compounds, complex things.

terkibbend (.—.) تركيببند P *lrnd.* long poem each stanza of which is followed by a refrain couplet, these couplets rhyming among themselves.

terkibî (.— —) تركيبى A *lrnd.* relating to composition; compound; composite; synthetic.

terkide (.—.) تركيده P *lrnd.* cracked, burst, torn. **—gi** (.—.—) P a splitting, a cracking.

terkikki 1 (.—) ترقيق A *lrnd.* 1. a making thin, slender or fine in substance. 2. a making the voice soft and gentle. 3. making an expression have a subtle meaning delicately conveyed. 4. a pronouncing with the sound of a lengthened vowel, a pronouncing with a half-closed mouth in reciting the Quran. 5. a reducing to slavery.

terkikki 2 (.—) تركيك A *lrnd.* 1. a causing a defect in speech or style. 2. a making thin or slender. 3. a making small in quantity or trifling in quality.

terkim (.—) ترقيم A *lrnd.* 1. a marking; a putting a number on. 2. a writing. **— et=** /ı/ to mark with a figure; to write.

terkin (.—) ترقين A *lrnd.* a canceling with some conventional mark; cancellation. **— et=** /ı/ to cancel, to cross out.

terkipbi تركيب |**terkib**| 1. a joining or compounding together so as to constitute one whole; a being compounded; composition. 2. a making a composite thing, a being made composite; a composite whole; compound; synthesis; mixture; structure. 3. a putting together words so as to form a composite or compound word or phrase; phrase; compound word. 4. a putting together letters so as to form a word or syllable; word or syllable so composed. 5. *log.* a putting together derivatively or syntactically two or more ideas in a single expression; derived or compound expression.

terkis (.—) ترقيص A *lrnd.* 1. a causing to dance or jump about. 2. a dandling a child. 3. a passing almost silently over a quiescent letter in reading the Quran and then strongly emphasizing a movent one (which is forbidden).

terkiş 1 (.—) ترقيش A *lrnd.* 1. an adorning, embellishing a discourse. 2. an interlarding discourse with exaggerations, lies or calumnies.

terkiş=ir 2 تركيشمك 1. to take turns riding pillion. 2. to follow one after the other.

terkiye ترقيه A *lrnd.* a causing to ascend or advance and make progress

terkiz (.—) تركيز A *lrnd.* a planting a spear upright.

terkos تركوس 1. the Istanbul municipal water supply. 2. *w. cap.* village and lake on the shore of the Black Sea near Istanbul, Derkos.

terkova, terkuva, terkuve تركوه A *anat.* collar bone.

terle=r ترلمك 1. to sweat, to perspire. 2. to be covered with dew (glass). 3. to start growing (mustache). 4. to be very tired. 5. to be embarrassed. **—me** *verbal n.* **—t=** /ı/ *caus. of* **terle=**.

terletici ترلتيجى 1. sudorific. 2. hard, fatiguing (work).

terli ترلى 1. sweating, perspiring. 2. covered with sweat or sweatlike moisture.

terlikgi ترلك 1. slippers; light shoes for indoor wear. 2. cloth skullcap worn under a headgear; night cap. 3. cloth or garment worn to prevent sweat from soiling other things, sweat-cloth under a saddle. 4. *prov.* a kind of light cloak (worn by women). **—çi** maker or seller of slippers.

terme ترمه a kind of wild radish.

termenti ترمنتى Gk *same as* **terementi**.

termid (.—) ترميد A *lrnd.* 1. a reducing to ashes. 2. a soiling or mixing with ashes.

termig (.—) ترميغ A *lrnd.* 1. a making food rich with fat. 2. an anointing.

termikki (.—) ترميك A *lrnd.* 1. an eyeing

termil

askance in anger or aversion. 2. a keeping body and soul together with the smallest possible amount of food. 3. a doing any act in the most perfunctory manner. 4. an interlarding with embellishment, exaggeration or falsehood.

termil (.—) تَرمیل A *lrnd.* 1. a sanding. 2. a tingeing, besmearing with blood. 3. a becoming a widow. 4. an interlarding with embellishment, exaggeration or falsehood.

termim (.—) تَرمیم A *lrnd.* a mending, patching, repairing; repairs. — **et=** /ı/ 1. to mend, patch, repair. 2. to set (a bone). —**ât** (.——) A repairs.

termizac (..—) تَرمِزاج P *lrnd.* unduly touchy or suspicious.

termometre F, **termometro** It (...'.) ترمومتره ترمومترو thermometer.

termos تَرموس G thermos flask.

termosifon ترموسیفون F bath stove. —**lu soğutma tertibatı** *auto.* convection cooling.

ternane (.—.) تَرنانه P *lrnd.* condiment eaten with bread.

ternim (.—) تَرنیم A *lrnd.*, same as **terennüm.**

ternin (.—) تَرنین A *lrnd.* 1. a twanging a bow; twang. 2. a crying out loudly, shrilly; shrill, vehement cry.

terniye تَرنیه A *lrnd.* 1. a causing to look intently, an attracting one's gaze. 2. a gladdening, pleasing, an interesting. 3. a crying out loudly, shrilly; shrill, vehement cry.

ternöv تَرنوو F Newfoundland dog.

ters 1 تَرس 1. reverse or back (of a thing). 2. wrong or reverse direction. 3. reverse, wrong, opposite. 4. inside out; upside down; inverted, introverted. 5. peevish, contrary, surly, wrong-headed. 6. perplexing, troublesome; unfortunate, ill-timed. 7. excrement. 8. *backgammon* dice. —**ine** on the contrary; invertedly; the wrong way. — **açı** *neol., geom.* opposite angle. — **akıllı** wrong-headed, eccentric. — **anla=** to misinterpret. — **bak=** to look sourly or in a hostile manner. — **baskı** *art* counter-proof. — **dön=** to get wrong. —**i dön=** to lose one's bearings; to become confused and bewildered. —**ine dön=** to become reversed; to take a bad turn. — **evirme** *neol., log.* contraposition. — **gel=** to be the wrong way about; to be in the opposite direction. — **git=** to go wrong, to turn out badly. **T— Maymun** a trademark of a good variety of Damascus steel with finely convoluted grain. —**inden oku=** 1. to misunderstand 2. to be very quick witted. — **orantılı** *neol., math.* inversely proportional. — **pers** 1. very inverted; all wrong; falling backwards; quite the reverse of what was desired. 2. disconcerted; disappointed. — **tarafından kalk=** to be in a bad mood; to be in a bad temper. — **ters bak=** to look sourly; to look disapprovingly. — **yön** *neol., astr.* retrograde, retrogressive. — **yüz et=** to reverse, to turn inside out (a suit of clothes). — **yüzü geri dön=** to come back empty-handed, to return disappointed.

ters 2 تَرس P *lrnd.* 1. fear, terror. 2 in fear; afraid; frightened.

tersa 1 (.—) تَرسا P *lrnd.* in fear, frightened.

tersa 2 (.—) تَرسا P 1. *lrnd.* Christian. 2. *lrnd.* heathen, unbeliever; fire-worshipper. 3. *myst.* a true convert.

tersabeçe (.—..) تَرساپچه P *lrnd.* 1. son of a Christian; pagan or unbelieving boy. 2. divine inspiration in the mind of a devotee. —**gân** (.—..—) P Christian children.

tersan (.—) تَرسان P *lrnd.* in fear, afraid, frightened. — **tersan** fearing, afraid.

tersane (.—..) تَرسانه It dockyard; maritime arsenal (especially that at Istanbul). — **emini** *Ott. hist.* supervisor of the dockyards. — **kethüdası** *Ott. hist.* secretary to the supervisor of the dockyards. — **umuru** *colloq.* very important work. — **zindanı** *Ott. hist.* prison of the galley slaves, the Bagnio.

tersaneli تَرسانه لی 1. attached to the maritime arsenal. 2. *Ott. hist.* naval officer.

tersayan (.——) تَرسایان P *lrnd.*, *pl. of* **tersa 2**.

tersayi (.——) تَرسایی P *lrnd.* quality and belief or acts of a heathen or a non-Muslim.

tersenbe تَرسنبه *archaic* disagreeable, peevish, quarrelsome. —**lik** disagreeableness of disposition.

tersende تَرسنده P *lrnd.* fearing; timid fearful.

tersengiz (..—) تَرسنگیز P *lrnd.* frightening.

tersgâr (.—) تَرسگار P *lrnd.* God-fearing, pious, devout. —**ân** (.——) P *pl.* —**i** (.——) P fear of God, piety.

tershane (.—.) تَرسخانه *colloq. for* **tersane**.

tersiⁱⁱ (.—) تَرصیع A 1. *rhet.* a joining together in a phrase the names of two or more things that have some conformity of meaning. 2. *rhet.* a composing rhymed prose in which every word of one clause is balanced by a similar word in the other; homophony. 3. *lrnd.* an ornamenting with pearls and precious stones. — **et=** /ı/ to set with pearls or precious stones. — **ma'tecnis** *rhet.* homophony and homonymy.

tersib (.—) تَرسیب A *lrnd.* a causing a sediment to precipitate; precipitation. — **et=** to deposit, precipitate. —**ât** (.——) A sediments.

tersif (.—) تَرصیف A *lrnd.* 1. a joining the parts of a thing compactly together. 2. a constructing a sentence lucidly and grammatically.

tersil (.—) تَرسیل A *lrnd.* a speaking or reading in a grave manner.

tersim (.—) تَرسیم A *lrnd.* 1. a drawing a

tersim figure, a writing. 2. a marking. — **et**= /ı/ to picture; to design, to draw; to mark. — **bişşems**, — **bizziya** photograph.

tersimât (.— —) ترسيمات A *lrnd.* drawings, writings.

tersimî (.— —) ترسيمى A *lrnd.* pertaining to designing or drawing. — **hendese** plane geometry.

tersin (. —) ترسين A *lrnd.* 1. a making sure and free from doubt. 2. a making strong.

tersinir *neol., phil.* reversible. —**lik** reversibility.

tersis (. —) ترصيص A *lrnd.* 1. a consolidating, a wedging together. 2. a soldering; a transferring into lead.

tersiye ترسيه A *lrnd.* 1. a lamenting, praising (the dead). 2. a poet's eulogizing a dead patron.

tersle=ʳ ترسلمك 1. /ı/ to scold; to answer harshly; to snub. 2. to dung; /ı/ to befoul with dung. —**n**= 1. to be in a bad temper; to behave in a peevish, contrary way. 2. to be snubbed. —**ndir**= /ı/ to cause to become peevish or cross.

terslikᵍⁱ ترسلك 1. a turning out to be the opposite of what was hoped. 2. a being reversed or wrong. 3. contrariness, vexatiousness. 4. peevishness, wrong-headedness, obstinacy.

tersnâkᵏⁱ (. —) ترسناك P *lrnd.* terrified, afraid; timid. —**î** (.— —) P fear, timidity.

terso, tersu (.′.) ترسو Gk *slang* Stop it! Shut up! Leave it alone! Drop it!

terşid (. —) ترشيد A *lrnd.* 1. a leading aright. 2. a deeming or pronouncing orthodox.

terşif (. —) ترشيف A *lrnd.* a sipping.

terşih (. —) ترشيح A *lrnd.* 1. a causing to ooze; filtration. 2. an educating from tender years, rendering qualified for any office. — **havuzu** filter bed.

terşiş (. —) ترشيش A *lrnd.* a splattering with drops of ink (pen).

tert ترت P *lrnd.* damage; damaged; ruin; ruined. — **bert** P reduced to ruin.

tertemiz (.′..) ترتميز absolutely clean.

terter ترتر *only in* — **tepin**= to kick and stomp.

tertere ترتره A *lrnd.* 1. moving, agitating, shaking backwards and forwards. 2. a shaking a drunken or sleeping man; shake, jolt. 3. a being garrulous; loquacity, talkativeness.

tertib 1 (. —) ترتيب A *lrnd., same as* **tertip**.

tertib 2 (. —) ترطيب A *lrnd.* 1. a moistening, a wetting. 2. a refreshing, enlivening.

tertibat (.— —) ترتيبات A *lrnd., pl. of* **tertib 1**, 1. arrangements; dispositions. 2. apparatus; installations.

tertibî (. — —) ترتيبى A *lrnd.* organizing; arranging.

tertibiye (.— ..) ترتيبيه A *lrnd.* type-setting for printing.

tertibkerde (.— ..) ترتيب كرده P *lrnd.* arranged, disposed, ordered or prescribed.

tertibsâz (. — —) ترتيب ساز P *lrnd.* arranger, one who orders.

tertil (. —) ترتيل A *lrnd.* 1. a chanting of the Quran in slow time. 2. a pronouncing distinctly and accurately; clear and distinct enunciation.

tertipᵇⁱ ترتيب [**tertib 1**] 1. an arranging or classifying in due order; arrangement, order; disposition. 2. a compounding; a making, preparing, composing, prescribing or planning a composition; composition; plan, project. 3. recipe, medical prescription. 4. a setting up type (for printing). 5. size of printed work, as quarto, octavo, *etc.*; format (of a book). 6. series; line; sequence; full edition. 7. *rhet.* an observing the natural order of sequence in the clauses of a sentence; an observing in presenting details the order already followed in a general statement. — **et**= 1. to arrange, put in order; to plan or prepare necessary things beforehand. 2. to compose; to organize. 3. to prescribe.

tertipçi ترتيبجى good at organizing; who is always planning; planner.

tertiple=ʳ ترتيبلمك /ı/ to organize, to arrange. —**n**= *pass.*

tertiplenme ترتيبلنمه 1. arrangement. 2. *mil.* disposition.

tertipli ترتيبلى 1. well-organized; well-prepared. 2. tidy, neat.

tertipsiz ترتيبسيز 1. unarranged, disarranged, confused. 2. without system; ill-prepared; badly planned. 3. untidy; disorderly.

tertipsizlikᵍⁱ ترتيبسيزلك 1. bad organization; lack of system. 2. confusion, disorder; untidiness.

tertümert ترت و مرت P *lrnd.* 1. in utter confusion and ruin. 2. dispersed, scattered; topsy turvy.

terütaze (.. —.) ترو تازه P *lrnd.* quite fresh; blooming.

terviⁱⁱ (. —) ترويع A *lrnd.* 1. a frightening, a terrifying. 2. a bewildering and enchanting through exceeding beauty.

tervic (. —) ترويج A *lrnd.* 1. a giving currency to, a making current. 2. a causing a plan to be accepted; a favoring or advocating a project; encouragement; advocacy (of a plan). — **et**= /ı/ 1. to make current. 2. to cause to be accepted; to advocate, encourage. —**ât** (.— —) A *pl.*

tervih (. —) ترويح A *lrnd.* 1. a causing to repose, a giving rest. 2. a perfuming. 3. an allowing a congregation to rest between two sections of a service, especially, in the supererogatory night-service of Ramazan. 4. a fanning.

5. a kind of stringed musical instrument resembling the dulcimer.

terviha (.—.) ترویحه A *lrnd.* 1. a single pause for rest and breath. 2. a single section of the supererogatory night service of Ramazan (consisting of four repetitions).

tervihât (.——) ترویحات A *lrnd.*, *pl. of* **tervih**.

tervik^(kı) (.—) ترویح A *lrnd.* 1. a straining, a filtering, a clarifying. 2. a spreading an awning; a spreading darkness (night).

terviye ترویه A *lrnd.* 1. a satisfying with something potable; a watering a plant and making it luxuriant. 2. a pondering, a reflecting. 3. a causing to relate what has been heard from another.

terviz (.—) ترویض A *lrnd.* 1. a turning a wilderness into a meadow, park or garden. 2. a breaking in and thoroughly training a colt. 3. a disciplining the mind.

terzeban (..—) ترزبان P *lrnd.* glib, ready of speech; eloquent. —i (..——) P, —lık readiness of speech, eloquence.

terzi ترزى |derzi| tailor, dressmaker.
— **sabunu** French chalk (soapstone).

terzihane (..—.) ترزخانه P 1. tailor's shop. 2. clothing factory.

terzik^(kı) 1 (.—) ترزيق A *lrnd.* 1. a feeding, a giving daily bread. 2. a giving as a part of the daily allowance.

terzik^(kı) 2 (.—) ترزيع P *lrnd.* a falsehood; nonsense.

terziktraz (.——) ترزيقطراز P *lrnd.* an inventor of nonsense and lies.

terzil (.—) ترزيل A *lrnd.* a rendering vile and contemptible, a treating with ignominy. — **et=** /ı/ to treat with ignominy; to humiliate before others; to ill-treat; to insult.

terzilik^(ği) ترزيلك tailoring; dressmaking.

terziliyat (.—.—) ترزيليات A *lrnd.* words uttered to humiliate or insult someone.

terzin (.—) ترزين A *lrnd.* a making or deeming grave, calm and sedate.

tesabi (.——) تصابى A *lrnd.* a declaring one's love openly.

tesabih (.——) تصابيح A *lrnd.*, *pl. of* **tesbih**.

tesabuk^(ku) (.——) تصابق A *lrnd.* a striving to get before and precede one another; a running, throwing, competing for a prize.

tesabür (.—.) تصابر A *lrnd.* a rushing upon or against one another.

tesadüf (.—.) تصادف A 1. a meeting by chance. 2. chance event; a happening, mere accident, coincidence. — **et=** /a/ 1. to meet by chance, to come across. 2. to coincide (with); to happen by chance; to fall (on such and such a date).

tesadüfât (.—.—) تصادفات A *lrnd.* coincidences; chances, events.

tesadüfen (.—'..) تصادفاً A by chance, by coincidence.

tesadüfî (.—.—) تصادفى A chance (event), fortuitous.

tesadüm (.—.) تصادم A *lrnd.* a colliding and striking against each other; collision, shock.
— **et=** to collide with one another. —**ât** (.—.—) A collisions.

tesagur (.—.) تصاغر A *lrnd.* a debasing oneself; a becoming contemptible.

tesahhun تسخن A *lrnd.* a becoming warm or hot.

tesahhur 1 تسخر A *lrnd.* 1. a mocking and making fun. 2. a making one work, an oppressing. — **et=** /ı/ to mock and make fun of.

tesahhur 2 تسحر A *lrnd.* a taking the supplementary meal called **sahur** before dawn during the Ramazan fast.

tesahub (.—.) تصاحب A a making oneself owner; a becoming a patron or protector. — **et=** /a/ 1. to take possession (of); to support, protect. 2. /a/ to claim to be the owner or the author (of). —**ât** (.—.—) A *pl.*

tesahül (.—.) تساهل A *lrnd.* 1. an acting indulgently towards one another. 2. a pretending to be easy and indulgent; a being careless or negligent. 3. an expressing oneself somewhat carelessly or ambiguously in dependence on information possessed by the person addressed. —**ât** (.—.—) A *pl.*

tesahüm (.—.) تساهم A *lrnd.* 1. a casting lots. 2. a mutually taking shares of a thing.

tesakkub تثقب A *lrnd.* a being pierced, perforated, worm-eaten. —**i lülü** perforation of pearls. —**ât** (...—) A *pl.*

tesakkuf تثقف A *lrnd.* 1. a being roofed or ceiled. 2. a becoming bishop.

tesakul^(lü) (.—.) تثاقل A *lrnd.* a being averse, a hanging back from; sluggishness; aversion.

tesakut (.—.) تساقط A *lrnd.* 1. a falling; a fall. 2. a falling gradually. 3. a throwing oneself on a person or thing. 4. a becoming of no effect, void.

tesakür (.—.) تساكر A *lrnd.* a feigning drunkenness.

tesaluh 1 تصالح A *lrnd.* a being reconciled together; mutual reconciliation.

tesaluh 2 تصالخ A *lrnd.* a pretending to be deaf.

tesalüb (.—.) تصالب A 1. *anat.* chiasma. 2. *lrnd.* cross-breeding. — **ettir=** /ı/ to cross-breed.

tesalüf (.—.) تصالف A *lrnd.* a being connected by affinity (as the husbands of two sisters).

tesalüm (.—.) تسالم A *lrnd.* a becoming at peace with one another, a being reconciled; mutual amity, concord.

tesami (.—.) تسامي A *lrnd.* 1. a contending for pre-eminence. 2. a being high or exalted.

tesamuᵘᵘ (.—.) تسامع A *lrnd.* 1. a mutually hearing of a person or thing from one another; a being generally heard of and notorious among the people. 2. a pretending to listen.

tesamuh, tesamüh (.—.) تسامح A 1. *lrnd.* an acting with feigned blindness to each other's shortcomings; condonation; tolerance. 2. *rhet.* a using allusive or deficient expressions or language through dependence on information possessed by the person addressed; looseness, ambiguity of expression. **—ât** (.—.—) A *pl.*

tesanüd (.—.) A, **tesanüt**ᵈᵘ تسانـد mutual support; cooperation; solidarity. **—iyc, —cülük** *phil.* solidarism.

tesarif (.——) تصاريف A *lrnd.* absolute commands; revolutions; changes, vicissitudes. **—i dehr** the world's circumstances.

tesaru'ᵘᵘ (.—.) تسارع A *lrnd.* a competing to be quick or quickest in some act.

tesaud تصاعد A 1. *lrnd.* an ascending. 2. *phys., chem.* sublimation.

tesaur تسعر A *lrnd.* a fire's blazing.

tesaüb (.—.) تثاؤب A *lrnd.* 1. a yawning; gape, yawn. 2. a being dronish, sluggish.

tesaül (.—.) تسائل A *lrnd.* 1. an asking one another. 2. a jointly asking or begging of another. **T— Suresi** *a name of the seventy-eighth sura of the Quran.*

tesavi (.——) تساوي A *lrnd.* a being equal to one another; equality, parity. **—i leyl ü nehar** *astr.* the equinox. **—i kuva** equality of powers. **—i nâkızeyn** *log.* antinomy.

tesayüf (.—.) تسايف A *lrnd.* a fighting together with swords.

tesbiⁱⁱ (.—.) تسبيع A *lrnd.* 1. a making into seven. 2. a making of seven parts or ingredients; a dividing into seven. 3. a doing an act seven times or the seventh time. 4. a composing a poem in stanzas of seven couplets or lines. 5. God's rewarding good sevenfold. **—an** (.—.) A dividing into seven. **—ât** (.——) A *pl.*

tesbih (.—) تسبيح A 1. *same as* **tespih**. 2. *lrnd.* a declaring or singing the praises of God; a litany of praise to God.

tesbihât (.——) تسبيحات A *lrnd.* ascriptions or litanies of praise to God.

tesbihiye (.———.) تسبيحية A *bot.*, Meliaceae.

tesbikᵏⁱ 1 (.—) تسبيك A *lrnd.* 1. an offering a prize to be competed for. 2. a giving the prize to a winner. 3. a winning a prize.

tesbikᵏⁱ 2 (.—) تسبيك A *lrnd.* a melting gold, silver, etc. and casting it in a mold. **—at** (.——) A *pl.*

tesbil (.—) تسبيل A *lrnd.* 1. a sending. 2. a trailing one's skirt on the ground. 3. a devoting property to pious uses.

tesbit (.—) تثبيت A 1. a making firm, fixed; a fixing or establishing, a proving, a demonstrating; a making valid, real, true, right. 2. stabilization; fixation. 3. a hindering; prevention. **— dâvası** *law* declaratory action. **— et=** /ı/ 1. to establish, stabilize; to fix. 2. to prove, confirm. 3. *mil.* to tie down (enemy).

tesciⁱⁱ (.—) تسجيع A *lrnd.* a composing in rhymed prose. **—ât** (.——) A rhythmic prose.

tescil (.—) تسجيل A an inscribing in the rolls of a court; registration. **— et=** /ı/ to register, record. **—ât** (.——) A State Registries.

tescin (.—) تسجين A *lrnd.* a putting in prison; imprisonment.

tescir (.—) تسجير A *lrnd.* 1. a causing to flow forth; a filling with water. 2. a providing an oven with fuel, a heating it.

tesciye تسجية A *lrnd.* a characterizing; characterization.

tesçil (.—) تسجيل *var. of* ‹tescil.

tesdid (.—) تسديد A *lrnd.* 1. a directing, a putting in the right direction. 2. a saying or doing what is right. 3. a stopping up, a barring.

tesdis (.—) تسديس A *lrnd.* 1. a dividing into six; a making six or hexagonal. 2. *lrnd.* a doing six times or for the sixth time. 3. *pros.* a composing a poem of stanzas of six distichs or hemistichs; poem composed in this manner. 4. *astr.* a planet's being in sextile aspect with another; sextile aspect. **—ât** (.——) A *pl.*

tesebbüb تسبب A *lrnd.* a causing, an employing means. **—en** (..'..) A as a reason or cause.

tesebbüt تثبت A *lrnd.* a being firm, cool, deliberate; firmness, coolness, steadiness, deliberateness.

teseccüd تسجد A *lrnd.* a prostrating oneself in worship.

teseddüc تسدع A *lrnd.* a lying. a weaving falsehood.

teseffüh تسفه A *lrnd.* a becoming a spendthrift or prodigal; dissolution.

teseffül تسفل A *lrnd.* 1. a descending; a being in the meanest or lowest place. 2. a becoming very mean and vulgar.

tesehhur تسخر A *lrnd.* 1. a mocking and making fun. 2. a making one work compulsorily. **— et=** to make fun of. **—ât** (...—) A *pl.* **—kâr** (...—) P buffoon. **—kârî** (...——) P buffoonery.

tesehhür تسحر A *lrnd.* a being awake.

tesekkün تسكن A *lrnd.* 1. a being calm and staid; calmness, staidness. 2. a becoming humble and submissive; humility, meekness. 3. a being poor and lowly; poverty, lowliness.

tesekkür نَسَكُّر A *lrnd.* a becoming drunk.
tesellâ (..—) نَسَلَّى نَسَلِّى A *poet.*, same as **teselli**.
teselli نَسَلِّى A a being consoled, comforted; consolation, comfort. **— bul=** to console oneself. **— et=** /ı/, **— ver=** /a/ to console, to comfort (somebody).
teselliâmiz (..———) نَسَلِّى آمِيز P *lrnd.* consoling, comforting, consolatory.
tesellibahş (..—.) نَسَلِّى بَخش P *lrnd.* comforting; consolatory.
tesellinâpezir (..——.—) نَسَلِّى نَاپَذِير P *lrnd.* inconsolable.
tesellipezir (..—.—) نَسَلِّى پَذِير P *lrnd.* consolable.
teselliyab (..——) نَسَلِّى يَاب P *lrnd.* who finds consolation.
teselliyat (...—) نَسَلِّيَات A *lrnd.*, pl. of **teselli**.
tesellüb نَسَلُّب A *lrnd.* a widow's divesting herself of finery.
tesellüf نَسَلُّف A *lrnd.* a taking or receiving part or whole payment in advance.
tesellüh نَسَلُّح A *lrnd.* a putting on or wearing arms or armor.
tesellül 1 نَسَلُّل A *lrnd.* a slipping quietly away, a withdrawing.
tesellül 2 نَسَلُّل A *med.* a having tuberculosis.
tesellüm نَسَلُّم A 1. a taking delivery; receipt, taking over. 2. a taking part or whole payment in advance. 3. *lrnd.* a declaring oneself free from or unconnected with. **— et=** /ı/ to take delivery. **— tecrübesi** full-power trials (of a ship for delivery).
teselsül نَسَلْسُل A 1. concatenation; a following in a continuous series like the links of a chain; *phil.* an uninterrupted chain of events or existence of successive things without beginning or end; sequence of events; *log.* a never-ending chain of premises necessary to prove a proposition; *lrnd.* tradition's passing uninterruptedly from narrator to narrator; uninterrupted tradition. 2. *law* joint liability. 3. *lrnd.* an acting or happening in succession; continuous succession, continuity; an acting or happening through the various successive grades of a series or hierarchy. **— et=** to follow in an uninterrupted series. **—ât** (...—) A *pl.* of **teselsül**.
tesemmi نَسَمِّى A *lrnd.* 1. a being named; a naming oneself, an asserting oneself to be so and so. 2. a becoming high, exalted.
tesemmüm نَسَمُّم A *lrnd.* a being poisoned. **— et=** to be poisoned (inadvertently).
tesemmün نَسَمُّن A *lrnd.* 1. a becoming fat; fatness. 2. a becoming wealthy; wealth.
tesenni (..—) نَسَنِّى A *lrnd.* a being bent, folded, doubled back; bend, fold.
tesennüh نَسَنُّه A *lrnd.* 1. a becoming moldy and musty (as bread or wine, from age). 2. a turning bad. 3. a being old and feeling the effects of age.
tesennün 1 نَسَنُّن A *lrnd.* 1. an adopting a habit or custom, especially the habitual practices of the Prophet Muhammad. 2. a being an observer of the Prophet's practices, a being a Sunni.
tesennün 2 نَسَنُّن A *med.* dentition.
teserri نَسَرِّى A *lrnd.* a keeping a female slave as a legal concubine.
teserrü نَسَرُّع A *lrnd.* a making haste, a being quick.
tesettür نَسَتُّر A *lrnd.* a being veiled, hidden, shrouded; concealment. **— et=** to veil oneself; to conceal oneself. **—i nisvân** the veiling of women.
teseüb نَسَؤُّب A *lrnd.* a being sleepy, sluggish, languid; a yawning; sleepiness, languor.
teseül نَسَؤُّل A *lrnd.* an asking alms; a begging, mendicancy. **— et=** to beg (as a beggar).
tesevvi (..—) نَسَوِّى A *lrnd.* 1. a being straight. 2. a being level with anything (ground).
tesevvüb نَسَوُّب A *lrnd.* 1. a performing an act deserving of reward. 2. a performing a supererogatory service of worship immediately after the incumbent service.
tesevvüd نَسَوُّد A *lrnd.* 1. a becoming a master, lord, prince. 2. a marrying and becoming the master of a house.
teseyyüb 1 نَسَيُّب A *lrnd.* a showing carelessness, lack of prudence in conduct of affairs; negligence, slackness. **— et=** to act negligently or thoughtlessly.
teseyyüb 2 نَسَيُّب A *lrnd.* a becoming a widow; a being divorced.
tesfif (.—) نَسْفِيف A *lrnd.* a grinding very fine, a reducing into powder (medicine).
tesfih (.—) نَسْفِيه A *lrnd.* a charging with folly, calling one a fool or ignorant.
tesfil (.—) نَسْفِيل A *lrnd.* a lowering, a causing to get low.
tesfir (.—) نَسْفِير A *lrnd.* a sending on a journey or campaign.
teshil (.—) نَسْهِيل A *lrnd.* 1. a making easy to manage or accomplish. 2. a making even or level. **— et=** /ı/ 1. to facilitate. 2. to level. **—ât** (.——) A facilities. **—en** (.—'.) A making easy, accomplishing.
teshin (.—) نَسْخِين A *lrnd.* a warming, a heating. **— et=** /ı/ to heat. **—ât** (.——) A heating installation.
teshir 1 (.—) نَسْخِير A 1. a fascinating, enchanting; fascination; enchantment. 2. *lrnd.* a causing to eat the supplementary meal at dawn during Ramazan. **— et=** /ı/ 1. to

enchant, to fascinate, to bewitch. 2. *lrnd.* to feed one with the meal called **sahur**.

teshir 2 (. —) تَسْخِير A *lrnd.* 1. a conquering, a taking by conquest; conquest, subjugation. 2. a compelling to work gratis. — **et=** /ı/ 1. to conquer. 2. to compel to work gratis. —**ât** (. — —) A conquests.

tes'id (. —) تَسْعِيد A a celebrating; celebration. — **et=** to celebrate (a feast).

te'sil (. —) تَأْسِيل A *lrnd.* 1. a causing to increase or prosper; a causing to take root. 2. a rendering important; a strengthening; a being firm. 3. a supporting one's family liberally. 4. a being wealthy, prosperity.

te'sim (. —) تَأْسِيم A *lrnd.* 1. a charging, accusing, convicting of crime. 2. sin, voluntary transgression of the law of God.

te'sir 1 (. —) A, **tesir** (— —) تَأْسِير 1. a producing an effect or impression; effect; impression; influence. 2. a touching, a moving (one's feelings). — **et=** /a/ 1. to effect; to cause an impression on, to influence. 2. to touch, to move.

tes'ir 2 (. —) تَسْعِير A *lrnd.* 1. a fixing the market price of a commodity, a pricing. 2. a causing a fire to blaze; a kindling the flames of war. 3. a stirring up animosity; a rousing to wrath.

te'sirat (. — —) تَأْسِيرَات A *lrnd.*, *pl. of* **te'sir 1**, impressions; effects, influences.

tesirli تَأْسِيرلِى 1. touching, moving. 2 impressive. 3. efficacious, efficient.

tesirsiz تَأْسِيرسِز 1. ineffective; without influence. 2. free, without being influenced. —**lik** inefficacy.

te'sis (. —) A, **tesis** (— —) تَأْسِيس 1. a laying a foundation; a basing (a matter on something). 2. foundation; establishment; legally recognized organization. — **et=** /ı/ to found, to establish, to institute; to base.

te'sisat (. — —) A, **tesisat** (— — —) تَأْسِيسَات institution, establishment; plant (industrial); installations.

te'siye تَأْسِيَة A *lrnd.* 1. an administering consolation; an exhorting to patience. 2. a reconciling.

teskere تَسْكَرَه [**deskere**] 1. litter; stretcher. 2. hand-barrow; bier. —**ci** stretcher-bearer.

teskıye تَسْقِيَة A *lrnd.* 1. a giving to drink. 2. a watering or irrigating; irrigation.

teskib (. —) تَسْقِيب A *lrnd.* 1. a piercing, perforating; perforation. 2. a making a fire or lamp burn up brightly.

teskif 1 (. —) تَثْقِيف A *lrnd.* 1. a straightening with an iron wrench. 2. a disciplining, teaching, educating; discipline, education, instruction.

teskif 2 (. —) تَسْقِيف A *lrnd.* 1. a roofing or ceiling. 2. a making a bishop.

teskil (. —) تَثْقِيل A *lrnd.* 1. a making heavy. 2. a causing to become disagreeable, burdensome, sluggish. 3. a causing to become indigestible and heavy on the stomach. 4. *Arabic gram.* a reduplicating a letter; gemination; a marking a letter with a **teşdid** sign. 5. the orthographical sign **teşdid**.

teskim (. —) تَسْقِيم A *lrnd.* 1. a making ill. 2. a declaring to be defective.

teskin (. —) تَسْكِين A 1. a calming, pacifying, making quiet. 2. a relieving, assuaging. 3. *lrnd.* a causing to dwell. 4. *Arabic gram.* a making a letter quiescent so as to end a syllable. — **et=** /ı/ 1. to calm, to pacify; to assuage. 2. *lrnd.* to cause to dwell. 3. *Arabic gram.* to make a letter end a syllable.

teskir (. —) تَسْكِير A *lrnd.* an intoxicating. — **et=** /ı/ to intoxicate, to make drunk.

teskit (. —) تَسْكِيت A *lrnd.* a silencing; a striking dumb.

teslif (. —) تَسْلِيف A *lrnd.* 1. a breakfasting; a giving a breakfast. 2. a sending before; a paying before due or in advance.

teslih 1 (. —) تَسْلِيح A *lrnd.* an arming; a furnishing with arms. — **et=** /ı/ to arm.

teslih 2 (. —) تَسْلِيخ A *lrnd.* 1. a having an animal skinned, a flaying. 2. a making the skin peel off.

teslihat (. — —) تَسْلِيحَات A *lrnd.*, *pl. of* **teslih 1**, armament.

teslil (. —) تَسْلِيل A *lrnd.* a drawing (a sword).

teslim (. —) تَسْلِيم A 1. a handing over, a delivering; delivery; payment. 2. a giving up, an admitting the futility of one's own argument; concession. 3. a surrendering, submitting; surrender, submission. 4. *lrnd.* a saving, a freeing from danger; salvation. 5. *lrnd.* a saluting with the formula **esselâmün aleyküm**. 6. *Or. mus.* ritornello of a **peşrev**, instrumental refrain. —! 1. Hands up! 2. I surrender; don't fire! — **al=** /ı/ to take over, to accept, assume responsibility (for). — **bayrağı çek=** *colloq.* to surrender; to be willing to accept anything. — **et=** /ı/ 1. to hand over, to deliver. 2. to give up, surrender. 3. to admit (an argument). 4. to pay over (money). — **ol=** to surrender, give oneself up. —**i ruh et=** to give up the ghost, to die. — **taşı** stone worn on the breast by Bektashi dervishes. — **ve tesellüm** 1. the handing over of an office to a successor. 2. delivery and receipt of goods, money, etc.

teslimat (. — —) تَسْلِيمَات A *lrnd.* 1. installments (of money, etc.). 2. deliveries of goods. 3. *lrnd.* salutations.

teslimi (. — —) تَسْلِيمِى A pertaining to, of the

teslimiyet

nature of a delivery, payment, concession or benediction.

teslimiyet (. — ..) تسليميت A *lrnd.* submission; resignation; concession.

teslis (. —) تثليث A *lrnd.* 1. trinity; *Christian rel.* doctrine of the Trinity. 2. a making into three; triplication. 3. a dividing into three. 4. a boiling until two-thirds have evaporated. 5. an asserting that only Abu Bekr, Umar and Osman were rightful caliphs. 6. a planet's being in trine aspect; trine aspect. 7. *Arabic gram.* inflecting a consonant with the three vowels; a marking a letter with three diacritical points. **T— ehli** believers in the Trinity, Christians.

tesliye تسلیه A *lrnd.* an offering consolation, a consoling, comforting; consolation. **— et=** /ı/ to console, to comfort.

tesliyet تسليت A *same as* **tesliye. —bahş** P consolatory; that consoles. **—kâr, —saz** (...—) P consolatory.

tesmi[ii] (. —) تسميع A *lrnd.* a causing to be heard; a making known or celebrated. **—at** (. — —) A *pl.*

tesmih (. —) تسميح A *lrnd.* 1. a straightening. 2. an acting considerately or kindly 3. a being gentle and submissive (animal).

tesmim (. —) تسميم A *lrnd.* a poisoning. **— et=** /ı/ to poison. **—en** (. —'.) A by poisoning.

tesmin 1 (. —) تسمين A *lrnd.* 1 a making a unit of eight. 2. a dividing into eight equal parts; a reducing to its eighth part. 3. a making octagonal. 4. a doing an act eight times. 5. a composing in stanzas of eight couplets or eight lines. 6. a setting a price or value. 7. a making costly.

tesmin 2 تسمين A *lrnd.* a fattening. **— et=** /ı/ to fatten.

tesmir 1 (. —) تسمير A *lrnd.* 1. a making a tree yield fruit. 2. a tree's forming fruit. 3. a making wealth increase.

tesmir 2 تسمير A *lrnd.* a nailing, a fastening with nails.

tesmit 1 (. —) تسميت A *lrnd.* a praying for another to be rightly directed; an invoking mercy from God on one who has sneezed.

tesmit[tı] **2** (. —) تسميط A *lrnd.* 1 a hanging by thongs; suspension. 2. a stringing beads. 3. a repeating the same rhyme four times in a couplet.

tesmiye تسميه A 1. naming, a giving a name. 2. a pronouncing the name of God over a thing as a blessing; a saying "**Bismillah**." **— et=** /ı/ to name, designate. **— olun=** to be named, called.

tesnid (. —) تسنيد A *lrnd.* a supporting with props.

tesnim (. —) تسنيم A *lrnd.* 1. *w. cap., name of a fountain or river in Paradise.* 2. a raising into the shape of a camel's hump or of a mound. 3. a showing the shape of a thing in profile or section.

tesniye تثنيه A 1. *Arabic gram.* a putting a word in the dual number; dual number. 2. *Arabic gram.* a marking with two diacritical points. 3. *lrnd.* a causing to be two, a doubling; a dividing into two; a halving; a doing an act twice, a repeating; repetition. 4. *lrnd.* a judging to be two, especially a holding the doctrine of duality; an asserting that Abu Bekr and Umar were the only rightful caliphs. 5. *lrnd.* a praising, eulogizing. **—i tağlibiye** *lrnd.* a dual masculine used to represent both a masculine and a feminine individual. **— zamiri** *gram.* dual pronoun.

tespih تسبيح |tesbih| prayer beads. **— ağacı** Margosa tree, bead tree, *bot., Melia Azadirachta;* common bladder nut, Anthony nut, *bot., Staphylea pinnata.* **— böceği** woodlouse. **— çek=** to tell one's beads. **—li** 1. having a string of prayer beads 2. *arch.* beading.

tespit تثبيت A *var. of* **tesbit.**

tesri[ii] (. —) تسريع A *lrnd.* a hastening, a causing to go fast or faster; acceleration **— et=** to accelerate. **—an** (. —'.) A hastening. **—at** (. — —) A *pl.*

tesrib 1 (. —) تسريب A *lrnd.* a blaming, reproving, reproaching with severity; blame, reprimand, reproach.

tesrib 2 (. —) تسريب A *lrnd.* a sending.

tesric (. —) تسريج A *lrnd.* 1. a saddling a horse. 2. a putting right, an arranging. 3. an embellishing. 4. a concocting a lie.

tesrih (. —) تسريح A *lrnd.* 1. a repudiating, divorcing one's wife. 2. a letting cattle go forth. 3. a causing to go to some distant place. 4. a loosing or combing out hair. 5. a poet's correcting his verses. **—i lihye** a letting one's beard grow.

tesrik[kı] (. —) تسريق A *lrnd.* 1. a stealing. 2. a deeming or pronouncing one a thief. **—at** (. — —) A *pl.*

tesrir (. —) تسرير A *lrnd.* a gladdening, a giving joy. **— et=** /ı/ to gladden. **—at** (. — —) A *pl.*

tesriye تسريه A *lrnd.* a banishing grief from the mind.

testere ('. ..) دسته ره [destere] saw; handsaw. **— balığı** sawfish. **— burun** goosander, saw-billed fish-eating duck.

testi تستى دستى |desti| pitcher, earthenware jug. **—yi doldur=** *colloq.* to accumulate money, to get rich. **— kebabı** a kind of stewed meat. **—yi kıran da bir suyu getiren de** There is no difference between the one who brings the water safely and the one who breaks the pitcher *said reproachfully when a deserving person is no better treated than an undeserving one.* — **kırılsa da kulpu elde kalır** A wealthy person can still be prosperous even though he may undergo some loss.

testir (. —) نَسْتِير A *lrnd.* a veiling a covering, draping, concealing.

testle=ʳ *neol.* /ı/ to test.

tesviⁱⁱ (. —) تَسَوُّء A *lrnd.* a finding fault with, a blaming.

tesvib (. —) تَشْوِيب A *lrnd.* 1. a rewarding; reward. 2. a performing a supererogatory service of worship immediately after an incumbent one. 3. a making signals. 4. a muezzin's calling the people to worship; a proclaiming the commencement of worship to the congregation.

tesvid (. —) تَسْوِيد A *lrnd.* 1. a making a rough draft of a document. 2. rough draft. 3. a blackening. 4. a disgracing, a being a source of disgrace. 5. a making master or lord. — **et=** /ı/ 1. to make a rough draft. 2. to blacken. —**at** (. — —) A rough drafts.

tesvif (. —) تَسْوِيف A *lrnd.* a putting one off with promises, a delaying, procrastinating. —**at** (. — —) A procrastinations.

tesvig (. —) تَسْوِيغ A *lrnd.* an allowing, permitting; a giving, bestowing.

tesvigat (. — —) تَسْوِيغَات A *lrnd.* magnificent present, especially one made to kings.

tesvikᵏⁱ 1 (. —) تَسْوِيك A *lrnd.* a driving, urging, inciting to act.

tesvikᵏⁱ 2 (. —) تَسْوِيك A *lrnd.* a brushing, cleaning the teeth with a tooth-brush (**misvak**).

tesvil (. —) تَسْوِيل A *lrnd.* 1. a falsely representing a thing to be good; delusion. 2. seductive suggestion or representation.

tesvilât (. — —) تَسْوِيلَات A *lrnd* delusion, misrepresentation. —**a kapıl=** to be taken in by a false appearance or representation. —**ı şeytaniye** Satan's suggestions, seductions and temptations.

tesvir 1 (. —) تَسْوِير A *lrnd.* 1. a decking with a bracelet. 2. a building a wall around a town. 3. a raising to high office and dignity.

tesvir 2 (. —) تَسْوِير A *lrnd.* 1. a stirring up, an exciting. 2. an investigating, studying; investigation, scrutiny, study.

tesviye تَسْوِيَة A 1. a making equal or level. 2. payment, settlement (of an account). 3. arrangement; adjustment. 4. a smoothing, planing; a fitting. 5. free pass (railway, etc., given to traveling soldiers). — **âleti** leveling-instrument. — **et=** /ı/ 1. to equalize, level. 2. to settle; to arrange. 3. to smooth, plane. — **hududu** contour line. — **münhanisi** leveling curve. — **ruhu** spirit level. — **sabiti** *astr.* value of division. —**i turabiye** leveling of the ground.

tesviyeci تَسْوِيَجِي fitter; one who levels the ground. —**lik** *mech.* fitting.

tesviyehane (. — .) تَسْوِيَخَانَة P workshop where boards are planed.

tesyar (. —) تَسْيَار A *lrnd.* a sending (a letter). — **et=** /ı/ to send, transmit a letter.

tesyib (. —) تَشْيِيب A *lrnd.* 1. a causing a woman to become single again after marriage. 2. a woman's becoming single again after marriage.

tesyil (. —) تَسْيِيل A *lrnd.* a causing to flow as a torrent.

tesyir (. —) تَسْيِير A *lrnd.* 1. a sending a letter. 2. a causing to walk or move.

teşabüh (. — .) تَشَابُه A *lrnd.* a resembling one another; mutual resemblance; similarity. —**ât** (. — . —) A similarities.

teşabükᵏᵘ (. — .) تَشَابُك A *lrnd.* 1. a becoming interlaced. 2. a being mixed up, complicated and embroiled together.

teşacür (. — .) تَشَاجُر A *lrnd.* 1. a being interlaced like the branches of a tree. 2. a contending or squabbling together; squabble.

teşahhus تَشَخُّص A *lrnd.* 1. a taking form as a visible object; personification. 2. a form's being more or less upright and visible or prominent. 3. an identifying, particularizing. — **et=** to take concrete form; to take the form of a person. — **ettir=** to personify. —**ât** (. . . —) A personifications.

teşaki (. — .) تَشَاكِي A *lrnd.* a complaining to or of one another.

teşakkukᵏᵘ تَشَقُّق A *lrnd.* a being cracked, split or cleft.

teşakül (. — .) تَشَاكُل A *lrnd.* a resembling or conforming to one another.

teşarükᵏᵘ (. — .) تَشَارُك A *lrnd* a being partners; partnership.

teşa'şuᵘᵘ تَشَعْشُع A *lrnd.* a sparkling; a being brilliant.

teşatüm (. — .) تَشَاتُم A *lrnd.* a reviling one another; mutual reproach.

teşaub 1 (. — .) تَشَاؤُب A *lrnd.* a splitting into branches.

teşa'ub 2 تَشَعُّب A *lrnd.* a being forked or branched; a branching, a dividing into branches; ramification; bifurcation. —**ât** (. . —) A ramifications.

teşa'ulⁱⁱ تَشَعُّل A *lrnd.* a being kindled.

teşaur (. — .) تَشَاعُر A *lrnd.* a pretending to be a poet.

teşaüm (. — .) تَشَاؤُم A *lrnd.* a drawing an evil omen from a thing or event; a taking sinister omen.

teşavür (. — .) تَشَاوُر A *lrnd.* a consulting and deliberating together.

teşaytun تَشَيْطُن A *lrnd.* a deporting oneself like Satan by being stubborn, proud and headstrong.

teşbiⁱⁱ (. —) تَشْبِيع A *lrnd.* a being almost satiated; a causing to be satisfied by food.

teşbib (. —) تَشْبِيب A *lrnd.* 1. a poet's stimulating interest by commencing a poem with a lively description of youth; a praising the beauty of one's beloved; a composing love songs or erotic poetry. 2. amatory exordium found in pre-Islamic Arabic poems; exordium of any modern eulogium. 3. a stirring up a fire to make it blaze.

teşbih (. —) تَشْبِيه A *poetry* 1. a likening, a comparing. 2. comparison, simile; parable. **— et=** /ı, a/ to compare, to liken. **—te hata olmaz** only for the sake of comparison; let it not be misunderstood. **—ât** (. — —) A *lrnd.* comparisons.

teşbikᵏⁱ (. —) تَشْبِيك A *lrnd.* an interweaving, interlacing.

teşbir (. —) تَشْبِير A *lrnd.* a measuring; a defining.

teşciⁱⁱ (. —) تَشْجِيع A *lrnd.* a giving courage, an emboldening, encouraging; encouragement. **— et=** /ı/ to encourage. **—ât** (. — —) A encouragements.

teşcin (. —) تَشْجِين A *lrnd.* a making sad, a grieving.

teşcir (. —) تَشْجِير A *lrnd.* a planting trees.

teşdid (. —) تَشْدِيد A *lrnd.* 1. a making firm, hard or severe; intensification; aggravation. 2. a redoubling (of efforts, etc.). 3. *Arabic gram.* a doubling a consonant, gemination, the orthographic sign " ّ " placed over single consonants to show that they are to be doubled in pronunciation. **— et=** /ı/ 1. to intensify, aggravate. 2. to redouble (efforts, etc.).

teşebbüh تَشَبُّه A *lrnd.* a being like in form or appearance, a resembling, being similar; similitude, likeness.

teşebbükᵏᵘ تَشَبُّك A *lrnd.* 1. a being reticulated. 2. a being perplexed; intricacy.

teşebbüs تَشَبُّث A 1. a taking firmly hold of a thing; enterprise; effort, initiative. 2. a setting earnestly to work at a thing, beginning with determination to persevere; initiative. 3. an attempting; attempt. **— et=** /a/ 1. to set to work (at), to undertake; to start (an enterprise, etc.). 2. to attempt. **—i şahsî** personal initiative.

teşebbüsât (. . . —) تَشَبُّثَات A *lrnd.* enterprises; efforts; attempts. **—ta bulun=** to take steps towards (doing something).

teşeccüⁱⁱ تَشَجُّع A *lrnd.* 1. a proving oneself brave by acts. 2. a pretending to be brave.

teşeddukᵏᵘ تَشَدُّق A *lrnd.* 1. a twisting the corners of the mouth while speaking, a mouthing. 2. a babbling, prating (pompously).

teşeddüdᵈᵘ تَشَدُّد A *lrnd.* 1. a being aggravated; a becoming more violent or severe; aggravation; intensity. 2. a becoming or being hard; a showing severity; rigors, hardship. **—ât** (. . . —) A *pl.*

teşeffi تَشَفِّي A *lrnd.* 1. a returning to calmness of mind (after anger), a being placid, pacified. 2. a becoming healed, cured; a seeking a cure or remedy. **—i sadr** a calming down after revenge.

teşeffuᵘᵘ تَشَفُّع A *lrnd.* an interceding, an acting as intercessor.

teşehhi تَشَهِّي A *lrnd.* a wishing, desiring eagerly; a becoming desirous.

teşehhüd تَشَهُّد A 1. *Isl. rel.* a making a profession of religion by testifying to the unity of God and apostleship of the Prophet Muhammad; a reciting the ascription of praise to God which ends with the formula **eşhedü-en-lâilâhe-illallah**. 2. *lrnd.* a seeking martyrdom, a wishing to become a martyr. **— et=** 1. *Isl. rel.* to recite the profession of faith of Islam. 2. *lrnd.* to wish to be a martyr. **— miktarı** a very short time, an instant.

teşekki (. . —) تَشَكِّي A *lrnd.* a complaining; complaint. **— et=** to complain; to grumble.

teşekkükᵏᵘ تَشَكُّك A *lrnd.* a being in doubt, a doubting.

teşekkül تَشَكُّل A 1. a being formed; formation. 2. organization; association. 3. an assuming the definitive shape of maturity or perfection. **— et=** 1. to be formed; to be constituted. **—i müstakim nazariyesi** *biol.* orthogenesis.

teşekkülât (. . . —) تَشَكُّلَات A *lrnd.* formations; associations.

teşekkür تَشَكُّر A a giving thanks; an expressing gratitude; a feeling gratitude; a thanking. **— ederim** Thank you. **— et=** /a/ to thank; to give thanks.

teşekkürât (. . . —) تَشَكُّرَات A *lrnd.* thanks.

teşelşül تَشَلْشُل A *lrnd.* 1. a flowing or coming drop by drop (water). 2. a trickling with blood (sword). **—ât** . (. . . —) A trickles.

teşemmüᵘᵘ تَشَمُّع A *lrnd.* a becoming waxed.

teşemmül تَشَمُّل A *lrnd.* 1. a being covered, concealed. 2. a putting on a wrapper which encloses the entire body.

teşemmüm تَشَمُّم A *lrnd.* 1. a smelling, a perceiving an odor. 2. a sniffing at a thing in order to catch its odor.

teşemmür تَشَمُّر A *lrnd.* 1. a preparing for work, being ready for work. 2. a tucking up the garments preparatory to work. 3. a being tucked up (sleeve, skirt).

teşemmüs تَشَمُّس A 1. *lrnd.* a being exposed to the sun; sunstroke. 2. insolation.

teşennüc نَشَنُّج A 1. *path.* a spasmodic contraction of a muscle; spasm, cramp, convulsion. 2. *lrnd.* to contract. **—ât** (...—) A spasms. corrugation. 3. *lrnd.* a becoming hopeless (matter). **— et=** 1. *path.* to become spasmodic. 2. *lrnd.* to contract. **—ât** (...—) A spasm. **—î** (...—) A *path.* spasmodic.

teşennüf تَشَنُّف A *lrnd.* an adorning oneself with earrings.

teşerruᵘᵘ تَشَرُّع A *lrnd.* 1. a conforming to the canonical law. 2. a becoming, or pretending to be, learned in the canon law.

teşerrüd تَشَرُّد A *lrnd.* 1. a fleeing suddenly through fear. 2. a being singular, opinionated, wedded to one's own ideas.

teşerrüf تَشَرُّف A a being honored. **— et=** to feel honored. **— ettim** I am honored (to meet you). **—ât** (...—) A *lrnd.*, *pl.*

teşetti تَشَتّي A *lrnd.* hibernation; a remaining during winter; a wintering.

teşettüt تَشَتُّت A *lrnd.* a being disunited, disintegrated, scattered; dispersal; disorder, confusion.

teşeümᵐᵘ تَشَؤُّم A *lrnd.* a drawing an evil augury. **— et=** 1. to draw an evil omen. 2. /dan/ to consider something as inauspicious.

teşevvukᵏᵘ تَشَوُّق A *lrnd.* 1. a being eager, desirous. 2. a manifesting a vehement desire; a pretending to be eager or desirous.

teşevvür تَشَوُّر A *lrnd.* a being perplexed, vexed or ashamed at something said or done by oneself; perplexity, vexation, shame.

teşevvüş تَشَوُّش A *lrnd.* a being complicated and doubtful in its bearings; confusion, disturbance. **—i hâfıza** *psych.* paramnesia. **—i kelimât** *psych.* paraphasia. **—i teheyyüci** *psych.* emotional crisis. **—i zihnî** *psych.* mental obscurity. **—ât** (...—) A disturbances.

teşeyyuᵘᵘ تَشَيُّع A *lrnd.* a professing to be of the Shia sect.

teşeyyuh تَشَيُّخ A *lrnd.* 1. a being middle-aged or old. 2. a feigning old age. 3. an assuming the character of a sheikh, an elder or a learned man; ostentatious pretense to honor or dignity.

teşeyyüd تَشَيُّد A *lrnd.* a being firmly built.

teşfiⁱⁱ (.—) تَشْفِيع A *lrnd.* 1. an accepting the intercession of one person for another; an interceding for. 2. an admitting the right of preemption.

teşfiye تَشْفِيَة A *lrnd.* a treating medically, a curing **— et=** /ı/ to cure. **—i sadr et=** to feel happy; to make someone feel happy.

teşhir (.—) تَشْهِير A 1. a making public or notorious; a publishing. 2. an exposing to the public view; exhibition. 3. an exposing an offender by parading him about and proclaiming his offense. 4. *lrnd.* a drawing (of the sword). **— cezası** punishment of the pillory. **— et=** /ı/ 1. to make public, divulge. 2. to expose to the public view, to exhibit; to pillory. **—i silâh et=** *lrnd.* to draw the sword. **—ât** (.——) A *pl.*

teşhis (.—) تَشْخِيص A 1. a diagnosing a malady; diagnosis. 2. a distinguishing the form of a thing; a recognizing; recognition; identification. 3. *lrnd.* a personifying; personification. **— et=** /ı/ 1. to identify, recognize. 2. to diagnose (a malady). **— koy=** to diagnose (a malady). **—ât** (..—) A *lrnd.* diagnoses.

teşhiye تَشْهِيَة A *lrnd.* a causing to desire; a rendering desirable and appetizing.

teşhiz (.—) تَشْحِيذ A *lrnd.* a sharpening (a sword). **—at** (.——) A *pl.*

teş'ib (.—) تَشْعِيب A *lrnd.* a dividing into forks, branches or ramifications. **—ât** (.——) A ramifications.

teş'il (.—) تَشْعِيل A *lrnd.* a kindling, lighting.

teş'ir (.—) تَشْعِير A *lrnd.* 1. a communicating, a making known; a publishing, proclaiming; communication. 2. a leading about town and proclaiming as bankrupt.

teşkıye تَشْقِيَة A *lrnd.* 1. a rendering miserable; an overcoming. 2. a causing to become a brigand.

teşkikᵏⁱ 1 (.—) تَشْقِيق A *lrnd.* a splitting, rending violently.

teşkikᵏⁱ 2 (.—) تَشْكِيك A *lrnd.* a causing to doubt, a making doubtful. **—ât** (.——) A *pl.*

teşkil (.—) تَشْكِيل A 1. a forming, organizing; formation; organization. 2 a putting into a shape; a shaping. 3. *lrnd.* a becoming confused and dubious (matter). 4. *lrnd.* an assuming the ultimate shape of maturity and perfection. **— et=** /ı/ 1. to form; to organize, to constitute. 2. to put into shape.

teşkilât (.——) تَشْكِيلات A organization; reorganization. **—ı esasiye kanunu** *pol.* Constitution.

teşkilâtçı تَشْكِيلاتْجِي organizer.

teşkilâtlan=ⁱʳ تَشْكِيلاتْلَن to become organized, to organize. **—dır=** /ı/ to organize.

teşkilâtlı تَشْكِيلاتْلِي organized.

teşmiⁱⁱ (.—) تَشْمِيع A *lrnd.* 1. a waxing, a soaking with beeswax. 2. a causing to excel.

teşmil (.—) تَشْمِيل A 1. an extending; extension; generalization. 2. *lrnd.* a covering oneself up in a cloak or wrap. 3. *lrnd.* a going along quickly, a being quick, a making haste. 4. *lrnd.* a taking a thing with the left hand. **— et=** /ı, a/ to extend (to), to include.

teşmim (.—) تَشْمِيم A *lrnd., same as* **teşemmüm**.

teşmir (.—) تَشْمِير A *lrnd.* 1. a tucking up one's garments or sleeves. 2. a being ready, alert. **—i sâid et=**, **—i sâk et=** a being ready for some accomplishment.

teşmis (.—) تشميس A *lrnd.* an exposing to the sun, insolation.

teşmit (.—) تشميت A *lrnd.* 1. *same as* **tesmit** 1. 2. a frustrating, a disappointing; frustration, disappointment.

teşne تشنه P *lrnd.* 1. thirsty, parched. 2. longing for.

teşneçeşm تشنه چشم P *lrnd.* hungry-eyed; with eager eyes.

teşnedil تشنه دل P *lrnd.* yearning, longing (person). **—ân** (..—) P *pl.* **—î** (...—) P longing, yearning.

teşnegân (..—) تشنگان P *lrnd.* those who are thirsty.

teşnegi (..—) تشنگى P *lrnd.* 1. thirstiness; parchedness; thirst. 2. a hankering after.

teşneleb تشنه لب P° *lrnd.* thirsty; parched-lipped. **—î** (...—) P thirstiness; thirst.

teşnelik[ġi] تشنه لك 1. thirstiness; thirst. 2. a being desirous to do something.

teşni[ii] (.—) تشنيع A *lrnd.* 1. a reviling or upbraiding as foul; a slandering. 2. slander, taunt, reproach, blame. **—ât** (.——) A vituperations.

teşnic (.—) تشنيج A *lrnd.* a causing to contract as in a spasm.

teşnif (.—) تشنيف A *lrnd.* 1. a decking with earrings. 2. an ornamenting with flowers or flowery expressions.

teşnifsâz (.——) تشنيف ساز P *lrnd.* 1. who decks a girl with earrings. 2. who uses flowery forms of expression. 3. who decorates with flowers.

teşri[ii] (.—) تشريع A *pol.* 1. a laying down or setting forth the law, a legislating; legislation. 2. *lrnd.* a making a road plain. 3. *lrnd.* a making an animal go into the water to drink. 4. *lrnd.* a pointing a weapon at one. 5. *lrnd.* a composing with two or more rhymes in each hemistich or clause; poem, sentence or phrase with two or more rhymes in each hemistich or clause.

teşrid (.—) تشريد A *lrnd.* 1. a driving away; a causing to take flight and run away. 2. a making one notorious or exposing him. **— et=** /ı/ 1. to drive or frighten away. 2. to decry or expose.

teşrif (.—) تشريف A 1. a conferring honor or rank; an ennobling or exalting; honor. 2. polite visit, arrival; departure. **— buyur=** /a or ı/ to come to visit; to honor by visiting. **— et=** 1. to honor by one's presence. 2. /a or ı/ to come (to). 3. /dan/ to come (from). **— mi?** Must you be going so soon? **— nereye?** Where are you going?

teşrifat (.——) تشريفات A 1. ceremonies; ceremonial. 2. official etiquette, protocol.

3. *w. cap.* department of the Foreign Office concerned with ceremony.

teşrifatçı تشريفاتجى master of ceremonies.

teşrifatî (.———) تشريفاتى A *lrnd.* 1. pertaining to ceremonial. 2. *same as* **teşrifatçı**.

teşrih (.—) تشريح A 1. dissecting; dissection; anatomy. 2. anatomically prepared skeleton; any anatomical preparation. 3. *lrnd.* a cutting up much or into very thin slices. 4. *lrnd.* a minutely commenting on a literary work. **— et=** /ı/ 1. to dissect. 2. to examine minutely. **— ilmi** anatomy. **—i marazî** pathological anatomy.

teşrihât (.——) تشريحات A *lrnd.* dissections.

teşrihhane (.——.) تشريحخانه P dissecting room.

teşrihî (.——) تشريحى A anatomical.

teşriî (.——) تشريعى A *pol.* legislative. **— kuvvet** legislative power. **— masuniyet** immunity of legislators.

teşrik[ki] 1 (.—) تشريك A *lrnd.* 1. a making partner or sharer in anything. 2. a deeming anything as partner to God. **— et=** /ı/ to make partner, to associate. **—i mesai** cooperation, joint effort.

teşrik[kı] 2 (.—) تشريق A *lrnd.* 1. a turning the face eastwards; a tending towards the east, reaching into the east. 2. a being fair and beautiful. 3. a reciting the usual formula **Allahüekber** at the end of a service of worship and especially at the end of each service of worship during Kurban Bayram and on the day immediately preceding that feast. 4. an exposing flesh in thin slices to the sun's rays to dry.

Teşrin (.—) تشرين A *name of two months of the solar year.* **—i evvel** October. **—i sani** November.

teşt تشت P *prov.* basin, large basin.

teştit (.—) تشتيت A *lrnd.* a dispersing, separating, scattering.

teşvik[ki] تشويق A an urging, inciting to some act; incitement; encouragement. **— et=** /ı/ to encourage; to incite. **—i sanayi** *lrnd.* stimulation of industries. **—at** (.——) A *lrnd.* encouragements.

teşvikkâr (.——) تشويقكار P *lrnd.* encouraging.

teşviş (.—) تشويش A *lrnd.* 1. a confusing or complicating (a matter). 2. a disturbing, troubling, rendering uneasy and uncomfortable. **— et=** /ı/ to confuse, to disorder. **—ât** (.——) A *pl.*

teşyi[ii] (.—) تشييع A 1. a seeing someone off. 2. a following (a funeral). **— et=** /ı/ 1. to accompany (a departing guest), to see someone off. 2. to follow a funeral.

teşyid (.—) تشييد A *lrnd.* a building strongly and firmly; a strengthening, consolidating. **— et=** /ı/ to strengthen, consolidate. **—ât** (.——) A *pl.*

teşyin (. —) تشيين A *lrnd.* a subjecting to disgrace and dishonor.

tetabuu̇ (. — .) تتابع A 1. *lrnd.* a being consecutive, uniform, proportional, gradual; uninterrupted succession; uniform progression; proportional modification. 2. *rhet.* concatenation of nouns and adjectives.

tetabuk^{ku} (. — .) تطابب 1. *lrnd.* a conforming; conformity; accord. 2. *gram.* concord. **—i elvan** *biol.* mimetism. **— et=** /a/ to correspond (to), to conform with. **—at** (. —. —) A *pl.*

tetafful تطفل A *lrnd.* an acting as a sponging parasite.

tetali (. — —) تتالى A *lrnd.* a following in succession; succession.

tetanos (. .' .) تتانوز F *path.* tetanus.

tetarük^{kü} (. — .) تتارك A *lrnd.* a mutual forsaking or abstaining from; mutual abandonment or abstention.

tetavül^ü (. — .) تطاول A *lrnd.* 1. a lengthening; extension. 2. an oppressing; oppression, tyranny, usurpation. 3. an exalting oneself (especially from pride); haughtiness, arrogance. **—ât** (. —. —) A *pl.*

tetayür (. — .) تطاير A *lrnd* 1. a flying about in all directions (as leaves in the wind). 2. the clouds' overspreading the whole sky. 3. a volatilizing; volatilization. 4. a growing over-tall.

tetbiⁱⁱ (. —) تتبيع A *lrnd.* 1. a pursuing, following; a searching diligently, investigating, exploring. 2. a causing to be followed by others of a similar kind.

tetbib (. —) تتبيب A *lrnd.* a causing to lose or be lost, killed, destroyed; an injuring, destroying.

tetbin (. —) تتبين A *lrnd.* 1. a speaking or acting with critical acumen, a making a subtle distinction. 2. a being critically discriminating; shrewdness, sagacity, discrimination.

tetebbu^{uu}, **tetebbü**^{üü} تتبع A *lrnd.* a following up carefully, pursuing, studying or investigating; search, pursuit; study; investigation; research **— et=** /1/ to study, investigate.

tetebbuât (. . . —) تتبعات A *lrnd.* studies, scientific researches.

tetelli تتلى A *lrnd.* a following up with pertinacity.

tetellu^{uu} تتلع A *lrnd.* a stretching the neck and raising up the head.

Teter تتر A *lrnd.* the Tatars.

teterbû (. . —) تتربو P *lrnd., same as* **tetrebu.**

Teteri (. . —) تتری A *lrnd., same as* **Tatari 1.**

teterrüb تترب A *lrnd.* a being soiled with dust.

teterrüf تترف A *lrnd.* a being in ease and luxury.

teterrüh تترح A *lrnd.* a being sad or anxious; disquietude, unhappiness.

tetevvüc تتوج A *lrnd.* 1. a being crowned; coronation. 2. a putting on or wearing a crown. **— et=** to be crowned.

teteyi تتی *prov.* stutterer. **—len=** to stutter. **—lendir=** /1/ to cause to stutter. **—lik** a stuttering.

teteyyüm تتيم A *lrnd.* a being slavishly in love.

te'tid (. —) تأتيد A *lrnd.* a firmly establishing, strengthening, corroborating.

tetik^{ği} تتيك 1. quick, sharp, vigilant, agile. 2. nice, delicate, fine. 3. trigger (of a gun). **—ini bozma=** to keep a cool head. **—te bulun=** to be vigilant. **— davran=** to be quick, sharp in adopting a measure of offense or precaution. **—te dur=**, **—te ol=**, **— üzerinde ol=** to be vigilant.

tetiklen=^{ir} تتيكلن 1. to be on one's guard. 2. to become fine and delicate. **—dir=** /1/ *caus.*

tetiklik^{ği} تتيكليك 1. sharpness of wits, readiness against surprise; promptness, agility. 2. delicateness, fineness of workmanship.

tetimmat (. . —) تتمات A *lrnd., pl. of* **tetimme**, supplements; accessories; accompaniments; complementary parts.

tetimme تتمه A *lrnd.* 1. a necessary appendage requisite to completeness. 2. complement, supplement, addendum. 3. *Ott. hist.* school preparing for higher **medrese** education.

tetire تتره *var. of* **kitre**, gum tragacanth.

te'tiye تأتيه A *lrnd.* a causing to come; a making right, smooth and easy; a facilitating.

tetkik^{kı} (. —) تتقيق A *same as* **tedkik.**

tetliye تتليه A *lrnd.* 1. a following. 2. a following a service of devotion by a supererogatory service. 3. a reciting a portion of the Quran. 4. a performing.

tetmim (. —) تتميم A 1. *lrnd.* a finishing, perfecting, consummating; completion, consummation. 2. *lrnd.* a killing. 3. *lrnd.* a hanging beads or charms upon an infant. 4. *rhet.* pleonasm. **— et=** /1/ to complete, finish, consummate. **—ât** (. — —) A *pl.*

tetre تتره *var. of* **tetri**, 1. sumach, *bot.*, *Rhus cotinus*. 2. *same as* **tetrebu.**

tetrebu, tetrebuh (. . —) تترهبو P *lrnd.* joke, practical joke; a jesting, jocularity.

tetri (. —) تتری P *lrnd., same as* **tetre**¹.

tetrib (. —) تتريب A *lrnd.* 1. a soiling, sprinkling with dust. 2. a being or becoming poor. 3. a being very rich.

tetrif (. —) تتريف A *lrnd.* 1. a causing to be in ease and luxury. 2. a making luxurious, dissolute, proud, unthankful, disobedient and rebellious against man or God; a corrupting; corruption, perversion.

tetrih (. —) تَسْرِيح A *lrnd.* a making sad or anxious.

tetris (. —) تَتْرِيس A *lrnd.* a making one arm himself with a shield.

tetsiⁱⁱ (. —) تَتْسِيع A *lrnd.* a making a thing nine or nine parts; a dividing into nine parts.

tetvibe تَتْوِبَة A *lrnd.* 1. a repenting of sin, a turning to God; repentance. 2. God's accepting repentance.

tetvic (. —) تَتْوِيج A *lrnd.* 1. a crowning; coronation. 2. an investing one with any head-covering or ornament. — **et**= /ı/ to crown. —**ât** (. — —) A *pl.*

tetvih (. —) تَتْوِيه A *lrnd.* 1. a turning one from the right way, a causing to lose the way. 2. a killing.

tetyim (. —) تَتْيِيم A *lrnd.* an enslaving through love, a making inextricably involved.

tev تَو P *lrnd.* 1. heat, warmth. 2. light. 3. fold; coat; stratum.

tevabiⁱⁱ (. —.) تَوَابِع *lrnd., pl. of* **tabi 1**, 1. followers. 2. dependents; dependencies. 3. consequences. 4. words not in use by themselves but always following certain other words, *as in* **ev bark**. —**i ayyuk** the stars β, ، ، ، Aurigae.

tevabil (. —.) تَوَابِل A *lrnd.* spices, seasoning used in cooking.

tevabit (. — —) تَوَابِيت A *lrnd., pl. of* **tabut**.

tevacüd (. —.) تَوَاجُد A *lrnd.* a saint's being in ecstasy; ecstasy; rapture.

tevacüh (. —.) تَوَاجُه A *lrnd.* a being face to face.

tevadᵈᵈⁱ (. —) تَوَادّ A *lrnd.* a loving one another; mutual affection.

tevaduᵘᵘ (. —.) تَوَادُع A *lrnd.* 1. a making peace with one another; reconciliation. 2. a saying good-bye to each other.

tevafi (. —.) تَوَافِى A *lrnd.* 1. an acting towards each other as is required; mutual faithfulness. 2. a company's being complete and all present.

tevafukᵏᵘ (. —.) تَوَافُق A *lrnd.* 1. a being in agreement with one another; agreement; compatibility; conformity; congruence. 2. a having a common measure greater than unity (numbers); commensurability. — **et**= /a/ to agree (with), conform (to), correspond (to). —**at** (. — . —) A *pl.*

tevafür (. —.) تَوَافُر A *lrnd.* a being abundant, a becoming multitudinous. —**ât** (. — . —) A *pl.*

tevaggulˡᵘ (. —.) تَوَغُّل A *lrnd.* 1. a being preoccupied with something. 2. a going away to a great distance. — **et**= /la/ to be engrossed in. —**ât** (. . . —) A preoccupations.

tevahhud تَوَحُّد A *lrnd.* 1. a being single, sole, unique, unparalleled; unity. 2. a being without a companion; isolation.

tevahhuş تَوَحُّش A *lrnd.* 1. a being frightened; a being wild and timid (like a wild animal); fright; timidity. 2. a being vacant and desolate; solitude. — **et**= to be frightened and wild.

tevakan (. . —) تَوَقَان A *lrnd.* a desiring ardently; desire. —**i nefs** lusts of the flesh, longing of the carnal man.

tevakiⁱⁱ (. . —) تَوَاقِيع A *lrnd., pl. of* **tevki**.

tevakki تَوَقِّى A *lrnd.* a taking care of oneself; a being on one's guard against something; caution. — **et**= /dan/ to beware of.

tevakkuᵘᵘ تَوَقُّع A *lrnd.* an expecting anything to be done or to happen; expectation, hope. — **et**= to look forward to the occurrence of an event. —**ât** (. . . —) A expectations.

tevakkud تَوَقُّد A *lrnd.* a fire's burning, blazing.

tevakkuf تَوَقُّف A 1. a stopping, standing still. 2. a tarrying, staying, sojourning in a place; stay, sojourn. 3. *lrnd.* a depending on something. — **et**= 1. to stop, to stay. 2. *lrnd.* /a/ to depend on, to require (thought, time, etc.). — **mahalli** stopping place (streetcar). —**ât** (. . . —) A stops.

tevakkur تَوَقُّر A *lrnd.* a being modest, sedate, grave; gravity, sedateness; dignity, honor.

tevakuᵘᵘ (. —.) تَوَاقُع A *lrnd.* 1. a successively falling, a being precipitated in succession. 2. a successively happening; succession.

tevakuf (. —.) تَوَاقُف A *lrnd.* a standing opposite or opposed to each other.

tevakuh (. —.) تَوَاقُح A *lrnd.* 1. a being proud, arrogant; pride, arrogance. 2. a being obstinately perverse; obstinate perversity.

tevakül (. —.) تَوَاكُل A *lrnd.* a deputing one another to act as agent or representative of each other.

tevakül-ül kavaim (. — . . . . —.) تَوَاكُل القَوَائِم A *lrnd.* a horse's legs' refusing each to act and deputing its duty to its fellow, a putting duty upon one who is hardly able to do it.

tevali (. —.) تَوَالِى A *lrnd.* a following or being behind each other in succession; uninterrupted series and succession — **et**= to follow in uninterrupted succession. — **üzere** in an uninterrupted series, successively.

tevalüd تَوَالُد A *lrnd.* a generating one another; a begetting; generation.

tevan (. —) تَوَان P *var. of* **tuvan**.

tevançe (. —.) تَوَانْچِه P *var. of* **tepançe**.

tevani (. —.) تَوَانِى A *lrnd.* an acting listless; listlessness, languor.

tevari (. —.) تَوَارِى A *lrnd.* a being or going behind something so as to be hidden; a concealing oneself; concealment.

tevarih (. — —) تَوارِيخ A *lrnd*, *pl. of* **tarih**, books of annals, histories. **— ehli** historians.

tevarüd (. — .) تَوارُد A *lrnd*. 1. an arriving; succession, arrival. 2. a coinciding; coincidence. 3. unintentional composition of the same verse by two different poets. **— et=** to arrive in succession. **—ât** (. — . —) A *pl. of* **tevarüd**.

tevarüs (. — .) تَوارُث A a successively inheriting; successive inheritance; devolution. **— et=** /ı/ to inherit. **—ât** (. — . —) A *pl. of* **tevarüs**.

tevasi (. — .) تَواصي A *lrnd*. an exhorting one another; mutual exhortation.

tevasuf (. — .) تَواصُف A *lrnd*. a describing, recounting or relating to one another.

tevasuk^ku (. — .) تَواثُق A *lrnd*. an entering into obligations, contracts or oaths with one another.

tevasul^lü (. — .) تَواصُل A *lrnd*. 1. a joining on to one another; conjunction. 2. a meeting one another; meeting; union, reunion. 3. a becoming friends with each other, concord. **—ât** (. — . —) A *pl*.

tevasüb (. — .) تَواثُب A *lrnd*. a springing up and attacking one another.

tevatu^uu (. — .) تَواطُؤ A *lrnd*. 1. an agreeing and consenting together. 2. a mutually coinciding.

tevatuh (. — .) تَواطُح A *lrnd*. people's quarreling or fighting with one another.

tevatus (. — .) تَواطُس A *lrnd*. 1. *same as* **tevatuh**. 2. waves dashing against each other.

tevatür (. — .) تَواتُر A 1. hearsay, generally current report. 2. *lrnd*. consensus of various reporters of a tradition; something confirmed, unanimous report. 3. *lrnd*. a continual cropping up of successive acts or events with slight intervals; a following in succession; succession, continuation. **— et=** to be talked of in public and always in one sense. **— ile malûm ol=** to be known by a general consensus of reporters. **—i nefes** difficulty of breathing; panting, gasping. **— olunduğuna göre** according to general report. **—ât** (. — . —) A *pl of* **tevatür**.

tevatüren (. —' . .) تَواتُراً A *lrnd*. by common report. **— sabit** known to all.

tevaud 1 (. — .) تَواعُد A *lrnd*. a making promises to one another.

teva'ud 2 تَوَعُّد A *lrnd*. threatening, menacing, terrifying.

teva'ur تَوَعُّر A *lrnd*. 1. a being difficult to deal with or bear. 2. a being perplexed through not properly understanding what is said; perplexity, embarrassment.

tevazi (. — .) تَوازي A *lrnd*. 1. a being side by side on the same line. 2. a being parallel to one another; parallelism.

tevazu^uu (. — .) تَواضُع A a humbling oneself; humility; modesty, lack of conceit. **—ât** (. — . —) A *lrnd*., *pl*.

tevazukâr (. — . —) تَواضُعكار P *lrnd*. modest. **—âne** (. — . — .) P *lrnd*. modest; modestly. **—î** (. — . — —) P, **—lık** modesty.

tevazün (. — .) تَوازُن A *lrnd*. a being of equal weight, equilibrium. **— et=** to balance one another.

tevazüniyat (. — . . —) تَوازُنيات A *phys*. statics.

tevazzu^uu تَوَضُّؤ A *lrnd*. a performing a Muslim canonical ablution.

tevazzuh تَوَضُّح A *same as* **tavazzuh**.

tevb تَوب A *lrnd*. a repenting of and renouncing sin, a returning to God.

tevbe تَوبة A *lrnd*., *same as* **tövbe**.

tevbih (. — .) تَوبيخ A *lrnd*. a scolding, blaming, reprimanding; rebuke, reprimand. **— et=** /ı/ to rebuke, reprimand. **—ât** (. — —) A *pl. of* **tevbih**.

tevbihen (. —'.) تَوبيخاً A *lrnd*. rebuking.

tevbihkâr (. — —) تَوبيخكار P *lrnd*. reproachful.

tevcib (. — .) تَوجيب A *lrnd*. 1. a causing to be incumbent and obligatory. 2. a holding or pronouncing obligatory.

tevcih (. — .) تَوجيه A 1. a turning or directing toward. 2. a conferring an office; appointment. 3. *lrnd*. an explaining or accounting for. 4. *rhet*. a composing a phrase that will admit of opposite explanations; a speaking ambiguously; ambiguity. 5. *lrnd*. a fastening on an expression of an adversary in order to controvert or modify it. 6. *lrnd*. an attributing actions as they naturally occur in fact. **— et=** /a/ 1. to turn towards. 2. to direct one's words or looks towards. 3. to confer (an office or rank). 4. to nominate. **—i muhal** *rhet*. a making the impossible occur in a composition. **— olun=** to be awarded (a decoration or post of honor). **—i vaki** a using personification in accordance with actual fact.

tevcihât (. — — .) تَوجيهات A *lrnd*. appointments.

tevdi^ii (. — .) تَوديع A 1. a committing the custody and safekeeping of another. 2. a handing or giving over. 3. *com*. deposit, lodgment. 4. *lrnd*. a committing to the protection of God when parting, a saying good-by. **— et=** /ı, a/ 1. to entrust (an affair or secret). 2. to deposit (money). 3. to commit to the charge of another. 4. to present, tender. 5. *lrnd*. to bid good-by. **T— Sûresi** a name of the 110th sura of the Quran.

tevdiat (. . —) تَوديعات A *lrnd*. deposits (in a bank, etc.).

tevdien (. —' .) تَوديعاً A *lrnd*. entrustingly.

teveccü^üü (. — .) تَوَجُّع A *lrnd*. 1. a being in pain; suffering. 2. a feeling sorry for another. **—ât** (. . . —) A *pl*.

teveccüd نوجّد A *lrnd.* 1. a becoming spiritually enraptured; ecstasy. 2. a being grieved or anxious. 3. a being in suffering and uneasiness.

teveccüh توجّه A 1. a being favorably inclined toward; favorable inclination; favor, kindness, good will. 2. a turning towards; a looking toward; a going toward. 3. a turning the attention toward. 4. a turning in heart and mind toward God. 5. *lrnd.* a falling to the share of a person. —**ünüz** You are too kind; you flatter me. **— et=** /a/ 1. to turn (towards); to turn one's attention (to). 2. to face. 3. to fall to one's lot (duty). 4. to address oneself to God.

teveccühât (...—) توجّهات A *lrnd.* favors, kindness.

teveccühkâr (...—) توجّهكار P *lrnd.* favorable; kindly.

teveddu^uu توّدع A *lrnd.* 1. a receiving a thing committed to one's safekeeping. 2. a being bid good-by; a being committed to God's safekeeping.

teveddüd توّدد A *lrnd.* a displaying love or friendship; a gaining the love of another; affection, friendship.

teveffi توفّي A *lrnd.* 1. a receiving one's due in full; receipt in full. 2. a receiving to himself (as God the souls of the just).

teveffuk^ku توفّق A *lrnd.* 1. a being successful; success. 2. nick of time, favorable conjuncture.

teveffüd توفّد A *lrnd.* a place's towering, overlooking other places.

teveffür توفّر A *lrnd.* 1. a showing all respect and consideration. 2. a being abundant or numerous; abundance.

tevehhüc توهّج A *lrnd.* a fire's blazing up.

tevehhüd توهّد A *lrnd.* a lying with.

tevehhül توهّل A *lrnd.* a causing one to err.

tevehhüm توهّم A *lrnd.* an imagining, fancying; unfounded apprehension or foreboding. **— et=** /ı/ to imagine (something that is not there). **—ât** (...—) A *pl.*

tevehhüs توهّس A *lrnd.* a working with care and perseverance, a persevering in an occupation.

tevek^gi تيك دكك ديكك تكاك *prov.* vine stock; any slip or stock newly planted or about to be planted.

tevekkel توكّل [**tevekkül**] *colloq.* who leaves things to chance; resigned.

tevekkeli توكّلى [*based on* **tevekkül**] *colloq.* by chance; without reason. **— değil** It was not without reason that...; it was not for nothing that...

tevekküd توكّد A *lrnd.* a being firm, fixed; firmness.

tevekkül توكّل A a putting one's trust in God; resignation. **— et=** to put one's trust in God; to be resigned.

tevekküllü توكّلى who trusts to God in all his concerns.

tevekkültü alallâh (.... ..—) توكّلت على الله A I have put my trust in God. So help me God.

tevekkün توكّن A *lrnd.* 1. a building or taking possession of a nest. 2. a settling in a home.

tevelli تولّى A *lrnd.* 1. a taking a person as friend, protector or protegé. 2. an attending to anyone's concerns; an undertaking a matter. 3. a turning one's back on a person or thing; a turning back; a going away. 4. a becoming ruler or governor.

tevellüd تولّد A a being born; birth. **— et=** to be born; to arise or spring from. **—i mütevâli** *biol.* epigenesis.

tevellüdât (...—) تولّدات A *lrnd.*, *pl.* of **tevellüd**.

tevellüdlü تولّدلى born (in such and such a year).

tevellüh تولّه A *lrnd.* a being lost with wonder or perplexity; amazement. **—ât** (...—) A *pl.*

tevelvül تولول A *lrnd.* a raising an outcry; a making a great noise; clamor, hubbub. **—ât** (...—) A *pl.*

tev'em توأم A *lrnd.* 1. twin; pair; similar. 2. a fellow pearl or star. **—i muahhar** *astr.* Pollux. **—i mukaddem** *astr.* Castor.

tev'emân (..—) توأمان A *lrnd.* twins.

tev'emî (..—) توأمى A *lrnd.* twinhood, twinship.

tev'emiyet توأميت A *lrnd.* twinhood.

teverru^uu تورّع A *lrnd.* a piously abstaining from unlawful and doubtful acts; pious abstention.

teverruk^ku تورّق A *lrnd.* foliation. **—at** (...—) A *pl.*

teverrut تورّط A *lrnd.* a falling into an abyss; difficulty or destruction.

teverrüd تورّد A *lrnd.* an arriving; arrival.

teverrüm تورّم A *path.* a swelling; tumefaction; tuberculosis. **— et=** 1. to become tubercular. 2. to swell, to form a tumor.

teverrüs تورّث A *lrnd.* an inheriting.

tevessuh توسّخ A *lrnd.* a being soiled; dirtied.

tevessuk^ku توسّق A *lrnd.* 1. a being firm; immovability. 2. a trusting, depending on.

tevessü^uu توسّع A *lrnd.* 1. a being spacious, wide, extensive; extension, expansion; spaciousness. 2. a term's being comprehensive; comprehensiveness. **— et=** to expand. **—ât** (...—) A *pl.* of **tevessü**.

tevessüb توسّب A *lrnd.* 1. a jumping, springing, especially in attack. 2. a pouncing on spoil.

tevessüd توسّد A *lrnd.* 1. a leaning, reclining or lying on a cushion. 2. a studying diligently. 3. a going to sleep over a study through sloth.

tevessüen (..'..) توسّعا A *lrnd.* extensively.

tevessül توسّل A *lrnd.* an endeavoring to

recommend oneself to the favor of God. — et= /a/ 1. to approach; to have recourse to. 2. to take steps to, to have in hand; to proceed.

tevessülât (. . . —) توسّلات A *lrnd., pl. of* **tevessül.**

tevessülen (. .'. .) توسّلاً A *lrnd.* having recourse to; approaching.

tevessüm توسّم A *lrnd.* a figuring correctly to oneself, a forming a correct idea.

tevessün توسّن A *lrnd.* a stealing upon (a woman) asleep.

tevessi توشّى A *lrnd.* grey hairs' being sprinkled over one's head, beard, etc.

tevessuh توشّح A *lrnd.* 1. a decking, adorning with ornaments. 2. a wearing a sash or baldrick over one shoulder and around the body. 3. a girding on a sword. —ât (. . . —) A *pl.*

tevettür توتّر A *phys.* tension. —i a'sâb *med.* nervous tension. —lü having tension (high or low).

teveyyül توّل A *lrnd.* a lamenting; an imprecating, woe. —ât (. . . —) A *pl.*

tevezzüüü توزّع A *lrnd.* 1. a sharing out and distributing; distribution. 2. a being distributed and shared out. —î (. . . —) A *phil.* distributive.

tevezzür توزّر A *lrnd.* 1. a taking a burden on oneself. 2. a becoming vizier to a sovereign.

tevfakᵏᶦ (. —) توفاق A *lrnd.* nick of time; a favorable conjuncture.

tevfid (. —) توفيض A *lrnd.* a sending as ambassador or envoy.

tevfikᵏᶦ (. —) توفيق A *lrnd.* 1. divine guidance and assistance. 2. God's making one successful; a prospering; prosperity; success. 3. an adapting one thing to another; adaptation. — et= /i/ to adapt; to cause to agree. —ı hareket et= /a/ to conform to. — ver= to grant guidance and success (God).

tevfikan (. —'.) توفيقاً A /a/ in accordance or conformity with.

tevfikat (. — —) توفيقات A *lrnd.* divine guidance and assistance

tevfir (. —) توفير A *lrnd.* 1. a causing to become numerous or abundant; abundance, increase. 2. a respecting, a considering.

tevfiye توفية A *lrnd.* a paying a debt in full.

tevhid (. —) توحيد A 1. *lrnd.* a causing to become one; unification. 2. *rel.* a holding or pronouncing to be one sole and unique without a fellow, (said especially of God); monotheism; recitation of prayers and the monotheistic formula. 3. *lrnd.* a causing to become without a companion; a causing to be one sole. — ehli those who believe in the oneness of God, especially the Muslims. — et= /i/ to unite. —i içtihad *law* combining the legal opinions (of various legists together); giving a final award or decision. — ilmi study of monotheism. —i mesai cooperation. — mezhebi monotheism. T— Sûresi *a name of the 112th sura of the Quran.* —ât (. — —) A *pl. of* **tevhid.**

tevhidhane (. — — .) توحيدخانه P *myst. orders* great hall where the sema' is performed in some of the Mevlevi lodges.

tevhil (. —) توحيل A *lrnd.* a frightening, terrifying.

tevhim (. —) توهيم A *lrnd.* 1. a throwing into doubt. 2. a judging or pronouncing a person to have imagined a thing without foundation. —ât (. — —) A *pl.*

tevhin (. —) توهين A *lrnd.* 1. a causing to become weak; a debilitating. 2. a looking upon one as weak; a despising. —ât (. — —) A *pl.*

tevhiş (. —) توحيش A *lrnd.* 1. a causing to become timid like a wild beast; a frightening. 2. a making empty and desolate like a wilderness. —ât (. — —) A *pl.*

te'vib (. —) تأويب A *lrnd.* 1. a returning home. 2. a reciting the praises of God.

te'vid 1 (. —) تأويد A *lrnd.* a bending or crooking a thing.

tev'id 2 (. —) توعيد A *lrnd.* a threatening, menacing; threat, intimidation. — et= to threaten, to menace. —ât (. — —) A *pl. of* **tev'id.**

te'vih (. —) تأويه A *lrnd.* a crying out ah, alas!

tev'ikᵏᶦ (. —) توعيق A *lrnd.* a preventing, opposing, delaying; opposition, hindrance, delay.

te'vil (. —) A, **tevil** (— —) تأويل 1. an explaining a word or expression by some slight but real analogy; an explaining away. 2. forced interpretation. — et= /i/ to explain something away; to put a forced construction on.

te'vilât (. — —) تأويلات A *lrnd., pl. of* **te'vil.**

te'vilî (. — —) تأويلى A *lrnd.* explanatory; having the nature of a forced interpretation.

te'vilsiz تأويلسز that cannot be explained away.

tevir 1 توير *prov.* sort, kind. — türlü all kinds.

tev'ir 2 (. —) توعير A *lrnd.* 1. a causing to become difficult to deal with or bear. 2. a bothering, perplexing, embarrassing.

te'viye تأوية A *lrnd.* 1. a seeking a place of rest or abode, a going or returning to. 2. a sheltering; a taking one to a shelter.

tevkᵏᶦ توق A *lrnd.* a becoming desirous; a longing; desire, lust.

tevkiⁱⁱ (. —) توقيع A 1. *Ott. hist.* the Sultan's signature (tugra); imperial rescript. 2. *lrnd.* a causing to occur, a bringing about; an ordering. —i refi-i hümayûn the sublime signature of the Sultan. —ci *same as* **tevkiî**

tevkid 1 (. —) توكيد A 1. *lrnd.* a causing to become firm, fixed; an establishing firmly.

tevkid

2. *gram.* a corroborating a word by another word which adds to its force; word used as a corroborative.

tevkid 2 (.—) تورکیب A *lrnd.* a lighting a fire. —**ât** (.——) A *pl.*

tevkif (.—) توقیف A 1. a causing to be detained or kept in custody; a being detained; detention, custody; arrest. 2. *lrnd.* a causing to stand. 3. *lrnd.* the pilgrims' assembling and standing according to the rule at any one of the holy stations at Mecca. — **et**= /ı/ 1. to detain, arrest, stop. 2 to deduct (sum of money). 3. *lrnd.* to cause to stand. — **müzekkeresi** warrant of arrest.

tevkifât (.——) توقیفات A *lrnd.* 1. deductions (from wages, etc.); stoppages of pay. 2. arrests.

tevkifhane (.——.) توقیفخانه P place of custody of arrested persons, house of detention.

tevkiî (.——) توقیعی A *Ott. hist.* official who drew the Sultan's signature. —**i divan-i hümayûn** *same as* **tevkiî**.

tevkil (.—) توکیل A *lrnd.* a deputing a person as one's agent, representative or attorney. — **et**= /ı/ to appoint as representative, attorney or deputy.

tevkir (.—) توقیر A *lrnd.* an honoring, a treating with respect and deference; respect, deference. — **et**= /ı/ to show honor to; to treat with respect. —**ât** (.——) A *pl. of* **tevkir**.

tevkit (.—) توقیت A *lrnd.* 1. a fixing a limit in time for a thing. 2. a fixing the time for an occurrence.

tevlid (.—) تولید A 1. a causing to bring forth; a giving birth; production. 2. a causing, producing. 3. *lrnd.* an acting as midwife. — **et**= /ı/ 1. to create; to cause. 2. to give birth to. 3. *lrnd.* to act as midwife to. —**ât** (.——) A births.

tevlih (.—) تولیه A *lrnd.* a causing to be lost in wonder or perplexity.

tevliye تولیه A *lrnd.*, *same as* **tevliyet**.

tevliyet تولیت A *lrnd.* 1. an appointing a person administrator of an estate in mortmain; appointment of a **mütevelli**; office of **mütevelli**. 2. an appointing a person ruler of a province.

tevliyetname (...—.) تولیتنامه P *lrnd.* patent of appointment of a **mütevelli**.

Tevrat (.—) تورات A 1. the Pentateuch. 2. the Bible. —**î** (.——) A *lrnd.* biblical.

tevriiⁱⁱ (.—) توریح A *lrnd.* a causing to abstain or withdraw; an abstaining, keeping off.

tevrih (.—) تورخ A *lrnd.* 1. a dating a document. 2. a giving the date of. —**ât** (.——) A *pl.*

tevrikᵏⁱ (.—) توریین A *lrnd.* foliation. —**ât** (.——) A *pl.*

tevrim (.—) تورم A *lrnd.* 1. a causing a part of the body to swell. 2. a making angry. 3. a causing to become tubercular. —**i enf** (*lit.*, a puffing out the nose) 1. a being proud, supercilious; pride, haughtiness. 2. a putting one in a passion.

tevris (.—) توریث A *lrnd.* 1. a causing to become heir to another; a causing to be inherited. 2. a stirring up a fire.

tevriye توریه A *lrnd.* 1. a hiding one thing behind another. 2. a shielding, a protecting behind oneself; protection. 3. a using an ambiguous word (with the object that its more unusual sense shall be understood). 4. a striking fire from a flint. — **üzere söyle**= to speak in hints. —**li** ambiguous, containing hints.

tevriyet (.—) توریت A *lrnd.*, *same as* **tevriye**.

Tevriz (.—) توریز P *archaic, geog.* Tabriz.

tevsen توسن P *lrnd.* untrained animal, especially: wild, intractable horse.

tevsiⁱⁱ (.—) توسیع A an enlarging, extending; enlargement, extension. — **et**= /ı/ to enlarge, to extend. —**ât** (.——) A *lrnd.*, *pl. of* **tevsi**.

tevsi'a توسعه A *lrnd.* spaciousness, wideness, extensiveness.

tevsid (.—) توسید A *lrnd.* a causing one to recline on a cushion.

tevsih (.—) توسیخ A *lrnd.* a soiling, dirtying. — **et**= /ı/ to soil with filth.

tevsikᵏⁱ (.—) توثیق A 1. a confirming, proving. 2. a making firm or trustworthy. — **et**= /ı/ to confirm, prove; to substantiate; to prove by documentary evidence. —**ât** (.——) A *lrnd.* documentation.

tevsil (.—) توسیل A *lrnd.* 1. a striving to obtain nearness and access. 2. a seeking the favor of God by good works.

tevsim (.—) توسیم A *lrnd.* 1. a naming, a giving a name. 2. a branding with a hot iron; a marking in any manner. 3. the body of Mecca pilgrims having arrived at the time and season appointed. —**ât** (.——) A *pl.*

tevşiⁱⁱ (.—) توشیح A 1. *lrnd.* a putting a border as an ornament. 2. *lrnd.* a twisting cotton into a roll preparatory to spinning; a winding yarn about the hand before winding it on a bobbin. 3. *rhet.* a concluding a proposition with a general term (to which is added an explanation in particular).

tevşih (.—) توشیح A *lrnd.* 1. an attiring (a lady, etc.) in a sash or baldric worn over one shoulder across the body. 2. a composing with two or more rhymes in each hemistich or clause. 3. a commencing a clause or a distich with a word the sense of which determines the end of the clause. 4. a composing a piece in which the first letters of the several clauses or distichs form a word; a composing an acrostic. 5. a form in religious music. —**ât** (.——) A *pl.*

tevşikᵏ¹ (. —) تَوْشِيم A *lrnd.* 1. a cutting in pieces. 2. a dividing, dispersing, scattering.

tevşim تَوْشِيم A *lrnd.* a tattooing. —**ât** (. — —) A tattoos.

tevtid (. —) تَوْتِيد A *lrnd.* 1. a firmly fixing, driving in, as a stake, etc. 2. a being firmly driven in and fixed. 3. a becoming as stiff as a post.

tevtir (. —) تَوْتِير A *lrnd.* a stringing a bow.

tevvab (. —) تَوَّاب A *lrnd.* 1. who is much given to repentence, who turns often to God; penitent. 2. God (who turns from His wrath on the repentence of sinners).

tevziⁱⁱ (. —) تَوْزِيع A 1. a distributing in shares or portions; distribution. 2. delivery (of letters, etc.). — **et=** /ı/ to distribute. — **tablosu** *elec.* switchboard. —**ât** (. — —) A distribution; postal deliveries.

tevzig (. —) تَوْزِيغ A *biol.* a foetus' being fully formed.

tevzii (. — —) تَوْزِيعِى A *gram.* distributive.

tevzin (. —) تَوْزِين A *lrnd.* 1. a balancing. 2. an undertaking after mature consideration. — **et=** /ı/ to balance. —**i mesai** *phil.* socialization of labor.

teyakkun تَيَقُّن A *lrnd.* an ascertaining; an acquiring or possessing knowledge that is free from doubt; certainty; conviction. — **et=** to be convinced of (something), to ascertain. —**ât** (. . . —) A certain knowledge.

teyakkuz تَيَقُّظ A *lrnd.* 1. a being awake; vigilance. 2. a becoming watchful; watchfulness, caution; circumspection. — **et=** to be awake; to be on one's guard. —**ât** (. . . —) A *pl.*

teybis (. —) تَيْبِيس A *lrnd.* a drying; desiccation. — **et=** /ı/ to dry, desiccate.

teyebbüsˢⁱⁱ تَيَبُّس A *lrnd.* a drying, becoming dry. —**ât** (. . . —) A *pl.*

teyel تَيَل a felling on the edges of a seam; coarse sewing, tacking.

teyelle=ʳ تَيَلَّه /ı/ to sew coarsely, to tack. —**n=** *pass.* —**t=** /ı/ *caus.*

teyelli تَيَلِّى tacked.

teyelti تَيَلْتِى *same as* **teğelti.**

teyemmüm تَيَمُّم A *rel.* 1. ritual ablution with sand or earth in default of water. 2. *lrnd.* a looking longingly at something one cannot have. 3. *lrnd.* a forming a resolve. — **et=** to perform a canonical ablution with dust or sand. —**ât** (. . . —) A *pl.*

teyemmün تَيَمُّن A *lrnd.* a regarding as lucky. — **et=** to regard as lucky; to rejoice in something as a piece of good luck. —**ât** (. . . —) A *pl.*

teyemmünen (..'..) تَيَمُّناً A *lrnd.* as a token of good luck; as an act of piety.

teyessür تَيَسُّر A *lrnd.* 1. a being easy and facile. 2. a becoming attained or accomplished; achievement. —**ât** (. . . —) A *pl.*

teyh تَيْه A *lrnd.* 1. desert; deserted country. 2. a leaving or losing one's way.

teyha (. —) تَيْهَا A *lrnd.* vast and utterly desolate (land), trackless (district).

teyhan (. —) تَيْهَان A *lrnd.* 1. proud. 2. strayed, astray.

teyhur (. —) تَيْهُور A *lrnd.* 1. proud. arrogant. 2. sheltered, level spot. 3. cliff in a sandhill. 4. wave.

te'yid (. —) A, **teyid** (— —) تَأْيِيد A 1. a strengthening, confirming, corroborating; corroboration; confirmation. 2. *lrnd.* a helping, supporting; help, support. — **et=** /ı/ to strengthen; to corroborate, confirm.

te'yidât (. — —) تَأْيِيدَات A *lrnd.* 1. corroborations. 2. help, support. —**ı Rabbaniye, —ı samadaniye** *lrnd.* Divine aid several times afforded.

te'yiden (. —'.) تَأْيِيداً A *lrnd.* confirming.

te'yidî (. — —) تَأْيِيدِى A *law* confirmatory. — **muameleler** confirmatory acts

teyin تَيِين *prov.* squirrel, *zool.*, *Sciurus europaeus.*

te'yis (. —) تَأْيِيس A *lrnd.* a causing to despair. — **et=** /ı/ to drive to desperation.

teykiz (. —) تَيْقِيظ A *lrnd.* a waking; a making vigilant.

teymim (. —) تَيْمِيم A *lrnd.* a causing to perform ritual ablution with sand or earth.

teymin (. —) تَيْمِن A *lrnd.* 1. a congratulating or wishing luck. 2. a going to the right.

teys تَيْس A *lrnd.* he-goat; male ibex.

teysir (. —) تَيْسِير A *lrnd.* a causing to be easy of accomplishment, a facilitating. —**ât** (. — —) A *pl.*

teytim (. —) تَيْتِيم A *lrnd.* a causing to become an orphan, an orphaning.

teyun تَيُون *var. of* **teyin.**

teyyar 1 (. —) تَيَّار A *lrnd.* 1 that spurts blood violently (as a vein when cut). 2. that prances in going. 3. puffed up with pride.

teyyar 2 (. —) تَيَّار A *lrnd.* 1. waves, flow, flood. 2. movement, tendency. —**ât** (. — —) A *pl.*

teyze تَيْزَه maternal aunt. — **kadın** procuress.

teyzezade تَيْزَه زَادَه cousin (child of a maternal aunt).

tez 1 تَز [*tiz 1*] quick; quickly, promptly. — **beri*.** — **canlı** 1. energetic. 2. impatient; restless. — **elden** without delay, in haste; quickly.

tez 2 تَز F 1. thesis. 2. question, matter.

tezaccür تَضَجُّر A *lrnd.* a being oppressed and weary in mind, grieved, vexed or disgusted; vexation, grief, disgust.

tezad (. —) تضاد A *same as* **tezat**.
tezahhüf تزحّف A *lrnd.* a crawling gently along; a drawing near each other to battle.
tezahhük^{kü} تضحّك A *lrnd.* a laughing with effort or affection
tezahhül تزحّل A *lrnd.* a going away, receding, retreating.
tezahhür تزخّر A *lrnd.* a being full to overflowing. boisterous and agitated (as a great river in flood or the sea at high tide).
tezahrüf تزخرف A *lrnd.* an adorning oneself.
tezahüd (. —.) تزاهد A *lrnd* a shunning, an avoiding.
tezahüf (. —.) تزاحف A *lrnd.* a marching in troops to join one another.
tezahüm (. —.) تزاحم A *lrnd.* a crowding on one another. **—ât** (. —. —) A *pl*.
tezahür (. —.) تظاهر A 1. a being manifest, visible; manifestation. 2. *lrnd.* an aiding or supporting one another. **— et=** to become manifest, to appear.
tezahürât (. —. —) تظاهرات A public demonstration; ovation.
tezakir (. —.) تذاكر A *lrnd.*, *pl.* of **tezkere**.
tezakkum تزقّم | *based on* **zıkkım** | *joc.* a stuffing oneself with food (used ironically).
tezakür (. —.) تذاكر A *lrnd.* 1. a mutually discussing; discussion, conference. 2. a mutually calling to mind. a remembering one another; mutual remembrance.
tezamm^{mmı} (. —) تذامّ A *lrnd.* a dispraising or blaming one another.
tezamüm (. —.) تذامم A *lrnd., same as* **tezam**.
tezamür (. —.) تذامر A *lrnd.* an inciting one another to fight in battle.
tezarrub تضرّب A *lrnd.* 1. a hitting oneself often or violently. 2. a thing's agitating itself, dashing its parts together; agitation, commotion.
tezat^{dı} تضاد | **tezad** | 1. a being opposed, contrary or repugnant to one another; mutual opposition; contrast; contradiction; incompatibility. 2. antithesis. **— ve tevad** mutual enmity and mutual amity.
teza'ub تتعّب A *lrnd.* 1. a being quick; quick, lively. 2 a being angry.
tezauf 1 (. —.) تضاعف A *lrnd.* a being two or several-fold greater; a being doubled. **— et=** to be doubled; to increase. **—i şahsiyet** *psych.* dual personality.
teza'uf 2 (. —.) تضعّف A *lrnd.* 1. a becoming weak; weakness. 2. a showing weakness. 3. a deeming or treating one as weak.
tezaüm 1 (. —.) تزاعم A *lrnd.* a conversing together.
teza'üm 2 تزعّم A *lrnd.* an asserting falsely or erroneously; a telling a lie.

teza'ür تزعّر A *lrnd.* a being alarmed or horrified
tezavuk^{ku} (. —.) تذاوق A *lrnd.* a tasting, a trying by taste.
tezavüc (. —.) تزاوج A *lrnd.* 1. a giving and taking in intermarriage, a pairing together. 2. phrases, words or letters' pairing by resemblance of sound or shape.
tezavül (. —.) تزاول A *lrnd.* a vying with each other; competition, rivalry.
tezavür (. —.) تزاور A *lrnd.* 1. a visiting one another. 2. a turning away, a deviating; deviation. **—ât** (. —. —) A *pl.*
tezayüd^{dü} (. —.) تزايد 1. an increasing, growing; increase, augmentation, growth. 2. *lrnd.* peoples' bidding against each other at an auction, etc. **— et=** to increase, multiply. **—ât** (. —. —) A *lrnd., pl.*
teza'zu^{uu} تزعزع A *lrnd.* a being shaken, rocked or agitated; agitation, commotion.
tezberi تزبرى *prov.* 1. soon. 2. easily.
tezbib 1 (. —.) تذبيب A *lrnd.* 1. a violently repelling. 2. an exerting oneself to the utmost.
tezbib 2 (. —.) تزبيب A *lrnd.* 1. a converting grapes into raisins. 2. a foaming at the mouth. 3. the sun's turning red when near setting.
tezbid (. —) تزبد A *lrnd.* 1. a foaming or frothing. 2. a carding or ginning cotton.
tezbih (. —.) تذبيح A *lrnd.* 1. a slaughtering many. 2. a worshipper's bowing his head lower than his waist.
tezbil (. —.) تزبيل A *lrnd.* a manuring land.
tezbir 1 (. —.) تزبير A *lrnd.* 1. a writing. 2. a reading without hesitation.
tezbir 2 (. —.) تزبير A *lrnd.* a writing or inscribing. **—ât** (. —. —) A writings, inscriptions.
tezebbüd تزبّد A *lrnd.* 1. a foaming or creaming. 2. a foaming at the mouth. 3. a becoming angry. 4. a taking an oath without hesitation.
tezebzüb تذبذب A *lrnd.* 1. a being tossed about, a waving; agitated movement; confusion, disorder. 2. a being very uncertain; a being changeable; capricious; caprice. 3. a dangling and swinging up and down or to and fro. **—ât** (. . . —) A vacillations.
tezehhüd تزهّد A *lrnd.* a becoming ascetic, a leading a life of self-mortification.
tezehhür تزهّر A *lrnd.* a flowering; efflorescence.
tezek^{ği} تزك dried dung (used as fuel).
tezekki تزكّى A *lrnd.* 1. a being purified. 2. a thriving and growing. 3. a being very pious. 4. a paying the legal alms tax (**zekât**); an almsgiving.
tezekkür تذكّر A *lrnd.* 1. a talking over in consultation; discussion; consultation. 2. a

seeking to recall to mind, trying to remember. 3. a bearing in mind; remembrance. 4. a noun's becoming masculine. — **et=** 1. to discuss, consider. 2. to remember, to recall to mind. —ât (...—) A discussions.

tezellük[ku] تَزَلُّك A lrnd. 1. a slipping, sliding. 2. a being slippery; slipperiness.

tezellüc, tezellüh تَزَلُّج تَزَلُّح A lrnd. 1. a slipping. 2. a having one's foot slip.

tezellül تَزَلُّل A lrnd. a becoming humble and submissive; an abasing oneself; abasement. — **et=** to demean oneself. —ât (...—) A humiliations.

tezelzül تَزَلْزُل A 1. lrnd. a being shaken, convulsed, agitated; a quaking, trembling; agitation, commotion, convulsion; shock. 2. rhet. a changing the vowel point of one letter so as completely to alter the sense of the word. — **et=** to be agitated; to quake, to be shaken. —ât (...—) A agitations; shocks; convulsions.

tezemmül تَزَمُّل A lrnd. a wrapping, covering oneself up.

tezemmüm تَزَمُّم A lrnd. a dreading blame and reproach and so avoiding what may bring them upon one.

tezemmür تَزَمُّر A lrnd. a becoming angry and raising the voice in reproach

tezemzüm تَزَمْزُم A lrnd. a muttering; mutter.

tezenduk تَزَنْدُك A lrnd. a being a Magian or atheist; an entertaining heretical notions.

tezene تَزَنَه same as **tazene**.

tezennüb تَزَنُّب A lrnd. an imputing a sin or fault; a charging falsely.

tezerri تَزَرِّي A lrnd. a blaming, chiding, reproaching.

tezerv تَزَرْو P lrnd. pheasant. —î (.—) P manners and gait of a pheasant; pertaining to the pheasant.

tezevvuk[ku] تَزَوُّق A lrnd. 1. a tasting little by little. 2. an experiencing little by little. —ât (...—) A pl.

tezevvüc تَزَوُّج A lrnd. a taking a wife; matrimony. — **et=** to marry —**i harici** sociol. exogamy. —ât (...—) A pl.

tezevvüd تَزَوُّد A lrnd. a providing oneself with provisions, a laying in store

tezevvür تَزَوُّر A lrnd. a speaking falsehood in order to deceive.

tezeyyüd تَزَيُّد A lrnd. 1. an increasing, a becoming more. 2. an exaggerating in discourse; exaggeration.

tezeyyün تَزَيُّن A lrnd. 1. an adorning oneself. 2. a being adorned. — **et=** to adorn oneself.

tezeyyünât (...—) تَزَيُّنَات A lrnd. ornaments.

tezfit (.—) تَزْفِيت A lrnd. a painting over with pitch, a tarring, calking.

tezgâh (.—) تَزْگَاه [**destgâh**] 1. loom. 2. workbench; counter. 3. shipbuilding yard. 4. workshop. 5. machine-tool. — **başı yap=** slang to have a drink at a bar. — **kur=** 1. to set up a place of business or of work, a bar, etc. 2. to arrange a plot or intrigue.

tezgâhçı تَزْگَاهْچِي 1. one who works at a loom. 2. maker of looms.

tezgâhdar (.——) تَزْگَاهْدَار P one who serves at a counter, salesman, shop assistant.

tezgâhdarlık[ğı] تَزْگَاهْدَارْلِك service at a counter, assistantship at a shop. — **et=** 1. to act as a shop assistant, salesman. 2. slang to talk somebody around coaxingly or flatteringly.

tezgâhla=[r] تَزْگَاهْلَه /ı, a/ 1. to arrange or make ready to be worked at. 2. to fit out with the requirements for working; to equip, to set up in business. 3. to make ready —**n=** pass. —**t=** /ı, a/ caus. of **tezgâhla=**.

tezgâhtar تَزْگَاهْتَار var. of **tezgâhdar**.

tezhib (.—) تَذْهِيب A lrnd. same as **tezhip**. —ât (.——) A lrnd. examples of gilding.

tezhip[bi] (.—) تَذْهِيب |**tezhib**| a gilding; an inlaying with gold. —**çi** gilder.

tezik=[ir] تَزِك prov. 1. to run. 2. to go astray.

te'zin (.—) تَأْذِين A lrnd. 1. a proclaiming the call to worship. 2. a proclaiming publicly. 3. a granting leave, giving permission.

tezkâr (.—) تَذْكَار A lrnd. 1. a bearing in mind; remembrance. 2. a recalling to mind, reminiscence; mention. — **et=** /ı/ to call to mind, to mention.

tezkere تَذْكِرَه A |**tezkire**| 1. short note or letter; memorandum. 2. official certificate or receipt. 3. soldier's discharge papers. 4. biographical memoir. — **al=** to receive one's discharge papers; to be discharged (soldier). —**sini eline ver=** /ın/ to fire (an employee). — **mumu** soft preparation of wax used instead of common sealing-wax for securing letters temporarily.

tezkereci تَذْكِرَجِي 1. Ott. hist. official charged with the duty of writing official memoranda. 2. discharged soldier; reservist.

tezkerelik[ği] تَذْكِرَلِك 1. paper used for official notes. 2. soldier due for discharge.

tezkir (.—) تَذْكِير A 1. lrnd. a reminding. 2. gram. a making masculine. 3. lrnd. an admonishing, advising. —ât (.——) A remembrances; reminders.

tezkire تَذْكِرَه A lrnd. 1. same as **tezkere**. 2. reminder, memorial, souvenir. —**i evvel** Ott. hist. first secretary to the Grand Vizier. —**i sani** Ott. hist. second secretary to the Grand Vizier.

tezkiretülevliyâ (......—) تَذْكِرَةُ الأَوْلِيَا A lrnd. biography of the saints.

tezkiretüşşuarâ تَذْكِرَةُ الشُّعَرَا A lrnd. biography of poets.

tezkiye 1 تَزْكِيه A *lrnd.* 1. a purifying; purification. 2. a deeming or pronouncing good and righteous; praise. 3. part of the Muslim funeral ceremony where the Hodja asks the congregation to confirm the deceased's good qualities. 4. a giving or taking the legal alms or tithe of anything (so as to purify it for use by its owner). 5. an investigating the antecedents of a witness in order to know whether his testimony is receivable; a pronouncing a witness to be acceptable. 6. a causing to thrive and grow. 7. a fitting an animal for food by slaughtering it in a canonical manner. 8. "even" in the game of odd or even. —**si bozuk** who has a bad reputation. —**sini düzelt**= /ın/ to reform oneself. — **et**= /ı/ 1. to purify. 2. to clear someone's character. 3. to ascertain the antecedents and character of a witness. 4. to slaughter canonically.

tezkiye 2 تَزْكِيه A *lrnd.* 1. a making burn brightly. 2. a medicine's sharpening the faculties. — **et**= /ı/ 1. to trim (a fire or lamp). 2. to sharpen a faculty.

tezlen=ir تَنَ اْمْلَنْ 1. to become quick or hasty. 2. to make haste; to be impatient. —**dir**= /ı/ *caus.*

tezlikği 1 تَيْنْ لِك speed; haste; impatience.

tezlikki (.—) تَنْلِيسِي A *lrnd.* 1. a making smooth and slippery; a causing to slide and slip. 2. a sharpening, a whetting. 3. a polishing.

tezlil (.—) تَنْلِيل A *lrnd.* a causing to be submissive and humble; a humiliating. — **et**= /ı/ to humiliate, vilify, insult. —**ât** (.——) A humiliations.

tezmil (.—) تَنْمِيل A *lrnd.* 1. a wrapping up, a covering (another) in a garment. 2. a concealing, a hiding; concealment.

tezmim 1 (.—) تَنْمِيم A *lrnd.* a blaming much.

tezmim 2 (.—) تَنْمِيم A *lrnd.* a putting a leading rein on a camel.

tezmir 1 (.—) تَنْمِير A *lrnd.* an inciting by reproaches or taunts.

tezmir 2 (.—) تَنْمِير A *lrnd.* a playing the flute, a piping.

teznib (.—) تَنْنِيب A *lrnd.* 1. an adding an appendage or tail. 2. a making hang down like a tail. 3. a returning in a sort of appendix to matters previously treated. 4. appendage; addenda. —**ât** (.——) A *pl.*

tezniye تَنْنِيه A *lrnd.* 1. a committing adultery or fornication. 2. a holding or pronouncing one guilty of adultery.

tezrif 1 (.—) تَنْرِيف A *lrnd.* 1. a shedding tears copiously. 2. an exaggerating.

tezrif 2 (.—) تَنْرِيف A *lrnd.* 1. an increasing, an augmenting. 2. a being profuse or diffuse; an exaggerating. 3. a driving away, a repelling. 4. a driving in, an introducing or inserting.

tezrim (.—) تَنْرِيم A *lrnd.* 1. an interrupting, cutting short. 2. a cutting one off from good or prosperity.

tezrir (.—) تَنْرِير A *lrnd.* a putting buttons to a garment; a buttoning.

tezriye تَنْرِيه A *lrnd.* 1. the wind's blowing dust about. 2. a winnowing. 3. a sitting on the ground. 4. a praising.

tezvib (.—) تَنْوِيب A *lrnd.* 1. a melting. 2. an adorning with a forelock. —**ât** (.——) A *pl.*

tezvic (.—) تَنْوِيج A *lrnd.* 1. a causing to take a wife. 2. a giving in marriage, a causing to marry. 3. a coupling or pairing one thing with another. — **et**= /ı/ to unite in matrimony; to cause to marry. —**ât** (.——) A *pl.*

tezvid (.—) تَنْوِيد A *lrnd.* a furnishing one with provisions and necessaries, a provisioning, equipping.

tezvikki 1 (.—) تَنْوِيك A *lrnd.* a causing to be tasted or experienced.

tezvikki 2 (.—) تَنْوِيك A *lrnd.* 1. a gilding by means of quicksilver. 2. an ornamenting with a painted figure. 3. ornament; ornamentation in gilt or paint on iron or steel.

tezvika (.—.) تَنْوِيقَه A *lrnd.* a single ornament in gilt or paint.

tezvil (.—) تَنْوِيل A *lrnd.* an obliterating; an annihilating.

tezvir (.—) تَنْوِير A 1. a falsifying a narrative with a premeditated lie. 2. willful misrepresentation; falsehood, deceit. 3. malicious instigation.

tezvirât (.——) تَنْوِيرَات A *lrnd., pl. of* **tezvir**. —**ta bulun**= to engage in malicious misrepresentations.

tezviren (.—'.) تَنْوِيرًا A *lrnd.* maliciously, with falsehood.

tezviye تَنْوِيه A *lrnd.* 1. a causing to go into a corner, cell, hermitage or retreat. 2. an investing with the garb or shape of (so and so). 3. a preparing a speech in one's mind.

tezyid (.—) تَنْيِيد A an increasing; multiplying, amplifying; augmentation, increase. — **et**= /ı/ to increase, multiply. —**ât** (.——) A *lrnd.* augmentations.

tezyif (.—) تَنْيِيف A 1. a deeming contemptible. 2. a mocking, a vilifying, a satirizing a person; derision, mockery; satire. 3. *lrnd.* a falsifying, corrupting or tampering with a document or saying; falsification. 4. *lrnd.* a pronouncing a coin spurious or of bad alloy. 5. *lrnd.* a making, pronouncing or allowing one's blood to be shed with impunity. — **et**= /ı/ 1. to deride, caricature. 2. to hold in contempt. —**ât** (.——) A *lrnd.* vilifications.

tezyil 1 (.—) تَنْيِيل A 1. *lrnd.* an adding

an appendix or supplement. 2. *rhet.* an appending a clause to a sentence in the same words or sense in order to fix the attention. 3. *prosody* an inserting a letter of prolongation between two consonants of a final syllable. 4. *lrnd.* an adding a skirt or train to a garment. **— et=** /ı/ to add as a supplement or appendix.

tezyil 2 (. —) تَزْيِيل A *lrnd.* a separating, scattering, dispersing.

tezyin (. —) تَزْيِين A 1. an adorning, embellishing, decorating, beautifying; ornamentation, embellishment, decoration. 2. a being an ornament, beauty, grace, honor to a person or thing. 3. *lrnd.* a causing to appear beautiful, good, desirable. 4. *lrnd.* God's endowing a person with faculties, wealth, etc. **— et=** /ı/ to adorn, embellish or endow.

tezyinat (. — —) تَزْيِينَات A adornments, ornamentations.

tezyinî (. — —) تَزْيِينِى A decorative.

tı 1 ط name of the nineteenth letter of the Ottoman alphabet.

-tı 2 دى *cf.* -**dı 2**.

-tı 3 دى *cf.* =**dı 3**.

-tı 4, -ti, -tu, -tü دى attached to bisyllabic onomatopoetics ending in -l or -r, e. g. **gürültü, inilti, patırtı,** *forms a noun.*

tıbᵇᵇⁱ طبّ A *lrnd., same as* **tıp. —ı adlî** forensic medicine, medical jurisprudence. **—ı ruhani** *myst.* spiritual medicine.

tıbaᵃ¹ **1** (. —) طباع A *lrnd.* natural quality, property or constitution; nature, temperament, disposition.

tıbaᵃ¹ **2** (. —) طباع A *lrnd., pl. of* **tab 3**, natural qualities.

tıbaa, tıbaatᵗⁱ (. — .) طباعت طباع A *lrnd.* 1. a printing. 2. the art of forging swords or molding earthen pots.

tıbahat (. — .) طباخت A *lrnd.* cookery.

tıbakᵏ¹ **1** (. —) طباق A *lrnd.* an agreeing, fitting, matching, conforming to; agreement, conformity.

tıbakᵏ¹ **2** (. —) طباق A *lrnd., pl. of* **tabak 1**, 1. things which fit others; lids. 2. plates; dishes; flat, shallow vessels. 3. folds; strata.

tıbben (. ′.) طبّاً A medically.

tıbbî (. —) طبّى A medical; therapeutic.

tıbbiye طبّيه A medical school, college of medicine. **—li** medical student.

Tıbhane (. — .) طبخانه P *Ott. hist.,* name of the first medical school in Istanbul in 1827.

tıbkᵏ¹ طبق A *lrnd.* 1. thing exactly corresponding with another, a counterpart; match. 2. exact correspondence and coincidence.

tıbkan (. ′.) طبقاً A *lrnd.* as an exact counterpart; in exact correspondence.

tıfalˡⁱ (. —) طفال A *lrnd., pl. of* **tafl**, young and tender children.

tıfılᶠˡⁱ طفل *var. of* **tıfl.**

tıfl طفل A *lrnd.* 1. infant; child. 2. infantile person. 3. young animal. 4. spark of fire. **—i cihelruze** (*lit.*, infant of forty days) Adam (whose clay was kneaded forty days before being shaped). **—i Hindu** (*lit.*, child of the Hindu) figure of oneself seen reflected in the eye of another; pupil of the eye. **—i ma'sum** innocent child (not responsible for sin). **—i meşime** wine from a skin. **—i şirhare** suckling infant. **—i zebandan** intelligent child.

tıflâne (. — .) طفلانه P *lrnd.* infantile; in a childish manner.

tıfle طفله A *lrnd.* baby girl.

tıfliyet طفليت A *lrnd.* infancy, childhood.

tığ 1 تيغ [**tiğ**] 1. crochet needle. 2. bodkin, awl. 3. knitting needle. 4. plane-iron. **— gibi** slender but strong and active, wiry. **— kalem** graver, burin. **— örgüsü** crochet.

tığ=ᵃʳ **2** تيغمك *slang* to slip away.

tığla=ʳ تيغلامق 1. /a/ to lance (the skin). 2. /ı/ to pierce (with a needle). 3. /ı/ *slang* to slaughter (animal). 4. to give a piercing pain (wound).

tığteber تيغ تبر broke, bankrupt.

tıhalˡⁱ (. —) طحال A *lrnd.* spleen, milt.

tıhalî (. — —) طحالى A *lrnd.* pertaining to the spleen, splenetic.

tıhanet (. — .) طحانت A *lrnd.* occupation of a miller, grinding.

tıkᵏ¹ **1** طيق sharp noise from a blow of a hard substance on another, tick, click. **— tık vur=** to tap with a ticking sound.

tık=ᵃʳ **2** تقميق /ı, a/ to thrust, squeeze or cram (into).

-tık 3 دك *cf.* -**dık 1.**

=**tık 4** دك *cf.* =**dık 2.**

=**tık 5** دك *cf.* =**dık 3.**

tıka=ʳ طيقامق /ı/ to stuff up; to plug; to gag.

tıkabasa طيقاباصا crammed full.

tıkaçᶜ¹ طيقاج 1. stopper, plug of cloth. 2. gag. **—lı** plugged; furnished with a stopper.

tıkalı طيقالو stopped up, choked up, obstructed or plugged.

tıkan=ʳ طيقانمق 1. to be stopped up. 2. to choke; to be suffocated. 3. to lose one's appetite.

tıkanıkᵏ¹ طيقانيق 1. stopped up. 2. choked. **—lık** 1. a being stopped up. 2. a choking; suffocation. 3. *mil.* interruption of communications. 4. lack of appetite.

tıkat=ʳ طيقاتمق /ı, a/ *caus. of* **tıka=.**

=**tıkça** دكچه *cf.* =**dıkça.**

tıkıl=ʳ طيقيلمق to be crammed, squeezed, thrust into.

tıkın=ʳ طيقينمق to stuff oneself; to eat in haste; to gulp down one's food.

tıkır طقير 1. imitates a rattling or

tıkırda=

clinking or tapping noise. 2. *slang* money, coins. **—ına gir=** to take a favorable turn. **—ında git=** to go well (affairs). **— para** clinking money. **— tıkır** with a clinking or rattling noise. **— tıkır işle=** to go perfectly (clock), to go like clockwork. **—ına uydur=**, **—ını uydur=** to put into good order. **—ı yolunda** doing well, prospering; happy.

tıkırda=ʳ طیقرد امھ to make a rattling and clinking noise. **—t=** /ı/ *caus.*

tıkırdı, tıkırtı طیقردی a rattling or clinking sound. **—lı telgraf âleti** sounder (telegraphy).

tıkış=ʳ طیقشم to be crammed or squeezed together. **—tır=** /ı/ *caus.* 1. to cram into a small space. 2. to bolt (food).

tıkız طیقز 1. fleshy; hard. 2. tightly packed together.

tıklım tıklım طیقلم طیقلم 1. filled to overflowing; brimful. 2. crammed or squeezed together. **— dol=** to be crammed with people (bus, etc.).

tıknaz طیقناز plump, fat. **—lık** plumpness.

tıknefes طیقنفس 1. short of breath, asthmatic. 2. shortness of breath, asthma.

tıksır=ʳ طیقسیرمھ to sneeze with the mouth shut.

tıksırık⁶¹ طیقسیریق a suppressed sneeze.

=tıkta د قده *cf.* =dıkta.

=tıktan başka د قدن باشقھ *cf.* =dıktan başka.

=tıktan sonra د قدن صوکره *cf.* =dıktan sonra.

tıl طلع A *lrnd.* accurate knowledge, intelligence.

tılâ 1 (. —) طلا P *lrnd.* 1. gold prepared for writing or painting. 2. gold writing or painting. 3. pure gold. 4. gold coin. 5. gold thread.

tılâ 2 (. —) طلاء A *lrnd.* unguent; ointment. **— et=** to smear, anoint with an unguent.

tılâ⁽ᵃ⁾ 3 (. —) طلاع A *lrnd.* a contemplating, studying or learning; consideration; study.

tılâb (. —) طلاب A *lrnd.* a seeking; search; object sought.

tılâduz (. — —) طلادوز P *lrnd.* embroiderer with gold. **—î** (. — — —) P gold embroidery.

tılâkâr (. — —) طلاکار P *lrnd.* gilder.

tılâkârî (. — — —) طلاکاری P 1. quality, art and business of a worker in gold. 2. goldsmith's work; illuminated work in gold.

tılâlⁱⁱ (. —) طلال A *lrnd., pl. of* **tal** 2.

tılâvet (. — .) طلاوت A *lrnd., same as* **talâvet**.

tılel طلل A *lrnd., pl. of* **tal** 2.

tılısım طلسم *var. of* **tılsım**.

tılsım طلسم A 1. talisman, charm, magical spell. 2. remedy; means; strong influence. **— boz=** to break a spell. **—ı bozuldu** The spell is broken; he (it) no longer has any influence.

tılsımât (. . —) طلسمات A *lrnd.* spells, talismans; remedies. **— ilmi** *lrnd.* science of talismans.

tılsımlı طلسملی having a charm or spell; spellbinding.

-tım 1 دم *cf.* **-dım 1.**

=tım 2 دم *cf.* **=dım 2.**

tımar تیمار [**timar**] 1. any kind of care and attentive service rendered to a helpless or needy man or animal; attention to a sick man or animal. 2. dressing of wounds. 3. grooming a horse. 4. pruning of trees; tilling the earth, tending plants; agriculture. 5. *Ott. hist.* small military fief. **—da** *Ott. hist.* sent for medical care (a sick person belonging to the palace). **— et=** /ı/ 1. to groom. 2. to attend to what needs help or care. **— fırçası** curry comb. **— sipahisi** man-at-arms holding a **tımar** fief.

tımarcı تیمارجی 1 holder of a fief. 2. *obs.* attendant or nurse at a hospital. 3. groom or stable-boy.

tımarhane (. . — .) تیمارخانھ P lunatic asylum. **— kaçkını** escaped lunatic; crazy person.

tımarhaneci تیمارخانھ جی 1. a director, guard, etc. of an asylum. 2. person who has to humor a person who is mentally abnormal. **—nin gözü kör olsun** Damn the asylum guard (for letting you escape); you ought to be locked up!

tımarî (. — —) تیماری P *Ott. hist.* pertaining to the fief system.

tımarla=ʳ تیمارلھ to attend to what needs help; to clean, to feed, to cultivate. **—n=** *pass.*

tımarlı تیمارلی 1. cared for, cleaned, fed, cultivated, etc. 2. having a fief.

tımarsız تیمارسز 1. neglected; not cleaned; not fed; uncultivated. 2. having no fief; unprovided for. **— gez=** to go about in untidy clothes.

tın 1 طین a tinkling sound.

tın=ᵃʳ 2 طینمھ 1. to make a sound (usually used in a negative form). 2. to take notice, to notice, to say or do something expressive of attention or observation. 3. *slang* to disclose; to inform. **—maz melâike** *iron.* quiet, aloof; noncommittal.

-tın 3 دڭ *cf.* **-dın 1.**

=tın 4 دڭ *cf.* **=dın 2.**

tınab (. —) طناب A *lrnd.* 1 tent-rope; any rope. 2. tendon. **—ı subh** rays of the sun at dawn.

tınaz طیناز stack of hay or grain. **— gibi** a whole heap of.

tınbâr (. —) طنبا A *lrnd., same as* **tambur**.

tıngadak (. ′ . .) طنغ داق *colloq.* suddenly and with a ring or crash. **— düştü** It fell with a crash (pottery).

tıngılda=ʳ طنغلدامھ to tinkle. **—t=** /ı/ *caus.*

tıngır طڭر 1. tinkling or clanging sound of metals. 2. *slang* rich miser (as continually counting money). 3. *slang* stone-broke. 4. completely empty. — **elek tıngır tas** *colloq.* having hardly any furniture; bare and empty. — **mıngır** imitates the sound of metallic things knocking together. — **tıngır** 1. same as **tıngır mıngır**. 2. cash down. 3. completely empty.

tıngırda=ʳ طڭردامـﻚ 1. to tinkle, clink, clang. 2. *slang* to die. —**t**= /ı/ *caus.*

tıngırtı طڭردى 1. clinking, clanging noise. 2. noisy conviviality. 3. *slang* sexual intercourse. —**lı** clanging, noisy.

-tınız 1 دڭز *cf.* **-dınız 1**.

=**tınız 2** دڭز *cf.* =**dınız 2**.

tınla=ʳ طڭلامـﻚ to tinkle, ring, clink (metal, etc.). —**t**= *caus.*

tınnet طنت A *lrnd.* tone; timbre.

tıpᵇᵇ¹ طب |tıb| medicine, therapeutics.

tıpa (.ʹ.) طپا stopper, cork. —**yı at**= to go into a fury; to get mad.

tıpatıp (.ʹ..) طپا طپ exactly; absolutely. — **uy**= to fit exactly. — **yetiş**= to arrive exactly on time.

tıpırda=ʳ طپردامـﻚ 1. to make a noise as of drops falling. 2. to walk with little noise. 3. to go pit-a-pat (heart).

tıpırdı, tıpırtı طپردى the sound of drops falling or of light footsteps.

tıpır tıpır طپر طپر imitates the sound of drops falling.

tıpış tıpış طپش طپش imitates the noise of small steps of a child. — **git**= to walk with small steps; to go willingly. — **yürü**= to run about with a pattering sound; to toddle.

tıpkı (.ʹ.) طپقى |tıbk| exactly like; in just the same way. —**sı** exactly like it; the very image of. — **tıpkısına** *colloq.* exactly fitting; very similar. — **basım** *neol.* facsimile.

-tır 1 در *cf.* **-dır 1**.

=**tır 2** در *cf.* =**dır 2**.

tırabzan طرابزان It hand rail; banister. — **babası** 1. newel; post with knob at the end of a banister. 2. father who has no influence over his children.

tırad (.—) طراد A *lrnd.* 1. a driving one another away or striving to do so; an engaging in strife; an encounter, strife, battle. 2. a chasing, hunting wild animals. 3. hunting-spear, javelin.

tırakᵍ¹ طراق bang; clink. — **tırak** bang bang; clinking, clinkingly.

tıraka (..ʹ.) طراقه *slang* 1. fear. 2. bullying; showing off. —**lı** coward.

tıramola (...ʹ.) طرامولـه *var.* of **tiramola**.

tırandaz تراندار *colloq., var.* of **tirendâz**.

tırar (.—) طرار A *lrnd., pl.* of **turre**.

tıraş تراش |Persian .—| 1. shaving; shave; haircut. 2. hair which grows between shaves. 3. *slang.* teasing, joking lies; boring talk; bragging. —**ı ağar**= to age, to become old. — **et**= /ı/ 1. to shave. 2. to cut. 3. *slang* to tell lies to, to take someone in. 4. *slang* to bore with idle talk. —**ı gel**= to need a shave. — **ol**= to shave, to get a shave or a haircut. —**a tut**= to detain someone by idle talk; to buttonhole somebody. —**ı uzamış** needing a shave.

tıraşçı تراشجى *slang* boring talker; braggart; swindler.

tıraşla=ʳ تراشلامـﻚ 1. to prune; to thin out trees. 2. *slang* to bore by idle talk; to buttonhole. 3. *bookbinding* to trim.

tıraşlı تراشلى 1. needing a shave. 2. shaved, clean shaven, unbearded.

tıraz 1 (.—) طراز P *lrnd.* 1. embroidery made with gold or silk thread; embroidery. 2. adornment. 3. style; way; form; manner. 4. badge; slogan.

-tıraz 2 (.—) طراز P *lrnd.* ornamenting, adorning, embroidering, *e. g.,* **dibacetıraz**, prologue writer, **asartıraz** historiographer.

tırazende (.—..) طرازنده P *lrnd.* who composes or ornaments; decorator, embroiderer.

tırfıl طرفيل Gk trefoil; clover.

Tırhala (.ʹ..) ترخاله *geog.* Trikala.

Tırhallı ترخاللى 1. native of Trikala. 2 *l. c., only in* **tırhallı bir halli** No individual can escape a calamity that befalls the entire group.

tırhandil طرخانديل Gk large fishing boat. — **postaları** filling transoms, stern frames.

tırıkᵍ¹ طريق imitates the noise of two hard things striking against each other (*usually used with* **tırak**). — **tırak**, — **tırık** clinkingly, clatteringly.

tırıkla=ʳ طريقلامـﻚ *slang* /ı/ to steal.

tırıl طريل 1. naked; thinly clad. 2. stone broke. 3. drone, sluggard. — **tırıl** shivering

tırılda=ʳ طريلدامـﻚ *same as* **tırıldan**=.

tırıldan=ʳ طريلدانمـﻚ to make a continued or repeated chattering, grumbling or purring noise.

tırılla=ʳ طريللامـﻚ 1. to shiver with cold. 2. to be broke.

tırıllıkᵍ¹ طريللك a being stone broke.

tırınkᵍ¹ طرنك a ringing sound. — **para say**= to pay down money as with a jingle.

tırıs طريس trot; gentle canter (horse). — **git**= to trot. — **gider bana** I don't care at all.

tırkaz طرقاز *prov.* bar behind a door to keep it shut.

tırkazla=ʳ طرقازلامـﻚ /ı/ to bolt or bar (a door). —**t**= *caus.*

tırkazlı طرقازلى 1. barred; bolted. 2. having a bar.

tırla=ʳ طرلامـﻚ 1. to purr. 2. *slang* to run away. 3. *slang* to die. 4. *school slang* to fail.

tırma=ᵣ طرماس *obs.* to drag along with the claws or with a hook.

tırmakᵍ¹ طرماق *same as* **tırmık**.

tırmala=ᵣ طرمالامس 1. to scratch, claw, wound with the nails or claws. 2. to worry, vex, annoy. 3. to offend (the ears, the taste). **—n=** *pass.* **—t=** /ı, a/ *caus. of* **tırmala=**.

tırman=ᵣ طرمانمق 1. to cling with the claws or the finger tips. 2. /a/ to climb (tree, mountain, etc.). **—dır=** /ı/ *caus.*

tırmaş=ᵣ طرماشمق 1. to climb by the claws, fingers or toes, etc. 2. to be very insistent and persistent in trying to get something. **—ıl=** *pass.* **—tır=** /ı/ *caus. of* **tırmaş=**.

tırmıkᵍ¹ طرمیق 1. scratch. 2. small, sharp claw (as that of a cat) 3. rake; harrow. 4. drag-hook.

tırmıkla=ᵣ طرمیقلامق /ı/ to scratch, rake, harrow.

tırnakᵍ¹ طرناق 1. fingernail; toenail. 2. claw; hoof. 3. ejector (of a gun). 4. fluke (of an anchor). 5. *mech.* catch. 6. quotation mark. 7. *jewelry* claw. **—ına benzeme=** /ın/ to be very inferior to. **— çekici** claw-hammer. **—ı dibinde** 1. close at hand. 2. counted down and paid at once (money) **—ları dökül=** to work very hard, to spend all one's energy. **— göster=** to show one's claws; to threaten. **— iliştir=** 1. to hook a claw slightly into a thing. 2. to get one's finger into a matter. **— işareti** quotation marks. **—larını kes=** /ın/ 1. to cut the nails. 2. to deprive of the power of offense. **— kesintisi** nail parings. **— keski** crosscut chisel. **—ının kiri bile olamaz** He couldn't be even the dirt in his finger-nails. He is not fit to lick his boots. **— otu** mouse-ear hawkweed, *bot., Hieracium pilosella.* **— pabucu** *naut.* anchor shoe. **— pidesi** *prov.* thin, round flat cake of household bread ornamented with impressions from the fingers or fingernails. **—ını sök=** /ın/ 1. to pull out the fingernails. 2. to torture; to leave in great torment. **— sürüştür=** to rub one's nails against each other in order to provoke a fight between two persons. **— tak=** /a/ to intend to punish a person. **— ucu** *naut.* peak; anchor bill. **—ın varsa başını kaşı** If you want your work done, do it yourself. **—' yalmanı** *same as* **tırnak ucu**. **—larını yaptır=** to have a manicure. **— yarası** a scratch, any wound where a flap of skin is left hanging. **— ye=** to bite one's nails. **— yeri** 1. nail scratch. 2. weak point in one's character open to malicious notice.

tırnakçı طرناقجی *slang* pickpocket; thief.

tırnakla=ᵣ طرناقلامق /ı/ to scratch with the nails.

tırnaklı طرناقلی 1. having nails or claws. 2. spiked (wheel).

tırnaksız طرناقسز *slang* opportunist.

tırpan تربان دربان طربان Gk 1. scythe. 2. surgical trepan. **— at=** /a/ to exterminate; to destroy. **—la biç=** /ı/ to mow by hand.

tırpana (..´.) طربانه Gk sting ray, *zool., Trygon pastinoca;* skate (fish), *zool., Raja batis.*

tırpanla=ᵣ طربانلامق /ı/ to mow; to mow down.

tırtıkᵍ¹ طرطیق 1. unevenness. 2. raw spot. **— tırtık** 1. uneven; jagged. 2. fleecy (cloud).

tırtıkçı طرطیقجی *slang* pickpocket; rogue.

tırtıkla=ᵣ طرطیقلامق /ı/ 1. to pull to pieces; to pluck. 2. *slang* to steal.

tırtıklı طرطیقلی rough, uneven; jagged.

tırtıl ترتیل طرطیل 1. caterpillar. 2. chenille, tufted cord. 3. milling (of a coin). 4. knurl. 5. perforation (of a stamp). 6. *slang* parasite, sponger. **— baklava** *Ott. hist.* chain of rhomboidal links found on the outer edge of some Eastern coins.

tırtıllan=ᵣ طرطیللنمش to become full of caterpillars (tree).

tırtıllı طرطیللی having a milled edge. **— tekerlek** caterpillar wheels.

tırtır 1 طرطیر F *chem.* tartar. **— hamızı** Tartaric acid.

tırtır 2 طرطیر *zool.* ichneumon fly.

tıs طس goose's hiss. **—!** Hush! **— deme=** not to make the slightest noise; not to raise the slightest objection.

tısla=ᵣ طسلامق to hiss like a goose; to spit like a cat.

tıyn (—) طین A *Irnd.* mud, clay; earth. **—i asfer** yellow ochre. **—i ebyaz** chalk. **—i hikmet** *chem.* luting. **—i mahtûm** Lemnian earth.

tıynet طینت A temperament, disposition; natural character. **—i pâk** good character, fine disposition. **—siz** of low character.

-ti 1 دی cf. **-tı 4.**

-ti 2 دی cf. **-dı 2.**

=ti 3 دی cf. **=dı 3.**

ti 4 نی *mil.* a bugle call. **— çek=** to sound a bugle call. **— işareti** a bugle call.

tib (—) طیب A *Irnd.* perfume, scent; odoriferous substance.

Tibe (—.) طیبه A *Isl. rel.* the Well of Zemzem.

tibet (—.) طیبت A *Irnd.* a being willing; consent. **—i nefs ile** willingly, cheerfully.

tibn تبن A *Irnd.* straw; powdered straw or chaff used as fodder. **—i Mekke** camel's hay, geranium grass, *bot., Cymbopogon schoenanthus.* **—i** (.—) A straw color.

tibr طبر A *Irnd.* 1. gold. 2. silver. 3. gold or silver in grains or nuggets just from the mine before it is touched by the fire or the hammer.

tibyan (.—) تبیان A *Irnd* a making clear

and plain; a setting forth or exposing; declaration, exposition.

tic (—), **tican** (— —) تِيج يَجان A lrnd., pl. of **tac**.

Ticanî (— — —) يَجانٰى A 1. adherent of a dervish order founded in North Africa. 2. reactionary, fanatical person.

ticaret (. —.) تِجارَت A 1. trade, commerce. 2. profit (in trade). **— borsası** grain market. **— bırak=** colloq. to yield a profit; to return profit. **— et=** 1. to engage in commerce. 2. to earn, to make a profit. **— hukuku** commercial law. **— mahkemeleri** commercial courts. **T— Odası** Chamber of Commerce. **— sicili** registration with the Chamber of Commerce.

ticaretgâh (. —. —) تِجارَتگاه P lrnd. center of commerce; business quarter.

ticarethane (. —. —.) تِجارَتخانه P 1. business house; firm. 2. place where a man has his business.

ticarî (. — —) تِجارى A commercial. **— defterler** account books. **— mümessil** authorized agent. **— senetler** negotiable instruments. **— vekâlet** authorized agency.

tifo تِيفو It typhoid fever.

tiftik[gi] تِفتِك [Persian **taftik**] 1. mohair. 2. fine soft wool (clipped from sheep in the spring). 3. med. lint. **— gibi** very soft. **— keçisi** Angora goat. **— tiftik et=** /ı/ to unravel, to pull into threads.

tiftiklen=[ir] تِفتِكلَنمك to become unravelled or frayed. **—dir=** caus.

tifüs (. '.) تِيفوس F path. typhus.

tig (—) تِيغ P lrnd. 1. sword; swordlike weapon; razor; lancet. 2 peak of a mountain; anything erect and lofty. 3. ray of light; tongue of flame. **—i âbdâr** tempered or keen sword. **—i âteşbar** a flaming sword. **—i âftab** beam or ray of sunlight. **—i bâtın** unforeseen and sudden calamity; divine punishment. **—i bürran** sharp sword. **—i dudesti** hard fighting. **—i Efrasiyab** (lit., Efrasyab's sword) beam of light seen in a goblet of wine. **—i gûştin** (lit., sword of flesh) the tongue. **—i Hindî** sword made in India or of Indian steel. **—i kûh** mountain peak. **—i seher** break of day. **—i sitem** sword of oppression. **—i teber şâhı levend** broke, bankrupt. **—i tiz** sharp sword. **—i zeban** sharp words.

tigbend (—.) تِيغبند P lrnd. 1. sword belt. 2. man girded with a sword.

tigdâr (— —) تِيغدار P lrnd. sword bearer.
tigzeban (—. —) تِيغزبان P lrnd. sharp tongued.
tigzen (—.) تِيغزن P lrnd. swordsman. **—i asman**, 1. the planet Mars. 2. dawn, sunrise, the sun.

tih (—) تِيه A lrnd. 1. wilderness; desolate place. 2. pride; vain boasting. **T— Vadisi** the Tih valley at the foot of Mount Sinai.

Tihame (. —.) تِهامه A lrnd. 1. a name of Mecca. 2. the low country along the east shore of the Red Sea.

tihu (— —) تِيهو P lrnd. grey partridge, zool., Perdix cinereus.

tik[ki] 1 تِك F 1. a twitching. 2. mannerism.
tik[ki] 2 تِك E teak tree, bot., Tectona grandis.

-tik 3 دِك تِك cf. **-dık** 1.
=tik 4 دِك تِك cf. **=dık** 2.
=tik 5 دِك تِك cf. **=dık** 3.
=tikçe دِكچه تِكچه cf. **=dıkça**.

tike تِكه prov. 1. piece, patch. 2. particle. **— tike** patched.

tikel neol., phil. partial, part.

tiken تِكن prov., same as **diken**.

tikke تِكه A lrnd. string passed through the hem in the upper part of drawers or trousers and tied round the waist.

tiksin=[ir] تِكسِنمك /dan/ to be disgusted (with), to be sickened (by); to loathe. **—dir=** /ı, dan/ caus.

tiksinti تِكسِنتى disgust, loathing. **— duy=** to be disgusted.

=tikte دِكته تِكته cf. **=dıkta**.
=tikten başka دِكتن باشقه تِكتن باشقه cf. **=dıktan başka**.
=tikten sonra دِكتن صوڭره تِكتن صوڭره cf. **=dıktan sonra**.

tilâl[li] (. —) تِلال A lrnd., pl. of **tel 2**.

tilâvet (. —.) تِلاوت A lrnd. a reading or chanting (especially the Quran). **— et=** to read or chant as a religious exercise. **— iskemlesi** lectern. **— odası** special room where the Mevlevi dervishes chant the Quran.

tilka تِلقا A lrnd. 1. space in front; side. 2. meeting, encounter. 3. presence of a person.

tilki تِلكى 1. fox. 2. cunning person; sly fellow. **—nin dönüp dolaşıp geleceği yer kürkçü dükkânıdır** proverb After all his wanderings the fox will end up in the furrier's shop. You can't escape it; you will come back to the place where you belong. **— kuyruğu** 1. ringworm. 2. evil suggestion of the mind. 3. meadow foxtail grass, bot., Alopecurus pratensis. **— masalı** false tale, yarn. **— taşağı** lizard orchis, bot., Orchis hircina. **— tırnağı** spotted orchis, purple orchis, bot., Orchis mascula. **— tilkiliğini anlatıncaya kadar post elden gider** proverb By the time the fox has proved that he is really a fox he will have lost his fur. A person can have a lot of trouble before the truth is understood. **— üzümü** fox grape, bot., Paris incompleta; black nightshade, hound's berry, bot., Solanum nigrum.

tilkileş=[ir] تِلكيلَشمك to become crafty.
tilkilik[gi] تِلكيليك craftiness, slyness.

tille تِلّه P *lrnd.* 1. landing at the foot of a staircase. 2. mounting-block
tilmiz (. —) تلميذ [telmiz] disciple.
-tim 1 دِم *cf.* **-dım 1.**
=tim 2 دِم *cf.* **=dım 2.**
tim 3 تيم E sports team.
timam (. —) تمام A *lrnd.* full length of a night.
timar (— —) تيمار P *same as* **tımar.**
timas (— —) تيماس P *lrnd.* thicket, jungle.
timi تيمى *obs.* 1. a kind of gipsy game. 2. swelling (caused by the bite of an insect).
timsah تمساح A crocodile.
timsal (. —) تمثال A 1. symbol; model, example. 2. *lrnd.* picture, image, representation. **—i mücessem** the very image; personification.
timsalger (. —) تمثالگر P *lrnd.* artist, painter, sculptor.
-tin 1 دِن *cf.* **-dın 1.**
=tin 2 دِن *cf.* **=dın 2.**
tin 3 (—) تين A *lrnd. fig.* **T— Suresi** a name of the ninety-fifth sura of the Quran.
tin 4 *neol., phil.* spirit; soul.
tinbal (. —), **tinbale** (. —.) تنبال A *lrnd.* short, squat, dwarfish; dwarf.
tingoz تنگوز *slang* cuff, box on the ears.
tini (— —) طينى A *lrnd.* 1. of clay; like clay; clayish. 2. natural, inborn (quality).
-tiniz 1 دِكِز *cf.* **-dınız 1.**
=tiniz 2 دِكِز *cf.* **=dınız 2.**
tinka (. .) تنقه tench, *zool., Tinca tinca.*
tinnin (. —) تنّين A *lrnd.* 1. dragon, great serpent. 2. intersection of the ecliptic or of the path of any planet and the equinoctial constellation Draco. **—i felek** milky way.
tinsel *neol., phil.* spiritual; moral. **—cilik** spiritualism.
tin tin تين تين *colloq.* toddlingly; slowly (walking). **— yürü=** to toddle (baby); to toddle along briskly (very old man); to move with unexpected agility
tinyoloz تنيولوز *slang* 1. slovenly; untidy. 2. idler.
tip تيپ F 1. type 2. queer specimen.
tipi تيپى blizzard, snowstorm.
tipik تيپيك F typical.
tipile= تيپيله مك to blow a blizzard; to snow heavily.
-tir 1 دِر *cf.* **-dır 1.**
=tir= 2 دِرلك *cf.* **=dır= 2.**
tîr 3 (—) تير P *lrnd.* 1. arrow. 2. thunderbolt. 3. any long and straight pole or stick of timber, as a mast or yard of a ship, ridgepole; bow of a violin. 4. discharge of a gun; shot, ball (when fired). 5. share, lot. 6. equal, mate (in a pair). 7. the planet Mercury. 8. the river Tigris. **—i kaza** misfortune; death. **— ü keman** 1. bow and arrow. 2. the glance and eyelashes of the beloved. **—i seher** 1. daybreak. 2. sigh. **—i tazallum** the lament or prayer of one oppressed. **—i terazu** arm of a balance.
tiraj تيراژ F circulation (of a newspaper).
tiraje (— —.) تيراژه P *lrnd.* rainbow.
tirak (. —) تيراك *same as* **tiryak.**
tiramola (. . .) تيراموله It *naut.* 1. haul (on a rope). 2. Let go and haul! About ship! 3. a kind of capstan. **— et=** to tack ship; to go about.
tirandaz تيرانداز [tirendaz] *colloq.* 1. trim, well dressed. 2. dexterous, skillful.
tiras (. —), **tirase** (. —.) تيراس A *lrnd., pl. of* **türs.**
tirbaran (— — —) تيرباران P *lrnd.* 1. shower of arrows. 2. act of shooting arrows in continued volleys.
tirbuşon تيربوشون F corkscrew.
tirdan (— —) تيردان P *lrnd.* quiver. **—lık** *obs.* quiver.
tire 1 تيره 1. sewing cotton. 2. cotton.
tire 2 تيره F *print.* dash, hyphen.
tire 3 (— .) تيره P *lrnd.* 1. dark, gloomy. 2. obscure; dark or deep (color). 3. opaque, cloudy. 4. turbid. 5. unhappy, wretched; inauspicious; evil.
tire 4 (— .) تيره A *lrnd.* omen, augury, ill omen.
tire 5 (— .) تيره P *lrnd.* 1. anger; grief, pain, uneasiness. 2. shame, modesty.
tirebaht (— . .) تيره بخت P *lrnd.* whose outlook is unpromising.
tirebâtın (— . — .) تيره باطن P *lrnd.* 1. whose heart is in gloom. 2. malignant, perverse.
tiredil (— . .) تيره دل P *lrnd.* 1. ignorant; dark; stolid. 2. malignant, perverse.
tiregi (— . —) تيره گى P *lrnd.* 1. darkness, gloom. 2. dark shade of a color. 3. turbidity, opacity. 4. sombreness of disposition.
tiregûn (— . —) تيره گون P *lrnd.* muddy, turbid.
tirehal (— . —) تيره حال P *lrnd.* in evil plight; unhappy, wretched.
tirek (— .) تيرك P *lrnd.* 1. small arrow, bolt or wand. 2. shooting pain.
tiremağz (— . .) تيره مغز P *lrnd.* stupid; stolid.
tirementi تيره منتى *var. of* **terementi.**
tirendaz (— . —) تيرانداز P *lrnd.* 1. archer. 2. *same as* **tirandaz. —ân** (— . — —) P archers. **—î** (— . — —) P, **—lık** quality or act of an archer; archery.
tirenti (. . .) تيرنتى It *naut.* fall (of a pulley); boat-falls.
tirerey (— . .) تيره رى P *lrnd.* improvident; thoughtless. **—i** (— . . —) P improvidence.
tireşeb (— . .) تيره شب P *lrnd.* dark night.
tirezamir (— . . —) تيره ضمير P *lrnd.* whose conscience is dark.

tirfil 1 تيرفيل [tırfıl] clover, *bot.*, *Trifolium*.
tirfil 2 تيرفيل It *naut.* 1. a kind of tackle; runner. 2. skid; round wooden bars used to move heavy loads.
tirfillen=ᶦʳ تيرفيللنمك to become threadbare.
tirger (—.) تيرگر P *lrnd.* arrow maker. —**î** (—.—) P arrow-making.
tirhal (.—) ترحال A *lrnd.* journey, departure.
tirhos تيرهوس Gk a kind of anchovy, *zool.*, *Engraulis encrasicholus*.
tirilde=ᶦʳ تيريلده مك to quiver; to shiver.
tiril tiril تيريل تيريل shivering, trembling.
tiringe (..'.) ترنفه ترينگه It *same as* **tringa**.
tirişko (.'.) ترشقو *slang* lie; false, made up (story, etc.).
tiritᵈᶦ تريت [**terit**] 1. bread soaked in gravy. 2. *colloq.* feeble old man. —**leş=** to become old and feeble.
tiriz تريز ديرز تيريز It 1. lath, batten. 2. *arch.* molding. 3. *dressmaking* piping. 4. warp-threads of cloth.
tirkeş (—.) تيركش P *lrnd.* quiver.
tirlin تيرلين F drawing-pen.
tirpidin, tirpit تيرپيدين تيرپيت small mattock.
tirsi ترسي تيرسي Gk shad, *zool.*, *Alosa*.
tirşe (—.) ترشه 1. pale green; of a delicate pea-green color. 2. vellum; parchment.
tir tir تير تير in — **titre=** to tremble like an aspen leaf; to be greatly frightened.
tiryakᵏᶦ **1** ترياك درياق ترياق P *lrnd.* 1. theriaca, antidote to poison. 2. panacea; sovereign remedy. 3. wine. 4. opium. —**ı Farsî** bezoar stone. —**ı faruk**, —**ı farukî** antidote against poisons. —**ı rustaiyan** garlic. —**ı Türkî** 1. asphaltum. 2. panacea reputed to be prepared by smothering a child in honey and keeping it unopened for a hundred and twenty years.
tiryakᵏᶦ **2** (.—) ترياق A *lrnd.* 1. theriac. 2. antidote.
tiryakî (.——) ترياكى P 1. addicted to alcohol, tobacco, opium, etc; addict. 2. tiresome, difficult person. —**si ol=** /ın/ to be much given (to).
tiryakilikᵍᶦ ترياكيلك a being addicted to something; thing to which one is addicted; obsession; smoking.
tirzen (—.) تيرزن P *lrnd.* shooting arrows; archer.
tis'a تسعه A *lrnd.* 1. nine. 2. ninth day of a month. — **mia** nine hundred.
tisele=ʳ تيسله مك to drizzle.
tis'in (.—) تسعين A *lrnd.* ninety.
tişe (—.) تيشه P *lrnd.* 1. axe, adze. 2. stone-mason's pick.
titiz تيتيز 1. peevish, captious; hard to please; irritable. 2. fastidious, sensitive. 3. meticulous, particular, extremely careful; very neat and tidy.

titizlen=ᶦʳ تيتيزلنمك 1. to be tiresome and hard to please. 2. to become annoyed and cross.
titizlikᵍᶦ تيتيزلك 1. peevishness, captiousness, irritability. 2. a being too punctilious or fastidious; pedantry; fastidiousness. 3. extreme accuracy, great attention to detail. 4. delicacy, sensitivity.
titre 1 تتره تيتره *same as* **kitre**.
titre=ʳ **2** تتره مك تيتره مك دتره مك د تره مك to shiver, tremble, quiver, quake, vibrate.
titrekᵍᶦ تتره ك دتره ك 1. trembling, shaky; tremulous. 2. artificial flower of jewels on a slender spiral stem. 3. *name of a certain wild flower.* — **kavak** aspen, trembling poplar, *bot.*, *Populus tremula*.
titreme تتره مه دتره مه ديترمه 1. a shaking, trembling; vibration. 2. a shaking from ague; ague.
titreş=ᶦʳ تتره شمك ديترشمك تيتره شمك to shiver, tremble, quake or vibrate together. —**im** *neol.* vibration. —**tir=** *caus.*
titret=ᶦʳ تتره تمك د تره تمك تيتره تمك 1. to cause to tremble, shiver or quake. 2. to terrify. —**il=** *pass.*
titsin=ᶦʳ تتسنمك تيتسنمك د تسنمك *same as* **tiksin=**. —**dir=** /ı, dan/ *caus.*
tiyatro (..'.) تياترو It 1. theater. 2. drama, play. —**cu** *colloq.* 1. theater owner. 2. actor.
tiz 1 (—) تيز P 1. high-pitched. 2. *mus.* high (of a note), designing the upper octave of an instrumental or vocal range. 3. *lrnd.* sharp, keen-edged; pointed. 4. *lrnd.* pungent, piquant in taste or smell. 5. *lrnd.* quick, fleet, speedy; deft. 6. *lrnd.* irritable, violent in disposition. — **buselik** the note b″. — **çargâh** the note c″. — **evc** *obs.* the note f‴. — **neva** the note d‴. — **saba** the note d‴. — **segâh** the note b″.
tiz 2 تيز *slang* buttocks.
tizâb (——) تيزاب P *lrnd.* aquafortis, nitric acid.
tizbin (——) تيزبين P *lrnd.* sharp-sighted.
tizcekᵍᶦ تيزجك *archaic* quickly.
tizçeşm (—.) تيزچشم P *lrnd.* quick-sighted.
tizdest (—.) تيزدست P *lrnd.* clever-handed, dexterous.
tizekᵏᶦ تيزك P *lrnd.* somewhat pungent.
tizfehm (—.) تيزفهم P *lrnd.* of quick understanding.
tizî (——) تيزى P *lrnd.* 1. sharpness, keenness, trenchancy. 2. strength, pungency. 3. quickness, fleetness; speed; deftness. 4. readiness, promptness. 5. irritableness.
tizintikalᶫᶦ (—..—) تيز انتقال P *lrnd.* quick of comprehension, intelligent.
tizlikᵍᶦ تيزلك *abstr. n.* of **tiz 1**.
tizmeşreb (—..), **tizmizac** (—.—) تيزمشرب تيزمزاج

tiznâ P *lrnd.* 1. hasty, irritable, passionate. 2. hot, choleric.
tiznâ (— —) تیزنا P *lrnd.* the cutting edge of a sword.
tizpâ (— —) تیزپا P *lrnd.* swift-footed, fleet.
tizper (—.) تیزپر P *lrnd.* swift of wing.
tizpervaz (—.—) تیزپرواز P *lrnd.* swift of flight.
tizreftar (—.—) تیزرفتار P *lrnd.* quick paced. **— olanın pâyına dâmen dolanır** (*lit.* He who rushes gets tangled in his robe.) Haste may cause delay.
tizrev (—.) تیزرو P *lrnd.* swift paced, rapid.
tiztab[b'ı] (—.) تیزطبع P *lrnd.* quick, hasty, impetuous, fiery in disposition.
tizvir (— —) تیزویر P *lrnd.* acute, quick, ingenious; very sharp, intelligent.
tizzeban (—.—) تیززبان P *lrnd.* glib-tongued, eloquent.
toğdarı طوغدارى طوبیدارى طوغدرى *prov.* greater bustard, *zool.,* Otis tarda.
toğrul طوغرول gerfalcon.
tohaf توهاف *same as* **tuhaf 1.**
tohta[r] طوهتامه *var. of* **tokta**[r].
tohum تخم توهم [tuhm] 1. seed; grain. 2. semen. 3. germ. 4. eggs (of insects). 5. lineage, family, dynasty. **— at** to sow. **— bağla** to go to seed, to form seed. **—a çek** 1. to go to seed. 2. to become overgrown. **—u dökül** to cease being fertile. **— ek** to sow seed. **—a kaç** 1. to go to seed. 2. *colloq.* to become too old; to lose the charm of youth. **— saç** to scatter seed (especially of sedition or discontent). **— ver** to yield seed.
tohumlan[ır] توهمرلنمش 1. to form seed, to go to seed. 2. to become seed. **—dır** /ı/ *caus.*
tohumlu توهمرلى seeded, that has seed. **— bitkiler** *neol.,* Spermatophyta.
tohumluk[ğu] توهملىك 1. seed kept for sowing; suitable for seed. 2. kept for breeding. 3. garden bed; receptacle for seed. 4. *slang* old (person), wizened. **— buğday** seed wheat.
tok[ku] طوق 1. satiated; filled, full. 2. deep (voice). 3. closely woven, thick (cloth). **— açın halinden anlamaz** A well-fed person cannot imagine the distress of a hungry person. **— ağırlamak güç olur** (*lit.* It is hard to feast one whose belly is full.) It is hard to do a favor to one who does not really need it. **— evin aç kedisi** well off but still not satisfied. **— gözlü** contented; not covetous. **— karnına** immediately after a meal. **— ol** to be full, satiated with food. **— satıcı** reluctant seller, one who has no need to sell. **— ses** deep voice. **— sözlü** who does not mince his words, outspoken. **— tut** to be filling (food).
toka 1 (.'.) طوقه توقه تقه buckle.

toka 2 (.'.) طوق It 1. clash or touch of glasses when drinking healths. 2. a shaking hands. **— et** 1. to shake hands. 2. to clink glasses. 3. /ı, a/ *slang* to give, to pay.
tokaç[cı] طوقاج 1. mallet. 2. stick (for beating out washing). **—la** /ı/ to beat out washing with a laundry stick.
tokalaş[ır] طوقالاشمق /la/ to shake hands.
tokat[dı] طوقات 1. blow, slap. 2. *prov.* hollow, low-lying piece of ground among hills. 3. a style of backgammon. **— aşket**, **— at** /a/ to slap, to hit (with open hand). **— çak** /a/ *slang* to slap. **— yapıştır** /a/ to slap. **— ye** to be slapped.
tokatla[r] طوقاتلامق /ı/ to slap.
tokaz توقاز *prov., same as* **tokuz.**
toklu طوقلى طوقلو توقلو 1. having pendent glands (goat). 2. yearling lamb.
tokluk[ğu] طوقلىق 1. thickness, density (of cloth). 2. satiety; fullness.
tokmak[ğı] طوقماق توقماق 1. mallet; beetle (implement). 2. door-knocker. 3. clapper (of a bell). 4. wooden pestle. 5. block of wood (used as a seat). 6. ball of flour. **— gibi** chubby. **— baş** goby.
tokmakçı طوقماقچى *slang* gigolo.
toksin توقسین F toxin.
tokta[r] طوقتامه *prov.* to fix, settle, establish oneself.
toktağan *neol.* perennial, lasting. **— karlar** perennial snow.
tokuç[cu] طوقوج *prov.* 1. stick (for beating out washing). 2. block-head.
tokur طوقور *prov.* having a protruding forehead (person). **— alınlı** with a protruding forehead.
tokurcun طوقورجین *prov.* 1. thatched stack of hay, grain, etc. 2. *a kind of game played with small stones or shells.*
tokurda[r] طوقوردامه to make a bubbling noise. **—t** /ı/ to make bubble (a nargile).
tokurtu طوقورتى bubbling noise of a nargile.
tokuş[ur] طوقوشمق /la/ to butt one another; to collide. **—tur** /ı/ 1. to cause to collide. 2. to clink (glasses). 3. to cannon (billiards).
tokuz طوقوز thick, closely woven (cloth).
tolga 1 توغه *archaic* helmet.
tolga 2 توله *same as* **tavulga.**
toloz توله Gk arched or groined vault.
tolu دولو *prov. for* **dolu 3.**
tolun 1 تولون *archaic, same as* **dolun.**
tolun 2 طولون طولون *prov.* temple; prominence between the temple and the ear.
tomağa طوماغه wooden ball fastened to a hawk's foot so that he cannot fly away.
tomak[ğı] طوماق 1. *prov.* wooden ball. 2. *prov.* a kind of short and heavy boot formerly worn

by horsemen. 3. *archaic* thick stick used for a certain game.

tomal=ⁱʳ طومالو *same as* **domal**=.

tomalan طومالان *same as* **domalan**.

tomalıçᶜⁱ طومالیج *same as* **domalıç**.

tomalıkᵏⁱ طومالق *prov.* prominent; turgid.

tomanıçᶜⁱ طومانج *same as* **domanıç**.

tomar طومار ، تومار Gk 1. roll or scroll (of paper, etc.). 2. cylindrical object. 3. *artillery* rammer. —**ı devril**= (*lit.*, for one's roll to be rolled up) to die. — **oku** arrow having a fireball in place of the point.

tombadız طومبادیز *prov.* very fat, like a ball.

tombakᵏⁱ طومباق ، تومباق gold-plated copper; copper-zinc alloy.

tombala (.ˈ..) طومبولا It lotto.

tombalakᵏⁱ طومبالاق round as a ball; plump.

tombay طومبای *same as* **dombay**.

tombaz طومبار 1. a kind of flat-bottomed, undecked barge or lighter. 2. punt. 3. pontoon. 4. buoy for mooring.

tomrukᵏᵘ طومروق ، تومروق 1. bud (on a plant). 2. heavy log (from the main trunk of a tree). 3. stocks (in which a culprit's feet are fastened); single heavy log fastened to the leg of a prisoner. 4. large stone, square boulder. 5. prison. — **ağası** *Ott. hist.* warden of a prison. —**a at**= /ı/ to cast into prison. —**a vur**= /ı/ to put into the stocks.

tomruklan=ⁱʳ طومروقلنمك to put forth buds, to bud.

tomruklu طومروقلی 1. having buds, budded. 2. confined in a lockup or in the stocks; chained in a chain-gang.

tomşukᵏᵘ طومشوق *archaic* curved beak.

tomşur=ᵘʳ طومشرمك *archaic* to feed a bird by putting food into its beak.

tomurcukᵏᵘ طومورجق bud.

tomuş=ᵘʳ طومشمك *archaic* /ı/ to clean one another's feathers with their beaks (birds).

ton 1 طون F canned tunny. — **balığı** tunny, *zool.*, *Thunnus*.

ton 2 طون F ton.

ton 3 طون F 1. *mus.* tone. 2. manner. 3. color quality or value; tone, tint, shade. — **değiştirme** 1. to change one's manner. 2. *print.* to change color and become darker (after drying).

tonaj طوناژ F tonnage.

tondura (..ˈ.) طوندوره F *geog.* tundra.

tonel طونل *var. of* **tünel**. — **geç**= *slang* to be absent-minded.

tonga (.ˈ.) طونغه *slang* deceit, trap, trick. —**ya bas**=, —**ya düş**=, —**ya otur**= to fall into a trap, to be deceived.

tonilato (..ˈ..) طونیلاطو It tonnage; ton. —**luk** having a tonnage of; a ton's weight of.

tonlukᵏᵘ طونلق of so many tons.

tonoz 1 طونوز [**toloz**] *arch.* vault.

tonoz 2 طونوس ، طونوز Gk *naut.* a warping by means of an anchor. — **demiri** kedge anchor. — **et**= to warp (a ship).

tonoz 3 طونوز Gk tunny. — **balığı** tunny.

tonton طون طون darling.

top 1 طوب ، توب 1. ball; knob; round. 2. collected together; in a mass; a whole; the whole lot, all. 3. a whole piece of cloth from the loom. 4. ball; gun, cannon; artillery. —**tan***. —**u** *colloq.* all of it, all of them, the whole lot. — **ağaç** 1. neatly trimmed round tree. 2. snowball tree, *bot.*, *Viburnum opulus*. —**un ağzında** the one most in danger. — **akasya** globe-headed acacia. — **altı** terreplein of a fort. — **ambarı** lower deck of an old line-of-battle ship. — **arabası** 1. guncarriage in field artillery. 2. *slang* testicle. — **at**= 1. to fire a gun. 2. to become bankrupt. 3. *slang* to fail in class. — **u at**= *same as* **top at**= ²,³. — **atan***. — **ateşi** gunfire, artillery fire. — **atımı** 1. a cannon's range. 2. a single cannon-shot. — **bindir**= to limber (up). — **çakmağı** lock of a cannon. — **çehre** 1. round face. 2. round faced. — **çeker***. — **et**= /ı/ to collect in a mass. — **falyası** touch-hole of a cannon. — **fonyası** friction primer for a cannon. — **gibi** 1. like a ball; like a cannon. 2. without delay or hesitation. 3. willynilly, without question. — **gibi git**= to go posthaste. — **gibi gürle**= 1. to make a great noise; to shout at the top of one's voice. 2. to brag; to exaggerate greatly, especially in self-praise. — **gibi patla**= 1. to come like a thunderbolt. 2. to become suddenly furious. — **gürlemesi** roar of a cannon. — **haznesi** chamber of a gun. — **kandil** round shaped chandelier. — **koğuşu** timber platform or slide for a cannon. — **kundağı** gun carriage (as used on board ship or in a permanent battery). — **kur**= to draw up artillery for action. — **kuyruğu** 1. breach of a cannon. 2. cascabel of a cannon. — **lâhana** drum-head cabbage, *bot.*, *Brassica oleracea*. — **lombarı** porthole in a ship. — **mazgalı** embrasure in a battery. — **menzili** *same as* **top atımı**. — **mıhla**= to spike a cannon. — **nişangâhı** sight of a cannon. — **ol**= 1. to become collected together in a mass; to be in a mass. 2. to be round, globular. 3. to form into a ball. — **otu** 1. charge of powder for a cannon. 2. brag, big words. — **oyunu** 1. ball game. 2. artillery fight. — **patla**= 1. to get fired (cannon). 2. to commence (hostilities). — **sakal** short, thick beard. — **salata** cabbage lettuce, *bot.*, *Lactuca sativa*. — **takımı** 1. subdivision of a battery of artillery. 2. complement of men, horses, tools, etc. for one cannon. — **talimi** artillery drill. — **tomarı** rammer or sponge of a cannon. — **top** 1. in groups. 2. in lumps; in masses. **—u topu***. **—a tut**= to bombard. **— tüfek** arms, weapons. **— yastığı** bed, quoin or wedge to support a cannon. **— yekûn** in all, totally. **— yekûn harb** total war. **— yoluna git**= 1. to be uselessly sacrificed. 2. to be spent or lost.

top 2 طوپ *prov.* 1. window. 2. camel fodder.

topaçᶜⁱ طوپاچ 1. top (plaything), teetotum. 2. thick rounded part of a Turkish oar. 3. round, globose. 4. short and fat. **— gibi** sturdy (child). **— tuğla** very thick brick.

topakᵍⁱ طوپاق 1. roundish lump. 2. inner side of a horse's fetlock. 3. short and fat.

topal طوپال توپال 1. lame; cripple. 2. one leg of which is too short (four-legged stool). **— eşekle kervana karış**= (*lit.*, to join a caravan with a lame donkey) to undertake something with inadequate means.

topalakᵍⁱ **1** طوپالاق توپالاق round lump; ball-shaped.

topalakᵍⁱ **2, topalan** طوپالاق توپالان buckthorn, *bot., Rhamnus chlorophorus globosus.* **— kökü** muskroot.

topalla=ʳ طوپاللامق to limp. **—n**= to become lame.

topallıkᵍⁱ طوپاللق lameness.

toparla=ʳ طوپارلامق /ı/ to collect together; to pack up; *mil.* to roll up.

toparlakᵍⁱ طوپارلاق طوپارله 1. round, globose. 2. *mil.* limber (of a gun). **— hesap** in round numbers.

toparlan=ʳ طوپارلانمق *pass. of* **toparla**=, 1. to be collected together. 2. to pull oneself together.

topatan طوپاتان an early elongated melon.

topaz طوپاز F topaz.

topçeker طوپ چكر large gunboat; tractor for pulling guns.

topçu طوپچی 1. artilleryman; gunner; the artillery. 2. *slang* bankrupt. 3. *school slang* one who fails the examinations (and therefore repeats the class). **— askeri** artilleryman; artillery corps. **— ayvası** a variety of quince. **—başı** *Ott. hist.* 1. Master-General of Artillery. 2. head-gunner; gunner.

topçulukᵍᵘ طوپچیلك gunnery; duties and profession of a gunner.

tophane (. —.) طوپخانه P *Ott. hist.* 1. arsenal. 2. factory where cannons are manufactured. **T—i Âmire** Imperial Arsenal of Ordnance and Artillery. **— güllesi** *school slang* zero.

topikᵍⁱ طوپیك Arm *cookery* balls of chickpeas.

topla=ʳ طوپلامق /ı/ 1. to collect; to gather. 2. to gather up, to pick up; to call together (council, troops, etc.); to convene; to sum up. 3. /ı/ to tidy up; to clear away. 4. to put on weight.

toplaçᶜⁱ *neol., phys.* collector.

toplam *neol., math.* total. **—lar toplamı** grand total.

toplama طوپلامه 1. *verbal n. of* **topla**=. 2. *math.* addition. **— kampı** concentration camp.

toplan=ʳ طوپلانمق 1. *pass. of* **topla**=. 2. to come together, assemble, collect. 3. to regain one's health; to put on flesh. 4. to come to a head (boil). 5. to pack up (one's belongings). **—ıl**= *same as* **toplan**= ².

toplantı طوپلانتی assembly, gathering, meeting.

toplardamar *neol., anat.* vein.

toplaş=ʳ طوپلاشمق طوپلشمق 1. to gather together; to come together. 2. to get hard lumps in it (soup, in cooking). **—tır**= /ı/ *caus.*

toplat=ʳ طوپلاتمق 1. /ı, a/ *caus. of* **topla**=. 2. /ı/ to seize (issue of newspaper, book). **—ıl**= *pass.*

toplu طوپلی طوپلو 1. having a knob or round head. 2. compact; collected together in a mass. 3. well-arranged, tidy. 4. plump. 5. collective. 6. pin. **— ateş** *mil.* concentrated fire. **— iğne** pin. **— rehin** collective charge, collective mortgage.

toplulukᵍᵘ طوپلولوق طوپلولك 1. a being collected together; compactness. 2. community. 3. a being plump. 4. tidiness. **— ismi** *neol., gram.* collective noun.

toplum *neol.* society, community. **—bilim** sociology. **—culuk** socialism. **—daş** *sociol.* fellow, associate, socius. **—laştır**= /ı/ to socialize. **—sal** social.

toprakᵍⁱ طوپراق طوپراغ 1. earth, soil; ground. 2. land; territory, country. 3. earthen, earthenware; made of clay. 4. *slang* heroin. **—ına ağır gelmesin** I hope it won't weigh heavy on him, *said when criticizing a dead person.* **— altı** 1. *geol.* subsoil; substratum. 2. underground. **—a bak**= to be nearing death. **— bastı** tax on goods or persons entering a town. **—ı bol olsun** (*lit.* May his earth be abundant.) May he rest in peace (used for a non-Muslim). **— boşaltma** clearing (away), removal (of excavated material). **— boya** paint in powder form. **— doldurma** a filling up, filling in, packing (with earth, etc.). **— doyursun gözünü** He won't be satisfied till he is dead (said of a very rapacious person). **—a gir**= 1. to be buried. 2. to enter a territory. **— işi** earthenware. **— kap** earthenware vessel. **T— Ofis** governmental wheat purchasing agency. **— rengi** earth color. **— sahibi** landowner. **—a veril**= to be delivered to one's rest, to be buried. **— yol** dirt road.

toprakla=ʳ طوپراقلامق /ı/ 1. to cover with earth. 2. to soil with earth. **—n**= *pass.*

topraklı طوپراقلی 1. mixed, adulterated or soiled with earth. 2. having land (peasant).

topraksız طوپراقسز landless, having no land to cultivate (peasant).
toptan طوپتان 1. wholesale; in the lump. 2. collectively; in all.
toptancı طوپتانجى wholesaler. —**lık** wholesale trading.
Toptaşıⁿⁱ طوپ طاشى name of a district in Istanbul where there was a well-known lunatic asylum; lunatic asylum. —**na göndermeli** He ought to be shut up.
toptopuz طوپ طوپوز strong, healthy (little child).
topukᵍᵘ 1. heel; ankle. 2. fetlock. 3. heel (of a shoe); *naut.* heel (of a mast). 4. *geog.* bar (of a river). —**una bas=** /ı/ to follow closely at one's heels. — **çal=** to brush the fetlock of one foot with the shoe of the opposite foot (horse). — **çatlat=** (*lit.*, to crack the ankles) to go fast or far. — **demiri** hinge-pin (of a door). — **kemiği** ankle bone. — **siniri** tendon or sinew of the ankle; the peroneus tendon behind the outer ankle.
topu topu طوپى طوپى in all; all told.
topuz 1. mace (for use in battle). 2. globular knob (on a stick). 3. knot of hair. 4. short, thick (man). — **altında** by compulsion. —**lu** 1. armed with a mace. 2. having a knob, knobbed.
tor 1 طور 1. net. 2. tissue. — **ağ** fine-meshed fishing net. —**a düş=** *colloq.* to be cheated.
tor 2 طور 1. raw, inexperienced. 2. wild, unbroken (horse). — **tay** unbroken, wild colt.
torakᵍⁱ 1 طوراق charcoal pit; kiln.
torakᵍⁱ 2 طوراق Sl *prov.* dried skim milk.
toraman طورامان 1. young, wild and untamed. 2. robust young man. 3. pet animal. 4. penis.
torba طوربه 1. bag. 2. *anat.* scrotum. 3. cyst. 4. *bookbinding* paper jacket (of a book). —**dakiler** something hitherto unsuspected in a man's nature. **bir — kemik** *colloq.* (*lit.*, a bag of bones) 1. skinny, very thin. 2. without a whole bone in his body, beaten to a jelly. — **oğlanı** *Ott. hist.* young Janissary in training. — **yoğurdu** yogurt strained in a bag.
torbalan=ⁱʳ طوربالانمق to become baggy.
torbalı طوربالى having a bag.
torgay طورغاى *prov.* lark.
torikᵍⁱ طوريك 1. large bonito, *zool., Pelamys sarda*. 2. *slang* brain; intelligence. — **akını** rush of large bonitos. —**ini çalıştır=** *slang* to use one's brain. —**ini kaşı=** *slang* to think.
torina (..´.) طورينه kingfish, *zool., Tampris luna*.

torla=ʳ طورلامق *archaic* /ı/ to make up in a bundle, to gather together.
torlakᵍⁱ طورلاق 1. unbroken colt. 2. wild youth.
torlan=ⁱʳ طورلانمق 1. *pass. of* **torla=**. 2. to become a net or tissue. 3. to become wild and intractable.
torlukᵍᵘ 1 طورلوق *archaic* 1. mud hut. 2. charcoal kiln.
torlukᵍᵘ 2 طورلوق wildness, untamedness.
torna (´.) طورنه It lathe. — **aynası** potter's wheel; lathe chuck. — **et=** /ı/ to turn (on a lathe). —**cı** lathe operator.
tornavida (..´.) طورناويدا It screwdriver; turn-screw.
tornistan (..´.) طورنيستان E 1. *naut.* stern-way. 2. *naut.* Astern! 3. a turning inside out (suit of clothes). 4. a going back (on one's word, plan, etc.). — **et=** 1. *naut.* to go astern. 2. to go back on one's word.
torno (´.) طورنو It 1. turning lathe. 2. *naut.* block (of a tackle).
Toros (..) طوروس *geog.* Taurus Mountains.
torpido (..´.) طورپيدو E *naut.* torpedo. — **kovanı** torpedo tube. — **muhribi** destroyer.
torpil طورپيل F 1. mine (explosive). 2. torpedo 3. *slang* pull, influence. 4. *slang* a big lie. — **balığı** campfish, torpedo.
torpille=ʳ طورپيلله /ı/ 1. to torpedo. 2. *school slang* to fail in class.
tortop طورطوپ quite round.
tortu طورطو 1. deposit; dregs; sediment; precipitate. 2. the lowest kind or part (of a thing). —**lu** having sediment; turbid. —**suz** free from sediment, clear.
torun طورون 1. grandchild. 2. two-year-old camel. — **torba sahibi ol=**, — **tosun sahibi ol=** to have children and grandchildren.
tos طوس a blow with the head or horns. — **vur=** /a/ to butt.
tosbağa طوسباغه tortoise.
tosla=ʳ طوسلامق 1. /ı/ to butt. 2. /a/ to have a slight collision, to pitch (ship). 3. /ı, a/ *slang* to pay, to give back. 4. /dan/ *school slang* to fail (an examination).
tostoparlakᵍⁱ (..´..) طوس طوپارلاق quite round.
tosun طوسون [**tevsen**] 1. young bull. 2. fine robust young man. — **gibi** robust and healthy.
tosuncukᵍᵘ طوسونجق large new-born baby.
toşar=ⁱʳ طوشارمق *prov.* 1. to be puffed up. 2. to become prominent (breast).
toto 1 طوطو sweepstakes based on soccer.
toto 2 طوطو *slang* buttocks.
toy 1 طوى 1. greater bustard, *zool., Otis tarda*. 2. greenhorn, raw, inexperienced; "green"; amateur.
toy 2 طوى *archaic* feast, banquet.

toyağa, toyaka طویاقه طویاغ *prov.*, same as **toyka**.
toygar طویغار crested lark, *zool.*, *Galerita cristata*.
toyka طویقه *prov.* stout stick, cudgel.
toyla=ʳ طویلامق *archaic* /ı/ to give a banquet; to entertain.
toylukᵍᵘ طویلق inexperience; rawness.
toz 1 طوز 1. dust; powder. 2. like dust; in powder form. 3. *slang* heroin. **— ağacı** aspen, *bot.*, *Populus tremula*. **— al=** to dust. **—unu al=** *slang* to beat, to thrash someone. **— altın** gold dust. **— bezi** duster, dust cloth. **—a boğ=** /ı/ to raise up a cloud of dust. **— duman** full of dust, clouded by dust. **—dan dumandan ferman okunma=** to be in a chaotic state. **—u dumana karıştır=**, **—u dumana kat=** 1. to raise clouds of dust. 2. to make a great ado; to create confusion. 3. to act or move very rapidly. **— et=** to raise the dust. **— inci** a seed pearl. **— kondurma=** /a/ (*lit.*, to allow no dust to settle on a thing) not to allow anything to be said against; not to pay attention to any criticism of. **— kopar=** to kick up dust. **— koparan** 1. very dusty place. 2. whirlwind of dust. **— ol=** 1. to become dust. 2. *slang* to run away, to disappear. **— pembe** pale pink. **— pembe gör=** /ı/ to see (the world) through rose colored glasses. **— silk=** to beat out the dust, to dust. **—unu silk=** to give someone a dusting. **— şeker** granulated sugar. **—a toprağa bula=** /ı/ to cover with dust and dirt. **—u toprağa kat=** same as **tozu dumana kat=**. **— tozut=** to raise the dust. **— varak** art gold leaf.
toz 2 طوز 1. level spot. 2. base, foundation, *as in* **kulak tozu**.
toz=ᵃʳ **3** طوزمق 1. *used only in* **gezip toz=**. 2. *archaic* to run.
toza=ʳ طوزامق *archaic* 1. to raise the dust. 2. to run away, to flee.
tozakᵍᵘ طوزاق *archaic* 1. storm of dust, whirlwind of dust. 2. any dry small thing that blows about like dust. 3. down; bracts, stipules, filaments (vegetable or animal).
tozaklan=ʳ طوزاقلانمق to produce or become covered with down or filaments.
tozaklı طوزاقلی covered with down or downy filaments.
tozan=ʳ طوزانمق same as **toza=**.
tozar=ʳ طوزارمق *archaic* 1. to become dust; to go to powder. 2. to drizzle.
tozat=ʳ طوزاتمق /ı/ *caus.* of **toza=**.
tozla=ʳ طوزلامق /ı/ to sprinkle powder or dust (upon); to cover with dust.
tozlan=ʳ طوزلانمق to become dusty. **—dır=** /ı/ *caus.*

tozlaş=ʳ طوزلاشمق 1. to become powder or dust. 2. to drizzle. **—ma** 1. *verbal n.* 2. *neol.*, *bot.* pollination.
tozlu طوزلو dusty.
tozlukᵍᵘ طوزلق 1. gaiter. 2. anything used as a protection against dust. 3. dusty place; place for dust.
tozu=ʳ طوزومق same as **toza=**.
tozuntu طوزونتی 1. any fine thing like dust. 2. cloud of dust blown about. 3. very fine drizzling rain.
tozuş=ᵘʳ طوزوشمق to raise dust together as in a scramble.
tozut=ᵘʳ طوزوتمق 1. to raise dust. 2. to go too far, to become unreasonable. 3. *slang* to go mad.
töhmet تهمت A suspicion that someone is guilty of a crime; guilt, offense; imputation.
töhmetlendir=ʳ تهمتلندرمك /ı/ to have under suspicion; to call guilty.
töhmetli تهمتلی under suspicion; guilty.
töhmetsiz تهمتسز not suspected; innocent.
tökezi=ʳ, **tökezle=**ʳ توكزه‌مك توكزلمك to stumble.
tömbeki تنباكی It Persian tobacco (smoked in hookahs).
töre توره custom; rule; law. **—bilim** *neol.* ethics. **—dışı** *neol.* amoral.
törel *neol.* moral; ethical. **—lik** morality. **—siz** amoral, immoral. **—sizlik** immorality.
tören *neol.* ceremony; celebration. **—li** ceremonious; ritual.
törpü طورپو rasp.
törpüle=ʳ طورپولمك to rasp, to file. **—n=** *pass.* **—t=** /ı, a/ *caus.* of **törpüle=**.
tös توس Back! said to horses, in backing them.
töskür=ᵘʳ توسكرمك *archaic* /ı/ to back (horses, etc.).
töskürt=ᵘʳ توسكورتمك *archaic* /ı/ to drive back, to scatter (an enemy).
töskürü توسكورو *archaic* backwards.
tövbe توبه [**tevbe**] repentance; vow not to repeat an offense. **—!** Enough! **T— Ayları** the major and minor months of repentance, i. e., the lunar months **Cemaziyülevvel** and **Cemaziyülâhır**. **—yi boz=** to go back on one's vow. **— et=** /a/ to repent having done something and vow not to do it again. **— istiğfar et=** to repent and ask God's forgiveness. **—ler olsun!** I'll never do it again. **T— Suresi** a name of the ninth sura of the Quran. **—ler tövbesi** 1. I promise myself never to do it again. Never again! 2. Good Heavens!
tövbegüzâr (...—) توبه‌گذار P *lrnd.* who vows never to sin again.
tövbekâr (..—) توبه‌كار P penitent. **— kadın** reformed prostitute. **—î** (..——) P *lrnd.* penitence.

tövbeli تَوْبَه لِى penitent; under a vow not to sin again or not to do a certain thing again.
tövbesiz تَوْبَه سِز who has not repented, impenitent.
tövbeşiken تَوْبَه شِكَن P lrnd. who breaks a vow of repentance.
töz 1 تَوْز same as **toz 2**.
töz 2 تَوْز prov., same as **tös**.
töz 3 neol., phil. substance; essence. **—cülük**, substantialism. **—el** substantial.
Trablus طَرابُلس [**Tarabulus**] geog. Tripoli.
Trablusgarb طَرابُلُس غَرب geog. Tripoli (in Lybia); Tripolitania.
Trablusşam طَرابُلُس شَام geog. Tripoli (in Lebanon).
Trabzon طَرابُزُون geog. Trebizond. **— hurması** persimmon.
trafikᵍⁱ تَرافِيك F traffic. **— memuru** traffic policeman.
trahom طَراخُوم F trachoma.
trahoma (..'.) تَراخُومَه Gk dowry (of a non-Muslim).
trahunya, trakonya (..'.) طَراخُونيَه Gk greater weever fish, zool., Trachinus draco.
Trakya ('.) تَراكيَا Gk geog. Thrace. **—lı** Thracian.
trampa ('.) تَرامبَه It barter; exchange. **— et=** to exchange. **—cı** barterer, peddler who sells by barter for rags and old wares.
trampete (.'.) تَرامبِتَه F side drum.
tramplen تَرامبلَن F spring-board.
tramvay تَرامواى F 1. streetcar, trolley. 2. a kind of card game. **—cı** trolley driver.
trança ('.) تَرانجَه It a kind of sea bream, pagrus, zool., Pagrus ehrenbergii.
trank تَرانك imitates the clanking of metal (usually in connection with the payment of cash).
transit تَرانسِت F transit; passage of goods without paying custom dues; through (traffic). **— geç=** chauffeur's slang to drive on without paying attention to traffic signs.
transmisyon تَرانسمِسيُون F mech. transmission; drive. **— iç kavraması** inner drive joint. **— mili** propeller shaft.
transport تَرانسپُرت F 1. transport. 2. transport ship.
traş تَراش var. of **tıraş**.
trata ('.) طَراطَه It naut. light cutter; small fishing smack.
travers تَراوَرس F railway sleeper. **—e çık=** to sail to windward by tacking.
traz (—) طَراز A lrnd. 1. an embroidering with silk or gold thread; embroidery. 2. motto.
tren تِرَن F train.
tribün تِريبُون F platform; tribune.
triko تِريكُو F tricot; knitted wear; knitted fabric.
trikotaj تِريكُوتاج F knitting; knitted work.
trilyon تِريليُون F trillion, a million million.

trimestr تِريمِستر F school term; trimester.
tringa تِرينغَه It 1. naut. gammoning. 2. slang smart, chic.
trinket, trinketa (..'.) تِرينكَت It naut. ship's foresail.
trinketin, trinketina تِرينكَتين It naut. fore stay sail.
tripo تِريپُو F slang gambling den.
trişin تِريشين F trichina (worm).
tropika 1 (..'.) طَرُوپيقا It path. estivo-autumnal fever.
tropika 2 طَرُوپيقا It astr. tropic.
tropikalⁱⁱ طَرُوپيقال F tropical.
trotuvar طَرُوتُوار F sidewalk; pavement.
tröst تَرُوست F com. trust.
trup تَرُوپ F troupe; theatrical company.
tu 1 (—) تُو interjection expressing disgust, pooh!
=**tu 2** دى cf. =**dı 2**.
=**tu 3** دى cf. =**dı 3**.
-**tu 4** دى cf. **-tı**.
tu 5 (—) تُو P lrnd. fold, ply.
tuam طَعام A lrnd., pl. of **tu'me**.
tûba 1 (—.) طُوبَى A lrnd. 1. w. cap., name of a tree in Paradise, a branch of which will enter the mansion of each inhabitant, with flowers and ripe fruit of every imaginable kind. 2. blessedness (in the life to come); God's favor; Paradise and its joys. 3. happiness, good fortune.
tûba 2 (—.) طُوبَى A lrnd. 1. good, excellent. 2. better; best; most agreeable.
tubûlⁱⁱⁱ (.—) طُبُول A lrnd., pl. of **tabl**.
tuçᶜᵘ تُوچ var. of **tunç**.
tude (—.) تُودَه P lrnd. heap, mound. **— be tude, — ber tude** in heaps.
tufacı تُوفَه جى slang thief, burglar. **—lık** theft, burglary.
tufala=ʳ تُوفَالا slang /ı/ to steal, pinch, pilfer.
tufan (——) طُوفان A 1. flood; violent rainstorm. 2. w. cap. the Flood. **T—ı Nuh** 1. the Flood. 2. very ancient time.
tufeyl طُفَيل A lrnd. 1. infant, a small child. 2. uninvited guest. 3. intruder, parasite, feast-hunter. 4. w. cap., name of a poet of Kufah who used to go uninvited to wedding feasts.
tufeylaniyet (..—..) طُفَيلانيَت A commonsalism, symbiosis.
tufeylî (..—) طُفَيلى A sponging parasite; sponger; toady. **—yat** (...—) biol. parasitology. **—yet** A toadying.
tufeylülarais (....—.), **tufeylüla'ras** (....—) طُفَيل الأعراس A lrnd. sponging parasite.
tufuᵘᵘ **1** (.—) طُفُوء A lrnd. a being extinguished, a going out (fire); extinction.
tufu 2 (.—) تُفُو P lrnd. spittle.

tufûh (. —) طفوع A *lrnd.* a being brimful or overflowing.
tufûlᵘ̈ (. —) طفول A *lrnd., pl. of* **tıfl**. **—âne** (. — —.) P childish.
tufûlet (. —.), **tufûliyet** (. —..) طفولت طفوليت A *lrnd.* infancy, childhood.
tugat (. —) طغات A *lrnd., pl. of* **tâgi**.
tugay *neol., mil.* brigade.
tuğ طوغ *Ott. hist.* horsetail (attached to a helmet or flag-staff as a sign of rank). **— çık=** 1. to go forth (standard). 2. to take the field (a general). **— ver=** to confer horsetails (high rank for a pasha).
tuğcu طوغجى *Ott. hist.* bearer of the horse-hair pennant.
tuğamiral *neol.* rear-admiral.
tuğbay *neol.* brigadier.
tuğgeneral *neol.* brigadier general.
tuğkeşân (. . —) طوغكشان P *Ott. hist.* bearers of the Sultan's horsetails.
tuğla (́.) طوغلا brick. **— harmanı** brickyard. **— ocağı** brick kiln. **—cı** brickmaker; brick seller.
tuğlu طوغلى wearing a crest of horsehair. **— turna** the crowned crane, *zool.*, *Balearica pavonina*.
tuğra 1 طغرا | **tuğra 2** | *Ott. hist.* the Sultan's monogram; the imperial signature. **— çek=** to write the Sultan's monogram over a document.
tuğra 2 طغرا P *lrnd., same as* **tuğra 1**. **—yı garrâyı sultanî** the illustrious imperial cypher.
tuğrakeş (. —.) طغراكش P *lrnd.* employee in the office where the imperial monogram was inscribed on documents.
tuğralı طغرالى ornamented, emblazoned with the imperial monogram.
tuğranüvis (. . . —) طغرانويس P *lrnd.* one who writes the Sultan's monogram over a document.
tuğrayî (. —.) طغرائى A *same as* **tuğrakeş**.
tuğulğa طغلغه *archaic* helmet.
tuğyan (. —) طغيان A *lrnd.* 1. insubordination, rebellion. 2. an overflowing, flooding; a breaking bounds. **— et=** 1. to overflow. 2. to rebel.
tuh ته *interjection expressing regret*: What a shame! What a pity! Too bad!
tuhaf 1 تحف | **tuhaf 2** | 1. comical, amusing, funny; queer, ridiculous. 2. curious, odd. 3. *lrnd.* uncommon, rare. **—!** How strange! How curious! That's odd! **—ıma gitti** It seemed odd to me. **— ol=** to be embarrassed; to feel strange. **— şey** *same as* **tuhaf!**
tuhaf 2 تحف A *lrnd., pl. of* **tuhfe**.
tuhafçı تحافى *obs., same as* **tuhafiyeci**.
tuhafiye تحافيه small articles, clothing accessories. **—ci** seller of clothing accessories.
tuhaflıkᵍ̈ᵢ تحافلى a being odd or funny.

— et= to do or say funny things. **bir —ım var** I don't feel well.
tuhal (. —) طحال A *lrnd.* disease of the spleen.
tuham تحم A *lrnd., pl. of* **tuhme 1**.
tuhamat (. . —) تحمات A *lrnd., pl. of* **tuhme 1**.
tuhfe تحفه A *lrnd.* 1. gift, present. 2. excellent, rare thing worthy of being presented, rarity, choice thing. 3. *a title of many books*.
tuhm تحم P *lrnd., same as* **tohum**.
tuhmdân (. —) تحمدان P *lrnd.* 1. receptacle for seed. 2. bed in a garden. 3. nursery-ground.
tuhme 1 تحمه P *lrnd.* 1. seed. 2. man's stock or lineage.
tuhme 2 تحمه A *lrnd.* disagreement of food with the stomach, indigestion, dyspepsy. **—zede** P dyspeptic.
tuhmriz (. —) تحمريز P *lrnd.* 1. a sower of seed. 2. an omelet.
tuhr طهر A *lrnd.* 1. cleanness, cleanliness. 2. the canonical cleanness of a woman.
tuhut (. —) تحوت A *lrnd., pl. of* **taht 1**.
-tuk 1 دك cf. **-dık 1**.
=tukᵍᵘ **2** دك cf. **=dık 2**.
=tuk 3 دك cf. **=dık 3**.
tuka تقا A *lrnd.* 1. a fearing, shunning. 2. piety, the fear of God.
tûlᵘ̈ (—) طول A *geog., lrnd.* longitude; length. **—i beled** longitude of a place. **— dairesi** meridian. **—i emel** *lrnd.* worldly ambition. **—i emel sahibi** worldly minded. **—i kevkeb** celestial longitude of a star. **—i mevc** *phys.* wave length. **—i ömür** *lrnd.* length of life. **— saati** ship's chronometer. **—i zaman** *lrnd.* length of time.
tulâ (— —) طولى A *lrnd.* 1. longer; longest. 2. any one of the longer chapters of the Quran.
tûlâni (— — —) طولانى A *lrnd.* longitudinal; in length.
tulen (—́.) طولاً A *lrnd.* in length; lengthwise.
tulga طولغه *same as* **tuğulga**.
tullâb (. —) طلاب A *lrnd., pl. of* **tâlib**.
tulûᵘᵘ (. —) طلوع A 1. a rising (of the sun or a star). 2. *lrnd.* an appearing (of a tooth, etc.). 3. birth (of an idea). **—i fecr** *lrnd.* the first break of day. **— ve gurub** the rising and setting of any heavenly body.
tulûat (. — —) طلوعات A 1. popular theater (where the actors improvise). 2. *lrnd.* sudden ideas; improvisations. **—cı** actor who improvises.
tulukᵍᵘ طلوك *prov., same as* **tulum**.
tulum طولوم 1. skin made into a bag (to hold water, etc. or used

as a float for a raft). 2. overalls. 3. tube (for toothpaste, etc.). 4. pair of fur squares (for making into a cloak). 5. bagpipe. — **çık=** to achieve one's purpose. — **çıkar=** to flay off a skin or hide. — **gibi** swollen all over; as fat as a pig. — **peyniri** a kind of cheese made in a skin.

tulumba (..'.) طولومبه طولومبه تلومبه طولمبه طلومبا 1. pump. 2. fire engine. 3. waterspout. — **bakracı** sucker of a pump. — **çek=** to pump. — **kolu** pump-handle, pump brake. — **tatlısı** sweet (made of pastry soaked in syrup).

tulumbacı طولومباجی *Ott. hist.* 1. member of one of the old independent fire brigades. 2. rough, rowdy (person). 3. unmannerly youth. — **koğuşu** 1. dormitory for firemen. 2. street gang. — **lık** 1. quality or functions of a fireman. 2. behavior of a rowdy.

tulumlular *neol., zool.,* Ascones.

-tum 1 دُمْ *cf.* **-dım 1.**
=tum 2 دُمْ *cf.* **=dım 2.**
tum=[ar] **3** طومحم *prov.* 1. to dive into the water. 2. to stoop, to bend over.
tum 4 طوم *prov.* heap, mound.
tu'm 5 طعم A *lrnd.* taste; flavor.
tuman 1 طومان تومان *prov.* long wide drawers or trousers. — **paça** trousers or drawers with very wide legs not gathered round the ankles by strings. — **paça gez=** to go about in drawers; to be in undress.
tuman 2 (——) تومان P *lrnd.* 1. ten thousand. 2. division of an army originally ten thousand strong. 3. *a gold coin of Persia.* 4. county or district originally paying ten thousand sequins land tax.
tuman=[ir] **3** تومانس *archaic* to stand out prominently.
tumaninet (.——.) طمانینت طمأنینت A *lrnd.* serenity of mind, quiet, tranquillity.
tumba ('.) طومبا It 1. a tumbling into bed (of children). 2. a turning upside down. 3. dump truck. — **düş=** to throw oneself down full length.
tu'me طعمه A *lrnd.* 1. thing seized as food, prey. 2. gain, earnings. 3. morsel, a mouthful; food; bait. — **i mâr u mûr** a prey to snakes and ants. — **i şimşir, — i tir** a prey to the sword.
tumturak[gı] طمطراق [*Persian* ..—] magnificence, pomp, display; pompous speech.
tumturaklı طمطراقلی bombastic; pompous; high-flown.
-tun 1 دُنْ *cf.* **-dın 1.**
=tun 2 دُنْ *cf.* **=dın 2.**
tun 3 طون *only in* **tundan tuna** from place to place; hither and thither. **—dan tuna düş=** to wander around in strange places, to go about as a stranger.

Tuna طونه *geog.* the Danube.
tunç[cu] تونج طونج bronze.
Tunus تونس [*Arabic* —.] *geog.* Tunis. — **gediği** thing got without trouble; rich woman married for her money. —**lu** Tunisian.
-tunuz 1 دُكْز *cf.* **-dınız 1.**
=tunuz 2 دُكْز *cf.* **=dınız 2.**
tur 1 طور F tour, promenade.
Tur 2 (—) طور A *lrnd.* 1. Mount Sinai. 2. Mount Tabor. 3. *l. c.* mountain. 4. *l. c.* courtyard. — **Sûresi** *a name of the fifty second sura of the Quran.*
=tur 3 در *cf.* **=dır 1.**
=tur= 4 درسز *cf.* **=dır= 2.**
tura 1 طورا *var. of* **tuğra.**
tura 2 طوره 1. *a game played with a knotted handkerchief.* 2. beater of leather or a leatherheaded stick used for drums. 3. *lrnd.* roll of paper; skein (of silk, etc.); coil (of rope). — **oyunu** *a game in which the handkerchief is used to beat an adversary.* — **saçak** *arch.* narrow eaves.
turab (.—) تراب A *same as* **türab.**
turaç[cı] طوراج francolin, *zool.,* Francolinus francolinus.
turala=[r] توره لمود طوره لمو to make into a coil. —**n=** to coil up. —**t=** /1, a/ *caus. of* **turala=.**
Turan (——) توران طوران Turan. —**cılık** Pan-Turanism. —**î** (———) P Turanian.
turb ترب *same as* **turba.**
turba ('.) تربا F *chem., bot.* turf; peat (for fuel). —**lık** peat bog; peaty.
turef طرف A *lrnd., pl. of* **turfe.**
tureng (—.) تورنگ A *lrnd.* pheasant.
turfa طرفه A 1. not kosher. 2. unclean; not fresh (food). 3. curiosity. — **ol=** to fall into disgrace, to be despised.
turfala=[r] طورفه لامو /1/ to despise, to treat with contempt.
turfanda (...) ترفنده طرفانه طرفنده [*Persian* **türfende**] 1. early fruit or vegetables. 2. *joc.* novice, new. —**cı** raiser or seller of early fruit or vegetables. —**lık** garden for growing early fruit, etc.
turfe طرفه A 1. *same as* **turfa.** 2. *lrnd.* new, strange, curious or prized thing; a curiosity. 3. *lrnd.* comical or quaint thing, act, word or manner.
turfegî (..—) طرفگی P *lrnd.* newness, rarity; comicalness; quaintness.
turfeneva (...—) طرفه نوا P *lrnd.* rare and curious thing; unprecedented.
Turhalli تورخالی *var. of* **Tırhallı.**
turhan طرخان *archaic* 1. noble man; chief, prince. 2. *w. cap.,* man's name.
Turî (——) توری P *lrnd.* Turanian.

turist توریست F 1. tourist. 2. *slang* guest who stays overnight (in a house). — **mevkii** inexpensive class (accommodations).

turistikᵍⁱ توریستیك F 1. available to tourists. 2. luxury quality; most expensive rate.

turizm توریزم F tourism.

Turla طورلا obs. the river Dniester.

turna طورنا تورنه طورنه crane, *zool.*, *Megalornis grus*. — **ayağı** ranunculus, crowfoot, *bot.*, *Ranunculus*. — **balığı** pike, *zool.*, *Esox lucius*; needlefish, *zool.*, *Belone vulgaris*. — **gagası** stork's bill, *bot.*, *Erodium gruinum*; adder's-tongue, fox geranium, *bot.*, *Geranium Robertianum*. — **geçidi** spring storm. — **gözü** color of a crane's eye, light yellow. — **gözü gibi** clear yellow. — **yı gözünden vurmak** to hit the mark; to do a good stroke of business. — **katarı** 1. a flock of cranes. 2. a procession of people. — **katarı gibi** *colloq.* in a line; in perfect order. — **kırı** ash-gray color. — **ol=** *gambler's slang* to lose.

turnacı طورناجى *Ott. hist.* 1. keeper of the cranes at the imperial palace. 2. member of the seventy-third regiment of Janissaries.

turne طورنه F tour.

turnike طورنیكه F turnstile.

turnsolⁱᵘ, **turnusol**ⁱᵘ طورنوسول F 1. dyer's croton; turnsole (purple dye). 2. *chem.* litmus paper.

turnuva طورنووا tourney, tournament.

turp طورپ تورپ توربه توربی [**türb 1**] radish, *bot.*, *Raphanus sativus*. — **gibi** sturdy, robust, healthy and strong, hale and hearty. —**giller** *neol.*, *bot.*, *Cruciferae*.

turrakᵏⁱ (.—) طرّا A *lrnd.*, *pl.* of **tarık**.

turre طرّه A *lrnd.* 1. a lock of hair, forelock. 2. a roll of any tissue. 3. ball of silk wound from cocoons. 4. border of land; border of a cloth or garment; an edging. 5. indication, trace; sequel.

Tursina (— — —) طورسینا A *geog.* Mount Sinai.

turşulukᵍᵘ (.—.), **turşruyî** (.——) ترشرولى ترشرویی P *lrnd.* quality or act of looking stern and morose; sternness of visage, moroseness of look.

turşu 1 طورشو ترشى تورشو [**türşî**] 1. pickle. 2. exhausted, very weary. 3. *slang* very drunk. — **gibi** very weary. — **kesil=** 1. to turn sour. 2. to go bad (food). 3. to become slack, to have no energy. — **kur=** to pickle. —**sunu kur=** 1. to pickle. 2. to keep indefinitely; to spoil by not using. —**sunu kur** Pickle it! *said in anger to one who has refused to give something*. — **lâpası** sour rice boiled soft. — **ol=** *same as* **turşu kesil=**. — **suratlı**, — **yüzlü** sour faced.

turşu=ʳ **2** ترشى to turn sour; to become acid.

turşucu ترشجى طورشوجى maker and seller of pickles. —**luk** pickle making and selling.

turşula=ʳ ترشلى /ı/ to pickle. —**n=** to be pickled; to become a pickle. —**t=** /ı, a/ *caus.*

turşulu ترشلى طورشولو prepared, mixed or flavored with pickles.

turşulukᵍᵘ ترشلى طورشولى material suitable for pickling.

turta (.'.) طورطه It cake.

turuf (.—) طروف A *lrnd.*, *pl.* of **taraf**.

turukᵏᵘ طرق A *lrnd.*, *pl.* of **tarik 1**.

turuncu تورنجى orange color.

turunçᶜᵘ تورنج ترنج طورنج P Seville orange, bitter orange, *bot.*, *Citrus aurantium*, *Citrus vulgaris*.

tuş 1 طوش F key of a piano, typewriter, etc.

tuş 2 (—) توش P *lrnd.* 1. sustenance, nutriment enough to maintain life. 2. body. 3. strength, power, vigor.

tuşdan (— —) توشدان P *lrnd.* traveller's provision bag or basket.

tuşe (—.) توشه P *lrnd.* 1. traveller's provisions. 2. food sufficient for a meal. —**i râh** provisions for a journey. —**dân** (—.—) P *same as* **tuşdân**.

tuşmalⁱⁱ (— —) توشمال P *lrnd.* butler.

tut 1 (—) توت A *lrnd.*, *same as* **ut 1**.

tut=ᵃʳ **2** طوتمق توتمق 1. /ı/ to hold; to hold on to; to catch; to take; to keep, to retain, to preserve; to stop, to detain; to capture; to make prisoner; to come (on), to attack one (illness or pain); to go to the head (wine, etc.); *slang* to infuriate. 2. /ı/ to hold up steadily; to support; *slang* to have as wife; to take the part (of), to favor; to keep, obey (command, etc.). 3. /ı/ to engage (servant); to hire (house, etc.); to occupy, take up, fill (space); to spread, to reach (district); to stop up, close up, choke up. 4. /ı/ to contain, hold (quantity, etc.); to restrain, to govern. 5. /ı/ to agree with, tally with. 6. to esteem, account, reckon, to suppose. 7. to take root; to take (seeds, grafts, vaccination, etc.); to succeed, to assume some particular desired condition; to take effect (curse); to stick, to adhere. 8. to hold on, endure, last. 9. to amount to, to reach (sum of money, account, etc.). 10. to begin (rain, etc.). —**uyor musun?** *slang* Do you have any cash? — **kelin perçeminden** hopeless *said of one from whom due reparation for a wrong cannot be expected or who cannot be held responsible*. —**alım ki** Let's suppose that... —**tuğunu kopar=** to succeed in every attempt.

tuta طوتا *archaic* on account; sum stopped on account of a claim. — **al=** to stop as an offset to a claim (a sum).

tutaçᶜⁱ طوتاج *prov.* 1. pot holder. 2. pincers, tongs (used in a laboratory).

tutakᵍ¹ طوتاق *prov.* 1. handle. 2. pot holder. 3. pincers, tongs. 4. hostage.

tutam طوتام 1. amount that can be grasped by the fingers, pinch. 2. small handful. 3. handle. 4. *archaic* behavior. — **tutam** in small handfuls; in bunches.

tutamakᵍ¹ طوتاماق 1. anything to be taken hold of; handle. 2. support. 3. proof, evidence. 4. habitual custom. 5. means of livelihood. 6. anything to be adversely criticized. — **bul=** to find a pretext. — **noktası** something to catch hold of. — **ver=** to afford a pretext.

tutamla=ʳ طوتاملامق /ı/ 1. to measure by handfuls. 2. to take as a handful.

tutamlı طوتاملى 1. that has a handle. 2. who has a grasp. 3. who has a constant practice or habit.

tutanakᵍ¹ *neol.* minutes (of a business meeting).

tutar طوتار 1. total, sum. 2. epilepsy, seizure, fit. 3. holding, seizing.

tutarakᵍ¹ طوتاراق 1. fit, seizure. 2. kindling wood, tinder. —**ı tut=** to have a seizure; to have a fit of obstinacy.

tutarıkᵍ¹ طوتاريق epilepsy. —**lı** epileptic.

tutarlı *neol.* logically consistent, congruous.

tutarsız *neol.* inconsistent, incongruous.

tutaş طوتاش *archaic* touching, adjacent, contiguous.

tutekᵏⁱ (—.) توتك P *lrnd.* 1. parrot. 2. shepherd's pipe.

tuti (——) طوطى P *lrnd.* 1. parrot. 2. young and pretty woman. —**i gûya** talking parrot. —**i mûcizegû** parrot that announces miracles. —**i şekerha** 1. sugar-chewing parrot. 2. sweet-spoken beautiful woman.

Tutiname (———.) طوطى نامه P *lrnd.* Parrot-tales (name of a famous book).

tutivar (———) طوطيوار P *lrnd.* 1. parrotlike. 2. eloquent; delicate.

tutiyan (———) طوطيان P parrots.

tutkal طوتقال glue; sizing; size. — **gibi** sticky (used of a person one can't get rid of).

tutkalla=ʳ طوتقالامق /ı/ to glue, to size. —**n=** *pass.*

tutkallı طوتقالى glued, sized.

tutku *neol., psych.* passion. —**lu** passionate.

tutkun طوتقون 1. /a/ affected by; given to. 2. /a/ in love with. 3. dupe; prey; deceived; duped; caught. 4. stopped up, impeded. 5. seized, captured. 6. prisoner, captive; affected with some kind of disease (paralysis, cramp, etc.). 7. eclipsed; eclipse. — **avla=** to hunt for a dupe. — **ver=** to be the victim of a surprise; to be caught.

tutkunlukᵍᵘ طوتقونلق passion; love.

tutma طوتمه 1. *verbal n.* of **tut=** 2. 2. arrest, detention. 3. *phil.* inhibition. 4. *prov.* farm hand.

tutmaçᶜ¹ طوتماج *prov.* fresh-made pastry cut in strips and cooked with meat and yogurt.

tutsakᵍ¹ طوتساق 1. captive, prisoner (of war). 2. *prov.* pawn. —**lık** captivity.

tuttur=ᵘʳ طوتدرمق 1. /ı, a/ *caus.* of **tut=** 2. 2. /ı/ to keep bothering somebody to do something (like a spoiled child); to insist. —**abildiğine sat=** /ı/ to sell for as high a price as he can get from any particular customer.

tutu طوتو *archaic* 1. pledge, pawn, deposit. 2. stake, wager; prize. — **ko=** 1. to put down stakes or a wager. 2. to offer a prize. — **ver=** 1. to give a pledge, to leave a deposit. 2. to give in pledge.

tutukᵍᵘ طوتوق 1. slow, hesitant; shy, timid. 2. embarrassed; tongue-tied; stuttering. 3. stopped up; impeded. 4. paralyzed; having had a stroke. 5. *slang* in love with.

tutuklu طوتقلى prisoner; under arrest.

tutuklukᵍᵘ طوتوقلق timidity; difficulty in talking.

tutul=ᵘʳ طوتولمق 1. *pass.* of **tut=** 2. 2. /a/ to fall in love with, to be struck with. 3. /a/ to be angered. 4. to stutter, to be tongue-tied. —**ma** *verbal n.*

tutum 1 طوتوم 1. manner, conduct, procedure. 2. economy, thrift.

tutum 2 طوتوم *archaic* sumach, *bot.*, Rhus cotinus.

tutumlu طوتوملى thrifty.

tutun=ᵘʳ طوتنمق 1. /ı/ to apply to oneself. 2. /a/ to hold (on), cling; to take a hold. —**ma** *verbal n.*

tuturukᵍᵘ طوتوروق *prov.* chip; kindling.

tutuş 1 طوتوش *verbal n.* of **tut=** 2.

tutuş=ᵘʳ **2** توتشمك 1. to catch hold of one another; to quarrel. 2. to catch fire, to burn, to be on fire. 3. to flare up (in anger). —**ma** *verbal n.* —**tur=** /ı/ *caus.* to set on fire.

tutya (.'.) طوطيا [Arabic —.—] zinc.

tuvalet تواليت F 1. cleaning up for going out to a social gathering. 2. make-up. 3. dressing table. 4. woman's evening gown. 5. lavatory, toilet.

tuvan (.—) توان P *lrnd.* 1. powerful, strong, mighty. 2. power, strength.

tuvana (.——) توانا P *lrnd.* strong, mighty, powerful.

tuvanger (.—.) توانگر P *lrnd.* wealthy, influential.

tuveys طويس A *lrnd.* little peacock.

tuyûr (.—) طيور A *lrnd., pl.* of **tair, tayr**.

tuz توز salt. —**u biberi** necessary addition. — **biber ek=** /a/ to make things worse; to be the last straw. —**u biberi yerinde**

tuzak

properly seasoned; nothing lacking, all right. — **buz ol=** 1. to be scattered into pieces. 2. to be in vain. —**la buz ol=** to be smashed to bits; to be utterly routed. — **ek=** /a/ to add salt (to). — **ekmek** 1. favor, charity. 2. bonds of friendship. 3. bread and salt. — **ekmek haini** ungrateful to a benefactor. — **ekmek hakkı** gratitude towards a benefactor. —**u kuru** well off, in easy circumstances; without worries. — **ruhu** hydrochloric acid.

tuzak[gi] طوزاق trap. —**a düş=** to fall into a trap. — **kur=** /a/ to lay a trap (for somebody). —**çı** cheat.

tuzcu طوزجى seller of salt.

tuzla 1 (..́.) طوزلا طوزلا نوزلا نوزلا saltpan; salt mine. — **tavası** evaporator in saltworks.

tuzla=[r] **2** طوزلامق نوزلامق /ı/ to salt; to pickle in brine. —**yım da kokma** You fool! You must be out of your head!

tuzlak[gi] طوزلاق نوزلاق 1. land impregnated with salt, from which salt is or could be obtained. 2. *same as* **tuzla 1**.

tuzlama طوزلامه 1. *verbal n. of* **tuzla= 2**. 2. salted; pickled in brine.

tuzlan=[ır] طوزلانمق نوزلانمق 1. to be salted. 2. to become salt.

tuzlat=[ır] طوزلاتمق نوزلاتمق /ı, a/ *caus. of* **tuzla= 2**.

tuzlu طوزلو نوزلو 1. salted; salty. 2. pickled. 3. expensive. — **balgam** *med.* scrofula; scurvy. —**ya mal ol=** to be expensive. — **mantar** puffball, *bot.*, *Lycoperdon*. —**ya otur=** to cost a lot. — **su** salt-water; brine.

tuzluca (..́.) طوزلوجه 1. somewhat salty. 2. rather expensive.

tuzluk[gu] طوزلوق نوزلوق salt-shaker, saltcellar.

tuzluluk[gu] طوزلولوق saltiness, salinity.

tuzsuz طوزسز 1. saltless; unsalted. 2. insipid.

tü 1 تو 1. sound or act of spitting. 2. expression of disgust.

tü 2 تو *P lrnd.* thou.

-tü 3 دى *cf.* **-tı 4**.

-tü 4 دى *cf.* **-dı 2**.

=tü 5 دى *cf.* **=dı 3**.

tüb توب *F same as* **tüp**.

tüberküloz توبركولوز *F med.* tuberculosis.

tüccar (.—) تجار *A* merchant. — **malı** merchandise. —**lık** trade.

tüfek[gi], **tüfenk**[gi] تفنك تفنك *P* gun, rifle. — **arpacığı** front sight of a gun. — **at=** to fire a rifle; to shoot. — **boşalt=** to discharge a gun. — **burgusu** wormer for withdrawing the charge of a gun. — **çat=** to pile arms. — **çubuğu** ramrod (for a gun). — **deliği** bore of a gun. — **demiri** gun barrel. — **dipçiği** butt of a gun. —**i duvara daya=** *colloq.* to be exhausted. — **falyası** touchhole of a gun. — **fitili** match of a matchlock gun. — **karşılığı** steel of a flintlock gun. — **kayışı** shoulder strap of a gun. — **kesmesi** slug. — **kılıfı** gun case. — **korkuluğu** trigger-guard. — **kundağı** gunstock. — **kuyruğu** tail of a gun barrel (screwed to the stock). — **memesi** nipple of a rifle. — **namlusu** gun barrel. — **nişangâhı** hind sight of a gun. — **otu** *obs.* gunpowder. — **patlaması** a breaking out of war. — **patlamaksızın** without war. — **saçması** small shot. — **talimi** drill in using arms. — **tanesi** bullet. — **yuvarlağı** bullet.

tüfekçi تفكجى 1. gun-maker. 2. *Ott. hist.* guard at the Imperial Palace. 3. *slang* communist.

tüfekendaz (...—) تفنك انداز *P lrnd.* musketeer.

tüfekhâne (..—.) تفنكخانه armory.

tüfeklik[gi] تفنكلك armory; gun-stand.

tüffah (.—) تفاح *A lrnd.* apple.

tüffaha (.—.) تفاحه *A lrnd.* a single apple.

tüffahülarz (.—..) تفاح الارض *A lrnd.* potato; Jerusalem artichoke.

tüffahülhüb (.—..) تفاح الحب *A lrnd.* tomato.

tüh توه *exclamation expressing regret or annoyance.* — **sana!** Shame on you!

tühame تهامه *same as* **tuhme 2**.

tühem تهم *A lrnd., pl. of* **töhmet**.

tühut (.—) تهوت *A lrnd., pl. of* **taht 2**, people of the lowest rank, the rabble.

-tük 1 دك *cf.* **-dık 1**.

=tük[gü] **2** دك *cf.* **=dık 2**.

=tük 3 دك *cf.* **=dık 3**.

=tükçe دكجه *cf.* **=dıkça**.

tüken=[ir] توكنمك to be exhausted; to come to an end; to give out. —**mez** 1. inexhaustible. 2. a kind of syrup (made of fruit juice to which water is constantly added). 3. ball-point pen.

tüket=[ir] توكتمك /ı/ to exhaust; to use up; to spend. —**il=** *pass*

tüketim *neol.* consumption.

=tükte دكته *cf.* **=dıkta**.

=tükten başka دكتن باشقه *cf.* **=dıktan başka**.

=tükten sonra دكتن صكره *cf.* **=dıktan sonra**.

tükrük[gü] توكروك *same as* **tükürük**.

tükür=[ür] توكورمك /ı/ to spit; to spit out. —**düğünü yala=** to eat one's words. —**t=** *caus.* /ı, a/

tükürük[gü] توكوروك spittle, saliva. — **bezleri** salivary glands. — **hokkası** spittoon. — **kâğıdı** paper guard held under the hand when writing. — **otu** Star-of-Bethlehem, *bot., Ornithogalum stachyoides*. — **yere düşme=** to be extremely cold (so as to freeze one's spittle). — **ünü yut=** to gulp (with desire for something delicious).

tükürükle=[r] توكوركله /ı/ to wet with saliva.

tül تل *F* tulle.

tülbent[di] تلبند [**dülbend**] muslin; gauze. — **kuru yuncaya kadar** in a very short time. — **ağası**

Ott. hist. court officer of the wardrobe.
— lâlesi white tulip, bot., *Tulipa stellaia*.
tüle=ʳ توله مك prov. to moult.
tülek⁼ᵍⁱ توه لك prov. 1. chicken coop. 2. *same as* **tünek**. 3. a bird's molting season and condition. 4. young bird that has reached its first molt. 5. refuge. 6. power, reach, opportunity. 7. sly; cheat; coward. **—ini bul=, —ine gel=** /ın/ to come into one's power, to come within one's reach. **— yeri** 1. lair or bed of a wild animal; perch of a domesticated bird. 2. covert used by hunters.
tüleng تنگ P lrnd. need, occasion; wish, desire, inclination.
tülengî (..—) تنگى P lrnd. needy person; beggar; supplicant.
tüm 1 توم 1. whole; entire. 2. prov. round (thing); mound.
-tüm 2 ـم cf. **-dım 1**.
=tüm 3 ـم cf. **=dım 2**.
tüm=ᵉʳ 4 تومل *same as* **tümel= 1**.
tümamiralⁱⁱ *neol.* vice-admiral.
tümbek⁼ᵍⁱ توم بك prov. 1. small round thing; mound. 2. small earthenware drum.
tümbelek⁼ᵍⁱ توم بلك long earthenware drum or tomtom.
tümbültü توم بلتى *archaic* 1. bundle or large saddlebag put on a horse's back. 2. saddlebag on which a man mounts.
tümceleme *neol.*, *phil.* reintegration.
tümdengelim *neol.*, *log.* deduction.
tümel=ⁱʳ **1** توملك *archaic* to be protuberant, to rise as in a mound.
tümel 2 *neol.*, *log.* universal. **—ler** the universals.
tümen تومن 1. great number, great heap. 2. ten thousand. 3. *mil.* division. 4. toman (a Persian gold coin). **— tümen** in vast numbers.
tümevarım *neol.*, *log.* induction. **—sal** inductive.
tümgeneralⁱⁱ *neol.*, *mil.* major-general.
tümle=ʳ *neol.* /ı/ to complete.
tümleç⁼ᶜⁱ *neol.*, *log.*, *gram.* the complement.
tümlen=ⁱʳ *neol.* to be completed.
tümler *neol.*, *math.* complementary.
tümör تومور F *path.* tumor.
tümsek⁼ᵍⁱ تومسك 1. small mound; protuberance. 2. prominent, protuberant, convex. **—lik** protuberance.
tümsel=ⁱʳ توملك 1. to rise (out of the ground). 2. to become round; to be protuberant.
tün 1 تون *only in* **— aydın** Good evening; Good night.
-tün 2 دك cf. **-dın 1**.
=tün 3 دك cf. **=dın 2**.
tünd تند P lrnd. 1. violent, strong, fierce. 2. irritable, hasty. 3. impetuous. **— ü tiz** swift.
tündbâd (.—) تندباد P lrnd. whirlwind; violent wind.

tünder تندر P lrnd. thunder.
tündhuy (.—) تندخوى P lrnd. 1. hasty, obstinate. 2. violent in disposition, irritable.
tündî (.—) تندى P lrnd. 1. violence, fierceness. 2. impetuosity. 3. irritability, hastiness. 4. moroseness.
tündinan تندعنان P lrnd. hard-bitted (horse); unmanageable; fast-going (horse).
tündlicam, tündlikâm (..—) تندلجام P lrnd. hard-mouthed (horse); fleet (horse).
tündmizac (..—) تندمزاج P lrnd. of hasty temper.
tündpervaz (..—) تندپرواز P lrnd. swift-flying.
tündreftar (..—) تندرفتار P lrnd. swift of pace, fleet.
tündrev تندرو P lrnd. swift-going.
tündru (.—) تندرو P lrnd. grim, morose; austere.
tündzeban (..—) تندزبان P lrnd. eloquent, fluent.
tüne=ʳ تونه مك to perch (bird).
tünek⁼ᵍⁱ تونك perch (in a chicken coop). **—le=** *same as* **tüne=**.
tünel تونل F tunnel. **— geç=** *slang* to be absent-minded.
-tünüz 1 دكڭز cf. **-dınız 1**.
=tünüz 2 دكڭز cf. **=dınız 2**.
tüpᵇᵘⁱ توب [**tüb**] 1. tube. 2. *chem.* test tube. **—lük** tube-holder.
tür 1 *neol.*, *biol.* 1. species; genus. 2. kind, sort.
=tür 2 در cf. **=dır 1**.
=tür= 3 در cf. **=dır 2**.
tür'a ترعه A lrnd. 1. opening through which water flows; canal or channel for water. 2. door, gate. 3. step, stair.
türab (.—) تراب A lrnd. 1. earth, dust. 2. district, territory. **—i hâlik** white arsenic, arsenic trioxide.
türaba (.——) ترابا A *only in* **Ħaraben türaba** tumbledown, utterly ruined.
türabî (.——) ترابى A pertaining to dust or earth; earthy.
türb 1 ترب P lrnd., *same as* **turp**.
türb 2 ترب A lrnd. earth, dust.
türbe تربه A 1. tomb, grave; mausoleum. 2. lrnd. earth, dust; soil.
türbedâr (..—) تربه دار P lrnd. keeper of a mausoleum. **—î** (..——) P, **—lık** office, quality and duties of a **türbedâr**.
türbet تربت A *poet.*, *same as* **türbe**.
türbin توربین F *mech.* turbine.
türbiye تربیه A lrnd. 1. related to earth or dust. 2. dust-colored, reddish-brown.
türe 1 توره *same as* **töre**.
türe=ʳ 2 تورمك 1. to spring up suddenly; to come into existence; to appear. 2. to increase and multiply.
türedi توره دى 1. one who has sprung up

from anywhere; upstart; parvenue. 2. bandit; rebel; vagabond.

türet=ⁱʳ نُورَتْمَك /ı/ caus. of **türe= 2.**

Türkᵏᵘ تُرك A 1. Turk; the Turks; Turkish. 2. *lrnd.* beautiful boy or girl, the belovéd. — **aksağı** *mus.* a fast rhythmic pattern of five beats (*same as* **süreyya**). **—i aşkar** *poet.* the planet Mars. **—i çarh** *lrnd.* 1. the planet Mars. 2. the sun. **—i çeşm** *lrnd.* a beautiful, predatory eye. **—i Çin** *lrnd.* the sun. **—i felek** 1. the sun. 2. Mars. **—i muarbid** *poet.* the planet Mars. **—i nimruz** *lrnd.* the sun. **—i pencümin** *lrnd.* the planet Mars. **—i rüstayan** *lrnd.* garlic. **—i sultan şükûh** *lrnd.* the world-illuminating sun. **—i taze** *lrnd.* 1. a young Turk. 2. a beautiful young boy or girl. 3. *myst.* a well of spiritual joy suddenly springing up in the heart of a devotee.

Türkân (.—) تُركان P *lrnd.* the Turks. **—ı çarh** *poet.* the seven planets.

Türkâne (.—.) تُركانه P *lrnd.* 1. Turk-like, like a Turk. 2. beautiful, lovely.

Türkânî (.——) تُركانى P *Ott. hist.* a kind of full upper garment worn by women.

Türkçe (.'.) تُوركچه 1. the Turkish language; in Turkish. 2. in the Turkish manner and fashion. **—si** in plain Turkish; the long and short of it. **— bilmez** dull of understanding. **— bilmez Allahtan korkmaz** (*lit.*, who neither knows Turkish nor fears God) barbarian. **—yi kaybet=** (*lit.*, to lose one's Turkish) to be utterly bewildered. **— söyle=** 1. to speak in Turkish. 2. to say a thing bluntly. **—yi unuttur=** /a/ to bewilder one.

Türkçeleş=ⁱʳ تُوركچەلشمك to become Turkish; to be translated into Turkish. **—tir=** /ı/ to put into Turkish.

Türkçü تُوركچى Turkist, defender of the superiority of the Turkish race and tradition. **—lük** doctrine of the Turkists.

Türkî (.—) تُركى A *lrnd.* Turkish; a single Turk. **— hicaz** *mus.* a **makam** starting like **hicaz** but ending on g' instead of a'.

Türkistan (..—) تُركستان P *geog.* Turkistan.

Türkiyat (..—) تُركيات A *lrnd.* study of things Turkish, Turcology.

Türkiye تُركيه A *geog.* Turkey. **— Cumhuriyeti** the Turkish Republic. **—li** belonging to or originating from Turkey.

Türkleş=ⁱʳ تُركلشمك to become Turkish; to adopt Turkish habits; to become like a Turk. **—tir=** /ı/ *caus.* to Turkify.

Türklükᵍᵘ تُركلك 1. the quality of being a Turk. 2. the Turkish community.

Türkmen تُركمن P Turkoman.

Türkmenistan (...—) تُركمنستان P land of the Turkomans.

türksüvar (..—) تُرك سُوار P *lrnd.* who rides well like a Turk, horseman.

türktaz (.—) تُركتاز P *lrnd.* who makes predatory raids like a Turk; predatory raid. **—î** (.——) P plundering excursion conducted with rapidity.

türkü تُركى folk song. **— çağır=** to sing a song. **—sünü çağır=** /ın/ to sing the praises of a person, to laud. **— söyle=** to sing. **— yak=** to compose a song.

türlü تُرلو 1. sort, kind, variety. 2. a number of different kinds. 3. a meat and vegetable stew. **—sü** all kinds. **bir —** *cf.* **bir 1. —sünü gör=** to have varied experience of a thing. **— türlü** of all sorts, various.

türrehat, türrühat (..—) تُرَّهات A *lrnd.* nonsense; idle tales, vain words.

türs تُرس A *lrnd.* shield. **—î** (.—) A 1. pertaining to a shield; peltate, scutiform. 2. shield-bearer; maker or seller of shields.

türş تُرش P *lrnd.* 1. sour, acid. 2. morose, cynical, crabbed in disposition or in expression. 3. disagreeable, unpleasant. **— ü şirin** 1. sour and sweet. 2. unpleasant and pleasant.

türşbâ (.—) تُرشبا P *lrnd.* soup acidulated with vinegar or lemon.

türşî (.—) تُرشى P *lrnd.* 1. sourness, acidity. 2. crabbedness, moroseness of look or disposition. 3. disagreeableness, unpleasantness. 4. pickles; pickle.

türşmizac (..—) تُرشمزاج P *lrnd.* sour-tempered, harsh.

türşru (.—) تُرشرو P *lrnd.* sour-faced, morose. **—luk** *abstr. n.*

türşruy (.—) تُرشروى P *lrnd.*, *same as* **türşru**. **—î** (.——) P *abstr. n.*

türşşirin (.——) تُرش شيرين P *lrnd.* mixed sour and sweet; sour-sweet.

türştabᵇ'¹ تُرشطبع P *lrnd.* sour-tempered, morose.

türşta'm تُرشطعم P *lrnd.* sour tasting, tart.

türus (.—) تُروس A *lrnd.*, *pl.* of **türs**.

türü=ʳ *neol.*, *phil.* to emanate.

türüm *neol.* 1. genesis, creation. 2. *phil.* emanation.

türünc تُرنج P *lrnd.*, *same as* **turunç**.

tüsˢᵘ تُسع A *lrnd.* ninth, ninth part.

tüskür=ᵘʳ, **tüskürt=**ᵘʳ تُوسكرمك، تُوسكُرتمك *archaic* 1. to back a horse. 2. to repulse (an enemy).

tüskürü تُوسكُرى *archaic* backwards, retreatingly.

tüslen=ⁱʳ تُوسلنمك *archaic* to have faint beginnings of a beard on the face.

tüslü تُوسلو *archaic* downy.

tüt=ᵉʳ تُوتمك to give out smoke (chimney); to smoke; to fume.

tütsü تُوتسى 1. fumigation; fumigant.

2. incense; the use of incense to avert the evil eye.
tütsüle=ʳ نوتسله‌مك /ı/ to cure by smoking (meat, etc.); to fumigate. **—n**= /ı/ pass.
tütsülü نوتسولى fumigated, smoked.
tüttür=ᵘʳ نوتته‌ورمك نوتته‌مك دوته‌ورمك دته‌رمك /ı/ 1. caus. of **tüt**=. 2. to smoke (cigarette or pipe).
tütün نوتون دتون دتن دوتن ستون نوتن
1. tobacco. 2. smoke; vapor. 3. bloom of ripe fruit. **— balığı** smoked fish. **—ü çık**= to give off smoke (thing). **—ü doğru çık**= to go on as well as possible (matter). **— iç**= to smoke (tobacco). **— kesesi** tobacco pouch.
tütüncü نوتونجى 1. tobacconist. 2. grower of tobacco. **— kâğıdı** thin coarse wrapping paper. **—lük** 1. tobacconist's business. 2. tobacco culture.
tütünle=ʳ نوتونله‌مك /ı/ to cure by smoking. **—n**= /ı/ pass.
tüvan (.—) توان P same as **tuvan**.
tüveyc توه‌يج A bot. corolla. **—ât** (..—) A pl.
tüy 1 توى 1. feather; down; quill (from a bird's wing). 2. hair. **— at**= to change feathers or fur. **— dik**= /a/ to be the last straw. **—leri diken diken ol**= to shudder; to stand on end (hair). **— dök**= to shed fur; to molt. **— döken** slang razor. **— dökümü** a shedding of the coat of fur; a molting. **—ü düz**= 1. to get the hair or coat in good condition. 2. to put on an improved appearance (said of one rising from poverty). **— gibi** as light as a feather. **— kabası** in spite of appearance nothing but skin and bone. **—lerini kabart**= to bristle up the hair or feathers. **— kalem** quill pen. **— kalemi** quill of a feather. **—ü öt**= 1. to shine, to be sleek, to be in good condition (animal's coat). 2. to shiver with cold (animal). **—ü tüsü yok** The hair has not sprouted on his cheeks. **—lerim ürperdi** My hair stood on end. **— yol**= to pluck feathers.
tüy=ᵉʳ 2 نوىكلمك slang to slip away, to flee; archaic to fly up. **—dür**= /ı/ 1. caus. 2. to steal.
tüylen=ⁱʳ نوىلنمك 1. to grow feathers. 2. to start to grow a beard. 3. colloq. to be well-feathered, to grow rich. **—dir**= /ı/ caus.
tüylü نوىلى نوىسل نوىكلى 1. feathered; feathery. 2. furred; furry. 3. downy. **— deve** young of a female African and a male Bactrian camel.
tüysüz نوىسز 1. unfeathered; unfledged. 2. young. **— şeftali** nectarine.
tüze neol. justice; equity.
tüzel neol. legal. **— kişiler** law juristic persons, corporate body.
tüzükᵍᵘ neol. rules and regulations (of a society, etc.).

U

u, U 1 twenty-fifth letter of the alphabet.
-uⁿᵘ 2 cf. **-ı** 2.
-u 3 cf. **-ı** 3.
-u 4 cf. **-u** 4.
ubab (.—) عباب A lrnd. main stream of a torrent; the ocean.
=**uban**, =**üben** obs., vars. of =**ıp**, etc.
ubaş (.—), **ubaşe** (.—.) اباش P lrnd. rabble, mob.
ubbad (.—) عبّاد A lrnd., pl. of **âbid** 1.
ubbar (.—) عبّار A lrnd., pl. of **âbir** 1.
ubeyd عبيد A lrnd. 1. little slave or servant. 2. humble worshipper. 3. w. cap., a mans name.
ubeydâne (..—.) عبيدانه P lrnd. like a little slave.
Ubeydiye عبيديه A hist. the Ubaidite sect.
Ubeydiyun (...—) عبيديون A hist. the Fatimid Caliphs of Egypt.
ubud (.—) عبود A lrnd., pl. of **abd**.
ubudiyet (.—..) عبوديت A 1. devotion to God with faith and obedience. 2. a serving; servitude, slavery. **— arzet**= to be respectfully ready to serve; to present one's respects to a superior.

ubur (.—) عبور A *lrnd.* 1. a passing; passage. 2. a crossing. **— et=** to pass; to cross.
ubus (.—), **ubuset** (.—.) عبوس ، عبوست A *lrnd.* a being sour-faced; grimness; scowl.
uc اوج 1. tip, point; extremity, end. 2. steel pen, pen point, nib. 3. *Ott. hist.* frontier. 4. *archaic* cause, motive. **—unu altına kaçır=** to be declining in quality (work, through slackness or mismanagement); to be headed toward bankruptcy. **—unda bir şey var** There is some secret purpose behind it. **— beyi** *early Ott. hist.* commander of a border area, margrave. **—u bucağı bulunmaz**, **—u bucağı yok** endless, vast, unending. **—unu bul=** to find a clue for a thing; to find a way of bringing something to a successful conclusion. **—u bulunmaz** 1. having no limit; endless. 2. insolvable, difficult. **—u dokun=** /a/ to involve or effect one; to entail. **—u düğmeli meç** a tipped foil; foil with button on the end for fencing. **—unu göster=** to drop a hint (of something advantageous as an inducement). **—unu kaçır=** /ın/ to lose the thread of a matter. **—u ortası belli değil** /ın/ It is hard to see how to tackle this matter. **—unu ortasını bul=** /ın/ to get to the bottom of a matter; to solve a matter. **—unda para var** /ın/ There is money to be made out of it. **— uca** 1. end to end. 2. barely. **—tan uca** from one end to the other. **— uca gel=** to be just enough. **—u ucuna getir=** to make both ends meet. **— ver=** 1. to appear. 2. to sprout, to grow. 3. to come to a head (boil).
uca اوجا *archaic* buttocks. **— kemiği** 1. coccyx. 2. hip-bone, ilium.
ucab (.—) عجاب A *lrnd.* very wonderful or pleasing.
ucalet (.—.) عجالت A *lrnd.* 1. anything that is ready and at hand; anything hastily procured and set before a guest. 2. manual.
ucaleten (.—'..) عجالةً A *lrnd.* hastily.
ucb عجب A *lrnd.* vanity, conceit, self-admiration.
uclu اوجلو 1. pointed. 2. having a nib in it (pen-holder).
ucme, ucmet عجمة A 1. barbarous pronunciation of Arabic; barbarism. 2. speech impediment.
ucra (.—) اوجرا *same as* **ücra**.
ucsuz اوجسز 1. without a point. 2. with no nib (pen-holder). **— bucaksız** vast, endless. **=ucu** اوجى *cf.* **=ıcı**.
u'cube (.—.) A, **ucube** (——.) اعجوبه 1. strange thing; monstrosity; a wonder. 2. *lrnd.* curiosity.
ucun ucun اوجن اوجن bit by bit.
ucuz اوجز ، اوجوز cheap, low-priced. **— al=** to buy cheaply. **— etin yahnisi yavan olur** *proverb* You can't get a valuable thing cheaply. **— kurtul=** to get off lightly; to escape cheaply. **— sat=** 1. to sell cheaply. 2. to think something easy to get or do; to undervalue. **— ver=** to sell cheaply.
ucuzcu اوجوزجى 1. who sells cheaply. 2. bargain hunter.
ucuzla=[r] اوجوزلر to become cheap, to go down in price. **—t=** /ı/ to reduce the price (of).
ucuzluk[ğu] اوجوزلق 1. cheapness. 2. place where living is cheap; time of cheapness and plenty.
uç[cu] 1 اوج *same as* **uc**.
uç=[ar] 2 اوچمق 1. to fly; to rise in the air. 2. to evaporate. 3. to fall (from a great height). 4. fade away, to disappear. 5. to go with great speed. 6. to act outrageously; to go beyond all bounds. 7. to be wild (with joy, etc.). 8. *slang* to walk away, to disappear; to get stolen. **— baba torik** *slang* Come on now! You're talking nonsense! **—an daire** flying saucer. **—an kale** flying fortress *name of a large airplane.* **— kırlangıç** flying gurnard, *zool.*, *Dactylopterus volitans*. **—an kuşa borçlu** in debt to everybody. **—sa da kuş değil** *colloq.* No matter what happens I won't go back on my word; I insist in any case.
uçak[ğı] 1. *neol.* airplane. 2. *archaic* climbing plant. **—la** by air; by airmail. **—savar** *neol.* anti-aircraft.
uçar اوچار flying; volatile. **—a at=** to shoot at birds on the wing.
uçarı اوچارى dissolute. **— çapkın** debauchee, rake. **— takımından** scoundrel. **—lık** dissoluteness.
uçkun 1 اوچقن *archaic* spark.
uçkun=[ur] 2 اوچقنمق *prov.* to be frightened; to get startled.
uçkur اوچقر broad band for holding up trousers or drawers; a waist-string. **—lu** having a waist-band. **—luk** seam for passing a band through top of trousers.
uçlan=[ır] اوچلنمق *slang* /ı/ to pay; to give; to return.
uçma اوچمه *verbal n. of* **uç=** 2.
uçmak[ğı] اوچماغ ، اوچمق *archaic* heaven, paradise.
uçmaklı اوچمقلى *archaic* of heaven (angel or soul), heavenly.
uçmaklık[ğı] اوچمقلق *archaic* destined to go to heaven (soul).
uçucu اوچوجى 1. flying. 2. volatile.
uçuk[ğu] 1 اوچوك ، اوچق 1. cold sore, herpes. 2. *archaic* infantile convulsions. **— tutmuş** person seized with epilepsy or convulsions.
uçuk[ğu] 2 اوچوك faded, pale. **— benizli** pale-faced.
uçukla=[r] اوچوقلامس to have a cold sore come on a lip.

uçun=ᵘʳ اوچینمك archaic 1. to be startled. 2. to be poised for flight (bird).

uçur=ᵘʳ ا اوچورمك اوچرمك 1. /ı/ caus. of **uç**=, to fly (airplane). 2. to cut off with a single stroke, to chop off, to lop off. 3. slang to exaggerate; to boast (about); to praise excessively. 4. slang to turn out (person), to drive away. 5. slang to lie; to steal. 6. slang to have something stolen.

uçurma اوچورمه ا /ı/ 1. verbal n. of **uçur**=. 2. same as **uçurtma**. 3. idle brag; exaggeration.

uçurt=ᵘʳ اوچورتخد اوچرتخد 1. /ı/ same as **uçur**=. 2. /ı, a/ caus. of **uçur**=.

uçurtma اوچورتمه kite (toy).

uçurum ا اوچورم اوچرم اوچیروم 1. precipice; abyss. 2. very steep place. —**un kenarında** in danger, ready to fall. —**lu** precipitous.

uçuş=ᵘʳ 1 اوچشمك 1. to fly together, to fly in a flock. 2. to fly about; to flap the wings and fly noisily.

uçuş 2 اوچیش 1. flight, flying. 2. flight (of an airplane). — **meydanı** airport; air strip. — **yolu** trajectory.

ud 1 (—) عود A lute, an instrument with six pairs of strings played with a plectrum.

ud 2 (—) عود A lrnd., same as **öd** 2.

udalⁱⁱ (. —) عضال A lrnd. 1. troublesome, almost incurable (disease). 2. troublesome, serious or important (business).

udhiye ضحيه A lrnd. 1. ram sacrificed at the Muslim Festival of Sacrifice. 2. the festival called Kurban Bayramı.

udhuke (. —) ضحكه ا A lrnd. ridiculous thing, jest, joke, laughable affair.

udhume (. —) ضحمه ا A lrnd. padding of petticoats; bustle.

udî (— —) عودى A a player of the **ud**.

udulⁱⁱ 1 (. —) عدوال A lrnd. a swerving, deviating; deviation.

udulⁱⁱ 2 (. —) عدول A lrnd. 1. pl. of **âdil** 1, 2. 2. can. law competent and disinterested (witnesses).

udvan (. —) عدوان A lrnd. enmity, hate; antipathy.

uf اف ا expression of boredom, annoyance or fatigue. — **puf de**= to sigh, to express annoyance.

ufacıkᵍⁱ (.'. .) اوفاجق اوفهجه ا very small, tiny. — **tefecik** insignificant; tiny, small.

ufakᵍⁱ اوفه ا اوفاق 1. small, little. 2. small thing; small fragment of a thing. — **göster**= to look younger than one is. — **para** change. — **tefek** 1. small; of no account. 2. small and short (person). 3. trifles, small things. — **tefek gör**= to regard as of no account. — **ufak doğra**= 1. to cut into small pieces. 2. slang not to exaggerate too much; not to go too far (words, etc.). — **yonca** lesser yellow trefoil, bot., Trifolium procumbens.

ufakla=ʳ اوفاقلمك اوفه قلمك ا archaic 1. to make smaller; to reduce in size. 2. to break up or crumble. —**n**= pass. —**t**= caus. of **ufakla**=.

ufaklıkᵍⁱ اوفه قلق ا 1. smallness, littleness. 2. change. 3. slang lice.

ufal=ᵘʳ اوفالمك to become small; to grow small; to diminish.

ufala=ʳ اوفالمك ا /ı/ 1. to reduce in size; to break into small pieces. 2. to crumble; to break up. —**n**= pass. —**nma** 1. verbal n. of **ufalan**=. 2. disaggregation. —**t**= /ı, a/ caus. of **ufala**=.

ufalt=ᵘʳ اوفالتمك /ı/ to reduce in size. —**ıl**= pass.

ufan=ᵘʳ اوفانمك 1. to be broken up small, to be crumbled. 2. to crumble away; to disintegrate.

ufantı اوفانتی broken fragments; crumbs.

ufarakᵍⁱ اوفارق ا tiny; very small.

ufat=ʳ اوفاتمك /ı/ same as **ufalt**=. —**ıl**= pass.

ufkᵏᵘ فق ا A lrnd., same as **ufuk**. —**i âlâ** myst. the last stage of the soul. —**i mübin** myst. the last stage of the heart. —**i şâm** horizon of the evening.

ufkan (.'.) فقا ا A lrnd. horizontally.

ufkî (. —) فقى ا A horizontal.

ufkur=ᵘʳ اوفقورمك archaic to heave a deep, sigh-like breath through pain (animal). —**t**= /ı/ caus.

ufla=ʳ اوفلمك to say "oof!" expressing boredom or annoyance. —**yıp pufla**= to keep saying "oof!" —**t**= /ı/ caus.

ufukᶠᵏᵘ فق ا |ufk| horizon.

ufûlⁱⁱ (. —) فول ا A lrnd., same as **üfûl**.

ufunet (. —) عفونت A lrnd. 1. a being putrid, a becoming fetid. 2. putrefaction; putrid smell; inflammation.

ufunetlen=ⁱʳ عفونتلنمك to putrefy; to become inflamed and putrid. —**dir**= caus.

ufunetli عفونتلی putrefying; putrid; stinking (of an inflamed wound).

ufuset (. —.) عفوصت A lrnd. astringent acridity. —**li** astringently acrid.

uglûtat (. — —) اغلوطات A lrnd., pl. of **uglûte**.

uglûte (. —.) اغلوط A lrnd. doubtful question, anything that may mislead a person; anything liable to error or misapprehension.

ugniye اغنيه A lrnd. song; hymn; canticle.

Ugniyetül Agani (. . . . . — — —) اغنية الاغانی A Bib. The Song of Songs.

uğla=ʳ اوغلمك اوغلدمك ا same as **uğulda**=.

uğra=ʳ 1 اوغرامك 1. /a/ to stop in passing (at a place); to stop by, drop by, drop in, to look in. 2. /a/ to meet, encounter; to meet with (an accident); to suffer (illness); to undergo (a

uğra change); to be possessed (by an evil spirit). 3. to dart out, to rush out suddenly; to bulge out (eyes).

uğra 2 وغرا prov. flour sprinkled to prevent the dough from sticking while preparing pastry.

uğrak[tr] اوغراغى much frequented place, meeting place, crossroad.

uğraş 1 اوغراش archaic struggle, fight. **— et=** to fight, to struggle. **— yeri** battlefield.

uğraş=[tr] **2** اوغراشمق 1. /la/ to struggle, to fight with one another. 2. to try hard, to take great pains. 3. /la/ to work at (something), to be working against (someone). **—tır=** 1. /ı, la/ caus. 2. /ı/ to cause annoyance to, to disturb.

uğrat=[tr] اوغراتمق 1. /ı, a/ caus. of **uğra= 1**. 2. /dan/ to send away (from business, etc.).

uğru اوغرى archaic robber, thief.

uğrula=[tr] اوغرولمق archaic to steal.

uğrulayın اوغريلين archaic like a thief; stealthily.

uğruluk[tru] اوغرولوق archaic theft.

uğrun اوغرين prov. stealthily, secretly. **— uğrun** secretly.

uğulda=[tr] اوغولدامق 1. to hum; to buzz. 2. to howl (wind).

uğultu اوغولتى a humming, a buzzing noise; a singing in the ears.

uğur 1 اوغور good omen; good luck; auspiciousness, luckiness. **—u açık** lucky. **— ola, —lar olsun** Good luck! Good journey! (said to one departing).

uğur[tru] **2** اوغور prov. 1. way, direction. 2. front. **—una, —unda** for the sake of; for the benefit of, for.

uğurla=[tr] اوغورلامق /ı/ to wish someone good luck; to bid Godspeed to someone, to see someone off (on a journey).

uğurlu اوغورلو lucky; auspicious. **— kademli** bringing good luck, a happy omen.

uğursa=[tr] اوغورسامق /ı/ to consider something to be a good omen, to regard as lucky.

uğursuz اوغورسز 1. inauspicious; bringing bad luck; ill-omened. 2. rascal. **—luk** ill omen, a being unlucky.

uğuştur=[tr] اوغوشدرمق /ı/ same as **oğuştur=**.

uhciye, uhcüve احجيه A lrnd. enigma, riddle, puzzle.

uhde عهده A lrnd. obligation; charge; duty, responsibility. **—sine geçir=** to charge someone with the duty, etc. (of). **—sinden gel=** /ın/ to carry out the task (of), to discharge the duty of. **—sinde ol=** /ın/ to be entrusted (with, to), to be in charge (of).

uhra اخرى A lrnd. another, other; not the first or first-named.

uhrevî (..—) اخروى A lrnd. pertaining to the next world. **— ve dünyevî** relating to the present and the future world.

uhreviyat (...—) اخرويات A lrnd. things pertaining to the next world.

uht اخت A lrnd. sister. **—an** (.—), **—eyn** A two sisters.

uhud (.—) عهود A lrnd., pl. of **ahd**.

uhuvvet اخوت A lrnd. 1. brotherly feeling; brotherhood. 2. affection; sincerity.

uhuvvetkâr (...—) اخوتكار P lrnd. affectionate; brotherly. **—âne** (...——.) P in a brotherly manner.

=uk ك cf. **=k 2**.

ukab (.—) عقاب A lrnd. 1. eagle. 2. a black standard of the Prophet. 3. astr. Aquila. **—ı ahenin minkar** iron-beaked eagle; pole-axe. **—ı çerh** astr. Aquila. **—ı hamam** death. **—ı melâ** 1. the desert eagle; the kite. 2. evil, calamity. **—ân** (.——) A pl.

ukabî (.——) عقابى A lrnd. pertaining to the eagle, aquiline.

ukad عقد A lrnd., pl. of **ukde**.

ukalâ (..—) عقلا A 1. wiseacre, smart aleck. 2. lrnd., pl. of **âkil 2**. **— dümbeleği** colloq. pretentious; quack; wiseacre.

ukalâlık[tr] عقلالق quality of a wiseacre; pretence of being clever; conceitedness; wisecrack. **— sat=, — tasla=** to lay claim to being clever.

ukam (.—) عقام A lrnd. 1. unrelenting, ruthless. 2. incurable (disease). 3. perverse; terrible, distressing.

ukama (..—) عقما A lrnd., pl. of **akim**.

ukara (..—) قراء A lrnd. versed in the art of reading, reciting or chanting the Quran.

Ukâz (.—) عكاظ A lrnd. the famous annual three-week fair anciently held near Mecca. **—î** (.——) A of or referring to the fair of **Ukâz**.

ukba عقبى A lrnd. 1. the next world; future state, eternity. 2. reward, requital; return. 3. end, rear, latter part of a thing or time.

ukde عقده A lrnd. 1. knot; tie. 2. anat. node, gland, ganglion. 3. sore subject; something that sticks in the throat. 4. difficulty, impediment to the arrangement of a matter. 5. node in the orbit of a planet. 6. joint, articulation; bone between two joints. **—i a'râs** the marriage tie. **—i derûn** unending regret. **— kal=** to have coolness remain between two people. **—i lisan** tongue-tiedness. **—i re's** the ascending node of a planet. **—i süflâ** descending node. **—i tulû** longitude of node. **—i ulya** ascending node. **—i zeneb** descending node.

ukdegîr (..—) عقده گير P lrnd. which becomes tangled, beset with difficulty.

ukdekûşa (...—) عقده كشا P lrnd. 1. who unties knots. 2. resolver of difficulties.

ukdelen= عقدلنمك to become knotted or tangled.
ukdetan (..—), **ukdeteyn** عقدتان عقدتين A lrnd. the two nodes in the orbit of a planet.
ukdevî (..—) عقدوى A anat. ganglionic. **— devir** astr. nodal revolution.
ukdî (.—) عقدى A sc. nodal.
ukhuvan (..—) اخوان A lrnd. camomile, bot., Anthemis nobilis.
ukiye اوقیه [Arabic ——.] obs. ounce, forty dirham weight.
Uklidis اقلیدس F obs. Euclid.
ukm 1 عقم A lrnd., pl. of **akim**.
ukm 2 عقم A lrnd., var. of **akm**.
ukmî (.—) عقمى A lrnd., var. of **akmi**.
uknum (.—) اقنوم A lrnd. 1. basis, root; substance. 2. a person of the Trinity.
ukr عقر A lrnd. 1. barrenness, sterility. 2. a woman's dower, especially compensation paid by a man who deflowers a woman through mistaken identity.
ukre عقره A lrnd. fief, a grant of land.
ukubât (.—) عقوبات A lrnd., pl. of **ukubet**.
ukubet (.—.) عقوبت A 1. retribution; punishment (especially in the next world). 2. torture, torment. **—e uğra=** to be punished severely.
ukubetli عقوبتلى painful.
ukud 1 (.—) عقود A lrnd., pl. of **akd**. **U— Sûresi** a name of the fifth sura of the Quran. **—i ticariye** commercial contracts.
ukud 2 (.—) عقود A lrnd., pl. of **ıkd**, necklaces.
ukûf (.—) عكوف A lrnd. 1. a persevering assiduously; a persisting willfully. 2. remaining in solitude for devotional exercises.
ukuk^ku (.—) عقوق A lrnd. a being undutiful to parents; filial ingratitude.
ukul 1 (.—) عقول A lrnd., pl. of **akl 1**.
ukul 2 (.—) عقول A lrnd., pl. of **akl 2**.
=ul= لم cf. **=ıl=**.
ulâ 1 (——) اولى اول A lrnd. first; earliest.
ula=^r **2** اولامق archaic to join one thing to another.
Ulah اولاخ obs. Wallachian. **—ça** (..'.) the Wallachian language.
ulak^kı اولاق 1. courier; messenger. 2. archaic near, at hand; neighbouring. **—lık** 1. the duties or quality of a courier. 3. horse (suitable for a courier).
ulal=^ır اولالمق archaic to become a powerful man. **—t=** /ı/ caus.
ulam اولام prov. group; troop. **— ulam** in groups; in troops.
ulama اولامه 1. consecutive; uninterrupted; linked together. 2. neol. supplement, addition. 3. ling. contraction, crasis. **— yonca** horsetail, bot., Equisetum.
ulan 1 اولان [oğlan] slang 1. Hey, fellow! Hey, son! 2. You rascal.

ulan=^ır **2** اولانمق pass. of **ula= 2**.
ulaş=^ır **1** اولاشمق /a/ 1. to reach, to arrive at. 2. to come into contact with; to meet.
ulaş 2 اولاش archaic junction; apposition; contiguity.
ulaşık^kı اولاشق اولاشمش اولاشى 1. archaic reaching; touching; joining. 2. arrived.
ulaşım اولاشم 1. verbal n. of **ulaş= 1**. 2. communication.
ulaştır=^ır اولاشدیرمق اولاشتیرمق اولاشترمق /ı, a/ caus. of **ulaş= 1**, to convey, communicate; to bring (to a place).
ulaştırı اولاشدیرى اولاشتیرى archaic consecutively; uninterruptedly.
ulaştırma اولاشدیرمه 1. verbal n. of **ulaştır=**. 2. communication. **U— Bakanlığı** Ministry of Communications and Transport.
ulat=^ır اولاتمق archaic /ı, a/ caus. of **ula= 2**.
ulbe علبه A lrnd. 1. milking bowl; case; coffer. 2. bot. capsule.
uleb علب A lrnd., pl. of **ulbe**.
ulema (..—) علماء A 1. doctors of Muslim theology, ulema. 2. lrnd. learnéd men. **—dan bir zat** a personage of the corps of legal counsellors of Islam; a learnéd man. **— feracesi** cloak worn out-of-doors on ceremonial occasions by doctors of the Canon Law of Islam. **— ve fukaha** the learnéd in science and in the Canon Law. **—yi rüsum** Ott. hist. hierarchy of theological scholars. **—yi ullâm** the learned counsellors in the Canon Law.
ulemaperver (..—..) علماپرور P lrnd. patron of learned men (said of a sovereign).
ullâm (.—) علّام A lrnd., pl. of **âlim 1**.
ulleyk^kı علیق A lrnd. 1. any twining, climbing plant, as bindweed, etc. 2. common bramble, blackberry, bot., Rubus fruticosus. 3. raspberry, bot., Rubus idoeus.
ulu 1 اولو 1. great; large; big. 2. great man. **— ağaç** big, tall tree. **— kum** waves of a groundswell at sea. **— orta*. — yol** archaic main street, highway.
ulu=^r **2** اولومق to howl (dog).
ulû 3 (——) اولو A lrnd. possessors, masters, men endowed with (some quality or property), as in **ulûl'azm, ulûl'emr**.
ul'ube (.—.) اعروبه A lrnd. 1. game. 2. amusement. 3. trick done to amuse or deceive.
Uludağ اولوداغ geog. Mount Olympus, Bithynian Olympus (near Bursa).
ulûf^fü (.—) الوف A lrnd., pl. of **elf**.
ulûfe (.—.) علوفه A 1. lrnd. provender. 2. Ott. hist. sum paid to a soldier for the fodder of his horse. **—ci** same as **ulufehâr**.
ulufeciyân علوفه جیان Ott. hist. paid soldiers. **—ı yemîn** name given to the first of the two regular cavalry corps. **—ı yesâr** name given to the second of the two regular cavalry corps.

ulufehâr (. — . —) علوفه خوار P lrnd. member of the old cavalry corps.
uluğ اولوغ archaic, same as **ulu 1**.
uluhiyet (. — ..) الوهیت A same as **üluhiyet**.
ulûk^ku (. —) علوك A lrnd. 1. a suspending; suspension. 2. a catching and clinging to a thing. 3. a being caught, sticking fast. 4. a having a hold, concern, relation to a thing; hold, concern, relation. 5. a being or becoming attached in love; attachment; love. 6. a conceiving, becoming pregnant; conception. **—a gel=** to become pregnant.
ulula=^r اولولامس اولولی to extol; to reverence; to magnify; to honor. **—n=** 1. to be honored; to be exalted. 2. to be puffed up. **—t=** caus. of **ulula=**.
ulûl'azm اولوالعزم A lrnd. masters of determination, i. e., certain prophets distinguished by Muslims as highest in rank.
ulûlebsar (... —) اولوالابصار A lrnd. men of discernment, sagacious, penetrating.
ulûlelbab (... —) اولوالالباب A lrnd. people of sense; prudent, intelligent.
ulûlemr اولوالامر A lrnd. rulers; masters; leaders.
ulûluk^gu اولولی 1. greatness; eminence; might; honor. 2. goodness; beneficence. 3. grand deed; memorable action.
ulûm (. —) علوم A lrnd., pl. of ilm sciences. **—i akliye** sciences invented human reason, inductive or experim sciences. **—i akliye ve nakliye ve riyazıye** speculative, practical and mathematical sciences. **—i âliye** exegetics and Hadith. **—i cüz'iye** special sciences as branches of the general all-comprising science of divine origin. **—i diniye** theology. **—i edebiye** the disciplining sciences, the humanities, Arabic grammar, rhetoric, logic, poetry and mathematics. **— u fünûn** arts and sciences. **—i garibe** occult sciences. **—i külliye** universal science comprised in divine revelation. **—i mezmume** unlawful sciences, as necromancy. **—i nakliye** traditionary, scriptural sciences entitled to belief on inspired authority. **—i nefsaniye** noology; noological sciences. **—i riyaziye** mathematics. **—i tabiiye** natural sciences. **—i tâlimiye** mathematics.
uluma اولومه verbal n. of **ulu= 2**.
uluorta اولواورته 1. openly; clearly; without reserve; rashly; recklessly. 2. unfounded, gratuitous (assertion).
ulus اولوس 1. nation, people. 2. archaic tribe, especially one of the four great Turanian tribes.
ulusal neol. national.
uluslararası neol. international.
uluş=^ur اولوشمك to howl together in packs (wolves, etc.).
uluttarik^ki (... —) اولوالطریق A lrnd. instituters and successive chiefs of an order of dervishes;
priors, abbots or other chiefs of religious orders.
ulüv^vvü علو A lrnd. a being high, a becoming elevated; greatness, highness; elevation. **—i cenâb** noblemindedness, magnanimity. **—i cenân** ambition of aspiration. **—i himmet** high aspirations. **—i mekân** highness of place or rank. **—i şân** grandeur.
ulvan (. —) علوان |unvan| haughtiness, pride. **— sat=** to be arrogant, to put on airs.
ulvî (. —) علوی A 1. high; lofty, sublime; celestial. 2. lrnd. pertaining to the upper or higher regions.
ulviyan (.. —) علویان A lrnd. the planets Jupiter and Saturn.
ulviyât (.. —) علویات A lrnd. superior things, sublimities.
ulviyet علویت A lrnd. superiority; loftiness; sublimity.
ulya علیا A lrnd. higher; highest; very high.
-um 1 م cf. **-ım 3**.
um=^ar 2 اومك اومید /1/ to hope, hope for; to expect. **—madığın taş baş yarar** (lit. It is the unexpected stone that wounds the head.) You never know what a person considered unimportant can do.
umacı اوماجی ogre, bogey man (to frighten children).
umaça اوماجه prov. 1. rump-bone on one side; lowest vertebra in the spine of man. 2. stump left behind in the earth when a tree is felled.
umde عمده A lrnd. 1. principle. 2. prop, support, buttress. 3. person who is the main prop and stay (of an institution or cause).
Umdetülislâm (....—) عمدة الاسلام A the support of Islam, a title of Imam Gazali.
umduha (. — .) امدوحه A lrnd. thing worthy of eulogy.
-umdur 1 ـمدر cf. **-ımdır**.
umdur=^ur 2 اومدرمك /1, a/ caus. of **um= 2**.
umhuza (. — .) محوضه A lrnd. sincere good advice; faithful counsel.
umk^ku عمق A lrnd. depth; thickness (as opposed to length and width).
umkan (. .) عمقاً A lrnd. in depth; in thickness.
umma اوما A 1. verbal n. of **um= 2**. 2. prov. a longing for; illness caused by an unsatisfied longing for something (usually food). **— illetine uğrat=** /1/ colloq. to disappoint some one greatly. **—ya uğra=** colloq. to expect something in vain, to be disappointed.
ummadık^ğı اوممادیق unexpected.
ummâl (. —) عمّال A lrnd., pl. of **âmil 4**.
umman (. —) عمّان A 1. ocean. 2. lrnd., w. cap. the Indian Ocean.
umran (. —) عمران A lrnd. 1. a being in

good condition, well built (house). 2. a being well cultivated and prosperous (country). 3. prosperity.

umranî (. — —) عمرانى A *lrnd.* pertaining to the good condition and prosperity of the land. **—yet** (. — ..) A state of good or flourishing cultivation.

umre عمره A *lrnd.* minor pilgrimage to Mecca (at any time of the year).

umsan=ᶦʳ اومسانى *prov.*, same as **umsun=**.

umsulukᵍᵘ اومسلق *prov.* 1. frustration, disappointment. 2. swelling or illness caused by an unsatisfied longing for some particular food (especially pregnant women).

umsun=ᵘʳ اومسنى *prov.* to yearn (for), to long for something intensely and desperately.

umsunukᵍᵘ اومسنق *prov.*, same as **umsuluk**.

umu اومى *prov.* hope, expectation, desire.

umuh (. —), **umuhet** (. — .) عموهت A *lrnd.* a being perplexed; bewilderment.

umukᵏᵘ (. —) عموك A *lrnd.*, *pl. of* **umk**.

umul=ᵘʳ اومولى *pass. of* **um=** 2. **—mıyan hal** *law* accident.

umum (. —) عموم A 1. universal; all. 2. the public; people in general. **—a açıktır** open to all, free entry. **—a açık yer** open to the public; public place. **— ve husus** universality and speciality (of a thing). **— millet** the whole nation. **— muvacehesinde** publicly, before everyone. **— müdür** director-general, general manager. **— üzre** universally; commonly.

umumen (. —ʹ .) عمومًا A generally; universally.

umumet (. — .) عمومت A *lrnd.* a being a paternal uncle; quality or relation of a paternal uncle.

umumhane (. — — .) عمومخانه P brothel.

umumî (. — —) عمومى A general; universal; common; public. **— âdâba mugayyir fiiller** *law* indecent assault; sexual offense. **— af** amnesty, general pardon. **— efkâr** public opinion. **— emniyet** public security. **— harb** world war. **— heyet** general assembly. **— hıfzısıhha hukuku** public health legislation. **— hukuk** common law. **— mağazalar** bonded warehouses. **— menfaatlere hâdim cemiyetler** public welfare associations; public utility companies. **— müfettişlik** inspector-generalship. **— seferberlik** general mobilization.

umumilikᵍᶦ عموميلك universality, generalness.

umumiyat (. — . —) عموميات A *lrnd.* general subjects.

umumiyet (. — ..) عموميت A universality; generality. **— itibariyle** on the whole, as a whole; generally speaking. **—le** in general.

umun=ᵘʳ اومنى *prov.*, same as **um=** 2.

umur 1 امر [**umur 2**] matter of importance, concern. **—umda değil** I don't care. **— et=** to make a fuss over nothing. **— etme=** not to trouble about something. **—a gel=** *colloq.* to care, to worry (about something).

umur 2 (. —) امور A *lrnd.* affairs; matters. **—i âdiye** ordinary affairs, usual happenings. **—i adliye** judicial affairs. **—i akliye** matters which are treated or decided by reasoning. **—i âmme** 1. general matters. 2. public affairs. **—i beytiye** domestic affairs. **—i cümhur** national affairs. **—i dahiliye** domestic affairs (of the nation). **—i devlet** affairs of state. **—i dünyeviye ve uhreviye** affairs of this life and of the future; matters temporal and spiritual. **—i hariciye** foreign affairs. **—i hayriye** charitable works. **— ve husus** matters and affairs. **—i maliye** financial affairs. **—i memure** official duties. **—i milkiye** administrative affairs of the State. **—i mutammirat** overwhelming affairs. **—i seyfiye** military matters. **—i sıhhiye** sanitary matters. **—i tıbbiye** medical matters, therapeutics. **—i zaptiye** police matters. **—i zâtiye** personal affairs. **—i zihniye** matters for the mind.

umuraşina (. — — . —) امورآشنا P *lrnd.* efficient in business, good businessman. **—yân** (. — — . — —) P *pl.*

umurat (. — —) امورات A *lrnd.*, *pl. of* **umur**.

umurdide (. — — .) امورديده P *lrnd.* experienced in business.

umursa=ʳ امورساما /ı/ to be concerned about; to consider important. **—n=** *pass.* to become a matter of concern.

umut اميد |ümid| *prov.* hope; expectation.

-umuz مز *cf.* **-mız**.

umyan (. —) عميان A *lrnd.*, *pl. of* **âma 2**.

-un 1 اڭ *cf.* **-ın 3**.

=un 2 اڭ *cf.* **=ın 4**.

-un 3 ڭ *cf.* **-ın 6**.

-un 4 اڭ *cf.* **-ın 5**.

=un= 5 *cf.* **=n=** 2.

-un 6 *cf.* **-ın 4**.

un 7 اون flour; meal. **—a bula=** to dredge in flour. **—umu eledim eleğimi duvara astım** (*lit.* I've sifted my flour and hung up my sieve.) I've finished with this sort of thing; I've done it all before; I'm too old. **— helvası** sweet prepared with flour, butter and sugar. **— ufak** as fine as flour.

un=ᵃʳ 8 اوكمك *same as* **on=** 2.

unal=ᶦʳ اوكالمق *archaic* to heal up; to be cured.

unar=ᶦʳ اوكارمق *same as* **onar=** 2.

unat (. —) عنات A *lrnd.*, *pl. of* **âni 4**.

=unca نجه *cf.* **=ınca**.

=uncak نجك *cf.* **=ıncak**.

=uncayadek نجه دك *cf.* **=ıncayadek**.

=uncaya kadar نجه يه قدار *cf.* **=ıncaya kadar**.

=uncaz نجز *cf.* **=ıncaz**.

uncu 1 اونجى' flour merchant.
-uncu 2 نجى cf. **-ncı**.
=**uncuya kadar** نجه يه تاداره var. of =**uncaya kadar**.
-undu 1 ندى cf. **-ndı**.
=**undu 2** ندى cf. =**ındı 2**.
unf عنف A lrnd. roughness; harshness; violence.
unfen (´.) عنفاً A lrnd. roughly; violently.
unfi (.—) عنفى A lrnd. rough, harsh; violent.
unfuvan عنفوان A lrnd. first bloom of beauty or youth. —**i civani**, —**i şebab** first bloom of youth.
unk[ku] عنق A lrnd. neck.
unkud (.—) عنقود A lrnd. bunch, cluster.
unla=[r] اونلامق /ı/ to sprinkle with flour. —**t=** /ı/ caus.
unlu اونلو prepared with flour; floury,
unmadık[gı] اونكمادق 1. incurable; that will not heal. 2. unlucky person.
unmaz اونماز 1. that will not heal. 2. incorrigible; unlucky.
unnab (.—) عنّاب A lrnd. 1. jujube, bot., Zizyphus jujuba. 2. lotus fruit and tree, bot., Zizyphus lotus. —**i** (.—.—) A 1. pertaining to the jujube. 2. of a dark chestnut color.
unnet عنّت A lrnd. sexual impotence.
unsur عنصر A 1. element. 2. root; origin. 3. component part. —**i** (..—) A elemental.
=**untu** نتى cf. =**ntı**.
-unu نى cf. **-ı 3**.
unud (.—) عنود A lrnd. a being obstinate or perverse; perversity, obstinacy.
unulmaz اونولماز same as **unmaz**.
unut=[ur] اونوتمق /ı/ 1. to forget. 2. to overlook; to neglect.
unutkan اونوتغان اونتقان forgetful. —**lık** forgetfulness.
unutma اونوتمه verbal n. of **unut=**.
unutmabeni اونوتمه بنى forget-me-not, bot., Myosotis palustris.
unuttur=[ur] اونوتدرمق اونوتدرمه /ı, a/ caus. of **unut=**.
unutucu اونوتوجى forgetful.
unutul=[ur] اونوتولمق pass. of **unut=**.
=**unuz 1** كز cf. =**ınız 2**.
-unuz 2 كز cf. **-nız**.
unvan (..—) عنوان A 1. title (of rank or dignity). 2. heading, superscription. 3. address (on a letter). 4. show, parade; pride. —**sat=** to give oneself out as; to put on airs. —**tezkeresi** trade license. —**i ticaret** trade name. —**ver=** to give polish to a thing, to set off.
unvanlı عنوانلى 1. bearing the title of. 2. entitled. 3. who gives himself airs.
-up ب cf. **-ıp**.
upuygun اوپويغون quite adequate.
upuzun اوپوزون 1. quite long. 2. very tall.

=**ur= 1** ر cf. =**ır= 2**.
ur 2 اور 1. wen; tumor; goiter. 2. excrescence.
ur=[ur] اورمق archaic, var. of **vur=**.
ur 4 (—) اور A lrnd., pl. of **a'ver 1**.
urağan اوراغان F hurricane.
urasa عراسا prov. silly tale; superstition; spell, charm.
urat 1 (.—) عرات A lrnd., pl. of **ârî 1**.
urat=[ır] **2** اوراتمق archaic /ı/ to devour.
urat=[ır] **3** اوراتمق archaic /ı/ to cause to be reaped.
uraze (.—.) عراضه A lrnd. 1. present brought by a traveler as a memento. 2. present, gift given to a guest; meal offered to a guest.
urba اوربا prov., var. of **ruba 1**.
Urban (.—) عربان A lrnd. Bedouin Arabs.
urcan (.—) عرجان A lrnd., pl. of **a'rec 1**.
urcet عرجت A lrnd. a walking with a limp; lameness.
urcun (.—) عرجون A lrnd. stump of a bunch of dates left on the tree when the bunch is cut off; bunch of dates (dry).
urdur=[ur] اوردرمق /ı, a/ archaic, same as **vurdur=**.
urefa (..—) عرفا A lrnd., pl. of **arif 2**, adepts, experts; adepts in spiritual mysteries or occult science; the wise, the holy.
urgan اورغان Gk stout rope; rope. —**cı** maker or seller of ropes.
urgun اورغون archaic, var. of **vurgun**.
urkub (.—) عرقوب A lrnd. 1. great tendon of the calf and heel, Achilles tendon. 2. projection of a mountain. 3. w. cap., name of a man notorious for breach of promise. 4. knotty point, difficulty.
urlan=[ır] اورلانمق 1. to become a wen or a varicose vein. 2. to become affected with a wen or a varicose vein. —**dır=** /ı/ caus.
urlu اورلو having a wen or a varicose vein.
urne عرنه A lrnd. disease in the heel of a beast of burden causing the hair to fall and the foot to crack; scratches.
urs عرس A lrnd. 1. wedding ceremony and bridal procession. 2. wedding feast.
ursuf (.—) عرصوف A lrnd. 1. longitudinal rib of a camel-packsaddle. 2. a binding sinew between two vertebrae of a camel. 3. nasal bone.
Urşelim (..—) اورشليم Heb lrnd. Jerusalem.
urub اوروب colloq., var. of **rub' 1**.
uruba اوروبا prov., var. of **ruba**.
urubet (.—.) عروبت A lrnd. quality of a genuine Arab; Arabian character.
urubiyet (.—..) عروبيت A lrnd., same as **urubet**.
uruc (.—) عروج A lrnd. an ascending,

mounting or climbing; ascent; ascension. — et= to ascend. U—i İsa Ascension of Christ.

uruk=ᵏᵘ 1 اورون ٔ اورون ٔ اورون archaic subdivision of a small Turkish tribe; clan.

urukᵏᵘ 2 (. —) عروق A *lrnd., pl. of* ırk.

urul=ᵘʳ اورولمق prov., var. of vurul=.

Urum اورم colloq., var. of **Rum** 1.

urun=ᵘʳ اورونمق 1. archaic, var. of vurun=. 2. archaic to wear.

urupᵇᵘ اوروب ٔ اورب [rub 1] prov. 1. quarter; fourth part. 2. eighth part of an old measure called endaze.

Urus اوروس colloq., var. of **Rus**.

uruş 1 اورش archaic, var. of vuruş 1.

uruş=ᵘʳ 2 اورشمق ٔ اوروشمق archaic, var. of vuruş= 2. —tur= /I/ caus.

uruş 3 (. —) عروش A lrnd., pl. of arş 2.

uruz (. —) عرض A lrnd., pl. of araz 5. —i cesed accidents and ailments of the body.

urva اروه ٔ اروا same as uğra 2. — saç= to dredge with flour.

urvala=ʳ اورولمق to dredge with flour.

urve عروه A 1. lrnd. loop for a button. 2. lrnd. loop-shaped handle; semicircular flap or flange serving as a handle. 3. anat. ansa. —i vuska same as urvetülvuska.

urvetülvuska عروة الوثقى A lrnd. (lit., the firmest, strongest handle) the faith of Islam.

ury عرى A lrnd. 1. a being nude, nudity; bareness. 2. a being free from defect.

uryan (. —) عريان A lrnd., same as üryan.

us اوص A archaic 1. mind, intelligence, wisdom; right state of mind; discretion. 2. good behavior. —u git= to go out of one's senses. — pahası 1. experience. 2. price paid for wisdom; troubles by which wisdom is gained. —a vur= /I/ to reason.

usalâ (. . —) اصلا A lrnd., pl. of asil 1.

usan 1 اوصانه ٔ اوصان archaic state of tired disgust caused by the continual repetition of the same thing; tedium, boredom.

usan=ᵘʳ 2 اوصانمق /dan/ to become tired of and disgusted with what was once liked; to become bored or disgusted (with).

usançᶜⁱ اوصانج 1. boredom, tedium. 2. boring, tedious. — gel= /dan/ to be bored (by). — ver= /a/ to cause boredom.

usandır=ᵘʳ اوصاندرمق /I, dan/ caus. of usan= 2.

usandırıcı اوصاندرجی boring, tedious.

usanıkᵍⁱ اوصانق tired of, disgusted with; bored.

usanma اوصانمه verbal n. of usan= 2.

usare (. —) عصاره A sap; expressed juice (of a fruit). —i mideviye physiol. gastric juice.

usat (. —) عصاة A lrnd., pl. of âsi 1.

usbuᵘᵘ اصبع A lrnd. 1. finger. 2. inch; digit.

usefa (. . —) عسفاء A lrnd., pl. of asîf 2.
useybat (. . —) عصيبات A lrnd., pl. of useybe.
useybe عصيبه A bot. fiber of a leaf.
usfur (. —) عصفر A lrnd. sparrow, lark, finch or similar small bird.
uskumru (. .' .) اسقومری Gk mackerel. zool., Scomber scomber.
uskuna (. .' .) اسقونه It naut. schooner.
uskunca (. .' .) اسقونجه It sponge (for a gun).
uskur اسقور E screw, propeller; screw-driven ship.
uskut اسکت A slang Quiet!
uskuta (. .' .) اسقوطه It naut. sheet, clew.
uskutla=ʳ اسکتلامق /I/ slang to shut up.
uslamlama neol., phil. reasoning.
uslan=ᵘʳ اوصلانمق to become sensible, discreet, well-behaved; to come to one's senses. —dır= caus.
uslat=ᵘʳ اوصلاتمق /I/ same as uslandır=.
uslu اوصلو 1. well-behaved; good (child); sensible. 2. quiet (horse). — akıllı sober-minded, quiet, steady. — otur= to sit still, keep quiet. —luk a being well-behaved or sensible.
usr عسر A lrnd. 1. a being difficult, arduous, irksome; difficulty, irksomeness. 2. a being straitened; straits, poverty. 3. a being harsh in manner; harshness, moroseness.
usret عسرت A lrnd. difficulty; straitness, distress, poverty. —i bevl med. strangury. —i teneffüs med. asthma.
usta اوستا ٔ اوستا [üstâd] 1. master (of a trade or craft); master workman. 2. craftsman; foreman; overseer. 3. skilled; clever; experienced. 4. Ott. hist. woman superintendent of servants and slaves. 5. Ott. hist. lesser officer of the Janissaries. — çık= to finish one's apprenticeship and become a master workman. — işi work of a master, any work of art well done. — kadın lady superintendent of a department in a palace. — ol= 1. same as usta çık=. 2. to be an adept (at anything).
ustabaşı اوستاباشی foreman, head workman.
ustakârî (. . — —) اوستاکاری P lrnd. work of a master; masterpiece, anything well done or made.
ustalıkᵍⁱ اوستالق ٔ اوستالوق 1. mastery (of a trade or craft). 2. proficiency. 3. masterstroke. — sat= 1. to make a display of ability or shrewdness. 2. to pretend to have ability.
ustalıklı اوستالقلی masterly; cleverly made; cunningly devised.
ustunçᶜᵘ اوستنج obs., surg. portable case of instruments.
ustura (. '.), (. .' .) اوستره ٔ استره P 1. razor. 2. slang strong drink). 3. slang false (news). — çalıştır= slang to tell a lie. — tut=, — tutun= to use a razor, to shave.

usturlâb اسطرلاب A astrolabe.
usturmaça (...'.) استرمجه It naut. fender, collision mat.
usturpa (..'.) اوسترپا اسطرپا It naut. mop of rope ends; scourge.
usturuplu اوستروپلی slang striking, impressive; right, decent.
usûl[lü] 1 (.—) اصول |usul 3| 1. method; system; plan. 2. procedure. 3. mus. rhythmic pattern, rule which regulates the metric structure of a composition; a realization of the rule which occasionally joins the melodic line as a rhythmic-melodic formula. — dairesinde in the recognized way. —i defter bookkeeping. — erkân manner and behavior. —i fahte mus. a rhythmic pattern of ten beats. — hukuku law of procedure. —i muhakeme judicial procedure. — vur= to beat time (in Turkish music).
usul 2 اصول |usul 1| prov. gently, carefully, quietly. —la*. — usul gently, slowly. — yürü Walk slowly.
usûl[lü] 3 (.—) اصول A lrnd., pl. of asıl 1, 1. roots, origins, fundamentals; essentials. 2. elements, first principles. 3. law ancestors. —i fıkıh bases of the canon law of Islam. — ve fürû 1. fundamentals and subdivisions of a science. 2. ancestors and posterity. —i hendese elements of geometry.
usulcacık[ğı] (..'..) اصولجه same as usullacık.
usulî (.—.—) اصولی A lrnd. methodical. —yat (..—.—) A methodology.
usuliyun (..—.—) اصولیون A 1. lrnd. scholars of canon law, ulema.
usulla (..'.) اصوللا carefully, gently; slowly.
usullacık[ğı] (..'..) اصوللجه gently, quietly; very slowly.
usûllü اصوللی 1. methodical; systematic. 2. quiet, poised, gentle.
usulsüz اصولسز 1. unsystematic; irregular. 2. contrary to rules. — tevdi law irregular deposit. —lük irregularity.
usûr 1 (.—) عثور A lrnd. a stumbling upon, a becoming aware of by chance.
usur 2 (.—) عصور A lrnd., pl. of asır 1, 2.
us'us عصعص A anat. rump bone, coccyx
=uş 1 cf. =ış 1.
uş[ssu] 2 عش A var. of aş 3.
uş 3 اوش prov. Oh! How funny!
uşacık[ğı] اوشجیق archaic 1. small child. 2. tiny, small.
uşak[ğı] 1 اوشاق اشاق 1. male servant; shop assistant. 2. prov. boy, youth, child. 3. archaic small, tiny. — devşek prov. 1. wife and children. 2. odds and ends, trifles. — kapan golden eagle, zool., Aquila chrysaetos; black vulture, zool., Vultur monachus; bearded vulture, lammergeier, zool., Gypaetus barbatus. — köpek obs. puppy. — kullan= to employ servants. — tut= to engage a man servant.
uşak[kı] 2 عشا P gum ammoniac, bot., Ammoniacum.
uşaklık[ğı] اوشاقلق 1. profession of a man servant. 2. servitude. 3. prov. childhood. 4. prov. womb.
uşan=[ır] اوشنمق archaic to be broken into pieces.
uşat=[ır] اوشاتمق archaic /ı/ to break a thing small.
uşb عشب lrnd. herbs, herbage.
uşkun اوشقون prov. a kind of wild rhubarb, bot., Rheum rhaponticum.
uşşak[kı] 1 (.—) عشاق P Or. mus. one of the two or three most common simple makams.
uşşak[kı] 2 (.—) عشاق A lrnd., pl. of âşık 1.
ut[du] 1 عود var. of ud 1.
ut[du] 2 اود prov. shame, shamefulness.
ut=[ar] 3 اوتمق archaic, same as üt= 1.
utan=[ır] اوتانمق اوتنمق 1. to be ashamed, to feel ashamed. 2. to be shy and bashful; to blush with shame or embarrassment.
utanacak[ğı] اوتاناجق 1. shameful, disgraceful. 2. capable of being ashamed; causing one to be ashamed.
utanç[cı] اوتانج shame, modesty; bashfulness.
U— Duvarı the Berlin Wall.
utandır=[ır] اوتاندیرمق اوتاندرمق /ı/ caus. of utan=.
utandırıcı اوتاندیریجی 1. shameful; disgraceful. 2. confusing.
utangaç[cı] اوتانغاج اوتانغاج اوتنج bashful, shy; shamefaced. —lık bashfulness.
utangan اوتانغان اوتنغن same as utangaç.
utanık[ğı] اوتانیق اوتانق same as utangaç. —lık abstr. n.
utanış, utanma اوتانیش اوتانمه verbal n. of utan=.
utanmaz اوتانماز اوتنمز shameless; impudent. —lık impudence; shamelessness.
Utarid (.—.) عطارد A lrnd. 1. the planet Mercury. 2. l. c. mercury.
utaridfıtnet (.—.—..) عطارد فطنت P lrnd. of mercurial intelligence, sagacious, clever.
utaridnisab (.—..—) عطارد نصاب P lrnd. equal in eminence to Mercury.
utas (.—) عطاس A lrnd. 1. a sneezing; sneeze. 2. dawn's breaking; dawn.
utaş (.—) عطاش A lrnd. insatiable thirst.
utat (.—) عتات A lrnd., pl. of âti 2.
uteha (..—) عتهاء A lrnd., pl. of âtih.
uteka (..—) عتقاء A lrnd., pl. of atîk 3.
utelâ (..—) عتلاء A lrnd., pl. of atîl.
utku neol. victory, triumph.
utufet (.—.) عطوفت A lrnd., same as atufet.
utul=[ur] اوتلمق prov. to lose in a game.

utüd عتد A *lrnd.*, *pl. of* **atad**.
utüvᵛᵛᵘ عتّر A *lrnd.* a being proudly disobedient and rebellious; pride, disobedience, rebellion.
uv⁼ᵃʳ اوومسه *same as* **ov**⁼.
uvacıkᵏⁱ اواجه ا وومجه *archaic*, *same as* **ufacık**.
uvakᵏⁱ اواى ا ووه ا ووه *archaic*, *same as* **ufak**.
uvala⁼ʳ اوغالي ا ووالمى *same as* **ovala**⁼.
uvan⁼ⁱʳ اوا نمى ا و نمى *archaic*, *same as* **ufan**⁼.
uvat⁼ⁱʳ اوا نمى ا و نمى *archaic*, *same as* **ufat**⁼.
uvdur⁼ᵘʳ اوغندرمه ا وغندرمه *same as* **ovdur**⁼.
uvertür اورتور F 1. *mus.* overture. 2. beginning, commencement.
uvuştur⁼ᵘʳ اوغشدر مه اووشدر مه *same as* **ovuştur**⁼.
uvvakᵏⁱ عتّى A *lrnd.*, *pl. of* **aik**.
uy⁼ᵃʳ اومسه /a/ 1. to suit; to answer. 2. to fit; to match; to be seemly, proper. 3. to agree; to confirm. 4. to adapt oneself; to harmonize. 5. to follow, to listen (to). 6. to be arranged or settled; to come about; to come right. —**up ulaş**⁼ to follow a person with abuse.
uya اوبا ا ومه *archaic* 1. stupid; imbecile. 2. idle.
uyak⁼ⁱʳ اومانى *archaic* to set (sun).
uyan 1 اومان ا *same as* **oyan**.
uyan⁼ⁱʳ **2** اومانمى 1. to wake up; to awake. 2. to burn up (fire, lamp). 3. to revive, to come to life 4. to start growing (plants). 5. to be aroused (into activity, prosperity, etc.).
uyandır⁼ اوياندير مه ا ومانديرمه /ı/ to waken, wake (someone), up.
uyandırıcı اومانديريجى awakening; arousing; stimulating.
uyandırma اومانديرمه *verbal n. of* **uyandır**⁼.
uyanıkᵏⁱ اومانق ا ومانيق 1. awake; vigilant, wary. 2. sharp, smart; quick (in taking advantage).
uyanıklıkᵏⁱ اومانقلق 1. a being wide awake; vigilance. 2. sharpness, smartness.
uyanış, uyanma اومانش ا ومانمه *verbal nouns of* **uyan**⁼ 2.
uyar 1 اومار ا 1. fitting; convenient. 2. comfortable. 3. like, resembling. —**ı yok** /ın/ incomparable.
uyar⁼ⁱʳ **2** اومار مه ا ومارمه /ı/ 1. *prov.* to wake up; to arouse. 2. *neol.* to warn; to remark. 3. *neol.* to excite, to stimulate. —**an** stimulant, stimulus. —**ıcı** stimulant, stimulus. —**ıl** *pass. of* **uyar**⁼. —**ma** *verbal n of* **uyar**⁼. —**t** /ı/ *caus. of* **uyar**⁼.
uydur⁼ᵘʳ اويديرمه ا و يديرمه 1. *caus. of* **uy**⁼. 2. to invent, to make up. 3. to find a way of doing or getting something. 4. to corrupt, to seduce. 5. to invent, concoct (tale, calumny, etc.). 6. *vulg.* to have carnal connection with.
uydurma اويديرمه 1. *verbal n. of* **uydur**⁼.

2. invented; false; made-up (story, excuse, etc.).
3. arranged in any way.
uydurmasyon اويديرماسيون *slang* invention, fable; made-up, concocted. —**cu** *slang* liar.
uydurt⁼ᵘʳ اويدير تمى /ı, a/ *caus. of* **uydur**⁼.
uydurukᵍᵘ اويديرمه *colloq.* invention; lie; concocted.
uydurul⁼ᵘʳ اويديرلمى *pass. of* **uydur**⁼.
uygar *neol.* civilized. —**laş**⁼ to be civilized. —**lık** civilization.
uygu *neol.* 1. proportion; convenience. 2. correspondence. —**la** /ı/ to carry out; to apply; to arrange. —**lama** application.
uygun اويغون ا 1. appropriate; in accord; fitting. 2. agreeable; favorable; in tune. 3. cheap, reasonable (price). 4. just right. — **rüzgâr** fair wind.
uygunlukᵍᵘ اويغونلقى 1. a being appropriate or fitting; agreeableness; favorableness. 2. reasonableness, cheapness of price.
uygunsuz اويغونسز unsuitable; unseemly. — **kadın** prostitute. — **vaziyette** in an incriminating situation.
uygunsuzlukᵍᵘ اويغونسزلقى unsuitability; unseemliness; impropriety; bad behavior.
uyhu اويحو ا و يحو *archaic*, *same as* **uyku**.
uyku اويقو 1. sleep; nap. 2. sleepiness. —**sunu aç**⁼ /ın/ to shake off one's drowsiness. —**su açıl**⁼ /ın/ to come out of sleepiness, to feel wide awake. —**su ağır** heavy sleeper. —**sunu al**⁼ to have a good night's rest. — **bas**⁼ to be overcome by sleep. —**su başına vur**⁼, — **beynine sıçra**⁼ to feel very restless because of lack of sleep. — **çek**⁼ to sleep, to sleep deeply. —**su dağıl**⁼ /ın/ *same as* **uykusu açıl**⁼. — **durak yok** There is no peace or rest whatsoever. —**su gel**⁼ /ın/ to feel sleepy. — **gözünden ak**⁼ to be very sleepy, not to be able to keep one's eyes open. —**su hafif** light sleeper. — **hastalığı** sleeping sickness. — **ilâcı** sleeping medicine. —**su kaç**⁼ /ın/ not to be able to sleep, to lose one's sleep. —**dan kalk**⁼ to wake up. — **kestir**⁼ to have a nap. —**su kırıl**⁼ not to be able to go to sleep again after waking up. —**da ol**⁼ 1. to be sleeping. 2. to be inactive (affairs). — **sersemliği** drowsiness. — **uyu**⁼ to sleep. —**m var** I am sleepy. —**ya var**⁼ to go to sleep. —**ya yat**⁼ to lie down to sleep. — **zamanı** bed-time.
uykucu اويقوجى fond of sleep; great sleeper.
uykulu اويقولى sleepy.
uykulukᵍᵘ اويقولقى 1. sweetbread of a lamb. 2. scurf (on the hands or head of an infant).
uykusuz اويقوسز sleepless. — **ko**⁼ /ı/ 1. to

uykusuzluk

keep awake. 2. to prevent from sleeping (as a mode of torture).

uykusuzluk[gu] اويقوسزلوق sleeplessness, insomnia. — **çek**= to suffer from sleeplessness.

uykuzen اويقوزن [uyku + zen] lrnd. great sleeper.

uylaşım neol., phil. convention.

uyluk[gu] اويلوك thigh. — **kası** neol., anat. femoral muscle. — **kemiği** anat. thigh bone, femur.

uyma اويمه 1. verbal n. of **uy**=. 2. neol., phil. adaptation.

uyruk[gu] neol. subject, citizen. —**luk** citizenship.

uysal اويسال 1. conciliatory, easy-going. 2. weak-minded; who always agrees with everyone. —**lık** weakness in yielding; docility; credulousness.

uyu=[r] اويومق 1. to sleep; to go to sleep. 2. to be negligent or slothful. 3. to come to a standstill; to make no progress. 4. to clot, to coagulate. —**ma, çuval ağzı aç!** slang Wake up!

uyub (.—) عيوب A lrnd., pl. of **ayb**.

uyuk[gu] اويوك archaic scarecrow.

uyukla=[r] اويوقلامق to doze. —**t**= /ı/ caus.

uyum اويوم 1. act of accord. 2. neol., gram. harmony. 3. neol., phys. accommodation.

uyuma اويومه verbal n. of **uyu**=.

uyun (.—) عيون A lrnd., pl. of **ayn** 3.

uyundu اويونده archaic, same as **uyuntu** 2.

uyuntu اويونتى 1. lacking in initiative, indolent, lazy. 2. archaic follower, dependent; parasite.

uyur اويور sleepy; lethargic; dormant, still. —**gezen**, —**gezer** neol. somnambulist. —**gezerlik** somnambulism.

uyuş=[ur] 1 اويوشمق /la/ to come to a mutual understanding, agreement, conformity.

uyuş=[ur] 2 اويوشمق 1. to become numb or insensible. 2. to relax, ease, slacken (pain etc.).

uyuşma اويوشمه verbal n. of **uyuş**= 1, 2.

uyuşmazlık[gı] اويوشمازلق difference; disagreement; discord.

uyuştur=[ur] اويوشدرمق caus. of **uyuş**= 2.

uyuşturan اويوشدران 1. benumbing. 2. the electric ray (fish), zool., Torpedo torpedo.

uyuşturucu اويوشديرجى that benumbs or deadens. — **ilâç** anodyne, narcotic. — **maddeler** narcotic substances, narcotics.

uyuşuk[gu] اويوشوك 1. numbed; insensible. 2. indolent, lazy. —**luk** numbness, insensibility; indolence, laziness.

uyut=[ur] اويوتمق /ı/ caus. of **uyu**=. —**ma** verbal n. —**ucu** soporific. —**ul**= pass. of **uyut**=.

uyuz اويوز 1. itch (in man); mange (in dogs); scab (in cattle). 2. having the itch; mangy; scabby. 3. weak, incapable, sluggish. — **merhemi** sulfur ointment. — **ol**= 1. to have the itch, mange or scab. 2. to be persistently irritated beyond endurance. 3. colloq. to be penniless. — **otu** scabious, bot., Scabiosa arvensis; devil's bit scabious, bot., Succisa pratensis.

uyuzlan=[ır] اويوزلنمق slang to become irritated; to become suspicious.

uyuzlu اويوزلو afflicted with the itch, mange or scab.

-uz 1 اوز cf. **-ız**.

uz 2 اوز 1. good. 2. able, adroit, clever. 3. fitting, seemly. 4. shrewd, quick. 5. quiet, well-behaved. 6. excellence, suitability.

uza=[r] اوزامق 1. to stretch; to grow longer; to extend, to lengthen. 2. to be prolonged. 3. to become remote in time. 4. to go to a distance. 5. to grow tedious, tiresome, irksome. 6. to be late in some act.

uzak[gı] اوزاق 1. distant, remote, far off (in time or space); distant place; the distance. 2. improbable; unlikely. 3. contrary, not in accordance. —**a** into the distance. — **düş**= to be far (from one another).

uzakça (...) اوزاقچه rather far off, somewhat distant.

uzaklaş=[ır] اوزاقلاشمق to recede into a distance; to be far away. —**ma** verbal n. —**tır**= /ı/ to remove.

uzaklık[gı] اوزاقلق 1. distance; remoteness. 2. difference. 3. absence from a beloved one.

uzaktan اوزاقدن from far off. — **akraba** distant relative. — **bak**= /a/ to look on from a distance; to take no part. — **merhaba** a distant, formal greeting. — **tanı**= /ı/ to know by sight. — **uzağa** very distant, far away.

uzâl[li] (.—) عضال A lrnd. 1. difficult, intractable, insurmountable. 2. difficult to cure (disease).

uzam (—) عظام A lrnd. very great, vast.

uzama 1 اوزامه verbal n. of **uza**=.

uzamâ 2 (..—) عظما A lrnd., pl. of **azîm 1**.

uzan=[ır] اوزانمق 1. to be prolonged or extended. 2. to stretch oneself out. 3. to expand. 4. to exceed one's rights. —**ma** verbal n.

uzat=[ır] اوزاتمق 1. to extend, to stretch out. 2. to postpone. 3. to prolong, to make tedious or tiresome; to be prolix; to be importunate. 4. to allow to grow long (hair, beard). —**mıyalım** to cut a long story short. —**ıl**= pass. of **uzat**=. —**ma** verbal n. of **uzat**= —**tır**= /ı, a/ caus. of **uzat**=.

uzay neol. space. — **eğrisi** math. space curve. — **gemisi** space ship.

uzayış اوزايش verbal n. of **uza**=.

uzbet عزبت A lrnd. a being single; celibacy.

uzd عضد *var. of* **adud**.
-uzdur ـُدُر *cf.* **-ızdır**.
uzema (..—) عُضَماء A *same as* **uzama 2**.
uzhuke (.—.) اُصْحُوكَه A *lrnd.* ridiculous thing; laughingstock.
uzlaş=ır اوزلاشمق ' to come to an agreement or understanding; to be reconciled (with). **—ıl**= *pass*. **—ma** *verbal n*. **—tır**= /ı/ to reconcile.
uzlet عزلت A *lrnd.* a retiring into; a becoming a devotional recluse; solitude; isolation.
uzletgâh (..—) عزلتگاه P *lrnd.* place of retirement; hermitage.
uzletgüzin (...—) عزلتگزين P *lrnd.* hermit, recluse.
uzletnişin (...—) عزلتنشين P *lrnd.* who lives the life of a recluse.
uzlukᵍᵘ اوزلوك ' *archaic* 1. goodness, excellence. 2. ability, cleverness. 3. shrewdness; quickness; wit.
uzlule (.—.) اُضْلوله A *lrnd.* an erring; error.
uzm عظم A *lrnd.* 1. magnitude, greatness. 2. assumed grandeur, arrogance; pride. 3. size. 4. main part or body of a thing.
uzmâ (.—) عُظْماء A *lrnd.* very great; greatest.
uzman *neol.* specialist, expert. **—lık** speciality, expertness.
uzubet 1 (.—.) عُزوبت A *same as* **uzbet**.
uzubet 2 (.—.) عُذوبت A *lrnd.* a being sweet and pleasant, sweetness, agreeableness.
uzud عضد A *var. of* **adud**.
uzun اوزون 1. long; tall. 2. in detail. **— atla**= running broad jump, long jump. **— bacaklılar** *zool., Grallae*. **— biber** long pepper, *bot., Capsicum*. **— boylu** 1. tall (person). 2. long, lengthy; at length. **— dilli** indiscreet in speech. **— eşek** game of leap-frog. **— et**= to hold forth at great length; to argue at length. **— etme** 1. That's enough, don't keep on talking about it. 2. Oh, come on! Don't act like that. **— hava** a form of folk music used without a rhythmic pattern. **— hayvan** snake. **— hikâye** long story, long affair. **— kafalı** *biol.* dolichocephalic. **— kulaktan haber al**= to get news in a very roundabout way. **— kulaklı** long-eared; donkey, ass. **— kuyruklu baştankara** long tailed titmouse, *zool., Aegithalos caudatus*. **— lâfın kısası** the long and the short of it, in short **— otur**= to sit with outstretched legs, to sit in a posture half lying down. **— tut**= 1. to drag out (a job, etc.). 2. /ı/ to hold for a long time; to prolong; to tell in great detail. **— uzadiye** at great length; extensively. **— uzun** at length. **— yol** long road; long journey; great distance. **—ca** (...) somewhat long or tall.
uzunlukᵍᵘ اوزونلوك ' 1. length; lengthiness. 2. height. **— ölçüsü** measure of length, measure of distance.
uzuvᶻᵛᵘ عضو [**uzv**] member (body); organ; limb.
uzv عضو A *same as* **uzuv**.
uzvî (.—) عضوى A *sc.* organic; pertaining to a member of the body. **—yet** A organism.
uzzalˡⁱ (.—) عُزّال A *Or. mus.* a simple **makam** belonging to the **hicaz** group.

Ü

ü, Ü 1 *twenty-sixth letter of the alphabet.*
-ü 2 *cf.* **-ı 2.**
-ü^{nü} **3** *cf.* **-ı 3.**
-ü 4 *cf.* **-ı 4.**
übab (. —) آ باب *A lrnd.* enormous wave, tidal wave, mountainous billow; flood.
übbehet تمحصّ *A lrnd.* magnificence, grandeur, glory.
übbehetlû (...—) تحمتصّه *lrnd.* grand, glorious, excellent, *second title of an ex-grand vizier.* — **devletlû** grand and illustrious (ex-grand vizier).
-üben *cf.* **-uban.**
übhet تحمصّ *cf.* **übbehet.**
übud (. —) ابرد *A lrnd., pl. of* **ebed**, future eternities.
übüvvet ابروتّ *A lrnd.* fatherhood, paternity.
ücac (. —) اجاع *A lrnd.* brackish water; bitter.
ücra اجرى remote; out of the way; solitary.
ücret اجرت *A* 1. pay, wage; fee. 2. cost (of postage, telegram, etc.); price (of a railway ticket).
ücretli اجرتلى wage-earner; employed for pay.
ücretsiz اجرتسز unpaid; without payment; gratis, free.
ücur (. —) اجور *A lrnd., pl. of* **ecr**, 1. fees, remunerations; rewards. 2. dowers, dowries given to wives by their husbands.
ücurat (. — —) اجورات *A lrnd.* scales of salary; salaries, fees, etc.
=ücü جى *cf.* **=ıcı.**
üç اوچ three. — **adım (atlama)** *sports* hop, skip and jump. — **ambarlı** three-decker (man-of-war). — **ambarlı süvarisi** first class senior post-captain. — **as'la mahkûm ol=** *slang* to be compelled to listen to somebody's bragging.

— **aşağı beş yukarı** after some haggling. — **aşağı beş yukarı dolaş=** to pace up and down anxiously or aimlessly. — **ayaklı** tripod. **Ü— Aylar** the three sacred months of Islam (Rejeb, Shaban, Ramazan). — **başlı kas** *anat.* triceps. —**e beşe bakma=** not to be fussy (in a bargain). —**te bir** a third, one third. — **buçuk** 1. three and a half. 2. a small number, a handful. — **buçuk at=** *slang* to be very frightened. — **buçuk cahil** a handful of ignoramuses. — **çatal** 1. three-pronged fork; trident. 2. three-forked. — **çifte kayık** rowboat with three pairs of oars. — **dilimli kemer** *arch.* trefoil arch. — **dilli** trilingual. — **dilli makara** three-sheaved block. — **direkli** 1. three-columned (building). 2. three-poled (tent). 3. three masted. — **etek, — etekli** a long robe with the back divided from the two front panels by vertical gores (worn over shalvars). — **göbek** three generations. — **hal kanunu** *phil.* law of the three states. —**te iki** two thirds. — **kardeş** three-peaked mountain. — **kat** 1. triple quantity. 2. threefold. 3. three-storied. — **köşe** triangle; triangular. — **misli** threefold. — **otuzunda** in his nineties; nonagenarian. — **parmak** three-fingered starfish. — **taşlı dolmen** *archaeol.* trilithon. — **tuğlu Paşa** *Ott. hist.* Pasha of three pennants, vizier. — **yol ağzı** junction of three roads.
üçer اوچر three each; three at a time. — **üçer** three by three, by threes.
üçgen *neol., geom.* triangle.
üçle= اوچله مك /ı/ 1. to make three; to divide by three. 2. to make of three strands (rope). 3. to hire a farm for a third of the produce.
üçleme اوچله مه 1. *verbal n. of* **üçle=**. 2. triple;

triad. 3. three-stranded (rope). — **yonca** white trefoil, *bot.*, *Trifolium repens*.

üçleş=ᵗʳ اوپەشمك ' to amount to three. **—tir**= /ı/ *caus*.

üçlü اوچلو ' 1. consisting of three. 2. marked with the number three.

üçlükᵍᵘ اوچلك ' 1. of the value of three (piasters). 2. for three persons (coffee, etc.).

üçüncü اوچنجى ' third. — **şahıs** third person (party); *gram*. the third person. **—lük** a being third; third place.

üçüz اوچوز ' 1. triplets; a triplet. 2. tripartite; three-branched.

üçüzlü اوچوزلى ' 1. triple. 2. bearing triplets. 3. three-branched. — **taret** *navy* turret with three guns.

üdeba (..—) ادبا ' A *lrnd.*, pl. of **edib**.

üf اوف ' expression of impatience or disgust, ugh.

üfle=ʳ اوفلمك ' 1. to blow, puff, pant. 2. /a/ to blow upon. 3. /ı/ to blow out (candle); to blow up (toy balloon); to blow (musical instrument). **—me** *verbal n.* **—n**= *pass. of* **üfle**=. **—t**= /ı, a/ *caus. of* **üfle**=.

üftade (.—.) افتاده ' P *lrnd.* 1. fallen; prostrate. 2. in misery, poor, degraded. 3. in love; captive. — **gân** (.—.—) P *pl.* **—gi** (.—.—) P *same as* **üftadelik**.

üftadelikᵍᵘ افتاده لك ' 1. prostration, poverty. 2. captivity; captivity by love; fondness.

üftan (.—) افتان ' P *lrnd.* falling; he who falls. — **hîzan**, — **ü hîzan** falling and rising (as a wounded fugitive might do); creeping along slowly, limping.

üfteri اوفترى ' Gk brake fern, *bot.*, *Pteris*.

üftüendaz (...—) افت واندار ' P *lrnd.* (lit., a falling and springing up) a moving with ease, graceful motions; graceful springing motion.

üftühiz (..—) افت وخير ' P *lrnd.* 1. a falling down and rising again; a stumbling pace. 2. an undulating motion, a working alternately up and down. 3. a middle course between haste and slowness.

üfûlᵘ (.—) افول ' A *lrnd.* 1. a sinking; a declining; a setting. 3. extinction; death.

üf'ule افعل ' A *psych.* function. **—vî** (...—) A *functional*.

üfür=ʳ اوفورمك ' 1. /a/ to blow (into or upon). 2. /ı/ to blow up (with the breath). 3. /a/ to cast a spell (upon), to cure by breathing on. **—t**= /ı, a/ *caus.*

üfürükᵍᵘ اوفوروك ' a breathing on a sick person to cure him.

üfürükçü اوفوركچى ' person who professionally claims to cure by breathing (on a sick person). **—lük** profession of an **üfürükçü**.

üfürül=ᵘʳ اوفورلمك ' *pass. of* **üfür**=.

üfürümᵐᵘ اوفوروم ' *obs.* a single act of blowing; puff; blast.

üfürümlükᵍᵘ اوفورملك ' thing special to a puff or a blast. — **nâciz şey** an insignificant thing.

üfüründü اوفورندى ' anything blown about or away with the breath.

üfürüş اوفورش ' 1. *verbal n. of* **üfür**=. 2. a single puff.

üğendire Gk, **üğendirek**ᵍᵘ اوكندرك ' *sa*. as **üvendire**.

üğrü, **üğrüle**=ʳ اوكرولمك ' *prov.* to swing; to rock (cradle).

üğü اوكى ' *prov.* owl.

üğürtle=ʳ اوكرتلمك ' *archa*. *same as* **öğürtle**=.

ühciyye, **ühcüvve** اهجيه ' A *lrnd.* poetic satire or lampoon.

=**ük** *cf.* =**k** 2.

ükle اكله ' A *lrnd.* 1. a mouthful; morsel; meal; food. 2. loaf of bread. 3. means of subsistence; source of income. 4. detraction; backbiting.

ükrume (.—.) اكرومه ' A *lrnd.* a noble, generous or magnanimous action.

ükzube (.—.) اكزوبه ' A *lrnd.* lie; calumny.

=**ül** *cf.* =**l**=.

üleş 1 اولش ' *archaic* that which is shared out; portion; share; part; lot.

üleş=ᵗʳ 2 اولشمك ' /ı/ to divide with another; to go shares. **—tir**= /ı, a/ *caus.* to distribute; to share out.

ülfet الفت ' A 1. familiar intercourse; familiarity; friendship. 2. familiar habit. — **et**= /la/ to be on sociable and familiar terms.

ülfetger الفتگر ' P *lrnd.* one who is sociable, friendly. **—i** (...—) P *lrnd.* sociability; social intercourse; friendship.

ülhüvve الهوه ' A *lrnd.* plaything, toy.

ülger اولگر ' |Persian **ruygar**| *archaic* right side (fabric).

ülke اولكه ' country; territory; province; region, district.

ülker اولكر ' the Pleiades. — **fırtınası** storm of the (heliacal rising of) the Pleiades (about the fifth of June).

ülkü *neol.* ideal. **—cü** idealist. **—cülük** idealism.

ülser السر ' F *path.* ulcer.

ültimatom الثيماتوم ' F *pol.* ultimatum.

ültraviyole الترايوله ' F *phys.* ultraviolet. — **ışınları** ultraviolet rays.

ülûf (.—) الوف ' A *lrnd.*, pl. of **elf**.

ülûhiyet (..—..) الوهيت ' A *lrnd.* nature and essence of God, deity; divinity.

ülü اولى ' *archaic*, same as **ülüş**.

ülüfer اولوفر ' *var. of* **nilufer**.

ülüş اولش ' 1. *archaic* portion, share; part, lot. 2. *prov.* gift, present. 3. *prov.* alms.

-üm 1 ﺃُﻡْ cf. -ım 3.
üm^{mmü} 2 ﺃُﻡّ A lrnd. 1. mother. 2. source; origin. 3. main body of a composite whole. Ü—i Dünya same as Ümmüddünya. —i hammûr the present life. —i leylâ wine. —i mirzem the chilly north wind. —i veled same as ümmülveled.
-ümdür cf. -ımdır.
=üme= cf. =ıma=.
ümem ﺃُﻣَﻢْ A lrnd., pl. of ümmet. —i salife people of bygone ages.
ümena (..—) ﺃُﻣَﻨﺎ A lrnd., pl. of emin, 1. men entrusted with property (as stewards, keepers, custodians, trustees). 2. legally credible witnesses; trustworthy witnesses. 3. w. cap., a name for the Melâmiye sect.
ümera (..—) ﺃُﻣَﺮﺍ A lrnd., pl. of emîr 2.
ümid (.—) ﺃﻣﻴﺪ P lrnd., same as ümit.
ümidbahş (.—.) ﺃﻣﻴﺪﺑﺨﺶ P lrnd. 1. that gives hope; giver of hope; God. 2. hopeful.
ümidbeste (.—..) ﺃﻣﻴﺪﺑﺴﺘﻪ P lrnd. who has fixed his hope on something.
ümidgâh (.——), ümidgeh (.—.) ﺃﻣﻴﺪﮔﺎﻩ ﺃﻣﻴﺪﮔﻪ P lrnd. place of hope or refuge; person on whom hope is fixed.
ümidvar (.——) ﺃﻣﻴﺪﻭﺍﺭ P lrnd. hopeful; supported by hope. —î (.———) P hopefulness; hope.
ümit^{di} ﺃﻣﻴﺖ |ümid| hope; expectation; thing hoped for; source or cause of hope. — bağla= to set hope (upon). Ü— Burnu geog Cape of Good Hope. — dünyası It's good to be hopeful. — et= /ı/ 1. to hope; to expect. 2. to be hopeful. — kes= /dan/ to cease hoping; to abandon hope. — ver= /a/ to offer hope; to encourage.
ümitlen=^{ir} ﺃﻣﻴﺘﻠﻦ to be hopeful; to conceive hopes. —dir= /ı/ to make hopeful, give hope.
ümitli ﺃﻣﻴﺘﻠﻰ hopeful.
ümitsiz ﺃﻣﻴﺘﺴﺰ hopeless. —lik hopelessness.
ümmat (.—) ﺃﻣّﺎﺕ A lrnd., pl. of üm 2.
ümmehat (..—) ﺃﻣّﻬﺎﺕ A lrnd., pl. of üm 2. —ı esma the four chief names of God. —ı süfliye the inferior elements (fire, air, water and earth). —ı ulviye the superior elements (i. e. the three sources of human actions: soul, mind and passions).
ümmehatül Müslimin (..—...—) A lrnd. wives of the Prophet Muhammad (eleven in all).
ümmet ﺃﻣّﺖ A community (of the same religion); people, nation. —i âhir zaman lrnd. the Muslims. —i davet lrnd. people invited by a prophet. —i icabet lrnd. people who obey a prophet's call; religious community whose prayers God answers favorably; the Muslims. —i İsa the Christians. —i Muhammed the Muslims. —i Musa Israelites; Jews. —i nâciye lrnd. people saved from hell, true believers in all ages of the world. —i vasat lrnd. the people of Islam.

ümmetullah (...—) ﺃﻣّﺖ ﺍﻟﻠّٰﻪ A lrnd. people of God, all human kind.
ümmi (.—) ﺃﻣّﻰ A 1. illiterate. 2. ignorant. Ü—i Gûya, Ü—i Sadık the Prophet Muhammad.
ümmiyâne (.——.) ﺃﻣّﻴﺎﻧﻪ P lrnd. in an ignorant way, illiterately.
ümmiyet ﺃﻣّﻴﺖ A lrnd. illiteracy.
ümmüddem ﺃﻡّ ﺍﻟﺪّﻡ A path. aneurism.
ümmüddimağ ﺃﻡّ ﺍﻟﺪّﻣﺎﻍ A anat. dura mater or the whole envelope of the brain.
Ümmüddünya ﺃﻡّ ﺍﻟﺪّﻧﻴﺎ A lrnd. Baghdad.
ümmülecsad (...—) ﺃﻡّ ﺍﻻﺟﺴﺎﺩ A lrnd. mercury.
ümmülevtar (...—) ﺃﻡّ ﺍﻻﻭﺗﺎﺭ A lrnd. the lowest string of a lute.
ümmülfezail (...—.) ﺃﻡّ ﺍﻟﻔﻀﺎﺋﻞ A lrnd. science; wisdom.
ümmülhabais (...—) ﺃﻡّ ﺍﻟﺨﺒﺎﺋﺚ A lrnd. (lit., mother of vices) wine.
ümmülkitab (...—) ﺃﻡّ ﺍﻟﻜﺘﺎﺏ A lrnd. (lit., mother of the book) 1. verses of the Quran that have a perfectly clear meaning. 2. a name of the first chapter of the Quran. 3. the heavenly original of the Quran, the Preserved Tablet (Levhi Mahfuz). 4. Primordial Wisdom. 5 the very essence of God.
ümmülkura (...—) ﺃﻡّ ﺍﻟﻘﺮﻯ A lrnd. Mecca.
Ümmülkur'an (...—) ﺃﻡّ ﺍﻟﻘﺮﺁﻥ A lrnd. first sura of the Quran.
Ümmülmüminin (....—) ﺃﻡّ ﺍﻟﻤﺆﻣﻨﻴﻦ A lrnd., title given to each one of the Prophet's wives.
Ümmülmüslimîn (....—) ﺃﻡّ ﺍﻟﻤﺴﻠﻤﻴﻦ A lrnd. 1. a title given to each one of the wives of the Prophet Muhammad. 2. Aisha, wife of the Prophet.
ümmülveled ﺃﻡّ ﺍﻟﻮﻟﺪ A lrnd. slave mother to her owner's child.
ümmünnücum (...—) ﺃﻡّ ﺍﻟﻨﺠﻮﻡ A lrnd. 1. the Milky Way. 2. the sky; the sun.
ümmürre's ﺃﻡّ ﺍﻟﺮﺃﺱ A lrnd. 1. envelope of the brain; pia mater; dura mater. 2. brain; encephalon.
ümmürrezail (...—.) ﺃﻡّ ﺍﻟﺮﺫﺍﺋﻞ A lrnd. ignorance.
Ümmürruhm ﺃﻡّ ﺍﻟﺮﺣﻢ A lrnd. Mecca.
ümmüssema (...—)ﺃﻡّ ﺍﻟﺴﻤﺎﻭﺍﺕ A lrnd. the Milky Way.
ümmüssibyan (...—) ﺃﻡّ ﺍﻟﺼﺒﻴﺎﻥ A lrnd. infantile convulsions.
ümniye ﺃﻣﻨﻴﻪ A lrnd. desire, wish, hope, aspiration.
ümumet (.—.) ﺃﻣﻮﻣﺖ A lrnd. maternity.
ümur (.—) ﺃﻣﻮﺭ A same as umur.
-ümüz cf. -müz.
-ün 1 cf. -ın 3.
=ün 2 cf. =ın 4.

-ün 3 cf. -ın 5.
-ün 4 cf. -ın 6.
=ün= 5 cf. =n= 2.
-ün 6 cf. -n 4.
ün 7 اونگ ' 1. fame, reputation. 2. voice, sound, cry. — sal= to become famous.
ünas (.—) اناس ' A lrnd., pl. of ins, insan 2.
ünbub (.—), ünbube (.—.) انبوب ' A lrnd. 1. same as enbube. 2. internodal tube or joint of a reed, etc. 3. spear, lance. 4. road, path, way.
=ünce cf. =ınca.
=üncek cf. =ıncak.
=ünceyedek cf. =ıncayadek.
=ünceye kadar cf. =ıncaya kadar.
=üncez cf. =ıncaz.
-üncü cf. -ncı.
=üncüye kadar var. of =ünceye kadar.
ünde=ᵣ archaic, same as ünle=.
-ündü 1 cf. -ndı.
=ündü 2 cf. =ındı.
üneyiş=ⁱʳ archaic to become obstinate and intractable.
üniforma (...'.) F uniform.
üniversite F university. — muhtariyeti university autonomy.
ünle=ᵣ prov. 1. to cry out; to give out a sound. 2. to sing.
ünlem neol., gram. interjection.
ünlen=ⁱʳ archaic to make a noise; to sound; to echo.
ünlet=ⁱʳ /ı/ caus. of ünle=.
ünlü famous; honored; renowned.
ünnab (.—) A lrnd., same as hünnap.
ünne=ᵣ prov., same as ünle=.
üns A lrnd. 1. a being sociable, friendly, intimate; sociability; familiarity; intimacy. 2. a becoming tame (animal); tameness. — tut= to be associated with.
ünsa A lrnd. female; feminine.
ünsiyet A familiarity; a being on friendly terms with someone. — et= /la/ to be intimately acquainted with.
ünşude (.—.) A lrnd. piece of poetry recited among the people.
-üntü cf. -ntı.
ünuf (.—) A lrnd., pl. of enf.
ünusi (.—.) A lrnd. feminine. —yet (.—..) A femininity.
-ünü cf. -ı 3.
=ünüz 1 cf. =ınız 2.
-ünüz 2 cf. -nız.
=üp cf. =ıp.
=ür=ⁱʳ 1 cf. =ır= 2.
ür=ⁱʳ 2 prov. to blow.
ürcufe (.—.) A lrnd. false rumor.

ürcuhe (.—.) A lrnd. 1. swing. 2. seesaw.
ürcuze (.—.) A lrnd. poem in the meter called recez.
ürcüvan (..—) A same as ercevan.
Ürdibihişt (.—..) P lrnd. the second Persian month in mid-spring, April.
Ürdün A geog. Jordan.
üre 1 F biochem. urea.
üre=ᵣ 2 to increase in numbers, to multiply.
üreğen neol. productive; prolific.
ürem neol. 1. increase. 2. fin. interest.
üreme verbal n. of üre= 2, reproduction, procreation.
üremi F path. uremia.
üren=ⁱʳ 1 archaic to multiply and become numerous.
üren 2 neol. generation, progeny.
üret=ⁱʳ /ı/ to breed, to raise.
üretim neol. production.
ürgün archaic full to overflowing, overstuffed.
ürk=ᵣᵣ /dan/ to be frightened; to start with fear; to shy (horse).
ürkek^{gi} timid, fearful; shy, easily frightened. —lik timidity; shyness.
ürkme verbal n. of ürk=.
ürkü archaic, same as ürküntü.
ürküntü sudden fright; panic.
ürküt=ʳʳ /ı/ caus. of ürk=, to frighten, to scare, to startle.
Ürmüz, Ürmüzd P same as Hürmüz.
ürper=ⁱʳ to shiver, to have one's hair stand on end. —me verbal n. —t= /ı/ caus.
ürperti shiver, shudder.
ürü=ᵣ to howl and bark; to bay at the moon.
ürün neol. product.
üründü archaic select, choice.
üründüle=ᵣ to choose the best. —n= caus.
üryan (.—) A naked; bare.
üryanî (.——) A a kind of thin-skinned plum; plum or prune skinned and dried.
üs^{ssü} A 1. lrnd. base; basis; foundation. 2. military installation. 3. lrnd. root, stock, origin, source (of anything). 4. math. exponent, index. —sü bahrî naval base. —sü mizanı doldur= to reach the required standard (in an examination). — rakamı index (in algebra showing the power of a term).
üsbuᵘᵘ (.—) A lrnd. week. —î (.——) A weekly.
üsera (..—) A lrnd., pl. of esir 1. — kampı, — karargâhı prisoner-of-war camp.

Üsküdar (..—) اسكدار‎ geog. Uskudar, a suburb of Istanbul.

üsküfᶠᵘ اسكف‎ ، اسكوف‎ ، اوسكوف‎ Gk 1. *prov.* knitted bonnet. 2. *Ott. hist.* knitted cap with a tassel (worn by officers of the Janissaries). 3. *archaic* falcon's hood. 4. wire-covering, wind-protector for the bowl of a nargile. **—lü doğan** moor buzzard, marsh harrier, *zool., Circus aeruginosus.*

üskül اوسكل‎ ، اسكول‎ ، اسكل‎ ، اوسكل‎ Gk *prov.* combed flax, fine flax in the fiber.

üskülü اوسكلى‎ Gk *prov., same as* **üskül. — bez** very fine linen cloth.

üsküre اوسكره‎ |*Persian* **uskura**| *prov.* tinned copper bowl (for soup, etc.).

üslûb (. —) اسلوب‎ A *lrnd., same as* **üslûp.**

üslûpᵇᵘ اسلوب‎ |**üslûb**| 1. manner; form; style of writing. 2. method, mode, fashion. 3. *mus.* scale of a **makam. —a getir=, —a sok=** /ı/ to bring into shape or form; to arrange. **—lu** orderly; regular; well-arranged. **—suz** irregular; uncouth.

üslükᵍᵘ اسلك‎ |**üstlük**| *prov.* 1. coat; frock. 2. veil; kerchief; wrap, covering.

üsr اسر‎ A *lrnd.* retention of urine, strangury.

üsret عسرت‎ *same as* **usret.**

üsruş (. —) اسروش‎ P *lrnd.* 1. angel, archangel, especially Gabriel. 2. pleasant voice. 3. the seventeenth day of the month.

üsrüb سرب‎ P *lrnd.* 1. lead. 2. custom-house transit seal. **—î** (..—) P 1. leaden; lead-like. 2. greyish.

üssül hareke اصل الحركه‎ A *mil.* base of operations.

üst اوست‎ 1. upper or outside surface. 2. top of anything; superior; upper; uppermost. 3. space over a thing. 4. clothing; *Ott. hist.* fur coat with double sleeves worn by viziers and other high officials. 5. remainder; change (money). 6. address (of a letter). **—e*. —te** above; on to. **—ten** 1. from the top. 2. superficially. **—ü** the top of it. **—ünde** on top of it; on; over; with, *e. g.,* **üstümde para yok** I have no money. **—tündeler** He is upset. **—ünden** from the top of; from the surface. **—üne** on top of; on; over. **—ü açık** 1. open at the top. 2. obscene. **—ünüze afiyet** May you have good health, *said while talking about some illness.* **—e al=** /ı/ to put on the upper surface. **—ten al=** to talk or behave in a superior manner. **—üne al=** /ı/ 1. to take upon oneself. 2. to put on (clothes). 3. to take as being directed against oneself (a remark, etc.). 4. to row ahead. **—ünden at=** /ı/ to try to avoid, to get rid of. **—üne at=** /ı, ın/ to lay the blame on. **—üne bir bardak su iç=** /ı/ to give up hope (of recovering a debt, etc.). **—üne bas=** to hit the nail on the head. **— baş*. —ü başı dökül=** to be in rags. **—üne başına et=** 1. to foul its clothing (child). 2. /ın/ *vulg.* to curse and swear violently, to abuse severely. **— başa geç=** to take the foremost place; to sit in the place of honor. **—üne bırak=** 1. to attribute to someone. 2. to quit, to give up. **—üne bir iki güneş doğ=** *colloq.* to have several days pass by. **—üne çevir=** /ı, ın/ to turn over to; to transfer to. **— çık=** to win. **—e çık=** to pretend to be innocent. **—üne çık=** to come to the top; to get the better of. **— deri*. —ünden dökül=** to be unbecoming, not to suit well (clothes). **—ünde dur=** /ın/ to concentrate (on); to stress, emphasize; to follow up with interest. **—üne düş=** /ın/ 1. to be deeply interested in. 2. to be persistent, to urge. 3. to fall on, to attack; to fall to. **— eşik** the upper lintel, lintel of a door frame. **—üne evlen=** /ın/ to take an additional wife. **— fırçası** clothes brush. **—ünden geç=** /ın/ to violate (a woman). **—üne geçir=** /ı/ *same as* **üstüne çevir=.** **— gel=** to surpass, to prevail. **—e gel=** 1. to come to the surface. 2. *colloq.* to put on weight. **—üne gel=** /ın/ to turn up, to appear when one is doing something (with a suggestion that the appearance will bring either good or bad luck). **—ünü gör=** to menstruate. **—üne gül koklama=** /ın/ to be faithful (to one's beloved). **—üne güneş doğma=** to rise up early every morning. **— hakkı** the right to build over another's property. **—ümüzden ırak** Far be it from us! Heaven forbid! **— insan** *neol.* superman. **—üme iyilik sağlık** *colloq.* Heaven forbid! Good heavens! **—ünde kal=** /ın/ to be left to the highest bidder (in an auction); to be saddled with. **—ü kapalı** in a roundabout way; not frank. **—üne kırıl=** /ın/ *colloq.* to be overfond of, to be exaggeratedly interested in. **—ünü kirlet=** to foul one's clothes (child). **—e koy=** 1. to place at the top. 2. to add (a sum) to a former sum. **—üne mal etme=** /ı/ not to take the responsibility (for); to be uninterested (in); to take no account of, not to worry (about). **—üne otur=** /ın/ *colloq.* not to restore (a borrowed thing), to keep. **—ü örtülü** *same as* **üstü kapalı. — perdeden konuş=** to speak in a high pitch; to brag. **—üne pervane ol=** /ın/ to love greatly, to be completely attached (to). **—ünüze sağlık** *same as* **üstünüze afiyet. —üne sıçra=** /ın/ 1. to jump, leap or spring upon. 2. to attack by leaping upon one. 3. to splash, spurt or fly upon or over one. **—üne soğuk su iç=** /ın/ *same as* **üstüne bir bardak su iç=. —ünüze şifalar** *same as* **üstünüze âfiyet. — tarafı** /ın/ 1. the rest (of), the remainder. 2. the upper part or side (of). **— tetik** notch of the double-cock in a gunlock; full-cock notch of a gun. **— tetiğe al=** /ı/ to double-cock.

—üne titre= /ın/ to love someone so tenderly that one is always on tenterhooks about him. —üne toz kondurma= /ın/ to consider above blame. —üne uğra= /ın/ to attack, assault or harass. — üste one on top of the other; one right after the other. —üne var= /ın/ to keep on at (someone). —üme varma 1. Don't bother me; leave me alone; don't insist. 2. Don't come near me. —e ver= to give in addition; to suffer loss in a business transaction. —e vur= to raise one's bid; to add to the price. — yan next door; a little farther on. —üne yap= /ın/ to make over something to (someone). —üne yaşa= /ın/ to outlive (someone). —üne yat= same as üstüne otur=. —üne yor= /ı/ to take as directed against oneself (remark, etc.). —üne yürü= /ın/ to march against, to attack.

üstad (. —) اوستاد ' P 1. master; teacher; expert. 2. w. cap., title or form of address for a writer. — ve amatör professional and amateur.

üstadâne (. — —.) اوستادانه ' P lrnd. masterly; in a masterly fashion.

üstadî (. — —) اوستادى ' P lrnd. quality or act of a master or teacher; cleverness; art.

üstah (. —) اوستاخ ' P lrnd. impudent, audacious, unblushing, insolent, bold.

üstaz (. —) اوستاذ ' |üstad| lrnd. same as üstad.

üstbaş اوست باش ' dress, attire; clothes. — ara= to search one's clothes. — çıkar= to undress. — dökül= to be in rags.

üstderi neol., anat. epidermis.

üste اوسته ' 1. on the top; to the top. 2. further; in addition. —sinden gel= /ın/ to succeed, to cope (with a matter).

üsteğmen neol., mil. first lieutenant.

üstele=[r] اوسته لمك 1. /ı/ to dwell upon something (with regret or desire); to insist. 2. /ı/ to put on top (of something else), to add. 3. to recur (illness). 4. to increase, rise, grow high; to become dominant. —me verbal n. relapse.

üstelik[gi] اوسته لك ' furthermore, in addition.

üstlük[gü] اوسلك ' 1. quality of being uppermost; thing that is naturally uppermost, lid, veil, muffler, cover. 2. same as üslük. 3. colloq. dessert.

üstsubay neol., mil. senior officer.

üstur (. —), üsture (. —.) اوسطوره ' A lrnd. legend; myth; anecdote.

üsturevi (. — —.) اوسطوروى ' A legendary; mythical.

üstübeç[ci] اوستبيج , اوسطوبج ' white lead. — merhemi ointment of lead carbonate.

üstübü اوستوبى , اوستبو ' var. of üstüpü.

üstühan, üstühvan (.. —) اوستخوان ' P lrnd. 1. bone. 2. stone, pip (in fruit). 3. noble.

üstühvanbüzürg (.. — ..) اوستخوان بزرگ ' P (lit., big boned) nobly born.

üstühvanpâre (.. — —.) اوستخوان پاره ' P lrnd. a piece of bone.

üstühvanrend, üstühvanreng (.. —.) اوستخوان رند ,اوستخوان رنگ ' P same as üstühvanrüba.

üstühvanrüba (.. — . —) اوستخوان ربا ' P lrnd. a kind of large eagle which feeds upon or carries off bones; the Huma, whose shadow is considered auspicious.

üstün 1 اوستون , اوستن ' superior; dominant; victorious. — gel= to come out on top; to be victorious.

üstün 2 اوستون ' Arabic script vowel point indicating an a, e.

üstünkörü اوستن كورى ' superficial; only on the surface; superficially.

üstünle=[r] اوستنلمك ' /ı/ 1. to mark a consonant with the vowel point for a, e. 2. to pronounce a consonant as followed by an a, e.

üstünlük[gü] اوستنلك ' superiority.

üstüpü اوستوپو , اوستوپى ' Gk 1. oakum; tow. 2. mop (for cleaning guns). 3. flax fiber for spinning. —le= /ı/ to fill with oakum or tow; to caulk. —lü prepared, coated, soiled with tow or oakum.

üstüvan (.. —) اوستوان ' P lrnd. firm, solid; trustworthy.

üstüvane (.. — .) اوسطوانه ' A geom. cylinder; cylindrically shaped thing. Ü— ehli lrnd. the Stoics.

üstüvanî (.. — —) اوسطوانى ' A cylindrical.

üstüyar (.. —) اوستوار ' P same as üstüvan. —î. (.. — —) P firmness; stability; strength; solidity, constancy.

üsud (. —) اسود ' A lrnd., pl. of esed.

=üş 1 شش ' cf. =ış 1.

üş=[er] 2 اوشمك ' /a/ to flock (to a place).

üş 3 اوش ' archaic here; now.

üşbu اوشبو ' archaic, same as işbu.

üşek[gi] اوشك ' prov., var. of vaşak.

üşen=[ir] اوشنمك ' 1. /a/ to be too lazy to do something; not to take the trouble to do a thing; to do with reluctance. 2. archaic to be harassed or annoyed; to be frightened. 3. prov. to be tickled.

üşenç[ci] اوشنج ' 1. habitually too lazy to act. 2. laziness, slothfulness.

üşendir=[ir] اوشندرمك ' /ı/ to cause to be lazy.

üşengeç[ci], üşengen اوشنگج , اوشنگن ' lazy, slothful.

üşenik[gi] اوشنك ' too lazy and indifferent to act. —lik laziness, sloth.

üşkûfe (. —.) اشكوفه ' P lrnd. 1. flower, blossom; bud. 2. a vomiting, spewing.

üşkûh (.—) اُشكوه P *lrnd.* majesty; pomp; grandeur.

üşne اُشنه P *lrnd.* a kind of tree moss, *used as a perfume, bot., Muscus arboreus.*

üşniye اُشنيه A *bot.* algae.

üşnûşe (.—.) اُشنوشه P *lrnd.* a sneeze.

üşr عشر A *lrnd., same as* **üşür 1**. **—î** (.—) A pertaining to tithes; titheable.

üştür اُشتر P *lrnd.* camel. (*See also* **şütür**.) **—ban** (..—) P *lrnd.* camel driver.

üşü=ᵉʳ اُوشومك اُوشيمك 1. to feel cold; to shiver with cold. 2. to catch cold. **—me** *verbal n.*

üşüntü اُوشنتى اُوشونتى a flocking together; crowd; mob. **— et=** to run and crowd together in haste; to make a mob.

üşürˢʳᵘ 1 عشر |uşr| *same as* **öşür.**

üşür=ᵘʳ 2 اُوشيرمك 1. *caus. of* **üş= 2**, to collect together; to gather into a crowd. 2. /ı, a/ to cause to make a concerted attack.

üşüş=ᵘʳ اُوشوشمك /a/ 1. to crowd together. 2. to make a concerted attack. **—tür=** /ı, a/ *caus.*

üşüt=ᵘʳ اُوشيتمك اُوشوتمك /ı/ *caus. of* **üşü=**, 1. to cause to feel cold. 2. to catch cold. **—tür=** /ı/ to cause someone to catch cold.

üt=ᵉʳ 1 اُوتمك *prov.* /ı/ to win in a game.

üt=ᵉʳ 2 اُوتمك *prov.* /ı/ 1. to singe. 2. to hold to the fire.

ütme اُوتمه wheat or corn held to the fire to have the husk come off.

ütrüc اُترج A *lrnd.* citrons; the citron, *bot., Citrus medica.* **—e** A citron. **—î** (..—) A citron-colored, citron-flavored (thing).

ütü اُوتو 1. flatiron, iron. 2. crease (made by ironing). 3. an ironing; the ironing. **— tut=** that can be ironed (cloth).

ütücü اُوتوجى ironer. **— lük** the occupation of an ironer.

ütüle=ʳ اُوتولمك /ı/ 1. to iron. 2. to singe. **—me** *verbal n.* **—n=** *pass.* **—t=** *caus.*

ütülü اُوتولى 1. ironed. 2. singed.

ütüme اُوتومه *prov.* roasted fresh wheat.

ütüv اُوتو *same as* **etüv.**

üvendire اُوكندره |üğendire| ox-goad.

üvey 1 اُوكى step. **— ana** stepmother. **— baba** stepfather. **— oğul** stepson.

üvey=ⁱʳ 2 اُوكمك *archaic* to coo (as a dove).

üveyikᵍⁱ, **üveyk**ᵍⁱ اُويك اُويگك stock dove, *zool., Columba oenas.* **— kırı** dove-grey (horse).

üveylikᵍⁱ اُويلك step-relationship.

üvez 1 اُوز اُوز common service tree, *bot., Sorbus domestica.*

üvez 2 اُوز اُورن *prov.* mosquito; sandfly; midge.

üvvab (.—) اوّاب A *lrnd., pl. of* **aib**, who turn or return to God in prayer or penitence.

üye *neol.* 1. member (of a society). 2. *anat.* organ. **—lik** membership.

üyez اُيز *archaic, same as* **üvez 2**.

=üyor *cf.* **=yor 3**.

üyükᵍᵘ اُويوك *archaic, same as* **hüyük**.

üyyab (.—) اُيّاب A *lrnd., pl. of* **aib**.

-üz 1 اُز *cf.* **-ız**.

üz=ᵉʳ 2 اُوزمك /ı/ 1. to hurt the feelings (of); to treat with harshness; to cause worry. 2. to cause to break down (from grief or anxiety). 3. to strain to the breaking point; to break.

üz=ᵉʳ 3 اُوزمك *prov., same as* **yüz= 4**, **yüz= 5**.

-üzdür *cf.* **-ızdır**.

üzengi اُوزنگى stirrup. **— ağası** *Ott. hist.* a lord who walked at the stirrup of the Sultan. **— kayışı** stirrup strap. **— kemiği** *anat.* stirrup bone, stapes.

üzengile=ʳ اُوزنگيلمك /ı/ to spur with the stirrup (horse, etc.). **—t=** /ı, a/ *caus.*

üzer- اُوزر *only with possessive suffix,* 1. upper. 2. space about the top or directly over a thing. 3. anything that is upon the surface of a thing. 4. back. 5. address of a letter. 6. dress, attire. 7. charge, obligation, duty. 8. remainder, change (money).

üzere اُوزره 1. *after infinitive* on condition of; for the purpose of. 2. *after infinitive* at the point of, just about to. 3. *archaic* on, upon; according to. 4. *archaic* on the subject of.

üzerinde اُوزرنده on, over, about (him, her, it). **— dur=** /ın/ to consider; to dwell (on a subject). **— kal=** /ın/ to remain on him, to remain as a debt or sin to the charge of him.

üzerinden اُوزرندن from on (him). **— at=** /ı/ to cast off from oneself. **— dökül=**, **— düş=** not to fit well, to look untidy (clothes).

üzerine اُوزرينه on to, over, about (him, her, it). **— al=** /ı/ to take it upon oneself (to do something), to undertake. **— at=** /ı, ın/ to throw on (someone) (blame, etc.). **— bırak=** /ı, ın/ to leave (some task to someone), to charge (someone with some task). **— düş=** 1. to persist. 2. to harass by insisting. **— kalk=** to rise up against one. **— titre=** /ın/ to love someone so tenderly that one is always on tenterhooks about him; to be in a quiver of emotion over a person or thing. **— yürü=** /ın/ 1. to march to an attack; to assault. 2. to attack one with verbal abuse.

üzerlikᵍⁱ اُوزرلك 1. harmal, *bot., Peganum harmala.* 2. harmal seeds (used as fumigant).

üzeyn اُزين A *anat.* auricle.

üzgeçᶜⁱ اُوزگچ rope ladder.

üzgü اُوزگى *prov.* oppression; cruelty.

üzgün اُوزگون 1. anxious, worried. 2. weak, invalid, ill. **— balığı** dragonet, *zool., Callionymus* **—lük** anxiety, worry.

üzlet عزلت A *lrnd., same as* **uzlet**.

üzn اذن A lrnd. 1. ear. 2. appendage shaped more or less like an ear; lobe; handle.

üzre اوزره ٠ same as üzere.

üzül=ür اوزولمك pass. of üz= 2, 1. to be worn out. 2. to be weakened by illness. 3. to be sorry or worried. 4. to regret having been unable to do something.

üzüm اوزوم grape. — asması grape vine. —ün çöpü armudun sapı var de= (lit., to say that the grapes have stems and pears have stalks) to be too pedantic about things, to find fault with everything. — derimi vintage. — kütüğü vinestock. — mengenesi press for expressing grape juice; wine-press. — salkımı a bunch of grapes. — suyu 1. grape juice. 2. wine; raki. — üzüme baka baka kararır proverb (lit. A grape darkens by watching other grapes.) A person gets to be like his associates. A person learns by example. (Often applied in a derogatory sense.) —ünü ye de bağını sorma (lit. Eat your grapes and don't ask what vineyard they come from.) Enjoy the benefit of it and don't ask embarrassing questions. —cü seller of grapes. —lü with grapes or raisins.

üzün znü اذن var. of üzn.

üzüntü اوزونتى anxiety, worry; dejection; fatigue.

üzüntülü اوزونتيلى 1. anxious; worried. 2. tedious; requiring great care and pains.

üzüntüsüz اوزونتيسز carefree; easy; comfortable.

V

v, V the twenty-seventh letter of the Turkish alphabet.

va 1 (—) وا A lrnd. Oh! Ah! Listen! Alas!

va- 2 وا P lrnd. back; again; away, e. g., vagirifte, vaistade, vakerde.

vabeste (—..) وابسته P lrnd. /a/ bound, related, connected; dependent; depending on. —gân (—..—) P pl.

vacib (—.) واجب A lrnd., same as vacip.

vacibat (—.—) واجبات A lrnd., pl. of vacibe.

vacibe (—..) واجبه A lrnd. incumbent duty, obligation. —i zimmet duty.

vacibüleda (—...—) واجب الاداء A lrnd. necessary to be discharged (duties).

vacibülittiba'ı (—....—) واجب الاتباع A lrnd. (a rule) that must be obeyed.

vacibüliz'an (—...—) واجب الاذعان A lrnd. imperatively worthy of compliance.

vacibülkatl'ı (—...) واجب القتل A lrnd. deserving death.

vacibülkaza (—...—) واجب القضاء A lrnd. payment of which is an obligation (debt); a just debt.

Vacibülvücud (—...—) واجب الوجود A lrnd. whose existence is a necessity, self-existent, God.

vacibürriaye (—...—.) واجب الرعايه A lrnd. worthy of kind consideration, deserving to be honored or obeyed.

vacid (—.) واجد A lrnd. 1. who creates; the Creator. 2. who finds, finder. 3. who perceives. 4. who goes into an ecstasy.

vacip bi (—.) واجب |vacib| necessary; proper; due; incumbent; bounden (duty).

vaciz (—.) واجز A lrnd. short, terse, laconic; epitomized (speech).

vacüda (—.—) واجدا P lrnd. entirely separated, apart.

va'd 1 وعد A lrnd., same as vaid 1. — et=*.

vad 2 (—) واد P lrnd. son.

vâdâde (—.—.) واداده P lrnd. given back, restored.

va'de A, vâde (—.) وعده 1. fixed term or date. 2. maturity (of a bill, etc.). 3. death. 4. lrnd. promise. —si geçmiş of which the date of payment has expired, overdue (check,

vâdeli etc.). **—si gel=** 1. to fall due. 2. to live one's last hour. **— ile borç et=** to borrow with a fixed date for payment. **—ci** one who habitually promises for performance at a future time.

vâdeli وعده لى payable at a specified future date, having a fixed term (debt, bill, draft, etc.). **— alış veriş** time bargain. **— borç** debt with a fixed time until payment. **— mevduat** deposit account which can only be withdrawn after a definite period, time deposit.

vâdesiz وعده سز without any specified date for payment. **— istikraz** banking call-loan. **— mevduat** deposit which can be drawn at sight, demand deposit.

vâdet=[der] وعد اتمك /ı/ to promise.

vadi 1 (—.) وادى A 1. valley. 2. stream in a valley. 3. manner; tenor, sense, subject of a saying, e. g., **o vadide** in that sense, to that effect; **her vadiden** on every subject. **V—i Eymen** lrnd. Valley where the burning bush appeared to Moses. **—i hâmuşan** lrnd. (lit., valley of the silent ones) grave; burial ground. **—i haşr** lrnd. valley of the Last Judgment. **—i hayret** lrnd. bewilderment, utter confusion of ideas. **—i kadim** lrnd. the old manner. **V—i Kebir** geog. the river Guadalquivir in Spain. **V—i Mecnun** lrnd., name of the desert where Majnun lived.

vadi[ii] **2** (—.) وادع A lrnd. 1. who leaves alone; who does not oppose. 2. who leaves a thing as a trust or deposit. **—an** (—́..) A without opposition.

vafi (—.) وافى A lrnd. 1. abundant, much, many. 2. sufficient. 3. that fulfills a promise, who performs an undertaking. **— ve kâfi** enough and to spare.

vafid (—.) وافد A lrnd. 1. envoy, ambassador. 2. that leads a flock (animal or bird).

vafir (—.) وافر A 1. lrnd. many, numerous; much, abundant, plentiful. 2. pros. meter characterized by the combination of trochee and anapest (.—..—/.—..—/.——).

vafiren (—́..) وافراً A lrnd. abundantly; numerously.

vaftiz وافتيز وافتيس Gk baptism. **— anası** godmother. **— babası** godfather **— et=** /ı/ to baptize.

vaga (.—) وغا A lrnd., same as **vega**.

vagadet (.—.) وغادت A lrnd. a being puny, weak and feeble-minded.

vagd[di] وغد A lrnd. 1. vile, low-down. 2. weak, puny, feeble-minded person. 3. servant; slave. 4. boy, lad, youth.

vagirifte (—...) واگرفته P lrnd. 1. who has taken a thing away or back. 2. taken away or back.

vagon واغون F railway car.
vagonli (...) واغونلى F sleeping-car.
vah 1 (—) وا A 1. Oh! Alas! 2. sorrow; sighing. **— vah!** Hard luck! What a pity! Too bad!
vah 2 (—) وا A lrnd. O! Beautiful! Excellent!
vah 3 (—) واح A lrnd. oasis.
vaha (—.) واحه A oasis.
vahal[hli] وحل A lrnd. mud, mire.
vahalgâh (..—) وحلگاه P lrnd. marshy place, bog.
vahalnâk[ki] (..—) وحلناك P lrnd. muddy.
vaham 1 (.—) وحام A lrnd. 1. longing of a pregnant woman for any particular food. 2. depraved appetite; a being difficult and untractable.
vaham 2 وحم A lrnd. 1. a pregnant woman's longing; anything for which a pregnant woman longs. 2. a craving.
vahamet (.—.) وخامت A a being fraught with serious consequences; gravity, seriousness (of a situation). **— kesbet=** to become serious, to grow critical (situation). **—li** fraught with serious consequences; grave.
vâ hasretâ وا حسرتا A lrnd. Alas!, Woe is me.
vahat (——) واحات A lrnd., pl. of **vaha**.
vâ hayfâ وا حيفا A lrnd. Alas!, Woe is me.
vahd[di] وحد A lrnd. a being alone; single, unique; solitude; uniqueness.
vahdani (.—.) وحدانى A lrnd. pertaining to the sole One, to God. **—ye** (.—..) A the doctrine of monotheism. **—yet** (.—..) A the unity of God.
vahdet وحدت A a being alone, solitary or unique; singleness; solitariness; uniqueness; unity. **—i fikr** psych. monoideism. **—i vücud** monotheism.
vahdetârâm (..——) وحدت آرام P lrnd. restful place.
vahdetgâh (..—) وحدت گاه P lrnd. solitary place where one can be alone.
vahdetgüzin (...—) وحدت گزين P lrnd. living in seclusion; recluse.
vahdethane (..—.) وحدت خانه P private room or cell, abode of a recluse.
vahdetiye وحدتيه A lrnd. monism.
Vahdetname (..—.) وحدت نامه P title of a famous poetical work by a celebrated Sufi of the fifteenth century called Abdürrahim Efendi (written 1460 A.D. — H. 865).
vahhab (.—) وهاب A lrnd. 1. one who bestows; liberal, munificent. 2. All-Bountiful (a title of God).
Vahhabi (.——) وهابى A Wahhabi, follower of the sect founded by Abdulwahhab. **—ye** (.—..) A the Wahhabi sect. **—yun** (.—.—) A the Wahhabis.

vahhac (.—) وقّاج A *lrnd.* flaming furiously, burning, blazing.
vahham (.—) وهّام A *lrnd.* suspicious, distrustful; given to imagining things.
vahi (—.) واهى A *lrnd.* silly, futile; weak; false.
vahib (—.) واهب A *lrnd.* who gives as a grace; giver, bestower; liberal, munificent. —**i biminnet** who grants favors ungrudgingly.
Vahibülâmâl (—..——) واهب الامال A *lrnd.* Granter of our wishes, God.
Vahibülhâcât (—..——) واهب الحاجات A *lrnd.* Bestower of necessities, God.
Vahibülvücud (—...——) واهب الوجود A *lrnd.* Granter of existence, God.
vahid 1 (—.) واحد A 1. one; unique, sole. 2. the One God. **V—i Hakikî** the True One, God. —**e irca et**= /ı/ to reduce to one. —**i kıyasi** unit of measurement.
vahid 2 (.—) وحيد A *lrnd.* one, single, unique. —**i dehr**, —**i zaman** paragon of the age.
vahiden (—'..) واحداً A *lrnd.* 1. one at a time; separately. 2. by oneself, individually. — **ba'de vahidün** one after another. — **vahiden** one by one, separately, singly.
vahidi (—.—) واحدى A *lrnd.* pertaining to one, to a sole or unique thing. —**yet** (—...) A unity.
vahidülasr (—..—) واحد العصر A *lrnd.* the unique one of the age.
vahim 1 (.—) وخيم A 1. grave, dangerous, serious. 2. *lrnd.* disagreeable; unhealthful, indigestible.
vahim 2 (—.) واهم A *lrnd.* who thinks, imagines a thing not in accordance with facts.
vahime (—..) واهمة A *lrnd.* imagination, fancy. —**si galib** imaginative (person).
vahin (—.) واهن A *lrnd.* weak, powerless; silly, feeble.
vahiy[hyi] وحى |**vahy**| *lrnd.* divine inspiration; God's revelation (to a prophet).
vahiyât (—.—) واهيات A *lrnd., pl.* of **vahiye**, nonsensicalities, absurdities, trifles.
vahiye (—..) واهية A *lrnd.* silly, futile, weak, false.
vahl[li] وحل A *lrnd.* mud, mire. —**dar** (.—) P muddy, miry.
vahş وحش A *lrnd.* 1. wild beast; fierce animal. 2. desolate wilderness. —**i ıssız** desolate wilderness.
vahşan (.—) وحشان A· *lrnd.* who avoids company; gloomy, sad, melancholy.
vahşet وحشت A 1. wildness, savageness. 2. gloom, melancholy. 3. terror, fear. 4. wilderness; solitude.
vahşetâbâd (..——) وحشت آباد P *lrnd.* solitary and frightful place.

vahşetâgin (..——) وحشت آگين P *lrnd.* very solitary, dreadful.
vahşetâmiz (..——) وحشت آميز P *lrnd.* frightful, dreadful; unpleasant.
vahşetâver (..—.) وحشت آور P *lrnd.* frightening, dreadful.
vahşetengiz (...—) وحشت انگيز P *lrnd.* which excites fear; frightful.
vahşetgâh (..—) وحشتگاه P *lrnd.* lonely, terrifying spot.
vahşetnâk[ki] (..—) وحشتناك P *lrnd.* solitary and frightening place.
vahşetzâr (..—) وحشت زار P *lrnd.* wild and solitary place.
vahşi (.—) وحشى A 1. wild, savage; brutish, bestial. 2. shy, man-fearing. 3. *anat.* lateral, outer (side).
vahşice (.—'.) وحشيجه 1. wild, brutal, savage. 2. in a wild, brutal or savage way.
vahşilik[ği] وحشيلك wildness; savageness, bestiality, brutality.
vahşiyane (.——.) وحشيانه P *lrnd., same as* **vahşice**.
vahşiyet (.—) وحشيت A *lrnd., same as* **vahşilik**.
vahşûr (.—) وحشور P *lrnd.* prophet.
vahy وحى A *lrnd., same as* **vahiy**. — **et**= /ı, a/ to inspire; to reveal. **V—i münzel** the Quran.
vaız[va'zı] وعظ [**va'z 2**] sermon; admonition.
va'id[va'di] **1** وعد [**va'd 1**] promise. —**inde dur**=, —**e vefa et**= to abide by one's promise, to fulfill one's promise.
vaid 2 (.—) وعيد A *lrnd.* a threatening, predicting anything bad; threat, menace.
vaidleş=[ir] وعدلشمك /la/ to promise mutually.
vaistade (—.—.) وا استاده P *lrnd.* who has stood back, aside.
vaiz (—.) واعظ A one who admonishes; preacher. —**ân** (—.—) P, —**în** (—.—) A *pl.* —**lik** duty or function of a preacher.
vajgûn (——), **vajgûne** (——.) واژگون, واژگونه P *lrnd.* 1. inverted, preposterous, contrary; reversed, opposite. 2. unfortunate.
vak[kı] وقع A *lrnd.* 1. standing, consideration, esteem enjoyed; respect, regard. 2. high place; cliff. 3. sound of a blow or collision; collision.
vak'a وقعة A 1. event, occurrence; *archaic* event of historical importance (such as a great battle). 2. *path.* case, occurrence, incident (of a disease). **V—i Fil** *early Arabic hist.* the event of the Elephant (a Yemenite attack on Mecca). **V—i Hayriye** *Ott. hist.* the abolition of the Janissaries by Mahmud II. **V—i Timur** the invasion by Tamerlane.
vakaa (—..) واقعا A *same as* **vakıa 2**.
vakahat (.—.) وقاحت A *lrnd.* 1. a being impudent, brazen-faced; impudence. 2. a being hard, firm; hardness, firmness, solidity.

vak'anüvis (...—) وقعه نویس P *lrnd.* annalist; historian.

vakar (.—) وقار [vekar] a being staid, calm, dignified; steadiness, gravity; dignity; dignified calmness.

vakayiⁱⁱ (.—.) وقائع A *lrnd.*, *pl.* of **vakia, vâkıa 2**, 1. events; calamities. 2. battles. **— kâtibi** *Ott. hist.* clerk who kept a register of events.

vakayiname (.—.—.) وقایعنامه P *lrnd.* chronicle.

vakayinigâr (.—..—) وقایعنگار P *lrnd.* annalist, chronicler, historian.

vakerde (—..) واکرده P *lrnd.* 1. who has separated, disjoined a thing. 2. separated, disjoined.

vaketa (.'.) واکته It cow-hide, calf-skin leather.

vakf 1 وقف A *lrnd.* 1. same as **vakıf 1**. 2. a causing one to stop and stand still; a standing, stopping, staying. 3. a making a pause in reading. 4. a checking, stopping or keeping back. **— et=***.

vakfe وقفه A *lrnd.* stop; pause; interval.

vakfet=ᵈᵉʳ وقف اتمك 1. /ı/ to devote to a pious foundation (property); to devote or dedicate (oneself or time to some purpose). 2. *lrnd.* to stop, to stand still.

vakfi (.—) وقفى A *lrnd.* 1. belonging to a pious bequest. 2. pertaining to a stop or pause.

vakfiye وقفیه A *law* deed of trust of a pious foundation.

vakfname (.—.) وقفنامه P *lrnd.*, same as **vakıfname**.

vakfon وقفون German silver.

vakıⁱⁱ (—.) واقع A *lrnd.*, same as **vaki 1**.

vakıa 1 (—..) واقعا A in fact, actually; it's true that; indeed.

vakıa 2 (—..) واقعه A 1. fact; occurrence, event. 2. *lrnd.* accident, sudden calamity; battle, fight. 3. *lrnd.* dream, vision. 4. *lrnd.* end of the world and general resurrection, Day of Judgment. **— gör=** 1. to witness an event or a catastrophy. 2. to have a dream.

vakıât (—.—) واقعات A *lrnd.*, *pl.* of **vakıa 2**.

vakıf 1 وقف |**vakf 1**| pious foundation; wakf.

vâkıf 2 (—.) واقف A 1. /a/ aware (of), cognizant; wide awake. 2. *law* donor to a pious foundation. 3. *lrnd.* that stops a thing, makes it stand still; that stands still, waits. **— gözlerle** with appraising eyes. **— ol=** 1. /a/ to be aware (of), to be cognizant (of a thing). 2. *lrnd.* to stop, stand still, wait. **—âne** (—.—.) P *lrnd.* intelligently, with knowledge. **—iyet** (—..) A, **—lık** cognizance, information; knowledge, experience.

vakıfname (..—.) وقفنامه |**vakfname**| *lrnd.* deed of trust.

vakiⁱⁱ **1** (—.) واقع A' 1. happening, taking place. 2. true, actual; existing. 3. situated, lying. 4. what actually happens; reality. 5. *lrnd.* falling, fallen; descending; alighting from the air. **—i hal** the actual state of the case. **— ol=** 1. to happen, befall. 2. to be, to be situated.

vaki 2 (—.) واقى A *lrnd.* that guards and protects; protecting; protective; protector.

vakia (.—.) وقیعه A *lrnd.* 1. battle; calamity. 2. event. 3. slander, disparagement.

vakiiyet (—...) وقعیت A *lrnd.* actuality, reality; existence.

vakir (.—) وقیر A *lrnd.* injured by a blow.

vakitᵏᵗⁱ وقت [vakt] 1. time; space or point of time. 2. hour; season. 3. leisure; circumstances. 4. means, ability. **bir —** 1. once, once upon a time. 2. one time; one season. **—iyle***. **—i âhar** *lrnd.* another time. **— akşamlıdır** There's an end to time; the end may come at any time; death is always here. **—ini al=** /ın/ to take someone's time. **— geçir=** to pass the time; to occupy oneself with something. **—i gelmiş** 1. its time has come. 2. The end has come. **—i gurubi** *same as* **vakti zevali**. **—i hacet** *lrnd.* time of need. **—i hacette** when needed; on occasion. **—i hakiki** *astr.* apparent time. **—i hâl** *lrnd.* the present time; the present conjuncture. **— ü hal** time and circumstance; time and place. **—i hali yerinde** well off, in easy circumstances. **—ler hayrolsun** Good day. **—i hazer** peacetime. **— kazan=** to gain time. **— kolla=** 1. to bide one's time. 2. to watch for a favorable opportunity. **— nakittir** *proverb* Time is money. **—i nücumi** *astr.* sidereal time. **—i olma=** 1. not to have time. 2. not to be disposed to do. **—ini öldür=** to kill time. **—i saadet** *lrnd.* the period of the Prophet Muhammad's lifetime. **—i sefer** *lrnd.* wartime. **bir vakitten sonra** after a certain space of time. **—ini şaşma=** to be punctual. **—i şerifler hayrolsun** Good day. **— vakit** from time to time; at times. **—i vasati** *astr.* mean time. **—ini ye=** /ın/ to waste somebody's time. **—im yok** 1. I have no time. 2. I don't have the means. 3. *colloq.* I am not feeling well. **—i zevali** *astr.* meridian time, mean time. **—i zuhr** *lrnd.* noontime; time of noontide devotions.

vakitli وقتلى done at the right time; in due season. **— vakitsiz** in season and out of season; at all sorts of times.

vakitsiz وقتسز 1. unseasonable; inopportune; at the wrong time. 2. premature, untimely.

vakkad (.—) وقاد A *lrnd.* 1. bright, lucid, burning; brilliant, sparkling. 2. very easily ignited. 3. very perspicacious; skillful, intelligent.

vakkas (.—) وقاص A *lrnd.* fighter, warrior.

vakr وَقْر A *lrnd.* 1. a being deaf; deafness. 2. an injuring, a knocking a piece out of a thing; crack, fissure.

vaktⁱⁱ وَقْت A *same as* **vakit**.

vakta (.ˈ.), **vakta ki** (.ˈ.) وَقْتَنا ، وَقْتَا كِه P *lrnd.* at the time when; when the time had come that…

vakten (.ˈ.) وَقْتًا A *lrnd.* 1. in respect of time. 2. at a time. — **minel evkat** at some time; at no time.

vaktiyle وَقْتِيلَه 1. in the past, once; at one time. 2. at its proper time.

vakud (.—) وَقُود A *lrnd.* fuel; anything with which a fire is kindled.

vak'ulhicab (.ˈ.ˈ—) وَقْعُ الحِجاب A *lrnd.* (lit., the falling of the veil) death (after which repentance will not avail).

vakum وَقُوم L 1. vacuum. 2. vacuum oil.

vakur (.—) وَقُور A *lrnd.* grave, dignified.

vakurâne (.——) وَقُورانه P *lrnd.* 1. grave or dignified (behavior, etc.). 2. in a grave or dignified manner.

vaküşade (—.—.) واكُشاده P *lrnd.* 1. who has opened. 2. wide open.

vakvakᵏⁱ 1 (.—) وَقْواق A *lrnd.* 1. coconut-palm, *bot., Cocos nucifera.* 2. a mythical tree whose fruit was shaped like a man. 3. quacking of ducks. 4. coward, timid.

vak vakᵏⁱ 2 وَقْوان ، وَقْواى P 1. Quack, quack! 2. consecutive quacking or croaking.

vakvaka وَقْوَقَه A *lrnd.* a making a confused repeated noise.

vâlâ 1 (——) والا P *lrnd., same as* **bâlâ 3**.

vala 2 [**vale**] والا *prov.* headkerchief; dress with a veil.

vâlâi (———) والائى P *lrnd.* highness; superiority.

vâlâcâh (———) والا جاه P *lrnd.* of high standing, high of rank.

vâlâkad (———.) والا قد P *lrnd.* tall.

vâlâkadr (———.) والا قدر P *lrnd.* highly esteemed.

vâlânijad (———.—) والا نِژاد P *lrnd.* of noble birth, noble.

vâlâşân (———) والا شان P *lrnd.* highly honored.

vâlâyi (———) والائى *var. of* **vâlâi**.

valde والده A *var. of* **vâlide**. — **çeşmesi** *colloq.* help, kindness; protection; income.

vale 1 واله F *cards* jack, knave.

vale 2 (—.) واله P *lrnd.* a very fine kind of silk gauze.

valf والف E valve.

vali 1 (—.) والى A governor of a province, vali.

valiⁱⁱ 2 (—.) والع A *lrnd.* lying, who speaks falsehood; liar.

vâlid (—.) والد A *lrnd.* that begets, generates; begetter; father. —**ân** (—.—) A the parents, father and mother.

vâlide (—..) والده A mother. **V— Sultan** *Ott. hist.* mother of the reigning sultan.

vâlideyn (—..) والدين A *lrnd.* parents.

vâlidiyet (—…) والديت A *lrnd.* parenthood.

vâlih (—.) واله A *lrnd.* bewildered, confused, distracted (with terror or grief). —**âne** (—.—.) P in a confused manner.

valilikᵏⁱ واليلك 1. quality, office, functions of a governor. 2. province ruled over by a governor.

valiyan (—.—) واليان P *lrnd., pl. of* **vali 1**.

valiz والز F suitcase, valise.

vallah (.ˈ.) والله A and God; by God! — **velik'ad** May paralysis seize me (if what I say is not true).

vallahi (.ˈ.) والله A 1. by God; I swear it is so. 2. for God's sake.

vallâhü a'lem (..ˈ…) والله اعلم A *rel. formula* God knows what is true.

vals 1 والس F waltz.

Vals 2 والس F *geog.* Wales.

valyoz والبوز Gk *same as* **balyoz 2**.

vam 1 (—) وام P *lrnd.* debt, loan; claim. —**i zemin** atoms of earth of which the human body is composed, man's corporeal body.

vam- 2 (—) وام P *lrnd.* relating to a loan, e. g., **vamdar, vamhah**.

vamande (——.) وامانده P *lrnd.* who has remained behind; worn out and unable to proceed; straggler.

vamandegân (——.—) وامانده گان P *lrnd.* tired. —**ı beyt** those who remain at home.

vamcû (——) وام جو P *lrnd.* searching for a loan.

vamdar (——) وامدار P *lrnd.* 1. debtor. 2. creditor.

vamhah (——) وام خواه ، وام خواه P *lrnd.* 1. creditor. 2. borrower.

vâmıkᵏⁱ (—.) وامق A *lrnd.* 1. enamored; lover. 2. *w. cap., man's name;* the lover of Azra (in a famous Oriental romance). 3. *mus.* a makam.

vami (—.) وامى P *lrnd.* 1. indebted, in debt. 2. distressed, unfortunate.

vampir وامپير F 1. vampire. 2. vampire bat, *zool., Vampirus spectrum.*

vamsitan (—.—) وامستان P *lrnd.* 1. borrower; debtor; buyer on credit. 2. creditor.

Van 1 وان *geog.* Van. — **azmanı**, — **azması** a very large kind of cat.

-van 2 وان *same as* **-ven**.

-van 3 (—) وان P *lrnd., same as* **-ban 5**, as in **bahçevan**.

vani (—.) وانى A *lrnd.* worn out, broken down, languid, fatigued.

vanihade (—.—.) وانهاده P *lrnd.* put away, set apart.

vanilya (..'.) مُرَانِيليا وَانِلْيه Sp vanilla, the fruit pods of *Vanilla planifolia*. **— çiçeği** heliotrope, *bot.*, *Heliotropium peruvianum*. **— fidanı** common vanilla, *bot.*, *Vanilla planifolia*.
vantilâtör وَانْتِيلَاتُور F ventilator; fan. **— kayışı** fan belt.
vantrilok[gu] وَانْتِرِيلُوك F ventriloquist.
vantuz وَانْتُوز F 1. *med.* cupping-glass. 2. sucker (of an octopus).
vapes (—.) وَاپَس P *lrnd.* behind, back; afterwards, then, again.
vapor It, **vapur** وَاپُور 1. steamer; steamship; ferry. 2. *slang* very drunk person. **— tombazı** mooring-buoy for steamers.
var 1 وَار 1. existent; present; at hand, available; ready; there is; there are. 2. *following possessed subjects* to have, *e. g.*, **Babam var** I have a father. **Parası var mı?** Does he have money? **Sizde sabır var** You have patience. 3. belongings; possessions; wealth. **— mısın?** *colloq.* 1. I dare you to do it! I bet you can't do it. 2. Will you? How about it? **— mı bana yan bakan!** *exclamation of challenge* Who can stand against me? How dare you! **— et=** /ı/ to give existence to, to create. **— evi** a wealthy house, a well-to-do family. **— evi kerem evi** *proverb* Where there is wealth there is generosity. **— kuvvetiyle** with all possible force; with all his strength. **— ol=** to exist. **— ol!** Good for you! Well done! How good of you! Hurray! **— olma** *phil.* existence, being. **— olsun** 1. Let him be present or existent. 2. Long may he live! **—ını tüket=** to exhaust all his means. **— yemez** miserly. **— yok** 1. barely, *e. g.*, **beş yaşında var yok** barely five years old. 2. in poor condition. 3. in a small quantity; between existence and non-existence. **—ı yoğu** all that he has. **bir bir yok** at one moment there, at another not there; transitory, uncertain. **—sa... yoksa...** to have no eyes except for, *e. g.*, **varsa o yoksa o** He has no eyes or ears except for her, he talks of nothing but her. **bir —mış bir yokmuş** once upon a time; ephemeral. **—la yok arası** very slight. **—a yoğa karış=** to poke one's nose into everything. **—ını yoğunu kaybet=** to lose one's all.
var=[ır] **2** وَار /a/ 1. to arrive (at), to reach, to attain. 2. to go towards, to approach, approximate. 3. to succeed in understanding. 4. to result, to end in. 5. to get married (woman). **—!** Go! Advance. Go on. **—an*. —sın*. — babana selâm söyle** *indicates confusion or bewilderment* Words fail me! **—an iki** That makes two. That's number two. **— istediğini yap** Do whatever you like (a challenge). Do your worst. **— işine git** Mind your own business. **—ıncaya kadar** up to, to. **—a vara** gradually; in the course of time. **—arak vararak kurbağa olur** If he goes on croaking he will become a frog (said in derision of a vain youth).
var 3 (—) وَار same as **bar 5**.
-var 4 (—) وَار P *lrnd.* 1. possessing, having, *as in* **ümitvar**. 2. resembling, like, *as in* **zerrevar**. 3. fitting, befitting, *as in* **şahvar**.
varagele وَارَه گله *naut.* pass-rope; ferry.
varak[gı] **1** وَرَه [**varak 2**] 1. metal beaten into leaf; gold or silver leaf. 2. sheet of paper. 3. stamped coin.
varak[kı] **2** وَرَه A *lrnd.* leaf; petal. **—ı mihr ü vefâyı kim okur kim dinler** (*lit.* Who reads and who listens to a letter of love and faithfulness?) Nobody is paying any attention.
varaka وَرَقَه A *lrnd.* 1. a single leaf or petal. 2. a single sheet of paper; note, letter, dispatch; document.
varakçı وَرَقْچِي worker in gold leaf, gilder. **— kursağı** gold-beater's skin.
varaki (..—) وَرَقِي A *lrnd.* leaf-like; pertaining to a leaf.
varakla=[r] وَرَقْلَمَه /ı/ to ornament with gold leaf. **—n=** 1. to be ornamented or covered with gold leaf. 2. to become a leaf; to come into leaf (plant). **—t=** /ı, a/ *caus. of* **varakla=**.
varaklı وَرَقْلِي 1. ornamented with gold leaf, gilded. 2. leafed.
varakpare (..—.) وَرَقْپَارَه P *lrnd.* scrap of paper; worthless document; rag (contemptuous term for newspaper).
varan وَارَان only in such phrases as **varan iki** (and other numbers) That makes two. That's number two.
varda (.'.) وَارْدَا It 1. Look out! Keep clear. Make way. 2. guard, watch. **— topu** warning or signal gun (forbidding ships to enter a harbor or the Straits).
vardabandıra (...'..) وَارْدَابَانْدِيرَه It *naut.* signalman.
vardacı وَارْدَاجِي 1. guard, watchman. 2. *Ott. hist.* man who ran in front of a great person to clear the way; guard who shouted out "Varda!" to clear the way for a horse-drawn streetcar. 3. promoter or propagandist (in a bad sense). **— kulübesi** sentry-box.
vardafogo (...'.) وَارْدَافُوغُو It slow-match-rod; linstock. **— fitili** slow-match of tow, port-fire-match.
vardakavo (...'.) وَارْدَاقَاوُو It *naut.* guest-rope or warp.
vardakosta (...'..) وَارْدَاقُوسْتَه It 1. coast-guard. 2. *slang* fat but imposing person.
vardamana (...'.) وَارْدَامَانَه It *naut.* guard-rope on board ship.

vardapruva (...ˊ.) وارداپیروه It cannon pointing right ahead in a ship.

vardasol واردا صول It *naut.* side-awning.

vardavela, vardavele (...ˊ.) وارداوه‌له وارداوه‌لو It manrope of a ship's yard.

vardır=" واردیرمك /ı, a/ *caus. of* **var=** 2. **—ıl=** *pass.*

vardiya (ˊ..) واردیا It *naut.* watch. **— bekle=** to have the watch.

vardiyan (..—) واردیان It quarantine guard.

vardolos, vardula واردولوس واردولا Gk welt of a shoe.

vare •ˊ- P *lrnd., same as* **var** 4.

varefte (—..) وارفته P *lrnd.* that has gone away; of whom something has gone away; deprived. **—i basar** blind.

varekᵍⁱ واره‌ك F seaweed, kelp, *bot., Alga marina.*

varen, varenc (—.) وارنج P *lrnd.* the elbow.

vareste (—..) وارسته P *lrnd.* 1. free, exempt; void (of). 2. that has escaped and got away. **—i iştibah** void of doubt, certain. **—i külfeti ihticac** (*lit.,* free from the troublesome task of adducing proofs) self-evident. **—gi** (—..—) P liberation.

vargel وارگل *mech.* shaper. **— tezgâhı** shaper.

varış 1 وارش 1. *verbal n. of* **var=** 2. 2. quickness of perception. **—ına gelişim** reciprocity. **—ına gelişim, tarhanana bulgur aşım** (*lit.* You visit me, I come to you; in return for your soup, I give you porridge.) As you treat others, so will they treat you. **— gidiş** a coming and going; familiarity.

varış=" 2 وارشمك *archaic* to pay mutual visits, to frequent.

varışat (..—) وارشات [*based on* **varış** 1] a mode of comprehending a subject; cleverness, quickness of comprehension. **—lı** clever, quick at comprehending.

varışlı وارشلی *archaic* clever, quick of comprehension. **—lık** cleverness.

-vari (—.—) واری P similar to, like, *e. g.,* **haçvari.**

varid (—.) وارد A *lrnd.* that which arrives or happens; probable; admissible. **— değildir** It is unlikely to happen. **— ol=** /a/ to arrive; to reach. **— ü sâdır** who comes and who goes; arriving and departing (people).

varidat (—.—) واردات A 1. revenues, income. 2. *lrnd.* sudden thoughts, inspirations. **— kalemi** *Ott. hist.* office registering tax revenues. **—çı, —î** (—.—) *Ott. hist.* director of a tax revenue office.

varide (—..) وارده A *lrnd.* 1. sudden thought. 2. incoming papers. **— defteri** register of incoming documents.

varidin (—.—) واردین A *lrnd., pl. of* **varid.** **— ü sâdırîn** those who come and those who go.

varil واریل Gk barrel, cask.

varis 1 (—.) وارث A 1. heir, inheritor; inheriting. 2. *lrnd.* God, the heir to all. **— ol=** /a/ to be heir, to inherit.

varis 2 واریس F *path.* varix; varicose vein.

varisülenbiya (—....—) وارث‌الانبیا A *lrnd.* (*lit.,* heir to the prophets) expounder of the canon law.

variyet واریت [*based on* **var** 1] wealth, riches; income. **—li** well-to-do, wealthy.

varlıkᵍⁱ وارلق 1. existence, being, self, personality. 2. wealth, riches; possessions. 3. easy circumstances. 4. presence (as opposed to absence). **—a darlık olmaz** Wealth makes many things possible. **— göster=** 1. to make one's presence felt. 2. to achieve something. **— içinde yaşa=** to live in easy circumstances. **— içinde yokluk** scarcity in spite of wealth (said when a wealthy person suffers from scarcity). **— vergisi** capital tax; property tax. **—lı** well-to-do, rich.

varma (..ˊ) وارمه *verbal n. of* **var=** 2. **— limanı** port of destination.

varoluşçulukᵍᵘ *neol., phil.* existentialism.

varoş واروش Hung suburb.

varsağı وارساغی 1. a folk music form. 2. a kind of scimitar.

varsakᵍⁱ وارساك *obs.* 1. *same as* **varsağı** ². 2. stone-cutter's axe or mattock.

varsam, varsan وارسام وارسان lesser weever (fish), sting fish, *zool., Trachinus vipera.*

varsın (..ˊ) وارسین let him..., *e. g.,* **— gelsin** Let him come if he likes. **— okumasın** It doesn't matter whether he studies or not.

Varşava, Varşova (.ˊ..) وارشاوه وارشوه *geog.* Warsaw.

varta (ˊ.) ورطه A 1. abyss. 2. great peril. 3. danger or difficulty in which one is embarrassed. **—yı atlat=** to escape great danger.

varun (——), **varune** (——.) وارون وارونه P *lrnd.* 1. inverted, turned upside down. 2. thrown down, demolished; unfortunate. 3. perverse, inauspicious.

varyete واریته F 1. variety show. 2. variety theater.

varyos واریوس Gk *same as* **balyoz** 2.

vasab وصب A *lrnd.* a being sick; sickness; ailment.

vasat وسط A 1. middle; average. 2. middling, mediocre. 3. environment, circle; medium.

vasati (..—) وسطی A 1. central, middle. 2. mean, average. **—sini al=** /ın/ to take the average of. **— hata** *astr.* mean error. **— öğle** *astr.* mean noon. **— zaman** mean time.

vasaya (.—.ˊ) وصایا A *lrnd., same as* **vesaya.**

vasf وصف A *same as* **vasıf** 1.

vasfen (.'.) وَصْفًا A *lrnd.* by way of description or praise.

vasfet=der وَصْفَتْمَكْ /ı/ 1. to describe. 2. to commend, eulogize.

vasfi (.—) وَصْفِى A *gram.* qualitative.

vasıb (—.) وَاصِب A *lrnd.* 1. long-continuing, never-ending, everlasting. 2. assiduous, persistent.

vasıfsh 1 وَصْف [vasf] 1. quality. 2. a describing; description. 3. eulogy, a praising. 4. *gram.* epithet, adjective. —a gelmez indescribable. —ı mümeyyiz *lrnd.* distinguishing quality, characteristic. —ı terkibî *gram.* 'compound adjective.

vasıf 2 (—.) وَاصِف A *lrnd.* who describes or qualifies; who eulogizes.

vasıflan=ır وَصْفَلَنْمَكْ to be qualified; to take the character of. —dır= /ı/ *caus.* —dırma qualification.

vâsıl 1 (—.) وَاصِل A 1. *lrnd.* arriving, joining; touching, in contact. 2. *lrnd.* that joins or connects things; conjunctive. 3. *myst.* who is joined with God in the spirit. — ol= /a/ 1. to arrive; to reach. 2. to join one's beloved.

vasılsh 2 وَصْل A *var.* of vasl.

vâsıla (—..) وَاصِلَه A *phil.* adventitious.

vâsılin (—.—) وَاصِلِين A *pl., myst.* those who have joined with God in spirit.

vâsıt (—.) وَاسِط A *lrnd.* middle; central; intermediary.

vasıta (—..) وَاسِطَه A 1. means; channel. 2. intermediary, go-between. 3. means of transportation. —sıyla 1. by means of. 2. in care of (address on a letter). —sız without intermediary; direct.

vasiii 1 (—.) وَاسِع A *lrnd.* 1. extensive, wide. 2. abundant, copious. 3. the All-Comprehending God.

vasi 2 (.—) وَصِى A *law* 1. executor, trustee; guardian. 2. who enjoins; who bequeaths, testator.

vasid (.—) وَصِيد A *lrnd.* 1. threshold; porch, area before a door. 2. *w. cap.* cave of the Seven Sleepers near Ephesus.

vasif (.—) وَصِيف A *lrnd.* 1. servant boy or girl. 2. servant.

vasikkı (—.) وَاثِق A *lrnd.* 1. trusting, reliant; secure, confiding. 2. firm, strong.

vasil (.—) وَصِيل A *lrnd.* one's constant companion; intimate (friend).

vasilikgi وَصِيلَك *law* executorship; trusteeship, guardianship.

vasimezheb (—...) وَاسِعْمَذْهَب P *lrnd.* too tolerant in matters of morals, lax.

vasistas وَاسِسْتَاس F transom.

vasitiı (.—) وَسِيط A *lrnd.* 1. man of primary importance among his people; highest in rank, dignity or kind. 2. mediator; arbiter.

vasiyet وَصِيَت A 1. will, testament. 2. a making a last will and testament; a bequeathing. 3. last request of a dying person. 4. *lrnd.* an enjoining, advising or commanding; injunction; advice; command. — et= 1. to bequeath; to give as one's last injunction. 2. to enjoin, advise or command.

vasiyetname (...—.) وَصِيَتْنَامَه P written will; last will and testament.

vaslii وَصْل A *lrnd.* a joining; meeting; union; attainment. —et= to unite; to join, to connect. —î (.—) A pertaining to junction or union.

vasm وَصْم A *lrnd.* 1. a splitting, cracking; a breaking (without separation of parts). 2. knot in wood. 3. flaw, defect; reproach, disgrace.

vasmet وَصْمَت A *lrnd.* 1. a feeling of languor and debility. 2. flaw, defect; blemish.

vassad (.—) وَصَّاد A *lrnd.* weaver, interweaver, knitter, netter.

vassaf (.—) وَصَّاف A *lrnd.* one noted for a power of description; good word-painter.

vassalii وَصَّال F vassal. —lik vassalage.

vaşakgı وَاشَاق وَشَاق [veşak] 1. lynx; especially the pardine lynx, *zool., Lynx pardina.* 2. fur of the lynx.

Vaşington وَاشِينْغْتُن 1. *geog.* Washington. 2. navel orange. — portakalı navel orange. — tipi *slang* eccentric; very fashionable.

vat 1 وَاتْ F *phys.* watt.

-vat 2 (—) وَاتْ cf. -at 3.

vatan وَطَن A one's native country, motherland. —ı kurtar= *slang* to manage the situation.

vatandaş وَطَنْدَاش 1. compatriot; fellow countryman. 2. citizen, subject. —lık citizenship; allegiance; a being a compatriot.

vatanî (..—) وَطَنِى A pertaining to one's native land; patriotic.

vatanperver وَطَنْپَرْوَر P patriotic; patriot. —lik love of one's country, patriotism.

vatansız وَطَنْسِز stateless. —lık statelessness.

vatar وَطَر A *lrnd.* a necessary or important thing, a thing which lies at the heart; necessity.

vatıd (—.) وَاطِد A *lrnd.* 1. that makes firm. 2. firm, solid; established.

vati 1 (.—) وَطِى A *lrnd.* 1. a trampling, treading under foot; trodden or pressed down smooth. 2. a smoothing and making level; trodden or used till soft and yielding. 3. pliant, tractable. 4. having sexual relations with.

vati 2 (.—) وَاطِى A *lrnd.* 1. that treads. 2. that has sexual relations with.

vatid (.—) وَطِيد A *lrnd.* firm, tight, immovable.

vatm وَطْم A *lrnd.* 1. a trampling, treading under foot. 2. a letting down a veil.

vatman واتمان F driver of a street-car.

vatoz واطوز ، واطوزه Gk 1. stingray, *zool.*, *Dasyatis pastinaca*. 2. common skate, *zool.*, *Raja batis*.

vatvat (. —) واطواط A *lrnd.* 1. mountain swallow. 2. bat, *zool.*, *Vespertilio* and other genera. 3. coward.

vatvata وطوطه A *lrnd.* 1. a speaking indistinctly as though twittering. 2. a being weak; powerlessness.

vav (—) و ، واو *name of the letter* و (the twenty-ninth letter of the Ottoman and Persian alphabets; twenty-sixth letter of the Arabic alphabet; in chronograms it has the numerical value of 6).

vaveylâ واويلا A *lrnd.* 1. Alas! Woe is me! 2. cry of horror or lament. **—yı kopar=** to raise a cry of horror or lament.

vavi (— —) واوى A *lrnd.* pertaining to the letter و .

vay (—) واى *interjection expressing surprise or regret* Oh! Alas! **— anam!** Oh! How queer! **— başım!** Oh, my poor head! **— başına!** Damn him! **— canına!** How amazing! **— sen misin?** Is that you?

vaya (——) وايا P *lrnd.* a want, need; business.

vayavay (———) واياواى P *lrnd.* cry; the uproar of combatants.

vaye (. —) وايه P *lrnd.* 1. part, portion, lot. 2. *same as* **vaya**. 3. sense, weight, importance of a word. **—dar** (—. —) P who participates; having a share. **—gir** (—. —), **—mend** (—. .) P one who participates.

vaz[z'1] **1** وضع A *same as* **vazı 1**. **— ü hareket** behavior.

va'z 2 وعظ A *same as* **vaız**. **— ü nasihat** admonition; sermon (advice).

vazaat[ti] (. —.) وضاعت A *lrnd.* a being low, humble; lowliness, humility.

vazaif (. —.) وظائف A *lrnd.*, pl. of **vazife**.

vaz'an (.'.) وضعاً A *lrnd.* 1. in position, according to position. 2. by or in arrangement.

vazayi (. —.) وضائع A *lrnd.*, pl. of **vazia**.

va'zet=[der] **1**, **vâzet=**[der] **1** وعظ ایتمك to admonish, to preach.

vaz'et=[der] **2** وضع ایتمك /ı/ 1. to put, to place. 2. to lay (foundation). 3. to impose (tax).

vazgeç=[er] وازگچمك /dan/ to give up; to cease from; to abandon (a project). **—ir=** /ı/. *caus.*

vazgeçti وازگدی [bazgeşt] difference or dispute (that has passed between two persons). **—si ol=** to have a difference or dispute. **—lik** *colloq.* misunderstanding; offense; enmity.

vazgel=[ir] وازگلمك *archaic, same as* **vazgeç=**.

vazgûn (——), **vazgûne** (——.) وازگون ، وازگونه

P *lrnd.* 1. turned upside down, inverted. 2. perverted, perverse.

vazı[z'1] **1** وضع [vaz 1] *lrnd.* 1. a putting down or laying. 2. a placing, depositing. 3. an imposing (a tax). 4. an arranging; arrangement. 5. a staking a thing as a wager. 6. attitude, manner, behavior. 7. posture; gesture; position. **—ı esas** the laying of a foundation. **—ı haml** parturition. **—ı haml et=** to give birth. **—ı yed***.

vâzı[u] **2** (—.) واضع A *lrnd.* 1. who lays down or institutes. 2. who places, puts a thing. **—ı kanun** *law* legislator.

vâzıh (—.) واضح A open, clear, manifest. **— idrâk** *psychol.* apperception. **—an** (—'. .) A clearly. **—ât** (—. —) A *lrnd.* evidences; things clear as daylight.

vâzıulimza (—. . . —) واضع الامضا A *lrnd.* signatory.

vaz'ıyed وضع ید A *law* seizure. **— et=** /a/ 1. to confiscate. 2. *lrnd.* to take up a matter.

vaz'i 1 (. —.) وضعى A *law* pertaining to position, resulting from attitude, conduct, etc.

vazi[ii] **2** (. —.) وضیع A *lrnd.* lowly, humble.

vazia (. —.) وضیعه A *lrnd.* 1. loss or reduction in capital invested in trade. 2. tax, duty. 3. anything lowered, abated or deducted. 4. book in which are inscribed the sayings of wise men.

vazife (. —.) وظیفه A 1. duty; obligation, task. 2. homework, classwork (of a student). 3. function, charge. 4. *lrnd.* salary; pension; school fees. **—si mi?** What does he care! **— edin=**, . **— et=** to care, to mind; to be interested. **—i hal** duty imposed on one by circumstances. **—i kimyeviye** chemical function.

vazifedar (. —. —) وظیفه دار P *lrnd.* charged with an official duty; competent authority.

vazifehar (. —. —), **vazifehor** (. —. .) وظیفه خور ، وظیفه خوار P *lrnd.* pensioner; salaried, dependent.

vazifeli وظیفه لی in charge; on duty; engaged.

vazifesiz وظیفه سز 1. without an official duty. 2. who neglects his work, careless, slack.

vazifeşinas (. —. . —) وظیفه شناس P dutiful; conscientious.

vazifeten (. —'. .) وظیفةً A *ex officio*, by virtue of office.

vazime (. —.) وضیمه A *lrnd.* 1. funeral banquet. 2. a body of two or three hundred men. 3. a body of guests.

vâzin (—.) وازن A *lrnd.* of just weight.

vaziyet وضعیت A 1. position; situation. 2. attitude. **— al=** 1. *mil.* to stand at attention. 2. to take sides, to state one's position.

vazo (.'.) وازو It *.* vase.

vazzah (. —) وضاح A *lrnd.* 1. clear, bright; evident, manifest. 2. fair skinned; handsome, good-looking.

ve ‎وَ‎ A 1. and, also, too. 2. or; but. 3. *lrnd.* by (in an oath). — **aleykümüsselâm** And unto you also be peace! *said in reply to the salutation* **selâmünaleyküm**. — **ba'dehü** *lrnd.* and then. — **bes***. — **gayri zalike**, — **gayruhu** *lrnd.* etcetera. — **illâ** *lrnd.* and if not, or otherwise. — **illâfelâ** *lrnd.* and if not, then, not; otherwise not. — **keza** *lrnd.* and in like manner; and likewise. — **kıs alâ hâzâ***. — **lâkin***. — **lehu eyzan** *lrnd.* by the same author (or composer). — **rahmetullahü aleyh** *lrnd.* May he rest in peace. — **saire** (abbreviated v.s.) etcetera, etc.

veba (. —) ‎وَبا‎ A 1. plague, pestilence; any epidemic fatal disease. 2. murrain. —**î** (. — —) A *lrnd.* pestilential, pertaining to the plague or a pestilence.

vebalⁱⁱ (. —) ‎وَبال‎ A 1. sin (that will be punished in the next world). 2. evil consequence. 3. *lrnd.* anything painful; heaviness; hurtfulness. —**i boynuna** on his (your) head be it; the responsibility is his. —**ini çek=** to be punished for; to undergo the consequence of.

vebalet (. —.) ‎وَبالت‎ A *lrnd., same as* **vebal**.

vebalı (. —.) ‎وَبالى‎ 1. plague-stricken. 2. having the infection of the plague.

veballi ‎وَباللى‎ that will be punished in the next world.

veber ‎وَبَر‎ A *lrnd.* fur, hair.

ve bes ‎وَبَس‎ P *lrnd.* and enough; and quite enough too.

vebîl (. —) ‎وَبيل‎ A *lrnd.* 1. unhealthy, unwholesome; dangerous, hurtful. 2. heavy, severe, vehement (blow, etc.). 3. thick staff; heavy stick.

vebr ‎وَبر‎ A *lrnd.* Syrian coney, zool., *Hyrax syriacus.*

vecaᵃⁱ ‎وَجع‎ A *lrnd.* pain; colic; ache. —**i cenb** *path.* pleurodynia.

vecah (. —) ‎وَجاه‎ A *lrnd.* the place opposite or facing one, the immediate presence of a person.

vecahet (. —.) ‎وَجاهت‎ A *lrnd.* 1. a being of a noble or pleasing presence; respect; dignity, authority. 2. beauty, comeliness. —**li** beautiful, handsome; of a pleasing or imposing aspect.

vecaib (. —.) ‎وَجائب‎ A *lrnd., pl. of* **vecibe**.

veca'li ‎وَجَعْلى‎ painful, in pain.

vecazet (. —.) ‎وَجازت‎ A *lrnd.* 1. a being laconic, terse or abrupt (saying); shortness, terseness, abruptness. 2. a being laconic in speech.

vecd ‎وَجد‎ A 1. a being in a state of rapture or ecstasy; ecstasy, rapture; a being intensely moved by an emotion such as love, grief or rage; intense excitement or emotion of love, grief or anger. 2. *lrnd.* a being rich; wealth, riches.

vecdâver (. —.) ‎وَجدآور‎ P *lrnd.* ecstatic; causing rapture.

vecdefza (. . —) ‎وَجدافزا‎ P *lrnd.* increasing rapture.

vecdî (. —) ‎وَجدى‎ A *lrnd.* ecstatic.

vecedtü (. .'.) ‎وَجدتُ‎ A *lrnd.* (*lit.* I have found it.) a lucky find, good thing; tidbit. —**sü yok** There is nothing worth finding in it.

vecel ‎وَجل‎ A *lrnd.* fear, terror.

vecem ‎وَجم‎ A *lrnd.* a being silent from fear or sullenness.

vecenat (. . —) ‎وَجنات‎ A *lrnd., pl. of* **vecne**.

vecer ‎وَجر‎ P *lrnd.* decree of a judge; official legal opinion.

vecerger ‎وَجرگر‎ P *lrnd.* official expounder of the law, chief justice, mufti.

vech ‎وَجه‎ A *lrnd.* 1. face. 2. surface (of a thing). 3. side of a solid body. 4. direction, bearing. 5. manner; road, path. 6. cause, reason, means. 7. sense; view; true sense; right view. —**i ahar** in a different way, in another manner. —**i ahsen** the best method. —**i arazbar** *Or. mus.* a **makam** composed two centuries ago. —**i arz** face of the earth; surface of the ground. —**i hâl** mode of living, state of one's circumstances. —**i icmalî** succinct manner. **bir — ile** in some way. —**i maaş** maintenance, subsistence. —**i memuriyet** means, method, authority for the office. —**i meşruh üzere** in the manner described. —**i muharrer üzere** as written or (previously) detailed. —**i müvecceh** duly adjusted, correct manner. —**i şer'i** canonical reason; canonical method. —**i tafsili** detailed manner. —**i tesmiye** reason for naming.

veche ‎وَجهه‎ A *same as* **veçhe**. — **ver=** /a/ to direct.

vechen (.'.) ‎وَجهًا‎ A *lrnd.* 1. in face; by face. 2. in some way or manner. — **minelvücuh** 1. somehow or other. 2. *negative* by no manner or means; in no shape.

vecheyn ‎وَجهين‎ A *lrnd.* two faces, sides, directions.

vechî (. —) ‎وَجهى‎ A *anat.* pertaining to a face; facial.

veciⁱⁱ 1 (. —) ‎وَجيع‎ A *lrnd.* painful; pained.

veciⁱⁱ 2 ‎وَجع‎ A *lrnd.* pained, suffering; sick.

vecibe (. —.) ‎وَجيبه‎ A *lrnd.* 1. obligation; needful thing; due. 2. money allowance or pension. —**i zimmet** one's unquestionable duty.

vecihᶜʰⁱ 1 ‎وَجه‎ *var. of* **vech**.

vecih 2 (. —) ‎وَجيه‎ A *lrnd.* of pleasing aspect; prepossessing.

vecih 3 (. —) ‎وَجيه‎ A *lrnd.* 1. chief, prince. 2. noble-looking, handsome man.

vecihî (. — —) ‎وَجيهى‎ A *lrnd.* pertaining to a chief or to a handsome man.

vecil ‎وَجل‎ A *lrnd.* timid; frightened.

vecim 1 مُرْحِم A lrnd. silent from disgust or fear.
vecim 2 (.—) مُبِمّ A lrnd. very hot, sultry.
vecitᵈⁱ وَجِدَ var. of **vecd**.
veciz (.—) وَجِيز A laconic, terse.
vecize (.—.) وَجِيزَه A terse saying; epigram, aphorism.
vecne وَجْنَه A lrnd. prominent part of the cheek; cheek-bone, cheek.
vecnî (.—) وَجْنِى A anat. pertaining to the cheek-bone; zygomatic.
vecz وَجْز A lrnd. 1. laconic; short, brief. 2. ready in giving. 3. nimble, agile.
veçhe وَجْهِه [veche] direction; side. — **ver=** /a/ to direct.
vedᵈᵈⁱ وُدّ A lrnd. 1. a loving, being a loving friend; love; friendship. 2. loving friend, lover.
vedaᵃⁱ **1** (.—) وَدَاع A a leave-taking; farewell. — **et=** /a/ to bid farewell to, to say good-by. —**a git=** /a/ to pay someone a farewell visit.
vedaᵃⁱ **2** وَدَع A cowry shells, zool., Concha veneris.
ved'a 3, vedaa وَدَعَه A lrnd. a single cowry shell.
vedaatᵗⁱ (.—.) وَدَاعَت A lrnd. 1. deposit, trust. 2. a being quiet, tranquil; tranquility, repose. —**iyle** by means of; through the medium of.
vedad (.—) وَدَاد A lrnd. love; friendship.
vedai (.——) وَدَاعِى A lrnd. pertaining to a farewell.
vedalaş=ⁱʳ وَدَاعِتْشْمَك /la/ to say good-by to each other, to take leave of.
vedaname (.——.) وَدَاعْنَامَه P farewell letter.
vedayi (.—.) وَدَايِع A lrnd., pl. of **vedia**.
veddua (..—) وَالدُّعَاء A lrnd. With my blessing (at the end of a letter).
vedec وَدَج A lrnd., same as **vidac**.
vediⁱⁱ **1** (.—) وَدِيع A lrnd. quiet, tranquil, at rest.
vediⁱⁱ **2** (.—) وَدِيع A law 1. compact, agreement, covenant. 2. one charged with a deposit, depositary.
vedia (.—.) وَدِيعَه A lrnd. 1. thing deposited or given into safekeeping. 2. compact or agreement. 3. w. cap., woman's name.
vedid (.—) وَدِيد A lrnd. very loving, affectionate; lover; friend.
vedide (.—.) وَدِيدَه A 1. lrnd. affectionate, friend. 2. w. cap., woman's name.
vedr وَدْر A lrnd. a being dead drunk; unconsciousness.
vedre وَدْرَه Sl prov. milk pail.
vedud (.—) وَدُود A lrnd. 1. very loving, very affectionate. 2. the All-loving God.
vefa (.—) وَفَاء A fidelity; loyalty; constancy in love; faithfulness. — **et=** 1. to be true, faithful in performing an obligation. 2. to suffice. — **hakkı** law right to repurchase.
vefadar (.——) وَفَادَار P same as **vefakâr**.
—**î** (.———) P, —**lık** fidelity, loyalty, constancy.
vefakâr (.——) وَفَاكَار P faithful, loyal, constant.
vefasız وَفَاسِز unfaithful, disloyal, untrustworthy. —**lık** faithlessness.
vefaşiar (.—.—) وَفَاشِعَار P lrnd., same as **vefakâr**.
vefat (.—) وَفَات A death; decease. — **et=** to die. — **ilm ü haberi** death certificate.
vefaz وَفَض A lrnd. a going along at a rapid rate; haste, hurry.
vefd وَفْد A lrnd. 1. an arriving, coming (as an ambassador to a king). 2. peak of sand on the ridge of a sandhill. **V— Partisi** the Wafd Party (in Egypt).
vefi (.—) وَفِى A lrnd. 1. sufficient, ample, abundant. 2. faithful (to an engagement).
vefikᵏⁱ (.—) وَفِيق A lrnd. 1. companion, associate; friend. 2. agreeing, conforming.
vefiyat (..—) وَفِيَات A lrnd., pl. of **vefat**, deaths; mortality.
vefkᵏⁱ وَفْق A lrnd. 1. a suiting, fitting, agreeing; agreement, conformity. 2. a kind of charm or talisman composed of a written formula (folded square or in triangular form or rolled). —**i dilhah üzere** according to the wishes of the heart. —**i murad üzere** as desired. —**i rubai** talisman in four lines of four words each. —**i südasi** geomantic square or talisman of six compartments each way. —**i sülâsi** talisman of three squares to the side.
vefret وَفْرَت A lrnd. abundance. —**le** abundantly.
vega (.—) وَغَا A lrnd. battle, strife; clamor, tumult.
veh وَه P lrnd. Oh! Alas! Strange!
vehb وَهْب A lrnd. a giving, bestowing; grant, gift.
vehbi (.—) وَهْبِى A lrnd. 1. bestowed by God; due to God's generosity. 2. natural, inborn; innate. 3. w. cap., man's name. **V—nin kerrakesi** cf. **anlaşıldı Vehbinin kerrakesi**. —**ye** A phil. innatism.
vehc وَهْج A lrnd. a burning, blazing (fire); heat of fire.
vehde وَهْدَه A lrnd. valley, hollow, declivity.
vehecan (..—) وَهَجَان A lrnd., same as **vehc**.
vehen وَهَن A lrnd. a being weak, unequal to; weakness, insignificance; baseness.
rehf وَهْف A lrnd. 1. a putting forth leaves (tree), a flourishing (plant). 2. a coming within reach, an approaching, drawing near.
vehham (.—) وَهَّام A lrnd., same as **vahham**.

vehic (. —) دُ ثَمَيْحٍ A *lrnd.* fierceness of fire; heat, blaze.

vehilʰˡⁱ دُ نَصْ A *lrnd.* very timorous; frightened; trembling.

vehimʰᵐⁱ دُ ثَمْ [vehm] a fearing, foreboding; groundless fear.

vehl دُ نَصْ A *lrnd.* a misunderstanding, mistaking.

vehle دُ نَصْ A *lrnd.* 1. first surprise at an unexpected event; first cognizance of a matter. 2. moment, instant. **—i ulâda** at the first onset, for the first moment.

vehleten (´..) دُ نَصْة A *lrnd.* for the first moment, just at first.

vehm دُ ثَمْ A *lrnd.* 1. same as **vehim**. 2. a surmising, conjecturing; surmise, conjecture ultimately proving false. 3. a mistaking, falling into error in opinion; error. 4. the surmising faculty, the imagination. 5. illusion, delusion. **—i havas** *psych.* illusion.

vehmet=ᵈᵉʳ دُ ثَمْ اِيتْنَك 1. to forebode, to fear. 2. to surmise, conjecture. 3. to mistake; to have the illusion that.

vehmî (. —) دُ ثَمِى A *lrnd.* imaginary; conjectural. **—yat** (..—) A imaginary things; groundless forebodings; conjectures.

vehmnâkᵏⁱ (. —) دُ ثَمْناك P *lrnd.* given to forebodings.

vehn دُ ثَصْ A *lrnd.*, same as **vehen**.

vehub (. —) دُ نَصْب A *lrnd.* habitually munificent, liberal.

vekâlet (. —.) دُ كَاَت A 1. a being an agent or representative of another; attorneyship; proxy. 2. Ministry. **— emrine alın=** to be temporarily removed from office, to be suspended. **— et=** /a/ 1. to represent someone. 2. to act as agent or attorney for someone. **—i ticariye** *com.* mercantile agency. **—i uzma** *Ott. hist.* the office of Grand Vizier. **— ver=** /a/ to give someone the right of representing.

vekâleten (. —´..) دُ كَاَتَة A as representative or deputy of another; by proxy.

vekâletname (. —.—.) دُ كَاَتْنَامَ P power of attorney, proxy.

vekâletpenah (. —..—) دُ كَاَتْپَنَاه P *Ott. hist.* the Grand Vizier.

vekar (. —) دُ نَاَر A *lrnd.* 1. same as **vakar**. 2. *lrnd.* calm, sedate, dignified. **—lı** grave, dignified; sedate, calm. **—sız** lacking in dignity or seriousness. **—sızlık** lack of dignity.

vekayiⁱⁱ (. —.) دُ نَاَيِع A same as **vakayi**.

ve kıs alâ haza (. . . — —) دُ نَسْ عَلَى هَذَا A *lrnd.* (*lit.* And measure upon this, and judge by this.) And so on accordingly; you can imagine the rest.

vekil (. —) A, **vekil** دُ كِيل 1. agent; representative; deputy; attorney; proxy. 2. Minister of State. **—i devrî** *lrnd.* attorney appointed irrevocably. **—i efrad** *lrnd.* attorney for one special matter. **— et=** /ı/ to appoint as one's representative. **—i mutlak** 1. *lrnd.* attorney with unlimited power. 2. *Ott. hist.* Chief Minister of an absolute sovereign; the Grand Vizier. **—i müseccel** *lrnd.* attorney duly attested and registered. **— ol=** /a/ to represent or act as deputy for someone. **—i şer'** *lrnd.* attorney appointed in due canonical form.

vekilharc (. —.) دُ كِيلْخَرج P steward or major-domo (in a great house).

vekillikᵏⁱ دُ كِيلِّك 1. quality or duties of a **vekil**. 2. agency; attorneyship.

vekir (. —), **vekire** (. —.) دُ كِير، دُ كِيرَه A *lrnd.* housewarming party.

vekn, vekne دُ كْن، دُ كْنَه A *lrnd.* 1. bird's nest. 2. a sitting on eggs (bird).

vekr دُ كْر A *lrnd.* bird's nest.

vekre دُ كْرَه A *lrnd.* 1. bird's nest. 2. house-warming party.

velâᵃⁱ (. —) دَلَاء A *lrnd.* 1. nearness, propinquity; kinship, relationship. 2. proprietorship.

velâdet (. —.) دَلاَدَت [vilâdet] *lrnd.* birth.

velâhu دَلَاه A *lrnd.* and to him…, also by him. **— aydan** also by the same author.

velâkin (. —.) دَلَكِن A but still, but yet.

velâyet (. —.) دَلاَيَت A 1. *law* guardianship; trusteeship. 2. *lrnd.* sanctity, holiness; sainthood. 3. *lrnd.* a being an aid or protector; aid, protection. 4. *lrnd.* a being ruler and governor; sovereignty; rule. 5. *lrnd.* a being closely connected with another in love and friendship.

velâyim (. —.) دَلاَيِم A *lrnd.*, pl. of **velime**.

veled دَلَد A 1. *slang* bastard; rascal. 2. *lrnd.* child; progeny; issue. **—i ekber** the eldest son. **—i mader behata** *lrnd.* illegitimate child. **—i mânevi** adopted child. **—i sulbî** one's own child. **—i zina** 1. bastard. 2. rascal.

veledülgıyye دَلَدُالغِيَّة A *lrnd.* bastard.

veledüsseyibeyn دَلَدُالسَّيِّبَين A *lrnd.* child whose parents have both had former spouses.

veleh دَلَه A *lrnd.* 1. a being distracted with emotion; a becoming afflicted or impatient from love or grief; stupefaction; violent emotion. 2. a being frightened; fear, terror. **— gel=** /a/ to become distracted. **— getir=** to be distracted.

velehan (..—) دَلَهَان A *lrnd.*, same as **veleh**.

velehzede دَلَهْزَدَه P *lrnd.* struck, distracted; angry, passionate.

velena (. ´.) دَلَنَا It *naut.* staysail.

velençe, velense دَلَنْچَه P Sp a kind of thick blanket; horse-rug.

velestralya (. . . ´.) دَلَسْتَرَالْيَه It *naut.* staysail, trysail.

velev ولو A even if, even though. **— ki** even if.

velfecri والفجر A *name of the eighty-ninth sura of the Quran which begins with this word, used in the phrase* **gözleri velfecri oku=** to give the impression of being very astute and wide-awake.

velhan (. —) ولهان A *lrnd.* bewildered; distractedly in love.

velhasıl (.' — .) والحاصل A in short.

veli 1 (. —) ولى A 1. protector, guardian (of a child etc.). 2. saint, friend of God. 3. *lrnd.* comrade, companion, one's trusted friend. 4. *lrnd.* near relation, one's next of kin. 5. *lrnd.* lord, sovereign. 6. *lrnd.* near, contiguous, adjoining. **— i baid** *lrnd.* a distant relation who is next of kin. **— i cinayet** *lrnd.* the next of kin entitled to retaliate for offenses. **— i dem** *lrnd.* he who is entitled to claim blood for blood shed. **V — i Hamîd** *lrnd.* God, the Praiseworthy, the One nearest to man. **V — i Müttakin** *lrnd.* God, who is near to those who fear Him. **— i nasîr** *lrnd.* 1. a friend who assists. 2. God, who helps His elect.

veli 2 (. —) ولى P *lrnd.* and but.

veliahd (. — .) وليعهد A heir to a throne, heir apparent.

velice (. — .) وليجه A *lrnd.* intimate, confidential friend; near, adjacent.

velid (. —) وليد A *lrnd.* 1. new-born child, infant. 2. son, lad, child. 3. home-born slave child.

velik (. —), **velikin** (. — .) وليكن P *lrnd.* but.

velilik[ti] ولىليك 1. qualities and duties of a guardian; guardianship. 2. quality of a saint.

velime (. — .) وليمه A *lrnd.* wedding feast; banquet.

velinimet ولنعمت A benefactor; patron. **— i biminnet** *lrnd.* benefactor who does not scold one.

veliye وليّه A *lrnd., fem. of* **veli 1**.

veliullah (. — . .) ولى الله [Arabic . — . —] *lrnd.* saint.

velosipet, velospit ولوسپيت F bicycle.

velûd (. —) ولود A *lrnd., same as* **velût**. **— iyet** (. — . .) A prolificacy; productivity.

velût[du] (. —) ولود [**velûd**] prolific; productive.

velvâl[li] (. —) ولوال A *lrnd.* 1. grief, anguish. 2. lament; cry of one weeping or threatening.

velvele ولوله A 1. outcry; clamor; hubbub. 2. *obs.* flourish of trumpets. 3. *lrnd.* a lamenting vociferously. 4. *Or. mus.* subdividing the beats of a rhythmic pattern to make a more complex pattern. **— çıkar=** to invoke a quarrel. **— kopar=** to set up an outcry; to scream, to shriek. **— ye ver=** /ı/ to cause a tumult and confusion.

velveleci ولولهجى person who is fond of noise and clamor.

velveleendaz (. . . . —) ولوله انداز P *lrnd.* that raises an outcry.

velyet[der] ولىيتل to follow in succession.

vemezan (. . —) وميضان A *lrnd., same as* **vemz**.

vemk[kı] ومق A *lrnd.* a loving; love.

vemz ومض A *lrnd.* a gleaming, flashing slightly (lightning).

-ven ون *archaic* I am..., *as in* **benven** I am.

Venedik[gi] ونديك *geog.* Venice. **— li** Venetian.

veni ونى A *lrnd.* a being torpid, languid, slow; slowness, languor.

venim (. —) ونيم A *lrnd.* excrement of a fly, flyblow.

ventil ونتيل F valve; cork.

vento (.' .) ونتو It *naut.* 1. guy rope. 2. vang of a peak. 3. topping lift of a boom.

Venüs ونوس F *myth., astr.* Venus.

ver=[ir] 1 ورمك 1. to give; to deliver. 2. to pay. 3. to sell. 4. to offer. 5. to attribute. 6. to suffer (losses). 7. to teach. 8. *added to another verb* just, quickly, with ease, *e. g.,* **geliverdi** He just came; **kapıyı açıver** Would you mind opening the door? **— Allahım ver!** Give more, o God, give more! (said when it is raining). **— elini Boğaziçi** We decided to go up the Bosphorus (and off we went). **— yansın et=** *colloq.* to destroy without mercy.

-ver 2 ور P *lrnd.* possessing, possessed of, *e. g.,* **tâcver**.

ver 3 ور P *lrnd.* and if.

vera 1 (. —) وراء A *lrnd.* 1. back part, rear, back surface (of a thing). 2. the space immediately behind a person or thing. **— dan** from behind. **— sı** its rear. **— ya** to the back part, to the rear. **— i perdei hafa** behind the veil of secrecy, hidden. **— yı zahrına at=** /ı/ to throw behind one's back; to take no heed.

vera[aı] **2** ورع A *lrnd.* 1. an abstaining or avoiding; caution. 2. an abstaining from what is unclean or sinful. 3. a being modest, pious, chaste.

vera 3 ورا A *lrnd.* God's creatures, the whole creation; mankind.

vera[aı] **4** (. —) وراع A *lrnd.* 1. a being a coward; cowardice. 2. a being of no account.

veraat[ti] (. — .) وراعت A *lrnd.* 1. *same as* **vera 4**. 2. a being poor. 3. an abstaining or desisting, *esp.* from what is divinely prohibited; fear of God.

Verarud (. — —) وراءرود P *lrnd., geog.* Transoxiana, Turkistan.

veraset (. — .) وراثت A a being or becoming

veraya (.—.) ورایا A *lrnd.*, pl. of **vera** 3.
Verazrud (.——) ورازرود P *lrnd.*, same as **Verarud**.
verb وَرْب A *lrnd*. 1. den of a wild beast. 2. orifice of a hole or burrow. 3. space between two ribs. 4. space between the index finger and the thumb. — **ve intikal vergisi** *law* death duties.
verçi ورچى P *lrnd*. and although.
verd 1 وَرْد A *lrnd*. 1. rose. 2. blossom; flower.
verd 2 وَرْد A *lrnd*. 1. darkish chestnut (horse). 2. w. cap., *name of one of the seven horses of the Prophet Muhammad*. 3. tawny lion. — **i ağbes** dun-colored horse.
verde وَرْدَه A *lrnd*. 1. a single flower. 2. one rose or variety of rose.
verdene وَرْدَنَه P *lrnd*. 1. a special kind of short rolling pin very thick in the center. 2. axle-tree pivot.
verdî (.—) وَرْدى A *lrnd*. 1. pertaining to the rose. 2. rose-colored.
verdir=[ir] ويرديرمك وَرْديرمك /ı, a/ *caus. of* **ver**= 1. —**il**= *pass*. —**t**= /ı, a/ *same as* **verdir**=.
verdiye وَرْدِيَّه A *bot.*, Rosaceae.
vere وَرَه Sl *Ott. hist.* capitulation, surrender. — **bayrağı** flag of surrender. — **kâğıdı** treaty of capitulation; written surrender. — **ver**= to capitulate.
verecek[ği] ويرَه جَك debt. —**li** debtor.
vereh وَرَه A *lrnd*. 1. a being foolish, stupid; silliness. 2. a being dazed with fear.
verek[ki] وَرَك A *anat*. hip or haunch-bone, ischium. —**i** (..—) A pertaining to the hipbone.
verem وَرَم A 1. tuberculosis. 2. tuberculous. 3. *lrnd*. swelling, tumor. — **aşısı** inoculation against tuberculosis. — **ol**= to contract tuberculosis. —**li** tuberculous.
verese وَرَثَه A *lrnd*. inheritors.
veresi ويرَسى *obs.*, same as **veresiye**.
veresiye ويرَسِيَه on credit. — **al**= to buy on credit. —**yi kes**= to stop selling on credit. — **tekâlif** *mil.* requisition without payment. — **ver**= /ı/ to sell on credit.
veret=[der] ويرَه يَتمك *slang* /a/ to keep on hitting, to give several blows to.
verev وَرَو *tailor*. oblique; diagonal, slanting.
vergi ويرگى 1. gift, present; talent given by God. 2. tax, tribute; duty. — **beyannamesi** tax return, tax statement. — **hukuku** legislation on tax and duties. — **matrahı** tax assessment. — **mükellefi** taxpayer. — **ol**= /a/ to be special (to), to be the speciality (of). — **tahakkuku** tax assessment. — **tahsildarı** tax-collector. — **tarhet**= to impose a tax, to levy.
vergili ويرگيلى 1. gifted, talented. 2. generous, munificent; bountiful.
veri 1 *neol*. datum.
veri[ii] 2 وَرِع A *lrnd*. God-fearing, who piously abstains from sin.
veri[ii] 3 (.—) وَرِع A *lrnd*. that abstains or desists; abstinent, chaste.
verici ويريجى 1. radio transmitter. 2. who or which gives.
verid (.—) وَريد A *anat*. vein, especially, jugular vein. — **iltihabı** phlebitis. —**i şiryanî** pulmonary vein. —**î** (.——) A pertaining to veins, venous.
veril=[ir] ويريلمك *pass. of* **ver**= 1. —**me emri** /a/ order for payment of government money.
verim ويريم 1. produce; yield; output; return; profit. 2. *mech*. efficiency.
verimli ويريملى productive; profitable. —**lik** productivity.
verimsiz ويريمسز that yields little or no produce, unfruitful.
verimkâr (..—) ويريمكار *only in* — **ol**= /ı/ to show willingness to give.
veriş 1 ويريش *verbal n. of* **ver**= 1.
veriş=[ir] 2 ويريشمك *archaic* /ı/ to give to one another, to exchange.
veriştir=[ir] ويريشديرمك *colloq*. /a/ to utter abuse, to swear at.
verka (.—) وَرْقا A *lrnd*. 1. stock dove, *zool*., Columba oenas. 2. off-white colored, dingy. 3. sterile, rainless (season).
verkaç ويركاچ *sports* pass and run maneuver.
verne وَرْنَه P *lrnd*. and if not, or otherwise.
vernik[ği] ورنيك Gk varnish. —**le**= /ı/ to varnish.
verniye ورنيه *mech*. vernier scale.
veronika (...'.) وَرونيقا It speedwell, *bot.*, Veronica anagaloides.
verz 1 وَرْز P *lrnd*. 1. a making or doing, work, occupation. 2. task, lesson, practice. 3. agriculture, husbandry. 4. country, land; field; plot.
-verz 2 وَرْز P *lrnd*. who does or practices, e. g., **abverz**, **ihlâsverz**.
verzan (.—) وَرْزان P *lrnd*. who does or practices.
verze وَرْزَه P *lrnd.*, *same as* **verz** 1.
verziş وَرْزِش P *lrnd*. a doing or practicing; endeavor, exertion.
verzişkâr (..—) وَرْزِشكار P *lrnd*. industrious. —**âne** (..——) P industriously. —**î** (..——) P industriousness.
verzkâr (.—)' وَرْزكار P *lrnd*. farmer, plowman.
vesacet (.—.) وَثاجَت A *lrnd*. a being firm and stout; firmness, stoutness.

vesah وَسَخ A *lrnd.* dirt, filth.
vesahülüzn وَسَخ الاُذن A *lrnd.* earwax.
vesaid (.—.) وَسَائِد A *lrnd.*, pl. of **visade**.
vesaikᵏⁱ (.—.) وَسَائِق A *lrnd.*, pl. of **vesika**.
vesail (.—.) وَسَائِل A *lrnd.*, pl. of **vesile**.
vesait (.—.) وَسَائِط A 1. means of transportation, vehicles. 2. *lrnd.*, pl. of **vasıta**, means, ways. **—i nakliye** means of transport, transportation.
vesakatᵗⁱ (.—.) وَثاقت A *lrnd.* a being firm, tight, strong; firmness, tightness; reliability.
vesalet (.—.) وَسَالَت A *lrnd.* a being a means or pretext.
vesam (.—), **vesamet** (.—.) وَسَام وَسَامَت A *lrnd.* a being beautiful, handsome, elegant; comeliness.
vesatatᵗⁱ, **vesatet** (.—.) وَسَاطَت A *lrnd.* 1. a being a mediator; mediation. 2. a being a means; intermediary. 3. a being a central object among the people. **—iyle** by means of him; through him. **— et=** to act as an intermediary; to be a channel or means.
vesavis (.—.) وَسَاوِس A *lrnd.*, pl. of **vesvese**. **—i şeytaniye** diabolical suggestions.
vesaya (.—.) وَصَايَا A *lrnd.*, pl. of **vasiyet**.
vesayet (.—.) وَصَايَت A 1. *law* executorship; trusteeship. 2. *lrnd.* injunction, warning.
vesb, veseban (..—) وَثب شَبَان A *lrnd.* a springing, jumping, leaping.
vesen 1 وَثَن A *lrnd.* idol.
vesen 2 وَسَن A *lrnd.* a being sleepy; drowsiness.
veseni (..—) وَثَني A *lrnd.* idolatrous; idolator.
vesiⁱⁱ (.—) وَسِيع A *lrnd.* wide, vast; ample, abundant.
vesic (.—) وَثِيج A *lrnd.* firm and stout.
vesikᵏⁱ (.—) وَثِيق A *lrnd.* firm, strong, secure; trustworthy.
vesika (.—.) وَثِيقَة 1. document; title-deed; document proving identity. 2. ration-card. 3. *lrnd.* anything in which one places confidence. **— ile** by coupon (rationed). **—lı** licensed (prostitute).
vesile (.—.) وَسِيلَه A 1. means; cause. 2. pretext. 3. opportunity. 4. *lrnd.* rank, favor and intimacy with a sovereign. **— buldukça** on any pretext. **bir —i hasene ile** taking advantage of an excellent opportunity. **bir — ile** by some means, under some pretext.
vesilecû (.—.—) وَسِيلَه جُو P *lrnd.* who seeks a pretext; who is on the lookout for an opportunity.
vesilehâh (.—.—) وَسِيلَه خواه P *lrnd.* who looks for an opportunity.
vesîm (.—) وَسِيم A *lrnd.* pretty, handsome, comely, elegant.
vesîr (.—) وَسِير A *lrnd.* plump and soft.

vesm 1 وَسم A *lrnd.* 1. a branding (man or beast); a tattooing. 2. sign, mark, brand.
vesm 2 وَسم A *lrnd.* a breaking, bruising, pounding, treading upon.
vesme وَسمَه A *lrnd.* 1. indigo with which skin or cloth is dyed. 2. brand impressed with a hot iron. **—dâr** (..—) P branded, marked.
vesnan (.—) وَسنَان A *lrnd.* sleepy, slumbering, dozing.
vesnet وَسنَت A *lrnd.* a being sleepy; sleepiness, drowsiness.
vesselâm (..—) وَالسَّلَام A 1. So that's that! So that's an end of the matter. 2. *lrnd.* and peace be (upon you); with cordial greetings (a letter ending). **—ı âlâ men ittebealhüda** *lrnd.* and peace be upon all who follow right guidance (a kindly conclusion to a Muslim's letter to a non-Muslim).
vestiyer وَستِيَر F cloak-room; coat-peg.
vesvas (.—) وَسواس A *lrnd.* 1. Satan (as the suggester of doubt and sin). 2. evil doubt or suggestion. 3. any faint sound made in moving (by a hunter).
vesvese وَسوَسَه A 1. secret fear, anxiety. 2. preoccupation; scruple. **— et=** to be inwardly unhappy or anxious, to have misgivings.
vesveseendaz (.…—) وَسوَسَه اَنداز P *lrnd.* who suggests fear, doubts or sin.
vesveseli وَسوَسَه لى having anxiety or scruple.
-veş وَش P *lrnd.* resembling, like, as in **mehveş**.
veşakᵏⁱ وَشَق P *lrnd.*, same as **vaşak**.
veşelan (..—) وَشَلَان A *lrnd.*, same as **veşl**.
veşice (.—.) وَشِيجَه A *lrnd.* matted rootlets of a plant.
veşime (.—.) وَشِيمَه A *lrnd.* enmity, grudge.
veşl وَشل A *lrnd.* a flowing, trickling or dripping.
veşm وَشم A *lrnd.* 1. a tattooing. 2. tattooed figure on the skin.
veşy وَشى A *lrnd.* 1. a painting, printing, staining, dying (cloth). 2. cloth of various colors; color or painting of a garment. 3. lying, coloring a story with falsehood; a bearing mischievous tales. 4. graining on a sword-blade. 5. specks of gold in ore.
vetair (.—.) وَتَائِر A *lrnd.*, pl. of **vetire**.
veted وَتَد A 1. *anat.* the tragus (of the ear); sphenoid bone. 2. *Arabic pros.* prosodic unit consisting of three consonants. 3. *astr.* each one of the four cardinal points or signs of the ecliptic at any given moment. 4. *myst.* any one of the four chief saints in the earthly hierarchy who rule the east, west, north or south quarters of the earth (as the representative of the inferior of the two imams who act

veter

under the Qutb or Ghauth, the supreme head of the order). 5. *lrnd.* stake; peg; tent-peg. **—i sâlikân** a chief saint of the mystics. **—ân** (..—) A tragi of the two ears. **—î** (..—) A sphenoid.

veter وتر 1. *anat.* tendon, sinew. 2. *geom.* chord of an arc; hypotenuse of a right-angled triangle. 3. *lrnd.* bowstring; string of a musical instrument. **—i kaime** *geom.* hypotenuse. **—i kavs** *geom.* chord of an arc. **—i zaviye** *geom.* side opposite an angle; the subtending side.

vetere وترة A *lrnd.* 1. septum of the nose; edge of the nostril. 2. space between the tip of the nose and the mustache. 3. middle groove in an archery bow. 4. the choicest part of anything.

vetih (.—) وتيح A *lrnd.* small in quantity and low-priced; trifling, insignificant.

vetin وتين A *lrnd.* aorta.

vetire (.—.) وتيرة A 1. *sc.* process, phenomenon. 2. *lrnd.* path, track, way. 3. *lrnd.* mode, manner, method. 4. *lrnd.* septum.

veya ويا or. **— aksine** or vice versa.

veyahut (.—.) وياخود P or.

veyh ويح A *lrnd.* Too bad! I'm sorry!

veyl ويل A *lrnd.* Too bad!

veys ويس A *lrnd.* poverty; want; need.

Veyselkarani (...—) ويس القرني A name of a renowned follower of the Prophet Muhammad, used in the phrase **Yemen ellerinde Veyselkarani** completely lost, utterly at a loss.

vezᶻⁱ وزع A *lrnd.* a restraining, checking, prohibiting; restrained.

vezaa وزعة A *lrnd.* princes, rulers, governors; those who restrain.

vezaat (.—.) وضاعت A *lrnd.*, same as *vazaat*.

vezaif (.—.) وظائف A *lrnd.*, same as *vazaif*.

vezân (.—) وزان P *lrnd.* blowing (wind). **— ol=** to blow (wind).

vezanet (.—.) وزانت A *lrnd.* prudence, sagacity, sobriety of judgment.

vezaret (.—.) وزارت A *hist.* quality, office, function of a vizier; vizierate. **—i uzma** *lrnd.* the office of the Grand Vizier.

veziden (.—.) وزيدن P *lrnd.* 1. a blowing (the wind). 2. a growing (herbage or hair).

vezidengâh (.—.—) وزيدنگاه P *lrnd.* windy place.

vezime (.—.) وزيمة A *lrnd.* gift; gift made to the Kaaba of Mecca.

vezinᶻⁿⁱ **1** وزن [vezn] 1. *poet.* meter. 2. *lrnd.* a weighing; weight. 3. *lrnd.* an estimating.

vezîn 2 (.—) وزين A *lrnd.* weighty, solid, sound (judgment).

vezir (.—) وزير A 1. *hist.* vizier; minister. 2. *chess* queen. **—i âzam** the Grand Vizier. **— inciri** name of a large green fig. **— kapısı** the Grand Vizier's office. **— karakulağı** title of the confidential messenger of the Grand Vizier.

vezirâne (.——.) وزيرانه P pertaining to, suitable to a vizier; grand.

vezirî (.——) وزيرى A vizierial, special to a vizier. **— kıt'a** tall folio (book size).

vezirlikᵍⁱ وزيرلك office and duties of a vizier.

vezme وزمه P *lrnd.* winter.

vezmebâd (..—) وزمه باد P *lrnd.* which begins to blow about the end of winter.

vezn وزن A *lrnd.*, same as *vezin 1*.

vezndâr (.—) وزندار P *lrnd.* of full weight; of just weight.

vezne وزنه A 1. cashier's office, cashier's window; pay-office, treasury. 2. *lrnd.* balance, gauge. 3. *lrnd.* powder flask; priming pan of a gun. **— boşaltan** a species of wild duck very hard to kill. **—ci** maker or seller of balances or scales.

veznedâr (..—) وزنه دار P treasurer; cashier. **—lık** 1. functions of a cashier. 2. treasury.

vezniyet وزنيت A *lrnd.* momentum.

vezzan (.—) وزان A *lrnd.* one who weighs, weigher.

vıcıkᵍⁱ وجيك viscid; gooey; sticky; dirty. **— vıcık** expresses the squelching noise of walking through thick mud; sticky and dirty. **— vıcık et=** same as **vıcıkla=**.

vıcıkla=ʳ وجيقلامق /ı/ to make sticky, etc.

vıkᵏⁱ وق squeak, expressing the noise made by someone in distress. **— deme=** not to make a single squeak.

vıkla=ʳ وقلامق 1. to moan under a burden. 2. to squeak.

vıkr وقر A *lrnd.* load, heavy burden.

vınla=ʳ وينلامق to buzz; to hum.

vır ور whir, whiz. **— vır** imitates continuous and exasperating talk. **— vır başının etini ye=** /ın/ to keep on nagging at someone. **— vır et=** to whir and buzz about; to nag.

vırılda=ʳ, **vırıldan=**ʳ ويريلدامق ويريلدانمق 1. to talk incessantly; to keep complaining querulously. 2. to make a loud or repeated whirring.

vırıltı ويريلدى 1. a whirring; buzzing noise. 2. tiresome talk; nagging; quarrelsomeness.

vırla=ʳ ويرلامق 1. to whir or buzz; to murmur. 2. to nag.

vız ويز buzz; whizzing sound. **— gel=** *colloq.* to be a matter of indifference. **— gelir tırıs gider** *colloq.* I don't care at all. **— savuş=** to slip away like an arrow.

vızılda=ʳ ويزيلدامق 1. to buzz, hum. 2. keep on complaining. **—n=** same as **vızılda=**.

vızıltı ويزيلدى 1. buzzing or whirring noise. 2. a querulous complaining.

vızır وزير وزر ويزر a humming or buzzing sound. — **vızır** with a whiz or buzz, *imitating the whirring of a machine and used to describe something that can easily and quickly be done.*
vızırda=ᵣ ويزردامس to make a great whizzing. **—t=** *caus.*
vızırtı ويزيرتى whizzing noise.
vızla=ᵣ ويزلامس وزلامس to whizz. **—t=** /ı/ *caus.*
via (.—) وعاء A 1. *anat.* blood vessel. 2. *lrnd.* receptacle of any kind.
vicah (.—) وجاه A *lrnd.* a being face to face; personal presence.
vicahen (.—´.) وجاهاً A *lrnd.* face to face; in the presence of; not by default.
vicahî (.——) وجاهى A *lrnd.* done in the presence of someone.
vical (.—) وجال A *lrnd.*, *pl. of* **vecil**.
vicar (.—) وجار A *lrnd.* 1. den (of a hyena etc.). 2. cavern hollowed out by water.
vicd وجد A *lrnd.* a being wealthy, rich.
vicdan (.—) وجدان A 1. conscience. 2. *lrnd.* rapture, ecstasy. 3. *lrnd.* intense love, grief or anger. — **azabı** pangs of conscience. — **hürriyeti** religious freedom.
vicdanen (.—´.) وجداناً A 1. in accordance with one's conscience. 2. with rapture and ecstasy.
vicdanî (.——) وجدانى A 1. pertaining to conscience. 2. *lrnd.* pertaining to ecstasy. **—yat** (.—.—) A *lrnd.* states, acts or visions belonging to a condition of intense excitement.
vicdanlı وجدانلى conscientious, honest.
vicdansız وجدانسز without a conscience; unscrupulous. **—lık** lack of conscience; unscrupulousness.
vidᵈᵈⁱ ودّ A *lrnd.* love, friendship, benevolence.
vida (.´.) ويده It screw.
vidac (.—) وداج A *anat.* jugular vein. **—i gair** internal jugular. **—i zâhir** external jugular. **—î** (.——) A pertaining to the jugular vein.
vidala=ᵣ 1 ويدالامس to screw; to screw down.
vidalâ 2 (.´.) ويدالا *var. of* **videle**.
vidalı ويدالى ويدالو screwed. — **civata** screw bolt.
videle (.´.) ويده له ودله It box-calf; calfskin.
vifakᵏⁱ (.—) وفاق A *lrnd.* a mutually agreeing; concord, agreement.
viğlâ, **viğle** ويغلر Gk observation post of a fishing station. **—cı** lookout at a fishing station.
vihad (.—) وهاد A *lrnd.*, *pl. of* **vehde**.
viham (.—) وهام A *lrnd.* a craving (as of a pregnant woman).

vije (—.) ويژه P *lrnd.* 1. pure, unadulterated. 2. sincere, unmixed. 3. holy.
vijegân (—.—) ويژگان P *lrnd.* intimate friends.
vikaᵃⁱ (.—) وقاع A *lrnd.* 1. a rushing upon (an enemy); fighting. 2. copulation, coition.
vikâf (.—) وكاف A *lrnd.* cushion used instead of a saddle; pack-saddle.
vikaye (.—.) وقايه A *lrnd.* 1. a protecting, guarding; protection. 2. anything that serves to protect; prophylaxis. — **et=** /dan/ to protect (from), to ward (off).
vikayet (.—.) وقايت A *lrnd.*, *same as* **vikaye**.
vikont ويقونت F viscount.
vikontes ويقونتس F viscountess.
vilâ (.—) ولاء A *lrnd.* 1. a mutually loving; mutual love and affection; friendship. 2. a continuing, following on without intermission; succession.
vilâd (.—) ولاد A *lrnd.* a bearing children; a being begotten or born; generation; birth.
vilâdet (.—.) ولادت A *lrnd.*, *same as* **velâdet**.
vilâdi (.——) ولادى A *lrnd.* inborn, congenital.
vilâf (.—) ولاف A *lrnd.* 1. a becoming familiar, intimate; familiarity, friendship. 2. a flashing incessantly (lightning). 3. an animal's cantering; canter.
vilâyat (.——) ولايت A *lrnd.*, *pl. of* **vilâyet**.
vilâyet (.—.) ولايت A 1. province governed by a vali, vilayet. 2. one's native country; one's native place. 3. *same as* **velâyet**. 4. *lrnd.* guardianship; stewardship. 5. *lrnd.* friendship. 6. *lrnd.* spiritual nearness to God. **—li** of such and such a **vilâyet**; fellow countryman.
vildan (.—) ولدان A *lrnd.*, *pl. of* **velid**.
villâ (.´.) ويلا It villa, suburban residence.
vinç ونج E crane, winch.
vir (—) وير P *lrnd.* intellect, intelligence, mind.
vira 1 ويرا It Pull away! — **et=** to heave away; to pull away.
vira 2 (.´.) ويرا [vira 1] continuously. — **konuşuyor** talking incessantly. — **vira** incessantly, continuously.
viraj ويراژ F curve of a road, bend. — **al= *slang*** to lie. **bir —ı dön=** to go around a bend.
viran (——) ويران P 1. ruined, in ruins. 2. devastated, laid waste. — **olası hanede evlâd ü ayâl var** I have a wife and family in that cursed house, *i. e.* My hands are tied, *used as an excuse for one's inaction.*
virane (——) ويرانه P 1. a building in ruins; ruins. 2. plot of land on which a house has been destroyed by fire. **—lik** place of ruins.
viranger (——.) ويرانگر P *lrnd.* that ruins or devastates; ruinous, destructive.

virani (– – –) ویرانی P *lrnd.* ruin, desolation.
viranlıkğı ویرانلغی a being a ruin; ruin, ruins.
vird 1 ورد A *lrnd.* 1. a portion of the Quran recited daily. 2. constantly repeated saying. 3. an arrival at a watering place; a drink of water. 4. intermittent fever; day of the access of such fever. **—i zeban et=** /ı/ to repeat constantly.
vird 2 ورد P *lrnd.* disciple, pupil, follower; apprentice.
virdet=der ورد ایتمك /ı/ to repeat constantly.
virgül ویرگول F comma.
visab 1 (. —) وثاب A *lrnd.* cushion, mattress; couch; sofa, chair.
visab 2 (. —) وثاب A *lrnd.* a springing, bounding, leaping; spring, bound, leap.
visad (. —), **visade** (. —.) وساد وساده A *lrnd.* cushion, pillow.
visakkı (. —) وثاق A *lrnd.* 1. band, ligature, tie. 2. a pledging one's faith; an entering into a confederacy.
visalli (. —) وصال A meeting; lover's union.
visam 1 (. —) وسام A *lrnd.* mark with which cattle are branded.
visam 2 (. —) وسام A *lrnd., pl. of* **vesim, vesime.**
visayet (. —.) وصایت A *lrnd., same as* **vesayet.**
viski ویسکی E whisky.
visvas (. —) وسواس A *lrnd., same as* **vesvas.**
vişah (. —) وشاح A *lrnd.* ornamented or jeweled baldric.
vişakkı (. —) وشاق P *lrnd.* handsome slave youth. **—an** (. — —) P *pl.* **—an-ı çemen** young plants and flowers; rose bushes.
vişam (. —) وشام A *lrnd., pl. of* **veşm.**
vişayat (. — —) وشایات A *lrnd., pl. of* **vişayet.**
vişayet (. —.) وشایت A *lrnd.* 1. a playing the spy, whispering, informing against, accusing. 2. mischievous spying or talebearing; calumny, slander.
vişnab (. —) وشناب [based on **vişne+ab**] 1. *lrnd.* drink made from syrup of the morello (sour) cherry. 2. a variety of large sour cherry.
vişne (. .) وشنه Sl sour cherry. **— çürüğü** purplish brown color.
vitamin ویتامین F *physiol.* vitamin. **—li** with vitamins added. **—sizlik hastalığı** *path.* avitaminosis.
vites ویتس F *auto.* gear; gears. **—le** in gear. **— değiştir=** to shift gears. **— kolu** gearshift. **— kutusu** gear box.
vitirtri وتر *var. of* **vitr.**
vitr وتر A *lrnd.* 1. odd, single or unique thing. 2. *service of worship performed between night and morning.* 3. *name of the eve of the Muslim Festival of Sacrifice.* 4. blood money, claim for bloodshed; *jus talionis,* retaliation of like for like in a case of bloodshed.

vitren (. .) وترا A *lrnd.* singly. **— vitren.** singly, one by one.
vitrin ویترین F shopwindow. **— yap=** to decorate the shopwindow, to arrange things attractively.
viya (. .) ویا It *naut., order to steer straight after altering course.* Steady!
viyakkı ویاق squawk. **— viyak** squawking. **—la=** to squawk.
Viyana ویانا *geog.* Vienna.
viyola (. . .) ویوله It *mus.* viola.
viyolon ویولون F violin.
viyolonsel ویولونسل F violoncello.
viza, vize ویزه F visa (of a passport). **—lı,** **—li** with a visa.
vizita, vizite (. . .) ویزیته It 1. medical visit; visit. 2. doctor's fee.
vizon ویزون F mink, mink fur.
vizr وزر A *lrnd.* 1. a carrying, bearing a burden; load; charge. 2. a sinning; sin.
vodvil (. .) وودویل F vaudeville.
volan ولان F 1. flywheel. 2. *auto.* steering wheel.
voli ولی Gk 1. space covered by a cast of a circular fishing net. 2. *slang* successful stroke of business. **— çevir=** to cast a net. **— vur=** *slang* to make a successful speculation.
volkan ولقان F volcano.
volta (. .) ولته It 1. *naut.* a round turn (knot); tack. 2. *colloq.* a turn in walking up and down. **—sını al=** *slang* to run away; to beat it. **— et=** 1. to tack about; to beat or ply to windward, to cruise about. 2. *slang* to walk up and down. 3. *slang* to beat about the bush. **— vur=** *same as* **volta et=.**
voltalı ولتالی It *naut.* upper foot-hook timbers in the hull of a ship.
vonoz ونوس Gk young mackerel or bonito.
votka (. .) وتقه Russ vodka.
voynukku وینوك Sl *Ott. hist.* non-Muslim serving as horse groom in the Ottoman army.
voyvo (. .) وویو *slang, exclamation used in making fun of somebody.*
voyvoda (. . .) ویوده Sl vaivode, a kind of mayor or governor.
v. s. *abbrev. for* **ve saire.**
vuhuş (. —) وحوش A *lrnd., pl. of* **vahş.**
vukiye وقیه A *lrnd., same as* **okka.**
vukuuu وقوع A 1. event; occurrence. 2. *lrnd.* a falling from a height; fall. **— bul=,** **—a gel=** to occur, to happen; to take place. **—i hal** *lrnd.* the facts. **—u halinde** in case of occurrence, if ... happens. **—u vardır** There is a precedent. This has happened before.
vukuat (. — —) وقوعات A 1. events, incidents. 2. cases (of trouble, crime, etc.).

vukud (.—) وقود A *lrnd.* a being kindled; ignition; combustion.

vukuf (.—) وقوف A 1. an acquiring or possessing knowledge of a thing; knowledge; information. 2. *lrnd.* a stopping and coming to a standstill; stop, halt. — **kesbet=** /a/ to get information about, to inquire into. —ı **tammı ol=** to have a thorough knowledge of. —**cu** *prov.* curious, inquisitive.

vukufdar (.——)ِ وقوفدار P informed of, knowing.

vukufiyet (.—..) وقوفيت A quality of being aware of a subject; knowledge.

vukuflu وقوفلى well-informed; knowledgeable, well-up (in a matter).

vukufsuz وقوفسز without knowledge; ignorant; badly informed. —**luk** lack of information; ignorance.

vuladika ولاديقه Sl metropolitan, archbishop.

vulikᵍⁱ ولیک Gk a swift kind of pirate boat, polacca.

vur=ᵘʳ وورمق 1. /a/ to strike, to hit; to knock. 2. /ı, a/ to hit something against something; to put one thing on another. 3. /ı/ to hit and kill, to shoot dead. 4. /ı, a/ to apply (paint). 5. /ı/ to chafe, gall, blister. 6. /ı/ to steal (pickpocket); to swindle. 7. /a/ to take (a road or direction). 8. to beat down on (sun). 9. /a/ to penetrate into (wind, light, etc.). 10. /a/ to pretend to be, to make believe. 11. *chauffeurs' slang* to drink. — **abalıya** Attack the weak. Put the blame on someone who can't defend himself. — **dedikse öldür demedik ya** I told you to hit him, not to kill him. I didn't ask you to go to the extreme. — **deyince öldür=** to exceed one's orders or advice. — **patlasın çal oynasın!** squandering money on pleasure; going on a spree. — **tut** 1. tumult, confusion. 2. bargaining hard.

vurdumduymaz وورديم دويماز (*lit.* I hit him but he didn't feel it) insensitive; thick-skinned; blockhead.

vurdur=ᵘʳ وورديرمك /ı, a/ *caus. of* **vur=**.

vurgu وورغى *ling.* accent, stress. —**lu** stressed.

vurgun وورغون 1. struck; hit. 2. /a/ in love with; enamored. 3. booty; good stroke of business; profiteering. — **vur=** to make a successful speculation, to make a good deal.

vurguncu وورغونجى speculator, profiteer. —**luk** profiteering.

vurgunlukᵍᵘ وورغونلغى condition of one who has been struck, hurt or afflicted; affliction.

vurul=ᵘʳ وورولمق 1. *pass. of* **vur=**. 2. /a/ to fall in love (with).

vurun=ᵘʳ وورونمق 1. to beat oneself. 2. to mourn deeply.

vuruş 1 وورش 1. *verbal n. of* **vur=** 2. blow; fight.

vuruş=ᵘʳ **2** وورشمق to fight with one another, to strike each other. —**tur=** 1. /ı/ *caus.* 2. *slang* to drink together.

vuslat وصلت A 1. union (with one's beloved); conjugal union. 2. *lrnd.* a meeting; conjunction; communion of friends.

vusta وسطى A *lrnd.* middle, central. —î (..—) A pertaining to the middle.

vustanî (.——) وسطانى A *lrnd.* middle, central.

vusulˡü (.—) وصول A *lrnd.* an arriving; arrival; junction; union. —**ünde** on his arrival. — **bul=** /a/ to arrive.

vusulpezir (.—.—) وصول پذير P *lrnd.* that arrives, arrived.

vusum (.—) وصوم A *lrnd., pl. of* **vasm**.

vuzuᵘᵘ **1** (.—) وضوع A *lrnd.* a humbling oneself; humility.

vuzu 2 (.—) وضوء A *lrnd.* a performing a canonical partial ablution; religious ablution. — **et=** to perform the canonical ablution.

vuzugâh (.——) وضوگاه P *lrnd.* 1. place for ablution. 2. toilet.

vuzuh (.—) وضوح A a being clear, evident, manifest; clearness; clarity (of speech, etc.). —**suzluk** lack of clarity, obscurity.

vüceha (..—) وجها A *lrnd., pl. of* **vecih 3**.

vücubᵇᵘ (.—) وجوب A *lrnd.* 1. a being obligatory, necessary; obligation, duty; necessity. 2. a being incumbent (as a religious duty). 3. a setting (the sun). 4. a dying; death.

vücubî (.——) وجوبى A *lrnd.* 1. pertaining to imperative obligation. 2. *gram.* necessitative.

vücudᵈü **1** (.—) وجود A *lrnd.* 1. *same as* **vücut**. 2. a finding, discovering, procuring. —**i aynî** real existence.

vücudᵈü **2** (.—) وجود A *lrnd., pl. of* **vecd, vicd**.

vücudî (.——) وجودى A *lrnd.* pertaining to existence. —**ye** (.—..) A *phil.* pantheism.

vücudpezir (.—.—) وجودپذير P *lrnd.* made, accomplished.

vücuh (.—) وجوه A *lrnd.* 1. *pl. of* **vech**. 2. (*no singular*) notables; *colloq.* chief man. —**i memleket** the chief men of the place.

vücum (.—) وجوم A *lrnd.* 1. a being afflicted, vexed, silent with grief or anger. 2. a being disgusted.

vücutᵈü وجود [vücud 1] 1. the human body. 2. being, existence. — **bul=** to come into existence, to arise. —**tan düş=** to fail in health. —**a gel=** *same as* **vücut bul=**. —**a getir=** /ı/ to bring into being, to produce; to create. — **sağlığı** bodily health. — **ver=** /a/ 1. to give existence to a thing, to create or produce it. 2. to give importance to a trifling thing. — **yor=** to wear oneself out, to become worn out. —çe bodily, physically. —lü large in body, heavily built. —süz 1. bodiless; non-existent. 2. small, weak, tiny.

vücuz (. —) وجيز A *lrnd.* a being ready, short, brief, laconic (in speech); readiness, promptness.

vüd[dü] وُدّ A *lrnd.*, same as vid.

vüdea (. . —) وُدَعا A *lrnd.*, pl. of vedi 1.

vüfud 1 (. —) وُفود A *lrnd.* a coming, arriving (as an ambassador to a king); arrival.

vüfud 2 (. —) وُفود A *lrnd.*, pl. of vafid, vefd.

vüfur (. —) وُفور A *lrnd.* a being full, complete, abundant; multitude, plenty, abundance.

vühufet (. —.) وُحوفت A *lrnd.* a being long and luxuriant (herbage or black hair).

vühul[lü] (. —) وُحول A *lrnd.*, pl. of vahl.

vücûlide (. — —.) وُجوليده P *lrnd.* 1. that has disturbed. 2. disturbed, confused.

vükelâ (. . —) وُكلا A *Ott. hist.*, pl. of vekil. —i devlet cabinet ministers, the Government. — heyeti council of Ministers, Cabinet. —lık post of minister.

vükûb (. —) وُكوب A *lrnd.* 1. a being assiduous, attentive (to business). 2. gradual progress.

vülât (. —) وُلات A *lrnd.*, pl. of vali 1.

vülû[ûu] (. —) وُلوع A *lrnd.* a desiring eagerly, being given to, intent on; desire, avidity, greed.

vülûb (. —) وُلوب A *lrnd.* 1. an arriving at, reaching; arrival. 2. an entering; entrance. 3. a making haste; haste.

vülûc (. —) وُلوج A *lrnd.* a going in, entering, penetrating; entrance, penetration. — ü huruc entrance and exit.

vülûdiyet (. —. .) وُلوديت A *lrnd.* 1. infancy, tenderness of age. 2. inhumanity, cruelty.

vülûğ (. —) وُلوغ A *lrnd.* lapping (dog).

vüreyd وُريد A *anat.* small jugular vein.

vüreyk[kı] وُريق A *lrnd.* small leaf.

vüreyka وُريقة A *lrnd.* a single leaf. —t (. . —) A *pl.*

vürud[dü] (. —) وُرود A *lrnd.* an arriving; arrival. —ünde on his arrival; on the arrival (of papers, post, etc.). — et= to arrive.

vürûk[kü] (. —) وُروك A *lrnd.* 1. a lying on the side. 2. a turning the hip when about to dismount. 3. an alighting or sojourning.

vüs وُسع A *lrnd.* 1. power, ability. 2. competence of means, wealth.

vüs'at[tı] وُسعت A *lrnd.* 1. a being wide, extensive, ample; spaciousness, ampleness, largeness; extent. 2. abundance; capacity; means. 3. convenience, opportunity, leisure. —ine göre as far as one's means or capacity allows. —i hâl easy circumstances. —li spacious; extensive.

vüsema (. . —) وُسماء A *lrnd.*, pl. of vesîm.

vüska وُثقى A *lrnd.* firmer, firmest, very firm.

vüsub (. —) وُثوب A *lrnd.* a leaping, jumping, bounding.

vüsûk[kü] (. —) وُثوق A *lrnd.* 1. a having a firm trust and confidence; trust, confidence. 2. a being trustworthy; trustworthiness; authenticity, confirmation. 3. strength, firmness, steadfastness. — bul= to be confirmed.

vüşum (. —) وُشوم A *lrnd.*, pl. of veşm.

vüzera (. . —) وُزراء A *lrnd.*, pl. of vezir.

vüzub (. —) وُزوب A *lrnd.* a flowing; flow.

Y

y, Y 1 *the twenty-eighth letter of the Turkish alphabet.*

-y-, =y= 2 *consonant joining a suffix beginning with a vowel to a stem ending with a vowel.*

ya 1 ىَا ی *name of the letter* ی (the thirty-first letter of the Ottoman and Persian alphabets and twenty-eighth of the Arabic; in chronograms and mathematical formulas it has the numerical value of 10).

ya 2 (—) یَا 1. Yes, indeed. 2. then so. 3. Can it be? Don't forget. 4. After all. — **ben ne yapayım** Well then, what shall I do? — **duyarsa** Yes, but what if he hears (about it)? — **gitmezse** And if he doesn't go, what then? — **öyle mi?** Oh, is that so?

ya 3 (—) یَا A Oh. O. — **Allah!** *same as* **yallah.** — **hey!** O and alas! — **heyi bas=** *colloq.* to raise a shout together while singing in a group. — **hey de=** *colloq.* to say "Let's get going", *when starting on a hard job.* — **Mevlâ** Alas! O Lord! — **Mevlâsını al=** to draw forth from one the ejaculation **ya Mevlâ** in gratitude for assistance; to act as one pleases regardless of what others will think or say. — **Rabbi!** O Lord! Oh my God! — **Sabûr!** O patient (God)! Heaven grant me patience! — **Sabûr çek=** to repeat the word **ya Sabûr** in order to overcome anger or impatience.

ya 4 یَا P either; or. — **ben ya sen** either I or you. The clash of viewpoints cannot be bridged. — **bu deveyi gütmeli ya bu diyardan gitmeli** (*lit.*, One either has to drive this camel or leave this country.) If you wish to get on well, you have to adjust yourself to your surroundings. — **devlet başa ya kuzgun leşe** Either sovereignty (good fortune) to his head or the ravens to his corpse, *said to indicate* struggle for victory and death. — **herrü ya merrü** *colloq.* Sink or swim. Let's go ahead with it; it may succeed, it may fail. — **huyundan ya suyundan** Blood will tell; traces of one's family heritage will show up in some way or another. — **taht ya tahta** the throne or a bier.

yaafir (. — —) یَعَافِیر A *lrnd., pl. of* **ya'fur.**
yaalil (. — —) یَعَالِیل A *lrnd., pl. of* **ya'lûl.**
ya'amir (. — —) یَعَامِیر A *lrnd., pl. of* **ya'mur.**
yaasib (. — —) یَعَاسِیب A *lrnd., pl. of* **ya'sûb.**

-yab (—) یَاب P *lrnd.* 1. that finds, *as in* **şerefyab.** 2. which, of which (so and so) is found, *as in* **kâmyab.**

yaba یَبَا یَابَا wooden fork (with three to five prongs for winnowing, carrying hay, etc.).

yabala=ʳ یَابَالَمَق /ı/ to winnow or carry with a wooden fork. —**n=** *pass.* —**t=** /ı, a/ *caus.*

yaban یَبَان یَابَان [P — —] 1. desert, wilderness. 2. wild; savage. 3. *prov.* stranger; the world of strangers (beyond the family or social circle). (*cf.* **biyaban**). — **adamı** savage. —**ın adamı** inconsiderate person. — **arısı** bumblebee, *zool., Bombus.* — **asması** wild vine, white bryony, *bot., Bryonia dioica or alba.* —**a at=** /ı/ to cast behind one's back, to pay no attention to. — **defnesi** laurustinus, wild bay tree, *bot., Viburnum tinus.* — **domuzu** wild boar, *zool., Sus scrofa.* — **enginarı** cardoon, prickly artichoke, *bot., Cynara cardunculus.* — **eriği** wild plum, sloe. — **eşeği** zebra, wild ass, *zool., Asinus onager.* — **fesleğeni** pennyroyal, *bot., Mentha Pulegium.* —**a git=** 1. to go to a stranger. 2. to go for nothing. — **gülü** dog-rose, *bot., Rosa canina.* — **havucu** parsnip, *bot., Pastinaca sativa; or Pastinaca sekakul.* — **inciri** wild fig, caprifig bot., *Ficus carica*. — **keçisi** wild goat, ibex, zool., *Capra hircus*. — **kedisi** wild cat. zool., *Felis sylvestris*. — **kendenesi** black. fetid horehound, bot., *Ballota nigra*. — **keteni** water hemp, hemp weed, bot., *Eupatorium cannabinum*. —**ın köpeği** a poor man, an outcast. — **marulu** wild lettuce, bot., *Lactuca virosa*. — **maydanozu** cow parsley, wild parsley, bot., *Anthriscus sylvestris*. — **mersini** butcher's broom, bot., *Ruscus aculeatus*. — **mürveri** dwarf elder, danewort, bot., *Sambucus ebulus*. — **pancarı** wild beet, bot., *Oenothera fruticosa*. — **pelini** common mugwort, bot., *Artemisia campestris*. — **pırasası** white horehound, bot., *Marrubium vulgare*. — **saparnası** wild sarsaparilla, bot., *Smilax aspera*. — **sıçanı** lemming, zool., *Lemmus lemmus*. — **sineği** gadfly, zool., *Tabanus bovinus*. —**a söyle=** archaic to talk nonsense. — **sümbülü** harebell, wood hyacinth, bot., *Scilla nonscripta*. — **tavuğu** jungle fowl, zool., *Gallus sonneratii*. — **tavusu** peacock pheasant, zool., *Polyplectron napoleonis;* argus pheasant, zool., *Argus giganteus*. — **teresi** cardamine, cressonnette, bot., *Cardamine pratensis*. — **turpu** horseradish, bot., *Armoracia lapathifolia*. — **yasemini** woody nightshade, bittersweet, bot., *Solanum dulcamara*. — **yulafı** haver, wild oat, bot., *Avena fatua*.

yabancı يابانجى يا بنجى stranger; foreigner; foreign. — **cisimler** *path.* foreign bodies. —**sı ol=** /ın/ not to be familiar (with); to be a stranger. —**lık** a being a stranger or foreigner.

yabani (. — —) يا باني P 1. belonging to the desert or wilds; untamed, wild. 2. boorish, unmannerly. — **adaçayı** wood sage, wild sage, bot., *Salvia sylvestris*. — **akdiken** common buckthorn, bot., *Rhamnus*. — **bitotu** lousewort, red rattle, bot., *Pedicularis sylvatica*. — **dereotu** wild dill, bot., *Anethum sylvestris*. — **gül** same as **yabangülü**. — **hardal** wild mustard, charlock, bot., *Brassica kaber*. — **kekik** wild thyme, creeping thyme, bot., *Thymus serpyllum*. — **kiraz** wild cherry, bot., *Cerasus avium*. — **kumru** rock-dove, zool., *Columba livia*. — **lâhana** sea cabbage, sea kale, bot., *Crambe maritima;* cabbage flowered moricandia, bot., *Moricandia arvensis*. — **menekşe** dog-violet, bot., *Viola canina*. — **mercanköşk** sweet marjoram, knotted marjoram, bot., *Origanum marjorana*. — **nar çiçeği** balaustina flowers. — **yasemin** same as **yaban yasemini**. — **yonca** wild clover, zigzag trefoil, bot., *Trifolium medium;* common saintfoin, bot., *Onobrychis sativa*.

yabanilikᵏⁱ يابانيلك wildness, boorishness.
yabanlıkᵏⁱ يابانلق 1. visiting clothes; one's best clothes. 2. wild place. 3. wildness.

yabantırakᵏⁱ يا بنتراق dill, anethum, bot., *Anethum graveolens*.
yâbende (—..) يا بنده P *lrnd.* one who finds or attains, finder, discoverer.
yabis (—.) يابس A *lrnd.* dry; naturally dry.
yâbisât (—.—) يابسات A *lrnd.* dry things.
yâbismizac (—..—) يابس مزاج P *lrnd.* of a dry temperament; dull.
yacan=ⁱʳ ياجامق *prov.* 1. to be weary. 2. /dan/ to shy away (from); to hesitate. 3. *archaic* /ı/ to withhold. —**dır=** /ı/ *caus.*
yâd 1 (—) ياد P *lrnd.* remembrance, recollecting; mention. —**a getir=** to call to mind. —**ı şebâbet** remembrances of youth.
yad 2 ياد only in — **elde** in a foreign land; away from home. — **eller** strange lands.
yadbud (—— —) يادبود P *lrnd.* remembrance, commemoration; souvenir.
yaddar (—— —) يادار P *lrnd.* one who remembers or recollects; mindful, remembering.
yaddaşt (—— —) ياداشت P *lrnd.* 1. thing borne in mind; memorandum, note. 2. recollection.
yâde (—.) ياده P *lrnd.* 1. memory, remembrance. 2. reminder, fee given as a reminder.
yâdes (—.) يادس [Persian *yâd ast*] same as **lâdes**.
yâdet=ᵈᵉʳ (—..) يادايتمك /ı/ to remember, recollect; to remember and talk about; to mention.
yadırga=ⁱʳ يادرغامق /ı/ 1. to regard as a stranger; to find something strange or odd. 2. to cry at a stranger (child). —**n=** *pass.*
yâdigâr (—.—) يادگار P 1. keepsake; souvenir. 2. scoundrel, trickster; notorious.
Yafa يافه *geog.* Jaffa. — **portakalı** navel orange.
yâfe (—.) يافه P *lrnd.*, same as **yave 1**.
yâfedarî (—.— —) يافه داري P *lrnd.* idle talk.
yâfederay (—..—) يافه دراي P *lrnd.* idle talker, brag.
Yafet (—.), **Yafis** (—.) يافت يافث A *Bib.* Japhet.
yafta (.'.) يافته [**yafte 1**] 1. label. 2. placard (especially one hung round the neck of a condemned person and describing his crime).
yafte 1 (—.) يافته P *lrnd.* 1. who has found or discovered. 2. that has reached, attained, achieved. 3. found, discovered.
-yafte 2 (—.) يافته P *lrnd.* found, that may be found, *e. g*, **şerefyâfte**.
ya'fur (.—) يعفر A *lrnd.* 1. young deer, fawn. 2. dun-colored deer. 3. a division or hour of the night. 4. *w. cap.*, name of a donkey on which the Prophet Muhammad often rode.
yağ 1 يا غ 1. oil; fat. 2. butter. 3. grease; ointment. — **asitleri** *chem.* fatty acids. — **bağla=** to put on fat. — **bal** excellent; desirable. —**ıyla balıyla** (*lit.*, with its butter

and its honey) with all its goodly accompaniments; having all that is desirable. **— ve baldan kelimât et=** to talk in a sweet and persuasive manner. **— bal olsun** I hope you'll enjoy it (food). **— balığı** catfish, *zool.*, *Silurus*. **— basınç göstergesi** *neol.*, *auto.* oil pressure indicator. **— başı** the finest and clearest oil which rises to the top. **— bezi** *anat.* sebaceous gland. **— bula=** /a/ to spread butter or oil (on). **— çek=** to toady. **—ı eri=** 1. to melt (fat of a thing). 2. to lose strength (an organ of the body). **— gibi git=**, **— gibi kay=** to move smoothly (car, etc.). **— karteri** *auto.* crankcase. **—dan kıl çeker gibi** with the greatest of ease. **— ölçü çubuğu** *auto.* oil gauge rod. **— pompası** *auto.* oil pump. **— sür=** /a/ 1. to spread butter (on bread etc.). 2. to rub oil upon, to anoint. **— süzgeci** *auto.* oil filter. **— tomarı** swab for greasing the bore of a gun. **— tulumu** *humorous* very fat (person). **— yak=** 1. to burn oil. 2. to scald butter before adding it to cooked food. **— yedir=** to work oil into the pores of a substance; to oil. **— yuvarı** *biol.* greasy globule.

yağ=ʳ 2 يَغْمُر يَا غَمُر to rain; to be poured out in abundance.

yağan=ʳ يَغْمُر يَا prov. 1. to brag about some evil design. 2. to have malice aforethought; to make a criminal attempt.

yağcı يَا غَمَجِي 1. dealer in oils, butter or the like. 2. one whose occupation is to lubricate machines, lubricator. 3. *slang* unctuous person. 4. *prov.* circumcisor.

yağcılıkᵗⁱ يَا غَمَجِيلِك 1. trade of a dealer in fats or oils. 2. toadying. **— et=** *slang* to fawn, to toady.

yağdan (.—), **yağdanlık**ᵗⁱ يَا غَدانلك oil-can.

yağdır=ʳ يَا غَدِيرِسَ /ı/ *caus. of* **yağ=** 2. **—ıl=** *pass.* **—t=** /ı/ *caus. of* **yağdır=**.

yağfiru (.ʹ..) يَغْفِر A *lrnd.* May He (God) blot out the sins (of). May He pardon.

yağfirullahü (.ʹ..—.) يَغْفِرُ اللهُ A *lrnd.* May God pardon.

yağhane (.—.) يَا غَخانَ P oil mill; butter factory; creamery.

yağı يَا غَمِي prov. 1. enemy; alien. 2. strange; stranger. **— ve bağı** *lrnd.* in active rebellion against a state or sovereign.

yağılaş=ʳ يَا غَيلاش /la/ to be at swords; to fight.

yağımcur يَا غَمَجُر archaic a kind of hot drink prepared with grape molasses and sesame meal.

yağımsı يَا غَمَسِي oily; greasy.

yağın=ʳ يَا غَمِن prov. 1. *same as* **yağan=**. 2. to occupy oneself seriously with a thing; to take it seriously; to be very angry.

yağır يَغْمِر يَغْمِر يَا غَمِر 1. withers of a horse; gall or sore on the withers or back of a beast; saddle-gall. 2. galled in the withers or back. **— ol=** to be galled in the withers or back.

yağış يَا غَمِش يَا غَمِش 1. *verbal n. of* **yağ=** 2. 2. precipitation. **—lı** rainy, showery.

yağız يَا غَمِز يَا غَمِز يَا غَمِز 1. black (horse). 2. swarthy, very dark (man). **— doru** brown (horse) with black mane and tail.

yağla=ʳ يَا غَلَسَ /ı/ 1. to oil; to butter. 2. to grease, to lubricate. 3. *slang* to flatter. 4. *slang* to grease the palm of, to bribe; to cause to make money. **—yıp balla=** /ı/ 1. to butter and sweeten with honey. 2. to paint in glowing colors; to praise. **—n=** *pass. of* **yağla=**. **—t=** /ı/ *caus. of* **yağla=**.

yağlavi (.——) يَغْلَوِي P *lrnd.* frying pan with a long handle.

yağlı يَا غَلِي 1. fat; greasy; oily. 2. dirty with grease. 3. *colloq.* rich, free with money. 4. profitable. **— ballı ol=** /la/ to be on the sweetest of terms (with each other). **— boya** 1. oil paint. 2. *slang* Make way. **— çarık** *slang* full purse, full pocket. **— fener** lantern made of oiled paper or cloth. **— kâğıt** 1. oil paper. 2. tracing paper. **— kapı** *colloq.* rich employer. **— kireç** fat lime. **— kuyruk** milch cow; profitable business. **— lokma** a rich windfall. **— maden kömürü** fat coal, bituminous coal. **— müşteri** 1. profitable customer. 2. *iron.* hard bargainer. **— paçavra** a kind of fireball used in ancient warfare. **— simit** a bread ring made with shortening.

yağlıkᵗⁱ يَا غَمْلِك 1. napkin; handkerchief. 2. headkerchief. **—çı** dealer or seller of handkerchiefs.

yağma 1 (.ʹ.) يَا غَمَا يَغْمَا P 1. booty, loot. 2. sack of a town, pillage. 3. scramble; anything to be scrambled for. **—!** It is all booty! Rush and grab! **— et=** /ı/ to sack, pillage, loot; to plunder. **— Hasan'ın böreği** Grab Hasan's pie! *phrase used to describe an irresponsible waste of other people's money.* **— yok** You can't fool me. You can't get away with that.

yağma 2 يَا غَمَا *verbal n. of* **yağ=** 2.

yağmacı يَا غَمَجِي pillager, looter, plunderer. **—lık** pillage, plundering.

yağmager (.—.) يَغْمَاگَر P *lrnd.* plunderer, pillager. **—ân** (.—.—) P *pl.* **—î** (.—.—) P, **—lik** pillage, plundering.

yağmaî (.——) يَغْمَائِي P *lrnd.* like plunder.

yağmur يَغْمُر يَا غَمُر rain. **— boşan=** to pour heavily. **—dan kaçarken doluya tutul=** (*lit.*, while trying to escape from rain to get into a hail storm) out of the frying-pan into the fire. **— kesil=** to stop raining. **— kuşu** plover. **— olsa kimsenin tarlasına yağmaz** If he were

yağmurca

rain itself, he would not fall on anyone's field, *used to describe any uncharitable and disobliging person.* **— suyu** rain water. **— yağ=** to rain. **— yağarken küpü doldur=** (*lit.,* to fill one's jar while it rains) to benefit by a good opportunity. **— ye=** to get wet through (in the rain).

yağmurca یاغمورجه 1. fallow deer, *zool., Dama dama.* 2. spotted young of any wild quadruped.

yağmurla= یاغمورلن to become rainy.
yağmurlu یاغمورلو rainy.
yağmurluk[tu] یاغمورلق 1. raincoat. 2. roof over a doorway.

yağrık[tı] یاغریك *prov.* chopping block.

yağrın, yağrını یاغرین *prov.* withers, space between the shoulder blades and the neck.

yağsız یاغسز 1. without fat or oil. 2. skim milk or cheese.

yah یخ P *lrnd.* ice.
yahâb (.—) یخ آب P *lrnd.* ice water, water cooled with ice.
yahâver (.—.) یخ آور P *lrnd.* covered with ice; possessed of ice.
yahbeste یخ بسته P *lrnd.* bound with ice, frozen.
yahbur یخبور A *lrnd.* a young bustard, a male bustard.
yahçe یخچه P *lrnd.* 1. icicle. 2. hail; hailstone.
yahey (—.) یا هی *exclamation expressing a feeling of comfort.*
yahmum (.—) یحموم A *lrnd.* 1. black or dark thing. 2. smoke.
yahmur (.—) یحمر A *lrnd.* wild ass.
yahni یخنی P meat stew with onions. **— kapan** *colloq.* smart boy (half affectionately). **—lik** 1. stew meat. 2. *slang* fool, imbecile.
yahpare (.—.) یخ پاره P *lrnd.* a piece of ice.
yahşi یخشی pretty; agreeable, good. **— yaman** pretty or ugly; good or bad.
yahte (—.) یاخته P *lrnd.* 1. drawn (sword). 2. taught, educated. 3. chamber. 4. wine; small wine jar. 5. like, resembling.
yahtemil یحتمل A *lrnd.* It is possible. **— ki** perhaps, possibly.
yahtı, yahtu یختی *archaic* light. **—lı, —lu** lighted; brilliant.
yahu (—'.) یا هو A 1. See here! *expresses impatience.* 2. O God! **— dün niçin gelmedin?** Why didn't you come yesterday (said reproachfully). **— neredesin?** Where on earth are you? **— yapma!** Please don't!
yahud 1 (——) یا هود P *lrnd., same as* **yahut.**
Yahud 2 (.—) یهود A *lrnd.* the Jews.
Yahuda (.—.) یهودا A *Bib.* Judah.
Yahudân (.——) یهودان P *lrnd.* the Jews.
Yahudâne (.——.) یهودانه P *lrnd.* 1. Jewish.

2. *hist.* a patch of yellow cloth ordered to be worn by Jews as a distinctive mark.

Yahudhane (.——.) یهودخانه P Jewish quarter.
Yahudi یهودی [*Arabic* .——] Jew; Jewish. **— baklası** Egyptian lupin, *bot., Lupinus termis.* **— kalpağı** earth nut, pig nut, *bot., Conopodium denudatum.* **— pazarlığı** hard bargaining. **— züğürtleyince eski defterleri karıştırır** When a Jew is hard up he searches his old accounts, *often used of one who refers to his past achievements or wealth, etc. to fill up his present lack of the same.* **— zülfü** very exaggerated, dangling side curls of hair. **—ce** 1. Spanish as spoken by Sephardi Jews. 2. Jewish, like a Jew. **—lik** 1. quality of a Jew. 2. Jewish method of business; stinginess.

Yahudiyan (.———) یهودیان P *lrnd., pl. of* **Yahudi.**
Yahudiyâne (.———.) یهودیانه P *lrnd.* Jewish.
yahut (—.) یا هود [**yahud 1**] or; else; otherwise.
Yahya یحیی A *Quranic* John the Baptist.
yai (——) یا ی A *lrnd.* pertaining to the letter ی .
yais (—.) یائس A *lrnd.* despairing, desperate, hopeless.
yak=[ar] **1** یاقمق /ı/ 1. to burn, to scorch, to singe. 2. to light; to set on fire. 3. to destroy by fire. 4. to blight (vegetation). 5. to inflame with love. 6. to apply (henna, poultice). 7. *slang* to dupe; to hurt deeply, to destroy. 8. to compose (a folk song).
yak=[ar] **2** یاقمق *archaic* /ı/ to cause to draw near.
yaka یاقا 1. collar. 2. edge, bank, shore. 3. *naut.* edge or corner of a sail. **—sı açılmadık** unusual, unheard of. **—sı açılmadık küfür** an unusual and obscene oath. **—sı açılmadık söz** (*lit.,* a saying whose collar has not been opened) a novel idea or saying. **—sına asıl=** /ın/ *same as* **yakasına yapış=.** **—dan at=** /ı/ to get rid of. **—mı bırak** Leave me in peace. **—sını bırakma=** /ın/ not to let someone go. **— bir tarafta paça bir tarafta** dishevelled. **— devşir=** to draw together one's garment in token of respect. **—yı ele ver=** to be caught or arrested. **—dan geçir=** /ı/ to adopt (an infant). **— halatı** *naut.* bolt-rope of a sail. **— ısır=** to express horror; to say "God forbid!" **— kavra=** to plead earnestly. **—yı kurtar=** to escape. **— paça** dragging by force. **— paça et=** /ı/ to seize by the collar and trousers and chuck out. **— paça kavra=** (*lit.,* to grasp the collar and trouser legs), to entreat earnestly. **—yı sıyır=** /dan/ to escape. **— silk=** /dan/ to be disgusted, fed

up (with). —**dan tut=** /ı/ 1. to seize, to lay hands on; to keep hold of. 2. to hold responsible. — **yakaya gel=** to come to blows, to seize each other by the collar. —**sına yapış=** /ın/ to hold responsible; to force someone to do something. — **yırtık at** horse with a line of crisp, curly hair in front of its neck and chest.

yakala=ᴵʳ باقلامق يغالامو /ı/ 1. to collar, to seize, to get hold of (in any way); to apprehend; to catch; to find. 2. to hold responsible. —**ma** 1. verbal n. 2. arrest. —**n=** pass of **yakala=**. —**t=** /ı, a/ caus. of **yakala=**.

yakalıkᵇᴵ باقلامى يغالاوى 1. cloth suitable for a collar. 2. removable collar; collar of a shirt.

yakamoz يغاموز باقاموز Gk phosphorescence in the sea.

yakar=ᴵʳ باقارمه يغارمه /a/ 1. to implore. 2. to beg piteously or whiningly. —**t=** /ı, a/ caus.

yakaza يقظه A lrnd. wakefulness; state of being awake.

yakazet (. —.) يقاظت A lrnd. a being awake, watching or vigilant; wakefulness, vigilance.

yakı باقى يقى 1. cautery. 2. blister; blister-plaster. — **aç=** /a/ to apply a cautery. — **nohudu** 1. chickpea placed in a skin opening to keep it open. 2. small ball of orris root used to keep an artificial wound open. — **otu** 1. fireweed, rose-bay, bot., Epilobium angustifolium. 2. the reed Calamagrostis epigeios or Arundo calamagrostis. — **vur=**, — **yapıştır=** /a/ same as **yakı aç=**.

yakıcı باقيجى burning, smarting; biting (to the taste).

yakıl=ᴵʳ باقيلمه يغيلمه 1. pass. of **yak=** 2. 2. to pour out one's woes.

yakılı باقيلى يغيلى lighted, burning.

yakım باقم يغم 1. act of lighting or burning. 2. prov. a kind of popular ballad.

yakın باقن يقين 1. near (in place or time). 2. neighborhood, nearby place. 3. recent time; near future. 4. from near at hand; closely, thoroughly. —**da** 1. near by. 2. in the near future. 3. recently. —**larda** same as **yakında**. —**akraba** close relative, near relation. —**dan alâkadar** closely interested. — **âmir** mil. immediate superior. —**dan bil=** to be closely acquainted with. — **dost** intimate friend. —**a getir=** /ı/ 1. to bring near. 2. to magnify (telescope). — **hısım** same as **yakın akraba**. — **muharebe** mil. close action. — **zamanda** 1. not long ago, recently. 2. soon, in a short time.

yakınlaş=ᴵʳ باقينلاشمه يغينلاشمى to draw near, to approach. —**tır=** /ı, a/ caus.

yakınlıkᵇᴵ باقينلى nearness, proximity. — **göster=** /a/ to show sympathy and concern.

yakış 1 باقيش يغش verbal n. of **yak=** 1.

yakış=ᴵʳ 2 باقيشمى يغشى 1. /a/ to be suitable or becoming, to be proper, to befit. 2. to look good, to be good looking.

yakışıkᵇᴵ باقيشى يغشى 1. suitability; most suitable way. 2. apparent truth, plausibility. 3. beauty. — **al=** to be suitable. — **almaz** It is not proper to do.

yakışıklı باقيشقلى 1. handsome, comely. 2. suitable, becoming; well set up.

yakışıksız باقيشقسز unsuitable, unbecoming; ugly. —**lık** unsuitability; unbecoming appearance.

yakıştır=ᴵʳ باقيشديرمه يغشديرمى 1. /ı, a/ caus. of **yakış=** 2. 2. /ı, a/ to think something is becoming to a person. 3. /ı, a/ to expect (something of a person). 4. chauffeurs' slang to drink between jobs. —**ıp takıştır=** to embellish, decorate. —**ıp uydur=** /ı/ to invent something suitable to the occasion.

yakıt neol. fuel.

yakin (. —) يقين A lrnd. 1. sure and certain knowledge; firm belief; certainty. 2. religious certitude based on revelation. — **bil=** /ı/ to know of a certainty. — **hâsıl et=** to become certain.

yakinen (. —ʹ.) يقيناً A lrnd. for certain, positively.

yakinî (. ——) يقينى A lrnd. known with certainty. —**yat** (. —. —) A certainties; things known or believed absolutely.

yaklaş=ᴵʳ باقلاشمه يغلاشمى /a/ 1. to draw near; to approach; to approximate. 2. to resemble. —**tır=** /ı, a/ caus. of **yaklaş=**.

yakma باقمه يغمى 1. verbal n. of **yak=** 1. 2. produced by burning.

yaktır=ᴵʳ باقديرمه يغديرمى /ı, a/ caus. of **yak=** 1. —**ıl=** pass.

yaktin (. —) يقطين A lrnd. gourd or similar creeper.

Ya'kub (. —) يعقوب A Bib. 1. Jacob. 2. James.

Ya'kubi (. ——) يعقوبى A Jacobite.

yakut 1 (—.) ياقوت [Arabic ——] ruby. —**i ahmer** lrnd. red gem, ruby. —**i hâm** lrnd. 1. unpolished ruby. 2. lips of a beauty. —**i kebud** lrnd. blue gem, sapphire. — **macunu** electuary of rubies. —**i müzab**, —**i revan** lrnd. 1. red wine. 2. tears of blood; blood. —**i rümmani** lrnd. a precious kind of ruby. —**i serbeste** poet. 1. mouth of a mistress. 2. lips closed in silence. —**i seyyâl** lrnd. precious stone of fine water. —**i zerd** lrnd. 1. yellow gem. 2. the sun.

Yakut 2 ياقوت the Yakut people (of northeastern Siberia). —**ça** the Yakut language.

yakzan (. —) يقظان A lrnd. 1. waking, awake. 2. wakeful, watchful, vigilant; provident.

yal 1 يال 1. bright, shining. 2. smooth, level.

yal 2 يال prov. mash prepared for dogs, dog food (made of flour and bran).

yâlⁱⁱ 3 (—) يال P lrnd. 1. neck; root of the neck; the withers (in a horse, etc.). 2. horse's mane. 3. power, strength. **— ü bâl** height and form; beauty and strength. **— ü bâl sahibi** handsome and well set up; well-to-do. **— ü kûpal** stout neck and shoulders.

yala=ʳ يالامق /ı/ 1. to lick with the tongue; to lick up. 2. to sweep over (a place, as of artillery fire). 3. to graze (the surface of). 4. to erase (with the tongue).

yalabı=ʳ يالابيمق prov. to shine; to glitter, sparkle; to twinkle.

yalabıkᵉⁱ يالابيق .يالابى prov. 1. shining, shiny; glittering; gorgeous. 2. sheen; glitter, sparkle.

yalakᵉⁱ يالاق .يالغ trough; drinking basin (at a fountain). **— taşı** stone trough where cattle are watered.

yalama يالاما 1. verbal n. of **yala**=. 2. mech. worn off by friction, loose. 3. erosion, abrasion. 4. sore. 5. art shading; washing, tinting (of a drawing). **—cı** slang toady, sycophant.

yalan 1 يالان 1. lie, falsehood. 2. false, deceitful. **—dan*. — at**= to lie, to tell lies. **— çık**= to turn out untrue. **çıkar**= to spread false rumors. **—ını çıkar**= /ın/ to show up someone's lies; to give the lie (to someone). **— dolan** lies and frauds; deceits and subterfuge. **— dünya** same as **yalancı dünya**. **—a sap**= to have recourse to lying. **— söyle**= to tell lies, to lie. **—ını tut**= /ın/ to catch someone in his lying. **— yanlış** false, erroneous; carelessly, superficially. **— yere şehadet** law false evidence. **— yere yemin** perjury. **— yere yemin et**= to perjure oneself.

yalan=ʳ 2 يالانمق 1. pass. of **yala**=. 2. to lick oneself. 3. to get a little profit (out of something).

yalancı يالانجى 1. liar. 2. false; imitated, not real, deceptive. 3. deceitful; imitation. **— ayaklar** biol. pseudopodia. **— çıkar**= /ı/ to prove someone to be a liar; to make someone look like a liar. **— çiçek** artificial flower. **— dolma** grape-leaves or vegetable stuffed with rice and stewed with oil. **— dünya** the false world, the transitory life. **—nın evi yanmış da kimse inanmamış** proverb The liar's house burned but nobody believed it. A liar is not believed even when he tells the truth. **— inci** artificial pearl. **—nın mumu yatsıya kadar yanar** A liar's candle only burns till bedtime. A lie has only a short life. **—sı ol**= /ın/ to repeat something heard of another not being sure whether it is true or not. **— öd ağacı** Indian aloe tree, agalloch, bot., Aloexylon agallochum. **— pehlivan** not quite such a fine fellow as he makes out; mock hero. **— safran** safflower, bastard saffron, false saffron, bot., Carthamus tinctorius. **— şahid** false witness. **— taş** false jewel.

yalancıktan يالانجقتن superficially; not meaning it; in pretense.

yalancılıkᵉⁱ يالانجيلق lying, mendacity.

yalandan يالاندن not seriously; only for appearance; superficially. **— söyle**= not to mean what one says. **— yıka**= /ı/ to wash superficially.

yalanla=ʳ يالانلامق /ı/ to deny, to contradict.

yalapᵇⁱ يالاب .يالاب prov. sparklingly, flashingly. **— yalap** in a sparkling manner. **— yalap ak**= to flow glittering away.

yalat=ⁱʳ يالاتمق /ı, a/ caus. of **yala**=.

yalavaçᶜⁱ يالاواج .يالواج archaic messenger; prophet.

yalayıcı يالايجى licking; grazing. **— ateş** mil. grazing fire, fire with a flat trajectory.

yalaz, yalaza, yalazı يالاز .يالازا .يالازى prov. flame.

yalazlan=ⁱʳ يالازلانمق to flame up, blaze up.

yalçı يالچى archaic, same as **alçı**.

yalçın يالچين smooth and bare; rugged; steep; slippery. **— kaya** smooth, slippery rock; cliff.

yaldıra=ʳ يالديرامق prov. to shine brightly, to gleam.

yaldırakᵉⁱ يالديراق .يالديراك bright, brilliant, shining.

yaldız يالديز 1. gilding. 2. superficial finish; false decoration, false show. 3. superficial accomplishment. **— altını** 1. gilding gold, pure gold. 2. Venetian ducat. **—dan ibaret** superficial. **—ı sıyır**= to put forth one's real nature. **— taklidi** imitation gilding, lacquer.

yaldızcı يالديزجى 1. gilder. 2. one who does superficial work. **—cılık** gilding.

yaldızla=ʳ يالديزلامق /ı/ 1. to gild. 2. to put a false finish (to). **—n**= pass. **—t**= /ı, a/ caus. of **yaldızla**=.

yaldızlı يالديزلى .يالديزلو 1. gilt; lacquered. 2. falsely adorned. **— hap** sugar-coated pill, bitter or evil news given gently or in a sweet manner. **— kâğıt** 1. gilt paper. 2. writing paper flecked with gold. **— kükürt** crude antimony sulfide.

yale (—.) يال P lrnd. horn.

yalelli (—.٠.) يللى 1. Arab song. 2. orgy; amusement. **— gibi** unending, monotonous.

yaleyt (—.), **yaleyte** (—..) ياليت A lrnd. I wish, would that!

yalgım, yalgın يالغم .يالغين archaic 1. glitter, luster. 2. flame; blaze; glow. 3. mirage.

yalı 1 يالى Gk 1. shore; beach. 2. waterside residence. 3. naut. waterway along the side of a ship's deck. **— boyu** shore, beach. **— boyunca git**= to go along the seashore. **— çamı** large pine, Corsican pine, bot., Pinus laricio. **— çapkını** kingfisher, zool., *Alcede atthis*. — **kazığı** *colloq.* tall thin person. **Y— Köşkü** *Ott. hist.* one of the buildings of the Palace (scrapped in the 19th century). — **kütüğü** *naut.* any one or the whole of the timbers on the side of a ship's deck along which the waterway runs, covering board. — **mevsimi** summer season. — **uşağı** one born and bred by the seaside.

yalı 2 يالى *archaic, same as* **yele**.

yalım 1 يالم 1. blade (of a sword). 2. beveled cutting edge. 3. stock; kind; nature. 4. *prov.* rock; cliff. **—ı alçak** 1. of which the edge is poor. 2. of base nature, mean; miserly.

yalım 2 يالم flame, glitter; lightning.

yalın 1 يالين ,ياين ,يالنك 1. bare, bared, stripped; naked (sword). 2. single (fold). — **ağaç** 1. tree that sheds its bark naturally. 2. barked tree. — **ayak** barefoot. — **ayak başı kabak** bareheaded and barefoot, in rags. — **hal** *neol., gram.* nominative case; uninflected form. — **kat** 1. single fold, not double. 2. superficial, shallow. 3. having a veneer. — **kat gül** single rose. — **kılıç** 1. drawn sword. 2. having a drawn sword. — **yüz** an unveiled face.

yalın 2 يالنك ياين يالين *prov.* 1. flame. 2. steep rocky slope. 3. flash; glitter; lightning.

yalınca, yalıncak يالنجى ياينجه *prov.* 1. all alone. 2. naked; bare. 3. poor.

yalıngaç يالنغاج *same as* **yelengeç**.

yalınız يالكز *same as* **yalnız**.

yalınla= يالينكمك 1. *prov.* to set aflame. 2. to blaze, to flame. 3. to flash, to glitter. **—n**= *pass.* **—t**= /ı/ 1. *caus. of* **yalınla**=. 2. to light (lamp).

yalil'aceb (—'…) ياعجيب A *lrnd.* How strange!

yallah يالله [*ya Allah*] Come here. Go away. Get going. — **yallah** at most.

yalman يالمان 1. the pointed cutting part of a weapon. 2. steep and jagged mountain peak. — **kaya** smooth-faced cliff or peak of rock.

yalmar= يالمارمق *archaic* to lick over and swallow whole.

yalmend (—.) يالمند P *lrnd.* master of a family, head of the house.

yalnız 1 (.'.) يالكز only; but. — **ve yalnız** exclusively, simply, solely.

yalnız 2 يالكز alone, solitary. — **başına** alone, by oneself, single-handed. **—ca** (..'.) alone, by oneself. **—lık** loneliness.

yalpa (.'.) يالپا the rolling of a ship at sea. — **vur**= 1. to roll heavily (ship). 2. to sway about, to lurch (drunken man).

yalpak يالپاق *prov.* 1. friendly. 2. untidy, slovenly. **—lık** 1. friendliness. 2. untidiness.

yalpuk يالپوك *archaic* shallow and agitated (water).

yaltak يالتاق fawning; sycophantic; cringing.

yaltaklan= يالتاقلنمق to fawn or cringe; to flatter obsequiously.

yaltaklık يالتاقلق fawning, cringing, flattery.

ya'lûl (.—) يعلول A *lrnd.* 1. bubble on water. 2. small fleecy cloud. 3. clear pool of running water. 4. camel with two humps.

yalvaç يالواج *same as* **yalavaç**.

yalvâne (——.) يالوانه P *lrnd.* swallow; small water-bird.

yalvar= يالوارمق /a/ to beg; to entreat; to implore. **—ıcı** entreating, imploring. **—ış**= to entreat, implore together (several persons). **—t**= /ı, a/ *caus. of* **yalvar**=.

yam يام Mong *archaic* 1. post-horse; post-driver. 3. post-driver's cloak.

yama 1 ياما patch. — **gibi dur**= to look out of place as though it did not belong. — **küçük delik büyük** The means are insufficient for the end. — **vur**= /a/ to put on a patch.

yama= 2 ياماسق /ı/ 1. to patch. 2. to stitch on. 3. to impose (someone or something on someone).

yamacı ياماجى 1. patcher; repairer (of clothes, boots, etc.). 2. skinflint.

yamaç ياماج slope of a hill; side. **—lı** uneven, with a rising slope.

yamak ياماق 1. assistant. 2. *Ott. hist.* locally hired soldier at a detached fort. — **terliği** pointed cloth slipper.

yamala= ياماسق /ı/ to patch. **—n**= *pass.*

yamalı ياما لى 1. patched. 2. with scars on the face.

yaman 1 يامان 1. capable, intelligent, efficient. 2. bad, disagreeable. 3. strong, violent, cruel.

yaman= 2 يامانمق 1. *pass. of* **yama**= 2. 2. /a/ to install oneself, to get a footing. 3. /a/ to settle down (in a job, etc.). 4. /a/ to foist oneself on (someone). **—dır**= /ı, a/ *caus.*

yamat= يامانمق *caus. of* **yama**= 2.

yamcı يامجى *archaic* driver and tender of post-horses.

yamçı يامچى 1. thick rough cape. 2. felt saddle cover.

yamık ياميق *prov.* bent, crooked.

yampırı, yampiri, yampürü يامپورى *same as* **yanpiri**.

yamrı yumru يامرى يومرى gnarled, uneven and lumpy.

ya'mur (.—) يعمور A *lrnd.* kid; small sheep.

yamyam يام يام cannibal. **—lık** cannibalism.

yamyassı يام ياصى flat, very flat.

yan 1 يان 1. side; flank. 2. vicinity

(of a thing). 3. presence (of a person). 4. direction, bearing. **—a*. —dan** from the side; sideways; in profile. **bir —dan** from one side, on one side. **—ıma** to my side, towards me. **—ımda** 1. at my side; by me. 2. *archaic* in my opinion. **—ımdan** from my side; from me. **—ında** 1. at his (your) side; by him (you). 2. /ın/ in comparison with. 3. *archaic* in his (your) opinion. **—ına adam al=** to take a man or men with him or into his employ. **— ağrısı** pain in the side; pleurisy. **—ına al=** to take into one's service. **— at=** to enjoy oneself lazily; to stretch oneself at ease. **— ateşi** *mil.* flanking fire, enfilade. **— bak=** to look askance, to cast unfriendly looks. **— bakış** 1. coquettish or roguish look. 2. an angry look. **— bakışı** *archaic* 1. side view. 2. profile. **— baksan kabahat** Every little error is brought up against me. **— bas=** *slang* to have one's hopes dashed; to be deceived. **—ı başında** at his very side, close by him; next to it. **—ına bırakma=** /ın/ not to leave unpunished. **—ından bile geçmemiş** /ın/ It has no likeness or connection (with it) whatsoever. Far from it, *said when a person fails to show good manners.* **— cebime koy** Put it in my side pocket, *said when one pretends not to want something while eagerly desiring to have it.* **— cümle** *gram.* subordinate clause. **—dan çarklı** 1. paddlewheel boat. 2. *slang* slow-going vehicle. 3. *slang* tea served with the sugar brought in the saucer (in a coffee house). **— çiz=** 1. to sneak off. 2. /ı/ to pretend not to see; to pay no heed; to shirk. **— duruşu** side view, profile. **—dan fırlama** *slang* scoundrel. **— gel=** to take one's ease, to make oneself comfortable. **— gelip zevke bak=** to be at ease and enjoy life. **— gözle** with the corner of the eye. **— gözle bak=** /a/ 1. to look at someone out of the corner of the eye. 2. to look at someone or something with evil intentions. **— hareketi** *mil.* flank movement. **— hücumu** *mil.* flank attack. **—ına kal=** to remain unpunished. **—ında kal=** 1. to stay with him, to remain in his possession. 2. to remain unpunished. **—ı kara*. — kemiği** *biol.* parietal bone. **— kes=** *archaic* to cut purses, to pick pockets. **— kesici*. —ına koyma=** /ın/ not to leave unpunished. **— mevzii** *mil.* flank position. **— müfrezesi** *mil.* flank company. **— omurgaları** *naut.* bilge logs. **—ında otur=** to sit down by him; to lodge with him. **—ına salavatla varılır** a proud and quick-tempered person, *to whom approach is made with fear and inward prayer.* **— salla=** *slang* not to pay attention, not to care. **—ı sıra** by his side. **— taarruzu** *mil.* flank attack. **—ına varılmaz** 1. unapproachable. 2. very expensive.

— ver= /a/ to lean to one's side (against a thing). **— yan** sideways, sidelong. **— yana** side by side; side to side. **bir —dan bir yana** from one side to the other. **— yan bak=** to look sideways with anger or evil intention. **— yat=** to lean over to one side. **— yelken** fore-and-aft-sail. **— zaviyesi** *mil.* horizontal training.

yan= 2 1. to burn, to be consumed by fire; to be alight. 2. to catch fire, to ignite. 3. to be burnt, scorched, over-roasted. 4. to be blighted (by heat or cold). 5. to be painful, to hurt; to be very thirsty. 6. to be ruined, to be done for; to become not valid or forfeited; to lose one's turn (in a game). 7. /a/ to feel grieved or sorry (for); to be consumed with passion (for). **—dım Allah diye bağır=** to be in great distress or suffering. **—ıp tutuş=** to burn with great passion. **—ıp yakıl=** to pour out one's woes piteously. **—a yana** complaining bitterly.

yân 3 (—) P *lrnd.* incoherent, unintelligible language; reverie of a fanatic, raving of one in a delirium; trance.

yana 1. /dan/ toward, e. g., **karadan yana** toward the shore. 2. /dan/ concerning, e. g., **paradan yana** as for money. 3. *archaic, same as* **yan** 1. **bir —a at=** to throw aside, to set aside.

yanak 1. cheek. 2. fur from the cheeks of animals. **— dibi** fur below the cheek-fur; fur composed of pieces from that part alone. **—ından kan damlıyor** His cheeks are ruddy with health. **— yumrucuğu** cheekbone.

yanal *neol., math.* lateral. **— çizgi** *biol.* lateral line. **— yükseklik** *geom.* apothem. **— yüzey** *geom.* lateral surface.

yanar inflammable. **— dağ** volcano. **— döner** shot (silk, etc.).

yanaş= /a/ 1. to draw near, approach. 2. to come alongside (ship). 3. to accede (to a request). 4. to incline, seem willing. 5. *mil.* to come close (to).

yanaşık adjacent, contiguous. **— nizam** *mil.* close order. **—lık** contiguity.

yanaşılmaz unapproachable, inaccessible.

yanaşma 1. *verbal n. of* **yanaş=**. 2. casual laborer.

yanaştır= /ı, a/ *caus. of* **yanaş=**.

yanay *neol.* 1. profile; side-face. 2. sidewise.

yanaz *prov.* peevish, spoiled. **—lan=** 1. to disagree; to object. 2. to become peevish or spoiled. **—lık** peevishness.

yanbeki *prov.* 1. athwart, in a sidelong position. 2. done while lying on the side.

yanbolu *slang* stupid, fool.

yancık[ı] يا نجىس يا نجى *archaic* flank armor; flank bag. **—lı** full and fleshy in the muscles of the thigh (horse).

yandık[ı] يا ندك ينـدك camel thorn, *bot.*, *Alhagi camelorum;* the plant *Alhagi mororum.*

yandır=[ır] يا ندير مـق ينـديـرمـق /ı/ *colloq.* to cause to burn; to burn.

yâne (—.) يانه P *lrnd.* mortar.

yangabuç[cu] يا نغابوج *colloq.* lopsided; distorted.

yangın يانغين يانغن 1. conflagration, fire. 2. burnt; burning. 3. smarting; suffering. 4. victim (of a fire); madly in love. 5. *prov.* fever. **— bombası** incendiary bomb. **— çengeli** large iron hook on a pole. **—dan çıkmış gibi** destitute. **— çıkar=** to start a fire; to cause a fire. **—a git=** to go in great haste. **— işareti** signal to announce a fire. **— köşkü, — kulesi** lookout station for fires, fire tower. **—a körükle git=** to add fuel to the flames. **—dan mal kaçırır gibi** showing unnecessary excitement or haste. **— sigortası** fire insurance. **— topu** gun fired as a signal when a fire breaks out. **— tulumbası** hand fire pump. **— var!** Fire!

yanı يانى *same as* **yanu.**

yanık[ı] 1 يانيق يانق 1. burn, scald. 2. burned, scorched; singed. 3. tanned. 4. blight; blighted. 5. lighted, turned on (electric light, etc.). 6. piteous, doleful, touching, pathetic. **— âşık** lover distracted with his passion, passionate lover. **Y— Kale** *Ott. hist.* Györ (Hungary), *a frontier fortress of the Ottoman Empire for a long time.* **— kara** *archaic, same as* **yanıkara.** **— kok=** to smell of burning; to have a smoky flavor. **— rüzgâr** wind that subsides quickly. **— ses** touchingly sweet voice. **— söyle=** to speak in a brokenhearted tone. **— yağı** ointment for burns. **— yanık** in a moving way.

yanık=[ır] 2 ينقمق *prov.* to complain, to whine.

yanıkara يانى قارا painful subcutaneous tumor, bubo of plague.

yanıklık[ı] يانقلق 1. state of what is burned, scorched, singed; burn, scald. 2. suffering, anguish, dolefulness.

yanıl=[ır] يانيلمق to err, make a mistake; to go wrong; to miss.

yanılmaz يانلماز who does not err; infallible; unfailing.

yanılt=[ır] يانيلتمق /ı/ *caus. of* **yanıl=.**

yanıltmaca يانيلتماجه 1. riddle based on a pun. 2. misleading argument; fallacy.

yanıltmaç[cı] يانيلتماج 1. tongue-twister. 2. puzzle.

yanın يانين sideways, sidelong. **— kıçın** sideways and backwards. **— yanın** *prov.* May you die! (curse). **— yanın git=** to go sideways.

ya'ni A, **yani** 1 (—.) يعنى that is to say; i. e.; namely; to say it another way.

Yani 2 (—́.) يانى Gk John.

yani[i] 3 (—.) يانع A *lrnd.* 1. ripe (fruit). 2. red, ruddy; rosy.

yankesici يانكسيجى pickpocket.

yankı يانقى يانكو يانغو يانقو 1. echo. 2. reaction. **—ca** *neol., psych.* echolalia.

yankıla=[r] يانقيلامق /ı/ to echo. **—n=** to echo. **—ndır=** /ı/ *caus. of* **yankıla=, yankılan=.**

yanla=[r] يانلامق to move sideways, to sidle. **—ya yanlaya yürü=** to go along sideways.

yanlış يانليش يانلش 1. error, blunder, mistake. 2. wrong, incorrect, erroneous. 3. *obs.* formidable, terrible (man). **— bakışlı** *obs.* ferocious-looking, menacing. **—ını çıkar=** /ın/ to find out one's mistakes. **— doğru cetveli** list of errata. **— herif** *obs.* a terrible fellow, not to be trifled with. **— hesap Bağdat'tan döner** It is never too late to correct a mistake. **— kapı çal=** (*lit.,* to knock at the wrong door) to be out in one's reckoning, to miscalculate. **— yere** wrongly, falsely.

yanlışlık[ı] يانليشلق mistake, error, blunder. **— et=** to make a mistake, to blunder.

yanma يانمه *verbal n. of* **yan=** 2.

yanpırı يانپيرى 1. leaning to one side; distorted; crooked. 2. awkward; crabwise. **—lık** distortion, awkwardness.

yanpiri, yanpürü يانپيرو يانپيرى *same as* **yanpırı.**

yansı 1 يانسى leaning to one side, lopsided.

yansı=[r] 2, **yansıla=**[r] يانسيمق يانسيلامق 1. to lean to one side. 2. *prov.* to imitate; to mimic.

yanşa=[r] يانشامـق *prov.* to be talkative, indiscreet; to blab.

yanşak[ğı] يانشاق يانشاغى *prov.* talkative, garrulous.

yanşal=[r] يانشالمق *prov., same as* **yanşa=.**

yanu يانو *prov.* lament; complaint; curse.

yap 1 يا پ gently, noiselessly; slowly. **— yap büyü=** to grow by degrees. **— yap yürü=** to walk with slow steps.

yap=[ar] 2 يـاپـمـق /ı/ 1. to do; to make. 2. to construct; to build; to arrange. 3. to set to rights; to make good. 4. to make ready. 5. to soothe, conciliate. 6. *archaic* to close, to shut. **—ma!** Oh don't! Incredible! **—acağımı ben bilirim!** You just see what I'll do (a threat). **—acağını yap!** Do your worst! **—acağını yaptı** He did all the harm he could.

yapa يا پا *slang* mustache.

yapağı, yapak[ğı] يا پاغى يا پاغ wool, especially the wool of a sheep shorn in the spring (as opposed to **yün,** the shorter wool of an autumn-shorn sheep). — **belediyesi** Ott. hist. commuted tax. **—cı, —çı** wool merchant. **—lı** well fleeced (sheep); woolen.

yapalakᵍ¹ يا پالاق . يا پا لاق . يالپو eagle owl, zool., Bubo bubo.

yapayalnız (..´..) يا پا يَكْنِز absolutely alone, quite alone.

yapça يا پچه . يا پجه archaic rather gently, softly or slowly. **— söyle=** to speak gently, modestly, submissively. **— yapça** continually or repeatedly and gently. **—cık** very gently and softly.

yapı يا پى 1. building, edifice. 2. build (of the body); structure (of any composite whole). **— mimarisi** architectonics.

yapıcı يا پجى 1. maker, builder; constructor. 2. creative; constructive.

yapıkᵍ¹ يا پيق . يا ينه . يا پورە 1. archaic horse-blanket. 2. archaic a kind of shaggy cape. 3. archaic beauty spot of gold or jewels stuck on a bride's face. 4. prov. kerchief; scarf.

yapıl=ᶦʳ يا پيلمق pass. of **yap=** 2.

yapılı يا پيلى . يا پيلو built, constructed; made.

yapılış, yapılma يا پيليش . يا پلمه verbal n. of **yapıl=**.

yapın=ᶦʳ يا پنمق archaic 1. to have made for oneself (clothes, etc.). 2. to prepare oneself to do something. 3. to pretend; to put on airs; to assume an affected manner. 4. to become wealthy.

yapıncakᵍ¹ 1 يا پنجاق a variety of white grape (from the village of **Yapıncak**).

yapıncakᵍ¹ 2 يا پنجاق 1. rug (to protect a horse from rain). 2. a kind of shaggy coat.

yapındır=ᶦʳ يا پندرمق /ı/ 1. archaic, caus. of **yapın=**. 2. slang to have a drink.

yapınış يا پنيش affected air, hypocritical manners.

yapırgan يا پرغان archaic 1. petal. 2. ray, floret of a composite flower.

yapış 1 يا پيش verbal n. of **yap=** 2.

yapış=ᶦʳ يا پيشمق /a/ 1. to stick, to adhere. 2. to stick to one (as a bore). 3. to set about doing something. 4. to grab, to clasp with both hands; to lay hold of. **—a kal=** to remain sticking; to stick to.

yapışıcı يا پيشيجى same as **yapışkan**.

yapışıkᵍ¹ يا پيشيق stuck on, attached; adhering. **— adam** a man one cannot get rid of, bore. **— kardeşler** Siamese twins. **— kulaklı** having ears laid flat to the head.

yapışkan يا پيشقان 1. sticky, adhesive. 2. persistent, pertinacious, importunate. 3. prov. bird lime. **— otu** common pellitory, bot., Parietaria officinalis. **—lık** stickiness; pertinacity.

yapışma يا پيشمه 1. verbal n. of **yapış=** 2. 2. sticking, clinging (thing).

yapıştır=ᶦʳ يا پيشديرمق /ı, a/ 1. caus. of **yapış=** 2. 2. to say something in quick reply. 3. to apply a thing closely or violently to another. **—ıl=** pass.

yapıştırma يا پيشديرمه 1. verbal n. of **yapıştır=**. 2. thing stuck on. 3. transfer (picture). 4. ornaments stuck on a bride's face.

yapış yapış يا پيش يا پيش sticky.

yapkın يا پقين 1. wealthy, rich. 2. intoxicated, drunk.

yapma (..´) يا پمه 1. verbal n. of **yap=** 2. 2. made, done. 3. artificial, false. 4. sham; pretended, feigned. **— bebek** pretty but soulless and cold girl or woman. **— diş** false tooth, artificial tooth.

yapmacıkᵍ¹ يا پمه جيق 1. artificial, feigned. 2. false. 3. affectation.

yapracıkᵍ¹ يا پراجيق little leaf or flake.

yaprakᵍ¹ يا پراق . يا پراك 1. leaf; grape-leaf. 2. sheet of paper; flake. 3. layer. 4. breadth of canvas (in a sail). **— aşısı** graft by budding; budding. **— ayası** border or edge of a leaf. **— biti** aphid; plant-louse. **— dolması** stuffed grape-leaves. **— dökümü** fall of the leaves, autumn. **— halı** rug made of several pieces sewn together. **— kur=** to pickle grape-leaves. **— sarması** same as **yaprak dolması**. **— sigara** cigar. **— tütün** tobacco in the leaf. **— yaprak** in leaves; in layers.

yapraklan=ᶦʳ يا پراقلنمق . يا پراكلنمق 1. to come into leaf. 2. to become flaky, to form into thin strata. 3. to flap in the wind (sail or flag).

yapraklı يا پراقلو . يا پراكلى 1. leafed; leafy. 2. flaked, flaky. 3. ornamented with leaf patterns. **— demir** scaled iron. **— makas** auto. springs.

yapraksız يا پراقسز . يا پراكسز 1. leafless. 2. bare (tree).

yaprıkᵍ¹ يا پريق archaic, same as **yapık**.

yaprıkçıyan (...—) يا پريقجيان Ott. hist. makers of horse-blankets (personnel of the Royal Stables).

yaptır=ᶦʳ يا پديرمق . يا پتيرمق /ı, a/ caus. of **yap=** 2. **—ıl=** pass.

yaptırım neol. 1. verbal n. of **yaptır=**. 2. sanction.

yaptırma يا پتيرمه verbal n. of **yaptır=**.

yapyalnız (..´..) يا پيا لكز same as **yapayalnız**.

yârʳ¹ 1 (—) يا ر P 1. friend; lover; one's beloved. 2. helper. **— ü ağyar** lrnd. friend and foe; all the world. **—i cân** lrnd. the beloved. **—i gâr** lrnd. (lit., friend of the Cave) 1. Abubekr (afterwards the first caliph). 2. intimate friend; companion in adversity. **—dan mı geçmeli serden mi?** Is it better to give up one's love or to sacrifice one's own interest? **—i kadîm** an old friend. **— ol=** /a/ 1. to be loving friends with one another.

2. to be a helping friend, to assist. — **olup bâr olma**= to be a friend without making oneself burdensome. **—i vefadar** *lrnd.* loyal friend. **— ü yaver ol**= *lrnd.* to help and favor one another.

yar 2 يار precipice, abyss. **—dan at**= /ı/ 1. to throw from a precipice. 2. to lead into deep trouble. **—dan uç**= 1. to fall down a precipice. 2. to get entangled in deep trouble. **— yıkıntısı** 1. the talus of a cliff. 2. any sudden overwhelming misfortune.

yar 3 يار *archaic* saliva.

yar 4 يار *archaic* public cry, proclamation.

yar=ᵃʳ **5** يارمه /ı/ 1. to split, rend, cleave, cut through. 2. *mil.* to break through.

yara 1 يارا ، يارە 1. wound; sore; cut; rent. 2. boil; scar. 3. pain, sorrow; injury, hurt. **— aç**= 1. to wound. 2. to hurt. **— bağı** surgical bandage. **— bere** wounds and bruises; all wounds and bruises. **—yı deş**= to open a wound; to touch a sore spot. **—sına dokun**= /ın/ to touch someone on his tender spot. **— fitili** surgical tent. **— işle**= to discharge (boil). **— kabuğu** scab of a wound. **— otu** squarestalked St. John's wort, *bot.*, *Hypericum quadrangulum.* **— sargısı** bandage. **— süngeri** proud flesh in a sore. **— topla**= 1. for a boil to come to head. 2. for a hurt to become intense. **—ya tuz biber ek**=, **—ya tuz ek**=, **—ya tuz saç**= to put salt on a wound, to increase another's pain by one's words.

yârâ 2 (— —) يارا P *lrnd.* 1. strength, force, power of resistance. 2. boldness, courage. **—yi sühan** ability of speech.

yara=ʳ **3** يارامه /a/ 1. to be serviceable; to be of use; useful. 2. to be suitable.

ya Rab, ya Rabbi يا رب ، يا ربي A O Lord; O my Lord.

Yaradan ياردان the Creator; creating. **—a kurban olayım!** *expression of admiration on seeing a beautiful child, etc.* **—a sığınırım!** I take refuge in God! God help me! **—a sığınıp vur**= to strike a violent blow.

yaradılış ياراديليش ، ياردلش 1. creation. 2. nature, temperament; constitution.

yarakᵗⁱ يارق ، برنه ، چ 1. *archaic* arms; armor. 2. *archaic* provisions; necessaries; tool, implements. 3. *vulg.* phallus.

yarakla=ʳ ياراقلامق *archaic* /ı/ 1. to equip with arms, provisions or necessaries. 2. to prepare. **—n**= *pass.*

yarala=ʳ يارا ، ياره لامق /ı/ 1. to wound. 2. to hit (a ship with a shell). **—n**= *pass.* **—t**= /ı, a/ *caus. of* **yarala**=.

yaralı يارالى ، يارە لى 1. wounded. 2. sore, ulcerated. 3. marked, notched.

yaramaz ياراماز 1. useless; good-for-nothing. 2. naughty. **—a odun!** For a good-for-nothing, the cudgel (should be ready).

yaramazlıkᵗⁱ يارامازلق 1. uselessness. 2. naughtiness. 3. rudeness, bad behavior.

yârân 1 (— —) ياران P *lrnd.*, *pl. of* **yâr 1**, friends; lovers. **—ı bâsafâ** friends of enjoyment and pleasure. **— gayreti** favoritism. **—ı safâ** pleasure companions.

yaran=ʳ **2** يارنمق /a/ 1. to make oneself useful; to offer one's services. 2. to curry favor; to pay polite but insincere attention.

yarane (— — .) يارانه P *lrnd.* special to a loving friend; friendly; affectionate.

yaranış, yaranma يارانش ، يارانمه 1. a currying favor. 2. polite attention.

yarar يارار 1. useful. 2. capable; brave. 3. use; advantage. **—lı** useful. **—lık** 1. usefulness, capability. 2. courage.

yarasa ياراسا ، يار صه ، يارسه bat, *zool.*, *Vespertilio*, etc. **—lar** *neol.* bats, *zool.*, *Chiroptera.*

yaraş=ʳ يارشمق ، يراشمق /a/ 1. to be suitable; to be pleasing in appearance. 2. to harmonize, to go well with.

yaraşıkᵗⁱ يارشيق ، يراشيق 1. pleasing appearance; suitability. 2. elegance. **— almaz** It is unsuitable. **—lı** suitable; pleasing in appearance; elegant. **—lık** elegance, suitability. **—sız** unsuitable; unpleasing.

yaraştır=ʳ ياراشديرمه ، يراشديرمه /ı, a/ to make suit; to deem suitable; invent (a lie).

yarat=ʳ ياراتمق /ı/ to create; to give existence to.

yaratan ياراتان *same as* **yaradan**.

yaratıcı ياراتجى creative; creating.

yaratıkᵗⁱ *neol.* creature.

yaratıl=ʳ ياراتلمق *pass. of* **yarat**=.

yaratılış ياراتلش *same as* **yaradılış**.

yaratma ياراتمه *verbal n. of* **yarat**=.

yarbay *neol.* lieutenant colonel.

yarda (ˊ.) ياردە It yard (measure).

yardakᵗⁱ ياردق ، يارداق ، چ assistant, mate; accomplice.

yardakçı ياردقچى helper; accomplice. **—lık** aid; complicity.

yardım ياردم help, aid, assistance. **— et**= /a/ to help, to succor. **—ına yetiş**= /ın/ to come to the aid of.

yardımcı ياردمجى 1. helper, assistant. 2. auxiliary. **— fiil** auxiliary verb. **— hücreler** *bot.*, *synergidae*. **— kuvvet** *mil.* auxiliaries; reinforcement. **—sız** without a helper; without assistance.

yardımlaş=ʳ ياردملشمق to help one another. **—ma** *verbal n.*

yardır=ʳ ياردرمق ، يارديرمه /ı, a/ *caus. of* **yar**= 5.

yare (— .) ياره *poet.*, *same as* **yara 1**.

yaren (—.) يارن *var. of* **yârân 1.** —**lik** friendly conversation or joking.

yarga (´.) يارغا *Sl prov.* one-year-old chicken.

yargı يارغو يارغى 1. *neol.* lawsuit. 2. *archaic* decision in a court of law. 3. *archaic* a splitting; split, fragment. — **yeri** law court. —**cı** 1. litigant. 2. judge, arbitrator.

yargıç[cı] *neol.* judge.

yargıla=ʳ *neol., law* /ı/ to hear a case; to try; to judge.

Yargıtay *neol.* Supreme Court of Appeal.

yarı يارى half. — **beline kadar** to the waist. —**da bırak**= /ı/ to discontinue, to interrupt. — **buçuk***. — **çekili bayrak** half-masted flag. — **deli** half-crazy; unbalanced. — **gece***. — **gölge** *astr.* penumbra. — **inme** *path.* hemiplegy. —**da kal**= to be left half finished, to be broken off in the middle. — **yarıya** halfway; on a fifty-fifty basis, taking equal shares. — **yolda** on the way, before we arrived. — **yolda bırak**= /ı/ to leave half finished; to give up before completion.

yarıbuçuk[tu] يارى بوچوق 1. small; insufficient. 2. only about half. — **askerle** with only a handful of soldiers.

yarıcı 1 يارجى 1. who splits, wood-chopper. 2. who breaks through the enemy's line.

yarıcı 2 يارجى one who works another's land for half the income, share-cropper.

yarıgece يارى گجه midnight; at midnight.

yarık[kı] يارق يارك 1. split, cracked, cleft. 2. crack, fissure.

yarıl=ır يارلمق *pass. of* **yar**= 4.

yarıla=ʳ يارلامق /ı/ 1. to be halfway through (job or period). 2. to be halfway to (a place). —**n**= *pass.* —**t**= /ı, a/ *caus. of* **yarıla**=.

yarım يارم half. —**da** at half past twelve. — **ada***. — **adam** invalid, cripple. — **ağızla** not seriously meant (as of an invitation). — **akıl** mentally weak. — **ay** half-moon, crescent. — **tabya** *fort.* demilune lunette. — **baş ağrısı** migraine. — **elma gönül alma** *proverb* A very small kindness may win a heart. — **kan** halfbreed. — **kârgir** half masonry and half timber. — **küre** hemisphere. — **kürk** fur jacket. — **pabuç**, — **pabuçlu** 1. pauper; vagabond. 2. prostitute. — **porsiyon** *slang* small, feeble (person). — **saat** half an hour. — **sağ** *mil.* half-right. — **setre** jacket. — **sol** *mil.* half-left. — **uyku** state of half-sleep. — **yamalak** 1. perfunctory; only half (done). 2. incompletely.

yarımada يارم آطه peninsula.

yarımca يارمجه *path.* migraine, hemicrania.

yarımcı يارمجى *same as* **yarıcı 2**.

yarımla=ʳ يارملامق /ı/ 1. to halve. 2. to half-finish. 3. to be half through. —**n**= *pass.* —**t**= /ı, a/ *caus. of* **yarımla**=.

yarımlık[ğı] يارملق 1. half-piaster piece. 2. *prov.* hernia, rupture.

yarımşar يارمشار a half each.

yarın (´.) يارن يارين tomorrow; the morrow. — **değil öbür gün** the day after tomorrow. —**cı** procrastinator.

yarındası يارنداسى *prov.* next day.

yarınki[nı] يارنكى of tomorrow.

yarış 1 يارش race, competition.

yarış 2 يارش *verbal n. of* **yar**= 5.

yarış=ʳ 3 يارشمق to race; to compete.

yarışçı يارشجى competitor.

yarışma يارشمه competition.

yarıştır=ır يارشدرمق /ı/ *caus. of* **yarış**= 3.

yârî (— —) يارى P *lrnd.* 1. friendship, intimacy. 2. assistance, aid; kindness; favor. — **kıl**= /a/ *archaic* to help; to show mercy. —**ci** *archaic* helper.

yariger (— — .) ياريگر P *lrnd.* helper, ally, assistant.

yarlığ يارليغ *archaic* command, edict; decree.

yarlığa=ʳ يارليغامق *archaic* to pardon sins, to show mercy (God). —**n**= *pass.*

yarlık[ğı] 1 يارلق *same as* **yarlığ**.

yarlık[ğı] 2 (—.) يارلق *archaic* charity, kindness; aid.

yarlık[ğı] 3 يارلق place of cliffs or precipices.

yarma يارمه 1. act of splitting. 2. cleft, fissure. 3. *mil.* breakthrough. 4. railway cutting. 5. large coarse man. 6. coarsely ground (wheat etc.). — **gibi** hugely built (person). — **muharebesi** battle aiming at a breakthrough. — **şeftali** freestone peach.

yarmala=ʳ يارمه لامق /ı/ to cut or tear in halves lengthwise.

yarmend (—.) يارمند P *lrnd.* 1. friendly. 2. helpful, useful. —**î** (—.—) P aid, assistance.

yarnâme (— — .) يارنامه P *lrnd.* one's record of good deeds (kept by the recording angels); good act, good name.

yarpuz يارپوز pennyroyal, *bot.*, Mentha Pulegium.

yarres (—.) يارس P *lrnd.* who comes to the relief of another; an aid or help.

yarsız يارسز friendless. —**lık** friendlessness.

yas 1 ياس [ye's] mourning (for the dead). — **tut**= to be in mourning.

yas=ar 2 ياصمق *archaic* 1. to flatten; to level. 2. to slacken.

yasa 1 ياسا *archaic, neol.* law; code of laws.

yasa=ʳ 2 ياساماق *archaic* 1. to make laws; to govern, to control. 2. to arrange, to put straight. 3. to prepare or get ready; to make.

yasakᵗⁱ
1. prohibition; interdict. 2. forbidden, prohibited. 3. *archaic* law, code of laws. **—ı Cengiz** *lrnd.* the code of laws of Jinghiz Khan. **— çıkar=** to publish an edict of prohibition. **— et=** /ı/ to forbid. **— sav=** 1. to serve in case of need; to be better than nothing. 2. to do something merely to comply with a rule.

yasakçı ياساقجى *Ott. hist.* a man who went in front to clear the way for a great person; guard for an ambassador or consul.

yasakla=ʳ ياساقله /ı/ to prohibit; to deprive of. **—n=** *pass.*

yasakname (..—.) ياساقنامه *Ott. hist.* code of laws.

yasama ياسامه 1. *verbal n. of* **yasa=** 2. 2. *law* legislation. **—lı** legislative.

yasavul ياساول يساول يصاول ياصاول 1. *Ott. hist.* official charged with the arrangement of state processions. 2. *archaic* guard.

yasem (—.), **yasemen** (—..) ياسمن P *lrnd., same as* **yasemin.**

yasemin (—.—) ياسمين P jasemin, *bot., Jasminum officinale.*

Yasin (——) ياسين A the thirty-sixth sura of the Quran.

yasla=ʳ ياصله /ı, a/ to support; to bolster up. **—n=** /a/ to lean against something; to support oneself.

yaslı ياسلى in mourning.

yasmıkᵗⁱ ياصمق *prov.* lentil.

yassı 1 ياصى flat and wide. **— burunlu** flat-nosed. **— kadayıf** small cakes of batter soaked in syrup. **— kulaklı** flat-eared.

yassı 2 ياصى *same as* **yatsı.**

yassıl=ʳ, **yassılan=**ʳ, **yassılaş=**ʳ ياصيلن ياصيلش to become flat and wide.

yassılıkᵗⁱ ياصيلق flatness; broadness of surface.

yassılt=ʳ ياصيلت /ı/ to flatten; to make flat and wide.

yasta=ʳ ياصده archaic, *same as* **yasla=.** **—n=** *same as* **yaslan=.**

yastağaçᶜⁱ ياصداغاج bream. 2. *same as* **yastığaç.**

yastığaçᶜⁱ ياصديغاج *prov.* board for rolling out pastry, bread-board.

yastıkᵗⁱ ياصدق 1. pillow, bolster; cushion. 2. pad. 3. nursery bed (garden). 4. ship or boat's fender. **bir —a baş koy=** to get married. **— dik=** to sow seed in a bed. **— kılıfı** pillowcase. **bir —ta koca=** to have a long married life. **— toprağı** fine, prepared earth for a seed bed. **— yüzü** pillowcase.

yastım ياصدم *prov.* flat; squat; flat-nosed. **—lık** flatness, squatness.

ya'sûb (.—) يعسوب A *lrnd.* 1. queen bee. 2. prince, chief, noble.

Ya'sûb-ül-mü'minin (.—...—) يعسوب المؤمنين A the Caliph Ali.

yaş 1 ياش 1. wet; damp, moist. 2. fresh. 3. wetness, moisture. 4. tears. 5. *slang* difficult, fearful, bad (person, place or thing). **— akıt=** to shed tears. **—a bastır=** /ı/ to deceive, cheat. **—lara boğul=** to have a flow of tears. **— dök=** to shed tears. **—ını içine akıt=** to hide one's grief. **— incir** fresh fig. **— odun** green wood. **— tahtaya bas=** to be cheated, to be taken in.

yaş 2 ياش age, years (of a person). **—ında** 1. in his ......th year, *e. g.,* **on yaşında** in his tenth year, nine years old. 2. ... years old, *e. g.,* **on yaşında** ten years old. **—ını al=** to advance in age. **— bastı** Old age has come. **—ını başını almış** of mature years. **—ına başına bakmadan** regardless of his age. **bir —ıma daha girdim!** I am astonished! I am older and wiser; I have learnt something from this. **— günü** birthday. **— haddi** age limit; retirement age. **—ı ne başı ne** He is too young.

Yaş 3 ياش *geog.* Jassy (in Rumania).

yaşa=ʳ ياشامق 1. to live; to know how to live. 2. to thrive, prosper. **—!** Long live! **—dık** We are in luck. **—sın!** Long live! Long may he live! **—nmış** true to life.

yaşar=ʳ ياشارمق 1. to become wet. 2. to become fresh. **—t=** /ı/ *caus.*

yaşat=ʳ ياشاتمق /ı/ 1. *caus. of* **yaşa=.** 2. to keep alive, to let prosper. **—ıl=** *pass. of* **yaşat=.**

yaşayış ياشايش manner of living; life; livelihood.

yaşdaş ياشداش of the same age.

yaşın 1 ياشن *archaic* secret. **— yaşın** secretly.

yaşın=ʳ **2** ياشنمق *archaic* to be hidden, covered or veiled.

yaşıt ياشيت of the same age.

yaşlan=ʳ ياشلنمق to grow old. **—dır=** /ı/ *caus.*

yaşlı 1 ياشلى wet; suffused with tears.

yaşlı 2 ياشلى aged; advanced in years. **— başlı** of mature years. **—ca** getting on in years; oldish.

yaşlıkᵗⁱ ياشلق 1. wetness. 2. damp weather. 3. greenness, juiciness.

yaşlılıkᵗⁱ ياشليلق old age; advanced years.

yaşmakᵗⁱ ياشماق 1. veil (worn by Oriental women). 2. curtain or screen for a fireplace.

yaşmakla=ʳ ياشمقلامق /ı/ to veil. **—n=** to be veiled, to put on the veil; to become nubile.

yaşmaklı ياشمقلى 1. veiled. 2. nubile.

yaşmaklıkᵗⁱ ياشمقلق material suitable for a yaşmak.

yaşmaksız ياشمقسز without a veil; unveiled. **— gez=** to go about unveiled.

yaştaş ياشداش *same as* **yaşdaş.**

yat 1 يا طا ات *archaic* armor; arms, weapons. **— yarak** arms and all necessaries.
yat 2 يات yacht.
yat 3 يات *archaic, same as* **yad 2.**
yat 4 يات *archaic* 1. method; manner. 2. skill, dexterity.
yat=ᵗʳ **5** ياتمق 1. to lie down; to go to bed; to be in bed. 2. to pass the night. 3. to be bedridden. 4. to become flat. 5. to lie at anchor (ship). 6. to stay in prison. 7. /a/ to lie on; to lean towards; to agree to. 8. *archaic, following another verb* to continue doing, *e. g.*, **koşup yat=** to go on running. **— borusu** *mil.* taps.
yatağan ياتاغان heavy curved knife, yataghan.
yatakᵗⁱ ياتاق 1. bed; couch; mattress. 2. lair. 3. anchorage, berth. 4. bearing (of a shaft). 5. chamber (of a gun). 6. receiver of stolen goods. 7. screen (for illicit enterprise). 8. place of congregation; mart. 9. river bed; ore bed. 10. space between the hind legs of a horse. **— bağı** large square of cloth in which to tie up bed and bedding. **— çarşafı** bed sheet. **—lar çek=** /ı/ to want to go to bed, to be very tired. **—lara döşen=** to be bedridden. **—a düş=** to take to one's bed. **—ı geniş** wide in the tread of the hind legs (horse). **—a gir=** to go to bed. **— liman** big harbor (for a fleet). **— odası** bedroom. **— sal=**, **— ser=** *prov.* to spread a bed. **— takımı** complete set of bedding. **—a yat=** 1. to go to bed. 2. to take to bed. **— yorgan yat=** to be sick in bed.
yatakhane (..—.) ياتاقخانه dormitory.
yataklı ياتاقلى 1. furnished with a bed; having beds. 2. deep-channeled (river). **— bıyık** trained mustache. **— vagon** wagon-lit, sleeping-car, sleeper.
yataklıkᵗⁱ ياتاقلق 1. bedstead; place for storing beds. 2. a being a receiver of stolen goods. 3. for (so many) beds. **— hasta** ill enough to have to go to bed. **— kadın** only fit to go to bed with (said contemptuously of a woman).
yatalakᵗⁱ ياتالاق bedridden.
yatay *neol.* horizontal; horizontal line.
yatı ياتى 1. a lying down; a going to bed. 2. place where one rests; halting place. **— mektebi** boarding school.
yatıkᵗⁱ ياتيق 1. leaning to one side. 2. gently rising (ground). 3. *prov.* flat bottle; very squat and shallow bottle or vessel. **— yollu top** gun with a flat trajectory.
yatılı ياتيلى 1. boarding (school). 2. boarder (student). **— mektep** boarding school.
yatım ياتيم 1. a lying down, leaning, or lying at anchor. 2. compliance, yielding.
yatımlı ياتيملى 1. level, smooth. 2. leaning. 3. compliant.

yatır 1 ياتور *prov.* 1. place where a saint is buried. 2. saint. **— çeşme** saint's tomb with a fountain.
yatır=ᵗʳ **2** ياتورمق /ı, a/ 1. to lay something down; to fell; to floor; to strike down. 2. to put to bed. 3. to deposit (in a bank); to invest. 4. to cause to heel over (ship).
yatırım *neol.* deposit; investment.
yatırma ياتورما 1. *verbal n. of* **yatır=** 2. 2. laid down. 3. deposited, laid away. **— mağazası** depot for commercial goods, warehouse. **— paraçol** 1. breast-hook in a ship's timbers. 2. horizontal knee to a ship's deck-beam.
yatısız ياتيسز day student (at a school); not accepting boarders (school).
yatış 1 ياتيش *verbal n. of* **yat=** 5.
yatış=ᵗʳ **2** ياتيشمق to calm down; to become quiet.
yatışıkᵗⁱ ياتيشيق calmed, calm; tranquil, submissive.
yatıştır=ᵗʳ ياتيشديرمق /ı/ to calm, to tranquilize.
yatkı ياتقى *archaic* crease, fold.
yatkın ياتقين 1. laid down; leaning to one side, inclined. 2. that has lain too long, deteriorated, stale. 3. well broken in (horse). 4. accustomed (hand). **—lık** a being accustomed; familiarity; habit.
yatlı ياتلى archaic 1. armed. 2. strange; stranger; alien. 3. inimical; noxious. 4. miserable; wretched; bad.
yatma ياتمه *verbal n. of* **yat=** 5.
yatsı ياتسى prayer said by Muslims two hours after sunset. **— namazı** *same as* **yatsı**. **—dan sonra ezan oku=** to do something too late or at an unsuitable moment.
Yaukᵏᵘ (. —) يعوث *A lrnd., name of an ancient Arabian idol.*
yava ياوه *archaic* 1. strange; stranger. 2. hostile; enemy. 3. lost; astray. 4. wild (beast).
yavan ياوان 1. plain, dry (food without fat or butter); tasteless, insipid. 2. unpleasant, disagreeable. **— çorba** plain rice soup, boiled rice.
yavanla=ᵗʳ ياوانلمق *slang* to be flat broke.
yavanlaş=ᵗʳ ياوانلاشمق to become tasteless or insipid.
yavanlıkᵗⁱ ياوانلق 1. a being dry or without fat or oil; insipidness. 2. disagreeableness.
yavaş ياواش 1. slow. 2. gentle, mild; soft (sound). 3. docile. **—!** Watch out! Be careful! **— gel** Steady; don't brag. **— konuş=** to talk in a low voice. **— söyle=** 1. to speak in a low voice. 2. to speak slowly. **— tütün** mild tobacco. **— yavaş** slowly, gradually. **— yürü=** to walk slowly; to walk quietly.

yavaşa یاواشه یواش [lâvaşa] *prov.* blacksmith's barnacles.

yavaşca, yavaşcacıkᵗⁱ (..'..) یاواشجهٖ یواشجهٖ یواشجن gently, slowly.

yavaşı=ʳ یاواشیمق *archaic* to become slow, mild, gentle, submissive. —t= /I/ *caus.*

yavaşla=ʳ یاواشلامق یواشلمق 1. to become slow or mild; to slow down. 2. to lose force (rain). —t= /I/ *caus.*

yavaşlıkᵗⁱ یاواشلق یواشلق slowness; gentleness; mildness.

yavaştır=ʳ یاواشدیرمق *archaic* /I/ 1. to slow down. 2. to render soft or mild. 3. to train or acclimatize.

yave (—.) یاوه P 1. foolish talk. 2. silly, commonplace. 3. *lrnd.* lost; ruined. 4. *lrnd.* worthless, futile. — **söyle**= 1. to talk nonsense. 2. to talk in vain.

yaveci یاوه جی *Ott. hist.* official charged with the apprehension of runaway slaves.

yavegi (—.—) یاوه گی P *lrnd.* 1. worthlessness. 2. plundering.

yavegû (—.—) یاوه گو P *lrnd.* who babbles nonsense; idle or silly talker.

yâvend (—.) یاوند P *lrnd.* king, monarch. **—ân** (—.—) P *pl.*

yaver (—.) یاور P 1. helping; helper. 2. assistant; aide-de-camp. **—i ekrem** general of the highest degree in the Palace. **—i fahrî** honorary aide-de-camp to the Sultan. **—i harb** aide-de-camp. **—ân** (—.—) P *pl.* **—î** (—.—) P 1. help; favor. 2. functions of an aide-de-camp. **—lik** status and duties of an aide-de-camp.

yavesenc (—..) یاوه سنج P *lrnd.*, same as yavegû.

yavetaz (—.—) یاوه تاز P *lrnd.* 1. who runs about uselessly; idle, worthless person. 2. who babbles nonsense.

yavı یاوی [yave] *archaic* 1. lost; astray. 2. vain, worthless. — **kıl**= to lose.

yavlakᵗⁱ یاولاق *archaic* much.

yavru یاورو 1. the young (of an animal or bird). 2. one's child; *affectionate term for any child*. 3. cub, chick. 4. *school slang* small and well behaved schoolboy or girl. **—m!** My child! My darling! **— ağzı** light rose color. **— at**= to have an abortion (animal). **— çıkar**= to hatch out chicks (bird).

yavrucakᵗⁱ یاوروجق poor little child; poor little dear.

yavrucukᵗᵘ یاوروجك little one; little darling.

yavrula=ʳ یاورولامق to bring forth young. **—t**= /I/ *caus.*

yavrulu یاورولی 1. with young. 2. with a wicket in it (gate).

yavsı یاوسی 1. *prov.* tick; horsefly. 2. *archaic* somewhat strange, wild or savage.

yavşakᵗⁱ یاوشاق *prov.* nit, nits (of lice).

yavşan یاوشان 1. *archaic* thorny, spiny. 2. wormwood. **— ağacı** shrubby wormwood, *bot.*, *Artemisia absinthium*. **— otu** wormwood of Judea, *bot.*, *Artemisia Judaiea;* water pumpernel, *bot.*, *Veronica Beccabunga*.

yavukᵗᵘ یاووق یاوق *prov.* 1. token of betrothal; betrothal. 2. near. 3. lost; astray.

yavukla=ʳ یاووقلامق /I, a/ to give a token of betrothal. **—n**= to become engaged (to).

yavuklu یاووقلی 1. betrothed, engaged. 2. beloved.

yavuz یاووز یاوز 1. *prov.* stern, ferocious; inflexible. 2. good; excellent; efficient; resolute. **— göz** *archaic* evil eye. **— hırsız ev sahibini bastırır** A bold thief will bluff the owner of the house, *said of one who is in the wrong but who carries the day by bluff*. **Y— Selim** *Ott. hist.* Sultan Selim I.

yavuzlukᵗᵘ یاووزلوق 1. sternness, inflexibility; cruelty. 2. *prov.* goodness, excellence, good nature.

yay 1 یای 1. bow (of an archer); bow for playing a stringed instrument. 2. anything shaped or curved like a bow. 3. simple straight or curved spring. 4. *astr.* the constellation Sagittarius. **— bağrı** inner side of a bow. **— boşalt**= 1. to unstring a bow. 2. to discharge an arrow. **— burcu** the zodiacal sign Sagittarius. **— burcu vakti** period of a month before the winter solstice. **—a çile geçir**= to put a string to a bow. **— doldur**= 1. to bend an archery bow. 2. to draw back or set a spring. **— kas**= to stretch a bow to the utmost. **— kaşlı** having arched eyebrows. **— kirişi** string of a bow. **— kur**= to string or bend a bow. **—a küşad ver**= to break in an archery bow, to use it gently for a time when new. **— sırtı** the back of a bow. **— ucu** horn of a bow. **—lar üstü** screen and fittings over the headrails on each side of a ship's head.

yay=ᵃʳ **2** یایمق /I/ 1. to spread, to scatter. 2. to disseminate. 3. to publish. 4. to churn. 5. to lead to pasture (cattle).

yay 3 یای *archaic* summer.

yaya یایا 1. on foot; pedestrian. 2. of little account; without skill. 3. *Ott. hist.* foot soldier; regiment of foot soldiers. **— başı** *Ott. hist.* head of the enfeoffed foot soldiers of a province. **— bırak**= /I/ to be superior (to); to leave behind. **— kal**= 1. to be compelled to go on foot (for want of horse or vehicle). 2. to be in a difficult situation, to get oneself into a mess. **— kaldın tatar ağası!** Now you are stranded. You are in trouble. You are on the wrong track. **— kaldırımı** sidewalk. **— seğirdimi** banquette of a fortification. **— yolu** foot path; sidewalk.

yayak¹ یایاق یایا بایە archaic on foot, pedestrian.

yayan یایان same as yaya. — **yapıldak** prov. barefooted and traveling on foot.

yaydır=ᵗʳ یایدرمق /ı, a/ caus. of **yay**= 2.

yaygara یایغارە shout; outcry, clamor. —**yı bas**=, —**yı kopar**= to raise an outcry; to make a great to-do about nothing. —**cı** noisy; brawling, noisy person, brawler; crybaby; loud (in taste).

yaygı یایغی something spread out as a covering; blanket for spreading out on the ground to sit on.

yaygın یایغین 1. widespread. 2. phil. diffused.

yayıkᵗ¹ 1 یایق spread out; broad, wide. — **yayık** dawdling; drawling one's words.

yayıkᵗ¹ 2 یایق churn. — **yağı** churned butter. — **yay**= to make butter.

yayıl=ᵗʳ یایلمق 1. pass. of **yay**= 2. 2. to spread; to spread out. —**ma** verbal n.

yayım neol. publication. —**la**= to publish.

yayın 1 neol. 1. distribution; diffusion. 2. publication.

yayın 2 یایین sheatfish, zool., Silurus glanis.

yayın=ᵗʳ 3 یاینمق prov. 1. to fly back, to fly to one side, to rebound. 2. to avert one's eyes from a terrible object. —**dır**= /ı/ caus.

yayınevi یاین اوی publishing house.

yayka=ᵗ یایقامق prov., same as **yıka**=.

yayla 1 (.´.) یایلە یایلا 1. high plateau. 2. summer camping ground. — **buzu** natural block ice (from a glacier). — **çiçeği** Mexican tea, wormseed, bot., Chenopodium ambrosioides. — **kuşu** brown owl, zool., Surnium aluco.

yayla=ʳ 2 یایلامق 1. to pass the summer in the mountains. 2. to graze.

yayla=ᵗ 3 یایلامق /ı/ to apply a bow or spring; to furnish with a bow or spring.

yaylakᵗ¹ یایلاق same as yayla 1. — **resmi** Ott. hist. tax collected on flocks when moving to summer pastures.

yaylakıye یایلاقیە rent paid for a **yaylak**.

yaylan=ᵗʳ یایلانمق 1. to become furnished with a bow or spring. 2. to rock as though on a spring. 3. slang to go away. —**dır**= /ı/ caus.

yaylı یایلی 1. armed with a bow. 2. having springs. 3. carriage with springs. — **tambur** a kind of tambur played with a bow.

yaylım یایلیم 1. a spreading or stretching. 2. volley. — **ateş** volley; drum-fire.

yayma یایمە 1. verbal n. of **yay**= 2. 2. small trader's stall. —**cı** small trader (whose goods are spread out on a tray).

yayvan یایوان 1. broad; spreading out. 2. slack. — **burunlu** broad-nosed. — **yayvan gül**= to laugh uproariously. — **yayvan konuş**= to drawl. —**lık** broadness.

yaz 1 یاز 1. summer. 2. archaic spring. —**a çık**= to reach the summer season. — **kış** in summer and winter.

yaz=ᵃʳ 2 یازمق 1. to write; to inscribe. 2. to register; to enroll (for military service). 3. to adorn, embellish (the face of a bride). 4. as an auxiliary verb =**a yaz**= cf. =**ayaz**= 2. 5. prov. to spread. —**ıp boz**= /ı/ 1. to give an order and then countermand it. 2. to be capricious. — **boz tahtası** school slate. —**ıp çiz**= /ı/ to set down in writing.

yazar neol. writer.

yazdeh (—.) یازدە P lrnd. eleven. —**üm** (—..) P eleventh.

yazdır=ᵗʳ یازدیرمق /ı, a/ caus. of **yaz**= 2. —**ıl**= pass. —**t**= /ı, a/ caus. of **yazdır**=. —**tıl**= pass.

yazgı neol., phil. predestination.

yazı 1 یازی 1. writing; inscription. 2. handwriting; calligraphy. 3. manuscript. 4. written article. 5. destiny, decree of Providence. —**yı çıkar**= to be able to decipher handwriting. — **dili** literary language. —**ya dök**= /ı/ to express in writing. —**ya gelme**= not to be fit for writing down. — **makinası** typewriter. — **odası** office, writing room. —**yı sök**= same as yazıyı çıkar=. — **tahtası** blackboard. — **taşı** slate. — **mı tura mı?** Heads or tails?

yazı 2 یازی prov. plain; flat place.

yazıcı یازیجی scribe, professional writer of letters and petitions; clerk. —**lık** clerkship.

yazıhane (..—.) یازیخانە 1. office. 2. writing table, desk.

yazıkᵗ¹ یازق یازیق 1. a pity; a shame. 2. Deplorable! What a pity! What a shame! 3. archaic providence, judgment; calamity. 4. archaic sin, guilt. —**ı gel**= prov. /a/ to pity, to be sorry (for). — **oldu** It was a pity that this happened. —**lar olsun!** Shame! — **sana!** 1. Shame on you! 2. I pity you.

yazıklan=ᵗʳ یازقلانمق archaic to pity; to be sorry for.

yazıklı یازقلی archaic sinner, guilty.

yazıksız یازقسیز archaic innocent.

yazıl=ᵗʳ یازیلمق pass. of **yaz**= 2. —**an bozulmaz** What is decreed cannot be changed.

yazılı یازیلی 1. written; inscribed, registered. 2. decreed by Fate, destined. — **hukuk** statute law. — **orkinos** bluefin tuna, zool., Thunnus thynnina. — **şekil** law written form.

yazılış یازیلیش method of writing; spelling.

yazın (.´.) یازین in summer; during the summer.

yazış 1 یازیش manner of writing.

yazış=ᵣ 2 باىشمك /la/ to write to one another; to correspond. **—ma** *neol.* correspondence. **—tır=** /ı, a/ *caus.* of **yazış=**.

yazıt *neol.* inscription.

yazla=ʳ بازلامق 1. to pass the summer in a place. 2. to become summery, to warm up (weather). **—t=** /ı/ *caus.*

yazlı یازلی باغلی *only in* **yazlı kışlı**, summer and winter alike.

yazlıkᵗⁱ یازلیق 1. suitable for the summer. 2. summer clothing. 3. rent for the summer.

yazma یازما 1. *verbal n. of* **yaz=** 2. 2. written, manuscript. 3. hand painted or hand printed kerchief or bedspread. 4. hand painted.

yazmacı یازمه جی 1. dealer in hand painted kerchiefs, etc. 2. one who paints or prints fine muslin. **—lık** profession of a **yazmacı**.

-ydı 1 یدی *cf.* **-dı 1**.

=ydı 2 یدی *cf.* **=dı 2**.

ye 1 ی *same as* **ya 1**.

ye=ʳ 2 یمك یماك /ı/ 1. to eat. 2. to feed. 3. to consume. 4. to dissipate. 5. to suffer (affliction, beating, etc.). 6. to take (bribe). 7. to corrode. 8. *slang* to kill; to smash. **—mez** *slang* cunning; he can't be deceived. **—yip bitir=** /ı/ to consume utterly, to exhaust. **—yip iç=** to eat and drink. **—me de yanında yat** Don't eat it, rather lie beside it, *said of a delicious food almost too good to touch*. **—yip yat=** to keep on eating; to live lazily.

yebab (.—) یباب A *lrnd.* ruined, devastated.

yebruh (.—) یبروح A *lrnd.* mandrake, *bot.*, *Mandragora officinarum*.

yebruhussanem (.—...) یبروح الصنم A *same as* **yebruh**.

yebs یبس A *lrnd.* a being or becoming dry; dryness.

Ye'cuc (.—) یاجوج A Gog. **— ve Me'cuc** 1. *Bib.* Gog and Magog. 2. *name of a dwarf people supposed to appear at the Day of Judgment*.

yed 1 ید A *lrnd.* 1. hand. 2. possession. 3. assistance, favor. 4. power; authority. **—i adil** depositary, trustee. **—i beyza** 1. the white hand of Moses (Exodus IV: 6 and Quran VII: 105); miracle. 2. favor, benefit or kindness freely and heartily bestowed. **—i emin** *same as* **yedi adil**. **—i kudret** the hand of power, Providence. **—i müeyyed** sustained power (divine). **—i tasarruf** possession, power of disposal. **—i tûlâ** power; capability.

yed=ᵉʳ 2 یدمك /ı/ to lead or tow with a rope.

yedbeyed, yeden biyed ید بید یداً بید A *lrnd.* from hand to hand, direct.

yede یده *archaic* piece of jade used in rain magic. **— taşı** jade.

yedekᵗⁱ یدك 1. halter. 2. tow-rope. 3. led animal; reserve horse. 4. reserve; substitute. 5. spare part. 6. spare, in reserve. **—e al=** /ı/ 1. to take in tow, to tow. 2. to take as reserve (horse). **— at** led horse. **—e bin=** to mount one's spare horse. **— çek=**, **—e çek=**, **—te çek=** /ı/ *same as* **yedeğe al=**. **— demir** spare anchor. **—e gel=** to be quiet and tractable when led (horse). **— ipi** tow rope. **— keşan** *Ott. hist.* thirty servants in charge of the Sultan's spare horses. **— parça** spare part. **— subay** supplementary officer, reserve conscript officer. **—e ver=** /ı/ to have (a horse) led, to have (a boat) towed.

yedekçi یدکچی man who leads a spare horse; man who tows a boat. **— yolu** towpath.

yedekli یدکلی 1. on a lead; in tow. 2. having a spare horse. 3. provided with a spare part.

yedeklikᵗⁱ یدکلك serving as a reserve or spare part.

yedeyn یدین A *lrnd.* two hands.

yedi یدی seven. **Y—ler** the Seven Sleepers. **Y— Adalar** the Ionian Islands. **— başlı**, **— başlı yılan** 1. seven-headed hydra. 2. venemous woman; dangerous man. **— buçuk** *name of a card game*. **— canlı** having seven lives, invincible. **— düvel** *colloq.* all the Western world. **— iklim dört bucak** everywhere. **Y— kardeş** *prov.* Big Dipper, Great Bear. **— karındaş** *archaic* succession of great billows. **— kubbeli hamam kur=** to build castles in the air. **Y— Kule** Castle of the Seven Towers (in Istanbul). **— mahalle** many people. **— parmak** tormentil, *bot.*, *Potentilla Tormentilla*. **— suda yıka=** (lit., to wash in seven waters) to cleanse with extra care. **— veren***. **Y— Yârlar** the seven stars of the Big Dipper. **—sinden yetmişine kadar** everybody.

yediger یدیگر the seven stars in the Big Dipper.

yedil=ᵢʳ یدیلمك *pass. of* **yed=** 2.

yedili یدیلی 1. having seven parts, etc. 2. of seven kurush. 3. the seven (of a suit of cards).

yedilikᵗⁱ یدیلك 1. costing, weighing or measuring seven. 2. *obs.* clothes given to the bride by the bridegroom (to be worn on the seventh day of the marriage).

yedinci یدنجی seventh.

yedir=ᵢʳ یدیرمك /ı, a/ 1. *caus. of* **ye=** 5. 2. to let eat, to give to eat. 3. to feed, to spoon-feed (a child). 4. to let absorb (shortening).

yedirme یدیرمه 1. *verbal n. of* **yedir=**. 2. stop-leak, preparation of hemp, lime and oil (used to make a watertight joint in pipes).

yedirt=ᵢʳ یدیرتمك /ı, a/ 1. *caus. of* **yedir=**. 2. *caus. of* **ye=** 5.

yedişer یدیشر seven each; seven at a time.

yediveren يدى ورن 1. any prolific plant. 2. plant producing several crops a year.
yegâh (. —) يگاه P Or. mus. one of the oldest **makams**. — **perdesi** mus. the note d.
yegân (. —) يگان P lrnd. singly; one by one; individually. — **yegân** one by one.
yegâne (. — .) يگانه P sole, unique. **Y—i A'sâr** (lit., the unique one of all ages) the Prophet Muhammad.
yegânegi (. — . —) يگانگى P lrnd. 1. unity; singleness. 2. union, concord. 3. uniqueness.
yegânegû (. — . —) يگانگو P lrnd. monotheist. —**yân** (. —. ——) P monotheists. —**yî** (. —. ——) P monotheism.
yegânelikᵍⁱ يگانه لك uniqueness; unity.
yeğ يگ archaic better, profitable.
yeğen يگن nephew; niece.
yeğin 1 يگين archaic 1. victorious; active; violent. 2. prov. much.
yeğin⁼ⁱʳ **2** يگينمك prov. to make a strenuous or painful effort in rising. —**dir**⁼ /ı/ caus.
yeğinlikᵍⁱ يگينلك 1. prov. victory; violence. 2. neol., phil. intensity.
yeğni يگنى same as **yeyni**.
yeğrekᵍⁱ يگرك archaic, better, preferable.
yeisʸᵉˢⁱ يأس [ye's] a despairing; despair.
yekᵏⁱ يك P 1. lrnd. one. 2. dice one. — **at yek mızrak** alone; having nobody. — **başına** all alone. — **defa** lrnd. once. — **nazarda** at a single glance; for the first moment. — **ve nim sâz** mus. tuned to tones and half tones, i. e. with strings for a complete chromatic scale. — **yek** one by one, singly. — **zarbdan** at a single stroke, with one blow. — **zerre** in negative sentence in the least, one iota.
yekâheng (. — .) يكآهنگ P lrnd. in unison.
yekâvâz (. — —) يكآواز P lrnd. with one voice; in unison.
yekâviz (. ——) يكآويز P lrnd. a kind of dagger; short, broad sword.
yekâyekᵏⁱ (. — .) يكايك P lrnd. 1. one by one. 2. suddenly; all at once. 3. one opposed to another.
yekbadû (. ——) يكبادو P lrnd. deuce-ace at dice.
yekbâr (. —), **yekbâre** (. — .) يكبار ـ يكباره P lrnd. once; all at once. —**gi** (. — . —) P for once only.
yekberg يكبرگ P lrnd. having only one leaf.
yek-be-yekᵏⁱ يك بيك P lrnd. one by one.
yekcâ (. —) يكجا P lrnd. together, in one place.
yekcan (. — —) يكجان P lrnd. one soul, friend.
yekcihet يكجهت P lrnd. having the same object or direction; unanimous. —**î** (. . . —) P unanimity, concord.
yekçend يكچند P lrnd. a few.
yekçeşm يكچشم P lrnd. 1. one-eyed. 2. purblind; who considers only the exterior.
yekdâne (. — .) يكدانه P lrnd. 1. single-grained; in a single mass. 2. incomparable gem. 3. necklace.
yekdem يكدم P lrnd. 1. one moment; one breath. 2. for an instant.
yekdeme يكدمه P lrnd. momentary.
yekdest يكدست P lrnd. 1. entire; whatever can be lifted with one hand. 2. joining hands, cooperating.
yekdiğer (. — .) يكديگر P lrnd. one another, each other, e. g., **yekdiğerinden ayrılmak zor** It is hard to be separated from one another.
yekdil يكدل P lrnd. of one heart or mind.
yekdile يكدله P lrnd. single-hearted.
yekdilî (. . —) يكدلى P lrnd. concord, accord, unanimity.
yekdu (. —) يكدو P deuce-ace at dice.
yeke 1 يكه Gk tiller of a rudder; yoke of a rudder.
yeke 2 يكه P lrnd. 1. one, singular, unique. 2. at once, together.
yekemel يكامل P lrnd. having the same purpose.
yekendaz (. . —) يكانداز P lrnd. 1. small arrow. 2. perpendicular river bank. 3. equal, even.
yekesbe يكاسبه P lrnd. 1. having but one horse. 2. one who rides alone.
yekesüvar (. . . —) يكسوار P lrnd., same as **yeksüvar**.
yeketaz (. . —) يكتاز P lrnd., same as **yektaz**.
yekin⁼ⁱʳ يكينمك prov., same as **yeğin**⁼ **2**.
yekkalem يكقلم P lrnd. 1. written all by the same hand; written off without a stop. 2. straightway; at one stroke.
yeknasakᵍⁱ يكنسق P 1. in a single row; uniform. 2. monotonous. — **buzlar** ice-floes. —**lık** uniformity; monotony.
yekpare (. — .) يكپاره P of a single piece, all of a piece.
yekran (. —) يكران P lrnd. 1. horse of pure blood. 2. roan horse with white mane and tail.
yekrek يكرك P lrnd. better, preferable.
yekreng P, **yekrenk**ᵍⁱ يكرنگ lrnd. 1. all of one color. 2. of the same mind. 3. constant, faithful.
yekru (. —) يكرو P lrnd. 1. sincere, pure. 2. having one face only.
yekruze (. — .) يكروزه P lrnd. 1. of one day's duration. 2. ephemeral.
yeksale (. — .) يكساله P lrnd. of one year, yearling.

yeksan (. —) كَسان P 1. equal; level; together. 2. *lrnd.* of the same appearance, alike.

yekser يَكسَر P *lrnd.* 1. from end to end. 2. all together, all at once. 3. alone.

yeksere يَكسَرَه P *lrnd.* all together, all at once.

yeksu (. —) يَكسُو P *lrnd.* on one side, to one side; aside.

yeksüvar (. . —) يَكسُوار P *lrnd.* 1. one who rides alone fearing nothing. 2. lone horseman.

yekşebe يَكشَبه P *lrnd.* 1. thing one night old. 2. that lasts only one night.

yekşenbih يَكشَنبه P *lrnd.* Sunday.

yekta (. —) يَكتا P *lrnd.* 1. single, sole, unique; matchless. 2. of a single fold, single; simple.

yektaz (. —) يَكتاز P *lrnd.* 1. that runs once only, that runs alone. 2. who charges the foe singlehanded.

yekten يَكتَن 1. all at once. 2. without any reason.

yekûn (. —) يَكون A total; sum. — **çek=** *colloq.* to end up. — **çek** /a/ Enough of that! Stop talking!

yeküm يَكُم P *lrnd.* first, the first.

yekvücud (. . —) يَكوجود P *lrnd.* united; one (with).

yekzeban (. . —) يَكزبان P *lrnd.* unanimous; with one voice.

yel 1 يَل 1. wind; the wind. 2. flatulence, wind-breaking. 3. rheumatism. — **değirmeni** windmill. — **gibi gel=** to slip in unobserved. — **mumu** a kind of flambeau with several wicks. — **üfürdü sel götürdü** The wind blew and the water carried (the boat); easily and without effort. —**e ver=** /ı/ 1. to scatter to the winds. 2. to destroy. — **yeper git=** to go running like the wind. — **yeperek***. — **yutan***.

yel 2 يَل P *lrnd.* hero; champion; brave.

yel=er **3** يَلَك *prov.* to run swiftly; to run about restlessly. —**ip yepir=** to run along or about.

yelân (. —) يَلان P *lrnd.*, *pl.* of **yel 2**.

yelda (. —) يَلدا P *lrnd.* longest night of the year.

yeldir=ir يَلدر *caus.* of **yel= 3**.

yeldirme يَلدِرمه a kind of light cloak worn by women.

yele يَله mane (of a horse).

yeleğen يَلَغَن *prov.* that naturally runs about much; street dog.

yelekği **1** يَلَك 1. waistcoat, vest. 2. wing-feather, pinion. 3. feather of an arrow.

yelekği **2** يَلَك camel one year old.

yelekle=r يَلَكله /ı/ to feather (an arrow). —**t=** /ı, a/ *caus.*

yelekli يَلَكلی 1. feathered, pinioned. 2. waistcoated.

yeleli يَلَلی maned (animal). — **kurt** hyena.

yelem يَلَم *same as* **yelim 1**.

yelengeçci يَلَنگَچ any tree that sheds its bark naturally.

yelim 1 يَليم mucilage; gum. — **kara** birdlime.

yelim 2 يَليم *archaic* swift movement; a running. — **yeperek** at full speed.

yelimle=r يَليمله /ı/ *archaic* 1. to smear with a sticky substance. 2. to fasten with gum, paste, or glue.

yeliş=ir يَلِش *archaic* to run with one another, to run all together.

yelişikği يَلِشِك *archaic* 1. sticky, glutinous. 2. tiresome, slow in leaving (guest).

yelken يَلكَن sail. — **aç=** to hoist sail. —**i aşağı al=** to unbend a sail. — **bezi** sail cloth. —**i çevir=** *colloq.* to change the subject. —**i fora et=** to loosen a sail before setting it. — **gemisi** sailing vessel. —**leri indir=** to lower sails. — **kürek** 1. with oars and sail. 2. with all speed. —**i mayna et=** to lower a sail with speed. —**leri suya indir=** to humble oneself, to knuckle under.

yelkenci يَلكَنجی 1. sailor (on a sailing vessel). 2. sail maker.

yelkenle=r يَلكَنله 1. to go along under sail. 2. *slang* to go away.

yelkenli يَلكَنلی 1. fitted with sails. 2. sailboat. —**ler** *neol.* sailfishes.

yelkovan يَلكووان 1. minute hand of a watch. 2. weathercock. 3. eaves-board. 4. smoke-cowl. 5. the Manx shearwater, *zool.*, *Puffinus puffinus*. 6. *archaic* irresponsible, unsteady person.

yelle=r يَلله /ı/ 1. to blow upon; to fan. 2. *prov.* to incite, to stir up.

yellen=ir يَللَن 1. to be blown upon. 2. to break wind.

yelli يَللی 1. windy. 2. flatulent. 3. rheumatic. — **mantar** puffball, *bot.*, *Lycoperdon pratense*.

yelloz يَللوز *slang* whore.

yelme يَلمه *prov.* 1. tight-fitting garment (with slits on each side of the skirt). 2. *verbal n.* of **yel= 3**.

yelpaze (. — .) يَلپازه fan. — **kulak** large, spreading ear. — **merdiven** short spiral staircase. — **yeltek** giddy; whose mind is carried away by every novelty.

yelpazele=r يَلپازه‌له /ı/ to fan. —**n=** to fan oneself.

yelpikği يَلپِك *prov.* severe asthma. — **ol=** to suffer an attack of asthma.

yelte=r يَلته *archaic* /ı/ to incite, entice, urge.

yeltekği يَلتَك *archaic* restless; who runs after novelties.

yelteklen=ᴵʳ تسكلنمك to become a frivolous, restless gadabout.

yelten=ᴵʳ ىلتنمك /a/ to strive or dare to do something beyond one's powers or rights.

yelve يلوه 1. woodcock. 2. green finch, *zool.*, *Chloris chloris*.

yelyeperekᵍⁱ يليپرك headlong; hurriedly; in great haste. — **yelken kürek** in a great hurry.

yelyutan يليوتان 1. white-bellied swift, *zool.*, *Apus melba*. 2. a disease in horses.

yem 1 يم 1. fodder; grain, swill. 2. bait. 3. priming of a muzzle-loading gun. — **as=** to hang up a bait. — **baha** *Ott. hist.* fodder tax (tax collected for providing army forage). — **borusu** 1. *mil.* bugle call for horse fodder. 2. empty promise. — **borusunu çal=** to put someone off by empty promises. — **dök=** /a/ 1. to give food or fodder. 2. to make empty promises. — **kestir=** to stop and feed the horses.

yemᵐⁱ **2** يم A *lrnd.* the ocean; sea. —**mi kerem** having kindness as wide as the ocean.

yemam (. —) يمام A *lrnd.* turtledove; wild pigeon.

Yemani (. — —) يمانى A *lrnd.* pertaining to Yemen.

yeme يمه verbal n. of **ye=** 2.

yemekᵍⁱ يمك 1. food; meal. 2. dish or course of food. 3. dinner, supper. — **ağırlaşmış** The food has gone bad. — **borusu** bugle call for food. — **çıkar=** to serve food. — **seç=** to have a preference for certain kinds of food; to be choosy in eating. — **ver=** to give a dinner. — **ye=** to eat, to have one's dinner or supper.

yemekhane يمكخانه dining-hall.

yemekle=ʳ يمكله /ı/ *archaic* to feed, to supply with food.

yemekli يمكلى 1. with food; with a meal. 2. of (so many) courses or dishes.

yemeklikᵍⁱ يمكلك 1. serving as food; edible. 2. thing destined to be food. 3. money for food.

yemeksiz يمكسز without food; without a meal.

Yemen يمن A *geog.* Yemen. — **kahvesi** the true Mocha coffee. — **zafranı** dyer's-weed, dyer's rocket, yellow seed, *bot.*, *Reseda Luteola*.

yemeni يمنى 1. a kind of light shoe (worn by peasants). 2. colored cotton handkerchief, headkerchief. —**li** wearing a **yemeni**.

yemin (. —) يمين A 1. oath. 2. *lrnd.* the right hand; the right side or direction. — **boz=** to violate an oath. — **et=** to swear, to take an oath. — **etsem başım ağrımaz** I can say it with a clear conscience, *meaning that the speaker is telling a half-truth*. — **ettir=** /a/ to administer an oath. — **ver=** /a/ to entreat with oaths. — **ü yesar** right and left, the right hand and the left.

yeminen (. — .) يمينا A *lrnd.* 1. on the right. 2. by oath.

yeminli يمينلى prevented by an oath from doing something.

yemiş يميش 1. fruit; fruits. 2. *prov.* figs. — **ver=** to bear fruit. —**çi** fruit grower or seller.

yemişli يميشلى fruit bearing. — **defne** cherry-laurel, *bot.*, *Prunus Laurocerasus*.

yemişlikᵍⁱ يميشلك fruit garden; fruit store; fruit dish.

yemle=ʳ يملمك /ı/ 1. to bait (a hook or trap). 2. to prime (gun). 3. to entice.

yemleme يملمه 1. *verbal n. of* **yemle=**. 2. bait. 3. a fuse leading to the charge of a mine. 4. alluring word.

yemlikᵍⁱ يملك 1. suitable for food, fodder (for animals). 2. trough, manger. 3. nose-bag. 4. bribe. 5. an easy prey (in gambling).

yemneten (.′ . . .) يمنة A *lrnd.* on the right; to the right. — **ü yesreten** on the right and left.

yemyeşil يمیشیل very green.

yen 1 ين sleeve; cuff. — **kapağı** very long cuff covering the whole hand. — **öp=** *Ott. hist.* to kiss the cuff of the sleeve of the Sultan as an act of homage (the sleeve of the royal mantel being spread along the throne to a distance from the sovereign's person). —**leri sıva=** to tuck up the cuffs; to prepare for work.

yen=ᵉʳ **2** ينمك /ı/ 1. to overcome, to conquer. 2. to be victorious. 3. to win (at a game).

yen=ᴵʳ **3** ينمك *pass. of* **ye=** 2.

yenabiⁱⁱ (. — —) ينابيع A *lrnd.*, *pl. of* **yenbû**.

yenbûᵘᵘ (. —) ينبوع A *lrnd.* spring, source, fountain.

yenç=ᵉʳ ينجمك /ı/ 1. to pull, to tighten; to shake. 2. *archaic* to hurt the feelings of; to injure.

yendir=ᴵʳ يندرمك /ı/ *caus. of* **yen=** 3.

yenge ينگه 1. a woman's sister-in-law or aunt-in-law. 2. elderly woman who helps and attends a bride.

yengeçᵉˡ ينگچ crab. — **gibi** like a crab; awkward, distorted man. — **gözü** 1. crab's eye. 2. medicinal crab's eyes.

yengi ينگى *prov.*, *same as* **yeni**.

yeni ينى 1. new; recent. 2. raw, inexperienced. 2. recently. —**den** over again from the beginning, afresh, anew. **Y— Ahit** *Bib.* the New Testament. — **ay** new moon; new month. — **ayak** just learning to walk. — **bahar***. — **baştan** over again, anew, afresh. **Y— Cami** the New Mosque (in Istanbul). **Y— çeri***. — **çıkma âdet** a new fashion, new fad.

— dünya*. —den yap= /ı/ to do over again. —den yeniye over again, over anew.

yenibahar کنی طاری. allspice.

yenice (...') ینیجہ fairly new or recent. — eleğim, seni nerelere asayım My new sieve, where can I hang you up? *said when one is very fussy over something new.* Y— Hisar *Ott. hist.* an earlier name for Anadolu Hisarı.

Yeniçeri ینیچری 1. *Ott. hist.* Janissary. 2. swashbuckler, bully. — ağası 1. Commander in chief of the Janissaries. 2. a very strict and domineering person. — ocağı the whole corps of the Janissary forces. — traşı *obs.* a rough-and-ready haircut. — ustası lieutenant in a Janissary regiment.

Yeniçerilik[ki] ینیچریلک 1. quality and functions of a Janissary. 2. blustering disturbance of the peace.

yenidünya ینی دنیا 1. *w. cap.* the New World, America. 2. Japanese medlar, loquat, *bot.*, *Eriobotrya japonica*; medlar tree, Dutch medlar, *bot.*, *Mespilus germanica*. 3. glass ball (used as an ornament in a room). — belesanı balsam of copaiba.

yenik[ki] ینیك ینیجك ینیناك place nibbled or gnawed by insects, etc.; moth-eaten place.

yenil=[ir] 1 ینیلمك ینجگلمك ینلك *pass.* of **ye**= 2. —ir yutulur şey değil not to be stomached, intolerable.

yenil=[ir] 2 ینیلمك *pass.* of **yen**= 3.

yenile=[r] ینیلہمك ینیلہمك /ı/ to renew; to renovate. —n= *pass.* —ş= to become new. —ştir= /ı/ *caus.* —t= /ı, a/ *caus.* of **yenile**=.

yenilgi *neol.* defeat.

yenilik[ki] ینیلك 1. newness; novelty. 2. rawness, inexperience. — korkusu *psych.* misoneism. —çi one who favors novelty.

yenir ینیر۔ ینیر۔ edible.

yenirce ینیرچه۔ ینیرجہ canker of trees.

yeniş=[ir] ینیشمك 1. to try to beat one another. 2. to wrestle; to fight; to grapple. —eme= to tie.

yenli ینلی having sleeves.

yepelek[ki] یپلك۔ یپلاك archaic running along quickly or in starts.

yeper=[ir] یپرمك archaic to run quickly or in starts; to rush about in confusion.

yepyeni ('..) یپ ینی brand-new, spick and span.

yer 1 یر۔ یر۔ 1. the earth. 2. surface of the earth; ground. 3. place; space. 4. landed property. 5. situation, employment. 6. mark (left behind by a thing). —de on the ground; on the earth. bir —de 1. in a place, somewhere. 2. *in negative sentence* nowhere. 3. (both) in the same place. —inde 1. in its place; suitable. 2. to the point, well put. 3. correct, right. — aç= to make a place; to make room. — al= 1. to take one's place; to occupy a place. 2. to take up position; to take part. 3. to buy an estate. —ini al= /ın/ to take another person's place; to replace. — altı*. —inden ayrıl= to leave, quit one's place. —e bak= 1. to look down on the ground. 2. to cast down one's eyes through modesty or shame. —e bakar sly, sneaking. —e bakar yürek yakar not so innocent as he looks, artful dodger. —e bat= 1. to sink into the ground. 2. to perish. —le beraber level with the ground. —le bir et= /ı/ to wreck altogether. —den bitme short, squat. — bul= to get a job. —ini bul= 1. to be carried out (order or assignment). 2. to find his right job (man). — cücesi short and small but very cunning. —e çal= /ı/ to knock down. — çamı ground pine, yellow bugle, *bot.*, *Ajuga Chamaepitys*. — çekimi*. —in dibi depths of the earth. —in dibine geç= to be thoroughly ashamed. —e düş= 1. to fall to the ground. 2. to be disregarded (command). — edin= to find a job or place to live. — elması*. — eşeceği, — eşeği a kind of wood louse, *zool.*, *Oniscus asellus*. — et= 1. to leave a mark. 2. to impress, to make an impression. — fesleğeni common marjoram, *bot.*, *Origanum vulgare*. — fıstığı*. —e geç=, —lere geç= to feel ready to sink into the earth with shame. —ine geç= /ın/ to replace (somebody). —e geçsin! May he perish! —ine gel= to come into place; to come out right. —ine getir= /ı/ to carry out (an order, etc.). — göçeni, — göçkeni mole, *zool.*, *Talpa europaea;* shrew mouse, *zool.*, *Sorex araneus.* —le gök bir olsa no matter what happens, even if the heavens fall. —den göğe kadar very much, greatly. —e göğe koyama= /ı/ to honor greatly. — götürmez which the land cannot hold or sustain; innumerable. —ini ısıt= to settle in a place; to keep one's seat warm. — incisi bulb or grain brought from Mecca and used medicinally. — kabuğu*. — kabul etmez great sinner (whom even the earth will reject at death). —de kal= not to be appreciated. — katı ground floor. — kayması landslide. —ine ko=, —ine koy= /ı, ın/ to replace (something by something). — koyu *archaic* flat on the ground. — kökü *prov.* carrot, *bot.*, *Daucus Carota*. —in kulağı var Walls have ears. — meşesi wall germander, *bot.*, *Tencrium chamaedrys*. — mürveri danewort, dwarf elder, *bot.*, *Sambucus ebulus*. —ine otur= to be well fixed in its place; to fit well; to settle (building). —inde rahat *mil.* At ease. —inden oyna= 1. to get out of place. 2. to get worked up. —i ölç= 1. to measure land. 2. to fall full length on the ground. — öp= to kiss the ground (in front of a very great personage). — **pırasası** black horehound, *bot.*, *Ballota nigra*. — **sakızı** 1. mineral pitch, bitumen. 2. gum of a kind of *Acarna*. — **sarmaşığı** seaside calystegia, *bot.*, *Calystegia soldanella*. — **sarsıntısı** earthquake. —**inde say**= to mark time; to make no progress. —**den selâm** a very respectful salute. —**e ser**= /ı/ to knock down, to beat; to subdue. —**ini sev**= to flourish (plant). — **sıçanı** 1. bank vole. 2. mole. — **sofrası** cloth spread on the ground for a meal; low table for meals. —**i soğumadan** shortly after leaving one's place. — **solucanı** earthworm, *zool.*, *Lumbricus terrestris*. — **şakayıkı** common wild peony, *bot.*, *Paeonica officinalis*. — **tut**= 1. to fill or occupy a place. 2. to reserve a place. —**ini tut**= /ın/ to fill the place of another as a substitute. **bir —i tutma**= to feel weak, to feel shaky. —**i var** There is a valid reason for it. It is fully called for. —**ine var**= 1. to go to his place; to fit exactly into a prepared place. 2. to be duly carried out. — **ver**= /a/ to give place to; to cause to happen. —**e vur**= /ı/ 1. to dash to the ground. 2. to defeat; to discredit. —**den yapma** very short (person). — **yatağı** bed made on the floor. —**le yeksan** leveled to the earth; thoroughly ruined. —**inde yeller esiyor** (*lit*. Winds blow in its place.) He (it) is gone for good. — **yer** in places; here and there. —**den yere** from one place to another. —**den yere vur**= /ı/ to throw violently to the ground. — **yıldızı** talc, mica. —**i yok** It is uncalled for. It is out of place. — **yurt** place to live in, home. —**i yurdu belirsiz** homeless, vagrant. — **yüzü***.

yer=ᵉʳ 2 /ı/ 1. to blame, to criticize. 2. to loathe; to shrink from. —**ip yenc**= *archaic* to criticize and pull to pieces.
yeraa (.—.) A *lrnd*. 1. reed; reed pen. 2. firefly, glowworm. 3. small fly that settles on the eyes. —**yı müsakkab** pipe, flute.
yeraacünban (.—..—) P *lrnd*. writer.
yeraazen (.—..) P *lrnd*. writer.
yerabiᵘ (.——) A *lrnd*., *pl*. of **yerbu**.
yerakan (..—) A *lrnd*. 1. jaundice, icterus. 2. a disease of grain. —**ı ahdar** green jaundice.
yeraltıⁿⁱ 1. under the earth, hidden, subterranean, underground. 2. tunnel. 3. underground chamber. — **suyu** *geol*. subterranean water.
yerbuᵘᵘ (.—) A *lrnd*. jerboa.
yerçekimi *neol.*, *phys*. gravitation.
yerelması 1. Jerusalem artichoke, *bot.*, *Helianthus tuberosus*. 2. potato, *bot.*, *Solanum tuberosum*. 3. truffle, *bot.*, *Tuber cibarium*; morel, *bot.*, *Morcella esculenta*.
yerfıstığıⁿⁱ peanut, *bot.*, *Arachis hypogaea*.

yerhamu (.'..) A *rel. formula* May he have mercy.
yerhamühüllah (..'...) A *rel. formula* May God have mercy on him. May he rest in peace.
yerhamükallah (..'...) A *rel. formula* May God have mercy on you, *said to one sneezing*.
yerin=ⁱʳ /a/ 1. to feel regret for; to be sorry about. 2. to loathe; to feel disgust. —**ip ağla**= to long and weep for some unattainable thing.
yerkabuğuⁿᵘ *geol*. crust (of the earth).
yerleş=ⁱʳ 1. to settle down; to become established. 2. to get into a job or office. 3. to settle (building).
yerleşikᵍⁱ settled; established.
yerleştir=ⁱʳ /ı, a/ *caus*. of **yerleş**=. —**il**= *pass*. of **yerleştir**=.
yerli 1. local; indigenous. 2. native; native resident. 3. fixed in a place, settled, rooted. 4. permanent, regular. — **çit** permanent hedge, quickset hedge. — **dolap** built-in cupboard. — **kulu** *Ott. hist*. volunteer Janissary. — **mahsul** home product. — **mal** local product. — **yerinde** in its proper place. — **yerine** 1. each to his post. 2. into its proper place.
yerlilikᵍⁱ 1. a belonging to a place. 2. immovability; rootedness. 3. indigenousness.
yermagan (..—) P *lrnd*., same as **armağan**.
yersiz 1. without a home. 2. out of place.
yeryüzüⁿᵘ face of the earth, the world. —**nde** on the face of the earth; over the globe. —**nde öyle bir şey yok** There is no such thing in the world.
ye's A *same as* **yeis**.
yesa *archaic for* **yasak**.
yesar (.—) A *lrnd*. 1. ease, facility. 2. wealth, riches. 3. left, left hand.
yesaren (.—'.) A *lrnd*. on the left; to the left; from the left.
yesaret (.—.) A *lrnd*. 1. ease, facility. 2. wealth, riches, comfort.
yesavul *same as* **yasavul**.
yeser A *lrnd*. 1. who works easily; easy. 2. attainable, attained. —**î** (..—) A easy, facile.
yesir 1 (.—) *var*. of **esir 1**.
yesir 2 (.—) A *lrnd*. 1. easy, not difficult. 2. little, small, trifling.
yesreten (.'..) A *lrnd*. on the left; to the left.
Yesrib A *hist.*, ancient name of Medina.
yestehle= *slang* to go to the toilet.

Yesuᵘᵘ (.—) يَسوعُ A lrnd. Jesus.
yesur (.—) يَسور A lrnd. much given to gambling, a confirmed gambler.
yeşb يَشب A lrnd. jasper.
yeşem يَشم A lrnd. jasper; porphyry; jade.
yeşer⁼ⁱʳ يَشَرمك to become green, to sprout. **—t**⁼ /ı/ caus.
yeşil يَشِل ـ يَشِـ 1. green. 2. verdant. 3. fresh. 4. slang hundred lira note. **— ağaçkakan** green woodpecker, zool., Picus viridis. **Y— Ay** the Green Crescent (Turkish temperance society). **— bağa** tree frog, zool., Hyla arborea. **— baş** mallard drake, zool., Anas platyrhynchos. **Y— Bayrak** Ott. hist. one section of the Ottoman cavalry. **— biber** green pepper, unripe fruit of capsicum annuum. **Y— Deniz** geog. Sea of Mekran. **— ispinoz** greenfinch, zool., Chloris chloris. **— keler** green lizard. **— kurbağa** tree frog. **Y— Ordu** hist. a leftist movement active at the time of the foundation of the first Turkish Republic. **— ot** green fresh herb; green grass. **bir — yaprak** poor man's present, a single green leaf. **—imsi, —imtrak** greenish.
yeşillen⁼ⁱʳ يَشِلَنمك 1. to become green; to be freshened. 2. slang /ı/ to be amorously excited (by). **—dir**⁼ /ı/ caus.
yeşilli يَشِلى mixed with green.
yeşillikᵏⁱ يَشِللك 1. greenness. 2. meadow. 3. green vegetable, greens.
yeşillikçi يَشِللكجى Ott. hist. attendant of the Court kitchen gardens.
yeşim يَشم A jade.
yeşkᵏⁱ يَشك P lrnd. any one of the four canine teeth of a beast.
yet⁼ᵉʳ يَتمك 1. to suffice, to be enough. 2. /a/ to reach, to attain. 3. to arrive at maturity, perfection.
yetama (.—.) يَتامى A lrnd., pl. of **yetim**.
yeteme يَتمه A lrnd., pl. of **yetim**.
yetenekᵏⁱ neol., psych. efficiency, capacity.
yeter يَتر 1. that suffices, sufficient. 2. Enough! **—lik** neol. competence, capacity, qualification. **—sizlik** neol. insufficiency, inadequacy.
yetim (.—) يَتيم A 1. orphan; fatherless child. 2. lrnd. single, solitary; rare, unique. **—âne** (.— — .) P like an orphan.
yetime (.—.) يَتيمه A lrnd. 1. orphan girl. 2. priceless pearl.
yetimhane (.— — .) يَتيمخانه P orphanage.
yetimî (.— —) يَتيمى A lrnd. pertaining to an orphan or orphans. **—yet** (.— ..) lrnd., same as **yetimlik**.
yetimlikᵏⁱ يَتيملك quality of an orphan; orphanhood.
yetin⁼ⁱʳ يَتنمك /la/ to be contented with.

yetir⁼ⁱʳ يَتِرمك ـ يَتِرمك /ı/ 1. caus. of **yet**⁼. 2. archaic to cause to reach or attain.
yetiş⁼ⁱʳ يَتِشمك 1. /a/ to reach; to attain; to arrive; to catch (a train, etc.); to have lived long enough to have seen (a person or event). 2. to attain maturity, to grow up; to grow (plant); to be brought up. 3. to be ready or on hand in time. **—in!** Help! **—me!, —meyesi!** May you (he) never grow up! a curse.
yetişme يَتِشمه 1. verbal n. of **yetiş**⁼. 2. arrived; arrived at full growth, ripeness, or perfection.
yetişmiş يَتِشمش 1. arrived. 2. mature, grown up.
yetiştir⁼ⁱʳ يَتِشتِرمك 1. /ı, a/ caus. of **yetiş**⁼. 2. to convey (news), to send (information). 3. /ı/ to breed (animals). 4. to train (personnel, specialists). **—ici** 1. breeder (of animals). 2. spreader of rumors. **—il**⁼ pass. of **yetiştir**⁼
yetki neol. 1. authority, power. 2. competence; qualification. **—li** competent, qualified, authoritative.
yetkin neol. perfect. **—lik** perfection.
yetmiş يَتمش seventy. **— işi bitmiş** He is too old. **—er** seventy each. **—inci** seventieth.
yetmişli يَتمشلى 1. containing seventy. 2. Ott. hist. belonging to the seventieth regiment of Janissaries.
yetmişlikᵏⁱ يَتمشلك 1. of the value of seventy kuruşh, paras, liras. 2. weighing seventy (kilos, etc.). 3. seventy years old; a person of seventy.
yevakit (.— — —) يَواقيت A lrnd., pl. of **yakut** 1.
yevm يَوم A lrnd. day. **Y—i Adha** the Feast of Sacrifice. **Y—i Arefe** the day passed by the pilgrims at Mount Arafat before the slaughter of sacrifices, the ninth of Dhulhijja. **Y—i Bedr** early Isl. hist. the day of the Battle of Badr and the battle itself. **—ün cedid rızkün cedid** A living from hand to mouth. **—i cem'** (lit., day of the assembly) 1. same as **Yevmi Arefe**. 2. Day of Resurrection. **—i elest** the day of creation when the interrogation "Am I not your Lord?" was put to Adam (and through him to his posterity) by the Creator. **Y—i Ficar** Isl. hist. battle in which the Prophet Muhammad was present as a young man. **—i kamerî** astr. lunar day. **—i me'ad** the Day of Resurrection. **—i mezalim** Day of Judgment. **—i nücumî** astr. sidereal day. **—i şems** astr. solar day. **Y—i Tahlâkullimem** Arab. hist. (lit. Day of the Shaving of the Side-locks.) name of a battle fought before Islam. **—i telâki** day of mutual meetings, Day of Resurrection.
yevmen (.'.) يَومًا A lrnd. on a certain day. **— beter** worse every day. **— feyevmen** A from day to day; daily. **— mineleyyam** A on a certain day, one day.
yevmî (.—) يَومى A lrnd. daily.

yevmiye 1 يَوْمِيَّة [Arabic .—.] daily pay; day's wages, daily fee.

yevmiye 2 يَوْمِيَّة com. journal. **— defteri** com. daybook, journal. **—ye geçir=** /ı/ to enter or record in the journal. **— kaydı** journal entry. **— tut=** to keep a journal.

yevmüddin (..—) يَوْمُ الدِّين A lrnd. day of the last judgment, Judgment Day.

yevmülahır يَوْمُ الْآخِر A lrnd. Day of Judgment.

yevmül'arz يَوْمُ الْعَرْض A lrnd. Day of Judgment.

yevmülâşura (..———) يَوْمُ الْعَاشُورا A lrnd. the tenth of Muharrem when Noah left the Ark, and when Husayin was killed at Karbalâ.

yevmülba's يَوْمُ الْبَعْث A lrnd. Day of Resurrection.

Yevmülcemel يَوْمُ الْجَمَل A Isl. hist. battle of the Camel when Aisha, widow of the Prophet Muhammad, commanded the insurgents against Ali near Basra (A.H. 35).

yevmülfasl[ıı] يَوْمُ الْفَصْل A lrnd. Judgment Day.

yevmülfeth يَوْمُ الْفَتْح A lrnd. 1. day of the Conquest of Mecca. 2. Judgment Day.

yevmülfeza[sı] يَوْمُ الْفَزَع A lrnd. (lit., the day of fear) Day of Judgment.

yevmülfurkan (...—) يَوْمُ الْفُرْقَان A lrnd. (lit., the day of the test) the day of the battle at Badr (A.H. 2).

yevmülhaşr يَوْمُ الْحَشْر A lrnd. Day of Resurrection.

yevmülhiyac (...—) يَوْمُ الْهِيَاج A lrnd. day of excitement, battle.

yevmülhuruc (...—) يَوْمُ الْخُرُوج A lrnd. Day of Resurrection.

yevmül'idad (...—) يَوْمُ الْعِداد A lrnd. 1. a recurring solemn day or festival. 2. day of death. 3. Day of Judgment.

yevmülkar[rm] يَوْمُ الْقَرّ A lrnd. day of the quiet halt by the pilgrims at Mina on the road to Mecca.

yevmülkıyam (...—) يَوْمُ الْقِيَام A lrnd. Day of Resurrection.

yevmülmisak[ki] (..——) يَوْمُ الْمِيثَاق A lrnd. Day of Judgment.

yevmülmizan (..——) يَوْمُ الْمِيزَان A lrnd. Last Judgment.

yevmünnahr يَوْمُ النَّحْر A lrnd. tenth of Dhulhijja when victims are slaughtered at **Kurban Bayramı**.

yevmünnefr يَوْمُ النَّفْر A lrnd. Day of the Rush from Mina towards Mecca; the day of sacrifices at the Feast of **Kurban Bayramı**.

yevmünneşr يَوْمُ النَّشْر A lrnd. Day of Resurrection.

yevmürreci[ı] (...—) يَوْمُ الرَّجِيع A lrnd. the day and the treacherous Affair of the Pool in A.H.3.

yevmürruus (...—) يَوْمُ الرُّؤُوس A lrnd. second day of Bayram when the heads of the victims sacrificed for the great Bayram are eaten.

yevmüşşek[kki] يَوْمُ الشَّكّ A lrnd. a day at the end of Shaban on which uncertainty exists as to whether the new moon of the first of Ramazan has appeared.

yevmüttenad (....—), **yevmüttenadi** (...—.) يَوْمُ التَّنَاد A lrnd. Day of Resurrection.

yevmütterviye يَوْمُ التَّرْوِيَة A lrnd. the day of providing water; the eighth day of Dhulhijja when the Mecca pilgrims provide themselves with water for the visit to Mina; or, when Abraham pondered on the sacrifice he was commanded to make of his son.

yey يَيْ same as **yeğ**.

yeygi يَيْگِى prov. food.

yeyinti يَيِنْتِى same as **yiyinti**.

yeyni يَيْنِى prov. light, easy. **—lik** flippancy.

yeyrek[ki] يَيْرَك same as **yeğrek**.

Yezd يَزْد P 1. geog. Yazd. 2. lrnd. God.

Yezdan (.—) يَزْدَان P lrnd. 1. God. 2. Zoroastrianism, name of the spirit who is the principle of good opposed to Ahriman the originator of evil. **—î** (.——) P 1. divine. 2. good. **—perest** (.—..) P worshipper of God.

yezek[kı] يَزَك P lrnd. advanced guard, sentinel or scout.

Yezid (.—) يَزِيد 1. name of men, especially of the second Caliph of the dynasty of the Ummaiads, son of Muawiya. (For having instigated the murder of the Caliph Ali's two sons, his name is cursed by Muslims.) 2. l. c. impious; cruel; vile fellow. **—î** (.——) A Yazidi. **—iye** (.—..) A the Yazidi sect.

yeziş يَزِش P lrnd. prayer, supplication.

yezişgâh (..—) يَزِشْگَاه P lrnd. place of prayer, oratory.

yezişhan (..—) يَزِشْخَان P lrnd. Zoroastrian priest who recites prayers; orator.

yezit[di] يَزِت [yezid] colloq., an insulting name, expressing crude disapproval.

yığ—[ar] يِغْمِش /ı/ 1. to collect in a heap; to pile up. 2. to accumulate, to hoard. 3. to mass, to concentrate (troops). 4. archaic to prevent, to stop. **—dır=** /ı, a/ caus. **—ıcı** 1. one who accumulates, hoards. 2. archaic obstacle. **—ıl=** pass. of **yığ=**. **—ılı** heaped, piled up.

yığın 1 يِغِن 1. heap, pile. 2. crowd. **bir —** a great deal. **— yığın** in heaps.

yığın=[ır] يِغِنْمِش archaic 1. to collect or mass together spontaneously. 2. to be concentrated.

yığınak[kı] يِغِنَاق 1. neol., mil. concentration. 2. archaic heap, pile; mass, collection; heaped, piled up.

yığınlık[kı] يِغِنْلِق archaic crowd, mass.

yığıntı يِغِنْتِى 1. things piled up in a

heap; heap, pile. 2. accumulation. 3. crowd. **-lı** full of heaps; heaped, massed.

yığış 1 *verbal n. of* **yığ=**.

yığış= 2 -/la/ to crowd together. **-ık** crowded. **-tır=** /ı/ *caus. of* **yığış=** 2.

yık= /ı/ 1. to pull down; to knock down, to demolish. 2. to throw down; to ruin, to overthrow. 3. to unload (animal). 4. to hurt (the feelings), to cause (someone) to be cast down. 5. /ı, a/ to heap on to another's shoulders (anything disagreeable).

yıka= /ı/ 1. to wash; to rinse; to cleanse. 2. to develop (films).

yıkama *verbal n. of* **yıka=**. — **makinası** washing machine.

yıkan= 1. *pass. of* **yıka=**. 2. to wash oneself, to have a bath. **-ış, -ma** *verbal n. of* **yıkan=**.

yıkat= /ı, a/ *caus. of* **yıka=**.

yıkıcı 1. destructive. 2. breaker (of old ships), demolisher (of buildings). 3. junk-dealer.

yıkık 1. demolished, razed; fallen down. 2. ruined (person), dilapidated (building).

yıkıl= 1. *pass. of* **yık=**. 2. to collapse, to fall down; to become decrepit. 3. to take oneself off, to clear out. **— git!** Clear out! **-ma, -ış** *verbal nouns of* **yıkıl=**.

yıkım 1. ruin. 2. bankruptcy.

yıkıntı 1. heap of ruins; debris. 2. act of ruining, ruination. **— ol=** /a/ to be great damage.

yıkkın 1. in ruins, about to collapse. 2. ruinous. **-lık** ruin.

yıktır= /ı, a/ *caus. of* **yık=** 2. **-ıl=** *pass.*

yıl 1 year. **— çıbanı** *path.* Aleppo button. **— dönümü** anniversary. **— on iki ay** through the whole year, continuously, incessantly. **— uğursuzundur** "The times belong to the crooks," *said when undeserving people get money or position.* **—lar yılı** for a very long time.

yıl= 2 /dan/ to be afraid; to dread.

yılan 1. snake, serpent. 2. ungrateful man, spiteful person. **—a ağı veren** the salamander, *zool., Salamandra maculosa.* **— balığı** eel, *zool., Anguilla anguilla.* **— başı** 1. panther cowry, *zool., Cypraea pantherina;* helmet-shell, *zool., Cassis.* 2. barbary ragwart, *bot., Othonna cheirifolia.* **—ın başını ez=** to smash serpent's head; to defeat. **— çıyan** snakes and all kinds of vermin. **— deliği** snake's burrow. **— dili** a kind of long, slender rowboat. **— dilli** snake-tongued; who talks maliciously and bitterly.

— gibi snake-like; treacherous; repulsive. **— gibi sok=** 1. to bite like a snake. 2. to hurt the feelings bitterly. **— gömleği** snakeskin; slough of a serpent. **— hikâyesi** a long-winded story; something that never ends. **— kabağı** snake gourd, *bot., Trichosanthes anguina.* **— kavı** slough of a snake. **— kemiği** *obs.* guilt which keeps torturing a person. **— kökü** meadow clary, snakeweed, *bot., Salvia pratensis.* **—ın kuyruğuna bas=** to arouse the spite of a venomous and powerful person. **— otu** gentian, *bot., Gentiana lutea.* **— oynatma** snake charming. **—a sarıl=** to grasp or clutch at a serpent (said of one in great difficulty). **— sokması** snakebite. **— taşı** stone supposed to cure snakebites. **— yastığı** wake-robin, cuckoopint, *bot., Arum maculatum.* **Y— Yılı** name of the sixth year in the old Eastern Turkish cycle of twelve. **—cı** snake charmer.

yılancık 1. a little snake. 2. *med.* erysipelas. **— taşı** stone supposed to cure erysipelas. **—çı** person who cures erysipelas by incantations.

yılancıl sacred ibis, *zool., Threshkiornis aethiopica.*

yılankavi spiral, winding.

yılbaşı the new year; New Year's Day.

yıldır= /ı/ *caus. of* **yıl=** 2.

yıldıra= *archaic* 1. to glitter, to gleam. 2. to flash (as lightning).

yıldıragan, yıldırak *archaic* 1. which glitters or sparkles. 2. lightning.

yıldırım thunderbolt, lightning. **— cezası** fine levied on the spot, automatic fine. **— çarpmış** struck by lightning. **— gibi** swift as a thunderbolt. **— harbi** lightning war, Blitzkrieg. **— telgrafı** urgent telegram. **—la vurulmuşa döndü** He was thunderstruck (with terror).

yıldız 1. star. 2. movie star. 3. Pole star. 4. north. 5. destiny. 6. *print.* asterisk. 7. *w. cap., same as* **Yıldız Sarayı.** **— akması** flight of a shooting star, meteor. **—ı barış=** /la/ to be on good terms, to get on (with). **— böceği** firefly; glowworm. **— çiçeği** dahlia. **—ı dişi** sympathetic, popular. **—ı düşkün** ill-fated. **— kayması** *same as* **yıldız akması.** **— kurdu** glowworm, *zool., Lampyris noctiluca.* **—ı parlak** whose star is in the ascendant, lucky. **— poyraz** the north-north-east point of the compass. **Y— Sarayı** Imperial Palace on the hills overlooking the Bosphorus. **— tabya** *mil.* star fort. **— taşı** aventurine. **— uçması** *same as* **yıldız akması.** **— yağmuru** meteoric shower. **— yeli** north wind.

yıldızlı یلدزلی 1. set with stars, starred. 2. ornamented with stars.

yılgın یلغین cowed, daunted; frightened. —**lık** a being cowed.

yılık[a] یلیك prov. 1. crooked, bent. 2. frightened, daunted, cowed. 3. cross-eyed. —**lık** terror, state of one frightened or cowed.

yılış=ır یلشمق to grin unpleasantly; to smile impudently.

yılışık[a] یلشیك sticky; importunate; grinning unpleasantly. —**lık** stickiness.

yılkı یلقی prov. 1. herd of brood mares and stallions with their colts loose in the fields. 2. a wild, unbroken horse or colt.

yılla=ʳ یللامق 1. to be a year (in one place). 2. same as **yıllan**=.

yıllan=ır یللانمق 1. to be a year or several years old, to take on years. 2. to remain for several years. 3. to grow old. 4. to drag on for a long time. —**mış şarap** very old wine.

yıllat=ır یللاتمق /ı/ caus. of **yılla**=.

yıllık[a] یللیك 1. one year old, (so many) years old. 2. one year's rent; a year's salary. 3. yearbook, annual; annals. —**çı**, —**lı** 1. who receives a yearly salary. 2. who pays a yearly rent. 3. servant paid by the year.

yılma یلمه 1. verbal n. of **yıl**=. 2. prov. gentle slope downwards.

yılmaz یلماز 1. undaunted; not to be cowed. 2. dreadnought.

yır=ar 1 یرمق /ı/ prov. to tear, rend, split, burst.

yır 2 یر prov., slang song; folk song.

yıra=ʳ یرامق prov. to become thin and scraggy (horse).

yırak[a] یراك prov. 1. same as **ırak** 1. 2. thin and scraggy (horse).

yırandır=ır یراندرمق prov., caus. of **yıra**=.

yırık[a] یریك prov. torn, rent.

yırıl=ır یریلمق prov. to tear, split, burst; to be torn or split.

yırın=ır یرینمق prov. to tear oneself, to rend one's own clothes; to strive and struggle.

yırla=ʳ یرلامق prov. to sing.

yırt=ar یرتمق /ı/ 1. to tear, to rend, to slit; to burst. 2. to tear to pieces. 3. to break in (horse). 4. to assault, violate (the person).

yırtıcı یرتیجی tearing, rending; rapacious. —**lar ayası** water crowfoot, bot., Ranunculus aquatilis. — **hayvan** beast of prey. — **kuş** bird of prey.

yırtık[a] یرتیك 1 torn, rent. 2. ragged, tattered. 3. broken in (horse). 4. shameless, brazen-faced. — **pırtık** all in pieces; in rags.

yırtıl=ır یرتیلمق 1. pass. of **yırt**=.

2. to struggle desperately, to tear oneself (for something). 3. /ı/ slang to pay, to give back.

yırtın=ır یرتینمق 1. to shriek in desperation or fear. 2. to be fearfully perturbed. 3. to struggle hopelessly.

yırtış=ır یرتشمق to claw at each other; to scratch one another's faces.

yırtlak[a] یرتلاك gaping as though torn (eye, etc.).

yırtlaz یرتلاز prov. 1. slit; hare-lipped. 2. everted (eyelid). 3. shameless, unblushing.

yırtmaç[a] یرتماج slit in a garment.

yırttır=ır یرتدرمق /ı, a/ caus. of **yırt**=.

yısa یسا It same as **yisa**.

yiğirmi یگرمی archaic, same as **yirmi**.

yiğit[di] یگیت 1. young man; fine manly youngster. 2. hero. 3. brave, stouthearted. —**başı** Ott. hist. man responsible for carrying out the regulations of a guild. —**çe** bravely, valiantly.

yiğitlen=ir یگیتلنمك 1. to grow up. 2. to become brave; to pluck up courage. —**dir**= /ı/ caus.

yiğitlik[a] یگیتلیك courage, pluck; heroism. — **çıbanı** pustules that break out on the face in youth; acne. —**e leke sürme**= to save one's face.

yiğren=ir یگرنمك archaic, same as **iğren**=.

yine یینه 1. again. 2. yet, but yet; still. 3. besides, moreover. — **görüşürüz inşallah** I hope we'll meet again.

yinile=ʳ, **yinilen**=ir یینیلمك prov. to become light, lighter; to become easy.

yirmi یرمی twenty. — **altı** a card game. — **bir** cards twenty-one. — **yaş dişi** wisdom tooth. —**li** costing, weighing, measuring twenty. —**lik** 1. of the value, weight, length of twenty. 2. twenty para or twenty-kurush piece. —**lik bir genç** a twenty-year-old youth. —**nci** twentieth. —**şer** twenty each; twenty at a time.

yisa یسا It Hoist away! Pull! Heave ho! — **beraber** All together, pull! — **et**= /ı/ 1. to hoist. 2. to force. — **yisa** 1. with force, with all one's might. 2. the very most.

yit=er 1 یتمك prov. 1. to be lost; to disappear. 2. to go astray. 3. to go to ruin.

yit=er 2 یتمك prov. for **it**= 2.

yitik[a] یتیك prov. 1. lost. 2. astray.

yitir=ir یتیرمك prov. /ı/ to lose.

yitkin یتكین archaic lost.

yiv یو 1. groove, chamfer; stripe. 2. rifling (of a gun). 3. hem. —**li** grooved; chamfered; rifled.

yiyecek[a] ییه جك 1. edible. 2. food.

yiyegen ییگن archaic 1. that eats much or voraciously. 2. who takes bribes; who embezzles.

yiyesi بیاسی ـ ـیبسی archaic food. — **eyle=** to give a dinner or banquet.

yiyi 1 ییگی ـ ییه ـ ییی edible; food.

yiyi 2 ییی archaic smell. — **duy=** to be aware of a smell, to smell.

yiyi=ʳ **3** ییمك archaic 1. to perceive a smell. 2. to give off a smell.

yiyici ییجی ـ یـ ییجی 1. who eats; glutton; greedy. 2. corroding (sore). 3. who takes bribes. 4. mordant, caustic. —**lik** bribery, corruption, subornation.

yiyil=ⁱʳ یـ یلمك ـ یلمك archaic 1. to be eaten. 2. to be edible.

yiyili یـ یلی ـ ییلی eaten; nibbled; gnawed; worn away.

yiyim ییم ـ یـ ییم 1. act of eating. 2. a single quantity eaten. — **yeri yap=** /ı/ to use a thing or person for one's profit for a long time.

yiyinti ییـ نتی ـ یـ ینتی anything edible; foodstuff.

yiyiş یـ ییش ـ ییش verbal n. of **ye=** 2.

yo (—) یو exclamation of rejection, etc., Oh, no! Don't!

yobaz یوبار 1. dangerous religious fanatic. 2. big, coarse; boor. 3. student in lower grades of a religious school; epithet jokingly applied to a country bumpkin when he first arrived at one of the old religious schools. —**lık** 1. bigotry, fanaticisim. 2. boorishness.

yoğ 1 یوغ archaic, same as **yok**.

yoğ=ᵃʳ **2** یوغمق to thicken, curdle, clot.

yoğrul=ᵘʳ یوغرولمق pass. of **yoğur=**.

yoğsul یوغسول archaic, same as **yoksul**.

yoğun یوغون 1. prov. thick; fat; big. 2. prov. coarse, gross, unmannered. 3. prov. stupid. 4. neol., phys. dense.

yoğuna یوغنه archaic vainly; for nothing. — **değildir** It is not for nothing. — **ver=** to give for nothing, to sell for a mere trifle.

yoğunlaş=ıʳ یوغونلشمق prov. 1. to become fat, boorish or stupid. 2. neol., phys. to become dense.

yoğunlukᵍᵘ یوغونلق 1. prov. thickness, stoutness; boorishness; stupidity. 2. neol., phys. density.

yoğur=ᵘʳ یوغورمق /ı/ to knead.

yoğurtᵈᵘ **1** یوغورت yogurt. — **çal=** to make yogurt. — **gibi** thick, curdled, clotted. — **mayası** ferment of yogurt, old curd used in preparing fresh yogurt. — **otu** cheese rennet, yellow bedstraw, bot., Gallium verum. —**u üfliyerek ye=** (lit., to blow upon one's yogurt before eating it) to be unnecessarily cautious because of a former bad experience.

yoğurt=ᵘʳ **2** یوغورتمق ـ یوغردمك /ı, a/ caus. of **yoğur=**.

yoğurtçu یوغورتجی maker or seller of yogurt.

yoğurtlu یوغورتلو prepared, mixed or served with yogurt.

yoğuruş یوغورش verbal n. of **yoğur=**.

yoh یوح prov. for **yok**.

yohsul یوخسول ـ یوخسل ـ یخسل archaic for **yoksul**.

yokᵍᵘ, ᵏᵘ یوق 1. non-existent; absent; not present; there is not. 2. following possessed subject not to have, e. g., **vaktim yok** I don't have time. 3. isolated no, a refusal to a request or negative answer to a question. 4. on the other hand; in the opposite case, e. g., **verirse iyi, yok vermedi, o zaman zorla al** If he gives it, all right; but if he doesn't, then take it by force. 5. at head of each statement in a series it expresses disbelief, e. g., **yok başı ağrıyormuş, yok dişi sızlarmış**... Now he complains of a headache, then of a toothache... —**tan** from nothing; having no cause. — **canım!** colloq. 1. Absolutely not! I refuse! 2. You don't say! Unbelievable! — **de=** to reject, to deny. — **değildir** There are (is); it exists. — **deve**, — **devenin başı** impossible, unbelievable. — **et=***. — **oğlu yok** non-existent; impossible to find. — **ol=** to be annihilated, to cease to exist. — **pahasına** for a mere song; for nothing — **yere** without reason; uselessly. — **yok** Everything can be found, you can get whatever you wish.

yoket=ᵈᵉʳ یوق ایتمك /ı/ to destroy utterly.

yokla=ʳ یوقلامق /ı/ 1. to feel with the fingers or hand. 2. to examine, inspect, search. 3. to try, to test. 4. to visit (a sick person). —**ya yoklaya git=** to feel one's way along.

yoklama یوقلامه 1. verbal n. of **yokla=**. 2. examination, test; inspection. 3. roll-call. 4. call-up (of recruits). —**cı** military inspector; official in charge of the personnel records of a military unit.

yoklan=ıʳ, **yoklanıl=**ıʳ یوقلانمق pass. of **yokla=**.

yoklaştır=ıʳ یوقلاشدیرمق /ı/ to feel, to search minutely.

yoklat=ıʳ یوقلاتمق /ı, a/ caus. of **yokla=**. —**ıl=** pass.

yoklayış یوقلایش verbal n. of **yokla=**.

yoklukᵍᵘ یوقلوق 1. absence; non-existence. 2. lack; poverty.

yoksa (ʹ.) یوقسه 1. if not; otherwise; or; or else. 2. followed by negation but not, e. g., but not now. 3. I wonder if, e. g., — **gelmiyecek mi?** Perhaps he is not coming after all.

yoksul یوقسول 1. possessing nothing, destitute. 2. in need of; lacking. — **bayırsa çanağı bayırmaz** archaic, proverb (lit. When

yoksun

a pauper grows rich his dish does not become bountiful.) A man raised from poverty is always stingy. **—luk** destitution.

yoksun *neol.* deprived.

yoksuz بوڭسز *prov.*, same as **yoksul**.

yokuş بوقوش بوقش 1. rise, ascent, slope. 2. rising (ground). **— aşağı** downhill. **— yukarı** uphill. **—lu** rising (ground); sloping upwards.

yol 1 يول 1. road, path, way; street; passage. 2. channel, canal. 3. means, medium. 4. course, manner, method, system; behavior. 5. rule, law. 6. journey. 7. rate of speed. 8. stripe, line. **bir —** *prov.* once. **—una** /ın/ for, for the sake of. **—unca** in its proper way or manner. **—unda** 1. /ın/ for the sake of. 2. in order, going as it should. 3. in the sense that, to the effect that. **—iyle** /ın/ 1. by way of; via. 2. properly, duly. **— aç=** 1. to open a road. 2. /a/ to be the cause (of). **—unuz açık olsun!** Have a good journey! Bon voyage! **— ağzı** entrance to a road. **— al=** 1. to acquire momentum, to get up speed. 2. to advance. **—dan ayrıl=** to leave the road, to get out of the road. **— azığı** provisions for a journey. **— bağla=** *archaic* to control the road. **—una bak=** /ın/ to await someone's arrival. **—unu bağla=** /ın/ to cut off someone's retreat. **—unu bekle=** /ın/ 1. to lie in wait (for). 2. to wait for. **— bil=** 1. to know the way; to know how to do something. 2. to know how to behave. **— bilir** who knows how to comport himself or how things should be done; well-mannered; adroit. **— bilmez** one who does not know how to go or act, unmannerly, awkward, maladroit. **—unu bul=** /ın/ to find a way of doing something. **bir —unu bul=** to accomplish a thing in some way or another; to get a thing done somehow. **—a çık=** to set out on a journey or way. **bir —a çık=** to lead to the same end. **—dan çık=** 1. to be derailed. 2. to go astray, to go bad. **—una çık=** /ın/ 1. to meet by chance. 2. to go to meet (a traveler). **—a çıkar=** /ı/ 1. to set on his (its) way. 2. to see off. **—undan çıkar=** /ı/ to mislead, to pervert. **—a düş=** to set out on a journey. **—lara düş=** to set out in search of someone (especially in an emergency). **—u düş=** /ın/ 1. to happen to go that way. 2. to be the right moment (for). **—a düzül=** to start off (on a journey). **— emri** *Ott. hist.* a kind of passport given to a traveler in Turkey requiring protection and post horses for him. **— eri** *archaic* traveler; fellow traveler. **— erkân** social conventions. **— erkân bil=** 1. to know the ways and proper manner (of society, court, office). 2. to have good manners. **— et=** 1. to go along at a good rate of speed.

2. /ı/ to go very often (to a place). **— evlâdı** person admitted to a religious order by the sheikh. **— geçen** building with two entrances, used as a passage way; thoroughfare, place where many people pass through. **—a gel=** 1. to come around, to think better of something. 2. to come to reason, to listen to advice. **—a getir=** /ı/ to bring someone around to the right view or course; to bring to reason, to persuade. **—a gir=**, **—una gir=** to come right somehow. **— git=** to advance (on one's way). **—a git=** to go on a journey. **— görün=** /a/ to be necessary for one to go on a journey. **— göster=** /a/ to show the way, to guide. **— gösteren** guide. **— harcı** travel expenses. **— harçlığı** travel expenses. **—a hazır** ready to sail. **— iz bil=** to know the rules of social behavior. **— kâğıdı** *Ott. hist.* 1. passport, pass. 2. *mil.* route. **—dan kal=** to be kept back, to be detained. **—larda kal=** to be delayed on the road. **—u kapa=** to block the road. **—unu kaybet=** to lose one's way. **— kes=** to waylay on the road, to stage a holdup. **—unu kes=** /ın/ to stop someone. **— kesme** highway robbery, brigandage. **—dan ko=** *archaic* to prevent, detain, delay. **—a koy=** *archaic* /ı/ to see off. **—una koy=** /ı/ to set right. **—undan koy=** /ı/ to prevent, detain, delay. **—a koyul=** to start off. **— mükellefiyeti** obligation to work on road construction. **— oğlu** member of a dervish order. **— ol=** to become a precedent, to cause the beginning of a habit. **—a revan ol=** to start off (on a journey). **—u sapıt=** 1. to take a wrong turning. 2. to turn into another road. 3. to go astray. **—a sok=** /ı/ to put to rights. **— sök=** to force a way and break through. **— şaş=** to fork; to take another direction (road). **—u şaşır=** to lose the way, to go astray. **—unu şaşır=** 1. to lose one's way. 2. to go bad. **— tası** 1. metal cup for drinking water. 2. traveler's food box (with several metal dishes fastened together). **— tezkeresi** *Ott. hist.* passport, pass. **— tut=** to take a road. **— uğrağı** place lying on one's road. **— üslûp** mode, manner. **— üstü*.** **— ver=** /a/ 1. to give passage, to make way. 2. to discharge, dismiss from service. 3. to give a horse his head. 4. to open the way (to), to cause. **— vur=** to waylay along a road, to stage a hold-up. **—a vur=** *colloq.* /ı/ to see someone off (on a journey). **— yarağı** *archaic* all necessities for a journey. **—a yat=** same as **yola gel=**. **— yol** 1. striped; in lines. 2. divided by various roads. **— yordam** manners, behavior. **— yürü=** to walk on a road, to go walking.

yol=^{ar} **2** يولمق 1. to pluck, to pluck out by the root. 2. to tear out. 3. to strip bare. 4. to

despoil, to rob; *slang* to extract money out of someone at gambling.
yolakʰ يولق *prov.* 1. path, narrow way. 2. manner, behavior.
yolcu يولجى 1. traveler; passenger. 2. child about to be born. 3. one at the point of death. 4. prostitute. — **et=** /ı/ to see off (a traveler). — **geçir=** to accompany someone on the start of a journey, to see him off. — **ol=** 1. to be about to travel. 2. to be a passenger. — **yolunda gerek** A traveler's place is on the road; one should stick to what he is doing.
yolculukᵗᵘ يولجيلق traveling, travel, journey. — **düş=** to have to go on a journey. — **ne zaman?** When do you set out on your journey?
yoldaş يولداش 1. fellow traveler; comrade. 2. companion, friend. 3. *Ott. hist.* fellow Janissary. —**lık** 1. a being a fellow traveler. 2. comradeship, companionship, fellowship.
yoldur=ᵘʳ يولديرمق /ı, a/ *caus. of* **yol=** 2.
yolla=ʳ يوللامق /ı/ to send; to dispatch; to send off.
yollama يوللامه 1. *verbal n. of* **yolla=**. 2. freight department of a railway. 3. military transport service. 4. large beam of building timber.
yollan=ᵘʳ يوللانمق 1. *pass. of* **yolla=**. 2. to advance, to acquire speed or momentum. 3. to be provided with roads. 4. to become regular, conformable to rule.
yollat=ᵘʳ يوللاتمق /ı, a/ *caus. of* **yolla=**.
yollu يوللى 1. having (such and such) roads. 2. having (such and such) a way or manner. 3. striped. 4. proper, correct, regular. 5. fast (ship, etc.). 6. of the nature of, by way of. 7. *slang* of suspect character, improper (woman). — **yolsuz işler** irregular actions.
yollukᵗᵘ يوللق provisions for a journey; travel funds.
yoloz يولوز *colloq.* hairless, beardless.
yolsuz يولسز 1. roadless; trackless. 2. irregular, contrary to law or custom. 3. *Ott. hist.* banned by his guild (tradesman as punishment for some fault). 4. without speed (ship, car). — **erkânsız** who acts in an irregular manner, contrary to principles. —**luk** 1. irregularity; impropriety. 2. *Ott. hist.* punishment of a tradesman.
yolukᵗᵘ يولوق plucked; hairless. —**luk** bareness, hairlessness.
yolun=ᵘʳ يولنمق 1. *pass. of* **yol=** 2. 2. to tear one's hair (with grief). —**dur=** /ı/ to cause to tear one's hair (with grief).
yoluntu يولنتى 1. hair shaved or cut off. 2. pluckings.
yoluş 1 يولش *verbal n. of* **yol=** 2.
yoluş=ᵘʳ 2 يولشمق /la/ to pluck each other.
yolüstüⁿᵘ يول اوستى 1. lying on one's road (place). 2. looking on the road (window).

yom يوم *archaic* luck; good luck. — **ver=** to bless, to ask for a blessing on. — **yor=** to take an augury.
yoma يوما Gk *naut.* shroud or cable-laid rope. — **bağı** carrick bend. — **bükümü** 1. cable-laid rope. 2. cable-laid, plain-laid (rope), hawser-laid.
yomlu يوملى *archaic* 1. lucky, fortunate. 2. auspicious.
yomsuz يومسز *archaic* unlucky; inauspicious.
yon=ᵃʳ يونمق /ı/ *same as* **yont=** 2.
yonca يونجه clover; any trifoliaceous plant used as fodder; trefoil; lucern.
yoncalı يونجه لى 1. mixed with clover. 2. fragrant like clover. — **kav** fragrant touchwood or punk.
yonga يونغه chip, chipping; kindling.
yongar يونغار *archaic* a kind of small three-stringed lute.
yonma يونمه *same as* **yontma**.
yontᵈᵘ 1 يونت 1. wild, unbroken mare. 2. water wagtail. — **kuşu** water wagtail, *zool.*, *Motacilla*. — **yılı** seventh year in the old Turkish cycle of twelve.
yont=ᵃʳ 2 يونتمق /ı/ 1. to cut, chip into shape; to dress by cutting (stone). 2. to pare (nails). 3. to sharpen (pencil).
yontma يونتمه 1. *verbal n. of* **yont=** 2. 2. chipped, cut. — **taş** dressed stone. — **taş devri** palaeolithic age.
yonttur=ᵘʳ يونتديرمك /ı, a/ *caus. of* **yont=** 2. —**ul=** *pass.*
yontul=ᵘʳ يونتلمق *pass. of* **yont=** 2.
yontulmamış يونتلممش 1. not chipped or hewn. 2. rough, uneducated, unrefined.
yonul=ᵘʳ يونلمق *pass. of* **yon=**.
yonuntu يوننتى fragmentary cuttings, chips, parings.
yor=ᵃʳ 1 يورمق /ı/ to tire, weary, fatigue.
yor=ᵃʳ 2 يورمق /ı, a/ 1. to interpret a dream or omen. 2. to presage; to attribute.
=yor 3 يور (he is)... -ing, *e. g.*, **uyuyor** He is sleeping.
yordam يوردام 1. agility; dexterity. 2. levity; disdain; pride. —**lı** 1. agile; dexterous. 2. frivolous; proud.
yordur=ᵘʳ يورديرمك /ı, a/ *caus. of* **yor=** 2.
yorga يورغه 1. jogtrot. 2. going at a jogtrot. — **git=** to go along at a jogtrot.
yorgala=ʳ يورغه لامق to go at a jogtrot. —**t=** /ı, a/ *caus. of* **yorgala=**.
yorgan يورغان quilt. — **çarşafı** upper sheet commonly basted to the quilt. — **gitti kavga bitti** The dispute is ended, *said when the subject of a dispute no longer exists*. —**ına göre ayağını uzat=** to stretch out one's feet according to the length of the cover. — **iğnesi** quilting-needle. —**a sarıl=** to roll oneself up

in a quilt. **— yüzü** outer covering of a quilt. **—cı** quilt-maker.

yorganla= يورغانلامق /ı/ to cover or furnish with a quilt. **—n=** pass.

yorganlıkᵏⁱ يورغانلق 1. suitable for making quilts. 2. material for making quilts.

yorgun يورغون tired, weary, worn out. **— argın** dead tired. **— düş=** to be worn out.

yorgunlukᵏᵘ يورغونلق weariness, fatigue. **— al=** to rest from one's fatigue, to take a rest. **— çıkar=** to rest. **— kahvesi** coffee to revive one when tired.

yort=ᵃʳ يورتمق 1. *slang* to go restlessly about as a vagrant; to rove about. 2. *archaic* to travel about on horseback. 3. *archaic* to trot (animal). **—ma** *verbal n.*

yortu يورطى Gk Christian feast.
yorucu يوروجى tiring, fatiguing, wearisome.
yorul=ᵘʳ 1 يورلمق *pass. of* **yor=** 1.
yorul=ᵘʳ 2 يورلمق *pass. of* **yor=** 2.
yorult=ᵘʳ يورلتمق /ı/ *archaic, same as* **yor=** 1.
yorum *neol.* 1. interpretation of a dream or omen. 2. a counting as auspicious. **—cu** commentator. **—la=** /ı/ *neol.* to comment on, to explain.

yosma يوصمه 1. pretty, graceful; attractive. 2. pretty and attractive person; coquette. **—m** My pet. **—lık** gracefulness, charm.

yosun يوصون moss. **— bağla=** to become covered with moss. **—lu** mossy, covered with moss. **—lu gül** moss rose.

yoz يوز *prov.* 1. untrained; wild. 2. simple-minded. 3. single (flower). **— yer** barren land.

yozlaş=ᵘʳ يوزلاشمق to become wild; to lose qualities that have been acquired.

yön يون 1. direction, quarter. 2. regard, relation. **bir —den** in one respect. **— tut=** 1. to take a direction. 2. to adopt a course. **—deş** *neol., geom.* corresponding.

yönel=ⁱʳ يونلمك /a/ 1. to incline or turn (towards). 2. to be directed (towards). **—t=** /ı, a/ to direct (toward). **—tim** *neol.* orientation.

yönet=ⁱʳ *neol.* /ı/ to administer, to direct; to manage.

yönetim *neol.* direction, administration, management. **— kurulu** council of managers. **—li** manageable; navigable.

yönetmelikᵏⁱ *neol.* governing statute; book of instructions; drill book, regulation.

yönlü يونلى 1. directed or turned towards. 2. *prov.* suitable, fitting.

yönseme *neol., psych.* tendency.
yönsüz يونسز *archaic* unsuitable, unfitting.
yöntem *neol.* method, way.

yöre يوره 1. *prov.* side; neighborhood. 2. *neol.* suburb.

Yörükᵏᵘ يورك *same as* **Yürük**.
yörünge *neol.* 1. course taken (by a thing). 2. orbit; trajectory.

yuf (—) يوف 1. *interjection expressing scorn and disgust.* 2. empty, vain. 3. lost, ruined, destroyed. **— borusunu çal=** 1. to boo. 2. to destroy; to curse and wish to destroy. **— çek=** /a/ to boo; to insult. **— ervahına!** damn! **— oku=** /a/ *same as* **yuf borusunu çal=**. **— ol=** to go to the winds; to be destroyed. **— sana!** Shame on you!

yufka يوفقه 1. thin; weak. 2. poor; powerless. 3. thin layer of dough; wafer; unleavened bread in thin sheets. **— yürekli** compassionate, softhearted.

yufkalıkᵏⁱ يوفقهلق 1. flour suitable for flake pastry. 2. thinness; poverty. 3. softheartedness.

yuğ (—) يوغ P. *lrnd.* yoke.
yuğur=ᵘʳ يوغورمق *same as* **yoğur=**.
yuh 1 يوه *interjection expressing anger and displeasure, sound used by a crowd booing.*
yuh 2 (—) يوه A *lrnd.* the sun.
yuha 1 يوها *shout of contempt or derision,* Shame on you! **— çek=** /a/, **—ya tut=** /ı/ to hold up to derision; to hoot.
yuha 2 (— —) يوها *same as* **yuh 2**.
yuhala=ʳ يوهالامق /ı/ to hold up to derision; to hoot.
Yuhanna (— . .) يوحنا A *Bib.* John.

yukarda يوقارده on high; above; overhead; upstairs.

yukardan يوقاردن from above. **— al=** to behave in a condescending manner. **— aşağı** from above downwards; completely, from head to foot. **— kop=** to set out with a very high figure (in beginning a negotiation).

yukarı يوقارى 1. high; upper; top. 2. above; upwards; on high; up. 3. upper or topmost part. **—dan** *same as* **yukardan**. **— kat** upper story of a house. **—ya yığ=** /ı/ to exaggerate.

yulaf يولاف [alef] oats; oat, *bot., Avena sativa*.

yular يولار halter. **bir —ı eksik** He needs a halter. He is a donkey. **—lı keser** large double-handed adze with an iron brace to strengthen its cutting blade.

yum=ᵃʳ يوممق to shut, to close (eye), to clench (fist).

yumakᵏⁱ يوماق ball (of wool, string, etc.).
yumakla=ʳ يوماقلامق /ı/ to wind into a ball. **—n=** 1. to become a ball. 2. to swell.

yumru يومرى 1. round, globular. 2. round thing; tumor; boil. 3. *bot.* tubercle. **— burun** bottlenose. **— cüsseli** round bodied.

yumrucakᵏⁱ يومرجق *same as* **yumurcak**.

yumrukᵘ يومرق ،يحرون ،يومرون 1. fist. 2. blow with the fist. — at= to hit. —u çak= /ı/ to hit, to beat. — göster= /a/ to threaten with the fist. —una güven= to trust one's physical strength. — hakkı with the force of one's fist, by force. — kavgası fist fight. —larını sık= to clench the fists; to threaten with the fists.

yumrukla=ʳ يومرقلامق 1. to hit with the fist. 2. to pound with the fist, knead. —n= pass. —t= /ı, a/ caus. of **yumrukla=**.

yumruklukᵘ يومرقلق used in **bir yumrukluk canı var** One blow and he is a dead man.

yumrul=ᵘʳ, **yumrulan=**ᵘʳ يومرولنمق ،يومرولمق to become swollen or lumpy.

yumrulukᵘ يومرولق roundness; swelling (of a boil).

yumşa=ʳ يومشامق same as **yumuşa=**.

yumşakᵗⁱ يومشاق ،يومشى ،يومشاق same as **yumuşak**.

yumukᵘ يوموق 1. closed by swelling (eye); half shut (eye). 2. plump; soft.

yumul=ᵘʳ يوملمق to become closed (the eye, by swelling).

yumulu يوملو shut, closed (eye or fist).

yumur=ᵘʳ يومرمق /ı/ archaic to deform, misshape.

yumurcakᵗⁱ يومرجاق ،يومرجاق 1. child; brat; naughty. 2. obs. bubo; plague. — ol= obs. to be stricken by the plague.

yumurda يومرده archaic for **yumurta**.

yumurta يومرطه 1. egg. 2. spawn. 3. darning egg. — akı the white of an egg. — bir kardeş children of the same mother. —yı çalka= 1. to turn its eggs (hen). 2. to beat an egg. —dan daha dün çıkmış newly fledged but acting like a grownup. — kabuğunu beğenmemiş The egg did not like its own shell, said of one who runs down those who brought him up or educated him. — kapıya dayanınca, — kapıya gelince 1. at the very last minute. 2. when the situation has become serious. —ya kulp takan (lit., who puts handles on eggs) one who invents pretexts. — ökçeli ayakkabı shoes with oval high heels (worn by town roughs). — patlıcanı white eggplant. — sarısı yolk. — tokuş= to play at knocking hard-boiled eggs against each other. — zarı tough fibrous membrane enclosing the white and yolk of an egg. —cı seller of eggs. —lı 1. that has eggs. 2. that lays (hen); brooding (bird).

yumurtalıkᵗⁱ يومرطلق 1. ovary. 2. egg cup.

yumurtla=ʳ يومرطلامق /ı/ 1. to lay eggs; to spawn. 2. to invent (a story); to blurt out, say something indiscreet. —n= to be laid (eggs). —t= /ı/ caus. of **yumurtla=**.

yumuş يومش prov. 1. service, work; duty. 2. order, command. — oğlanı boy servant.

yumuşa=ʳ يومشامق 1. to become soft. 2. to become pliant or yielding; to calm down.

yumuşacıkᵗⁱ يومشاجق very soft or mild.

yumuşakᵗⁱ يومشاق 1. soft; mild; yielding. 2. soft part (of anything). — ağızlı that takes the bit easily (horse). — başlı docile. — yüzlü too kind to refuse.

yumuşakçalar neol., zool., Mollusca.

yumuşaklıkᵗⁱ يومشاقلق softness; mildness; gentleness.

yumuşat=ᵘʳ يومشاتمق /ı/ 1. to soften. 2. to appease; to mitigate. —ıl= pass.

yun=ᵘʳ يونمق prov. to wash oneself; to bathe.

yunakᵗⁱ يوناق prov. 1. wash-house; place for washing clothes on a river bank. 2. public bath.

Yunan (——) يونان A 1. Greece. 2. the Greek nation. —ca ancient Greek or modern Greek (as spoken in Greece).

Yunanî (———) يوناني A 1. pertaining to ancient Greece. 2. Greek; the Greek language. —yân (————) P the Greeks.

Yunanistan (——.—) يونانستان P geog. Greece.

Yunanlı يوناني Greek.

yund يوند same as **yont** 1.

yundciyan يوندجيان Ott. hist. attendants of the Imperial stables.

Yunus (—.) يونس A Bib. and Quranic the prophet Jonah; Jonah. — balığı porpoise, zool., Phocaena phocaena; common dolphin; grampus, zool., Delphinus delphis.

yura يوره prov. lower slopes and skirts of a mountain; steep slope.

yurdu يوردى ،يوردو prov. 1. eye of a needle. 2. hole, sight-hole. —lu iğne needle.

yurtᵈᵘ يورد ،يورت 1. native country. 2. home; habitation. 3. student dormitory. 4. estate. — tut= 1. to adopt as home. 2. to settle.

yurtlan=ᵘʳ يورتلنمق 1. to settle (in a place). 2. to cease being a nomad and live a settled existence. 3. to acquire an estate. —dır= /ı/ caus.

yurtlukᵗⁱ يورتلق estate, domain. — ocaklık vechile Ott. hist. by way of domain-land and family possession.

yurtsever neol. patriotic. —lik patriotism.

yurtsuz يورتسز homeless.

yurttaş يورتداش fellow countryman, compatriot. —lık common citizenship. —lık bilgisi civics.

Yusuf (—.) يوسف A Joseph. — efendi tangerine. —i sânî Irnd. a second Joseph, a very beautiful boy.

yusufçukᵗⁱ يوسفجق 1. turtle-dove, zool., Streptopelia turtur. 2. dragonfly, zool., Libellula variegata.

Yusufî (—.—) يوسفي peaked turban (formerly worn by great personages). — sarık a form of turban worn by sultans with a cap covered with scarlet cloth.

yusyumru (´..) يوصیومرو very swollen, round.

yusyumşak[¹] يوصیومشاق very soft.

yusyuvarlak[¹] (´...) يوصیوارلاق very round.

Yuşa[ⁿ¹] (—.) يوشع A Bib. Joshua.

yut=[ⁿʳ] يوتمق /ı/ 1. to swallow; to gulp down; to devour. 2. to swallow (an insult); to endure in silence (injury). 3. to believe (a lie); to swallow (a tall story). 4. to win (at cards). 5. to appropriate wrongfully. 6. to swallow whole, take on faith. 7. to know well and in detail, to learn very well (lesson).

yutkun=[ⁿʳ] يوتقونمق to swallow one's spittle; to gulp in suppressing one's emotions.

yutma يوتمه 1. verbal n. of **yut**=. 2. swallowed; duped; beaten. 3. neol., biol. deglutition.

yuttur=[ⁿʳ] يوتدرمق to sell (a lie); to talk into accepting (a ruse). —**maca** joke made so cleverly that the person to whom it is directed will not get it. —**ul**= pass. of **yuttur**=.

yutucu يوتیجی 1. who swallows or devours. 2. who wins (at cards).

yutul=[ⁿʳ] يوتلمق pass. of **yut**=.

yuva يووا 1. nest; home. 2. socket; seating (of a valve). — **boz**= to break up a home. — **kur**= to build a nest; to set up a home. —**sını yap**= /ın/ to give someone a scolding, to teach someone a lesson.

yuvacı يوواجی Ott. hist. provider and raiser of hunting birds for the Court.

yuvak[¹] يواق prov. cylinder.

yuvala=[ʳ] 1 يووالامق /ı/ to nest; to make a nest.

yuvala=[ʳ] 2 يووالامق archaic, same as **yuvarla**=.

yuvalak[¹] يووالاق archaic, same as **yuvarlak**.

yuvalan=[ⁿʳ] يووالانمق to become provided with a nest or socket.

yuvar neol., biol. globule, corpuscle.

yuvarla=[ʳ] يووارلامق /ı/ 1. to rotate; to roll. 2. to roll up; to roll along. 3. to swallow greedily. 4. to utter (a lie). 5. to toss off (glass of wine). 6. to turn out of office.

yuvarlak[¹] يووارلاق 1. round, spherical, globular. 2. ball; marble. 3. limber of a gun. 4. cylinder of a printing press. — **bağ** neol., anat. round ligament. — **hesap** round figure.

yuvarlaklaş=[ⁿʳ] يووارلاقلاشمق to become round or globular. —**tır**= /ı/ caus.

yuvarlaklık[¹] يووارلاقلق roundness.

yuvarlan=[ⁿʳ] يووارلانمق 1. to revolve, turn round. 2. to roll along; to topple over. 3. to lose one's job, to be fired. 4. to be tormented (by grief or worry). 5. slang to die suddenly. —**ıp git**= to worry along somehow.

yuvarlat=[ⁿʳ] يووارلاتمق /ı/ 1. to cause to rotate. 2. to make round.

yuz (—) يوز P lrnd. cheetah, zool., Acinonyx jubatus. —**ân** (——) P pl.

yübuset (.—.) يبوست A lrnd. a being dry; dryness.

yüce يوجه 1. high. 2. exalted (person or position). 3. high place. 4. monumental. **Y— Divan** High Court.

yücel 1 يوجل same as **yüce**.

yücel=[ⁿʳ] 2 يوجلمك to become high, to rise.

yücelen=[ⁿʳ] يوجەلنمك to become high or exalted.

yücelik[¹] يوجەلك 1. height; loftiness. 2. exalted rank.

yücelt=[ⁿʳ] يوجەلتمك /ı/ caus. of **yücel**=. —**il**= pass. of **yücelt**=.

yüğrük[ᵏᵘ] يوگرك prov. fast going, fleet. —**lük** fleetness.

yüğür=[ⁿʳ] 1 يوگورمك prov. 1. to run, to go fast. 2. to make a charge, attack or incursion. 3. to make an accusation or vituperation.

yüğür=[ⁿʳ] 2 يوگورمك prov. to mate (female animal with a male animal).

yük[ᵏᵘ] يوك 1. load, burden. 2. heavy task or responsibility. 3. cargo; pile of bedding. 4. large cupboard for bedding. 5. Ott. hist. sum of one hundred thousand kurush. 6. archaic fetus, embryo, unborn young. —**ünü al**= 1. to become crowded. 2. to take all it can hold. —**ün altından kalkama**= to find one's duties too much for one. — **arabası** wagon. — **beygiri** pack horse. — **götür**= 1. to carry a load. 2. to bear, support, endure a load or weight. —**te hafif pahada ağır** light but valuable. — **hayvanı** pack animal. — **ol**= /a/ to be a burden on a person. —**ünü tut**= to become rich. —**ü üzerinden at**= to decline or shift a responsibility. — **vur**= /a/ to load (an animal). — **yık**= to unload, to throw off the loads of animals. —**ünü yukarıya yığ**= archaic to ask a high price. —**ünü yüklenmiş** wealthy.

yükle=[ʳ] يوكلەمك /ı, a/ 1. to load. 2. to throw the blame (on). 3. to impute; to attribute.

yüklem neol., gram., log. predicate; attribute.

yükleme يوكلەمە verbal n. of **yükle**=. — **müddeti** lay days, loading days.

yüklen=[ⁿʳ] يوكلەنمك 1. pass. of **yükle**=. 2. /ı/ to shoulder (a burden). —**il**= same as **yüklen**=.

yüklet=[ⁿʳ] يوكلەتمك /ı, a/ 1. to place a load on; to load (ship, etc.). 2. to impose (duty, expense). 3. to impute, attribute. —**en** shipper. —**tir**= /ı, a/ caus. of **yüklet**=.

yüklü يوكلو 1. loaded, laden; burdened. 2. pregnant. 3. overburdened with work. 4. in debt. 6. colloq. rich. 7. slang drunk.

yüklük[su] 1. large cupboard or closet for bedding. 2. porter's knot.
yüksek[si] 1. high; elevated; tall. 2. loud (voice). 3. high altitude. —**ten at**= to boast. — **atlama** high jump. —**ten bak**= /a/ to look down upon. —**lerde dolaş**= to aim high, to be ambitious. — **döşlü** *prov.* high-shouldered. — **kabartma** *art* high relief. —**ten kop**= to set out with great pretensions. — **okul** institution of higher education. — **öğretim** *neol.* higher education. — **perdeden konuş**= 1. to talk in a high pitch. 2. to talk big; to talk challengingly. — **sesle oku**= to read aloud. —**ten uç**= to be ambitious or presumptious. — **ustura** *slang* big lie. — **üstlüklü at** tall horse. — **yığ**= same as **yükünü yukarıya yığ**=.
yükseklik[si] height, elevation, altitude.
yüksel=[ir] 1. to mount; to rise; to rise high. 2. to be promoted. 3. to gain the open sea (ship). —**iş**, —**me** *verbal n.*
yükselt=[ir] /ı/ *caus.* of **yüksel**=. —**me** 1. *verbal n.* 2. *neol.*, *phil.* sublimation.
yükserek[si] somewhat higher.
yüksü=[r] archaic for **yüksün**=.
yüksük[su] thimble. —**le ölç**= /ı/ to dole out stingily. — **otu** foxglove, *bot.*, *Digitalis purpurea*.
yüksün=[ür] 1. to show dissatisfaction when charged with some task, to fret under a duty, to regard as burdensome. 2. *prov.* to begrudge, to envy, to be jealous (of), to grudge giving or fulfilling a promise.
yüküm *neol.* burden; obligation, liability. —**lü** obligatory, compulsory.
yükün=[ür] archaic to bow or kneel (before someone).
yüle=[r], **yület**=[ir] /ı/ *prov.* to sharpen, whet, grind.
yülgü archaic razor.
yülü=[r] *prov.* /ı/ to shave off with a razor.
yülüğen *prov.* razor.
yülük[su] *prov.* shaven; smooth.
yülün=[ür] *prov.* to be shaved with a razor.
yülüt=[ür] /ı, a/ *prov.*, *caus.* of **yülü**=.
yülüyücü *prov.* barber.
yümn A *lrnd.* a being lucky; prosperity.
yümna A *lrnd.* right (hand); the right hand.
yümni (.—) A *lrnd.* pertaining to prosperity or auspiciousness.
yümum (.—) A *lrnd.*, *pl.* of **yem** 2.
yümün[mnü] *var.* of **yümn**.
yün wool; woolen. — **çorap** wool socks or stockings. — **iplik** wool yarn; worsted.

yüncülük[sü] wool production; wool trade.
yünle=[r] /ı/ 1. to furnish, coat, pad with wool. 2. to deprive of wool.
yünlen=[ir] to become woolly; to be frayed.
yünlü 1 1. woolen. 2. woolly. 3. woolen cloth. 4. coated, padded with wool.
yünlü 2 *prov.* fishing net.
yünlük[sü] *Ott. hist.* the part of a Janissary hat where a plume or aigrette was placed.
yünül[lü] *prov.* light; easy. —**let**= /ı/ to consider as light and unimportant.
yürek[gi] 1. heart. 2. *colloq.* stomach. 3. center of the affections. 4. courage, boldness. 5. *cards* hearts. —**ten** sincerely, heartfelt. — **acısı**, —**ler acısı** heart-breaking (event or condition). —**i açık** simple-hearted; ingenuous; sincere. — **ağrısı** pain in the heart; stomach ache. —**i ağzına gel**= /ın/ to be suddenly frightened. —**i at**= to have palpitations. —**i bayıl**= to be very hungry. — **berkliği** hardness of heart. —**ini boşalt**= to make a clean breast of it. — **burması** stomach cramps, colic. —**i cız et**=, —**i cızla**= to be moved with great compassion. —**i çarp**= same as —**i at**=. — **çarpıntısı** 1. palpitation of the heart. 2. misgivings. —**i çek**= to wish to have, to desire. —**i dar** impatient. — **dayanmaz** unbearable; heart-breaking. —**i delik** full of woes. —**ine derd ol**= to have a troubled feeling (about something). — **dol**= to be full of complaint and bitterness. —**i dolu** having a persistent grudge. —**ini dök**= same as **yüreğini boşalt**=. —**i ezil**= to feel sudden hunger. —**i ferahla**= to feel relieved. —**i geniş** easy-going, unworried. —**i hop et**=, —**i hopla**= to feel one's heart jump for joy or fear. —**ine in**= /ın/ to be struck with great fear, agitation or shame. —**ine işle**= to feel deeply (words). —**i kabar**= 1. to be nauseated. 2. to suffer trouble or pain. —**ini kaldır**= to upset or excite someone thoroughly; to make feel nauseated. —**i kalk**= to be alarmed; to be very upset; to feel nauseated. —**ine kar yağ**= /ın/ to suffer a pang of jealousy. — **karası** wickedness, depravity. —**i karar**= to be dismayed, to feel hopeless. —**i katı** 1. hard-hearted. 2. obdurate, obstinate. — **katıl**= 1. to suffer greatly. 2. to gasp for breath. — **katılığı** hardness of heart. —**i kop**= to suffer fear or pain greatly. —**ine od düş**= same as **yüreği yan**=. —**i oyna**= to have a fluttering of the heart; to have misgivings. —**i parçalan**= /ın/ to feel very sorry (for someone). —**i pek** stout-hearted. —**ini pek tut**= to hold on to one's courage. — **perdesi** *anat.* pericardium. — **Selânik!** *colloq.* coward. —**i serinle**= to feel relieved. —**i sıkıl**= to

Red 80.

feel depressed or bored. —i sızla= to be greatly sorry (for someone). —i söyle= to be brave. —ine su serpil= to be refreshed or comforted. — sür= prov. to have diarrhea. —i şiş= to feel greatly bored (from long discussion). —i tüken= to wear oneself out (in trying to explain something). —ini tüket= 1. caus. of yüreği tüken=. 2. same as yüreği tüken=. — ver= /a/ to hearten, to give courage. —i yağ bağla= to drink deeply of happiness; to feel very happy. —inin yağı eri= /in/ 1. to desire intensely. 2. to feel greatly sorry or anxious. —i yan= 1. to be grieved; to feel pity. 2. to meet with disaster. — yarası great sorrow. —i yaralı stricken with sorrow or disaster. —i yufka easily moved, compassionate.

yüreklen=[ir] to take heart, to become emboldened. —dir= /ı/ caus.

yürekli brave, bold, stout-hearted. —lik stout-heartedness, courage.

yüreksiz 1. faint-hearted, timid. 2. apathetic, lukewarm. —lik faint-heartedness, timidity; lukewarmness.

yürü=[r] 1. to walk; to move, to go in any way or direction. 2. to advance, to make progress. 3. to march (army). 4. to hurry along. 5. slang to die.

yürüğen archaic 1. walking or moving fast. 2. sharp.

yürük[gü] 1. active, that goes fast, fleet. 2. w. cap. nomad. 3. w. cap., Ott. hist. a class of Janissary soldiers. — aksak mus. a rhythmic pattern. — sema'î mus. 1. a rhythmic pattern with six beats. 2. a form of vocal music sung just before the instrumental piece at the end of a fasıl. — sofyan mus. a rhythmic pattern.

yürükân (..—) P lrnd., pl. of yürük.

yürüme 1. verbal n. of yürü=. 2. walk; pace.

yürürlük[gü] neol., law a being in force; validity. —e geç= to become effective. —e koy= /ı/ to make effective.

yürüt=[ür] /ı/ 1. caus. of yürü=. 2. slang to walk off with, to steal. 3. slang to fire, to dismiss. 4. neol. to put into force. —me verbal n. —ül= pass. of yürüt=. —üm neol. execution, a carrying out.

yürüyüş 1. verbal n. of yürü=. 2. gait; march; assault. — kapısı wicket gate.

yüsr A lrnd. 1. facility. 2. wealth; riches; ease.

yüsra A lrnd. 1. more or most easy; more or most affluent. 2. left (hand); left handed.

yüz 1 hundred; one hundred. —ü devir= 1. to pass the hundredth year. 2. to drink off a hundred dirhems of wine at once. —de*. — yıl*. —ler neol., arith. hundreds. —lerce, —lerle by hundreds, in hundreds; in great numbers.

yüz 2 1. face. 2. surface; outer covering of a thing. 3. face or right side (of a thing). 4. boldness; effrontery. —de successful; triumphant. —den 1. on the surface. 2. superficial. —ünde /ın/ on, on the surface of. —ünden for the sake of, on account of. —ü açıl= to flourish, to become beautiful. —ünü ağart= to do honor (to). — akı personal honor. —ünden akıyor /ın/ It is obvious that he... You can see by his looks that... —ü ak alnı pak pure and honest, without blemish. —ü ak olsun! Bless him! phrase expressing gratitude. — aklığı freedom from shame or disgrace, serenity of honest pride. —ü astarı belirsiz of doubtful character. —üne at= /ın/ to cast in one's face (act), to reproach or taunt one (with some deed). —üne bağır= /ın/ to shout at. — bağla= to form cream (milk). —üne bakılacak gibi, —üne bakılır good looking. —üne bakma= /ın/ 1. not to pay attention to. 2. to be cross with. —üne bakmağa kıyılmaz very beautiful. —üne bakılmaz ugly, horrible. — berkliği impudence. —ü boyalı gelin gibi kal= (lit., to keep rigid like a bride with a painted face) to look foolish. — bul= to be emboldened; to become presumptuous; to be spoiled (by kind treatment). — bulunca astar ister If you give him an inch he will take a mile. —ünden çek= /ın/ to suffer at the hands of. — çevir= /dan/ to be estranged, to turn away from. —e çık= 1. to come to the surface. 2. to be insolent; to maintain a position arrogantly. —ü davul derisi (lit. His face is a drum's skin.) He is brazen-faced. —ünden düşen bin parça olur sour-faced, frowning terribly. —ünü eğ= to frown. — ekşit= to make a sour face, to look cross. — et= /ı/ 1. prov. to hand something over. 2. to face up (two boards that are to be joined together). —e gel= same as yüze vur=. —e gelen select, superior. — geri dön= to face about, to turn around; to retreat. — göre just to please or flatter. — görümü, — görümlüğü customary present given by a bridegroom to his bride on first seeing her unveiled face. — göster= to put in an appearance; to show up. — göz a being too familiar. —ünü gözünü aç= to open one's eyes, to initiate (a child) to knowledge about sex. —üne gözüne bula=, —üne gözüne bulaştır= /ı/ (lit., to besmear face and eyes) to spoil or disarrange thoroughly through incapacity, to make a mess of something, to fail. — göz ol= /la/ to become too intimate when one would like to keep his distance. **—e gül=** to feign friendship, to dissimulate scorn or hate. **—ü gül=** to be happy or delighted. **—ünü güldür=** /ın/ to make happy. **—ünden kan damlıyor** rosy-cheeked; very healthy. **—üne kan gel=** to recover one's health. **—ü kara** one who in the past has done something to be ashamed of, disgraced, in disgrace. **—üne kara dürt=** to throw one's lie into one's face. **— karası** dishonor, disgrace, shame. **—üne karşı** to one's face. **—ü kasap süngeri ile silinmiş** brazen-faced, who has no sense of shame, thoroughly unashamed. **—ünü kızart=** 1. to overcome one's natural reluctance (in asking a favor). 2. /ın/ to cause someone to blush. **— kızartıcı** shameful, disgusting. **—ünü kızdır=** *same as* **yüzünü kızart=**. **—ü kibrit gibi oldu** His face became sallow. **—ü koyu**, **—ü koyun***. **— maskarası** mask. **—ünden oku=** /ı/ 1. to read on sight (as opposed to reciting by heart). 2. to understand from one's face. **—ü olma=** 1. not to have the face (to), not to dare. 2. to be unable to refuse; to be unable to face. **—ü pek** brazen-faced, shameless. **—ü sıcak** sympathetic, attractive. **—ü soğuk** dour. **— suyu** honor, self-respect. **— suyu dök=** to degrade oneself. **—ü suyu hürmetine** /ın/ out of respect (to) someone; thanks (to) him. **—ü sulu** *archaic* 1. whose face is fresh and lovely. 2. honest, honorable. **— surat hak getire**, **— surat mahkeme duvarı** *colloq.* brazen-faced, unashamed. **— sür=** /a/ to pay humble respect (to a superior), to prostrate oneself humbly (before). **—ü teneke kaplı** brazen-faced, shameless. **— tut=** /mağa/ to begin; to take a turn towards. **—ü tutma=** to feel ashamed to do (something); to shrink (from an act). **—üm tutmaz** I can't bring myself (to do or say so and so). **— üstü***. **— ver=** /a/ to be indulgent (to), to spoil; to give encouragement. **— verince astar ister** If you give him an inch he will take a mile. **— vur=** /a/ to apply (to), to refer (to); to have recourse (to). **—üne vur=** /ın/ to cast (something) in (a person's) teeth; to reproach (someone) with something. **— yastığı** pillow. **—ünü yaz=** /ın/ to decorate the face (of a bride). **— yazdır=** to cause a face to be painted, decorated. **— yazısı** decoration stuck on to the face of a village bride. **— yazıcı** woman who paints and embellishes faces. **—ü yazılı kal=** to remain untouched. **—ü yerde** modest, humble. **—ü yere gel=** to feel ashamed of somebody. **—ü yok** 1. He hasn't got the face! He doesn't dare! He is ashamed of himself. 2. One can't hold out against, *e. g.*, **sıcağa yüzüm yok** I can't face the heat. **—ü yumuşak** too kind to refuse. **— yüze** face to face. **— yüze bak=** to meet, to look each other in the face.

— yüze gel= /la/ to come face to face with, to meet. **— yüzden utanır** It is easier for people to be reconciled when they come face to face.

yüz=[er] 3 بوزمك to swim; to float.

yüz=[er] 4 بوزمك /ı/ 1. to flay; to skin. 2. to despoil. **—dük yüzdük kuyruğuna geldik** The main job is done; the lesser one will easily be done. A little patience, we are nearly there.

yüzbaşı بوزباشى captain (army). **—lık** rank of captain.

yüzbeyüz بوزبيوز face to face.

yüzde بوزده percent; percentage; rate. **— beş** five percent. **— nisbeti** percentage. **— yüz** one hundred percent. **—lik** percentage.

yüzdür=[ür] 1 بوزدرمك /ı/ 1. *caus.* of **yüz=** 3. 2. to float. 3. *slang* to send or drive away.

yüzdür=[ür] 2 بوزدرمك /ı, a/ *caus.* of **yüz=** 4.

yüzdürme بوزدرمه *verbal n.* of **yüz=** 3. **— kabiliyeti**, **— kuvveti** buoyancy.

yüzdürül=[ür] بوزدرولمك *pass.* of **yüzdür=** 1.

yüzer 1 بوزر a hundred each; a hundred at a time. **— yüzer** by the hundreds.

yüzer 2 بوزر that swims. **— havuz** floating dock.

yüzerlik[ği] بوزرلك *prov., same as* **üzerlik**.

yüzey *neol.* surface.

yüzgeç[ci] بوزكج 1. swimming; floating; knowing how to swim; swimmer. 2. fin; float (of a seaplane). **—lik** quality of a swimmer.

yüzle=[r] بوزله مك /ı/ to accuse openly, to make open reproaches, to put on the spot. **—n=** *pass.*

yüzleş=[ir] بوزلشمك /la/ to meet face to face; to be confronted with one another. **—tir=** /ı, a/ to confront. **—tiril=** *pass.*

yüzlü 1 بوزلى with (such and such) a face or surface. **— yüzlü** unashamedly.

yüzlü 2 بوزلى having a hundred.

yüzlük[ğü] 1 بوزلك cover or protection for the face.

yüzlük[ğü] 2 بوزلك 1. costing, worth or weighing one hundred. 2. a hundred lira bill. 3. bulb of 100 watts.

yüzlülük[ğü] بوزلىلك state of having (such and such) a face.

yüzsüz بوزسز 1. brazen-faced, shameless. 2. having no case (pillows). **—lük** shamelessness, effrontery.

yüzücü بوزجى 1. swimmer. 2. flayer.

yüzük[ğü] بوزوك ring. **— çevir=** to play the **yüzük oyunu**. **—ü geri çevir=** to break off an engagement. **— oyunu** a parlor game (resembling the English "Up Jenkins"). **— parmağı** ring finger, the fourth finger.

yüzükoyu, yüzükoyun بوزى قويو بوزى قويون

يوزی طوبین face downwards, lying on one's face; upside down. — düş= to fall down flat on the face. — kapan= 1. to throw oneself flat on the face. 2. to trip and fall flat.

yüzül=ᵘʳ يوزیلمك pass. of **yüz**= 4.

yüzüncü يوزنجی hundredth.

yüzüstü يوزاوستی 1. face downwards. 2. as things are, incomplete. — bırak= /ı/ to leave things as they are in an incomplete condition. — kapan= to be prostrate with one's face on the ground.

yüzyıl neol. century.

Z

z, Z the twenty-ninth letter of the alphabet.

za 1 (—) زا‌ name of the letter ز (the thirteenth letter of the Ottoman and Persian alphabets and eleventh letter of the Arabic; in chronograms it has the numerical value of 7).

za 2 (—) ظا‌ name of the letter ظ (the twentieth letter of the Ottoman and Persian alphabets and seventeenth of the Arabic; in chronograms it has the numerical value of 900).

-za 3 (—) زا P lrnd. that gives birth to, bringing forth, producing, as in **fitneza, nadireza, nükteza, sühenza**.

zaafᶻᵃ'ᶠⁱ ضعف [za'f 1] weakness, feebleness, infirmity; weak spot, foible.

zaafallah iktidarehu (. — . — . . — . .) ضاعف الله اقتداره A rel. formula May God increase his power.

zaafet (. —.) ضعافت A lrnd. a being or becoming weak; weakness.

zaafir (. —.) زعافر A lrnd., pl. of za'feran.

zaamet (. —.) زعامت A same as zeamet.

zabab (. —) ضباب A lrnd. mist, fog.

zabıtᵖᵗᵘ **1** ضبط [zabt] minutes (of a meeting), protocol, proceedings. — tut= to take minutes.

zâbıt 2 (—.) ضابط A lrnd. that holds and restrains.

zâbıta (. —..) ضابطه A 1. police. 2. lrnd. organization, order; rule. — memuru police magistrate; policeman.

zâbıtalıkᵍⁱ ضابطه لك matter for the police; person whom only the police can deal with.

zabıtname (. . —.) ضبطنامه [zabtname] lrnd. 1. minutes (of a meeting). 2. proceedings; protocol.

zabi ظبی A lrnd. wild buck, gazelle.

zâbih (—.) ذابح A lrnd. that slaughters by cutting the throat of a sacrifice; sacrificer.

zâbit (—.) ضابط A 1. officer. 2. lrnd. capable of command, who can keep discipline. — nâmzedi gentleman cadet.

zâbitân (—. —.) ضابطان P officers. —ı aklâm senior clerks in public offices.

zabitlikᵍⁱ ضابطلك rank, status and duties of an officer; commission.

zabt ضبط A lrnd. 1. a holding firmly; a firm hold. 2. a taking possession of, a conquering. 3. a restraining, controlling, mastering. 4. a seizing by violence; seizure. 5. a grasping, understanding. 6. a taking down in writing. — ü rabt orderliness; discipline.

zabtiye ضبطیه same as zaptiye. Z— Nazırı Ott. hist. Minister of Public Security. Z— Nezareti Ott. hist. Ministry of Public Security.

zabtname (. . —.) ضبطنامه P same as zabıtname.

zabtsız ضبطسز not under firm rule and restraint. —lık disorder from lack of firm rule.

zabuᵘᵘ ضبع A lrnd. hyena, especially female hyena.

Zabül (—.) زابل P lrnd., name of a country and people formerly occupying a part of Afghanistan. —î (—. —) P of the people or country of Zabul.

Zabülistan (—. . —) زابلستان P the region including Kabul, and Ghaznin, the native country of Rustem.

zaby ظبی A lrnd. wild buck, gazelle.

zac 1 (—) زاج P iron or zinc sulfate. —i Kıbrıs iron sulfate. — yağı sulfuric acid.

zacᶜᶜⁱ **2** ضجیج A lrnd. a crying out in distress.

zacce ضجة A lrnd. a cry; a clamor; uproar.

zacir (—.) زاجر A *lrnd.* 1. who chides and compels. 2. prohibitive.

zacirat (—.—) زاجرات A *Isl. rel.* 1. angels that compel the clouds. 2. passages of the Quran containing threats and prohibitions.

zacire (—..) زاجره A *lrnd.* 1. *same as* **zacir**¹. 2. rebuke, threat.

zaciyet (—..) زاجیت A *lrnd.* the quality of vitriol.

zad 1 ضاد A *name of the letter* ض (the eighteenth letter of the Ottoman and Turkish alphabets, and fifteenth of the Arabic alphabet; in chronograms it has the numerical value of 800).

zad 2 (—) زاد A *lrnd.* 1. stock of provisions. 2. good works (as a store laid up for Judgment day). —**ı sefer** provisions for a journey. —**ve yarak** *archaic* provisions and necessities. —**ü zevad** provisions and supplies.

zad 3 (—) زاد P *lrnd.* anything born. —**ü bûd** 1. all that has been, is or will be. 2. goods and chattels. —**ı dil** *Or. mus.* **makam** no longer extant, first used in the seventeenth century.

-zad 4 (—) زاد P *lrnd.* born of (so and so); free; noble, *e. g.*, **nevzad, perizad**.

zad^(ddı) **5** ضدّ A *lrnd.* 1. a getting the better, gaining a case (in law). 2. a turning one back or away.

zadallahu kadrehu (—.—. ...) زاد الله قدره A *rel. formula* May God raise him to a high degree.

zadallahu mecdehu (—.—. ...) زاد الله مجده A *rel. formula* May God increase his honor.

zade 1 (—.) زاده P 1. born; noble. 2. son.

-zade 2 زاده P son of, *e. g.*, **haramzade, şehzade**.

zadegân (—.—) زادگان P 1. nobles; noble. 2. the nobility and gentry. — **alayı** *slang* rascal, vagabond. — **hâkimiyeti** aristocracy. —**ı ilmiye** *Ott. hist.* sons of scholars of high position. —**lık** nobility of birth, aristocracy.

zadegi (—.—) زادگی P *lrnd.* noble birth.

zadelik^(81) زاده لك noble birth.

zadmerd (—.) زادمرد P *lrnd.* noble-minded man; valiant; generous.

za'f 1 ضعف A *lrnd., same as* **zaaf**. —**ı asabi** neurasthenia. —**ı basar** weakness of sight. —**ı kalb** 1. weakness of heart. 2. pusillanimity. —**ı mizac** feeble health. —**ı pirî** weakness caused by old age. —**ı te'lif** *gram.* a making a pronoun precede the noun to which it relates.

za'f 2 ضعف A *lrnd.* a killing on the spot.

za'f 3 ذعف A *lrnd.* 1. a poisoning. 2. a dying quickly or suddenly.

zafair (.—.) ضفائر A *lrnd., pl. of* **zafire**.

zafer ظفر A a being successful, an attaining to; success, attainment; accomplishment; victory. — **bul**= to be successful or victorious.

za'feran (..—) زعفران A *lrnd.* 1. saffron. 2. iron rust. —**ı âhen**, —**ı hadid** sesquioxide of iron, crocus powder. —**ı Yemen** saffron of Yemen, *bot.*, Memecylon tinctorium; dyer's weed, *bot.*, Reseda Luteola. —**î** (..——) A mixed or colored with saffron; like saffron.

zaferbu (..—) ظفربو P *lrnd.* that promises success or victory.

zafername (..—.) ظفرنامه P eulogy praising a victory; article written about a victory.

zaferrehber ظفررهبر P *lrnd.* victorious.

zaferyab (..—) ظفریاب P *lrnd.* successful; victorious.

zâfir (—.) ظافر A *lrnd.* victorious, conquering; conqueror.

zafire (.—.) ضفیره A *lrnd.* braided lock, hair twisted or plaited.

za'fiyet A, **zafiyet** (—..) ضعفیت 1. weakness, debility; thinness. 2. tuberculosis.

zağ 1 (—) زاغ P *lrnd.* 1. carrion crow, *zool.*, Corvus corone. 2. rook, *zool.*, Corvus frugilegus. 3. horn of an archery bow. —**ı siyah** inauspicious person.

zağ 2 (—) زاغ *prov.* very keen edge; keenness of edge (of a sword). — **ver**= /a/ to whet.

zağan 1 (——) زاغان P *lrnd.* crows, rooks.

zağan 2 زغن P *lrnd.* black kite, *zool.*, Milvus migrans.

zağanos 1 زاغنوس Gk 1. edible sea-crab, *zool.*, Cancer pagarus. 2. *same as* **çağanoz**.

zağanos 2, zağanoz زاغنوس hunting owl trained like a falcon.

zağar زغار hound.

zağara زغاره [zıhâre] fur collar (of a coat).

zağarcı زغارجی *Ott. hist.* 1. Imperial houndsman, keeper of the Sultan's hounds. 2. Janissary serving in the 64th regiment. — **başı** commander of the 64th Janissary regiment.

zağbeçe (—..) زاغبچه P *lrnd.* young rook or crow.

zağçeşm (—..) زاغچشم P *lrnd.* blue-eyed.

zağine ضغینه A *lrnd.* hatred.

zağla= ضغا /1/ 1. to give a keen edge to. 2. to polish (sword, knife). —**t**= /1/ *caus.*

zağs ضغث A *lrnd.* 1. bunch, bundle; faggot. 2. medley, jumble.

zağsız ضغسز dull, blunt.

zağzağa زغزغه A *lrnd.* nonsense.

zahair (.—.) ذخائر A *lrnd., pl. of* **zahire 1**.

zahairullah (.—..—) ذخائرالله A *lrnd.* God's store of saints on earth.

zahamet (..—.) ضخامت A *lrnd.* a being big, large; bigness. —**li** big, large.

zahf ضعف A *lrnd.* 1. a creeping; a dragging

itself along (animal). 2. an army marching against the enemy; a numerous army.

zahırʰʳⁱ ظهر A *var. of* **zahr** 2.

zâhib (—.) ذاهب A *lrnd.* 1. who goes, follows, travels along. 2. who forms or follows (a doctrine). 3. who supposes, forms an idea. **— ol=** /a/ 1. to follow (a doctrine). 2. to incline (to an idea), to surmise.

zâhid (—.) زاهد A *lrnd.* piously abstemious, ascetic. **—i huşk** 1. a rigid ascetic (without divine love in his heart). 2. hypocrite, dissembler.

zâhidâne (—.—.) زاهدانه P pertaining to an ascetic, ascetic.

zâhidî (—.—) زاهدى P asceticism for religious reasons; piety.

zâhidnihad (—..—) زاهدنهاد P *lrnd.* of an ascetic temperament.

zahif 1 (—.) زاحف A *lrnd.* creeping, crawling.

zahif 2 (—.) زاخف A *lrnd.* boasting, vainglorious, proud.

zahife (—..) زاحفه A *zool.* reptile.

zahikᵏⁱ 1 (—.) ذاهق A *lrnd.* 1. that goes away, departs. 2. that fades away, disappears, comes to naught; vanishing, perishing.

zahikᵏⁱ 2 (—.) ضاحك A *lrnd.* 1. laughing, smiling. 2. that appears; conspicuous.

zahil 1 (—.) ذاهل A *lrnd.* forgetful, unmindful, neglectful; willfully careless.

zahil 2 (—.) زاهل A *lrnd.* who withdraws from evil and trouble; who is tranquil at heart.

zahil 3 (—.) زاحل A *lrnd.* 1. who goes away or remains at a distance; distant. 2. that lags, hangs back; backward. 3. fatigued, exhausted.

zahir 1 (—.) ظاهر [**zahir 2**] apparently, clearly, evidently.

zahir 2 (—.) ظاهر A *lrnd.* 1. outward, external; outside, exterior (of a thing). 2. apparent, plain, self-evident; outward circumstances of a thing; the visible world. 3. the words and acts of a man. 4. the Manifest One (a title of God). 5. successful; victorious, dominant. **—e bak=** to look at the exterior circumstances only. **— ve batın** external and internal, outer appearance and inward qualities. **—i bâtınına muvafık** whose outward words and acts correspond with his inward sentiments. **— ol=** to be or become evident. **—i şehirde** on the outskirts of the town.

zahir 3 (.—) ظهير A *lrnd.* helper, supporter, backer.

zahir 4 (—.) زاخر A *lrnd.* 1. boiling up and overflowing. 2. full, swelling (sea); raging, violent. 3. liberal; luxuriant.

zahir 5 (—.) زاهر A *lrnd.* 1. shining, bright. 2. blooming, in bloom.

zahir 6 (.—) ظصير A *lrnd.* a twisting of the guts with griping and discharge of blood, dysentery.

zahirbin (—.—) ظاهربين P *lrnd.* who sees only the outside of things, superficial.

zahire 1 (.—.) ذخيره A store of grain or provisions; provisions. **— ambarı** granary. **— nâzırı** *Ott. hist.* superintendent of grain and provisions.

zahire 2 (—..) ظاهره A *lrnd.* 1. exterior; the outside of a thing. 2. apparent. 3. those who help a person.

zâhiren (—..) ظاهراً A 1. outwardly, to outward appearance. 2. *lrnd.* by heart, from memory. **— kıraat et=** *lrnd.* to recite by heart.

zahiri (—.—) ظاهرى A 1. external, outward 2. *phil.* phenomenal. **— görünüm** *phys.* image. **—yât** (—..—) A outward appearances.

zahiriyet (—...) ظاهريت A *lrnd.* quality of that which is external, visible or predominant; manifestation, externality.

zahirperest (—...) ظاهرپرست P *lrnd.* who esteems externals highly; superficial observer.

zahiye (—..) ضاحيه A *lrnd.* 1. distant province, border land. 2. open country; desert. 3. outer exposed part, especially, exposed to the sun.

zahiyeten (—'...) ضاحية A *lrnd.* openly, publicly.

zahlᵘ 1 ذحل A *lrnd.* 1. blood revenge, retaliation for homicide; blood feud. 2. revenge for any wrong; enmity, hatred; grudge.

zahlᵘ 2 زحل A *lrnd.* a keeping back or aloof, a withdrawing, vanishing.

zahm 1 زخم P *lrnd.* 1. blow (with a weapon), wound, bruise. 2. a stroke on an instrument. **—i çeşm** the evil eye. **—i hançer** a dagger blow.

zahm 2 ضخم A *lrnd.* big, large.

zahmdar (—.) زخمدار P *lrnd.* hurt, wounded, struck.

zahme 1 زخمه P *lrnd.* plectrum (of a stringed musical instrument).

zahme 2 زخمه stirrup strap.

zahmet زحمت A trouble; difficulty; distress; fatigue. **— buyurdunuz** You have put yourself to great trouble. **— çek=** to suffer trouble or fatigue. **—ine değdi** It was worth the trouble. **— et=**, **—e gir=** to go to a lot of trouble, to inconvenience oneself. **—e koş=** /ı/, **—e sok=** /ı/, **— ver=** /a/ to occasion trouble, to cause trouble.

zahmetli زحمتلى troublesome; painful; difficult; fatiguing.

zahmetsiz زحمتسز free from trouble; easy. **—ce** easily; without trouble.

zahmhâr (.—) زخمخوار P *lrnd.* wounded, hurt.
zahmhurde زخم خورده P *lrnd.* hurt, wounded.
zahmkâr (.—) زخمكار P *lrnd.* wounding, hurting. —**î** a being hurt; mortal wound.
zahmnâk^kı (.—) زخمناك P *lrnd.* wounded, struck.
zahmres زخمرس P *lrnd.* wounding, piercing.
zahmzede زخم زده P *lrnd.* hurt, wounded.
zahmzen زخمزن P *lrnd.* wounding, piercing.
zahr 1 ذخر A *lrnd.* a laying up in store.
zahr 2 ظهر A *lrnd.* 1. the back; the space behind one's back; the back of a book. 2. outer and visible form (of a thing); the letter, text, words of a saying. 3. outside or upper side of the hand, foot, etc. 4. stay or support for one's back. 5. burden on one's back.
zahre ظهره *colloq., var. of* **zahire 1.**
zahrî (.—) ظهری A *lrnd.* 1. pertaining to the back, dorsal. 2. pertaining to the exterior, external. —**ye** A label or title put on the outside of a document.
zaıf^za'fı ضعف [za'f 1] *same as* **zaaf.**
zaib (—.) ذائب A *lrnd.* 1. melting, melted; dissolving, dissolved; liquified, fluid. 2. flowing, running down. 3. suffused with tears (eye).
zaibülmâl (—..—) ذائب المال A *lrnd.* chattle property, especially livestock.
zaibünnefs (—...) ذائب النفس A *lrnd.* dull of intellect, stupid.
zaid (—.) زائد A 1. *math.* plus; above zero. 2. *lrnd.* additional; redundant, superfluous. — **işareti** the plus sign.
zaide (—..) زائده A *lrnd.* 1. servile letter. 2. *anat.* lobe of an organ, process of a bone.
zaif (.—) ضعیف A *lrnd., same as* **zayıf.**
zaifâne (.—.) ضعیفانه P *lrnd.* pertaining to one who is weak or poor; weakly, poorly.
zaife (.—.) ضعیفه A 1. weak woman. 2. woman; wife.
zaik^kı (—.) ذائق A *lrnd.* who or which tastes, taster.
zaika (—..) ذائقه A *physiol.* faculty of taste.
zail (—.) زائل A 1. *lrnd.* declining; that goes away, that disappears; disappearing. 2. *lrnd.* transitory, passing; perishable; that no longer exists; past. — **ol**= to go away; to disappear.
zaim 1 (—.) زائم A *lrnd.* having a fief.
zaim 2 (.—) زعیم A *Ott. hist.* 1. holder of a large military fief. 2. *law* surety.
zair (—.) زائر A *lrnd.* visitor; pilgrim.
zak^kı (—) زاغ P *lrnd.* the young of anything. — **ü zik** children; noise, uproar.
zakan ذقن A *lrnd.* chin; beard.
zâkdân (——) زاقدان P *lrnd.* womb; matrix.
zâki 1 (—.) ذاكی A *lrnd.* 1. bright, shining. 2. pungent.
zâki 2 (—.) زاكی A *lrnd.* 1. pure, undefiled;

good, virtuous, devout. 2. that thrives, grows; flourishing, thriving.
zakir (—.) ذاكر A *lrnd.* 1. dervish performing the **zikr** in a **tekke.** 2. who tells, narrates, recites from memory, especially who recites the names and praises of God. 3. who commits to memory; who remembers. —**başı** dervish leading the service. —**în** (—.—) A *pl. of* **zakir.** —**lik** quality or act of a chanter. —**un** (—.—) A *pl. of* **zakir.**
zakkum (.—) زقّوم A 1. oleander, *bot.*, *Nerium oleander.* 2. a tree that grows in hell (mentioned in the Quran). 3. very bitter. 4. food of the damned.
zakon زاقون Sl *slang* way, manner.
zâl^ıı 1 (—) ذال *name of the letter* ذ (the eleventh letter of the Ottoman and Persian alphabets and the ninth of the Arabic; in mathematical formulas it has the numerical value of 700; it is used as the abbreviation of the month **Zilhicce**).
zâl^ıı 2 زال P 1. *lrnd.* old, decrepit, white-haired. 2. *lrnd.* old hag. 3. *w. cap.*, name of a legendary Persian prince, father of Rustem. —**i bedfial** (*lit.*, the evil old hag) the world, fortune. **Z—i destan** Zal, the hero. **Z—i Kûfe** the old woman of Kufa out of whose oven the waters of the deluge issued without injuring her. **Z—i Medain** the old woman of Ctesiphon, whose hut was enclosed in the palace of Nushirevan. — **oğlu*.** —**i pir** a very decrepit old man. —**i ra'na** the world, fortune. —**i zaman** time, the world (considered as an old woman). **Z—i zer** Zal, the hero.
zalâl^ıı (.—) ظلال A *lrnd.* thing that shades, awning, cloud, etc.
zalâm (.—) ظلام A *lrnd.* 1. darkness; the dark. 2. oppression.
zaleme (...) ظلمه A *lrnd., pl. of* **zâlim.**
zalike (—..) ذالك A *lrnd.* that.
zalil (.—) ظلیل A *lrnd.* shady (place).
zalim (—.) ظالم A unjust; tyrannical; cruel; tyrant. —**âne** (—.—.) P unjust, tyrannical, cruel. —**în** (—.—) A *pl. of* **zalim.** —**lik** cruelty, oppression, tyranny.
zallâm (.—) ظلّام A *lrnd.* very unjust, tyrannical; great oppressor.
zalma ظلما A *lrnd.* dark night; darkness.
Zâloğlu (—..) زال اوغلی 1. *a name of Rustem.* 2. type of a very strong man.
zalûm (.—) ظلوم A *lrnd.* very unjust, tyrannical.
zam^mmı ضمّ A 1. addition; an adding; sum or quantity added. 2. *lrnd.* a gathering, collecting together. 3. *lrnd.* a pronouncing a consonant with the vowel **u, ü**; this vowel and its sign.

zama (.—) ضماء A *lrnd.* a being very thirsty; thirst.

zamaim (.—.) ضمائم A *lrnd.*, pl. of **zamime**.

zamair (.—.) ضمائر A *lrnd.*, pl. of **zamir 1**.

zaman 1 (.—) زمان A 1. time; period; epoch; era. 2. proper season; opportunity. 3. present life. 4. *gram.* tense. **bir —, bir —lar** at one time; formerly, once. **—ında** 1. in his day. 2. in its season; at the right time. **—la** in the course of time. **— adamı** opportunist. **— aşımı** *neol., law* prescription. **Z—ı Cahiliyet** pre-Islamic times. **—ı hâl** *lrnd.* the present time; *gram.* present tense. **—ın hükümdarı** the ruler of the day, the then ruler. **—ı mazi** *lrnd.* bygone time; *gram.* the past tense. **—la mukayyed akid** transaction on account. **—ı müstakbel** *lrnd.* future time; *gram.* future tense. **—a uy=** to conform to the exigencies of the day, to adopt an opportunistic attitude. **— zaman** occasionally, from time to time. **— zarfı** *gram.* adverb of time. **— ü zemin** conditions of time and place.

zaman 2 (.—) ضمان A *lrnd.* guarantee, surety.

zamane (.—.) زمانه P 1. the age; the present time. 2. fortune. **— adamı** opportunist. **— çocukları** children of today; modern youth.

zamanen (.—´.) زمانًا A *lrnd.* according to the time; as regards time.

zamanî (.——) زمانى A *lrnd.* 1. pertaining to time, temporal. 2. temporary, transitory. 3. a mortal; man.

zamaniyan (.———) زمانيان P *lrnd.* people of the world.

zamansız (.—.) زمانسز 1. untimely; inappropriate. 2. that affords no time or delay.

zama ظمى A *lrnd.* a being very thirsty; thirst.

zambak⁽ᵍⁱ⁾ زنبك same as **zanbak**.

zami ظمى A *lrnd.* thirsty.

zamil (—.) زامل A *lrnd.* that goes along briskly under a load and leaning to one side.

zamile (—..) زامله A *lrnd.* 1. beast of burden. 2. bundle, pack on one side of a beast.

zamime (.—.) ضميمه A *lrnd.* 1. added, appended. 2. addition; supplement.

zamimeten (.—´..) ضميمةً A *lrnd.* in addition; by way of supplement.

zamin (—.) ضامن A *law* surety, guarantee; who stands surety, guarantor. **— ol=** /a/ to be a guarantee, to make oneself responsible (for). **—lik** suretyship.

zamir 1 (.—) ضمير A 1. *gram.* pronoun. 2. *lrnd.* heart; inner consciousness; secret thought. **—ine gir=** /ın/ *lrnd.* to enter somebody's mind (a thought).

zamir 2 (—.) زامر A *lrnd.* one who plays a pipe or lute.

zamirî (.——) ضميرى A *lrnd.* 1. mental. 2. cordial. 3. pronominal.

zamk⁽ᵏⁱ⁾ زمك [samg] glue, paste, gum.

zamkinos زمكينوس *slang* a running away. **— et=** to run away.

zamkla=ʳ زمقلهمك /ı/ to mix, smear or fasten with gum; to gum. **—n=** *pass.* **—t=** /ı, a/ *caus.* of **zamkla=**.

zamklı زمقلى gummed.

zamme ضمّه A *lrnd.* the sign ' in Arabic grammar.

zammet=ᵈᵉʳ ضم ايتمك /ı/ to add, to increase.

zampara زنپاره [zenpâre] womanizer, rake.

zamparalık⁽ᵍⁱ⁾ زنپاره لك debauchery; running after women. **—a çık=, — et=** to run after women.

zanⁿⁿⁱ ظن A 1. opinion. 2. surmise; suspicion. **—ımca** in my opinion. **—ındayım** I am of the opinion (that). **—ı galib** *lrnd.* the prevailing opinion; the fairly certain presumption. **—ıma göre** in my opinion.

zanaatᵗⁱ صناعت [sınaat] craft; handicraft.

zanbak⁽ᵍⁱ⁾ زنبق A lily, any liliaceous flowering plant.

zanet=ᵈᵉʳ ظن ايتمك same as **zannet=**.

zangırda=ʳ زنغردامق to have the teeth chatter through fear; to tremble; to clank, to rattle. **—t=** /ı/ *caus.*

zangırtı زنغردى a clanging, rattling noise.

zangır zangır زنغر زنغر trembling; with the teeth chattering; making a clanking or rattling noise. **— titre=** to shake and tremble violently.

zangoçᶜᵘ زنغوچ Arm verger of a church.

zani (—.) زانى A *lrnd.* who commits adultery, adulterer; adulterous. **—ye** (—..) A adulteress.

zanka (´.) زانقه Sl horse-drawn sleigh.

zanlı *neol., law* defendant, accused.

zannet=ᵈᵉʳ ظن ايتمك to think, to suppose.

zanni (.—) ظنّى A *lrnd.* conjectural, surmised. **—yat** (..—) A conjectures; suppositions.

zan sipas (—.—.) زن سپاس P *lrnd.* after that.

zanu (——) زانو P *lrnd.* knee. **— bezanu** knee to knee; side by side; opposite. **— bezemin** kneeling.

zanuzede (——..) زانوزده P *lrnd.* who has bent the knee in reverence.

zanuzen (———.) زانوزن P *lrnd.* who bends the knee in reverence.

zaparta (.´.) زاپارتا *var.* of **saparta**.

zapt ضبط *var.* of **zabt**.

zaptet=ᵈᵉʳ ضبط ايتمك /ı/ 1. to hold firmly, to seize; to take possession of, to conquer. 2. to restrain, to master. 3. to grasp, to understand. 4. to take down in writing.

zaptiye ضبطيه [zabtiye] gendarmerie; gendarme.

zapturapt ضبط و ربط [zabt ü rabt] orderliness, discipline.
zar 1 زار 1. membrane; film. 2. thin skin (of an onion).
zar 2 زار 1. die; dice. 2. *slang* joy, pleasure. — **at**= to throw dice. —**ım kaçtı** *slang* I am out of spirits. — **tut**= to cheat in throwing dice.
zar 3 ظار *colloq.*, *var. of* **zahir 1**.
zar 4 (—) زار P *lrnd.* 1. weeping bitterly. 2. miserable, sorrowing; piteous. 3. thin, wan, meager. 4. bitter weeping. — **ü nizar** wretched and meager. — **zar** 1. utterly miserable, completely wretched. 2. most miserably, wretchedly.
-zar 5 (—) زار P *lrnd.* place abounding in as in **çemenzar, lâlezar**.
zar[rr] **6** (—) ضار A *lrnd.* that harms or injures. —**ı nâfî** the Injurer who also gives benefit, *i. e.* God.
zar[rr] **7** ضرّ A *lrnd.* a harming, injuring; harm.
zar[r¹] **8** ضرع A *lrnd.* udder; teat of milch cattle.
zarafet (.—.) ظرافت A a being ingeniously graceful in thought, diction or act; elegance, grace, delicacy; *archaic* joke, play on words. —**li** graceful, elegant.
zarar ضرر A 1. damage, injury. 2. harm; harmfulness. 3. *com.* loss. — **bedeli** compensation for damages. — **çek**= to suffer harm or loss. — **et**=, — **gör**= to suffer harm; to lose. —**a karşı sigorta** insurance against damage. —**ı lahm** *Ott. hist.* Government subsidy for the meat price for Janissaries. —**la mukabele** *law* retortion. —**ı ol**= /a/ to be injurious, objectionable (for someone); to do harm, to do an injury (to somebody). — **öde**= to pay compensation for damages. —**ına sat**= /ı/ to sell at a loss. —**ı telâfi etme** *com.* recoup. — **ver**= /a/ to cause harm or loss. —**ı yok** It doesn't matter; never mind. — **ve ziyan** damages.
zarardide (..—.) ضرردیده P *lrnd.* who has suffered injury or loss. —**gân** (..—.—) P *pl.*
zararlaş[r] ضررلشـ to go shares in a loss.
zararlı ضررلی 1. harmful, 2. who suffers harm. — **çık**= /dan/ to come out the loser.
zararsız ضررسز 1. harmless; innocent. 2. safe, unhurt. 3. not so bad; pretty good.
zarazar (— — —) زازار P *lrnd.* continuously or totally wretched.
zarb ضرب A *arith.* multiplication. —**et**= /ı, la/ to multiply.
zarbhane (.—.) ضربخانه *same as* **darbhane**.
zarbuzan ضربزن *var. of* **darbezen**.
zare (—.) زاره P *lrnd.* wretchedness, misery; plaint, moan.
zareban (..—) ضربان *same as* **daraban**.
zarf ظرف A 1. receptacle. 2. envelope; cover; wrap. 3. case; sheath. 4. metal container for a porcelain coffee cup. 5. *gram.* adverb. —**ında** during; within. — **ile mazruf** 1. outward appearance and inner substance. 2. style and content (of a book). —**ı mekân** *gram.* adverb of place. —**ı zaman** *gram.* adverb of time.
zarfçı ظرفچی *slang* trickster who places an envelope on the road and then exacts money from the finder.
zarfi (.—) ظرفی A *lrnd.* 1. pertaining to a receptacle. 2. adverbial. —**yet** A nature or functions of a receptacle.
zarfla=[r] ظرفلا /ı/ to put into an envelope (letter).
zargana (.'..) زارغنه Gk needlefish, *zool.*, *Belone vulgaris*.
zarî 1 (— —) زاری P *lrnd.* 1. wretchedness, misery. 2. weeping, wailing.
zari[ıı] **2** (—.) زارع A *lrnd.* who sows seed; who cultivates; farmer.
zari 3 (—.) زاری A *lrnd.* 1. that propels and scatters. 2. that sows, sprinkles, scatters.
zariyat (—.—) زاریات A *lrnd.* quick scattering (winds). — **Suresi** *a name of the fifty-first sura of the Quran*.
zarib (—.) ضارب A *lrnd.* 1. that strikes or beats. 2. who stamps, coins (money).
zarif (.—) ظریف A 1. graceful, elegant; delicate. 2. witty, clever.
zarifâne (.—.) ظریفانه P graceful, witty; cleverly; elegant.
zarife (.—.) ظریفه A *lrnd.* 1. elegant thing, witty saying. 2. prostitute.
zariflik[81] ظریفلك elegance, delicacy.
zarih (—.) ضریح A *lrnd.* tomb, sepulcher.
zarir (—.) ضریر A *lrnd.* 1. blind; paralyzed. 2. harmed, injured.
zariyane (—.—.) زاریانه P *lrnd.* 1. plaint, lament. 2. subject of complaint.
zari zari (—.—.) زاری زاری [*based on* **zar 4**] *only in* — **ağla**= to weep bitterly.
zarla=[r] زارلا /ı/ to cover over with a canvas or with a tapestry. —**n**= *pass.* —**t**= /ı, a/ *caus. of* **zarla**=.
zarnâl[ıı] (— —) زارنال P *lrnd.* who weeps or moans bitterly. —**î** (— — —) P subdued wailing.
zarra 1 (.—) ضرّاء A *lrnd.* 1. bad, distressing state, weakness, disease, grief, poverty. 2. calamity, punishment.
zarra 2 ضرّة A *lrnd.* woman whose husband has more than one wife.
zarrab (.—) ضرّاب A *lrnd.* 1. one who strikes or hits much. 2. coiner of money.
zarrabhane (.—.) ضرّابخانه P *lrnd.* mint.
zarrat (.—) ضرّات A *lrnd., pl. of* **zarra 2**.

zarta (´.) ضرط A fart. —yı çek= slang 1. to fart. 2. to die.
zartçı ضرطجى slang boaster, braggart.
zartzurt ظارت زورت colloq., imitates loud and domineering words. — et= to give orders or to talk in a loud and blustering manner.
zarurat (.——) ضرورات A lrnd., pl. of zaruret.
zaruret (.—.) ضرورت A 1. need, want, necessity; requirement. 2. poverty, indigence. — hâlinde in case of necessity. —inde kal= to be obliged to, to be under the necessity of. —i vezn pros. requirement of the meter.
zaruri (.——) ضرورى A 1. necessary, requisite, indispensable. 2. unavoidable; involuntary. — masraflar necessary expenses.
zaruriyat (.—.—) ضروريات A lrnd. indispensable things.
zaruriyet (.—..) ضروريت A lrnd. indispensability.
zarzavat زرزوات same as zerzevat.
zar zor زار زور willy-nilly; barely.
zat 1 (—) ذات A 1. person, individual; personality. 2. essence, substance. —a ait belonging to the individual; personal. —ı âlileri, —ı âliniz your exalted person (polite for you). —ı âlii sipehsâlârileri Ott. hist. Your excellency, title used in addressing the Minister of War. —ı devletleri lrnd. their prosperous person, used in politeness for he or they or you. —ı envat lrnd., name of a sacred tree of the pagan Arabs. —ı evtar lrnd. stringed instrument. — işleri personnel affairs. Z—ı Kibriya lrnd. God. —ı kürsi astr. Cassiopeia. —a mahsus 1. personal, not transferable. 2. confidential. —ı mesele lrnd. the essence of the matter, the real point. —ı misem lrnd. possessed of beauty, beautiful. — ü sıfat lrnd. essence and attributes, substance and properties. Z—ı Şahane Your Majesty, His Majesty. —ı şefe lrnd. word; speech. —ı şimal lrnd. left hand side or direction.
zat- 2 (—) ذات A possessor of, endowed with, suffering in, as in zatülcenb, zatürree.
zaten (—´.) ذاتاً A 1. essentially; in any case; as a matter of fact. 2. lrnd. personally, in person.
za'ter زعتر [sa'ter] A var. of sa'ter.
zati 1 (——) ذاتى A 1. essential; original, natural. 2. personal. — eşya personal effects.
zati 2 (—.) ذاتى colloq. for zaten.
zatiyat (—.—) ذاتيات A lrnd. personal matters, personal questions.
zatülbasair (—..—.) ذات البصائر A lrnd. the mind.
zatülbeyn (—..) ذات البين A lrnd. relation existing between two or among many in respect of good or ill will; concord, friendship, union.
zatülcenb (—..) ذات الجنب A path. pleurisy.

Zatülceyş (—..) ذات الجيش A lrnd., name of a valley near Medina.
zatülhareke (—....) ذات الحركة A lrnd. automatic. —lik automatism.
zatülkebed (—...) ذات الكبد A path. inflammation of the liver.
zatülvadkayn (—...) ذات الودقين A lrnd. 1. shower blown in two opposite directions. 2. calamity that comes on one from two directions.
zatülvedaⁿ¹ (—...) ذات الودع A lrnd. 1. Noah's ark. 2. the Kaaba of Mecca in pagan times. 3. any ancient Arabian idol.
zatürree, zatürrie (—...) ذات الرئة A path. pneumonia.
zatüssudur (—..—.) ذات الصدور A lrnd. thoughts.
zatüzzevc (—..) ذات الزوج A lrnd. having a husband, married woman.
zav ضو A lrnd. light, effulgence.
zavabıt (.—.) ضوابط A lrnd. regulations, rules, precepts.
zavahir (.—.) ظواهر A lrnd., pl. of zahir 1, zahire 2, 1. outside; visible parts; appearance. 2. dwelling outside Mecca and in the surrounding country (Kuraish Arabs). —i kurtar= to save appearances; to save face.
zavallı زواللى 1. miserable, wretched; unlucky. 2. transitory, fading, fleeting. —! Poor man!
zaver (—.) زاور P lrnd. 1. strength, might, power, ability. 2. the planet Venus.
zavil زاويل A Or. mus. a compound makam composed about six centuries ago.
zaviye (—..) زاويه A 1. geom. angle. 2. cell (of a recluse); lodge (of dervishes). 3. lrnd. corner of a house, room, or building. —i basite geom. superficial angle. —i hadde geom. acute angle. —i humul lrnd. oblivion. —i kaime geom. right angle. —i katıa geom. inscribed peripheral angle in the segment of a circle. —i küreviye geom. spherical angle. —i meyite mil. dead angle. —i mücesseme geom. solid angle. —i münferice geom. obtuse angle. —i müsattaha geom. superficial angle. —i müsteviye geom. plane angle.
zaviyedar (—..—) زاويه دار P lrnd. keeper of a cell, recluse.
zaviyetan (—..—) زاويتان A geom. two angles. —ı mütebadiletan geom. alternate angles. —ı mütekabiletan geom. opposite angles.
Zavuş (—.) زاوش P lrnd. the planet Jupiter.
zay'a ضيعه A lrnd. 1. estate or plot of land. 2. occupation, calling, business.
zayende (—..) زاينده P lrnd. 1. that gives birth. 2. that is born.
zayet=ᵈᵉʳ (—..) ضايع A var. of zayi et=.

zayf ضيف A *lrnd.* guest.
zayıf ضعيف [zaif] 1. weak, thin; infirm; weakly. 2. of little weight or authority.
zayıfla= ضعيفله to become enfeebled; to become thin or weak; to lose weight. —t= /ı/ *caus.*
zayıflık[fı] ضعيفلق 1. weakness, debility. 2. thinness, emaciation.
zayi[iı] (—.) ضايع A 1. lost, gone. 2. perished; destroyed. 3. *lrnd.* vain, useless, profitless. — et= /ı/ to lose. — geçir= /ı/ to waste (one's life, time). — ol= to be lost, to perish. —inden ver= to issue a duplicate of a lost document.
zayiat (—.—) ضايعات A losses. — ver= to suffer casualties. — verdir= /a/ to inflict losses.
zayiçe (—..) زايچه P *lrnd.* horoscope; astronomical table. —sine bak= /ın/ to work out someone's horoscope.
zayiş (—.) زايش P *lrnd.* 1. a giving birth, a bringing forth. 2. a being born.
zayk[kı] ضيق A *lrnd.* 1. a being narrow, a becoming contracted, oppressed, difficult. 2. narrowness, contraction; oppression; difficulty.
zaykünnefes ضيق النفس [zıykünnefes] same as tıknefes.
zaykussadr ضيق الصدر path. asthma.
zayol=[ur] ضايع اولمق *var. of* **zayi ol=**.
zayyık[kı] ضيّق A *lrnd.* 1. narrow, strait. 2. close, miserly.
zayyıkülhabl ضيّق الحبل A *lrnd.* narrow in attachments or interests.
zayyıkuzzıra (....—) ضيّق الذراع A *lrnd.* powerless.
ze ز same as **za 1**.
zeamet (.—.) زعامت A 1. *Ott. hist.* large fief. 2. *lrnd.* responsibility, surety. — sipahisi yeoman of a large fief.
zeb[bbi] ذبّ A *lrnd.* a driving away, repelling or expelling, a resenting insult or injury.
zebad (.—) زباد A *lrnd.* 1. civet, the perfume of the civet cat. 2. the civet cat.
zebaih (.—.) ذبايح A *lrnd., pl. of* **zebiha**.
zeban 1 (.—) زبان P *lrnd.* 1. tongue; language, speech. 2. style of expression; idiom, dialect. 3. a means of expression. 4. anything tonguelike, as a flame or the point of a weapon. —a al= /ı/ to mention, to speak about. —a düş= to become a topic for comment; to be talked about. —a getir= /ı/ 1. to cause to be commonly talked about. 2. to mention. —i hal 1. the mute language of an action or condition. 2. the mute language of communion with God. —i kal spoken language.
-zeban 2 (.—) زبان P *lrnd.* tongued, *e. g.,* **ateşzeban, düzeban.**

zebanâver (.——.) زبان آور P *lrnd.* eloquent, fluent.
zebandân (.——) زبان دان P *lrnd.* 1. who knows a language or languages, linguist. 2. intelligent.
zebandıraz (.—.—) زبان دراز P *lrnd.* 1. long-tongued. 2. insolent; intemperate in speech. —î (.—.——) P, —lık insolence, intemperance of speech.
zebane (.—.) زبانه P *lrnd.* anything shaped like a tongue, as a flame, the point of a weapon, a tenon or a point of land. —keş (.—..), —paş (.—.—) P flaming, throwing out flames.
zebangez (.—.) زبان گز P *lrnd.* acrid, pungent.
zebangir (.——) زبان گير P *lrnd.* 1. that seizes the tongue. 2. pungent, acrid. — sal= to send out parties to capture prisoners for information.
zebani (.—.) زبانى A 1. demon of hell; cruel monster. 2. *lrnd.* champion who goes forth to single combat. —ye (.—..) A *pl. of* **zebani**.
zebanran (.——) زبان ران P *lrnd.* eloquent.
zebanzed (.—.) زبان زد P *lrnd.* commonly used in speech.
zebed زبد A *lrnd.* 1. foam, froth. 2. scum, dross. —î (..—) A pertaining to foam, of the nature of foam.
zebedülbahr[ri] زبد البحر A *lrnd.* 1. sea foam. 2. cuttle-fish bone.
zebedülkamer زبد القمر A *lrnd.* moonstone, selenite.
zebellâ (..—), **zebellâyi** (..——) زبلاى [based on Arabic] *colloq.* 1. huge; thick-set. 2. huge man.
zeber زبر P *lrnd.* 1. top or upper part of a thing. 2. the upper direction. 3. *Arabic script* the vowel-point for **a, e**.
zeberced زبرجد A 1. chrysolite; beryl. 2. pale bluish green. —î (...—) A 1. of chrysolite. 2. pale bluish green.
zeberdest زبردست P *lrnd.* 1. who has or gets the upper hand, superior; victorious. 2. higher, more exalted. —î (...—) P superiority, upperhandedness.
zeberî (..—), **zeberin** (..—) زبرى P *lrnd.* upper, uppermost, highest.
zebh ذبح A *lrnd.* 1. a cutting of the throat. 2. ritual slaughter. —et= /ı/ to slaughter ritually (an animal).
zebhiye زبحيه A *Ott. hist.* tax on slaughtered animals.
zebib زبيب A *lrnd.* raisins, currants; dried figs.
zebih[bhi] **1** ذبح A *var. of* **zebh**.
zebih 2 (.—) ذبيح A *lrnd.* 1. slaughtered, sacrificed. 2. *w. cap., a name given to Ishmail son of Abraham (Muslim equivalent of Isaac).*
zebiha (.—.) ذبيحه A *lrnd.* victim,

zebil

slaughtered or to be slaughtered, for food or in sacrifice.

zebil زبیل *colloq., var. of* **sebil**.

zebr زبر A *lrnd.* 1. a writing, inscription, letter or book. 2. knowledge, understanding, comprehension.

zebun (. —) زبون P *lrnd.* 1. weak, helpless. 2. exhausted, worn out. —**î** (. — —) P infirmity, indisposition, weakness.

zebunküş (. — .) زبونکش P *lrnd.* who oppresses the weak or defenseless; cruel and cowardly. —**âne** (. — . — .) P cruelly. —**î** (. — . —) P oppression of the weak; cowardly cruelty.

zebunla=ʳ, **zebunlaş**=ⁱʳ زبونلامق، زبونلاشمق to become weak and emaciated. —**t**= *caus. of* **zebunla**=.

zebunlukᵗᵘ زبونلوق weakness; helplessness.

Zebur (. —) زبور A 1. *Quranic* the Psalms of David. 2. *l. c.* writing; book. 3. *myst.* material manifestations of God's power in the world.

zebzebe زبزبه A *lrnd.* 1. a being agitated; agitation. 2. a waving of anything in the air, motion.

zeccac (. —) زجّاج A *lrnd.* maker or seller of glassware.

zecirᶜʳⁱ زجر *var. of* **zecr**.

zecr زجر A *lrnd.* 1. restraining; chiding; a forbidding, restraint. 2. a compelling to work unwillingly; compulsion; violence.

zecren (. ́ .) زجرًا A *lrnd.* with violence; forcibly.

zecrî (. —) زجری A *lrnd.* restrictive, prohibitory; compulsory; violent; forcible. — **tedbirler** *pol.* sanctions; coercive measures. —**ye** tax on alcoholic liquor.

zed 1 زد P *lrnd.* a striking, a beating. — **ü hurd** battle, conflict.

zed 2 زد P *lrnd.* that has struck.

-zed 3 زد P *lrnd.* struck, *e. g.* **zebanzed**.

zede 1 زده P *lrnd.* 1. that has struck.

-zede 2 زده P struck; stricken, *e. g.* **felâketzede, kazazede**.

-zedegân (. . —) زدگان P *lrnd., pl. of* **-zede 2**, *e. g.* **harikzedegân**.

zedele= زدله مك، زده له مك to damage by striking; to maltreat; to bruise; to batter. —**n**= *pass.* —**t**= /ı/ *caus. of* **zedele**=.

zefir 1 (. —) زفیر A *lrnd.* 1. deep-drawn breath, deep sigh; expiration. 2. roar of a fire.

zefir 2 زفیر E *lrnd.* zephyr cloth; zephyr shirting.

zehab (. —) ذهاب A *lrnd.* 1. *same as* **zehap**. 2. a going away, departure. 3. a following, adopting a course of action. 4. a going, pacing along, through or over a thing or place; motion; passage. —**ı bâtıl** vain belief or supposition.

—**ı hilâfına** /ın/ contrary to the belief held by... — **ü iyab** a going and coming.

zehadet (. — .) زهادت A *lrnd.* a practicing asceticism; ascetic abstinence. —**li** ascetic.

zehapᵇⁱ (. —) ذهاب [**zehab**] belief; imagination.

zeheb ذهب A *lrnd.* gold. —**î** (. . —) A golden.

zehi (. —) زهی P *poet.* 1. Excellent! Well done! 2. Alas! 3. What a...! —**hayal!** What an illusion!

zehirʰʳⁱ زهر [**zehr 1**] 1. poison; anything very bitter. 2. grief, anxiety, care. 3. anything very disagreeable, bitter. 4. very keen or sharp thing. — **et**= /ı, a/ to spoil a thing thoroughly. — **gibi** 1. very bitter. 2. very keen or sharp. — **yut**= 1. to swallow poison. 2. to brood over grief, rage, or envy. — **zakkum** like poison, very bitter. — **zakkum olsun** May you be punished! — **zemberek** very bad or poisonous.

zehirle=ʳ زهرلمك /ı/ 1. to poison. 2. to subject a person to something excessively disagreeable. 3. to spoil a person's mind by evil suggestions. —**n**= *pass.* —**t**= /ı, a/ *caus. of* **zehirle**=.

zehirli زهرلی 1. poisonous, venomous. 2. poisoned (food).

zehr 1 زهر P *lrnd., same as* **zehir**. —**i katil** deadly poison.

zehr 2 زهر A *lrnd.* 1. flowers, blossoms, bloom. 2. flowering plants.

zehra (. —) زهرا A *lrnd.* 1. white and beautiful; fair-skinned; bright, shining, luminous. 2. lustrous, clear (pearl). 3. *w. cap., a name of Fatima, daughter of the Prophet Muhammad*.

zehrab (. —) زهراب A *lrnd.* 1. poisoned water, liquid poison. 2. any water made nauseously bitter. 3. tears of grief. —**ı ecel** the bitter cup of death.

zehrabe (. — .) زهرابه P *lrnd., same as* **zehrab**.

zehralûd (. — —) زهرآلود P *lrnd.* mixed with poison; very bitter; poisoned.

zehramiz (. — —) زهرآمیز P *lrnd.* mixed with poison, poisoned (drink).

Zehravan (. — .) زهروان A *lrnd.,* the second and third suras of the Quran.

zehrbar (. —) زهربار P *lrnd.* poison-scattering; poisonous, very bitter.

zehrdade (. — .) زهرداده P *lrnd.* to whom poison has been given, imbued with poison.

zehrdar (. —) زهردار P *lrnd.* poisonous, venomous; poisoned, infected.

zehrdaru (. — —) زهردارو P *lrnd.* antidote against poison; bezoar.

zehre 1 زهره A *lrnd.* 1. flower, blossom. 2. flowering plant. 3. the pleasures and comforts of life; beauty, grace.

zehre 2 زهره P *lrnd.* 1. gall bladder; gall, bile. 2. power, ability, daring, spirit.

zehreçakᵏⁱ (. — —) زهرهچاک P *lrnd.* 1. whose gall bladder has burst (through fear). 2. broken-hearted.

zehredár (..—) زهردار P lrnd. brave, valiant.
—ân (..——) P pl.
zehrefşan (..—) زهرافشان P lrnd. diffusing poison.
zehreterakᵏⁱ (...—) زهره ترياك P lrnd., same as **zehreçak**.
zehrhand زهرخند P lrnd. forced smile, grim, ghastly laugh; smiling bitterly, forcedly, or sardonically.
zehrî (.—) زهری A lrnd. pertaining to flowers or plants.
zehrnâkᵏⁱ (.—) زهرناك P lrnd. 1. poisonous, venomous. 2. containing poison; poisoned (food, dagger).
zehrülhacer زهرالحجر A lrnd. rock moss; lichen.
zehukᵏᵘ (.—) زهوك A lrnd. that passes away, transitory, perishing.
zeir (.—) زئر A lrnd. growl or roar of a lion.
zekâ 1 (.—) ذكا A sharpness of intelligence, quickness of mind; intelligence; perspicacity.
zekâ 2 (.—) زكا A lrnd. 1. growth and increase, thriving. 2. righteousness.
zekâb (.—) زكاب P lrnd. writing ink.
zekât 1 (.—) زكات A 1. Isl. rel. alms (prescribed by Islam, generally one fortieth of one's income); tax for helping the poor. 2. lrnd. purity; purification; righteousness. 3. lrnd. growth and increase, thriving.
zekât 2 (.—) زكات A lrnd. 1. a purifying a beast for food (by slaughter in a canonical manner). 2. canonical purification of anything for use. **— et=** /ı/ to slaughter (a beast in a canonical manner).
zekâvet 1 (.—.) ذكاوت A lrnd. sharpness of intelligence, quickness of perception, acuteness of understanding.
zekâvet 2 (.—.) زكاوت A lrnd., same as **zekâ 2**.
zeker ذكر A 1. anat. the male organ. 2. lrnd. male; masculine.
Zekeriya (...—) زكريا A Bib. and Quranic Zachariah. **— sofrası** meal of various sorts of dried fruit etc. which forty friends prepare during **Şaban** and to which guests are invited, and at which the host makes a solemn wish.
zekevat (..—) زكوات A lrnd., pl. of **zekât 1**.
zeki 1 (.—) ذكی A sharp, quick-witted, intelligent.
zeki 2 (.—) زكی A lrnd. 1. pure, virtuous, chaste. 2. growing, thriving, prospering; well grown.
zel 1 ذل var. of **zâl 1**.
zelˡˡ **2** زلّ A lrnd. 1. a slipping, sliding, falling. 2. an erring, blundering in speech, a slip of the tongue. 3. a going or passing away.
zelak زلق A lrnd. 1. a slipping. 2. slippery place.

zelaka زلقه A lrnd. slippery place.
zelâlet 1 (.—.) ذلالت A lrnd. 1. a being submissive and tractable; submissiveness. 2. a being humble or abject; humility, abasement.
zelâlet 2 (.—.) ضلالت A lrnd., same as **dalâlet**.
zelâzil (.—.) زلازل A lrnd., pl. of **zelzele**.
zelber زلبر [Persian **serbar**] prov. small bundle added to the proper load of a beast of burden.
zelel زلل A lrnd. 1. a slipping, stumbling; slip; slippery. 2. an erring; error; deficiency.
zelem زلم A lrnd. 1. arrow used in gambling or casting lots (by the ancient Arabians). 2. strong, active boy.
zelifen (.—.) زليفن P lrnd. threat, menace; terror, fear, dread.
Zeliha (.—.) زليخا [Züleyha] wife of Potiphar.
zelil (.—) ذليل A 1. low, base, contemptible. 2. humbled, abased, despicable. **—âne** (.——.) P meanly, abasedly.
zelka زلقه A lrnd. a slip.
zellât (.—) زلّات A lrnd., pl. of **zelle**.
zelle, zellet زلّه زلّت A lrnd. 1. food taken from a banquet. 2. slip. 3. lapse, error, sin.
zelûl (.—) ذلول A lrnd. submissive, tractable, quiet.
zelzâlˡˡ (.—) زلزال A lrnd., same as **zilzâl**.
zelzele زلزله A earthquake. **Z— Suresi** a name of the ninth sura of the Quran.
zelzelenüvis (....—) زلزله نويس P lrnd. seismograph.
zemᵐᵐⁱ **1** ذمّ A blame, censure; disparagement. **— ü kadih dâvası** law action for libel.
zem 2 زم P lrnd. cold; frost.
zemaim (.—.) ذمائم A lrnd., pl. of **zemime**.
zeman (.—) زمان A same as **zaman 1**.
zemane (.—.) زمانه P lrnd., same as **zamane**.
zemanesâz (.—.—) زمانه ساز P lrnd. who suits himself to the times, time-server; turncoat. **—î** (.—.——) P time-serving, hypocrisy.
zemaneseyr (.—..) زمانه سير P lrnd. traveling fast; transitory.
zemanî (.——) زمانی A lrnd., same as **zamani**.
zemazim (.—.) زمازم A lrnd., pl. of **zemzeme**.
zemberekᵏⁱ زنبرك [zenburek] 1. spring (of a watch). 2. spring door-latch. **— aşığı** tumbler of a crossbow. **—i boşal=** /ın/ to lose control of oneself and laugh long and unrestrainedly. **— marazı** a certain fatal disease that attacks camels. **—çi** Ott. hist. Janissary serving in the 82nd regiment. **—li** fitted with a spring.
zembil زنبيل [zenbil] basket (woven of rushes or palm-leaves). **—i kitman** lrnd. conceal-

ment, secrecy. —ci maker or seller of rush baskets. —li carrying a rush basket.

zemen زَمَن A lrnd., same as zaman 1. Z—i Tahzir Arabic hist. the Time of the Subdivision (of the territory north from Medina when the Jews were a second time expelled and debarred).

zemheri زَمهَرى colloq., var of zemherir. —zürefası joc. one who wears very inadequate clothes in winter.

zemherir (..—) زَمهَرير A lrnd. intense cold; the depths of winter. —î (..——) A intensely cold.

zemim (.—) ذَميم A lrnd. reprehensible; disparaged.

zemime (.—.) ذَميمة A lrnd. act or quality to be blamed or reprehended; vice, misdemeanor, crime.

zemin (.—) زَمين P 1. the earth, the world. 2. ground; surface of the earth. 3. ground (of a design); background. 4. subject-matter (of a discourse). 5. meaning, sense. 6. mus. the music of the first line of a song. — aç= same as zemin hazırla=. — hattı base line, ground line (perspective). — hazırla= /a/ to prepare the way for something. — katı ground floor. —i mürde lrnd. unoccupied land; waste ground. — testeresi fretsaw. —i üftade lrnd. land which has lain fallow for a time. — ü zaman conditions of time and place.

zeminbus (.——) زَمينبوس P lrnd. kissing the ground; making a very low bow. —î (.———) P act of kissing the ground.

zemindar (.——) زَميندار P lrnd. 1. one who owns land. 2. zamindar, a kind of feudal baron in India. —an (.———) P pl. —î (.———) P lrnd. zamindari, the jurisdiction of a zamindar.

zemingir (.——) زَمينگير P lrnd. 1. that clings to the earth. 2. paralytic, bedridden. —î (.———) P lrnd. 1. pertaining to the earth or ground. 2. earthy.

zeminkâr (.——) زَمينكار P lrnd. who has recourse to subterfuge in talking, who tries to avoid the main question. —âne (.———.) P lrnd. evasive, typical of one who makes excuses or finds pretexts.

zeminkûb (.——) زَمينكوب P lrnd. (lit., which beats the ground) horse, camel, etc.

zeminlerze (.—..) زَمينلرزه P lrnd. earthquake, the shock of an earthquake.

zeminpeymay (.—.—) زَمينپيما P lrnd. 1. surveyor. 2. traveler.

zemistan (..—) زَمستان P lrnd. winter, cold season. —î (..——) P wintery. —iye Ott. hist. Janissary's winter allotment of cloth for a coat.

zemmam (.—) ذَمّام A lrnd. slanderer, disparager.

zemmet=der ذَمَّت /ı/ to censure, to slander, to denigrate.

zemzem 1 زَمزَم A 1. w. cap. famous well in the court of the Kaaba at Mecca. 2. copious, abundant, plenteous (well, water). Z— Kuyusuna işe— (lit., to urinate into the Well of Zemzem) to do something monstrous merely to acquire notoriety. — suyu water from the Well of Zemzem. —le yıkanmış gibidir a perfect paragon compared with most of them.

zemzem 2 زَمزَم P lrnd., same as zemzeme 2.

zemzeme 1 زَمزَمه P lrnd. 1. a chanting; chant; recitation. 2. prayer or litany of the Zoroastrians (as muttered in recitation); w. cap., name of a book attributed to Zoroaster. 3. soft whispering, flattering speech. 4. Or. mus. another term for kürdî.

zemzeme 2 زَمزَمه A lrnd. 1. rolling, pealing, reverberating (thunder). 2. a lion's growling; a horse's whinnying. 3. a dove's cooing.

zemzemle= زَمزَملَمَك /ı/ 1. to sprinkle with water from Zemzem (corpse). 2. to sip (water).

-zen 1 زَن P lrnd. 1. that thrusts, that hurls or shoots a weapon, as in darbzen. 2. who cuts, cuts off, cuts down, as in rahzen. 3. who strikes, who beats, as in tablzen. 4. who performs an act by a sudden pressure, in the sense of coining money, printing a stamp, applying one thing to another, etc., as in sikkezen. 5. who speaks or sings, as in lafzen, nârezen.

zen 2 زَن P lrnd. 1. woman; lady; wife. 2. effeminate man. — ü şuy man and wife.

zenaat صَناعت same as zanaat.

zenabil (.——) زَنابيل A lrnd., pl. of zenbil.

zenabir (.——) زَنابير A lrnd., pl. of zenbûr.

zenadikkı (.—.), zenadika (.—..) زَناديق A lrnd., pl. of zındık.

zenah زَنَخ P lrnd. 1. the chin, dimple in the chin. 2. talk, especially idle words; public rumor. 3. muzzle of an animal.

zenahdan (..—) زَنَخدان P 1. lrnd. the chin. 2. myst. the favor of God.

zenahzen زَنَخزَن P lrnd. idle talker, boaster, braggart.

zenan 1 (.—) زَنان P lrnd., pl. of zen 2.

-zenan 2 (.—) زَنان P lrnd., pl. of -zen 1.

zenane (.—.) زَنانه P lrnd. 1. peculiar to women. 2. women's apartments in an eastern house.

zenanir (.——) زَنانير A lrnd., pl. of zünnar.

zenb زَنب A lrnd. fault, offense, sin, disobedience to God. —i Suhr the fault of Suhr, unappreciated service.

zenbil (.—) زَنبيل A lrnd., same as zembil.

zenbûr (.—) زَنبور A lrnd. wasp, hornet.

—i asel honey-bee, bee. —e (. —.) A black bee; hornet.

zenburek^kı (. —.) زنبورك P lrnd. 1. little wasp. 2. a kind of small sharp arrowhead; arrow with a sharp head. 3. same as zemberek.

zenburî (. — —) زنبورى P lrnd. reticulated; like a honeycomb.

zenc زنج A lrnd. the Ethiopians.

zencar (. —) زنجار [jengâr] lrnd. rust, verdigris.

zencebil (.. —) زنجبيل A lrnd. 1. same as zencefil. 2. name of a drink of the Arabs; any delicious beverage. 3. a fountain of paradise. —i Acem camel thorn, bot., Alhagi maurorum. —i kilâb a kind of origanum fatal to dogs. —i Şamî elecampane, bot., Inula Helenium.

zencefil زنجفيل [zencebil] ginger. —li mixed or flavored with ginger.

zencerf زنجرف P cinnabar, vermilion. —î (.. —) P 1. containing vermilion. 2. like vermilion, red.

zenci (. —) زنجى A 1. Ethiopian. 2 Negro.

Zencibar زنجبار [Arabic ..—] same as Zengibar.

zencir (. —) زنجير P 1. lrnd., same as zincir. 2. Or. mus. the longest rhythmic pattern, with 120 beats. —i adalet, —i dâd a chain reputed to have been attached to a bell in the palace of Nushirevan, by which any sufferer could appeal directly to the king for justice. —i murabba a rhythmic pattern. —i Nuşirevan same as zenciri adalet.

zencirbend (. — .) زنجيربند P lrnd. chained; fettered.

zencire (. —.) زنجيره P lrnd. 1. anything resembling a chain. 2. edging of silk or gold lace. 3. chain-pattern as a border (round a picture, etc.).

zencirek (. — .) زنجيرك P lrnd. 1. small chain. 2. chain-pattern; strokes excellently formed in writing or in sculpture.

zencirî (. — —) زنجيرى P lrnd. 1. pertaining to a chain, chained. 2. fit to be chained, mad, insane. —yân (. — — —) P violently insane people.

Zencistan (.. —) زنجستان P country of the Negroes.

zenciye زنجيه A lrnd. Negress.

zençe زنچه P harlot.

zend 1 زند A lrnd. 1. either of the two bones of the forearm. 2. fire drill, fire stick.

Zend 2 زند P the Zendavesta. — dili Zend, the Zend language.

Zendabesta (. —. —) زنداﺑﺴﺘﺎ P the Zendavesta.

zendaka زندقه A lrnd. 1. belief in the two principles of light and darkness; ditheism. 2. atheism, impiety, heresy.

zendan (. —) زندان [zend 1] lrnd. 1. two bones of the forearm. 2. wooden apparatus for striking fire.

Zendavesta (. —. —) زنداوستا P the Zendavesta.

Zendbaf (. —) زندباف P lrnd. 1. reciter of the Zendavesta; priest of the Magi. 2. l. c. nightingale.

Zendce زندجه in Zend.

Zendesta (.. —) زندستا var. of Zendavesta.

Zendhan (. —) زندخوان P same as Zendbaf.

Zendî (. —) زندى A lrnd. 1. pertaining to the Zendavesta. 2. Zoroastrian; fire-worshipper.

zendost زندوست [Persian .—] lrnd. fond of women; rake.

zene زنه P same as zenne.

zeneb زنب A lrnd. 1. tail. 2. retinue, following. —i cedi astr. the star δ Capricorni. —i kaytus the star β Ceti.

zenec زنج A lrnd. a suffering from thirst; burning thirst.

zenek^kı زنك P lrnd. a little woman.

zeng زنگ P lrnd. 1. rust. 2. verdigris. 3. tarnish. 4. film of dirt. 5. gum of the eyes. 6. bell; noise made by clapping the hands. 7. black people of eastern Africa; Ethiopia. —i dil care, sorrow. —i hava cloudiness, mistiness of the weather; darkness.

zengâr (. —) زنگار P lrnd. 1. verdigris. 2. rust or tarnish.

zengârbeste (. — ..) زنگاربسته P same as zengbeste.

zengârhurde (. — ..) زنگارخرده P lrnd. rust-eaten.

zengârî (. — —) زنگارى P 1. rust-colored. 2. rustiness.

Zengbar (. —) زنگبار P same as Zengibar.

zengbeste زنگبسته P lrnd. rusted; tarnished.

Zengi (. —) زنگى P lrnd. Ethiopian; Negro.

Zengibar (.. —) زنگبار [Zengbar] geog. Zanzibar.

zengin زنگين rich, wealthy; wealthy man. —ce (. . .') rather rich.

zenginle=^r, zenginleş=^ir زنگينلشمك to become rich.

zenginlik^ki زنگينلك riches, wealth.

zengûle (. —.), zengül, zengüle Or. mus. an old simple makam in the Hicaz group.

zenne زنه [zene] P 1. the female sex; female. 2. male taking a female part (in the old Turkish theater). 3. female (clothes, etc.). — terzisi women's tailor. —ci seller of women's clothes.

zennelik^ki زنه لك 1. womanhood. 2. a taking a female part (actor).

zenpare (. —.) زنپاره P lrnd., same as zampara.

zer 1 زر P lrnd. 1. gold. 2. money, coin of any kind. 3. yellow. 4. light-skinned. 5. myst. orders vigils, fastings, long-continued devotion. —i destefşar gold reduced to a soft state and capable of being wrought by hand. **—i gül** pollen. **—i mahbub** *Ott. hist.* gold coin of twenty-five kurush. **—i mahi** fish scale. **—i muştefşar** *same as* **zeri destefşar. —i nergis** petals of the narcissus. **—i surh** 1. pure gold. 2. gold as money, gold coin. **—i şükûfe** essence of a flower.

zerʳ¹ **2** زَرع *A lrnd.* 1. a sowing seed; a cultivating. 2. sown seed; seed for sowing. 3. sown field; crop of plants from sown seed. **— et=***.

zerab (.—) زَراب *P lrnd.* 1. gold-water. 2. gold ink or gold dissolved in *aqua regia* for gilding. 3. gold-colored wine.

zerabî (.——) زَرابي *A lrnd., pl. of* **zerbî**.
zeraiⁱⁱ (.—.) زَرايع *A lrnd., pl. of* **zeria** 2.
zerari (.——) زَراري *A lrnd., pl. of* **zürriyet**.
Zeratüşt (.—.) زَرَاتُشت *P lrnd.* Zoroaster. **—name** (.—.—.) *P* book of the Life of Zoroaster.

zeravend (.—.) زَراوَند *P lrnd.* aristolochia, birthwort, *bot., Aristolochia.* **—i Şami** round birthwort.

zerbaf (.—) زَرباف *P lrnd.* 1. weaver of cloth of gold. 2. cloth of gold, brocade.

zerbeft زَربفت *P lrnd.* woven with gold, gold brocade.

zerbî (.—), **zerb**ⁱve زَربي *A lrnd.* cushion, carpet, spread out to serve as a couch.

zerd 1 زَرد *P lrnd.* 1. yellow; pale, wan. 2. yellow bay (horse).

zerd 2 زَرد *A lrnd.* coat of mail, link-armor.
zerdab (.—) زَرداب *P lrnd.* 1. safflower-water. 2. bile. 3. pus or yellow matter running from a wound. 4. white wine.

zerdali زَردالي [**zerdalû**] wild apricot, *bot., Prunus armeniaca.*

zerdalû (.——) زَردالو *P lrnd., same as* **zerdali**.

zerdava, zerdave زَرداوه beach martin; beach martin's fur. **— fırça** artist's paint brush.

zerdbur (.—) زَردبور *P lrnd.* bright yellow bay (horse).

zerdçub (.—), **zerdçube** (.—.) زَردچوب *P lrnd., same as* **zerdeçal**.

zerde زَرده *P* 1. dish of sweetened rice colored with saffron (served especially at weddings). 2. *lrnd.* yellow water of safflower. 3. *lrnd.* bile. 4. *lrnd.* yoke of an egg. 5. *lrnd.* yellow bay horse.

zerdecav, zerdeçal, zerdeçöp زَردچاو, زَردچال [**zerdçub**] turmeric, *bot., Curcuma longa.*

zerdegûş (..—) زَردگوش *P lrnd., same as* **zerdguş**.

zerdfam (.—) زَردفام *P lrnd.* yellow, yellowish.
zerdgûş (.—), **zerdgûşe** (.—.) زَردگوش

P lrnd. 1. hypocritical; hypocrite. 2. pliant, subservient. 3. pusillanimous.

zerdî (.—) زَردي *P lrnd.* yellowness.
zerdiye زَرديه *A lrnd.* coat of mail; link-armor.
zerduz (.—) زَردوز *P lrnd.* 1. embroiderer. 2. embroidered; fastened with golden nails.

Zerdüşt زَردُشت *P* Zoroaster. **—î** (..—) *P* Zoroastrian.

zerefşan (..—) زَرَافشان *P lrnd.* scattering gold.
zerekᵏⁱ زَرك *P lrnd.* 1. a little piece of gold. 2. gold leaf.

zeren زَرن *var. of* **zerin**.
zerendud (..—) زَرَاندود *P lrnd.* gilded, gilt, overlaid with gold.

zer'et=ᵈᵉʳ زَرع ايتمك to sow.
zerger زَرگر *P lrnd.* goldsmith. **—î** (..—) *P* craft and art of a goldsmith.

zergûn (.—) زَرگون *P lrnd.* of the color of gold.

zerharid (..—) زَرخَريد *P lrnd.* purchased as a slave; bought with gold or money.

zerî 1 (.—) زَري *P lrnd.* golden, of or like gold.

zeriⁱⁱ **2** (.—) زَريع *A lrnd.* 1. sown. 2. what grows in the fields spontaneously from stray seeds.

zeriⁱⁱ **3** (.—) زَريع *A lrnd.* intercessor.
zeria 1 (.—.) زَريعه *A lrnd.* 1. means of attainment. 2. pretext, motive, course.

zeria 2 (.—.) زَريعه *A lrnd.* 1. seed that is or may be sown. 2. state or act from which a consequence springs; cause, motive, reason.

zerin (.—) زَرين *P lrnd.* 1. golden, of or like gold. 2. gilt, gilded.

zerinalem (.—..) زَرين علم *P lrnd.* marked with gold, embroidered or woven with figures of gold.

zerine (.—.) زَرينه *P lrnd., same as* **zerin**.
zerinizar (.—.—) زَرين عذار *P lrnd.* sallow-faced, pale-faced.

zerinkadeh (.—..) زَرين قدح *P lrnd.* white and yellow narcissus, jonquil, *bot., Narcissus jonquilla.*

zerinkâse (.—.) زَرين كاسه *P lrnd.* the sun.
zerinkülâh (.—.—) زَرين كلاه *P lrnd.* 1. wearing a golden helmet. 2. golden, like gold; the sun.

zerinsedef (.—..) زَرين صدف *P lrnd.* the sun.
zerinşâh (.——) زَرين شاه *P* (*lit.,* the golden branch) reed pen.

zer'iyat (..—) زَرعيات *A lrnd.* sowing; crop; cultivation.

zerkᵏⁱ **1** زَرق *A* 1. *med.* injection. 2. *lrnd.* a spearing or stabbing with a spear. 3. *lrnd.* an eyeing one intently, especially with a view to perverting him from the true faith. 4. *lrnd.* a turning towards any object (the eye).

zerkᵏⁱ **2** زَرق *P lrnd.* hypocrisy.
zerka (.—) زَرقاء *A lrnd.* 1. light-blue, sky-

blue. 2. blue, green or gray (eye); blue, green or gray eyed.

zerkâr (. —) زرکار P lrnd. anything golden or gilded. —î (. ——) P embroidered with gold.

zerkeş زرکش P lrnd. gold-wire drawer.

zerkeşide (.. —.) زرکشیده P lrnd. done over with gold; gilt.

zerket=der زرکتمك /1/ med. to inject.

zerkfürüş (.. —) زرقروش P lrnd. hypocrite; hypocritical.

zerkûb (. —) زرکوب P lrnd. gold-beater.

zerkûft (. —) زرکوفت P lrnd. inlaid with gold by hammering.

zerkun (. —) زرکون A lrnd. red lead, vermilion.

zermehçe زرمهچه P lrnd. small golden or gilded crescent at the point of a banner or spear.

zernisar (.. —) زرنثار P lrnd. that scatters gold.

zernişan (.. —) زرنشان P lrnd. inlaid with gold (by hammering). **—ger** (.. —.) P inlayer with gold.

zerraı (. —) زراع A lrnd. 1. sower; farmer. 2. sower of strife.

zerrad (. —) زراد A lrnd. 1. maker or seller of coats of mail. 2. strangler.

zerrakı (. —) زراق A lrnd. a very deceitful man; hypocrite; sycophant, rogue.

zerraka (. —.) زراقه A lrnd. 1. a kind of syringe formerly used for throwing burning naphtha into besieged places. 2. medical injection.

zerrat (. —) زرات A lrnd., pl. of **zerre**.

zerre زره A atom; mote; minute particle. **— kadar** in the slightest degree. **—nin zerresi** absolutely none.

zerrebin (.. —) زربین P lrnd. 1. microscope. 2. keen-eyed.

zerrece (..'.) زرهجه as much as an atom, very small.

zerrevâr (.. —) زرهوار P lrnd. humble, lowly; insignificant.

zerrevî (.. —) زرهوی P lrnd. atomic.

zerrin (. —) زرین P 1. jonquil, bot., Narcissus jonquilla. 2. lrnd. golden, like gold. **— kadeh** jonquil, bot., Narcissus jonquilla.

zerrişte زرشته P lrnd. gold thread.

zersay (. —) زرسای P lrnd. 1. that rubs or rubs up gold; gold-beater, preparer of gold for painting. 2. slab on which gold is rubbed up.

zersaz (. —) زرساز P lrnd. goldsmith.

zerşinas (.. —) زرشناس P lrnd. banker, money-changer; goldsmith.

zertar (. —) زرتار P lrnd. made of gold thread, gold embroidered. —î (. ——) P cloth of gold.

zerur (. —) زرور A lrnd. 1. anything pounded small and sprinkled (as salt or drugs).

2. powdered Calamus aromaticus (used as a perfume).

zervarakı زرورق P lrnd. gold leaf.

zerver زرور P lrnd. rich, wealthy.

zeryun (. —) زریون P lrnd. 1. gold colored. 2. cheerful; green and pleasant. 2. anemone.

zerzavat, zerzevat زرزوات [sebzevat] vegetables. **— bahçesi** kitchen garden. **—cı** vegetable grocer.

zevacir (. —.) زواجر A lrnd., pl. of **zacire**.

zevad (. —), **zevade** (. —.) زواده P lrnd. provisions in stock.

zevahif (. —.) زواحف A lrnd., pl. of **zahife**.

zevahir (. —.) زواهر A same as **zavahir**.

zevaid (. —.) زوائد A lrnd. 1. pl. of **zaide**. 2. net accrual of a pious foundation.

zevalli (. —) زوال A 1. decline; decadence; adversity. 2. lrnd. a disappearing; disappearance; cessation; failure; fading away. 3. lrnd. the sinking of the sun after noon; noon. **— bilmez** that knows no decay; eternal. **— bul**= to decline, pass away (an empire, etc.). **—i vasati** lrnd. mean noon.

zevalî (. —.) زوالی A lrnd. reckoned from noon, e. g., **zevalî saat dört** 4:00 p.m.

zevalnâpezir (. ———.—) زوالناپذیر P lrnd. permanent, imperishable.

zevalpezir (. —.—) زوالپذیر P lrnd. transitory; subject to decline.

zevalsiz زوالسز unfading; everlasting, permanent.

zevamil (. —.) زوامل A lrnd., pl. of **zamile**.

zevan (. —) زوان P lrnd., same as **zeban** 1.

zevane (. —.) زوانه P lrnd. 1. tongue. 2. tongue of a balance. 3. same as **zıvana**.

zevani (.. —.) زوانی A lrnd., pl. of **zaniye**.

zevarikı (. —.) زوارق A lrnd., pl. of **zevrak**.

zevat (. —) زوات A lrnd. persons, personalities. **—ı a'lâm** 1. signals, obelisks, milestones, posts. 2. women with special names or aliases; women watched by the police. **Z—ı Hamim** the suras 40 to 46 of the Quran.

zevaya (. ——) زوایا A lrnd., pl. of **zaviye**.

zevb زوب A lrnd. 1. a melting, dissolving; liquefaction. 2. a flowing; liquid; fluid. 3. clarified liquid honey. 4. tears' running down. 5. a wasting away (flesh).

zevbaa زوبعه A lrnd. 1. demon, djinn. 2. whirlwind, tornado. 3. evil.

zevc زوج A lrnd. 1. same as **zevç**. 2. one of a pair, mate; pair, couple.

zevcat (. —.) زوجات A lrnd., pl. of **zevce**.

zevce زوجه A lrnd. wife.

zevceyn زوجین A lrnd. a married couple, man and wife.

zevcî (. —) زوجی A lrnd. marital; matrimonial.

zevciyet زوجیت A lrnd. the married state, matrimony.

zevcülferd زوج الفرد A lrnd. even number that

zevcüzzevc ازدواج الزوج A *lrnd.* even number that is a power of two.

zevç[cI] زوج [zevc] husband, consort.

zeveban (..—) ذويان A *lrnd.,* same as zevb [1, 2, 5].

zevil- ذوىال A *lrnd.* masters of, possessors of. —hayat (...—) A living things. —ihtiram (....—) A most honored. —iktidar (....—) A powerful. —itibar (....—) A in the highest esteem. —ukul (...—) A rational creatures.

zevk[kI] ذوق A 1. sense of taste; taste; flavor. 2. good taste. 3. delight, pleasure, enjoyment; fun, amusement. 4. appreciation (of a thing). 5. voluptuousness, sensuality. 6. *myst.* blissful perception of God's presence. — al= /dan/ to find pleasure in, to enjoy. —e al= /ı/ to make fun of. —e bak= to strive after pleasure. —ine bak Enjoy yourself. —i bedii *lrnd.* esthetic pleasure. —ini boz= /ın/ to spoil someone's pleasure. — bul= to find pleasure (in doing something). —ini çıkar= /ın/ to enjoy something to the full. — ehli 1. man of pleasure. 2. man of taste. — et= to enjoy oneself. —ine gel= /ın/ *prov.*, —ine git= to appear odd, amusing or pleasant to one. — için for fun. —i lâya'bar inexpressible delight. —ine mecbur, —ine meclûb *lrnd.* voluptuary. —ini okşa= /ın/ to please. —inde ol= to be enjoying or amusing oneself. — ü safa, — ve safa pleasure, amusement. —i selim good taste. —i selim sahibi a man of taste. — sür= to amuse or enjoy oneself. — u tarab*. —e var= 1. to give oneself up to pleasure. 2. to enjoy. —ine var= /ın/ to appreciate something. — ver= /a/ to give pleasure or amusement.

zevkidil ذوق دل P *Or. mus.* a compound **makam** rarely used.

zevkî (.—) ذوقى A *lrnd.* pertaining to amusement, pleasing, fun; amusing; pleasant.

zevkiyat (..—) ذوقيات A *lrnd.* amusing things or occupations, amusements.

zevklen=[ir] ذوقلن 1. to amuse oneself. 2. /la/ *colloq.* to mock (at), to make fun (of), to poke fun (at). —dir= /ı/ *caus.*

zevkli ذوقلى 1. pleasant, amusing, delightful. 2. with good taste.

zevksiz ذوقسز 1. tasteless; ugly, in bad taste. 2. insipid, dull, flat; unpleasant. —lik bad taste.

zevkutarab ذوق وطرب A 1. *lrnd.* pleasure and enjoyment. 2. *Or. mus.* a compound **makam** not now in frequent use.

zevkyab (.—) ذوقياب P *lrnd.* who enjoys or finds pleasure. — ol= /dan/ to take pleasure in.

zevra (.—) زورا A *lrnd.* 1. bent, crooked, distorted. 2. archery bow. 3. *w. cap.* the town of Baghdad. 4. *w. cap.* bend of the river Tigris at Baghdad.

zevrak[kI] زورق A *lrnd.* 1. boat; ship. 2. a kind of dervish cap shaped like a boat. 3. the closed handle of a jug. 4. carina or keel of a papilionaceous flower. —çe P small boat.

zevrakî (..—) زورقى A *lrnd.* 1. pertaining to a boat, boat-shaped. 2. a kind of boat-shaped dervish cap. 3. boatman.

zevraklı زورقلى very pompous and magnificent.

zevrakülbeled زورق البلد A *lrnd.* (*lit.,* boat of the desert) camel.

zevvakîn (.—) ذواقين A *Ott. hist.* the Sultan's food tasters.

zevzek[gI] زوزك silly; giddy; talkative.

zevzeklen=[ir] زوزكلنمك to behave in a silly manner; to say stupid things.

zevzeklik[gI] زوزكلك silly, flighty behavior; senseless chatter.

zeybak[kI] زيبق A *lrnd.* mercury. —î (..—) A pertaining to mercury, mercuric.

zeybek[gI] زيبك 1. Turk from southwestern Anatolia in traditional costume. 2. dance music of western Anatolia composed in the **aksak** and **oynak** rhythmic patterns. 3. *Ott. hist.* a kind of light infantryman. — havası music accompanying the **Zeybek** dance. — oyunu a kind of folk dance.

zeybekçe (.'.) زيبكجه in the manner of the zeybeks.

zeyc زيج A *lrnd.* astronomical tables.

Zeyd زيد A name used in fatvas to designate a hypothetical person, John Doe.

zeyegan (..—) زيغان A *lrnd.,* same as zeyg.

zeyf زيف A *lrnd.* spurious, base (coin).

zeyg زيغ A *lrnd.* 1. an inclining; a deviating from the right way. 2. a becoming dim (eyesight). 3. a declining from the meridian (sun).

zeyil[yII] ذيل [zeyl] appendix, addendum; postscript; supplement.

zeyl ذيل A *lrnd.* 1. same as zeyil. 2. *lrnd.* skirt; train; tail. 3. *lrnd.* base, foot of a mountain.

zeylen ('.) ذيلا A *lrnd.* by way of appendix, as a postscript.

zeylnâme (.—.) ذيلنامه P *lrnd.* 1. supplement, annex. 2. additional policy.

zeyn زين A *lrnd.* ornament; adornment; embellishment.

zeyrek[gI] زيرك [zirek] intelligent, wide awake. —lik intelligence.

zeyt زيت A *lrnd.* 1. olive oil. 2. any kind of expressed oil. —i 'azb sweet oil, olive oil. —î (.—) A pertaining to oil.

zeytin نَزِيْتِين نَزِيْتُون [zeytun] olive. — **koruğu** green, unripe olives. — **yağı** olive oil. — **yağı gibi üste çık**= to come off best; to get the better of an argument. —**ci** dealer in olives. —**lik** olive grove.

zeytun (. —) زَيْتُون A lrnd., same as zeytin.

zeytunî (. — —) زَيْتُونِى A 1. olive green. 2. pertaining to the olive. —**ye fasilesi** bot., Oleaceae.

zeyyâl[u] (. —) ذَيَّال A lrnd. 1. long-skirted; long-tailed. 2. who swaggers in his walk. 3. prancing, curveting (horse).

zı ظ same as za 2.

zıba[ar] 1 (. —) ضِبَاع A lrnd., pl. of zabu.

zıba 2 (. —) ظِبَاء A lrnd., pl. of zabi.

zıb'an ضِبْعَان A lrnd. male hyena.

zıbar[ır] زِبَار 1. to become torpid from drink. 2. contemptuously to go to bed, to sleep; to die.

zıbın زِبُون 1. quilted jacket for a baby. 2. prov. a kind of shirt or jacket; a kind of garment with three flaps.

zıcret ضَجْرَت A lrnd., same as zucret.

zıd[ddı] ضِدّ A same as zıt.

zıddan (. —) ضِدَّا A lrnd. the two opposites. —**ı lâyecteme'an** lrnd. opposites that never unite.

zıddî (. —) ضِدّى A lrnd. pertaining to the contrary.

zıddiyet ضِدِّيَّت A 1. opposition, repugnance, antipathy. 2. contrast.

zı'f ضِعْف A lrnd. 1. the double of any number. 2. any multiple of a number. 3. a member or part of the body. 4. any blank space in a book or writing.

zıfan (. —) ضِيفَان A lrnd., pl. of zayf.

zıfr ظُفْر A lrnd. 1. fingernail, toenail. 2. hoof; bird's claw, talon. 3. a disease of the eye. —**î** (. —) A pertaining to the fingernail.

zığn ضِغْن A lrnd. hate, rancor, grudge.

zıh زِه P 1. edging; border. 2. fillet. 3. molding. 4. crease. 5. braid down the side of trousers. 6. lrnd. bowstring.

zıhare (. — .) ضِهَارَه A lrnd. face, outer side of a garment.

zıhla=[r] زِهلَمَك /ı/ 1. to edge with piping, fillet or border. 2. lrnd. to string (a bow).

zıhlı زِهلى 1. edged with cord or a fillet. 2. lrnd. strung (bow).

zıkkım زَقُّوم [zakkum] colloq. 1. food (when referred to in an angry manner). 2. raki.

zıkkımlan=[ır] زَقُّومْلَانْمَق to stuff oneself with food, expression used in anger or contempt.

zıl[llı] ظِلّ A 1. lrnd. shadow, shade; astr. umbra. 2. lrnd. protection. 3. lrnd. phantom, specter. 4. lrnd. representative. 5. math. tangent. —**ı kavs** tangent of an arc. —**ı ma'kus** versed tangent, a shadow of a horizontal style on a vertical plane. —**ı memdûd** lengthening shadow. —**ı zalil** l. deep shade. 2. protection of a powerful superior.

zılâl[li] (. —) ضِلَال A lrnd. 1. pl. of zıl, shadows, shades. 2. pl. of zulle, shading or protecting things.

zılâm (. —) ظِلَام lrnd., pl. of zulm.

zılf ظِلْف A lrnd. 1. cloven hoof. 2. cloven-footed animal.

zılgıt زِلْغِيت [based on Arabic] slang threat; scolding. — **ver**= /a/ to scold. —**ı ye**= to get a scolding.

zıllî (. —) ظِلِّى A lrnd. 1. pertaining to a shadow or to a shade. 2. math. tangential.

zılliyet ظِلِّيَّت A lrnd. 1. nature, the quality of shadow or shade. 2. the quality of sovereignty as being the shadow of God on earth.

zılliyetpenâh (. . . . —) ظِلِّيَّتْ پَنَاه P lrnd. abode of God's shadow on earth, i. e. the Sovereign. —**î** (. . . . — —) P 1. sovereignty. 2. sovereign.

Zıllullah (. . —) ظِلُّ اللّٰه A lrnd. the Shadow of God, a title of the Caliph. —**i filarz** the Shadow of God on earth, title of the Sultan as Caliph of Islam.

zımad (. —), **zımade** (. — .) ضِمَاده A lrnd. 1. fillet; bandage. 2. any medicinal application, poultice, plaster, ointment.

zıman (. —) ضِمَان A lrnd., same as zaman 2.

zımar (. —) ضِمَار A lrnd. uncertainty, a thing not looked upon with certainty or hope, e. g., an enterprise whose profit is in doubt.

zımba (.'.) زِمْبَا drill; punch.

zımbala=[r] زِمْبَالَامَق /ı/ 1. to drill, punch. 2. slang to stab. —**t**= /ı, a/ caus.

zımbalı زِمْبَالى perforated; with a hole punched in it.

zımbırdat=[ır] زِمْبِرْدَاتْمَق /ı/ 1. to twang. 2. to strum (on a stringed instrument).

zımbırtı زِمْبِرْتى colloq. 1. a twanging or strumming noise. 2. trifle, worthless thing.

zımn ضِمْن A lrnd. 1. inside of any container. 2. view, object, purpose (contemplated or implied by a word or act). 3. idea, concept, subject; tenor (of a letter or book). —**ında** with a view to; for the purpose of. —**ı mektupta** in the course of the letter.

zımnen (.'.) ضِمْنًا A by implication; between the lines; tacitly. — **anlat**= /ı, a/ to imply. — **itiraf ediyorlar** They practically confess.

zımnî (. —) ضِمْنى A implied, indirectly or tacitly understood. — **irade izharı** implied declaration of will.

zımpara زِمْپَاره [Persian sumbade] emery. — **kâğıdı** emery paper; sandpaper.

zıncan زِنْجَان same as sincan.

zındık[kı] زِنْدِيق [Arabic . —] 1. misbeliever; atheist. 2. heretic; impious; hypocritical.

zındıkî (..—) زنديقى A *lrnd.* impiety, heresy. —yet (..—.) A *lrnd.* atheism.

zındıklık^(ħ) زنديقلق atheism.

zıngadak^(ħ) (ʹ..) زنغه دق *colloq.* all of a sudden.

zıngıl زنغيل *same as* zıngır.

zıngılda= زنغلداسى *same as* zıngırda=.

zıngırda= زنغرداسى to tremble violently; to rattle. —t= /ı/ *caus.*

zıngırtı زنغردى زنغرتى rattling or trembling noise.

zıngır zıngır زنغر زنغر زنغير زنغير *imitates the noise of violent trembling.*

zınk^(ħ) زنق *imitates the noise of a moving thing brought to an abrupt standstill.* — diye dur= to come to a violent stop.

zınnet ضنّت A *lrnd.* 1. stinginess, avarice. 2. that by which one sets great store; one's treasure.

zıp زيب suddenly, all of a sudden; pop! — çıktı upstart. — çıktı bir halde dressed in a ridiculous manner. — diye çık= to pop up suddenly. — zıp sıçra= to jump about wildly.

zıpır زيبير 1. harebrained; madcap. 2. who jumps and frisks about. — deli frantic madman.

zıpka زپقه a kind of tight-fitting trousers.

zıpkın زپقين fish spear; harpoon.

zıpla= زپلاسى to jump, to hop, to skip or bounce about. —t= /ı/ *caus.*

zıppadak^(ħ) (ʹ...) زيپاده ق suddenly, unexpectedly; with one bound. — dur= to come to a standstill, to stop suddenly.

zıpzıp زپزپ marble (plaything).

zır زر 1. a buzzing or whizzing sound. 2. buzzing, whirring. — zır vızla= to buzz. — zır zırla= to cry incessantly, to keep whining.

zırar (.—) ضرار A *lrnd.* 1. a harming one another. 2. a contending with or opposing one another.

zırdava زرداوه *var. of* zerdava.

zırdeli زردلى raving mad.

zırgam (.—) ضرغام A *lrnd.* lion.

zırh زره [Persian zirih] 1. armor. 2. crease; braid down the side of trousers. —ı Davudi *lrnd.* mail-armor made by David. — giy= to put on or wear armor. — halkası a link of chain armor. — kapla= to armorplate (a ship).

zırhbâf (.—) زره باف P *lrnd.* maker of chain or scale armor.

zırhcâme (.—.) زره جامه P *lrnd.* coat of mail.

zırhdâr (.—) زره دار P *lrnd.* clad in mail.

zırhdûz (.—) زره دوز P *lrnd.* 1. who makes link or scale armor. 2. that pierces through armor.

zırhkaba (..—) زره قبا P *lrnd.* coat of mail.

zırhkürte زره كرته P *lrnd.* frock of mail.

zırhlı زرهلى 1. armored; armor-plated. 2. battleship.

zırhpûş (.—) زره پوش P *lrnd.* clothed in mail or any other military garment.

zırılda= زرلداسى to keep up an incessant chatter or clatter. —n= to keep chattering to oneself; to keep up a wearisome muttering. —t= /ı/ *caus. of* zırılda=.

zırıltı زرلتى زرلدى 1. continuous chatter or clatter; squabble. 2. *slang* dirty, silly, useless. 3. noisy mechanism, source of noise. 4. contraption.

zırıl zırıl زرل زرل in streams. — ağla= to weep loudly and incessantly. — ak= to flow in rivulets.

zırla= زرلاسى 1. to keep up a continuous noise. 2. to bray. 3. to weep (used contemptuously).

zırlak^(ħ) زرلاق 1. noisy, bawling. 2. cricket (insect).

zırnık^(ħ) زرنيق [Persian .—] orpiment; yellow arsenic. — bile alamazsın You won't get anything (out of him). — bile vermez He won't give a thing.

zırp, zırpadak^(ħ) زرپ suddenly.

zırtapoz زرتاپوز *slang* crazy.

zırtullahı kermani (..—. .——) زرت الله كرمانى *colloq.* crazy.

zırtzırt زرت زرت *colloq.* frequently, at unexpected or unsuitable times.

zırva زروه [Persian ——] 1. silly chatter; nonsense. 2. sheep's trotters stewed with garlic. 3. a kind of rice pudding. — tevil götürmez It is no use trying to make sense out of foolish talk.

zırvala= زروالاسى to talk nonsense.

zırzop زرزوپ *colloq.* crackbrained; silly fool. —luk silliness.

zıt^(ddı) ضد [zıd] 1. the contrary; the opposite. 2. opposition; detestation. 3. person or thing disliked, detested. —ına bas= /ın/ to do something to spite someone. —ına git= /ın/ to act contrary to the wishes of; to oppose. — güt= to nourish hatred or opposition. —ı ol= 1. to dislike something. 2. to appear abhorrent to a person.

zıtlık^(ħ) ضدلق contrariness, opposition.

zıvana زوانه [zevane] 1. lining tube of a mouthpiece to a Turkish tobacco pipe; projecting portion of the joint of any tube. 2. appendage more or less shaped like a tongue; tenon of a mortise; projecting heel of a door or gate; pivot. 3. paper tube used as a cigarette holder. —dan çık= to be befuddled; to be in a rage. — testeresi tenon saw.

zıvanalı زوانه لى having a paper tube or mouthpiece at the end (cigarette).

zıya 1 (.—) ضيا A *same as* ziya.

zıyaᵃ¹ 2 (.—) ضياع A lrnd. loss. —ı ebedî eternal loss. —ı elem med. analgesia. —ı hâfıza psychiatry loss of memory, amnesia. —ı his med. anesthesia. —ı intizam psych. ataxia. —ı irade psych. loss of will power, abulia. —ı kelâm psych. loss of speech, aphasia. —ı kıraat psych. word blindness, alexia. —ı şahsiyet psych. depersonalization. —ı tahrir psych. loss of ability to write, agraphia.

zıyaᵃ¹ 3 ضيع A lrnd., pl. of zay'a, estates or plots of land.

zıykᵏ¹ ضيق A lrnd., same as zayk.

zıykünnefes ضيق النفس A same as zayküннefes.

zıypakᵏ¹ زيباك [zibak] prov. slippery.

zi 1 زِ P lrnd. from; than.

zi 2 (—) ذي A lrnd. possessor; person or thing qualified, as in zihayat, zikıymet.

ziab (.—) ذئاب A lrnd., pl. of zi'b 1.

ziamet (.—.) زعامت A lrnd., same as zeamet.

zi'b 1 ذئب A lrnd. wolf. —i Yusuf scapegoat.

zib 2 (—) زيب P lrnd. 1. embellishment, adornment, ornament. 2. grace, elegance, beauty.

ziba (——) زيبا P lrnd. 1. beautiful, elegant; ornamental. 2. of a bright rose or pink color.

zibahû (———) زيباضمير P lrnd. praiseworthy of disposition.

zibak زيبك A lrnd., same as zeybak.

ziban (.—) زيبان P lrnd. beautiful, elegant; ornamental, decked.

zibaver (——.) زيباور P lrnd. that beautifies, ornaments.

zibayi (———) زيبايي P lrnd. beauty, loveliness, gracefulness.

zibayiş (——.) زيبايش P lrnd. embellishment, ornamentation, decoration.

zibende (—..) زيبنده P lrnd. that ornaments and adorns.

zibha ذبحة A lrnd. 1. mumps. 2. croup.

zibidi زيبيدى زيبيت oddly dressed; eccentric, crazy; upstart.

zibil زبل [Arabic zibl] prov. 1. dung, manure. 2. rubbish, sweepings. —ci garbage collector.

zibr زبر A lrnd. a writing; inscription; letter; scripture.

zic (—) زيج A lrnd. 1. same as zeyc. 2. book of astronomical tables.

zicacet (.—.) زجاجت A lrnd. occupation of a dealer in glassware.

-zida (.—), -ziday (.—.) زدای P lrnd. that polishes or removes tarnish; wiping, cleaning, as in, gamzida.

zidayende (.—..) زدآينده P lrnd. that wipes, cleans. —i gam remover of anxiety.

zide- (·.) زيد A lrnd., in formulas of blessing May it be increased.

zidefazlühü زيد فضله A lrnd. May his virtue increase.

zideilmihü زيد علمه A lrnd. May his wisdom increase.

zidekadrühü زيد قدره A lrnd. May his value increase.

zidemecdühü زيد مجده A lrnd. May his glory increase.

zidude (.—..) زدوده P lrnd. 1. polished away, removed (tarnish, etc.). 2. polished, cleaned, brightened.

zifaf (.—) زفاف A nuptial ceremony, marriage. — gecesi first night after marriage. — odası bridal chamber.

zifir زفير [zehir] 1. deposit in a pipe stem. 2. bitter. 3. dark. —i (..—) A pitch black; very dark. —li begrimed.

zifos زفوس 1. splash of mud. 2. useless, in vain. —at= /a/ 1. to annoy, to tease. 2. to backbite, to slander. — ye= to be bespattered with mud.

zift زفت A 1. pitch, tar. 2. pitch black; very bitter. —in pekini yesin, — yesin Let him starve for all I care. —î (.—) A lrnd. pertaining to pitch; like pitch; mixed with pitch, made of pitch.

ziftle=ᵗʳ زفتلمك /ı/ to daube with pitch.

ziftlen=ᵗʳ زفتلنمك 1. pass. of ziftle=. 2. colloq. to overeat; to eat, consume, squander. 3. to put to one's own use (not too honestly).

ziftli زفتلى daubed with pitch; pitchy; containing pitch.

zigan (——) زغان A lrnd., pl. of zağ 1.

zihaf (.—) زحاف A pros. any modification of the measure of a foot; a dropping of one letter between two others. —ât (.——) A pl.

ziham (.—) زحام A lrnd. a crowding and pressing on one another; crowd, throng.

zihayat (—.—) ذي حيات A lrnd. alive, living.

zihgir (.—) زهگير P lrnd. archer's thumb stall.

zihi (.—) زهى P lrnd., same as zehi.

zihinʰⁿⁱ ذهن [zihn] 1. mind, intelligence; intellect. 2. memory. — aç= to stimulate the mind. — açıklığı sharpness of mind. —ini boz= 1. /ın/ to make one suspicious. 2. /la/ to be crazy about something. —i bulan= to be confused. —ini bulandır= /ın/ to make one suspicious. — bulanıklığı psych. mental dimness. —im durdu My mind ceased to work; I couldn't take anything in. —i evvel joc. very intelligent. —e gir= to be understood. — hesabı mental arithmetic. — karış= to be confused. —ini karıştır= /ın/ to confuse someone. —ini kurcala= 1. to occupy one's mind. 2. to strain one's mind. — meşguliyeti preoccupation of mind. — sarfet= /a/ to apply the mind to something. — seviyesi mental

level. —e sığ═ to be comprehensible. —i takıldı /a/ His attention was caught, *by some striking fact or knotty point.* —inde tut═ /ı/ to bear in mind. —i yat═ to become convinced, to admit. — yor═, —ini yor═ to think hard, to rack one's brains. — yorgunluğu mental fatigue. —siz lacking intelligence.
zihle═ʳ زهله ماك *lrnd.* /ı/ *same as* zıhla═.
zihli زهلى *same as* zıhlı.
zihn ذهن A *same as* zihin.
zihnen (.́.) ذهنا A mentally, in one's mind. — hesab et═ /ı/ to reckon in one's head.
zihni (.—) ذهنى A 1. pertaining to the mind; mental; intellectual. 2. *phil.* ideal. — iltibas *lrnd.* mental confusion. — takyid *lrnd.* mental reservation.
zihniyat (..—) ذهنيات A *lrnd.* intellectual matters.
zihniye ذهنيه A *phil.* conceptualism, intellectualism.
zihniyet ذهنيت A mentality.
zikıymet (—..) ذى قيمت A *lrnd.* precious, valuable; costly.
zikir^(kri) ذكر [zikr] 1. *rel.* a mentioning; mention. 2. *rel.* a praising God with recitation of litanies; formula of litanies, formula or litany of praise; the act of glorifying God; dervish religious service, litanies. 3. *lrnd.* a bearing in one's mind; remembrance, recollection. —i âti vechiyle *lrnd.* as explained below. —i celi *lrnd.* a public recitation of the attributes of God. —i cemil *lrnd.* honorable mention, praise. —i cüz ve iradei kül *rhet.* a mention of a part to signify the whole. —iniz geçti You were mentioned, *expression of politeness.* —i hafi *lrnd.* recitation of the attributes of God without audible expression. —i hakim *lrnd.* divine or divinely inspired saying or passage. —i hâl ve iradei muhal 1. that form of metonymy where the abstract is put for the concrete or the particular for the general. 2. *rhet.* the kind of metonymy in which the thing contained is put for that which contains it. — halkası circle of devotees assembled with a leader to chant praises to God.
zikr ذكر A *lrnd., same as* zikir. — bilkalb silent recital (without audible expression). — billisan oral recital.
zikra ذكرى A *lrnd.* 1. remembrance, reminiscence; mention. 2. recitation; declaration; invocation. 3. admonition, exhortation; advice.
zikran (.—) ذكران A *lrnd.* commemoration; anniversary.
zikret═^(der) ذكر ايتمك 1. /ı/ to mention. 2. to chant religious formulas or prayers.
zikrhan (.—) ذكرخوان P *lrnd.* who recites the names of God.

zikrolun═^(ur) ذكر اولنمق to be mentioned.
zikzak^h زيقزاق F zigzag. —vari (..——) zigzagging.
zil 1 زيل 1. cymbal; bells on a tambourine. 2. gong; bell, electric bell. 3. *slang* hungry. — gibi 1. very thin; starving with hunger. 2. always in motion. — gibi sarhoş blind drunk. — takın═ to make merry. — takıp oyna═ to give oneself over to merriment. — zurna, — zurna sarhoş riotously drunk.
zil 2 ذل A *lrnd.* 1. a being submissive; submissiveness; tractability. 2. gentle kindness and consideration.
zilâl^li (.—) ذلال A *lrnd., pl. of* zelil.
Zilhicce ذى الحجة A *name of the twelfth month of the Arabian year.*
Zilkade ذى القعدة A *name of the eleventh month of the Arabian year.*
zillet ذلت A *lrnd.* abasement, degradation.
zilli زيللى 1. with cymbals or bells; having a bell. 2. *slang* badly behaved; quarrelsome. — bebek doll which when squeezed strikes cymbals. — daire tambourine with small cymbals on its rim. —yi kır═ *slang* to eat. — maşa forked tongs with cymbals at the end, used as rhythmic instruments in dance music. —yi şişir═ *slang* to have a good meal.
zilsiz زيلسيز without a bell, cymbals or castanets. — oyna═ to dance for joy.
zilyed ذى اليد A *lrnd.* owner, possessor; holder. — bulun═ /a/ to be in possession of a thing. —lik ownership.
zilzâl^li (.—) زلزال A *lrnd.* causing to tremble (earth); earthquake.
zilzen زيلزن P player of the cymbals.
zimam 1 (.—) زمام A *lrnd.* 1. leading rein; reins. 2. cord by which anything is fastened. —i idare the reins of government.
zimam 2 (.—) زمام A *lrnd.* 1. protection, safeguard, indemnity (resulting from a covenant); honor, reputation. 2. an undertaking an engagement; compact, covenant.
zimamdar (.——) زمامدار P *lrnd.* one who holds the reins (of government); statesman; leader. —ân (.———) P *pl.*
zimem ذمم A *lrnd., pl. of* zimmet. —ât (..—) A *pl.* debts.
zimmet ذمت A 1. charge; debt. 2. debit side (of an account). 3. duty; obligation. 4. *Ott. hist.* duty of tribute and obedience owed to the State by a non-Muslim subject. —inde to his charge, *e. g.,* —inde yüz lira alacağım var He owes me a hundred liras. — ehli *Ott. hist.* non-Muslim subject of the Ottoman Empire. —ine geçir═ /ı/ to embezzle. —i himmet *lrnd.* thing incumbent upon one. —te kal═

to be owing. —i tebriye edildi He has received the cancellation of his debt.

zimmi (.—) ذمّى A Ott. hist. non-Muslim subject.

zin (—) زين P lrnd. saddle.

zina (.—) زنا A adultery; fornication.

zinab 1 (.—) زنب A lrnd., pl. of **zeneb**.

zinab 2 (.—), **zinabe** (.—.) زناب، زنابه A lrnd. 1. tail, extremity of anything. 2. outer corner of the eye. 3. sequel, consequence. 4. lower or lowest part of a valley; extreme point to which a valley stream flows. 5. tail rope of an animal.

zinad (.—) زناد A lrnd. steel for striking fire.

zinai (.——) زنائى A lrnd. pertaining to adultery or fornication.

zinakâr (.———) زناكار P lrnd. adulterous. —**î** (.————) P, —**lık** adultery; fornication.

zincab زنجاب var. of **sincab**.

zincef زنجف [Persian **sincef**] border, edging or binding on the edge of a cloth or garment. —**li** edged, bordered, bound.

zincifre (..˙.) زنجفره [sincefre] cinnabar, vermilion.

zincir زنجير P 1. chain; fetters. 2. phil. succession, series. 3. log. endless series of connected propositions as proof or argument. — **baklası** link of a chain. —**den boşan**= to act like a madman. — **çek**= 1. to draw or carry a chain. 2. to trace a chain-like design. —**e çek**= /ı/ to chain, to fetter (person). — **gomena** naut. chain-cable. — **halkası** link of a chain. — **kesir** math. continued fraction. —**i kopar**= to lose all control of oneself. —**ini kopar**= to run amok (madman). —**ini sürü**= to drag one's chain after one. —**e vur**= /ı/ to chain, to put (someone) in chains.

zincirle= زنجيرله /ı/ 1. to chain. 2. to connect in a series or chain.

zincirleme زنجيرلمه 1. verbal n. 2. in a continuous series. 3. a proceeding continuously.

zincirlen=ⁱʳ زنجيرلن pass. of **zincirle**=.

zincirli زنجيرلى 1. provided with a chain; chained. 2. in a continuous manner; linked. 3. madman or prisoner in chains. 4. Ott. hist. a gold coin. — **kuyu** 1. well worked by a wellsweep and chain. 2. w. cap., name of a district in Istanbul.

zincirlikⁱⁱ زنجيرليك naut. locker.

zindan (.—) زندان P 1. prison; dungeon. 2. dark place; very dark. — **gibi** very dark or dismal. —**ı hâmûşân** lrnd. the grave. **Z— Kapısı** one of the city gates of Istanbul (on the Golden Horn).

zindanî (.——) زندانى P lrnd. 1. pertaining to a prison. 2. jailor. 3. prisoner.

zinde زنده P 1. alive, active, energetic. 2. living, alive, vital. 3. vigilant, watchful. 4. alive with divine love. 5. lrnd. bleeding or suppurating (wound). 6. lrnd. night passed in work, pleasure or devotions (without sleep).

zindebad (..—) زنده باد P lrnd. Long live ...! Bravo!

zindedar (..—) زنده دار P lrnd. 1. keeping alive, wakeful. 2. who makes a place alive with his activities.

zindedil زنده دل P lrnd. live-hearted; pious.

zindegân (..—) زندگان P lrnd. the living. —**î** (..——) P 1. life; pleasant, joyous life. 2. means of life, livelihood, sustenance.

zindegi (..—) زندگى P lrnd. vitality; life.

zindekûn زنده كن P lrnd. who or which vivifies.

zindelikⁱⁱ زنده لك life, animation, activity, briskness.

zinderûd (..—) زنده رود P obs. a makam related to **Isfahan**.

zinefzar (—.—) زين افزار P lrnd. saddle-gear, especially, such arms and armor as were formerly carried on the saddle.

zinger (—.) زينگر P lrnd. saddler.

zinhar 1 (——) زنهار P lrnd., same as **zinhar 2**.

zinhar 2 (.—) زنهار P 1. Beware! 2. by no means; lrnd. by all means. 3. lrnd. protection, safeguard, safe-conduct. 4. lrnd. abstinence, continence. — **ve zinhar!** Beware, take care!

zinharhah (.——) زنهارخواه P lrnd. who asks for mercy; refugee.

zinharhar (.——) زنهارخوار P lrnd. who breaks his promise, treacherous.

zinharî (.——) زنهارى P lrnd. who is under protection or safe-conduct; refugee; a non-Muslim living in a Muslim country.

zinkûhe (—.) زين كوهه P lrnd. saddlebow; cantle of a saddle.

zinpuş (—.) زين پوش P lrnd. ornamental covering of a saddle.

zinsaz (——) زين ساز P lrnd. saddler.

zinsipes (—..) زين سپس P lrnd. henceforth, henceforward.

zir (—) زير P lrnd. 1. lowest portion; under part; bottom of a thing. 2. below, beneath, lower. 3. top string (of a lute). — **ü bâlâ** up and down; high and low. — **ü bem** the top string and the bass string (of a lute). —**i idaresinde** /ın/ under the direction (of). — **ü zeber** 1. below and above. 2. upside down. — **ü zeber et**= /ı/ to turn upside down.

zira 1 (——) زيرا P because; inasmuch as, by reason that, since.

ziraⁱⁱ **2** (.—) زراع A 1. obs. cubit. 2. lrnd. forearm and hand; the long bone of the forearm.

ziraatⁱⁱ (.—.) زراعت A a cultivating; agriculture. — **ehli** 1. agriculturist. 2. farmers, tillers of the soil. —**çi** agriculturist.

ziraî (.——) زراعی A agricultural.

zirdest (—.) زیردست P lrnd. 1. inferior place or position. 2. antagonist who gets the worst of the encounter. 3. dependent, subject, tributary; servant; serf. —**î** (—.—) P obedience, submission.

zire (—.) زیره P lrnd. cummin, bot., *Cuminum cyminum*. —**i Rumi** black cummin, bot., *Nigella sativa*.

zirefgend (—..) زیرافکند P Or. mus. an ancient compound **makam** now very rare.

zirek^ki (—.) زیرک P lrnd., same as **zeyrek**. —**î** (—.—) P, —**lik** sharpness, shrewdness, intelligence.

zireksar (—.—) زیرک‌سار P lrnd. quick-witted, intelligent.

zirgüle زیرگوله P same as **zengüle**.

ziribad (—.—) زیرباد P lrnd. leeward side or direction; leeward.

zirîn (——) زیرین P lrnd. lower; inferior; down, below.

zirman زرمان slang powerfully built, huge (man).

zirmeşk^ki (—.) زیرمشق P lrnd. small portfolio held in the left hand to support a sheet of paper when writing.

zirpuş (——) زیرپوش P lrnd. underclothing, anything worn under a garment.

ziruh (——) ذی‌روح A lrnd. 1. alive. 2. animate object.

zirve زروه A summit; peak; apex. —**toplantısı** pol. summit meeting.

zirzemin (—.—) زیرزمین P lrnd. subterranean; buried.

zist (—) زیست P lrnd. living, life, existence.

zişan (—.—) ذیشان A lrnd. honorable, glorious.

zişt زشت P lrnd. 1. hideous, ugly, unsightly. 2. unseemly; obscene.

ziştgû (.—) زشت‌گو P lrnd. foul-mouthed.

zişthah (.—) زشت‌خواه P lrnd. enemy.

ziştthu (.—) زشت‌خو P lrnd. bad-tempered. —**yi** (.—.) P badness of temper.

ziştî (.—) زشتی P lrnd. ugliness; unseemliness.

ziştrû (.—) زشت‌رو P lrnd. ugly-faced. —**yî** (——) P ugliness of face.

ziştsiret (.—.) زشت‌سیرت P lrnd. morally bad; ill-mannered.

ziver (—.) زیور P lrnd. 1. ornament. 2. trinket. 3. any embellishment.

zivoma (.'..) زیوما carpenter's square.

ziy^yi زی A lrnd. 1. guise, garb, costume. 2. form, shape. 3. aspect, appearance.

ziya (.—) ضیا A light. —**ver**= to give out light.

ziyad (.—) زیاد P lrnd. 1. abundance; increase; excess. 2. name of one of the seven games of backgammon.

ziyadar (.——) ضیادار P lrnd. 1. luminous; well-lighted (room). 2. illuminated.

ziyade (.—.) زیاده A 1. more; much; too much. 2. increase, augmentation. 3. too; very. 4. excessive; superfluous. 5. lrnd. surplus; excess. 6. lrnd. residue, remainder. —**siyle** to a great degree; largely. — **olsun** lit., May it be extra for you, used in declining an invitation to partake of food. —**ce** (.—.') rather more, somewhat.

ziyadecû (.—.—) زیاده‌جو P lrnd. who seeks for increase, covetous; avaricious.

ziyadelen=^ir, **ziyadeleş**=^ir زیاده‌لنمك to increase; to become excessive.

ziyadelik^ki زیاده‌لك abundance; excess.

ziyafeşan (.—.—) ضیافشان P lrnd. scattering light.

ziyafet (.—.) ضیافت A feast, banquet; dinner party. — **çek**=, — **ver**= /a/ to give a banquet.

ziyagüster (.—..) ضیاگستر P lrnd. light-diffusing; luminous.

ziyaî (.——) ضیائی A lrnd. pertaining to or consisting of light, luminous.

ziyalan=^ir ضیالانمك to become illumined, to derive light. —**dır**= caus. /ı/.

ziyan (.—) زیان P 1. loss; damage. 2. hurt, harm, injury. —**ına** at a loss. — **çek**=, — **et**=, — **gör**= to suffer loss or damage, to suffer prejudice. — **öde**= to pay damages. — **sebil ol**= to be wasted. — **ver**= to cause injury or loss. —**ı yok** Never mind.

ziyankâr (.——) زیانکار P wasteful. —**lık** wastefulness.

ziyanlı زیانلی injured; who suffers loss.

ziyansız زیانسیز 1. harmless. 2. not so bad, pretty good.

ziyapaş (.——) ضیاپاش P lrnd. light-diffusing, luminous.

ziyaret (.—.) زیارت A 1. a paying a visit; visit. 2. voluntary pilgrimage. 3. same as **ziyaretgâh**. — **et**= 1. to pay a visit. 2. to perform a voluntary pilgrimage. —**e git**= to go on a visit.

ziyaretçi زیارتچی 1. visitor. 2. pilgrim.

ziyaretgâh زیارتگاه P lrnd. a much visited place; place to which a pilgrimage is made.

ziynet (—.) زینت A ornament; decoration; adornment; jewelry. — **altını** ornamental gold coin. — **ver**= /a/ to give grace or beauty.

ziynetle= زینتله‌مك /ı/ to adorn, embellish.

ziynetlen=^ir زینتلنمك to become adorned, embellished.

ziynetli زینتلی ornamented, embellished.

ziynetsiz زینتسیز unadorned, plain.

zizefun (—.—) زیزفون A lrnd. linden, bot., *Tilia europaea*.

zobu زوبو *Ott. hist.* an apprentice under one of the aghas in the household of a grandee.

zoka (´.) زوقه It 1. fishhook; artificial bait; spinner. 2. *slang* trick; trap. —**yı yut**= *slang* to be duped.

zokula= زوقولامق *prov., same as* **zonkla**=.

zom 1 زوم drunk.

zom 2 زوم *slang* perfected, mature (person). — **ol**= to get very drunk.

zonkla= زونقلامق to throb with pain.

zolota (´.) زولوطه Sl *Ott. hist.* an ancient coin.

zor زور P 1. hard, difficult; fatiguing; difficulty; with difficulty; only just. 2. strength; force; might. 3. violence; compulsion, constraint. —**la** by force; with difficulty. —**u altında kal** *same as* **zora gel**=. — **belâ** by great effort, after great trouble. — **çek**= to suffer violence, difficulty or disease. — **gel**= to seem hard, to appear difficult. —**a gel**= to be forced or constrained. —**a gelme**= not to withstand hardship; to eschew hard work. —**la güzellik olmaz** It's no use forcing it. —**u ne?** /ı/ What's the matter with him? What's the trouble? What does he want? Why should he do it? (He is not obliged to.) — **nikâh** forced marriage. —**unda ol**= to be obliged to. —**u zoruna** with great difficulty.

zoraki (.—.) زوراكى P forced; involuntary; under compulsion; by force. —**lik** a forced thing.

zorba زوربا [zorbaz] 1. who uses force; rebel; bully. 2. violent; brutal. — **kesil**= to become a rebel, mutinous, unruly. —**lık** the use of force; violence; bullying.

zorbaz (.—) زورباز P *lrnd.* 1. who exerts his strength; who uses violence. 2. rebel; rioter; rebellious. —**î** (.——) P, —**lık** rebellion; mutiny; violence.

zorger زورگر P *lrnd.* athlete, hero, champion.

zorhane (.—.) زورخانه P *lrnd.* school for athletic exercises, gymnasium.

zorkâr (.—) زوركار P *lrnd.* doing violence; arduous.

zorla= زورلامق 1. to force; to use force. 2. to exert one's strength. 3. to handle roughly; to misuse. 4. to oblige; to urge strongly. —**n**= *pass.* —**ş**= to grow difficult, to become harder.

zorlu زورلو 1. strong; violent. 2. powerful, influential.

zorluktu زورلق difficulty, arduousness. —**ları yen**= to overcome difficulties.

zormend زورمند P *lrnd.* 1. strength. 2. robust, powerful, strong. —**î** (..—) P, —**lik** strength, power, courage.

zorunlu *neol., phil.* necessary.

zu- 1 (—) ذو A *lrnd.* possessor, owner, master; one who has or occupies a thing; one that is endowed with, qualified with a thing, *as in* **zufünun, zukâhil, zuşucun.**

zu 2 (—) ضو A *lrnd.* light, radiance.

zuaf (.—) زعاف A 1. *lrnd.* that kills quickly or instantly; poison. 2. *obs., w. cap.* Zouave. 3. *obs.* headgear worn by the Zouave.

zuafa (..—) ضعفا A *lrnd., pl. of* **zaif.**

zuama (..—) زعما A *lrnd., pl. of* **zaim.**

zucret ضجرت A *lrnd.* distress; annoyance.

zud (—) زود P *lrnd.* 1. quick, swift, speedy. 2. soon; quickly; at once.

zudaşna (———) زودآشنا P *lrnd.* quick to make acquaintance, soon intimate.

zudaşti (———) زودآشتى P *lrnd.* quick to make peace, placable.

zudazud (———) زودازود P *lrnd.* quickly in succession, readily.

zudendaz (—.—) زودانداز P *lrnd.* 1. that throws or shoots quickly. 2. thrown out hastily, extempore (word).

zudhışm (—.) زودخشم P *lrnd.* quickly angered, hasty (man).

zudhiz (—.) زودخيز P *lrnd.* 1. early-rising. 2. active. 3. early maturing (plant).

zudî (——) زودى P *lrnd.* quickness, celerity.

zudnevis (—.—) زودنويس P *lrnd.* who writes quickly; rapid writer.

zudres (—.) زودرس P *lrnd.* 1. that arrives or happens quickly. 2. that comes early to maturity.

zudter (—.) زودتر P *lrnd.* quicker, more speedily; as soon as possible.

zufünun (—.—) ذوفنون A *lrnd.* learned.

zufr ظفر A *lrnd., same as* **zıfr.**

zuhaf (.—) زحاف A *lrnd., same as* **zuaf.**

zuhr 1 ظهر A *lrnd.* noon; time of noon worship.

zuhr 2 ذخر A *lrnd.* provisions laid up for future use; store.

zuhrî (.—) ظهرى A *lrnd.* pertaining to noon time. —**yet** *abstr. n.*

zuhrüf زخرف A *lrnd.* 1. gold. 2. adornment, as a piece of jewelry, or the furniture of a room. 3. varnished tale, falsehood, anything intended to deceive; adorned falsehood; exaggeration. **Z— Suresi** *a name of the forty-third sura of the Quran.*

zuhûr 1 (.—) ظهور A 1. a becoming manifest, evident, visible; appearance; a happening, coming to pass; coming into being. 2. a becoming conspicuous, powerful or famous. — **et**= 1. to appear; to come to pass; to come into existence. 2. to become a man of note. —**a gel**= to happen. —**a getir**= /ı/ to cause to happen, to bring to pass.

zuhûr 2 (.—) ظهور A *lrnd., pl. of* **zahr 2.**

zuhurat (.——) ظهورات A 1. sudden occurrences; chance events; unexpected events; the turn of events. 2. unexpected expenses. —a tâbi ol= to depend on events; to conform to events. — tatarı extraordinary courier carrying urgent dispatches.

zuhuri (.—–) ظهوری A 1. lrnd. pertaining to chance occurrence, occasional. 2. w. cap., name of a clown in the old Turkish theater. —ye çıkar gibi dressed in a ludicrous manner. Z— kolu name of a theatrical company of the orta oyunu theater.

zukâhil (—–.) ذوكاهل A lrnd. having plenty of backbone, a man not to be trifled with.

zukak[kı] (.—) زقاق A lrnd., same as **sokak**. —î (.——) A pertaining to the street.

zukeserat (—..—) ذوكسرات A lrnd. one who habitually loses in trade.

zula et=[der] زولا ات=[slang] slang to steal, to rob.

zulbüyut (—.—) ذوالبيوت A lrnd. of high lineage.

Zulcelâl (—.—) ذوالجلال A rel. the Lord of majesty and glory.

Zulektaf (—..—) ذوالاكتاف A lrnd. (lit., he of the shoulder-blades) Shapur, son of Hurmuz, legendary king of Persia who punished rebel Arabs by cutting out their shoulder blades.

zulemat (..—) ظلمات A lrnd., same as **zulmat**.

Zulevtad (—.—) ذوالاوتاد A lrnd. Pharaoh.

Zulfakar, Zulfıkar (—.—) ذوالفقار A lrnd., name of the Caliph Ali's famous sword. In popular representations it has two blades and two points.

zulhicreteyn (—...) ذوالهجرتين A lrnd. any companion of the Prophet Muhammad who accompanied him at both emigrations.

Zulihsan (—.—) ذوالاحسان A lrnd. the Lord of Grace, God.

Zulkadir[dri] (—..) ذوالقدر [Zulkadr] man's name. — oğulları hist., name of a dynasty that ruled in southeastern Anatolia in the fifteenth century.

Zulkadr (—.—) ذوالقدر A lrnd. the Possessor of Might.

Zulkarneyn (—..) ذوالقرنين A lrnd. (lit., the two-horned one) 1. Alexander the Great. 2. Es-Sa'b al-Himyari. 3. a person referred to in the Quran.

Zulku'de (—..) ذوالقعده A lrnd., same as **Zilka'de**.

zulle ظله A lrnd. anything that shades or protects.

zulm ظلم A lrnd., same as **zulüm**.

zulmaaşeyn (—.—.) ذوالمعاشين A biol. Amphibia.

zulmani (.——) ظلمانى A lrnd. 1. pertaining to darkness; dark. 2. obscure. —yet (.—..) A obscurity; shadedness.

zulma'niyeyn (—...) ذوالمعنيين A lrnd. a word with two distinct meanings.

zulmat (.—) ظلمات A lrnd., pl. of **zulmet** 1.

zulmeani (—.—.) ذوالمعانى A lrnd. with three or more meanings (word).

zulmen ('.) ظلما A lrnd. wrongfully; cruelly.

zulmet 1 ظلمت A lrnd. darkness; the dark.

zulmet=[der] 2 ظلم ا يتمك /a/ to do a wrong to; to treat unjustly or cruelly; to tyrannize.

zulmetenduz (...—) ظلمت اندوز P lrnd. very dark.

zulmi (.—) ظلمى A lrnd. pertaining to wrong, wrongful; tyrannical, unjust.

zulminen (—..) ذوالمنن A lrnd. giver of ungrudged gifts, bountiful, God.

zulumba, zulumpad زولومبا [Persian **zurumba, zurumbad**] zedoary (aromatic root), bot., Curcuma zedoaria.

zulüm[lmü] ظلم [zulm] wrong; oppression, cruelty.

zulümkâr (..—) ظلمكار P lrnd. oppressive; tyrannical, cruel. —âne (..——.) P tyrannically. —î (..——) P cruelty.

zulvecheyn (—..) ذوالوجهين A lrnd. anything that faces in two directions.

zulyed (—.) ذواليد A lrnd., same as **zilyed**.

zu'm زعم A lrnd. unfounded opinion; false assumption. —unca according to his own views. —î (.—) A assumed as true without authority.

zu'miyat (.——) زعميات A lrnd. matters based on supposition.

zumur (.—) ضمور A lrnd. 1. a being lean, a becoming thin; leanness, thinness. 2. same as **dumur**.

Zunnahle (—..) ذوالنخل A lrnd. Christ as having been born at the foot of a date palm.

Zunnun (——) ذوالنّون A lrnd. 1. the prophet Jonah. 2. by-name of a celebrated Arabic mystic. 3. name of a certain sword. —eyn (——.) A name of a certain sword.

Zunnureyn (——.) ذوالنّورين A lrnd. (lit., Possessor of the two Glories.) surname of the Caliph Othman, who successively married the Prophet Muhammad's two daughters.

zunun (.—) ظنون A lrnd., pl. of **zan** 1.

zûr (.—) زور A lrnd. lie, falsehood.

Zurah (.—) ضراح A lrnd., name of the celestial Kaaba which corresponds to the Kaaba in Mecca.

zurefa (..—) ظرفاء A same as **zürefa**.

zurna زورنا [surna] 1. a primitive double-reed instrument played with a drum in folk music. 2. the saury or skipper, zool., Scomberesox saurus. 3. slang big nose. —cı player of the **zurna**.

zurnapa زرناپا [Persian .——] lrnd. giraffe.

zurnazen زرنازن [sûrnazen] lrnd. player of the **zurna**.

zuruᵘᵘ ضروع A *lrnd., pl. of* **zar** 8.
zurub (.—) ضروب A *lrnd., pl. of* **zarb.** **—i Acem** Persian locutions or idiomatic expressions. **—i emsal** proverbs. **—ât** (.——) A *pl.*
zuruf (.—) ظروف A *lrnd., pl. of* **zarf.**
zuşücun (—.—) ذو شجون A *lrnd.* complicated, intricate.
Zuttavlˡ (—.) ذوالطول A *lrnd.* the Possessor of superiority or beneficence, a name of God.
zuumᶻᵘ'ᵐᵘ ذعم A *var. of* **zu'm.**
zuyuf (.—) ضيوف A *lrnd., pl. of* **zayf.**
zü (—) ذو A *lrnd., same as* **zu** 1.
züabat (.——) ذوابات A *lrnd., pl. of* **züabe.**
züabe (.—.) ذوابه A *lrnd.* 1. lock, tress of hair hanging down. 2. horse's forelock. 3. pendulous tassel. 4. lash of a whip; any pendulous appendage.
zübab (.—) ذباب A *lrnd.* 1. flies; the fly. 2. black speck in the iris of the eye of a horse. 3. sharp edge or point of a sword or of any weapon. **—e** (.—.) A a single fly.
zübâlˡ (.—) ذبال A *lrnd.* lamp wicks. **—e** (.—.) A single candle wick.
zübdᵈᵘ ذبد A *lrnd.* 1. fresh butter. 2. cream.
zübde ذبده A *lrnd.* 1. cream; the cream of anything. 2. the choicest portion of a thing; quintessence. **Z—i Kâinat** the Prophet Muhammad.
zübdetülefazil (.....—.) زبدة الافاضل A *lrnd.* an eminent man of learning.
zübed ذبد A *lrnd., pl. of* **zübde.**
zübeyde ذبيده A *lrnd.* small portion of froth, cream, or butter.
zübûlˡ (.—) ذبول A *lrnd.* 1. a languishing, withering. 2. a gradually but fatally sinking into exhaustion; fatal collapse. 3. an old man's losing flesh and withering in the due course of nature.
zübur (.—) زبور A *lrnd., pl. of* **zibr,** books.
zücac (.—) زجاج A *lrnd.* glass. **—e** (.—.) A a single article or piece of glass.
zücacî (.——) زجاجى A *lrnd.* 1. glassy, vitreous. 2. pertaining to or resembling glass. 3. worker or dealer in glass.
zücaciye (.—..) زجاجيه A glassware.
zücaciyet (.—..) زجاجيت A vitreousness, glassiness.
züğürtᵈᵘ زوگورت ذوگورت destitute; bankrupt; poor; moneyless. **— tesellisi** cold comfort, sour grapes.
züğürtleˢ زوگورتلمك to become destitute; to go bankrupt.
züğürtlükᵏᵘ زوگورتلك indigence; bankruptcy; a being moneyless. **—ten kazın=** to suffer extreme poverty.
Zühalˡ زحل A *astr.* Saturn.

zühd زهد A *lrnd.* pious asceticism. **— ü takva** asceticism.
zühhad (.—) زهاد A *lrnd., pl. of* **zahid.**
Zühre زهره A 1. Venus. 2. the first night of the new moon. **—i Zehra** *lrnd.* Venus.
zührecebin (...—) زهره جبين P *lrnd.* with a brow like Venus.
zühreruh زهره رخ P *lrnd.* whose cheek is as beautiful as Venus.
zühresuz (..—) زهره سوز P *lrnd.* who is so beautiful that Venus is consumed by jealousy.
zühret زهرت A *lrnd.* beautiful whiteness, fairness, brightness, beauty.
zührevi (..—) زهروى A venereal. **— hastalıklar** venereal diseases.
zühukᵏᵘ (.—) زهوق A *lrnd.* a passing away, perishing, vanishing.
zühulˡ (.—) زهول A *lrnd.* a being forgetful or neglectful; negligence; omission; forgetfulness.
zühulen (.—'.) زهولاً A *lrnd.* by error; through forgetfulness.
zühur (.—) زهور A *lrnd.* 1. a being bright; brightness. 2. a being beautiful and blooming; beauty, bloom.
zühüvᵛᵛᵘ زهو A *lrnd.* brightness and bloomingness.
zükâm, zükkâm (.—) زكام A *path.* cold in the head, catarrh. **—ı daimî** chronic catarrh. **—ı hınzır** scrofulous catarrh. **— ol=** to catch a cold in the head. **—lı** suffering from a cold in the head.
zükran (.—) ذكران A *lrnd., pl. of* **zeker,** males.
zükûr (.—) ذكور A *lrnd., pl. of* **zeker,** males. **— ve inas** men and women.
zükûret (.—.) ذكورت A *lrnd.* quality of a male, manhood.
zükûrî (.——) ذكورى A *lrnd.* pertaining or special to males, masculine (thing). **—yet** (.—..) A virility, quality of a male; masculinity.
zülˡ ذل A degradation; humiliation. **—i süal** the degradation of begging.
zülâlˡ (.—) زلال A 1. *poet.* pure, cold, pleasant to drink (water). 2. *chem.* albumin. **—î** (.——) A albuminous.
zülâm (.—) زلام A *lrnd.* poor and needy. **—lık** poverty, need.
zülbiye زلبيه *var. of* **zülubiye.**
Züleyha زليخا P *same as* **Zeliha.**
zülf زلف P *lrnd.* 1. *same as* **zülüf.** 2. aigrette. 3. *myst.* the very essence of the Godhead; proximity to God; doubts and difficulties of the spiritual life or anything that interposes between the heart of man and God. **—i arus** flower bunches of the caracalla bean, *bot., Phaseolus caracalla.* **—i cerrar** a ravishing lovelock. **—i**

zülfe hata the veil of error. **—i İbrahim** a single lovelock on the cheek of a beauty (compared to Abraham in Nemrud's fire). **—i siyah kula dun** (horse) with a black mane. **—i yâr** the beloved one's curl. **—i yâre dokun=** to touch a tender spot; to bring up a touchy subject; to rouse one's jealousy or anger. **—i zemin** 1. darkness of night. 2. carnal element in man's nature. 3. earthly trial and suffering.

zülfe زلف A lrnd. 1. a small lovelock. 2. step, station, grade. 3. first part or watch of the night.

zülfgâh (.—) زلفگاه P lrnd. part of the cheek where the lovelock hangs.

Zülfikar (—.—) ذوالفقار A same as Zulfıkar.

zülûbiye (.—..) زلوبيه [Arabic zalabiya] cake made with honey and almonds.

zülüf[ra] زلف زولوف [zülf] side lock of hair, lovelock.

zülüflü زلفلى 1. having lovelocks. 2. wearing a tasseled cap. **— baltacı** Ott. hist. a class of palace guards.

zümbül زنبل زمبل [sünbül] colloq. for şümbül.

zümer زمر A lrnd., pl. of zümre. **Z— Suresi** name of the thirty-ninth sura of the Quran.

zümre زمره A party, body; set of people; group; class. **— dersi** a body of studies embracing different subjects. **—i düveliye** lrnd. a group of states or Powers.

zümrevi (..—) زمروى A belonging to a certain group or class.

zümrüdüanka (....—) زمرد عنقاء [simurgi anka] fairy tales a mythical bird of enormous size. **— gibi ismi var cismi yok** existing only by name, imaginary.

zümrüt[dü] زمرد [zümürrüd] emerald. **— gibi** emerald-like.

zümürrüd زمرد A lrnd., same as zümrüt. **—fam** (...—) P, **—gûn** (...—) P emerald-colored. **—î** (...—) P, **—în** (...—) P emerald green.

zünnar (.—) زنّار A 1. Isl. hist. rope girdle worn by Christians. 2. path. shingles, herpes zoster. 3. myst. sincerity of a saint, love for God. 4. lrnd. the essence of the Godhead. 5. poet. ringlets of a mistress.

zünub (.—) ذنوب A lrnd., pl. of zenb, offenses, sins. **—at** (.——) A categories of sins.

zünuc (.—) زنوج A lrnd., pl. of zenci.

züppe زديه 1. affected person, dandy. 2. affected, snobbish.

züppelik[ği] زديه لك affectation; snobbery.

zürafa, zürafe (.—.) زرافه A a giraffe, zool. Giraffa camelopardalis.

zürare (.—.) ذرارة A lrnd. particle, mote, dust that flies about or falls.

zürdeva زرد وا same as zerdava.

zürefa (..—) ظرفاء A 1. Lesbian. 2. lrnd., pl. of zarif.

zürra[aı] (.—) زرّاع A lrnd., pl. of zâri 2.

zürriyet زريّت A 1. issue, progeny, descendants. 2. child, children.

züru[uu] (.—) زروع A lrnd., pl. of zer' 2, sown fields; sown seeds.

züvvar (.—) زوّار A lrnd., pl. of zair.

züyuf (.—) زيوف A lrnd., pl. of zeyf, base money, spurious coins.

züyûl[lü] (.—) ذيول A lrnd., pl. of zeyl.

züyut (.—) زيوت A lrnd., pl. of zeyt, oils.

züzuniyet (.—..) ذو ظنية final word, conclusion.

FARMINGDALE PUBLIC LIBRARY
3 1736 00300 7657

DOES NOT CIRCULATE